DICTIONARY OF WOMEN WORLDWIDE:

25,000 Women through the Ages

DICTIONARY OF WOMEN WORLDWIDE:

25,000 Women through the Ages

Volume 2
M-Z

Anne Commire, Editor
Deborah Klezmer, Associate Editor

YORKIN PUBLICATIONS

THOMSON

GALE

Detroit • New York • San Francisco • New Haven, Conn. • Waterville, Maine • London • Munich

THOMSON
GALE

Dictionary of Women Worldwide: 25,000 Women through the Ages

Yorkin Publications Staff
Anne Commire, *Editor*
Deborah Klezmer, *Associate Editor*
Eileen O'Pasek, *Editorial Assistant*
Chetna Chopra, Jennifer Jue-Steuck, Bronwyn
Law-Viljoen, Catherine Powers, Elizabeth
Renaud, Andy Smith, Mary Staub, *Contributors*

Project Editor
Margaret Mazurkiewicz

Editorial Support Services
Emmanuel T. Barrido, Luann Brennan

Rights Acquisitions Management
Jackie Jones, Kim Smilay

Imaging
Lezlie Light, Christine O'Bryan

Composition
Evi Seoud

Product Design
Jennifer Wahi

Manufacturing
Rita Wimberley

LIBRARY OF CONGRESS CATALOGING-IN-PUBLICATION DATA

Dictionary of women worldwide : 25,000 women through the ages / Anne Commire, editor ;
Deborah Klezmer, associate editor.
    p. cm.
        Includes bibliographical references.
        ISBN 0-7876-7585-7 (set hardcover : alk. paper) –
        ISBN 0-7876-7676-4 (vol 1 : alk. paper) –
        ISBN 0-7876-7677-2 (vol 2 : alk. paper) –
        ISBN 1-4144-1861-2 (vol 3 : alk. paper)
        1. Women–Biography–Dictionaries.
        I. Commire, Anne. II. Klezmer, Deborah.

CT3202.D53 2006
920.72–dc22

2006008290

British Library Cataloguing-in-Publication Data
A catalogue record for this book is available from the British Library

This title is also available as an e-book
ISBN 0-7876-9394-4
Contact your Thompson Gale sales representative for ordering information.

Printed in the United States of America
10 9 8 7 6 5 4 3 2

CONTENTS

INTRODUCTION

The idea for *Dictionary of Women Worldwide* (*DWW*) began while we were editing the 17-volume set of reference books entitled *Women in World History* (*WIWH*). While frequently turning to dictionaries for help, we were startled by the paucity of women included. In one oft-used biographical dictionary under 5% were women. Other biographical dictionaries had the same or less. It soon became clear that as long as women's entries had to compete with each other for the small percentage of pages set aside for them in traditional dictionaries, these sources were nearly useless to readers looking for a more balanced view of history.

And did those women included in conventional biographical dictionaries get short shrift? Let us approximate the ways. In one recent edition, Abigail Adams was allotted around 25 words, Rosa Bonheur, Empress Theodora, Hypatia, Charlotte Corday, Aspasia, Berthe Morisot, Anna Comnena, between 30 and 40, Mary Cassatt, Dorothea Dix and Anne Boleyn, around 50, Teresa of Avila, 75, and Rosa Luxemburg, 80. As for the men: Halsford Mackinder was allotted around 80 words, Charles Parry, Vincas Kreve and August Kotzebue, over 100, Gebhard Blucher, over 200, Charles I, over 400, Oliver Cromwell, over 600, and Napoleon, over 900. Richard Milhous Nixon, well over 400, was a great deal longer than Indira Gandhi, around 100, Empress Maria Theresa, around 125, Catherine II the Great, around 150, Queen Victoria, around 250, and Elizabeth I, 350.

Dictionary of Women Worldwide is a single source for researching women of any time period and any field of endeavor. It can answer a question quickly, saving users an afternoon slog on the Internet. Since the advent of the Web, conventional wisdom would have us believe that the women in *DWW* can be found quickly and easily in cyberspace. Would that were true; it would certainly have made our job easier. To make the most of the Internet, name variations, correct spellings, dates and personal information are vital. Being multilingual also helps. As well, the Internet has a kind of now-you-see-it-now-you-don't quality. Sites that were there yesterday, loaded with information, vanish like vapor. (Remember those in-depth personal accounts of athletes for the Sydney Olympics? Gone now.) "The average lifespan of a Web page today is 100 days," noted Brewster Kahle of the Internet Archive in San Francisco in 2003. Our goal was to produce a work that would allow the user to verify facts, answer ready reference questions, and begin to research a woman in less time than it takes to log on.

Because of the subject matter, the entries for *DWW* had to be longer than those found in a standard dictionary. For women, the personal is indeed the political. Who the king married is not traditionally required; who the queen married is. In an entry for Eleanor Dulles, listing her brother is essential. In an entry for John Foster Dulles, listing his sister is annoyingly optional. Names of husbands are also important; these are names that the women often went by in public and private life (e.g., Mrs. John Drew). More often than not, after time-consuming sleuthing, we only found a death date for an entrant after uncovering one or all of her married names. We also came across numerous duplicate entries in other biographical dictionaries, women who were listed under two different names, because without personal information it was impossible to see the duplication.

Realizing the influence that such name variations have had in fracturing women's historical identities was one of the greatest lessons we learned while editing *Women in World History*. The genealogical charts we produced for that work are also included in this volume for reasons best explained in the following excerpt from the introduction of *WIWH*. The excerpt addresses two of the most difficult challenges involved in an undertaking like *Dictionary of Women Worldwide:* sorting out and cross-referencing the myriad names given to historical women and naming the nameless.

Throughout the ages, fathers and sons have been scrupulously documented in historical records; for mothers and daughters, birth and death dates are often unknown and approximated. Many cultures do not even count daughters as children. The king's daughter was often treated with the same indifference as the daughter of a tavern owner. But, like certain Soviet leaders who made an art form of airbrushing discredited colleagues from the photographic record, history has occasionally left in a hand or an elbow by mistake. We encountered one historic tome that solemnly noted: "Ariadne was a 5th-century Byzantine empress and daughter of the childless Leo I." Leo had no sons. Records of Eliza Lynch, a major figure in the cultural and political development of Paraguay, scrupulously list her children with dictator Francisco Solano López: "Jan (b. 1855); Enrique (b. 1858); Federico (b. 1860); Carlos (b. 1861); Leopoldo (b. 1862); Miguel (b. 1866); and three daughters, names unknown."

For expediency, historians have eliminated what they perceive to be the secondary storyline. When a woman is known to exist historically, she has often been the casualty of streamlining. The secret to good writing is brevity. "The Holy Roman emperor Otto I arranged a marriage for his son Otto II to a Byzantine empress" is much more readable than "Empress Adelaide of Burgundy and Holy Roman emperor Otto I arranged a marriage for their son Otto II to Theophano, a Byzantine empress."

In the world's text, women have been relegated to common nouns (the queen, the princess, the sister of Charles IV, the duchess of Carlisle) and possessive pronouns ("and his daughter," "and his mother," "and his wife"). In many accounts that chronicle the early years of the 20th century, this phrase appears: "The 1914 assassination of Archduke Franz Ferdinand and his wife led directly to World War I." (Worse, in most reports Archduchess Sophie Chotek's death goes unmentioned; Franz Ferdinand dies alone.) Michael Collins storms the barricade during the Easter rising, and Michael Collins is named; Constance Markievicz and Winifred Carney storm the same barricade, and they are referred to as "two women activists." The often-used phrase "Einstein and his wife" (he had two) evokes an image of a disheveled genius and a drab, faceless woman when, in fact, Mileva Einstein-Maric did the computations for his theory of relativity.

We were determined not to leave a mother, wife, duchess or daughter unturned. Take Ingeborg. Our morning would start simply enough; then we would read: "After his marriage at Amiens, on August 14, 1193, Philip II Augustus, king of France, took a sudden aversion to his 18-year-old Danish bride and sought a divorce." Well, there it was. Obviously, by her marriage to Philip II Augustus, the Danish bride was a queen of France, but who was she? From one source, we learned that she was on good terms with the ensuing French kings; from another, that she lived peacefully, gaining a reputation for kindness. From a third, that she died highly esteemed but, as in the previous sources, nameless, either in 1237 or 1238. Within an hour, we had her name: Ingeborg. By mid-morning, we learned that Ingeborg was the daughter of Waldemar I the Great, king of Denmark. No mother mentioned. Now we had a nameless Danish queen, and a barely named French one.

To give complete and accurate information on Ingeborg, we needed her mother, but while pouring through Palle Lauring's *A History of Denmark,* we read in passing that Philip Augustus "had threatened to cast off his first wife." Another ball in the air. Now we had a nameless Danish queen, one barely named daughter, and an unnamed first wife. By noon, we had uncovered Isabella, first wife of Philip and daughter of Baldwin V, count of Hainault. No mother mentioned. Unfortunately, we had also uncovered a third wife, known only as the mother of Philip Hurepel. Now we had the aforementioned twosome, a newly named first wife, and an unknown third. By mid-afternoon, we gleaned that the mother of Philip Hurepel was named Agnes; she was also the mother of the nonessential Marie. By late afternoon, we had a headache. The results of our day's exploration can be found under the names Agnes of Meran (d. 1201), Ingeborg (c. 1176-1237/38), Isabella of Hainault (1170-1190), and Marie of France (1198-c. 1223). As far as we were able to ascertain, Ingeborg's mother was either Sophie of Russia or Richezza of Poland. No one knows for sure. These were not idle chases. Often the woman off-handedly referred to as the "queen-regent" or "queen mother" turned out to be someone of major import, like Catherine de Medici or Eleanor of Aquitaine. A towering stack of books would eventually straighten out these problems, but the quantity needed will not be found in a small library collection.

The majority of the time, when we did find the woman for whom we were looking, she didn't have one name; she had five or six. Unlike most men whose various names have been sifted down over time to one or two, Holy Roman Empress Agnes of Poitou strolls through the history books as Agnes of Aquitaine, Agnes of Guienne, Agnes of Bavaria, or Agnes of Germany. The dowager empress of China, in her various transliterations, is known as Cixi or Tz'u-hsi, Tse-Hi, Tsu-Hsi, Tze Hsi, Tzu Hsi, Tsze Hsi An, Yehonala, Xiaoqin Xian Huanghou, Xi Taihou, Nala Taihou, Lao Fuoye, or Imperial Concubine Yi. Running down these names easily added years to the project, but we had no choice. Otherwise, the same woman would be scattered throughout our series as Yolande of Brienne on page 29, Jolanta on page 403, and Isabella II of Jerusalem on page 1602.

Name changes that accompany marriage added to the difficulty. Women from outside Russia took on Russian names when they married tsars; one minute they're Sophia Augusta Frederika, princess of Anhalt-Zerbst, the next minute they're Catherine II the Great. East Germany's Christa Rothenburger won the Olympic gold medal in speedskating in 1984. In 1992, she won the silver medal as Christa Luding. In some books, Alice Guy Blache can be found under B; in others, Alice Guy-Blache is found under G. Then there's the longtime bugbear: Mrs. John D. Rockefeller. Which one? Mrs. John D. the 1st, the 3rd, or junior? So often, the dreaded, "the philanthropist, Mrs. Reid," stopped us cold. Is that Mrs. Ogden Mills Reid or Mrs. Whitelaw Reid?

We were not alone in our exasperation. "How are you listing Etta Palm?," queried one of our French historians about an assignment: "As *Palm, Etta Aelders? Palm Aelders, Etta?* or Palm d'Aelders, Etta? My best sources call her Etta Palm d'Aelders, but I'll put her under Palm because she's more widely known to English audiences as Etta Palm. Whew! You'd think there would be more uniformity in these matters."

Researching the lives of Roman women in Republican times was also daunting. Free Roman men had three or four names: the praenomen or given name, the nomen or family name, and sometimes the cognomen or distinguishing name: thus, Gaius Julius Caesar. The women,

however, were given only one name, the feminine form of the family name. That is why the daughters of Julius Caesar and his sister are all named Julia. Only Julia. Historians have taken to qualifiers like Julia Minor and Julia Major, but it has not solved the problem. Five of the Julias can be found in *Women in World History* [and *Dictionary of Women Worldwide*], as well as all eight Cleopatras (Cleopatra VII is the famous one), five Arsinoes, seven sisters Bonaparte, seven Beatrice d'Estes, numerous Euphrosynes, Eurydices, Eudocias, Theopanos, Theodoras, Zoes, Faustinas, and Flavias, many Sforzas and Viscontis, and all 35 women named Medici.

Eventually, we picked up speed. With the material we had accumulated, we could begin to answer our own questions more readily and find the women more quickly. Out of necessity, we were using Women in *World History* as a primary reference source, long before it was completed.

We were also using our charts. Women are rarely included on existing genealogies. A Chinese journalist recalled being handed a copy of her family tree which stretched back 3,000 years. "Not one woman was included on the tree," she noted, "not a mother, a sister, a daughter, a wife." For expediency, women have been left off charts which, while following the male line, are difficult enough to read without adding a cadre of women. When women do appear because of their regal status, usually only their sons are noted on the ancestral line below. In one case, a son was included who had died at age six, while his surviving sister, who had become queen of a neighboring country, was missing.

Determined to come up with an easy-to-use cast list, we set about giving one name to each woman on the world stage as she made her entrances and exits throughout the series. In order to do this, we needed to make our own charts, settle on a name for the subject, and add dates if known. Without identifying dates, five Margarets of Austria all look alike. Thought was given to imposing a rational system on the names, but problems outweighed the advantages. One commonly used data base made a stab at it by changing all Catherines to Katherine. Thus, they had Katherine the Great. Whenever possible, we have tried to use the name by which the subject has been most clearly identified in historical contexts. In so doing, the inconsistencies arise. A Spanish historian might call a queen Isabella; an English historian might call the same queen Elizabeth; a French and German historian, Elisabeth; a Russian historian, Elizaveta.

If the women were difficult for us to locate without knowing the exact name used, we knew the task would be even more difficult for our readers. For this reason, we offer many avenues to find the women sought: by the charts, by indexing, by cross-referencing of collective name variants (*Rejcka. Variant of Ryksa.*), by cross-referencing of name variations within the entries (*Gonzaga, Eleanor [1534-1594]. See Eleanora of Austria.*), and by cross-referencing of titles (Pembroke, countess of. See Clifford Anne [1590-1676].).

We began to rely so heavily on our genealogical charts—all 85 of them—that we decided to put them in the front of Volume I [in both *WIWH* and *DWW*], alphabetized by country. If a woman is bolded on the chart, she appears in her own entry under the name given. Sometimes her sketch will just be personal data, but as Rutger's Kay Vandergrift notes: "The first step for those who are the 'others' in traditional history is to prove their very existence."

We envisioned a series heavily focused on international women, many of whom were enormously important, even revered in their own countries, though seldom known in the United States. Most books in the U.S. cover only American women; by so doing, they isolate women's accomplishments to the last 200 years and neglect about 3,000 years of women's history. An international emphasis, however, did not prove easy. Since much of the information and many of the primary sources we needed for our research were not available in

English, we asked professors to undertake translations. More than 300 contributors, from over 20 nations, participated in the *WIWH* project [and their contributions are reflected in *DWW*].

Readers will inevitably find omissions and inequities in length. We invite suggestions for inclusion in every area from our readers. We have also spent years checking our facts. Nonetheless, because women have been ignored historically, the record is replete with inaccuracies which have been given widespread circulation. Thus, there will be errors in these volumes. We welcome suggestions and corrections.

Anne Commire
Deborah Klezmer

M

MAC AND MC. *Names beginning with the prefix Mac and Mc are listed in alphabetical order.*

MA KUM-JA (1955—). Korean volleyball player. Born Aug 24, 1955, in South Korea. ❖ At Montreal Olympics, won a bronze medal in team competition (1976).

MA XIANGJUN (1964—). Chinese archer. Born Oct 30, 1964, in China. ❖ At Barcelona Olympics, won a silver medal in team round (1992).

MA YANHONG (1963—). Chinese gymnast. Born July 5, 1963, in China. ❖ At World championships, won a gold medal (1979) and a silver (1981), in uneven bars; at Los Angeles Olympics, won a bronze medal in team all-around and shared gold medal with Julianne McNamara in uneven bars (1984).

MA YING. Chinese softball player. Born in China. ❖ Won a silver medal at Atlanta Olympics (1996).

MAACAH (fl. 1000 BCE). Canaanite princess. Name variations: Maachah. Dau. of Talmai, king of Geshur (nation northeast of the Sea of Galilee); one of the wives of David, Israelite king (r. 1010–970 BCE); children: Absalom; Tamar. ❖ See also *Women in World History.*

MAACAH (fl. 931 BCE). Biblical woman. Name variations: Maachah; Michaiah. Dau. of Abishalom; 3rd wife of Rehoboam, king of Judah (r. 931–913 BCE); children: sons Abijah, Attai, Ziza, and Shelomith. ❖ Characterized as a strong-willed woman, retained her position as queen-mother for many years, until her grandson Asa had her removed. ❖ See also *Women in World History.*

MAACHAH (fl. 1575 BCE). Biblical woman. Fl. around 1575 BCE; concubine of Caleb, one of 12 men sent out by Moses to assess the Promised Land.

MAAKAL, Jenny (1913—). South African swimmer. Name variations: Jennie Maakal. Born Aug 2, 1913, in South Africa. ❖ At Los Angeles Olympics, won a bronze medal in the 4x100-meter freestyle (1932); was only included in South African team if she would pay her own expenses; her widowed mother took a loan on their house.

MAANSDATTER, Katherine (1550–1612). Swedish paramour. Born Nov 6, 1550; died Sept 13, 1612; m. Eric XIV (1533–1577), king of Sweden (r. 1560–1568, deposed in 1568), July 4, 1568; children: Henry; Sigrid (b. 1566, who m. Henry Tott and Niels Natt); Gustav (b. 1568); Henry (b. 1570); Arnold (b. 1572). ❖ Was mistress, then wife, of King Eric of Sweden.

MAAR, Dora (1907–1997). French artist, model and mistress. Born Theodora Markovitch, Nov 22, 1907, in Tours, France; died July 16, 1997; buried in Clamart, south of Paris; only child of Yugoslavian father (architect) and French mother; studied painting in Paris at École d'Art Décoratif, Académie de Passy, Académie Julien, and with André Lhote. ❖ Mistress and model for Picasso, whose countenance adorns the walls of museums and pages of art books throughout the world; was the subject of numerous of Picasso's portraits, including *Bust of a Seated Woman,* which sold at auction for $3 million (1995); studied painting, then took up surrealist photography; had 1st exhibition at Galerie de Beaune in Paris (1937); met Pablo Picasso (1936); during their 10-year affair, sat for scores of his portraits, including *Dora in a striped blouse, Dora with cigarette holder, portrait of Dora, 1937* and *portrait of Dora, 1944,* then lived alone, a legendary recluse, working at her own painting. ❖ See also James Lord, *Picasso and Dora* (Farrar, 1993); and *Women in World History.*

MAAS, Annelies (1960—). Dutch swimmer. Name variations: Annelies Kraus-Maas; Annelies Kraus. Born Jan 25, 1960. ❖ At Moscow Olympics, won a bronze medal in 4x100-meter freestyle relay (1980).

MAAS-FJETTERSTROM, Marta (1873–1941). Swedish textile designer. Name variations: Märta Måås-Fjetterstrøm or Fjetterstroem; MMF. Born 1873 in Sweden; died 1941. ❖ One of the leading figures in the textile art scene, began career as an artist, creating a series of works that were exhibited in museums and galleries throughout the world; contributed greatly to the development of the modernist carpet by rethinking weaving methods, including mixed flatweave and knotting techniques, and using more organic patterns; was a master of form, line and composition; had her own weaving workshop in Båstad, just north of Malmö (1919–41), where she created more than 600 designs under the signature MMF; works are now sought by collectors.

MAASS, Clara (1876–1901). American nurse. Born in East Orange, NJ, June 28, 1876; died in Las Animas, Cuba, Aug 24, 1901; interred in East Orange; dau. of B. Maass (father) and H.A. Maass (mother); graduated from Newark German Hospital Training School for Nurses, 1895. ❖ Served in Spanish-American War (1898); at age 25, volunteered for yellow fever immunity experiments being conducted by Walter Reed for US Yellow Fever Commission, Cuba (1901), and died 10 days later, the only woman and only American to succumb. At time of her death, *The New York Times* noted: "No soldier in the late war placed his life in peril for better reasons than those which prompted this faithful nurse to risk hers." Newark German Hospital Training School for Nurses was renamed in her memory; inducted into Hall of Fame of the American Nurses' Association; US post office issued a memorial stamp. ❖ See also *Women in World History.*

MAATHAI, Wangari (1940—). Kenyan ecologist and activist. Name variations: Wangari Muta Maathai or Maathi. Born April 1, 1940, in Nyeri, Kenya; Mount St. Scholastica College, BS in biology, 1964; University of Pittsburgh, MS in anatomy and tissue culture; University of Nairobi, PhD, 1971, the 1st woman in East and Central Africa to earn a doctorate; m. businessman, 1969 (div. mid-1970s); children: 3. ❖ Nobel peace laureate, became the 1st woman to lecture, teach, and later serve as anatomy department head at University of Nairobi (1976); ran for Parliament but was disqualified on a technicality (late 1970s); planted 7 trees in a Nairobi park on World Environment Day to start Green Belt Movement (June 5, 1977), which called upon women to plant trees to help provide wood and improve soil conditions (the movement had 80,000, mostly female members in Kenya by 1997 and had reached 30 additional African nations); hoping to improve conditions in Kenya, became involved in politics (beginning late 1980s), leading to harassment from the government; led protest against destruction of forest outside Nairobi and construction of 62-story office tower in Uhuru Park; served as visiting fellow at Yale University's Global Institute for Sustainable Forestry (Jan 2002); elected to Parliament (Dec 2002); appointed deputy minister for Kenya's Ministry of Environment, Natural Resources, and Wildlife (Jan 2003) by newly elected Kenyan President Mwai Kibabi; won Nobel Peace Prize (2004), the 1st African woman to win the award; writings include *The Green Belt Movement* (1985) and *The Green Belt Movement: Sharing the Approach and the Experience* (1988). Received Woman of the Year Award (1983), Right Livelihood Award (1984), Windstar Award for the Environment (1988), Woman of the World Award (1989), Goldman Environmental Prize (1991), and Jane Addams International Women's Leadership Award (1993).

MAATHI, Wangari (1940—). See Maathai, Wangari.

MÄÄTTÄ, Pirkko (1959—). Finnish cross-country skier. Name variations: Pirkko Maatta. Born Mar 7, 1959, in Kuusamo, Finland. ❖ Won a bronze medal at Sarajevo Olympics (1984) and Calgary Olympics (1988), both for 4x5km relay.

MABEL OF BURY ST. EDMUNDS (fl. 1230). English professional embroiderer. Fl. 1230 in London, England. ❖ Her name is found frequently in the royal treasury records of King Henry III (r. 1216–1272), having been given several important commissions by the king himself. ❖ See also *Women in World History*.

MABLEY, Jackie (1894–1975). African-American comedian. Name variations: Moms Mabley. Born Loretta Mary Aiken, 1894, in Brevard, NC; died in White Plains, NY, May 23, 1975; dau. of Jim Aiken (businessman); never married; children: 5, including Christine, Yvonne, Bonnie and Charles. ❖ The 1st black female comedian to gain widespread recognition, left home at 14 and moved to Cleveland; began entertainment career in Pittsburgh (c. 1910); changed name to Jackie Mabley soon after; performed on Chitlin' Circuit (c. 1910–23), developing act; debuted at Connie's Inn in NY (1923), where career took off; performed regularly at black venues from then on; by 1939, was a regular at Apollo Theater in Harlem; performed in several Broadway shows, including *Fast and Furious* and *Swinging the Dream*; was a regular on radio show "Swingtime at the Savoy"; discovered by white audiences (1960s), began releasing comedy records, including *Moms Mabley—The Funniest Woman in the World, Now Hear This, Moms Mabley at the U.N.*, and more than 20 others; made tv debut (1967) on all-black comedy special "A Time For Laughter" (ABC); appeared on several tv variety shows, including "The Ed Sullivan Show," "The Flip Wilson Show," and "The Smothers Brothers Comedy Hour"; appeared at Copacabana and Carnegie Hall in NY and at Kennedy Center in Washington, DC; starred in film *Amazing Grace* (1974). Was a member of NAACP and a guest at White House Conference on Civil Rights (1966). ❖ See also *Women in World History*.

MABLEY, Moms (1894–1975). *See Mabley, Jackie.*

MAC AND MC. *Names beginning with the prefix Mac and Mc are listed in alphabetical order.*

MACADAMS, Roberta (1881–1959). *See Price, Roberta Catherine MacAdams.*

MACANDREW, Jennie (1866–1949). New Zealand pianist, organist, music teacher, and conductor. Name variations: Jennie West. Born Sept 6, 1866, in Dunedin, New Zealand; died on Dec 24, 1949, at Titirangi, New Zealand; dau. of George Richard West (music shop proprietor) and Mary Elizabeth (Newman) West (music teacher); m. Arthur William Macandrew (telegraph engineer), 1900. ❖ Made 1st public appearance at 11; studied in London and returned to New Zealand, where she taught music at Otago Girls' High School and later at private college (1883); also served as pianist, organist, and conductor at various churches in addition to performing numerous solo concerts. ❖ See also *Dictionary of New Zealand Biography* (Vol. 2).

MACAPAGAL-ARROYO, Gloria (1947—). *See Arroyo, Gloria Macapagal.*

MACARDLE, Dorothy (1889–1958). Irish historian, novelist, and drama critic. Name variations: often wrongly spelled McCardle. Born Dorothy Margaret Macardle in Dundalk, Co. Louth, Ireland, Mar 7, 1889; died in Drogheda, Co. Louth, Dec 23, 1958; dau. of Sir Thomas Callan Macardle, KBE, DL, and Minnie Lucy (Ross) Macardle; attended Alexandra College, Dublin; University College, Dublin, BA with 1st Class Honors, 1911. ❖ Had distinguished academic career at Alexandra College, where she also participated in philanthropic activities; after graduating from University College, returned to Alexandra to teach, and maintained a close connection with it for the rest of life; during Irish war of independence (1919–21), worked as a publicist for Sinn Fein and for a time lived in same house as Maud Gonne and Charlotte Despard; worked for republican publicity but was arrested after civil war had broken out (1922); released from prison (1923); published *Tragedies of Kerry* (1924), one of her most famous books; wrote several plays, one of which, *Dark Waters*, was performed at Gate Theater (1932); also published volumes of short stories; when Eamon de Valera founded Fianna Fail, was elected to the 1st executive (1926) and became drama critic and regular feature writer on his newspaper, the *Irish Press* (1931); was also a frequent broadcaster on Irish radio; published *The Irish Republic* (1937), a massive chronicle which for decades was the standard reference work on the period; saw 2 of her novels, *Uneasy Freehold* and *The Uninvited*, made into successful films; during WWII, worked for refugee causes, resulting in *Children of Europe* (1949); was vice-president of Irish Association for Civil Liberties (late 1940s). ❖ See also *Women in World History*.

MACARTHUR, Elizabeth (1767–1850). English diarist and letter writer. Name variations: Elizabeth Veale Macarthur. Born Elizabeth Veale in 1767 (some sources cite 1768 or 1769), in Devon, England; died in Australia, 1850; dau. of Richard Veale (farmer) and Grace (Hatherley) Veale; m. John Macarthur (Scottish soldier), 1788, in England; children:

9, one of whom died in infancy; grandmother of Elizabeth Macarthur-Onslow (1840–1911). ❖ Pioneer in the Australian wool industry, accompanied husband to Botany Bay in NSW, Australia (1788); with husband, established Elizabeth Farm at Camden Park (1793), founded initial colonial wool trade, and was 1st to establish sheep farming in NSW; while husband lived in exile for 8 years because of participation in Rum Rebellion (1809–17), ran wool business in correspondence with him; was responsible for increasing flocks and expanding sales to English market, establishing NSW as a noted wool-producing region, and founding Australian wool industry overall; retired as manager of Elizabeth Farm (1817) upon husband's return; following his death (1834), again managed wool operation with sons. ❖ See also *Women in World History*.

MACARTHUR, Ellen (1976—). British sailor. Born July 8, 1976, in Derbyshire, England. ❖ At 18, sailed alone around Britain; won her class on an Open 50 in Route Du Rhum transatlantic race (1998, 2003), setting a record of 13 days, 13 hrs., 31 mins., 47 secs. (2030); won Europe 1 New Man Star (2000); placed 2nd overall in the Vendée Globe, the 2nd fastest cirumnavigation in the history of the event (2000–01); broke the round-the-world record in 71 days, 14 hrs., 18 mins. and 22 secs. (Nov 28, 2004–Feb 7, 2005). Named Yachtsman of the Year; named Member of the British Empire (2002). ❖ See also autobiography *Ellen MacArthur: Taking on the World* (2003).

MACARTHUR, Mary (1930–1949). American actress. Born Feb 15, 1930, in New York, NY; died Sept 22, 1949, age 19, of polio, in NYC; dau. of Charles MacArthur (playwright) and Helen Hayes (actress, 1900–1993); sister of James MacArthur (actor); graduate of American Academy of Dramatic Arts. ❖ Made stage debut with mother in *Alice Sit-By-the-Fire* in New Hope, PA; toured with Lillian Gish in *The Marquise*; was resident ingenue at Olney (MD) Theater for 2 seasons; appeared with mother in *Good Housekeeping* on summer tour (1949).

MACARTHUR, Mary Reid (1880–1921). Scottish trade unionist. Name variations: Mary Reid Anderson; Mary Reid MacArthur. Born Mary Reid Macarthur in Glasgow, Scotland, 1880; died of cancer in 1921; dau. of a Conservative Glasgow draper; attended Glasgow Girls' High School, followed by a year of study in Germany, 1896; m. Will C. Anderson, 1911; children: 2, one of whom died at birth. ❖ Was a member of the Shop Assistants' Union (1901); served as president of Scottish National District of the Union (1902); as secretary of Women's Trade Union League (WTUL, 1903–21), is credit with revitalizing the WTUL, vastly increasing its membership and its clout; was a delegate to International Congress of Women (1904, 1908); was founder and 1st president of National Federation of Working Women (1906); established and served as editor of journal *Woman Worker* (1907–09); was a member of National Council of the Independent Labour Party (1909–12) and Central Committee of Women's Training and Employment (1914–18); was a Labour candidate for Parliament (1918). ❖ See also *Women in World History*.

MACARTHUR-ONSLOW, Elizabeth (1840–1911). Australian property owner and businesswoman. Born May 8, 1840, at Camden Park, Menangle, NSW, Australia; died Aug 2, 1911, while visiting England; only child of James Macarthur and Emily (Stone) Macarthur; granddau. of Australian wool industry pioneers Elizabeth Macarthur (1767–1850) and John Macarthur; m. Arthur Alexander Walton Onslow (navy captain), Jan 31, 1867 (died 1882); children: 6 sons, 2 daughters. ❖ With father's death (1867), inherited a share in Camden Park as well as valuable real estate elsewhere in the state; established profitable dairies and a central creamery at Camden Park (1892); also planted mulberry trees at the estate to use in breeding silkworms for raw silk, and was a member of the Women's Cooperative Silk-Growing and Industrial Association and the Victorian Silk Culture Association; converted family estate into a corporation (1899), naming her children as shareholders and thus consolidating the fortune. ❖ See also *Women in World History*.

MACAULAY, Catharine (1731–1791). British historian and political activist. Name variations: Catherine or Catharine Macaulay-Graham; Catherine Graham Macaulay; Catherine Sawbridge Macaulay. Born Catharine Sawbridge, April 2, 1731, at Olantigh, the family estate near Wye, Kent, England; died in Binfield, Berkshire, June 22, 1791, of a long illness; dau. of John Sawbridge (wealthy country gentleman) and Elizabeth Wanley Sawbridge (heiress); largely self-educated; m. Dr. George Macaulay (Scottish physician), June 1760 (died 1766); m. William Graham, 1778; children: (1st m.) Catharine Sophia Macaulay, born sometime between 1760 and 1766. ❖ Controversial British historian, political radical, and champion of women's education who was an ardent supporter of America in

18th-century England; moved to London following marriage (1760); published 1st volume of *History of England* (1763), a bombshell that elicited reactions from admiration to ridicule, since, according to the thinking of the time, women were not capable of understanding or writing history; published 7 additional vols. intermittently until 1783; moved to Bath (1774); corresponded with a number of American leaders such as John Adams and James Otis, a leader of opposition to British rule (1770s); spent 1 year in America, including 10 days at Mount Vernon with the Washingtons (1784–85); published *Letters on Education With Observations on Religious and Metaphysical Subjects* (1790), a vol. of "letters" to a fictitious friend which sums up her philosophies on topics ranging from human nature to the institutionalized church and Christianity, good government, cruelty to animals, penology, the problem of pain and evil, relations between the sexes, intellectual abilities of women, and the education of children; was one of the most famous women in England. ❖ See also Bridget Hill, *The Republican Virago: The Life and Times of Catharine Macaulay, Historian* (Oxford U. Press, 1992); and *Women in World History*.

MACAULAY, Rose (1881–1958). British novelist, poet, historian, journalist, literary critic, anthologist, travel writer, and broadcaster. Name variations: Emilie Macaulay; Dame Rose Macaulay. Born Emilie Rose Macaulay, Aug 1, 1881, in Rugby, England; died Oct 30, 1958, in London of coronary thrombosis; dau. of Grace Mary (Conybeare) Macaulay and George Campbell Macaulay (literary critic and translator); Somerville College, Oxford University, 1900–03. ❖ Known for her caustic wit, satirical comedy, and, in later life, religious quest, published 1st novel *Abbots Verney* (1906), followed by *The Furnace* (1907), *The Secret River* (1909) and *The Valley Captives* (1911), all of which asserted the values of conventional lifestyles and virtuous behavior; had popular success with 10th novel, *Potterism* (1920); was central to London literary world (1922–58), with such novels as *Mystery at Geneva* (1922), *Told by an Idiot* (1923), *Orphan Island* (1924), *Crewe Train* (1926), *Keeping Up Appearances* (1928) and *Staying With Relations* (1930); published 2 collections of essays, *A Casual Commentary* (1925) and *Catchwords and Claptrap* (1926); began to write regular column, "Notes on the Margin," for *Time and Tide* (1932) and weekly column, "Marginal Comments," for *The Spectator* (1936); published 23 novels of social satire and moral quest, a critical biography of Milton, 5 books of criticism, 4 books of history and travel, 2 vols. of poetry, an anthology, plus numerous book reviews and essays (1906–56); was a frequent BBC radio performer (1934–54). Won Femina-Vie Heureuse Prize for *Dangerous Ages* (1921); won James Tait Black Prize for *The Towers of Trebizond* (1956); named Dame Commander of the British Empire (1958). ❖ See also (letters) *Letters to a Friend: 1950–1952* (1961), *Last Letters to a Friend: 1952–1958* (1962), *Letters to a Sister* (1964); Jane Emery, *Rose Macaulay: A Writer's Life* (John Murray, 1991); Contance Babington Smith, *Rose Macaulay* (Collins, 1972); and *Women in World History*.

MACBETH, Lady (fl. 1020–1054). See Gruoch.

MACBRIDE, Maud Gonne (1866–1953). See Gonne, Maud.

MACCOLL, Kirsty (1959–2000). English singer and songwriter. Born Oct 10, 1959, in London, England; died Dec 18, 2000, in Cozumel, Mexico; dau. of Ewen MacColl (folk musician); m. Steve Lillywhite (music producer), 1984 (div. 1997); children: 2 sons. ❖ Collaborated with Rolling Stones, Talking Heads, and Van Morrison, among others, and was known for witty but moving songs; signed with Stiff Records at 16; had unsuccessful debut single "They Don't Know" (1979), which became hit for Tracey Ullman in UK (1983); mixed country, rockabilly, and pop in "Chip Shop" and *Desperate Character* (1981); had one of UK's biggest Christmas hits, "Fairytale of New York" (1987), a duet with the Pogues' Shane McGowan; released 1st US album, *Kite* (1989), then *Electric Landlady* (1991), both featuring collaborations with guitarists Johnny Marr, Mark E. Nevin, and Marshall Crenshaw; released *Titanic Days* (1993) and *Galore* (1995); made guest appearances on recordings, including for Billy Bragg (late 1990s); released *Tropical Brainstorm* and *What Do Pretty Girls Do?* (2000), a collection of BBC radio sessions (recorded 1989–95).

MACDONALD, Annette (1944—). See Av-Paul, Annette.

MACDONALD, Barbara K. (1957—). American musician. Name variations: Barbara K., Timbuk 3. Born Oct 4, 1957, in Wausau, WI; m. Pat MacDonald (musician), 1983 (div. 1997). ❖ With husband, formed alternative-pop duo Timbuk 3 in Madison, WI (1984), for which she sang, played guitar, violin, mandolin, and harmonica; using pre-recorded tracks on boombox for rhythm section, released *Greetings from Timbuk 3* (1986), which included hit single, "The Future's So Bright, I Gotta Wear

Shades"; other albums include *Eden Alley* (1988), *Big Shot in the Dark* (1991), and *A Hundred Lovers* (1995); after divorce, continued to perform in Austin clubs as Barbara K.

MACDONALD, Betty (1908–1958). American humorist. Name variations: Anne Bard; Betty Bard MacDonald; Betty Heskett MacDonald. Born Anne Elizabeth Campbell Bard, Mar 26, 1908, in Boulder, CO; died Feb 7, 1958, in Seattle, WA; dau. of Darsie Campbell Bard (mining engineer) and Elsie Tholimar (Sanderson) Bard; sister of Mary Bard (1904–1970, writer); attended University of Washington in Seattle; m. Robert Eugene Heskett, 1927 (div.); m. Donald Chauncey MacDonald, April 24, 1942; children: (1st m.) Anne Elizabeth Heskett; Joan Sydney Heskett. ❖ Writer whose life provided material for several humorous, bestselling autobiographical books; operated small chicken farm with 1st husband (1927–31); pursued business career (1931–43); began writing career (1943); published bestseller *The Egg and I* (1945); also published *The Plague and I*, *Anybody Can Do Anything*, and *Onions in the Stew* (1948–55); published several children's books in "Mrs. Piggle-Wiggle" series (1947–57). ❖ See also *Women in World History*.

MACDONALD, Blossom (1895–1978). American actress. Name variations: Marie Blake; Blossom Rock. Born Edith Blossom MacDonald, Aug 21, 1895, in Philadelphia, PA; died Jan 14, 1978, in Woodland Hills, CA; sister of Elsie MacDonald and Jeanette MacDonald (1903–1965, actress); m. Clarence Rock (actor), 1926 (died 1960). ❖ Toured with husband in vaudeville; made films under name Marie Blake (1938–48), including *Mannequin, Love Finds Andy Hardy, Calling Dr. Kildare, Blind Alley, Secret of Dr. Kildare* and *Mourning Becomes Electra*; under name Blossom Rock, best known as grandmama in tv series "The Addams Family."

MACDONALD, Christie (1875–1962). American musical-comedy star. Born 1875; died July 25, 1962, in Fairfield, CT; children: Christie Fanton. ❖ Made stage debut in *Puritania* (1892); had greatest success in Victor Herbert's operettas *The Spring Maid* and *Sweethearts* which he wrote for her; other plays include *Erminie, Princess Chic, The Toreador, Champagne Charlie, An English Daisy, Miss Hook of Holland* and *The Belle of Mayfair*; also appeared in all-star revival of *The Mikado*.

MACDONALD, Cordelia Howard (1848–1941). See Howard, Cordelia.

MACDONALD, Elaine (1943—). Scottish ballerina. Born 1943 in Tadcaster, Scotland; trained with Olivia Morley in Scarborough and Louise Brown in York; attended Royal Ballet School (1958). ❖ Joined Western Theater Ballet (1964); traveled with company and director Peter Darrell to Glasgow (1969), becoming founding member of Scottish Ballet as well as leading ballerina (1969–89); premiered many original pieces choreographed by Darrell, including *Sun Into Darkness* (1966), *Beauty and the Beast* (1969), *Tales of Hoffmann* (1972), *Mary, Queen of Scots* (1976) and *Five Ruckert Songs* (1978); performed outside Scotland as well, dancing leads in *La Sylphide, Giselle* and *Swan Lake*; served as artistic controller of company (1988–89) after Darrell's death; appointed associate artistic director of Northern Ballet Theater (1990). Awarded Officer of British Empire (OBE, 1983).

MACDONALD, Elizabeth Roberts (1864–1922). Canadian poet and short-story writer. Name variations: Jane Elizabeth Gostwycke Roberts; Elizabeth Roberts; Elizabeth Roberts MacDonald. Born Jane Elizabeth Gostwycke Roberts, Feb 17, 1864, in the rectory of Westcock, New Brunswick; died Nov 8, 1922, in Ottawa; dau. of George Goodridge Roberts (Anglican cleric) and Emma (Wetmore) Bliss; sister of Sir Charles G.D. Roberts; graduate of University of New Brunswick; married cousin Samuel Archibald Roberts MacDonald, 1896 (sep. 1914); children: 3, including C. Goodridge Roberts (poet). ❖ Taught at School for Blind in Halifax (1890–92); published 1st collection, *Poems* (1888); with brothers, published *Northland Lyrics* (1899); released her major work, *Dream Verses and Others* (1906); was a prominent member of Canadian Authors' Association and Women's Suffrage Association.

MACDONALD, Finula (fl. 1569–1592). Queen of Tirconnell (or Tir Chonaill). Name variations: (nickname) Inghean Dubh; Finula O'Donnell. Fl. between 1569 and 1592; dau. of James MacDonald of Isla and Agnes (Campbell) MacDonald; m. Hugh O'Donnell, king of Tirconnell or Tir Chonaill, in 1569; children: Hugh Roe O'Donnell, known as Red Hugh (1572–1602, who m. Finula O'Neill); Ruaidhrí O'Donnell (1575–1608); daughter Nuala O'Donnell (fl. 1608–1617); and at least 2 other sons; grandmother of Mary Stuart O'Donnell. ❖ See also *Women in World History*.

MACDONALD, Fiona (1974—). Scottish curler. Name variations: Fiona Brown. Born Fiona Brown, Dec 9, 1974, in Paisley, Scotland; m. Ewan MacDonald. ❖ Won World Jr. championship (1993); won a team gold medal for curling at Salt Lake City Olympics (2002).

MACDONALD, Flora (1722–1790). Scottish heroine. Born Fionnghal nighean Raonuill'ic Aonghais Oig, an Airidh Mhuillinn (Gaelic for "Flora, dau. of Ranald, son of Aungus, Younger of Milton"), in 1722; died 1790; dau. of Ranald Macdonald of Milton, South Uist, and Marian Macdonald; m. Allan Macdonald (key figure in the fight to save North Carolina for the king), 1750; children: 2 daughters (including Anne) and 5 sons (including Charles, Alexander, and James). ❖ Ferried Bonnie Prince Charlie out of danger to the Isle of Skye after the failure of his rebellion against George II (1746); was imprisoned in the Tower of London (1746–47), but Londoners soon began to treat her not as a traitor or conspirator but as a romantic heroine; was freed as part of the terms of a General Indemnity (1747); facing hard times, immigrated to North Carolina with husband and bought a large plantation, "Killiegray," consisting of 70 acres of arable fields and a group of orchards (1774); when Revolutionary War began, was a staunch opponent of the Revolution and defender of King George III; was riding with husband the day his column was ambushed at the Battle of Moore's Creek Bridge and he and their sons were taken prisoner (1776); reunited with husband in NY (1778), spent winter in Nova Scotia followed by return to Scotland (1779). ❖ See also Hugh Douglas, *Flora Macdonald: The Most Loyal Rebel* (Sutton, 1993); and *Women in World History*.

MACDONALD, Frances (1874–1921). English-born artist and designer. Born Frances Macdonald, 1874, in Glasgow, Scotland; died 1921; sister of Margaret Mackintosh (1865–1933); studied at Glasgow College of Art; m. J.L. Herbert MacNair (painter), 1899. ❖ A member of the Glasgow group, painted portraits and figurative subjects; with sister, opened a studio (1894) and worked with stained glass, metal, embroidery, and illustration; exhibited in Vienna (1900) and at Turin (1902); following marriage, moved to Liverpool, teaching arts and crafts there at the university; returned to Glasgow (1907) where she taught various crafts. ❖ See also *Women in World History*.

MACDONALD, Georgiana (1840–1920). English painter. Name variations: Lady Georgiana Burne-Jones. Born 1840; died 1920; dau. of Rev. George Macdonald (not the writer) and Hannah Macdonald; sister of Alice Macdonald (1837–1910), who was the mother of Rudyard Kipling, Agnes Macdonald (1843–1906), who married painter Edward Poynter, and Louisa Macdonald (1845–1925), who was the mother of Prime Minister Stanley Baldwin; studied drawing at Government School of Design, Gore House; m. painter Edward Burne-Jones (1833–1898), 1860; children: Philip Burne-Jones (1861–1926, portrait painter) and Margaret Burne-Jones Mackail (1866–1953, who m. John William Mackail); grandmother of Angela Thirkell (writer). ❖ Worked in woodcuts and was a close friend of George Eliot (Mary Anne Evans). ❖ See also Ina Taylor, *Victorian Sisters* (1987).

MACDONALD, Irene (1933–2002). Canadian diver. Born Nov 22, 1933, in Hamilton, Ontario, Canada; died June 2002 in Lower Mainland, Canada. ❖ At Melbourne, won a bronze medal in springboard (1956), capturing Canada's 1st Olympic medal in diving; at Empire Games, won a bronze medal (1954) and a silver medal (1958); was 15-time Canadian champion, 6-time US champion, and 2-time Mexican champion; was a tv sports analyst for CBC (1976–88) and also a coach. Inducted into Canadian Sports Hall of Fame (1981).

MACDONALD, Isabella (1809–1857). Canadian wife of John A. Macdonald. Born 1809; died Dec 28, 1857; m. John A. Macdonald (prime minister of Canada, 1867–73, 1878–91), Sept 1, 1843; children: John Alexander (1847–1848), Hugh John Macdonald (1850–1929, MP 1891–93). ❖ Died before husband took office; was an invalid for much of their married life.

MACDONALD, Jane Elizabeth Gostwycke (1864–1922). *See MacDonald, Elizabeth Roberts.*

MACDONALD, Jeanette (1903–1965). American light-opera singer and actress. Name variations: Jeanette MacDonald Raymond. Born Jeanette Anna MacDonald in Philadelphia, PA, June 18, 1903; died while preparing for open heart surgery, Jan 14, 1965, in Houston, TX; sister of actress Blossom MacDonald; m. Gene Raymond (actor), 1937. ❖ At 4, appeared in "mini operas" (1907); toured East Coast summer resorts with Al White's "Six Sunny Song Birds" (1914); joined sister Blossom in *The Demi-Tasse Revue* in NYC (1919); quit school to appear in

Broadway's *The Night Boat* (1920); after several small parts, played a lead in *A Fantastic Fricassee* and had a secondary career in modeling (1922); received star billing in *Yes, Yes, Yvette* (1927); while appearing in title role of Broadway's *Angela*, made screen test at Paramount in NY (1928–29); starred in movie *The Love Parade* (1929); after several films with Paramount and Fox, signed with MGM and made *Naughty Marietta* with Nelson Eddy, one of the 100 top-grossing films in history (1935); made 7 more pictures with Eddy in next 6 years: *Rose Marie* (1936), *Maytime* (1937), *The Girl of the Golden West* (1938), *Sweethearts* (1938), *New Moon* (1940), *Bitter Sweet* (1940) and *I Married an Angel* (1942); toured in concert (1939); debuted as Juliette in Gounod's opera, *Romeo et Juliette*, in Montreal (1943); other films include *San Francisco* (1936), *Broadway Serenade* (1939), *Smilin' Through* (1941) and *Follow the Boys* (1944). ❖ See also *Women in World History*.

MACDONALD, Katherine (1881–1956). American silent-film star. Born Katherine Agnew MacDonald, Dec 14, 1881, in Pittsburgh, PA; died June 4, 1956, in Santa Barbara, CA; sister of Mary MacLaren (1896–1985, actress). ❖ Known as the "American Beauty"; films include *The Squaw Man, The Thunderbolt, Headin' South, The Infidel, The Notorious Miss Lisle, Refuge, The Beautiful Liar* and *New Loves for Old*. Rumored to be the mistress of Woodrow Wilson.

MACDONALD, Lady (1836–1920). *See Macdonald, Susan Agnes.*

MACDONALD, Linsey (1964—). Scottish runner. Name variations: also seen as Linsey MacDonald. Born Feb 14, 1964, in Dunfermline, Scotland. ❖ At Moscow Olympics, won a bronze medal in 4x400-meter relay (1980); won UK 400-meter indoor championship (1985).

MACDONALD, Lucy Maud (1874–1942). *See Montgomery, Lucy Maud.*

MACDONALD, Marcia (1865–1947). *See Hill, Grace Livingston.*

MACDONALD, Margaret (1865–1933). *See Mackintosh, Margaret.*

MACDONALD, Margaret (c. 1907–1956). English philosopher. Born in England c. 1907, an abandoned child; had surgery at St. Thomas Hospital in London, to treat a heart condition, but died in recovery, Jan 7, 1956; fellow of Girton College, Cambridge University, 1932; granted PhD, Bedford College, by 1938. ❖ Was a lecturer at St. Hilda's College, Oxford University, from 1938; edited the academic philosophy journal *Analysis;* writings include notes from Ludwig Wittgenstein's lectures and discussions, published as *The Blue and Yellow (or Brown) Books,* and *Art and Imagination* (1953).

MACDONALD, Margo (c. 1948—). Scottish politician. Born c. 1948. ❖ Formerly MP for Govan; served as president of the Edinburgh University Federation of Student Nationalists; was SNP deputy leader (1974–79); as an Independent, elected to the Scottish Parliament for Lothians.

MACDONALD, Noel (1915—). Canadian basketball player. Name variations: Noel MacDonald Robertson. Born 1915 in Mortlach, Saskatchewan, Canada; m. Harry Robertson, 1939 (hockey player). ❖ Played 135 games for the powerful Edmonton Grads (1933–39), scoring 1,874 points for a 13.9 per game average, the best in the club's history; named captain (1936). Inducted into Canadian Sports Hall of Fame.

MACDONALD, Susan Agnes (1836–1920). Canadian first lady. Name variations: Baroness Macdonald of Earnscliffe; Lady Macdonald. Born Susan Agnes Bernard, Aug 24, 1836, in Jamaica; died Sept 5, 1920; buried in Highgate Cemetery, England; dau. of Theodora Foulks Bernard and T.J. Bernard (member of Privy Council, Island of Jamaica); m. John A. Macdonald (prime minister of Canada, 1867–73, 1878–91), Feb 16, 1867 (died June 6, 1891); children: Margaret Mary Theodora Macdonald (1869–1933). ❖ Second wife of John A. Macdonald, headed a movement for the establishment of an art museum and industrial college; following husband's death, moved back to England.

MACDONALD OF EARNSCLIFFE, Baroness (1836–1920). *See Macdonald, Susan Agnes.*

MACDOWELL, Marian (1857–1956). American arts colony founder. Name variations: Marian Griswold Nevins MacDowell; Marian Griswold MacDowell; Mrs. Edward MacDowell. Born Marian Griswold Nevins, Nov 22, 1857, in New York, NY; died in Los Angeles, California, Aug 23, 1956; dau. of David Henry Nevins (banker and broker) and Cornelia (Perkins) Nevins; briefly attended school in New London, Connecticut, but was largely educated by father; m. Edward Alexander MacDowell (1st internationally known American composer), July 9, 1884 (died 1908); no children. ❖ Was the founder and tireless champion for nearly half a century of the MacDowell Colony, America's premier artists' colony, in Peterborough, New Hampshire. ❖ See also *Women in World History.*

MACDOWELL, Susan Hannah (1851–1938). *See Eakins, Susan Hannah.*

MACEDONIA, queen of.
See Thessalonike (c. 345–297 BCE).
See Statira III (fl. 324 BCE).
See Phila II (c. 300 BCE–?).
See Nicaea (fl. 300 BCE).

MACENTEE, Maire (b. 1922). *See Mhac An tSaoi, Máire.*

MACEO, Mariana Grajales de (1808–1893). *See Grajales, Mariana.*

MACEWEN, Gwendolyn (1941–1987). Canadian poet, novelist, short story and children's writer. Born Gwendolyn Margaret MacEwen, Sept 1, 1941, in Toronto, Ontario, Canada; died Nov 30, 1987, in Toronto; dau. of Alick James MacEwen and Elsie Doris (Mitchell) MacEwen; m. poet Milton Acorn (div.); m. Nikos Tsingos (Greek singer), 1971 (div. 1978). ❖ At 17, published 1st poem in *The Canadian Forum*; helped edit the journal *Moment* (1960–62); published 1st two chapbooks of poetry, *Selah* and *The Drunken Clock* (1961); established reputation as a poet with *A Breakfast for Barbarians* (1966) and *The Shadow-maker* (1969); published a novel about Egyptian pharaoh Akhenaton, *King of Egypt, King of Dreams* (1971), the poetry collections *The Armies of the Moon* (1972), *Magic Animals* (1975), and *The Fire-Eaters* (1976), as well as the travel documentary *Mermaids and Ikons: A Greek Summer* (1978); served as writer in residence at University of Western Ontario (1984–85) and University of Toronto; published what critics regard as the most complete synthesis of her canon, *The T.E. Lawrence Poems* (1982), followed by *Afterworlds* (1987). Received DuMaurier Gold and Silver Awards (1983) and Governor-General's Award for Poetry (1970, 1987). ❖ See also *Women in World History.*

MACFADDEN, Gertrude (c. 1900–1967). American actress. Name variations: Mickey MacFadden. Born c. 1900; died June 3, 1967, age 67, in Hollywood, CA; m. Harry Dornan; children: 3 sons. ❖ With her sister, performed as the MacFadden Sisters in vaudeville and Ziegfeld Follies; appeared in several films.

MACFADDEN, Mickey (c. 1900–1967). *See MacFadden, Gertrude.*

MACFALL, Frances E. (1854–1943). British novelist. Name variations: Frances Elizabeth MacFall, McFall, or M'Fall; Frances Bellenden-Clarke; Frances Elizabeth Clarke; (pseudonym) Sarah Grand. Born Frances Elizabeth Bellenden-Clarke in Donaghadee, Co. Down, Northern Ireland, 1854; died in Bath, Calne, Wiltshire, May 12, 1943; dau. of Edward John Bellenden-Clarke (lieutenant in Royal Navy) and Margaret Bell (Sherwood) Bellenden-Clarke; m. David MacFall (army surgeon), 1870 (sep.); children: 1 son. ❖ Spent formative years in Northern Ireland, then went to live with mother's family in England after father's death (1861); eloped at 16 with an army surgeon 23 years her senior, a widower with 2 children; with husband, traveled to Hong Kong and the Far East for 5 years, then returned to England; completed 1st novel *Ideals* (1888), under pseudonym Sarah Grand; with profits from *Ideals*, permanently separated from husband; established reputation with 2 feminist novels, *The Heavenly Twins* (1893) and *The Beth Book* (1898); was extremely active in the suffrage campaign, joining the Women Writers' Suffrage League; later works include *Adnam's Orchard* (1912) and *The Winged Victory* (1916); moved to Bath (1920), where she was elected mayor for 6 separate terms. ❖ See also *Women in World History.*

MACFARLANE, Edith Mary (1871–1948). New Zealand community worker. Name variations: Edith Mary Durrieu. Born Edith Mary Durrieu, May 20, 1871, at Torquay, Devonshire, England; died on Dec 2, 1948, in Auckland, New Zealand; dau. of Louis Adolphus Durrieu (accountant) and Marianne (Feltham) Durrieu; m. James Buchanan Macfarlane (mercantile firm owner), 1890; children: 6. ❖ Immigrated as child to New Zealand (c. 1873); active in patriotic and welfare societies formed during World Wars I and II; remained active in New Zealand Branch of British Red Cross Society, Victoria League, and Auckland Women's Patriotic League, and organized numerous charitable benefits; also member of free kindergarten movement for many years. Received Order of British Empire (1919). ❖ See also *Dictionary of New Zealand Biography* (Vol. 3).

MACGIBBON, Harriet (1905–1987). American stage, tv, and screen actress. Name variations: Harriet E. MacGibbon. Born Oct 5, 1905, in Chicago, IL; died Feb 8, 1987, in Beverly Hills, CA; m. Charles C. White (died); m. William R. Kane (div.). ❖ Made Broadway debut in *Beggar on Horseback* (1928), followed by *Ringside, The Marriage Bed, Houseparty, Midnight, The Inside Story, Our Betters, Lightnin'* and *The Ladies of the Corridor*, among others; probably best remembered as Mrs. Drysdale on tv series "Beverly Hillbillies."

MACGILL, Elsie (d. 1980). Canadian aeronautical engineer and feminist. Name variations: Elizabeth MacGill; E.G. MacGill; (incorrectly) McGill. Born Elizabeth Gregory MacGill; died 1980; dau. of Helen Gregory MacGill (1871–1947) and James H. MacGill; married 1943 but continued to use maiden name. ❖ The 1st woman to graduate in electrical engineering from University of Toronto (1927) and 1st woman to graduate from University of Michigan's master's program in aeronautical engineering (1929), was hired by Fairchild Aircraft Ltd in Montreal (1934); worked as chief aeronautical engineer for the Canadian Car and Foundry Co., where she designed the Maple Leaf Trainer, possibly the 1st airplane designed by a woman; during WWII, was the engineer in charge of Canadian production of the Hawker Hurricane fighter plane at Fort William, Ontario, with a staff of 4,500; after the war, started her own business as a consulting aeronautical engineer in Toronto, was a prominent member of Toronto Business and Professional Women's Club, and campaigned on issues involving paid maternity leave, day-care facilities, and liberalization of abortion laws; published biography of her mother, *My Mother the Judge* (1955). Received Gzowski Medal of Engineering Institute of Canada (1941) and an award for Meritorious Contribution to Engineering from Society of Women Engineers (1953); awarded Order of Canada (1971).

MACGILL, Helen Gregory (1871–1947). Canadian feminist and lawyer. Name variations: (incorrect) Helen McGill; Helen Gregory-Flesher; Helen Flesher. Born Helen Gregory into a socially prominent family in Hamilton, Ontario, Canada, 1871; died 1947; Trinity College, Toronto, BA, 1888, the only woman to graduate in that year's class; m. Dr. Lee Flesher (died 1901); m. James H. MacGill, 1902; children: (1st m.) 2 sons; (2nd m.) Elsie MacGill (d. 1980, aeronautical engineer). ❖ The 1st woman judge in British Columbia, served on the British Columbia juvenile court (1917–29, 1934–45); also served on the national level as a member of the Minimum Wage Board (1918), and as chair of the Mother's Pension Board (1920–21); founded the Vancouver Women's Press Club and University Women's Club; helped found the Vancouver Women's Building, and was active in welfare reform and women's rights issues throughout life. ❖ See also *Women in World History.*

MACGILL, Moyna (1895–1975). Irish actress. Name variations: Moyna McGill. Born Charlotte "Chattie" Lillian McIldowie, Dec 10, 1895, in Belfast, Ireland; died Nov 25, 1975, in Santa Monica, CA; m. Reginald Denham (director), 1919 (div. 1924); m. Edgar Lansbury (lumber merchant), 1924 (died 1935); children: (1st m.) Isolde Denham (b. 1920, actress); (2nd m.) Angela Lansbury (b. 1925, actress); twins Edgar and Bruce Lansbury (producers). ❖ Made London stage debut in *Love in a Cottage* (1918); appeared in many London stage productions before moving to US; films include *Gaslight, Frenchman's Creek, Picture of Dorian Gray, Black Beauty, Green Dolphin Street* and *Kind Lady.*

MACGILLAVRY, Carolina H. (1904–1993). Dutch crystallographer. Born Carolina Henriette MacGillavry, Jan 22, 1904, in Amsterdam, Netherlands; died May 9, 1993; dau. of Donald MacGillavry (neurosurgeon); Amsterdam's Gemeente University, PhD in chemistry, 1937. ❖ The 1st woman elected to the Dutch Academy of Sciences (1950), conducted important research on the Harker-Kasper equations, but failed to receive proper recognition (compared to Jerome Karle, winner of the Nobel Prize for work in the same area); began career assisting A. Smits at the Laboratory for General and Inorganic Chemistry in Amsterdam (1932–34); coedited *International Tables for X-ray Crystallography* (1948–66) and *Nederlandsch Tijdschrift voor Natuurkunde* (Dutch journal for natural science, 1942–59); at Gemeente University, served as a lecturer (1946–50), professor (1950–72) and emeritus professor (from 1972); worked with Ray Pepinsky at the Alabama Polytechnic Institute (1949).

MACGOYE, Marjorie Oludhe (1928—). Kenyan poet and novelist. Born 1928 in Southampton, England; studied at Royal Holloway and Birckbeck College; m. D.G.W. Oludhe-Macgoye (member of the Luo tribe); children: 4. ❖ Went to Kenya as missionary bookseller (1954); married a Kenyan and took citizenship (1964); works, which often focus on the tensions between British and African cultures, include *Growing up at Lima School* (1970), *Murder in Majengo* (1972), *Song of Nyarloka* (1977), *The Story of Kenya* (1986), *Street Life* (1987), *The Present*

Moment (1987) and *Homing In*; won the Sinclair Prize for *Coming to Birth* (1986).

MACGRATH, Leueen (1914–1992). English-born actress and playwright. Name variations: Leueen Kaufman; Mrs. George S. Kaufman. Born July 3, 1914, in London, England; died Mar 27, 1992, in London; m. Christopher Burn (div.); m. Desmond Davis (div.); m. Stephen Quinto (div.); m. George S. Kaufman (playwright), 1949 (div. 1957); m. Stephen Goodyear, 1962 (div.). ❖ Made 1st stage appearance in London in *Beggars in Hell*, followed by *The Night Club Queen, The Laughing Woman, Tovarich, No Exit, Pride and Prejudice, Lucretia, French Without Tears, Saloon Bar, Blossom Time* and *Edward, My Son*, among others; made Broadway debut in *Edward, My Son* (1948), followed by *The Enchanted, High Ground, Tiger at the Gates, Potting Shed*, among others; off-Broadway, appeared in *The Seagull* and *Tribute to Lili Lamont*; with husband George S. Kaufman, wrote *Small Hours, Fancy Meeting You Again* and *Silk Stockings*.

MACGRAW, Ali (1938—). American actress and model. Born Alice MacGraw, April 1, 1938, in Pound Ridge, NY; m. Bob Evans (producer), 1969 (div. 1972); m. Steve McQueen (actor), 1973 (div. 1978); children: Josh Evans (actor). ❖ Began career as fashion model; made film debut in *A Lovely Way to Die* (1968), followed by *Goodbye Columbus, The Getaway, Convoy, Players, Just Tell Me What You Want* and *Natural Causes*; on tv, appeared in the mini-series "The Winds of War" and "Dynasty." Nominated for Oscar as Best Actress for *Love Story* (1970). ❖ See also autobiography *Moving Pictures* (1991).

MACGREGOR, Esther Miller (1874–1961). Canadian novelist. Name variations: Mary Esther MacGregor; Esther Miller; (pseudonym) Marian Keith. Born Mary Esther Miller, 1874, in Rugby, Ontario, Canada; died 1961; dau. of John Miller; m. Rev. Donald C. MacGregor (minister of the Orillia Presbyterian church), 1909. ❖ Taught in Central School in Orillia; wrote religious biographies and novels, including *The Silver Maple* (1906), *The Black Bearded Barbarian: The Life of George Leslie Mackay of Formosa* (1912) and *Little Miss Melody* (1927).

MACGREGOR, Sue (1941—). English radio presenter. Name variations: Susan Katriona MacGregor. Born Aug 30, 1941, in Oxford, England; raised in South Africa; educated in Geneva at École de Commerce and in England at House of Citizenship. ❖ BBC radio broadcaster, began career in South Africa, hosting "Woman's World" (1962–67); returned to London and worked on BBC's "World at One," "World This Weekend" and "PM," before beginning 15-year position as announcer-producer on "Woman's Hour" (1972–87); also worked on "Tuesday Call" (1973–86) and her own radio series, "Conversation Piece" (1978–94); was host of news and current affairs program "Today" (1984–2002) and appeared on tv with "Around Westminster" (1990–92); continued working intermittently after retirement, presenting "A Good Read" and "The Reunion" (2004). Made Officer of British Empire (OBE, 1992) and Commander of British Empire (CBE, 2002). ❖ See also Sue MacGregor, *Women of Today* (Headline, 2002).

MACHADO, Gilka (1893–1980). Brazilian poet. Name variations: Gilka da Costa de Melo Machado. Born Mar 12, 1893, in Rio de Janeiro, Brazil; died 1980 in Rio de Janeiro; m. Rodolfo de Melo Machado (died 1923). ❖ Worked for Rio Railway Co.; poetry collections include *Cristais partidos* (1915), *Estado de alma* (1917), *Poesias: 1915–1917* (1918), *Mulher nu* (1922), *Meu glorioso pecado* (1928), *Sublimação* (1938), and *Velha poesia* (1965). Won Machado de Assis Prize from Academia Brasileira de Letras (1979).

MACHADO, Luz (1916–1999). Venezuelan poet, essayist and journalist. Name variations: Luz Machado de Arnao; (pseudonym) Agata Cruz. Born Mar 2, 1916, in Bolivar, Venezuela; died 1999. ❖ Studied law, philosophy, and literature; worked as journalist and was member of *Viernes* Group of poets; writings include *Variciones en tono de amor* (1943), *La espiga amarga* (1950), *Cartas al señor tiempo* (1959), *La casa por dentro* (1965), *La ciudad instantanea* (1969), *Retratos y tormentos* (1973), and *Crónicas sobre Guyana, 1946–68* (1984); epic poem "Canto al Orinoco" (1953) translated into French. Received National Literature Prize (1987).

MACHAR, Agnes Maule (1837–1927). Canadian poet, biographer and short-story writer. Name variations: (pseudonym) Fidelis. Born 1837 in Kingston, Ontario, Canada; died 1927; dau. of Rev. John Machar (Presbyterian minister) and Margaret Machar. ❖ Social activist, worked for labor reform, temperance, and women's rights; wrote poetry, Christian stories, and patriotic and historical books; writings include

Lays of the 'True North' and Other Canadian Poems (1899) and *Roland Graeme, Knight: A Novel of Our Time* (1892); was also a watercolorist.

MACHEL, Graca (1946—). Mozambian lawyer, revolutionary and first lady. Name variations: Graca Mandela. Born Graca Simbine, 1946, in rural Mozambique; dau. of farmers; attended Lisbon University in Portugal; m. Samora Machel (founding president of Mozambique, 1975–86), 1975 (died in plane crash 1986); m. Nelson Mandela (president of South Africa), July 1998; children: (1st m.) Josina and Malengane (also raised 5 children from Samora's 3 other wives). ❖ Lawyer and freedom fighter, joined Frelimo Party (1973) which advocated independence from Portuguese colonial rule; with independence won, served as minister of education in Mozambique (1975–89); served as president of Foundation of Community Development and chair of National Organization of Children of Mozambique; supervised UN report on "The Impact of Armed Conflict on Children" (1997).

MACHNOW, Emy (1897–1974). Swedish swimmer. Born Sept 1, 1897, in Sweden; died Nov 23, 1974. ❖ At Antwerp Olympics, won a bronze medal in 4x100-meter freestyle relay (1920).

MACIEL MOTA, Miraildes (1978—). Brazilian soccer player. Name variations: known as Formiga. Born Mar 3, 1978, in Salvador, Brazil. ❖ Midfielder, won a team silver medal at Athens Olympics (2004).

MACINGHI, Alessandra (1406–1469). *See Strozzi, Alessandra.*

MACINNES, Helen (1907–1985). Scottish novelist. Name variations: Helen Clark; Helen Clark MacInnes; Helen Highet. Born Helen Clark MacInnes, Oct 7, 1907, in Glasgow, Scotland; died Sept 30, 1985, in New York, NY; dau. of Donald MacInnes and Jessica (McDiarmid) MacInnes; Glasgow University, MA, 1928; diploma in librarianship, University College, London, 1931; m. Gilbert Highet (classical scholar), 1932 (died 1978); children: 1 son. ❖ Known as the "Master Teller of Spy Stories," wrote 21 novels that detail a world of international adventure not dissimilar to her own globe-trotting exploits; immigrated to US (1937); wrote 1st novel *Above Suspicion* (1941), an immediate bestseller, followed by *Assignment in Brittany* (1942), *While Still We Live* (1944), *Horizon* (1945), *Rest and Be Thankful* (1949), *I and My True Love* (1953), *Decision at Delphi* (1960), *The Venetian Affair* (1963) and *Ride a Pale Horse* (1984); became US citizen (1951). ❖ See also *Women in World History*.

MACIVER, Loren (1909–1998). American artist. Born Loren Newman, Feb 2, 1909, in New York, NY; died May 3, 1998, in NY, NY; dau. of Charles Augustus Paul Newman and Julia MacIver Newman; m. Lloyd Frankenberg (poet), 1929 (died 1975). ❖ Acclaimed for her half-abstract landscapes, city views, and close-ups of inanimate objects, all rendered with luminous color, achieved 1st measure of fame while working on NY Federal Arts Project (1936–39); had 1st solo show (1938), at Marian Willard's East River Gallery, and a 2nd show at Pierre Matisse Gallery, which would continue to represent her until it closed 50 years later; among best-known pieces were *Hopscotch* (1940), *Oil Slick* (1940), *The Violet Hour* (1943), *Pushcart* (1944), *Tree* (1945), *Puddle* (1945), *Taxi* (1951), *Cathedral* (1949), *Dublin and Environs* (1950) and *Venice* (1949). ❖ See also *Women in World History*.

MACK, Helen (1913–1986). American actress. Name variations: Helen McAvity; Helen Macks. Born Helen McDougall, Nov 13, 1913, in Rock Island, IL; died Aug 13, 1986, in Beverly Hills, CA; m. Thomas McAvity (died 1974). ❖ Began as a child star on stage and in silent films on East Coast; played leads and 2nd leads in talkies; films include *Zaza, Strange Holiday, My Girl Friday, All of Me, Melody Cruise, The Last Train from Madrid, Gambling Ship* and *Son of Kong*; co-authored the play *The Mating Dance* under married name, Helen McAvity.

MACK, Louise (1874–1935). Australian novelist and children's writer. Name variations: Mary Louise Mack Leyland. Born Marie Louise Hamilton Mack, 1874, in Hobart, Tasmania; died 1935; sister of Amy Mack (1876–1939, writer). ❖ Traveled in Europe; during WWI, served as the 1st women's war correspondent, filing from Belgium for the London *Daily Mail* and *Evening News* (1914), then published *A Woman's Experience in the Great War* (1915); later returned to Sydney; fiction for girls, which drew on her school experiences, includes *The World is Round* (18996), *Teens* (1897), *Girls Together* (1898), *Children of the Sun* (1904), *Teens Triumphant* (1933), and *The Maiden's Prayer* (1934); collaborated with Ethel Turner on girls' magazine *The Parthenon* and wrote "A Woman's Letter" for the literary journal *Bulletin*.

MACK, Marion (1902–1989). American actress and producer. Born Joey Marion McCreery, April 9, 1902, in Mammoth, Utah; died May 1, 1989, in Costa Mesa, CA; m. Louis Lewyn (producer), 1924 (died 1969). ❖ Co-starred as Annabelle Lee with Buster Keaton in *The General*; with husband, produced a series of shorts, including "Voice of Hollywood" and "Hollywood on Parade."

MACK, Nila (1891–1953). American actress, radio writer and producer. Name variations: Nila Mac. Born Nila Mac, Oct 24, 1891, in Arkansas City, Kansas; died Jan 20, 1953, in New York, NY; dau. of Carl Mac (engineer) and Margaret (Bowen) Mac; m. Roy Briant (actor and screenwriter), Mar 20, 1913 (died 1927). ❖ Radio producer who introduced the concept of having parts played by children on children's shows, began career as an actress with traveling repertory companies, including Alla Nazimova troupe; also worked in vaudeville and wrote scripts for films; performed on Broadway in *Eva the Fifth* (1928) and *Buckaroo* (1929); joined CBS in NYC, performing in Radio Guild productions, and in "Nit-Wits" and "Night Club Romances" (1929); was program director of Arkansas City radio station; was director of CBS radio's children's program, "The Adventures of Helen and Mary" (renamed "Let's Pretend" in 1934), and wrote adaptations, mostly of stories of Brothers Grimm, Hans Christian Andersen, and Arabian Nights, for shows (1930–53). "Let's Pretend" won almost 60 awards, including George Foster Peabody Award (1943).

MACK, Ruth (1897–1946). *See Brunswick, Ruth Mack.*

MACKAILL, Dorothy (1903–1990). English actress. Born Mar 4, 1903, in Hull, Yorkshire, England; died Aug 12, 1990, in Honolulu, HI; m. Lothar Mendes (director), 1926 (div. 1928); m. Neil Miller (singer), 1931 (div. 1934); m. Harold Patterson (orchid grower), 1934 (div. 1938). ❖ Began career as London show girl, then appeared in Ziegfeld Follies; made film debut in *The Face at the Window* (1920) and often co-starred with Jack Mulhall; other films include *The Fighting Blade, Chickie, The Lotus Eater, Joanna, The Streets of New York, Lady Be Good, The Man Who Came Back, The Dancer of Paris, Curtain at Eight* and *Bulldog Drummond at Bay*; retired and moved to Hawaii (1937), where she later made guest appearances on tv series "Hawaii Five-O."

MACKAY, Catherine Julia (1864–1944). New Zealand journalist and cook. Name variations: Catherine Julia Bilston, Katrine Mackay. Born Nov 12, 1864, at Merino, Australia; died Mar 28, 1944, at Christchurch, New Zealand; dau. of George Yarra Bilston (innkeeper) and Ellen Augustine (McElligott) Bilston; m. John William Mackay (auctioneer), 1890 (died 1919); children: 1 son, 1 daughter. ❖ Began writing career early, publishing novel, *Eve's Sacrifice*, serially in *Australian Journal*, in addition to several novelettes and short stories in *Australian, Hamilton Spectator* and *Sydney Bulletin* by age 17; worked as journalist at *Auckland Weekly News* (early 1900s); joined daily *New Zealand Times* in Wellington (1908); worked as cook on several North Canterbury sheep stations (1920s); returned to journalism, editing women's columns "Cookery Chats" and "Mutual Help" for *Weekly Press* (1926); published best-selling *Practical Home Cookery Chats and Recipes* (1929); also worked briefly for *New Zealand Life and Home Magazine* and contributed to numerous journals under nearly 20 pseudonyms. ❖ See also *Dictionary of New Zealand Biography* (Vol. 4).

MACKAY, Elizabeth (c. 1845–1897). New Zealand homemaker. Name variations: Elizabeth Ormiston. Born Elizabeth Ormiston, between 1842 and 1847, in Scotland; died Feb 1, 1897, at Trentham, New Zealand; dau. of Walter Ormiston (shepherd) and Mary (McKenzie) Ormiston; m. Robert Mackay (shepherd), 1862; children: 9, including Georgina Mackay and Jessie Mackay (poet). ❖ Immigrated with husband to New Zealand (1863); endured many privations, including living in a sod hut for 5 years; isolated while husband was away for long periods; daughter Jessie Mackay would later write about those early years. ❖ See also *Dictionary of New Zealand Biography* (Vol. 2).

MACKAY, Elizabeth Ann Louisa (1843–1908). New Zealand farmer, feminist, and inventor. Name variations: Elizabeth Ann Budge. Born Elizabeth Ann Budge, Jan 23, 1843, at Godmanchester, Huntingdonshire, England; died Aug 24, 1908, at Nelson, New Zealand; dau. of Matthew Budge (laborer) and Ann (Church) Budge; m. Robert Mackay, 1868; children: 1. ❖ Immigrated to New Zealand (1863); farmed an isolated piece of land with husband and owned 125 acres of her own; voiced feminist views and worked to address community's needs such as improved roads and fencing; later applied for patents for rheumatism ointment and for cooking utensil similar to saucepan/colander. ❖ See also *Dictionary of New Zealand Biography* (Vol. 2).

MACKAY, Jessie (1864–1938). New Zealand poet. Born Dec 15, 1864, in Rakaia Gorge, Canterbury, New Zealand; died Aug 23, 1938, in Christchurch, New Zealand; dau. of Robert Mackay (manager of a sheep station) and Elizabeth Ormiston Mackay (c. 1845–1897); sister of Georgina Mackay; never married; no children. ❖ The 1st significant native-born poet of New Zealand, worked as a journalist and was active in the suffrage movement in Christchurch; campaigned for prohibition, penal reform, and women's rights; writings, which were well known during her lifetime but later dismissed by critics, include *The Spirit of the Rangatira and Other Ballads* (1889), *The Sitter on the Rail and Other Poems* (1891), *From the Maori Sea* (1908), *Land of the Morning* (1909), *The Bride of the Rivers and Other Verses* (1926), *The Girl of the Drift* (1928), and *Vigil* (1935). ❖ See also *Dictionary of New Zealand Biography* (Vol. 2).

MACKAY, Katrine (1864–1944). *See Mackay, Catherine Julia.*

MACKAY, Maria Jane (1844–1933). New Zealand midwife and nurse. Name variations: Maria Jane Taylor. Born Maria Jane Taylor, July 21, 1844, on Norfolk Island, Australia; died on Feb 5, 1933, in Te Aroha, New Zealand; dau. of Thomas Taylor (convict guard) and Margaret (O'Sullivan) Taylor; m. John Joseph Mackay (farmer), 1862 (died 1908); children: 16. ❖ Immigrated with family to New Zealand (1846); managed family farm while husband was away guarding settlement (1860s); moved to East Tamaki farm after 1863, losing property (1890s); supported family by working as midwife and nurse to mining families in Karangahake and Waikino. ❖ See also *Dictionary of New Zealand Biography* (Vol. 2).

MACKAY, Mary (1855–1924). *See Corelli, Marie.*

MACKAY, Mona Innis (1892–1959). *See Tracy, Mona Innis.*

MACKAY, Nancy (1929—). Canadian runner. Born April 6, 1929. ❖ At London Olympics, won a bronze medal in the 4x100-meter relay (1948).

MACKELLAR, Dorothea (1885–1968). Australian poet. Born Isobel Marion Dorothea Mackellar on July 1, 1885, in Sydney, Australia; died Jan 14, 1968, in Paddington, Australia; dau. of Sir Charles Kinnaird Mackellar (physician and parliamentarian) and Marion (Buckland) Mackellar; attended lectures at Sydney University. ❖ Famed creator of "My Country," wrote many poems celebrating Australian countryside; 1st published poem, "Core of My Heart," appeared in London's *Spectator* (1908); created 1st draft of "My Country" while homesick in England, publishing it in the *Spectator* and later revising and including it in 1st published collection *The Closed Door* (1911); fell in love with English poet Patrick Chalmers; returned to Australia and sent letter telling of parents' permission to wed but it was lost in mail (Chalmers married another); continued to write and travel (1920s–30s), publishing work in well-known journals including *Harper's Magazine* and Sydney *Bulletin*; with Ruth Bedford, produced 3 novels; poetry collections include *The Witchmaid, Dreamharbour* and *Fancy Dress*. Awarded Officer of British Empire (OBE, 1968). ❖ See also *I Love a Sunburnt Country: The Diaries of Dorothea Mackellar* (1990); Adrienne Howley, *My Heart, My Country: The Story of Dorothea Mackellar* (U. of Queensland Press, 1990).

MACKENZIE, Ada (1891–1973). Canadian golfer. Name variations: Ada MacKenzie. Born Oct 30, 1891, in Toronto, Ontario, Canada; died Jan 25, 1973, in Richmond Hill, Ontario. ❖ Won Canadian Women's open five times (1919, 1925, 1926, 1933, 1935); won 9 Ontario Ladies' Open titles, 10 Toronto District Women's Open titles, and 8 Canadian Ladies' Senior G.A. championships; named Canada's Oustanding Women Athlete (1933); dominated women's golf in Canada; founded the Toronto Ladies' Golf and Tennis Club, the 1st women's golf club in the world (1924), allowing women to play seriously. Was 1st woman inducted into Canadian Golf Hall of Fame; also inducted into Ontario Golf Hall of Fame.

MACKENZIE, Gisele (1927–2003). Canadian singer. Born Gisele Marie-Louise LaFleche, Jan 10, 1927, in Winnipeg, Manitoba, Canada; died Sept 5, 2003, in Burbank, CA; attended Royal Conservatory of Music in Toronto; m. Robert Klein (div.); m. Robert J. Shuttleworth, 1958 (div.); children: (2nd m.) Gigi Downs and Mac Shuttleworth. ❖ Best known for regular appearances as a vocalist on tv's "Your Hit Parade" (1953–57); also starred on "The Gisele MacKenzie Show" (1957–58) and had hit record "Hard to Get"; made frequent guest appearances on "The Jack Benny Program," among others.

MACKENZIE, Jane (1825–1893). Canadian first lady. Born Jane Sym, Mar 22, 1825, in Perthshire, Scotland; died Mar 30, 1893; m. Alexander

MacKenzie (prime minister of Canada, 1873–1878), June 17, 1853 (died April 17, 1892).

MACKENZIE, Jean Kenyon (1874–1936). American missionary and writer. Born Jan 6, 1874, in Elgin, IL; died Sept 2, 1936, in New York, NY; dau. of Robert Mackenzie (pastor, president of San Francisco Theological Seminary [1909–11]) and Lydia Ann (McLeod) Mackenzie. ❖ Volunteered as Presbyterian missionary to German colony of Kamerun (1904–14); published 1st article in long association with *Atlantic Monthly* (1914); published 1st book, *Black Sheep: Adventures in West Africa* (1916); returned for 18-month stint in Kamerun (1916); short story "Exile and Postman" (1917) became minor classic. Books include *An African Trail* (1917), *The Story of a Fortunate Youth* (1920), *African Clearings* (1924), *The Trader's Wife* (1930), and poetry collection *The Venture* (1925).

MACKENZIE, Maria Elizabeth Frederica Stewart- (1783–1862). *See Stewart-Mackenzie, Maria.*

MACKENZIE, Midge (1938–2004). English filmmaker and feminist. Born Margaret Rose Mackenzie, Mar 6, 1938, in London, England; died Jan 28, 2004; briefly married to Peter Jepson-Henry (antiques dealer); lived with Frank Cvitanovich (Canadian director), 1967–76; children: (with Cvitanovich) Alexander (died 1978). ❖ Documentary filmmaker who chronicled and championed feminism, was best known for her highly successful documentary *Shoulder to Shoulder* shown on BBC2 (1975); filmed a Boston women's collective, which included Betty Friedan and Kate Millett, for *Women Talking*; made a documentary for Amnesty about abuses against women; taught film history at Harvard (1980); other documentaries include *I Stand Here Ironing* (1980), based on the stories of Tillie Olsen, and *Prisoners of Childhood* (1991), inspired by the books of Alice Miller.

MACKENZIE, Regla (1971—). *See Bell, Regla.*

MACKILLOP, Mary Helen (1842–1909). Australian religious leader and founder. Name variations: Mother Mary of the Cross; Mary Helen McKillop. Born Maria Ellen MacKillop, Jan 15, 1842, in Fitzroy, Melbourne, Australia; died Aug 8, 1909, in Sydney, Australia; dau. of Alexander MacKillop and Flora (MacDonald) MacKillop; educated in Melbourne public schools. ❖ Became the 1st sister in a new religious order, the Sisters of St. Joseph of the Sacred Heart (1866), the 1st such established on Australian soil by Australians; elected superior general (1875); continued to work to advance both her order and the cause of Catholic education throughout the region until her death; devoted much of her life to those who had been discarded by most of society, including rural and urban poor children, street people, prostitutes, ex-convicts, and unmarried mothers. ❖ See also *Women in World History.*

MACKIN, Catherine (1939–1982). American journalist. Name variations: Cassie Mackin. Born Catherine Patricia Mackin in Baltimore, MD, Aug 28, 1939; died in Towson, MD, Nov 20, 1982; dau. of Francis Michael Mackin and Catherine Gillooly Mackin; University of Maryland, BA, 1960; selected as a Nieman fellow in 1967 and enrolled in Harvard University's "Great Lectures" program. ❖ Began journalism career at Washington bureau of Hearst family newspapers; joined staff of Washington's NBC affiliate, WRC-TV (1969), where she spent 2 years as an investigative reporter and anchored a local news broadcast; while remaining based in Washington, took on responsibilities of a general assignment reporter for the network (1971–73); won national recognition (1972) when she became the 1st female tv floor reporter at the national political conventions; worked as a congressional correspondent for NBC (1973–77), concentrating on the Senate; was hired by ABC as a Washington correspondent (1977). ❖ See also *Women in World History.*

MACKINLAY, Jean Sterling (1882–1958). English actress. Born in 1882 in London, England; died Dec 15, 1958; m. E. Harcourt Williams (actor and director), 1908. ❖ Made stage debut (with F.R. Benson) in *Coriolanus* (1901), followed by *If I Were King, When a Man Marries, The Gay Lord Quex, A Pair of Spectacles, Arms and the Man* and *King Henry V* (as Katherine), among others; achieved more success with a series of dramatic and folksong recitals; was prominently associated with the movement for Children's Theatre in England and staged a series of children's matinees every Christmas for 27 years.

MACKINNON, Catherine A. (1946—). American feminist writer. Born Oct 1, 1946, in Minneapolis, Minnesota; Smith College, BA, 1968; Yale Law School, JD, 1977; Yale University, PhD, 1987. ❖ Legal scholar who pioneered legal claim for sexual harassment as a form of sex discrimination and published 1st book, *Sexual Harassment of Working Women: A Case of Sex Discrimination* (1979), was ultimately vindicated when US Supreme Court declared sexual harassment to be a form of discrimination (1986); with Andrea Dworkin, wrote *Pornography and Civil Rights* (1988); helped Women's Legal Education and Action Fund to craft approaches which were adopted by Supreme Court of Canada with regards to sexual equality (1989), pornography (1992), and hate speech (1991); published *Feminism Unmodified: Discourses on Life and Law* (1987) and *Toward a Feminist Theory of the State* (1989); became professor of law at University of Michigan Law School (1990) and visiting professor at University of Chicago Law School (1997); also taught at Yale, Harvard, Stanford, Minnesota, UCLA, Osgoode Hall in Toronto and University of Basel in Switzerland; provided *pro bono* co-counsel for Croatian and Muslim women and children seeking remedies under international law for Serbian genocidal sexual atrocities (1990s), winning damage award of $745 million (2000); served as co-director for Lawyers Alliance for Women (LAW) Project of Equality Now; also wrote *Only Words* (1993), *In Harm's Way: The Pornography Civil Rights Hearings* (edited with Andrea Dworkin, 1998) and *Sex Equality* (2001).

MACKINNON, Joanna (1878–1966). New Zealand nurse. Name variations: Joanna Murray. Born Nov 12, 1878, in Balmeanach, on island of Skye, Scotland; died Aug 26, 1966, in Dunedin, New Zealand; dau. of John MacKinnon (fisherman) and Jane (Finlayson) MacKinnon; m. James Dingwall Murray (firefighter), 1908; children: 2 sons. ❖ Worked as an attendant at a mental hospital (1902–05); requested by Frederic Truby King to teach mothers his methods of modifying cow's milk for infant feeding (1905); became integral figure in nascent infant-welfare movement in Dunedin (a formalized system based on her work was proposed by governor, Lord Plunket, and Lady Victoria Plunket, 1908); became 1st Plunket nurse in New Zealand and received the 1st medal; helped found Society for the Promotion of the Health of Women and Children (later the Plunket Society). ❖ See also *Dictionary of New Zealand Biography* (Vol. 3).

MACKINTOSH, Anne (1918–1976). *See Elder, Anne.*

MACKINTOSH, Elizabeth (1896–1952). *See Tey, Josephine.*

MACKINTOSH, Margaret (1865–1933). English-born artist. Name variations: Margaret MacDonald. Born Margaret MacDonald in Staffordshire, England, 1865; died 1933; sister of Frances MacDonald (1874–1921); studied at Glasgow College of Art; m. Charles Rennie Mackintosh (1868–1928, Scottish architect, designer and watercolorist), 1900. ❖ Known for her watercolors, stained glass, and book illustration, worked closely with sister; following marriage, collaborated with husband on much of his work, especially in textile design; exhibited widely on the Continent and won the Diploma of Honor at Turin International Exhibition (1902).

MACKLIN, Madge (1893–1962). American geneticist. Name variations: Madge Thurlow Macklin. Born Madge Thurlow, Feb 6, 1893, in Philadelphia, PA; died Mar 14, 1962, in Ontario, Canada; dau. of William Thurlow (engineer) and Margaret (De Grofft) Thurlow; Goucher College, AB, 1914; Johns Hopkins, MD, 1919; m. Charles Macklin (physician), 1918 (died 1959); children: Carol (b. 1919), Sylva (b. 1921) and Margaret Macklin (b. 1927). ❖ Following marriage, moved to London, Ontario, where she began research in genetics and assisted husband with histology classes at Western Ontario University; despite 23-year career at the university, was never promoted beyond assistant professor; through her research, which analyzed statistics culled from family histories and scientific studies, demonstrated the value of genetics in diagnosis, therapy, prognosis, and prevention of disease; using controlled data, provided evidence that both hereditary and environmental factors contribute to various kinds of cancer; controversially, also became a supporter of the eugenics movement, seeing it as a form of preventive medicine, and was a founder of Canadian Eugenics Society (1930); when the university did not renew her appointment (1945), became an associate in cancer research at Ohio State University; elected president of the American Society for Human Genetics (1959). Awarded Elizabeth Blackwell Medal of American Medical Women's Association (1957). ❖ See also *Women in World History.*

MACKS, Helen (1913–1986). *See Mack, Helen.*

MACKWORTH, Margaret (1883–1958). *See Rhondda, Margaret.*

MACLAINE, Shirley (1934—). American actress, dancer and writer. Born Shirley MacLean Beaty, April 24, 1934, in Richmond, VA; dau. of Ira Owens Beaty and Kathlyn Beaty; sister of Warren Beatty (actor);

m. Steve Parker, 1954 (div. 1982); children: Stephanie "Sachi" Parker (b. 1956, actress). ❖ Began career in the chorus of several Broadway shows; came to prominence when she went on for Carol Haney in *Pajama Game* (1954); made film debut in *The Trouble with Harry* (1955), followed by *Hot Spell, Around the World in 80 Days, Ocean's 11, Can-Can, The Matchmaker, Sweet Charity, Two for the Seesaw, The Children's Hour, Being There, Steel Magnolias* and *Guarding Tess*, among others; books include *You Can Get There from Here, Out on a Limb, Dancing in the Light* and *Going Within*; active in politics. Was nominated for Oscar as Best Actress for *Some Came Running* (1958), *The Apartment* (1960), *Irma La Deuce* (1963), *The Turning Point* (1977), and finally won for *Terms of Endearment* (1983); nominated for Oscar for Best Documentary for *The Other Half of the Sky: A China Memoir* (1975); shared Best Actress prize at Venice for *Madame Sousatska*. ❖ See also autobiography *Don't Fall Off the Mountain* (1970).

MACLAREN, Mary (1896–1985). American silent-screen actress. Name variations: Mary McLaren. Born Jan 19, 1896, in Pittsburgh, PA; died Nov 9, 1985, in Los Angeles, CA; sister of Katherine MacDonald (1891–1956, actress); m. Col. George Herbert Young. ❖ Made film debut as star of *Shoes*, under Lois Weber's direction (1916); other films include *The Mysterious Mrs. M, The Three Musketeers, The Wild Goose, Across the Continent, Outcast, On the Banks of the Wabash, The Dark Swan* and *The Uninvited Guest*; ended her days in poverty.

MACLEAN, Elizabeth (1903–1996). See Roland, Betty.

MACLEAN, Hester (1859–1932). New Zealand nurse, hospital matron, editor, and writer. Born Feb 25, 1859, in Sofala, New South Wales, Australia; dau. of Harold Maclean (goldfields commissioner) and Emily (Strong) Maclean. ❖ Trained as nurse at Royal Prince Alfred Hospital, Sydney (1893); worked as private nurse before becoming matron of Kogarah Cottage Hospital, Melbourne (1897); was a sister at Women's Hospital, Melbourne (1897), matron (1900–04); served as matron of Queen Victoria Hospital for Women and Children (1899–1900) and matron of Bay View Asylum, Sydney (1905–06); secured post of assistant inspector of hospitals in New Zealand's Department of Hospitals and Charitable Aid (1906–23); active in Australasian and Victorian Trained Nurses' associations; instrumental in merging New Zealand's various nursing associations into New Zealand Trained Nurses' Association (1909); during WWI, worked with New Zealand Army Nursing Service, escorting 1st nurses to Egypt (1915); responsible for drafting Nurses and Midwives Registration Act (1925); edited and published nursing journal, *Kai Tiaki* (guardian, 1908). Royal Red Cross medal (first class) (1917); Florence Nightingale Medal (1920). ❖ See also autobiography, *Nursing in New Zealand* (1932) and *Dictionary of New Zealand Biography* (Vol. 3).

MACLEAN, Ida Smedley (1877–1944). English biochemist. Born Ida Smedley, June 14, 1877, in Birmingham, England; died Mar 2, 1944; studied at Newnham College, Cambridge, on a Gilchrist Scholarship, 1896–99; m. Dr. Hugh Maclean (University of London medical professor), Mar 28, 1913. ❖ The 1st woman staff member of Manchester University chemistry department, was also the 1st woman formally admitted to London Chemical Society (1920), after rallying for women to be permitted to join; researched optical properties of organic compounds while working as an assistant lecturer and demonstrator at Victoria College, Manchester University (1906–10); was a fellow at Lister Institute for Preventive Medicine Research (1910–14); served as a founding member (1907) and as president (1929–35) of British Federation of University Women; studied the functions of fatty acids in animals and fat synthesis in carbohydrates. Received American Association of University Women's Ellen Richards Prize (1915).

MACLEAN, Kate (1958—). Scottish politician. Born 1958 in Dundee, Scotland. ❖ As a Labour candidate, elected to the Scottish Parliament for Dundee West (1999); was a member of the Justice and Home Affairs Committee (1999–2001).

MACLEAN, Katherine (1925—). American science-fiction writer. Name variations: Katherine Anne MacLean. Born Jan 22, 1925, in Glen Ridge, NJ; m. Charles Dye, 1951 (div. 1952); m. David Mason, 1956 (div. 1962); m. Carl West. ❖ Works, which often explore implications of medical and scientific experimentation, include *Unclean Sacrifice* (1958), *The Diploids and Other Flights of Fancy* (1962), *The Man in the Bird Cage* (1971), *Missing Man* (1975), *Dark Wing* (with Carl West, 1979), *The Trouble With You Earth People* (1980), and *The Second Game* (1981). Won Nebula Award (1971).

MACLEAN, Letitia Elizabeth (1802–1838). See Landon, Letitia Elizabeth.

MACLEAN, Vida (1881–1970). New Zealand nurse and hospital matron. Born Vida Mary Katie MacLean, Nov 4 1881, at Whangaehu, near Wanganui, New Zealand; died July 1, 1970, in Wanganui; dau. of Finlay McLean (farmer) and Julia (Williamson) McLean. ❖ Trained as nurse at Wanganui Hospital (1909); served as nurse throughout WWI, attached to New Zealand Expeditionary Force in Samoa, and New Zealand Army Nursing Service in Egypt (1914–15); matron of New Zealand General Hospital (1917); matron of Trentham Military Hospital (1918–20); managed Malifa private hospital in Wellington (1920); matron of Mothercraft Home in Wellington (1925) and Karitane Hospital in Auckland (1927); trained nurses and supervised work of Plunket Society (1929); joined Indian Military Nursing Service (1938). Received Royal Red Cross medal, second class (1916), first class (1918). ❖ See also *Dictionary of New Zealand Biography* (Vol. 3).

MACLEHOSE, Agnes (1759–1841). Scottish correspondent. Name variations: Agnes M'Lehose; Clarinda. Born Agnes Craig in 1759 in Glasgow, Scotland; died 1841 in Edinburgh; dau. of Andrew Craig, an Edinburgh surgeon; grandniece of Colin Maclaurin (1698–1746, mathematician and natural philosopher); m. James Maclehose (Glasgow lawyer), in 1776 (sep. 1780). ❖ After separation from husband (1780), moved to Edinburgh where she met poet Robert Burns (1787); corresponded with him under the name Clarinda until 1794. Their correspondence was published in 1843.

MACLEISH, Martha Hillard (1856–1947). American educator and community leader. Name variations: Martha Hillard. Born Aug 17, 1856, in Hadlyme, CT; died Dec 19, 1947, in Chicago, IL; dau. of Elias Brewster Hillard (minister) and Julia (Whittlesey) Hillard; m. Andrew MacLeish (partner in department-store firm Carson Pirie Scott & Co.), Aug 2, 1888; children: 2 daughters, 3 sons, including Archibald MacLeish (poet). ❖ Was assistant in mathematics at alma mater Vassar College; served as principal of Rockford (IL) Seminary (1884–88); formed West Side branch of Visiting Nurse Association in Chicago; was early contributor to school that became University of Chicago; served as board member, vice-president, and president of Woman's Baptist Foreign Missionary Society of the West; after its merger with another group, served as vice-president for home administration of Woman's American Baptist Foreign Mission Society. ❖ See also *Martha Hillard MacLeish (1856–1947)* (privately published, 1949).

MACLEOD, Mrs. Alick (1847–1937). See Martin, C.E.M.

MACLEOD, Banda (1898–1919). See MacLeod, Juana-Luisa.

MACLEOD, Charlotte (1852–1950). Canadian nurse. Born Nov 11, 1852, in New Brunswick, Canada; died Oct 21, 1950. ❖ The 1st chief superintendent of Victorian Order of Nurses (VON) in Canada, pursued a teaching career for 15 years before becoming a nurse; graduated from Waltham Training School for Nurses in Waltham, MA (1891); began studying nurse education in Britain (1896), where she met with Florence Nightingale; at Waltham School, created 1st home nursing course in US, which became the foundation of the public health nursing education field; invited by Canada's Lady Aberdeen to create the 1st Canadian visiting nursing service (1898), founded VON; traveled for over 6 years to establish VON district offices across Canada; returned to MA (1906) to form and direct the Boston Instructive Visiting Nurses Association's Training School for Visiting Nurses; led and helped the Brattleboro Mutual Aid Association's Training School for Attendants in Vermont (1909–12); had several short-term positions as superintendent and acting matron at various institutions (1913–14); retired to Winchendon, MA (1917).

MACLEOD, Jaime (1976—). American snowboarder. Born Dec 18, 1976, in Concord, NH. ❖ Won gold (2001), silver (Winter 2000), and bronze (Winter 1999) in Slopestyle at X Games; other 1st-place finishes include: Yahoo Big Air and Style, Okemo, VT, in Slopestyle (2000); US Open, Stratton, VT, in Big Air (2000); and Yahoo Big Air, Breckenridge, CO, in Big Air (2002).

MACLEOD, Juana-Luisa (1898–1919). Daughter of Mata Hari. Name variations: Jeanne-Louise; called "Non" or Banda or Bandda MacLeod or Macleod. Born Juana-Luisa MacLeod in Toempoeng, Dutch East Indies, 1898; died Aug 9, 1919; dau. of Captain John MacLeod and Margaretha Zelle (Mata Hari). ❖ After parents separated (1902), lived briefly with mother until abducted by father (1903) who kept her mother from contacting her; died mysteriously and unexpectedly on eve of departure for her 1st teaching assignment in the Dutch East Indies, at 21. ❖ See also *Women in World History*.

MACLEOD, Margaretha (1876–1917). *See Zelle, Margaretha.*

MACLEOD, Mary (c. 1615–c. 1706). Scottish poet. Born Mairi nighean Alasdair Ruaidh (Mary the Daughter of Red Alasdair), c. 1615, in Rodel, Harris, Scotland; died c. 1706 in Dunvegan, Scotland; dau. of Alasdair Ruadh na Droighnach. ❖ First Gaelic poet to compose court poetry in vernacular diction, lived in court of MacLeod chief Sir Roderick Mór; was exiled from court after Restoration but recalled upon accession of Sir Norman of Bernera. Only 16 Gaelic poems extant, published in J. Mackenzie, *The Beauties of Gaelic Poetry and Lives of the Highland Bards* (1907) and in J.C. Watson, *Songs of Mary MacLeod* (1934).

MACLEOD, Sheila (1939—). Scottish science-fiction writer. Born Mar 23, 1939, on Isle of Lewis, Scotland; m. Paul Jones (actor), 1963 (div.). ❖ Wrote reviews and articles for various newspapers and magazines, including *The Evening Standard, The Observer, The Times Literary Supplement,* and *Vogue;* novels include *The Moving Accident* (1968), *The Snow-White Soliloquies* (1970), *Letters From the Portuguese* (1971), *Xanthe and the Robots* (1976), *Circuit-Breaker* (1977) and *Axioms* (1984); also wrote 2 teleplays, "They Put You Where You Are" (with Paul Jones, 1965) and "God Speed Co-operation" (1985), and work of criticism, *D.H. Lawrence's Men and Women* (1985). ❖ See also autobiography *The Art of Starvation: An Adolescent Observed* (1981).

MACMAHON, Aline (1899–1991). American actress. Born May 3, 1899, in McKeesport, PA; died Oct 12, 1991, in NY from pneumonia; graduate of Erasmus Hall and Barnard College; m. Clarence S. Stein (architect), 1928 (died 1975). ❖ Made Broadway debut in *The Mirage* (1921), followed by *Grand Street Follies, Artists and Models* (1925), *Beyond the Horizon* (1926), *Winter Bound* (1929) and *The Eve of St. Mark* (1942), among others; made film debut as Edward G. Robinson's secretary in *Five Star Final* (1931), for which she won glowing reviews; other films include *The Heart of New York* (1932), *Once in a Lifetime* (1932), *Gold Diggers of 1933* (1933), *Big-Hearted Herbert* (1934), *Babbitt* (1934), *Ah Wilderness!* (1935), *The Mighty McGurk* (1947), *The Search* (1948), *Cimarron* (1960), *I Could Go on Singing* (1963) and *All the Way Home* (1963); continued to work in theater and was also seen on tv. Nominated for Academy Award for Best Supporting Actress for *Dragon Seed.* ❖ See also *Women in World History.*

MACMANUS, Anna Johnston (1866–1902). Irish writer. Name variations: Mrs. Anna Johnston; Mrs. Seumas MacManus (sometimes seen as Seamus MacManus); (pseudonym) Ethna Carbery. Born Anna Johnston in Ballymena, Co. Antrim, 1866; died 1902 (some sources cite 1911); m. Seumas MacManus (1869–1960, poet). ❖ Credited with influencing the early Sinn Fein movement, wrote poetry that was 1st published in the journals *Nation* and *United Ireland,* then in a collection called *The Four Winds of Eirinn* (1902); in conjunction with a Belfast workingmen's club, founded the monthly newspaper *Northern Patriot* with Alice Milligan; following a dispute with the club, founded *Shan Van Vocht* (1896), which she edited until 1899; was also active in Inghinidhe na héireann, which offered free classes in music, dance, and drama, and purportedly motivated William Butler Yeats to start the Irish National Theater.

MACMILLAN, Chrystal (1871–1937). Scottish feminist and pacifist. Born in Edinburgh, Scotland, in 1871; died in 1937; educated at St. Leonard's School, St. Andrews, and Edinburgh University; also studied in Berlin. ❖ On behalf of women Scottish graduates, became the 1st woman to address the House of Lords (1908), arguing for their right to vote for parliamentary candidates to the Scottish Universities seat; joined National Union of Suffrage Societies, serving as its leader for a number of years until she resigned in opposition to proposals for protective legislation for women; founded Open Door Council which espoused the elimination of legal restrictions on women (1923); named president of Open Door International for the Economic Emancipation of the Woman Worker (1929); as a pacifist, was a major organizer for The Hague Congress (1915) and secretary of International Alliance of Women (1913–23); ran unsuccessfully as a Liberal candidate for the Edinburgh election (1935).

MACMILLAN, Maureen (1943—). Scottish politician. Born 1943 in Oban. ❖ As a Labour candidate, elected to the Scottish Parliament for Highlands and Islands (1999).

MACMILLAN, Shannon (1974—). American soccer player. Born Shannon Ann MacMillan, Oct 7, 1974, in Syosset, NY; attended University of Portland. ❖ Won a team gold medal at Atlanta Olympics (1996) and a team silver at Sydney Olympics (2000); won a team gold at World Cup (1999); was a founding member of the Women's United Soccer Association (WUSA); signed with San Diego Spirit (2001). Won Hermann Award and named Soccer America Player of the Year (1995). ❖ See also Jere Longman *The Girls of Summer* (HarperCollins, 2000).

MACMONNIES, Mary Fairchild (1858–1946). *See Low, Mary Fairchild.*

MACMURCHY, Helen (1862–1953). Canadian physician. Born Jan 7, 1862, in Toronto, Canada; died Oct 8, 1953, in Toronto; dau. of Marjorie Jardine (Ramsay) MacMurchy and Archibald MacMurchy; Ontario Medical College for Women, MD, 1901. ❖ As chief of the Canadian Department of Health's Division of Child Welfare (1920–34), discovered that Canada had a high maternal mortality rate and thus wrote the successful "Blue Books" series to educate women about the birth process; was Toronto General Hospital's 1st woman intern.

MACMURCHY, Marjory (1869–1938). Canadian journalist. Name variations: Lady Marjory Willison. Born Marjory Jardine Ramsay MacMurchy, 1869, in Canada; died Dec 15, 1938. ❖ Was literary editor of *The News,* book reviewer for Canadian dailies, and wrote a regular column for several newspapers called "Politics for Women"; served as president of Canadian Women's Press Club (1909–13) and secretary of the Ontario Unemployment Commission; published work in Toronto *Saturday Night, Harper's Bazaar,* and *The Bohemian;* wrote *The Women–Bless Her* (1916) and *Women of Today and Tomorrow* (1919), and the children's books *The Child's House* and *The Longest Way Round* (1937), among others.

MACNAGHTEN, Anne (1908–2000). British violinist. Name variations: Anne Catherine Macnaghten. Born Aug 9, 1908, in Londonderry, England; died Dec 31, 2000. ❖ Studied at Leipzig Conservatory and formed women's string quartet (1932) which gave many concerts and broadcasts; with Iris Lemare and Elisabeth Lutyens, founded concert series to promote contemporary music (many well-known composers had debuts through series which became known as New Macnaghten Concerts).

MACNAMARA, Jean (1899–1968). Australian doctor and scientist. Name variations: Annie Jean Connor; Jean Connor. Born in Beechworth, Victoria, Australia, April 1, 1899; died Oct 13, 1968; dau. of John Macnamara (court clerk) and Anne Fraser Macnamara; educated at Melbourne's Presbyterian Ladies' College; University of Melbourne, MBBS, 1922, MD, 1925; m. Joseph Ivan Connor (dermatologist), Nov 19, 1934 (died 1955); children: 2 daughters. ❖ Championed the use of an immune serum to treat pre-paralytic patients with polio and helped pave the way toward the development of the Salk vaccine with her discovery that more than one strain of the polio virus existed; named clinical assistant to the outpatients' physician at Royal Children's Hospital (1926) and at the same time established a private practice specializing in treatment of polio (poliomyelitis); served as a consultant and medical officer to Poliomyelitis Committee of Victoria (1925–31). Named Dame Commander of the Order of the British Empire (DBE, 1935). ❖ See also *Women in World History.*

MACNEISH, June (1924—). *See Helm, June.*

MACOMBER, Mary Lizzie (1861–1916). American artist. Born in Fall River, MA, Aug 21, 1861; died in Boston, MA, Feb 4, 1916; studied drawing in Fall River with Robert S. Dunning and for a year at school of Boston Museum of Fine Arts. ❖ Opened a studio in Boston; known for her Pre-Raphaelite style, produced such paintings as *Love Awakening Memory* (1891) and *Love's Lament* (1893); exhibited over 20 paintings at annual National Academy of Design shows (1889–1902); won Dodge Prize at National Academy exhibition in NY for *St. Catherine* (1897); after a fire destroyed much of her work (1903), traveled to England, Netherlands, and France to view the works of the great masters; returned home strongly influenced by Rembrandt; notable later paintings were *Night and Her Daughter* and *Memory Comforting Shadow.* ❖ See also *Women in World History.*

MACONACHIE, Bessie. Northern Ireland politician. Name variations: Elizabeth Maconachie. Born Elizabeth Hamill. ❖ Began career as a schoolteacher; representing the Unionist Party for Queen's University, Belfast, sat in the Northern Ireland House of Commons (1953–69).

MACONACHIE, Elizabeth. *See Maconachie, Bessie.*

MACONAQUA (1773–1847). *See Slocum, Frances.*

MACONCHY, Elizabeth (1907–1994). British composer. Name variations: Dame Elizabeth Maconchy. Born Elizabeth Maconchy in Boxbourne, Hertfortshire, England, Mar 19, 1907; died in 1994; attended Royal College of Music in London, 1923–29, studying under Charles Wood and Ralph Vaughn Williams; m. William Lefanu, 1930; children: 2 daughters, one of whom is the composer Nicola Lefanu (b. 1947). ❖ Composer of works for orchestra, chamber orchestra, opera and voice, whose unique style, combining the best in modern and classical techniques, has been a great influence on modern music both in Great Britain and internationally; was a star pupil at Royal College of Music (1923); won the Blumenthal and Sullivan scholarships, and the Octavia Traveling Scholarship (1929); successfully premiered *The Land,* a suite of 4 numbers written for a large orchestra, at one of London's famous Promenade Concerts (1930); with Elizabeth Lutyens, Anne Macnaghten, and Iris Lemare, founded the Macnaghten-Lemare concerts, which strongly favored women composers; by mid-20s, had her work performed by major orchestras in England and Europe; began to concentrate increasingly on the composition of string quartets (1933), writing 13 of them within next 5 decades and becoming the English composer most associated with the form; wrote 3 one-act operas, several choral pieces, and several pieces for children's voices, including *Samson* and *The King of the Golden River* (1957–67); experimented with vocal works in *Ariadne, Epyllion,* and *The Leaden Echo and the Golden Echo*; composed hundreds of works, which were increasingly performed and recorded. Won Edwin Evans Prize (1948), L.C.C. Prize for overture *Proud Thames* (1953) and GEDOK International prize (1961); received Radcliffe award (1969); became Commander of the Order of the British Empire (CBE, 1977) and Dame of the British Empire (DBE, 1987). ❖ See also *Women in World History.*

MACOVICIUC, Camelia (1968—). Romanian rower. Born Jan 3, 1968, in Bucharest, Romania. ❖ Won a gold medal for lightweight double sculls at Atlanta Olympics (1996).

MACPHAIL, Agnes (1890–1954). Canadian politician. Name variations: originally "MacPhail," changed the spelling to "Macphail" in 1925. Born Agnes MacPhail in Proton Township, Grey Co., southwestern Ontario, Canada, Mar 24, 1890; died in Toronto, Feb 13, 1954; dau. of Henrietta Campbell MacPhail and Dougald MacPhail; never married; no children. ❖ The 1st woman elected to Canada's federal Parliament, was a tireless defender of the rights of the disadvantaged through a political career spanning 3 decades; taught school in rural areas and became involved with a growing farmers' movement (1910–20); joined United Farm Women of Ontario (UFWO), organizing local chapters and publicizing goals of UFO; was soon a popular activist in rural Ontario; elected as a UFO candidate for Southeast Grey (1919) to the Parliament of Canada; fought for the rights and dignity of the disadvantaged, including women's rights and prisoner reform; embraced a form of moderate socialism, supporting motions for better old-age pensions and government health insurance; consequently, was an instrumental figure in the creation of Canada's Social Democratic Party (later the New Democratic Party); was a delegate at founding convention of Cooperative Commonwealth Federation (CCF); spoke out frequently on foreign affairs, was an active member of the Women's International League, and was appointed to League of Nations as Canada's 1st woman delegate (1929); went on extensive speaking tours throughout Canada and US; won 4 successive elections, remaining the representative for Southeast Grey until 1940; ran successfully as a CCF candidate for York East in the Ontario provincial election (1943), becoming one of the 1st female MPPs (members of provincial parliament) in Ontario legislature; won back her seat (1948). A bust of Macphail was unveiled in the federal Parliament (1955). ❖ See also Terry Crowley, *Agnes Macphail and the Politics of Equality* (Lorimer, 1990); Stewart and French, *Ask No Quarter: A Biography of Agnes Macphail* (Longmans, 1959); Doris Pennington, *Agnes Macphail, Reformer* (Simon & Pierre, 1989); and *Women in World History.*

MACPHAIL, Katherine Stewart (1888–1974). Scottish doctor. Born Katherine Stewart Macphail, 1888, in Coatbridge, Lanarkshire, Scotland; died 1974 in Scotland; dau. of a physician; graduate of Glasgow University Medical School, 1911. ❖ A doctor in Yugoslavia during WWI and WWII, worked with the Scottish Women's Hospital Unit in Salonika and then the Serbian Army headquarters; founded (1919) and worked at the Anglo-Yugoslav Children's Hospital in Belgrade until 1933; organized Sremska Kamenitsa, a surgical tuberculosis children's hospital on the Danube at Kamenica; during WWII, was interned by the Italians (1941–43); led the Save the Children Fund medical relief unit in Yugoslavia (1944); practiced 2 more years at her Belgrade Hospital (1945–47) before retiring to Scotland. Received many decorations from the Yugoslavian government; awarded the Russian Red Cross Insignia (1932).

MACPHERSON, Jay (1931—). Canadian poet. Name variations: Jean Jay Macpherson. Born June 13, 1931, in London, England; attended University College, London, McGill University, and University of Toronto. ❖ Taught English at Victoria College, University of Toronto (1957–96); works, which often explore religious and philosophical themes, include *Nineteen Poems* (1952), *O Earth Return* (1954), *The Boatman* (1957), *Welcoming Disaster* (1974), and *Poems Twice Told: The Boatman and Welcoming Disaster* (1981); also published *Four Ages of Man: The Classical Myths* (1962) and *The Spirit of Solitude: Conventions and Continuity in Late Romance* (1982); did illustrations for *Poems Twice Told.* Won Governor General's Award for *The Boatman.* ❖ See also Lorraine Weir, *Jay Macpherson and Her Works* (ECW Press, 1989–90).

MACPHERSON, Jeanie (1887–1946). American screenwriter, actress, and director. Name variations: Jean du Rocher or J. DuRocher Macpherson; Jeannie Macpherson. Born May 18, 1887, in Boston, MA; died Aug 26, 1946, in Los Angeles, CA; dau. of Evangeline Tomlinson and John Sinclair Macpherson. ❖ One of the 1st women to become a screenwriter and director, began acting in films (1908), appealing directly to D.W. Griffith for her 1st role; became a lead actress for Universal Studio, where she also directed and wrote many two-reelers; began writing exclusively (1915), eventually becoming a screenwriter for Cecil B. De Mille; over the course of their 27-year relationship, worked with him on most of his silent films, including *Joan the Woman* (1916), *Something to Think About, The Affairs of Anatol* and *Adam's Rib*; was also an aviator and apparently the only woman to pilot a plane for the noted stunt flyer, Lieutenant Locklear. ❖ See also *Women in World History.*

MACPHERSON, Margaret Louisa (1895–1974). New Zealand journalist and writer. Name variations: Margaret Louise Kendall. Born June 19, 1895, in Headingley, Leeds, England; died Sept 14, 1974, in Kaitaia, New Zealand; dau. of Alfred Sunderland Kendall (linen draper) and Fannie (Gibson) Kendall; m. Alfred Sinclair Macpherson (draftsman), 1916 (div. 1925); m. W.T. Albert (journalist), c. 1940s (ended, 1949); children: 7. ❖ Wrote women's column, "Wahine," in *Maoriland Worker*; edited progressive weekly, *Northlander* (1920s); traveled to Australia, US, Britain, and Malta (1930s); rebuked by George Bernard Shaw for her complaint that New Zealand lacked artistic culture, followed his advice to take a trip throughout the country and then wrote *Antipodean Journey* (1937); published *I Heard the Anzacs Singing* (1942); wrote children's story, *New Zealand Beckons* (1952); returned to New Zealand (1960s) and wrote series of columns entitled "Margaret Meditates" in *Northland Age.* ❖ See also *Dictionary of New Zealand Biography* (Vol. 4).

MACPHERSON, Michelle (1966—). Canadian swimmer. Born May 11, 1966. ❖ At Los Angeles Olympics, won a bronze medal in the 4x100-meter medley relay (1984).

MACPHERSON, Wendy (1968—). American bowler. Born Jan 28, 1968, in Walnut Creek, CA. ❖ At 14, rolled a 300 game; at 18, won the BPAA US open; at 20, won the WIBC Queens (1988), then won it again (2000, 2003); joined LPBT tour (1986) and was Rookie of the Year; as of 2004, won over 20 tournaments, including 6 majors.

MACQUARIE, Elizabeth (1778–1835). Scottish-born diarist. Born Elizabeth Campbell, 1778, in Airds, Scotland; died 1835 in Scotland; dau. of John Campbell; m. Lachlan Macquarie (1762–1824, governor of New South Wales in Australia [1809–1821]), before 1809. ❖ When husband was appointed governor of NSW in Australia, accompanied him to his posting and recorded the journey in *Diary of Journey from England to New South Wales 1809*; counseled him on ticklish matters of state and supported him in disputes he had with a variety of factions in NSW; displayed particular concern for women convicts and was interested in ensuring that all people, including the colony's Aboriginal inhabitants, were treated equitably by the state; returned to Scotland (1822). A prominence overlooking Sydney Harbor is called Mrs. Macquarie's Chair. ❖ See also Lysbeth Cohen, *Elizabeth Macquarie* (1979); and *Women in World History.*

MACRINA (327–379). Byzantine composer, singer, teacher, saint and founder. Name variations: Makrina. Born in Caesarea (modern-day Kayseri), capital of Cappadocia, 327 CE; died 379; 1 of 10 children of Basil (distinguished lawyer and professor of rhetoric in Cappadocia) and Emmelia; granddau. of Macrina the Elder; sister of Peter, bishop of Sebaste, Basil the Great (329–379), bishop of Caesarea, whose authority extended over 11 provinces of Asia Minor, and Gregory of Nyssa (335–387), one of the fathers of the Eastern Church. ❖ The founder of a religious community for women in the Eastern Church, was a strong supporter of orthodox Christianity as delineated by the Nicene Creed; at 12, when chosen fiancé died, renounced all future suitors; became deaconess of the church of St. Sophia in Byzantium; on family estate at Annesi, founded a small community of religious women, where she taught the scriptures, established a hospital, and encouraged the renunciation of wealth, rank, and all pleasures of the body, the beginning of monasticism; following mother's death, raised and educated younger brother Peter who became bishop of Sebaste; during a conversation he explored at length in *Concerning the Soul and the Resurrection,* urged brother Gregory of Nyssa to play an expanded role in the spread of Christianity; wrote both the text and music of many songs performed in her convent. ❖ See also *Women in World History.*

MACROBERT, Rachel (1884–1954). Scottish-American baroness and geologist. Name variations: Lady Rachel or Rachael MacRobert; Rachel Workman; baroness of Crawnmore and Cromar. Born Rachel Workman, 1884, in Worcester, MA; died Sept 1, 1954, at Alastrean House, her home in Tarland, Aberdeenshire, Scotland; dau. of Dr. William Hunter Workman and Fanny Workman (1859–1925, explorer); studied political economy and geology at University of Edinburgh; conducted postgraduate work (mineralogy and petrology) in Oslo, Norway; m. Sir Alexander MacRobert, baronet of Crawnmore and Cromar and founder of the British India Corporation, 1911 (died 1922); children: 3 (all died: 2 while serving in RAF, 1 in a flying accident). ❖ One of the Geological Society of London's 1st 8 female fellows (elected, 1919), moved to India with Sir Alexander MacRobert after marriage (1911); researched in the Kolar goldfields; published a paper about calcite and igneous rocks (1911) and a paper about rocks from the Eildon Hills in Roxburghshire (1914); after husband's death (1922), became director of the British India Corporation; served as an Aberdeen justice of peace; directed the Scottish Chamber of Agriculture; was a president of British Friesian Cattle Society; during WWII, donated funds to the Royal Air Force (RAF) to purchase planes and a Stirling bomber named "MacRobert's Reply" (1941); established the MacRobert Reply Association to assist Scottish youth organizations (1945).

MACRUARI, Amy (fl. 1300s). Lady of the Isles. Fl. in the 1300s; dau. of Roderick Macruari; m. John Macdonald, 1st Lord of the Isles; children: John Macdonald; Godfrey Macdonald, lord of Uist; Ronald Macdonald.

MACSWINEY, Mary (1872–1942). Irish politician. Born Mar 27, 1872, in Surrey, England; died Mar 7, 1942; dau. of John MacSwiney and Mary Wilkinson; sister of Annie MacSwiney, Sean MacSwiney (TD) and Terence MacSwiney (lord mayor of Cork). ❖ Began career as a secondary schoolteacher; was a founder member of Inghinidhe na héireann and Cumann na mBan (1914–33), serving as 1st president (Cork) and national vice-president; dismissed from teaching after arrest and imprisonment for national activities (1916); joined the women's suffrage movement and Sinn Féin (1917); was a pioneer of the language revival movement in Cork; following death of brother Terence from a hunger strike, replaced him in the 2nd Dáil (parliament) for Cork (1921); was appointed 1 of 12 members of Éamon de Valera's Council of State (1922); imprisoned but released after a hunger strike (1922); was an anti-Treaty abstentionist in 3rd and 4th Dáil (1922–27); espoused Republican cause until her death. ❖ See also Charlotte H. Fallon *Soul of Fire: A Biography of Mary MacSwiney* (Mercier, 1986).

MACTAGGART, Fiona (1953—). English politician and member of Parliament. Born Sept 12, 1953, in London, England; dau. of Sir Ian Mactaggart and Rosemary Belhaven Mactaggart; Kings College, BA; Goldsmiths College, MA in education. ❖ Served as lecturer in primary education, Institute of Education (1992–97); representing Labour, elected to House of Commons for Slough (1997, 2001, 2005); became parliamentary under secretary for Race Equality, Community Policy and Civil Renewal, then parliamentary secretary, Home Office.

MACTIER, Kate (1975—). Australian cyclist. Born Mar 23, 1975, in Melbourne, Australia; attended Royal Melbourne Institute of Technology. ❖ Won the Australian road title (2001); placed 2nd in World championships at 3,000-meter indiv. pursuit (2003 and 2004); won silver medal at Athens Olympics for 3,000-meter individual pursuit in cycling (2004). Named Australian Female Track Cyclist of the Year (2003).

MACTIER, Susie (1854–1936). New Zealand novelist and poet. Born Susan Seaman, 1854, in New Zealand; died 1936. ❖ Sometimes called the Takapuna Lake Poet, though she published only 1 volume of poetry; novels include *A Far Countrie* (1901), *The Hills of Hauraki* (1908) and *Miranda Stanhope* (1911).

MACURDY, Grace Harriet (1866–1946). American Greek scholar and teacher. Born Grace Harriet Macurdy, Sept 15, 1866, in Robbinston, Maine; died Oct 23, 1946, in Poughkeepsie, NY; dau. of Simon Angus Macurdy (carpenter) and Rebecca Bradford (Thomson) Macurdy; graduate of Society for Collegiate Instruction of Women (later Radcliffe College), 1888; studied at University of Berlin, 1899–1900; Columbia University, PhD, 1903. ❖ Respected Greek scholar, began teaching career at Cambridge School for Girls (1888); at Vassar College, appointed instructor of Greek (1893), associate professor (1903), full professor (1916), and chair of the department (1920), a post she held until her retirement (1937); scholarly writings include 5 books: *The Chronology of the Extant Plays of Euripides* (1905), *Troy and Paconia* (1925), *Hellenistic Queens* (1932), *Vassal-Queens and Some Contemporary Women in the Roman Empire* (1937) and *The Quality of Mercy* (1940); during WWII, worked for Greek and British relief. Awarded British King's Medal (1946). ❖ See also *Women in World History.*

MACVICAR, Martha (1925–1971). *See Vickers, Martha.*

MACWHINNEY, Linda (1888–1951). *See Kearns-MacWhinney, Linda.*

MACY, Anne Sullivan (1866–1936). American teacher and activist for the blind. Name variations: Anne or Annie Sullivan; Anne Mansfield Sullivan. Born Joanna Sullivan in Feeding Hill, MA, April 14 (some sources cite April 13), 1866; died in Forest Hills, NY, Oct 20, 1936; dau. of Thomas (Irish immigrant farmer) and Alice (Cloesy) Sullivan; m. John Macy (writer, Harvard professor, and Helen Keller's literary agent), May 2, 1905 (sep. 1914); no children. ❖ Best known as the lifelong teacher and companion of Helen Keller, experienced failing eyesight at 8; spent 4 years in the state poorhouse in Tewksbury; entered Perkins School for the Blind in Boston (1880); while there, regained much of her sight after a series of operations; graduated at head of her class (1886); traveled to Tuscumbria, Alabama, to be governess to the unruly 7-year-old known as Helen Keller, who had been stricken blind and deaf in infancy; using a manual alphabet, spelled out words into Helen's hand; after many weeks, was successful in teaching her that the movements she felt in her hand were the names of objects; became as devoted to Keller as Keller was to her. ❖ See also Nella Braddy, *Anne Sullivan Macy* (Doubleday, 1933); Helen Keller, *Teacher* (Doubleday, 1955); Joseph P. Lash, *Helen and Teacher* (Delacorte, 1980); and *Women in World History.*

MACY, Gertrude (1904–1983). American producer, writer, and manager. Born 1904 in CA; died Oct 18, 1983, in New York, NY. ❖ Began career as assistant stage manager on *The Age of Innocence* (1928), eventually becoming general manager for Katharine Cornell; produced *One for the Money, Forever is Now, The Happiest Years* and *I Am a Camera,* among others.

MACY, Robin Lynn (1958—). American musician and singer. Name variations: Dixie Chicks; Domestic Science Club; Big Twang. Born Robin Lynn Macy, Nov 27, 1958, in Sunnyvale, CA. ❖ As vocalist and guitar player, helped form the country-music group Dixie Chicks in Dallas, TX (1989); with group, made Grand Ole Opry debut (1991); left group after 2nd album; recorded 2 albums with Domestic Science Club; joined Big Twang, a bluegrass group. Albums include (with Dixie Chicks) *Thank Heavens for Dale Evans* (1990) and *Little Ol' Cowgirl* (1992); (with Domestic Science Club) *Domestic Science Club* (1993) and *Three Women* (1996).

MACY-HOOBLER, Icie. *See Hoobler, Icie Macy.*

MADAGASCAR, queen of.
See Ranavalona I.
See Ranavalona II.
See Ranavalona III.

MADAME BLANCHE (1855–1875). *See Whiteside, Jane.*

MADAME MÈRE (1750–1836). *See Bonaparte, Letizia.*

MADAME ROYALE.
See Jeanne of Nemours (d. 1724).
See Marie Thérèse Charlotte (1778–1851).

MADAME SANS-GÊNE (fl. 1764–after 1820). *See Lefebvre, Catherine.*

MADAR, Olga (1915–1996). American labor activist. Name variations: Olga Marie Madar. Born May 17, 1915, in Sykesville, PA; died May 16, 1996; Michigan Normal School (later Eastern Michigan University), degree in physical education, 1938. ❖ Employed at Ford Willow Run bomber plant (beginning 1941); served as Detroit Parks and Recreation Commissioner (1958–66); was the 1st woman elected to United Automobile Workers (UAW) International Executive Board as member-at-large (1966); was the 1st woman elected vice president of UAW (1970); played significant part in launching Michigan Women's Political Caucus and the Network for Economic Rights; elected national president of Coalition of Labor Union Women (1974); known particularly for work to end discrimination against women and minorities. Inducted into Michigan Women Hall of Fame (1989) and Labor's International Hall of Fame (2004). ❖ See also The Olga Madar Collection, Walter P. Reuther Library of Labor & Urban Affairs, Wayne State University.

MADARY, Ilona (1916—). Hungarian gymnast. Born June 23, 1916, in Hungary. ❖ At Berlin Olympics, won a bronze medal in team all-around (1936).

MADDALENA. Variant of Magdalena.

MADDALENA OF CANOSSA (1774–1833). Saint. Name variations: Magdalena. Born in Verona in 1774; died in 1833. ❖ Founded the congregation of the Daughters of Charity, an order that taught the peasants and cared for the sick. Feast day is April 10.

MADDEN, Beezie (1963—). American equestrian. Born Nov 20, 1963; lives in Cazenovia, NY. ❖ On Authentic, won silver medal for team jumping at Athens Olympics (2004).

MADDEN, Katherine Cecil (1875–1911). See Thurston, Katherine.

MADDERN, Merle (1887–1984). American actress. Born Nov 3, 1887; died Jan 15, 1984, in Denver, CO; niece of Jack London (novelist). ❖ Appeared in NY in Nice People, Enchanted April, Trial of Mary Dugan, The Sea Gull, Antigone, Land's End, Romeo and Juliet, Hedda Gabler and The Druid Circle, among many others.

MADDERN, Minnie (1865–1932). See Fiske, Minnie Maddern.

MADDOX, Mary (1827–1919). See Hames, Mary.

MADDOX, Rose (1925–1998). American country singer. Born Aug 15, 1925, in Alabama; died April 15, 1998, in Ashland, Oregon; sister of Cal, Henry, Dan, Fred and Cliff Maddox; children: Donnie (died 1982). ❖ With brothers, formed The Maddox Brothers and Rose band (1937), popular performers in 1940s; hits included "Philadelphia Lawyer," "Tramp on the Street" and "Whoa, Sailor"; after group split up (1956), began solo career and had such hits as "Sing a Little Song of Heartache," "Gambler's Love," "Kissing My Pillow" and "Bluebird, Let Me Tag Along"; named Top Female Country Vocalist (1963); nominated for Grammy for CD $35 and a Dream (1996).

MADELBERTE (fl. 7th c.). Saint and abbess. Name variations: Madelberta. Fl. in 7th century; dau. of St. Vincent Madelgaire and St. Wandru (d. 688); sister of Aldetrude, abbess of Maubeuge. ❖ Succeeded sister as abbess of Maubeuge, a convent founded by their aunt, Saint Aldegund. Feast day is Sept 7.

MADELEINE (1914–1944). See Khan, Noor Inayat.

MADELEINE (b. 1982). Duchess of Halsingland and Gastrikland. Name variations: Madeleine Bernadotte. Born Madeleine Therese Amelie Josephine Bernadotte, June 10, 1982; dau. of Silvia Sommerlath (1943—) and Carl XVI Gustavus (b. 1946), king of Sweden (r. 1973—).

MADELEINE DE LA TOUR D'AUVERGNE (1501–1519). Duchess of Urbino and mother of Catherine de Medici. Name variations: Madeleine de Medici; Madeleine of Auvergne; Madeline of Auvergne. Born 1501; died of puerperal fever, April 28, 1519, 3 days after birth of her only child; dau. of John de la Tour, count of Auvergne, and Jane of Bourbon-Vendome (d. 1511); sister of Anne de la Tour (c. 1496–1524); m. Lorenzo de Medici, duke of Urbino, on June 13, 1518 (also died in 1519); children: Catherine de Medici (1519–1589).

MADELEINE DE SAINT-NECTAIRE (fl. 1575). French soldier. Name variations: Comtesse de Miremont; Countess of Miremont. Fl. around 1575. ❖ The leader of a company of 60 Huguenot cavaliers, distinguished herself during French civil wars by defending her château at Miremont, in the Limousin, against Catholic invasion. ❖ See also Women in World History.

MADELEINE OF ANHALT-ZERBST (1679–1740). Duchess of Saxe-Gotha-Altenburg. Name variations: Magdalena Augusta of Anhalt-Zerbst. Born Madeleine Augusta, Oct 13, 1679; died Oct 11, 1740; dau. of Charles William (b. 1652), prince of Anhalt-Zerbst, and Sophie of Saxe-Weissenfels (b. 1654); m. Frederick II, duke of Saxe-Gotha-Altenburg; children: Frederick III, duke of Saxe-Gotha (b. 1699); Wilhelm or William, duke of Saxe-Gotha (b. 1701); John August (b. 1704); Augusta of Saxe-Gotha (1719–1772).

MADELEINE OF AUVERGNE (1501–1519). See Madeleine de la Tour d'Auvergne.

MADELEINE OF FRANCE (1443–1486). Queen of Hungary and Bohemia. Name variations: Madeleine de France; Magdalen. Born 1443; died 1486; dau. of Charles VII the Victorious (1403–1461), king of France (r. 1422–1461), and Marie of Anjou (1404–1463); m. Ladislas V (or VI) Posthumus (1440–1457), king of Hungary (r. 1444–1457) and Bohemia (r. 1452); m. Gaston de Foix, vicomte de Castelbon and prince of Viane or Viana; children: (2nd m.) Francis, king of Navarre; Catherine de Foix (c. 1470–1517); possibly Anne de Foix (fl. 1480–1500).

MADELEINE OF FRANCE (1520–1537). French princess. Name variations: Madeleine Valois; Madeleine de France; Magdelaine de France. Born Aug 10, 1520, in St. Germain-en-Laye, near Paris, France; died at age 17 at Holyrood, Edinburgh, Scotland, July 7, 1537; interred at Holyrood; elder dau. of Francis I, king of France (r. 1515–1547), and Claude de France (1499–1524); m. James V (1512–1542), king of Scots (r. 1513–1542), Jan 1, 1537, at Notre Dame, Paris, France. ❖ See also Women in World History.

MADELEINE SOPHIE BARAT (1779–1865). See Barat, Madeleine Sophie.

MADELEVA, Sister Mary (1887–1964). American religious educator, poet, and college administrator. Name variations: Sister Madeleva; Mary Evaline Wolff; Sister Madeleva Wolff. Born Mary Evaline Wolff, May 24, 1887, in Cumberland, WI; died July 25, 1964, in Boston, MA; dau. of August Wolff (harness maker) and Lucy (Arntz) Wolff; St. Mary's College, BA, 1909, MA, 1918; University of California at Berkeley, PhD, 1925; post-graduate study at Oxford University, 1933–34. ❖ The 1st woman religious to receive a doctorate from Berkeley, served as 1st dean and president of College of St. Mary-of-the-Wasatch in Salt Lake City, Utah (1925–33); served as president of St. Mary's College, Notre Dame (1934–1961); writings include: Knights Errant and Other Poems (1923), Chaucer's Nuns and Other Essays (1925), Penelope and Other Poems (1927), A Question of Lovers and Other Poems (1935), The Happy Christmas Wind (1936), Gates and Other Poems (1938), Four Girls (1941), Lost Language and Other Essays (1951), The Last Four Things (1959) and Conversations with Cassandra (1961). ❖ See also memoir My First Seventy Years (1959); and Women in World History.

MADELINE. Variant of Madeleine.

MADEMOISELLE, La Grande (1627–1693). See Montpensier, Anne Marie Louise d'Orleans, duchess de.

MADEMOISELLE DE X (1650–1724). See La Force, Charlotte-Rose de Caumont de.

MADGE. Variant of Margaret.

MADGETT, Naomi Long (1923—). African-American poet, professor, publisher, and editor. Name variations: Naomi Witherspoon; Naomi Cornelia Long. Born Naomi Cornelia Long, July 5, 1923, in Norfolk, VA; dau. of Clarence Marcellus Long (minister) and Maude (Hilton) Long (teacher); Virginia State College, BA, 1945; Wayne State University, MEd., 1956; International Institute for Advanced Studies, PhD, 1980; m. Julian F. Witherspoon, 1946 (div. 1949); m. William Harold Madgett, 1954 (div. 1960); m. Leonard Patton Andrews, 1972 (died 1996); children: (1st m.) Jill Witherspoon (b. 1947). ❖ Published Songs of a Phantom Nightingale (1941), a collection of poems; on marriage, moved to Detroit (1946), where she worked as a reporter for African-American weekly, The Michigan Chronicle; began teaching in Detroit school system (1955); published 2nd collection, One and the Many (1956), which included one of her most important poems, "Refugee"; released 3rd collection, Star by Star (1965); taught 1st African-American literature course offered in Detroit school system (1965); became assistant professor at Eastern Michigan University (1968), where she would remain until her retirement as professor emeritus (1984); other poetry collections include Pink Ladies in the Afternoon

(1972), *Exits and Entrances* (1978), *Octavia* (1988) and *Remembrances of Spring* (1993). Received American Book Award and Governor's Arts Award (both 1993). ❖ See also *Women in World History.*

MADIKIZELA-MANDELA, Winnie (1934—). South African anti-apartheid activist. Name variations: Winnie Nomzamo Mandela; Winnie Mandela. Born Sept 26, 1934, in Pondoland, South Africa; m. Nelson Mandela (later president of South Africa), 1958 (div. 1996); children: 2. ❖ Regarded as one of the foremost heroes of the anti-apartheid struggle, studied social science and worked as social worker at Baragwanath Hospital; received degree in international relations from University of Witwatersrand; participated in demonstrations and was arrested, imprisoned, and banned many times; became active in Women's League of African National Congress (ANC) and, after Nelson Mandela's imprisonment, was regarded as spokeswoman for ANC; was severely restricted, imprisoned for 12 months for breaking banning order, and rearrested several times on same charge; banned to town of Brandfort (1976); returned to live in Soweto (1986) and became embroiled in legal controversy over killing of child by her bodyguards; in new government, was appointed minister of arts, culture, science, and technology but dismissed following allegations of corruption; remained popular despite conviction of fraud and theft (2003). Awarded Third World Prize (1985).

MADINA, Stefka (1963—). Bulgarian rower. Born Jan 23, 1963, in Bulgaria. ❖ At Seoul Olympics, won a bronze medal in double sculls (1988).

MADISON, Cleo (1883–1964). American silent-film actress and director. Born Mar 26, 1883, in Chicago, IL; died in Hollywood, CA, Mar 11, 1964. ❖ One of the 1st women directors in the film industry, began as an actress in films for Universal (1913); became involved in serials and made a number of films with Lon Chaney; had over a dozen films to her credit by the time she achieved stardom with a double role as twin sisters in the serial, *The Trey O' Hearts* (1914); headed her own production company; wrote, directed and starred in *Her Bitter Cup* (1916), one of the earliest films to take the women's suffrage movement as its theme; continued to direct herself in films until 1921, when a nervous breakdown forced her to take a hiatus; returned to make a handful of films, the last of which was released in 1925; was involved as an actress or director in at least 80 silent films. ❖ See also *Women in World History.*

MADISON, Dolley Payne (1768–1849). American first lady. Name variations: often spelled Dolly; Dorothea Payne Madison. Born Dolley Payne, May 20, 1768, in Guilford Co., NC; died in Washington, DC, July 12, 1849; dau. of John Payne (planter and a businessman) and Mary (Coles) Payne; m. John Todd Jr., Jan 7, 1790 (died Oct 24, 1793); m. James Madison (president of US, 1809–1817), Sept 15, 1794 (died June 28, 1836); children: (1st m.) John Payne Todd (b. Feb 29, 1792); William Temple Todd (1793–1793). ❖ Socialite who as first lady became a famous Washington host, moved with family to VA (1769); moved to Philadelphia with family, after parents, staunch Quakers, had freed all their slaves (1783); first husband and infant son died during yellow fever epidemic (1793); married James Madison (1794), then serving as a congressman from Virginia in US House of Representatives; moved to Washington, DC, after he became secretary of state (1801); husband inaugurated as president (1809); as first lady, exercised social leadership in ways that most of her predecessors had not; held regular Wednesday receptions, known as "Mrs. Madison's levees," and made certain that all guests were properly greeted; was an excellent conversationalist with wide-ranging interests, though she deliberately avoided partisan politics; played a significant role in the planning and execution of refurbishing the White House; during War of 1812, rescued portrait of George Washington, just before the British invaders burned the White House (Aug 24, 1814); returned to VA after James Madison's presidential term ended (1817); following husband's death, moved from VA to Washington, DC (1837), where she lived for rest of life with niece Anna Payne; attended laying of Washington Monument cornerstone (July 1848). ❖ See also Anthony, Katharine, *Dolly Madison: Her Life and Times* (Doubleday, 1949); Virginia Moore, *The Madisons* (McGraw, 1979); Ethel Arnett, *Mrs. James Madison: The Incomparable Dolley* (Piedmont, 1972); and *Women in World History.*

MADISON, Dorothea Payne (1768–1849). See Madison, Dolley.

MADISON, Helene (1913–1970). American swimmer. Born June 19, 1913, in Madison, WI; died of cancer, Nov 27, 1970; m. Art Jarrett (bandleader, div.); m. Billy Rose (theatrical producer); m. once more. ❖ Won an indiv. gold medal in the 100 meters, a gold medal in the 400 meters, and a team gold medal in the 4x100m free-style relay, all at

Los Angeles Olympics (1932); held 26 world freestyle records in distances from 50 yards to one mile; won 14 world free-style championships at a variety of distances (1930–32); played Jane opposite Glenn Morris' Tarzan in *Tarzan's Revenge.* Named Associated Press Female Athlete of the Year (1931); named to International Swimming Hall of Fame and US Olympic Hall of Fame. ❖ See also *Women in World History.*

MADONELLA (1666–1731). See Astell, Mary.

MADONNA. See Mary the Virgin.

MADONNA (1958—). American musician. Born Madonna Louise Veronica Ciccone, Aug 16, 1958, in Bay City, Michigan; studied dance at University of Michigan in Ann Arbor; m. Sean Penn (actor), 1985 (div. 1989); m. Guy Ritchie (film director), 2001; children: (with Carlos Leon) Lourdes (b. Oct 1996); (with Ritchie) Rocco (b. 2000). ❖ Controversial and provocative, generated both adulation and criticism of her music and frequently changing style; was singer and drummer in band, Breakfast Club; had 1st club hit, "Everybody" (1982) in New York City; released debut album, *Madonna* (1983), selling more than 5 million copies; released *Like a Virgin* (1984), earning hits with title track and "Material Girl"; had hits with songs from films in which she acted, such as "Crazy for You" (*Vision Quest,* 1985), "Into the Groove" (*Desperately Seeking Susan,* 1985), "Hanky Panky" (*Dick Tracy,* 1990) and "Don't Cry for Me Argentina" (*Evita,* 1996); other hit songs include "Papa Don't Preach" (1986), "Like a Prayer" (1989), "Vogue" and "Justify My Love" (1991), "I'll Remember" from film *With Honors* (1994), and "Frozen" (1998); albums include *True Blue* (1986), *The Immaculate Collection* (1990), *Bedtime Stories* (1994) and *Music* (2000); released book of photographs, *Sex;* wrote children's book, *The English Roses* (2003); was among 1st pop stars to draw public attention to AIDS.

MADONNA OF THE SCREEN, The (1889–1955). See Joyce, Alice.

MADRID, duchess of. See Margaret of Parma (1847–1893).

MADSEN, Gitte (1969—). Danish handball player. Born Mar 24, 1969, in Denmark. ❖ Won a team gold medal at Atlanta Olympics (1996); won team European championships (1996) and World championships (1997); retired (1997).

MAEDA, Echiko (1952—). Japanese volleyball player. Born Jan 31, 1952, in Japan. ❖ At Montreal Olympics, won a gold medal in team competition (1976).

MAEDER, Clara Fisher (1811–1898). See Fisher, Clara.

MAEHATA, Hideko (1914–1995). Japanese swimmer. Born May 20, 1914, in Japan; died Feb 24, 1995. ❖ Won a silver medal at Los Angeles Olympics (1932) and a gold medal at Berlin Olympics (1936), both for 200-meter breaststroke; was the 1st Japanese woman to medal in Olympic swimming and one of the 1st swimmers to use the butterfly stroke, which was controversial at the time. ❖ See also *Women in World History.*

MAENDLI, Lesley (1966—). See McNaught, Lesley.

MAES, Nelly (1941—). Belgian politician. Born Feb 25, 1941, in Sinaai. ❖ Was a member of the Flemish Parliament (1995–98); vice-chair, Group of the Greens/European Free Alliance; elected to 4th and 5th European Parliament (1994–99, 1999–2004).

MAESA, Julia (c. 170–224 CE). See Julia Maesa.

MAFALDA. *Variant of Matilda.*

MAFALDA (c. 1197–1257). Portuguese princess. Born c. 1197; died May 1, 1257, in Arouca, Lisbon, Portugal; dau. of Douce of Aragon (1160–1198) and Sancho I (1154–1211 or 1212), king of Portugal (r. 1185–1211 or 1212); m. Enrique also known as Henry I (1184–1252), king of Castile (annulled in 1216).

MAFALDA OF HESSE (1902–1944). Italian-born princess. Name variations: Princess Mafalda of Savoy; landgravine of Hesse. Born Mafalda Maria Elizabeth, princess of Savoy, Nov 19, 1902, in Rome, Italy; died Aug 29, 1944, in Buchenwald concentration camp; dau. of Elena of Montenegro (1873–1952) and Victor Emmanuel III (1869–1947), king of Italy (r. 1900–1946); sister of Giovanna of Italy (1907–2000) and Maria of Savoy (b. 1914); m. Philip (b. 1896), landgrave of Hesse, Sept 23, 1925; children: Maurice Frederick (b. 1926), prince of Hesse; Henry William (b. 1927); Otto Adolf (b. 1937); Elizabeth Marguerite Elena (b. 1940), princess of Hesse (who m. Friedrich Carl, count of

Oppersdorf). ❖ Daughter of the king and queen of Italy, died in a concentration camp during WWII, accused of poisoning Hitler ally, Tsar Boris III of Bulgaria. ❖ See also *Women in World History.*

MAFALDA OF PORTUGAL (c. 1149–1173). *See Matilda of Portugal.*

MAFALDA OF SAVOY.
See Matilda of Maurienne (c. 1125–1157).
See Mafalda of Hesse (1902–1944).

MAFFETT, Debra Sue (c. 1957—). Miss America. Name variations: Debra Wilson. Born Debra Sue Maffett c. 1957 in Cut-N-Shoot, Texas; graduate of Lamar University; m. Buster Wilson (songwriter and music publisher). ❖ Named Miss America (1983), representing California; hosted, wrote and produced numerous network, cable and syndicated shows, as well as music albums; co-hosted "The New Harvest" for the Inspirational Network.

MAGAFAN, Ethel (1916–1993). American painter and muralist. Born in Chicago, IL, Oct 10, 1916; died 1993; dau. of Petros Magafan, also seen as Peter J. Magafan, and Julia (Bronick) Magafan; twin sister of artist Jenne Magafan; studied at Colorado Springs Fine Arts Center; m. Bruce Currie (artist), June 30, 1946; children: Jenne Magafan Currie. ❖ With sister, was hired by Frank Mechau to work as an assistant on some of his mural projects; commissioned to create 1st mural, *Wheat Threshing* (1937), for the Auburn, Nebraska, post office; with sister, exhibited a number of easel-size paintings at least 7 times and jointly produced the large-scale mural, *Mountains and Snow,* for boardroom of the Social Security Building (later known as the Health, Education, and Welfare Building) in Washington, DC; produced murals into her late 60s, for the US Senate Chamber, Recorder of Deeds Building in Washington, DC, and post offices at Wynne, AR, Mudill, OK, and Denver, CO. Received Tiffany Foundation award (1950s), Childe Hassam Purchase award from Academy of Arts and Letters (1970), Altman prize from National Academy of Design, as well as Hallgarten Award, and Edwin Austin Abbey Mural Award (1980). ❖ See also *Women in World History.*

MAGAFAN, Jenne (1916–1952). American painter and muralist. Born in Chicago, IL, Oct 10, 1916; died in Woodstock, NY, in 1952; dau. of Petros Magafan, also seen as Peter J. Magafan, and Julia (Bronick) Magafan; twin sister of artist Ethel Magafan; studied at Colorado Springs Fine Arts Center; m. Edward Chavez (artist). ❖ With sister, was hired by Frank Mechau to work as assistants on some of his mural projects; had 1st major commission, the mural *Western Town,* for post office in Helper, Utah; with sister, exhibited a number of easel-size paintings and jointly produced the large-scale mural, *Mountains and Snow,* for the boardroom of the Social Security Building in Washington, DC. Received Tiffany Foundation award (1950s). ❖ See also *Women in World History.*

MA-GCIG LAB-SGRON (c. 1055–c. 1149). Tibetan Buddhist master. Name variations: Magcig Labsgron. Born in Labphyi, Tibet, possibly in 1055; died 1149; taught by Skyo-ston Bsod-nams Bla ma and Grwa-pa Mngon-shes; children: (with an Indian Tantric yogin) 5; her son or grandson, Thod-smyon Bsam-grub, was an accomplished mediator. ❖ The most eminent female Buddhist master in Tibetan history, professed that she gave up all regard for personal appearance and social convention to become a Gcod practitioner; was vilified when she ran off with an Indian Tantric yogin; lived in Kong-po for many years, and gave birth to 5 children before leaving her family to study with famed Indian teacher of the Zhi-byed tradition, Pha Dam-pa Sangs-rgyas; retired to Mt. Zangs-ri Mkhar-dmar, living in retreat for the rest of life; also wrote a treatise on the Gcod meditational practice, which is comprised of indigenous pre-Buddhist ideas and the Prajnaparamita and Mahamudra doctrines she studied with Pha Dam-pa; had many disciples, including her son or grandson, whom she purportedly cured of epilepsy; remains a source of inspiration for new liturgies and lineages.

MAGDALEN. *Variant of Madeleine.*

MAGDALEN (fl. early 1st c.). *See Mary Magdalene.*

MAGDALENA (1532–1590). German princess. Born in Innsbruck, Aug 14, 1532; died in Hall, Tyrol, Dec 10, 1590; dau. of Anna of Bohemia and Hungary (1503–1547) and Ferdinand I, Holy Roman Emperor (r. 1556–1564); possibly m. the duke of Neuburg.

MAGDALENA (fl. late 1500s). Countess Palatine. Fl. in late 1500s; dau. of Mary (1531–1581) and William V, duke of Cleves (r. 1539–1592); sister of Maria Eleonora (1550–1608), duchess of Prussia; m. John I,

Count Palatine of Zweibrucken; children: John II, Count Palatine of Zweibrucken.

MAGDALENA AUGUSTA OF ANHALT-ZERBST (1679–1740). *See Madeleine of Anhalt-Zerbst.*

MAGDALENA SYBILLA (1587–1659). Electress of Saxony. Name variations: Magdalene Sibylle of Brandenberg; Magdelene Sibylle Hohenzollern. Born Jan 9, 1587 (some sources cite Dec 31, 1586); died Feb 22 (some sources cite Feb 12), 1659; dau. of Maria Eleanora (1550–1608) and Albert Frederick (b. 1553), duke of Prussia; sister of Anna of Prussia (1576–1625); m. John George I (1585–1656), elector of Saxony, July 29, 1607; children: Marie Elizabeth of Saxony (1610–1684); John George II, elector of Saxony (b. 1613); August, duke of Saxe-Weissenfels (b. 1614); Magdalena Sybilla (1617–1668).

MAGDALENA SYBILLA (1617–1668). Danish royal. Name variations: Magdalene Sibylle of Saxony. Born Dec 23, 1617; died Jan 6, 1668; dau. of Magdalena Sybilla (1587–1659) and John George I (1585–1656), elector of Saxony; m. Christian Oldenburg (1603–1647, son of Christian IV, king of Denmark), Oct 5, 1634.

MAGDALENA SYBILLA OF HOLSTEIN-GOTTORP (1631–1719). Duchess of Mecklenburg-Gustrow. Name variations: Magdalene Sibylle of Holstein-Gottorp. Born Nov 24, 1631; died April 22, 1719; dau. of Marie Elizabeth of Saxony (1610–1684) and Frederick III, duke of Holstein-Gottorp; m. Gustav Adolf, duke of Mecklenburg-Gustrow, Dec 28, 1654; children: Marie of Mecklenburg-Gustrow (1659–1701); Louise of Mecklenburg-Gustrow (1667–1721).

MAGDALENE (fl. early 1st c.). *See Mary Magdalene.*

MAGDALENE OF BRANDENBURG (1582–1616). Landgravine of Hesse-Darmstadt. Born Jan 7, 1582; died May 4, 1616; dau. of Elizabeth of Anhalt (1563–1607) and John George (1525–1598), elector of Brandenburg (r. 1571–1598); m. Louis V, landgrave of Hesse-Darmstadt, on June 5, 1598; children: Anne-Eleanor of Hesse-Darmstadt (1601–1659); George II (b. 1605), landgrave of Hesse-Darmstadt.

MAGDALENE OF OLDENBURG (1585–1657). Princess of Anhalt-Zerbst. Name variations: Magdalene von Oldenburg. Born Oct 6, 1585; died April 14, 1657; dau. of John XVI (b. 1540), count of Oldenburg, and Elizabeth von Schwarzburg (b. 1541); m. Rudolf, prince of Anhalt-Zerbst, Aug 31, 1612; children: John (b. 1621), prince of Anhalt-Zerbst.

MAGDALENE OF SAXONY (1507–1534). Princess of Saxony. Born Mar 7, 1507; died Jan 28, 1534; dau. of Barbara of Poland (1478–1534) and George the Bearded (b. 1471), duke of Saxony; m. Joachim II Hector (1505–1571), elector of Brandenburg (r. 1535–1571), Nov 6, 1524; children: John George (1525–1598), elector of Brandenburg (r. 1571–1598).

MAGDALEN WOMEN (c. 1820s–early 1970s). Irish women. ❖ In Ireland, Magdalen women, so called in reference to Mary Magdalene, were thousands of unwed mothers, orphans, and ex-prostitutes, who were confined to convents, where they worked as unpaid launderers until their deaths, when they were buried in unmarked graves on convent grounds. ❖ See also *Women in World History.*

MAGDELAINE DE FRANCE (1520–1537). *See Madeleine of France.*

MAGDELENE. *Variant of Magdalena or Magdalene.*

MAGEE, Joni (1941—). American obstetrician and gynecologist. Name variations: Joni Lahr Magee. Born Joni Lahr, 1941, in Philadelphia, PA; attended New York University and University of Pennsylvania; Medical College of Pennsylvania, MD, 1968; married and div.; children: at least 3. ❖ Influenced by personal childbirth experiences with insensitive physicians, encouraged physicians to educate themselves about the perspectives and needs of female patients; interned in pediatrics at Philadelphia's Presbyterian Hospital and served as a resident of internal medicine at Medical College of Pennsylvania; worked as a resident at Philadelphia's Jefferson Hospital (1971–76); employed full-time at Booth Maternity Center (from 1976); maintained a Merion Station (PA) practice.

MAGEE, Martha Maria (d. 1846). Irish philanthropist. Born Martha Maria Stewart in Lurgan, Co. Armagh, Northern Ireland; died 1846; m. William Magee (Presbyterian minister), 1780 (died 1800). ❖ After husband and brothers died (1800), inherited what was then considered a fortune; on her death, bequeathed a sum of £20,000 sterling to be used for the construction and endowment of Magee College to educate and train Irish Presbyterian ministers (it is now part of University of Ulster).

MAGEE, Samantha (1983—). American rower. Born July 10, 1983, in Hartford, CT; attended Stanford University. ❖ Won a silver medal for coxed eights at Athens Olympics (2004); won 2 World Cups for coxed eights (2004).

MAGER, Manuela (1962—). East German pairs skater. Born July 11, 1962, in Dresden, East Germany. ❖ With Uwe Bewersdorf, won a bronze medal at Lake Placid Olympics (1980); left East Germany before reunification and moved to Starnberg.

MAGERAS, Georgia Lathouris (1867–1950). Greek midwife. Name variations: Magerou, the Greek Midwife. Born Georgia Lathouris, 1867 in Achladokambos, Greece; died of leukemia in 1950; m. Nick "Niko" Mageras (an Austrian, died 1946); children: 7. ❖ With husband, moved to Snaketown, Utah, a community with other Greek immigrant families; treated immigrant male workers and was particularly good at caring for broken bones; as a midwife, boasted a perfect record (0 deaths); was adamant about sanitation and cleanliness when delivering; cared for both mother and child patients until the baby was baptized; assisted physicians and actively worked into her late 70s.

MAGEROU (1867–1950). See Mageras, Georgia Lathouris.

MAGERS, Rose (1960—). African-American volleyball player. Born June 25, 1960, in Big Spring, TX; attended University of Houston. ❖ Won a team bronze medal at World championships (1982); at Los Angeles Olympics, won a silver medal in team competition (1984).

MAGGIE. Variant of Margaret.

MAGILL, Helen White (1853–1944). See White, Helen Magill.

MAGNANI, Anna (1908–1973). Italian actress. Born Mar 7, 1908, in Rome, Italy; died Sept 26, 1973, in Rome; dau. of Marina Magnani, from Romagna; father unknown, except that he was from Calabria; m. Goffredo Alessandrini (director), 1935 (annulled 1950); children: (with actor Massimo Serato) son, Luca Alessandrini (b. 1942). ❖ For a time, reigned as Italy's best-known screen presence in theaters around the world; studied at Rome's Academy of Dramatic Art while earning living as nightclub singer; began appearing in plays and variety shows (mid-1920s); made 1st film appearance in *Scampolo* (1927), though she did not receive recognition as a film actress until 1941, in Vittorio De Sica's *Teresa Venerdi*; became international star with appearance in Rossellini's *Roma, città aperta* (*Open City*, 1945), which has often been called the opening salvo of Italian neo-realism; was given American Board of Review's Best Foreign Actress award (1946); appeared in *La Voce Umana* (The Human Voice) and *Il Miracolo* (The Miracle); also starred in Visconti's *Bellissima* and Renoir's *La Carrozza Doro*; continued to work steadily in film and tv until her death; other films include *Un Uomo ritorna* (1946), *Davanti a lui tremava tutta Roma* (1946), *Il Bandito* (1946), *Abbasso la Ricchezza* (1946), *Lo Sconosciuto di San Marino* (1947), *Quartetto Pazzo* (1947), *L'Onorevole Angelina* (1947), *Assunta Spina* (1947), *Molti Sogni per le Strade* (1948), *Vulcano* (1950), *Camicie rosse* (1952), *Siamo Donne* (1953), *Suor Letizia* (1956), *Nella Città l'Inferno* (1958), *The Fugitive Kind* (1960), *Made in Italy* (1965), *The Secret of Santa Vittoria* (1969) and *Fellini's Roma* (1972). Won Academy Award for performance in screen adaptation of Williams' *The Rose Tattoo* (1955); nominated for Best Actress for *Wild Is the Wind* (1957). ❖ See also *Women in World History.*

MAGNES, Frances (1919—). American violinist. Born Frances Shapiro in Cleveland, Ohio, April 27, 1919. ❖ At 14, made debut with Cleveland Orchestra under Artur Rodzinski; toured America with Busch Chamber Players (1945–46); made recordings with Ernö Dohnányi and New York Philharmonic Orchestra; was 1st to perform and record Stefan Wolpe's Violin Sonata (1949) and Tibor Serly's Sonata (1950); increasingly appeared with Westchester Symphony Orchestra where she was concert-master (1960s). ❖ See also *Women in World History.*

MAGNUS (d. 1676). Sunksquaw of the Narragansett tribe. Name variations: Matantuck; Quaiapan; Old Queen. Born in area now known as Rhode Island, during middle 1600s; died 1676, near Warwick, RI; m. Mriksah. ❖ A member of the powerful Narragansetts, led her tribe into battle during King Philip's War (1675–76); when the Narragansetts were defeated, was taken prisoner and executed as a warrior with 90 of her tribe. ❖ See also *Women in World History.*

MAGNUSSEN, Karen (1952—). Canadian figure skater. Name variations: Karen Magnussen Cella. Born April 4, 1952, in North Vancouver, British Columbia, Canada; m. Toby Cella. ❖ Won a silver medal at Sapporo Olympics (1972), the only Canadian to medal at the games; at World championships, won a bronze (1971), silver (1972), and gold medal (1973); was 5-time Canadian champion (1968–73); turned to coaching. Awarded Order of Canada (1973); inducted into Canadian Sports Hall of Fame (1973).

MAGOFFIN, Susan Shelby (1827–c. 1855). American diarist. Born Susan Shelby in Arcadia, KY, July 30, 1827; died in Barrett's Station, MO, c. 1855; m. Samuel Magoffin, 1845; children: 2 daughters. ❖ The 1st white woman to travel the Santa Fe Trail, kept a written record of the journey, which was published as *Down the Santa Fe Trail and Into Mexico: The Diary of Susan Shelby Magoffin, 1846–1847* (1926). ❖ See also *Women in World History.*

MAGOGO KA DINIZULU, Constance (1900–1984). South African composer, singer, ugubhu player. Name variations: Princess Magogo. Born in Nongoma, South Africa, 1900; died in Durban, Nov 21, 1984; dau. of Chief Dinuzulu Ka Cetshwayo; m. Chief Mathole Shenge Buthelezi; children: son, Chief Mangosuthu Buthelezi, was chief minister of KwaZulu. ❖ Princess whose songs were connected with Zulu life and history, learned the Zulu musical repertoire from mother and grandmothers, memorizing songs that date back to 18th century; learned to play the *ugubhu*, a musical bow, the *umakhweyana* bow, and the European autoharp; became primary wife of Chief Mathole and had son Mangosutho Buthelezi, who would become a powerful figure in South African politics like his parents; continued to sing and compose songs of a court and ceremonial nature and also sang traditional songs; made recordings (1939); as an authority, was frequently consulted on knowledge of Zulu music and served as musical consultant for the film *Zulu*. ❖ See also *Women in World History.*

MAGONI, Paoletta (1964—). Italian Alpine skier. Born Sept 14, 1964, in Selvino, Italy. ❖ Won a gold medal for slalem at Sarajevo Olympics (1984); placed 7th for slalom at Calgary Olympics (1988); won a bronze medal for slalom at World championships (1985).

MAGRI, Lavinia Warren (1841–1919). See Warren, Lavinia.

MAGRUDER, Julia (1854–1907). American novelist. Born Sept 14, 1854, in Charlottesville, VA; died June 9, 1907, in Richmond, VA; dau. of Allan Bowie Magruder (lawyer) and Sarah (Gilliam) Magruder; niece of John Bankhead Magruder (US army officer). ❖ Anonymously published 1st novel, *Across the Chasm* (1885), about the need for reconciliation between North and South which attracted much attention, but none of her subsequent works received as much fanfare; also wrote *The Princess Sonia* (1895), *A Magnificent Plebeian* (1888), *Struan* (1899), *A Heaven-Kissing Hill* (1899), and *A Sunny Southerner* (1901), among others.

MAGUIRE, Joan (1936—). See Tewkesbury, Joan.

MAGUIRE, Mairead (b. 1944). See Corrigan, Mairead.

MAHALATH. See Bashemath.

MAHALDE. Variant of Matilda or Maud.

MAHAPAJAPATI (fl. 570 BCE). Indian nun. Name variations: Mahaprajapati; Mahaprajapati Gautami; Gautami Mahapajapati. Fl. c. 570 BCE in Nepal, near the Indian border; younger sister of Maya; m. Suddhodana or Suddhodanaa (who was also m. to her sister Maya); aunt and foster mother to Prince Siddhartha Gautama or Gautami, also known as the Buddha (c. 563–483 BCE). ❖ Became a nun. ❖ See also *Women in World History.*

MAHARANI or MAHARANEE OF GONDWANA. See Durgawati (d. 1564).

MAHARANI or MAHARANEE OF GURRAH. See Durgawati (d. 1564).

MAHARANI or MAHARANEE OF JAIPUR. See Gayatri Devi (b. 1919).

MAHARANI or MAHARANEE OF JHANSI. See Lakshmibai (c. 1835–1858).

MAHAULT. Variant of Matilda or Maud.

MAHAUT. Variant of Matilda, Maud, and Mahout.

MAHAUT (c. 1270–1329). Countess of Artois. Name variations: Matilda of Artois; Mahout or Mahaut Capet; Mahaut of Artois; Mahaut of Burgundy; Mahaut of Flanders. Pronunciation: Mah-o. Born c. 1270 in Artois; died in Paris, Nov 27, 1329, of a sudden illness; dau. of Robert II, count of Artois, and Amicie de Courtenay (d. 1275), both high-ranking members of the French nobility; m. Othon also known as Otto IV, count palatine of Burgundy, in 1285; children: Jeanne I of Burgundy (c. 1291–1330, queen of France); Blanche of Burgundy (1296–1326, queen of France); Robert (born c. 1299); Jean (born c. 1300, died in infancy). ❖ One of the most important women in France during early 14th century, utilized her social standing to be an active participant in the politics and culture of French courtly society; inherited the county of Artois at father's death (1302); became regent for her son as count of Burgundy when her husband died (1303); saw eldest daughter Jeanne I of Burgundy marry Philip, 2nd son of King Philip of France (1306 or 1307); saw daughter Blanche of Burgundy marry Charles, another son of the French king (1307); continued to administer her feudal holdings in Artois and Burgundy; daughters were involved in a scandal of adultery at the French court for which Blanche was imprisoned and Jeanne was acquitted (1314); son Robert died, leaving her as sole heir to the county of Artois (Sept 1317); was cleared by her son-in-law, King Philip V of France, of charges of sorcery and treason (Oct 1317); her claims to the county of Artois were upheld by Philip V against counter-claims brought by her nephew, Robert (1318). ❖ See also *Women in World History.*

MAHAUT I (r. 1215–1242). Ruler of Bourbon. Name variations: Dame Mahaut. Heir of Archimbaud or Archambaud V, ruler of Bourbon (r. 1116–1171); m. Gautier de Vienne, ruler of Bourbon (r. 1171–1215); m. Gui II de Dampierre, in 1242; children: (2nd m.) 2 daughters, Mahaut II de Dampierre (1234–1266) and Agnes de Dampierre (1237–1288). ❖ After husband's death (1215), ruled for 27 years, until 2nd marriage (1242). ❖ See also *Women in World History.*

MAHAUT II DE DAMPIERRE (1234–1266). Countess of Tonnerre. Name variations: Baroness Mahaut; countess of Tonnere; Mahaut II de Bourbon. Born in 1234; died in 1266 (some sources cite 1262); dau. of Mahaut I (r. 1215–1242) and her 2nd husband Gui II de Dampierre; sister of Agnes de Dampierre; m. Eudes de Bourgogne or Eudes (1230–1266), count of Nevers, in 1248; children: Yolande of Burgundy (1248–1280); Marguerite de Bourgogne (1250–1308); Alix of Burgundy (1251–1290, who m. John I, count d'Auxerre and Tonnerre). ❖ Succeeded to the throne of Bourbon upon death of Baron Archambaud VII (1249); succeeded grandmother, Countess Mahaut de Courtenay, who ruled Nevers (1182–1257); ruled Bourbon (1249–1262) and Nevers (1257–1266). ❖ See also *Women in World History.*

MAHAUT DE BOULOGNE (c. 1103–1152). See *Matilda of Boulogne.*

MAHAUT DE CHATILLON (d. 1358). Countess of Valois. Name variations: Mahaut of Chatillon; Mahaut de Chatillon-Saint-Pol; Matilda of Chatillon or Châtillon; Matilda of Chatillon. Died Oct 3, 1358; possibly dau. of Gaucher de Chatillon, lord of Crevecoeur, count of Porcien, constable of France since 1302; possibly dau. of Guido III, count of St. Pol; became third wife of Charles I (1270–1325), count of Valois (son of Philip III the Bold, king of France), in June 1308; children: Isabelle of Savoy (d. 1383); Blanche of Valois (c. 1316–?). ❖ Charles' 1st wife was Margaret of Anjou (c. 1272–1299); his 2nd was Catherine de Courtenay (d. 1307).

MAHAUT DE COURTENAY (d. 1257). Countess and ruler of Nevers. Died in 1257; dau. of Pierre de Courtenay and Countess Agnes de Nevers (r. 1181–1192); m. Count Hervé de Donzy, in 1199 (died 1226); m. Guy de Forez. ❖ Reigned (1192–1257); succeeded by her granddaughter Mahaut II de Dampierre (1257).

MAHAUT DE DAMMARTIN OR DAMMARATIN (d. 1258). See *Matilda de Dammartin.*

MAHAUT LOUVAIN (1224–1288). See *Maude of Brabant.*

MAHAUT OF ARTOIS (c. 1270–1329). See *Mahaut.*

MAHAUT OF BURGUNDY (d. 1202). Countess of Auvergne. Name variations: Mahaut de Bourgogne; Matilda of Burgundy. Died July 22, 1202; dau. of Eudes II (1118–1162), duke of Burgundy (r. 1143–1162), and Marie of Blois (1128–1190); m. Robert IV, count of Auvergne.

MAHAUT OF BURGUNDY (c. 1270–1329). See *Mahaut.*

MAHAUT OF FLANDERS (c. 1270–1329). See *Mahaut.*

MAHBUBA (fl. 9th c.). Arabian poet and singer. Born in al-Basra (now Iraq); flourished 840s–860s. ❖ Became the property of a man of al-Taif who taught her poetry and how to play the lute and sing; given to Mutawakki (r. 847–861) as a gift when he ascended the throne as

caliph; when Mutawakki was murdered (861), became the property of Wasif al-Turki who had initiated the assassination; continued to mourn the slain caliph and was thrown in prison; saved from death by a Turkish captain, went to Baghdad; is the only historical female singer to appear in *The Thousand and One Nights.* ❖ See also *Women in World History.*

MAHER, Ellen (1799–1878). See *Maher, Mary Cecilia.*

MAHER, Granny (1893–1959). See *McDonald, Hedwick Wilhelmina.*

MAHER, Hedwick Wilhelmina (1893–1959). See *McDonald, Hedwick Wilhelmina.*

MAHER, Kim (1971—). American softball player. Born Sept 5, 1971, in Vietnam; grew up in CA. ❖ Won a team gold medal at Atlanta Olympics (1996).

MAHER, Mary Cecilia (1799–1878). New Zealand nun, teacher, and social worker. Name variations: Ellen Maher. Born Ellen Maher, Sept 13, 1799, in Co. Kilkenny, Ireland; died Oct 10, 1878, in Auckland, New Zealand; dau. of John Maher (farmer) and Adelaide Maher; St. Leo's Convent, Carlow, Ireland. ❖ Took vows (1840); was among 1st group of women religious to arrive in New Zealand (1850); administered existing schools, later founded a boarding school for girls from affluent families, and school for Maori girls; tended to social needs of community during goldrush period in Auckland; established new convent for Auckland Sisters of Mercy (1862). ❖ See also *Dictionary of New Zealand Biography* (Vol. 1).

MAHER, Robyn (1959—). Australian basketball player. Born Robyn Gull, Oct 6, 1959, in Ballarat, Australia; m. Thomas Maher (basketball coach). ❖ Was captain of the Opals (1989–99); as captain, won a team bronze medal at Atlanta Olympics (1996); with husband, was instrumental in Australia's rise to world prominence in women's basketball as player and administrator. Was Australia's WNBL MVP (1984) and Defensive Player of the Year (1993); received Maher medal (1988, 1990–91).

MAHLAH. Biblical woman. Eldest of 5 daughters of Zelophehad, of the Manasseh tribe. ❖ When father died without male heirs, requested permission from Moses, along with her 4 sisters, to inherit father's property; was granted the request, with the stipulation that the sisters marry within their father's tribe (afterwards, Moses' judgment concerning the inheritance became general law).

MAHLER, Alma (1879–1964). Austrian music composer and diarist. Name variations: Alma Mahler-Gropius; Alma Mahler-Werfel. Born Alma Marie Schindler, Aug 31, 1879, in Vienna, Austria; died in New York, NY, Dec 11, 1964; dau. of (Emil) Jakob Schindler (Viennese painter) and Anna Bergen (or von Bergen) Schindler (singer); m. Gustav Mahler, Mar 9, 1902 (died 1911); m. Walter Gropius, Aug 18, 1915 (div. 1920); m. Franz Werfel, July 6, 1929 (died 1945); children: (1st m.) Maria Mahler (1902–1907); Anna Mahler, known as Gucki (b. 1904); (2nd m.) Manon Gropius (1916–1935); (with Franz Werfel) Martin (1918–1920). ❖ Though she had her own set of gifts as a composer, is most prominent for her role as the companion—married and otherwise—of some of the most talented men on the European cultural scene from close of 19th through 1st half of 20th century; studied counterpoint with Josef Labor, noted Vienna organist; composed serious music and pursued a career in musical world; at 19, became romantically involved with Gustav Klimt (1898); married Gustav Mahler (1902), who insisted that she give up her work as a composer; began love affair with Walter Gropius (1910); following death of husband, began love affair with Oscar Kokoschka (1912); married Gropius (1915); began love affair with Franz Werfel (1917), the last and also the greatest love of her life; went into exile from Austria with Werfel (1938); settled in US (1941); began work on autobiography (1945) which was published as *And the Bridge is Love* (1958); became US citizen (1946). ❖ See also Françoise Giroud, *Alma Mahler or the Art of Being Loved* (trans. by R.M. Stock, Oxford U. Press, 1991); Susanne Keegan, *The Bride of the Wind: The Life and Times of Alma Mahler-Werfel* (Secker & Warburg, 1991); Karen Monson, *Alma Mahler: Muse to Genius* (Houghton, 1983); and *Women in World History.*

MAHLER, Hedwig (1867–1950). See *Courths-Mahler, Hedwig.*

MAHLER, Maria (1895–1942). See *Leichter, Käthe.*

MAHON, Alice (1937—). English politician and member of Parliament. Born Alice Bottomley, Sept 28, 1937; m. 2nd husband Tony Mahon. ❖ Representing Labour, elected to House of Commons for Halifax (1992, 1997, 2001); left Parliament (2005).

MAHONEY, Ernestine (1910–2000). *See Howard, Jean.*

MAHONEY, Mary Eliza (1845–1926). African-American nurse. Name variations: Mary Elizabeth Mahoney. Born Mary Elizabeth Mahoney, April 15 (some sources cite April 16, others May 7), 1845, in Dorchester, MA; died Jan 4, 1926; dau. of Charles Mahoney and Mary Jane (Steward) Mahoney; New England Hospital for Women and Children, RN, 1879; never married; no children. ❖ At 18, began working at New England Hospital for Women and Children as a cook and scrubber; at 33, was finally accepted as a student nurse (1878); became 1st black woman in US to earn a nursing degree (1879); supported the efforts of Martha Minerva Franklin, who founded the National Association of Colored Graduate Nurses (NACGN, 1908), and delivered welcoming address at association's 1st annual convention (1909); awarded lifetime membership in NACGN and became the group's national chaplain (1911); moved to NY (1911) and became supervisor of Howard Orphan Asylum for Black Children in Kings Park, LI, where she remained until her retirement (1922). ❖ See also *Women in World History.*

MAHONY, Bertha (1882–1869). *See Miller, Bertha Mahony.*

MAHONY, Marion (1871–1961). American architect. Name variations: Marion Mahony Griffin; Marion Lucy Griffin; Mrs. Walter Burley Griffin. Born Marion Lucy Mahony, Feb 14, 1871, in Chicago, IL; died Aug 10, 1961, in Chicago; dau. of Jeremiah Mahony (schoolteacher and journalist) and Clara (Perkins) Mahony (principal); Massachusetts Institute of Technology, degree in architecture, 1894; m. Walter Burley Griffin (architect), 1911 (died 1937); no children. ❖ Became the 1st woman licensed to practice architecture in Illinois (1896) and began working with Frank Lloyd Wright in his Oak Park studio; one of her greatest skills, during her time with Wright and later, was as a delineator (or artist) of architectural plans; executed the designs for the *Ausgeführte Bauten und Entwurfe von Frank Lloyd Wright* (also called the Wasmuth Portfolio, 1910), which brought Wright his 1st significant international recognition; during Wright's absence in Europe, designed the David Amberg House in Grand Rapids, MI (1909–11), the Adolph Mueller House in Decatur, IL (1910), and an unexecuted house for Henry Ford; went into partnership with husband, and her work was a major factor in his winning a commission to design Canberra, the new capital city of Australia (1912); lived in Australia (1914–35), and designed Castlecrag, a self-contained community on banks of Sydney Harbor; following husband's death (1937), returned to Chicago where she established her own practice and remained active for another 20 years. ❖ See also *Women in World History.*

MAHOUT. *See Variant of Mahaut.*

MAHRINGER, Erika (1924—). Austrian Alpine skier. Name variations: Riki Mahringer; Erika Spiess-Mahringer; Riki Spiess. Born Nov 16, 1924, in Austria; m. Ernst Spiess (member of the Austrian ski national team); children: Uli Spiess (b. 1955, skier) and Nicola Werenigg-Spiess (b. 1958, skier). ❖ Member of the Austrian national team (1947–54); won bronze medals for combined and slalom at St. Moritz Olympics (1948); opened a ski school in Mayrhofen (1954).

MAHUPUKU, Maata (1890–1952). New Zealand literary inspiration. Name variations: Maata Mahupuku McGregor, Maata Mahupuku Asher. Born April 10 (1890, in Greytown, Wairarapa, New Zealand; died on Jan 15, 1952, in Palmerston North, New Zealand; dau. of Richard (Tiki) William Mahupuku (sheepfarmer) and Emily (Sexton) Mahupuku; m. George Steward McGregor (farmer), 1907, div. 1914; m. Thomas Asher (landowner), 1914, div. 1932; children: (1st m.) 1 son, 2 daughters; (2nd m.) 2 daughters. ❖ Friend of Katherine Mansfield and inspiration for story, "Kezia and Tui" (1916), and unfinished novel, *Maata,* published posthumously. ❖ See also *Dictionary of New Zealand Biography* (Vol. 3).

MAHY, Margaret (1936—). New Zealand children's writer. Born Mar 21, 1936, in Whakatane, New Zealand; dau. of Francis George (builder) and May (Penlington) Mahy (teacher); University of New Zealand, BA, 1958; children: Penelope Helen and Bridget Frances. ❖ Graduated from University of Canterbury and attended New Zealand Library School, Wellington; became children's librarian at Christchurch City Libraries; wrote tv scripts, poems, plays, and picture books for children; works include *The Procession* (1961), *A Lion in the Meadow* (1969), *The Wind Between the Stars* (1976), *The Changeover* (1984), *Memory* (1987), *Tick Tock tales* (1993), *The Other Side of Silence* (1996), *Alchemy* (2002), and *Dashing Dog* (2002). Received Esther Glenn Medal from New Zealand Library Association for *A Lion in the Meadow* (1969), *The First*

Margaret Mahy Story Book (1973) and *The Haunting* (1983); won Carnegie Medal for *The Haunting* (1982).

MAHZOLINI, Anna (1716–1774). *See Manzolini, Anna Morandi.*

MAIA (fl. c. 100 BCE). *See Iaia.*

MAIATITSA (1898–1990). *See Bunzel, Ruth.*

MAIDEN QUEEN, the (1533–1603). *See Elizabeth I.*

MAIDMENT, Ellen Wright (1836–1885). *See Blackwell, Ellen Wright.*

MAID OF ANTIOCH (c. 255–c. 275). *See Margaret of Antioch.*

MAID OF NORWAY (c. 1283–1290). *See Margaret, Maid of Norway.*

MAID OF ORLEANS (c. 1412–1431). *See Joan of Arc.*

MAID OF SARAGOSSA OR ZARAGOZA (1788–1857). *See Agostina.*

MAID OF THE MILL (1864–1934). *See Jermy, Louie.*

MAIER, Ulrike (1967–1994). Austrian skier. Born Oct 22, 1967, in Rauris, Austria; killed Jan 29, 1994, during a World Cup downhill race in Garmisch-Partenkirchen, Germany. ❖ Won World championships for Super-G (1989, 1991); placed 5th overall at World Cup (1992–93).

MAIERHOFER, Ine (1976—). *See Poetzl, Ine.*

MAIGA-KA, Aminata (1940—). Senegalese novelist. Name variations: Rokhayatou Aminata Maïga Ka. Born Jan 11, 1940, in St-Louis, Senegal; studied in Senegal, France, and US; m. Abdou Anta Ka; children: 6. ❖ Worked as English teacher and then filled several high level positions in UNESCO and Senegalese government; served as technical advisor to Ministry of Education, member of Central Committee of Socialist Party, and Senegalese Cultural Attaché in Rome, Italy; works include *La voie du salut suivi de Le miroir de la vie* (1985), *En votre nom au mien* (1989), and *Brisures de vies* (1998).

MAIHI, Rehutai (1895–1967). New Zealand tribal leader, journalist, newspaper publisher and editor, and politician. Name variations: Nellie Nathan, Rehutai Netana, Nell Rehutai Nathan, Rehutai Gilberd. Born Sept 16, 1895, at Whakapara, near Whangarei, New Zealand; died Aug 12, 1967, at Kawakawa, New Zealand; dau. of Netana Maihi (bushman) and Te Paea Nehua; m. Stanley Gilberd (contractor, d. 1967), 1933; children: 1 daughter. ❖ Edited *Northlander* newspaper (1920s); wrote for Kawakawa *Luminary* and *Northland Age* under pen-name Nellie Nathan; founded Maori-language newspaper, *Aotearoa,* 1932; was the 1st Maori woman to run for Parliament (1935). ❖ See also *Dictionary of New Zealand Biography.*

MAIJ-WEGGEN, Hanja (1943—). Dutch politician. Name variations: Johanna R.H. Maij-Weggen. Born Dec 29, 1943, in Emmen, Netherlands; attended AZVU nurses school, Amstelveen; studied social pedagogy at Amersterdam Municipal University. ❖ Member of Dutch delegation to UN (1977–78); as a member of the European People's Party (Christian Democrats) and European Democrats (EPP), elected to 1st, 2nd, 3rd, 4th and 5th European Parliament (EP, 1979–86, 1986–90, 1990–94, 1994–99, 1999–2004); served as vice-chair of the EPP Group in the EP (1986–89) and minister of Transport and Public Works (1989–94). Awarded European Schuman medal (1989); named Knight of the Order of the Netherlands (1994).

MAIJ-WEGGEN, Johanna R.H. (1943—). *See Maij-Weggen, Hanja.*

MAILER, Jeanne (1928—). *See Campbell, Lady Jeanne.*

MAILING SOONG (1897–2003). *See Song Meiling.*

MAILLART, Ella (1903–1997). Swiss-French writer, traveler, skier, and yacht racer. Name variations: Ella K. Maillart; Kini. Pronunciation: MY-ar. Born Ella Katherine Maillart, 1903, in Geneva, Switzerland; died in her mountain chalet in Chandolin, Switzerland, Mar 27, 1997; dau. of middle-class parents, her father was a fur-trader; never married; no children; spent winter months in Geneva, summer months in Alpine village of Chandolin. ❖ Perhaps one of the last great 20th-century travelers to explore Asia before the onslaught of modern tourism, whose many travel narratives introduced Western readers to new, challenging perspectives on previously unexplored cultures, learned to sail on Lake Geneva as a child; captained and organized 1st Swiss women's field hockey team; represented Switzerland in single-handed yacht competition in Paris Olympics (1924), the only woman among 17 entrants; sailed to Crete with all-woman crew (1925); traveled to Berlin and later Moscow (1930) to study filmmaking; became a 4-year member of international Swiss ski team, trekking to then-Soviet Caucuses, then-Soviet Central Asia, Peking, Tibet, Afghanistan, and India (1930s–40s). Writings include *Turkestan Solo: One Woman's Expedition from the Tien Shan to the Kizil Kum* (*Des Montes Celestes aux Sables Rouges*, 1938), *Forbidden Journey: From Peking to Kashmir* (*Oasis Interdites*, 1937), *Gypsy Afloat* (1942), *Cruises and Caravans* (1942), *The Cruel Way* (1947), *Ti-Puss* (1951) and *Land of the Sherpas* (1955). ❖ See also *Women in World History.*

MAILLÉ, Jeanne-Marie de (1331–1414). French prophet. Born 1331 into aristocratic family in Touraine region; died 1414. ❖ Grew up under the guidance of an erudite Franciscan monk; influenced by the lives of the saints, obtained an agreement from husband at the time of their marriage (1347 or 1348), that the union would not be consummated; after husband's death (1362), lived as a recluse, 1st settling in Tours and then moving near a Franciscan monastery (1386); in a life divided between prayer and care of the poor and sick, had visions and apparitions of Mary the Virgin and St. Francis; prophesied that the Great Schism would be brought to an end by a Franciscan (1396), a prophecy that came true in 1409, with the election of Pope Alexander V; despite hermit's life, kept close links with aristocratic families of Touraine and Vendée, exerting spiritual influence on the members of the same aristocratic circle who were later supporters of Joan of Arc; met Charles VI privately and also reproached Queen Isabeau of Bavaria, who was mistress of the king's brother, Louis of Orleans.

MAILLET, Antonine (1929—). Canadian novelist. Born May 10, 1929, in Bouctouche, New Brunswick, Canada; attended universities of Montreal and Laval. ❖ Works, which draw on Acadian history, language, and folklore, include *Pointe-aux-Coques* (1958), *La Sagouine* (1971, trans. into English with same title, 1979), *Don L'Original* (1972, trans. as *The Tale of Don L'Original*), *Crache à Pic* (1984, trans. as *The Devil is Loose!* 1986), *Le Huitième Jour* (1986, trans. as *On the Eighth Day,* 1989), *Les Confessions de Jeanne de Valois* (1992), and *Le Chemin Saint-Jacques* (1996). Won Prix Goncourt for *Pélagie-la-Charrette* (1979, trans. as *Pélagie: The Return to a Homeland,* 1983); received Governor General's Award (1972) and Le Prix Québec-Paris (1975); named Companion of the Order of Canada and Officer of the Ordre National du Québec.

MAILLY, Louise Julie de Mailly-Nesle, Comtesse de (1710–1751). French mistress of Louis XV. Name variations: Comtesse de Mailly; countess of Mailly. Born 1710; died 1751; dau. of Louis, marquis de Nesle (whose family name was Mailly) and Madame de Nesle (lady-in-waiting to Queen Marie Leczinska); sister of Pauline, marquise de Vintimille (1712–1741), Marie Anne de Mailly-Nesle, Duchesse de Châteauroux (1717–1744), and the Duchesse de Lauraguais; m. her 1st cousin. ❖ During her 4-year relationship with Louis XV, actually loved him. ❖ See also *Women in World History.*

MAILLY-NESLE, Marie Anne de (1717–1744). See *Châteauroux, Marie Anne de Mailly-Nesle, Duchesse de.*

MAIMUNAH BINT AL-HARITH (fl. 7th c.). Wife of Muhammad. Sister-in-law of Muhammad's uncle Abbas; widowed; m. Muhammad, 629. ❖ See also *Women in World History.*

MAIN, Janet (c. 1819–1892). See *Donald, Janet.*

MAIN, Marjorie (1890–1975). American actress. Born Mary Tomlinson, Feb 24, 1890, in Acton, IN; died in Los Angeles, CA, April 10, 1975; dau. of Rev. Samuel Tomlinson and Mary (McGaughey) Tomlinson; attended Knickerbocker Hall, Franklin College, and Hamilton College; studied dramatics in Chicago and NY; m. Stanley L. Krebs (psychologist), Nov 2, 1921 (died 1934); no children. ❖ Veteran of Broadway stage and some 80 movies, including the popular "Ma and Pa Kettle" series, was one of the finest character actresses of her time; made NY debut at Palace Theater, appearing in a comedy skit with W.C. Fields; made Broadway debut in *Cheating Cheaters* (1916), followed by *Yes or No* (1917); after husband's death (1934), returned to Broadway in breakthrough role of Mrs. Martin, mother of a gangster, in *Dead End* (1935), which ran for a year; followed that with another showy part in *The Women* (1936); turned to film (1937), finding her niche in a series of comedies, many with Wallace Beery; films include *Dead End* (1937), *Stella Dallas* (1937), *Test Pilot* (1938), *Three Comrades* (1938), *Angels Wash Their Faces* (1939), *The Women* (1939), *Another Thin Man* (1939), *Susan and God* (1940), *The Trial of Mary Dugan* (1941), *Barnacle Bill* (1941), *Honky Tonk* (1941), *Heaven Can Wait* (1943), *Meet Me in St. Louis* (1944), *Murder He Says* (1945), *The Harvey Girls* (1946), *The*

Wistful Widow of Wagon Gap (1947), *The Long Long Trailer* (1954), and *Friendly Persuasion* (1956). Nominated for Academy Award for *The Egg and I* (1947). ❖ See also *Women in World History.*

MAIN, Mrs. (1861–1934). See *Le Blond, Elizabeth.*

MAINE, countess of.
See *Rothild (c. 871–c. 928).*
See *Matilda of Château-du-Loir.*
See *Ermentrude (d. 1126).*
See *Jeanne of Lorraine (1458–1480).*

MAINES, Natalie (1974—). American musician. Name variations: Dixie Chicks. Born Oct 14, 1974, in Lubbock, TX; dau. of Lloyd Maines (producer and steel guitarist); married (div. 1999); m. Adrian Pasdar (actor), June 2000. ❖ Joined country-music group Dixie Chicks (1995), as vocalist and guitar player; with group, released back-to-back multi-platinum Grammy-winning country albums: *Wide Open Spaces* (1998) and *Fly* (1999).

MAINTENON, Françoise d'Aubigné, Marquise de (1635–1719). French marchioness and paramour. Name variations: Madame or Mlle Maintenon. Born Nov 27, 1635, in Niort Prison, Poitou, France; died April 15, 1719, at St. Cyr; interred at St. Cyr; dau. of Constant d'Aubigné and Jeanne de Cardilhac; married poet Paul Scarron, 1652 (died 1660); m. Louis XIV (1638–1715), king of France (r. 1643–1715), June 12, 1683 or 1684; no children. ❖ The 2nd wife of Louis XIV, was born Catholic but educated by a Protestant aunt until age 7; lived with family in French West Indies (1645–47); at 12, given into the care of another aunt, was sent to an Ursuline convent where she was educated in the Catholic faith; following husband's death, lived a quiet, though far from isolated, life in a convent (1660–68); became nurse and governess of Louis XIV's illegitimate children, the product of his liaison with Madame de Montespan; made a marquise (1675); appointed lady-in-waiting to the dauphine (1679); became Louis' mistress (1680); after the queen died (1683), entered into a morganatic marriage with the king, but was never crowned queen of France; had a positive influence on Louis and was soon accepted by most of his family as well as his legitimate children; set up school for girls at St. Cyr (1686); retired to St. Cyr after death of Louis (1715). ❖ See also H.C. Barnard, *Madame de Maintenon and Saint-Cyr* (Black, 1934); M. Cruttwell, *Madame de Maintenon* (Dutton, 1930); Charlotte Haldane, *Madame de Maintenon: Uncrowned Queen of France* (Constable, 1970); and *Women in World History.*

MAIQUES DERN, Ana (1967—). Spanish field-hockey player. Born Sept 3, 1967, in Spain. ❖ At Barcelona Olympics, won a gold medal in team competition (1992).

MAIR, E.K. (1862–1893). See *Sperrey, Eleanor Catherine.*

MAIR, Eleanor Catherine (1862–1893). See *Sperrey, Eleanor Catherine.*

MAIRET, Ethel (1872–1952). English weaver. Born 1872 in Barnstaple, England; died 1952; m. 2nd husband Philip Mairet. ❖ Inspired by a visit to Ceylon (1903–06), began studying with Charles Robert Ashbee Robert and the Guild of Handcrafts; by 1911, was weaving in Devon, before establishing Gospels, her Ditchling-based workshop in Sussex that became a worldwide hub for weavers.

MAITLAND, Agnes Catherine (1850–1906). English educator. Born April 12, 1850; died Aug 19, 1906. ❖ As the principal of Somerville College, Oxford (1889–1906), was responsible for increasing enrollment, developing a tutorial system, and the construction of a college library; was also the author of the highly popular *Rudiments of Cookery,* as well as novels.

MAITLAND, Clover (1972—). Australian field-hockey player. Born Mar 14, 1972, in Maryborough, Queensland, Australia. ❖ Won team gold medals at Atlanta Olympics (1996) and Sydney Olympics (2000).

MAITLAND, Elizabeth (1626–1698). See *Murray, Elizabeth.*

MAITLAND, Mrs. Lauderdale (d. 1961). See *Alexander, Janet.*

MAIZTEGUI, Laura. Argentinean field-hockey player. Name variations: Laurita Maiztegui. Born in Argentina. ❖ Won a team silver medal at Sydney Olympics (2000).

MAJEROVÁ, Marie (1882–1967). Czech novelist, feminist, and politician. Name variations: Marie Majerova; Marie Stivinová; Marie Tusarová; (pseudonym) Marie Bartosova or Bartosová. Born Marie Bartosová in Úvaly, Austria (now Czech Republic), Feb 1, 1882; died in Prague, Jan 16, 1967. ❖ Published 1st poem, "Písen" (A Song,

1901), voicing the frustrations of many working-class mothers; during next several years, lived in Paris, Vienna and Prague, completing her education and becoming active in feminist and Social Democratic movements; published 1st novel, the largely autobiographical *Panenství* (Virginity, 1907); was at 1st attracted to doctrines of social anarchism, ideals clearly reflected in 1st collection of short stories, *Povídky z pekla* (Stories from Hell, 1907); finding anarchist ideals inadequate, joined Czech Social Democratic Party (1908); published novels *Náměstí Republiky* (Place de la République, 1914) and *Nejkrásnejsí svet* (The Most Beautiful of Worlds, 1920); became a founding member of Czechoslovak Communist Party (1921) and issued a collection of short stories, *Muckeny* (The Women Martyrs); published the work which is generally considered her masterpiece, *Siréna* (The Factory Siren, 1935), a sweeping epic that traces 3 generations in the lives of the Hudecs, a Czech working-class family; presented a portrait of proletarian life in novella *Havírská balada* (Ballad of a Miner, 1938); after WWII, was hailed as one of her nation's artistic giants and awarded title of National Artist of Czechoslovakia (1947); became well known throughout Communist bloc, with translations of her major works appearing in Russian-, German-, and even Chinese-language editions. ❖ See also *Women in World History.*

MAJOLI, Iva (1977—). Croatian tennis player. Born Aug 12, 1977, in Zagreb, Croatia. ❖ Turned pro (1991); won singles title at Roland Garros (1997), beating Martina Hingis; won Paris Indoors double championship (2001).

MAJOR, Clare Tree (d. 1954). English-born actress, director, and theater founder. Name variations: Clare Tree. Born Clare Tree; died 1954; grandniece of Ellen Tree. ❖ Moved to US (1914); joined Washington Square Theater Co.; became director of Princess Theater (NY); established and ran Clare Tree Major School of the Theatre in NY (1923–54), which included a children's theater with a number of companies touring each summer.

MAJOR, Ethel Lillie (1890–1934). English poisoner. Born 1890; hanged at Hull Jail, Dec 19, 1934; m. Arthur Major, June 1, 1918; children: Auriel (illeg.) and Lawrence (b. 1919). ❖ Gave birth out of wedlock to daughter Auriel (c. 1914), and to avoid scandal her parents declared the child to be theirs; married Arthur Major (1918), who insisted that she tell him the name of Auriel's father, but she refused and marriage deteriorated; after husband died of strychnine poisoning (May 23–24, 1934) as did a dog to whom she had fed scraps, was tried for murder at Lincoln Assizes (Nov 1934) and found guilty.

MAJOR, Maeghan (1984—). American wakeboarder. Born Jan 3, 1984, in Springfield, MO. ❖ Won many major wakeboarding titles including 1st place finishes at Wakeboard Worldchampionship (1999 and 2000), X Games (1999), Gravity Games (2000), US Wakeboard Nationals (2000), 41st US Masters (2000), and World Cup (2000), Pro Wakeboard Tour, Detroit, MI (2002).

MAJSTOROVIC, Biljana (1959—). Yugoslavian basketball player. Born Dec 31, 1959, in Yugoslavia. ❖ At Moscow Olympics, won a bronze medal in team competition (1980).

MAKAR, Nancy Hogshead- (1962—). *See Hogshead, Nancy.*

MAKARE (c. 1515–1468 BCE). *See Hatshepsut.*

MAKAROVA, Elena (1951—). Russian short-story writer. Name variations: Elena Grigorevna Makarova. Born 1951; dau. of Inna Lisnianskaya (poet, b. 1928). ❖ Taught art to children in Moscow (1980s); co-curated exhibition of art by children from Terezin concentration camp and published *Friedl Dicker-Brandeis: Vienna 1898–Auschwitz 1944*; stories, which reflect experiences of young women struggling for self-expression, include "Treasure," "Herbs from Odessa," and "Uncle Pasha" stories.

MAKAROVA, Inna (1928—). Russian actress. Born Inna Vladimirovna Makarova, July 28, 1928, in Taiga, Russia; children: (with actor-director Sergei Bondarchuk) Natalya Bondarchuk (b. 1950, actress). ❖ Appeared in over 30 films, including *Molodaya gvardiya* (1948), *Dimitrovgradtsy* (1956), *Vysota* (1957), *Devchata* (1961), *Zhenitba Balzaminova* (1964) and *Prestupleniye i nakazaniye* (1969), shown in US as *Crime and Punishment.* ❖ See also *Red Women on the Silver Screen.*

MAKAROVA, Natalia (1940—). Russian ballerina. Born in Leningrad (now St. Petersburg), Russia, Nov 21, 1940; studied ballet at Vaganova School, 1953–59; trained with Natalia Dudinskaya at Leningrad Choreographic School; m. Edward Karkar (businessman), 1976; children:

son Andre Michael (b. 1978). ❖ At 13, entered famed Vaganova School of Ballet; joined Kirov Ballet (1959) and rose quickly to rank of ballerina; created sensation when she danced in *Giselle* in Kirov's 1st appearance at London's Covent Garden (1961); toured US with Kirov, dancing in such classic Russian ballets as *Aurora* and as Odette/Odile in *Swan Lake*; awarded Gold Medal at 2nd International Ballet Competition at Varna, Bulgaria (1965); while performing with Kirov in London, requested political asylum (Sept 4, 1970); signed with NY's American Ballet Theater (ABT), making debut in *Giselle* (1970); danced a number of roles during years at ABT; began lengthy relationship with Royal Ballet of London, appearing in *Swan Lake, Giselle, The Sleeping Beauty, Les Sylphides, Manon, Song of the Earth, Concerto, Cinderella, A Month in the Country, Voluntaries, Dances at a Gathering, Serenade, Elite Syncopations, Rituals, Checkmate* and *Les Biches*; gave last performance with Royal Ballet (1989) in Kenneth MacMillan's modern version of *Romeo and Juliet*; appeared as guest dancer with leading ballet companies of the world, including Roland Petit's Ballets de Marseille, Paris Opera Ballet, National Ballet of Canada, Stuttgart Ballet, Royal Danish Ballet, London Festival Ballet, and Bejart's Ballet of the 20th Century; staged full-length production of *La Bayadere,* making the ABT the 1st company in the West to present this work (1980). Received Tony Award and Laurence Olivier Award for Best Actress in a Musical for *On Your Toes.* ❖ See also *A Dance Autobiography* (1979); and *Women in World History.*

MAKAROVA, Tamara (1907–1997). Russian actress and teacher. Born Aug 13, 1907, in St. Petersburg, Russia; died in Jan 1997; graduated from Leningrad Theatrical Institute, 1930; m. Sergei Gerasimov (film director, died 1985). ❖ While a student at Leningrad Theatrical Institute, began a film career closely aligned with husband; starred in *Seven Brave Men, Big Earth, The Young Guards* and *To Love a Man*; began teaching, eventually becoming a professor at the State Institute of Cinematographers (1958).

MAKARYEVA, Nadiezhda (1925—). Soviet spy. Name variations: Nadiezhda Mikhailovna Makaryeva; Marianne Koch. Born 1925 in Kharkov, Russia. ❖ Trained at Soviet spy school Prakhovka for 10 years and became known as Marianne Koch; sent initially to West Berlin (1958) then established a cover in Frankfurt-am-Main by setting up a Secretarial Service Bureau (1958); organized spy network in part by blackmailing ex-Nazis into cooperation; gathered information about West German installations and was also active in the American sector in West Germany; when her espionage network was running smoothly and could be taken over by a less valuable spy, was recalled to the Soviet Union and likely reassigned.

MAKAVEEVA, Petkana (1952—). Bulgarian basketball player. Born Oct 4, 1952, in Bulgaria. ❖ Won a bronze medal at Montreal Olympics (1976) and a silver medal at Moscow Olympics (1980), both in team competition.

MAKEBA, Miriam (1932—). South African Xosa singer and activist. Born Zenzile Makeba, Mar 4, 1932, in Prospect, South Africa; attended Kimerton Training Institute in Pretoria; m. James Kubay; m. singer Sonny Pillay (div.); m. Hugh Masekela (trumpeter and bandleader), 1964 (div. 1968); m. Stokely Carmichael (Black Panther activist), 1968 (div.); m. Bageot Bah (airline executive, div.); children: (1st m.) daughter Bongi (died at 35). ❖ One of Africa's greatest vocalists, began career as domestic worker in Johannesburg; toured South Africa, Rhodesia (Zimbabwe) and Belgian Congo (Republic of Congo) with Black Mountain Brothers (1954–57); starred in semi-documentary *Come Back Africa,* about apartheid (1959); decided not to return to Africa while attending the film's premiere at Venice Film Festival (1959); had passport invalidated by South African government, making a return impossible; obtained permission to enter US (1959); put African music on international map (1960s); performed at birthday celebration for President John F. Kennedy (1963); saw her recordings banned in South Africa (1963) and career harmed by marriage to Black Panther activist, Stokely Carmichael (1968); moved with husband to Guinea, West Africa, and continued to perform on international circuit; served as UN delegate from Guinea; won Dag Hammarskjold Peace Prize for work against apartheid (1986); after living in exile for 30 years, was welcomed back to her homeland in the post-apartheid era; appeared with Paul Simon on his Graceland tour (1987); released CD *Homeland* for Putumayo records (2000). ❖ See also autobiography (with James Hall) *Makeba: My Story* (New American Library, 1987); and *Women in World History.*

MAKEDA (fl. 10th c. BCE). *See Sheba, Queen of.*

MAKEMSON, Maud Worcester (1891–1977). American astronomy professor and writer. Name variations: Maud W. Makemson. Born Maud Worcester, Sept16, 1891, in Center Harbor, NH; died Dec 25, 1977, in Weatherford, TX; dau. of Ira Eugene Worcester and Fannie Malvina Davisson Worcester; attended Radcliffe, 1908–09; University of California, AB in astronomy, 1925, AM in astronomy, 1927, PhD in astronomy, 1930; m. Thomas Emmet Makemson, Aug 7, 1912 (div. July 1919); children: Lavon, Donald, Harris. ❖ Noted for her work in archaeoastronomy and astrodynamics, was a newspaper reporter for *Arizona Gazette* (1917–21); was assistant professor of mathematics, Rollins College (1931–32); served as assistant professor of astronomy, chair of astronomy department, director of observatory, Vassar College (1932–57); was research astronomer and lecturer, University of California, Los Angeles (1959–64); was consultant, Consolidated Lockheed-California (1961–63); moved to Texas (1965) and became a NASA consultant at Applied Research Laboratories of General Dynamics in Fort Worth; devised a method for astronauts to navigate on the moon without using radio or radar. ❖ See also *Women in World History.*

MAKEPEACE, Joan.
See Joan (1210–1238).
See Joan of the Tower (1321–1362).

MAKHFI (1639–1702). *See Zeb-un-Nissa.*

MAKHINA, Antonina (1958—). Soviet rower. Born Mar 1958 in USSR. ❖ At Moscow Olympics, won a silver medal in single sculls (1980).

MAKHUBU, Lydia (1937—). Swazi medical researcher and chemist. Name variations: Lydia Phindile Makhubu. Born July 1, 1937, at the Usuthu Mission in Swaziland; studied mathematics and chemistry at Pius XII College in Lesotho Co., Swaziland (BS, 1963); University of Alberta, MA, 1967; University of Toronto, PhD in medicinal chemistry, 1973; m. Daniel Mbatha (surgeon); children: 2. ❖ First Swazi woman to earn a doctorate and one of the 1st females in southern Africa to serve as a high-ranking university official, studied at University of Alberta, Edmonton, on a Canadian Commonwealth scholarship; at University of Swaziland, worked as lecturer in chemistry department (1973), senior lecturer (1979), dean of science faculty (1976–80), full professor (1980), pro-vice-chancellor (1978), and vice-chancellor (1988); established and served as president of Royal Swaziland Society of Science and Technology (1977); served as co-founder (1989), president (1993), and first chair of Third World Organization of Women in Science (TWOWS); studied and preserved medical effects and chemical nature of plants used by Swazi healers; was 1st woman to head Association of Commonwealth Universities (1989–90).

MAKIN, Bathsua (1608–1675). English educator. Name variations: Basua. Born Bathsua Pell, c. 1608, in Southwick, Sussex, England; died c. 1675; dau. of Henry Reginald (Sussex rector); sister of John Pell (1610–1685), eminent mathematician; m. Richard Mackin or Macking. ❖ Served as a tutor for the daughters of Charles I, including Elizabeth Stuart; after Elizabeth's death (1650), returned to the private sector as governess until she established a school of her own in London; met and befriended Anna Maria van Schurmann (1646), and the two kept up a lively correspondence; blending her ideas and that of Schurmann's, published an anonymous polemic, *An Essay to Revive the Antient Education of Gentlewomen in Religion, Manners, Arts and Tongues* (1673). ❖ See also *Women in World History.*

MAKOGONOVA, Irina (1959—). Soviet volleyball player. Born Nov 12, 1959, in USSR. ❖ At Moscow Olympics, won a gold medal in team competition (1980).

MAKRAY, Katalin (1945—). Hungarian gymnast. Born April 5, 1945, in Hungary. ❖ At Tokyo Olympics, won a silver medal in uneven bars (1964).

MAKRINA (327–379). *See Macrina.*

MAKSIMOVIC, Desanka (1898–1993). Serbian writer. Name variations: Maksimović. Born in Rabrovica near Valjevo, Serbia, May 16, 1898; died in Belgrade, Feb 12, 1993; dau. of Mihailo Maksimovic (schoolteacher) and Draginja Petrovic Maksimovic; graduate of University of Belgrade, 1924; attended Sorbonne, 1925; m. Sergej Nikiforovic Slastikov. ❖ Doyenne of Serbian poets, had a writing career of verse, short stories, translations, children's books and novels that spanned 7 decades; began to contribute poetry to Belgrade's influential journal, *Srpski knjizevni glasnik* (Serbian Literary Herald); published 1st collection of poems (1924); appointed professor at Belgrade's elite First High

School for Girls (1925) and taught there until retirement from teaching (1953); during German occupation of Yugoslavia, wrote defiant poetry, but could only publish several children's books; at war's end, released the collection *Pesnik i zavicaj* (The Poet and His Native Land, 1946) which includes the well-known "Krvava bajka" (A Legend of Blood), a requiem for the schoolboys of Kragujevac who were massacred by the Germans; though a traditionalist and certainly not a Marxist, was elected to the Serbian Academy of Sciences and Arts (1959); created what is generally regarded as her best work, the collection *Trazim pomilovanje* (*I Seek Clemency*), about the need for a moral renaissance (1964); received Special Vuk Award for Lifetime Achievement (1975), only the 2nd artist so honored; published *Letopis Perunovih potomaka* (A Chronicle of Perun's Descendants, 1976); at 90, issued new collection of poems, *Pamtiću sve* (I Shall Remember Everything, 1988); also translated writings by Chekhov, Dostoyevsky, Pushkin, Anna Akhmatova and Balzac. ❖ See also *Women in World History.*

MALABARBA, Germana (1913–2002). Italian gymnast. Born Nov 19, 1913, in Italy; died 2002. ❖ At Amsterdam Olympics, won a silver medal in team all-around (1928).

MALAGA, Natalia (1964—). Peruvian volleyball player. Born Jan 26, 1964, in Peru. ❖ At Seoul Olympics, won a silver medal in team competition (1988).

MALAIKA, Nazik al- (1923–1992). Iraqi poet and critic. Name variations: Nazik al-Mala'ika. Born in 1923; died in 1992; dau. of Salma al-Malaika (1908–1953, poet); graduate of Higher Teachers' College, in Baghdad, Iraq. ❖ One of Iraq's leading poets and critics, taught Arabic literature at University of Mosul in Iraq and at University of Kuwait; by 1978, had published 7 vols. of poetry and 3 vols. of poetic criticism; her poem "Cholera" (1947), written during the cholera epidemic in Egypt, broke with the classical verse forms and initiated the New Movement in Arabic poetry. ❖ See also *Women in World History.*

MALAIKA, Salma al- (1908–1953). Iraqi poet. Name variations: Umm Nizar. Born 1908 in Iraq; died 1953; children: Nazik al-Malaika (Iraqi poet, 1923–1992). ❖ Wrote poetry about various subjects, including the Kilani uprising against the British, the Baghdad revolution of 1948, the tragedy of Palestine, and the Iraqi poet Jamil Sidqi al-Zawhi who championed women's rights; also wrote feminist verse; work collected and published as *Song of Glory* (1965) with introduction by daughter Nazik al-Malaika.

MALAK HIFNI NASSIF (1886–1918). *See Nassif, Malak Hifni.*

MALAKHOVSKAYA, Natalia (1947—). Russian feminist. Name variations: Nataliia or Natalya Malakhovskaia; Anna Natalia Malakhovskaya; Anna-Nataliia Malakhovskaia. Born 1947; graduated from faculty of letters in Leningrad, 1973. ❖ Worked as teacher but became involved in underground feminist movement; formed illegal women's organization Club Maria, and with Tatyana Mamonova, Natalia Goricheva, and Yulia Voznesenskaya, wrote *samizdat* publication *Women and Russia* about women's domestic oppression and state's failure to provide maternity and childcare; expelled from USSR with the 3 other writers (1980), settled in Vienna.

MALASPINA, Ricciarda. Princess of Massa. Name variations: Ricciarda Cybo. Married Lorenzo Cybo or Cibo.

MALATESTA (fl. 1504–1505). Lyons courtesan. Fl. between 1504 and 1505. ❖ Not to be confused with Francesca da Rimini (d. 1285?) who was infamously killed by husband Gianciotto Malatesta in a "crime of honor."

MALATESTA, Anna (fl. 15th c.). Noblewoman of Mantua. First wife of Rodolfo Gonzaga (1451–1495); his 2nd wife was Caterina Pico (d. 1501).

MALATESTA, Battista da Montefeltro (1383–1450). Italian scholar. Name variations: Battista da Montefeltro. Born Battista da Montefeltro in 1383; died 1450; dau. of Antonio, count of Urbino; m. Galeazzo Malatesta; children: 1 daughter; granddaughter Constanza Varano also became known for her scholarship. ❖ Had an extremely unhappy marriage; after husband was assassinated as a despot, retained an intellectual friendship with his father; taught philosophy and received much admiration from the professors; became a Sister of the Franciscan Order of Saint Claire. ❖ See also *Women in World History.*

MALATESTA, Elisabetta. *See Montefeltro, Elisabetta.*

MALATESTA, Francesca (d. 1285?). *See Francesca da Rimini.*

MALATESTA, Ginevra (1414–1440). *See Este, Ginevra d'.*

MALATESTA, Margherita (d. 1399). *See Gonzaga, Margherita.*

MALATESTA, Michelina (1300–1356). *See Michelina of Pesaro.*

MALATESTA, Paola (1393–1453). *See Gonzaga, Paola.*

MALATESTA, Parisina. *See Este, Parisina d'.*

MALATESTA, Polissena. *See Sforza, Polissena.*

MALATO, Giusy (1971—). **Italian water-polo player.** Born July 9, 1971, in Italy. ❖ At World championships, won team gold medals (1998, 2001); center forward, won a team gold medal at Athens Olympics (2004).

MALAVESSE. *See David, Catherine*

MALCHUGINA-MIKHEYEVA, Galina (1962—). **Soviet runner.** Name variations: Galina Mikheyeva. Born Dec 17, 1962, in USSR. ❖ Won a bronze medal at Seoul Olympics (1988) and a silver medal at Barcelona Olympics (1992), both in 4x100-meter relay.

MALCOLM, Emilie Monson (1829/30–1905). **New Zealand writer.** Name variations: Emilie Monson Wilton. Born Emilie Monson Wilton, c. 1829 or 1830, in England; died June 10, 1905, in Avondale, Auckland, New Zealand; dau. of Colonel Wilton (retired British army officer); m. Neill Malcolm (barrister), 1848 (died 1898); children: 10. ❖ Immigrated to New Zealand (1851); following failed farming ventures, established homestead with family on abandoned property, petitioning government to survey and grant title to it; when petitions were ignored and property was included in allotment for new settlers, was finally allowed to purchase homestead; published pamphlet based on her diaries, *My Own Story.* ❖ See also *Dictionary of New Zealand Biography* (Vol. 1).

MALCOLM, Fanny (1852–1934). *See Osborne, Fanny.*

MALCOLM, Isabella (1850–1926). *See May, Isabella.*

MALCOLM, Margaret (1848–1938). *See Caro, Margaret.*

MALCOLM, Sarah (c. 1710–1733). **Irish-born murderer.** Born in Ireland c. 1710 (some sources cite 1711); executed in London, England, Mar 7, 1733. ❖ Was executed for the infamous "Temple Murders," having killed her elderly mistress and 2 other servants in a murderous rampage (1733). ❖ See also *Women in World History.*

MALCOMSON, Ruth (1906–1988). **Miss America.** Name variations: Ruth M. Schaubel. Born Ruth Malcomson, April 16, 1906, in PA; died May 25, 1988, in Delaware, PA; m. Carl Schaubel. ❖ Named Miss Philadelphia and crowned Miss America (both 1924). ❖ See also Frank Deford, *There She Is* (Viking, 1971).

MALE, Carolyn Therese (1966—). **Australian politician.** Born May 7, 1966, in Nambour, Australia. ❖ Teacher; as a member of the Australian Labor Party, elected to the Queensland Parliament for Glass House (2001).

MALEEVA, Magdalena (1975—). **Bulgarian tennis player.** Pronunciation: ma-LAY-vuh. Born April 1, 1975, in Sofia, Bulgaria; dau. of Youlia Berberian (her coach) and George Maleev; sister of Manuela and Katerina Maleeva (both tennis players). ❖ Won singles jr. championship at US Open (1990); won 3 singles titles (Chicago, Moscow and Oakland, 1995); won 14 career singles titles.

MALEEVA, Manuela (1967—). **Bulgarian tennis player.** Born Feb 14, 1967; dau. of Youlia Berberian (her coach and 9-time Bulgarian women's-singles tennis champion) and George Maleev (electronics professor); sister of Katerina and Magdalena Maleeva (both tennis players); m. François Fragnière. ❖ At Seoul Olympics, won a bronze medal in singles (1988); on WTA Tour, was ranked among the top 10 in the world for 10 years.

MALESZEWSKA, Maria (1913—). *See Kwadzniewska, Maria.*

MALET, Lucas (1852–1931). *See Kingsley, Mary St. Leger.*

MALETZKI, Doris (1952—). **East German runner.** Born June 11, 1952, in East Germany. ❖ At Montreal Olympics, won a gold medal in the 4x400-meter relay (1976).

MALGHERITA. *Italian variant of Margaret.*

MALGORZATA (fl. 1290s). **Queen of Poland.** Fl. in the 1290s; dau. of Albert, duke of Brandenburg; fourth wife of Przemysl II (1257–1296), king of Poland (r. 1290–1296).

MALIBRAN, Maria (1808–1836). **French-born Spanish soprano.** Name variations: María Malibran; Maria Garcia or García. Born María Felicità García, Mar 24, 1808, in Paris, France; died Sept 23, 1836, in Manchester, England; eldest dau. of Manuel del Popolo Vicente García also known as Manuel Garcia (1775–1832, the tenor); mother's name unknown; sister of Pauline Viardot (1821–1910, mezzo-soprano); studied with father and Giuditta Pasta; m. François Eugène Malibran (merchant), 1826 (sep. 1827, annulled 1836); m. Charles de Bériot, 1836; children: (with de Bériot) Charles Wilfred de Bériot (b. 1830) and a daughter (b. 1832) who died at birth. ❖ One of the world's 1st international superstars, made stage debut in Naples at age 5 in Paër's *Agnese* (1813); made London debut as Rosina in *Il barbiere di Siviglia* (Barber of Seville, 1825); joined father's troupe on tour of US (1825–26), quickly becoming America's 1st prima donna, appearing in *Otello, Romeo, Don Giovanni, Tancredi, Cenerentola,* and in 2 operas written by her father, *L'amante astuto* and *La Figlia dell' aria*; was also a consummate actress, a quality which was somewhat rare for the period; made Paris debut in *Semiramide* (1828) and, for the next 8 years, followed one triumph with another; made Teatro alla Scala debut as Bellini's Norma (1834); while in London, was thrown from a horse and dragged some distance (April 1836), receiving head injuries from which she never fully recovered, though she continued to perform; died that September, age 28. ❖ See also H. Bushnell, *Maria Malibran: A Biography of a Singer* (University Park, 1979); A. Fitzlyon, *Maria Malabran* (1987); A. Pougin, *Marie Malibran: histoire d'une cantatrice* (1911); and *Women in World History.*

MALINA, Judith (1926—). **American theatrical director and actress.** Born June 4, 1926, in Kiel, Germany; raised in US; dau. of a German rabbi; m. Hannon Resnikov; m. Julian Beck, 1948 (died Sept 14, 1985); children: 1. ❖ Studied at New School University under Erwin Piscator and made debut at Cherry Lane Theater, NY; with Julian Beck, founded Living Theater (1947) which was dedicated to collective improvisation and anarcho-pacifist stance, became increasingly political in 1950s, and won Obie for Jack Gelber's play about drug addiction *The Connection* (1959); starred in several commercial films, including *The Addams Family* (1991) and *Household Saints* (1993). Living Theater toured successfully in Europe but, facing financial and legal trouble in US, closed (1963) and moved to London and then Europe; company returned to US (1968), toured Brazil (1970s), and settled in France (1975); productions include *The Brig* (1963), *Paradise Now* (1968), *The Legacy of Cain* (1971) and *Masse Mensch* (1980).

MALINCHE (c. 1500–1531). **Indian translator, interlocutor, and mistress.** Name variations: La Malinche; Doña Marina; Malintzin; Marina Malintzin; Mallinalli Tenepal; Martina; Marina de Jaramillo; Mariana. Born a Totonac Indian in village of Painala in southeastern Mexico, probably c. 1500; died near Orizaba, 1531; m. Juan de Jaramillo, 1523, after 4 years of a semiofficial liaison with Hernán Cortés; children: (with Cortés) Martín (b. 1520). ❖ Mistress of Hernán Cortés, was sold into slavery by her family and taken southward to the Maya-speaking Tabasco region (1512); together with 19 other Indian women, was given as a gift to the Spanish conquerors of Tabasco (1519); began a personal and political relation with Cortés, acting as his translator and confidant with all of the Indian groups (1519); gave birth to Martín and uncovered a major anti-Spanish plot at Cholula (1520); with the fall of the Aztec capital Tenochtitlán (Aug 1521), went from translator and diplomat to a minor member of a rather large entourage of women surrounding Cortés; was commanded by Cortés to marry Juan Jaramillo, an old though not very reputable associate of the captain (1523); caught in an unhappy marriage, retired into obscurity, finally dying near Orizaba (1531); aided immeasurably in forwarding the Spanish conquest of the Aztec Empire. ❖ See also *Women in World History.*

MALINOVSKA, Valentina. **Soviet spy.** Name variations: Valentina Nikolayevna or Nikolevna Malinovska; Greta Nielsson. Born in USSR. ❖ Entered Soviet spy school Prakhovka (1944), where she trained for 10 years, then assumed new identity as a Swede named Greta Nielsson; smuggled into Sweden (1954), traveled to Copenhagen and entered into arranged marriage to a Dane in order to gain Danish citizenship; opened a gift shop which served as a front for espionage activities; developed spy network which included 17 operational agents and informers (by 1955); focused primarily on NATO installations as well as other military and technical secrets; in danger of being discovered, received signal from Moscow to go into hiding; by the time counter-intelligence discovered the truth about her, had successfully eluded arrest; her network caused significant damage to Western security and defense.

MALINTZEN, Marina (c. 1500–1531). *See Malinche.*

MALIPIERO, Giovanna Dandolo (fl. 1457). *See Dandolo, Giovanna.*

MALISON, Joyce (c. 1935—). American golfer. Name variations: Joyce Ziske. Born c. 1935 in Milwaukee, WI; m. Tom Malison (bowling proprietor), 1961 (died 1993); children: 3 sons. ❖ Was Wisconsin state champion (1952–54); won North and South Invitational and Palm Beach Amateur (1954); member Curtis Cup team (1954); joined LPGA tour (1955); won Syracuse Open (1956), Howard Johnson Invitational, and Wolverine Open, Western Open and Hoosier Celebrity (1960); runner-up US Women's Open (1960).

MALLABER, Judy (1951—). English politician and member of Parliament. Born Judy Mallaber, July 10, 1951. ❖ Representing Labour, elected to House of Commons for Amber Valley (1997, 2001, 2005).

MALLESON, Joan (1900–1956). English doctor. Name variations: Joan Graeme Malleson; (pseudonym) Medica. Born Joan Graeme Billson, June 3, 1900; died of a coronary thrombosis (blood clot) in Fiji, en route back to Britain, May 14, 1956; m. Miles Malleson (actor-playwright, 1888–1969), 1920s. ❖ Family planning expert in Britain, served on the executive committee of the Family Planning Association; became qualified as a doctor at Charing Cross Hospital (1925) and was influenced by the psychologist and writer Havelock Ellis; encountered many patients with sexual challenges while working for the Holborn Borough Council and the West End Hospital for Nervous Diseases; worked as a medical officer at the clinic for sexual difficulties at the North Kensington Women's Welfare Centre; employed as a medical officer at University College Hospital's Obstetrics Department contraceptive clinic; on a professional exchange, had been visiting New Zealand when she died. Wrote *The Principles of Contraception: A Handbook for GPs* (1935) and *Problems of Fertility in General Practice* (with J. Stallworthy, 1953).

MALLESWARI, Karnam (1975—). Indian weightlifter. Born June 1, 1975, in Srikakulam, Andhra Pradesh, India; sister of Narasimha "Krishna" Malleswari (weightlifter). ❖ Won World championship (1995) and Asian championships (1995, 1996); won a bronze medal for 63–69kg at Sydney Olympics (2000), the 1st Indian woman to win an Olympic medal. Received Arjuna Award (1995), Rajiv Gandhi Khel Ratna (1996), Padma Shri (1997).

MALLET-JORIS, Françoise (1930—). Belgian-French novelist. Name variations: Francoise Mallet-Joris. Born Françoise Lilar, July 6, 1930, in Antwerp, Belgium; dau. of Suzanne Lilar; educated in US and at Sorbonne. ❖ Feminist and existentialist, was awarded the Prix Femina for *L'Empire Céleste* (1958, *Café Céleste*, 1959); other writings, most of which have been translated into English, include the bestselling *Le Rempart des béguines* (1951), published in US as *The Illusionist* (1952), as well as *Les Mensonges* (1956, *House of Lies*, 1957), *Lettres à moi-même* (1963), *Les signes et les prodiges* (1966), *La maison de papier* (1970), and *La Tristesse du Cerf-Volant* (1988); served as member of jury of Prix Femina; was elected president of Académie Goncourt (1973). ❖ See also autobiography, *Signs and Wonders* (Farrar, 1967).

MALLINGER, Mathilde (1847–1920). Croatian soprano. Born in Zagreb, Feb 17, 1847; died in Berlin, Germany, April 19, 1920; studied in Prague with Gordigiani and Vogl, in Vienna with Loewy. ❖ Made debut in Munich as Norma (1866), remaining there until 1868, singing Elsa, Elisabeth, and the first Eva; appeared in Berlin (1869–82); retired from stage (1882) and taught singing in Prague, where one of her students was Lotte Lehmann. ❖ See also *Women in World History.*

MALLIORI, Minerva Melpomeni (1952—). Greek politician. Born Aug 30, 1952, in Patras, Greece. ❖ Played an active role in the struggle against the dictatorship in Greece and was arrested by security forces; served as president of Organization against Drugs (OKANA) and adviser to the Mental Health Section and expert of the WHO on Mental Health Issues, Drugs, and AIDS (1987—); as a European Socialist, elected to 5th European Parliament (1999–2004).

MALLON, Mary (1867–1938). American cook. Name variations: Typhoid Mary; Mrs. Brown; Marie Breshof. Born, she said, in America in 1867; died North Brother Island, Nov 11, 1938 (left no record of her past, nor would she allow her photograph to be taken, though one or two exist). ❖ As the 1st known symptom-free carrier of the typhoid bacilli, was a 9-year nightmare for New York City's Department of Health; unknowingly contributed to the spread of typhoid, earning the name Typhoid Mary. ❖ See also Judith Walzer Leavitt, *Typhoid Mary: Captive to the Public's Health* (Beacon, 1996); and *Women in World History.*

MALLON, Meg (1963—). American golfer. Born April 14, 1963, in Natick, MA; attended Ohio State University. ❖ Joined tour (1987); won US Women's Open and LPGA championship (1991); won PING/Welch's championship (1993); won Sara Lee Classic (1993, 1996, 1999); won Cup Noodles Hawaiian Ladies Open (1996); won Star Bank LPGA Classic (1998); won Subaru Memorial (1999); won Wegmans Rochester International and du Maurier Classic (2000); crossed the $5 million mark in career earnings (2000); won Bank of Montreal Canadian Women's Open (2002); again won US Women's Open and LPGA championship (2004), with the greatest final round by a winner in 59-year history of the Open (6-under 65). Inducted into Ohio State Athletic Hall of Fame (1996).

MALLORY, Boots (1913–1958). American stage and screen actress. Name variations: Patricia Mallory. Born Oct 22, 1913, in New Orleans, LA; died Dec 1, 1958, in Santa Monica, CA; m. Herbert Marshall (actor). ❖ Made film debut (1932), followed by *Handle with Care, Humanity, Hello, Sister, Sing Sing Nights* and *Powder Smoke Range,* among others.

MALLORY, Mrs. Franklin (1884–1959). *See Mallory, Molla.*

MALLORY, Molla (1884–1959). Norwegian tennis player. Name variations: Anna Margrethe Bjurstedt; Molla Bjurstedt; Mrs. Franklin Mallory. Born Anna Margrethe Bjurstedt, Mar 1884, in Oslo, Norway; died Nov 22 (some sources cite Nov 21), 1959, in Norway; m. Franklin Mallory (stockbroker), 1919 (died 1934). ❖ Won the Norwegian national championship 8 times; at Stockholm Olympics, won a bronze medal in singles (1912); won 8 US singles championships, more than any other woman in history (1915–18, 1920–22, and 1926); with Eleanora Sears, won the doubles championship (1916 and 1917); won mixed doubles, with Ian Wright (1917) and with Bill Tilden (1922 and 1923); also played for the US 5 times in the Wightman Cup and came in 2nd at the World Hard Court championship (1921). Inducted into International Tennis Hall of Fame (1958). ❖ See also *Women in World History.*

MALLORY, Patricia (1913–1958). *See Mallory, Boots.*

MALLOWAN, Agatha Maria (1890–1976). *See Christie, Agatha.*

MALMFRID OF RUSSIA (fl. 1100s). Queen of Denmark. Fl. in the early 1100s; m. Erik Emune, king of Denmark (r. 1134–1137).

MALMSTRÖM, Cecilia (1968—). Swedish politician. Born May 15, 1968, in Stockholm, Sweden. ❖ Member of the People's Party Executive (1997—) and the Swedish section of the European Movement (1996—); as a member of the European Liberal, Democrat and Reform Party, elected to 5th European Parliament (1999–2004).

MALO, Gina (1909–1963). American theatrical performer. Born Janet Flynn, June 1, 1909, in Cincinnati, Ohio; died Nov 30, 1963, in New York, NY. ❖ Trained at Albertina Rasch's studio in New York City, then danced in *George White's Scandals of 1926*; toured Paris with Rasch precision ballet dancers, appearing at Moulin Rouge; remained in Paris, dancing in *Broadway* and *The New Moon*; returned to US as "a famous French chanteuse," replacing Lili Damita in *Sons O'Guns*; starred in many British productions, including *The Cat and the Fiddle* and *On Your Toes*; also performed as dramatic and comic actress on stage and in such films as *Strike It Rich* (1933), *Lily of Killarney* (1934) and *Over She Goes* (1937).

MALONE, Annie Turnbo (1869–1957). African-American entrepreneur. Name variations: Annie Turnbo; Annie Turnbo-Malone. Born Annie Minerva Turbo in Metropolis, IL, Aug 9, 1869; died of a stroke, May 10, 1957; dau. of Robert Turnbo and Isabella (Cook) Turnbo; married a man named Pope, 1903; m. Aaron Malone, 1914 (div. 1927); no children. ❖ Pioneer in black beauty culture, learned the cosmetics business with help of older sister; by 1900, had developed several hair-care products for African-American women: straighteners, growers, and hair oils; moved to St. Louis (1902), where she began to sell her products, enlisting other women to help; opened 1st shop to showcase her wares (1904), naming the business Poro; by 1917, had built a million-dollar complex called Poro College, encompassing a beauty school, barbershops, manufacturing plant, theater, bakery, auditorium, and hospitality facilities, which became the social center for blacks in St. Louis. ❖ See also *Women in World History.*

MALONE, Bernie (1948—). Irish politician and lawyer. Born Bernie O'Brien, Mar 26, 1948, in Clontarf, Dublin, Ireland; m. Frank Malone, 1972. ❖ Representing Labour, elected member of the European Parliament for Dublin (MEP, 1994–99, 1999—).

MALONE, Dorothy (1925—). American actress. Born Dorothy Eloise Maloney, Jan 30, 1925, in Chicago, IL; attended Southern Methodist University; m. actor Jacques Bergerac, 1959 (div. 1964); m. Robert Tomarkin, 1969 (div. 1969); m. Charles Huston Bell, 1971 (div. 1974); children: (1st m.) Mimi and Diane. ❖ Signed by RKO, played several small roles under Dorothy Maloney before moving to Warner Bros. (1945) and changing name to Malone; played leading lady roles for the next decade, developing into a fine dramatic actress; films include *The Big Sleep* (1946), *Torpedo Alley* (1953), *Pushover* (1954), *Young at Heart* (1954), *Battle Cry* (1955), *Artists and Models* (1955), *Pillars of the Sky* (1956), *Tension at Table Rock* (1956), *Man of a Thousand Faces* (1957), *Tip on a Dead Jockey* (1957), *The Tarnished Angels* (1958), *Too Much Too Soon* (1958), *Fate Is the Hunter* (1964) and *Winter Kills* (1979); had a long run on hit tv series "Peyton Place" (1964–69). Won Academy Award for Best Supporting Actress for *Written on the Wind* (1956).

MALONE, Maicel (1969—). African-American runner. Name variations: Maicel Malone-Wallace. Born Dec 6, 1969, in Indianapolis, IN; attended Arizona State University, 1991–95. ❖ At World championships, won gold medals for 400 meters and 4x400-meter relay (1993); won a gold medal for the 4x100-meter relay at Atlanta Olympics (1996); was the 1st female to win the NCAA indoor and outdoor 400m title and the TAC 400m title in the same season.

MALONEY, Kristen (1981—). American gymnast. Born Mar 10, 1981, in Hackettstown, NJ. ❖ Won Heathrow Cup (1993), Foxsport Challenge, International Team Championships and Pacific Alliance (1998), and American Classic (1997, 1998); won US nationals (1998, 1999); won a gold medal for balance beam at Goodwill Games (1998); placed 4th for team all-around at Sydney Olympics (2000).

MALONEY, Lucia (c. 1950–1978). American classical Indian dancer. Born c. 1950 in Chappaqua, NY; died Sept 21, 1978, in London; m. Nedd Williard. ❖ Studied classical Indian dance at University of Wisconsin, University of Delhi, and with teachers throughout India; throughout the world, performed solo recitals in Bharata Natyam, considered the oldest and most important of 8 Indian classical dance styles.

MALPEDE, Karen (1945—). American writer. Born June 29, 1945, in Wichita Falls, Texas; dau. of Joseph James Malpede (accountant) and Doris Leibschutz (radio commentator); sister of John Malpede (performance artist); University of Wisconsin, BA, 1967; Columbia University, MFA, 1971; m. George Bartenieff (actor-playwright), 1994; children: Carrie Sophia Hash. ❖ Published *People's Theater in America* (1972), beginning long-standing association with Open Theater and Living Theater; produced 1st play, *A Lament for Three Women* (1979); wrote extensively on theater, theater history and theater as tool for social action in such works as *Women in Theater: Compassion and Hope* (1983); published *A Monster Has Stolen the Sun and Other Plays* (1987) and *Women on the Verge: Seven Avant-Garde Plays* (1993), among others; conducted interviews with 9/11 survivors through Oral History and Memory Project at Columbia University (2001); with husband, wrote Obie Award-winning play *I Will Bear Witness*, based on Holocaust diaries of Victor Klemperer (2001).

MALRAUX, Clara (c. 1897–1982). French novelist, critic, and translator. Name variations: Clara Malraux-Goldschmidt. Born Clara Goldschmidt around 1897; died Dec 15, 1982, in Paris, France; 1st wife of Andre Malraux (b. 1901, writer and politician). ❖ Published travelogues of journeys with husband; also wrote 6 vols. of her memoirs, including *When We Were Twenty, The End of the Beginning* and *The Sound of Footsteps*; trans. Virginia Woolf's *A Room of One's Own* into French; combined fiction with autobiography to portray a woman's struggle for equality in novel *Portrait de Grisélidis* (1945).

MALTBY, Margaret E. (1860–1944). American physicist and educator. Name variations: Minnie Maltby; Margaret Eliza Maltby. Born Minnie Maltby, Dec 10, 1860, in Bristolville, Ohio; died May 3, 1944, in New York, NY; dau. of Edmund Maltby and Lydia Jane (Brockway) Maltby; Oberlin College, BA, 1882, MA, 1891; attended Art Students League, 1882–83; Massachusetts Institute of Technology, BS, 1891; University of Göttingen, Germany, PhD, 1895; never married; children: Philip

Randolph Meyer (adopted 1902). ❖ While at MIT, was a physics instructor at nearby Wellesley (1889–93); was 1st American woman to receive a PhD from University of Göttingen in Germany (1895); was research assistant for Friedrich Kohlrausch, president of Physikalisch-Technische Reichsanstalt in Charlottenburg, Germany (1898–99); returned to US to work in theoretical physics at Clark University with A.G. Webster; began long association with Barnard College (1900), serving as instructor in chemistry until transferring to physics department (1903), then serving as adjunct professor until 1913, and assistant professor and chair of department (1913–31); was listed in 1st edition of *American Men and Women of Science* (1906); served on fellowship committee of American Association of University Women (AAUW, 1912–29), chairing the organization (1913–24). ❖ See also *Women in World History.*

MALTHACE (fl. 40 BCE). Biblical woman and queen of Judea. Fl. around 40 BCE; 3rd of 10 wives of Herod the Great (73–4 BCE), king of Judea; children: Herod Archelaus II (d. before 18 CE), ethnarch of Judea; Herod Antipas (d. after 40 CE), tetrarch of Galilee who m. Herodias. ❖ Samaritan who was briefly queen of Judea.

MALUKHINA, Anna (1958—). Soviet shooter. Born Dec 21, 1958, in USSR. ❖ At Seoul Olympics, won a bronze medal in air rifle (1988).

MALYON, Eily (1879–1961). English-born character actress. Born Eily Sophie Lees-Craston, Oct 30, 1879, in London, England; died Sept 26, 1961, in South Pasadena, CA; dau. of Harry Lees-Craston and Agnes Thomas (actress). ❖ Began career on stage; made film debut in *Born to Love* (1931), followed by 80 films, including *Great Expectations* (as Sarah Pocket), *Clive of India, A Tale of Two Cities* (as Mrs. Cruncher), *The Little Princess, On Borrowed Time, Young Tom Edison, The Seventh Cross* and *Paris Underground*; probably best-remembered as the Housekeeper in *Going My Way.*

MAMA CASS (1941–1974). See Elliot, Cass.

MAMAEA, Julia (c. 190–235). See Julia Mamaea.

MAMA JAEL (1939—). See Mbogo, Jael.

MAMA-OCLLO (fl. around 12th c.). Co-founder and queen of the Incan Empire. Name variations: Mama Ocllo; Mama Oello Huaco; Mana-Ocllo; Mana Ocllo; Mama-baco; Coya (queen). Probably born c. the 12th century; died in Cuzco, in what is now Peru; according to Incan mythology, was the dau. of the Sun, whose wife was his sister the Moon; possibly had 3 sisters (names unknown) and 4 brothers, one of whom was Manco Capac (co-founder and 1st ruler of the Incan empire); m. Manco Capac; children: daughter Mama Cora (later queen of Inca Empire); son Sinche Roca (later ruler of Inca Empire). ❖ Founded with brother the great Incan Empire and selected the site for the holy city of Cuzco; taught the women of her people the arts of spinning and weaving; to ensure the purity of the royal line, married brother and began the Incan ruling dynasty. ❖ See also *Women in World History.*

MAMAS AND THE PAPAS, The.
See Elliot, Cass.
See Phillips, Michelle.

MAMLOK, Ursula (1928—). German-born American composer. Born in Berlin, Germany, Feb 1, 1928; only child of Dorothy Lewis and John Lewis; m. Dwight Mamlok, 1949. ❖ Escaped from Nazi Germany to Ecuador (1939); based on her compositions, received a full scholarship at Mannes School of Music where she studied with George Szell; studied with Roger Sessions for a year; received scholarship to study at Manhattan School of Music; premiered *Variations for Solo Flute* at Carnegie Hall (1961); gained considerable attention with her String Quartet (1962); composed *Sonar Trajectory* (1966), an electronic composition which was not performed until 1984; continued her work with the help of many commissions as well as grants from the National Endowment for the Arts and the CUNY Faculty Research Foundation, and a Martha Baird Rockefeller Recording Grant. ❖ See also *Women in World History.*

MAMMAEA, Julia (c. 190–235). See Julia Mamaea.

MAMO (1914–1986). See Clark, Mamo.

MAMOSHINA, Glafira Adolfovna (c. 1870–1942). Russian children's writer and poet. Name variations: Glafira Adol'fovna Mamoshina; (by marriage) Gloria Einerling and Gloria Guseva-Orenburgskaia; (pseudonym) G.A. Gálina, G.A. Galina or G. Galina. Born c. 1870 in Russia; died 1942. ❖ Worked in telegraph office (1890–96); banned from St Petersburg for 1 year for reading poem about government repression of student activism; published *Poems* (1902) and *Pre-Dawn Songs* (1906) and 2 collections of fairytales (1903, 1909); poems widely anthologized and published in newspapers; also wrote poem on Boer War, which became folksong, and had poems set to music by Rachmaninov and Glière.

MAN, Judith (fl. 1640s). British translator. Flourished 1640s; dau. of Peter Man. ❖ Translated John Barclay's political-allegorical romance, *An Epitome of the History of Faire Argenis and Polyarchus by N. Coéffeteau* (1640).

MANA OCLLO. *See Mama-Ocllo.*

MANA-ZUCCA (1887–1981). American pianist, operatic singer, and composer. Name variations: Mana Zucca. Born Gizella Augusta Zuckerman in New York, NY, Dec 25, 1887; died in Miami Beach, FL, Mar 8, 1981; educated in Europe; m. Irwin M. Cassel, Sept 22, 1921; children: Marwin Shepard Cassel. ❖ After studying piano with Alexander Lambert, made debut at 7 with NY Philharmonic Orchestra in Carnegie Hall; at 13, embarked on European tour which lasted 4 years; in Berlin, studied piano with Leopold Godowsky and composer Feruccio Busoni; in London, studied composition with Hermann Spielter; in Paris, studied singing with Von Zur Muehlen; appeared as lead soprano in Lehar's *Count of Luxembourg* (1914); changed name (1916), dropping 1st name and rearranging syllables in surname; wrote over 1,100 published pieces, many of these lyrical songs to her own texts, and composed 2 operas and a ballet score; premiered her Piano Concerto (1919) and Violin Concerto (1955); also wrote memoirs and accounts of European travels. ❖ See also *Women in World History.*

MANAHAN, Anna Anderson (1902–1984). *See Anderson, Anna.*

MANAUDOU, Laure (1986—). French swimmer. Born Oct 9, 1986, in Villeurbanne, France. ❖ Won a bronze medal for 100-meter backstroke and gold medals for 400-meter and 800-meter freestyle at Athens Olympics (2004).

MANCE, Jeanne (1606–1673). Canadian colonizer and founder. Name variations: Jeanne de Mance. Pronunciation: Jan Monce. Born Jeanne Mance in late 1606 (baptized, Nov 12, 1606) in Langres, France; died in Montreal, Canada, June 18, 1673; dau. of Charles Mance (lawyer) and Catherine Émonnot Mance; never married; no children. ❖ One of the early colonizers of Canada, who is credited as the founder of the Hôtel Dieu hospital and the co-founder of Montreal, 1st worked as a nurse in France attending to victims of war and plague (1635–36); immigrated to New France and played a critical role in the fortunes of the colonies (1641); along with Paul de Maisonneuve, is credited with being the founder of Montreal (1642); was instrumental in the colony's survival, advising the governor and securing financial aid, including funds to stave off Iroquois attack (1651); was also given sole responsibility for establishing a hospital and worked tirelessly over the years overseeing its construction and administration, while providing nursing care to the colonists; as well, arranged for the establishment of an order of nursing sisters at the hospital, thereby ensuring its independence and survival after her death (the hospital, the Hôtel Dieu, still exists in Montreal); journeyed to France and returned with nursing sisters to Montreal (1658); was present at the founding of the Church of Notre Dame (1673). ❖ See also J.K. Foran, *Jeanne Mance: Her Life* (Herald Press, 1931); Marie-Claire Daveluy, *Jeanne Mance* (Fides, 1962); and *Women in World History.*

MANCHESTER, Marianne Allen (1852–1911). *See Tasker, Marianne Allen.*

MANCHESTER, Melissa (1951—). American musician. Born Feb 15, 1951, in Bronx, New York, NY; attended High School of Performing Arts. ❖ Began singing jingles at 15; was staff writer at Chappell Music (late 1960s); discovered by Bette Midler and accompanist, Barry Manilow, while playing in NYC clubs, and signed as backup singer (1971); got record contract in 6 months and released debut, *Home to Myself* (1973), with songs co-written by Carole Bayer Sager; had 1st hit, "Midnight Blue," from 3rd album, *Melissa* (1975); gained wide following with release of Peter Allen and Sager's "Don't Cry Out Loud" (1979); co-wrote Kenny Loggins and Stevie Nicks' hit duet, "Whenever I Call You Friend"; became 1st performer to have 2 Academy Award-nominated film themes, "Ice Castles" and "The Promise" (1980); had biggest hit with "You Should Hear How She Talks About You" (*Hey Ricky*, 1982), and won Grammy for Best Female Vocal Performance; other albums include *Tribute* (1989), *If My Heart Had Wings* (1995), *Joy* (1998), and with Peabo Bryson and Roberta Flack, *Colors of Christmas* (late 1990s);

also acted in Bette Midler film, *For the Boys*, and tv series, *Blossom;* starred in touring revue, *Andrew Lloyd Webber–Music of the Night.*

MANCINI, Evelina (1849–1896). Italian poet and novelist. Name variations: Evelina Cattermole Mancini; (pseudonym) Contessa Lara. Born Evelina Cattermole (also seen as Kattermole) in 1849 in Florence, or possibly Cannes, Italy; grew up in Florence; killed in 1896; dau. of Guglielmo Cattermole (consul to Cannes) and Elisa Sandusch Cattermole; m. Eugenio Mancini, 1871. ❖ Notorious for her passions, had a relationship with writer Mario Rapisardi, had another lover who was killed by her husband in a duel, and was killed by her lover Giuseppe Pierantoni; writings include *Canti e ghirlandi* (1867), *Versi* (1883), *E ancora versi* (1886), *Nuovi versi* (1897), and *L'innamorata.*

MANCINI, Hortense (1646–1699). Duchess of Mazarin. Name variations: Hortense de la Porte; Duchesse de Mazarin. Born in Rome in 1646 (some sources cite 1640); died in Chelsea, England, 1699; 4th dau. of Laurent also seen as Lorenzo Mancini and a mother (maiden name Mazarini or Mazarino) who was the sister of Cardinal Jules Mazarin (chief minister to Louis XIV); sister of Olympia (c. 1639–1708), Marie Mancini (1640–1715), Marie-Anne Mancini (1649–1714), Laure Mancini (1635–1657); cousin of Anne-Marie Martinozzi (1637–1672) and Laura Martinozzi; m. Marquis de La Meilleraye and Mayenne, who was elevated by the cardinal to the duke of Mazarin. ❖ One of the most beautiful and flamboyant women in Europe, walked out on her miserable marriage to the duke of Mazarin who forced her to perform severe penances for her sins—real or imagined—and had squandered her sizeable dowry; her petitions for return of her property went unacknowledged by Louis XIV; after a brief dalliance with the duke of Savoy and an order by a French court to return to her husband, fled to England (1675) where she became the mistress of Charles II of England for a short term. ❖ See also *Women in World History.*

MANCINI, Laura (1823–1869). Italian poet. Born Laura Beatrice Oliva in Naples in 1823; died in Florence, Italy, July 17, 1869; m. Pasquale Stanislaus Mancini (b. 1817, Italian diplomat and jurist). ❖ Best-known for her patriotic poems. ❖ See also *Women in World History.*

MANCINI, Laure (1635–1657). Duchess of Mercoeur. Name variations: Laura Mancini; Duchesse de Mercoeur. Born in Rome in 1635 (some sources cite 1636); died in Paris, France, Feb 8, 1657; 1st dau. of Laurent also seen as Lorenzo Mancini and a mother (maiden name Mazarini or Mazarino) who was the sister of Cardinal Jules Mazarin (chief minister to Louis XIV); sister of Olympia Mancini (c. 1639–1708), Marie Mancini (1640–1715), Hortense Mancini (1646–1699), and Marie-Anne Mancini (1649–1714); cousin of Anne-Marie Martinozzi (1637–1672) and Laura Martinozzi; m. Louis de Vendôme, duc de Mercoeur (grandson of Henry IV and Gabrielle d'Estrees), in 1651; children: Louis Joseph, duc de Vendome (1654–1712, well-known French soldier who conquered Barcelona and fought his cousin Prince Eugene of Savoy, son of Olympia Mancini, in the War of the Spanish Succession). ❖ See also *Women in World History.*

MANCINI, Marie (1640–1715). Princess of Colonna. Name variations: Marie de Mancini. Born 1640 (some sources cite 1639); died 1715 (some sources cite 1714); 3rd dau. of Laurent also seen as Lorenzo Mancini and a mother (maiden name Mazarini or Mazarino) who was the sister of Cardinal Jules Mazarin (1602–1661, chief minister to Louis XIV); sister of Olympia Mancini (c. 1639–1708), Laure Mancini (1635–1657), Hortense Mancini (1646–1699), Marie-Anne Mancini (1649–1714); cousin of Anne-Marie Martinozzi (1637–1672) and Laura Martinozzi; m. the prince of Colonna, connétable de Naples (High Constable of Naples), in 1661. ❖ When Louis XIV of France fell in love with her, was sent away by uncle Jules Mazarin; married prince of Colonna on the rebound (1661), but soon left him and returned to France where she was shut up in a convent by Louis; lived in Spain for most of her life, then returned to France where she died in obscurity. ❖ See also *Mémoires de Madame la Connétable de Colonna* (1678); and *Women in World History.*

MANCINI, Marie-Anne (1649–1714). Duchess de Bouillon and salonnière. Born 1649; died 1714; 5th dau. of Laurent also seen as Lorenzo Mancini and the sister (maiden name Mazarini or Mazarino) of Cardinal Jules Mazarin (chief minister to young Louis XIV); sister of Olympia Mancini (c. 1639–1708), Marie Mancini (1640–1715), Hortense Mancini (1646–1699), Laure Mancini (1635–1657); cousin of Anne-Marie Martinozzi (1637–1672) and Laura Martinozzi; m. Godfrey Maurice de la Tour, duke of Bouillon (soldier), in 1662. ❖ Though renowned for her literary salon and patronage of La Fontaine, was accused of being involved with Catherine Deshayes (La Voisin) in the

"Affair of the Poisons," and was banished from France (1680); her innocence was later proven.

MANCINI, Olympia (c. 1639–1708). Princess of Savoy-Carignan, countess of Soissons, and mistress of Louis XIV. Name variations: Olympe or Olympie; comtesse de Soissons; countess of Soissons. Born c. 1639; died in Brussels in 1708; 2nd dau. of Laurent also seen as Lorenzo Mancini and the sister (maiden name Mazarini or Mazarino) of Cardinal Jules Mazarin (chief minister to young Louis XIV); sister of Marie-Anne Mancini (1649–1714), Marie Mancini (1640–1715), Hortense Mancini (1646–1699), Laure Mancini (1635–1657); cousin of Anne-Marie Martinozzi (1637–1672) and Laura Martinozzi; m. Eugene Maurice de Savoie-Carignan, prince of Savoy-Carignan, in 1657 (died 1673); children: Louis (who served in the army of Baden); Prince Eugene of Savoy (1663–1736). ❖ Had a youthful romance with Louis XIV; later embroiled in the "Affair of the Poisons," fled France to the Netherlands and eventually died in poverty in Brussels. ❖ See also *Women in World History.*

MANDAME, Mary (fl. 1639). American colonial. Flourished c. 1639 in Plymouth, MA. ❖ The 1st woman forced to wear a prominent mark on her clothing for a sexual offense, was convicted of "dallyance" with a Native American (1639) and sentenced to be publicly whipped and wear a badge of shame on her left sleeve.

MANDEL, Maria (1912–1948). Austrian war criminal. Born in Münzkirchen, Upper Austria, on Jan 10, 1912; sentenced to death on Dec 22, 1947; executed Jan 24, 1948, in Cracow; did not attend high school. ❖ SS head of women at Auschwitz II (Birkenau), began working as a supervisor at Ravensbrück (1939) and gained a reputation as one of the cruelest of the female SS guards there; appointed female Oberaufseherin (head supervisor) of Auschwitz II (1942); became known to the prisoners as "the beast"; captured (1945), was placed on trial at Cracow and sentenced to death (1947). ❖ See also *Women in World History.*

MANDEL, Miriam (1930–1982). Canadian poet. Born Miriam Minovitch in 1930 in Rockglen, Saskatchewan, Canada; committed suicide, Feb 13, 1982, in Edmonton; University of Saskatchewan, BA; m. Eli Mandel (div. 1967); children: 2. ❖ Won Governor General's Award for Poetry for *Lions at Her Face* (1973); other works include *Station 14* (1977), *Where Have You Been* (1980), and *The Collected Poems of Miriam Mandel* (ed. Sheila Watson, 1984).

MANDELA, Graca (1946—). See *Machel, Graca.*

MANDELA, Winnie (1934—). See *Madikizela-Mandela, Winnie.*

MANDELSTAM, Nadezhda (1899–1980). Russian memoirist. Name variations: Nadezhda Mandelshtam or Mandel'shtam; Nadezhda Yakovlevna; Nadezhda Yakolevna Mandelstam; Nadezheda. Born Nadezhda Khazina, Oct 31,· 1899, in Saratov, Russia; died Dec 29, 1980, in Moscow, USSR; dau. of Yakov Khazin (physician) and physician mother (name unknown); m. Osip Mandelstam (b. 1891, poet), in 1921, 1922, or 1924 (died in a Siberian labor camp in 1938). ❖ Was responsible for the preservation of husband Osip Mandelstam's poetry; when husband was punished for criticizing Stalin, went into exile in the Urals with him (1934–37); returned to Moscow, but lived continually under surveillance by the government; wrote the memoirs *Hope Against Hope* and *Hope Abandoned* (1970), chronicling the years of terror following Stalin's rise to power. ❖ See also Beth Holmgren, *Women's Works in Stalin's Time: On Lidiia Chukovskaia & Nadezhda Mandelstam* (Indiana U. Press, 1993); and *Women in World History.*

MANDER, Jane (1877–1949). New Zealand teacher, journalist, and novelist. Name variations: Manda Lloyd; Mary Jane Mander. Born Mary Jane Mander, April 9, 1877, at Ramararma, New Zealand; died Dec 20, 1949, at Whangarei, New Zealand; dau. of Francis Mander (farmer) and Janet (Kerr) Mander. ❖ Taught at Devonport, Otahuhu, and Newton West primary schools (1890s); edited and reported for *Northern Advocate* until 1906; wrote for Sydney *Maoriland Worker* under pseudonym Manda Lloyd (1907 and 1910); traveled to England and America, where she contributed to *New Republic,* and worked for American Red Cross during WWI; published novels that addressed social issues: *The Story of a New Zealand River* (1920), *The Passionate Puritan* (1922), *The Strange Attraction* (1923), *Allen Adair* (1925), *The Besieging City* (1926) and *Pins and Pinnacles* (1928); also contributed to Christchurch *Sun* and Auckland *Sun;* was a founding member of PEN New Zealand Center and executive member of New Zealand Women Writers' and Artists' Society. ❖ See also *Dictionary of New Zealand Biography* (Vol. 4).

MÄNDLI, Lesley (1966—). See *McNaught, Lesley.*

MANDRELL, Barbara (1948—). American country singer and musician. Born Barbara Ann Mandrell, Dec 25, 1948, in Houston, Texas; dau. of Irby Mandrell and Mary Ellen Mandrell; sister of Louise Mandrell and Irlene Mandrell; m. Ken Dudney (drummer), 1967; children: Kenneth, Jaime and Nathaniel. ❖ Became highly adept at playing steel guitar at young age; toured with Red Foley, Johnny Cash, Patsy Cline and Tex Ritter; formed group with family at age 14, with mother on bass, father on vocals and guitar, and future husband Ken Dudney on drums; signed with Columbia (1969), enlisting sisters as back-up singers to form group Do-Rites, and had 1st chart hit with cover of Otis Redding's "I've Been Loving You Too Long"; scored 1st of many top-40 hits with "Playing Around with Love" (1970) and partnered successfully with singer David Houston; joined Grand Ole Opry (1972); had series of hits, including "Midnight Oil" (1970s); with ABC/Dot Records had 4 #1 hits, including "I Was Country When Country Wasn't Cool" (1981), and received several industry awards; starred on NBC-TV in *Barbara Mandrell and the Mandrell Sisters* (1980–82); released gospel album *He Set My Life to Music* (1982); was in head-on car crash (1984); returned to music after recovering, but focused on live performances rather than recording; received over 75 major awards, including Country Music Association's Female Vocalist of the Year (1979, 1981) and Entertainer Of the Year (1980, 1981), and 1 Grammy; starred in NBC Movie of the Week "The Wrong Girl" (1999). ❖ See also autobiography *Get to the Heart: My Story* (Bantam, 1990).

MANÈS, Gina (1893–1989). French actress. Name variations: Gina Manes. Born April 7, 1983, in Paris, France; died Sept 6, 1989, in Toulouse, France. ❖ Made film debut in *L'homme sans visage* (1919), followed by *La nuit rouge, La main qui a tué, Napoléon* (as Josephine), *Sables, Synd, Quartier Latin, Nuits de princes, Grock, Pax, Divine, Mayerling, Le mort, S.O.S. Sahara, La Bella Otero, Les carnets du Major Thompson* and *Bonaparte et la révolution* (as Josephine), among others; probably best remembered for performance in title role of Feyder's *Du sollst nicht ehebrechen* (*Thérèse Raquin,* 1928); retired from the screen to run a restaurant and acting school in Morocco.

MANG, Veronique (1984—). Cameroon-born French runner. Born Dec 15, 1984, in Douala, Cameroon. ❖ Moved to France (1995); won a bronze medal for the 4x100-meter relay at Athens Olympics (2004).

MANGAKAHIA, Meri Te Tai (1868–1920). New Zealand tribal leader and suffragist. Name variations: Meri Te Tai. Born Meri Te Tai, c. May 22, 1868, near Whakarapa, on Holianga Harbor, New Zealand; died Oct 10, 1920, at Panguru, New Zealand; dau. of Re Te Tai and Hana Tera; m. Hamiora Mangakahia, late 1880s or early 1890s (died 1918); children: 2 sons, 2 daughters. ❖ Came into contact with suffrage movement through New Zealand's Women's Christian Temperance Union; as the 1st recorded Maori woman to address Parliament, pressed for rights of participation of women in choosing its members (1893); maintained active role in Maori politics. ❖ See also *Dictionary of New Zealand Biography* (Vol. 2).

MANGANO, Silvana (1930–1989). Italian film actress. Born April 21, 1930, in Rome, Italy; died from a heart attack following surgery for lung cancer, 1989; dau. of a Sicilian railroad worker and an Englishwoman; m. Dino De Laurentiis (film producer), 1949 (sep. 1983); children: son Frederico De Laurentiis, film producer (died 1981), and 3 daughters, one of whom, Raffaella De Laurentiis, is also a film producer. ❖ Trained as a dancer, entered films as a teenager after winning title of Miss Rome; rocketed to fame as the voluptuous lead in *Riso Amaro* (*Bitter Rice,* 1949); other films include *Anna* (1951), *L'Oro di Napoli* (*Gold of Naples,* 1954), *Ulisse* (*Ulysses,* 1954), *La Tempesta* (*Tempest,* 1958), *Jovanka e l'Altri* (*Five Branded Women,* 1960), 1960), *Barabba* (*Barabbas,* 1961), *Una Vita difficile* (*A Difficult Life,* 1961), *La Mia Signora* (1964), *Le Streghe* (*The Witches,* 1967), *Edipo Re* (*Oedipus Rex,* 1967), *Teorema* (1968), *Morte a Venezia* (*Death in Venice,* 1971), *Il Decameron* (*The Decameron,* 1971) and *Dune* (1984). ❖ See also *Women in World History.*

MANGESHKAR, Lata (1929—). Indian singer. Name variations: Anandadhan or Anandaghan; Anand Ghar. Born Sept 28, 1929, in Indore, Madhya Pradesh, India; dau. of Dinanath Mangeshkar (theatrical company owner and classical singer, died 1942) and Shudhhamati Mangeshkar; sister of Meena Mangeshkar, Asha Bhosle Mangeshkar, Usha Mangeshkar, Hridaynath Mangeshkar; studied with father, classical scholar Amanat Ali Khan Bhindibazarwala, Ustad Amanat Khan Devaswale, and Pandit Tulsidas Sharma. ❖ Credited with having the world's most recorded voice, 1st acted in films (1942–48); made breakthrough as playback singer in movie *Majboor* (1948) and followed with hits in 4 more films (1949), becoming the singing voice of actresses in over 2,000 musical films during 36-year career; composed for several movies under pseudonym Anand Ghar (1950–65) and has also produced several films over course of career; experienced phenomenal success, rendering over 40,000 songs in 20 Indian languages, including "Uthaye Ja Unke Situm" (*Andaaz*, 1949), "Rasik Balma" (*Chori Chori*, 1956), "Bedardi Balma" (*Arzoo*, 1966), "Ae Dil-e-Nadan" (*Razia Sultan*, 1980) and "Jiya Jale" (*Dil Se*, 1998); received Bharatha Rathna, the highest civilian honor, by the Government of India. ❖ See also Harish Bhimani, *In Search of Lata Mangeshkar* (South Asia Books, 1995).

MANGOLTE, Babette (c. 1945—). French cinematographer. Born c. 1945 in France. ❖ Regarded as one of most important and innovative cinematographers and filmmakers of late 20th century, was one of the 1st women accepted at L'Ecole Nationale de la Photographie et de la Cinématographie; began career editing several films, including Marcel Hanoun's *L'Automne*, before moving to New York (1970); became involved in downtown art scene and was director of photography for 2 films by Yvonne Rainer and 5 films by Chantal Akerman; taught 16mm filmmaking at Pratt Institute and won Prix de la Lumière at Toulon Film Festival (1975) for own film *What Maisie Knew*; other films, many shown at major festivals, include *The Camera: Je* (1977), *The Sky on Location, Visible Cities* (1991), *Four Pieces by Morris* (1993) and *Les Modèles de Pickpocket*.

MANIANI-TZELILI, Miréla (1976—). See *Manjani-Tzelili, Miréla*.

MANICOM, Jacqueline (1938–1976). Guadeloupean novelist and midwife. Born 1938 in Guadeloupe; died 1976. ❖ Studied law and medicine and became midwife; with husband, founded Guadeloupe Association for Family Planning; led a movement to legalize abortion and was co-founder of Choisir (Choice); novels include *Mon examen de blanc* (My Exam in Whiteness, 1972) and *La Graine: Journal d'une Sage-Femme* (The Seed: The Diary of a Midwife, 1974).

MANIGAULT, Ann Ashby (1703–1782). American diarist. Born 1703 in South Carolina; died 1782. ❖ From age 53, kept diary of busy social life in Charleston, sections of which were included in *Extracts from the Journal of Mrs Ann Manigault 1754–1781*.

MANIKARNIKA (c. 1835–1858). See *Lakshmibai*.

MANINA, Tamara (1934—). Soviet gymnast. Born Sept 16, 1934, in USSR. ❖ At Melbourne Olympics, won a bronze medal in teams all-around, portable apparatus, silver medals in balance beam and vault, and a gold medal in team all-around (1956); at Tokyo Olympics, won a silver medal in balance beam and a gold medal in team all-around (1964).

MANIOUROVA, Gouzel (1978—). Russian wrestler. Born Jan 24, 1978, in Saransk, USSR. ❖ Won European championships for 72kg freestyle (2004) and a silver medal for 72kg freestyle at Athens Olympics (2004).

MANJA, Salmi (b. 1939). See *Rashid, Saleha Abdul*.

MANJANI, Miréla (1976—). Greek javelin thrower. Name variations: Mirela or Miréla Tzelili; Mirela Manjani; Mirela Manjani-Tzelili; also seen as Mirella Maniani-Tzelili. Born Miréla Tzelili, Dec 21, 1976, in Dirrahio, Albania; divorced. ❖ Won a gold medal at World championships (1999 and 2003) and at European championships (2002); won a silver medal at Sydney Olympics (2000) and a bronze medal at Athens Olympics (2004).

MANKIEWICZ, Rose (1913–1958). See *Stradner, Rose*.

MANKILLER, Wilma (1945—). Native American activist and tribal leader. Name variations: Wilma Pearl Mankiller. Born Nov 18, 1945, in Tahlequah, OK; dau. of Charlie Mankiller (full-blooded Cherokee) and Irene Mankiller (of Dutch-Irish heritage); attended Skyline Junior College in San Bruno, CA, and San Francisco State College; Union for Experimenting Colleges and Universities, BA, 1977; graduate studies at University of Arkansas, 1979; m. Hector Hugo Olaya de Bardi, 1962 (div. 1974); m. Charlie Soap, c. 1987; children: (1st m.) Felicia (b. 1964), Gina (b. 1966). ❖ Became involved with Native Americans who set about reclaiming Alcatraz Island (1969), asserting ownership based on an old treaty guaranteeing the reversion of unused government land to the tribe; spent 5 years establishing a defense fund for the Pit River tribe's battle to reclaim ancestral lands from Pacific Gas and Electric Co.; hired by Cherokee Nation, served as community development director (1977–83), then appointed principal organizer of a grant-funded revitalization project; became deputy chief of the Cherokee Nation (1983); took over as

principal chief (1985); was reelected (1987); retired (1994). Received Donna Nigh First Lady Award from Oklahoma Commission for Status of Women (1985), American Leadership Award from Harvard University (1986), John W. Gardner Leadership Award (1988); inducted into Oklahoma Women's Hall of Fame (1986), Oklahoma Hall of Fame, and Women's Hall of Fame (1994). ❖ See also autobiography, *Mankiller: A Chief and Her People* (1984); and *Women in World History*.

MANKIN, Helen Douglas (1894–1956). American politician. Name variations: Helen Douglas. Born Sept 11, 1894, in Atlanta, GA; died July 25, 1956; dau. of Hamilton Douglas (lawyer and founder of Atlanta Law School) and Corinne (Williams) Douglas (teacher and lawyer); sister of Jean Douglas; Rockford College, AB, 1917; Atlanta Law School, LLB, 1920; m. Guy Mark Mankin (engineer), 1927; children: (stepson) Guy Jr. ❖ US congressional representative, state assemblywoman, and lawyer who was the 1st woman elected to Congress from Georgia; joined American Women's Hospital Unit during WWI and drove an ambulance in France for 13 months; admitted to Georgia bar (1920); opened own law firm (1924); a Democrat, served as representative to the Georgia legislature (1937–46), being re-elected 4 times; won a special election for US House of Representatives (1946), though publicly mocked because she had black support; though she ran again in 1946 primaries and won the popular vote, lost when her opponent claimed victory under an obscure county-unit system, a system revived to nullify African-American votes. ❖ See also Lorraine N. Spritzer, *The Belle of Ashby Street: Helen Douglas Mankin and Georgia Politics* (U. of Georgia Press, 1982); and *Women in World History*.

MANKOVA, Svetlana (1962—). Soviet handball player. Born Dec 1, 1962, in USSR. ❖ At Seoul Olympics, won a bronze medal in team competition (1988).

MANLEY, Delarivier (1663–1724). See *Manley, Mary de la Rivière*.

MANLEY, Dorothy (1927—). English runner. Name variations: Dorothy Gladys Hall. Born Dorothy Gladys Manley, April 29, 1927, in London, England. ❖ Trained as a high jumper, before becoming a sprinter; was Essex County 100-yards champion (1947, 1948, 1949); won 100-meters silver medal at London Olympics (1948). ❖ See also *Women in World History*.

MANLEY, Effa (1900–1981). American entrepreneur and civil-rights activist. Born Effa Brooks, Mar 27, 1900, in Philadelphia, PA; died in Los Angeles, CA, April 16, 1981; m. and div. a man named Bush, sometime between 1916 and 1932; m. Abraham L. Manley, June 15, 1933 (died 1952); m. Charles Alexander, mid-1950s (div.). ❖ As co-owner of the powerful Newark Eagles black baseball club, exerted a major influence on the game of baseball (1930s–40s) and used the games to promote civil-rights causes; was the first woman elected to baseball's Hall of Fame. ❖ See also James Overmyer, *Effa Manley and the Newark Eagles* (Scarecrow, 1993); and *Women in World History*.

MANLEY, Elizabeth (1965—). Canadian figure skater. Name variations: Liz Manley. Born Aug 7, 1965, in White Rock, British Columbia, Canada. ❖ Became the 1st Canadian woman to land a triple jump combination in competition (1979); was 3-time Canadian champion (1985, 1987, 1988); won Skate Canada (1986); won a silver medal at Calgary Olympics and at World Championships (1988). Awarded the Order of Canada; inducted into Skate Canada Hall of Fame (2001). ❖ See also autobiography *Thumbs Up!: The Elizabeth Manley Story*.

MANLEY, Liz (1965—). See *Manley, Elizabeth*.

MANLEY, Mary de la Rivière (1663–1724). English author and playwright. Name variations: Delarivier Manley; Mary de la Riviere Manley; Dela Manley; Mrs. Manley Delarivière. Born 1663 in England; died 1724 in England; dau. of Sir Roger Manley (high-ranking British officer and writer); married cousin John Manley (dissolved because he was already married); lived with Barbara Villiers, duchess of Cleveland (c. 1641–1709). ❖ Broke new ground in a number of literary areas; said to have been the 1st Englishwoman to work as a political journalist, the 1st to author a bestseller, and the 1st to be arrested because of something she had written: *Secret Memoirs and Manners of Several Persons of Quality of Both Sexes From the New Atalantis, an Island in the Mediterranean* (1709), a satiric diatribe against the opposition Whig Party; also wrote several plays and succeeded Jonathan Swift as editor of the *Examiner*, a popular Tory publication. ❖ See also *Women in World History*.

MANMATI (d. 1619). Rajput princess. Name variations: Jodha Bai; Manmati Jodha Bai. Born in India; died April 18, 1619; dau. of

Raja Udai Singh of Jodhpur (r. 1583–1595); 2nd wife of Jahangir (1569–1627), Mughal emperor (r. 1605–27), 1588; children: Parwiz (1589–1626); Shah Jahan (1592–1666), Mughal emperor (r. 1628–1658); Bahar Banu (d. 1653).

MANN, Aimee (1960—). American musician. Born Sept 8, 1960, in Richmond, VA; studied bass at Berklee College of Music; m. Michael Penn (singer and songwriter), Dec 29, 1997. ❖ Joined Boston punk group, Young Snakes; with guitarist Robert Holmes, drummer Michael Hausman, and keyboardist Joey Pesce, formed band, 'Til Tuesday (1982), which won music contest and recording deal; with band, released debut album, *Voices Carry* (1985), with hit title song, and unsuccessful album, *Everything's Different Now* (1988), then disbanded; after 5 years, disentangled self from band's Epic Records contract and released critically acclaimed solo album, *Whatever* (1993); signed with Geffen Records and released 2nd album, *I'm with Stupid* (1995); joined husband in Acoustic Vaudeville Tour; recorded many songs for soundtrack of film, *Magnolia* (1999); released *Bachelor No. 2* on own label, SuperEgo (2000).

MANN, Carol (1941—). American golfer. Born Carol Ann Mann, Feb 3, 1941, in Buffalo, NY. ❖ Won the Vare Trophy (1968) with an average score of 72.04, a record which remained for a decade; won the Western Junior championship (1958) and the Women's Western (1964); won USGA Open (1965); won 10 tournaments (1968) and 8 tournaments (1969); won Lawson's Open, Border Classic, George Washington Classic, and Dallas Civitan (1975); carded 200 strokes for 54 holes in LPGA competition at Canongate Country Club in Palmetto, GA (1978), to win the Lady Carling. ❖ See also *Women in World History.*

MANN, Elisabeth (1918–2002). German-born writer and environmentalist. Name variations: Elisabeth Mann Borgese. Born April 24, 1918, in Munich, Germany; died Feb 8, 2002, while on vacation in St. Moritz, Switzerland; lived in Halifax, Nova Scotia; became US citizen (1941), then took Canadian citizenship (1983); dau. of Thomas Mann (1875–1955, novelist) and Katia or Katja (Pringsheim) Mann; sister of Erika Mann (1905–1969, writer), Monika Mann, Angelus Gottfried (known as Golo) Mann, Klaus Mann, and Michael Mann; received diploma from Conservatory of Music in Zurich, 1938; m. Giuseppe A. Borgese (professor), 1939 (died 1952); children: Angelica Borgese and Domenica Borgese. ❖ Political scientist and writer of fiction and oceanic yearbooks, founded the International Oceans Institute based in Malta; an expert on maritime law, helped organize the international Peace in the Oceans Conference (1970), which would result in the UN Law of the Seas treaty (1982); joined faculty at Dalhousie University in Halifax (1979), 1st as a political science professor, then as an adjunct law professor.

MANN, Erika (1905–1969). German writer, journalist, and actress. Born Erika Julia Hedwig Mann in Munich, Germany, Nov 9, 1905; died in Zurich, Switzerland, Aug 27, 1969; dau. of Thomas Mann (1875–1955, novelist) and Katia or Katja (Pringsheim) Mann; sister of Elisabeth Mann (1918–2002, writer), Monika Mann, Angelus Gottfried (known as Golo) Mann, Klaus Mann, and Michael Mann; m. Gustaf Gründgens, 1926 (div. 1929); m. W.H. Auden (1907–1973, poet), 1935, in a marriage of convenience that gave her citizenship. ❖ Using biting satire to attack Nazism, was a thorn in the side of the Third Reich with her cabaret *Die Pfeffermühle* (The Peppermill) which toured Europe (1933–36); after coming to US (1936), set out to alert Americans to the growing threat of fascism; collaborated with brother Klaus on such books as *Escape to Life* (1939), *School for Barbarians: Education under the Nazis* (1939), *The Lights Go Down* (1940) and *The Other Germany* (1940); as a journalist, reported on the London Blitz and from the battlefields of North Africa, France and Germany; in postwar years, finding the Cold War hysteria increasingly difficult to deal with, moved to Switzerland (1951); served as literary assistant to famous father, Thomas Mann, during last years of his life. ❖ See also *Women in World History.*

MANN, Erika (1950—). German politician. Born Nov 2, 1950, in Leipzig; attended University of Hannover. ❖ As a European Socialist, elected to 4th and 5th European Parliament (1994–99, 1999–2004); chaired the delegation to the European Economic Area Joint Parliamentary Committee (EEA).

MANN, Harriet (1831–1918). See *Miller, Olive Thorne.*

MANN, Ida (1893–1983). English ophthalmologist. Name variations: Ida Caroline Mann; Mrs. Gye or Mrs. W.E. Gye. Born Ida Caroline Mann, Feb 6, 1893, in West Hampstead, London, England; died Nov 18, 1983; dau. of Ellen (Packham) Mann and Frederick Mann (civil servant);

m. William Ewart Gye (professor), 1944 (died 1952). ❖ Oxford University's 1st woman professor and Britain's 1st Ophthalmology professor, began career as the 1st woman consultant at Moorfields Eye Hospital (London); entered London School of Medicine for Women (1914); received clinical training at St. Mary's Hospital in Paddington; assisted professor E.S. Frazer with embryological studies; as a surgeon, worked at several institutions, including Elizabeth Garrett Anderson Hospital (1922–25), Central London Ophthalmic Hospital (1925–27), Royal London Ophthalmic Hospital in Moorfields (1927–49) and Royal Free Hospital (1928–39); at Oxford University, served as a Margaret Ogilvie Reader (1941–46) and as an Ophthalmology professor (1942–49); led Ministry of Supply's ophthalmic research team (1940–45) to study the effects of gases on the eye (worked with biochemist Antoinette Pirie); introduced the slit lamp, which allowed ophthalmologists to see inside an eye, to England; due to husband's heart condition, immigrated to Perth (1949); served as consultant ophthalmologist for Western Australia Public Health Department (1951–76); treated and studied eye conditions of Aborigine patients; granted membership to many organizations, including the Royal College of Surgeons (fellow); wrote *The Development of the Human Eye* (1928), *The Science of Seeing* (with Pirie, 1946) and *The Cockney and the Crocodile* (1962). Named Commander of the Order of the British Empire (1954) and Dame Commander of the Order of the British Empire (1980).

MANN, Mary Peabody (1806–1887). American educator. Born Mary Tyler Peabody in Cambridgeport, MA, Nov 16, 1806; died Feb 11, 1887; dau. of Nathaniel and Elizabeth Palmer Peabody (1778–1853); sister of Sophia Peabody Hawthorne (1809–1871) and Elizabeth Palmer Peabody (1804–1894); aunt of Rose Hawthorne Lathrop (1851–1926); m. Horace Mann, 1843 (died 1859); children: Horace Mann Jr. (b. 1844); George Combe Mann (b. 1845); Benjamin Pickman Mann (b. 1848). ❖ One of the notable Peabody sisters, replaced sister Elizabeth Palmer Peabody in a teaching position in Maine, then joined her to open a dame school in Boston; following husband's death (1859), rejoined Elizabeth in Boston and helped promote the new kindergarten movement. ❖ See also Louise Hall Tharp, *The Peabody Sisters of Salem* (Little, Brown, 1950); and *Women in World History.*

MANN, Rhonda Fleming (1922—). See *Fleming, Rhonda.*

MANN, Shelley (1937—). American swimmer. Born Oct 15, 1937, in Arlington, VA. ❖ Crippled by polio (1943); won U.S. national championship (1951); was the 1st woman to win a gold medal in the inaugural 100-meter butterfly at Melbourne Olympics (1956), and also went home with a silver medal in the 4x100-meter freestyle relay; held records in backstroke, freestyle, individual medley, and butterfly. Inducted into Swimming and Diving Hall of Fame (1966). ❖ See also *Women in World History.*

MANNER, Eeva-Liisa (1921–1995). Finnish poet, playwright, novelist, and translator. Name variations: (pseudonym) Anna September. Born in Helsinki, Finland, Dec 5, 1921; died in Helsinki, Jan 1995; dau. of Leo Johannes Manner and Elsi Irene Kukkonen Manner; never married. ❖ Leading figure in the modernist movement, worked for a publishing firm (1944–46) before turning to writing and translating to support herself; published *Kuin tuuli tai pilvi* (Like the Wind or the Cloud, 1949); received recognition with publication of verse collection *Tämä matka* (This Journey, 1956) which would appear in 5 editions by 1964 and change the course of Finnish literature; other writings include *Tyttö taivaan laiturilla* (The Girl on the Pier of Heaven, novel, 1951), *Varokaa, voittajat* (Beware, Victors, novel 1972), *Eros ja Psykhe* (Eros and Psyche, verse drama, 1959), *Uuden vuoden yö* (New Year's Eve, play, 1965), and poetic dramas *Toukokuun lumi* (Snow in May, 1966) and *Poltettu oranssi* (Burnt-Out Ocher, 1968). Won Michael Agricola Prize and Alexis Kivi Prize. ❖ See also *Women in World History.*

MANNERING, Mary (1876–1953). English-born stage actress. Name variations: Florence Friend. Born Florence Friend, April 29, 1876, in England; died Jan 21, 1953, in Los Angeles, CA; m. James K. Hackett (actor, div.); m. Frederick E. Wadsworth (industrialist). ❖ Under real name Florence Friend, made London debut as Zela in *Hero and Leander* (1892); as Mary Mannering, made US debut opposite James K. Hackett in *The Courtship of Leonie* (1896); starred in *Trelawny of the Wells, The Lady of Lyons, Janice Meredith, The Walls of Jericho, Judith, The House of Cards* and *The Garden of Allah.*

MANNERS, Catherine (1785–1845). See *Stepney, Catherine.*

MANNERS, Lady Diana (1892–1986). See *Cooper, Diana Duff.*

MANNERS, Martha (1924–1977). English dancer. Born April 24, 1924, in England; died Mar 28, 1977, in New York, NY; m. Nicholas DeRose (died). ❖ Made professional debut at 14; performed with Marquis de Cuevas Co. and Ballet Russe; danced as soloist with Russian Opera Ballet and Metropolitan Opera Ballet, NY; held teaching positions at Newark Ballet Academy (NJ), Birmingham Civic Ballet (AL), and Birmingham Southern College (AL); taught private classes in New York City.

MANNERS, Mrs. (1785–1845). See Stepney, Catherine.

MANNES, Clara Damrosch (1869–1948). American pianist, educator, and founder. Born Dec 12, 1869, in Breslau, Prussia (now Wroclaw, Poland); died Mar 16, 1948, in New York, NY; dau. of Leopold Damrosch (musician and musical conductor) and Helene (von Heimburg) Damrosch; sister of Walter Damrosch (1862–1950) and Frank Damrosch (1859–1937), both musical directors; attended private schools in NY City, to which her family moved in 1871; began study of piano at 6; continued musical studies in Dresden, Germany (1888–89); m. David Mannes (violinist), June 1898 (died 1959); children: Leopold Mannes; Maria von Heimburg Mannes (1904–1990), writer known as Marya Mannes. ❖ Best known as co-founder with husband of NY's David Mannes Music School (now the Mannes College of Music), where she served as co-director until her death. ❖ See also Women in World History.

MANNES, Marya (1904–1990). American writer and social commentator. Name variations: Marya Mannes Blow; (pseudonym) Sec. Born Maria von Heimburg Mannes, Nov 14, 1904, in New York, NY; died Sept 13, 1990, in San Francisco, CA; dau. of David Mannes (violinist and co-founder of Mannes College of Music) and Clara Damrosch Mannes (1869–1948, pianist and co-founder of Mannes College of Music); m. Jo Mielziner (theatrical designer), 1926 (div. 1931); m. Richard Blow (artist), 1937 (div. 1943); m. Christopher Clarkson, 1948 (div. 1966); children: (2nd m.) David Jeremy Blow. ❖ Achieved renown as a writer on a variety of political and cultural matters, but may be best remembered for her incisive portrait of the postwar American psyche; was hired as features editor at Vogue magazine (1933); during WWII, worked for US government in Office of Strategic Service, forerunner of Central Intelligence Agency, and also wrote a series of articles for The New Yorker; was associated with Glamour for several years; published 1st book, Message from a Stranger (1948); began to write pieces for The Reporter under pen name "Sec." (1952); published collection of satirical poetry Subverse (1959); worked as tv and radio commentator (1960s–70s), beginning with a stint as host of tv program "I Speak for Myself" (1959); also wrote columns for McCall's and The New York Times. Won George Polk Memorial Award for magazine criticism (1958). ❖ See also autobiography, Out of My Time (1971); and Women in World History.

MANNHEIM, Lucie (1899–1976). German actress. Born April 30, 1899, in Berlin, Germany; died July 28, 1976, in Braunlage, Germany; m. Marius Goring (actor), 1941. ❖ Made stage debut as Käthie in Old Heidelberg (1920), then appeared as Ännchen in Jugend, Lulu in Erdgeist, and Hedwig in The Wild Duck; was principal actress of the Berlin Theater (1924–30), playing Nora in A Doll's House, Juliet in Romeo and Juliet, Puck in A Midsummer Night's Dream, Irina in The Three Sisters, and title role in Hannele; also appeared in musicals, comedies, and farces, and in plays under other managements, including Arms and the Man, The Trial of Mary Dugan and Liebestrank; expelled by Nazis, made London debut to great success in title role in Nina; during WWII, broadcast frequently to Germany with BBC European service; toured in Germany (1947), then translated and directed in Berlin (1949), appearing there in The Corn is Green, The Rose Tattoo, Rats, Power of Darkness, Look Homeward Angel, Tonight at 8:30 and La voix humaine; made over 25 films, including Danton, The 39 Steps, Hotel Reserve and So Little Time. Received Order of Merit (1953) and Grand Cross of the Order (Bonn, Germany, 1959); nominated Berlin State Actress for services to the theater (1963).

MANNIN, Ethel (1900–1984). British author and political activist. Born Ethel Edith Mannin in Clapham, London, England, Oct 11, 1900; died in Devon, England, Dec 5, 1984; dau. of Robert Mannin and Edith Gray Mannin; m. J.A. Porteous, 1919; m. Reginald Reynolds, 1938; children: (1st m.) daughter, Jean Porteous. ❖ Pacifist, anarchist, and supporter of the Palestinian cause, published 1st novel Martha (1922) and went on to publish 94 additional books, including numerous novels as well as travel reports that often served as political tracts; found her voice as a writer with Sounding Brass (1924), a satire of the advertising world which was a commercial and critical success; produced 30 novels by 1952 including Privileged Spectator (1939), Red Rose (1941) and Late Have I Loved Thee (1948); also wrote The Living Lotus (1956), The Road to Beersheba (1963),

The Night and Its Homing (1966), The Midnight Street (1969) and The Late Miss Guthrie (1976); nonfiction includes Confessions and Impressions (1930), Commonsense and the Child (1931), South to Samarkand (1936), Commonsense and the Adolescent (1937), Women and the Revolution (1938), Connemara Journal (1947), German Journey (1948), A Lance for the Arabs: A Middle East Journey (1963) and This Was a Man (1952), a work about her father. ❖ See also Sunset over Dartmoor: A Final Chapter of Autobiography (1977); and Women in World History.

MANNING, Anna Amelia (1845–1931). See Comfort, Anna Manning.

MANNING, Anne (1807–1879). English novelist. Born in London, England, Feb 17, 1807; died in Tunbridge Wells, England, Sept 14, 1879; dau. of William Oke Manning (insurance broker for Lloyd's) and Joan Whatmore (Gibson) Manning (dau. of the principal surveyor of the London Docks and a distant cousin of Charles and Mary Lamb); never married. ❖ Wrote 1st book, A Sister's Gift (1826), followed by The Village Belle (1838), and The Maiden and Married Life of Mary Powell (1849), the novel for which she is probably best known; was also an occasional contributor to Sharpe's Magazine. ❖ See also Women in World History.

MANNING, Hope (1912–2004). See Manning, Irene.

MANNING, Irene (1912–2004). American stage and screen actress and lyric soprano. Name variations: Hope Manning. Born Incz Harvuot, July 17, 1912, in Cincinnati, Ohio; died of congestive heart failure, May 28, 2004, in San Carlos, CA; m. Clinton H. Green. ❖ Under name Hope Manning, made stage debut as Margot in The Desert Song (1935), then starred in low-budget westerns opposite Gene Autry; as Irene Manning, signed with Warner's and appeared in such films as Yankee Doodle Dandy, The Big Shot, The Desert Song, Shine on Harvest Moon, The Doughgirls and Hollywood Canteen; made NY stage debut in The Day Before Spring (1945) and London film debut in I Lived in Grosvenor Square (1945).

MANNING, Katharine (1904–1974). American modern dancer and teacher. Born Nov 11, 1904; died Aug 13, 1974, in Chicago, IL. ❖ Trained at Denishawn school in New York City under Doris Humphrey and Charles Weidman; danced in original cast of Humphrey-Weidman Concert Group, where she appeared in numerous premieres, including Humphrey's Water Study (1928), The Shakers (1930) and With My Red Fires (1936), and Weidman's Happy Hypocrite (1931), Color Harmony (1930) and Quest (1936); taught at University of Chicago.

MANNING, Leah (1886–1977). English politician. Name variations: Dame Leah Perrett Manning. Born Elizabeth Leah Perrett, April 14, 1886, in Rockford, Illinois; died Sept 15, 1977, in England; dau. of Charles William Perrett and Harriett Margaret Tappin; great-granddau. of Methodist philanthropist Susan Tappin; graduate of Homerton College, Cambridge; m. William Manning, 1914. ❖ Colorful left-wing politician of 1930s, joined Labour Party and Fabian Society; an ardent trade unionist, became president of National Union of Teachers (1929); elected to represent East Islington in House of Commons (1930), but then lost seat (1931) and lost contest for Sunderland seat 4 years later (1935); served as Labour NEC (1931–32); campaigned for Republican cause during Spanish Civil War and published What I Saw in Spain (1933); served as secretary to Spanish Medical Aid Committee (1936) in defiance of Labor Party's position of non-interference; continued to support anti-Franco forces, helping to evacuate Basque children to Britain (1937) and bearing witness to bombing of Guernica; returned to Spain (1938) and wrote report on hospitals where British doctors and nurses were working; became Labor Party candidate for Epping and won seat (1945); published Growing Up (1948); defeated in 1950, attempted unsuccessfully to regain seat (1951, 1955). Named Dame of British Empire (DBE, 1966). ❖ See also autobiography, A Life for Education (1970).

MANNING, Madeline (1948—). American runner. Name variations: Madeline Mims. Born Jan 11, 1948, in Cleveland, Ohio. ❖ At Mexico City Olympics, won a gold medal in 800 meters (1968); at Munich Olympics, won a silver medal in 4x400-meter relay (1972); during 14-year career, won gold medals at World University Games (1966) and Pan American Games (1967), and 7 outdoor and 5 indoor AAU championships.

MANNING, Maria (c. 1821–1849). English murderer. Name variations: Marie Manning; Maria de Roux; Marie deRoux; Maria Manning DeRoux. Born Maria de Roux in 1821 (some sources cite 1825), in Lausanne, Switzerland; died by hanging, Nov 13, 1849, in London,

England; m. Frederick George Manning, in 1847. ❖ The inspiration for a character in Charles Dickens' *Bleak House* whose much-publicized crime, conviction, and public execution enthralled Victorian England. ❖ See also *Women in World History.*

MANNING, Marie (c. 1873–1945). American columnist and reporter. Name variations: Marie Manning Gasch; (pseudonym) Beatrice Fairfax. Born Jan 22, c. 1873 (all sources are estimates, and include 1875 and 1878), in Washington, DC; died in Washington, DC, Nov 28, 1945; dau. of Michael Charles Manning (War Department employee) and Elizabeth (Barrett) Manning; m. Herman Eduard Gasch, 1905; children: Oliver Gasch; Manning Gasch. ❖ The 1st American newspaper advice columnist, began writing features for the "women's page" of *New York Evening Journal* (1897), primarily concerning household and beauty tips; having suggested the creation of a separate column to respond to letters requesting personal assistance, launched 1st "Letters from the Lovelorn" column under pen name "Beatrice Fairfax" (July 20, 1898) and was an instant success; became known for dispensing matter-of-fact advice regarding courtship and problems in love, with far less obligatory sentiment than was the norm; continued to write news articles for the paper under real name; also wrote fiction published in *Harper's*, and published 2 novels, *Lord Allingham, Bankrupt* (1902) and *Judith of the Plains* (1903); a longtime suffragist, was a founding member of the Women's National Press Club. ❖ See also *Women in World History.*

MANNING, Mary (1906–1999). Irish playwright. Name variations: Mary Manning Howe; Mary Adams. Born Mary Manning, June 30, 1906, in Dublin, Ireland; died 1999 in Cambridge, MA; dau. of Fitzmaurice Manning and Susan Bennett Manning; attended Morehampton House School and Alexandra College, Dublin; studied at Abbey Acting School; m. Mark DeWolfe Howe Jr. (Harvard Law School professor), 1935 (died 1967); m. Faneuil Adams, 1980; children: (1st m.) Susan Howe (b. 1937, writer); Fanny Howe (b. 1940, writer); Helen Howe (who m. Christopher Braider). ❖ Lived in US from 1930s and helped found Poets' Theater in Cambridge, MA; novels and plays include *Storm Over Wicklow* (1933), *Happy Family* (1934), *Lovely People* (1953), *The Last Chronicles of Ballyfungus* (1978) and *Go, Lovely Rose* (1989); adapted Joyce's *Finnegans Wake* (1955), which was filmed by Mary Ellen Bute and won prize at Cannes International Film Festival (1965).

MANNING, Olivia (1908–1980). English novelist. Name variations: Jacob Morrow. Born Olivia Manning, Mar 2, 1908, in Portsmouth, England; died of a stroke suffered in Ryde, Isle of Wight, July 23, 1980; elder child of Lieutenant-Commander Oliver Manning, R.N. (retired) and Olivia (Morrow) Manning; attended Portsmouth Grammar School and Portsmouth Technical College; m. Reginald (Reggie) Donald Smith, 1939. ❖ Novelist whose best-known works are 2 trilogies dealing with WWII, moved to London (1926); published 1st novel *The Wind Changes* (1937); spent war years in Bucharest, Athens, Cairo and Jerusalem (1939–46); published 1st book of short stories *Growing Up* (1948); published 1st book of the Balkan trilogy, *The Great Fortune* (1960), followed by *The Spoilt City* (1962) and *Friends and Heroes* (1965); published the Levant Trilogy: *The Danger Tree* (1977), *The Battle Lost and Won* (1978), and *The Sum of Things* (1980). The *Balkan Trilogy* was successfully serialized on tv as "The Fortunes of War," starring Emma Thompson, Kenneth Branagh and Ronald Pickup (1987). Made Commander of the British Empire (1976). ❖ See also *Women in World History.*

MANNOURY D'ECTOT, Madame de (fl. 1880). French novelist. Name variations: Vicomtesse de Coeur-Brulant. Born in France. ❖ Entertained artists and writers at chateau near Argenton and opened matrimonial agency; wrote erotic works *Les Cousines de la colonelle* (1880) and *Le Roman de Violette.*

MANNY, Anne (b. 1355). Countess of Pembroke. Name variations: Anne Hastings. Born c. 1355; dau. of Walter Manny, 1st baron Manny (d. 1372), and Margaret (c. 1320–1400), duchess of Norfolk; m. John Hastings, 2nd earl of Pembroke (1347–1375); children: John Hastings, 3rd earl of Pembroke (1372–1389).

MANOLACHE, Ionela (1976—). See *Tirlea-Manolache, Ionela.*

MANOLIU, Lia (1932–1998). Romanian track-and-field athlete. Born April 25, 1932, in Chisnau, Romania; died Jan 9, 1998, in Bucharest; graduated from college in Bucharest with a degree in electrical engineering. ❖ Participated as a discus thrower in 6 Olympic Games (1952–72), winning a bronze medal in Rome (1960) and Tokyo (1964) and a gold medal in Mexico City (1968); was the oldest woman in Olympic

history to win a gold medal in a track-and-field event; named president of Romanian Olympic Committee, becoming only the 3rd woman worldwide to head a national Olympic committee (1990). ❖ See also *Women in World History.*

MANOS, Aspasia (1896–1972). Queen of the Hellenes. Born Sept 4, 1896, in Athens, Greece; died Aug 7, 1972, in Venice, Italy; dau. of Colonel Petros Manos and Maria Argyropoulos; m. Alexander I, king of the Hellenes, Nov 4, 1919; children: Alexandra (1921–1993), queen of Yugoslavia.

MANOY, Mina (1885–1926). See *Arndt, Hermina.*

MANRIQUE PEREZ, Silvia (1973—). Spanish field-hockey player. Born Mar 1973. ❖ At Barcelona Olympics, won a gold medal in team competition (1992).

MANSBERGER, Margarita Nelken (1896–1968). See *Nelken, Margarita.*

MANSEL, Lucy (c. 1830–1915). New Zealand social leader. Born in 1830 or 1831, in Co. Clare, Ireland; died Jan 22, 1916, at Greerton, New Zealand; dau. of Robert Mansel (military officer) and Maria (Armstrong) Mansel. ❖ Raised in England and later lived on Isle of Wight, immigrated with 6 nephews to New Zealand following their father's death (1884); purchased and renovated 320-acre estate southwest of Tauranga, where she raised her nephews (1884); became active in social and cultural life of area, helping to establish memorial church on battle site of Gate Pa (1900). ❖ See also *Dictionary of New Zealand Biography* (Vol. 2).

MANSENÉE, Desle la (c. 1502–1529). French victim of the Inquisition. Name variations: Desle la Mansenee. Born c. 1502; executed Dec 18, 1529, in Anjeux, France; married. ❖ Prosecuted on unsubstantiated claims, adamantly insisted that she was innocent of all charges (1529); subjected to squassation, a method of torture that was a mainstay of the Inquisition, confessed to anything, including a disclosure that the devil had promised to make her rich if she would reject Jesus Christ; was convicted of murder, heresy, and renunciation of the Catholic faith, then hanged at Anjeux and her body burned. ❖ See also *Women in World History.*

MANSFIELD, Arabella (1846–1911). American lawyer. Name variations: Arabella A. Mansfield; Arabella Aurelia Babb Mansfield. Born Belle Aurelia Babb, May 23, 1846, near Sperry Station, IA; died Aug 2, 1911, in Aurora, IL; dau. of Miles Babb (farmer) and Mary (Moyer) Babb (farmer); earned undergraduate degree from Iowa Wesleyan University, 1866, MA, 1870, LLB, 1872; m. John Melvin Mansfield (professor of natural history), June 23, 1868 (died 1894); no children. ❖ Taught English and history at Iowa Wesleyan; passed bar exam with high marks and was admitted to Iowa bar (1869), becoming the 1st woman lawyer in America; though she never practiced as a lawyer, became involved in suffrage cause (1870s) and was one of the founders of Iowa Woman Suffrage Society; was dean of the art, then music school at Indiana Asbury University, renamed DePauw University. ❖ See also *Women in World History.*

MANSFIELD, Jayne (1933–1967). American actress. Born Vera Jayne Palmer in Bryn Mawr, PA, April 19, 1933; died near New Orleans, LA, June 29, 1967; dau. of Herbert Palmer (attorney) and Vera Palmer; attended Parkland High School in Dallas, TX, University of Texas, University of California at Los Angeles, and Southern Methodist University in Dallas; m. Paul Mansfield, May 6, 1950 (div. 1956); m. Mickey Hargitay (bodybuilder), Jan 13, 1958 (div. 1964); m. Matt Cimber (film producer and director), 1964 (sep. 1966); children: (1st m.) Jayne Marie Mansfield (b. 1950); (2nd m.) Miklos Hargitay (b. 1958), Zoltan Hargitay (b. 1960), and Mariska Hargitay (b. 1964, actress); (3rd m.): Anthony Richard Cimber (b. 1965). ❖ One of Hollywood's leading sex symbols (1950s–60s), won a small part in a Dallas presentation of *Death of a Salesman*; moved to California (1954); after an appearance in *Playboy* (1955), appeared in 1st film *Illegal* and tv series "Casablanca"; made successful Broadway debut in *Will Success Spoil Rock Hunter?* (1956), followed by 1st film for Fox *The Girl Can't Help It* (1957), which was a box-office smash; reprised Broadway role in Fox's film version of *Rock Hunter* (1957); other films include *Kiss Them for Me* (1957), *The Loves of Hercules* (1960) and *A Guide for the Married Man* (1967). ❖ See also *Women in World History.*

MANSFIELD, Katherine (1888–1923). New Zealand-born writer of short stories, poems, sketches, and reviews, letters, journals, and translations. Name variations: Kathleen Beauchamp; Kathleen Beauchamp Bowden; Kathleen Murry; Catherine, Katharina, Kathie

Schonfeld; (pseudonyms) Katherine Mansfield, K.M. Born Kathleen Mansfield Beauchamp, Oct 15, 1888, in Wellington, New Zealand; died Jan 9, 1923, in Fontainebleu, France; dau. of Harold Beauchamp (banker) and Annie Burnell (Dyer) Beauchamp; attended Queen's College in London; m. George C. Bowden, Mar 2, 1909 (div. April 29, 1918); m. John Middleton Murry, May 3, 1918; no children. ❖ Gained fame as a writer who helped to shape emerging themes and methods in modern fiction; gained notoriety as a woman who dispensed with notions of traditional female roles and sexual behavior; spent childhood in Wellington except for 5 years on outskirts at Karori; attended state schools in Wellington (1895–99) and private school (1899–1903); attended Queen's College in Harley Street, London (1903–06); returned to Wellington and published several pieces in the *Native Companion*; returned to London (1908) to pursue a career in music or writing; m. George Bowden (1909), and left him the same day; pregnant by another man, went to Bavaria and suffered a miscarriage; returned to London (1910); began writing as Katherine Mansfield in periodicals; published her 1st book of stories, *In a German Pension* (1911); met John Middleton Murry (1912) and began relationship that continued until her death; diagnosed as tubercular (1918); div. from George Bowden (Apr) and married Murry (May 1918); published *Prelude;* subsequently moved to Italy, France, and Switzerland, at times accompanied or visited by Murry, in search of a healthful climate; had a very productive period of writing (1920–22); began radium treatments (1922) and entered Gurdjieff Institute in Fontainebleu, France (Oct 1923), where she died. Other writings include *Bliss and Other Stories* (1921), *The Garden Party and Other Stories* (1922), *The Dove's Nest and Other Stories* (1923). ❖ See also *Journal of Katherine Mansfield* (1954); Antony Alpers, *The Life of Katherine Mansfield* (Viking, 1980); Jeffrey Meyers, *Katherine Mansfield* (New Directions, 1978); Claire Tomalin, *Katherine Mansfield: A Secret Life* (Viking, 1987); and *Women in World History*.

MANSFIELD, Martha (1899–1923). American actress. Name variations: Martha Early, Martha Ehrlich. Born Martha Ehrlich, July 14, 1899, in Mansfield, Ohio; died Nov 30, 1923, on movie set when her dress caught fire while filming *The Warrens of Virginia* in San Antonio, TX. ❖ Began career as a Ziegfeld girl; films include *Dr. Jekyll and Mr. Hyde* (as Millicent Carew), *Broadway Bill, Civilian Clothes, Till We Meet Again, Potash and Perlmutter* and *Youthful Cheaters.*

MANSFIELD, Portia (1887–1979). American dancer and choreographer. Name variations: Portia Mansfield Swert. Born Nov 19, 1887, in Chicago, IL; died Jan 29, 1979, in Carmel, CA; trained at Smith College and with Charlotte Perry, Luigi Albertieri, Louis Chalif, and others. ❖ Taught social dance classes in Omaha and Chicago; founded several summer schools in Colorado with Charlotte Perry, most notably Perry-Mansfield School of the Theater and Dance (c. 1913–57) where teachers over the years included Doris Humphrey, Hanya Holm, Charles Weidman, and Helen Tamiris.

MANSILLA, Daniel Garcia (1838–1892). *See Mansilla de García, Eduarda.*

MANSILLA DE GARCÍA, Eduarda (1838–1892). Argentinean novelist, playwright and short-story writer. Name variations: (pseudonyms) Daniel García Mansilla, Alvar. Born 1838 in Buenos Aires, Argentina; died 1892; m. Manuel Rafael García (diplomat). ❖ Published 1st novel, *El médico de San Luis* (1860), which was based on Goldsmith's *The Vicar of Wakefield*, under son's name (Daniel García Mansilla); traveled with diplomat husband in US and Europe; held salon for writers and intellectuals in Buenos Aires; other works include *Lúcia Miranda* (1860), *Pablo où la vie dans les pampas* (1869), *La marquesa de Altamira* (1881), and *Creaciones* (1883).

MANSOUR, Agnes Mary (c. 1931–2004). American nun and welfare worker. Name variations: Sister Agnes Mary Mansour. Born c. 1931; died Dec 17, 2004, at a Sisters of Mercy assisted-living facility in Farmington Hills, Michigan. ❖ A Roman Catholic nun for 30 years, headed the Michigan welfare agency that oversaw Medicaid funding for abortions for the poor; when given the ultimatum from the Vatican to resign as Department of Social Services director or be dismissed from Sisters of Mercy (Mar 1983), asked to be released from vows; believed that as long as abortion was legal, poor women should have the same access as those who could afford it. Inducted into Michigan Women's Hall of Fame (1988).

MANSOUR, Joyce (1928–1987). English-born novelist and poet. Born 1928 in England of Egyptian parents; lived in France; died 1987. ❖ Works include *Les Gisants satisfaits* (1958), *Les Rapaces* (1960), *Carré blanc* (1965), *Ça* (1970), and *Faire signe au machiniste* (1977).

MANTELL, Mrs. Robert B. (c. 1889–1971). *See Hamper, Geneviève.*

MANTLE, Winifred Langford (1911–1983). British young-adult and romance writer. Name variations: (pseudonyms) Jan Blaine, Anne Fellowes, Frances Lang, and Jane Langford. Born Winifred Langford Mantle, Feb 15, 1911, in Staffordshire, England; died Nov 13, 1983, in Wolverhampton, Staffordshire; dau. of Joseph Langford Mantle and Florence (Fellows) Mantle. ❖ Published novels for juveniles and adults, including *Happy is the House* (1951), *The Secret Fairing* (1956), *The Keys of Heaven* (1958), *The Leaping Lords* (1963), *The Painted Cave* (1965), *Winter at Wycliffe* (1968), *The Tower of Remicourt* (1971), *The Inconvenient Marriage* (1974), *The Vanishing Bridegroom* (1980), and *To Be a Fine Lady* (1985).

MANTON, Irene (1904–1988). English botanist. Born April 17, 1904, in London, England; died May 31, 1988; younger dau. of George Manton (dental surgeon); sister of Sidnie Manton (1902–1979, zoologist); Girton College, Cambridge, MA in botany, 1926, PhD, 1930, DSc, 1940. ❖ The Linnean Society of London's 1st woman president and the creator of the squash technique (to count chromosomes more efficiently), studied with Professor Otto Rosenberg at University of Stockholm (1926–27); worked as assistant lecturer (1928–30) and lecturer (1930–46) at University of Manchester; employed as botany professor at University of Leeds (1946–48); discovered new species of watercress; with help of cryptogramic botany professor W.H. Lang, studied fern development, including *Osmunda regalis* (royal fern); discovered the thylakoid structure of chloroplasts and details of cell ultrastructure; was honorary research fellow in Electron Microscopy at Lancaster University (1971–88); developed large collection of original art works; bequeathed nearly £250,000 to Linnean Society of London.

MANTON, Sidnie (1902–1979). English zoologist. Name variations: Mrs. Harding. Born Sidnie Milana Manton, May 4, 1902, in London, England; died Jan 2, 1979; elder dau. of George Manton (dental surgeon); sister of Irene Manton (1904–1988); Girton College, Cambridge, PhD, 1928, ScD, 1934; m. Dr. John Philip Harding (keeper of zoology at British Museum), 1937; children: 1 daughter, 1 son. ❖ Visited Tasmania (1928) and participated in an exploration of the Great Barrier Reef, making advanced studies in arthropods; served as director of studies in natural science at Girton (1935–42), then held positions of staff fellow (1942–45) and research fellow (1945–48); was elected a fellow of the Royal Society (1948); was appointed a reader (instructor) in zoology at King's College in London (1949), where she remained until 1960; her research, much of which focused on evolution, added significantly to the knowledge of invertebrates, and she became eminent in the fields of arthropod embryology and functional morphology; published her most comprehensive work, *The Arthropods: Habits, Functional Morphology and Evolution* (1977). Received Linnaean Gold Medal (1963) and Frink Medal of the Zoological Society (1977). ❖ See also *Women in World History*.

MANTUA, duchess of.
See Gonzaga, Margherita (1510–1566).
See Catherine of Habsburg (1533–1572).
See Eleonora of Austria (1534–1594).
See Medici, Eleonora de (1567–1611).
See Medici, Caterina de (1593–1629).
See Gonzaga, Isabella (fl. 1600s).
See Margaret of Savoy (fl. 1609–1612).

MANTUA, marquesa of.
See Gonzaga, Paola (1393–1453).
See Barbara of Brandenburg (1422–1481).
See Margaret of Bavaria (1445–1479).
See Este, Isabella d' (1474–1539).

MANUELA (1847–1933). *See Uzès, Anne, Duchesse d'.*

MANUS, Rosa (1881–1942). Dutch feminist. Name variations: Rosette. Born Rosette Suzanne Manus, Aug 20, 1881, in Amsterdam, Netherlands; died 1942 at Ravensbrück concentration camp in Germany; dau. of Henry Philip Manus (merchant in tobacco) and Soete Vita Israel; attended secondary girls' school and boarding school in Switzerland; never married. ❖ With Mia Boissevain, organized a major exhibition on the status of women (1913), was an advocate of women's suffrage, women's rights and the worldwide peace movement, and active in aiding war refugees; was active in the International Woman Suffrage Alliance from 1908 (known as the International Alliance of Women since 1926); organized an exhibition on the position of women, entitled "Woman 1813–1913"; was a member of the women's committee to help mobilized families during WWI; served as secretary of the Dutch Association for Woman Suffrage; served as vice-president of the International Woman Suffrage Alliance (1923) and as secretary of the Peace Committee of the International Alliance of Women (1926); was a member of the Women's Disarmament Committee of International Organizations; served as secretary of the International Peace Congress of the Rassemblement Universel pour la Paix (RUP) in Brussels (1936); was active in helping Jewish refugees (1933–42); co-founded the International Archive of the Women's Movement (IAV) in Amsterdam, Netherlands (1935); arrested in Amsterdam by the Gestapo (1941), was brought to a prison in Scheveningen, and afterwards transported to Ravensbrück. ❖ See also *Women in World History.*

MANZINI, Gianna (1896–1974). Italian novelist and journalist. Name variations: wrote about fashion under the names "Vanessa" and "Pamela." Born Mar 24, 1896, in Pistoia, Tuscany, Italy; died in Rome, Aug 31, 1974; dau. of Giuseppe Manzini (watch repairer); degree in modern literature from University of Florence; m. Bruno Fallaci (journalist), 1929 (div.). ❖ Published 1st novel *Tempo innamorato* (The Time of Love) to critical acclaim (1928), followed by short-story collections, *Incontro col falco* (Meeting with a Falcon, 1929) and *Casa di riposo* (Rest Home, 1934); moved to Rome (c. 1936); won praise for *Lettera all'editore* (Letter to the Publisher, 1945); received prestigious literary award, Premio Viareggio, for autobiographical novel *La Sparviera* (The Sparrow-Hawk, 1956); won Naples Prize and published *Allegro con disperazione* (Allegro with Despair, 1965); considered one of the premier practitioners of a style known as *prosa d'arte* (artistic prose), a form that combined the lyrical beauty of poetry with a narrative, sometimes surreal, structure. ❖ See also *Women in World History.*

MANZOLINI, Anna Morandi (1716–1774). Italian anatomist. Name variations: Anne Manzolini; Anna Morandi; Anna Mahzolini or Mohzolini. Born Anna Morandi in Bologna, Italy, 1716; died in Bologna in 1774; m. Giovanni Manzolini (professor of anatomy), in 1736; children: 6. ❖ When husband became too ill to fulfill his lecturing duties at University of Bologna, received permission from the school to step into his place; because of her comprehensive knowledge of anatomy and her effective teaching style, was appointed lecturer of anatomy in her own name upon husband's death (1760), then elected to a professorship (1766); with word of her work spreading, subsequently lectured in Russia, where she was made a member of the Russian Royal Scientific Society, and in Britain, where she was made a member of the Royal Society. ❖ See also *Women in World History.*

MAO, Madame (1914–1991). *See Jiang Qing.*

MAO FUMEI (1892–?). First wife of Chiang Kai-shek. Name variations: Mao Fu-mei. Born 1892; became 1st wife of Chiang Kai-shek, in 1909 (div. 1921); children: Zhang Jingguo (Chiang Ching-kuo), later president of Republic of China (Taiwan). ❖ At 17, entered into an arranged marriage with 14-year-old Chiang Kai-shek, whom she had never seen.

MAR, Anna (1887–1917). *See Brovar, Anna Iakovlevna.*

MAR, countess of.
See Helen (fl. 1275).
See Bruce, Christian (d. 1356).
See Marr, Margaret (d. after 1384).

MAR, Frances, Countess of (1690–1761). English countess. Name variations: Lady Mar. Born Frances Pierrepont in 1690; died 1761; 2nd dau. of Evelyn Pierrepont, earl of Kingston, and Lady Mary Pierrepont (dau. of William Fielding, earl of Denbigh); m. John Erskine, 6th or 11th earl of Mar, July 20, 1713 (died 1732); children: Frances Erskine (b. 1715). ❖ Sister of the well-known woman of letters Lady Mary Wortley Montagu, married a Scottish Jacobite, followed him into exile, and fell victim to severe depression which incapacitated her for much of her life. ❖ See also *Women in World History.*

MAR, Sabrina (1970—). American gymnast. Born May 31, 1970; University of California at Los Angeles, BS in physiology, 1993; married in 2000; children: Noah (b. 2001). ❖ Won US nationals (1985) and Pan American Games (1987); came in 3rd all-around at the American Classic (1986); as an animator, worked on "South Park" (1997–2002). Inducted into US Gymnastics Hall of Fame (2004).

MARA, Adele (1923—). American actress, singer and dancer. Born Adelaide Delgado, April 28, 1923, in Highland Park, Michigan; sister of Luis Delgado (actor); m. Roy Huggins (screenwriter and tv director),

c. 1952 (died 2002); children: 3 sons. ❖ Began career as a singer and dancer with the Xavier Cugat Orchestra; films include *Navy Blues, Alias Boston Blackie, Wake of the Red Witch, Angel in Exile, Sands of Iwo Jima, Back from Eternity* and *The Big Circus.*

MARA, Gertrud (1749–1833). German soprano. Name variations: Gertrude Elizabeth Mara; Gertrud Elisabeth Mara; Madame Mara. Born Gertrud Elisabeth Schmeling in Cassel, Germany, Feb 23, 1749; died in Revel or Reval (present-day Tallinn), Russia, Jan 20, 1833; studied violin; studied with Paradisi in London and Hiller at Leipzig; m. Johann Mara (cellist), 1773 (div. 1799). ❖ One of the 1st opera singers to become internationally famous, made a successful debut in Dresden (c. 1767) and was selected by Frederick II the Great to become a court singer in Berlin, much to the consternation of Mozart who deplored her singing; left the court (1778) and toured the Continent, enjoying a celebrated rivalry with Luiza Todi; sang in London (1784–91), notably at the Haymarket and chiefly music by Handel; moved to Moscow (1803); returned to London (1816). ❖ See also *Women in World History.*

MARA, La (1837–1927). *See Lipsius, Marie.*

MARACCI, Carmelita (1911–1988). Spanish-trained American dancer and choreographer. Born in Montevideo, Uruguay (some sources claim Goldfield, Nevada), 1911; died 1988; studied ballet and Spanish dance in California; taught dance in Los Angeles. ❖ Made professional debut in Los Angeles, CA (1930); appeared with her own group, weaving Spanish techniques into her style of dance with fine castanet and heel work; choreographed solos: *Viva Tu Madre, Nightingale and the Maiden, Etude, Cantine, Fandanguillo, Gavotta Vivace*; trios: *Another Fire Dance, Sonate, Portrait in the Raw España, Flamenco*; group dances: *Narrative of the Bull Ring* and *Suite*; as well as the ballet *Circo de España* for the Ballet Theater in 1951; was a long-time friend of Agnes de Mille; taught ballet to Gerald Arpino, Erik Bruhn, Leslie Caron, Cynthia Gregory, Robert Joffrey, Allegra Kent, Carmen de Lavallade and Jerome Robbins.

MARACINEANU, Roxana (1975—). French-Romanian swimmer. Born May 7, 1975, in Bucharest, Romania. ❖ At LC World championships, won gold medal for 200-meter backstroke (1998); at LC Europeans, won gold medal for 200-meter backstroke (1999); won silver medal for 200-meter backstroke at Sydney Olympics (2000).

MARAGALL VERGE, Elisabeth (1970—). Spanish field-hockey player. Born Nov 25, 1970. ❖ At Barcelona Olympics, won a gold medal in team competition (1992).

MARAINI, Dacia (1936—). Italian novelist and short-story writer. Born Nov 13, 1936, in Florence, Italy; dau. of Fosco Maraini; lived with Alberto Moravia. ❖ Celebrated Italian writer and intellectual, has been a progressive political activist for over 40 years; writings, which often focus on feminist themes or experiences of childhood, include *La vacanza* (The Holiday, 1962), *L'eta del malessere* (The Age of Discontent, 1963), *Crudeltà all'aria aperta* (Cruelty in the Open, 1966), about her relationship with her father, *A memoria* (1967), *Mio marito* (1968), *Lettere a Marine* (1981), *Il treno per Helsinki* (1984), *Isolina* (1985), *La lunga vita di Marianna Ucria* (The Long Life of Marianna Ucria or The Silent Duchess, 1990), which won the Campiello Prize, *Voci* (1994), *Un clandestino a bordo* (1996), *Dolce* (1997) and *Buio* (1999), a collection of short stories which won the Strega Prize; wrote *Donna in guerra* (1975), widely considered a manifesto of Italian feminism; has also written novels, poetry, essays, screenplays and plays, including *Il ricatto a teatro* (1970), *Maria Stuarda* (1975), *I sogni di Clitennestra* (1981) and *Veronica, meretrice e scrittora* (1991). ❖ See also Bruce Merry, *Women in Modern Italian Literature: Four Studies Based on the Work of Grazia Deledda, Alba De Céspedes, Natalia Ginzburg & Dacia Maraini* (James Cook University of North Queensland, 1990).

MARANGONI, Clara (1915—). Italian gymnast. Born Nov 13, 1915, in Italy. ❖ At Amsterdam Olympics, won a silver medal in team all-around (1928).

MARANHÃO, Heloísa (1925—). Brazilian novelist, playwright and short-story writer. Name variations: Heloisa Maranhao; Heloísa dos Reis Maranhão. Born 1925 in Brazil. ❖ Worked as translator and drama professor; probably best known for novel *Lucrécia* (1980); other works include *Paixão de terra* (1957), *Negra Bá* (1959), *Tiradentes* (1970), *Castelo interior e moradas* (1973), *Inês de Castro, a rainha morta* (1975), *A Cobra* (1977), *Florinda* (1982), *Dona Leonor Teles* (1985), *A rainha de Navarra* (1986), and *Adriana* (1990).

MARARED (fl. 1173). Princess of Gwynedd. Fl. around 1173; dau. of Madog ap Maredudd, king of Powys, and Susan of Powys (dau. of the king of Gwynedd and Angharad); m. Iorwerth Drwyndwn, prince of Gwynedd; children: Llywelyn II the Great (1173–1240), Ruler of All Wales.

MARATTI ZAPPI, Faustina (c. 1680–1745). Italian poet. Born c. 1680 in Rome, Italy; died 1745; dau. of Carlo Maratta and Francesca Gommi; m. Giovambattista Felice Zappi, 1705 (died 1719). ❖ Poetry, which explores her personal experiences and includes *canzoni,* madrigals, sonnets, and elegies, has been published with husband's in the collection *Rime dell'avvocato Giovanni Battista Felice Zappi e di F. Maratti sua consorte* (1723, 1736).

MARBLE, Alice (1913–1990). American tennis player. Born Sept 13, 1913, in Beckwith, CA; died Dec 13, 1990, in Los Angeles, CA; m. Joseph Crowley, 1942 (died 1944). ❖ Won California women's singles title (1933); after collapsing on court and being diagnosed with tuberculosis, spent 18 months at a sanatorium; won US singles championship (1936), the 1st of 4 (1936–40), not only in singles but doubles and mixed doubles; won singles, doubles and mixed doubles at Wimbledon (1939); during WWII, was recruited by US government to spy on Nazis while teaching tennis clinics in Europe as a cover, and was instrumental in discovering where the Third Reich had hidden much of its stolen wealth, information that was used at Nuremburg Trials (1945–46); spoke out strongly against decision to bar African-American player Althea Gibson from US National championship games (1950); generally credited with being the 1st woman to adopt the aggressive court strategy previously practiced only by male players. Inducted into Tennis Hall of Fame (1964) and International Sportsman's Hall of Fame (1967). ❖ See also autobiography (with Dale Leatherman) *Courting Danger* (St. Martin's, 1991) and Sue Davidson, *Changing the Game: The Stories of Tennis Champs Alice Marble and Althea Gibson* (Seal, 1997); and *Women in World History.*

MARBLE, Mary (d. 1965). American musical-comedy star. Died Feb 5, 1965, age 91, in East Islip, LI, NY; m. John W. Dunne (producer). ❖ Was in vaudeville as part of the team, Chip and Marble; from 1890s, appeared in such musicals as *Off the Earth, Milk White Flag, Babes in Toyland, Dream City* and *Green Pastures;* retired (1931).

MARBURY, Elisabeth (1856–1933). American author's representative, producer, and theatrical manager. Name variations: Bessie or Bess Marbury. Born in New York City, June 19, 1856; died in NY, Jan 22, 1933; privately educated, mostly by her father; never married; lived with Elsie de Wolfe, 1887–1926. ❖ Co-produced *Little Lord Fauntleroy* on Broadway (1888) and began managing the career of its author, Frances Hodgson Burnett; became English and American representative for the Société de Gens de Lettres (1891), a French writers' organization, and began to handle English-speaking rights for French playwright Victorien Sardou; would also represent the US interests of Georges Feydeau, Edmond Rostand, Ludovic Halévy, George Bernard Shaw, James M. Barrie, Jerome K. Jerome, and such American clients as Rachel Crothers and Clyde Fitch; attained prominence in NY as a producer of plays and musical comedies, including *Love o' Mike* (1916) with music by Jerome Kern, and *See America First* (1916), with music by Cole Porter; was responsible for American careers of Vernon and Irene Castle; co-founded the Colony Club, the 1st women's social club in NY. Was twice decorated by French government for services rendered to French authors. ❖ See also autobiography *My Crystal Ball* (1923); and *Women in World History.*

MARCARI OLIVA, Hortencia (1959—). Brazilian basketball player. Name variations: Hortencia de Fatima Marcari Oliva; known in Brazil simply as Hortencia or Hortência or the "Queen." Born Sept 23, 1959, in Potirendaba, Brazil. ❖ Once considered one of the best players in the world, won a team gold medal at World championships (1994), gold at South American championships (1978, 1981, 1986, 1989, 1993), and a team silver medal at Atlanta Olympics (1996); became a basketball commentator for Brazilian tv. Inducted into Women's Basketball Hall of Fame in Texas (2002).

MARCELLA OF ROME (c. 325–410). Roman founder. Name variations: Marcella. Born between 325 and 335; died in 410 or 411; dau. of Albina; married briefly. ❖ With her mother and Principia, retired to her house on Rome's Aventine Hill to live by a rule adapted from the monastic foundations of the East, knowledge of which circulated in Rome thanks to the efforts of Athanasius, bishop of Alexandria; as time passed, her fame grew among the women of Rome, and many were driven to join her in a life of seclusion, probably the 1st organized community in the West

consisting of Christian women living according to a religious rule; met with Jerome when he visited Rome between 382 and 385 and took the opportunity to pose a number of philological and exegetical questions about Christian scripture; when Rome was sacked by the Visigoths (410), was sought out by their king Alaric as a probable possessor of hidden wealth; subjected to torture, died of her wounds. ❖ See also *Women in World History.*

MARCELLA THE ELDER (fl. 25 BCE). Roman noblewoman. Born between 54 and 40 BCE; fl. around 25 BCE; dau. of Octavia (c. 69–11 BCE) and G. Marcellus (Roman consul); niece of Gaius Julius Caesar Octavianus also known as Octavian or Augustus, Roman emperor; was 1st wife of Marcus Agrippa (Augustus demanded that Agrippa divorce Marcella to marry Augustus' daughter Julia [39 BCE–40 CE]).

MARCELLA THE YOUNGER (fl. 20 BCE). Roman noblewoman. Born between 54 and 40 BCE; fl. around 20 BCE; dau. of Octavia (c. 69–11 BCE) and G. Marcellus (Roman consul); niece of Gaius Julius Caesar Octavianus also known as Octavian or Augustus, Roman emperor.

MARCELLINA (fl. 4th c.). Saint. Fl. during 4th century; dau. of the praetorian prefect of the Gauls; sister of Satyrus and Saint Ambrose. ❖ Upon death of father, is believed to have returned to Rome with her mother and 2 brothers, one of whom, Ambrose, would become a well-known saint; on feast of Epiphany (335), received the virgin's veil in Church of St. Peter; remained close to Ambrose, corresponding with him frequently and relying on him to counsel her through difficult periods. Feast day is July 17. ❖ See also *Women in World History.*

MARCET, Jane (1769–1858). English scientist and school mistress. Name variations: Jane Haldimand or Jane Haldimond; Jane Haldimand Marcet or Jane Haldimond Marcet; Margaret Bryan. Born in 1769, in London, England; died in London, June 28, 1858; dau. of Anthony Francis Haldimand (merchant) and Jane Haldimand; m. Alexander John Gaspard Marcet (physician), in 1799 (died 1822); children: 3. ❖ On marriage, became a part of a social circle that included many prominent and learned members of English society, among them Harriet Martineau, Mary Fairfax Somerville, and Thomas Malthus; encouraged by friends and husband to write a "beginner's" text on chemistry, anonymously published *Conversations on Chemistry: Intended More Specifically for the Female Sex* (1805), an instant success which centered around a dialogue between a woman teacher and two young female students; wrote numerous other books intended for young women, and some for young people in general, a number of which followed the same successful formula, including *Conversations on Political Economy* (1816), *Conversations on Natural Philosophy* (1819) and *Conversations on Vegetable Physiology* (1829). ❖ See also *Women in World History.*

MARCH, Anne. See Woolson, Constance Fenimore.

MARCH, countess of.
See Dunbar, Agnes (c. 1312–1369).
See Montacute, Philippa (fl. 1352).
See Dunbar, Christine (c. 1350–?).
See Mortimer, Philippa (1355–1382).
See Holland, Alianor (c. 1373–1405).
See Mortimer, Catherine (fl. 1402).
See Stafford, Anne (d. 1432).

MARCH, Eve (1910–1974). American actress. Born Sept 27, 1910, in Fresno, CA; died Sept 19, 1974, in Hollywood. CA. ❖ Films include *How Green Was My Valley, Curse of the Cat People, Killer McCoy, Adam's Rib* and *The Sun Shines Bright.*

MARCH, Mrs. Frederic (1901–1988). See Eldridge, Florence.

MARCH, Susana (1918–1991). Spanish poet and novelist. Born Jan 28, 1918, in Barcelona, Spain; died 1991; m. Ricardo Fernández de la Reguera. ❖ Novels include *Nido de vencejos* (1943), *Canto rodado* (1944), *Nina* (1949), and *Algo muere cada día* (1955); poetry collections include *Rutas* (1938), *Ardiente voz* (1946), *La pasión desvelada* (1946), *El viento* (1951), *Los poemas del hijo* (1970), and *Poemas de la Plaza Real* (1987); with husband, published *Episodios nacionales contemporáneos* (1963–72).

MARCHAL, Arlette (1902–1984). French actress. Born Jan 29, 1902, in Paris, France; died Feb 9, 1984, in Paris. ❖ Won a beauty contest; made film debut in *Mon p'tit* (1922), followed by *Madame Sans-Gêne, Venetian Lovers, The Cat's Pajamas, Diplomacy, Blonde or Brunette, Wings, A Gentleman in Paris, Figaro, La poule, Le petit roi, La femme idéale, Don*

Quichotte, Entente cordiale, The Elusive Pimpernel and *Sans laisser d'adresse*, among others.

MARCHAL, Lynda (1946—). *See La Plante, Lynda.*

MARCHAND, Collette (1925—). French theatrical and ballet dancer. Name variations: Colette Marchand. Born April 29, 1925, in Paris, France. ❖ Danced 1 season at Paris Opéra Ballet and Metropolitan Ballet, most notably in works by Serge Lifar; joined Roland Petit's Ballets de Paris, appearing in his *L'Oeuf à la Coque, Les Demoiselles de la Nuit, Carmen, Ciné-Bijou,* among others; performed in numerous Paris revues including *Two on the Aisle* (1951) and *Plein Fue* 1954), and in John Houston's film, *Moulin Rouge* (1953).

MARCHAND, Corinne (1937—). French actress. Born Dec 4, 1937, in Paris, France. ❖ Began career as a photographic model and nightclub singer; made credited film debut as Wanda in *Arrêtez le massacre* (1959), followed by *Lola, Nunca pasa nada, Les Sultans, Du mou dans la gâchette, Arizona Colt, Borsalino, Liza, Travels with my Aunt, Attention bandits!, Le client* and *Les palmes de M. Schutz,* among others; probably best remembered for title role in *Cleo de cinq à Sept* (*Cleo from 5 to 7,* 1962).

MARCHAND, Inga Fung (1979—). *See Brown, Foxy.*

MARCHAND, Nancy (1928–2000). American stage, tv, and screen actress. Born June 19, 1928, in Buffalo, NY; died June 18, 2000, in Stratford, CT; m. Paul Sparer (actor, died 1999). ❖ Made NY stage debut (1951); starred in the original tv version of "Marty"; films include *The Bachelor Party, Tell Me That You Love Me Junie Moon, The Hospital, The Bostonians, Jefferson in Paris* and *Sabrina;* at time of death, had recurring role as Livia Soprano on "The Sopranos." Won Obie for performance off-Broadway in "The Balcony"; won 4 Emmys for portrayal of publisher Margaret Pynchon on "Lou Grant."

MARCHAND, Valérie (1980—). *See Hould-Marchand, Valérie.*

MARCHANT, Bessie (1862–1941). British author. Name variations: Elizabeth Comfort; Bessie Marchant Comfort; (pseudonym) John Comfort. Born Dec 12, 1862, in Petham, Kent, England; died in Charlbury, Oxfordshire, England, Nov 10, 1941; dau. of William Marchant (farmer) and Jane (Goucher) Marchant; m. Jabez Ambrose Comfort (minister), Dec 28, 1889 (died 1915); children: Constance (1891). ❖ Prolific author, wrote juvenile adventure fiction that was remarkable for the daring and cleverness of her young heroines; in her nearly 150 published titles, introduced readers to far-away locales and exotic escapades, a fact made perhaps even more remarkable because she never ventured far from the English countryside where she spent her 78 years; writings include *The Old House by the Water* (1894), *Yuppie* (1898), *Cicely Frome, The Captain's Daughter* (1900), *A Heroine of the Sea* (1903), *Athabasca Bill* (1906), *Juliette, The Mail Carrier* (1907), *A Countess from Canada* (1910), *A Girl of the Northland* (1912), *A Girl Munitions Worker* (1916), *A Dangerous Mission* (1918), *The Fortunes of Prue* (1923), *Millicent Gwent, Schoolgirl* (1926), *How Nell Scored* (1929), *Erica's Ranch* (1934), *Nancy Afloat* (1936) and *Waifs of Woolamoo* (1938). ❖ See also *Women in World History.*

MARCHANT, Catherine (1906–1998). *See Cookson, Catherine.*

MARCHANT, Maria Élise Allman (1869–1919). New Zealand school principal. Born Oct 28, 1869, at Wellington, New Zealand; died Nov 15, 1919, at Invercargill, New Zealand; dau. of John William Allman Marchant (surveyor) and Maria Élise (Wright) Marchant; Canterbury College, BA, 1892, MA, 1894. ❖ Served as principal of Otago Girls' High School (1895–1911) and superintendent of Anglican Children's Home, Ponsonby (1914–15); served as founding headmistress of Church School for Girls (later St Mary's Diocesan School), Stratford (1915–17); established Bishopscourt hostel for women students, Christchurch (1917–18); helped found St John's Girls' School, Invercargill (1918–19). ❖ See also *Dictionary of New Zealand Biography* (Vol. 3).

MARCHENKO, Anastasiia Iakovlevna (1830–1880). Russian novelist, poet and short-story writer. Name variations: Anastasiia Márchenko; (pseudonym) T. Ch. Born 1830; died 1880; m. military officer named Kir'iakov. ❖ Stories, which reflect life in St Petersburg and are often tales of unrequited love, include "The Governess" and "Around and About"; novellas published under title *Travel Notes*; also published 4 novels, poetry, and other short prose works.

MARCHESI, Blanche (1863–1940). French-born soprano. Name variations: Baroness A. Caccamisi. Born in Paris, France, 1863; died 1940; dau. of Marchese della Rajata Castone, a political refugee who adopted

the *nom de théâtre* Salvatore Marchesi (1822–1908, Italian baritone and composer) and Mathilde Marchesi (1826–1913); educated in Vienna, Frankfort, and Paris; m. Baron Caccamisi. ❖ Made 1st professional appearance in Berlin (1895) as a concert singer; toured England and Europe; sang in operas at Covent Garden, Prague, Brussels, and elsewhere; appeared before Queen Victoria and Queen Alexandra of Denmark, as well as the courts of Brussels and Germany; was painted by Sargent, Shannon, and other well-known artists; opened the largest private academy of singing in London. ❖ See also *Women in World History.*

MARCHESI, Mathilde (1821–1913). German mezzo-soprano and voice teacher. Name variations: Mathilde de Castrone Marchesi; Mlle Graumann. Born Mathilde Graumann at Frankfort-Am-Main, Germany, Mar 26 (also seen as Mar 20 and 24), 1826 (some sources cite 1821, but 1826 seems more probable); died in London, England, Nov 17, 1913; studied in Vienna and Paris and was highly educated; m. Marchese della Rajata Castone, a political refugee who adopted the *nom de théâtre* Salvatore Marchesi (1822–1908, Italian baritone and composer), 1852; children: daughter Blanche Marchesi (1863–1940, concert and opera singer). ❖ Persuaded to take up music as a profession by Mendelssohn, studied in Paris under Manuel Garcia; took lessons in acting from Joseph-Isidore Samson; as Mlle Graumann, made debut as a mezzo-soprano concert singer in London (1849) and then on the Continent; became a teacher of singing, 1st as professor at Vienna Conservatory (1854–61, 1868–78), then Paris (1861–64) and Cologne (1865–68); established École Marchesi in Paris (c. 1881), maintaining a salon that would become one of the most important circles of musical life in the city until 1908; became celebrated for the great opera singers who studied with her, among them Etelka Gerster, Mary Garden, Nellie Melba, Emma Eames, Emma Calvé, Sibyl Sanderson, Selma Kurz, and Frances Alda. Awarded Golden Cross of Merit with the Crown from emperor of Austria, and gold medals for Arts and Sciences from royals of Italy, England, Saxony, Prussia and Russia. ❖ See also autobiography *Marchesi and Music: Passages from the Life of a Famous Singing Teacher* (Harper, 1898); and *Women in World History.*

MARCIA (fl. c. 100 BCE). *See Iaia.*

MARCIA (fl. 100 BCE). Roman noblewoman. Fl. around 100 BCE; dau. of Q. Marcius Rex; m. Gaius Julius Caesar; children: Gaius Julius Caesar Maior (praetor in 85 BCE, who m. Aurelia); Julia (d. 68 BCE, who m. Gaius Marius); Sextus Julius Caesar (consul in 91 BCE); grandmother of Roman emperor Julius Caesar (101–44 BCE).

MARCIA (fl. 177–192 CE). Imperial concubine. Fl. in late 2nd century, between 177 and 192 CE. ❖ After the banishment of Empress Bruttia Crispina (177), became mistress of Marcus Aurelius Commodus, the Roman emperor; said to have been a Christian, became influential after the death of Commodus' longtime friend and chamberlain Cleander (189); played a leading role with Eclectus and Aemilius Laetus, in the plot to murder Commodus (192). ❖ See also *Women in World History.*

MARCIA (fl. 1357). *See Marzia.*

MARCIANA (fl. 98–117 CE). *See Ulpia Marciana.*

MARCINKIEWICZ, Jadwiga (1912–1990). *See Wajs, Jadwiga.*

MARCOS, Imelda (1929—). Philippine politician and first lady. Born Imelda Romualdez, July 2, 1929, in Tacloban, Leyte Province, Philippines; 1st of 6 children of Vicente Orestes Romualdez and Remedios Trinidad Romualdez; m. Ferdinand Edralin Marcos (b. 1917, president of the Philippines, 1965–1986), May 1, 1954 (died Sept 28, 1989); children: Marie Imelda ("Imee") Marcos; Ferdinand Marcos Jr.; Maria Victoria Irene Marcos. ❖ Ruled with husband and amassed a fortune through corruption and the skimming of public funds (1965–86); became first lady of the Philippines (Dec 30, 1965); legalized as head of state in event of death or illness by Presidential Decree 731 (June 7, 1975); was virtual ruler of the Philippines (after 1979) because of husband's failing health; played the US against the USSR to gain increasing aid; became legendary for her conspicuous consumption (1980s) and was associated with the thousands of shoes found in her wardrobe; with husband, tried to fight off the Aquinos and their followers (1983–86); forced into exile (1986); returned to Philippines (1991); during husband's 20 years in office as president of the Philippines, was at the center of power, exercising dictatorial powers on her own authority. ❖ See also Katherine W. Ellison, *Imelda: Steel Butterfly of the Philippines* (McGraw-Hill, 1988); Carmen Navarro Pedrosa, *Imelda Marcos* (St. Martin's, 1987); Beth Day

Romulo, *Inside the Palace: The Rise and Fall of Ferdinand and Imelda Marcos* (Putnam, 1987); and *Women in World History*.

MARCUS, Adele (1905–1995). American pianist and teacher. Born in Kansas City, MO, in 1905; died in NY City, May 3, 1995; studied with Josef Lhévinne in New York and with Artur Schnabel in Berlin. ❖ Won Naumburg Award (1929); though she performed often in public, was best known for her years of work at Juilliard where she taught some of the 20th century's finest pianists, including Byron Janis, Agustin Anievas, Tedd Joselson, Santiago Rodriguez, Stephen Hough and Horacio Gutierrez. ❖ See also *Women in World History*.

MARCUS, Marie (1914–2003). American jazz pianist. Name variations: Marie Brown, Marie Doherty. Born Marie Eleanor Doherty, Mar 25, 1914, in Roxbury, Massachusetts; died Oct 10, 2003, in Hyannis, Massachusetts; attended New England Conservatory of Music; m. Jack Brown (singer), 1937 (div.); m. Bill Marcus (trumpet player, lawyer), 1945 (died 1964); children: Jack Brown, William Marcus (jazz pianist), Mary Liles, Barbara Marcus. ❖ Protégée of Fats Waller, worked in New York clubs under name Marie Doherty (1930s), eventually working for mobster Dutch Schultz in Kean's Steakhouse; played for such jazz greats as Nat King Cole, Willy the Lion and Duke Ellington; began playing at midtown jazz haunts like the Swing Club on 52nd Street; formed 13-piece, all-male band, Marie Doherty and her Gentlemen of Swing; took job at Coonamessett Club in Falmouth on Cape Cod (1942); became fixture of Cape Cod jazz scene and never returned to New York; formed Cape Cod Jazz Society; also fell in love with dixieland; joined Preacher Rollo and the Five Saints (1950s) and made numerous albums with the Saints.

MARCUS, Ruth Barcan (1921—). American philosopher. Born Ruth Barcan in NY City, Aug 2, 1921; dau. of Samuel Barcan and Rose (Post) Barcan; New York University, BA, magna cum laude, 1941; Yale University, MA, 1942, PhD, 1946; m. Jules Marcus; children: James Spencer Marcus; Peter Webb Marcus; Katherine Hollister Marcus; Elizabeth Post Marcus. ❖ One of the few women who began to make forays into academic philosophy in the 20th century, was research assistant at Institute for Human Relations (1945–46) and visiting professor at Northwestern University (1950–53, 1959); served as assistant and then associate professor, Roosevelt University, Chicago (1956–59, 1960–63); was professor of philosophy, University of Illinois (1964–70); was head of the Department of Philosophy, University of Illinois (1964–68); was professor of philosophy, Northwestern University (1970–73) and Reuben Post Halleck Professor of Philosophy, Yale University (1973–1992), then emeritus. ❖ See also *Women in World History*.

MARDEN, Adrienne (1909–1978). American tv and screen actress. Born Sept 2, 1909, in Cleveland, Ohio; died Nov 9, 1978, in Los Angeles, CA; children: 2 daughters. ❖ Films include *13 Hours by Air, Star for a Night, Dangerous Crossing, Walk on the Wild Side, The Sound and the Fury, The Shrike* and *Birdman of Alcatraz*; frequently appeared on tv.

MARDEN, Anne (1958—). American rower. Born June 12, 1958; Princeton University, BA in economics, 1981; married; children: 1. ❖ At Los Angeles Olympics, won a silver medal in quadruple sculls with coxswain (1984); at Seoul Olympics, won a silver medal in single sculls (1988); moved to England.

MARDRUS, Lucie Delarue (1880–1945). See *Delarue-Mardrus, Lucie*.

MARE, Mary Florence (1914–1997). See *Spooner, Molly*.

MARECKOVA, Eva (1964—). Czech gymnast. Born May 18, 1964, in Detva, Czechoslovakia. ❖ Won Czech nationals (1977, 1978, 1980, 1981), Dynamo Spartakiade (1977), Trnava International (1979) and Rome Grand Prix (1982); placed 4th team all-around at Moscow Olympics (1980).

MAREK, Martha Lowenstein (1904–1938). Austrian murderer. Born Martha Lowenstein in Vienna, Austria, 1904; beheaded in Vienna, Dec 6, 1938; educated at finishing schools in France and England; m. Emil Marek, 1924 (died 1932); children: 1 daughter, 1 son. ❖ Killed husband, daughter, aunt and an elderly woman named Kittenberger with thallium, a rare and poisonous chemical compound, to collect on their insurance; received the death penalty (1938). ❖ See also *Women in World History*.

MARERI, Filippa (c. 1190–1236). Saint. Name variations: Philippa Mareria. Born c. 1190, in Rieti valley, along the valley of the Salto River that marked the border between territory of St. Peter and Kingdom of Naples; died Feb 16, 1236; dau. of Imperatrice Mareri and Filippo Mareri, prince of Cicolano. ❖ Franciscan nun—belonging

to the family of the Counts Mareri, feudatories of Cicolano—who was the founder of the nunnery of St. Peter of Molito, the 1st Franciscan settlement in the territory of Naples. ❖ See also *Women in World History*.

MARETSKAYA, Vera (1906–1978). Soviet actress. Born in Moscow, Russia, July 1, 1906; died in Aug 17, 1978, in Moscow. ❖ Studied acting at Moscow's Bakhtangova Studio; made stage debut (1924), followed by silent-film debut in *The Tailor from Torzhok* (1925); achieved a measure of fame with help of Soviet propaganda machine, primarily undertaking stock comedic characters; achieved stardom as the revolutionary heroine in the films *The Generation of Conquerors* (1936) and *Member of the Government* (1939); admired for the maturity and depth of her performances, also starred in talking version of Maxim Gorky's *Mother* (1955), among others. ❖ See also *Women in World History*.

MARFA. *Russian form of Marta or Martha.*

MARFAN, Magdalena (1903–1968). See *Petit, Magdalena*.

MARGALOT, Mercedes (1975—). Argentinean field-hockey player. Born Maria Mercedes Margalot, May 28, 1975, in Buenos Aires, Argentina. ❖ Defender, won a team silver medal at Sydney Olympics (2000) and a team bronze medal at Athens Olympics (2004); won Champions Trophy (2001), World Cup (2002), and Pan American Games (2003).

MARGARET. *Variant of Marguerite.*

MARGARET (fl. 1000s). Queen of Scots. Fl. in the 1000s; m. Donalbane or Donelbane also known as Donald III (c. 1033–1099), king of the Scots (r. 1093–1098); children: Bethoc (who m. Hadria of Tynedale).

MARGARET (d. 1209). Queen of Norway. Name variations: Margaret Ericsdottir. Died in 1209; dau. of Erik or St. Eric IX, king of Sweden (r. 1156–1160), and Kristina; m. Sverre (c. 1152–1202), king of Norway (r. 1177–1202), in 1185; children: Christine Sverresdottir (d. 1213, who m. Philip, king of Bagler); Erling.

MARGARET (d. 1228). Countess of Huntingdon. Name variations: Margaret Dunkeld. Died in 1228; dau. of Maude of Chester (1171–1233) and David Dunkeld, 1st earl of Huntingdon; m. Alan, lord of Galloway, in 1209; children: Christian (d. 1246, who m. William de Forz); Devorgilla (d. 1290, who m. John Balliol).

MARGARET (d. 1270). Queen of Norway. Name variations: Margaret Skulisdottir. Died in 1270; dau. of Jarl Skule; m. Haakon IV the Elder (1204–1263), king of Norway (r. 1217–1263), May 25, 1225; children: Haakon the Younger (b. 1232), king of Norway (co-r. 1232–1257); Magnus VI the Law-mender (1238–1280), king of Norway (r. 1263–1280); Christine of Norway (1234–1262, who m. Felipe of Castile, archbishop of Seville); Olav (b. 1227). ❖ Haakon IV was 1st married to Kanga.

MARGARET (d. 1275). Countess of Bar. Died Nov 23, 1275; dau. of Henry II, count of Bar, and Philippa de Dreux (d. 1240); m. Henry V the Blond, count of Luxemburg (r. 1226–1281); children: Henry VI (1240–1288), count of Luxemburg (r. 1281–1288); Walram of Luxemburg; Philippine of Luxemburg (d. 1311).

MARGARET (1240–1275). Queen of Scots. Born Sept 29 (some sources cite Oct 5), 1240, in Windsor, Berkshire, England; died at Cupar Castle, Fife, Scotland, Feb 26, 1275; buried at Dunfermline, Fife, Scotland; eldest dau. of Henry III (1206–1272), king of England (r. 1216–1272), and Eleanor of Provence (c. 1222–1291); sister of Edward I Longshanks (1239–1307), king of England (r. 1272–1307); Beatrice (1242–1275), duchess of Brittany; Edmund Crouchback (c. 1245–1296), earl of Lancaster; and Katherine Plantagenet (1253–1257); m. Alexander III (1241–1286), king of Scotland (r. 1249–1286), Dec 26, 1251; children: Margaret of Norway (1261–1283, who m. Eric II Magnusson, king of Norway); Alexander (1264–1284); David (1273–1281). ❖ At 11, married 10-year-old Alexander III, future king of Scotland; was confined to Edinburgh castle by his guardians and only released by the intercession of her parents. ❖ See also *Women in World History*.

MARGARET (1275–1318). Duchess of Brabant. Name variations: Margaret Plantagenet. Born Sept 11, 1275, at Windsor Castle, in Windsor, Berkshire, England; died in 1318 in Brussels, Belgium; interred at the Collegiate Church of St. Gudule, Brussels; dau. of Edward I Longshanks (b. 1239), king of England (r. 1272–1307), and Eleanor of Castile (1241–1290); m. John II (1275–1312), duke of Brabant

(r. 1294–1312), on July 9, 1290, in Westminster Abbey; children: John III (b. 1300), duke of Brabant (r. 1312–1355).

MARGARET (c. 1320–1400). Duchess of Norfolk. Name variations: Countess of Norfolk; Margaret Plantagenet; Margaret Segrave; Margaret Manny. Born c. 1320; died Mar 24, 1400; dau. of Thomas of Brotherton, earl of Norfolk, and Alice Hayles; m. John Segrave, 3rd baron Segrave, in 1327; m. Walter Manny, 1st baron Manny, around 1354; children: (1st m.) Anne Segrave (d. c. 1377); Elizabeth Segrave (1338–1399); (2nd m.) Anne Manny.

MARGARET (1346–1361). English princess. Name variations: Margaret Plantagenet; Margaret Hastings. Born July 20, 1346, in Windsor, Berkshire, England; died, age 15, after Oct 1, 1361; buried at Abingdon Abbey, Oxfordshire, England; dau. of Philippa of Hainault (1314–1369) and Edward III (1312–1377), king of England (r. 1327–1377); m. John Hastings (1347–1375), 2nd earl of Pembroke, in 1359, in Reading, Berkshire, England.

MARGARET (1395–1447). Duchess of Bavaria. Name variations: Margarethe. Born June 26, 1395, in Vienna; died Dec 24, 1447, in Burghausen; dau. of Johanna of Bavaria (c. 1373–1410) and Albrecht also known as Albert IV (1377–1404), duke of Austria (r. 1395–1404); sister of Albert V (1397–1439), duke of Austria (r. 1404–1439), king of Hungary (r. 1437); king of Bohemia (r. 1438) and Holy Roman emperor as Albert II (r. 1438–1439).

MARGARET (1912–1993). Duchess of Argyll. Name variations: Margaret Campbell; Margaret Whigham; Margaret Sweeney also seen as Sweeny. Born Dec 1, 1912; died July 25, 1993; dau. of George Hay Whigham (Scottish textile millionaire); m. Charles Sweeney (American stockbroker and golfer), in 1933; m. Ian Douglas Campbell (1903–1973), 11th duke of Argyll, Mar 22, 1951 (div. 1963); children: (1st m.) Frances Helen Sweeney (who m. David Manners, duke of Rutland). ❖ Well-known debutante, famed for her beauty, was immortalized in Cole Porter's "You're the Top" with the lines: "You're Mussolini,/ You're Mrs. Sweeney,/ You're Camembert"; was accused by duke of Argyll of "multiple adultery," and her fame turned into notoriety. ❖ See also *Women in World History.*

MARGARET (1949—). Romanian princess in exile. Name variations: Margaret Hohenzollern; Margarita von Hohenzollern-Sigmaringen; Margaret Duda. Born Mar 26, 1949, in Lausanne, Switzerland; dau. of Michael, king of Romania (r. 1927–1930 and 1940–1947) and Anne of Bourbon-Parma (b. 1923); married Radu Duda, Sept 21, 1997. ❖ Father was deposed two years before her birth.

MARGARET, Ann (1941—). *See Ann-Margret.*

MARGARET, Countess of Salisbury (1473–1541). *See Pole, Margaret.*

MARGARET, Lady (1443–1509). *See Beaufort, Margaret.*

MARGARET, Maid of Norway (c. 1283–1290). Child-queen of Scotland. Name variations: Margaret of Norway; Margaret Ericsdottir. Born before April 1283 in Tönsberg, Norway; died, age 8, Sept 26, 1290, en route to Kirkwall, Orkney, Scotland; buried in Bergen, Norway; dau. of Margaret of Norway (1261–1283) and Eirik the Priest-Hater also known as Eric II Magnusson (1268–1299), king of Norway (r. 1280–1299); granddau. of Alexander III, king of Scotland (r. 1249–1286). ❖ At 3, succeeded grandfather Alexander III, king of Scotland (1286); was affianced to Prince Edward (future Edward II, king of England), but mysteriously died at sea en route to the Orkneys from Bergen, Norway, by way of the North Sea (1289); her death left Scotland without a monarch, prompting a bitter conflict, the 1st Interregnum, between the families of Bruce and Balliol for the throne.

MARGARET, Princess (1930–2002). *See Margaret Rose.*

MARGARET, Saint.
See Margaret of Antioch (c. 255–c. 275).
See Margaret, St. (c. 1046–1093).
See Margaret of Hungary (1242–1270).
See Margaret of Cortona (1247–1297).

MARGARET, St. (c. 1046–1093). Saint and Saxon princess. Name variations: Saint Margaret; Margaret Atheling; Margaret of Scotland. Born sometime in 1046 in Hungary; died in Scotland in Edinburgh Castle, Nov 16, 1093; buried in Dunfermline, Fife, Scotland; dau. of Edward the Exile also known as Edward the Atheling (1016–1057, son of Edmund II Ironside) and Agatha of Hungary (c. 1025–?); well educated; m. Malcolm III Canmore or Caennmor, king of Scots (r. 1057–1093), c. 1070;

children: Edward (d. 1093); Edmund, king of Scots (r. 1094–1097); Edgar, king of Scots (r. 1098–1107); Ethelred, abbot of Dunkeld; Alexander I (1077–1124), king of Scots (r. 1107–1124); David I (b. around 1084), king of Scots (r. 1124–1153); Matilda of Scotland (1080–1118); Mary of Atholl (d. 1116, mother of Matilda of Boulogne [c. 1103–1152]). ❖ With family, returned to England at the behest of her great-uncle, Edward III the Confessor (1057); spent 9 years at Edward's court; escaped to Scotland after the Conquest of England (1067); following marriage to Malcolm III of Scotland (c. 1070), worked hand-in-hand with husband in the governance of the kingdom and exercised considerable power and influence; conducted a revival of church discipline and reform, establishing religious orders based on the rule of St. Benedict; performed spiritual and charitable exercises; left an influential legacy of equally pious sons and daughters; held several conferences of clerics (1070–93); was canonized by Pope Innocent IV (Sept 16, 1249). ❖ See also T. Ratcliffe Barnett, *Margaret of Scotland: Queen and Saint* (Oliver & Boyd, 1926); Lucy Menzies, *St. Margaret, Queen of Scotland* (Dent, 1925); and *Women in World History.*

MARGARET I OF DENMARK (1353–1412). Queen of Denmark. Name variations: (Danish) Margrete, Margrethe I, Margareta; Margaret of Denmark, Margaret Valdemarsdatter or Valdemarsdottir; Margaret Waldemarsdatter or Waldemarsdottir; "Semiramis of the North." Born in 1353; died board her royal ship anchored in Flensburg's harbor on Oct 28, 1412; 2nd dau. of Valdemar IV also known as Waldemar IV Atterdag, king of Denmark (r. 1340–1375), and Queen Helvig of Denmark (sister of Waldemar III, duke of Schleswig); sister of Ingeborg (1347–1370); m. Haakon VI (1338–1380), king of Norway (r. 1355–1380), king of Sweden (r. 1362–1364), in 1363; children: Olaf or Oluf (born at the royal castle of Oslo in 1370), king of Denmark (r. 1376–1387), king of Norway (r. 1380–1387). ❖ One of Scandinavia's greatest monarchs, unified Denmark, Norway, and Sweden by the Union of Kalmar; reigned as queen of Denmark (1387–97), queen of Norway (1388–1405), and regent of Sweden (1389–1412); at death of father Waldemar IV (1375), persuaded the council of the realm to elect son Olaf as king of Denmark and appoint herself guardian; when Olaf inherited kingdom of Norway at death of her Norwegian husband Haakon VI (1380), became guardian for that country as well; at Olaf's sudden death (1387), was declared "Denmark's proxy and guardian"; was made regent for life by Norwegians, and even the Swedes allied with her to rid themselves of their German-born king; to ensure royal succession in all 3 countries, adopted her sister's 6-year-old grandson, Erik of Pomerania, who was crowned king in each of the Scandinavian kingdoms (1397), while she remained regent; summoned the Union of Kalmar which unified the 3 Nordic countries, Denmark, Norway and Sweden (1397); maintained rulership till her death (1412). ❖ See also *Women in World History.*

MARGARET II OF DENMARK (b. 1940). *See Margrethe II.*

MARGARET ATHELING (c. 1046–1093). *See Margaret, St.*

MARGARET BALLIOL.
See Balliol, Margaret (c. 1255–?).
See Balliol, Margaret (fl. 1300s).

MARGARET BEATRICE (1872–1954). Landgravine of Hesse-Cassel. Name variations: Margaret Hohenzollern. Born Margaret Beatrice Feodore or Feodora, April 22, 1872, in Potsdam, Brandenburg, Germany; died Jan 22, 1954, in Kronberg; dau. of Victoria Adelaide (1840–1901) and Frederick III (1831–1888), emperor of Germany (r. 1888), king of Prussia (r. 1888); m. Frederick Charles, landgrave of Hesse-Cassel, on Jan 25, 1893; children: Frederick Victor (b. 1893); Maximilian (b. 1894); Philip (b. 1896), landgrave of Hesse; Wolfgang (b. 1896); Richard (b. 1901); Christopher of Hesse-Cassel (1901–1943).

MARGARET BEAUFORT (1443–1509). *See Beaufort, Margaret.*

MARGARET BERNADOTTE (1934—). Swedish royal. Name variations: Margaret Ambler; Margaretha. Born Margaret Desiree Victoria, Oct 31, 1934, at Haga Castle, Stockholm, Sweden; dau. of Gustavus Adolphus (1906–1947), duke of Westerbotten, and Sybilla of Saxe-Coburg-Gotha (1908–1972); sister of Carl XVI Gustavus, king of Sweden; m. John Kenneth Ambler, on June 30, 1964; children: Sybilla Louise Ambler (b. 1965); Charles Edward Ambler (b. 1966); James Patrick Ambler (b. 1969).

MARGARET BRUCE.
See Bruce, Margaret (c. 1286–?).

See Bruce, Margaret (1296–1316).
See Bruce, Margaret (d. 1346).

MARGARET BURGO (d. 1303). *See Margaret de Burgh.*

MARGARET CAPET (1158–1198). *See Margaret of France.*

MARGARET CAPET (d. 1271). French princess. Name variations: Margaret of Brabant; Marguerite. Died at an early age in 1271; dau. of Margaret of Provence (1221–1295) and Louis IX, king of France (r. 1226–1270); sister of Philip III the Bold (1245–1285), king of France (r. 1270–1285); m. John I (c. 1252–1294), duke of Brabant, around 1270. ❖ Two years after Margaret Capet's death, John I married Margaret of Flanders (d. 1285).

MARGARET CAPET.
See Margaret of Burgundy (1290–1315).
See Margaret of Artois (d. 1382).

MARGARET CHRISTOFSDOTTIR (c. 1305–1340). Danish princess. Born c. 1305; died in 1340; dau. of Euphemia of Pomerania (d. 1330) and Christopher II (1276–1332), king of Denmark (r. 1319–26, 1330–32); became 1st wife of Louis V the Brandenburger (1316–1361), duke of Bavaria (r. 1347–1361), in Dec 1324. ❖ Louis' 2nd wife was Margaret Maultasch (1318–1369).

MARGARET CLEMENTINE (1870–1955). Princess of Thurn and Taxis. Name variations: Margarethe; Margaret Clementine of Habsburg-Lotharingen. Born July 6, 1870; died in 1955; dau. of Clotilde of Saxe-Coburg-Gotha (1846–1927) and Archduke Josef Karl Ludwig also known as Joseph Charles Louis (1833–1905); m. Albert Maria, 8th prince of Thurn and Taxis; children: Franz Joseph (b. 1893), 9th prince of Thurn and Taxis; Charles Augustus (b. 1898), prince of Thurn and Taxis.

MARGARET DE BURGH (c. 1193–1259). Scottish princess and duchess of Kent. Name variations: Princess Margaret; Margaret Dunkeld. Born c. 1193; died in 1259; interred at Church of the Black Friars, London; dau. of William I the Lion, king of Scots (r. 1165–1214), and Ermengarde of Beaumont (d. 1234); m. Hubert de Burgh, 1st earl of Kent, on June 19, 1221; children: Magota de Burgh (died young); Margaret de Burgh (c. 1226–1243).

MARGARET DE BURGH (c. 1226–1243). English noblewoman. Born c. 1226; died in 1243 (some sources cite Nov 1237); dau. of Hubert de Burgh, 1st earl of Kent, and Margaret de Burgh (c. 1193–1259); m. Richard de Clare, 6th earl of Hertford and 2nd earl of Gloucester, in 1232 (div.). ❖ Was married to 10-year-old Richard de Clare, then count of Gloucester, when she was 6; died at age 17.

MARGARET DE BURGH (d. 1303). Countess of Ulster. Name variations: Margaret Burgo. Died in 1303; dau. of John de Burgh; m. Richard de Burgh the Red (c. 1259–1326), 2nd earl of Ulster (r. 1271–1326) and 4th earl of Connaught, before Feb 27, 1280; children: Elizabeth de Burgh (d. 1327, queen of Scots); Matilda de Burgh (d. 1315, who m. Gilbert de Clare, earl of Gloucester); John, earl of Ulster; Sir Edmund de Burgh; Lady Joan de Burgh (who m. Thomas FitzGerald, 2nd earl of Kildare, and John Darcy, Lord Darcy of Naith); Katherine de Burgh (d. 1331, who m. Maurice Fitzgerald, 1st earl of Desmond); Aveline de Burgh (who m. John de Birmingham); Alianore de Burgh (who m. Thomas, Lord Multon).

MARGARET DE CHATILLON (d. 1404). *See Marie of Guise.*

MARGARET DE CLARE (fl. 1280–1322). *See Clare, Margaret de.*

MARGARET DE FOIX (d. 1258). Queen of Navarre. Name variations: Marguerite de Foix; Margaret of Foix; Margaret of Bourbon. Died April 13, 1258; dau. of Archibald also known as Archimbaud or Archambaud VIII of Bourbon; became 3rd wife of Teobaldo or Theobald I (1201–1253), king of Navarre (r. 1234–1253, also known as Theobald IV of Champagne), in 1232; children: Theobald II (1237–1270), king of Navarre (r. 1253–1270); Enrique or Henry I (c. 1240–1274), king of Navarre (r. 1270–1274). ❖ Theobald I was also married to Gertrude of Metz and Agnes of Beaujeu.

MARGARET DE FOIX (fl. 1456–1477). *See Marguerite de Foix.*

MARGARET DEL BALZO (fl. 15th c.). Countess of St. Pol. Married Peter of Luxemburg, count of St. Pol; children: Louis St. Pol, count of St. Pol; Jacquetta of Luxemburg (c. 1416–1472).

MARGARET DE MÂLE.
See Margaret of Brabant (1323–1368).
See Margaret of Flanders (1350–1405).

MARGARET DE ROHAN (1397–1428). Viscountess de Rohan. Name variations: Margaret de Dreux. Born in 1397; died in 1428; dau. of John IV de Montfort, 5th duke of Brittany (r. 1364–1399) and Joanna of Navarre (c. 1370–1437); m. Alan de Rohan, viscount de Rohan.

MARGARET DE ROHAN (fl. 1449). Countess of Angoulême. Name variations: Marguerite de Rohan. Fl. around 1449; m. John Valois (1404–1467), count of Angoulême, in 1449; children: Charles Valois (1459–1496), count of Angoulême; grandmother of Francis I, king of France.

MARGARET DUNKELD (1261–1283). *See Margaret of Norway.*

MARGARET HABSBURG.
See Margaret of Austria (1480–1530).
See Margaret of Austria (c. 1577–1611).

MARGARET LE BRUN (d. 1283). French noblewoman. Died in 1283; dau. of Isabella of Angoulême (1186–1246), queen of England, and Hugh X, count of Lusignan; m. Raymond VII, count of Toulouse (div. 1245); m. Aymer, viscount of Thouars; m. Geoffrey, seigneur de Chateaubriand; children: (1st m.) Joan of Toulouse (d. 1271).

MARGARET LOUVAIN (1323–1368). *See Margaret of Brabant.*

MARGARET-MARY OF HUNGARY (c. 1177–?). Eastern Roman empress. Born c. 1177; death date unknown; dau. of Anne of Chatillon-Antioche (c. 1155–1185) and Bela III, king of Hungary (r. 1173–1196); sister of Emeric I, king of Hungary (r. 1196–1204), and Andrew II (1175–1235), king of Hungary (r. 1205–1235); married the widowed Isaac II Angelus, Eastern Roman emperor (r. 1185–95 and 1203–04); m. Boniface of Montferrat; children: (1st m.) Alexius IV Angelus (d. 1204), emperor of Byzantium (r. 1203–1204); Irene Angela of Byzantium (d. 1208, who m. Philip of Swabia); (2nd m.) Demetrius of Thessalonica.

MARGARET MAULTASCH (1318–1369). German ruler of Tyrol and Carinthia. Name variations: Margarete, countess of Tirol or Tyrol and duchess of Carinthia; Margaret of Carinthia; Margaretha Maultasch or Maultasche; Margarete von Karnten or Kärnten. Born in 1318 somewhere in Germany; died in Vienna in 1369; dau. of Henry of Carinthia, king of Bohemia (r. 1306–1310) and duke of Tyrol, and Anna of Bohemia; granddau. of Meinhard II; m. Johann also known as John of Bohemia or John Henry of Luxemburg, margrave of Moravia (brother of Charles IV, Holy Roman emperor), in 1330 (marriage annulled 1342); m. Ludwig also known Louis V (1316–1361), duke of Bavaria and margrave of Brandenburg (r. 1347–1361), in 1342; children (2nd marriage) Meinhard, margrave of Brandenburg and duke of Bavaria (r. 1361–1363). ❖ Known for her intelligence and political skills, was one of the most efficient and well-respected rulers of her day; became countess of Tyrol and duchess of Carinthia after father's death and governed those territories (1335–69); used the charge of witchcraft as the means of extricating herself from 1st marriage, then married Louis of Bavaria (1342); successfully defended her lands from the encroachments of a land-hungry emperor, Charles IV; initiated several reform policies which strengthened the central government and encouraged commercial trade in towns; tried, albeit unsuccessfully, to protect the Jews living in Tyrol from persecution; ceded Tyrol to Rudolf of Habsburg after death of son (1363); retired to Vienna (1363) and died there (1369). ❖ See also Lion Feuchtwanger, *The Ugly Duchess* (Viking, 1928); and *Women in World History*.

MARGARET OF ALSACE (c. 1135–1194). Countess of Hainault and ruler of Flanders. Name variations: Margareta of Alsace; Marguerite. Born c. 1135; died Nov 15, 1194; dau. of Sybilla of Anjou (1112–1165) and Theodore of Alsace (also known as Didrik, Dietrich, or Thierry), count of Flanders (r. 1128–1157); sister of Philip of Alsace, count of Flanders (r. 1157–1191); m. Baudouin also known as Baldwin V, count of Hainault (Baldwin VIII of Flanders); children: Isabella of Hainault (1170–1190); Baudouin also known as Baldwin IX (1171–1205), count of Flanders and Hainault (r. 1195–1205), also crowned Baldwin I, emperor of Constantinople; Yolande of Courtenay (d. 1219), empress of Constantinople; Philip of Namur. ❖ Succeeded brother Philip of Alsace as ruler of Flanders when he died (1191).

MARGARET OF ANGOULÊME (1492–1549). Queen of Navarre, poet, and writer. Name variations: Margaret of Angouleme; Margaret of

France; Margaret or Marguerite of Navarre; Marguerite of France; Marguerite d'Navarre; Marguerite de Navarre; Marguerite d'Angoulême or Marguerite of Angouleme; Margaret of Orleans; Margaret of Valois; duchess of Alençon or Alencon; duchess of Berry. Pronunciation: ON-gyou-lame. Born in castle of Angoulême, April 11, 1492; died in castle of Odos-in-Bigorre, near Tarbes, Dec 21, 1549; buried in the cathedral of Lescar; dau. of Charles de Valois-Orléans (1460–1496), count of Angoulême, and Louise of Savoy (1476–1531); sister of Francis I, king of France (r. 1515–1547); m. Charles, duke of Alençon, Oct 9, 1509, at Blois; m. Henry II (1517–1555), king of Navarre, on Jan 24, 1527, at St. Germain-sur-Laye; children: (2nd m.) Jeanne d'Albret (1528–1572), later queen of Navarre; son Jean (died Christmas Day 1530, aged 5 months); twins (b. 1542, died within hours). ❖ Patron of reformers and humanists and author of *The Heptaméron*, who, with brother and mother, formed the renowned *trinité*, which ruled over the French court in early 16th century; acted as mother's deputy, traveling many miles, serving as mediator and messenger, most notably in Spain during brother's captivity (1525); sought solace in matters spiritual through her correspondence over many years with Guillaume Briçonnet; became a friend and supporter of those who saw the need for reform in the church, defending them and protecting them during periods of persecution; inspired and encouraged brother to form the Collège de France, and helped to ensure the survival of the Renaissance in France; was a prolific writer, both of letters, personal and official, and of poetry; is most remembered for *The Heptaméron*, which she wrote to amuse brother Francis during his last illness. Not to be confused with the notorious Margaret of Valois, queen of Navarre (1553–1615), who is sometimes also referred to as Margaret of Angoulême. ❖ See also Samuel P. Putnam, *Marguerite of Navarre* (1936); A. Mary F. Robinson, *Margaret of Angoulême, Queen of Navarre* (1886); and *Women in World History*.

MARGARET OF ANGOULÊME (1553–1615). *See Margaret of Valois.*

MARGARET OF ANJOU (c. 1272–1299). Countess of Valois. Name variations: Margaret of Valois; Marguerite of Anjou-Sicily. Born c. 1272; died Dec 31, 1299; dau. of Marie of Hungary (d. 1323) and Charles II (1254–1309), duke of Anjou (r. 1285–1290), king of Naples and Anjou (r. 1285–1309); sister of Blanche of Naples (d. 1310), Robert the Good, king of Naples (r. 1309–1343), and Lenore of Sicily (1289–1341); m. Charles of Valois also known as Charles I (1270–1325), count of Valois (son of Philip III the Bold, king of France), Aug 16, 1290; children: Philip VI of Valois (1293–1350), king of France (r. 1328–1350); Jeanne of Valois (c. 1294–1342, mother of Philippa of Hainault). ❖ Charles of Valois' 2nd wife was Catherine de Courtenay (d. 1307); their daughter, also called Jeanne of Valois (b. 1304), married Robert III of Artois. Charles' 3rd wife was Mahaut de Chatillon (d. 1358).

MARGARET OF ANJOU (1429–1482). Queen of England. Name variations: Margaret d'Anjou; Marguerite d'Anjou. Born Mar 23, 1429 (some sources cite 1430), at Château Keure in Lorraine (France); died Aug 25, 1482, at Château de Dampierre in Anjou (France); dau. of René I the Good, duke of Anjou and titular king of Sicily, Hungary, and Naples, and Isabelle of Lorraine (1410–1453); sister of Yolande of Vaudemont (1428–1483); m. Henry VI, king of England (r. 1422–1461, 1470–1471), on April 22, 1445, in Titchfield, England; children: Edward, prince of Wales (Oct 13, 1453–1471). ❖ One of the most well known of English queens and a principal player in the Wars of the Roses, was crowned queen of England (May 1445); founded Queen's College at Cambridge University (1448); was the leader of the party of Lancaster, and fought against Yorkists for many years, though in the end unsuccessfully, to restore to her husband and her son their right to rule England (1456–71); fled to Scotland after Yorkist seizure of throne (1461); met final defeat in Battle of Tewkesbury (1471); returned to Anjou (1476). ❖ See also J.J. Bagley, *Margaret of Anjou, Queen of England* (Jenkins, 1948); Jacob Abbott, *History of Margaret of Anjou, Queen of Henry VI of England* (Harper, 1861); and *Women in World History*.

MARGARET OF ANJOU (1553–1615). *See Margaret of Valois.*

MARGARET OF ANTIOCH (c. 255–c. 275). Saint. Name variations: Marina of Antioch; Margarete or Margaret the Dragon Slayer; Maid of Antioch. Born at Antioch in Pisidia c. 255; beheaded c. 275 at Antioch; dau. of Aedisius or Aedesius (high-ranking pagan priest). ❖ Converted to Christianity by her childhood nurse, was driven from the house by an outraged father; became a shepherd in the countryside; captured the attention of the prefect Olybrius, who wished to make her his bride; was imprisoned by Olybrius when she apprised him of her faith; while in

prison, is said to have performed a series of miracles, not the least of which was subduing a dragon which tried to devour her; was eventually beheaded. Feast day is July 20. ❖ See also *Women in World History*.

MARGARET OF ANTIOCH-LUSIGNAN (fl. 1283–1291). Regent of Tyre. Fl. between 1283 and 1291; dau. of Henry of Antioch and Isabella of Cyprus (fl. 1230s); sister of Hugh III, king of Cyprus (r. 1267–1284), king of Jerusalem (r. 1268–1284); m. John of Montfort, lord of Tyre.

MARGARET OF ARTOIS (d. 1382). Countess of Artois. Name variations: Marguerite of Artois; Margaret Capet; Joan. Reigned as countess of Artois from 1361 to 1382. Died in 1382; dau. of Philip V the Tall (c. 1294–1322), king of France (1316–1322), and Jeanne I of Burgundy (c. 1291–1330); m. Louis I (d. 1346), count of Flanders (r. 1322–1346); children: Louis II de Male (1330–1384), count of Flanders and Artois (r. 1346–1384). ❖ As countess of Artois, reigned (1361–82). After her death, the county of Artois merged with that of Flanders, which had belonged to her husband Louis.

MARGARET OF ATTENDULI (1375–?). Italian military leader. Name variations: Margherita Sforza; Margaret of Attendolo; Margaret Attenduli. Born in 1375 in Italy; date of death unknown; dau. of Romagna peasants; sister of Muzio Attenduli or Attendolo (c. 1369–1424), founder of Italy's famous Sforza family. ❖ An aggressive politician and military leader, played an important role in her family's political games. ❖ See also *Women in World History*.

MARGARET OF AUSTRIA (fl. 1200s). German queen. Fl. in 1200s; m. Henry VII (d. 1242), king of Germany (r. 1219–1235); children: Frederick and Henry.

MARGARET OF AUSTRIA (1480–1530). Duchess of Savoy. Name variations: Marguérite; Marguerite d'Autriche; Margaret Hapsburg; Duchess of Savoy and regent of the Netherlands. Born in Brussels, Belgium, Jan 11, 1480; died in Malines, Nov 30 or Dec 1, 1530; dau. of Maximilian I, Holy Roman emperor (r. 1493–1519) and king of Germany, and Mary of Burgundy (1457–1482); sister of Philip I the Fair (also called the Handsome [1478–1506], husband of Juana La Loca); stepdau. of Bianca Maria Sforza (1472–1510) of Milan; engaged to future Charles VIII of France, in 1482; m. Infante Juan also known as John of Spain (1478–1497), Spanish crown prince and son of Ferdinand and Isabella I, April 3, 1497 (he died a few months later on Oct 4); m. Philibert II, duke of Savoy (1497–1504), in 1501; children: none. ❖ At 3, married the 12-year-old Dauphin Charles (VIII), crown prince of France (1483); when Louis XI died two months later, became queen to Charles' king; returned to the Low Countries and her father Maximilian after Charles had marriage annulled (1491); when 3rd husband Philibert showed little interest in governing his domains, willingly managed his affairs; her true public career began at age 27, when she was named regent of the Netherlands and guardian of her nephew Charles, later Charles V (1507); remained regent (1507–15, 1519–30) and was a chief player in European politics for the rest of her life; with Louise of Savoy, negotiated the treaty of Cambrai, known as the "Ladies Peace" (1529) between France and the Netherlands; helped to introduce the energy and aesthetic values of the Italian Renaissance to Northern Europe. ❖ See also Eleanor E. Tremayne, *The First Governess of the Netherlands: Margaret of Austria* (Putnam, 1908); and *Women in World History*.

MARGARET OF AUSTRIA (1522–1586). *See Margaret of Parma.*

MARGARET OF AUSTRIA (c. 1577–1611). Queen of Spain. Name variations: Archduchess Margarete of Styria; Margaret Habsburg. Born c. 1577 (some sources cite 1584); died of puerperal fever in 1611; dau. of Karl also known as Charles (youngest son of Emperor Ferdinand I, founder of the Austrian branch of the House of Habsburg), archduke of Styria (located in southeastern Austria and Slovenia) and Mary of Bavaria (dau. of the duke of Bavaria); sister of Holy Roman emperor Ferdinand II (1578–1637); cousin of Rudolf II, Holy Roman emperor, king of Hungary and Bohemia (present-day Czech Republic) and archduke of Austria; m. Philip III (1578–1621), king of Spain (r. 1598–1621), in 1599; children: 7, including Maria Anna of Spain (1606–1646, who m. Ferdinand III, king of Bohemia and Hungary); Anne of Austria (1601–1666); Philip IV (1605–1665), king of Spain (r.1621–1665). ❖ See also *Women in World History*.

MARGARET OF BABENBERG (fl. 1252). Queen of Bohemia and duchess of Austria. Fl. around 1252; dau. of Leopold VII, one of several claimants to the title of duke of Austria (r. 1250–1253); 1st wife of

Otakar or Ottokar II (b. 1230?), king of Bohemia (r. 1253–1278), duke of Austria and Styria (r. 1252–1276).

MARGARET OF BADEN (d. 1457). German noblewoman. Died Oct 24, 1457; dau. of James I of Baden, margrave of Baden; became 1st wife of Albert Achilles (1414–1486) also known as Albert III (1414–1486), elector of Brandenburg (r. 1470–1486), in 1446; children: John Cicero (1455–1499), elector of Brandenburg (r. 1486–1499). ❖ Albert's 2nd wife was Anne of Saxony (1437–1512).

MARGARET OF BADEN (1932—). Grand duchess of Baden. Name variations: Margarita Alice Scholastica, grand duchess von Baden; Margarita of Baden. Born Margaret Alice Thyra Victoria Mary Louise Scholastica, July 14, 1932, in Salem, Baden, Germany; dau. of Berthold (b. 1906), margrave of Baden, and Theodora Oldenburg (1906–1969, sister of Prince Philip of England); m. Tomislav Karadjordjevic (1928–2000) also known as Prince Tomislav (brother of Peter II, king of Yugoslavia), on June 5, 1957 (div. 1981); children: Prince Nicholas (b. 1958); Catherine also seen as Princess Katarina (b. 1959).

MARGARET OF BAVARIA (fl. 1390–1410). Duchess of Lorraine. Fl. between 1390 and 1410; m. Charles II, duke of Lorraine; children: Isabelle of Lorraine (1410–1453), queen of Naples.

MARGARET OF BAVARIA (d. 1424). Duchess of Burgundy. Died in 1424 (some sources cite 1426); dau. of Albert I, duke of Bavaria (r. 1353–1404); m. John the Fearless (1371–1419), duke of Burgundy (r. 1404–1419), on April 12, 1385; children: Philip III the Good (1396–1467), duke of Burgundy (r. 1419–1467); Margaret of Burgundy (d. 1441); Mary of Burgundy (c. 1400–1463, who m. Adolf I of Cleves); Joan (d. around 1413); Isabella of Burgundy (d. 1412, who m. Oliver, count of Penthièvre); Catherine (who m. Louis, duke of Guise); Anne Valois (c. 1405–1432, who m. John, duke of Bedford); Agnes of Burgundy (d. 1476, who m. Charles I, duke of Bourbon).

MARGARET OF BAVARIA (1445–1479). Marquesa of Mantua. Name variations: Margherita of Bavaria; Margherita Gonzaga. Born in 1445; died in 1479; m. Frederigo also known as Federico Gonzaga (1441–1484), 3rd marquis of Mantua (r. 1478–1484); children: Chiara Gonzaga (1465–1505); Francesco Gonzaga (1466–1519), 4th marquis of Mantua (r. 1484–1519, who m. Isabelle d'Este); Sigismondo (1469–1525, cardinal); Elisabetta Montefeltro (1471–1526); Maddalena Sforza (1472–1490); Giovanni (1474–1523, who m. Laura di Giovanni Bentivoglio).

MARGARET OF BLOIS (d. 1404). See Marie of Guise.

MARGARET OF BOHEMIA (d. 1212). See Dagmar of Bohemia.

MARGARET OF BOURBON (d. 1258). See Margaret de Foix.

MARGARET OF BOURBON (d. 1483). Duchess of Savoy. Name variations: Marguerite de Bourbon. Born Margaret de Beaujeu; died in 1483; sister of Pierre de Beaujeu, who was married to Anne of Beaujeu (1460/61–1522); m. Philip II, count of Bresse, later duke of Savoy; children: Louise of Savoy (1476–1531); Philibert II (1478–1504, who m. Margaret of Austria [1480–1530]); Charles II the Good of Savoy, duke of Savoy; Philippe, marquis of Saluzzo; René, count of Villare and Tende.

MARGARET OF BRABANT (d. 1311). Holy Roman empress. Name variations: Marguerite of Brabant. Died in 1311; m. Henry of Luxemburg also known as Henry VII (c. 1274–1313), Holy Roman emperor (r. 1308–1313), in 1292; children: Mary of Luxemburg (1305–1323, who m. Charles IV, king of France); John Limburg (1296–1346), count of Luxemburg and king of Bohemia (r. 1310–1346).

MARGARET OF BRABANT (1323–1368). Countess of Flanders. Name variations: Margaret Louvain; Margaret de Mâle; Margaret of Male or Mâle. Born in 1323; died in 1368; dau. of John III (1300–1355), duke of Brabant (r. 1312–1355), and Marie of Evreux (d. 1335); sister of Joanna of Brabant (1322–1406) and Marie of Guelders (1325–1399); m. Louis II de Male (1330–1384), count of Flanders and Artois (r. 1346–1384); children: Margaret of Flanders (1350–1405, who m. Philip the Bold, duke of Burgundy).

MARGARET OF BRANDENBURG (c. 1450–1489). Duchess of Pomerania. Name variations: Margaret von Brandenburg. Born c. 1450; died in 1489; dau. of Catherine of Saxony (1421–1476) and Frederick II (1413–1471), elector of Brandenburg (r. 1440–1470, abdicated); m. Bogislav X also known as Boleslav X (b. 1454), duke of Pomerania, on Sept 20, 1477.

MARGARET OF BURGUNDY (1290–1315). Queen of Navarre and France. Name variations: Margaret Capet; (Fr.) Marguerite of Bourgogne. Born in 1290; died Aug 14, 1315, in Château Gaillard, France; dau. of Robert II (1248), duke of Burgundy, and Agnes Capet (1260–1327, dau. of Louis IX of France); sister of Jeanne of Burgundy (1293–1348, 1st wife of Philip VI of France); m. Louis X the Headstrong (1289–1316), king of France (r. 1314–1316), on Sept 23, 1305 (annulled before Aug 1315); children: Joan II of Navarre (1309–1349). ❖ After a 10-year marriage, was convicted of adultery, imprisoned, then smothered to death (1315). ❖ See also Women in World History.

MARGARET OF BURGUNDY (d. 1441). Duchess of Guienne. Died in 1441; dau. of Margaret of Bavaria (d. 1424) and John the Fearless (1371–1419), duke of Burgundy (r. 1404–1419); m. Louis (d. 1415), duke of Guienne; m. Arthur III of Brittany (1393–1458), count of Richmond, duke of Brittany (r. 1457–1458).

MARGARET OF BURGUNDY (c. 1376–1441). Countess of Hainault and Holland. Name variations: Margaret Valois; Margaret of Ostrevent, countess of Ostrevent. Born c. 1376; died in 1441; dau. of Philip the Bold (1342–1404), duke of Burgundy (r. 1363–1404), and Margaret of Flanders (1350–1405); sister of John the Fearless, duke of Burgundy (r. 1404–1419); m. Count William VI (d. 1417), count of Hainault and Holland (r. 1404–1417), on April 12, 1385; children: Jacqueline of Hainault (1401–1436).

MARGARET OF BURGUNDY (1446–1503). See Margaret of York.

MARGARET OF CARINTHIA (1318–1369). See Margaret Maultasch.

MARGARET OF CLEVES (fl. early 1400s). Duchess of Bavaria. Fl. in the early 1400s; m. William II, duke of Bavaria (r. 1397–1435); children: Adolph, duke of Bavaria (r. 1435–1441).

MARGARET OF CONNAUGHT (1882–1920). Swedish royal. Name variations: Margaret Saxe-Coburg; Margaret of Sweden; Crown Princess Margaret of Sweden; Margaret Victoria of Sweden. Born Jan 15, 1882, in Bagshot Park, Surrey, England; died May 1, 1920, in Stockholm, Sweden; dau. of Arthur Saxe-Coburg, duke of Connaught, and Louise Margaret of Prussia (1860–1917); granddau. of Queen Victoria of England; m. Gustavus VI Adolphus (1882–1973), king of Sweden (r. 1950–1973), June 15, 1905, at St. George's Chapel, Windsor Castle, England; children: Gustav Adolphus, duke of Westerbotten (1906–1947); Sigvard (1907–); Ingrid of Sweden (b. 1910, who m. Frederick IX, king of Denmark); Bertil (b. 1912), duke of Halland; Charles John, duke of Dalecarlia (b. 1916). ❖ Following her death, Gustavus VI Adolphus married Louise Mountbatten.

MARGARET OF CONSTANTINOPLE (1202–1280). See Margaret of Flanders.

MARGARET OF CORIGLIANO (fl. 14th c.). Neapolitan noblewoman. Married Louis of Durazzo; children: Charles III, king of Naples (r. 1382–1386), king of Hungary as Charles II (r. 1385–1386).

MARGARET OF CORTONA (1247–1297). Saint and Franciscan nun. Name variations: "The Magdalene of Cortona." Born in Alviano (Laviano), near Chiusi, in Tuscany, in 1247; died in Cortona, in Tuscany, Feb 22, 1297; children: (with the lord of Montepulciano) one son. ❖ Lived with the lord of Montepulciano as his mistress for 9 years and had a son; when he was assassinated by robbers, was overcome by shock and contrition; eventually arrived at the Franciscan convent in Cortona where, barefoot, with a rope around her neck, begged to be admitted as a penitent into the order; was permitted to take the habit of the Third Order of St. Francis (1272); prayed before the image of Christ, and it is said that he bowed his head in forgiveness; from that time on, was regarded as "the Magdalene of Cortona"; is often depicted with a small dog, usually a spaniel, at her feet. Feast day is Feb 22. ❖ See also Women in World History.

MARGARET OF DENMARK.
See Estrith (fl. 1017–1032).
See Margaret I of Denmark (1353–1412).

MARGARET OF DENMARK (1456–1486). Queen of Scotland. Born June 23, 1456; died July 14, 1486, in Stirling, Scotland; buried in Cambuskenneth Abbey, Stirling; dau. of Christian I (1426–1481), king of Denmark, Norway, and Sweden (r. 1448–1481), and Dorothea of Brandenburg (1430–1495); m. James III (1451–1488), king of Scotland (r. 1460–1488), on July 13, 1469; children: James IV (1473–1513), king of Scotland (r. 1488–1513); James Stewart (1476–1504), archbishop of St. Andrews; Alexander Stewart, earl of Mar and Garioch; John Stewart (1479–1503), earl of Mar and Garioch.

MARGARET OF FLANDERS (1202–1280). Countess of Flanders. Name variations: Black Meg; Margaret of Constantinople; Marguerite of Flanders; Marguerite de Flandre. Born in 1202 in Flanders; died in 1280 in Flanders; dau. of Baudouin also known as Baldwin IX, count of Flanders (and emperor of Constantinople as Baldwin I), and Marie of Champagne (d. 1203); sister of Johanna of Flanders (c. 1200–1244); m. Bourchard d'Avesnes of Hainault, in 1212 (annulled around 1215); m. William de Dampierre, around 1223 (died before 1245); children: (1st m.) 2 sons; (2nd m.) 3 sons, including Guy de Dampierre, later count of Flanders, and 2 daughters (names unknown). ❖ Religious founder and great contributor to the commercial growth of 13th century, inherited the county of Flanders after sister Johanna died (1245); was soon engaged in a 10-year war with her d'Avesnes sons (1st marriage) and her Dampierre sons (2nd marriage) over which son was her legal heir; with peace restored, turned her attention toward the welfare of the towns and people under her rule; became a respected founder of religious establishments, favoring the Dominicans, for whom she established a house at Ypres and one at Douai; corresponded with Thomas Aquinas on questions of moral rule; also promoted the trade of her region, helping to bring more commerce and money into her capital trading city of Bruges. ❖ See also *Women in World History.*

MARGARET OF FLANDERS (d. 1285). Duchess of Brabant. Name variations: Margaret of Brabant. Died in 1285; dau. of Guy of Flanders (probably Guy de Dampierre, later count of Flanders, son of Margaret of Flanders [1202–1280]); became 2nd wife of John I (c. 1252–1294), duke of Brabant, in 1273; children: a son who died. ❖ John I's 1st wife was Margaret Capet (d. 1271).

MARGARET OF FLANDERS (1350–1405). Countess of Flanders, duchess of Burgundy, and countess of Artois and Nevers. Name variations: Margaret de Mâle; Margaret of Male or Mâle; Margaret II, countess of Flanders; (Fr.) Marguerite de Flandre. Reigned as countess of Flanders (r. 1384–1405); countess of Artois and Nevers. Born 1350; died Mar 16, 1405, in Arras; dau. of Margaret of Brabant (1323–1368) and Louis II de Male, count of Flanders and Artois (r. 1346–1384); m. Philippe de Rouvre, count of Artois, Mar 21, 1356 or 1357; m. Philip the Bold (1342–1404), duke of Burgundy (r. 1363–1404), in 1369; children: John the Fearless (1371–1419), duke of Burgundy (r. 1404–1419); Antoine also known as Anthony, duke of Brabant (d. 1415); Philip (d. 1415), count of Nevers; Margaret of Burgundy (c. 1376–1441); Catherine of Burgundy (1378–1425); Mary of Burgundy (d. 1428). ❖ When father died (1384), inherited Flanders and Artois, and the cities of Antwerp and Malines. ❖ See also *Women in World History.*

MARGARET OF FOIX.
See Margaret de Foix (d. 1258).
See Marguerite de Foix (fl. 1456–1477).

MARGARET OF FRANCE (1158–1198). Queen of Hungary. Name variations: Margaret Capet. Born in 1158; died in 1198 in Acre (Akko), now Israel; dau. of Constance of Castile (d. 1160) and Louis VII (c. 1121–1180), king of France (r. 1137–1180); m. six-year-old Henry Plantagenet (1155–1183), known as the Young King (son of Henry II and Eleanor of Aquitaine), count of Anjou and duke of Normandy, Nov 2, 1160; became 2nd wife of Bela III (1148–1196), king of Hungary (r. 1173–1196), in 1185 or 1186; children: (1st m.) William (stillborn).

MARGARET OF FRANCE (c. 1282–1318). Queen-consort of England. Name variations: Marguerite of France; Margaret of Westminster. Born c. 1282 (some sources cite 1279) in Paris, France; died Feb 14, 1318 (some sources cite 1317); buried at Christ Church, Newgate, London; interred at Grey Friars Church, Newgate, London; dau. of Philip III the Bold (1245–1285), king of France (r. 1270–1285), and Marie of Brabant (c. 1260–1321); half-sister of Philip IV, king of France (r. 1285–1314) and Blanche of France (c. 1266–1305); aunt of Isabella of France (1296–1358); became 2nd wife of Edward I Longshanks, king of England (r. 1272–1307), Sept 10, 1299 (also seen as 1298); children: Thomas (b. 1300), earl of Norfolk; Edmund of Woodstock (1307–1330), earl of Kent; Margaret (b. 1306, died young); Eleanor (1306–1311); (stepson) Edward II, king of England (r. 1307–1327). ❖ At 16, married Edward I Longshanks, king of England, while he was at war with Scotland (1299); became a much-admired and beloved queen; when she accompanied husband on campaigns, was known to intercede with him to save lives and forgive debts; was instrumental in the building of London's Grey Friars Church where she was buried following her death at 36. ❖ See also *Women in World History.*

MARGARET OF FRANCE.
See Margaret of Angoulême (1492–1549).
See Margaret of Savoy (1523–1574).
See Margaret of Valois (1553–1615).

MARGARET OF GENEVA (fl. late 1100s–early 1200s). Countess of Savoy and poet. Born in late 1100s; m. Thomas I, count of Savoy (troubadour); children: Amadeus IV (b. 1197), count of Savoy; Thomas (b. 1199), count of Flanders; Beatrice of Savoy (d. 1268); Peter II (b. 1203), count of Savoy; Philip (b. 1207); Boniface, archbishop of Canterbury; and 3 others.

MARGARET OF GERMANY (1237–1270). Landgravine of Thuringia and ancestor of house of Saxe-Coburg-Gotha. Born Feb 1237; died Aug 8, 1270; dau. of Frederick II, Holy Roman emperor (r. 1215–1250), and Isabella of England (1214–1241, Holy Roman empress and dau. of King John of England); m. Albert, landgrave of Thuringia; children: Frederick, margrave of Meissen and Thuringia.

MARGARET OF HAINAULT (d. 1342). Countess of Artois. Name variations: Margarete of Hainault; Margaret of Hainaut. Died Oct 18, 1342; dau. of John II, count of Hainault and Holland, and Philippine of Luxemburg (d. 1311); became 3rd wife of Robert II, count of Artois, in 1298.

MARGARET OF HOLLAND (d. 1356). Countess of Hainault and Holland. Died in 1356; dau. of William III the Good, count of Holland and Hainault, and Jeanne of Valois (c. 1294–1342, sister of Philip VI, king of France); sister of Philippa of Hainault (1314–1369) and Joan of Hainault (c. 1310–?); became 2nd wife of Louis III, duke of Bavaria (r. 1294–1347), king of the Romans (r. 1314–1328), also known as Ludwig IV of Bavaria or Louis IV, Holy Roman emperor (r. 1314–1347); children: Louis the Roman, also known as Louis the Younger (1330–1365), elector of Brandenburg (r. 1350–1365); William V, duke of Bavaria (r. 1347–1358), count of Holland (r. 1354–1358), count of Hainault (r. 1356–1358); Albert I, count of Holland (r. 1353–1404); Otto V (1341–1379), elector of Brandenburg (r. 1365–1373). ❖ Louis IV's 1st wife was Beatrice of Silesia.

MARGARET OF HUNGARY (1242–1270). Dominican nun, saint, and mystic. Name variations: Saint Margaret of Hungary. Born in 1242 in Dalmatia; died Jan 18, 1270, in what is now Budapest, Hungary; dau. of Béla IV (b. 1206), king of Hungary (r. 1235–1270), and Queen Maria Lascaris (fl. 1234–1242); never married; no children. ❖ Though the daughter of a king, made formal religious vows at 12; determined to receive no special favors because of her royal birth, subjected herself to the most menial and squalid tasks as an expression of her devotion to God; was so weakened by her extreme asceticism, in particular her frequent fasts and refusal to sleep, that she died at age 28. Feast day is Jan 26. ❖ See also *Women in World History.*

MARGARET OF HUNTINGDON (c. 1140–1201). Duchess of Brittany and countess of Hereford. Born c. 1140; died in 1201; interred at Sawtrey Abbey, Huntingdonshire; dau. of Adelicia de Warrenne (d. 1178) and Henry Dunkeld, 1st earl of Huntingdon; sister of Malcolm IV and William I the Lion, both kings of Scotland, David Dunkeld, 1st earl of Huntingdon, and Ada Dunkeld (c. 1145–1206); m. Conan IV, duke of Brittany, in 1160; m. Humphrey de Bohun, constable of England, in 1175; children: (1st m.) Constance of Brittany (1161–1201); (2nd m.) Henry de Bohun, 5th earl of Hereford (r. 1200–1220); Maud de Bohun (who m. Henry de Oilly).

MARGARET OF KENT (1327–before 1352). English royal. Name variations: Margaret Plantagenet; Margaret d'Albret. Born in 1327; died before 1352; dau. of Edmund of Woodstock (1307–1330), 1st earl of Kent, and Margaret Wake of Liddell (c. 1299–1349); sister of Joan of Kent (1328–1385); m. Amanco d'Albret (also known as Amaneus d'Albret).

MARGARET OF LANCASTER (1443–1509). *See Beaufort, Margaret.*

MARGARET OF LIMBURG (d. 1172). Duchess of Lower Lorraine. Died in 1172; m. Godfrey III of Brabant, duke of Brabant and Lower Lorraine (r. 1142–1190), in 1155 (died 1190). ❖ Godfrey's 2nd marriage was to Imagina von Loon (d. 1214/20).

MARGARET OF LORRAINE (1463–1521). Duchess of Alençon. Name variations: Blessed Margaret of Lorraine, duchess of Alencon; Marguerite de Lorraine. Born in 1463; died Nov 1, 1521; dau. of Yolande of Vaudemont (1428–1483) and Ferrey de Vaudemont also known as Frederick, count of Vaudemont; m. René (d. 1492), duke of Alençon, on May 14, 1488; children: Charles, duke of Alençon (who m. Margaret of Angoulême [1492–1549]); Françoise d'Alencon (who m. Charles, duke of Vendome, and Francis II, duc de Longueville); Anne d'Alencon (who m. William VII, marquis of Montferrat). ❖ Widowed at 29, continued to fulfill her duties as duchess of Alençon until her son came of age; then became a Poor Clare at the convent of Argentan. Feast day is Nov 2.

MARGARET OF LORRAINE.
See Marguerite of Lorraine (c. 1561–?).
See Marguerite of Lorraine (fl. 1632).

MARGARET OF MÂLE.
See Margaret of Brabant (1323–1368).
See Margaret of Flanders (1350–1405).

MARGARET OF NAPLES (fl. late 1300s). Queen of Naples. Dau. of Marie of Naples and Charles of Durazzo; m. Charles III of Durazzo (1345–1386), king of Naples (r. 1382–1386), also ruled Hungary as Charles II (r. 1385–1386); children: Ladislas I, king of Naples (r. 1386–1414); Joanna II of Naples (1374–1435).

MARGARET OF NAVARRE (fl. 1154–1172). Queen of Sicily and regent of Naples and Sicily. Name variations: Margherita. Queen of Sicily, 1154–1166; regent, 1166–1172; death date unknown; dau. of Garcia IV, king of Navarre (r. 1134–1150), and Marguerite de l'Aigle (d. 1141); m. William I the Bad (1120–1166), king of Naples and Sicily (r. 1154–1166), in 1150; children: William II the Good (1153–1189), king of Naples and Sicily (r. 1166–1189, who m. Joanna of Sicily); Henry. ❖ Was one of the few queens of Norman Sicily to have played a significant political role in the kingdom, in part due to husband's inertia; when he died (1166), faced the challenge of governing as regent and struggled to impose order on a nearly chaotic situation, with the European barons conspiring to undermine the monarchy's power and Sicily's myriad ethnic and religious groups. ❖ See also Women in World History.

MARGARET OF NAVARRE.
See Margaret of Angoulême (1492–1549).
See Margaret of Valois (1553–1615).

MARGARET OF NORWAY (1261–1283). Queen of Norway. Name variations: Margaret Dunkeld; Margaret of Scotland. Born Feb 28, 1261, in Windsor Castle, Windsor, Berkshire, England; died April 9, 1283, in Tönsberg, Norway; buried in Bergen, Norway; dau. of Alexander III (b. 1241), king of Scotland (r. 1249–1286), and Margaret, queen of Scots (1240–1275); m. Eirik the Priest-Hater also known as Eric II Magnusson (1268–1299), king of Norway (r. 1280–1299), Aug 31, 1281; children: Margaret, Maid of Norway (c. 1283–1290).

MARGARET OF NORWAY (c. 1283–1290). See Margaret, Maid of Norway.

MARGARET OF ORLEANS.
See Marguerite of Orleans (d. 1466).
See Margaret of Angoulême (1492–1549).

MARGARET OF OSTREVENT (c. 1376–1441). See Margaret of Burgundy.

MARGARET OF PARMA (1522–1586). Duchess of Parma. Name variations: Margaret of Austria; Margaret or Margherita de Medici; (Italian) Margherita de Parma; (German) Margarete von Österreich; (Spanish) Marguerite of Spain. Born sometime in 1522 in the Netherlands; died in 1586 in Italy; illeg. dau. of Charles V (1500–1558), Holy Roman emperor (also known as Charles I, king of Spain) and Johanna van der Gheenst; half-sister of Philip II, king of Spain, and Joanna of Austria (1535–1573); m. Alexander also known as Alessandro de Medici, in 1534 (died 1535); m. Ottavio Farnese, duke of Parma, in 1540; children: (2nd marriage) Alessandro Farnese (also known as Alexander). ❖ Illegitimate daughter of Charles V, who ruled the Netherlands as regent for 8 years, was educated in the Netherlands by 2 female regents: Margaret of Austria (1480–1530) and Mary of Hungary (1505–1558); lived in Italy after 1st marriage; appointed regent of the Netherlands by Philip II (1559); frugal in her habits, intelligent and good natured, was well liked, but Philip's indecisiveness severely undercut her ability to govern as effectively as possible; efforts to govern successfully were also thwarted by Philip's

intransigence over enforcing the heresy laws, since her policy was to follow public opinion, which was lenient towards heretics as long as they did not disturb the peace; when Philip sent the duke of Alva to establish a "new order" which would not tolerate any dissent, abdicated as regent (1567); returned to Netherlands for short regency (1580); died in Italy (1586). ❖ See also Women in World History.

MARGARET OF PARMA (b. 1612). Duchess of Parma. Name variations: Margherita of Parma; Margherita de Medici; Margaret de Medici; Margaret Farnese. Born in 1612; dau. of Cosimo II de Medici (1590–1620), grand duke of Tuscany (r. 1609–1620), and Maria Magdalena of Austria (1589–1631); m. Odoardo or Edward Farnese, duke of Parma (1612–1646, r. 1622–1646), in 1628.

MARGARET OF PARMA (1847–1893). Duchess of Madrid. Born Jan 1, 1847; died Jan 29, 1893; dau. of Louise of Bourbon-Berry (1819–1864) and Charles III, duke of Parma; m. Charles, duke of Madrid, on Feb 4, 1867; children: Blanche of Bourbon (1868–1949); Elvira of Bourbon (1871–1929); Beatrix of Bourbon (b. 1874, who m. Fabrizio, prince Massimo); Alicia of Bourbon (b. 1876, who m. Friedrich, prince of Schönburg-Waldenburg, and Lino del Prete).

MARGARET OF POMERANIA (d. 1282). Queen of Denmark. Name variations: Margaret of Pommerania. Died in Dec 1282; dau. of Sambor, duke of Pomerania; m. Christopher I (1219–1259), king of Denmark (r. 1252–1259), in 1248; children: Eric V (or VII) Clipping (b. around 1249), king of Denmark (r. 1259–1286); Valdemar also known as Waldemar; Niels; Matilda Christofsdottir (died c. 1300, who m. Albert III, margrave of Brandenburg); Margaret Christofsdottir (died c. 1306, who m. John II, count of Holstein). ❖ Following husband's death (1259), was regent for her son Eric V during his minority.

MARGARET OF PROVENCE (1221–1295). Queen of France. Name variations: Marguerite de Provence; Marguerite of Provence. Born in Provence in 1221 (some sources cite 1219); died in 1295 in France; dau. of Raymond Berengar IV (some sources cite V), count of Provence, and Beatrice of Savoy (d. 1268); sister of Eleanor of Provence (c. 1222–1291), Sancha of Provence (c. 1225–1261), and Beatrice of Provence (d. 1267, who m. Charles of Anjou, brother of Louis IX); m. Louis IX, also known as Saint Louis (1214–1270), king of France (r. 1226–1270), in May 1234; children: 11, including Philip III the Bold (b. 1245), king of France (r. 1270–1285); John, count of Nevers; Robert (1256–1317), count of Clermont; Isabella Capet (who m. Theobald of Navarre); Margaret Capet (d. 1271, who m. John of Brabant); Agnes Capet (1260–1327); Blanche of France (1253–1321, who m. Ferdinand of Castile). ❖ When husband left Paris to lead the Seventh Crusade (c. 1244), accompanied him at his request; also accompanied him on the Eighth Crusade (1270), where he died in battle at Tunis. ❖ See also Women in World History.

MARGARET OF SAVOY (d. 1483). Countess of St. Paul. Name variations: Marguerite de Savoie. Died Mar 9, 1483; dau. of Anne of Lusignan and Louis I, duke of Savoy (r. 1440–1465); m. Peter also known as Pierre II, count of St. Paul (r. 1476–1482); children: Marie of Luxemburg (d. 1546).

MARGARET OF SAVOY (1523–1574). Duchess of Savoy. Name variations: Margaret of France; Marguerite de France or Marguerite de Savoie; Marguerite of Berry, duchess of Berry. Reigned from 1550 to 1574. Born in 1523; dau. of Francis I, king of France (r. 1515–1547), and Claude de France (1499–1524); sister of Henry II, king of France (r. 1547–1559); sister-in-law of Catherine de Medici; m. Emmanuel Philibert (1528–1580), 10th duke of Savoy (r. 1553–1580), June 1559; children: Charles Emmanuel I (1562–1630), duke of Savoy (r. 1580–1630). ❖ Called the Minerva of France, wrote verses and was a patron of the young school of poets led by Pierre de Ronsard; cherished by brother Henry II, king of France, was offered the Piedmont as her dowry in marriage. ❖ See also Women in World History.

MARGARET OF SAVOY (fl. 1609–1612). Duchess of Mantua. Name variations: Margherita of Savoy. Fl. between 1609 and 1612; dau. of Catherine of Spain (1567–1597) and Charles Emmanuel I the Great, duke of Savoy (r. 1580–1630); sister of Victor Amadeus I (1587–1637), duke of Savoy (r. 1630–1637); m. Francis also known as Francesco Gonzaga (1586–1612), 5th duke of Mantua (r. 1612); children: Maria Gonzaga (1609–1660, who m. Carlo, count of Rethel); Louis also known as Ludovico (1611–1612); Maria Margherita Gonzaga (b. 1612).

MARGARET OF SAVOY (1851–1926). Queen of Italy. Name variations: Margherita of Savoy; Margherita de Savoia. Born in 1851; died in 1926;

dau. of Elizabeth of Saxony (1830–1912) and Ferdinand of Savoy (1822–1855), duke of Genoa; m. her cousin Humbert I or Umberto I (1844–1900, son of Marie Adelaide of Austria and Victor Emmanuel II), king of Italy (r. 1878–1900); children: Victor Emmanuel III (1869–1947), king of Italy (r. 1900–1946, abdicated). ❖ A proud woman, entered into a dynastic and loveless marriage with cousin Umberto I who ascended the throne as the 2nd king of Italy in 1878; husband was assassinated at Monza by an anarchist (1900); a fervent nationalist and religious to the point of bigotry, lived long enough to back Benito Mussolini in his rise to power. ❖ See also *Women in World History.*

MARGARET OF SAXONY (c. 1416–1486). Duchess and electress of Saxony. Name variations: Margarethe. Born in 1416 or 1417 in Wiener Neustadt; died Feb 12, 1486, in Altenburg; dau. of Cimburca of Masovia (c. 1396–1429) and Ernest (d. 1424, son of Leopold III of Austria); m. Frederick II the Gentle (1412–1464), duke and elector of Saxony; children: Anne of Saxony (1437–1512); Ernest of Saxony (b. 1441), elector of Saxony; Albert the Bold (b. 1443), duke of Saxony.

MARGARET OF SAXONY (1449–1501). Electress of Brandenburg. Born in 1449; died July 13, 1501; dau. of William III the Brave of Saxony (b. 1425), duke of Luxemburg, and Anne of Austria (1432–1462); m. John Cicero (1455–1499), elector of Brandenburg (r. 1486–1499), Aug 25, 1476; children: Joachim I Nestor (1484–1535), elector of Brandenburg (r. 1499–1535); Anna of Brandenburg (1487–1514); Ursula of Brandenburg (1488–1510).

MARGARET OF SAXONY (1469–1528). Duchess of Brunswick. Name variations: Margaret of Saxony Wettin. Born Aug 4, 1469; died Dec 7, 1528; dau. of Ernest of Saxony (b. 1441), elector of Saxony; sister of Christina of Saxony (1461–1521), queen of Norway and queen of Denmark; m. Henry (1466–1532), duke of Brunswick (r. 1471–1532), Feb 27, 1487; children: Otto III of Luneburg; Ernest the Pious (b. 1497), duke of Luneburg; Francis, duke of Brunswick.

MARGARET OF SAXONY (1840–1858). Princess of Saxony. Born May 24, 1840; died Sept 15, 1858; dau. of Amalia of Bavaria (1801–1877) and Johann also known as John (1801–1873), king of Saxony (r. 1854–1873); became 1st wife of Karl Ludwig also known as Charles Louis (1833–1896), archduke of Austria, Nov 4, 1856. Charles Louis' 2nd wife was Maria Annunziata (1843–1871); his 3rd was Maria Theresa of Portugal.

MARGARET OF SCOTLAND.
See Margaret, St. (c. 1046–1093)
See Margaret of Norway (1261–1283).

MARGARET OF SCOTLAND (1424–1445). Scottish poet. Name variations: Margaret Stuart or Stewart; Marguerite Stuart; Marguerite d'Écosse. Born in Scotland, Dec 25, 1424; died in Chalons, Champagne, France, Aug 16, 1445; eldest dau. of James I, king of Scotland (r. 1406–1437), and Joan Beaufort (c. 1410–1445); m. Louis XI (1423–1483), king of France (r. 1461–1483), June 24, 1436; no children. ❖ It is said that her marriage to Louis was so wretched that when she died at 22, her parting words were: "Oh! fie on life! Speak to me no more of it."

MARGARET OF SPAIN (1651–1673). *See Margaret Theresa of Spain.*

MARGARET OF SWEDEN (1882–1920). *See Margaret of Connaught.*

MARGARET OF THOUARS (r. 1365–1377). *See Marguerite de Thouars.*

MARGARET OF TURENNE (fl. 12th c.). Countess of Angoulême. Married Aimar IV, count of Limoges; m. Guillaume also known as William IV Taillefer, count of Angoulême (r. 1140–1178); children: (2nd m.) Vulgrin III Taillefer, count of Angoulême (1178–1181); William; Ademar.

MARGARET OF VALOIS.
See Margaret of Anjou (c. 1272–1299).
See Margaret of Angoulême (1492–1549).

MARGARET OF VALOIS (1553–1615). Queen of Navarre. Name variations: Marguerite of Valois or Marguerite de Valois; Marguerite d'Angoulême; Margaret of Angoulême or Angouleme; Margaret or Marguerite of Anjou; Margaret of France; Margaret of Navarre; Queen Margot. Born May 14, 1553, at St. Germain-en-Laye; died of pneumonia, Mar 27, 1615, in Paris; 3rd dau. of Henry II, king of France (r. 1547–1559), and Catherine de Medici (1519–1589); sister of Francis II (r. 1559–1560), Charles IX (r. 1560–1574), Henry III (r. 1574–1589), all kings of France, and Elizabeth of Valois (1545–1568), queen of Spain; m. Henry of Navarre (future Henry IV, king

of France, r. 1589–1610), Aug 18, 1572 (div., Dec 1599); no children. ❖ French princess who was the sister of 3 French kings and the 1st wife of Henry of Navarre, the future King Henry IV; educated at French royal court; at 19, became queen of Navarre (1572) in a marriage intended to end more than 10 years of religious civil wars in France but instead sparked the St. Bartholomew's Day Massacre (she was Catholic, he was a leader of the Huguenots); estranged from Henry for most of her marriage; one of the most accomplished and beautiful women in France, held court with poets, musicians, and philosophers whom she dazzled and charmed; was forced into a 19-year exile by her brother, King Henry III (1586–1605); returned to Paris (1605). ❖ See also Charlotte Haldane, *Queen of Hearts: Marguerite of Valois ("La Reine Margot") 1553–1615* (Constable, 1968); *La Reine Margot* (film), starring Jeanne Moreau (1954); *Queen Margot* (film), starring Isabelle Adjani (1994); and *Women in World History.*

MARGARET OF VENDÔME (fl. 16th c.). Duchess of Nevers. Name variations: Margaret of Vendome. Married Francis II, duke of Nevers (d. 1595); children: Jacques, duke of Nevers (r. 1562–1563); Henrietta of Cleves, duchess of Nevers (r. 1564–1601); and 2 other daughters.

MARGARET OF WESTMINSTER (c. 1282–1318). *See Margaret of France.*

MARGARET OF YORK (1446–1503). Duchess of Burgundy and religious patron. Name variations: Margaret Plantagenet; Margaret of Burgundy; Margeret. Born into House of York, May 3, 1446, at Fotheringhay Castle in Yorkshire, England; died Nov 28, 1503, in Malines, Flanders; interred at Church of the Cordeliers, Malines; dau. of Richard Neville (b. 1411), duke of York, and Cecily Neville (1415–1495); sister of Edward IV (1442–1483), king of England (r. 1461–1470, 1471–1483), George (d. 1478), duke of Clarence, Richard III (1452–1485), king of England (r. 1483–1485), Edmund (d. 1460), earl of Rutland, Edward (d. 1471), prince of Wales, Elizabeth de la Pole (1444–1503), wife of John de la Pole, duke of Suffolk); became 3rd wife of Charles the Bold (1433–1477), duke of Burgundy (r. 1467–1477), July 3, 1468; no children. ❖ Well educated and pious, is primarily remembered as a patron of the church, especially the Order of Poor Clares; gave generously of her substantial wealth to support and establish religious institutions; was also an avid book collector. ❖ See also Christine Weightman, *Margeret of York, Duchess of Burgundy 1446–1503* (St. Martin, 1989); and *Women in World History.*

MARGARET OF YPRES (fl. 1322). Surgeon of Paris. Fl. in 1322 in Paris. ❖ Built a successful practice using her empirical knowledge and common-sense methods; caught in the ban on unlicensed physicians issued by the faculty of University of Paris (1322), was arrested for practicing without a degree but not held for long. ❖ See also *Women in World History.*

MARGARET ROSE (1930–2002). English royal princess. Name variations: Princess Margaret Rose; Margaret Windsor; Margaret Armstrong-Jones; countess of Snowdon. Born Aug 21, 1930, in Glamis Castle, Tayside, her mother's ancestral home in Scotland; died Feb 9, 2002; 2nd dau. of Albert Frederick Arthur George, 13th duke of York, later known as George VI, king of England (r. 1936–1952), and Elizabeth Bowes-Lyon (b. 1900); sister of Elizabeth II, queen of England (r. 1952—); educated privately by governesses and at a small school at Windsor Castle; m. Anthony Armstrong-Jones, earl of Snowdon (photographer), May 6, 1960 (div. 1978); children: David Armstrong-Jones (b. Nov 3, 1961), Viscount Linley; Sarah Armstrong-Jones (b. May 1, 1964). ❖ At 21, fell in love with father's equerry, Group Captain Peter Townsend, a divorced man with whom marriage was out of the question; was forced to give him up; marriage in 1960 ended in a bitter divorce (1978), the 1st in the royal family since Henry VIII legally parted from Anne of Cleves. ❖ See also Anne Edwards, *Royal Sisters* (Morrow, 1990); and *Women in World History.*

MARGARET SAXE-COBURG (1882–1920). *See Margaret of Connaught.*

MARGARET SOPHIE (1870–1902). Duchess of Wurttemberg. Name variations: Margarethe Sophie. Born May 13, 1870, in Artstettn, Lower Austria; died Aug 24, 1902, in Gmunden, Lower Austria; dau. of Maria Annunziata (1843–1871) and Karl Ludwig also known as Charles Louis (1833–1896), archduke of Austria; sister of Franz Ferdinand (who was assassinated in 1914).

MARGARET THE DRAGON SLAYER (c. 255–c. 275). *See Margaret of Antioch.*

MARGARET THERESA OF SPAIN (1651–1673). Holy Roman empress. Name variations: Margaret of Spain; Maria Teresa or Maria Theresa of Spain; Margarita Teresa de España; Margareta Teresa; Infanta Margarita; Empress of Germany. Born July 12, 1651; died Mar 12, 1673; dau. of Philip IV (1605–1665), king of Spain (r. 1621–1665), and Maria Anna of Austria (c. 1634–1696); sister of Charles II, king of Spain (r. 1665–1700); half-sister of Maria Teresa of Spain (1638–1683); became 1st wife of Leopold I (1640–1705), Holy Roman emperor (r. 1658–1705), Dec 12, 1666; children: Maria Antonia (1669–1692); Ferdinand Wenzel (1667–1668); John Leopold (1670–1670). ❖ Was married to Leopold I to strengthen political and dynastic ties between the Spanish and Austrian Habsburgs. ❖ See also *Women in World History*.

MARGARET TUDOR (1489–1541). Queen of Scotland. Born Nov 28, 29, or 30, 1489, at the Palace of Westminster, England; died of "palsy" (probably a stroke) at Methven Castle, Perthshire, Scotland, Oct 18, 1541; buried in Carthusian Abbey of St. John, Perth, Scotland; eldest dau. of Henry VII, king of England (r. 1485–1509) and Elizabeth of York (1465–1503); sister of Henry VIII, king of England (r. 1509–1547) and Mary Tudor (1496–1533); grandmother of Mary Stuart, Queen of Scots (1542–1587); great-grandmother of James VI, king of Scotland (r. 1567–1625), who was king of England as James I (r. 1603–1625); m. James IV (1473–1513), king of Scotland (r. 1488–1513), by proxy at Richmond Castle, Surrey, England, Jan 25, 1502, and in person at Holyrood Abbey, Edinburgh, Scotland, Aug 8, 1503; m. Archibald Douglas, 6th earl of Angus, on August 6, 1514, at Kinnoul Church near Perth (div. 1525); m. Henry Stewart, 1st Lord Methven, Mar 3, 1528; children (1st m.) 6, of whom only 2, James V (1512–1542), king of Scotland (r. 1513–1542) and Alexander (1514–1515), duke of Ross, lived for more than one year; (2nd m.) Margaret Douglas (1515–1578), afterwards countess of Lennox. ❖ While living in constant fear for her life and the lives of her children, strived within the complicated diplomatic and power struggles of Renaissance Europe to keep peace between Scotland and England; was crowned queen of Scotland (Aug 8, 1503); on James IV's death on Flodden Field (1513), became regent of Scotland and guardian of the baby James V; after a secret marriage to earl of Angus, was forced (1515) to give up both the regency and the young king to John Stewart, duke of Albany (1515); escaped to England and gave birth to her daughter at Harbottle Castle in Northumberland (1515); held with little respect by either side, was used and betrayed as it suited their best interests; nevertheless continued to fight to keep her son's throne secure, changing sides as seemed expedient; after lengthy, frustrating negotiations, divorced Angus (Aug 1525) and married Henry Stewart and with him became James V's chief adviser; tried unsuccessfully to divorce Henry Stewart; became alienated from her son as he sank into a depression following the deaths of his sons and heirs; interceded with Henry VIII for her daughter, Margaret Douglas (1536), after her daughter's ill-advised marriage with Lord Thomas Howard; died alone and unmourned at age 52. ❖ See also Patricia H. Buchanan, *Margaret Tudor, Queen of Scots* (Scottish Academic Press, 1985); and *Women in World History*.

MARGARET VALDEMARSDATTER or VALDEMARSDOTTIR (1353–1412). *See Margaret I of Denmark.*

MARGARET VALOIS (c. 1376–1441). *See Margaret of Burgundy.*

MARGARET WAKE OF LIDDELL (c. 1299–1349). Duchess of Kent. Name variations: Baroness Wake of Lydell. Born Margaret Wake c. 1299; died Sept 29, 1349; dau. of John Wake, 1st baron Wake of Liddell; m. Edmund of Woodstock (1307–1330), 1st earl of Kent (son of Edward I Longshanks, king of England), in 1325; children: Margaret of Kent (1327–before 1352); Edmund (c. 1327–1331 or 1333), 2nd earl of Kent; Joan of Kent (1328–1385); John (1330–1352), 3rd earl of Kent.

MARGARET WALDEMARSDATTER or WALDEMARSDOTTIR (1353–1412). *See Margaret I of Denmark.*

MARGARETA. *Variant of Margaret.*

MARGARETA LEIJONHUFVUD (1514–1551). Queen of Sweden. Name variations: Lejonhufvud. Born Jan 1, 1514; died Aug 26, 1551; became 2nd wife of Gustavus I Adolphus Vasa (1496–1560), king of Sweden (r. 1523–1560), in 1536; children: John III (1537–1592), king of Sweden (r. 1568–1592), who m. Catherine Jagello, sister of Sigismund II, king of Poland); Katharina (1539–1610, who m. Edward, count of East Friesland); Cecilie (1540–1627, who m. Christopher, margrave of Baden); Magnus, duke of East Gotland (b. 1542); Karl (b. 1544); Anna Marie (1545–1610, who m. George John of Veldenz); Sten (b. 1546); Sophie (1547–1611, who m. Magnus, duke of Saxe-Luneburg);

Elizabeth (1549–1597, who m. Christopher of Mecklenburg); Charles IX (1550–1611), king of Sweden (r. 1604–1611). Gustavus I's 1st wife was Katarina of Saxe-Lüneburg; his 3rd was Katarina Stenbock.

MARGARETE. *Variant of Margaret.*

MARGARETE OF PRUSSIA (1872–1954). *See Margaret Beatrice.*

MARGARETE OF STYRIA (c. 1577–1611). *See Margaret of Austria.*

MARGARETE VON KARNTEN (1318–1369). *See Margaret Maultasch.*

MARGARETHA. *Variant of Margaret.*

MARGARETHA OF SWEDEN (1899–1977). Swedish royal. Name variations: Margaretha Bernadotte. Born Margaretha Sophie Louise on June 25, 1899; died in 1977; dau. of Ingeborg of Denmark (1878–1958) and Charles of Sweden; sister of Martha of Sweden (1901–1954, who m. the future Olav V, king of Norway) and Astrid of Sweden (1905–1935); m. Axel Christian George Oldenburg, May 22, 1919; children: George (b. 1920); Flemming (b. 1922).

MARGARETHE. *Variant of Margaret.*

MARGARETHE (1370–c. 1400). Margravine of Moravia. Born c. 1370; died after 1400; dau. of Virida Visconti (1350–1414) and Leopold of Habsburg also known as Leopold III (1351–1386), archduke of Austria, Styria, and Carniola, co-emperor of Austria (r. 1365–1379).

MARGARETHE OF VÄSTERGÖTLAND (fl. 1100). Danish royal. Name variations: Margaret of Vastergotland. Fl. around 1100; 1st wife of Niels, king of Denmark (r. 1104–1134). Niels' 2nd wife was Ulfhild.

MARGARETS, The Three. *See Margaret of Angoulême (1492–1549); Margaret of Savoy (1523–1574); and Margaret of Valois (1553–1615).*

MARGARIT, Elena (1936—). *See Niculescu-Margarit, Elena.*

MARGARITA. *Variant of Margaret and Marguerite.*

MARGARITA MARIA (1939—). Spanish crown princess. Born Mar 6, 1939, in Anglo-American Hospital, Rome, Italy; dau. of Maria de las Mercedes (1910–2000) and John or Juan (1913–1993), count of Barcelona; sister of Juan Carlos I (1938—), king of Spain (r. 1975—); m. Carlos Zurita y Delgado, on Oct 12, 1972; children: Alfonso Juan (b. 1973); Maria Sofia Zurita y de Borbón (b. 1975).

MARGE (1905–1993). *See Buell, Marjorie Henderson.*

MARGERET. *Variant of Margaret.*

MARGHERITA. *Italian variant of Margaret.*

MARGHERITA, La (c. 1683–1746). *See Épine, Margherita de l'.*

MARGHERITA OF ITALY (1851–1926). *See Margaret of Savoy.*

MARGHERITA OF PARMA (b. 1612). *See Margaret of Parma.*

MARGHERITA OF SAVOY (1851–1926). *See Margaret of Savoy.*

MARGHERITA OF TARANTO (fl. 1300s). *See Balliol, Margaret.*

MARGHERITA PALEOLOGO (1510–1566). *See Gonzaga, Margherita.*

MARGHIERI, Clotilde (1897–1981). Italian novelist and essayist. Name variations: Clotilde Betocchi Marghieri. Born 1897 in Naples, Italy; died 1981; attended University of Florence. ❖ Achieved popular and critical success with such works as *Vita in villa* (1963), *Le educande di Poggio Gherardo* (1963), *Il segno sul braccio* (1970), which were collected as *Trilogia* (1982); wrote the bestselling novel *Amati enigmi* (1974), which won the Viareggio Prize; also contributed to *Il Mondo* and *Corriere della Sera* and won several other prizes. ❖ See also *A Matter of Passion: Letters of Bernard Berenson and Clotilde Marghieri* (U. of California Press, 1989).

MARGO (1918–1985). Mexican-American actress. Born Marie Marguerita Guadalupe Teresa Estela Bolado Castilla y O'Donnell in Mexico City, Mexico, May 10, 1918; died from a brain tumor, July 17, 1985, at home in Pacific Palisades, CA; m. Francis Lederer (actor), 1937 (div. 1940); m. Eddie Albert (actor), Dec 6, 1945; children: (2nd m.) Edward Albert (actor) and 1 adopted daughter; became US citizen (1942). ❖ At 9, was dancing professionally; by 12, was performing with Xavier Cugat's band at Waldorf Astoria; made film debut starring in *Crime Without Passion* (1934); starred on Broadway and in the film of *Winterset* (1935, 1936), now considered one of her best roles; other films include *Lost Horizon* (1937), *Miracle on Main Street* (1940), *The Leopard Man* (1943), *Viva Zapata* (1952), *I'll Cry Tomorrow* (1955) and *Who's*

Got the Action? (1962); on stage, also appeared in *Masque of Kings* (1937) and *A Bell for Adano* (1944). ❖ See also *Women in World History.*

MARGOLIN, Janet (1943–1993). American actress. Born July 25, 1943, in New York, NY; died Dec 17, 1993, in Los Angeles, CA; m. Jerry Brandt, 1968 (div. 1970); m. Ted Wass (actor). ❖ Made Broadway debut in *Daughter of Silence* (1961); made film debut as star of *David and Lisa* (1962); other films include *The Greatest Story Ever Told, Bus Riley's Back in Town, Nevada Smith, Enter Laughing, Take the Money and Run* and *Annie Hall.*

MARGOT. *Variant of Margaret or Marguerite.*

MARGOT (1553–1615). *See Margaret of Valois.*

MARGRETE. *Danish variant of Margaret.*

MARGRETHE I OF DENMARK (1353–1412). *See Margaret I of Denmark.*

MARGRETHE II (1940—). Queen of Denmark. Name variations: Margaret II or Margrete II; Daisy. Born Margrethe Alexandrine Thorhildur Ingrid, April 16, 1940, in Copenhagen, Denmark; dau. of Frederick IX, king of Denmark (r. 1947–1972), and Queen Ingrid of Sweden (b. 1910); sister of Princess Benedikte (b. 1944) and Princess Anne-Marie Oldenburg (b. 1946), ex-queen of Greece; graduated from Danish and English primary and secondary schools, attended the universities of Copenhagen and Aarhus, Cambridge University, and Sorbonne; m. Count Henri or Henrik of Laborde De Montpezat, in 1967; children: Crown Prince Frederik (b. 1968) and Prince Joachim (b. 1969). ❖ Popular queen of the constitutional monarchy of Denmark who has reigned since 1972, works closely with her government and has numerous social and diplomatic engagements in Denmark as well as abroad; is considered one of the best-educated monarchs of Europe. ❖ See also *Women in World History.*

MARGRETHE OF DENMARK (1895–1992). *See Oldenburg, Margaret.*

MARGRIET FRANCISCA (1943—). Dutch princess. Name variations: Margaret. Born Jan 19, 1943; dau. of Juliana (b. 1909), queen of the Netherlands (r. 1948–1980), and Prince Bernard of Lippe-Biesterfeld; sister of Queen Beatrix of the Netherlands (b. 1938) and Irene Emma (b. 1939); m. Pieter von Vollenhoven, in 1967.

MARGUERITE. *Variant of Margaret.*

MARGUERITE (r. 1218–1230). Countess of Blois. Eldest dau. of Thibaut or Theobald V, count of Blois and Chartres (r. 1152–1218), and possibly Alice, countess of Blois (1150–c. 1197); m. Gauthier d'Avesnes. ❖ Following father's death (1218), ruled Blois with 3rd husband, Gauthier d'Avesnes; died (1230) and was succeeded by Marie de Chatillon.

MARGUERITE (1905–2004). *See Villameur, Lise.*

MARGUERITE D'ANGOULÊME. *See Margaret of Angoulême (1492–1549).*

MARGUERITE D'AUTRICHE (1480–1530). *See Margaret of Austria.*

MARGUERITE DE BOURGOGNE (1250–1308). Queen of Naples and Sicily and countess of Tonnerre. Name variations: Margaret of Burgundy, countess of Tonnere. Born in 1250; died Sept 4, 1308, in Tonnerre; dau. of Mahaut II de Dampierre (1234–1266) and Eudes (1230–1266), count of Nevers; m. Charles I of Anjou, king of Naples (r. 1268–1285) and Sicily (r. 1266–1282), on Nov 18, 1268. ❖ Charles I's 1st wife was Beatrice of Provence (d. 1267).

MARGUERITE DE BRABANT (c. 1192–?). Countess of Guelders. Name variations: Margaretha. Born c. 1192; dau. of Henry I (1165–1235), duke of Brabant, and Maude of Alsace (1163–c. 1210); m. Gerhard III of Gelre or Geldeland, ruler of the Netherlands (d. 1229); children: Otto II, called Otto the Lame (b. around 1220). ❖ On death of Gerhard III, ruler of the Netherlands, was guardian for her ruling son Otto II the Lame (1229–1234).

MARGUERITE DE BRESSIEUX (d. 1450). French noble and warrior. Died 1450 in France. ❖ Along with several other noblewomen, was raped by the soldiers of Louis de Chalons when they invaded her father's castle; joined in the battle against Louis with the other women; was mortally wounded and died soon after; celebrated for her bravery. ❖ See also *Women in World History.*

MARGUERITE D'ÉCOSSE (1424–1445). *See Margaret of Scotland.*

MARGUERITE DE DUYN (d. 1310). *See Oignt, Marguerite d'.*

MARGUERITE DE FLANDRE (1350–1405). *See Margaret of Flanders.*

MARGUERITE DE FOIX (d. 1258). *See Margaret de Foix.*

MARGUERITE DE FOIX (fl. 1456–1477). Duchess of Brittany. Name variations: Margaret of Foix; Marguerite of Foix; Margaret de Dreux; Margaret of Dreux. Fl. between 1456 and 1477; dau. of Francis I (b 1414), duke of Brittany, and Isabel Stewart (d. 1494); m. François or Francis II, duke of Brittany (r. 1458–1488); children: Anne of Brittany (c. 1477–1514); and possibly one other daughter.

MARGUERITE DE L'AIGLE (d. 1141). Queen of Navarre. Died May 25, 1141; dau. of Gilbert de l'Aigle and Julienne du Perche; m. Garcia IV the Restorer, king of Navarre (r. 1134–1150); children: Sancho VI (d. 1194), king of Navarre (r. 1150–1194); Blanche of Navarre (d. 1158, who m. Sancho III, king of Castile); Margaret of Navarre (fl. 1154–1172). Garcia's 2nd wife was Urraca of Castile (d. 1179).

MARGUERITE DE NAVARRE (1492–1549). *See Margaret of Angoulême.*

MARGUERITE DE PROVENCE (1221–1295). *See Margaret of Provence.*

MARGUERITE DE SAVOIE (1523–1574). *Margaret of Savoy.*

MARGUERITE DE THOUARS (r. 1365–1377). Joint ruler of Dreux. Name variations: Margaret of Thouars. Reigned (1365–77); dau. of Simon de Thouars, ruler of Dreux (r. 1355–1365); sister of Peronelle de Thouars. ❖ Was co-parcener of Dreux with brother Peronelle de Thouars, until they sold the fief to Charles VI, king of France (1377–78).

MARGUERITE D'OIGNT (d. 1310). *See Oignt, Marguerite d'.*

MARGUERITE LOUISE OF ORLEANS (c. 1645–1721). Grand duchess of Tuscany. Name variations: Marguerite Louise de Medici. Born c. 1645; died in Paris, France, in Sept 1721; dau. of Gaston d'Orleans (1608–1660), duke of Orléans (brother of Louis XIII), and Marguerite of Lorraine (fl. 1632); 1st cousin of Louis XIV, king of France; stepsister of Anne Marie Louise d'Orléans, Duchesse de Montpensier (1627–1693); m. Cosimo III de Medici (1642–1723), grand duke of Tuscany (r. 1670–1723), in April 1661; children: Ferdinand (1663–1713); Anna Maria Luisa de Medici (1667–1743, who m. John William of the Palatinate); Giovan or Gian Gastone (1671–1737). ❖ Against her will and loving another, married Cosimo de Medici (1661); began to hate all things Italian; balked at learning the language and begged the French king to let her enter a convent rather than remain in Tuscany; after 13 years in Tuscany, returned to France and settled at the convent of Montmartre, near Paris; became a popular member of the French court; a brilliant conversationalist with a biting wit, amused Louis XIV with her ridicule of things Tuscan. ❖ See also *Women in World History.*

MARGUERITE OF BOURGOGNE (1290–1315). *See Margaret of Burgundy.*

MARGUERITE OF FLANDERS.
See Margaret of Flanders (1202–1280).
See Margaret of Flanders (1350–1405).

MARGUERITE OF FOIX (fl. 1456–1477). *See Marguerite de Foix.*

MARGUERITE OF FRANCE.
See Margaret of France (c. 1282–1318).
See Margaret of Angoulême (1492–1549).

MARGUERITE OF HAINAULT (d. 1310). *See Porete, Marguerite.*

MARGUERITE OF LORRAINE (c. 1561–?). Duchess of Joyeuse. Name variations: Margaret of Lorraine; Margaret of Vaudemont-Lorraine; Madame de Joyeuse. Born c. 1561; dau. of Nicolas of Lorraine, count of Vaudemont, and Marguerite d'Egmont; sister of Louise of Lorraine (1554–1601), queen of France, and Philippe-Emmanuel, duc de Mercoeur; m. Anne, duc de Joyeuse (governor of Normandy), in 1581; married M. de Luxembourg.

MARGUERITE OF LORRAINE (fl. 1632). Duchess of Orléans. Name variations: Margaret of Lorraine. Fl. in 1632; sister of Charles IV, duke of Lorraine (r. 1624–1675, sometimes referred to as Charles III); became 2nd wife of Gaston d'Orleans (1608–1660), duke of Orléans (brother of Louis XIII, king of France), in Jan 1632; children: Marguerite Louise of Orleans (c. 1645–1721); Françoise d'Orleans (fl. 1650); stepmother of Anne Marie Louise d'Orléans, Duchesse de Montpensier (1627–1693). ❖ Gaston's 1st wife was Marie de Bourbon (1606–1627).

MARGUERITE OF NAVARRE (1492–1549). *See Margaret of Angoulême.*

MARGUERITE OF ORLEANS (d. 1466). Countess of Étampes. Name variations: Margaret of Orleans or Margaret of Orléans; Marguerite de Orléans; countess of Etampes or Estampes or d'Etampes. Died in 1466; dau. of Valentina Visconti (1366–1408) and Louis (1372–1407), duke of Orléans; m. Richard of Brittany also known as Richard Montfort, count of Etampes or d'Etampes (d. 1438); sister-in-law of Joanna of Navarre (c. 1370–1437); children: Francis II, duke of Brittany (r. 1458–1488); Catherine of Brittany (1428–c. 1476).

MARGUERITE PORETE (d. 1310). See Porete, Marguerite.

MARGUERITES, Les Trois. See Margaret of Angoulême (1492–1549); Margaret of Savoy (1523–1574); and Margaret of Valois (1553–1615).

MARGULIS, Lynn (1938—). American microbiologist and geneticist. Name variations: Lynn Sagan. Born Lynn Alexander, Mar 5, 1938, in Chicago, IL; dau. of Morris and Leona Alexander; University of Chicago, BA, c. 1957; University of Madison, MA in zoology and genetics, 1960; University of California, Berkeley, PhD in evolution of cells, 1965; m. Carl Sagan (physicist), 1957 (div. c. 1966); m. Thomas N. ("Nick") Margulis (crystallographer), 1967 (div. 1980); children: (1st m.) Dorion and Jeremy Sagan; (2nd m.) Zachary and Jennifer Margulis. ❖ Creative and prolific biologist, researcher, and writer, began studying at University of Chicago at age 15; supported "serial endosymbiosis theory," which argued that simple microorganisms carried genetic information; published research in *Journal of Theoretical Biology* (1966), which expanded to a book, *Origin of Eukaryotic Cells* (1970), later republished as *Symbiosis in Cell Evolution* (c. 1981); was professor at Boston University (1977); elected to National Academy of Science (1983); appointed Distinguished University Professor (1988) at University of Massachusetts, Amherst; supported James E. Lovelock's Gaia theory of Earth as single living organism.

MARIA. *Variant of Marie and Mary.*

MARIA (fl. 700s). Byzantine empress. Fl. in the 700s; m. Leo III the Iconoclast, Byzantine emperor (r. 717–741); children: Constantine V Kopronymus, Byzantine emperor (r. 741–775); Anna (who m. Artabasdus).

MARIA (fl. 995–1025). Dogaressa of Venice. Name variations: Maria Arpad; Maria of Hungary. Fl. between 995 and 1025; dau. of Geza (d. 997), prince of Hungary (r. 970–997), and Sarolta (fl. 900s); sister of Judith of Hungary and King Stephen I of Hungary (d. 1038); m. Otto Orseolo, doge of Venice; children: Peter (d. 1046), king of Hungary (r. 1038–1041, 1041–1046).

MARIA (fl. 1200s). Byzantine princess. Name variations: Maria Lascaris. Fl. in the 1200s; dau. of Helen Asen of Bulgaria and Theodore II Lascaris, emperor of Nicaea (r. 1254–1258); m. Nicephorus I of Epirus (d. 1296). Nicephorus was also m. to Anna Paleologina-Cantacuzene.

MARIA, Dowager Countess of Waldegrave (1736–1807). See Walpole, Maria.

MARIA, Mother (1891–1945). See Skobtsova, Maria.

MARIA I OF BRAGANZA (1734–1816). Queen of Portugal. Name variations: María I Braganza; María I of Braganza; María Francisca. Born María Francisca Isabel Josefa Antonia Gertrudes Rita Joana, Dec 17, 1734, in Lisbon, Portugal; died in Rio de Janeiro, Brazil, Mar 20, 1816; interred at Basilica of Estrela, Lisbon; dau. of José I also known as Joseph I Emanuel (1714–1777), king of Portugal (r. 1750–1777), and Maria Ana Victoria (1718–1781); m. her uncle, Pedro or Peter III (1717–1786), king of Portugal (r. 1777–1786), on June 6, 1760; children: José or Joseph (August 21, 1761–1788), prince of Beira; John de Paula (1763–1763); João or John VI (b. May 13, 1767), king of Portugal (r. 1816–1826); Mariana Victoria (1768–1788); Maria Clementina (1774–1776); Maria Isabel (1776–1777). Heir and successor: John VI (João VI). ❖ First queen to rule Portugal, who ended the despotic regime of the Marquis of Pombal, her father's chief minister, and reigned during a period of relative peace and prosperity before succumbing to mental illness; on death of father, became queen (Feb 24, 1777); let Pombral retire to his estate; moderate politically, guided a far-reaching reform of Portuguese monastic houses, fostered road- and canal-building, sought greater independence from Great Britain and a rapprochement with Spain, steered a neutral course during England's war with its American colonies, transformed University of Coimbra library into a public institution and ordered that the faculty be drawn from all disciplines rather than only from theology, ordered a review of Portuguese laws which had not been codified for 2 centuries, created the Royal Academy of Sciences, 18 schools for girls in Lisbon, and founded a

house for abandoned children; husband died (1786); son, Crown Prince Joseph, died (1788); daughter Mariana Victoria died (1788); her mental illness forced Prince John to become regent (1792); distraught, struggled on, only to confront the French Revolution, which cost the head of more than one monarch; began suffering from acute depression and nightmares; declared incurably insane, and John, her only surviving child, reluctantly elevated to prince-regent (July 15, 1799); with French invasion of Portugal (1807), fled with Portuguese royal family and court to Brazil (1807–08); died in Brazil (1816). ❖ See also *Women in World History.*

MARIA II DA GLORIA (1819–1853). Queen of Portugal. Name variations: María II da Glória. Born April 4, 1819, in Rio de Janeiro, Brazil; died in Lisbon, Nov 15, 1853; eldest child of Peter IV, king of Portugal (r. 1826), also known as Pedro I, emperor of Brazil (r. 1822–1831), and the Archduchess Leopoldina of Austria (1797–1826); m. Prince August of Leuchtenburg also known as Auguste Beauharnais (1810–1835), Jan 28, 1835 (died 2 months later); m. Ferdinand of Saxe-Coburg-Gotha (1816–1885), also known as Ferdinand II of Portugal, duke of Saxony, April 9, 1836; children: Pedro de Alcântara (1837–1861), later known as Pedro V or Peter V, king of Portugal (r. 1853–1861); Luis Filipe (1838–1889), later known as Luís I or Luis I, king of Portugal (r. 1861–1889); João or John (1842–1861), duke of Beja; Maria Anna of Portugal (1843–1884); Antonia of Portugal (1845–1913); Fernando or Ferdinand (1846–1861), duke of Coimbra; Augusto or August (1847–1889); plus Maria (1840–1840), Leopoldo (1849–1849), Maria (1851–1851), and Eugénio (1853–1853), who died at birth. ❖ Ruled as a symbol of constitutional monarchy during an era of intense strife between Portuguese conservatives and liberals; father began rule as Emperor Pedro I in Brazil (1822); mother died (1826); with death of John VI (1826), father was acclaimed king of Portugal but abdicated in her favor; at 9, was sent to Europe, but father's brother Michael was acclaimed king (1828); returned to Brazil (1829); father abdicated as Brazilian emperor (1831); returned to France with father who began to wage war with Michael (1831); when Michael was finally defeated and forced into permanent exile, arrived in Lisbon (1833); declared of age to rule (1834); father died (1834), leaving her a nation devastated by intermittent warfare since 1807 and a government in financial crisis; a political moderate committed to constitutional rule, faced repeated controversy and crisis from both the right and left; during September Revolution (1836), took refuge with family in Belém; gave approval to the new constitution, which was acceptable to both Septembrists and Chartists (1838); when Septembrists resurfaced, sought support within the military to impose a new ministry against the will of Parliament, effectively polarizing the nation and touching off a bloody civil war (Oct 6, 1846); saw the beginning of "Regeneration" (1851). ❖ See also *Women in World History.*

MARIA ALEXANDROVNA (1824–1880). *See Marie of Hesse-Darmstadt.*

MARIA AMALIA (1724–1730). Austrian princess. Born in 1724; died in 1730; younger sister of Maria Theresa of Austria (1717–1780); dau. of Charles VI (1685–1740), Holy Roman emperor (r. 1711–1740), and Elizabeth Christina of Brunswick-Wolfenbuttel.

MARIA AMALIA (1746–1804). Duchess of Parma. Name variations: Amelia; Maria Amalie. Born Feb 26, 1746, in Vienna; died June 18, 1804, in Prague; dau. of Maria Theresa of Austria (1717–1780) and Francis I, Holy Roman emperor (r. 1745–1765); niece of Maria Amalia (1724–1730); sister of Maria Carolina (1752–1814), Joseph II, emperor of Austria and Holy Roman emperor (r. 1765–1790), Maria Christina (1742–1798), Elizabeth of Austria (1743–1808), Leopold II, Holy Roman emperor (r. 1790–1792), and Marie Antoinette (1755–1793), queen of France; m. Ferdinand I (1751–1802), duke of Parma (r. 1765–1802), on July 19, 1769; children: Caroline of Parma (1770–1804); Louis I (1773–1803), duke of Parma (r. 1801–1803); Marie Antoinette (1774–1841, Ursuline abbess); Charlotte of Parma (1777–1813); Philipp of Parma (1783–1786); Louise (1787–1789).

MARIA AMALIA (1782–1866). Queen of France. Name variations: Amélie; Maria Amélie or Marie Amélie, or Marie-Amelia of Bourbon; Maria Amalia of Naples; Marie Amélie of Sicily; Marie Amelie de Bourbon. Born in Caserta, April 26, 1782; died Mar 24, 1866, in Esher, Surrey, England; dau. of Ferdinand I, king of the Two Sicilies (r. 1816–1825), also known as Ferdinand IV, king of Naples and Sicily (r. 1759–1806, 1815–1825), and Maria Carolina (1752–1814); m. Louis Philippe I (1773–1850), king of France (r. 1830–1848), Nov 25, 1809; children: Ferdinand (1810–1842); Louise d'Orleans

(1812–1850); Marie d'Orleans (1813–1839, who m. Alexander, duke of Württemberg); Louis, duke of Nemours (1814–1896); Fransisca (1816–1818); Clementine of Orleans (1817–1907, who m. Augustus, prince of Coburg); Francis, prince of Joinville (1818–1900); Charles (1820–1828); Henry, duke of Aumale (1822–1897); Antoine, duke of Montpensier (1824–1900). ❖ See also *Women in World History.*

MARIA AMALIA OF SAXONY (1724–1760). Queen of Spain. Name variations: Marie-Amelia Saski. Born Nov 24, 1724; died Sept 27, 1760; dau. of Frederick Augustus II (1696–1763), elector of Saxony (r. 1733–1763), also known as Augustus III, king of Poland (r. 1733–1763), and Marie Josepha (1699–1757); m. Carlos III also known as Charles III (1716–1788), king of Spain (r. 1759–1788), also known as Charles IV, king of Naples and Sicily (r. 1735–1759), June 19, 1738; children: Marie Elizabeth (1740–1742); Marie Josepha (1742–1742); Marie Elizabeth (1743–1749); Marie Josepha (1744–1801); Maria Louisa of Spain (1745–1792, who m. Leopold II, emperor of Austria); Philipp Anton (b. 1747); Charles IV (1748–1819), king of Spain (r. 1788–1808); Marie Therese (1749–1750); Ferdinand IV (1751–1825), king of Naples and Sicily (r. 1759–1806, 1815–1825), later known as Ferdinand I, king of the Two Sicilies (r. 1816–1825); Gabriel (b. 1752); Marie Anna (1754–1755); Anton (b. 1755); Franz Xaver (b. 1757). ❖ See also *Women in World History.*

MARIA ANA OF AUSTRIA (1683–1754). *See Maria Antonia of Austria.*

MARIA ANA VICTORIA (1718–1781). Queen and regent of Portugal. Name variations: Mariana Victoria or Vitória; Maria Ana Victoria of Spain; Marianna Victoria; Maria Anna of Spain; Marie-Anne Bourbon; Marie Anne of Spain. Regent of Portugal (1776–1777). Born Jan 31, 1718, in Madrid; died Jan 15, 1781, at Ajuda Palace, Lisbon; interred at Sao Francisco de Paula, Lisbon; dau. of Elizabeth Farnese (1692–1766) and Philip V, king of Spain (r. 1700–1724, 1725–1746); sister of Ferdinand VI and Louis I, kings of Spain; m. José Manuel also known as Joseph I Emanuel, king of Portugal (r. 1750–1777), on Jan 19, 1729; children: Maria I of Braganza (1734–1816); Maria Ana Francisca (1736–1813); Maria Francisca Dorotea (1739–1771); daughter (1741–1741, stillborn); daughter (1742–1742, stillborn); Maria Francisca Benedicta (1746–1829, who m. José Francisco Xavier, prince of Beira).

MARIA ANNA (1718–1744). Austrian princess. Born in 1718; died in 1744; younger sister of Maria Theresa of Austria (1717–1780); dau. of Charles VI (1685–1740), Holy Roman emperor (r. 1711–1740), and Elizabeth Christina of Brunswick-Wolfenbuttel.

MARIA ANNA OF AUSTRIA (c. 1634–1696). Queen and regent of Spain. Name variations: Maria of Austria; Marie-Anne of Austria; Mariana de Austria; Mariana of Austria; Mariana Teresea of Austria. Born Dec 24, 1634 or 1635; died May 16, 1696; dau. of Ferdinand III, king of Hungary and Bohemia, Holy Roman emperor (r. 1637–1657), and Maria Anna of Spain (1606–1646); became 2nd wife of Philip IV (1605–1665), king of Spain (r. 1621–1665), on Nov 8, 1649; children: Margaret Theresa of Spain (1651–1673); Charles II the Bewitched (1661–1700), king of Spain (r. 1665–1700). ❖ When husband died (1665), named regent for 4-year-old son Charles II, known as Charles the Bewitched; depended heavily upon counsel of Fernando Valenzuela and especially of her confessor, the German Jesuit Johann Eberhard Nithard, causing resentment among Spanish courtiers; gave up the regency when Charles turned 14 (1675). ❖ See also *Women in World History.*

MARIA ANNA OF BAVARIA (1574–1616). Queen of Bohemia and Hungary. Name variations: Mary; Mary Anne of Bavaria; Marie-Anne of Bavaria. Born Dec 12, 1574, in Munich; died Mar 8, 1616, in Graz; became 1st wife of Ferdinand II, king of Bohemia and Hungary (r. 1578–1637), Holy Roman emperor (r. 1619–1637), April 23, 1600; children: Maria Anna of Bavaria (1610–1665, who m. Maximilian, elector of Bavaria); Ferdinand III (1608–1657), king of Bohemia and Hungary, and Holy Roman emperor (r. 1637–1657); Cecilia Renata of Austria (1611–1644). ❖ Ferdinand II's 2nd wife was Eleonora I Gonzaga (1598–1655).

MARIA ANNA OF BAVARIA (1610–1665). Electress of Bavaria. Born Jan 13, 1610, in Graz; died Sept 25, 1665, in Munich; dau. of Maria Anna of Bavaria (1574–1616) and Ferdinand II, king of Bohemia and Hungary (r. 1578–1637), Holy Roman emperor (r. 1619–1637); sister of Ferdinand III (1608–1657), king of Bohemia and Hungary, and Holy Roman emperor (r. 1637–1657); m. Maximilian, elector of Bavaria (r. 1623–1651); children: Ferdinand Maria (1636–1679), elector of Bavaria.

MARIA ANNA OF BAVARIA (1660–1690). Dauphine of France. Name variations: Marie Christine, dauphine or dauphiness of France; Marie-Anne; Mary Anne Christine of Bavaria; Marie-Anne Christine-Victoire of Bavaria. Born Marie Anne Christine Victoire de Baviere, Nov 17, 1660; died April 20, 1690, in France; m. Louis (1661–1711), le Grand Dauphin (son of Louis XIV, king of France), on Mar 17, 1680; children: Louis (1682–1712), duke of Burgundy; Philip V (1683–1746), king of Spain (r. 1700–1724, 1724–1746); Charles (1685–1714), duke of Berry.

MARIA ANNA OF NEUBERG (1667–1740). Queen of Spain. Name variations: Maria Anna of Bavaria-Neuberg. Born in Dusseldorf on Oct 28, 1667; died July 16, 1740; dau. of Philip Wilhelm or Philip William, Elector Palatine of the Rhine, and Elizabeth Amalia of Hesse (1635–1709); sister of Maria Sophia of Neuberg (1666–1699); 2nd wife of Charles II the Bewitched (1661–1700), king of Spain (r. 1665–1700), May 4, 1690; no children. ❖ Was married to Charles II of Spain to strengthen Austria's influence at the Spanish court against France; exercised great influence over her mentally deficient husband but lacked any significant group of political supporters; when Charles' health declined, and France and Austria began intriguing to pick his successor, did everything possible to swing the decision in the Habsburgs' favor; remained in Spain and supported the Austrian cause during War of the Spanish Succession (1701–13); was the heroine of Victor Hugo's *Ruy Blas.* ❖ See also *Women in World History.*

MARIA ANNA OF PORTUGAL (1843–1884). Portuguese princess. Name variations: Maria Ana or Maria Anna of Saxe-Coburg-Gotha. Born July 21, 1843, in Lisbon, Portugal; died Feb 5, 1884, in Dresden; dau. of Maria II da Gloria (1819–1853) and Ferdinand of Saxe-Coburg-Gotha; m. George (1832–1904), king of Saxony (r. 1902–1904), on May 11, 1859; children: Frederick Augustus III (1865–1932), king of Saxony (r. 1904–1918, abdicated in 1918); Maria Josepha of Saxony (1867–1944); John George; Maximilian.

MARIA ANNA OF SAVOY (1803–1884). Empress of Austria. Name variations: Marianna of Savoy. Born Maria Anna Caroline Pié on Sept 19, 1803, in Turin; died May 4, 1884, in Vienna; dau. of Maria Teresa of Austria (1773–1832) and Victor Emmanuel I (1759–1824), king of Sardinia (r. 1802–1821, abdicated); m. Ferdinand I the Good (1793–1875), emperor of Austria (r. 1835–1848), on Sept 5, 1823; children: Louise (1821–1823); Charles III (1823–1854), duke of Parma (r. 1849–1854).

MARIA ANNA OF SAXONY (1795–1865). Grand duchess of Tuscany. Born May 27, 1795; died Jan 3, 1865, at Brandeis Castle in Bohemia; 2nd wife of Ferdinand III (1769–1824), grand duke of Tuscany (r. 1790–1802 and 1814–1824). ❖ Ferdinand's 1st wife was Louisa Amelia (1773–1802).

MARIA ANNA OF SAXONY (1799–1832). Grand duchess of Tuscany. Name variations: Marie Anna of Saxony. Born Nov 15, 1799, in Dresden, Germany; died Mar 24, 1832, in Pisa; 1st wife of Leopold II (1797–1870), grand duke of Tuscany (r. 1824–1859), on Nov 16, 1817; children: (2nd marriage) 3 daughters, including Augusta of Tuscany (1825–1864, who m. Luitpold of Bavaria).

MARIA ANNA OF SAXONY (1836–1859). *See Anna Maria of Saxony.*

MARIA ANNA OF SPAIN (1606–1646). Holy Roman empress and queen of Bohemia. Name variations: Maria of Austria; Maria of Hungary; Infanta Maria. Born Aug 18, 1606, in Madrid, Spain; died May 13, 1646, in Linz; dau. of Margaret of Austria (c. 1577–1611) and Philip III (1578–1621), king of Spain (r. 1598–1621); sister of Anne of Austria (1601–1666) and Philip IV (1605–1665), king of Spain (r. 1621–1665); became 1st wife of Ferdinand III (1608–1657), king of Bohemia (r. 1627–1646), king of Hungary (r. 1625), Holy Roman emperor (r. 1637–1657), on Feb 20, 1631; children: Ferdinand (1633–1654); Maria Anna of Austria (c. 1634–1696, who became the 2nd wife of Philip IV, king of Spain); Leopold I, Holy Roman emperor (r. 1658–1705). ❖ Ferdinand's 2nd wife was Maria Leopoldine (1632–1649); his 3rd was Eleonora II Gonzaga (1628–1686).

MARIA ANNUNZIATA (1843–1871). Princess of Sicily and archduchess of Austria. Name variations: Annunciata of Sicily; Maria Annuziata of Bourbon and the Two Sicilies; María Annunciata of Bourbon-Naples; Maria Annunziata of Naples. Born Mar 24, 1843, in Naples; died May 4, 1871, in Vienna; dau. of Theresa of Austria (1816–1867) and Ferdinand II, king of the Two Sicilies (r. 1830–1859); became 2nd wife of Karl Ludwig also known as Charles Louis (1833–1896), archduke of Austria, on Oct 21, 1862 (drank from the river Jordan while on a pilgrimage and died from an intestinal infection); children: Francis

Ferdinand also known as Franz Ferdinand (1863–1914), archduke of Austria (assassinated with wife Sophie Chotek at Sarajevo in 1914); Otto (1865–1906), who m. Maria Josepha of Saxony); Ferdinand Karl (1868–1915, who became known as Ferdinand Burg when he renounced his title in 1911); Margaret Sophie (1870–1902). ❖ Charles Louis was also married to Margaret of Saxony (1840–1858) and Maria Theresa of Portugal (1855–1944).

MARIA ANNUNZIATA (1876–1961). Austrian royal. Name variations: Miana. Born July 31, 1876, in Reichenau an der Rax; died April 8, 1961, in Vaduz; dau. of Maria Theresa of Portugal (1855–1944) and Karl Ludwig also known as Charles Louis (1833–1896), archduke of Austria.

MARIA ANTONIA (1669–1692). Electress of Bavaria. Name variations: Maria Antonieta or Antoinette. Born in 1669; died in 1692; dau. of Leopold I, Holy Roman emperor (r. 1658–1705), and Margaret Theresa of Spain (1651–1673); m. Maximilian II Emmanuel (1662–1726), elector of Bavaria (r. 1679–1726), in 1685; children: Joseph Ferdinand, electoral prince of Bavaria (d. 1699). ❖ Following Maria Antonia's death in 1692, Maximilian married Cunigunde Sobieska, the mother of Charles VII, Holy Roman emperor.

MARIA ANTONIA OF AUSTRIA (1683–1754). Queen of Portugal and archduchess of Austria. Name variations: Marie-Anne of Austria; Maria Ana. Born Maria Antonia Josefa in Linz, Austria, Sept 7, 1683; died Aug 14, 1754; dau. of Leopold I, Holy Roman emperor (r. 1658–1705), and his third wife, Eleanor of Pfalz-Neuburg (1655–1720); m. Joao or John V (1689–1750), king of Portugal (r. 1706–1750), in 1708; children: Pedro (1712–1714); Maria Barbara of Braganza (1711–1758, who m. Ferdinand VI, king of Spain); José or Joseph I (1714–1777), king of Portugal (r. 1750–1777); Carlos (1716–1736); Pedro or Peter III (d. 1786), king of Portugal (r. 1777–1786); Alexander (1723–1728). ❖ To strengthen an alliance with Portugal during War of the Spanish Succession, was married to John V (1708); governed as regent on 2 occasions: when the king secluded himself at Vila Viçosa suffering from depression (1716) and when he became very ill (1742); intermittently governed as regent until his death, despite the fact that her son Joseph was already an adult; when John died (1750), helped launch the governmental career of Sebastião José de Carvalho e Melo, the future marquis of Pombal (he would govern as virtual dictator of Portugal from 1756 to 1777). ❖ See also *Women in World History*.

MARIA ANTONIA OF AUSTRIA (1724–1780). Princess of Bavaria, electress of Saxony, and German composer, pianist, harpsichordist, poet, singer, composer, and patron of the arts. Name variations: Maria Antonia Walpurgis; (pseudonym) ETPA (Ermelinda Talea Pastorella Arcada). Born in Munich, Germany, on July 18, 1724; died in Dresden on April 23, 1780; dau. of Karl Albert also known as Charles VII Albert (1697–1745), elector of Bavaria (r. 1726–1745), later known as Charles VII, Holy Roman emperor (r. 1742–1745); sister of Maximilian III Joseph, elector of Bavaria (r. 1745–1777); m. Friedrich Christian also known as Frederick Christian (1722–1763), elector of Saxony (r. 1763), on June 20, 1747; children: Frederick Augustus III (1750–1827), elector of Saxony (r. 1763–1806), also known as Frederick Augustus I the Just, king of Saxony (r. 1806–1827); Anthony Clement I (1755–1836), king of Saxony (r. 1827–1836); Maximilian (b. 1759), duke of Saxony (who m. Caroline of Parma). ❖ Was taught piano by Giovanni Ferrandini; studied composition and singing with Nicola Porpora and Johan Adolf Hasse; a writer and poet, composed her own music and libretto for operas in which she sang, while some of her works were set to music by Graun, Ferrandini, Hasse, Risteri, and Nauman; was also a painter, rendering her own self-portrait; as a patron of the arts, supported Gluck when he produced *Orpheus and Euridice* in Munich.

MARIA ANTONIA OF NAPLES (1784–1806). Neapolitan princess. Name variations: Antonia of Sicily; Antoinette; Princess of Asturias. Born in 1784; died under mysterious circumstances in 1806; dau. of Maria Carolina (1752–1814), queen of Naples and the Two Sicilies, and Ferdinand IV (1751–1825), king of Naples (r. 1759–1806, 1815–1825), later known as Ferdinand I, king of the Two Sicilies (r. 1816–1825); sister of Maria Amalia (1782–1866, who m. Louis Philippe, king of France); became 1st wife of Ferdinand, prince of Asturias (the future Ferdinand VII, king of Spain, r. 1813–1833), in 1802; no surviving children. ❖ See also *Women in World History*.

MARIA ANTONIA OF PORTUGAL (1862–1959). Duchess of Bourbon-Parma. Born Nov 28, 1862, in Bronnbach; died May 14, 1959, in Luxembourg; dau. of Adelheid (1831–1909) and Miguel also known as Michael I (1802–1866), king of Portugal (r. 1828–1834); m.

Robert, duke of Bourbon-Parma, on Oct 15, 1884; children: Adelaide of Parma (b. 1885, a nun); Sixtus (b. 1886); Franz Xaver (b. 1889); Francisca Josephe (b. 1890, a nun); Zita of Parma (1892–1989); Felix (b. 1893), prince consort; René Charles (b. 1894), prince of Bourbon-Parma; Maria Antonia of Parma (b. 1895); Isabella of Parma (b. 1898); Ludwig (b. 1899); Henriette of Parma (b. 1903); Gaëtan (b. 1905).

MARIA ANTONIA OF SICILY (1814–1898). Grand duchess of Tuscany. Name variations: Antonietta of Bourbon-Two Sicilies; Maria Antonia of Bourbon-Two Sicilies. Born Dec 19, 1814, in Palermo; died Nov 17, 1898, in Orth, near Gmunden; dau. of Marie Isabella of Spain (1789–1848) and Francis I, king of the Two Sicilies (r. 1825–1830); m. Leopold II (1797–1870), grand duke of Tuscany (r. 1824–1859), June 7, 1833; children: 10, including Maria Isabella (1834–1901, who m. Francesco, count of Trapani); Ferdinand IV (1835–1908), grand duke of Tuscany; Charles Salvator (1839–1892, who m. Maria Immaculata of Sicily); Maria Ludovica (1845–1917, who m. Charles of Isenburg-Birstein); Louis Salvator (1847–1915); John Nepomucen (1852–1891, who renounced rights in 1889 and took the name Johann Orth); and 4 others who died young. ❖ Leopold's 1st wife was Maria Anna of Saxony (1799–1832).

MARIA ANTONIA OF SPAIN (1729–1785). Duchess of Savoy. Name variations: Marie Antoinette of Spain; Mary of Spain; (Spanish) Maria Antoineta Fernanda; (Italian) Maria Antonia Ferdinanda. Born Marie Antoineta Fernanda, Nov 17, 1729; died Sept 19, 1785; dau. of Elizabeth Farnese (1692–1766) and Philip V, king of Spain (r. 1700–1724, 1725–1746); m. Victor Amadeus III (1726–1796), duke of Savoy (r. 1773–1796), May 31, 1750; children: 12, including Charles Emmanuel IV (1751–1819), duke of Savoy (r. 1796–1802); Joseph Benedict; Marie Josephine of Savoy (d. 1810, who m. Louis XVIII, king of France); Maria Charlotte of Sardinia (c. 1761–c. 1786); Maria Teresa of Savoy (1756–1805, who m. Charles X, king of France); Victor Emmanuel I (1759–1824), king of Sardinia (r. 1802–1821); Charles Felix, duke of Genoa (r. 1821–1831).

MARIA ANTONIA WALPURGIS (1724–1780). *See Maria Antonia of Austria.*

MARIA AUGUSTA OF THURN AND TAXIS (1706–1756). Duchess of Wurttemberg. Born Aug 11, 1706; died Feb 1, 1756; dau. of Anselm Franz, prince of Thurn and Taxis; m. Charles I Alexander (1684–1737), duke of Wurttemberg (r. 1733–1737), on May 1, 1727; children: Charles Eugene (1728–1793), duke of Wurttemberg (r. 1737–1793); Louis Eugene (1731–1795), duke of Wurttemberg (r. 1793–1795); Frederick II Eugene (1732–1797), duke of Wurttemberg (r. 1795–1797).

MARIA BARBARA OF BRAGANZA (1711–1758). Queen of Spain. Name variations: Marie-Barbara of Portugal; Barbara of Braganza or Barbara de Bragança; Maria Barbara, Marie-Barbara, or Mary Barbara; Marie Magdalena Barbara; Maria Magdalena Josepha de Bragança. Born in Lisbon, Dec 4, 1711; died Aug 27, 1758, in Aranjuez; dau. of Joao V also known as John V, king of Portugal (r. 1706–1750), and Maria Antonia of Austria (1683–1754); sister of Joseph I (1714–1777), king of Portugal (r. 1750–1777), and Peter III (d. 1786), king of Portugal (r. 1777–1786); m. Fernando or Ferdinand VI el Sabio (1713–1759), king of Spain (r. 1746–1759), Jan 20, 1729; children: none. ❖ Became a tool of dynastic diplomacy (1725) when father betrothed her to Ferdinand (VI) of Spain, a son of Spanish monarch Philip V; was married (1729); fell in love with husband and he, in turn, became very reliant upon her; following Philip's death (1746), ruled with husband over a period of relative prosperity and tranquility; since husband lacked the energy or will to govern, managed the government with such royal ministers as the Marquis of Ensenada and José de Carvajal; her ties to the Portuguese crown proved valuable to the negotiation of the Treaty of Limits (1750), which adjusted the boundaries between the Iberian nations' South American colonies; adored sacred music, which she also composed, and was especially remembered as the patron of the Italian opera star Farinelli (Carlos Broschi), who performed often at court. ❖ See also *Women in World History*.

MARIA BEATRICE OF MODENA (1750–1829). Duchess of Massa and Carrara. Name variations: Archduchess Beatrice of Modena; Maria Beatrice d'Este; Beatrix of Modena-Este; Maria Riccarda; Maria Beatrix Riccarda of Este; Mary Beatrice of Modena. Born April 6 or 7, 1750, in Modena; died Nov 14, 1829, in Vienna; dau. of Hercules also known as Ercole III d'Este (1727–1803), duke of Modena; m. Archduke Ferdinand (1754–1806, governor general of Lombardy in Milano and son of Maria Theresa of Austria [1717–1780]), on Oct 15, 1771; children: Maria

Teresa of Austria (1773–1832, who m. Victor Emmanuel I, king of Sardinia); Josepha (1775–1777); Maria Leopoldina (1776–1848, who m. Charles Theodore of Bavaria); Francis IV (1779–1846), duke of Modena (r. 1814–1846); Ferdinand (1781–1850); Maximilian Joseph (1782–1863); Maria Antonia (1784–1786); Charles (1785–1809); Maria Ludovica of Modena (1787–1816, who m. Francis I, emperor of Austria).

MARIA BEATRICE OF MODENA (1824–1906). Spanish royal. Name variations: Beatriz of Austria Este; Marie Beatrix of Modena. Born Feb 13, 1824, in Modena; died Mar 18, 1906, in Gorz; dau. of Franz or Francis IV (1779–1846), duke of Modena (r. 1814–1846) and Maria Beatrice of Sardinia (1792–1840); m. the infante Juan de Borbon also known as John of Bourbon or John of Molina (1822–1887), on Feb 6, 1847; children: Charles (b. 1848), duke of Madrid; Alphonse Carlos (b. 1849), duke of San Jaime.

MARIA BEATRICE OF SARDINIA (1792–1840). Duchess of Modena. Name variations: Beatrix of Modena-Este; Maria Beatrice of Modena; Maria Beatrix of Savoy. Born Maria Beatrice Victoire Josephine on Dec 6, 1792; died Sept 15, 1840; dau. of Maria Teresa of Austria (1773–1832) and Victor Emmanuel I (1759–1824), king of Sardinia (r. 1802–1821, abdicated); m. Franz or Francis IV (1779–1846), duke of Modena (r. 1814–1846), on June 20, 1812; children: Therese of Bourbon (1817–1886); Francis V (1819–1875), duke of Modena (r. 1846–1859, who m. Adelgunde of Bavaria); Ferdinand (1821–1849, who m. Elizabeth [1831–1903], dau. of Archduke Joseph); Maria Beatrice of Modena (1824–1906, who m. the infante Juan de Borbon).

MARIA CANTACUZENE (fl. 1300s). Byzantine princess. Fl. in the 1300s; dau. of Irene Asen and John VI Cantacuzene, emperor of Nicaea (r. 1347–1354); m. Nicephorus II of Epirus.

MARIA CAROLINA (1752–1814). Queen-consort of Naples and Sicily. Name variations: Maria of Austria; Marie Caroline; Mary Carolina or Mary Caroline; Maria Karolina. Born Aug 13, 1752, in Vienna, Austria; died Sept 7 or 8, 1814, in Vienna, Austria; 13th of 16 children of Empress Maria Theresa of Austria (1717–1780, queen of Hungary, Bohemia and the Netherlands, archduchess of Austria) and Francis I, Holy Roman emperor (r. 1745–1765), also known as Francis Stephen of Lorraine, grand duke of Tuscany; sister of Marie Antoinette (1755–1793); m. Ferdinand IV (1751–1825), king of Naples (r. 1759–1806, 1815–1825), later known as Ferdinand I, king of the Two Sicilies (r. 1816–1825), May 13, 1768; children: Maria Teresa of Naples (1772–1807); Louisa Amelia (1773–1802), grand duchess of Tuscany; Anna (1775–1780); Carlo or Charles (1776–1778); Gennaro (d. 1789); Carlo or Charles (d. 1789); Leopold; Carlo Alberto or Charles Albert (d. 1798); Francis I (1777–1830), king of the Two Sicilies (r. 1825–1830); Maria Amalia (1782–1866), later queen of France (r. 1830–1848); Christine of Bourbon (1779–1849); Maria Antonia of Naples (1784–1806); and 6 others who did not survive to adulthood. ❖ Queen-consort who exercised the real power behind the throne; crowned queen of Naples and Sicily on marriage to Ferdinand I (1768); dominated her passive, uneducated husband; within a few years of marriage, was ruling the country in Ferdinand's name; 1st 20 years of joint reign were extremely successful and marked by several efforts to reform and modernize Naples; last 20 years were clouded by the results of the French Revolution, including the execution of her sister Marie Antoinette, the temporary occupation of Naples by Jacobin forces, and finally the annexation of Naples as part of the Napoleonic empire; died at the very end of the Napoleonic wars, just before Naples was restored to her husband by the Congress of Vienna. ❖ See also Catherine Mary Charlton Bearne, *A Sister of Marie Antoinette: The Life-Story of Maria Carolina, Queen of Naples* (Dutton, 1907); and *Women in World History.*

MARIA CHARLOTTE OF SARDINIA (c. 1761–c. 1786). Princess of Savoy. Name variations: possibly Caroline. Born c. 1761; died c. 1786; dau. of Maria Antonia of Spain (1729–1785) and Victor Amadeus III, duke of Savoy (r. 1773–1796); m. Anthony I Clement of Saxony (1755–1836), king of Saxony (r. 1827–1836), Oct 24, 1781. ❖ Anthony Clement married his 2nd wife, Theresa (1767–1827), in 1787.

MARIA CHRISTINA (1742–1798). Archduchess and governor-general of Austrian Netherlands. Name variations: Maria Cristina; Marie Christine, stattholder or stadholder of the Netherlands; (nickname) Mimi. Born May 13, 1742, in Vienna; died June 24, 1798, in Vienna; dau. of Maria Theresa of Austria (1717–1780) and Francis I, Holy Roman emperor (r. 1745–1765); sister of Marie Antoinette (1755–1793), Maria Carolina (1752–1814), and Joseph II, Holy Roman emperor (r. 1765–

1790); m. Albert, duke of Saxony-Teschen. ❖ Quick-minded, was governor-general of the Austrian Netherlands (present-day Belgium), during her brother Joseph II's reign as Holy Roman emperor.

MARIA CHRISTINA (1947—). Dutch princess. Name variations: Maria-Christina; Maria Christina of Marijke. Born Feb 18, 1947; dau. of Juliana (b. 1909), queen of the Netherlands (r. 1948–1980), and Prince Bernard of Lippe-Biesterfeld; sister of Queen Beatrix of the Netherlands (b. 1938) and Irene Emma (b. 1939); m. Jorge Guillermo (Cuban-born New York teacher of deprived children), in 1975.

MARIA CHRISTINA I OF NAPLES (1806–1878). *See Maria Cristina I of Naples.*

MARIA CHRISTINA OF AUSTRIA (1858–1929). Queen and regent of Spain. Name variations: Maria Cristina of Habsburg Lorraine; Marie-Christine of Austria; Christina of Spain. Born in Moravia, July 21, 1858; died Feb 9, 1929; dau. of Charles Ferdinand (1818–1874), archduke of Austria, and Archduchess Elizabeth; became 2nd wife of Alfonso or Alphonso XII (1857–1885), king of Spain (r. 1875–1885), on Nov 29, 1879; children: Maria de las Mercedes (1880–1904); Maria Teresa (1882–1912, who m. Ferdinand of Bavaria); Alfonso also known as Alphonso XIII (1886–1941), king of Spain (r. 1886–1931). ❖ Was pregnant when husband died (Nov 25, 1885); gave birth to future Alphonso XIII (May 17, 1886); governed as regent for 17 years, presiding over Spain's fragile constitutional monarchy until her son was old enough to rule; worked as an impartial arbiter between the conservatives and the liberals. ❖ See also *Women in World History.*

MARIA CHRISTINA OF BOURBON (1779–1849). *See Christine of Bourbon.*

MARIA CHRISTINA OF MARIJKE (b. 1947). *See Maria Christina.*

MARIA CHRISTINA OF SAXONY (1779–1851). Duchess of Savoy-Carignan. Name variations: Marie of Saxony. Born in 1779; died in 1851; m. Charles Emmanuel (1770–1800), duke of Savoy-Carignan (r. 1780–1800); children: Charles Albert, king of Sardinia (r. 1831–1849).

MARIA CLEMENTINA OF AUSTRIA (1777–1801). Florentine princess. Name variations: Clementina of Austria; Marie Klementine. Born April 4, 1777, in Florence; died Nov 15, 1801, in Naples; dau. of Leopold II (1747–1792), count of Tuscany, ruler of Florence (r. 1765–1790), Holy Roman emperor (r. 1790–1792), and Maria Louisa of Spain (1745–1792); m. Francis I, later king of the Two Sicilies (r. 1825–1830); children: Caroline of Naples (1798–1870, who m. the duke of Berri); Ferdinand (b. 1800). ❖ Francis I's 2nd wife was Marie Isabella of Spain (1789–1848).

MARIA COMNENA (fl. 1090s). Byzantine princess. Dau. of Irene Ducas (c. 1066–1133) and Alexius I Comnenus, Byzantine emperor (r. 1081–1118); sister of Anna Comnena (1083–1153/55).

MARIA COMNENA (fl. 1100s). Queen of Jerusalem. Name variations: Mary Comnena. Fl. in the 1100s; 2nd wife of Amalric I (1136–1174), king of Jerusalem (r. 1162–1174); m. Balian II of Ramla; children: (1st marriage) Isabella I of Jerusalem (d. 1205); (2nd marriage) Helvis (who m. Reginald of Sidon, lord of Sidon); Margaret (who m. Hugh of Tiberias and Walter of Caesarea). ❖ Amalric's 1st wife was Agnes of Courtenay (1136–1186).

MARIA CRISTINA (1911–1996). Spanish princess. Name variations: Infanta. Born Dec 12, 1911, at Royal Palace, Madrid, Spain; died Dec 23, 1996, at Villa Giralda, Madrid; dau. of Ena (1887–1969) and Alphonso XIII (1886–1941), king of Spain (r. 1886–1931); m. Enrico Eugenio, 1st count of Marone, on June 10, 1940; children: Victoria Marone (b. 1941, who m. José Carlos Alvarez de Toledo y Gross, 8th count of Villapeterna); Giovanna Marone (b. 1943, who m. Jaime Galobart y Satrústegui and Luis Angel Sanchez Merlo y Ruiz); Maria Teresa Marone (b. 1945, who m. José Ruiz de Arana y Montalvo, 5th marques of Brenes); Anna Sandra Marone (b. 1948, who m. Gian Carol Stavro Santarosa).

MARIA CRISTINA I OF NAPLES (1806–1878). Queen and regent of Spain. Name variations: María Cristina; Maria Cristina of Naples or María Christina I of Naples; Cristina of Naples; Christina of Naples; Marie-Christine of Sicily; Maria Cristina de Borbón or Bourbon. Born in Naples, Italy, April 27, 1806; died at Havre, France, Aug 22 or 23, 1878; dau. of Francis I, king of the Two Sicilies (r. 1825–1830), and Marie Isabella of Spain (1789–1848); dau. of Francis I, king of the Two Sicilies

(r. 1825–1830), and Marie Isabella of Spain (1789–1848); sister of Teresa Cristina of Bourbon (1822–1889, empress of Brazil); became 4th wife of Ferdinand VII, king of Spain (r. 1813–1833), Dec 11, 1829; secretly m. a soldier named Agustín Fernando Muñoz y Sánchez in an irregular ceremony on Dec 28, 1833; children: (1st marriage) Isabella II (1830–1904) and Luisa Fernanda (1832–1897); (2nd marriage) four more. ❖ Ferdinand VII's 1st wife was Maria Antonia of Naples (1784–1806); his 2nd was Maria Isabel of Portugal (1797–1818); his 3rd was Maria Josepha of Saxony (1803–1829).

MARIA CRISTINA OF HABSBURG LORRAINE (1858–1929). *See Maria Christina of Austria.*

MARIA CRISTINA OF SICILY (1877–1947). Archduchess of Austria. Name variations: Maria Cristina of Bourbon-Sicily. Born April 10, 1877; died Oct 4, 1947, in St. Gilgen; dau. of Antonia von Trapani (b. 1851) and Alphonse of Sicily (1841–1934), count of Caserta; m. Peter Ferdinand (1874–1948), archduke or grand duke of Austria, on Nov 8, 1900; children: Gottfried also known as Godfrey (1902–1984, who m. Dorothea of Bavaria); Helene (1903–1924); George (1905–1952, who m. Marie Valerie of Waldburg-Zeil); Rosa of Austria (1906–1983).

MARIA DA FONTE (fl. 1846). *See Maria de Fonte.*

MARIA DA GLORIA (1819–1853). *See Maria II da Gloria.*

MARIA DA GLORIA (1946—). Princess of Orleans-Braganza. Born Dec 13, 1946, in Petropolis, Brazil; dau. of Peter Gonzaga (Prince Peter of Orleans and Braganza) and Maria de la Esperanza (b. 1914); m. Alexander Karadjordjevic (son of Peter II, king of Yugoslavia), July 1, 1972 (div. 1985); m. Ignacio Medina y Fernandez, 21st duke of Segorbe, on Oct 24, 1985; children: (1st marriage) Peter (b. 1980); twins Philip and Alexander (b. 1982).

MARIA DAL POZZO (fl. 19th c.). Duchess of Aosta. First wife of Amadeo also known as Amadeus of Savoy, duke of Aosta, king of Spain (r. 1871–1873); children: Emmanuel (who m. Helen of Bourbon); Victor; Louis. Amadeus' 2nd wife was Marie Laetitia (1866–1890).

MARIA DE FONTE (fl. 1846). Portuguese dissenter. Name variations: Maria da Fonte Arcada; Maria of Fonte. Fl. 1846. ❖ When the liberal Portuguese government tried to carry out a series of reforms, among which was a law forbidding (on sanitary grounds) the burial of bodies within churches (1846), led a number of peasant women who opposed the new burial ordinance, causing a riot which led to a civil war. ❖ See also *Women in World History.*

MARIA DÉIA or MARIA DÉIA DE NENEM (c. 1908–1938). *See Bonita, Maria.*

MARIA DEI CONTI D'AQUINO (fl. 1300s). Princess. Name variations: Fiammetta. Illeg. dau. of Robert the Good, duke of Anjou, king of Naples (r. 1309–1343). ❖ Beloved by Boccaccio, was portrayed by him under the name Fiammetta.

MARIA DE LA ESPERANZA (1914—). Princess of the Two Sicilies. Born June 14, 1914; dau. of Louise of Orleans (1882–1952) and Carlos, prince of Bourbon-Sicily, also known as Charles (1870–1949), prince of the Two Sicilies; sister of Maria de las Mercedes (1910–2000); m. Pedro de Alcantra, prince of Grao Para, also known as Peter Gonzaga (Prince Peter of Orleans and Braganza); children: Maria da Gloria (1946—).

MARIA DE LA PAZ (1862–1946). Spanish princess. Name variations: María. Born in 1862; died in 1946; dau. of Isabella II (1830–1904), queen of Spain, and Francisco de Asiz or Asis; m. Louis Ferdinand of Bavaria (b. 1884).

MARIA DE LAS MERCEDES (1860–1878). Queen of Spain. Born in 1860; died in 1878; dau. of Antoine, duke of Montpensier (1824–1900), and Luisa Fernanda (1832–1897); became 1st wife of Alfonso also known as Alphonso XII (1857–1885), king of Spain (r. 1875–1885), in 1878. ❖ Alphonso married his 2nd wife, Maria Christina of Austria (1858–1929), in 1879.

MARIA DE LAS MERCEDES (1880–1904). Queen infanta of Spain. Name variations: Maria Mercedes. Born Sept 11, 1880; died Oct 17, 1904; dau. of Maria Christina of Austria (1858–1929) and Alphonso XII (1857–1885), king of Spain (r. 1875–1885); sister of Alphonso XIII (1886–1941), king of Spain (r. 1886–1931); m. Carlos, prince of Bourbon-Sicily, also known as Charles or Charles of Bourbon (1870–1949), conti de Caserta, prince of the Two Sicilies, on Feb 14, 1901; children: Alphonse of Bourbon-Sicily (b. 1901); Ferdinand (b. 1903);

Isabella of Bourbon-Sicily (b. 1904, who m. John, count Zamoyski). Charles of Bourbon's 2nd wife was Louise of Orleans (1882–1952). ❖ When father died without a male heir (Nov 25, 1885), was named queen at age 5; when mother gave birth to a boy (May 17, 1886), was succeeded by him on the day of his birth.

MARIA DE LAS MERCEDES (1910–2000). Countess of Barcelona. Name variations: Mercedes of the Two Sicilies; Maria Mercedes; Maria-Mercedes; Maria Mercedes of Bourbon; María de Borbón; princess of Bourbon-Sicily. Born Maria de la Mercedes Christine Januaria Isabel Louise Caroline Victoria, Dec 23, 1910, in Madrid, Spain; died Jan 2, 2000, in her residence on the Canary Island of Lanzarote; dau. of Carlos, prince of Bourbon-Sicily, also known as Charles of Bourbon (1870–1949), prince of the Two Sicilies, and Louise of Orleans (1882–1952); m. John or Juan (1913–1993), also known as Juan de Borbón y Battenberg, count of Barcelona, Oct 12, 1935; children: Maria del Pilar (b. 1936); Juan Carlos I (b. 1938), king of Spain (r. 1975—); Margarita Maria (b. 1939); Alfonso or Alphonso (1940–1956, who died in a shooting accident).

MARIA DEL OCCIDENTE (c. 1794–1845). *See Brooks, Maria Gowen.*

MARIA DEL PILAR (1936—). Duchess of Badajoz. Name variations: Maria de Pilar Bourbon; Maria de Bourbon or Maria of Bourbon. Born July 30, 1936, in Cannes, France; dau. of Maria de las Mercedes (1910–2000) and John or Juan (1913–1993), count of Barcelona; sister of Juan Carlos I (b. 1938), king of Spain (r. 1975—); m. Louis de la Torre Gómez-Acebo, duke of Estrada; children: Fatima Simoneta Gomez-Acebo (b. 1968); Juan (b. 1969); Bruno (b. 1971); Beltran (b. 1973); Fernando (b. 1974).

MARIA DE MOLINA (d. 1321). Queen-regent of Castile and Leon. Name variations: Maria of Molina; Mary of Molina. Born between 1260 and 1270 in Spain; died July 1, 1321, in Castile; dau. of Alphonse Castilla de Molina and Mayor Alfonsa de Meneses; m. cousin Sancho IV the Fierce (1258–1295), king of Castile and Leon (r. 1284–1296), July 1281 or 1282; children: Isabel de Limoges (1283–1328); Ferdinand IV, king of Castile and Leon (r. 1296–1312, who m. Constance of Portugal); Alfonso (1286–1291); Enrique (1288–1299); Pedro (1290–1319), regent of Castile; Felipe or Philip (1292–1327); Beatrice of Castile and Leon (1293–1359, who m. Alphonso IV of Portugal). ❖ When husband died, retained her authority as regent of the kingdom in her young son's name; proved to be a successful regent, a difficult accomplishment given the great number of would-be usurpers of the Castilian throne that she was forced to war against; when son died (1312), was called upon by the people of Castile to restore order and to act again as regent, this time for her infant grandson Alphonso XI. ❖ See also *Women in World History.*

MARIA DE PADILLA (c. 1496–1531). *See Padilla, Maria Pacheco.*

MARIA DE PORTUGAL (1521–1577). Infanta of Portugal. Name variations: Maria of Portugal. Born June 8, 1521, in Lisbon; died Oct 10, 1577, in Lisbon; dau. of Manuel I the Fortunate (1469–1521), king of Portugal (r. 1495–1521), and Eleanor of Portugal (1498–1558); half-sister of João also known as John III, king of Portugal; never married; no children. ❖ See also *Women in World History.*

MARIA DE SANCTO PAULO (1304–1377). *See Marie de St. Pol.*

MARIA DE VENTADOUR (b. 1165). Literary patron and poet of France. Name variations: Marie de Ventadorn. Born 1165 in Turenne; died after 1221 in Ventadour; dau. of Raimon II of Turenne and Helis de Castelnau; m. Ebles V, viscount of Ventadour, around 1183 (separated 1221); children: two sons. ❖ Patron of the Provençal troubadours, also composed poetry; supported several important male troubadours at her court, among them Gui d'Ussel. ❖ See also *Women in World History.*

MARIA DO CÉU (1658–1753). Portuguese poet and abbess. Name variations: Maria do Ceu or Maria do Ceo; Sor Maria do Ceo del Cielo; Sor Maria del Cielo; (pseudonym) Sor Marina Clemencia. Born Sept 11, 1658, in Lisbon, Portugal; died 1753; dau. of Antonio d'Eça and Catherine de Távora (twin sister of Isabel da Silva). ❖ At 18, entered the Franciscan convent of N.S. da Esperanza in Lisbon (June 27, 1676); was an abbess on 2 occasions; wrote poetry and prose, including *Preciosa I* (1731) and *Enganos do Bosque, Desenganos do Rio* (Errors of the Forest, Disillusionments of the River, 1741); also wrote 5 plays under the title *Trionfo do Rosario* (1740); often wrote in Spanish.

MARIA DOROTHEA OF AUSTRIA (1867–1932). Duchess of Orléans. Born June 14, 1867; died April 6, 1932; dau. of Clotilde of Saxe-Coburg-Gotha (1846–1927) and Archduke Josef Karl Ludwig also known as

Joseph Charles Louis (1833–1905); m. Louis Philippe (1869–1926), duke of Orléans, on Nov 5, 1896.

MARIA DUCAS (fl. 1070–1081). *See Maria of Alania.*

MARIA ELEANORA (1550–1608). Duchess of Prussia. Name variations: Marie Eleonore of Jülich-Cleves; Marie Eleonore von Julich-Kleve. Born June 15, 1550; died May 23, 1608; dau. of Mary (1531–1581) and William V, duke of Cleves (r. 1539–1592); m. Albert Frederick (b. 1553), duke of Prussia, on Oct 14, 1573; children: Anna of Prussia (1576–1625, who m. John Sigismund, elector of Brandenburg); Marie Hohenzollern (1579–1649); Albert Frederick (b. 1580); Sophie Hohenzollern (1582–1610); Eleonore Hohenzollern (1583–1607); Wilhelm Friedrich (b. 1585); Magdalena Sybilla (1586–1659, who m. John George, elector of Saxony).

MARIA ELEONORA OF BRANDENBURG (1599–1655). Queen of Sweden. Name variations: Maria Eleanora Hohenzollern. Born Nov 11, 1599; died Mar 28, 1655; dau. of John Sigismund (1572–1619), elector of Brandenburg (r. 1608–1619), and Anna of Prussia; sister of George William, elector of Brandenburg (r. 1619–1640); m. Gustavus II Adolphus (1594–1632), king of Sweden (r. 1611–1632), on Nov 25, 1620; children: Christine (1623–1624); Christina of Sweden (1626–1689). ❖ See also *Women in World History.*

MARIA ELISABETH (1680–1741). Stadholder of the Netherlands. Born Dec 13, 1680, in Linz; died Aug 26, 1741, in Mariemont Castle near Morlanwelz, Hennegau; dau. of Eleanor of Pfalz-Neuburg (1655–1720) and Leopold I of Bohemia (1640–1705), Holy Roman emperor (r. 1658–1705).

MARIA FRANCISCA OF SULZBACH (fl. 18th c.). Bavarian noblewoman. Married Frederick Michael (died 1767); children: Maximilian I Joseph, elector of Bavaria (r. 1799–1805), king of Bavaria (r. 1805–1825).

MARIA GABRIELE OF BAVARIA (1878–1912). Bavarian princess. Born Oct 9, 1878; died Oct 24, 1912; dau. of Maria Josepha of Portugal (1857–1943) and Charles Theodore also known as Karl Theodor "Gackl" (1839–1909), duke in Bavaria [*sic*]; became 1st wife of Rupprecht also known as Rupert, crown prince of Bavaria, Aug 10, 1900; children: Luitpold (b. 1901); Irmingard (1902–1903); Albert (b. 1905), duke of Bavaria; Rudolf (b. 1909).

MARIA HEDWIG, Sister (b. 1919). *See Walter, Silja.*

MARIA HENRIETTA OF AUSTRIA (1836–1902). Queen of the Belgians. Name variations: Marie Hendrika; Marie Henriette or Marie-Henriette. Born Aug 23, 1836, in Ofen; died Sept 19, 1902, in Spa, Belgium; dau. of archduke Joseph of Austria (1776–1847) and Maria of Wurttemberg (1797–1855); m. Leopold II, king of the Belgians, Aug 22, 1853; children: Stephanie of Belgium (1864–1945); Leopold (d. 1869); Louise of Belgium (1858–1924, who m. Philip of Saxe-Coburg-Gotha); Clementine of Belgium (1872–1955).

MARIA IMMACULATA (1878–1968). Duchess of Wurttemberg. Name variations: Maria Immakulata. Born 1878; died 1968; dau. of Charles Salvator of Tuscany (1839–1892) and Maria Immaculata of Sicily (1844–1899).

MARIA IMMACULATA OF SICILY (1844–1899). Austrian archduchess. Name variations: Maria Immakulata. Born April 14, 1844, in Caserta; died Feb 18, 1899, in Vienna; dau. of Theresa of Austria (1816–1867) and Ferdinand II, king of the Two Sicilies (r. 1830–1859); m. archduke Karl Salvator also spelled Charles Salvator of Tuscany (1839–1892); children: 7, including Leopold Salvator (1863–1931, who m. Blanche of Bourbon) and Maria Immaculata (1878–1968).

MARIA INNOCENTIA, Sister (1909–1946). *See Hummel, Berta.*

MARIA ISABEL FRANCISCA (1851–1931). Princess of Spain. Name variations: Princess Isabel, the infanta; Maria Isabel Francisca; Isabella of Spain; countess of Girgenti. Born Dec 20, 1851; died April 23, 1931; dau. of Isabella II (1830–1904), queen of Spain, and probably a young officer, José Ruíz de Arana; tutored by Frances Calderón de la Barca (1804–1882); m. Gaetano also known as Caetano de Borbón (1846–1871), count of Girgenti (distant cousin), May 13, 1868. ❖ See also *Women in World History.*

MARIA ISABEL OF PORTUGAL (1797–1818). Portuguese princess. Name variations: Marie-Isabel Braganza; Isabella of Portugal. Born May 19, 1797, at Queluz; died Dec 26, 1818, in Madrid; dau. of Carlota

Joaquina (1775–1830) and John VI (1767–1826), king of Portugal (r. 1816–1826); became 2nd wife of Fernando or Ferdinand VII (1784–1833), king of Spain (r. 1813–1833), Sept 29, 1816; sister of Peter or Pedro IV, king of Portugal, and Michael I, king of Portugal. ❖ Ferdinand VII's 1st wife was Maria Antonia of Naples (1784–1806); his 3rd was Maria Josepha of Saxony (1803–1829); his 4th was Maria Cristina I of Naples (1806–1878). ❖ See also *Women in World History.*

MARIA ISABELLA (1834–1901). Countess of Trapani. Name variations: Isabella; Maria Isabella of Tuscany. Born May 21, 1834, in Florence, Italy; died July 14 or 16, 1901, in Burgenstock; dau. of Leopold II (1797–1870), grand duke of Tuscany (r. 1824–1859) and Maria Antonia of Sicily (1814–1898); m. Francesco also known as Francis of Sicily (1827–1892), count of Trapani, April 10, 1850.

MARIA ISABELLA (1848–1919). Countess of Paris. Name variations: Isabella d'Orleans; Isabella of Orleans. Born Sept 21, 1848; died April 23, 1919; dau. of Antoine (1824–1900), duke of Montpensier, and Luisa Fernanda (1832–1897); m. Louis Philippe (1838–1894), count of Paris, April 30, 1864; children: Marie-Amelie of Orleans (1865–1951, who m. King Charles I of Portugal); Helene (b. 1871, who m. Emanuel Philibert, duke of Aosta); Karl (b. 1875); Isabella of Orleans (b. 1878); Jacob (b. 1880); Louise of Orleans (1882–1952, who m. Charles of Bourbon, prince of the Two Sicilies); Louis Philippe (1869–1926, who m. Maria Dorothea of Austria); Ferdinand, duke of Montpensier (d. 1924).

MARIA JOSEPHA OF AUSTRIA (1699–1757). *See Marie Josepha.*

MARIA JOSEPHA OF BAVARIA (1739–1767). Empress of Austria. Name variations: Josepha of Bavaria. Born Mar 20, 1739, in Munich; died of smallpox, May 28, 1767, in Vienna; became the unhappy 2nd wife of Joseph II (1741–1790), emperor of Austria (r. 1765–1790) and Holy Roman emperor (r. 1765–1790).

MARIA JOSEPHA OF PORTUGAL (1857–1943). Princess of Portugal. Name variations: Marie-José Bragança von Wittelsbach; Infanta of Portugal. Born Mar 19, 1857; died Mar 11, 1943; dau. of Adelheid (1831–1909) and Miguel also known as Michael I (1802–1866), king of Portugal (r. 1828–1834); m. Karl Theodor "Gackl" (1839–1909), April 29, 1874; children: Elizabeth of Bavaria (1876–1965); Maria Gabriele of Bavaria (1878–1912).

MARIA JOSEPHA OF SAXONY (1803–1829). Queen of Spain. Name variations: Mary Josepha. Born Dec 6, 1803; died May 17, 1829; dau. of Caroline of Parma (1770–1804) and Maximilian of Saxony, duke of Saxony (r. 1830–1838); became 3rd wife of Ferdinand VII, king of Spain (r. 1813–1833), Oct 20, 1819; no children. ❖ Ferdinand VII's 1st wife was Maria Antonia of Naples (1784–1806); his 2nd was Maria Isabel of Portugal (1797–1818); his 4th was Maria Cristina I of Naples (1806–1878).

MARIA JOSEPHA OF SAXONY (1867–1944). Archduchess of Austria. Name variations: Marie Josepha of Saxony. Born May 31, 1867, in Dresden; died May 28, 1944, at Wildenwart Castle, Upper Bavaria; dau. of Maria Anna of Portugal (1843–1884) and George (1832–1904), king of Saxony (r. 1902–1904); m. Otto (1865–1906, son of Charles Louis and Maria Annunziata), archduke of Austria, Oct 2, 1886; children: Karl also known as Charles I (1887–1922), emperor of Austria (r. 1916–1918, who m. Zita of Parma); Maximilian (1895–1952, who m. Frances of Hohenlohe).

MARIA JULIANA OF BRUNSWICK (1729–1796). Queen of Denmark and Norway. Name variations: Queen Juliana; Juliana Bevern; Juliane Marie of Brunswick-Wolfenbüttel; Marie of Brunswick; Maria Juliana of Brunswick-Wolfenbuttel. Born Juliana Mary, Sept 4, 1729, in Wolfenbuttel, Germany; dau. of Ferdinand, duke of Brunswick; died Oct 10, 1796, in Fredensborg, Denmark; became 2nd wife of Frederick V, king of Denmark and Norway (r. 1746–1766), July 8, 1752; children: Frederic (1753–1805, who m. Sophia of Mecklenburg [1758–1794]); stepmother of Christian VII, king of Denmark and Norway (r. 1766–1808). ❖ Frederick V's 1st wife was Louise of England (1724–1751). ❖ See also *Women in World History.*

MARIA-KYRATZA ASEN (fl. late 1300s). Empress of Nicaea. Fl. in the late 1300s; dau. of Ivan Alexander; m. Andronicus IV Paleologus, emperor of Nicaea (r. 1376–1379); children: John VII Paleologus (d. 1408), emperor of Nicaea (r. 1390). ❖ When husband tried to overthrow his father, was thrown into prison along with blinded husband

and their infant son; supposedly rubbed salve into his eyes and restored his sight.

MARIA LASCARIS (fl. 1200s). *See Maria.*

MARIA LASCARIS (fl. 1234–1242). Queen of Hungary. Name variations: Mary Lascaris; Laskaris. Fl. between 1234 and 1242; dau. of Theodore I Lascaris, emperor of Nicaea (r. 1204–1222) and probably Anna Angelina (dau. of Alexius III, Byzantine emperor); m. Bela IV, king of Hungary (r. 1235–1270); children: Cunegunde (1234–1292); Stephen V, king of Hungary (b. 1239, r. 1270–1272); Margaret of Hungary (1242–1270). ❖ Bela IV's 2nd wife was Saint Salome of Hungary (1201–c. 1270).

MARIA LESCZINSKA (1703–1768). *See Marie Leczinska.*

MARIA LEOPOLDINA (1776–1848). Electress of the Palatine. Name variations: Maria Leopoldine; Leopoldine. Born Dec 10, 1776, in Milan; died June 23, 1848, in Wasserburg; dau. of Maria Beatrice of Modena (1750–1829) and Archduke Ferdinand (1754–1806, son of Maria Theresa of Austria [1717–1780]); sister of Francis IV, duke of Modena (r. 1814–1846); m. Charles IV Theodore of Bavaria, elector of the Palatine, Feb 15, 1795; m. Ludwig, count of Arco, Nov 14, 1804.

MARIA LEOPOLDINA OF AUSTRIA (1797–1826). *See Leopoldina of Austria.*

MARIA LEOPOLDINE (1632–1649). Queen of Bohemia and Holy Roman empress. Name variations: Maria Leopoldina. Born April 6, 1632, in Innsbruck; died July 7, 1649, in Vienna; dau. of Claudia de Medici (1604–1648) and Leopold V (1586–1632), archduke of Austrian Tyrol or Tirol; 2nd wife of Ferdinand III (1608–1657), king of Bohemia (r. 1627–1646), king of Hungary (r. 1625), Holy Roman emperor (r. 1637–1657). ❖ Ferdinand III's 1st wife was Maria Anna of Spain (1606–1646), the mother of three of his children. His 3rd was Eleonora II Gonzaga (1628–1686).

MARIA LEOPOLDINE (1776–1848). *See Maria Leopoldina.*

MARIA LOUISA OF SAVOY (1688–1714). *See Marie Louise of Savoy.*

MARIA LOUISA OF SPAIN (1745–1792). Holy Roman empress, empress of Austria, and grand-duchess of Tuscany. Name variations: Marie-Louise Bourbon; Maria Ludovica; infanta Maria Ludovica of Bourbon-Spain. Born Nov 24, 1745, in Naples; died May 15, 1792, in Vienna; dau. of Charles III, king of Spain (r. 1759–1788), also known as Charles IV, king of Naples and Sicily (r. 1735–1759), and Maria Amalia of Saxony (1724–1760, dau. of Augustus III of Poland); m. Leopold II (1747–1792), count of Tuscany, ruler of Florence (r. 1765–1790), Holy Roman emperor (r. 1790–1792); children: Ferdinand III (1769–1824), grand duke of Tuscany; Alexander Leopold (1772–1795); Theresa (1767–1827); Francis II (1768–1835), last Holy Roman emperor (r. 1792–1806), also known as Francis I, emperor of Austria (r. 1804–1835); Maria Anna (1770–1809); Maria Clementina of Austria (1777–1801); Maria Amalia (1780–1798); John (1782–1859), vicar-general; Joseph (1776–1847), archduke Palatine of Hungary; Anthony Victor (1779–1835); Rainer (1783–1853), viceroy of Lombardy; Louis (1784–1864); Rudolf (1788–1831), cardinal-archbishop of Olmutz.

MARIA LUDOVICA (1798–1857). Tuscan noblewoman. Name variations: Marie Louise or Marie Luise. Born Aug 30, 1798, in Florence, Italy; died June 15, 1857, in Florence; dau. of Ferdinand III, grand duke of Tuscany (r. 1790–1802 and 1814–1824) and Louisa Amelia (1773–1802); sister of Leopold II, grand duke of Tuscany (r. 1824–1859).

MARIA LUDOVICA (1845–1917). Tuscan noblewoman. Name variations: Maria Luisa. Born Oct 31, 1845, in Florence, Italy; died Aug 27, 1917, in Hanau; dau. of Leopold II, grand duke of Tuscany (1797–1870, r. 1824–1859) and Maria Antonia of Sicily (1814–1898); m. Charles of Isenburg-Birstein.

MARIA LUDOVICA OF MODENA (1787–1816). Empress of Austria. Name variations: Maria Ludovica Beatrix. Born Dec 14, 1787, inMonza; died April 7, 1816, in Verona; dau. of Archduke Ferdinand (1754–1806, son of Maria Theresa of Austria [1717–1780]) and Maria Beatrice of Modena (1750–1829); became 3rd wife of Franz or Francis II, Holy Roman emperor (r. 1792–1806), also known as Francis I, emperor of Austria (r. 1804–1835), Jan 6, 1808.

MARIA LUISA OF ETRURIA (1782–1824). Queen of Etruria (Tuscany). Name variations: Luisa, Regent of Etruria, Duchess of Lucca; Marie Louise and María Luisa of Spain. Born in Madrid, Spain;

on July 6, 1782; died Mar 13, 1824; dau. of Charles IV, king of Spain (r. 1788–1808), and Maria Luisa Teresa of Parma (1751–1819); sister of Carlota Joaquina (1775–1830) and Ferdinand VII, king of Spain (r. 1813–1833); m. Louis de Bourbon also known as Louis I (1773–1803), duke of Parma (r. 1801–1803), Aug 25, 1795; children: Charles Louis (1799–1803), duke of Parma; Louise of Parma (1802–1857). ❖ Upon death of husband (1803), became regent of Etruria for son; lost her kingdom (1807); failing in an attempt to flee to England (1811), was imprisoned in a Roman cloister until 1814; after fall of Napoleon (1815), was granted province of Lucca by Congress of Vienna; ruled as duchess of Lucca until her death.

MARIA LUISA TERESA OF PARMA (1751–1819). Queen of Spain. Name variations: María or Maria Louisa Teresa of Parma; Marie-Louise of Parma; Maria Luisa of Parma; Maria Luisa of Spain; Marie Louise Therese; Luisa Maria Teresa. Born Dec 9, 1751; died Jan 2, 1819; dau. of Philip de Bourbon (1720–1765, duke of Parma and son of Elizabeth Farnese), and Louise Elizabeth (1727–1759, dau. of Louis XV of France); m. Charles IV (1748–1819), king of Spain (r. 1788–1808), on Sept 4, 1765; children: Carlota Joaquina (1775–1830); Maria Luisa of Etruria (1782–1824); Ferdinand VII (1784–1833), king of Spain (r. 1813–1833); Charles or Carlos Maria Isidro or Don Carlos (1788–1855); Francisco de Paula (1748–1865), duke of Cadiz; Maria Amalia (1779–1798, who m. Anton Pascal de Bourbon); Marie Isabella of Spain (1789–1848). ❖ Wife of Charles IV and mother of Ferdinand VII, whose support of an alliance with Napoleon helped weaken the Spanish monarchy; championed the unpopular Manuel de Godoy; when Napoleon forced the abdication (May 1808) of both her husband and son in favor of his brother Joseph Bonaparte, went into exile in France. ❖ See also *Women in World History.*

MARIA MADDALENA DE' PAZZI (1566–1607). *See Mary Magdalen of Pazzi.*

MARIA MAGDALENA (1689–1743). Bohemian princess. Born Mar 26, 1689, in Vienna; died May 1, 1743, in Vienna; dau. of Eleanor of Pfalz-Neuburg (1655–1720) and Leopold I of Bohemia (1640–1705), Holy Roman emperor (r. 1658–1705).

MARIA MAGDALENA OF AUSTRIA (1589–1631). Grand duchess of Tuscany. Name variations: Maria Maddalena; Maria Maddalena of Austria; Maria Maddalena de Medici; Marie-Madelaine. Born Oct 7, 1589, in Graz; died Nov 1, 1631, in Passau; dau. of Mary of Bavaria (1551–1608), duchess of Styria, and Charles (1540–1590), archduke of Styria; sister of Ferdinand II, king of Bohemia and Hungary (r. 1578–1637), Holy Roman emperor (r. 1619–1637), Margaret of Austria (c. 1577–1611), Anna of Styria (1573–1598), and Constance of Styria (1588–1631); m. Cosimo II de Medici (1590–1620), grand duke of Tuscany (r. 1609–1620), on Oct 19, 1608; children: Ferdinand II (1610–1670), grand duke of Tuscany (r. 1620–1670); Maria Cristina de Medici (1610–1632, twin sister of Ferdinand II); Giovanni Carlo, cardinal (1611–1663); Margaret of Parma (b. 1612, who m. Edward Farnese, duke of Parma); Mattia or Mattias (1613–1667); Francesco (d. 1634); Anna de Medici (b. 1616, who m. Ferdinand of Austrian Tyrol); Leopoldo (1617–1675), cardinal. ❖ Exceptionally well educated, showed considerable interest in contemporary art and the intellectual movement known as humanism; fit in fairly well in the culturally refined, ostentatious Medici court in Florence, and seems to have gotten along well with husband; following his death (1620), shared regency for young son with Christine of Lorraine. ❖ See also *Women in World History.*

MARIA MALIUTA (d. 1605). *See Maria Skuratova.*

MARIA MERCEDES (1910–2000). *See Maria de las Mercedes.*

MARIA NAGAIA (d. 1612). Empress of Russia. Name variations: Maria Nagoy; Martha. Died July 20, 1612; dau. of Theodor Nagaia (minor landowner); became the 7th wife of Ivan IV the Terrible (1530–1584), tsar of Russia (r. 1533–1584), Sept 1580; children: Demetrius also known as Dmitri (b. 1583, killed in 1591). Ivan IV had previously m. Anastasia Romanova (d. 1560), Maria of Circassia (d. 1369), Marta Sobakin (d. 1571), Anna Koltoskaia (d. 1626), Anna Vassiltschikov, and Vassilissa Malentieva. ❖ Wed Ivan IV; when he died and his son Theodore (from a previous marriage) succeeded as tsar (1584), planned a coup with family to place her son Dmitri on the throne; was arrested and eventually forced to live in a nunnery, where she took the name Martha; after son died in a freak accident, chose to back Dmitri the Pretender for a time. ❖ See also *Women in World History.*

MARIA NIKOLAEVNA (1819–1876). Duchess of Leuchtenburg. Name variations: Nicholiava; Maria Romanov; duchess of Leuchtenberg. Born Aug 6, 1819; died Feb 21, 1876; eldest dau. of Nicholas I (1796–1855), tsar of Russia (1825–1855), and Charlotte of Prussia (1798–1860); sister of Alexander II, tsar of Russia, Olga of Russia (1822–1892), and Alexandra Nikolaevna (1825–1844); m. Maximilian de Beauharnais also known as Maximilian (1817–1852), duke of Leuchtenburg, July 14, 1839; m. Gregory Alexandrovna, count Stroganov, Nov 16, 1856; children: (1st marriage) George (b. 1852), count of Leuchtenburg.

MARIA OF ALANIA (fl. 1070–1081). Byzantine empress. Name variations: Mary of Alania, Maria Ducas. Born into the tribe of Alan, located in what is now southern Russia; dau. of the king of Georgia; m. Michael VII Ducas, emperor of Byzantium (r. 1071–1078); m. Nicephorus III Botaneiates (Botoniates), emperor of Byzantium (r. 1078–1081), in 1708; children: (1st marriage) Constantine Ducas (who was at one time betrothed to Anna Comnena). ❖ When 1st husband abandoned the throne to take up monastic vows, was abandoned also; agreed to marry Nicephorus III Botaneiates to safeguard the possible succession of her son Constantine, then age 4; when Nicephorus named Synadenus successor instead of Constantine, threw her energy to the Comneni and aided Alexius I's royal ambitions. ❖ See also *Women in World History.*

MARIA OF ALEXANDRIA (fl. 1st, 2nd, or 3rd c.). *See Mary the Jewess.*

MARIA OF AMNIA (fl. 782). Byzantine empress. Name variations: Maria of Armenia. Fl. around 782; 1st wife of Constantine VI Porphyrogenitus (b. 771), emperor of Byzantium (r. 780–797); children: Euphrosyne (c. 790–c. 840, who m. Byzantine emperor Michael II of Amorion). ❖ Was chosen to be the wife of Constantine VI by winning a beauty contest held by Irene of Athens; because she had been forced on him, was hated by Constantine and later compelled to withdraw to a nunnery.

MARIA OF ANJOU (1371–1395). *See Maria of Hungary.*

MARIA OF ARAGON (fl. 1311). Sicilian princess. Fl. in 1311; dau. of Blanche of Naples (d. 1310) and James II or Jaime, king of Sicily and Aragon (r. 1291–1327); m. Peter, regent of Castile, in Dec 1311; children: Blanche of Castile (c. 1320–1375).

MARIA OF ARAGON (1403–1445). Queen of Castile and Leon. Name variations: María; Mary Trastamara. Born in 1403; died Feb 18, 1445, in Villacastin; dau. of Ferdinand I, king of Aragon (r. 1412–1416), and Eleanor of Albuquerque (1374–1435); became 1st wife of Juan II also known as John II (1404–1454), king of Castile and Leon (r. 1406–1454), Aug 4, 1420; children: Catalina of the Asturias (1422–1424); Leonor of the Asturias (1423–1425); Enrique also known as Henry IV (1425–1474), king of Castile and Leon (r. 1454–1474, who m. Blanche of Navarre and Joanna of Portugal); Maria of Castile (1429–1430). ❖ John II's 2nd wife was Isabel of Portugal (1428–1496, mother of Isabella I).

MARIA OF ARAGON (fl. 1440). Marquesa of Ferrara. Name variations: Maria d'Este. Fl. around 1440; m. Leonello (1407–1450), 13th marquis of Ferrara. ❖ Leonello's 1st wife was Margherita Gonzaga (1418–1439).

MARIA OF ARMENIA (fl. 1300). Byzantine empress. Name variations: Xene. Fl. in the early 1300s; m. Michael IX Paleologus (d. 1320), Byzantine emperor, co-emperor of Nicaea (r. 1295–1320); children: Andronicus III, emperor of Nicaea (r. 1328–1341); Manuel; Theodora Paleologina (who m. Theodore Svetoslav and Michael Shishman); Anna (who m. Thomas of Epirus and Nicholas Orsini).

MARIA OF AUSTRIA (1505–1558). *See Mary of Hungary.*

MARIA OF AUSTRIA (1584–1649). Austrian royal. Born June 16, 1584, in Innsbruck; died Mar 2, 1649, in Innsbruck; dau. of Anna Caterina Gonzaga (1566–1621) and Ferdinand II, archduke of Austria; sister of Anna Gonzaga (1585–1618).

MARIA OF AUSTRIA (1752–1814). *See Maria Carolina.*

MARIA OF BAVARIA (1805–1877). Queen of Saxony. Born in 1805; died in 1877; dau. of Maximilian I Joseph, elector of Bavaria (r. 1799–1805), king of Bavaria (r. 1805–1825), and Caroline of Baden (1776–1841); twin sister of Sophie of Bavaria (1805–1872); sister of Elizabeth of Bavaria (1801–1873, who m. Frederick William IV of Prussia); 2nd wife of Frederick Augustus II (1797–1854), king of Saxony (r. 1836–1854). ❖ Frederick Augustus' 1st wife was Caroline of Austria (1801–1832).

MARIA OF BAVARIA (1841–1925). *See Maria Sophia Amalia.*

MARIA OF BAVARIA (1872–1954). Duchess of Calabria. Name variations: Marie of Bavaria. Born July 6, 1872; died June 10, 1954; dau. of Maria Teresa of Este (1849–1919) and Louis also known as Ludwig III (1845–1921), king of Bavaria (r. 1913–1918); m. Ferdinand Pio (1869–1934), duke of Calabria, on May 31, 1897; children: Maria Antoinette (b. 1898); Maria Cristina (b. 1899); Roger (1901–1914); Barbara (1902–1927, who m. Franz Xaver of Stolberg-Wernigerode); Lucia (b. 1908); Urraca (b. 1913).

MARIA OF BYZANTIUM (fl. 12th c.). Queen of Hungary. Married Stephen IV, king of Hungary (r. 1162–1163).

MARIA OF CASTILE (1401–1458). Queen of Aragon, Naples, and Sicily. Name variations: María of Castile; Mary Trastamara; infanta of Castile. Born Nov 14, 1401, in Segovia; died Sept 7, 1458 (some sources cite 1457), in Valencia; dau. of Catherine of Lancaster (1372–1418) and Enrique also known as Henry III (1379–1406), king of Castile (r. 1390–1406); m. Alfonso or Alphonso V the Magnanimous (1396–1458), king of Aragon (r. 1416–1458), king of Sicily as Alphonso I (r. 1443–1458), in Valencia, Aragon, on June 12 or 13, 1415; children: none (Ferdinand or Ferrante I of Naples [b. 1423, r. 1458–1494] was Alphonso V's illeg. son). ❖ Talented monarch and an able administrator, who ruled Aragon successfully for a quarter of a century, wed cousin Alphonso V, king of Aragon (1415); during husband's absence, was viceroy of Aragon (1421–24); negotiated truce between the armies of Aragon and Castile (July 1, 1429); with Alphonso king of Naples, was viceroy of Aragon (1434–58); urged neutrality in conflict between Navarre and Castile (July 1444); signed peace treaty with Castile (May 16, 1454); proved herself both on the battlefield and in the council chamber; was a deft negotiator, and initiated policies which benefited the common people of Aragon and fostered economic growth; a generous patron of the arts, also favored monastic reform. ❖ See also *Women in World History.*

MARIA OF CASTILE (1482–1517). Queen of Portugal. Name variations: Maria of Castile or Marie of Castile; Mary Trastamara. Born June 29, 1482, in Cordoba; died Mar 7, 1517, in Lisbon; dau. of Ferdinand II, king of Aragon, and Isabella I (1451–1504), queen of Castile (r. 1468–1504); became 2nd wife of Miguel also known as Manuel I the Fortunate (1469–1521), king of Portugal (r. 1495–1521), on Oct 30, 1500; children: Luiz (1506–1555), duke of Beja; Isabella of Portugal (1503–1539); Beatrice of Portugal (1504–1538, who m. Charles II of Savoy); Fernando (1507–1534), duke of Guarda; Alfonso (1509–1540), archbishop of Lisbon; Enrique or Henry (1512–1580), cardinal of Portugal; Duarte (b. 1515, who m. Isabella of Braganza); Joao also known as John III, king of Portugal (r. 1521–1557, who m. Catherine [1507–1578], sister of Charles V); Maria (1513–1513); Antonio (1516–1516). ❖ See also *Women in World History.*

MARIA OF CIRCASSIA (d. 1569). Russian empress. Name variations: Maria Tscherkaski. Died Sept 1, 1569; dau. of Temrink Tscherkaski; became 2nd wife of Ivan IV the Terrible (1530–1584), tsar of Russia (r. 1533–1584), Aug 1561; children: Vassilli (1563–1563). ❖ See also *Women in World History.*

MARIA OF CORDOVA (d. 851). Saint and martyr of the Roman Catholic Church. Born in Cordova, Spain; died Nov 24, 851; sister of the deacon Valabonse. ❖ A Christian, went into hiding following the death of her brother; decided to face the authorities with Flora of Cordova and was martyred with her. ❖ See also *Women in World History.*

MARIA OF HABSBURG (1528–1603). *See Marie of Austria.*

MARIA OF HUNGARY (fl. 995–1025). *See Maria.*

MARIA OF HUNGARY (1371–1395). Queen of Hungary and Bohemia. Name variations: Maria of Anjou; Mary of Anjou. Born in 1371 in Hungary (some sources cite 1370); died May 17, 1395, in Hungary (some sources cite 1392); dau. of Louis I the Great, king of Hungary (r. 1342–1382), king of Poland (r. 1370–1382), and Elizabeth of Bosnia (c. 1345–1387); sister of Jadwiga (1374–1399), queen of Poland (r. 1384–1399); became 1st wife of Sigismund I (1368–1437), margrave of Brandenburg, king of Bohemia (r. 1419–1437), duke of Luxemburg (1419–1437), king of Hungary (r. 1387–1437), and Holy Roman emperor (r. 1410–1437), in Oct 1385. ❖ When father died (1382), inherited Hungary at age 17; ruled well with husband, making important alliances and preserving the empire for 12 years; died suddenly after a fall from her horse at 29; was greatly mourned. ❖ See also *Women in World History.*

MARIA OF HUNGARY (1606–1646). *See Maria Anna of Spain.*

MARIA OF JULICH-BERG (fl. 1515). Duchess of Cleves. Name variations: Marie of Julich; Mary of Jülich-Berg-Ravensburg. Fl. around 1515; dau. of William III (or IV), duke of Juliers, and Sybilla of Brandenburg; m. John III, duke of Cleves (r. 1521–1539); children: Sybilla of Cleves (1514–1554); Anne of Cleves (1515–1557), who m. Henry VIII, king of England); William IV (or V), duke of Cleves (r. 1539–1592); Amelia of Cleves (1517–1586).

MARIA OF KIEV (d. 1087). Queen of Poland. Name variations: Dobronega Maria. Born before 1015; died in 1087; dau. of Vladimir I, grand prince of Kiev (r. 980–1015) and one of his nine wives; sister of Yaroslav I the Wise, grand prince of Kiev (r. 1019–1054); m. Kazimir or Casimir I the Restorer (1015–1058), king of Poland (r. 1038–1058), in 1043; children: Boleslaw II Szczodry also known as Boleslaus II the Bold, king of Poland (r. 1058–1079); Wladyslaw I or Ladislas Herman (1043–1102), king of Poland (r. 1079–1102); Swietoslava (who m. Vratislav, king of Bohemia); Mieszko.

MARIA OF KIEV (d. 1146). Princess of Kiev. Died in 1146; dau. of Gyseth (fl. 1070) and Vladimir II Monomakh or Monomach (1053–1125), grand prince of Kiev (r. 1113–1125); m. Leo Diogenes of Byzantium (d. 1116).

MARIA OF KIEV (d. 1179). *See Marie of Kiev.*

MARIA OF MACEDONIA (d. around 864). Macedonian wife of Basil I. Born in Macedonia; died c. 864; 1st wife of Basil I the Macedonian, Byzantine emperor (r. 867–886); children: Constantine (crowned as co-emperor on Jan 6, 869, but died young in 879). ❖ Basil's 2nd wife was Eudocia Ingerina.

MARIA OF MECKLENBURG-SCHWERIN (1854–1920). Grand duchess. Name variations: Grand duchess Vladimir; Mary of Mecklenburg-Schwerin. Born Mary or Maria Alexandra Elizabeth Eleanor on May 14, 1854; died Sept 6, 1920; dau. of Frederick Francis II, grand duke of Mecklenburg-Schwerin; m. Vladimir Alexandrovitch (son of Alexander II, tsar of Russia, and Marie of Hesse-Darmstadt), Aug 16, 1874; children: Cyril Vladimorovitch (1876–1938); Boris (1877–1943); Andrew (1879–1956); Helena of Russia (1882–1957).

MARIA OF MOLINA (d. 1321). *See Maria de Molina.*

MARIA OF MONTPELLIER (1181–1213). Queen of Aragon. Name variations: Marie of Montpellier or Montpelier; Mary of Montpellier or Montpelier. Born in 1181 (some sources cite 1182); died in 1213 (some sources cite 1219); dau. of Guillaume or Guillem or William VIII, lord of Montpellier, and Eudocia of Byzantium (niece of the Byzantine emperor Manuel I Comnenus); m. Barral, viscount of Marseilles, in 1192 (died 1192); m. Bernard IV, count of Comminges, in 1197 (Maria was repudiated and sent home in 1201); m. Pedro or Peter II, king of Aragon (r. 1196–1213), in 1204; children: daughter Sancia; Jaime or James I the Great of Catalonia (1208–1276), king of Aragon (r. 1213–1276); two other daughters (names unknown). ❖ Devoted her short life to protecting her inheritance, the town of Montpellier, from greedy husbands and rebellious city nobles, to preserve it for her son who became James I, king of Aragon. ❖ See also *Women in World History.*

MARIA OF NAVARRE (fl. 1340). Queen of Aragon. Fl. around 1340; 1st wife of Pedro IV also known as Peter IV the Ceremonious (b. 1319), king of Aragon (r. 1336–1387). ❖ Peter IV's 2nd wife was Eleanor of Portugal (1328–1348); his 3rd was Eleanor of Sicily (d. 1375).

MARIA OF PORTUGAL (1313–1357). Queen of Castile and Leon. Name variations: Mary Henriques, Enriques or Enriquez. Born in 1313; died Jan 18, 1357, in Evora; interred in Seville, Spain; dau. of Beatrice of Castile and Leon (1293–1359) and Alphonso IV, king of Portugal (r. 1325–1357); m. Alphonso XI (1311–1350), king of Castile and Leon (r. 1312–1350), in Sept 1328; children: Fernando (1332–1333); Pedro el Cruel also known as Peter I the Cruel (1334–1369), king of Castile (r. 1350–1369). ❖ See also *Women in World History.*

MARIA OF PORTUGAL (1538–1577). Duchess of Parma. Name variations: Maria Farnese. Born Dec 8, 1538, in Lisbon; died July 18, 1577, in Parma; dau. of Isabella of Braganza (c. 1512–1576) and Duarte (1515–1540), duke of Guimaraes; m. Alexander also known as Allesandro Farnese, duke of Parma, in Nov 1565; children: Ranuccio I (1569–1622), duke of Parma (r. 1592–1622).

MARIA OF PRUSSIA (1825–1889). Queen of Bavaria. Name variations: Marie of Prussia. Born Marie Hedwig on Oct 15, 1825, in Berlin; died at the castle of Hohenschwangau on May 18, 1889; dau. of Mary of Hesse-Homburg (1785–1846) and William (son of Frederick William II, king of Prussia, and Frederica of Hesse); niece of Frederick William III of Prussia; m. her cousin Maximilian II (1811–1864), king of Bavaria (r. 1848–1864), on Oct 12, 1842; children: Ludwig II (1845–1886), the mad king of Bavaria (r. 1864–1886); Otto (1848–1886), king of Bavaria (r. 1886–1913).

MARIA OF SAVOY (fl. 1400s). Duchess of Milan. Fl. in the early 1400s; m. Filippo Maria Visconti (1392–1447), duke of Milan (r. 1402–1447). ❖ Filippo had an illegitimate daughter, Bianca Maria Visconti (1423–1470), with Agnes del Maino.

MARIA OF SAVOY (1914—). Italian princess. Name variations: Marie of Savoy; Maria di Savvia. Born Maria Francesca di Savoia-Carignano, Dec 26, 1914; dau. of Elena of Montenegro (1873–1952) and Victor Emmanuel III (1869–1947), king of Italy (r. 1900–1946, abdicated); sister of Mafalda of Hesse; m. Louis Charles of Bourbon, 1939; children: 4.

MARIA OF SICILY (d. 1402). Queen of Sicily. Name variations: Mary of Sicily. Reigned from 1377 to 1402 (some sources cite 1401); died in 1402; dau. of Frederick III the Simple, king of Sicily (r. 1355–1377) and Constance of Aragon (c. 1350–?); m. Martin I the Younger, king of Sicily (r. 1390–1409); children: one son (d. 1402). ❖ Following death of her father (1377), came to the throne in name only; abducted from her castle (1390), was forced to marry her cousin (son of Martin I, king of Aragon), so that he might become king of Sicily (1392).

MARIA OF THE PALATINATE. *See Anna Maria of the Palatinate.*

MARIA OF TREBIZOND (d. 1439). Byzantine empress. Name variations: Maria Komnene or Comneni of Trebizond. Died in 1439; 3rd wife of John VIII Paleologus (1391–1448), emperor of Nicaea and Byzantine emperor in exile (r. 1425–1448). ❖ See also *Women in World History.*

MARIA OF TVER (c. 1440–1467). Grand Princess of Moscow. Born in 1440 or 1442, in Tver, a town northwest of Moscow; died April 22, 1467; dau. of Prince Boris of Tver and Anastasia of Mojaisk (d. 1451); betrothed to Ivan III when she was six; m. Ivan III (1440–1505), tsar of Russia (r. 1462–1505), on June 2, 1452; children: Ivan the Younger (1456–1490), prince of Moscow (r. 1471–1490, who m. Helene of Moldavia). ❖ See also *Women in World History.*

MARIA OF WALDECK (1857–1882). Princess of Waldeck and Pyrmont. Name variations: Marie of Waldeck and Pyrmont. Born May 23, 1857; died April 30, 1882; dau. of George II Victor, prince of Waldeck and Pyrmont, and Helen of Nassau (1831–1888); became 1st wife of William II (1848–1921), king of Wurttemberg (r. 1891–1918, abdicated), Feb 15, 1877; children: Pauline of Wurttemberg (1877–1965), who m. Frederick, prince of Wied); Ulrich (b. 1880). ❖ William II married his 2nd wife, Princess Charlotte of Schaumburg-Lippe (1864–1946), April 8, 1886.

MARIA OF WURTTEMBERG (1797–1855). Archduchess of Austria. Name variations: Maria Dorothea. Born Nov 1, 1797; died Mar 30, 1855; dau. of Henrietta of Nassau-Weilburg (1780–1857) and Ludwig Frederick Alexander, duke of Wurttemberg; m. Joseph, archduke of Austria, Aug 24, 1819; children: Elizabeth (1820–1820); Archduchess Elizabeth (1831–1903); Alexander (b. 1825); Joseph (b. 1833); Maria Henrietta of Austria (1836–1902).

MARIA PADILLA (1335–1365). *See Marie de Padilla.*

MARIA PALEOLOGINA (fl. 1271–1279). Tsarina of Bulgaria. Name variations: Maria Palaeologina. Flourished around 1278 and 1279; dau. of Eulogia Paleologina; niece of Michael VIII Paleologus, emperor of Byzantium (r. 1261–1282); became 2nd wife of Constantine Tich, tsar of Bulgaria (r. 1257–1277), around 1271; m. Ivajlo, tsar of Bulgaria (r. 1278–1279), around 1277. ❖ See also *Women in World History.*

MARIA PIA (1847–1911). Queen of Portugal. Name variations: Marie-Pia; Maria Pia of Italy; Maria Pia de Savoie. Born in Turin on Oct 16, 1847; died July 5, 1911, in Stupinigi, Italy, from heart disease; dau. of Victor Emmanuel II, king of Italy (r. 1849–1878), and Marie Adelaide of Austria (1822–1855); m. Luis or Louis I (1838–1889), king of Portugal (r. 1861–1889), Sept 27, 1862 (some sources cite Oct 6); children: Carlos or Charles I (1863–1908), king of Portugal (r. 1889–1908); Afonso also known as Alfonso Henrique (1865–1920), duke of Oporto. ❖ Rarely intervened in government affairs, preferring to devote her energies to charitable works, but did press for the abolition of slavery in the

Portuguese colonies, which occurred in 1868; with republican revolution (1910), went into exile. ❖ See also *Women in World History*.

MARIA SKURATOVA (d. 1605). Tsarina of Russia. Name variations: Maria Maliuta; Mary of Malyuta; Maria Godunov, Godunova or Godunovna; Maria Gudunov; Maria Skurateva. Born Maria Maliuta-Skuratova; killed in 1605; dau. of Grigorii Maliuta-Skuratov or Skuratev (leader of Ivan IV's terror squad); m. Boris Godunov (1552–1605), tsar of Russia (r. 1598–1605), in 1570; children: (daughter) Xenia Godunova (1582–1622); Fyodor or Fedor Borisovich also known as Theodore II (1589–1605), tsar of Russia (r. 1605).

MARIA SOBIESKA (1702–1735). *See Sobieski, Clementina.*

MARIA SOPHIA AMALIA (1841–1925). Duchess in Bavaria and last queen of the Two Sicilies. Name variations: Maria of Bavaria. Born Oct 4, 1841; died Jan 19, 1925; dau. of Maximilian Joseph, duke of Bavaria, and Ludovica (1808–1892); sister of Elizabeth of Bavaria (1837–1898), empress of Austria and Hungary; m. Francesco II also known as Francis II (1836–1894), king of the Two Sicilies (r. 1859–1861), Feb 3, 1859; children: Marie Christine (1869–1870). ❖ Was briefly queen of the Two Sicilies (1859–61), before Italy was united under Victor Emmanuel II.

MARIA SOPHIA OF NEUBERG (1666–1699). Queen of Portugal. Name variations: Marie-Sophia; Maria Sophia of Palatinate. Born August 6, 1666, in Neuberg; died Aug 4, 1699, in Lisbon, Portugal; dau. of Philip Wilhelm or Philip William, elector Palatine of the Rhine (r. 1667–1706), and Elizabeth Amalia of Hesse (1635–1709); sister of Maria Anna of Neuberg (1667–1740); became 2nd wife of Pedro or Peter II, king of Portugal (r. 1667–1706), Aug 11, 1687; children: John of Portugal (1668–1688); John V (1689–1750), king of Portugal (r. 1706–1750); Francisco (b. 1691); Antonio Francisco (b. 1695); Teresa (1696–1704); Manuel (b. 1697); Francisca Josefa of Portugal (1699–1736).

MARIA TELLES (d. 1379). *See Telles, Maria.*

MARIA TERESA (1882–1912). Spanish princess. Born in 1882; died in 1912; dau. of Maria Christina of Austria (1858–1929) and Alfonso or Alphonso XII (1857–1885), king of Spain (r. 1875–1885); m. Ferdinand of Bavaria (1884–1958), in 1906.

MARIA TERESA OF AUSTRIA (1773–1832). Queen of Sardinia. Name variations: Maria-Theresa. Born Nov 1, 1773; died Mar 29, 1832; dau. of Maria Beatrice of Modena (1750–1829) and Archduke Ferdinand of Austria (1754–1806, son of Maria Theresa of Austria [1717–1780]); m. Victor Emmanuel I (1759–1824), king of Sardinia (r. 1802–1821, abdicated), on April 25, 1789; children: Maria Beatrice of Sardinia (1792–1840), who m. Francis IV, duke of Modena); Theresa of Savoy (1803–1879), who m. Charles, duke of Parma); Maria Anna of Savoy (1803–1884), who m. Ferdinand I, emperor of Austria); Christina of Sardinia (1812–1836), who m. Ferdinand II of Naples).

MARIA TERESA OF ESTE (1849–1919). Queen of Bavaria. Name variations: Maria Theresa; Maria Theresa of Modena. Born July 2, 1849, in Brunn; died Feb 3, 1919, in Schloss, Wildenwart; interred at Dom Church, Munich, Germany; dau. of Ferdinand (1821–1849), archduke of Austria-Este (r. 1835–1848), and Archduchess Elizabeth (1831–1903); m. Louis III also known as Ludwig III (1845–1921), king of Bavaria (r. 1913–1918), on Feb 20, 1868; children: 11, including Rupert (1869–1955), and Maria of Bavaria (b. 1872).

MARIA TERESA OF NAPLES (1772–1807). Holy Roman empress. Name variations: Maríe-Thérèse of Bourbon-Naples; Maria Teresa of the Two Sicilies; Maria Theresa of Naples; empress of Austria. Born June 6, 1772, in Naples; died in childbirth on April 13, 1807, in Vienna; dau. of Maria Carolina (1752–1814) and Ferdinand I, king of the Two Sicilies (r. 1816–1825), king of Naples and Sicily as Ferdinand IV (r. 1759–1806, 1815–1825); became 2nd wife of Francis I (1768–1835) emperor of Austria (r. 1804–1835), also known as Francis II, Holy Roman emperor (r. 1792–1806), on Sept 19, 1790; children: Marie Louise of Austria (1791–1847), who became 2nd wife of Napoleon I Bonaparte); Ferdinand I the Good (1793–1875), emperor of Austria (r. 1835–1848); Caroline (1794–1795); Caroline (1795–1799); Leopoldina of Austria (1797–1826), who m. Pedro I of Brazil); Clementine of Austria (1798–1881); Joseph (b. 1799); Caroline of Austria (1801–1832), who m. Frederick Augustus II of Saxony); Francis Charles (1802–1878), who m. Sophie of Bavaria); Mari Anna (1804–1858); Johann (b. 1805); Amalie (1807–1807). Holy Roman emperor Francis II had 4 wives: Elizabeth of Wurttemberg (1767–1790), Maria Teresa of Naples, Maria Ludovica of Modena (1787–1816), and Caroline Augusta of Bavaria (1792–1873).

MARIA TERESA OF SAVOY (1756–1805). Queen of France. Name variations: Marie Thérèse; Maria Theresa of Sardinia; Clotilde of Savoy. Born in 1756; died in 1805; dau. of Maria Antonia of Spain (1729–1785) and Victor Amadeus III (1726–1796), duke of Savoy (r. 1773–1796); m. Charles X (1757–1830), king of France (r. 1824–1830, abdicated); children: Louis XIX (1775–1844), duke of Angoulême; Charles Ferdinand (1778–1820), duke of Berry.

MARIA TERESA OF SPAIN (1638–1683). Queen of France. Name variations: Marie Theresa or Thérèse; Marie Therese of Austria; Marie-Thérèse of Spain; Maria Theresa; Maria Teresa; Marie-Theresa; Infanta of Spain. Born at the Escorial, Spain, Sept 20, 1638; died of blood poisoning on July 30, 1683, at Versailles, France; interred at St. Denis; dau. of Philip IV (1605–1665), king of Spain (r. 1621–1665), and his 1st wife Elizabeth Valois (1602–1644, sister of Louis XIII); m. and became queen-consort of Louis XIV (1638–1715), king of France (r. 1643–1715), June 9, 1660; children: 6, only one of whom survived her, Louis (1661–1711), le grand dauphin. ❖ The year before her marriage to Louis XIV, signed the Treaty of the Pyrenees, renouncing any claim to Spanish succession. ❖ See also *Women in World History*.

MARIA TERESA OF SPAIN (1651–1673). *See Margaret Theresa of Spain.*

MARIA TERESA OF THE TWO SICILIES (1772–1807). *See Maria Teresa of Naples.*

MARIA TERESA OF TUSCANY (1801–1855). *See Maria Theresa of Tuscany.*

MARIA THE JEWESS. *See Mary the Jewess.*

MARIA THERESA OF AUSTRIA (1717–1780). Holy Roman empress. Name variations: Maria Theresia (German spelling). Pronunciation: tay-RAY-zee-ah. Born May 13, 1717, in Vienna, Austria; died Nov 29, 1780, in Vienna; dau. of Charles VI, Holy Roman emperor (r. 1711–1740), and Elizabeth Christina of Brunswick-Wolfenbuttel (1691–1750); educated at home by Jesuit tutors; m. Francis Stephen, duke of Lorraine, later Holy Roman emperor (r. 1745–1765) as Francis I; children: 16, of whom 6 died before the age of 17, including Johanna (d. 1762) and Josepha (d. 1767); those surviving to adulthood include: Joseph II (1741–1790) emperor of Austria (r. 1765–1790), who succeeded his mother and became Holy Roman emperor; Leopold II (1747–1792), grand duke of Tuscany, Holy Roman emperor (r. 1790–1792); Maximilian Francis (who became elector of Cologne); Maria Carolina (1752–1814, who m. into the Bourbon family and became queen of Naples and the Two Sicilies); Maria Amalia (1746–1804, who m. the duke of Parma); Marie Antoinette (1755–1793, who m. Louis XVI and became queen of France); Elizabeth of Austria (1743–1808, who became abbess in Innsbruck); Ferdinand (1754–1806, who was governor general of Lombardy in Milano and m. Maria Beatrice of Modena); Maria Christina (1742–1798, who m. Duke Albert of Saxony-Teschen and became duchess and governor-general of Austrian Netherlands); Maria Anna (who became abbess of Klagenfurt). ❖ Habsburg monarch who ascended a throne threatened on all sides, repulsed most of her adversaries, and instituted a series of social and administrative reforms largely credited with ensuring the survival of the Habsburg empire through the 19th century; succeeded to her father's hereditary domains (1740), which she was forced to defend against an overwhelming armed coalition in the Austrian Succession War (1740–48); led the anti-Prussian coalition during the Seven Years' War (1756–63); participated with Prussia and Russia in the First Polish Partition (1772); intervened to end the Bavarian Succession War (1778–79), promoted by her son, Holy Roman Emperor Joseph II; with aid of 2 highly capable ministers, Counts Haugwitz and Kaunitz, instituted far-reaching reforms in virtually every domain of public life, the most durable of which were the foundation of a progressive educational system and the modernization of the realm's administrative structure; therefore, considered an "enlightened despot" by some, but not all, scholars. ❖ See also Robert Pick, *Empress Maria Theresa: The Earlier Years, 1717–1757* (Harper & Row, 1966); Edward Crankshaw, *Maria Theresa* (Atheneum, 1986); and *Women in World History*.

MARIA THERESA OF MODENA (1849–1919). *See Maria Teresa of Este.*

MARIA THERESA OF PORTUGAL (1855–1944). Archduchess of Austria. Name variations: Maria Teresa da Imaculda. Born Aug 24, 1855, in Kleinheubach; died Feb 12, 1944, in Vienna, Austria; dau. of Michael I (or Miguel), king of Portugal (r. 1828–1834) and Adelheid (1831–1909); became 3rd wife of Karl Ludwig also known as Charles Louis (1833–1896), archduke of Austria and governor of Tirol (r. 1855–

1861), on July 23, 1873; children: Elisabeth Amalia (b. 1878, who m. Aloys, prince of Liechtenstein); Maria Annunziata (1876–1961).

MARIA THERESA OF SARDINIA (1756–1805). *See Maria Teresa of Savoy.*

MARIA THERESA OF SPAIN (1638–1683). *See Maria Teresa of Spain.*

MARIA THERESA OF SPAIN (1651–1673). *See Margaret Theresa of Spain.*

MARIA THERESA OF SPAIN (1726–1746). French dauphine and infanta of Spain. Name variations: Marie Therese de Bourbon; Mary Theresa; Marie Raphaëlle or Marie Raphaelle of Spain. Born Marie-Thèrése Raphaele de Bourbon, June 11, 1726; died 4 days after giving birth to a girl on July 22, 1746, at age 20; dau. of Philip V (b. 1683), king of Spain, and Elizabeth Farnese (1692–1766); became 1st wife of Louis le dauphin (1729–1765, father of Louis XVI), on Feb 23, 1745; children: one girl (name unknown). ❖ Louis the Dauphin's 2nd wife was Marie Josephe of Saxony (1731–1767).

MARIA THERESA OF TUSCANY (1801–1855). Queen of Sardinia. Name variations: Maria Teresa of Austria; Archduchess Therese of Austria; Teresa of Tuscany; Theresa of Modena; queen of Savoy-Piedmont. Born Mar 21, 1801, in Vienna, Austria; died Jan 12, 1855; dau. of Ferdinand III, grand duke of Tuscany (r. 1790–1802 and 1814–1824) and Louisa Amelia (1773–1802); sister of Leopold II, grand duke of Tuscany (r. 1824–1859); m. Charles Albert (1798–1849), prince of Carignano and king of Sardinia (r. 1831–1849); children: Victor Emmanuel II, king of Italy (r. 1849–1878, who m. Marie Adelaide of Austria); Ferdinand (who m. Elizabeth of Saxony).

MARIA THERESA OF WURTTEMBERG (1934—). Countess of Clermont. Name variations: Maria-Theresa of Württemberg. Born Nov 12, 1934; dau. of Philip Albert of Wurttemberg and Rosa (1906–1983), duchess of Wurttemberg; married Henri or Henry of Clermont (b. 1933), count of Clermont, in 1957; children: Marie Isabelle (b. 1959), Francis Henri (b. 1961), Blanche Elisabeth (b. 1962), Jean Carl (b. 1965) and Eudes (b. 1968).

MARIAMME. *Variant of Mariamne.*

MARIAMNE (fl. 1st c.). Saint and Biblical woman. Flourished in the 1st century. ❖ After Jesus' ascension, accompanied the apostle Philip to teach the gospel to the Scythians at Hieropolis, then carried the Gospel to Lycaonia. Feast day is Feb 17.

MARIAMNE THE HASMONIAN (c. 60–c. 29 BCE). Wife of Herod the Great. Name variations: Mariamme the Hasmonaean. Born c. 60 BCE; executed around 29 BCE; dau. of Alexandra (d. 27 BCE) and Alexander (d. 49 BCE); granddau. of Hyrcanus II; became 2nd wife of Herod the Great, 37 BCE; children: Alexander and Aristobulus (both born c. 35 BCE); grandchildren: Herod of Chalcis and Herod Agrippa I. ❖ As Herod's favorite wife, was bitterly opposed by his 1st wife Doris and his sister Salome, whose partisans took every opportunity to blacken Mariamne's name; because of rumors, was executed for adultery.

MARIANA. *Variant of Maria or Marie.*

MARIANA DE AUSTRIA (c. 1634–1696). *See Maria Anna of Austria.*

MARIANA DE PAREDES (1618–1645). Ecuadoran saint. Born in Quito, Ecuador, in 1618; died in Quito in 1645. ❖ Longed to be a Dominican nun; instead, lived the life of a contemplative in the house of her relatives; when an earthquake hit Quito (1645), died after she "offered herself as a victim to divine justice for the deliverance of the city." The Republic of Ecuador conferred on her the title of "national heroine." Feast day is May 26.

MARIANA OF JESUS (1565–1624). Saint. Born in 1565; died in 1624. ❖ Was the founder of the discalced (barefoot) nuns of Our Lady of Mercy in Spain. Feast day is April 17.

MARIANA VICTORIA (1768–1788). Portuguese princess. Born Mariana Ana Victoria, Dec 15, 1768; died of smallpox in 1788, shortly after giving birth; dau. of Maria I of Braganza (1734–1816) and Pedro or Peter III (1717–1786), king of Portugal (r. 1777–1786); m. Gabriel Antonio Francisco of Spain.

MARIANI, Felice (1954—). Italian judoka. Born July 8, 1954, in Italy. ❖ At Montreal Olympics, won a bronze medal in half-lightweight 65 kg (1976).

MARIANNE OF MOLOKAI, Mother (1838–1918). *See Cope, Mother Marianne.*

MARIANNE OF THE NETHERLANDS (1810–1883). Princess of the Netherlands. Born May 9, 1810; died May 29, 1883; dau. of Frederica Wilhelmina of Prussia (1774–1837) and William I (1772–1843), king of the Netherlands (r. 1813–1840, abdicated in 1840); m. Albert (1809–1872), prince of Prussia, Sept 14, 1830 (div. 1849); children: Charlotte (1831–1855, who m. Bernard II, duke of Saxe-Meiningen); Albert (b. 1837); Elizabeth (1840–1840); Alexandrine (1842–1906, who m. William, duke of Mecklenburg-Schwerin). ❖ Prince Albert's 2nd wife was Rosalie von Rauch (1820–1879), countess of Hohenau.

MARIC, Ljubica (1909–2003). Serbian conductor and composer. Born in Kragujevac, Serbia, Mar 18, 1909; died in 2003. ❖ Studied under J. Slavenski at Music School in Belgrade and under Josef Suk and Alois Haba at Prague Conservatory; also studied conducting under Nikolai Malko; during WWII, fought the Nazis as a partisan; at war's end, began teaching; came to the Music Academy of Belgrade (1957). ❖ See also *Women in World History.*

MARíC, Mileva (1875–1948). *See Einstein-Maríc, Mileva.*

MARICICH, Linda (1960—). *See Fratianne, Linda.*

MARIE. *French form of Maria and Mary.*

MARIE (fl. 13th c.). English nun and writer. Born in England. ❖ May have been a nun at Chatteris in Cambridgeshire which was connected with Ely; wrote Anglo-Norman verse life of St. Audrey (Etheltrhith, 630–679), former abbess of Ely, which was adapted from the Latin version contained in *History of Ely* by the monk Thomas; was one of 3 women known to have written Anglo-Norman religious poetry.

MARIE (1393–1438). Prioress of Poissy. Name variations: Mary Valois; Marie de Bourbon; Mary de France or Mary of France. Born in 1393; died in 1438; dau. of Charles VI, king of France (r. 1380–1422), and Isabeau of Bavaria (1371–1435); sister of Catherine of Valois (1401–1437); Isabella of Valois (1389–c. 1410, who m. Richard II, king of England), and Charles VII, king of France (r. 1422–1461).

MARIE (1876–1940). Greek princess. Name variations: Mary Oldenburg. Born Mar 3, 1876; died Dec 13, 1940; dau. of George I, king of the Hellenes, and Olga Constantinovna (1851–1926); m. George Michaelovitch (grandson of Tsar Nicholas I of Russia); children: 2.

MARIE (1900–1961). Queen of Yugoslavia. Name variations: Mignon; Maria or Mary Hohenzollern; Marie of Rumania. Born Jan 9, 1900, at Schloss Friedestein, in Gotha, Thuringia, Germany; died June 22, 1961, in London, England; dau. of Ferdinand I, king of Romania (r. 1914–1927), and Marie of Rumania (1875–1938); m. Alexander I (1888–1934), king of Yugoslavia (r. 1921–1934), on June 8, 1922 (he was assassinated by a Croatian in Marseilles, France, on Oct 9, 1934); children: Peter II (1923–1970), king of Yugoslavia, who m. Alexandra Oldenburg); Prince Tomislav Karadjordjevic (1928–2000); Andrej Karadjordjevic (b. 1929).

MARIE, abbess of Romsey (d. 1182). *See Marie of Boulogne.*

MARIE, empress (1824–1880). *See Marie of Hesse-Darmstadt.*

MARIE (1899–1918). Russian grand duchess. Name variations: Mary Nicholaevna. Born Marie Nicholaevna Romanov (Romanoff or Romanovna) on June 26, 1899, in Peterhof, Russia; executed with her family by the Bolsheviks on July 16–17, 1918, at Ekaterinburg, in Central Russia; dau. of Alexandra Feodorovna (1872–1918) and Nicholas II (tsar of Russia); never married; no children. ❖ See also *Women in World History.*

MARIE, grand duchess of Russia (1847–1928). *See Marie Feodorovna.*

MARIE, Jeanne (1809–1875). *See Héricourt, Jenny Poinsard d'.*

MARIE, princess of Orleans (1813–1839). *See Marie of Württemberg.*

MARIE, Teena (1956—). American musician. Born Mary Christine Brockert, Mar 5, 1956, in Santa Monica, CA; attended Santa Monica College for 1 year; children: daughter, Alia. ❖ Began singing professionally at 8; signed with Motown (1977) and made debut album, *Wild and Peaceful* (1979), which included hit R&B single, "I'm a Sucker for Your Love"; released successful singles "I Need Your Lovin'" (1980) and "Square Biz" (1981); nominated for Grammy for Best Female R&B Vocal Performance (1981); successfully sued Motown Records for non-payment of royalties, setting precedent of "Teena Marie Law," which bans record companies from holding performers to contracts if their recordings are not released (1981); signed with Epic Records; released *Starchild* (1984), which included her only Top-20 pop single, "Lovergirl"; other albums include *Emerald City* (1986), *Naked to the World* (1988) and *Ivory* (1990); scored hits "Ooo La La La" and "Work It" (1988); started own label, Sara, and released *Passion Play* (1994) and *Black Rain* (2000).

MARIE-ADELAIDE D'ORLEANS (1698–1743). *See Louise-Adelaide.*

MARIE ADELAIDE OF AUSTRIA (1822–1855). Queen of Sardinia and Italy. Name variations: Adelaide of Austria; Maria Adelaide di Asburgo-Lorena. Born June 3, 1822; died Jan 20, 1855; dau. of Rainer, archduke of Austria, and Elizabeth of Savoy-Carignan; m. Victor Emmanuel II, king of Italy (r. 1849–1878), April 12, 1842; children: Carlo Alberto also known as Charles Albert; Oddone Eugenio; Maria Pia (1847–1911), who m. the king of Portugal); Clotilde of Savoy (1843–1911); Amadeus (b. 1845), king of Spain (r. 1870–1873); Humbert I also known as Umberto I (1844–1900), king of Italy (r. 1878–1900, assassinated); Vittorio Emanuele also known as Victor Emmanuel (b. 1855). ❖ Won respect as a pious, charitable woman known for her kindliness to the poor.

MARIE ADELAIDE OF LUXEMBURG (1894–1924). Grand duchess of Luxemburg. Name variations: Maria Adélaïde; Marie Adélaïde, Marie Adelaide, Marie-Adelaide. Born June 14, 1894; died Jan 24, 1924; dau. of William IV (1852–1912), grand duke of Luxemburg, and Marie-Anne of Braganza; sister of Charlotte (1896–1985), grand duchess of Luxemburg. ❖ Reigned (1912–19); unpopular, was forced to abdicate in favor of sister Charlotte. ❖ See also *Women in World History.*

MARIE ADELAIDE OF SAVOY (1685–1712). Duchess of Burgundy. Name variations: Marie Adélaïde; Marie-Adelaide of Savoy; Maria Adelaide, Duchesse de Bourgogne. Born Dec 6, 1685; died Feb 12, 1712; dau. of Anne-Marie d'Bourbon-Orleans (1669–1728) and Victor Amadeus II (1666–1732), duke of Savoy (r. 1675–1713), king of Sicily (r. 1713–1718) and Sardinia (r. 1718–1730); m. Louis (1682–1712), duke of Burgundy (grandson of Louis XIV), on Dec 7, 1697; children: Louis Bourbon (1704–1705), duke of Brittany; Louis XV (1710–1774), king of France (r. 1715–1774). ❖ See also Charles Elliott, *Princess of Versailles: The Life of Marie Adelaide of Savoy* (1993); and *Women in World History.*

MARIE ALEXANDRA OF BADEN (1902–1944). German royal. Name variations: Zahringen. Born Mary Alexandra Thyra Victoria Louise Carol Hilda, Aug 1, 1902, in Salem, Baden, Germany; killed in an air raid, age 42, on Jan 29, 1944, in Frankfurt-am-Main, Germany; dau. of Maximilian, margrave of Baden, and Marie-Louise Guelph (1879–1948); m. Wolfgang of Hesse-Cassel, Sept 17, 1924.

MARIE ALEXANDROVNA (1853–1920). Russian grand duchess and duchess of Edinburgh. Name variations: Maria or Mary Alexandrovna, Mary Romanov; Grand Duchess of Russia. Born Oct 17, 1853, in St. Petersburg, Russia; died Oct 24, 1920, in Zurich, Switzerland; dau. of Alexander II (1818–1881), tsar of Russia (r. 1855–1881), and Marie of Hesse-Darmstadt (1824–1880); sister of Alexander III, tsar of Russia (r. 1881–1894); m. Alfred Saxe-Coburg (1844–1900), duke of Edinburgh, on Jan 23, 1874; children: Alfred Saxe-Coburg (b. 1874); Marie of Rumania (1875–1938); Victoria Melita of Saxe-Coburg (1876–1936); Alexandra Saxe-Coburg (1878–1942); Beatrice of Saxe-Coburg (1884–1966).

MARIE AMÉLIE (1782–1866). *See Maria Amalia.*

MARIE-AMELIE OF ORLEANS (1865–1951). Queen of Portugal. Name variations: Amalia of Paris; Amélia or Amélie; Amelia of Orleans. Born Sept 28, 1865, in Twickenham, Middlesex, England; died Oct 25, 1951, at Château de Bellevue, Le Chesnay, Versailles; dau. of Louis Philippe (1838–1894), count of Paris, and Maria Isabella (1848–1919); m. Carlos also known as Charles I (1863–1908), king of Portugal (r. 1889–1908), on May 22, 1886; children: Luis Filepe also known as Louis Philippe (1887–1908), duke of Braganza; Maria Ana of Portugal (1887–1887); Manuel II (1889–1932), king of Portugal (r. 1908–1910). ❖ Founded the Carriage Museum (1905) and dedicated much of her time to the campaign against tuberculosis; was present when her husband and son Louis Philippe were assassinated (Feb 1, 1908); accompanied son Manuel into exile in England, though she later took up residence at Versailles. ❖ See also *Women in World History.*

MARIE ANGELIQUE, Mere. *See Arnauld, Jacqueline.*

MARIE-ANNE DE LA TRÉMOUILLE (c. 1642–1722). Princess of the Ursins. Name variations: Madame or Princess des Ursins; Marie Anne Ursins; Anne Marie de la Trémouille, Duchess of Bracciano; Marie-Anne de la Tremouille; Marie-Anne Orsini. Probably born 1642 (perhaps as early as 1635); died in Rome on Dec 5, 1722; eldest child of Louis de la Trémouille, marquis of Noirmoutier, and Julie Aubry; m. Adrien-Blaise de Talleyrand, prince of Chalais, July 5, 1659 (died 1670); m. Flavio deglio Orsini, duke of Bracciano, on Feb 17, 1675 (died April 5, 1698); no known children. Appointed *camarera mayor* (1701); dismissed and exiled (Dec 1714). ❖ Ambitious French aristocrat who headed the household of Queen Marie Louise of Savoy, wife of Philip V of Spain, and wielded great political influence during the War of the Spanish Succession. ❖ See also Maud Cruttwell, *The Princess des Ursins* (Dutton, 1927); Constance Hill, *The Story of the Princess des Ursins in Spain (Camarera-Mayor)* (John Lane, 1906); and *Women in World History.*

MARIE-ANNE OF AUSTRIA (1683–1754). *See Maria Antonia of Austria.*

MARIE-ANNE OF BRAGANZA (1861–1942). Princess of Portugal. Name variations: Maria Anna of Portugal. Born July 13, 1861, in Bronnbach; died July 31, 1942, in New York; dau. of Adelheid (1831–1909) and Miguel also known as Michael I (1802–1866), king of Portugal (r. 1828–1834); m. William IV (1852–1912), grand duke of Luxemburg (of the House of Nassau), on June 21, 1893; children: Marie Adelaide of Luxemburg (1894–1924); Hilda (b. 1897, who later m. Prince Adolf of Schwartzenberg); Antoinette of Luxemburg (1899–1954, who m. Crown Prince Rupprecht of Bavaria); Elisabeth (1901–1950, who m. Prince Ludwig-Philipp of Thurn and Taxis); Sophie of Nassau (1902–1941); and Charlotte, Grand Duchess of Luxemburg (1896–1985).

MARIE ANNUNZIATA OF NAPLES (1843–1871). *See Maria Annunziata.*

MARIE ANTOINETTE (1755–1793). Queen of France. Name variations: Marie-Antoinette; Madame Veto. Born in Vienna, Austria, Nov 2, 1755; died by the guillotine in Paris, France, Oct 16, 1793; dau. of Francis Stephen of Lorraine, grand duke of Tuscany, also known as Francis I, Holy Roman emperor (r. 1745–1765), and Maria Theresa of Austria (1717–1780), empress of the Habsburg domains; sister of Maria Carolina (1752–1814), Joseph II, emperor of Austria and Holy Roman emperor (r. 1765–1790), Maria Christina (1742–1798), Elizabeth of Austria (1743–1808), Leopold II, Holy Roman emperor (r. 1790–1792), and Maria Amalia (1746–1804); m. Louis XVI, king of France (r. 1774–1792), in 1770; children: 1st daughter, Princess Marie Thérèse Charlotte (1778–1851), was exchanged by the Revolutionary government to the Court of Vienna and grew up to be the duchess of Angoulême; the 1st dauphin, Louis Joseph (1781–1789); the 2nd dauphin, Louis Charles (b. 1785), imprisoned during the Revolution, was proclaimed "Louis XVII" by royalists, and apparently died in prison in 1795; Princess Sophie Beatrix (1786–1787). ❖ Austrian-born queen of France whose misfortune was to be the wife of Louis XVI when that monarch was overthrown in the French Revolution of 1789, and whose poor judgment and provocative behavior led to her execution in the name of the Revolution; was raised at the Schonbrunn palace and indifferently educated; betrothed to the dauphin of France, the future Louis XVI (1769) to reinforce the alliance between the House of Habsburg and the House of Bourbon; married the dauphin (1770); engaged in court intrigues and flirtations until outbreak of French Revolution (1789); failed in attempted flight from France with the king (June 1791); arrested by revolutionaries (1792) and tried before Revolutionary Tribunal (Oct 14, 1793). ❖ See also Stefan Zweig, *Marie Antoinette: The Portrait of an Average Woman* (Viking, 1933); Carolly Erickson, *To the Scaffold: The Life of Marie-Antoinette* (Morrow, 1991); Joan Haslip, *Marie Antoinette* (Weidenfeld & Nicolson, 1987); and *Women in World History.*

MARIE ANTOINETTE OF SPAIN (1729–1785). *See Maria Antonia of Spain.*

MARIE AUGUSTINE DE LA COMPASSION (1820–1893). *See Jamet, Marie.*

MARIE-BARBARA OF PORTUGAL (1711–1758). *See Maria Barbara of Braganza.*

MARIE CAROLINE (1752–1814). *See Maria Carolina.*

MARIE CAROLINE FERDINANDE LOUISE OF NAPLES (1798–1870). *See Caroline of Naples.*

MARIE CASIMIR (1641–1716). Queen of Poland. Name variations: Maria Casimira; Marie Casimere d'Arquien; Marie de la Grange d'Arquien; Marie Casimire de la Grange d'Arquien; Marysienka; Marie Kazimiere or Kazimierz; Marie Sobieski. Born in 1641 in Nevers, France; died Jan 30, 1716, in Blois, France; dau. of Henri, marquis d'Arquien, and Françoise de la Chatre (governess to Louise Marie de Gonzague); m. John Zamoyski (Polish noble), in 1658 (died 1665); m. Jan III also known as John III Sobieski (1624–1696), king of Poland (r. 1674–1696), in 1655; children: Constantine Sobieski; Alexander Sobieski; Teresa Sobieski also known as Cunigunde Sobieska; James Sobieski (who m. Hedwig Wittelsbach); grandchildren: Clementina Sobieski (1702–1735, who m. James Francis Edward, the Old Pretender). ❖ Raised in the Polish royal court at Warsaw, became Queen Louise Marie de Gonzague's favorite maid of honor; developed a friendship with John (III) Sobieski, a Polish noble who was quickly emerging as a great military leader; following 1st husband's death (1665), married Sobieski in a secret ceremony only 3 weeks later, for which criticism would follow her throughout her life; aided husband in his successful campaign to be king (1673); was never popular with her subjects, though husband enjoyed great popularity; when he became incapacitated, acted as unofficial regent of Poland from 1692 until his death in 1696; on husband's death, moved to Rome; participated actively in the court life of Rome's elite and was often at the Vatican, where she enjoyed the friendship of Pope Clement XI. ❖ See also *Women in World History.*

MARIE-CECILE HOHENZOLLERN (1942—). Prussian royal. Name variations: Marie-Cecile of Oldenburg. Born Mary Cecily Kira Victoria Louise on May 28, 1942; dau. of Louis Ferdinand, prince of Prussia, and Kira of Russia (1909–1967); m. Frederick Augustus of Oldenburg, Dec 3, 1965; children: 3.

MARIE CHRISTINE OF BAVARIA (1660–1690). *See Maria Anna of Bavaria.*

MARIE CLOTILDE (d. 1794). Saint. Died in 1794. ❖ Was mother superior at an Ursuline convent at Valenciennes; caught in the upheaval of the French Revolution, became a political and religious martyr, as did the 32 sisters under her supervision. Feast day is Oct 23. ❖ See also *Women in World History.*

MARIE CLOTILDE (1759–1802). Queen of Sardinia. Name variations: Clotilde or Clothilde; Clotilde de France or Clotilde of France; Marie-Clotilde. Born Sept 23, 1759; died Mar 7, 1802; dau. of Marie Josèphe of Saxony (1731–1767) and Louis (1729–1765), dauphin of France; sister of Louis XVI, king of France (r. 1774–1792); m. Charles Emmanuel IV, king of Sardinia (r. 1796–1802), on Sept 6, 1775.

MARIE D'AUTRICHE.
See Mary of Hungary (1505–1558).
See Marie of Austria (1528–1603).

MARIE DE BOURBON (fl. 1350s). French noblewoman and prioress of Poissy. Flourished in the 1350s at convent of Poissy, France; dau. of Isabelle of Savoy (d. 1383) and Pierre or Peter I (1311–1356), duke of Bourbon (r. 1342–1356); sister of Jeanne de Bourbon (1338–1378), queen of France; never married; no children. ❖ Was closely connected to the royal house of France through her sister who married Charles V; was given to the Dominican convent of Poissy (near Paris) when she was only four; took the vows of a nun at 17 and remained at Poissy the rest of her life; became a highly respected prioress. ❖ See also *Women in World History.*

MARIE DE BOURBON (fl. 1440s). Duchess of Calabria. Dau. of Agnes of Burgundy (d. 1476) and Charles I, duke of Bourbon (r. 1434–1456); m. John II (1424–1470), duke of Calabria; children: Nicholas, duke of Anjou (1448–1473).

MARIE DE BOURBON (1606–1627). Duchess of Auvergne and Montpensier. Name variations: Duchess of Auverne. Born in 1606; died in childbirth around May 29, 1627; dau. of Henri, duke of Montpensier (ruler of Auvergne, 1602–08), and Henriette de Joyeuse; m. Gaston d'Orléans (1608–1660), duke of Orléans (brother of Louis XIII, king of France), Aug 1626; children: Anne Marie Louise d'Orléans, duchesse de Montpensier (1627–1693). ❖ Sole heiress of the Montpensier family, inherited father's rule (1608); died while giving birth to Anne Marie Louise d'Orléans, duchess de Montpensier, who inherited her rule and her fabulous wealth. ❖ See also *Women in World History.*

MARIE DE BOURBON (fl. 18th c.). Princess of Carignan. Married Thomas Francis, prince of Carignan or Carignano (died 1656); children: Emmanuel Philibert (1628–1709); Eugene (d. 1673, who m. Olympia Mancini).

MARIE DE BOURGOGNE. *Variant of Mary of Burgundy.*

MARIE DE BRABANT (c. 1530–c. 1600). French poet. Born c. 1530 in France; died c. 1600 in France; dau. of John of Brabant (Jean de Brabant); m. Claude de Tourotte. ❖ Somewhat of a moralist, composed epistles against what she considered the lewd and scandalous behavior of French women of the lower classes; also translated foreign works in verse into French, achieving a considerable reputation; published *A Declaration of the Spirit of the Faithful Soul* (1602) as well as her translation of the *Song of Songs.*

MARIE DE CHAMPAGNE (1145–1198). Countess of Champagne. Name variations: Marie, countess of Champagne; Marie of Champagne; Mary of Champagne; Mary Capet; Mary of France; possibly, Marie de France. Born in 1145; died in 1198; dau. of Eleanor of Aquitaine (1122–1204) and Louis VII, king of France (r. 1137–1180); sister of Alice (1150–c. 1197), countess of Blois; m. Henry I, count of Champagne, around 1164; children: Henry I, king of Jerusalem (Henry II of Champagne); Theobald III, count of Champagne; Marie of Champagne (c. 1180–1203); Scholastica of Champagne (d. 1219). ❖ A literary patron, commissioned courtly romances from poets like Chretien de Troyes. Some think that the woman known only as Marie de France, who wrote many popular *lais* (story-songs), was either Marie of Champagne or Emma de Gatinais, an illegitimate sister of Henry II and thus Eleanor of Aquitaine's sister-in-law.

MARIE DE CHAMPAGNE (c. 1180–1203). *See Marie of Champagne.*

MARIE DE CHATILLON (r. 1230–1241). Countess of Blois and Chartres. Died in 1241; m. Hugues de Chatillon, count of Saint-Pol; children: son Jean de Chatillon, count of Blois and Chartres (r. 1241–1279); granddaughter: Jeanne de Chatillon, countess of Blois and Chartres (r. 1279–1292). ❖ Inherited Blois on the death of Marguerite, countess of Blois (1230); ruled until 1241.

MARIE DE COURTENAY (fl. 1215). Empress of Byzantium. Name variations: Marie or Mary of Courtenay; dau. of Yolande of Courtenay (d. 1219) and Pierre II also known as Peter II of Courtenay, emperor of Constantinople; 3rd wife of Theodore I Lascaris, Byzantine emperor (r. 1204–1222); no children. ❖ See also *Women in World History.*

MARIE DE FRANCE (c. 1140–1200). French writer. Name variations: Marie of France. Specifics of Marie's life are not known with certainty. She was born c. 1140 and died c. 1200; she was French but lived in England in the late 12th century, at, or associated with, the court of Henry II and Eleanor of Aquitaine; she may have been an abbess; wrote fables, a religious tract, and courtly short stories (called *lais*). ❖ French writer who lived and worked in England and is most famous for her short tales dealing with romantic love and court life; had a marked influence on medieval literature; developed a distinctive stylistic technique and was innovative in her use of Celtic plots and motifs woven together with Classical imagery; created memorable female characters who relied on their intellectual, moral and physical faculties to create a world receptive to their interior needs; writings include *Fables, Lais,* and *The Purgatory of Saint Patrick.* Some theorize that she was Emma de Gatinais, the illeg. dau. of Geoffrey of Anjou (which would make her a half-sister to Henry II), and that she later became abbess of Shaftesbury where early manuscript copies of her *lais* were found; others have speculated that she was a nun at Reading, or Isabel of Beaumont, or one of the daughters of Stephen of Blois, or Marie de Champagne (dau. of Eleanor of Aquitaine and Louis VII of France). ❖ See also Paula Clifford, *Marie de France: Lais* (1982); Emanuel J. Mickel, *Marie de France* (1974); and *Women in World History.*

MARIE DE FRANCE (d. 1335). *See Marie of Evreux.*

MARIE DE GONZAGA (1611–1667). *See Louise Marie de Gonzague.*

MARIE DE L'INCARNATION (1566–1618). *See Acarie, Barbe.*

MARIE DE L'INCARNATION (1599–1672). French educator and founder. Name variations: Marie de L'Incarnation; Mary of the Incarnation; Marie Guyard or Marie Guyart. Born Marie Guyard or Guyart on Oct 28, 1599, at Tours, France; died April 30, 1672, in Quebec City, New France (Quebec, Canada); 3rd child of Florent Guyart (master baker) and Jeanne Michelet; educated at elementary religious school in Tours; m. Claude Martin, in 1617; children: Claude (b. 1619). ❖ Founder of the Ursuline Order in New France, had a mystical experience (Mar 24, 1620), which convinced her to enter holy orders; joined the novitiate of the Ursuline order of nuns in Tours (1625); took final vows (1633); claimed that God told her to go to New France (modern-day Quebec, Canada) to build a house for Jesus and Mary; set sail with 2 other Ursuline nuns (May 4, 1639); by 1642, had raised enough funds to allow her and her sisters to build an impressive convent (though it was destroyed by fire 3 years later); abetted by Jesuit brothers, helped draw up the 1st constitution for the colony of New France (1646); became fluent in several native languages and eventually wrote the 1st French-Algonquin and French-Iroquois dictionaries as well as a catechism in Iroquois that was extensively used by Jesuit missionaries; wrote a series of religious tracts of which the *École Sainte: Explication des Mystères de la Foi* (1633–35) came to be considered one of the best and most important catechisms ever written in the French language; composed *Relation Autobiographique,* an open and honest account of her life and the principal spiritual influences upon it (1654). ❖ See also Agnes Repplier, *Mère Marie of the Ursulines: A Study in Adventure* (1931); and *Women in World History.*

MARIE DE MEDICI or MEDICIS (c. 1573–1642). *See Medici, Marie de.*

MARIE DE PADILLA (1335–1361). Royal mistress. Name variations: Maria Padilla; Marie Padilla. Born in 1335 (some sources cite 1333); died July 1361 (some sources cite 1365), in Seville, Spain; dau. of Diego or Juan García de Padilla and Meria de Henestrona also seen as María González de Hinestrosa; secretly m. Pedro el Cruel also known as Peter the Cruel (1334–1369), king of Castile and León (r. 1350–1369), in 1353; children: Constance of Castile (1354–1394, who m. John of Gaunt); Isabel of Castile (1355–1392, who m. Edmund of Langley, duke of York); Beatriz of Castile (1354–1369); Juan (1355–1405, who m. Elvira de Eril); Alfonso (1359–1362). Peter also m. Blanche of Bourbon (c. 1338–1361), in 1353. ❖ Began a relationship with Peter the Cruel (1350 or 1351); lacked sufficient rank to marry him, but status as royal mistress brought her social and economic benefits; showed little interest in becoming involved in the political disputes surrounding the court. ❖ See also *Women in World History.*

MARIE DE ST. POL (1304–1377). Countess of Pembroke and religious founder. Name variations: Marie de St. Paul; Marie of St. Paul; Marie de Saint-Pol; Mary of St. Pol; Maria de Sancto Paulo. Born in 1304 in France; died in 1377 in Pembroke, England; dau. of Guy IV de Châtillon, count of St. Pol, and Mary of Brittany; m. Aymer de Valence, earl of Pembroke, around 1320 (d. 1324); children: none. ❖ By age 20, was a childless widow living in England with great estates both there and in France; was an important patron of the Franciscan order of nuns (called Poor Clares or Minoresses) and founded the still-extant Pembroke College at Cambridge (1347). ❖ See also *Women in World History.*

MARIE D'OIGNIES (1177–1213). *See Mary of Oignies.*

MARIE D'ORLEANS (1813–1839). Duchess of Wurttemberg and artist. Name variations: Marie of Wurttemberg; Marie of Württemberg; Marie, Princess of Orléans; Marie of Orleans. Born in Palermo on April 12, 1813; died Jan 2, 1839; dau. of Maria Amalia (1782–1866) and Louis Philippe I (1773–1850), king of France (r. 1830–1848); m. Alexander (1804–1881), duke of Württemberg, Oct 17, 1837. ❖ A talented painter and sculptor, is best known for her statue of Joan of Arc at Versailles. ❖ See also *Women in World History.*

MARIE D'SAVOY-NEMOURS (d. 1724). *See Jeanne of Nemours.*

MARIE DU COEUR DE JÉSUS (1829–1893). *See Barbier, Adèle Euphrasie.*

MARIE ELIZABETH OF SAXONY (1610–1684). Duchess of Holstein-Gottorp. Born Nov 22, 1610; died June 24, 1684; dau. of Magdalena Sybilla (1587–1659) and John George I (1585–1656), elector of Saxony; m. Frederick III, duke of Holstein-Gottorp, Feb 21, 1630; children: Sophie Auguste (b. 1630); Magdalena Sybilla of Holstein Gottorp (1631–1719); Christian Albrecht, duke of Holstein-Gottorp (b. 1641); Augusta Maria of Holstein-Gottorp (1649–1728, who m. Frederick VII, margrave of Baden-Durlach).

MARIE FEODOROVNA (1759–1828). *See Sophia Dorothea of Wurttemberg.*

MARIE FEODOROVNA (1847–1928). Russian empress. Name variations: Princess Dagmar of Denmark; Maria Feodorovna or Fyodorovna or Fedorovna; Mary Feodorovna or Fyodorovna or Fedorovna; Mary Oldenburg; Minny; Maria. Born Marie Sophia Frederika Dagmar, Nov 26, 1847, at Gule Palace in Copenhagen, Denmark; died at Hvidore Villa near Copenhagen, Denmark, Oct 13, 1928; 2nd dau. of Prince Christian of Schleswig-Holstein-Sönderborg-Glücksburg, later Christian IX, king of Denmark (r. 1863–1906), and Louise of Hesse-Cassel (1817–1898); sister of Frederick VIII (1843–1912), king of Denmark (r. 1906–1912), Alexandra of Denmark (1844–1925), queen of England, Thyra Oldenburg (1853–1933), and William of Denmark, who was elected king of the Hellenes as George I (r. 1863–1913); m. Alexander III (1845–1894), tsar of Russia (r. 1881–1894); children: Nicholas II (1868–1918), tsar of Russia (r. 1894–1917); Alexander (1869–1870); George (1871–1894, died of tuberculosis); Xenia Alexandrovna (1876–1960); Michael (1878–1918, who m. Natalia Sheremetskaia); Olga Alexandrovna (1882–1960). ❖ Known as the "Lady of Tears," lived through the assassination of her brother, King George I of Greece, the premature death of her husband, the abdication of her son, Tsar Nicholas II, and the execution of many members of her family during the Bolshevik Revolution; married Grand Duke Alexander Alexandrovitch (1866); became empress of Russia at his coronation as Alexander III (1881); headed the Russian Red Cross; became dowager empress following Alexander III's death (1894); was a prisoner of the Bolshevik Revolution (1917–19); escaped from Russia and embarked for England after WWI Armistice (1919); took permanent residence in Denmark (1919–28); won the admiration and respect of the world. ❖ See also autobiographies *Education of a Princess* (Viking, 1931) and *A Princess in Exile* (Viking, 1932); E.E.P. Tisdale, *Marie Feodorovna: Empress of Russia* (Day, 1958); and *Women in World History.*

MARIE FEODOROVNA (1876–1936). *See Victoria Melita of Saxe-Coburg.*

MARIE FRANÇOISE OF SAVOY (1646–1683). Queen of Portugal. Name variations: Maria Francisca Luisa de Savoie; Maria Francisca Isabel of Savoy. Born Marie de Savoie-Nemours, June 21, 1646; died Dec 27, 1683; dau. of Charles Amedeé of Savoy (who was killed in a celebrated duel with his brother-in-law, François de Vendome, duke of Beaufort) and Elizabeth de Bourbon; sister of Jeanne of Nemours (d. 1724); m. Afonso or Alphonso VI (1643–1683), king of Portugal (r. 1656–1667), on August 2, 1666 (annulled in 1668); m. his brother Pedro or Peter II (1648–1706), king of Portugal (r. 1667–1706), on April 2, 1668; children: (2nd m.) Isabel Luisa Josefa (1669–1690).

MARIE-ILEANA (1933–1959). Granddaughter of Marie of Rumania. Name variations: Marie Ileana Habsburg. Born Dec 18, 1933, in Modling, Austria; killed in a plane crash on Jan 11, 1959, in Rio de Janeiro, Brazil; dau. of Anthony, archduke of Austria, and Ileana (b. 1909).

MARIE ISABELLA OF SPAIN (1789–1848). Queen of Sicily. Name variations: Maria Isabel. Born July 6, 1789; died Sept 13, 1848; dau. of Maria Luisa Teresa of Parma (1751–1819) and Charles IV (1748–1819), king of Spain (r. 1788–1808); became 2nd wife of Francis I, king of Sicily (r. 1825–1830), on Oct 6, 1802; m. Franz de Balzo, on Jan 15, 1839; children: (1st marriage) Louisa Carlotta of Naples (1804–1844); Maria Cristina I of Naples (1806–1878); Ferdinand II (1810–1859), king of the Two Sicilies (r. 1830–1859); Maria Antonia of Sicily (1814–1898); Marie Amalie (1818–1857, who m. Sebastian de Bourbon); Caroline of Sicily (1820–1861); Teresa Cristina of Bourbon (1822–1889, who m. Pedro II of Brazil); Francesco, count of Trapani (1827–1892). ❖ Francis I's 1st wife was Maria Clementina of Austria (1777–1801).

MARIE JOSÉ OF BELGIUM (1906–2001). Belgian princess and queen of Italy. Name variations: Marie Jose of Belgium; Maria-José or Marie-Jose; countess of Sarre. Born Aug 3, 1906; died Jan 27, 2001, in Geneva; dau. of Albert I (1875–1934), king of the Belgians (r. 1909–1934), and Elizabeth of Bavaria (1876–1965); attended boarding school in Florence; m. Humbert II also known as Umberto II (1904–1983), king of Italy (r. 1946, for 34 days), on Jan 8, 1930; children: Maria Pia (b. 1934); Victor Emmanuel (b. 1937); Maria Gabriella (b. 1940); Beatrice (b. 1943). ❖ Married into Italian House of Savoy (1930); worked tirelessly as inspector general of the Red Cross; while popular with Italians, never won the respect and trust of her father-in-law, King Victor Emmanuel III, who bristled at her reputation of being the only ruler in the House of Savoy; estranged from husband and father-in-law, lived in an apartment in the Palazzo del Quirinale in Rome (1940–43), a clandestine center of the movement against Benito Mussolini where she received emissaries from the political underground in Rome and Vatican City; became an important factor in the overthrow of Mussolini. ❖ See also *Women in World History.*

MARIE JOSEPHA (1699–1757). Queen of Poland. Name variations: Marie Josephine; Maria Josepha of Austria; Marie Josephe. Born Dec 8, 1699; died Nov 17, 1757; dau. of Joseph I (1678–1711), Holy Roman emperor (r. 1705–1711), and Wilhelmina of Brunswick (1673–1742); m. Frederick Augustus II (1696–1763), elector of Saxony (r. 1733–1763), also known as Augustus III, king of Poland (r. 1733–1763), on August 20, 1719; children: Frederick Christian (1722–1763), elector of Saxony (r. 1763); Maria Amalia of Saxony (1724–1760), who m. Charles III, king of Spain); Marie Josephe of Saxony (1731–1767, who m. Louis, dauphin of France).

MARIE JOSEPHE OF SAXONY (1731–1767). French royal. Name variations: Marie Josèphe; Marie or Maria Josepha of Saxony; Marie-Josephe de Saxe; Marie Josephine. Born Nov 4, 1731; died Mar 13, 1767; dau. of Frederick Augustus II (1696–1763), elector of Saxony (r. 1733–1763), also known as Augustus III, king of Poland (r. 1733–1763), and Marie Josepha (1699–1757); became 2nd wife of Louis the Dauphin of France (1729–1765), on Feb 9, 1747; children: duke of Burgundy (1751–1761); duke of Aquitaine (1753–1754); Louis XVI (1754–1793), king of France (r. 1774–1792); Louis XVIII (1755–1824), king of France (r. 1814–1824); Charles X (1757–1836), king of France (r. 1824–1830); Marie Clotilde (1759–1802, who m. Charles Emmanuel IV of Sardinia); Madame Élisabeth (1764–1794). ❖ Louis the Dauphin's 1st wife was Maria Theresa of Spain (1726–1746).

MARIE JOSEPHINE OF SAVOY (d. 1810). Countess of Provence. Name variations: Josephine Louise of Savoy; Marie Joséphine; Louise Benedicta; Maria Josepha Louisa; Joséphine. Died in 1810; dau. of Maria Antonia of Spain (1729–1785) and Victor Amadeus III (1726–1796), duke of Savoy (r. 1773–1796); m. Louis Stanislas Xavier, count of Provence, who later became Louis XVIII (1755–1824), king of France (r. 1814, 1815–1824), in 1771. ❖ Died in exile in England (1810), before Louis took the throne, and was buried in Westminster Abbey with all the pomp befitting a queen.

MARIE LAETITIA (1866–1890). Duchess of Aosta. Born Marie Laetitia Eugenie, Dec 20, 1866; died Oct 25, 1890; dau. of Prince Napoleon (Plon-Plon) and Clotilde of Savoy (1843–1911); m. Amadeo also known as Amadeus of Savoy (b. 1845), duke of Aosta, king of Spain (r. 1871–1873), on Sept 11, 1888; children: Umberto also known as Humbert or Humberto (b. 1889), count of Salemi. ❖ Amadeus' 1st wife was Maria dal Pozzo.

MARIE LECZINSKA (1703–1768). Queen of France. Name variations: Marie, Maria, or Mary Leszczynska; Maria Lesczinska. Pronunciation: (French) Lek-ZON-skah. Born June 23, 1703, in Breslau, Silesia, Poland; died June 24, 1768, in Versailles, France; dau. of Stanislaw also known as Stanislaus I Leczinski or Leszczynski (d. 1766), duke of Lorraine (r. 1737–1766), king of Poland (r. 1704–1709); m. Louis XV (1710–1774), king of France (r. 1715–1774), on Sept 5, 1725; children: 10, including (twin daughters) Louise Elizabeth (1727–1759) and Henriette (1727–1752); Louis le dauphin (1729–1765, father of Louis XVI); Adelaide (1732–1800); Victoire (1733–1799); Sophie (1734–1782); Louise Marie (1737–1787). ❖ Following father's banishment from Poland (1709), settled in Alsace as a destitute exile; won the right to marry Louis with the help of Madame de Prie (who assumed she would be grateful and grant favor) after spirited competition between 40 princesses; came to the throne with neither beauty, possessions, nor connections. ❖ See also *Women in World History.*

MARIE LEOPOLDINA or LEOPOLDINE (1797–1826). *See Leopoldina of Austria.*

MARIE LESCZINSKA (1703–1768). *See Marie Leczinska.*

MARIE LOUISE (1695–1719). Duchess of Berry. Name variations: Mary Bourbon-Orleans; duchesse de Berri; Marie-Louise d'Orleans. Born Aug 20, 1695; died July 21, 1719; dau. of Philip Bourbon-Orléans (1674–1723), 2nd duke of Orléans (r. 1701–1723), and Françoise-Marie de Bourbon (1677–1749); m. Charles (1686–1714), duke of Berri or Berry, on July 6, 1710; married a von Rioms in 1716.

MARIE LOUISE (1872–1956). Princess. Name variations: Marie Louise of Schleswig-Holstein. Born Franziska Josepha Louise Augusta Marie Christiana Helena, Aug 12, 1872, in Windsor, Berkshire, England; died Dec 8, 1956, in London; dau. of Christian of Schleswig-Holstein-

Sonderburg-Augustenburg and Helena (1846–1923, dau. of Queen Victoria); m. Prince Aribert of Anhalt, July 6, 1891 (marriage annulled, 1900). ❖ After marriage was annulled, returned to England and devoted life to charitable and artistic causes; was heavily involved in the creation of Queen Mary of Teck's Dolls' House. ❖ See also autobiography *My Memories of Six Reigns* (1956).

MARIE LOUISE (1879–1948). Margravine of Baden. Name variations: Marie Louise Guelph. Born Mary Louise Victoria Caroline Amelia Alexandra Augusta Fredericka on Oct 11, 1879, in Gmunden, Austria; died Jan 31, 1948, in Salem, Baden, Germany; dau. of Ernest Augustus, 3rd duke of Cumberland and Teviotdale, and Thyra Oldenburg (1853–1933); granddau. of George V, king of Hanover; m. Maximilian, margrave of Baden, on July 10, 1900; children: Marie-Alexandra of Baden (1902–1944); Berthold, margrave of Baden (1906–1963).

MARIE LOUISE ALBERTINE OF LEININGEN-HEIDESHEIM (1729–1818). Landgravine of Hesse-Darmstadt. Name variations: Princess George. Born in 1729; died in 1818; m. imperial lieutenant field marshal Prince George William, landgrave of Hesse-Darmstadt (1722–1782); children: Frederica of Hesse-Darmstadt (1752–1782); Charlotte of Hesse-Darmstadt (1755–1785).

MARIE LOUISE D'ORLEANS (1662–1689). Queen-consort of Spain. Name variations: Marie Louise of Orleans or Orléans; Marie-Louise Bourbon-Orleans; Maria Luisa de Orleans, Maria Luisa de Borbon. Born April 26 (some sources cite Mar 27), 1662; died Feb 12, 1689; dau. of Henrietta Anne (1644–1670) and Philip also known as Philippe I (1640–1701), 1st duke of Orléans (r. 1660–1701); m. Charles II (1661–1700), king of Spain (r. 1665–1700), Aug 31, 1679 (some sources cite Nov 19); no children. ❖ To strengthen peace between Spain and France, was wed to Charles II of Spain, who was mentally deficient; comported herself with dignified piety, occasionally ruling for husband, but governmental councils generally determined policy; her death, at 27, occasioned rumors that she had been poisoned, though little evidence substantiated the allegation.

MARIE LOUISE D'ORLEANS (1695–1719). *See Marie Louise.*

MARIE LOUISE D'ORLEANS (1750–1822). Duchess of Bourbon. Name variations: Princess de Bourbon; duchesse de Bourbon. Born Louise-Marie-Thérèse d'Orleans on July 9, 1750; died Jan 13, 1822; dau. of Louisa Henrietta de Conti (1726–1759) and Louis Philippe (1725–1785), 4th duke of Orléans (r. 1752–1785); m. Louis-Joseph, duke of Bourbon (later Prince de Condé in 1818), April 24, 1770 (div. 1780).

MARIE-LOUISE GONZAGA or GONZAGUE (1611–1667). *See Louise Marie de Gonzague.*

MARIE LOUISE OF AUSTRIA (1791–1847). Empress and regent of France and duchess of Parma. Name variations: Maria Louisa or Maria Luisa; Marie-Louise; Marie-Louise of France; Marie-Louise Habsburg; Mary Louise of Austria. Archduchess of Austria (1814–1847). Born in Vienna, Austria, Dec 12, 1791; died in Parma, Italy, Dec 17, 1847; dau. of Francis II, Holy Roman emperor (r. 1792–1806), who was king of Austria as Francis I (r. 1804–1835), and Maria Teresa of Naples (1772–1807); sister of Ferdinand I, emperor of Austria (r. 1835–1848), and Leopoldina of Austria (1797–1817); daughter-in-law of Letizia Bonaparte (1750–1836); became 2nd wife of Napoleon I, emperor of France (r. 1804–1815), in 1810; m. Count Adam Adalbert von Neipperg, in 1821; m. Count Charles de Bombelles, in 1834; children: (1st marriage) Napoleon II (1811–1832), also known as the duc de Reichstadt, king of Rome; (2nd marriage) two. ❖ Was married to Napoleon I for the purpose of producing an heir and in hopes of establishing a bond between his regime and the Habsburgs, one of Europe's oldest royal houses; when he went into exile on island of Elba (1814), returned home to father and was granted sovereignty over Parma, Piacenza and Guastalla; was a liberal ruler. ❖ See also *Women in World History.*

MARIE LOUISE OF BULGARIA (1933—). Bulgarian princess. Born Jan 13, 1933, in Sofia, Bulgaria; dau. of Boris III, king of Bulgaria, and Giovanna of Italy (b. 1907); m. Charles Vladimir Ernst, prince of Leiningen, Feb 14, 1957 (div. 1968); m. Bronislav Chrobok, Nov 16, 1969, in Toronto, Ontario, Canada; children: (1st m.) Boris of Leiningen (b. 1960); Hermann of Leiningen (b. 1963); (2nd m.) Alexandra Nadpichida Hrobok; Pavel Alister Hrobok.

MARIE LOUISE OF FRANCE (1727–1759). *See Louise Elizabeth.*

MARIE-LOUISE OF FRANCE (1791–1847). *See Marie Louise of Austria.*

MARIE LOUISE OF ORLEANS.
See Marie Louise d'Orleans (1662–1689).
See Marie Louise (1695–1719).

MARIE LOUISE OF PARMA.
See Louise Elizabeth (1727–1759).
See Maria Luisa Teresa of Parma (1751–1819).

MARIE LOUISE OF PARMA (1870–1899). Queen of Bulgaria. Name variations: Maria Louisa of Parma; Mary of Parma. Born Jan 17, 1870; died Feb 1, 1899; dau. of Robert (b. 1848), duke of Bourbon-Parma, and Pia of Sicily (1849–1882); m. Ferdinand I (1861–1948), king of Bulgaria (r. 1887–1918, abdicated), on April 20, 1893; children: Boris III (1894–1943), king of Bulgaria (r. 1918–1943); Cyril (b. Nov 17, 1895); Eudoxia (b. Jan 17, 1898); Nadejda of Bulgaria (b. 1899, who m. Albert Eugene of Württemberg). ❖ Ferdinand's 2nd wife was Eleanora of Reuss.

MARIE LOUISE OF SAVOY (1688–1714). Queen of Spain. Name variations: Maria Louisa; María Luisa Gabriela; María Luisa Gabriel of Savoy; Louise Marie. Born María Luisa Gabriela in Savoy, Italy, on Sept 17, 1688 (some sources cite 1687); died Feb 14, 1714; dau. of Anne-Marie d'Bourbon-Orleans (1669–1728) and Victor Amadeus II (1666–1732), duke of Savoy (r. 1675–1713), king of Sicily (r. 1713–1718) and Sardinia (r. 1718–1730); sister of Marie Adelaide of Savoy (1685–1712), duchess of Burgundy (mother of Louis XV of France); became 1st wife of Philip V (1683–1746), king of Spain (r. 1700–1724, 1725–1746), Nov 2, 1701; children: Luis or Louis I (Aug 25, 1707–Aug 1724), king of Spain (r. 1724–1724); Felipe (1712–1719); Ferdinand VI (b. Sept 23, 1713), king of Spain (r. 1746–1759). ❖ Was 13 when chosen by Louis XIV to marry Philip of Anjou (future Philip V of Spain), in part because of Savoy's strategic location in France's struggle with Austria to control Italy; exerted considerable influence over husband while being significantly influenced by Marie-Anne de la Trémouille; reign was overshadowed by War of the Spanish Succession; acted as regent while Philip was away on military campaign and had to abandon Madrid when the enemy occupied it (1706); her youth, energy, and kindliness made her more popular among Spaniards than Philip's 2nd wife, Elizabeth Farnese. ❖ See also *Women in World History.*

MARIE LOUISE OF SCHLESWIG-HOLSTEIN (1872–1956). *See Marie Louise.*

MARIE MAGDALENA BARBARA (1711–1758). *See Maria Barbara of Braganza.*

MARIE MELITA OF HOHENLOHE-LANGENBURG (1899–1967). Duchess of Schleswig-Holstein-Sonderburg-Glucksburg. Born Jan 18, 1899, in Langenburg, Germany; died Nov 8, 1967, in Munich, Bavaria, Germany; dau. of Ernest, 7th prince of Hohenlohe-Langenburg, and Alexandra Saxe-Coburg (1878–1942); m. Wilhelm Fredrich also known as Frederick, duke of Schleswig-Holstein-Sonderburg-Glucksburg, Feb 15, 1916; children: Hans (1917–1944); William (1919–1926); Peter, duke of Schleswig-Holstein-Sonderburg-Glucksburg (b. 1922); Marie-Alexandra of Schleswig-Holstein-Sonderburg-Glucksburg (b. 1927).

MARIE OF AGREDA (1602–1665). *See Agreda, Sor María de.*

MARIE OF ANHALT (1898–1983). Princess of Prussia. Name variations: Marie Auguste von Anhalt. Born June 10, 1898, at Schloss Ballenstedt; died May 22, 1983, at Essen; dau. of Eduard Georg Wilhelm, duke of Anhalt, and Marie of Saxe-Altenburg, duchess of Saxony; m. Joachim Francis Humbert, prince of Prussia, Mar 11, 1916; m. Johann Michael, baron von Löen or Loen, Sept 27, 1926 (div. 1935); children: (1st m.) Charles Francis Joseph (b. 1916), prince of Prussia.

MARIE OF ANJOU (1404–1463). Queen of France. Name variations: Marie d'Anjou; Mary of Anjou; Mary d'Anjou. Born in 1404 in Angers, France; died in 1463 at Amboise, France; dau. of Louis II (1377–1417), duke of Anjou and king of Sicily, and Yolande of Aragon (1379–1442); sister of King René I the Good, duke of Anjou and Lorraine (husband of Isabelle of Lorraine); m. Charles VII (1403–1461), king of France (r. 1422–1461), Dec 18, 1422; children: 14, including Louis XI (1423–1483), king of France (r. 1461–1483); Jean (b. 1426); Catherine de France (1428–1446, who m. Charles the Bold); Jacques (b. 1432); Jeanne of Bourbon (1434–1482, who m. John II of Bourbon); Yolande of France (1434–1478, who m. Amadeus of Savoy); Marguerite (1437–1438); Marie (1437–1439); Charles of Berri (1446–1472); Radegonde (b. 1445); Madeleine of France (1443–1486, who m. Ladislas Posthumus); and adopted daughter Louise de Laval. ❖ At 9, was betrothed to the Dauphin Charles (1414); at 18, wed (1422); was prevented from developing a close relationship with husband because of her mother, who exercised enormous sway over Charles personally and politically; had 14 children, only 6 of whom survived to adulthood, including future king Louis XI; was particularly involved in their education, unlike many queens who left child-rearing to servants and tutors; also devoted herself to charitable works; with mother's death, husband came under the influence of Agnes Sorel, a lady in the queen's entourage. ❖ See also *Women in World History.*

MARIE OF ANTIOCH (d. 1183). Byzantine empress and regent. Name variations: Mary of Antioch; Maria of Antioch. Born before 1149, possibly in the 1130s; died in 1183; dau. of Constance of Antioch (1128–1164) and Raymond I of Poitiers, prince of Antioch; sister of Bohemund III, prince of Antioch (r. 1163–1201); 2nd wife of Manuel I Comnenus or Komnenos (c. 1120–1180), Byzantine emperor (r. 1143–1180); children: Alexius II Comnenus (c. 1168–1183), emperor of Byzantium (r. 1180–1183). ❖ When husband died (1180), became regent for 11-year-old Alexius, but her pro-Western policies and indulgence of corrupt favorites made her unpopular; after Andronicus I Comnenus compelled Alexius to sign a death warrant for her, then had himself crowned co-emperor, was strangled to death. ❖ See also *Women in World History.*

MARIE OF AUSTRIA (1505–1558). *See Mary of Hungary.*

MARIE OF AUSTRIA (1528–1603). Holy Roman Empress. Name variations: Maria or Mary of Hapsburg; Marie d'Autriche. Born June 21, 1528, in Madrid, Spain; died Feb 26, 1603, in Villamonte, Spain; dau. of Holy Roman Emperor Charles V (Charles I of Spain) and Isabella of Portugal (1503–1539); sister of Phillip II, king of Spain (r. 1556–1598), and Joanna of Austria (1535–1573); half-sister of Margaret of Parma (1522–1586); m. Maximilian II, Holy Roman emperor (r. 1564–1576); children: Anne of Austria (c. 1550–1580, who m. Philip II of Spain); Rudolf II (1552–1612), Holy Roman emperor (r. 1576–1612); Elisabeth of Habsburg (1554–1592, who m. Charles IX); Matthew (1557–1619), king of Bohemia, also known as Matthias, Holy Roman emperor (r. 1612–1619); Archduke Ernst (governor of some Austrian duchies). ❖ See also *Women in World History.*

MARIE OF BADEN (1817–1888). Duchess of Hamilton and princess of Zahringen. Born Oct 11, 1817; died Oct 17, 1888; dau. of Stephanie de Beauharnais (1789–1860) and Charles Ludwig, grand duke of Baden; m. William Alexander, 11th duke of Hamilton, on Feb 23, 1843; children: William Alexander (b. 1845), 12th duke of Hamilton; Charles George (b. 1847), earl of Selkirk; Mary Victoria (b. 1850), Lady Douglas-Hamilton.

MARIE OF BLOIS (d. 1404). *See Marie of Guise.*

MARIE OF BOULOGNE (d. 1182). Countess of Boulogne and abbess of Romsey. Name variations: Marie, Abbess of Romsey; Mary, countess of Boulogne; countess of Mortain; countess of Mortaigne. Born c. 1136; died in 1182 (some sources cite 1181) in St. Austrebert, Montreuil, France; interred at St. Austrebert; dau. of Matilda of Boulogne (c. 1103–1152) and Stephen of Blois (c. 1096–1154), later king of England (r. 1135–1154); sister of Eustace IV and William II (also known as Guillame II); m. Matthew I (Matthieu d'Alsace), count of Boulogne, c. 1160 (annulled 1169); children: daughter Ide d'Alsace (c. 1161–1216); Maude of Alsace (1163–c. 1210). ❖ Became prioress of Lillechurch, then abbess of Romsey before succeeding brothers as ruler of Boulogne (1159); because of inheritance, was abducted by Matthew I of Alsace and forced by her cousin King Henry II to marry Matthew, in order to secure an alliance; after 9 years of marriage, was allowed to return to religious life (1169). ❖ See also *Women in World History.*

MARIE OF BRABANT (c. 1260–1321). Queen of France. Name variations: Mary Louvain; Mary of Brabant; Marie de Brabant. Born c. 1260 (some sources cite 1254); died in 1321; dau. of Henry III (d. 1261), duke of Brabant, and Adelaide of Burgundy (d. 1273); became 2nd wife of Philip III the Bold (1245–1285), king of France (r. 1270–1285), in 1274; children: Louis of Evreux (d. 1319); Margaret of France (c. 1282–1318, who m. Edward I, king of England). ❖ Philip's 1st wife was Isabella of Aragon (1243–1271).

MARIE OF BRABANT (fl. 1250). Countess Palatine. Fl. around 1250; 1st wife of Ludwig also known as Louis II the Stern (1229–1294), count Palatine (r. 1253–1294), duke of Bavaria (r. 1255–1294). ❖ Louis' 2nd wife was Anna of Silesia.

MARIE OF BRANDENBURG-KULMBACH (1519–1567). Electress of the Palatinate and duchess of Simmern. Name variations: Marie von Brandenburg-Kulmbach. Born Oct 11, 1519; died Oct 31, 1567; dau. of Suzanne of Bavaria (1502–1543) and Casimir, margrave of Brandenburg; m. Frederick III the Pious (1515–1576), duke of Simmern and elector of the Palatinate (r. 1559–1576), on Oct 21, 1537; children: Louis VI (b. 1539), elector of the Palatinate; Elizabeth of Wittlesbach (1540–1594). ❖ Following Marie of Brandenburg-Kulmbach's death, Frederick III married Amalie von Neuanahr on April 25, 1569.

MARIE OF BRUNSWICK (1729–1796). See Maria Juliana of Brunswick.

MARIE OF BULGARIA (c. 1046–?). Bulgarian princess. Name variations: Maria of Bulgaria. Born c. 1046; death date unknown; possibly dau. of King Samuel of Bulgaria; possibly sister of Catherine of Bulgaria; m. Andronicus Ducas (general, known as the traitor of Manzikert); maternal grandmother of Anna Comnena; children: two sons and three daughters, including Irene Ducas (c. 1066–1133).

MARIE OF CHAMPAGNE (1145–1198). See Marie de Champagne.

MARIE OF CHAMPAGNE (c. 1180–1203). Countess of Flanders and Hainault. Name variations: Maria of Champagne; Mary of Champagne. Born c. 1180; died during an epidemic while on crusade in 1203; dau. of Marie de Champagne (1145–1198) and Henry I, count of Champagne; m. Baudouin also known as Baldwin IX (1171–1206), count of Flanders and Hainault (crowned Baldwin I of Constantinople), in 1186; children: Johanna of Flanders (c. 1200–1244), countess of Belgium; Margaret of Flanders (1202–1280).

MARIE OF CLEVES (1426–1486). Duchess of Orléans and poet. Name variations: Mary of Cleves; Marie de Clèves; Marie Clèves, Marquise d'Isles; Anne de Cleves; Anne of Cleves. Born Sept 19, 1426, in France; died Aug 23, 1486 (some sources cite 1487); dau. of Adolph or Adolf IV, duke of Cleves; became 3rd wife of Charles Valois (1391–1465), duke of Orléans, in 1441; children: Louis XII (1462–1515), king of France (r. 1498–1515); Marie of Orleans (d. 1493, who m. Jean de Foix, comte d'Etampes); Anne of Orleans (d. 1491), abbess of Fontevrault. Charles' 1st wife was Isabella of Valois (1389–c. 1410); his 2nd was Bonne of Armagnac (d. 1415). ❖ In court of Burgundy, played host to visiting poets. Only 2 *rondeaux* extant.

MARIE OF DREUX (1391–1446). Duchess of Alençon. Name variations: Mary of Dreux; Mary de Dreux; duchess of Alencon. Born 1391; died 1446; dau. of John IV de Montfort, 5th duke of Brittany (r. 1364–1399) and Joanna of Navarre (c. 1370–1437); m. John I, duke of Alençon.

MARIE OF EVREUX (d. 1335). Duchess of Brabant. Name variations: Marie de France or Marie of France; Mary of Evreux. Died in 1335; dau. of Louis, count of Evreux; m. John III the Triumphant (1300–1355), duke of Brabant (r. 1312–1355), around July 19, 1311; children: Margaret of Brabant (1323–1368); Joanna of Brabant (1322–1406); Marie of Guelders (1325–1399); John of Brabant (1327–1335); Henry of Brabant (d. 1349); Godfrey of Brabant (d. after Feb 1352). Her husband John III had many illegitimate children, including John Brant; William Brant; John van Veen; Joanna (who m. Costin von Raenst); Jeanette (who m. Godfrey van der Dilft); Marie van Veen (a nun in Brussels who died in 1394); Arnold van der Hulpen (who m. Elisabeth Moedels); Henry van der Hulpen; Margareta van der Hulpen (who m. Bernardus van der Spout and Walter de Melin); Barbe van Ophem (a nun who died in 1354); Nikolaus de Sweerthere; Nikolaus de Werthusen; Henry of Brussels; John van Linden; John van Overysche; Dionysius van Louvain; Katharina (who m. Godefroy de Henri-Chapelle); another daughter who m. Winand de Henri-Chapelle; another daughter who m. Clerembaut de Hauterive.

MARIE OF FRANCE (c. 1140–1200). See Marie de France.

MARIE OF FRANCE (1198–c. 1223). Duchess of Brabant. Name variations: Maria de France. Born in 1198; died Aug 15, 1223 or 1224; dau. of Philip II Augustus, king of France (r. 1180–1223), and Agnes of Meran (d. 1201); m. Philip of Namur (son of Margaret of Alsace and brother of Baldwin IX); became 2nd wife of Henry I (1165–1235), duke of Brabant, April 22, 1213; children: 2 daughters.

MARIE OF FRANCE (1344–1404). Countess of Bar. Born 1344; died 1404; dau. of Bona of Bohemia (1315–1349) and John II the Good (1319–1364), king of France (r. 1350–1364); m. Robert I, duke of Bar.

MARIE OF GASCONY (d. 1399). See Robine, Marie.

MARIE OF GUELDERS (1325–1399). Duchess of Guelders. Name variations: Countess of Gelderland. Born in 1325; died in 1399 (some sources cite 1398); dau. of John III (1300–1355), duke of Brabant (r. 1312–1355), and Marie of Evreux (d. 1335); m. Reginald also known as Renaud III (1333–1371), duke of Guelders, in 1347.

MARIE OF GUISE (d. 1404). Countess of Guise. Name variations: Margaret of Blois; Margaret de Chatillon or Châtillon; Marie of Blois. Died in 1404; dau. of Charles de Chatillon, count of Blois; m. Louis I (1339–1384), count of Provence, duke of Anjou, king of Naples, Sicily and Jerusalem (r. 1360–1384), in 1360; children: Louis II (1377–1417), duke of Anjou and king of Sicily; Charles, count de Roucy; Marie of Anjou (d. 1370).

MARIE OF GUISE (1515–1560). See Mary of Guise.

MARIE OF HAINAULT (fl. 1300). Countess of Clermont. Name variations: Marie of Hainaut. Fl. around 1300; m. Louis I the Grand (1270–1342), count of Clermont; children: Pierre or Peter I (1311–1356), duke of Bourbon; Jacques I or James I (1315–1361), comte de la Marche.

MARIE OF HESSE-DARMSTADT (1824–1880). Empress of Russia. Name variations: Mariia Aleksandrovna or Alexandrovna; Mary of Hesse-Darmstadt; Princess Wilhelmine (before 1841), Empress Marie; Empress Marie of Russia. Born Princess Maximilienne Wilhelmine Auguste Sophie Marie on July 27, 1824, in Hesse-Darmstadt; died of tuberculosis on May 22, 1880 (o.s.) in St. Petersburg; illegitimate dau. of Baron August Ludwig de Senarclans-Grancy (a minor state official) and Princess Wilhelmine of Baden (1788–1836); education uncertain; m. Alexander II, tsar of Russia (r. 1855–1881), in 1841; children: Alexandra or Aleksandra (1842–1849); Nicholas (1843–1865); Alexander III (1845–1894), tsar of Russia (r. 1881–1894); Vladimir (b. 1847, who m. Maria of Mecklenburg-Schwerin); Aleksei (1850–1908, who m. Alexandra Zhukovskaya); Marie Alexandrovna (1853–1920); Sergei or Sergius (1857–1905, who m. Ella); Paul (1860–1919, who m. Alexandra Oldenburg [1870–1891]). ❖ Intelligent and progressive, was raised in German duchy of Hesse-Darmstadt (1824–40); lived in St. Petersburg as wife of Alexander II (1841–80); as empress of Russia (1855–80), was a liberal and stabilizing influence on her weak-willed husband; was also the victim of court intrigue and of Alexander's philandering; active in numerous charitable activities, served as president of the Russian Red Cross and fostered better education for women; spent the last 15 years of her life in poor health and undeserved humiliation. ❖ See also Women in World History.

MARIE OF HOHENZOLLERN-SIGMARINGEN (1845–1912). Countess of Flanders. Born Nov 17, 1845; died Nov 26, 1912; dau. of Charles Anthony I of Hohenzollern-Sigmaringen (1811–1885), prince of Romania, and Josephine of Baden (1813–1900); sister of Carol I, king of Romania (r. 1881–1914); m. Philip (1837–1905), count of Flanders, in 1867; children: Baudouin (1869–1891); twins Henrietta of Belgium (1870–1948, who m. Emmanuel of Orléans) and Josephine (1870–1871); Josephine of Belgium (1872–1958, who m. Charles Anthony II of Hohenzollern-Sigmaringen); Albert I (1875–1934), king of the Belgians (r. 1909–1934).

MARIE OF HUNGARY (d. 1323). Queen of Naples and Anjou. Name variations: Maria; Mary of Hungary. Born in Hungary; died Mar 25, 1323; dau. of Stephen V, king of Hungary (r. 1270–1272) and Elizabeth of Kumania (c. 1242–?); m. Charles II the Lame (1254–1309), duke of Anjou (r. 1285–1290), king of Naples (r. 1285–1309), in 1270; children: Charles Martel of Hungary; Blanche of Naples (d. 1310, who m. James II of Aragon); Robert the Good, king of Naples (r. 1309–1343); Philip of Tarento (d. 1332); Margaret of Anjou (c. 1272–1299); Lenore of Sicily (1289–1341, who m. Frederick II of Sicily); John of Gravina (who m. Agnes of Perigord).

MARIE OF KIEV.
See Maria of Kiev (d. 1087).
See Maria of Kiev (d. 1146).

MARIE OF KIEV (d. 1179). Grand princess of Kiev. Died in 1179; dau. of Christina of Sweden (d. 1122) and Mstislav I (b. 1076), grand prince of Kiev (r. 1125–1132); sister of Ingeborg of Russia, Izyaslav II also known as Yziaslav II, prince of Kiev (r. 1146–1154), and Irene of Kiev; m. Vsevolod II, grand prince of Kiev; children: Svyatoslav also known as Sviatoslav III, prince of Kiev; Jaroslav also known as Yaroslav (b. 1139), prince of Kiev.

MARIE OF LEININGEN (1907–1951). See Marie of Russia.

MARIE OF LUSIGNAN (d. 1260). Countess of Eu. Died Oct 1, 1260, in Melle, Poitou; interred at Fourcarmont Abbey; dau. of Yolande de Dreux (d. 1238) and Raoul III de Lusignan, count of Eu; m. Alfons de Brienne, count of Eu, in 1249; children: John de Brienne, count of Eu.

MARIE OF LUXEMBURG (fl. 16th c.). Duchess of Brittany. Name variations: Luxembourg. Dau. of Sebastian of Luxembourg, duke of Penthièvre; m. Philippe-Emmanuel (1548–1602), duc de Mercoeur, brother of Louise of Lorraine; children: at least a daughter. ❖ As father's only heir, inherited the duchy of Brittany, which she and her husband governed.

MARIE OF LUXEMBURG (d. 1546). Countess of Vendome. Died April 1, 1546; dau. of Margaret of Savoy (d. 1483) and Peter also known as Pierre II, count of St. Paul (r. 1476–1482); m. Jacques de Romont, in 1460; m. François also known as Francis of Bourbon, count of Vendôme, on Sept 8, 1487; children: (2nd m.) Charles (b. 1489), duke of Vendome; Francis (b. 1491), duke of St. Pol; Antoinette of Bourbon (1494–1583).

MARIE OF MECKLENBURG (fl. 1380). Danish royal. Name variations: Marie von Mecklenburg. Flourished in 1380; dau. of Ingeborg (1347–1370) and Henry, duke of Mecklenburg; m. Vratislav or Vratislas of Pomerania (d. 1394); children: Erik VII of Pomerania (c. 1382–1459), king of Denmark, Norway, and Sweden (r. 1397–1438); Catherine of Pomerania (d. 1426, who m. Johan or John of Bavaria).

MARIE OF MECKLENBURG-GUSTROW (1659–1701). Duchess of Mecklenburg-Strelitz. Name variations: Marie von Mecklenburg-Güstrow. Born July 19, 1659; died Jan 16, 1701; dau. of Magdalena Sybilla (1617–1668) and Christian Oldenburg (1603–1647, son of Christian IV, king of Denmark); m. Adolf Frederick II, duke of Mecklenburg-Strelitz, on Sept 24, 1684.

MARIE OF MONTFERRAT (d. 1212). Queen and regent of Jerusalem. Name variations: Maria or Mary of Montferrat; Marie de Montferrat; Maria La Marquise; Mary la Marquise of Jerusalem. Died in 1212; dau. of Conrad of Montferrat, king of Jerusalem (r. 1190–1192), and Isabella I of Jerusalem (d. 1205); m. John of Brienne also known as John I de Brienne, king of Jerusalem (r. 1210–1225), emperor of Constantinople (r. 1228–1237), in 1210; children: Yolande of Brienne (1212–1228), queen of Jerusalem. ❖ Was queen under a regency (1205–12). ❖ See also *Women in World History*.

MARIE OF NAPLES (fl. 1300s). Heir to the throne of Naples. Flourished from 1320s to 1350s; dau. of Charles of Calabria and Marie of Valois; sister of Joanna I of Naples (1326–1382); granddau. of Robert the Good, king of Naples (r. 1309–1343); m. Charles of Durazzo; m. Philip II of Constantinople; children: (1st marriage) Margaret of Naples (who m. Charles III of Durazzo, king of Naples, r. 1382–1386, who ruled Hungary as Charles II, r. 1385–1386).

MARIE OF NASSAU (1841–1910). Princess of Wied. Born July 5, 1841; died June 22, 1910; dau. of Louise (1808–1870) and Frederick Orange-Nassau (son of William I of the Netherlands); m. William (1845–1907), 5th prince of Wied, on July 18, 1871.

MARIE OF ORLEANS (d. 1493). Countess of Étampes. Name variations: Marie de Orléans; countess of Etampes or Estampes or d'Etampes. Died in 1493; dau. of Marie of Cleves (1426–1486) and Charles Valois (1391–1465), duke of Orléans; m. Jean de Foix, comte d'Etampes.

MARIE OF ORLEANS (1813–1839). See *Marie d'Orleans*.

MARIE OF PONTHIEU (d. 1251). See *Joanna of Ponthieu*.

MARIE OF RUMANIA (1875–1938). Queen of Romania and English princess. Name variations: Marie of Romania; Marie of Roumania; Mary of Saxe-Coburg; Marie of Saxe-Coburg-Gotha; called Missy by her family. Born Marie Alexandra Victoria of Saxe-Coburg, Oct 29, 1875, at family country home in Eastwell Park, Kent, England; died July 18, 1938, at Castle Pelesch, Sinaia, Romania, of an intestinal hemorrhage; dau. of Prince Alfred Saxe-Coburg, duke of Edinburgh (son of Queen Victoria) and Grand Duchess Marie Alexandrovna (dau. of Alexander II of Russia); sister of Alexandra Saxe-Coburg (1878–1942), Beatrice of Saxe-Coburg (1884–1966), duchess of Galliera, and Victoria Melita of Saxe-Coburg (1876–1936); m. Ferdinand I of Hohenzollern-Sigmaringen (1865–1927), king of Romania (r. 1914–1927), on Jan 10, 1893; children: Carol II (1893–1953), king of Romania (r. 1930–1940); Elisabeth (1894–1956); Marie (1900–1961, also known as Mignon); Nicholas (1903–1978); Ileana (1909–1991); Mircea (1913–1916). ❖ One of the most colorful and influential monarchs of the early 20th century, married the heir to the Romanian throne and played an important role in the affairs of her adopted country during and immediately after WWI; spent portion of early years in Malta (1885–89); moved with family to Duchy of Coburg in Germany, where Prince Ferdinand of Hohenzollern-Sigmaringen became heir to Romanian throne (1889); married him (1893); during Romanian peasant revolt, began longstanding love affair with Barbo Stirbey, a noble and prominent leader in the country's economy (1907); performed relief work when Romania fought 2nd Balkan War against Bulgaria (1913), obtaining permission from the king to personally administer one of the cholera camps; following German invasion (1916), became a heroine-queen, one of few effective leaders in her country; directed the Romanian Red Cross, worked long hours setting up relief efforts, and personally worked in the nation's bulging military hospitals; conducted mission to Paris Peace Conference (1919); gained worldwide fame; toured US, beginning with a ticker-tape welcoming parade in NY (1926); widowed by death of Ferdinand (1927). ❖ See also autobiography *The Story of My Life* (1934); Terence Elsberry, *Marie of Roumania: The Intimate Life of a Twentieth Century Queen* (St. Martin, 1972); Hannah Pakula, *The Last Romantic: A Biography of Queen Marie of Roumania* (Simon & Schuster, 1984); and *Women in World History*.

MARIE OF RUMANIA (1900–1961). See *Marie*.

MARIE OF RUSSIA (1907–1951). Princess of Leiningen. Name variations: Mary Cyrillovna; Marie of Leiningen. Born Feb 2, 1907, in Coburg, Bavaria, Germany; died Oct 27, 1951, in Madrid, Spain; dau. of Cyril Vladimirovitch (son of Tsar Alexander II of Russia) and Victoria Melita of Saxe-Coburg (1876–1936); m. Charles, 6th prince of Leiningen, on Nov 25, 1925; children: seven, including Emrich, 7th prince of Leiningen (b. 1926); Charles (b. 1928); Kira of Leiningen (b. 1930); Margaret of Leiningen (b. 1932); Matilda of Leiningen (b. 1936); Frederick (b. 1938).

MARIE OF SALERNO (fl. 1000s). Countess of the Principate. Flourished around 1000s; m. William, count of the Principate (d. 1080); children: Robert, count of the Principate (r. 1080–1099); Tancred (who fought under Roger I in Sicily and received lands of the country of Syracuse); Richard (who was with Bohemund in Antioch in 1096); Rainald (who was with Bohemund in Antioch in 1096).

MARIE OF SAVOY-NEMOURS (d. 1724). See *Jeanne of Nemours*.

MARIE OF SAXE-COBURG-GOTHA (1875–1938). See *Marie of Rumania*.

MARIE OF SAXE-WEIMAR-EISENACH (1808–1877). Princess of Prussia. Born Feb 3, 1808; died Jan 18, 1877; dau. of Marie Pavlovna (1786–1859) and Charles Frederick, duke of Saxe-Weimar; m. Charles Hohenzollern, prince of Prussia, on May 26, 1827; children: Frederick Charles (b. 1828), prince of Prussia; Marie Louise Anne (1829–1901, who m. Alexis William, landgrave of Hesse); Anne Frederica (1836–1918).

MARIE OF SWABIA (c. 1201–1235). German princess. Name variations: Marie de Swabia; Marie von Hohenstaufen. Born c. 1201 in Constantinople; died in 1235; dau. of Irene Angela of Byzantium (d. 1208) and Philip of Swabia (c. 1176–1208), Holy Roman emperor (r. 1198–1208); sister of Beatrice of Swabia (1198–1235) and Cunigunde of Hohenstaufen; became 1st wife of Henry II (1207–1248), duke of Brabant (r. 1235–1248), before August 22, 1215; children: Maude of Brabant (1224–1288); Henry III (b. 1233), duke of Brabant (r. 1248–1261). ❖ Henry II's 2nd wife was Sophia of Thuringia (1224–1284).

MARIE OF VALOIS (fl. 14th c.). Neapolitan noblewoman. Married Charles of Calabria (son of Robert the Good, king of Naples); children: Joanna I of Naples (1326–1382) and Marie of Naples.

MARIE OF WURTTEMBERG (1813–1839). See *Marie d'Orleans*.

MARIE PADILLA (1335–1365). See *Marie de Padilla*.

MARIE PAVLOVNA (1786–1859). Russian royal and duchess of Saxe-Weimar. Name variations: Mary Pavlovna; Princess Mary. Born Feb 15, 1786; died June 23, 1859; dau. of Paul I (1754–1801), tsar of Russia (r. 1796–1801), and Sophia Dorothea of Wurttemberg (1759–1828); sister of Anna Pavlovna (1795–1865) and Helena Pavlovna (1784–1803); m. Charles Frederick, duke of Saxe-Weimar, on Aug 3, 1804; children: Marie of Saxe-Weimar-Eisenach (1808–1877); Augusta of Saxe-Weimar (1811–1890, who m. Wilhelm I, emperor of Germany); Charles Alexander (b. 1818).

MARIE PAVLOVNA (1890–1958). Duchess of Sodermanland. Name variations: Mary Pavlovna Romanov. Born Marie Pavlovna on April 6, 1890; died Dec 13, 1958; dau. of Paul Alexandrovitch (son of Alexander II, tsar of Russia) and Alexandra Oldenburg (1870–1891); m. William Bernadotte, duke of Sodermanland (son of Gustavus V, king of Sweden, and Victoria of Baden), May 3, 1908 (div. 1914); m. Serge Michailovitch, count Putiatin, Sept 6, 1917 (div. 1924); children: (1st m.) Lennart Gustaf, count of Wisborg (b. 1909).

MARIE POVEKA (1887–1980). See Martinez, Maria Montoya.

MARIE RAPHAELLE OF SPAIN (1726–1746). See Maria Theresa of Spain.

MARIE SOPHIE OF HESSE-CASSEL (1767–1852). Queen of Denmark. Name variations: Marie Sofie Frederikke of Hesse-Cassel. Born Oct 28, 1767, in Hanau; died Mar 21, 1852, in Amalienborg, Copenhagen, Denmark; dau. of Louise of Denmark (1750–1831) and Charles of Hesse-Cassel, regent of Schleswig-Holstein; sister of Louise of Hesse-Cassel (1789–1867); m. Frederick VI, king of Denmark (r. 1808–1839), on July 31, 1790; children: Christian (1791–1791); Marie Louise (1792–1793); Caroline (1793–1881, who m. Frederick Ferdinand, prince Oldenburg); Louise (1795–1795); Christian (1797–1797); Louise Juliane (1802–1802); Frederica Maria (1805–1805); Wilhelmine (1808–1891, who m. Frederick VII, king of Denmark).

MARIE STUART (1542–1587). See Mary Stuart.

MARIE THÉRÈSE CHARLOTTE (1778–1851). Duchess of Angoulême. Name variations: Marie Therese Charlotte; Marie-Thérèse-Charlotte; Madame Royale; Filia Dolorosa, the Modern Antigone; Comtesse de Marnes. Born at Versailles, France, Dec 19, 1778; died of pneumonia on Oct 19, 1851, in Austria; dau. of Louis XVI (1754–1793), king of France (r. 1774–1792), and Marie Antoinette (1755–1793); educated at French court; m. Louis Antoine de Bourbon (1775–1844), duke of Angoulême, in 1799. ❖ Eldest daughter of Louis XVI and Marie Antoinette, who survived her parents and lived most of her life in exile; was imprisoned with family in the Temple (1792); mother and father guillotined (1793), but only learned of mother's death 18 months after the event; released from prison (1795); kept a journal detailing her experiences; married duke of Angoulême (1799); lived in exile with uncle Louis XVIII in various European countries (1799–1814); returned with Louis when he was restored to French throne (1814); lived a quiet life in Paris (1814–29), with her own court at the Tuileries; with the revolution in Paris and abdication of Charles X and duke of Angoulême (1830), spent remaining years in exile once more. ❖ See also Elizabeth Powers, The Journal of Madame Royale (Walker, 1976); Joseph Turquan, Madame Royale: The Last Dauphine (Unwin, 1910); Alice Curtis Desmond, Marie Antoinette's Daughter (Dodd, 1967); and Women in World History.

MARIE-THÉRÈSE DE SOUBIRAN (1834–1889). Founder of the Society of Mary Auxiliatrix. Born May 16, 1834, at Castelnaudary (Aude), France; died June 7, 1889, in Paris, France; beatified by Pius XII in 1946. ❖ At 14, took a vow of chastity, began to eat nothing but bread and water, and slept on a board; after spending some time in a convent in Ghent, established her own congregation, which eventually came to be known as the Society of Mary Auxiliatrix. ❖ See also Women in World History.

MARIE THERESE OF AUSTRIA (1638–1683). See Maria Teresa of Spain.

MARIE THERESE OF BOURBON (fl. 19th c.). Princess of Hohenzollern. Married William (1864–1927), prince of Hohenzollern; children: Augusta Victoria (1890–1966, who m. Manuel II, king of Portugal).

MARIE THERESE OF SPAIN (1638–1683). See Maria Teresa of Spain.

MARIE VALERIE (1868–1924). Archduchess of Austria. Name variations: Marie Valérie. Born 1868; died 1924; dau. of Elizabeth of Bavaria (1837–1898) and Franz Josef also known as Francis Joseph, emperor of Austria (r. 1848–1916); m. Francis (Franz) Salvator, archduke of Tuscany; children: Elisabeth Franziska, known as Ella Salvator (1892–1930); Franz Karl Salvator (1893–1918); Hubert Salvator (1894–1971); Hedwig Salvator (1896–1970); Theodor Salvator (1899–1978); Gertrud Salvator (1900–1962); Maria Salvator (1901–1936); Klemens Salvator (1904–1974); Mathilde Salvator (b. 1906).

MARIE VETSERA (1871–1889). See Vetsera, Marie.

MARIETTA (fl. 1430s). Mistress of the king of Cyprus. Born in the Greek city of Patras; mistress of John II, the Lusignan king of Cyprus (r. 1432–1458); children: illeg. son, James II the Bastard, king of Cyprus (b. in either 1440 or 1441); possibly mother of Anne of Lusignan. ❖ See also Women in World History.

MARIIA. Variant of Maria.

MARIIA, Mother (1891–1945). See Skobtsova, Maria.

MARILLAC, Louise de (1591–1660). Saint and founder. Name variations: Madame le Gras. Born in Paris, France, on August 15, 1591; died of gangrene on Mar 15, 1660; dau. of Louis de Marillac (counselor to Parliament) and his 2nd wife Marguerite (le Camus) de Marillac; m. Antoine le Gras, in 1613 (died 1626); children: 1 son. ❖ Following husband's death (1626), became a nun; under guidance of St. Vincent de Paul, founded Sisters of Charity (1633), which would establish hospitals for the poor and mentally afflicted; elevated to superior-general (1668). Feast day is Mar 15. ❖ See also Women in World History.

MARIN, Gladys (1941–2005). Chilean revolutionary and politician. Name variations: Gladys Marin Millie. Born July 16, 1941, in Curepto, Chile; died of a brain tumor, Mar 6, 2005, in Santiago, Chile; dau. of Adriana (schoolteacher) and Heraclio (farmer); attended Escuela Normal in Santiago; m. Jorge Muñoz (Santiago Communist party secretary), 1959 ("disappeared" under police custody, 1976); lived with Julio Ugas (journalist); children: sons. ❖ Communist leader who spearheaded the fight against the military dictatorship of Pinochet (1973–90), began career working on unsuccessful presidential campaign for socialist Salvador Allende (1958); elected to Congress, becoming Chile's youngest parliamentarian (1965); after the Pinochet coup (1973), broadcast a message of defiance, then went into exile (1974); slipped back into Chile to develop the resistance (1978); was instrumental in creating the Manuel Rodriguez Patriotic Front (FPMR) to foment popular rebellion (1980); resurfaced from clandestinity (1990); elected general secretary of Communist Party (1994); continued to vocally oppose Pinochet, resulting in brief imprisonments and beatings; stood as the 1st Communist Party presidential candidate since 1932 (1999); elected party president (2002), the 1st woman to lead a political party in Chile; was a national figure, respected by all parties, at the time of her death. ❖ See also autobiography, La Vida Es Hoy (Life is Today, 203).

MARIN, Maguy (1951—). French dancer and choreographer. Born June 2, 1951, in Toulouse, France; studied classical ballet at Toulouse Conservatoire; trained with Nina Vyroubova in Paris and at Maurice Béjart's Mudra school in Brussels. ❖ Performed with Strasbourg Opéra Ballet in France (late 1960s) and with the Chandra group, Brussels, directed by Micha van Hoecke; danced with Béjart's Ballet du XXIème Siècle in Brussels (starting 1972) and choreographed 1st work Yu-ku-ri for company (1976); with Daniel Ambash, founded Le Ballet Théâtre de l'Arche, Créteil, in France (1978), which was renamed Campagnie Maguy Marin (1984) and later evolved into Centre Chorégraphique National (1990); has choreographed works for Paris Opéra Ballet, Lyon Opéra Ballet, Dutch National Ballet, Nederlands Dans Theater, and others; awards include 1st prizes at Nyon Choreography Competition (1977) and Bagnolet Festival International Choreography Competition (1978), and Grand Prix National de Chorégraphie, France (1983); works most often described as Tanztheater (dance-theater) for inclusion of aural, vocal and visual facets. Major works include La jeune fille et la mort (Death and the Maiden, 1979), Cante (1980), May B. (1981), Babel Babel (1982), Hymen (1984), Cendrillon (Cinderella, 1985), Groosland (1990), and Coppélia (1993).

MARÍN DEL SOLAR, Mercedes (1804–1866). Chilean poet. Name variations: Mercedes Marin del Solar. Born 1804 in Santiago, Chile; died Dec 21, 1866, in Santiago; dau. of José Gaspar Marín and Luisa Recabarren; children: Amelia de Claro (poet) and Enrique del Solar (b. 1844, poet). ❖ Learned French, literature, and studied philosopher Andrés Bello; established reputation with a poem on the death of General Portales (1837); influenced by Spanish-Cuban writer Gertrúdis Gómez de Avellaneda; works include Canto fúnebre al la muerte de don Diego Portales (1837); her collected poems were published posthumously (1874) by son.

MARINA (c. 1500–1531). See Malinche.

MARINA (1938—). See Vlady, Marina.

MARINA CLEMENCIA, Sor (1658–1753). See Maria do Céu.

MARINA OF ANTIOCH (c. 255–c. 275). See Margaret of Antioch.

MARINA OF GREECE (1906–1968). Duchess of Kent. Name variations: Marina Oldenburg; Marina of Kent; Dame Marina. Born Dec 13, 1906, in Athens, Greece; died Aug 27, 1968, at Kensington Palace, London, England; dau. of Helena of Russia (1882–1957) and Prince Nicholas (Oldenburg) of Greece (uncle of England's Prince Philip); sister of Olga Oldenburg (1903–1981) and Elizabeth Oldenburg (1904–1955); m. George Windsor (1902–1942), 1st duke of Kent, Nov 29, 1934; children: Edward Windsor (b. 1935), 2nd duke of Kent; Princess Alexandra of Kent (b. 1936); Prince Michael of Kent (b. 1942). ❖ Husband died in a plane crash (1942); during WWII, served as commandant, and later chief commandant, of the Women's Royal Naval Service (WRNS); was also colonel-in-chief of the Queen's Own Royal West Kent Regiment and Corps of Royal Electrical and Mechanical Engineers; was a chancellor of Kent University and a patron of National Association for Mental Health; also served as president of Royal National Lifeboat Institution and of All England Lawn Tennis Club. Named Grand Cross of the British Empire (GBE, 1937) and Grand Cross of the Royal Victorian Order (GCVO, 1948).

MARINA OF KENT (1906–1968). See Marina of Greece.

MARINDA (c. 1678–1715). See Monck, Mary.

MARINE GIRLS. See Thorn, Tracey.

MARINESCU, Alexandra (1981—). Romanian gymnast. Born Mar 19, 1981, in Bucharest, Romania. ❖ Won Jr. European championships (1994, 1996), Hapoel Games (1995); at World championships, won gold medals for team all-around (1995, 1997) and a silver medal for balance beam (1996); at Atlanta Olympics, won a bronze medal for team all-around (1996); forced to retire because of scoliosis (1998).

MARINESCU-BORCANEA, Tecla (1960—). Romanian kayaker. Born Jan 1960 in Romania. ❖ At Los Angeles Olympics, won a gold medal in K4 500 meters (1984).

MARINETTI, Benedetta Cappa (1897–1977). Italian essayist and painter. Name variations: Benedetta; Benedetta Cappa. Born Benedetta Cappa, Aug 14, 1897, in Rome, Italy; died in Venice in 1977; sister of Arturo Cappa; studied painting with Giacomo Balla; m. F(ilippo) T. Marinetti (father of futurism), 1923 (died 1944); children: 3 daughters, Vittoria (b. 1927), Ala (b. 1928), and Luce (b. 1932). ❖ Proponent of Futurism, produced 2 bodies of work for the movement, in painting and literature; with husband, worked on developing the theory of "Tactilism" and experimented with collage and mixed media to create tactile works; regularly exhibited paintings, notably at Venice Biennale (1926, 1930, 1934, 1936) and Rome Quadrienniale; became a leader in the Futurist Aeropittura style of painting; wrote 1st experimental novel, Le forze umane (Human Forces, 1924); other works include Viaggio di Gararà (Garara's Journey, 1931), and Astra e il sottomarino (Astra and the Submarine, 1935).

MARINOFF, Fania (1890–1971). Russian-born actress. Name variations: Fania Van Vechten. Born Mar 20, 1890, in Odessa, Russia; died Nov 16, 1971, in Englewood, NJ; m. Carl Van Vechten (critic, author, and photographer). ❖ At age 8, made stage debut in Denver (1898); made NY debut in A Japanese Nightingale (1903), followed by You Never Can Tell, Streets of New York, Pillars of Society, Judgment Day, Within the Law, Arms and the Man, The Tempest and The Charlatan.

MARINOVA, Mila (1974—). Bulgarian rhythmic gymnast. Born June 3, 1974, in Sofia, Bulgaria. ❖ Was Bulgarian National champion, won the Julieta Shishmanova Cup, and placed 2nd at the Goodwill Games (1990); placed 3rd at European Cup (1991); won a bronze medal at US nationals (2000).

MARINOVA, Tereza (1977—). Bulgarian triple jumper. Born Sept 5, 1977, in Pleven, Bulgaria. ❖ Won a gold medal at Sydney Olympics (2000).

MARINOVA, Zornitsa (1987—). Bulgarian rhythmic gymnast. Born Jan 6, 1987, in Veliko, Bulgaria. ❖ Won team all-around bronze medal at Athens Olympics (2004).

MARIO, Queena (1896–1951). American soprano and writer. Name variations: wrote under names Queen Tillotson and Florence Bryan. Born Queena Mario Tillotson, Aug 21, 1896, in Akron, Ohio; died in NY, May 28, 1951; studied singing with Oscar Saenger and Marcella Sembrich; m. Wilfred Pelletier (conductor at Metropolitan Opera), Nov 23, 1925 (div. 1936). ❖ Worked as a columnist for leading NY papers under names Queen Tillotson and Florence Bryan; made singing debut with San Carlo Opera in Tales of Hoffmann (1918); remained with San

Carlo for 2 seasons, singing the roles of Violetta, Lucia, Gilda, and Juliet, then joined Scotti Grand Opera Co. for 2 seasons; debuted at Metropolitan (1922) as Micaëla in Carmen; remained with Met for next 15 years, singing over 20 leading roles in Italian, French, and German operas; received acclaim for interpretations of Inez, Aennchen, Ah-Yoe, and Sophie, but became best known for performance of Gretel in Humperdinck's Hansel and Gretel, in the 1st full performance to be broadcast on radio from stage of the Met (Christmas Day, 1931), and again at her farewell performance (1938); made guest appearances with San Francisco Opera (1923–24, 1929–30), where she won particular acclaim as the Child in premiere of Ravel's L'Enfant et les Sortilèges (1930); retired and taught such singers as Rose Bampton and Helen Jepson; also wrote successful murder mystery, Murder in the Opera House. ❖ See also Women in World History.

MARION. Variant of Mary and Miriam.

MARION, Frances (1888–1973). American screenwriter. Name variations: (pseudonym for westerns) Frank M. Clifton. Born Marion Benson Owens in San Francisco, CA, Nov 18, 1888; died May 12, 1973, of an aneurysm; dau. of Len Douglas Owens (in advertising business) and Minnie Benson Hall Owens; m. Wesley de Lappe, Oct 23, 1906 (div. 1911); m. Robert Dickson Pike (industrialist), Nov 14, 1911 (div. 1917); m. Fred Thomson, Nov 2, 1919 (died 1928); m. George Hill, Jan 1930 (div. 1931); children: (3rd m.) Fred Thomson Jr. (b. Dec 8, 1926); (adopted) Richard Gordon Thomson (1927). ❖ Won Academy Award for Screenwriting for her original story The Big House (1930), the 1st female writer to win an Oscar; won 2nd Academy Award for The Champ; served as vice president and only woman on the 1st board of directors of the Screen Writers Guild; wrote over 100 produced films, including Rebecca of Sunnybrook Farm, Pollyanna, A Little Princess, and a dozen others for Mary Pickford; also penned The Foundling, Humoresque, The Love Light, Smilin' Through, Within the Law, Toll of the Sea, The Dramatic Life of Abraham Lincoln, The Red Mill, Son of the Shiek, Bringing up Father, Anna Christie, Stella Dallas, Poor Little Rich Girl, Dinner at Eight, Camille and Min and Bill. ❖ See also autobiography, Off With Their Heads (1972); Cari Beauchamp, Without Lying Down: Frances Marion and the Powerful Women of Early Hollywood (Scribner, 1997); and Women in World History.

MARIS, Mona (1903–1991). Argentinean-born actress. Born María Capdevielle, Nov 7, 1903, in Buenos Aires, Argentina; died Mar 23, 1991, in Buenos Aires; m. Clarence Brown (director, div.); m. Herman Rick (Dutch millionaire), 1960 (div. 1969). ❖ Educated in France, began film career in Britain and Germany; made US film debut in The Apache (1925); other films include The Little People, Die Leibeigenen, Rutschbahn, Romance of the Rio Grande, Under a Texas Moon, The Arizona Kid, Seas Beneath, Secrets, No dejes la puerta abierta, White Heat, Tres amores, El cantante de Napoles, Underground, My Gal Sal, Berlin Correspondent, The Falcon in Mexico, The Avengers and Camila.

MARISCOTTI, Hyacintha (d. 1640). Saint. Died at Viterbo in 1640. ❖ Was ordered into the religious life as a Franciscan nun at Viterbo against her wishes; for 10 years, remained indifferent to her surroundings; was eventually converted and became a distinguished saint. Feast day is Jan 30.

MARISOL (1930—). Venezuelan-American artist and portrait sculptor. Name variations: Marisol Escobar. Pronunciation: Mah-ree-SOLE Acekoh-BARR. Born Marisol Escobar, May 22, 1930, in Paris, France; dau. of Gustavo Escobar (wealthy real-estate broker) and Josefina Hernandez Escobar; attended Catholic and boarding schools until age 11, Westwood School for Girls in Los Angeles, Jepson School, École des Beaux-Arts in Paris, Art Students League in NY, Hans Hofmann's painting schools in NY and Provincetown, MA, New School for Social Research; never married; no children. ❖ Noted for her use of multimedia assemblages and monumental scale, established her reputation in the art world following a solo exhibition at prestigious Stabler Gallery (1962); because of her mask of taciturnity, became known as the "Latin Garbo" and was famous for her long periods of silence; work brought to life people from all classes, from Family from the Dust Bowl to the stereotyped women in The Party to Britain's Royal Family; targeted political leaders for social analysis such as Lyndon Baines Johnson and Francisco Franco; starred in one of Andy Warhol's underground films The Kiss; other works include Babies, and The Generals (from 1962 exhibition), Lick My Bicycle Tire (1974), Pablo Picasso (1977), and The Last Supper (1983). ❖ See also Nancy Grove, Magical Mixtures: Marisol Portrait Sculpture (Smithsonian, 1991); and Women in World History.

MARITAIN, Raïssa (1883–1960). Russian-born French writer. Name variations: Raissa Maritain; Raïssa Oumancoff, Oumançoff, Oumansov, or Oumansoff. Born Raïssa Oumansov in Rostov on the Don, Russia, Sept 12, 1883; died in Paris, France, Nov 4, 1960; dau. of Ilia Oumansoff and Issia Oumansoffa; sister of Véra Oumansoff (also spelled Oumancoff or Oumançoff, d. 1959); with family, immigrated to Paris (1893); studied at Sorbonne; m. Jacques Maritain (1882–1973), Nov 26, 1904. ❖ Wife and collaborator of philosopher Jacques Maritain, who played a key role with husband in the revival of Catholic intellectual life and advocated for a modern rekindling of the thoughts of the medieval philosopher St. Thomas Aquinas; wrote a number of books, including 4 vols. of poetry, 2 vols. of memoirs (*We Have Been Friends Together* [1942], and *Adventures in Grace* [1945]), and the posthumously published *Notes on the Lord's Prayer* (1964) and *Raïssa's Journal* (1974); also wrote *Liturgy and Contemplation* with husband. ❖ See also John M. Dunaway, ed. *Exiles and Fugitives: The Letters of Jacques and Raïssa Maritain, Allen Tate, and Caroline Gordon* (Louisiana State U. Press, 1992); and *Women in World History*.

MARITZA, Sari (1910–1987). German actress. Born Patricia Detering Nathan, Mar 17, 1910, in Tientsin, China; died July 1987, in US Virgin Islands; dau. of a British father (a major) and Austrian mother. ❖ Came to prominence in Germany in *Bomben auf Monte Carlo* (*Monte Carlo Madness*, 1931); brought to Hollywood to star in *Forgotten Commandments* (1932), followed by *Evenings for Sale, The Water Gipsies, A Lady's Profession, International House, The Right to Romance, Her Secret* and *Crimson Romance*; retired from the screen (1934).

MARIYA. Variant of Maria.

MARJA. Variant of Maria.

MARJORIE. Variant of Margery or Marjory.

MARJORIE OF CARRICK (c. 1254–1292). Scottish royal. Name variations: Marjory or Marjorie, Countess of Carrick. Born c. 1254; died before Oct 27, 1292; dau. of Neil, 2nd earl of Carrick, and Margaret Stewart; m. Adam, 3rd earl of Carrick, before Oct 4, 1266; m. Robert Bruce, earl of Carrick, in 1271; children: Robert Bruce (1274–1329) also known as Robert the Bruce and Robert I, king of Scotland (r. 1306–1329); Edward Bruce (d. 1318), king of Ireland; Thomas Bruce (d. 1307); Isabel Bruce (c. 1278–1358, who m. Eric II, king of Norway); Alexander (d. 1307); Nigel (d. 1306); Mary Bruce (fl. 1290–1316); Christian Bruce (d. 1356, who m. Gratney, 7th earl of Mar, and Christopher Seton and Andrew Moray of Bothwell); Matilda Bruce (who m. Hugh Ross, 4th earl of Ross); Margaret Bruce (d. 1346, who m. William de Carlyle).

MARJORY. Variant of Margery or Marjorie.

MARJORY (fl. 13th c.). Daughter of the king of Scots. Name variations: Marjorie; Marjory Dunkeld; Marjory Durward. Illegitimate dau. of Alexander II (1198–1249), king of Scotland (r. 1214–1249), and an unknown mistress; m. Alan Durward.

MARJORY (d. 1244). Countess of Pembroke. Name variations: Marjory Dunkeld; Margaret; Marjory Marshall. Died Nov 17, 1244; interred at Church of the Black Friars, London; dau. of William I the Lion, king of Scots (r. 1165–1214), and Ermengarde of Beaumont (d. 1234); m. Gilbert Marshall, 4th earl of Pembroke, Aug 1, 1235.

MARK, Mary Ellen (1940—). American photojournalist. Born Mar 20, 1940, in Philadelphia, Pennsylvania; University of Pennsylvania, BFA, 1962, MA in photojournalism, 1964; m. Martin Bell (filmmaker and photographer). ❖ World renowned photographer of social documentaries, traveled extensively for over 3 decades to produce photo-essays of such subjects as Mother Teresa in Calcutta, brothels in Bombay, inmates in a mental hospital in Oregon, childrens' wards in Ethiopia, and runaway children in Seattle which became the basis for the film *Streetwise*; served as contributing photographer to *The New Yorker*; published photo-essays in *Life, New York Times Magazine, Paris-Match, Rolling Stone* and *Vanity Fair*, among others; books include *Passport* (1974), *Ward 81* (1979), *Falkland Road* (1981), *A Cry for Help* (1996), *Mary Ellen Mark: American Odyssey* (1999) and *Twins* (2003). Received Cornell Capa Award. ❖ See also *Mary Ellen Mark: 25 Years*.

MARKANDAYA, Kamala (1924–2004). See Taylor, Kamala Purnaiya.

MARKEN, Jane (1895–1976). See Marken, Jeanne.

MARKEN, Jeanne (1895–1976). French stage and screen actress. Name variations: Jane Marken. Born Jane Krab, Jan 13, 1895, in Paris, France; died Dec 1, 1976, in Paris. ❖ Made film debut in *La course aux millions* (1912); appeared in leads and supporting roles under such directors as Gance, Renoir, Carné, Duvivier, Guitry, Becker, and Germaine Dulac; films include *La Dame aux Camélias, Beethoven, Gueule d'amour, Hôtel du Nord, Paradis perdu, Les enfants du paradis, L'Idiot, Le secret de Mayerling, Chéri, Les compagnes de la nuit, Et Dieu . . . créa la femme* and *Le miroir à deux faces*.

MARKEY, Enid (1891–1981). American radio, stage, tv and screen actress. Born Feb 22, 1891, in Dillon, CO; died Nov 15, 1981, in Bay Shore, NY; m. George W. Cobb (exec. American Can Co.). ❖ Became a contract player for Thomas Ince (1913); was 1st Jane to Elmo Lincoln's Tarzan in *Tarzan of the Apes* (Louise Lorraine was 2nd) and appeared opposite William S. Hart in several films; was 1st actress to ride bareback and use a six-shooter (*The Darkening Trail*); other films include *Civilization, Snafu, The Naked City, Take One False Step* and *The Boston Strangler*; on Broadway, appeared in *Up in Mabel's Room, Barnum Was Right, Sisters of the Chorus, Morning's at Seven, Ah Wilderness!, Sweet Charity, Mrs. McThing* and *Ballad of the Sad Cafe*, among many others.

MARKEY, H.K. (1913–2000). See Lamarr, Hedy.

MARKGRAF, Kate (1976—). See Sobrero, Kate.

MARKHAM, Beryl (1902–1986). English-born aviator. Born Beryl Clutterbuck, Oct 26, 1902, in Ashwell, Leicestershire; died Aug 4, 1986; dau. of Charles Baldwin Clutterbuck (British army officer and farmer) and Clara Agnes (Alexander) Clutterbuck; raised on a ranch in British East Africa; m. Captain Alexander Laidlaw "Jock" Purves (British army officer and farmer), Oct 15, 1919 (div. 1925); m. Mansfield Markham (wealthy aristocrat and landowner), Sept 3, 1927 (div. 1942); m. Raoul Schumacher (writer), Oct 15, 1942 (div. 1960); children: (2nd m.) Gervase. ❖ Famous adventurer and accomplished horse trainer and bush pilot who is most widely known for her record-breaking solo flight from east to west across the Atlantic in 1936 and her bestselling memoir *West with the Night*; brought to Kenya to join father (1905); mother left for England (1906); began career as horse trainer (1921); pursued career as pilot (1929); flew the Atlantic solo (1936) from England to Nova Scotia; moved to California (1938) where she worked as a consultant for film industry as well as working on memoir *West with the Night* and short stories; returned to Kenya (1949) to resume career as a horse trainer where she won top trainer's award for 5 years, then Kenya Derby for 6 years: moved to South Africa (1967) where she continued her career as a trainer but with limited success; returned to Kenya for the last time (1969); lived in semi-poverty until *West with the Night* was republished (1983) to great acclaim and popularity; royalties allowed her freedom from poverty. ❖ See also Mary S. Lovell, *Straight On Till Morning: The Biography of Beryl Markham* (St. Martin, 1987); Errol Trzebinski, *The Lives of Beryl Markham* (Norton, 1993); and *Women in World History*.

MARKHAM, Helen Deane (1917–1966). See Deane, Helen Wendler.

MARKHAM, Mary (c. 1584–1659). See Frith, Mary.

MARKHAM, Pauline (d. 1919). English pantomime performer. Born Pauline Margaret Hill in East End of London, England; died Mar 20, 1919, in New York, NY. ❖ Considered a great beauty, made professional debut at Manchester Theater in England in role of Oberon (1865); toured US with Lydia Thompson's pantomime group, performing in *Ixion, the Man in the Moon,* among others; appeared as Stalacta in revival of *The Black Crook* in NY (1868); performed mainly in US from then on, most notably in *Chow Chow* (1872), *H.M.S. Pinafore*, and *East Lynne*; published memoirs (1871).

MARKHAM, Violet Rosa (1872–1959). English public servant. Born in Chesterfield, England, 1872; died 1959; dau. of a Chesterfield colliery owner; granddau. of Sir Joseph Paxton, architect who designed London's Crystal Palace; m. James Carruthers (lieutenant colonel), 1915 (died 1936). ❖ Joined Liberal Party and, from 1914, served on the Central Committee on Women's Training and Employment, which she chaired for numerous years; was also a member of executive committee of National Relief Fund; was a member of Industrial Court (1919–46); elected mayor of Chesterfield (1927); joined Assistance Board (1934), serving as deputy chair (1937–46); was a member of the Appeals Tribunal on Internment (1939–45) and chaired the Investigation Committee on Welfare of Service Women (1942). ❖ See also autobiography *Return Passage* (1953); and *Women in World History*.

MARKIEVICZ, Constance (1868–1927). Irish revolutionary. Name variations: Countess de Markiewicz; Constance Gore-Booth. Pronunciation: Mark-ee-vitz. Born Constance Georgina Gore-Booth at Buckingham Gate, London, England, Feb 4, 1868; died in Dublin, Ireland, July 15, 1927, of peritonitis; dau. of Sir Henry Gore-Booth of Sligo, Ireland, and Georgina Mary Hill of Yorkshire, England; sister of Eva Gore-Booth (1870–1926); educated privately and at Julien's of Paris, France, 1897–99; m. Count Casimir Dunin-Markievicz, Sept 29, 1900; children: Maeve Alys (b. Nov 14, 1901). ❖ Revolutionary who was both symbol and exemplar of the crucial role played by many active, though less visible, women in Irish nationalist politics between 1909 and 1922; founded Fianna na hEireann (1909), an explicitly militaristic body whose aim was the overthrow of the establishment; joined labor movement during Great Lockout in Dublin (1913); fought in Dublin during 1916 rebellion as a lieutenant in Irish Citizen Army; sentenced to death but reprieved, and spent year in prison; elected to 1st Dail Eireann (1919); the only woman appointed to the Dail's "cabinet" or "government," was the 1st ever Irish secretary for labour; along with Cabinet colleagues and most of the Dail, became a fugitive member of a fugitive administration, spent 2 more periods in prison and was released only after hostilities ceased in July 1921; opposed Anglo-Irish Treaty of 1921 and played active part in civil war (1922–23). ❖ See also Jacqueline Van Voris, *Constance de Markievicz: In the Cause of Ireland* (U. of Massachusetts Press, 1967); Anne Haverty, *Constance Markievicz: Irish Revolutionary* (Pandora, 1988); Ann Marreco, *The Rebel Countess* (Weidenfeld & Nicolson, 1967); and *Women in World History*.

MARKO, Jadwiga (1939—). Polish volleyball player. Born April 1939 in Poland. ❖ Won a bronze medal at Tokyo Olympics (1964) and a bronze medal at Mexico City Olympics (1968), both in team competition.

MARKOVA, Alicia (1910–2004). English-born ballerina. Name variations: Lilian Alicia Marks; Dame Alicia Markova. Pronunciation: Mar-COVE-ah. Born Lilian Alicia Marks in Finsbury, North London, Dec 1, 1910; died Dec 2, 2004, in Bath, England; dau. of Arthur Marks (mining engineer) and Eileen Barry Marks; studied dance with Serafima Astafieva, 1921–25; never married; no children. ❖ One of the most eminent dancers of the 20th century, was a pioneer in the formation of British ballet; began career as dancer in pantomime (1920); received 1st offer to dance in a production by Diaghilev (1921); joined Diaghilev's Ballets Russes and danced 1st solo role in *Le Rossignol* (1925); joined Old Vic-Sadler's Wells ballet (1933); gave 1st performance of *Giselle* (1934); formed Markova-Dolin Ballet (1935); joined Ballet Russe de Monte Carlo and made debut in America (1938); joined Ballet Theatre (1941); appeared in Broadway show *The Seven Lively Arts* (1943–44); with Dolin, founded the London Festival Ballet and promoted interest in classical dance in Great Britain (1950); gave final performance (1962); announced retirement; served as ballet director, Metropolitan Opera (1963–69); taught at University of Cincinnati (1970–74); presented tv series on BBC (1981); was given gala birthday celebration at Sadler's Wells (1990); noted for title roles in *The Dying Swan*, *The Firebird* and *La Sylphide*, as well as Juliet in *Romeo and Juliet*, Odette-Odile in *Swan Lake*, Sugar-Plum Fairy in *The Nutcracker*, and Swanhilda in *Coppélia*. Received Order of the British Empire (OBE, 1953) and Dame of the British Empire (DBE, 1963). ❖ See also autobiography *Markova Remembers* (Hamish Hamilton, 1986); Maurice Leonard, *Markova: The Legend* (Hodder & Stoughton, 1995); and *Women in World History*.

MARKOVA, Olga (c. 1969—). Russian marathon runner. Born c. 1969 in St. Petersburg, USSR. ❖ Won Boston Marathon (1992, 1993).

MARKOVA, Olga (1974—). Russian figure skater. Born Jan 22, 1974, in Leningrad, USSR. ❖ Turned pro (1998).

MARKOVA, Olga. Ukrainian opera singer. Name variations: Olga Markova-Mikhailenko or Mikailenko. Born in USSR; graduate of Kiev Conservatory, 1989. ❖ Joined the Shevchenko Opera and Ballet Company in Kiev (1989); became soloist with the State Academic Mariinsky Theatre (1990).

MARKOVA, Vera (1932—). *See Vancurova, Vera.*

MARKOVIC, Mirjana (1942—). Serb politician. Name variations: Mira; Dr. Mirjana Milosevic. Born July 10, 1942, in the village of Brezane; dau. of Moma Markovic (high-ranking Communist) and Vera Miletic; received undergraduate degree from Belgrade University; University of Nis, PhD in sociology; m. Slobodan Milosevic (later president of Serbia and then of Yugoslav Federal Republic), Mar 14, 1965 (died 2006); children: daughter Marija Milosevic (b. 1965); son Marko Milosevic (b. 1976). ❖ Founder and president of the modern Marxist party Yugoslav United Left (YUL) and wife of Slobodan Milosevic, former president of the Yugoslav Federal Republic, was characterized as a "Balkan Lady Macbeth"; taught Marxist sociology at Belgrade University; with husband's rise to power (1980s), served as his main adviser, though she remained in the background and was seldom seen at political events; began to emerge into limelight (1990), the year after husband was elected president of Serbia, founding the Yugoslav United Left, an alliance of some 20 Communist groups aligned with the Socialist Party of Serbia, which was a kind of Mafia, doling out favors to high-ranking businessmen; when the Bosnian crisis threatened husband's standing, began writing a column in fashionable bi-weekly magazine *Duga*, using it to both humanize and defend him (1993). ❖ See also *Women in World History*.

MARKOVIC, Vera (1931—). Yugoslavian ballet dancer. Born 1931 in Zagreb, Yugoslavia. ❖ Began performing with Zagreb National Ballet (1945), where she was principal dancer for many years under Margaret Froman, then Pino and Pia Mlakar, and Dmitri Parlic; had principal roles in Froman's *Romeo and Juliet* and *The Legend of Ohrid*, and Mlakar's *Devil in the Village*.

MARKOVICH, Mariia Aleksandra (1834–1907). *See Vilinska, Mariya.*

MARKS, Hertha (1854–1923). *See Ayrton, Hertha Marks.*

MARKS, Josephine (1874–1922). *See Peabody, Josephine Preston.*

MARKS, Nora (1863–1942). *See Atkinson, Eleanor.*

MARKS, Rita (c. 1908–1976). American theatrical dancer. Born c. 1908; died Nov 11, 1976, in Hollywood, FL. ❖ Trained in tap and acrobatics and other dance forms with Ned Wayburn and Jack Blue in NY; made professional debut at 16; danced with touring company of *No, No, Nanette*, and later on Broadway in same production (1925); performed as specialty dancer in *Yes, Yes, Yvette* (1927), *Grand Street Follies* (1928–29), *New Moon* (1928), and *Music in the Air* (1932).

MARKUS, Erzsebet (1969—). Hungarian weightlifter. Name variations: Erzsebet Peresztegine Markus. Born Erzsebet Peresztegine in 1969 in Hungary. ❖ Won European championship (1998); won a silver medal for 63–69kg at Sydney Olympics (2000).

MARKUS, Fanny (1811–1889). *See Lewald, Fanny.*

MARKUSHEVSKA, Galyna (1976—). Ukrainian handball player. Born July 16, 1976, in Ukraine. ❖ Won a team bronze medal at Athens Olympics (2004).

MARLATT, Abby (1916—). American civil-rights activist. Born 1916 in Kansas; granddau. of Rev. Washington Marlatt (pioneer settler in Kansas) and Julia Ann (Bailey) Marlatt; niece of Abby L. Marlatt (1869–1943); Kansas State University, BS, University of California, Berkeley, PhD. ❖ Became associate professor at University of Kansas (1945); became director of School of Home Economics at University of Kentucky (1956); assisted students in nonviolent protests, including sit-ins, to challenge discrimination against blacks in Lexington, KY; assisted in negotiations that led to desegregation of public accommodations; helped form Lexington Chapter of Congress on Racial Equality; inducted into Kentucky Civil Rights Hall of Fame (2001).

MARLATT, Abby L. (1869–1943). American home economist. Born Abby Lillian Marlatt on Mar 7, 1869, in Manhattan, Kansas; died June 23, 1943, in Madison, WI; only dau. and youngest of 5 children of Rev. Washington Marlatt (Methodist minister and pioneer settler in Kansas) and Julia Ann (Bailey) Marlatt; Kansas State Agricultural College, BS, 1888, MS in chemistry, 1890; also attended Brown University. ❖ Organized department of domestic economy at Utah State Agricultural College (now Utah State University) and served as professor there (until 1894); organized department of home economics at Manual Training (later Technical) High School (Providence, RI); served as chair (1903) and vice president (1907) of Lake Placid Conference on Home Economics; organized courses in home economics at University of Wisconsin (1909) and served as director of home economics there for 30 years; served as vice-president of American Home Economics Association (1912–18). The high academic standards she set for home economics students at University of Wisconsin were then followed by many US schools.

MARLBOROUGH, duchess of.
See Churchill, Sarah Jennings (1660–1744).
See Churchill, Henrietta (1681–1733).

See Churchill, Fanny (1822–1899).
See Vanderbilt, Consuelo (1877–1964).

MARLEY, Cedella (1967—). Jamaican singer, musician and actress. Name variations: Ziggy Marley and the Melody Makers. Born Aug 23, 1967, in Kingston, Jamaica; dau. of Bob Marley (reggae musician) and Rita Marley (reggae musician); sister of David "Ziggy" Marley (reggae musician) and Stephen Marley; half-sister of Sharon Marley Prendergast (singer). ❖ With brothers and half-sister Sharon, formed Ziggy Marley and the Melody Makers in Kingston, Jamaica (1979) and recorded single, "Children Playing in the Streets"; with Melody Makers, signed contract with EMI America and released pop reggae album, *Play the Game Right* (1985); with band, moved to Virgin Records and released *Conscious Party* (1988), with the hit, "Tomorrow People"; acted in films *The Mighty Quinn* (1989), *Joey Breaker* (1993), and *Kla$h* (1995); other albums released with Melody Makers include *One Bright Day* (1989), *Jahmekya* (1991), *Joy and Blues* (1993), *Fallen Is Babylon* (1997) and *Spirit of Music Chant* (1999).

MARLEY, Rita (1946—). Cuban-born reggae singer. Born Alpherita Constantia Anderson, July 25, 1946, in Santiago, Cuba; grew up in Kingston, Jamaica; m. Bob Marley (reggae singer), 1966 (died May 11, 1981); children: Stephen Marley, Cedella Marley (b. 1967), David "Ziggy" Marley (b. 1968) and Stephanie Marley (Bob Marley fathered 7 other children out of wedlock). ❖ Performed as lead singer for a group called the Soulettes (1964); had several solo hits in Jamaica; with Marcia Griffiths and Judy Mowatt, was part of trio, I-Threes, that backed Bob Marley; moved to Ghana, where she set up a foundation to help children orphaned by AIDS; her own children comprise Ziggy Marlowe & the Melody Makers. ❖ See also memoir *No Woman No Cry* (2004).

MARLEY, Sharon (1964—). *See Prendergast, Sharon Marley.*

MARLITT, Eugenie (1825–1887). German novelist. Name variations: Eugenie John; E. Marlitt. Born in Arnstadt, Thuringia, Dec 5, 1825; died in Arnstadt, June 22, 1887; her father was a portrait painter. ❖ At 17, was sent by foster mother, the princess of Schwarzburg-Sondershausen, to Vienna to study vocal music; after appearing in concert in Leipzig, Linz, and Graz, became deaf and was obliged to give up music career; lived for 11 years at court of the princess, but ultimately took up residence in Arnstadt; beginning with *Die zwölf Apostel* (The Twelve Apostles, 1865), published all works initially in journal *Die Gartenlaube*; other writings include *Goldelse* (Gold Else), *Blaubart* (Blue Beard), *Das Geheimniss der alten Mamsell* (The Old Mamsell's Secret, all 1868), *Thüringer Erzählungen* (Thuringian Tales, 1869), *Reichsgräfin Gisela* (Countess Gisela, 1879), *Heideprinzesschen* (The Moorland Princess, 1872), *Die zweite Frau* (The Second Wife, 1874), *Im Haus des Kommerzienrats* (In the House of the Counselor, 1877) and *Im Schillingshof* (1879).

MARLOWE, Charles (1863–1932). *See Jay, Harriett.*

MARLOWE, Julia (1866–1950). English-born actress. Name variations: earliest stage name, Fanny Brough; performed as Julia Marlowe from 1887; also known as Mrs. Robert Taber (1894–1900), then Mrs. Edward H. Sothern (from 1911); Julia Marlowe Sothern. Born Sarah Frances Frost (family changed name to Sarah Frances Brough), Aug 17, 1866, at Upton Caldbeck, near Keswick, Cumberlandshire, England; died in New York, NY, Nov 12, 1950; dau. of farmers; m. Robert Taber (actor), 1894 (div. 1900); m. E.H. Sothern (1859–1933, actor), Aug 17, 1911 (died Oct 28, 1933). ❖ One of the most popular Shakespearean actresses on the American stage of her day, was brought to US as a child of 4 (1870); made 1st stage appearance in a children's performance of *H.M.S. Pinafore*, in Vincennes, Ohio, under name Fanny Brough (1878); appeared in *Rip Van Winkle*, *Macbeth*, *Romeo and Juliet*, *Richard III*, *The Chimes of Normandy*, *The Hunchback*, *Pygmalion and Galatea* (in repertory, 1878–84); made NY debut in *Ingomar* (1887); made subsequent appearances *inter alia* in *Twelfth Night*, and *As You Like It* (1887), *The Rivals* (1896), *Countess Valeska* (1898), *Barbara Frietchie* (1899), *When Knighthood Was in Flower* (1901), *The Hunchback* (1904), *The Sunken Bell* and *Gloria* (1907); teamed with future husband E.H. Sothern for *Romeo and Juliet* (1904) and, except for a brief hiatus in 1907–09, they became for 20 years the most important acting team in US and leading interpreters of Shakespearean roles on the American stage; subsequently appeared in repertory in *Romeo and Juliet*, *The Taming of the Shrew*, *Hamlet*, *Twelfth Night*, *Macbeth*, *The Merchant of Venice*, *Jeanne d'Arc*, *John the Baptist*, and in revivals of *The Sunken Bell*, *When Knighthood Was in Flower*, etc.; retired from the stage (1924). ❖ See also Charles Edward Russell, *Julia Marlowe: Her Life and Art* (1926); E.H. Sothern, *Julia Marlowe's Story* (1954); and *Women in World History*.

MARLOWE, June (1903–1984). American actress. Name variations: June Sprigg. Born Gisela Valaria Goetten, Nov 6, 1903, in St. Cloud, MN; died Mar 10, 1984, in Burbank, CA; m. Rodney S. Sprigg (film executive), 1932. ❖ Was the heroine in Rin-Tin-Tin films, the teacher Miss Crabtree in "Our Gang" comedies, and appeared in Laurel and Hardy's 1st picture; other films include *Find Your Man*, *Clash of the Wolves*, *The Old Soak*, *Life of Riley*, *Foreign Legion* and *Slave Girl*; also appeared in a number of German and Argentinean films; retired at time of marriage.

MARLOWE, Katharine (1941—). *See Allen, Charlotte Vale.*

MARLOWE, Missy (1971—). Belgian-born gymnast. Born Melissa Marlowe, 1971, in Belgium; m. Joe Clausi (football player). ❖ Placed 3rd all-around at Champions All (1984); won American Classic (1985, 1986, 1987, 1988), Kips Invitational (1986); won a silver medal in all-around, gold in uneven bars, and bronze in balance beam at US nationals (1987).

MARLOWE, Nora (1915–1977). American actress. Born Sept 5, 1915, in Worcester, MA; died Dec 31, 1977, in Los Angeles, CA; m. James McCallion (actor). ❖ Films include *An Affair to Remember*, *North by Northwest*, *I'll Cry Tomorrow*, *Thomas Crown Affair* and *Westworld*; appeared as Flossie Brimmer in tv series "The Waltons."

MARLY, Florence (1918–1978). Czech actress, writer, and producer. Name variations: Hana Smekalova. Born Hana Smekalova, June 2, 1918, in Obrnice, Czechoslovakia (now Czech Republic); died Nov 9, 1978, in Glendale, CA; studied at Sorbonne; m. Count Degenhard von Wurmbrand; m. Pierre Chenal (French film director, div.). ❖ Began career in France in *Alibi*; moved to US during WWII; films include *Sealed Verdict*, *The Damned*, *Tokyo Joe*, *Undersea Girl*, *Doctor Death* and *Games*; throughout career, had lead or supporting parts in French, American, Czech, and Argentinean films; wrote, produced, and starred in the short *Spaceboy: A Cosmic Love Affair*, which won an award at Cannes (1973).

MARMEIN, Irene (1894–1972). American concert dancer. Born Feb 4, 1894, in or around Chicago, IL; died Sept 9, 1972, in Schenectady, NY; dau. of Anna Egleton; sister of Miriam and Phyllis Marmein (dancers). ❖ Trained and performed with sisters under mother's direction; with sisters, appeared on Keith circuit (1915) and became headliners (1919); the 1st to retire from performing, taught and directed in Schenectady, NY, where she was in charge of the family school.

MARMEIN, Miriam (1897–1970). American concert dancer. Born July 28, 1897, probably in or around Chicago, IL; died Aug 17, 1970, in Schenectady, NY; dau. of Anna Egleton; sister of Irene and Phyllis Marmein (dancers). ❖ Began appearing on Keith circuit as a class act with sisters (1915); choreographed numerous trio acts with sisters, then went on to create own works for another 20 years, including *With a Terpsichorean Bow to Mrs. Erskine* (1931) and *Chef d'Orchestre* (1936); taught with sisters at family studio in Schenectady, NY.

MARMEIN, Phyllis (1908–1994). American concert dancer. Born July 4, 1908, probably around Chicago, IL; died June 23, 1994, in Schenectady, NY; dau. of Anna Egleton; sister of Irene and Miriam Marmein (dancers). ❖ Performed concert and vaudeville acts with sisters, including Egyptian, Indian, Chinese, and trio tandem dances; moved to Schenectady, NY, to teach ballet at family-run studio after retirement from performance career; served as director of Schenectady Civic Ballet.

MARMONT, Louise (1967—). Swedish curler. Born May 22, 1967, in Sweden. ❖ Won gold medals at World championships (1995, 1992); won a bronze medal for curling at Nagano Olympics (1998); placed 6th at Salt Lake City Olympics (2002); retired (2002).

MARNI, Jeanne (1854–1910). *See Marnière, Jeanne.*

MARNIÈRE, Jeanne (1854–1910). French novelist and playwright. Name variations: Jeanne Marniere; (pseudonym) Jeanne Marni. Born 1854 in France; died 1910; married (husband died 1858). ❖ Began career as an actress; early work appeared in journals and was subsequently published in volume form by Ollendorf; often focused on lack of independence of French women; writings include *La Femme de Silva* (1887), *L'Amour coupable* (1889), *Comment elles se donnent* (1895), *Les Enfants qu'elles ont* (1897), *Celles qu'on ignore* (1899), *Pierre Tisserand* (1907) and *Souffrir* (1909); was on the first jury of the Prix Femina.

MARNO, Anne (1931—). *See Bancroft, Anne.*

MARON, Monika (1941—). East German novelist. Born Monika Iglarz, June 1941, in Berlin, Germany; stepdaughter of Karl Maron, hard-line

Stalinist who served as head of the People's Police in GDR, then minister of the Interior, 1955–63. ❖ With mother and aunt, moved from West to East Berlin (1951); became a journalist with East Berlin newspaper *Wochenpost;* had an uneasy relationship with the Stasi and work was banned (1978); published 1st novel, *Flugasche* (Flight of Ashes, 1981), in West Germany (1981), followed by *Die Überläuferin* (The Defector, 1986); immigrated to Hamburg (1988); other works include *Animal triste* (1996), *Pawels Briefe* (1999) and *Endmoränen* (2002). Won Kleist Prize for *Stille Zeile Sechs* (Silent Close No. 6, 1992).

MARONEY, Susan Jean (1974—). Australian long-distance swimmer. Name variations: Susie Maroney. Born 1974 in Sydney, Australia; sister of twin brother Sean Maroney (died 2002). ❖ Won US championship in endurance swimming (25 kilometers, 1989); swam English Channel in record time (1990); became 1st Australian to double cross the English Channel, setting a new record of 17 hours, 14 minutes (1991); became the 1st woman to swim the 107 miles from Cuba to Florida, in 24 hours and 31 min. (1997); swam the 128 miles from Jamaica to Cuba (1999); swam from Mexico to Cuba (1999); set 6 world records over an 18-year career; retired (2003). Inducted into International Swimming Hall of Fame. ❖ See also *Women in World History.*

MAROS, Magda (1951—). Hungarian fencer. Born Nov 4, 1951, in Hungary. ❖ At Montreal Olympics, won a bronze medal in team foil (1976); at Moscow Olympics, won a bronze medal in team foil and a silver medal in indiv. foil (1980).

MAROSI, Paula (1936—). Hungarian fencer. Born Nov 3, 1936, in Hungary. ❖ Won a gold medal at Tokyo Olympics (1964) and a silver medal at Mexico City Olympics (1968), both in team foil.

MAROT, Helen (1865–1940). American labor activist. Born in Philadelphia, PA, June 9, 1865; died of heart attack in New York, NY, June 3, 1940; dau. of Charles Henry Marot (bookseller and publisher) and Hannah Griscom Marot; educated in Quaker schools; never married; no children. ❖ Involved in some of the most significant union actions of the early 20th century, was especially concerned with improving working conditions for women and abolishing the practice of child labor; co-founded private library in Philadelphia (1897); hired by US Industrial Commission to investigate custom tailoring trades in Philadelphia (1899); became executive secretary of National Women's Trade Union League in NY (1906); devoted herself to writing about labor causes (1913); served on US Industrial Relations commission (1914–16); joined editorial board of the *Masses* (1917); writings include *Handbook of Labor Literature* (1899), *American Labor Unions* (1914) and *Creative Impulse in Industry* (1918). ❖ See also *Women in World History.*

MAROTHY-SOLTESOVA, Elena (1855–1939). Czechoslovakian novelist and literary critic. Name variations: Elena Maróthy-Soltesová; Elena Soltesova; Elena Marothy-Soltes. Born Elena Maróthy, Jan 6, 1855, in Krupina, Slovakia; died Feb 11, 1939, in Martin, Slovakia; dau. of Daniel Maróthy (1825–1878, romantic poet). ❖ Pioneered Slovak women's movement and was influenced by Slovak national movement; served as chair of women's society Živena, and worked for involvement of women in reform movements; wrote novels *Proti prúdu* (1894) and *Moje deti* (1923–24); also wrote short stories, essays, reviews, and the memoir *70 rokov života* (70 Years of Life, 1925); edited magazine *Živena* (1910–22) and was the 1st female Slovak literary critic.

MAROZIA CRESCENTII (885–938). Ruler of Rome. Name variations: Marotia; Marozia the Senatrix. Reigned from 928 to 932. Born 885 in Rome; died 938 in Rome; dau. of Theophylact Crescentii also known as Theophylacte (governor of the Roman senate) and Theodora of Rome; m. Alberic I of Spoleto, margrave of Camerino and prince of Rome (d. 928); m. Marquis Guido also known as Guido of Tuscany and Guy of Tuscany (d. 932); m. Hugo also known as Hugh of Provence, king of Italy (r. 926–932); children: at least 2 sons, Alberic II, prince of the Romans, and John, later Pope John XI, and a daughter Bertha. ❖ Highly intelligent, with a keen mind for politics, controlled the papal court for 4 years; married 3 times, was reputed to have had numerous lovers, and outlived each of her husbands; reportedly was also the long-term mistress of Pope Sergius III, who granted her authority in Rome; after giving birth to son John (c. 908), gained power in her own name, supported by the wealth she had inherited from husbands; upon father's death (c. 920), became head of the household and assumed the titles *senatrix* and *patrician,* becoming the omnipotent ruler of Rome; after death of 1st husband Alberic I (928) and with the help of stepson and new husband Marquis Guido of Tuscany, overthrew and imprisoned Pope John X and took control of the papacy; was instrumental in electing two stopgap popes, the short-lived Leo VI and Stephen VII, until her son John was prepared to succeed as John XI (931). ❖ See also *Women in World History.*

MARPHA (1664–1716). Empress of Russia. Name variations: Marpha Apraxin. Born Marpha Matveyovna Apraxin in 1664; died Jan 11, 1716; dau. of Matvey Apraxin; m. Feodor also known as Theodore III (1661–1682), tsar of Russia (r. 1676–1682), Feb 14, 1682. Theodore's first wife was Agraphia Grushevski (1662–1681). ❖ Since Theodore died on April 27, 1682, Marpha was only empress for two months.

MARQUAND, Nadine (1934—). *See Trintignant, Nadine.*

MARQUARDT, Melissa (1983—). American wakeboarder. Born Dec 16, 1983, in Mission Viejo, CA. ❖ Placed 4th in Freeride at X Games (Summer 2002) and 1st in Freeride at Vans Triple Crown, Pensacola, FL (2002); won silver in Freeride at Gravity Games (2002); ranked 4th in Freeride for World Cup Year End Ranking (2002); won silver in Wakeboarding (Freestyle) at X Games (Summer 2003).

MARQUET, Mary (1895–1979). Russian-born actress. Born April 14, 1895, in St. Petersburg, Russia; died Aug 29, 1979, in Paris, France, after a fall. ❖ Made stage debut (1912), traveling with Paul Porel, then appeared in *Les Trois Mousquetaires* (1914), *Les Cathédrales, L'Aiglon, L'Homme à la rose, La Bataille* and *La Dolorès;* joined Comédie Française (1923) and appeared there in most of the classical revivals and original plays, most notably *Le Maitre de son Coeur, Christine, Madame Quinze, Andromaque, Bajazet, Athalie, Phèdre* and *Le soulier de satin;* made many films, including *Sapho, Si Versailles m'était conté* (as Mme de Maintenon), *Paris canaille, Au voleur, Landru, Arsène Lupin contre Arsène Lupin, Phèdre* and Fellini's *Casanova.*

MARQUETS, Anne de (1533–1588). French nun and poet. Born 1533 in Normandy; died May 11, 1588. ❖ At 9, entered the order of St. Dominic at the royal monastery in Poissy; probably took the veil (1548); attended conference at Poissy (1561), convened by ecclesiastics to resolve religious differences, where she addressed the delegates with poems and prayers which were later published as *Sonets, prieres et devises* (1562); published translation of works of Flaminio, *Divines poesies* (1569), as well as a collection of poetry dedicated to Margaret of Valois, and a collection of sonnets (1605); was celebrated by the poet Ronsard.

MARQUIS, Gail (1956—). African-American basketball player. Born Gail Annette Marquis, Nov 18, 1956, in Queens, NY. ❖ At Montreal Olympics, won a silver medal in team competition (1976); won a team silver at World University games (1977); played professionally with NY Stars (1979–80) and NJ Gems (1980–91); often does guest sports commentary for tv networks.

MARR, Lady. *See Mar, Frances, Countess of (1690–1761).*

MARR, Margaret (d. after 1384). Countess of Mar. Name variations: Margaret Douglas. Died after 1384; m. William Douglas (c. 1327–1384), 1st earl of Douglas; children: James Douglas (c. 1358–1388), 2nd earl of Douglas. William Douglas' 2nd wife was Margaret, countess of Angus.

MARR, Sally (1906–1997). American comedian and talent agent. Born Sadie Kitchenberg in Jamaica, New York, 1906; died in Los Angeles, California, Dec 14, 1997; m. Mickey Schneider (div.); m. Tony Viscarra; children: Lenny Bruce (1926–1966, the comedian). ❖ Probably best known as the flamboyant mother of comedian Lenny Bruce, worked as a standup comedian, performing in nightclubs, doing impersonations of James Cagney and Humphrey Bogart; known for her bawdy act and free lifestyle, remained active in entertainment world throughout most of life; instrumental in managing son's career, also worked as a talent agent and is credited with discovering comics Cheech and Chong, Sam Kinison, and Pat Morita; appeared in the films *Every Little Crook and Nanny* (1972), *Fire Sale* (1977), *House Calls* (1978), *Cheech and Chong's Nice Dreams* (1981) and *The Devil and Max Devlin* (1981). ❖ See also Broadway play *Sally Marr . . . and Her Escorts,* starring Joan Rivers, which was based on her life (1994); and *Women in World History.*

MARRACK, Philippa (1945—). British-American immunologist. Name variations: Pippa Marrack. Born June 18, 1945, in Ewell, England; Cambridge University, BA, 1967, PhD, 1970; m. John W. Kappler, 1974; children: James and Kate Kappler. ❖ Studied immune system at Cambridge; married research partner John W. Kappler while at University of California, San Diego; with husband, cofounded Denver-based National Jewish Center for Immunology and Respiratory Medicine (1979) and studied substances seen as foreign to immune cells called superantigens; worked as professor at University of Colorado Health Science Center; elected to National Academy of Sciences; received Feodor Lynen Medal (1990) and William B. Coley Award (1991).

MARRIOTT, Alice Sheets (1907–2000). American entrepreneur. Born Alice Sheets, Oct 19, 1907, in Salt Lake City, Utah; died April 17, 2000, in Washington, DC; graduate of University of Utah, 1927; m. J. Willard Marriott, 1927; children: J.W. Marriott Jr. and Richard. ❖ With husband, co-founded and built the hotel empire, Marriott Corporation, which was originally a nine-stool root beer stand in Washington DC; served 2 terms on board of John F. Kennedy Center for Performing Arts; was vice chair of Republican National Committee (1965–76). ❖ See also J.W. Marriott Jr. *The Spirit to Serve: Marriott's Way* (1997).

MARRIOTT, Anne (1913–1997). Canadian poet and short-story writer. Name variations: occasionally published under Joyce McLellan. Born Joyce Anne Marriott, 1913, in Victoria, British Columbia, Canada; died 1997 in Vancouver, British Columbia; m. Gerald McLellan, 1947 (died 1974); children: (adopted) 3. ❖ Co-founded modernist literary magazine *Contemporary Verse* (1941); worked as journalist, edited scripts for National Film Board, and produced radio documentaries; published *The Wind, Our Enemy* (1939), *Salt Marsh* (1942), *Sandstone and Other Poems* (1945), *Countries* (1971), *The Circular Coast* (1981), *This West Shore* (1981), *Letters from Some Islands* (1986) and *Aqua* (1991). Won Governor General's Award for *Calling Adventurers!* (1941).

MARRIOTT, Ida (1865–1943). See Lee, Ida.

MARRON, Eugenie (1899–1999). American sportswoman. Born Nov 22, 1899, in Jersey City, NJ; died Aug 16, 1999, in West Palm Beach, FL; Columbia University, BA and MA; studied art with Alexander Archipenko; m. Louis E. Marron (real-estate developer). ❖ The 1st woman to catch a giant bluefin, came into angling career through husband; spent 30 years traveling with him on fishing expeditions from Nova Scotia to Hong Kong, picking up records along the way; in the seas of the Humboldt Current off Chile, reeled in a world-record 772-pound broadbill (1954); also assisted in research at Massachusetts Institute of Technology and University of Miami on the central nervous system of the giant squid. ❖ See also autobiography *Albacora: The Search for the Giant Broadbill* (Random, 1957); and *Women in World History*.

MARRON, Marie-Anne Carrelet de (1725–1778). See Carrelet de Marron, Marie-Anne.

MARRYAT, Florence (1837–1899). British novelist. Name variations: Mrs. Florence Church; Mrs. Lean. Born July 9, 1837, in Brighton, England; died Oct 27, 1899, in London; 6th dau. of 4 sons and 7 daughters of Frederick Marryat (1792–1848, novelist) and Catharine (Shairp) Marryat; sister of Augusta, Blanche and Emilia Marryat (all writers); m. Colonel T. Ross Church, 1854 (div.); m. Colonel Francis Lean, 1879. ❖ Published father's correspondence (1872) and edited *London Society* (1872–76); traveled extensively in India with first husband and worked as speaker, entertainer, and journalist; published almost 60 novels, including *Temper* (1859), *Love's Conflict* (1865), *"Gup": Sketches of Anglo-Indian Life and Character* (1865), *No Intentions* (1874), *A Star and A Heart* (1879), *Peeress and Player* (1883), *The Spirit World* (1894) and *The Folly of Allison* (1899).

MARS, Ann Françoise (1779–1847). French actress. Name variations: Mlle Mars; Anne Françoise Hippolyte Boutet. Born Anne Françoise Hippolyte Boutet in 1779; died 1847; dau. of Jacques Marie Boutet (1745–1812, actor and playwright under name of Monvel) and a mother who was also an actor. ❖ Made stage debut in childhood, using the name Ann Françoise Mars; came to prominence with portrayal of a deaf-mute in *The Abbé del'Epée* (1803); was soon the premier comic actress of her day and a favorite of Napoleon; for 30 years, was without rival in sophisticated comedy, successful in every part she attempted, including that of the title role in *Mlle de Belle-Isle* (1839), in which, though then 60, she appeared as a young woman of 20; though she had some of her greatest triumphs in modern plays, much preferred the dramas of the old school, especially the comedies of Molière and Marivaux, retired (1841).

MARS, Mlle. See Mars, Ann Françoise (1779–1847).

MARS, Nancy (b. 1920). See Freedman, Nancy.

MARSCHLINS, Meta Salis- (1855–1929). See Salis-Marschlins, Meta.

MARSDEN, Karen (1962—). Australian field-hockey player. Born Nov 28, 1962, in Perth, Australia. ❖ Goalkeeper; won a team gold medal at Atlanta Olympics (1996).

MARSDEN, Kate (1859–1931). British nurse. Name variations: Katherine Marsden. Born Katherine Marsden, 1859, in Edmonton, North London, England; died 1931 in England; dau. of J.T. Marsden (solicitor). ❖ Trained at Snell's Park and Tottenham Hospital; traveled to Bulgaria to tend soldiers in Russo-Turkish war (1877); went to New Zealand (1884) and became Lady Superintendent of Wellington Hospital; returned to England and was invited to St Petersburg to receive medal from Russian Red Cross (1890); with friend Anna Field, traveled to northern Russia to nurse lepers; journeyed for 3 months under arduous conditions and reached Viluisk where she visited leper colonies; reported journey in Moscow and raised money for lepers to open hospital in Viluisk; made Free Life Fellow of Royal Geographic Society (1916). Story of travels recounted in *On Sledge and Horseback to Outcast Siberian Lepers* (1893) and *My Mission to Siberia: A Vindication* (1921).

MARSH, Jean (1934—). English stage, tv and screen actress and writer. Born Jean Lyndsay Torren Marsh, July 1, 1934, in London, England; m. Jon Pertwee (div.). ❖ Made stage debut in English rep; made NY debut in John Gielgud's production of *Much Ado About Nothing*, remaining for the 3-year run; returning to London, appeared in "Dr. Who"; co-created and starred as Rose in "Upstairs, Downstairs" (1971–75), co-created "The House of Elliot" (1991), and was a regular on "9 to 5" (1982–83); films include *The Roman Spring of Mrs. Stone*, *Jane Eyre*, *Frenzy*, *The Eagle Has Landed*, *The Changeling*, *Return to Oz* and *Willow*.

MARSH, Joan (1913–2000). American actress. Name variations: Dorothy Rosher. Born Nancy Ann Rosher, July 10, 1913, in Porterville, CA; died Aug 10, 2000, in Ojai, CA; dau. of Charles Rosher, Sr. (cinematographer); m. Charles Belden (div.); m. John D.W. Morrill, 1943. ❖ Made film debut as a child, appearing in several Mary Pickford silents as Dorothy Rosher; returned to films (1930) as Joan Marsh; films include *All Quiet on the Western Front*, *That's My Boy*, *Three-Cornered Moon*, *Rainbow Over Broadway*, *Many Happy Returns*, *Anna Karenina*, *Charlie Chan on Broadway*, *Idiot's Delight* and *Road to Zanzibar*.

MARSH, Mae (1895–1968). American actress. Name variations: Mary Marsh. Born Mary Warne Marsh, Nov 9, 1895, in Madrid, NM; died Feb 13, 1968, in Los Angeles, CA; dau. of Charles Marsh (auditor for Santa Fe Railroad) and Mary (Warne) Marsh; educated at Convent of the Sacred Heart, Hollywood; sister of Marguerite Loveridge; m. Louis Lee Arms, Sept 21, 1918; children: Mary Arms (b. 1919); Brewster Arms (b. 1925); Marguerite Arms (b. 1928). ❖ Appeared in both *The Birth of a Nation* and *Intolerance*, 2 of the most important early works in US cinema; landed a job on a one-reel silent film by Mack Sennett (1912); signed by D.W. Griffith to his Biograph studio, had 1st break in *Man's Genesis*; worked with Griffith at several different studios until 1916, appearing in such roles as Apple Pie Mary in *Home Sweet Home* (1914), Flora Cameron in the controversial *The Birth of a Nation* (1915), and the "Dear Little One" in *Intolerance* (1916); became the original "Goldwyn Girl," making 13 films with the studio, only 2 of which, *Polly of the Circus* and *The Cinderella Man* (both 1917), she considered worthwhile; after a brief run on stage in English comedy *Brittie*, moved to England for a fresh start and soon became extremely popular there for performances in *Flames of Passion* (1922) and *Paddy the Next Best Thing* (1923); reclaimed place in film spotlight in Griffith's *The White Rose*, one of her most successful films; with advent of talkies, appeared in cameo roles in more than 100 films, nearly a 3rd of them directed by John Ford. ❖ See also *Women in World History*.

MARSH, Margaret Mitchell (1900–1949). See Mitchell, Margaret.

MARSH, Marian (1913—). Trinidad-born actress. Name variations: Marilyn Morgan, Violet Adams. Born Violet Ethelred Krauth, Oct 17, 1913, in Trinidad, West Indies; sister of Jean Fenwick (b. 1910, actress); m. Albert Scott, 1938; m. Clifford Henderson, 1960 (died 1984). ❖ Raised in Boston; made film debut under name Marilyn Morgan in *Young Sinners* (1929); as Marian Marsh, starred as Trilby opposite John Barrymore in *Svengali* (1931); other films include *The Mad Genius*, *Road to Singapore*, *Five Star Final*, *Rebecca of Sunnybrook Farm*, *The Black Room*, *A Girl of the Limberlost*, *Murder by Invitation* and *House of Errors*.

MARSH, Mrs. (1791–1874). See Marsh-Caldwell, Anne.

MARSH, Ngaio (1895–1982). New Zealand-born novelist. Name variations: Ngaio Edith Marsh; Edith Marsh; Dame Ngaio Marsh. Pronunciation: 1st name is pronounced "nye o." Born Edith Ngaio Marsh, April 23, 1895, in Merivale, Christchurch, New Zealand; died

Feb 18, 1982, in Canterbury, New Zealand; dau. of Henry Edmund Marsh (a bank clerk) and Rose Elizabeth (Seager) Marsh; attended Canterbury University College School of Art (1915–20). ❖ One of 20th-century's foremost writers of detective fiction, began career as an actress, appearing on stage in Australia and New Zealand for several years; also wrote or co-wrote plays; was a producer and director of stage dramas in New Zealand, many of them classics from the Shakespearean repertoire, and often incorporated the world of actors, rehearsals, and curtain calls into her plots; published *A Man Lay Dead* (1934), introducing the urbane Detective Roderick Alleyn, who would reappear in much of her work; set most of her novels—such as *Death in a White Tie* (1938), *Final Curtain* (1947), *Spinsters in Jeopardy* (1953), *Clutch of Constables* (1968), and *Grave Mistake* (1978)—on the playgrounds of the rich and idle: English country house parties or the French Riviera; wrote over 30 books and consistently won critical acclaim for her prose, characterizations, and insight into social mores; spent much of her adult life divided between homes in her native land and London. Named a Dame Commander of the British Empire (1966). ❖ See also autobiography, *Black Beech and Honeydew* (1965); B.J. Rahn, *Ngaio Marsh: The Woman and Her Work* (Scarecrow Press, 1995); and *Women in World History.*

MARSH-CALDWELL, Anne (1791–1874). British novelist. Name variations: Anne Caldwell; Ann Marsh-Caldwell or Anne Caldwell Marsh; Anne Marsh; Mrs. Marsh. Born Anne Caldwell, 1791 in Newcastle-under-Lyme, Staffordshire, England; died Oct 5, 1874, in Linley Wood, Talke, Staffordshire; dau. of James Caldwell and Elizabeth Stamford Caldwell; m. Arthur Cuthbert Marsh, 1817; children: 7. ❖ Novelist of domestic fiction who began publishing with encouragement and assistance of Harriet Martineau; published 1st story, "The Admiral's Daughter," to sensational success; works include *The Old Men's Tales: "The Deformed" and "The Admiral's Daughter"* (1834), *Emily Wyndham* (1846), *Tales of the First French Revolution* (1849), *Aubrey* (1854), *The Rose of Ashurst* (1857), and *Lords and Ladies* (1866).

MARSHALL, Brenda (1915–1992). American actress. Born Ardis Anderson, Sept 29, 1915, on Negros Island, Philippines; died July 30, 1992, in Palm Springs, CA; m. Richard Gaines (div. 1940); m. William Holden (actor), 1941 (div. 1970). ❖ Leading player in such films as *The Sea Hawk, South of Suez, Espionage Agent, The Constant Nymph, Something for the Boys, Whispering Smith* and *The Iroquois Trail.*

MARSHALL, Catherine (1914–1983). American author. Name variations: Catherine LeSourd; Mrs. Peter Marshall. Born Sarah Catherine Wood, Sept 27, 1914, in Johnson City, TN; died Mar 18, 1983, in Boynton Beach, FL; dau. of John Ambrose Wood (minister) and Leonora (Whitaker) Wood; Agnes Scott College, BA, 1936; m. Peter Marshall (1902–1949, Presbyterian minister and chaplain of US Senate), Nov 4, 1936; m. Leonard Earle LeSourd (editor and publisher), Nov 14, 1959; children: (1st m.) Peter John Marshall. ❖ Following death of 1st husband Peter Marshall, produced 2 of the bestselling works of nonfiction of 1950s: a collection of husband's sermons entitled *Mr. Jones, Meet the Master,* and *A Man Called Peter*; also wrote *Christy* (1967) and *The Helper* (1980). ❖ See also film *A Man Called Peter* (1955); and *Women in World History.*

MARSHALL, Clara (1847–1931). American physician and educator. Born May 8, 1847, in London Grove Township, Chester Co., PA; died Mar 13, 1931, in Bryn Mawr, PA; dau. of Pennock and Mary (Phillips) Marshall (both Quakers); graduate of Woman's Medical College in Philadelphia, 1875; attended Philadelphia College of Pharmacy, 1876, the 1st woman admitted there. ❖ Served as demonstrator in materia medica and practical pharmacy (beginning 1875), professor of materia medica and therapeutics (until 1905), and dean (1888–1917) of Woman's Medical College of Pennsylvania; had private practice; was 1st woman staff member of Philadelphia Hospital (1882–95); as the attending physician (from 1886) of the Philadelphia House of Refuge girls' department, was one of the 1st woman doctor staff members of a state charitable institution; writings include *The Woman's Medical College of Pennsylvania:An Historical Outline* (1897).

MARSHALL, Eva. *See Braose, Eve de.*

MARSHALL, Frances (1900–2004). *See Partridge, Frances.*

MARSHALL, Mrs. Frank (1839–1895). *See Cavendish, Ada.*

MARSHALL, Isabel (1200–1240). Countess of Hertford and Gloucester. Name variations: Isabel de Clare. Born Oct 9, 1200, at Pembroke Castle, Dyfed, Wales; died in childbirth on Jan 19 (some sources cite 15 or 17), 1240, at Berkkhamsted Castle, Hertfordshire, England; interred at Beaulieu Abbey, Hampshire; dau. of William Marshall, 1st earl of Pembroke, and Isabel de Clare (c. 1174–1220), countess of Pembroke; m. Gilbert de Clare, 5th earl of Hertford, 1st earl of Gloucester, Oct 9, 1217; m. Richard of Cornwall (1209–1272), earl of Cornwall, king of the Romans (r. 1227–1272), on Mar 30, 1231; children: (1st m.) Amicia de Clare (1220–1283); Richard de Clare (1222–1262), 6th earl of Hertford, 2nd earl of Gloucester; Isabel de Clare (1226–1254); Sir William de Clare (b. 1228); Gilbert de Clare (b. 1229, a priest); Agnes de Clare; (2nd m.) John (1232–1233); Isabel (1233–1234); Henry of Almayne (1235–1271); Nicholas (1240–1240). ❖ Following her death, Richard of Cornwall married Sancha of Provence (c. 1225–1261), then Beatrice von Falkestein (c. 1253–1277).

MARSHALL, Joyce (1913—). Canadian novelist, translator and short-story writer. Born 1913 in Montreal, Canada. ❖ Educated at McGill University and was writer-in-residence at Trent University and in Vaughan Township, Ontario; works include *Presently Tomorrow* (1946), *Lovers and Strangers* (1957), and *A Private Place* (1975); trans. works by Gabrielle Roy, including *Cet Eté qui Chantait* as *Enchanted Summer* (1976), which was awarded Canada Council Translation Prize.

MARSHALL, Kirstie (1969—). Australian freestyle skier. Born April 21, 1969, in Melbourne, Australia. ❖ Known in Australia as the "First Lady of Skiing," began career as a gymnast; placed 7th in aerials at Albertville (1992); won World Cup aerials (1992); carried the flag for Australia at Lillehammer Oympics and finished 6th (1994); won a gold medal for aerials at World championships (1997), the 1st Australian to ever win a winter-sports world title; introduced the triple twisting double-back somersault.

MARSHALL, Lois (1924–1997). Canadian soprano. Born Lois Catherine Marshall in Toronto, Ontario, Canada, Jan 29, 1924; died in Toronto, Feb 19, 1997; m. Weldon Kilburn (her voice coach), 1968. ❖ Won top award in "Singing Stars of Tomorrow" and the Eaton Graduating Scholarship (1950); won the coveted Naumburg Award and made NY debut at Town Hall (1952); appeared with NBC Symphony Orchestra under baton of Arturo Toscanini in Beethoven's *Missa solemnis* (1953) and was featured in a subsequent recording; debuted with London Philharmonic (1956); toured USSR (1958); primarily a concert artist, was one of Canada's leading sopranos (1950s–60s) and continued to perform with major international orchestras throughout 1970s. ❖ See also *Women in World History.*

MARSHALL, Margaret (1949—). Scottish opera singer. Name variations: Margaret Anne Marshall. Born Jan 4, 1949, in Stirling, Scotland; attended Royal Scottish Academy of Music and Drama; studied with Edna Mitchell, Peter Pears and Hans Hotter. ❖ Won 1st prize at International Competition in Munich (1974); gave concerts throughout Europe and made recital debut at Wigmore Hall (1975); made Festival Hall debut singing in Bach's *St. Matthew Passion* (1976); gave operatic debut in Florence as Euridice in *Orfeo ad Euridice,* conducted by Riccardo Muti (1978); performed for 1st time in US with Boston Symphony Orchestra (1980) and appeared with Chicago Symphony, New York Philharmonic and in Philadelphia with Sir Neville Mariner; made acclaimed appearance as Countess in *Figaro* at Covent Garden (1980); debuted in Salzburg and at La Scala in Milan, singing Fioriligi in *Cosi fan Tutte* (which she recorded for EMI, 1982); appeared for 1st time with Vienna State Opera as Mozart's Countess (1988); also performed for Scottish Opera in such roles as Pamina and Countess and with Royal Scottish National Orchestra in Britten's *War Requiem* and Strauss' *Four Last Songs.* Awarded Officer of British Empire (OBE, 1999).

MARSHALL, Maud (d. 1248). Countess of Warrenne and Surrey. Name variations: Maud de Warrenne; Maud Marshal. Died April 4, 1248; dau. of Isabel de Clare (c. 1174–1220) and William Marshall (b. 1146), 4th earl of Pembroke; sister of Sybilla Marshall; m. Hugh Bigod, 3rd earl of Norfolk (r. c. 1200–1225) and earl marshall of England; m. William de Warrenne, 6th earl of Warrenne and Surrey (r. 1202–1240), before Oct 13, 1225; children: (1st m.) Roger Bigod (c. 1212–1270), 4th earl of Norfolk; Hugh Bigod, Justiciar of England; Isabel de Bigod (who m. Gilbert de Lacy and John FitzGeoffrey, justiciar of Ireland); Sir Ralph Bigod; William Bigod; (2nd m.) John de Warrenne (b. 1231), 7th earl of Warrenne and Surrey; Isabel de Warrenne (d. 1282).

MARSHALL, Niní (1903–1996). Argentinean actress. Name variations: Nini Marshall "Catita." Born Marina Esther Traverso, June 1, 1903, in Buenos Aires, Argentina; died Mar 18, 1996, Buenos Aires; m. Felipe Edelemann, 1921 (div.); m. Carmelo Santiago (sep. 1968); m. Marcelo Salcedo (div.). ❖ Famed comic actress, made film debut as Catita in

Mujeres que trabajan (1938); starred in *Cándida* (1939); other films include *Hay que educar a Niní* (1940), *Cándida millonaria* (1941), *La Mentirosa* (1942), *Carmen* (1943), *Madame Sans-Gêne* (1945), *Una Gallega en México* (1949), *Catita es una dama* (1956) and *Escándalo en la familia* (1967).

MARSHALL, Paule Burke (1929—). African-American novelist and short-story writer. Born Paule Burke, April 9, 1929, in Brooklyn, NY; dau. of Samuel and Ada Burke (both immigrants from Barbados); Brooklyn College, BA, 1953; attended Hunter College; m. Kenneth E. Marshall, 1957 (div. 1963); m. Nourry Menard (Haitian businessman), 1970; children: (1st m.) Eran-Keith. ❖ Began career on *Our World* magazine (1955); published autobiographical 1st novel, *Brown Girls, Brownstones* (1959) to good reviews; other works include a collection of novellas, *Soul Clap Hands and Sing* (1961), the novels *The Chosen Place, the Timeless People* (1969) and *Praisesong for the Widow* (1983), as well as *Reena and Other Stories* (1983) and *Daughters* (1991); became distinguished chair in creative writing at New York University.

MARSHALL, Penny (1942—). American actress and director. Born Carole Penny Marshall, Oct 15, 1942, in Bronx, New York; dau. of Anthony "Tony" (Marschiarelli) Marshall (industrial filmmaker) and Marjorie Ward (dance instructor); sister of Gary Marshall (tv director) and Ronny Hallin; attended University of New Mexico; m. Michael Henry, 1961 (div. 1963); m. Rob Reiner (actor, director), 1971 (div. 1980); children: Tracy Reiner. ❖ Comedic actress and director with working-class persona, made film debut in *How Sweet It Is* (1968); was Oscar Madison's secretary on tv series "The Odd Couple" (1970–75); with Cindy Williams, appeared on "Happy Days" (1974), then had spinoff "Laverne and Shirley" (1976) which became wildly popular and aired for 7 years; directed "Tracey Ullman Show," several tv movies, and 1st film, *Jumping Jack Flash* (1986), starring Whoopi Goldberg; had box-office hit with *Big* (1988), the 1st woman to direct a movie that grossed over $100 million; directed *Awakenings* (1990), which received 3 Academy Award nominations, followed by *A League of Their Own* (1992); won American Comedy Award for Creative Achievement (1992); directed and produced several other films including *Calendar Girl* (1993), *Getting Away with Murder* (1996), *Risk* (2003), *Riding in Cars with Boys* (2001) and *Bewitched* (2005).

MARSHALL, Mrs. Peter (1914–1983). See *Marshall, Catherine.*

MARSHALL, Sheina (1896–1977). Scottish marine bioligist. Name variations: Sheina Macalister Marshall; S.M. Marshall. Born April 20, 1896, Rothesay, on island of Bute, off westcoast of Scotland; died April 7, 1977; dau. of a general practitioner who was founder of Buteshire Natural History Society; University of Glasgow, BS, 1919, DSc, 1934. ❖ An expert on the copepod *Calanus* (a major herring food source), 1st studied planktonic marine crustaceans; as a researcher for Scottish Marine Biological Association (SMBA) Laboratory (1922–77), studied feeding and habits of copepods; investigated conditions and effects of a section of Loch Striven with Andrew Picken Orr; joined C.M. Yonge's Great Barrier Reef expedition (1927); with Orr and A.G. Nicholls, studied Loch Striven's *Calanus* population and herring development (1934–35); during WWII, researched agar gel production for government; studied *Calanus* egg production and *Calanus* nitrogen excretion; researched zooplankton feeding and respiration in La Jolla, CA (1970–71); elected fellow of Royal Society of Edinburgh (1963); appointed SMBA's 1st honorary fellow. Received Order of the British Empire (1966).

MARSHALL, Susan (1958—). American choreographer and dancer. Born Oct 17, 1958, in Pensacola, FL; attended Juilliard School of Music, 1976–78. ❖ Founded performing group Susan Marshall and Company and began working as choreographer (1982); premiered 1st full-length choreography *Interior With Seven Figures* at Brooklyn Academy of Music (1988); choreographed works for Boston Ballet, Dallas Ballet, Frankfurt Ballet, Montréal Danse, Lyon Opéra Ballet, and others; received 2 New York Dance and Performance (Bessie) awards (1985, 1997) and American Choreographer award (1988). Major works include *Contenders* (1990), *Fields of View* (1994), *Spectators at an Event* (1994), *Les Enfants terribles: Children of the Game*, a dance-opera in collaboration with composer Philip Glass (1996), and *The Most Dangerous Room in the House* (1998).

MARSHALL, Sybilla (fl. 1230). Countess of Derby. Name variations: Sibyl Marshal. Flourished around 1200; dau. of Isabel de Clare (c. 1174–1220) and William Marshall (b. 1146), 4th earl of Pembroke; sister of Maud Marshall (d. 1248); m. William de Ferrers, 6th earl of Derby; children: Agnes de Ferrers (d. 1240, who m. William de Vesci);

Isabel de Ferrers (d. 1260); Maud de Ferrers (d. 1299); Sibyl de Ferrers; Jean de Ferrers (d. 1267); Agatha de Ferrers (d. 1306).

MARSHALL, Trudy (1922–2004). American actress. Born Feb 14, 1922, in Brooklyn, NY; died May 23, 2004, in Century City, CA; m. Phillip Raffin, 1944 (died 1982); children: Judy Holston, Bill Raffin, Deborah Raffin (b. 1953, actress). ❖ Began career as a model; films include *Secret Agent of Japan*, *Footlight Serenade*, *Springtime in the Rockies*, *Crash Dive*, *Heaven Can Wait*, *The Sullivans*, *The Dolly Sisters*, *Dragonwyck*, *Sentimental Journey*, *The Fuller Brush Man* and *Full of Life*.

MARSHALL, Mrs. Tully (1875–1979). See *Fairfax, Marion.*

MARSHALL-WHITE, Mrs. (1839–1936). See *White, Emily Louisa Merielina.*

MARSMAN, Margot (1932—). Dutch swimmer. Born Feb 9, 1932, in Netherlands. ❖ At London Olympics, won a bronze medal in the 4x100-meter freestyle relay (1948).

MARSON, Aileen (1912–1939). Egyptian-born actress. Born Aileen Pitt-Marson, Sept 13, 1912, in Alexandria, Egypt; died after giving birth to twins, May 4, 1939, in London, England. ❖ Made stage debut in London as Mary in *The Third Degree* (1932), then toured in South Africa with Leontine Sagan; made West End debut as Mattea in *Cabbages and Kings* (1933), followed by *Ten Minute Alibi* (succeeding Jessica Tandy), *The Wind and the Rain*, *They Do These Things in France* and *Vicky* (title role), among others; films include *The Merry Men of Sherwood* (as Maid Marian), *Black Mask*, *The Tenth Man*, *Living Dangerously* and *Spring Handicap*.

MARSON, Una (1905–1965). Jamaican poet and playwright. Born 1905 in Jamaica; died 1965; attended Hampton School, Malvern. ❖ Lived in England (1932–36, 1938–45); worked as secretary for League of Coloured People, London, and to Emperor Haile Selassie during his exile; worked for Women's International League for Peace and Freedom and International Alliance of Women; founded Reader's and Writer's Club in Jamaica; worked for BBC World Service and launched "Caribbean Voices" program; worked as journalist, publisher, and social worker in Jamaica; published poetry collections *Tropic Reveries* (1930), *Heights and Depths* (1932), *The Moth and the Star* (1937), and *Towards the Stars* (1945); plays include *At What a Price* (1932), *London Calling* (1937) and *Pocomania* (1938).

MARTA. *Italian form of Martha.*

MARTEL, Adeloga (fl. 775). Frankish abbess and founder. Flourished in France; dau. of Charles Martel (c. 690–741), mayor of Austrasia and Neustria (r. 714–741), and possibly Sunnichild (d. 741); granddau. of Alphaida (c. 654–c. 714); never married; no children. ❖ Showing an early inclination towards holy work, was allowed to enter a convent rather than be used as a marriage pawn in a political alliance; was soon elected abbess; throughout life, was renowned for her learning and devotion to serving God through charitable works; founded numerous churches and communities for women.

MARTEL, Gisela (d. 919). See *Gisela Martel.*

MARTEL, Judith (c. 844–?). Countess of Flanders and queen-consort. Name variations: Princess Judith. Born c. 844; death date unknown; dau. of Charles I the Bald, king of France (r. 840–877), also known as Charles II, Holy Roman emperor (r. 875–877), and Ermentrude (d. 869); became 2nd wife of Ethelwulf, king of Wessex and the English (r. 839–858), on Oct 1, 856; then m. Ethelwulf's son Ethelbald (c. 834–860), king of Wessex and the English (r. 855–860), in 858 or 860 (annulled); m. Baldwin I (d. 879), count of Flanders (r. 862–878), in 863; children: (3rd m.) Charles of Flanders; Baldwin II (d. 918), count of Flanders (r. 878–918); Ralph (b. 865), count and abbott of Cambrai; Gunhilda of Flanders; (stepchildren) Alfred the Great, king of the English (r. 871–899). ❖ Contrary to tradition, was crowned queen-consort at 13 when she married Ethelwulf (856), a deed that would cause problems some years later; following husband's death and an annulled 2nd marriage, was abducted by, and married to, Baldwin I. ❖ See also *Women in World History.*

MARTEL, Matilda (943–c. 982). See *Matilda Martel.*

MARTEL DE JANVILLE, Comtesse de (1850–1932). French novelist. Name variations: Comtesse de Mirabeau; (pseudonym) Gyp. Born Sybille Gabrielle Marie Antoinette de Riquetti de Mirabeau at Château de Koëtsal, Morbihan, in Brittany, c. 1850; died in Neuilly in 1932; dau. of Comtesse de Mirabeau (1827–1914, journalist and novelist) and

Comte Arundel Joseph de Mirabeau (died 1860); descendant of Gabriel-Honoré Riqueti, Count Mirabeau (1749–1791). ❖ Known to millions under pseudonym Gyp, wrote for *La Vie Parisienne* and *La Revue des Deux Mondes*; created several well-known characters (notably Paulette, Loulou, and le petit Bob) who appeared in her writings; humorous novels include *Autour de mariage* (1883), *Sans voiles* (1885), *Autour du divorce* (1886), *Bob au salon* (1888–90), *C'est nous qui sont l'histoire* (1890), *Passionette* (1891) and *Mariage de Chiffon* (1894). ❖ See also *Women in World History*.

MARTELL, Claudia (1903–1992). *See Wolff, Victoria.*

MARTELLI, Camilla (fl. 1570s). Grand duchess of Tuscany. Name variations: Camilla de Medici. Fl. in 1570s; mistress, then wife, of Cosimo I de Medici, grand duke of Tuscany (1519–1574), c. 1571; children: Giovanni de Medici (d. 1621); Virginia d'Este (who m. Cesare d'Este, duke of Modena). ❖ Cosimo's 1st wife was Eleonora de Medici (1522–1562).

MÄRTEN, Lu (1879–1970). German poet, essayist and playwright. Name variations: Lu Marten or Maerten. Born 1879; died 1970. ❖ Became internationally famous with play *Bergarbeiter* (Miners, 1909); wrote an account of her childhood in *Torso: Das Buch eines Kindes* (Torso: The Book of a Child, 1909); joined Communist Party (1920); turned to writing essays which focus on socialist and feminist themes; writings include *Meine Liedsprachen* (1906), *Die Frau als Künstlerin* (1914), and *Revolutionäre Dichtung in Deutschland* (1920); also wrote children's stories.

MARTEN GARCIA, Maritza (1963—). Cuban track-and-field athlete. Born Aug 16, 1963, in Cuba. ❖ At Barcelona Olympics, won a gold medal in discus throw (1992).

MARTENS, Adelaide (1845–1930). *See Hicks, Adelaide.*

MARTENS, Camille (1976—). Canadian rhythmic gymnast. Born June 1, 1976; m. Patrick Yam (physician) 1997. ❖ Won Canadian nationals (1989); won a gold for team and silver for all-around at Commonwealth Games (1994).

MARTENS, Maria (1955—). Dutch politician. Born Jan 8, 1955, in Doetinchem, Netherlands. ❖ Served as secretary, Netherlands Overseas Mission Council (1984–88), study secretary, Association of Catholic Social Organizations (1988–99), and chair, European Forum of National Committees of the Laity (1996–2000); as a member of the European People's Party (Christian Democrats) and European Democrats (EPP), elected to 5th European Parliament (1999–2004).

MARTENSSON, Agneta (1961—). Swedish swimmer. Born July 31, 1961, in Sweden. ❖ At Moscow Olympics, won a silver medal in 4x100-meter freestyle relay (1980).

MARTHA (1877–1941). *See Polson, Florence Ada Mary Lamb.*

MARTHA AND MARY OF BETHANY (fl. early 1st c. CE). Biblical women. Name variations: Sisters of Bethany; some think Mary of Bethany and Mary Magdalene are one and the same. Flourished in the early 1st century CE; sisters of Lazarus. ❖ Followers of Jesus who frequently used the sisters' home in Bethany as a retreat; when Lazarus died, went into a deep grief; four days later, admonished Jesus for not coming sooner to help him (Jesus then brought Lazarus back to life). ❖ See also *Women in World History*.

MARTHA AND THE VANDELLAS. *See Reeves, Martha (b. 1941).*

MARTHA DE FREITAS (1958—). Norwegian royal. Born April 5, 1958, in Rio de Janeiro, Brazil; dau. of Jose Marie Gomes de Freitas and Maria Bernadette Aragao Carvalho; m. Haakon Lorentzen (grandson of Olav V of Norway), April 14, 1982; children: one.

MARTHA OF DENMARK (c. 1272–1341). Queen of Sweden. Name variations: Margaret of Denmark; Margaret Eriksson. Born c. 1272; died Mar 2, 1341; dau. of Eric V, king of Denmark (r. 1259–1286) and Agnes of Brandenburg (d. 1304); sister of Eric VI Menved (1274–1319), king of Denmark (r. 1286–1319), and Christopher II (1276–1332), king of Denmark (r. 1319–1326 and 1330–1332); m. Birger also spelled Berger (d. 1321), king of Sweden (r. 1290–1318, deposed 1318), Nov 25, 1298; sister-in-law of Ingeborg (c. 1300–1360); children: Magnus Bergersson (b. 1300); Eric Bergersson; Agnes Bergersdottir; Katherina Bergersdottir.

MARTHA OF SWEDEN (1901–1954). Crown princess of Norway. Name variations: Crown Princess Martha or Märtha; Martha Bernadotte. Born Martha Sophia Louise Dagmar Thyra, Mar 28, 1901, in Stockholm, Sweden; died April 5, 1954, in Oslo, Norway; dau. of Charles of Sweden (1861–1951) and Ingeborg of Denmark (1878–1958); sister of Astrid of Sweden (1905–1935, queen of the Belgians); m. Olav V, king of Norway (r. 1957–1991, and son of Haakon VII), on Mar 21, 1929; children: Ragnhild Oldenburg (b. 1930); Astrid Oldenburg (b. 1932); Harold or Harald V, king of Norway (b. 1937, r. 1991—). ❖ Died 3 years before husband was crowned king of Norway.

MARTHA THE NUN (1560–1631). Founder of the Romanovs. Name variations: Marta the Nun; Xenia Chestov or Shestov; Martha Romanov. Born in 1560; died Jan 27, 1631; dau. of Ivan Shestov; m. Fedor also known as Theodore the Metropolitan (1558–1663), also known as the Monk Philaret or Theodore Romanov; children: Mikhail also known as Michael III (1596–1645), tsar of Russia (r. 1613–1645). ❖ Could claim descent from Rurik, the 7th century founder of the Russian monarchy; when son Michael (III) became a candidate for tsar of Russia, extrapolated a promise from the notification committee that his reign would be supported by all Russia (thus, a new dynasty was founded—the Romanovs). ❖ See also *Women in World History*.

MARTHE OR MARTHON. *French form of Martha.*

MARTIA. *Variant of Marcia.*

MARTIA (fl. c. 100 BCE). *See Iaia.*

MARTIN, Agnes (1912–2004). Canadian-born American artist. Born Agnes Bernice Martin, Mar 22, 1912, in Macklin, Saskatchewan, Canada; died Dec 16, 2004, in Taos, NM; dau. of Malcolm Ian Martin and Margaret (Kinnon) Martin; immigrated to US, 1932, naturalized citizen, 1940; attended Western Washington College, 1932, Columbia University, 1941–42, 1951–52; University of New Mexico, BFA, 1954. ❖ Developed the "grid" style for which she became famous; had 1st solo exhibition in NY (1958); after 1964, paintings often consisted of canvas or paper entirely covered by a grid, as in *Little Sister* (1962), *Orange Grove* (1965) and *Desert* (1966); inducted into American Academy and Institute of Arts and Letters (1989); held major retrospective exhibitions in Europe (1991) and US (1992); was a featured artist at Whitney Biennial (1995); wrote *The Perfection Underlying Life* and *The Untroubled Mind* and produced the film *Gabriel* (1976). Received Alexej von Jawlensky Prize from city of Wiesbaden, Germany (1991) and Oskar Kokoschka Prize from Austrian government (1992); won the Golden Lion Award for her contribution to contemporary art at Venice Biennale (1997). ❖ See also Barbara Haskell, *Agnes Martin* (Whitney Museum of Art, 1992); and *Women in World History*.

MARTIN, Ann (1757–1830). *See Taylor, Ann Martin.*

MARTIN, Anne Henrietta (1875–1951). American pacifist and suffragist. Name variations: (pseudonym) Anne O'Hara. Born in Empire City, NV, Sept 30, 1875; died in Carmel, CA, April 15, 1951; University of Nevada (Reno), AB, 1894; Stanford University, BA, 1896, MA in history, 1897. ❖ Founded University of Nevada history department (1897) and was its head until 1903; elected president of the state suffragists, successfully led the movement for Nevada women to win the vote (1914); was the 1st woman to run for US Senate (1918 and 1920), polling 20% of Nevada's votes; moved to Carmel, CA, where she became active in the Women's International League for Peace and opposed America's involvement in WWII.

MARTIN, Mrs. Bell (1815–1850). *See Martin, Mary Letitia.*

MARTIN, Camilla (1974—). Danish badminton player. Born Mar 23, 1974, in Frederiksberg, Denmark. ❖ Won Danish nationals (1991–2003); won Danish Open (1994, 1997, 1998, 1999), Indonesian Open (2000), Korean Open (2000, 2001); won World championship (1999); won a silver medal for singles at Sydney Olympics (2000).

MARTIN, Catherine (1847–1937). *See Martin, C.E.M.*

MARTIN, C.E.M. (1847–1937). Australian novelist and journalist. Name variations: Catherine Edith Macauley; Catherine Edith Macauley Martin; Catherine Martin; (pseudonym) Mrs. Alick Macleod. Born Catherine Edith Macauley, 1847, in Isle of Skye, Scotland; m. Frederick Martin. ❖ Migrated with family to South Australia (1855); ran girls' school in Mount Gambier before marriage; under name Mrs. Alick Macleod, published *An Australian Girl* (1894); also wrote *The Silent Sea* (1892), *The Old Roof-Tree* (1906), and *The Incredible Journey* (1923), and published *The Moated Grange* in serial form.

MARTIN, Claire (1914—). Canadian novelist and translator. Born 1914 in Quebec City, Quebec, Canada; m. Roland Faucher, 1945. ❖ Worked for CKCV Radio in Quebec and Radio-Canada, Montreal; served as president of Société des Écrivains Canadiens-Français; lived in France for 10 years and returned to Canada (1982); works include *Avec ou sans amour* (1958), *Doux-amer* (1960), *Quand j'aurai Payé ton Visage* (1962), *Dans un Gant de Fer* (1965), *La Joue droite* (1966), and *Moi, je n'étais qu'espoir* (1972); translated works of Margaret Laurence, Robertson Davies, and others into French. Made Officer of Order of Canada (1984).

MARTIN, Dorcas Eglestone (fl. 16th c.). British writer. Born in England. ❖ Translated French book of devotions and religious instructions, printed in Thomas Bentley's *Monuments of Matrones* under title *An Instruction for Christians conteining a fruitful and godlie exercise, as well in wholsome and fruitfull praiers, as in reverend discerning of Gods holie Commandements and Sacraments.*

MARTIN, Emma (1812–1851). British feminist and writer. Name variations: Emma Bullock. Born Emma Bullock in 1813 in Bristol, England; died of tuberculosis in 1851; m. Isaac Martin; children: 4. ❖ Joined Particular Baptists and set up Ladies Seminary at 18; moved to London and became active in Owenite circles; became well known for public lectures on education and women's rights, and for igniting controversy through attacks on traditional marriage and religion; traveled widely as lecturer but settled in London and became midwife. Published *The Most Common Female Complaints* (1848), translations of Guiccardini and Boccaccio, and novel *The Exiles of Piedmont.*

MARTIN, Gael (1956—). Australian track-and-field athlete. Name variations: Gael Mulhall; Gael Mulhall-Martin. Born Gael Mulhall, Aug 27, 1956, in Australia. ❖ At Los Angeles Olympics, won a bronze medal in the shot put (1984); at national championships, placed 1st in the shot put (1976–81, 1983–87); after Pacific Conference Games (1981), was put under suspension for failing a drug test.

MARTIN, George Madden (1866–1946). *See Martin, Georgia.*

MARTIN, Georgia (1866–1946). American writer. Name variations: George Madden Martin. Born Georgia May Madden, May 3, 1866, in Louisville, KY; died Nov 30, 1946, in Louisville; dau. of Frank Madden and Anne Louise (McKenzie) Madden; sister of Eva Madden (writer and journalist); m. Attwood Reading Martin, June 15, 1892. ❖ Leading figure in Louisville-based Authors Club, published 1st story in *Harper's Weekly* (1895); earned widespread attention for 2nd book, *Emmy Lou: Her Book and Heart* (1902), a collection of stories originally published in *Youth's Companion* and *McClure's Magazine*; published *Children in the Mist*, on the life of blacks in the South (1920); helped found (1919) and served on board (1920–34) of Commission on Interracial Cooperation; despite relatively enlightened racial and social views, opposed federal legislation on woman suffrage, child labor, or lynching.

MARTIN, Hannah (1830–1903). New Zealand writer. Name variations: Hannah White. Born Hannah White, May 18, 1830, in Durham, England; died Dec 5, 1903, in Auckland, New Zealand; dau. of Francis White (timber merchant) and Jane (Angus) White; m. Édouard Philippe Martin (missionary), 1856 (died 1910); children: 5. ❖ Immigrated with family to New Zealand (1835); lived privileged life in close contact with Maori; spent 7 years on Viwa in Figi Islands where husband ran Wesleyan Missionary Press before returning to Auckland (c. 1863); memoirs, *Grandma Martin's Story*, reveal positive aspects of childhood in colonial missionary enclave. ❖ See also *Dictionary of New Zealand Biography* (Vol. 1).

MARTIN, Helen (1909–2000). African-American stage, tv, and screen actress. Born July 23, 1909, in St. Louis, MO; died Mar 25, 2000, in Monterey, CA. ❖ Films include *Cotton Comes to Harlem, Death Wish, Repo Man, Hollywood Shuffle, A Rage in Harlem, Doc Hollywood, Beverly Hills Cop III, Kiss the Girls* and *Bullworth*; had recurring role of Pearl Shay on tv series "227" (1985–90).

MARTIN, Janet (c. 1819–1892). *See Donald, Janet.*

MARTIN, Joan (1899–1962). *See Adler, Polly.*

MARTIN, Lady (1817–1898). *See Faucit, Helena Saville.*

MARTIN, LaVonna (1966—). African-American runner. Name variations: LaVonna Martin-Floréal or Floreal. Born LaVonna Ann Martin, Nov 18, 1966, in Ohio; attended University of Tennessee, 1984–88. ❖ Won gold medal in 100-meter hurdles at Pan Am Games (1987); at Barcelona Olympics, won a silver medal in 100-meter hurdles (1992).

MARTIN, Lillien Jane (1851–1943). American psychologist. Born Lillie Jane Martin, July 7, 1851, in Olean, NY; died Mar 26, 1943, in San Francisco, CA; dau. of Russell Martin (merchant) and Lydia Hawes Martin (college matron); Vassar College, BA, 1880; University of Göttingen, Germany, PhD, 1898; never married; no children. ❖ Taught botany, physics and chemistry at Indianapolis High School (1880–89), then was vice-principal and science department head at Girls' High School in San Francisco (1889–94); became 1st woman to enroll in science department at University of Göttingen in Germany (1894); accepted assistant professorship at Stanford University (1899), named full professor (1911), and was head of psychology department (1915–16), the 1st woman to head an academic department at that university; published 4 technical vols. on psychology in German (1899–1914); became 1st American to be awarded an honorary PhD from Germany's University of Bonn (1913); at 65, forced to retire from Stanford, served as president of California Society for Mental Hygiene (1917–20); founded nation's 1st guidance clinics for preschoolers, at Polyclinic and Mt. Zion hospitals in San Francisco (1920); opened Old Age Center in San Francisco (1929); wrote *Salvaging Old Age* (1930) and *Sweeping the Cobwebs* (1933); at 87, journeyed by boat up Amazon River (1939). ❖ See also Miriam Allen deFord, *Psychologist Unretired: The Life Pattern of Lillien J. Martin* (Stanford U. Press, 1948); and *Women in World History.*

MARTIN, Lisa (1960—). *See Ondieki, Lisa.*

MARTIN, Lynn (1939—). American politician. Born Judith Lynn Morley, Dec 26, 1939, in Evanston, IL; dau. of Lawrence Morley and Helen (Hall) Morley; University of Illinois, Urbana, BA, 1960; m. John Martin (engineer), 1960 (div. 1978); m. Harry Leinenweber (US district court judge), 1987; children: (1st m.) Julia Martin; Caroline Martin. ❖ US Republican congressional representative and secretary of labor, began career as a teacher; served as member of Winnebago Co. Board (1972–76); was a member of Illinois House of Representatives (1977–79) and Illinois Senate (1979–80); was a delegate to Illinois State Republican Convention (1980); elected to 97th and 4 succeeding Congresses (1981–91); appointed to the influential Budget Committee where she served for 3 Congresses; outspoken, skilled and confident, won election as vice chair of Republican Conference in the House (1984 and 1986), the 1st time a woman had held a position in the congressional Republican Party's hierarchy; delivered vice-presidential nomination speech at national convention (1984); a fiscal conservative but a social moderate, was a supporter of abortion rights and Equal Rights Amendment; stood but was not elected to US Senate (1990); served as secretary of labor under George Bush (1991–93); was professor at J. Kellogg Graduate School of Management at Northwestern University (1993—) and fellow at Harvard University's Kennedy School of Government. ❖ See also *Women in World History.*

MARTIN, Maria (1796–1863). American artist. Name variations: Maria (Martin) Bachman. Born July 3, 1796, in Charleston, South Carolina; died Dec 27, 1863, in Columbia, South Carolina; dau. of John Nicholas Martin (Lutheran minister) and Rebecca Murray Martin; m. her widowed brother-in-law, John Bachman (Lutheran minister and naturalist), in 1848; no children. ❖ One of the best nature artists of 19th century, created flower and plant backgrounds for many of Audubon's bird paintings, including some of the most popular prints from *Birds of America*; also contributed drawings of Carolina reptiles to John Edward Holbrook, who used them in his 5-vol. work *North American Herpetology* (1836–1842). ❖ See also *Women in World History.*

MARTIN, Marianne (1961—). American cyclist. Born 1961 in Fenton, Michigan. ❖ Won the 1st Tour de France for women (1984).

MARTIN, Marion (1908–1985). American stage and screen actress. Born Marion Suplee, June 7, 1908, in Philadelphia, PA; died Aug 13, 1985, in Santa Monica, CA. ❖ Made Broadway debut in *Lombardi, Ltd.* (1927), followed by *Shady Lady, Ziegfeld Follies of 1933*, George White's *Scandals* and *New Faces of 1936* (replacing Gypsy Rose Lee); made film debut in *Sinners in Paradise* (1938); other films include *Youth Takes a Fling, The Storm, Suspense, Cinderella Jones, Queen of Burlesque, Angel on My Shoulder, Come to the Stable, Boom Town, Girls of the Big House* and *Tales of Manhattan*; retired (1950).

MARTIN, Mary (1905–1983). *See Renault, Mary.*

MARTIN, Mary (1907–1969). British painter and sculptor. Born Mary Balmford in 1907, in Kent, England; died in 1969; educated at Goldsmiths School of Art and Royal College of Art in London; m. Kenneth Martin (artist), 1930; children: 2, including Paul Martin (artist). ❖ Abandoning representational art (1940s), started painting geometrical shapes, simply arranged; along with husband and artists Anthony Hill and Victor Pasmore, created what became known as the post-war Constructivist movement; her growing interest in abstraction led to relief sculpting; also received commissions on numerous architectural structures, including fountains and large wall constructions. ❖ See also *Women in World History.*

MARTIN, Mary (1913–1990). American actress, singer, dancer. Born Mary Virginia Martin, Dec 1, 1913, in Weatherford, TX; died of cancer in Rancho Mirage, California, Nov 4, 1990; m. Benjamin Hagman, 1930 (div. c. 1936); m. Richard Halliday (story editor at Paramount), 1940; children: (1st m.) Larry Hagman (b. 1931, actor); (2nd m.) Heller Halliday (b. 1941). ❖ Major Broadway star, began career in nightclubs in Los Angeles; made Broadway debut in Cole Porter's *Leave It to Me* (1938), introducing "My Heart Belongs to Daddy"; starred in *One Touch of Venus* (1943), then *Annie Get Your Gun*; created roles of Nellie Forbush in Rodgers and Hammerstein's *South Pacific* (1949), Peter Pan in Jerome Robbins' musical production of *Peter Pan* (1954), and Maria von Trapp in *The Sound of Music* (1959); had another hit with *I Do! I Do!* (1966); appeared in such films as *Rage of Paris* (1938), *The Great Victor Herbert* (1939), *New York Town* (1941), *Kiss the Boys Goodbye* (1941), *Birth of the Blues* (1941), *Star Spangled Rhythm* (1942), *Night and Day* (1946) and *Main Street to Broadway* (1953). ❖ See also autobiography *My Heart Belongs* (Morrow, 1976); and *Women in World History.*

MARTIN, Mother Mary (1892–1975). Irish founder. Name variations: Mary Martin. Born in 1892, in Glenageary, Co. Dublin, Ireland; died Jan 27, 1975, in the hospital she had founded in Drogheda, Co. Louth, Ireland; father was a timber merchant; educated at Sacred Heart Convent, Leeson Street, Dublin, and Holy Child College, Harrogate, Yorkshire, England; never married; no children. ❖ Advocated for permission from Roman Catholic Church to allow women's religious orders to perform medical work; once permission was granted by Pope Pius XI (1936), founded a religious order, the Medical Missionaries of Mary, in Drogheda that has since opened hospitals in Spain, Italy, US, and throughout Africa; was the 1st woman to be made a freeman of Drogheda (1966) and the 1st woman to be inducted into the honorary fellowship of Royal College of Surgeons, Ireland (RCSI). ❖ See also *Women in World History.*

MARTIN, Mary Ann (1817–1884). New Zealand teacher and writer. Name variations: Mary Ann Parker. Born Mary Ann Parker, July 3, 1817, in London, England; died Jan 2, 1884, in Devon, England; dau. of William Parker (cleric) and Ann Parker; m. William Martin (barrister), 1841 (died 1880). ❖ Immigrated to New Zealand, to join husband who had been appointed chief justice of New Zealand (1842); a semi-invalid, helped to establish hospital and dispensary service for Maori at Taurarua; taught younger boys at St John's College (1858); returned to England following wars of 1860s. Several of her diary entries formed basis of series of articles in Charlotte Yonge's magazine, *Monthly Packet,* and were included in Martin's posthumously published *Our Maoris.* ❖ See also *Dictionary of New Zealand Biography* (Vol. 1).

MARTIN, Mary Letitia (1815–1850). Irish novelist. Name variations: Mrs. Bell Martin; Princess of Connemara. Born Harriet Mary Letitia Martin at Ballinahinch Castle, Co. Galway, Ireland, Aug 25, 1815; died in childbirth in NY, Nov 7, 1850; only child of Thomas Barnewall Martin (MP); granddau. of "Humanity Dick" Martin; m. Arthur Gonne Bell, in 1847. ❖ Turned to writing for monetary support; chief works are *St. Etienne, a Tale of the Vendean War* (1845) and *Julia Howard: A Romance* (1850). ❖ See also *Women in World History.*

MARTIN, Mary Steichen (1904–1998). See *Calderone, Mary Steichen.*

MARTIN, Millicent (1934—). English actress and singer. Born June 8, 1934, in Romford, Essex, England; m. Ronnie Carroll (div.); m. Norman Eshley. ❖ Made London debut at the Royal Opera House, Covent Garden, in the children's chorus of *The Magic Flute* (1948); made NY debut as Nancy in *The Boyfriend* (1954); back in London, came to prominence as Maisie in *Expresso Bongo* (1958) and Cora in *The Crooked Mile* (1959); other plays include *The Dancing Heiress, The Lord Chamberlain Regrets* (revue), *State of Emergency* and *Our Man Crichton*; made film debut in *Libel* (1959), followed by *The Horsemasters, Invasion Quartet, Nothing But the Best, Those Magnificent Men in Their Flying Machines, Alfie* and *Stop the World I Want to Get Off*; on tv, starred on "That Was the Week That Was" (1962), "Mainly Millicent" (1966), "From a Bird's Eye View" (1971), "Downtown" (1986) and "Moon and Son" (1992); also appeared regularly on "Days of Our Lives" and "Frasier."

MARTIN, Nana (1915–1989). See *Woodbury, Joan.*

MARTIN, Patricia J. (1928—). American advertising executive. Born June 25, 1928, at Croton-on-Hudson, NY. ❖ Served as editor at Warner-Hudnut, NY; served as director of marketing support at Parke-Davis division of Warner-Lambert (1959–85); with Joan Lipton, formed Martin and Lipton Advertising, Inc.; served as president of American Advertising Federation (AAF, 1969–71); was the 1st woman named chair of AAF (1981); received Matrix Award for women in communications (1982) and Barton A. Cummings Gold Medal for outstanding volunteer service with AAF (1997).

MARTIN, Rebecca (1882–1953). See *Love, Ripeka Wharawhara.*

MARTIN, Rhona (1966—). Scottish curler. Name variations: Mrs. Merton. Born Oct 12, 1966, in Irvine, Scotland, Great Britain. ❖ Won a silver medal at the European championships (1998); named Scottish Ladies champion (2000); (as skip) won a team gold medal for curling at Salt Lake City Olympics (2002). Given the Frances Brodie Award (2000), for female sportsmanship at World championships.

MARTIN, Sara (1884–1955). African-American blues singer. Name variations: Sarah Dunn Martin; Margaret Johnson; Sally Roberts. Born June 18, 1884, in Louisville, KY; died of a stroke, May 24, 1955, in Louisville; m. William Myers (marriage ended); m. Hayes Withers. ❖ As a teenager, performed in vaudeville in Louisville; took her act to Chicago (c. 1915), then New York City (c. 1920); attracted the notice of Clarence Williams, African-American composer; as one of the 1st female blues singers to record, made initial set of records with Okeh (1922), including "Uncle Sam Blues," "A Green Gal Can't Catch On," "Achin' Heart Blues," and "Sugar Blues," which become a classic; also recorded on Columbia label with her own group, Brown Skin Syncopators (1922); recorded again on Okeh label with Eva Taylor, Shelton Brooks, and Fats Waller (1923) and later recorded with guitarist Sylvester Weaver; toured with Waller (1922–23) and with W.C. Handy Band (1923) on the Theatre Owners Booking Association (TOBA) circuit; appeared in many 1920s revues, theatrical shows, and musicals, singing everything from traditional 12-bar and 16-bar blues to vaudeville comedy songs and foxtrots; sang on radio (1924, 1927) and in film *Hello Bill* (1927); appeared with Mamie Smith in *The Sun-Tan Frolics* in NYC (1929); began singing gospel music with Thomas Dorsey (1931), touring Chicago-area churches (1932). ❖ See also *Women in World History.*

MARTIN, Steffi. See *Walter-Martin, Steffi.*

MARTIN, Stella (1902–1974). See *Heyer, Georgette.*

MARTIN, Mrs. Theodore (1817–1898). See *Faucit, Helena Saville.*

MARTIN, Violet (1862–1915). Irish writer. Name variations: Martin Ross. Born Violet Florence Martin, June 11, 1862, at Ross House, Oughterard, Co. Galway, Ireland; died Dec 21, 1915, in Cork, Ireland; dau. of James Martin and Anna Selina (Fox) Martin; sister of Robert Martin (journalist and writer of some prominence); educated at home and briefly at Alexandra College, Dublin; never married; no children. ❖ Writer, who collaborated with cousin E. Somerville (under name Martin Ross) on novels and other writings which chronicled the declining fortunes of their class, the Anglo-Irish gentry, in the decades before Irish independence; spent early years at Ross; after father's death (1872), moved with family to Dublin and also spent some time in England; 1st met cousin Edith Somerville (1886); returned to Ross (1888) but stayed frequently at Edith's family home in Castletownshend; published 1st collaborative novel, *An Irish Cousin* (1889), which received good reviews; published *The Real Charlotte* (1893), considered the best work; published *Some Experiences of an Irish R.M.* (1899), an enormous success; after mother's death (1906), lived at Castletownshend permanently; health deteriorating following a serious accident (1898); died from a brain tumor (1915). Writings include *Through Connemara in a Governess Cart* (1893), *In The Vine Country* (1893), *Further Experiences of an Irish R.M.* (1908), *In Mr Knox's Country* (1915), *Irish Memories* (1917), *Mount Music* (1919), *Wheeltracks* (1923), *The Big House of Inver* (1999), *The States through Irish Eyes* (1930). ❖ See also Maurice Collis, *Somerville and Ross: A Biography* (Faber, 1968); John Cronin, *Somerville and Ross* (Bucknell U. Press, 1972); *The Selected Letters of Somerville and Ross* (ed. by Gifford Lewis, Faber, 1989); and *Women in World History.*

MARTIN, Vivian (1893–1987). American stage actress. Born July 22, 1893, in Grand Rapids, Michigan; died Mar 16, 1987, in New York, NY; m. William Jefferson; m. Arthur Samuels. ❖ Made stage debut as a child; made Broadway debut in *The Only Son* (1911); other plays include

Just Married, The Wild Westcotts, Puppy Love, Hearts Are Trumps and *Mrs. Dane's Defense*; films include *The Girl from Home, Giving Becky a Chance, Little Miss Optimist, The Sunset Trail* and *Molly Entangled*; managed her own theatrical company.

MARTÍN GAITE, Carmen (1925—). Spanish novelist and historian. Name variations: Carmen Martín Gaite. Born in Salamanca, Spain, Dec 8, 1925; graduated of University of Salamanca, 1948; m. Rafael Sánchez Ferlosio (a writer), 1953 (div. 1987); children: 2. ❖ Began to establish a reputation as one of Spain's foremost writers with publication of short novel *El balneario* (*The Spa*) (1954), which won the Gijón Prize, in part for innovatively combining fantastic and realistic elements; won Nadal Prize, Spain's most prestigious literary award, for novel *Entre visillos* (*Behind the Curtains*, 1958); other novels include *Ritmo lento* (1962), *Retahílas* (1974), *Fragmentos de interior* (1976), and *El cuarto de atrás* (1978), which received Spain's National Literature Prize and is her most widely acclaimed work. ❖ See also *Women in World History*.

MARTIN-SPENCER, Lilly (1822–1902). American painter. Name variations: Angelique Marie Martin. Born Angelique Marie Martin, 1822, in Exeter, Devon, England, to parents of French descent; died 1902 in Poughkeepsie, New York; m. Benjamin Spencer (tailor, painter of stereoptican slides), 1844 (died 1890); children: 13. ❖ Immigrated to US (1830), settling in Marietta, Ohio, where parents worked to establish utopian co-operative society and were deeply involved in Fourierist movement; studied art with Sala Bosworth and Charles Sullivan; caught attention of prominent Chicagoan, Nicholas Longworth (1841); trained in Cincinnati with John Insco Williams and James Henry Beard; sold art through Western Art-Union (1847), experiencing some success; moved to NY, where popularity continued to grow, and ultimately settled with family in Newark; depicted humor and sentiment in popular works which offer unique window onto 19th-century domestic life; produced 500 pieces, many of which were reproduced as popular engravings and lithographs.

MARTINA (fl. 600s). Byzantine empress. Flourished during the 600s; 2nd wife of uncle Herakleos also known as Heraclius I of Carthage, Byzantine emperor (r. 610–641); children: 10, including Heraklonas also known as Heraclonas II, Byzantine emperor (r. 641). ❖ Traveled with husband on his campaigns, and gave birth to some of their children at far-flung military outposts; had such influence over husband that before his death was able to secure a joint kingship for their 15-year-old son Heraclonas II; was taken into custody by enemy factions who cut out her tongue and banished her with son to island of Rhodes. ❖ See also *Women in World History*.

MARTINDALE, Hilda (1875–1952). British civil servant. Born in London, England, 1875; died 1952; dau. of William Martindale (merchant) and Louisa (Edwards) Martindale (1839–1914, suffragist and educational advocate); sister of Louisa Martindale (well-known obstetrician and gynecologist); educated at Royal Holloway College and Bedford College in London. ❖ Secured a position in civil service as a factory inspector; wrote an influential report on lead poisoning suffered by workers in brick factories (1903); rose steadily through the ranks of the civil service, obtaining posts of senior lady inspector (1908), superintending inspector (1921), and deputy chief inspector (1925); named director of women establishments in the Treasury Department (1933), one of the 1st women to secure a position in highest ranks of the civil service; retired (1937) and published several books, including *Women Servants of the State, 1870–1938* (1938), *One Generation to Another* (1944), which was about her family, and *Some Victorian Portraits* (1948). Awarded Order of the Commander of the British Empire (1935). ❖ See also *Women in World History*.

MARTINEAU, Harriet (1802–1876). English writer. Born Harriet Martineau, June 12, 1802, in Norwich, England; died at Ambleside, in Lake District, June 27, 1876; dau. of Thomas Martineau (textile manufacturer) and Elizabeth (Rankin) Martineau; educated at Reverend Isaac Perry's school, 1813–15; never married; no children. ❖ Author of fiction, reviews, travel writings, and religious, philosophical, and sociological essays, who was an advocate for women's rights, education, the abolition of slavery, and other liberal and radical causes of the 19th century, grew up in Norwich in middle-class family of Unitarian faith; led unhappy childhood beset by fears, illnesses, and onset of deafness at 12; sent from home at 15 to relatives in Bristol for 15 months, and came under the influence of philosophical traditions of Locke, Hartley, and Priestley; published 1st writings in the Unitarian journal, the *Monthly Repository* (1822–23); following father's death and an engagement that

ended with death of fiancé, contributed to household support 1st through needlework and eventually by her writing (1826); gained fame by popularizing principles of political economy through a series of didactic narratives (1832–34); traveled extensively in US (1834–36); became a strong advocate of abolitionism and women's rights; established reputation as a social analyst through writings on her American travels; suffered a period of invalidism (1839–44), from which she announced her cure through mesmerism; settled in Lake District (1845) where she continued to write, lectured to working classes, and established a model farm and low-income housing; traveled to Near East (1846–47); published *Household Education* and most important historical work, *The History of the Thirty Years' Peace 1816–1846* (1849); declared final break with religious faith (1851); following a recurrence of illness (1855) from which she did not expect to recover, wrote her *Autobiography*; continued writing to support herself until incapacitated by illness (1866). ❖ See also Valerie Kossew Pichanick, *Harriet Martineau: The Woman and Her Work, 1802–76* (U. of Michigan Press, 1980); and *Women in World History*.

MARTINELLI, Elsa (1932—). Italian actress. Born in Grosseto, Italy, Jan 13, 1932; married Count Franco Mancinelli Scotta di San Vito, 1957; children: Cristiana Mancinelli (actress). ❖ Worked as a barmaid and model before being discovered by Kirk Douglas, who launched her film career in his movie *The Indian Fighter* (1955); graced Italian and international films throughout 1960s, in such movies as *La Risaia* (*Rice Girl*, 1956), *Four Girls in Town* (1957), *Ciao Ciao Bambina* (1959), *La Notte Brava* (1959), *Un Amore a Roma* (1960), *Hatari* (1962), *The Pigeon That Took Rome* (1962), *Rampage* (1963); *The V.I.P.s* (1963), *La Fabuleuse Aventure de Marco Polo* (*Marco the Magnificent*, 1967), *Sept fois Femme* (*Woman Times Seven*, 1967), *Les Chemins de Kathmandou* (1969), *Il Garofano Rosso* (1976), *Pygmalion 88* (1988) and *Once Upon a Crime* (1991). ❖ See also *Women in World History*.

MARTINENGOU, Elisavet Moutza- (1801–1832). See *Moutza-Martinengou, Elisavet*.

MARTINES, Julia (1932—). See *O'Faolain, Julia*.

MARTINEZ, Conchita (1972—). Spanish tennis player. Born Concepción Martinez Bernat, April 16, 1972, in Monzón, Aragon, Spain. ❖ Turned pro (1988); won Wimbledon singles title (1994), the 1st Spanish woman to win that event; won Austrian Open (1991, 1992), Italian Open (1993–96), Polish Open (1999), German Open (1998, 2000); won a silver medal for doubles at Barcelona Olympics (1992), bronze medal for doubles at Atlanta Olympics (1996), and silver medal for doubles at Athens Olympics (2004); won 700th career match (April 2004); led Spain to 5 Fed Cups.

MARTINEZ, Estibaliz. Spanish rhythmic gymnast. Born in Spain. ❖ Won a team gold medal at Atlanta Olympics (1996).

MARTINEZ, Maria (1886–1951). See *Cadilla de Martínez, Maria*.

MARTINEZ, Maria Montoya (1887–1980). Tewa potter. Name variations: Marie. Signed work: Poh've'ka, Marie, Marie & Julian (1923–1922); Marie & Santana (1943–1956); Marie Poveka (Pond Lily); and Maria/Popovi (1956–1971). Born Poh've'ka or Pond Lily (Tewa) or Maria Antonita Montoya (Spanish) in the Tewa Pueblo P'owo'ge, or Place Where the Waters Meet (in Spanish: San Ildefonso, New Mexico) April 5, 1887; died July 21, 1980, in Santa Fe, New Mexico; dau. of Reyecita Pena and Tomas Montoya; attended St. Catharine's Indian School (Santa Fe, New Mexico); m. Julian Martinez, 1904 (died 1943); children: Adam Martinez (who m. Santana Roybal Martinez); Juan Diego Martinez; Popovi Da Martinez (died 1971); Felip Martinez; and daughter and son who died in infancy. ❖ Potter, known primarily for developing matte black-on-black ware, who was the key figure in 20th-century revival of Pueblo pottery, survived epidemic that decimated Pueblo population (c. 1890); participated with husband Julian in "Anthropology Exhibit" at St. Louis World's Fair (1904); with Julian, joined archaeological excavation of the Pajarito Plateau at Tyuonyi and Frijoles Canyons under Dr. Edgar L. Hewett (1908); began reproduction of ancient Frijoles pottery, originally polychrome; employed at Museum of New Mexico (1909–10); experimented with black-on-black ware (1910–12); developed black ware; exhibited at San Diego World's Fair (1912–15); discovered matte-on-black ware method (1919–21); developed pottery-making as full-time industry (1921–22); exhibited at Chicago World's Fair (1934); demonstrated pottery-making at San Francisco World's Fair with Julian (1939); husband died (1943); worked with Santana Martinez (1943–1956); worked with son, Popovi Da

Martinez (1956–1971). Won many awards including New Mexico Arts Commission Governor's Award for Outstanding Service to the Arts (1974); retrospective exhibition, "Maria: The Legend, The Legacy," presented by Wheelwright Museum, NM (June 1980). ❖ See also Alice Marriott, *Maria: The Potter of San Illdefonso* (U. of Oklahoma Press, 1948); Susan Brown McGreevey, *Maria: The Legend, The Legacy* (Sunstone, 1982); Susan Peterson, *The Living Tradition of Maria Martinez* (Kodansha, 1977); and *Women in World History.*

MARTINEZ, Marianne (1744–1812). Austrian composer, patron, pianist, harpsichordist, singer, and teacher. Name variations: Marianne von Martinez. Born Anna Caterina Martines in Vienna, Austria, May 4, 1744; died in Vienna, Dec 13, 1812; father was Spanish in origin and master of ceremonies to the Papal Nuncio. ❖ Friend and associate of Haydn and Mozart, grew up in a house of musicians, including Joseph Haydn and Pietro Metastasio; taught harpsichord by Haydn; studied compostion with Porpora, Bonno and Hasse; wrote large church works; composed around 200 pieces, including 4 symphonic masses, 6 motets, and 3 litanies for choir and orchestra; had one of her masses, probably her 3rd, performed at the court chapel (1761); when Joseph II became king and reinstated rule against women speaking, that is "singing," in church, lost chance for public performances in Austria; continued to compose anyway and fame continued to spread; admitted to the Philharmonic Academy of Bologna (1773); became acquainted with the young Amadeus Mozart in Vienna (many believe he modeled his 1768 Mass, K. 139, on one of her works); opened a singing school in her home (1796) and trained many professional singers. ❖ See also *Women in World History.*

MARTINEZ, Vilma (1943—). Mexican-American attorney and civil-rights activist. Born Vilma Socorro Martinez, Oct 17, 1943, in San Antonio, TX; University of Texas, BA, 1964; Columbia University, LLB, 1967; married; children: 2 sons. ❖ Influential Chicana, was staff attorney for the NAACP Legal Defense Fund; served on the Advisory Committee to US Commission on Civil Rights; was board member for Legal Defense Fund of National Organization of Women (NOW); co-founded and served as president and general counsel of the Mexican-American Legal Defense and Educational Fund (MALDEF, 1973–82); became a partner in law firm of Munger, Tolles and Olson in Los Angeles (1982), where she specializes in civil litigation.

MARTINEZ ADLUN, Maybelis (1977—). Cuban volleyball player. Born June 12, 1977, in Cuba. ❖ Won a team bronze medal at Athens Olympics (2004).

MARTÍNEZ SIERRA, Maria de la O (1874–1974). Spanish novelist. Born 1874 in San Millán de la Cogolla, Spain; died 1974; m. Gregorio Martínez Sierra. ❖ Works, written with husband, include *Almas ausentes* (1900), *Pascua florida* (1903), and *Tú eres la paz* (1906).

MARTINI, Virginia (1908–1996). *See Cherrill, Virginia.*

MARTINO, Angel (1967—). American swimmer. Name variations: Angel Myers. Born Angel Myers, April 27, 1967, in Americus, GA; graduate of Furman University, 1989; m. Mike Martino (swimmer), 1989. ❖ Placed 1st at national NCAA Division II swim meets (1986); became 1st American woman to swim 100-meter freestyle in under 55 seconds (1988); won a bronze medal for the 50-meter freestyle and a gold medal for the 4x100-meter freestyle relay at Barcelona Olympics (1992); set world record for the 100-meter backstroke (1993); won gold medals for 4x100-meter freestyle relay and 4x100-meter relay and bronze medals for 100-meter freestyle and 100-meter butterfly at Atlanta Olympics (1996).

MARTINOD, Marie (c. 1984—). French skier. Born c. 1984 in Aime, France. ❖ Placed 1st in Superpipe at US Open (2003) and 2nd in Superpipe at X Games Global championship (2003).

MARTINOZZI, Anne-Marie (1637–1672). Niece of Cardinal Jules Mazarin. Name variations: Princesse de Conti. Born 1637; died 1672; dau. of Hieronymus Martinozzi also seen as Girolamo Martinozzi and Laura Margaret Mazarini (sister of Cardinal Jules Mazarin, chief minister to the young Louis XIV); sister of Laura Martinozzi; cousin of Laure Mancini (1635–1657), Olympia Mancini (c. 1639–1708), Marie Mancini (1640–1715), Hortense Mancini (1646–1699), and Marie-Anne Mancini (1649–1714); m. the prince de Conti (brother of Louis II de Bourbon, the Great Condé), 1654. ❖ Became a Jansenist and devoted herself to piety.

MARTINOZZI, Laura (fl. 1658). Duchess of Modena. Name variations: Laura d'Este. Flourished around 1658; dau. of Hieronymus Martinozzi also seen as Girolamo Martinozzi and Laura Margaret Mazarini (who was the sister of Cardinal Jules Mazarin, chief minister to the young Louis XIV); sister of Anne-Marie Martinozzi (1637–1672); cousin of Laure Mancini (1635–1657), Olympia Mancini (c. 1639–1708), Marie Mancini (1640–1715), Hortense Mancini (1646–1699), and Marie-Anne Mancini (1649–1714); m. Alphonse d'Este (heir of the duke of Modena), in 1656; children: Mary of Modena (1658–1718), queen of England; Francis II, duke of Modena. ❖ Was regent of Modena for 12 years following death of husband Alphonse d'Este.

MARTINSEN, Bente (1972—). Norwegian cross-country skier. Name variations: Bente Skari. Born Sept 10, 1972, in Oslo, Norway; dau. of Odd Martinsen (Olympic gold medalist in 40K cross-country relay, 1968). ❖ Won the World Cup overall (1999, 2000, 2003); won a bronze medal in the 5km and a silver medal for the 4x5km relay at Nagano Olympics (1998); won a gold medal in the 10km, a silver medal in the 4x5km classical/free and a bronze medal in the 30km at Salt Lake City (2002), the 1st Norwegian woman to win an Olympic cross-country gold medal.

MARTINSON, Helga Maria (1890–1964). *See Martinson, Moa.*

MARTINSON, Moa (1890–1964). Swedish writer and feminist. Name variations: Helga Svartz. Born Helga Maria Svartz, Nov 2, 1890, in Vårdnäs, suburb of Norrköping, Sweden; died in Södertälje, Sweden, Aug 5, 1964; dau. of Kristina Svartz (unmarried textile-factory worker); father unknown; spent 1 semester at Fogelstad Women Citizens College; m. Karl L. Johansson (after publication of marriage banns in 1911), April 1922 (committed suicide, 1928); m. Harry Martinson, Oct 3, 1929 (div. 1940); children: (1st m.) Olle (b. 1910); Tore (b. 1911); Erik (b. 1913); Manfred (b. 1914); Knut (b. 1916). ❖ Proletarian-feminist, political activist, syndicalist sympathizer and experimental modernist writer whose literary reputation has been overshadowed by husband's fame as a poet; spent 1st seven years in slum foster homes; quit school (1903); became syndicalist union organizer (1921); resumed education at college level (1924); received 1st literary recognition in exchange of letters with Elise Ottesen-Jensen published in Swedish newspaper *Arbetaren* (1922); saw publication of 1st novel *Women and Appletrees* (1933); traveled to Soviet Union (1934); won Sweden's De Nois Prize for Literature (1944); became a figure widely adored by Swedish populace; published poetry, essays and novels (1933–59), including *Sallys söner* (Sally's Sons, 1934), *Rågvakt* (Rye Watch, 1935), *Mor gifter sig* (1936, Eng. tr. *My Mother Gets M.,* 1988), *Drottning Grågyllen* (Queen Grågyllen, 1937), *Kyrkbröllop* (1938, Eng. tr. *Church Wedding), Kungens rosor* (The King's Roses, 1939), *Vägen under stjärnorna* (The Journey Under the Stars, 1940), *Brandliljor* (Firelilies, 1941), *Den osynlige älskaren* (The Invisible Lover, 1943), *Livets fest* (Life's Celebration, 1949), *Du är den enda* (You Are the Only, 1952), *Kvinnorna på Kummelsjö* (The Women at Kummelsjö, 1955), *Klockor vid Sidenvägen* (Bells at Sidenvägen, 1957), and *Hemligheten* (The Secret, 1959). ❖ See also correspondence, manuscripts, papers and memorabilia located at Martinson's home, Johannedal, in Osmo, Sweden, now a museum; and *Women in World History.*

MARTINSSON, Barbro. Swedish cross-country skier. Born in Sweden. ❖ Won silver medals for 3x5km relay at Innsbruck Olympics (1964) and Grenoble Olympics (1968).

MARTIUS, Hedwig (1888–1966). *See Conrad-Martius, Hedwig.*

MARTO, Lucia (1907–2005). *See Lucia, Sister.*

MARTYN, Constance Palgrave (1864–1942). *See Abraham, Constance Palgrave.*

MARTYN, Edith How- (1875–1954). *See How-Martyn, Edith.*

MARUCHA (1944–1991). Cuban photographer, cartoonist, and graphic designer. Born Maria Eugenia Haya in 1944, in Havana, Cuba; died in Havana in 1991; studied at Instituto Cubano de Arte e Industria Cinematográfica, 1962–63, Biblioteca Nacional de José Marti, 1964–65, and with painter Raúl Martínez, 1965–66; studied philology at Havana University, 1972–78; m. Mario García Joya (director of photography at Instituto Cubano de Arte e Industria Cinematografía); children: Mayitín and María. ❖ Was a photographer for Chamber of Congress in Havana (1970–78); served as researcher and script supervisor for filmmaker Tomás Gutierrez Alea (1975–78); was a member of the Unión Nacional de Escritores y Artistas Cubanos; played a key role in organizing the Coloquio de Fotografía Latinoamericana in Havana (1984). Won 1st prize from Salon of University of Havana (1978).

MARUOKA, Hideko (1903–1990). Japanese writer. Born 1903 in Japan; died 1990. ❖ Wrote *The Problems of Women Farmers in Japan* (1937) and co-edited 10-vol. *Archive Series of Women's Issues in Modern Japan* (1976–80).

MARVALICS, Gyorgyi (1924—). See *Szekelyne-Marvalics, Gyorgyi.*

MARVELETTES.
See Anderson, Katherine.
See Cowart, Juanita.
See Dobbins, Georgia.
See Horton, Gladys.
See Young, Wanda.

MARWEDEL, Emma (1818–1893). American educator. Born Emma Jacobina Christiana Marwedel, Feb 27, 1818, in Münden, near Göttingen, Germany; died Nov 17, 1893, in San Francisco, CA; dau. of Capt. Heinrich Ludwig Marwedel and Jacobina (Brokmann) Marwedel. ❖ Became 1st director of Girls' Industrial School (Hamburg, 1867–68); published *Warum bedürfen wir weibliche Gewerbeschulen? und wie sollen sie angelegt sein?* (1868); with encouragement from Elizabeth Palmer Peabody, immigrated to US; established women's cooperative industrial school (Long Island, NY, 1870), private school with kindergarten and Froebelian teacher-training classes (Washington, DC, 1871), California Model Kindergarten and the Pacific Model Training School for Kindergartners (Los Angeles, CA, 1876), and Pacific Kindergarten Normal School (San Francisco, CA); served as leading founder (1879) and 1st president of California Kindergarten Union.

MARWICK, Tricia (1953—). Scottish politician. Born Nov 5, 1953, in Fife, Scotland. ❖ Elected to the SNP National Executive; elected to the Scottish Parliment for Mid Scotland and Fife; named the Shadow Minister of Local Government.

MARX, Eleanor (1855–1898). See *Marx-Aveling, Eleanor.*

MARX, Jenny von Westphalen (1814–1881). German political theorist. Name variations: Jenny von Westphalen. Born Johanna Bertha Julie Jenny von Westphalen, Feb 12, 1814, in Salzwedel, Germany; died in London, Dec 2, 1881; dau. of Johann Ludwig von Westphalen (Prussian civil servant) and Caroline Heubel von Westphalen; perhaps attended a private Catholic school in Trier; m. Karl Marx (1818–1883, philosopher, economist and sociologist who wrote *The Communist Manifesto*), June 19, 1843; children: Jenny Marx (1844–1883); Laura Marx (1845–1911); Edgar Marx (1846–1855); Heinrich Marx (1849–1850); Franziska Marx (1851–1852); Eleanor Marx-Aveling (1855–1898), and an unnamed last child who died shortly after birth, July 6, 1857. ❖ Prussian of aristocratic lineage who married her childhood playmate Karl Marx and became his lifelong companion in the struggle for socialism; moved with family to Trier (1816); confirmed as a Protestant (1828); secretly engaged to Karl Marx (1836); married him and moved to Paris (1843); joined husband in a commitment to the emancipation of the working class and the abolition of capitalism, giving to the socialist cause her unremunerated services as financial manager, organizational secretary, scribe and critic; expelled from Paris, moved to Brussels (1845); became Brussels secretary of Communist correspondence committees (1848); arrested by Belgian police, returned to Paris (Mar 1848); moved to Cologne and became secretary of German Workers Party (summer 1848); took up residence in London (1849); finished copying *Capital* (1867); was the unsung orchestrator at the center of one of the key command posts of the 19th-century European revolutionary movement: the Marx home, which served as a meeting place and headquarters. ❖ See also H.F. Peters, *Red Jenny: A Life with Karl Marx* (Allen & Unwin, 1986); and *Women in World History.*

MARX, Laura (1845–1911). Daughter of Karl and Jenny Marx. Name variations: Laura Lafargue. Born Jenny Laura Marx (all of the Marx daughters carried the name "Jenny") in 1845; committed suicide in 1911 (her husband died by his own hand that same year); dau. of Jenny von Westphalen Marx (1814–1881) and Karl Marx (1818–1883, philosopher, economist and sociologist who wrote *The Communist Manifesto*; sister of Jenny Marx (1844–1883) and Eleanor Marx-Aveling (1855–1898); m. Paul Lafargue (1842–1911); children: 3, all died as infants. ❖ See also Ronald Florence, *Marx's Daughters* (Dial, 1975); and *Women in World History.*

MARX, Susan Fleming (1908–2002). American actress, dancer and politician. Name variations: Susan Fleming. Born Feb 19, 1908, in New York, NY; died Dec 22, 2002, in Rancho Mirage, CA; m. Adolpho "Harpo" Marx (comedian), Sept 28, 1936 (died Sept 28, 1964); children: (adopted) 4. ❖ Appeared in the Ziegfeld Follies; in films, starred opposite John Wayne in *Range Feud* and as W.C. Fields daughter in *Million Dollar Legs* (1932); became a Palm Springs politician and activist.

MARX-AVELING, Eleanor (1855–1898). English political activist. Name variations: Eleanor Marx. Born Jenny Julia Eleanor Marx (all of the Marx daughters carried the name "Jenny"), Jan 16, 1855, in London, England; committed suicide at 42, Mar 31, 1898, in London; dau. of Karl Marx (1818–1883), founder of Marxism, and Jenny von Westphalen Marx (1814–1881); sister of Jenny Marx (1844–1883) and Laura Marx (1845–1911); tutored by father and by Friedrich Engels; took courses at South Hampstead College for Ladies; not legally married, but maintained long-term household and "free marriage" with socialist and freethinker Edward Aveling. ❖ Youngest daughter of Karl Marx, who worked much of her adult life to fulfill the vision of her father and to create a labor party in England; was questioned by French authorities during visit to France (1870); accepted teaching job at Brighton (1873); engaged to Hippolyte Prosper Olivier Lissagaray (1882); joined W.M. Hyndman's Democratic Federation and seceded from the organization a short time later (1884); toured US with Edward Aveling (1886–87); helped organize May Day demonstration for an 8-hour working day (1890); helped found the Independent Labour Party and was elected to the party's 1st executive committee (1893); rejoined the Democratic Federation (1895); was made financially independent from provision in Engels' will (1895). Writings and translations include *The Factory Hell* (1885), (with Edward Aveling) *The Woman Question* (1886), (trans.) Hippolyte Prosper Olivier Lissagaray's *History of the Commune of 1871* (1886), (trans.) Gustav Flaubert's *Madame Bovary* (1886), (trans.) Georgi Plekhanov's *Anarchism and Socialism* (1887), (trans.) Henrik Ibsen's *An Enemy of Society* (1888), *The Working Class Movement in England: A Brief Historical Sketch* (1896), and (edited) Karl Marx's *Value, Price, and Profit* (1898). ❖ See also Ronald Florence, *Marx's Daughters* (Dial, 1975); Yvonne Knapp, *Eleanor Marx* Vol. I: *Family Life (1855–1887)* and Vol. II: *The Crowded Years (1884–1898)* (Lawrence & Wishart, 1972, 1976); Chushichi Tsuzuki, *The Life of Eleanor Marx: 1855–1898: A Socialist Tragedy* (Clarendon, 1967); and *Women in World History.*

MARY. *Variant of Maria.*

MARY (1278–1332). Princess and nun of Amesbury. Name variations: Mary Plantagenet. Born Mar 11, 1278, in Windsor, Berkshire, England; died in 1332 in Amesbury, Wiltshire, England; dau. of Edward I Longshanks, king of England (r. 1272–1307), and Eleanor of Castile (1241–1290). ❖ Because the Catholic Church pressured her mother to offer one of her daughters to God, entered a nunnery at Amesbury at 7 where her fraternal grandmother, dowager-queen Eleanor of Provence acted as her guardian; traveled and was often at court. After her death, Dominican friar Nicholas Trevet composed an Anglo-Norman chronicle for her which became a principal source for Chaucer's *Man of Law's Tale.*

MARY (1344–1362). English princess. Born Mary Plantagenet. Born Oct 10, 1344, in Waltham, Hampshire, England; died of a form of sleeping sickness at age 17 in 1362; buried at Abingdon Abbey, Oxfordshire, England; dau. of Philippa of Hainault (1314–1369) and Edward III (1312–1377), king of England (r. 1327–1377); m. John IV, duke of Brittany (r. 1364–1399), in summer 1361, in Woodstock, Oxfordshire, England. ❖ See also *Women in World History.*

MARY (1531–1581). Duchess of Julich-Cleves-Berg. Name variations: Maria. Born May 15, 1531, in Prague; died Dec 11, 1581, at Hambach Castle; dau. of Anna of Bohemia and Hungary (1503–1547) and Ferdinand I, Holy Roman emperor (r. 1558–1564); m. William V of Cleves, duke of Juliers (r. 1539–1592); children: Maria Eleanora (who m. Albert Frederick, duke of Prussia); John William, duke of Cleves (r. 1592–1609); Anna (who m. Philip Louis, count Palatine of Neuberg); Magdalena (who m. John I, count Palatine of Zweibrucken).

MARY (1718–1794). Countess of Bute. Name variations: Lady Bute; Mary Wortley Montagu or Wortley-Montagu; Mary Stuart. Born in Feb 1718; died 1794; dau. of Mary Wortley Montagu (1689–1762) and Edward Wortley Montagu; m. John Stuart (1713–1792), 3rd earl of Bute (a powerful politician and secretary of state); children: Louisa Stuart (1757–1851, writer).

MARY (1776–1857). Duchess of Gloucester. Name variations: Mary Guelph; Mary Hanover; Princess Mary. Born April 25, 1776, at

St. James's Palace, London, England; died April 30, 1857; buried at St. George's Chapel, Windsor, England; fourth dau. of George III, king of England, and Charlotte of Mecklenburg-Strelitz; m. William, 2nd duke of Gloucester and Edinburgh, July 22, 1816.

MARY (1897–1965). Princess Royal of England and countess of Harewood. Name variations: Mary Lascelles. Born Victoria Alexandria Alice Mary on April 25, 1897, in York Cottage, Sandringham, Norfolk, England; died Mar 28, 1965, in Harewood House, Leeds, West Yorkshire, England; dau. of George V, king of England (r. 1910–1936), and Mary of Teck (1867–1953); m. Henry Lascelles (1882–1947), 6th earl of Harewood, on Feb 28, 1922; children: George Lascelles, 7th earl of Harewood (b. 1923); Gerald Lascelles (b. 1924).

MARY (b. 1964). Romanian princess. Name variations: Mary Hohenzollern. Born July 13, 1964, in Copenhagen, Denmark; dau. of Michael I (b. 1921), king of Romania (r. 1927–1930, 1940–1947), and Anne of Bourbon-Parma (b. 1923).

MARY, Countess of Boulogne (d. 1182). See Marie of Boulogne.

MARY, Countess of Falconberg or Fauconberg (1636–1712). See Cromwell, Mary.

MARY, Countess of Rosse (1813–1885). See Parsons, Mary.

MARY, Crown Princess (1972—). See Donaldson, Mary.

MARY, Queen (1867–1953). See Mary of Teck.

MARY, Queen of Scots (1542–1587). See Mary Stuart.

MARY, Saint (20 BCE–40 CE). See Mary the Virgin.

MARY I (1516–1558). English queen. Name variations: Bloody Mary; Mary Tudor; Mary the Catholic. Born Mary Tudor at Greenwich Palace, near London, England, Feb 18, 1516; died at St. James's Palace in London, Nov 17, 1558; buried in Westminster Abbey, London; dau. of Henry VIII, king of England (r. 1509–1547), and the Spanish princess Catherine of Aragon (1485–1536, youngest child of Ferdinand of Aragon and Isabella I [1451–1504]); ascended throne, July 1553; m. Philip II, king of Spain (r. 1556–1598), and king of Portugal as Philip I (r. 1580–1598), on July 25, 1554; no children. ❖ Queen of England (1553–1558), who restored Roman Catholicism as the established religion of England and was popularly known as Bloody Mary; passed from childhood into adolescence under a darkening cloud as her father became increasingly desperate to beget a legitimate male heir to the throne; was restored officially to royal succession directly behind Edward (1544); upon Henry VIII's death (1547), inherited a number of estates; when Edward's regime embarked upon a course of radical religious reform, defiantly held public masses in contravention of First Act of Uniformity (1549); provided a visible focus for conservative religious dissent by riding to court with a retinue of 130, each holding a rosary (1551); when Edward died (1553), proclaimed her own accession and commanded the obedience of the Privy Council and of the towns and counties of the realm; had a resolve and impracticality which hampered the effectiveness of her 3 great aims: the restoration of England to the Roman Catholic fold, the accomplishment of her long-delayed marriage, and the production of an heir who could ensure the continuation of England's Catholic regime; chose to marry Philip (II) of Spain, raising fears that Protestantism would be endangered and English interests subordinated to the Spanish Habsburgs, which precipitated Wyatt's Rebellion (1554); redoubled her efforts to stamp out the Protestant heresy: imprisoned prominent Protestants, including Thomas Cranmer, shut down Protestant printers and had Protestant refugees from the Continent expelled, deprived married clergy of their livings, affirmed the traditional Catholic doctrine of the Eucharist, and had Parliament repeal all ecclesiastical legislation passed after 1529, in return for which the papal legate granted absolution to the kingdom and welcomed "the return of the lost sheep" back to Rome (300 Protestant martyrs were convicted of heresy and burned, persecution which only stiffened Protestant opposition). ❖ See also D.M. Loades, Mary Tudor: A Life (Blackwell, 1989); Robert Tittler, The Reign of Mary I (Longman, 1991); and Women in World History.

MARY II (1662–1694). Queen of England. Name variations: Mary Stewart or Stuart. Reigned 1689–1694; born April 30, 1662, at St. James's Palace, London, England; died of smallpox on Dec 28, 1694, at Kensington Palace, London; interred at Westminster Abbey, London; dau. of James, duke of York, later James II, king of England (r. 1685–1688), and Anne Hyde (1638–1671); sister of Anne (1665–1714), queen of England (r. 1702–1707), queen of Scotland (r. 1702–1707), queen of Britain (r. 1702–1714); educated under Protestant guidelines, apart from

parents; m. William III, prince of Orange (r. 1672–1702), later William III, king of England (r. 1689–1702), on Nov 4, 1677; children: three who died stillborn. ❖ Raised by a Protestant governess at the demand of her uncle Charles II, became 2nd in line to English throne behind her Catholic father (1671); married to William III of Orange, Hereditary Stadholder and military leader of the Dutch United Provinces, spent 12 years in Holland at Dutch royal court (1677–89); when Charles II died (1685), her father ascended to the throne and soon began alienating much of the political community not only for his increasing favoritism towards Catholics, but for his tendencies to practice arbitrary rule; became queen of England during the "Glorious Revolution" after father was deposed by English Parliament (1688); refused to accept the throne unless husband shared the royal title with her; in the early years of her reign, was not very involved in governmental affairs; during war with France, acted as regent for William on 4 separate occasions (1690–94), handling these periods of regency with political skill and strength; came to be admired and respected. ❖ See also Hester Chapman, Mary II, Queen of England (Cape, 1953); Elizabeth Hamilton, William's Mary: A Biography of Mary II (Hamilton, 1972); Henri and Barbara van der Zee, William and Mary (Macmillan, 1973); and Women in World History.

MARY ADELAIDE (1833–1897). Duchess of Teck. Name variations: Mary Adelaide Guelph; Fat Mary. Born Mary Adelaide Wilhelmina Elizabeth on Nov 27, 1833, in Hanover, Lower Saxony, Germany; died Oct 27, 1897, at White Lodge, Richmond Park, Surrey, England; dau. of Adolphus Guelph, 1st duke of Cambridge, and Augusta of Hesse-Cassel (1797–1889); m. Francis, 1st duke of Teck, on June 12, 1866; children: Mary of Teck (1867–1953); Adolphus, 1st marquess of Cambridge (1868–1927); Francis of Teck (1870–1910); Alexander of Teck, earl of Athlone (1874–1957).

MARY ALEXANDROVNA (1853–1920). See Marie Alexandrovna.

MARYAM THE EGYPTIAN (fl. 7th c.). One of the wives of Muhammad. Name variations: Mary the Egyptian; Mary of Egypt. Married Muhammad in 629 CE. ❖ Christian slave sent to Muhammad by the Byzantine governor of Egypt; may have been one of Muhammad's chief sources for Christianity whose knowledge of which betrays a superficial acquaintance of the faith as it was practiced in Egypt. ❖ See also Women in World History.

MARYAN (1847–1927). See Descard, Maria.

MARY AVIS (1527–1545). See Mary of Portugal.

MARY BARBARA (1711–1758). See Maria Barbara of Braganza.

MARY BARBARA, Sister (1910–2003). See Bailey, Barbara Vernon.

MARY BERNARD, Sr. (c. 1810–1895). See Dickson, Mary Bernard.

MARY BOSOMWORTH (c. 1690–c. 1763). See Musgrove, Mary.

MARY CAROLINE (1752–1814). See Maria Carolina.

MARY DE BOHUN (1369–1394). First wife of Henry IV. Name variations: Mary Bohun; Mary of Bohun. Born 1369; died in childbirth on July 4, 1394, at Peterborough Castle, Cambridgeshire, England; buried at Leicester; dau. of Humphrey de Bohun, earl of Hereford, and Joan Fitzalan (d. 1419); sister of Eleanor Bohun (1366–1399, who m. Thomas of Woodstock); m. Henry Bolingbroke, later Henry IV, king of England (r. 1399–1413); children: Henry (1387–1422) also known as Prince Hal, later Henry V, king of England (r. 1413–1422); Thomas, duke of Clarence (1388–1421); John, duke of Bedford (1389–1425); Humphrey, duke of Gloucester (1390–1447); Blanche (c. 1392–1409, who m. Louis, duke of Bavaria); Philippa (1394–1430, who m. Eric VII, king of Denmark). ❖ Died a few years before husband became king of England as Henry IV (he then married Joanna of Navarre [c. 1370–1437]).

MARY DE COUCY (c. 1220–c. 1260). Queen of Scots. Name variations: Marie de Coucy; Mary de Couci; Mary di Coucy; Mary of Coucy. Born c. 1220; died c. 1260; interred at Newbottle, Scotland; dau. of Enguerrand de Coucy, 3rd baron de Coucy, and Mary de Montmirel-en-Brie; became 2nd wife of Alexander II (1198–1249), king of Scots (r. 1214–1249), May 15, 1239; m. Jean de Brienne, before June 6, 1257; children: (1st m.) Alexander III (1241–1286), king of Scots (r. 1249–1286); (2nd m.) Blanche of Brienne (who m. William II de Fiennes). ❖ Alexander II's 1st wife was Joan (1210–1238).

MARY DE COUCY (fl. 1370). English royal. Fl. around 1370; dau. of Enguerrand VII, lord of Coucy and earl of Bedford, and Isabella

(1332–1382, dau. of Philippa of Hainault and King Edward III); sister of Philippa de Coucy.

MARY DE MEDICIS (c. 1573–1642). *See Medici, Marie de.*

MARY DE MONTHERMER (1298–after 1371). Duchess of Fife. Born in 1298; died after 1371; dau. of Joan of Acre (1272–1307) and Ralph Monthermer, earl of Gloucester and Hertford; m. Duncan Fife (1285–1353), 10th earl of Fife (r. 1288–1353), in Nov 1307; children: Isabel of Fife (c. 1332–1389).

MARY DE PADILLA (1335–1361). *See Marie de Padilla.*

MARY ELIZABETH, Mother (1784–1882). *See Lange, Elizabeth Clovis.*

MARY-ELIZABETH OF PADUA (1782–1808). Duchess of Brunswick. Name variations: Mary Elizabeth of Padua Zähringen. Born Sept 7, 1782; died April 20, 1808; dau. of Amalie of Hesse-Darmstadt (1754–1832) and Charles Louis of Padua (b. 1755), prince of Padua and Baden; m. Major-General Frederick William (1771–1815), duke of Brunswick (r. 1806–1815), Nov 1, 1802; children: Charles Frederick (b. 1804); William Maximilian (b. 1806), duke of Brunswick.

MARY FEODOROVNA (1847–1928). *See Marie Feodorovna.*

MARY HABSBURG (1528–1603). *See Marie of Austria.*

MARY HENRIETTA (1631–1660). *See Mary of Orange.*

MARY HENRIQUES (1313–1357). *See Maria of Portugal.*

MARY KATHARINE, Mother (1858–1955). *See Drexel, Mary Katharine.*

MARY LOUVAIN (c. 1260–1321). *See Marie of Brabant.*

MARY MAGDALEN OF PAZZI (1566–1607). Saint. Name variations: Maria Maddalena de' Pazzi. Born Catherine in 1566; died 1607; dau. of Florentine nobles. ❖ At 12, vowed not to marry; at 18, entered the Carmelite Monastery of Santa Maria degli Angeli; endured corporal and spiritual sufferings which she had asked of God; was beatified by Pope Urban VIII (1626) and canonized by Alexander VIII (1670). Feast day is May 29, and a church in Florence bears her name.

MARY MAGDALENE (fl. early 1st c. CE). Biblical woman. Name variations: Mariam; Mariamne or Mariamme, Mariham; Maria or Maryam; Maria Magdalene; the Magdalene; the Magdalen; Mary of Magdala or Magdalo. ❖ Disciple of Jesus, ranked with the apostles because of her role at the resurrection, who, for much of Western history, has been thought to be a repentant prostitute; based on the 4 Gospels of the New Testament, was born in late 1st century BCE in Magdala on the lake of Galilee; after being cured of "seven devils" by Jesus, became a disciple, was with Jesus at the crucifixion, and came to anoint his dead body on Easter morning; was the 1st to discover the empty tomb and to see the risen Christ; because she announced the resurrection to the other disciples, is called "apostle to the apostles"; according to legend, ended her days as a solitary hermit in France about 50 CE. By the 6th century, in the West the Magdalene was conflated with Mary of Bethany and with the repentant sinner in Luke 7 (assumed to be a prostitute), who, on encountering and anointing Jesus, reformed and devoted herself to his ministry. ❖ See also Susan Haskins, *Mary Magdalen: Myth and Metaphor* (Harcourt, 1993); Sandra M. Rushing, *The Magdalene Legacy: Exploring the Wounded Icon of Sexuality* (Bergin & Garvey, 1994); and *Women in World History.*

MARY OF AGREDA (1602–1665). *See Agreda, Sor María de.*

MARY OF ALANIA (fl. 1070–1081). *See Maria of Alania.*

MARY OF ANJOU (1371–1395). *See Maria of Hungary.*

MARY OF ANJOU (1404–1463). *See Marie of Anjou.*

MARY OF ANTIOCH (d. 1277). Princess of Antioch. Died in 1277; dau. of Melisande and Bohemund IV, prince of Antioch. ❖ When she died (1277), left her claims to Charles of Anjou, king of Sicily.

MARY OF ATHOLL (d. 1116). Countess of Boulogne. Name variations: Mary Dunkeld. Died May 31, 1116; buried at Bermondsey Abbey, London, England; dau. of Malcolm III, king of Scots (r. 1057–1093), and Saint Margaret (c. 1046–1093); m. Eustace III, count of Boulogne (brother of Baldwin I, king of Jerusalem), in 1102; children: two, including Matilda of Boulogne (c. 1103–1152).

MARY OF BADEN (1834–1899). Princess of Leiningen. Born Nov 20, 1834; died Nov 21, 1899; dau. of Leopold, grand duke of Baden, and Sophia of Sweden (1801–1865); m. Ernest, 4th prince of Leiningen, on Sept 11, 1858; children: two, including Emich, 5th prince of Leiningen (1866–1939).

MARY OF BATTENBERG (1852–1923). Aunt of Earl Mountbatten of Burma. Born July 18, 1852; died in 1923; dau. of Alexander of Hesse-Darmstadt and Julie von Hauke (1825–1895); aunt of Lord Louis Mountbatten, Earl Mountbatten of Burma.

MARY OF BAVARIA (1551–1608). Duchess of Styria and Austria. Name variations: Maria of Bavaria. Born Mar 21, 1551; died April 29, 1608; dau. of Anna of Brunswick (1528–1590) and Albert V (d. 1579), duke of Bavaria; m. Karl also known as Charles of Styria (1540–1590), archduke of Styria; children: Katharina Renea, known as Renata (1576–1595); Margaret of Austria (c. 1577–1611), who m. Philip III, king of Spain); Ferdinand II (1578–1637), king of Bohemia and Hungary (r. 1578–1637), Holy Roman emperor (r. 1619–1637); Leopold V, archduke of Austrian Tirol (d. 1632, who m. Claudia de Medici); Maximilian Ernst (1583–1616); Maria Magdalena of Austria (1589–1631, who m. Cosimo II, duke of Tuscany); Anna of Styria (1573–1598, who m. Sigismund III of Poland); Gregoria Maximiliane (1581–1597); Eleonore (1582–1620); Constance of Styria (1588–1631, who m. Sigismund III, king of Poland).

MARY OF BETHANY (fl. early 1st c. CE). *See Martha and Mary of Bethany.*

MARY OF BRABANT (c. 1191–c. 1260). Countess of Brabant and Holy Roman empress. Name variations: Marie of Brabant; Marie de Brabant. Born c. 1191; died after Mar 9, 1260; dau. of Henry I (1165–1235), duke of Brabant, and Maude of Alsace (1163–c. 1210); became 2nd wife of Otto IV of Brunswick (c. 1183–1218), earl of York, count of Ponthieu, duke of Bavaria, and Holy Roman emperor (c. 1198–1214), in 1213 or 1214 (Otto was deposed in 1215); children: none. ❖ When Countess Matilda de Dammartin died (1258), ruled Brabant briefly for that year. ❖ See also *Women in World History.*

MARY OF BURGUNDY (c. 1400–1463). Duchess of Cleves. Born c. 1400; died in 1463; dau. of Margaret of Bavaria (d. 1424) and John the Fearless (1371–1419), duke of Burgundy (r. 1404–1419); sister of Anne Valois (c. 1405–1432), duchess of Bedford, Agnes of Burgundy (d. 1476), Philip the Good, duke of Burgundy (r. 1419–1467), and Margaret of Burgundy (d. 1441); m. Adolphus also known as Adolf I, duke of Cleves; children: John I, duke of Cleves (r. 1448–1481).

MARY OF BURGUNDY (d. 1428). Duchess of Savoy. Died in 1428; dau. of Margaret of Flanders (1350–1405) and Philip the Bold (1342–1404), duke of Burgundy (r. 1363–1404); m. Amadeus VIII, duke of Savoy; children: Louis I, duke of Savoy.

MARY OF BURGUNDY (1457–1482). Duchess of Burgundy, countess of Flanders, and archduchess of Austria. Name variations: Marie of Burgundy; Marie de Bourgogne; Maria van Bourgund; Duchess of Burgundy and Luxemburg; Queen of the Low Countries; (sometimes incorrectly known as Margaret of Burgundy because she has historically been confused with her stepmother Margaret of York). Born in Brussels on Feb 13, 1457; died Mar 27, 1482, at the Prinsenhof in Ghent; dau. of Charles the Bold, the last Valois duke of Burgundy (r. 1467–1477), and his 2nd wife, Isabelle of Bourbon (d. 1465); became 1st wife of Maximilian I of the Habsburgs (1459–1519), archduke of Austria, and Holy Roman emperor (r. 1493–1519), in 1477 (by proxy on April 22, and in person on August 18); children: Philip the Handsome also known as Philip I the Fair (1478–1506), who m. Juana La Loca); Margaret of Austria (1480–1530, duchess of Savoy, regent of the Netherlands); Frederic (b. Sept 1481 and lived only a few months). Maximilian I, who had many illeg. children, also m. Bianca Maria Sforza (1472–1510). ❖ Fought to save her land from France and preserved what was to become the modern country of Belgium; was inaugurated duchess of Burgundy and countess of Flanders (Feb 16, 1477); became archduchess of Austria upon marriage to Maximilian; had she lived, would have become empress of Austria. ❖ See also G.P.R. James, *Mary of Burgundy; or, the Revolt of Ghent* (Routledge, 1903); and *Women in World History.*

MARY OF BUTTERMERE (d. 1837). *See Robinson, Mary.*

MARY OF CLEOPHAS. Saint and Biblical woman. Name variations: ❖ Mary Cleophas; Mary, the wife of Clopas. Sister or close relative of Mary the Virgin; children: possibly James of Jerusalem and Joseph (called the brothers of Jesus in Mark 6.3). ❖ Followed Jesus to Calvary, was present at his burial, and saw him after he had risen. Feast day is April 9.

MARY OF CLEVES (1426–1486). *See Marie of Cleves.*

MARY OF COUCY (c. 1220–c. 1260). *See Mary de Coucy.*

MARY OF EGYPT (d. 430). Saint and Christian ascetic. Name variations: Mary the Egyptian. Born in Egypt; died in 430, in the desert of Palestine, near the river Jordan; often confused with Mary Magdalene. ❖ According to legend, left home at 12, embarking on a dissolute life in Alexandria; at 29, accompanied a group of Libyans who were going to Jerusalem to witness the Exaltations of the Cross; arriving in the Holy City, sought to join the crowd going into the temple, but found herself rooted to the ground; saw a light, telling her that her sinful ways prevented her from entering, followed by a vision of Mary the Virgin; was told to Cross Jordan to find peace; crossed the Jordan as instructed, taking with her 3 loaves of bread; remained in the desert for the next 47 years, eating only roots and herbs and communing with God; was visited in the desert by St. Zosimus to whom she related the story of her life; as he was leaving, requested that he return to her on Holy Thursday of the following year to bring her the Eucharist (the monk kept his promise but found that she had since died, and as he began to dig a grave, a lion appeared and with his paw assisted the monk). Feast day is April 2.

MARY OF EGYPT. *See Maryam the Egyptian (fl. 7th c.).*

MARY OF FRANCE.
See Marie de France (c. 1140–1200).
See Mary Tudor (1496–1533).

MARY OF GUELDERS (d. 1405). Duchess of Juliers. Name variations: Mary of Gueldres. Died in 1405; dau. of Sophia of Malines (d. 1329) and Renaud, also known as Rainald or Reginald II the Black Haired (d. 1343), duke of Guelders (also known as count of Gelderland), count of Zutphen; m. William VI (d. 1393), duke of Juliers.

MARY OF GUELDERS (1433–1463). Queen of Scotland. Name variations: Mary of Gelders; Mary of Gueldres; Mary of Gelderland; Marie von Geldern. Born July 3, 1433, in Holyrood Abbey, Edinburgh, Scotland (some sources cite Guelders, the Netherlands); died Dec 1, 1463, in Scotland; interred in Holy Trinity Church, Edinburgh; dau. of Arnold, duke of Guelders, and Catherine of Cleves (1417–1479); m. James II (1430–1460), king of Scotland (r. 1437–1460), on July 3, 1449; children: James III (1451–1488), king of Scotland (r. 1460–1488); Margaret Stewart (fl. 1460–1520); Alexander Stewart (c. 1454–1485), 1st duke of Albany; David, earl of Moray (died in infancy); David (c. 1454–1456); John (c. 1456–1479), earl of Mar and Garioch; Mary Stewart (c. 1451–1488). ❖ Became a great supporter and patriot of her adopted country, playing an important role in Scotland's continuous wars against English rule; after husband died (1460), maintained the Scottish campaigns against the British as regent of Scotland for young son, James III; a capable strategist and leader, headed the siege of several northern English towns and conquered the town of Berwick; was a prominent political force in Scotland throughout her regency and even beyond, and was rewarded by the Scots' loyalty to her rule; founded the Church of the Holy Trinity in Edinburgh (1462).

MARY OF GUISE (1515–1560). Queen of Scotland. Name variations: Mary of Lorraine; Mary of Guise-Lorraine; Marie of Guise; (Fr.) Mary de Guise, duchess of Longueville. Pronunciation: Geez or Geese. Born Nov 20 (some sources cite 22), 1515, in Castle Bar-le-Duc, Lorraine, in northern France; died in Edinburgh Castle, Scotland, on June 10 or 11, 1560; buried in Rheims, Champagne, France; dau. of Claude I, duke of Guise, and Antoinette of Bourbon (1494–1583); m. Louis II d'Orleans, duke of Longueville, on August 4, 1534; m. James V (1512–1542), king of Scotland (r. 1513–1542), on May 9, 1538; children: (1st marriage) François III also known as Francis III (b. Oct 30, 1535), duke of Longueville; Louis (b. August 4, 1537); (2nd marriage) James Stewart (b. May 22, 1540), 5th duke of Rothesay; Arthur Stewart (b. April 24, 1541), duke of Albany (also referred to in some sources as Robert); Mary Stuart (1542–1587), Queen of Scots. ❖ French-born queen of Scotland who fought to retain the throne for her daughter, Mary Stuart, against Scottish nobles and Protestant reformers; educated at Pont-au-Mousson convent; presented at court of Francis I of France (1531); crowned queen of Scots (Feb 22, 1540); widowed and assumed title queen dowager (Dec 14, 1542); was thrust to the center of a political and religious struggle to control the regency of her child Mary Stuart; appointed head of advisory council to Scottish governor (1544); while at war with Henry VIII of England (1543–48), organized French troops at siege sites and gave a stirring speech before her armies for what was to be one of the final battles of the war; because of a countermove from the English, was forced to remove herself and daughter to the fortified castle of Stirling; managed to arrange a treaty with France that secured the marriage of her daughter

to Francis, the dauphin of France (later Francis II), leaving the English outmaneuvered, not on the battlefield but through diplomacy; made diplomatic visit to France (1550); with political position strengthened, appointed regent of Scotland (April 12, 1554). ❖ See also Rosalind K. Marshall, *Mary of Guise* (Collins, 1977); and *Women in World History*.

MARY OF HABSBURG (1528–1603). *See Marie of Austria.*

MARY OF HANOVER (1849–1904). Hanoverian princess. Born Mary Ernestine Josephine Adolphine Henrietta Theresa Elizabeth Alexandrina on Dec 2, 1849, in Hanover, Lower Saxony, Germany; died June 4, 1904, in Gmunden, Austria; dau. of George V (b. 1819), king of Hanover, and Mary of Saxe-Altenburg (1818–1907).

MARY OF HESSE-CASSEL (1723–1772). English princess royal. Name variations: Mary, Princess of Hesse; Mary Guelph; Mary Hanover. Born Feb 22 (some sources cite Mar 5), 1723, at Leicester House, St. Martin's, London, England; died in Hanau on Jan 14, 1772; dau. of George II (1683–1760), king of Great Britain and Ireland (r. 1727–1760) and Caroline of Ansbach (1683–1737); m. Frederick II, landgrave of Hesse-Cassel or Kassel, on June 28, 1740; children: William (b. 1741); William IX, elector of Hesse (b. 1743); Charles of Hesse-Cassel (1744–1836); Frederick III (1747–1837), landgrave of Hesse-Cassel. ❖ When husband became a Catholic (1754), separated from him and lived with her children at Hanau.

MARY OF HESSE-CASSEL (1796–1880). Grand duchess of Mecklenburg-Strelitz. Born Jan 21, 1796; died Dec 30, 1880; dau. of Frederick III, landgrave of Hesse-Cassel, and Caroline of Nassau-Usingen; m. George, grand duke of Mecklenburg-Strelitz, Aug 12, 1817; children: four, including Frederick (1819–1904), grand duke of Mecklenburg-Strelitz.

MARY OF HESSE-HOMBURG (1785–1846). Princess of Prussia. Born Oct 13, 1785; died April 14, 1846; dau. of Frederick Louis, landgrave of Hesse-Homburg, and Caroline of Hesse-Darmstadt (1746–1821); cousin of Louis II, grand duke of Hesse-Darmstadt; m. William (1783–1851, son of Frederick William II, king of Prussia, and Frederica of Hesse), prince of Prussia, on Jan 12, 1804; children: Frederica (1805–1806); Frederick (b. 1811); Adalbert (b. 1811), admiral in the Prussian navy; Elizabeth Hohenzollern (1815–1885); Waldemar (b. 1817), Prussian major general; Maria of Prussia (1825–1889, who m. Maximilian II, king of Bavaria).

MARY OF HUNGARY (1371–1395). *See Maria of Hungary.*

MARY OF HUNGARY (1505–1558). Queen of Hungary and regent of the Netherlands. Name variations: Marie of Austria or Marie d'Autriche; Maria of Hungary; Maria of Castile; Mary Habsburg or Hapsburg. Born in 1505 in the Netherlands; died in 1558 in the Netherlands; dau. of Philip of Burgundy also known as Philip I the Fair, king of Castile and Léon (r. 1506), and Juana La Loca (1479–1555) of Aragon, queen of Castile; sister of Ferdinand I and Charles V, both Holy Roman emperors, and Catherine (1507–1578), Eleanor of Portugal (1498–1558), and Elisabeth of Habsburg (1501–1526); m. Lajos also known as Louis II (1506–1526), king of Hungary (r. 1516–1526), around 1520; no children. ❖ Served as regent of the Netherlands for 27 years; was reared by aunt, Margaret of Austria, who had taken over the government of the Netherlands for Mary's brother Charles (later Holy Roman Emperor Charles V); at 7, was betrothed to Prince Louis (II) Jagellon, heir to throne of Hungary; at 15, left the Netherlands for Hungary, where she and Louis were married; husband was killed in battle (1526); named regent in the Netherlands for brother Charles V (1531); proved to be an astute choice, for she was a wise, thoughtful ruler, interested in promoting the welfare of her subjects; enjoyed great popularity among her people (1531–58). ❖ See also *Women in World History*.

MARY OF JERUSALEM. Biblical woman. Children: John, also called Mark, possibly one of the writers of the four gospels (Acts 12:12). ❖ A resident of Jerusalem, was the mother of John whose other name was Mark, thought by the 2nd-century Christian writer Papias to be one of the writers of the four gospels; was apparently of some wealth and influence, as her large and well-staffed house became a meeting place for the early Christians of Jerusalem, and it was there that the disciples gathered following the release of the Apostle Peter who had been imprisoned by Herod Antipas.

MARY OF LORRAINE (1515–1560). *See Mary of Guise.*

MARY OF LUXEMBURG (1305–1323). Queen of France. Name variations: Marie of Luxemburg. Born in 1305; died of puerperal fever around 1323 near Bourges, France; eldest dau. of Margaret of Brabant (d. 1311) and Henry VII, Holy Roman emperor (r. 1308–1313); became 2nd wife of Charles IV the Fair (1294–1328), king of France (r. 1322–1328), on Sept 21, 1322.

MARY OF MAGDALA (fl. early 1st c. CE). *See Mary Magdalene.*

MARY OF MECKLENBURG-SCHWERIN (1854–1920). *See Maria of Mecklenburg-Schwerin.*

MARY OF MODENA (1658–1718). Queen of England. Name variations: Mary Beatrice; Mary Beatrice d'Este; Mary Beatrice Eleanora d'Este; duchess of York. Born Mary Beatrice Eleanor on Oct 5 (some sources cite Sept 25), 1658, at the Ducal Palace, Modena, Italy; died of cancer, May 7 or 8, 1718, at Château St. Germain-en-Laye, near Paris, France; interred at the Abbey of Visitation of St. Mary, Chaillot, France; dau. of Alphonso IV or Alfonso IV, duke of Modena, and Laura Martinozzi; became 2nd wife of James (1633–1701), duke of York, later James II, king of England (r. 1685–1688, deposed), on Nov 21, 1673; children: Catherine (1675–1675); James Francis Edward Stuart (1688–1766), duke of Cornwall, known as the Old Pretender; Isabel (1676–1681); Elizabeth (1678–1678); Charlotte (1682–1682); Louise (1692–1712); six others died at birth or in infancy of smallpox. ❖ As a 15-year-old Italian Catholic from the duchy of Modena, was betrothed to James, duke of York (later James II), causing an uproar in England's Parliament and a wave of anti-Catholic hysteria (1671); husband became king (1685) and was highly unpopular, as his brief reign was predominantly concerned with furthering the cause of Catholicism; in 15 years, had 3 children who died in infancy, and many happily assumed her childbearing years and threat of a Catholic heir were over; gave birth to a boy, James Francis Edward Stuart (June 1688), who was destined to be known throughout his years as the Old Pretender because enemies invented and popularized the story that her pregnancy had been a pretense and the boy was smuggled into the royal bed in a warming pan by Jesuits; with baby, preceded husband on his flight to France during the "Glorious Revolution." ❖ See also *Women in World History.*

MARY OF MOLINA (d. 1321). *See Maria de Molina.*

MARY OF MONTPELIER (1181–1213). *See Maria of Montpellier.*

MARY OF MUNSTER (d. 570). *See Ita of Ireland.*

MARY OF NAZARETH (20 BCE–40 CE). *See Mary the Virgin.*

MARY OF OIGNIES (1177–1213). Belgian holy woman. Name variations: Marie d'Oignies; Blessed Mary d'Oignies. Born in 1177 in Nivelles (Brabant), Belgium; died in 1213 in Belgium; married. ❖ Though married at 14, felt so strongly that she had a religious vocation that she persuaded husband to abstain from sexual intimacy; with husband, worked with patients at a leper colony; began to live as a Beguine, part of an informal order of women who dedicated themselves to public service; had mystical visions which she revealed and interpreted to people while preaching on the streets of Belgian cities; traveled with reformer preacher Jacques de Vitry for some time and helped him write his sermons; separating permanently from husband, joined the St. Nicholas convent at Oignies (c. 1207); revered after death as a popular saint, though she was never canonized. Feast day is June 23.

MARY OF ORANGE (1631–1660). Princess of Orange and princess royal. Name variations: Mary Stuart; Mary Henrietta. Named princess royal around 1642. Born Nov 4, 1631, at St. James's Palace, in London, England; died of smallpox on Dec 24, 1660, at Whitehall, London; interred at Westminster Abbey, London; dau. of Henrietta Maria (1609–1669) and Charles I (1600–1649), king of England (r. 1625–1649); m. William II (1625–1650), prince of Orange (r. 1647–1650), May 2, 1648; children: William III (1650–1702), prince of Orange (r. 1672–1702), king of England (r. 1689–1702).

MARY OF PORTUGAL (1527–1545). Portuguese princess. Name variations: Maria of Portugal; Mary Avis. Born Oct 15, 1527, in Coimbra; died four days after giving birth on July 12, 1545, in Valladolid, Castile and Leon, Spain; dau. of João III or John III the Pious, king of Portugal (r. 1521–1557), and Catherine (1507–1578, dau. of Philip I of Spain); m. Philip II (1527–1598), king of Spain (r. 1556–1598), and king of Portugal as Philip I (r. 1580–1598), on Nov 12, 1543; children: Charles (1545–1568).

MARY OF ST. POL (1304–1377). *See Marie de St. Pol.*

MARY OF SAXE-ALTENBURG (1818–1907). Queen of Hanover. Name variations: Marie Alexandrina. Born Alexandrina Mary Wilhelmina Katherine Charlotte Theresa Henrietta Louise Pauline Elizabeth Fredericka Georgina on April 14, 1818, in Hildburghausen,

Germany; died Jan 9, 1907, in Gmunden, Austria; dau. of Joseph, duke of Saxe-Altenburg, and Amelia of Wurttemberg (1799–1848); sister of Alexandra of Saxe-Altenburg (1838–1911); m. George V, king of Hanover, on Feb 18, 1843; children: Ernest Augustus, 3rd duke of Cumberland and Teviotdale (1845–1923); Fredericka of Hanover (1848–1926); Mary of Hanover (1849–1904).

MARY OF SAXE-COBURG (1875–1938). *See Marie of Rumania.*

MARY OF TECK (1867–1953). Queen of England. Name variations: Queen Mary; May of Teck; Victoria Mary of Teck; duchess of York; princess of Wales. Born Victoria Mary Augusta Louise Olga Pauline Claudine Agnes on May 26, 1867, in Kensington Palace, London, England; died Mar 24, 1953, at Marlborough House, London; dau. of Francis, duke of Teck, and Mary Adelaide (1833–1897); betrothed to Albert Saxe-Coburg, duke of Clarence and Avondale (son of Edward VII and Alexandra of Denmark), in 1891; m. George, duke of York, later George V, king of England (r. 1910–1936), on July 6, 1893; children: Edward VIII (1894–1972), duke of Windsor; Albert, later George VI (1895–1952), king of England (r. 1936–1952); Mary (1897–1965), princess royal; Henry Windsor (1900–1974), 1st duke of Gloucester; George (1902–1942), 1st duke of Kent; John Windsor (1905–1919). ❖ Beloved queen of early 20th-century England and grandmother of Elizabeth II; betrothed to duke of Clarence, the future king of England (1891), but he died (1892); married duke of York (1893); gave birth to 1st child (1894); became princess of Wales (1901); crowned queen of England (1911); became queen mother and saw son abdicate throne (1936); her devotion to duty, loyalty to the monarchy, and genuine courtesy to, and interest in, her subjects were legendary; survived the crises of 2 world wars, unexpected deaths in the family, and an unprecedented abdication. ❖ See also James Pope-Hennessy, *Queen Mary 1867–1953* (Knopf, 1960); and *Women in World History.*

MARY OF THE CROSS, Mother (1842–1909). *See MacKillop, Mary Helen.*

MARY OF THE CROSS, Sister (1792–1879). *See Jugan, Jeanne.*

MARY OF THE INCARNATION.
See Acarie, Barbe (1566–1618).
See Marie de l'Incarnation (1599–1672).

MARY OF WURTTEMBERG (1799–1860). Duchess of Saxe-Coburg-Gotha. Name variations: Marie of Wurttemberg; Mary von Württemberg. Born Sept 17, 1799, in Coburg, Bavaria, Germany; died Sept 24, 1860, in Gotha, Thuringia, Germany; dau. of Alexander, duke of Wurttemberg, and Antoinette Saxe-Coburg (1779–1824); cousin of Queen Victoria; became 2nd wife of Ernest I (1784–1844), duke of Saxe-Coburg-Gotha, Dec 23, 1832. ❖ Ernest I's 1st wife was Louise of Saxe-Gotha-Altenburg (1800–1831).

MARY PLANTAGENET (1278–1332). *See Mary.*

MARY PLANTAGENET (1467–1482). English princess. Born in Aug 1467 in Windsor, Berkshire, England; died May 23, 1482, in Greenwich, London; buried in St. George's Chapel, Windsor; dau. of Edward IV (1442–1483), king of England (r. 1461–1470, 1471–1483), and Elizabeth Woodville (1437–1492).

MARY ROMANOV (1853–1920). *See Marie Alexandrovna.*

MARY STEWART.
See Stewart, Mary (c. 1451–c. 1488).
See Stewart, Mary (d. 1458).
See Mary Stuart (1542–1587).
See Mary II (1662–1694).

MARY STEWART, countess of Buchan (d. 1465). *See Stewart, Mary.*

MARY STUART (1542–1587). Queen of Scots. Name variations: Mary, Queen of Scots; Mary Stewart; dauphine of France. Born Dec 8, 1542, at Linlithgow, Lothian, Scotland; beheaded by order of Elizabeth I for treason at Fotheringhay Castle, Northamptonshire, England, Feb 8, 1587; dau. of James V, king of Scotland (r. 1513–1542), and Mary of Guise (1515–1560); m. Francis, dauphin of France, later Francis II, king of France (r. 1559–1560), April 24, 1558; m. Henry Stuart, duke of Albany, Lord Darnley, July 29, 1565; m. James Hepburn, 4th earl of Bothwell, May 15, 1567; children: (2nd m.) James (1566–1625), king of Scotland as James VI (r. 1567–1625) and king of England as James I (r. 1603–1625). ❖ Queen who lived in the turbulent period of the Counter-reformation and became caught up in scandals which ended her reign and resulted in her execution by Elizabeth I; proclaimed queen of

Scotland 6 days after her birth, with the death of her father James V; at age 5, was betrothed to the dauphin of France, Francis, and sent to France to be brought up in the French court; was queen of France during the brief reign of husband Francis II (1559–60); following death of Francis, went back to Scotland to claim birthright; married Henry Stuart, Lord Darnley (1565); son James born (1566); under bizarre circumstances, husband Darnley strangled (Feb 1567); within months of murder, married the earl of Bothwell, who was widely believed to have been the perpetrator; because these actions provoked a widespread rebellion, had to abdicate the Scottish throne in favor of her son and flee to England (1567); remained in England for almost 20 years, becoming the focus of many Catholic plots against the life of Queen Elizabeth I; though her degree of participation in plots is still debated by historians, was ordered to stand trial and executed for treason, since Elizabeth eventually became convinced of Mary's duplicity (1587). ❖ See also Ian B. Cowan, *The Enigma of Mary Stuart* (Gollancz, 1971); Gordon Donaldson, *Mary Queen of Scots* (English Universities Press, 1974); Antonia Fraser, *Mary Queen of Scots* (1969); and *Women in World History*.

MARY STUART.
    See Mary of Orange (1631–1660).
    See Mary II (1662–1694).

MARY THE CATHOLIC (1516–1558). *See Mary I.*

MARY THE EGYPTIAN.
    See Mary of Egypt (d. 430).
    See Maryam the Egyptian (fl. 7th c.).

MARY THE JEWESS. *See also Miriam the Prophet.*

MARY THE JEWESS (fl. 1st, 2nd or 3rd c.). Hebrew alchemist. Name variations: Maria the Jewess; Miriam the Jewess; Maria Prophetissa; Maria of Alexandria; Miriam the Prophet; Miriam the Prophetess. Born in Alexandria, Egypt, in the 1st, 2nd, or 3rd century CE. ❖ A shadowy historical figure, is often erroneously identified as Miriam the Prophet, the sister of Moses; as an alchemist, left behind enough fragments of her writings to establish for herself a revered place in scientific antiquity; is considered one of the founders of alchemy, and in a 17th-century text is listed as one of the 12 sages of alchemy. ❖ See also *Women in World History*.

MARY THE VIRGIN (20 BCE–40 CE). Biblican woman. Name variations: Maria; Miriam; Mary of Nazareth; the Virgin Mary. Born approximately 20 BCE in Roman Palestine; died about 40 CE; dau. of Anne and Joachim; m. Joseph (a carpenter of Nazareth); children: Jesus of Nazareth (c. 6 BCE/4 CE–c. 27/37 CE). James of Jerusalem and Joseph (called the brothers of Jesus in Mark 6.3), might be the sons of Joseph from a previous marriage, while some contend they were actually sons of another Mary, possibly Mary of Cleophas, the sister of the Virgin. ❖ Mother of Jesus of Nazareth and the most important Christian saint who is thought by some to be the most perfect of women as well as held to be an intercessor between God and mortals and dispenser of all graces; though relatively inactive in the New Testament narrative, her centrality in Western religious and cultural history significantly outstrips her role in the Gospel stories. From the Gospels we learn that Mary, a young Jewish woman, lived in Nazareth, a town in Galilee; was betrothed to a carpenter named Joseph; before the wedding took place, was visited by an angel of the Lord who told her she had been chosen to bear the son of the Most High (the Annunciation); when the time of delivery was near, traveled with husband to Bethlehem in order to register for the census; unable to find a place in the inn, slept in the stable; there, in fulfillment of a prophecy in Isaiah 7.14, was delivered of a child; wrapped him in swaddling clothes and used a manger for his crib. ❖ See also Sally Cunneen, *In Search of Mary* (1996); Maria Warner, *Alone of Her Sex: The Myth and the Cult of the Virgin Mary* (Knopf, 1976); Hilda Graef, *Mary: A History of Doctrine and Devotion* (1963–65); Mary Clayton, *The Cult of the Virgin Mary in Anglo-Saxon England* (Cambridge U. Press, 1990); and *Women in World History*.

MARY TRASTAMARA.
    See Maria of Castile (1401–1458).
    See Maria of Aragon (1403–1445).
    See Maria of Castile (1482–1517).

MARY TUDOR (1496–1533). Queen of France. Name variations: Mary of France; Duchess of Suffolk. Born Mary Tudor on Mar 18, 1496, in Richmond-upon-Thames, Surrey, England; died June 26, 1533, in Westhorpe, Suffolk; buried at Bury St. Edmunds, Suffolk; dau. of Henry VII, king of England (r. 1485–1509), and Elizabeth of York

(1466–1503); sister of Henry VIII, king of England (r. 1509–1547); m. Louis XII (1462–1515), king of France (r. 1498–1515), Oct 9, 1514 (died Jan 1515); m. Charles Brandon (1484–1545), 1st duke of Suffolk (r. 1514–1545), May 13, 1515; children: Henry Brandon (1516–1534), earl of Lincoln; Frances Brandon (1517–1559, mother of Lady Jane Grey); Eleanor Brandon (c. 1520–1547). Charles Brandon was also m. to Anne Browne (d. 1511), Margaret Neville (b. 1466), and Catharine Bertie (1519–1580). ❖ Sister of Tudor king Henry VIII, married Louis XII, king of France (1514); widowed (1515); wed in secret Charles Brandon, duke of Suffolk, which raised the ire of brother, now king of England (1515); joined brother and Francis I of France near Calais in a place referred to as the Field of the Cloth of Gold for a lavish ceremonial alliance between the two longtime enemy nations (1520). ❖ See also *Women in World History*.

MARY TUDOR (1516–1558). *See Mary I.*

MARY TUDOR (1673–1726). Countess of Derwentwater. Born in 1673; died in 1726; illeg. dau. of Moll Davies and Charles II (1630–1685), king of England (r. 1661–1685); m. Edward Radclyffe, 2nd earl of Derwentwater (1655–1705); m. Henry Graham of Levens (d. 1707); m. James Rooke.

MARZIA (fl. 1357). Italian noblewoman and military leader. Name variations: Marcia. Fl. in 1357 in Italy; m. Francesco Ordelaffi, lord of Forli; children: son and daughter. ❖ Became one of husband's most trusted allies in his struggle against papal rule; with about 400 troops, held the town of Cesena against papal soldiers' attacks for several months, despite the siege laid on the town. ❖ See also *Women in World History*.

MARZOUK, Zahia (1906–1988). Egyptian social worker. Born 1906; died 1988; had two sisters; studied in London; studied in America at Harvard Graduate School of Education, 1933–35; married. ❖ One of her nation's 1st trained social workers, was the 1st Egyptian woman to study in US; opened Egypt's 1st schools of social work in Alexandria and Cairo (1935 and 1936), which led to the creation of Egypt's Ministry of Social Affairs (1938); worked as a psychiatric social worker at Ministry of Education, the only woman there; convened a formal conference on population issues which enjoyed the sponsorship of the Egyptian Medical Association (Muslim conservatives disapproved of her presence at the conference, and when she began her lecture she was pelted with tomatoes and eggs); founded the Alexandria Family Planning Association, the 1st association of its kind in Egypt. ❖ See also *Women in World History*.

MASAKAYAN, Liz (1964—). American volleyball player. Born Dec 31, 1964, in Santa Monica, CA. ❖ Was 2-time NCAA All-American; was a member of Olympic volleyball team at Seoul (1988); won bronze medal at World championships (1999). Won Broderick Award (1984); inducted into UCLA Hall of Fame. ❖ See also Christina Lessa, *Women Who Win* (Universe, 1998).

MASAKO (1963—). Japanese crown princess. Born Masako Owada, Dec 9, 1963, in Tokyo, Japan; dau. of a diplomat; graduate of Harvard University, 1985; attended University of Tokyo and Balliol College at Oxford University; m. Crown Prince Naruhito (son of Emperor Akihoto), June 9, 1993; children: daughter Princess Aiko (b. Dec 1, 2001). ❖ The second commoner married into the Japanese imperial household, grew up in Moscow, New York and Tokyo because of her father's diplomatic postings; began career in Japan's Ministry of Foreign Affairs (1987); with the constant pressure of producing an heir, suffered from a miscarriage (Dec 1999) which left her depressed; since her marriage, has maintained a low profile.

MASAKO HOJO (1157–1225). *See Hōjo Masako.*

MASARYK, Alice Garrigue (1879–1966). Czech sociologist and social activist. Name variations: Alice Garrigue Masaryková. Born in Vienna, Austria, May 3, 1879; died in Chicago, IL, Nov 29, 1966; eldest child of Thomas Garrigue Masaryk (1850–1937), president of the Czechoslovak Republic (1918–35), and Charlotte Garrigue Masaryk (1850–1923); sister of Herbert and Jan Masaryk (1886–1948, a diplomat and Czech foreign minister), and Olga Garrigue Masaryk; Charles University (Prague), doctoral degree in philosophy, 1903; never married. ❖ Eminent sociologist and social activist, made 1st trip to US (1904), where she worked at University of Chicago Social Settlement (UCSS), becoming acquainted with a number of leading social reformers, including Jane Addams and UCSS director Mary McDowell; returning to Prague (1905), taught in girls' schools; during WWI, because of father's importance in Czech nationalist movement, was incarcerated in Vienna for 8 months, until a massive campaign from abroad secured her release; after father took office as president of Czechoslovak Republic (1918), often substituted for ailing mother as first lady, retaining this role after mother's death (1923) and until father's retirement (1935); appointed president of Czechoslovak Red Cross (1919), a post in which she would remain for fully 2 decades; became a member of the Executive Committee of International Red Cross (1930); during 1920s, was one of the best-known women in the world in the fields of sociology and social welfare and presided over the 1st International Conference of Social Work (1928). ❖ See also Zbynek Zeman, *The Masaryks: The Making of Czechoslovakia* (Tauris, 1990); and *Women in World History.*

MASARYK, Charlotte Garrigue (1850–1923). First lady of Czechoslovakia. Name variations: Charlotta Garrigue Masaryková; "Charlie" Garrigue. Born in Brooklyn, NY, Nov 20, 1850; died at her country house at Lány, near Prague, on May 13, 1923; dau. of Rudolph Garrigue and Charlotte Lydia (Whiting) Garrigue; had 10 siblings; m. Thomas Garrigue Masaryk (1850–1937), president of Czechoslovak Republic (1918–35); children: daughters, Alice Garrigue Masaryk (1879–1966), Eleanora (died shortly after her birth in 1889), and Olga Garrigue Masaryk; sons Herbert Garrigue Masaryk and Jan Masaryk (1886–1948, diplomat and Czech foreign minister). ❖ American-born wife of Czech nationalist, who played an active role in Czech public life during the decades before 1914, encouraging women to fully utilize their talents and engage in political activity; wed the progressive Thomas Masaryk who replaced his middle name Vlastimil with her maiden name (1878); though she often remained behind the scenes in husband's career, was an enthusiastic advocate of women's rights; joined the Social Democratic Party—rather than husband's Realist Party—because of its ongoing and militant support of the rights of workers, as well as its feminist platform (1905); after husband was elected president of Czechoslovakia (1918), spent the next years in seclusion, because her health had been shattered both physically and psychologically during WWI (husband had been sentenced to death in absentia, daughter Alice had been imprisoned for 8 months, son Herbert had died from typhus while working in a refugee camp, and son Jan had been captured while attempting to flee abroad and drafted into the Imperial and Royal Austrian Army as punishment). ❖ See also Zbynek Zeman, *The Masaryks: The Making of Czechoslovakia* (Tauris, 1990); Mila Veger, *Czechoslovakia's American First Lady* (trans. by Brackett Lewis, Masaryk Institute, 1939); and *Women in World History.*

MASHAM, Abigail (1670–1734). English confidante of Queen Anne. Name variations: Baroness Masham of Otes. Born Abigail Hill in 1670; died Dec 6, 1734; dau. of Francis Hill, wealthy merchant of London; married Samuel Masham, a page at Court, in 1707. ❖ Was given a position in Queen Anne's household at Sarah Churchill's request; proved attentive and eager to please; when Sarah's relationship with Anne began deteriorating, supplanted Sarah as royal favorite; became involved in the intrigues of Court, especially those in favor of the Tories and the exiled House of Stuart. ❖ See also *Women in World History.*

MASHAM, Damaris (1658–1708). English scholar. Name variations: Lady Masham; Damaris Cudworth; Philoclea. Born Damaris Cudworth in England on Jan 18, 1658; died April 20, 1708; buried in Bath Abbey; dau. of Ralph Cudworth (1617–1688, a philosopher) and Damaris (Cradock) Cudworth; studied under her father and John Locke; m. Sir Francis Masham, 3rd baronet, of Oates (or Otes), Essex, in 1685; children: Francis Cudworth Masham (b. 1686). ❖ Wrote over 40 letters to the philosopher John Locke who often addressed her as Philoclea; also corresponded, almost exclusively on the topic of philosophy, with Gottfried Wilhelm Leibniz; wrote *A Discourse Concerning the Love of God* (1690), *Occasional Thoughts in Reference to a Virtuous or Christian Life* (1705), an essay on Locke for the *Great Historical Dictionary*, and a biography of Locke in *La Bibliotheque Universelle* (1704). ❖ See also *Women in World History.*

MASHIN, Draga (1867–1903). *See Draga.*

MASINA, Giulietta (1920–1994). Italian actress. Born Giulia Anna Masina, Feb 22, 1920, in San Giorgio di Piano, Italy; died of lung cancer, Mar 23, 1994, in Rome; dau. of Gaetano Masina (1st violinist with Milan's Teatro Scala); grew up under tutelage of her aunt Giulia Pasqualin; m. Federico Fellini (director), 1943; children: 1 son (b. 1945, died in infancy). ❖ Award-winning actress who earned international recognition for her portrayal of Gelsomina in *La Strada*, 1st appeared as an actress while at university in Rome, performing with the school's drama society and attracting professional attention with her performance in a radio play written by Federico Fellini (1942); married Fellini (1943); won Best

Supporting Actress award at Venice Film Festival for her work in *Senza Pietà* (*Without Pity*, 1948), and Best Actress for her performance in Fellini's *Le Notti di Cabiria* (*The Nights of Cabiria*), at the Cannes Film Festival (1956); became an icon of Italian tv and cinema (1970s), though her only recognition outside her own country was mainly due to her work with Fellini; films include *Paisà/Paisan* (1946), *Luci del Varietà* (*Variety Lights*, 1951), *Persiane chiuse* (1951), *Europa 51* (1952), *Lo Sceicco Bianco* (*The White Sheik*, 1952), *Donne proibite* (1953), *Il Bidone* (*The Swindle*, 1955), *Fortunella* (1958), *Nella Città l'Inferno* (1958), *La Grande Vie* (1960), *Landru* (1972), *Giulietta degli Spiriti* (*Juliet of the Spirits*, 1965), *Non Stuzzicate la Zanzara* (1967), *The Madwoman of Chaillot* (1969), *Frau Holle* (1985), *Ginger e Fred* (*Ginger and Fred*, 1986) and *Aujourd'hui Peut-Etre* (1991). ❖ See also *Women in World History.*

MAŠIOTENE, Ona (1883–1949). Lithuanian feminist and nationalist. Name variations: Ona Masiotene. Born Ona Brazauskaité in Slavenae, Lithuania, 1883; died 1949; attended the Advanced School of Moscow. ❖ Attended the Advanced School of Moscow and developed an interest in the feminist movements of Western Europe; upon return to Vilnius (1905), founded Alliance of Lithuanian Women; subsequently represented the Alliance at Russian Women's National Congress and remained active in the women's movement until outbreak of WWI (1914); founded Lithuanian Women's Freedom Association (1917), which campaigned for the independence of Lithuania; founded and became president of Council of Lithuanian Women (1929), and wrote a history of the role of Lithuanian women in politics and nationalist movements, *Moteru politnis ir valstybiniai tautiskas darbas*, the last volume of which was published in 1937.

MASKELL, Virginia (1936–1968). English actress. Born Feb 27, 1936, in Shepherd's Bush, London, England; died Jan 25, 1968, by suicide, in Stoke, Mandeville, England; m. Geoffrey Shakerley; children: 2 sons. ❖ Films include *Virgin Island, The Man Upstairs, Jet Storm, Suspect, Doctor in Love, Only Two Can Play* and *Interlude.*

MASKOVA, Hana (1949–1972). Czech figure skater. Name variations: Hana Masková. Born Sept 26, 1949, in Prague, Czechoslovakia; killed in auto accident near Vouvray, France, Mar 31, 1972. ❖ Won a bronze medal at Grenoble Olympics (1968) and a gold medal at European championships (1968).

MASLAKOVA-ZHARKOVA, Lyudmila (1952—). Soviet runner. Born July 26, 1952, in USSR. ❖ Won a bronze medal in Mexico City Olympics (1968), bronze medal in Montreal Olympics (1976), and silver medal in Moscow Olympics (1980), all for 4x100-meter relay.

MASLOVA, Nesta (c. 1912–1995). *See Toumine, Nesta.*

MASLOW, Sophie (1911—). American modern dancer and choreographer. Born Mar 22, 1911, in New York, NY. ❖ Joined Martha Graham's company (1931), where she created numerous roles for 12 years in, among others, *Tragic Patterns* (1933), *American Lyric* (1937), *Letter to the World* (1940) and *Deaths and Entrances* (1943), in which she danced with Graham and Jane Dudley as one of the Brontë sisters; choreographed numerous works for New Dance League in NY, including *Prelude to a May Song* (1935) and *Women of Spain* (1937); formed dance trio with Jane Dudley and William Bales and continued to create works for this group— as well as for its outgrowth New Dance Group—for another 12 years; staged many opera works, including *Three Wishes for Jamie* (1956) and *The Machinal* (1960) for New York City Opera; served as president of New Dance Group. Works of choreography include *Themes for a Slavic People* (1934), *Prelude to a May First Song* (1935), *Ragged Hungry Blues* (1937), *Runaway Rag* (1937), *Melancholia* (1941), *Dust Bowl Ballads* (1941), *Folksay* (1942), *Festival* (1949), *The Village I Knew* (1950), *Neither Rest nor Harbor* (1968) and *Ladino Suite* (1969).

MASNADA, Florence (1968—). French Alpine skier. Born Dec 16, 1968, in Vizille, France. ❖ Won a bronze medal for the combined at Albertville Olympics (1992); won the bronze medal for the downhill at Nagano Olympics (1998); won a bronze medal for combined at World championships (1999).

MASON, Alice Trumbull (1904–1971). American artist. Name variations: Alice Trumbull; Alice Mason. Born 1904 in Litchfield, Connecticut; died in 1971 in New York, NY; attended National Academy of Design (1924–28); studied with Arshile Gorky at the Grand Central Art Galleries; studied at Atelier 17 (1944–47); m. Warwood Mason (ship's captain), 1928 (one source cites 1930); children: 1 son (died 1958); Emily Mason Kahn (artist). ❖ Important abstract painter in the movement to introduce European-centered abstract art into the canon of serious American painting, began to receive recognition only after her death; started painting in earnest (1928) after a trip through Greece and Italy, where she saw the links between the flat color fields of modern European abstract art and the formal structures of classical Byzantine art; became a founding member of the American Abstract Artists group (1936); held a number of executive positions within the organization, including president, and remained an active member until 1963; also belonged to Federation of Modern Painters and Sculptors, and to 14 Painters/Printmakers group; held 1st solo show (1942), at Museum of Living Art. Two years after her death, the 1st retrospective of her work was held at the Whitney Museum of American Art. ❖ See also *Alice Trumbull Mason: Etchings and Woodcuts* (Taplinger, 1985); and *Women in World History*.

MASON, Ann (c. 1898–1948). American stage actress. Born c. 1898 in VA; died Feb 6, 1948, in NYC. ❖ Plays include *The Last Warning, The Acquittal, Fly Away Home* and *John Loves Mary*.

MASON, Biddy (1818–1891). African-American philanthropist and entrepreneur. Name variations: Bridget Mason. Born into slavery Aug 15, 1818, in Georgia or Mississippi; died Jan 15, 1891, in Los Angeles, CA; children: Ellen Mason Owens; Ann Mason; Harriet Mason. ❖ At birth, was the property of Mississippi plantation owners, Robert and Rebecca Crosby Smith; became a well-regarded midwife; at 20, became a mother herself with the 1st of 3 daughters (Robert Smith may have been the father); when Robert Smith converted to the Mormon faith and decided to move to the Utah Territory (1847), traveled the 2,000 miles from Mississippi on foot; when Smith moved to California (unaware it prohibited slavery), was freed by the court along with other members of her family; quickly gained renown as an excellent midwife, assisting at hundreds of births of African-Americans, whites and Native Americans of all social classes; after 10 years, bought her own home on Spring Street, one of the 1st African-American women to own property in Los Angeles; became well known in Los Angeles for her relief aid to people of all colors, and visited the city jails frequently; with Charles Owens, hosted a meeting at her home of what became the founding congregation of the First African Methodist Episcopal Church of Los Angeles (1872); her homestead has been preserved as a historical site. ❖ See also *Women in World History*.

MASON, Bobbie Ann (1940—). American novelist and short-story writer. Born May 1, 1940, in Mayfield, KY; dau. of Wilburn A. (dairy farmer) and Christianna (Lee) Mason; University of Kentucky, BA, 1962; State University of New York at Binghamton, MA, 1966; University of Connecticut, PhD, 1972; m. Roger B. Rawlings (writer), 1969. ❖ Works include *Shiloh and Other Stories* (1982), *In Country* (1985), which was filmed, *Spence and Lila* (1988), *Love Life: Stories* (1989), *Feather Crowns: A Novel* (1993), and *Zigzagging Down a Wild Trail: Stories* (2001). Won PEN/Hemingway Award for *Shiloh and Other Stories*.

MASON, Christine (1956—). See Larson-Mason, Christine.

MASON, Elizabeth (d. 1712). English murderer. Born at Melton Mowbray, Leicestershire, England; hanged at Tyburn, June 18, 1712. ❖ Lived in London with godmother Jane Scoles and a Mrs. Cholwell; thinking to inherit godmother's estate, poisoned Scoles with arsenic (Easter-week, 1712), but failed in 2 attempts to kill Cholwell; arrested for death of Scoles, to which she confessed on April 30; sentenced to death at her trial (1712).

MASON, Lisa (1982—). English gymnast. Born Feb 26, 1982, in Milton Keynes, England. ❖ Won Camberley International (1996), Coupe Mosane (1997); won GBR championships (1997, 1998); won a gold medal for vault at Commonwealth Games (1998).

MASON, Lucy Randolph (1882–1959). American labor activist and social reformer. Born Lucy Randolph Mason at "Clarens" on Seminary Hill near Alexandria, VA, July 26, 1882; died in Atlanta, GA, May 6, 1959; dau. of Landon Randolph Mason (1841–1923, Episcopal minister) and Lucy (Ambler) Mason (1848–1918; sister of Anna, Ida, John, Landon and Randolph Mason; never married. ❖ Drawn to the feminist movement, became the industrial secretary of Richmond's Young Women's Christian Association (YWCA) 1914, the 1st woman to be appointed to such a position in any Southern state; used her new post to educate working women and carry on lobbying activities for legislation that would bring about major reforms of women's working conditions, including an 8-hour day and restriction of night work; joined Union Label League, which urged consumers to purchase only union-made products; came to attention of Samuel Gompers, head of American

Federation of Labor (AFL), and was named Virginia chair of the Committee on Women in Industry of the wartime National Advisory Committee on Labor (1917); began working on behalf of National Consumers' League (NCL) as director of the fledgling Southern Council on Women and Children in Industry (1931); wrote pamphlet *Standards for Workers in Southern Industry* that would prove to be of considerable influence; moved to NY City to succeed Florence Kelley as NCL general secretary (1932); began working for Congress of Industrial Organizations (CIO, 1937); for 16 years, worked as public-relations officer for CIO, striving to change Southern attitudes toward labor unions; playing a significant role in the slow but steady growth of Southern liberalism, was involved in the work of such organizations as the Southern Policy Committee, Southern Conference for Human Welfare, and Southern Regional Council. ❖ See also John A. Salmond, *Miss Lucy of the CIO: The Life and Times of Lucy Randolph Mason, 1882–1959* (U. of Georgia Press, 1988); and *Women in World History*.

MASON, Marge (1918–1974). American golfer. Born Jan 17, 1918, in Paterson, NJ; died Nov 5, 1974, in Teaneck, NJ. ❖ Won 6 New Jersey state titles and 14 Garden State titles; won the Metropolitan (1960); won USGA Women's Senior championship (1967).

MASON, Marsha (1942—). American actress. Born April 3, 1942, in St. Louis, Missouri; m. Gary Campbell, 1965 (div. 1970); m. Neil Simon, 1973 (div. 1981). ❖ Began career on stage; had regular role on "Love of Life" (1971–72); won an Oscar nomination for *Cinderella Liberty* (1973); met Neil Simon while rehearsing play *The Good Doctor* and starred on film in his *Chapter Two* (1979), a semi-autobiographical account of their courtship; also starred in *The Goodbye Girl* (1977), *The Cheap Detective* (1978), *Only When I Laugh* (1981) and *Max Dugan Returns* (1983).

MASON, Monica (1941—). South African ballet dancer. Born Sept 6, 1941, Johannesburg, South Africa; married and divorced. ❖ Trained early on in Johannesburg, with Ruth Ingelstone, Reina Berman, and Frank Staff; danced in Staff's company as adolescent; moved to England to train at Royal Ballet and soon joined its professional company (1958), performing in both classical repertory and contemporary works; became principal (1967); created roles for Kenneth MacMillan's *The Rite of Spring* (1962), *Manon* (1974), *The Four Seasons* (1975), and *Rituals* (1975), among others; received acclaim for performances in works by Jerome Robbins' *Dances at a Gathering* and George Balanchine's *Ballet Imperial* and *Serenade*; became head of the Royal Ballet (Dec 2002).

MASON, Pamela (1918–1996). English actress, author and talk-show host. Name variations: Pamela Kellino. Born Pamela Ostrer, Mar 10, 1918, in Westgate-on-Sea, Kent, England; died June 29, 1996, in Beverly Hills, CA; dau. of Isidore Ostrer (head of family that controlled Gaumont British studios); m. Roy Kellino (director, producer and cinematographer, div. 1940); m. James Mason (actor), 1941 (div. 1964); children: Morgan and Portland Mason Schuyler (1948–2004, actress and writer). ❖ Under Pamela Kellino, appeared on Broadway with James Mason in *Bathsheba* (1947); on tv, appeared on "The James Mason Show" (1956) and had 2 talk shows of her own: "The Pamela Mason Show" (1965) and "The Weaker(?) Sex" (1968).

MASON, Shirley (1900–1979). American stage and screen actress. Name variations: Leonie Flugrath. Born Leonie Flugrath, June 6, 1900, in Brooklyn, NY; died July 27, 1979, in Los Angeles, CA; sister of Viola Dana (actress) and Edna Flugrath (actress); m. Bernard J. Durning (died 1923); m. Sidney Lanfield (director). ❖ Made film debut in *At the Threshold of Life* (1911); appeared in over 90 films, including *The Seven Deadly Sins, Treasure Island, The Talker, The Awakening of Ruth* (title role), *Lord Jim, Sweet Rosie O'Grady, Vanity Fair* and *So This is Paris*.

MASON-BROWN, Michele (1939—). Australian track-and-field athlete. Name variations: Michele Mason; Michele Brown. Born July 3, 1939, in NSW, Australia. ❖ At Tokyo Olympics, won a silver medal in the high jump (1964); became the 2nd woman in the world to clear 6 feet when she set a Commonwealth record.

MASOTTA, Paula Karina (1972—). Argentinean field-hockey player. Born June 15, 1972, in Argentina. ❖ Won a team silver medal at Sydney Olympics (2000).

MASSARI, Lea (1933—). Italian screen actress. Name variations: Léa Massari. Born Anna Maria Massatani, June 30, 1933, in Rome, Italy. ❖ Starred in such French and Italian films as *Proibito, Auferstehung, Il colosso di rodi, Una vita difficile, Le quattro giornate di Napoli, Llanto por*

un bandido, L'Insoumis, Le Soldatesse, Il giardino delle delizie, Céleste, Le silencieux, Le fils, Violette & François, La flambeuse, Viagio d'amore and most memorably as Anna in Antonioni's *L'Avventura* (1960) and Clara Chevalier in Louis Malle's *Murmur of the Heart* (1971); on tv, starred in "Anna Karenina" (1974), among others.

MASSARY, Fritzi (1882–1969). Austrian-born actress and operetta star. Born Friederika Massaryk (or Massarik), Mar 21, 1882, in Vienna, Austria; died Jan 30, 1969, in Beverly Hills, CA; dau. of Leopold Massaryk and Hermine (Herzfeld) Massaryk; m. Max Pallenberg (comic actor, died in air crash 1934); children: Liesl Frank (1903–1979, married to author Bruno Frank). ❖ Made stage debut in Vienna in a revue, then appeared in the title role of Leo Fall's operetta *The Empress*, followed by title roles in *Madame Pompadour, The Gypsy Princess, The Rose of Stamboul*, and *The Spanish Nightingale*; because of her husband's Jewish heritage was forced to flee Germany (1933); made London debut in *Operette* (1938); retired (1938).

MASSEE, May (1881–1966). American editor. Born May 1, 1881, in Chicago, IL; died Dec 24, 1966, at home in New York City; dau. of Francis Spink Massee and Charlotte Maria (Bull) Massee; attended state normal school in Milwaukee; enrolled at Wisconsin Library School in Madison; attended Armour Institute in Chicago for 2 years; never married. ❖ Editor and children's literature specialist who was instrumental in establishing high critical standards for children's books; became editor of *The Booklist* (1913); sought out by Doubleday, created the country's 2nd children's book publishing department (1919), remaining there until 1933; founded Viking Press' children's book department (1933), where she served as editor and director for 27 years; willing to take risks, published some of the 1st children's books with minority protagonists; trans. and published German author Eric Kästner's *Emil and the Detectives,* the success of which led other publishers to seek children's books by foreign authors; edited 10 children's books that won Newbery Medals and 4 that won Caldecott Medals. ❖ See also *Women in World History.*

MASSEN, Osa (1916–2006). Danish-born actress. Name variations: Stephanie Paull. Born Aase Madsen, Jan 13, 1916, in Copenhagen, Denmark; died Jan 2, 2006, in Santa Monica, California; m. Allan Hersholt, 1938; m. Dr. Harvey Cummins, 1947. ❖ Starred or was featured in Hollywood films of the 1940s, including *Honeymoon in Bali, Honeymoon for Three, A Woman's Face, You'll Never Get Rich, The Devil Pays Off, Iceland, Jack London, Background to Danger, The Master Race, The Cry of the Werewolf, Tokyo Rose, Deadline at Dawn, Strange Journey, Night Unto Night, Rocketship X-M* and *Outcasts of the City.*

MASSERONI, Daniela (1985—). Italian rhythmic gymnast. Born Feb 28, 1985, in Trescore Balneario, Italy. ❖ Won team all-around silver medal at Athens Olympics (2004).

MASSET, Louise (c. 1863–1900). French-English murderer. Name variations: Louisa Masset. Born 1863; hanged at Newgate prison, Jan 9, 1900. ❖ Tried at Old Bailey for killing her illegitimate 3-year-old son Manfred (1899); found guilty and condemned to death, reportedly confessed while in her cell; the 1st person to be executed in Britain in 20th century (Jan 9, 1900), was buried in unmarked grave.

MASSEVITCH, Alla G. (1918—). Soviet astrophysicist. Born Alla Genrikohovna Massevitch, Oct 9, 1918, in Tbilisi, capital of the Georgian Republic (now Georgia); dau. of Genrikh Massevitch (lawyer) and Natalie (Zhgenty) Massevitch (nurse); University of Moscow, degree in physics, 1941; candidate's degree (equivalent of a PhD) from Sternberg State Astronomy Institute in Moscow, 1946; m. Joseph Friedlander (metallurgical engineer), 1941; children: Natalie Friedlander. ❖ Astrophysicist, university professor, and vice-president of the USSR's Academy of Science, who organized and administered a network of stations that tracked movements of Soviet Sputniks; became a lecturer in astrophysics at University of Moscow (1946); named vice president of Astronomical Council of the Academy of Sciences (1952); when the Council was assigned the task of tracking space vehicles (1957), trained leaders for a network of 70 tracking stations throughout USSR and had them in place when *Sputnik I* was launched (Oct 4); became a spokeswoman for Soviet science abroad, making trips to almost every European country and US; served as chair of tracking group of International Committee on Space Research; elected a foreign member of Britain's Royal Astronomical Society (1963); was vice president of the Institute for Soviet-American Relations; authored 2 books on stellar evolution and published over 60 papers, mainly in the *Astronomical Journal of the USSR.* ❖ See also *Women in World History.*

MASSEY, Christina Allan (1863–1932). New Zealand political host. Name variations: Christina Allan Paul. Born Jan 11, 1863, in Forbes, New South Wales, Australia; died April 19, 1932, in Wellington, New Zealand; dau. of Walter Paul (miner) and Christina (Allan) Paul; m. William Ferguson Massey (farmer and politician), 1882 (died 1925); children: 7. ❖ Served as political host after husband was elected to Parliament (1894), then prime minister (1912); active in fund-raising and social services during WWI; was the 1st woman in New Zealand to be appointed Dame Grand Commander of British Empire (1926). Named Commander of British Empire (1923) and Dame Grand Commander of British Empire (1926). ❖ See also *Dictionary of New Zealand Biography* (Vol. 3).

MASSEY, Debbie (1950—). American golfer. Name variations: Deborah Massey. Born Nov 5, 1950, in Grosse Pointe, Michigan. ❖ Won 4 major events (1974); member of Curtis Cup and World Cup teams (1974); won 3 consecutive Canadian Amateurs (1974–76); won Western Amateur (1972, 1975) and Eastern Amateur (1975); joined LPGA tour and was named Rookie of the Year (1977); won Mazuno Japan Classic (1977), Wheeling Classic (1979), Women's British Open (1980 & 1981) and Mazda Japan Classic (1990); retired from LPGA tour (1995).

MASSEY, Edith (1918–1984). American actress. Born May 28, 1918, in New York, NY (some sources cite Baltimore, MD); died Oct 24, 1984, in Los Angeles, CA. ❖ Character actress, films include *Multiple Maniacs, Pink Flamingos* (as Mama Edie), *Female Trouble, Polyester, Desperate Living* and *Mutants from Space*; worked with John Waters and was the subject of the biographical short film "Love Letter to Edie."

MASSEY, Estelle (1901–1981). *See Osborne, Estelle Massey.*

MASSEY, Ilona (1910–1974). Hungarian-born American actress. Name variations: Ilona Hajmassy. Born Ilona Hajmássy in Budapest, Hungary, June 16, 1910 (some sources cite 1912); died in Bethesda, MD, Aug 20, 1974; m. Nick Szavazd, 1935 (div.) 1936; m. Alan Curtis (actor), in 1941 (div. 1942); m. Charles Walker (jeweler); m. Donald S. Dawson (air force general), 1955; became US citizen (1946). ❖ Began career in Viennese music halls; made 2 films in Austria, *Knox aus die lustigen Vagabonden* and *Der Himmel auf Erden* (1935); signed with MGM and was teamed with Nelson Eddy in *Rosalie* (1937); starred in some of the international espionage tales that were a staple of the WWII years, including *International Lady* (1941) and *Invisible Agent* (1942); also appeared in *Frankenstein Meets the Wolf Man* and on Broadway in *Ziegfeld Follies* (both 1943); was intensely involved in anti-Communist political circles in Southern California; retired (1959) but remained active in the Hungarian expatriate community. ❖ See also *Women in World History.*

MASSIMI, Petronilla Paolini (1663–1726). Italian poet and writer. Name variations: Fidalma Partenide (as member of the Arcadia Academy). Pronunciation: Pet-ro-KNEE-la Pay-o-LEE-nee Mah-SEE-mee; Fee-DAHL-ma Pahr-tuh-NEE-dee. Born Petronilla Paolini in Tagliacozzo, Abruzzo, in 1663; died 1726; dau. of Baron Francesco Paolini (owner of Marsica) and Silvia Argoli (noblewoman); at 10, married Marquis Francesco Massimi. ❖ An admired member of the Arcadian Academy, whose work is noted for its sharp defense of women and anticipation of gender theory; while a small child, father was murdered in an ambush; with mother, fled to Rome, taking refuge at the court of Pope Clement X; received an excellent education during the time she spent at the boarding school of the Convent of the Holy Spirit, but at age 10 was removed from the convent and married to a nephew of the pope, a callous soldier with the title of marquis; after the death of one of her sons, reentered the Convent of the Holy Spirit, where she wrote the works for which she is known; writings include *Non disdire alla Donna gli esercizi letterari e cavallereschi* (no date), *Oratorio per la morte del Redentore* (1697), *La corona poetica rinterzata in lode di Clemente XI* (1701), *Canzoni epitalamiche* (1704), *Le Muse in gala* (1704), *I giuochi olimpici* (1705), and "Note sul Simposio di Platone," in *Prose delgi Arcadi* (Tome III). ❖ See also *Women in World History.*

MASSINGHAM, Dorothy (1889–1933). English actress and playwright. Born Dec 12, 1889, in Highgate, England; died Mar 30, 1933. ❖ Made stage debut at Liverpool Rep as Kalleia in *The Perplexed Husband* (1912) and London debut as Claire in *Great Catherine* (1913); appeared with the Birmingham Rep, Everyman Theatre, and the Old Vic; wrote such plays as *Glass Houses, The Goat, Washed Ashore, Not in Our Stars* and *The Haven.*

MASSY, Annie (1867–1931). Irish marine biologist. Name variations: Annie Letitia Massy; Anne L. Massy or A.L. Massy. Born 1867 in Ireland; died April 16, 1931. ❖ Self-educated, internationally recognized mollusk expert, studied cephalopods (squid); corresponded with and identified and described many specimens for several museums as a biologist (1901–31) for Department of Agriculture and Technical Instruction's Fisheries Division in Dublin; as an amateur ornithologist, was the 1st to record redstarts nesting in Ireland (Powerscourt Deer Park, 1885); served as a secretary of Irish Society for Protection of Birds (ISPB, later Irish Wildbird Convervancy, 1926) and was 1 of its 1st members; fought for successful passage of Wild Birds Protection Act (1930); was a member of the Conchological Society of Great Britain and Ireland.

MASSY-BERESFORD, Monica (1894–1945). English-born Danish heroine. Name variations: Monica Wichfeld, Monica de Wichfeld. Born Monica Emily Massy-Beresford in London, England, July 12, 1894; died in Waldehim, Germany, Feb 27, 1945; daughter of George (Irish landowner and sportsman) and Alice (Mulholland) Massy-Beresford (dau. of the wealthy Lord Dunleath); grew up in County Fermanagh on Lough Erne in northern Ireland; tutored at home, attended a girls' school in Dresden, Germany, for 1 year; married Jorgen de Wichfeld (Danish aristocrat), June 15, 1916; children: Ivan (b. 1919); Varinka Wichfeld-Muus (1922–2002, Danish resistance leader); Viggo (b. 1924). ❖ Heroine of the Danish Resistance in WWII, married Jorgen de Wichfeld, a man 11 years her senior, whose father, as chamberlain to Christian X, had just inherited some 3,000 acres of Denmark's richest farmland and the country estate Engestofte, the family seat; settled at Engestofte, on the island of Lolland (1922); gave up her British passport for her Danish one; upon the death of her father (July 1924), her mother moved into a large villa at Rapallo, a small seaside town near Genoa in Italy; when the family finances took a turn (1923–24), began to spend late autumn, winter and early spring in Italy or southern France, and April thru Oct at Engestofte; knew everybody; played tennis with Clementine Churchill, dined with Tallulah Bankhead, lunched with Edwina Mountbatten; also worked closely with Free Denmark and Britain's Special Operations Executive (SOE) in sabotage activities; arrested by the Germans (1944), was sentenced to death for refusing to give information about her involvement in the Resistance and about her contacts (May 13, 1944), the 1st time since the Middle Ages that a woman was condemned to death in Denmark; sentence commuted to life, but she died in prison of tuberculosis in Waldheim (Feb 1945). ❖ See also Christine Sutherland, *Monica: Heroine of the Danish Resistance* Farrar, Straus, 1990.

MASTENBROEK, Rie (1919–2003). Dutch swimmer. Name variations: Hendrika or Ria Mastenbroek or Mastenbroeck. Born Hendrika Wilhelmina Mastenbroek, Feb 26, 1919, in Rotterdam, Netherlands; died Nov 6, 2003, in Rotterdam; married thrice; children: 3. ❖ Won 3 gold medals and 1 silver at European championships (1934); at age 17, won gold medals for the 100-meter freestyle at 1:05.9, 400-meter freestyle at 5:26.4, and 4x100-meter freestyle relay as well as a silver medal for the 100-meter backstroke at Berlin Olympics (1936). Inducted into International Swimming Hall of Fame (1968).

MASTER, Edith (1932—). American equestrian. Born Aug 25, 1932, in US. ❖ At Montreal Olympics, won a bronze medal in team dressage (1976).

MASTERKOVA, Svetlana (1968—). Russian runner. Born Jan 17, 1968, in Achinsk, Siberia, USSR; children: Anastasiya (b. Mar 1995). ❖ Won gold medals for 1,500 meters and 800 meters at Atlanta Olympics (1996); at European championships, won a gold in the 1,500 meters (1998); at World championships, won a gold in the 1,500 and a bronze in the 800 meters (1999).

MASTERS, Margaret (1934—). Australian golfer. Name variations: Margaret Ann Masters; Margee Masters. Born Oct 24, 1934, in Swan Hill, Victoria, Australia. ❖ Won the New Zealand Open (1956); South African Women's Open (1957) and Australian Ladies's Open (1958); won Australia's Victoria Open five times (1959–63); won Canadian Women's Amateur (1964); joined LPGA tour in US and was Rookie of the Year (1965).

MASTERS, Olga (1919–1986). Australian journalist, novelist and short-story writer. Born 1919, NSW, Australia; died 1986; children: 7. ❖ Began 26-year career in journalism (1959), working for several newspapers; began writing fiction when nearly 60; writings, which are often critical of position of women and children in Australian society, include *The Home Girls* (1982), *Loving Daughters* (1984), *A Long Time Dying* (1985), *Amy's Children* (1987) and *The Rose Fancier* (1988); collection of journalism pieces *Reporting Home* published posthumously (1990).

MASTERS, Sybilla (d. 1720). American inventor. Name variations: Sabella or Isabella Masters. Born Sybilla Righton, possibly in Bermuda (date and place unknown); died, possibly in Philadelphia, Aug 23, 1720; dau. of William Righton (mariner, merchant, and plantation owner) and Sarah Righton, both Quakers; m. Thomas Masters (planter and prosperous Quaker merchant), between 1693 and 1696 (died 1723); children: Sarah; Mary (Mercy?); Thomas; William (3 or perhaps 4 others died in infancy). ❖ Was the 1st American inventor to own a patent; journeyed to England and came home with British Patents #401 (1715), for an improved method for grinding corn, and #403, for a new way for weaving, staining, and decorating straw hats (1716), though the patents were issued to her husband on her behalf. ❖ See also *Women in World History*.

MASTERS, Virginia (b. 1925). See *Johnson, Virginia E.*

MASTON, June (1928—). Australian runner. Name variations: June Maston Ferguson. Born Mar 11, 1928, in NSW, Australia. ❖ Won a silver medal in London Olympics in the 4x100-meter relay (1948).

MASTROIANNI, Flora (1926–1999). See *Carabella, Flora.*

MASUBUCHI, Mariko (1980—). Japanese softball player. Born Jan 24, 1980, in Japan. ❖ Won a team silver medal at Sydney Olympics (2000).

MATA HARI (1876–1971). See *Zelle, Margaretha.*

MATAIRA, Katarina Te Heikoko (1932—). New Zealand children's writer. Born 1932 in New Zealand. ❖ Active in promotion of Maori language and culture especially among children; worked for Maori Language Commission and Broadcasting Corporation of New Zealand; works include *Maui and the Big Fish* (1972), *Maori Legends for Young New Zealanders* (1975), *Te Atea* (1975), and *The Oxford Maori Picture Dictionary* (1978); later works written mostly in Maori.

MATALIN, Mary (1953—). American political consultant. Born Mary Jo Matalin, Aug 19, 1953, in Chicago, IL; Western Illinois University, BA in political science, 1978; attended Hofstra University Law School; m. James Carville (Democratic political consultant), 1993; children: 2 daughters. ❖ Political strategist, moved to Washington, DC, to work at the Republican National Committee (1981); was political director for George Bush's reelection campaign (1992); assisted George W. Bush in his election bid for the presidency; served as senior advisor to US vice-president Dick Cheney (2001–03); was host of CNN's "Crossfire" and co-hosted CNBC's "Equal Time"; joined HBO's "K Street" (2003); wrote *Letters to My Daughters* (2004). ❖ See also memoir (with Carville) *All's Fair: Love, War and Running for President* (1994).

MATAMOROS, Mercedes (1851–1906). Cuban poet. Name variations: Mercedes Matamoros y del Valle; (pseudonym) Ofelia. Born 1851 in Cuba; died 1906. ❖ Published essays, poetry, and translations of poetry of Victor Hugo, Lord Byron, and others into Spanish; wrote *Poesías completas* (1892), *Armonías cubanas* (1897) and *Sonetos* (1902).

MATANTUCK (d. 1676). See *Magnus.*

MATAYER, Odette (1912–1995). See *Sansom, Odette.*

MATCHLESS ORINDA, the (1631–1664). See *Philips, Katharine.*

MATEFI, Eszter. Hungarian handball player. Born in Hungary. ❖ Won a team bronze medal at Atlanta Olympics (1996).

MATELD OR MATELDA. *Variant of Matilda.*

MATENE, Ripeka (1882–1953). See *Love, Ripeka Wharawhara.*

MATENGA, Huria (1840/42–1909). New Zealand tribal leader and landowner. Name variations: Ngarongoa Katene, Nga Hota. Born Ngarongoa Katene, c. 1840 and 1842, at Whakapuaka (near Nelson), New Zealand; died April 24, 1909, at Whakapuaka, New Zealand; dau. of Wikitoria Te Amohau and Wiremu Katene Te Puoho; m. Hemi Matenga Wai-punahau. ❖ Born to pacifist parents who were leaders of Whakapuaka, married into highly regarded family with extensive land holdings; gained prominence after rescuing shipwrecked crew (1863); inherited rights to nearly 18,000 acres of land following father's death and spent most of her life fighting petitions to the land. ❖ See also *Dictionary of New Zealand Biography* (Vol. 1).

MATERA, Barbara (1929–2001). English-born costumer and costume designer. Born Barbara Gray, July 16, 1929, in Hythe, Kent, England;

died Sept 13, 2001, in New York, NY; m. Arthur Matera. ❖ Costumer for New York City Ballet, American Ballet Theater, Metropolitan Opera, Broadway and film, moved to US (1960); with husband, founded Barbara Matera Ltd. (1968); produced costumes for such films as *The Great Gatsby, Death on the Nile, The Age of Innocence, Moonstruck* and *Indiana Jones and the Temple of Doom*; on Broadway, outfitted over 100 shows, including *Follies, A Chorus Line, A Little Night Music, La Cage aux Folles, Dreamgirls, Sunday in the Park with George, The Lion King,* and *Angels in America.*

MATERNA, Amalie (1844–1918). Austrian soprano. Born July 10, 1844, in St. Georgen, Austria; died Jan 18, 1918, in Vienna, Austria; m. K. Friedrich (actor). ❖ Made professional debut in a performance of Suppé's *Light Cavalry* in Graz (1864); was prima donna of Austrian court opera in Vienna (1869–96); selected by Richard Wagner to sing the part of Brünnhilde in 1st complete performance of his *The Ring of the Niebelung,* in Bayreuth (1876); also performed the part of Kundry in debut of Wagner's opera, *Parsifal* (1882); toured US and made debut at NY's Metropolitan Opera (1884–85); retired from the stage (1900), then taught singing in Vienna. ❖ See also *Women in World History.*

MATEROA, Heni (1852/56?–1930). *See Carroll, Heni Materoa.*

MATEVUSHEVA, Svitlana (1981—). Ukrainian sailor. Born July 22, 1981, in Ukraine. ❖ Won a silver medal for Yngling class at Athens Olympics (2004), a debut event.

MATHÉ, Carmen (1938—). English ballet dancer. Born Margaret Matheson, Nov 3, 1938, in Dundee, Scotland; trained with Margaret Craske. ❖ Danced with Grand Ballet du Marquis de Cuevas (late 1950s); performed in US with Ballet Theater for 1962 season; returned to London, where she had successful career with Festival Ballet for 8 years, performing featured roles in *Les Sylphides, The Nutcracker, Petrouchka, The Sleeping Beauty,* and others; performed once more in US with National Ballet in Washington, DC, during the company's final years (c. 1970–75); moved to Chicago, IL, where she continued to perform as well as teach dance classes.

MATHER, Margrethe (c. 1885–1952). American photographer. Born c. 1885, in or near Salt Lake City, Utah; died 1952 in Glendale, CA. ❖ Met noted photographer Edward Weston (1912) and established an "essentially platonic" working and personal relationship that would last for nearly 2 decades, sharing a highly respected studio in Glendale, near Los Angeles; producing portraits and other images, as well as working with interior decorators, was included in several photography exhibits and eventually took over the Glendale Studio. ❖ See also *Women in World History.*

MATHER, Winifred Holt (1870–1945). *See Holt, Winifred.*

MATHERS, Helen (1853–1920). English novelist. Name variations: Helen Buckingham Mathers; Helen Reeves; Mrs. Henry Reeves; (pseudonym) David Lyall. Born at Crewkerne, Somerset, England, Aug 26, 1853; died in London, England, Mar 11, 1920; dau. of Thomas Mathers (country gentleman) and Maria Buckingham Mathers; m. Henry Albert Reeves (orthopedic surgeon), 1876 (died 1914); children: Phil. ❖ At 13, went away to the Chantry School, where her writing ability landed her in a class with students who were much older; worked so hard at her studies that she had a physical breakdown, causing partial deafness which was to last entire life; published 1st story in illustrated monthly magazine *Belgravia* (1872), followed by autobiographical 1st novel, issued anonymously, *Comin' Thro' the Rye* (1875), which sold over 35,000 copies and was translated into many languages; other writings include *Cherry Ripe!* (1877), *Land o' the Leal* (1878), *As He Comes up the Stair* (1878), *My Lady Greensleeves* (1879), *Jock o' Hazeldean* (1884), *Murder or Manslaughter* (1885) and *The Fashion of this World* (1886). ❖ See also *Women in World History.*

MATHESON, Elizabeth (1866–1958). Canadian physician. Name variations: Elizabeth Beckett Scott Matheson; Elizabeth Scott Matheson. Born Elizabeth Beckett Scott, 1866, near Campbellford, Ontario, Canada; died Jan 1958; dau. of Elizabeth Scott and James Scott (Scottish immigrants); m. John Grace Matheson (missionary), Dec 1891 (died 1915); children: 9, including Ruth Matheson Buck (b. 1905, writer). ❖ Pioneer physician in Canada's Northwest, studied for 1 year at Women's Medical College in Kingston, Ontario; taught in central India for Presbyterian Board of Missions of Toronto until malaria forced her return to Canada; established (with John Grace Matheson) and taught at the Onion Lake mission in Saskatchewan; graduated from Ontario Medical College for Women in Toronto (1898); practiced freely as an unregistered physician until registered physician immigrants from England settled in the Onion

Lake region (1903); pursued courses at the Manitoba Medical College in Winnipeg to prepare for the medical licensing exam (1904); cared for patients within a 100-mile radius of Onion Lake for 16 years (after receiving an official medical license); served as 1 of 2 women medical inspectors for the Winnipeg public schools (1918–20); retired (1941). ❖ See also Ruth Matheson Buck, *The Doctor Rode Side-Saddle* (McClelland & Stewart).

MATHEW, Sarah Louise (c. 1805–1890). New Zealand diarist. Born Sarah Louise Mathew, c. 1805 (baptized, Nov 19, 1805), in London England; died Dec 14, 1890, in Kent, England; dau. of Richard Mathew and Ann Constant (Strange) Mathew; m. Felton Mathew (cousin), 1832 (died 1847). ❖ Left England to marry cousin who was appointed town surveyor of Windsor, NSW, Australia (1831); relocated to Bay of Islands, New Zealand (1839); accompanied husband on most of his travels and captured perceptions of colonial settlements in diary entries, later published as *The Founding of New Zealand.* ❖ See also *Dictionary of New Zealand Biography* (Vol. 1).

MATHEWS, Ann Teresa (1732–1800). American nun and religious founder. Name variations: Sister Bernardina Teresa Xavier of St. Joseph; Mother Bernardina. Born Ann Teresa Mathews in 1732, in Charles Co., MD; died June 12, 1800, in Port Tobacco, MD; dau. of Joseph Mathews (farmer) and Susannah (Craycroft) Mathews; never married. ❖ Better known as Mother Bernardina, was head of the 1st Roman Catholic religious order for women in US; at 22, journeyed to Hoogstraeten, Belgium, to enter a convent (convents were banned in Maryland); joined the English order of the Discalced (Barefoot) Carmelites and took vows (1755), becoming Bernardina Teresa Xavier of St. Joseph; elected prioress of her order (1774); after American Revolution (1783) and the lifting of restrictions on Catholic worship in Maryland, sailed for America with Frances Dickinson (Sister Clare Joseph) and founded the 1st convent in US at Chandler's Cove, Maryland, later moved to Port Tobacco. ❖ See also *Women in World History.*

MATHEWS, Carmen (1914–1995). American stage and tv actress. Name variations: Carmen Sylva Mathews. Born May 8, 1914, in Philadelphia, PA; died Aug 31, 1995, in West Redding, CT. ❖ Made stage debut at Stratford Memorial Theatre in England (1936), subsequently appearing there as Lady Mortimer in *Henry IV (Part I)*, Ophelia in *Hamlet* and the Queen in *Richard III*; appeared often on Broadway, in such plays as *Hamlet, Richard II, Harriet, The Cherry Orchard, Man and Superman, My Three Angels, Holiday for Lovers, The Yearling, Delicate Balance, Dear World, Ambassador* and *Morning's at 7*; appeared off-Broadway in *Sunday in the Park with George*; also played leads in many teleplays; film credits include *Butterfield 8, Rage to Live* and *Sounder.*

MATHEWS, Lucia Elizabeth (1797–1856). *See Vestris, Lucia.*

MATHEWS, Marlene (1934—). Australian runner. Name variations: Marlene Matthews; Marlene Willard; Marlene Judith Mathews-O'Shea. Born Feb 14, 1934, in NSW, Australia. ❖ At Melbourne Olympics, won a bronze medal in the 200 meters and a bronze medal in the 100 meters (1956); set 6 world records; won gold medals in both sprints at the Commonwealth Games (1958).

MATHEWS, Vera Laughton (1888–1959). British military officer. Name variations: Vera Laughton. Born Vera Elvira Sibyl Maria Laughton in London, England, Sept 25, 1888; died in London, Sept 25, 1959; dau. of Sir John Knox Laughton (naval historian) and Maria Josefa di Alberti Laughton; attended Convent of St. Andrew at Streatham; was also educated in Tournai, Belgium; attended King's College, London; m. Gordon Dewar Mathews, 1924; children: 1 daughter; 2 sons. ❖ Served in British Women's Royal Naval Service (WRNS, 1917–19) and as editor of the organization's journal, *The Wren*, for many years; also worked as a journalist, writing primarily for *The Ladies' Field* and *Time and Tide*; served as director of WRNS during WWII; unique among the directors of Britain's 3 women's services during the war, remained in her post from the start to the end of the conflict; retired from WRNS (1946). Created Commander of British Empire (CBE, 1942) and Dame of British Empire (DBE, 1945). ❖ See also autobiography *Blue Tapestry* (Hollis & Carter, 1948); and *Women in World History.*

MATHIESON, Catherine (1818–1883). New Zealand dairy producer. Name variations: Catherine Johnstone. Born Catherine Johnstone, Dec 11, 1818, in Dumfriesshire, Scotland; died Sept 14, 1883, in Pukehiki, New Zealand; dau. of Thomas Johnstone and Jean (Bryden) Johnstone; m. John Mathieson, 1851 (died 1887); children: 3. ❖ Immigrated to Dunedin, New Zealand (1858); leased farm and purchased cows, providing milk, butter, and cheese to Dunedin community; helped to found Otago Peninsula Co-operative Cheese Factory (1871). ❖ See also *Dictionary of New Zealand Biography* (Vol. 1).

MATHIEU, Simone (1908–1980). French tennis player. Born Simone Passemard, Jan 31, 1908, in Neuilly-sur-Seine, France; died 1980; married name was Mathieu. ❖ Won French junior championship (1926); won French mixed doubles with Damien Mitic (1927) and Yvon Petra (1938); won Wimbledon doubles with Elizabeth Ryan (1933, 1934) and Billie Yorke of England (1937); won French doubles with Elizabeth Ryan (1933, 1934), Billie Yorke (1936, 1938), and Jadwiga Jedrejowska of Poland (1939); was runner-up for the French singles title (1929, 1932–33, 1935–37); was runner-up in US doubles with Jedrejowska (1938).

MATHIEU, Susie. American public relations director. Born in US. ❖ Served as assistant sports information director for St. Louis University, MO; became public relations director for St. Louis Blues of National Hockey League, as 1st female public relations director in major-league professional hockey (1977); served as vice president for marketing for St. Louis Blues.

MATHIEU, Véronique (1955—). French politician. Born Oct 28, 1955, in Nancy, France. ❖ Served as deputy secretary of the Chasse, Pêche, Nature, Traditions Party (CPNT, 1998); representing Group for a Europe of Democracies and Diversities (EDD), elected to 5th European Parliament (1999–2004).

MATHILDA. *Variant of Matilda.*

MATHILDA (1925–1997). Duchess of Argyll. Name variations: Mathilda Campbell; Mathilda Heller; Mathilda Mortimer. Born Mathilda Costner Mortimer in Geneva, Switzerland, on August 20, 1925; died in Paris, France, on June 6, 1997; dau. of Stanley Mortimer of Litchfield, Connecticut; m. Clemens Heller (div. 1961); m. Ian Douglas Campbell (1903–1973), 11th duke of Argyll, on June 15, 1963 (died 1973). ❖ Of American parentage but raised in France by grandparents, wed the 11th duke of Argyll (1963), following his notorious split with wife number three, Margaret (d. 1993).

MATHILDE. *Variant of Matilda.*

MATHILDE (1820–1904). Princess of Westphalia and salonnière. Name variations: Mathilde Bonaparte. Born Mathilde Laetitia Wilhelmine Bonaparte on May 27, 1820; died in 1904; dau. of Jerome Bonaparte (1784–1860), king of Westphalia (youngest brother of Napoleon), and Catherine of Wurttemberg (1783–1835); sister of Prince Napoleon (Plon-Plon) and niece of Napoleon I, emperor of France; m. Count Demidoff, a Russian count (separated 1845). ❖ Was extremely influential during the 2nd Empire because of her close friendship with her cousin Napoleon III; held a salon at her country house in Saint-Gratien as well as in Paris which was frequented by writers and artists, including Flaubert, Gautier, Edmond de Goncourt, and Sainte-Beuve.

MATHILDE DE MAYENNE (fl. 12th c.). Duchess of Burgundy. Died after 1162; m. Hugh II (b. 1085), duke of Burgundy (r. 1102–1143), around 1115; children: Clemence of Burgundy (b. 1117, who m. Henri III de Donzy); Eudes II (b. 1118), duke of Burgundy; Gauthier, archbishop of Besancon (b. 1120); Hugh (b. 1121); Robert (b. 1122), bishop of Autun; Henri (b. 1124), bishop of Autun; Raymond (b. 1125); Aigeline of Burgundy (d. 1163, who m. Hugo I, count of Vaudemont); Sibylle of Burgundy (1126–1150); Ducissa of Burgundy (b. 1128, who m. Raymond de Grancey); Mathilde of Burgundy (b. 1130, who m. William VII, lord of Montpellier); Aremburge of Burgundy (b. 1132), became a nun.

MATHILDE OF BAVARIA (1843–1925). Countess of Trani. Born Sept 30, 1843; died June 18, 1925; dau. of Ludovica (1808–1892) and Maximilian Joseph (1808–1888), duke of Bavaria; m. Louis of Sicily (1838–1886), count of Trani, on June 5, 1861; children: Maria Theresia (1867–1909), who m. William, prince of Hohenzollern.

MATHILDE OF BELGIUM (1973—). Crown princess of Belgium. Name variations: Duchess of Brabant. Born Mathilde Marie Christine Ghislaine d'Udekem d'Acoz, Jan 20, 1973, in Ukkel, Belgium; oldest of 5 children of Count Patrick d'Udekem d'Acoz and Countess Anne Marie Komorowski; m. Crown Prince Philippe of Belgium (b. 1960), Dec 4, 1999; children: Elisabeth (b. 2001). ❖ Popular princess, spent her childhood at the castle of Losange, Vilers-la-Bonne-Eau in Flemish Bastenaken; was a speech therapist working with autistic children before marrying into the royal family.

MATHILDIS. *Variant of Matilda.*

MATHIS, June (1892–1927). American actress, screenwriter, and scenarist. Born in Leadville, CO, in 1892; died in 1927 in Hollywood, CA. ❖ Hired as a scenarist to adapt theatrical and literary works for silent movies at Goldwyn's Metro studios (1918); became head of script department (1919); lobbied to adapt *The Four Horsemen of the Apocalypse* for the screen and insisted the picture star Rudolph Valentino, then an unknown actor; when the film was released to great success (1921), joined Famous Players Studio, where she adapted *The Sheik* and wrote the script for *Blood and Sand* (1922), both starring Valentino; became head of story division at Goldwyn Studio (1923); for the now-merged MGM, collaborated with Alla Nazimova on *Salome* (1922); was then assigned to rewrite, re-edit, and reduce director Eric von Stroheim's epic film *Greed* from 24 reels to 10, a task which was completed in 1923; by 1925, had become so indispensable to MGM that Samuel Goldwyn insured her life for $1 million and she was assigned to write the script and scenarios for the studio's new epic, *Ben-Hur.* ❖ See also *Women in World History.*

MATHISON, Melissa (1950—). American screenwriter. Born June 3, 1950, in Los Angeles, CA; dau. of Richard Mathison (West Coast bureau chief for *Newsweek*); m. Harrison Ford (actor), 1983 (div. 2004); children: Malcolm and Georgia Ford. ❖ Wrote screenplays for *The Black Stallion* (1979), *E.T.* (1982), (adaptation) *The Indian in the Cupboard* (1995) and *Kundun* (1997).

MATIDIA I (d. 119 CE). Roman noblewoman. Died in 119 CE; dau. of Ulpia Marciana and C. Salonius Matidius Patruinus; niece of Trajan, the Roman emperor; m. L. Vibius Sabinus; children: Sabina (88–136 CE); Matidia II. ❖ Mother of the Empress Sabina, was present at the death of Trajan (117). When she died and was deified (119), Hadrian delivered her funeral oration.

MATIDIA II (fl. 110 CE). Roman noblewoman. Fl. around 110 CE; dau. of Matidia I (d. 119 CE) and L. Vibius Sabinus; sister of Sabina (88–136 CE).

MATIJASS, Julia (1973—). German judoka. Born Sept 22, 1973, in Lyubino, USSR. ❖ Won 48kg A Tournament at Prague (2003); won a bronze medal for 48kg at Athens Olympics (2004).

MATIKAINEN, Marjo (1965—). Finnish cross-country skier and politician. Name variations: Marjo Matikainen-Kallström or Kallstrom. Born Marjo Tuulevi Matikainen, Feb 3, 1965, in Lohja, Finland. ❖ Won a bronze medal for the 4x5km relay at Sarajevo Olympics (1984); won gold, silver, and bronze medals in national cross-country skiing championships (1987, 1989); won a gold medal in the 5km cross-country event and bronze medals for the 10km and 4x5km relay at Calgary Olympics (1988); retired from competitive skiing to study engineering (1989); named vice-chair of Finnish Olympic Committee (2000); as a member of European People's Party (Christian Democrats) and European Democrats (EPP), elected to 4th and 5th European Parliament (1994–99, 1999–2004) and named vice-chair of Delegation to the European Economic Area Joint Parliamentary Committee (EEA). Awarded the Finnish Sports Gold Cross (1998).

MATILDA. *Variant of Mathilda, Mathilde, or Maud.*

MATILDA (fl. 680s). Queen of Austrasia. Born an Anglo-Saxon princess and flourished in the 680s; m. Saint Dagobert II, Merovingian king of Austrasia (r. 674–678); children: Saints Adela (d. 735) and Irmina (d. 716?); Clothaire or Lothair IV (c. 682–719), king of Neustria (r. 716–719).

MATILDA (fl. 1100s). Duchess of Brittany. Born Fl. in the 1100s; illeg. dau. of Henry I (1068–1135), king of England (r. 1100–1135), and Sybilla Corbett; sister of Sybilla, queen of Scots (d. 1122); m. Conan III, duke of Brittany; children: Hoel Fergaunt, count of Nantes (d. 1158); Bertha of Brittany (d. 1163).

MATILDA (1046–1115). *See Matilda of Tuscany.*

MATILDA (d. 1252). Countess of Winchester. Died in 1252; 3rd wife of Roger de Quincy. ❖ A patron of the arts, backed Matthew Paris, the chronicler and artist of St. Albans.

MATILDA (1813–1862). Grand duchess of Hesse-Darmstadt. Born Aug 30, 1813; died May 25, 1862; dau. of Louis I Augustus also known as Ludwig I (1786–1868), king of Bavaria (r. 1825–1848, abdicated), and Theresa of Saxony (1792–1854); m. Louis III (1806–1877), grand duke of Hesse-Darmstadt, on Dec 26, 1833.

MATILDA, Empress (1102–1167). Holy Roman empress. Name variations: Aaliz, Aethelic, or Adela; Lady of England; Empress Maud, Mathilda or Matilda of England; Matilda Augustus of England; Mold. Born Matilda Alicem Feb 7, 1102, in Winchester, Hampshire, England; died at Rouen, duchy of Normandy, France, Sept 10, 1167; dau. of Henry I (1068–1135), king of England (r. 1100–1135), and Queen Matilda of Scotland (1080–1118); m. Henry V (1081–1125), Holy Roman emperor (r. 1106–1125), on Jan 7, 1114 (d. 1125); m. Count Geoffrey of Anjou, on June 17, 1128; children: (2nd m.) Henry II, king of England (r. 1154–1189, who m. Eleanor of Aquitaine); Geoffrey de Gatinais (Geoffrey IV of Anjou), count of Nantes (r. 1134–1157); William de Gatinais, count of Poitou (r. 1136–1164). ❖ Daughter and heir of King Henry I of England, who waged a 15-year civil war to establish her right to rule the kingdom of England and the duchy of Normandy; betrothed to Henry V, Holy Roman emperor (1109); married him (1114); widowed childless (1126); returning to England, found her father's realm in the midst of a deepening succession crisis; named heir by father who required that all his barons swear a solemn oath in support (1126); was allied with the house of Anjou through marriage to Geoffrey Plantagenet (1128); saw barons swear fealty to her a 2nd time as her father's heir (1131); gave birth to future King Henry II of England (1133); saw fealty sworn a 3rd time after birth of 2nd son (1134); began struggle to secure holdings in Normandy after death of her father (1135); failed in appeal to 2nd Lateran Council to recognize her right to the English throne (1139); waged war against Stephen of Blois for English throne (1139–54); her failed quest for the English crown allowed her son's peaceful ascent to it; returned to Normandy, where she frequently acted as regent for her son (1148). ❖ See also Marjorie Chibnall, *The Empress Matilda: Queen Consort, Queen Mother and Lady of the English* (Blackwell, 1991); and *Women in World History.*

MATILDA, Empress (c. 1103–1152). *See Matilda of Boulogne.*

MATILDA, Rosa (c. 1772–1825). *See Dacre, Charlotte.*

MATILDA, Saint (c. 892–968). *See Matilda of Saxony.*

MATILDA I (c. 1031–1083). *See Matilda of Flanders.*

MATILDA AUGUSTUS OF ENGLAND (1102–1167). *See Matilda, Empress.*

MATILDA BRUCE.
See Bruce, Matilda (c. 1285–c. 1326).
See Bruce, Matilda (d. 1353).

MATILDA DE BLOIS (d. 1120). Countess of Chester. Name variations: Maud of Blois; Matilda of Blois. Born c. 1100; drowned, along with her husband and sister Lucy de Blois, in the wreck of the *White Ship* on Nov 25, 1120, in Barfleur, Normandy, France; dau. of Stephen Henry of Blois, count of Blois, and Adela of Blois (1062–c. 1137); sister of Stephen of Blois (c. 1096–1154), later king of England (r. 1135–1154); m. Richard d'Avranches (1094–1120), 2nd earl of Chester, in 1115.

MATILDA DE BURGH (d. 1315). Countess of Hertford and Gloucester. Name variations: Matilda de Clare. Died in 1315 (some sources cite 1320); interred at Tewkesbury Abbey, Gloucester; dau. of Richard de Burgh the Red (c. 1259–1326), 2nd earl of Ulster (r. 1271–1326) and 4th earl of Connaught, and Margaret de Burgh (d. 1303); m. Gilbert de Clare, 8th earl of Hertford, 4th earl of Gloucester, on Sept 29, 1308, at Waltham Abbey, Essex; associated with John de Birmingham; children: John de Clare (b. 1312).

MATILDA DE CHATILLON (d. 1358). *See Mahaut de Chatillon.*

MATILDA DE DAMMARTIN (d. 1258). Countess of Dammartin, countess of Boulogne. Name variations: Mahaut de Dammartin or Dammaratin; Mahault; Matilda of Dammartin or Dammaratin; Matilde. Died 1258 (some sources cite 1257); dau. of Ide d'Alsace (c. 1161–1216), countess of Boulogne, and Reinaldo, count of Dammartin; m. Philippe Hurpel, count of Clermont, in 1216; m. Alphonso III, future king of Portugal (r. 1248–1279), c. 1238; children: (1st marriage) Jeanne de Clermont; (2nd m.) Robert (b. 1239, died in infancy). ❖ A wealthy heiress (the richest in France, according to some estimates), married the future Alphonso III who was residing at the court of Louis VIII (1238); when Alphonso returned home to claim the throne (1948), was left in France without protest; but when Alphonso tried to wed Beatrice of Castile and Leon (1253), sought redress from Pope Alexander IV, who excommunicated Alphonso.

MATILDA MARTEL (943–c. 982). Queen of Burgundy. Born 943; died c. 982; dau. of Gerberga of Saxony (c. 910–969) and Louis IV, king of France (r. 936–954); m. Conrad the Pacific, king of Burgundy (r. 937–993); children: Bertha of Burgundy (964–1024); Rudolf III (b. 970), king of Burgundy.

MATILDA OF ANJOU (1107–1154). Duchess of Normandy and abbess. Name variations: Isabel de Gatinais; sometimes referred to as Alice. Born in 1107; died in 1154 in Fontevraud, Anjou, France; dau. of Fulk V, count of Anjou and king of Jerusalem, and Ermentrude, countess of Maine (d. 1126); m. William the Atheling, duke of Normandy, in June 1119 (d. 1120). ❖ At the time of her death, was the abbess of Fontevraud.

MATILDA OF ARTOIS (c. 1270–1329). *See Mahaut.*

MATILDA OF BAVARIA (fl. 1300s). Bavarian princess. Fl. in the 1300s; dau. of Beatrice of Silesia and Louis III, duke of Bavaria (r. 1294–1347), also known as Ludwig IV of Bavaria and Louis IV, Holy Roman emperor (r. 1314–1347); sister of Louis V (1315–1361), margrave of Brandenburg (r. 1347–1361), who m. Margaret Maultasch) and Stephen II, duke of Bavaria (r. 1363–1375).

MATILDA OF BOULOGNE (c. 1103–1152). Queen of England and countess of Boulogne. Name variations: Mahaut de Boulogne; Empress Maud; Empress Matilda. Born c. 1103 in Boulogne (France); died May 3, 1152 (some sources cite 1151), at Heningham Castle, Kent, England; buried at Faversham Abbey, Kent; dau. of Eustace III, count of Boulogne, and Mary of Atholl, princess of Scotland (d. 1116); niece of Matilda of Scotland (1080–1118); cousin of Empress Matilda (1102–1167); m. Stephen of Blois (c. 1096–1154), later king of England (r. 1135–1154), around 1120; children: Baldwin (c. 1126–1135); Eustace IV (c. 1130–1153), count of Boulogne; William (1134–1159), earl of Warrenne and Surrey (who m. Isabel de Warrenne [c. 1137–1203]); Matilda (c. 1133–c. 1135); Marie of Boulogne (d. 1182). ❖ Played an important role in the English civil war fought between her husband and Empress Matilda of England; at 17, married Stephen of Blois who claimed the throne of England as a descendant of William the Conqueror; intelligent and daring, became husband's most significant ally in the bloody war against Matilda who had inherited the throne as King Henry's heir and daughter; planned battle strategies and even led troops; a skilled politician and negotiator, mediated an alliance with Scotland, but was willing to resort to kidnapping and blackmail when negotiations failed; when husband was taken prisoner by Matilda's allies, captured Robert of Gloucester and agreed to free him on Stephen's release. ❖ See also *Women in World History.*

MATILDA OF BOULOGNE (1163–c. 1210). *See Maude of Alsace.*

MATILDA OF BRANDENBURG (d. 1261). Duchess of Brunswick-Luneburg. Died June 10, 1261; dau. of Albert II, duke of Brandenburg (r. 1205–1220); m. Otto I Puer also known as Otto the Child (1204–1252), duke of Brunswick-Luneburg (r. 1235–1252), in 1228; children: Albert I (b. 1236), duke of Brunswick; John, duke of Brunswick-Luneburg; Helene of Brunswick-Luneburg (d. 1273).

MATILDA OF CANOSSA (1046–1115). *See Matilda of Tuscany.*

MATILDA OF CHÂTEAU-DU-LOIR (fl. 12th c.). Countess of Maine. Married Elias I, count of Maine; children: Ermentrude, countess of Maine (d. 1126).

MATILDA OF CHESTER (1171–1233). *See Maude of Chester.*

MATILDA OF ENGLAND.
See Matilda of Flanders (c. 1031–1083).
See Matilda, Empress (1102–1167).

MATILDA OF ENGLAND (1156–1189). Duchess of Bavaria and Saxony. Name variations: Matilda, duchess of Saxony. Born in Windsor Castle, Windsor, Berkshire, England, in June 1156; died in Brunswick, Germany, on June 28, 1189 (one source cites 1198); buried in Brunswick Cathedral, Lower Saxony, Germany; dau. of Eleanor of Aquitaine (1122–1202) and Henry II, king of England (r. 1154–1189); m. Henry XII also known as Henry V the Lion (1129–1195), duke of Saxony and Bavaria (r. 1156–1195), on Feb 1, 1168; children: Henry Welf, count palatine of the Rhine; Otto IV of Brunswick (c. 1175–1218), earl of York, count of Ponthieu, duke of Bavaria, and Holy Roman emperor (r. 1198–1214); William of Winchester (1184–1213), duke of Brunswick-Luneburg. ❖ When husband refused to submit to forfeiture of his lands to the emperor Frederick I Barbarossa, and the town of

Brunswick in Lower Saxony was besieged (1180), appealed to the emperor's chivalry and the siege was ended; with husband, sought refuge in England. ❖ See also *Women in World History*.

MATILDA OF ESSEN (949–1011). Abbess of Essen. Born in 949; died in 1011; dau. of Ida of Swabia (d. 986) and Liudolf also known as Ludolf (980–957), duke of Swabia (r. 948–957).

MATILDA OF FLANDERS (c. 1031–1083). Queen of England. Name variations: Matilda or Matilda I; Matilda of England. Born in Flanders around 1031; died in Normandy on Nov 3, 1083; dau. of Baldwin of Lisle also called Baldwin V le Debonnaire (c. 1012–1067), count of Flanders (r. 1035–1067), and his 2nd wife Adela Capet (c. 1010–1097, dau. of Robert II and sister of Henry I, kings of France); sister of Judith of Flanders (1032–1094) and Baldwin VI, count of Flanders; m. William of Normandy (c. 1027–1087), later William I the Conqueror, duke of Normandy (r. 1035–1087), king of England (r. 1066–1087), in 1051 or 1053; children: Robert III also seen as Robert II Curthose (c. 1054–1134), duke of Normandy (r. 1087–1106); Richard (c. 1055–d. between 1069 and 1075), duke of Bernay; Cecilia (c. 1059–1126), abbess of Holy Trinity in Caen; Adeliza (c. 1066?); William II (c. 1060–1100), king of England; Constance (c. 1066–1090); Adela of Blois (c. 1062–1137, countess of Blois and Chartres, who m. Stephen Henry, count of Blois); Agatha (betrothed to Harald or Harold II, king of the English, but died unm.); Henry I (1068–1135), king of England (r. 1100–1135); and perhaps a Matilda (mentioned in *Domesday Book*, but nothing further is known). ❖ Played a significant part in the political affairs of the period, especially in Normandy; born into the powerful ruling family of Flanders, was closely related, through her mother, to the ruling house of France; despite opposition of papacy, married William, duke of Normandy (1051 or 1053) and spent much of the rest of her life in the duchy; assisted William in administering the area and acted as his regent when he was absent; following William's conquest of England (1066), became queen of England and was crowned (1068); was a powerful, wealthy woman who was generous in her endowment of the church; had 9 or 10 children, including 2 future kings; an astute and independent administrator of her own considerable fortune, was also a generous patron of the Church and a skilled negotiator on its behalf; may also have been involved in the creation of the magnificent Bayeux Tapestry. ❖ See also *Women in World History*.

MATILDA OF GERMANY (d. before 1044). Queen of France. Died before 1044; 1st wife of Henry I, king of France (r. 1031–1060); children: Hugh the Great (b. 1057), count of Vermandois. ❖ Henry's 2nd wife was Anne of Kiev (1024–1066).

MATILDA OF GUELDERS (d. 1380). Princess of Guelders. Name variations: Matilda of Gueldres. Died in 1380; dau. of Sophia of Malines (d. 1329) and Renaud, also known as Rainald or Reginald II the Black Haired (d. 1343), duke of Guelders (also known as count of Gelderland), count of Zutphen; stepdau. of Eleanor of Woodstock (1318–1355); m. Godfrey, count of Hennenburg; m. John, duke of Cleves; m. John, count of Chatillon.

MATILDA OF HABSBURG (1251–1304). Duchess of Bavaria and countess Palatine. Name variations: Mathilda or Mathilde of Hapsburg. Born in 1251; died Dec 22, 1304, in Munich; dau. of Rudolf I (1218–1291), king of Germany (r. 1273), Holy Roman emperor (r. 1273–1291), and Anna of Hohenberg (c. 1230–1281); sister of Albert I (b. 1250), Holy Roman emperor (r. 1298–1308 but not crowned); sister of Catherine of Habsburg (c. 1254–1282) and Clementia of Habsburg (d. 1293); 3rd wife of Louis II the Stern (1229–1294), count Palatine (r. 1253–1294), duke of Bavaria (r. 1255–1294); children: Ludwig, also known as Louis IV (1287–1347), Holy Roman emperor (r. 1314–1347); Rudolf or Rudolph I (b. 1274), duke of Bavaria (1294–1317), Elector Palatine (r. 1294–1319).

MATILDA OF LEININGEN (b. 1936). German royal. Name variations: Matilda Bauscher. Born Jan 2, 1936, in Wurzburg, Bavaria, Germany; dau. of Marie of Russia (1907–1951) and Charles, 6th prince of Leiningen; m. Charles Bauscher, on Nov 25, 1961; children: Ulf (b. 1963); Berthold (b. 1965); John (b. 1971).

MATILDA OF MAURIENNE (c. 1125–1157). Queen of Portugal. Name variations: Mafalda of Savoy; Matilda of Savoy. Born c. 1125; died Nov 4, 1157, in Coimbra, Portugal; dau. of Amadeus III of Maurienne and Savoy and Matilde of Vienne (d. after 1145); m. Alfonso or Alphonso Henriques also known as Alphonso I, count of Portugal (r. 1112–1139), king of Portugal (r. 1139–1185); children: Henrique (b. 1147, died young); Urraca of Portugal (c. 1151–1188); Sancha (c. 1153–c. 1160);

Sancho I (1154–1211 or 1212), king of Portugal (r. 1185–1211 or 1212); Joao or John (b. around 1156, died young); Teresa of Portugal (1157–1218, who m. Philip of Flanders); Matilda of Portugal (c. 1149–1173, who m. Alphonso II, king of Aragon).

MATILDA OF NARBONNE (d. after 1348). Castilian royal. Name variations: Mafalda de Narbonne. Died after 1348; dau. of Sibylle de Foix and Aimery IV, vicomte of Narbonne; m. Alphonso de la Cerda (c. 1270–1327), Infant of Castile, after 1294; children: Luis de la Cerda, prince of Canary Islands; Margarita de la Cerda (c. 1300–1330, who m. Felipe de Castile, sn de Cabrera); Ines de la Cerda (c. 1302–1362, who m. Fernando Rodriquez de Villalobos); Juan Alfonso; Maria de la Cerda (b. 1306, who m. Alfonso Melendez de Guzman); Alfonso de la Cerda.

MATILDA OF NASSAU (fl. 1285–1310). Countess Palatine. Fl. between 1285 and 1310; m. Rudolf or Rudolph I of Bavaria, count Palatine (r. 1294–1319) and duke of Upper Bavaria; children: Adolph the Simple (1300–1327), count Palatine (r. 1319–1327); Rudolph II (1306–1353), count Palatine (r. 1327–1353); Rupert I (1309–1390), count Palatine (r. 1353–1390).

MATILDA OF NORTHUMBERLAND (c. 1074–1131). Queen of Scotland. Born c. 1074; died in 1131; buried at Scone, Perth, Tayside, Scotland; dau. of Judith of Normandy (c. 1054–after 1086) and Waltheof II, earl of Huntingdon and Northampton; m. Simon, earl of Northampton, c. 1090; m. David I the Saint (c. 1084–1153), king of Scotland (r. 1124–1153), in 1113 or 1114; children: (1st marriage) Simon (b. after 1103), earl of Huntington; St. Waldef (b. around 1100), abbot of Melrose; Matilda of Northampton (d. 1140, who m. Robert FitzRichard); (2nd marriage) Malcolm (b. around 1114); Henry (c. 1115–1152), 1st earl of Huntingdon (r. 1136–1152); Claricia; Hodierna (died young).

MATILDA OF PORTUGAL (c. 1149–1173). Queen of Aragon. Name variations: Mafalda of Portugal; Mathilde de Bourgogne. Born c. 1149; died in 1173; dau. of Alphonso Henriques also known as Alphonso I, count of Portugal (r. 1112–1139), king of Portugal (r. 1139–1185), and Matilda of Maurienne (c. 1125–1157); sister of Teresa of Portugal (1157–1218), Urraca of Portugal (c. 1151–1188), and Sancho I, king of Portugal (r. 1185–1211); became 1st wife of Alphonso II (1152–1196), king of Aragon (r. 1162–1196), count of Barcelona (r. 1162–1196), and count of Provence as Alphonso I (r. 1166–1196), in 1160. ❖ At 11, married Alphonso II, king of Aragon, but died 13 years later, age 24. Following her death, Alphonso married Sancha of Castile and Leon (d. 1208).

MATILDA OF QUEDLINBURG (c. 953–999). Abbess of Quedlinburg and regent of Germany. Name variations: Mathilda. Born c. 953; died in 999 at Quedlinburg monastery, Germany; dau. of Emperor Otto I (912–973), king of Germany, and refounder of the Holy Roman empire (r. 936–973), and Adelaide of Burgundy (931–999); sister of Otto II (955–983), Holy Roman emperor (r. 973–983); never married; no children. ❖ As a girl, was allowed to enter a convent rather than marry; highly educated by the nuns of Quedlinburg, especially in the areas of medicine and history, also showed a talent for artistic work, and became well known for her exquisite embroidery; was eventually elected abbess and, under her rule, Quedlinburg became famous for its production of richly embroidered clothing for clerics and altar cloths, some of which still exist; was pulled out of the convent to act as regent for nephew Otto III (c. 980), along with mother Adelaide and sister-in-law Theophano (c. 955–991); became an excellent leader, even sending an army to defeat an enemy invasion (983); when Otto came of age, returned to Quedlinburg.

MATILDA OF RINGELHEIM (c. 892–968). *See Matilda of Saxony.*

MATILDA OF SAVOY (c. 1125–1157). *See Matilda of Maurienne.*

MATILDA OF SAXONY (c. 892–968). Holy Roman empress, queen of Germany, and saint. Name variations: Maud; Matilda of Germany; Matilda of Ringelheim; St. Matilda. Born c. 892 (some sources cite 895) in Saxony; died Mar (some sources cite May) 14, 968, in Quedlinburg, Germany; dau. of Dietrich, count of Ringelheim, and Reinhild of Denmark; became 2nd wife of Henry I the Fowler (c. 876–936), king of Germany, Holy Roman emperor (r. 919–936), in 909; children: Otto I the Great (912–973), king of Germany (r. 936–973), Holy Roman emperor (r. 962–973); Henry I the Quarrelsome (918–955), duke of Bavaria (r. 947–955, who m. Judith of Bavaria); Bruno (925–965), archbishop of Cologne; Gerberga of Saxony (c. 910–969); Hedwig (c. 915–965, who m. Hugh the Great). Henry I the Fowler was 1st married to Hatheburg. ❖ Was married to Henry the Fowler, heir of the duke of

Saxony (909); spent little time with husband, who after being elected to the German throne (919) spent most of his days at war; established a pious, quiet and intellectual court; converted 3 of her 5 dower towns into religious communities, including Quedlinburg and Nordhausen, later renowned as centers of learning; when husband died (936), favored younger son Henry I the Quarrelsome over Otto for succession, which cost her Otto's trust; though he allowed her to remain at his court for several years, was accused of wasting royal income with her generous charity to the poor; eventually reconciled with son and returned to court, taking up her charitable works once more and even acting as regent for Otto during his absences; was canonized shortly after her death. ❖ See also *Women in World History*.

MATILDA OF SAXONY (978–1025). Countess Palatine. Born in 978 in Saxony, Germany; died Nov 4, 1025; dau. of Theophano of Byzantium (c. 955–991) and Otto II (955–983), Holy Roman emperor (r. 983–983) and king of Germany (r. 973–983); m. Ezzo of Palatine, count Palatine, around 992; children: Richesa of Lorraine (d. 1067), queen of Poland; possibly 9 others.

MATILDA OF SCOTLAND (1080–1118). Queen of England. Name variations: Matilda Dunkeld; Mahalde; Edith Matilda of England, Maud; Good Queen Molde. Born Edith Matilda in 1080; died in Westminster, London, May 1, 1118; buried in Westminster Abbey; dau. of Malcolm III, king of the Scots (r. 1057–1093), and St. Margaret (c. 1046–1093); became 1st queen of Henry I (1068–1135), king of England (r. 1100–1135), on Nov 11, 1100 (his 2nd wife was Adelicia of Louvain, 1103–1151); children: Euphemia (b. 1101, died in infancy); Empress Matilda (1102–1167); William Atheling (1103–1120), duke of Normandy; Richard (d. 1120). ❖ See also *Women in World History*.

MATILDA OF TUSCANY (1046–1115). Ruler of Tuscany. Name variations: Matilda of Canossa; Matelda, Mathilda, or Mathildis. Born in 1046, somewhere in northern Italy (month, day, and place unknown); died July 15 or 24, 1115, at the monastery of Polirone in northern Italy; dau. of Boniface II, margrave of Canossa and Tuscany, and Beatrice of Lorraine (c. 1020–1076); m. Godfrey III the Hunchback (her stepbrother), in 1069 (died 1076); m. Welf V of Bavaria (c. 1073–1120), in 1089 (separated by 1097); children: (1st marriage) probably one child who died in infancy (birthdate unknown). ❖ Powerful ruler of extensive lands in Tuscany and Lombardy-Emilia (Italy), who was the most loyal and courageous supporter of the papal cause during the lengthy dispute between the popes and the German emperors known as the Investiture Conflict; born into a powerful Italian family during a time of political turmoil (relations between the German emperors and the Papacy were heading towards a crisis, and the rulers of states within the empire were forced to choose between the 2 warring sides); inherited sizeable and wealthy territories and soon showed her preference for the papal cause; was asked by Henry IV to intervene with Pope Gregory VII in the famous incident at Canossa (1077); devoted her life to the support, moral, financial and military, of the popes and earned the title "handmaiden of St. Peter"; had two brief and unhappy marriages and no children who survived beyond infancy. ❖ See also Nora Duff, *Matilda of Tuscany: La Gran Donna D'Italia* (London, 1909); and *Women in World History*.

MATILDE. *Variant of Matilda.*

MATILDE OF VIENNE (d. after 1145). Countess of Savoy. Died after 1145; m. Amadeus III, count of Savoy (r. 1103–1148), c. 1120; children: Matilda of Maurienne (c. 1125–1157); Humbert III, count of Savoy (b. 1136).

MATIYEVSKAYA, Yelena (1961—). Soviet rower. Born Mar 1961 in USSR. ❖ At Moscow Olympics, won a silver medal in quadruple sculls with coxswain (1980).

MATOAKA (c. 1596–1617). *See Pocahontas.*

MATOKO, Hani (1873–1957). *See Hani, Motoko.*

MATOUSKOVA-SINOVA, Matylda (1933—). Czech gymnast. Name variations: Matylda Sinova. Born Mar 29, 1933, in Czechoslovakia. ❖ Won a bronze medal at Helsinki Olympics (1952) and a silver medal at Rome Olympics (1960), both in team all-around.

MATOVA, Nonka (1954—). Bulgarian shooter. Born Oct 20, 1954, in Bulgaria. ❖ At Barcelona Olympics, won a silver medal in smallbore rifle 3 positions (1992).

MATSNER, Sidonie (1881–1974). *See Gruenberg, Sidonie.*

MATSUDA, Noriko (1952—). Japanese volleyball player. Born Mar 5, 1952, in Japan. ❖ At Montreal Olympics, won a gold medal in team competition (1976).

MATSUI, Yayori (1934–2002). Japanese journalist and activist. Born April 12, 1934, in Kyoto, Japan; died Dec 27, 2002, in Tokyo; dau. of Chinese Christian missionaries; attended college in Minnesota and Paris. ❖ Joined the newspaper staff of *Asahi Shimbun* (1961), pursuing, among other stories, Japan's use of thalidomide; after being posted by Asahi in Singapore (1981), fought for greater Japanese disclosure of its sexual enslavement of Asian women during WWII; returned to Japan (1985); retired from Asahi (1994); as an activist, founded Asian Women in Solidarity (1976), Tokyo's Asia-Japan Women's Resource Center (1995), Violence Against Women in War-Network, Japan (1998), which was the principal sponsor of the Women's International War Crimes Trial (2000), and the Women's Museum (2006), an archive documenting the violence against women during conflicts throughout the world. Author of *Women in New Asia: From Pain to Power* (St. Martin's, 2000).

MATSUKATA, Haru (c. 1915–1998). *See Reischauer, Haru.*

MATSUMOTO, Naomi (1968—). Japanese softball player. Born 1968 in Japan. ❖ Won a team silver medal at Sydney Olympics (2000).

MATSUMURA, Katsumi (1944—). Japanese volleyball player. Born Mar 8, 1944, in Japan. ❖ Won a gold medal at Tokyo Olympics (1964) and a silver medal at Munich Olympics (1972), both in team competition.

MATSUMURA, Yoshiko (1941—). Japanese volleyball player. Born Dec 9, 1941, in Japan. ❖ At Tokyo Olympics, won a gold medal in team competition (1964).

MATSUOKA MOTO (1873–1957). *See Hani, Motoko.*

MATSUTANI, Miyoko (1926—). Japanese children's writer. Born 1926 in Tokyo, Japan. ❖ Won Association of Writers of Children's Literature Prize for New Writer; works, which often draw upon Japanese folklore, include *The Child Who Became a Shell* (1951), *Taro, The Child of a Dragon, Two Iidas*, and 15-vol. *Collection of Matsutani Miyoko* (1971–72).

MATTESON, Ruth (1909–1975). American stage actress. Born Dec 8, 1909, in San José, CA; died Feb 5, 1975, in Westport, CT; m. Arthur Pierson (div.); m. Curt Peterson (adv. exec.). ❖ Made NY stage debut as Kathie Starr in *Geraniums in My Window,*; other plays include *Symphony, Wingless Victory, Barchester Towers, Parnell, What a Life!, Male Animal, Merry Widow, Antigone, Park Avenue, Clutterbuck* and *The Happiest Millionaire*; was a regular on radio's "The Aldrich Family" and appeared on tv.

MATTHEWS, Burnita S. (1894–1988). American jurist. Born Burnita Shelton in Burnell, Mississippi, Dec 28, 1894; died in Washington, DC, April 25, 1988; dau. of Burnell Shelton and Laura Drew (Barlow) Shelton; National University Law School, LLB, 1919, LLM, 1920, LLD, 1950; m. Percy Ashley Matthews, April 28, 1917. ❖ Founded her own legal practice in Washington, DC, though she was denied membership in the local law association due to her gender; became a lawyer for the National Women's Party and played a leading role in expanding the legal rights of women; appointed by President Harry S. Truman to Federal District Court for District of Columbia (1949), the 1st woman in America to serve as a federal district judge. ❖ See also *Women in World History*.

MATTHEWS, Mrs. Charles (1797–1856). *See Vestris, Lucia.*

MATTHEWS, Donna (1971—). British singer. Name variations: Elastica. Born Dec 2, 1971, in Newport, Wales. ❖ As guitarist and vocalist, was a founding member of English punk-influenced pop band Elastica (1992); with band, released debut album *Elastica* (1995) which reached #1 in UK; left band after 1st album.

MATTHEWS, Eliza Jane (1862–1938). *See Pudney, Elizabeth Jane.*

MATTHEWS, Janet (1965—). Canadian-born snowboarder. Born Dec 30, 1965, in Toronto, Ontario. ❖ Became snowboarding competitor (1997); won gold (Summer 1998) and bronze (Summer 1999 and Winter 1999) at X Games in Big Air; won silver at Gravity Games in Big Air (2000); other 1st-place finishes include: Vegetate (1998); Bud Light Big Air in CA and WA (both 1998); and Bored Stiff (1998).

MATTHEWS, Jessie (1907–1981). British actress and dancer. Born Jessie Margaret Matthews, Mar 11, 1907, in Soho district of London, England; died of cancer, Aug 20, 1981; m. Henry Lytton Jr. (actor), 1926 (div.

1931); m. Sonnie Hale (actor), 1931 (div. 1944); m. Brian Lewis, 1945 (div. 1959). ❖ Began training in classical ballet (1917); made theatrical debut in *Bluebell in Fairyland,* in London (1919); starred in *Charlot's Revue of 1926;* famed in both England and US (1920s–30s), starred in such shows as *Earl Carroll's Vanities,* with which she toured US (1927), and Cole Porter's *Wake Up and Dream,* in which she introduced "Let's Do It"; was perhaps best known for her performance in Rodgers and Hart's *Ever Green* (1930); appeared in such films as *This England* (1923), *There Goes the Bride* (1932), *Friday the Thirteenth* (1933), Alfred Hitchcock's *Waltzes from Vienna* (1933), *The Good Companions* (1933), *Evergreen* (1934), *Gangway* (1937), *Sailing Along* (1938); *Tom Thumb* (1958) and *The Hound of the Baskervilles* (1977); had last starring role in *Wild Rose* (1942); was a regular on radio soap opera "Mrs. Dale's Diary" (1961–66); made last stage appearance, as Duchess of Berwick in *Lady Windermere's Fan,* which toured US (1978). Received Order of the British Empire (OBE, 1970). ❖ See also autobiography (with Muriel Burgess) *Over My Shoulder* (1974); and *Women in World History.*

MATTHEWS, Kelly (1982—). American inline skater. Born Jan 20, 1982, in Hoboken, NJ. ❖ Won silver in Street (Summer 1999) and bronze in Park (Summer 2000) at X Games; won bronze in Street at Gravity Games (2000); ranked 3rd in Street for ASA year-end ranking (2000).

MATTHEWS, Margaret (1935—). African-American track-and-field athlete. Name variations: Margaret Matthews Wilburn. Born Margaret Rejean Matthews, Aug 5, 1935, Griffin, GA; m. Jesse Wilburn (Tennessee State football running back). ❖ Won the broad jump title in the national outdoor AAU meet (1957); at AAU, was the 1st American woman to leap 20 feet in the broad jump (1958); won the AAU broad jump title (1957, 1958, 1959); won a bronze medal in the 4x100-meter relay at Melbourne Olympics (1956); was a member of the famed Tennessee Tigerbelles. ❖ See also *Women in World History.*

MATTHEWS, Marlene (1934—). See Mathews, Marlene.

MATTHEWS, Mary (c. 1690–c. 1763). See Musgrove, Mary.

MATTHEWS, Victoria (1954—). Canadian bishop. Born in Toronto, Canada, in 1954; educated at Trinity College, University of Toronto, BA, 1976, ThM, 1987; Yale University Divinity School, MDiv (Divinity), 1979. ❖ Began career as an assistant curate at Church of St. Andrew in Scarborough, Ontario (1979), serving there until 1983; served as an incumbent at parishes of Georgina, York-Simcoe (1983–87), and at All Souls, Lansing, York-Scarborough (1987–94); also served as regional dean at Deanery of York Mills, Ontario (1989–94) and as suffragan (assistant) bishop of the Diocese of Toronto (1994); was named bishop of Edmonton, Diocese of Edmonton (1997), the Anglican Church of Canada's 1st woman diocesan bishop. ❖ See also *Women in World History.*

MATTHEWS, Victoria Earle (1861–1907). African-American author and journalist. Name variations: (pseudonym) Victoria Earle. Born Victoria Earle Smith in Fort Valley, GA, May 27, 1861; died of tuberculosis in New York City, Mar 10, 1907; dau. of Caroline Smith, a slave; according to family oral history, her birth father was her mother's slave-owner; attended Grammar School 48 in New York City; m. William Matthews (carriage driver), 1876; children: son Lamartine. ❖ Wrote stories of her childhood for the *Waverly* magazine, *New York Weekly* and *Family Story Paper;* freelanced for various newspapers in Brooklyn and Manhattan, including *The New York Times, New York Herald Tribune* and *Brooklyn Eagle;* became a full-time journalist for *New York Age;* founder and 1st president of the Woman's Loyal Union, was also instrumental in forming women's clubs in New York City and Boston and was on the executive board of the National Federation of Afro-American Women. ❖ See also *Women in World History.*

MATTHIASDOTTIR, Louisa (1917–2000). Icelandic painter. Name variations: Ulla Matthiasdottir. Born 1917 in Reykjavik, Iceland; died Feb 24, 2000 in Delhi, NY; dau. of a surgeon; studied painting in Copenhagen, then in Paris with Marcel Gromaire and in US with Hans Hofmann; m. Leland Bell (painter), 1944 (died 1991); children: daughter Temma Bell (painter). ❖ Came to US (1942); merging many styles, had 1st solo show at Jane Street Gallery in NY (1948); work included portraits and self-portraits, still lifes and interiors, as well as the coastal landscape of Iceland.

MATTHIJSSE, Margriet (1977—). Dutch sailor. Name variations: Matthysse. Born April 29, 1977, in Rotterdam, Netherlands. ❖ Won a silver medal at Atlanta Olympics (1996) and a silver medal at Sydney

Olympics (2000), both for single-handed dinghy (Europe); won World championship (1999); won 3 European titles in the Europe class.

MATTHISON, Edith (1875–1955). English actress. Born Edith Wynne Matthison, Nov 23, 1875, in Birmingham, England; died September 23, 1955; dau. of Henry Matthison and Kate (Wynne) Matthison; m. Charles Rann Kennedy (playwright). ❖ Shakespearean actress and leading lady for Sir Henry Irving and Herbert Beerbohm Tree, made stage debut at Blackpool in *The School Girl* (1896); came to prominence as Violet Oglander in *The Lackey's Carnival* (1900); made NY debut in *Everyman* (1902) and remained there for 2 years, appearing as Viola in *Twelfth Night* and Kate Hardcastle in *She Stoops to Conquer;* on return to England, was engaged by Irving to tour as Portia to his Shylock in *Merchant of Venice* which then opened at the Drury Lane (1905); often played both sides of the Atlantic, appearing in *King Henry VIII* and *Merry Wives of Windsor* with Beerbohm Tree in New York (1916) and as Francesca da Rimini in *The Salutation* in London (1926); was a great success in America, appearing as Hamlet (1930); also performed in many of husband's plays.

MATTHYSSE, Margriet (1977—). See Matthijsse, Margriet.

MATTINGLY, Marie (1878–1943). See Meloney, Marie Mattingly.

MATTLER, Heike (1958—). See Schulter-Mattler, Heike.

MATTOCKS, Isabella (1746–1826). English actress. Name variations: Isabella Hallam; Mrs. George Mattocks. Born Isabella Hallam in 1746; died in Kensington, England, June 25, 1826; dau. of Lewis Hallam (d. 1756, a comedian) and Mrs. Lewis Hallam (actress, 1st name unknown, who died in 1774); m. George Mattocks who became a theater manager in Liverpool. ❖ At 4, played children's parts at Covent Garden; a comedian and singer, was noted for her portrayals of chambermaids and old women.

MATTO DE TURNER, Clorinda (1854–1909). Peruvian novelist, playwright and essayist. Name variations: (pseudonym) Carlota Dumont, also seen as Carlotta Dumont. Born 1854 in Peru; died 1909. ❖ Influenced by Ricardo Palma, wrote *Tradiciones cusqueñas* (Traditions of Cuzco, 1884–86); also wrote *Aves sin nido* (Birds without a Nest, 1889), the 1st indigenous novel of contemporary Indian life, *Indole* (1890), *Hima-sumac* (1892), *Leyendas y recortes* (1893), *Hernecia* (1893), and *Borealis, minaturas y porcelanas* (1902); was one of the most important woman writers of 19th-century Latin America.

MATTOX, Martha (1879–1933). American screen actress. Born June 19, 1879, in Natchez, Mississippi; died May 2, 1933, in Sidney, NY. ❖ Made film debut (1913); other films include *Huckleberry Finn* (1920), *The Hero, Penrod and Sam, Maytime, East Lynne, Torrent, The Rainmaker, The Cat and the Canary, The Little Shepherd of Kingdom Come, Murder by the Clock, The Monster Walks, So Big, Haunted Gold* and *Bitter Tea of General Yen.*

MATULA, Cheryl (c. 1979—). See Ezzell, Cheryl.

MATUSCSAKNE-RONAY, Ildiko (1946—). Hungarian fencer. Name variations: Matuscak-Ronay. Born Mar 25, 1946. ❖ At Munich Olympics, won a silver medal in team foil (1972).

MATUSZEWSKA, Halina (1900–1989). See Konopacka, Halina.

MATUTE, Ana Maria (1926—). Spanish novelist. Name variations: Ana María Matute Ausejo. Born in Barcelona, Spain, in 1926; m. Ramón Eugenio de Goicoechea, in 1954 (div. 1963); children: Juan Pablo (b. 1956). ❖ Important novelist of the post-Civil War era, completed *Pequeño teatro* as a teenager (1943), which she later revised and published (1954); published 1st novel *Los Abel* (1948), exploring the conflict between Cain and Abel, to understand Spain following the Civil War; wrote prolifically, publishing novels, short stories, and children's books, and her trilogy, *Los Mercaderes,* received acclaim both at home and abroad, as did *Olvidado Rey Gudu* (1974). Won Spain's most prestigious literary awards, including the Nadal Prize and the Cervantes National Literature Prize. ❖ See also Janet Winecoff Díaz, *Ana María Matute* (Twayne, 1971); Margaret. E.W. Jones, *The Literary World of Ana Maria Matute* (1970); and *Women in World History.*

MATVEEVA, Novella Niklayevna (b. 1934). See Matveyeva, Novella Niklayevna.

MATVEYEVA, Novella Niklayevna (1934—). Russian poet. Name variations: Novella Nikolaevna Matvéeva. Born 1934 in Pushkin, Russia. ❖ Published 1st collection of poems, *Lirika* 1961; also published *Korablik* (The Little Boat, 1963) and *Dusha veshchey* (The Soul of Things, 1966).

MATYAS, Auguszta. Hungarian handball player. Born in Hungary. ❖ Won a team bronze medal at Atlanta Olympics (1996).

MATZ, Evelyn (1955—). East German handball player. Born Nov 22, 1955, in East Germany. ❖ Won a silver medal at Montreal Olympics (1976) and a bronze medal at Moscow Olympics (1980), both in team competition.

MATZENAUER, Margaret (1881–1963). Hungarian contralto, soprano and mezzo-soprano. Name variations: Margarete or Margarette. Born June 1, 1881, in Temeszvar, Hungary; died May 19, 1963, in Van Nuys, CA; studied in Graz with Januschowsky; studied in Berlin with Mielke and Franz Emerich, and in Munich with Ernst Preuses; married 3 times. ❖ Possessed of a stupendous contralto voice, sang roles for mezzo-soprano or soprano as well; debuted in Strasbourg as Puck in Weber's *Oberon* (1901); was featured in Wagnerian soprano roles with the Hofoper in Munich (1904–11), made Metropolitan Opera debut as Amneris in *Aida,* with Toscanini conducting (1911); was featured at the Metropolitan for the next 18 years, during which she successfully portrayed Leonore, the 3 Brünhildes, Kundry, Isolde, Donna Elvira, Selika, Orfeo, Carmen, and Delilah; made Covent Garden debut (1914); retired and became a teacher (after 1938). ❖ See also *Women in World History.*

MATZINGER, Polly (1947—). American immunologist. Born July 21, 1947; dau. of a Dutch resistance fighter and a former nun; studied science at University of California, Davis; University of California, San Diego, PhD. ❖ Joined (1989) and heads laboratory at National Institute of Allergy and Infectious Diseases (NIAID) of the National Institutes of Health in Bethesda, MD; partnered with neighboring laboratory colleague Ephraim Fuchs to test new "danger theory" (described first in 1994) that immune system reacts to danger, not to "foreignness" (1989); searched for methods to stop immune system attacks on grafted tissues without debilitating entire bodily systems.

MAUBEUGE, abbess of.
See Aldegund (c. 630–684).
See Aldetrude (fl. 7th c.).
See Madelberte (fl. 7th c.).

MAUD. *Variant of Matilda, Mathilda, Maude, Mold.*

MAUD (1869–1938). Queen of Norway. Name variations: Maud Saxe-Coburg. Born Maud Charlotte Mary Victoria on Nov 26, 1869, in London, England; died Nov 20, 1938, in London; dau. of Edward VII, king of England (r. 1901–1910), and Alexandra of Denmark (1844–1925); m. Haakon VII, king of Norway (r. 1905–1957), on July 22, 1896; children: Olav V (1903–1991), king of Norway (r. 1957–1991). ❖ Queen Maud Land in Antarctica was named in her honor.

MAUD, Empress.
See Matilda, Empress (1102–1167).
See Matilda of Boulogne (c. 1103–1152).

MAUD CARINTHIA (c. 1105–1160). Countess of Champagne and Blois. Name variations: Maud of Carinthia. Born c. 1105; died in 1160; dau. of Inglebert II, duke of Carinthia, and Uta of Passau; m. Theobald II, count of Champagne and Blois, in 1123; children: Henry I (d. 1181), count of Champagne (who m. Marie de Champagne); Theobald V, count of Blois (who m. Alice, Countess of Blois); Stephen, count of Sancerre; William of Rheims, cardinal; Adele of Champagne (1145–1206).

MAUD CHAWORTH (1282–c. 1322). *See Chaworth, Maud.*

MAUD DE BOHUN.
See Bohun, Maud (fl. 1240s).
See Bohun, Maud (fl. 1275).

MAUD DE BRAOSE.
See Braose, Maud de (d. 1211).
See Mortimer, Maud (c. 1229–1301).

MAUD DE KEVILIOC (1171–1233). *See Maude of Chester.*

MAUD DE ST. WALERIE (d. 1211). *See Braose, Maud de.*

MAUD OF LUSIGNAN (d. 1241). Countess of Hereford and Essex. Born Maud d'Eu; Maud de Lusignan. Died Aug 14, 1241; interred at Llanthony Priory, Gloucester; some sources say she was the dau. of Isabella of Angouleme (1186–1246) and Hugh X, count of Lusignan; others say she was the dau. of Ralph de Lusignan and Alice d'Eu (d. 1246), countess of Eu; m. Humphrey Bohun (1200–1275), 2nd earl of Hereford, 1st earl of Essex (some sources cite 6th earl of Hereford and Essex [r. 1220–1275]), and constable of England; children: Maud Bohun (fl. 1240s); Humphrey Bohun (d. 1265, who m. Eleanor de Braose). ❖ Humphrey Bohun was also married to Maud of Avenbury (d. 1273).

MAUD OF MANDEVILLE (d. 1236). Countess of Essex. Name variations: Maud de Mandeville or Mandville; countess of Hereford. Acceded as countess of Essex on Jan 8, 1226; died Aug 27, 1236; dau. of Geoffrey, 4th earl of Essex (r. 1199–1213), and Beatrice de Say (d. before 1197); m. Humphrey Bohun, 1st earl of Hereford (some sources cite 5th earl of Hereford); m. Roger de Daunteseye (div. 1233); children: (1st m.) Henry; Humphrey Bohun (1200–1275), 2nd earl of Hereford, 1st earl of Essex (some sources cite 6th earl of Hereford and Essex [r. 1220–1275]).

MAUD OF NORMANDY (d. 1017). Countess of Blois, Champagne and Chartres. Name variations: Matilda. Died in 1017; dau. of Richard I the Fearless (d. 996), duke of Normandy (r. 942–996), and Gunnor of Denmark (d. 1031); m. Eudes also spelled Odo I, count of Blois, Champagne, and Chartres (r. 978–995); children: Theobald II also known as Thibaut II, count of Blois, Champagne, and Chartres (r. 995–1004).

MAUD OF NORWAY (1869–1938). *See Maud, queen of Norway.*

MAUD PLANTAGENET (c. 1310–c. 1377). Countess of Ulster. Born c. 1310; died c. 1377 in Campsey Abbey, Suffolk, England; dau. of Henry, 3rd earl of Lancaster, and Maud Chaworth (1282–c. 1322); m. William de Burgh, 3rd earl of Ulster, around 1330; m. Ralph de Ufford; children: (1st m.) Elizabeth de Burgh (1332–1363); (2nd marriage) Maud de Vere. ❖ Became a nun at Campsey Abbey (c. 1348).

MAUD PLANTAGENET (1335–1362). Countess of Hainault and Holland. Name variations: Matilda; Maud Stafford. Born April 4, 1335 (some sources cite 1339); died April 10, 1362, in England; dau. of Henry (b. 1306), 1st duke of Lancaster, and Isabel Beaumont (d. 1368); sister of Blanche of Castile (1341–1369); m. Ralph Stafford, Lord Stafford, on Nov 1, 1344; m. William V, duke of Bavaria (r. 1347–1358), count of Holland (r. 1354–1358), count of Hainault (r. 1356–1358), in 1352.

MAUDE, Caitlín (1941–1982). Irish poet. Name variations: Caitlin Maude. Born 1941 in Connemara, Ireland; died 1982. ❖ Worked as teacher, singer, and translator; was active in Gaeltacht civil-rights movement; poems, all written in Irish, collected posthumously as *Caitlín Maude, Dánta* (1984); wrote play with Michael Hartnett, *An Lasair Choille,* and made recording of folk-songs and readings, *Caitlín* (1975).

MAUDE, Clementina, Lady Hawarden (1822–1865). *See Hawarden, Clementina.*

MAUDE, Margery (1889–1979). English-born actress. Born April 29, 1889, in Wimbledon, England; died Aug 7, 1979, in Cleveland, Ohio; dau. of Cyril Maude (celebrated actor-manager) and Winifred Emery Maude (d. 1924); m. Joseph Warren Burden. ❖ Made London debut as Cynthia in *D'Arcy of the Guards* (1910); joined Herbert Beerbohm Tree's Co., appearing as Titania in *Midsummer Night's Dream* (1911); made NY debut with father's company on their US and Canadian tour in *The Second in Command* and *Grumpy* (1913); other plays include *Lady Windermere's Fan, Paganini, The Old Foolishness, The Two Mrs. Carrolls, O Mistress Mine, The School for Scandal* (in London's All-Star revival), *Searchlights* and *My Fair Lady*; films include *You're Never Too Young* and *The Birds and the Bees*; also appeared on radio and tv.

MAUDE, Sibylla Emily (1862–1935). New Zealand hospital matron, district nurse, and social worker. Born Aug 11, 1862, in Christchurch, New Zealand; died July 12, 1935, in Christchurch; dau. of Thomas William Maude and Emily Catherine (Brown) Maude. ❖ Trained as nurse in England and administered large surgical ward in Middlesex Hospital, London (1889); returned to New Zealand and served as matron of Christchurch Hospital (1892–96); established medical treatment center and dispensary for the poor (1896); gained support of District Nursing Association (1901); returned to London to train in obstetrics (1901); raised money to build TB sanatorium at New Brighton (1904); coordinated nursing efforts during influenza pandemic (1918); ran soup kitchen for undernourished children (1920s); active in Canterbury branch New Zealand Trained Nurses' Association, becoming president (1912), Made OBE (1934). ❖ See also *Dictionary of New Zealand Biography* (Vol. 2).

MAUDE OF ALSACE (1163–c. 1210). Duchess of Brabant. Name variations: Matilda of Boulogne. Born in 1163 at Pas-de-Calais, France; died c. 1210 or 1211; dau. of Matthew I (Matthieu d'Alsace), count of Boulogne, and Marie of Boulogne (d. 1182); m. Henry I (1165–1235), duke of Brabant, in 1179; children: Godfrey de Brabant (b. 1186); Marle de Brabant (b. 1188); Mary of Brabant (c. 1191–c. 1260); Marguerite de Brabant, countess of Guelders (c. 1192–?); Alix de Brabant also known as Adelaide of Brabant (b. 1194); Mathilde de Brabant (b. 1200, who m. Floris IV, count of Holland); Henry II (1207–1248), duke of Brabant. ❖ Following her death, Henry I married Marie of France in 1213.

MAUDE OF BRABANT (1224–1288). Countess of Artois. Name variations: Mahaut Louvain; Matilde de Brabant. Born in 1224; died Sept 29, 1288; dau. of Henry II, duke of Brabant, and Marie of Swabia (c. 1201–1235); sister of Henry III (1233–1261), duke of Brabant; m. Robert I the Good (1216–1250), count of Artois (r. 1237–1250), on June 14, 1237; m. Guion de Chastillon, count of St. Pol; children: (1st marriage) Robert II (1250–1302), count of Artois; Blanche of Artois (c. 1247–1302, who m. Henry I, king of Navarre, and Edmund the Crouchback, 1st earl of Lancaster); (2nd marriage) Beatrice of Chastillon (d. 1304, who m. John de Brienne, count of Eu).

MAUDE OF CHESTER (1171–1233). Countess of Huntingdon. Name variations: Maud de Kevilioc or de Keveliock; Maud Dunkeld; Matilda of Chester. Born in 1171; died Jan 6, 1233; dau. of Hugh de Kevilioc, 3rd earl of Chester (some sources cite 6th earl of Chester), and Bertrada of Evreux; m. David (c. 1144–1219), earl of Huntingdon (r. 1185–1219), Aug 26, 1190; children: 7, including Margaret (d. 1228, who m. Alan of Galloway); Isabella (1206–1251, who m. Robert Bruce); Ada Dunkeld (c. 1195–after 1241); Robert (died young); Henry (died young); John of Chester (c. 1207–1237), earl of Chester (r. 1232–1237).

MAUDUIT, Louise (1784–1862). French artist. Name variations: Madame Hersent. Born Louise Marie Jeanne Mauduit, 1784, in France; died 1862; m. Louis Hersent (French painter, 1777–1860). ❖ A pupil of Meynier, graduated from portraits to history and genre paintings, one of which, *Louis XIV visits Peter the Great*, was purchased for the Royal Collection in Versailles; ran a studio to teach other women artists; did painting *Portrait of Pauline Bonaparte* (1806); exhibited in the Salons (1810–24).

MAUER, Renata (1969—). Polish shooter. Name variations: Renata Mauer-Rózanska or Rozanska. Born April 23, 1969, in Kryczki, Nasielsk, Poland. ❖ Won a gold medal for 10m air pistol (40 shots) and a bronze medal for 50m rifle 3 positions at Atlanta Olympics (1996); won a gold medal for 50m rifle 3 positions at Sydney Olympics (2000); won Polish championship 21 times. Named Best Polish Sportsperson of the Year (1996).

MAUERMAYER, Gisela (1913–1995). German discus thrower. Name variations: Maürmayer. Born Nov 24, 1913, in Germany; died Jan 9, 1995. ❖ Heaved the discus 158′6′ to set a world record that remained unbroken for 12 years; won a gold medal for discus at Munich Olympics (1936); became a schoolteacher and high-ranking member of the Nazi women's organization; following WWII, lost job because of Nazi affiliation; returned to school, receiving a doctoral degree from Zoological Institute of Munich University, specializing in study of ants.

MAULE, Annabel (1922—). English actress. Born Sept 8, 1922, in London, England; dau. of Donovan Maule (director and manager) and Mollie Shiells; sister of Robin Maule (actor); m. Douglas Dickson (div.). ❖ Made stage debut as Cupid in *Love is the Best Doctor* (1934), followed by *The Children's Hour, Jane Eyre, First Stop North, As Good as a Feast, Less Than Kind, Dark Summer* and *The Day After Tomorrow*, among others; served in WRNS during WWII; took over management and appeared in a variety of lead roles at father's theater in Nairobi (1962–64), then became artistic director (1968), managing director (1971), and chair (1973); appeared as Lady Byrne in film *Out of Africa*. Named Member of the British Empire (MBE, 1975).

MAULTASCH, Margaret (1318–1369). See *Margaret Maultasch*.

MAUNDER, Annie Russell (1868–1947). Irish astronomer. Born Annie Scott Dill Russell in 1868 in Co. Tyrone, Ireland; died 1947; dau. of W.A. Russell (Anglican vicar); attended Victoria College in Belfast; graduate of Girton College in Cambridge, 1889; m. Edward Maunder (astronomer), 1895. ❖ At Girton College, named Senior Optime in the Mathematical Tripos (1889), the highest honor ever granted to a woman at Girton; secured a position at Royal Observatory at Greenwich, measuring and examining photographs of sunspots; despite growing prominence, was

denied admission to Royal Astronomical Society (1892); became 1st editor of *Journal of the British Astronomical Society* (1894); her work on sunspots and her photographic survey of the Milky Way galaxy secured her a place in the history of science; with husband, published *The Heavens and Their Story*, a history of astronomy (1908); was inactive as a scientist (1898–1915), then worked at Royal Observatory (1915–20), and edited the *Journal of the British Astronomical Society* (1917–30).

MAUNDER, Maria (1972—). Canadian rower. Born Mar 19, 1972, in St. John's, Newfoundland, Canada. ❖ Won a silver medal for coxed eights at Atlanta Olympics (1996).

MAUPIN, d'Aubigny (c. 1670–1707). French mezzo-soprano and duelist. Name variations: Julie d'Aubigny Maupin; Julie, Chévalier de Maupin; Mlle de Maupin; Mlle d'Aubigny; Aubigny Maupin. Born Julie d'Aubigny in Paris, c. 1670 (some sources cite 1673); died Nov 1707, probably in a suburb of Paris, perhaps in Provence; dau. of Gaston, Sieur d'Aubigny; m. Jean Maupin, c. 1687. ❖ Flamboyant French singer, renowned bisexual, and notorious sword duelist; was the 1st mezzo-soprano in French opera to play leading roles; was mistress of the Comte d'Armagnac (c. 1685–87); moved to Marseille, where she sang at Academy of Music (c. 1687–89); condemned by Parlement of Aix for taking a lover from a convent (c. 1689), made her way to Paris, fighting and singing (c. 1689–90); debuted at Paris Opera as Pallas in *Cadmus et Hermione* (1690); fled to Brussels, where she became mistress of the elector of Bavaria (1696–98); was possibly in Spain (c. 1698); starred at Paris Opera (1698–1705), in such roles as Minerve in *Thésée* (1698), Cidippe in *Thétys et Pelée* (1699), Cérès in *Proserpine* (1699), Clymène in *Phaéton* (1702), Scylla in *Arcis et Galathée* (1702), Médée in *Médus, Roi de Mèdes* (1702), Clorinde in *Tancrède* (1702), Pénélope in *Ulysse et Pénélope* (1703), Cassiope in *Persée* (1703), title role in *Armide* (1703), Madness in *Le Carnival et la Folie* (1704), Junon in *Isis* (1704), Diane in *Iphigénie et Tauride* (1704) and Isabelle in *La Vénitienne* (1705); had liaison with Marquise de Florensac (1703–05); left the stage and took up religious pursuits (1705–07); as a duelist, apparently fought only men, and on an equal footing. ❖ See also *Women in World History*.

MAURA, Carmen (1945—). Spanish actress. Born Carmen García Maura, Sept 15, 1945, in Madrid, Spain; great-niece of politician Antonio Maura; m. Francisco Forteza (lawyer), 1964 (div. 1970); children: 2. ❖ International star, gained initial fame on tv, working as presenter for popular "Esta Noche" (Tonight) and "Encantada de Conocerte" (Delighted to Meet You, 1970s); made 1st film appearance in successful *Tigres de Papel* (1977); came to prominence in comic roles in such films as *Sal Gorda* (Rock Salt, 1984), *Sé Infiel y No Mires con Quién* (Be Unfaithful and Don't Look with Whom, 1985) and *Tata Mía* (My Daddy, 1986); worked on 7 films with Pedro Almodóvar, including *Pepi, Luci Bom y otras Chicas del Montón* (Pepi, Luci, Bom and Other Girls from the Heap, 1980) and *Mujeres al Borde de un Ataque de Nervios* (Women on the Verge of a Nervous Breakdown, 1988), for which she won European Film Award for Best Actress; appeared in Carlos Saura's *¡Ay Carmela!* (1990), Techiné's *Alice y Martín* (1998) and Iglesia's *La Comunidad* (Common Wealth, 2000); won Goya Award (1988, 1990, 2000) and European Film Festival's Best Actress Award for *¡Ay Carmela!* (1990); on tv, appeared in "Cervantes" (mini-series, 1980), "A las Once en Casa" (At Home at 11, series, 1998), and "Famosos y Familia" (series, 1999); other films include *El Espíritu* (The Spirit, 1969), *Don Juan* (1974), *¿Qué He Hecho Yo para MercerEsto?* (What Have I Done to Deserve This?, 1984), *Matador* (1986), *Sur la Terre Comme au Ciel* (Between Heaven and Earth, 1992), *Cómo Ser Mujer y No Morir en el Intento* (How to Be a Woman and Not Die Trying, 1991), *El Palomo Cojo* (The Lame Pigeon, 1995), *El Cometa* (The Comet, 1999), *Carretera y Manta* (To The End of the Road, 2000), *Arroz y Tartana* (Rice and Tartana, 2003) and *Reinas* (Queens, 2005).

MAURER, Lea (1971—). See *Loveless, Lea*.

MAURESMO, Amelie (1979—). French tennis player. Born July 5, 1979, in Saint-Germain-en-Laye, France. ❖ Was runner-up at Australian Open (1999) and semi-finalist at Wimbledon and US Open (2002); won a silver medal for singles at Athens Olympics (2004); won the Italian Open (2004, 2005); ranked WTA #1 in the world (Sept 2004); won WTA championship (2005) and Australian Open (2006); announced that she was gay (1999).

MAUREY, Nicole (1925—). French tv and screen actress. Born Dec 20, 1935, in Bois-Colombes, France. ❖ Made film debut as Solange in *Le cavalier noir* (1945); starred in such films as *Blondine, Little Boy Lost, Les compagnes de la nuit, The Secret of the Incas, Napoléon* (as Mme Tallien),

The Constant Husband, The Bold and the Brave, Me and the Colonel, The Scapegoat, High Time, Don't Bother to Knock, The Day of the Triffids, Gloria and *Chanel Solitaire.*

MAURI, Rosita (1856–1923). Spanish ballet dancer. Born Sept 15, 1856, in Rens, Barcelona, Spain; died 1923 in Paris, France. ❖ Made debut in Majorca (1866); danced with Teatro Principale of Barcelona (1871); was a principal dancer in Vienna, Paris, and at major Italian opera houses such as Teatro Reggio di Turino and Teatro alla Scala in Milan; debuted at Paris Opéra (1878), where she created roles in such works as Louis Mérante's *Korrigane* (1880), *La Farrandole* (1883), and *Yedda* (1885), and Josef Hansen's *La Tempête* (1889), *La Rêve* (1890), *La Maladetta* (1893) and *l'Etoile* (1897); best known for her mime work as Fenella in *La Muette di Portici.*

MAURICE, Mary (1844–1918). American actress. Name variations: Mrs. Mary Maurice. Born Nov 15, 1844, in Morristown, Ohio; died April 30, 1918, in Port Carbon, PA. ❖ Known as the 1st "perfect" screen mother, appeared with Vitagraph (1910–18); films include *My Old Dutch, The Seventh Son, Sins of the Mothers, The Battle Cry of Peace, The Goddess* and *Rose of the South.*

MAURITZ, Anja (1968—). See Fichtel, Anja.

MAURIZIO, Anna (1900–1993). Polish-born Swiss apiculturist. Born in Poland of Swiss parents (father was a professor of botany) in 1900; died at Liebefeld, near Bern, Switzerland, July 24, 1993; never married. ❖ In a scientific career that spanned more than 50 years, established a reputation as one of the world's leading apiculturists, publishing many pioneering studies of various aspects of the life cycle of bees and the factors that influence their ability to produce honey. ❖ See also *Women in World History.*

MAUROY, Magda (1894–1990). See Julin-Mauroy, Magda.

MAURY, Antonia (1866–1952). American astronomer. Pronunciation: MAW-ree. Born Antonia Caetana de Paiva Pereira Maury, Mar 21, 1866, in Cold Spring, New York; died Jan 8, 1952, in Dobbs Ferry, New York; dau. of Mytton Maury (an Episcopal minister) and Virginia (Draper) Maury; sister of Carlotta Maury (1874–1938); Vassar College, BS, astronomy, 1887; never married. ❖ Noted for her contributions to stellar spectral classification and the study of spectroscopic binaries, served intermittently as an assistant, Harvard College Observatory (1888–96, 1918–35); was a science teacher, Gilman School, Cambridge, MA (1891–94); worked as teacher and lecturer (1896–1918); as a classifier of stellar spectra, was a central figure in Henry Draper Catalogue project, discovering that the traditional classification scheme of assigning letters of the alphabet to classes of differing spectral line strengths was inadequate to explain the complexity of the structure being seen; was custodian at Draper Park Observatory Museum (1935–38). Received Annie J. Cannon Prize, American Astronomical Society (1943). ❖ See also *Women in World History.*

MAURY, Carlotta (1874–1938). American paleontologist. Born Carlotta Joaquina Maury in Hastings-on-Hudson, New York, 1874; died in Yonkers, NY, 1938; dau. of Mytton Maury (Episcopal minister) and Virginia (Draper) Maury; sister of noted astronomer Antonia Maury (1866–1952); graduated from Radcliffe College, 1894; Cornell University, PhD, 1902. ❖ Published *A Comparison of the Oligocene of Western Europe and the Southern United States* (1902); worked as an assistant in department of paleontology at Columbia University (1904–06), then lectured in paleontology (1909–12); served as a paleontologist with Louisiana Geological Survey (1907–09); undertook 1st field study (1910); retained by Royal Dutch Shell Petroleum Company as a consulting paleontologist and stratigrapher (1910), a post she would hold until her death; served as professor of geology and zoology at Huguenot College, University of the Cape of Good Hope, in South Africa (1912–15); named official paleontologist to Brazil (1914); published a number of papers and reports on her specialties of fossil faunas and Antillean, Venezuelan, and Brazilian stratigraphy, and organized a geological expedition to Dominican Republic (1916). ❖ See also *Women in World History.*

MAUTEBY, Margaret (1423–1484). See Paston, Margaret.

MAVIA (c. 350–c. 430 CE). Queen of the Saracens. Name variations: Mania; Mawia; Mawia, Queen of Syria. Born c. 350 CE on the southern or southwestern coast of Arabia; died c. 430 CE; dau. of a Saracen chief; probably married a Roman military commander named Victor; children: possibly Mavia. ❖ Elevated to the status of "phylarch," a nomadic chieftain whose status was recognized by Rome (378); was so honored because of the strategic nature of the territory over which her people ranged, and because the Romans needed allies to help provide for the defense of Constantinople; lived up to her end of the bargain, providing troops which helped to repel the Goths from the walls of Constantinople; when the Romans did not live up to their promises, led a revolt against them (378), the 1st large-scale attack upon Roman territory by a Roman phylarch of Arabian extraction. ❖ See also *Women in World History.*

MAVROGENOUS, Manto (d. 1848). Greek freedom fighter. Died 1848. ❖ Was living in the city of Trieste, then part of the Austro-Hungarian Empire, when the Greeks rose in revolt against the Ottoman Empire (1821); immediately moved to Aegean island of Mykonos, where she used her wealth to raise and maintain an army of guerilla fighters and outfit 2 warships for the Greek cause; personally led forces in battle on a number of occasions; awarded rank of lieutenant general by Greek revolutionary leadership, was celebrated in poems and stories during the war, and portraits painted by her contemporaries still survive. ❖ See also *Women in World History.*

MAVROKORDATOU, Alexandra (1605–1684). Greek intellectual. Born in Constantinople in 1605; died in prison in 1684; married and div. twice; children: at least 1 son. ❖ Following a period of study of classical history, literature, and philosophy, founded Greece's 1st literary salon, which attracted both Greek and international intellectuals, and eventually produced many notable Greek politicians and artists; ran afoul of Turkish authorities late in life (1683) and died in prison. ❖ See also *Women in World History.*

MAWIA (c. 350–c. 430 CE). See Mavia.

MAX-THEURER, Elisabeth (1956—). See Theurer, Elisabeth.

MAXIMOVA, Ekaterina (1939—). Soviet ballet dancer. Name variations: Ykaterina Maximova. Born Feb 1, 1939, in Moscow, Russia. ❖ Studied at school of Bolshoi Ballet under Elizaveta Gerdt; joined Bolshoi where she continued to perform throughout career; performed as Marie in Yuri Grigorovich's *The Nutcracker* (1966), as a principal in his *Spartacus,* as Katerina in his *The Stone Flower,* and had numerous other principal parts, including in Les Sylphides.

MAXTONE GRAHAM, Joyce (1901–1953). British author. Name variations: (incorrectly) Joyce Maxtone-Graham; (pseudonym) Jan Struther. Born Joyce Anstruther, June 6, 1901; died July 20, 1953, in New York City; dau. of Dame Eva Anstruther (writer); m. Anthony Maxtone Graham, in 1923 (div.); m. Adolf Kurt Placzek, in 1948; children: (1st m.) James Anstruther Maxtone Graham (b. 1924, a writer); Janet Maxtone Graham; Robert Maxtone Graham. ❖ Obtained 1st writing job as a contributor to the court page of London *Times,* using pseudonym Jan Struther to differentiate herself from mother; published 1st book, *Betsinda Dances and Other Poems* (1931) and soon had a devoted following; wrote *Mrs. Miniver,* a semi-autobiographical series of sketches on family life during wartime that was a tremendous commercial success upon its release (1939); during WWII, lectured throughout US on behalf of British War Relief; also published *The Glass Blower* (1940) and edited *Women of Britain* (1941); remained in US, becoming a member of the library staff at Columbia University. ❖ See also *Women in World History.*

MAXWELL, Alice Heron (1860–1949). New Zealand preservationist. Born Oct 9, 1860, in Kilmore, Victoria, Australia; died July 24, 1949, in Te Papa, New Zealand; dau. of Andrew Maxwell (minister) and Euphemia Ballingall (Johnston) Maxwell. ❖ Preserved historic Te Papa mission station and grounds, renamed The Elms, through sale of own land and through fund-raising events; opened property to visitors (mid-1920s); broadcast a series of interviews about The Elms (1920s) which were published as *Memories of a Mission House* (1942). ❖ See also *Dictionary of New Zealand Biography* (Vol. 3).

MAXWELL, Anna Caroline (1851–1929). American nursing educator. Born Mar 14, 1851, in Bristol, NY; died Jan 2, 1929, in New York, NY; dau. of John Eglinton Maxwell (minister) and Diantha Caroline Brown; graduate of Boston City Hospital Training School for Nurses (1880). ❖ Served as superintendent of Training School for Nurses of the Massachusetts General Hospital (1881–89); was superintendent of nurses at St. Luke's Hospital in NY; founded (1892) and served as head (to 1921) of nurses' training school at Presbyterian Hospital in NY; with Amy E. Pope, wrote *Practical Nursing* (1907); established and worked for nursing service in Georgia during Spanish-American War (1898); advocated creation of Army Nurse Corps and designation of officer rank for nurses in armed forces; throughout career, set high standards in nursing education and procedures, which contributed to improvement in professional status of nurses.

MAXWELL, Caroline Elizabeth Sarah, Lady Stirling (1808–1877). *See Norton, Caroline.*

MAXWELL, Constantia (1886–1962). Irish historian. Born Constantia Elizabeth Maxwell in Dublin, Ireland, Aug 24, 1886; died at Pembury, Kent, England, Feb 6, 1962; dau. of Patrick W. Maxwell (ophthalmic surgeon) and Elizabeth (Suckling) Maxwell; sister of Euphan Maxwell, the 1st woman ophthalmic surgeon in Ireland; educated at St. Leonard's School, St. Andrew's, Scotland, Trinity College, Dublin and Bedford College, University of London. ❖ Entered Trinity College, University of Dublin (1904), the 1st year it accepted women, and was soon marked out as one of the most brilliant of the distinguished women who took advantage of the change of regulations; became the 1st woman member of the academic staff when she was appointed lecturer in modern history at Trinity (1909); served as lecturer in history (1909–39), professor of economic history (1939–45), and Lecky Professor of modern history (1945–51), the 1st woman to hold a full-time chair in Trinity; was a member of the Irish Academy of Letters; writings include *Irish History from Contemporary Sources* (1923), *Dublin under the Georges* (1936), *Country and Town in Ireland under the Georges* (1940), *A History of Trinity College, Dublin* (1946) and *The Stranger in Ireland, from the reign of Elizabeth to the Great Famine* (1954). ❖ See also *Women in World History.*

MAXWELL, Elsa (1883–1963). American hostess. Born May 24, 1883, in Keokuk, Iowa; died Nov 1, 1963, in New York City; dau. of James David Maxwell and Laura (Wyman) Maxwell; never married; no children. ❖ In the years before WWI, was esteemed as a hostess by high-living American expatriates and wealthy Europeans, 1st in Venice and later on French Riviera; moved to Hollywood, where she made a number of short films, including *Elsa Maxwell's Hotel for Women, Elsa Maxwell's Public Deb Number One* and *The Lady and the Lug;* launched a radio program, "Elsa Maxwell's Party Line" (1942), chronicling the comings and goings of the rich and famous; wrote a nationally syndicated gossip column, appeared in the wartime revue *Stage Door Canteen,* and was a frequent guest on Jack Paar's "The Tonight Show." ❖ See also autobiography *R.S.V.P.* (1954); and *Women in World History.*

MAXWELL, Florida Scott- (1883–1979). *See Scott-Maxwell, Florida.*

MAXWELL, Mrs. John (1835–1915). *See Braddon, Mary Elizabeth.*

MAXWELL, Kate (fl. 1886). American frontier woman. Name variations: "Cattle Kate." Flourished around 1886; married a man named Maxwell. ❖ Operated a gambling hall, saloon, dance hall and brothel in Bessemer, Wyoming; known as Cattle Kate, is often confused with Ellen Watson. ❖ See also *Women in World History.*

MAXWELL, Lois (1927—). Canadian actress. Name variations: Lois Hooker, Lois Maxwell-Marriott. Born Lois Hooker, Feb 14, 1927, in Kitchener, Ontario, Canada; m. Peter Churchill Marriott. ❖ Began career on a Canadian children's radio program; made film debut in *A Matter of Life and Death* (1946), followed by *That Hagen Girl, Corridor of Mirrors, The Decision of Christopher Blake, The Dark Past, The Crime Doctor's Diary* and *Kazan;* went to Italy (1950) and made 2 films; moved to England, appearing there in numerous movies and as Miss Moneypenny in 14 of the James Bond films; retired (1989). Won Golden Globe as Most Promising Newcomer (1947).

MAXWELL, Marilyn (1921–1972). American tv and screen actress and band singer. Born Marvel Marilyn Maxwell, Aug 3, 1921, in Clarinda, IA; died Mar 20, 1972, in Beverly Hills, CA; m. John Conte (actor), 1944 (div. 1947); m. Andy McIntyre, 1949 (div. 1950); m. Jerry Davis (screenwriter), 1954 (div. 1960). ❖ Initially a band singer, made film debut in *Stand By for Action* (1942), as a contract player for MGM; other films include *Presenting Lily Mars, As Thousands Cheer, DuBarry Was a Lady, Between Two Women, The Show-Off, Lemon-Drop Kid, Champion* and *Summer Holiday;* also appeared in tv series "Bus Stop" (1961–62).

MAXWELL, Mary (fl. 1715). Countess of Traquair. Name variations: Lady Traquair; Lady Traquir; Mary Stuart. Flourished around 1715; dau. of Robert Maxwell, 4th earl of Nithsdale, and Lady Lucy Douglas; sister-in-law of Winifred Maxwell (1672–1749); m. Charles Stuart, 4th earl of Traquir or Traquair; children: Charles Stuart, 5th earl of Traquair; John Stuart, Lucy Stuart; Anne Stuart; Mary Stuart; Catherine Stuart (who m. William Maxwell, 6th earl of Nithsdale).

MAXWELL, Mary Elizabeth (1835–1915). *See Braddon, Mary Elizabeth.*

MAXWELL, Mary Sutherland (1910–2000). *See Rabbani, Ruhiyyih.*

MAXWELL, Susie (1941—). *See Berning, Susie Maxwell.*

MAXWELL, Vera (c. 1892–1950). American actress and dancer. Born c. 1892 in New York, NY; died May 1, 1950, in NY, NY. ❖ Made stage debut as a member of a Ned Wayburn feature act, *The Broilers of 1908;* often cast as a show girl, appeared in numerous productions of *Ziegfeld Follies* (1909–16); other Broadway appearances include *Winsome Widow, The Pink Lady* and *The Century Girl;* also had a successful career as a ballroom dancer, partnering with Wallace McCutcheon and John Jarrott, and performed in vaudeville as well; opened cabarets in NY and Paris; retired (1928).

MAXWELL, Vera (1901–1995). American fashion designer. Name variations: Huppe. Born April 22, 1901; died in Rincon, Puerto Rico, in Jan 15, 1995. ❖ A popular designer of sportswear, known as the American Coco Chanel, designed women's clothes for endurance and comfort as well as chic; created the prototype of the jumpsuit for Rosie the Riveter during WWII; clients included Lillian Gish, Martha Graham, Pat Nixon and Rosalynn Carter.

MAXWELL, Winifred (1672–1749). Countess of Nithsdale. Name variations: Winifred Herbert; Lady Winifred Nithsdale. Born Winifred Herbert in 1672; died 1749; dau. of William Herbert (1617–1696), 1st marquis of Powis or Powys, 3rd baron Powis or Powys, and Elizabeth Somerset; m. William Maxwell (1676–1744), 5th earl of Nithsdale, 1699; children: William Maxwell, 6th earl of Nithsdale; Anne Maxwell. ❖ Famed for her daring rescue of husband William Maxwell from the Tower of London, where he was imprisoned while awaiting execution for his participation in the Jacobite rebellion (1715). ❖ See also *Women in World History.*

MAXWELL-PIERSON, Stephanie (1964—). American rower. Born Jan 4, 1964, in Somerville, NJ; attended Cornell University. ❖ At Barcelona Olympics, won a bronze medal in coxless pairs (1992).

MAY. *Variant of Mary.*

MAY, Abby W. (1829–1888). American activist and suffragist. Name variations: Abigail Williams May. Born Abigail Williams May, April 21, 1829, in Boston, MA; died Nov 30, 1888, in Boston; dau. of Samuel May (hardware merchant and woolen manufacturer) and Mary (Goddard) May; 1st cousin of Abba May Alcott, mother of Louisa M. Alcott. ❖ Worked as secretary and chair of executive committee (1862–66) for New England's Women's Auxiliary Association of the US Sanitary Commission; served as trustee of Tuskegee Institute (1882–88); was a founder (1868) and president (1877–79) of New England Women's Club; elected to but denied seat on Boston School Committee (1873); lobbied successfully for legislation to permit women to serve on Boston School Committee (passed 1874), then served 2 terms (1874–78); appointed to MA state Board of Education (1879–88). ❖ See also Ednah Dow Cheney, *Memoirs of Lucretia Crocker and Abby W. May* (1893).

MAY, Ada (1898–1978). *See Weeks, Ada May.*

MAY, Catherine Dean (1914–2004). American politician. Name variations: Catherine Dean Bedell. Born Catherine Dean Barnes on May 18, 1914, in Yakima, WA; died June 4, 2004, in Rancho Mirage, CA; dau. of Charles Henry Barnes and Pauline (Van Loon) Barnes (both real estate brokers); graduated from Yakima Valley Junior College, 1934; University of Washington, Seattle, BA, 1936, MEdn, 1937; studied speech at University of Southern California, 1939; m. John O. May, Jan 1943 (div.); m. Donald W. Bedell, Nov 14, 1970; children: (1st m.) James C. May; Melinda E. May. ❖ Six-term Republican member of US House of Representatives, became a writer and assistant commentator for NBC in New York City (1944); ran successfully as a Republican candidate for Washington state legislature (1952), in which position she served until 1958; won the seat for the 4th district (1958), the 1st woman from Washington state elected to the US House; served on Committee on the District of Columbia, Committee on Atomic Energy, and Committee on Agriculture, where she quickly gained a reputation as an advocate of the protection and improvement of farm incomes; co-sponsored joint resolutions to create a US World Food Study and Coordinating Commission and a Select Committee on Standards and Conduct (1967); voted against the party majority on numerous occasions; appointed to US International Trade Commission by President Richard Nixon (1971), serving in that capacity until 1981; named a Special Consultant to the president on the 50 States Project by Ronald Reagan (1982). ❖ See also *Women in World History.*

MAY, Doris (1902–1984). American silent-screen actress. Name variations: Doris Lee. Born Oct 15, 1902, in Seattle, WA; died May 12, 1984, in Camarillo, CA; m. Wallace MacDonald (western actor). ❖ Films include *The Foolish Age, Peck's Bad Boy, The Rookie's Return, Boy Crazy, The Common Law, The Gunfighter* and *Faithful Wives.*

MAY, Doris (1917—). *See May, Pamela.*

MAY, Edna (1875–1948). American musical-comedy star. Born Edna May Pettie, Sept 2, 1875, in Syracuse, NY; died Jan 1, 1948, in Lausanne, Switzerland; m. Oscar Lewisohn, 1907. ❖ Made 1st NY stage appearance in *Santa Maria* (1895); scored international fame as Violet Gray in *The Belle of New York* (1897); other plays include *The Girl from Up There, The School Girl* and *The Catch of the Season*; made last stage appearance in London in title role of *Nelly Nell* (1907).

MAY, Elaine (1932—). American actress, director, playwright, and screenwriter. Name variations: Elaine Berlin, Esther Dale. Born Elaine Berlin, April 21, 1932, in Philadelphia, PA; dau. of Jack Berlin (Yiddish stage actor); m. Marvin May (div.); m. Sheldon Harnick (div.); children: Jeannie Berlin (b. 1949, actress). ❖ As a child, toured in plays with her father; worked in improvisation at Chicago's Second City where she met Mike Nichols and enjoyed a huge success when they teamed for nightclubs, tv, recordings and their own Broadway show *An Evening with Mike Nichols and Elaine May* (1960); wrote such plays as *A Matter of Position, Not Enough Hope* and *Adaptation*; films include *Enter Laughing, Luv, California Suite* and *In the Spirit*; made writing and directing debut with *A New Leaf* (1971), followed by *The Heartbreak Kid, Mikey and Nicky* and *Ishtar*; reteamed with Nichols to write *The Birdcage* (1996).

MAY, Fiona (1969—). English-Italian long jumper. Born Dec 12, 1969, in Slough, England. ❖ Began competing for Italy (1994); at World championships, won gold medals (1995, 2001), a silver (1999), and a bronze (1997), equalling the record established by Heike Drechsler in 1993 for 4 medals at Worlds; won silver medals at Atlanta Olympics (1996) and Sydney Olympics (2000).

MAY, Geraldine (1895–1997). American military leader. Born Geraldine Pratt, April 21, 1895, in Albany, New York; died Nov 2, 1997, in Menlo Park, CA; dau. of Louis W. Pratt and Geraldine (Schuyler) Pratt; University of California at Berkeley, BA, 1920; member of 1st graduating class of Women's Army Auxiliary Corps, 1942; m. Albert May (contractor), 1928 (died 1945). ❖ One of the 1st female officers in the American military, was commissioned a second lieutenant in the Women's Army Auxiliary Corps (1942); made captain (April 1943), then major (Nov 1943); made lieutenant colonel (May 1945); became director of the Women's Army Corps (Jan 1947) and the 1st director of the Women's Air Force (WAF) with the passage of the Women's Armed Services Integration Act of 1948; retired (1951). ❖ See also *Women in World History.*

MAY, Gisela (1924—). German singer and actress. Born in Wetzlar, Germany, May 31, 1924; dau. of Ferdinand May (1896–1977), well-known playwright and author) and Käthe (Käte) Mettig May (1898–1969, successful actress). ❖ Began acting (1942) and became a permanent member of the ensembles of the Deutsches Theater (1951) and the Berliner Ensemble (1962), 2 of East Berlin's leading theaters; regarded for a generation as the foremost singing actress of the German Democratic Republic, was also a major dramatic actress; continued to perform after the unification of the 2 German states (1990); among her most famous roles was that of Mother Courage in Brecht's play of the same name; regarded by many as the greatest interpreter of the songs of Brecht, Kurt Tucholsky, Kurt Weill, and Hanns Eisler. Awarded the Arts Prize of GDR (1959); won Grand Prix du Disque for recording of Kurt Weill's *Die Sieben Todsünden* (*The Seven Deadly Sins*, 1967). ❖ See also Dieter Kranz, *Gisela May, Schauspielerin und Diseuse: Bildbiographie* (Henschelverlag, 1988); and *Women in World History.*

MAY, Isabella (1850–1926). New Zealand temperance worker, suffragist, and dress reformer. Name variations: Isabella Malcolm. Born Isabella Malcolm, June 22, 1850, in Hoxton, London, England; died May 1, 1926, at Kingston upon Thames, England; dau. of Andrew Wilson Malcolm (brewer's clerk) and Jemima Crawford (Souter) Malcolm; sister of Kate Sheppard (suffragist); m. Henry Ernest May (draper), 1879; children: 2 daughters, 2 sons. ❖ Immigrated with family to New Zealand (1869); worked with sister Kate Sheppard to promote women's suffrage; active in New Zealand Women's Christian Temperance Union (WCTU); member of Rational Dress Society, London; elected to first committee of Christian Ethical Society (1890);

served as president of Canterbury Women's Institute (1897); founding member of Lyceum Club; relocated to China before settling permanently near London (c. 1900). ❖ See also *Dictionary of New Zealand Biography* (Vol. 3).

MAY, Misty (1977—). American volleyball player. Born July 30, 1977, in Santa Monica, CA; dau. of Butch May (beach volleyball player) and Barbara May (tennis and beach volleyball player); cousin of Taylor Dent (tennis player); attended Long Beach State University; m. Matt Treanor (Florida Marlins catcher), Nov 13, 2004. ❖ Played collegiate volleyball at Long Beach State where she was a part of the NCAA championship team (1998); with Kerri Walsh, won World championship (2003, 2005) and had a 59-match winning streak going into the Athens Olympics, where they won a gold medal for beach volleyball (2004).

MAY, Pamela (1917–2005). Trinidad-born ballet dancer. Name variations: Doris May. Born Doris May, May 30, 1917, in San Fernando, Trinidad, BWI; died June 6, 2005; dau. of Reginald Henry May and Hilda (Curtis) May; m. Painton Sidney Cowen (died); m. Charles Howard Gordon; children: (1st m.) son; (2nd m.) daughter. ❖ Trained by Ninette de Valois at Sadler's Wells Ballet School; made stage debut in ballet *Alice in Wonderland* (1930); 1st soloed in the *pas de trois* in *Swan Lake* (1934); with Sadler's Wells appeared successfully in *Orpheus and Eurydice, The Gods Go a'Begging, Les Patineurs, Checkmate* (created role of Red Queen), *The Prospect Before Us* (created role of Mlle Theodore), *Horoscope* (created role of the Moon), *Carnaval, Dante Sonata, The Sleeping Princess, Les Sylphides, Le Lac des Cygnes, Coppelia, Symphonic Variations* (premiere), and *Cinderella* (created role of Fairy Godmother); appeared in the ballet sequence in film *Escape Me Never*; taught at Royal Ballet School for many years.

MAY, Sophie (1833–1906). *See Clarke, Rebecca Sophia.*

MAY, Theresa (1956—). English politician and member of Parliament. Born Theresa Brasier, Oct 1, 1956; dau. of Rev. Hubert Brasier and Zaidee Brasier; m. Philip John May, 1980. ❖ As a Conservative, ran unsuccessfully for House of Commons for Durham North West (1992) and Barking (1994); named chair of Conservative Party; elected to House of Commons for Maidenhead (1997, 2001, 2005).

MAY, Valerie (c. 1915/16—). Australian phycologist. Born c. 1915/16; University of Sydney, BS, 1936, MS in chemistry and botany, 1939; m. Ern Jones (University of Sydney staff member), 1940; children: 4. ❖ Algae expert, began work for Commonwealth Scientific Industrial Research Organisation (CSIRO) Fisheries Division in Cronulla (1940); as a volunteer and (later) honorary custodian of cryptograms at National Herbarium of New South Wales (1960–86), studied freshwater environments and marine algae (e.g., Rhodophyta or red seaweeds) and investigated the causes of farm stock deaths due to Cyanobacteria (blue-green algae) found in water; recognized as a water quality and toxic algae expert, published many articles in Australian journals; elected honorary research associate of Royal Botanic Gardens (1987).

MAYA (d. around 563 BCE). Indian princess. Died c. 563 BCE at Lumbini (in modern-day Nepal); elder sister of Mahapajapati; m. Suddhodanaa or Suddhodana (a noble prince of the Gautama [Gotama] clan, belonging to the Sakyas tribe who lived on the border of India and Nepal); children: Prince Siddhartha Gautama, also known as the Buddha (c. 563–483 BCE). ❖ See also *Women in World History.*

MAYAWATI (1956—). Indian politician. Name variations: Behenji (means sister); Ms. Mayawati. Born Jan 15, 1956, in Badalpur village of Ghaziabad, Uttar Pradesh, India, into the low-caste Hindu Jatav, or Chamar, community; like many Dalit women, has only one name; graduate of Delhi University; never married. ❖ Began career as a schoolteacher; in Uttar Pradesh, as a member of the Bahujuan Samaj Party, became the 1st Dalit woman to serve as chief minister of an Indian State (1995); returned (1997 and 2002); elected to Parliament (1996).

MAYBRICK, Florence Elizabeth (c. 1853–1941). American woman convicted in Liverpool of murder. Name variations: Florie. Born in Alabama, c. 1853; died in US, 1941; m. James Maybrick, 1881; children: 2. ❖ Resided in Liverpool with English husband James Maybrick, a hypochondriac who regularly dosed himself with various substances including arsenic; after he died (May 11, 1889) and arsenic was found in his body, arrested for his murder; tried in Liverpool (July 1889), received death sentence (Aug 7), which was commuted to life imprisonment; served 15 years before release (1904) and penned the autobiography *Mrs. Maybrick's Own Story; My Fifteen Lost Years* (1904). Due to a host of factors, many have maintained her innocence.

MAYCON (1977—). *See dos Santos, Andreia.*

MAYER, Bronwyn. Australian water-polo player. Name variations: Bronwyn Smith. Born in Balmain, Sydney, Australia; cousin of Taryn Woods (water-polo player). ❖ Won a team gold medal at Sydney Olympics (2000).

MAYER, Constance (c. 1778–1821). French painter. Name variations: Marie Françoise Constance Mayer; Marie-F-Constance Mayer Lamartiniere. Born in 1775 or 1778, in Paris, France; committed suicide on May 27, 1821; dau. of a customs official; studied art privately in Paris with J.B. Suvee and Jean-Baptiste Greuze. ❖ Exhibited in the Salons beginning in 1796, and was then invited by painter Pierre-Paul Prud'hon to work in his atelier; from 1802 on, assisted Prud'hon and executed her own paintings; her hand is evident in several of works signed by Prud'hon, including *Innocence Seduced by Love* and *The Dying Laborer*; though her paintings belonged to the traditional genre that was expected in the Salons during this era, exhibited a distinctive talent for conveying animated personalities and lively scenes; commissioned by Empress Josephine to paint *The Sleep of Psyche*, which was exhibited at the 1806 Salon under title *The Sleeping Venus with Cupid Caressed and Wakened by Zephyrs*; paintings are held in private collections and in collections of Louvre in Paris, Wallace Collection in London, Baltimore Museum of Art, and museums of Dijon and Nancy, France, among others. ❖ See also *Women in World History.*

MAYER, Diana K. (c. 1947—). American executive. Born c. 1947. ❖ Joined corporate development department at Citicorp (1971) and became director of 3 Citicorp subsidiaries (by 1974); became 1st woman vice president of Citicorp (1974); named administrative vice president in money management division of Marine Midland Bank of NY (1981), then senior vice president.

MAYER, Emilie (1821–1883). German composer, sculptor, and opera director. Born in Friedland, Mecklenburg, May 14, 1821; died in Berlin, April 10, 1883; studied under Carl Loewe; studied counterpoint under B.A. Marx and orchestration under Wieprecht. ❖ Co-director of the Berlin Opera, whose instrumental works were frequently performed in Germany and Central Europe, gave a successful concert of her own works (1850) which included a concert overture, string quartet, setting of Psalm 118 for chorus and orchestra, 2 symphonies and some piano solos; received gold medal of art from queen of Prussia, Elizabeth of Bavaria; was also a talented sculptor.

MAYER, Helene (1910–1953). German-Jewish fencer. Name variations: Hélène Mayer. Born Helene Mayer, Dec 20, 1910, in Offenbach, Germany; died Oct 15, 1953, in Heidelberg, Germany; sister of Eugen Mayer (champion fencer); m. Erwin Falkner von Sonnenburg, 1952 (died 1980). ❖ Won German foil championship at 14 (1925); won a gold medal at Amsterdam Olympics at 17 (1928); won European championships (1929, 1931); expelled from Offenbach Fencing Club for being half Jewish, excluding her from competition (1933); after international outcry, was allowed to compete at Berlin Olympics and won a silver medal (1936); won US indoor championships (1934–35, 1937–39, 1941–42, 1946). ❖ See also *Women in World History.*

MAYER, Irene. *See Selznick, Irene Mayer.*

MAYER, Jacquelyn (c. 1942—). Miss America. Name variations: Jacquelyn Mayer Townsend. Born Jacquelyn Jeanne Mayer c. 1942 in Sandusky, Ohio; attended Northwestern University; married; children: 2. ❖ Named Miss America (1963), representing Ohio; suffered a stroke (1970); following a 90% recovery, traveled the nation as a motivational speaker and produced videos for the American Heart Association. Inducted into the Ohio Women's Hall of Fame. ❖ See also Frank Deford, *There She Is* (Viking, 1971).

MAYER, Maria Goeppert (1906–1972). German-American physicist. Name variations: Maria or Marie Goeppert-Mayer; Göppert, Geoppart, or Geoppert. Pronunciation: GER-pert MAY-er. Born Maria Gertrud Käte Göppert, June 28, 1906, in Kattowitz, Upper Silesia (now Katowice, Poland); died in San Diego, California, Feb 20, 1972, of a pulmonary embolism; dau. of Friedrich Göppert (pediatrician and professor of medicine at Georgia Augusta University in Göttingen) and Maria Wolff Göppert (schoolteacher and musician); Georgia Augusta University, PhD, 1930; m. Joseph Edward Mayer, Jan 18, 1930; children: Maria Anne Mayer (b. 1933); Peter Conrad Mayer (b. 1938). ❖ Was the 1st woman to win the Nobel Prize for Physics (1963), for her explanation of the nuclear shell model theory; sailed for US (1931); became a naturalized citizen (1933); worked as "volunteer associate" at Johns Hopkins University (1931–39); despite attitudes against hiring women, was lecturer in chemistry at Columbia University (1939–45); was a research physicist for Substitute Alloy Materials Project (1942–45); served as senior physicist for Institute for Nuclear Studies and Argonne National Laboratory at the University of Chicago (1945–59); published theory of nuclear shell model in *Physical Review* (1948); co-wrote *Statistical Mechanics* (1940) and *Elementary Theory of Nuclear Shell Structure* (1955); was the 5th woman elected to National Academy of Sciences (1956); named professor and given salary at University of California at San Diego (1959–72); became 1st woman to win the Nobel Prize for theoretical physics when she was awarded the honor along with Hans Jensen and Eugene P. Wigner for their research on the structure of atomic nucleia (1963); overcame the obstacles of being a woman in the world of theoretical science and a German immigrant in the US in 1930s to rise to the top of her field. ❖ See also *Women in World History.*

MAYFAIR, Mitzi (1914–1976). American theatrical dancer. Born June 6, 1914, in Fulton, KY; died May 1976 in Tucson, AZ; m. Charles Henderson (movie studio executive), 1944. ❖ Performed on Broadway as Hal Le Roy's exhibition ballroom partner in *Ziegfeld Follies of 1931* and continued to perform with him in a series of musical film shorts for Vitaphone (1931–34); tap-danced on Broadway in *Take a Chance* (1932), *Calling All Stars* (1934), *At Home Abroad* (1935), and others; films include *Paramount on Parade* (1930), *Tip, Tap, Toe* (1932), and *Four Jills in a Jeep* (1944); also performed for USO during WWII.

MAYFREDA DE PIROVANO (d. 1300). Italian heretic. Killed in 1300 in Milan; never married; no children. ❖ A close friend and follower of the heretical sect leader Guglielma of Milan, continued preaching for 8 years after his death; was eventually arrested, condemned, and burned at the stake as a heretic. ❖ See also *Women in World History.*

MAYHAR, Ardath (1930—). American science-fiction and short-story writer. Name variations: (pseudonyms) Frank Cannon; John Kildeer. Born Ardath Hurst, Feb 20, 1930, in Timpson, TX; m. Joe Mayhar, 1958; children: 4. ❖ Published western novels but mostly known as writer of science fiction, focusing on telepathy and other mind powers; best known for *Exile on Vlahil* (1984), also wrote *How the Gods Wove in Kyrannon* (1979), *The Seekers of Shar Nuhn* (1980), *Warlock's Gift* (1982), *Lords of the Triple Moons* (1983), *The World Ends in Hickory Hollow* (1985), *Island in the Lake* (1993), *Passage West* (1994), *The Savage Land* (1995) and *A Road of Stars* (1998).

MAYHEW, Kate (1853–1944). American stage actress. Born Sept 2, 1853, in Indianapolis, IN; died June 16, 1944, in NYC. ❖ Appeared on stage for more than 75 years in over 500 productions; made NY debut in *My Neighbor's Wife* at Niblo's Gardens (1873); later appeared with Edward O. Sothern, father of E.H. Sothern, in *The American Cousin*; created title role in Bret Harte's *M'Liss* (1878).

MAYLING SOONG (b. 1898). *See Song Meiling.*

MAYNARD, Anna Maria (1791–1855). *See Chapman, Anna Maria.*

MAYNARD, Frances (1861–1938). *See Greville, Frances Evelyn.*

MAYNARD, Mary (c. 1938—). American labor leader. Born c. 1938. ❖ Served as truck driver for Pittston Coal Co.; the only female member of United Mine Workers of America (UMWA) in Rum Creek, WV, became its president, making her the 1st woman president of a local union (1977).

MAYNE, Ethel Colburn (1865–1941). British novelist and short-story writer. Name variations: Frances E. Huntley; Ethelind Colburn Mayne. Born Ethelind Frances Colburn Mayne, Jan 7, 1865, in Co. Kilkenny, Ireland; died April 30, 1941, Torquay, Devon, Ireland; dau. of Charles Edward Bolton Mayne and Charlotte Emily Henrietta (Sweetman) Mayne. ❖ Published short stories in literary magazine *Yellow Book* and was its assistant editor; stories and novels, which deal with position of women in society, include *Jessie Vandeleur* (1902), *The Fourth Ship* (1908), *Byron* (1912), *One of Our Grandmothers* (1916), and *A Regency Chapter: Lady Bessborough and Her Friendships* (1939); also translated several works, including *The Lessons of Raoul Pugno* by Raoul Pugno (1911), *Madame de Pompadour* by Marcelle Tinayre (1925), *The Forest Ship: A Book of the Amazon* by Richard Bermann (1930), and *Byron and the Need of Fatality* by Charles du Bos (1932).

MAYNE, Janet (c. 1819–1892). *See Donald, Janet.*

MAYNE, Margo (1938–2004). *See McLennan, Margo.*

MAYNOR, Dorothy (1910–1996). African-American concert soprano. Name variations: Dorothy Leigh Mainor; Dorothy L. Maynor; Dorothy Maynor-Rooks. Born Sept 2 (some sources cite Sept 3), 1910, in Norfolk, VA; died Feb 19, 1996, in West Chester, PA; dau. of John Mainor (minister) and Alice (Jeffries) Mainor; Hampton Institute, BS, 1933; Westminster Choir College, BMus, 1935; m. Shelby Albright Rooks (Presbyterian minister), 1942. ❖ Became soloist with Westminster Choir (1935); moved to NY (1935); made professional debut at NYC's Town Hall (1939); debuted at Carnegie Hall (1941); won acclaim for her classical repertoire and for her renderings of African-American spirituals and recorded oratorio and opera on the Victor music label; was the 1st African-American to perform in the concert hall of the Library of Congress; during WWII, often sang for armed forces on board military ships, and also soloed with the Philadelphia Symphony, NY Philharmonic Orchestra, Boston Symphony, and Chicago Symphony; performed at Harry Truman's presidential inauguration (1948); toured Europe (1949); retired from the stage (1963); founded Harlem School for the Arts (1964); though never offered a contract with a leading opera house because of skin color, was invited to join the board of the Metropolitan Opera (1975), becoming the 1st African-American so honored. ❖ See also *Women in World History.*

MAYO, Katherine (1867–1940). American novelist. Born Jan 24, 1867, in Ridgway, PA; died Oct 9, 1940, in Bedford Hills, NY; dau. of James Henry Mayo and Harriet Elizabeth Ingraham; longtime companion of heiress M. Moyca Newell. ❖ Lived in Dutch Guiana for 8 years during father's search for gold (from 1899); worked as research assistant for Oswald Garrison Villard for biography of John Brown; met (1910) and traveled with M. Moyca Newell; lobbied for state police force in NY (1917); published 1st book, *Justice to All,* with introduction by Theodore Roosevelt (1917); published several magazine articles and books, the most famous of which was *Mother India* (1927), which tended to paint an unsubstantiated portrait of gender behavior among Hindus; her writings often advocated for "the voiceless underdog" and argued against independence for developing nations (e.g., India and Phillippines); other books include *The Isles of Fear* (1925), *Slaves of the Gods* (1929), *Volume Two* (1931) and *Soldiers What Next!* (1934).

MAYO, Margaret (1882–1951). American actress and playwright. Born Lilian Clatten, Nov 19, 1882, in Brownsville, IL; died Feb 25, 1951, in Ossining, NY; m. Edgar Selwyn (div.). ❖ Began career as an actress, debuting in NY in *Thoroughbred* (1896); retired from the stage (1903) and turned to writing plays, including *The Winding Way, The Austrian Dancer, Nip and Tuck, Polly of the Circus, The Debtors, Baby Mine, Behind the Scenes, The Flirt, The Wall Street Girl* (with husband), *Twin Beds, His Bridal Night, Heads Up* (with Zellah Covington), *Being Fitted, Prisoner of the World,* and *The White Way* and *Loving Ladies* (both with Aubrey Kennedy); also adapted *Under Two Flags, The Jungle* and *The Marriage of William Ashe.*

MAYO, Mary Anne (1845–1903). American farm organizer. Name variations: Mary Anne Bryant Mayo. Born Mary Anne Bryant, May 24, 1845, near Battle Creek, Michigan; died April 21, 1903; m. Perry Mayo, April 1865. ❖ Became effective organizer for the Patrons of Husbandry (called the Grange) and traveled through Michigan in various capacities to promote work of the Grange; emphasized full participation of women and children in Grange organizations and Farmers' Institute meetings; effected creation of women's department (1897) at Michigan State Agricultural College (now Michigan State University).

MAYO, Sara Tew (1869–1930). American physician. Born Sara Tew Mayo, May 26, 1869, near Vidalia, LA; died Mar 7, 1930, in New Orleans, LA, from angina pectoris; dau. of Emma (Tew) Mayo and George Spencer Mayo; graduate of Woman's Medical College of Pennsylvania, 1898. ❖ One of the 1st practicing female physicians in the American south, founded (with Elizabeth Bass and other women physicians) the South's only all-women-managed hospital, the New Orleans Dispensary for Women and Children (1905, renamed the New Orleans Hospital and Dispensary for Women and Children by 1908, then Sara Mayo Hospital), in large part because of the sexist employment policies apropos of women physicians in New Orleans at the time; served as a president (1st 2 years) and as a treasurer; denied admittance on the basis of gender to the Orleans Parish Medical Society until 1913; served as physician at St. Anna's Asylum; was staff member of Touro Infirmary and Baptist Hospital; maintained extensive private practice throughout career, specializing in surgery, obstetrics, and gynecology; was the 1st medical woman in New Orleans to be awarded the New Orleans *Times-Picayune* "Loving Cup" for outstanding civic service (1910).

MAYO, Virginia (1920–2005). American actress. Born Virginia Clara Jones on Nov 30, 1920, in St. Louis, MO; died Jan 17, 2005, in Thousand Oaks, CA; m. Michael O'Shea (actor), 1947 (died 1973); children: 1. ❖ Began career as a show girl; made film debut in *Jack London* (1943); during WWII, starred in a number of films designed for US military personnel abroad, including *Stand for Action* (1942) and *Salute to the Marines* (1943); was often cast as a foil opposite such comedians as Danny Kaye and Bob Hope; most critically acclaimed roles were in the Academy Award-winning classics *The Best Years of Our Lives* (1946) and *The Secret Life of Walter Mitty* (1947); other films include *The Kid From Brooklyn* (1946), *The Girl from Jones Beach* (1949), *Always Leave Them Laughing* (1949), *The West Point Story* (1950), *The Flame and the Arrow* (1950), *Painting the Clouds With Sunshine* (1951), *Captain Horatio Hornblower* (1951), *The Silver Chalice* (1955), *Won Ton Ton, The Dog Who Saved Hollywood* (1976) and *French Quarter* (1977).

MAY OF TECK (1867–1953). See *Mary of Teck.*

MAYOR, Flora M. (1872–1932). British novelist and short-story writer. Name variations: F.M. Mayor; (pseudonym) Mary Stafford. Born Flora Macdonald Mayor, Oct 20, 1872, in Kingston upon Thames, Surrey, England; died Jan 28, 1932, in Hampstead, London; dau. of Rev. Joseph Mayor (professor of moral philosophy at King's College) and Jessie Grote Mayor (musician and linguist); had identical twin sister, Alice Mayor; attended Newnham College, Cambridge. ❖ Began acting career which ended after illness; became a semi-invalid; never married and often used spinsterhood as theme for novels; works explore late-Victorian morality and inner lives of female characters; published *Mrs. Hammond's Children* under name Mary Strafford (1901), followed by *The Third Miss Symons* (1913), *The Rector's Daughter* (1924), considered her best work, *The Squire's Daughter* (1929), and *The Room Opposite and Other Tales of Mystery and Imagination* (1935).

MAYREDER, Rosa (1858–1938). Austrian painter, writer, sociologist, feminist, and peace activist. Born Rosa Obermayer, Nov 30, 1858, in Vienna, Austria; died Jan 19, 1938, in Vienna; dau. of Franz Obermayer (restaurant owner) and Marie Obermayer; attended Institute for Girls and Sophie Paulus' School, both private girls' schools in Vienna; studied painting with Hugo Darnaut; m. Karl Mayreder (architect), 1881 (died 1935). ❖ Along with Marianne Hainisch, Marie Lang, and Auguste Fickert, is remembered as one of the founders of the Austrian feminist movement; studied painting and exhibited her landscapes and flower paintings at Vienna *Künstlerhaus*; for many years, wrote art criticism for a Vienna newspaper under pseudonym Franz Arnold; published collection of short stories, *Aus meiner Jugend (From my Youth,* 1896); became active in feminist movement (1894); helped write the "Petition to the Austrian Parliament against the Official Sanctioning of Houses of Prostitution"; began co-editing the journal *Dokumente der Frauen (Documents of Women,* 1900); elected vice president of Allgemeiner Österreichischer Frauenverein, one of Vienna's largest women's organizations (1903), of which she had been a co-founder with Fickert; addressed feminism in 1st novel *Idole, Geschichte einer Liebe (Idols, A Love Story,* 1899); published a volume of essays in cultural philosophy, *Zur Kritik der Weiblichkeit (Contributions to a Critique of Womanhood,* 1905), followed by *Geschlecht und Kultur (Gender and Culture,* c. 1914); at 3rd congress of International Women's League for Peace and Freedom, was elected vice president of Austrian branch (1921); also became a fervent pacifist and antimilitarist. An Austrian 500 schilling banknote bearing her likeness was issued in her honor (1997). ❖ See also *Women in World History.*

MAYRÖCKER, Friederike (1924—). Austrian poet, novelist and children's writer. Name variations: Friederike Mayrocker or Mayroecker. Born Dec 20, 1924, in Vienna, Austria. ❖ Was associated with experimental Vienna Group and became known for the baroque, hallucinatory quality of her writing; prose works include *Larifari, Ein konfuses Buch* (1956), *Minimonsters Traumlexikon* (1968), *Aus einem Stein entsprungen* (1989), and *Heiligenanstalt* (1994); poetry includes *Texte* (1966), *Fantom Fan Rowohlt Reinbek* (1971), *Drei Hörspiele* (1975), *Die Abschiede* (1980), *Reise durch die Nacht* (1984), *Entfachung* (1990), *Kabinett Notizen nach James Joyce* (1995), and *Magische Blätter V* (1999); children's works include *Sinclair Sofokles der Babysaurier* (1971) and *ABC-Thriller* (1992); non-fiction includes *Requiem für Ernst Jandl* (2001). Won International Prize of The America Awards (1997).

MAYSON, Isabella Mary (1836–1865). See *Beeton, Isabella Mary.*

MAYUMI AOKI (1953—). See *Aoki, Mayumi.*

MAYWOOD, Augusta (1825–1876). American ballet dancer. Name variations: Augusta Williams. Born 1825, probably in New York City; died in Lemberg, Austrian Galicia (now Lvov, Poland), Nov 3, 1876; dau. of Henry August Williams (itinerant English actor) and Martha Bally (English actress); stepdau. of Robert Maywood (manager of Chestnut Street Theater in Philadelphia); m. Charles Mabille (dancer), 1840 (sep. 1848); m. Carlo Gardini (physician, journalist, and impresario), 1858 (sep. 1864); children: (with Mabille) Cecile Augusta Mabille (b. 1842); (with Pasquale Borri) Paul Maywood (b. around 1847); one who died young (b. 1864). ❖ The 1st American ballet dancer to achieve critical acceptance in Europe, made stage debut (1837) and NY debut (1838); with mother, sailed for Paris (1838); made Paris debut in *Le Diable boîteux* (1839); underage, caused scandal when she ran off with another dancer from the Opera, Charles Mabille (1840); leaving daughter and husband, relocated to Vienna (1845), where she began a successful engagement at Kaerntnertor Theater; made debut at La Scala (1848), where she won enormous acclaim and steady engagements; was named La Scala's *prima donna assoluta* (1853), the company's highest honor, for her interpretations of classic ballets such as *Giselle* and *La Gypsy*; devised a ballet version of *Uncle Tom's Cabin*; also danced as Rita Gauthier (Alphonsine Plessis) in 1st Italian production of *La Dame aux Camélias*; was the 1st woman to tour with her own company of dancers and technicians, which made performances run much more smoothly; a legitimate star in Europe, consistently avoided returning to US; retired from stage (1858) and married Carlo Gardini; founded a school of ballet in Vienna. ❖ See also *Women in World History*.

MAYY ZIYADA (1886–1941). *See Ziyada, Mayy.*

MAZARIN, duchess of (1646–1699). *See Mancini, Hortense.*

MAZARIN'S NIECES. *See Mancini, Laure (1635–1657); Martinozzi, Anne Marie (1637–1672); Mancini, Olympia (c. 1639–1708); Mancini, Marie (1640–1715); Mancini, Hortense (1646–1699); Mancini, Marie-Anne (1649–1714); Martinozzi, Laura.*

MAZEAS, Jacqueline (1920—). French track-and-field athlete. Born Oct 10, 1920, in France. ❖ At London Olympics, won a bronze medal in the discus throw (1948).

MAZEPPA (1835–1868). *See Menken, Adah Isaacs.*

MAZINA, Maria (1964—). Russian-Jewish fencer. Name variations: Mariya Mazina. Born April 18, 1964, in Moscow, Russia. ❖ Won a bronze medal at Atlanta Olympics (1996) and a gold medal at Sydney Olympics (2000), both for team épée.

MAZIY, Svetlana (1968—). Ukrainian rower. Name variations: Svetlana Mazy. Born Jan 30, 1968, in Kiev, Ukraine; married. ❖ Won a silver medal in quadruple sculls at Seoul Olympics (1988) and Atlanta Olympics (1996); came in 4th at Sydney Olympics (2000); at World championships, won silver medals in quadruple sculls (1989, 1990, 1999) and bronze medals (1987, 1994, 1997).

MAZUMDAR, Sucheta (1908–1974). *See Kripalani, Sucheta.*

MAZURANIC, Ivana Brlic (1874–1938). *See Brlić-Mažuranić, Ivana.*

MAZY, Svetlana (1968—). *See Maziy, Svetlana.*

MAZZETTI, Enrica von Handel (1871–1955). *See Handel-Mazzetti, Enrica von.*

MBANDE, Jinga (c. 1580s–1663). *See Njinga.*

MBANGO ETONE, Françoise (1976—). Cameroonian track-and-field athlete. Born April 14, 1976, in Cameroon. ❖ Breaking the African record at 15.30, won a gold medal for triple jump at Athens Olympics (2004), the 1st Cameroon woman to win an Olympic gold.

MBOGO, Jael (1939—). Kenyan politician. Name variations: Mama Jael; Jael Ogombe Mbogo. Born 1939 in Rift Valley Province, Kenya. ❖ Trained as stenographer; became a member of Nairobi City Council; studied economics in US and then worked with women's political party in Tanzania; returned with family to Nairobi (1965) and joined women's organization Maendeleo wa Wanawake; with 4 other women, founded FORD-Kenya Party and became its organizing secretary; became secretary general of Freedom from Hunger; was a candidate in the general elections (1974 and 1997).

MC AND MAC. *Names beginning with the prefix Mac have been separated from Mc and are listed earlier in alphabetical order.*

McAFEE, Mildred Helen (1900–1994). *See Horton, Mildred McAfee.*

McALEESE, Mary (1951—). Irish politician, barrister, broadcast journalist, and president of Ireland. Born Mary Leneghan, June 27, 1951, in Belfast, Northern Ireland; m. Martin McAleese, 1976; children: Emma (b. 1982) and twins Justin and SaraMai (b. 1985). ❖ Became a barrister (1973); called to the Northern Ireland Bar (1974), specializing in criminal and family law; was Reid Professor of Criminal Law, Criminology and Penology, Trinity College, Dublin (1975–79, 1981); joined the Irish television service, RTE (1979), as a current affairs journalist and co-host; campaigned to have ban on abortion added to Constitution and ban on divorce retained, but supported such liberal causes as women in the priesthood and homosexual law reform; appointed director of Institute on Legal Studies at Queen's University, Belfast (1987); appointed pro-vice-chancellor at Queen's (1994), the 1st woman to hold this position; elected president of Ireland (1997), the 1st born in Northern Ireland.

McALISKEY, Bernadette Devlin (1947—). Irish activist. Name variations: Bernadette Devlin; Bernadette Devlin-McAliskey. Pronunciations Mack-AL-is-KEE. Born Bernadette Josephine Devlin at Cookstown, Co. Tyrone, Northern Ireland, April 23, 1947; dau. of John James Devlin and Elizabeth Bernadette Devlin, both of Cookstown; educated at St. Patrick's Academy, Dungannon, Co. Tyrone, and at Queen's University, Belfast; m. Michael McAliskey, April 23, 1973; children: Roisin McAliskey (b. Aug 1971); Deirdre McAliskey (b. 1976); Fintan McAliskey (b. 1979). ❖ Irish socialist republican, who was a prominent and well-remembered figure in 1960s civil-rights campaign in Northern Ireland, became a founder-member of the People's Democracy movement (1968); took part in the civil-rights march from Belfast to Derry (Jan 1969); elected to British House of Commons and sat for Mid-Ulster constituency (1969–74); unsuccessfully contested European election (1979) and Irish Republic's election (1982); narrowly survived assassination attempt (1981); campaigned against extradition from Irish Republic to Northern Ireland (1987–88); was opposed to the Downing Street Declaration of Dec 1993; continued to take an active part in socialist republican politics; as the popular champion of nationalist Derry during the ferment of 1969–70, became a living symbol both of Northern Ireland's most intractable political problems and of the need for, and inevitability of, change. ❖ See also autobiography *The Price of My Soul* (Deutsch, 1969); G.W. Target, *Bernadette* (Hodder & Stoughton, 1975); and *Women in World History*.

McALISKEY, Roisin (1971—). Irish activist. Born Aug 1971; dau. of Bernadette Devlin McAliskey and Michael McAliskey. ❖ Ill and pregnant, was jailed in connection with an Irish Republican Army mortar attack on a British army base in Osnabrueck, northwest Germany (1997). ❖ See also *Women in World History*.

McALLAN, Jessie Marguerite (c. 1855–1937). *See Williamson, Jessie Marguerite.*

McALLISTER, Anne Hunter (1892–1983). Scottish speech therapist. Born 1892 in Biggar, Lanarkshire, Scotland; died 1983; Glasgow University, BEd, DSc. ❖ Pioneer in speech training and therapy, began career teaching in city schools in Glasgow; joined staff of what would later become Jordanhill College of Education (1919); earned education degree from Glasgow University as well as PhD for research into speech training and pathology; began assisting at educational pioneer William Boyd's clinic (1926); established Glasgow School of Speech Therapy (1935) and was among founders of College of Speech Therapists, which serves as British professional headquarters of speech therapy.

McALLISTER, Mary H. (1947—). *See McAllister, Susie.*

McALLISTER, Susie (1947—). American golfer. Name variations: Mary H. McAllister. Born Aug 27, 1947, in Beaumont, TX. ❖ Turned pro (1971); won Wheeling Classic (1975); plays on Women's Senior tour.

McALPINE, Rachel (1940—). New Zealand poet, novelist and playwright. Born 1940 in Fairlie, New Zealand; Victoria University, BA in Education. ❖ Taught at Doshisha Women's University in Kyoto, Japan; as a writer, became known for lyrical verse and facility for dialogue in plays and novels; poetry includes *Lament for Ariadne* (1975), *Stay at the Dinner Party* (1977), *Recording Angel* (1983), and *Thirteen Waves* (1986); plays include *The Stationary Sixth Form Poetry Trip* (1980), *Driftwood* (1985), and *Power Play* (1990); novels include *The Limits of Green* (1986), *Running Away from Home* (1987), and *Farewell Speech* (1990).

McANDREWS, Agnes (1907–1974). *See Geraghty, Agnes.*

McAULEY, Catherine (1778–1841). Irish religious founder. Name variations: (incorrectly) Catherine McCauley. Born in Ballymun, Co. Dublin, Ireland, in 1778 (some sources cite 1781); died in Dublin, Nov 11, 1841; dau. of James McAuley and Elinor (Conway) McAuley. ❖ Irish nun who founded the Institute of Our Lady of Mercy (Sisters of Mercy), 1st opened a house on Baggot Street, Dublin (1827), to serve as a school for poor children and a shelter for homeless young women; as a preliminary to founding her own order of nuns (1830), entered the Presentation Convent at George's Hill in Dublin to serve her novitiate; took final vows (1831) and within days the new Institute of Our Lady of Mercy was established; her Sisters of Mercy soon proved their value when a cholera epidemic broke out (1832) and they took charge of one of the temporary hospitals at the request of Board of Health; faced enormous problems in the early years of the Sisters of Mercy, including the myriad difficulties in establishing new foundations in Ireland and Britain, lack of money, poor health, and continuing problems with certain Catholic church leaders, but overcame most of them by her determination, practicality and good humor; founded 11 convents in Ireland and Britain. ❖ See also *The Correspondence of Catherine McAuley, 1827–41* (Sisters of Mercy, 1989); Roland Burke Savage, *Catherine McAuley: The First Sister of Mercy* (Gill, 1949); Mary C. Sullivan, *Catherine McAuley and the Tradition of Mercy* (Four Courts, 1995); and *Women in World History.*

McAULEY, Mary Ludwig Hays (1754–1832). See *McCauley, Mary Ludwig Hays.*

McAULEY, Sarah (c. 1817–1898). See *Dougherty, Sarah.*

McAULIFFE, Christa (1948–1986). American educator and space pioneer. Born Sharon Christa Corrigan, Sept 2, 1958, in Boston, MA; died in space shuttle, Jan 28, 1986; dau. of Edward C. Corrigan (accountant) and Grace George Corrigan (teacher); attended Framingham State College, BA, 1970, Bowie State College, MEd, 1978; m. Steve James McAuliffe, Aug 23, 1970; children: Scott (b. 1976) and Caroline (b. 1979). ❖ First private American citizen selected to fly in space and 1st civilian to die on the space shuttle, taught in several Maryland and New Hampshire schools and developed a women's history course (1970–85); won NASA's Teacher-in-Space competition (1985); killed on space shuttle *Challenger* (Jan 28, 1986). ❖ See also Grace George Corrigan, *A Journal for Christa* (1993); and *Women in World History.*

McAULIFFE-ENNIS, Helena (1951—). Irish politician. Name variations: Helena McAuliffe Ennis. Born Helena McAuliffe, April 1, 1951, in Miltownpass, Co. Westmeath, Ireland; dau. of Timothy McAuliffe (senator). ❖ Quit the Labour Party to join the Progressive Democrats (1985), then returned to Labour (1988); elected to the Seanad from the Cultural and Educational Panel (1983–87).

McAVAN, Linda (1962—). English politician. Born Dec 2, 1962, in Bradford, West Yorkshire, England. ❖ As a European Socialist, elected to 4th and 5th European Parliament (1994–99, 1999–2004) from UK.

McAVITY, Helen (1913–1986). See *Mack, Helen.*

McAVOY, May (1901–1984). American silent-film actress. Name variations: Mae McAvoy. Born Sept 18, 1901, in New York, NY; died after heart attack, April 26, 1984, in Sherman Oaks, CA; dau. of a livery-stable owner; m. Maurice G. Cleary (United Artists and Lockheed Aircraft executive), 1929 (div.); children: Patrick Cleary. ❖ Star of the silent-film era, was cast as an ingenue in *Hate* (1917), which led to steady work in Pathé studio's silent films; appeared in *Mrs. Wiggs of the Cabbage Patch* (1919); received good reviews for her work in *Sentimental Tommy* (1921), winning a contract with Paramount; over next few years, appeared in such films as *The Enchanted Cottage* (1924), *Lady Windermere's Fan* (1925), and *Ben-Hur* (1927), which cast her opposite Al Jolson in *The Jazz Singer*, the film that introduced spoken dialogue; also appeared in 1st British talkie, *The Terror* (1928), after which she dropped from sight. ❖ See also *Women in World History.*

McBEAN, Marnie (1968—). Canadian rower. Born Marnie Elizabeth McBean, Jan 28, 1968, in Vancouver, British Columbia, Canada. ❖ Along with Kathleen Heddle, won gold medals for coxless pairs and coxed eights at World championships (1991), gold medal in coxless pairs and a gold medal in coxed eights at Barcelona Olympics (1992), and a gold medal for double sculls and a bronze medal for quadruple sculls at Atlanta Olympics (1996). Inducted into Canadian Sports Hall of Fame (1997).

McBETH, Susan Law (1830–1893). American missionary. Born 1830 in Doune, Scotland; died May 26, 1893, in Mount Idaho, Idaho; dau. of Alexander McBeth (stonemason) and Mary (Henderson) McBeth. ❖ Invited by Presbyterian Board of Foreign Missions to do missionary work with Choctaw Indians (1858); with outbreak of Civil War having interrupted mission, taught at Fairfield University in Iowa; became 1 of 1st women agents for relief organization US Christian Commission (1863); helped establish and served as presiding head of home for working girls in St. Louis, MO (1866–73); returned to missionary work, this time with Nez Percé Indians in Idaho; took over job of preparing Indian men for ministry in Kamiah, Idaho, after death of Henry Harmon Spalding (1874); compiled but did not complete dictionary of Nez Percé language; taught at school for women established by sister and fellow missionary Kate McBeth. ❖ See also Kate C. McBeth, *The Nez Percés since Lewis and Clark* (Revell, 1908); Allen Conrad Morrill, *Out of the Blanket: The Story of Sue and Kate McBeth, Missionaries to the Nez Percés* (U. Press of Idaho, 1978).

McBRIDE, Clara (1905–1992). See *Hale, Clara.*

McBRIDE, Mary Margaret (1899–1976). American journalist, writer, and radio host. Name variations: (early radio name) Martha Deane. Born Nov 16, 1899, in Paris, MO; died in West Shokun, New York, April 7, 1976; dau. of Thomas Walker McBride (farmer) and Elizabeth (Craig) McBride; University of Missouri, BA, 1919. ❖ A fixture on American radio networks for 2 decades, worked for a few years at *New York Evening Mail*, where she was only the 2nd female writer to be hired; wrote articles for the *Saturday Evening Post, Good Housekeeping,* and other popular periodicals; wrote light-hearted travel guides with Helen Josephy (1929–32); began hosting radio program aimed at women for NY radio station, WOR (1934); hired by CBS Radio Network (1937) to air a show under own name; worked for NBC (1941–50), then jumped to ABC; extremely popular, interviewed noted celebrities of the day, broadcast from remote locations, and ad-libbed, a risky practice in the days of live radio; called "the First Lady of Radio," held 10th anniversary in Madison Square Garden for 25,000, and the 15th in Yankee Stadium for 40,000. Awarded medal for outstanding journalism from University of Missouri and medal from Woman's National Exposition of Arts and Industries (1936). ❖ See also autobiographies *How Dear to My Heart* (1940), *A Long Way from Missouri* (1959), and *Out of the Air* (1960); and *Women in World History.*

McBRIDE, Patricia (1942—). American ballet dancer. Born Aug 23, 1942, in Teaneck, NJ; m. Jean-Pierre Bonnefoux (dancer), 1973; children: son Chris; (adopted) Melanie. ❖ Studied at School of American Ballet; joined New York City Ballet (1959), became a principal (1961), and created many roles for George Balanchine, becoming one of his favorite dancers; had successful partnership with Edward Villella (1960s); retired from performance (1989); became associate director of North Carolina Dance Theater (1996).

McBRIDE, Rose (1879–1974). See *Graham, Rose.*

McCAFFERTY, Chris (1945—). English politician and member of Parliament. Born Chris Livesley, Oct 14, 1945; attended Footscray High School, Melbourne, Australia; also schooled in Manchester, UK; m. Michael McCafferty; m. David Tarlo. ❖ Representing Labour, was a member of House of Commons for Calder Valley (1997, 2001, 2005).

McCAFFREY, Anne (1926—). American science-fiction and short-story writer. Born April 1, 1926, in Cambridge, MA; dau. of George Herbert (city administrator and colonel, US army) and Anne D. (McElroy) McCaffrey; Radcliffe College, BA cum laude, 1947; graduate study in meteorology, University of City of Dublin; married Wright Johnson (in public relations), Jan 14, 1950 (div. 1970); children: Alec, Todd, Georgeanne. ❖ Works include *Restoree* (1968), *Dragonflight* (1968), *Dragonquest* (1971), *The Kilternan Legacy* (1975), *Dragonsong* (1976), *The Crystal Singer* (1981), *The Coelura* (1983), *Stitch in Snow* (1984), *Nerilka's Story* (1986), *All the Weyrs of Pern* (1991), *Freedom's Landing* (1996), *The Master Harper of Pern* (1998), *The Tower and the Hive* (1999), and *Nimisha's Ship* (1999). Won Hugo Award for Dragonflight (1967); won Nebula Award, Science Fiction Writers of America (1968). ❖ See also Gordon Benson Jr. and Phil Stephenson-Payne, *Anne McCaffrey, Dragonlady and More: A Working Bibliography* (Galactic Central, 1990).

McCALLUM, Heather (c. 1973—). See *Whitestone, Heather.*

McCAMBRIDGE, Mercedes (1916–2004). American actress. Born Carlotta Mercedes Agnes McCambridge, Mar 17, 1916, in Joliet, IL; died Mar 2, 2004, in LaJolla, CA; dau. of John Patrick McCambridge (farmer) and Marie (Mahaffry) McCambridge; Mundelein College, BA,

1937; m. William Fifield (writer), 1939 (div. 1946); m. Fletcher Markle (writer and director), 1950 (div. 1962); children: (1st m.) John Lawrence (died 1987). ❖ Stage, screen, and radio actress, appeared in numerous radio series, including "Inner Sanctum," "Abie's Irish Rose," "I Love a Mystery," "Bulldog Drummond," "Dick Tracy," and "The Thin Man"; starred in her own series on CBS radio, "Big Sister" (1945); signed with Columbia, made film debut in *All the King's Men* (1949) for which she won an Academy Award for Best Supporting Actress (1950); won acclaim for performances in *Johnny Guitar* (1954), *Giant* (1956), for which she received her 2nd Academy Award nomination, and *Suddenly, Last Summer* (1959); was the off-camera voice of the demon in *The Exorcist*. ❖ See also memoir *The Two of Us* (1960) and autobiography *The Quality of Mercy* (1981); and *Women in World History*.

McCANNON, Peggy Santiglia (1944—). *See Santiglia, Peggy.*

McCARDELL, Claire (1905–1958). American fashion designer. Born May 24, 1905, in Frederick, MD; died of cancer, Mar 22, 1958, in New York, NY; dau. of Adrian Leroy McCardell (banker and politician) and Frances (Clingan) McCardell; degree from New York School of Fine and Applied Arts (later Parsons School of Design), 1928; m. Irving Harris (architect), 1943. ❖ One of the foremost American sportswear designers of mid-20th century, moved to New York City (1925); traveled to Paris (1927); hired at Townley Frocks (1930), became its chief designer (1931), creating a line of "separates" that could be worn in various combinations for varying occasions; created designs for Hattie Carnegie's Workshop Originals line (1938–40); returned to Townley Frocks (1940) and became a partner there (1952); helped define what came to be called the "American Look." Received Coty Award from American Fashion Critics Association (1944). ❖ See also *Women in World History*.

McCARDLE, Dorothy (1889–1958). *See Macardle, Dorothy.*

McCARTHY, Arlene (1960—). Irish politician. Born Oct 10, 1960, in Belfast, Northern Ireland. ❖ As a European Socialist, elected to 4th and 5th European Parliament (1994–99, 1999–2004) from UK.

McCARTHY, Carolyn (1944—). American nurse and politician. Born Carolyn Cook, Jan 5, 1944, in Brooklyn, NY; grew up in Mineola, LI; dau. of Tom (boilermaker) and Irene Cook; trained at Glen Cove Nursing School; m. Dennis McCarthy (stockbroker), 1967; children: Kevin McCarthy (b. 1968). ❖ Was a registered nurse for over 30 years; husband was killed and son paralyzed when a crazed gunman shot indiscriminately on a Long Island commuter train (Dec 7, 1993); a lifelong Republican, turned the incident into a campaign against gun violence; as a Democrat, elected to US House of Representatives (1996), in her 1st race for public office; reelected (1998, 2000, 2002, 2004), representing Long Island's 4th Congressional District. ❖ See also (NBC-TV movie) "The Long Island Incident" (1998).

McCARTHY, Kathryn O'Loughlin (1894–1952). American politician. Born Kathryn Ellen O'Loughlin, April 24, 1894, near Hays, Kansas; died in Hays, Kansas, Jan 16, 1952; dau. of John O'Loughlin and Mary Ellen (McIntosh) O'Loughlin; Fort Hays State College (later Kansas State Teachers College), BS in Edn, 1917; University of Chicago Law School, JD, 1920; m. Daniel M. McCarthy (Kansas state senator), Feb 4, 1933. ❖ Opened her own law practice (1928); became active in the state Democratic Party and was elected to Kansas State House of Representatives (1931); elected to US House of Representatives (73rd Congress) from 6th District of Kansas (1932); a supporter of New Deal policies, also backed the Agriculture Adjustment Act; served on the Committee on Education, in which role she sought increased federal funding for vocational schools; lost bid for reelection (1934).

McCARTHY, Lillah (1875–1960). English actress and manager. Name variations: Lady Lillah Keeble; Lillah Granville-Barker. Born Sept 22, 1875, in Cheltenham, England; died April 15, 1960, in London; dau. of J. McCarthy, FRAS; sister of Daniel McCarthy (actor); great-aunt of Patricia Jessel; m. Harley Granville-Barker (playwright, director, trans., and writer), 1906 (div. 1918); m. Sir Frederick Keeble, 1920. ❖ Made London stage debut in *The Sign of the Cross* (1896); often toured with Wilson Barrett (1897–1904); appeared in the title role of *Nan*, as Lady Sybil in *What Every Woman Knows* (1908), as Margaret Knox in *Fanny's First Play* (1911), as Lavinia in *Androcles and the Lion* (1913) and starred in Shaw's *Man and Superman* and *Arms and the Man*, directed by Harley Granville-Barker; also worked with husband in his revolutionary series of Shakespearean productions at the Savoy Theater (1912–14); following divorce and remarriage (1920), left the stage. Named Officer of the

British Empire (OBE). ❖ See also autobiography *Myself as Friends* (1933).

McCARTHY, Marie Cecilia (1876–1943). *See Loftus, Cissie.*

McCARTHY, Mary (1912–1989). American critic, novelist, and journalist. Name variations: Mary McCarthy (1912–1933 and in her professional life throughout); Mary Johnsrud (1933–36); Mary Wilson (1937–45); Mary Broadwater (1948–60); Mary West (1961–89). Born Mary Therese McCarthy in Seattle, WA, June 21, 1912; died of lung cancer, Oct 25, 1989; dau. of Roy Winfield McCarthy and Therese (Preston) McCarthy; sister of Kevin McCarthy (actor); Vassar College, AB, 1933; m. Harold Johnsrud, 1933 (div. 1936); m. Edmund Wilson (writer), 1937 (div. 1945); m. Bowden Broadwater (writer and deputy headmaster), 1948 (div. 1961); m. James West (Public Affairs officer), April 15, 1961; children: (2nd m.) one son, Reuel K. Wilson (b. 1938). ❖ Leading literary critic, writer, and one of the nation's most prominent intellectuals whose sardonic social observations made her widely feared as well as much admired, 1st established herself as a hard-hitting and controversial literary critic, primarily for the *New Republic* and the *Nation;* found regular work and a circle of new friends at the *Partisan Review,* a journal of the anti-Communist left for which she became drama critic (mid-1930s); published 1st novel, *The Company She Keeps* (1942); with Edmund Wilson, had one of the most famous literary bad marriages of the 20th century; drew thinly veiled fictional versions of Wilson in many later novels, notably *The Groves of Academe;* published 2nd novel, *The Oasis* (1949), describing an intellectuals' commune; spent more and more time in Europe, culminating in 2 books about Italy, *Venice Observed* and *The Stones of Florence;* moved to Paris with James West (1962); gained fame with her most successful novel *The Group* (1963), a national bestseller which describes the fortunes of a circle of Vassar graduates in the 1930s, and depends heavily for characters and situations on her actual college friends; deplored America's role in Vietnam, writing *Vietnam, Hanoi, The Seventeenth Parallel* and *Medina;* returned to novels with *Birds of America* (1971) and *Cannibals and Missionaries* (1979), weaving, as before, episodes of her own life and those of her friends into imaginary dramatic settings. ❖ See also memoirs *Memories of a Catholic Girlhood* (1957), *How I Grew* (1987), and *Intellectual Memoirs: New York: 1936–1938* (1992); Doris Grumbach, *The Company She Kept* (Coward, 1967); Frances Kiernan, *Seeing Mary Plain* (Norton, 2000); Carol Brightman, *Writing Dangerously: Mary McCarthy and Her World* (Potter, 1992); and *Women in World History*.

McCARTHY, Mary Ann Recknall (1866–1933). New Zealand teacher, temperance reformer, and political activist. Born Aug 11, 1866, in Dunedin, New Zealand; died Oct 13, 1933, in Dunedin; dau. of Samuel McCarthy (locksmith) and Elizabeth Ann (Pyke) McCarthy. ❖ Trained at Dunedin Normal School and Dunedin Training College (early 1900s); assumed control of Waihao Downs School (1905–13); active in New Zealand Women's Christian Temperance Union (WCTU), becoming national superintendent for purity and moral education (1916); formed Dunedin branch of Women's International League (1917); represented New Zealand Section of Women's International League for Peace and Freedom (WILPF) at International Congress of Women in Zurich (1919); joined New Zealand Labor Party, spoke on its behalf and helped to establish new branches; also interested in internationalism and promotion of Esperanto. ❖ See also *Dictionary of New Zealand Biography* (Vol. 3).

McCARTHY, Maud (1858–1949). Australian-born nurse. Name variations: Dame Maud McCarthy; Emma Maud McCarthy. Born 1858 in Sydney, Australia; died 1949; dau. of William Frederick McCarthy. ❖ Traveled to England to train in nursing at the London Hospital (1858), then entered the nursing service of British armed forces; served in South Africa as an army nurse during Boer War (1899–1902); entered Queen Alexandra's Imperial Military Nursing Service, remaining in that post until 1910, when she was named principal matron of the War Office; at outbreak of WWI (1914), was named Matron-in-Chief of the British armies in France; headed the Territorial Nursing Service (1920–25). Created Dame Grand Cross of the Order of the British Empire (GBE, 1918).

McCARTHY, Patricia (1911–1943). American theater and film dancer. Name variations: McCarthy Sisters. Born Patricia Cook, 1911; died Jan 25, 1943, in New York, NY. ❖ Replaced Margaret McCarthy as one of the McCarthy Sisters and performed successfully in this dance team's Charleston-duet, considered unique for its all-female cast; with Dorothy McCarthy, appeared in *George White Scandals of 1927,* on the Keith circuit, and as flappers in numerous short subjects filmed in

Brooklyn studios; continued to perform for film after retirement of Dorothy McCarthy.

McCARTHY, Peggy (1956—). American rower. Born Mar 1956; attended University of Wisconsin, 1975–78. ❖ At Montreal Olympics, won a bronze medal in coxed eights (1976).

McCARTHY SISTERS. See McCarthy, Patricia (1911–1943).

McCARTNEY, Linda (1941–1998). American photographer and cookbook author. Name variations: Linda Eastman. Born Linda Louise Eastman on Sept 24, 1941, in Scarsdale, NY; died of breast cancer in Tucson, Arizona, April 17, 1998; dau. of Lee V. Eastman (entertainment lawyer) and Louise (Linder) Eastman; attended University of Arizona in Tucson; m. Joseph Melville See (geology student), c. 1960 (div. 1963); m. Paul McCartney (British musician and member of the Beatles), Mar 12, 1969; children: (1st m.) Heather See (potter); (2nd m.) Mary McCartney (photographer); Stella McCartney (fashion designer); James McCartney (musician). ❖ Discovered photography while attending University of Arizona; moved to NY with daughter (1965); began career as a photographer (1966), getting exclusive photos of Rolling Stones rock band; specialized in photos of pop and rock bands, often at the beginning of their careers; photographed the Beatles in London (1967); continued to pursue career as a rock photographer, with work published in magazines around the world, while conducting an on-and-off romance with Paul McCartney; moved to London to live with McCartney (1968); sang harmonies on husband's solo albums post-Beatles (1970–71); became a vegetarian in early 1970s, campaigned for animal rights until her death; sang and played keyboards despite no musical training with husband's band Wings (1971–80), and with husband's unnamed band (1980–97); published 1st cookbook (1989); launched McVege line of frozen vegetarian products (1991) which grew to sales of $50 million by 1998; 1st solo album, 20 years in the making, released posthumously; photographs appeared in 2 posthumous exhibits: in Liverpool, England, and as part of a traveling exhibit of *Rolling Stone* magazine covers (1998). ❖ See also Danny Fields, *Linda McCartney: A Portrait* (Renaissance, 2000); and *Women in World History*.

McCARTY, Mary (1923–1980). American actress and singer. Born Sept 27, 1923, in Winfield, Kansas; died April 30, 1980, in Westwood, CA. ❖ Began career in nightclubs; made Broadway debut as Eva in *Sleepy Hollow* (1948), followed by *Small Wonder, Miss Liberty, Bless You All, A Rainy Day in Newark, Follies* and *Chicago;* films include *Rebecca of Sunnybrook Farm, Keep Smiling, The Sullivans, The French Line, Babes in Toyland* and *My Six Loves;* appeared as Nurse Starch on tv's "Trapper John"; owned and operated her own nightclub in NY called Mary-Mary. Won Tony award for performance in *Anna Christie.*

McCARTY, Patti (1921–1985). American actress. Born Feb 11, 1921, in Healdsburg, CA; died July 7, 1985, in Honolulu, HI. ❖ Made several westerns with Buster Crabbe; other films include *You'll Never Get Rich, Under Age* and *She Knew all the Answers.*

McCAULEY, Catharine (1778–1841). See McAuley, Catharine.

McCAULEY, Diane (1946—). Australian politician. Born June 4, 1946, in Wondai. ❖ Representing National Party, served in the Queensland Parliament for Callide (1986–98); was coalition shadow minister for Local Government and shadow minister assisting the leaders on Women's Issues (1995–96); was minister for Local Government and Planning (1996–98).

McCAULEY, Mary Ludwig Hays (1754–1832). American revolutionary. Name variations: Molly Pitcher; Mary Hays; McAuley, M'Kolly, or McKolly. Born Mary Ludwig, Oct 13, 1754, near Trenton, New Jersey; died in Carlisle, Pennsylvania, Jan 22, 1832; dau. of John George Ludwig; illiterate, signed her name with an "X"; m. William Hays, probably on July 24, 1769 (died 1788); m. John McCauley, 1793 (died 1813); children (1st m.) John Ludwig Hays. ❖ Worked as domestic servant for the family of Dr. William Irvine, Carlisle, Pennsylvania (1769–77); joined husband's military unit as "camp follower" (1778); learned how to load and fire from observing husband during gunnery drills; at battle of Monmouth, in the heat of the conflict, took over husband's place as cannoneer when he was disabled (June 28, 1778); awarded army pension for life from state of Pennsylvania (1822); worked at odd jobs and as a domestic in Carlisle until her death (1832); not to be confused with Margaret Cochran Corbin. ❖ See also Samuel S. Smith, *A Molly Pitcher Chronology* (Philip Freneau Press, 1972); John B. Landis, *A Short History of Molly Pitcher. The Heroine of the Battle of Monmouth* (Cornman, 1905); and *Women in World History*.

McCLAIN, Katrina (1965—). African-American basketball player. Born Katrina Felicia McClain, Sept 19, 1965, in Washington, DC; dau. of Sara McClain and Edward McClain (A.M.E. minister and former Baltimore Colts running back); graduate of University of Georgia. ❖ Twice named All-American at University of Georgia; won team gold medals at FIBA World championships and Goodwill Games (1986) and Pan American Games (1987); won a team gold medal at Seoul Olympics (1988), a team bronze at Barcelona Olympics (1992), and a team gold at Atlanta Olympics (1996); played for Kyodo Petroleum in Japan (1988–91), then for ABA's Atlanta Glory. Named National Player of the Year and Southeast Conference Player of the Year (1987). ❖ See also *Women in World History*.

McCLELLAN, Catharine (1921—). American cultural anthropologist. Name variations: Catharine Hitchcock. Born Catharine McClellan, Mar 1, 1921, in York, PA; dau. of William Smith McClellan (vice president of a lumber mill) and Josephine Niles McClellan; graduate of Bryn Mawr College, 1942; University of California, Berkeley, PhD, 1950; m. John Hitchcock (anthropologist), 1974. ❖ Known primarily for work among peoples of Alaska and the Yukon Territory, studied with future field companion Frederica de Laguna at Bryn Mawr; during WWII, served in US Navy; taught at University of Washington (1952–56), Barnard College (1956–61), and University of Wisconsin (1961–83); with de Laguna, studied Tlingit Indians of Angoon (AK, 1950), peoples of Yukon Territory (Canada), Yakutat Tlingit and Atna Athapaskans (Copper River, AK, 1950s); worked with Alaskan Inuit; continued studies of Atna (1958–60); served as president of American Ethnological Society.

McCLEMENTS, Lyn (1951—). Australian swimmer. Name variations: Lynette McClements. Born May 11, 1951, in Nedlands, Western Australia. ❖ Captured state senior titles in the 100- and 200-meter butterfly stroke (1968); at Mexico City Olympics, won a gold medal in 100-meter butterfly and a silver medal in the 4x100-meter medley relay (1968).

McCLENDON, Rosalie (1884–1936). African-American actress. Name variations: Rose McClendon. Born Rosalie Virginia Scott, Aug 27, 1884, in Greenville, North Carolina; died of pneumonia, 1936; dau. of Sandy Scott and Tena (Jenkins) Scott; grew up in New York City; received a scholarship to study at American Academy of Dramatic Art, 1916; m. Dr. Henry Pruden McClendon (chiropractor and Pullman porter), 1904. ❖ Stage actress who combined wide-ranging theatrical talents with a desire to promote and advance black theater during the Harlem Renaissance; following marriage, spent next 10 years engaged in church work (1904–14); cast in 1st serious role in play *Justice* (1919); achieved critical acclaim for role in *Deep River* (1926); appeared in nearly every important African-American play staged in NY (1926–mid-1930s), including *In Abraham's Bosom* (1926), *Porgy* (1927), *The House of Connelly* (1931), *Never No More* (1932), *Black Souls* (1932), *Brainsweat* (1934), *Roll Sweet Chariot* (1934) and *Mulatto* (1935); began directing plays at Negro Experimental Theater in NY (early 1930s); with Dick Campbell, organized Negro People's Theater in Harlem (1935); fell ill with pleurisy (1935). ❖ See also *Women in World History*.

McCLENDON, Sarah (1910–2003). American journalist. Born July 8, 1910 in Tyler, Texas; died Jan 24, 2003, in Washington, DC; graduate of University of Missouri School of Journalism; m. John Thomas O'Brien (div.); children: Sally Newcomb MacDonald (linguist). ❖ As White House correspondent for over 50 years, was notorious for asking tough questions and demanding answers; began career in Texas with the *Tyler Courier-Times,* then *Tyler Morning Telegraph* and *Beaumont Enterprise;* was Washington correspondent for Philadelphia Daily News (1944–45); established the McClendon News Service (1946), for smaller newspapers; was accredited to cover the White House until the day she died. ❖ See also memoirs, *My Eight Presidents* (1977) and *Mr. President! Mr. President! My 50 Years of Covering the White House* (1996).

McCLINTOCK, Barbara (1902–1992). American biologist and geneticist. Born June 16, 1902, in Hartford, CT; died on Long Island, NY, Sept 2, 1992; dau. of Thomas Henry McClintock (physician) and Sara (Handy) McClintock; Cornell University, BS, 1923, MA, 1925, PhD in botany, 1927; never married. ❖ One of the geniuses in the history of genetics, who discovered the way genetic material moves and alters chromosomes, and therefore heredity, winning the Nobel Prize for her pioneering work, began studies of plant genetics at Cornell; worked with maize (Indian corn); began publishing research papers (1929); divided time conducting research for 2 years at Cornell University, University of

Missouri, and California Institute of Technology; received Guggenheim to work in Berlin at Kaiser Wilhelm Institute (1933); returned to US after witnessing rise of Nazism; worked in research at Cornell; became assistant professor at University of Missouri (1936), teaching and conducting research; became vice-president of Genetics Society of America (1939), then its 1st woman president (1944); began working at Cold Spring Harbor Laboratory on Long Island (1941); was on staff of Carnegie Institution (1941–67); experimented with chromosomes in maize (1940s), making many original discoveries; conducted experiments that led to her discoveries of "jumping genes," the movement of genes from one place to another in the chromosomes, which thus change the expected patterns of heredity; presented findings (1951), but the information was so contrary to the thinking at the time that her audience did not accept her theories; was vindicated in 1950s, when molecular biologists, using powerful new tools (crystallographic techniques and X-ray diffraction patterns), found the basic double helix structure of DNA, which comprises genes; trained Latin American cytologists in methods of conducting research of maize (1958–60); appointed Andrew White professor-at-large by Cornell University (1965); gained recognition for her discoveries (1970s); worked at Cold Spring Harbor Laboratory until end of life; while at Cold Spring Harbor, was listed in *American Men of Science,* and elected to National Academy of Science (only 2 other women had become members in 81 years). Received Kimber Genetics Award (1967), National Medal of Science (1970), Albert Lasker Basic Medical Research Award (1981), Wolf Foundation Prize from Israel (1981), (shared with Susumu Tonegawa) Horwitz Prize, Columbia University (1982), MacArthur Laureate Award, and Nobel Prize in Physiology or Medicine (1983). ❖ See also *The Discovery and Characterization of Transposable Elements: The Collected Papers of Barbara McClintock* (Garland, 1987); Evelyn Fox Keller, *A Feeling for the Organism: The Life and Work of Barbara McClintock* (Freeman, 1983); and *Women in World History.*

McCLUNG, Nellie L. (1873–1951). Canadian suffragist, temperance activist, politician, writer, and public speaker. Born Nellie Letitia Mooney, Oct 20, 1873, in Grey Co., Ontario; died Sept 1, 1951, at home outside Victoria, British Columbia; dau. of John Mooney and Letitia (McCurdy) Mooney; m. R.W. (Wes) McClung; children: 4 sons, 1 daughter. ❖ A crucial force in the fight for women's political and legal rights, began career as a schoolteacher in Manitoba; became actively involved in Manitou branch of Women's Christian Temperance Union (WCTU); published novel *Sowing Seeds in Danny* (1908), a bestseller in Canada; moved with family to Winnipeg (1911); helped found Political Equality League (PEL, 1912), one of several provincial associations dedicated to cause of female suffrage; held a mock parliament (1914), satirically reversing gender roles, which received much press and is considered the turning point of the Canadian suffrage movement; moved to Alberta (1914); as a Liberal, became a member of Alberta legislature (1921), supporting legislation for old-age pensions, mothers' allowances, factory regulation, minimum wages and birth control; with others, became involved in the now-famous "Persons Case" (1927), petitioning the prime minister to decide if the word "persons" included women, a major step towards ensuring female equality in Canadian society; became the 1st woman appointed to board of governors of the new Canadian Broadcasting Corporation (CBC, 1936); appointed a delegate to the League of Nations (1938); published an additional 15 books and many articles, most attaining wide readership. ❖ See also autobiographies *Clearing in the West* (1935) and *The Stream Runs Fast* (1945); Mary Lile Benham, *Nellie McClung* (Fitzhenry & Whiteside, 1984); Carol L. Hancock, *No Small Legacy* (Wood Lake, 1986); and *Women in World History.*

McCLURE, Tori Murden-. *See Murden, Tori.*

McCOLGAN-LYNCH, Elizabeth (1964—). Scottish runner. Name variations: Liz McColgan. Born Elizabeth McColgan, May 24, 1964, in Dundee, Scotland. ❖ At Commonwealth Games, won gold medals for 10,000 meters (1986, 1990) and 3,000 meters (1990); at Seoul Olympics, won a silver medal in the 10,000 meters (1988); won the Tokyo and NY Marathon (1991) and London Marathon (1996). Named Member of the British Empire (MBE). ❖ See also Adrianne Blue, *Queen of the Track: The Liz McColgan Story* (Gollancz).

McCOLLUM, Ruby (1915—). American murderer. Born in Live Oak, FL, in 1915; children: at least 1 daughter. ❖ As an African-American woman in the South before the civil-rights movement, suffered discrimination throughout life; was alleged to have been the mistress of a local white politician and had a child by him; convicted of murdering him

(1952), was saved from the death penalty through the efforts of a white attorney; after spending 2 years in the state penitentiary, was transferred to a mental hospital, from which she was eventually released into the custody of her daughter. ❖ See also William Bradford Huie, *Ruby McCollum: Woman in the Suwanee Jail.*

McCOMAS, Carroll (1886–1962). American stage and screen actress. Born June 27, 1886, in Albuquerque, NM; died Nov 9, 1962, in NYC. ❖ Began career in vaudeville as a whistler; made Broadway debut (1907); plays include *The Innocents, The Single Man, The Dollar Princess, Inside the Lines, The Devil's Disciple, Cyrano de Bergerac, Arms and the Man* and *The Stained Glass Window;* best remembered for her performance in title role of Pulitzer Prize-winning play *Miss Lulu Bett* (1920); films include *At the Rainbow's End* and *Where Love is King.*

McCOMBS, Elizabeth Reid (1873–1935). New Zealand political activist, social worker, and politician. Name variations: Elizabeth (Bessie) Reid Henderson. Born Elizabeth Reid Henderson, Nov 19, 1873, in Kaiapoi, NZ; died June 7, 1935, at Christchurch, NZ; dau. of Daniel Henderson and Alice (Connolly) Henderson; sister of Alice Henderson (missionary), Stella Henderson (journalist) and Christina Henderson (educator); m. James McCombs (MP), 1903 (died Aug 1, 1933); children: Terence McCombs (MP) and Patricia McCombs Foster; also raised 2 orphans. ❖ Involved with Women's Christian Temperance Union (WCTU) for many years; member of Canterbury Fabian Society; was 2nd woman to serve on Christchurch City Council (1921–35); became justice of the peace (1926); made 2 unsuccessful Labour Party bids for Parliament seat: for Kaiapoi (1928), for Christchurch North (1931); upon death of husband, replaced him (1933) for Lyttelton, the 1st woman elected to the New Zealand House of Representatives; was dedicated to women's rights and to the alleviation of the conditions of unemployed; died while in office (1935). ❖ See also *Dictionary of New Zealand Biography* (Vol. 4).

McCONNELL, Lulu (1882–1962). American actress and comedian. Born April 8, 1882, in Kansas City, MO; died Oct 9, 1962, in Los Angeles, CA. ❖ Began career in vaudeville; became a popular musical-comedy star of Broadway in such plays as *Poor Little Ritz Girl, Snapshots, Ziegfeld Follies, Peggy Ann, Ballyhoo* and *Bet Your Life;* was one of the delightfully dumb panelists on radio comedy show "It Pays to be Ignorant."

McCONNELL, Rosemary Lowe (1921—). *See Lowe-McConnell, Rosemary.*

McCONNELL, Suzanne (1966—). American basketball player. Born July 29, 1966; attended Pennsylvania State University. ❖ Won a gold medal at Seoul Olympics (1988) and a bronze medal at Barcelona Olympics (1992), both in team competition.

McCOO, Marilyn (1943—). American singer. Name variations: Fifth Dimension or 5th Dimension. Born Sept 30, 1943, in Jersey City, NJ; younger sister of Glenda Wina (actress); m. Billy Davis Jr., 1969. ❖ Began career as a fashion model; with LaMonte McLemore, Floyd Butler and Harry Elston, formed the Hi-Fi's and toured with Ray Charles' revue; with McLemore, Florence LaRue, Ron Townson and Billy Davis Jr., formed the Fifth Dimension and had 1st hit with "Go Where You Wanna Go" (1967); with group, had an even bigger hit with "Up, Up and Away" (1967), which garnered 4 Grammys, followed by "Stoned Soul Picnic" (1968), "Sweet Blindness" (1968), "Wedding Bell Blues" (1968), the medley from *Hair* ("Aquarius/Let the Sunshine In," 1969) and "(Last Night) I Didn't Get to Sleep at All" (1972); after marriage, worked with Davis as a duo (1975), releasing the hit "You Don't Have to Be a Star" (1976); co-hosted the tv show, "Solid Gold."

McCOOL, Courtney (1988—). American gymnast. Born April 1, 1988, in Kansas City, MO. ❖ Won a silver medal for team all-around at Athens Olympics (2004).

McCORD, Joan (1930–2004). American criminologist. Born Joan Fish, Aug 4, 1930, in New York, NY; died Feb 24, 2004, in Narberth, PA; Stanford University, PhD in sociology, 1968; m. William M. McCord (div.); m. Carl A. Silver; children: (1st m.) Geoffrey Sayre-McCord and Robert McCord. ❖ A professor at Temple University, saw the need to assess the results of social programs; amassed evidence which challenged the effectiveness of such social programs as boys' clubs, summer camps, Scared Straight and D.A.R.E.; was the 1st woman president of American Society of Criminologists; wrote many books and articles.

McCORD, Louisa S. (1810–1879). American writer, plantation owner, and defender of slavery. Name variations: Louisa Susannah Cheves

McCord; (pen name) L.S.M. Born Louisa Susannah Cheves, Dec 3, 1810, in Charleston, SC; died Nov 23, 1879, in Charleston; dau. of Langdon Cheves (lawyer and politician) and Mary Elizabeth (Dulles) Cheves; educated at Mr. Grimshaw's Academy; m. David James McCord (lawyer, journalist, and politician), May 2, 1840; children: Langdon Cheves McCord (b. 1841); Hannah Cheves McCord (b. 1843); Louisa Rebecca Hayne Smythe (b. 1845); 10 stepchildren. ❖ At an early age, became a staunch defender of slavery; at 20, took over Lang Syne, a cotton plantation near Columbia bequeathed to her by an aunt (1830), where she owned 200 slaves, and reportedly supervised a nursery for the children of field hands and trained some slaves to run a rudimentary plantation hospital; put her French to use to translate an economic treatise, *Sophismes Economiques* (Economic Sophism or Fallacy), that became an important part of the South's anti-tariff political platform (1848); wrote 5-act verse tragedy *Caius Gracchus* (1851); contributed to such political journals as the *Southern Quarterly Review*; unlike some defenders of slavery who considered it a necessary evil, thought slavery "a God-like dispensation, a providential caring for the weak, and a refuge for the portionless"; during Civil War, lost a son in battle, supervised a military hospital in Columbia that would later be encompassed by the campus of the University of South Carolina, and exhibited bravery under duress when the city was torched by Union troops. ❖ See also *Women in World History*.

McCORKLE, Susannah (1946–2001). American cabaret singer. Born Jan 4, 1946, in Berkeley, CA; jumped from her 16th-floor apartment in New York, NY, May 19, 2001; attended University of California at Berkeley; m. Dan DiNicola. ❖ Made 1st recording in London; performed at the Cookery in Greenwich Village; made several albums with Concord, which included classics by Cole Porter and George Gershwin; appeared at the Oak Room in the Algonquin Hotel in NY (1990–2001).

McCORMACK, Katheryn (1974—). Canadian ice-hockey player. Name variations: Kathy McCormack. Born Feb 16, 1974, in Blackville, New Brunswick, Canada; attended University of New Brunswick. ❖ Won a team silver medal at Nagano (1998), the 1st Olympics to feature women's ice hockey.

McCORMACK, Patty (1945—). American actress. Name variations: Patricia McCormack. Born Patricia Russo, Aug 21, 1945, in Brooklyn, New York. ❖ At 4, worked as a professional model; appeared in tv series "Mama" (1952–56); had most notable role, that of Rhoda Penmark, in both the stage (1954) and screen (1956) versions of Maxwell Anderson's *The Bad Seed*; briefly starred on her own tv show, "Peck's Bad Girl" (1959); played troubled teens in such films as *The Explosive Generation* (1961), *The Mini-Skirt Mob* (1968), *The Young Runaways* (1968) and *Bug* (1975); later appeared on tv sitcom "The Ropers" (1979–80).

McCORMICK, Alma. See Heflin, Alma.

McCORMICK, Anita (1866–1954). See Blaine, Anita McCormick.

McCORMICK, Anne O'Hare (1880–1954). American journalist. Name variations: Anne O'Hare. Born Anne Elizabeth O'Hare, May 16, 1880, in Wakefield, Yorkshire, England; died in New York, NY, May 29, 1954; dau. of Thomas O'Hare (life insurance employee) and Teresa Beatrice (Berry) O'Hare (writer and poet); College of St. Mary of the Springs, BA, Columbus, Ohio; m. Francis J. McCormick (engineer and importer), Sept 14, 1910. ❖ While on the staff at *The New York Times* (1922–35), was one of the most influential opinion-makers in the American press; made her reputation by covering the rise of fascism in Italy, correctly insisting that dictator Benito Mussolini was "the master voice" to which Italy was responding; published *Hammer and the Scythe: Communist Russia Enters the Second Decade* (1928), a firsthand account of the Soviet experiment; was appointed the 1st woman member of the editorial board of the *Times* (1935), a position she held for the remainder of her life; wrote 3 weekly columns, 1st called "In Europe," then "Affairs of Europe," then "Abroad," for the op-ed page (1936–54); interviewed most of the prominent political leaders of her day, including Joseph Stalin and Adolf Hitler. Won practically every major award in the field of journalism, including the Pulitzer Prize (1937). ❖ See also Marion Turner Sheehan, ed. *The World at Home: Selections from the Writings of Anne O'Hare McCormick* (Knopf, 1956); and *Women in World History*.

McCORMICK, Edith Rockefeller (1872–1932). Chicago socialite and patron of the arts. Name variations: Edith Rockefeller; Mrs. Harold McCormick. Born Edith Rockefeller, Aug 31, 1872, in Cleveland, Ohio; died of liver cancer, Aug 25, 1932, in Chicago, IL; dau. of John Davison Rockefeller (1839–1937, founder of Standard Oil Trust in Ohio and philanthropist) and Laura Celestia (Spelman) Rockefeller (1839–1915); briefly attended Rye (New York) Female Seminary; m. Harold Fowler McCormick (son of Nettie Fowler McCormick [1835–1923]), Nov 26, 1895 (div. 1921); children: John Rockefeller McCormick (died young); Fowler McCormick; Muriel McCormick; Editha McCormick (died young); Mathilde McCormick. ❖ One of the most eccentric of America's art patrons in the early decades of 20th century, was heiress to the Standard Oil fortune; ruled over Chicago society for many years and gave lavishly to her city's cultural institutions; in later years, became a student of Swiss psychoanalyst Carl Jung and even practiced psychology herself; over a 30-year span, probably gave away well over $10 million to various causes; helped found Chicago Opera Co. (1910). ❖ See also *Women in World History*.

McCORMICK, Mrs. Harold (1872–1932). *See McCormick, Edith Rockefeller.*

McCORMICK, Katharine Dexter (1875–1967). American philanthropist and advocate for women's reproductive freedom. Born Katharine Dexter, Aug 27, 1875, in Dexter, Michigan; died Dec 28, 1967, in Boston, Massachusetts; dau. of Wirt Dexter and Josephine (Moore) Dexter; Massachusetts Institute of Technology, BS in biology, 1904; m. Stanley Robert McCormick (son of Nettie Fowler McCormick [1835–1923]), Sept 1904 (died 1947); no children. ❖ Inherited family fortune (1894); became active in national suffrage moment (1909); for years, worked with Carrie Chapman Catt in the National American Woman Suffrage Association (NAWSA), and chaired its War Service Department during WWI; founded Neuroendocrine Research Foundation at Harvard Medical School (1927) and funded publication of the journal *Endocrinology*; began funding research into an oral contraceptive (1952) and because of her efforts, Enovid, the 1st oral contraceptive for women, came on the market and quite literally changed the world; funded the construction of 2 dormitories for women at MIT (1962 and 1968); left a $5 million bequest to Planned Parenthood Foundation of America. ❖ See also Armond Fields, *Katharine Dexter McCormick* (2003); and *Women in World History*.

McCORMICK, Katherine Medill (d. 1932). American socialite. Name variations: Kate Medill; Kate McCormick; Catherine Medill McCormick. Born Katherine Van Etta Medill; died 1932; dau. of Joseph Medill (1823–1899, proprietor and editor of Chicago *Tribune*); sister of Elinor (Nellie) Medill Patterson (d. 1933, mother of Eleanor Medill "Cissy" Patterson); m. Robert Sanderson McCormick (1849–1919, US diplomat and ambassador to Austria, Russia, and France); children: Joseph Medill McCormick (1877–1925, journalist and politician who m. Ruth Hanna McCormick); Robert (Bertie) Rutherford McCormick (1880–1955, editor of Chicago *Tribune*, who m. Amie Irwin Adams). ❖ Was the leading stockholder in the Chicago *Tribune*.

McCORMICK, Kelly (1960—). American diver. Name variations: Kelly McCormick Robertson. Born Feb 13, 1960, in Anaheim, CA; dau. of Glenn McCormick (diving coach) and Patricia (Keller) McCormick (diving champion). ❖ Won a silver medal at Los Angeles Olympics (1984) and a bronze medal at Seoul Olympics (1988), both on springboard; won 9 national titles, 2 Pan American gold medals, and a World Cup bronze medal. ❖ See also Christina Lessa, *Women Who Win* (Universe, 1998); and *Women in World History*.

McCORMICK, Nettie Fowler (1835–1923). American philanthropist and entrepreneur. Born Nancy Maria Fowler, Feb 8, 1835, in Brownville, NY; died July 5, 1923, in Lake Forest, IL; dau. of Melzar Fowler (merchant) and Clarissa (Spicer) Fowler; was schooled at 3 seminaries, including Genesee Wesleyan Seminary in Lima, NY; m. Cyrus McCormick (inventor and industrialist), Jan 26, 1858 (died 1884); children: Cyrus Hall McCormick II; Mary Virginia McCormick; Anita McCormick Blaine; Harold Fowler McCormick (who m. Edith Rockefeller McCormick); Stanley Robert McCormick (who m. Katharine McCormick). ❖ Chicago business leader and philanthropist who was one of the top American donors to the Presbyterian Church in 19th century, 1st served as husband's personal secretary for many years, and was an integral part of many important business decisions; widowed (1884), inherited a vast fortune; contributed to over 40 different educational institutions, including the McCormick Theological Seminary in Chicago; was also active in funding the World's Student Christian Federation and gave generously to religious conversion efforts by Protestant clerics around the globe; for over 3 decades, served in various capacities on the Woman's Board of the Presbyterian Mission of the Northwest, including treasurer, vice-president, and honorary vice-president; a Democrat, also donated sums to political campaigns, including the presidential candidacies of Woodrow Wilson (1912 and 1916). ❖ See also *Women in World History*.

McCORMICK, Patricia (1930—). American diver. Born Patricia Keller, May 12, 1930, in Seal Beach, CA; m. Glenn McCormick (diving coach), 1949; children: Kelly McCormick (diver). ❖ Became the 1st diver to win 5 US national championships; won gold medals in springboard and platform at Helsinki Olympics (1952) and gold medals in springboard and platform at Melbourne Olympics (1956), the only woman in Olympic diving history to achieve a "double-double," 2 gold medals in each of 2 consecutive Olympic Games; won 17 AAU titles. Named Associated Press Athlete of the Year and Sullivan Award winner (1956); was inaugural inductee into International Swimming Hall of Fame (1965); named to International Women's Sports Hall of Fame (1984); named to US Olympic Hall of Fame (1985). ❖ See also *Women in World History*.

McCORMICK, Ruth Hanna (1880–1944). American politician. Name variations: Ruth Hanna McCormick Simms. Born Ruth Hanna, Mar 27, 1880, in Cleveland, Ohio; died in Billings Hospital, Chicago, IL, Dec 31, 1944, of pancreatitis following a fall from a horse; dau. of Marcus Alonzo Hanna, known as Mark Hanna (US senator) and Augusta Rhodes Hanna; attended Miss Porter's School, Farmington, Connecticut; m. (Joseph) Medill McCormick (1877–1925, journalist and politician), 1903 (died 1925); m. Albert Gallatin Simms, 1932; children: (1st m.) Katrina "Triny" McCormick; Medill McCormick (d. 1938); Ruth "Bazy" McCormick. ❖ Prominent politician, who worked for suffrage, was elected "congressman-at-large," was nominated for the Senate, and managed the 1st presidential campaign of Thomas E. Dewey; moved to Chicago (1903) with husband Medill McCormick; founded women's division of National Civic Federation and Women's City Club of Chicago; served as chair of women's committee of Progressive Party in Chicago (1912); led successful suffrage campaign in Illinois (1913); served as chair of Congressional Committee of National American Woman Suffrage Association (1914); served as chair of Republican National Party Women's Executive Committee (1918–19); was Republican National Committeewoman for Illinois (1924); defeated 7 men in Republican primary for US "congressman-at-large" for Illinois, then won the election (1928), the 1st woman to win a state-wide election for national office; beat the incumbent senator, Charles S. Deneen, twice governor and undefeated in 38 years of public service, to become the 1st woman nominated for US Senate by a major party (1930), but lost the general election in the Democratic landslide; moved to Albuquerque, NM (1932); founded Manzano School and Sandia School for Girls (1932) and the Albuquerque June Music Festival (1942); was co-manager of preconvention presidential campaign of Thomas E. Dewey (1940). ❖ See also Kristie Miller, *Ruth Hanna McCormick: A Life in Politics 1880–1944* (University of New Mexico Press, 1992); and *Women in World History*.

McCORQUODALE, Barbara (1901–2000). *See Cartland, Barbara.*

McCOUBREY, Margaret (1880–1955). Scottish suffragist, trade unionist and economist. Born in Eldersley, Scotland, in 1880; died in Carnlough, Co. Antrim, Northern Ireland, in 1955; attended Manchester University; married. ❖ Moved to Belfast, Northern Ireland (1905); joined militant suffragist movement (1910); developed an interest in trade unionism, and served as general secretary of Cooperative Guild (1910–16); during WWI, was active in pacifist movement; elected Labour Party councilor for Dock Ward of Belfast (1920); contributed scholarly pieces to economic and trade-union periodicals, including *Co-op News* and *Wheat Sheaf*; moved to Carnlough, Co. Antrim (1933), to run Drumalla House, a nonprofit retreat for members of Belfast Girl's Club Union; remained active in politics and trade-union movement as an orator.

McCOY, Bessie (1888–1931). American theatrical dancer and singer. Name variations: Bessie McCoy Davis; The Yama Yama Girl. Born Elizabeth McAvoy in 1888; died Aug 16, 1931, in Bayonne, France; m. Cecil Clark (div. 1912); m. Richard Harding Davis (writer), 1912 (died 1916). ❖ Made theatrical debut in parents' vaudeville act; won great acclaim for performance in Broadway's *The Three Twins* (1908) where she danced and sang "The Yama-Yama Man," and was known as The Yama-Yama Girl thereafter; performed in *The Echo* (1910) and *Ziegfeld Follies of 1911*, and after marriage appeared as Bessie McCoy Davis in *Miss 1917* at Century Theater; performed as specialty dancer in *Greenwich Village Follies* (1919) and danced in Morris Gest's *Midnight Whirl* (1919) before retiring from stage.

McCOY, Elizabeth (1903–1978). American bacteriologist. Born in Madison, WI, 1903; died in Madison, 1978; dau. of Cassius McCoy (farmer) and Esther (Williamson) McCoy (nurse); received undergraduate degree and PhD in bacteriology (1929) from University of Wisconsin. ❖ Began career as assistant professor of bacteriology at University of Wisconsin (1930); became an authority on the bacteria of lake ecosystems; also studied butyl alcohol-producing bacteria, known as *clostridia*, and traveled to Puerto Rico to help the territorial government establish a butyl alcohol fermentation plant (this work led her to develop a new culture of *clostridia*, which she patented); created new strains of bacteria, including Strain X1612, a bacterium which made the production of penicillin for civilian use economically and scientifically feasible. ❖ See also *Women in World History*.

McCOY, Gertrude (1890–1967). American silent-film actress. Born June 30, 1890, in Sugar Valley, GA; died July 16, 1967, in Atlanta, GA; m. Duncan McRae (British actor), 1919. ❖ Was a NY Gibson Girl; in Hollywood, appeared in *The Blue Bird, The Working Girl, The Silent Witness* and *Winsome Winnie*, among others; also made films in Europe.

McCOY, Iola Fuller (1906–1993). American writer. Name variations: Iola Fuller. Born Jan 25, 1906, in Marcellus, Michigan; died April 12, 1993, in Littleton, CO; dau. of Henry Fuller and Clara (Reynolds) Fuller; University of Michigan, AB, 1935, AM in English, 1940, AMLS, 1962; m. 1st husband; m. Raymond McCoy (artist); children: (1st m.) Paul Goodspeed. ❖ Was an associate professor of English at Ferris State College (1964–69); started writing historical novels (late 1930s) and traveled extensively throughout Canada, Mexico, US, and Europe to gather research; novels include *The Loon Feather* (1940), about the history of Mackinac Island in Michigan, *The Shining Trail* (1943), a portrait of the Native American chief Black Hawk, *The Gilded Torch* (1958), about La Salle's discovery of the mouth of the Mississippi River, and *All the Golden Gifts* (1966), which details life in the court of King Louis XIV. Received Avery Hopwood Award for Creative Writing (1940) and Michigan Distinguished Alumni Award (1967).

McCOY, Irene (1892–1964). *See Gaines, Irene McCoy.*

McCOY, Memphis Minnie (1897–1973). *See Douglas, Lizzie.*

McCRACKEN, Elizabeth (c. 1865–1944). Irish suffragist. Born (pseudonym) L.A.M. Priestly. Born c. 1865; died in 1944. ❖ Gained renown as one of Ulster's leading advocates of women's suffrage; published numerous articles on women's suffrage under pseudonym L.A.M. Priestly; her books include *The Feminine in Fiction*.

McCRACKEN, Esther Helen (1902–1971). English actress and playwright. Name variations: Esther McCracken. Born Esther Helen Armstrong, June 25, 1902, in Newcastle-on-Tyne, England; died Aug 9, 1971; m. Angus McCracken (died in action in WWII, 1943); m. Mungo Campbell. ❖ Acted with the Newcastle Rep (1924–37); wrote such plays as *The Willing Spirit, Quiet Wedding Quiet Weekend* (which had over 1,000 performances), *Living Room, White Elephants, Cry Liberty* and *No Medals* (1944); with Patrick Kirwan, adapted Dodie Smith's *Dear Octopus* for the screen (1943).

McCRACKEN, Joan (1922–1961). American dancer and actress. Born Dec 31, 1922, in Philadelphia, PA; died Nov 1, 1961, in New York, NY; attended Catherine Littlefield's ballet school; m. Jack Dunphy (dancer, div.); m. Bob Fosse (dancer, director), 1951 (div. 1959). ❖ Began career with the Littlefield American Ballet (1934–35); danced with the Rockettes, the Eugene Loring Dance Co., and American Ballet; came to prominence in *Oklahoma!*; other credits include *Bloomer Girl, Billion Dollar Baby, Me and Juliet, Galileo, The Big Knife, Dance Me a Song* and *Angel in the Pawnshop*; on tv, starred in "Claudia: The Story of a Marriage" (1952); appeared on film in *Hollywood Canteen, Kiss Me Kate* and *Good News*; forced to retire because of heart condition (1954).

McCRACKEN, Mary Ann (1770–1866). Irish political feminist, radical, and philanthropist. Name variations: Mary McCracken. Born July 8, 1770, in Belfast, Co. Antrim, Ireland; died in Belfast, July 26, 1866; dau. of John McCracken (ship's captain and merchant) and Ann (Joy) McCracken; attended David Manson's Play School in Belfast; never married; children: none of her own, but cared for brother Harry's illeg. daughter Maria. ❖ Prominent in a range of charitable and reforming societies, started a small muslin manufacturing business with sister Margaret, soon after leaving school; shared brother Henry's interest in radical politics and social justice; attended his trial on charges of involvement in United Irishmen's rebellion of 1798, and accompanied him to his execution at the old Market House in Belfast (July 17, 1798); continued to assist former United Irishmen and their dependents, including Thomas Russell who was executed at Downpatrick (Oct 21, 1803); retired from business (c. 1815), embarking on a 2nd career as a philanthropist and social reformer; aware of the condition of workers and of poorest classes in Belfast, was a member of the ladies' committee of the Belfast Poorhouse (1814–16), the ladies' committee reconstituted (1827) and secretary (1832–51); was a member of the committee of the Ladies' Industrial School (1847–66), of Belfast Ladies' Clothing Society and of Society for the Relief of the Destitute Sick; involved in temperance and anti-slavery movements and in campaign to outlaw the use of climbing boys as chimney sweeps. ❖ See also Mary McNeill, *The Life and Times of Mary Ann McCracken, 1770–1866* (Figgis, 1960); and *Women in World History*.

McCRACKIN, Josephine Clifford (1838–1920). American writer and conservationist. Born Josephine Woempner, Nov 25, 1838, in Petershagen, Westphalia, Germany; died Dec 21, 1920, in Santa Cruz, CA; dau. of Georg Ernst Woempner and Charlotte (Hartman) Woempner; m. James A. Clifford (lieutenant in US army), Jan 1864 (died c. 1867); m. Jackson McCrackin, 1882 (died 1904). ❖ Inspired by travels in Southwest, began contributing stories to such periodicals as *Overland Monthly* and *Harper's Magazine* (1869); published collected stories as *Overland Tales* (1877), *Another Juanita* (1893), and *The Woman Who Lost Him* (1913); joined environmental conservation movement after fire destroyed CA ranch (1899); named vice-president-at-large of Sempervirens Club of California (forerunner of Save-the-Redwoods League); founded (1901) and served as president of Ladies' Forest and Song Bird Protective Association; was 1st woman member of California Game and Fish Protective Association. Lobbying of Sempervirens Club led to formation of California Redwood Park.

McCRAE, Georgiana Huntly (1804–1890). Australian diarist. Born 1804 in London, England; died 1890 in Australia; illeg. dau. of George, Marquis of Huntly, later 5th duke of Gordon, and Jane Graham; m. Andrew Murison McCrae (lawyer, squatter and gold fields magistrate), 1830 (died 1874); children: 9, including George Gordon McCrae (poet, 1833–1927). ❖ Was a professional portrait painter in Edinburgh, Scotland (1820s); immigrated to Australia (1841); became well known in Melbourne intellectual circles; journals supplemented by son George Gordon McCrae, edited by grandson, poet Hugh McCrae, were published as *Georgiana's Journal* (1934). ❖ See also Brenda Niall, *Georgiana* (1996).

McCRAY, Nikki (1971—). African-American basketball player. Born Dec 17, 1971, in Collierville, TN; University of Tennessee, BS, 1995. ❖ Guard; helped Tennessee Lady Vols get to NCAA tournament 4 years in a row (1992–95); joined Columbus Quest of American Basketball League (1996); won team gold medals at Atlanta Olympics (1996) and Sydney Olympics (2000); signed by Washington Mystics in WNBA (1998); drafted by Indiana Fever (2001). Named SEC Player of the Year (1994, 1995); named ABL's MVP (1996–97).

McCREA, Jane (c. 1752–1777). Young Hudson Valley woman murdered during American Revolution. Born c. 1752, near Bedminster (later Lamington), Somerset County, New Jersey; died of bullet wounds and scalping on July 27, 1777, near Fort Edward, New York; dau. of James McCrea (Presbyterian minister) and Mary (Graham) McCrea. ❖ While visiting a friend (July 27, 1777), was surprised by a party of Indians working on behalf of Burgoyne and the British; though the facts are murky, was shot while on horseback and then scalped; her death became a great sensation of the time and provoked intense sentiment against the British. ❖ See also *Women in World History*.

McCREEDY, Sally (1965—). *See McDermid, Sally.*

McCREERY, Maria (1883–1938). American suffragist and labor organizer. Name variations: Maud McCreery. Born Maria Maud Leonard, Feb 24, 1883, in Cedarburg, WI; died April 10, 1938, in Milwaukee, WI; dau. of Sylvester S. Leonard (stockbreeder and veterinary surgeon) and Anna (Reilly) Leonard; m. Rex Irving McCreery (lawyer), Nov 28, 1902 (div. June 1918); James Walter Walker (carpenter), Oct 17, 1923 (div. 1931); children: (1st m.) 1 son. ❖ Helped organize Political Equality League in Brown Co., WI; campaigned for suffrage throughout US (1912–17); suffered bout of TB (1917) and afterward redirected energies toward Socialist and labor causes; hired as woman's page editor at *Milwaukee Leader* (1917); wrote widely distributed pamphlet *How I Won My Fight Against Tuberculosis*; toured Midwest for labor and Socialist-oriented news service, Federated Press; became organizer for Amalgamated Clothing Workers of America in WI and IL; served as editor-in-chief of weekly *New Deal* (1934–36); was part of union negotiating team and counseled strike families during AFL's unionization campaign at Kohler Co.; was highly respected and effective worker in trade union labor movement in Wisconsin.

McCUE, Lillian de la Torre Bueno (1902–1993). American writer of historical mysteries. Name variations: (pseudonym) Lillian de la Torre. Born Lillian de la Torre Bueno in New York, NY, Mar 15, 1902; died in Colorado Springs, Colorado, Sept 13, 1993; graduate of New Rochelle College; Columbia, MA; Harvard-Radcliffe, MA; taught high school English; m. George McCue (English professor at Colorado College), 1932 (died 1984). ❖ Describing herself as a histo-detector, used scholarly research to delve into old crimes and scandals, especially those in 18th-century Britain, and arrive at her own modern solutions; also took real people and events and wove them into fictionalized plots; dismissed 12 theories on the 1753 disappearance of Elizabeth Canning, a maidservant near the Tower of London, and offered her own in 1st book *Elizabeth Is Missing or Truth Triumphant*; followed with a similar book, *Villainy Detected* (1947); her most popular fiction comprised a series of short stories about Samuel Johnson and James Boswell under title *Dr. Sam: Johnson, Detector*; was president of Mystery Writers of America.

McCULLERS, Carson (1917–1967). American novelist, playwright, and short-story writer. Born Lula Carson Smith in Columbus, Georgia, Feb 19, 1917; died in Nyack, NY, following massive cerebral hemorrhage, Sept 29, 1967; oldest child of Lamar Smith (watchmaker and jeweler) and Marguerite Waters Smith; sister of Margarita G. Smith (fiction editor for *Mademoiselle*); m. James Reeves McCullers, Sept 20, 1937 (div. 1941, remarried Feb 1945); no children. ❖ One of the most gifted and original writers to emerge from the American South in 1940s, whose haunting novels and stories about loneliness and frustrated love have long appealed to readers and critics throughout the world, had an attack of rheumatic fever which marked the beginning of a long struggle against debilitating illness (1932); left for NY to study at Juilliard (1934), but then took creative writing courses at Columbia University and New York University (1935–37); published "Wunderkind" in *Story* (Dec 1936); after marriage, moved to Charlotte and then Fayetteville, NC; published 1st novel, *The Heart Is a Lonely Hunter* (1940); lived on and off at a home in Brooklyn Heights, rented with such celebrities as W.H. Auden and Gypsy Rose Lee, who became lifelong friends (1940–42); published 2nd novel *Reflections in a Golden Eye* and suffered a stroke that temporarily impaired her vision (1941); published 4th novel, *The Member of the Wedding*, to universal acclaim (1946); suffered a 2nd stroke that left her paralyzed on left side (1947); unable to write, attempted suicide (1948); dramatized *The Member of the Wedding*, which was a huge success on Broadway (1950–51); lost confidence once more following suicide of husband (1953), sudden death of her mother (1955), and failure of her 2nd play, *The Square Root of Wonderful* (1957); helped by psychiatrist friend, Dr. Mary Mercer, was able to finish 5th and last novel, *Clock Without Hands* (1960); during remaining 7 years of life, wrote some stories and poems for *Harper's Bazaar* and other fashion magazines, and published a collection of children's verses, *Sweet as a Pickle, Clean as a Pig* (1964). ❖ See also Virginia Spencer Carr, *The Lonely Hunter: A Biography of Carson McCullers* (Doubleday, 1975); Richard M. Cook, *Carson McCullers* (Ungar, 1975); Judith Giblin James, *Wunderkind: The Reputation of Carson McCullers, 1940–1990* (Camden House, 1995); Margarita G. Smith, ed. *The Mortgaged Heart: Carson McCullers* (Houghton, 1971); Nancy B. Rich, *The Flowering Dream: The Historical Saga of Carson McCullers* (Chapel Hill, 1999); and *Women in World History*.

McCULLOCH, Catharine (1862–1945). American lawyer and suffragist. Name variations: Catharine Waugh McCulloch; Catharine Gouger Waugh McCulloch. Born Catharine Gouger Waugh, June 4, 1862, in Ransomville, New York; died of cancer, April 20, 1945, in Evanston, IL; dau. of Abraham Miller Waugh and Susan (Gouger) Waugh; attended Union College of Law, 1885–86; Rockford Female Seminary, BA, MA, 1888; m. Frank Hathorn McCulloch (lawyer), May 30, 1890; children: Hugh Waugh (b. 1891); Hathorn Waugh (b. 1899); Catharine Waugh (b. 1901); Frank Waugh (b. 1905). ❖ Became partner of Chicago firm of McCulloch & McCulloch (c. 1890); also became involved in women's suffrage; served as legislative superintendent of Illinois Equal Suffrage Association, and in that capacity wrote a suffrage bill that was not ratified by the state legislature for 20 years (it finally passed in 1913, giving Illinois women the right to vote in presidential elections some 7 years before 19th amendment made women's suffrage the law of the land); admitted to bar of US Supreme Court (1898); elected justice of the peace (1907); co-founded the Mississippi Valley Conference (1912); served as president of Women's Bar Association of Illinois (1916–20); was also longtime legal adviser to

Women's Christian Temperance Union (WCTU); named senior counsellor of Illinois Bar Association (1940); writings include *Mr. Lex* (1899) and *Bridget's Daughters* (1911). ❖ See also *Women in World History*.

McCULLOCH, Williamina (1844–1895). *See Dean, Williamina.*

McCULLOUGH, Colleen (1937—). Australian novelist. Born June 1, 1937, in Wellington, NSW, Australia; m. Ric Robinson. ❖ Worked as neurophysiologist in Sydney and established Department of Neurophysiology at Royal North Shore Hospital; practiced medicine in England and moved to Yale University's School of Medicine where she was early exponent of microsurgical techniques; works include *Tim* (1974), *The Thorn Birds* (1977), *An Indecent Obsession* (1981), *A Creed for the Third Millenium* (1985), *The Ladies of Missalonghi* (1987), *The First Man in Rome* (1990), *Song of Troy* (1999), *Morgan's Run* (2001), and *Touch* (2003).

McCULLOUGH, Myrtle Reed (1874–1911). *See Reed, Myrtle.*

McCULLY, Emily Arnold (1939—). American children's writer, novelist and illustrator. Name variations: Emily Arnold. Born July 1, 1939, in Galesburg, IL; dau. of Wade E. (writer) and Kathryn (Maher) Arnold (teacher); Brown University, BA, 1961; Columbia University, MA, 1964; m. George E. McCully (historian), June 3, 1961 (div. 1975); children: Nathaniel, Thaddeus. ❖ Worked in advertising and as a free-lance magazine artist (1961–67); began illustrating children's books (1966); won National Book Award for Meindert De Jong's *Journey from Peppermint Street* (1969); other illustrated works include *Hurray for Captain Jane!* (1972), *Ma nDa La* (1975) and *Edward Troy and the Witch Cat* (1979); after illustrating more than 100 books by other authors, completed her own, *Picnic,* a story about a family of mice told through watercolor paintings; followed this with a sequel, *First Snow* (1985); also wrote adult fiction, winning an O. Henry Award (1977) and publishing the novel *A Craving,* which was nominated for a National Book Award (1982).

McCUSKER, Joan (c. 1966—). Canadian curler. Born c. 1966 in Saltcoats, Saskatchewan, Canada. ❖ Won a gold medal for curling at Nagano Olympics (1998); with Team Schmirler, won the World championship (1993, 1994, 1997), the only 3-time winner in the history of the sport. ❖ See also *Gold on Ice* (Coteau, 1989).

McCUSKER, Marilyn Wehrie (1944–1979). American miner. Born Feb 2, 1944, in Utica, NY; died Oct 2, 1979, at Osceola Mills, PA. ❖ Sued Rushton Mining Co. at Osceola Mills, PA, which resulted in the hiring of the mining company's 1st female employees (including McCusker, 1977); worked as general laborer for Rushton; was the 1st woman to die in an underground mine in US, when a tunnel gave way above her (1979).

McCUTCHEON, Floretta (1888–1967). American bowler. Name variations: Mrs. Mac. Born Floretta Doty, July 22, 1888, in Ottumwa, IA; died Feb 2, 1967, in Pasadena, CA; m. Robert J. McCutcheon; children: Barbara McCutcheon. ❖ Challenged Jimmy Smith, world-champion bowler, to a 3-game set and defeated him 704 to 697 (1927); set up schools and organized leagues (1930–38); with the exception of Marion Ladewig, was perhaps the greatest woman bowler of all time. Inducted into Women's International Bowling Congress Hall of Fame (1956) and Colorado Sports Hall of Fame (1973). ❖ See also *Women in World History*.

McDANIEL, Hattie (1895–1952). African-American actress and singer. Born June 10, 1895, in Wichita, Kansas; died Oct 26, 1952, in Los Angeles, CA; dau. of Henry McDaniel (Baptist minister) and Susan (Holbert) McDaniel; sister of Etta McDaniel (actress); m. George Langford, 1922 (died 1922); m. Howard C. Hickman, 1938 (div. 1938); m. James Lloyd Crawford (real-estate agent), 1941 (div.); m. Larry C. Williams (interior decorator), 1949 (div. 1950). ❖ First African-American actress to win an Academy Award, sang on Denver radio station (1915); joined Pantages Circuit of vaudeville shows (1924); made film debut in *The Golden West* (1931); won Academy Award for Best Supporting Actress for *Gone With the Wind* (1940); cast in title role of "Beulah" for radio (1947); other films include *I'm No Angel* (1933) with Mae West, *Judge Priest* (1934), in which she sang with Will Rogers, *Alice Adams* (1935), *The Little Colonel* (1935) and *Show Boat* (1936); when accused of participating in the perpetuation of African-American stereotypes, replied "I'd rather play a maid than be a maid." ❖ See also *Women in World History*.

McDANIEL, Mildred (1933–2004). African-American track-and-field athlete. Name variations: Mildred McDaniel Singleton. Born Mildred

Louise McDaniel, Nov 4, 1933, in Atlanta, GA; died of cancer, Sept 30, 2004, in Pasadena, CA; attended Tuskegee Institute; m. Louis Singleton, 1958. ❖ Was AAU national high jump champion (1953, 1955, and 1956) and indoor champion (1955, 1956); won the high jump title at Pan American Games (1955) with a meet record; won the Olympic gold medal in high jump at Melbourne Olympics (1956), setting a world record with a jump of 5'9¼", and also won a bronze medal in 4x100-meter relay; taught physical education for 32 years in Pasadena schools. Inducted into National Track and Field Hall of Fame (1983) and Georgia Sports Hall of Fame. ❖ See also *Women in World History*.

McDERMID, Heather (1968—). Canadian rower. Born Oct 17, 1968, in Calgary, Alberta, Canada; attended Rice University. ❖ Won a silver medal at Atlanta Olympics (1996) and a bronze medal at Sydney Olympics (2000), both for coxed eights.

McDERMID, Sally (1965—). Australian softball player. Name variations: Sally McCreedy. Born Sally McDermid, June 6, 1965, in ACT, Australia. ❖ Third baseman, won bronze medals at Atlanta Olympics (1996) and Sydney Olympics (2000).

McDERMID, Sandra (1948—). *See Post, Sandra.*

McDERMID, Val (1955—). Scottish playwright, journalist and mystery writer. Born Valerie Lesley Campbell McDermid, June 4, 1955, in Kirkcaldy, Scotland; read English at St Hilda's College, Oxford; children: 1 son. ❖ Worked as journalist for such papers as *South Devon Times, The Sunday Independent,* and *Manchester Evening News*; works include *Report for Murder* (1987), *Common Murder* (1989), *Final Edition* (1991), *Kick Back* (1993), *The Wire in the Blood* (1997), *A Place of Execution* (1999), *The Last Temptation* (2002), *Hostage to Murder* (2003), and *The Torment of Others* (2004).

McDEVITT, Ruth (1895–1976). American stage and screen character actress. Born Ruth Shoecraft, Sept 13, 1895, in Coldwater, Michigan; died May 27, 1976, in Hollywood, CA; m. Patrick John McDevitt (died 1936). ❖ Made Broadway debut in *Young Couple Wanted* (1940), followed by *Goodbye in the Night, Arsenic and Old Lace, Harvey, Sleepy Hollow, Picnic, Solid Gold Cadillac, The Best Man* and *Absence of a Cello*; films include *The Parent Trap, Boys' Night Out, The Birds, Dear Heart, The Out of Towners, The Shakiest Gun in the West, An Angel in my Pocket* and *Change of Habit*; of her frequent tv appearances, was a regular in the series "Pistols and Petticoats" and the mother of Wally Cox on "Mr. Peepers."

McDONAGH, Isobel (1899–1982). Australian actress. Name variations: Marie Lorraine. Born Isobella Mercia McDonagh, Jan 3, 1899, in Sydney, NSW, Australia; died Mar 5, 1982, in London, England; dau. of Dr. J. McDonagh (resident doctor for J.C. Williams theater co.); sister of Paulette McDonagh (1901–1978) and Phyllis McDonagh (1900–1978); m. a wealthy banker. ❖ Became an established actress under stage name Marie Lorraine; was directed by sister Paulette in 4 films: *Those Who Love* (1926), *The Far Paradise* (1928), *The Cheaters* (1930) and the sound film, *Two Minutes Silence* (1933); helped form Sydney's Ensemble Theatre.

McDONAGH, Paulette (1901–1978). Australian filmmaker. Born Paulette DeVere McDonagh in Sydney, Australia, June 11, 1901; died Aug 30, 1978, in Sydney; dau. of Dr. J. McDonagh (resident doctor for J.C. Williams theater co.); sister of Isobel McDonagh (1899–1982) and Phyllis McDonagh (1900–1978). ❖ The 1st woman to write and direct silent films for the commercial cinema in Australia, wrote and helmed *Those Who Love* (1926), which starred her sister Isobel, who was already an established actress under the stage name Marie Lorraine; with sisters, made *The Far Paradise* (1928), a box-office success, followed by *The Cheaters,* which was naturalistic in style; made last film, *Two Minutes' Silence* (1933), a serious drama with an antiwar slant that was a financial disaster; went on to direct a series of documentaries, including a film about the legendary Australian race horse Phar Lap. With sisters, received the prestigious Langford Award from the Australian Film Institute (1978). ❖ See also *Women in World History*.

McDONAGH, Phyllis (1900–1978). Australian art director. Born Phyllis Glory McDonagh, Jan 7, 1900, in Sydney, NSW, Australia; died Oct 17, 1978, in Sydney; dau. of Dr. J. McDonagh (resident doctor for J.C. Williams theater co.); sister of Isobel McDonagh (1899–1982) and Paulette McDonagh (1901–1978). ❖ Served as art director and production manager on her sisters' films; moved to New Zealand and became a journalist.

McDONAGH, Siobhain (1960—). English politician and member of Parliament. Born Feb 20, 1960; dau. of Cumin and Breda Doogue McDonagh. ❖ Representing Labour, elected to House of Commons for Mitcham and Morden (1997, 2001, 2005).

McDONALD, Agnes (1829–1906). New Zealand accommodation-house keeper, nurse, and postmaster. Name variations: Agnes Carmont. Born Agnes Carmont, Sept 2, 1829, in Kirkcudbrightshire, Scotland; dau. of John Carmont and Elizabeth (Caven) Carmont; m. Hector McDonald (trader), 1854 (died 1878); children: 10. ❖ Immigrated to New Zealand (1850); when coach service began along coast between Wanganui and Wellington, established accommodation house with husband as a link between colonial settlers and Maori villagers (1858); served as nurse to local Maori; was postmaster (1883–94). ❖ See also *Dictionary of New Zealand Biography* (Vol. 1).

McDONALD, Ann (1862–1954). *See McVicar, Annie.*

McDONALD, Audra (1970—). African-American actress and singer. Born Audra Ann McDonald, July 3, 1970, in Berlin, Germany; grew up in Fresno, CA; graduate of Juilliard, 1993; m. Peter Donovan (bass player), 2000; children: Zoe Madeline Donovan (b. 2001). ❖ The only performer in theater history to win 3 Tony's for 1st 3 shows: *Carousel* (1994), *Master Class* (1996) and *Ragtime* (1998); had 1st starring role in *Marie Christine* (1999), for which she was nominated for a Tony; also won a Tony for *A Raisin in the Sun* (2004); on tv, appeared on "Having Our Say: The Delany Sisters' First 100 Years" (1999), "Annie" (1999) and "Wit" (2001); films include *Tea Time with Roy & Sylvia* (2003).

McDONALD, Beverly (1970—). Jamaican runner. Born Feb 15, 1970, in St. Mary, Jamaica; attended Texas Christian University. ❖ At World championships, won a gold medal for 4x100-meter relay (1991) and a silver medal for the 100 meters (1999); won a silver medal for 4x100-meter relay at Sydney Olympics (2000) and a gold medal for 4x100-meter relay at Athens Olympics (2004); placed 1st in the 200 meters at Super Grand Prix (2003).

McDONALD, Deborah (1954—). American equestrian. Born Aug 27, 1954, in Orange County, CA. ❖ At World Cup Final in Gothenburg, won indiv. dressage (2003); won a bronze medal for team dressage at Athens Olympics (2004).

McDONALD, Golden (1910–1952). *See Brown, Margaret Wise.*

McDONALD, Gabrielle Kirk (1942—). African-American lawyer and judge. Born 1942 in St. Paul, Minnesota; raised in Manhattan and Teaneck, NJ; attended Boston University, 1959–61, and Hunter College, 1961–63; graduate of Howard University School of Law, 1966 (finishing 1st in her class). ❖ Became staff lawyer for NAACP Legal Defense and Educational Fund; nominated by President Jimmy Carter to serve on US Court for the Southern District of Texas (1979), the 1st African-American to be appointed in Texas and the 3rd African-American federal judge in US; resigned from the court (1988), to resume private practice and to teach at Texas Southern University's Thurgood Marshall School of Law and St. Mary's School of Law; elected to a judgeship on the International War Crimes Tribunal for the Former Yugoslavia (1993); as chief judge, presided over the 1st full war crimes trial of the tribunal; reelected (1997), then was nominated and endorsed by the judges on the court to be president and presiding judge for next 2 years.

McDONALD, Grace (1918–1999). American dancer and actress. Born June 15, 1918, in Boston, MA; died Oct 30, 1999, in Scottsdale, AZ; sister of Ray McDonald (dancer, died 1959). ❖ Began career in a dancing act with her brother; films include *Dancing on a Dime, It Ain't Hay, Always a Bridesmaid, Murder in the Blue Room, Follow the Boys* and *Honeymoon Ahead.*

McDONALD, Hedwick Wilhelmina (1893–1959). New Zealand racehorse trainer. Name variations: Hedwick Wilhelmina Maher, Granny Maher. Born on April 28, 1893, at Hastings, New Zealand; died on Oct 5, 1959, at Palmerston North, New Zealand; dau. of John Maher (racehorse trainer) and Hedwick Wilhelmina (Douglass) Maher; m. Allan William McDonald (steeplechase jockey), 1929. ❖ First female professional racehorse trainer and one of New Zealand's most successful trainers (1924), produced the winner of 1938 Melbourne Cup. ❖ See also *Dictionary of New Zealand Biography* (Vol. 4).

McDONALD, Julie (1970—). Australian swimmer. Born Mar 14, 1970, in Australia. ❖ At Seoul Olympics, won a bronze medal in the 800-meter freestyle (1988).

McDONALD, Kim (1957–1986). *See Peyton, Kim.*

McDONALD, Marie (1923–1965). American actress and singer. Born Cora Marie Frye, July 6, 1923, in Burgin, KY; died of an overdose of pills, Oct 21, 1965, in Calabasas, CA; m. Richard Allord, 1940 (div.); m. Lou Bass; m. Vic Orsatti (div. 1947); m. Harry Karl, 1947 (div. 1954); m. Edward F. Calahan, 1962 (annulled 1962); m. Donald F. Taylor (film producer), 1964 (div. 1965). ❖ Nicknamed "The Body," began career as a showgirl, model, and bandsinger; films include *Guest in the House, It Started with Eve, Pardon My Sarong, Hit Parade of 1951* and *Promises! Promises!.*

McDORMAND, Frances (1957—). American actress. Born June 23, 1957, in Chicago, IL; raised in Monessen, Pennsylvania; adopted dau. of Vernon (Disciples of Christ minister) and Noreen McDormand (both Canadian-born); Bethany College, BA in theater, 1979; Yale University, MFA, 1982; m. Joel Coen (film director), 1984; children: 2. ❖ Nominated for Tony Award as Best Actress for performance in *A Streetcar Named Desire* (1988); won Academy Award as Best Actress for *Fargo* (1996); other films include *Blood Simple* (1984), *Mississippi Burning* (1988), *Paradise Road* (1997), *Madeline* (1998), *Wonder Boys* (2000), *Almost Famous* (2000), *The Man Who Wasn't There* (2001), *Something's Gotta Give* (2003) and *North Country* (2005), for which she was nominated for an Academy Award as Best Supporting Actress.

McDOUGALL, Adelaide (1909–2000). Cree midwife. Name variations: Adelaide Flett. Born April 4, 1909, in St.Theresa Point, Manitoba, Canada; died Nov 28, 2000, in St. Theresa Point; m. 1st husband (died); Charlie McDougall, April 3, 1931; children: (2nd m.) 11. ❖ Aboriginal midwife, assisted local Canadian midwives from a young age; began a thriving midwife practice at age 20 and delivered last baby, a great-grandson, around 1987; originated from and later served as an elder of the aboriginal Oji-Cree community; battled extreme weather conditions to reach patients, often burning birch bark as a light source while traveling during night. Was the 1st Canadian recipient (1999) of the Sage Femme Award from the Midwives' Alliance of North America.

McDOWELL, Anne E. (1826–1901). American publisher. Born in Smyrna, Delaware, June 23, 1826; died in Philadelphia, PA, 1901. ❖ Founded Philadelphia *Woman's Advocate*, a weekly newspaper, whose staff, including printers and typesetters, were all women (1855); was editor of women's department of Philadelphia *Sunday Despatch* (1860–71), then became editor of Philadelphia *Sunday Republic* (1871); created an organization to secure sickness and death benefits for employees of Wanamaker's department store (1884), and also founded the McDowell Free Library for women employed by Wanamaker's.

McDOWELL, Claire (1877–1966). American actress. Name variations: (pseudonym) Doris Carlton. Born Nov 2, 1877, in New York, NY; died Oct 23, 1966, in Hollywood, CA; m. Charles Hill Mailes (actor, died 1937). ❖ Appeared on stage; played dramatic leads in D.W. Griffith films for Biograph (1910–14); other films include *The Big Parade, Midsummer Madness, The Viking, Something to Think About, Ben-Hur, Tillie the Toiler, The Big House* and *Rebecca of Sunnybrook Farm*; retired (1937).

McDOWELL, Katharine Bonner (1849–1883). *See Bonner, Sherwood.*

McDOWELL, Mary Eliza (1854–1936). American social reformer. Born Nov 30, 1854, in Cincinnati, Ohio; died after a stroke, Oct 14, 1936, in Chicago, IL; dau. of Malcolm McDowell and Jane Welch (Gordon) McDowell; attended Elizabeth Harrison's kindergarten training school in Chicago, late 1880s. ❖ "Angel of the Stockyards" who helped to improve living conditions in Chicago's squalid meat-packing district, moved to Chicago (c. 1866); was active in relief efforts after Chicago Fire of 1871; served as national organizer for Women's Christian Temperance Union (c. 1887); was 1st director of University of Chicago Settlement House (1894); traveled to Europe to study sanitation plants (1911); appointed commissioner of Public Welfare (1923); retired from Settlement House (1929); fought big business and apathetic government to improve the lives of the poor and desperate. ❖ See also Caroline Hill, ed. *Mary McDowell and Municipal Housekeeping* (1929); and *Women in World History*.

McELDERRY, Margaret K. (1912—). American children's editor and publisher. Born in Pittsburgh, Pennsylvania, in 1912; graduated from Mt. Holyoke College, 1933. ❖ For 9 years, assisted Anne Carroll Moore at New York Public Library; during WWII, served in Office of War Intelligence in London (1944–45); became head of children's department of Harcourt Brace (1945), along with May Massee, Ursula Nordstrom, and Elizabeth Reilly, was largely responsible for shaping the field of modern children's literature; edited Mary Norton's classic *The Borrowers*, and was a champion of both picture books and stories by foreign authors at a time when few American publishers looked beyond their own shores; forced to retire (1972), moved to Atheneum, where she became the 1st children's editor to receive her own imprint; moved to Simon & Schuster, where she was still working at age 90. ❖ See also *Women in World History*.

McELHENNEY, Jane (1836–1874). *See Clare, Ada.*

McELMURY, Audrey (1943—). American cyclist. Name variations: Audrey Phleger; Audrey Levonas. Born Audrey Phleger in 1943; graduate of University of California at San Diego, 1965; m. Scott McElmury (div.); m. Michael Levonas (cyclist), 1971. ❖ Won US road racing and pursuit championships (1966, 1970); won World road race title (1969).

McELROY, Mary Arthur (d. 1916). White House hostess. Born Mary Arthur; died 1916; dau. of William Arthur (Baptist cleric); grew up in Fairfield, Vermont; sister of Chester Alan Arthur (US president); schooled at Emma Willard's Seminary; m. John Edward McElroy (insurance man), 1861. ❖ After death of Ellen Herndon Arthur, became the official White House host for brother Chester Arthur. ❖ See also *Women in World History*.

McENTIRE, Reba (1955—). American musician. Born Reba Nell McEntire, Mar 28, 1955, in Chockie, OK; dau. of Clark (rodeo steer roper) and Jacqueline McEntire; sister of Susie Luchsinger, also known as Susie McEntire (Christian musician); m. Charlie Battles, June 21, 1976 (div. 1987); m. Narvel Blackstock (guitarist), June 1989; children: Shelby Steven (b. 1990). ❖ While in high school, performed at nightclubs with siblings as Singing McEntires; drew attention singing "Star Spangled Banner" at National Rodeo Finals (1974) and signed with Mercury Records (1976); had 1st hit, "(You Lift Me) Up to Heaven" (1980); other hits include "Today All Over Again" (1981), "I'm Not That Lonely Yet" (1982) and "Just a Little Love" (1984); signed with MCA and career began to take off with such albums as *Whoever's In New England* (1986), *Rumor Has It* (1990), *Read My Mind* (1994), and *If You See Him* (1998), and hit songs "Little Rock" (1986), "I Know How He Feels" (1988), "Fallin' Out of Love" (1991), "Does He Love You" (1993), and "And Still" (1995); with husband, started company, Starstruck Entertainment (1988); lost 8 members of band in plane crash (1991); published *Comfort From a Country Quilt: Finding New Inspiration and Strength From Old-Fashioned Values* (1999); became hit on Broadway, starring in *Annie Get Your Gun* (2001); launched own tv series "Reba" (2001); films include *Tremors* (1990), *North* (1994), and *Forever Love* (1998). ❖ See also autobiography, *Reba: My Story* (1994).

McEWAN, Geraldine (1932—). English actress. Born Geraldine Mckeown, May 9, 1932, in Old Windsor, England; m. Hugh Cruttwell (principal of Royal Academy of Dramatic Art), 1953 (died 2002); children: 2. ❖ Intelligent, versatile actress at home in both classical and contemporary drama, made stage debut at 14 at Theatre Royal in Windsor; by 18, had starred in London's West End in several long-running productions; received 1st serious critical attention for performance in *The Member of the Wedding* (1958); acted with Shakespeare Memorial Theater, then joined Royal Shakespeare Co. (1961), appearing as Beatrice and Ophelia, among others; originated lead in Orton's *Loot* (1965); made NY debut in *School for Scandal* (1963) and went on to captivate Broadway with *The Private Ear and the Public Eye*, later receiving Tony Award nomination for performance in *The Chairs* (1998); won *Evening Standard* Best Actress Award for *The Rivals* (1983), BAFTA Best Actress Award for *Oranges Are Not the Only Fruit* (1991) and *Evening Standard* Best Actress Award for *The Way of the World* (1995); on tv, appeared on such shows as "The Prime of Miss Jean Brodie" (1978), "Barchester Chronicles" (1982) and as Agatha Christie's Miss Marple (2004); films include *The Dance of Death* (1968), *Henry V* (1989), *Titus* (1999) and *The Magdalene Sisters* (2002).

McEWEN, Anne (c. 1903–1967). Australian prime-ministerial wife. Born Anne Mills McLeod, c. 1903; died Feb 10, 1967, in Toorak; m. John McEwen (prime minister of Australia, 1967–68), Sept 21, 1921; no children. ❖ Active in the Country Party, campaigned in husband's federal elections; raised funds for local causes and was an active member of the Country Women's Association in Victoria; appointed a life governor of Melbourne's Prince Henry Hospital; heavily involved with the care of Royal Australian Air Force recruits while they trained at Point Cook throughout WWII; was a founding member of the White Wings

Auxiliary, a group formed to support the Women's Auxiliary Australian Air Force. Named Dame of the British Empire (1966).

McEWEN, Anne (1905–1962). *See Forbes-Robertson, Jean.*

McEWEN, Sarah Katherine (1882–1964). *See Ramsland, Sarah.*

McFALL, Frances E. (1854–1943). *See MacFall, Frances E.*

McFALL, Lauren (1980—). American synchronized swimmer. Born Feb 9, 1980, in Sacramento, CA. ❖ Won a team bronze medal at Athens Olympics (2004).

McFALLS, Jennifer (1971—). American softball player. Born Nov 10, 1971, in Grand Prairie, TX. ❖ Won a team gold medal at Sydney Olympics (2000).

McFARLAND, Beulah (c. 1898–1964). American theatrical dancer. Born c. 1898, in Des Moines, Iowa; died Aug 8, 1964, in Los Angeles, CA. ❖ Performed in 4 editions of *Ziegfeld Follies* in NY (starting 1918); best remembered for appearance as a "living curtain" in *Follies* (1922) where she and Eva Brady were attached to stage curtain with jeweled garters and rose along with it as the show began.

McFARLAND, Irene (fl. 1925). American aviator. Flourished c. 1925. ❖ The 1st woman to save her own life with a parachute, jumped from her plane in Cincinnati, Ohio, to test a self-opening parachute which jammed, then made safe landing with a second, standard army parachute (June 28, 1925); as a result, became the 1st woman member of the Caterpillar Club.

McFARLANE, Elaine (1942—). American singer. Name variations: Elaine "Spanky" McFarlane, Spanky, Mama Spanky, Spanky and Our Gang. Born June 19, 1942, in Peoria, IL. ❖ Sang with band, the New Wine Singers (early 1960s); became lead singer for folk-pop group, Spanky and Our Gang (1966), which had several hit songs, including "Sunday Will Never Be the Same" (1967) and "Like to Get to Know You" (1968); with group, spawned controversy with protest song, "Give a Damn" (1969), which was banned on numerous radio stations but later became part of public service announcement campaign; joined group, Mamas and Papas (1981); later sang with new lineup in Spanky and Our Gang.

McFARLANE, Tracey (1966—). American swimmer. Name variations: Tracey McFarlane-Mirande. Born July 20, 1966; attended University of Texas. ❖ At Seoul Olympics, won a silver medal in the 4x100-meter medley relay (1988).

McGAFFEY, Christine (1883–1970). *See Frederick, Christine.*

McGAHEY, Kathleen (1960—). American field-hockey player. Born Mar 1960. ❖ At Los Angeles Olympics, won a bronze medal in team competition (1984).

McGEE, Anita Newcomb (1864–1940). American physician and founder of the army nurse corps. Born Anita Newcomb, Nov 4, 1864, in Washington, DC; died Oct 5, 1940; dau. of Professor Simon Newcomb (astronomer at US Naval Observatory) and Mary Caroline (Hassler) Newcomb (dau. of Ferdinand Rudolph Hassler, founder and 1st superintendent of US Coast and Geodetic Survey); traveled and studied for 3 years in England and Switzerland, took special courses at Newnham College, Cambridge, and University of Geneva; Columbia, MD, 1892; took postgraduate course in gynecology at Johns Hopkins; m. William J. McGee (ethnologist), 1888; children: daughter Klotho (b. 1889); son Eric (b. 1902). ❖ During Spanish-American War (1898–1900), was acting assistant surgeon, the only woman officer in US Army, and established and had charge of the nurse corps division of the Surgeon-General's office, the Army Nurse Corps.

McGEE, Molly (1896–1961). *See Jordan, Marian.*

McGEE, Pamela (1962—). African-American basketball player. Born Pamela Denise McGee, Dec 1, 1962, in Flint, Michigan; twin sister of Paula McGee (basketball player). ❖ With sister Paula, Cynthia Cooper, and Cheryl Miller, led USC to NCAA championships (1983–84); at Los Angeles Olympics, won a gold medal in team competition (1984); played professionally for WNBA's Sacramento Monarchs and Los Angeles Sparks; named assistant coach for WNBA's Detroit Shock (2003).

McGEHEE, Helen (1921—). American modern dancer and choreographer. Born 1921 in Lynchburg, VA; trained at Randolph-Macon Women's University. ❖ Performed with Martha Graham company in NY, creating roles in *Night Journey* (1947), *Canticle for Innocent*

Comedians (1952), *Clytemnestra* (1958), *Phaedra* (1967), and *Cortege of Eagles* (1967), among others; taught at Juilliard.

McGENNIS, Marian (1953—). Irish politician. Born Nov 1953 in Dublin, Ireland; m. Bryan McGennis. ❖ Was one of the Taoiseach's nominees to the Seanad (1993); representing Fianna Fáil, elected to the 28th Dáil (1997–2002) for Dublin Central.

McGHEE, Carla (1968—). African-American basketball player. Born Mar 6, 1968, in Peoria, IL; graduate of University of Tennessee, 1990. ❖ Forward; played 3 years for Tennessee Lady Vols (1987, 1989–90); played professionally in Spain, Italy, Switzerland, and Germany (1990–94); won a team gold medal at Goodwill Games (1994); won a team gold medal at Atlanta Olympics (1996); played for the Orlando Miracles (1999–2002); signed with the Connecticut Sun (2003).

McGILL, Helen (1871–1947). See MacGill, Helen.

McGILL, Linda (1945—). Australian long-distance swimmer. Born 1945 in Queensland, Australia. ❖ Competed in 4 events in Olympic games (1964) but her best finish was 5th in 400-meter individual medley; crossed the Channel from France to England in 11:12 (1965), the 1st Australian to swim the channel; twice crossed France to England (1967), in times of 13.02 and 9:59 (then a new women's record); was also the 1st to swim around Hong Kong Island and across Port Phillip Bay, Victoria.

McGILL, Moyna (1895–1975). See MacGill, Moyna.

McGINLEY, Phyllis (1905–1978). American poet, author of children's books, and essayist. Born Phyllis McGinley, Mar 21, 1905, in Ontario, Oregon; died of a stroke, Feb 22, 1978, in New York, NY; dau. of Daniel McGinley (land speculator) and Julia Kiesel McGinley; graduate of University of Utah, 1927; m. Charles L. Hayden, 1937; children: Julia Elizabeth Hayden (b. 1939); Phyllis Louise "Patsy" Hayden (b. 1941). ❖ Pulitzer Prize-winning writer, was most recognized for her light verse describing suburban life in America (1930s–60s); taught school and worked in publishing before marriage; published 1st book of poetry, *On the Contrary* (1934), followed by *One More Manhattan* (1937) and *A Pocketful of Wry* (1940); published 1st children's book, *The Horse Who Lived Upstairs* (1944); published *The Love Letters of Phyllis McGinley*, which focused on the joys of suburban living and was one of her most popular collections of verse (1954); designated Columbia University's Phi Beta Kappa poet, wrote "In Praise of Diversity," one of her best-known works (1954); won Pulitzer Prize for *Times Three: Selected Verse from Three Decades* (1961); published essays, *The Province of the Heart* (1959) and *Sixpence in Her Shoe* (1964); an observer of humanity, her interests included everything from the qualities of sainthood to myths and social criticism. ❖ See also Linda Welshimer Wagner, *Phyllis McGinley* (Twayne, 1971); and *Women in World History*.

McGLEW, Phyllis (1894–1987). See Cilento, Phyllis.

McGRATH, Kathleen (1952–2002). American naval captain. Born June 4, 1952, in Columbus, Ohio; died of cancer, Sept 26, 2002, in Bethesda, MD; dau. of a US Air Force pilot; attended California State University at Sacramento; m. Lt-Commander Gregory Brandon; children: (adopted) son and daughter from Russia. ❖ An admiral in the US Navy, became the 1st woman to command a warship when she was named captain of the guided-missile frigate *USS Jarrett* (1998); while helming the *Jarrett*, patrolled the Gulf off Iraq.

McGRATH, Peggy (d. 1996). See Rockefeller, Margaret.

McGRAW, Eloise Jarvis (1915–2000). American children's writer. Born Dec 9, 1915, in Houston, Tex.; died Nov 30, 2000; raised in Oklahoma City; dau. of Loy Hamilton (merchant) and Genevieve (Scoffern) Jarvis; Principia College, BA, 1937; m. William Corbin McGraw (writer and filbert-grower), Jan 29, 1940 (died 1999); children: Peter Anthony, Lauren Lynn. ❖ In a writing span of over 50 years, won Newbery Honors for 3 books: *The Golden Goblet* (1961), *Moccasin Trail* (1952) and *The Moorchild* (1996); won an Edgar Award for *A Really Weird Summer* (1977) and an Edgar Award nomination for *Tangled Webb* (1993); other books include *Sawdust in His Shoes* (1950), *Crown Fire* (1951), *Master Cornhill* (1973), *The Money Room* (1981) and *Hideaway* (1983).

McGREGOR, Maata Mahupuku (1890–1952). See Mahupuku, Maata.

McGREGOR, Tammy (1975—). See Cleland, Tammy.

McGREGOR, Yvonne (1961—). English cyclist. Born April 9, 1961, in Wibsey, Bradford, England. ❖ Began career as a fell runner; took up riding at age 30 (1990); won Commonwealth Games championship for 25-kilometer points race (1994); placed 4th in pursuit at Atlanta Olympics (1996); won a bronze medal for indiv. pursuit at Sydney Olympics (2000); won the World championship for pursuit (2000); retired from international racing (2001); set a women's European hour record of 43.689km at Manchester (April 2002). Awarded an MBE (2001).

McGROARTY, Sister Julia (1827–1901). American nun, educator, and founder of Trinity College. Born Susan McGroarty, Feb 13, 1827, in Donegal, Ireland; died Nov 12, 1901, in Peabody, Massachusetts; dau. of Neil McGroarty and Catherine (Bonner) McGroarty; received teachers' training from the Sisters of Notre Dame de Namur; never married; no children. ❖ Immigrated to US (1831); began preparations to enter women's religious order (1846); took vows as Sister Julia (1848); served as mistress of boarders at the Academy of Notre Dame in Roxbury, MA (1854–60); was transferred to the post of superior of the Notre Dame order's Philadelphia school (1860), becoming the 1st American nun to hold that position; became provincial superior in Cincinnati with responsibilities for overseeing all 26 Notre Dame de Namur houses east of the Rocky Mountains (1887); set up an orphanage and established 14 new schools; battled great opposition to establish Trinity College, a college for women attached to the prestigious Catholic University of America in Washington, DC (1900). ❖ See also *Women in World History*.

McGRORY, Mary (1918–2004). American journalist. Born Aug 22, 1918, in Boston, Massachusetts; died April 21, 2004, in Washington DC; dau. of Edward Patrick McGrory (postal worker) and Mary (Jacobs) McGrory; Emmanuel College, BA, 1939; never married; no children. ❖ Nationally syndicated American columnist who in 1975 became the 1st woman to receive the Pulitzer Prize for commentary; worked in publishing (1939–42); joined *Boston Herald* staff as a secretary (1942), and became book reviewer; served as regular book reviewer for *Washington Star* (1947–54); became one of the most respected journalists in Washington, DC, covering McCarthy hearings (1954) and assigned to national desk; started 1st regular column (1960); won Pulitzer Prize for commentary on Watergate scandal (1975); wrote passionate columns against the Vietnam War which ran defiantly contrary to the *Star*'s pro-Vietnam editorial policy; covered Three Mile Island story (1979); after the *Star* folded, took a news position at the *Washington Post*; had column syndicated nationally (1985). Won George R. Polk Memorial Award (1962). ❖ See also *Women in World History*.

McGUGAN, Irene (1952—). Scottish politician. Born 1952 in Angus, Scotland. ❖ Was an activist for SNP for over 20 years; elected to the Scottish Parliament for North East Scotland.

McGUINNESS, Catherine (1934—). Irish politician, lawyer and judge. Born Catherine Ellis, Nov 14, 1934, in Dunmurry, Belfast, Northern Ireland; dau. of Robert Ellis (Church of England rector); m. Proinsías MacAonghusa. ❖ Served as a parliamentary officer for the Labour Party; when husband was expelled from the Labour Party (1967), resigned her post; qualified as a barrister (1977) and became an authority on family law; as an Independent, elected to Seanad in a by-election (1979) and served (1979–82, 1983–87); was the 1st woman judge of the Circuit Court (Dublin Circuit, 1994–96), of the High Court (1996–2000), and of the Supreme Court (2000—).

McGUINNESS, Norah (1901–1980). Irish artist. Born Norah Allison McGuinness in Derry, Northern Ireland, Nov 7, 1901; died in Monkstown, Co. Dublin, Nov 22, 1980; dau. of Joseph Allison McGuinness and Jessie McCleery McGuinness; attended Dublin Metropolitan School of Art and Chelsea Polytechnic; m. Geoffrey Taylor also known as Geoffrey Phipps (poet), 1925 (div. 1929, partially because of his affair with Laura Riding). ❖ Major proponent of modern movement in Ireland, won a 3-year scholarship to Dublin Metropolitan School of Art (1921), where she studied under Patrick Tuohy, Oswald Reeves, and Harry Clarke; published illustrations in magazines, which remained an important source of income throughout her life (1923–24); commissioned to illustrate Laurence Sterne's *A Sentimental Journey through France and Italy* (1925); worked at Abbey Theater, designing sets and costumes for W.B. Yeats' *Deirdre* and *The Only Jealousy of Emer* (1926); also conceived the garden scene for *The Importance of Being Earnest*; illustrated Yeats' *Stories of Red Hanrahan and the Secret Rose*; studied in Paris for 2 years with André Lhote and was influenced by the work of Braque, Lurçat, Dufy and Vlaminck; lived in London (1931–37), working mostly in landscapes; continued to design for the stage, most notably for Denis Johnston's *A Bride for the Unicorn* at Westminster Theater in London; had 1st exhibition in NY (1939) and regular exhibitions of her paintings in Dublin; became a considerable portrait artist, painting many of the leading cultural figures in Ireland; career took a major turn (1943–44), when she became a founder member of Irish Exhibition of Living Art, then president (1944–72); as such, became speaker for the modern movement in Ireland and its champion against the forces of reaction symbolized by Royal Hibernian Academy (RHA). Received Royal Dublin Society medal (1923) and Tailteann Competition medal (1924). ❖ See also *Women in World History*.

McGUIRE, Anne (1949—). Scottish politician and member of Parliament. Born Anne Long, May 26, 1949; m. Len McGuire, 1972. ❖ Representing Labour, elected to House of Commons for Stirling (1997, 2001, 2005); named parliamentary under-secretary of state, Scotland Office; named minister, Scotland Office.

McGUIRE, Dorothy (1916–2001). American actress. Born Dorothy Hackett McGuire, June 14, 1916, in Omaha, Nebraska; died Sept 13, 2001, in Santa Monica, CA; dau. of Thomas Johnson McGuire and Isabelle (Flaherty) McGuire; attended Pine Manor Junior College, c. 1936; m. John Swope (photographer), in 1943 (died 1979); children: son Mark Swope; daughter Topo Swope. ❖ Won coveted title role in *Claudia,* her 1st Broadway play (1940); made film debut in *Claudia* (1943) and went on to appear in a number of other critically acclaimed films, including *A Tree Grows in Brooklyn* (1944), *The Enchanted Cottage* (1945), *Claudia and David* (1946), and *The Spiral Staircase* (1946); other films include *Three Coins in the Fountain* (1954), *Old Yeller* (1957), *The Remarkable Mr. Pennypacker* (1959), *The Dark at the Top of the Stairs* (1960), and *The Greatest Story Ever Told* (1965); returned to Broadway in a revival of Tennessee Williams' *Night of the Iguana* (1973); also appeared on tv. Nominated for Academy Award for Best Actress for *Gentleman's Agreement* (1948). ❖ See also *Women in World History*.

McGUIRE, Edith (1944—). African-American track-and-field athlete. Name variations: Edith McGuire Duvall. Born Edith Marie McGuire, June 3, 1944, in Atlanta, GA. ❖ Won the 100 meters and long jump at the AAU indoor and outdoor meets and the 100 meters at the Pan American Games (1963); won the AAU 200 meters (1964–66); at Tokyo Olympics, won a gold medal for the 200 meters and silver medals for the 100 meters and 4x100-meter relay (1964); was a member of the famed Tennessee Tigerbelle team. ❖ See also *Women in World History*.

McGUIRE, Kathryn (1903–1978). American actress. Name variations: Kathryn Landy. Born Dec 6, 1903, in Peoria, IL; died Oct 10, 1978, in Los Angeles, CA; m. George Landy (talent agent, died 1955). ❖ Appeared opposite Buster Keaton in *The Navigator* and *Sherlock, Jr.*; made over 50 films, including *Crossroads of New York, The Shriek of Araby, Naughty But Nice, Lilac Time* and *The Long, Long Trail.*

McGUIRE, Linda (1949—). See Gustavson, Linda.

McGUIRE, Phyllis (1931—). American pop singer. Born Feb 14, 1931, in Middletown, Ohio; youngest sister of singers Christine McGuire (b. 1928) and Dorothy McGuire (b. 1930). ❖ With older sisters Christine and Dorothy, singing as the McGuire Sisters in the close three-part harmony, won a showdown on the popular "Arthur Godfrey Talent Hour" (1954); signed with Coral Records and had a hit with 1st single, "Goodnight, Sweetheart, Goodnight," (1954); followed that with "Sincerely," which reached No. 1 (1955); had several other top-10 hits, such as "Give Me Love," "Volare," "Theme from Picnic," "Delilah," "Tears on My Pillow" and "Sugartime" which reached No. 1 (1957); launched solo career, becoming successful on Las Vegas nightclub circuit and romantically linked with alleged crime figure Sam Giancana, who was later murdered (their affair was the basis for HBO's movie *Sugartime,* starring Mary-Louise Parker and John Turturro, 1995). ❖ See also *Women in World History*.

McHAFFIE, Catherine Ann (1870–1957). See Andersen, Catherine Ann.

McHUGH, Fanny (1861–1943). New Zealand midwife, nurse, shopkeeper, lecturer. Name variations: Fanny Balmer. Born Fanny Balmer, Aug 21, 1861, in Auckland, New Zealand; died on Dec 17, 1943, in Bombay, Auckland; dau. of William Balmer (soldier) and Margaret (McIntosh) Balmer; m. Henry Joseph McHugh (farmer), 1880 (died c. 1904); children: 1 daughter, 5 sons. ❖ Served as midwife and nurse to local residents of Turakina Valley (late 1880s); opened Turakina general store (1893); established maternity home at Manaia

(1907); joined New Zealand Volunteer Sisterhood to care for sick soldiers at Trentham and in Egypt (1914); returned to New Zealand after WWI and was appointed to health patrol with Department of Health (1919); also lectured on social hygiene until 1926. ❖ See also *Dictionary of New Zealand Biography* (Vol. 3).

McHUTCHESON, Elizabeth (1800–1892). See Sinclair, Elizabeth McHutcheson.

McILRAITH, Jane (1823–1911). See Deans, Jane.

McILWRAITH, Jean Newton (1859–1938). Canadian novelist and literary critic. Born 1859 in Hamilton, Ontario, Canada; died 1938. ❖ Works include children's books, 1 opera, and historical romances *The Curious Career of Roderick Campbell* (1901), *A Diana of Quebec* (1912), and *Kinsmen at War* (1927).

McINDOE, Mabel (1872–1956). See Hill, Mabel.

McINGVALE, Cynthia (1950—). See Potter, Cynthia.

McINTIRE, Barbara (1935—). American golfer. Name variations: Barbara Joy McIntire. Born Jan 12, 1935, in Toledo, Ohio. ❖ Won USGA Women's Amateur (1959, 1964); won British Women's Amateur (1960); member of Curtis Cup team (1958, 1960, 1962, 1964, 1966, 1972); captain of Curtis Cup squads (1976, 1998); served on USGA Women's Committee (1985–96) and was chair (1995). Received US Golf Association's Bob Jones Award (2000).

McINTOSH, Anne (1954—). English politician and member of Parliament. Born Anne McIntosh, Sept 20, 1954; m. John Harvey. ❖ Served as Member of European Parliament for Essex North East (1989–94) and Essex North and Suffolk South (1994–99); as a Conservative, elected to House of Commons for Vale of York (1997, 2001, 2005); named shadow minister of Transport.

McINTOSH, Caroline C. (1813–1881). Second wife of Millard Fillmore. Name variations: Caroline Fillmore. Born Caroline Carmichael, Oct 21, 1813, in Morristown, New Jersey; died Aug 11, 1881, in Buffalo, New York; dau. of Charles Carmichael (New Jersey merchant) and Temperance (Blachley) Carmichael; m. Ezekiel C. McIntosh (one of the builders of Mohawk and Hudson Railroad); m. Millard Fillmore (former US president), Feb 10, 1858; no children. ❖ See also *Women in World History*.

McINTOSH, Gail (1955—). New Zealand politician. Born Gail McIntosh, June 16, 1955, in Woodville, NZ; married. ❖ Was a taxi driver in Wellington, then a chartered accountant; served as National MP for Lyttelton (1990–93).

McINTOSH, Lyndsay (1955—). Scottish politician. Born 1955 in Glasgow, Scotland. ❖ Stood as candidate for Fallside at local elections (1992 and 1999); stood as candidate in 3 by-elections, Greenfaulds (1997), Condorrat (1998), and Whinhall (1998); as a Conservative and Unionist, elected to Scottish Parliament for Central Scotland.

McINTOSH, Madge (1875–1950). English actress and producer. Born April 8, 1875, in Calcutta, India; died Feb 19, 1950; m. W. Graham Browne (div.). ❖ Made stage debut in London as Peg Woffington in *Masks and Faces* (1893); toured with the companies of Ben Greet, Olga Nethersole, the Kendals, and Forbes-Robertson; also appeared in *Mademoiselle Mars, The Silver Link, Hamlet, The Virgin Goddess, The Great Conspiracy, The Blue Bird* and *A Fool There Was*; appointed director of Liverpool Rep (1914) and produced an 8-week season at King's, Hammersmith (1925); produced other plays and ran Madge McIntosh's Rep Co. at Theatre Royal, Huddersfield, Yorkshire; taught at Royal Academy of Dramatic Art (RADA).

McINTOSH, Maria (1803–1878). American novelist. Born Maria Jane McIntosh, 1803, in Sunbury, Liberty Co., GA; died Feb 25, 1878, in Morristown, NJ; dau. of Lachlan McIntosh (lawyer) and Mary (Moore) Maxwell. ❖ Under pen name Aunt Kitty, wrote series of children's books later collected into *Aunt Kitty's Tales* (1847); published 8 novels, the most successful of which was *Charms and Counter-Charms* (1848); critical of early woman's movement in non-fiction *Woman in America: Her Work and Her Reward* (1850), was known for sentimental fiction that espoused piety and virtue and periodically criticized abolition; also wrote *Conquest and Self-Conquest* (1843), *The Lofty and the Lowly* (1853), *Violet; or, The Cross and the Crown* (1856) and *Two Pictures* (1863).

McINTOSH, Millicent Carey (1898–2001). American educator and feminist. Born Millicent Carey, Nov 30, 1898, in Baltimore, MD;

died Jan 3, 2001, in Tyringham, MA; dau. of Anthony Morris Carey and Margaret Cheston (Thomas) Carey (both Quakers); niece of M. Carey Thomas; attended Bryn Mawr College and Johns Hopkins University; m. Dr. Rustin McIntosh (pediatrician), 1932; children: James, Kenneth, R. Carey, and J. Richard McIntosh and Susan Lloyd. ❖ Became an instructor at Bryn Mawr, then appointed dean of freshmen and acting dean of the college; served as headmistress of Brearley School (1930–47); became dean of Barnard College (1946), the 1st married woman to head one of the Seven Sisters schools, and was then given the title of president (1952); retired (1962); lectured widely on women, education and child-rearing.

McINTYRE, Elizabeth (1965—). American freestyle skier. Name variations: Liz McIntyre. Born April 5, 1965, in Hanover, NH. ❖ Won a silver medal for moguls at Lillehammer Olympics (1994); won World Cup for moguls (1988, 1993, 1996, 1997).

McINTYRE, Leila (1882–1953). American musical-comedy actress. Born Dec 20, 1882, in NYC; died Jan 9, 1953, in Los Angeles, CA; m. John Hyams (performer); children: Leila Hyams (1905–1977, actress). ❖ Appeared in vaudeville and musical comedies with her husband, including *The Girl of My Dreams*; films include *On the Level, Hurricane, The Prisoner of Shark Island* and *Captain Eddie.*

McINTYRE, Liz (1965—). See McIntyre, Elizabeth.

McINTYRE, Molly (c. 1886–1952). Scottish-born actress. Born c. 1886 in Glasgow, Scotland; died Jan 29, 1952, in NYC. ❖ Starred on Broadway in *Kitty MacKay*; other appearances include *Bunty Pulls the Strings* and *Expressing Willie.*

McINTYRE, Vonda N. (1948—). American science-fiction and short-story writer. Name variations: Vonda Neel McIntyre. Born Aug 29, 1948, in Louisville, KY. ❖ Contributed to *Star Trek* series; works, which explore feminist themes and usually have strong female protagonists, include *The Exile Waiting* (1975), *Superluminal* (1983), *The Bride* (1985), *Screwtop* (1989), *Transition* (1990), and *The Moon and the Sun* (1997). Received Nebula Award (1973, 1978) and Hugo Award (1979).

McISAAC, Shona (1960—). English politician and member of Parliament. Born Shona McIsaac, April 3, 1960; m. Peter John Keith. ❖ Magazine editor; representing Labour, elected to House of Commons for Cleethorpes (1997, 2001, 2005); named PPS to Jane Kennedy as minister of state, Northern Ireland Office.

McKAIN, Douglas Mary (1789–1873). New Zealand nurse, midwife, and landowner. Name variations: Douglas Mary Dunsmore. Born Douglas Mary Dunsmore, July 20, 1789, in Glasgow, Scotland; died April 3, 1873, in Eskdale, New Zealand; dau. of John Dunsmore (ale-house keeper) and Mary (Paterson) Dunsmore; m. William McKain, 1808 (died 1837); children: 13. ❖ Emigrated from London to New Zealand (1840); purchased land in town and leased cottages to immigrants (1850s); served as midwife and general nurse in Wellington for 20 years. ❖ See also *Dictionary of New Zealand Biography* (Vol. 1).

McKANE, Alice Woodby (1865–1948). African-American physician and educator. Name variations: Alice Woodby-McKane. Born Alice Woodby in 1865 in Bridgewater, Pennsylvania; died Mar 6, 1948; dau. of Charles Woodby and Elizabeth B. (Frazier) Woodby; Hampton Institute, 1883–86; Institute for Colored Youth in Philadelphia, 1888–89; Women's Medical College of Pennsylvania, MD, 1892; m. Cornelius McKane (physician), Feb 2, 1893; children: Cornelius Jr. (b. 1897), Alice Fanny (b. 1898), William Francis (b. 1902). ❖ Worked as resident physician and instructor at Haines Institute and privately taught a class on nursing; with husband, founded 1st training school for nurses in southeast Georgia (1893), then traveled to Monrovia, Liberia, where they helped organize health facilities; also co-organized and headed the department of women's diseases at Monrovia's 1st hospital; with husband, established McKane Hospital for Women and Children and Training School for Nurses in Savannah (1896); moved to Boston; published *The Fraternal Society Sick Book* (1913) and a book of poems, *Clover Leaves* (1914). ❖ See also *Women in World History.*

McKANE, Kitty (1896–1992). English tennis player. Name variations: Kathleen McKane, Kitty McKane Godfree, Kitty Godfree, Mrs. L.A. Godfree; (wrongly) Kathleen Godfrey. Born Kathleen McKane, May 7, 1896, in London, England; died June 19, 1992; m. Leslie A. Godfree (tennis player). ❖ At Antwerp Olympics, won a bronze medal in singles, a silver medal in mixed doubles–outdoors, and a gold medal in doubles (1920); at Paris Olympics, won a bronze medal in singles and a silver

medal in doubles (1924); lost to Suzanne Lenglen in the singles finals at Wimbledon (1923); won Wimbledon singles title (1924), beating Helen Wills Moody (Helen Newington Wills), and (1926), beating Lili de Alvarez; with husband, won Wimbledon mixed doubles (1926). Inducted into Tennis Hall of Fame (1978).

McKAY, Catherine (1842–1935). See Carran, Catherine.

McKAY, Flora (b. 1936). See Shearer, Jill.

McKAY, Heather (1941—). Australian squash player. Name variations: Heather Blundell. Born Heather Pamela Blundell, July 31, 1941, in Queanbeyan, New South Wales, Australia. ❖ Lost only 2 squash matches in 20 years and is recognized as one of the leading players of the game; won 1st Australian Amateur Squash championship title (1960); won 1st British Open title in the sport (1962); won the inaugural Women's World championship title (1976), then won again (1979); became a coach in Brisbane.

McKAY, Penny Dudleston (1952—). See Dudleston, Penny.

McKEAN, Olive (1915—). American swimmer. Born Aug 10, 1915. ❖ At Berlin Olympics, won a bronze medal in 4x100-meter freestyle relay (1936).

McKECHIN, Ann (1961—). Scottish politician and member of Parliament. Born Ann McKechin, April 22, 1961. ❖ Became solicitor in Glasgow (1983); representing Labour, elected to House of Commons at Westminster (2001, 2005), for Glasgow North.

McKECHNIE, Donna (1940—). American theatrical dancer. Born Nov 16, 1940, in Pontiac, Michigan; married briefly (1965); m. Michael Bennett, 1976 (div. 1977). ❖ Trained at Ballet Theater School in New York City; made Broadway debut in chorus of *How to Succeed in Business without Really Trying* (1961); danced opposite Michael Bennett on tv in "Hullaballo" (1965–66); appeared in *The Education of Hyman Kaplan* on Broadway and later in Bennett's *Promises, Promises* (1968), *Company* (1970) and as Cassie in *A Chorus Line* (1975), for which she won a Tony Award; also starred in *Sweet Charity*; began performing solo show *Inside the Music* (1997).

McKECHNIE, Marj (1939—). See Bond, Mary.

McKECHNIE, Sheila (1948–2004). Scottish consumer's advocate. Name variations: Dame Sheila McKechnie. Born Sheila Marshall McKechnie, May 3, 1948, in Falkirk, Scotland; died Jan 2, 2004; attended Edinburgh University; Warwick University, MA in industrial relations; lived with Alan Grant for her last 27 years. ❖ Leading force in the consumer movement, spent early years in the trade union movement (1972–85); served as director of Shelter (1985–94), then became director of the Consumers' Assocation (1995); served as president of the European Union Consumer Group (2001). Awarded an OBE (1995) for services to the housing and the homeless; made a dame (2001) for services to consumers.

McKEE, Georgette (1919–2003). See King, Andrea.

McKEE, Maria (1964—). American rock singer. Born Aug 17, 1964, in Los Angeles, California; half-sister of Brian Maclean (member of 60s band, Love). ❖ Known for powerful soprano voice and authoritative delivery, joined with Ryan Hedgecock to form Lone Justice (1982), performing initially as acoustic duo; added rhythm section and electric guitar and signed with Geffen Records; released 1st album *Lone Justice* to critical acclaim (1985) though limited commercial success; shuffled band's membership, keeping only Hedgecock and releasing *Shelter* (1986), again to limited success; released solo debut album, *Maria McKee* (1989); scored critical breakthrough with 2nd solo album, *You Gotta Sin to Get Saved* (1993), then broke from country-rock tradition, playing guitar as well as singing on *Life Is Sweet* (1996); contributed song "If Love Is A Red Dress (Hang Me in Rags)" to *Pulp Fiction* soundtrack (1996); released Lone Justice retrospective *The World Is Not My Home* (1999) and performed country folk on *Songcatcher* soundtrack (2001); other albums include *High Dive* (2003) *Maria McKee: Live in Hamburg* (2004) and *Peddlin Dreams* (2005).

McKELLAR, Georgina Burne (1832–1898). See Hetley, Georgina Burne.

McKENNA, Lesley (1974—). Scottish snowboarder. Born Aug 9, 1974, in Aviemore, Scotland. ❖ As skier, was British national champion (1994); started snowboarding at age 20 and went on to become known as Britain's top female Halfpipe competitor; placed 1st Overall in British championships (1997, 1998, and 1999); repeatedly ranked in World

Cup top 5; took 2nd in World Cup Halfpipe (2001); was 1st and only British competitor at Salt Lake City Winter Olympics (2002).

McKENNA, Margaret (c. 1837–1925). *See McKenzie, Margaret.*

McKENNA, Marthe (1893–1969). Belgian spy and novelist. Born Marthe Cnockaert in Belgium, 1893; died 1969; m. Jock McKenna (British soldier). ❖ Became a qualified nurse; during WWI, when pressed into service in military hospitals set up by the occupying Germans, became a spy, gathering information from her patients and their superior officers and passing it to Allied forces; eventually caught, was sentenced to death by a German military court, but the end of the war came before the sentence could be carried out. ❖ See also autobiography *I Was a Spy* (1953); and *Women in World History.*

McKENNA, Patricia (1957—). Irish politician. Born Mar 13, 1957, in Castleshane, Co. Monaghan, Ireland; m. Martin Gillen. ❖ Taught art in Dublin; became coordinator of the Green Party (1989), then advisor to the deputy; representing the Green Party, elected member of the European Parliament for Dublin (MEP, 1994–99, 1999–2004).

McKENNA, Rollie (1918–2003). American photographer. Born Rosalie Thorne in Houston, Texas, Nov 15, 1918; died June 15, 2003, in Northampton, MA; dau. of Henry Thorne (army pilot) and Bel (Bacon) Thorne; awarded undergraduate and graduate degrees from Vassar College; m. Henry Dickson McKenna (architect), April 27, 1945 (div. 1949); no children. ❖ Began career photographing architecture (1948), then moved into portraiture, becoming best known for her penetrating images of poets, artists, and musicians, including Robert Graves, Truman Capote, Sir Herbert Read, Elizabeth Bishop, Marianne Moore, Dame Edith Sitwell, Anne Sexton, Elizabeth Hardwick, W.H. Auden, Robert Frost, T.S. Eliot, Ezra Pound and Dylan Thomas, among many others. ❖ See also autobiography *Rollie McKenna: A Life in Photography* (Knopf, 1991); and *Women in World History.*

McKENNA, Rosemary (1941—). Scottish politician and member of Parliament. Born Rosemary Harvey, May 8, 1941; m. James Stephen McKenna, 1963. ❖ Representing Labour, elected to House of Commons for Cumbernauld, Kilsyth and Kirkintilloch East (1997, 2001, 2005). Awarded CBE.

McKENNA, Siobhan (1922–1986). Irish actress, director, and translator. Name variations: Siobhán McKenna; Siobhán Nic Cionnaith. Pronunciation: SHE-vawn. Born Siobhán McKenna, May 24, 1922, in Belfast, Northern Ireland; died Nov 16, 1986, in Dublin; dau. of Eoin McKenna (university professor) and Margaret (O'Reilly) McKenna; University College, Galway, BA (1st class honors), 1943; m. Denis O'Dea, Sept 1946; children: son Donnacha O'Dea (b. Aug 30, 1948). ❖ Celebrated for her interpretations of Shaw's *St. Joan* and Pegeen Mike in *Playboy of the Western World,* joined Abbey Theater and made debut in *Stiana* (1944); had 1st part in English in Tomelty's *The End House*; made film debut in *Hungry Hill* (1946); appeared in 2 plays in London, Olivier's production of Anouilh's *Fading Mansions* and Forsyth's *Heloïse* (1947); made directorial debut staging Shaw's *St. Joan* in Irish (1950); gave 1st performance in English of *St. Joan* (1953), one of her most famous roles; made US film debut in *The Chalk Garden* (1955), followed by *St. Joan* (1956) and *The Rope Dancers* (1957); at the Abbey, appeared in *The Loves of Cass Maguire* (1967) and as Ranevskaya in *Cherry Orchard* (1968), 2 of her finest performances; opened highly successful one-woman show, *Here Are Ladies,* in London (1970), dramatic vignettes featuring famous speeches by women in Irish literature including, most notably, Molly Bloom's soliloquy from *Ulysses;* also appeared in such films as *Doctor Zhivago;* achieved an international reputation as an actress both on stage and screen, but, unlike a previous generation of actors who had been trained at the Abbey Theater, she retained close links with Irish drama and continued to work regularly in Ireland until her death. ❖ See also Micheál Ó hAodha, *Siobhán: A Memoir of an Actress* (Brandon, 1994); and *Women in World History.*

McKENNA, Virginia (1931—). English stage and actress. Born June 7, 1931, in London, England; m. Denholm Elliott (actor), 1954 (div.); m. Bill Travers (actor), 1957 (died 1994). ❖ Made film debut in *The Second Mrs. Tanqueray* (1952), followed by *The Cruel Sea, Simba, A Town Like Alice, The Wreck of the Mary Deare, Ring of Bright Water* and *An Elephant Called Slowly,* among others; portrayed Violette Szabo in *Carve Her Name with Pride* (1958) and Joy Adamson in *Born Free* (1966); helped found the Born Free Foundation (1984) and opened a museum in Hereford dedicated to Szabo.

McKENNEY, Ruth (1911–1972). American author. Born Nov 18, 1911, in Mishawaka, Indiana; died July 25, 1972, in New York, NY; dau. of John Sidney McKenney and Marguerite (Flynn) McKenney (schoolteacher); sister of Eileen McKenney West (who m. novelist Nathanael West); attended Ohio State University; m. Richard Bransten (editor and historian who wrote under pseudonym Bruce Minton), Aug 12, 1937 (died 1955); children: Eileen Bransten; Thomas Bransten; (adopted her sister Eileen's child) Patrick West. ❖ Best known for her 1st book, *My Sister Eileen,* which was made into a Broadway play, 2 films, and a musical, also wrote *Industrial Valley* (1939), *The McKenneys Carry On* (1940), *Browder and Ford: For Peace, Jobs and Socialism* (1940), *Jake Home* (1943), *The Loud Red Patrick* (1947), *Love Story* (1950), *All About Eileen* (1952), *Far, Far From Home* (1954) and *Mirage* (1956), among others. ❖ See also *Women in World History.*

McKENZIE, Ella (1911–1987). American screen actress. Name variations: Lally McKenzie. Born April 9, 1911, in Oregon; died April 23, 1987, in Los Angeles, CA; dau. of Robert McKenzie (1880–1949, actor) and Eva McKenzie (1889–1967, actress); sister of Fay McKenzie (b. 1918, also credited as Fay Shannon) and Ida Mae McKenzie (actress); m. Billy Gilbert, 1937. ❖ With sister Ida Mae, appeared as a child actor in over 100 films with Charlie Chaplin, Edna Purviance, Bronco Billy and Ben Turpin.

McKENZIE, Eva B. (1889–1967). American screen actress. Name variations: Eva McKenzie; Mrs. McKenzie. Born Eva B. Heazlit, Nov 5, 1889, in Toledo, Ohio; died Sept 15, 1967, in Hollywood, CA; m. Robert McKenzie (1880–1949, actor); children: actresses Ida Mae McKenzie (1911–1986), Ella McKenzie (1911–1987), and Fay McKenzie (b. 1918, also credited as Fay Shannon). ❖ Made film debut (1915) and subsequently appeared in over 150 movies, including *With Love and Kisses, The Nightshirt Bandit, Rattling Romeo, Olaf Laughs Last* and *Wells Fargo Days.*

McKENZIE, Grace (b. 1903). English swimmer. Born July 8, 1903, in UK. ❖ Won a silver medal at Antwerp Olympics (1920) and a silver medal at Paris Olympics (1924), both in 4x100-meter freestyle relay.

McKENZIE, Henrietta Catherine (1908–1970). *See Angus, Rita.*

McKENZIE, Ida Mae (1911–1986). American actress. Name variations: Ida McKenzie. Born Jan 15, 1911 in OR; died June 29, 1986, in Los Angeles, CA; dau. of Robert McKenzie (1880–1949, actor) and Eva McKenzie (1889–1967, actress); sister of Ella McKenzie (1911–1987), and Fay McKenzie (b. 1918, also credited as Fay Shannon). ❖ With sister Ella, appeared as a child actor in over 100 films with Charlie Chaplin, Edna Purviance, Bronco Billy and Ben Turpin.

McKENZIE, Jane Robertson (1901–1964). *See McKenzie, Jean.*

McKENZIE, Jean (1901–1964). New Zealand diplomat. Name variations: Jane Robertson McKenzie. Born Jan 19, 1901, at Edendale, Southland, New Zealand; died July 1 or 2, 1964; dau. of Duncan McIntyre McKenzie (blacksmith) and Amy Evelyn (Swale) McKenzie. ❖ Worked as secretary at Invercargill Post Office and Public Works Department during WWI; employed by Main Highways Board in Wellington (1924), before becoming secretary to imperial affairs officer in prime minister's department (1926); part of New Zealand delegation to Canada (1930s); transferred to League of Nations section of trade commissioner's staff in London during WWII; transferred to New Zealand Legation in Washington, DC (1941), and was promoted to second secretary; posted as official secretary to Canberra (1943), and to London as delegate to 1st session of General Assembly of United Nations (1946); appointed chargé d'affaires at New Zealand Legation in Paris (1949), and was promoted to rank of minister—the 1st New Zealand woman to hold position of seniority in Overseas Service. ❖ See also *Dictionary of New Zealand Biography* (Vol. 4).

McKENZIE, Julia (1941—). English actress, singer and director. Born Feb 17, 1941, in Enfield, Middlesex, England; attended Guildhall School of Music and Drama; m. Jerry Harte. ❖ Appeared in numerous London musicals, including *Maggie May* (1965), *Mame* (1969), and *Guys and Dolls* (1982), but is probably best known for work in Sondheim's *Company* (1972), *Side by Side* (1977), *Follies* (1987) and *Into the Woods* (1990); also appeared in straight plays, notably *Schweyk in the Second World War* (1982), *The Norman Conquests* (1974), *Ten Times Table* (1979) and *Woman in Mind* (1986), for which she won the *London Evening Standard* Theater Award for Best Actress; made directorial debut with *Stepping Out* (1984) and followed with such plays as *Steel Magnolias* (1989) and *Putting It Together* (1992); on tv, starred in "Battle of the Sexes" (1976), "Maggie and Her" (1978), "That Beryl

Marston . . . !" (1981), "Fresh Fields" (1984–86) and "French Fields" (1989–91), "Adam Bede" (1992), "The Old Curiosity Shop" (1995) and "Death in Holy Orders" (2003); films include *Shirley Valentine* (1989) *Vol-au-vent* (1996) and *Bright Young Things* (2003). Won Laurence Olivier Award for Best Actress for *Guys and Dolls* (1983) and *Sweeney Todd* (1994); nominated for a Tony Award for *Side by Side by Sondheim* (1977).

McKENZIE, Lally (1911–1987). *See McKenzie, Ella.*

McKENZIE, Margaret (c. 1837–1925). New Zealand homemaker. Name variations: Margaret McKenna. Born Margaret McKenna, between 1836 and 1839, in Co. Tyrone, Northern Ireland; died Feb 13, 1925, in Dunedin, New Zealand; dau. of Hugh McKenna (farmer) and Alice (McConnell) McKenna; m. Daniel McKenzie (printer), 1868 (died 1920); children: 2 daughters, 1 son. ❖ Immigrated to New Zealand (1866); lived an isolated and impoverished existence, which also gave her much satisfaction; husband drove cattle while she remained home to sustain and educate children; after children left, moved with husband to Glenorchy (1903) and then Queenstown (1920). ❖ See also *Dictionary of New Zealand Biography* (Vol. 2).

McKENZIE, Regla (1971—). *See Bell, Regla.*

McKENZIE, Rhona (1901–1931). *See Haszard, Rhona.*

McKIERNAN, Catherina (1969—). Irish marathon runner. Born Nov 30, 1969, in Drumkeeran, Cornafean, Ireland; m. Darmien O'Reilly (RTE radio presenter), 2000. ❖ Won Ulster cross-country 3,000 meters (1986) and Irish Schools Cross-Country (1988); placed 2nd at the Boston marathon (1992); won the Berlin (1977), London (1998), and Amsterdam marathons (1998); won 4 silver medals in successive years in the World Cross Country championship (1992–95); won gold medals for the Europa Cup (1994) and European Cross-Country championships (1994).

McKILLOP, Mary Helen (1842–1909). *See MacKillop, Mary Helen.*

McKILLOP, Patricia (1956—). Zimbabwean field-hockey player. Born July 15, 1956, in Zimbabwe. ❖ At Moscow Olympics, won a gold medal in team competition (1980).

McKILLOP, Peggy (1909–1998). Australian aviator. Name variations: Peggy Kelman. Born Margaret Mary McKillop, April 6, 1909, in Glasgow, Scotland; died Dec 23, 1998, in Maroochydore, Queensland, Australia; dau. of Rose McKillop (an Australian) and William McKillop (MP in House of Commons, died c. 1910); m. Colin Kelman (grazier and aviator), 1936 (died 1964); children: John, Bill, Jane and (twins) Mary and Susan. ❖ After father died, returned with mother to Orange, NSW, as a baby; began flying (1931), gaining pilot's license (1932), then commercial license (1935); barnstormed for Nancy Bird in western NSW (1935); with husband, flew from London to Australia while pregnant (Dec 19–Jan 15, 1936); was Australian governor of the Ninety Nines.

McKIM, Ann (d. 1875). American namesake. Born Ann Bowly in Baltimore, MD; died 1875; m. Isaac McKim (1775–1838), Dec 21, 1808. ❖ Was the 1st woman to have a clipper ship named for her when husband built the *Ann McKim* (1833), considered the 1st true clipper ship.

McKIM, Ann (1912–1979). *See Dvorak, Ann.*

McKIM, Josephine (1910—). American swimmer. Born Jan 4, 1910, in Oil City, PA. ❖ At Amsterdam Olympics, won a bronze medal in the 400-meter freestyle (1928); at Los Angeles Olympics, won a gold medal the 4x100-meter freestyle relay (1932); during swimming career, set 6 world records and won 6 AAU national championships; was swimming double for Maureen O'Sullivan in *Tarzan and His Mate*. Inducted into International Swimming Hall of Fame (1991).

McKINLEY, Ida Saxton (1847–1907). American first lady. Born June 8, 1847, in Canton, Ohio; died May 26, 1907, in Canton; eldest dau. of James Asbury Saxton (banker) and Katherine (DeWalt) Saxton; m. William McKinley (1843–1901, president of US, 1897–1901), Jan 25, 1871; children: Katherine (b. 1871 and died before 4th birthday); Ida (b. 1873 and died 5 months later). ❖ By the time her husband won the presidency (1897), was a confirmed invalid, but made a brave effort to manage as many of the demanding duties of first lady as possible; assisted by a cane, accompanied husband on many of his travels, including his ill-fated trip to the Pan Am Exposition held in Buffalo (Sept 1901) when he was assassinated. ❖ See also *Women in World History.*

McKINLEY, Margaret (1844–1929). *See Gardner, Margaret.*

McKINNEY, Cynthia (1955—). African-American politician. Born Cynthia Ann McKinney, Mar 17, 1955, in Atlanta, GA; dau. of Billy McKinney (member of Georgia state house) and Leola McKinney (nurse); University of Southern California, BA in International Relations, 1978; Fletcher School of Law at Tufts, MA; m. Coy Grandison (div. 1990); children: Coy. ❖ Served in the Georgia State House of Representatives (1989–93); elected as a Democrat to US House of Representatives 103rd Congress (1993), the 1st black woman to serve in US House from Georgia; elected to 4 succeeding Congresses, serving Jan 3, 1993–Jan 3, 2003; a victim of political redistricting (2002), was defeated in 2002 Democratic primaries by Denise Majette; reelected to Congress (2005); was an advocate for voting rights, human rights and strengthening business ties between Africa and US; served on Armed Services Committee and International Relations Committee.

McKINNEY, Louise (1868–1931). Canadian suffragist and legislator. Name variations: often listed as one of the Alberta Five, also known as the Famous Five; Mrs. James McKinney. Born Louise Crummy in Frankville, Ontario, Canada, Sept 22, 1868; died in Claresholm, Alberta, Canada, 1931; m. James McKinney. ❖ Won election to Alberta Legislative Assembly as an NPL candidate (1917), and holds the distinction of being one of the 1st two women elected to a legislature in the British Empire; though defeated in her bid for reelection (1921) and retired from politics, remained an active orator and advocate of temperance and women's rights; with others, became involved in the now-famous "Persons Case" (1927), petitioning the prime minister to decide if the word "persons" included women, a major step towards ensuring female equality in Canadian society. ❖ See also *Women in World History.*

McKINNEY, Nina Mae (c. 1912–1967). African-American actress, singer, and dancer. Born Nina Mae McKinney, June 12, c. 1912 (some sources give dates as early as 1909 or as late as 1914), in Lancaster, SC; died in New York, NY, May 3, 1967; m. James Monroe, 1940 (div. 1941). ❖ Self-taught dancer and singer, won a place in chorus line of Lew Leslie's *Blackbirds*, a long-running all-black Broadway revue; discovered by Hollywood, appeared as Chick in MGM all-black musical *Hallelujah*, which made her a star; put under contract by MGM, turned down her only offers: maids and slave roles; toured Europe as jazz singer (1929–30), appearing at Chez Florence in Paris and Trocadero in London, as well as clubs in Dublin, Berlin, and Budapest; also starred with Paul Robeson in English film *Congo Road* (1931); returning to US, found a few roles in such films as *Safe in Hell* (1931), *Swan Boat* (1931) and *Reckless* (1935); returned to Europe for steadier work (1935–38); once again co-starred with Robeson, in London Films' *Sanders of the River* (1935); back in US, churned out a string of black-produced films, among them *Devil's Daughter*, *Mantan Messes Up*, *Gang Smashers* and *Gun Moll*; had a few small roles in white films, almost always as a maid, such as *Dark Waters* (1947); cast by Elia Kazan as the spiteful Rozelia in *Pinky* (1949), in which white actress Jeanne Crain won the lead role that might have seemed more suitable for the light-complexioned McKinney—that of a light-skinned black nurse who passes herself off as white; was the 1st African-American actress to win wide acceptance among white audiences and the 1st of her contemporaries to legitimize African-American culture, 1st in Europe and, later, in films produced by and for black American audiences. Inducted into Black Filmmakers' Hall of Fame (1978). ❖ See also *Women in World History.*

McKINNEY, Susan (1847–1918). *See Steward, Susan McKinney.*

McKINNEY, Tamara (1962—). American skier. Born Oct 16, 1962, in Lexington, KY; one of seven children of Rigan McKinney (d. 1981, veteran steeplechase rider) and Frances McKinney (d. 1988, ski instructor); sister of Sheila McKinney and Steve McKinney (both skiers). ❖ Took World Cup giant slalom title (1981); finished in top 4 in 7 of 12 races entered (1982); was 1st American to win World Cup overall (1983); won World Cup giant slalom (1983) and slalom (1984); won US national slalom championship (1984); won bronze medals in combined events at World championships (1985, 1987); took 1st place in World Cup races (1986); won a gold medal in combined event, World championship Alpine races (1989); competed in 2 Olympics (1980, 1984); was also an accomplished equestrian. ❖ See also *Women in World History.*

McKINNEY STEWARD, Susan (1847–1918). *See Steward, Susan McKinney.*

McKINNON, Betty (1924—). Australian runner. Name variations: Elizabeth McKinnon. Born 1924 in NSW, Australia. ❖ Won a silver medal at London Olympics (1948) in the 4x100-meter relay.

McKINNON, Emily Hancock (1873–1968). *See Siedeberg, Emily Hancock.*

McKISACK, May (1900–1981). Irish historian and educator. Born May McKisack, Mar 30, 1900, in Belfast, Northern Ireland; died Mar 14, 1981, in Oxford, England; dau. of Audley John McKisack and Elizabeth (McCullough) McKisack. ❖ Eminent historian of medieval English history, was educated at Somerville College, Oxford; taught at Liverpool University (1927–1935), Somerville, and Westfield College, University of London; held visiting professorship at Vassar College (1967–1968); published *Parliamentary Representation of the English Boroughs* (1932), *History as Education, an Inaugural Lecture* (1956), *The Fourteenth Century* (1959), and *Medieval History in the Tudor Age* (1971). ❖ See also F.R.H. Du Boulay and C.M. Barron, *The Reign of Richard II: Essays in Honour of May McKisack* (1971).

McKNIGHT, Kim. American skier. Born in US. ❖ Participated in speed skiing competitions including World Cup events; with snowmobiler Lisa Phillips, placed 2nd at Tesoro Arctic Man Ski & Sno-Go Classic (2000), combination ski and snowmobile race in Summit Lake, Alaska; cross trains with sports including mountain biking and wake boarding.

McKNIGHT, Marian (c. 1937—). Miss America. Name variations: Marian Conway; Marian McKnight Conway; Marian McKnight-Conway. Born Marian Ann McKnight c. 1937 in SC; attended Coker College; m. Gary Conway (actor); children: 2. ❖ Named Miss America (1957), representing South Carolina; as an actress, appeared on tv shows and in commercials; co-produced several motion pictures. Founded Carmondy McKnight, a vineyard and winery (1986). ❖ See also Frank Deford, *There She Is* (Viking, 1971).

McKOLLY, Mary (1754–1832). *See McCauley, Mary Ludwig Hays*

McLACHLAN, Ann (1862–1954). *See McVicar, Annie.*

McLACHLAN, Laurentia (1866–1953). English abbess and scholar. Name variations: Dame Laurentia McLachlan. Born Margaret McLachlan, Jan 11, 1866, in Coatbridge, Lanarkshire, England; died Aug 23, 1953, in Worcester, England; dau. of Henry McLachlan and Mary (McAleese) McLachlan; received education at Stanbrook Abbey under Benedictine clergy; never married; no children. ❖ Entered Benedictine order (1884); became subprioress (c. 1910), then abbess (1932); despite living cloistered in a Roman Catholic abbey in England for nearly 70 years, maintained lively friendships with renowned humanists, intellectuals, and writers, including George Bernard Shaw. ❖ See also D. Felicitas Corrigan, *The Nun, the Infidel, and the Superman* (U. of Chicago Press, 1985); and *Women in World History*.

McLACHLAN, Sarah (1968—). Canadian musician. Born Jan 28, 1968, in Halifax, Nova Scotia, Canada; m. Ashwin Sood (drummer), Feb 7, 1997; children: India Ann Sushil (b. April 6, 2002). ❖ Raised by adoptive parents, took piano, guitar, and voice lessons as child; sang for new-wave band, October Game, at age 17; released debut album, *Touch* (1988), which went gold in Canada, followed by *Solace* (1991); released *Fumbling Towards Ecstacy* (1993), inspired by trip to Cambodia and Thailand, which went triple platinum, and included hits "Possession" and "Good Enough"; released smash hit, *Surfacing* (1997), which produced hit singles, "Adia," "Angel" and "Building a Mystery," and won Grammy Awards for Best Female Pop Vocal Performance and Best Pop Instrumental Performance; started Lilith Fair, annual summer tour featuring women performers, which included Tracy Chapman, Jewel, Missy Elliott, Dixie Chicks, and Erykah Badu (1997–99); released triple platinum *Mirrorball* (1999), winning Grammy for Best Female Pop Vocal Performance (2000).

McLACHLIN, Beverley (1943—). Canadian chief justice. Born Sept 7, 1943, in Pincher Creek, Alberta, Canada; University of Alberta, MA, 1968, LLB, 1968; m. Roderick McLachlin (died); m. Frank E. McArdle, 1992; children: (1st m.) Angus. ❖ Called to the bar of Alberta (1969) and to the bar of British Columbia (1971); practised law (1969–75); professor at University of British Columbia (1974–81); appointed County Court of Vancouver (1981), Supreme Court of British Columbia (1981) and Court of Appeal of British Columbia (1985); appointed chief justice of the Supreme Court of British Columbia (1988); appointed to the Supreme Court of Canada (1989), then chief justice of Canada (Jan

7, 2000), the 1st woman to hold the position; member of the Privy Council of Canada.

McLAGLAN, Eleanor Southey Baker (1879–1969). *See Baker McLaglan, Eleanor Southey.*

McLAREN, Agnes (1837–1913). Scottish doctor. Born 1837 in Edinburgh, Scotland; died 1913. ❖ Began medical studies at 38 and became the 1st woman graduate in medicine at University of Montpellier in France (1878); practiced in Nice; converted to Catholicism at age 60 and set out to provide women doctors to Catholic missions; founded the 1st Catholic medical mission in India, St. Catherine's Hospital in Rawalpindi, now in Pakistan (1910); helped to achieve appointment of several women despite law banning women in religious orders from practicing medicine; work was continued by Anna Dengel and Joanna Lyons who founded the Society of Catholic Medical Missionaries (1925).

McLAREN, Anne Laura (1927—). Welsh biologist and geneticist. Name variations: Dame Anne McLaren; Dr. Anne McLaren; Anne Michie. Born Anne Laura Dorinthea McLaren, April 26, 1927, in Tal-y-cafn, Wales; dau. of Henry Duncan McLaren, 2nd Baron of Aberconway, and Christabel Melville MacNaghten; Lady Margaret Hall, University of Oxford, BS, PhD, 1952; m. Donald Michie (scientist), 1952 (div. 1959); children: Susan, Jonathan and Caroline Michie. ❖ Renowned scientist, best known for discovery and isolation of the embryonal carcinoma cell line, became the 1st female Christopher Welch scholar after conducting mini-research project in J.B.S. Haldane's laboratory at University College, London (UCL), on infestation of Drosophila with mites; with husband, worked with Peter Medawar at UCL, then moved to Royal Veterinary College (1955); moved to Institute of Animal Genetics to study superovulation and superpregnancy (1959) and went on to study immunoconception, DNA hybridization and skeletal characteristics (1960s–70s); served as director of Medical Research Council's Mammalian Development Unit at UCL (1974–92); involved with birth of 1st test-tube baby (1978); moved to Wellcome Trust/CR UK Institute of Cancer and Developmental Biology in Cambridge (1992), becoming honorary fellow (1996); served as member of Warnock Committee on Human Fertilization and Embryology, on Voluntary Licensing Authority for human in vitro fertilization and embryology, and was member of the UK Human Fertilisation and Embryology Authority that regulates IVF and human embryo research in UK; particularly concerned about ethical implications of genetic research, served on Nuffield Foundation's Bioethics Council and European Group on Ethics; invested as fellow of Royal Society (1975), served as its vice-president (1991–1996); was founding member of Academia Europaea and Academy of Medical Sciences. Named Dame of British Empire (DBE, 1993).

McLAREN, Louise Leonard (1885–1968). American labor educator. Name variations: Louise Leonard, Louise McLaren. Born Louise Leonard, Aug 10, 1885, in Wellsboro, PA; died Dec 16, 1968, in East Stroudsburg, PA; dau. of Fred Churchill Leonard (lawyer, US marshal, and bank president) and Estella (Cook) Leonard (schoolteacher); Vassar College, AB, 1907; Columbia University, AM, 1927; m. Myron McLaren (professor at St. John's College, Annapolis), 1930. ❖ Worked for Young Women's Christian Association, as industrial secretary in Wilkes Barre, PA (1914–18), and metropolitan industrial secretary in Baltimore, MD (1918–20), becoming national industrial secretary for the south (1920); formed committee of educators, industrial workers, and trade unionists (1926), to establish Southern Summer School for Women Workers in Industry (1927); served as director and organizer of school, traveling to recruit students and supporters, and educating women about impact of rapid industrialization (1927–44), and overseeing inclusion of men into school (1938); held teaching and research position with American Labor Education Service until retirement (1968).

McLAREN, Mary (1896–1985). *See MacLaren, Mary.*

McLAUCHLAN, Joy (1948—). New Zealand politician. Name variations: Marilyn Joy McLauchlan. Born Joy Quigley, May 9, 1948, in Geraldine, NZ; m. Alistair McLauchlan. ❖ Elected National MP for Western Hutt (1990); supported legislation for a mine-free South Pacific; served as deputy chair of committees (1993–96).

McLAUGHLIN, Audrey (1936—). Canadian politician. Born Nov 7, 1936, in Dutton, Ontario, Canada. ❖ Worked as a caseworker for Children's Aid Society of Metropolitan Toronto; was a teacher in Ghana, West Africa; moved to Yukon (1979); elected to House of Commons (July 20, 1987), the 1st New Democrat to represent Yukon, serving until 1997; became chair of the party caucus (1988), the 1st woman chair of the parliamentary caucus of any federal party in Canada; elected leader of the NDP (Dec 2, 1989), the 1st woman in Canadian history to lead a federal political party; sworn to the Privy Council (1991). ❖ See also memoir, *A Woman's Place: My Life and Politics* (Macfarlane, c. 1992).

McLAUGHLIN, Betty (1921–1975). *See Ryan, Sheila.*

McLAUGHLIN, Florence (1916—). Northern Ireland politician. Born Florence Patricia Alice Aldwell, June 23, 1916; dau. of Canon F. B. Aldwell; m. Major W. McLaughlin, 1937. ❖ Representing the Unionist Party, elected to House of Commons at Westminster (1955) for Belfast West; retired (1964). Made Officer of the British Empire (OBE, 1975).

McLAUGHLIN, M. Louise (1847–1939). American artist. Name variations: Mary Louise McLaughlin. Born 1847 in Cincinnati, Ohio; died 1939; attended McMicken School of Design in Cincinnati. ❖ Pioneering ceramic artist, developed underglazing techniques known as "faience," leading to new style known as "Cincinnati Limoges" or "Cincinnati Faience" ware; founded Cincinnati Art Pottery Club (1879) with Clara Newton and Laura Ann Fry; patented new method of decoration called "American Faience" (1895); became 1st to produce studio porcelain in US and 1st to discover technique for decorating under glaze, achieving considerable recognition in NY and Paris and winning several international awards; produced most successful work, Losanti (named after Cincinnati's original name, Losantiville), around 1901, using high-fired translucent porcelain carved and filled with delicate glazes; abandoned ceramics entirely at age 59 (1906); wrote several books on ceramic art, including *China Painting* (1887), the 1st manual on subject written in US by woman for women, launching china painting movement. ❖ See also Anita J. Ellis, *Ceramic Career of M. Louise McLaughlin* (Ohio U. Press, 2003).

McLAUGHLIN-GILL, Frances (1919—). American photographer and filmmaker. Born in New York, NY, 1919; twin sister of Kathryn Abbe; Pratt Institute, BFA, 1941; studied painting at New School for Social Research and Art Students League (1940–42); m. Leslie Gill (photographer and artist), 1948 (died 1958); children: 1 daughter, Leslie Gill (b. 1957, photographer). ❖ Won *Vogue* magazine's Prix de Paris contest (1941); served as a member of the photography staff of Condè Nast magazines (1944–54), photographing still lifes, portraits, celebrities, and fashion and travel shots for *Vogue, Glamour,* and *House and Garden,* among others; worked as independent film producer and director (1964–73), shooting tv commercials for major soap and cosmetics manufacturers; also produced short films. Received gold medal at International Film and TV Festival for film *Cover Girl: New Face in Focus* (1969).

McLEAN, Alice (1886–1968). American founder. Name variations: Alice T. McLean; Alice Throckmorton McLean; Alice Tinker. Born Mar 8, 1886, in New York, NY; died in Baltimore, Maryland, Oct 25, 1968; dau. of James T. McLean and Sara (Throckmorton) McLean; m. Edward Larocque Tinker (lawyer and writer), c. 1903 (div.); children: James McLean; Edward T. McLean. ❖ Founded American Women's Volunteer Services (1940) with membership reaching 325,000 nationwide by the end of the war in 1945; also founded National Clothing Conservation Program to address wartime fabric shortages (1944). ❖ See also *Women in World History.*

McLEAN, Annie Isabel (1868–1939). *See Fraser, Annie Isabel.*

McLEAN, Barbara (1903–1996). American film editor. Born Barbara Pollut, Nov 16, 1903, in Palisades Park, NJ; died Mar 28, 1996, in Newport Beach, CA; m. Gordon McLean; m. Robert Webb, 1951 (died 1990). ❖ Pioneer film editor for 20th Century-Fox, earned 1st film credit on *The Affairs of Cellini* (1934), followed by *The Mighty Barnum, Clive of India, Lloyd's of London, Seventh Heaven, In Old Chicago, Alexander's Ragtime Band, Stanley and Livingstone, The Rains Came, Chad Hanna, Tobacco Road, The Song of Bernadette, A Bell for Adano, The Dolly Sisters, Twelve O'Clock High, All About Eve, Niagara, The Snows of Kilimanjaro* and *The Robe,* among others; became head of Fox's editing division (1949); retired (1969). Nominated for 7 Academy Awards, won for work on *Wilson* (1944).

McLEAN, Evalyn Walsh (1886–1947). American socialite. Born Aug 1, 1886, in Denver, Colorado; died April 26, 1947, in Washington, DC; dau. of Thomas F. Walsh (a carpenter and gold miner) and Carrie Bell (Reed) Walsh; m. Edward Beale McLean, July 22, 1908 (sep. 1928); children: Vinson McLean (died young); John R. McLean; Edward Beale McLean; Evalyn Washington McLean Reynolds (died 1946). ❖ A

mining heiress and renowned Washington hostess best remembered for her extravagant soirées and profligate spending habits; also owned the storied Hope diamond, a 44.52-carat jewel rumored to bring bad luck to its owners. ❖ See also autobiography *Father Struck It Rich* (1936); and *Women in World History.*

McLEAN, Kathryn (1909–1966). American author and short-story writer. Name variations: Kathryn Forbes. Born in San Francisco, California, Mar 10, 1909; died May 15, 1966; dau. of Leon Ellis and Della (Jesser) Anderson; m. Robert McLean (contractor), 1926 (div., May 1946); children: Robert Jr. and Richard. ❖ Under pseudonym Kathryn Forbes, wrote her semi-autobiographical *Mama's Bank Account,* an episodic work centering around her Norwegian-American family stretching their earnings to pay expenses in turn-of-the-century San Francisco, which was produced on Broadway as *I Remember Mama* (1944) and evolved into a highly popular tv series (1949–57). ❖ See also *Women in World History.*

McLEAN, Mary Hancock (1861–1930). American physician. Born Mary Hancock McLean, Feb 28, 1861, in Washington, MO; died May 17, 1930; dau. of Mary C. (Stafford) McLean and Dr. Elijah McLean (physician); graduated from University of Michigan Medical School (1883) in the same class as Amelia Yeomans, the Canadian physician. ❖ One of the 1st practicing women physicians in St. Louis, Missouri, became assistant physician at St. Louis Female Hospital (1884), the 1st woman with an official position in a St. Louis hospital, where she investigated women's diseases; was the 1st woman admitted to the St. Louis Medical Society (1885); opened a private practice after overcoming many challenges; established an all-women-staffed free clinic for working-class women patients (1908); became an American College of Surgeons fellow and an American Medical Society member; practiced surgery until 1928.

McLEAN, Mary Jane (1866–1949). New Zealand school principal. Born April 4, 1866, at Timaru, New Zealand; died Feb 9, 1949, in Wellington; dau. of Duncan McLean (physician and surgeon), and Ann (le Ber) McLean; Montfleuri Girls' School, BA, 1888, MA, 1890. ❖ Appointed 1st assistant teacher of Timaru High School (1890); served as principal of Timaru Girls' High School (1898–1926); was a significant figure in establishment of Wellington East Girls' College (1925). Named Commander of the British Empire (1928). ❖ See also *Dictionary of New Zealand Biography* (Vol. 3).

McLEAN, Sarah (1856–1935). *See Greene, Sarah.*

McLELLAN, Joyce (1913–1997). *See Marriott, Anne.*

McLENNAN, Margo (1938–2004). English actress. Name variations: Margo McMenemy; Margo Mayne. Born Eileen Marguerite McMenemy, Feb 8, 1938, in Peckham, south London, England; died of cancer, July 28, 2004, in England; m. Tony Doonan (actor), 1962 (div. 1969); m. Rod McLennan (Australian actor), 1974; children: (1st m.) Nicola. ❖ Under name Margo McMenemy, began career skating in ice productions of 1950s; under Margo Mayne (1960s), turned to acting, appearing in West End hit, *Goodnight Mrs Puffin* (1961), among others; was also frequently seen on tv; married and moved to Australia; as Margo McLennan, was one of the original stars of the long-running Australian tv soap opera "Prisoner: Cell Block H"; was also seen on "All the Rivers Run"; films include *The Getting of Wisdom* (1977) and *The More Things Change* (1986); as Margo Lady McLennan, became empowered by the Commonwealth of Australia as an official marriage celebrant (2001); as such, became the 1st woman in the world to work as a celebrant of gay marriages.

McLENNAN, Mary (c. 1913—). *See Hirsch, Mary.*

McLEOD, Alice (b. 1937). *See Coltrane, Alice.*

McLEOD, Catherine (1921–1997). American actress. Born Catherine Frances McLeod, July 2, 1921, in Santa Monica, CA; died May 11, 1997, in Encino, CA; m. William Gerd (div. 1949); m. Don Keefer (actor), 1950. ❖ Played the lead in several Republic movies; films include *I've Always Loved You, Courage of Lassie, The Fabulous Texan* and *My Wife's Best Friend*; appeared as Claire Larkin on "Days of Our Lives" (1968–69).

McLEOD, Fiona (1957—). Scottish politician. Born 1957 in Glasgow, Scotland. ❖ As an SNP candidate, elected to the Scottish Parliament for West of Scotland (1999); serves as SNP deputy spokesperson on the Environment.

McLEOD, Mary Adelia (1938—). American bishop. Name variations: Mary Adelia McLeod. Born Sept 27, 1938, in Birmingham, Alabama; Smith College, LHD, 1994; University of Charleston, DD, 1996; m. Rev. Henry Marvin McLeod III, Nov 25, 1970. ❖ Ordained deacon (June 1980), then priest (Dec 1980); became 1st woman Episcopal Diocesan bishop in US (1993), serving as Bishop of Vermont (1993–2001); also the 2nd woman bishop elected in the world; was vocal and supportive of the gay and lesbian community in Vermont and backed same sex unions.

McLEOD, Mrs. (d. 1727). Scottish accused criminal. Name variations: also seen as M'Leoid. Hanged Mar 8, 1727, in Edinburgh, Scotland. ❖ Fashionable woman in mid-30s, who was tried for forgery in Scotland, where such an offense was then a capital crime (1726); maintained innocence to the end, but was found guilty and sentenced to death.

McLERIE, Allyn Ann (1926—). Canadian actress, singer and dancer. Born Dec 1, 1926, in Grand-Mère, Quebec, Canada; m. Adolph Green (lyricist), 1945 (div. 1953); m. George Gaynes (actor), 1953. ❖ Performed with San Carlo Opera Company (1942); danced in Agnes de Mille's *One Touch of Venus* (1943), Jerome Robbins' *On the Town* and appeared as Amy in Ray Bolger's *Where's Charley?* (1943); danced frequently with Ballet Theater (1950s) and on Broadway in works by Robbins, including *Miss Liberty* (1949) and *West Side Story* (1957); films include *Where's Charley?* (1951), *They Shoot Horses, Don't They* (1969), *Cinderella Liberty* (1973) and *All the President's Men* (1976); appeared frequently on tv.

McLISH, Rachel (1958—). Hispanic-American bodybuilder. Name variations: Rachael McLish. Born Rachel Livia Elizondo, June 21, 1958, in Harlington, Texas; dau. of Rafael and Rachel Elizondo; m. John McLish, 1989 (div. 1989); m. Ron Samuels (film producer), 1990. ❖ Helped to define the sport of bodybuilding for women, proposing power and strength as ultimate expressions of beauty; competed as bodybuilder for 4 years, winning inaugural US Bodybuilding championships (1980), 1st ever Ms. Olympia (1980, 1982), and Pro World (1982); parlayed fame into career in film and tv, appearing in *Getting Physical* (1984), *Aces: Iron Eagle III* (1992), and *Raven Hawk* (1996); also made successful exercise videos such as *Pumping Iron II: The Women* (1985) and *Rachel McLish: In Shape* (1996); wrote several books on bodybuilding and fitness including *Perfect Parts* (1987); left bodybuilding competition when the use of steroids became a factor, prompting her crusade against steriod use and drug abuse.

MC LYTE (1971—). African-American musician and singer. Name variations: Lana Moorer. Born Lana Michele Moorer, Oct 11, 1971, in Queens, NY. ❖ Known for street style, began rapping at 12; at 16, released debut single, "I Cram to Understand U (Sam)," through father's First Priority records; released *Lyte as a Rock* (1988) and *Eyes on This* (1989); became 1st rapper to perform in Carnegie Hall, appearing for AIDS benefit (1990); introduced elements of soul and R&B to new album, *Act Like You Know* (1991), which included rap hits "Poor Georgie" and "Eyes Are the Soul"; released *Ain't No Other* (1993), which returned to hard rap; with female rappers Lin Que and Kink Easy, began management company, Duke Da Moon (early 1990s); released gold single, "Keep On, Keepin' On"; released *Bad as I Wanna B* (1996), which included single "Cold Rock a Party"; appeared in film, *An Alan Smithee Film—Burn Hollywood Burn* (1997); released moderately successful album, *Seven & Seven* (1998); was 1st female hip hop artist to receive a gold record.

McMAHON, Brigitte (1967—). Swiss triathlete. Name variations: Brigitte McMahon-Huber. Born Brigitte Huber, Mar 25, 1967, in Switzerland; m. Michael McMahon. ❖ Won a gold medal at Sydney Olympics (2000).

McMAHON, Louise (1911–1997). *See Campbell, Louise.*

McMAHON, Sonia (1932—). Australian prime-ministerial wife. Born Sonia Rachel Hopkins, Aug 1, 1932; m. William McMahon (prime minister of Australia, 1971–72), Dec 11, 1965; children: Melinda (b. 1966), Julian (b. 1968), and Deborah (b. 1971). ❖ Was an occupational therapist; had youngest child, while husband was in office; known for social and charity work.

McMAIN, Eleanor Laura (1866–1934). American settlement worker and social worker. Born Mar 2, 1866, near Baton Rouge, LA; died May 12, 1934, in New Orleans; dau. of Jacob West McMain (dean and secretary of Louisiana State University) and Jane Josephine Walsh. ❖ Became

head resident of Kingsley House Settlement in New Orleans (1901); opened city's 1st vacation school (1902); oversaw expansion of Kingsley House to include children's summer retreat, athletics programs, drama programs, and courses for the blind; founded and served as 1st president of city's Woman's League, representing several local women's groups (from 1905); worked toward passage of compulsory education law (1910) and women and child labor laws (1906, 1908); traveled to spread concept of settlement house throughout US and Europe.

McMANN, Sara (1980—). American wrestler. Born Sept 24, 1980, in Takoma Park, MD. ❖ Won a silver medal for 63kg freestyle at Athens Olympics (2004).

McMANUS, Jane (1807–1878). *See Cazneau, Jane McManus.*

McMANUS, Liz (1947—). Irish politician and writer. Born Elizabeth O'Driscoll, Mar 1947, in Montreal, Canada; dau. of Tim O'Driscoll (head of Bord Fáilte); m. John McManus. ❖ Representing Democratic Left, elected to the 27th Dáil (1992–97) for Wicklow; returned to 28th Dáil (1997–2002), then, representing Labour, elected to 29th Dáil (2002); was minister with responsibility for Housing (194–97); also writes novels. Her novel *Acts of Subversion* (1990) was nominated for the Aer Lingus/*Irish Times* Award for new writing.

McMASTER, Elizabeth Jennet (1847–1903). Canadian nurse. Name variations: Elizabeth Jennet Wyllie. Born Elizabeth Jennet Wyllie, Dec 27, 1847, in Toronto, Ontario, Canada; died Mar 3, 1903, in Chicago, IL; dau. of Mary Ann (Reid) Wyllie and George Wyllie; graduate of Illinois Training School for Nurses in Chicago, 1891; m. Samuel Fenton McMaster, 1865; children: 4. ❖ Established the Toronto Hospital for Sick Children (1875), Canada's 1st children's hospital, and the Toronto Hospital for Sick Children's Training School for Nurses (1886); after newspaper owner John Ross Robertson donated funds to build a larger home for the Toronto Hospital for Sick Children (1883), became the 1st superintendent of the new building.

McMEIN, Neysa (1888–1949). American commercial illustrator and portraitist. Name variations: Marjory Edna McMein. Born Margary Edna McMein, Jan 24, 1888, in Quincy, Illinois; died May 12, 1949, in New York, NY; dau. of Harry Moran McMein (newspaper editor) and Isabelle Lee (Parker) McMein; attended School of the Art Institute of Chicago and Art Students League; m. John Gordon Baragwanath (engineer and writer), May 18, 1923; children: Joan Gordon Baragwanath. ❖ Perhaps the 1st female artist ever to be invited to the White House to execute a portrait of a sitting president, sold 1st drawing (1914) and 1st magazine cover (1915), to the *Saturday Evening Post*; did magazine covers for the best-known publications of the era, including *Collier's* and *Women's Home Companion*; pastel illustrations were on the covers of every issue of *McCall's* (1923–37); painted portraits of 2 sitting presidents, Warren G. Harding (c. 1922) and Herbert Hoover (c. 1931), and of many other well-known figures of the day, including Anne Morrow Lindbergh, Bea Lillie, Charlie Chaplin, Dorothy Parker, Edna St. Vincent Millay, and Janet Flanner. ❖ See also Brian Gallagher, *Anything Goes: The Jazz Age Adventures of Neysa McMein and Her Extravagant Circle of Friends* (Times Books, 1987); and *Women in World History*.

McMENEMY, Margo (1938–2004). *See McLennan, Margo.*

McMILLAN, Clara Gooding (1894–1976). American politician. Name variations: Clara Eloise McMillan. Born Clara Eloise Gooding on Aug 17, 1894, in Brunson, South Carolina; died Nov 8, 1976, in Barnwell, South Carolina; dau. of William James Gooding and Mary Emily (Webb) Gooding; attended Flora MacDonald College (Red Springs, NC), and Confederate Home College (Charleston, SC); m. Thomas Sanders McMillan (1888–1939, congressional representative), Dec 16, 1916 (died Sept 29, 1939); children: Thomas Sanders; James Carroll; William Gooding; Edward Webb; Robert Hampton. ❖ US representative in the 76th Congress (Nov 7, 1939–Jan 3, 1941), was chosen by House Democrats to finish late husband's Congressional term (1939); chose not to run for a 2nd term; was affiliated with National Youth Administration (1941); hired at Department of State (1946); retired from public service (1957). ❖ See also *Women in World History*.

McMILLAN, Ethel (1904–1987). New Zealand politician. Born Ethel Black, May 12, 1904, in Gisborne, NZ; died Aug 13, 1987; m. David Gervan McMillan (physician and MP, 1935–43), 1929 (died 1951); children: 2 sons. ❖ Represented Labour Party for North Dunedin (1953–63) and Dunedin North (1963–75); was the 1st woman in New Zealand to be a trustee of a savings bank (1960).

McMILLAN, Kathy (1957—). African-American track-and-field athlete. Born Kathy Laverne McMillan, Nov 7, 1957, in Raeford, NC; graduate of Tennessee State University. ❖ At Montreal Olympics, won a silver medal in the long jump (1976); won gold medals at AAU meet (1976) and Pan American Games (1979), both for long jump.

McMILLAN, Margaret (1860–1931). American-born English reformer. Born in New York, July 1860; died Mar 27, 1931; brought up in Inverness, Scotland; sister of Rachel McMillan (1859–1917). ❖ A pioneer of nursery schools, campaigned for medical inspection of schoolchildren and school clinics in the north of England; with sister, opened their 1st school clinic (1908), and their 1st open-air nursery in Deptford (1914). Named CBE (1917) and Companion of Honor (CH, 1930).

McMILLAN, Rachel (1859–1917). English educationalist. Born Mar 25, 1859, in New York; died Mar 25, 1917, in London, England; dau. of James McMillan and Jean McMillan (Scottish immigrants); sister of Margaret McMillan (1860–1931); attended Inverness High School. ❖ Educationalist and Christian Socialist who pioneered child health measures and pre-school education, was born in NY to parents who had emigrated from Inverness, Scotland (1840); following death of father and sister Elizabeth to scarlet fever (1865), returned to Scotland with mother and sister Margaret; joined sister in London (1888) and became junior superintendent in home for young girls; began contributing to *Christian Socialist* magazine; aided workers during 1889 London Dock Strike; toured industrial regions with sister, speaking at meetings and visiting homes of poor; joined Fabian Society, Labor Church, Social Democratic Federation and newly formed Independent Labor Party; joined Dr. James Kerr, Bradford's medical officer, in carrying out 1st medical inspection of elementary school children in Britain, publishing report on findings and campaigning for such radical innovations as installation of bathrooms and improved ventilation as well as free school meals; won election as Independent Labor Party candidate for Bradford School Board (1894); returned to London (1902) and joined Labor Party, working closely with leaders James Keir Hardie, George Lansbury and others; won passage of Provision of School Meals Act (1906); with sister, opened England's 1st school clinic in Bow (1908), followed by Deptford (1910), providing dental care and surgical aid; supported universal suffrage; started Rachel McMillan Open Air Nursery School and Training Center in Peckham (1914), which would become blueprint for future nursery schools; wrote *Child Labour and the Half Time System* (1896), *Early Childhood* (1900), *Education Through the Imagination* (1904) and *The Economic Aspects of Child Labour and Education* (1905).

McMILLAN, Terry (1951—). African-American writer and educator. Born Oct 18, 1951, in Port Huron, Michigan; dau. of Edward McMillan (sanitation worker) and Madeline Washington Tilman (factory worker); University of California at Berkeley, BA, 1979; Columbia University, MA; m. Jonathan Plummer; children: Solomon Welch. ❖ Bestselling novelist, published 1st story, "The End," while at Berkeley; published 1st book, *Mama* (1987), and took on task of marketing novel, contacting black organizations and book stores, earning high sales and critical acclaim; became associate professor at University of Arizona (1988); published 2nd novel *Disappearing Acts* (1990) to even greater success; served as judge for National Book Award for fiction (1990) and in same year edited *Breaking Ice* to introduce other black authors to readers; published bestselling novel *Waiting to Exhale* (1992), which was filmed, followed by *A Day Late and a Dollar Short*, which featured a character modeled after her mother (2001); had additional popular success with semi-autobiographical novel *How Stella Got Her Groove Back* (1996), which was also filmed (1998). ❖ See also Diane Patrick, *Terry McMillan: The Unauthorized Biography* (1999).

McMORDIE, Julia (1860–1942). Northern Ireland politician. Born Julia Gray, Mar 30, 1860, in Hartlepool, England; died April 12, 1942; dau. of Sir William and Dorothy Gray; m. R.J. McMordie (MP for East Belfast and Lord Mayor of Belfast), 1885 (died 1914). ❖ Was the 1st woman member of Belfast City Council (1917) and the 1st woman high sheriff of Belfast (1929); served as vice-president of Ulster Women's Unionist Council (1919–40); representing the Unionist Party for Belfast South, elected to the Northern Ireland House of Commons (1921–25); campaigned for more women police officers.

McMURRAY, Bette Clair (1924–1980). See Graham, Bette Nesmith.

McMURRY, Lillian Shedd (1921–1999). American blues producer. Born Lillian Shedd in Purvis, Mississippi, Dec 30, 1921; died of heart attack in Jackson, Mississippi, Mar 18, 1999; dau. of itinerant Southern musicians; studied law in Jackson, Mississippi; m. Willard McMurry (store manager), 1945 (died 1996); children: Vitrice McMurry. ❖ Founded Trumpet Records (c. 1950), producing the 1st recordings of 2 major Delta blues musicians, Sonny Boy Williamson and Elmore James, as well as recordings by such leading figures as Willie Love, Big Joe Williams, and Jerry McCain; inducted into Blues Hall of Fame (1998). ❖ See also *Women in World History*.

McNAB, Agnes Muir (1885–1964). See Bettjeman, Agnes Muir.

McNAB, Nancy Muir (1885–1964). See Bettjeman, Agnes Muir.

McNABB, Dinah. Northern Ireland politician. Born in Lurgan, Northern Ireland; m. Thomas G. McNabb. ❖ Representing Unionist Party for Armagh North, sat in the Northern Ireland House of Commons (1945–69); did not seek reelection due to ill health.

McNAIR, Denise (d. 1963). One of the Birmingham Four. Murdered Sept 15, 1963, age 11. ❖ With Cynthia Wesley (14), Addie Mae Collins (14), and Carol Robertson (14), was in the Sixteenth Street Baptist church basement in Birmingham, Alabama, preparing to attend Sunday school and the monthly Youth Day service, when a bomb went off, killing her and the others (Sept 15, 1963). ❖ See also Spike Lee documentary *4 Little Girls* (1998).

McNAIR, Winifred (1877–1954). English tennis player. Name variations: Winifred Slocock McNair. Born Aug 9, 1877, in UK; died Mar 28, 1954. ❖ Was runner-up at Wimbledon for singles and doubles (1913); at Antwerp Olympics, won a gold medal in doubles (1920).

McNALL, Belva (1830–1917). See Lockwood, Belva Bennett.

McNALLY, Eryl Margaret (1942—). Welsh politician. Born April 11, 1942, in Bangor, Gwynedd, Wales. ❖ Served as Constituency Labour Party secretary (1972–75) and County Labour Party secretary (1977–82); as a European Socialist, elected to 4th and 5th European Parliament (1994–99, 1999–2004) from UK.

McNALLY, Karen Cook (1940—). American geologist. Born 1940; grew up in Clovis, CA; attended Fresno State College; University of California, Berkeley, BS, 1971, MA, 1973, PhD in geophysics, 1976; m. (div. 1966); children: 2. ❖ Known for her contributions to seismic gap theory, a method used to predict earthquakes, was postdoctoral researcher, then associate professor at California Institute of Technology in Pasadena until 1986; worked with research teams that used seismic gap theory to predict Mexico's 7.8 quake (Nov 29, 1977) and Mexico City's 8.1 quake (Sept 19, 1985); established the country's national seismological network (1984); appointed professor of geophysics (1998) and director of Institute of Tectonics and Charles F. Richter Seismology Laboratory at University of California, Santa Cruz.

McNAMARA, Ann (c. 1857–1934). See O'Donnell, Ann.

McNAMARA, Julianne (1966—). American gymnast and actress. Name variations: Julianne McNamara Zeile. Born Oct 6, 1966 (also seen as Nov 10, 1965), in Flushing, NY; dau. of Australians; attended University of California at Los Angeles; m. Todd Zeile (major-league baseball player), 1989; children: 4. ❖ At World championships, placed 3rd in uneven bars and 7th in all-around, the highest an American woman gymnast had ever placed (1981); won American Cup, Australia Cup, Pacific Cup, and US Classic (1982); won US nationals (1980), then finished 2nd for the next 3 years; won a bronze in the vault at World Cup (1982); won silver medals in floor exercise and team all-around and shared a gold medal with Ma Yanhong for uneven bars at Los Angeles Olympics (1984); provided sports commentary and, as an actress, appeared in several movies and had a recurring role on tv's "Charles in Charge."

McNAMARA, Maggie (1928–1978). American actress. Born June 18, 1928, in New York, NY; died of an overdose of pills in New York, NY, Feb 18, 1978; m. director David Swift (div.). ❖ A fashion model while still in her teens, made Broadway debut (1951); later replaced Barbara Bel Geddes in *The Moon is Blue*, a comedy considered racy for its time; reprised the role on film (1953) and was nominated for Academy Award for Best Actress; starred in 2 more films, *Three Coins in the Fountain* (1954) and *Prince of Players* (1955), and also appeared in *The Cardinal* (1963), but lasting fame eluded her; returned to Broadway in *Step on a Crack* (1962); abandoned acting career and began working as a typist, but suffered from mental illness.

McNAUGHT, Lesley (1966—). Swiss equestrian. Name variations: Lesley McNaught-Mändli or Maendli. Born Feb 10, 1966, in Great

Britain. ❖ Won a team silver for jumping at Sydney Olympics (2000), on Dulf.

McNAUGHT, Rose (1893–1978). American nurse-midwife. Born Rose Madeline McNaught, Mar 6, 1893, in Holyoke, MA; died Aug 1978; dau. of Mary (Hurley) McNaught and William McNaught. ❖ The 1st practicing nurse-midwife in New York City, contributed to the development of America's 1st nurse-midwifery school; graduated from Army School of Nursing (1920); began assisting home births as a staff nurse at Lillian Wald's Henry Street Visiting Nurse Service in NYC (1922); became a nurse for Mary Breckinridge's Frontier Nursing Service in Leslie County, KT (1926); earned a certificate from York Road Lying-in-Hospital's midwifery program in London (1928); established the Lobenstine Midwifery Clinic and School in NYC (1932), the 1st US nurse-midwifery school, where she introduced nurse-midwifery to NY physicians, served as the state's 1st practicing nurse-midwife and was named the school and clinic's 1st supervisor; worked as a Maternity Center Association (MCA) consultant until 1962.

McNAUGHTON, Marion Turpie (d. 1967). *Turpie, Marion.*

McNEIL, Claudia (1917–1993). African-American actress. Born in Baltimore, Maryland, Aug 13, 1917; died in Englewood, New Jersey, Nov 25, 1993. ❖ A nightclub singer before making off-Broadway debut in Langston Hughes' *Simply Heavenly* (1957), is best known for her role as Lena Younger in *A Raisin in the Sun* on stage (1959) and screen (1961); portrayed Sister Margaret in a London production of *The Amen Corner* (1965), for which she was voted Best Actress of the Year; appeared in a variety of film and tv roles before returning to cabaret (1978).

McNEIL, Florence (1937—). Canadian poet, editor and children's writer. Born 1937 in North Burnaby, British Columbia, Canada; dau. of Gaelic-speaking immigrants from the Scottish Hebrides; University of British Columbia, BA and MA; married. ❖ Poetry collections include *A Silent Green Sky* (1967), *The Rim of the Park* (1972), *Ghost Towns* (1975), *A Balancing Act* (1979), *Barkerville* (1984) and *Swimming Out of History* (1991); also wrote children's books *Miss P. and Me* (1982) and *All Kinds of Magic* (1984).

McNEIL, Loretta T. (1907–1988). American runner. Born Jan 10, 1907; died Feb 24, 1988 in San Mateo, CA. ❖ At Amsterdam Olympics, won a silver medal in the 4x100-meter relay (1928).

McNEILL, Florence Marian (1885–1973). Scottish folklorist. Name variations: F. Marian McNeill. Born 1885 in St. Mary's Holm, Orkney, Scotland; died 1973 in Scotland; attended Glasgow University. ❖ Specialist in folklore and culinary history of Scotland, was born and brought up in Orkney, where her father, a university graduate in divinity and medicine, kept up many of the old customs; best known for *The Scots Kitchen* (1929), which examines Scottish culinary history, links it to France and includes many traditional recipes; also published only novel, *The Road Home* (1932), loosely based on her years in Glasgow and London; returned to folklore with *The Scots Cellar* (1956) and her comprehensive 4-vol. study, *The Silver Bough* (1957–68); also wrote *Hallowe'en* (1970).

McNEILL, Janet (1907–1994). Irish novelist, playwright and children's writer. Name variations: Janet Alexander. Born Janet McNeill, Sept 14, 1907 in Dublin, Ireland; dau. of William (minister) and Jeannie P. (Hogg) McNeill; University of St. Andrews, MA, 1929; m. Robert P. Alexander (civil engineer), 1933 (died); children: 4. ❖ Works include *A Child in the House* (1955), *The Other Side of the Wall* (1957), *As Strangers Here* (1960), *The Early Harvest* (1962), and *The Maiden Dinosaur* (1964). Works tell about life in Protestant Belfast from woman's perspective.

McNEILL, Pauline (c. 1967—). Scottish politician. Born c. 1967. ❖ Began career as a graphic designer; as a Labour candidate, elected to the Scottish Parliament for Glasgow Kelvin (1999).

McNULTY, Dorothy (b. 1908). *See Singleton, Penny.*

McNULTY, Faith (1918–2005). American novelist and nonfiction writer. Born Faith Trumbull Corrigan, Nov 28, 1918, in New York, NY; died April 10, 2005, in Wakefield, RI; dau. of Joseph Eugene Corrigan (judge); attended Barnard College, 1937–38; m. Charles M. Fair (writer), 1938 (div.); m. John McNulty (*New Yorker* writer), 1945 (died 1956); m. Richard H. Martin (theatrical prop designer), 1957 (died 1984); children: John McNulty. ❖ A *New Yorker* staff writer (1943–91), generally wrote about rural animals and country life, for adults and children, until she wrote about Francine Hughes in *The Burning Bed: The*

True Story of an Abused Wife (1980), which was filmed with Farrah Fawcett; also wrote *The Whooping Crane: The Bird That Defies Extinction* (1966), *How to Dig a Hole to the Other Side of the World* (1979) and *When I Lived with Bats* (1998).

McNULTY, Mrs. William. *See Tait, Agnes.*

McPARTLAND, Marian (1920—). English-born jazz pianist. Name variations: Marian Page. Born Margaret Marian Turner in Slough near Windsor, England, Mar 20, 1920; dau. of Frank Turner (civil engineer) and Janet (Payne) Turner (pianist); attended Guildhall School of Music, London; m. Jimmy McPartland, Feb 4, 1945 (div. then remarried 2 weeks before he died in 1991). ❖ Studied classical music before moving into jazz; toured English vaudeville theaters as pianist with Billy Mayerl (1941); toured with Britain's ENSA in Europe (1943) and with USO camp shows in France (1944); came to US (1946); formed group with husband, played with Billie Holiday; formed Marian McPartland Trio (1951); toured US nightclubs; played Hickory House in New York City (1952–60); performed with Benny Goodman (1963); founded Halcyon Records (1969); toured South America with Earl Hines and Teddy Wilson (1974); made numerous recordings; won Peabody Award for hosting her National Public Radio series "Piano Jazz" (1984); composed "Twilight World" and "Ambience"; albums include: *Ambience, Fine Romance, Now's the Time, Solo Concert at Haverford, Personal Choice,* and *In My Life.* Given lifetime achievement award from *Down Beat* (1994). ❖ See also autobiography *All in Good Time* (Oxford U. Press, 1987); and *Women in World History.*

McPAUL, Louise (1969—). Australian javelin thrower. Name variations: Louise McPaul-Currey. Born Jan 24, 1969, in Port Kembla, Australia. ❖ Placed 6th at World championships (1991); won Commonwealth Games (1994, 1998); won a silver medal at Atlanta Olympics (1996).

McPEAK, Holly (1969—). American volleyball player. Born May 15, 1969, in Hollywood, CA; attended University of California, Berkeley. ❖ Was the 1st women's professional beach volleyball player to earn over $1 million in prize money; placed 2nd overall in World Tour ranking (2004); with Elaine Youngs, won a bronze medal for beach volleyball at Athens Olympics (2004). Named AVP's Most Valuable Player (1993); named WPVA's Best Defensive Player (1995–97) and Rookie of the Year (1991).

McPHERSON, Aimee Semple (1890–1944). Canadian evangelical preacher. Born Aimee Kennedy in Ingersoll, Ontario, Canada, Oct 9, 1890; died in Oakland, CA, Sept 27, 1944; dau. of James Morgan Kennedy (Ontario farmer) and Minnie (Pearce) Kennedy (Salvation Army fund raiser); m. Robert Semple, 1908 (died in Hong Kong, 1910); m. Harold Stewart McPherson, 1912 (div. 1918); m. David Hutton, 1930 (div. 1935, on grounds of mental cruelty); children: (1st m.) Roberta Semple; (2nd m.) Rolf. ❖ The 1st woman evangelist to enjoy international renown, migrated to California (1918) and quickly made a name for herself in Los Angeles and along West Coast, preaching the Foursquare Gospel, a cheery credo of good health, family love, and wholesome simplicity; opened Angelus Temple, Los Angeles, then the largest religious building in US history, seating 5,300 worshippers (Jan 1, 1923); along with the Temple, created a music conservatory, a Bible college, and radio station KFSG, only the 3rd radio station to be licensed in Los Angeles; at height of her fame, claimed to have been kidnapped and tortured in the Mexican desert, but skeptical investigators maintained that she had been hiding out with a married lover (1926); became an important precursor of one side of the postwar evangelical revival, in addition to being a pioneer for women preachers and evangelical broadcasters. ❖ See also autobiography *The Story of My Life* (Word, 1973); Daniel Mark Epstein, *Sister Aimee* (Harcourt, 1993); and *Women in World History.*

McPHERSON, Heather (1942—). New Zealand poet and feminist. Born 1942 in New Zealand. ❖ With 3 other women, founded the feminist literary magazine *Spiral* (1976), which also developed into a publishing house and published works like Keri Hulme's *The Bone People*; often writes of her experiences as a lesbian; works include *A Figurehead, A Face* (1982) and *The Third Myth* (1986); also edited *Spiral 7: a collection of lesbian art and writing from Aotearoa New Zealand* (1992).

McPHETRIDGE, Louise (1905–1979). *See Thaden, Louise.*

McQUEEN, Butterfly (1911–1995). *See McQueen, Thelma.*

McQUEEN, Mary (1860–1945). New Zealand deaconess and social worker. Born July 13, 1860, in Ballarat, Victoria, Australia; died May

30, 1945, in Brisbane, Australia; dau. of John McQueen (farmer) and Catherine (McIntosh) McQueen. ❖ Trained at Presbyterian Deaconess Training Institute in Melbourne (1902); became parish deaconess at Knox Church, Dunedin (1902–07); helped found Presbyterian Social Service Association in Otago (1906); established Presbyterian Orphanage and Children's Home in Otago (1907). ❖ See also *Dictionary of New Zealand Biography* (Vol. 3).

McQUEEN, Thelma (1911–1995). African-American actress. Name variations: Thelma "Butterfly" McQueen. Born Thelma McQueen, Jan 8, 1911, in Tampa, FL; died in Augusta, GA, Dec 22, 1995, after suffering critical burns when a kerosene heater caught fire; father was a stevedore; mother was a domestic worker (names unknown); graduated New York City College, BA in Spanish, 1975; never married; no children. ❖ Best known for her role as Prissy in the film *Gone With the Wind*, made stage debut at New York City College (1935); made Broadway debut in *Brown Sugar* (1937) and movie debut in *Gone With the Wind* (1939); produced one-woman shows, *Butterfly McQueen and Friends* (1969) and *Prissy in Person* (1976); won Rosemary Award (1973) and Black Filmmakers Hall of Fame Award (1975); won Emmy Award for "The Seven Wishes of Joanna Peabody" (1979); wrote, produced, and starred in *Tribute to Mary Bethune* (1978); was active in the 50th anniversary celebration of release of *Gone With the Wind* (1989); other films include *The Women* (1939), *Affectionately Yours* (1941), *Cabin in the Sky* (1943), *I Dood It* (1943), *Since You Went Away* (1944), *Mildred Pierce* (1945), *Duel in the Sun* (1946), *Amazing Grace* (1974) and *Mosquito Coast* (1986); refused many demeaning roles, often to the detriment of her popularity with producers and film casters. ❖ See also *Women in World History*.

McQUILLAN, Rachel (1971—). Australian tennis player. Born Dec 2, 1971, in Merewether, NSW, Australia. ❖ At Barcelona Olympics, won a bronze medal in doubles (1992); became 1st Australian woman to reach Lipton quarterfinals (1995); upset Conchita Martinez in 3rd round of US Open (1997).

McRAE, Carmen (1920–1994). African-American jazz singer. Born Carmen McRae, April 8, 1920, in Brooklyn, NY; died after a stroke, Nov 10, 1994, in Beverly Hills, CA; m. Kenny Clarke (drummer), 1940s (div. 1947); m. Ike Isaacs (div.). ❖ At 17, won a talent contest at Apollo Theater with her smoky contralto; began singing in NY nightclubs; wrote "Dream of Life" for Billie Holiday; joined Benny Carter Orchestra (1944), then sang with Count Basie; signed with Decca (1954) and recorded the 1st of what would eventually be close to 2 dozen albums on various labels, including *Bittersweet, Woman Talk, Just a Little Lovin', The Great American Songbook, I'm Coming Home* and *Carmen Sings Monk*; sang with her own trio (1961–69); recorded duets with Betty Carter, the hugely successful "Take Five" with Dave Brubeck, a tribute album to Sarah Vaughan, versions of "God Bless the Child," "I've Got You Under My Skin," and Billy Joel's "New York State of Mind"; also appeared in several films, including *The Subterraneans* (1960), *Hotel* (1967) and *Monterey Jazz* (1968). Won *Down Beat* magazine's new singer award (1954); named master of jazz by National Endowment for the Arts (1993). ❖ See also *Women in World History*.

McRAE, Ellen (1932—). See Burstyn, Ellen.

McRAE, Francine (1969—). Australian softball player. Name variations: Frankie McRae. Born April 27, 1969, in Melbourne, Australia. ❖ Power hitter, won a bronze medal at Atlanta Olympics (1996).

McTEER, Maureen (1952—). Canadian lawyer, author, and first lady. Name variations: Maureen Clark. Born Maureen McTeer, Feb 27, 1952, in Cumberland, Ontario, Canada; m. (Charles Joseph) Joe Clark (prime minister of Canada, 1979–80), June 30, 1973; children: Catherine Jane Clark (b. 1976). ❖ Medical-law specialist and advocate for equality in Canada, lectured on such issues as education, health care, technology, and institutional change; chair of the Canadian Bar Association's Eastern and Central European Legal Programs; active member of the Canada-China Child Health Foundation; foreign advisor to the Tianjin Children's Hospital; author of *Tough Choices: Living and Dying in the 21st Century, Residences: Homes of Canada's Leaders*, and *Canada's Democracy and How It Works*.

McTIER, Martha (c. 1743–1837). Irish letter writer. Born Martha Drennan in Ireland c. 1743; died in 1837; sister of William Drennan (member of the United Irishmen); m. Samuel McTier (president of the 1st Belfast Society of United Irishmen). ❖ Through her association with brother and husband, met many of the leading Irish politicians and reformers of the day; maintained an extensive correspondence, and her

political commentary has proven valuable to historians studying Irish and British politics in the turbulent period around the turn of the 19th century.

McVEY, Lucille (1890–1925). See Drew, Lucille.

McVICAR, Annie (1862–1954). New Zealand politician and social-welfare worker. Name variations: Ann McLachlan, Ann McDonald. Born Ann McLachlan, Nov 4, 1862, near Kilmartin, Argyllshire, Scotland; dau. of Alexander McLachlan (laborer) and Lilly (McNair) McLachlan; m. Gordon McDonald (clerk), 1888 (died 1906); m. Alexander McVicar (engineer), 1906 (died 1922). ❖ Immigrated to New Zealand with 1st husband (1901); active in social and educational work in Wellington from 1906; executive member of New Zealand Society for the Protection of Women and Children; helped establish local branch of Plunket Society (1908); active in New Zealand Political Reform League (1913); served as Miramar borough councillor (1919 and 1921); was the 1st woman elected to Wellington City Council (1921); was a member of Wellington Hospital and Charitable Aid Board (1915–38); appointed justice of peace (1926); with funds from estate of Dr Edith Huntley, established Alexandra Maternity Hospital at Newtown (1927). Alliance française bronze medal (1916); Member of British Empire (1938). ❖ See also *Dictionary of New Zealand Biography* (Vol. 3).

McVIE, Christine (1943—). English rock singer. Name variations: Fleetwood Mac. Born Christine Anne Perfect, July 12, 1943, in Birmingham, England; dau. of Cyril (concert violinist) and Beatrice Perfect (faith-healing psychic); sister of John Perfect (entomologist); attended Birmingham University; m. John McVie (bass player), 1968 (div. 1976); m. Eddie Quintela (keyboard player), 1986 (div.). ❖ Member of legendary band Fleetwood Mac, 1st played bass with Sounds of Blue, with Andy Sylvester and Stan Webb (1964–65); joined Chicken Shack with same musicians (1966), playing keyboard; had 1st major success as songwriter and musician with "I'd Rather Go Blind" (1969); recorded solo album of own songs, *Christine Perfect*, earning Melody Maker's Best Female Vocalist Award (1968–69); joined Fleetwood Mac (1970), after several years of unofficial work as keyboardist and back-up singer, and recorded *Kiln House* with group in same year; with group, release several albums, including highly successful *Bare Trees* (1972) and *Mystery to Me* (1973); moved to California with band (1974), where she became its principal songwriter, with such hits as "Why," "Emerald Eyes" and "Come a Little Bit Closer"; added Lindsey Buckingham and Stevie Nicks to band after losing Bob Welch, and recorded phenomenally successful album *Fleetwood Mac* (1975), featuring hits "Rhiannon," "Say You Love Me" and "Over My Head"; with group, drew on personal troubles to record enormously successful *Rumours* (1977), which won Grammy Award for Album of the Year, and recorded 2 more smash-hit albums, *Tusk* (1979) and *Fleetwood Mac Live* (1980); had huge success with album *Mirage* (1982), featuring hits "Hold Me," "Gypsy," and "Love In Store"; released 2nd solo album (1984), scoring hit with "Got a Hold on Me"; went on solo tour before returning to recording studio with Fleetwood Mac for *Tango in the Night* (1987), featuring "Big Love," "Little Lies," "Seven Wonders" and "Everywhere," and additional album *Behind the Mask* (1990); left Fleetwood Mac after ill-fated *Time* album (1995), having spent almost 30 years with band, but reunited 1 last time for popular live album *Dance* (1997); released well-received solo album *In the Meantime* (2004). Inducted into Rock and Roll Hall of Fame (1998).

McWHINNEY, Madeline H. (1922—). American bank executive. Born Mar 11, 1922, in Denver, CO. ❖ Served as 1st president of First Women's Bank and Trust Company, NY (1974–76); served 30 years as economist with Federal Reserve Bank including positions as chief of Financial and Trade Statistics Division (1955–59), chief of Market Statistics Department (1960), and 1st woman vice president in Federal Reserve System (beginning 1965); was 1st woman president of New York University Graduate School of Business (1957–59); served as president of Dale, Elliott & Co., Inc. (1977–94); served as chair of Woman's Economic Round Table (1987/88); served New Jersey Supreme Court as member of Advisory Board on Professional Ethics (1983–98) and member of Investment Committee (beginning 1990).

McWHINNIE, Mary Alice (1922–1980). American scientist. Born Aug 10, 1922; died Mar 1980, in Downer's Grove, IL. ❖ International authority on krill, became 1st woman in National Science Foundation program to overwinter in Antarctica; studied biochemistry and metabolism of Antarctic krill at Palmer Station during austral summer

(1975–76); served as chief scientist at McMurdo Station; spent 10 years working offshore (as 1st American woman) on an Antarctic research ship.

McWILLIAMS, Jackie (1964—). Ulster field-hockey player. Born Feb 18, 1964, in Northern Ireland. ❖ Joined Randalstown Hockey Club at 14; at Barcelona Olympics, won a bronze medal in team competition (1992).

McWILLIAMS, Monica (1954—). Northern Ireland politician. Born April 28, 1954, in Kilrea, Co. Derry, Northern Ireland. ❖ Won a postgraduate scholarship to University of Michigan and became an urban planner in Detroit; returned to Northern Ireland (1978); became a lecturer, professor of social policy and women's studies, University of Ulster; active in the civil rights movement; was a founder member of Northern Ireland Women's Coalition (NIWC, 1996); representing NIWC, elected to the Northern Ireland Assembly for South Belfast (1998).

MDLULI, Labotsibeni (c. 1858–1925). See Labotsibeni Gwamile LaMdluli.

MEAD, Andrea (1932—). See Lawrence, Andrea Mead.

MEAD, Elizabeth Storrs (1832–1917). American educator. Born Elizabeth Storrs Billings, May 21, 1832, in Conway, Massachusetts; died Mar 25, 1917, in Coconut Grove, Florida; dau. of Charles Eugene Billings and Sally Williston (Storrs) Billings; attended Ipswich Female Seminary; m. Hiram Mead (minister and professor), Aug 5, 1858 (died 1881); children: Alice Edwards Mead; George Herbert Mead. ❖ The 1st president of Mt. Holyoke College, is credited with laying the foundation upon which much of Mt. Holyoke's modern reputation as a prestigious educational institution rests; moved to New York (1837); ran a girls' school in Massachusetts (c. 1852); moved to Ohio (1869); named president of newly created Mt. Holyoke College (1890); retired (1901). ❖ See also Women in World History.

MEAD, Kate Campbell (1867–1941). See Hurd-Mead, Kate Campbell.

MEAD, Lucia Ames (1856–1936). American writer, lecturer, and reformer. Name variations: Lucy True Ames; Lucia Ames. Pronunciation: Meed. Born Lucy Jane Ames, May 5, 1856, in Boscawen, New Hampshire; died in Boston, Massachusetts, of injuries suffered in a fall, Nov 1, 1936; dau. of Nathan Plummer Ames (farmer) and Elvira (Coffin) Ames; aunt of Mary Ware Dennett (1872–1947); graduate of Salem Normal School; m. Edwin Doak Mead (writer and reformer), Sept 29, 1898. ❖ Promoter of reform causes, including women's suffrage and world peace, began career as piano teacher (1875); offered courses for women on literature, history, and philosophy (1886); published novel, *Memoirs of a Millionaire* (1889); attended 1st peace conference, Lake Mohonk Conference on International Arbitration (1897); served as president of Massachusetts Woman Suffrage Association (1903–09); selected as peace committee chair, National American Woman Suffrage Association (1904) and National Council of Women (1905); wrote *Patriotism and the New Internationalism* (1906) and *Swords and Ploughshares* (1912); a leader of US peace movement, named national secretary, Woman's Peace Party (1915–18), and national secretary, US branch of Women's International League for Peace and Freedom (1919–21); lectured for National Council for the Prevention of War (1922–33); wrote *Law or War* (1928); her attempts to involve women's groups and individual women in the peace crusade, and her personal efforts to publicize antiwar sentiment among non-elites, render her among the most important American peace activists of late 19th and early 20th centuries. ❖ See also John M. Craig, *Lucia Ames Mead and the American Peace Movement* (Edwin Mellen, 1990); and *Women in World History*.

MEAD, Lynda Lee (c. 1939—). Miss America. Name variations: Lynda Lee Mead Shea. Born Lynda Lee Mead c. 1939 in Natchez, Mississippi; attended University of Mississippi; m. John Shea (physician); children: 3. ❖ Named Miss America (1960), representing Mississippi; owner and president of French Country Imports and Shea-Moore Design. ❖ See also Frank Deford, *There She Is* (Viking, 1971).

MEAD, Margaret (1901–1978). American anthropologist. Born Margaret Mead, Dec 16, 1901, in Philadelphia, Pennsylvania; died in New York, NY, Nov 15, 1978; dau. of Edward Sherwood Mead (economist) and Emily Fogg Mead (sociologist); attended DePauw University, 1919–20; Barnard College, AB, 1923; Columbia, MA, 1924, PhD, 1929; m. Luther Sheeleigh Cressman (Episcopal priest; later sociologist, archeologist), Sept 3, 1923 (div. 1928); m. Reo Franklin Fortune (anthropologist), Oct 8, 1928 (div. 1935); m. Gregory Bateson (anthropologist), Mar 13, 1936 (div. 1950); children (3rd m.): Mary Catherine Bateson

(b. 1939, anthropologist). ❖ The most prominent anthropologist in the world, traveled to Pago Pago, Samoa, to study adolescence among the Polynesians (1925); published *Coming of Age in Samoa* (1928), a bestseller that launched her into worldwide fame; went to the central island of the Great Admiralty archipelago, Manus (1928), settling in a village called Peri, to study the minds of primitive children, which produced *Growing Up in New Guinea* (1930); published *Sex and Temperament in Three Primitive Societies* (1935); appointed assistant curator of ethnology, American Museum of Natural History (1926), then associate curator (1942), curator (1964), curator emeritus (1969); appointed adjunct professor of anthropology, Columbia (1954–78); was professor of anthropology and chair, division of social sciences, Fordham University (1968–70); was visiting lecturer, department of psychiatry, school of medicine, University of Cincinnati (1957–58), and Menninger Foundation, Topeka (1959); wrote close to 30 books, including *And Keep Your Powder Dry: An Anthropologist Looks at America* (1942), *Balinese Character* (1942), *Male and Female: A Study of the Sexes in the Changing World* (1949), and *Culture and Commitment: A Study of the Generation Gap* (1970), edited a dozen more, contributed hundreds of articles, helped lead major professional associations, and was one of the most sought-after lecturers in the nation; built upon her celebrity status until at last she became a national oracle, pronouncing on all topics from Soviet child-rearing to Anglican liturgy. ❖ See also autobiographies *Blackberry Winter* (1972) and *Letters from the Field, 1925–1975* (Harper & Row, 1977); Robert Cassidy, *Margaret Mead: A Voice for the Century* (Universe, 1982); Jane Howard, *Margaret Mead* (Simon & Schuster, 1984); and *Women in World History*.

MEAD, Sylvia Earle (1935—). American marine biologist. Name variations: Sylvia Earle. Born Sylvia Alice Earle in Gibbstown, New Jersey, Aug 30, 1935; dau. of Lewis Reade (electrical contractor) and Alice Freas (Richie) Mead (nurse); Florida State University, BS, 1955; Duke University, MA, 1956, PhD, 1966; m. Giles W. Mead (ichthyologist and museum curator and later director of the Los Angeles County Museum of Natural History), 1967; children: daughter Gale Mead, 2 adopted children, and 3 stepchildren. ❖ One of the world's most respected aquanauts and marine scientists, served as an associate in botany at Los Angeles County Museum of Natural History, and held appointments at Harvard University, University of California at Berkeley, and University of Southern Florida; conducted systematic and ecological studies of marine plants, and the interrelationship between marine animals and plants, in the Gulf of Mexico, northwest Indian Ocean, and southeast Pacific; made history as the leader of the 5-member team of women aquanauts participating in the Tektite project of underwater research in the Great Lameshur Bay of the Virgin Islands (1970); participated in numerous other undersea operations, including one under the aegis of SCORE (Scientific Cooperative Operational Research Expedition), during which she successfully completed the longest and deepest lock-out dive ever done by a woman; surpassed her own record, surveying the ocean floor untethered at 2,500 feet; served as chief scientist of the National Oceanographic and Atmospheric Administration (NOAA); joined the Sustainable Seas Expedition (1998). Inducted into Women's Hall of Fame at Seneca Falls (2000). ❖ See also *Women in World History*.

MEADOWS, Audrey (1922–1996). American actress. Name variations: Audrey Cotter; Audrey Six. Born Feb 8, 1922, in Wuchang, China; died of lung cancer, Feb 3, 1996, in Los Angeles, CA; dau. of Francis James Meadows Cotter (missionary and minister) and Ida Taylor Cotter; younger sister of Jayne Meadows (b. 1920, actress); m. Randolph T. Rouse (builder), May 26, 1956 (div. 1958); m. Robert Six (airline executive), Aug 24, 1961 (died 1986); no children. ❖ Best remembered as the tart-tongued Alice Kramden in "The Honeymooners," moved to US (c. 1927); made stage debut as a singer at Carnegie Hall (c. 1938); moved to New York City (c. 1940); appeared on "The Jackie Gleason Show" (1952–55) and "The Honeymooners" (1955–57); won Emmy Award (1955); retired (1961); returned to tv on ABC sitcom "Too Close for Comfort" (1986). Named to Broadcasting Hall of Fame (1990). ❖ See also memoir *Love, Alice: My Life as a Honeymooner* (1994); and *Women in World History*.

MEADOWS, Jayne (1920—). American actress. Name variations: Jane Cotter; changed stage name to Jayne Meadows (c. 1946). Born 1920 in Wuchang, China; dau. of Francis James Meadows Cotter (missionary and minister) and Ida Taylor Cotter; sister of Audrey Meadows (1922–1996); m. Milton Krims (div.); m. Steve Allen (actor and comic), July 31, 1954; children: (2nd m.) William Christopher Allen. ❖ Stage and screen personality of 1950s, appeared on stage in *Spring Again* (1942),

Another Love Story (1943) and *Kiss Them for Me* (1945); films include *Undercurrent* (1946), *Lady in the Lake* (1947), *Song of the Thin Man* (1947), *The Luck of the Irish* (1948), *Enchantment* (1949) and *David and Bathsheba* (1951); on tv, was a panelist on popular quiz show *I've Got a Secret* (1952–58). ❖ See also *Women in World History.*

MEAGHER, Aileen (1910–1987). Canadian runner. Born Nov 26, 1910 in Nova Scotia, Canada; died Aug 1987. ❖ At Berlin Olympics, won a bronze medal in 4x100-meter relay (1936).

MEAGHER, Mary T. (1964—). American swimmer. Name variations: Mary Meagher Plant or Meagher-Plant. Born Mary Terstegge Meagher, Oct 27, 1964, in Louisville, KY. ❖ At US nationals (1981), set world records of 57.93 for 100-meter butterfly and 2:05.96 for 200-meter butterfly which went unbroken until 1999; won gold medals for the 100-meter butterfly, 200-meter butterfly, and 4x100-meter medley relay at Los Angeles Olympics (1984); won a bronze medal for the 200-meter butterfly and a silver medal for the 4x100-medley relay at Seoul Olympics (1988); won the World championship for 100-meter butterfly (1982) and 200-meter butterfly (1986).

MEAKER, Marijane (1927—). American novelist and children's writer. Name variations: M.J. Meaker; (pseudonyms) Ann Aldrich, Vin Packer, and M.E. Kerr. Born May 27, 1927, in Auburn, NY; dau. of Ellis R. (mayonnaise manufacturer) and Ida T. Meaker; attended Vermont Junior College, and New School for Social Research; University of Missouri, BA, 1949. ❖ Worked at several jobs, including assistant file clerk for E.P. Dutton (1949–50); became freelance writer (1949); wrote young adult fiction under pseudonym M.E. Kerr, including *Dinky Hocker Shoots Smack!* (1972), *If I Love You, Am I Trapped Forever?* (1973), *The Son of Someone Famous* (1974), *Is That You, Miss Blue?* (1975), *I'll Love You When You're More Like Me* (1977), *Gentlehands* (1978), *Little, Little* (1981), *What I Really Think of You* (1982) *I Stay Near You* (1985) and *Night Kites* (1987); as M.J. Meaker, wrote adult fiction and nonfiction; under pseudonym Ann Aldrich, wrote *We Walk Alone* (1955), *We Too Must Love* (1958) and *Take a Lesbian to Lunch* (1972), among others; under pseudonym Vin Packer, wrote crime novels for Gold Medal books. ❖ See also autobiography, *Me, Me, Me, Me, Me: Not a Novel* (1983) and *Highsmith: A Romance of the 1950s,* about her relationship with writer Patricia Highsmith.

MEALING, Philomena (1912–2002). Australian swimmer. Name variations: Philomena Alecia Mealing; Bonnie Mealing. Born July 28, 1912 (another source cites May 18, 1913), in Woolloomooloo, Australia; died Jan 1, 2002, in Sydney; married; children: Fraser and Denise. ❖ Broke World record for 100-meter backstroke with a time of 1:20.6 (Feb 1930); at Los Angeles Olympics, won a silver medal for the 100-meter backstroke (1932).

MEANS, Jacqueline (1936—). American priest. Name variations: Jacqueline Allene Means-Bratsch. Born Jacqueline Allene Ehringer in Peoria, Illinois, Aug 26, 1936; dau. of Theodore R. Ehringer and Minnett M. Ehringer; m. Delton Means (div. 1979); m. David H. Bratsch; children: (1st m.) Deborah Means; David Means; Delton Means; Patrick Means. ❖ Ordained a deacon in the Episcopal Church (1974), was assigned to All Saints', an inner-city parish in a racially mixed neighborhood of Indianapolis; was the 1st woman to be officially recognized as an ordained priest by the Episcopal Church in US (1977); advanced to position of associate pastor of St. John's Episcopal Church in Indianapolis (1982). ❖ See also *Women in World History.*

MEANS, Marianne (1934—). American reporter. Born Marianne Hansen, June 13, 1934, in Sioux City, IA; dau. of Ernest Maynard Hansen and Else (Andersen) Hansen; University of Nebraska, BA, 1956; m. 2nd husband James J. Kilpatrick (journalist). ❖ Began reporting on Washington politics for Washington bureau of Hearst newspapers (1959); served as 1st woman reporter assigned full time to White House (1961–65); became syndicated political columnist with King Features (1965); wrote *The Woman in the White House* (1963).

MEANY, Helen (1904–1991). American swimmer. Born Dec 15, 1904; died July 21, 1991. ❖ Participated in the Olympics (1920, 1924); won a gold medal for springboard diving at Amsterdam Olympics (1928); won 17 national AAU diving championships for the New York Women's Swimming Association; saw career end when she appeared in a water show unsanctioned by US Olympic Committee. Inducted into the Swimming and Diving Hall of Fame (1971). ❖ See also *Women in World History.*

MEARES, Anna (1983—). Australian cyclist. Born Sept 21, 1983, in Blackwater, Australia. ❖ Won 500-meter time trial at World championships (2004); at Athens Olympics, won a bronze medal for sprint and a gold medal for 500-meter time trial (2004), setting a track World record of 33.952.

MEARIG, Kim (1963—). American surfer. Born Kimberly Irene Mearig, Sept 10, 1963, in Apple Valley, CA; m. Brian Gruetzmacher (homebuilder). ❖ Won NSSA nationals and US nationals (1979); won ASP championship (1983–84).

MEARS, Elizabeth (1900–1988). American ballet and theatrical dancer and casting director. Name variations: Liz Mears; Elizabeth M. Jameson. Born Feb 23, 1900, in Chicago, IL; died April 18, 1988, in Danbury, CT; dau. of John Henry Mears (actor-manager and Broadway producer). ❖ Trained with Adolf Bolm, Andreas Pavley, and Serge Oukrainsky, ballet masters at Chicago Civic Opera; was featured in photographs illustrating Sergei Marinoff Home-Study Course in Russian Classical Dancing, a work she is often said to have ghost written; on Broadway, danced in *Judy* (1927), *Queen at Home* (1930) and *Singapore* (1932); retired from performance career (1934); was casting director for all programs on the Dumont Television Network.

MEARS, Helen Farnsworth (1872–1916). American sculptor. Born in Oshkosh, WI, Dec 21, 1872; died in New York, NY, Feb 17, 1916; dau. of John Hall Mears (dealer in farm implements) and Mary Elizabeth (Farnsworth) Mears (poet, essayist, and playwright, who published a book of poetry under name Nellie Wildwood); sister of Mary Mears (writer) and Louise Mears (book illustrator); briefly attended Art Students League, NY; apprentice to Augustus Saint-Gaudens; studied sculpture under Frederick MacMonnies in Paris; studied abroad with Alexander Charpentier and Denys Puech; never married; no children. ❖ At 20, received 1st commission: a statue of a woman and a winged eagle, *Genius of Wisconsin*, for Wisconsin Building at World's Columbian Exposition (1893), a work widely acclaimed; apprenticed with Augustus Saint-Gaudens, working in his studio for several years; set up a studio in Washington Square (1899); continued to tackle large-scale projects, including a full-length statue of Frances E. Willard (1905) for Statuary Hall in US Capitol rotunda; also did bas-reliefs of Saint-Gaudens and Edward MacDowell and busts of George Rogers Clark and Dr. William T.G. Morton; possibly best known for her ambitious, three-panel bas-relief *Fountain of Life*, which won medals in several competitions. ❖ See also *Women in World History.*

MEBARAK, Shakira (1977—). See Shakira.

MECHLIN, Leila (1874–1949). American art critic and editor. Born May 29, 1874, in Georgetown, Washington, DC; died May 6, 1949, in Washington, DC; dau. of Frederick Alexander Smith Mechlin (commission agent) and Cornelia Stout (Hyatt) Mechlin (painter); attended Corcoran School of Art. ❖ The 1st major woman art critic in US, became a founder of American Federation of Arts (1909) and later secretary (1912–33); served as art critic for *Washington Evening Star* and *Sunday Star* (1900–45); established and edited *American Magazine of Fine Arts* (originally *Art and Progress* [1st edition 1909]); was early advocate of National Art Gallery in Washington, DC; elected fellow of Royal Society of Arts, London (1940).

MECHTEL, Angelika (1943–2000). German novelist and short-story writer. Name variations: Angelika Eilers. Born Aug 26, 1943, in Dresden, Germany; died Feb 2000 in Cologne, Germany; dau. of Walter Mechtel (journalist) and Gisela Altendorf (actress); married and div.; children: Anke and Silke Eilers. ❖ Became editor of *Aspekte-Impulse* (1965) and *Publikation* (1972); as a member of Gruppe 61, took an interest in worker's literature; writings include *Die feinen Totengräber* (1968), *Die Blindgängerin* (1974), *Die Träume der Füchsin* (1978), and *Gott und die Liedermacherin* (1983).

MECHTHILD. *Variant of Mechtild.*

MECHTILD OF DRIESSEN (d. 1160). Saint. Died at the abbey of Driessen in 1160. ❖ A Bavarian Augustinian, was related to Frederick I Barbarossa (1123–1190), Holy Roman emperor and king of Germany. Feast day is July 6.

MECHTILD OF HACKEBORNE (1241–1298). Germany mystic. Born 1241; died 1298; sister of Gertrude of Hackeborne (1232–1292). ❖ The choir mistress of Helfta, had visions. An account of her revelations, compiled by 2 nuns, is titled *Liber specialis gratiae (Book of Special Grace)*. ❖ See also *Women in World History.*

MECHTILD OF HOLSTEIN (d. 1288). Queen of Denmark. Name variations: Mechtild von Holstein. Died in 1288; dau. of Adolf V, count of Holstein; m. Abel (1218–1252), king of Denmark (r. 1250–1252, killed), on April 25, 1237; children: Erik, duke of Schleswig; Valdemar also known as Waldemar, duke of Schleswig; Sophie Abelsdottir (b. around 1240, who m. Bernard, prince of Anhalt-Bernburg); Abel (b. 1252).

MECHTILD OF MAGDEBURG (c. 1207–c. 1282). German Christian mystic and Beguine. Name variations: Mechtild von Magdeburg; Mechthild von Magdeburg; Mechthild von Magdeburg; Mechtilde de Magdebourg. Born between 1207 and 1212 near Magdeburg in Lower Saxony (Germany); died in the convent at Helfta in 1282 (though some suggest her death might be as late as 1297). ❖ Wrote of the love affair between God and her soul; had religious experience (c. 1219); left home for Magdeburg (c. 1229 or 1230), where she led a semi-religious life as a Beguine; wrote the 1st 6 books of *The Flowing Light of the Godhead* (1250–70); retired to the Cistercian convent at Helfta (1270), and wrote book 7 of *The Flowing Light* before her death. When *The Flowing Light of the Godhead* was found in a monastery (1860), it was considered a major discovery: not only was it the 1st Christian mystical text known to be written by a man or a woman in the vernacular (or language of the common people) rather than in Latin, it also contained one of the 1st descriptions of a type of Christian devotion known as the Sacred Heart. German literary historians and theologians declared Mechtild of Magdeburg one of the 1st and best examples of the German mystic movement. ❖ See also Lucy Menzies, *The Revelations of Mechthild of Magdeburg (1210–1297) or the Flowing Light of the Godhead* (Longmans, 1953); and *Women in World History.*

MECHTILDE. *Variant of Mechtild.*

MECK, Nadezdha von (1831–1894). *See Von Meck, Nadezdha.*

MECKLENBURG, duchess of.
See Euphemia (1317–after 1336).
See Ursula of Brandenburg (1488–1510).
See Sophie of Holstein-Gottorp (1569–1634).
See Cecilia of Mecklenburg-Schwerin (1886–1954).
See Juliana (1909–2004).

MECKLENBURG-GUSTROW, duchess of.
See Elizabeth of Denmark (1524–1586).
See Anna Sophia of Prussia (1527–1591).
See Magdalena Sybilla of Holstein-Gottorp (1631–1719).

MECKLENBURG-SCHWERIN, duchess of.
See Anna of Brandenburg (1507–1567).
See Catherine of Mecklenburg-Schwerin (1692–1733).
See Louise of Saxe-Gotha (1756–1808).
See Caroline Louise of Saxe-Weimar (1786–1816).
See Alexandrina of Mecklenburg-Schwerin (1879–1952).

MECKLENBURG-SCHWERIN, grand duchess of.
See Alexandrine of Prussia (1803–1892).
See Anastasia Romanova (1860–1922).
See Alexandra Guelph (1882–1963).

MECKLENBURG-STRELITZ, duchess of.
See Marie of Mecklenburg-Gustrow (1659–1701).
See Elizabeth of Saxe-Hildburghausen (1713–1761).
See Frederica of Hesse-Darmstadt (1752–1782).
See Augusta Guelph (1822–1916).
See Romanov, Catherine (1827–1894).

MECKLENBURG-STRELITZ, grand duchess of.
See Charlotte of Hesse-Darmstadt (1755–1785).
See Mary of Hesse-Cassel (1796–1880).
See Elizabeth of Anhalt-Dessau (1857–1933).

MECOM, Jane Franklin (1712–1794). American home economist. Name variations: Jane Franklin. Born Jane Franklin, Mar 27, 1712, in Boston, MA; died c. May 9, 1794, in Boston; dau. of Josiah Franklin and Abiah Folger; sister of Benjamin Franklin (diplomat, writer and inventor); m. Edward Mecom (saddler), July 27, 1727 (died 1765); children: 8 sons, 4 daughters. ❖ Left for Rhode Island at beginning of siege of Boston (1775); escorted by and taken into home of younger brother Benjamin Franklin in Philadelphia (1775–77); returned to Boston and lived in home owned by him (1784); despite wide gap in education and economic status, maintained warm relationship with brother via

extensive correspondence; was periodically assisted by him financially and was bequeathed his Boston home.

MEDALEN, Linda (1965—). Norwegian soccer player. Born June 17, 1965, in Norway. ❖ Defender; won team championships at UEFA European (1993), FIFA Invitational (1988) and FIFA World Cup (1995); won a team bronze medal at Atlanta Olympics (1996); played for Asker in Norway (1992–98) and Nikko in Japan.

MEDEA (d. 1440). Queen of Cyprus. Died 1440; became the 1st wife of John II, the Lusignan king of Cyprus (r. 1432–1458), c. 1440. ❖ John II's 2nd wife was Helen Paleologina (c. 1415–1458).

MEDERS, Mary (1643–1673). *See Moders, Mary.*

MEDFORD, Kay (1914–1980). American stage, tv, and screen actress. Born Maggie O'Regin, Sept 14, 1914, in New York, NY; died April 10, 1980, in New York, NY. ❖ Made film debut in *The War against Mrs. Hadley* (1944); other films include *Swing Shift Maisie, Guilty Bystander, A Face in the Crowd, The Rat Race, Butterfield 8, Ensign Pulver, A Fine Madness, Funny Girl* and *Windows*; debuted on Broadway as Cherry in *Paint Your Wagon* (1951), followed by *Lullaby, Two's Company, John Murray Anderson's Almanac, Mr. Wonderful, A Hole in the Head, Carousel, Pal Joey, Bye Bye Birdie* and *Funny Girl*; was a regular on tv's "Dean Martin Show" (1970–01), among others.

MEDFORTH-MILLS, Helen (b. 1950). *See Helen, Princess.*

MEDHAVI, Ramabai (1858–1922). *See Ramabai, Pandita.*

MEDICA (1900–1956). *See Malleson, Joan.*

MEDICI, Alfonsina de (d. 1520). Florentine noblewoman. Name variations: Alfonsina Orsini. Born Alfonsina Orsini; died in 1520; m. Pietro the Unfortunate also known as Pietro de Medici (1471–1503), ruler of Florence, on May 22, 1488; children: Lorenzo de Medici, duke of Urbino (1492–1519); Clarice de Medici (1493–1528, who m. Filippo Strozzi). ❖ A daughter of the powerful Orsini family, was known to be haughty and showed an "unconcealed contempt" for the Florentines; was driven out of Florence with her equally unpopular husband, 2 infant children, and the rest of the Medici clan (Nov 9, 1494).

MEDICI, Anna de (1616–?). Italian princess. Born in 1616; dau. of Cosimo II de Medici (1590–1620), grand duke of Tuscany (r. 1609–1620), and Maria Magdalena of Austria (1589–1631); sister of Ferdinand II (1610–1670), grand duke of Tuscany; m. 1st cousin Ferdinand, archduke of Austrian Tyrol (son of Claudia de Medici); children: 1 daughter, Claudia Felicitas who m. Leopold I, Holy Roman emperor (r. 1658–1705). ❖ With husband, spent more time in Florence than in their duchy in the Austrian Tyrol, preferring the Tuscan court.

MEDICI, Anna Maria de (d. 1741). Grand duchess of Tuscany. Name variations: Anna Maria of Saxe-Lauenburg; Anne of Saxe-Lauenburg. Died in 1741; dau. of the duke of Saxe-Lauenburg; m. Philip of Neuberg, count Palatine (died); m. Giovan also known as Giovanni or Gian Gastone de Medici (1671–1737), grand duke of Tuscany (r. 1723–1737), in July 1697; no children. ❖ See also *Women in World History.*

MEDICI, Anna Maria Luisa de (1667–1743). Electress of the Palatinate. Name variations: Anna Maria Luisa of the Palatinate; Anna Maria Ludovica. Born 1667; died 1743; dau. of Cosimo III de Medici (1642–1723), grand duke of Tuscany (r. 1670–1723), and Marguerite Louise of Orleans (c. 1645–1721); m. John William of the Palatinate. ❖ Ruler, benefactor, and the last member of the famous Medici family, played a vital role in establishing Florence's modern status as an artistic and tourist center of Italy; was a political figure of great importance, taking over her father's administrative duties, including diplomatic negotiations; was a competent administrator and became a popular ruler; became renowned as a benefactor and art collector and made a gift of the entire Medici collection of art to the city of Florence. ❖ See also *Women in World History.*

MEDICI, Bianca de (fl. late 1400s). Sister of Lorenzo the Magnificent. Name variations: Bianca dei Pazzi. Flourished in the late 1400s; dau. of Piero or Pietro de Medici (1416–1469, a preeminent figure in Florence) and Lucrezia de Medici (1425–1482); sister of Lorenzo de Medici, the Magnificent (1449–1492), unofficial ruler of Florence; m. Guglielmo dei Pazzi.

MEDICI, Bianca de (1548–1587). *See Cappello, Bianca.*

MEDICI, Camilla de (fl. 1570s). *See Martelli, Camilla.*

MEDICI, Caterina de (c. 1462–1509). *See Sforza, Caterina.*

MEDICI, Caterina de (1593–1629). Duchess of Mantua. Name variations: Catherine de Medici; Caterina Gonzaga. Born in 1593; died in Siena of smallpox in 1629; dau. of Christine of Lorraine (c. 1571–1637) and Ferdinand I (1549–1609), grand duke of Tuscany (r. 1587–1609); sister of Claudia de Medici (1604–1648); m. Ferdinando also known as Ferdinand Gonzaga (1587–1626), 6th duke of Mantua, in 1617. ❖ Known for her piety, returned to Tuscany following death of husband, where she was made governor of Siena.

MEDICI, Catherine de (c. 1462–1509). *See Sforza, Caterina.*

MEDICI, Catherine de (1519–1589). Queen of France. Name variations: Catherine or Katherine de Médicis or Medicis; Catherine de' Médici or de' Medici; Caterina Maria Romola; Caterina de Medici or Caterina de Médicis. Pronunciation: (Italian) MEH-de-chee or MED-ee-chee; (French) MAY-dee-sees. Born in Florence, then an independent city-state in Italy, April 13, 1519; died in Blois, Anjou, France, Jan 5, 1589; dau. of Lorenzo de Medici (1492–1519), duke of Urbino (and grandson of Lorenzo the Magnificent) and French noblewoman Madeleine de la Tour d'Auvergne (1501–1519); m. Henry, duke of Orléans, the future Henry II, king of France (r. 1547–1559), Oct 28, 1533; children: Francis II (Jan 19, 1543–1560), king of France (r. 1559–1560); Elizabeth of Valois (1545–1568, queen of Spain); Claude de France (1547–1575); Louis (Feb 3, 1549–1550); Charles IX (June 27, 1550–1574), king of France (r. 1560–1574); Henry III (Sept 20, 1551–1589), king of France (r. 1574–1589); Margaret of Valois (May 14, 1553–1615); Hercule, later confirmed as Francis (b. Mar 18, 1555, later pronounced duke of Anjou but died in 1584 before he had an opportunity to ascend the throne of France); twins Jeanne and Victoire (b. June 24, 1556, died at birth, almost costing their mother's life). ❖ Influential queen mother who tried to put an end to the French Wars of Religion, alternating between attempts at encouraging peaceful coexistence between Catholics and Protestants and attempts to eliminate the Protestant minority; was a prisoner of the Florentine republic (1527–30); became queen of France (1547), as husband ascended to throne as King Henry II; when Henry II went to war against Spain, served as regent of France for the 1st time (1552); after death of Henry (1559), made regent for son Charles IX (1560); called the Colloquy of Poissy (1561); issued edicts favoring the toleration of French Protestantism (1562 and 1563), resulting in the start of the French Wars of Religion (1562) and later the St. Bartholomew's Day Massacre (1572); entered into peace negotiations with Henry of Bourbon, the Protestant king of Navarre (1578 and 1586). Though she had attempted toleration, the age was not tolerant. ❖ See also Jean Héritier, *Catherine de Medici* (trans. by Charlotte Haldane, St. Martin, 1963); Mark Strage, *Women of Power: The Life and Times of Catherine de' Medici* (Harcourt, 1976); Paul Van Dyke, *Catherine de Médicis* (2 vols., Scribner, 1924); and *Women in World History.*

MEDICI, Christine de (c. 1571–1637). *See Christine of Lorraine.*

MEDICI, Clarice de (c. 1453–1487). Florentine noblewoman. Name variations: Clarice Orsini. Born c. 1453; died in August 1487 (some sources cite 1488); came from a celebrated Roman noble family, the Orsinis; dau. of Jacopo also known as Giacomo Orsini of Monterotondo; m. Lorenzo de Medici, the Magnificent (1449–1492), unofficial ruler of Florence), June 4, 1469; children: (4 daughters) Lucrezia de Medici (b. around 1480, who m. Giacomo Salviati); Maddalena de Medici (d. 1519, who m. Franceschetto Cybo); Luisa or Luigia (who died before age 12); Contessina de Medici (who m. Piero Ridolfi); (3 sons) Pietro (1471–1503), who was briefly master of Florence upon his father's death and m. Alfonsina Orsini de Medici), Giovanni (1475–1521, who became Pope Leo X, r. 1513–1521); and Giuliano (1479–1516, who became duke of Nemours and m. Philiberta of Savoy). ❖ See also *Women in World History.*

MEDICI, Clarice de (1493–1528). Florentine noblewoman. Name variations: Clarice Strozzi; Clarice de Medici degli Strozzi. Born Clarice di Pietro de' Medici in 1493; died May 3, 1528; dau. of Pietro also known as Piero de Medici (1471–1503) and Alfonsina de Medici (d. 1520); granddau. of the Florentine ruler Lorenzo the Magnificent; m. Philip Strozzi also known as Filippo Strozzi, in 1508; children: 3 daughters, 7 sons. ❖ The subject of high praise by many historians and biographers, divided her time between the Strozzi palace in Florence and the papal palaces of Rome, where 1st her uncle Giovanni was pope as Leo X (1513–1521), and then her distant relative Guilio served as pope as Clement VII (1523–1534); had an excellent relationship with Leo X, who admired her as an intelligent and spirited woman (he is quoted as saying that it would

have been better for the Medici if she had only been born male so that she could lead the family); later instigated the expulsion of Pope Clement's supporters from the Medici Palace, showing the people of Florence that the "true" Medici did not support Clement and his harsh rule. ❖ See also *Women in World History.*

MEDICI, Claudia de (1604–1648). Princess of Urbino and regent of Austrian Tyrol. Name variations: Claude de' Medici; Claudia of Tuscany; Claudia della Rovere; archduchess of Austrian Tyrol. Born June 4, 1604, in Florence; died Dec 25, 1648, in Innsbruck; dau. of Ferdinand I de Medici (1549–1609), grand duke of Tuscany (r. 1587–1609), and Christine of Lorraine (c. 1571–1637); m. Federigo della Rovere, hereditary prince of Urbino, in 1620; m. Leopold V (1586–1632), archduke of Austrian Tyrol or Tirol, in 1625; children: (1st m.) Vittoria de Medici (d. 1694); (2nd m.) 2 sons and 2 daughters, including Ferdinand Karl or Ferdinand Charles, archduke of Austrian Tyrol (b. 1626, who m. his 1st cousin Anna de Medici); Isabella Clara (1629–1685); Sigmund Franz (1630–1665), archduke of Austrian Tyrol; Maria Leopoldine (1632–1649). ❖ When 2nd husband died, ruled as regent of Tyrol for her eldest son Ferdinand Karl (1632–46), and ruled well. ❖ See also *Women in World History.*

MEDICI, Contessina de (fl. 1400–1460). Florentine noblewoman. Name variations: Contessina de' Bardi. Born Contessina de Bardi (Contessina was her Christian name, not a title) in Florence; eldest dau. of Giovanni de Bardi (a partner in the Rome branch of the Bardi bank); m. Cosimo de Medici the Elder (1389–1464), also known as Pater Patriae, ruler of Florence (r. 1434–1464); children: Piero de Medici (1416–1469), ruler of Florence; Giovanni de Medici (1421–1463); Lorenzo. ❖ One of the matriarchs of the Medici family. ❖ See also *Women in World History.*

MEDICI, Contessina de (fl. 15th c.). Florentine noblewoman. Name variations: Contessina Ridolfi. One of four daughters of Lorenzo de Medici (1449–1492), the Magnificent, unofficial ruler of Florence, and Clarice de Medici (c. 1453–1487); m. Piero Ridolfi; children: Niccolo Ridolfi, cardinal.

MEDICI, Eleonora de (1522–1562). Italian noblewoman and warrior, duchess of Florence. Name variations: Eleonora of Toledo; Eleonore of Toledo; Eleonora da Toledo. Born in 1522; died of malarial fever in 1562; dau. of Pedro de Toledo (a rich Spanish viceroy at Naples and marquis of Villafranca); became 1st wife of Cosimo I or Cosmos de Medici (1519–1574), grand duke of Tuscany (r. 1569–1574), in 1543; children: 5 sons, Francesco (1541–1587); Giovanni, cardinal (d. 1562); Garzia (d. 1562); Ferdinand I (1549–1609); Pietro (1554–1604); and three daughters, Maria (b. 1540, died at 17); Isabella de Medici (1542–1576); Lucrezia de Medici (c. 1544–1561). ❖ While husband spent most of his career trying to defeat the House of Strozzi, was an active participant and a bold warrior; participated in the capture of the town of Siena (1554). ❖ See also *Women in World History.*

MEDICI, Eleonora de (1556–1576). Tuscan noblewoman. Name variations: Eleonore or Eleonora or Eleanora of Toledo; Eleonora di Toledo; Leonora. Born c. 1556; murdered in 1576; niece of Eleonora de Medici (1522–1562); m. Pietro de Medici (1554–1604), in 1571; children: Cosimo. ❖ As husband scandalized Florence with consecutive orgies and openly insulted her, fell in love with Bernardino Antinori; was killed by husband who also had Bernardino executed. ❖ See also *Women in World History.*

MEDICI, Eleonora de (1567–1611). Duchess of Mantua. Name variations: Eleonora Gonzaga. Born Eleonora de Medici in 1567; died in 1611; dau. of Joanna of Austria (1546–1578) and Francis or Francesco I de Medici (1541–1587), grand duke of Tuscany (r. 1574–1587); sister of Marie de Medici (c. 1573–1642); m. Vincenzo I (1562–1612), 4th duke of Mantua (r. 1587–1612), in 1583; children: Francesco (1586–1612), 5th duke of Mantua (r. 1612–1612); Ferdinando also known as Ferdinand (1587–1626), 6th duke of Mantua (r. 1612–1626); Margherita Gonzaga (1591–1632); Vincenzo II (1594–1627), 7th duke of Mantua (r. 1626–1627); Eleonora I Gonzaga (1598–1655). ❖ See also *Women in World History.*

MEDICI, Eleonora de (1591–1617). Tuscan noblewoman. Born in 1591; died, age 26, in Dec 1617; dau. of Christine of Lorraine (c. 1571–1637) and Ferdinand I de Medici (1549–1609), grand duke of Tuscany (r. 1587–1609); sister of Cosimo II de Medici (1590–1620), grand duke of Tuscany (r. 1609–1620). ❖ Was betrothed to Philip III, king of Spain, but he reneged on the agreement, and it is said that she died of a broken heart; portrait hangs in the Uffizi Gallery.

MEDICI, Eleonora de (fl. 1690). Tuscan noblewoman. Name variations: Eleonora Gonzaga. Flourished around 1690; m. Francesco Maria de Medici (1660–1711, who was cardinal until 1709).

MEDICI, Ginevra de (fl. 1450–1460). Florentine noblewoman. Name variations: Ginevra degli Alessandri. Born Ginevra degli Albizzi; m. Giovanni de Medici (1421–1463); children: 1 son who died in 1461 at age 9.

MEDICI, Ginevra de (fl. 15th c.). Tuscan noblewoman. Name variations: Genevra Cavalcanti; Ginevra d'Medici. Married Lorenzo de Medici (1395–1440); children: Pier or Piero Francesco (d. 1467).

MEDICI, Isabella de (1542–1576). Princess of Bracciano. Name variations: Isabella Orsini. Born in 1542; died in July 1576 by her husband's hand; dau. of Cosimo I de Medici (1519–1574), grand duke of Tuscany (r. 1569–1574), and Eleonora de Medici (1522–1562); m. Paolo Giordano Orsini, prince of Bracciano or Brachiano, in 1558. ❖ Married Paolo Giordano Orsini, the most powerful prince in Rome (1558); highly accomplished, beautiful and kind, captivated every heart but her husband's; was killed by husband who was spurred on by his lover Vittoria Accoramboni (1576); her fate brought down the house of Orsini. ❖ See also *Women in World History*.

MEDICI, Joanna de (1546–1578). *See Joanna of Austria.*

MEDICI, Laudomia de (fl. 1460s). Tuscan noblewoman. Name variations: Laudomia Accaiuoli or Acciaiuoli; Laudomia d'Medici. Born Laudomia Accaiuoli; flourished in 1460s; m. Pier or Piero Francesco d'Medici (d. 1467); children: Lorenzo (1463–1507); Giovanni (1467–1498).

MEDICI, Laudomia de (fl. 1530s). Tuscan noblewoman. Name variations: Laudomia Salviati; Laudomia Strozzi. Flourished in the 1530s; dau. of Pier Francesco de Medici (d. 1525) and Maria Soderini de Medici; sister of Lorenzino de Medici who assassinated Alessandro de Medici; m. Alemanno Salviati (died); m. Piero Strozzi. ❖ When Alessandro de Medici was assassinated by her brother Lorenzino (Jan 5, 1537), was innocent but implicated.

MEDICI, Lucrezia de (1425–1482). Italian businesswoman. Name variations: Lucrezia Tornabuoni. Born Lucrezia Tornabuoni (of an ancient aristocratic and powerful Florentine family) in 1425; died in 1482 in Florence; m. Piero "il Gottoso" de Medici also known as Piero or Pietro de Medici (1416–1469, a preeminent figure in Florence), about 1444; children: Lorenzo de Medici, the Magnificent (1449–1492, unofficial ruler of republican Florence during the Renaissance period, who was a poet, diplomatist, and celebrated patron of the arts); Giuliano (1453–1478); Bianca de Medici (who m. Guglielmo dei Pazzi); Nannina de Medici (who m. Bernardo Rucellai); Maria de Medici (who m. Lionetto de' Rossi). ❖ Contributed to the emerging prestige of the Medicis through her business acumen, her administrative skills, and her willingness to act as her husband's surrogate in negotiations and financial transactions. ❖ See also *Women in World History*.

MEDICI, Lucrezia de (b. around 1480). Tuscan noblewoman. Name variations: Lucrezia Salviati. Born Lucrezia Giovanni de Medici around 1480; dau. of Lorenzo de Medici (1449–1492), the Magnificent, and Clarice de Medici (c. 1453–1487); sister of Pope Leo X (1475–1521); m. Jacopo also known as Giacomo Salviati; children: Giovanni Salviati, cardinal; Maria Salviati (1499–1543, who m. Giovanni delle Bande Nere); Elena Salviati (who m. Jacopo V Appiani). ❖ See also *Women in World History*.

MEDICI, Lucrezia de (c. 1544–1561). Duchess of Ferrara. Born c. 1544; died in 1561; dau. of Cosimo I de Medici (1519–1574), grand duke of Tuscany, and Eleonora de Medici (1522–1562); 1st wife of Alfonso II (1533–1597), 5th duke of Ferrara and Modena (r. 1559–1597). Alfonso II's 2nd wife was Margherita Gonzaga (1564–1618). ❖ Though it was rumored that she was poisoned by husband because of infidelity, the story's origins have now been attributed to enemies of the house of Ferrara.

MEDICI, Luisa de (fl. 15th c.). Florentine noblewoman. Died before age 12; dau. of Lorenzo de Medici, the Magnificent (1449–1492), and Clarice de Medici (c. 1453–1487).

MEDICI, Maddalena de (d. 1519). Florentine noblewoman. Name variations: Maddalena Cybo, Cibo, or Cibò. Died at the villa of Careggi in 1519; eldest dau. of Lorenzo de Medici (1449–1492), the Magnificent, and Clarice de Medici (c. 1453–1487); m. Franceschetto or Francesco

Cybo (son of Pope Innocent VIII), on Jan 20, 1488; children: Innocenzo Cibò, cardinal; Lorenzo Cibò (who m. Ricciarda Malaspina, princess of Massa); Caterina Cibò, duchess of Camerino. ❖ See also *Women in World History*.

MEDICI, Maddalena de (1600–1633). Tuscan noblewoman and nun. Born in 1600; died in 1633; dau. of Christine of Lorraine (c. 1571–1637) and Ferdinand I de Medici (1549–1609), grand duke of Tuscany (r. 1587–1609); twin sister of Lorenzo de Medici (d. 1648). ❖ At 20, a few months after her brother Cosimo II's death in 1620, became a nun at the convent of the Crocetta.

MEDICI, Madeleine de (1501–1519). *See Madeleine de la Tour d'Auvergne.*

MEDICI, Margaret de.
See Margaret of Parma (1522–1586).
See Margaret of Parma (b. 1612).

MEDICI, Margherita de.
See Margaret of Parma (1522–1586).
See Margaret of Parma (b. 1612).

MEDICI, Marguerite Louise de (c. 1645–1721). *See Marguerite Louise of Orleans.*

MEDICI, Maria Cristina de (1610–1632). Tuscan noblewoman. Born in 1610; died at the villa of Poggio Imperiale at age 22 in August 1632; dau. of Maria Magdalena of Austria (1589–1631) and Cosimo II de Medici (1590–1620), duke of Tuscany (r. 1609–1620); twin sister of Ferdinand II (1610–1670), grand duke of Tuscany (r. 1620–1670).

MEDICI, Maria de (fl. late 1400s). Florentine noblewoman. Name variations: Maria de Rossi. Flourished in late 1400s; dau. of Piero "il Gottoso" de Medici also known as Piero or Pietro de Medici (1416–1469), a preeminent figure in Florence, and Lucrezia de Medici (1425–1482); sister of Lorenzo de Medici, the Magnificent (1449–1492), unofficial ruler of republican Florence during the Renaissance period; m. Lionetto de Rossi.

MEDICI, Maria de.
See Salviati, Maria (1499–1543).
See Medici, Marie de (c. 1573–1642).

MEDICI, Maria Magdalena de (1589–1631). *See Maria Magdalena of Austria.*

MEDICI, Maria Soderini de (fl. 16th c.). Tuscan noblewoman. Name variations: Maria Soderini. M. Pier Francesco de Medici the Younger (d. 1525); children: Lorenzino de Medici (1514–1548, who assassinated Alessandro de Medici in 1537); Laudomia de Medici (who m. Piero Strozzi); Maddalena de Medici (who m. Roberto Strozzi); and Giuliano, bishop of Beziers.

MEDICI, Marie de (c. 1573–1642). Queen of France. Name variations: (French with the "s" and accent) Marie de Médicis; (Italian without the "s" and accent) Maria de Medici or Marie de' Medici; also Mary de Medici. Pronunciation: MEH-de-chee. Born April 26, 1573 or 1574 in Florence, Italy; died July 3, 1642, in poverty and exile, in Cologne, Germany; youngest child of Francis or Francesco I de Medici (1541–1587), grand duke of Tuscany (r. 1574–1587), a scholar and patron of the arts, and Joanna of Austria (1546–1578); m. Henri also known as Henry IV the Great (1553–1610), king of France (r. 1589–1610) and Navarre, Oct 5, 1600; children: Louis XIII (1601–1643), king of France (r. 1610–1643); Elizabeth Valois (1602–1644, who m. Philip IV, king of Spain); Christine of France (1606–1663); Philippe (b. 1607); Gaston d'Orléans (1608–1660), duke of Orléans; Henrietta Maria (1609–1669, who m. Charles I, king of England). ❖ Member of the powerful Florentine family who became a queen of France, hungered for power in the tradition of her blood, and achieved it but only fleetingly, more for lack of wisdom than of spirit; married by proxy to King Henry IV of France and set out from Italy to meet new husband (1600); became regent to 9-year-old son, Louis XIII, the day after Henry's assassination (1610); given genuine responsibility, proved reasonable at making decisions and continuing Henry's policies, even when they were contrary to her own convictions; after murder and execution of her court favorites, was placed under house arrest at Blois (1617–19); escaped from Blois and was reconciled to the king by Cardinal Richelieu (1619); exiled again, after another confrontation with Cardinal Richelieu, followed by another escape (1630); exiled finally to Cologne, where her remains were held for a year after her death until her debts were paid. ❖ See also Louis Battifol,

Marie de Medicis and the French Court (Books for Library Press, 1970); and *Women in World History*.

MEDICI, Nannina de (fl. 15th c.). Florentine noblewoman. Name variations: Nannina Rucellai. Dau. of Piero de Medici (1416–1469) and Lucrezia de Medici (1425–1482); sister of Lorenzo de Medici, the Magnificent (1449–1492); m. Bernardo Rucellai.

MEDICI, Philiberta de (c. 1498–1524). See Philiberta of Savoy.

MEDICI, Piccarda de (fl. 15th c.). Matriarch of the House of Medici. Name variations: Piccarda Bueri. Buried next to her husband in the "Old Sacristy" in the church of San Lorenzo; m. Giovanni de Medici, known as Giovanni di Bicci de Medici (1360–1429 or 1428); children: Cosimo the Elder de Medici (1389–1464), ruler of Florence (r. 1434–1464); Lorenzo de Medici (1395–1440).

MEDICI, Semiramide de (fl. 1480s). Tuscan noblewoman. Name variations: Semiramide Appiani or Appiano. Flourished in 1480s; m. Lorenzo the Younger also known as Lorenzo "Popolano" de Medici (1463–1507); children: 3 sons, including eldest son Pier Francesco "the Younger" de Medici (died 1525, who m. Maria Soderini de Medici); and 2 daughters (names unknown).

MEDICI, Violante Beatrice de (d. 1731). Tuscan noblewoman and governor of Siena. Name variations: Violante of Bavaria; Violante Beatrice of Bavaria; Yolande. Died in 1731; m. Ferdinand de Medici (1663–1713, son of Cosimo III, grand duke of Tuscany, and Marguerite Louise of Orleans), in 1688; no children. ❖ Following husband's death, retired to Siena and was made governor there; when Gian Gastone de Medici became grand duke of Tuscany (1723), was installed as the social center of life at court and became extremely influential. For her patronage of the arts and the poor, Pope Benedict XIII bestowed on her the Golden Rose. ❖ See also *Women in World History*.

MEDICI, Virginia de (b. 1573?). See Este, Virginia d'.

MEDICI, Vittoria de (d. 1694). Grand duchess of Tuscany. Name variations: Vittoria della Rovere. Born Vittoria della Rovere; died in 1694; dau. of Claudia de Medici (1604–1648) and Federigo Ubaldo also known as Federigo della Rovere, hereditary prince of Urbino; married Ferdinand II de Medici (1610–1670), grand duke of Tuscany (r. 1620–1670), on April 6, 1637; children: Cosimino and Innominata (died young); Cosimo III de Medici (1642–1723), grand duke of Tuscany (r. 1670–1723); Francesco Maria de Medici (1660–1711, a cardinal until 1709, who m. Eleonora de Medici [fl. 1690]). ❖ The last descendant of the noble Rovere family, hereditary rulers of Urbino, inherited the duchy of Urbino on father's death and was raised to be the grand duchess of Tuscany as well; following husband's death (1670), played an important role in son Cosimo's administration. ❖ See also *Women in World History*.

MEDICINE, Beatrice A. (1923—). Native-American anthropologist, teacher, and author. Born on the Standing Rock Reservation, Wakpala, South Dakota, Aug 1, 1923 (some sources cite 1924); South Dakota State University, BS; Michigan State University, MA; University of Wisconsin-Madison, PhD; married and div.; children: 1 son, Clarence. ❖ A member of the Lakota (Sioux) Sihasapa tribe, took up the study of anthropology to better understand her Native American heritage; focused on the development of Native American family life and the role of women in Native American culture and society; taught at many leading centers of Native American studies, including San Francisco State College and the University of Calgary in Alberta, Canada. Was honored as the Sacred Pipe Woman of the revived Lakota Sun Dance (1977); received the Distinguished Service Award of American Anthropological Association (1991).

MEDICIS. *French variant of Medici.*

MEDINA, Patricia (1919—). English-born actress. Born July 19, 1919, in Liverpool, England; m. Richard Greene (actor), 1941 (div. 1952); m. Joseph Cotten, 1960 (died 1994). ❖ Made film debut in England in *Dinner at the Ritz* (1937); made US film debut in *The Secret Heart* (1946); other films include *The Foxes of Harrow, The Three Musketeers, The Fighting O'Flynn, Francis, Abbott and Costello in the Foreign Legion, The Lady and the Bandit, Valentino, Aladdin and His Lamp, Lady in the Iron Mask, Botany Bay, Sangaree, Phantom of the Rue Morgue, Mr. Arkadin, The Beast of Hollow Mountain, The Killing of Sister George* and *Timber Tramps*.

MEDINA SIDONIA, duchess of (1936—). See Alvarez de Toledo, Luisa Isabel.

MEDIO, Dolores (1914–1996). Spanish writer of social-realist fiction. Name variations: Dolores Medio Estrada. Born Dec 24, 1914, in Oviedo, Spain; died 1996 in Oviedo; dau. of Ramón Medio-Tuya y Rivero and Maria Teresa Estrada y Pastor. ❖ Just before Spanish Civil War began (1936), secured a teaching position, but conservatives caused her dismissal within a few months; published "Niña" (1945), which won a short-story prize; wrote for *El Domingo* (1945–65), a newspaper aimed at the lower class; also wrote novels, short stories, poetry and literary criticism; received the Nadal Prize, one of Spain's most prestigious literary awards, for *Nosotros los Rivero* (*We Riveros*, 1953); the following year, published *Compás de espera* (*Pause*) and *Mañana* (*Tomorrow*), then a biography of Isabella II (1966); her fiction was traditional narrative, which realistically examined the condition of Spain's common people; drew heavily on her own experiences in such works as *Diario de una maestra* (*Diary of a School Teacher*, 1961). ❖ See also Margaret E.W. Jones, *Dolores Medio* (Twayne, 1974); and *Women in World History*.

MEDVECZKY, Krisztina (1958—). Hungarian gymnast. Born April 14, 1958, in Hungary. ❖ At Munich Olympics, won a bronze medal in team all-around (1972).

MEE, Margaret (1909–1988). English botanical artist and traveler. Name variations: Margaret Ursula Mee. Born Margaret Ursula Brown, May 1909, in Chesham, Buckinghamshire, England; died Nov 30, 1988; attended Camberwell School of Art; m. Greville Mee (commercial artist). ❖ At 57, started career as a botanical artist; traveled extensively in the Brazilian Amazonia, collecting new species and making paintings of remarkable technical accuracy and delicate beauty; her renderings, executed in gouache, are the only verification left of some species of the area, which have since become extinct; was an outspoken crusader against destruction of the Amazonia.

MEECH, Matilda (c. 1825–1907). New Zealand shopkeeper. Name variations: Matilda Fisher, Matilda Sancto. Born Matilda Fisher, c. 1825 (baptized, June 12, 1825), in Kent, England; died Aug 10, 1907, at Clyde Quay, Wellington, New Zealand; dau. of James Fisher (fishmonger) and Sarah Fisher; m. John Sancto (bargeman), 1846 (died 1859); m. Henry Meech (shipwright), 1868 (died 1885); children: 6. ❖ Immigrated to New Zealand to join husband (1855); opened fruit shop and general store on Lambton Quay (1864); assisted 2nd husband in operating salt-water baths until his death, when she assumed full management of business. ❖ See also *Dictionary of New Zealand Biography* (Vol. 1).

MEEKE, Mary (d. 1816). British novelist. Name variations: Mrs. Mary Meeke; (pseudonym) Gabrielli. Born in Staffordshire, England; died 1816 in Staffordshire; m. Reverend Francis Meeke (cleric, died 1801). ❖ Writer of Gothic novels including *Count St. Blancard, or the Prejudiced Judge* (1795), *Anecdotes of the Altamont Family* (1800), *The Old Wife and the Young Husband* (1804), *Laughton Priory* (1809), *The Spanish Campaign; or, The Jew* (1815), and *The Birthday Present, of Pleasing Tales of Amusement and Instruction* (1830); translations include *Lobenstein Village* by Augustus La Fontaine (1804), *Elizabeth, or the Exiles of Siberia* by Sophie Cottin (1814), and *Solyman and Almena* by John Langhorne (1814).

MEENA (1956–1987). Afghan women's-rights activist and resistance leader. Born Feb 27, 1956, in Kabul, Afghanistan; assassinated Feb 4, 1987, in Quetta, Pakistan; attended a French school; married a doctor (killed, 1986); children: daughter and twins. ❖ Social activist, was dedicated to organizing and educating women; founded the Revolutionary Afghan Women's Association (RAWA, 1977) to work for democracy and social justice; began campaigning against Russian forces and their fundamentalist puppet regime (1979); launched bilingual magazine *Payam-e-Zan* (Women's Message, 1981); established Watan Schools for refugee children and a center in Pakistan where women could support themselves by selling handicrafts; represented the Afghan resistance movement at the French Socialist Party Congress; after husband was killed by fundamentalists (1986), fled to Pakistan where she continued RAWA's work in refugee camps; abducted and assassinated by agents of KHAD (Afghanistan branch of KGB), with help from fundamentalists. Her organization, RAWA, later took a stand against the Taliban's abuse of women. ❖ See also Melody Ermachild Chavis, *Meena: Heroine of Afghanistan* (2003).

MEER, Fatima (1928—). Indian South African anti-apartheid activist. Born Aug 28, 1928, in Durban, South Africa; dau. of Moosa Meer, editor of *Indian Views*, a weekly newspaper aimed at Gujarti-speaking Muslim communities; University of Natal, MA in sociology; m. Ismail Meer (1918–2000, South African Indian political activist); children, including Rashid Meer. ❖ Noted for dedication to non-violence, vehement defense of human rights, and commitment to racial integration and harmony, taught sociology at University of Natal (from 1959); participated in Defiance Campaign and helped to found Federation of South African Women (FEDSAW); was banned (1952–54); banned once more after election to presidency of FEDSAW and for trying to organize a rally for Steve Biko (1975); survived an assassination attempt (1976); her son Rashid was forced into exile (1976–86); was detained under Internal Security Act (1982) and prevented from traveling and publishing after release; wrote and produced dance drama *Ahimsa Ubuntu* (1995); founded and directed Institute for Black Research at University of Natal; wrote more than 40 books, including *Portrait of Indian South Africans, Apprenticeship of a Mahatma*, and *Higher Than Hope*. ❖ See also Ismail Meer, *A Fortunate Man–Ismail Meer* (2002).

MEES, Helga (1937—). West German fencer. Born July 12, 1937, in Germany. ❖ At Tokyo Olympics, won a bronze medal in team foil and a silver medal in indiv. foil (1964).

MEEUWSEN, Terry (1949—). Miss America and singer. Name variations: Terry Meeuwsen Friedrich. Born Terry Anne Meeuwsen, Mar 2, 1949, in DePere, Wisconsin; attended St. Norbert College; m. Andrew Friedrich; children: 7. ❖ Featured singer with the New Christy Minstrels; named Miss America (1973), representing Wisconsin; began co-hosting "The 700 Club" (1993). Author of devotional books.

MEFTAHEDDINOVA, Zemfira (1963—). *See Meftakhetdinova, Zemfira.*

MEFTAHEGYINOVA, Zemfira (1963—). *See Meftakhetdinova, Zemfira.*

MEFTAKHETDINOVA, Zemfira (1963—). Azerbaijani skeet shooter. Name variations: Meftakhedinova, Meftaheddinova, Meftahegyinova. Born 1963 in Baku, Azerbaijan; University at Azerbaijan, MA; divorced. ❖ Won a gold medal at Sydney Olympics (2000), the 1st year that women's skeet shooting was held as a separate event; won a European and World championship (2001); won a bronze medal at Athens Olympics (2004). Received Azerbaijan's highest civic award, the Shohrat (Fame) Order.

MEG. *Variant of Margaret.*

MEGALOSTRATA (fl. 6 BCE). Greek poet. Born in Greece. ❖ Spartan poet, was cited by lyric poet Alcman (7th c. BCE).

MEGYERINE-PACSAI, Marta (1952—). Hungarian handball player. Name variations: Marta Pacsai. Born Aug 29, 1952, in Hungary. ❖ At Montreal Olympics, won a bronze medal in team competition (1976).

MEHETABEL. Biblical woman. The dau. of Matred and the wife of Hadar (or Hadad), one of the kings of Edom.

MEHL, Gabriele (1967—). German rower. Born Feb 25, 1967, in Germany. ❖ At Barcelona Olympics, won a bronze medal in coxless fours (1992).

MEHLIG, Anna (1846–1928). German pianist. Born in Stuttgart, Germany, July 11, 1846; died in Berlin, July 26, 1928; a pupil of Liszt. ❖ One of Franz Liszt's many students, helped to preserve his style; enjoyed a successful career in Europe and America. ❖ See also *Women in World History*.

MEHR-UN-NISA, Mehrunnisa, or Mehrunnissa (1577–1645). *See Nur Jahan.*

MEHTA, Hansa (1897–1995). Indian legislator and activist for women's rights. Born Hansa Mehta, July 3, 1897, in Surat, Bombay, India; died 1995; dau. of Sir Manubhai Mehta (prime minister of Baroda and Bikaner) and Harshad Kumari M. Desai; granddau. of Ras Bahadur Nandshankar Mehta (novelist); Baroda College, degree in philosophy, 1918; attended London School of Economics; m. Dr. Jivraj Narayan Mehta (chief medical officer for state of Baroda), 1924; children: daughter Anjani and son Harshraj. ❖ Educator, justice of the peace, legislator and nonviolent revolutionary, was a member of the 1st session of the All-India Women's Conference (1927); for participating in Gandhi's civil disobedience campaign, spent 3 months in prison (1930) and 5 months (1941); elected to Bombay Legislative Council (1937, 1940), serving as parliamentary secretary to the Minister of Education and Health (1937–39); was Indian delegate to United Nations Commission on the Status of Women (1946); also served on UN Commission on Human Rights (1946), for which she presented a draft resolution for an international Bill of Rights (1947).

MEI (d. 1875). Queen of Cambodia. Reigned from 1835 to 1847; died 1875; dau. of Ang Chan, king of Cambodia (r. 1797–1835). ❖ On father's death (1835), inherited the Cambodian throne, but Cambodia was then controlled by Vietnam and she had little power; ruled for 12 years before she was deposed.

MEI-FIGNER, Medea (1859–1952). Italian soprano. Born Zoraide Amedea in Florence, Italy, in 1859; died July 8, 1952, in Paris; m. Nikolay Figner (tenor), 1889 (div. 1904). ❖ Sang in Italy, Spain, Russia and South America; performed at St. Petersburg Opera (1887–1912), creating 4 important Russian roles—Lisa in Tchaikovsky's *The Queen of Spades* and title role in his *Iolanta*, and Mascha in Napravnik's *Dubrovsky* and Francesca in his *Francesca da Rimini*; remained in Russia and taught after retirement (1923); best remembered for her close association with Tchaikovsky; eventually moved to Paris. ❖ See also *Women in World History*.

MEIGHEN, Isabel J. (1883–1985). Canadian first lady. Born Isabel J. Cox, April 18, 1883, in Granby, Quebec, Canada; died Sept 6, 1985; m. Arthur Meighen (prime minister of Canada, 1920–21, 1926–26), June 1, 1904 (div. Aug 5, 1960); children: Theodore Roosevelt (b. 1905), Max (b. 1908), Lillian (b. 1910).

MEIGNAN, Laetitia (1960—). French judoka. Born June 25, 1960, in France. ❖ At Barcelona Olympics, won a bronze medal in half-heavyweight 72 kg (1992).

MEIGS, Cornelia Lynde (1884–1973). American children's writer and educator. Name variations: (pseudonym) Adair Aldon. Born Dec 6, 1884, in Rock Island, Illinois; died Sept 10, 1973, in Hartford Co., Maryland; dau. of Montgomery Meigs and Grace Lynde Meigs; Bryn Mawr College, degree in English, 1908; never married; no children. ❖ Prolific writer, published a collection of short stories (1915) as *The Kingdom of the Winding Road*; over next 2 decades, produced 17 more juvenile novels and short-story collections, several of which she wrote under pseudonym Adair Aldon; also wrote many plays for young people, the 1st of which, *The Steadfast Princess*, won the Drama League prize (1915); taught English at Bryn Mawr (1932–50); edited and contributed to *A Critical History of Children's Literature*, a widely acclaimed landmark survey of English juvenile literature from premodern times (1953). Received Newbery Medal (1934) for *Invincible Louisa: The Story of the Author of Little Women*. ❖ See also *Women in World History*.

MEIJER, Elien (1970—). Dutch rower. Born Jan 25, 1970, in Utrecht, Netherlands. ❖ Won a gold medal at World championships (1994); won a silver medal for coxed eight at Sydney Olympics (2000).

MEIJI EMPRESS (1850–1914). *See Haruko.*

MEILI, Launi (1963—). American shooter. Born June 1963 in Washington; attended Eastern Washington University. ❖ At Barcelona Olympics, won a gold medal in smallbore rifle 3 positions (1992); won a bronze medal at World championships (1990); set 3 World shooting records and more than 100 national records.

MEILING, Soong (b. 1898). *See Song Meiling.*

MEINERT, Maren (1973—). German soccer player. Born Aug 5, 1973, in Duisburg, Germany; m. Andreas Guido, 1998. ❖ Forward; won a team bronze medal at Sydney Olympics (2000); won team European championship (2001); played for FCR Duisburg (1998) and Brauweiler-Pulheim (2000–01); signed with WUSA's Boston Breakers (2001). Selected a Breakers' MVP (2002).

MEINHOF, Ulrike (1934–1972). German journalist and political terrorist. Name variations: Ulrike Röhl, Rohl, or Roehl. Pronunciation: OOL-re-ka MINE-hawf. Born Ulrike Marie Meinhof, Oct 7, 1934, in Oldenburg, Germany; died May 8 or 9, 1976, while imprisoned in Stammheim, Stuttgart, the official cause of death given as suicide; dau. of Walter Meinhof (art historian) and Ingeborg Meinhof (teacher); MA in educational science, psychology and sociology; m. Klaus Rainer Röhl, 1961; children: (twin daughters) Bettina and Regine Röhl (b. 1963). ❖ Wrote on social issues but is mainly remembered as a leader of Germany's notorious Red Army Faction (RAF) or Baader-Meinhof Gang; was engaged in the anti-bomb movement (1958–59);

became journalist for leftist weekly magazine, *konkret* (1959), then chief editor (1960–64); published other articles in various media branches focusing on topics concerning fringe groups (to 1969); lectured at Free University of Berlin (1970); participated in liberation of Andreas Baader (May 1970); as Germany's most wanted female terrorist, was a fugitive and leader of the Red Army Fraction (RAF) until arrest (1972); was tried for aiding Baader's escape, found guilty, and sentenced to 8 years in prison; transferred to Stammheim prison to await the "Baader-Meinhof-Prozesse" (1975); died, allegedly by suicide (May 1976). ❖ See also *Women in World History*.

MEIR, Golda (1898–1978). Israeli politician. Name variations: Golda Mabovitch (in Russia); Goldie Mabovitch (in America); Goldie Meyerson or Myerson (after marriage); Golda Meir (from 1956). Pronunciation: May-EAR. Born Goldie Mabovitch, May 3, 1898, in Kiev, Russia; died in Jerusalem, Dec 8, 1978; dau. of Moshe Yitzhak Mabovitch (carpenter) and Bluma Mabovitch; attended schools in Milwaukee, Wisconsin, and Denver, Colorado; m. Morris Myerson or Meyerson, Dec 24, 1917 (sep. 1940); children: Menachem Meyerson also known as Menachem Meir (b. 1924); Sarah Meyerson Rehabi (b. 1926). ❖ Prime minister of Israel, the only woman to hold that position, who was a lifelong worker for the creation and preservation of a secular, socialist Israel; moved from Kiev, Russia, to Milwaukee, Wisconsin (1906); was a Zionist and labor activist and organizer in America, then Palestine; arrived in Tel Aviv (1921); elected to the Woman's Labor Council of Histadruth (trade union for Jewish workers in Palestine), and served as secretary of the Moetzet Hapoalot (Women's Labor Council, 1928); elected a delegate of the Ahdut Haavoda faction to the World Zionist Congress (1929); was chosen secretary of Histadruth's executive committee (1934); served as a Mapai (Israeli Workers Party) delegate to the international congresses (1939); named head of Histadruth's political department (1940); became president of the political bureau of the Jewish Agency (1946); signed the Proclamation declaring the creation of Israel, the new Jewish state (May 14, 1948); appointed Israel's minister to Moscow (1948); elected to 1st Knesset (Parliament) as a candidate of the Mapai Party, and appointed Israel's minister of labor and development (1949); served as ambassador to Soviet Union for Israel (1948–49); served as minister of labor (1949–56); served as chair of the Israeli delegation to UN General Assembly (1953–66); served as foreign minister (1956–65), as secretary general of the Mapai Party (1966–69), and as prime minister of Israel (1969–74). ❖ See also autobiography *My Life* (Putnam, 1975); Ralph G. Martin, *Golda: Golda Meir, the Romantic Years* (Scribner, 1988); Menachem Meir, *My Mother, Golda Meir* (Arbor House, 1983); Robert Slater, *Golda: The Uncrowned Queen of Israel* (Jonathan David, 1981); tv miniseries, "A Woman Called Golda," starring Ingrid Bergman (1982); and *Women in World History*.

MEIRELES, Cecília (1901–1964). Brazilian poet, writer and teacher. Name variations: Cecilia Meireles; Cecília Beneviles Meireles. Born in 1901 in Rio de Janeiro; died Nov 9, 1964, in Rio de Janeiro; m. Fernando Correia Dias (painter), 1921 (died 1935 or 1936); m. Heitor Grillo; children: (1st m.) 3 daughters. ❖ Considered Brazil's greatest Portuguese-language woman poet, trained to become a teacher but quickly branched out into journalism, contributing to magazines *Arvore Nova* and *Terra do Sol* (1919–27), and to the spiritualist periodical *Festa* (1927); published 1st book, *Espectros* (Ghosts, 1919); most popular works were *Viagém* (Voyage, 1939), which was awarded the Poetry Prize from the Brazilian Academy of Letters, and *Mar Absoluto* (Absolute Sea, 1942); also wrote *Romanceiro da Inconfidência* (Poet of the Inconfidence, 1953); was instrumental in founding the 1st children's library in Brazil (1934) and was a professor at a number of universities, including University of Texas and Federal University in Rio de Janeiro. ❖ See also *Women in World History*.

MEISEL-OLDAY, Hilde (1914–1945). *See Monte, Hilda.*

MEISELAS, Susan (1948—). American photojournalist. Born 1948 in Baltimore, MD; Sarah Lawrence College, BA in anthropology, 1970; Harvard University, MEd in visual education, 1971. ❖ Renowned photojournalist, began career as assistant film editor on Frederick Wiseman documentary, *Basic Training*; spent 3 summers traveling with striptease artists for book *Carnival Strippers* (1976); became Magnum Photo agency nominee (1976), associate (1977), full member (1980) and American vice president (1987); photographed civil war in Nicaragua (1977), resulting in her book *Nicaragua* (1979), and in El Salvador (1980s); over the years, worked for *The New York Times*, *London Times*, *Time*, *Geo* and *Paris Match*, among others; began a 6-year project on a visual history of Kurdistan (1992), then published *Kurdistan: In the Shadow of History* (1997). Awarded Robert Capa Gold Medal by Overseas Press Club.

MEISER, Edith (1898–1993). American actress. Born May 9, 1898, in Detroit, Michigan; died Sept 26, 1993, in New York, NY; m. Tom McKnight (div.). ❖ Made stage debut with Jessie Bonstelle's company in Detroit (1921); made Broadway debut as Matilda Mayhew in *The New Way* (1923), followed by *Fata Morgana*, *The Guardsman*, *He*, *The Strangler Fig* (which she also adapted), *Jupiter Laughs*, *Mexican Hayride*, *Sabrina Fair*, *Happy Hunting*, *The Unsinkable Molly Brown*, and many editions of the *Garrick Gaieties*; wrote the play *The Wooden O* and the novel *Death Catches Up with Mr. Kluck* (filmed as *Death on the Air*).

MEISHO (1624–1696). Japanese empress. Name variations: Meishō; Myojo-tenno; Myosho. Born in 1624 (some sources cite 1623); died 1696; dau. of Emperor Go-Mizunoo (also seen as Go-Mizuno-o) and Tokugawa Kazuko; had 1 sister; had 3 emperor brothers, Go-Komyo (r. 1643–1654, d. 1654), Gosai or Go-Sai (r. 1655–1663, d. 1685), and Reigen (r. 1663–1687, d. 1732); never married. ❖ The 109th sovereign of the Empire of Japan according to the traditional count, came to the throne as a child at the time of father's abdication (1629) and reigned until 1643. ❖ See also *Women in World History*.

MEISSNER, Katrin (1973—). East German swimmer. Born Jan 17, 1963, in East Germany. ❖ At Seoul Olympics, won a bronze medal in the 50-meter freestyle and gold medals in the 4x100-meter medley relay and the 4x100-meter freestyle relay (1988).

MEISSNER, Renate (1950—). *See Stecher, Renate.*

MEISSNITZER, Alexandra (1973—). Austrian Alpine skier. Born June 18, 1973, in Abtenau, Austria. ❖ Won 8 World Cup races to capture the slalom, giant slalom and overall World Cup titles (1998–99); at World championships, won gold medals in slalom, giant slalom and overall (1999) and a silver medal in downhill (2003); won a silver medal for giant slalom and a bronze medal for super-G at Nagano Olympics (1998); placed 4th in giant slalom and super-G at Salt Lake City Olympics (2002), won a bronze medal for super-G at Torino Olympics (2006).

MEISTER, Phyllis (1942—). *See Allbut, Phyllis.*

MEITNER, Lise (1878–1968). Austrian theoretical physicist. Pronunciation: MITE-ner. Born Lise Meitner in Vienna, Austria, Nov 7, 1878; died in Cambridge, England, Oct 27, 1968; dau. of Hedwig (Skovran) Meitner and Philip Meitner; sister of Walter Meitner who married the photographer Lotte Meitner-Graf; attended University of Vienna, 1902–06, awarded PhD; never married; no children. ❖ The 1st woman in Germany to hold the title professor, who made key contributions to the discovery of nuclear fission, enrolled in Max Planck's lectures, University of Berlin (1907); met Otto Hahn (Sept 28, 1907) and began collaboration; with Hahn, discovered thorium c (1908); joined Kaiser Wilhelm Institute for Chemistry (1912); became research assistant to Max Planck (1912); was X-ray technician in Austro-Hungarian Army (1914–18); appointed head of Department of Physics, Kaiser Wilhelm Institute for Chemistry (1918); with Hahn, discovered protactinium (1918); became a privatdozent, University of Berlin (1919); appointed Professor Extraordinary, University of Berlin (1926); was one of the 1st to report that positrons were formed by gamma rays (1933); worked with Hahn to confirm Fermi's thesis (1934); fled Nazi Germany (1938); joined Nobel Institute, Stockholm, Sweden (1938); identified nuclear fission (1939); refused to participate in the Manhattan Project (1942); was a visiting professor, Catholic University, Washington, DC (1946); retired from the Nobel Institute (1947); joined Royal Institute of Technology, Stockholm (1947); retired to Cambridge, England (1966). Received Leibnitz Medal of Berlin Academy of Sciences (1924), Lieber Prize of the Austrian Academy of Sciences (1925), City of Vienna's Prize in Science (1947), Max Planck Medal (1949), and Enrico Fermi Award (1966). ❖ See also Deborah Crawford, *Lise Meitner: Atomic Pioneer* (Crown, 1969); Ruth Lewin Sime, *Lise Meitner: A Life in Physics* (U. of California Press, 1996); and *Women in World History*.

MEKARSKA, Adèle (1839–1901). *See Mink, Paule.*

MEKEEL, Joyce (1931—). American composer, harpsichordist, pianist, anthropologist and professor. Born in New Haven, Connecticut, July 6, 1931; studied at Longy School of Music (1952–55) and with Nadia Boulanger at National Conservatory in France (1955–57); attended Yale School of Music (1957–60), where she studied harpsichord with Gustav Leonhardt and theory with David Kraehenbuehl; pursued further study at Princeton. ❖ Taught at New England Conservatory (1964–70), while also composing for Ina Hahn Dance Co.; appointed assistant professor of theory and composition at Boston University (1970), becoming involved with the university's electronic studio, which she directed; compositions include *Corridors of Dreams* (1972), *Serena* (1975) and *Alarums and Excursions* (1978). ❖ See also *Women in World History*.

MEKONS, The.
See Timms, Sally.
See Honeyman, Susie.

MEKSHILO, Eudokia. Russian cross-country skier. Name variations: Yevdoyka or Jedowkija Mekschilo. Born in USSR. ❖ Won a silver medal for 10km and a gold medal for 3x5km relay at Innsbruck Olympics (1964).

MEKSCHILO, Jedowkija. *See Mekshilo, Eudokia.*

MEKSZ, Aniko (1965—). Hungarian handball player. Born June 18, 1965, in Budapest, Hungary. ❖ Won a team bronze medal at Atlanta Olympics (1996).

MELANIA THE ELDER (c. 350–c. 410). Roman founder. Born c. 350; died around 410; granddau. of Antonius Marcellinus; grandmother of Melania the Younger; m. possibly Valerius Maximus (praetorian praefect), probably in 365; children: 3 sons, including Valerius Publicola (father of Melania the Younger). ❖ Founder of 2 of the earliest Christian religious communities, who left Rome for Egypt and Palestine, following the death of husband and 2 of her children, there to associate with the holy men and women of the monastic movement who dominated the Church of the period as priests, bishops, monks and nuns; visited both the influential See of Alexandria and the hermits of the desert, becoming fond of the theological writings of Origen; moved on to Jerusalem (late 370s), where she founded and endowed a convent for herself and a monastery in honor of Rufinus on the Mount of Olives; even as the weight of Church opinion began to swing toward the anti-Origenists, maintained her allegiance to Origen's interpretive assumptions, which eventually set her at odds with the likes of Jerome and Paula, both of whom had monastic communities of their own near Bethlehem; by about 399 with the controversy intense, returned to Rome, possibly to put forth (unsuccessfully) the case for Origen to granddaughter Melania the Younger. ❖ See also *Women in World History*.

MELANIA THE YOUNGER (c. 385–439). Roman ascetic and religious founder. Born c. 385; died in 439; dau. of Valerius Publicola (son of Melania the Elder) and Albina; m. Valerius Pinianus (son of Valerius Severus, the Roman prefect), around 399. ❖ An important patron of the early Christian Church, wed a distant relative at 14, the 17-year-old Christian Valerius Pinianus; with husband, renounced conjugal relations and began to experiment with an austere way of life, selling off vast estates in Italy and Spain; with husband and mother, went to North Africa and settled on land owned near Thagaste, the small hometown of St. Augustine, and endowed both a monastery and a convent; remained in North Africa for about 7 years, embracing more and more isolated asceticism; spent most of time in prayer, studying scripture, and copying books; fame begin to spread; with husband and mother, left Thagaste (417) to journey to the Holy Land; in Jerusalem, lived in a tiny cell constructed on the Mount of Olives, close to, but distinct from, the religious community which a generation before had been founded by Melania the Elder; when mother died (c. 430), abandoned social contact for a year, after which she founded a 2nd convent, situated on the Mount of Olives; after husband's death (c. 431), engaged in a 2nd period of mourning, this time for 4 years, after which she established a 2nd monastery, also on the Mount of Olives; set out for Constantinople, accompanied by, among others, the priest Gerontius who would write the chronicle of her life; her fame preceded her virtually everywhere she went; returned to Jerusalem and her cell on the Mount of Olives; when she died, was mourned not only by those living in her communities, but by all Christians, great as well as humble. ❖ See also *Women in World History*.

MELANIE (1947—). *See Schekeryk, Melanie.*

MELANIE B. (1975—). *See Brown, Melanie.*

MELANIE C. (1974—). *See Chisholm, Melanie.*

MELBA, Nellie (1861–1931). Australian opera singer. Name variations: Dame Nellie Melba; Helen Porter Armstrong. Born Helen Porter Mitchell, May 19, 1861, in Melbourne, Victoria, Australia; died of paratyphoid fever, Feb 23, 1931, in Sydney; studied singing with Pietro Cecchi, 1879–86, and Mathilde Maresi, 1886–87; m. Charles Armstrong, 1882 (div. 1900). ❖ First Australian prima donna, with a

voice like a nightingale, ruled Covent Garden for nearly 40 years; moved to London (1886); made opera debut as Gilda in *Rigoletto* at Théâtre Royale de la Monnaie, Brussels (1887); made Covent Garden debut as Lucia in *Lucia di Lammermoor* (1888); made 1st Australian tour (1902); co-founded Melba-Williamson Opera Co. (1911); gave Covent Garden farewell concert (1926); returned to Australia for farewell tour (1927); gave final opera performance (Aug 7, 1928); was seen frequently in such roles as Violetta in *La Traviata*, Juliette in *Roméo et Juliette*, Mimi in *La Bohème*, Marguerite in *Faust*, Ophelie in Thomas' *Hamlet*, Nedda in *Pagliacci*, Rosina in *The Barber of Seville*, and Desdemona in Verdi's *Otello*. Made Dame Commander of the British Empire (1918) and Dame Grand Cross of the British Empire (1927). ❖ See also autobiography *Melodies and Memories* (1925); John Hetherington, *Melba* (Cheshire, 1967); *Melba* (film), starring Patrice Munsel (1953); *Peach Melba: Melba's Last Farewell*, a play by Theresa Radic (Currency, 1990); and *Women in World History*.

MELBOURNE, Elizabeth (d. 1818). Viscountess Melbourne. Name variations: Lady Melbourne; Elizabeth Milbanke; Elizabeth Lamb. Born Elizabeth Milbanke; died in the spring of 1818; only dau. of Sir Ralph Milbanke, Bart., of Halnaby, in Yorkshire; m. Peniston Lamb, 1st viscount Melbourne; aunt of Anne Milbanke; children: four sons, including Peniston (1770–1805); (possibly with Lord Egremont) Henry William Lamb, 2nd viscount Melbourne (1779–1848); (possibly with George IV, king of England) George Milbanke (1784–1834); and Emily Lamb, countess of Cowper. ❖ Along with her importance in the story of Lord Byron, was one of the many mistresses of George IV, king of England. ❖ See also *Women in World History*.

MELBOURNE, Lady (1785–1828). *See Lamb, Caroline.*

MELENDEZ, Jolinda (1954—). American ballet dancer. Born Nov 17, 1954, in New York, NY. ❖ Trained at National Academy of Ballet under Thalia Mara, and at Kirov Ballet in Leningrad; joined American Ballet Theater (1972) and remained there throughout most of career performing in classical works including *Swan Lake*, *La Bayadère*, and *Giselle*; appeared in Alvin Ailey's *The River* and Frederick Ashton's *Les Patineurs*.

MELENDEZ RODRIGUEZ, Urbia. Cuban taekwondo player. Name variations: Urbia Melendez. Born in Cuba. ❖ Won a silver medal for -49kg at Sydney Olympics (2000).

MELESEND. *Variant of Melisande.*

MELIDONI, Aniopi (1977—). Greek water-polo player. Born Oct 11, 1977, in Athens, Greece. ❖ Won team silver medal at Athens Olympics (2004).

MELIEN, Lori (1972—). Canadian swimmer. Born May 11, 1972, in Calgary, Alberta, Canada; grew up in Brampton, Ontario; attended University of Calgary. ❖ At Seoul Olympics, won a bronze medal in the 4x100-meter medley relay (1988); won 11 national championships (1987–90).

MELIKOVA, Genia (c. 1930–2004). French-born ballerina and teacher. Born in France; died Mar 5, 2004, in New York, NY; trained with Lyubov Egorova, Anatole Vilzak and Igor Schwezoff. ❖ A leading ballerina with the Grand Ballet du Marquis de Cuevas (1954–62), was the 1st Western ballerina to perform with Rudolf Nureyev after his defection in 1961; also performed with London Festival Ballet and Grand Ballet Classique de France and at Radio City Music Hall and on Broadway; a noted ballet teacher, taught at Juilliard for 26 years, then at Randolph-Macon Woman's College (1996–2004).

MELINTE, Doina (1956—). Romanian runner. Born Dec 27, 1956, in Romania. ❖ At Los Angeles Olympics, won a silver medal in 1,500 meters and a gold medal in the 800 meters (1984).

MELISANDE (fl. 1100). French noblewoman. Flourished around 1100; m. Hugh of Rethel; children: Baldwin II, king of Jerusalem (r. 1118–1131).

MELISANDE (1105–1161). Queen-regnant of Jerusalem. Name variations: Melesend; Mélisande; Melissande; Melisend; Mélisende or Melisende; Melisinda, Mélisinde, or Melisinde. Born 1105 in Frankish principality of Jerusalem; died Nov 30, 1161, in Jerusalem; dau. of Baldwin II, count of Edessa, later king of Jerusalem (r. 1118–1131), and Morphia of Melitene; sister of Hodierna of Jerusalem (c. 1115–after 1162), Alice of Jerusalem (c. 1106–?), and Joveta of Jerusalem (1120–?); became 2nd wife of Count Foulques also known as Fulk V, count of

Anjou, king of Jerusalem (r. 1131–1143), June 2, 1129 (died 1143); children: Baldwin III (1130–1162), king of Jerusalem (r. 1143–1162); Amalric I (1136–1174), king of Jerusalem (r. 1162–1174). ❖ Queen-regnant and co-ruler of the principality of Jerusalem, was named heiress to the throne of Jerusalem (1128); married (1129); succeeded Baldwin II (1131), co-ruling with husband who, for next 5 years, strove to disempower her and retain all authority for himself; with the rebellion of Hugh of Le Puiset (1134), became a true co-ruler, as her father had planned, rather than as a consort only; revealed a talent for leadership and a clear understanding of importance of patronage—making gifts of land and title to her supporters in reward for loyalty (1136–43); also acted on behalf of her 3 sisters; established convent of Bethany (1138); widowed and was crowned as co-ruler with 13-year-old son (1143); when Christian-held city of Edessa fell to a besieging Muslim army (1144), sought help from the Christian kingdoms of Europe, resulting in 2nd crusade (1148) which was a complete fiasco; endured rebellion of son Baldwin III and division of kingdom (1152); reconciled and co-ruled (1153–1160); suffered stroke (1160). ❖ See also *Women in World History*.

MELISANDE (fl. 1200s). Princess of Antioch. Name variations: Melisinda. Fl. in 1200s; dau. of Isabella I of Jerusalem (d. 1205) and Aimery de Lusignan (brother of Guy de Lusignan) also known as Amalric II, king of Jerusalem (r. 1197–1205), king of Cyprus; m. Bohemund or Bohemund IV the One Eyed, prince of Antioch (r. 1201–1216, 1219–1233); children: Mary of Antioch (d. 1277). ❖ Bohemund IV also fathered Bohemund V and Henry of Antioch with other wives.

MÉLISENDE or MELISENDE. *Variant of Melisande.*

MÉLISINDA or MELISINDE. *Variant of Melisande.*

MELISSA (fl. around 3 BCE). Greek philosopher. Fl. in Greece between 500 and 100 BCE. ❖ Credited with being Pythagorean philosopher, may have come from Athens. Her letter to another woman, Clearete, is extant.

MELISSANTHI (c. 1907–c. 1991). Greek poet. Name variations: Eve Chougia; Hebe Chougia; Ivi Chougia; Eve Koúyia or Kouyia; Hebe Koúyia; Ivi Koúyia; Ivi Skandalakes; Ivi Skandhalaki; Ivi Koughia-Skandalaki; Skandalákis. Born Ivi Koughia (also seen as Kouyia) in Athens, Greece, April 7, 1907 (some sources cite 1910); died in Athens, Nov 9, 1991 (some sources cite 1990); m. Ioánnis (Giannes) Skandalákis (lawyer and politician from Lakonia who also authored a number of philosophical works), 1932. ❖ An essentially lyrical poet, published 1st collection, *Insect Voices* (1930), followed by *Prophecies* (1931), which established her as the 1st Greek woman poet to explore in modern terms some of the metaphysical dimensions of human existence; published 15 books of verse, a book of criticism, 2 books of translations of foreign poets (Pierre Garnier and Emily Dickinson), and 2 children's books (1930–86); also published translations of many other foreign authors including Claudel, Péguy, and Verlaine from the French, Rainer Maria Rilke and Nelly Sachs from the German, and Durrell, Wilde, Yeats, and Eliot (Mary Anne Evans) from the English; received the Athens Academy of Arts and Sciences Award for Poetry for *Return of the Prodigal* (1936); in *Itinerary* (1986), lamented the loss of a sense of the sacred in the modern world, which she saw as destroyed by the march of utilitarian pragmatism. Won numerous prizes, including Kostis Palamas Award, National Poetry Award, and Gold Cross of the Order of Deeds of Merit. ❖ See also *Women in World History*.

MELITA or MELITTA. *Variant of Melissa or Melusine.*

MELKI, Colette Anna (1931–1966). *See Grégoire, Colette Anna.*

MELL, Marisa (1939–1992). Austrian-born actress. Born Marlies Theres Moitzi, Feb 24, 1939, in Graz, Austria; died May 16, 1992, in Vienna, Austria; m. Pier Luigi Torri. ❖ Appeared in the ill-fated *Mata Hari* which closed before reaching Broadway (1967); made over 60 films, including *Masquerade, French Dressing, What's New Pussycat, Casanova '70, Diabolik, Casanova & Co., Anyone Can Play, Danger: Diabolik* and *Mahogany.*

MELLANBY, Helen (1911–2001). Scottish-Canadian zoologist and physician. Name variations: Agnes Helen Neilson Mellanby. Born Agnes Helen Neilson, June 7, 1911, in Montreal, Canada; died from pneumonia, May 26, 2001; London's University College, BS, 1931, PhD, 1937; University of Sheffield Medical School, MD, 1949; m. Dr. Kenneth Mellanby. ❖ Studied tsetse fly reproduction in Entebbe, Uganda (1935); at the Medical Research Council (MRC) in Mill Hill, London, studied the development of enamel teeth and the effects of maternal

vitamin deficiencies (1940–53); conducted clinical trials on influenza vaccines at National Institute for Medical Research during influenza outbreak of 1947; studied hypertension upon her return to clinical medicine (1953); opened a Leicester private practice; maintained lifelong connection to Scottish background and summered in a northern Scotland cottage after retirement. Writings include *Animal Life in Fresh Water: A Guide to British Fresh-water Invertebrates* (1938).

MELLANBY, May (1882–1978). English dental researcher. Name variations: May Tweedy or May Tweedy Mellanby; Lady Mellanby. Born May Tweedy, May 1, 1882, in London, England; died Mar 5, 1978; dau. of a shipowner; sister of Nora Edkins (1890–1977, physiologist who married Professor J.S. Edkins); Girton College, Cambridge, DSc, 1906; m. Sir Edward Mellanby (college lecturer), 1914 (died 1955). ❖ An expert on tooth decay and structure of teeth, spent early years in Russia; was research scholar and lecturer at University of London's Bedford College (1906–14); lectured in physiology at Chelsea and Battersea Polytechnics (1914–18); began conducting dental research (1918) for Medical Research Council (MRC) and was 1st to report (with Sir Edward Mellanby, 1918) that a fat-soluble vitamin is essential to the calcification of dental enamel; in Germany, researched the connection between the quality of bread consumed and the amount of dental decay (1934–38); lectured in Germany, Hungary, South Africa, France and US; served on MCR's Dental Disease Committee; assisted husband when he became MCR's secretary; became a Girton College honorary fellow (1958) and a University of Toronto Charles Mickle fellow (1935–36).

MELLER, Raquel (1888–1962). Spanish singer and actress. Born Francisca Marqués López, Mar 10, 1888, in Tarazona, Zaragoza, Aragon, Spain; died July 26, 1962, in Barcelona; m. Edmond Salac; m. Gomez Carillo. ❖ Made theater debut as Raquel Meller (1907) and became known as a "cuplés" (couplets) singer and music-hall entertainer; came to international prominence with such songs as "La Violetera," "Nena," "Flor de Te", "Mimosa," "Flor del Mal," and "El Relicario" (1922); appeared in NY at Empire Theater (1926) and made a triumphant tour of US and Europe, the 1st Spanish popular singer to succeed internationally; appeared in many films, including *Violettes impériales* and *Carmen.*

MELLGREN, Dagny (1978—). Norwegian soccer player. Born June 19, 1978, in Algard-Rogaland, Norway. ❖ Forward; won a team gold medal at Sydney Olympics (2000), scoring the final goal; signed with Atlanta Beat (2001).

MELLISH, Edith Mary (1861–1922). New Zealand deaconess and religious community founder. Born Mar 10, 1861, at Pailles, Moka, Mauritius; died May 25, 1922, at Christchurch, New Zealand; dau. of Edward Mellish (banker) and Ellen (Borrowes) Mellish. ❖ Assumed Anglo-Catholic parish work at St Andrew's Deaconess Community in London, and was admitted to community (1891); chosen by bishop of London to establish religious community of women in Christchurch (Community of the Sacred Name), immigrated to New Zealand (1893); established homes for unmarried women and orphaned children (early 1900s). ❖ See also *Dictionary of New Zealand Biography* (Vol. 2).

MELLON, Gwen Grant (1911–2000). American philanthropist. Born Gwen Grant, July 22, 1911, in Englewood, NJ; died Nov 29, 2000, in Miami, FL; graduate of the Shipley School and Smith College; studied topical medicine and hospital administration at Tulane University; m. John de Groot Rawson (div. 1942); m. Dr. William Larimer Mellon Jr., 1946 (died 1989); children: (1st m.) Michael and Ian Rawson and Jenifer Rawson Grant. ❖ With husband, founded and built a modern hospital that served an area with few medical facilities (1955), in Deschapelles, Haiti; learned Haitian Creole and ran the hospital until she died.

MELLON, Harriot (c. 1777–1837). English actress and duchess of St. Albans. Born c. 1777 in London, England; died in 1837; m. Thomas Coutts (a banker), 1815 (d. 1822); stepgrandmother of Angela Burdett-Coutts; m. William Aubrey de Vere, 9th duke of St. Albans, 1827. ❖ Made acting debut (1787); appeared at Drury Lane (1795–1815). ❖ See also *Women in World History*.

MELLON, Sarah Jane (1824–1909). English actress. Born Sarah Jane Woolgar in 1824; died 1909; m. Alfred Mellon (leading violinist with Royal Italian Opera in London and musical director at Adelphi and Haymarket theaters), in 1858. ❖ A versatile actress who could play comedy and tragedy, 1st appeared on stage at Plymouth (1836); began performing at the Adelphi (1843) and remained there for several years, most notably originating the part of Lemuel in Buckstone's *Flowers of the*

Forest (1847); played Florizel in *Perdita* (1856), Ophelia in *Hamlet* (1857), Catherine Duval in *The Dead Heart* (1850), Mrs. Cratchit in *A Christmas Carol* (1860), Anne Chute in *The Colleen Brown* (1860), and Mrs. O'Kelly in *The Shaughraun*; also created the part of Miss Sniffe in *A Bridal Tour* (1880); retired (1883).

MELLOR, Fleur (1936—). Australian runner. Born July 13, 1936, in NSW, Australia. ❖ Won a gold medal at the Melbourne Olympics in the 4x100-meter relay (1956).

MELMOTH, Charlotte (1749–1823). English-born actress. Born 1749 in England, probably London; died 1823 in US; when young, ran away with actor Courtney Melmoth (1749–1814, whose real name was Samuel Jackson Pratt and who later became a popular author, dramatist and bookseller); soon separated but continued to use his name. ❖ Began career in Dublin, London, and Edinburgh and enjoyed great success (1773); appeared at Covent Garden (1774) and Drury Lane (1776); came to prominence in NY as Euphrasia in *Grecian Daughter* with the American Company (1793); became well known for roles in such tragedies as *Macbeth*; acted with Chestnut Street Theatre, Philadelphia, and later opened school of English elocution in Brooklyn.

MELNIK, Faina (1945—). Ukrainian track-and-field athlete. Name variations: Faina Myelnik. Born June 1945 in the Ukraine. ❖ Won a gold medal for discus at Munich Olympics (1972) with a throw of 66.62 meters; was almost unbeatable (1971–75), setting the record 11 times, from 64.22 meters to 70.50 meters; 1st passed the 70-meter mark (August 20, 1975), in Zurich; won European championships (1971, 1974); finished 4th at Montreal Olympics (1976).

MELNIK, Olga (1974—). Russian biathlete. Born May 12, 1974, in Sovetskij, Russia. ❖ Won a silver medal for 4x7.5km relay at Nagano Olympics (1998).

MELNIKOVA, Antonina (1958—). Soviet kayaker. Born Feb 19, 1958, in USSR. ❖ At Moscow Olympics, won a bronze medal in K1 500 meters (1980).

MELNIKOVA, Elena. Russian biathlete. Born in USSR. ❖ Won a bronze medal for 3x7.5km relay at Albertville Olympics (1992).

MELNOTTE, Violet (1856–1935). English actress and theatrical manager. Name variations: Violet Melnotte-Wyatt; Violet Wyatt. Born Emma Solomon, May 2, 1856, in Birmingham, England; died Sept 17, 1935, in London; m. Frank Wyatt (actor, died 1926). ❖ Made stage debut in a pantomime in Hull (mid-1870s) and London debut as Fezz in *Bluebeard* (1876); performed regularly in comic opera and pantomime (1877–84); went into management, running the Avenue Theatre (1885), Comedy Theatre (1885–86) and Toole's Theatre, and produced plays at the Royalty; with husband, built and was the 1st proprietor of the Duke of York's Theatre, St. Martin's Lane, when it was known as the Trafalgar Square Theatre (1892–95), retaining ownership until her death; also owned the Amber Ale Brewery.

MELONEY, Marie (1878–1943). American journalist and editor. Name variations: Mrs. William Brown Meloney; Marie Mattingly; Missie. Born Marie Mattingly in Bardstown, Kentucky, Dec 8, 1878; died in Pawling, New York, June 23, 1943; dau. of Cyprian Peter Mattingly (physician) and Sarah Irwin Mattingly (1852–1934); educated privately by mother who was editor of *Kentucky Magazine* and taught at Washington College for Girls; m. William Brown Meloney (editor on New York *Sun*), June 1904. ❖ Leading American journalist, joined the staff of *Washington Post* as a reporter (1895), and then Washington Bureau of the Denver *Post* (1897–99); moving to NY, worked briefly for the *World* (1900) before signing on with the *Sun* (1901–04); was named editor of *Woman's Magazine* (1914–20), associate editor of *Everybody's* (1917–20), and editor of the *Delineator* (1921–26); became editor of New York *Herald Tribune*'s Sunday magazine (1926); named editor of *This Week* (1935).

MELPOMENE (fl. 1896). Greek marathon runner. Flourished c. 1896. ❖ At the 1st modern Olympic Games, though women were still forbidden from participating, went to the competition dressed as a man and managed to blend in among the 24-odd male runners as the race began; when officials barred her from entering the stadium for the final lap, completed the marathon by circling the outside of the stadium, finishing in four and a half hours. ❖ See also *Women in World History*.

MELTON, Nancy (1957—). *See Lopez, Nancy.*

MELUSINA or MELUSINE. *Variant of Melisande or Melisenda.*

MELVAINE, Alma (1912–1990). *See Lee, Alma Theodora.*

MELVILL, Elizabeth (c. 1571–1600s). *See Colville, Elizabeth.*

MELVILLE, Eliza Ellen (1882–1946). New Zealand lawyer, politician, and feminist. Born May 13, 1882, at Tokatoka, Northern Wairoa, New Zealand; died July 27, 1946, in Remuera, New Zealand; dau. of Alexander Melville (boatbuilder and farmer) and Eliza Annand (Fogerty) Melville (schoolteacher and governess). ❖ Received early legal training at Devore and Cooper firm in Auckland, and studied law at night at Auckland University College; became 2nd New Zealand woman to be admitted to Bar (1906) and 2nd to establish herself in practices (1909); instrumental in reviving feminist movement in 20th century; helped to form Young Women's Christian Association (YWCA) Women's Club, Auckland (1911); held office in Auckland Women's Club, New Zealand Society for Protection of Women and Children, Women's Forum, and Unemployed Women's Emergency Committee in Auckland; helped form Civic League to encourage women to run for office (1913); was 1st woman in New Zealand to be elected to city council, Auckland (1913–46); instrumental in reviving National Council of Women of New Zealand (NCW, 1917); founded Women to Wellington movement to encourage women to run for Parliament (1944). ❖ See also *Dictionary of New Zealand Biography* (Vol. 3).

MELVILLE, Elizabeth (c. 1571–1600s). *See Colville, Elizabeth.*

MELVILLE, June (1915–1970). English actress and theatrical manager. Born Sept 17, 1915, in Worthing, Sussex, England; died Sept 15, 1970; dau. of Frederick Melville and Jane (Eyre) Melville; m. John Elton Le Mesurier Halliley (div.). ❖ Made stage debut in *Puss in Boots* in Brixton (1931), eventually becoming stage manager (1936), then proprietor and manager of the Brixton Theater (1938); was leading lady with the Repertory Company at the Palace, Watford, subsequently becoming director of that theater.

MELVILLE, Rose (1873–1946). American actress. Born Jan 30, 1873, in Terre Haute, IN; died Oct 8, 1946, in Lake George, NY; sister of Ida Melville; m. Frank Minzey. ❖ With sister Ida, formed a traveling stock company, appearing in *Zeb* as Sis Hopkins, a character so successful that it was subsequently included in a number of New York plays, 20 films, and became a vaudeville showpiece (1894–1918); films include *A Leap Year's Wooing*, *Sis the Detective* and *The Bishop of the Ozarks*.

MEMM, Simone (1967—). *See Greiner-Petter-Memm, Simone.*

MEMMEL, Chellsie (1988—). American gymnast. Born June 23, 1988, in Milwaukee, WI. ❖ Won team World championship (2003).

MEMPHIS MINNIE (1897–1973). *See Douglas, Lizzie.*

MENCHIK, Vera (1906–1944). Russian-born Czech-British chess player. Name variations: Mencik; Vera Mencikova or Věra Menčíková; Vera Menchik-Stevenson; Vera Stevenson; Mrs. R.H.S. Stevenson. Born Vera Francevna Menchiková in Moscow, Feb 16, 1906; died in Kent, England, June 27, 1944; had Czech father and British mother; sister of Olga; coached by Hungarian grandmaster Geza Maroczy; m. R.H.S. Stevenson (secretary of British Chess Federation), 1937 (died 1943). ❖ Reigned as the women's World champion from 1927 until her death in a German bombing attack on Kent during WWII; moved with parents to Great Britain (1921); won 1st World championship for women sponsored by International Federation of Chess (FIDE, 1927); went on to win World championship at Hamburg, 7 points out of 8 games (1930), Prague, 8 of 8 (1931), Folkestone, 14 of 14 (1933), Warsaw, 9 of 9 (1935), Stockholm, 14 of 14 (1937), and Buenos Aires, 18 of 19 (1939), losing only 1 game out of the total of 83 games played. Czech Republic issued a commemorative postage stamp in her honor (1996). ❖ See also *Women in World History*.

MENCHÚ, Rigoberta (1959—). Mayan indigenous-rights activist. Name variations: Rigoberta Menchu; Rigoberta Menchú Tum or Menchú-Tum. Pronunciation: Ree-go-BER-ta Men-CHU. Born Jan 9, 1959, in Chimel, Guatemala; dau. of Vicente Menchú (peasant and political organizer) and Juana Tum (peasant midwife and healer); m. Angel Canil also seen as Angel Camile, Jan 1998; children: Mash Nahual J'a. ❖ Was born 5 years after one of the most traumatic events in Guatemalan history, the 1954 coup that overthrew the left-leaning government of Arbenz; at 8, began working full days picking coffee and cotton; went to Guatemala City as a 13-year-old, to work as a maid; father, who had become active in efforts to organize the Mayan peasantry to resist encroachments on community lands, was jailed for 14 months; when father became an organizer for the Committee of Peasant Unity (Comité de Unidad Campesina or CUC, mid-1970s), also joined it

(1979); during civil war, brother Petrocinio was tortured and murdered (Sept 1979); father died after massacre at the Spanish embassy (Jan 1980); mother tortured and murdered (April 1980); escaped to Mexico (1980); published *Me llamo Rigoberta Menchú* (*I, Rigoberta Menchú*, 1983); briefly arrested on her return to Guatemala (1988); awarded the Nobel Peace Prize (1992); headed United Nations' Decade of Indigenous Peoples (1993—). Although widely read and admired, her memoir also provoked controversy after the publication of *Rigoberta Menchú and the Story of All Poor Guatemalans* (1999), a book by anthropologist David Stoll which asserted that she exaggerated and even fabricated certain events. ❖ See also *Crossing Borders: An Autobiography* (Verso, 1998); and *Women in World History*.

MENCIA DE HARO (d. 1270). Queen of Portugal. Died in 1270; dau. of Diego Lopez, count of Vizcaya; m. Sancho II (1207–1248), king of Portugal (r. 1223–1248), around 1246.

MENCO, Sara (1920—). Dutch novelist. Name variations: Sara Voeten-Minco or Vöten Minco; (pseudonym) Marga Minco. Born Mar 31, 1920, in Ginneken, Netherlands; grew up in a Jewish family of 5 children in Breda; m. Bert Voeten, 1945 (died 1992). ❖ Went into hiding after parents and siblings were arrested in WWII; published the bestselling *Het bittere kruid* (Bitter Herbs, 1957), which chronicled her experiences; other writings include *De andere kant* (The Other Side, 1959), *Een leeg huis* (An Empty House, 1966), *De val* (The Fall, 1983), *De glazen brug* (The Glass Bridge, 1986) and *Nagelaten dagen* (1997).

MENCZER, Pauline (1970—). Australian surfer. Born May 21, 1970, in Sydney, Australia. ❖ Won World amateur title (1988) and World pro title (1993).

MENDELENYINE-AGOSTON, Judit (1937—). Hungarian fencer. Name variations: Judit Agoston. Born Jan 23, 1937, in Hungary. ❖ At Tokyo Olympics, won a gold medal in team foil (1964).

MENDELS, Josepha (1902–1995). Dutch novelist. Born July 18, 1902, in Groningen, Netherlands; died Sept 10, 1995, in Eindhoven, Netherlands. ❖ Was headmistress of learning center for Jewish girls; lived in Paris from 1936; novels often challenge orthodox Jewish background; works include *Rolien and Ralien* (1947), *Je vist het toch ...* (1948), *Als wind en rook* (1950), *Zoethout en etamien* (1956), *De speeltuin* (1970), *Welkom in dit leven* (1981), *Joelika en andere verhalen* (1986), and *Het rode kerkhof* (1987). Won Vijverberg Prize (1950) and Anna Bijns Prize (1986).

MENDELSSOHN, Dorothea (1764–1839). German-Jewish-born salonnière and writer. Name variations: Brendel Mendelssohn; Beniken Mendelssohn; Caroline Veit or Madame Veit; Dorothea Schlegel; Dorothea von Schlegel; Dorothea von Schlegel von Gottleben; Dorothea Mendelssohn Veit Schlegel. Born Brendel Mendelssohn in Berlin, Oct 24, 1764 (some sources cite 1763 or 1765); died in Frankfurt am Main, Aug 3, 1839; dau. of Moses Mendelssohn (1729–1786, Jewish philosopher) and Fromet Gugenheim Mendelssohn; sister of Henriette Mendelssohn (1768–1831); Rebekah Mendelssohn (born Reikel, later called Recha), Sara Mendelssohn, Sisa Mendelssohn, Abraham Mendelssohn, Hayyim Mendelssohn, Joseph Mendelssohn, Mendel Abraham Mendelssohn, and Nathan Mendelssohn; m. Simon Veit (sep. 1797, div.); m. Friedrich von Schlegel (1772–1829, Romantic theorist), in 1804; children: (1st m.) 2 daughters, both of whom died in infancy; sons, Johannes and Philipp Veit. ❖ Participated in the rapid emancipation and acculturation of Germany's Jewish elite, and, as the host of one of Berlin's most brilliant salons, situated herself at the very center of the emerging Romantic movement; initially founded a reading society, and this soon evolved into a full-scale literary salon where restless young Prussian nobles met equally restless daughters of wealthy Berlin Jewish families; in 1797, then mistress of one of the most popular of Berlin's 14 salons, left husband and began living with theorist Friedrich von Schlegel; divorced (1799); lived with Schlegel in Paris (1801–04); collaborated with Schlegel on a number of his literary projects and published a novel of her own, *Florentin* (1801), regarded by contemporary critics as a work of considerable artistic substance; published a translation of Germaine de Staël's *Corinne* (1807); married Schlegel and converted from Judaism to Lutheranism (1804), then Roman Catholicism (1808); moved to Vienna (1809); while Schlegel edited journals, resumed her role as a salonnière, presiding over a brilliant assemblage of writers, artists, and politicians which included such luminaries as Karoline Pichler and Joseph von Eichendorff. ❖ See also *Women in World History*.

MENDELSSOHN, Fanny (1805–1847). *See Mendelssohn-Hensel, Fanny.*

MENDELSSOHN, Henriette (1768–1831). German-Jewish-born teacher and salonnière. Name variations: Henrietta Mendelssohn; Marie Mendelssohn. Born Yente Mendelssohn in Berlin, Germany, 1768; died 1831; dau. of Moses Mendelssohn (1729–1786, Jewish philosopher) and Fromet Gugenheim Mendelssohn; sister of Dorothea Mendelssohn (1764–1839); Rebekah Mendelssohn (born Reikel, later called Recha), Sara Mendelssohn, Sisa Mendelssohn, Abraham Mendelssohn, Hayyim Mendelssohn, Joseph Mendelssohn, Mendel Abraham Mendelssohn, and Nathan Mendelssohn; never married. ❖ Became a teacher, moving 1st to Paris; while in Paris, established a salon that attracted most of that city's intellectual luminaries, including Madame de Staël, Benjamin Constant, Spontini, and her sister Dorothea Mendelssohn's lover—and later, husband—Friedrich von Schlegel. ❖ See also *Women in World History*.

MENDELSSOHN-HENSEL, Fanny (1805–1847). German composer and performer. Name variations: Fanny Cäcilie; Fanny Hensel; Fanny Mendelssohn; Fanny Cäcilia Mendelssohn; Fanny Mendelssohn-Bartholdy. Born Cäcilie Mendelssohn in Hamburg, Germany, Nov 14, 1805; died in Berlin, May 14, 1847; dau. of Abraham Mendelssohn (international banker) and Lea (Salomon) Mendelssohn (gifted amateur musician); m. Wilhelm Hensel (court painter), Oct 3, 1829; children: Sebastian (b. 1830). ❖ Composer whose works were increasingly performed and recorded in late 20th century and whose playing and compositions have been compared favorably to those of her more famous brother Felix Mendelssohn; became Fanny Mendelssohn-Bartholdy, converting with her family from Judaism to Protestantism at age 11, the same year she wrote her 1st musical composition (1816); sponsored the 1st of her musical salons while still in her teens (1822); after marriage, conducted large weekly musical salons which became highly influential in Berlin's musical and social circles; at age 40, despite brother's opposition, announced her intention to publish her compositions (1846); published some 60 of her several 100 compositions by the time of her death (1847). ❖ See also Marcia J. Citron, ed. and trans. *The Letters of Fanny Hensel to Felix Mendelssohn* (Pendragon, 1987); and *Women in World History*.

MENDENHALL, Dorothy Reed (1874–1964). American physician. Name variations: Dorothy Reed. Born Dorothy Reed, Sept 22, 1874 (some sources cite 1875), in Columbus, Ohio; died July 31, 1964, in Chester, Connecticut; dau. of William Pratt Reed (shoe manufacturer) and Grace (Kimball) Reed; Smith College, BL, 1895; Johns Hopkins Medical School, MD, 1900; m. Charles Elwood Mendenhall (physics professor), Feb 14, 1906; children: Margaret (1907–1907); Richard (1908–1910); Thomas Corwin (b. 1910); John Talcott (b. 1912). ❖ Pioneer in women's and children's health care, made important discovery in Hodgkin's disease research, proving conclusively that it was not a version of the infectious bacterial disease tuberculosis but a form of cancer affecting the lymphatic system (c. 1901); joined staff of New York Babies Hospital (1903); moved to Wisconsin (c. 1906); joined faculty of University of Wisconsin–Madison as a home economics lecturer (1914); began conducting research into infant mortality; set up Wisconsin's 1st infant welfare clinic (1915), in Madison; for next 2 decades, supervised this clinic and 4 like it; became medical officer for US Children's Bureau (1917); represented US at International Child Welfare Conference (1919); conducted study of childbirth practices in US and Denmark (1926–29). ❖ See also *Women in World History*.

MENDES, Gracia (1510–1569). *See Nasi, Gracia Mendes.*

MENDES, Jonna (1979—). American Alpine skier. Born Mar 31, 1979, in Heavenly, CA. ❖ Won US giant slalom championships (2001, 2002); won a bronze medal for super-G at World championships (2003).

MENDÈS, Judith (1845–1917). *See Gautier, Judith.*

MÉNDEZ, Josefina (c. 1940—). Cuban ballet dancer. Born c. 1940 in Havana, Cuba. ❖ Performed with Alicia Alonso's Ballet de Cuba and Ballet Nacional de Cuba in such classical works as *Giselle, Coppélia,* and *Swan Lake,* and contemporary works as José Lefebre's *Edipo Rey,* José Parés' *Un Concierto en Blanco y Negro,* and others; served as artistic director of Ballet Nacional de Cuba.

MENDL, Lady (1865–1950). *See de Wolfe, Elsie.*

MENDOZA, Amalia (1923–2001). Mexican mariachi singer. Name variations: La Tariacuri. Born 1923 in Michoacan, Mexico, into a family of musicians; died June 11, 2001, in Mexico City, Mexico; children: reared her nephew, Guillermo Valero Mendoza. ❖ Famed singer of mariachi ballads, whose career spanned 30 years, was one of the 1st women to become successful in the genre; began career singing duets with her sister Perla; launched solo career (1954), with recording of "Puñalada Trasera" ("Backstab"); came to prominence broadcasting over radio XEW; had such hits as "Echame la Culpa" ("Put the Blame on Me") and "Amarga Navidad" ("Bitter Christmas"); recorded about 36 albums, including *Las Tres Señoras* (1996).

MENDOZA, Ana de (fl. late 1400s). Portuguese mistress of John II. Flourished in the late 1400s; had liaison with Juan or John II (1455–1495), king of Portugal (r. 1481–1495); children: (with John II) Jorge de Lancastre, duke of Coimbra.

MENDOZA, Ana de (1540–1592). Spanish aristocrat and princess of Eboli. Name variations: Princesa de Eboli; princess of Eboli. Born in Cifuentes, near Guadalajara, Spain, in 1540; baptized on June 29, 1540; died Feb 2, 1592; dau. of Diego Hurtado de Mendoza, count of Mélito, and Catalina de Silva; m. Ruy Gómez de Silva (prince of Eboli and adviser to Philip II, king of Spain), on April 18, 1553 (died 1572); children: 10, including a daughter who m. the Duke of Medina Sidonia, commander of the Spanish Armada against England in 1588. ❖ As a Mendoza, was from one of Spain's great aristocratic families; following husband's death (1572), retired to a Carmelite convent she had founded in Pastrana, but her insistence on being accorded deference alienated the nuns there, who demanded that she leave; returned to court and became the intimate of Antonio Pérez, one of Philip II's secretaries and chief advisers (1576 or 1577); when Philip ordered Pérez's arrest (1579) for the assassination of Juan de Escobedo, was also imprisoned. ❖ See also *Women in World History*.

MENDOZA, Jean (1893–1978). *See Acker, Jean.*

MENDOZA, Jessica (1980—). American softball player. Born Nov 11, 1980, in Oxnard, CA; attended Stanford University. ❖ Outfielder, won World championship (2002); won team gold medal at Athens Olympics (2004).

MENDOZA, Juana B. Guitérrez de (1875–1942). *See Gutiérrez de Mendoza, Juana Belén.*

MENDOZA, Lydia (1916—). Mexican-American Tejano singer and guitarist. Name variations: La Cancionera. Born 1916 in Houston, Texas, into a well-known musical family. ❖ Launched career (1932), singing in the plazas of downtown San Antonio; came to prominence with such hits as "Mal hombre" (1934) and "Pero hay que triste"; recorded over 50 albums and over 200 songs; developed "Musician Nortena," a style of music that combines German folk accordion style with the traditional Mexican 12-stringed guitar. Received the National Heritage Award (1982) and National Medal of the Arts. ❖ See also *Lydia Mendoza: A Family Autobiography* (1993).

MENEBHI, Saïda (1952–1977). Moroccan poet. Born 1952 in Marrakech, Morocco; died 1977 in Casablanca, Morocco. ❖ Taught English in Rabat; joined National Union of Moroccan Students (UNEM) and Marxist-Leninist organization Ila Al Amam; arrested (1976) and sentenced to 7 years solitary confinement; died during prison hunger strike; poems and prose published as *Poèmes, Lettres, Ecrits de Prison* (1978).

MENEN (1899–1962). Empress of Ethiopia. Name variations: Menen Selassie; Wayzaro Menen. Born Menen Asfaw in Dessié, Ethiopia, Mar 1899; died after many years of ill health, Feb 15, 1962, in Addis Ababa, Ethiopia; dau. of Asfaw Mikael Ambassel (jantirar [ruler] of Anbassel or Ambassel) and Sehin Mikael (dau. of King Michael of Wollo and sister of Lij Iyasu); niece of Lij Eyasu also known as Lij Iyasu, king of Ethiopia; cousin of Amde Mikael; m. Lul Sagad (a Shewan noble) also known as Ras Leulseged Atnaf Seged (died 1916); m. Ras Tafari, later known as Haile Selassie I (1892–1975), emperor of Ethiopia (r. 1930–1974), on July 31, 1911, in Harar, Ethiopia; children: (1st m.) Gabre Iqziabher Asfa (b. 1909); (2nd m.) Princess Tenagne Worq also seen as Tenagnework (1912–2003); Asfa Wossen (1916–1997), known under title Meredazmatch (1931–1997), also 65th emperor of Ethiopia as Amha Selassie I (r. 1975–1997); Princess Zenabe Worq also seen as Zenebework (1918–1933); Princess Tsahai Worq also seen as Tsehai (1919–1942); Prince Makonnen (1923–1957); Prince Sahle Selassie (1931–1962). ❖ Crowned empress of Ethiopia upon the coronation of her husband as emperor (1930); remained a trusted advisor to her husband until her death. ❖ See also *Women in World History*.

MENENDEZ, Osleidys (1979—). Cuban javelin thrower. Born Nov 14, 1979, in Martia, Matanzas, Cuba. ❖ Won a bronze medal at Sydney Olympics (2000) and a gold medal at World championships (2001); won a gold medal at Athens Olympics (2004), with an Olympic record throw of 234:8.14; won 8 events in Golden League, Grand Prix and Super Grand Prix (2002–04).

MENERES, Maria Alberta (1930—). Portuguese poet and children's writer. Born Aug 25, 1930, in Vila Nova de Gaia, Portugal; m. E. M. Melo de Castro (poet); graduate of University of Lisbon. ❖ Worked as schoolteacher; produced children's program for Portuguese Radio and Television; edited several journals, reviews, and anthologies; poetry collections include *Intervalo* (1952), *A Palavra Imperceptivel* (1955), *Agua Memória* (1960), *Os Mosquitos de Suburna* (1967), and *O Jogo dos Silêncios* (1996); children's books include *Conversos com Versos* (1968), *Lengalenga do Vento* (1976), *Um Peixe no Ar* (1980), *Dez Dedos Dez Segredos* (1985), *O Mistério do Nevão Assombrado* (1989), *Corre, Corre, Pintainho* (1988), *O Meu Livro de Natal* (1991), and *Sigam a Borboleta!* (1996); with husband, edited *Antologia Novíssima Poesia Portuguesa* (1971).

MENESES, Juana Josefa de (1651–1709). Portuguese poet and religious writer. Name variations: Doña Juana Josefa de Meneses; condesa de Ericeira or countess of Ericeira. Born Sept 13, 1651, in Lisbon, Portugal; died Aug 26, 1709, in Lisbon; dau. of Fernando de Meneses, 2nd count of Ericeira; became the 3rd to hold the title in Ericeira; m. her uncle Luis de Meneses (who committed suicide in 1690); children: Francisco Javier de Meneses, 4th count of Ericeira. ❖ Published poem in Castilian, *Despertador de alma al sueño de la vida* (1695), plays *Dividido imperio de amor* and *El duelo de las finezas,* and 2 religious plays.

MENETEWAB (c. 1720–1770). Ethiopian empress and regent. Name variations: Mentuab; Berhan Magass (Glory of Grace). Regent of Ethopia (Gondar) from 1730 to 1760. Christened Welleta Georgis around 1720; died 1770; m. Emperor Baqaffa or Bakaffa, in 1720s (died 1729); children: Iyasu II (died 1755), emperor of Ethiopia. ❖ On death of husband (1729), was made regent of Ethiopia for her son Iyasu II; as he had little interest in ruling, controlled the government until his death (1755); known for her nepotism, managed to weaken the empire and endured many revolts by Ethiopian nobles; had grandson Ioas made emperor (1755), but gradually lost influence to her daughter-in-law's family; power ended at the time of Ioas' death (1769).

MENININHA, Mother (1894–1986). *See Nazaré, Maria Escolástica Da Conceição.*

MENININHA DO GANTOIS, Mae (1894–1986). *See Nazaré, Maria Escolástica Da Conceição.*

MENIS, Argentina (1948—). Romanian runner. Born July 19, 1948. ❖ At Munich Olympics, won a silver medal in the discus throw (1972); won Romanian nationals for discus (1971, 1973, 1975–79).

MENJOU, Verree (1904–1987). *See Teasdale, Verree.*

MENKEN, Adah Isaacs (1835–1868). American actress and poet. Name variations: Mazeppa. Born Adah Bertha Theodore, June 15, 1835, in Chartrain (now Milneburg), Louisiana; died of TB and peritonitis in Paris, France, Aug 10, 1868; dau. of Auguste Theodore (shopkeeper) and Marie Theodore; m. Alexander Isaac Menken (musician and dry goods salesman), Oct 3, 1856; m. John Carmel Heenan (prizefighter), Sept 3, 1859; m. Robert Henry Newell (writer and editor known by pen name Orpheus C. Kerr), Sept 24, 1862; m. James Paul Barkley, Aug 19, 1866; children: 1 died in infancy (b. 1860); Louis Dudevant Victor Emmanuel Barkley (later given new identity by adoptive parents). ❖ With her beauty and daring, was one of the great celebrities of her era; made 1st stage appearance as Pauline in *The Lady of Lyons,* Shreveport, LA (1857); made New Orleans debut as Bianca in *Fazio* (1857); made NY debut as Widow Cheerly in *The Soldier's Daughter* (1859); opened in Albany in her most famous role, as a Tartar boy in *Mazeppa,* an adaptation of Lord Byron's poem (1861), adding to the traditional climax of the play that called for the boy, stripped of his clothes and lashed to the back of a wild horse, riding up papier-maché cliffs into the clouds (rather, she rode a horse up a platform through the crowd, clad in skin-colored tights to appear naked); bought an impressive house, which became a center of NY intellectual life, and proved to be a brilliant host; made spectacular San Francisco debut in *Mazeppa* (1863); made London debut in *Mazeppa* (1864), taking about 2 dozen curtain calls; lived in London and Paris (late 1860s); made Paris debut in *The Pirates of the Savannah* (1866) and became a sensation; 8 days after her death, her collection of poems, *Infelicia* was published in London (1868). ❖ See also Allen Lesser, *Enchanting Rebel: The Secret of Adah Isaacs Menken* (Kennikat, 1947);

Paul Lewis, *Queen of the Plaza* (Funk & Wagnalls, 1964); and *Women in World History*.

MENKEN, Helen (1901–1966). American stage and radio actress. Born Dec 12, 1901, in New York, NY; died Mar 27, 1966, in New York, NY; m. Humphrey Bogart (actor, div.); m. Dr. Henry T. Smith (div.); m. George N. Richard. ❖ Made NY debut as a child actress in *Midsummer Night's Dream* (1906); starred in *Three Wise Fools, Seventh Heaven, The Old Maid, Mary of Scotland, The Makropoulos Secret, The Merchant of Venice, Hamlet, Julius Caesar* and *The Skin of Our Teeth*; starred on radio's "Second Husband" (1933–45); organized the Stage Door Canteen during WWII for American Theatre Wing (1942–46) and appeared as herself in film of the same name; served as president of Theatre Wing and organized its Antoinette Perry Awards.

MENKEN, Marie (1909–1970). American filmmaker, artist, and actress. Born 1909 in New York, NY; died Dec 29, 1970, in Brooklyn; m. Willard Maas (filmmaker). ❖ Created 1st film, *Visual Variations on Noguchi* (1945), in which statues of Isamu Noguchi appeared as if they were in motion through the innovative use of light; credited with freeing the movie camera from the tripod; films include *Hurry! Hurry!* (1957), *Faucets* (1960), *Arabesque for Kenneth Anger* (1961), *Eye Music in Red Major* (1961), *Mood Mondrian* (1961–63), *Go Go Go* (1963), *Andy Warhol* (1965), *Drips in Strips* (1965), *Excursion* (1968) and *Watts with Eggs* (1969).

MENKEN-SCHAUDT, Carol (1957—). American basketball player. Name variations: Carol Schaudt. Born Nov 23, 1957; attended Oregon State University, 1979–81. ❖ Set career scoring record at OSU with 2,243 points and was a Kodak All-American; at Los Angeles Olympics, won a gold medal in team competition (1984); played professionally in Italy.

MENOU, Mlle (c. 1642–1700). See Bejart, Armande.

MENSING, Barbara (1960—). German archer. Born Sept 23, 1960, in Herten, Germany. ❖ Won a silver medal for teams at Atlanta Olympics (1996) and a bronze medal for teams at Sydney Olympics (2000).

MENTEITH, countess of. See Graham, Margaret (d. 1380).

MENTEN, Maude (1879–1960). Canadian histochemist and pathologist. Born Maude Leonora Menten, Mar 20, 1879, in Port Lambden, Ontario, Canada; died July 26, 1960, in Leamington, Ontario; University of Toronto, BA, 1904, MB in Medicine, 1907, MD, 1911; University of Chicago, PhD, 1916. ❖ Was a fellow at Rockefeller Institute for Medical Research, studying effect of radium on tumors (1907–08); worked as demonstrator of physiology at University of Toronto; since women were not allowed to conduct research in Canadian universities, became research fellow at Rockefeller Institute and at Western Reserve University; joined Leonor Michaelis at University of Berlin to study enzyme kinetics (1912), resulting in the Michaelis-Menten Equation, which helped to shape field of biochemistry by providing scientists with manner in which to mathematically analyze observations and descriptions of biological reactions; went on to co-devise the now-standard method of isolating and describing protein behavior; joined faculty at University of Pittsburgh (1918); became assistant professor of pathology there (1923), then associate professor (1925), while serving as clinical pathologist at Children's Hospital of Pittsburgh, but did not receive promotion to full professor until 1949 (1 year before retirement); returned to Canada (1950) and conducted cancer research at Medical Institute of British Columbia (1951–54); inducted into Canadian Medical Hall of Fame.

MENTER, Sophie (1846–1918). German pianist. Name variations: Sofie Menter. Born in Munich, Germany, July 29, 1846; died in Munich, Feb 23, 1918; taught at St. Petersburg Conservatory, 1883–87. ❖ One of Liszt's best students, composed several pieces which were orchestrated by Tchaikovsky and which she played with him as conductor. ❖ See also *Women in World History*.

MENTUAB (c. 1720–1770). See Menetewab.

MENUHIN, Diana (1912–2003). English ballet dancer. Name variations: Lady Menuhin; Diana Gould. Born Diana Rosamond Constance Grace Irene Gould, Nov 12, 1912, in Belgravia, England; died Jan 25, 2003, in London, England; sister of Griselda Gould; sister-in-law of Hephzibah and Yaltah Menuhin; daughter-in-law of Marutha Menuhin; m. 2nd wife of Yehudi Menuhin (violinist), Oct 19, 1947 (died Mar 1999); children: 2 sons; 2 stepchildren. ❖ Began career as a ballet dancer, making professional debut in a private recital in Norwich; danced with Marie

Rambert company in early seasons, notably as the chief nymph in Nijinsky's *L'Après-midi d'un faune* and as Chiarina in Fokine's *Le Carnaval*; danced with George Ballanchine's Ballets in Paris and London (1933), then with the Markova–Dolin ballet; became lead dancer for the Arts Theatre Ballet (1940); guarded husband's talents and had an enormous impact on his career and causes. ❖ See also autobiography *Fiddler's Moll*.

MENUHIN, Hephzibah (1920–1981). American pianist. Born May 20, 1920, in San Francisco, California; died in London, England, Jan 1, 1981; dau. of Moshe Mnuchin (who would later change his name to Moshe Menuhin) and Marutha Menuhin (1896–1996); sister of Yaltah Menuhin (pianist) and the famous violinist Yehudi Menuhin (1916–1999); m. Lindsay Nicholas; m. Richard Hauser. ❖ A prodigy, gave 1st public performance as a pianist (1928); concertized widely in the US and Europe, often with her brother. ❖ See also Lionel Menuhin Rolfe, *The Menuhins: A Family Odyssey* (Aris, 1978); and *Women in World History*.

MENUHIN, Marutha (1896–1996). Russian-born mother of the renowned Menuhins. Born Marutha Sher in the Crimea, near Yalta, Russia, Jan 7, 1896; died Nov 15, 1996; dau. of Nahum Sher and Sarah Liba Sher; m. Moshe Mnuchin (who would later change his name to Moshe Menuhin), 1914; children: daughters, Hephzibah Menuhin (1920–1981, pianist); Yaltah Menuhin (b. 1921, pianist); son, Yehudi Menuhin (1916–1999, violinist); mother-in-law of Diana Menuhin. ❖ When it was discovered that all 3 of her children were talented musicians, quit her job to devote full time to their careers. ❖ See also Lionel Menuhin Rolfe, *The Menuhins: A Family Odyssey* (Aris, 1978); and *Women in World History*.

MENUHIN, Yaltah (1921–2001). American-born pianist. Name variations: Yalta Menuhin. Born in San Francisco, California, Oct 7, 1921; died at her London home, June 10, 2001; dau. of Moshe Menuhin and Marutha Sher Menuhin; sister of Yehudi Menuhin (1916–1999, violinist) and Hephzibah Menuhin (1920–1981); m. William Stix; m. Joel Ryce; children: 2 sons. ❖ Appeared worldwide as a soloist as well as an accompanist to leading instrumentalists. ❖ See also Lionel Menuhin Rolfe, *The Menuhins: A Family Odyssey* (Aris, 1978); and *Women in World History*.

MENZELLI, Elisabetta (c. 1860–c. 1929). Prussian ballet dancer and choreographer. Born c. 1860, in Bresslau, Prussia (now Poland); died c. 1929 in Los Angeles, CA; sister of Elena Menzelli; children: (adopted) Lola Menzelli (ballet dancer). ❖ With sister, worked at Pasqualli's Kinderballet in Berlin as child ballet dancers, as well as in Hamburg Stadtopera's premiere of *Il Trovato* and in St. Peterburg, Russia; at 16, joined Imperial Theater in Vienna, where she danced as Fenella in *Maisanello* (also called *The Dumb Girl of Portici*), a role she would also dance throughout US; toured with a German opera company and later with Italian opera company under Charles Mapleson in US; served as ballet master in Italy briefly before immigrating to US (1904); opened school in New York City where she taught ballet until 1923, then taught at McAdam Normal School in Los Angeles.

MENZELLI, Lola (c. 1898–1951). American ballet dancer. Born c. 1898 in Vienna, Austria; died Mar 11, 1951, in Chicago, IL; m. Senia Solomonoff (dancer), 1914; children: Marya Saunders (dancer). ❖ Danced at age 4 in German-language opera in New York City; worked as German-language actress until 1912; studied with Elisabetta Menzelli—who also adopted her—as of age 8; performed in numerous recitals throughout New York City organized by her mentor; danced in Weber and Field musicals, including *The Man with Three Wives* (1913); performed on tour with vaudeville ballet dancer Stafford Pemberton, also a student of Elisabetta Menzelli; danced in vaudeville and variety successfully in Europe and US; toured with husband for 15 years before retiring to FL.

MENZIES, Katherine (1914—). See Stammers, Kay.

MENZIES, Pattie (1899–1995). Australian prime-ministerial wife. Name variations: Dame Pattie Menzies. Born Pattie Maie Leckie, Mar 2, 1899, in Alexandria, Victoria, Australia; died Aug 30, 1995, in Canberra; dau. of John Leckie, a Deakinite Liberal, member of the federal parliament (1917–19), and United Australia Party senator; m. Robert Menzies (prime minister of Australia, 1939–41, 1949–66), Sept 27, 1920 (died 1978); children: Kenneth (b. 1922), Ian (b. 1923), and Heather Menzies (b. 1928). ❖ Widely respected and politically savvy, was considered crucial to her husband's success; did a makeover of The Lodge (the official prime-ministerial residence) and Government House in Canberra; was involved in the Free Kindergarten movement and served as president of a number of Women's Hopital Auxiliaries; accompanied her husband on many overseas tours. Awarded Dame Grand Cross of the British Empire (GBE, 1954), one of only 3 Australians to receive the award. ❖ See also Diana Langmore, *Prime Ministers' Wives* (McPhee Gribble, 1992).

MENZIES, Trixie Te Arama (1936—). Maori poet. Born 1936 in Wellington, New Zealand; attended Auckland University; m. Brian Menzies. ❖ Taught at Otahuhu College in Auckland; poetry, which combined feminism and Maori culture, published by branch of national Maori women's group Karanga; works include *Papakainga* (1988). Poems.

M.E.R. (1875–1975). *See Rothmann, Maria Elisabeth.*

MERAB (fl. 1000 BCE). Biblical woman. Eldest of the two daughters of King Saul and Ahinoam; sister of Michal (fl. 1000 BCE); m. Adriel of Abel-Meholab; children: five sons. ❖ In an arrangement brokered by her father King Saul, was betrothed to David following his victory over the giant Goliath; apparently took issue with the agreement, however, so David was given the hand of her younger sister Michal instead; later married Adriel of Abel-Meholab and gave birth to 5 sons, all of whom were put to death by the Gibeonites.

MERAH, Nouria (1970—). *See Benida, Nouria.*

MERANDE, Doro (1892–1975). American actress. Born Dorothy Matthews, Mar 31, 1892, in Columbia, Kansas; died Nov 1, 1975, in Miami, FL. ❖ Made NY stage debut in *Loose Moments* (1935); among numerous Broadway roles, appeared as Eulalie Mackecknie Shinn in *The Music Man* (1965) and Jenny in *The Front Page* (1969); film credits include *Our Town, Mr. Belvedere Rings the Bell, Seven Year Itch, Man with the Golden Arm, The Cardinal, Kiss Me Stupid* and *Hurry Sundown*; also appeared frequently on tv, with recurring roles in 2 series "Bringing Up Buddy" and "That Was the Week That Was."

MERARD DE SAINT-JUST, Anne-Jeanne-Félicité d'Ormoy (1765–1830). French novelist. Name variations: A.J.F. Merard de Saint-Just. Born 1765 in France; died 1830. ❖ Wrote *Les Quatre Ages de l'homme, poème* (1782), *Bergeries et opuscules* (1782), *Rosine et Colette* published in *Journal Littéraire de Nancy* (1784), *Mon journal d'un an* (1787), *Histoire de la baronne d'Alvigny* (1788), *La Corbeille de fleurs* (1795), *Démence de Mme de Panor* (1796), *Le Chapeau noir* (1799), *Le Petit Lavater, almanach* (1800), and *Six mois d'exil* (1805).

MERCADIER, Jeanne (1740–?). *See Baret, Jeanne.*

MERCÉ, Antonia (c. 1886–1936). Argentine-born dancer of Spanish ballet flamenco. Name variations: La Argentina; Antonia Merce. Born Antonia Mercé c. 1886 in Argentina; died in Bayonne, France, 1936. ❖ Moving to Europe, became La Argentina, the "first lady of the Spanish Ballet"; represented a change in flamenco, replacing its Gypsy (Roma) dance, accompanied by guitar, with ballet flamenco which combined various forms of dance, including classical, with large troupes for theatrical audiences; toured widely outside Spain, helping popularize her stylized flamenco among international spectators; her chief rival as "Queen of the Castenets" was another woman called "Argentinita," Encarnación Lopez.

MERCEDES OF THE TWO SICILIES (1910–2000). *See Maria de las Mercedes.*

MERCER, Beryl (1882–1939). English actress. Born Aug 13, 1882, in Seville, Spain; died July 28, 1939, in Santa Monica, CA; dau. of British parents; m. Maitland Sabrina Pasley. ❖ Made stage debut as a child in Yarmouth as little Willie Carlyle in *East Lynne* (1886); made London debut in *Two Little Vagabonds* (1896) and NY debut in *The Shulamite* (1906); other plays include *Her Point of View, The Lodger, A Lady's Name, The Old Lady Shows Her Medals, Out There, Dark Rosaleen, Queen Victoria,* and *Outward Bound*; films include *Mother's Boy, Three Live Ghosts, All Quiet on the Western Front, Seven Days' Leave, In Gay Madrid, The Matrimonial Bed, Outward Bound, Inspiration, East Lynne, Always Goodbye, Merely Mary Anne, Lena Rivers, Smilin' Through, Cavalcade, Berkeley Square, Change of Heart, Jane Eyre, The Little Minister* and *The Age of Indiscretion*.

MERCER, Frances (1915–2000). American actress. Born Oct 21, 1915, in New Rochelle, NY; died Nov 12, 2000, in Los Angeles, CA; dau. of Sid Mercer; m. G. Robert Fleming. ❖ Began career as a model; films include *Vivacious Lady, The Story of Vernon and Irene Castle, The Mad Miss Manton* and *Society Lawyer*; also appeared on tv in "Dr. Hudson's Secret Journal" (1955–57).

MERCER, Jacque (1931–1982). Miss America. Name variations: Jacque Curran. Born 1931 in Litchfield, Arizona; died 1982; graduate of Arizona State University; married briefly; m. Dick Curran (All-American football player and advertising exec.); children: 2. ❖ Named Miss America (1949), representing Arizona; married and divorced during her tenure, successfully lobbied that future Miss America's stay single the year of their reign; became a copywriter. ❖ See also Frank Deford, *There She Is* (Viking, 1971).

MERCER, Mabel (1900–1983). British-American nightclub singer. Born Feb 3, 1900, in Burton-on-Trent, Staffordshire, England; died April 20, 1984, in Pittsfield, MA; dau. of a black American jazz musician father (who died before she was born) and a white English actress mother. ❖ With cousins, was part of a music-hall act called The Five Romanys; went from English vaudeville circuit to performing in musical comedy on London stage; began appearing at Bricktop's, the legendary Parisian nightclub (c. 1931); arrived in NY (1941) and found longterm employment at Le Ruban Bleu (1938, 1941), Tony's (1942–49), Byline Room (1949–57), and the St. Regis Hotel, becoming indelibly associated with the vocal style known as parlando, a method of half-singing, half-speaking that emphasizes the emotional content in a song's lyrics; repertoire consisted mostly of Broadway tunes, including the works of Cole Porter, Rodgers and Hart, and later Stephen Sondheim; recorded a number of albums for Atlantic, including a tribute to Cole Porter and 2-record set *The Art of Mabel Mercer*. ❖ See also *Women in World History*.

MERCHANT, Natalie (1963—). American musician. Born Oct 26, 1963, in Jamestown, NY. ❖ Joined group, 10,000 Maniacs, at age 17, and gained huge following as lead vocalist; with band, signed contract with Elektra and released *The Wishing Chair* (1985), which, despite critical acclaim, was commercially unsuccessful; with band, released well-received *In My Tribe* (1987), which included chart singles "Like the Weather" and "What's the Matter Here"; released other albums with Maniacs including *Blind Man's Zoo* (1989) and *Our Time in Eden* (1992); left band to pursue successful solo career (1993); released 1st album, *Tigerlily* (1995), which included hit singles "Carnival," "Wonder," and "Jealousy"; released *Ophelia* (1998), which went to #8.

MERCHANT, Vivien (1929–1983). English actress. Born Ada Thompson, July 22, 1929, in Manchester, England; died Oct 3, 1982, in London, England, of cirrhosis of the liver; m. Harold Pinter (playwright), 1956 (div. 1980). ❖ Made stage debut as a child in *Jane Eyre* (1943); made London debut as a dancer in *Sigh No More* (1945); often appeared with the Donald Wolfit Shakespearean Co. (1947–50); other London plays include *The Wandering Jew, The Room, Judith, The Lover, Mixed Doubles, Old Times* and *Exiles*; made NY debut in *The Homecoming* with Royal Shakespeare Company (1967); films include *The Way Ahead, Accident, Frenzy* and *Under Milk Wood*; made frequent tv appearances; following divorce from Pinter and his subsequent marriage to Antonia Fraser, became a chronic alcoholic. Nominated for Oscar for Best Supporting Actress for performance in *Alfie* (1966).

MERCIA, countess of. *See Godiva (c. 1040–1080).*

MERCIA, queen of.
See Emma (fl. 600s).
See Ermenburga (fl. late 600s).
See Ostrith (d. 697).
See Cynewise (fl. 7th c.).
See Orthryth (fl. late 7th c.).
See Ermenilda (d. about 700).
See Cynethryth (fl. 736–796).
See Ethelswyth (c. 843–889).
See Ethelflaed (869–918).
See Elfwyn (c. 882–?).

MERCIANS, Lady of the. *See Ethelflaed (869–918).*

MERCIER, Euphrasie (1823–?). French murderer. Born 1823 in French province of Nord; died in a French prison after 1886. ❖ Working as a paid companion, killed Elodie Ménétret, buried her in the garden, and informed callers to the house that Ménétret had entered a convent (1883); was finally caught (1885). ❖ See also *Women in World History*.

MERCIER, Margaret (1937—). Canadian ballet dancer. Born 1937 in Montreal, Canada. ❖ Trained at Sadler's Wells Ballet under Ursula Moreton, Winifred Edwards, Lydia Kyasht, and Ailene Phillips; performed with Royal Ballet (1954–58) in such works as *Swan Lake* and *The Sleeping Beauty*; danced with Les Grands Ballets Canadiens (1958) in numerous repertory classics including *The Sleeping Beauty, The Nutcracker,* and *Don Quixote.*

MERCOEUR, duchess of. *See Mancini, Laure (1635–1657).*

MERCOEUR, Elisa (1809–1835). French poet and essayist. Born 1809 in Nantes, France; died 1835. ❖ Learned Latin, Greek, and enough English to begin giving lessons at 12; published 1st poems at 16 but later switched to literary journalism to earn living; poems, essays, and 1 play published as *Oeuvres complètes* (1843).

MERCOURI, Melina (1923–1994). Greek actress and politician. Name variations: Merkouri. Born Maria Amalia Mercouris in Athens, Greece, Oct 18, 1923; died Mar 6, 1994, in New York, NY; dau. of Irene and Stamatis Mercouris (member of the Greek Chamber of Deputies and minister of the interior); m. Panayiotis Harokopos, 1940; m. Jules Dassin (director), 1966; no children. ❖ Actress who achieved international stardom in the movies *Stella* and *Never on Sunday,* spent 7 years in exile while Greece was ruled by a right-wing military junta, then returned home to serve in Parliament and as minister of culture and science; as a teenager, enrolled in the Academy of the National Theater where she studied classical Greek tragedy for 3 years; after bit parts, starred on stage in *Mourning Becomes Electra, A Streetcar Named Desire,* and *The Seven Year Itch* before moving on to such movies as *Stella, He Who Must Die, Never on Sunday* and *Topkapi;* quickly became a star; fought vehemently against the anti-democratic colonels who staged a coup in Greece, forcing her into exile after they took power (1967); returned to Greece after the overthrow of the military regime and won a seat in Parliament, a rare accomplishment for a woman in Greece (1974); appointed minister of culture and science (1980), a position she held for 8 years. ❖ See also autobiography *I Was Born Greek* (Doubleday, 1971); and *Women in World History.*

MERCURIADE OF SALERNO (fl. 1200). Italian physician and professor. Fl. around 1200 (some sources cite the 14th century) in Salerno, Italy. ❖ Studied at the medical school at Salerno; specialized in the art of surgery and gained renown for her healing abilities; is believed to have written at least 4 treatises on medicine, concerning surgery and herbal treatments.

MERDAN, Jasna (1956—). *See Kolar-Merdan, Jasna.*

MEREAU-BRENTANO, Sophie (1770–1806). German poet and novelist. Born 1770; died in childbirth in 1806; m. Friedrich Mereau, professor of jurisprudence (div. 1801); m. Clemens Brentano (poet), 1803; sister-in-law of Bettine von Arnim (1785–1859). ❖ One of the leaders of the Romantic movement, translated major literary texts, notably those of Giovanni Boccaccio and Germaine de Staël; also published her own poetry in the important literary journals of the day, some of which she edited; in an acclaimed work, an appraisal of the 17th-century French intellectual Ninon de Lenclos, advocates women's erotic emancipation, a subject she also explored in her novels *Das Blüthenalter der Empfindung* (*The Blossoming of Sensitivity,* 1794) and *Amanda and Eduard* (1803). ❖ See also *Women in World History.*

MEREDITH, Dallas (1936—). *See Rothman, Stephanie.*

MEREDITH, Gwen (b. 1907). Australian playwright, scriptwriter and novelist. Name variations: Gwen Harrison; Gwenyth Valmai. Born Gwenyth Valmai Meredith, Nov 18, 1907, in Orange, NSW, Australia; dau. of George Meredith and Florence Meredith; University of Sydney, BA; m. Ainsworth Harrison, Dec 24, 1938. ❖ Owned Chelsea Bookshop (1932–39) and worked as freelance writer; began work for Australian Broadcasting Corporation (ABC, 1943), for which she wrote serials and documentaries, including "Blue Hills" which ran for 5,795 episodes in 27 years; works include *Wives Have Their Uses* (1944), *Great Inheritance* (1946), *The Lawsons* (1946), *Blue Hills* (1950), *Beyond Blue Hills* (1953), (with Ainsworth Harrison) *Inns and Outs* (1955), and *Into the Sun.* Appointed Member of the Order of the British Empire (MBE, 1967) and Officer of the Order of the British Empire (OBE, 1977).

MEREDITH, Iris (1915–1980). American actress. Name variations: Iris Shunn. Born June 3, 1915, in Sioux City, IA; died Jan 22, 1980, in Los Angeles, CA; children: daughter. ❖ Started career as a "Goldwyn Girl," then appeared in serial adventures and westerns; films include *Call of the Rockies, West of Cheyenne, The Spider's Web, The Man from Sundown, Those High Grey Walls, Thundering Frontier* and *The Kid Rides Again.*

MEREDITH, Louisa Anne (1812–1895). Australian botanist and poet. Name variations: Louisa Anne Twamley; Louisa Meredith; Mrs. Charles Meredith. Born Louisa Anne Twamley, July 20, 1812, in Birmingham, England; died Oct 21, 1895, in Victoria, Tasmania, Australia; dau. of Thomas Twamley (farmer and miller) and Louisa Anne (Meredith) Twamley; m. Charles Meredith (later member of Tasmanian Parliament), April 18, 1839; children: George (b. 1840); Charles (b. 1844); Owen (b. 1847); 1 son who died young. ❖ The 1st Australian woman to achieve literary renown in international circles, wrote popular travelogues and entertaining first-person accounts of life in Australia; published 1st book, *Poems* (1835); moved to NSW (1840) and published *Notes and Sketches of New South Wales* (1844); wrote 1st children's book (1860); compiled and illustrated several books about the plant and animal life in Australia; co-founded Tasmanian branch of Society for the Prevention of Cruelty to Animals (1878); granted government pension (1884); writings include *My Home in Tasmania* (1852), *Some of My Bush Friends in Tasmania* (1860), *Over the Straits: A Visit to Victoria* (1861), *Phoebe's Mother* (1869), *Our Island Home* (1879), *Tasmanian Friends and Foes, Feathered, Furred, and Finned: A Family Chronicle of Country Life* (1880) and *Waratah Rhymes for Young Australia* (1891). ❖ See also *Women in World History.*

MEREDYTH, Bess (1890–1969). American screenwriter. Born Helen MacGlashan, Feb 12, 1890, in Buffalo, NY; died July 13, 1969, in Woodland Hills, CA; m. Burton Leslie (annulled); m. Wilfred Lucas (div.); m. Michael Curtiz (Hungarian film director), 1929 (died 1962); children: John Meredyth Lucas. ❖ Began career as an extra for D.W. Griffith at Biograph; wrote scripts for some of the most notable silent and sound pictures of her era, including *Ben-Hur, The Sea Beast, Don Juan, The Little Shepherd of Kingdom Come, Strange Interlude, The Mighty Barnum* and *Under Two Flags.* ❖ See also *Women in World History.*

MERETE ULFSDATTER (fl. 1320–1370). Swedish noblewoman. Name variations: Marta Ulfsdottir. Born around 1320; dau. of St. Bridget of Sweden (1303–1373) and Ulf Gudmarsson (d. 1342), prince of Nericia, sister of Saint Catherine of Sweden (c. 1330–1381); children: Ingegerd, who became an abbess at Vadstena. ❖ See also *Women in World History.*

MEREZHKOVSKI, Zinaida Nikolaevna (1869–1945). *See Gippius, Zinaida.*

MERGLER, Marie Josepha (1851–1901). American physician and surgeon. Born Marie Josepha Mergler, May 18, 1851, in Mainstockheim, Bavaria; died of pernicious anemia, May 17, 1901, in Los Angeles, CA; dau. of Francis R. Mergler (physician) and Henriette (von Ritterhausen) Mergler. ❖ Immigrated to US with family (1853); grew up in Palatine, Illinois; graduated as class valedictorian from Woman's Medical College in Chicago, IL (1879); served as professor of medica materia and adjunct professor of gynecology at Woman's Medical College of Chicago; was 2nd woman on staff of Cook County Hospital (1882); became head physician and surgeon of Mary Thompson Hospital (1895); served as secretary of faculty and dean of faculty at Woman's Medical College (renamed Northwestern University Woman's Medical College); was professor of gynecology at Post-Graduate Medical School of Chicago (1895–1901); specializing in obstetrics, gynecology, and abdominal surgery, was 1 of the most respected women in American medicine at end of 19th century.

MERI, La (b. 1898). *See La Meri.*

MERIAN, Maria Sybilla (1647–1717). German-Dutch entomologist and artist. Born Maria Sybilla Merian in Frankfurt am Main, Germany, April 2, 1647; died in Amsterdam, Netherlands, Jan 13, 1717; dau. of Matthäus Merian (engraver and topographer) and his 2nd wife, Johanna (Heim) Merian; m. Johannes Graf, 1665 (div. c. 1686); children: Johanna Helena Graf; Dorothea Graf Gsell. ❖ Illustrator who helped establish the field of entomology, made drawings and writings preeminent in the field, and traveled extensively in South America gathering specimens for her work, was interested insects from early youth, especially in silkworms and their cocoons; worked as an artist, engraver, and manufacturer of paints; established reputation as an entomologist and scientific illustrator with *Florum Fasciculi tres* (Flower Collection in Three Parts, c. 1675–78); published illustrated treatise on caterpillars and their food supply, *The Miraculous Transformations of Caterpillars and Their Strange Flower Nourishment* (1679); published *Neues Blumenbuch* (1680); lived as member of Labadist Commune (1678–88); divorced husband and resumed using maiden name (1685 or 1686); did 127 illustrations for Joannes Goedaert's *Metamorphosis et historia naturalis insectorum* (1691); voyaged to Surinam in South America for scientific study and to illustrate her discoveries (1699–1701); published major scientific work, *Metamorphosis insectorum*

Surinamensium in 3 vols. (1705). ❖ See also Patricia Phillips, *The Scientific Lady: A Social History of Women's Scientific Interests 1520–1918* (St. Martin, 1990); and *Women in World History*.

MERICI, Angela (1474–1540). *See Angela of Brescia.*

MÉRICOURT, Théroigne de (1762–1817). *See Théroigne de Méricourt, Anne-Josèphe.*

MERILUOTO, Paivi (1952—). Finnish archer. Name variations: Päivi or Paeivi Aulikki Meriluoto; Paivi Meriluoto-Aaltonen. Born Feb 12, 1952, in Finland. ❖ At Moscow Olympics, won a bronze medal in double FITA round (1980).

MERIT-NEITH (fl. c. 3100 BCE). *See Mer-neith.*

MERIVALE, Viva (1887–1934). *See Birkett, Viva.*

MERIWETHER, Lee Ann (1935—). American actress. Born Lee Ann Meriwether, May 27, 1935, in Los Angeles, CA; attended City College of San Francisco; m. Frank Aletter (actor), 1958; m. Marshall Borden (actor); children: (1st m.) 2 daughters. ❖ Named Miss America (1955), representing California; appeared as Betty on tv's "Barnaby Jones" for 8 years; appeared as Mrs. Martin on "All My Children" for 2 years, and as the Catwoman in the 1st Batman movie; films include *Angel in My Pocket* and *The Legend of Lylah Clare.* ❖ See also Frank Deford, *There She Is* (Viking, 1971).

MERIWETHER, Louise (1923—). African-American biographer and novelist. Born May 8, 1923, in Haverstraw, NY; dau. of Marion Loyd Jenkins and Julia Jenkins; m. Angelo Meriwether; m. Earl Howe. ❖ Wrote novel *Daddy Was a Number Runner* (1970), and biographies *The Freedom Ship of Robert Smalls* (1971), *The Heart Man: Dr. Daniel Hale Williams* (1972), and *Don't Ride the Bus on Monday: The Rosa Parks Story* (1973).

MERK, Larisa (1971—). Russian rower. Born Mar 16, 1971, in Novosibirsk, USSR. ❖ Won a bronze medal for quadruple sculls at Sydney Olympics (2000); won World Cup gold medal for double sculls in Milan (2003); at World championships, won silver medal for quadruple sculls (1998) and silver medal for double sculls (2002).

MERKEL, Angela (1954—). German politician and physicist. Born July 17, 1954, in Hamburg, Germany; dau. of a Lutheran minister; University of Leipzig, PhD in physics, 1986; m. 2nd husband, a chemistry professor, 1999. ❖ Was a member of the Free German Youth in the German Democratic Republic (GDR, 1971–90); became a member of Demokratisher Aufbruch (1989); was assistant spokesperson for the last government of the GDR (1990); with unification, joined the Christian Democratic Union (CDW, 1990); elected to the German Parliament (Bundestag) from the state of Mecklenburg-Western Pomerania (1990); in a political career supported by Chancellor Helmut Kohl, served as federal minister for Women and Youth (1991–94), federal minister for Environment, Conservation and Nuclear Safety (1994–98), vice chair of CDU (1991–98), and CDU chair in the state of Mecklenburg-Western Pomerania (1993–2000); became chair of CDU (2000), heading the opposition in the Bundestag, became the 1st female chancellor of Germany (2005).

MERKEL, Una (1903–1986). American actress. Born Dec 10, 1903, in Covington, Kentucky; died Jan 2, 1986, in Los Angeles, CA; dau. of a traveling merchant; m. Ronald L. Burla (aviation designer), 1932 (div. 1946). ❖ As a teen, modeled for movie magazines, which led her to roles as an extra in motion pictures being filmed at various New York studios; had 1st speaking part in Broadway play *Two by Two* (1925); spent next few years in the cast of 2 long-running shows, *Pigs* and *Coquette;* made film debut as Ann Rutledge in D.W. Griffith's *Abraham Lincoln* (1930); appeared in such films as *Blonde Bombshell, 42nd Street, Cat's Paw, Riff-Raff, Saratoga, The Maltese Falcon, The Merry Widow, On Borrowed Time, The Parent Trap* and *Destry Rides Again,* in which she engaged in a memorable on-screen fight with Marlene Dietrich; returned to Broadway with *Three's a Family* (1944). Won Tony Award for performance in *The Ponder Heart* (1956); nominated for Academy Award for *Summer and Smoke* (1961). ❖ See also *Women in World History*.

MERKEN, Lucretia Wilhelmina van (1721–1789). Dutch poet and playwright. Name variations: Lucretia van Winter. Born Lucretia Wilhelmina van Merken, Aug 21, 1721, in Amsterdam, Netherlands; died Oct 24, 1789, in Leiden, Netherlands; m. Nicolaas Simon van Winter, 1768. ❖ Considered by contemporaries as one of the most important poets of her age, wrote such epic poems as *Het nut der tegenspoeden* (The Benefit of Adversities, 1762), *David* (12 vols., 1768),

and *Germanicus* (16 vols., 1768); wrote plays in French classical style, including *Beleg der stad leyden* (1774); also wrote 17 metrical psalms; published *Toneelpoezij* (1774–86) containing own and husband's plays; *De ware geluksbedeeling* appeared posthumously (1792); works reflect her Remonstrant Protestant sensibility, patriotism and late 18th-century classicism.

MERLE, Carole (1964—). French Alpine skier. Born Jan 24, 1964, in Super Sauze, France. ❖ Won a silver medal for super-G at Albertville Olympics (1992); at World championships, won a silver medal for giant slalom (1989), a silver medal for super-G (1991) and a gold medal for giant slalom (1993); placed 5th for giant slalom at Lillehammer Olympics (1994); won 4 World Cup super-G titles (1989–92) and 2 World Cup giant slalom titles (1992–93).

MERLENI, Irini (1982—). Ukrainian wrestler. Born Feb 8, 1982, in Minitskoye, Ukraine. ❖ Won World championships for 46kg freestyle (2000, 2001) and 48kg freestyle (2003); won European championship for 46kg (2001) and 48kg (2004); won a gold medal for 48kg freestyle at Athens Olympics (2004).

MERMAN, Ethel (1912–1984). American actress and singer. Born Ethel Agnes Zimmerman, Jan 16, 1912, in New York, NY; died in NY, Feb 15, 1984; m. William Smith, 1940 (div. 1941); m. Robert Levitt, 1941 (div. 1952); m. Robert Six, 1953 (div. 1960); m. Ernest Borgnine (actor), 1964 (div. 1964). ❖ With her powerful, exuberant singing style, made stage debut in *Girl Crazy* (1930), introducing song "I Got Rhythm"; appeared in George White's *Scandals,* introducing "Life Is Just a Bowl of Cherries," followed by *Anything Goes,* where she belted out "You're the Top," "Blow, Gabriel, Blow," and "I Get a Kick Out of You"; became a fixture of Broadway musical stage (1940s–50s), starring in original productions of such musicals as *Panama Hattie, Something for the Boys, Annie Get Your Gun, Call Me Madam* and *Gypsy;* films include *Follow the Leader* (1930), *The Big Broadcast of 1936* (1936), *Anything Goes* (1936), *Alexander's Ragtime Band* (1938), *Stage Door Canteen* (1943), *Call Me Madam* (1953), *There's No Business Like Show Business* (1954) and *It's a Mad, Mad, Mad, Mad World* (1963). ❖ See also autobiography (with George Eells) *Merman* (Simon & Schuster, 1978); and *Women in World History*.

MERMET, Karine (1974—). French gymnast. Born July 12, 1974, in France. ❖ Won Mediterranean Games (1991).

MERMEY, Fayvelle (1916–1977). American synagogue president. Born 1916; died 1977 in Larchmont, NY. ❖ Served as president of Reform Synagogue in Larchmont, NY (1960–62 and 1972–74), probably as 1st woman elected president of a synagogue; founded Women's Interfaith Seminary, Larchmont, NY; served as columnist and feature writer for *Mamaroneck Daily Times,* NY (1964–70).

MER-NEITH (fl. c. 3100 BCE). Queen of Egypt. Name variations: Meritneith or Merit-Neit; Meryet-Nit. Flourished around 3100 BCE. ❖ Early queen of Egypt and possibly regent on behalf of an underaged son; assumed by most scholars to have been a queen of ancient Egypt's 1st Dynasty and probable daughter of King Djer and mother of King Den. ❖ See also *Women in World History*.

MERNISSI, Fatima (1940—). Moroccan sociologist and educator. Born 1940 in Fez, Morocco. ❖ Grew up in harem with mother, grandmothers and sisters; received PhD in US and became professor of sociology at Université Mohammed V; served on editorial boards of several periodicals; studied *Qu'ran* and early Muslim thinkers and proposed that subordination of women does not fit into early Islam; works include *Beyond the Veil: Male-Female Dynamics in a Modern Moslem Society* (1975), *Doing Daily Battle: Interviews with Moroccan Women* (1988), *Le Harem Politique (Le Prophète et les femmes)* (1987), *Chahrazad n'est pas marocaine* (1988), *The Forgotten Queens of Islam* (1997) and *Islam and Democracy: Fear of the Modern World* (2002). ❖ See also memoir, *Dreams of Trespass: Tales of a Harem Girlhood* (1995).

MERO, Yolanda (1887–1963). Hungarian pianist. Born in Budapest, Hungary, Aug 30, 1887; died in New York, NY, Oct 17, 1963; studied with father and then with Augusta Rennebaum, who had been a pupil of Franz Liszt. ❖ Widely known on American concert stages, made 1st tour of the US with great success (1910).

MÉRODE, Cléo de (c. 1875–1966). French dancer and paramour. Name variations: Cleo de Merode. Born around 1875 (some sources cite 1873); died of arteriosclerosis, Oct 17, 1966, in Paris, France; studied with Joseph Hanssen at Paris Opéra. ❖ Celebrated dancer of the Belle

Epoque era and mistress of King Leopold II of the Belgians, joined Paris Opera corps de ballet (c. 1887); met King Leopold II (c. 1893); performed throughout Europe and starred at Opera Comique in Paris; made tour of US (1897); was known as "la ballerina des bandeaux" because of her chignon. ❖ See also autobiography (in French) *Le Ballet de Ma Vie* (1955); and *Women in World History*.

MEROVINGIANS, queen of the.
See Basine (fl. 465).
See Galswintha (d. c. 568).
See Fredegund (c. 547–597).
See Brunhilda (c. 533–613).
See Audovera (d. 580).

MERRALL, Mary (1890–1973). English actress. Name variations: Queenie Merrall. Born Jan 5, 1890, in Liverpool, England; died Aug 31, 1973; m. J.B. Hissey (div.); m. Ion Swinley (div.); m. Franklin Dyall (died). ❖ Made stage debut in the harlequinade of *Cinderella* (1907), followed by *Milestones, Just Like Judy, Other Times, The Speckled Band, The Green Cord, The Orphans, The Green Goddess, Loose Ends, Macbeth* (as Lady Macbeth), *Little Eyolf, The Woman in Room 13, The Master Builder, Ladies in Retirement* and *The Little Foxes*, among others; made over 35 films, including *Nicholas Nickleby* (as Mrs. Nickleby, 1947), *Badger's Green, The Belles of St. Trinian's* and *Bitter Harvest*; with husband Franklin Dyall, briefly assumed the management of the Abbey Theatre, Dublin.

MERRALL, Queenie (1890–1973). *See Merrall, Mary.*

MERRELL, Mary (1938—). American figure skater. Name variations: Mary Brennan. Born Mary Brennan, Nov 24, 1938, in Miami, FL; m. Grady Merrell (roller skating coach); children: Diane Merrell and Grady Merrell Jr. (both skaters). ❖ Won 6 national seniors titles (1959–61, 1964, 1966–67).

MERRET, Faustine (1978—). French windsurfer. Born Mar 13, 1978, in Brest, France. ❖ At World championships, won a silver medal for board (Mistral) in 2001 and bronze medals (2002, 2003, 2004); won a gold medal for board (Mistral) at Athens Olympics (2004).

MERRIAM, Charlotte (1906–1972). American actress. Born April 5, 1906, in Sheridan, IL; died July 10, 1972, in Los Angeles, CA. ❖ Lead player for Vitagraph and Christie comedies; films include *The Brass Battle, Captain Blood, Pampered Youth* and *The Candy Kid*.

MERRIAM, Florence (1863–1948). *See Bailey, Florence.*

MERRICK, Caroline (1825–1908). American suffragist and temperance reformer. Born Caroline Elizabeth Thomas, Nov 24, 1825, in East Feliciana Parish, LA; died Mar 29, 1908, in New Orleans, LA; dau. of David Thomas and Elizabeth Patillo; m. Edwin Thomas Merrick (lawyer and chief justice of Louisiana Supreme Court), Dec 3, 1840 (died 1897); children: 2 sons, 2 daughters. ❖ Publicly addressed Louisiana constitutional convention to ask for limited suffrage for women (1879); despite initial lack of conviction for the temperance issue, elected president of New Orleans branch of Woman's Christian Temperance Union (1882); established Portia Club, women's club which dealt with laws affecting women and children (1892); served as president of state woman suffrage association to 1900. ❖ See also autobiography *Old Times in Dixie Land: A Southern Matron's Memories* (1901).

MERRICK, Myra King (1825–1899). American physician. Born Myra King, Aug 15, 1825, in Hinckley, Leicestershire, England; died Nov 10, 1899, in Cleveland, Ohio; dau. of Elizabeth King and Richard King; graduate of Central Medical College, Rochester, NY, 1852; m. Charles H. Merrick (builder), June 1848; children: at least 2 sons. ❖ The 1st practicing woman physician in Cleveland, Ohio, moved with family to Cleveland (1841); studied privately with physicians Eli and Levi Ives; opened a Cleveland practice (Aug 1852); contributed to the formation of both a Cleveland hospital for women and children and a Cleveland women's medical school; during Civil War, managed husband's lumber business and sawmill and concurrently practiced medicine in rural North Eaton, Ohio; returned to Cleveland practice (1863); helped establish and served as professor (1867–71) and as president (1869–71) of the Cleveland Homeopathic Hospital College for Women; with other women physicians, founded and served as a dispensary president of the Cleveland Medical and Surgical Dispensary Society (1878–99), a free dispensary known as the "Open Door" (later the Women's and Children's Free Medical and Surgical Dispensary).

MERRIL, Judith (1923–1997). American science-fiction writer and anthologist. Name variations: Josephine Juliet Grossman; (pseudonyms) Ernest Hamilton, Cyril Judd, Rose Sharon, Eric Thorstein. Born Josephine Juliet Grossman, Jan 21, 1923, in New York City; died of heart failure on Sept 12, 1997, in Toronto, Ontario, Canada; dau. of Schlomo Grossman and Ethel (Hurwitch) Grossman; attended City College (now City College of New York), 1939–40; Rochdale College, BA, 1970; m. 3 times, once to Frederick Pohl (a science-fiction writer), 1949–53; children: Merril Zissman McDonald; Ann Pohl. ❖ One of the premier writers of science fiction in America during the genre's flourishing years after WWII, wrote stories and novels notable for their realistic characterizations of women; was hired at Bantam Books (1947); published 1st short story (1948); published 1st science-fiction novel *Shadow on the Hearth* (1950); edited 1st "Year's Best" anthology (1956); served as book editor and reviewer for *Magazine of Fantasy and Science Fiction* (1959–69); moved to Canada (1968); donated literary resources to Toronto Public Library (1970); other writings include *The Petrified Planet* (1953), *The Tomorrow People* (1960), *Out of Bounds* (1960), *Daughters of the Earth and Other Stories* (1968), *Survival Ship and Other Stories* (1973) and *The Best of Judith Merril* (1976). Received Canadian Science Fiction and Fantasy Award (1983). ❖ See also *Women in World History*.

MERRILL, Beth (1892–1986). American stage actress. Born Sept 9, 1892, in WI; died Feb 22, 1986, in Tenafly, NJ. ❖ Made Broadway debut as Adele in *Fashions for Men* (1922), followed by *The White Desert, Ladies of the Evening, Christmas Eve, The Lady Who Came to Stay, Autumn Hill* and *All My Sons*; retired (1947).

MERRILL, Dina (1925—). American actress. Born Nedenia Hutton, Dec 9, 1925, in New York, NY; youngest dau. of Marjorie Merriweather Post (heiress to Post cereal fortune) and E.F. Hutton (stockbroker and founder of the Wall Street firm); cousin of Barbara Hutton (1912–1979); attended George Washington University for 1 year; studied at American Academy of Dramatic Arts; m. Stanley F. Rumboug, Jr., 1946 (div. 1966); m. Cliff Robertson (actor), Dec 21, 1966 (div. 1989); m. Ted Hartley (actor and partner in their production company, RKO Pavilion), Nov 1989; children: (1st m.) Stanley Rumbough; Nina Rumbough; (2nd m.) Heather Robertson. ❖ Appeared on tv and on Broadway before making screen debut in *Desk Set* (1957); often cast as an American aristocrat, appeared in a number of other films, including *Operation Petticoat* (1959), *Butterfield 8* (1960), *The Sundowners* (1960), *The Courtship of Eddie's Father* (1963) and *Just Tell Me What You Want* (1980); also frequently appeared on tv, in guest spots on weekly series and in movies of the week. ❖ See also *Women in World History*.

MERRILL, Flora (1867–1921). *See Denison, Flora MacDonald.*

MERRILL, Gretchen (1925–1965). American figure skater. Name variations: Gretchen Gay. Born Nov 2, 1925, in Boston, MA; died April 16, 1965, in Windsor, CT, where she had been under treatment for emotional problems for the preceding 3 years. ❖ Was US figure-skating champion 6 consecutive years (1943–48), but lost her chance to win a world title when the Olympics were suspended for 12 years during and after WWII; placed 6th at St. Moritz Olympics (1948).

MERRILL, Jan (1956—). American runner. Name variations: Jan Merrill-Morin. Born June 18, 1956, in Waterford, CT; m. Jeff Morin (coaches track at Coast Guard Academy). ❖ Won US National indoor mile and 2-mile titles (1976); won 2 gold medals at Pan American Games and 2 US team 1st places at World Cross Country championships; set world records for 3,000 meters (indoors) at 8:57.3 (1978), 2 miles (outdoor) at 9:46.6 (1978), 2 miles (indoor) at 9:31.8 (1977) and 5,000 meters (outdoor) at 15:30.8 (1980).

MERRILL, Linda (1950—). *See Ashley, Merrill.*

MERRILL, Mary (1853–1924). American social-welfare worker. Name variations: Mary Sroufe Merrill. Born 1853 in Diamond Springs, CA; died 1924; m. John Francis Merrill, 1874; children: 6, 4 of whom survived to adulthood. ❖ Became San Francisco society leader; served as founder and member of many charitable organizations; served as president of San Francisco Red Cross; was a founder of Pacific Dispensary for Women and Children, San Francisco (1875, present-day Children's Hospital); served as director of San Francisco YWCA; served as 1st director of Asilomar, CA (1913–c. 1924).

MERRILL-PALMER, Lizzie (1838–1916). *See Palmer, Lizzie Merrill.*

MERRIMAN, Nan (1920—). American mezzo-soprano. Born Katherine-Ann Merriman, April 28, 1920, in Pittsburgh, PA; studied with Alexia Bassian and Lotte Lehmann. ❖ Made debut with Cincinnati Summer Opera (1942), Piccolo Scala (1955–56), and Glyndebourne (1956); was especially known for her portrayal of Dorabella in *Cosi fan tutte*, which she recorded twice; frequently sang with Toscanini's NBC Symphony broadcasts; among many recordings, lauded for performance of the contralto solos in Mahler's *Das Lied von der Erde*; also recorded American show tunes; retired (1965). ❖ See also *Women in World History*.

MERRITT, Anna Lea (1844–1930). American artist. Name variations: Anna Massey Merritt; Anna Massey Lea Merritt; Anna W. Lea Merritt. Born 1844 in Philadelphia, PA; died 1930; m. Henry Merritt (artist and critic), 1877 (died 1877); studied art for extended periods in both Rome and Dresden. ❖ Expatriate, was an accomplished portraitist and genre painter and one of the 1st women whose work was purchased by the British government, the allegorical *Love Locked Out*; made grand tour of Europe (1867); won medal at Philadelphia Centennial Exposition (1876); married and widowed (1877); began exhibiting at the annual salons of Royal Academy (1878); settled in Hurstborne Tarrant, England (1890); won medal at Chicago World's Columbian Exposition (1893); wrote 1st book *A Hamlet in Old Hampshire* (1902). ❖ See also *Love Locked Out: The Memoirs of Anna Lea Merritt*; and *Women in World History*.

MERRITT, Kim (c. 1955—). American marathon runner. Born c. 1955 in Racine, WI; attended University of Wisconsin–Parkside. ❖ Won the Boston Marathon (1976) and the New York City Marathon (1975).

MERRITT, Theresa (1924–1998). African-American actress and singer. Born Sept 24, 1924, in Emporia, VA; died June 12, 1998, in The Bronx, NY; m. Benjamin Hines, 1945; children: 4. ❖ Was a member of the Helen Way Singers (1950s) and did session singing, most notably "Early in the Morning" for Buddy Holly (1958); made Broadway debut in *Carmen Jones* (1943), followed by *Golden Boy, Tambourines to Glory, Trumpets of the Lord, Don't Play Us Cheap, Division Street, The Wiz* and *Mule Bone*; star of tv series "That's My Mama"; films include *They Might be Giants, The Goodbye Girl, All that Jazz, The Great Santini, The Best Little Whorehouse in Texas* and *The Serpent and the Rainbow*. Nominated for Tony Award as Best Actress for *Ma Rainey's Black Bottom* (1985); nominated for 2 Emmys.

MERRON, Gillian (1959—). English politician and member of Parliament. Born April 12, 1959, in London, England; University of Lancaster, BSc in Management Studies. ❖ Representing Labour, elected to House of Commons for Lincoln (1997, 2001, 2005); named assistant government whip, then government whip; Lords Commissioner, HM Treasury (2004).

MERRY, Ann Brunton (1769–1808). English-born actress. Name variations: Ann Brunton. Born Ann Brunton, May 30, 1769, in London, England; died June 28, 1808, in Alexandria, VA; dau. of John Brunton (manager of Theatre Royal in Norwich); m. Robert Merry (poet), Aug 1791 (died Dec 1798); m. Thomas Wignell (theater manager), 1803 (died 1803); m. William Warren, Aug 1806. ❖ Leading tragic actress of American stage, made debut in *The Grecian Daughter* (Bath, 1785); made London debut at Covent Garden in *The Roman Father* (1785); immigrated to US (1796) and made triumphant American debut in Philadelphia in *Romeo and Juliet* (1796); made NY debut in *Venice Preserved* (1797).

MERRY, Katharine (1974—). English runner. Born Sept 21, 1974, in Dunchurch, Warwickshire, England. ❖ Won a bronze medal for 400 meters at Sydney Olympics (2000).

MERSEREAU, Violet (1892–1975). American child actress of the silents. Born Oct 2, 1892, in New York, NY; died Nov 12, 1975, in Plymouth, MA; sister of Claire Mersereau (1894–1982, actress). ❖ Made stage debut as a child; billed the "Child Wonder," became a Universal IMP star (1914); films include *The Spitfire, The Avalanche, Little Miss Nobody, Nero, Luck* and *Lend Me Your Husband*.

M.E.R.T. (1870–1939). See *Tripe, Mary Elizabeth*.

MERTEN, Lauri (1960—). American golfer. Name variations: competed as Lauri Peterson (1983–87), Lauri Merten-Peterson (1988), then Lauri Merten; Lauri Merten Capano. Born in July 1960 in WI; raised in AZ; dau. of George Merten; m. 2nd husband Louis Capano Jr. (Wilmington, DE, developer and brother of Thomas Capano), 1994. ❖ Won Arizona

Match Play title (1980) and Western Collegiate AA championship (1980–81); won Rail Charity Classic (1983), Jamie Farr Toledo Classic (1984), and US Open (1993); had 8 top-10 finishes (1993).

MERTON, Rhona (1966—). See *Martin, Rhona*.

MERYET-NIT (fl. c. 3100 BCE). See *Mer-neith*.

MERZ, Sue (1972—). American ice-hockey player. Born April 10, 1972, in Greenwich, CT. ❖ Won a team gold medal at Nagano with one goal and two assists (1998), the 1st Olympics to feature women's ice hockey; won team silver medals at World championships (1990, 1992, 1994, 1999, 2000, 2001); won a team silver medal at Salt Lake City Olympics (2002). ❖ See also Mary Turco, *Crashing the Net: The U.S. Women's Olympic Ice Hockey Team and the Road to Gold* (HarperCollins, 1999); and *Women in World History*.

MESA LUACES, Liana (1977—). Cuban volleyball player. Born Dec 26, 1977, in Camagüey, Cuba. ❖ Placed 1st at World championship (1998); won a team bronze medal at Athens Olympics (2004).

MESEKE, Marilyn (1916–2001). Miss America. Name variations: Marilyn Hume; Marilyn Rogers. Born Oct 7, 1916, in Peru, Ohio; died Sept 12, 2001, in Mount Dora, FL; m. Stanley Hume (pilot in US Army Air Corps), Jan 1944 (died); m. Benjamin Rogers (pilot); children: (1st m.) 1 son. ❖ Named Miss Ohio and Miss America (1938); had a modeling career. ❖ See also Frank Deford, *There She Is* (Viking, 1971).

MESHCHERYAKOVA, Natalya (1972—). Soviet swimmer. Born June 1, 1972, in USSR. ❖ At Barcelona Olympics, won a bronze medal in 4x100-meter medley relay (1992).

MESHULLEMETH. Biblical woman. Married Manasseh, the 14th king of Judah; children: Amon, who succeeded his father to the throne.

MESKHI, Leila (1968—). Soviet tennis player. Born Jan 5, 1968, in Tbilisi, Georgia. ❖ At Barcelona Olympics, won a bronze medal in doubles (1992).

MESSALINA, Statilia (fl. 66–68 CE). Roman empress. Born of high birth and flourished around 66–68 CE; 3rd and last wife of Nero (37–68 CE). ❖ Wealthy and intelligent, survived Nero's death (68); though she intended to marry Marcus Salvius Otho (69), was prevented by his defeat at Bedriacum and subsequent suicide.

MESSALINA, Valeria (c. 23–48). Roman empress. Name variations: Messallina. Born in Rome c. 23 (date is speculative); executed for alleged treason in 48; dau. of M. Valerius Messalla Barbatus and Domitia Lepida, both members of the dynastic Julio-Claudian family; great-granddau. of Octavia (69 BCE–11 CE); m. Claudius, c. 38, who became Roman emperor in 41; children: daughter, Octavia (c. 39–62); son, Tiberius Claudius Caesar Germanicus, later named Britannicus. ❖ Attractive, clever, and self-involved, found herself near the center of political power in Rome; exploited every possibility to maintain her position, earning in the process a reputation for being cruel, manipulative, and sexually promiscuous; initiated scores of trials against people she wanted removed from circulation, including the seemingly loyal senator, Decimus Valerius Asiaticus; sought to undermine perceived rivals, including Agrippina the Younger and Julia Livilla; was executed for an alleged involvement in a plot to overthrow husband Emperor Claudius. ❖ See also *Women in World History*.

MESSENE (fl. early 12th c. BCE). Greek hero. Flourished in early 12th century BCE in Greece; dau. of King Triopas of Argos (most powerful Greek king of his day); m. Polycaon, younger son of Lelex, another powerful lord whose land would later be known as Laconia. ❖ Allegedly a figure of the Greek Bronze ("Mycenaean") Age prior to the Trojan war, possibly mythological, who convinced father and father-in-law to mount a joint military operation against the land which lay to the west of Laconia, so that it could be her husband's to rule (new realm was renamed "Messene" in her honor). ❖ See also *Women in World History*.

MESSENGER, Margaret (1948—). Viscountess Lascelles. Name variations: Margaret Lascelles. Born April 15, 1948, in Cheltenham, Gloucestershire, England; dau. of Edgar Messenger and Margaret (Black) Messenger; m. David Lascelles, viscount Lascelles, on Feb 12, 1979; children: Emily Lascelles (b. 1975); Benjamin Lascelles (b. 1978); Alexander Lascelles (b. 1980); Edward Lascelles (b. 1982).

MESSENGER-HARRIS, Beverly (1947—). American Episcopal rector. Name variations: Beverly Messenger Harris. Born April 29, 1947, in Buffalo, NY. ❖ Ordained as Episcopal priest (1977); became 1st woman rector of an Episcopal church when named to position at Gethsemane Episcopal Church, Sherrill, NY (1977–81); served as vicar for Gethsemane, St. John's (Oneida, NY) and Trinity (Canastota, NY) churches (1987–1991).

MESSERER, Sulamith (1908–2004). Russian ballerina and choreographer. Born Sulamith Mikhailovna Messerer, Aug 27, 1908, in Moscow, Russia; died June 3, 2004, in London, England; dau. of a Lithuanian Jewish dentist; sister of Asaf Messerer (1903–1992, ballet dancer) and Raissa Messerer (actress and mother of Maya Plisetskaya); m. Gregory Levitin (motorcyclist), 1947; children: Mikhail Levitin (dance teacher). ❖ The Bolshoi Ballet's prima ballerina for more than 20 years, began training there at 8, joined the company (1926), became prima ballerina (1928), and danced all the major roles; was especially acclaimed for Kitri in *Don Quixote*, Zarema in *The Fountain of Bakhchisarai* and Lise in *La Fille Mal Gardée*; she and her brother Asaf became the 1st Soviet dancers to be granted permission to perform in western Europe (1933); was instrumental in establishing classical ballet in Japan (1961); defected to Berlin with her son (1980), then settled in London, where she taught; also held the Soviet swimming record for the 100-meters crawl (1927–30). Became an OBE (2000).

MESSICK, Dale (1906–2005). American cartoonist. Name variations: changed name from Dalia to Dale, 1927, because of bias against women cartoonists among art editors. Born Dalia Messick in South Bend, IN, April 11, 1906; died April 5, 2005, in Sonoma County, CA; dau. of Cephas Messick (art teacher) and Bertha Messick (milliner); studied at Art Institute of Chicago; m. Everett George (div.); m. Oscar Strom (div.); children: (1st m.) Starr (Mrs. Jack Rohrman, b. 1942). ❖ Launched "Brenda Starr, Reporter" as a Sunday strip in several papers of the Chicago Tribune–New York News Syndicate (June 1940), which became a daily strip (1945); her creation, the red-headed news reporter, was the number one comic-strip heroine for 40 years, at one time appearing in over 100 papers in US, 5 foreign papers, and boasting a readership exceeding 40 million; retired (1980). ❖ See also *Women in World History*.

MESSINE, de la (1836–1936). See *Adam, Juliette la Messine*.

MESSMER, Magali (1971—). Swiss triathlete. Born Sept 9, 1971, in Switzerland. ❖ Won World Cup (1999); won a bronze medal at Sydney Olympics (2000).

MESSNER, Pat (1954—). Canadian water skier. Born Mar 17, 1954, in Ancaster, Ontario, Canada; dau. of Joe Messner (champion water skier). ❖ At Olympic Games, won 3rd in slalom as demonstration event (1972); at World championships, won a bronze medal (1975), silver medal (1977), and gold medal (1979), all in slalom.

MESTA, Perle (1889–1975). Washington hostess and US ambassador. Name variations: Pearl Reid Skirvin. Born Pearl Reid Skirvin, Oct 12, 1889, in Sturgis, Michigan; died of hemolytic anemia in Oklahoma City, OK, Mar 16, 1975; dau. of William Balser Skirvin (oil prospector) and Harriet Elizabeth (Reid) Skirvin; m. George Mesta (founder of Pittsburgh's Mesta Machine Co.), Feb 12, 1917 (died 1925); no children. ❖ With husband, moved to Washington DC during WWI, where career as a Washington socialite began; traveled extensively in Europe; following husband's death (1925), purchased a mansion in Newport, RI (1929); an active Republican, became a champion of women's rights; switched political allegiances (c. 1940), becoming the great ally of Harry Truman whose success ensured her success as a Washington scene-maker and party-giver; raised a great deal of money for Democratic Party coffers during 1948 elections; was named Envoy Extraordinary and Minister Plenipotentiary to Luxemburg (1948), only the 3rd female ambassador in US history; retired as ambassador (1953). ❖ See also autobiography (with Robert Cahn) *Perle: My Story* (1960), stage musical and film *Call Me Madam*, starring Ethel Merman, was loosely based on her life (1953); and *Women in World History*.

MESTRE, Audrey (1974–2002). French deep-sea diver and marine biologist. Born Aug 11, 1974, in St. Denis, France; died in La Romana, Dominican Repubic, Oct 12, 2002; attended La Paz University; m. Francisco "Pipin" Ferreras (freediver). ❖ In a practice dive off the coast of the Dominican Republic, reached a record depth of 170 meters (558 ft) without an air supply in the sport of "no limit" freediving (Oct 2002); died during her official attempt; in early years, moved to Mexico with family; began career as a scuba diver; started freediving, setting women's world records; became the 5th deepest freediver in the world with a depth of 125 meters (2000).

MESZAROS, Erika (1966—). Hungarian kayaker. Born June 24, 1966, in Hungary. ❖ Won a silver medal at Seoul Olympics (1988) and a gold medal at Barcelona Olympics (1992), both in K4 500 meters.

MESZAROS, Gabriella (b. 1913). Hungarian gymnast. Born Dec 14, 1913, in Hungary. ❖ At Berlin Olympics, won a bronze medal in team all-around (1936).

MÉSZÁROS, Márta (1931—). Hungarian screenwriter and film director. Name variations: Marta Meszaros. Born Sept 19, 1931, in Budapest, Hungary; dau. of Laszlos Mészáros and a mother who died while Mészáros was young; attended VGIK (Moscow Academy of Cinematographic Art); married a Romanian citizen, in 1957 (div. 1959); m. Miklos Jancso (director), c. 1966 (div.). ❖ Prolific filmmaker, achieved international renown for her thoughtful, incisive portrayals of life behind the former Iron Curtain; fled Hungary with family (1936); returned to Hungary (1946); made 1st short film (1954); moved to Romania (c. 1955); returned to Hungary (1959); joined Mafilm Group 4 (mid-1960s); made 1st feature film, *The Girl* (1968); won Berlin Film Festival Golden Bear award for *Adoption* (1975), won Fipresci Prize at Cannes Film Festival for *Nine Months* (1976); won Cannes Film Festival Special Jury Prize for the autobiographical *Diary for My Children* (1984); co-wrote and directed *The Last Soviet Star* (1991), the story of Liubov Orlova, and *Sisi*, a 26-segment series about the life of Empress Elizabeth of Bavaria (1837–1898) which was shown on Hungarian tv (1992); other films include *Don't Cry, Pretty Girls* (1970), *Riddance* (1973), *Two Women* (1977), *On the Move* (1979), *The Heiresses* (1980), *Mother and Daughter* (1981), *Land of Mirages* (1983), *Diary for My Loves* (1987), *Travel Diary* (1989), *Diary for My Father and Mother* (1990) and *Gypsy Romeo* (1991). ❖ See also Catherine Portuges, *Screen Memories: The Hungarian Cinema of Márta Mészáros* (Indiana U. Press, 1993); and *Women in World History*.

META. *Variant of Margaret.*

METALIOUS, Grace (1924–1964). American author. Name variations: Grace DeRepentigny Metalious. Born Grace de Repentigny in Manchester, New Hampshire, Sept 8, 1924; died Feb 25, 1964, of chronic liver disease; dau. of Alfred Abert de Repentigny (printer) and Laurette (Royer) de Repentigny; m. George Metalious, Feb 27, 1943 (div. Feb 25, 1958); m. T.J. Martin, Feb 28, 1958 (div. Oct 6, 1960); supposedly remarried George Metalious, Oct 8, 1960, but no record exists; children: (1st m.) Marsha Metalious Dupuis; Christopher Metalious; Cynthia Metalious. ❖ Had meteoric rise to fame with publication of *Peyton Place*, considered quite sexually explicit at the time, which explored, questioned, and challenged both 1950s restrictive and idealistic view of women's place in society and conformity in general; also wrote *Return to Peyton Place* (1959), *The Tight White Collar* (1960) and *No Adam in Eden* (1963). ❖ See also autobiography (with June O'Shea) *The Girl from "Peyton Place"* (Dell, 1965); Emily Toth, *Inside Peyton Place: The Life of Grace Metalious* (Doubleday, 1981); and *Women in World History*.

METCALF, Augusta (1881–1971). See *Metcalfe, Augusta Corson*.

METCALF, Harriet (1958—). American rower. Name variations: Harriet Morris-Metcalf. Born Harriet Metcalf, Mar 25, 1958; attended Mount Holyoke College. ❖ At Los Angeles Olympics, won a gold medal in coxed eights (1984); at World championships, won a bronze medal (1981) and a silver medal (1982) in coxed fours.

METCALFE, Alexandra (1903–1995). English reformer. Name variations: Lady Alexandra Metcalfe. Born Alexandra Curzon in 1903; died Aug 1995; dau. of Mary Leiter Curzon (1870–1906) and Lord George Curzon (1859–1925, a diplomat); m. Edward Dudley Metcalfe, equerry to the prince of Wales; children: twins (b. 1930). ❖ Became an advocate for children's welfare throughout the world. ❖ See also *Women in World History*.

METCALFE, Augusta Corson (1881–1971). American artist. Name variations: often wrongly spelled Metcalf. Born Augusta Isabella Corson, Nov 10, 1881, in Vermillion, Kansas; died May 1971 in Sayre, Oklahoma; dau. of Edward and Mary Corson; m. Jim Metcalfe, 1906 (left 1908); children: 1 son, Howard Metcalfe. ❖ Dubbed the "Sage Brush Artist," moved with family to Oklahoma's Indian Country (1886) and for a half century painted scenes of the area near Durham, where she spent most of her life; had a solo exhibition at the Oklahoma Art Center (1949) and a showing at Grand Central Galleries in New York (1958). Elected to Oklahoma's Hall of Fame (1968). ❖ See also *Women in World History*.

METCALFE, Evelyn (1893–1963). *See Scott, Evelyn.*

METELLA, Malia (1982—). **French swimmer.** Born Feb 23, 1982, in Cayenne, French Guiana. ❖ Won a silver medal for 50-meter freestyle at Athens Olympics (2004).

METHENY, Linda (1948—). **American gymnast.** Name variations: Linda Metheny Mulvihill. Born Aug 22, 1948 (some sources cite Aug 12, 1947), in Olney, IL; attended University of Illinois; m. Dick Mulvihill (her coach). ❖ Won Pentathlon Gym championships (1965), AAU championships (1966, 1968) and North American championships (1968); placed 6th team all-around at Mexico City Olympics (1968); won US national all-around (1966, 1968, 1970, 1971, 1972); won a record 5 gold medals at Pan American games (1967); became a coach.

METHOT, Mayo (1904–1951). **American stage and screen actress.** Born Mar 3, 1904, in Portland, OR; died June 9, 1951, in Multhomak, OR; m. Percy Morgan Jr. (div.); m. Humphrey Bogart (actor), 1938 (div. 1945). ❖ Made NY stage debut in *The Mad Honeymoon* (1922); other stage appearances include *The Song and Dance Man, Great Day* (introducing the song "More Than You Know"), *All the King's Men,* and *Torch Song;* films include *Corsair, Harold Teen, The Night Club Lady, Virtue, Women in Prison* and *Mr. Deeds Goes to Town;* left Hollywood following her divorce.

METNEDJENET (c. 1360–1326 BCE). *See Mutnedjmet.*

METODIEVA, Penka (1950—). **Bulgarian basketball player.** Born Oct 12, 1950, in Bulgaria. ❖ Won a bronze medal at Montreal Olympics (1976) and a silver medal at Moscow Olympics (1980), both in team competition.

METRAUX, Rhoda (1914–2003). **American cultural anthropologist.** Name variations: Rhoda Bubendey Metraux or Métraux. Born Rhoda Bubendey, Oct 18, 1914, in Brooklyn, NY; died Nov 26, 2003, in Craftsbury, VT; dau. of Frederick Bubendey (banker) and Anna Marie (Kappelmann) Bubendey; attended Packer Collegiate Institute; graduate of Vassar College, 1934; attended Yale University; m. Arthur B. Proctor III (army officer), c. 1934 (died c. 1936); m. Alfred Metraux (anthropologist), Mar 1941; children: (2nd m.) Daniel. ❖ Became research assistant to Margaret Mead; performed fieldwork in village of Tambunam in East Sepik Province of Papua New Guinea (3 trips between 1967 and 1972); with Mead, published *The Study of Culture at a Distance* (1953); with 2nd husband and Mead, lived in cooperative household; known particularly for work on culture at a distance.

METSCHUCK, Caren (1963—). **East German swimmer.** Born Sept 27, 1963, in Greifswald, East Germany; went to youth sports school in Rostock. ❖ At Moscow Olympics, won a silver medal in the 100-meter freestyle, gold medal in the 100-meter butterfly, gold medal in the 4x100-meter medley relay and gold medal in the 4x100-meter freestyle relay (1980); won a gold medal in 400-meter freestyle relay at World championships (1982); also won 8 European championships. Inducted into International Swimming Hall of Fame (1990).

METTE-MARIT (1973—). **Norwegian crown princess.** Born Mette-Marit Tjessem Hoiby, Aug 19, 1973; dau. of Marit Tjessem (bank officer) and Sven Olav Bjarte Hoiby (journalist); attended University of Oslo; m. Crown Prince Haakon, Aug 25, 2001; children: (with an Oslo man) Marius; Ingrid Alexandra (b. Jan 21, 2004, Norway's 1st female heir to the throne). ❖ A former waitress with an admitted history of "heavy partying" and a son from a previous relationship, wed in a glittering state ceremony (2001).

METZ, Karin (1956—). **East German rower.** Born Aug 21, 1956, in East Germany. ❖ At Montreal Olympics, won a gold medal in coxed fours (1976); at Moscow Olympics, won a gold medal in coxed eights (1980).

METZ, queen of.
See Suavegotta *(fl. 504).*
See Deoteria *(fl. 535).*
See Vuldetrade *(fl. 550).*

METZGER, Hélène (1889–1944). **French chemist and historian.** Name variations: Helene Metzger. Born 1889 in France; died in Auschwitz, 1944; m. Paul Metzger (professor of history and geography), 1913 (missing in action during WWI, Sept 1914). ❖ Studied mineralogy at Sorbonne and wrote doctoral thesis on evolution of crystallography; won Prix Bordin in philosophy for *Les concepts scientifiques;* directed library of history of science at Centre Internationale de Synthèse from 1939; during WWII, worked at Bureau d'Etudes Israëlites in Lyons; arrested by Nazis

(Feb 1944) and sent to Auschwitz; had important influence on scientific historians.

MEULAN, Elisabeth de (1773–1827). *See Guizot, Pauline.*

MEURDRAC, Catherine (1613–1676). *See Guette, Catherine de la.*

MEURDRAC, Marie (fl. 17th c.). **French chemist.** Born Marie Meurdrac in France; sister of Catherine de la Guette (memoirist). ❖ The 1st woman to write a book on chemistry, published *Accessible and Easy Chemistry for Women* (1666).

MEVEL, Valerie (1969—). *See Barlois, Valerie.*

MEW, Charlotte (1869–1928). **British poet and short-story writer.** Name variations: Charlotte Mary Mew. Born Charlotte Mary Mew, Nov 15, 1869, in London, England; died after ingesting poison, Mar 24, 1928, in London; dau. of Frederick Mew (architect) and Anne (Kendall) Mew; attended University College, London. ❖ Published 1st short story "Passed," in the *Yellow Book,* a journal illustrated by Aubrey Beardsley (1894); gradually began to achieve modest renown for fiction and poetry; published articles, essays, and reviews in such periodicals as *Temple Bar, New Statesman* and the *Nation;* father died (1898); published 1st book of poetry, *The Farmer's Bride* (1916) which was highly praised and reissued as *Saturday Market* in US (1921); received civil-list pension for contributions to English letters (1922); published *The Rambling Sailor* (1929). ❖ See also Penelope Fitzgerald, *Charlotte Mew and Her Friends* (1984); and *Women in World History.*

MEXIA, Ynes (1870–1938). **Mexican-American botanical explorer.** Name variations: Ynez Mexia. Born Ynes Enriquetta Julietta Mexia on May 24, 1870, in Georgetown section of Washington, DC; died of lung cancer, July 12, 1938, in Berkeley, California; dau. of Enrique Antonio Mexia (diplomat) and Sarah R. (Wilmer) Mexia; attended University of California, 1921–37; m. Herman E. de Laue, c. 1898 (died 1904); m. Augustin A. de Raygados, 1907 (div. c. 1908); no children. ❖ Botanical explorer whose research expeditions contributed greatly to the modern scientific classification of plants of the Americas, moved to San Francisco (1908); made 1st botanical expedition to collect plants (c. 1925), bringing back 500 plants, one of which, *Mimosa mexiae,* was named after her; journeyed to South America (1929), traveling 25,000 miles up Amazon River on a steamship, then another 5,000 miles by canoe; returned with over 65,000 specimens, mainly from Brazil and Peru (1932). ❖ See also *Women in World History.*

MEXICAN NUN, the (1651–1695). *See Juana Inés de la Cruz.*

MEXICO, empress of. *See Carlota (1840–1927).*

MEYEN, Janna (1977—). **American snowboarder.** Born Feb 12, 1977, in Torrance, CA. ❖ Won silver (Winter 2002) and gold (Winter 2003) in Slopestyle at X Games; other finishes include 2nd at Sims Invitational World Snowboard championships in Slopestyle (2000), 2nd at Chevy Grand Prix, Northstar-at-Tahoe, CA, in Big Air (2000), 2nd at World championships, Vail, CO, in Slopestyle (2002), and 1st at Vans Triple Crown, Sierra-at-Tahoe, CA, in Slopestyle (2002).

MEYER, Agnes (1887–1970). **American writer, social reformer, and newspaper publisher.** Name variations: Agnes Elizabeth Ernst Meyer; Agnes Ernst Meyer. Born Agnes Elizabeth Ernst on Jan 2, 1887, in New York, NY; died of cancer, Sept 1, 1970, in Mt. Kisco, NY; dau. of Frederic H. Ernst and Lucy M (Schmidt) Ernst; Barnard College, BA, 1907; attended the Sorbonne (Universite de Paris), c. 1908–09; attended Columbia University, 1911–12; m. Eugene Meyer (financier, presidential adviser, and later newspaper publisher), Feb 12, 1910 (died 1959); children: Florence Meyer Homolka; Elizabeth Meyer Lorentz; Katharine Graham (publisher); Ruth Meyer; Eugene Meyer III. ❖ Involvement in the family business, the *Washington Post,* helped make it one of the most influential newspapers in the nation; hired as the 1st woman reporter for *New York Sun* (1907); lived in Paris (1909); became involved in charity work (1912); was a delegate to Republican National Convention (1924); after husband purchased *Washington Post* (1933), became part-owner (1935); traveled to wartime England as a reporter for the *Post* (1942); played an active role in the paper's editorial content and wrote numerous features and series herself; began agitating for creation of cabinet department for social services (1944), resulting in eventual creation of federal Department of Health, Education, and Welfare (1953); was active in promoting veterans' issues and also a champion of desegregation; wrote for other publications, including *Collier's, The New York Times Book Review* and *Atlantic Monthly.* ❖ See also *Women in World History.*

MEYER, Annie Nathan (1867–1951). American author and founder. Name variations: Annie Nathan; Annie Florance Nathan. Born Anne Nathan in New York, NY, Feb 19, 1867; died in New York, NY, Sept 23, 1951; dau. of Robert Weeks Nathan (stockbroker and later a passenger agent for a railroad) and Annie Augusta (Florance) Nathan (d. 1878); younger sister of Maud Nathan (1862–1946); attended Columbia College, 1885–87; m. Alfred Meyer (physician), Feb 15, 1887; children: Margaret Meyer (1894–1923). ❖ Best remembered as a founder of Barnard College, the women's affiliate of Columbia University (1889), was also a prolific writer, turning out novels, plays, short stories, and essays in which she often extolled women's strengths and abilities, though her views did not extend to the vote; wrote 3 novels, an autobiography (1st published in 1935 as *Barnard Beginnings*, but revised into a chattier version, *It's Been Fun,* 1951), several books of nonfiction, and 26 plays, one of which, *The Advertising of Kate,* had a brief life on Broadway (1922); remained a trustee of Barnard (1893–1942) and played a role in recruiting black students. ❖ See also *Women in World History.*

MEYER, Antoinette. Swiss Alpine skier. Born in Switzerland. ❖ Won a silver medal for slalom at St. Moritz Olympics (1948).

MEYER, Debbie (1952—). American swimmer. Name variations: Deborah Meyer; Deborah Elizabeth Reyes. Born Deborah Elizabeth Meyer, Aug 14, 1952, in Haddonfield, NJ. ❖ Won gold medals for the 800-meter freestyle, 400-meter freestyle, and 200-meter freestyle at Mexico City Olympics (1968), becoming the 1st woman to win gold medals in 3 indiv. swimming events at the same Olympics and to set Olympic records in each race; won Pan American championships for 400 and 800 meters (1967); set 15 world records; retired (1970). Inducted into Women's Sports Foundation Hall of Fame (1987). ❖ See also *Women in World History.*

MEYER, Elana (1966—). South African runner. Born Oct 10, 1966, in Albertina, South Africa; attended Stellenbosch University; m. Michael Meyer (runner). ❖ Won a silver medal in the 10,000 meters at Barcelona Olympics (1992) and was a finalist in Sydney (2000); won World Cup in London for 10,000 meters (1994); finished 2nd in Boston Marathon (1995 and 1996); set world record in half-marathon (1:07.29, 1998), then broke her own record in Tokyo City Half (1:06.44, 1999); won over 20 South African titles in track, half-marathon, 15km, cross country, and marathon.

MEYER, Gertrud (1914—). German gymnast. Born July 13, 1914, in Germany. ❖ At Berlin Olympics, won a gold medal in team all-around (1936).

MEYER, Helen (1907–2003). American business executive and publisher. Born Helen Honig, Dec 4, 1907, in Brooklyn, NY; died April 21, 2003, in Livingston, NJ; m. Abraham J. Meyer (died 1993); children: Dr. Adele M. Brodkin and Robert L. Meyer. ❖ Began career as a clerk for George Delacorte at Dell Publishing (1924); became president of Dell (1944), the 1st woman to head a publishing firm; ran Delacorte, Dell and Dial Press with success for more than 30 years, then supervised their sale to Doubleday; retired (1978). Inducted into Publishers Hall of Fame (1986).

MEYER, Joyce (1943—). American preacher. Born Pauline Joyce Hutchison, June 4, 1943, in St. Louis, Missouri; m. 2nd husband David B. Meyer, 1966; children: 4. ❖ Began ministry (1980); became associate pastor at Life Christian Center in St. Louis, Missouri; started Joyce Meyer Ministries; launched radio broadcast "Life in The Word" and her own cable tv program "Life in The Word with Joyce Meyer," which became one of the world's largest television ministries; wrote over 60 books, including *Beauty for Ashes, The Root of Rejection, Battlefield of the Mind* and *The Word, The Name, The Blood.*

MEYER, Lucy (1849–1922). American religious writer, social reformer, physician, and founder. Name variations: Lucy Jane Rider Meyer; Lucy Rider Meyer. Born Sept 9, 1849, in New Haven, Vermont; died of Bright's disease, Mar 16, 1922, in Chicago, Illinois; dau. of Richard Dunning Rider (farmer) and Jane (Child) Rider; attended New Hampton Literary Institute, 1867; degree from Oberlin College, 1872; attended Woman's Medical College of Pennsylvania, 1873–75, and Massachusetts Institute of Technology, 1877–78; Women's Medical College of Chicago, MD, 1887; m. Josiah Shelly Meyer, May 23, 1885; children: son Shelly Rider. ❖ Prominent Methodist writer and founder of a training school for Methodist women social workers in Chicago, moved to Canada (c. 1868); taught freed slaves in North Carolina (c. 1869); became teacher at Oberlin College (early 1870s);

returned to Vermont (c. 1875); became principal of Troy Conference Academy (1876); moved to Illinois (1879); became secretary of the Illinois State Sunday School Association (1881); a leading figure in the American deaconess movement, co-founded 1st deaconess home in US (1885); founded journal for deaconesses (1886); formed the Methodist Deaconess Association (1908). ❖ See also *Women in World History.*

MEYER, Olga (1889–1972). Swiss novelist. Name variations: Olga Meyer-Blumfeld also seen as Blumenfeld. Born April 30, 1889, in Zurich, Switzerland; died Jan 29, 1972, in Zurich; dau. of a pastor. ❖ Worked as teacher in poor district of Zurich, where she wrote novels to educate pupils; published over 30 novels, including the popular *Anneli: Erlebnisse eines kleinen Landmädchens* (Anneli: Experiences of a Small Country Girl, 1918).

MEYERHOFF, Jane (1924–2004). American art collector. Born Jane Bernstein, 1924, in Baltimore, MD; died Oct 16, 2004, in Baltimore, MD; graduate of Goucher College; m. Robert Meyerhoff (home builder, developer art collector), 1945; children: Neil and John Meyerhoff and Rose Ellen Greene. ❖ With husband, assembled one of the most important US collections of late-20th-century art, which included the work of Jasper Johns, Ellsworth Kelly, Roy Lichtenstein, Robert Rauschenberg, Grace Hartigan and Frank Stella, then donated the entire collection to the National Gallery of Art (1987).

MEYEROWITZ, Theresa F. (1890–2002). See *Bernstein, Theresa Ferber.*

MEYERS, Ann (1955—). American basketball player and tv commentator. Name variations: Ann Meyers Drysdale. Born Mar 25, 1955, San Diego, CA; graduate of University of California, Los Angeles; m. Don Drysdale (Los Angeles Dodgers' pitcher and broadcaster), 1986 (died 1993); dau. of Bob Meyers (basketball guard for Marquette University and the Milwaukee Shooting Stars); sister of Dave Meyers (played basketball for UCLA and Milwaukee Bucks). ❖ Was the 1st high-school player to make the US National women's basketball team and the 1st woman to receive a full athletic scholarship from a major university; was the 1st 4-time All-American at UCLA and the 1st woman to sign a contract with a men's NBA team; won a team silver medal at Montreal Olympics (1976); became a tv sports commentator for ESPN and NBC. Won Broderick Cup; inducted into Basketball Hall of Fame. ❖ See also *Women in World History.*

MEYERS, Jan (1928—). American politician. Born July 20, 1928, in Lincoln, Nebraska; William Woods College, AFA, 1948; University of Nebraska, BA, 1951. ❖ Six term Republican US congressional representative from Kansas, was elected to Kansas legislature (1972), serving in the state house until 1984; elected to US House of Representatives (1984); during 1st term, served on Committee on Science and Technology as well as on Select Committee on Aging; following reelection (1986), served on prestigious Senate Committee on Foreign Affairs, where she focused on curtailing international drug trafficking; a strong proponent of Equal Rights Amendment (ERA) and a member of the Women's Congressional Caucus, also supported women's reproductive freedoms; served as vice-chair of the Energy and Environment Study Conference; retired from Congress (1996). ❖ See also *Women in World History.*

MEYERS, Mary (1946—). American speedskater. Born Mary Margaret Meyers, Feb 10, 1946, in US. ❖ Won a silver medal in a 3-way tie with Dianne Holum and Jennifer Fish for the 500 meters at Grenoble Olympics (1968).

MEYERSON, Golda (1898–1978). See *Meir, Golda.*

MEYFARTH, Ulrike (1956—). West German high jumper. Born May 4, 1956, in Köln-Rodenkirchen, West Germany; grew up in Munich. ❖ Won a gold medal for high jump at Munich Olympics (1972), the youngest competitor—male or female—to win an indiv. Olympic track-and-field event; won a gold medal for high jump at Los Angeles Olympics (1984), the oldest woman high-jump winner in Olympic history.

MEYGRET, Anne (1965—). French fencer. Born Feb 15, 1965, in France. ❖ At Los Angeles Olympics, won a bronze medal in team foil (1984).

MEYNELL, Alice (1847–1922). English poet and essayist. Born Alice Christiana Gertrude Thompson at Barnes, Surrey, England, Sept 22, 1847 (some sources cite Aug 17); died Nov 27, 1922; 2nd dau. of Thomas and Christiana Weller Thompson (concert pianist); younger sister of Elizabeth Thompson Butler (artist); m. Wilfred Meynell (journalist), 1877; children: 8, including Francis, Everard, and Viola Meynell (1886–1956). ❖ One of England's most thoughtful poets and insightful essayists, published 1st book of poems, *Preludes* (1875), with illustrations by her sister; with husband, edited and wrote for *The Pen* (1880), *The Weekly Register* (1881–98), and their monthly *Merry England* (1883–95); published 1st book of essays, *The Rhythm of Life* (1893); began writing weekly articles for *Pall Mall Gazette* (1894), some of which were collected as *The Color of Life* (1896); wrote for *The Spectator, Saturday Review, The Magazine of Art*, and *The Art Journal*, among others; though not a militant, was an active supporter of the women's suffrage movement. ❖ See also *Women in World History.*

MEYNELL, Alicia (fl. 1804–1805). English equestrian. Born around 1782; flourished 1804–05. ❖ Competed in a horse race over a 4-mile course at York, becoming the 1st woman known to have done so (1804); competed once again (1805), winning 2 races: the 1st, by default; the 2nd, by half a neck. ❖ See also *Women in World History.*

MEYNELL, Viola (1886–1956). English writer, poet, and biographer. Born Viola Meynell at Phillimore Place, Kensington, in 1886; died 1956; dau. of Alice Meynell (1847–1922, writer) and Wilfred Meynell (journalist); m. John Dallyn, 1922; children: 1 son. ❖ Published 1st novel, *Lot Barrow* (1913); produced 20 volumes of prose and poetry, as well as editing others, including selections from George Eliot (Mary Anne Evans); wrote a memoir of her mother, as well as one on her father's association with Francis Thompson, the poet; short stories, perhaps her best work, were collected (1957).

MEYNER, Helen Stevenson (1929–1997). American politician. Born Helen Day Stevenson, Mar 5, 1929, in New York, NY; died in 1997; was a distant cousin of Adlai Stevenson; attended Colorado Springs College, 1946–50; m. Robert B. Meyner (governor of New Jersey, 1953–62), 1957; children: 1 son (born and died Feb 11, 1970). ❖ US congressional representative (Jan 3, 1975–Jan 3, 1979), served as a Red Cross field worker in Korean War until 1952; began writing a weekly column for *Newark Star-Ledger* (1962); hosted tv interview program broadcast in NY and New Jersey (1965–68); began serving on New Jersey State Rehabilitation Commission (1971), in which capacity she continued into 1990s; elected to US Congress as a Democrat (1974); during 2 terms, served on the Committee on Foreign Affairs and played a significant role in international affairs; also served on Select Committee on Aging and Committee on the District of Columbia and backed the Equal Rights Amendment; was defeated in bid for a 3rd term (1978). ❖ See also *Women in World History.*

MEYNERT, Dora von Stockert- (1870–1947). See *Stockert-Meynert, Dora von.*

MEYSEL, Inge (1910–2004). German actress. Born May 30, 1910, in Berlin, Germany; died July 10, 2004, in Bullenhausen, Lower Saxony. ❖ Banned from the stage during the Nazi era because her father was Jewish, appeared in many popular tv shows after the war; earned nickname "Mother of the Nation" for her role as a concierge in tv series "Das Fenster zum Flur" ("The Window to the Floor," 1959–60).

MEYSENBURG, Malwida von (1816–1903). German salonnière and writer. Name variations: Malvida von Meysenburg. Born Oct 28, 1816 in Cassel, Germany; died 1903 in Rome, Italy. ❖ A socialist and supporter of 1848 Revolution, was forced to leave Berlin (1852); thereafter, lived in England, Paris, and Rome, conducting salons that attracted such luminaries as Giuseppe Garibaldi and Friedrich Nietzsche; during later years, greatly influenced French novelist Romain Rolland, with whom she shared stories about her famous circle of friends; writings are mostly autobiographical and include *Eine Reise nach Ostende* (*A Journey to Ostend*, 1849), and *Memoiren einer Idealistin* (1876), which was published in English as *Rebel in Bombazine: Memoirs of Malvida von Meysenburg* (1936).

MEYSEY-WIGLEY, Caroline (1801–1873). See *Clive, Caroline.*

MEZARI, Maddalena (c. 1540–1583). See *Casulana, Maddalena.*

MHAC AN TSAOI, Máire (1922—). Irish poet. Name variations: Maire MacEntee; Maire Cruise O'Brien. Born Maire MacEntee, 1922, in Dublin, Ireland; dau. of Sean MacEntee and Margaret MacEntee; studied French and English at University College, Dublin, and at Sorbonne, Paris; m. Conor Cruise O'Brien (writer and politician), 1962. ❖ Feminist writer, was called to the bar (1944) and later served with Department of Foreign Affairs in Dublin, France, Spain, and at UN; published *Cré na Mna Ti* (The Housewife's Credo, 1958); other writings include *Margabh na Saoire* (1956), *A Heart Full of Thought* (1959), *Codladh an Ghaiscigh* (1973), *An Galar Dubhach* (1980), and *An Cion go dtí Seo* (1987);

collaborated with husband on *A Concise History of Ireland* (1972). Received honorary degree from National University of Ireland and O'Shaughnessy Award for poetry (1988).

MIAHUAXOCHITL (d. 1551). See *Tecuichpo.*

MICAIA, Vera (1926—). See *de Sousa, Noémia.*

MICHAEL, Gertrude (1910–1965). American actress. Born Lillian Gertrude Michael, June 1, 1910, in Talladega, Alabama; died Dec 31, 1964, in Hollywood, CA. ❖ Made NY stage debut in Rachel Crother's *Caught Wet* (1931); films include *Wayward, Ann Vickers, I'm No Angel, Cleopatra, Murder at the Vanities* (as Rita Ross), *Just Like a Woman, Till We Meet Again, Flamingo Road, Caged* and *The Farmer's Daughter*; starred in *The Notorious Sophie Lang* series.

MICHAEL, Julia Warner (b. 1879). Bahamian poet. Born 1879 in the Bahamas. ❖ Published *A Memory of New Providence Island* (1909).

MICHAELIS, Hanny (1922—). Dutch poet and essayist. Born Dec 19, 1922, in Amsterdam, Netherlands; m. Gerard Reve (writer), 1948 (div. 1959). ❖ Jewish parents were killed during WWII (1943); worked as editor and translator of children's books and served on Amsterdam Arts Council (1957–84); published *Klein voorspel* (1949), *Water uit de rots* (1957), *Tegen de wind* (1962), *Onvoorzien* (1966), *De rots van Gibraltar* (1970), *Wegdraven naar een nieuw Utopia* (1971), *Selected Poems* (1984), *Hanny Michaelis over Gerard Reve* (1987), *Het ontkruid van de twijfel* (1989), *Verzamelde gedichten* (1996), and *Verst verleden* (2002); translations published in, among others, *Change of Scene: Contemporary Dutch and Flemish Poems in English Translation* (1969) and *Dutch Interior: Postwar Poetry of the Netherlands and Flanders* (1984). Awarded Anna Bijns Prize (1996).

MICHAËLIS, Karin (1872–1950). Danish novelist and short-story writer. Name variations: Michaelis; Karin Michaëlis Stangeland; Karin Michaëlis-Stangeland. Born Katharina Marie Bech-Brøndum at Randers, Denmark, Mar 20, 1872; died Jan 11, 1950, in Copenhagen; dau. of Jac Brøndum; mother's maiden name was Bech; sister of Baroness Dahlerup; educated in private schools and with tutors; m. Sophus Michaëlis (1865–1932, well-known Danish poet), c. 1893 (div. 1911); m. Charles Emil Stangeland (an American), 1912. ❖ Wrote more than 50 books; best-known novel was *The Dangerous Age: Letters and Fragments from a Woman's Diary* (*Den Farlige Alder*), which was serialized in the *Revue de Paris* (1911) before being published in hardcover and called by Proust, the "most sincere, the most complete, the most humble and the most disquieting feminine confession perhaps ever written"; also wrote the popular "Bibi" series for children, about an untamed girl who lives with her father and travels through Denmark. ❖ See also *Women in World History.*

MICHAELIS, Liane (1953—). East German handball player. Born April 23, 1953, in East Germany. ❖ At Montreal Olympics, won a silver medal in team competition (1976).

MICHAEL OF KENT (1945—). Czech-born English princess. Name variations: Marie-Christine von Reibnitz. Born Marie Christine Agnes Hedwig Ida von Reibnitz, Jan 15, 1945, in Karlovy Vary (Karlsbad), Czech Republic; dau. of Gunther von Reibnitz and Marie-Anne, countess Szapary; m. Tom Troubridge, in 1971 (annulled, 1978); m. Prince Michael of Kent (Michael Windsor), June 30, 1978; children: (2nd marriage) Frederick Windsor (b. 1979); Gabriella Windsor (b. 1981).

MICHAELSEN, Isabel Annie (1887–1938). See *Aves, Isabel Annie.*

MICHAIAH. *Variant of Maacah.*

MICHAL (fl. 1000 BCE). Biblical woman. Fl. about 1000 BCE; youngest of 2 daughters of Saul (1st king of the Jewish nation) and Ahinoam; sister of Merab; 1st wife of David (r. 1010–970 BCE); no children. ❖ With brother Jonathan, helped David escape assassination planned by her father. ❖ See also *Women in World History.*

MICHEL, Louise (1830–1905). French anarchist and writer. Name variations: "La Vierge Rouge" (The Red Virgin). Pronunciation: Mee-SHELL. Born Clémence-Louise Michel, May 29, 1830, in Vroncourt (Haute-Marne), France; died in Marseille of pneumonia and exhaustion, Jan 9, 1905; dau. of Marie-Anne (called Marianne) Michel (1808–1885), a servant, and an unknown father, probably Marie-Anne's master, Etienne-Charles Demahis, or (more likely) his son Laurent; took teacher's training for 3 months at Lagny in Madame Duval's school (1851) and at Chaumont (1851–52); never married. ❖ Anarchist and writer whose heroism during Paris Commune insurrection and subsequent imprisonments, and example of selfless devotion to her ideals, made her one of the most celebrated female revolutionaries of her time; founded and ran private schools off and on in Haute-Marne (1852–56); taught in private schools in Paris, gradually becoming interested in left-wing politics (c. 1856–70); was active during siege of Paris (Franco-Prussian War), running a school for poor children, taking part in demonstrations, and working on vigilance committees (1870–71); continued social work and teaching but also became a nurse and soldier during Paris Commune, was arrested and sentenced to deportation to a prison colony for life (1871); after imprisonment in France (1871–73), sent to New Caledonia, where she taught the native Kanakas until amnestied (1873–80); triumphantly returned to France, began a career of anarchist speech-making, and was imprisoned (1883–86); shot in the head at Le Havre by a would-be assassin (1888); arrested for incitement but released, then moved to London (1890); after a triumphal return to Paris, resided alternately in Paris and London, making frequent speaking tours in France until her death (1895–1905); return of her body to Paris for burial occasioned a huge but peaceful leftist demonstration (1905); wrote poetry throughout life. ❖ See also *Mémoires* (1886, English version, *The Red Virgin: Memoirs of Louise Michel*, ed. and trans. by Lowry and Gunter, U. of Alabama Press, 1981); Edith Thomas, *Louise Michel* (trans. by Williams, Black Rose Books, 1980); and *Women in World History*.

MICHEL, Micheline (b. 1922). *See Presle, Micheline.*

MICHELENA, Beatriz (1890–1942). American actress. Born Feb 22, 1890, in New York, NY; died Oct 10, 1942, in San Francisco, CA; sister of Vera Michelena (1884–1961, actress); m. George Middleton. ❖ Best remembered for her portrayal of Bret Harte heroines for the California Motion Picture Corp.; films include *Mrs. Wiggs of the Cabbage Patch*, *Salomy Jane*, *The Unwritten Law*, *The Heart of Juanita* and *The Flame of Hellgate*.

MICHELER, Elisabeth (1966—). German kayaker. Born April 30, 1966, in Germany. ❖ At Barcelona Olympics, won a gold medal in K1 slalom (1992).

MICHELINA OF PESARO (1300–1356). Saint. Name variations: Michelina Malatesta; Blessed Michelina. Born Michelina Matelli in Pesaro, in the Marches of Ancona, 1300; died June 19, 1356; m. Lord Malatesta, duke of Rimini, 1312 (died 1320); children: 1 who did not survive to adulthood. ❖ Married at 12 and widowed at 20, joined the Franciscans in their work; humbled herself and worked for the poor, despite family's growing objections; also devoted herself to the care of lepers, purportedly restoring some of them to health by kissing their leprous sores. Feast day is June 19. ❖ See also *Women in World History*.

MICHELLE VALOIS (1394–1422). Duchess of Burgundy. Name variations: Michelle de France. Born 1394; died July 8, 1422, in Ghent, Flanders, Belgium; dau. of Charles VI, king of France (r. 1380–1422), and Isabeau of Bavaria (1371–1435); sister of Charles VII (1403–1461), king of France (r. 1422–1461); became, around 1415, 1st wife of Philip the Good, duke of Burgundy (r. 1419–1467). Philip the Good later m. Bonne of Artois (d. 1425), then Isabella of Portugal (1397–1471).

MICHELMAN, Kate (1942—). American feminist and reproductive rights activist. Born Aug 4, 1942; grew up in Defiance, Ohio; married; children: 3 daughters. ❖ A specialist in early childhood development, with a particular emphasis on developmentally disabled children, developed a model milti-disciplinary diagnostic treatment program for developmentally disabled preschool children and their families which became a model throughout US; was executive director of Planned Parenthood in Harrisburg, PA; served as president of National Abortion Rights Action League, later known as NARAL Pro-Choice America (1985–2003).

MICHIE, Anne (1927—). *See McLaren, Anne Laura.*

MICHIKO (1934—). Empress of Japan. Born Michiko Shoda in Oct 1934; m. Akihito (b. 1933), emperor of Japan, in 1959; children: son Crown Prince Naruhito (b. 1960). ❖ The 1st commoner to marry a crown prince, was criticized for breast-feeding her babies, carrying them in public, and attempting to raise them herself; for years, had conflicts with mother-in-law Nagako, who sided with the traditionalists; possibly suffered the 1st of 2 nervous breakdowns (1963); when Japanese press accused her of being domineering toward her husband (1993), fell unconscious the following day and reputedly could not speak for the next 6 months. ❖ See also *Women in World History*.

MICHITSUNA NO HAHA (c. 936–995). Japanese diarist and poet. Name variations: Michitsuna no haha is Japanese for "Michitsuna's mother" (her personal name is not known). Born c. 936 in Japan; died 995; dau. of a provincial governor; m. Fujiwara Kaneie (became regent [986], then chancellor [989], died 990; his descendants by his principle wife [not Michitsuna no haha] would be *de facto* rulers of Japan); children: Fujiwara Michitsuna (955–1020). ❖ One of the most important writers of the Heian period in Japan, wrote journal *Kagero nikki* (The Kagero Diary, trans. into English as *The Gossamer Journal* or *The Gossamer Years*), a classic which documents her troubled marriage and life in the Japanese court; following husband's death, possibly become a Buddhist nun.

MICKELSON, Anna (1980—). American rower. Born Mar 21, 1980, in Seattle, WA; dau. of David and Denise Mickelson; attended University of Washington. ❖ Won a gold medal for coxed eights at World championships (2002); won a silver medal for coxed eights at Athens Olympics (2004); won 2 World Cups for coxed eights (2003 and 2004).

MICKEY and SYLVIA. *See Vanderpool, Sylvia.*

MICKLER, Ingrid (1942—). West German track-and-field athlete. Name variations: Ingrid Becker, Ingrid Mickler-Becker. Born Sept 26, 1942, in Geseke, West Germany. ❖ At Mexico City Olympics, won a gold medal in the pentathlon (1968); at Munich Olympics, won a gold medal in 4x100-meter relay (1972).

MICSA, Maria (1953—). Romanian rower. Born Mar 31, 1953, in Romania. ❖ At Montreal Olympics, won a bronze medal in quadruple sculls with coxswain (1976).

MIDA. *Variant of Ida.*

MIDDLETON, Alice (c. 1472–1545). *See More, Alice.*

MIDDLETON, Jane (1645–1692). *See Myddelton, Jane.*

MIDDLETON, Margaret (1556–1586). *See Clitherow, St. Margaret.*

MIDLER, Bette (1945—). American musician. Born Dec 1, 1945, in Paterson, NJ; grew up in Honolulu, Hawaii; attended University of Hawaii; m. Martin von Haselberg (commodities trader and performance artist), 1984; children: Sophie (b. 1986). ❖ Played small part in film, *Hawaii* (1966); appeared off-Broadway, then on Broadway in *Fiddler on the Roof*, with Barry Manilow on piano, sang and performed comedy routines at the Continental Baths in NYC, becoming cult figure (1970s); released gold debut album, *The Divine Miss M* (1972), which earned Grammy for Best New Artist; nominated for Academy Award for Best Actress for *The Rose* (1979) and also performed on soundtrack, which went platinum; wrote bestselling memoir, *A View From a Broad* (1980), and children's book, *The Saga of Baby Divine* (1983); acted in comedies, including *Ruthless People* (1986) and *Big Business* (1988); won Grammy for "Wind Beneath My Wings" from *Beaches* (1989), in which she also acted; nominated for Oscar for *For the Boys* (1991); other films include *Stella* (1990), *Scenes From a Mall* (1991), *The First Wives Club* (1996), and *What Women Want* (2000); other albums include *Songs for the New Depression* (1974), *Broken Blossom* (1977), *Bette of Roses* (1995), *Bathhouse Betty* (1998) and *Bette Midler Sings the Rosemary Clooney Songbook* (2003); performed in tv series, "Bette" (2000).

MIDORI (1971—). Japanese-born violinist. Born 1971 in Osaka, Japan; dau. of Setsu Goto (violinist); studied with her mother, then at Juilliard under Dorothy DeLay; Gallatin School of New York University, BA in psychology, 2000. ❖ Moved to US (1981); at 11, launched professional career when she performed the first movement of the Paganini Violin Concerto No. 1 with the New York Philharmonic and Zubin Mehta (Dec 1982), debuted with Philadelphia Orchestra and St. Paul Chamber Orchestra (1983), Toronto Symphony (1985); made the 1st of 2 recordings for Philips (1986); made legendary debut at Tanglewood with the Boston Symphony, Leonard Bernstein conducting (1987), breaking two E-strings but continuing unfazed on borrowed violins; signed with Sony Classical (1988), releasing the Grammy-nominated recording of the Paganini Caprices for Solo Violin, as well as her 20th anniversary album (2002), among many others; began giving master classes at Manhattan School of Music (2001); appeared in key concert halls throughout the world. Awarded Avery Fisher Prize (2001).

MIDTHUN, Kristin (1961—). Norwegian handball player. Name variations: Kristin Midthun Ihle. Born Feb 4, 1961, in Oslo, Norway. ❖ At Seoul Olympics, won a silver medal in team competition (1988).

MIEGEL, Agnes (1879–1964). German poet and short-story writer. Born in Königsberg, East Prussia (modern-day Kaliningrad, Russia), Mar 9, 1879; died in Bad Salzuflen, Oct 26, 1964; dau. of Gustav Adolf Miegel and Helene Wilhelmine Miegel. ❖ Writer whose books, set in East Prussia and written in the spirit of *Blut und Boden* (Blood and Soil) Romanticism, were popular with a nationalistic and conservative readership before, during, and after the Third Reich; published 1st book of poems, *Gedichte* (1901); wrote a number of ballads, including "Jane," "Lady Gwen" and "Die Nibelungen" (1902); published *Balladen und Lieder* (Ballads and Songs, 1907) to critical acclaim; received Kleist Prize (1916), which effectively proclaimed her Germany's most eminent poet of the day; covered cultural events for conservative Königsberg newspaper, *Ostpreussische Zeitung* (1920–26); published her longest prose work, *Geschichten aus Alt-Preussen* (Stories from Old Prussia, 1926); like most conservative Germans, threw her support to Nazis (1933); was elected to a Prussian Academy of the Arts (1933) and appointed a senator in German Academy of Poetry; received the Herder Prize (1936); joined Nazi Party (1937); published 1st postwar book, a small verse collection *Du aber bleibst in mir* (But You Remain in Me, 1949); edited her collected works, of which 6 vols. appeared in print (1952–55) and a 7th vol. appeared posthumously (1965). Depicted on a stamp issued by the post office of the German Federal Republic (1979). ❖ See also *Women in World History.*

MIETH, Hansel (1909–1998). American photographer. Name variations: Hansel Mieth Hagel; Johanna M. Hagel. Born April 9, 1909; died at a friend's home in Santa Rosa, California, Feb 14, 1998. ❖ Documented the Great Depression and World War II for *Time, Fortune,* and *Life* magazines.

MIEZA, Carmen (1931–1976). See Farrés, Carmen.

MIFTAKHUTDINOVA, Diana (1973—). Ukrainian rower. Name variations: Dina Myetaknudinova or Myftakhutdinova. Born Nov 2, 1973, in Ukraine. ❖ Won a silver medal for quadruple sculls at Atlanta Olympics (1996).

MIGLIACCIO, Lucia (1770–1826). Italian duchess. Name variations: Lucia Partanna; Duchess of Florida; duchess of Florida. Born 1770; died 1826; dau. of Vincent Migliaccio; m. Benedict Grifero, prince of Partanna, before 1814; became mistress, then wife (in a morganatic marriage), of Ferdinand IV (1751–1825), king of Naples and Sicily (r. 1759–1806, 1815–1825), later known as Ferdinand I, king of the Two Sicilies (r. 1816–1825). ❖ Ferdinand's 1st wife was Maria Carolina (1752–1814).

MIGLIETTA, Ethel (1912–1977). See Colt, Ethel Barrymore.

MIGNOT, Claudine Françoise (c. 1617–1711). French adventurer. Name variations: commonly called Marie. Born near Grenoble, at Meylan, around 1617; died Nov 30, 1711; m. Pierre des Portes d'Amblérieux (treasurer of the province of Dauphiny); m. François de l'Hôpital (a marshal of France); morganatic marriage with John Casimir, ex-king of Poland, in 1672. ❖ Married 3 wealthy men, and inherited 3 fortunes. The history of her life, freely revised, was the subject of a play by Bayard and Paul Duport, *Marie Mignot* (1829). ❖ See also *Women in World History.*

MIGUÉLEZ RAMOS, Rosa (1953—). Spanish politician. Name variations: Rosa Miguelez Ramos. Born Aug 27, 1953, in Ferrol, Spain. ❖ Served as mayor of Ares (1983–87) and as a deputy in the Galician Regional Parliament (1989–93), becoming director-general, Women's Issues, and chef de cabinet of the Minister of Labour; as a European Socialist, elected to 5th European Parliament (1999–2004).

MIHALY, Aneta (1957—). Romanian rower. Born Sept 23, 1957, in Romania. ❖ At Los Angeles Olympics, won a silver medal in coxed eights (1984).

MIHI-KI-TE-KAPUA (?–1872/80). New Zealand tribal composer and poet. Born at Ruatahuna; died c. 1872–1880, at Te Whaiti-nui-a-Toi. ❖ After her children had grown and her husband had died, composed songs about solitude and longing; was considered greatest composer of the Tuhoe and Mataatua. ❖ See also *Dictionary of New Zealand Biography* (Vol. 1).

MIHRI KHATUN (fl. 15/16th c.). Turkish poet. Fl. in late 15th and early 16th centuries in Turkey; believed to be in the court of Prince Ahmad, son of Bajazet or Bayazid II (r. 1481–1512). ❖ Wrote Persian odes (*ghazels*) in classical tradition, only 28 of which survive.

MIHRIMAH (1522–1575). Princess of the Ottoman Empire. Name variations: Mirhrimah. Born in Constantinople in 1522; died in Constantinople in 1575; only dau. of Roxelana (c. 1504–1558) and Suleiman or Suleyman the Magnificent (c. 1494–1566), sultan of the Ottoman Empire (r. 1520–1566); m. Rüstem, chosen by her mother as her father's vizier; children: Aysha Humashah. ❖ Along with mother and husband, formed a powerful coalition which influenced domestic and foreign politics; was the most powerful royal princess of the Ottoman Empire, especially after the death of her mother (1558), when she became Suleiman's closest advisor. ❖ See also *Women in World History.*

MIHR-UR-NISA (1577–1645). See Nur Jahan.

MIKAILENKO, Olga. See Markova, Olga.

MIKEY, Fanny (1931—). Argentinean-born actress. Born Dec 26, 1931, in Argentina; dau. of José Mikeaj (name changed to Mikey by immigration official); m. Gastón Dijan (div.); m. Pedro I. Martinez (Colombian actor). ❖ Acclaimed actor, director, theatrical manager, producer and promoter, was discovered at 15 while performing at a Jewish club and invited to act in a William Saroyan play; began taking acting classes at Argentine Hebrew Society and performed under director Reynaldo D'Amore and others; left theater for 2 years at behest of new husband Gastón Dijan, but ultimately left husband to return to stage; began performing title role in García Lorca's *Yerma* while working by day in factory; moved to Colombia to marry director Pedro I. Martinez; began acting and coordinating cultural activities in Cali, Colombia (1960s) with TEC (Cali Experimental Theater); helped build one of the 1st professional theatrical groups in Colombia, the Bogotá Popular Theater (TPB, 1970s), now one of Colombia's most important groups; founded La Gata Caliente (Hot Cat), the 1st Colombian "café concert" variety show; mounted political play *Mamá Colombia* as well as solo act *Oiganme* (Listen to Me); went on to participate as actress, producer, director, juror and special guest in such festivals as World Festival in Paris, International Festival of Drama in Caracas, Grand Mexico City Festival and Avignon Arts Festival; worked as director in France, Spain and Argentina; served as executive director for Bogotá Popular Theater for 7 years; has acted in many movies, including *Bolívar Soy Yo* (I Am Bolivar, 2002). Played key role in establishing many enduring cultural institutions and events, helping to initiate founding of National Theater (1978), creating ongoing major cultural event Bogotá Latin American Theater Festival (1988), which attracts groups from all over world, and founding with others the film production company Grupo Colombia Ltda (1994).

MIKHAILENKO, Olga. See Markova, Olga.

MIKHAYLOVA, Angelina (1960—). Bulgarian basketball player. Born June 1960 in Bulgaria. ❖ At Moscow Olympics, won a silver medal in team competition (1980).

MIKHAYLOVA, Maria (1866–1943). Russian soprano. Born June 3, 1866, in Kharkov; died Jan 18, 1943; studied at St. Petersburg Conservatory and in Paris with Saint-Yves-Bax and Milan with Ronconi. ❖ Internationally famous, made debut in St. Petersburg as Marguerite de Valois in *Huguenots* (1892), remaining there until 1912; toured Prague, Tokyo, Kiev, etc.; sang Zerlina, Juliette, Nannetta, Lakmé, and Lyudmila and was the 1st Electra in Tanayev's *Oresteia.*

MIKHAYLOVA, Snezhana (1954—). Bulgarian basketball player. Born Jan 29, 1954, in Bulgaria. ❖ Won a bronze medal at Montreal Olympics (1976) and a silver medal at Moscow Olympics (1980), both in team competition.

MIKHAYLOVSKAYA, Lyudmila (1937—). Soviet volleyball player. Born Nov 21, 1937, in USSR. ❖ At Mexico City Olympics, won a gold medal in team competition (1968).

MIKHEYEVA, Galina (1962—). See Malchugina-Mikheyeva, Galina.

MIKKELSEN, Henriette Roende (1980—). Danish handball player. Born Sept 21, 1980, in Denmark. ❖ Left wing, won a team gold medal at Athens Olympics (2004).

MIKKELSPLASS, Marit (1965—). Norwegian cross-country skier. Born Dec 20, 1965, in Norway. ❖ Won a silver medal for 4x5 km relay at Calgary Olympics (1988); won a silver medal for 30 km at Lillehammer Olympics (1994); won a silver medal for 4x5 km relay at Nagano Olympics (1998).

MIKULICH, Alena (1977—). Belarusian rower. Name variations: Yelena Mikulich. Born Feb 21, 1977, in Minsk, Belarus. ❖ Won a bronze medal for coxed eights at Atlanta Olympics (1996); won World championship for quadruple sculls (1999).

MIKULICH, V. (1857–1936). *See Veselítskaia, Lidiia.*

MIKULSKI, Barbara (1936—). American politician. Born July 20, 1936, in Baltimore, MD; dau. of Christine and William Mikulski; Mount St. Agnes College, BA, 1958; University of Maryland School of Social Work, MA in social work, 1965. ❖ Served on Baltimore City Council (1971–76); made unsuccessful bid for US Senate (1974); as a Democrat, elected to US House of Representatives (1977), followed by 4 succeeding Congresses (1977–87); elected to US Senate (1986), the 1st Democratic woman to hold a Senate seat not previously held by her husband; reelected (1992, 1998, 2004); elected secretary of the Democratic Conference for the 104th and 105th Congress (1994 and 1996), the 1st woman elected to a Democratic leadership position in the Senate; became a national leader on women's health care.

MILA, Adriana (fl. 1469–1502). Italian noblewoman. Name variations: Adriana da Mila, Adriana Milo, Adriana Orsini. Probably born in Rome; died after 1502; dau. of Pedro de Mila (a Catalan); 2nd cousin to Rodrigo or Roderigo Borgia; m. Ludovico Orsini (died before 1489); children: Orsino Orsini. ❖ Brought Lucrezia Borgia up from age 3 to age 13, supervising her education. ❖ See also *Women in World History.*

MILAN, duchess of.
See Este, Beatrice d' (d. 1334).
See Visconti, Catherine (c. 1360–1404).
See Maria of Savoy (fl. 1400).
See Visconti, Bianca Maria (1423–1470).
See Bona of Savoy (c. 1450–c. 1505).
See Isabella of Naples (1470–1524).
See Sforza, Bianca Maria (1472–1510).
See Este, Beatrice d' (1475–1497).
See Christina of Denmark (1521–1590).

MILANI, Milena (1922—). Italian novelist, poet and painter. Born 1922 in Savona, Italy. ❖ Contributed to many journals and periodicals and won several literary awards; works include *La storia di Anna Drei* (1947, trans. as *The Story of Anna Drei*), *Uomo e donna* (1952), *La ragazza di nome Giulio* (1964, trans. as *A Girl Called Jules*), *Italia sexy* (1967), *Io donna e gli altri* (1972), *Oggetto sessuale* (1977), *Mi sono innamorata a Mosca* (1980), and *L'angelo nero e altri ricordi* (1984).

MILANOV, Zinka (1906–1989). Croatian soprano. Born Mira Zinka Teresa Kunç in Zagreb, Croatia, May 17, 1906; died May 30, 1989, in NY; studied at Zagreb Academy with Milka Ternina, Maria Kostrencic, and Fernando Carpi; m. Predrag Milanov (theater director and actor), 1937 (div.); m. General Ljubomir Ilic, 1947. ❖ Renowned for her larger-than-life stage persona as well as for her powerful voice, made debut at Ljubliana Opera in *Il Trovatore* (1927); sang at Zagreb Opera (1928–35); performed widely throughout Yugoslavia, introducing opera to her country; engaged by Toscanini for his production of Verdi's *Requiem* at Salzburg (1937); debuted at Metropolitan Opera in *Il Trovatore* (1937) and was principal soprano there until the closing of the old Metropolitan (1966); debuted at Teatro all Scala (1950); retired (1966). ❖ See also *Women in World History.*

MILASHKINA, Tamara Andreyevna (1934—). Russian soprano. Born Sept 13, 1934, in Astrakhan; studied at Moscow Conservatory with Yelena Katulskaya. ❖ While still a student, was engaged as a soloist at Bolshoi Opera (1958); appeared as Lida in Verdi's *La battaglia di Legnano* at La Scala (1962), the 1st Soviet singer to perform there; was particularly well known for portrayal of Tchaikovsky heroines Tatyana, Lisa, and Mariya and was filmed as Feroniya in Rimsky-Korsakov's *Legend of the Invisible City of Kitezh* (1966); appeared in Prokofiev's *War and Peace* as Natasha and as Lyubka in *Semyon Kotko*; also sang at Metropolitan Opera. Made a National Artist of the USSR (1973). ❖ See also *Women in World History.*

MILBANK, Helen (1909–1997). *See Kirkpatrick, Helen.*

MILBANKE, Anne (1792–1860). English philanthropist. Name variations: Annabella; Lady Noel Byron. Born Anne Isabella Milbanke at Elmore Hall, Durham, May 17, 1792; died 1860; only child of Sir Ralph and Lady Milbanke; niece of Lady Elizabeth Melbourne; m. George Gordon Byron, Lord Byron, Jan 2, 1815 (sep. 1816); children: Ada Byron, countess of Lovelace (1815–1852). ❖ Following brief marriage to Lord Byron, founded a progressive industrial and agricultural school at Ealing Grove, based on theories of Swiss agriculturist Philipp

Fellenberg; also subsidized other educational institutes, including Mary Carpenter's Red House, a girls' reformatory (1854); a close associate of Barbara Bodichon, backed American abolitionists and Italian Republicans. ❖ See also E.C. Mayne, *Life and Letters of Anne Isabella, Lady Noel Bryon* (1929); Harriet Beecher Stowe, *Lady Byron Vindicated* (1870); and *Women in World History.*

MILBANKE, Elizabeth (d. 1818). *See Melbourne, Elizabeth.*

MILBRETT, Tiffeny (1972—). American soccer player. Born Oct 23, 1972, in Portland, OR; graduate of University of Portland, 1995. ❖ Won a team gold medal at Atlanta Olympics (1996) and a team silver at Sydney Olympics (2000); won a team gold medal at World Cup (1999), scoring 3 goals; was a founding member of the Women's United Soccer Association (WUSA); signed with the New York Power. Named US Soccer's Female Athlete of the Year (2000, 2001). ❖ See also Jere Longman *The Girls of Summer* (HarperCollins, 2000).

MILBURG (d. 722?). English saint and abbess. Name variations: Mildburga or Mildburh. Died around 722; dau. of Merowald or Merwald, king of Mercia, and Ermenburga, the abbess of Minster, sister of Mildgyth and Saint Mildred. ❖ Built a nunnery at Winwick or Wenlock (680) which was restored by the earl of Shrewsbury (1080). Feast day is Feb 23.

MILCAH. Biblical woman. One of the 5 daughters of Zelophehad, of the Manasseh tribe, given permission by Moses to share in their father's estate.

MILCAH. Biblical woman. Dau. of Haran; married Nahor; children: 8.

MILCH, Klara (1891—). Austrian-Jewish swimmer. Born May 24, 1891, in Austria; death date unknown. ❖ At Stockholm Olympics, won a bronze medal in the 4x100-meter freestyle relay (1912); was Austrian national champion in the 100-meter freestyle (1907–12), 100-meter breaststroke (1911), and 100-meter backstroke (1912–13).

MILCHINA, Lolita. Belarusian shooter. Name variations: Lolita Yevlevskaya-Milchina; Lolita Eulevskaya. Born in Belarus. ❖ Won a bronze medal for 25m pistol at Sydney Olympics (2000).

MILDBURGA or MILDBURH (d. 722?). *See Milburg.*

MILDENBURG, Anne Bahr (1872–1947). *See Bahr-Mildenburg, Anna.*

MILDER-HAUPTMANN, Anna (1785–1838). Austrian soprano. Name variations: Pauline Anna Milder-Hauptmann; Mme Milder. Born in Constantinople, Dec 13, 1785 (some sources cite 1781); died in Vienna, Austria, May 29, 1838. ❖ A well-known performer in early 19th-century Europe, was a pupil of Salieri; debuted at Theater an der Wien as Juno in Süssmayer's *Der Spiegel von Arkadien* (1803); sang all 3 versions of Beethoven's *Fidelio* (1805, 1806, and 1815); created title role in *Faniska* (1806) and *Médée* (1814), in its 1st Viennese production; moved to Berlin, where she played Emmeline in *Die Schweizerfamilie* by Weigl; at Berlin Hofoper, created Namouna in *Nurmahal* (1822); also created Irmengard in *Agnes von Hohenstaufen* (1829); returned to Vienna, where she sang until retirement (1836). ❖ See also *Women in World History.*

MILDGYTH (fl. early 700s). Mercian princess. Name variations: Mildgithe. Flourished early 700s; dau. of Merowald or Merwald, king of Mercia, and Ermenburga, abbess of Minster; sister of saints Mildred and Milburg; great-niece of Egbert, king of the English. ❖ Became a nun.

MILDMAY, Audrey (1900–1953). English lyric soprano. Born Audrey Louise St. John in Herstmonceux, Sussex, England, Dec 19, 1900; died in London, May 31, 1953; m. John Christie, 1931. ❖ Studied with Jani Strasser in Vienna; toured North America (1927–28); joined Carl Rosa Company, staying with that group until her marriage to a wealthy aristocrat (1931); with husband, designed an opera house on their estate at Glyndebourne which seated 311, and the Glyndebourne Festival was born; performed Susanna, Zerlina and Norina (1934–39); also appeared as Gretel, Micaëla, Olympia, Musetta, and Nedda; retired (1943). ❖ See also *Women in World History.*

MILDMAY, Grace (1553–1620). British diarist. Born Grace Sherrington, 1553, in Laycock Abbey, Wiltshire, England; died July 1620 in Apethorpe, Northamptonshire, England; 2nd dau. of Sir Henry Sherrington (Wiltshire landowner) and Lady Sherrington; m. Sir Anthony Mildmay (son of Sir Walter Mildmay, founder of Emmanuel College, Cambridge), 1567 (died 1671). ❖ Kept a journal (1570–1617) until husband's death, which was later published as *Lady Grace Mildmay's Journal and Papers.*

MILDRED. *Variant of Mildrid, Mildryth, or Mildthryth.*

MILDRED (d. 700?). English saint and abbess. Name variations: Mildryth or Mildthryth (*thryth* means commanding or threatening; thus, Mildthryth means "one who is gently or mildly strict"). Died around 700; dau. of Merowald or Merwald, king of Mercia, and Ermenburga, the abbess of Minster; sister of Mildgyth and Saint Milburg; great-niece of Egbert, king of the English. ❖ Sent to France, to the Abbey of Chelles, near Paris, where she took the veil and was tutored in ecclesiastical learning; persecuted by the abbess, returned to England, and was appointed abbess of her mother's newly founded Monastery of Minstre; proved to be a gentle, and humble leader. ❖ See also *Women in World History.*

MILDREDA. *Variant of Mildred, Mildryth, or Mildthryth.*

MILDRID. *Variant of Mildred, Mildryth, or Mildthryth.*

MILENA (1847–1923). Queen of Montenegro. Name variations: Milena Vukotich or Vukotic. Born April 22, 1847; died Mar 16, 1923; dau. of Peter or Petar Vukotic from Cevom (an influential member of the Senate); m. Nicholas Petrovic (1840–1921), prince of Montenegro (r. 1860–1910), king of Montenegro (r. 1910–1918), Sept 8, 1860; children: 9 daughters and 3 sons, including Zorka of Montenegro (1864–1890); Militza of Montenegro (1866–1951); Anastasia Petrovitch-Njegos (1868–1935); Daniel (1871–1939); Elena of Montenegro (1873–1952); Anna (who m. Francis of Battenberg); Mirko (who m. Natalia Constantinovich); Xenia (Ksenija); Vjera; Peter.

MILES, Debra (c. 1947—). *See Barnes, Debra Dene.*

MILES, Jearl (1966—). African-American runner. Name variations: Jearl Miles-Clark. Born Jearl Atawa Miles, Sept 4, 1966, in Gainesville, FL. ❖ At Barcelona Olympics, won a silver medal in 4x400-meter relay (1992); at World championships, won the 400 meters (1993); won US Outdoor 400-meter championship (1993, 1995, 1997, 2002) and 800-meter championship (1998, 1999); won US Indoor 800 meters (2001); won a gold medal at Atlanta Olympics (1996) and at Sydney Olympics (2000), both for the 4x100-meter relay.

MILES, Lizzie (1895–1963). American blues singer. Born Elizabeth Landreaux, Mar 31, 1895, in New Orleans, LA; died Mar 17, 1963, in New Orleans. ❖ Born on Bourbon Street, was a light-skinned Creole with a big voice; began to sing pop ballads, vaudeville standards, and jazz numbers in both French and English; performed with King Oliver and Kid Ory in New Orleans; worked in clubs and cabarets in Chicago, NY, and Paris, with an urbane and sophisticated style; recorded for Okeh label (1921), then Emerson, Columbia, and Victor; retired (1930s); made a comeback with Bob Scobey Band (1950s) and appeared at Monterey Jazz Festival (1958). ❖ See also *Women in World History.*

MILES, Sarah (1941—). English actress. Born Dec 31, 1941, in Ingatestone, Essex, England; sister of Christopher Miles (director, producer and screenwriter); attended Royal Academy of Dramatic Arts; m. Robert Bolt (screenwriter and playwright) 1967 (div. 1975); remarried Bolt, 1988 (died 1995); children: 1. ❖ Made auspicious film debut in *Term of Trial* (1962), followed by *The Servant* (1963) and *Those Magnificent Men in Their Flying Machines* (1965); caused a stir in *Blow Up* (1966); nominated for Best Actress Oscar for *Ryan's Daughter* (1970); other films include *The Man Who Loved Cat Dancing* (1973), *White Mischief* (1987) and *Hope and Glory* (1987); on stage, starred in *Vivat! Vivat! Regina!* (1971), among others. ❖ See also autobiographies *A Right Royal Bastard* (1993), *Serves Me Right* (1996) and *Bolt from the Blue* (1996).

MILES, Sylvia (1932—). American actress. Born Sept 9, 1932, in NYC; m. Ted Brown (NYC radio personality, div.). ❖ Appeared off-Broadway in *The Iceman Cometh* and *The Balcony*; made film debut in *Murder Inc.* (1971), followed by *The Last Movie, Heart, 92 in the Shade, Evil Under the Sun, Critical Condition, Spike of Bensonhurst, Wall Street, Crossing Delancey* and *She-Devil,* among others; made headlines when she dumped a plate of food on critic John Simon (1973). Nominated for Oscar as Best Supporting Actress for *Midnight Cowboy* (1969) and *Farewell My Lovely* (1975).

MILES, Vera (1929—). American screen actress. Born Vera May Ralston, Aug 23, 1929, in Boise City, OK; m. Robert Miles, 1948 (div. 1954); m. Gordon Scott (actor), 1954 (div. 1959); m. Keith Larsen (actor) 1960

(div. 1971); m. Bob Jones, 1973; children: (1st m.) Deborah Miles (b. 1950), Kelley Miles (b. 1952, actress); (2nd m.) Michael Scott; (3rd m.) Erik Larsen. ❖ Named Miss Kansas (1948); made film debut in *Two Tickets to Broadway* (1951); came to prominence in John Ford's *The Searchers* (1956) and Hitchcock's *The Wrong Man* (1957); other films include *Tarzan's Hidden Jungle, The FBI Story, Psycho, Back Street, The Man Who Shot Liberty Valance, A Tiger Walks, Those Calloways, Gentle Giant, Twilight's Last Gleaming, Psycho II, Brainwaves* and *Into the Night.*

MILEY, Marion (c. 1914–1941). American golfer. Born Marion Miley c. 1914 in Danvers, MA; killed by intruders who broke into her mother's Lexington Country Club apartment, Sept, 28, 1941, in Lexington, KY; dau. of Elsie Ego Miley (who was also shot, and died Oct 1, 1941). ❖ Won the Women's Western Amateur (1935, 1937); won the Trans-Mississippi Amateur (1935–36) and the Southern Amateur (1938–39). ❖ See also William J. Buchanan, *Execution Eve* (New Horizon, 1993).

MILFORD HAVEN, marchioness of. *See Victoria of Hesse Darmstadt (1863–1950).*

MILH AL-ATTARA (fl. 840s). Arabian singer. Flourished in the 840s; associated with Shariyya, the great Arabian singer. ❖ As a slave, was trained in the art of singing; became part of the court of Caliph al-Mutawakki (r. 847–861) in Samarra. ❖ See also *Women in World History.*

MILHOLLAND, Inez (1886–1916). *See Boissevain, Inez M.*

MILICENT or MILLICENT. *Variant of Melissa, Melita, or Melusine.*

MILÍTSYNA, Elizaveta Mitrofanovna (1869–1930). Russian short-story writer. Name variations: Militsyna. Born 1869 in Russia; died 1930. ❖ Published collected stories (1905) and 2 vols. of collected works (1910), which often dealt with village life and focused on rural poor; also wrote *Notes of a Nurse* (1916), about experiences as volunteer nurse during WWI, as well as *In A Prisoner-of-War Camp: From the Worlds of P.Z. Bakhmetov, Formerly Imprisoned.*

MILITZA OF MONTENEGRO (1866–1951). Princess of Montenegro. Name variations: Militza Petrovitch-Njegos; Milica. Born July 26, 1866; died Sept 5, 1951; dau. of Queen Milena (1847–1923) and Nicholas, prince of Montenegro (r. 1860–1910), king of Montenegro (r. 1910–1918); m. Peter Nicholaevitch (grandson of Tsar Nicholas I of Russia and Charlotte of Prussia), Aug 1889; children: 3.

MILL, Chris Evert (b. 1954). *See Evert, Chris.*

MILL, Harriet Taylor (1807–1858). *See Taylor, Harriet.*

MILLAIS, Pérrine (1893–1979). *See Moncrieff, Pérrine.*

MILLAR, Annie Cleland (1855–1939). New Zealand innkeeper and business executive. Name variations: Ann Cleland. Born Ann Cleland, Mar 15, 1855, at Coatbridge, near Glasgow, Scotland; died Mar 25, 1939, in Invercargill, New Zealand; dau. of Andrew Cleland and Mary (Masterton) Cleland; m. John Millar (baker), 1885 (died 1913); children: 9. ❖ Immigrated to New Zealand in her early 20s; when husband's bakery business failed, managed a private hotel (c. 1893–1900); leased and then purchased ACM Company Tea Rooms, which she managed (1900–16); also entered bread-baking industry, renamed A.C. Millars Ltd, which became a dynasty managed by generations of her descendants. ❖ See also *Dictionary of New Zealand Biography* (Vol. 3).

MILLAR, Gertie (1879–1952). English actress. Born Feb 21, 1879, in Manningham, Bradford, England; died April 25, 1952, in Chiddingford, England; m. Lionel Monckton (theatrical composer), 1902 (died); m. William Humble Ward (1867–1932), 2nd earl of Dudley, 1924 (died 1931). ❖ Made stage debut in Manchester, England, in a pantomime (1893); subsequently moved to London to play in musical comedies, including *The Toreador* (1901), *Our Miss Gibbs* (1909), *The Quaker Girl* (1910) and *A Country Girl* (1914); was known as London's premier "Gaiety Girl" by the mid-1920s.

MILLAR, Margaret (1915–1994). Canadian-born writer of mystery novels. Born Margaret Sturm, Feb 5, 1915, in Kitchener, Ontario, Canada; died Mar 26, 1994, at her home in Santa Barbara, CA; attended Kitchener-Waterloo Collegiate Institute; attended University of Toronto, 1933–36; m. Kenneth Millar (writer of detective novels under pseudonym Ross Macdonald), 1938 (died 1983); children: Linda Millar. ❖ Published 1st novel, *The Invisible Worm* (1941), introducing psychiatrist-detective Dr. Paul Prye, a central character in many succeeding novels, including *The Weak-Eyed Bat* (1942) and *The*

Iron Gates (1945); after WWII, moved to Santa Barbara, which she began to use as her fictional setting; worked as screenwriter for Warner Bros. (1945–46); won Edgar Award from Mystery Writers of America for *A Beast in View* (1955); served as president of Mystery Writers of America (1957–58); was active with husband in California's conservation movement (1960s) and collected wildlife observations in *The Birds and the Beasts Were There* (1968); won Edgar Allan Poe Award for *The Banshee* (1983); won Grand Master Award from Mystery Writers of America (1983); other writings include *The Devil Loves Me* (1942), *The Wall of Eyes* (1943), *Wives and Lovers* (1954), *A Stranger in My Grave* (1960), *How Like an Angel* (1962), *The Fiend* (1964), *Beyond This Point Are Monsters* (1970), *Ask For Me Tomorrow* (1976) and *Spider Webs* (1986).

MILLARD, Evelyn (1869–1941). English actress and manager. Name variations: Mrs. Coulter. Born Sept 18, 1869, in Kensington, England; died Mar 9, 1941; dau. of John Millard (teacher of elocution); m. Robert Porter Coulter; children: Ursula Millard (actress). ❖ Made stage debut in London as a walk-on in *The Dancing Girl* (1891), followed by *The Trumpet Call*, *The Masqueraders*, *Sowing the Wind*, *The Second Mrs. Tanqueray* and *Liberty Hall*, among others; came to prominence as Princess Flavia in *The Prisoner of Zenda* (1896); other plays include *The Adventure of Lady Ursula* (title role), *The Christian*, *Madame Butterfly* (as Cho-Cho-San), *Paolo and Francesca*, *The Unforeseen*, *His Majesty's Servant*, *Romeo and Juliet* (as Juliet), and *Othello* (as Desdemona); managed and appeared at the Garrick (1908–09).

MILLARD, Ursula (b. 1901). English actress. Born Sept 20, 1901, in London, England; dau. of R.P. Coulter and Evelyn Millard (actress); m. A. Warburton. ❖ Made stage debut in *The Pierrot of the Minute* (1921), followed by *Clothes and the Woman*, *The Pigeon*, *Pomp and Circumstance* and *East of Suez*.

MILLAY, Edna St. Vincent (1892–1950). American poet. Name variations: (pseudonym) Nancy Boyd. Born in Rockland, Maine, Feb 22, 1892; died of a heart attack at Steepletop, Oct 19, 1950; 1st of 3 daughters of Cora (Buzzelle) Millay (nurse) and Henry Tolman Millay (schoolteacher); sister of Norma Millay; graduate of Vassar, 1917; m. Eugen Boissevain (businessman), July 18, 1923 (died Aug 1949). ❖ Pulitzer Prize-winning poet, seen as exemplary of the "modern woman," whose work captured the spirit of the post-World War I generation, is probably best known for her early works, particularly "Renascence" (1912), *A Few Figs from Thistles* (1920), and *Second April* (1921), despite a writing career that spanned nearly 4 decades, and a canon that ranges from lyrics to verse plays and political commentary; also wrote *Aria da Capo* (1920), a verse play on the foolishness of war; is seen as among the most skilled of sonnet writers, especially with "Euclid alone has looked on Beauty bare" (1923) and the sequences "Epitaph for the Race of Man" (1934) and "Sonnets from an Ungrafted Tree" (1923); for most of the 20th century, was among the most widely known and read of all American literary figures; other writings include *The Lamp and the Bell* (1921), *Two Slatterns and a King* (1921), *The Ballad of the Harp-Weaver* (1922), *The Buck in the Snow and Other Poems* (1928), *Wine from These Grapes* (1934), *Conversation at Midnight* (1937), *Huntsman, What Quarry?* (1939), "There Are No Islands Any More" (1940), *Make Bright the Arrows: 1940 Notebook* (1940) and *The Murder of Lidice* (1942). ❖ See also Anne Cheney, *Millay in Greenwich Village* (U. of Alabama Press, 1975); and *Women in World History*.

MILLAY, Norma (d. 1986). American actress. Name variations: Norma Millay Ellis. Born in Maine; died May 14, 1986, age 92, at Steepletop, the Millay farm in Austerlitz, NY; sister of Edna St. Vincent Millay (poet, 1892–1950). ❖ Made Broadway debut in *The Saint* (1924), followed by *Desire Under the Elms*, *Patience*, *Love for Love*, *La Finta Giardiniera* and *Key Largo*; edited 2 of her sister's poetry collections (1950 and 1954).

MILLE, Agnes de (1905–1993). See de Mille, Agnes.

MILLER, Alice (1956—). American golfer. Born May 15, 1956, in Marysville, CA; Arizona State University, BS in Phys Ed, 1978. ❖ Won West Virginia Classic (1983, 1984); won Sarasota (1984); won four titles, including Nabisco Dinah Shore (1985); won Jamie Farr Toledo Classic (1991); served as president of LPGA Tour (1993).

MILLER, Alice (1923—). Polish-born psychoanalyst. Born 1923 in Poland; moved to Zurich, Switzerland; studied philosophy, sociology, and psychology and took her doctorate in 1953. ❖ Completed psychoanalytic training in Zurich; as a practicing psychoanalyst, was involved in teaching and training for more than 20 years; departed from Freudian theory in an attempt to understand abused and silenced children who later become destructive; published the widely read *Prisoners of Childhood*

(1979, later titled *The Drama of the Gifted Child*); wrote of Hitler's childhood in *For Your Own Good: Hidden Cruelty in Child-Rearing and the Roots of Violence*; also published *Thou Shalt Not Be Aware, Banished Knowledge*, and *Pictures of a Childhood* (2004), a collection of 66 of her watercolors.

MILLER, Alice Duer (1874–1942). American novelist and poet. Name variations: Mrs. Alice Miller. Pronunciation: DUE-er. Born Alice Duer in New York, NY, July 28, 1874; died in New York, Aug 22, 1942; dau. of James G.K. Duer and Elizabeth (Meads) Duer; graduate of Barnard College, 1899; m. Henry Wise Miller (Wall Street broker), Oct 1899; children: Denning. ❖ Probably best known for her long narrative poem, *The White Cliffs* (1940), essentially a novel in verse, which was a tribute to the people of Great Britain who had been under furious bombardment and the threat of invasion by the Germans since 1939; other writings include *The Modern Obstacle* (1903), *Calderon's Prisoner* (1903), *Less Than Kin* (1909), *Come Out of the Kitchen* (1916), *The Charm School* (1919), *The Reluctant Duchess* (1925), *Gowns by Roberta* (became the successful musical comedy *Roberta*, 1933), *Death Sentence* (1935), *The Rising Star* (1937), *Not for Love* (1937), *And One Was Beautiful* (1938) and *I Have Loved England* (1941). ❖ See also *Women in World History*.

MILLER, Anita (1951—). American field-hockey player. Born May 14, 1951; lived in Gladwyne, PA. ❖ At Los Angeles Olympics, won a bronze medal in team competition (1984).

MILLER, Ann (1919–2004). American dancer and actress. Name variations: Lucy Ann Collier; Lucille Ann Collier. Born Johnnie Lucille Collier on April 12, 1919 (she claimed 1923), in Chireno, Texas; died Jan 22, 2004, in Los Angeles, CA; dau. of John Alfred Collier (criminal lawyer) and Clara Collier; m. Reese Llewellyn Milner (millionaire industrialist), Feb 16, 1946 (div.); m. William Moss (Texas oilman), 1958 (div. May 1961); m. Arthur Cameron (Texas oil millionaire), 1961 (marriage annulled 1962); no children. ❖ Known for her rapid-fire tap dancing, starred in 40 motion pictures, numerous Broadway shows and national tours; made film debut in *New Faces of 1937*; appeared in a host of films for RKO, including *Stage Door* (1937), *Radio City Revels* (1938), and *Room Service* (1938), before leaving for NY to join the Three Stooges on stage in *George White's Scandals of 1939*; signed with Columbia to highlight minor musicals the studio churned out, including *Go West, Young Lady* (1941), *Reveille with Beverly* (1943), *Hey, Rookie* (1944), *Jam Session* (1944), *Eadie Was a Lady* (1945) and *Eve Knew Her Apples* (1945); was featured in *Easter Parade* (1948); signed with MGM and starred in *The Kissing Bandit* (1948), *On the Town* (1949), *Watch the Birdie* (1950), *Texas Carnival* (1951), *Small Town Girl* and *Kiss Me Kate* (1953); starred in *Mame* on Broadway (1969–70). Nominated for Tony Award for performance in *Sugar Babies* (1979). ❖ See also autobiography, *Miller's High Life* (1972); and *Women in World History*.

MILLER, Anna Riggs (1741–1781). British travel writer. Name variations: Anne Miller; Lady Anna Miller; Lady Riggs Miller. Born Anna Riggs, 1741, in England; died June 24, 1781, in Hot-Wells, Bristol, England; dau. of Edward Riggs and Margaret Piggott; m. Capt. John Miller (who adopted her maiden name with his own to become John Riggs Miller), 1765, became an Irish baronet, 1778; children: son and daughter. ❖ Traveled to Europe and wrote of impressions, especially of Italy; upon return to England, established salon which became popular amusement for literati visitors to Bath; noted also for donations to charity; contributed to and edited *Poetical Announcements at a Villa Near Bath* (1775, 1776, 1777, 1781); wrote *Letters from Italy, Describing the Manners, Customs, Antiquities, Paintings, of that Country, in the Years MDCCLXX and MDCCLXXI* (1776) and *On Novelty: and On Trifles, and Triflers* (1778).

MILLER, Anne (1741–1781). See Miller, Anna Riggs.

MILLER, Annie Jenness (b. 1859). American dress reformer, author and lecturer. Name variations: Anna Jenness Miller; Mrs. Jenness Miller. Born in the White Mountains of New Hampshire, Jan 28, 1859; dau. of Solomon Jenness and Susan (Wendell) Jenness (both of old New England stock); educated in Boston by private tutors; m. Conrad Miller, in 1887. ❖ Widely known as an advocate of dress reform for women, became editor and proprietor of the *Jenness Miller Monthly* (1885); books include *Mother and Babe* (1892) and *Creating a Home* (1896). ❖ See also *Women in World History*.

MILLER, Bebe (1950—). American dancer and choreographer. Born Beryl Adele Miller, Sept 20, 1950, in New York, NY; studied with Murray Louis at Henry Street Settlement, 1954–62; Earlham College,

BA, 1971; trained at Nikolais Dance Theater Lab, 1972–73; Ohio State University, MA in dance, 1975. ❖ Performed with Nina Wiener Company (1976–82) and toured with Dana Reitz Co. (1983); presented 1st choreography *Tune* (1978); known for including socio-political content in her creative works, founded Bebe Miller Co. (1984); was 1st American choreographer to work in South Africa after fall of apartheid; received 2 New York Dance and Performance (Bessie) awards (1986–87) and American Choreographer Award (1988). Major choreographies include the solo *Spending Time Doing Things* (1985); the trilogy of *Hell Dances* (1987–88), *The Hendrix Project* (1991) and *Cantos Gordos* (1994); the multimedia performance *Drummin': The Rhythms of Miami* (1997); and *Going to the Wall* (1998).

MILLER, Bertha Mahony (1882–1969). American bookseller, editor, children's literature specialist. Name variations: Bertha Mahony; Bertha Everett Mahony Miller; Bertha E. Miller. Born Bertha Everett Mahony in Rockport, Massachusetts, Mar 13, 1882; died of a stroke at her home in Ashburnham, Massachusetts, May 14, 1969; dau. of Daniel Mahony (railroad station passenger agent) and Mary Lane (Everett) Mahony (music teacher); m. William Davis Miller (president of a furniture concern), 1932; no children. ❖ Originator of the *Horn Book Magazine*, was assistant secretary, Women's Education and Industrial Union (WEIU), Boston (1906); opened Bookshop for Boys and Girls (1916); co-founded *Horn Book Magazine* (1924), the 1st American magazine to deal exclusively with children's literature; instituted innovative ideas to promote children's interest in reading and was responsible for the discovery and promotion of children's writers and artists. Received Constance Lindsay Skinner Award, Women's National Book Association (1955), American Library Association tribute (1959), and Regina Medal (1967). ❖ See also *Women in World History*.

MILLER, Caroline (1903–1992). American novelist. Born Aug 26, 1903, in Waycross, Georgia; died July 12, 1992, in North Carolina; dau. of Elias Pafford (schoolteacher and Methodist minister) and Levy Zan Hall Pafford; m. William D. Miller (her high school English teacher), 1921 (div. 1936); m. Clyde H. Ray Jr. (1937); children: (1st m.) William Dews Miller Jr. (b. 1927); twins George and Harvey Miller (b. 1929); (2nd m.) Clyde H. Ray III and Caroline Patience Ray. ❖ Southern novelist won Pulitzer Prize for bestselling book, *Lamb in His Bosom!* (1934), a work of historical realism about pioneer life in the Wiregrass region of Georgia; uncomfortable with her newfound celebrity, continued to write but did not publish often, except for the novel *Lebanon* (1944).

MILLER, Cheryl (1964—). African-American basketball player. Born Cheryl De Ann Miller, Jan 3, 1964, in Riverside, CA,; sister of Reggie Miller (NBA basketball player); graduate of University of Southern California. ❖ Led University of Southern California to successive NCAA championships (1983–84); won team gold medals at World University and Pan American Games (1983) and Goodwill Games (1986); won a team gold medal at Los Angeles Olympics (1984); coached WNBA Phoenix Mercury (1997–2000); was the 1st woman analyst to work on a nationally televised NBA game (1996) and did tv sports commentary for a number of networks. Named four-time All-American; won final four Most Valuable Player honors after tournaments (1983, 1984); named *Sports Illustrated* National Player of the Year (1985); won Wade Trophy (1986); inducted into Basketball Hall of Fame (1995). ❖ See also *Women in World History*.

MILLER, Colleen (1932—). American actress. Born Nov 10, 1932, in Yakima, WA; m. Ted Briskin, 1955 (div. 1975). ❖ Films include *The Las Vegas Story, Man Crazy, Playgirl, Four Guns to the Border, Man in the Shadow, The Purple Mask, The Rawhide Years, The Night Runner, Step Down to Terror* and *Gunfight at Comanche Creek*.

MILLER, Dorothy Canning (1904–2003). American museum curator. Born Dorothy Canning Miller, Feb 6, 1904, in Hopedale, Massachusetts; died July 11, 2003, in New York, NY; dau. of Arthur Barrett Miller and Edith Almena (Canning) Miller; Smith College, BA, 1925; attended New York University Institute of Fine Arts, 1926–27; m. Holger Cahill (curator and administrator), Aug 17, 1938. ❖ Appointed curator of painting and sculpture at the Museum of Modern Art, NY (1943), one of the few female curators in US at the time; began a series of groundbreaking exhibits (1943, 1946, 1952, and 1956) with such artists as Jackson Pollock, Mark Rothko, Clyfford Still, Morris Graves, Mark Tobey, Louise Nevelson, Jasper Johns, Robert Rauschenberg and Robert Indiana; became curator of museum collections (1947), a position she would hold for next 20 years; was a senior curator (1968–69). ❖ See also *Women in World History*.

MILLER, Elizabeth Smith (1822–1911). American reformer. Name variations: Lizzie or Libby Miller. Born Elizabeth Smith in Hampton, New York, Sept 20, 1822; died 1911; dau. of Gerrit Smith (prominent politician); cousin of Elizabeth Cady Stanton; m. Charles Dudley Miller (well-known NY lawyer), 1850. ❖ After years of feeling constrained in the long skirts of the day (1851), came up with an outfit that would allow her to prune and dig in her garden unfettered: Turkish trousers that became known as Bloomers; also wrote a bestselling cookbook, *In the Kitchen* (1875). ❖ See also *Women in World History*.

MILLER, Emily Huntington (1833–1913). American writer and reformer. Born Emily Clark Huntington, Oct 22, 1833, in Brooklyn, CT; died Nov 2, 1913, in Northfield, MN; dau. of Thomas Huntington (physician and cleric) and Paulina Clark Huntington; m. John Edwin Miller (teacher), Sept 5, 1860; children: 3 sons, 1 daughter. ❖ With other Methodist women, founded Evanston College for Ladies (1871), which later merged with Northwestern University; frequently lectured as part of the Chautauqua movement and served as president of Chautauqua Woman's Club; contributed to and was editor of Chicago youth magazine *Little Corporal*; served as president of Minneapolis Branch of Methodist Woman's Foreign Missionary Society (1883–89); was dean of women (1891–98), assistant professor of English literature (1891–90), and trustee at Northwestern University; contributed to such magazines as *Atlantic Monthly, Scribner's, Cosmopolitan*, and the Woman's Christian Temperance Union publication *Our Union*; books include *The Parish of Fair Haven* (1876), *Kathie's Experience* (1886) and *The King's Messengers* (1891).

MILLER, Emma Guffey (1874–1970). American feminist and Democratic party official. Name variations: Mary Emma Guffey, Emma Guffey, Emma Miller. Born Mary Emma Guffey on July 6, 1874, at Guffey Station, Westmoreland Co., PA; died Feb 23, 1970, in Grove City, PA; dau. of John Guffey (oil, gas, and coal businessman) and Barbaretta (Hough) Guffey; sister of Joseph Guffey (US senator); Bryn Mawr College, AB (1899); m. Carroll Miller (engineer, business executive, and government official), Oct 28, 1902 (died 1949); children: William Gardner III (b. 1905), twins John and Carroll, Jr. (b. 1908), and Joseph (b. 1912). ❖ Strong supporter of Franklin D. Roosevelt and Harry S. Truman, who also worked for suffrage movement, helped organize Democratic women's clubs into Pennsylvania Federation of Democratic Women (1920s); was a member of state executive board of League of Women Voters (1921–25) but resigned, objecting to nonpartisanship; joined Women's Organization for National Prohibition Reform (1929), serving on advisory council until 1933; elected delegate from ward to Democratic National Convention (1924); resigned from Daughters of the American Revolution to protest group's militarism (1930); held seat as Democratic National Committeewoman from PA (1932–1970); worked with Democratic National Committee in Washington, DC, but had disagreement with Eleanor Roosevelt over style of leadership of Women's Division (late 1930s); was advocate of Equal Rights Amendment, testifying before Senate Judiciary Committee (1938), and persuading Democratic Party to include amendment in party platform (1944); worked with National Woman's Party (1940s–50s), serving as chair (1960–65) and as life president (1965–70).

MILLER, Flora Whitney (b. 1897). *See Whitney, Flora Payne.*

MILLER, Florence Fenwick (1854–1935). British journalist and lecturer. Name variations: (pseudonym) Philomena. Born Florence Fenwick Miller, Nov 5, 1854, in London, England; died April 24, 1935, in Hove, Sussex, England; dau. of Captain John Miller and Eleanor (Fenwick) Miller; m. Frederick Alfred Ford. ❖ Entered Ladies' Medical College, London, and practiced obstetrics after graduating top student; became well known in England and US as platform speaker on women's issues; wrote "Ladies' Notes" for *Illustrated London News* for 33 years; edited periodicals *Outward Bound, Homeward Bound* and *Signal*; wrote *House of Life* (1878), *An Atlas of Anatomy* (1879), *Lynton Abbott's Children* (1879), *Animated Physiology for Elementary Schools* (1882), *Readings in Social Economy* (1883), *Harriet Martineau* (1884), *Hughes's Natural History Readers* (1884) and *In Ladies' Company* (1892).

MILLER, Freda (c. 1910–1960). American composer and pianist for dancers. Born c. 1910; died May 25, 1960, in New York, NY. ❖ Considered nearly as important as Louis Horst in the field of pianist and accompanist for traditional modern dancers, composed for numerous dancers, including Pauline Koner, Hanya Holm, Charles Weidman, John Butler and Helen Tamiris; upon her death, a series of

Freda Miller Memorial Concerts were hosted at 92nd Street YMHA in NYC where she had often played.

MILLER, Frieda S. (1889–1973). American labor reformer and government official. Born Frieda Segelke Miller in LaCrosse, Wisconsin, April 16, 1889; died of pneumonia, July 21, 1973, in New York, NY; dau. of James Gordon Miller and Erna (Segelke) Miller; Milwaukee-Downer College, BA, 1911; University of Chicago, graduate work, 1911–15; lifelong companion, Pauline Newman; children: Elizabeth (adopted 1923). ❖ Was executive secretary, Philadelphia Women's Trade Union League (WTUL, 1917–23); was a factory inspector for the International Ladies' Garment Workers Union (ILGWU, 1924–26); did private charity work (1926–29); served as director, Division of Women in Industry, New York Department of Labor (1929–38); was active in International Labor Organization (1930s–50s); served as labor commissioner for state of New York (1938–42); was special assistant on labor to ambassador to Great Britain, John G. Winant (1943); was director of Women's Bureau of US Department of Labor (1944–52); served as representative on United Nations' commission on International Union for Child Welfare (1960s); stressed need for labor laws, especially regarding mediation, to insure a positive and stable relationship between employer and employee. ❖ See also *Women in World History.*

MILLER, Gail. Australian water-polo player. Born in Queensland, Australia. ❖ Won a team gold medal at Sydney Olympics (2000).

MILLER, Harriet Mann (1831–1918). See Miller, Olive Thorne.

MILLER, Inger (1972—). African-American runner. Born June 12, 1972, in Los Angeles, CA; dau. of Lennox Miller (Jamaican sprinter and Olympic medalist); graduate of University of Southern California. ❖ Won a gold medal for the 4x100-meter relay at Atlanta Olympics (1996); at World Outdoor championships, won a gold medal for the 200 meters and a silver for the 100 (1999).

MILLER, Issette (fl. 1893). See Pearson, Issette.

MILLER, Jane (1945—). American ballet dancer. Born Mar 19, 1945, in New York, NY; trained at School of American Ballet in NY. ❖ Danced briefly with Pennsylvania Ballet in PA; joined National Ballet in Washington, DC, where she danced lead roles in numerous repertory works, including Humphrey's *The Shakers,* Franklyn's *Hommage,* and Fokine's *Les Sylphides;* made guest appearances with Harkness Ballet in Deakin's *Masque of the Red Death* and Nebrada's *Circle of Love;* served as co-artistic director of Eglevsky Ballet on Long Island, NY.

MILLER, Jessie Maude (1910–1972). Australian aviator. Name variations: Chubbie Miller; Mrs. Keith Miller. Born 1910 in Australia; died 1972 in London; m. Keith Miller. ❖ Better known in America than her native Australia, was among air racing's top women contestants; made international news for record-breaking 13,000-mile flight from London to Australia with airman Bill Lancaster (1927), whose love for her would become legendary (though Miller and Lancaster were both married, they became lovers as well as flying partners, spending much of late 1920s together in US); in Miami, fell in love with writer Charles Haden Clarke who died from gunshot wound to the head after apparently leaving suicide note; after Lancaster was arrested for Clarke's murder, stood by him through trial (Aug 1932), at which he was found not guilty. While he was attempting another record, Lancaster disappeared (1933) and was not found until French Army discovered the wreckage decades later in African desert (1962); as he waited to die, he made final entry in logbook diary which spoke of his love for "Chubbie."

MILLER, Jo-Ann (1958—). Australian politician. Born Aug 22, 1958, in Ipswich, Queensland, Australia; m. Neil Miller; children: Stephanie and Brianna Miller. ❖ As a member of the Australian Labor Party, won a by-election to Queensland Parliament for Bundamba (2000); named parliamentary secretary to the minister for Education (2001).

MILLER, Joyce D. (1928—). American labor activist. Born 1928 in Chicago, IL. ❖ Leading advocate for women trade unionists and working women, was the 1st woman elected to AFL-CIO executive council (1980); served as vice president of Amalgamated Clothing and Textile Workers Union (ACTWU) and president of Coalition of Labor Union Women; served as education director (in Pittsburgh, PA, and Chicago, IL) and social-services director for ACTWU.

MILLER, Kathy (1947—). See Switzer, Kathy.

MILLER, Katrina (1975—). Australian mountain biker. Born Sept 15, 1975, in Sydney, Australia. ❖ Won gold in Biker X (Winter 2000) and bronze in Speed (Winter 1998) at X Games; ranked 6th overall in Downhill in NORBA National Series (1998); won NORBA championship in Dual Slalom (1999).

MILLER, Lee (1907–1977). American photographer. Born Elizabeth Miller in Poughkeepsie, New York, 1907; died in Chiddingly, England, 1977; dau. of Theodore Miller (engineer and executive); studied painting, theatrical design and lighting at Art Students League, 1927–29; m. Aziz Eloui Bey (Egyptian businessman), 1934 (sep. 1939, div. 1947); m. Roland Penrose (English painter and art collector), 1947; children: (2nd m.) Antony Penrose. ❖ One of America's foremost women photographers, gave up a successful career as a fashion model to take up the camera; apprenticed with Man Ray (1929); starred in Jean Cocteau's film *The Blood of a Poet* (1930); served as head of *Vogue* magazine's London studios (1940–45), doing fashion layouts and general stories; also began a series of photographs documenting the London Blitz, which was published as *Grim Glory: Pictures of Britain Under Fire,* with text by Edward R. Murrow; became a war correspondent for *Vogue* (1945); accompanied Allied troops through Europe, recording the war in startling surrealistic photographs; at close of war, photographed Buchenwald and Dachau, and was inhabiting Hitler's apartment in Munich when his death was announced. ❖ See also Antony Penrose, *The Lives of Lee Miller* (1985) and *Lee Miller's War* (Little, Brown, 1992); Jane Livingston, *Lee Miller, Photographer* (1989); and *Women in World History.*

MILLER, Lucille (1930—). American murderer. Born 1930; m. Gordon E. "Cork" Miller. ❖ San Bernardino housewife, murdered husband in car fire (Oct 1964) and was linked shortly thereafter to murder of Elaine Hayton, wife of her lover Arthwell C. Hayton; sentenced to life imprisonment at California Institute for Women at Fontana; paroled several years later (1972).

MILLER, Marilyn (1898–1936). American musical-comedy actress. Born Sept 1, 1898 (some sources cite 1896), in Evansville, IN; died suddenly of acute infection in New York, NY, April 7, 1936; dau. of Edwin D. Reynolds (electrician) and Ada (Thompson) Reynolds; m. Frank Carter (actor), May 24, 1919 (died 1920); m. Jack Pickford (actor), July 30, 1922 (div. 1927); m. Chester L. O'Brien (chorus man), Oct 1, 1934; no children. ❖ At 4, joined eldest sister and parents as Mlle. Sugarplum in their vaudeville act "The Columbian Trio" (which eventually became "The Five Columbians") in Dayton, Ohio (1903); toured Midwest with the popular act for 10 years; appeared in Schubert revues: *The Passing Show of 1914, The Passing Show of 1915, The Show of Wonders* (1916), and *The Passing Show of 1917;* then appeared in *Fancy Free* and *Ziegfeld Follies* (1918); came to prominence starring in the musical comedy *Sally,* stopping the show singing "Look for the Silver Lining" (1920); other shows include *Peter Pan* (1924), *Sunny* (1925), *Rosalie* (1928), *Smiles* (1930) and *As Thousands Cheer* (1933); made film debut in *Sally* (1929), followed by *Sunny* (1930) and *Her Majesty, Love* (1931). ❖ See also film *Look for the Silver Lining,* starring June Haver (1949); and *Women in World History.*

MILLER, Olive Thorne (1831–1918). American nature writer and author of children's books. Name variations: Harriet Mann; Harriet M. Miller. Born Harriet Mann, June 25, 1831, in Auburn, New York; died Dec 25, 1918, in Los Angeles, California; dau. of Seth Hunt Mann (banker) and Mary (Holbrook) Mann; m. Watts Miller (businessman), Aug 15, 1854; children: Harriet Mabel Miller (b. 1856); Charles Watts Miller (b. 1858); Mary Mann Miller (b. 1859); Robert Erle Miller (b. 1868). ❖ One of the most popular writers on birds in her day, wrote hundreds of essays for children and nature sketches; best known for *A Bird-Lover in the West* (1894) and *With the Birds in Maine* (1904); also lectured on ornithology. ❖ See also *Women in World History.*

MILLER, Patricia (1927—). South African ballet dancer. Born 1927 in Pretoria, South Africa. ❖ Moved to England; joined Sadler's Wells Ballet (1947), where she created numerous roles in John Cranko's *Children's Corner* (1948), *Beauty and the Beast* (1949), *Pastorale* (1950), *Harlequin in April* (1951), *The Lady and the Fool* (1954), among others; moved back to South Africa (mid-1950s) and opened a dance studio in Capetown.

MILLER, Patsy Ruth (1904–1995). American actress in silent films and early talkies. Born Patricia Ruth Miller, June 22, 1904, in St. Louis, MO; died July 16, 1995, in Palm Desert, CA; sister of Winston Miller; m. Tay Garnett (director), 1929 (div. 1933); m. John Lee Mahin (screenwriter); m. Effingham S. Deans (died 1985). ❖ Appeared as Esmeralda in Lon Chaney's *Hunchback of Notre Dame* (1923); other films include *Camille* (with Valentino and Nazimova), *Omar the Tentmaker*, *This is Paris*, *Painting the Town*, *Beautiful but Dumb* and *Quebec*; wrote short stories, radio scripts, and a novel, *The Flanagan Girl* (1939). ❖ See also autobiography *My Hollywood—When Both of Us Were Young* (O'Raghailligh, 1988).

MILLER, Paula (1911–1966). See Strasberg, Paula.

MILLER, Perry. See Adato, Perry Miller.

MILLER, Ruth (1919–1969). South African poet. Born 1919 in Uitenhage, South Africa; died 1969. ❖ Taught English; won Ingrid Jonker Memorial Prize for 1st collection; works, which reflect influence of Jonker and Sylvia Plath, often convey sense of despair possibly brought about by death of her 14-year-old son; corresponded with poet Guy Butler and revealed awareness of violence of apartheid; writings include *Floating Island* (1965) and *Selected Poems* (1968). Selection of writings edited by Lionel Abrahams and published as *Ruth Miller: Poems, Prose, Plays* (1990).

MILLER, Sarah (1870–1960). See Heap, Sarah.

MILLER, Shannon (1977—). American gymnast. Born Mar 10, 1977, in Rolla, MO. ❖ Won Catania Cup (1990), Swiss Cup and Arthur Gander Memorial (1991), American Cup (1993), Pan American Games (1995), Reese's Cup (1997), and World University Games (1997); won US nationals (1993, 1996); at World championships, won silver medals for team all-around and uneven bars (1991), gold medals in all-around, uneven bars, and floor exercises (1993), and gold medals in all-around and balance beam (1994); at Barcelona Olympics, won a silver medal in balance beam, bronze medals in floor exercises, uneven bars, and team all-around, and a silver medal in indiv. all-around (1992); at Atlanta Olympics, won gold medals for team all-around and balance beam (1996).

MILLER, Sharon Kay (1941—). American golfer. Born Jan 13, 1941, in Marshall, Michigan; graduate of Western Michigan University. ❖ Won 2 Michigan state titles; joined LPGA tour (1966); won Corpus Christi Open (1973), Borden Classic (1974), and Tucson and Bob Hope Classics (1976); retired (1981); received LPGA National Teacher of the Year Award (1989); included on *Golf for Women* magazine's Top 50 Teachers (1999); plays on Women's Senior tour.

MILLER, Sheila Copps (1952—). See Copps, Sheila.

MILLER, Susanne (1915—). Bulgarian-born German historian. Born Susanne Strasser in Sofia, Bulgaria, May 14, 1915; dau. of an Austrian banker; studied at University of Vienna; University of Bonn, PhD, 1963; m. Horace Miller (Labour Party activist); m. Willi Eichler, leader of International Socialist League of Struggle (ISK). ❖ Leading historian of the German Social Democratic movement, whose research and persuasive arguments have earned her a worldwide reputation as a scholar, moved from Austria to London (1934); moved to Germany (1946); wrote a large number of books examining the complexities of the relationship between the Social Democratic movement and political power, including the difficulties of creating a democratic spirit in Germany; retired (1978) but remained active in German public life. ❖ See also *Women in World History*.

MILLER, Tammy (1967—). English field-hockey player. Born June 21, 1967, in UK. ❖ At Barcelona Olympics, won a bronze medal in team competition (1992).

MILLET, Cleusa (c. 1931–1998). Afro-Brazilian religious leader. Name variations: Mãe Cleusa do Gantois. Born c. 1931; died Oct 15, 1998; dau. of Alvaro MacDowell and Mãe (means mother) Menininha do Gantois or Mother Menininha, also known as Maria Escolástica da Conceição Nazareth or Maria Escolastica da Conceicao Nazare (the most important high priestess of Afro-Brazilian religion called Candomblé); children: 4 sons and 1 daughter, including Mônica and Zeno. ❖ Spent much of her childhood at the Gantois (Ilê Iya Omin Axé Iya Massé) *terreiro* or ritual center in Salvador, capital of the Brazilian state of Bahia; from a young age, learned from mother the songs, dances, and rituals associated with the worship of the *orixás* (animist divinities of African, especially Yoruban, origin); took over at Gantois (Sept 1987), the year after mother's death; officiated as *ialorixá* (high priestess) of Gantois until her death from a heart attack. ❖ See also *Women in World History*.

MILLETT, Kate (1934—). American writer, feminist, political activist and sculptor. Born Katherine Murray Millett, Sept 14, 1934, in St. Paul, Minnesota; dau. of James Albert Millett (engineer) and Helen (Feely) Millett (teacher); University of Minnesota, BA (magna cum laude), 1956; St. Hilda's College, Oxford, MA (1st class honors), 1958; Columbia University, PhD (with distinction), 1970; m. Fumio Yoshimura (sculptor), 1965 (div.); no children. ❖ Became actively involved in civil-rights movement (1960s) and was one of the early committee members of National Organization for Women (NOW, 1966); published *Sexual Politics* (1970), which was hailed as a manifesto on the inequity of gender distinctions in Western culture; made a documentary film about women, *Three Lives* (1971); published 1st autobiographical work, *Flying* (1974); was involved in feminist politics, particularly in demonstrations for Equal Rights Amendment (1970s); remained active in feminist and civil-rights issues and continued to work as a sculptor. ❖ See also *Women in World History*.

MILLICAN, Arthenia J. Bates (1920—). African-American novelist, folklorist and short-story writer. Name variations: Arthenia Bates Millican; Arthenia Millican. Born Arthenia Jackson, June 1, 1920, in Sumter, SC; sister of Calvin Shepard Jackson and Susan Emma (David) Jackson. ❖ Wrote PhD dissertation on James Wheldon Johnson (1972) and taught at Southern University in Baton Rouge; works include *Seeds Beneath the Snow* (1969) and *The Deity Nodded* (1973).

MILLIE. Variant of Emily.

MILLIEX, Tatiana Gritsi (1920—). See Gritsi-Milliex, Tatiana.

MILLIGAN, Alice (1866–1953). Irish writer and nationalist. Name variations: I.O.; Iris Olkyrn. Born Alice Letitia Milligan, Sept 14, 1866, in Omagh, Co. Tyrone, Ireland; died in Tyrcur, Omagh, April 13, 1953; dau. of Seaton Forest Milligan (businessman) and Charlotte (Burns) Milligan; sister of Charlotte Milligan Fox (1864–1916); educated at Methodist College, Belfast, and King's College, London. ❖ One of the 1st dramatists of the Celtic Twilight, who became an influential propagandist for the Irish nationalist movement in the early 20th century, co-founded, with Anna Johnston (Ethna Carbery), journals *Northern Patriot* and *Shan Van Vocht*; was a prolific contributor to various Irish journals; was an organizer for the Gaelic League; was a founder member of Ulster Anti-Partition Council; writings include (novel) *The Royal Democrat* (1893), (play) *The Last Feast of the Fianna* (1900), (poems) *Hero Lays* (1908), (with W.H. Milligan) *Sons of the Sea Kings* (1914), (play) *The Daughter of Donagh* (1920); (with Ethna Carbery and Seumas MacManus) *We Sang for Ireland* (1950); poems include, "Nocturne," "March Violets," "Lyrics in Memory of a Sea Lover," "The White Wave Following," "If This Could Be" and "When I Was a Little Girl." ❖ See also Sheila Turner Johnston, *Alice: A Life of Alice Milligan* (Colourpoint, 1994); and *Women in World History*.

MILLIGAN, Charlotte (1864–1916). See Fox, Charlotte Milligan.

MILLIGAN, Marilyn Elaine (1944—). See White, Marilyn Elaine.

MILLIKIN, Kerry. American equestrian. Born in Westport, MA; BS in Nursing, 1994. ❖ Competed with US equestrian team (1985–87); won the Rolex Kentucky International and Chesterland International 3-day events (1987), both on The Pirate; won an indiv. bronze medal for eventing at Atlanta Olympics (1996), on Out and About.

MILLIN, Sarah (1888–1968). Jewish South African writer. Born Sarah Gertrude Liebson, Mar 3, 1888, in Zagar, Lithuania; died July 6, 1968; dau. of Isaiah Liebson (businessman) and Olga (Friedmann) Liebson; earned music teacher's certificate, 1906; m. Philip Millin (lawyer), Dec 1, 1912 (died 1952). ❖ At height of career, achieved considerable fame and influence; immigrated to South Africa with family (Aug 1888); was obsessed with race and blood purity, themes that appeared again and again in her novels; published 1st novel *Adams Rest* (1922); published bestseller *God's Stepchildren* (1924) which would be used by the Nazis as part of their pro-Aryan propaganda; founded South Africa PEN writer's club (1928); published biography of Jan Smuts (1936) and became his confidante during WWII; campaigned for Ian Smith's government in Zimbabwe (1965); over 50 years, published more than 30 books, including *The Dark River* (1919), *The Jordans* (1923), *Mary Glenn* (1925), *The South Africans* (1926), *An Artist in the Family* (1928), *The Coming of the Lord* (1928), *The Fiddler* (1929), *The Sons of Mrs. Aab* (1931), *Cecil Rhodes* (1933), *Three Men Die* (1934), *What Hath a Man?* (1938), *The Dark Gods* (1941), *The Night is Long* (1941), *South Africa* (1941), *War Diary* (Vol. 1: *World Blackout*, 1944, Vol. 2: *The Reeling Earth*, 1945, Vol. 3: *The Pit of the Abyss*, 1946, Vol. 4: *The Sound of the Trumpet*, 1947,

Vol. 5: *Fire out of Heaven*, 1947, Vol. 6: *The Seven Thunders*, 1948), *The People of South Africa* (1951), *The Burning Man* (1952), *Two Bucks Without Hair* (1957) and *Goodbye, Dear England* (1965). ❖ See also Martin Rubin, *Sarah Gertrude Millin: A South African Life* (Donker, 1977); and *Women in World History*.

MILLINGTON, Jean (1949—). American guitarist. Name variations: Fanny. Born Jean Yolanda Millington, 1949, in Manila, Philippines; moved to California with family (1961); sister of June Millington. ❖ Helped form the group Fanny, the 1st all-female rock 'n' roll band to sign a contract with a major record label; released 1st album, *Fanny* (1970), followed by *Charity Ball* (1970), *Fanny Hill* (1972), and *Mothers Pride* (1973); quit the band (1975); with sister, recorded an album, *Ladies on the Stage*. ❖ See also *Women in World History*.

MILLINGTON, June (1950—). American guitarist. Name variations: Fanny. Born June Elizabeth Millington, 1950, in Manila, Philippines; moved to California with family (1961); sister of Jean Millington. ❖ Lead guitarist, helped form the group Fanny with her sister and Alice DeBuhr (drums); released 1st album, *Fanny* (1970), followed by *Charity Ball* (1970), *Fanny Hill* (1972), and *Mothers Pride* (1973); quit the band to make demo records and play background music for various bands (1973); with sister, recorded an album, *Ladies on the Stage*; involved in the women's-music movement, produced albums by such performers as Cris Williamson, Holly Near, and Mary Watkins. ❖ See also *Women in World History*.

MILLION DOLLAR MERMAID (1886–1975). *See Kellerman, Annette.*

MILLIS, Nancy (1922—). Australian microbiologist. Name variations: Nancy Fannie Millis. Born April 10, 1922, in Australia; University of Melbourne, MAgSc, 1946, MSc, 1948; University of Bristol, PhD, 1952. ❖ One of the Australian Academy of Technological Sciences 1st 2 women members, was employed at the Commonwealth Scientific Industrial Research Organisation (CSIRO) Forest Products Division; researched fermentation (1963) at University of Tokyo's Institute of Applied Microbiology; at University of Melbourne's Microbiology Department, served as a lecturer (began 1952), as reader (began 1968) and as microbiology professor (1982–87); served as a food advisor to China (1980); was president of Australian Society for Microbiology (1978–80); wrote the groundbreaking book *Biochemical Engineering* (1965). Made a Member of the Order of the British Empire (1977) and Companion of the Order of Australia (1990).

MILLMAN, Bird (1895–1940). American theatrical dancer and tightrope walker. Born Jennadean Engelmann, Oct 20, 1895, in Canon City, CO; died Aug 5, 1940, in Canon City; dau. of Dyke and Genevieve Millman (aerialists). ❖ Made professional debut at Hippodrome in New York City (1909); appeared on Keith and Orpheum circuits with Millman Trio, later billed Bird Millman and Her Company (as of 1915); performed intermittently in Barnum and Bailey Circus (1913–20); appeared on Broadway in *Ziegfeld Midnight Frolics* (1915–16) and *Greenwich Village Follies of 1921.*

MILLS, Alice (1986—). Australian swimmer. Born May 23, 1986, in Brisbane, Australia. ❖ Won a gold medal for 4x100-meter freestyle relay at Athens Olympics (2004), with a world record time of 54.75.

MILLS, Amy (c. 1949—). American conductor. Born c. 1949 in US. ❖ Became youngest and 1st woman commander and conductor of US Air Force Band and Orchestra, Washington, DC (1990); left active duty (1991); served as 1st woman music director of US Air Force Singing Sergeants, founded National Women's Symphony, Washington, DC (1992), and serves as music director; active as guest conductor, served as music director and conductor of La Crosse Symphony Orchestra, Wisconsin.

MILLS, Barbara (1940—). English lawyer. Name variations: Dame Barbara Mills, Barbara Jean Lyon. Born Barbara Jean Lyon, Aug 1940, in Chorley Wood, Hertfordshire, England; graduate of Lady Margaret Hall, Oxford University; m. John Mills (managing director of import company, John Mills Ltd.). ❖ Called to bar (1963); made recorder of Crown Court (1982) and Queens Counsel (1986); as Junior Treasury counsel to Central Criminal Court (1980s), gained notoriety for prosecution of Michael Fagin for breaking into bedroom of Elizabeth II; served as Department of Trade and Industry inspector under Financial Services Act (1986); named director of Serious Fraud Office (1990); became 1st woman to head Department of Public Prosecutions, presiding over its

rehabilitation and its transformation into one of England's highest profile law offices (1992–98); served as adjudicator for Inland Revenue and Customs and Excise, as trustee of Victim Support, and, since 2000, as non-executive director of Royal Free Hampstead teaching hospital. Created Dame of British Empire (DBE).

MILLS, Eleanor (1888–1922). American murder victim. Murdered on Sept 16, 1922, in New Brunswick, NJ; married to the church sexton. ❖ Episcopal choir singer, who was found brutally slain, along with her pastor, reputedly in a "lover's lane" (for which the pastor's wife was acquitted in the most sensational trial of 1926, and the case remains unsolved). ❖ See also *Women in World History*.

MILLS, Elizabeth (1868–1956). *See Platts-Mills, Daisy Elizabeth*

MILLS, Florence (1895–1927). African-American actress, singer and dancer. Born Florence Winfree, Jan 25, 1895 (some sources cite 1896), in Washington, DC; died of appendicitis in New York, NY, Nov 1, 1927; dau. of John Winfree and Nellie (Simons) Winfree; m. Ulysses Thompson (dancer and comedian). ❖ Beloved entertainer whose performances in musical theater productions like *Shuffle Along* and *Blackbirds* made her an international star and a popular figure of the Harlem Renaissance; by age 5, was winning dance contests; made 1st stage appearance at 8 in a Washington, DC, production of *Sons of Ham*; toured with Bonita Stage Co. as a "pickaninny" with the singing and dancing chorus; performed in the Mills Trio with sisters Olivia and Maude; later formed the Panama Trio with Ada Smith and Cora Green; toured with Tennessee Ten Co. in a trio with husband and Fredi Johnson; received important professional break with *Shuffle Along* (1921); performed in numerous other Broadway and Harlem productions, including *Dixie to Broadway* (1924) and *Blackbirds* (1926), which brought her international recognition. ❖ See also *Women in World History*.

MILLS, Hayley (1946—). English actress. Born April 18, 1946, in London, England; dau. of John Mills (actor) and Mary Hayley Bell (novelist and playwright); sister of Juliet Mills (actress); m. Roy Boulting (film director), 1971 (div. 1976); children: (with Boulting) Crispian Mills (b. 1973, singer); (with actor Leigh Lawson) Jason. ❖ As a child, made film debut opposite father in *Tiger Bay* (1959); signed with Disney, appeared in *Pollyanna* (1960), for which she won a special Juvenile Academy Award; other films include *The Parent Trap* (1961), *In Search of the Castaways* (1962), *Summer Magic* (1963), *Whistle Down the Wind* (1961), *The Chalk Garden* (1964), *The Moon-Spinners* (1964), *That Darn Cat!* (1965) and *The Trouble with Angels* (1966); also appeared in tv series "The Flame Trees of Thika" (1981), among others.

MILLS, Lorna H. (1916–1998). American bank president. Born Feb 5, 1916, at Long Beach, CA; died Dec 30, 1998, in Newport Beach, CA. ❖ As 1st woman president of a federally chartered savings and loan company, served as president and manager of Laguna Beach Federal Savings & Loan (1957–82); retained position after bank merged with Great American First Savings Bank (1982).

MILLS, Mary (1940—). American golfer. Name variations: Mary B. Mills. Born Jan 14, 1940, in Laurel, Mississippi; Millsaps College, 1962; Florida International University, MA in Landscape Architecture. ❖ Won 8 straight Mississippi state championships (1954–61); joined LPGA tour and named Rookie of the Year (1962); won USGA Women's Open (1963), LPGA championship (1964, 1973), and 8 other LPGA events; finished in top 20 (1963–74); retired from tour (1980); designs golf courses. Inducted into Mississippi Sports Hall of Fame (1988).

MILLS, Mary Hayley (1911—). *See Bell, Mary Hayley.*

MILLS, Melissa (1973—). Australian water-polo player. Name variations: Melissa Byram. Born Dec 26, 1973, in Sydney, Australia. ❖ Left driver, outside shot, won a team gold medal at Sydney Olympics (2000).

MILLS, Molly (1907–1981). *See Dwan, Dorothy.*

MILLS, Nikki (1960—). *See Payne, Nicola.*

MILLS, Phoebe (1972—). American gymnast. Born Nov 2, 1972, in Northfield, IL; sister of Nathan Mills (speedskater) and Jessica Mills (1989 World Jr. figure-skating champion). ❖ Began career as a speedskater; as a gymnast, won US nationals, American Cup, International Mixed Pairs, US Olympic Trials, and Mardi Gras Invitational (1988); at Seoul Olympics, won a bronze medal in balance beam (1988); took up diving, finishing as high as 23rd at US nationals (1993); coached snowboarding. Inducted into USA Gymnastics Hall of Fame (2000).

MILLS, Stephanie (1957—). African-American musician. Born Mar 22, 1957, in New York, NY; m. Jeffrey Daniels (singer for band, Shalamar), 1980 (div.); m. 3rd husband Mike Saunders (radio station program director). ❖ At 9, won talent competition at Harlem's Apollo Theater, which led to album with Paramount Records, role in Broadway play, *Maggie Flynn,* and appearances with Isley Brothers, and Spinners; played Dorothy in smash-hit all-black stage production of *The Wizard of Oz* (1975); released unsuccessful debut album, *For the First Time* (1976), on Motown; signed with 20th Century Records, released 1st hit, "What Cha Gonna Do With My Lovin'" (1979); had several hits, including "Sweet Sensation" (1980), "Two Hearts" (1981) and "I Have Learned to Respect the Power of Love" (1986); other albums include *Stephanie* (1981), *Home* (1989), and gospel album, *Personal Inspirations* (1995); appeared in musical theater productions of *Black Nativity* (1995) and *Ragtime* (1999).

MILLS, Susan Tolman (1825–1912). American educator. Born Susan Lincoln Tolman, Nov 18, 1825, in Enosburg, VT; died Dec 12, 1912, in Oakland, CA; dau. of John Tolman (tanner) and Elizabeth (Nichols) Tolman (died 1837); graduate of Mount Holyoke, 1845; m. Cyrus T(aggart) Mills (Presbyterian missionary), Sept 1848 (died 1884). ❖ Taught at Mount Holyoke Seminary (later College), which served as a model for her later educational activities; with husband, performed missionary work in Ceylon and Hawaiian Islands; with husband, purchased Ladies Seminary in Benicia, CA, which later became Mills Seminary then Mills College, the 1st women's college on the Pacific Coast; elected 1st president of Mills College (1890) and served for 19 years.

MILNE, Elizabeth Anne (1858–1926). *See Gard'ner, Elizabeth Anne.*

MILNE, Leslie (1956—). American field-hockey player. Born Oct 17, 1956, in US. ❖ At Los Angeles Olympics, won a bronze medal in team competition (1984).

MILNE, Mary Jane (1840–1921). New Zealand milliner and shopkeeper. Born Sept 16, 1840, in Co. Tyrone, Ireland; died April 4, 1921, in Remuera, New Zealand; dau. of James Stewart Milne (builder) and Margaret Fay (Dawson) Milne. ❖ Immigrated with family to New Zealand (1863); worked as head milliner at local softgoods emporium, where she gained experience in business management; established successful millinery, dressmaking, and drapery shop with sister in Auckland (1867); traveled to England and Europe for latest styles and materials. ❖ See also *Dictionary of New Zealand Biography* (Vol. 2).

MILNER, Brenda Atkinson (1918—). English-born Canadian psychologist. Born Brenda Atkinson Langford in Manchester, England, in 1918; Cambridge University, MA, 1949; attended Montreal Neurological Institute; McGill University, PhD, 1952. ❖ Pioneer in the discipline of neuropsychology, immigrated to Canada (1944); served concurrently at the Montreal Neurological Institute and as a professor at McGill University; is best known for her investigations into brain function, particularly how the brain structure creates new memory. Received Wilder Penfield Prize for Biomedical Research from the Province of Quebec (1993); named Officer of the Order of Canada (1984) and Officier de L'Ordre national du Québec (1995); received Gairdner Award (2005). ❖ See also *Women in World History.*

MILNER, Marion (1900–1998). English psychoanalyst, psychologist and author. Name variations: (pseudonym) Joanna Field. Born Marion Blackett, Feb 1, 1900, in London, England; died May 29, 1998; London University, BS in psychology; m. Dennis Milner (author and inventor, died 1954). ❖ Worked as a psychologist and later trained as a psychoanalyst; as a researcher for the Girl's Public Day School Trust (GPDST, 1935–38), investigated schools and wrote of creative solutions to help difficult students in the critically acclaimed *The Human Problem in Schools* (1938); believed that male qualities were overvalued in Western societies in comparison to female qualities; under pseudonym Joanne Field, published her reflections on inner transformations in *A Life of One's Own* (1934), *An Experiment in Leisure* (1937) and *On Not Being Able to Paint* (1950); also wrote *The Hands of the Living God* (1969), *The Suppressed Madness of Sane Men* (1987), *Eternity's Sunrise: A Way of Keeping a Diary* (1987) and *Bothered by Alligators.*

MILO, Adriana (fl. 1469–1502). *See Mila, Adriana.*

MILO, Sandra (1935—). Italian actress. Born Sandra Marini, Mar 11, 1935, in Milan, Italy (some sources cite Tunis, Tunisia). ❖ Star of Italian and French films, including *Lo Scapolo, Mio figlio Nerone, Les aventures d'Arsène Lupin, Le miroir à deux faces, Vita perdute, Erode il grande, Il Generale della Rovere, Le chemin des écoliers, Gli scontenti,*

Vanina Vanini (title role), *8½, The Visitor, Le voci bianche, Juliet of the Spirits, L'Ombrellone, Bang Bang, Grog* and *Camerieri.*

MILOLEVIC, Vesna (1955—). Yugoslavian handball player. Born Aug 29, 1955. ❖ At Moscow Olympics, won a silver medal in team competition (1980).

MILONIA CAESONIA (d. 41). Roman noblewoman. Murdered in 41; 4th wife of Caligula (12–41), Roman emperor (r. 37–41); children: (Julia) Drusilla (c. 37–c. 41). ❖ After Caligula's assassination, was killed as well, along with daughter Drusilla. ❖ See also *Women in World History.*

MILOSAVLJERIC, Ljubinka (1917—). Communist official and murderer. Born 1917. ❖ Assembled band of Communist partisan fighters during WWII; postwar, held high positions within Communist leadership, including minister of education in Serbian government, chief censor of Yugoslavia's press, and head of Control Commission; for killing ex-lover Momcilo Cupic (April 1955), was sent to an asylum.

MILOSEVIC, Bojana (1965—). Yugoslavian basketball player. Born Nov 29, 1965. ❖ At Seoul Olympics, won a silver medal in team competition (1988).

MILOSEVIC, Mirjana (b. 1942). *See Markovic, Mirjana.*

MILOSLAVSKAIA, Maria (1626–1669). Russian empress. Name variations: Miloslavskaya, Miloslavna, or Miloslavski. Born Maria Ilyanova Miroslavskaia in 1626; died Mar 3 or 4, 1669; born into the powerful Miloslavsky family of Russian nobles; dau. of Ilya Milosavsky; became 1st wife of Alexis I (1629–1676), tsar of Russia (r. 1645–1676), Jan 16, 1648; children: 14, including Eudoxia (died after 1706); Marpha (1652–1705, who became a nun); Dimitri (d. 1667); Alexis (1653–1670); Sophia Alekseyevna (1657–1704); Ivan; Fyodor also known as Theodore III (1661–1682), tsar of Russia (r. 1676–1682); Theodosia (1662–1676); Marie Romanov (1663–1723); Michael (1664–1669); Catherine Romanov (1669–1718); Anna Romanov (1655–1674); John also known as Ivan V (1666–1696), tsar of Russia (r. 1682–1689). ❖ Alexis' 2nd wife was Natalya Narishkina. ❖ See also *Women in World History.*

MILOSOVICI, Lavinia (1976—). Romanian gymnast. Name variations: Lavinia Milo_ovici. Born Lavinia Corina Milosovici, Oct 21, 1976, in Lugoj, Romania; m. Cosmin Vinatu (policeman). ❖ At Barcelona Olympics, won a gold medal in the vault, bronze medal in indiv. all-around, silver medal in team all-around, and gold medal in floor exercises (1992); was the 1st female gymnast since Vera Caslavska to win World and Olympic titles on every event; was the only female gymnast to win the Chunichi Cup 3 times (1992, 1993, 1995); at Atlanta Olympics, won bronze medals for team all-around and indiv. all-around (1996); took up race-car driving, placing 6th in her 1st rally (1999).

MILTO (fl. 415–370 BCE). *See Aspasia the Younger.*

MILTON, DeLisha (1974—). African-American basketball player. Born Sept 11, 1974, in Riceboro, GA; graduate of Florida University, 1997. ❖ Forward; drafted by Portland Power for ABL (1997); drafted by Los Angeles Sparks in 1st round (1999); won a team gold medal at Sydney Olympics (2000) and team gold medals at World championships (1998, 2003); won the Euro League championship playing with team Ekaterinburg in Russia (2003). Won Wade Trophy and named SEC Player of the Year (1997).

MILTON, Frances (c. 1779–1863). *See Trollope, Frances.*

MILTON, Gladys (1924–1999). African-American midwife. Name variations: Gladys Nichols. Born May 26, 1924, in Caney Creek, FL; died June 17, 1999, in Flowersview, FL; dau. of Lillie Mae (Anderson) Nichols and Lonnie Nichols; m. Huey Milton (former classmate); children: (out of wedlock) 2; (2nd m.) 5. ❖ Esteemed midwife, trained at the Florala Medical and Surgical Clinic; received a state of Florida midwifery license (Oct 1959); attended home births for 17 years in Covington County (AL) and in Walton and Okaloosa Counties (FL); attended to 3,000 births during career; was involved in an ongoing debate about who could practice midwifery, especially after the passage of the 1984 Midwifery Practice Act in the state of FL, making it difficult to become legally qualified. ❖ See also autobiography, *Why Not Me?* (1993).

MIMS, Madeline (1948—). *See Manning, Madeline.*

MIMS, Tairia (1981—). *See Flowers, Tairia.*

MIN (1851–1895). Queen of the Yi Dynasty in Korea. Name variations: Bin; Empress Min; Empress Myongsong; Empress Myungsong. Born Ja-young Min in 1851 (some sources cite c. 1840); assassinated by Japanese, Aug 20, 1895; m. Yi T'ae Wang also known as Kojong (1852–1919), king of Korea (r. 1863–1907), in Mar 1866; children: son Sunjong (b. 1874), the last king of Korea (r. 1907–1910). ❖ One of the most controversial figures in Korean history, was the *de facto* ruler of Korea because of husband's lack of interest in the day-to-day administration of his kingdom; ruled (1882–95) and showed considerable political skill; tried to avoid war with Japan by signing a diplomatic treaty (1876); fearing the growing imperialism of the Japanese, shifted policies to favor the Chinese; after the Sino-Japanese War (1894–95), vehemently opposed Japan's informal annexation of Korea; was assassinated by the Japanese (1895). ❖ See also Korean opera, *The Last Empress* (1997); and *Women in World History.*

MIN, Anchee (1957—). Chinese memoirist. Name variations: An Chee Min. Born 1957 in Shanghai, China. ❖ Spent 2 years doing hard labor on the Red Fire collective farm; became a leader of the Little Red Guards; played title role in the film version of Madame Mao's (Jiang Qing) *Red Azalea*; moved to US (1984); published her memoir *Red Azalea* (1993), about growing up during the Cultural Revolution; also wrote the novels *Katharine* (1997) and *Becoming Madame Mao* (2000).

MIN HYE-SOOK (1970—). Korean handball player. Born Mar 15, 1970, in South Korea. ❖ At Barcelona Olympics, won a gold medal in team competition (1992).

MINAICHEVA, Galina (1929—). Soviet gymnast. Born Dec 29, 1929, in USSR. ❖ At Helsinki Olympics, won a bronze medal in vault, silver medal in teams all-around, portable apparatus, and gold medal in team all-around (1952).

MINAMOTO, Sumika (1979—). Japanese swimmer. Born May 2, 1979, in Tokushima, Japan. ❖ Won a bronze medal for 4x100-meter medley relay at Sydney Olympics (2000).

MINCHIN, Alice Ethel (1889–1966). New Zealand teacher and librarian. Born Nov 5, 1889, at Waihou, Hokianga, New Zealand; died July 26, 1966, in Auckland; dau. of Charles Minchin and Edith (Fennell) Minchin; Auckland University College, BA, 1926. ❖ Taught at district high schools (early 1900s); became 1st librarian at Auckland University College (1918); lectured in classification and cataloging at New Zealand Library School in Wellington (1940s). ❖ See also *Dictionary of New Zealand Biography* (Vol. 4).

MINCK, Paule (1839–1901). See Mink, Paule.

MINCO, Marga (b. 1920). See Menco, Sara.

MINEA-SOROHAN, Anisoara (1963—). Romanian rower. Born Feb 1963 in Romania. ❖ At Los Angeles Olympics, won a gold medal in quadruple sculls with coxswain (1984); at Seoul Olympics, won a bronze medal in quadruple sculls without coxswain (1988).

MINER, Dorothy (1904–1973). American museum curator and art historian. Born Dorothy Eugenia Miner Nov 4, 1904, in New York, NY; died May 15, 1973, in Baltimore, MD; dau. of Roy Waldo Miner (Episcopalian minister, then marine biologist) and Anna Elizabeth (Carroll) Miner (previously Catholic nun); Barnard College, AB, 1926; attended Bedford College, University of London, late 1920s, and Columbia University, 1928–29. ❖ Joined Bedford College, London, as 1st Barnard International Fellow (1926); worked for Pierpont Morgan Library in NYC, preparing exhibition of illuminated manuscripts (1933–34); among the 1st few professionally trained art historians to be employed by American museums, worked for Walters Art Gallery in Baltimore, MD, as Keeper of Manuscripts and as curator of Islamic and Near Eastern Art (1934–73); co-authored, with Grace Frank, *Proverbes et Rimes* (1937), authored *Early Christian and Byzantine Art* (1947), edited *Studies in Art and Literature for Belle da Costa Greene* (1954), and published 1st children's coloring book based on medieval woodcuts, *Dragons and Other Animals* (1960); edited *Journal of the Walters Art Gallery* (1938–69) and numerous catalogs of Walters collections; received copy of festschrift, *Gatherings in Honor of Dorothy Miner* (1973).

MINER, Jan (1917–2004). American actress. Born Oct 15, 1917, in Boston, MA; died Feb 15, 2004, in Bethel, CT; m. Richard Merrell (actor and writer), 1953 (died 1988). ❖ Best known as Madge the Manicurist in Palmolive commercials, which she appeared in for 27 years, had a long career on NY stage; made debut in Boston in *Street Scene* (1945) and in NY as Maria Louvin in *Obligatoo* (1948); also

appeared in *Heartbreak House* and *The Heiress,* among others; films include *Lenny* and *Mermaids;* was frequently seen on tv.

MINER, Myrtilla (1815–1864). American educator. Born Mar 4, 1815, near Brookfield, New York; died Dec 17, 1864, in Washington, DC; dau. of Seth Miner (farmer) and Eleanor (Smith) Miner. ❖ Pioneer in education for African-American girls, opened the Colored Girls School in Washington, DC (Dec 3, 1851); despite local opposition, had many ardent supporters, particularly among Quakers; assembled a library of 1,500 books, and brought scholars in to give lectures; encouraged activities such as nature study, gardening, and astronomy and focused on training teachers; after the Civil War forced the school to close (1860), her supporters in Congress gained the school a charter as the Institution for the Education of Colored Youth (1863), renamed the Miner Normal School, but she did not live to see it reopened. ❖ See also Ellen O'Connor, *Myrtilla Miner: A Memoir,* 1885; and *Women in World History.*

MINER, Sarah Luella (1861–1935). American missionary and teacher. Born Oct 30, 1861, in Oberlin, Ohio; died Dec 2, 1935, in Tsinan, China; dau. of Daniel Irenaeus Miner and Lydia Jane (Cooley) Miner. ❖ Took teaching post at boys' high school, North China College, and theological seminary near Beijing, China (1888); remained in China during Boxer Rebellion, besieged in British legation (1900); served as principal of Bridgman Academy in Beijing (1903–13) and president of offshoot North China Union Women's College (1905–20); negotiated affiliation of and served as 1st dean of Women's College of Yenching University (1920–22); appointed acting dean of Women's Medical Unit of Shandong Christian University in Jinan (1923); published *Two Heroes of Cathay* (1903) and *China's Book of Martyrs* (1903).

MINERVINA (fl. 290–307). Roman consort. Name variations: Flourished around 290 to 307; consort, possibly 1st wife, of Constantine I the Great, Roman emperor (r. 306–337); children: Crispus (b. around 305); possibly Constantina (c. 321–c. 354). ❖ Was either dead or dismissed before Constantine's marriage to Fausta (d. 324), in 307. ❖ See also *Women in World History.*

MINEYEVA, Olga (1952—). Soviet runner. Born Oct 1952 in USSR. ❖ At Moscow Olympics, won a silver medal in 800 meters (1980).

MINIFIE, Susannah (c. 1740–1800). See Gunning, Susannah.

MINIJIMA, Kiyo (1833–1919). Japanese businesswoman and philanthropist. Name variations: Mrs. Kiyo Minijima. Born 1833; died 1919. ❖ Following husband's death (1897), invested in real estate and became the wealthiest woman in Japan. ❖ See also *Women in World History.*

MINK, Patsy (1927–2002). American politician. Name variations: Patsy Takemoto Mink; Patsy T. Mink. Born Patsy Matsu Takemoto, Dec 6, 1927, in Paia, Maui, Hawaii; died Aug 30, 2002, in Honolulu; dau. of Suematsu Takemoto and Mitama Tateyama Takemoto; University of Hawaii at Honolulu, BA in zoology and chemistry, 1948; earned law degree at University of Chicago, 1951; m. John Francis Mink (geologist); children: Gwendolyn Rachel (known as Wendy) Mink (professor of political science at University of California, Santa Cruz). ❖ US Democratic congressional representative from Hawaii, whose long political career centered on defending the rights of minorities and women, was elected to Hawaii House of Representatives (1956) and Hawaii state senate (1958); elected to US House of Representatives (1964); over next several years, served on Committee on Education and Labor, Committee on Interior and Insular Affairs, and Budget Committee; introduced or sponsored many acts such as the 1st child-care bill and legislation establishing programs like student loans, bilingual education, and Head Start; also worked for the successful passage of Title IX; as chair of Subcommittee on Mines and Mining, was lead author of the Strip-Mining Act and Mineral Leasing Act of 1976; was an early critic of the expansion of the American military presence in Vietnam; authored and sponsored the Women's Educational Equity Act in 1974; lost a bid for nomination to US Senate (1976); served as assistant secretary of state for oceans and international environmental affairs (1977–78) and as president of the Americans for Democratic Action; served on Honolulu City Council (1983–87); returned to US House of Representatives (1990); reelected (1992, 1994, 1996, 1998, 2000). ❖ See also *Women in World History.*

MINK, Paule (1839–1901). French revolutionary socialist, feminist, orator, and journalist. Name variations: Mink or Minck is a pseudonym of Adèle Paulina Mekarska. Pronunciation: pohl meenk. Born Adèle

Paulina Mekarska in Clermont-Ferrand (Puy-de-Dôme), France, Nov 9, 1839, to Polish exiles; died in Auteuil (Seine), April 28, 1901; dau. of Count Jean Nepomucène Mekarski and Jeanne-Blanche Cornelly de la Perrière; married to and separated from (at unknown dates) Prince Bohdanowicz (engineer); m. Maxime Négro (mechanic), 1881; children: (1st m.) Anna and Wanda (d. 1870); (with painter Jean-Baptiste Noro) Mignon and Jeanne-Héna; (2nd m.) Lucifer-Blanqui-Vercingetorix-Révolution (b. 1882, died in infancy) and Spartacus-Blanqui-Révolution (b. 1884, renamed Maxime by a civil tribunal). ❖ As a feminist orator and militant socialist republican, began public speaking on women's issues (1868); played a heroic role in Franco-Prussian War and Paris Commune uprising (1870–71); lived in Switzerland as a political refugee (1871–80); returned to France and aroused a storm at the socialist congress (1880); jailed following a demonstration (1881); joined Guesde's French Workers' Party (1882); opposed Hubertine Auclert on women's suffrage (1884); left the French Workers' Party, joined the Revolutionary Socialist Party (Blanquist) and Women's Solidarity, and ran for Parliament (1892–93); was an outspoken Dreyfusard during the Affair (1897–99); left Solidarity (1900). ❖ See also *Women in World History.*

MINKH, Irina (1964—). Soviet basketball player. Born April 16, 1964, in USSR. ❖ Won a bronze medal at Seoul Olympics (1988) and a gold medal at Barcelona Olympics (1992), both in team competition.

MINNE, Daniele (1939—). *See Amrane, Djamila.*

MINNELLI, Liza (1946—). American singer and actress. Born Mar 12, 1946, in Los Angeles, CA; dau. of Vincente Minnelli (director) and Judy Garland (actress and singer); half-sister of Lorna Luft; m. Peter Allen (singer), 1967 (div. 1972); m. Jack Haley Jr. (producer), 1974 (div. 1979); m. Mark Gero (sculptor), 1979 (div. 1992); m. David Gest, 2002 (div.). ❖ Began acting as child and appeared on stage with mother; came to prominence on Broadway in *Best Foot Forward* (1963), then won Tony Awards for *Flora, the Red Menace* (1965) and *The Act* (1977); won an Emmy for "Liza with a Z!" (1973); also appeared in *Minnelli on Minnelli* (1998); appeared in the film *The Sterile Cuckoo* (1969), for which she was nominated for an Academy Award; won an Oscar for performance as Sally Bowles in *Cabaret* (1972); other films include *Charlie Bubbles* (1967), *Tell Me That You Love Me, Junie Moon* (1970), *A Matter of Time* (1976), *New York, New York* (1977) and *Arthur* (1981).

MINNER, Ruth Ann (1935—). American politician. Born Jan 17, 1935, in Slaughter Neck, Sussex Co., Delaware; dau. of a sharecropper; m. Frank Ingram (died 1967); m. Roger Minner, 1969 (died 1991); children: 3 sons. ❖ Widowed with 3 sons (1967), landed a receptionist's job in the office of the Delaware governor; as a Democrat, spent 18 years in the state legislature; served as lieutenant governor (1993–2001); became the 1st woman governor of Delaware (2001).

MINNERT, Sandra (1973—). German soccer player. Born April 7, 1973, in Gedern, Germany. ❖ Defender; won team European championships (1995, 1997, 2001); won a team bronze medal at Sydney Olympics (2000) and Athens Olympics (2004); played with FFC Frankfurt; signed with Washington Freedom in WUSA professional league (2002); won FIFA World Cup (2003).

MINNIE. *Variant of Wilhemina.*

MINNIGERODE, Lucy (1871–1935). American nurse. Born Feb 8, 1871, near Leesburg, VA; died of a stroke, Mar 24, 1935; dau. of Charles and Virginia Cuthbert (Powell) Minnigerode. ❖ The 1st US Public Health Service (USPHS) superintendent of nurses, trained at the Bellevue Hospital Training School for Nurses in NYC (nursing diploma, 1899); worked as a private-duty nurse for 10 years; in Washington, DC, was superintendent of nurses at Columbia Hospital for Women and Children and at Episcopal Eye, Ear and Throat Hospital (1910–12); during WWI, was a supervisor with American Red Cross in Kiev, Russia (1914–15); served as Columbia Hospital for Women's director of nurses (1915–17); worked with American Red Cross Nursing Service (1917–19); appointed director of newly created USPHS department of nurses (1919); established and chaired the 1st American Nurses Association (ANA) section for government nurses; served as chair of the ANA committee of federal legislation (1923–28). Received the Cross of St. Anne (1915) from Czar Nicholas II.

MINOKA-HILL, Rosa (1876–1952). Native American physician. Name variations: Lillie Rosa Minoka-Hill; Lillie Rosa Minoka Hill; L. Rosa Minoka. Born Lillie Minoka, Aug 30, 1876, on St. Regis Reservation in New York State; died of a heart attack, Mar 18, 1952, in Fond du Lac,

Wisconsin; dau. of Joshua G. Allen (Quaker physician) and a Mohawk mother who died shortly after her birth; Woman's Medical College of Pennsylvania, MD, 1899; m. Charles Abram Hill (farmer), 1905 (died 1916); children: Rosa Melissa Hill (b. 1906); Charles Allan Hill (b. 1906); Norbert Seabrook Hill (b. 1912); Alfred Grahame Hill (b. 1913); Jane Frances and Josephine Marie Hill (twins, b. 1915). ❖ Graduated from medical school (1899); abandoned medical practice for marriage (1905); widowed (1916); when sole doctor left Oneida, Wisconsin (1917), became the community's only trained physician and continued her practice in Oneida for rest of life, varying fees according to a patient's ability to pay; named Outstanding American Indian of the Year by the Indian Council Fire, Chicago (1947); given honorary lifetime membership by State Medical Society of Wisconsin (1949). ❖ See also *Women in World History.*

MINOR, Virginia L. (1824–1894). American suffrage leader and Civil War relief worker. Born Virginia Louisa Minor, Mar 27, 1824, in Caroline Co., Virginia; died of liver disease, Aug 14, 1894, in St. Louis, Missouri; dau. of Warner Minor and Maria (Timberlake) Minor; m. Francis Minor (attorney), Aug 31, 1843; children: Francis Gilmer Minor (1852–1866). ❖ The 1st woman in Missouri to publicly support suffrage, was co-founder and president of Woman Suffrage Association there (1867–71); filed lawsuit against St. Louis registrar who had denied her voter registration, contending that a woman's right to vote as a citizen was already ensured by the Constitution and the 14th Amendment; lost lawsuit (1872), then lost again when Supreme Court upheld lower court ruling (1874); was president of St. Louis branch of National Woman Suffrage Association (1879–90) and St. Louis branch of National American Woman Suffrage Association (1890–92). ❖ See also *Women in World History.*

MINTER, Mary Miles (1902–1984). American actress. Name variations: Juliet Shelby. Born Juliet Reilly, April 1, 1902 (some sources cite 1898) in Shreveport, Louisiana; died of heart failure, Aug 4, 1984, in Santa Monica, California; dau. of Charlotte Shelby; m. Brandon O'Hildebrandt (died 1965). ❖ At 5, made stage debut as "Little Juliet Shelby," in Arnold Daly production of *Cameo Kirby*; signed with Metro (1915) and went on to star in minor films, including *Barbara Frietchie* (1915), *Dimples* (1916), and *The Ghost of Rosie Taylor* (1918); moved to Realart-Paramount (1918), where she starred in *Anne of Green Gables* (1919); also appeared in *The Trail of the Lonesome Pine* (1923); brief career was abruptly ended by scandal because of her association with William Desmond Taylor, a director who was murdered (Feb 1922), though she was not seriously suspected of the crime. King Vidor's conclusion that the murder was committed by Minter's mother Charlotte Shelby has now been accepted by many. ❖ See also *Women in World History.*

MINTON, Yvonne (1938—). Australian mezzo-soprano. Born Yvonne Fay Minton, Dec 4, 1938, in Sydney, Australia; studied with Marjorie Walker at Sydney Conservatory and with Henry Cummings and Joan Cross in London; m. William Barclay, 1965. ❖ Won Kathleen Ferrier prize and Hertogenbosch Competition (1961); debuted as Britten's Lucretia, London (1964); performed at Covent Garden (since 1965); debuted at Metropolitan Opera (1973) and Paris Opéra (1976); has performed in operas by Berg, Wagner, Bartók, Berlioz, Strauss, and Mozart. Named Commander of the Order of the British Empire (1980). ❖ See also *Women in World History.*

MINUS, Rene (1943—). American singer. Name variations: The Chantels. Born 1943. ❖ Sang with Arlene Smith, Lois Harris, Jackie Landry, and Sonia Goring in their Bronx, NY, parochial school choir and became 2nd soprano for their doo-wop group, The Chantels (formed 1956), one of 1st and most well-received girl groups; with group, released single "He's Gone" (1957), followed by the album *We Are the Chantels* (1958); had such hits as "Maybe" (1958), "Look in My Eyes" (1961) and "Well, I Told You" (1961); appeared with original group in reunion performances (1990s).

MINUZZO, Giuliana (1931—). *See Chenal-Minuzzo, Giuliana.*

MINYTHYIA (fl. 334 BCE). *See Thalestris.*

MIOLAN-CARVALHO, Marie (1827–1895). French soprano. Name variations: Marie Carvalho; Marie Carvalho-Miolan. Born Marie Caroline Felix-Miolan in Marseilles, France, Dec 31, 1827; died at Chateau-Puys, near Dieppe, France, July 10, 1895; studied with father F. Félix-Miolan, then in Paris with Duprez; m. Leon Carvalho (impresario), 1853. ❖ One of the most celebrated singers of her time, made debut as Isabella in *Robert le Diable* in Brest (1849); appeared with Paris Opera (1849–55, 1868–85) and created the roles of Marguerite, Baucis, Juliette, and Mireille for Gounod; also sang to great success in London (1860); retired (1885). ❖ See also *Women in World History.*

MIOU-MIOU (1950—). French actress. Name variations: Miou Miou. Born Sylvette Héry, Feb 22, 1950, in Paris, France; children: (with actor Patrick Dewaere) Angele (b. 1974); (with singer Julien Clerc) Jeanne. ❖ Made film debut in *La Cavale* (1971); won the César Award for Best Actress for *La dérobade* (1979); other films include *Les Valseuses* (1974), *Coup de foudre* (1983, released in US as *Entre Nous*), *Blanche et Marie* (1984), *La lectrice* (1988), *Milou en mai* (1990), *La totale!* (1991), *Tango* (1993), *Germinal* (1993), *Le Huitiéme jour* (1996), *Nettoyage à sec* (1997), *Tout va bien, on s'en va* (2000) and *Folle embellie* (2003).

MIR, Isabelle (1949—). French Alpine skier. Born Mar 2, 1949, in Saint Lary, France. ❖ Won a silver medal for downhill at Grenoble Olympics (1968); placed 4th for downhill at Sapporo Olympics (1972), at World championships, won a silver medal for downhill (1970); at World Cup, won 2 downhill titles (1968, 1970), placed 2nd overall (1968) and 3rd overall (1971).

MIRA BAI (1498–1547). Indian queen, poet, and songwriter. Name variations: Meera; Mirabai. Born in Merta, 1498; died in Dwarka, 1547 (some sources cite 1573); brought up in the court of her grandfather in the worship of the Hindu god Vishnu; m. Prince Bhoj Raj of Mewar, 1516 (died of wounds sustained in battle, 1521). ❖ Considered India's best-known woman poet, was a rebel in thought and religion, devoting her life to the worship of Krishna. Though her poems were written in Hindi, they were translated early into other Indian languages. ❖ See also *Women in World History.*

MIRABAL DE GONZÁLEZ, Patria (1924–1960). Dominican political activist and one of the Mirabal sisters. Name variations: Las Mariposas (The Butterflies). Born Patria Mercedes Mirabal, Feb 27, 1924; assassinated by command of Trujillo, dictator of the Dominican Republic, Nov 25, 1960; dau. of Enrique Mirabal and Mercedes Mirabal; had sisters Minerva, María Teresa, and Dedé; married; children: son, Nelson González Mirabal (became chief aide to the nation's vice president, Jaime David Fernandez Mirabal). ❖ Dominican Republic political activist who, in the generation after her death, was transformed into national martyr, feminist icon and revolutionary hero, along with sisters; joined the anti-Trujillo underground forces; having been involved with the failed revolt of June 1959, husband was arrested and imprisoned; along with sisters, was known within the underground Movimiento Revolucionario 14 de Junio (MR14J) by the code name of Mariposa (butterfly) and soon became known to agents of Trujillo's secret police; arrested, subjected to torture, and killed. ❖ See also Julia Alvarez, *In the Time of the Butterflies* (1994); and *Women in World History.*

MIRABAL DE TAVÁREZ, Minerva (1927–1960). Dominican political activist and one of the Mirabal sisters. Name variations: Las Mariposas (The Butterflies). Born Minerva Mirabal, Mar 12, 1927; assassinated by command of the dictator of the Dominican Republic, Generalissimo Rafael Leonidas Trujillo Molina, Nov 25, 1960; dau. of Enrique Mirabal and Mercedes Mirabal; graduated with high honors from National Autonomous University of the Dominican Republic; had sisters Patria, María Teresa, and Dedé; married; children: Minou Tavárez Mirabal (became deputy foreign minister of the Dominican Republic). ❖ At age 22, having turned down sexual overtures from Trujillo, was jailed and banned from continuing her law studies; joined the anti-Trujillo underground forces; having been involved with the failed revolt of June 1959, husband was arrested and imprisoned; along with sisters, was known within the underground Movimiento Revolucionario 14 de Junio (MR14J) by the code name of Mariposa (butterfly) and soon became known to agents of Trujillo's secret police; arrested, subjected to torture, and killed. ❖ See also Julia Alvarez, *In the Time of the Butterflies* (1994); and *Women in World History.*

MIRABAL DE GUZMÁN, María Teresa (1936–1960). Dominican political activist and one of the Mirabal sisters. Name variations: Las Mariposas (The Butterflies); Maria Teresa Mirabal; (nickname) Maté. Born María Teresa Mirabal on Oct 15, 1936; assassinated by command of Trujillo, dictator of the Dominican Republic, Nov 25, 1960; dau. of Enrique Mirabal and Mercedes Mirabal; had sisters Minerva, Patria, and Dedé; married. ❖ Joined the anti-Trujillo underground forces; having been involved with the failed revolt of June 1959, husband was arrested and imprisoned; along with sisters, was known within the underground

Movimiento Revolucionario 14 de Junio (MR14J) by the code name of Mariposa (butterfly) and soon became known to agents of Trujillo's secret police; arrested, subjected to torture, and killed. ❖ See also Julia Alvarez, *In the Time of the Butterflies* (1994); and *Women in World History.*

MIRABEAU, Comtesse de (1827–1914). French journalist and novelist. Name variations: Marie de Gonneville. Born Marie de Gonneville, 1827, in France; died 1914; m. Comte Arundel Joseph de Mirabeau (died 1860); children: Comtesse de Martel de Janville (1850–1932, writer). ❖ Wrote for *La Mode, Le Figaro* and *La Vie Parisienne*; also wrote *Les Jeunes Filles Pauvres* (1863), *Hélène de Gardannes* (1868), *Jane et Germaine* (1875), *Chut!!!* (1880) and *Coeur d'Or* (1896).

MIRABEAU MARTEL, Comtesse de (1850–1932). *See Martel de Janville, Comtesse de.*

MIRABELLA, Erin (1978—). American cyclist. Born May 18, 1978, in Kenosha, Wisconsin. ❖ Placed 1st overall in World Cup ranking for indiv. pursuit and scratch (2002); won a bronze medal for points race at Athens Olympics (2004).

MIRAMION, Madame de (1629–1696). French founder. Name variations: Marie Bonneau. Born in Paris, France, 1629; died in Paris, 1696. ❖ Founded the House of Refuge, the establishment of Ste.-Pélagie, and the original community of 12 young women which later became the Congrégation des Miramiones; became its superior and upon her death left her great fortune to this and other benevolent institutions.

MIRAMOVA, Elena (c. 1905—). Russian actress and ballet and theatrical dancer. Born c. 1905 in Tsaritsyn, Russia; trained in Seattle, WA, at Cornish School. ❖ As a ballet dancer, performed with ballet class act at age 16 on Northwest Pantages vaudeville circuit; worked mainly as a dramatic actress in Los Angeles in productions of *A Bill of Divorcement* and *Sister Beatrice*, and on Broadway in *The Affairs of Anatol, The Two Mrs. Carrolls,* and as the ballerina in *Grand Hotel*; wrote several plays, including *Dark Eyes* (1943).

MIRANDA, Carmen (1909–1955). Brazilian singer and actress. Born Maria do Carmo Miranda da Cunha, Feb 9, 1909, in Marco de Canavezes, near Oporto, Portugal; died in Los Angeles, CA, Aug 5, 1955; sister of Aurora Miranda da Cunha; m. David Sebastian, 1947. ❖ Immigrated to Brazil (1910); made 1st hit recording, "Taí" (1930); began appearing on stage in *bahiana* clothing: turban, wide-starched skirt, and heavy jewelry, with bare midriff and the typical sandals substituted by 5-inch platform heels, which became her trademark, especially after she appeared in Brazilian film *Banana da Terra* which featured the song-and-dance number "O que é que a bahiana tem?" ("What Does the Bahian Girl Have?," 1939); appeared on Broadway in *The Streets of Paris* (1939); became an international star in *Down Argentine Way* (1940); was chief Latin star in Hollywood's "Good Neighbor" films (1940–45); films include *That Night in Rio* (1941), *Week-End in Havana* (1941), *Springtime in the Rockies* (1942), *The Gang's All Here* (1943), *Four Jills in a Jeep* (1944), *Greenwich Village* (1944), *Something for the Boys* (1944), *Copacabana* (1947), *A Date With Judy* (1948) and *Scared Stiff* (1953). ❖ See also Martha Gil-Montero, *Brazilian Bombshell* (Fine, 1989); "Carmen Miranda: Bananas Is My Business," (documentary), 1st aired on PBS (1995); and *Women in World History.*

MIRANDA, countess of. *See Nilsson, Christine (1843–1921).*

MIRANDA, Isa (1909–1982). Italian actress. Born Inèes Isabella Sampietro in Milan, Italy, July 5, 1909; died of an infected bone fracture in Rome, July 8, 1982; trained for the stage at Milan Academy; m. Alfredo Guarini (film producer). ❖ One of Italy's leading actresses, was a bit player when she was selected by Max Ophuls to star in *La Signora di Tutti* (1934); went on to star in many Italian, German, French and British films, winning the Best Actress award at Cannes for performance in *Au-delà des Grilles*, released for English-speaking audiences as *The Walls of Malapaga* (1949); her US films included *Hotel Imperial* (1939) and *Adventure in Diamonds* (1940); also appeared on Italian stage and tv and was respected as a poet, novelist, and painter; other films include *Come le Foglie* (*Like the Leaves*, 1934), *Scipione l'Africano* (*Scipio Africanus*, 1937), *Una Donna fra due Mondi* (*Between Two Worlds*, 1937), *Malombra* (1942), *Zazà* (1943), *La Ronde* (1950), *Les sept Péchès capitaux* (*The Seven Deadly Sins*, 1952), *Rasputin* (1954); *Summer Madness* (*Summertime,* 1955), *Il Tesoro di Rommel* (1956), *The Yellow Rolls-Royce* (1964); *The Shoes of the Fisherman* (1968) and *Il Portiere di Notte* (*The Night Porter,* 1974).

MIRANDA, Patricia (1979—). American wrestler. Born June 11, 1979, in Manteca, CA; attended Stanford University. ❖ Won Pan American championships for 51kg freestyle (2002); won a bronze medal for 48 kg freestyle at Athens Olympics (2004).

MIRANDE, Tracey (1966—). See McFarlane, Tracey.

MIREILLE (1906–1996). French composer, singer and actress. Born Mireille Hartuch in Paris, France, Sept 30, 1906; died in Paris, Dec 29, 1996; m. Emmanuel Berl (noted editor), 1936 (died 1976). ❖ Author of more than 600 songs, started collaboration with lyricist Jean Nohain (1928), when their operetta *Fouchtra* was published; also a successful actress, appeared in operetta *Flossie,* and in a short film with Buster Keaton; after appearing in London at Café de Paris, starred on Broadway in *Manon la Crevette*; composed several film scores in Hollywood; had major breakthrough (1932) when the cabaret duo Pills et Tabet performed "Couchés dans le Foin" (Lying in the Hay), from *Fouchtra,* and almost overnight a new style in French popular music was born; over next decades, nearly all of France's popular singers would sing chansons crafted by the team of Mireille-Nohain, including Jacques Brel ("Le Petit Chemin"), Maurice Chevalier ("Quand un Vicomte"), Yves Montand ("Une Demoiselle sur une Balançoire"), and Maurice Sablon; began performing her own compositions (1934) and made numerous recordings; played an active role in French resistance during WWII; founded Petit Conservatoire de la Chanson (1954), the 1st attempt to teach the art of the French chanson. ❖ See also *Women in World History.*

MIREMONT, Anne d'Aubourg de La Bove, Comtesse de (1735–1811). French novelist. Name variations: Countess of Miremont. Born 1735 in France; died 1811. ❖ Wrote novel *Mémoires de madame la marquise de Crémy* (1766) and a work on women's education with course of lessons, *Traité de l'éducation des femmes* (7 vols., 1779–89).

MIREMONT, countess of.
See Madeleine de Saint-Nectaire (fl. 1575).
See Miremont, Anne d'Aubourg de La Bove, Comtesse de (1735–1811).

MIREMONT, Jacqueline de (fl. 16th c.). French poet. Born in France. ❖ Works include collection *Le Petit Nain qui combat le monde* which was followed by poem "La Part de Marie, soeur de Marthe"; also published play and several other collections of poetry.

MIRHRIMAH (1525–1575). See Mihrimah.

MIRIAM. *Variant of Mary.*

MIRIAM. Biblical woman. A dau. of Ezrah, of the tribe of Judah.

MIRIAM THE PROPHET (fl. c. 13th or 14th c. BCE). Hebrew prophet. Name variations: Miriam the Jewess; Miriam the Prophetess; Mary the Jewess; Mariam. Flourished in 13th or 14th century BCE; born in Alexandria, Egypt; died at Kadesh; dau. of Jochebed; sister of Moses and Aaron. ❖ Well-known Biblical figure, most often associated with her criticism of Moses and subsequent punishment by God, and with leading the Israelite women in song and dance after the escape from Egypt; is often commingled, or by some accounts erroneously confused, with an influential Alexandrian alchemist and inventor of the 1st, 2nd or 3rd century CE, Mary the Jewess, who is known by some of the same alternative appellations. ❖ See also *Women in World History.*

MIRIAM THE PROPHET (fl. 1st, 2nd, or 3rd c.). See Mary the Jewess.

MIRÓ, Pilar (1940–1997). Spanish film director. Name variations: Pilar Miro; Pilar Miro Romero. Born 1940 in Madrid, Spain; died of a heart attack, Oct 19, 1997, in Madrid; studied screenwriting at Spain's Official School of Cinematography. ❖ At 23, became Spain's 1st woman tv director (1963); released 1st feature film, *La Petición* (The Demand) (1976), which caused controversy due to its feminist themes; came to international prominence with *El Crimen de Cuenca* (The Cuenca Crime, 1979), which depicted the repressive measures of Spain's Guardia Civil and was banned in Spain; released *Gary Cooper que estas en los Cielos* (Gary Cooper Who Art in Heaven), an autobiographical film with a feminist slant (1980), followed by *Hablamos esta Noche* (Let's Talk Tonight, 1982); served as director general of Cinematography in Spanish Ministry of Culture (1982–86); released final feature film, *Werther* (1986). ❖ See also *Women in World History.*

MIROSHINA, Yelena (1974—). Soviet diver. Born June 5, 1974, in USSR. ❖ At Barcelona Olympics, won a silver medal in platform (1992).

MIRREN, Helen (1945—). English actress. Name variations: Dame Helen Mirren. Born Ilyena Lydia Mironoff, July 26, 1945, in Chiswick, London, England; dau. of English mother and Russian father (violinist with London Philharmonic Orchestra); sister of Catherine and Peter Mironoff; m. Taylor Hackford (producer and director), 1997. ❖ Possibly best known as Chief Inspector Jane Tennison on British series "Prime Suspect," began career at 18 as Cleopatra for National Youth Theater (1965); joined Royal Shakespeare Co. (1967) where she starred in numerous plays, including nontraditional portrayal of Lady Macbeth in Trevor Nunn's production of *Macbeth* (1974), as well as *The Roaring Girl* and *Antony and Cleopatra* (1984); made 1st film, *Herostratus* (1967), followed by Peter Hall's *A Midsummer Night's Dream* (1968), *Miss Julie* (1972), *The Age of Consent* (1969), *Savage Messiah* (1972), *Hamlet* (1976), *Caligula* (1979), *Blue Remembered Hills* (1979), *Excalibur* (1981), *White Nights* (1985), *Mosquito Coast* (1986), *The Cook, The Thief, His Wife and Her Lover* (1989), *Calendar Girls* (2004) and *Cal,* for which she won Best Actress Award at Cannes (1984); made Broadway debut as Natalya Petrovna in *A Month in the Country* (1995); won 3 BAFTA awards for series "Prime Suspect" (1990–2000); nominated for Best Actress Oscar for *The Madness of King George* (1995); won Golden Globe for *Losing Chase* (1996); won Emmy Award for *The Passion of Ayn Rand* (1999) and received 2nd Oscar nomination for *Gosford Park* (2001); nominated for Laurence Olivier Theatre Award for Best Actress for *Orpheus Descending* (2001) and *Mourning Becomes Electra* (2003); won Tony award for *Dance of Death* (2002). Created Dame of British Empire (DBE, 2003).

MISAKOVA, Miloslava (1922—). Czech gymnast. Born Feb 25, 1922, in Czechoslovakia. ❖ At London Olympics, won a gold medal in team all-around (1948).

MISELER, Carola (1962—). See Hornig-Miseler, Carola.

MISENER, Dorothy (1909–2002). See Jurney, Dorothy Misener.

MISERSKY, Antje (1967—). See Harvey, Antje.

MISEVICH, Vera (1945—). Soviet equestrian. Born April 10, 1945, in USSR. ❖ At Moscow Olympics, won a gold medal in team dressage (1980).

MISHAK, Valentina (1942—). Soviet volleyball player. Born Jan 16, 1942, in USSR. ❖ At Tokyo Olympics, won a silver medal in team competition (1964).

MISHENINA, Galina (1950—). Soviet rower. Born Aug 1950 in USSR. ❖ At Montreal Olympics, won a bronze medal in coxed fours (1976).

MISHINA, Masumi (1982—). Japanese softball player. Born Mar 12, 1982, in Kanagawa, Japan. ❖ Infielder, won a team bronze at Athens Olympics (2004).

MISHKOWSKY, Zelda Shneurson (1914–1984). Israeli poet. Name variations: Zelda Shneurson-Mishkowsky or Mishkovsky; (pseudonym) Zelda. Born 1914 in Chernigoff, Ukraine; died 1984 in Jerusalem, Israel; only dau. of a Hassidic family (father was a rabbi); attended Mizrachi Teacher's College (now Efrata College); married. ❖ Immigrated with family to Israel (1924), living first in Jaffa, then Jerusalem; taught in religious schools for girls in Jerusalem, Tel-Aviv, and Haifa; published 1st collection of poems, *Pnai* (Leisure, 1967); writings, containing mystical images, include *Ha-Carmel Ha-Ee Nir'a* (The Invisible Camel, 1971), and *Shirim Zelda* (Zelda's Poems, 1985). Won Bialik Prize for *Behold the Mountain and the Fire.*

MISHKUTENOK, Natalia (1970—). Belarusian pairs skater. Name variations: Mishkutunok; Mishkutionok. Born July 14, 1970, in Minsk, Belarus, USSR; m. Craig Shepherd (American hockey player). ❖ All with partner Artur Dmitriev (who would later skate with Oksana Kazakova), won European championships (1991–92) and World championships (1991–92); won gold medal at Albertville Olympics (1992), skating to "Liebestraum," and a silver medal at Lillehammer Olympics (1994); split up with Dmitriev (fall 1994).

MISME, Jane (1865–1935). French feminist journalist. Pronunciation: MEEM. Born Jeanne Maurice in France, 1865; died 1935; m. Louis Misme (Lyons architect), 1888; children: Clotilde (b. 1889). ❖ Began to write for *Le Figaro* and *Le Matin*; became involved in feminist activities when she joined Jeanne Schmahl's L'Avant-courrière (The Advance Messenger) as its secretary; was a regular contributor to Marguerite Durand's *La Fronde* (1897–1905), especially writing drama criticism—a novelty for a woman columnist—under the pen name "Jane"; with Mathilde Méliot, founded the weekly *La Française* (1906), which in time became the most important single publication in France devoted to women's life and issues, lasting to 1939; helped Cécile Brunschvicg organize Estates-General of Feminism (1929), which laid women's issues before the country in well-publicized campaigns; also presided over press section of National Council of French Women (CNFF) and was convener (1930–34) of the letters committee of International Council of Women; was arguably the greatest exemplar of a firm but moderate feminism, which she believed best suited France's case. ❖ See also *Women in World History.*

MISNIK, Alla (1967—). Ukrainian gymnast. Born Aug 27, 1967, in Kharkov, Ukraine, USSR. ❖ At European championships, won silver medals in uneven bars and floor exercise and a bronze medal in all-around (1981); won Moscow News and USSR Cup (1981), Ukrainian Spartakiade (1983).

MISS MALVINA (1830–1906). *See Florence, Malvina Pray.*

MIST, Augusta De (1783–1832). *See De Mist, Augusta.*

MISTINGUETT (1875–1956). French singer and dancer. Born Jeanne-Marie Bourgeois, April 5, 1875 (some sources cite 1873), in Enghien, France; died Jan 5, 1956, at her home near Paris. ❖ Made 1st appearance on music-hall stage at Casino de Paris (1893); with dancing partner Max Dearly, took Paris by storm with their *valse chaloupée,* which became known to English audiences as the "Apache Dance," 1st presented at Le Moulin Rouge (1909); starred in a musical extravaganza at Folies Bergère with Maurice Chevalier (1911); appeared in 14 silent movies (1913–16); by outbreak of WWI (1917), had become a popular Parisian music-hall performer, known for her elaborately produced shows with their earthy humor, gaudy costumes, and semi-nudity; shared same bill with Chevalier in *Paris Qui Danse* (1919), the start of a long series of *Paris Qui . . .* revues; in *Féerie de Paris* at Casino de Paris (1938), sang *Je Cherche un Millionaire,* which became the bestselling recording in France that year and sold more than 5 million copies by the time WWII erupted (1939); between the 2 world wars (1919–39), became France's best-known entertainer and attracted audiences in Britain and US as well; continued performing well into her 70s until ill health forced retirement from stage (1950s). ❖ See also autobiography *Mistinguett: Queen of the Paris Night* (Elek, 1954); David Bret, *The Mistinguett Legend* (Robson, 1990); and *Women in World History.*

MISTRAL, Gabriela (1889–1957). Chilean poet. Name variations: Lucila Godoy Alcayaga. Pronunciation: Gahb-ree-A-la Mee-STRAHL. Born Lucila Godoy Alcayaga, April 7, 1889, in Vicuña, Coquimbo, Chile; died Jan 10, 1957, in Hempstead, New York, of pancreatic cancer; dau. of Jerónimo Godoy Villanueva (poet, teacher and minstrel) and Petronila Alcayaga Rojas; awarded teaching certificate from Escuela Normal No 1 in Santiago, 1910; never married; no children. ❖ Nobel Prize-winning poet who was also a noted educator, humanist and social reformer, was strongly affected by boyfriend's suicide (1909); by 1911, writing was regularly featured in the Chilean press and also published in other Latin American countries; won major poetry prize, Juegos de Florales, for 3 "Sonnets of Death" (1914); began to use pseudonym Gabriela Mistral; served as director and professor of language at Liceo de Niñas (Girls' School, 1918–20) and Liceo No 6 in Santiago (1920–22); invited to Mexico to help in the reform, development, and restructuring of that country's public schools and libraries (1922); inaugurated the school "Gabriela Mistral" for young women; saw publication of *Desolación* (1922), heralded as a departure from modernism and foreign influences; named "Teacher of the Nation" by Chilean government (1923); attached to Committee of Arts and Letters of the League of Nations (1926–29); made consul to Naples (1932), Madrid (1933), and life consul (1935), by Chilean government; published *Tala* (The Felling, 1938); won Nobel Prize for Literature (1945), the 1st Latin American writer to be so honored; made triumphal return to Chile (1954); also published *Ternura* (Tenderness, 1924), and *Lagar* (Wine Press, 1954). ❖ See also Margot Arce de Vazquez, *Gabriela Mistral: The Poet and Her Work* (trans. by Helene Masslo Anderson, New York U. Press, 1964); and *Women in World History.*

MITCHEL, Jane (1820–1899). *See Mitchel, Jenny.*

MITCHEL, Jenny (1820–1899). Irish nationalist. Name variations: Jane Mitchel. Born Jane Verner in Co. Armagh, Ireland, 1820 (month and day unknown); died in Brooklyn, New York, Dec 31, 1899; dau. of James Verner and Mary Ward; educated at Miss Bryden's School, Newry, Co. Down, Ireland; m. John Mitchel (lawyer and Irish nationalist), Dec 12, 1836; children: 3 daughters, Isabel, Henrietta (d. 1863), and Minnie;

3 sons, James, John (d. 1864), and Willie (d. 1863). ❖ Moved to Dublin with husband (1845), when he became chief editorial writer for *The Nation,* the journal of the Young Ireland movement; with husband, was part of a brilliant circle of writers and poets and her hospitality became famous; after husband was found guilty of treason-felony and sentenced to 14 years' transportation in Tasmania (1848), set out with children to join him (Jan 1851); followed husband when he escaped to America (1853). ❖ See also Rebecca O'Conner, *Jenny Mitchel: Young Irelander* (O'Conner Trust, 1988); and *Women in World History.*

MITCHELL, Abbie (1884–1960). African-American singer and actress. Born Sept 25, 1884, in New York City; died Mar 16, 1960, in NYC; studied with Harry T. Burleigh and Emilia Serrano; m. Will Marion Cook (composer), 1899 (div. 1908); children: Marion Abigail Cook (b. 1900); Will Mercer Cook (b. 1903). ❖ Accomplished performer of international fame, made stage debut at 13 in *Clorindy: The Origin of the Cakewalk* (1898); appeared both in America and abroad (1899–1908), often in shows produced or composed by husband; won international acclaim when she appeared in vaudeville show *In Dahomey* before King Edward VII (1903), a play that sparked the cakewalk dance craze in London; sang for a time with Sissieretta Jones' Black Patti Troubadours; appeared at a command performance before Russian tsar Nicholas II (1908); was a featured actress with all-black stock company of Harlem's Lafayette Theater (1915–20); starred in Pulitzer Prize-winning *In Abraham's Bosom*; appeared with Helen Hayes in *Coquette* and in Langston Hughes' *Mulatto*; probably best remembered for roles as the original Clara in *Porgy and Bess* and as Addie in *The Little Foxes* (1939); taught voice at Tuskegee Institute (1931–34); served as executive secretary of Negro Actors Guild of America. ❖ See also *Women in World History.*

MITCHELL, Betsy (1966—). *See Mitchell, Elizabeth.*

MITCHELL, Elizabeth (1966—). American swimmer. Name variations: Betsy Mitchell. Born Jan 15, 1966; attended University of North Carolina and University of Texas at Austin. ❖ At Los Angeles Olympics, won a silver medal in the 100-meter backstroke and gold medal in the 4x100-meter medley relay (1984); at Seoul Olympics, won a silver medal in the 4x100-meter medley relay (1988); while at Univ. of Texas, won 7 NCAA titles; won 100-meter backstroke at Pan Pacific championships (1985), Goodwill Games (1990) and US Open (1985–87); at World championships (1986), set world record in 200-meter backstroke and won gold medal in 100-meter backstroke and silver in 200-meter backstroke; won 11 US national championships in 100-meter and 200-meter backstroke; was head swimming coach at Dartmouth (1990–96), then athletic director at the Laurel School in Ohio.

MITCHELL, Elyne (1913–2002). Australian children's writer. Born Elyne Chauvel, Dec 12, 1913, in Melbourne, Australia; died Mar 4, 2002, in Corryong, Victoria, Australia; dau. of Sir Harry Chauvel (military commander); m. Tom Mitchell, 1935 (died 1984); children: 4. ❖ Won Canadian downhill skiing championships (1938); with family, lived on a station on the upper Murray in the foothills of the Victorian Alps; works include the popular "Silver Brumby" series; also wrote articles and environmental books, including *Australia's Alps* (1942) and *Speak to the Earth* (1945). Received Medal of the Order of Australia (1988). ❖ See also memoir, *Chauvel Country* (1983).

MITCHELL, Ethel Catherwood (1910–1987). *See Catherwood, Ethel.*

MITCHELL, Gladys (1901–1983). British mystery writer. Name variations: (pseudonyms) Stephen Hockaby; Malcolm Torrie. Born April 19, 1901, in Oxfordshire, England; died 1983. ❖ Studied European history at University College, London; worked as schoolteacher for 40 years before becoming writer; works include *Speedy Death* (1929), *The Saltmarsh Murders* (1932), *Come Away Death* (1937), *The Rising of the Moon* (1945), *Groaning Spinney* (1950), *Twelve Horses and the Hangman's Noose* (1956), *The Nodding Canaries* (1961), *Lament for Letto* (1971), *The Whispering Knights* (1980) and *The Crozier Pharaohs* (1984).

MITCHELL, Hannah (1871–1956). British suffragist and politician. Born Hannah Webster, 1871, in Derbyshire, England; died 1956; dau. of John Webster (farmer); m. Gibbon Mitchell, 1895. ❖ Became active in socialist politics, trade-union movement, and women's suffrage movement; joined Women's Social and Political Union (1904), then, along with Charlotte Despard and others, moved to the new Women's Freedom League (1907); a pacifist, opposed British involvement in

WWI and spent the war years working for Women's Peace Council; after war, was elected to Manchester city council (1924). ❖ See also autobiography, *The Hard Way Up* (1956); and *Women in World History*.

MITCHELL, Jackie (1912–1987). American baseball player. Name variations: Virne Gilbert. Born Virne Beatrice Mitchell, Aug 29, 1912; died Jan 1987 in Fort Oglethorpe, GA; daughter of Joe Mitchell (physician); m. Eugene Gilbert. ❖ Was the 2nd woman ever to sign a men's minor-league baseball contract (Lizzie Arlington being the 1st); became a minor-league pitcher for Chattanooga Lookouts (Mar 1931), then struck out Babe Ruth and Lou Gehrig back-to-back in a controversial exhibition game between the Lookouts and New York Yankees (April 2, 1931); saw her contract rescinded one month later. ❖ See also *Women in World History*.

MITCHELL, Joan (1926–1992). American abstract painter. Born Feb 12, 1926, in Chicago, Illinois; died of lung cancer, Oct 30, 1992, in France; dau. of James Herbert Mitchell (physician) and Marion Strobel (poet and editor of *Poetry* magazine); attended Smith College, 1942–44; Art Institute of Chicago, BFA, 1947, MFA, 1950; studied briefly in NYC with Hans Hofmann; m. Barney Rossett (editor and founder of Grove Press), 1949 (sep. 1951). ❖ Considered one of the greatest abstract artists of her generation, was a member of The Club, founded by New York school of abstract expressionists, and took part in the influential Ninth Street Show (1951); had 1st one-woman show in NY (1952) and saw importance as a New York artist acknowledged by mid-1950s; continued to exhibit both at group and individual shows and spent time with a hard-drinking crowd of artists and writers, including Franz Kline, Willem de Kooning and Frank O'Hara; moved to France (1959), where she would remain until her death; lived initially in Paris, and soon began a relationship with Canadian-born Jean-Paul Riopelle, an abstract painter, that would last for 25 years; painted mostly large canvases, some in multiple panels; moved to Vétheuil (1968), near the Giverny garden of Claude Monet, where she painted a number of works inspired by sunflowers; a prolific painter, work is held in major museums and private collections both in America and Europe. ❖ See also Judith E. Bernstock, *Joan Mitchell* (Hudson Hills, 1997); Klaus Kertess, *Joan Mitchell* (Abrams, 1997); and *Women in World History*.

MITCHELL, Joni (1943—). Canadian singer and songwriter. Born Roberta Joan Anderson, Nov 1, 1943, in Fort Macleod, Alberta, Canada; m. Chuck Mitchell (musician), 1965 (div. 1967); m. Larry Klein (musician), 1982 (div. 1992); children: (with Brad MacMath) daughter, Kilauren Gibb (b. 1965). ❖ One of the most distinctive and influential figures in 20th-century popular music, suffered from polio at age 9; began performing at Depression Club in Calgary (1963); moved to Toronto, then to Detroit to perform as a folksinger; moved to NY and played at Café Au Go-Go (1967); toured England as the opening act for Incredible String Band (1967); wrote songs recorded by Tom Rush, Buffy Sainte-Marie, and Judy Collins ("Both Sides Now," 1968); recorded 1st album *Joni Mitchell* also known as *Song for a Seagull* (1968); released 2nd album, *Clouds*, featuring her version of "Both Sides Now" and "Chelsea Morning" (1968), which won the Grammy Award for Best Folk Performance; toured almost continually, playing at festivals and opening for Crosby, Stills and Nash; wrote generational anthem "Woodstock," recorded by Crosby, Stills and Nash (1970); released album *Ladies of the Canyon* (1970), enjoying 1st gold album and international success; released most acclaimed album, *Blue* (1971), followed by *For the Roses* (1972) which featured her 1st hit single ("You Turn Me On, I'm a Radio"); released *Court and Spark* (1974), an even bigger commercial success which included her 1st and, to date, only Top-10 single ("Help Me"); joined up with Bob Dylan's Rolling Thunder Review and appeared at the Band's farewell concert in San Francisco (1976) and in the documentary about the concert, *The Last Waltz*; released album *Hejira* (1976), her 7th consecutive gold album; released *Night Ride Home* (1991), followed by *Turbulent Indigo* (1994), which won Grammy Awards; over course of more than 30 years, recorded more than 20 albums; pushed boundaries of folk-rock genre; credited with creating confessional singer-songwriter genre; experimented with jazz, working with artists including Charles Mingus and Wayne Shorter; also painted and exhibited, creating art for all her albums (1980s–90s). Won Grammys (1974 and 1994); received *Billboard*'s Century Award (1995); inducted into Canada's Juno Hall of Fame (1981); inducted into Rock and Roll Hall of Fame and Songwriters' Hall of Fame (both 1997). ❖ See also *Women in World History*.

MITCHELL, Juliet (1934—). British feminist. Born 1934 in New Zealand; attended King Alfred School in London; received degree in English from St. Anne's College, Oxford; postgraduate study at Oxford. ❖ Moved with family to England (1944); became a lecturer at University of Leeds (1962); transferred to University of Reading (1965); published 1st book, *Women: The Longest Revolution* (1966); retired from academia to concentrate on writing and lecturing (1971); released 2nd book, *Women's Estate* (1972), followed by *Psychoanalysis and Feminism* (1974); renowned as an advocate of socialism and feminism, served on editorial boards of such periodicals as *New Left Review, Social Praxis* and *Signs;* collaborated with feminist Ann Oakley to edit *The Rights and Wrongs of Women*, a collection of essays (1976).

MITCHELL, Kelly Rickon (1959—). *See Rickon, Kelly.*

MITCHELL, Lucy (1845–1888). American archaeologist. Born Lucy Myers Wright, Mar 20, 1845, in Urmia, Persia (now Orūmīyeh, Iran); died in Lausanne, Switzerland, Mar 10, 1888; dau. of a missionary to Nestorian Christians; attended Mt. Holyoke Seminary; m. Samuel S. Mitchell (missionary), 1867. ❖ Spent formative years in Persia and gained a conversational ability in Syriac, Arabic, French, German and Italian; moved to US (1860); with husband, returned to Syria (1867) where she began work on a dictionary of modern Syriac; because of husband's failing health, moved to Rome, where she studied ancient art and by 1876 was giving lectures on Greek and Roman sculpture; despite lack of formal archaeological training, collaborated with noted archaeologists; published *A History of Ancient Sculpture* and a companion vol. of plates, *Selections from Ancient Sculpture* (1883); became the 2nd woman elected to the German Archaeological Institute (1884).

MITCHELL, Lucy Sprague (1878–1967). American educator and children's author. Born Lucy Sprague in Chicago, Illinois, July 2, 1878; died of heart attack, Oct 15, 1967; dau. of Otho Sprague (wholesale grocer) and Lucia (Atwood) Sprague; attended Radcliffe College; m. Wesley Clair Mitchell (1874–1948, economist), April 6, 1912 (died 1948); children: 4. ❖ Became the 1st dean of women at University of California at Berkeley, starting out as advisor to the dean (1903); with husband and Harriet Johnson (1916), founded the Bureau of Educational Experiments, later known as the Bank Street College of Education; was also responsible for its Writer's Laboratory, inviting publishing professionals to attend; published *Here and Now Story Book* (1921), widely recognized as a radical departure in the writing for children. ❖ See also memoir *Two Lives: The Story of Wesley Clair Mitchell and Myself* (Simon & Schuster, 1953); Joyce Antler, *Lucy Sprague Mitchell: The Making of a Modern Woman* (Yale U. Press, 1987); and *Women in World History*.

MITCHELL, Maggie (1832–1918). *See Mitchell, Margaret J.*

MITCHELL, Margaret (1900–1949). American author. Name variations: Peggy Mitchell; Peg Marsh. Born Margaret Munnerlyn Mitchell, Nov 8, 1900, in Atlanta, Georgia; died Aug 16, 1949, from injuries suffered when she was struck near her home by an automobile; dau. of Eugene Muse Mitchell (Atlanta lawyer) and Mary Isabel (Stephens) Mitchell, known as May Belle; m. Berrien "Red" Upshaw, Sept 2, 1922 (div. 1924); m. John Marsh, July 4, 1925; no children. ❖ Except for a year spent at Smith College in Massachusetts, spent nearly all her life in Atlanta, working for a time for the *Atlanta Journal* before an ankle injury forced her to leave the paper; during convalescence, began work on the 1st of what would be many drafts of her epic novel, *Gone With the Wind*, written over a period of 9 years; published *Gone With the Wind* (1936); won the Pulitzer Prize (1937); attended premiere of David O. Selznick's award-winning film of her book (1939); became an international celebrity, with her book translated into more than 2 dozen languages, before outbreak of WWII; was an outspoken advocate of authors' rights and pursued several legal actions through the courts to protect her rights to her novel. An earlier novella, *Lost Laysen*, was discovered (1994). ❖ See also Anne Edwards, *Road to Tara* (Ticknor & Fields, 1985); Darden Pyron, *Southern Daughter: The Life of Margaret Mitchell* (Oxford U. Press, 1991); Marianne Walker, *Margaret Mitchell & John Marsh: The Love Story Behind* Gone With the Wind (Peachtree, 1993); and *Women in World History*.

MITCHELL, Margaret J. (1832–1918). American actress. Name variations: Maggie Mitchell. Born Margaret Julia Mitchell in New York, NY, June 14, 1832; died at her home in New York City of a cerebral hemorrhage, Mar 22, 1918; dau. of Charles S. Mitchell (of Scottish birth) and Ann (Dodson) Mitchell (of English birth); half-sister of Mary Mitchell and Emma Mitchell, a child actress; m. for 1 week, in 1850s (div.); m. Henry T. Paddock (her manager), Oct 15, 1868 (div. 1888); m. Charles Mace, known as Charles Abbott (actor); children: (1st m.) Julian Mitchell; (2nd m.) Fanchon Paddock; Harry M. Paddock. ❖ Played child parts on stage before she was 5; made NY debut as an adult (1851), as Julia in *The Soldier's Daughter*; originated the part of Fanchon, in *Fanchon the Cricket* (1860), which she played for many years, and with which her name is permanently associated; was also known for such roles as Jane Eyre, Mignon, Little Barefoot, Pearl of Savoy, and Nan the Good-for-Nothing; retired (1892).

MITCHELL, Maria (1818–1889). American astronomer and educator. Born Maria Mitchell, Aug 1, 1818, on Nantucket, Massachusetts; died June 28, 1889, in Lynn, Massachusetts; dau. of William Mitchell (cooper, teacher, and astronomer) and Lydia (Coleman) Mitchell; attended her father's school; attended academy of Cyrus Peirce; never married. ❖ One of the best-known faculty members at Vassar College, was born into a family of Quakers; at 12, recorded a solar eclipse with father (1831); was librarian at Nantucket Athenaeum for 20 years; assisted father with the Coast Survey and made thousands of accurate observations; left Quaker religion (1843); discovered a new comet (1848) and was awarded a gold medal by the king of Denmark; elected to American Academy of Arts and Sciences in Boston; appointed one of the original computists for the new *American Ephemeria and Nautical Almanac* (1849); elected to American Association for the Advancement of Science (1850); moved to Lynn, Massachusetts, with widowed father (1861); enticed by Matthew Vassar to join the faculty at Vassar College where he built the 3rd largest observatory in the country for her; taught at Vassar (1865–88); was the 1st woman elected to American Philosophical Society (1869); elected vice-president of the American Social Science Association (1873); one of the founders of Association for the Advancement of Women (AAW, 1873), served as president (1875–76) and chaired the science committee until her death. ❖ See also Phebe Mitchell Kendall, ed. *Maria Mitchell: Life, Letters, and Journals* (Lee & Shepard, 1896); Helen Wright, *Sweeper in the Sky: The Life of Maria Mitchell First Woman Astronomer in America* (Macmillan, 1949); and *Women in World History*.

MITCHELL, Marion (1876–1955). New Zealand singer and political hostess. Name variations: Marion Davis. Born Oct 19, 1876, in Wellington, New Zealand; died May 5, 1955, in Auckland; dau. of Walter Mitchell (bootmaker and amateur musician) and Fanny Maria Wheatland (Waters) Mitchell; m. Ernest Hyam Davis (brewer and mayor), 1899; children: 1 daughter, 1 son. ❖ Made professional singing debut at 14, in Tom Pollard's juvenile opera company (1891); became overnight success, and mastered wide repertoire of light and comic operatic roles; retired from company to raise family and became involved in several civic and charitable activities when husband became mayor of Auckland (1935). ❖ See also *Dictionary of New Zealand Biography* (Vol. 2).

MITCHELL, Martha (1918–1976). American public figure. Born Martha Elizabeth Beall, Sept 2, 1918, in Pine Bluff, Arkansas; died May 31, 1976, in New York, NY; dau. of George Virgil Beall (cotton broker) and Arie (Ferguson) Beall (teacher); graduate of University of Miami, 1942; m. Clyde Jennings Jr., 1946 (div. 1957); m. John Newton Mitchell (US attorney general), 1957; children: (1st m.) Clyde Jay Jennings (b. 1947); (2nd m.) Martha Elizabeth Jr., called Marty Mitchell (b. 1961). ❖ Controversial and outspoken public figure, helped bring down the Nixon administration during Watergate scandal; as wife of John Mitchell, Nixon's US attorney general, began to eavesdrop on phone calls between husband and the president; spoke vehemently, ingenuously, and frequently to the press about almost everything: desegregation, education, politicians, the Supreme Court, often in opposition to administration policies; probably the most famous Cabinet wife in US history, became a strident critic of Nixon and his administration's "dirty tricks," while administration officials told the press that her claims were the ravings of a sick woman; as the full Watergate story began playing out (1973), earned some sheepish respect from those who had dismissed her stories. The year after she died, in a tv interview with David Frost, Nixon commented: "If it hadn't been for Martha, there would have been no Watergate." ❖ See also Winzola McLendon, *Martha: The Life of Martha Mitchell* (Random House, 1979); and *Women in World History*.

MITCHELL, Michelle (1962—). American diver. Name variations: Michelle Mitchell-Rocha. Born Jan 10, 1962; attended Arizona State University. ❖ Won a silver medal at Los Angeles Olympics (1984) and a silver medal at Seoul Olympics (1988), both in platform.

MITCHELL, Nikole. Jamaican runner. Born in Jamaica. ❖ Won a bronze medal for 4x100-meter relay at Atlanta Olympics (1996).

MITCHELL, Olivia (1947—). Irish politician. Born July 1947, in Birr, Co. Offaly, Ireland; m. James Mitchell. ❖ Representing Fine Gael, elected to the 28th Dáil (1997–2002) for Dublin South; returned to 29th Dáil (2002).

MITCHELL, Rhea (1890–1957). American silent-film actress. Born Dec 10, 1890, in Portland, OR; found murdered in her apartment, Sept 16, 1957, in Hollywood, CA. ❖ Appeared opposite such stars as William S. Hart, Tom Mix, King Baggott, and Bert Lytell; films include *D'Artagnan*, *The Goat*, *Good Women*, *The Other Kind of Love* and *Modern Youth*.

MITCHELL, Roma (1913–2000). Australian feminist, lawyer, politician, and judge. Name variations: Dame Roma Mitchell. Born Roma Flinders Mitchell in Adelaide, Australia, Oct 2, 1913; died Mar 5, 2000; dau. of Harold Mitchell (lawyer) and Maude Mitchell; graduate of Adelaide University; admitted to the bar, 1934; never married; no children. ❖ The 1st woman governor of an Australian state, had a career focused on criminal law, women's rights and human rights; was appointed 1st female Queen's Counsel (1962); became the 1st female Supreme Court judge (1965); was appointed founding chair of the Australian Human Rights Commission (1981); became the 1st female chancellor of a university (1983); became the governor of South Australia, the 1st female state governor (1991). Made Dame Commander of the Order of the British Empire (1982); made Companion in the Order of Australia (1991); awarded Commander of the Royal Victoria Order (2000). ❖ See also *Women in World History*.

MITCHELL, Ruth (c. 1888–1969). American author and adventurer. Born c. 1888; died in Belas, Portugal, Oct 24, 1969; dau. of John Lendrum Mitchell (US congressional representative, 1891–93, and senator, 1893–99) and Harriet Danforth (Becker) Mitchell; sister of William "Billy" Mitchell (1879–1936, brigadier general and advocate of uses of air power in modern warfare); m. Stanley Knowles; children: Ruth and John Knowles. ❖ With husband, lived in England during WWI; launched *Friendship Travel Magazine* for children which soon had 50,000 subscribers; took up photography and was sent to Albania (1938) by *Illustrated London News* to cover wedding of King Zog and Queen Geraldine; was living in Yugoslavia when the Balkans were drawn into WWII; appeared in newspaper stories across US (April 2, 1941), described as having been sworn in as 1st American woman member of the Komitaji, a near-legendary group of Serbian guerilla fighters later called Chetniks; was arrested by Germans in Belgrade (April 6, 1941) but claimed to have managed to hide Chetnik papers; accused of spying and sentenced to death, persuaded judges to consider US public opinion; was released (along with 184 other Americans in exchange for German nationals living in US) and repatriated home (1942); became an indefatigable defender of the Yugoslav Chetnik cause in US and published *The Serbs Choose War* (1943); found a receptive intellectual home in the pages of *The American Mercury*, a journal of the extreme Right; published biography of her famous brother, *My Brother Bill* (1953). Much remains unexplained regarding her activities in the Balkans before and after April 1941. ❖ See also *Women in World History*.

MITCHELL, Yvonne (1925–1979). British actress. Born Yvonne Joseph in London, England, July 7, 1925; died of cancer, Mar 24, 1979, in London; m. Derek Monsey (died 1979). ❖ Made stage debut at 14; rose to prominence with the Old Vic, portraying roles as varied as Ophelia in *Hamlet* and Eliza Doolittle in *Pygmalion*; one of Britain's leading stage performers (1940s–50s), also worked in film and tv, becoming well known for her "anguished" roles; won British Film Award for performance in *The Divided Heart* (1954) and a Berlin Festival Award for *Woman in a Dressing Gown* (1957); other films include *Queen of Spades* (1949), *Children of Chance* (1951), *Turn the Key Softly* (1953), *Escapade* (1955), *Tiger Bay* (1959), *Sapphire* (1959), *Conspiracy of Hearts* (1960), *The Trials of Oscar Wilde* (1960) and *The Great Waltz* (1972); also wrote plays and novels. ❖ See also autobiography, *Actress* (1957)

MITCHELL-TAVERNER, Claire (1970—). Australian field-hockey player. Born June 17, 1970, in Melbourne, VIC, Australia. ❖ Forward/midfielder, won a team gold medal at Sydney Olympics (2000).

MITCHISON, Naomi (1897–1999). Scots-English novelist, poet, and playwright. Name variations: Lady Mitchison. Born Naomi Margaret Haldane, Nov 1, 1897, in Edinburgh, Scotland; died Jan 11, 1999, at her home on the Mull of Kintyre in Scotland; dau. of Louisa Kathleen (Trotter) Haldane and John Scott Haldane, known as J.S. Haldane (physiologist and philosopher); sister of J.B.S Haldane (geneticist and philosopher); niece of Elizabeth Haldane (1862–1937); attended St. Anne's College in Oxford; m. Gilbert Richard Mitchison (created a

Baron [Life Peer], 1964), Feb 1916 (died 1970); children: Geoff, Dennis, Murdoch (who m. social historian Rosalind Mitchison), Lois Mitchison, Avrion and Valentine Mitchison. ❖ Writer who sought to delineate women's adventure-quest in fiction as well as in private and political life, voicing women's issues in the socialist wing of the Labor Party in London during 1930s, in Scotland as a major writer in the Scottish Renaissance, and as a Scottish nationalist during 1940s–50s; was elected to Argyll Co. Council (1945–48 and 1953–65); appointed to Highland and Island Advisory Panel (1947–65), and to Highlands and Islands Development Council (1966–76); historical and political fiction includes *The Conquered* (1923), *When the Bough Breaks and Other Stories* (1924), *Cloud Cuckoo Land* (1925), *The Corn King and the Spring Queen* (1931), *We Have Been Warned* (1936), *The Blood of the Martyrs* (1939), *The Bull Calves* (1947), *Lobsters on the Agenda* (1952), and *Early in Orcadia* (1987); science and fantasy fiction includes *Beyond This Limit* (1935), *The Fourth Pig* (1936), *Memoirs of a Spacewoman* (1962), *Solution Three* (1975), *The Vegetable War* (1980) and *Not By Bread Alone* (1983); also wrote poetry and plays. Awarded Order of British Empire (1985). ❖ See also memoirs: *Vienna Diary* (1934); *Return to the Fairy Hill* (1966); *Small Talk: Memoirs of an Edwardian Childhood* (1973); *All Change Here: Girlhood and Marriage* (1979); *You May Well Ask: A Memoir 1920–1940* (1979); *Mucking Around* (1981); *Among You Taking Notes: Wartime Diary 1939–45* (ed. Dorothy Sheridan, 1985); Jill Benton, *Naomi Mitchison: A Biography* (Pandora, 1992); and *Women in World History.*

MITCHISON, Rosalind (1919–2002). English feminist historian. Born Rosalind Mary Wrong, April 11, 1919, in Manchester, England; died Sept 19, 2002, in Edinburgh, Scotland; dau. of Murray Wrong (Oxford mathematician); granddau. of George Mackinnon Wrong (Canadian historian); graduated with double 1st from Lady Margaret Hall, Oxford; m. Murdoch Mitchison (professor of cell biology and zoology at Edinburgh University and son of Naomi Mitchison), 1947; children: 1 son, 3 daughters. ❖ Was assistant lecturer in history at Manchester University (1943–46); collaborated with Leah Leneman on *Girls in Trouble* and *Sex in the City* (1948), pioneering contributions to history of sexuality in Scotland; at Edinburgh University, was assistant lecturer (1954–57), lecturer in social and economic history (1967–76) and professor of social history (1981–86); wrote *The Life of Sir John Sinclair* (1962); published the acclaimed *A History of Scotland* (1970), which became a standard history text; also wrote *British Population Change since 1869* (1977), *Lordship and Patronage: Scotland 1603–1745* (1983), *People and Society in Scotland, 1760–1830* (1988) and *The Old Poor Law of Scotland: The Experience of Poverty, 1574–1845* (1999); was leader of Scottish feminist historians.

MITFORD, Deborah (1920—). English socialite, businesswoman, and duchess of Devonshire. Name variations: Debo; Deborah Cavendish, Duchess of Devonshire. Born Deborah Vivian Mitford in 1920; dau. of David Freeman-Mitford, 2nd Baron Redesdale, and Sydney Bowles; sister of Nancy Mitford (1904–1973), Jessica Mitford (1917–1996), Diana Mitford (b. 1910), and Unity Mitford (1914–1948); m. Andrew Cavendish, duke of Devonshire, April 19, 1941 (his brother William married Kathleen Kennedy, elder sister of John F. Kennedy); children: Emma Cavendish (b. 1943); Peregrine Cavendish (b. 1944); Sophia Cavendish (b. 1957); 3 other children died at birth. ❖ Unlike her rebellious sisters, avoided politics and became an entrepreneur, running food, book, and garden furniture shops at Chatsworth and wrote a book about Chatsworth entitled *The House*. ❖ See also Jonathan and Catherine Guinness, *The House of Mitford* (Hutchinson, 1984); and *Women in World History.*

MITFORD, Diana (1910–2003). English socialite. Name variations: Lady Diana Mosley. Born June 17, 1910; died Aug 11, 2003, in Paris, France; dau. of David Freeman-Mitford, 2nd Baron Redesdale, and Sydney Bowles; sister of Nancy Mitford (1904–1973), Jessica Mitford (1917–1996), Deborah Mitford (b. 1920), and Unity Mitford (1914–1948); m. Bryan Guinness (later Lord Moyne), Jan 1929 (div. 1934); m. Sir Oswald Mosley (politician and founder of British Union of Fascists), 1936 (died 1980); children: (1st m.) Jonathan Guinness; Desmond Guinness; (2nd marriage) Alexander Mosley; Max Mosley. ❖ Married an heir to the Guinness brewing fortune before she was 20; at 23, met Oswald Mosley, a Labour politician who had settled on Fascism to save England from its economic woes; became a staunch believer and fell in love with Mosley; left family to become his mistress; became friendly with Adolf Hitler, whom she greatly admired, and had no difficulty in accepting the Nazi attitude towards Jews; following death of Oswald's 1st wife Cynthia Mosley, was married secretly in Berlin at house of Josef and Magda

Goebbels; at start of WWII, returned to England with husband as national pariahs; was arrested as a "dangerous woman" and spent over 3 years (1940–43) in Holloway prison without trial. ❖ See also autobiography *A Life of Contrasts* (1977); Jonathan and Catherine Guinness, *The House of Mitford* (Hutchinson, 1984); Jan Dalley, *Diana Mosley* (Knopf, 2000); and *Women in World History.*

MITFORD, Jessica (1917–1996). British-born American writer. Name variations: Decca. Born Jessica Lucy Mitford in Batsford Mansion, Gloucestershire, England, on Sept 11, 1917; died July 23, 1996, at her home in Oakland, California; dau. of David Freeman-Mitford, 2nd Lord Redesdale, and Sydney Bowles; sister of Nancy Mitford (1904–1973), Deborah Mitford (b. 1920), Diana Mitford (b. 1910), Unity Mitford (1914–1948), Pamela Mitford (b. Nov 25, 1907), and Thomas Mitford (born Jan 1909; killed in action 1945); eloped with cousin Esmond Romilly, Feb 1937 (killed in action 1941); m. Robert Treuhaft, June 21, 1943; children: (1st m.) Julia Romilly (1937–1938); Constancia ("Dinky") Romilly (b. 1940); (2nd m.) Benjamin Treuhaft (b. 1946). ❖ Radical and "muckraking" writer, whose bestseller, *The American Way of Death* (1963), led to reforms of US funeral industry; immigrated to America (1939); naturalized (1944); spent most of adult life in US and lived good-humoredly at the center of a succession of controversies; was active in Communist Party USA, mostly to dismantle the legal structure of racism (1946–58); appeared before House Committee on Un-American Activities (HUAC); left party on revelations of Stalin's atrocities; was active in civil-rights movement; writings include *The Trial of Dr. Spock* (1969), *Kind and Usual Punishment* (1973), *Poison Penmanship: The Gentle Art of Muckraking* (1979), *Grace Had an English Heart* (1988), *The American Way of Birth* (1992), and (posthumously) *The American Way of Death Revisited* (1998). ❖ See also autobiographies *Daughters and Rebels* (1960) and *A Fine Old Conflict* (1977); Jonathan and Catherine Guinness, *The House of Mitford* (Hutchinson, 1984); and *Women in World History.*

MITFORD, Mary Russell (1787–1855). English author. Born Mary Russell Mitford, Dec 16, 1787, in Alresford, Hampshire, England; died in Swallowfield, Berkshire, Jan 10, 1855; dau. of George Mitford (medical practitioner) and Mary (Russell) Mitford; never married; no children. ❖ Writer whose evocation of the English countryside has proved the most lasting aspect of her many writings; moved with her family between Alresford, Lyme Regis and Reading before settling in the vicinity of the latter town for the remainder of her life; began to write poetry in late teens, then drama and country sketches in early 30s; wrote prolifically, often through pressure to earn an income; in later life, had the reputation of a "bluestocking" who knew many of the leading authors of her day; writings include *Our Village* (5 vols, 1824–32) and *Belford Regis: Sketches of a Country Town* (1835). ❖ See also memoirs *Recollections of a Literary Life; or Books, Places and People* (1852); Marjorie Astin, *Mary Mitford: Her Circle and Her Books* (Douglas, 1930); Henry Chorley, *The Letters of Mary Russell Mitford* (Bentley, 1870); Constance Hill, *Mary Russell Mitford and Her Surroundings* (John Lane, 1920); Vera Watson, *Mary Russell Mitford* (Evans, 1949); and *Women in World History.*

MITFORD, Nancy (1904–1973). English writer. Born Nancy Freeman Mitford in London, England, Nov 28, 1904; died of fibromyositis, June 30, 1973; dau. of David Freeman-Mitford, Lord Redesdale, and Sydney Bowles; sister of Jessica Mitford (1917–1996), Diana Mitford (b. 1910), Deborah Mitford (1920—), and Unity Mitford (1914–1948); m. the Hon. Peter Rodd, Nov 1933 (sep. 1945, div. 1958); had long relationship with Fabrice, duc de Sauveterre (hero of the French resistance). ❖ Comic novelist of the 1st rank, settled in Paris, then Versailles, following WWII and a failed marriage, where she remained for the rest of her life; was the author of several satirical novels known for their biting wit, including *Love in Cold Climate* (1949), *The Blessing* (1951), *Noblesse Oblige* (1956), *Don't Tell Alfred* (1960) and *Pursuit of Love* (1945), which verged on the autobiographical and sold over 1 million copies; also wrote 4 historical biographies: *Madame de Pompadour* (1953), *Voltaire in Love* (1957), *The Sun King* (1966) and *Frederick the Great* (1970), as well as a sardonic book about her sister Unity and the British Union of Fascists, *Wigs on the Green*. ❖ See also Harold Acton, *Nancy Mitford* (Harper & Row, 1975); Charlotte Mosley, ed. *Love from Nancy: The Letters of Nancy Mitford* (Houghton, 1993); Jonathan and Catherine Guinness, *The House of Mitford* (Hutchinson, 1984); and *Women in World History.*

MITFORD, Unity (1914–1948). English socialite and Nazi sympathizer. Name variations: Bobo. Born Unity Valkyrie Mitford, Aug 8, 1914; died May 28, 1948; dau. of David Freeman-Mitford, 2nd Baron Redesdale, and Sydney Bowles; sister of Nancy Mitford (1904–1973), Jessica

Mitford (1917–1996), Diana Mitford (b. 1910), and Deborah Mitford (b. 1920). ❖ Became infatuated with the Nazi movement, befriended Hitler, then shot herself in the head when her beloved England and Germany went to war (1934–39); brain-damaged, regressed to the mental age of an 11-year-old; died 9 years later, having contracted a severe bout of meningitis from the old bullet wound. ❖ See also Jonathan and Catherine Guinness, *The House of Mitford* (Hutchinson, 1984); and *Women in World History*.

MITIC, Vukica (1953—). Yugoslavian basketball player. Born Dec 1953 in Yugoslavia. ❖ At Moscow Olympics, won a bronze medal in team competition (1980).

MITOVA, Silvia (1976—). Bulgarian gymnast. Born June 29, 1976, in Sofia, Bulgaria; dau. of Maya Balgoeva (3-time Bulgarian national champion gymnast); m. J. Arthur Hutchinson. ❖ Was 4-time Bulgarian national champion; won a bronze medal for floor exercises at the European Cup (1991) and a bronze medal for vault at European championships (1992); won Dutch Open and Sofia International (1991).

MITRYUK, Natalya (1959—). Soviet handball player. Born Nov 26, 1959, in USSR. ❖ At Seoul Olympics, won a bronze medal in team competition (1988).

MITSCHERLICH, Andrea (1961—). *See Schöne, Andrea Mitscherlich.*

MITSUYA, Yuko (1958—). Japanese volleyball player. Born July 29, 1958, in Japan. ❖ At Los Angeles Olympics, won a bronze medal in team competition (1984).

MITSUYE YAMADA (b. 1923). *See Yamada, Mitsuye.*

MITTERMAIER, Rosi (1950—). German Alpine skier. Name variations: Rosi Mittermaier-Neureuther. Born Aug 5, 1950, in Reit im Winkel, West Germany, near the Austrian border; sister of Evi Mittermaier (skier who came in 8th in the giant slalom in the 1976 Olympics). ❖ Won World Cup overall and slalom (1976); won gold medals for downhill and slalom and a silver medal for the giant slalom at Innsbruck Olympics (1976); at World championships, won a gold medal for combined (1976). ❖ See also *Women in World History*.

MITTERMAYER, Tatjana (1964—). German moguls skier. Born July 26, 1964, in Prien, Germany. ❖ Placed 1st at European Cup and Calgary Olympics (1988); won a silver medal for freestyle moguls at Nagano Olympics (1998).

MITTERRAND, Danielle (1924—). First lady of France and human-rights activist. Born Danielle Gouze in 1924; m. François Mitterrand (president of France, 1981–95, died Jan 8, 1996); children: 2 sons. ❖ An important and committed human-rights activist, became well known for her work on behalf of the Kurdish citizens of Iraq; founded France Libertés, a humanitarian organization that agitated foreign governments with its outspoken support for dissidents and ethnic minorities (1986). ❖ See also *Women in World History*.

MITTS, Heather (1978—). American soccer player. Born June 9, 1978, in Cincinnati, Ohio; attended University of Florida. ❖ Won a team gold medal at Athens Olympics (2004).

MIURA, Ayako (1922–1999). Japanese novelist. Born April 25, 1922, in Asahikawa, Hokkaido, Japan; died Oct 12, 1999; m. Miura Mitsuyo. ❖ Works, influenced by strong Christian beliefs, include *Hyôten* (1964, trans. as *Freezing Point*, 1986), *Shiokari tôge* (1968, trans. as *Shiokari Pass*, 1968), *Hosokawa Garasha fujin* (1975), *Deiryû chitai* (1977), and *Inochi aru kagiri* (1995).

MIURA, Hanako (1975—). Japanese gymnast. Born Mar 28, 1975, in Hiroshima, Japan. ❖ Won Japan nationals (1993); placed 12th for team all-around at Atlanta Olympics (1996).

MIURA, Tamaki (1884–1946). Japanese soprano. Born Feb 22, 1884, in Tokyo, Japan; died May 26, 1946, in Tokyo; studied with Junker in Japan, then with Petzold and Sarcoli in Germany. ❖ Recognized as Japan's 1st international opera star, made debut in Gluck's *Euridice* in Tokyo (1909); appeared at London Opera House (1915), with Chicago Civic Opera (1918), and in Rome (1921); toured US with Naples opera company (1924); premiered Aldo Franchetti's *Namiko-San*, written specifically for her, at Chicago Civic Opera (1925). ❖ See also *Women in World History*.

MIXER, Elizabeth (fl. 1707–1720). American writer. Born into devout Puritan family in Ashford, MA. ❖ Experienced visions as teenager that were transcribed and published as *An Account of Some Spiritual Experiences and Raptures* (1736).

MIYAJIMA, Keiko (1965—). Japanese volleyball player. Born Sept 24, 1965, in Japan. ❖ At Los Angeles Olympics, won a bronze medal in team competition (1984).

MIYAMOTO, Emiko (1937—). Japanese volleyball player. Born May 10, 1937, in Japan. ❖ At Tokyo Olympics, won a gold medal in team competition (1964).

MIYAO, Tomiko (1926—). Japanese novelist. Born 1926 in Kochi prefecture, Japan; dau. of a geisha and geisha master. ❖ Works include *An Oar* (1973), based on the life of her mother, as well as *Yokiro, Mai,* and *Kinone.* Won the Naoki Prize for *A Koto with One String* (1978).

MIZOGUCHI, Noriko (1971—). Japanese judoka. Born July 23, 1971, in Japan. ❖ At Barcelona Olympics, won a silver medal in half-lightweight 52 kg (1992).

MIZUTA, Tamae (1929—). Japanese historian and feminist. Born 1929 in Tokyo, Japan. ❖ Taught economics at Nagoya University and wrote works on feminism which influenced women's liberation theory in Japan; writings include *A History of Women's Liberation Thought* (1979).

M'KOLLY, Mary (1754–1832). *See McCauley, Mary Ludwig Hays*

M'LACHLAN, Jessie (c. 1834–1899). Scottish servant convicted of murder. Born c. 1834 in Scotland; died in Huron, Michigan, Jan 1, 1899. ❖ Worked in household of Glasgow accountant John Fleming; when a fellow servant, Jessie M'Pherson, was found hacked to death with a cleaver (July 7, 1862), was arrested for the murder, after pawning some silver which had been stolen from the household around the time of the killing; was found guilty in a trial noted for its bias and lack of hard evidence; sentence commuted to life imprisonment; released after 15 years (1877); died in America (1899). She claimed that the dying M'Pherson, whom she had tended, had accused John Fleming's father of attempted sexual assault.

MLADOVA, Milada (c. 1918—). American ballet dancer. Born Milada Mráz, c. 1918, in Oklahoma City, OK. ❖ Trained in NY with Edward Caton and Aubrey Hitchens, and under Olga Preobrazhenska and Bronislava Nijinska in Los Angeles and Paris; joined Ballet Russe de Monte Carlo (1939) where she performed in Platt's *Ghost Town,* Massine's *Nobilissima Visione, Gaité Parisienne,* and *Bacchanale,* and Balanchine's *Jeu de Cartes* and *Serenade,* among others; also created role in Ashton's *Devil's Holiday;* performed on Broadway in *The Merry Widow* and *The Man Who Came to Dinner;* appeared in nightclubs (1940s–50s); films include *Atlantis, The Eternal Melody,* and *Night and Day.*

MLAKAR, Pia (1908–2000). Yugoslavian ballet dancer and choreographer. Born Pia Scholz, Dec 28, 1908, in Hamburg, Germany; died in 2000; m. Pino Mlakar (ballet dancer, b. 1907). ❖ Trained under Rudolf von Laban and Elena Poljaka in Belgrade, where she met future husband; performed with him in numerous opera ballets throughout Europe, including Darmstadt, Dessau, Zurich, and Munich (1930s–40s); returned to Yugoslavia at end of WWII and taught in Slovenia; created numerous works with husband, including the much acclaimed *Der Teufel im Dorf* (1935), *Josefslegende* (1941), and *The Little Ballerina* (1947), as well as *Prometheus* (1935), *Verklungene Feste* (1941), *Jeu de Cartes* (1953) and *Legend of Ohrif* (1978).

MLAKAR, Veronika (1935—). Yugoslavian ballet dancer. Born Dec 8, 1935, in Zurich, Switzerland; dau. of Pino and Pia Mlakar (both ballet dancers and choreographers); trained by parents. ❖ Debuted and danced at Munich State Opera (1952–56), creating role in Rosen's *La Dame à la Licorne* (1953) and performing in *Coppélia* and *Jeu de Cartes,* among others; danced with company of Roland Petit, performing in his *La Chambre, The Lady and the Moon, Contrepointe,* and others; moved to US (1958) where she performed with Chicago Opera Ballet in works by Ruth Page; with American Ballet Theater, created role in Robbins' *Les Noces* (1965) and was featured in numerous Tudor works such as *Dark Elegies, Pillar of Fire, Echoing of Trumpets,* and *Jardin Aux Lilas.*

MLECZKO, A. J. (1975—). American ice-hockey player. Born Allison Jaime Mleczko, June 14, 1975, in Nantucket, MA; attended Harvard University. ❖ Led Harvard Crimson to a 22–1 record and the American Women's College Hockey Alliance National championship during senior year; named Patty Kazmaier Award winner for most outstanding player as well as the player of the year in Ivy League and the ECAC (1999); won team gold medal at Nagano (1998), the 1st Olympics to feature women's ice hockey; won silver medals at World championships (1997, 2000, 2001); won a silver medal at Salt Lake City Olympics (2002). ❖ See also Mary Turco, *Crashing the Net: The U.S. Women's Olympic Ice Hockey Team and the Road to Gold* (HarperCollins, 1999); and *Women in World History.*

MMANTHATISI (c. 1780–c. 1836). Tlokwa leader. Born c. 1780 in the present Orange Free State, South Africa; died c. 1836; married tribal chief; children: at least several sons. ❖ Following husband's death (1817), became tribal regent for 13-year-old son, with complete responsibility for leading the Tlokwa; planned military operations, though she did not personally participate in any of their battles with the Boers and Zulus, and her warriors were legendary for their ferocity; after much fighting, led her tribe to Lesotho, out of the reach of both Boers and Zulus. ❖ See also *Women in World History.*

MNISHEK, Marina (c. 1588–1614). *See Mniszek, Marina.*

MNISZCHÓWNA, Marina (c. 1588–1614). *See Mniszek, Marina.*

MNISZEK, Marina (c. 1588–1614). Russian empress. Name variations: Marina Mnizek; Marina Mniszech, Mnizeck, Mnishek, Mniszchówna, or Muizeck. Born Marina Mniszek in Sambor, Poland, c. 1588; died in Kaluga, Russia, 1614; dau. of Jerzy (George) Mniszek (palatine of Sandomierz) and Jadwiga Tarlówna; m. Demetrius the False also known as Dmitry or Dmitri the 1st Pretender, tsar of Russia (r. 1605–1606), in 1606; m. Dmitri the 2nd Pretender, in 1608; m. Ivan M. Zarutski; children: (2nd m.) Ivan (b. 1611). ❖ Daughter of a Polish noble who became empress of Russia as the wife of Tsar Dmitri the Pretender during the Time of Troubles in the 17th century; before marriage, arrived in Moscow with a large, boisterous and arrogant Polish cortege and exhibited the unimperial behavior of an overindulged teenager, which she was (May 2, 1606); as an unconverted Roman Catholic foreigner, angered Russians with her marriage and coronation; when a mob stormed the tsar's apartments and murdered her unpopular husband (May 17, 1606), hid during the attack under the ample skirts of Pani Kazanowska, a Polish lady-in-waiting; was forced to renounce all claims to the title of empress; on way home to Poland with father, was seized by forces loyal to a 2nd false Dmitri (Dmitri the Second Pretender) who had raised an army and established a rebel government in Tushino, near Moscow; recognized the new pretender as her husband Tsar Dmitri and became pregant; when he was killed (1610), fell in love with Don Cossack leader Ivan Mikhailovitch Zarutski; son Ivan born (1611); with Zarutski, tried to advance the candidacy of Ivan to Russian throne; was eventually brought to Moscow in chains (1614); son was hanged; died shortly thereafter, probably from grief, in a prison in Kolomna. Most Russians believed she possessed supernatural powers. ❖ See also *Women in World History.*

MNIZEK, Marina (c. 1588–1614). *See Mniszek, Marina.*

MNOUCHKINE, Ariane (1938—). French theater director. Born Mar 3, 1938, in Boulogne-sur-Seine, France; attended Oxford University and the Sorbonne. ❖ At the Sorbonne, formed student theater group (1959); traveled to Cambodia and Japan (1962); upon return to Paris, founded collective Théâtre du Soleil (1964), a troupe that studied mime and various theatrical traditions, including commedia dell'arte and kabuki; when French government donated disused munitions warehouse to her company, had a permanent home; collaborated with writer Hélène Cixous to create several works, including *L'Indiade ou l'Inde de leurs rêves* (1986). Other works of Théâtre du Soleil include *1789* (1970), *L'Age d'or* (1975), and *Mephisto* (1979).

MNTWANA, Ida (1903–1960). South African activist. Name variations: Ida Flyo Mntwana, Mtwana or Mtwa. Born 1903; died 1960; worked as a dressmaker. ❖ Elected 1st president of the African National Congress Women's League (1949); helped organize South African women's participation in demonstrations, marches, boycotts, strikes and civil disobedience especially over the issue of passes; with need for an autonomous organization to advocate for women's issues, signed invitation for inaugural conference of the Federation of South African Women (FSAW, 1953); served as 1st National president of FSAW (1954–56); was one of the defendants in the marathon Treason trials (1956–1961); when South Africa's Women's Monument, built to honor the vital part women played in the fight against apartheid, was unveiled (Aug 9, 2000), was among those women cited as "torchbearers." ❖ See also *Women in World History.*

MO HUILAN (1979—). Chinese gymnast. Born July 19, 1979, in Guilin, Guanxi province, China; fraternal twin sister of Mo Huifang (gymnast).

❖ Won gold medals in vault, bars, beam, floor and team all-round at Asian Games (1994); won China Cup (1995); won a gold medal for balance beam and silver medals for team all-around and uneven bars at World championships (1995); won Chinese National (1996); at Atlanta Olympics, won a silver medal for vault (1996); won East Asian Games and Thailand Gymnastics Open and tied for 1st at World Gymnastics in Bangkok (1997); was the 1st female to perform a Gaylord salto on uneven bars. Appeared as Sang Lan in a 20-part tv series, then starred in "The Mo Huilan Show" (2002).

MØBERG, Anette (1971—). *See Hoffman, Anette.*

MOBLEY, Mamie Till (1921–2003). African-American educator and civil-rights activist. Name variations: Mamie E. Mobley; Mamie Till or Mamie Till-Mobley. Born Mamie Carthan, Nov 23, 1921, in Webb, Mississippi; grew up in Chicago; died Jan 6, 2003, in Chicago, IL; dau. of John and Alma Carthan; m. Louis Till, Oct 14, 1940 (sep. 1942, executed in Italy, 1945); m. Gene "Pink" Bradley, c. 1952 (div. c. 1954); married once more; children: Emmett Till (b. 1941). ❖ For 50 years, sought justice for her son, who was murdered at age 14 and thrown into a river in Mississippi because he supposedly whistled at a white woman (1955); demanded his disfigured body be displayed in an open coffin in his hometown of Chicago, causing the spark that ignited the civil-rights movement; taught in Chicago Public Schools for 26 years; championed children in poor neighborhoods and spoke out against racial injustice. ❖ See also memoir (with Chris Benson) *Death of Innocence* (Random House, 2004).

MOBLEY, Mary Ann (1939—). American actress. Born Mary Ann Mobley, Feb 17, 1939, in Brandon, Mississippi; attended University of Mississippi; m. Gary Collins (actor); children: daughter Mary Clancy Collins (MGM tv executive). ❖ Named Miss America (1959), representing Mississippi; went on to a successful acting career in tv and on Broadway; filmed hour-long documentaries on plight of children who are victims of war and deprivation. ❖ See also Frank Deford, *There She Is* (Viking, 1971).

MOCANU, Diana (1984—). Romanian swimmer. Born Diana Iuliana Mocanu, July 19, 1984, in Braila, Romania. ❖ Won gold medals for 100- and 200-meter backstroke at Sydney Olympics (2000); at LC World championships, won a gold medal for 200-meter backstroke (2001).

MOCEANU, Dominique (1981—). American gymnast. Born Sept 30, 1981, in Hollywood, CA. ❖ Won US nationals (1995); won Visa Challenge (1995) and Goodwill Games (1998); at World championships, won a silver medal for balance beam and a bronze medal for team all-around (1995); at Atlanta Olympics, won a gold medal for team all-around (1996).

MOCHIZUKI, Noriko (1967—). Japanese gymnast. Born July 16, 1967, in Shizuoka, Japan. ❖ Won Japanese nationals (1984, 1985); placed 6th for team all-around at Atlanta Olympics (1996).

MOCK, Jerrie (1925—). American aviator. Name variations: Mrs. Russell C. Mock. Born Geraldine Lois Fredritz, Nov 22, 1925, in Newark, Ohio; dau. of Timothy J. Fredritz and Blanche (Wright) Fredritz; attended Ohio State University, majoring in aeronautical engineering, 1943–45; m. Russell C. Mock, Mar 21, 1945; children: Roger, Gary, and Valerie. ❖ Began flying lessons (1957) and received pilot's license (1958); became 1st woman to fly solo around the world (April 17, 1964), in 29 days, 11 hours, and 59 minutes (including 21 stopovers), during which she flew 22,858.8 miles in a Cessna 180; in course of this flight, also became the 1st to fly alone across Pacific Ocean from west to east, the 1st to fly a single-engine plane across the Pacific in either direction, and the 1st woman to fly solo from coast to coast by going around the world; appointed to post of vice-chair of FAA's Women's Aviation Advisory Committee; having set a total of 21 world records in aviation, retired from flying (Nov 1969) to become a missionary in New Guinea. Received FAA's Gold Medal Award from President Lyndon B. Johnson (1964).

MODEL, Lisette (1901–1983). Austrian-born photographer. Name variations: Elise Seybert; Lisette Stern. Pronunciation: Moh-DELL. Born Elise Amelie Felicie Stern, Nov 10, 1901, in Vienna, Austria; died Mar 30, 1983, in New York, NY; dau. of Victor Hypolite Josef Calas Stern, later Seybert (Viennese doctor), and Françoise Antoinette Felicite (Picus) Stern (French clerk); m. Evsei (Evsa) Konstantinovich Model (Russian painter), Sept 7, 1937, in Paris; no children. ❖ When young, developed a strong passion for music, seriously studying piano and voice; lived in

Paris (1926–33); took up photography; half-Jewish, immigrated to US (NY) with rise of Nazism (1938); captivated by energy of city streets, photographed in Wall Street and on the Bowery, as well as in the city's cabarets and cafes; had 1st works purchased by Museum of Modern Art (1940); began photographing window displays on Fifth Avenue, exploring the theme of American glamour; signed contract with *Harper's Bazaar* (1941) and also contributed to *Look;* became US citizen (1944); began teaching at New School for Social Research (1951); held exhibitions in Tokyo, Ottawa, Venice, Australia, Paris, and Germany (1980–81); had retrospective, *Lisette Model: A Celebration of Genius*, at Parsons Exhibition Center, NYC (1983); images were often controversial, contradictory, and political in nature; explored the social landscapes of both pre-World War II Europe and postwar America, and probed the inner landscapes of the subjects of her portraiture. ❖ See also *Lisette Model* (Aperture, 1979), *Lisette Model: Portfolio* (Graphics International, 1976), and *Lisette Model: A Retrospective* (New Orleans Museum of Art, 1981); Ann Thomas, ed. *Lisette Model* (National Gallery of Canada, 1990); and *Women in World History*.

MODENA, duchess of.
See Este, Virginia d' (b. 1573?).
See Martinozzi, Laura (fl. 1658).
See Charlotte-Aglae (1700–1761).
See Maria Beatrice of Sardinia (1792–1840).
See Adelgunde of Bavaria (1823–1914).

MODERS, Mary (1643–1673). English adventurer. Name variations: Mary Meders; Mary Carleton; also known as the German Princess. Born Jan 11, 1643 (some sources cite 1633, 1634 or 1642), in Canterbury, England; died by hanging, Jan 2, 1673, in Tyburn, England; dau. of a chorister at Canterbury Cathedral; married a man named Stedman; m. a man named Day, in Dover; m. John Carleton, c. 1663; children: (1st m.) 2 who died young. ❖ Celebrated and later hanged for her fraudulent exploits, was charged with bigamy, but 1st husband did not appear at the trial and she was set free; went to Germany and worked in a Cologne brothel; returned to England (1663); married a 3rd time; charged with bigamy, but 1st two husbands did not appear at trial and was again set free; by now quite famous in England, became a success on stage (1663) and wrote tracts defending herself from accusations; convicted of robbery and transported to Jamaica as punishment; escaped back to England, discovered, and hanged for returning from transportation (1673). The incident became famous and was recorded in plays and stories, including *The Case of Mary Carleton* (1663), *A True Account* (1663), and *An Historical Narrative.* ❖ See also Ernest Bernbaum, *The Mary Carleton Narratives, 1663–73* (Ayer); and *Women in World History*.

MODERSOHN-BECKER, Paula (1876–1907). German painter. Name variations: Paula Becker; Paula Modersohn-Becker. Born Paula Becker in Dresden, Germany, Feb 8, 1876; died in Worpswede of a heart attack following childbirth, Nov 21, 1907; dau. of Carl Woldemar Becker (civil engineer) and Mathilde von Bültzingslöwen Becker; studied art in London (1892), Berlin (1897–98), and Paris (1900–07); m. Otto Modersohn, May 25, 1901; children: Mathilde Modersohn (b. 1907); (stepdaughter) Elspeth Modersohn. ❖ Painter whose striking and imaginative pictures moved beyond the naturalism and realism of late 19th-century German art to make her a pioneer of German Expressionism at the start of the 20th century; settled in artists' colony at Worpswede (1898); had 1st public exhibit of her painting (1899); on 1st trip to Paris, met Rainer Maria Rilke (1900); on 2nd trip, met Auguste Rodin (1903); made 3rd trip (1905); estranged from husband, started 4th (and most extended stay in Paris), gave 2nd exhibit of her painting, reconciled with husband (1906); returned to Worpswede, became pregnant, rendered final paintings; lived only 31 years and sold only 1 painting, nonetheless produced 400 paintings and 1,000 drawings, which were forceful, important works of art; paintings include *Elspeth* (1902), *Clara Rilke-Westhoff* (1905), *Self-Portrait on her Sixth Wedding Day* (1906) and *Self-Portrait with Camellia Branch* (1907). ❖ See also *The Letters and Journals of Paula Modersohn-Becker* (trans. by J. Diane Radycki, Scarecrow, 1980); Gillian Perry, *Paula Modersohn-Becker: Her Life and Work* (Harper & Row, 1979); Gunter Busch, ed. *Paula Modersohn-Becker: The Letters and Journals* (Northwestern, 1990); and *Women in World History*.

MODESTA OF TRIER (d. about 680). Saint. Died c. 680; niece of Ida of Nivelles; cousin of St. Gertrude of Nivelles (626–659). ❖ Founded the monastery of Horren, at Trier, in the buildings of the ancient public granary (*borreum*). Feast day is Oct 6.

MODEVA, Mariyka (1954—). Bulgarian rower. Born April 4, 1954, in Bulgaria. ❖ Won a silver medal at Montreal Olympics (1976) and a silver medal at Moscow Olympics (1980), both in coxed fours.

MODJESKA, Helena (1840–1909). Polish-born actress. Name variations: Modrejewska or Modrzejewi; Countess Bozenta or Countess Chlapowski. Born Jadwiga Opid, Oct 12, 1840, in Cracow, Poland; died April 9, 1909, on Bay Island (Modjeska Island), California; dau. of Michael Opid (music teacher) and Jozefa Benda Opid; educated at St. Joseph Convent school; m. Gustav Sinnmayer who later called himself Gustav Modrzejewski; m. Count Bozenta Chlapowski, Sept 12, 1868; children: (1st m.) Rudolph (b. 1861), Marylka (1862–1865). ❖ Polish patriot, who gained fame as a major interpreter of Shakespearean plays for 19th-century US audiences, sought to use her career to advance the cause of Polish independence from foreign rule; made professional debut in Poland (1861); established acting company with husband (1862); began performing at Cracow theater (1865); performed at Warsaw Imperial Theater (1868); arrived in US and settled with husband in area of Anaheim, California (1876); made US debut in San Francisco (1877); made debuts in NY, Boston, and Washington, DC (1877); performed in London and Paris (1878); became US citizen (1883); made professional tour of Poland and England (1884–85); banned from further appearances in Russian-occupied Poland (1894); played benefit at NY's Metropolitan Opera (1905); famed for performances in *Adrienne Lecouvreur, As You Like It, Romeo and Juliet* and *Camille.* ❖ See also autobiography *Memories and Impressions of Helena Modjeska* (Blom, 1910); Arthur Coleman, *Wanderers Twain: Modjeska and Sienkiewicz* (Cherry Hill, 1964); Marion Moore Coleman, *Fair Rosalind: The American Career of Helena Modjeska* (Cherry Hill, 1969); Antoni Gronowicz, *Modjeska* (Yoseloff, 1956); Susan Sontag, *In America* (Farrar, 2000, novel loosely based on Modjeska's life); and *Women in World History*.

MÖDL, Martha (1912–2001). German mezzo-soprano and soprano. Born Mar 22, 1912, in Nuremberg, Germany; died Dec 17, 2001, in Stuttgart, Germany; studied with Klinck-Schneider at Nuremberg Conservatory. ❖ Began as a performer of light mezzo-soprano repertory, then moved into more dramatic Wagnerian roles; made debut as Hänsel in Nuremberg (1942); sang mezzo roles in Düsseldorf (1945–49) and Hamburg Staatsoper (1947–55); made Covent Garden debut as Carmen (1949); debuted at Bayreuth as Kundry in *Parsifal* (1951); remained at Bayreuth and later performed Isolde and Brünnhilde (1951–67); debuted at Metropolitan Opera (1957); recorded the *Walküre* with conductor Wilhelm Furtwängler for EMI before recording the entire Ring cycle with the same conductor, a touchstone for all modern interpretations; returned to roles in her natural mezzo range (1960s). ❖ See also *Women in World History*.

MODOTTI, Tina (1896–1942). Italian photographer and activist. Name variations: Tina Modotti Mondina. Born Assunta Adelaide Luigia Modotti, Aug 16, 1896, in Udine, Italy; died Jan 5, 1942, in Mexico City, Mexico; dau. of Giuseppe Modotti (mason) and Assunta Modotti; m. Roubaix de L'Abrie Richey (American poet and painter), 1917 (died 1922); no children. ❖ Important 20th-century photographer, was also an ardent revolutionary and Communist Party member; immigrated to US (1913); lived in Los Angeles following marriage (1917); appeared in several films (1920–21); met photographer Edward Weston (1920) and began liaison (1921); following death of husband, moved to Mexico with Weston as assistant, apprentice, model and mistress (1922); took 1st serious photograph in Mexico (1923); began to specialize in portraits, still lifes, architecture, and documentary photographs (1926); started contributing to Mexican magazines *Formas* and *Mexican Folkways*; joined Communist Party (1927); met Italian political activist Vittorio Vidali (June 1927); was much in demand, with requests from the Pacific International Salon of Photographic Art, *British Journal of Photography*, and New York City's *Creative Art* magazine; began affair with Cuban revolutionary Julio Antonio Mella (June 1928); witnessed Mella's assassination (Jan 1929); though not involved, was arrested, then deported following assassination attempt on Mexican president (Feb 1930); moved to Soviet Union (fall 1930); abandoned photography in favor of revolutionary party work (1931); left Soviet Union, was barred from entering Spain and moved to Paris (1934); joined Vidali in Spain (1935); active in Spanish Civil War (1936–39); returned to Mexico as a refugee (April 1939). ❖ See also Mildred Constantine, *Tina Modotti: A Fragile Life* (Chronicle, 1993); Patricia Albers, *Shadows, Fire, and Snow: The Life of Tina Modotti* (Clarkson Potter, 1999); Margaret Hooks, *Tina Modotti: Photographer and Revolutionary* (Harper, 1993); Sarah M. Lowe, *Tina Modotti: Photographs* (Abrams, 1995); and *Women in World History*.

MODTHRYTH (fl. 520). German princess and warrior. Name variations: Modthrith. Born in Germany; dau. of the king of a Germanic tribe. ❖ Well schooled in the art of warfare, proved a formidable foe to the men who challenged her or perhaps even, it is reported, dared seek her hand in marriage.

MODWENNA (d. 518). Saint. Name variations: Moninne. Died in Dundee, 518; buried at Burton-on-Trent; dau. of the king of Iveagh. ❖ Said to have been blessed by St. Patrick, was an Irish princess who founded churches at Louth, Wexford, Kileevy, Armagh, Swords, and the Aran Islands; also journeyed "with other maidens" to England where she established churches from Warwickshire to Dundee, Scotland.

MOE, Karen (1952—). American swimmer. Name variations: Karen Thornton. Born Jan 22, 1952, in Del Monoe, the Philippines; grew up in Orinda, CA; attended UCLA; m. Mike Thornton. ❖ Set world record in 200-meter butterfly (1970); at Munich Olympics (1972), was the 1st American woman to win a gold medal for the 200-meter butterfly; placed 4th at Montreal Olympics for 200-meter butterfly and retired (1976); won 18 US national championships; became head coach at University of California.

MOEBIUS, Sabine (1957—). *See John-Paetz-Moebius, Sabine.*

MOEHRING, Anke (1969—). East German swimmer. Name variations: Anke Möhring. Born Aug 28, 1969, in East Germany. ❖ At Seoul Olympics, won a bronze medal in the 400-meter freestyle (1988).

MOELLER-GLADISCH, Silke (1964—). East German runner. Name variations: Silke Gladisch; Silke Moller or Möller. Born June 20, 1964, in East Germany. ❖ At Seoul Olympics, won a silver medal in the 4x100-meter relay (1988).

MOE MOE (1944–1990). *See Daw San San.*

MOEN, Anita (1967—). *See Moen-Guidon, Anita.*

MOEN-GUIDON, Anita (1967—). Norwegian cross-country skier. Name variations: Anita Moen Guidon; Anita Moen. Born Anita Moen, Aug 31, 1967, in Trysil, Norway. ❖ Won a silver medal for 4x5 km relay at Lillehammer Olympics (1994); won a silver medal for 4x5 km relay and a bronze for 15 km mass at Nagano Olympics (1998); won a silver medal for the 4x5 km relay and a bronze medal for the 1.5 km sprint at Salt Lake City Olympics (2002).

MOERDRE, Berit. *See Mørdre, Berit.*

MOERO (fl. 4th–3rd BCE). Byzantine poet. Name variations: Myro. Married Andromachus (surnamed Philologus); children: the grammarian and tragic poet Homerus. ❖ Wrote epic, elegiac and lyric poems. Two Greek epigrams and 10 lines of epic hexameter are extant.

MOFFAT, Gwen (1924—). British mountaineer. Born Gwen Goddard in Brighton, England, July 1924; m. Gordon Moffat, 1949; m. Johnnies Lees, 1952 (div. 1969); children: Sheena (b. 1949). ❖ Was the 1st qualified female rock climbing and mountaineering guide in Britain. ❖ See also memoir *Space Beneath my Feet* (Hodder & Stoughton, 1961); and *Women in World History.*

MOFFATT, Laura (1954—). English politician and member of Parliament. Born Laura Field, April 9, 1954; m. Colin Moffatt. ❖ Representing Labour, elected to House of Commons for Crawley (1997, 2001, 2005); named PPS to Lord Irvine of Lairg as Lord Chancellor.

MOFFATT, Mary (1820–1862). *See Livingstone, Mary Moffatt.*

MOFFATT, Mary Smith (1795–1870). British missionary to Africa. Born Mary Smith, 1795, in New Windsor, England; died 1870 in England; dau. of James Smith and Mary (Gray) Smith; m. Robert Moffatt (missionary), Dec 27, 1819; children: 10, including Mary Moffatt Livingstone (1820–1862, who m. the explorer David Livingstone), and several who died. ❖ At 24, sailed to South Africa, where she married in Cape Town (1819); with husband, journeyed 600 miles inland to Kuruman, in Cape Province, to set up their mission (1820), remaining there until 1870. ❖ See also *Women in World History.*

MOFFITT, Billie Jean (b. 1943). *See King, Billie Jean.*

MOFFO, Anna (1932–2006). American soprano. Born Anna Moffo, June 27, 1932, in Wayne, PA; died Mar 9, 2006, in New York, NY; studied at Curtis Institute of Music with Giannini-Gregory and at Rome's Accademia di Santa Cecilia with Luigi Ricci and Mercedes Llopart; m. Mario Lanfranchi (film director and later her manager), 1957 (div. 1972);

m. Robert Sarnoff (RCA chair), 1974 (died 1997). ❖ Internationally renowned for voice and beauty, made stage debut in Spoleto as Norina in *Don Pasquale* (1955); appeared at La Scala in *Falstaff* (1957); made US debut as Mimi in *La Bohème* with Lyric Opera of Chicago (1957); made Metropolitan Opera debut as Violetta in *La Traviata* (1959); returned to Met to sing 3 new roles: Gilda in *Rigoletto,* Adina in *L'Elisir d'Amore,* and the slave girl Liù in *Turandot* (1960–61); enjoyed a 17-year run with the Met, during which time she gave 220 performances in 18 operas; had her own tv series in Italy, "The Anna Moffo Show" (1960–73); also appeared in over 20 films (including several in which she played straight dramatic roles), and made numerous recordings, including *La Traviata, Madame Butterfly, La Rondine,* and *La Bohème* with Maria Callas; began singing the heavier Verdi roles (late 1970s), such as Leonora in *Il Trovatore* and Lina in *Stiffelio,* then added the title role in Bellini's *Norma* (1991). ❖ See also *Women in World History.*

MOFFORD, Rose (1922—). American politician. Born Rose Perica, June 10, 1922, in Globe, Arizona; dau. of John and Frances Perica; m. T.R. "Lefty" Mofford (founder of the Phoenix Police Dept.), 1957. ❖ Served as secretary of state (1977–87); became 1st woman governor of Arizona on the heels of impeachment of Governor Evan Mecham (1987); serving until 1991, rescinded controversial appointments by her predecessor and provided much-needed stability; did not run for reelection.

MOGADOR, Céleste (1824–1909). *See Chabrillan, Céleste de.*

MOGGRIDGE, Jackie (1922–2004). English aviator. Born Dolores Teresa Sorour, Mar 1, 1922, in Pretoria, South Africa; died Jan 7, 2004; married Lt-Colonel Reginald Moggridge, 1945 (died 1997); children: 2 daughters. ❖ Wartime Air Transport Auxiliary (ATA) pilot, 1st soloed at age 16 in South Africa; moved to England and took a flying course at Witney Aeronautical College (1939); during WWII, joined the Women's Auxiliary Air Force and became a radar operator; transferred to the ATA and ferried more than 63 types of aircraft from the factories to the squadrons; later flew jet aircraft as an officer in the Women's Royal Air Force Volunteer Reserve and became an airline captain for Channel Airways. ❖ See also memoir, *Woman Pilot* (1957).

MOHAWK PRINCESS, The (1861–1913). *See Johnson, E. Pauline.*

MOHL, Mary (1793–1883). English salonnière. Name variations: Madame Mohl. Born Mary Clarke, 1793; died 1883; educated in a convent school; m. Julius Mohl (orientalist), 1847. ❖ For 40 years, held a salon in Paris that was attended by the city's literati, including Juliette Récamier and Chateaubriand.

MOHOLY, Lucia (1894–1989). Czech photographer and filmmaker. Name variations: Lucia Moholy-Nagy. Born Lucia Schultz or Schulz in Karlin, Austria-Hungary, 1894; died in Zurich, Switzerland, 1989; graduate of Prague University, 1912; m. László Moholy-Nagy (photographer and artist), 1921 (sep. 1929, div.). ❖ While husband was a member of Bauhaus school of architecture in Weimar, was an apprentice in Ecknar photographic studio (1923–24); followed Bauhaus school when it moved to Dessau and compiled a series of photographic portraits of its teachers and associates (1925); moved to Berlin (1929), where she shot photographs of husband's stage designs; served as curator of historical section of Stuttgart *Film und Foto* exhibition (1930); moved to Paris (1933), then London (1934), where she opened a photographic portrait studio; wrote a history of photography (1939); became British citizen (1940); moved to Switzerland (1959). ❖ See also *Women in World History.*

MOHOLY-NAGY, Sibyl (1903–1971). German-born American architectural historian and critic. Born Dorothea Maria Pauline Alice Sibylle Pietzsch in Dresden, Germany, Oct 29, 1903 (some sources cite 1893); died in New York, NY, Jan 8, 1971; dau. of Martin and Fanny Clauss Pietzsch; studied at universities of Frankfurt am Main and Leipzig; m. Lazzlo also seen as Laslo or László Moholy-Nagy (1895–1946, Hungarian-born design teacher at Bauhaus), 1932 (died 1946); children: Claudia Moholy-Nagy and Hattula Moholy-Nagy. ❖ Major voice in the field of architectural history and criticism in America, began career in Germany as head of the dramatic department of Tobis motion-picture syndicate, working with future husband to produce a series of cinema classics: *Berliner Stilleben* (Berlin Still Life), *Marseille Vieux Port* (The Old Port of Marseille, 1929), *Ein Lichtspiel: Schwarz, Weiss, Grau* (Lightplay: Black, White, Gray, 1930) and *Grossstadt-Zigeuner* (Gypsies of the Metropolis, 1932); with the Nazi threat, moved with husband to London (1935), then US (1937); hired to head the humanities division at School of Design in Chicago (1941), taught courses in architectural history, theory and practice; was an associate professor of art at Bradley

University (1947–49); published *Moholy-Nagy: Experiment in Totality* (1950); lectured at University of California, Berkeley (1949–51); became professor of history of architecture at NY's Pratt Institute (1951); wrote several other books. Named "critic of the year" by American Institute of Architects (1971). ❖ See also *Women in World History*.

MOHR, Nicholasa (1935—). Puerto Rican-American novelist and short-story writer. Born 1935 in Harlem, NY; dau. of Puerto Rican immigrants; attended New School for Social Research and Brooklyn Museum of Art School. ❖ Began career as a painter before writing short stories, primarily for young adults; works, which reflect experiences of Puerto Ricans living in US, include *Nilda* (1973), *In Nueva York* (1977), *Going Home* (1986), *Nicholasa Mohr: Growing Up Inside the Sanctuary of My Imagination* (1994), *Old Letvia and The Mountain of Sorrows* (1996), and *A Matter of Pride and Other Stories* (1997).

MÖHRING, Anke (1969—). *See Moehring, Anke.*

MOHUN, Elizabeth (fl. 14th c.). Countess of Salisbury. Name variations: Elizabeth Montacute. Dau. of John Mohun, 2nd baron Mohun of Dunster, and Joan Mohun; sister of Philippa Mohun (d. 1431); m. William Montacute (1328–1397), 2nd earl of Salisbury; children: William Montacute (d. 1382).

MOHUN, Joan (fl. 14th c.). Baroness Mohun of Dunster. Name variations: Joan Burghersh. Born Joan Burghersh; dau. of Bartholomew Burghersh, 3rd baron Burghersh, and Elizabeth Verdon; m. John Mohun, 2nd baron Mohun of Dunster; children: Philippa Mohun (d. 1431); Elizabeth Mohun, countess of Salisbury.

MOHUN, Philippa (d. 1431). Duchess of York. Name variations: Died July 17, 1431; buried in Westminster Abbey; dau. of John Mohun, 2nd baron Mohun of Dunster, and Joan Mohun; sister of Elizabeth Mohun, countess of Salisbury; m. Edward Plantagenet, 2nd duke of York, in 1396 (d. 1415).

MOHZOLINI, Anna (1716–1774). *See Manzolini, Anna Morandi.*

MOILLON, Louise (1610–1696). French still-life painter. Born in 1610 (some sources cite 1615, others 1609) in Paris; died 1696 in Paris; dau. of Nicolas Moillon (painter and picture dealer) and Marie Gilbert; m. Etienne Girardot (wood merchant), 1640; children: at least 3. ❖ A pioneer of the still-life genre in France, worked primarily with studies of fruit, though she also occasionally painted vegetables; also successfully integrated human figures within the still-life composition in several of her paintings, notably *The Fruit Seller* (1629) and *At the Greengrocer* (1630). ❖ See also *Women in World History*.

MOINEAU, Môme (1905–1968). *See Benitez-Rexach, Lucienne.*

MOIR, Margaret (1941—). New Zealand politician. Born Margaret Putt, Sept 9, 1941, in Kimberley, South Africa; m. Derek Moir (plumber), 1963. ❖ Elected National MP for West Coast (1990).

MOISANT, Matilde (c. 1877–1964). American aviation pioneer. Name variations: Tudy, Tillie. Pronunciations: MOY-sant or MWAH-zawnt. Born Matilde Josephine Moisant in Manteno, Illinois, c. 1877 or 1878; died in La Crescenta, California, 1964; dau. of Medore Moisant and Josephine (Fortier) Moisant; never married; no children. ❖ The 2nd American woman to receive a pilot's license, was a partner of her brothers Alfred and John in the Moisants' airfield, flight school, plane factory and air circus; earned pilot's license after 32 minutes of instruction (1911); led an air circus in Mexico in the midst of a revolution (1911); was a member of the Early Birds association; after a crash—the 5th of her career—at Wichita Falls, Texas (April 14, 1912), retired from flying and spent the remainder of her life in Los Angeles and La Crescenta. Won Rodman Wanamaker Trophy (altitude record for women, Sept 24, 1911). ❖ See also Doris L. Rich, *The Magnificent Moisants* (Smithsonian Institution Press, 1998); and *Women in World History*.

MOÏSE, Penina (1797–1880). Jewish-American hymn writer. Name variations: Penina Moise. Born April 23, 1797, in Charleston, South Carolina; died Sept 13, 1880, in Charleston; dau. of Abraham Moïse (storekeeper) and Sarah Moïse; never married; no children. ❖ A devout Jew, was a member of Charleston's Congregation Beth Elohim and began serving as superintendent of its Sunday School (1842); wrote verses on Jewish themes and composed hymns for the synagogue's services, which were published as *Hymns Written for the Use of Hebrew Congregations* (1856) and are still included in Jewish hymnals. ❖ See also *Women in World History*.

MOISEEVA, Irina (1955—). Russian ice dancer. Name variations: Irina Moiseyeva. Born June 3, 1955, in Moscow, Russia. ❖ With Andrei Minenkov, won the World championships (1975, 1977), a silver medal at Innsbruck Olympics (1976) and a bronze medal at Lake Placid Olympics (1980).

MOISEIWITSCH, Tanya (1914–2003). British stage and costume designer. Pronunciation: Moy-ZAY-e-vich. Born Dec 3, 1914, in London, England; died Feb 19, 2003, in London; dau. of Benno Moiseiwitsch (concert pianist) and Daisy Kennedy (violinist); m. Felix Krish (RAF pilot), during World War II (died); no children. ❖ One of Britain's foremost set and costume designers, designed 1st production, for *The Faithful*, at Westminster Theatre, London (1934); designed over 50 productions for Abbey Theatre in Dublin (1936–39); moved to Q Theatre, London (1939); took part in 1st production in West End, with *The Golden Cuckoo* (1940); designed sets at Oxford Playhouse (1941–44), then Old Vic's Liverpool Playhouse company, where she designed the acclaimed production of *Uncle Vanya*, starring Laurence Olivier; with Tyrone Guthrie, was responsible for some of the foremost British stage productions of postwar period, including *Cyrano de Bergerac* (1946) and *Peter Grimes* (1947); designed the wedge-shaped "apron" stage for Stratford Theatre Festival in Ontario, Canada (1952); designed sets and costumes for productions in Britain and US and for annual festivals in Stratford, Edinburgh, and Piccolo Teatro, Milan, among others (from 1955). Named Commander of British Empire (1976). ❖ See also *Women in World History*.

MOISEYEVA, Irina (1955—). *See Moiseeva, Irina.*

MOLANDER, Karin (1889–1978). Swedish screen actress. Born May 20, 1889, in Stockholm, Sweden; died Sept 3, 1978, in Vardinge, Stockholm; m. Gustaf Molander (director, screenwriter), 1910 (div. 1918); m. Lars Hanson (actor), 1922 (div. 1965). ❖ Star of early Swedish silents, films include *Halvblod* (Half-Breed), *The Red Tower*, *Kärlek och journalistik* (released in US as *Love and Journalism*), *Hennes Kungliga höghet*, *Thomas Graals bästa film*, *Tösen från Stormytorpet* (released in US as *Girl from Stormy Croft*), *Vem sköt?*, *Thomas Graals bästa barn*, *Synnöve Solbakken* (title role), *Surrogatet*, *Erotikon*, *Fiskebyn*, *Bomben* and *Gabrielle*.

MOLD or MOLDE. *Variant of Matilda or Maud.*

MOLDEN, Paula (1887–1951). *See Preradovic, Paula von.*

MOLESWORTH, Martha (1577–1646). English writer. Name variations: Martha Moulsworth. Born Martha Dorsett, Nov 10, 1577, probably in Oxford, England; died autumn 1646, probably in Hoddesdon, Hertfordshire, England; dau. of Robert Dorsett (died 1580, tutor to Sir Philip Sidney); raised by maternal grandparents; m. Nicholas Prynne (London goldsmith), 1598 (died c. 1604); Thomas Thorowgood (draper), 1605 (died 1615); Bevil Molesworth (goldsmith), 1619; children: (1st m.) Richard and Martha Prynne (died young); (3rd m.) Bevil Molesworth (died young). ❖ Wrote one of the earliest autobiographical poems in the English language, "Memorandum" (1632), which protests inferiority of women's education.

MOLESWORTH, Mary (c. 1678–1715). *See Monck, Mary.*

MOLESWORTH, Mary Louisa (1839–1921). English novelist and children's author. Name variations: Mrs. Molesworth; Louisa Molesworth or Louise Molesworth; (pseudonym) Ennis Graham. Born Mary Louisa Stewart, May 29, 1839 (some sources cite 1838), in Rotterdam, Holland; died July 20, 1921, in London, England; dau. of Charles Augustus Stewart and Agnes Janet (Wilson) Stewart; m. Major Richard Molesworth (career military man), 1861 (sep. 1879); children: Violet (1863–1869); Cicely (b. 1863); Juliet (b. 1865); Olive (b. 1867); Richard Walter Stewart (died young, 1869); Richard Bevil (b. 1870); Lionel Charles (b. 1873). ❖ Popular and acclaimed author of children's literature, novels and short stories in Victorian England, published 1st romance novel, *Lover and Husband* (1870); began writing books for children, and had great success with the 1st, *Tell Me a Story* (illus. by Walter Crane, 1875); continued to write at least 1 to 3 books each year for several decades, most of them for children; wary of morality tales, then common fodder for children's books, created stories for children that did not attempt to strike the fear of God into them; her *Carrots: Just a Little Boy* (1876) and *The Cuckoo Clock* (1877) sold thousands of copies; also wrote popular ghost stories. ❖ See also Roger Lancelyn Green, *Mrs. Molesworth* (Bodley Head, 1961); and *Women in World History*.

MOLIK, Alicia (1981—). Australian tennis player. Born Jan 27, 1981, in Adelaide, Australia. ❖ Won Moorilla International (2003) and Nordea Nordic Light Open (2004); won a bronze medal for singles at Athens Olympics (2004).

MOLIN-KONGSGARD, Anne (1977—). Norwegian snowboarder. Born Nov 12, 1977, in Kongsberg, Norway. ❖ Won silver medal in Halfpipe at Gravity Games, Mammoth Mountain, CA (2000); placed 3rd in Halfpipe at Vans Triple Crown, Mount Seymour, BC (2000), and bronze medal in Superpipe at X Games Global championship (2003).

MOLINARI, Susan (1958—). American politician. Born Mar 27, 1958, in Staten Island, NY; dau. of US congressional representative Guy Victor Molinari; State University of New York, Albany, BA, 1980, MA, 1982; m. Bill Paxon (US congressional representative); children: Susan Ruby Paxon (b. 1996). ❖ US congresswoman, served on Republican National Committee (1983–84); served on NY City Council as minority leader (1986–90); elected to the 101st Congress by special election (Mar 20, 1990), and to 4 succeeding Congresses; a moderate, served on Committee on Public Works and Transportation, Committee on Small Business, Committee on Resources and the Environment, and Committee on the Budget, and was a co-founder of Republicans for Choice; gave the keynote address at Republican National Convention (1996); resigned (1997); was a CBS tv anchorwoman (1998–99); received a visiting fellowship to Harvard University's Kennedy School of Government (1999); formed lobbying group with Michael McCurry, former White House chief of staff (1999); with Elinor Burkett, wrote *Representative Mom: Balancing Budgets, Bill and Baby in the US Congress* (1999). ❖ See also *Women in World History.*

MOLINES, Catherine (d. 1452). *See Howard, Catherine.*

MOLL CUTPURSE (c. 1584–1659). *See Frith, Mary.*

MOLLENHAUER, Paula (1908–1988). German track-and-field athlete. Born Dec 22, 1908, in Germany; died July 7, 1988. ❖ At Berlin Olympics, won a bronze medal in discus throw (1936).

MOLLER, Lorraine (1955—). New Zealand long-distance runner. Born June 1955 in Putaruru, New Zealand; lives in Boulder, CO. ❖ Moved to US (1979); won Boston Marathon (1984); won Avon World championship; won Osaka International for 3 consecutive years (1986, 1987, 1988); at Barcelona Olympics, won a bronze medal in the marathon (1992), then competed in 3 more Olympics; retired from competition (1996).

MØLLERUP, Mette (1931—). Danish ballet dancer. Name variations: Mette Mollerup. Born Nov 25, 1931, in Copenhagen, Denmark; trained privately with aunt, Asta Møllerup, and later at school of Royal Danish Ballet. ❖ Joined Royal Danish Ballet (1950), appearing in range of works, including Bournonville revivals and Balanchine's *Symphony in C, La Somnambule,* and *Apollo;* appeared in Birgit Cullberg's *Medea* and also in Alfred Rodrigues' *Blood Wedding;* retired (1969).

MOLLEY, Captain (1751–c. 1800). *See Corbin, Margaret.*

MOLLISON, Amy (1903–1941). *See Johnson, Amy.*

MOLLISON, Ethel (1875–1949). *See Kelly, Ethel.*

MOLLOY, Cate (1955—). Australian politician. Name variations: Cathryn Molloy. Born May 11, 1955, in East Melbourne, Victoria, Australia. ❖ Nurse; as a member of the Australian Labor Party, elected to the Queensland Parliament for Noosa (2001).

MOLLOY, Georgiana (1805–1842). Australian botanist. Born Georgiana Kennedy, May 23, 1805, near Carlisle in Cumberland, England; died April 8, 1842, at Busselton, Western Australia, of complications following birth of 7th child; dau. of David Kennedy (country gentleman) and Mrs. Kennedy (1st name unknown), nee Graham (country gentlewoman); m. Captain John Molloy (thought to be illeg. son of the duke of York), 1829; children: 7. ❖ Amateur botanist and pioneer of the remote southwest region of Western Australia, whose collections of native Australian flora were the finest to arrive in Britain during her day; spent childhood in the Border country in genteel circumstances; upon marriage, immigrated to Swan River Colony (present-day Western Australia) to settle 1st in remote Southwest corner at Augusta, and 9 years later in slightly larger settlement of Busselton, 80 miles north; lived in isolated and relatively primitive conditions; lost 1st-born child, a daughter, several days after birth; lost 3rd-born child, a son, at 19 months; struggled out of grief by collecting native Australian flora, sending thousands of seeds and plant specimens to Captain Mangles, gentleman horticulturist, in London, over a 5-year period. ❖ See also Alexandra Hasluck, *Portrait with Background: A Life of Georgiana Molloy* (Oxford U. Press, 1979); William Lines, *An All Consuming Passion* (Allen & Unwin, 1994); and *Women in World History.*

MOLNAR, Andrea (1975—). Hungarian gymnast. Born Mar 3, 1975, in Hungary. ❖ Won a gold medal for floor and a bronze for vault at European Cup (1993); placed 9th in team all-around at Atlanta Olympics (1996).

MOLNARNE-BODO, Andrea (1934—). Hungarian gymnast. Born Aug 1934 in Hungary. ❖ At Helsinki Olympics, won a bronze medal in teams all-around, portable apparatus, and silver medal in team all-around (1952); at Melbourne Olympics, won a silver medal in team all-around and a gold medal in teams all-around, portable apparatus (1956).

MOLONY, Helena (1884–1967). Irish nationalist, actress, and labor leader. Born in Dublin, Ireland, Jan 1884; died in Dublin, Jan 28, 1967; never married. ❖ Greatly respected throughout the trade union movement, joined Inghinidhe na hEireann (Daughters of Ireland, 1903), becoming involved in teaching, acting, and radical political activism; became editor of *Bean na hEireann* (The Irishwoman), monthly paper of Inghinidhe (1908); joined the Abbey Theatre company (1909), working with them, off and on, for several years; having taken a leading part in protests against the visit of King George V and Queen Mary of Teck to Dublin (1911), was arrested and charged with high treason, a highly dramatic charge which was later reduced to "using language derogatory to His Majesty"; while performing at the Abbey (1913), became involved in the "Lock-Out," which saw thousands of Dublin workers, striking for better pay and conditions, locked out of their jobs by employers; with James Connolly, helped resuscitate the demoralized labor movement, reviving the Workers' Cooperative and reorganizing the Irish Women Workers' Union (IWWU); became secretary of IWWU; joined Irish Citizen Army and Cumann mBan (League of Women, 1914); was arrested after the Easter Rising and was one the last women prisoners to be released (Dec 1916); took an active role in struggle for independence, continuing to work for Cumann na mBan and Sinn Fein; elected to executive of the Dublin Trades Council (1929) and president of Irish Trade Union Congress (1937). ❖ See also *Women in World History.*

MOLSA, Tarquinia (1542–1617). *See Molza, Tarquinia.*

MOLTON, Flora (1908–1990). American blues and jazz singer and guitarist. Born in Louisa Co., VA, Mar 12, 1908; died in Washington, DC, May 31, 1990. ❖ Moved to Washington, DC (1937); supported herself by singing and playing on city streets; became a fixture in Washington's gospel and blues scene, playing guitar and singing in clubs and cabarets, influencing the local jazz scene for over 50 years. ❖ See also *Women in World History.*

MOLZA, Tarquinia (1542–1617). Italian philosopher and musician. Name variations: Tarquinia Molsa; Tarquinia Molza Porrina. Born Nov 1, 1542, in Modena, Italy; died 1617 in Modena; dau. of Cavaliero Camillo Molza and Isabella Colomba Molza; granddau. of poet Francesco Maria Molza; m. Paolo Porrino, 1560 (died 1579); no children. ❖ Italian beauty, wit, writer, composer, singer, musician and scholar, who lived and worked in Modena and Ferrara, was also a student of natural philosophy; as the eldest and most experienced of the women musicians at the court of Alfonso II d'Este, 5th duke of Ferrara (1583–89), was one of the court's leading intellects; was so respected by the Roman Senate that she was voted Roman citizenship to her and her heirs in perpetuity (1601).

MONA AL-HUSSEIN (1941—). *See Gardiner, Antoinette.*

MONA LISA (1474–?). *See del Giocondo, Lisa.*

MONAMI, Dominique (1973—). *See van Roost, Dominique.*

MONBART, Marie-Joséphine de Lescun (1758–1800). French novelist and essayist. Name variations: Madame Sydow. Born 1758 in France; died 1800; lived in Germany. ❖ Writings, which were often published in Berlin, include *Les loisirs d'une jeune dame* (1776), *Sophie, ou l'education des filles* (1777), *De l'education d'une princesse* (1781), *Lettres taitiennes* (1786), and *Mélanges de littérature.*

MONCEAUX, Marquise de (1573–1599). *See Estrées, Gabrielle d'.*

MONCHA. *Irish form of Monica.*

MONCK, Mary (c. 1678–1715). British poet. Name variations: Mary Molesworth; Mary Monk; (pseudonym) Marinda. Born Mary

Molesworth, c. 1678, in England; died 1715 in Bath, England; dau. of Robert Molesworth, Viscount Molesworth, and Letitia Molesworth (daughter of Richard, Lord Coote of Colooney, Ireland); m. George Monck (MP from 1703 to 1713). ❖ Wrote *Poems and Translations upon Several Occasions* (1716); best known poem is "Verses written on her Death-bed at Bath to her husband in London"; also translated Latin, Italian, and Spanish poetry.

MONCKTON, Mary (1746–1840). Irish salonnière and countess of Cork and Orrery. Born 1746 in Galway, Ireland; died in Co. Cork, Ireland, 1840; dau. of John Monckton, 1st Viscount Galway; m. Edmund Boyle, 7th earl of Cork, 1786. ❖ Following marriage, entertained some of the finest writers of late 18th and early 19th centuries, including George Gordon, Lord Byron, Sir Walter Scott, and playwright Richard Brinsley Sheridan. It has been speculated that the characters of Lady Bellair in Benjamin Disraeli's *Henrietta Temple* and Mrs. Leo Hunter in Charles Dickens' *Pickwick Papers* were based on her.

MONCKTON, Valerie (1918–2003). *See Goulding, Valerie.*

MONCRIEFF, Gladys (1892–1976). Australian actress and operatic singer. Born Gladys Lillian Moncrieff, April 13, 1892, in Bundaberg, Queensland, Australia; died Feb 8, 1976, in Gold Coast, Queensland; dau. of Amy Lambell (singer) and Reginal Moncrieff (pianist); m. Thomas Henry Moore; lived with Elsie Wilson. ❖ Made stage debut in Sydney as Josephine in *H.M.S. Pinafore* (1915) and subsequently played lead roles in all the Gilbert and Sullivan operas; came to prominence as Teresa in *The Maid of the Mountain*, followed by *Maytime, The Merry Widow, The Chocolate Soldier, The Belle of New York, Ma Mie Rosette* and the title role in *Rio Rita*; made London debut in title role of *Riki-Tiki* (1926); hugely popular in Australia (known as "Our Glad"), also sang on radio on "Gladys Moncrieff Show"; took hiatus from performing after being seriously injured in an auto accident (1938–42).

MONCRIEFF, Pérrine (1893–1979). New Zealand ornithologist, conservationist, and writer. Name variations: Pérrine Millais. Born Feb 8, 1893, in London, England; died Dec 16, 1979, at Wakapuaka, near Nelson, New Zealand; dau. of Everett Millais and Mary St Lawrence (Hope-Vere) Millais; m. Malcolm Matthew Moncrieff, 1914; children: 2 sons. ❖ Immigrated to New Zealand (1921); was a founding member of New Zealand Native Bird Protection Society (1923) and joined Royal Australasian Ornithologists' Union (RAOU); wrote *New Zealand Birds and How to Identify Them* (1925); contributed papers to RAOU's *Emu*, and articles to *Birds* and newspapers, including *Nelson Evening Mail*; active in numerous campaigns to save native bush and bird species, donating land and establishing Nelson Bush and Bird Society (1928); president of Nelson Institute and of Nelson Philosophical Society; initiated Girl Guides movement in Nelson; became justice of peace and honorary ranger for departments of Internal Affairs and Lands and Survey; published historical novel, *The Rise and Fall of David Riccio* (1976). Received Loder Cup (1953); made officer of Dutch Order of Orange-Nassau (1974); awarded CBE (1975). ❖ See also *Dictionary of New Zealand Biography* (Vol. 4).

MONEGUNDE (fl. 6th c.). Saint. Name variations: Monegund. Born in Chartres, France. ❖ Led the life of a recluse in Chartres and then in Tours, near the tomb of St. Martin of Tours. Feast day is July 2; Bishop Gregory of Tours wrote her biography.

MONEYMAKER, Kelly (1965—). American singer. Name variations: Exposé. Born June 4, 1965, in Fairbanks, Alaska. ❖ Replaced Gioia Carmen Bruno in vocal trio Exposé for group's 3rd album *Exposé* (1992), which included the hit "I'll Never Get Over You (Getting Over Me)"; started own indie label Midnite Sun Records and released solo albums, including *Like a Blackbird* and *Through the Basement Walls.*

MONGELLA, Gertrude (1945—). Tanzanian educator, politician, diplomat, and activist. Name variations: Gertrude Ibengwe Mongella. Born Sept 13, 1945, on Ukerewe, an island in Lake Victoria, Tanganyika (now United Republic of Tanzania); degree in education from Dar es Salaam University, 1970; married; children: 1 daughter, 3 sons. ❖ Internationally known for her efforts to improve the status of women, taught at Changombe Teachers College, Tanzania (1970–75); served as curriculum developer at Institute of Adult Education, Tanzania (1975–78); became one of few female members of Chama Cha Mapinduzi (Revolutionary Party); was a legislative council member (1975–82) and central committee member (1982–87); served as school inspector of Eastern Zone School District (1981–82); appointed minister of state (1982); served as head of

department of social welfare (1982–91), minister of lands, natural resources, and tourism (1985–87), and minister without portfolio (1987–91); represented Tanzania at numerous international conferences (1980s); appointed High Commissioner to India (1991); member, board of trustees of United Nations' International Research and Training Institute for the Advancement of Women (INSTRAW); served as secretary-general, Fourth United Nations World Conference on Women (1992–95). ❖ See also *Women in World History.*

MONICA (331–387). Saint and mother of St. Augustine. Name variations: St. Monica. Born in or near Thagaste (in modern Algeria) in 331; died at Ostia (in modern Italy) in 387; buried at Ostia, though her sanctified remains were later removed to Rome; m. Patrick also known as Patricius; children: probably 4, sons, Navigius and Saint Augustine of Hippo (354–430, one of the most important figures in history of Christian theology), and 2 daughters (names unknown). ❖ Orthodox Christian, who agonized over Augustine's spiritual health until he fully embraced her faith, only shortly before she died; while nominally deferring to husband, became a figure of note in local Christian community, to which she introduced her children; after death of husband (372), followed son Augustine to monitor his spiritual growth, but he rejected his Christian upbringing to dabble in philosophy and religious experimentation; when Augustine left for Italy (383) and secured for himself an appointment to teach rhetoric in Milan (384), followed him to Milan (385); joined religious community of Ambrose, orthodox bishop of Milan and perhaps the most intellectually commanding Christian thinker of his generation, and fell under the spell of his charisma; under Ambrose's influence, abandoned many of the "primitive" Christian traditions she had learned in Africa; introduced son to Ambrose who then took baptism and was transformed; with son, set sail for Africa to establish a secluded community dedicated to serious study of scripture; en route, while resting in Ostia, engaged in a tender conversation with son, long remembered and later depicted by him as a notable cap to their occasionally tempestuous relationship and a prophecy of her own death; slipped into a coma 5 days later and died. ❖ See also *Women in World History.*

MONICA (1978—). *See de Paula, Monica Angelica.*

MONICA (1980—). African-American musician. Name variations: Monica Arnold. Born Monica Denise Arnold, Oct 24, 1980, in Atlanta, GA. ❖ By age 10, was touring with gospel choir, Charles Thompson and the Majestics; at 12, was discovered by Rowdy Records producer, Dallas Austin; released debut album, *Miss Thang* (1995), which included hit singles "Don't Take It Personal (Just One of Dem Days)," "Like This and Like That," and "Why I Love You So Much"; graduated from high school with 4.0 average; signed modeling contract; released album, *The Boy Is Mine* (1998), whose title song, duet with Brandy, became 3rd-highest-selling single ever in Hot 100; other hit songs include "The First Night" (1998) and "Angel of Mine" (1999); appeared in films *Boys and Girls* (2000) and *Love Song* (2000).

MONINNE (d. 518). *See Modwenna.*

MONIQUE. *French form of Monica.*

MONK, Maria (1816–1849). Canadian writer. Born June 1, 1816 (some sources cite 1817), probably in St. John's, Quebec, Canada; died Sept 4, 1849 (some sources cite 1850), in New York, NY; dau. of William Monk (army barracks yard orderly) and Isabella (Mills) Monk; may have married twice; children: 2 daughters. ❖ Nominal author of a lurid and controversial anti-Catholic book, was confined for a time at a Catholic institution for prostitutes, located near Montreal's Hôtel Dieu Hospital and Convent and run by Hôtel Dieu nuns; at 18, was discovered to be pregnant and forced to leave (1834); met and presumably became mistress of Reverend William K. Hoyt, an anti-Catholic zealot who enlisted the aid of several fomenters associated with the *American Protestant Vindicator*, an anti-Catholic newspaper, to write Monk's "autobiography": *Awful Disclosures of Maria Monk, As Exhibited in a Narrative of Her Sufferings during a Residence of Five Years as a Novice and Two Years as a Black Nun, in the Hotel Dieu Nunnery at Montreal* (1836). ❖ See also *Women in World History.*

MONK, Mary (c. 1678–1715). *See Monck, Mary.*

MONK, Meredith (1942—). American choreographer and dancer. Born Meredith Jane Monk, Nov 20, 1942, in Lima, Peru; studied Dalcroze movement when young; Sarah Lawrence College, BA, 1964; studied dance with Mia Slavenska, Merce Cunningham, Martha Graham, and at the Ruth Mata–Eugene Hari studio and the Joffrey

School. ❖ Performed with Judson Dance Group in NY (1960s), mainly in her own works; founded interdisciplinary arts group, The House (1968), where she remains artistic director, chief choreographer and composer; began including own musical compositions and film sequences in choreography early on; also composed independent scores, mainly for vocalists, such as *Our Lady of Late* (1973); directed independent video and film projects, including *Turtle Dreams* (1983) and *Book of Days* (1989); works are often described as operas of the future; major choreographies include *Duet with Cat's Scream and Locomotive* (1966), *Education of the Girlchild* (1973), *Quarry* (1976), *Recent Ruins* (1979), *Atlas: An Opera in Three Parts* (1991); independent scores include *Raw Recital* (1970), *Fear and Loathing in Gotham* (1975), *Dolmen Music* (1980), and *Turtle Dreams* (1980–81). Won 3 Obie awards (1972, 1976, 1985), New York Dance and Performance (Bessie) award (1985), and Samuel H. Scripps American Dance Festival award (1996); received MacArthur Foundation fellowship (1995). ❖ See also Deborah Jowitt, *Meredith Monk* (1997).

MONKMAN, Phyllis (1892–1976). English theatrical ballet dancer. Born Jan 8, 1892, in London, England; died 1976. ❖ Made debut as child performer in pantomimes at Prince of Wales Theatre (c. 1904); performed at Gaiety Theatre where she was featured in *The Belle of Mayfair* (1907), *The Quaker Girl* (1910), *The Monte Carlo Girl* (1912), and others; was principal dancer at Alhambra Theater (1913–16), dancing opposite Harry Pilcer in *5064 Gerrard* and *Keep Smiling!*; appeared in numerous West End musicals, including *See-Saw* (1912), *The Sunshine Sisters* (1930), and several editions of *The Co-Optomists*; retired as a dancer (c. 1935), but continued to work as comedian thereafter.

MONNET, Marie Moreau (1752–1798). French short-story writer. Born 1752 in La Rochelle, France; died 1798. ❖ Wrote *Contes orientaux* (1772), *Histoire d'Abdal Mazour* (1784), *Lettres de Jenny Bleinmore* (1787) and *Essai en vers* (1788); also contributed to *Mercure*.

MONNIER, Adrienne (c. 1892–1955). French bookseller, writer, and publisher. Born c. 1892; committed suicide in France on June 19, 1955, a victim of Mènière's syndrome (aural disturbances of inner ear); dau. of Clovis Monnier; elder sister of Marie Monnier; companion of bookseller Sylvia Beach. ❖ Founded Maison des Amis Livres (The House of the Friends of Books, 1915), where she sold works of significant new French writers; bookshop became a French literary center, frequented by the likes of André Gide, Jean Schlumberger, Paul Valéry, Jean-Paul Fargue, Erik Satie, Valéry Larbaud and Jules Romain; was also responsible for the French language publication of *Ulysses* and the costly, short-lived magazine *Le Navire d'Argent*. ❖ See also autobiography *The Very Rich Hours of Adrienne Monnier* (trans. by Richard McDougall, Bison, 1996); and *Women in World History*.

MONNOT, Marguerite (1903–1961). French songwriter. Born Marguerite Angèle Monnot, May 28, 1903, in Decize Nièvre, France; died Oct 12, 1961, in Paris; dau. of Marius Monnot (blind organist and composer); studied organ and composition with father; studied piano with Alfred Cortot and harmony with Nadia Boulanger. ❖ At 3, made debut as a pianist; also began writing compositions at young age; moved to US and cut short performing career; as a composer, scored 1st hit with "L'Etranger" for Annette Lajon, receiving Grand Prix du Disque from French Academy (1935); worked with lyricist and cabaret pianist Raymond Asso, writing melody for many hits, including "Mon legionnaire," 1st sung by Marie Dubas and later Edith Piaf; collaborated with Piaf on "L'Hymne à l'amour" and "C'etait un jour de fête," with Charles Dumont on "Les Amants d'un jour," with René Rouzaud on "La goualante du pauvre Jean" (rerecorded by Les Baxter as "The Poor People of Paris") and with Henri Contet on "Ma mome, Ma p'tite môme," all sung by Piaf; had huge success with musical *Irma la Douce* (1960), for which she was nominated for a Tony Award; with lyricist George Moustaki, wrote the hit "Milord"; other songs include "Paris Méditerranée," "J'ai dansé avec l'amour," "C'est un monsieur trés distingué," "Tu es partout," "C'est à Hambourg," "Le petite monsieur triste," and "Escale."

MONOD, Sarah (1836–1912). French philanthropist and feminist. Pronunciation: mo-NO. Born 1836; died 1912; dau. of a pastor. ❖ Was a field-hospital nurse during Franco-Prussian War (1870–71), long the editor of *La Femme* (1878—), and a leading participant in many philanthropic enterprises and social causes, from promoting world peace and public health to combating juvenile delinquency, alcoholism, pornography, and prostitution; founded the Versailles Conferences (1891), which annually brought together leaders of Protestant women's charitable organizations; at Paris Exposition (1900), presided over Second Congress of Feminine Works and Institutions (June 18–27), for which the Versailles Conference had taken the initiative; was the 1st president of National Council of French Women (CNFF), an umbrella federation of many kinds of women's organizations. ❖ See also *Women in World History*.

MONPLAISIR, Emma (1918—). Martiniquan novelist. Born 1918 in French Antilles; dau. of a French mother and Martiniquan father; grew up in Martinique. ❖ Works include *Cric Crac Martinique* (1957), *La Fille du Caraïbe* (1960), *Martinique et ses danses* (1962), and *Christophe Colomb chez les Indiens*.

MONROE, Eliza Kortright (1786–1840). American first daughter. Name variations: Eliza Monroe Hay. Born Dec 5, 1786 (some sources cite 1787) in Fredericksburg, VA; died 1840 in Paris, France; buried in Pere LaChaise Cemetery, Paris; dau. of James Monroe (1758–1831, 5th US president) and Elizabeth (Kortright) Monroe (1768–1830); sister of Maria Hester Monroe (1803–1850); m. Judge George Hay (conducted the prosecution for treason of Aaron Burr), 1808 (died 1830); children: Hortensia Hay (who married Nicholas Lloyd Rogers). ❖ With mother, changed White House customs to promote the formal atmosphere of European courts.

MONROE, Elizabeth (1768–1830). American first lady. Born Elizabeth Kortright, June 30, 1768, in New York, NY; died Sept 23, 1830, in Oak Hill, Virginia; dau. of Hannah (Aspinwall) Kortright and Captain Laurence Kortright (merchant and a founder of New York Chamber of Commerce); sister of Hester Kortright Gouverneur; m. James Monroe (later president of US), Feb 16, 1786; children: Eliza Kortright Monroe (1786–1840) and Maria Hester Monroe (1803–1850); and a son who died in infancy. ❖ First lady (1817–1825) who had enjoyed success as a diplomat's wife but whose years in the White House were marred by ill health and misunderstanding; for 17 years, while husband served as legislator, governor of Virginia, and ambassador to France, England and Spain, accompanied him to his foreign posts and gained a reputation as an elegant, charming hostess; suffering from rheumatism by the time husband was elected president (1817), curtailed social duties and greeted guests with European formality, sitting on a raised platform; was thought to be haughty and aloof; is credited, however, with restoring the executive mansion with the addition of exquisite French imports, providing an elegant backdrop for state occasions. ❖ See also *Women in World History*.

MONROE, Harriet (1860–1936). American poet, essayist, and periodical founder. Born Harriet Monroe, Dec 23, 1860, in Chicago, Illinois; died Sept 26, 1936, in Arequipa, Peru; dau. of Henry S. Monroe (a lawyer) and Martha Mitchell Monroe; sister of Lucy Monroe Calhoun and Dora Monroe Root; graduated high school from Visitation Convent of Georgetown in Washington, DC, 1879; never married; no children. ❖ Publisher who revived enthusiasm for verse through the pages of *Poetry,* the magazine she founded and edited until her death; served as art critic and travel writer for the *Chicago Tribune* and other papers; was commissioned to write the official poem ("Columbian Ode") for the dedication of Chicago's World Columbian Exposition (1892); founded the spectacularly successful *Poetry: A Magazine of Verse* (1912), offering poets "a chance to be heard" by an audience that regarded poetry as art not filler, promising to publish the best poetry regardless of style or source, and pledging to regard poets as professionals and pay authors for their work; stunned the American audience with the work of Hamlin Garland, Conrad Aiken, Ezra Pound, Rupert Brooke, Marianne Moore, Robert Frost, Amy Lowell, Vachel Lindsay, Hilda Doolittle (H.D.), T.S. Eliot, William Butler Yeats, William Carlos Williams, e.e. cummings, and others; introduced Americans to new artistic movements such as Imagism. ❖ See also Ellen Williams, *Harriet Monroe and the Poetry Renaissance: The First Ten Years of Poetry, 1912–22* (U. of Illinois Press, 1977); and *Women in World History*.

MONROE, Jessica (1966—). Canadian rower. Born May 31, 1966, in Palo Alto, CA; moved to Canada (1972). ❖ At Barcelona Olympics, won a gold medal in coxed eights and a gold medal in coxed fours (1992); won a silver medal for coxed eights at Atlanta Olympics (1996).

MONROE, Maria Hester (1803–1850). American first daughter. Name variations: Mrs. Samuel L. Gouverneur; Hester Kortright Gouverneur. Born 1803 in Paris, France; died 1850 in Oak Hill, VA; dau. of James Monroe (5th US president) and Elizabeth (Kortright) Monroe (1768–1830); sister of Eliza Kortright Monroe (1786–1840); m. Samuel Laurence Gouverneur (member of NY State legislature and postmaster of NYC), 1820 (died 1867); children: James Monroe Gouverneur (1822–1865); Samuel Laurence Gouverneur (1826–1880); Elizabeth

Kortright Gouverneur (1824–1868). ❖ Was the 1st daughter of a US president to be married in the White House (Mar 9, 1820).

MONROE, Marilyn (1926–1962). American actress. Name variations: Norma Jeane Mortonson or Mortensen; Norma Jean Mortonson; Norma Jeane Baker. Born June 1, 1926, in Los Angeles, CA; died of a drug overdose, Aug 4, 1962, in Los Angeles; dau. of Gladys Baker Mortonson (also seen as Mortensen) and possibly C. Stanley Gifford (salesman); m. Jim Dougherty, June 19, 1942 (div. 1946); m. Joe DiMaggio (baseball player), Jan 14, 1954 (div. autumn 1954); m. Arthur Miller (playwright), June 29, 1956 (div. Jan 1961); no children. ❖ One of the last stars of the Hollywood studio system and the most enduring of American cultural icons, whose appeal and allure have extended far beyond her brief life, was hired as a freelance model (1943) and appeared on covers of over 30 magazines within a year; signed with 20th Century-Fox (1946), but had no say over early roles in such films as *Dangerous Years* and *Scudda-Hoo! Scudda-Hay!* (both 1948); signed with Columbia (1949), but contract lapsed; unemployed, posed nude for $50; won a small part in Marx Brothers' *Love Happy* (1950), the 1st film to capture her high-pitched, childlike voice that would become her trademark, and her sensual walk; received positive reviews for *The Asphalt Jungle* (1950); became "pin-up girl" of choice and appeared on cover of *Look* magazine (1951); made a dozen "B" movies in succession, most of them forgettable, except for *Don't Bother to Knock* (1952); had breakout year (1953), with classic performance as Lorelei Lee in *Gentlemen Prefer Blondes*, followed by *How to Marry a Millionaire*; made *River of No Return* (1954), *There's No Business Like Show Business* (1954) and *The Seven Year Itch* (1955); moved to NY to study with Lee Strasberg at Actors Studio; filmed *Bus Stop* (1956), *The Prince and the Showgirl* (1957), *Some Like it Hot* (1958), *Let's Make Love* (1960) and *The Misfits* (1961); became acquainted with John F. Kennedy (to whom she so famously sang "Happy Birthday"); was fired from *Something's Got to Give* (1962), then found dead 2 months later (it is possible, though not probable, that she did not give herself the last dose). ❖ See also Norman Mailer, *Marilyn* (Grosset, 1973); Gloria Steinem, *Marilyn* (Holt, 1986); Barbara Leaming, *Marilyn Monroe* (Crown); Anthony Summers, *Goddess: The Secret Lives of Marilyn Monroe* (Macmillan, 1985); and *Women in World History*.

MONS, Anna (d. 1714). Russian paramour. Born Anna Mons, probably in Moscow, during 1670s; died in Moscow, Aug 1714; dau. of Johann Mons (sometimes seen as Monst or Munst), a German innkeeper in Moscow; no formal education; m. M. de Kaiserling (Keyserling), 1711; mistress of Peter I the Great (1672–1725), tsar of Russia (r. 1682–1725), from 1691 to 1703; no known children. ❖ Longtime mistress of Tsar Peter I the Great of Russia (1691–1703), who, through greed and jealousy, lost his affection as well as many of the perquisites he had bestowed upon her. ❖ See also *Women in World History*.

MONSERDÀ DE MACÍA, Dolors (1845–1919). Spanish novelist. Name variations: Dolors Monserda de Macia. Born 1845 in Catalonia, Spain; died 1919. ❖ Wrote realist novels about problems of working class and corruption in upper classes of Catalan society.

MONSTIERS-MÉRINVILLE, Marquise des (1863–1909). *See Caldwell, Mary Gwendolin.*

MONTACUTE. *Variant of Montagu.*

MONTACUTE, Alice (c. 1406–1463). Duchess of Salisbury. Name variations: Alice Neville. Born c. 1406; died 1463; dau. of Thomas Montacute, 4th earl of Salisbury, and Eleanor Holland (c. 1385–?); m. Richard Neville, 1st earl of Salisbury, before 1428; children: Richard Neville (1428–1471), earl of Warwick (known as Warwick the Kingmaker); Thomas Neville (d. 1460); John Neville (1431–1471), marquess of Montagu; George Neville (c. 1433–1476), archbishop of York; Ralph Neville; Robert Neville; Joan Neville (who m. William Fitzalan, 13th earl of Arundel); Cecily Neville (who m. Henry Beauchamp, duke and 6th earl of Warwick, and John Tiptoft, 1st earl of Worcester); Alice Neville (who m. Henry Fitzhugh, 5th Lord Fitzhugh of Ravensworth); Eleanor Neville (who m. Thomas Stanley, earl of Derby); Catherine Neville (who m. William Bonville, Lord Harrington, and William Hastings, Lord Hastings); Margaret Neville (who m. John de Vere, 13th earl of Oxford, and William Hastings, Lord Hastings).

MONTACUTE, Anne (d. 1457). Duchess of Exeter. Name variations: Anne Hankford; Anne Holland; Anne of Salisbury. Died Nov 28, 1457; interred at St. Katherine by the Tower, London; dau. of John Montacute, 3rd earl of Salisbury, and Maud Montacute; m. Richard Hankford (1397–1430); became 3rd wife of John Holland (1395–1447), duke of Huntington (r. 1416–1447), duke of Exeter (r. 1443–1447); children: (1st m.) Anne Hankford (1431–1485); Thomasine Hankford, Baroness Fitz-Waryn (1422–1453). ❖ *The Complete Peerage* makes it clear that John Holland's 1st wife Anne Stafford (d. 1432) was the mother of Anne Holland and not Anne Montacute as shown in other sources. John Holland's 2nd wife was Beatrice of Portugal (d. 1439).

MONTACUTE, Eleanor (c. 1385–?). *See Holland, Eleanor.*

MONTACUTE, Elizabeth. *See Mohun, Elizabeth.*

MONTACUTE, Joan (fl. 1300s). Countess of Suffolk. Name variations: Joan de Ufford. Dau. of Edward Montacute, Baron Montacute, and Alice Plantagenet (d. 1351, granddau. of Edward I, king of England); m. William de Ufford (c. 1330–1382), 2nd earl of Suffolk.

MONTACUTE, Margaret (fl. 1400s). Baroness Ferrers of Groby. Name variations: Margaret de Montagu. Dau. of John Montacute, 3rd earl of Salisbury, and Maud Montacute (fl. 1380s); m. William Ferrers (d. 1445), 5th baron Ferrers of Groby. ❖ William Ferrers' 2nd wife was Philippa Clifford, the mother of Henry Ferrers (d. 1394).

MONTACUTE, Maud (fl. 1380s). Countess of Salisbury. Name variations: Maud de Montagu; Maud Fraunceys. Born Maud Francis or Maud Fraunceys; m. John Montacute, 3rd earl of Salisbury; children: Anne Montacute (d. 1457), duchess of Exeter; Thomas Montacute, 4th earl of Salisbury (1388–1428); Margaret Montacute, Baroness Ferrers of Groby.

MONTACUTE, Philippa (fl. 1352). Countess of March. Name variations: Philippa Mortimer. Dau. of William Montacute, 1st earl of Salisbury, and Katharine Grandison; m. Roger Mortimer (1328–1359), Baron Mortimer of Wigmore and 2nd earl of March; children: Edmund Mortimer (1352–1381), 3rd earl of March and earl of Ulster.

MONTAGU. *Variant of Montacute.*

MONTAGU, Elizabeth (1720–1800). British socialite and author. Name variations: Elizabeth Robinson in York, Oct 2, 1720; died in London, Aug 25, 1800; eldest dau. of Matthew Robinson (Yorkshire landowner) and Elizabeth Drake Robinson (Cambridge heiress); sister of Sarah Scott (1723–1795, then a well-known novelist); cousin by marriage of Lady Mary Wortley Montagu (1689–1762); education supervised by her grandfather Dr. Conyers Middleton, a Cambridge scholar; m. Edward Montagu (scholar), 1742 (died 1775); children: John (1743–1744). ❖ One of London's foremost intellectual hostesses, was an early member of the Bluestocking Circle; began giving receptions in her famous Chinese Room (1748), with such guests as Margaret Cavendish Harley, countess of Oxford, Elizabeth Carter, Catherine Talbot, Elizabeth Vesey, Mary Delany, Fanny Boscawen, Anna Seward, Hester Chapone, Edmund Burke, Joshua Reynolds, Lord Lyttelton, David Garrick, Fanny Burney, and Hannah More, as well as Samuel Johnson, Horace Walpole and, once, King George III; for 50 years, despite all competitors, remained the preeminent host of intellectual gatherings in London; was the anonymous author of *Essay on the Writings and Genius of Shakespeare* (1769) and 3 dialogues in Lyttelton's *Dialogues of the Dead* (1760). Her nephew, Matthew Montagu, oversaw publication of her letters, which ran to 4 vols. (1809 and 1813). ❖ See also *Women in World History*.

MONTAGU, Elizabeth (1909–2002). English actress. Born Sept 26, 1909, in London, England; died May 2002 in Hampshire, England; dau. of Lord Montagu of Beaulieu and Lady Cecil (Kerr) Montagu. ❖ Made stage debut with the Newcastle Rep in *Well Caught* (1932); made London debut as Nadine Browning in *Beggars in Hell* (1933); other plays include *Other People's Lives*, *Private Room*, *Dark Horizon*, *Viceroy Sarah* and *Mesmer*.

MONTAGU, Helen (1928–2004). Australian-born theatrical producer. Born April 21, 1928, in Sydney, Australia; died Jan 1, 2004, in London, England; dau. of an Australian banker; attended University of Sydney and Central School of Speech and Drama in London; m. Russell Willett (psychologist), 1953; children: Amanda, Sara, Louisa and Johnnie. ❖ The 1st woman to become a major West End producer, began career as an actress; became casting director (1965), then general manager at the Royal Court; was managing director of the play-production company, HM Tennent (1975–77); became head of Backstage Productions (1977), then formed her own company, Helen Montagu Productions; produced a diverse crop of plays, including Lindsay Anderson's production of *The Seagull* (1975), Ben Travers' *The Bed Before Yesterday* (1975), Zeffirelli's *Filumena* (1977), *42nd Street* (1989), *Hot Shoe Shuffle* (1994) and *Prisoner: Cell Block H* (1995).

MONTAGU, Lady Mary Wortley (1689–1762). English aristocrat and intellectual. Name variations: Mary Wortley-Montagu. Born Mary Pierrepont in London, England, May 1689; died of breast cancer, Aug 21, 1762; eldest dau. of Evelyn Pierrepont, earl of Kingston, and Lady Mary Pierrepont (dau. of William Fielding, earl of Denbigh); privately tutored and self taught; cousin by marriage to Elizabeth Montagu (1720–1800); m. Edward Wortley Montagu, Aug 1712; children: Edward Wortley Montagu (1713–1776, author and traveler); Mary, Countess of Bute (b. 1718). ❖ Self-taught aristocrat of keen intelligence and sparkling wit, whose most enduring legacy can be found in her hundreds of surviving letters which incisively describe the mores of English high society, the mysteries of the East, and the life of an aristocratic exile in 18th-century Italy and France; showed a passion for learning in childhood and acquired considerable skill in languages, including Latin, though she had little formal instruction; pressured by father to marry a man of suitable social status, eloped to marry the man she loved, at age 23 (1712); accompanied husband to a diplomatic posting in Turkey (1716), taking her young son and giving birth to her daughter before they returned to England (1718); fell deeply in love with a young Italian scholar, Francesco Algarotti (1736) and left England to be with him; spent the next 22 years on the Continent, returning to England 8 months before she died (1762); letters and poetry published only after her death, bringing her literary fame. ❖ See also *Letters of the Right Honourable Lady M—y W—y M—e: Written during her Travels in Europe, Asia and Africa . . . .* (2 vols., T. Cadell, 1789); Robert Halsband, *The Life of Lady Mary Wortley Montagu* (Oxford U. Press, 1961); Cynthia Lowenthal, *Lady Mary Wortley Montagu and the Eighteenth Century Familiar Letter* (U. of Georgia Press, 1994); and *Women in World History.*

MONTAGU-DOUGLAS-SCOTT, Alice (1901–2004). Duchess of Gloucester. Name variations: Princess Alice, duchess of Gloucester. Born Alice Christabel Montagu-Douglas-Scott on Dec 25, 1901; died Oct 29, 2004, at Buckingham Palace; dau. of John Montagu-Douglas-Scott, 7th duke of Buccleuch and Queensbury, and Margaret Bridgeman; m. Henry Windsor (1900–1974), 1st duke of Gloucester (3rd son of George V and Mary of Teck), Nov 6, 1935; children: William Windsor also known as Prince William of Gloucester (1941–1973); Richard Windsor (b. 1944), 2nd duke of Gloucester. ❖ Helped lift morale on homefront during WWII; lived in Australia with husband while he was governor general there (1945–47); returned to England and maintained official duties until her death. ❖ See also *The Memoirs of Princess Alice, Duchess of Gloucester* (1983).

MONTALBA, Clara (1842–1929). English artist. Born in Cheltenham, England, 1842; died 1929; dau. of Antony Montalba and Emiline Montalba; studied with Eugene Isabey in Paris for 4 years; sister of artists Henrietta Skerrett Montalba (1856–1893), Ellen Montalba (fl. 1868–1902), and Hilda Montalba (d. 1919). ❖ Landscape and marine painter, made associate of London Society of Painters in Water Colors (1874) and of Belgian Society (1876); lived in Venice for many years, painting several Venetian scenes.

MONTALBA, Henrietta Skerrett (1856–1893). English sculptor. Born in London, England, 1856; died in Venice, Sept 14, 1893; dau. of Antony Montalba and Emiline Montalba; sister of Clara Montalba (1842–1929), Ellen Montalba (fl. 1868–1902), and Hilda Montalba (d. 1919); studied at South Kensington, at the Belle Arti in Venice, and with Jules Dalou in London. ❖ Excelling in portrait and "fancy" busts, had 1st exhibition at Royal Academy (1876); did a portrait bust of Robert Browning in terracotta (1883); other works include *A Dalecarlian Peasant Woman, The Raven,* and *A Venetian Boy Catching a Crab* (1893), which was exhibited in London and at International Exhibition in Chicago.

MONTALCINI, Rita Levi (b. 1909). See *Levi-Montalcini, Rita.*

MONTANA, Patsy (1909–1996). American country-and-western singer. Born Rubye Blevins in Jesseville, Arkansas, 1909; died of heart failure, May 3, 1996, in San Jacinto, CA. ❖ The 1st successful woman in country-and-western music and the 1st female country singer to dress in full cowgirl regalia (boots, hat, and fringe), was known for yodeling songs; was also the 1st to sell over 1 million records, with her own composition, "I Want to Be a Cowboy's Sweetheart" (1936); got her start on WLS "National Barn Dance" in Chicago, becoming a 15-year program mainstay with the Prairie Ramblers; had a great influence on the style of many women singers who followed, including that of Patsy Cline. ❖ See also *Women in World History.*

MONTANARIA (fl. 1272). Bolognese illuminator. Flourished in Bologna, Italy. ❖ A manuscript calligrapher, is referred to as "Montanaria, wife of Onesto" in a business contract dated 1272 from Bologna, the flourishing intellectual center of Italy in the 13th century.

MONTANCLOS, Marie-Emilie Maryon de (1736–1812). French journalist, feminist and playwright. Name variations: Mme de Montaclos; Baronne de Prinzen or Princen. Born 1736 in Aix, France; died 1812; married (died); married (legally sep.). ❖ Succeeded Catherine Michelle de Maisonneuve as editor of *Journal des Dames* (1774), where she defended rights of women to education and independence, criticized frivolity of court, and re-evaluated motherhood as important role for women; plays include *Le choix des fées* (1782), *Le fauteuil* (1799), *Robert le bossu* (1799), *Alison et Sylvain* (1803), and *La Bonne maîtresse* (1804); prose writing published as *Oeuvres diverses* (1791); several pieces published in newspapers during Revolution and signed Madame de M. may have been written by her.

MONTANSIER, Marguerite (1730–1820). French actress, theater manager and salon hostess. Name variations: Marguerite Brunet; Mademoiselle or Mlle Montansier. Born Marguerite Brunet, Dec 19, 1730, in Bayonne, France; died July 13, 1820, in Paris; studied at Convent of Ursulines of Bordeaux; m. Honoré Bourdon de Neuville (actor). ❖ Prominent figure during ancien régime and after French Revolution, lived with an aunt who owned a fashionable shop named Montansier; taking the name, began an unsuccessful career as an actress; with support of Queen Marie Antoinette, became manager of Théâter de Versailles (1768), then built a new theater at Versaille, Théâter Montansier; opened several provincial theaters and effectively controlled all theatrical productions in northern France; went to Paris at outbreak of Revolution, where she presided over salon situated in the foyer of her Theatre National in the Palais-Royal; accused of being a Royalist, was imprisoned for 10 months (1794) but saved from guillotine during 9th Thermidor coup; opened the Variétés Montansier theatre (1795); was given the task of reorganizing the Italian opera by Napoleon; dominated Parisian theatre life for over 50 years.

MONTE, Hilda (1914–1945). German-Jewish journalist and anti-Nazi activist. Name variations: Eva Schneider; Hilde Meisel-Olday. Born Hilde Meisel in Vienna, Austria, July 31, 1914; shot in Feldkirch while trying to escape, April 18, 1945; had marriage of convenience with John Olday (British anarchist writer and artist). ❖ In exile in England, contributed articles to *The Vanguard, Tribune, Left News* and other radical journals; during WWII, published several well-received books, including *Help Germany to Revolt!* (1942), written with Hellmut von Rauschenplat, and *The Unity of Europe* (1943); joined a group that included Josef Kappius and others who trained for OSS secret missions on the Continent (1944); went to Switzerland in order to enter Nazi Germany, establishing contacts in Swiss Tessin region with members of Austrian Resistance (1944); using alias Eva Schneider, was captured in Feldkirch (Austrian Vorarlberg) on Austro-German border (1945), during final weeks of the war. ❖ See also *Women in World History.*

MONTEALEGRE, Felicia (d. 1978). Costa Rican-born stage and tv actress. Name variations: Felicia Bernstein. Born in Costa Rica; died June 16, 1978, in East Hampton, LI, NY; m. Leonard Bernstein (composer, conductor). ❖ Made stage debut in Chile; arrived in NYC (1944); appeared in such plays as *If Five Years Pass, Swan Song, Merchant of Venice, International Set, Henry V, Pelleas and Melisande, The Little Foxes* and *Poor Murderers;* on tv, starred opposite Charlton Heston in "Of Human Bondage" for "Studio One" (1949), among others.

MONTEFELTRO, Elisabetta (fl. 15th c.). Noblewoman of Urbino. Name variations: Elisabetta Malatesta. Dau. of Federigo Montefeltro, duke of Urbino, and Battista Sforza (1446–1472); m. Roberto Malatesta.

MONTEFELTRO, Elisabetta (1471–1526). Duchess of Urbino. Name variations: Elisabetta Gonzaga; Elisabeth or Elizabeth Gonzaga. Born in 1471; died in 1526; dau. of Frederigo also known as Federico Gonzaga (1441–1484), 3rd marquis of Mantua (r. 1478–1484), and Margaret of Bavaria (1445–1479); sister of Francesco Gonzaga, Maddalena Sforza (1472–1490), and Chiara Gonzaga (1465–1505); sister-in-law of Isabella d'Este (1474–1539); m. Guidobaldo Montefeltro (1472–1508), duke of Urbino. ❖ As the younger sister of Marchese Francesco Gonzaga, ruler of Mantua, showed considerable interest in the arts as well as in humanist scholarship; at 17, married the 16-year-old duke of Urbino; led a court which was widely known for its magnificence, and for the talent of the artists and scholars it attracted and patronized, including Unico Aretino and Pietro Bembo, both of whom became famous for their poetry, much of which was dedicated to her; maintained a close relationship with her sister-in-law Isabella d'Este, marchioness of Mantua; following husband's death (1508), remained at the center of Urbino's intellectual and social life for the rest of her days; is best known from the descriptions of her in the Renaissance treatise on the aristocracy, Castiglione's *The Book of the Courtier*. ❖ See also *Women in World History*.

MONTEFELTRO, Giovanna (fl. 15th c.). Noblewoman of Urbino. Name variations: Giovanna della Rovere. Dau. of Federigo Montefeltro, duke of Urbino, and Battista Sforza (1446–1472); m. Giovanni della Rovere (1458–1501); children: Francesco Maria della Rovere (1490–1538, who m. Eleonora Gonzaga [1493–1543]).

MONTEFELTRO, Isotta (1425–1456). *See Este, Isotta d'.*

MONTEMAYOR, Alice Dickerson (1902–1989). Mexican-American civic leader and painter. Name variations: Alicia Dickerson Montemayor; (pseudonym) ADMonty or Admonty. Born Alice Dickerson, Aug 6, 1902, in Laredo, TX; died May 13, 1989, in Laredo; dau. of John Randolph Dickerson and Manuela (Barrera) Dickerson; m. Francisco Montemayor, Sept 8, 1927; children: 2 sons. ❖ Was a social worker in Webb Co. (1934–49), working with Mexican Americans; elected 2nd national vice-president general of the League of United Latin American Citizens (LULAC, 1937), the 1st woman to hold a national office not specifically designated for women; became the 1st woman associate editor of *LULAC News*; also served as director of Junior LULAC; signing her works ADMonty or Admonty, began to establish herself as a folk artist (1974) and had many solo shows.

MONTENEGRO, queen of. *See Milena (1847–1923).*

MONTEREY, Carlotta (1888–1970). *See O'Neill, Carlotta.*

MONTES, Lola (1818–1861). *See Montez, Lola.*

MONTESI, Wilma (1932–1953). Italian model and murder victim. Born in Rome, Italy, 1932; died in Rome, April 1953. ❖ A 21-year-old model whose unsolved murder set off a chain of events that nearly destroyed the government of Italian prime minister Mario Scelba. ❖ See also *Women in World History*.

MONTESINO, Violante (1601–1693). *See Violante do Céu.*

MONTESPAN, Françoise, Marquise de (1640–1707). French royal mistress. Name variations: Athénaïs or Athenais; Madame de Montespan. Pronunciation: Fran-SWAHZ mar-KAY-sa der MOHN-TES-PAH. Born Françoise de Rochechouart de Mortemart, Oct 5, 1640, in the Château de Lussac near Lussac-les-Châteaux (Vienne); died at Bourbon-l'Archambault (Allier), May 27, 1707, probably of heart disease and an overdose of emetic; dau. of Gabriel de Rochechouart, marquis (later duke) de Mortemart, and Diane de Grandseigne (d. 1666); sister of Gabrielle de Rochechouart (abbess); educated at Convent of Sainte-Marie at Saintes (Charente-Maritime); m. Louis-Henry de Pardaillan de Gondrin, marquis de Montespan, 1663; children: (with husband) Marie-Christine (1663–1675), Louis-Antoine, marquis (later duke) d'Antin (1665–1736); (with Louis XIV, king of France [r. 1643–1715]) Louise (1669–1672), Louis-Auguste de Bourbon (1670–1736), duke of Maine, Louis-César de Bourbon (1672–1683), count of Vexin, Louise-Françoise de Bourbon (1673–1743), countess of Nantes, Louise-Marie-Anne de Bourbon (1674–1681), countess of Tours, Françoise-Marie de Bourbon (1677–1749), countess of Blois, Louis-Alexandre de Bourbon (1678–1737), count of Toulouse. ❖ Brilliant mistress of Louis XIV, during his most successful years, who lived a life of splendor, scandal, and sincere repentance; came to court (1660); married the Marquis de Montespan (1663); became Louis XIV's mistress (1667); shared Louis during the "Reign of the Three Queens" (1668–74); separated from husband (1674); under Church pressure, ceased sexual relations with Louis (1675–76); probably ceased relations with Louis permanently (1678); secretly implicated in the Poisons affair (1680–81); for over 30 years (1660–91), was a striking presence at the court of France's Sun King, and for at least 11 (1667–78), had been its true queen; took over supervision of the Daughters of Saint Joseph (1681); left the court (1691); founded Hospice of the Holy Family (1693); transferred the Hospice to her Château d'Oiron (1703). ❖ See also H. Noël Williams, *Madame de Montespan and Louis XIV* (Scribner, 1910); and *Women in World History*.

MONTESSON, Charlotte Jeanne Béraud de la Haye de Riou, marquise de (1737–1805). Duchess of Orléans. Name variations: Charlotte de la Haye. Born in Paris of an old Breton family, 1737 (some sources cite 1736); died Feb 8, 1805 (some sources cite 1806); dau. of Johann Béraud de la Haye; m. Jean Baptiste, marquis de Montesson, c. 1754 (d. 1769);

m. Louis Philippe (1725–1785), 4th duke of Orléans (r. 1752–1785), July 29, 1773. Louis Philippe's 1st wife was Louisa Henrietta de Conti (1726–1759). ❖ Following 1st husband's death (1769), attracted the attention of Louis Philippe, duke of Orléans, whom she secretly married (1773) with authorization of King Louis XV; for husband's amusement, wrote and acted in several plays, including *Mme de Chazelle*; imprisoned for some time during the Terror but released after the fall of Robespierre, became a close friend of Empress Josephine and was a prominent figure at the beginning of the empire; poetry was published as *Mélanges de poésie* (1782); plays appeared in 7 vols. as *Oeuvres anonymes* (1782–85), though only 12 copies were printed.

MONTESSORI, Maria (1870–1952). Italian doctor, scientist and pioneer children's educator. Pronunciation: Mont-ES-OR-ee. Born Maria Montessori, Aug 31, 1870, in Chiaravalle, near Ancona, Italy; died May 6, 1952, at Noordwijk-on-Sea, Holland; only child of Alessandro Montessori (soldier and civil servant) and Renilde Stoppani; University of Rome, Doctor of Medicine, 1890; never married; children: Mario (b. 1898 or 1901). ❖ Enormously influential educator of children, qualified as the 1st female MD to be licensed in Italy (1896); appointed an assistant doctor in Rome University's psychiatric clinic (1896); served as 1st director of Orthophrenic school, which provided facilities to train teachers in special needs of retarded children; named chair of anthropology at Rome University (1904), while continuing her medical practice in various clinics and hospitals throughout city; assumed responsibility for a small school for younger children (aged 3 to 6) in San Lorenzo quarter of Rome (1906); over next 3 years, became convinced that there were certain important and identifiable characteristics of childhood which were hidden or denied by traditional educational methods and began to develop her "Montessori Method"; published series of books in Italian (1909), seeking to explain the apparent success of her methods, books that were translated into over 20 languages; became an international celebrity, receiving numerous requests to tour abroad and lecture; book *The Montessori Method: Scientific Pedagogy as Applied to Child Education in the "Children's Houses"* was published in US (1911), attracting widespread interest and becoming a bestseller; conducted cross-country series of lectures in US (1914), then returned to California (1915) to organize the 1st special training courses for teachers; her ideas found increasingly enthusiastic support throughout the world; in Italy, because she refused to require children to wear a special uniform and give the fascist salute each morning, saw all her schools and centers closed (1934); spent war years in India. ❖ See also Rita Kramer, *Maria Montessori* (U. of Chicago Press, 1976); E.M. Standing, *Maria Montessori: Her Life and Work* (Mentor, 1954); and *Women in World History*.

MONTEZ, Lola (1818–1861). Irish-born dancer, actress, courtesan and adventurer. Name variations: Maria-Dolores Porris y Montes; Marie de Landsfeld Heald; Lolla Montes; Mrs. Eliza Gilbert; Countess of Landsfeld. Born Maria Dolores Eliza Rosanna Gilbert in Limerick, Ireland, 1818; died Jan 17, 1861, in New York, NY; dau. of Edward Gilbert (Irish officer in British army), and a mother, name unknown, who was the illeg. dau. of Irish noble Charles Oliver; m. Thomas James, July 23, 1837 (div. 1842); m. George Trafford Heald, 1849 (died 1851); m. Patrick Purdy Hull, July 2, 1853 (sep. soon after); no children. ❖ Legendary figure, was taken to India as an infant (1819); sent to Scotland for her education after father's death and mother's remarriage (1826); moved to Bath (1830); eloped and moved to India with 1st husband (1837); returned to England and obtained a divorce (1842); made stage debut in London billed as "Donna Lola Montez of the Teatro Real in Seville," performing a dance called "El Oleano," which would remain in her repertoire throughout stage career (1843); aware of the value of publicity, was skilled at keeping her name in the papers; had affair with Franz Liszt (1843–45); was mistress of King Ludwig I of Bavaria, enjoying remarkable power behind the throne (1846–48); immigrated to America and made NY stage debut (1851); toured eastern US in a play based on her German adventures, *Lola Montez in Bavaria* (1852–53); following San Francisco debut, performed in California mining camps (1853); following 3rd marriage, took up residence in Grass Valley, CA (1853–55); made Australian stage tour (1855); made lecture tour of Ireland and England (1858–59); returned to NY (late 1859); felled by a stroke (1860). ❖ See also Edmund D'Auvergne, *Lola Montez: An Adventuress of the Forties* (Laurie, 1909); Horace Wyndham, *The Magnificent Montez: From Courtesan to Convert* (1935); Bruce Seymour, *Lola Montez: A Life* (Yale U. Press, 1996); and *Women in World History*.

MONTEZ, Maria (1918–1951). Spanish actress. Born Maria Africa Vidal de Santo Silas, June 6, 1918, in Dominican Republic; drowned in her bath, possibly after a heart attack, Sept 7, 1951, in France; dau. of a Spanish consular official stationed in Dominican Republic; m. William McFeeters, 1932 (div. 1939); m. Jean-Pierre Aumont (actor), 1943; children: (2nd m.) Tina Aumont, also known as Tina Marquand (b. 1946). ❧ Made screen debut in *The Invisible Woman* (1940); appeared in numerous adventure movies that often included camels or pirates, such as *Arabian Nights* (1942, in which she played Scheherazade), *Ali Baba and the Forty Thieves* (1944), and *Tangier* (1946); moved to Europe, where she acted in a number of action films. ❧ See also *Women in World History*.

MONTEZ, Minnie (1836–1914). *See Leslie, Miriam Folline Squier.*

MONTFORT, Amicia (fl. 1208). Countess of Leicester. Name variations: Amicia Beaumont; Amice of Montfort. Dau. of Robert Beaumont (1130–1190), 3rd earl of Leicester, and Patronil de Gremtemesnil; m. Simon (IV) Montfort (c. 1150–1218), earl of Leicester; children: Simon (V) Montfort (c. 1208–1265), earl of Leicester.

MONTFORT, countess of (c. 1310–c. 1376). *See Jeanne de Montfort.*

MONTFORT, Eleanor de.
See Eleanor of Montfort (1215–1275).
See Eleanor of Montfort (1252–1282).

MONTFORT, Elizabeth (1954—). French politician. Born June 29, 1954, in Nantes, France. ❧ Served as vice-chair of the Auvergne Regional Council (1998) and as a member of the MPF (Mouvement pour la France) Executive Committee (1995); as an Independent or Non-attached (NI), elected to 5th European Parliament (1999–2004).

MONTFORT, Jeanne de (c. 1310–c. 1376). *See Jeanne de Montfort.*

MONTGOMERY, Charlotte (1958—). Swedish golfer. Name variations: Charlotte Montgomery-Brostedt. Born Aug 24, 1958, in Stockholm, Sweden; attended Arizona State University. ❧ Won French Junior (1977); won European Junior (1979); won European (1979, 1981); won North and South (1979); turned pro (1981); won World Cup (indiv. 1981).

MONTGOMERY, Cora (1807–1878). *See Cazneau, Jane McManus.*

MONTGOMERY, countess.
See Bauer, Karoline (1807–1877).
See Clifford, Anne (1590–1676).

MONTGOMERY, Elizabeth (1933–1995). American actress. Born April 15, 1933, in Los Angeles, CA; died of colon cancer, May 18, 1995, in Beverly Hills, CA; dau. of Robert Montgomery (actor) and Elizabeth (Allen) Bryan Montgomery (actress known as Elizabeth Allen); studied acting at American Academy of Dramatic Arts, NY; m. Frederick Gallatin Cammann, 1954 (div. 1955); m. Gig Young (actor), 1957 (div. 1963); m. William Asher (producer), 1963 (div. 1974); m. Robert Foxworth (actor), in 1993; children: (3rd m.) William Jr.; Robert; Rebecca. ❧ Star of ABC's "Bewitched" (1964–72), made 1st stage appearance at 5, as the wolf in a French-language production of *Little Red Riding Hood*; made tv debut in an episode of father's NBC series "Robert Montgomery Presents" (1951) and had several stage roles as ingenues, notably in *Late Love* (1953), for which she received *Theatre World*'s Daniel Blum Award for most promising newcomer; starred as Samantha Stephens on "Bewitched," the #1 show for 4 of its 8 years, which brought her 5 of her 9 Emmy nominations; continued to work regularly in tv, appearing in 19 made-for-tv movies over 2 decades. Nominated for Emmy awards for "The Rusty Heller Story" on "The Untouchables" (1961), "A Case of Rape" (1974), "The Legend of Lizzie Borden" (1975) and "The Awakening Land" (1978). ❧ See also *Women in World History*.

MONTGOMERY, Florence (1871–1950). *See Arliss, Florence.*

MONTGOMERY, Goodee (1906–1978). American-born actress. Born Mar 28, 1906, in St. Joseph, MO; died June 5, 1978, in Hollywood, CA; m. Frank McDonald (film and tv director); children: son. ❧ Films include *Up the River, Lightnin', Charlie Chan Carries On* and *Stolen Harmony*.

MONTGOMERY, Helen Barrett (1861–1934). American civic reformer, foreign mission worker, and philanthropist. Born Nellie Barrett, July 31, 1861, in Kingsville, Ohio; died Oct 19, 1934, in Summit, New Jersey; dau. of Adoniram Judson Barrett (school principal and Baptist minister) and Emily (Barrows) Barrett (teacher); attended Livingston Park Seminary; Wellesley College, BA, 1884; Brown University, MA;

m. William A. Montgomery (businessman), Sept 6, 1887; children: Edith. ❧ The 1st woman to translate the Greek New Testament into contemporary English, *The Centenary Translation of the New Testament* (1924), taught at Rochester (NY) Free Academy (1884–85) and Wellesley Preparatory School, Philadelphia (1885–87); organized a large Bible study class for women (1888), which she taught for 44 years; was licensed to preach by Lake Avenue Baptist Church in Rochester (1892); became 1st president of Women's Educational and Industrial Union of Rochester; was president of New York State Federation of Women's Clubs (1896–97); elected to Rochester school board (1899); served as 1st president of Women's American Baptist Foreign Mission Society (1914–24); worked to open University of Rochester to female students; elected president of Northern Baptist Convention (1921), the 1st woman to be elected to a position of such prominence in any major Christian denomination; was a delegate to Baptist World Alliance, Stockholm Congress (1923); also wrote extensively. ❧ See also *Women in World History*.

MONTGOMERY, Jemima (1807–1893). *See Tautphoeus, Baroness von.*

MONTGOMERY, Lucy Maud (1874–1942). Canadian author. Name variations: Maud Montgomery. Born Lucy Maud Montgomery, Nov 30, 1874, in Clifton, Prince Edward Island, Canada; died in Toronto, Ontario, Canada, April 24, 1942; dau. of Hugh John Montgomery (entrepreneur) and Clara (Woolner Macneill) Montgomery; attended Prince of Wales College, obtaining a teacher's license, and Dalhousie University, 1895–96; m. Reverend Ewan Macdonald, July 1911; children: Chester (b. 1912); Hugh Alexander (stillborn, 1914); Stuart (b. 1915). ❧ World-renowned author of *Anne of Green Gables* and over 20 juvenile books and stories, who immortalized Canada's Prince Edward Island (P.E.I.) and the childhood experience, lived with maternal grandparents on P.E.I. (1876–91); composed 1st poem (1883); published 1st poem (1890); taught for 3 years; was a newspaper columnist for 1 year; wrote and took care of aging grandmother (1902–11); published *Anne of Green Gables* (June 1908); wrote 8 more books around the character of Anne Shirley, one of the most beloved children in fiction (1908–39); became fellow of Royal Society of the Arts (1923); by the time of her death, had published over 21 books of fiction and countless stories and poems, and *Anne of Green Gables* had sold more than 1 million copies and was circulating the world in over 11 languages in book, movie, play or stage form (1942). Invested with Order of the British Empire (1935). ❧ See also Wilfrid Eggleston, ed. *The Green Gables Letters* (Ryerson, 1960); Mollie Gillen, *Lucy Maud Montgomery* (Fitzhenry & Whiteside, 1978); Mary Rubio and Elizabeth Waterston, *The Selected Journals of L.M. Montgomery* (Vols. I–III, Oxford U. Press, 1987); and *Women in World History*.

MONTGOMERY, Margaret (fl. 1438). Countess of Lennox. Married John Stewart of Darnley, 1st earl of Lennox, in 1438 (d. around 1495); children: Matthew, 2nd earl of Lennox (d. 1513).

MONTGOMERY, Mary (fl. 1891–1914). Irish artist and metalworker. Flourished between 1891 and 1914 in Fivemiletown, Co. Tyrone, in what is now Northern Ireland; married a landowner; studied metalworking in London. ❧ Traveled to London to study repoussé metalwork (1891); work shown at Home Arts and Industries Exhibition (HAIE) at the Albert Hall (1893); received numerous awards for her metalwork from the HAIE, Royal Dublin Society, and Cheltenham and Bristol exhibitions; returned to Fivemiletown, where she established her own metalworking school and organized annual exhibitions. ❧ See also *Women in World History*.

MONTGOMERY, Peggy (1917—). American actress and writer. Name variations: Baby Peggy; Diana Serra Cary. Born Peggy Montgomery in Rock Island, Illinois, Oct 26, 1917; dau. of a screen extra and stuntman; m. Gordon "Freckles" Ayres (member of the cast of the Our Gang comedies); m. Robert Cary (painter); children: Mark. ❧ Popular child star (1920s), was featured in many 2-reelers and over a dozen films, including *Peggy Behave* (1922), *The Darling of New York* (1923), *Captain January* (1924), *The Hollywood Reporter* (1926), *Prisoners of the Storm* (1926), *The Sonora Kid* (1927), *Arizona Days* (1928), *West of Santa Fe* (1928) and *Having a Wonderful Time* (1938); retired from the screen (1939); became a journalist, contributing to *American Heritage, Esquire* and *The Saturday Evening Post*; under name Diana Serra Cary, published *The Hollywood Posse: The Story of a Gallant Band of Horsemen Who Made Movie History* (1975) and *Hollywood Children* (1979), on the life of child stars.

MONTHERMER, Margaret (fl. 1350). Baroness Monthermer. Dau. of Thomas Monthermer, 2nd baron Monthermer, and Margaret Monthermer, baroness Monthermer; m. John Montacute; children: John Montacute (c. 1350–1400), 3rd earl of Salisbury.

MONTIEL, Sarita (1928—). Spanish singer and actress. Name variations: Sara Montiel. Born María Antonia Abad Fernández in Campo de Criptana, Ciudad Real, Spain, Mar 10, 1928; m. Anthony Mann (film director), 1957 (annulled 1963). ❖ Popular in the Spanish-speaking world, appeared in numerous movies in her native Spain and in Mexico beginning 1940s; made 4 Hollywood films, including *That Man from Tangier* (1953), *Vera Cruz* (1954), *Serenade* (1956) and *Run of the Arrow* (1957), in which her voice was dubbed by Angie Dickinson; returned to Spain (1957); had greatest success on screen with the hugely popular *El Último Cuplé*; appeared on stage and tv (1980s). ❖ See also *Women in World History*.

MONTIERO, June (1946—). African-American singer. Name variations: The Toys. Born July 1, 1946, in Queens, NY. ❖ With Barbara Harris and Barbara Parritt, formed R&B group, The Toys in Queens, NY (1960s) and had huge hit single, "A Lover's Concerto," based on Bach's "Minuet in G"; with group, also had hits "Attack" (1966) and "Sealed With a Kiss" (1968); appeared on tv's "American Bandstand" and "Shindig!" and in film, *It's a Bikini World* (1967); after group disbanded (1968), went on to do session work.

MONTIFAUD, Marc de (1848–1912). See *Chartroule, Marie-Amelie.*

MONTIJO, Eugenie de (1826–1920). See *Eugenie.*

MONTILLET, Carole (1973—). French Alpine skier. Born April 7, 1973, in Grenoble, France; sister of Christele Montillet (competes in skeleton). ❖ Won the 1st World Cup race after 10 years on circuit (2001); won a gold medal for downhill at Salt Lake City Olympics (2002).

MONTMINY, Anne (1975—). Canadian diver. Name variations: Anne Katherine Montminy. Born Jan 28, 1975, in Montreal, Canada. ❖ Won gold medals at Commonwealth Games and Pan American Games (1995), both for 10-meter platform; won a silver medal for synchronized platform diving and a bronze for 10-meter platform at Sydney Olympics (2000).

MONTOLIEU, Pauline (1751–1832). Swiss novelist and translator. Name variations: Madame Polier de Bottens; Baronne Isabelle de Montolieu. Born Isabelle Pauline Polier de Bottens, 1751, in Lausanne, Switzerland; died 1832; m. Benjamin de Crousaz, 1769 (died 1775); m. Baron de Montolieu, 1786. ❖ Wrote novels *Caroline de Litchfield* (1786), *Cécile de Rodeck*, and *Alice*; published many translations of German and French works, including *The Swiss Family Robinson* (1813) to which she wrote a sequel (1824).

MONTORIOL I PUIG, Carme (1893–1966). Spanish playwright, poet, novelist and feminist. Name variations: Carme Montoriol. Born 1893 in Catalonia, Spain; died 1966; lived in Barcelona. ❖ Works, which often focus on family relationships, include plays *L'abisme* (1933) and *L'huracà* (1935), and novel *Teresa o la vida amorosa d'una dona* (1932); an active feminist during Second Republic, ceased to write after Franco regime prohibited use of Catalan.

MONTORO, duchess of (1762–1802). See *Cayetana, Maria del Pilar Teresa.*

MONTOUR, Isabelle (1667–c. 1750). Canadian-born Indian interpreter. Name variations: Madame Montour; Elisabeth Montour; also called Madame La Chenette or Madame Tichenet. Born Elisabeth Couc, 1667, possibly in Trois-Rivieres, Quebec, Canada; died c. 1750, possibly near Harper's Ferry, PA; dau. of Pierre Couc (called Lafleur, soldier and interpreter) and Marie Miteouagamegoukoue; sister of Louis Couc (called Montour, who was stabbed in 1709 by 2 Frenchmen after trying to persuade them not to go to war against the Five Nations); m. Joseph Germaneau (also seen as Germano), 1684; m. Outoutagon; lived with Etienne de Vernard de Bourgmont (ex-commandant at Detroit); m. a Carundawana chief known as Big Tree or Onneiout (who took the name Robert Hunter to honor Governor Robert Hunter), killed in 1729; children: at least 2 sons, 1 or 2 daughters. ❖ Known as a half-breed, followed the Indian way of life; acted as Indian interpreter for English for conference between New York governor Robert Hunter and Iroquois chiefs or Five Nations (1711); traveled with Col. Peter Schuyler to Onondaga (now Syracuse, NY) to dissuade the Five Nations from sending warriors to North Carolina to aid the Tuscarora in their war against the English (1712); settled in Pennsylvania and served as interpreter at conferences in Philadelphia between Iroquois and Pennsylvania governor Patrick Gordon (1727, 1728, 1734).

MONTPENSIER, Anne Marie Louise d'Orléans, Duchesse de (1627–1693). French duchess and memoirist. Name variations: The Grand or Grande Mademoiselle, The Great Mademoiselle; La Grande Mademoiselle; Mlle d'Orleans Montpensier. Born May 29, 1627, at the Louvre in Paris, France; died in Paris, April 5, 1693; dau. of Gaston d'Orléans (1608–1660), duke of Orléans (brother of Louis XIII, king of France, and known as "Monsieur"), and Marie de Bourbon (1606–1627), duchesse de Montpensier ("Madame"); never married; no children. ❖ Heiress and participant in the Fronde who provided in her memoirs a personal account of the splendor of the courts of Louis XIII and Louis XIV; born and raised in the court of Louis XIII; actively participated in a civil disturbance known as the Fronde against Cardinal Mazarin (Mar–Oct 1652); while exiled at St. Fargeau (1652–57), wrote her memoirs; returned to the court of Louis XIV (1657); courted and almost married the duke de Lauzun (1666–70). ❖ See also Victoria Sackville-West, *Daughter of France: The Life of Anne Marie Louise d'Orléans, Duchesse de Montpensier, 1627–1693, La Grande Mademoiselle* (Doubleday, 1959); Francis Steegmuller, *La Grande Mademoiselle* (Hamish Hamilton, 1955); and *Women in World History*.

MONTPENSIER, duchess of.
See *Catherine of Guise (1552–c. 1594).*
See *Marie de Bourbon (1606–1627).*
See *Montpensier, Anne Marie Louise d'Orléans, duchess de (1627–1693).*
See *Louise Marie of Bourbon (1753–1821).*

MONTRELAY, Michèle. French psychoanalyst. Name variations: Michele Montrelay. Lives in Paris, France. ❖ Influenced by work of Jacques Lacan, was a training member of the École Fredienne de Paris (1965–80); works include *L'Ombre et le Nom* (1977) and *Le physicien et le réel.*

MONTSENY, Federica (1905–1994). Spanish anarchist, feminist and writer. Name variations: Frederica Montseny y Mañé. Pronunciation: Fay-day-REE-kah Mont-SAY-nee (in Spanish); Mun-SEIN or Moon-SAYN (in Catalonian). Born Federica Montseny, Feb 12, 1905, in Madrid, Spain; died in Toulouse, France, Jan 14, 1994; dau. of Juan Batista Montseny y Carret (used pseudonym Federico Urales), and Teresa Mañé (used pseudonym Soledad Gustavo); educated at home; m. Germinal Esgleas, 1930; children: Vida (b. around 1934); Germinal (b. 1938); Blanca (b. 1942). ❖ One of the most important anarchists and one of the most important women during Spanish Civil War (1936–39), edited, published and wrote for *La Revista Blanca* (1923–36), a distinguished anarchist journal; joined secret anarchist organization FAI (Iberian Anarchist Federation) (1928, 1927 or 1933); served on the Anti-Fascist Militia Committee, Barcelona (July 1936); appointed minister of health and public assistance of the Spanish Republic (Nov 4, 1936), the 1st woman to hold a ministerial post in Spanish history, and transformed a second-rate ministerial portfolio into a 1st-rate position; was instrumental in making Spain the 1st country in Europe, outside the Soviet Union, to possess a system of safe and legal abortions; arrived in Barcelona to mediate fighting between anarchists and others, and the Communists (May 5, 1937); resigned from the government (May 16, 1937); testified in favor of the political prisoners arrested in Barcelona (Oct 1937); when Franco began his final offensive, fled Barcelona with family and journeyed to France (Jan–Feb 1939); arrested by police of Vichy France, but court of Limoges rejected Spanish government's extradition request (Nov 1941); published the weekly *CNT* in Toulouse (after 1939); returned to Barcelona from exile (April 27, 1977). ❖ See also memoir in Spanish *Seis Años de mi vida, 1939–1945* (Galba, 1978); and *Women in World History*.

MONTVID, A. S. (b. 1845). Russian short-story writer. Name variations: Aleksandra Stanislavovna Montvid; (pseudonym) A.S. Shabel'skaia or Shabelskaia. Born 1845 in Ukraine; death date unknown. ❖ Published a collection of stories as "Pencil Sketches," about life in Ukrainian villages (1880s–90s); stories include "Paraska," "Naked Lady," "Nagornoe" and "The Legend."

MONVOISIN, Catherine (d. 1680). See *Deshayes, Catherine.*

MOODIE, Geraldine (1853–1945). Canadian photographer. Born Geraldine Fitzgibbons in Ottawa, Ontario, Canada, 1853; died in Calgary, Alberta, Canada, 1945; m. John Douglas Moodie (officer in Royal Canadian Mounted Police, then governor of Hudson's Bay Co.). ❖ Began photographing Native Americans and frontierspeople she encountered near Battleford, Saskatchewan (1890s); accompanied husband on an expedition to the Arctic (1904–06); traveled to England to photograph coronation of King George V (1911), then returned to the Arctic (1915). ❖ See also *Women in World History*.

MOODIE, Susanna (1803–1885). British-born Canadian writer. Name variations: Susanna Strickland; Susanna Strickland Moodie. Born Susanna Strickland, Dec 6, 1803, in Suffolk, England; died April 8, 1885, in Toronto, Canada; 6th dau. of Thomas Strickland (retired manager of Greenland Dock) and Elizabeth (Homer) Strickland; sister of writers Agnes Strickland (1796–1874), Elizabeth Strickland (1794–1875), Jane Margaret Strickland (1800–1888), Catherine Parr Traill (1802–1899), and Samuel Strickland; m. John Wedderburn Dunbar Moodie (writer and officer), April 1831; children: 7, 2 of whom died young. ❖ Youngest of England's literary Strickland sisters, began career following father's death (1818); wrote sketches, stories, poems, and moral and historical stories for children, published in periodicals of the day; met Thomas Pringle, who introduced her to a group of London writers (1820s); submitted short sketches to *La Belle Assemble* (1827–29); immigrated with husband to Canada (1832); during 8 years of pioneer life in Ontario, submitted material to US, Canadian, and English journals; was a principal contributor to Montreal's *Literary Garland* (1838–50); with husband, edited *The Victoria Magazine* (1847–48); published successful *Roughing It in the Bush* (1852) and *Life in the Clearings* (1853); followed with *Mark Hurdlestone* (1853) and *Flora Lyndsay* (1854); published last novel (1875). ❖ See also Margaret Atwood, *The Journals of Susanna Moodie* (1972); and *Women in World History*.

MOODY, Agnes Claypole (1870–1954). English-American zoologist. Name variations: Agnes Claypole or Agnes Mary Claypole. Born Agnes Mary Claypole, Jan 1, 1870, in Bristol, England; died 1954 in Berkeley, CA; dau. of Jane (Trotter) Claypole and Edward Waller Claypole (British professor at Buchtel College and a founder of journal, *American Geologist*); twin sister of Edith Jane Claypole (1870–1915, physiologist and pathologist); Buchtel College, PhD, 1892; Cornell University, MS, 1894; University of Chicago, PhD, 1896; m. Dr. Robert Orton Moody (University of California anatomy professor), 1903. ❖ Dedicated scientist and professor who, despite gender obstacles, managed a successful career in academia; was employed as a Wellesley College zoology instructor (1896–98); at Cornell University, worked as a histology and embryology assistant (1898–1900) and was the 1st woman to instruct laboratory classes that were mandatory for all students; was an instructor (1900–03) at Throop Polytechnic Institute (later California Institute of Technology) in Pasadena; lectured in sociology (1918–23) at Mills College in Oakland, CA; elected to Berkeley City Council (1923). Starred in the 1st–7th editions of *American Men of Science* as one of the 1,000 best scientists in America.

MOODY, Anne (1940—). African-American memoirist. Born Sept 15, 1940, in Wilkinson Co., Mississippi; dau. of Fred and Elnire (Williams) Moody; attended Natchez Junior College; Tougaloo College, BS, 1964; m. Austin Stratus (div. 1969); children: Sascha. ❖ A civil-rights activist, worked for CORE in 1960s and took part in Freedom Summer; was civil rights project coordinator at Cornell University (1964–65); published autobiography, *Coming of Age in Mississippi* (1968), to great acclaim; also wrote *Mr. Death: Four Stories* (1975).

MOODY, Deborah (c. 1583–c. 1659). Early American colonist. Name variations: Lady Deborah Moody. Born Deborah Dunch in Avebury, Wiltshire, England, c. 1583 (some sources cite 1580, some cite 1600); died in Gravesend, New Netherland, c. 1659; dau. of Walter Dunch and Deborah (Pilkington) Dunch; granddau. of James Pilkington, bishop of Durham; m. Henry Moody of the manor of Garesdon, Wiltshire, Jan 20, 1605 or 1606; children: Henry. ❖ Following death of husband and a conflict with English authorities, immigrated to American colonies (1639); lived in Massachusetts until a disagreement with authorities over religious convictions prompted her to move in 1643 to Dutch province of New Netherland (now Brooklyn, NY); there, received land grant and established Gravesend, the 1st colonial settlement established and run by a woman; is credited with designing areas known today as Midwood, Coney Island, Sheepshead Bay, and Bensonhurst. ❖ See also *Women in World History*.

MOODY, Mrs. D. L. (1842–1903). *See Moody, Emma Revell.*

MOODY, Elizabeth (1737–1814). British poet. Name variations: Mrs. Moody; (pseudonyms) Aretina; Eliza; Miss G; The Muse of Surbiton; Sappho. Born April 1737 in Kingston, Surrey, England; died Dec 10, 1814, in London, England; dau. of Edward Greenly and Mary Shepherd Greenly; m. Reverend Christopher Lake Moody. ❖ Encouraged by

husband, published poems in periodicals; became 1st female reviewer for *Monthly Review* (1789); published a collection of poems in *Poetic Trifles* (1798).

MOODY, Emma Revell (1842–1903). British-born wife of American evangelist Dwight L. Moody. Name variations: Mrs. D.L. Moody. Born Emma Revell in 1842 in London, England; died 1903 (some sources cite 1902) in Northfield, Massachusetts; dau. of Fleming Revell and Emma (Manning) Revell; m. Dwight L. Moody (Congregationalist evangelist), 1862; children: Emma; W.R.; Paul. ❖ Accompanied husband as he traveled and preached throughout the country (they had no permanent home until their last years). ❖ See also Emma Moody Powell, *Heavenly Destiny*; and *Women in World History*.

MOODY, Mrs. F. S. (1905–1998). *See Wills, Helen Newington.*

MOODY, Heather (1973—). American water-polo player. Born Aug 21, 1973, in Green River, WY; attended San Diego State University. ❖ Center, won a team silver medal at Sydney Olympics (2000) and a team bronze at Athens Olympics (2004); won World championship (2003).

MOODY, Helen Wills (1905–1998). *See Wills, Helen Newington.*

MOODY, Mrs. (1737–1814). *See Moody, Elizabeth.*

MOON HYANG-JA (1972—). South Korean handball player. Name variations: Hyang-ja Moon. Born May 5, 1972, in South Korea. ❖ Won a team gold medal at Barcelona Olympics (1992) and a team silver medal at Atlanta Olympics (1996).

MOON KYEONG-HA (1980—). South Korean handball player. Born May 29, 1980, in South Korea. ❖ Won a team silver at Athens Olympics (2004).

MOON KYUNG-JA (1965—). Korean basketball player. Born Aug 14, 1965, in South Korea. ❖ At Los Angeles Olympics, won a silver medal in team competition (1984).

MOON, Lorna (1886–1930). Scottish-American writer. Name variations: Nora Wilson Low. Born Helen Nora Wilson Low, June 16, 1886, in Strichen, Aberdeenshire, Scotland; died of TB, May 1, 1930, in Albuquerque, New Mexico; dau. of Charles Low (hotelier); m. William Hebditch (jewelry salesman); m. Walter Moon; children: (1st m.) 1; (2nd m.) 1; (with William De Mille, brother of Cecil B. De Mille) Richard De Mille (b. 1922). ❖ Grew up in Strichen, where her father owned the Temperance Hotel; met and married William Hebditch, who was staying there, and moved with him to Alberta, Canada; set off for Winnipeg with new beau Walter Moon, who introduced her to journalism; traveled to Hollywood and wrote scripts for MGM, including *Mr. Wu*, starring Lon Chaney, which was huge success; befriended Frances Marion and Anita Loos; contributed tales about Strichen (called Pitouie in stories) to magazines; published successful collection of short stories *Doorways in Drumorty* (1926), depicting the foibles of villagers in Strichen, which alienated folks back home; wrote bestselling novel *Dark Star* (1929). ❖ See also Richard De Mille, *My Secret Mother: Lorna Moon* (Farrar, 1998).

MOON, Lottie (1840–1912). American missionary. Born Charlotte Diggs Moon, Dec 12, 1840, in Crowe, VA; died Dec 24, 1912, in Kobe, Japan; dau. of Edward Harris Moon (plantation owner) and Anna Maria (Barclay) Moon; Hollins College, BA, 1856; Albermarle Female Institute, MA, 1861; never married; no children. ❖ Southern Baptist missionary to China and founder and namesake of the Lottie Moon Christmas Offering, had religious conversion (1859); assisted elder sister Orianna, one of the South's 1st female physicians, in Civil War hospitals (1861); with friends, established a school for girls in Cartersville, Georgia (1870); joined younger sister Edmonia in China (1873); moved to more remote villages (1885), centering her mission at Pingtu, an area no missionary had spent time in before; returned to America on furlough (1891–93), spreading word of her work; because of Boxer Rebellion, moved to Fukuola, Japan (1900), returning to China (1901); remained in China during Russo-Japanese War (1904–05) and 1911 Chinese rebellion against the Manchu Dynasty; set sail for San Francisco (1912), but died aboard ship in harbor of Kobe, Japan, on Christmas Eve; is best remembered for the Christmas offering which bears her name, begun by her pleas for assistance and nurtured by the Southern Baptist Woman's Missionary Union. ❖ See also Una Roberts Lawrence, *Lottie Moon* (1927); and *Women in World History*.

MOON PIL-HEE (1982—). South Korean handball player. Born Dec 2, 1982, in South Korea. ❖ Won a team silver at Athens Olympics (2004).

MOONEY, Julie (1888–1915). American theatrical dancer. Born 1888 in New York, NY; died Mar 6, 1915, in New York, NY; sister of dancer Gypsy Mooney. ❖ Performed tap and soft-shoe dances in musical comedies and revues (1893–1920); danced in *The Earl and the Girl* (1905), *His Majesty* (1907), *The Merry-Go-Round* (1908), and others; with younger sister Gypsy, performed in Gus Edwards' *School Days* (1909) and *Song Revue* (1911).

MOONEY, Mary (1958—). Irish politician. Born Dec 1958 in Dublin, Ireland. ❖ Representing Fianna Fáil, elected to 25th Dáil (1987–89) for Dublin South Central; member and vice-chair of Oireachtas Joint Committee on Women's Rights (1987–89).

MOONEY, Ria (1904–1973). Irish actress, teacher, director, and producer. Born Catherine Marea (one source cites Maria) in Dublin, Ireland, 1904; died in Dublin, Jan 3, 1973; studied dance at Madame Rock's Dancing Academy and art at Metropolitan School of Art, both Dublin; never married; no children. ❖ The 1st woman producer at the Abbey Theatre, began acting at 6; sang with Rathmines and Rathgar Musical Society in her teens; invited to join Abbey Theatre, Dublin (1924); selected by Sean O'Casey to play Rosie Redmond in premiere of *The Plough and the Stars* (1926); toured England and US with Molly Allgood; made US acting debut (1927); joined Eva Le Gallienne at New York's Civic Repertory Theatre, serving as assistant director of plays (1928–34); joined Edwards-MacLiammóir company at Gate Theatre Company, Dublin (1934); produced verse plays at Abbey and Peacock Theatres for Austin Clarke's Dublin Verse-Speaking Society/ Lyric Theatre Company; appointed teacher at Abbey School of Acting (Aug 1935); directed Abbey's experimental Peacock Theatre (1937); directed Gaiety Theatre School of Acting, Dublin (1944); was a producer at Abbey Theatre (1948–63). ❖ See also *Women in World History.*

MOOR, Agnes (1591–1656). *See More, Agnes.*

MOORE, Alice Ruth (1875–1935). *See Dunbar-Nelson, Alice.*

MOORE, Ann (1950—). English equestrian. Born Aug 20, 1950, in Great Britain. ❖ At Munich Olympics, rode Psalm to a silver indiv. medal in Grand Prix jumping (1972).

MOORE, Annabelle (1878–1961). *See Annabelle.*

MOORE, Anne Carroll (1871–1961). American librarian, lecturer, writer, and children's book critic. Born Anne Carroll Moore, July 12, 1871, in Limerick, Maine; died Jan 20, 1961, in New York, NY; dau. of Luther Sanborn Moore (lawyer) and Sarah Hidden (Barker) Moore; attended Limerick Academy, 1881–89; attended Bradford Academy for Women, Bradford, Massachusetts, 1889–91; attended Pratt Institute Library School, Brooklyn, 1895–96. ❖ Pioneer in the field of children's librarianship, became head of new children's department at Pratt Institute (1897); helped establish and was 1st chair of Club of Children's Librarians, American Library Association (1900); became supervisor of children's division of New York Public Library (NYPL, 1906), where she revolutionized children's library practices, expanded storytelling, and initiated book review programs; helped establish Children's Book Week, also began reviewing children's literature for *The Bookman* (1918); issued annual list of "Children's Books Suggested as Holiday Gifts" (1918–41); edited "The Three Owls" column of criticism in *New York Herald Tribune* (1924–30); retired from NYPL (1940); accepted position with University of California at Berkeley graduate school of librarianship (1941). Received 1st Constance Lindsay Skinner Gold Medal (1940) and Regina Medal (1960). ❖ See also autobiography *My Roads to Childhood* (1961); Frances Clarke Sayers, *Anne Carroll Moore* (Atheneum, 1972); and *Women in World History.*

MOORE, Aubertine Woodward (1841–1929). American writer and translator. Name variations: Aubertine Woodward; (pseudonym) Auber Forestier. Born Annie Aubertine Woodward, Sept 27, 1841, in Montgomery Co., PA; died Sept 22, 1929, in Madison, WI; dau. of Joseph Janvier Woodward (publisher) and Elizabeth Graham (Cox) Woodward; m. Samuel Hughes Moore (contractor), Dec 22, 1887. ❖ Translated 2 German-language novels by Robert Byr (Robert von Bayer), *Sphinx; or, Striving with Destiny* (1871) and *The Struggle for Existence* (1873); moved into home of Rasmus Bjørn Anderson, professor of Scandinavian languages at University of Wisconsin, to learn Norwegian language (1879); published trans. of German epic poem Nibelungenlied, *Echoes from Mist-Land, or The Nibelungen Lay,*

Revealed to Lovers of Romance (1880); published *The Spell-Bound Fiddler,* trans. of novel by Norwegian writer Kristofer Janson (1880); worked with Anderson to translate 7 novels by Norwegian poet Bjørnstjerne Bjørnson; taught music at Madison Musical College (1900–12); published compilations including *Norway Music Album* (1881), *For My Musical Friend* (1900), *Faustina, a Venetian Queen of Song* (1918), and essay collection *For Every Music Lover* (1902).

MOORE, Audley (1898–1997). African-American activist. Name variations: Queen Mother Audley Moore. Born Audley Eloise Moore, 1898, in New Iberia, Louisiana; died May 2, 1997, in Brooklyn, NY; dau. of Henry Moore (sheriff's deputy) and St. Cyr Moore; completed 3rd grade; married; children: 1 son. ❖ Organizer for civil rights, women's rights, and Pan-African nationalism, was a driving force behind many economic and political efforts to better the lives of African-Americans for over 80 years; joined Marcus Garvey's Universal Negro Improvement Association, supporting his "Back to Africa" movement (1920s); with husband and sisters, settled in NYC's Harlem (1922); founded Harriet Tubman Association to organize poorly paid domestic workers; was a member of Communist Party (1933–50), because of its advocacy of voters' rights and civil rights; returning to Louisiana (1950), became an advocate for poor people in the South and formed Universal Association of Ethiopian Women, Inc.; was the founder of World Federation of African People and a founding member, with sister Lorita, of Ethiopian Orthodox Church of North and South America, of which she became an abbess in 1969; was also a founding member of Congress of African Peoples (1970) and of Republic of New Africa, in part a result of her many visits to Africa; in later years, concentrated on the issue of reparation for slavery, while also campaigning to establish a national monument in memory of Africans who died during the centuries in which slavery was legal in US; earned title "Queen Mother" from Ashanti people in Africa. ❖ See also *Women in World History.*

MOORE, C. L. (1911–1987). American science-fiction writer. Name variations: Catherine Lucille Moore; (pseudonyms) Lawrence O'Donnell; Lewis Padgett. Born Catherine Lucille Moore, Jan 24, 1911, in Indianapolis, IN; died April 7, 1987, in Hollywood, CA; dau. of Otto Newman Moore and Maude Estelle Jones; m. Henry Kuttner, 1949 (died 1958); m. Thomas Reggie, 1960. ❖ Forerunner of feminist science-fiction writers (1970s), who created the characters Northwest Smith and Jirel of Jory; solo works include *Judgement Night* (1952), *Doomsday Morning* (1960), and short-story collections *Shambleau and Others* (1953), *Jirel of Joiry* (1969), and *The Best of C. L. Moore* (1975); collaborated with husband under 17 pseudonyms for such works as *The Day He Died* (1947), *Fury* (1950), *Well of the Worlds* (1953), *Earth's Last Citadel* (1964), *The Time Axis* (1965), *The Mark of Circe* (1971), and short-story collections *A Gnome There Was* (1950), *Ahead of Time* (1953), *No Boundaries* (1955), and *Clash by Night* (1980), among others.

MOORE, Catherine Lucille (1911–1987). *See Moore, C.L.*

MOORE, Charlotte Emma (1898–1990). *See Sitterly, Charlotte Moore.*

MOORE, Clara (1824–1899). American writer. Name variations: (pseudonyms) Clara Moreton, Mrs. Bloomfield-Moore, Mrs. H.O. Ward. Born Clara Sophia Jessup, Feb 16, 1824, in Philadelphia, PA; died Jan 5, 1899, in London, England; dau. of Augustus Edward Jessup (mineralogist and paper manufacturer) and Lydia Eager (Mosley) Jessup; m. Bloomfield Haines Moore, Oct 27, 1842 (died 1878); children: 1 son, 2 daughters. ❖ Served as corresponding secretary of and raised war-relief money for Women's Pennsylvania Branch of US Sanitary Commission; was financial backer of so-called inventor John Ernst Worrell Keely to 1895; published several works of poetry and fiction, one of the more successful being novel *On Dangerous Ground, or Agatha's Friendship: A Romance of American Society* (1876); found widespread and longstanding audience with publication of *Sensible Etiquette of the Best Society* (1878), which went through 20 editions.

MOORE, Cleo (1928–1973). American actress. Born Oct 31, 1928, in Baton Rouge, LA; died Oct 25, 1973, in Inglewood, CA; sister of Mara Lea (actress); m. Palmer Long (son of politician Huey Long), 1944 (div. 1944); m. Herbert Heftler, 1961. ❖ Made film debut in *Congo Bill* (1948), followed by *Rio Grande Patrol, Bright Leaf, Gambling House, This Side of the Law, On Dangerous Ground, Women's Prison* and *Hit and Run* among others; ran unsuccessfully for governor of Louisiana (1956).

MOORE, Colleen (1900–1988). American actress. Born Kathleen Morrison, Aug 19, 1900, in Port Huron, Michigan; died Jan 25, 1988, in Paso Robles, CA; m. John McCormick (production head of 1st

National films), 1923 (div. 1930); m. Albert P. Scott (stockbroker), 1932 (div. 1934); m. Homer P. Hargrave (stockbroker), 1937 (died 1966); m. Paul Maginot (building contractor), 1982; children: 1 son. ❖ Popular star of the silent-movie era, with a trademark Dutch boy bob, signed with D.W. Griffith's Triangle-Fine Arts (1917); left Triangle (1918) and had 1st leads in *A Hoosier Romance* and *Little Orphan Annie*; signed with 1st National (1923), where she made breakthrough film *Flaming Youth* (1923), followed by *Painted People* (1924) and *The Perfect Flapper* (1924); having proven her comic ability, turned to drama in 1st film version of Ferber's *So Big* (1925); returned to lighter fare with *Sally* (1925) and *Irene* (1926); other silents include *Orchids and Ermine* (1927) and *Lilac Time* (1928); made 1st talking picture, *Smiling Irish Eyes* (1929), followed by *Footlights and Fools* (1929), *The Power and the Glory* (1933), *The Scarlet Letter* (1934); did not make a smooth transition into talkies and retired from films (1934); published *Colleen Moore's Doll House*, about her extraordinary collection of miniatures. ❖ See also autobiography, *Silent Star* (1968); and *Women in World History*.

MOORE, Constance (1919–2005). American actress and band singer. Born Jan 18, 1919, in Sioux City, Iowa; died Sept 16, 2005, in Los Angeles, California; m. John Maschio (her agent), 1937; children: 2. ❖ Began career as a band singer and on radio; starred on Broadway in *By Jupiter*; made film debut in *Prescription for Romance* (1937), followed by *Buck Rogers* (serial), *You Can't Cheat an Honest Man, Charlie McCarthy—Detective, Framed, Argentine Nights, Take a Letter Darling, Show Business, Atlantic City, Earl Carroll Vanities, In Old Sacramento, Earl Carroll Sketchbook, Hit Parade of 1947* and *Spree*, among others; on tv, co-starred with Robert Young in "Window on Main Street" (1961–62).

MOORE, Decima (1871–1964). English actress and singer. Name variations: Lady Moore-Guggisberg; Lady Guggisberg. Born Lilian Decima Moore, Dec 11, 1871, in Brighton, Sussex, England; died Feb 18, 1964, in Kensington, England; dau. of Emily (Strachan) Moore and Edmund Henry Moore; sister of Bertha Moore, Jessie Moore (actress and singer), Eva Moore (actress); aunt of Jill Esmond (actress); m. Cecil Ainslie Walker-Leigh (actor), 1894 (div. 1901); m. Sir F. Gordon Guggisberg (governor of British Guiana), 1905 (died 1930). ❖ Created role of Casilda in *The Gondoliers* (1889), then appeared as Polly in *Captain Billy*, before leaving the Savoy; then appeared in *Miss Decima, A Pantomime Rehearsal, The Maelstrom, Rosencrantz and Guildenstern, The Wedding Eve, The White Silk Dress* and *Dorothy* (title role); accompanied 2nd husband to West Africa (1905); toured Australia and America. Named Commander of the British Empire (CBE, 1918), for services in founding and running a military services' leave club in Paris during WWI. ❖ See also memoir (written with husband) *We Two in West Africa* (Heinemann, 1909).

MOORE, Elisabeth H. (1876–1959). American tennis player. Born Mar 5, 1876, in Brooklyn, NY; died Jan 22, 1959. ❖ Won US national singles titles (1896, 1901, 1903, 1905); won US women's doubles with Juliette Atkinson (1896) and with Carrie B. Neely (1903) and mixed doubles with Wylie C. Grant (1904).

MOORE, Elizabeth (1826–1913). *See Horrell, Elizabeth.*

MOORE, Ellie Durall (1940—). American businesswoman. Name variations: Ellie Brown. Born Eleanor Bennett Durrall, Feb 11, 1940, in Central City, KY; m. John Y. Brown Jr. (Kentucky governor who later married tv host Phyllis George, 1979, and Jill Louise Brown, 1998), 1960 (div. 1977); m. Robert Moore; children: 3, including John Young Brown III (Kentucky Secretary of State). ❖ Established majority stock ownership in Kentucky Colonels team of American Basketball Association and became head of team's 5-woman governors board (1973); received Kentucky Woman of the Year Award (1973).

MOORE, Erin O'Brien (1902–1979). *See O'Brien-Moore, Erin.*

MOORE, Eva (1870–1955). English actress. Born Feb 9, 1870, in Brighton, East Sussex, England; died April 27, 1955, in Maidenhead, Berkshire, England; dau. of Emily (Strachan) Moore and Edmund Henry Moore; sister of Jessie Moore and Decima Moore (both actress-singers) and Bertha Moore; m. H.V. Esmond, 1891 (died 1922); children: Jack Esmond; Jill Esmond (1908–1990, actress and 1st wife of Laurence Olivier). ❖ Made stage debut in London in *Proposals* (1887) and subsequently had highly successful stage and screen career in London before arriving in Hollywood (1931); films include *The Law Divine, The Crimson Circle, Chu Chin Chow, Motherland, Brown Sugar, The Old Dark House* (as Rebecca Femm), *Just Smith, House of Dreams, Jew Suss, Vintage Wine, The Bandit of Sherwood Forest* and *Of Human Bondage.*

MOORE, Grace (1898–1947). American singer of opera, musical comedy, and concerts. Born Mary Willie Grace Moore, Dec 5, 1898, in Slabtown, TN; died in plane crash at Copenhagen, Denmark, Jan 26, 1947; attended Ward-Belmont School for Girls, Nashville, 1916–17, Wilson-Greene School of Music, 1917–19; m. Valentin Parera (Spanish film actor), 1931. ❖ Made operatic debut, singing an aria from *Aïda* at Washington's National Theater (1919); made Broadway debut in *Hitchy Koo* (1920), followed by Irving Berlin's *Music Box Review* (1923); studied opera in Europe (1925–28); debuted as Mimi in *La Bohème* at Metropolitan Opera (1928); established herself as a vocal star on American radio when she appeared on NBC's "General Motors Hour"; appeared in 1st Hollywood film *A Lady's Morals* (1931), a biography of Jenny Lind; during depression, turned to light opera and vaudeville and made frequent appearances on radio; appeared in film *One Night of Love* (1934) which made her a box-office star; began a regular half-hour radio broadcast on NBC (1935), popularizing the song, "Ciribiribin"; debuted in London to great success (1935); made goodwill tours of Latin America (1940–41); went on wartime USO tours (1942–45). Awarded France's Legion of Honor (1939). ❖ See also autobiography *You're Only Human Once* (Garden City, 1946); Rowena Farrar, *Grace Moore and Her Many Worlds* (Cornwall, 1982); and (film) *So This is Love* (1953); and *Women in World History*.

MOORE, Ida (1882–1964). American stage and screen character actress. Born Mar 1, 1882, in Altoona, Kansas; died Sept 26, 1964, in Los Angeles, CA. ❖ Made film debut in *Lightnin'* (1925), followed by *To Each His Own, The Egg and I, Johnny Belinda, Ma and Pa Kettle, Roseanna McCoy, The Lemon Drop Kid, Show Boat, Scandal at Scourie, The Country Girl, Desk Set* and *Rock-a-Bye Baby*, among others.

MOORE, Isabel (1863–1921). *See Button, Isabel.*

MOORE, Isabella (1863–1921). *See Button, Isabel.*

MOORE, Isabella (1894–1975). Scottish swimmer. Born Oct 23, 1894, in Scotland; died Mar 7, 1975. ❖ At Stockholm Olympics, won a gold medal in the 4x100-meter freestyle relay (1912).

MOORE, Jane Elizabeth (1738–?). British poet and memoirist. Born 1738 in London, England. ❖ Published *Genuine Memoirs* (1786) and *Miscellaneous Poems on Various Subjects* (1796).

MOORE, Jessie (1865–1910). English actress. Born 1865 in Brighton, Sussex, England; died Nov 28, 1910, in London; dau. of Emily (Strachan) Moore and Edmund Henry Moore; sister of Bertha Moore, Decima Moore (actress and singer) and Eva Moore (actress); aunt of Jill Esmond (actress); m. Cairns James (D'Oyly Carte baritone). ❖ Toured with D'Oyly Carte (1889–91), appearing as Yum-Yum in *The Mikado*, Elsie Maynard in *The Yeomen of the Guard*, and Gianetta in *The Gondoliers*; replaced younger sister Decima Moore at the Savoy as Polly in *Captain Billy* (1891); subsequently appeared in comedy and light operas (1892–1905), most notably as Theresa in *The Mountebanks*.

MOORE, Juanita (1922—). African-American actress. Born Oct 19, 1922, in Los Angeles, CA. ❖ Notable character actress, nominated for an Academy Award for Best Supporting Actress for performance in *Imitation of Life* (1959); appeared frequently in supporting roles in films and on tv (1950–80); other films include *Lydia Bailey* (1952), *Affair in Trinidad* (1952), *Witness to Murder* (1954), *Women's Prison* (1955), *Ransom* (1956), *A Band of Angels* (1957), *Tammy Tell Me True* (1961), *A Raisin in the Sun* (1961), *Walk on the Wild Side* (1962), *Papa's Delicate Condition* (1963), *The Singing Nun* (1966), *Rosie* (1968), *Thomasine and Bushrod* (1974) and *Two Moon Junction* (1988). ❖ See also *Women in World History*.

MOORE, Julia A. (1847–1920). American poet. Born Julia Ann Davis, Dec 1, 1847, in Plainfield, Michigan; died 1920; m. Frederick Franklin Moore, 1864; children: 10. ❖ Known as "The Sweet Singer of Michigan," inspired Mark Twain's character Emmeline Grangerford in *The Adventures of Huckleberry Finn*; published sentimental poetry in collections *The Sweet Singer of Michigan Salutes the Public* (1876, republished as *The Sentimental Song Book*) and *A Few Words to the Public* (1878).

MOORE, Lilian (1909–2004). American poet, editor and children's book writer. Born Lilian Levenson, Mar 17, 1909, in New York, NY; died July 20, 2004, in Seattle, WA; dau. of Sarah (Asheron) Levenson and Aaron Levenson; Hunter College, BA, 1930; graduate study at Columbia University; m. 2nd husband William Moore; m. Sam Reavin, 1969 (died); children: (2nd m.) Jonathan Moore. ❖ Worked as elementary schoolteacher in New York City; became staff member of NYC Bureau of Educational Research (1937); became the 1st editor of Arrow Book Club for Scholastic Book Services (1957), then editor of special book project (history and biography series, 1968–69); also worked as editor of easy reader series in Wonder Books Division of Grosset & Dunlap and as series editor for Thomas Y. Crowell; helped make children's books more affordable, and worked to combat racial stereotypes in children's literature; helped establish the Council on Interracial Books for Children; books include *Old Rosie, the Horse Nobody Understood* (1952), *The Terrible Mr. Twitmeyer* (1952), *Sam's Place: Poems from the Country* (1973), *I'll Meet You at the Cucumbers* (1988), and the "Little Racoon" series.

MOORE, Lillian (1911–1967). American dancer and choreographer. Born 1911 in Chase City, VA; died July 29, 1967, in New York, NY. ❖ Performed with American Ballet at Metropolitan Opera in NYC in works by Balanchine (until 1938) and Romanoff (1939–42); danced with Fokine Ballet (1940), where she performed in *Polovtsian Dances from Prince Igor* and *Les Sylphides*; created own works for solo concert recitals, such as *Terpsichore* (1934), *The Amazon* (1942), *30 Years in a Dancer's Life* (1947) and *Tentative Tango* (1952); taught at High School of Performing Arts and American Ballet Center, where she also directed the apprentice program which evolved into the charter company of the City Center Joffrey Ballet; often wrote articles about American and Danish dance history, which were collected in *Artists of the Dance* (1938) and *Images of the Dance* (1965).

MOORE, Maggie (1847–1929). American-born actress and singer. Name variations: Mrs. J.C. Williamson. Born Margaret O'Sullivan, July 10, 1847, in San Francisco, CA; died Mar 15, 1926; m. J. C. Williamson (actor and producer), 1872 (div. 1899, he then m. Mary Weir, 1899); m. Harry R. Roberts (actor), 1902. ❖ Made stage debut in San Francisco (1871), then appeared with husband J.C. Williamson as Lizzie Stofel in the huge hit *Struck Oil*; made stage debut in Sydney, Australia, in the same part (1874), then repeated the success in London (1876), followed by *Fool of the Family, The Colleen Bawn, The Chinese Question* and *Our Boarding House*; settled in Australia (1879), appearing there as Josephine in *H.M.S. Pinafore*, Bettina in *La Mascotte*, Katisha in *The Mikado*, then starred in *Meg the Castaway* (1924).

MOORE, Marianne (1887–1972). American poet, editor, and scholar. Born Marianne Craig Moore, Nov 15, 1887, in Kirkwood, Missouri; died in New York, NY, Feb 5, 1972; dau. of John Milton Moore and Mary (Warner) Moore (English teacher, died 1947); attended Metzger Institute, Pennsylvania; Bryn Mawr College, BA, 1909; graduate of Carlisle Commercial College, 1910; never married; no children. ❖ A shaping force in the American Modernist tradition, submitted poems to college literary magazine, *Tipyn o'Bob* (1907–10); cultivated an interest in 17th-century prose writers who remained influences on her work; traveled abroad (1911); taught and coached at US Indian School in Carlisle, PA (1911–15); published 1st poem, a satire on war, in the *Egoist* and other poems in *Poetry* (1915); work reviewed in *Egoist* by H.D. (1916); began keeping a notebook that became a storehouse of ideas for poems (1916); moved with mother to NY (1918); worked as private tutor, secretary, and assistant in Hudson Park branch of New York Public Library; became part of a circle that included Wallace Stevens and William Carlos Williams; became acting editor of the *Dial* (1925–29); moved with mother from Greenwich Village to Brooklyn (1929), where she lived for nearly 40 years; became critic and reviewer of works by many of her contemporaries (1920s); met Elizabeth Bishop (1934) and began a correspondence that lasted until her death; began translation of La Fontaine's *Fables* (1945); threw out the 1st baseball at Yankee Stadium (1968); continued to write and translate until shortly before her death; writings include *Poems* (1921), *Observations* (1924), *Selected Poems* (1935), *The Pangolin and Other Verse* (1936), *What Are Years* (1941), *Nevertheless* (1944), *Predilections* (1955), *Like a Bulwark* (1956), *O to Be a Dragon* (1959) and *Tell, Me, Tell Me: Granite, Steel, and Other Topics* (1966). Won Pulitzer Prize (1951), National Book Award (1951), Bollingen Award (1953), and National Medal for Literature (1968). ❖ See also Bonnie Costello, *Marianne Moore: Imaginary Possessions* (Harvard U. Press, 1981); Donald Hall, *Marianne Moore: The Cage and the Animal* (Western, 1970); Charles Molesworth, *Marianne Moore: A Literary Life* (Atheneum, 1990); and *Women in World History*.

MOORE, Marjorie (1917–1997). See *Reynolds, Marjorie*.

MOORE, Mary (1861–1931). See *Wyndham, Mary*.

MOORE, Mary Emelia (1869–1951). New Zealand missionary. Born Mar 7, 1869, at Dunedin, New Zealand; died May 17, 1951, at Dunedin; dau. of Charles Moore (saddler) and Mary (Stewart) Moore; University of Otago, BA, 1893. ❖ Sent by Church of Scotland to establish mission in Ichang (Yichang) district on Yangtze Kiang (Chang Yangtze) River, in China (1897) which she ran until 1932; opened girls' boarding school in Ichang (c. 1900); established own refuge at Ichang, where she helped poor and disabled women and children and helped establish prisoners' aid society (1932–38); because of Japanese invasion, was forced to evacuate to New Zealand until 1940, when she returned to China and retired at Ching Tu; evacuated to India, then to Scotland, and finally to New Zealand (1950). ❖ See also *Dictionary of New Zealand Biography* (Vol. 3).

MOORE, Mary Tyler (1936—). American stage, tv and screen actress. Born Dec 29, 1936, in Brooklyn, NY; m. Dick Meeker, 1955 (div. 1961); m. Grant Tinker (NBC executive), 1962 (div. 1981); m. Dr. Robert Levine, 1983; children: (1st m.) Richie Meeker (died 1980). ❖ Made tv debut as an elf in a Hotpoint commercial (1955) and co-starred on "The Dick Van Dyke Show" (1961–66); with husband Tinker, founded MTM Enterprises (1969) which produced, among others, "Lou Grant," "Hill Street Blues," "St. Elsewhere," "The Bob Newhart Show," and "WKRP in Cincinnati"; appeared on "The Mary Tyler Moore Show" (1970–77); films include *Thoroughly Modern Millie, Don't Just Stand There, What's So Bad About Feeling Good, Change of Habit, Six Weeks, Just Between Friends, Flirting with Disaster* and *Keys to Tulsa*; active for animal rights. Nominated for an Oscar as Best Actress for *Ordinary People* (1980); received a Special Tony for Broadway performance in *Whose Life Is It Anyway?* (1980); won 5 Emmys. ❖ See also autobiography, *After All* (1995).

MOORE, Mollie Evelyn (1844–1909). See *Davis, Mollie Moore*.

MOORE, Mrs. (1916–2000). See *Gynt, Greta*.

MOORE, Mrs. Owen (1897–1983). See *Perry, Katherine*.

MOORE, Queen Mother Audley (1898–1997). See *Moore, Audley*.

MOORE, Sara Jane (1930—). American would-be assassin. Born Sara Jane Kahn (Moore is her mother's maiden name), Feb 15, 1930, in Charleston, WV; married 4 men (one of them twice), including John Aalberg; children: 4, including (with Aalberg) Frederick. ❖ Was a nursing school dropout, Women's Army Corps recruit, and accountant; turned to revolutionary politics in her 40s; recruited by FBI to collect information about Patty Hearst kidnapping (1974), but cover was blown; to reestablish radical credentials, stood outside a San Francisco hotel and fired a .38 revolver at President Gerald Ford, missing her target when a bystander, Oliver Sipple, grabbed her arm (Sept 22, 1975); escaped from Alderson Federal Prison for Women, where she was serving a life sentence, but was apprehended 25 miles away (1979); transferred to federal prison in Pleasanton, CA. Moore's attempt on Ford's life came just 17 days after Lynette "Squeaky" Fromme had tried to assassinate him; like Moore, Fromme also made a prison break from Alderson, before being apprehended 2 days later (1987).

MOORE, Terry (1929—). American screen actress and producer. Name variations: Jan Ford, Judy Ford, Helen Koford. Born Helen Luella Koford, Jan 7, 1929, in Los Angeles, CA; m. Glenn Davis (football player), 1951 (div. 1952); m. Stuart Cramer, 1959 (div. 1972); m. Richard Carey, 1979; also claimed to have been secretly married to Howard Hughes for which the Hughes estate paid a settlement. ❖ Was a child model; at 11, made film debut in *Maryland* (1940); tried various screen names for next 6 films before settling on Terry Moore (1948); films include *The Return of October, The Great Rupert, The Barefoot Mailman, Mighty Joe Young, Beneath the 12-Mile Reef, King of the Khyber Rifles, Daddy Long Legs, Bernadine, Peyton Place, Waco* and *Double Exposure*; co-produced and wrote story for *Beverly Hills Brats* (1989). Nominated for Oscar for *Come Back Little Sheba* (1952).

MOORE-GUGGISBERG, Lady (1871–1964). See *Moore, Decima*.

MOORE SITTERLY, Charlotte (1898–1990). See *Sitterly, Charlotte Moore*.

MOOREHEAD, Agnes (1900–1974). American actress. Born Dec 6, 1900, in Clinton, MA; died April 30, 1974, in Rochester, MN; dau. of John Moorehead (Presbyterian minister) and Mary Mildred (McCauley) Moorehead (professional singer); Muskingum College, BA, 1928; University of Wisconsin, MA; graduate of American Academy of Dramatic Arts, 1929; m. John Griffith Lee (actor), June 6, 1930 (div.

1952); m. actor Robert Cist (div. 1958); children: (adopted) son, Sean (b. 1949). ❖ Character actress of incredible range, nominated for 4 Academy Awards, began career in NY in small roles in Theater Guild productions; during Depression, turned to radio, taking part in thousands of shows, including "The March of Time," "The Shadow," and several daytime soaps; recruited for Orson Welles' Mercury Players, moved with the group to Hollywood (1940); had small but pivotal roles in 2 of Welles' early films: *Citizen Kane* (1941), as Kane's mother, and *The Magnificent Ambersons* (1942), for which she won New York Film Critics Award and was nominated for an Academy Award; back on radio, starred on "Sorry, Wrong Number" (1943) and played Cora Dithers on "Blondie"; received 3 additional Academy Award nominations for work in *Mrs. Parkington* (1944), *Johnny Belinda* (1948), and *Hush Hush . . . Sweet Charlotte* (1964); made over 60 other films; was part of the First Drama Quartet's dramatic reading of *Don Juan in Hell* (1951–54); appeared in one-woman show, *The Redhead,* later revised to *Come Closer, I'll Give You an Earful;* appeared as Endora on tv series "Bewitched" (1963–71). Won Emmy for an episode in "Wild, Wild West." ❖ See also Warren Sherk, *Agnes Moorehead: A Very Private Person* (1976); and *Women in World History.*

MOORER, Lana (1971—). *See MC Lyte.*

MOORHEAD, Sarah Parsons (fl. 1741–1742). American poet. Lived in Boston, MA. ❖ Poems include *To the Rev. James Davenport on His Departure from Boston* (1742) and "Lines . . . Dedicated to the Rev. Mr. Gilbert Tennent," both written to balance excesses of the Great Awakening in Boston.

MOOSDORF, Johanna (1911–2000). German poet and novelist. Born July 12, 1911, in Leipzig, Germany; died June 21, 2000; m. Paul Bernstein (writer), 1932 (died 1944). ❖ Husband died in Auschwitz; moved with the group to West Berlin from East Germany (1950); works, which deal with fascism and position of women in male-dominated society, include *Brennendes Leben* (1947), *Flucht nach Afrika* (1952, trans. as *Flight to Africa*), *Die Nachtigallen schlagen im Schnee* (1953), *Nebenan* (1961, trans. as *Next Door*), *Die Andermanns* (1969) and *Die Freundinnen* (1977).

MORA, Constancia de la (1906–1950). Spanish political activist. Name variations: Connie; Constancia de la Mora y Maura. Pronunciation: Con-STAN-thee-ah day lah Mor-ah ee Mau-rah. Born Constancia de la Mora y Maura in Madrid, Spain, Jan 28, 1906; died as a result of injuries received in auto accident in Guatemala, Jan 26, 1950; dau. of Germán de la Mora (managing director of one of the most important electric companies in Madrid) and Constancia Maura (dau. of Prime Minister Antonio Maura); attended St. Mary's Convent School of Cambridge, 1920–23; m. Manuel Bolín, May 1927 (div. 1932, one of the 1st divorces of Spanish Republic); m. Ignacio Hidalgo de Cisneros (diplomat), 1933; children: (1st m.) Constancia María de Lourdes Bolín Maura (known as "Luli"). ❖ Spanish activist during Spanish Civil War (1936–39) who held position of Censor for Foreign Press Bureau and was instrumental in the organization of the Joint Anti-Fascist Refugee Committee during WWII; when rebel forces staged a military coup against the legally elected government (July 1936), starting Spanish Civil War, joined the Spanish Communist Party (PCE, 1936); became an active member of National Committee of Antifascist Women, the central governing organ of AMA, the National Organization of Anti-Fascist Women; worked with the Ministry of Justice for the Protection of Minors; directed a hospice for abandoned or orphaned children; ordered by the Committee for the Protection of Minors to leave the capital, due to intense bombings of Madrid (autumn 1936); evacuated, along with her 650 charges, to the Mediterranean city of Alicante and oversaw colonies for evacuated children; established a convalescent home for wounded aviators in Alicante; evacuated daughter to USSR; was the only woman to join the staff of censors of the Foreign Press Bureau in Valencia, the new capital of the Republic (1937); visited various fronts; attended International Anti-Fascist Writers Conference in Valencia; evacuated with rest of Republican government to coastal city of Barcelona (1937); promoted to chief of the Foreign Press Bureau—the only woman to hold this position in Spanish history (1938); accompanied the foreign minister to Geneva where they pleaded the Spanish cause before League of Nations Assembly (May 1938); left Barcelona for Figueras (Jan 1939); evacuated to France (Feb 1939); set up makeshift press agency in Toulouse and became impromptu speaker for the government of the Spanish Republic; left for US to ask for military and humanitarian aid for Spanish cause (Feb 1939); after Franco declared his victory over Spanish Republic, relocated with family to Cuernavaca, Mexico (1940); was instrumental

in the operation of the Joint Anti-Fascist Refugee Committee (1940–45). ❖ See also autobiography *In Place of Splendor* (1939); and *Women in World History.*

MORACE, Carolina (1964—). Italian soccer player. Born Feb 5, 1964, in Venice, Italy. ❖ A soccer legend in Italy, voted one of the nation's top women in history, had a 20-year playing career, winning 12 Italian League titles with 8 different clubs, scoring more than 500 goals; as captain of the national team, scored 105 goals in international play; was the 1st woman to coach an Italian men's professional team (1999), then became head coach of the women's national team; does commentary on soccer matches for Telemontecarlo (TMC) and is a qualified lawyer.

MORALES, Hilda (1946—). American ballet dancer. Born June 17, 1946, in the Bronx, NY; raised in Santurce, Puerto Rico; trained at School of American Ballet. ❖ Danced a "Snowflake" as apprentice in New York City Ballet's *The Nutcracker;* joined Pennsylvania Ballet (1965) where she danced in Balanchine repertory as well as in such contemporary works as John Butler's *Ceremony* (1968) and *Journeys* (1970); performed with American Ballet Theater (1972–73) in Ailey's *The River,* Baryshnikov's *The Nutcracker* and Tudor's *Jardin aux Lilas,* among others.

MORAN, Dolores (1924–1982). American actress. Born Jan 27, 1924, in Stockton, CA; died Feb 5, 1982, in Woodland Hills, CA. ❖ Films include *Yankee Doodle Dandy, Old Acquaintance, To Have and Have Not, Hollywood Canteen* and *The Horn Blows at Midnight.*

MORAN, Gussie (1923—). American tennis player. Name variations: Gertrude Augusta Moran; "Gorgeous Gussie" Moran. Born Gertrude Augusta Moran in 1923 (some sources cite 1922, others 1924) in Santa Monica, CA; married twice. ❖ Won Seabright mixed-doubles crown with Pancho Segura (1946) and National Clay Court Doubles with Mary Arnold Prentiss (1947); made the Top Ten of Tennis list (1947); won 3 titles (mixed doubles, women's doubles, and women's singles) at National Indoor Tennis championships (1949); caused a stir by wearing lace-trimmed panties as part of her outfit during Wimbledon tournament (1949); became a radio host in California (1972). ❖ See also *Women in World History.*

MORAN, Lois (1907–1990). American actress. Name variations: Lois Moran Young. Born Lois Darlington Dowling, Mar 1, 1907 (some sources cite 1908), in Pittsburgh, Pennsylvania; died July 13, 1990, in Sedona, Arizona, of cancer; dau. of Roger Dowling and Gladys (Evans) Dowling; educated at Lycée de Tours, France; m. Clarence M. Young (assistant secretary of commerce and later Pan Am executive), 1935; children: 1 son. ❖ Raised in France, trained as a dancer and performed with the Paris National Opera for 2 years (1922–24); also appeared in 2 French films; made US film debut in *Stella Dallas* (1925), starring Mrs. Leslie Carter; made over 25 films then retired from the screen (1931) to return to the stage; scored some success in stage musicals, notably on Broadway in *Of Thee I Sing* (1931), then abandoned career to marry; taught drama and dance at Stanford University and appeared on tv series "Waterfront" (1953–56). The character of Rosemary in F. Scott Fitzgerald's novel *Tender Is the Night* is said to be based on her. ❖ See also *Women in World History.*

MORAN, Margaret (1955—). English politician and member of Parliament. Born Margaret Moran, April 24, 1955, in East London, England, to Irish parents; attended St. Mary's College of Education and Birmingham University. ❖ Representing Labour, elected to House of Commons for Luton South (1997, 2001, 2005); became assistant government whip (2003); was responsible for the Womenspeak project to link Parliamentarians and survivors of domestic violence.

MORAN, Mary Nimmo (1842–1899). American landscape etching artist. Name variations: Mary Nimmo. Born May 16, 1842, in Strathaven, Lanarkshire, Scotland; died of typhoid fever, Sept 25, 1899, in East Hampton, New York; dau. of Archibald Nimmo (weaver) and Mary Nimmo; m. Thomas Moran (artist), 1862; children: Paul Nimmo Moran (b. 1867); Mary Scott Moran; Ruth Bedford Moran. ❖ At 5, immigrated with family to US, settling in Crescentville, PA; following marriage, exhibited some of work at Pennsylvania Academy of Fine Arts and National Academy of Design in New York City; moved to Newark, NJ, and often sketched the surrounding countryside (such as *Newark From the Meadows*); began etching (early 1870s); elected to New York Etching Club (1880); invited to exhibit with Royal Society of Painter-Etchers in London (1881); became foremost American woman in the etching field. Received diploma and medal for etchings at World's

Columbian Exposition in Chicago (1893). ❖ See also *Women in World History*.

MORAN, Patsy (1903–1968). American comedic actress. Born Oct 12, 1903, in PA; died Dec 10, 1968, in Hollywood, CA; m. John Strock. ❖ Appeared in over 30 films, many of them with Laurel and Hardy.

MORAN, Peggy (1918–2002). American screen actress. Born Mary Jeanette Moran, Oct 23, 1918, in Clinton, IA; died Oct 25, 2002, in Camarillo, CA, as a result of injuries from auto accident; dau. of Earl Moran (artist) and Louise Moran (Denishawn dancer); m. Henry Koster (director), 1942 (died 1988). ❖ Made film debut in *Boy Meets Girl* (1938), followed by *Ninotchka, The Mummy's Hand, Rhythm of the Saddle, Trail of the Vigilantes, Spring Parade, Argentine Nights, One Night in the Tropics, Horror Island, Flying Cadets, Drums of the Congo* and *King of the Cowboys,* among others.

MORAN, Polly (1884–1952). American comic actress. Born Pauline Theresa Moran, June 28, 1884, in Chicago, Illinois; died Jan 25, 1952, in Los Angeles, CA; m. 2nd husband Martin T. Malone, 1933; children: (adopted) son. ❖ Began career in vaudeville, then crossed over into films (c. 1913); appeared in numerous silent shorts with Mack Sennett before returning to the stage (1918); reemerged in feature films (1920s), playing comic character roles; was particularly noted for a series of films that she made with Marie Dressler during early sound era, including *Reducing, Politics* (both in 1931), and *Prosperity* (1932); other films include *The Affairs of Anatol* (1921), *The Callahans and the Murphys* (1927), *Bringing Up Father* (1928), *Rose-Marie* (1928), *While the City Sleeps* (1928), *The Hollywood Revue* (1929), *Way Out West* (1930), *Alice in Wonderland* (1933), *Ladies in Distress* (1938), *Tom Brown's School Days* (1940), *Adam's Rib* (1949) and *The Yellow Cab Man* (1950). ❖ See also *Women in World History*.

MORANDINI, Giuliana (1938—). Italian novelist and literary critic. Born 1938 in Udine, Italy. ❖ Frequently published critical essays in Italian newspapers and magazines; scholarly works include *E allora mi hanno rinchiusa* (1977, Then They Locked Me Up), on the condition of women in mental asylums, and *La voce che è in lei* (The Voice Within Her, 1980), a study on women writers; other writings include *I cristalli di Vienna* (1978, Cut Glass from Vienna), *Caffè specchi* (1983, trans. as *The Café of Mirrors*), *Angelo e Berlino* (1987, An Angel in Berlin), *Da te lontano* (1989, Far From You) and *Giocando a Dama con la Luna* (1996).

MORANI, Alma Dea (1907–2001). American plastic surgeon. Born in New York, NY, Mar 21, 1907; died Jan 27, 2001, in Philadelphia, PA; dau. of Salvatore Morani (sculptor) and Amalia (Gracci) Morani; New York University, BS, 1928; Woman's Medical College, MD, 1931. ❖ The 1st female member of the American Society of Plastic and Reconstructive Surgeons, interned at St. James Hospital, Newark (1931–32); was surgeon resident, Woman's Medical Hospital, Philadelphia (1932–35); had private practice at St. Louis University (1946–47); fellow in plastic surgery, University of Washington Medical School (1946–47); private practice in plastic surgery, Philadelphia (1948 on); associate surgeon, Roxborough Memorial Hospital (1940 on), Woman's Hospital (1938 on); chief of plastic surgery, St. Mary's Hospital (1948 on); professor of clinical surgery, Woman's Medical College (1950 on).

MORANTE, Elsa (1912–1985). Italian writer. Pronunciation: Moe-RANT-Tay. Born Aug 18, 1912, in Rome, Italy; died of a heart attack in Rome, Nov 25, 1985; dau. of Irma Poggibonsi Morante (descendant of a Jewish family in Modena) and legally the dau. of Augusto Morante (Sicilian schoolteacher); probably the dau. of Francesco Lo Monaco; largely self-educated, but some sources indicate that she studied briefly at University of Rome; m. Alberto Moravia (writer), 1941 (sep. 1962). ❖ One of Italy's most distinguished writers during mid-20th century, used techniques of "magic realism" to explore the way in which individuals have been shaped by the pains and traumas of childhood; published 1st short stories (1935–36); met Alberto Moravia (1936); went into hiding to evade fascist police (1943); published 1st novel, *Menzogna e sortilegio* (*House of Liars*) and won Viareggio prize (1948); won Strega prize (1957); published *L'isola di Arturo* (*Arturo's Island,* 1959); wrote bestseller *La storia* (*History: A Novel,* 1974), the most popular Italian novel since Giuseppe di Lampedusa's *The Leopard*; won Prix Medicis for *Aracoeli* (1982); attempted suicide (1983, some authorities place this in 1984); also wrote poetry *Il mondo salvato dai ragazzini* (*The World Saved by Little Children,* 1968) and *Alibi* (*Alibi*) and short stories *Il gioco segreto* (*The Secret Garden,* 1941) and *Lo scialle andaluso* (*The Andalusian Shawl,* 1963). ❖ See also *Maledetta benedetta* (*Cursed and Blessed*), a family

history by brother Marcello Morante (1986); posthumous publication of her diary (1989); and *Women in World History*.

MORAS, Karen (1954—). Australian swimmer. Name variations: Karen Moras Stephenson. Born Jan 1954 in Australia. ❖ At Mexico City Olympics, won a bronze medal in 400-meter freestyle (1968); won 3 Commonwealth gold medals (1970).

MORATA, Fulvia Olympia (1526–1555). Italian scholar. Name variations: also seen as Olympia Fulvia Morata. Born in Ferrara in 1526; died in Heidelberg, Germany, Oct 25, 1555; dau. of Fulvio Pellegrino Morata (humanist scholar, who was once duke of Ferrara); had at least 2 brothers and 2 sisters; educated at home by brothers, in Latin at the court of Ferrara by Chilian Senf, and through self-study; m. Andrea (or Andrew) Grunthler. ❖ While still in teens, was writing in Latin and Greek, emulating the classical literary styles and composing critical philosophical essays; was welcomed at the court of Renée of France (1510–1575), duchess of Ferrara, as a companion for Renée's daughter, Princess Anne of Ferrara; because of religious intolerance, moved with husband to Schweinfurt, Franconia, where he had secured a position as physician to a garrison of Spanish troops; continued her studies, which had become wholly focused on religion; in an ensuing war (1553), fled Schweinfurt and died soon after; orations, letters, and poems, published as *Opera Omnia* (1580) and in monograph form by Caroline Bowles Southey (1834). ❖ See also *Women in World History*.

MORATH, Inge (1923–2002). Austrian-born photographer. Born Inge Mörath, May 27, 1923, in Graz, Austria; died Jan 30, 2002, in New York, NY; graduate of University of Berlin, 1944; dau. of scientists; m. Arthur Miller (playwright), 1962; children: Rebecca Miller (b. 1962, filmmaker and painter). ❖ Internationally known photographer and photojournalist, bought a Leica and began working as an assistant and researcher for photographer Henri Cartier-Bresson (1953–54); became a member of Magnum Photos (1955); began traveling widely (1955), resulting in such books as *De la Perse à l'Iran* (*From Persia to Iran,* 1958), *Tunisie* (1961), *In Russia* (1969), *Chinese Encounters* (1979), and *Russian Journal* (1991); photographed the 1st Chinese production of *Death of a Salesman,* published as *Salesman in Beijing* (1984); work has been published in such magazines as *The Saturday Evening Post, Life, Paris-Match, Vogue,* and *Picture Post,* and exhibited in numerous galleries and major museums, including Metropolitan Museum of Art, Chicago Art Institute, Kunsthaus in Zurich, Union of Photojournalists in Moscow, and Inge Morath Museum for Photography in Saxony, Germany; also known for her photographic portraits of artists and political personalities. Received Medal of Honor from City of Vienna; received Great Austrian State Prize for Photography (1992). ❖ See also *Inge Morath: Life as a Photographer* (Keyahoff, 1999); and *Women in World History*.

MORAVCOVA, Martina (1976—). Slovakian swimmer. Born Jan 16, 1976, in Piestany, Slovakia; University of Economics, Bratislava, 1994–95; Southern Methodist University, Dallas, MA in Applied Economics, 2000. ❖ At SC European championships, won gold medals for 200-meter freestyle (1998, 1999, 2000, 2001), 100-meter butterfly (1998, 2000, 2001), 100-meter indiv. medley (1998, 1999, 2000, 2001) and 200-meter indiv. medley (1999); at SC World championships, won a gold medal for 200-meter freestyle (1999), and 100-meter indiv. medley (1999, 2000, 2002) and 200-meter indiv. medley (1999) and 100-meter butterfly (2002); won silver medals for 100-meter butterfly and 200-meter freestyle at Sydney Olympics (2000).

MORAWETZ, Cathleen Synge (1923—). American mathematician. Born Cathleen Synge, May 5, 1923, in Toronto, Canada; dau. of John Light Synge (mathematician) and Eleanor Mabel Allen Synge; m. Herbert Morawetz (chemist), Oct 28, 1945; children: 4. ❖ Became naturalized US citizen (1950); served as research associate (from 1952), professor (from 1965), and director (from 1984) of New York University's Courant Institute of Mathematical Sciences (1st woman head of an American mathematical institute); served as chair of women's committee of American Mathematical Society; named Outstanding Woman Scientist by Association for Women in Science; was the 2nd woman elected president of American Mathematical Society (1995); was the 1st woman awarded National Medal of Science for mathematics (highest honor in science and technology in US).

MORAY, countess of.
See Gruaidh.
See Ross, Euphemia (d. 1387).
See Stewart, Marjorie (d. after 1417).

MORDAUNT, Miss (1812–1858). *See Nisbett, Louisa Cranstoun.*

MORDECAI, Pamela (1942—). Jamaican-born poet, editor and children's writer. Born 1942 in Jamaica; m. Martin Mordecai. ❖ Worked as English teacher, radio broadcaster, and film interviewer; employed as publications officer for School of Education at University of West Indies; with husband, established Sandberry Press in Kingston; edited journals and poetry anthologies; work focuses on development of language arts in Carribean; poems published in anthologies *The Caribbean Poem* (1976) and *Ambakaila* (1976) and in journals including *Savacou*, *Jamaica Journal*, and *Caribbean Quarterly*; edited *Caribbean Quarterly* and contributed to *Jamaica Woman*.

MØRDRE, Berit. Norwegian cross-country skier. Name variations: Berit Mordre or Moerdre; Berit Mordre-Lammedal; Berit M. Lammedal. Born in Norway. ❖ Won gold medals for 10 km and 3 x 5 km relay at Grenoble Olympics (1968); won a bronze medal for 3 x 5 km relay at Sapporo Olympics (1972).

MORDVINOVA, Vera Aleksandrovna (1895–1966). *See Aleksandrovna, Vera.*

MORE, Agnes (1591–1656). British translator. Name variations: Dame Agnes More or Moor. Born 1591, possibly in Bampton Co., Oxon, England; died Mar 14, 1656, in Cambrai, Flanders; dau. of John More of Bampton Co., Oxon; great-great-granddau. of Sir Thomas More; cousin of John Donne and Gertrude More. ❖ Entered recusant English Benedictine Abbey of Our lady of Consolation at Cambrai in Flanders (1623); trans. work of mystical theology of Jeanne de Cambry as *The Building of Divine Love As Translated by Dame Agnes More, Transcribed from the 17th Century Manuscript.*

MORE, Alice (c. 1472–1545). English gentlewoman who was the 2nd wife of Thomas More. Name variations: Alice Middleton; Lady Alice More. Born c. 1472; died in 1545; m. a man named Middleton (died 1509); became 2nd wife of Thomas More (1478–1535, English scholar and statesman who was slain for his opposition to detaching England from the spiritual authority of the Roman Catholic Church), in 1511; children: (1st marriage) one daughter, Alice; 4 stepchildren. ❖ Presided with famous (or infamous, depending on the chronicler) efficiency over one of the most illustrious households in 16th-century England. ❖ See also Ruth Norrington, *In the Shadow of a Saint: Lady Alice More* (Kylin, 1985); and *Women in World History.*

MORE, Gertrude (1606–1633). British poet and spiritual writer. Name variations: Helen Gertrude More. Born Helen Gertrude More, Mar 25, 1606, in Low Leyton, Essex, England; died of smallpox, Aug 17, 1633, in Cambrai, Flanders; dau. of Cresacre More and Elizabeth Gage More; sister of Bridget More (abbess); great-great-granddau. of Sir Thomas More; cousin of John Donne and Agnes More. ❖ Poet and spiritual writer, became a nun at English Benedictine Abbey of Our lady of Consolation at Cambrai in Flanders, which was financed by her father; influenced by Augustine Baker, her writings emphasize the interior life, comtemplative prayer, and freedom of conscience.

MORE, Hannah (1745–1833). English playwright, novelist, and tract writer. Born Hannah More at Stapleton, Gloucestershire, England, Feb 2, 1745; died in Clifton, Sept 7, 1833; dau. of Jacob More (schoolmaster) and Mary Grace More; never married; no children. ❖ Writer whose talents were turned to evangelism within the Anglican Church, agitation against human slavery, and education for the working classes, despite fame and the promise of an honored place among the most accomplished citizens of the Republic of Letters; displaying intelligence at an early age, could read by age 4 and became proficient in the study of the classics; taught school with her sisters at Bristol and began to write (after 1757); ended long engagement with a Mr. Turner, a merchant (1773); published *The Search after Happiness* (1773); had 1st play, *The Inflexible Captive,* presented at Bath (1774); associated with David Garrick and other literary figures (after 1773); acclaimed for her play *Percy* which was performed in London (1777–78); at home in the cultivated company of Georgian England, also saw its imperfections, its indifference to the lot of the poor, its complicity in human bondage, and its rejection of what she regarded as its essential heritage, the Christian religion; departed London and began religious writing at Cowslip Green, near Bristol (after 1779); published *Thoughts on the Importance of the Manners of the Great to General Society* (1788); opened 1st Sunday school in Cheddar (1789); published *The Slave Trade* (1790), *Village Politics* (1792) and *Coelebs in Search of a Wife* (1809). ❖ See also Mary Alden Hopkins, *Hannah More and Her Circle* (Longmans, 1947); Henry Thompson, *Life*

of Hannah More with Notices of her Sisters (Cadell, 1838); and *Women in World History.*

MORE, Helen Gertrude (1606–1633). *See More, Gertrude.*

MORE, Jane Colt (c. 1488–1511). English gentlewoman who was the 1st wife of Thomas More. Name variations: Jane Colte. Born Jane Colt c. 1488; died 1511; eldest of three daughters of John Colt of Essex, a family friend of Thomas More; became 1st wife of Thomas More (1478–1535, English scholar and statesman), 1505; children: Margaret More Roper (1505–1544); Elizabeth More Daunce or Dancy (b. around 1506, who m. William Daunce on Sept 29, 1525, the same day her sister Margaret married); Cecily More Heron (b. around 1507, who m. Giles Heron in 1522); John More (who m. Anne Cresacre in 1529). ❖ An uneducated country girl at the time of her marriage, was instructed in art and music by husband and trained to match his own tastes; rebelled but eventually made peace. ❖ See also *Women in World History.*

MORE, Mary (d. 1713/15). British writer. Born in England; died c. 1713. ❖ Wrote the polemical work *The Woman's Right, or Her Power in a Greater Equality to Her Husband proved than is allowed or practised in England* (c. 1674).

MORE ROPER, Margaret (1505–1544). *See Roper, Margaret More.*

MOREAU, Janet (1927—). American runner. Name variations: Janet Moreau Stone. Born Oct 26, 1927, in Pawtucket, Rhode Island; attended Boston University on a swimming scholarship. ❖ At Helsinki Olympics, won a gold medal in 4x100-meter relay (1952).

MOREAU, Jeanne (1928—). French actress. Born Jan 23, 1928, in Paris, France; dau. of French father Anatole Moreau (restaurateur) and English mother Kathleen (Buckley) Moreau (entertainer); sister of Michelle Moreau; trained at Paris Conservatory of Dramatic Art; m. Jean-Louis Richard (actor), 1949 (div. 1951); m. William Friedkin (director) 1977 (div. 1978); children: (1st m.) son, Jérôme. ❖ An icon of the French cinema's postwar renaissance, made stage debut in small part in *La Terrasse du Midi* at Avignon (1947); scored immediate triumph as Veroushka in Comédie Française production of *A Month in the Country* (1947); offered 4-year contract, became youngest paid actress in history of Comédie Française; received 3rd billing in 1st film, *Dernier Amour* (Last Love, 1948); played gun molls, prostitutes, and scandalous mistresses (1948–57); was a huge hit in *L'heure Eblouissante* (The Dazzling Hour) at Théâtre Nationale Populaire (1953); was at forefront of French dramatic theater (mid-1950s) with performances in such plays as *La Machine Infernale, Pygmalion,* and *Cat on a Hot Tin Roof;* teamed with Louis Malle for *Ascenseur pour L'Echafaud* (Frantic, 1957), the opening salvo of the French cinema's New Wave, followed by the explosive *Les Amants* (The Lovers, 1958); did a cameo for Truffaut's 1st film, *Les Quatre Cent Coups* (*The 400 Blows,* 1959), launching her most productive period on film in a string of *nouvelle vogue* classics: Michelangelo Antonioni's *La Notte* and, most famously, Truffaut's *Jules et Jim* (1963); also appeared in Ritt's *Five Branded Women,* Welles' *The Trial* and *Chimes at Midnight,* Losey's *Eva,* and Buñuel's *Le Journal d'une Femme de Chambre* (*The Diary of a Chambermaid*); wrote and directed 1st film, *Lumière* (Light, 1975) and turned her memories of WWII into her 2nd, *L'Adolescente* (1978); returned to the stage in *Le Récit de la Servante Zerline* (Zerline's Story) in a performance hailed throughout Europe; other films include *Les Liaisons dangereuses* (1959), *Le Train* (1964), *The Yellow Rolls-Royce* (1964), *Viva Maria* (1965), *Great Catherine* (1968), *Chére Louise* (1972), *Les Valseuses* (1974), *Souvenirs d'en France* (1975), *Querelle* (1982), *La Truite* (1982), *Le Miraculé* (1987), *La Femme Nikita* (1990), *Until the End of the World* (1992), *Map of the Human Heart* (1992) and *The Summer House* (1994). Received award from Cannes Film Festival for *Moderato Cantabile* (1960); won Crystal Award for Best Actress for *Jules et Jim;* awarded the Moliére as Best Actress for *Le Récit de la Servante Zerline* (1988); won César Award as Best Actress for *La Vielle qui Marchait dans la Mer* (The Old Woman Who Walked in the Sea, 1992). ❖ See also Marianne Gray, *La Moreau: A Biography of Jeanne Moreau* (Little, Brown, 1994); and *Women in World History.*

MOREAU, Mady (1928—). French diver. Born May 1, 1928, in France. ❖ At Helsinki Olympics, won a silver medal in springboard (1952).

MOREAU DE JUSTO, Alicia (1885–1986). Argentine feminist and politician. Name variations: Alicia Moreau. Pronunciation: ah-LEE-seeah mo-ROW day HOOS-toe. Born Alicia Moreau, Oct 11, 1885, in London, England; died in Buenos Aires, Argentina, 1986; dau. of Armando Moreau (journalist and influential member of the Argentine

Socialist Party) and María Denampont de Moreau; attended Colegio Nacional Central (Central National College, 1906, Facultad de Medicina, Universidad de Buenos Aires (Medical School, University of Buenos Aires, 1907–14; m. Juan Bautista Justo, 1922 (died 1928); children: Juan, Luís, and Alicia. ❖ Noted feminist, fighter for the right of women to vote, medical doctor, writer, editor, and political activist who was a leader in the Socialist Party; founded La Unión Nacional Feminista (National Feminist Union, 1918) and the Socialist Women's Suffrage Committee (1930); served as editor of Socialist newspaper, *La Vanguardia* (1956–62) and was elected to the party's executive board (1958); in an attempt to reunify a divided Socialist Party, created and presided over the Confederación Socialista Argentina (Argentine Socialist Confederation, 1975); died in her 101st year, after a lifetime that encompassed the entire history of socialism and feminism in Argentina; writings include *La emancipación civil de la mujer* (The Civil Emancipation of Woman, 1919), *El feminismo en la evolución social* (Feminism in Social Evolution, 1911), *La mujer en la democracia* (The Woman in a Democracy, 1945), *El socialismo de Juan B. Justo* (The Socialism of Juan B. Justo, 1946), and *Socialismo y la mujer* (Socialism and the Woman, 1946). ❖ See also *Women in World History*.

MOREIRA DE MELO, Fatima (1978—). Dutch field-hockey player. Name variations: Fatima Moreira. Born July 4, 1978, in Rotterdam, Netherlands. ❖ Won a team bronze medal at Sydney Olympics (2000) and a team silver at Athens Olympics (2004); won Champions Trophy (2000) and European championship (2003).

MOREL, Madame de (fl. 16th c.). *See Loynes, Antoinette de.*

MORELLA, Constance A. (1931—). American politician. Name variations: Connie Morella. Born Constance Albanese Morella, Feb 12, 1931, in Somerville, MA; education: Boston University, AB; American University, MA. ❖ Was a professor of English at Montgomery College (1970–85); elected to Maryland General Assembly (1978); represented Maryland's 8th Congressional District in US House of Representatives (1987–2003); served as a senior member of the House Committee on Science and chaired one of its panels, the Subcomittee on Technology (1995–2000); was also on the Committee on Government Reform and chaired the Subcommittee on the District of Columbia; was chair of the Congressional Caucus for Women's Issues; appointed by the president to serve as US Permanent Representative to the Organization for Economic Cooperation and Development (OECD, 2003).

MOREMAN, Marjorie. English gymnast. Born in UK. ❖ At Amsterdam Olympics, won a bronze medal in team all-around (1928).

MORENCY, Barbe-Suzanne-Aimable Giroux de (1770–?). French novelist. Name variations: Barbe Giroux de Morency; Madame G. de Morency; Madame or Mme Bertrand Quinquet. Born 1770 in France; death date unknown. ❖ Published *Illyrine, ou l'écueil de l'inexpérience* (1799–1800), detailing the life of a courtesan during the Reign of Terror, which appears to be the 1st novel with a 1st-person erotic narrative written by a woman; also wrote *Lise, ou les hermites du Mont-Blanc* (1801), *Rosellina, ou les méprises de l'amour et de la nature* (1801), *Euphémie, ou les suites du siège de Lyon* (1802), *Orphana, ou les enfants du hameau*, and *Zephira et Figdella, ou les débutantes dans le monde* (1806).

MORENO, Luisa (1906–1992). Latina labor organizer and civil-rights activist. Born in Guatemala, Aug 30, 1906; died in Guatemala, 1992; graduate of Convent of the Holy Names, Oakland, California, mid-1920s; married to a Mexican artist by 1928 (div. by mid-1930s); children: 1 daughter. ❖ Worked as a journalist in Mexico for a Guatemalan newspaper (late 1920s); immigrated to US (1928); after briefly working in garment trade in NY (early 1930s), became an organizer for Needle Trades Workers International; became organizer for American Federation of Labor (AFL) and (after 1936) for Congress of Industrial Organizations (CIO); was co-founder of El Congreso de Pueblos que Hablan Espanol (National Congress of Spanish Speaking Peoples, 1938); was an organizer and international vice president, United Cannery, Agricultural, Packing, and Allied Workers of America (UCAPAWA, 1941–47); appointed to California Fair Employment Practices Commission during WWII; made vice president, California CIO (1945); facing deportation from US (the Tenney Commission, a state-level forerunner to the national anti-Communist hysteria of 1950s, was determined to deport labor and political radicals), left her adopted homeland in protest and returned to Guatemala (1949); became an active supporter of the democratic government of Jacobo Arbenz; moved to Mexico after the overthrow of the Arbenz government (1954);

participated in the revamping of the Cuban education system after 1959 revolution. ❖ See also *Women in World History*.

MORENO, Marguerite (1871–1948). French actress. Name variations: Marguérite Moréno; Marguerite Heap. Born Marguerite Monceau, Sept 15, 1871, in Paris, France; died July 14, 1948, in Touzac, Lot, France. ❖ Made stage debut with Comédie Française (1890); a noted actress of stage and screen, made last stage appearance in title role of *La Folle de Chaillot* (*The Madwoman of Chaillot*); appeared in over 80 films, including *Chérie* (1930), *Le cordon bleu* (1931), *Miche* (1932), *Le Chasseur de chez Maxim's* (1933), *Casanova* (1934), *Les Misérables* (1934), *Mes tantes et moi* (1936), *Gigolette* (1936), *La Fessée* (1937), *Les Perles de la couronne* (1937), *La Dame de pique* (1937), *Secrets* (1943), *Carmen* (1945) and *L'Idiot* (1946). ❖ See also *Memories of My Life* (1948).

MORENO, Patricia (1988—). Spanish gymnast. Born Jan 7, 1988, in Madrid, Spain. ❖ Won a silver medal for floor exercise at Athens Olympics (2004).

MORENO, Rita (1931—). Puerto Rican actress, singer, and dancer. Name variations: Rosita Moreno; Rosita Cosio. Born Rosa Dolores Alverio, Dec 11, 1931, in Humacao, Puerto Rico; m. Leonard Gordon (physician), 1965; children: Fernanda Luisa (actress). ❖ Had to endure many years cast as "Latin spitfire" or "Indian princess," images that were frequently the only roles available for Hispanic actresses; made film debut as a delinquent in *So Young, So Bad* and signed with MGM (1950); had minor roles in 25 movies, the most notable of which were *The Toast of New Orleans* and *Pagan Love Song* (1950); dropped by MGM but continued as a freelancer, usually appearing as the Latin vamp in such films as *The Fabulous Señorita* (1952), *Cattle Town* (1952), *Latin Lovers* (1953), and *Jivaro* (1954); also played an Arab in *El Alamein* (1953) and a Native American in *Fort Vengeance* (1953) and *The Yellow Tomahawk* (1954); signed with 20th Century-Fox; sang in *Garden of Evil* (1954), did a Marilyn Monroe takeoff in *The Lieutenant Wore Skirts* (1955), and was cast as a Burmese slave girl in *The King and I* (1956); got 1st break with supporting role of Anita in film version of *West Side Story* (1961); appeared on stage in *Summer and Smoke* (1961) and *Cry of Battle* (1963); starred in *She Loves Me* in London and *The Sign in Sidney Brustein's Window* in NY (1964); received excellent reviews for performance in *The Rose Tattoo* in Chicago (1968); returned to film in *The Night of the Following Day* (1969), followed by *Marlowe* (1969), *Popi* (1969), and *Carnal Knowledge* (1971); began appearing on CTW's "Electric Company" (1971); appeared on Broadway as Googie Gomez in *The Ritz* (1975), followed by film version (1976); other movies include *The Boss's Son* (1979), *Happy Birthday, Gemini* (1980) and *The Four Seasons* (1981); was the only performer to win all 4 of the entertainment world's major awards. Won a Golden Globe (1962) and Academy Award for Best Supporting Actress (1961), both for *West Side Story*; won a Grammy Award (1972) for "The Electric Company"; won Emmy Award for "Out to Lunch" (1975) and "The Muppet Show" (1977); won Tony Award for Best Supporting Actress for *The Ritz* (1975); won Emmy Award for Outstanding Lead Actress for "The Rockford Files" (1978); received Sarah Siddons Award (1985) and Hispanic Heritage Award (1990). ❖ See also Susan Suntree, *Rita Moreno* (Chelsea House, 1993); and *Women in World History*.

MORENO, Virginia R. (1925—). Filipino poet and playwright. Born 1925 in the Philippines. ❖ Became the 1st director of Film Center at University of Philippines; published collection of poems, *The Batik Maker and Other Poems*; her verse drama *Itim Asu* (The Onyx Wolf) was staged in 1972 and later turned into a full-length ballet.

MORENO, Yipsi (1980—). Cuban hammer thrower. Born Nov 19, 1980, in Camagüey, Cuba. ❖ Won World championships (2001, 2003); won a silver medal at Athens Olympics (2004). Named Cuban Sportswoman of the Year (2003).

MOREN VESAAS, Halldis (1907–1995). *See Vesaas, Halldis Moren.*

MOREROD, Lise-Marie (1956—). Swiss Alpine skier. Born April 16, 1956, in Les Diablerets, Switzerland. ❖ At 15, became Swiss champion in the giant slalom (1972); at World championships, placed 3rd for slalom (1974) and 2nd for giant slalom (1978); placed 4th for giant slalom at Innsbruck Olympics (1976); won a World Cup overall (1977), the 1st Swiss woman to do so.

MORESBY, Louis (c. 1862–1931). *See Beck, Elizabeth Louisa.*

MORESEE, Sophie (1962—). *See Moresee Pichot, Sophie.*

MORESSEE-PICHOT, Sophie (1962—). French fencer. Name variations: Moressée; also seen as Moresee. Born April 3, 1962, in Sissonne, France. ❖ Won a gold medal team épée at Atlanta Olympics (1996).

MORETE, Maraea (1844–1907). New Zealand tribal leader and writer. Name variations: Maria Morris. Born Maria Morris, July 24, 1844, at either Whakaari or Waikokopu, New Zealand; died Oct 8, 1907, on tribal land at Ruangarehu, Te Karaka; dau. of William Morris (whaler) and Puihi (tribal leader of Te Aitanga-a-Mahaki); attended Wesleyan Native Institution, Auckland; m. Pera Taihuka, 1863 (died 1868); children: 1; (with local farmer, J.B. Poynter) 1 (b. around 1873). ❖ Captured by followers of guerilla fighter, Te Kooti (1868); escaped and later appeared as witness before Supreme Court in Wellington, at trials of Te Kooti's followers; recorded autobiographical recollections, *Reminiscences.* ❖ See also *Dictionary of New Zealand Biography* (Vol. 1).

MORETON, Clara (1824–1899). *See Moore, Clara.*

MORETON, Ursula (1903–1973). English ballet dancer. Born Mar 13, 1903, in Southsea, England; died June 24, 1973, in London. ❖ Danced with Tamara Karsavina in London (1920); taught at Ninette de Valois' Academy of Choreographic Arts and appeared in numerous de Valois premieres, including *Les Petits Riens* (1928), *Hommages aux Belle Viennoises* (1929) and *Narcissus and Echo* (1932); performed with Camargo Society and Vic-Wells troupe, where she danced in works by de Valois, Ashton and Fokine; upon retirement from performance career (1946), taught and co-directed at Sadler's Wells Theater Ballet; served as principal of Royal Ballet School (1952–68).

MORETT, Charlene (1957—). American field-hockey player. Born Dec 5, 1957, in Aldan, PA; graduate of Pennsylvania State University, 1979. ❖ At Los Angeles Olympics, won a bronze medal in team competition (1984); became head coach of women's field hockey at Penn State (1987).

MORGAN, Agnes Fay (1884–1968). American biochemist. Born Jane Agnes Fay, May 4, 1884, in Peoria, Illinois; died of a heart attack, July 20, 1968, in Berkeley, California; dau. of Patrick John Fay (laborer who later became a builder) and Mary (Dooley) Fay; attended Vassar College; University of Chicago, BS, 1904, MS, 1905, PhD, 1914; m. Arthur Ivason Morgan, 1908; children: Arthur Ivason Jr. (b. 1923). ❖ Pioneer in the development of home economics as a scientific discipline, taught chemistry at Hardin College, Mexico, MO (1905–06), University of Montana (1907–08), and University of Washington, where she organized an honor society for women in chemistry (1910–12); began teaching at University of California at Berkeley (1915), became full professor (1923), professor of home economics and biochemistry (1938–54), department chair (1923–54); played a major role in transforming the field of home economics by making chemistry an integral part of the curriculum; also did pioneering research on the biochemistry of vitamins. Received Garvan Medal from American Chemical Society for work on vitamins (1949); received Borden Award from American Institute of Nutrition (1954). ❖ See also *Women in World History.*

MORGAN, Ann Haven (1882–1966). American zoologist and conservationist. Name variations: (nickname) Mayfly Morgan. Born Anna Haven Morgan, May 6, 1882, in Waterford, CT; died of stomach cancer, June 5, 1966, at home in South Hadley, MA; elder dau. of Stanley Griswold Morgan and Julia (Douglass) Morgan; attended Wellesley College, 1902–04; Cornell University, AB, 1906, PhD, 1912; never married; no children. ❖ Worked as assistant and instructor of zoology, Mt. Holyoke College (1906–09); received doctorate with a dissertation on the biology of mayflies (1912); became associate professor at Mt. Holyoke (1914), served as chair of the zoology department (1916–47), and became full professor (1918), a position she retained until her retirement in 1947; was instrumental in reforming the science curriculum in schools and colleges to include ecology and conservation courses; wrote *Field Book of Ponds and Streams: An Introduction to the Life of Fresh Water* (1930), *Field Book of Animals in Winter* (1939), and *Kinships of Animals and Man: A Textbook of Animal Biology* (1955). ❖ See also *Women in World History.*

MORGAN, Anna (1851–1936). American educator. Born Feb 24, 1851 in Fleming, New York; died of coronary sclerosis, Aug 27, 1936, in Chicago, Illinois; dau. of Allen Denison Morgan (gentleman farmer who served briefly in New York legislature) and Mary Jane (Thornton) Morgan; studied elocution at Hershey School of Music, 1877. ❖ Chicago teacher who raised the standards of study for theater and speech during late 19th and early 20th centuries, 1st gained renown as dramatic reader with naturalistic style (early 1880s); brought many advanced plays and staging ideas to Chicago; opened school of dramatic arts, the Anna Morgan Studios, in Chicago's Fine Arts Building (1899); fostered cultural growth in Chicago (early 1900s); was one of the founders of the Little Room, a loose organization whose members included Harriet Monroe, Hamlin Garland, and Henry B. Fuller; was instrumental in preparing the way for the "little theater" movement in US; writings include *An Hour with Delsarte* (1889) and *The Art of Speech and Deportment* (1909). ❖ See also autobiography *My Chicago* (1918); and *Women in World History.*

MORGAN, Anne (1873–1952). American philanthropist and social worker. Born Anne Tracy Morgan in New York, NY, July 25, 1873; died Jan 29, 1952; youngest child of John Pierpont Morgan (1837–1913, financier) and Frances Louisa (Tracy) Morgan; sister of J.P. Morgan (1867–1943); never married; no children. ❖ With Elisabeth Marbury and Florence Jaffray Harriman, founded and was an early officer of the Colony Club (1903); also devoted herself to the woman's department of the National Civic Federation; a believer in trade unions, supported shirtmakers' strikes (1909 and 1910); during WWI, established a home for the wounded in Versailles and became active in American Fund for French Wounded; after war, founded American Committee for Devastated France; organized American Friends of France (Comité Americain de Secours Civil, 1938). Received Croix de Guerre with palm; made Commander of the French Legion of Honor (1932), then the only American woman to have received the decoration. ❖ See also *Women in World History.*

MORGAN, Barbara (1900–1992). American artist and photographer. Born Barbara Brooks Johnson in Buffalo, Kansas, 1900; died in Tarrytown, New York, 1992; graduate of University of California, Los Angeles, 1923; m. Willard Morgan (writer and photographer), 1925 (died 1967); children: Douglas (b. 1932); Lloyd (b. 1935). ❖ Famed for her innovative dance photographs, became interested in recording dancer's movements after seeing Martha Graham Dance Co. perform (1935); in her images of Graham, and in later photographs of dancers Doris Humphrey, Charles Weidman, Erick Hawkins, José Limón, and Merce Cunningham, captured the vitality of the American modern dance movement of 1930s and 1940s, and changed the course of American dance photography; published *Martha Graham: Sixteen Dances in Photographs* (1941), for which she won the American Institute of Graphic Arts Trade Book Clinic Award; also produced 2nd volume of photographs, *Summer Children* (1951); had one-woman exhibitions at Institute of American Indian Art (Santa Fe), Pasadena Art Museum, Museum of Modern Art (NY), George Eastman House, and National Museum of Dance (Saratoga Springs, NY). ❖ See also *Women in World History.*

MORGAN, Claire (1921–1995). *See Highsmith, Patricia.*

MORGAN, Claudia (1912–1974). American stage, radio, and screen actress. Born June 12, 1912, in Brooklyn, NY; died Sept 17, 1974, in NY, NY; dau. of Ralph Morgan (actor); m. Talbot Cummings (div.); m. Robert Shippee (div.); m. Ernest Chappell (div.); m. Kenneth Loane. ❖ Made stage debut on tour in *Gypsy April* (1928); made NY debut as Sally Lawrence in *Top o' the Hill* (1929); other plays include *Dancing Partner, Accent on Youth, On Stage, The Man Who Came to Dinner, Ten Little Indians, Venus Observed* and *The Apple Cart*; on radio, portrayed Nora Charles in "The Thin Man" series (1942–48) and Carolyn Kramer in "The Right to Happiness" (1943–60); also appeared frequently on tv, including "Edge of Night" (1958–59), and in films, among them *Once in a Lifetime* and *The World of Henry Orient.*

MORGAN, Eluned (1967—). Welsh politician. Name variations: Mair Eluned Morgan. Born Feb 16, 1967, in Cardiff, Wales. ❖ As a European Socialist, elected to 4th and 5th European Parliament (1994–99, 1999–2004) from UK.

MORGAN, Frances Louisa (1845–1924). American philanthropist and society matron. Name variations: Mrs. J. Pierpont Morgan. Born Frances Louisa Tracy, May 15, 1845; died Nov 16, 1924; dau. of Charles Tracy (lawyer) and Louisa Kirkland Tracy; m. J. Pierpont Morgan (1837–1913, financier), May 31, 1865; children: Louisa Pierpont Morgan Satterlee (b. Mar 10, 1866); J.P. Morgan (1867–1943, who m. Jane Norton Grew Morgan); Juliet Morgan Hamilton (b. July 1870); Anne Morgan (1873–1952). ❖ See also *Women in World History.*

MORGAN, Helen (1900–1941). American singer and actress. Born Helen Morgan (birth name sometimes given as Helen Riggins), Aug 21,

1900; birthplace variously given as Danville, IL, and Toronto, Ontario, Canada; died Oct 5, 1941, of cirrhosis of the liver; dau. of Lulu Morgan and probably Thomas Morgan; m. Maurice Mashke Jr., 1933 (div. 1935); m. Lloyd Johnson, 1941. ❖ Began singing in small Chicago cabarets, establishing a reputation as a torch singer; in NY, became connected with 3 of the city's most popular clubs—Helen Morgan's 54th Street Club, Chez Morgan, and Helen Morgan's Summer Home; appeared for 2 seasons in George White's *Scandals,* followed by his revue *Americana* (1926), in which she sang "Nobody Wants Me"; singing "My Bill" and "Can't Help Loving That Man of Mine," became a Broadway star with creation of the role of Julie in *Show Boat* (1927), which she recreated on screen (silent and talkie versions) and in a Broadway revival (1932); other films include *Applause* (1930), *Roadhouse Nights* (1930), *You Belong To Me* (1934), *Marie Galante* (1934), *Go Into Your Dance* (1935), and *Frankie and Johnny* (1936); had active nightclub career in NY and Chicago speakeasies during prohibition and was acquitted of federal charges filed under the Volstead Act after several raids; career declined afterward due to health problems brought on by alcoholism. ❖ See also Gilbert Maxwell, *Helen Morgan* (Hawthorn, 1974); (film) *The Helen Morgan Story,* starring Ann Blyth (1957); and *Women in World History.*

MORGAN, Helen (1966—). English field-hockey player. Born July 20, 1966, in UK. ❖ At Barcelona Olympics, won a bronze medal in team competition (1992).

MORGAN, Mrs. J. P. (1868–1925). See Morgan, Jane Norton Grew.

MORGAN, Mrs. J. Pierpont (1845–1924). See Morgan, Frances Louisa.

MORGAN, Jane Norton Grew (1868–1925). American socialite. Name variations: Mrs. J.P. Morgan. Born Jane Norton Grew, Sept 20, 1868; died Aug 14, 1925; dau. of Henry Sturgis Grew and Jane (Wigglesworth) Grew; m. J.P. Morgan (1867–1943, banker and son of Frances Louisa Morgan and J. Pierpont Morgan), Dec 1890; children: Junius Spencer Morgan (b. 1892); Jane Norton Morgan (b. 1893); Frances Tracy Morgan (b. 1897); Henry Grew Morgan (b. 1900). ❖ See also *Women in World History.*

MORGAN, Jane (1924—). American pop singer. Born Florence Catherine Currier, May 3, 1924, in Newton, MA; dau. of Bertram Currier (cellist with the Boston Pops) and Olga Currier (concert singer and pianist); graduate of Juilliard; m. Jerry Weintraub (film producer); children: 3 daughters. ❖ Began career in Europe, where she had success; during 1950s, had a series of hit singles, including "Fascination" (1957) and "The Day the Rain Came Down."

MORGAN, Jaye P. (1931—). American pop singer. Born Mary Margaret Morgan, Dec 3, 1931, in Mancos, CO; sister of singing brothers, Duke, Bob, Charlie and Dick Morgan. ❖ Was a band singer with the Frank DeVol orchestra; had 1st hit single with "Life Is Just a Bowl of Cherries" (1951), followed by "The Longest Walk" and "That's All I Want from You"; became a regular vocalist on tv's "Stop the Music" (1955), then had her own program, "The Jaye P. Morgan Show" (1956); became known for her sassy ways on "The Gong Show" (1976–80).

MORGAN, Joan (1905–2004). English actress and writer. Name variations: (pseudonyms) Iris North and Joan Wentworth Wood. Born Feb 1, 1905, in Kent, England; died July 22, 2004, in Henley-on-Thames, Oxfordshire, England; dau. of Sidney Morgan (film director) and Evelyn Wood (actress). ❖ Silent screen star, began acting at age 8; made film debut in *The Cup Final Mystery* (1913); appeared in title role of *Little Dorrit* (1920), followed by *A Lowland Cinderella* (1921), *The Road to London* (1921), *Swallow* (1922), *Shadow of Egypt* (1923) and *A Window in Piccadilly* (1928), among many others; made only 1 talkie, *Her Reputation* (1931); under pseudonym Joan Wentworth Wood, wrote 10 screenplays, including *The Callboy Mystery, Chelsea Life* and *The Minstrel Boy*; wrote several books, including *Citizen of Westminster, Ding Dong Dell* and *The Hanging Wood*; also wrote the successful play *This Was a Woman* (1944); began converting old buildings into homes which resulted in *The Casebook of Capability Morgan* (1965).

MORGAN, Julia (1872–1957). American architect. Born Jan 20, 1872, in San Francisco, California; died Feb 2, 1957, in San Francisco from a series of strokes; dau. of Charles Bill Morgan and Eliza Woodland (Parmelee) Morgan; 1st woman to enroll in the College of Engineering at University of California, Berkeley; received diploma in Civil Engineering, 1894; 1st woman accepted in department of architecture at École des Beaux-Arts, Paris, France, and received certificate, 1902; passed California state exam and became the state's 1st certified woman

architect, 1904. ❖ Designed over 700 buildings but is best known for creating a modern-day castle for millionaire William Randolph Hearst; moved West with parents where father hoped to make a fortune in silver mines (1878); formed a lasting friendship with cousin Lucy Thornton and Thornton's architect husband Pierre Lebrun, the 1st to influence her; in senior year, studied under Bernard Maybeck; accepted at École des Beaux-Arts (Oct 1898); met William Randolph Hearst (1903) which led to the most flamboyant architectural creation of her career, the Hearst Castle (1919–39); over a span of 47 years, designed El Campanil (Bell Tower) at Mills College, Oakland (1903–04), library at Mills College (1905–06), reconstruction after the earthquake and fire of the Fairmont Hotel, San Francisco (1906–07), Methodist Chinese Mission, San Francisco (1907–10), St. John's Presbyterian Church and Sunday School, Berkeley (1908–10), Kings Daughters Home for Incurables, Oakland (1908–12), Asilomar YWCA Conference Center, Pacific Grove, CA (1913–28), and Honolulu YWCA buildings, Honolulu (1925–26), among others. ❖ See also Sara Holmes Boutelle, *Julia Morgan, Architect* (Abbeville, 1988); Richard W. Longstreth, *Julia Morgan: Architect* (Architectural Heritage Association, 1977); and *Women in World History.*

MORGAN, Julie (1944—). Welsh politician and member of Parliament. Born Julie Edwards, Nov 2, 1944; m. Rhodri Morgan (MP), 1967. ❖ Began career as a social worker; representing Labour, elected to House of Commons for Cardiff North (1997, 2001, 2005).

MORGAN, Kay Summersby (1908–1975). See Summersby, Kay.

MORGAN, Marilyn (1913—). See Marsh, Marian.

MORGAN, Marion (c. 1887–1971). American choreographer. Born c. 1887; died 1971; grew up in California; graduate of Yale School of Drama, 1934; lived with Dorothy Arzner, 1930–71; married; children: Roderick (died 1930s). ❖ Founded the Marion Morgan Dancers which toured on the vaudeville circuit (1916–mid-1920s), before working on Hollywood soundstages; appeared in *Don Juan* (1926), *Up in Mabel's Room* (1926), *A Night of Love* (1926), *The Masked Woman* (1926), as well as Dorothy Arzner's 1st 3 films: *Fashions of Women, Ten Modern Commandments,* and *Get Your Man.*

MORGAN, Mary Kimball (1861–1948). American Christian Science teacher. Born Nellie May Kimball, Dec 8, 1861, in Janesville, WI; died Oct 13, 1948, in Elsah, IL; dau. of Freeman Aaron Kimball and Helen Maria (Chapin) Kimball; m. William Edgar Morgan (dry goods dealer), Dec 15, 1885 (died 1935); children: 2 sons. ❖ Helped organize 1st Christian Science church in St. Louis, MO; became authorized Christian Science practitioner (1896); opened school primarily for children of Christian Science families, the Principia (1898); oversaw addition of high school branch, 2-year college (1910), and 4-year liberal arts college (1932); appointed president emeritus of the Principia (1938). ❖ See also Edwin S. Leonard Jr., *As the Sowing: The First Fifty Years of The Principia* (1948).

MORGAN, Maud (1903–1999). American artist. Name variations: Maud Cabot. Born Maud Cabot in New York, NY, Mar 1, 1903; died in Boston, MA, Mar 14, 1999; dau. of Francis Higginson Cabot and Maud (Bonner) Cabot; studied under Hans Hoffmann; m. Patrick Morgan (artist), c. 1930 (sep. c. 1957, div. 1980); children: 1 daughter, 1 son. ❖ An icon of the Boston art world for over 50 years, began painting (c. 1927) and launched career in New York (1930s), exhibiting alongside abstract expressionists Jackson Pollock, Barnett Newman, and Mark Rothko. ❖ See also autobiography *Maud's Journey: A Life from Art* (1995); and *Women in World History.*

MORGAN, Michèle (1920—). French actress. Name variations: Michele Morgan. Born Simone Roussel, Feb 29, 1920, in Neuilly-sur-Seine, France; m. William Marshall (American actor), 1942 (div. 1949); m. Henri Vidal (French actor), 1950 (died 1959); children: (1st m.) Michael. ❖ One of France's most acclaimed actresses, studied drama and dance as a child; began appearing in small film roles (1935); came to stardom in Allégret's *Gribouille* (1937), followed by *Orage* (The Storm, 1938), *Quai des Brumes* (Port of Shadows, 1938), *L'Entraîneuse* (The Trainer, 1939) and *Les Musiciens du ciel* (Heaven's Musicians, 1940); by start of WWII, was among the most popular screen personalities in France (1939); spent much of the war in Hollywood, making several films which were generally mediocre (1939–45), including *Joan of Paris* (1942), *Two Tickets to London* (1943) and *Passage to Marseilles* (1944); returned triumphantly to French screen (1946), winning Best Actress award at Cannes for work in *La Symphonie Pastorale*; maintained active international screen career (1940s–70s), in such films as *The Fallen Idol* (1948), *The Naked Heart* (1949), *Fabiola* (1951), *Les Grande Manoevres* (1956) and *Lost Command* (1964); served as president of Cannes Film Festival (1971); was a member of board of directors of France's government-owned tv channel, FR3, and began accepting tv work (her series *Le Tiroir Secret* was a huge success); appeared on stage in *Cherie* (1982), which ran for 246 performances in Paris, and the Italian-French comedy *Tutti stanno benne* (Everybody's Fine, 1990). Named Chevalier of the French Legion of Honor (1969); made an officer of France's National Order of Merit (1975). ❖ See also autobiography (with Marcelle Routier) *Avec ces yeux-la* (Editions Laffont, 1977, published in English as *With Those Eyes*); and *Women in World History*.

MORGAN, Robin (1941—). American feminist, essayist and actress. Born Jan 29, 1941, in Lake Worth, FL; grew up in Mount Vernon, NY; dau. of Faith Berkley Morgan; attended Columbia University; m. Kenneth Pitchford (poet), 1962; children: son Blake Morgan-Pitchford. ❖ Began career as a child actress, coming to prominence as Dagmar in tv series, "Mama" (1950–56); participated in Civil Rights Movement (1960s), then was an early member of the Women's Liberation movement, becoming a prominent speaker for cultural feminism; edited *Sisterhood is Powerful* (1970) and published collections of essays, including *Going Too Far* (1978), *The Anatomy of Freedom* (1982), *The New Woman* (1984), *Sisterhood is Global* (1984) and *The World of a Woman: Feminist Dispatches 1968–1991* (1992); poetry includes *Monster* (1972) and *Lady of the Beasts* (1976); served as editor-in-chief of *Ms* magazine (1989–93).

MORGAN, Sally (1951—). Australian Aboriginal writer and artist. Born Sally Milroy, Jan 18, 1951, in Perth, Western Australia, of Palku descent; University of Western Australia, BA, 1974; Western Australian Institute of Technology, post-graduate diploma in psychology and library studies; m. Paul Morgan, 1972; children: 3. ❖ Unaware of aboriginal heritage until age 15, having been told that family came from India, began researching family's story, traveling north to Pilbara area of Western Australia where her grandmother was born (1983); overwhelmed by grandmother Nan's story, published bestselling *My Place* (1987), which won Australian Human Rights Award for Literature; published 2nd book, a biography of her grandfather, *Wanamurraganya: The Story of Jack McPhee* (1989); began painting as well, holding exhibitions, winning prizes and selling paintings, some of which are displayed in Australian National Gallery and collected in *The Art of Sally Morgan* (1996); also illustrated such children's books as *Little Piggies* (1991) and *Hurry Up Oscar* (1993); wrote play *Sistergirl*, 1st performed at Festival of Perth (1992); served as director of Center for Indigenous History and the Arts at University of Western Australia.

MORGAN, Sandra (1942—). Australian swimmer. Name variations: Sandra Morgan-Beavis. Born June 6, 1942, in Australia. ❖ At age 14 years, 6 months, won a gold medal in the 4x100-meter freestyle relay at the Melbourne Olympics (1956).

MORGAN, Sydney (1780–1859). Irish novelist. Name variations: Miss Sydney Owenson; Lady Morgan. Born Sydney Owenson near Dublin, Ireland, on Christmas Day, 1780 (some sources cite 1783); died April 14, 1859; dau. of Robert Owenson (actor) and a mother, name unknown; worked as a governess (1798–1800); m. Sir Charles Morgan (eminent physician), 1812; no children. ❖ At 21, began professional writing career with a vol. of poems (1801) and a collection of Irish tunes, for which she composed the words; published 1st novel *St. Clair* (1804), which attracted attention, followed by *The Wild Irish Girl* (1806), a book that made her reputation; following marriage, moved from Dublin to London; published a detailed study of France under the Bourbon restoration (1817); was one of the most vivid and hotly discussed literary figures of her generation. ❖ See also W.H. Dixon, ed. *Lady Morgan's Memoirs: Autobiography, Diaries, and Correspondence*; W.J. Fitzpatrick, *Lady Morgan: Her Career, Literary and Personal*; and *Women in World History*.

MORGANTINI, Luisa (1940—). Italian politician. Born Nov 5, 1940, in Villadossola, Italy. ❖ One of the founders of the Women in Black antiwar movement and the international network, Women for Peace in Conflict Zones; representing the Confederal Group of the European United Left/Nordic Green Left (GUE/NGL), elected to 5th European Parliament (1999–2004). Awarded Israeli "Women in Black" Peace Prize (1996).

MORGENSTERN, Lina B. (1830–1909). German social reformer. Born Lina Bauer, Nov 25, 1830, in Breslau, Germany, of Jewish parents; died Dec 16, 1909, in Berlin; married Dr. Theodore Morgenstern; children: 5.

❖ Founded the Berlin Kindergarten Association and served as its president (1860–66); established the Public Kitchens in Berlin to relieve economic distress; also founded a society for the protection of illegitimate children, and an academy for the instruction of young women in practical arts; was the author of a number of books on domestic and educational subjects.

MORGNER, Irmtraud (1933–1990). East German novelist and feminist. Born Aug 22, 1933, into working-class family in Chemnitz, Germany; died May 6, 1990, in Germany; University of Leipzig, BA, 1956; m. Joachim Schreck, 1956 (div. 1970); m. Paul Weins (poet and writer), 1971 (div. 1977); children: David Schreck (b. 1967). ❖ Was assistant editor for a literary magazine published by German Democratic Republic Writers Federation in East Berlin (1956–58); published *The Signal Stands on Travel* (1959) and *A House at the Edge of the City* (1962), which conformed to the strictures of Communist realism; disillusioned with socialism, wrote novel *Rumba auf einen Herbst* (*Rumba on an Autumn*), which was banned by state censors (1965) and published posthumously (1992); broke free of conventions to create satirical iconoclastic novels, such as *Wedding in Constantinople* (1968) and *Gauklerlegende* (1970); with 2nd husband, moved to Paris (1971), then Soviet Union (1974); published most famous novel *Trobadora Beatriz* (1974), for which she won Heinrich Mann Prize; divorced 2nd husband (1977) after discovering that he was turning over information on literary friends to Stasi officials; awarded German Democratic Republic's National Prize for Literature (1978); traveled to US, giving readings at many universities (1984); received Hroswitha of Gandersheim Literary Award (1985); lived to see German reunification but soon died of cancer after prolonged illness; also wrote *Das heroische Testament: Roman in Fragmenten* (The Heroic Will: Novel in Fragments, 1966), *Amanda: A Witch Novel* (1983), *Die Hexe im Landhaus: Gespräch in Solothurn* (1984, The Witch in the Country House).

MORGUE, Efua Theodora (1924–1996). *See Sutherland, Efua Theodora.*

MORI, Mari (1903–1987). Japanese novelist and essayist. Born 1903 in Tokyo, Japan; died 1987; father was Mori Ogai (1862–1922, writer); sister of Mori Annu (later Kobori Annu, b. 1909). ❖ Published essay collection, *My Father's Hat* (1957), which won the Japanese Essayist Club Prize; novels include *The Forest for Lovers* (1961) and *The Room Filled with Sweet Honey* (1975), which won the Tamura Tashika Prize.

MORICO, Lucia (1975—). Italian judoka. Born Dec 12, 1975, in Fano, Italy. ❖ Won a bronze medal for 78kg at Athens Olympics (2004).

MORIN, Micheline (fl. 1930s). French mountaineer. Sister of Jean Morin (mountaineer); sister-in-law of Nea Morin. ❖ With Nea Morin and Alice Damesme, traversed the Meije in the Dauphine Alps (the last major peak in the Alps to be climbed) *encordée féminine* (women-rope only), the 1st all-female traverse of the Meije (1933).

MORIN, Jan (1956—). *See Merrill, Jan.*

MORIN, Nea (1906–1986). British mountaineer. Born Nea Barnard, 1906; died 1986; father was a member of the Alpine Club; m. Jean Morin (mountaineer), 1928 (killed on a mission with the Free French forces, 1943); sister-in-law of climber Micheline Morin; children: Denise (b. 1931); Ian (b. 1935). ❖ Arguably one of the greatest British female mountaineers between World Wars I and II, made 1st all-female traverse of the Meije (1933); made 1st all-female ascent of the Aiguilles de Blaitière (1934); made 1st ascent of "Nea" on Clogwyn Y Grochan; was president of Ladies' Alpine Club (1947); was president of the Pinnacle Club (1954); with Janet Adam Smith, translated Maurice Herzog's *Annapurna* (1952), R. Frison-Roche's *The Last Crevasse* (1952), Bernard Pierre's *A Mountain Called Nun-Kun* (1955), and Giusto Gervasutti's *Gervasutti's Climbs* (1957). ❖ See also (autobiography) *A Woman's Reach* (Eyre 7amp; Spottiswoode, 1968); and *Women in World History*.

MORIN DU MESNIL, Anne Louise (1730–1783). *See Elie de Beaumont, Anne Louise.*

MORINI, Erica (1904–1995). Austrian-born American violinist. Born in Vienna, Austria, Jan 5, 1904; died of heart failure in New York, NY, Nov 1, 1995; dau. of a music teacher; m. Felice Siracusano (Sicilian diamond broker who died in 1985). ❖ By 5, was performing in public; studied with father before entering Vienna Conservatory at 7; debuted in Vienna (1916); over the years performed with the Leipzig Gewandhaus Orchestra and Berlin Philharmonic Orchestra; at 20, received a 198-year-old violin, the Davidoff Stradivarius, from father (1924); made NY debut at

Carnegie Hall with Metropolitan Opera Orchestra, then spent 3 years in US; returned to Europe to concertize until 1938, when she became one of the many Jewish musicians to flee Central Europe with advent of Nazis; settled in NY; became US citizen (1943); during career, toured US, South America, Australia, and the Far East, before retiring (1976), a victim of arthritis in her fingers. ❖ See also *Women in World History.*

MORIO, Maiko (1967—). Japanese gymnast. Born Feb 18, 1967, in Kawasaki City, Kanagawa, Japan. ❖ Won All-Japan championships (1982), Japan nationals (1982, 1983), and NHK Cup (1983, 1984, 1986); placed 6th team all-around at Los Angeles Olympics (1984) and 12th team at Seoul Olympics (1988).

MORISAKI, Kazue (1927—). Japanese poet. Born April 20, 1927, in Kumamoto, Japan. ❖ During youth, lived in Korea and in coal-producing district of northern Kyushu; works, which reflect concerns about discrimination and oppression of laborers, especially women, include *Makkura* (1961), *Dai-san no sei* (1965), *Karayuki-san* (1976), and *Inochi hibikiau* (1998); founded magazine *Sâkuru Mura* with Tanigawa Gan and Ueno Eishin.

MORISHITA, Yoko (1948—). Japanese ballet dancer. Born Dec 7, 1948, in Hiroshima, Japan. ❖ Trained at Tachibana Ballet School and with Asami Maki in Tokyo; performed in Asami Maki company (late 1960s) in *Swan Lake, Giselle, Sleeping Beauty, Nutcracker,* among others; as guest dancer, appeared with numerous US companies, including American Ballet Theater (1977), and with London Festival Ballet (1979).

MORISON, Harriet (1862–1925). New Zealand feminist and labor activist. Born Harriet Russell Morison in Magherafelt, Co. Londonderry, Ireland, probably June 1862; died Aug 19, 1925, at home in New Lynn, New Zealand; dau. of Margaret Clark Morison and James Morison (master tailor); never married; no children. ❖ Moved to New Zealand (1874); worked in garment trade and established 1st women's union, Tailoresses' Union (1889); served as secretary of union and became factory inspector (1906); worked for Labour Department as head of Women's Employment Bureau (1908–13); also worked as suffragist, temperance worker, and in Unitarian Church as chair of church committee.

MORISON, Patricia (1914—). American stage and screen actress and singer. Born Eileen Patricia Augusta Fraser Morison, Mar 19, 1914, in New York, NY; dau. of William R. Morison (playwright-actor) and Selena Carson Morison (talent agent). ❖ Made NY debut as Helen in *Growing Pains* (1933), followed by *The Two Bouquets, Allah Be Praised!,* and a 2-year run as the lead in *Kiss Me Kate* (1948–50); made film debut in *Persons in Hiding* (1939); other films include *The Song of Bernadette, The Fallen Sparrow, Song without End* (as George Sand), *Lady on a Train, Tarzan and the Huntress, Song of the Thin Man* and *The Prince of Thieves.*

MORISOT, Berthe (1841–1895). French painter. Born Berthe Marie Pauline Morisot, Jan 14, 1841, in Bourges, France; died in Paris, Mar 2, 1895, of pneumonia; dau. of (Edme) Tiburce Morisot (civil servant) and Marie-Joséphine-Cornélie Thomas; studied privately under a number of artists, including Camille Corot; m. Eugène Manet (landowner), Dec 22, 1874 (died April 13, 1892); children: Julie Manet (b. Nov 14, 1878). ❖ One of the most talented and prominent members of the Impressionist movement, moved to Passy on outskirts of Paris (1855); began drawing lessons with sister Edma (1857); registered as a copyist at the Louvre (1858); exhibited with sister at Paris Salons (1864–68); executed 1st major work, *Thatched Cottage in Normandy,* one of earliest examples of her developing Impressionist style (1865); met Manet, who would become her closest colleague for many years (1868); produced 2 of her finest early works, *The Harbour at Lorient* and *Young Woman at a Window* (1869); exhibited alone (1870, 1872, 1873); sold 1st 4 works (1872), to Paul Durand-Ruel; rendered one of her best-known works, *The Cradle* (1872); participated in 1st Impressionist exhibition (1874), 2nd (1876), 3rd (1877), 5th (1880), 6th (1881), 7th (1882), and 8th (1886); with birth of daughter (1878), found her principle model for life; produced one of her best-known and most often reproduced works, *In the Dining Room* (1886); exhibited with Les XX in Brussels, and was included in Durand-Ruel's NY Impressionist exhibition (1887); held 1st solo exhibition (1892); exhibited with Le Libre Esthetique in Brussels (1894); other representative works include *Mother and Sister of the Artist* (1870), *Catching Butterflies* (1873), *At the Ball* (1875), *Psyche* (1876) and *Summer's Day* (1879); works are contained in over a dozen collections in major museums, including Chicago Art Institute, Tate Gallery (London), Metropolitan Museum of Art (NY), Musée du Louvre (Paris), Doria Pampli (Rome) and National Gallery of Art (Washington, DC). ❖ See also Adler and Garb, *Berthe Morisot*

(Phaidon, 1987); Armand Fourreau, *Berthe Morisot* (trans. by H. Wellington, Bodley Head, 1925); Anne Higonnet, *Berthe Morisot* (Harper & Row, 1990); Julie Manet, *Growing Up With the Impressionists* (Sotheby's, 1987); Jean Dominique Rey, *Berthe Morisot* (trans. by S. Jennings, Bonfini, 1982); and *Women in World History.*

MORISSETTE, Alanis (1974—). Canadian musician. Name variations: Alanis Nadine Morissette. Born Alanis Nadine Morissette, June 1, 1974, in Ottawa, Canada. ❖ Was the youngest person, at 21, to earn Album of the Year Grammy with *Jagged Little Pill,* which became one of the highest selling albums ever; began to play piano at 6; wrote 1st song at 9; at 10, acted on Nickelodeon's "You Can't Do That on Television"; released single, "Fate Stay With Me" (1987); released moderately successful dance-pop albums *Alanis* (1991) and *Now Is the Time* (1992); moved to LA (1994), and partnering with producer and songwriter Glen Ballard, wrote songs for rock album, *Jagged Little Pill* (1995), which included hits, "You Oughta Know," "Hand in My Pocket" and "Ironic," making her international star; won 4 Grammy Awards; released moderately successful Eastern-music-influenced *Supposed Former Infatuation Junkie* (1998), which included song "Thank U", won 2 Grammys, including Best Rock Song, for song, "Uninvited," from soundtrack of *City of Angels* (1998); played God in film *Dogma* (1999); released live album, *MTV Unplugged* (1999); films include *Jay and Silent Bob Strike Back* (2001) and *De-Lovely* (2004); other albums include *Feast On Scraps* (2002), *Under Rug Swept* (2002) and *So-Called Chaos* (2004).

MORITA, Kimie (1958—). Japanese volleyball player. Born Feb 27, 1958, in Japan. ❖ At Los Angeles Olympics, won a bronze medal in team competition (1984).

MORITS, Yunna (1937—). Ukrainian-born poet. Name variations: Iunna Petrovna Morits; Yunna Pinkhusovna Morits. Born 1937 in Kiev, Ukraine, of Jewish parents; evacuated from Kiev with the Nazi advance; studied at Gorky Literary Institute in Moscow. ❖ Influenced by Marina Tsvetaeva, published 1st vol. of poetry, *Razgovor o shchastye* (Talk of Happiness, 1957); other collections include *Mys zelaniya* (Cape of Desire, 1961), *Loza* (The Vine, 1970) and *Surovoy nityu* (With a Course Thread, 1974); also published translations of work by Jewish poet M. Toif.

MORKIS, Dorothy (1942—). American equestrian. Born Dec 29, 1942; lived in Dover, MA. ❖ At Montreal Olympics, won a bronze medal in team dressage (1976).

MORLACCHI, Guiseppina (1836–1886). Italian-born ballet dancer. Born Oct 8, 1836, in Lainate, Italy; died July 23, 1886, in Billerica, MA; dau. of Antonio Morlacchi and Maria (Raimondi) Morlacchi; m. John ("Texas Jack") Burwell Omohundro (cowboy, hunter, government scout, and actor), Aug 31, 1873 (died 1880). ❖ Debuted at Carlo Felice Theatre in Genoa, Italy (1856); made 1st American appearance at Banvard's Opera House and Museum in New York City in *The Devil's Auction* (1867); performed in NY and Boston in such productions as *Esmeralda, The Seven Dwarfs, The French Spy, La Bayadère, L'Almée,* and *The Nymphs of the Forest;* played 1st speaking role (as Dove Eye) in Ned Buntline's successful Western drama *The Scouts of the Prairie* in Chicago (1872); introduced US audiences to her trademark dance, the French cancan. ❖ See also Herschel C. Logan, *Buckskin and Satin* (1954).

MORLAND, Mary (d. 1857). See Buckland, Mary Morland.

MORLAY, Gaby (1893–1964). French stage and screen actress. Born Blanche Fumoleau, June 8, 1893, in Angers, Frances (some sources cite Biska, Algeria); died July 4, 1964, in Nice. ❖ Popular star of French silents and talkies, began career on Paris stage in *Les Cloches de Corneville* (1912); made film debut in *La vacance de Max (1913),* followed by *L'Agonie des aigles, Faubourg Montmartre, Le bois sacré, Son dernier Rôle, Les nouveaux messieurs, Ariane jeune fille russe, Mélo, Il était une fois, Le scandale, Jeanne, Giuseppe Verdi, Le roi, Les amants terribles, Nuits de feu, Hercule, Entente cordiale, Le destin fabuleux de Désirée Clary* (title role), *Mademoiselle Béatrice, Farandole, Dernier métro* and *Gigi,* among others; probably best remembered for performance in *Le voile bleu (The Blue Veil,* 1942); following WWII, suffered a career setback because of marriage to a minister in the Vichy cabinet.

MORLEY, Karen (1905–2003). American actress. Born Mabel (also seen as Mildred) Linton, Dec 12, 1909, in Ottumwa, IA; died Mar 8, 2003, in Woodland Hills, CA; m. Charles Vidor (director), 1932 (div. 19430; m. Lloyd Gough. ❖ Made film debut in *Inspiration* (1931); other films include *The Sin of Madelon Claudet, Mata Hari, Arsene Lupin, Outcast, Gabriel Over the White House, Dinner at 8, The Littlest Rebel, Our Daily Bread, Beloved Enemy, The Last Train from Madrid, Scarface, M* and *Pride* *and Prejudice*; career ended abruptly during McCarthy era when she was blacklisted for refusing to testify against others before House Un-American Activities Committee (1952); ran unsuccessfully for lieutenant governor of NY State on American Labor Party ticket (1954).

MORLEY, Mrs. (1665–1714). *See Anne, queen of England.*

MORLEY, Ruth (1925–1991). Austrian-born costume designer. Born Ruth Miriam Birnholz, Nov 19, 1925, in Vienna, Austria; died Feb 12, 1991, in The Bronx, NY; children: Melissa Hacker and Emily Hacker (both filmmakers). ❖ Came to US as a Kindertransport refugee during WWII; began career designing for the stage; also designed for such films as *Never Love a Stranger, The Hustler, Lilith, A Thousand Clowns, Diary of a Mad Housewife, The Front, Taxi Driver, Kramer vs. Kramer, Little Miss Marker, Tootsie, Parenthood* and *Ghost,* and for Diane Keaton in *Annie Hall,* which launched a fashion trend. Nominated for Oscar for *The Miracle Worker* (1962). ❖ See also Melissa Hacker's documentary *My Knees Were Jumping: Remembering the Kindertransports* (1996).

MORODER, Karin (1974—). Italian skier. Born Nov 30, 1974, in Bolzano, Italy. ❖ Won a bronze medal for 4x5km relay at Nagano Olympics (1998).

MOROZOVA, Natalia (1973—). Soviet volleyball player. Name variations: Natalya. Born Jan 28, 1973, in USSR. ❖ Won a team silver medal at Barcelona Olympics (1992) and a team silver medal at Sydney Olympics (2000).

MOROZOVA, Theodosia (d. 1675). Russian noblewoman. Name variations: Boyarina Feodosia Morozova. Born in Russia; died 1675 in Moscow; eldest dau. of Boyar Sokovnin; sister of Princess Eudocia Urusova; m. Gleb Morozov (died); sister-in-law of Boris Morozov (tutor to Alexis I); related by marriage to the empress, Maria Miloslavskaia; children: son. ❖ Held an important position at court; became a devoted follower of Avvakum (1664); because of her newfound religious convictions, refused to attend the wedding of Tsar Alexis I to Natalya Narishkina (1671); was arrested as an Old Believer, interrogated and thrown in a Kremlin dungeon, because she was opposed to church reforms initiated by Patriarch Nikon; her sister was imprisoned as well; when Tsar Alexis I offered to release her if she'd agree not to proselytize, refused (1671); was put on an extreme regimen and died in a convent; considered a saintly woman by traditionalists. Subject of a famous painting by Vasily Surikov, where she is being led off to exile on a wooden sledge.

MORPETH, Lady (1783–1858). *See Cavendish, Georgiana.*

MORPHIA OF MELITENE (fl. 1085–1120). Queen of Jerusalem. Name variations: Morphia of Melitin. Flourished between 1085 and 1120; born an Armenian noble; m. Baldwin II, king of Jerusalem (r. 1118–1131); children: Melisande (1105–1160), queen-regnant of Jerusalem; Hodierna of Jerusalem (c. 1115–after 1162), countess and regent of Tripoli; Alice of Jerusalem (b. around 1106); Joveta of Jerusalem (b. 1120).

MORPHISE (1737–1814). *See O'Murphy, Marie-Louise.*

MORPURGO, Rachel (1790–1871). Jewish poet. Born Rachel Luzzatto in Trieste, 1790; died 1871; was related to the famous philosopher and cabbalist Haim Moses Luzzatto and writer-scholar Samuel David Luzzatto; educated privately; m. Jacob Morpurgo, c. 1819; children: 4. ❖ At 18, began her lifelong occupation with poetry, which she wrote in Hebrew; her collected letters and poems were published in the vol. *Rachel's Harp.* ❖ See also *Women in World History.*

MORRELL, Ottoline (1873–1938). English patron of the arts, salonnière, antiwar activist, and memoirist. Name variations: Lady Ottoline Morrell. Born Ottoline Violet Anne Cavendish-Bentinck, June 16, 1873, in London, England; died April 21, 1938, in London; dau. of Lt.-General Arthur Bentinck and Augusta Mary Elizabeth (Browne) Bentinck (later Baroness Bolsover); attended St. Andrews University, Scotland, 1897, and Somerville College, Oxford, 1899; m. Philip Morrell, Feb 8, 1902 (died 1943); children: (twins) daughter Julian Morrell and son Hugh (b. May 18, 1906, Hugh died 3 days later). ❖ Titled English aristocrat who spurned her illustrious lineage to become a patron of budding literary and artistic talents of early 20th century; was eccentric, flamboyant, possessive, generous, and unconventional—a tall, imposing figure dressed in gaudy, ornate costumes that drew curious stares even on the streets of London; successfully campaigned on behalf of husband Philip Morrell for Parliament (1907); held salon on Bedford Square, London (1908–15); began affair with

Augustus John (1908), then Henry Lamb (1909); met Lytton Strachey (1909); began affair with Bertrand Russell (1911); bought Garsington Manor (1913); met D.H. and Frieda Lawrence (1914); held salon on Gower Street, London (1928–38); traveled to India (1935). ❖ See also Robert Gathorne-Hardy, ed. *Ottoline, The Early Memoirs 1873–1915* (Vol. 1, 1963) and *Ottoline at Garsington, 1915–1918* (Vol. 2, 1974); Sandra Jobson Darroch, *Ottoline: The Life of Lady Ottoline Morrell* (Coward, 1975); Miranda Seymour, *Ottoline Morrell: Life on a Grand Scale* (Sceptre, 1993); and *Women in World History.*

MORRICE, Jane (1954—). Northern Ireland politician and journalist. Born May 11, 1954, in Belfast, Northern Ireland. ❖ Was a Brussels-based journalist with French press agency and contributed to BBC World Service (1980–86); was a founder member of Northern Ireland Women's Coalition (NIWC, 1996); representing NIWC, elected to the Northern Ireland Assembly for North Down (1998); named deputy speaker (2000).

MORRIS, Anita (1943–1994). American stage, tv, and screen actress. Born Anita Rose Morris, Mar 14, 1943, in Durham, NC; died Mar 3, 1994, in Los Angeles, CA; m. Grover Dale (director), 1973. ❖ Began career in American Mime Theater; came to theatrical prominence in Broadway musical *Nine* (1982); films include *The Hotel New Hampshire, Absolute Beginners, Ruthless People, Bloodhounds of Broadway* and *Radioland Murders.*

MORRIS, Betty (1948—). American bowler. Born May 10, 1948, in Sonora, CA. ❖ Won WPBA National (1973), Women's Open (1977), WIBC all events (1976, 1979) and WIBC singles (1979, 1980); named Bowler of the Year (1974, 1977, 1987); bowled 2 perfect games on same day (June 2, 1976).

MORRIS, Clara (1847–1925). American actress. Born Mar 17, 1847 (some sources cite 1846 or 1848), in Toronto, Ontario, Canada; died of chronic endocarditis, Nov 20, 1925, in New Canaan, Connecticut; dau. of Charles La Montagne (French-Canadian cab driver) and Sarah Jane Proctor (servant); m. Frederick C. Harriott, Nov 30, 1874; no children. ❖ Moved to Ohio with mother while young; was a ballet girl in stock company of Cleveland Academy of Music (1860–69); made NY debut (1870) in *Man and Wife,* directed by Augustin Daly; starred in a number of his other productions, including *No Name, Delmonico's, Alixe, Jezebel,* and *Madeleine Morel*; proclaimed the greatest "emotional" actress of her time for portrayal of Cora in *L'Article 47* (1872); leaving Daly (1873), won praise for performance in title role of *Camille* (1874); also appeared in *Miss Multon* (1876), *The New Leah* (1875), *Jane Eyre* (1877) and *The New Magdalen* (1882); toured extensively; after retirement, gave lectures and contributed many articles on acting and theater to *McClure's, Century,* and other magazines (1900–06); books include *A Silent Singer* (1899), *A Pasteboard Crown* (1902), *Left in Charge* (1907), *New East Lynne* (1908), *A Strange Surprise* (1910), *Dressing-Room Receptions* (1911), and the children's book, *Little Jim Crow* (1900). ❖ See also her 3 vols. of personal reminiscences and thoughts: *Life on the Stage* (1901), *Stage Confidences* (1902), and *The Life of a Star* (1906); and *Women in World History.*

MORRIS, Estelle (1952—). English politician and member of Parliament. Name variations: Rt. Hon. Estelle Morris. Born June 17, 1952; dau. of Pauline Morris and Rt. Hon. Charles Morris (MP); attended Coventry College of Education. ❖ Was a teacher in Coventry; was a member of Warwick District Council (1979–91), serving as leader of the Labour group for 7 years; representing Labour, elected to House of Commons for Birmingham Yardley (1992); appointed Opposition whip (1994) and Opposition Spokesperson on Education and Employment (1995); was School Standards minister at Department for Education and Employment (1997–98); promoted to minister of State (1998); was secretary of state of Education (2001–02); became Arts minister (2003) and voted minister of the year (2003); left Parliament (2005).

MORRIS, Esther Hobart (1814–1902). American suffragist and politician. Name variations: Esther Hobart McQuigg Slack Morris. Born Esther Hobart McQuigg, Aug 8, 1814, near Spencer, Tioga Co., NY; died April 2, 1902, in Cheyenne, Wyoming; dau. of Daniel McQuigg and Charlotte (Hobart) McQuigg; m. Artemus Slack (civil engineer), Aug 10, 1841 (died 1845); m. John Morris (merchant and storekeeper); children: (1st m.) Edward Archibald (b. 1842); (2nd m.) John (died in infancy), Robert and Edward (twins, b. 1851). ❖ The 1st American woman to hold an official government position, moved with son to Peru, IL (1845), following death of 1st husband; remarried; moved to Wyoming Territory, where she promoted the cause of women's suffrage (1869); appointed justice of the peace for South Pass City, Wyoming (1870), the 1st woman ever to hold such a position; left husband and moved to Laramie (1871); was briefly on the ballot for state representative (1873); left Wyoming for NY but later returned and settled in Cheyenne (by 1890). Statues honoring her were placed in Statuary Hall in US Capitol and in the state house in Cheyenne (1960). ❖ See also *Women in World History.*

MORRIS, James (1926—). *See Morris, Jan.*

MORRIS, Jan (1926—). British travel writer. Name variations: James Morris. Born James Morris, 1926, in Somerset, England; attended Lancing Colege and Oxford University; m. Elizabeth Tuckniss, 1949. ❖ Worked for London *Times* as foreign sub-editor and for *The Guardian*; began to work independently as travel writer, traveling to more than 70 major cities around world by early 1960s; had gender-change operation (1972), as recounted in *Conundrum* (1974), and began publishing under name Jan Morris (1973); travel books include *The Market of Seleukia* (1957), *South African Winter* (1958), *Cities* (1963), *The Presence of Spain* (1964), *Travels* (1976), *Journeys* (1984), *Locations* (1992), *Fifty Years of Europe: An Album* (1997), and *Trieste and the Meaning of Nowhere* (2001); historical works include trilogy *Pax Britannica* (1968, 1973, 1978) which was published under name James Morris.

MORRIS, Jane Burden (1839–1914). English model. Born Jane Burden, 1839, in Oxfordshire, England; died in 1914; dau. of a stablehand; sister of Bessie Burden; m. William Morris (writer and artist), in 1859; children: Jenny Morris and May Morris. ❖ Considered a Pre-Raphaelite stunner, began career modeling for Dante Gabriel Rossetti, then modeled for William Morris; was sickly throughout life.

MORRIS, Janet E. (1946—). American science-fiction and short-story writer. Name variations: Janet Ellen Morris. Born May 25, 1946, in Boston, MA; m. Chris Morris, 1972 (div. 1975). ❖ Works include *High Couch of Silistra* (1977), *The Carnellian Throne* (1979), *Earth Dreams* (1982), *The 40-minute War* (with Chris Morris, 1984), *Kill Ratio* (with David Drake, (1987), *Kings in Hell* (with C.J. Cherryh, 1987), *Storm Seed* (with Chris Morris, 1990), *The Stalk* (with Chris Morris, 1994), and *ARC Riders* (with David Drake, 1995); also contributed short stories to anthologies and magazines.

MORRIS, Jenny (1972—). Australian field-hockey player. Born Sept 20, 1972, in Australia. ❖ Defender; won team gold medals at Atlanta Olympics (1996) and Sydney Olympics (2000).

MORRIS, Margaret (1890–1981). English theatrical dancer and choreographer. Born Mar 10, 1890, in London, England; died 1981. ❖ Made performance debut as specialty dancer in Plymouth, England, in a Christmas pantomime; moved to London and performed in numerous Ben Greet productions, including *Midsummer Night's Dream* (1901); choreographed incidental dances for several shows such as Marie Brena's revival of *Orpheus* (1910) and Herbert Tree's *Henry VIII* (1911); opened 2 dance studios (1909, 1918); after retiring from performance career (1925), developed own movement theories, inspired by Duncan and Rudolf Steiner, and worked as dance therapist; founded Scotland's 1st professional dance company, the Celtic Ballet (1950s), based on natural movements (Margaret Morris Movement); helped inspire the modern dance movement. ❖ See also Margaret Morris, *My Life in Movement* (1970).

MORRIS, Margaret Hill (1737–1816). American diarist. Born 1737 in Burlington, NJ; died 1816; children: 4. ❖ A widow, kept a journal which was addressed to her sister, and later published as *Private Journal of Margaret Morris* (1836), of events in Burlington, NJ, surrounding Revolutionary war (1776–78); described difficulty of remaining neutral as demanded by her Quaker faith.

MORRIS, Maria (1844–1907). *See Morete, Maraea.*

MORRIS, Mary (1895–1970). American stage star. Born June 24, 1895, in Swampscott, MA; died Jan 16, 1970, in New York, NY; married twice. ❖ Made NY stage debut in *The Clod* (1916); also appeared in *Fashion, Cross Roads, Camille, Double Door, Within the Gates,* as Abbie Putnam in *Desire Under the Elms* and Mrs. Connelly in *The House of Connelly*; was on the faculty of Carnegie Tech and American Shakespeare Festival Academy and appeared in films.

MORRIS, Mary (1915–1988). English stage, tv, and screen actress. Born Dec 13, 1915, in Suva, Fiji Islands; died Oct 14, 1988, in Aigle, Switzerland; studied at Royal Academy of Dramatic Art. ❖ Made London stage debut (1936); films include *Prison without Bars, Pimpernel Smith, Major Barbara, Thief of Bagdad, The Man from Morocco, Undercover* and *The Spy in Black.*

MORRIS, May (1862–1938). English designer. Born Mary Morris, Mar 25, 1862, in England; died 1938 in London; dau. of William Morris (early proponent of Arts and Crafts movement) and Jane Burden Morris; sister of Jenny Morris (embroiderer); studied with father, mother and aunt, Bessie Burden. ❖ Accomplished embroiderer and designer of jewelry, wallpaper and fabrics as well as central figure in Arts and Crafts movement, took over direction of Morris & Co.'s embroidery department (1885); assisted father in promoting cause of socialism (1880s–90s) and was active in Socialist League; taught embroidery at Central School of Arts & Crafts in London and at Birmingham's Municipal School of Art, becoming leading figure in male-dominated Arts and Crafts movement (late 1800s); lectured on embroidery and jewelry in US as well; devoted much of later career to documenting work of father. Edited and published *The Collected Works of William Morris* (24 vols., 1910–15), and *William Morris, Artist, Writer, Socialist* (2 vols., 1934). ❖ See also Jan Marsh, *Jane and May Morris: A Biographical Story, 1839–1938* (Rivers Oram Press, 1986).

MORRIS, Pamela (1906–2002). English publisher. Born Nov 10, 1906, in England; grew up in Paris; died Oct 20, 2002; m. John Morris, 1925. ❖ With husband and C.J. Greenwood, founded the publishing house of Borriswood; translated George Bernanos' *Diary of a Country Priest,* which established the firm's reputation; also published Archibald Macleish's *Land of the Free*; when the house was bought by Bodley Head, taught English as a foreign language at Oxford; with Anne Dreydel, founded the Oxford English Centre, which later became St. Clare's Hall.

MORRIS, Rocq (1913–1995). *See Ballesteros, Mercedes.*

MORRIS-METCALF, Harriet (1958—). *See Metcalf, Harriet.*

MORRISON, Adrienne (1889–1940). American actress and literary agent. Born Mabel Adrienne Morrison in New York, NY, Mar 1, 1889; died Nov 20, 1940; m. Richard Bennett (actor), Nov 8, 1903; m. Eric Pinker; children: (1st m.) actresses Constance (1904–1965), Barbara (1906–1958), and Joan Bennett (1910–1990). ❖ See also *Women in World History.*

MORRISON, Ann (1916–1978). American actress. Born April 9, 1916, in Sioux City, IA; died April 18, 1978, in Woodland Hills, CA; children: 1 daughter, 2 sons. ❖ Radio, tv stage and film actress; films include *Walls of Jericho, House of Strangers, People Will Talk, Battle Circus* and *The Brothers Karamazov*; appeared as Mrs. Nelson on "General Hospital" (1971).

MORRISON, Annie Christina (1870–1953). New Zealand headmistress. Born Feb 27, 1870, at Onehunga, Auckland, New Zealand; died Aug 31, 1953, in Auckland; dau. of Donald Morrison and Christina (Ross) Morrison; Auckland University College, MA, 1893. ❖ Served as 1st headmistress of Epsom Girls' Grammar School (1917–29), which became largest secondary girls' school in New Zealand; contributed significantly to girls' secondary education by adding more practical work and athletic programs. ❖ See also *Dictionary of New Zealand Biography* (Vol. 3).

MORRISON, Harriet (1862–1925). *See Morison, Harriet.*

MORRISON, Melissa (1971—). African-American hurdler. Born July 9, 1971, in Kannapolis, NC; Appalachian State University, BS. ❖ Won a bronze medal for 100-meter hurdles at Sydney Olympics (2000) and Athens Olympics (2004); won the US Indoor title for 60-meter hurdles (2002); placed 1st in 100-meter hurdles at Super Grand Prix (2003).

MORRISON, Toni (1931—). African-American novelist. Born Chloe Anthony Wofford, Feb 18, 1931, in Lorain, Ohio; dau. of George Wofford and Rahmah Willis Wofford; Howard University, BA; Cornell University, MA in English; m. Harold Morrison (Jamaican architect), 1958 (div. 1964); children: Harold Ford Morrison and Slade Kevin Morrison. ❖ Major contemporary novelist whose writing is a means of reclaiming her people's past; grew up poor in midwestern steel town of Lorain, Ohio; began career as a professor, 1st at Texas Southern University and then at Howard University; began working as a textbook editor for Random House in Syracuse, NY (1965); moved to New York City (1967) to become a senior editor, publishing the work of other African-American writers; continued adjunct university teaching alternately at Yale, Bard College and SUNY at Purchase; published 1st novel,

The Bluest Eye (1970), followed by *Sula* (1973) and *Song of Solomon* (1977); left NYC to live on a houseboat on Hudson River (1979); after publication of *Tar Baby* (1981), was elected to American Academy and Institute of Arts and Letters; made the cover of *Newsweek* (1981), the 1st African-American woman to do so since writer and folklorist Zora Neale Hurston in 1943; ended career in publishing (1984) when she accepted the Albert Schweitzer Professorship of the Humanities at SUNY at Albany; published highly acclaimed novel, *Beloved* (1987); accepted professorship in the Humanities at Princeton University (1989) in African-American studies and creative writing; published *Jazz* and 1st book of essays, *Playing in the Dark: Whiteness and the Literary Imagination* (1992); also wrote *Paradise* (1998), children's book, *The Big Box* (1999), *Love* (2003) and the opera *Margaret Garner* (2003). Won National Book Critics Circle Award (1977); Named Distinguished Writer of 1978 by American Academy of Arts and Letters; appointed by President Carter to National Council on the Arts (1980); won Pulitzer Prize for *Beloved* (1988); received Chianti Ruffino Antico Fattore International Award in Literature (1990); received Nobel Prize for Literature (1993), the 1st African-American to win the coveted award. ❖ See also Danille Taylor-Guthrie, ed. *Conversations with Toni Morrison* (U. Press of Mississippi, 1994); Wilfred D. Samuels, *Toni Morrison* (Twayne, 1990); and *Women in World History*.

MORROW, Doretta (1927–1968). American actress and singer. Born Doretta Marano, Jan 27, 1927, in New York, NY; died Feb 28, 1968, in London, England; cousin of Vic Damone (singer); m. 3rd husband Albert E. Hardman; children: (3rd. m.) daughter. ❖ Debuted on stage in *The Red Mill* (1946); played Marsinah in musical version of *Kismet* (1953); appeared in only one film, *Because You're Mine,* opposite Mario Lanza.

MORROW, Elizabeth Cutter (1873–1955). American author and educator. Born Elizabeth Reeve Cutter in Cleveland, Ohio, May 29, 1873; died Jan 23, 1955; dau. of Charles Long and Annie E. (Spencer) Cutter; graduate of Smith College, 1896; further studied at Sorbonne and in Florence, Italy; m. Dwight W. Morrow (US Senator and ambassador to Mexico), June 16, 1903; children: Anne Morrow Lindbergh (b. 1906); Elisabeth Reeve Morgan (d. 1934); Constance Cutter Morrow; Dwight Morrow Jr. ❖ After husband was appointed ambassador to Mexico, wrote many articles about the Mexican scene and 5 children's books; became acting president of Smith (1939), the 1st woman to head the college since its founding; was deeply opposed to the isolationist views of her famous son-in-law. ❖ See also *Women in World History*.

MORROW, Jane (1890–1925). See Drew, Lucille.

MORROW, Simmone (1976—). Australian softball player. Born Oct 31, 1976, in Cowell, South Australia; attended University of South Australia. ❖ Outfielder, won a team bronze medal at Sydney Olympics (2000) and a team silver medal at Athens Olympics (2004).

MORROW, Suzanne. Canadian pairs skater. Born in Canada. ❖ With partner Wallace Diestelmeyer, won Canadian nationals (1947, 1948), North American championships (1947), and a bronze medal at St. Moritz Olympics and World championships (1948), the 1st Canadian pair to win Olympic and World medals.

MORROW, Virginia Tighe (1923–1995). See Tighe, Virginia.

MORSE, Ella Mae (1925–1999). American pop vocalist. Born Sept 12, 1925, in Mansfield, TX; died Oct 16, 1999, of respiratory failure in Bullhead City, AZ; dau. of George Morse (drummer) and Ann Morse (played ragtime in husband's dance band); m. Dick Showalter (bandleader), 1939 (div. 1944); m. a doctor, 1946 (div. 1953); m. Jack Bradford, 1958. ❖ Began singing with father's band (1934) claiming to be 19, got job with Jimmy Dorsey Band (1939); joined band of Freddie Slack, a former pianist with Dorsey who was then working at Pacific Square Ballroom in San Diego; with Slack's band, made 1st recording on Capitol, the hit *Cow-Cow Boogie* (1942); signed with Capital as a soloist, remaining with the company for next 15 years, following up with many more hits, including "Mister Five by Five," "House of Blue Lights," "Shoo Shoo, Baby," "No Love, No Nothin'," and "Milkman, Keep Those Bottles Quiet"; became known for her engaging mixture of boogie-woogie, blues, jazz, swing and country; also appeared in several films, including *Reveille with Beverly* (1942), *Ghost Catchers* (1944), *South of Dixie* (1944) and *How Do You Do* (1945); took several years off to start a family; recorded million-seller comeback hit *The Blacksmith Blues* (1952); recorded last album, *The Morse Code* (1959). ❖ See also *Women in World History*.

MORSKOVA, Natalya (1966—). Soviet handball player. Born Jan 17, 1966, in USSR. ❖ Won a bronze medal at Seoul Olympics (1988) and a bronze medal at Barcelona Olympics (1992), both in team competition.

MORTELL, Marie Corridon (1930—). See Corridon, Marie.

MORTEMARTE, Marie-Madeleine-Gabrielle de (1645–1704). See Rochechouart, Gabrielle de.

MORTENSEN, Karin (1977—). Danish handball player. Name variations: Karin Ørnhøj (Ørnhoj or Oernhoej) Mortensen. Born Sept 26, 1977, in Denmark. ❖ Goalkeeper, won a team gold medal at Sydney Olympics (2000) and at Athens Olympics (2004).

MORTIMER, Adeline (1825–1917). See Billington, Adeline.

MORTIMER, Agnes (fl. 1347). Countess of Pembroke. Name variations: Agnes Hastings. Flourished in 1347; dau. of Roger Mortimer (c. 1287–1330), 1st earl of March, and Joan Mortimer; m. Laurence Hastings (c. 1320–1348), 1st earl of Pembroke; children: John Hastings (1347–1375), 2nd earl of Pembroke.

MORTIMER, Alianor (c. 1373–1405). See Holland, Alianor.

MORTIMER, Angela (1932—). English tennis player. Name variations: Angela Mortimer Barrett. Born Florence Angela Margaret Mortimer, April 21, 1932, in Plymouth, Devon, England; m. John Edward Barrett (Davis Cup player and captain). ❖ Partially deaf, won the singles finals at Wimbledon (1961); lost the Wimbledon final to Althea Gibson (1958); won the French (1955), the Australian (1958) and Wimbledon doubles (1955); was a member of the Wightman Cup team for 6 years. Inducted into International Tennis Hall of Fame (1993).

MORTIMER, Anne (1390–1411). Countess of Cambridge. Name variations: Lady Anne Mortimer. Born Dec 27, 1390 (some sources cite 1388); died in childbirth, Sept 1411; dau. of Roger Mortimer (1374–1398), 4th earl of March, and Alianor Holland (c. 1373–1405); m. Richard of York also known as Richard of Conisbrough, 2nd earl of Cambridge, c. May 1406 (died 1415); children: Isabel (1409–1484, who m. Thomas Grey and Henry Bourchier, 1st earl of Essex); Richard Plantagenet (1411–1460), 3rd duke of York. ❖ Chief heir to the rights of her great-grandfather Lionel, duke of Clarence, died, age 21, shortly after giving birth to her son Richard Plantagenet, 3rd duke of York, who would be the father of English kings Edward IV and Richard III.

MORTIMER, Anne (d. 1432). See Stafford, Anne.

MORTIMER, Babe or Barbara (1915–1978). See Paley, Babe.

MORTIMER, Beatrice (d. 1383). English noblewoman. Name variations: Beatrice de Braose. Died Oct 16, 1383; dau. of Roger Mortimer (c. 1287–1330), 1st earl of March, and Joan Mortimer; m. Edward Plantagenet (grandson of Edward I, king of England), around 1327; m. Thomas de Braose, Lord Brewes, around 1334; children: Beatrice de Braose (who m. William, Baron Say); John de Braose (a knight); Thomas de Braose (a knight); Peter de Braose; Elizabeth de Braose; Joan de Braose.

MORTIMER, Catherine (c. 1313–1369). Countess of Warwick. Name variations: Catherine Beauchamp; Katherine Beauchamp. Born c. 1313; died Aug 1369; dau. of Roger Mortimer (c. 1287–1330), 1st earl of March, and Joan Mortimer; m. Thomas Beauchamp (c. 1313–1369), 3rd earl of Warwick, in 1328; children: Guy (d. 1369); Thomas, 4th earl of Warwick (1339–1401); Reynburne; William, lord of Abergavenny (d. 1419); John; Roger; Hierom; Maud Beauchamp; Philippa Stafford (fl. 1368–1378); Alice Beauchamp; Joan Beauchamp; Isabel Beauchamp; Margaret Beauchamp (who became a nun at Shouldham on death of husband); Agnes Beauchamp; Juliana Beauchamp; Catherine Beauchamp (nun at Wroxhall, Warwickshire).

MORTIMER, Catherine (d. before 1413). Countess of March. Name variations: Lady Mortimer; Katherine; Catherine Glendower. Born Catherine Glendower; died before Dec 1413; dau. of Owen Glendower and Margaret Glendower; m. Edmund Mortimer (1376–1438), 5th earl of March, 1402. ❖ Was the daughter of Owen Glendower and wife of Edmund Mortimer, both rebels against the crown during Wars of the Roses; is portrayed as Lady Mortimer in Shakespeare's *Henry IV, Part I.*

MORTIMER, Dorothy (1898–1950). American actress. Born 1898; died Feb 15, 1950, in New York, NY. ❖ Appeared on Broadway with Leo Ditrichstein in *The King, Parlor Bedroom and Bath* and *Just Married.*

MORTIMER, Eleanor (c. 1395–1418). English noblewoman. Name variations: Eleanor Courtenay. Born c. 1395; died, age 23, in 1418; dau. of Roger Mortimer (1374–1398), 4th earl of March, and Alianor Holland; m. Edward Courtenay (admiral of the fleet and son of Edward, 3rd earl of Devon), c. 1409.

MORTIMER, Elizabeth (1371–1417). *See Percy, Elizabeth.*

MORTIMER, Isabel (fl. 1267). Countess of Arundel. Name variations: Isabel Fitzalan; Isabella Mortimer. Dau. of Roger Mortimer (d. 1282), baron Wigmore, and Maud Mortimer (c. 1229–1301); m. John Fitzalan (d. 1272), earl of Arundel; m. Ralph d'Arderne; m. Robert Hastings; children: (1st m.) Richard Fitzalan (1267–1302), 6th earl of Arundel; possibly Eleanor Fitzalan Percy (who m. Henry Percy, 1st baron Percy).

MORTIMER, Joan (fl. 1300). Baroness Wigmore. Name variations: Joan de Genville, Genevill or Geneville. Born Joan de Genville; m. Roger Mortimer (c. 1287–1330), 8th baron Wigmore, 1st earl of March; children: 8, including Edmund (d. 1331), 3rd baron Mortimer of Wigmore; Catherine Mortimer (c. 1313–1369), countess of Warwick; Agnes Mortimer (fl. 1347), countess of Pembroke; Beatrice Mortimer (d. 1383).

MORTIMER, Margaret (d. around 1296). Countess of Oxford. Died c. 1296; interred at Grey Friars, Ipswich; dau. of Maud Mortimer (c. 1229–1301) and Roger Mortimer (d. 1282), lord of Wigmore; m. Robert de Vere, 6th earl of Oxford; children: Thomas de Vere (b. around 1282).

MORTIMER, Mary (1816–1877). American teacher and principal. Born Dec 2, 1816, in Trowbridge, Wiltshire, England; died July 14, 1877, in Milwaukee, WI; dau. of William Mortimer (blacksmith) and Mary (Pierce) Mortimer. ❖ Became involved with Catharine Beecher's project to train teachers and open nonsectarian schools for women in West; was superintendent of instruction, normal course teacher, and 1st principal of Normal Institute and High School of Milwaukee (later Milwaukee Female College, 1850–57); served as principal of seminary in Baraboo, WI (1859–63); returned to run Milwaukee Female College (1866–74); was principal founder of Woman's Club of Wisconsin (1876). ❖ See also Minerva Brace Norton, *A True Teacher: Mary Mortimer* (1894).

MORTIMER, Matilda (1925–1997). *See Mathilda, duchess of Argyll.*

MORTIMER, Maud (c. 1229–1301). Baroness Wigmore. Name variations: Maud de Braose. Born c. 1229; died in 1301; dau. of William de Braose, lord of Abergavenny, and Eve de Braose; granddau. of Reginald, baron de Braose; m. Roger Mortimer (d. 1282), lord of Wigmore; children: Ralph Mortimer; Edmund Mortimer (d. 1303), 1st lord Mortimer; Roger Mortimer (d. 1336); William Mortimer; Geoffrey Mortimer; Isabel Mortimer (who m. John Fitzalan); Margaret Mortimer.

MORTIMER, Penelope (1918–1999). Welsh novelist. Name variations: Ann Temple; Penelope Dimont; Penelope Ruth Mortimer. Born Sept 19, 1918, in Rhyl, North Wales; died in Oct 1999 at a hospice in London, England; dau. of Arthur F.G. Fletcher (cleric) and Amy Caroline Fletcher; attended Central Educational Bureau for Women in London and University of London; m. Charles Dimont, 1937 (div. 1949); m. John Clifford Mortimer (playwright and lawyer), 1949 (div. 1972); children: (1st m.) Madelon, Caroline, Julia, Deborah; (2nd m.) Sally and Jeremy. ❖ Published 1st novel, *Johanna* (under name Penelope Dimont), shortly before marriage to writer John Mortimer (1947); published popular novel, *The Pumpkin Eater* (1962); received Whitbread Award for nonfiction for *About Time* (1979); became well known for *Queen Elizabeth: A Life of the Queen Mother,* a controversial biography which included a portrayal of Elizabeth Bowes-Lyon's romantic life before marriage to future king George VI (1986); also wrote (novel) *Daddy's Gone A-Hunting* (1958), (novel) *Long Distance* (1974), (novel) *The Handyman* (1983), *Queen Mother: An Alternative Portrait of Her Life and Times* (1995), *Saturday Lunch with the Brownings* (1960), (with John Mortimer) *Bunny Lake Is Missing* (screenplay, 1965), and *Portrait of a Marriage* (screenplay, 1990). ❖ See also *About Time: An Aspect of Autobiography* (1979); and *Women in World History.*

MORTIMER, Philippa (fl. 1352). *See Montacute, Philippa.*

MORTIMER, Philippa (1355–1382). Countess of Ulster and March. Name variations: Philippa Plantagenet; Philippa of Clarence. Born August 16, 1355, in Eltham, Kent, England; died Jan 5, 1382 (some sources cite Jan 7, 1378); buried at Wigmore, Hereford and Worcester, England; dau. of Lionel of Antwerp and Elizabeth de Burgh (1332–1363); m. Edmund Mortimer, 3rd earl of March, in 1368; children: Elizabeth Percy (1371–1417); Roger Mortimer (1374–1398), 4th earl of March; Philippa Mortimer (1375–1401); Edmund Mortimer (1376–1438), 5th earl of March; John Mortimer (d. 1422).

MORTIMER, Philippa (1375–1401). Countess of Arundel. Name variations: Philippa Fitzalan; Philippa Poynings. Born Nov 21, 1375, in Ludlow, Shropshire, England; died Sept 24, 1401, in Halnaker, West Sussex, England; dau. of Edmund Mortimer, 3rd earl of March, and Philippa Mortimer (1355–1382); m. John Hastings (1372–1389), 3rd earl of Pembroke, c. 1385 (died 1389); m. Richard Fitzalan (1346–1397), 9th earl of Arundel, around 1390 (died 1397); m. Thomas Poynings (d. 1429), 5th baron St. John; children: (2nd m.) 1.

MORTON, Azie Taylor (c. 1936–2003). African-American government official. Born c. 1936; died Dec 7, 2003, in Austin, TX; graduate of Huston-Tillotson College, 1956; m. James Morton (died Jan 2003); children: Virgie Floyd and Stacey Hurst. ❖ Served on President John F. Kennedy's Committee on Equal Employment Opportunity; was an observer for presidential elections in Haiti, Senegal and the Dominican Republic; appointed by Jimmy Carter, was the only African-American to serve as US treasurer (1977–81).

MORTON, Clara (c. 1882–1948). American actress. Born c. 1882; died May 2, 1948, in Detroit, Michigan. ❖ Was a member of the internationally known comedy team, the Four Mortons, along with her father, mother, and brother.

MORTON, Elsie K. (1885–1968). *See Morton, Katherine E.*

MORTON, Katherine E. (1885–1968). New Zealand journalist, writer, and radio commentator. Name variations: Elsie K. Morton. Born Katherine Elizabeth Morton, Oct 5, 1885, in Melrose, Devonport, Auckland, New Zealand; died on Aug 21, 1968, at Auckland; dau. of William Edmund Morton (accountant) and Elizabeth Ayerst (Bishop) Morton. ❖ Contributed articles to *New Zealand Herald* under name Elsie Morton (early 1900s); became reporter and popular feature writer for *Herald* (1916); published selection of her articles, *Along the Road* (1928); traveled throughout Europe, Middle East, and North America (1930s); made popular lecture tours throughout New Zealand and broadcast talks on radio program, "The Friendly Road," which she compiled and published with articles about her travels in *A Message from England* (1942), *Far Horizons* (1943), and *Sunrise at Midnight* (1948); most successful book was *Cruises of Sunday Island* (1957). ❖ See also *Dictionary of New Zealand Biography* (Vol. 4).

MORTON, Lucy (1898–1980). English swimmer. Name variations: Lucy Heaton. Born Feb 23, 1898; died Aug 26, 1980; attended Collegiate School for Girls, Blackpool. ❖ Won a gold medal in the 200-meter breaststroke at the Paris Olympics (1924) with a time of 3:33.2. ❖ See also *Women in World History.*

MORTON, Margaret (1968—). Scottish curler. Born Jan 29, 1968, in Mauchline, Scotland. ❖ Placed 4th at European (1999) and World championships (2000); (vice-captain) won a team gold medal for curling at Salt Lake City Olympics (2002).

MORTON, Martha (1865–1925). American playwright. Born Oct 10, 1865, in New York, NY; died Feb 18, 1925, in NY, NY; sister of Michael Morton (playwright); m. Hermann Conheim. ❖ Wrote such plays as *Helene* (aka *The Refugee's Daughter*), *The Merchant* (1890), *Geoffrey Middleton Gentleman, Brother John, Christmas, The Bachelor's Romance, His Wife's Father, The Fool of Fortune* (1896), *The Sleeping Partner, Her Lord and Master, The Illusion of Beatrice,* and *The Three of Hearts* (1915).

MORTON, Rosalie Slaughter (1876–1968). American physician. Born Rosalie Slaughter, Oct 28, 1876, in Lynchburg, VA; died May 5, 1968, in Winter Park, FL; dau. of Mary Haines (Harker) Slaughter and John Flavel Slaughter (lawyer and banker); graduate of Woman's Medical College of Pennsylvania, 1897; m. George B. Morton Jr. (attorney), Sept 5, 1905. ❖ The 1st woman faculty member at 2 medical schools (New York Polyclinic Hospital and Post-Graduate Medical School, 1912–18, and Columbia University's College of Physicians and Surgeons, 1916–18), supported the women physicians' involvement during WWI; conducted postgraduate studies in Europe (from 1899) and India (6 months studying the bubonic plague); established a Washington, DC, private practice (1902); after marriage (1905), moved to and practiced in NYC; established the Social Service Department of the New York Polyclinic Hospital and Post-Graduate Medical School (1917); named a special American Red Cross commissioner for the Serbian army (WWI, 1916); appointed chair of the War

Service Committee (later became the American Women's Hospital Service) to provide care in war-torn nations (1917); moved to Winter Park, FL (1930), where she practiced; lectured in Europe, Africa and Australia; invented a surgical shoe, a treatment lamp and adjustable bed-lifting blocks. ❖ See also autobiography, *A Woman Surgeon* (1937).

MORUEDI (b. 1911). *See Kiengsiri, Kanha.*

MOSCHINE (fl. 4 BCE). Athenian poet. Name variations: Moschine of Athens; Moschine the Athenian. Born in Athens; fl. around 325 BCE; children: Hedyle (poet). ❖ Of her work, nothing is extant.

MOSCOSO, Mireya (1946—). Panamanian politician. Name variations: Mireya Elisa Moscoso Rodriguez de Arias; on 2nd marriage, Mireya Moscoso de Gruber. Born Mireya Elisa Moscoso Rodriguez, July 1, 1946; earned an interior design diploma from Miami Dade Community College; m. Arnulfo Arias (president of Panama, died 1988); married once more, 1991–97 (div.). ❖ Representing the Democratic Alliance, made an unsuccessful bid for the presidency of Panama (1994); representing the Arnulfista Party, was the 1st woman president of Panama (1999–2004).

MOSDALE, Virginia (1907–1967). *Hill, Virginia.*

MOSEKA, Aminata (1930—). *See Lincoln, Abbey.*

MOSELY-BRAUN, Carol (b. 1910). *See Braun, Carol Mosely.*

MOSER, Ana (1968—). Brazilian volleyball player. Name variations: Ana Beatriz Moser. Born Aug 14, 1968, in Brazil. ❖ Outside hitter, won team World Grand Prix (1994, 1996, 1998); won South American championship (1991, 1995, 1997); won a team bronze medal at Atlanta Olympics (1996). Named Best Server at Barcelona Olympics (1992).

MOSER, Christina (1960—). West German field-hockey player. Born Sept 23, 1960, in Germany. ❖ At Los Angeles Olympics, won a silver medal in team competition (1984).

MOSER, Franziska (1966–2002). *See Rochat-Moser, Franziska.*

MOSER, Mary (1744–1819). German-born flower painter. Born in Germany, 1744; died 1819; dau. of a Swiss gold-chaser and enameller; educated in England. ❖ As a child, was exhibiting her flower paintings at the Society of Artists; by 20, was elected a founder member of Royal Academy, along with one other woman, Angelica Kauffmann, and exhibited there (1768–90); was paid £900 to decorate one of the rooms at Frogmore for Queen Charlotte of Mecklenburg-Strelitz (1744–1818), wife of George III. ❖ See also *Women in World History.*

MOSER-PROELL, Annemarie (b. 1953). *See Proell-Moser, Annemarie.*

MOSES, Anna "Grandma" (1860–1961). American artist. Name variations: Grandma Moses. Born Anna Mary Robertson, Sept 7, 1860, near Greenwich, New York; died Dec 13, 1961, in Hoosick Falls, NY; dau. of Russell King Robertson and Margaret (Shanahan) Robertson (dau. of Irish immigrants); educated sporadically in local country schools; m. Thomas Salmon Moses (farmer), Nov 9, 1887 (died 1927); children: 10 (5 died in infancy), including Anna (d. 1932), Winona, Hugh, Forrest and 1 other son. ❖ Farmwife who became a nationally renowned painter of traditional scenes while in her 70s; always painted or drew, finding inspiration in the scenes around her, though in literal terms she often used Currier & Ives for ideas, or half-tones from newspapers and magazines; her technique was to apply separate brush strokes, as one would use embroidery floss, to create a three-dimensional effect; at age 75, began to paint seriously (1935); had 1st one-woman show at New York City's Galerie St. Etienne (Oct 1940); soon saw her paintings in high demand; became an American icon, appearing on radio and tv; completed approximately 2,000 paintings; was the subject of nearly 150 solo shows and another 100 group exhibitions; primary works include *Apple Pickers, Sugaring Off, Out for the Christmas Trees, Catching the Thanksgiving Turkey, The Old Oaken Bucket, The Old Checkered House, Black Horses* and *From My Window.* ❖ See also autobiography *My Life's History* (1952); *Grandma Moses: American Primitive* (Dryden, 1946); Jane Kallir, *Grandma Moses: The Artist Behind the Myth* (Wellfleet, 1982); William H. Armstrong, *Barefoot in the Grass: The Story of Grandma Moses* (Doubleday, 1971); and *Women in World History.*

MOSES, Dorothy Sydney (1904–1986). *See Alexander, Dorothy.*

MOSES, Grandma (1860–1961). *See Moses, Anna "Grandma."*

MOSES or MOSEY, Phoebe Anne (1860–1926). *See Oakley, Annie.*

MOSHEIM, Grete (1905–1986). German stage actress. Name variations: Greta Mosheim. Born Jan 8, 1905, in Berlin, Germany; died Dec 29, 1986, in New York, NY. ❖ Prominent German actress, began career with Max Reinhardt (1925–32), making stage debut in *Des Esels Schatten* (1925), then playing the lead in *Der Sprechende Affe* to great success; other plays include *Widower's Houses, Artisen* and *Marcelin Fredelin*; toured Germany, Switzerland, Austria, etc., with her own company; made London debut in *Two Share a Dwelling* (1935) and Broadway debut in *Letters to Lucerne* (1941); other NY plays include *Street Scene, Phaedra, The Fairy, Waterloo Bridge, Faust* and *Calico Wedding*; succeeded Lotte Lenya in *The Threepenny Opera*; films include *The Car of Dreams.*

MOSHER, Clelia Duel (1863–1940). American physician. Born Clelia Duel Mosher, Dec 16, 1863, in Albany, NY; died Dec 22, 1940, in Palo Alto, CA; dau. of Sarah (Burritt) Mosher and Cornelius Duel Mosher (physician); cousin of Eliza Maria Mosher (1846–1928, physician); Stanford University, AB, 1893, MA, 1894; graduate of Johns Hopkins University School of Medicine, 1900. ❖ Externed as Dr. Howard Kelly's gynecological assistant at the Johns Hopkins Hospital dispensary; at Stanford University, worked as a hygiene instructor (1894–96), as a professor of personal hygiene (from 1910), as a women's medical advisor (from 1910), as the Roble Gymnasium director (from 1910) and as a professor of hygiene (associate from 1922, professor from 1928); advocated deep-breathing and isometric exercises, later known as "the moshers"; patented and coinvented a posture-analyzing device, the schematograph (1915); conducted an unpublished longitudinal survey of women's sexual habits that refuted traditional Victorian notions of women's sexuality; attributed menstrual disorders to poor posture, psychology, inactivity and poor breathing habits. Wrote the popular book, *Woman's Physical Freedom* (3rd ed., 1923), and many journal articles.

MOSHER, Eliza Maria (1846–1928). American physician and educator. Born Oct 2, 1846, in Cayuga Co., New York; died of pneumonia and a cerebral thrombosis, Oct 16, 1928, in New York, NY; dau. of Augustus Mosher and Maria (Sutton) Mosher; cousin of Clelia Duel Mosher (physician); completed preparatory course plus an extra year of study at Friends' Academy in Union Springs, NY; entered New England Hospital for Women and Children as an intern apprentice, 1869; University of Michigan, MD, 1875; never married; no children. ❖ Had private practice in Poughkeepsie, NY (1875–77); appointed resident physician at Massachusetts Reformatory Prison for Women (1877), then superintendent (1880); established hospital facilities there and dealt with the medical, surgical, and dental care of the prisoners; forced to resign after accidental injury (1883); returned to private practice with Dr. Lucy M. Hall, with whom she alternated semesters as resident physician and associate professor of physiology and hygiene at Vassar College (1883–87); organized medical training course at Union Missionary Training Institute (1888); became dean of women and professor of hygiene at University of Michigan (1896), but resigned due to ill health (1902); maintained private practice and gave lectures for rest of life; served as senior editor of the *Medical Women's Journal* (1905–28), and was a founder of the American Posture League. ❖ See also *Women in World History.*

MOSKALENKO, Larisa (1963—). Soviet yacht racer. Born Jan 3, 1963, in USSR. ❖ At Seoul Olympics, won a bronze medal in the 470 class (1988).

MOSKOWITZ, Belle (1877–1933). American politician. Name variations: Belle Israels. Born Belle Lindner, Oct 5, 1877, in New York, NY; died in New York, Jan 2, 1933, of complications following a fall; dau. of Isidor Lindner (watchmaker and cantor) and Esther (Freyer) Lindner; m. Charles Israels, Nov 11, 1903 (died 1911); m. Henry Moskowitz, Nov 22, 1914; children: (1st m.) Carlos, Miriam, Josef. ❖ One of the most influential women in politics during 1920s, was a reform advocate and principal campaign advisor for NY governor Alfred E. Smith; worked as a program director at Educational Alliance (1900–03); did social work, lobbying, and public relations for United Hebrew Charities, Council of Jewish Women, and New York State Conference of Charities and Corrections (1903–09), for which she was named a vice-president (1908), the 1st woman to so serve in the male-dominated organization; was active in the dance-hall reform movement (1908–13); served as a labor negotiator for Dress and Waist Manufacturers Association (1913–16); was executive secretary of Governor Alfred E. Smith's Reconstruction Committee (1919–21); was director, Industrial and Education Department, Universal Film Co. (1920–22); was publicity director, Democratic State Committee (1923–28), and primary political consultant to Smith, especially on presidential campaigns of 1924 and

1928; was owner-director of Publicity Associates (1928–33). ❖ See also Elisabeth Israels Perry, *Belle Moskowitz: Feminine Politics and the Exercise of Power in the Age of Alfred E. Smith* (Oxford U. Press, 1987); and *Women in World History.*

MOSLEY, Benita Fitzgerald (1961—). See Fitzgerald, Benita.

MOSLEY, Cynthia (1898–1933). English socialite. Name variations: Lady Cynthia Mosley; Cimmie Mosley, Cynthia Curzon. Born Cynthia Curzon on August 28, 1898; died in 1933; dau. of Mary Leiter Curzon (1870–1906), vicereine of India) and Lord George Curzon (1859–1925, diplomat and viceroy of India); m. Sir Oswald Mosley (1896–1980), 6th baronet. ❖ Like her mother before her, died young. Husband, Fascist leader Sir Oswald Mosley, would marry Diana Mitford in 1936 and go on to become a national pariah.

MOSLEY, Diana (b. 1910). See Mitford, Diana.

MOSLEY, Tracey (1973—). Australian softball player. Born Sept 25, 1973, in Sydney, Australia. ❖ Catcher, shortstop, and third base, won a team silver medal at Athens Olympics (2004).

MOSOLOVA, Vera (1875–1949). Russian ballet dancer and teacher. Born April 19, 1875, possibly around Moscow; died Jan 29, 1949, in Moscow, Russia. ❖ Performed with Bolshoi Ballet in Moscow and Maryinsky Ballet in St. Petersburg; moved back to Moscow where she performed in numerous works by Alexander Gorsky, including *Raymonda, Le Corsair, La Esmeralda*, and *The Sleeping Beauty*; danced at Alhambra Theatre in London in Gorsky's *Dance Dream*; taught at Bolshoi Ballet School after retirement from performance career where her students made up the 1st generation of Soviet dancers and included Igor Moiseyev and Asaf and Sulamith Messerer.

MOSQUERA MENA, Mabel (1969—). Colombian weightlifter. Born July 1, 1969, in Quibdo, Colombia. ❖ Won a bronze medal for 53 kg at Athens Olympics (2004).

MOSQUINI, Marie (1899–1983). American actress. Name variations: Marie De Forest. Born Dec 3, 1899, in Los Angeles, CA; died Feb 21, 1983, in Los Angeles; m. Lee De Forest (inventor of the audion vacuum tube, a key component of all major communications, including radio, telephone, radar and tv), 1930 (died 1961). ❖ Began career as secretary to Hal Roach (1916); became a well-regarded supporting player to Will Rogers, Charlie Chase and Snub Pollard; films include *Sold at Auction, Going to Congress, Genevieve* and *Seventh Heaven.*

MOSS, Cynthia (1940—). American zoologist. Born Cynthia Moss, July 24, 1940, in Ossining, NY; dau. of Julian Moss (publisher) and Lillian Moss; Smith College, BA in philosophy, 1962. ❖ Celebrated for her significant, long-term elephant research and conservation efforts, worked as *Newsweek* reporter and researcher; visited and worked at British researcher Ian Douglas-Hamilton's elephant camp in Tanzania (c. 1967–70); wrote for *Life* and *Time*; studied more than 1,600 elephants in one of last undisturbed elephant herds in Africa, as founder and director of Amboseli Elephant Research Project at Kenya's Amboseli National Park (1972); funded research in large part by Washington DC-based African Wildlife Foundation (AWF); worked with Joyce Poole (1976), a former Kenya Wildlife Service employee; honors include Smith College medal for alumnae achievement (1985), Friends of the National Zoo and the Audubon Society's conservation award. ❖ See also *Elephant Memories: Thirteen Years in the Life of an Elephant Family* (Morrow, 1988).

MOSS, Emma Sadler (1898–1970). American pathologist. Born 1898 in Pearlington, Mississippi; died April 30, 1970, at Charity Hospital, New Orleans, LA. ❖ Began career as medical technologist at Charity Hospital, New Orleans, LA (1910); became head of department of pathology at Charity Hospital (1940); established 1st medical technology training program to require baccalaureate degree (1941); served as president of American Society for Clinical Pathology (1955–56), the 1st woman president of a major medical society; taught in Department of Pathology and Bacteriology at Louisiana State University; specialized in parasitology and fungus diseases; known largely for contributions in medical education; with Albert Louis McQuown. writer of *Atlas of Medical Mycology* (1953).

MOSS, Kate (1974—). English model. Born Jan 16, 1974, in Croydon, Surrey, England; sister of Nick Moss (model); children: (with magazine publisher Jefferson Hack) Lola Hack. ❖ Supermodel, who generated controversy in early years because of her waif-like thinness, began modeling at 14; appeared on covers of *Allure, Harper's Bazaar, Arena, Elle,* and *Vogue* and in ads for Burberry, Dolce and Gabbana, Gianni Versace, L'Oreal, Yves Saint Laurent and most famously Calvin Klein; appeared in tv documentary "Models Close-Up," in BBC comedy series "French and Saunders," and MTV's "Fashionably Loud" and "Choose or Lose"; also appeared in music videos for Johnny Cash, Primal Scream and Elton John, among others; won "VH1" fashion awards (1996, 1997). ❖ See also memoir, *Kate* (1995); Katherine Kendall, *Kate Moss: Model of Imperfection* (Chamberlain, 2004).

MOSS, Marjorie (c. 1895–1935). English ballet and exhibition ballroom dancer. Born c. 1895, possibly in London, England; died of tuberculosis, Feb 3, 1935, in Palm Spring, CA; m. Edmund Goulding (English-born film director), 1931. ❖ Danced for Katti Lanner and Malvina Cavallazzi at Empire Theater as soloist, understudy, and corps member; with George Fontana, had great success as a ballroom dancer throughout Europe (1924–32) and appeared in such shows as *Sunny* (1925), *International Revue* (1930), *Sweet and Low* (1930), and *I'm Much Obliged* (1936); also appeared with Fontana at Hotel Metropole, at Café de Paris, and Kit Kat Club in London, as well as at Central Park Casino in NYC where they soon became the most famous dance team in US (1930); retired on marriage.

MOSSETTI, Carlotta (1890–?). English theatrical ballet dancer. Born Sept 23, 1890, in London, England. ❖ Debuted at Alhambra Theatre, London, in *Paquita* (1908); worked frequently *en travestie* representing male characters in numerous ballets, including Fred Farren's *Sylvia* (1911), Edouard Espinosa's *Europe* (1914), Alfred Majilton's *Pastorale* (1915), and others at Empire Theatre, London; opened studio in London where she trained precision troupes for pantomime and variety shows; did choreography for *Lilac Time* (1922) and *Angelo* (1923).

MOSSON, Louise Berta (1884–1962). See Hanson-Dyer, Louise.

MOSTEL, Kate (1918–1986). American actress and author. Name variations: Kathryn Harkin. Born Oct 8, 1918; died Jan 22, 1986, in New York, NY; m. Zero Mostel (actor), 1944; children: Tobias Mostel; Josh Mostel (actor). ❖ Under name Kathryn Harkin, made 1st stage appearance as a child; Broadway credits include *The Bird Cage, The Ladies of the Corridor* and *Three Men on a Horse.*

MOSTEPANOVA, Olga (1968—). Soviet gymnast. Born Olga Vasilyevna Mostepanova, Jan 3, 1968, in Moscow, Russia. ❖ Won the Blume Memorial (1982) and USSR Cup (1984); won a gold medal for balance beam, a team gold, and silver medals for indiv. all-around and floor exercises at World championships (1983) and a team gold (1985); won the Alternate Games at Olomouc (1984), scoring a perfect 40.00 in the all-around; placed 3rd (1982) and 2nd (1984) at USSR nationals. Merited Master of Sport in Artistic Gymnastics.

MOSZUMANSKA-NAZAR, Krystyna (1924—). Polish composer and pianist. Born in Lwow, Poland, Sept 5, 1924; studied composition under S. Wiecowicz and piano under J. Hoffman at State Music College in Cracow. ❖ Appointed to faculty of State Music College in Cracow (1964), eventually becoming a professor of composition and vice-rector; served as president of the Cracow section of the Union of Polish Composers (1962–71); wrote numerous pieces for orchestra and chamber orchestra.

MOTA, Rosa (1958—). Portuguese marathon runner. Born June 29, 1958, in northern town of Foz do Douro near city of Oporto, Portugal. ❖ Won the Portuguese championship for both the 1,500 and 3,000 meters (1975, 1976); won European championship (1982); won a bronze medal for marathon at Los Angeles Olympics (1984); won a World championship for marathon (1987); won a gold medal for marathon at Seoul Olympics (1988), the 1st Portuguese athlete to win a medal at the Olympic games and the 1st Portuguese woman to win the gold; won Boston marathon (1987, 1988, 1990). Twice named Female Runner of the Year by *Runner's World.* ❖ See also *Women in World History.*

MOTEN, Etta (1901–2004). African-American actress and singer. Name variations: Etta Moten Barnett. Born Etta Moten, Nov 5, 1901, in Weimer, Texas; died Jan 2, 2004, in Chicago, IL; dau. of a Methodist minister; University of Kansas, BS, 1931; married her high school teacher when young (div.); m. Claude Barnett (founder of Associated Negro Press), 1934 (died 1967); children: (1st m.) 3, including Sue Ish. ❖ Broke color barriers with small parts in 2 films, *Flying Down to Rio*, where she sang "The Carioca," and *Gold Diggers of 1933*, singing a chorus of "Remember the Forgotten Man"; invited by Eleanor Roosevelt, was the 1st black woman to sing at the White House; starred on Broadway in

Porgy and Bess (1942); had her own radio show on NBC's WMAQ in Chicago for many years.

MOTEN, Lucy Ellen (1851–1933). American educator. Name variations: Lucy Ella Moten. Born 1851 in Fauquier County, VA; died Aug 24, 1933, in New York, NY; dau. of Benjamin Moten and Julia (Withers) Moten; Howard University Medical College, MD, 1897. ❖ Served as principal of Miner Normal School in Washington, DC (1883–1920), appointed on recommendation of Frederick Douglass; during 37-year tenure, trained nearly all teachers working in black elementary schools in DC area.

MOTH, Sophie Amalie (fl. 1670s). Danish royal mistress. Dau. of Paul Moth, count Samsoë; children: (with Christian V) Christian von Gyldenlow or Gyldenlove (1674–1703). ❖ Associated with Christian V, king of Denmark.

MOTHER LALLA (b. 1355). *See Lal Ded.*

MOTLEY, Constance Baker (1921–2005). African-American lawyer, politician, and judge. Name variations: Constance Baker; Connie Motley. Born in New Haven, Connecticut, Sept 14, 1921; died Sept 29, 2005, in New York, NY; dau. of Willoughby Alba Baker and Rachel (Huggins) Baker; attended Fisk University, 1941–42; transferred to New York University, graduating 1943; entered Columbia Law School, 1943, graduated, 1946; m. Joel Motley, 1946; children: Joel Jr. ❖ Became a lawyer to facilitate the idea that the 14th Amendment's "equal protection" clause might be further applied to the issues of racial inequality in America; worked for the NAACP Legal Defense and Education Fund (1946–63), the legal arm of the civil-rights movement; was the 1st woman to join the Defense Fund which at that time included just 3 other lawyers: Robert Carter, Edward Dudley, and Thurgood Marshall; participated in some of the most groundbreaking cases in civil-rights history, including *Brown v. Board of Education*; also defended James Meredith in his historic case against University of Mississippi; was a member of New York State House of Representatives (1964–65), the 1st black woman to serve in the state legislature; served as Manhattan Borough president (1965–66); nominated by Robert F. Kennedy, was confirmed as federal district court judge (1966). Inducted into Women's Hall of Fame in Seneca Falls, NY (1995). ❖ See also *Women in World History.*

MOTOKO HANI (1873–1957). *See Hani, Motoko.*

MOTOS ICETA, Teresa (1963—). Spanish field-hockey player. Born Dec 29, 1963, in Spain. ❖ At Barcelona Olympics, won a gold medal in team competition (1992).

MOTOYOSHI, Miwako (1960—). Japanese synchronized swimmer. Born Dec 21, 1960, in Japan. ❖ At Los Angeles Olympics, won a bronze medal in duet and a bronze medal in solo (1984).

MOTT, Lucretia (1793–1880). American Quaker minister, abolitionist, and women's rights activist. Name variations: Lucretia Coffin Mott. Born Lucretia Coffin, Jan 3, 1793, on Nantucket Island, Massachusetts; died Nov 11, 1880, at Roadside, Pennsylvania; dau. of Thomas Coffin Jr. (sea captain and merchant) and Anna (Folger) Coffin; sister of Martha Coffin Wright (1806–1875); attended private Quaker schools; secondary education at Nine Partners, a Quaker boarding school in Dutchess County, NY; m. James Mott Jr., April 10, 1811; children: Anna Mott; Thomas Mott (d. 1817); Maria Mott; Thomas Coffin Mott; Elizabeth Mott (d. 1865); Martha Mott. ❖ One of the 1st to advocate equal rights for women and a major abolitionist, was appointed assistant teacher (1808); was officially recognized as Quaker minister (1821), taking advantage of her position to challenge Quaker rules of discipline she believed to be unfair; during a schism within the Society of Friends, became a "Hicksite" (1827); organized female anti-slavery society in Philadelphia (1833), one of the 1st women's political groups in the country; helped organize 1st Anti-Slavery Convention of American Women in NY (1837); as America's leading female abolitionist, appointed delegate to World Anti-Slavery Convention in London (1840), though female delegates were excluded from the convention proceedings and relegated to the balcony; joined Elizabeth Cady Stanton and 3 other women to help organize 1st Woman's Rights Convention, Seneca Falls, NY (1848); served as president of American Equal Rights Association (1866–68); was president of Pennsylvania Peace Society (1870–80). ❖ See also Margaret Hope Bacon, *Valiant Friend: The Life of Lucretia Mott* (Walker, 1980); Otelia Cromwell, *Lucretia Mott* (Russell & Russell, 1958); and *Women in World History.*

MOTT, Nikki (1976—). *See Hudson, Nikki.*

MOTTE, Claire (1937—). French ballet dancer. Born Dec 21, 1937, in Belfort, France. ❖ Trained with Carlotta Zambelli and Serge Lifar at Paris Opéra Ballet and danced there throughout performance career; created roles in Serge Lifar's *Chemin de la Lumière* (1957), Michel Descombey's *Bacchus et Ariadne* (1967), and Roland Petit's *Turangalila* (1968), among others; danced opposite Jean-Pierre Bonnefous in Corelli's *Lament* and was featured in works by Balanchine and Georges Skibine; retired (1979).

MOTTEVILLE, Françoise Bertaut de (c. 1621–1689). French memoir writer. Name variations: Madame de Motteville; Madame Langlois de Motteville. Born Françoise Bertaut c. 1621; died 1689; dau. of Pierre Bertaut (gentleman of the king's chamber) and a Spanish mother (who was friend and private secretary of Anne of Austria); niece of bishop-poet Jean Bertaut (1552–1611); m. Nicolas Langlois, seigneur de Motteville, president of Chambre des Comptes of Rouen, 1639 (died 1641). ❖ Was lady-in-waiting for Anne of Austria (1642–66); through all the intrigues and troubles of the Fronde, remained devoted to her mistress, eschewing party ties or interests; was also a friend of Henrietta Maria of England; chief work is her *Mémoires pour servir à l'histoire d'Anne d'Autriche*, which are in effect a history of Anne of Austria. ❖ See also *Women in World History.*

MOUCHARD, Marie-Anne-Françoise (1737–1813). *See Beauharnais, Fanny de.*

MOUKHATCHEVA, Lubov. *See Mukhacheva, Lubov.*

MOULD, Mrs. David (1947—). *See Coakes, Marion.*

MOULSWORTH, Martha (1577–1646). *See Molesworth, Martha.*

MOULTON, Barbara (1915–1997). American bacteriologist. Born 1915 in Chicago, IL; died 1997; dau. of Harold Moulton (president of Brookings Institute); attended Smith College and the University of Vienna; University of Chicago, AB, 1937; George Washington University, MA, 1940, MD, 1944; m. E. Wayne Brown Jr., Mar 30, 1962. ❖ Known for her testimony before the Kefauver congressional subcommittee, which investigated the drug industry's questionable practices (e.g., bribing government officials for easy drug approval), taught anatomy at George Washington University (1947–48); was instructor of antibiotic medicine at University of Illinois (1953); served assistant medical director at Chicago Municipal Contagious Disease Hospital (1953); was director of US Food and Drug Administration's division of New Drugs (1955–60); at Federal Trade Commission's Bureau of Deceptive Practices, worked as a medical officer in Division of Scientific Opinions (1961–79).

MOULTON, Louise Chandler (1835–1908). American writer and literary hostess. Born Ellen Louise Chandler, April 10, 1835, in Pomfret, CT; died of Bright's disease, Aug 10, 1908, in Boston, MA; dau. of Lucius Lemuel Chandler and Louisa Rebecca (Clark) Chandler; attended Christ Church Hall in Pomfret; graduate of Emma Willard's Troy (NY) Female Seminary, 1855; m. William Upham Moulton (editor and publisher of *The True Flag*, a Boston literary journal), Aug 27, 1855; children: Florence Moulton; 1 son died in infancy. ❖ Published collection of poems and sketches as *This, That and the Other* (1854), which sold some 20,000 copies; praised for 2nd book, *Juno Clifford*, which rapidly established her as an important figure in Boston literary circles; in years that followed, published many verses, stories and sketches in *Godey's Lady's Book, Atlantic Monthly, Scribner's, Harper's Bazaar,* and other magazines; published children's stories in several vols. of *Bed-Time Stories* (1874–80) and another book of poetry to excellent reviews (1877); became known for her Friday salons, which were frequented by Julia Ward Howe, Annie Adams Fields, Sarah Orne Jewett, Harriet Prescott Spofford, Henry Wadsworth Longfellow, John Greenleaf Whittier, James Russell Lowell, Oliver Wendell Holmes and Ralph Waldo Emerson; was Boston literary correspondent for *New York Tribune* (1870–76), then *Boston Sunday Herald* (1887–91), introducing US readers to new poets and writers, especially the Pre-Raphaelites and French Symbolists; spent 6 months of each year in London and much of her travel was documented in *Random Rambles* (1881) and *Lazy Tours in Spain and Elsewhere* (1896); published another vol. of verse, *In the Garden of Dreams* (1889), which confirmed her reputation. ❖ See also *Women in World History.*

MOUNSEY, Tara (1978—). American ice-hockey player. Born Mar 12, 1978, in Concord, NH; attended Brown University. ❖ Won Outstanding Performance Award for US at IIHF Pacific Women's Hockey championship (1996); won a team gold medal at Nagano

(1998), the 1st Olympics to feature women's ice hockey; won team silver medals at World championships (1997, 1999); won a team silver medal at Salt Lake City Olympics (2002). ❖ See also Mary Turco, *Crashing the Net: The U.S. Women's Olympic Ice Hockey Team and the Road to Gold* (HarperCollins, 1999); and *Women in World History.*

MOUNSEY, Yvonne (c. 1921—). South African ballet dancer. Born c. 1921 in Pretoria, South Africa. ❖ Trained locally and in Paris with Olga Preobrazhenska and Lyubov Egorova; moved to US where she worked at School of American Ballet (NY); performed with touring companies of Ballet Russe de Monte Carlo and Original Ballet Russe in US (1940s), performing featured parts in numerous classical repertory works such as *Les Sylphides, Swan Lake,* and *Giselle;* danced with New York City Ballet (1949–59), appearing in Balanchine's *Prodigal Son* and Robbins' *The Cage* (1951), and creating roles in Robbins' *Age of Anxiety* (1950) and Balanchine's *La Valse* (1951) and *The Nutcracker* (1954), among others; returned to South Africa (1959) where she was one of the founding members of Johannesburg Ballet; became director of Westside Ballet in Santa Monica, CA.

MOUNTBATTEN, Edwina Ashley (1901–1960). Countess Mountbatten of Burma who was vicereine of India. Name variations: Lady Mountbatten of Burma. Born Edwina Cynthia Annette Ashley in London, England, Nov 28, 1901; died Feb 21, 1960, in Jesselton, North Borneo; dau. of Colonel Wilfred William Ashley, baron Mount Temple of Lee (member of Parliament), and Maud (Cassel) Ashley; maternal granddau. of Ernest Cassel, financial advisor to King Edward VII; attended Alde House, Aldeburgh, Suffolk; m. Lord Louis Mountbatten, July 18, 1922; children: Patricia Mountbatten (b. 1924); Pamela Mountbatten (b. 1929). ❖ Married Lord Louis Mountbatten, a cousin of British royal family and officer in royal navy (1922); began an intense period of global travel (1928), visiting the archaeological digs at Persepolis, trekking over the Andes, examining Inca ruins in Machu Picchu and studying Mayan civilization in the Yucatan; with outbreak of WWII, joined St. John Ambulance Association (1939), quickly rising to position of Ambulance president for London, Hampshire, and Isle of Wight; toured US with husband, to thank those who had aided the British war effort (1941); traveled to France (1944), where the Red Cross and the Brigade were charged with inspecting French and Allied hospitals, inspections that subsequently took her to northern Europe, Italy, and Southeast Asia; became part of husband's "Operation Zipper," which involved rescue and recovery of hundreds of thousands of Allied soldiers from Japanese prisoner-of-war camps; when husband was appointed viceroy of India, was a great asset as vicereine of this volatile country (1947–48); also began a close, how close is in dispute, 14-year relationship with India's prime minister Jawaharlal Nehru. ❖ See also Richard Hough, *Edwina: Countess Mountbatten of Burma* (Morrow, 1984); Janet Morgan, *Edwina Mountbatten: A Life of Her Own* (Scribner, 1991); and *Women in World History.*

MOUNTBATTEN, Irene (1890–1956). Marquise of Carisbrooke. Name variations: Irene Denison. Born Irene Frances Adza Denison, July 4, 1890, in London, England; died July 16, 1956, in London; dau. of William Denison, 2nd earl of Londesborough, and Lady Grace Fane; m. Alexander Mountbatten, marquess of Carisbrooke, July 19, 1917; children: Iris Mountbatten (1920–1982).

MOUNTBATTEN, Pamela (1929—). Daughter of the earl and countess of Burma. Name variations: Pamela Hicks. Born Pamela Carmen Mountbatten, April 19, 1929, in Barcelona, Spain; dau. of Louis Mountbatten, earl of Burma, and Edwina Ashley Mountbatten (1901–1960); m. David Hicks (interior designer), Jan 1960 (died 1998); children: Edwina Hicks (b. 1961); Ashley Hicks (b. 1963); India Hicks (b. 1967).

MOUNTBATTEN, Patricia (1924—). Daughter of the earl and countess of Burma. Name variations: Patricia Knatchbull; Baroness Romsey. Born Patricia Edwina Mountbatten, Feb 14, 1924, in London, England; dau. of Louis Mountbatten, earl of Burma, and Edwina Ashley Mountbatten (1901–1960); m. John Knatchbull, 7th baron Brabourne, Oct 26, 1946; children: Norton Knatchbull (b. 1947); Lord Romsey; Michael-John (b. 1950); Joanna Knatchbull (b. 1955); Amanda Knatchbull (b. 1957); Philip (b. 1961); Timothy (b. 1964); Nicholas (1964–1979); and one other.

MOUNTFORD, Kali (1954—). English politician and member of Parliament. Born Jan 12, 1954, in Crewe, England; married; children: 2. ❖ Representing Labour, elected to House of Commons for Colne

Valley (1997, 2001, 2005); was a member of the Social Security Select Committee (1998–99) and Treasury Select Committee (2001–03).

MOUNTFORT, Susanna (c. 1667–1703). *See Verbruggen, Susanna.*

MOURNING DOVE (c. 1888–1936). Native American writer. Name variations: Christal Quintasket; Christine Quintasket; Humishuma. Born 1888 (some sources cite 1882, 1884, or 1885), near Bonner's Ferry, Idaho; died of influenza, Aug 8, 1936, in Medical Lake, Washington; dau. of Joseph Quintasket and Lucy (Stuikin) Quintasket; attended Sacred Heart convent school; attended business school, 1913–15; m. Hector McLeod, 1909 (marriage ended); m. Fred Galler, Sept 8, 1919; no children. ❖ Pioneering folklorist and novelist of the Inland Northwest, is widely hailed as the 1st Native American woman to write a novel; began using pen name "Mourning Dove" (1912); met Lucullus V. McWhorter (1914), archaeologist and scholar of Native American culture, who encouraged her to write both Okanogan folktales for posterity as well as fiction; taught school in British Columbia (c. 1917); published 1st novel *Cogewea, The Half-Blood: A Depiction of the Great Montana Cattle Range* (1927); founded Colville Indian Association (1930); also wrote *Coyote Stories* (1933). ❖ See also Jay Miller, ed. *Mourning Dove: A Salishan Autobiography* (U. of Nebraska Press, 1990); and *Women in World History.*

MOUSKOURI, Nana (1934—). Greek pop and jazz singer. Born Ioanna Mouskouri, Oct 13, 1934, in Crete, Greece; studied classical singing at Athens Conservatory of Music for 8 years; m. Yorgos (George) Petsilas, 1961 (div. 1975); m. André Chapelle (music producer), Jan 2003. ❖ Participated in the 1st Greek Song Festival, winning 1st and 2nd prize with songs "Kapou Iparchi i Agapi Mou" and "Aster! Asterak!" (1959); won 1st prize in Barcelona for presentation of "Xipna Agapi Mou" (1960); won Golden Lion for appearance in documentary film *Greece Land of Dreams* (1961); had 1st gold album with *Weisse Rosen aus Athen* (White Rose of Athens, 1961); with Quincy Jones, recorded album *The Girl from Greece Sings* (1962); with Michel Legrand, recorded *Les Parapluies de Cherbourg;* with Harry Belafonte, recorded *An Evening with Belafonte and Mouskouri* (1963); with her trademark glasses, was an international star, selling over 300 million albums; in UK, had own tv show, "Presenting Nana Mouskouri" (1968–70); representing the Conservatives, was a member of the European Parliament (1994–99).

MOUTAWAKIL, Nawal El (1962—). *See El Moutawakel, Nawal.*

MOUTZA-MARTINENGOU, Elisavet (1801–1832). Greek poet, translator and playwright. Born 1801 in Zakinthos, Greece; forced to marry, died in childbirth 1832; dau. of a wealthy noble; children: 1. ❖ As a child, studied Ancient Greek and Latin; began writing plays and poems; translated Homer's *Oddyssey* and Aeschylus's *Prometheus;* wrote 2 treatises, on economics and on art of poetry; autobiography was published by her son (1881). Except for autobiography (My Story), all her work was lost in a fire after earthquake in Zakinthos (1953).

MOVSSESSIAN, Vicki (1972—). American ice-hockey player. Born Victoria Movsessian, Nov 6, 1972, in Lexington, MA. ❖ Won a team gold medal at Nagano (1998), the 1st Olympics to feature women's ice hockey; won a team silver medal at World championships (1997). ❖ See also Mary Turco, *Crashing the Net: The U.S. Women's Olympic Ice Hockey Team and the Road to Gold* (HarperCollins, 1999).

MOWAT, Helen McRae (1850–1926). *See Stace, Helen McRae.*

MOWATT, Anna Cora (1819–1870). American playwright and actress. Name variations: Mrs. William Fouchee Ritchie; "Lily." Born Anna Cora Ogden, Sept 12, 1819, in Bordeaux, France; died July 27, 1870, in St. Margaret's Wood, Twickenham, England; dau. of Samuel Gouverneur Ogden (merchant and member of distinguished New York family) and Eliza (Lewis) Ogden; m. James Mowatt, Oct 1834 (died 1851); m. William Fouchee Ritchie (newspaper editor of Richmond, Virginia), 1854. ❖ Author of *Fashion,* the 1st American comedy of manners, who also defied convention as the 1st woman of her privileged class to become a professional actress, sailed for NY with family (1826); at 15, secretly married James Mowatt (1834); composed an epic poem of 130 stanzas, "Pelayo or the Cavern of Cavadonga," which was published by Harpers' under pen name "Isabel" and gained considerable attention; made successful debut as an elocutionist, giving poetry readings in Boston (1841); began to contribute articles to magazines; became the 1st American woman to write for the professional stage when her play *Fashion,* a good-natured satire on pretensions of NY's newly rich, opened in NY (Mar 1845); made triumphant debut as actress in NY in Bulwer-Lytton's *The Lady of Lyons* (1845); pursued highly successful career in US and England (1845–54); was especially praised for performances as Shakespeare's Beatrice and Rosalind; was a charter and active member of Mount Vernon Association to preserve George Washington's home. ❖ See also autobiography *Mimic Life: The Autobiography of an Actress* (Ticknor & Fields, 1854); Eric Wollencott Barnes, *The Lady of Fashion: The Life and the Theatre of Anna Cora Mowatt* (Scribner, 1954); Mildred Allen Butler, *Actress In Spite of Herself: The Life of Anna Cora Mowatt* (Funk & Wagnalls, 1966); and *Women in World History*.

MOWATT, Judy (1952—). Jamaican reggae singer. Name variations: also recorded under the names Julie-Ann, Julien and Jean. Born 1952 in Kingston, Jamaica. ❖ One of reggae's leading female vocalists for a quarter of a century, joined the singing trio Gaylettes, also know as the Gaytones (1967), with Beryl Lawson and Merle Clemonson; following split, went solo and had a string of hits, including "I Shall Sing"; formed her own label, Ashandan; with Rita Marley and Marcia Griffiths, formed the trio, I-Threes (1974), doing backup vocals for Bob Marley and the Wailers, and recording "Jah Live," among others; her album "Black Woman" is considered one of the finest female albums made in Jamaica; was nominated for a Grammy.

MOWBRAY, Alison (1971—). English rower. Born Feb 1, 1971, in Derby, England; attended Liverpool University; Cambridge University, PhD in molecular biology. ❖ Won a silver medal for quadruple sculls at Athens Olympics (2004).

MOWBRAY, Anne (1472–1481). Young bride of the duke of York. Born Dec 10, 1472, in Framlingham, Suffolk, England; died Jan 16, 1481, age 8, in Greenwich, London, England; buried at Westminster Abbey, London; coffin later removed and reburied next to her mother's grave at Aldgate; reinterred in Westminster in 1965; dau. of John Mowbray, 4th duke of Norfolk, and Elizabeth Talbot (dau. of John, earl of Shrewsbury); m. Richard Plantagenet, duke of York (Prince in the Tower), Jan 15, 1478.

MOWBRAY, Elizabeth.
See Segrave, Elizabeth (1338–1399).
See Fitzalan, Elizabeth (d. 1425).

MOWBRAY, Isabel (fl. late 1300s). Baroness Ferrers of Groby. Name variations: Isabel Ferrers. Dau. of Thomas Mowbray (c. 1362–1399), 1st duke of Norfolk, and Elizabeth Fitzalan (d. 1425); m. Henry Ferrers; children: Elizabeth Ferrers, baroness Ferrers of Groby.

MOWBRAY, Margaret (fl. 1400). English aristocrat. Name variations: Margaret de Mowbray; Margaret Howard. Flourished in the 1400s; dau. of Thomas Mowbray (c. 1362–1399), 1st duke of Norfolk, and Elizabeth Fitzalan (d. 1425); m. Robert Howard, before 1420; children: John Howard (1420–1485), 1st duke of Norfolk (r. 1483–1485); Margaret Howard (who m. Thomas Danyell, baron of Rathwire); Catherine Howard (d. after 1478, who m. Edward Neville, baron Abergavenny).

MOWBRAY, Mary Ann (1822–1873). *See Cotton, Mary Ann.*

MOWLAM, Mo (1949–2005). English politician. Name variations: Marjorie Mowlam. Born Marjorie Mowlam, Sept 1949, in Watford, England; died Aug 19, 2005; Ph.D., University of Iowa; m. Jon Norton. ❖ Representing Labour, was elected to Parliament for Redcar (1987), later becoming a member of the House of Commons Public Accounts Committee and the party's ruling National Executive committee; was an opposition frontbench spokeswoman for various departments (1988–97) and a member of the shadow cabinet (1992–97); as a key member of Tony Blair's cabinet, served as secretary of state for Northern Ireland (1997–2001), making her, in effect, chief minister of the province; negotiated the introduction of home rule; served as minister of the Cabinet Office and chancellor of the Duchy of Lanchester (1999–2001); stepped down from Parliament (June 2001). ❖ See also autobiography *Momentum* (Hodder & Stoughton, 2002).

MOXIE GIRL, The (1896–1989). *See Ostriche, Muriel.*

MOXON, Margaret (1808–1891). *See Kissling, Margaret.*

MOYA, Idalmis (1971—). *See Gato, Idalmis.*

MOYD, Pauline. Canadian geologist. Lives in Napean, Ontario, Canada; m. Louis Moyd. ❖ Explored mineral deposits in US and Canada, searching for aluminum and uranium; conducted research into concrete materials; became 1st woman to conduct symposium of American Institute of Mining, Metallurgical and Petroleum Engineers (AIMMPE, 1957); lobbied at AIMMPE convention for more significant efforts to interest woman students in fields of mining and metallurgy.

MOYER, Diane (1958—). American field-hockey player. Born July 29, 1958, in US. ❖ At Los Angeles Olympics, won a bronze medal in team competition (1984).

MOYES, Patricia (1923–2000). Irish mystery writer. Name variations: Patricia Pakenham-Walsh; Patricia Moyes Haszard. Born Patricia Pakenham-Walsh, Jan 19, 1923, in Bray, Ireland; died Aug 2, 2000, in Virgin Gorda, British Virgin Islands; dau. of Ernst Pakenham-Walsh (judge) and Marion Boyd Pakenham-Walsh; m. John Moyes (photographer), 1951 (div. 1959); m. John S. Haszard (official of the International Court of Justice), 1962 (died 1994). ❖ Was assistant to Peter Ustinov for 8 years; translated Anouilh's play *Leocadia* as *Time Remembered*, which was produced on Broadway (1957); was an assistant editor for British *Vogue* (1958–62); introduced Chief Superintendent Henry Tibbet and Emmy, a sleuthing couple, in *Dead Men Don't Ski* (1959); other novels include *Down Among the Dead Men* (1961), *Murder Fantastical* (1967), *Season of Snows and Suns* (1971), *The Coconut Killings* (1977), *A Six-Letter Word for Death* (1983), and *Twice in a Blue Moon* (1993).

MOYET, Alison (1961—). English musician and singer. Name variations: Genevieve Alison-Jane Moyet. Born Genevieve Alison-Jane Moyet, June 18, 1961, in Billericay, Essex, England. ❖ Partnered with Vince Carter, sang in technopop duo Yazoo (known as Yaz in US, early 1980s); with Carter, released album *Upstairs at Eric's* (1982), which included dance-club hits, "Don't Go," "Only You," and "Situation," and album, *You and Me Both* (1983); released debut solo album *Alf* (1984), which sold over 1.5 million copies in England; released *Raindancing* (1987), which entered UK charts at #2, followed by *Hoodoo* (1991), which included Grammy-nominated single "It Won't Be Long," and *Essex* (1993); released greatest hits collection, *Singles* (1995), which entered UK charts at #1 and went double platinum; released *The Best of Yaz* (1999).

MOYLAN, Mary-Ellen (1926—). American ballet dancer. Born 1926 in Cincinnati, Ohio. ❖ Danced on scholarship at School of American Ballet in New York City where she also performed in Balanchine's premiere of *Ballet Imperial* (1942); performed with Ballet Russe de Monte Carlo, most notably in Balanchine's *Serenade*, *Concerto Barocco*, and *Night Shadow*; appeared on Broadway in Balanchine's *Rosalinda* (1940s) and *The Chocolate Soldier* (1947); danced with Ballet Theater (as of 1950), where she was featured in Lichine's *Helen of Troy*, Taras' *Designs with Strings*, Fokine's *Les Sylphides*, and others; was solo ballerina at Metropolitan Opera in New York City (mid-1950s) before retiring.

MOYLAND, Monica (1860–1939). *See Ros, Amanda.*

MOYNIHAN, Mary (c. 1903—). Irish murderer. Born c. 1903 in Ireland. ❖ At age 15, employed as servant to Jeremiah and Nora Horgan in Kanturk, Co. Cork (1918); after Nora was murdered (Sept 9, 1922), tried and convicted for the crime (Dec 1924); when sentenced to death, accused Jeremiah (thought to be her lover) of the murder; had sentence commuted to life imprisonment.

MOYNIHAN-CRONIN, Breeda (1953—). Irish politician. Name variations: Breeda Moynihan. Born Breeda Moynihan, Mar 1953, Killarney, Co. Kerry, Ireland; dau. of Michael Moynihan (TD, Kerry South, 1981–87); m. Daniel C. Cronin. ❖ Representing Labour, elected to the 27th Dáil (1992–97) for Kerry South, replacing her father who had retired; returned to 28th Dáil (1997–2002) and 29th Dáil (2002); appointed chair of the Oireachtas Committee on Tourism, Sport, and Recreation (2000).

MOZART, Constanze (1762–1842). German musician and wife of Mozart. Name variations: Constanze von Nissen; Constanze Weber or Constanze Weber Mozart. Born Constanze Weber, Jan 5, 1762, in Zell, Germany; died 1842 in Salzburg; dau. of Fridolin Weber (court musician) and Cecilia Weber; sister of Josepha Hofer (c. 1758–1819), Aloysia Lange (1761–1839), and Sophie Weber (1763–1846); m. Wolfgang Amadeus Mozart (the composer), Aug 4, 1782; m. Georg Nikolaus von Nissen, June 26, 1809; children: (1st m.) Raimund Leopold (b. 1783, died young); Carl Thomas (b. 1784); Johann Thomas (b. 1786, died young); Theresa (b. 1787, died young); Anna Maria (b. 1789, died young); Franz Xaver (b. 1791). ❖ Trained as a singer and pianist; met Mozart (1777) when he became a boarder in the Weber household, but he 1st fell in love with her older sister, Aloysia Lange; wed Mozart (1782) and had a loving marriage; sang opera roles or accompanied him on the piano while he was composing and occasionally performed publicly in Vienna in productions of his work; suffered from poor health brought on by her frequent pregnancies (1788–90); following husband's sudden death (1791), was sole possessor of his many unpublished manuscripts, and her efforts to protect his work were critical in establishing his permanent fame; with sister Aloysia, undertook a successful concert tour of northern German states (1795). ❖ See also *Women in World History.*

MOZART, Maria Anna (1751–1829). Austrian musician. Name variations: Marianne Mozart; also known as Nännerl or Nannerl. Born July 30 or 31, 1751, in Salzburg, Austria; died Oct 29, 1829, in Salzburg; dau. of Leopold Mozart (violinist, composer, and theorist) and Anna Maria Mozart; sister of Wolfgang Amadeus Mozart (composer); m. Johann Baptist Franz von Berchtold zu Sonnenburg, 1784; children: at least one son. ❖ Also a musical prodigy, was 5 years older than her famous brother; received top billing during their early tours as a sister-brother act, performing for the elector of Bavaria in Munich and for Empress Maria Theresa in Vienna; unlike Wolfgang, did not rebel against their father; became a piano teacher. ❖ See also Emily Anderson, ed. *The Letters of Mozart and His Family* (1985); and *Women in World History.*

MOZEE, Phoebe Anne Oakley (1860–1926). *See Oakley, Annie.*

MOZZONI, Anna Maria (1837–1920). Italian socialist and women's rights advocate. Born in Milan, 1837; died in Rome, 1920. ❖ A leading figure in the early years of the modern feminist movement in Italy, launched what she termed the "risorgimento delle donna," or the "renaissance of women"; espoused socialism and workers' rights; founded La Lega promotrice degli interessi femminili in Milan; in response to new governmental laws that rescinded some civil-rights gains won in a 1789 revolution, wrote a manifesto that petitioned the Italian government on 18 points regarding women's rights at home, in school, and in the workplace; for years, presented petitions to the government to allow women the right to vote, and spoke and wrote on a number of topics concerning women and public morals; published *La liberazione delle donne* and *L'indegna schiavitù.*

M'RABET, Fadéla (1935—). Algerian writer and feminist. Name variations: Fadela M'rabet or Mrabet. Born 1935 in Constantine, Algeria; graduate of University of Algiers. ❖ A leading voice for feminism in Algeria, 1st worked with father at Algerian state radio station, where she was responsible for a woman's program; published 1st book, *La Femme algérienne* (1962), a collection of interviews with women concerning the Algerian war for independence, followed by *Les algériennes* and *L'Algérie des illusions* (1973).

MROCZKIEWICZ, Magdalena (1979—). Polish fencer. Name variations: Magda. Born Aug 28, 1979, in Poland. ❖ Won a silver medal for team foil at Sydney Olympics (2000).

M. THEOPHANE, Sister (1913–1993). *See Reinders, Agnes.*

MUAMMER, Latife (1898–1975). *See Hanim, Latife.*

MUCHINA, Vera (1889–1953). *See Mukhina, Vera.*

MUCIA (fl. 80 BCE). Third wife of Pompey. Related to the Mucii Scaevolae and the Caecilii Metelli; became 3rd wife of Gnaeus Pompeius Strabo, also known as Gnaeus Pompeius Magnus or Pompey the Great (106–48 BCE, Roman general and consul), in 80 BCE (div. c. 63 BCE); children: (sons) Gnaeus Pompeius Magnus Junior and Sextus Pompeius Magnus Pius; (daughter) Pompeia. ❖ Married Pompey soon after the death of his 2nd wife Aemilia. Pompey was also married to Antistia (dau. of Publius Antistius), Julia (d. 54 BCE), and Cornelia (c. 75–after 48 BCE). ❖ See also *Women in World History.*

MUCKE, Manuela (1975—). German kayaker. Born Jan 30, 1975, in Lutherstadt, Wittenberg, Germany. ❖ Won a gold medal at Atlanta Olympics (1996) and a gold medal at Sydney Olympics (2000), both for K4 500 meters; won 4 World championship gold medals.

MUCKELT, Ethel (c. 1900—). British figure skater. Born c. 1900 in UK. ❖ With Sydney Wallwork, placed 5th in pairs competition at Antwerp Olympics (1920); won a bronze medal for singles at Chamonix Olympics (1924); with John ("Jack") F. Page, placed 4th for pairs at Chamonix (1924) and 7th at St. Moritz Olympics (1928) and won the British Pair title 9 times.

MUDGE, Isadore (1875–1957). American librarian. Born Isadore Gilbert Mudge, Mar 14, 1875, in Brooklyn, NY; died May 16, 1957, in Baltimore, MD; dau. of Alfred Eugene Mudge (lawyer) and Mary Gilbert (Ten Brook) Mudge; Cornell University, PhB, 1897; New York State Library School, BLS, 1900. ❖ Worked at University of Illinois at Urbana as reference librarian and assistant professor, teaching reference work and book selection (1900–03); was head librarian at Bryn

Mawr College (1903–07); with close companion Minnie Earle Sears, published *Thackeray Dictionary* (1910) and *George Eliot Dictionary* (1924); became editor of *Guide to Reference Books,* issued by American Library Association (ALA, 1910), and compiled editions 3–6 (1917, 1923, 1929, 1936); created annual review of new reference books for *Library Journal* (1911–29); worked at Columbia University as reference librarian (1911–41), creating outstanding reference library, and taught at School of Library Services (1926–42), becoming associate professor (1927). ALA established Isadore Gilbert Mudge Citation, annual award for "distinguished contribution to reference librarianship" (1958).

MUECKE, Ada (1871–1929). *See Crossley, Ada.*

MUEHE, Lotte (1910–1981). German swimmer. Name variations: Lotte Mühe. Born Jan 24, 1910, in Germany; died Jan 10, 1981. ❖ At Amsterdam Olympics, won a bronze medal in the 200-meter breaststroke (1928).

MUELLER, Anna-Maria (1949—). *See Müller, Anna-Maria.*

MUELLER, Clara (1861–1905). *See Müller, Clara.*

MUELLER, Claudia (1974—). German soccer player. Name variations: Muller or Müller. Born May 21, 1974, in Germany. ❖ Forward; won a team bronze medal at Sydney Olympics (2000).

MUELLER, Emilia (1951—). *See Müller, Emilia Franziska.*

MUELLER, Gabi. Swiss kayaker. Name variations: Gabi Müller or Muller. Born in Switzerland. ❖ Won a silver medal for K4 500 meters at Atlanta Olympics (1996).

MUELLER, Irina (1951—). East German rower. Name variations: Irina Müller. Born Oct 10, 1951, in East Germany. ❖ At Montreal Olympics, won a gold medal in coxed eights (1976).

MUELLER, Kerstin (1969—). German rower. Name variations: Kerstin Müller. Born June 1969 in Germany. ❖ At Barcelona Olympics, won a gold medal in quadruple sculls without coxswain (1992).

MUELLER, Leah Poulos (1951—). American speedskater. Name variations: Leah Poulos; Lean Poulos-Mueller. Born Leah Poulos, Oct 5, 1951, in Berwyn, IL; m. Peter Mueller (speedskater). ❖ At World sprint championships, won gold medals (1974, 1979) and silver medals (1976, 1977, 1980); won a silver medal for 1,000 meters at Innsbruck Olympics (1976); won silver medals for 1,000 and 500 meters at Lake Placid Olympics (1980).

MUELLER, Martina (1980—). German soccer player. Born April 18, 1980, in Kassel, Germany. ❖ Won FIFA World Cup (2003); won a team bronze medal at Athens Olympics (2004).

MUELLER, Mary (c. 1819–1902). *See Müller, Mary Ann.*

MUELLER, Petra (1965—). East German runner. Name variations: Petra Müller. Born July 18, 1965, in East Germany. ❖ At Seoul Olympics, won a bronze medal in the 4x400-meter relay and a silver medal in the 400 meters (1988).

MUELLER, Romy (1958—). East German runner. Name variations: Romy Müller. Born July 26, 1958, in East Germany. ❖ At Moscow Olympics, won a gold medal in 4x100-meter relay (1980).

MUELLER, Silke (1978—). German field-hockey player. Born Nov 23, 1978, in Germany. ❖ Won a team gold medal at Athens Olympics (2004).

MUELLER, Susanne (1972—). German field-hockey player. Born May 12, 1972, in Germany. ❖ At Barcelona Olympics, won a silver medal in team competition (1992).

MUELLEROVA, Milena (1923—). Czech gymnast. Born June 1923 in Czechoslovakia. ❖ At London Olympics, won a gold medal in team all-around (1948).

MUENCHOW, Kirsten (1977—). *See Münchow, Kirsten.*

MUENTER, Friederike (1765–1835). *See Brun, Friederike.*

MUENZER, Lori-Ann (1966—). Canadian cyclist. Born May 21, 1966, in Toronto, Ontario, Canada. ❖ Won 2 World Cup sprints (2001); won a gold medal for sprint at Athens Olympics (2004).

MUGABE, Sally (1932–1992). Ghanaian-born Zimbabwean political leader. Name variations: also known as "Amai," Mother of the Nation. Born Sarah Francesca Hayfron in Accra, Gold Coast (now Ghana), 1932;

died in Harare, Zimbabwe, Jan 27, 1992; had twin sister Edith; m. Robert Mugabe (1st prime minister and executive president of Zimbabwe); children: son, Nhamodzenyika. ❖ The first lady of a newly independent Zimbabwe for nearly a dozen years, began career as a teacher; with husband, moved from Ghana to white-governed Rhodesia (1961), where she became a political activist, organizing women's protests which were soon banned; was placed under house arrest; went to Tanzania (1963), then Ghana, then London, while husband was imprisoned for 10 years for "subversive speech"; reunited with freed husband in Mozambique (1974); continued struggle against Ian Smith's Rhodesian regime for next 5 years; as wife of a key leader of the Zimbabwe African National Union (ZANU), was already filling the role of the yet-to-be-born nation's "Amai" (mother in the Shona language); with husband, returned in triumph to Rhodesia (1980), where he become the 1st prime minister of the Republic of Zimbabwe; though husband now wielded immense power, continued to exercise at least some restraint when it came to perceptions of her own power, diplomatically avoiding the appearance of any interest on her own part; assumed post of secretary of ZANU Women's League (1989); public image was one of dedication to charitable and relief activities, which included founding a national Child Survival Foundation; charmed visiting dignitaries with a combination of natural grace and spontaneity; was an activist first lady, giving countless speeches, appearing at official ceremonies, and visiting schools and hospitals; soon after independence, was diagnosed as suffering from kidney failure and for 11 years endured regular dialysis treatments. ❖ See also *Women in World History*.

MUGARI, Joice (1955—). *See Mujuru, Joyce.*

MUGO, Micere Githae (1942—). Kenyan poet, playwright and educator. Born 1942 in Baricho, Kirinyaga District, Kenya; University of Makerere, Uganda, BA; University of New Brunswick, Canada, MA, PhD. ❖ Joined staff at University of Nairobi (1973), becoming the 1st female dean of the Faculty of the Arts (1978); exiled from Kenya for political reasons (1982), became a citizen of Zimbabwe (1984); taught in US, Canada, and Zimbabwe; works, which reflect Marxism and are concerned with conditions in Kenya and other African countries, include *My People, Sing!* (1976), *Daughter of My People* (1976), *The Long Illness of Ex-Chief Kiti* (1976), (with Ngugi wa Thiong'o) *The Trial of Dedan Kimathi* (1976), *Visions of Africa: The Fiction of Chinua Achebe, Margaret Laurence, Elspeth Huxley and Ngugi wa Thiong'o* (1978), and *My Mother's Poem and Other Songs: Songs and Poems* (1994).

MUGOSA, Ljiljana (1962—). Yugoslavian handball player. Born April 10, 1962, in Yugoslavia. ❖ At Los Angeles Olympics, won a gold medal in team competition (1984).

MUGOSA, Svetlana (1964—). Yugoslavian handball player. Born Nov 13, 1964, in Yugoslavia. ❖ At Los Angeles Olympics, won a gold medal in team competition (1984).

MÜHE, Lotte (1910–1981). *See Muehe, Lotte.*

MUHLBACH, Louise or Luise (1814–1873). *See Mundt, Klara Müller.*

MU-IAN (fl. 5th c.). *See Hua Mu-Lan.*

MUIR, Dick (1930—). *See Robertson, Grace.*

MUIR, Elizabeth (d. before 1355). Duchess of Atholl. Name variations: Elizabeth Mure; Elizabeth of Rowallan. Died before 1355; dau. of Adam Muir (or Mure) of Rowallan; became 1st wife of Robert II (1316–1390), earl of Atholl, earl of Strathearn (r. 1357–1390), king of Scots (r. 1371–1390), c. 1349; children: John Stewart of Kyle, later known as Robert III, king of Scots (1337–1406, who m. Annabella Drummond); Walter Stewart, earl of Fife (r. 1362–1363); Robert Stewart, 1st duke of Albany (1339–1420, who m. Muriel Keith); Margaret Stewart (who m. John MacDonald, 1st lord of Isles); Alexander Stewart, 1st earl of Buchan, known as the Wolf of Badenach; Marjorie Stewart (who m. John Dunbar, 1st earl of Moray, and Alexander Keith of Grantown); Elizabeth Stewart (who m. Thomas de la Haye); Isabel Stewart (who m. James Douglas, 2nd earl of Douglas, and John Edmondstone); Jean Stewart (who m. John Keith, Sir John Lyon, and James Sandilands of Calder); Katherine Stewart (who m. Sir Robert of Restalrig). ❖ Robert II's 2nd wife was Euphemia Ross (d. 1387).

MUIR, Esther (1903–1995). American stage and screen actress. Born Mar 11, 1903, in Andes, NY; died Aug 1, 1995, in Mt. Kisco, NY; m. Busby Berkeley (director-choreographer), 1929 (div. 1931); m. Sam Coslow (producer-composer, div. 1948); children: Jacqueline Coslow (actress). ❖ Appeared on Broadway in such shows as *Greenwich Village Follies*,

Earl Carroll Vanities, International Revue and *My Girl Friday!*; films include *A Dangerous Affair, So This is Africa, The Bowery, Fury, City Girl* and *Stolen Paradise*; was wallpapered by the Marx Brothers in *A Day at the Races.*

MUIR, Florabel (1889–1970). American reporter and columnist. Born May 6, 1889, in Rock Springs, WY; died April 27, 1970, in Cheviot Hills, CA. ❖ Veteran reporter and Hollywood columnist, also wrote screenplay for *Fighting Youth* (1935).

MUIR, Gladys Elinor (1901–1964). *See Watkins, Gladys Elinor.*

MUIR, Helen (1920–2005). English biochemist. Born Isabella Helen Mary Muir, Aug 20, 1920, in UK; died Nov 28, 2005; Oxford University, MA, 1944, PhD, 1947, DSc, 1973. ❖ Contributor of influential research on osteoarthritis, researched the chemical composition of ligaments and joints (1950s); discovered the protoglycan molecule (acts as a shock absorber); while exploring methods to slow osteoarthritis, discovered that injury can trigger the disease; at Kennedy Institute of Rheumatology in London, headed the Biochemistry Division (1966–86) and, as the institute's director (1977–90), garnered international recognition for the institution; served on editorial boards of *Journal of Orthopaedic Research, Annals of the Rheumatic Diseases,* the *Biochemical Journal* and *Connective Tissue Research*; opened Cell Matrix Research's Welcome Centre in Manchester (Mar 1996); was the 1st woman council member of Medical Research Council (1973–77); appointed a fellow of Royal Society (1977), a foreign member of Royal Swedish Academy of Sciences (1989), and honorary member of American Society of Biological Chemists (1982). Named Commander of Order of the British Empire (1981).

MUIR, Jean (1911–1996). American actress. Born Jean Muir Fullarton, Feb 13, 1911, in New York, NY; died at a nursing home in Mesa, Arizona, Sept 23, 1996. ❖ Began career on Broadway stage (1930); was offered a contract with Warner Bros. on strength of her performance in the play *Saint Wench* (1933); films include *Oil for the Lamps of China* (1935), *A Midsummer Night's Dream* (1935), *Stars Over Broadway* (1935), *White Fang* (1936), *Fugitive in the Sky* (1936), *Her Husband's Secretary* (1937), *The Outcasts of Poker Flat* (1937), *Dance Charlie Dance* (1937), *The Lone Wolf Meets a Lady* (1940) and *The Constant Nymph* (1941); left Hollywood to concentrate on stage career; while playing the role of the mother on "The Aldrich Family" tv series (1950), was named a Communist sympathizer by the infamous Red Channels newsletter, a publication that listed rumored Communists; though she vehemently denied the charges, lost her job and was blacklisted; afterward, suffered a long bout of alcoholism, then returned to Broadway and tv (1960s); began teaching in drama department at Stephens College (1968).

MUIR, Jean (1928–1995). British fashion designer. Born Jean Elizabeth Muir, 1928, in London, England; died of cancer, May 28, 1995, in London; educated at Dame Harper School, Bedford, England, 1945–50; m. Harry Leuckert, 1955. ❖ Concentrating on elegant and stylish tailoring instead of fashion's latest whim, designed clothing known for its quality and classic appeal; worked as a fashion sketcher at Liberty's department store, London (1952–55); was a designer for Jacqmar (1955) and Jaeger dress and knitwear collections (1956–63), both London; was a founder-director, Jane and Jane fashion company, London (1962–66); founder-partner, with Harry Leuckert, and chief designer of her own design firm, Jean Muir Ltd (from 1966). Created a Commander of Order of the British Empire (CBE, 1984). ❖ See also autobiography *Jean Muir* (London, 1981); and *Women in World History*.

MUIR, Willa (1890–1970). Scottish novelist and translator. Name variations: Willa Johnstone Anderson Muir; (pseudonym) Agnes Neill Scott. Born Wilhelmina or Williamina Johnstone Anderson, Mar 13, 1890, in Montrose, Angus, Scotland; died May 22, 1970, in London, England; dau. of Peter Anderson and Elizabeth Pray Anderson; attended St. Andrews University; m. Edwin Muir (poet), 1918 (died 1959); children: Gavin (b. 1927). ❖ Taught classics and educational psychology in London; translations with husband include *The Island of the Great Mother* by G. Hauptmann (1925), *The Ugly Duchess* by L. Feuchtwanger (1927), *The Life of Eleanora Duse* by E.A. Reinhardt (1930), *The Sleepwalkers* by H. Broch (1932), *Three Cities* by S. Asch (1933), *The Queen's Doctor* by R. Neumann (1936), and *America* (1938) and *In a Penal Settlement*, both by Kafka (1948); also wrote novels and essays, and *Living with Ballads*. ❖ See also memoir *Belonging* (1968).

MUIR-WOOD, Helen (1895–1968). English paleontologist. Name variations: Helen Marguerite Muir-Wood. Born Feb 1895, in London, England; died Jan 16, 1968; University of London's

Bedford College, BA, 1918; attended University College, London 1918–19. ❖ Brachiopods specialist (a marine invertebrates phylum), researched brachiopods in Middle and Upper Paleozoic rocks; at the British Museum, worked as a part-time curator (1919), assistant (1920–55) and deputy keeper (1955–65); with Dr. G.A. Cooper of Smithsonian Institution, wrote *Morphology, Classification and Life Habits of the Productoidea (Brachiopoda)* in 1960; received Geological Society's Lyell Medal (1958).

MUIS, Marianne (1968—). Dutch swimmer. Born July 28, 1968, in the Netherlands; twin sister of Mildred Muis. ❖ At Seoul Olympics, won a silver medal in the 4x100-meter freestyle relay (1988).

MUIS, Mildred (1968—). Dutch swimmer. Born July 28, 1968, in the Netherlands; twin sister of Marianne Muis. ❖ At Seoul Olympics, won a silver medal in the 4x100-meter freestyle relay (1988).

MUIZECK, Marina (c. 1588–1614). See Mniszek, Marina.

MUJANOVIC, Razija (1967—). Yugoslavian basketball player. Born April 15, 1967, in Yugoslavia. ❖ At Seoul Olympics, won a silver medal in team competition (1988).

MUJURU, Joyce (1955—). Zimbabwean guerilla fighter. Name variations: Mrs. "Teurai Ropa" Nhongo (meaning "Spill-blood" Nhongo); Teurai Ropa Nhongo; Teurai-Ropa Nhongo; Teurai Ropa Nhongo; Joice Mugari; Joice or Joyce Nhongo; Joice Mujuru, Mrs. J. Mujuru. Born Joice Murari, April 15, 1955; m. Rex Nhongo (deputy head of Mugabe's ZANLA forces [aka Tapfumaneyi Rex Nhongo Mujuru; aka Solomon Mujuru]); children: 3. ❖ Under the name Teurai-Ropa Nhongo, was a member of General Staff of ZANLA at 18 and camp commander of the women's detachment of largest guerilla camp in Mozambique at 21, during Zimbabwe's war of liberation in Rhodesia; the most famous guerilla in the ZANLA forces, famed as a fierce fighter, was sought by Rhodesian security troops; gave birth to daughter during raid of camp Chimoio; as minister of Youth, Sport, and Recreation, became Zimbabwe's 1st and youngest woman Cabinet minister in Mugabe government soon after independence (1980); served as minister of Community Development and Women's Affairs (1980–85), minister of State by the Prime Minister (1985–88), minister of Community Development, Cooperatives and Women's Affairs (1988–92), resident minister and governor–Mashonaland Central (1992–96), minister of Information, Post and Telecommunication (1996–97), and minister for Rural Resources and Water Development (1997–2004); became vice-president of Zimbabwe (2004).

MUKAI, Chiaki (1952—). Japanese astronaut. Born May 6, 1952, in Tatebayashi, Gunma Prefecture, Japan; Keio University School of Medicine, PhD in medicine, 1977, PhD in physiology, 1988; m. Mako Mukai. ❖ Japan's 1st female astronaut, became board certified as a cardiovascular surgeon (1989); was a visiting scientist at Division of Cardiovascular Physiology, Space Biomedical Research Institute, NASA (1987–88); became research instructor at Baylor (1992); was a visiting associate professor of Department of Surgery at Keio University School of Medicine, Tokyo (1992–98), then promoted to visiting professor (1999); was selected as one of three Japanese Payload Specialist candidates (1985); was on the Columbia mission (July 8–23, 1994); was a member of the Discovery crew 10-day mission (Oct 29–Nov 7, 1998).

MUKHACHEVA, Lubov. Russian cross-country skier. Name variations: Lyubov Moukhatcheva. Born in USSR. ❖ Won a gold medal for 3x5km relay at Sapporo Olympics (1972).

MUKHERJEE, Bharati (1938—). Indian-born novelist and short-story writer. Born July 27, 1938, in Calcutta, India; dau. of Bina Mukherjee and Sudhir Lal; University of Iowa, PhD, 1969; m. Clark Blaise, 1963; children: 2. ❖ Moved with husband to Canada; after 14 years in Canada, immigrated to US (1980); taught at University of California, Berkeley; works include *The Tiger's Daughter* (1971), *Wife* (1975), *Days and Nights in Calcutta* (1977), *Darkness* (1985), *Middleman and Other Stories* (1988), *Jasmine* (1989), and *The Holder of the World* (1993). Awarded National Book Critics Circle Award for Fiction for *Middleman and Other Stories.*

MUKHINA, Elena (1960—). Soviet gymnast. Name variations: Yelena Mukhina. Born June 1, 1960, in Moscow, USSR. ❖ Placed 2nd at European championships, USSR Cup, USSR nationals (1977); won the USSR nationals and World championship (1978); broke her leg in competition (1979); competing at the demand of her coach, without sufficient time to heal, fell once more in competition and was paralyzed from the neck down (1980). ❖ See also documentary "More than a Game" (1991).

MUKHINA, Vera (1889–1953). Soviet Russian sculptor. Name variations: Vera Muchina; also known just as Mukhina. Born Vera Ignatevna Mukhina in Riga, Russian Empire (now Latvia), July 1, 1889; died in Moscow, Oct 6, 1953; studied with Ilya Mashkov and Nikolai Sinitsyna, then at Emile-Antoine Bourdelle's studio at the Académie de la Grande Chaumiere in Paris; dau. of Ignaty Mukhin; m. Alexei Zamkov; children: 1 son. ❖ Noted internationally for her monumental stainless steel work *Worker and Collective Farm Woman (Kolkhoznitsa),* which stood 24 meters high on top of the Soviet Pavilion at International Exposition in Paris (1937), produced 1st mature work of sculpture, *Flame of the Revolution* (1922), a memorial to Bolshevik leader Yakov Sverdlov; collaborated with Alexandra Exter to produce designs for film *Aelita,* and also worked closely with Exter in field of theatrical design; sculpted *Yulia* and *Wind* and her popular bronze, *The Peasant Woman* (1927), commemorating the 1st decade of Soviet rule; became a member of USSR Academy of Arts (1947) and a member of its Presidium (1953); concerned during her final years about the toll taken on the arts by Stalinist dictates to produce only orthodox works of Socialist Realism, spoke in favor of artistic creativity in her last address before the Academy of Arts; received many awards from the Soviet state, including Order of the Red Banner (1938), and Stalin Prizes (1941, 1943, 1946, 1951, and 1952); also designated a People's Artist of the USSR. Soviet postage stamp was issued to commemorate the centenary of her birth (June 25, 1989). ❖ See also *Women in World History.*

MUKODA, Kuniko (1929–1981). Japanese essayist and short-story writer. Born Nov 28, 1929, in Tokyo, Japan; killed in airplane crash, Aug 22, 1981, on a trip to Taiwan. ❖ Began career as a tv scriptwriter; works include *My Father's Letter of Apology* (1978) and *Memory of Cards* (1980), about her bout with cancer, for which she won the Naoki Prize; also wrote short stories, *The Name of the Flower.*

MULALLY, Teresa (1728–1803). Irish educator. Born in Pill Lane, Dublin, Ireland, 1728; died 1803 in Dublin. ❖ Worked as a milliner for several years before she retired around 1762 to devote herself to charitable work; founded the 1st Catholic school for poor girls in Dublin (1766) and an orphanage (1771), which was eventually handed over to the Presentation Order which she introduced into Dublin (1794); though she did not take vows, managed the affairs of the school and convent until her death.

MU-LAN or MULAN (fl. 5th c.). See Hua Mu-Lan.

MULDER, Eefke (1977—). Dutch field-hockey player. Born Oct 13, 1977, in Nijmegen, Netherlands. ❖ Midfielder, won a team silver medal at Athens Olympics (2004).

MULDER, Elisabeth (1904–1987). Spanish novelist and poet. Name variations: Elisabeth Mulder Pierluisi; Elisabeth Mulder de Dauner. Born Elisabeth Mulder Pierluisi, 1904, in Barcelona, Spain, of a South American mother and Dutch-born father; died Nov 28, 1987, in Barcelona; married Ezequiel Dauner, 1921 (died 1931). ❖ Works, often about an impossible love, include *Crepúsculo de una ninfa* (1942), *Preludio de la muerte* (1946), and *Luna de la máscaras* (1958); was also a translator; said to have had a fleeting but passionate relationship with Ana Maria Sagi, poet, journalist and national champion in the javeline throw, who helped launch the women's sports movement in Barcelona (1932).

MULDOWNEY, Shirley (1940—). American drag racer. Name variations: Cha Cha Muldowney. Born Shirley Rocque, June 19, 1940, in Schenectady, NY; m. Jack Muldowney, 1956 (div. 1972). ❖ Was the 1st woman to qualify for a national event in Top Fuel (1974), the 1st woman to win a National Hot Rod Association event title (1976), and the 1st woman to be selected for Auto Racing All American Team. ❖ See also Christina Lessa, *Women Who Win* (Universe, 1998), and Jane Duden, *Shirley Muldowney* (Crestwood House, 1988); *Heart Like a Wheel* (113 min. film), starring Bonnie Bedelia (1982); and *Women in World History.*

MULENGA, Alice (1924–1978). Zambian prophet and founder of the Lumpa Church. Name variations: Alice Lenshina; Alice Lenshina Mulenga; Alice Mulenga Mubusha; Lenshina. Born Alice Mulenga in 1924 (one source cites 1927); died in prison, 1978. ❖ As Lenshina (meaning "regina" or "queen"), founded Zambia's most well-known independent church; launched movement (1953), when she underwent either a near-death experience or, as she believed, actual death and resurrection, accompanied by revelations commanding her to proselytize a new religion; rapidly attracted followers and gained a reputation as a healer and a prophet; founded the Lumpa Church (c. 1954); after Northern Rhodesia became the independent republic of Zambia (1964), was arrested (1965) and the church was banned; died while in prison (1978). ❖ See also *Women in World History.*

MULFORD, Wendy (1941—). British poet, literary critic and feminist. Born 1941 in Wales. ❖ Joined Communist Party of Great Britain and became active in women's peace movement; works include *Bravo to Girls and Heroes* (1977), *Reactions to Sunsets* (1980), and *Late Spring Next Year* (1987); with Denise Riley, wrote *No Fee: A Line or Two for Free* (1978); edited *The Virago Book of Love Poetry* (1991).

MULHALL, Gael (1956—). *See Martin, Gael.*

MULHOLLAND, Clara (d. 1934). Irish novelist. Born in Belfast, Ireland, in mid-19th century; died in Littlehampton, England, 1934; attended boarding schools in England and Belgium. ❖ Wrote 1st novel (1880); wrote children's books as well, including *Percy's Revenge* (1888), *In a Roundabout Way* (1908) and *Sweet Doreen* (1915).

MULHOLLAND, Rosa (1841–1921). Irish novelist. Name variations: Lady Gilbert; (pseudonym) Ruth Murray. Born in Belfast, Ireland, 1841; died in Dublin, Ireland, 1921. ❖ Met Charles Dickens, who encouraged her to write and published her early stories in his periodical *Household Words*; released 1st novel, *Dunmara* (1864), under pseudonym Ruth Murray; went on to produce novels for next 50 years, including *The Wild Birds of Killeevy* (1883), *Marcella Grace* (1886) and *A Fair Emigrant* (1889).

MULIN CHI (b. 1934). *See Liu, Nienling.*

MULKERNS, Val (1925—). Irish novelist and short-story writer. Born 1925 in Dublin, Ireland. ❖ Was Mayo Co. library's first writer-in-residence; wrote weekly column for *Evening Press* (1968–83); was assistant editor of literary magazine *The Bell* (1950s); works include *A Time Outworn* (1951), *A Peacock Cry* (1954), *Antiquities* (1978), *A Friend of Don Juan* (1979), *An Idle Woman* (1980), *The Summerhouse* (1984), and *Very Like a Whale* (1986); edited *New Writings from the West.*

MULKEY, Kim (1962—). American basketball player and coach. Name variations: Kim Mulkey-Robertson. Born Kim Mulkey, May 17, 1962, in Hammond, LA; attended Louisiana Tech; m. Randy Robertson; children: Makenzie and Kramer. ❖ At Los Angeles Olympics, won a gold medal in team competition (1984); coached at Louisiana Tech for 15 years (1985–2000); became head basketball coach at Baylor (2000).

MULLANY, Kate (1845–1906). American labor leader. Born 1845 in Ireland; died Aug 17, 1906, in Troy, NY. ❖ Came to US with parents and settled in Troy, NY; went to work washing, starching and ironing clothes at the nation's 1st commercial laundry; organized and led the all-female Collar Laundry Union (1864), which remained an organized force in the industries of Troy for more than 5 years; was the 1st female appointed to a labor union's national office (1868); her house became a National Historic Landmark in Troy, NY (2005). Inducted into the Women's Hall of Fame at Seneca Falls, NY (2000).

MULLEN, Barbara (1914–1979). American stage, tv, and screen actress. Born June 9, 1914 in Boston, MA; died Mar 9, 1979, in London, England; m. John Taylor. ❖ Appeared as dancer and singer in vaudeville (1917–34); moved to London (1934); made London stage debut in *Bar Sinister* (1939), then appeared often as Miss Marple and also in the title role in *Jeannie* which she reprised on film; other films include *The Challenge, Kidnapped, Thunder Rock, A Place of One's Own, You Can't Beat the Irish, So Little Time* and *It Takes a Thief;* on tv, had recurring role of Janet in "Dr. Finlay's Casebook"; was director of Pilot Films and Falcon Productions. ❖ See also her book of reminiscences *Life is My Adventure.*

MULLENS, Priscilla (c. 1602–c. 1685). *See Alden, Priscilla.*

MÜLLER, Anna-Maria (1949—). East German luge athlete. Name variations: Mueller or Muller; Anna M. Muller. Born Feb 23, 1949, in East Germany. ❖ Won a gold medal for singles at Sapporo Olympics (1972).

MÜLLER, Clara (1860–1905). German poet and novelist. Name variations: Clara Muller or Mueller; Clara Mueller-Jahnke. Born Feb 5, 1860, in Lenzen, near Belgard, in Eastern Pomerania; died Nov 4, 1905 in Berlin-Wihelmshagen, Germany; dau. of a Protestant minister (died 1873); m. Oskar Jahnke, 1902. ❖ Taught, then edited left-wing journals; poems, which express sympathy toward workers' movement, include "Fabrikausgang" (1899) and "Den Ausgesperrten" (1907); wrote autobiographical novel *Ich bekenne* (I Confess, 1904).

MÜLLER, Claudia (1974—). *See Mueller, Claudia.*

MULLER, Doris Kopsky. *See Kopsky, Doris.*

MÜLLER, Emilia Franziska (1951—). German politician. Name variations: Emilia Mueller. Born Sept 28, 1951, in Schwandorf, Germany. ❖ Worked at the Institute for Biochemistry, Microbiology, and Genetics (1988–97) and the Institute for Physiology (1997–99), both at the University of Regensburg; as a member of the European People's Party (Christian Democrats) and European Democrats, elected to 5th European Parliament (1999–2004).

MÜLLER, Gabi. *See Mueller, Gabi.*

MULLER, Gertrude (1887–1954). American businesswoman and inventor. Born Gertrude Agnes Muller, June 9, 1887, in Leo, Indiana; died of cancer, Oct 31, 1954, in Fort Wayne, Indiana; dau. of Victor Herbertus Muller (businessman) and Catherine (Baker) Muller; attended International Business College in Fort Wayne. ❖ Pioneer in auto-crash product safety testing, worked at General Electric Co. (1904–10); was assistant to the president and later assistant manager of Van Arnam Manufacturing Co.; designed folding child's toilet seat, then founded Juvenile Wood Products Co. (1924); designed 1st child's car seat and was one of the 1st to conduct auto-crash safety studies; was a guest at White House Conference on Highway Safety (1954). ❖ See also *Women in World History.*

MÜLLER, Irina (1951—). *See Mueller, Irina.*

MULLER, Jennifer (1949—). American modern dancer and choreographer. Born Oct 16, 1949, in Yonkers, NY; trained at Juilliard School. ❖ Performed in numerous New York companies of Pearl Lang, Sophie Maslow, and Manuel Alum; joined José Limón's company where she danced in *Missa Brevis, Comedy, The Moor's Pavanne, The Winged,* and others; danced in premiere's of Louis Falco's *Huescape* (1968), *Timewright* (1969), *Caviar* (1970), *Sleepers* (1971), and others; served as associate director and choreographer for Falco's troupe, creating such works as *Nostalgia* (1971); choreographed for other dance companies, including Netherlands Dance Theater and Repertory Dance Theater of Utah; formed own company, Jennifer Muller and The Works (1975). Also choreographed *Rust-Giocometti Sculpture Garden* (1971), *Sweet Milkwood and Blackberry Bloom* (1971), *Tub* (1973), *Biography* (1974), *Four Chairs* (1974), *An American Beauty Rose* (1974), *Beach* (1976), *Predicament for Five* (1977) and *Lovers* (1978).

MÜLLER, Kerstin (1969—). *See Mueller, Kerstin.*

MÜLLER, Mary Ann (c. 1819–1902). New Zealand feminist. Name variations: Mary Muller or Mueller; (pseudonym) Femina. Born Mary Ann Wilson in London, prob 1819 or 1820; died July 18, 1901, at Blenheim, NZ; m. James Whitney Griffiths (chemist), Dec 16, 1841 (died); m. Stephen Lunn Müller (doctor with 4 children), Dec 5, 1851 (died 1891); children: (1st m.) 2. ❖ Pioneer suffragist, immigrated to NZ (Aug 1849); under the pseudonym Femina, published articles in local newspaper arguing for emancipation and women's suffrage; wrote *An Appeal to the Men of New Zealand* (1869), the 1st pamphlet on the women's vote published in New Zealand; owing to disapproval of husband, had to work in secret; became a member of London suffrage society and campaigned for such reforms as Married Women's Act (1884); revealed identity long after husband's death (1898). ❖ See also *Dictionary of New Zealand Biography* (Vol. 1).

MÜLLER, Petra (1965—). *See Mueller, Petra.*

MÜLLER, Renate (1907–1937). German stage and screen actress. Name variations: Renate Muller or Mueller. Born April 26, 1907, in Munich, Germany; died after a fall from a third-story window, Oct 10, 1937; dau. of the editor-in-chief of the *Münchener Zeitung* and a painter. ❖ Studied with Max Reinhardt (1924–25); began appearing in Berlin at Lessing Theater, where one of her 1st roles was that of Fanny Elssler in *L'Aiglon* (1926); cast in 1st film *Peter der Matrose* (Peter the Sailor, 1928); appeared opposite Emil Jannings in *Liebling der Götter* (Darling of the Gods, 1930); had best-known role in *Die Privatsekretärin* (Office Girl, 1931); under contract to UFA, made numerous well-received films, including 1934's *Viktor und Viktoria* (a 1980s remake starred Julie Andrews); though one of her nation's most well-known stars, consistently avoided meeting Hitler despite formal invitations to the Chancellory; also avoided propaganda films until pressured into making *Togger* (1937); committed suicide under suspicious circumstances (1937). ❖ See also *Women in World History.*

MÜLLER, Romy (1958—). *See Mueller, Romy.*

MÜLLER, Rosemarie (1949—). German politician. Born Jan 15, 1949, in Ludwigsburg, Germany. ❖ Chaired Nieder-Olm SPD (Social Democratic Party, 1989–99); as a European Socialist, elected to 5th European Parliament (1999–2004).

MÜLLER-PREIS, Ellen (b. 1912). *See Preis, Ellen.*

MULLER-SCHWARZE, Christine. American psychologist. Utah State University, PhD; m. Dietland Muller-Schwarze. ❖ Studied penguin behavior in Antarctica (beginning 1969) as 1st woman to work with US Antarctic Research Program; with husband, surveyed 24 rookeries on the peninsula and 26 additional rookeries on Antarctic islands. Mapmakers of US government named an island near Palmer Station after her.

MULLIGAN, Mary (1960—). Scottish politician. Born 1960 in Liverpool, England; University of Manchester, BA; married; children: 2 sons, 1 daughter. ❖ As a Labour candidate, elected to the Scottish Parliment for Linlithgow (1999).

MULLIN, Sharon Ritchie (c. 1937—). *See Ritchie, Sharon.*

MULLINIX, Siri (1978—). American soccer player. Born Siri Lynn Mullinix, May 22, 1978, in Denver, CO. ❖ Goalkeeper; won a silver medal at Sydney Olympics (2000); signed with Washington Freedom (2001).

MULLINS, Aimee (c. 1973—). American paralympian and model. Born c. 1973 in Allentown, PA; attended Georgetown University. ❖ Born without fibula bones in shins, had to have double amputation below the knee; became world record holder in the 100 meter and long jump and national record holder in 200 meter (1996). Named Disabled Athlete of the Year (1997). ❖ See also Christina Lessa, *Women Who Win* (Universe, 1998).

MULLINS, Priscilla (c. 1602–c. 1685). *See Alden, Priscilla.*

MULOCK, Dinah Maria (1826–1887). *See Craik, Dinah Maria Mulock.*

MULRONEY, Mila (1953—). Canadian first lady. Born Mila Pivnicki, July 15, 1953, in Sarajevo, Yugoslavia; dau. of Dimitrije Pivnicki (Montreal psychiatrist); m. (Martin) Brian Mulroney (prime minister of Canada, 1984–93), May 26, 1973; children: Caroline (b. 1974), Benedict (b. 1976), Mark (b. 1979), and Nicholas (b. 1985). ❖ Served as honorary chair of the Canadian Cystic Fibrosis Foundation. ❖ See also Sally Armstrong's *Mila* (1992).

MULSO, Hester (1727–1801). *See Chapone, Hester.*

MULVANY, Josephine (1901–1967). New Zealand weaver. Name variations: Josephine Glasgow. Born Mar 6, 1901, in Parnell, Auckland, New Zealand; died Oct 6, 1967, at Christchurch, New Zealand; dau. of Thomas John Mulvany and Mary (Reilly) Mulvany; sister of Sybil Mary Mulvany; m. William Charles Daniel Glasgow, 1936; children: daughters. ❖ Traveled with sister to Britain and trained at London School of Weaving (1927); worked under trade name, Taniko Weavers, at Newmarket, Auckland (1928–36). ❖ See also *Dictionary of New Zealand Biography* (Vol. 4).

MULVANY, Sybil Mary (1899–1983). New Zealand weaver. Name variations: Sybil Mary Wright. Born May 7, 1899, in Parnell, Auckland, New Zealand; died Mar 28, 1983, at Whangarei, New Zealand; dau. of Thomas John Mulvany and Mary (Reilly) Mulvany; sister of Josephine Mulvany; m. Selwyn Harding Wright (engineer), 1935; children: 1 son. ❖ Traveled with sister to Britain and trained at London School of Weaving (1927); and worked under trade name Taniko Weavers, at Newmarket, Auckland (1928–36). ❖ See also *Dictionary of New Zealand Biography* (Vol. 4).

MULVIHILL, Linda (1948—). *See Metheny, Linda.*

MUMFORD, Mary Bassett (1842–1935). American education and social reformer. Name variations: Mary Bassett. Born Mary Eno Bassett, May 9, 1842, in CT; died May 9, 1935, in New Britain, CT; dau. of Ozias Buell Bassett (farmer and magistrate) and Emeline (Eno) Bassett; m. Joseph Pratt Mumford (bank cashier), May 9, 1866 (died 1915); children: 5 children. ❖ Published children's book *Hilda Dart; A Born Romp* (1871), later reissued as *A Regular Tomboy* (1913); served as chair of educational committee, director, and president of New Century Club (1889–92), Philadelphia-based women's organization; elected to sectional school board for local district (1882); was 2nd woman selected to be ward representative to Philadelphia central Board of Public Education (1889); co-founded Civic Club of Philadelphia (1893) and General Federation of Women's Clubs (1890); worked with Pennsylvania Congress of Mothers to establish juvenile courts, mothers' clubs, and day nurseries; elected to (1891) and served as president (1893–1912) of board of corporators of Woman's Medical College of Pennsylvania.

MU'MININ, Umm al- (c. 613–678). *See A'ishah bint Abi Bakr.*

MUMMHARDT, Christine (1951—). East German volleyball player. Born Dec 27, 1951, in East Germany. ❖ At Moscow Olympics, won a silver medal in team competition (1980).

MUMTAZ MAHAL (c. 1592–1631). Indian empress. Name variations: Arjemand or Arjumand Banu; Nawab Aliya. Pronunciation: MOOM-taz mah-HALL. Born c. 1592, probably in India; died after giving birth to 14th child, June 7, 1631, in Burhanpur, India; dau. of Asaf Khan (noble and prime minister in court of Mughal emperor Jahangir); m. Prince Khurram, later known as Shah Jahan (3rd son of Jahangir and his successor as Mughal emperor), in April 1612; children: 8 sons, including Huralnissa (1613–1616), Dara Shikoh (b. 1615), Shuja (b. 1616) and Aurangzeb (Oct 23, 1618–1707, who succeeded Shah Jahan as Mughal emperor), and 6 daughters, including Jahanara (1614–1681) and Roshanara (b. 1617). ❖ Indian empress of Persian extraction who is buried in the Taj Mahal, the most beautiful mausoleum—and, according to many, the most beautiful building—in the world; married Prince Khurram at the instigation of her father, who wanted to advance her fortunes at the expense of Jahangir's empress (1612); became Khurram's constant companion for next 19 years, earning the title Mumtaz Mahal (Jewel of the Palace) when he took the Mughal throne under the name of Shah Jahan (1628). ❖ See also *Women in World History.*

MUNA AL-HUSSEIN (1941—). *See Gardiner, Antoinette.*

MÜNCHOW, Kirsten (1977—). German hammer thrower. Name variations: Kirsten Muenchow or Munchow. Born Jan 21, 1977, in Auetal-Rehren, Germany. ❖ Won a bronze medal at Sydney Olympics (2000).

MUNCK, Ebba (1858–1946). Countess of Wisborg. Name variations: Ebba Henrietta of Fulkila. Born Ebba Henrietta Munck on Nov 15, 1858; died Oct 16, 1946; dau. of Carl Jacob Munck; m. Oscar Charles Augustus (son of the king of Sweden), count of Wisborg, Mar 15, 1888; children: Countess Maria Sophia Henrietta Bernadotte (1889–1974); Carl Oscar (b. 1890), count of Wisborg; Countess Sophia Bernadotte of Wisborg (1892–1936, who m. Carl Marten, baron Fleetwood); Countess Elsa Victoria Bernadotte of Wisborg (b. 1893, who m. Carl Cedergren); Count Folke Bernadotte (Jan 2, 1895–1948), count of Wisborg (a humanitarian who, having engineered the Red Cross and prisoner exchange with Nazi Germany, in turn saving many Jews, was assassinated).

MUNDA, Constantia (fl. early 17th c.). British writer. Fl. in early 1600s in England. ❖ Wrote *The Worming of Mad Dogge: Or, A Soppe For Cerberus The Jaylor of Hell. No Confutation but a Sharpe Redargution of the bayter of Women* (1617) in response to John Swetnam's misogynist pamphlet *The Arraignment of Women.*

MUNDINGER, Mary O. (1937—). American nurse. Name variations: Mary O'Neil Mundinger. Born Mary O'Neil, April 27, 1937, in Fredonia, NY; dau. of Dorothy and Thomas O'Neil; University of Michigan, BS, 1959, Columbia University, MA, 1974, PhD, 1981; m. Paul Mundinger (biology professor); children: 4. ❖ Dean of Columbia University's School of Nursing, began career as director of United Hospital's Nursing Education Department in Port Chester, NY (1971–77); at Columbia, was a nursing professor, director of the nursing graduate program (1982–83), associate professor (1983–86), associate dean of administrative affairs (1984–85), assistant dean of Faculty of Medicine (1986), then became dean School of Nursing (1986); led the creation (1997) of Columbia's Advanced Practice Nurse Association (a health care clinic run by nurse practitioners who collaborate with, instead of follow, physicians); served as a health-care reform advisor to President Bill Clinton and to Senator Edward Kennedy.

MUNDT, Klara Müller (1814–1873). German novelist. Name variations: (pseudonym) Luise or Louise Mühlbach. Born Klara Müller in Neubrandenburg, Germany, Jan 2, 1814; died in Berlin, Sept 26, 1873; m. Theodore Mundt (1808–1861, novelist and critic), 1839. ❖ Under pseudonym Luise Mühlback, published 1st novel (1839), followed by a long series of historical romances which earned her a large audience and a large fortune; was a prominent figure in literary circles, with a salon that brought Fanny Lewald, among others, to the attention of high society; an advocate of women's suffrage and changes in the social position of women, was a frequent participant in reform movements and wrote many essays on social questions; wrote more than 50 novels, some multivolume, comprising nearly 100 vols., including her best-known historical novels: *Aphra Behn* (3 vols., 1849), *Frederick the Great and his Court, Joseph II and His Court, Henry VIII and Catharine Parr, Louisa of Prussia and Her Times, Marie Antoinette and her Son, The Empress Josephine* and *The Thirty Years' War.*

MUNDT, Kristina (1966—). East German rower. Born Jan 25, 1966, in East Germany. ❖ Won a gold medal at Seoul Olympics (1988) and a gold medal at Barcelona Olympics (1992), both in quadruple sculls without coxswain.

MUNIA ELVIRA (995–1067). Queen of Navarre. Name variations: Munia Mayor Sanchez. Born 995; died 1067; dau. of Sancho, count of Castile, and Urraca (d. 1025); m. Sancho III the Great (c. 991–1035), king of Navarre (r. 970–1035); children: Garcia III, king of Navarre (d. 1054). ❖ Two other children were born to Sancho III the great and Sancha de Aybar: Ferdinand or Fernando I, king of Castile and Leon; Ramiro I, king of Aragon.

MUNK, Kirsten (1598–1658). Danish queen-consort of Christian IV. Name variations: Christine, countess of Schleswig-Holstein. Born July 6, 1598; died April 19, 1658, in Odense; dau. of Ludwig Munk, count of Schleswig-Holstein; m. Christian IV (1577–1648), king of Denmark and Norway (r. 1588–1648), Dec 31, 1615; children: 12, including Leonora Christina Ulfeldt (1621–1698). ❖ Was banished from court for having committed adultery, an incongruous charge considering Christian's own reputation for promiscuity. ❖ See also *Women in World History.*

MUNK, Susanne (1967—). *See Lauritsen, Susanne.*

MUNKHBAYAR, Dorzhsuren (1969—). Mongolian shooter. Born July 29, 1969, in Mongolia. ❖ At Barcelona Olympics, won a bronze medal in sport pistol (1992).

MUNN, Meg (1959—). English politician and member of Parliament. Born Aug 24, 1959, in England; dau. of Lillian (Seward) Munn and Reginald Edward Munn (representative); m. Dennis Bates, 1989. ❖ Served as a senior social worker for Nottingham County Council (1990–92), district manager for Barnsley Metropolitan Council (1992–96), children's services manager for Wakefield Metropolitan District Council (1996–99), and asst. dir. of City of York Council (1999–2000); representing Labour, elected to House of Commons at Westminster (2001, 2005) for Sheffield Heeley; named parliamentary undersecretary of Trade and Industry (2005).

MUÑOZ, Jimena (c. 1065–1128). Spanish royal mistress. Name variations: Munoz, Muñiz, or Múñoz. Born c. 1065; died 1128; probably dau. of Count Monnio (Muño) Muñiz and Velasquita, an aristocratic couple from region of Bierzo; began liaison with Alphonso VI (c. 1030–1109), king of Castile and Leon, c. 1080; children: Elvira (who m. Raymond IV of Toulouse, count of St. Giles, and died after 1151); Teresa of Castile (c. 1080–1130), countess of Portugal. ❖ Mistress of Alphonso VI, was an important figure in Castile (c. 1100), because her daughter Teresa of Castile laid the groundwork for Portuguese independence and because Alphonso VI appointed Jimena to political positions rarely accorded a woman who was not part of royalty. ❖ See also *Women in World History.*

MUÑOZ, Mercedes (1895–1973). *See Negron Muñoz, Mercedes.*

MUNOZ CARRAZANA, Aniara (1980—). Cuban volleyball player. Born Jan 24, 1980, in Cuba. ❖ Won a team bronze medal at Athens Olympics (2004).

MUNOZ MARTINEZ, Almudena (1968—). Spanish judoka. Born Nov 4, 1968, in Spain. ❖ At Barcelona Olympics, won a gold medal in half-lightweight 52 kg (1992).

MUNRO, Alice (1931—). Canadian short-story writer. Born Alice Laidlaw, July 10, 1931, in Wingham, Ontario, Canada; attended University of Western Ontario, 1949–51; m. James Munro, 1951 (div. 1972); m. Gerald Fremlin, 1976; children: (1st m.) Sheila (b. 1953), Jenny (b. 1957), Sarah (b. 1966). ❖ Highly regarded short-story writer, ran a bookstore with 1st husband in Victoria, British Columbia; collections include *Dance of the Happy Shades* (1968), which won the Governor General's Award for Fiction, *Something I've Been Meaning to Tell You* (1974), *The Moons of Jupiter* (1982), *The Progress of Love* (1986), *Friend of My Youth* (1990), *Open Secrets* (1994), *The Love of a Good Woman* (1996), and *Hateship, Friendship, Courtship, Loveship, Marriage* (2001);

also wrote the novel *Lives of Girls and Women* (1971); stories published in *The New Yorker, Atlantic Monthly, Paris Review,* among others. Received Lannam Literary award and W.H. Smith award.

MUNRO, Janet (1883–1945). *See Fraser, Janet.*

MUNRO, Janet (1934–1972). English actress. Born Sept 28, 1934, in Blackpool, Lancashire, England; died Dec 6, 1972, in London; dau. of a stage comedian; m. Tony Wright (actor), 1956 (div. 1961); m. Ian Hendry (actor), 1963 (div. 1971). ❖ Grew up on British tv; made British film debut in *Small Hotel* (1957); starred in Hollywood debut in *Darby O'Gill and the Little People* (1959); other films include *Third Man on the Mountain, Swiss Family Robinson, Day the Earth Caught Fire, Bitter Harvest* and *Mr. Sebastian.*

MUNRO, Janet Henderson (1883–1945). *See Fraser, Janet.*

MUNRO, Mimi (1952—). American surfer. Born in Daytona, Fl; surfed at Ormond Beach. ❖ Won 3 consecutive Florida State championships and 3 consecutive East Coast championships; retired at age 15. Inducted into Surfing Hall of Fame.

MUNRO, Thalia (1982—). American water-polo player. Born Mar 8, 1982, in Santa Barbara, CA; attended University of California, Los Angeles. ❖ Won World championship (2003); won a team bronze medal at Athens Olympics (2004).

MUNRO, Vicki Keith- (1959—). *See Keith, Vicki.*

MUNSEL, Patrice (1925—). American opera singer. Born Patrice Beverly Munsel, May 14, 1925, in Spokane, WA; studied with William Herman and Renato Bellini; coached in operatic roles by Giacomo Spadoni; m. Robert C. Schuler, 1952. ❖ Became the youngest winner of the popular radio show "Metropolitan Auditions of the Air," singing the "Mad Scene" from *Lucia di Lammermoor* and walking away with a contract with the Metropolitan; at 18, was also the youngest singer to debut with the Metropolitan Opera (1943), performing the role of the courtesan Philine in *Mignon;* other early roles included Olympia in *Tales of Hoffmann* and Gilda in *Rigoletto;* eventually found a comfortable niche with the Met while developing a parallel concert and recording career; also became a popular radio entertainer and played the title role in the film *Melba* (1953), based on the life of Nellie Melba; performed with the Met until late 1950s, then concentrated on musical comedy. ❖ See also *Women in World History.*

MUNSON, Audrey (1891–1996). American artists' model. Born Audrey Marie Munson, June 8, 1891, in upstate New York; died Feb 20, 1996, in Ogdensburg, NY. ❖ One of the most popular nude female models of the Beaux-Arts school, moved to New York City with mother; posed for more civic art commissions in NY than any other model in a 10-year period; despite a lack of acting ability, appeared in 2 films which contained nude scenes, *Inspiration* (1915), one of the highest grossing films of its day, and *Purity* (1916); was committed to a mental institution at age 39, where she spent the last 65 years of her life. ❖ See also Rozas and Gottehrer, *American Venus: The Extraordinary Life of Audrey Munson, Model and Muse* (1999).

MUNSON, Mrs. Curtis (1899–1984). *See Cummings, Edith.*

MUNSON, Edith Cummings (1899–1984). *See Cummings, Edith.*

MUNSON, Elizabeth (1838–1912). *See Sangster, Margaret.*

MUNSON, Ona (1894–1955). American actress and singer. Born Owena Wolcott, June 16, 1894, in Portland, OR; died Feb 11, 1955, from overdose of sleeping pills in New York, NY; m. Eddie Buzzell (director), 1927 (div.); m. Stewart McDonald, 1941 (div. 1947); m. Eugene Berman, 1949 (div. 1955). ❖ At 4, made vaudeville debut on Northwest circuit; traveled with one of Gus Edwards' Kiddy acts for 10 years; at 18, appeared in title roles of *Tip-Toes* and *No, No, Nanette* on tour (1925); an ingenue star, replaced Louise Groody in "Nanette" on Broadway; starred in Broadway drama and musicals, introducing the song "You're the Cream in My Coffee" in *Hold Everything* (1927); was also seen in *Manhattan Mary, Pardon My English, Hold Your Horses, Petticoat Fever* and *Ghosts;* films include *Going Wild, Wagons Westward, The Cheaters, Dakota* and *The Red House;* best remembered for her performance as Belle Watling in *Gone with the Wind;* on radio, replaced Claire Trevor as Lorelie Kilbourne on "Big Town" (1940–42).

MÜNTER, Gabriele (1877–1962). German artist. Name variations: Gabriele Munter. Pronunciation: GAH-bree-el MUHn-ter. Born Feb 19, 1877, in Berlin, Germany; died May 19, 1962, in Murnau; dau. of

Carl Friedrich Münter (dentist) and Wilhelmine (Scheuber) Münter; attended Lyceum for Girls in Koblenz; private art lessons from Herford art organization "Malkiste," the Düsseldorf professor Willy Spatz, and from sculptor Hermann Küppers in Bonn; attended classes at Ladies Academy of Association of Women Artists in Munich and Phalanx School in Munich; never married. ❖ Co-founder of the Blue Rider movement, one of the most important schools of 20th-century German Expressionist art, moved from Berlin to Herford, Germany, with family (1878), then lived in Bad Oeynhausen before moving to Koblenz (1884); enabled by inheritance from mother to chart own course in art (1897), toured and visited US (1898–1900); met Vassily Kandinsky, the beginning of a long-term personal and professional relationship (1902); had 1st solo exhibition at Cologne (1908); was a founding member, with Kandinsky, of the New Artists Association of Munich (1909); purchased house in Murnau, with separate section for Kandinsky (1909); along with Kandinsky, resigned from New Artists Association and formed the "Blue Rider" (1911); participated in 1st Blue Rider exhibition (1911); exhibited 84 paintings in 12th exhibition of *Der Sturm* gallery in Berlin (1913); participated in an exhibition of "Expressionist painting" in Dresden and Breslau (1914); with advent of WWI, traveled with Kandinsky to Switzerland, then took up residence in Stockholm (1915); held 1st exhibition of paintings in Stockholm (1915); moved to Copenhagen (1917); held exhibition of 93 oil paintings and 18 reverse-glass paintings in Copenhagen (1919); returned to Berlin and learned of Kandinsky's remarriage (1920); exhibited paintings with Associated Women Artists of Berlin (1926); began life with journalist and freelance art historian Johannes Eichner (1929); submitted paintings, unsuccessfully, to Nazi-sponsored exhibition of "Great German Art" (1933); was subject of criticism by the Nazi Bavarian Minister of Arts (1937); hid much of her work from Nazi government (1937–45) and from occupying American troops (1946); saw reputation rise in the postwar years and was hailed as one of the few remaining members of the Blue Rider; had some of her works featured in a Blue Rider retrospective show in Munich (1949); was the subject of a show prepared by Eichner which toured German cities for 4 years (beginning 1950); 1st exhibitions of her work in US were held in Los Angeles and NY (1960–61); was a pioneer of German Expressionist art in the early years of 20th century, art which used intense colors and strong lines to depict her own subjective reactions to still lifes and landscapes. ❖ See also Reinhold Heller, *Gabriele Münter: The Years of Expressionism* (Prestel, 1997); Anne Mochon, *Gabriele Münter: Between Munich and Murnau* (Harvard U. Press, 1980); and *Women in World History*.

MÜNTER, Friederike (1765–1835). *See Brun, Friederike.*

MUNZ, Diana (1982—). American swimmer. Born June 19, 1982, in Chagrin Falls, Ohio; attended John Carroll University. ❖ Won a gold medal for 800-meter freestyle relay and a silver medal for 400-meter freestyle at Sydney Olympics (2000); at World championships, placed 1st in 4x200-meter freestyle relay (2001, 2003); at Pan Pacific Games, won gold medals for 400-meter freestyle, 800-meter freestyle, 1,500-meter freestyle (2002); won a bronze medal for 800-meter freestyle at Athens Olympics (2004).

MURADYAN, Nina (1954—). Soviet volleyball player. Born Aug 17, 1954, in USSR. ❖ At Montreal Olympics, won a silver medal in team competition (1976).

MURASAKI SHIKIBU (c. 973–c. 1015). Japanese novelist and poet. Name variations: Lady Murasaki. Pronunciation: Moo-rah-SAH-kee Shee-KEE-boo. Born c. 973 (some sources cite 970, 974, or 975) in Rozanji, Kamigyo-ku, Japan; died c. 1015 (some sources cite 1014 or 1025), in Japan; dau. of Fujiwara no Tametoki (court official) and an unknown mother; m. Fujiwara no Nobutaka (court official), c. 998; children: a daughter, Masako or Kenshi (sources differ as to her name), known later as Daini no Sanmi (999–after 1078) ❖ Writer whose greatest accomplishment, *The Tale of Genji*, is both the world's oldest known novel and an insightful portrait of the life of the imperial court of Heian Japan—the country's "golden age"; traditionally thought to have begun work on *The Tale of Genji*, widely considered the greatest masterpiece that Japanese literature has ever produced, sometime after the death of husband of the plague (1001); entered imperial service as a lady-in-waiting to the Empress Shoshi (c. 1005–06); compiled her *Diary* and composed poems (c. 1008–10). ❖ See also Richard Bowring, *Murasaki Shikibu: Her Diary and Poetic Memoirs* (Princeton U. Press, 1982); and *Women in World History*.

MURAT, Caroline (1782–1839). *See Bonaparte, Carolina.*

MURAT, Princess Eugène (1878–1936). French princess. Name variations: Violette Ney; Violette Murat (also seen as Violet). Born Violette Jacqueline Charlotte Ney d'Elchingen, Sept 9, 1878, in Rocquencourt, France; died July 19, 1936, in Paris, France; m. Prince Eugene Louis Michel Joachim Napoleon Murat (son of Prince Louis Napoleon Murat and Eudocia Michailovna Somova), April 26, 1899; children: Prince Pierre Murat (1900–1948). ❖ Wealthy eccentric in turn-of-the-century France, who was well-known in artistic circles and a friend of Marie Laurencin, Berenice Abbott, Germaine Tailleferre and Winnaretta Singer.

MURAT, Henriette Julie de (1670–1716). French memoirist, short-story writer and novelist. Name variations: Henriette de Castelnau; Henriette-Julie de Castelnau, Comtesse de Murat. Born Henriette de Castelnau, 1670, in Brest, Brittany; died Sept 24, 1716; dau. of Marquis de Castelnau; m. Count de Murat, 1686. ❖ Orphaned at early age, came to Paris at 16 on marriage to the Count of Murat (1686); wrote stories and fairytales as part of Countess d'Aulnoy's circle, including "Bearskin"; became involved in slander case when a tale she wrote was recognized as a slightly veiled account of King Louis XIV's mistress, and was exiled to Loches (1694–1715), during which time she wrote memoirs published as *Mémoires de Madame la Comtesse de M* (1697); allowed to return to Paris only after Louis died (1715), but died 1 year later.

MURAT, Isabella (b. 1900). *See Isabella of Guise.*

MURAT, Violette (1878–1936). *See Murat, Princess Eugène.*

MURATOVA, Kira (1934—). Soviet film director. Name variations: Kira Korotkova. Born Nov 5, 1934, in Soroca, Romania (now Moldova); lives in Ukraine; m. Aleksandr Muratov (div.). ❖ Made film debut with *U krutogo yara* (On the Steep Cliff, 1962); films, which tend to deal with universal themes in a socialist-realist style, include *Korotkiye vstrechi* (Brief Encounters, 1967), *Dolgie provody* (Long Goodbyes, 1971), *Russia* (1972), *Poznavaya belyy svet* (Getting to Know the Big Wide World, 1979), *Astenicheskiy sindrom* (The Aesthenic Syndrome, 1989), *Uvlecheniya* (Passions, 1994), which was awarded the Nika, *Tri istorii* (Three Stories, 1997), *Lyst do Ameryky* (Letter to America, 1999) and *Chekhovskie motivy* (Chekhov's Motives, 2002).

MURATOVA, Sofiya (1929—). Soviet gymnast. Born July 13, 1929, in USSR. ❖ At Melbourne Olympics, won bronze medals in uneven bars, indiv. all-around, and teams all-around, portable apparatus, and a gold medal in team all-around (1956); at Rome Olympics, won a bronze medal in balance beam, silver medals in indiv. all-around and vault, and a gold medal in team all-around (1960).

MURAVYOVA, Countess (1864–1910). *See Komissarzhevskaya, Vera.*

MURDAUGH, Angela (1940—). American nurse-midwife. Name variations: Sister Mary Angela Murdaugh; Sister Angela Murdaugh. Born Mary Angela Murdaugh, Sept 15, 1940, in Little Rock, Arkansas; dau. of Mary Angela (Graviss) Murdaugh (labor and delivery nurse) and George Earl Murdaugh (aeronautics factory worker); St. Louis University School of Nursing and Allied Health, BS; Columbia University, MS in maternity nursing, 1971. ❖ A leader in nurse-midwifery who established (May 1972) and directed one of the 1st freestanding birth centers in the nation and the 1st freestanding birth center in the state of TX (Nurse-Midwifery Services at Su Clinica Familiar in Raymondville, TX); created (1983) and directed the Holy Family Services Birth Center in Weslaco, TX; served as a Franciscan Sister of Mary for more than 35 years; was the 1st full-time president of American College of Nurse-Midwives (ACNM, 1981–83); served at Mary Breckinridge's Frontier School of Midwifery and Family Nursing in KY (1988–90); successfully negotiated with the state of TX to recognize certified nurse-midwives as reimbursable providers for Medicaid clients.

MURDEN, Tori (1963—). American rower. Name variations: Tori Murden McClure. Born 1963 in Louisville, Kentucky; dau. of Albert Murden (educator) and Martha Murden; undergraduate degree from Smith College, 1985; graduate degree from Harvard Divinity School, 1989; law degree from University of Louisville; m. Mac McClure. ❖ Became the 1st woman and the 1st American to row solo across the Atlantic (Dec 3, 1999), having made the 3,000-mile journey from the Canary Islands to Fort-du-Bas, Guadelupe, in 81 days, 7 hours, and 31 minutes, just 8 days longer than the record set in 1970 by Britain's Sidney Genders; was also the 1st woman to reach the summit of Lewis Nunatak in Antarctica and was one of a 9-person team to ski 750 miles to the geographic South Pole, the 1st American to do so. ❖ See also *Women in World History*.

MURDOCH, Iris (1919–1999). English moral philosopher and novelist. Name variations: Dame Iris Murdoch. Born Jean Iris Murdoch, July 15, 1919, in Dublin, Ireland; died in Oxford, England, Feb 8, 1999; dau. of Irene Alice (Richardson) Murdoch (singer) and Wills John Hughes Murdoch (civil servant); received early education at Froebel Educational Institute, London, and Badminton School, Bristol; attended Somerville College, Oxford University, 1938–42; m. John Bayley (literary critic and Oxford professor), 1956; no children. ❖ Prominent 20th-century moral philosopher, as well as a gifted, prolific, and widely acclaimed novelist, worked as temporary wartime civil servant (assistant principal) in the Treasury (1942–44, 1944–46); worked with refugees, 1st in Belgium, then Austria, where she was assigned to a camp for displaced persons; received Sarah Smithson Studentship in Philosophy, Newnham College, Cambridge (1947–48); named fellow at St. Anne's College, Oxford, and appointed as university lecturer (1948), where she taught until 1963 when she was named honorary fellow; was a lecturer at Royal College of Art (1963–67); published 1st novel *Under the Net* (1954); her prodigious output of 25 novels and several plays was directed toward the elaboration of a moral vocabulary for a post-theistic age; while not a Christian believer, embraced a religious picture of human beings as fallen, as, in some sense, sinful, and in need of transcendence; writings include *The Flight From the Enchanter* (1955), *The Sandcastle* (1957), *The Bell* (1958), *A Severed Head* (1961), *An Unofficial Rose* (1962), *The Unicorn* (1963), *The Italian Girl* (1964), *The Red and the Green* (1965), *The Time of the Angels* (1966), *The Nice and the Good* (1968), *Bruno's Dream* (1969), *A Fairly Honorable Defeat* (1970), *An Accidental Man* (1971), *A Word Child* (1975), *Henry and Cato* (1976), *Nuns and Soldiers* (1980), *The Philosopher's Pupil* (1983), *The Message to the Planet* (1989), *The Green Knight* (1993) and *Jackson's Dilemma* (1995). Made honorary member of the American Academy of Arts & Sciences (1975); won James Tait Black Memorial Prize (1973) for *The Black Prince*; won Whitbread Literary Award (1974) for *The Sacred and Profane Love Machine*; won Booker McConnell Prize (1978) for *The Sea, the Sea* and was shortlisted for the Booker for *The Good Apprentice* (1985) and *The Book and the Brotherhood* (1987); made Dame of the Order of the British Empire (1987). ❖ See also John Bayley, *Elegy for Iris* (St. Martin, 1998) and *Iris and Her Friends* (Norton, 1999); A.S. Byatt, *Iris Murdoch* (Longman, 1976); Peter J. Conradi, *Iris Murdoch: The Saint and the Artist* (St. Martin, 1986); Deborah Johnson, *Iris Murdoch* (Indiana U. Press, 1987); and *Women in World History*.

MURDOCH, Nina (1890–1976). Australian journalist, writer, and poet. Name variations: sometimes used pen name Manin. Born Madoline Murdoch, Oct 19, 1890, in Melbourne, Australia; died April 16, 1976, in Camberwell, Australia; dau. of John Andrew Murdoch (law clerk) and Rebecca (Murphy) Murdoch; attended Sydney Girls' High School, 1904–07; m. James Duncan Mackay Brown (journalist), Dec 19, 1917; no children. ❖ Joined staff of *Sydney Sun* (1914), as one of its 1st female reporters; published *Songs of the Open Air*, a book of verse (1915); moved to Melbourne (1922), where she worked for *Sun News-Pictorial* and was 1st woman allowed to cover Senate debates; traveled alone through England and Europe (1927) and subsequently wrote *Seventh Heaven, A Joyous Discovery of Europe* (1930), the 1st of her 4 travel books; wrote "Miss Emily" trilogy: *Miss Emily in Black Lace* (1930), *Portrait of Miss Emily* (1931), and *Exit Miss Emily* (1937); with inauguration of Australian Broadcasting Commission (ABC, 1932), managed children's programming, pioneering the "Argonauts' Club." ❖ See also *Women in World History*.

MURDOCK, Margaret (1942—). American Olympic shooting champion. Born Margaret L. Thompson, Aug 25, 1942, in Topeka, Kansas; attended nursing school, specializing as an anesthetist; graduate of Kansas State University, 1965; children: at least one. ❖ The 1st female member of a US Olympic shooting team and the 1st woman to win a medal in an Olympic shooting competition, won a silver medal in the small-bore rifle competition at Montreal Olympics (1976); previously, had won a gold medal at Pan-American Games with a World record (1967), the 1st time a woman had ever surpassed the men's record in any sport; set many individual and team records in her sport and won 14 World team championships, 7 individual World championships, and 5 Pan American gold medals; is the only woman ever ranked in the world's top-ten shooters list of the International Shooting Union. ❖ See also *Women in World History*.

MURE, Elizabeth (d. before 1355). *See Muir, Elizabeth.*

MURFIN, Jane (1893–1955). American playwright and screenwriter. Born Oct 27, 1893, in Quincy, Michigan; died Aug 10, 1955, in Los Angeles, CA; m. Donald Crisp (actor and director), 1932 (div. 1944). ❖ Began career as a playwright, co-writing with Jane Cowl, the hugely successful Broadway play *Smilin' Through* (1919), in which Cowl also starred; began writing a series of "Strongheart" scripts, starring her pet German shepherd (1922); became the 1st female supervisor at RKO studios (1934); wrote the script for *What Price Hollywood?* (1932), the original version of the story that later became *A Star is Born*; co-wrote film adaptation of *Alice Adams* (1935), which starred Katharine Hepburn; other screen credits include *The Silver Cord* (1933), *Ann Vickers* (1933), *Spitfire* (1934), *The Little Minister* (1934), *Roberta* (1935), *Come and Get It* (1936), *I'll Take Romance* (1936), *The Shining Hour* (1938), *The Women* (1939), *Stand Up and Fight* (1939), *Pride and Prejudice* (1940), *Flight for Freedom* (1943) and *Dragon Seed* (1944). ❖ See also *Women in World History*.

MURFREE, Mary N. (1850–1922). American novelist and short-story writer. Name variations: (pseudonyms) R. Emmet Dembry, Charles Egbert Craddock (1878–85). Born Mary Noailles Murfree, Jan 24, 1850, at Grantland plantation near Murfreesboro, TN; died July 31, 1922, in Murfreesboro; dau. of William Law Murfree (lawyer and plantation owner) and Fanny Priscilla (Dickinson) Murfree; attended Chegaray Institute, 1867–69; never married; no children. ❖ Writing fiction set in the Tennessee mountains, became one of the most popular authors of her day; published "Flirts and Their Ways," in *Lippincott's* under pseudonym R. Emmet Dembry (1874), followed by *The Dancin' Party at Harrison's Cove* in *Atlantic Monthly* (1878), under Charles Egbert Craddock; as Craddock, published 8 stories as *In the Tennessee Mountains* (1884), an instant success that contributed greatly to the local-color movement in American fiction; in quick succession, wrote *Where the Battle Was Fought* (1884), *The Prophet of the Great Smoky Mountains* (1885), and *Down the Ravine* (1885), a boys' story serialized by *Wide Awake* magazine; revealed identity (1885), and her popularity increased further; published novels *In the Clouds* (1886) and *The Despot of Broomsedge Cove* (1888), and was acclaimed on a par with such local colorists as Sarah Orne Jewett and Bret Harte; published *In the "Stranger People's" Country* (1891), now considered her most fully realized novel. ❖ See also Richard Cary, *Mary N. Murfree* (Twayne, 1967); and *Women in World History*.

MURIA, Anna (1904–2002). Spanish novelist and journalist. Name variations: Anna Murià i Romani. Born 1904 in Barcelona, Spain; died in Terrassa, 2002; m. Agustí Bartra (Catalan poet). ❖ Was exiled from Spain for political reasons (1939) but eventually returned to Catalonia (1970); works include *Joana Mas* (1933), *La Peixera* (1938), *Res no és veritat, Alicia* (1984), and *Aquest serà el principi* (1985).

MURIE, Margaret (1902–2003). American conservationist and author. Name variations: Mardy Murie. Pronunciation: MYUR-ee. Born Margaret Elizabeth Thomas, Aug 18, 1902, in Seattle, Washington; died Oct 19, 2003, in Moose, Wyoming; was the 1st woman to graduate from University of Alaska; m. Olaus Murie (biologist and longtime director and president of the Wilderness Society), 1924; children: Martin Murie, Donald Murie, and Joanne Murie Miller. ❖ Grew up in a log cabin in Alaska; with husband, moved to Wyoming to study elk migrations (1930s); with husband, helped preserve millions of acres in Alaska and throughout US by encouraging the creation of the Arctic National Wildlife Refuge (1962) and passage of the Wilderness Act (1964); wrote *Island Between* (1977) and (with husband) *Wapiti Wilderness* (1966). Her Wyoming Home, Murie Ranch, was declared a National Historic District (1997). Received the Audubon Medal (1980), John Muir Award (1983), and Presidential Medal of Freedom from President Bill Clinton (1998). ❖ See also autobiography, *Two in the Far North* (1962).

MURIELLA. *Variant of Muriel.*

MURIELLA (fl. 1000). Frankish noblewoman. Flourished around the year 1000; 1st wife of Tancred of Hauteville; children: William "Bras de Fer" (died in 1046 in Italy); Drogo (murdered in 1051 in Italy); Humphrey (died 1057, leader at Civitatee in 1053); Geoffrey, count of Loritello; Serlo.

MURNAGHAN, Sheelagh (1924–1993). Northern Ireland barrister and politician. Name variations: Sheelagh Mary Murnaghan. Born May 26, 1924, in Dublin, Ireland; died Sept 14, 1993; granddau. of George Murnaghan (Nationalist MP at Westminster for Mid-Tyrone, 1895); grandniece of John Morrogh (MP for Cork at Westminster, 1895). ❖ Was Northern Ireland's 1st woman barrister; representing Queen's University, Belfast, was the only Liberal MP ever elected to

Northern Ireland's Stormont Parliament (1961–69); for many years, was the voice of the poor on human rights and civil liberties issues, on women's rights and economic development, and on the rights of the homeless; served on the first Northern Ireland Community Relations Commission (1969–72) and the Whitelaw Advisory Commission (1972); chaired the National Insurance and Industrial Relations Tribunals.

MURPHY, Brianne (1933–2003). American cinematographer. Born Geraldine Brianne Murphy, April 1, 1933, in London, England, to Irish-American parents; died Aug 20, 2003, in Puerto Vallarta, Mexico; moved to US with family (1939); attended Pembroke College (now Brown University); m. Jerry Warren (film producer, div.); m. Ralph Brooke (died 1963). ❖ The 1st woman permitted into Hollywood features union as a director of photography, was admitted to the International Cinematographers Guild (1973); became the 1st woman to be director of photography at a major studio feature with Anne Bancroft's *Fatso* (1980); became the 1st woman invited to join the American Society of Cinematographers (1980); her cinematography for tv included "Little House on the Prairie," "Trapper John MD" and "In the Heat of the Night"; won a Daytime Emmy (1978) and nominated for 3 other Emmys; shared an Academy Award of Merit for the invention of a camera vehicle with safety features to protect technicians.

MURPHY, Bridey (1923–1995). See Tighe, Virginia.

MURPHY, Dervla (1931—). Irish travel writer. Born Nov 23, 1931, in Cappoquin, Co. Waterford, Ireland; attended Ursuline Convent in Waterford; children: Rachel (b. Dec 1968, who often cycled with mother). ❖ Set out on 1st bicycle trip (1963) and followed it with many more bicycle tours, cycling in India to work with Tibetan refugees; writings, which often address international political problems, include *Full Tilt: Ireland to India with a Bicycle* (1965), *The Waiting Land* (1967), *In Ethiopia with a Mule* (1968), *On a Shoestring to Coorg: An Experience of South India* (1976), *Eight Feet in the Andes* (1983), *Changing the Problem: Post-Forum Reflections* (1984), *Cameroon with Egbert* (1989), *The Ukimwi Road: From Kenya to Zimbabwe* (1993), *South From the Limpopo: Travels Through South Africa* (1997), and *Through the Embers of Chaos: Balkan Journeys* (2003). ❖ See also autobiography *Wheels within Wheels* (1979).

MURPHY, Edna (1899–1974). American actress. Born Elizabeth Edna Murphy, Nov 17, 1899, in New York, NY; died Aug 3, 1974, in Santa Monica, CA; m. Mervyn LeRoy (film director), 1927 (div. 1933). ❖ Became a top NY model; appeared on screen (1919–32), in such films as *Live Wires, Nobody's Bride, The White Moth, Lena Rivers, College Days* and *Modern Daughters.*

MURPHY, Emily (1868–1933). Canadian magistrate, writer, and social reformer. Born Emily Gowan Ferguson, Mar 14, 1868, in Cookstown, Ontario, Canada; died at home, Oct 26, 1933, in Edmonton, Alberta, Canada; dau. of Isaac Ferguson (prominent businessman) and Emily (Gowan) Ferguson; attended private Bishop Strachan School for Girls, 1883–87; m. Arthur Murphy, Aug 24, 1887; children: Kathleen (b. 1888); Evelyn; Madeleine (1893–1894); Doris (1896–1902). ❖ Social reformer, author, and 1st female magistrate in the British Empire, who initiated and led the famous "Persons Case"—a landmark case in the battle for women's rights in Canada, began writing career while traveling in Europe (1898–1900); published 1st book (1901); moved from Ontario to the West (1903); appointed 1st female magistrate in British Empire (1916); formed famous "Alberta Five" to petition the Supreme Court for an interpretation of a constitutional point which asked, "Does the word Persons in Section 24 of the BNA Act of 1867 include female persons?" (1927); when the 1st ruling declared that "women" were not included in the word "persons" (1928), appealed to the Privy Council in London; was victorious in the "Persons Case" (1929); retired from the bench (1931); writings include *Impressions of Janey Canuck Abroad* (1901), *Janey Canuck in the West* (1910); *Open Trails* (1912), *Seeds of Pine* (1914); *The Black Candle* (1922) and *Bishop Bompas* (1929). ❖ See also Christine Mander, *Emily Murphy: Rebel* (Simon & Pierre, 1985); Byrne Hope Sanders, *Emily Murphy: Crusader* (Macmillan, 1945); Donna James, *Emily Murphy* (Fitzhenry & Whiteside, 1977); and *Women in World History.*

MURPHY, Janice (1942—). Australian swimmer. Born Oct 19, 1942, in Australia. ❖ At Tokyo Olympics, won a silver medal in 4x100-meter freestyle relay (1964).

MURPHY, Juliette (1903–1973). See Johnson, Julie.

MURPHY, Lizzie (1894–1964). American baseball player. Born Mary Elizabeth Murphy, April 13, 1894, possibly in Warren, RI; died July 27, 1964; m. Walter Larivee, 1937 (died). ❖ Pioneer American baseball player, played first base for Ed Carr's All-Stars of Boston in the men's league (1918–35) and hit a single off Satchel Paige during a barnstorming game; played in Fenway Park, in a charity game pitting the Boston Red Sox against a group of American League and New England All-Stars (1922); played another major league exhibition game (1928), this time with the National League All-Stars against the Boston Braves, making her the 1st woman to play for a major league team in an exhibition game and the 1st person, man or woman, to play with both American League and National League All-Star teams. ❖ See also *Women in World History.*

MURPHY, Marie Louise (1737–1814). See O'Murphy, Marie-Louise.

MURPHY, Mary (1931—). American actress. Born Jan 26, 1931, in Washington DC; m. Dale Robertson (actor, div.). ❖ Made film debut in *The Lemon Drop Kid* (1949), followed by *Carrie, Main Street to Broadway, Sitting Bull, The Desperate Hours, The Maverick Queen, Live Fast Die Young, The Electronic Monster, Harlow* and *Junior Bonner,* among others; probably best remembered for lead performance opposite Marlon Brando in *The Wild One* (1954); later ran an art gallery.

MURPHY, Sara (1883–1975). American expatriate. Born Sara Wiborg, Nov 7, 1883, in Cincinnati, Ohio; died Oct 10, 1975, in Arlington, VA; dau. of Frank Bestow Wiborg (a wealthy industrialist); educated in Germany and at the Spence School; m. Gerald Murphy (painter and later president of Mark Cross Co.), 1916 (died 1964); children: Honoria Murphy Donnelly, and 2 sons, Patrick and Baoth, who died in 1930s. ❖ Wealthy expatriate American, living in Paris with husband, who became the center of a social circle that included a number of major artists and writers of the Lost Generation; resided in Cap d'Antibes (1917–31), then moved to the Hamptons, on Long Island; with husband, served as the basis for the characters Nicole and Dick Diver in F. Scott Fitzgerald's *Tender is the Night.* ❖ See also Calvin Tomkins, *Living Well is the Best Revenge* (1971); Honoria Donnelly with Richard Billings, *Sara & Gerald: Villa America and After* (1983); Amanda Vail, *Everybody Was so Young: Gerald and Sara Murphy, a Lost Generation Love Story* (1998).

MURPHY, Sarah Ellen Oliver (1864–1939). See Snow, Sarah Ellen Oliver.

MURRAY, Alice Rosemary (1913—). See Murray, Rosemary.

MURRAY, Anna Maria (1808–1899). Irish-Australian novelist. Name variations: Anna Maria Bunn. Born Anna Maria Murray, 1808, in Balliston, Co. Limerick, Ireland; died 1899; 2nd child of Catholic parents Terence Murray (army paymaster) and Ellen Fitzgerald Murray (died young); sister of Terence Murray (politician); m. Captain George Bunn (shipowner and whaler), 1829 (died 1840); children: 2. ❖ With father and brother, moved to Australia (1827) and remained there until death; after father died (1835), began to write; published anonymously *The Guardian: A Tale by an Australian* (1838), the 1st novel published by a woman in Australia; kept her secret until just before she died at 81, confessing to her only living son William.

MURRAY, Anne (1945—). Canadian musician and pop singer. Name variations: Morna Anne Murray. Born Morna Anne Murray, June 20, 1945, in Springhill, Nova Scotia, Canada; dau. of James Carson Murray (surgeon) and Marion Murray (nurse); attended University of New Brunswick, 1960s; m. Bill Langstroth, 1975 (sep. 1998); children: Will and Dawn Langstroth. ❖ Named Canada's Country Female Vocalist of the Year (1979–86); 1st sang on Canadian tv shows, "Sing Along Jubilee" and "Let's Go" (1960s); released debut album, *Snowbird* (1970), whose title track became the 1st single by a Canadian female performer to go gold; appeared frequently on Glen Campbell's tv show and recorded *Anne Murray/Glen Campbell* (1971); released hit *Danny's Song* (1973); other hits include cover of John Lennon and Paul McCartney song, "You Won't See Me" (1974), "Love Song" (1975), and "I Just Fall in Love Again" (1979); released platinum *Let's Keep It That Way* (1978), which included hits "You Needed Me" and "Walk Right Back"; released platinum albums *New Kind of Feeling* (1979) and *Anne Murray's Greatest Hits* (1980); won Best Female Country Vocal Performance Grammy for "A Little Good News" (1983); other albums include *Heart Over Mind* (1984), *As I Am* (1988), *You Will* (1990), *Croonin'* (1993) and *All of Me* (2005, released in Canada as *I'll Be Seeing You*); other hit singles include "Just Another Woman in Love" (1984), "Time Don't Run Out on Me" (1985), and "Feed This Fire" (1990); won 3 other Grammys.

MURRAY, Annie (c. 1852/53–1910). See Yates, Ngawini.

MURRAY, Mrs. D. L. (1889–1960). *See Eyles, Leonora.*

MURRAY, Elaine (1954—). Scottish politician. Born Dec 22, 1954, in Edinburgh, Scotland; Edinburgh University, BSc in chemistry, 1976; married; children: 3. ❖ Formerly a research scientist and a lecturer with Open University; as a Labour candidate, elected to the Scottish Parliment for Dumfries (1999).

MURRAY, Elizabeth (1626–1698). Countess of Dysart and duchess of Lauderdale. Name variations: Bess; Elizabeth Maitland; Lady Lauderdale. Born Sept 28, 1626, in St. Martin-in-the-Fields, England; died June 5, 1698 (some sources cite 1697), in Richmond, England; dau. of William Murray, 1st earl of Dysart, and Catherine Bruce; m. Lionel Tollemache, in 1648; m. John Maitland, duke of Lauderdale, in 1672; children: (1st marriage) Lionel (b. 1649); Thomas (b. 1651); Elizabeth Tollemache (b. 1659); Catherine Tollemache (b. 1661); William (b. 1662). ❖ Inherited Ham House (1655), along with the title countess of Dysart; a royalist, struck up a surprising friendship with Oliver Cromwell (early 1650s); as a leading social hostess with Cromwell's trust, was able to continue her secret political activities with those working to bring back the monarchy, a group of nobles calling themselves the Sealed Knot; following Cromwell's death (1658) and the return of Charles II (1660), was recognized for her efforts on behalf of the monarchy and financially rewarded by the new king. ❖ See also Doreen Cripps, *Elizabeth of the Sealed Knot: A Biography of Elizabeth Murray, Countess of Dysart* (Roundwood, 1975); and *Women in World History.*

MURRAY, Elizabeth (1871–1946). American comedic actress. Born April 25, 1871; died Mar 27, 1946, in Philadelphia, PA. ❖ Appeared in *Madame Sherry, Watch Your Step, High Jinks, Cohan Revue of 1918, Good Night Paul, Sidewalks of New York,* and *Madame Capet*; starred in vaudeville and appeared in such films as *Little Old New York* and *The Bachelor Father.*

MURRAY, Elizabeth (1940—). American painter. Born 1940 in Chicago, IL; Art Institute of Chicago, BFA; Mills College, MFA; m. Bob Holman (poet). ❖ Pioneer in painting, broke with the art-historical tradition of "illusionistic" space in two dimensions; her paintings jut out from the wall on complex-shaped canvases and are sculptural in form and expressionistic in style; was 1st exhibited in NY in a show at the Whitney (1972); had over 60 solo exhibits (1972–2005); work is featured in many collections, including the Walker Art Center, MoMA, Guggenheim, Whitney, Hirshhorn, Art Institute of Chicago and Museum of Contemporary Art in Los Angeles; taught at Art Institute of Chicago, Princeton, Yale and Bard College, among others.

MURRAY, Helen McKenzie (1896–1963). *See Black, Helen McKenzie.*

MURRAY, Joanna (1878–1966). *See MacKinnon, Joanna.*

MURRAY, Judith Sargent (1751–1820). American essayist, playwright, poet and feminist. Name variations: (pseudonyms) Constantia, Mr. Vigilius, and Honora. Born May 1, 1751, in Gloucester, Massachusetts; died July 6, 1820, in Natchez, Mississippi; dau. of Winthrop Sargent (shipowner and merchant) and Judith (Saunders) Sargent; tutored with brother as he prepared to attend Harvard College; m. John Stevens (sea captain and trader), Oct 3, 1769 (died 1786); m. John Murray (minister and founder of Universalist Church in America), Oct 1788; children: (2nd m.) George (b. 1789, died young); Julia Maria (b. 1791). ❖ Considered North America's 1st important feminist, wrote essays to express her growing concerns regarding issues generated by the American Revolution: human rights, liberty, and, by extension, the status of women; published 1st essay "Desultory Thoughts upon the Utility of Encouraging a Degree of Self-Complacency, Especially in Female Bosoms" in *Gentleman and Lady's Town and Country Magazine* under pseudonym "Constantia" (1784); 1st husband died in West Indies (1786); married John Murray (1788); published poems in *Massachusetts Magazine* as well as essay series "The Gleaner" (1792–94); wrote failed plays *The Medium* (1795) and *The Traveller Returned* (1796); published *The Gleaner* in 3 vols. (1798); edited and published husband's *Letters and Sketches of Sermons* (1812–13); edited and published husband's autobiography *Records of the Life of the Rev. John Murray, Written by Himself, with a Continuation by Mrs. Judith Sargent Murray* (1816). ❖ See also *Women in World History.*

MURRAY, Katharine Stewart- (1874–1960). *See Stewart-Murray, Katharine.*

MURRAY, Katherine (1894–1974). American actress and singer. Name variations: Katherine Shoninger. Born Mar 12, 1894; died Aug 12, 1974, in Rye, NY; m. Frederick Shoninger. ❖ Appeared in NY in *The Quaker* and several editions of the *Ziegfeld Follies.*

MURRAY, Kathleen (d. 1969). American actress. Died Aug 24, 1969, age 41, in New York, NY; m. Joseph Beruh (producer-manager). ❖ Began career at age 6; on stage, appeared in *Leave It to Jane, Maybe Tuesday, A Swim in the Sea, Purple Dust, Summer and Smoke, The Enchanted* and *An Ordinary Man*; on tv, starred in title role of "Kitty Foyle" (1958).

MURRAY, Kathryn (1906–1999). American entrepreneur. Born Kathryn Kohnfelder in Jersey City, New Jersey, Sept 15, 1906; died in Honolulu, Hawaii, Aug 6, 1999; dau. of Abraham Kohnfelder (newspaper advertising executive); m. Arthur Murray (ballroom dancer and businessman), c. 1924 (died 1991); children: twin daughters, Jane and Phyllis Murray. ❖ With husband, established a chain of dance studios utilizing the "magic step" teaching technique, a series of dotted lines, arrows, and outlines of shoes, diagramming a particular dance; worked hand-in-hand with husband and had a commanding role in the business, serving as executive vice president and writing the training manual for its numerous franchises; hosted tv show "The Arthur Murray Party" (1950–60); co-wrote *My Husband, Arthur Murray* (1960) and *Family Laugh Lines* (1966). ❖ See also *Women in World History.*

MURRAY, Leonora (1889–1960). *See Eyles, Leonora.*

MURRAY, Lilian (1871–1960). English dental surgeon. Name variations: Lilian Lindsay. Born Lilian Murray in London, England, July 24, 1871; died in Jan 31, 1960; Edinburgh Dental Hospital and School, LDS, 1895; m. Robert Lindsay (dental surgeon), 1905. ❖ The 1st woman to qualify as a dental surgeon in England, set up practice at 69 Hornsea Rise in north London; elected 1st woman president of the British Dental Association (1946). ❖ See also *Women in World History.*

MURRAY, Mae (1885–1965). American silent-film actress. Born Marie Adrienne Koenig, May 10, 1885, in Portsmouth, VA; died 1965; dau. of Austrian and Belgian immigrants; m. 3rd husband, Robert Z. Leonard (director), 1918 (div. 1925); m. 4th husband Prince David Mdivani, 1925 or 1926 (div. 1933); children: (4th m.) Koran. ❖ At 21, appeared on Broadway in *About Town*; performed in several Ziegfeld Follies productions; made screen debut in *To Have and to Hold* (1916); became a major silent-film star, giving best performance in Erich von Stroheim's *The Merry Widow* (1925); other films include *Sweet Kitty Bellairs* (1916), *The Dream Girl* (1916), *The Big Sister* (1916), *On With the Dance* (1920), *Peacock Alley* (1921), *Broadway Rose* (1922), *Jazzmania* (1923), *Mademoiselle Midnight* (1924), *The Masked Bride* (1925), *Valencia* (1926), *Bachelor Apartment* (1931) and *High Stakes* (1931). ❖ See also autobiography *The Self-Enchanted* (1959); and *Women in World History.*

MURRAY, Margaret (1863–1963). British archaeologist. Born in Calcutta, India, July 13, 1863; died Nov 13, 1963; dau. of Anglo-Irish parents (father was a merchant, mother a missionary); University College London, degree in linguistics. ❖ Though advanced degrees in archaeology were largely restricted to men, was allowed to enroll in Sir Flinders Petrie's Egyptology classes at University College and participate in his excavations at Abydos (1890s); by 1895, was teaching elementary hieroglyphics; began teaching at University College (1902), becoming assistant (1909), lecturer (1921), and assistant professor (1922); following retirement (1932), undertook an archaeological dig in Palestine; writings include *The Splendour that was Egypt* (1931) and *The Genesis of Religion.* ❖ See also autobiography *My First Hundred Years*; and *Women in World History.*

MURRAY, Ngawini (1852/53?–1910). *See Yates, Ngawini.*

MURRAY, Patty (1950—). American politician. Born Oct 10, 1950, in Bothell, Washington; Washington State University, BA, 1972; m. Rob Murray, 1972; children: Randy and Sara. ❖ While lobbying against cuts in funding for parent-child education programs, was told by a legislator that she could not make a difference because she was "just a mom in tennis shoes" (1980); served in the Washington State Senate (1988–92); became the 1st woman to serve in the US Senate from Washington state (1992); reelected (1998 and 2004), serving as the highest-ranking Democrat of the Senate Transportation Appropriations subcommittee; the daughter of a disabled WWII veteran, was the 1st woman to serve on the Senate Veterans Affairs Committee; helped write and pass the Violence Against Women Act (1994); focuses on women, children and the environment.

MURRAY, Pauli (1910–1985). African-American civil rights and women's rights activist, lawyer, Episcopal priest, poet, and educator.

Name variations: Anna Pauline Murray. Born Anna Pauline Murray, Nov 20, 1910, in Baltimore, Maryland; died July 1, 1985, of cancer in Pittsburgh, PA; dau. of William Henry Murray (public school teacher and principal) and Agnes (Fitzgerald) Murray (nurse, died 1914); Hunter College, BA, 1933; Howard University, LLB cum laude, 1944; University of California, Berkeley, LLM, 1945; Yale University, JD, 1965; General Theological Seminary, MDiv cum laude, 1976; m. "Billy," 1930 (annulled). ❖ Committed to justice, was among the architects of the legal strategy that toppled some of the pillars of racism and sexism in America; after college, worked for Works Progress Administration (WPA) in Workers' Education Project; arrested on segregated bus (1940); served as field secretary for Workers' Defense League; worked with National Association for the Advancement of Colored People (NAACP) and Congress on Racial Equality (CORE) during law school; was 1st black deputy attorney general of California (1946); ran for New York City Council on Liberal Party ticket (1949); was associate attorney at Paul, Weiss, Rifkind, Wharton and Garrison, in NY (1956–60); was a senior lecturer, Ghana School of Law (1960–61); was a member of the President's Commission on the Status of Women (1961–62); was a founding member of National Organization for Women (NOW, 1966); served as vice-president, Benedict College, South Carolina (1967–68); was a professor at Brandeis University (1968–73); ordained to Episcopal priesthood (1977); retired from ministry (1984); wrote *Proud Shoes: The Story of an American Family* (1956) and *Dark Testament and Other Poems* (1970). ❖ See also autobiography *Song in a Weary Throat: An American Pilgrimage* (1987); and *Women in World History*.

MURRAY, Rosemary (1913–2004). English chemist and educator. Name variations: Dame Rosemary Murray. Born Alice Rosemary Murray, July 28, 1913, in Newbury, England; died Oct 8, 2004; dau. of Admiral A.J.L. Murray and Ellen Maxwell Spooner; granddau. of William A. Spooner (New College Oxford warden and spoonerism namesake); Oxford University, BS, 1934, PhD in chemistry, 1939. ❖ Joined the Women's Royal Navy Service (1942–46); at Girton College, Cambridge, served as a lecturer (1946–54), as a fellow (1949) and as a tutor (1951); demonstrated in chemistry at Cambridge University (1947–52); served as the 1st president of New Hall, Cambridge (1964–81) and the 1st woman vice-chancellor of Cambridge University (1975–77); appointed to numerous leadership positions, including director of Midland Bank (1978–84), city of Cambridge justice of the peace (1953–83), Cambridgeshire deputy lieutenant (from 1982), Lockwood Committee for Higher Education (Northern Ireland) member and the sole woman member of the Armed Forces Pay Review Body (1972–84); wrote *New Hall, 1954–1972: The Making of a College* (1980). Made Dame Commander of the Order of the British Empire (DBE, 1977).

MURRAY, Ruby (1935–1996). Irish pop singer. Born in Belfast, Northern Ireland, Mar 1935; died of liver cancer in Torquay, England, Dec 17, 1996. ❖ At 19, moved to England (1953); within months, recorded "Heartbeat" which sold 200,000 copies; followed that with "Softly, Softly," "Happy Days and Lonely Nights," "Let Me Go Lover" and "If Anyone Finds This I Love You" (all 5 were on Britain's Top 20 in the same week in 1955, a record still unbroken). ❖ See also Joan Moules, *Ruby Murray* (Evergreen, 1995); and *Women in World History*.

MURRAY, Ruth (1841–1921). See Mulholland, Rosa.

MURRAY, Susanna (1870–1970). See Hanan, Susanna.

MURRAY, Yvonne (1964—). Scottish runner. Born Oct 1964 in Musselburgh, near Edinburgh, Scotland. ❖ Won the Scottish championships for 3,000 meters (1982); at European championships, won a silver medal (1986) and a gold medal (1990), both for 3,000 meters; at Commonwealth Games, won a bronze medal (1986) and a silver medal (1990), both for 3,000 meters, and a gold medal for 10,000 meters (1994); at Seoul Olympics, won a bronze medal in 3,000 meters (1988); won a gold medal at World Indoor championships for 3,000 meters (1993); won the BUPA Festival of Road Racing for 5,000 meters (1993); at World championships, won a gold medal for 3,000 meters (1994). Awarded MBE (1990).

MURRELL, Christine (1874–1933). British physician. Born 1874; died 1933; London University, MD, 1905. ❖ Began general practice; became member of Marylebone Health Society and during WWI served in Women's Emergency Corps; elected to Council of British Medical Association (1924) and became president of Medical Women's Federation (1925); was the 1st woman elected to membership of

General Medical Council of Great Britain (1933). Wrote *Womanhood and Health* (1923).

MURRELL, Hilda (c. 1906–1984). English anti-nuclear activist. Born c. 1906 in UK; died Mar 21, 1984. ❖ Well-known activist, was found dead near her ransacked home in Shrewsbury (Mar 24, 1984), just before she was to present a paper on the hazards of nuclear waste to the Sizewell-B nuclear power station inquiry. Though a laborer from Shrewsbury (Andrew George) was given a life sentence for the murder (May 6, 2005), there are still those who strongly believe in a conspiracy. ❖ See also Judith Cook, *Who Killed Hilda Murrell?* (1985).

MURRELL, Vera (b. 1906). See Tanner, Vera.

MURRY, Kathleen (1888–1923). See Mansfield, Katherine.

MURSKA, Ilma Di (1836–1889). See Di Murska, Ilma.

MURTFELDT, Mary (1848–1913). American entomologist. Born in New York, NY, 1848; died 1913; studied at Rockford College in Illinois, 1858–60. ❖ Lived in Missouri; worked as a local assistant in US Department of Agriculture's Bureau of Entomology (1868–77), making important contributions to her field; astute in both entomology and botany, discovered how insects affect the pollination of certain plants, and also chronicled the life histories of recently discovered and little-known insects and how they affected their host plants. ❖ See also *Women in World History*.

MURZINA, Elena (1984—). Russian rhythmic gymnast. Born June 15, 1984, in Sverdlovsk, USSR. ❖ Won 3 group competition events at World championships (2003); won team all-around gold medal at Athens Olympics (2004).

MUSA, Gilda (1926–1999). Italian novelist, essayist and poet. Born 1926 in Rome, Italy; died Feb 26, 1999; studied German in Heidelberg and English at Cambridge. ❖ Translated German poetry into Italian; worked as literary reviewer for *Paese Sera*; well-known for poetry and science-fiction novels, works include *Il porto inquieto* (An Unquiet Haven, 1953), *Amici e nemici* (Friends and Enemies, 1961), (poetry) *Berliner Mauer* (Berlin Wall, 1967), *La notte artificiale* (False Night, 1965), *Strategie* (1968), (poetry) *Lettere senza francobollo* (Letters with No Stamp, 1972), *Giungla domestica* (The Domestic Jungle, 1972), *Marinella Super* (1978), and *Esperimento donna* (Woman Experiment, 1979).

MUSCARDINI, Cristiana (1948—). Italian politician. Born Nov 6, 1948, in Cannobio, Italy. ❖ Member of Alleanza nazionale (AN) political executive; was a member of Italian Parliament (1983–87); representing Union for Europe of the Nations Group (UEN), elected to 4th and 5th European Parliament (1994–99, 1999–2004).

MUSE LIMONADIÈRE, La (1714–1784). See Bourette, Charlotte Rouyer.

MUSE OF SURBITON, The (1737–1814). See Moody, Elizabeth.

MUSGRAVE, Thea (1928—). Scottish composer and conductor. Born Thea Musgrave in Barnton, Edinburgh, Scotland, May 27, 1928; attended Moreton Hall, Shropshire; University of Edinburgh, BMus, 1950; studied with Hans Gal, Mary Grierson, and Sidney Newman, and at Paris Conservatoire with Nadia Boulanger and Aaron Copland; m. Peter Mark (violist and conductor), 1971. ❖ One of the most important composers of 20th century, composed *A Tale for Thieves*, a ballet based on Chaucer's *The Pardoner's Tale* (1953); wrote the large-scale composition *Cantata for a Summer's Day*, which proved to be her 1st major success at its premiere at Edinburgh International Festival (1955); wrote 1st short opera, *The Abbot of Drimock*, based on a Scots Border tale, and composed *Five Love Songs* for soprano and guitar (1955); during this period, was experimenting with both tonal and atonal music; composed *Colloquy* for violin and piano and *Trio* for flute, oboe, and piano (1960); received commissions from City of Glasgow, BBC, opera houses, ballet companies, and colleges; set out on new course with 1st full-length opera, *The Decision*, described as dramatic-abstract, which was hailed as a turning point in music when it was 1st performed (1967); followed this with Chamber Concertos No. 2 and No. 3 (1966); published Concerto for Clarinet and Orchestra (1968); became interested in electronic music, making use of a prerecorded electronic tape in *Beauty and the Beast*, a 2-act ballet (1968–69); followed that with highly successful 3-act chamber opera *The Voice of Ariadne* (1972–73) which also used taped sound; made 8 broadcasts on UK's Radio 3, entitled "End or Beginning" (1973); composed and wrote libretto for 4th opera, *Mary Queen of Scots* (1975–77), which premiered at Edinburgh Festival; while living in US, wrote

6th opera, *Harriet: A Woman Called Moses*, focusing on Harriet Tubman, which premiered in Norfolk under husband Peter Mark's direction and was subsequently performed by Royal Opera in London; began conducting her own works; became the 3rd woman to conduct the Philadelphia Orchestra and the 1st to conduct one of her own compositions; also conducted New York City Opera, BBC Symphony Orchestra, and London's Royal Philharmonic Orchestra. Became 1st British composer to win Lili Boulanger prize (1952); received Koussevitzky Award (1972). ❖ See also *Women in World History*.

MUSGROVE, Mary (c. 1690–c. 1763). Creek interpreter and entrepreneur. Name variations: Mary Bosomworth; Mary Matthews; Coosaponakeesa. Born near Muskogee (Creek) town of Coweta, c. 1690; died in English colony of Georgia, c. 1763; dau. of regal Creek woman (name unknown) and an English man, possibly Henry Woodward or Edward Griffin (traders); educated in Pon Pon, South Carolina; m. Johnny Musgrove, 1717 (died 1735); m. Jacob Matthews, 1735; m. Thomas Bosomworth, 1744; no children. ❖ Influential intermediary between the Muskogee (Creek) tribe and English colonists, and successful trader and landowner, made claims against Georgia based on her status among Creeks and ownership of certain Creek lands; was possibly a Beloved Woman of the Creeks; established successful trading centers in Georgia colony; was Creek interpreter, negotiator and diplomat for James Oglethorpe and Trustees of Georgia Colony (1733–47); served as interpreter for Methodism founder-evangelist John Wesley (1736); engaged in legal battle with colonial government over ownership of three coastal islands and other property given to her by Creeks (1747–62). ❖ See also Helen Todd, *Mary Musgrove: Georgia Indian Princess* (Seven Oakes, 1981); and *Women in World History*.

MUSI, Maria Maddalena (1669–1751). Italian singer. Name variations: Known as La Mignatta (the leech). Born in Bologna, June 18, 1669; died in Bologna, May 2, 1751; dau. of Antonio Musi and Lucrezia Mignati; m. Pietro degli Antoni. ❖ One of the highest paid singers of her era, was extremely popular with audiences throughout Italy; given an annual salary by Ferdinand Carlo Gonzaga, duke of Mantua (1689), along with title "virtuosa," sang in Sabadini's *Teodora clemente*, Legrenzi's *Giustino*, and Perti's *Siracusano* (1689); in Naples, received a salary of 500 Spanish doubloons (1696–1700, 1702); retired (1726). ❖ See also *Women in World History*.

MUSIDORA (1884–1957). French actress, director, and producer. Name variations: Musidora Lasseyne; Juliet Musidora. Born Jeanne Roques, Feb 23, 1884 (some sources cite 1889), in Paris, France; died Dec 11, 1957, in Paris; father was a musician and philosopher and mother was a feminist who founded literary journal *Le Vengeur* in 1897; attended Jullian Academy of Fine Arts and Schommer Studio; m. Dr. Clement Marot, 1927 (div. 1944); children: Clement Marot. ❖ Cinema star and pioneering producer-director, abandoned painting for the stage (1910), appearing at the Star Theater in a vaudeville comedy sketch; joined Mount Parnasse troupe of actors and adopted stage name "Musidora"; made screen debut (1913), in *Les Misères de l'Aiguille* (The Sorrows of the Needle); appeared in 15 films (1914), including *Le Colonel Bontemps* and *La Ville de Madame Tango*; came to prominence, costumed in a black full-body leotard, in Louis Feuillade's surreal *Les Vampires* (1915); turned to producing and directing with Colette's *Minne, or L'Ingénue Libertine* (1915), followed by *Le Malliot Noir* (The Black Leotard, 1917) and *La Flamme Cachée* (1918); directed several films (1920s) and many stage productions (1930s–40s); directed and starred in last film, *La Magique Image* (1950); turned to writing, publishing many articles on cinema as well as poetry, a play, and 2 novels. ❖ See also *Women in World History*.

MUSSER, Tharon (1925—). American lighting designer. Born Tharon Myrene Musser, Jan 8, 1925, in Roanoke, Virginia; dau. of George C. Musser (cleric) and Hazel (Riddle) Musser; Berea College, BA, 1945; Yale University, MFA, 1950; never married. ❖ One of a trio of pioneering women lighting designers, lit 1st Broadway show: the premiere of O'Neill's *Long Day's Journey into Night* (1956); credits mounted quickly, and came to include everything from Shakespeare to musical comedy; worked with American Shakespeare Festival, Dallas and Miami opera companies, Mark Taper Forum, and American Ballet Theater; lit all of Neil Simon's plays since *Prisoner of 2nd Avenue* (1971) and designed an impressive list of musicals; won 1st Tony Award for *Follies* (1971) and 2nd for *A Chorus Line* (1975), for which she used the prototype LS8, the 1st computerized memory lighting board employed on Broadway; won 3rd Tony for *Dreamgirls* in which she used moving lights, yet another innovation. Received a Lifetime in Light Award from *Lighting*

Dimensions magazine (1990) and Wally Russell Award for Outstanding Lifetime Achievement (1995). ❖ See also *Women in World History*.

MUSSEY, Ellen Spencer (1850–1936). American lawyer, reformer, and founder. Born Ellen Spencer, May 13, 1850, in Geneva, Ohio; died of a cerebral hemorrhage, April 21, 1936, in Washington, DC; dau. of Platt Rogers Spencer (proponent of widely used Spencerian script) and Persis (Duty) Spencer; attended Cornell University; m. Reuben Delavan Mussey (attorney), June 14, 1871 (died 1892); children: 2 sons. ❖ Admitted to the bar of the District of Columbia (1893), practiced alone and in occasional partnership in probate and commercial law; argued before US Supreme Court (1896), and before US Court of Claims (1897); also worked in international law, serving as counsel to the Swedish and Norwegian consulates for 25 years; was involved in passage of the Married Women's Act, a bill which gave women guardianship rights over their children and property equal to those of their husbands (1896); with Emma M. Gillett, formed the Washington College of Law (1898), which accepted both women and men; served as dean of the law school (1898–1913); drafted and helped pass the Cable Act, which ended the automatic loss of citizenship for American women who married citizens of other countries (1922). ❖ See also *Women in World History*.

MUSSOLINI, Alessandra (1962—). Italian actress and politician. Born Dec 30, 1962, in Italy; dau. of Anna Maria Scicolone (younger sister of Sophia Loren) and Romano Mussolini (jazz musician and 3rd son of Benito Mussolini); granddau. of Benito Mussolini; earned a degree in medicine and surgery, 1993; m. Mauro Floriani, 1989; children: Caterina, Clarissa and Romano. ❖ Began career as an actress and posed topless in *Playboy*; representing the Movimento Sociale Italiano (MSI), elected to Italian Parliament (Italian Chamber of Deputies) in a Naples constituency (1992); became a member of the Alleanza Nazionale (National Alliance); when a leader of her party condemned her grandfather, resigned from Alleanza Nazionale but retained her seat in the Italian Parliament (Nov 2003); founded Libertà d'Azione (Freedom of Action–LdA) and was elected to the European Parliament (2004).

MUSSOLINI, Edda (1910–1995). *See Ciano, Edda.*

MUSSOLINI, Rachele (1891–1979). *See Guidi, Rachele.*

MUSTONEN, Kaija (1941—). Finnish speedskater. Born Aug 4, 1941, in Finland. ❖ Won a silver medal for the 1,500 meters and a bronze for the 1,000 meters at Innsbruck Olympics (1964); won a gold medal for 1,500 meters and a silver for the 3,000 meters at Grenoble Olympics (1968).

MUSUMECI, Maddalena (1976—). Italian water-polo player. Born Mar 26, 1976, in Italy. ❖ At World championships, won team gold medals (1998, 2001); center back, won a team gold medal at Athens Olympics (2004).

MUTAFCHIEVA, Vera P. (1929—). Bulgarian writer and historian. Name variations: Vera Moutafchieva. Born Vera Petrova Mutafchieva in Sofia, Bulgaria, Mar 28, 1929; dau. of Petûr Mutafchiev (1883–1943, historian) and Nadezhda Trifonova Mutafchieva (historian); Historical Institute of the Bulgarian Academy of Sciences, MA, 1958, PhD, 1978; m. Jossif Krapchev; m. Atanas Slavov; children: 2 daughters. ❖ Historian whose research concentrates on Ottoman rule in the Balkans, while novels deal with phases of Bulgaria's national evolution, published 1st study in Ottoman history (1960), followed by almost 70 books and articles over a 30-year span; though historical works were highly specialized and intended only for experts, quickly gained a reputation that extended beyond Bulgaria; while working at Sofia's Institute of Balkan Studies (1963–79), also began to write historical fiction, incorporating original historical documents into plots and experimenting with narrative and dialogue; hired as a professor at the national Institute of Literature (1979); after the collapse and repudiation of Communism in Bulgaria (1989), used her prestige to help bring about a successful transition to an open society; writings include *Letopis na smutnoto vreme: Roman v dve chasti* (Chronicle of the Times of Turbulence, 1965–66) and *Poslednite Shishmanovtsi* (The Last Shishmans, 1969); also adapted 2 of her novels, *Zemya zavinagi* (Land Forever, 1980) and *Nepalnotie* (Under Age, 1981), into film scripts and wrote the script for *Khan Asparukh* (released in US as *The Glory of Khan* 1981), based on her novel *Preredcheno ot Pagane* (Pagane's Prophecy, 1980). Received Gottfried von Herder Prize from University of Vienna (1980), Georgi Dimitrov Award (1981), City of Sofia Prize (1986), and John Panitsa Award (1995). ❖ See also *Women in World History*.

MUTAYYAM AL-HASHIMIYYA (fl. 8th c.). Arabian singer and poet.
Born in al-Basra (now Iraq) during Abbasid period. ❖ Unlike many
female Arabian singers, was a freed woman; studied with Ibrahim al-
Mausili, his son Ishaq, and Badhl; famed for both music and poetry, sang
at the court of caliphs al-Mamun (r. 813–833) and al-Mu'tasim (833–
842) before singing for Ali ibn Hisham. ❖ See also *Women in World
History.*

MUTEMWIA (fl. 1420–1411 BCE). Egyptian regent. Possibly dau. of
Tjuya and Yuya who were of high social standing; sister of Tiy
(c. 1400–1340 BCE); concubine of pharaoh Thutmose IV; mother of
Amenhotep III for whom she ruled as regent until he was of age.

MUTNEDJMET (c. 1360–1326 BCE). Egyptian queen. Name variations:
Eji; Metnedjenet, Mutnedjme, or Mutnodjmet. Born c. 1360 BCE;
possibly died in childbirth in 1326 BCE; parents unknown; sister of
Nefertiti; m. Haremheb (a general). ❖ Great Hereditary Princess and
Mistress of Upper and Lower Egypt, was an Egyptian queen of the New
Kingdom and probably the last surviving member of the enigmatic family
of Queen Nefertiti, her sister; lent legitimacy to rule of husband, the
general Haremheb, who seized the throne upon the death of King Aye,
successor of Tutankhamun; is depicted in equal size with husband in a
large statue group now in the Turin Museum. ❖ See also *Women in
World History.*

MUTOLA, Maria (1972—). Mozambique runner. Born Maria De Lurdes
Mutola, Oct 27, 1972, in Maputo, Mozambique. ❖ Did not lose an
800-meters race for almost 4 years (1992–95); won World championship
for 800 meters (1993, 2001); won a gold medal for the 800 at
Commonwealth Games (1998, 2002); won a bronze medal at Atlanta
Olympics (1996) and a gold medal at Sydney Olympics (2000), both for
the 800 meters.

MUUS, Varinka Wichfeld- (1922–2002). *See Wichfeld-Muus, Varinka.*

MUZAKOVA, Johanna (1830–1899). *See Svetla, Caroline.*

MUZIO, Christine (1951—). French fencer. Born May 10, 1951, in
France. ❖ Won a silver medal at Montreal Olympics (1976) and a
gold medal at Moscow Olympics (1980), both in team foil.

MUZIO, Claudia (1889–1936). Italian soprano. Born Claudina Muzio,
Feb 7, 1889, in Pavia, Italy; died May 24, 1936, in Rome; studied with
Annetta Casaloni in Turin and Viviani in Milan. ❖ Made debut at
Teatro alla Scala as Desdemona (1913–14), followed by Covent Garden
(1914) and Metropolitan Opera (1916), remaining there until 1922;
appeared in Chicago (1922–32), sharing 9 seasons with Rosa Raisa,
and at Teatro alla Scala (1926–27); made more than 30 recordings for
EMI (1911–35); was the 1st Turandot of Buenos Aries. ❖ See also E.
Arnosi, *Claudia Muzio* (Buenos Aires, 1987); and *Women in World
History.*

MVUNGI, Martha. Tanzanian novelist and short-story writer. Born into
the Bena tribe but spent early years among the Hehe; educated at
universities of Edinburgh and Dar-es-Salaam. ❖ Worked as researcher
in Dar-es-Salaam and teacher in southern Tanzania; became principal
secretary, Ministry of Education, and senior lecturer, at University of
Dar-es-Salaam; works, influenced by oral traditions of Tanzania, include
Three Solid Stones (1975), *Hana Hatia*, and *Yasin in Trouble* (1990).

MYANT MYANT AYE. *See Lwin, Annabella.*

MYATT, Beryl (1923—). *See Platt of Writtle, Baroness.*

MYBURGH, Jeanette (1940—). South African swimmer. Born Sept 16,
1940, in South Africa. ❖ At Melbourne Olympics, won a bronze medal
in the 4x100-meter freestyle relay (1956).

MYBURGH, Natalie (1940—). South African swimmer. Born May 15,
1940, in South Africa. ❖ At Melbourne Olympics, won a bronze medal
in the 4x100-meter freestyle relay (1956).

MYDANS, Shelley (1915–2002). American journalist and writer. Born
Shelley Smith, May 20, 1915, in Palo Alto, California; died Mar 7, 2002,
in New Rochelle, NY; dau. of Everett Smith (professor of journalism);
m. Carl Mydans (photojournalist), in June 1938; children: Seth (journal-
ist) and Shelley. ❖ Began working as journalist for *Life* magazine (1939);
was correspondent in Manila, Europe and Far East; while covering
Douglas MacArthur's buildup in the Philippines with husband during
WWII, spent 12 months in custody of the Japanese; wrote novel *Open
City* about experiences (1945); also wrote *Thomas: A Novel of the Life,
Passion, and Miracles of Becket* (1965), (with Carl Mydans) *The Violent*

Peace: A Report on Wars in the Postwar World (1968), and *The Vermilion
Bridge* (1980). ❖ See also *Women in World History.*

MYDDELTON, Jane (1645–1692). English noblewoman. Name variations: Jane Middleton. Born 1645; died 1692; dau. of Sir Robert
Needham; m. Charles Myddelton, 1660. ❖ A rival of Barbara Villiers,
was known as the great beauty of Charles II's time, and those who came
under her spell included a French noble from Grammont, the duke of
Montagu, the duke of York, and Edmund Waller.

MYELNIK, Faina (1945—). *See Melnik, Faina.*

MYERS, Angel (b. 1967). *See Martino, Angel.*

MYERS, Carmel (1899–1980). American actress. Born April 4, 1899, in
San Francisco, CA; died Nov 9, 1980, in Los Angeles, CA; cousin of
director Mark Sandrich; dau. of a rabbi; sister of Zion Myers (director);
m. Ralph H. Blum (attorney), 1929; m. Al Schwalberg (died); m. once
more; children: Ralph Blum (writer). ❖ Appeared in over 50 films
(1916–76), including *Beau Brummell, Broadway after Dark, Babbitt,
Tell It to the Marines, Broadway Scandals, Show of Shows, Svengali, Ben-
Hur, Countess of Monte Cristo* and *Whistle Stop*; hosted an early tv talk
show, "The Carmel Myers Show" (1951–52).

MYERS, Caroline Clark (c. 1888–1980). American teacher and editor.
Born c. 1888; died July 3, 1980, at Boyds Mill, PA; m. Garry Cleveland
Myers. ❖ With husband, developed methods and materials to teach
reading to illiterate soldiers during WWI and became 1st woman hired as
a teacher by US Army (1917); with husband, founded the periodical
Highlights for Children (1946) and served as managing editor; became
chair of the board (1971).

MYERS, Dee Dee (1961—). American journalist and press secretary.
Born Margaret Jane Myers, Sept 1, 1961, in Providence, RI; raised in
Valencia, CA; sister of Betsy Myers (feminist activist); m. Todd Purdum
(journalist); children: Katherine (b. 2000). ❖ Served as White House
press secretary for the 1st two years of the Clinton administration (Jan 20,
1992–Dec 22, 1994), the 1st female to hold that position; with Mary
Matalin, hosted tv show "Equal Time"; became a consultant on "The
West Wing" and a contributor for MSNBC.

MYERS, Hannah E. (1819–1901). *See Longshore, Hannah E.*

MYERS, Paula Jean (1934—). American diver. Name variations: Paula
Jean Myers-Pope; Paula J. Pope. Born Nov 11, 1934, in La Verne, CA;
attended University of Southern California. ❖ At Helsinki Olympics,
won a silver medal in platform (1952); at Melbourne Olympics, won a
bronze medal in platform (1956); at Rome Olympics, won a silver medal
in springboard and a silver medal in platform (1960); won 11 AAU
national championships; won gold medals for springboard and platform
at Pan American games (1959).

**MYERS, Phoebe (1866–1947). New Zealand teacher, education refor-
mer, and writer.** Born June 13, 1866, in Nelson, New Zealand; died
June 2, 1947, in Wellington; dau. of Judah Myers (merchant) and Eve
(Solomon) Myers; Canterbury College, BA, 1890. ❖ Taught at Hunt
and Petone district and Wellington high schools before joining staff at
Victoria College (1906–12); worked to improve education services for
women; helped to form Wellington Women Teachers' Association
(1901); contributed article, "Influence of Home and Social Education
on Child-Welfare," to Dunedin *Evening Star,* which was later republished as booklet; helped to organize branch of British Red Cross Society
and Women's National Reserve of New Zealand, and was founding
president of Wellington Crippled Soldiers' and Sailors' Hostel during
WWI; retired from teaching (1921); represented New Zealand at League
of Nations as substitute delegate on welfare of women and children, and
was 1st woman to represent her country at League of Nations (1929);
appointed justice of peace (1931). ❖ See also *Dictionary of New Zealand
Biography* (Vol. 3).

MYERS, Viola (1928—). Canadian runner. Born 1928 in Canada. ❖ At
London Olympics, won a bronze medal in the 4x100-meter relay (1948).

**MYERSON, Bess (1924—). American tv personality and political
appointee.** Born in New York, NY, 1924; dau. of Louis Myerson
(house painter) and Bella Myerson; Hunter College, BA, 1945; m.
Allan Wayne (businessman), Oct 1946 (div. 1957); m. Arnold Grant
(entertainment lawyer), 1962 (div. and rem., div. again in 1970); children: (1st m.) Barra Grant. ❖ Made history as the 1st Jewish Miss
America (1945); won a spot as host on tv game show "The Big Payoff"
(1951) and was a regular panelist on popular game show "I've Got a

Secret" (1958–67); served as NYC Commissioner of Consumer Affairs (1969–73), orchestrating one of the most progressive (and aggressive) consumer protection programs the city had known; took active role in mayoral campaign of Edward Koch (1977); was appointed Commissioner of Cultural Affairs (1983); while professional life soared, endured 2 painful divorces, was arrested for shoplifting, suffered ovarian cancer and a stroke, and was involved in a number of ill-fated relationships, including a love affair with Andy Capasso, a married sewer contractor, which led to her arraignment on charges of bribery, conspiracy and obstruction of justice (1988); was later acquitted. ❖ See also Susan Dworkin, *Miss America, 1945: Bess Myerson's Own Story* (Newmarket, 1987); Shana Alexander, *When She Was Bad*; and *Women in World History*.

MYERSON, Golda (1898–1978). See Meir, Golda.

MYETAKNUDINOVA, Dina. See Miftakhutdinova, Diana.

MYIA (fl. 6th c. BCE). Pythagorean philosopher. Born in Crotona, Italy, and flourished around 6th century BCE; dau. of Pythagoras of Samos (philosopher, mathematician, politician, and spiritual leader) and Theano (Pythagorean philosopher); sister of Arignote, Damo, Telauges and Mnesarchus; educated at the School of Pythagoras; married Milon of Crotona (also known as Milo, Mylon, and Meno, a famous athlete and a leading Pythagorean). ❖ Is known for her *Letter to Phyllis*, in which she advises a friend on the practice of rearing an infant, recommending that the caretaker (the mother) be even-tempered and moderate—the Pythagorean prescription in all practical matters. ❖ See also *Women in World History*.

MYKLEBUST, Merete (1973—). Norwegian soccer player. Born May 16, 1973, in Norway. ❖ Forward; won a team bronze medal at Atlanta Olympics (1996).

MYLES, Lynda (1947—). Scottish film and tv producer. Born May 2, 1947, in Arbroath, Angus, Scotland; Edinburgh University, BA in philosophy. ❖ Served as director of Edinburgh Film Festival (1973–1980), the 1st woman to hold that position; co-wrote *Movie Brats* (1979) with Michael Pye; served as curator at Pacific Film Archive at University of California (1980–82); received British Film Industry special award for services to film (1981); returned to UK (1982) and began career as movie producer and consultant; served briefly as senior vice-president of European Production for Columbia Pictures and subsequently worked for BBC; produced *Defense of the Realm* (1985), *The Snapper* (1993) and the BAFTA Award-winning *The Commitments* (1991).

MYLLER, Riita (1956—). Finnish politician. Born July 12, 1956, in Joensuu, Finland. ❖ Member of the Finnish Parliament (1987–95) and the Finnish group in the International Parliamentary Union (IPU, 1987–95); as a European Socialist (PSE), elected to 4th and 5th European Parliament (1994–99, 1999–2004) and named vice-chair of the PSE Group (1996).

MYLONAKI, Anthoula (1984—). Greek water-polo player. Born June 10, 1984, in Chania, Greece. ❖ Won team silver medal at Athens Olympics (2004).

MYOJO-TENNO (1624–1696). See Meisho.

MYONGSONG (1851–1895). See Min.

MYOSHO (1624–1696). See Meisho.

MYOUNG BOK-HEE (1979—). South Korean handball player. Born Jan 29, 1979, in South Korea. ❖ Won a team silver at Athens Olympics (2004).

MYRA. *Variant of Mira or Myrrha.*

MYRDAL, Alva (1902–1986). Swedish sociologist, social activist, and government figure. Pronunciation: Moor-DOLL. Born Jan 31, 1902, in Uppsala, Sweden; died Feb 1, 1986, in Stockholm, Sweden; dau. of Albert Jansson Reimer and Lowa (Larsson) Reimer; graduate of University of Stockholm, 1924; further graduate study in Britain, Germany, US, and Switzerland, 1925–31; University of Uppsala, MA 1934; m. Gunnar Myrdal (economist), Oct 8, 1924; children: son Jan

Myrdal (b. 1928); daughters, Sissela Myrdal Bok (b. 1934) and Kaj Myrdal (b. 1936). ❖ Noted Swedish sociologist and UN official who won the Nobel Peace Prize for her work in the cause of international disarmament; met Gunnar Myrdal (1919); went on a study tour of US (1929–30); suffered severe illness during stay in Switzerland (1931–32); worked as psychologist at a Swedish prison (1932–34); published 1st book, *Crisis in the Population Problem* (1934); served as adviser to Swedish government on housing and population (1935); founded Training College for Nursery and Kindergarten Teachers (1936); edited Labor party journal (1936–38); resided in US (1938–40, 1941–42); was a Swedish representative to International Labor Organization conference in Paris (1946); appointed director of Department of Social Affairs, United Nations (1949); appointed director of Division of Social Sciences, UNESCO (1951); was Swedish ambassador to India (1955–61); published *The Game of Disarmament* (1976); widely recognized as an authority on early childhood education, urged that youngsters be given a loving environment in which their individual differences were respected and cultivated. Won Albert Einstein Peace Prize (1980); won Nobel Peace Prize (1982). ❖ See also Sissela Bok, *Alva Myrdal: A Daughter's Memoir* (Addison-Wesley, 1991); and *Women in World History*.

MYRMAEL, Marit. Norwegian cross-country skier. Name variations: Marit Myrmel. Born in Norway. ❖ Won a bronze medal for 4x5km relay at Lake Placid Olympics (1980).

MYRMEL, Marit. See Myrmael, Marit.

MYRO. See Moero.

MYRTALE (c. 371–316 BCE). See Olympias.

MYRTEL, Hera (b. 1868). French murderer and novelist. Name variations: Héra Myrtel or Hera Myrtel Jacques; Hera Bessarabo. Born Marie-Louise Victorine Grônes in Lyons, France, Oct 25, 1868; m. Paul Jacques, 1894 (died 1914); m. Charles Bessarabo; children: (1st m.) Paule. ❖ First husband was found shot to death (Mar 5, 1914) and thought to have committed suicide; published successful romantic novel under name Héra Myrtel and became a somewhat recognized literary figure; fired shot that killed her 2nd husband (July 30, 1920), and with help of daughter Paule placed his body in a trunk which was shipped to Nancy; when both were tried for murder (Feb 15, 1921), was implicated by daughter in the killing; found guilty and received 20-year sentence while daughter went free.

MYRTIL, Odette (1898–1978). French-born actress, singer, designer, and violinist. Born June 28, 1898, in Paris, France; died Nov 18, 1978, in Doylestown, PA; m. Bob Adams (div.); m. Stanley Logan (died); children: Roger Adams. ❖ Fluent in French and English, debuted on stage as a violinist in Paris (1911); made NY stage debut in *The Follies* (1914), followed by a long theatrical career in US in such plays as *Vogues of 1924*, *The Love Song*, *Countess Maritza*, *White Lilacs*, *The Red Mill* and *Saratoga Trunk*; films include *Dodsworth*, *Kitty Foyle*, *Girl from Scotland Yard*, *Yankee Doodle Dandy*, *Reunion in France*, *Assignment in Brittany* and *Here Comes the Groom*; was also a well-known dress designer in Beverly Hills, then opened her own restaurant, Inn Chez Odette, in New Hope, PA (1961).

MYRTIOTISSA (1883–1968). See Dracopoulou, Theony.

MYRTIS (fl. early 5th c. BCE). Boeotian poet. Born in early 5th century BCE, probably in Boeotia. ❖ The earliest known Boeotian poet, taught the craft of poetry to Pindar and Corinna; her contemporary fame was enough to attract some of the best poetic talent of her time to her school. ❖ See also *Women in World History*.

MYSIE. *Variant of Margaret.*

MYSKINA, Anastasia (1981—). Russian tennis player. Born July 8, 1981, in Moscow, Russia. ❖ Won singles championship at Roland Garros (2004).

MYSTAKIDOU, Elisavet (1977—). Greek taekwondo player. Born Aug 14, 1977, in Yiannitsa, Greece. ❖ Won a silver medal in 67 kg at Athens Olympics (2004).

N

N (1828–1865). *See Khvoshchinskaia, Sofia.*

N., Olga (1828–1894). *See Èngelgardt, Sofia Vladimirovna.*

NAAMAH. Biblical woman. Sister of Tubal-Cain.

NAAMAH (fl. 900 BCE). Biblical woman. Dau. of the king of Ammon; one of 700 wives of Solomon (c. 985–c. 925 BCE), last king of the united 12 tribes of Israel; children: Rehoboam, also seen as Rehabam, king of Israel. ❖ One of the 700 wives of Solomon (I Kings 11:3), was apparently the only one to bear him a son.

NAARAH. Biblical woman. Second of 2 wives of Ashur, of the tribe of Judah.

NACI, Gracia (1510–1569). *See Nasi, Gracia.*

NADDEZHDA. *Variant of Nadezhda, Nadiezhda, Nadia or Nadya.*

NADEJA or NADEJDA. *Variant of Nadezhda, Nadia, or Nadya.*

NADEJDA MICHAELOVNA (1896–1963). Countess of Torby. Born 1896; died 1963; dau. of Michael Michaelovitch (grandson of tsar Nicholas I) and Sophia, countess of Torby; m. George Mountbatten, 2nd marquess of Milford Haven, 1916; children: Tatiana and David.

NADEJDA OF BULGARIA (1899–1958). Duchess of Wurttemberg. Name variations: Princess of Bulgaria. Born Nadejda Klementine Maria Pia Majella, Jan 30, 1899; died Feb 15, 1958; dau. of Marie Louise of Parma (1870–1899) and Ferdinand I (1861–1948), king of Bulgaria (r. 1887–1918, abdicated); m. Albrecht also known as Albert Eugene, duke of Wurttemberg; children: Ferdinand Eugen (b. 1925); Margareta Louise (b. 1928, who m. the viscount de Sheringon); Eugen Eberhard (b. 1930), duke of Wurttemberg; Alexander Eugen (b. 1933); Sophie of Wurttemberg (who m. Antonio Ramoo Baudena).

NADEN, Constance Caroline Woodhill (1858–1889). English poet and philosopher. Born Jan 24, 1858, in Edgbaston, near Birmingham, England; died Dec 23, 1889; dau. of an architect; educated at a Unitarian day school in Edgbaston; studied science at Mason College under Herbert Spencer. ❖ On death of grandfather, inherited a large sum of money, which enabled her to travel throughout Turkey, Palestine, Egypt and India (1887); settled in London (1888) and began giving talks on philosophy; with Robert Lewins, developed a philosophical system known as "Hylo-Idealism," a form of monistic positivism; writings include *Songs and Sonnets of Springtime* (1881) and *A Modern Apostle and Other Poems* (1887); her essays (*Induction and Deduction*), edited by Lewins, was published posthumously (1890).

NADEZHDINA, Nadezhda (1908–1979). Soviet ballet dancer and folk dancer. Born June 3, 1908, in St. Petersburg, Russia; died 1979 on tour in Germany. ❖ Danced with Bolshoi Ballet in Moscow, performing character roles; moved into folk dance, concentrating on traditional dance from Soviet nations; founded Beryozhka Dance Ensemble (1948), which she served as director until her death.

NADIA. *Variant of Nadezhda or Nadya.*

NADIG, Marie-Thérèse (1954—). Swiss Alpine skier. Name variations: Marie-Therese Nadig. Born Mar 8, 1954, in Tannebolden, Switzerland. ❖ Won Olympic gold medals in the downhill and giant slalom in Sapporo, Japan (1972); won Olympic bronze medal in the downhill at Lake Placid, New York (1980); won the World Cup overall (1981), downhill (1980, 1981), giant slalom (1981), and combined (1981). ❖ See also *Women in World History.*

NADJA (c. 1900–1945). American interpretative dancer. Name variations: Beatrice Wanger. Born Beatrice Wanger, c. 1900, in San Francisco, CA; died Mar 15, 1945, in New York, NY. ❖ Trained at school of Florence Flemming Noyes in New York City; taught classes at schools in NY and London; moved to Paris where she made performance

debut at Théâtre Mogador in Cora Laparcie's *Lysistrata* (1924); created and performed recitals (often set to poems by Dante Gabriel Rosetti and G. Constant Lounsberry) at Théâtre Esotérique and other popular venues; returned to US (1937) and taught at studio of Albertina Rasch in NY.

NADON, Amelie (1983—). *See Goulet-Nadon, Amelie.*

NADYA. *Variant of Nadezhda or Nadia.*

NAGAIA, Maria (d. 1612). *See Maria Nagaia.*

NAGAKO (1903–2000). Empress of Japan. Name variations: Princess Nagako; Nagako Kuni; Showa empress. Born in Tokyo, Japan, Mar 6, 1903; died in Tokyo, June 16, 2000; eldest dau. of Prince Kuni no Miya Kunihiko, also known as Kuni Kuniyoshi (field marshal and member of the Fushimi house), and Princess Chikako Kuni (from the noble family of Shimazu, who ruled over the feudal clan of Satsuma); graduated from girls' middle school department of Gakushuin; m. Hirohito (Emperor Showa), emperor of Japan (r. 1926–1989), Jan 26, 1924 (died Jan 7, 1989); children: Princess Shigeko (1925–1961, who m. the son of Prince Higashikuni, the 1st postwar prime minister); Princess Kazuko (b. 1927); Princess Atsuko (b. 1929); Crown Prince Akihito (b. 1933), later emperor of Japan (r. 1989—); Prince Masahito (b. 1935); Princess Takako (b. 1939); another daughter, born in the 1920s, died within a year. ❖ A member of the Satsuma clan, was criticized during her 6-year betrothal to Crown Prince Hirohito for not being a Fujiwara (1918–24); became empress of Japan (1926); enthroned with husband (1928), the 1st time an empress-consort took part in such a ceremony; became Japan's "most endearing public figure," lending warmth to formal occasions; served as honorary president of Japanese Red Cross Society; a talented artist, was also known for her Japanese-style paintings, which she signed with the name Toen. ❖ See also *Women in World History.*

NAGEIKINA, Svetlana (1965—). *See Nagejkina, Svetlana.*

NAGEJKINA, Svetlana (1965—). Russian cross-country skier. Name variations: Svetiana or Swetlana Nageikina, Nagcykina, or Nagueikina. Born Feb 13, 1965, in Belarus. ❖ Won a gold medal for 4 x 5 km relay and placed 4th for 10 km at Calgary Olympics (1988).

NAGEL, Anne (1915–1966). American actress. Born Anne Dolan, Sept 30, 1912 (some sources cite Sept 29), in Boston, MA; died July 6, 1966, in Hollywood, CA; m. Ross Alexander (actor), 1933 (died 1937); m. Lt. James H. Keenan, 1941 (div. 1951). ❖ Debuted in *I Loved You Yesterday* (1933) and continued to work in film for 3 decades; appeared in such movies as *Stand Up and Cheer, Escape By Night, The Spirit of West Point, The Green Hornet* (series), *My Little Chickadee, Women in Bondage* and *Murder in the Music Hall.;* had a notable turn as Madame Gorgeous in *Never Give a Sucker an Even Break.*

NAGEYKINA, Svetlana (1965—). *See Nagejkina, Svetlana.*

NAGIRNAYA, Yekatarina (1949—). *See Kuryshko-Nagirnaya, Yekatarina.*

NAGLE, Nano (1718–1784). Irish philanthropist. Name variations: Honora Nagle. Born Honora Nagle in 1718 (some sources incorrectly cite 1728) at Ballygriffin, Co. Cork, Ireland; died at South Presentation Convent, Cork, April 26, 1784; dau. of Garret Nagle (a gentleman) and Ann (Mathew) Nagle; educated in France. ❖ In defiance of penal legislation, established a number of poor schools and other charitable projects in Cork, introduced the Ursuline Order to Ireland, and founded her own congregation, the Presentation Order, which set a precedent for the involvement of nuns in social work; entered a convent in France as a postulant but, convinced that her vocation lay in Ireland, returned home permanently (c. 1748); opened her 1st school for poor girls (c. 1755); had 7 such schools, all in Cork (by 1769); launched other enterprises which included an almshouse for old women, and sick visiting and missionary work among the poor; invited the Ursuline Order to Ireland; opened 1st convent in Cork (1771); finding the Ursulines were prevented by their vows of enclosure from taking over all of her charitable projects, established her own congregation, the Sisters of the Charitable Instruction, later the Presentation Order (1775); received the religious habit as Sister St. John of God (1776); took her final vows and confirmed as superior of the congregation (1777). ❖ See also T. J. Walsh, *Nano Nagle and the Presentation Sisters* (1959); and *Women in World History*.

NAGLER, Lotte (1917–1943). *See Salomon, Charlotte.*

NAGRÓDSKAIA, Evdokiia (1866–1930). Russian writer. Name variations: Evdokiia Nagrodskaia; Evdokia Nagrodskaia or Nagrodskaya. Born Evdokiia Apollonovna Golovacheva in Russia in 1866; died 1930; dau. of Avdot'ia Panáeva (c. 1819–1893, fiction and memoir writer) and Apollon Golovachev (journalist); married. ❖ Published debut novel, the bestseller *The Wrath of Dionysus* (1910), which created an uproar for its exploration of sexual and gender disorientation and mothers trying to balance family and career; immigrated to France with husband following 1917 Revolution in Russia, where her works had lost favor in the changing political climate; published the historical trilogy *The River of Time* (1924–26). ❖ See also *Women in World History*.

NAGUEIKINA, Svetlana (1965—). *See Nagejkina, Svetlana.*

NAGY, Agnes Nemes (1922–1991). *See Nemes Nagy, Agnes.*

NAGY, Aniko. Hungarian handball player. Name variations: Anikó. Born in Hungary. ❖ Won a team bronze medal at Atlanta Olympics (1996) and a team silver medal at Sydney Olympics (2000).

NAGY, Annamaria (1982—). Hungarian fencer. Born Sept 3, 1982, in Hungary. ❖ Won a gold medal for indiv. épée at Athens Olympics (2004).

NAGY, Ilona (1951—). Hungarian handball player. Born Jan 21, 1951, in Hungary. ❖ At Montreal Olympics, won a bronze medal in team competition (1976).

NAGY, Käthe von (1909–1973). *See Von Nagy, Käthe.*

NAGY, Margit (1921—). *See Sandorne-Nagy, Margit.*

NAGY, Marianna. Hungarian pairs skater. Born in Hungary. ❖ With László Nagy, won bronze medals at Oslo Olympics (1952) and Cortina Olympics (1956); at World championships, won bronze medals (1950, 1953, 1955); won a gold medal at European championship (1950, 1955).

NAGY, Marianna (1957—). Hungarian handball player. Born Aug 30, 1957, in Hungary. ❖ At Montreal Olympics, won a bronze medal in team competition (1976).

NAGY, Timea (1970—). Hungarian fencer. Born Aug 22, 1970, in Budapest, Hungary. ❖ Won a gold medal for indiv. épée at Sydney Olympics (2000); won 5 team World championships.

NAGY, Zsuzsanna (1951—). Hungarian gymnast. Born Nov 14, 1951, in Hungary. ❖ At Munich Olympics, won a bronze medal in team all-around (1972).

NAHEED, Kishwar (1940—). Pakistani poet and journalist. Born 1940 in Bulandshahr, Uttar Pradesh, India; Punjab University, MA in Economics. ❖ Family moved to Lahore, Pakistan, after Partition (1947); published poems in several anthologies; wrote daily column for *Jang* and edited literary magazine *Mah-i naw*; served as director general of Pakistan National Council of the Arts; works include *Lab-i-goya* (1968), *Benam musafat* (1971), *Nazmen* (1975), and *Dasht-i qais men Lail'a* (2001). Collection of poems translated into English by Baidar Bakht and Derek M. Cohen as *The Price of Looking Back* (1987).

NAHIENAENA (c. 1815–1836). Hawaiian princess. Born c. 1815; died Dec 30, 1836; dau. of Keopuolani (c. 1778–1823) and Kamehameha I the Great (1758–1819), king of Hawaii (r. 1810–1819); sister of Liholiho known as Kamehameha II (1797–1824), king of Hawaii (r. 1819–1824) and Kauikeaouli (1814–1854), later known as Kamehameha III, king of Hawaii (r. 1824–1854); trained under the missionaries; m. brother Kauikeaouli (Kamehameha III), 1834; m. Leleiohoku (chief), 1836. ❖ When mother died, was entrusted to the mission in Lahaina for her Christian education and to the Hawaiian chiefs for "moral guidance," splitting her allegiance in two very different ways; as was customary, married her brother Kauikeaouli (Kamehameha III, 1834), but despaired when neither the court nor the missionaries would recognize the nuptials. ❖ See also *Women in World History*.

NAHRGANG, Elaine Tanner (1951—). *See Tanner, Elaine.*

NAIDU, Sarojini (1879–1949). Indian poet and politician. Name variations: Sarojini Chattopadhyaya; Nayadu or Nāyadu. Born Feb 13, 1879, in Hyderabad, India; died Mar 2, 1949, in Lucknow, India, after suffering a head injury; dau. of Aghorenath Chattopadhyaya (doctor and principal of Nizam's College, Hyderabad) and Varada Sundari (Devi) Chattopadhyaya (also seen as Shrimati Sundari Devi); m. Govindurajulu Naidu (doctor), Dec 1898; children: Jayasurya Naidu; Padmaja Naidu; Ranadheera Naidu; Lilamani Naidu. ❖ One of the most influential women in India in the 20th century, is known equally for her lyric works in English that celebrate the Indian spirit, her association with Mohandas Gandhi, Nehru, and other leaders of the Indian independence movement, and her own role as a politician in colonial and post-independence India; born the eldest daughter of the highly educated Chattopadhyay family (1879); matriculated with a 1st Class and honors at Madras (1891); traveled to England to study at King's College, London, and at Girton College, Cambridge (1895–98); health permanently damaged by a breakdown (1896); published 1st volume of poetry, *The Golden Threshold* (1905); won Kaiser-i-Hind Gold Medal from Government of India (1908); sailed to England for medical treatment and became an associate of Mohandas Gandhi (1914); entered national politics as speaker for women's education and rights and Hindu-Muslim unity (1915); returned Kaiser-i-Hind Gold Medal in protest over Jallianwala Bagh massacre (colonial repression of Indian freedom movement); elected president of Indian National Congress (1925) and All India Women's Conference (1930); jailed for independence activities (1930–31, 1932–33, 1942–43); elected president of Asian Relations Conference, New Delhi (1947); served as governor of province of Uttar Pradesh, India (1947–49); writings include *Songs* (1896), *The Golden Threshold* (1905), *The Bird of Time* (1912), *The Gift of India* (1914–15), *The Broken Wing* (1917), *The Soul of India* (1917) and *The Sceptred Flute: Songs of India* (c. 1928). ❖ See also Izzat Yar Khan, *Sarojini Naidu, the Poet* (S. Chand, 1983); Padmini Sathianadhan Sengupta, *Sarojini Naidu: A Biography* (Asia Publishing House, 1966); and *Women in World History*.

NAIMUSHINA, Elena (1964—). Soviet gymnast. Name variations: Yelena Naymushina. Born Nov 19, 1964, in Krasnoyarsk, Siberia, Russia. ❖ Was Jr. Siberian champion (1977); placed 2nd in Chunichi Cup and 3rd at USSR nationals (1978); won a silver all-around at Champions All (1979); won the bronze medal at USSR Cup, medaled on two events at USSR championships, placed 3rd at Moscow News, won gold on beam at World Cup (all 1980); at Moscow Olympics, won a gold medal in team all-around (1980). The film *Elena Naimushina: A Videosymphony* aired on CBS (1981).

NAIR, Mira (1957—). Indian film director, screenwriter and producer. Pronunciation: Nair rhymes with fire. Born Oct 15, 1957, in Bhubaneswar, Orissa, India; dau. of a government administrator; attended Delhi University and Harvard University; m. Mahmood Mamdani (Ugandan political scientist); children: Zohran. ❖ Began career as an actress; turned to making documentaries, including *India Cabaret*, a study of a group of Bombay strippers which won the American Film Festival Award for Best Documentary (1985); produced and directed 1st feature film, *Salaam Bombay!* (1988), which won awards at Cannes and an Academy Award nomination for Best Foreign Film; produced and directed 1st English-language film, *Mississippi Masala* (1991), which won 3 awards at Venice Film Festival; produced and directed *Monsoon Wedding* which won the Golden Lion at Venice Film Festival (2001); other films include *Kama Sutra* (1996), (for tv) *Hysterical Blindness* (2002) and *Vanity Fair* (2004).

NAIRNE, Baroness (1788–1867). *See Elphinstone, Margaret Mercer.*

NAIRNE, Carolina (1766–1845). Scottish poet and songwriter. Name variations: Lady Caroline Nairne; Carolina Oliphant; Baroness Nairne; also seen as Nairn; (pseudonyms) B.B., Mrs. Bogan of Bogan, and Scottish Minstrel. Born Carolina Oliphant, Aug 16, 1766, at Gask in Perthshire, Scotland; died Oct 26, 1845, at Gask; dau. of Laurence Oliphant and Margaret (Robertson) Oliphant; m. her cousin Major William Murray Nairne, later 5th Baron of Nairne, 1806 (died 1829); children: William Nairne (1808–1837). ❖ Wrote 1st lyric, "The Pleuchman" (The Plowman, 1792), inspired by poet Robert Burns; traveled with brother to England, where she wrote what is possibly her most famous lyric, "Land o' The Leal" (1798), a song about homesickness; an excellent lyricist, wrote many celebrated Jacobite songs and humorous ballads under name "B.B." (Mrs. Bogan of Bogan); among her most popular Jacobite songs were "The Hundred Pipers," "Wha'll be King but Charlie?" and "Charlie is my darling," which was still a well-known folk song in 20th century; shortly before death, agreed to permit publication of her poems as *Lays From Strathearn*. ❖ See also memoir *Life and Songs* (1869); and *Women in World History*.

NAITO, Emi (1979—). Japanese softball player. Born Oct 6, 1979, in Fukuoka, Japan. ❖ Infielder, won a team silver medal at Sydney Olympics (2000) and a team bronze at Athens Olympics (2004).

NAKADA, Kumi (1965—). Japanese volleyball player. Born Sept 3, 1965, in Japan. ❖ At Los Angeles Olympics, won a bronze medal in team competition (1984).

NAKAJIMA, Riho (1978—). Japanese synchronized swimmer. Born 1978 in Japan. ❖ Won a team bronze medal at Atlanta Olympics (1996).

NAKAJIMA SHOEN (1863–1901). See *Kishida Toshiko*.

NAKAJIMA TOSHIKO (1863–1901). See *Kishida Toshiko*.

NAKAMURA, Kiharu (1913–2004). Japanese geisha. Born Kazuko Ihara Yamamoto, 1913, on the island of Hokkaido, Japan; grew up in Tokyo; died Jan 5, 2004, in Jackson Heights, Queens, NY; dau. of a physician; m. Shintaro Ota (Japanese diplomat, div.); married Masaya Nakamura (photographer, div.); children: son Masakatsu Ota. ❖ Former geisha, one of the few to learn English, entertained distinguished visitors in Tokyo, such as Charlie Chaplin, Babe Ruth and Jean Cocteau; wrote 10 books, including a bestselling memoir of her experiences, *Edokko Geisha Ichidai-ki* (*The Memoir of a Tokyo-born Geisha*, 1983); was also the 1st woman in Japan to gain a pilot's license; moved to NY (1956), where she became a well-known consultant for plays and films about her profession. A tv mini-series based on her life was broadcast in Japan.

NAKAMURA, Mai (1979—). Japanese swimmer. Born July 16, 1979, in Niigata, Japan. ❖ At Pan Pacific Games, won gold medals for 100-meter backstroke (1997, 1999) and 200-meter backstroke (1997); at SC World championships, won gold medals for 100- and 200-meter backstroke (1999); won a silver medal for 100-meter backstroke and a bronze for 4 x 100-meter medley relay at Sydney Olympics (2000).

NAKAMURA, Reiko (1982—). Japanese swimmer. Born May 17, 1982, in Japan. ❖ Placed 2nd at SC World championships for 200-meter backstroke (2002); won a bronze medal for 200-meter backstroke at Athens Olympics (2004).

NAKAMURA, Taniko (1943—). Japanese gymnast. Born Mar 23, 1943, in Japan. ❖ At World championships, won a bronze medal for team all-around (1962); at Tokyo Olympics, won a bronze medal in team all-around (1964).

NAKANISHI, Yuko (1981—). Japanese swimmer. Born April 24, 1981, in Osaka, Japan; attended Kinki University. ❖ Won a bronze medal for 200-meter butterfly at Athens Olympics (2004).

NAKAO, Miki (1978—). Japanese swimmer. Born June 25, 1978, in Nagasaki, Japan. ❖ Won a bronze medal for 200-meter backstroke at Sydney Olympics (2000).

NAKATINDI, Princess (c. 1943—). Zambian politician. Name variations: Princess Nakatindi Wina. Born Nakatindi Miriam Nganda, c. 1943, in Lealui; dau. of Princess Nakatindi (1923–1972); granddau. of Yeta III (1871–1946), litunga of the Lozi and paramount chief of Borotseland; m. Sikota Wina (chair of MMD); children: daughter Mbile Wina; son Wina Wina. ❖ The 1st woman to run in a Zambia general election, was also the 1st to be an MP (1964); served as parliamentary secretary of Labour and Social Development (1964–68), minister of State for Tourism (1992–93), minister of Community Development and Social Welfare (1993–98); unlawfully imprisoned along with 100 others by President Chiluba (early 1998), in connection of the 1997 coup attempt; released for lack of evidence (Dec 1998); was national chair of Women's Affairs Committee of the ruling Movement for Multiparty Democracy (MMD, 1997–2002).

NAKAYAMA YOSHIKO (1834–1907). See *Yoshiko*.

NAKIC, Danira (1969—). Yugoslavian basketball player. Born July 22, 1969, in Yugoslavia. ❖ At Seoul Olympics, won a silver medal in team competition (1988).

NÁKOU, Lilika (1903–1989). Greek novelist and essayist. Name variations: Lilika Nakou. Born 1903 in Athens, Greece; died 1989. ❖ Lived in Switzerland and France before returning to Greece (1930); studied philosophy and piano and worked as piano teacher; knew many intellectuals, including Gide, Einstein, de Unamuno, and Rolland; works, which reflect socialist and feminist concerns, include *The Deflowered Maiden* (1931), *Parastratiméni* (1935), *Children's Hell* (1944), *Madame Doremi* (1953), and *Nausika* (1954).

NAKOVA, Dolores (1957—). Bulgarian rower. Born June 15, 1957, in Bulgaria. ❖ At Moscow Olympics, won a bronze medal in quadruple sculls with coxswain (1980).

NAKSHEDIL SULTANA (c. 1762–1817). See *De Rivery, Aimee Dubucq*.

NALA TAIHOU (1835–1908). See *Cixi*.

NALDI, Nita (1897–1961). Italian-American silent-screen actress. Born Anita Donna Dooley, April 1, 1897, in New York, NY; died Feb 17, 1961, in New York, NY; m. J. Searle Barclay, 1929 (died 1945). ❖ A leading lady of 1920s, came to prominence in the Ziegfeld Follies; in Hollywood, was typecast as a screen siren in such silents as *Dr. Jekyll and Mr. Hyde* (1920), *The Unfair Sex* (1922), *Blood and Sand* (1922), *The Ten Commandments* (1923), *Cobra* (1925), *A Sainted Devil* (1925), *The Marriage Whirl* (1926) and *The Lady Who Lied* (1927); retired from film with advent of talkies. ❖ See also *Women in World History*.

NALKOWSKA, Zofia (1884–1954). Polish novelist and salonnière. Name variations: Zofja; Zofia Gorzechowski-Nalkowska; Zofia Rygier-Nalkowska; Nalkovskoi. Born in Warsaw, Russian Poland, Nov 10, 1884; died in Warsaw, Dec 17, 1954; dau. of Waclaw Nalkowski (1851–1911, geographer and publicist); m. Leon Rygier. ❖ Leading member of the "psychological school" in interwar Polish literature, who presided over a preeminent literary salon in Warsaw, 1st published verse in *Chimera* (1898); starting in her 20s, published a series of novels, including *Kobiety* (Women, 1906), *Rówiesnice* (Contemporaries, 1909), *Narcyza* (Narcissa, 1910), *Ksiaze* (The Prince, 1910) and *Weze i róze* (Serpents and Roses, 1915), and story collections *Koteczka, czyli biale tulipany* (Pussycat, or the White Tulips, 1909) and *Lustra* (Mirrors, 1913); following WWI, published novels *Hrabia Emil* (Count Emil, 1920) and *Charaktery* (Characters, 1922), both of which were more rooted in real life than earlier works; exploring good and evil, pleased critics with 1923 novel *Romans Teresy Hennert* (Teresa Hennert's Love Affair); became active in organizations protesting the police-state tactics of Pilsudski rule; was a co-founder of Zwiazek Zawodowy Literatów Polskich (Trade Union of Polish Writers) and active in PEN; a leader of Poland's literary underground during German occupation (1940s), supported the creation of a Socialist society in Poland after 1945; was a member of the Glowna Komisja Badania Zbrodni Niemieckich (Main Commission for the Investigation of German War Crimes); elected deputy to the Sejm; other writings include the novels *Dom nad lakami* (The House Beyond the Meadows, 1925), *Choucas* (Choucas, 1927), and *Niedobra milosc* (The Wrong Kind of Love, 1928), *Granica* (The Border, 1935), *Niecierpliwi* (The Impatient Ones, 1939), *Wezly zycia* (Knots of Life, 1948), and 2 plays: *Dom kobiet* (A House of Women, 1930) and *Dzien jego powrotu* (The Day of His Return, 1931). Awarded State Prize of Polish People's Republic (1953). ❖ See also *Women in World History*.

NALL, Anita (1976—). American swimmer. Born July 24, 1976, in Baltimore, MD. ❖ At Barcelona Olympics, won a bronze medal in the 200-meter breaststroke, a silver medal in the 100-meter breaststroke, and a gold medal in the 4 x 100-meter medley relay (1992).

NAM EUN-YOUNG (1970—). Korean handball player. Born Mar 20, 1970, in South Korea. ❖ At Barcelona Olympics, won a gold medal in team competition (1992).

NAMAKELUA, Alice K. (1892–1987). Hawaiian composer, guitarist, singer. Born in Honolulu, Hawaii, Aug 12, 1892; died April 1987 in Hauula, Honolulu. ❖ Named the person who contributed the most to Hawaiian music by the Hawaiian Music Foundation (1972), composed over 180 songs and taught them to children, in order to ensure that Hawaiian culture would endure. ❖ See also *Women in World History*.

NAMBA, Yasuko (1949–1996). Japanese mountain climber. Born Feb 7, 1949, in Japan; died May 10, 1996, on Mount Everest; m. Kenichi Namba. ❖ Scaled 6 of the highest peaks in the world; became the 2nd Japanese woman to reach the top of Mount Everest, but died on the descent, along with 7 others, when a sudden storm with hurricane force winds swept the peak. ❖ See also Jon Krakauer, *Into Thin Air* (1998).

NAMJOSHI, Suniti (1941—). Indian poet, novelist and feminist. Born 1941 in Mumbai, India; dau. of Captain Manohar Vinayak Namjoshi (test pilot killed in a crash, 1953) and Sarojini (née Naik Nimbalkar) Namjoshi; studied at universities of Poona and Missouri; McGill University, Canada, PhD; became a Canadian citizen. ❖ Held teaching posts in India and at Toronto University in Canada and Exeter University in England; work draws on oral story-telling tradition and often gives fairytales a feminist turn; poetry collections include *The Jackass and the Lady* (1980), *The Authentic Life* (1983), *Flesh and Paper* (1986), and *Because of India* (1989); prose works include *Feminist Fables* (1981), *The Conversations of Cow* (1985), *Aditi and the One-Eyed Monkey* (1986), *The Blue Donkey Fables* (1989), *The Mothers of Maya Diip* (1989), and *Saint Suniti and the Dragon* (1993); with mother, translated poems of Marathi poet Govindagraj into English (1968).

NAMPEYO (c. 1860–1942). Hopi-Tewa potter. Name variations: Nampayu; The Old Woman; Snake Woman, Snake Girl or Tsu-mana. Born Nampeyo on the Hopi 1st Mesa called Hano, northeast Arizona, c. 1860; died July 20, 1942, in Hano; dau. of Kotsakao, also called Qo-tca-ka-o (Tewa woman of the Corn Clan), and Kotsuema also called Qots-vema (Hopi man of the Snake Clan); m. Kwivioya, 1879 (marriage annulled); m. Lesou, 1881 (died 1932); children: (2nd m.) 4 daughters, Kwe-tca-we, Ta-wee, Po-pong-mana (potter known as Fanny), and Tu-hi-kya; 1 son, Qoo-ma-lets-tewa (died 1918). ❖ The finest Hopi potter of her generation, who single-handedly started what became a renaissance in Hopi pottery, was drawn to ancient (Sikyatki) pottery (1892); her skills were discovered by visiting anthropologists, Dr. Jesse W. Fewkes and Walter Hough of the Smithsonian (1895–96); had 1st exhibition of pottery at Field Museum in Chicago (1898); exhibited and sold pottery through Fred Harvey's (commercial trading post), Grand Canyon, Arizona (1907); held 2nd exhibition in Chicago (1910); continued working while passing on techniques that began "Sikyatki Revival" in pottery throughout Hopi tribe though she was blind by 1920. ❖ See also Barbara Kramer, *Nampeyo and Her Pottery* (1996); and *Women in World History*.

NAMUMPAM (c. 1650–1676). *See Wetamoo.*

NANA YAA ASANTEWAA (c. 1850–1921). *See Yaa Asantewaa.*

NANCY, Miss (1915–1997). *See Claster, Nancy.*

NANDI (c. 1760s–1827). Zulu queen. Born in 1760s in what is now South Africa; died 1827; m. Zulu chief Senzangakhona (or Senzangakhoma), c. 1787; children: at least 1 son, Shaka (born c. 1787), Zulu chief. ❖ Around 1787, had an illicit affair with Senzangakhona and gave birth to Shaka, who would later become one of the greatest Zulu chiefs; though Senzangakhona then married her, was condemned by the Zulu and the Langeni, both because of her pregnancy and because she and her husband were considered too closely related to be married; forced out with son, found refuge with the Mthethwa (Mtetwa) people, whose chief Dingiswayo was in the process of creating a powerful military state; after son became chief (c. 1815), was enormously powerful. ❖ See also *Women in World History*.

NANETTE, Baby (1920—). *See Fabray, Nanette.*

NANNY (fl. 1730s). Afro-Jamaican chieftainess. Date of birth and death unknown and most details of life are little more than tantalizing fragments. ❖ Key leader of the Maroons, descendants of escaped slaves who maintained their freedom by successfully waging guerilla warfare against white planters, was a formidable military tactician; enjoyed a reputation of having slain British soldiers in battle with her own hands and was said to have the power to summon forth supernatural forces on behalf of her people; her military exploits lived on in the oral traditions of Jamaica's black population, both free and slave, well into 19th century; since Jamaica achieved its independence (1962), has been celebrated as one of the island nation's historical giants. ❖ See also *Women in World History*.

NANSEN, Betty (1873–1943). Danish actress. Born Betty Anna-Marie Muller, Mar 19, 1873, in Copenhagen, Denmark; died Mar 15, 1943, in Copenhagen. ❖ Was a celebrated stage and screen star in Denmark before coming to US to star for Fox (1914); made 6 silent pictures, including *Anna Karenina* (1915), after which she returned to Denmark.

NANTHILDE (610–642). Queen of Austrasia and the Franks. Name variations: Nantilde. Born in 610; died in 642; became 2nd wife of Dagobert I (c. 606–639), king of Austrasia (r. 623–628), king of the Franks (r. 629–639), in 629; children: Clovis II (634–657), king of Neustria and Burgundy (r. 639–657), king of the Franks (r. 639–657). Dagobert's 1st wife was Ragnetrude.

NANYE'HI (1738–1822). Tribal leader. Name variations: called Nancy Ward by the English; (tribal nickname) Tsistu-na-gis-ka (Wild Rose); known as the Ghigan or Ghi-gan (Beloved Woman); also referred to as Ghi-ga-u and Agiyagustu (Honored Woman). Born Nanye'hi (derivative of tribal name for "spirit people"), a member of the Ani-wa-yah or Wolf Clan, c. 1738, in the Cherokee capital, Chote, located on Little Tennessee River; died spring 1822 at Womankiller Ford, near Benton, Tennessee; dau. of Tame Doe of the Wolf Clan, and an unidentified member of Delaware Nation; m. Kingfisher of the Ani-Ka-Wi, or Deer Clan, early 1750s (died 1755); m. Bryan Ward, late 1750s; children: (1st m.) Fivekiller (or Hiskyteehee) and Catharine; (2nd m.) Elizabeth Ward. ❖ The last Ghigan of the Tsa-la-gi or Cherokee Nation, was head of the Woman's Council, member of the Council of Chiefs, and the only woman to speak on behalf of a native nation during treaty negotiations; distinguished herself in battle with the Creek Indians (1755); was invested with the office of Ghigan, essentially assuming the responsibility of the most important position in the Cherokee Nation at age 17 (1755); used powers of the Ghigan to save the lives of settlers (1776); led the Cherokee Nation in treaty negotiations (1781); participated in negotiating the Treaty of Hopewell with the colony of South Carolina (1785); lobbied to keep Cherokee land intact (1817); lost her homeland in the Hiwassee Purchase and relocated to Womankiller Ford (1819); was the last Cherokee to hold the title "Beloved Woman." ❖ See also *Women in World History*.

NAOMI (fl. 1100 BCE). Biblical woman. Name variations: Noemi. Born in Bethlehem, in Judah; m. Elimelech; mother-in-law of Ruth; children: Mahlon (who m. Ruth); Chilion (who m. Orpah). ❖ Made her home in Bethlehem with husband and sons, until the great famine forced the family to migrate to Moab, east of the Dead Sea; over next 10 years, lost both husband and sons, after which she made plans to return to her homeland, accompanied by daughter-in-law Ruth. ❖ See also *Women in World History*.

NAPIER, Geills (1937—). Canadian first lady. Born Geills McCrae Kilgour, Dec 23, 1937, in Winnipeg, Manitoba, Canada; m. John Napier Turner (prime minister of Canada, 1984–84), May 11, 1963; children: Elizabeth (b. 1964), Michael (b. 1965), David James (b. 1968), and Andrew (b. 1971).

NAPIER, Sarah (1745–1826). *See Lennox, Sarah.*

NAPIERKOWSKA, Stacia (1886–1945). French dancer. Name variations: Stanislawa Napierkowska. Born Dec 16, 1886, in Paris, France (some sources cite Constantinople); died May 11, 1945, in Paris; studied at National Academy, Paris. ❖ Made stage debut at Opéra Comique, Paris, in the ballet *Jeux Athlétiques* (1907), followed by *Jaunes, Raymonde, Griselidis, Les Drames Sacrés, Izeyl, Kosacks!, La Tragique Histoire d'Hamlet, La Reine Flammette* and *Les Ailes*; made London debut at the Palace (1911); films include *Messaline, Notre Dame de Paris* (as Esmeralda), *Semiramis* (title role), *Les Vampires*, and Jacques Feyder's *L'Atlantide* (as Queen Antinea).

NAPLES, grand duchess of. *See Louisa Amelia (1773–1802).*

NAPLES, queen of.
See Beatrice of Savoy (fl. 1240s).
See Marguerite de Bourgogne (1250–1308).
See Marie of Hungary (d. 1323).
See Joanna I of Naples (1326–1382).
See Margaret of Naples (fl. late 1300s).
See Joanna II of Naples (1374–1435).
See Maria of Castile (1401–1458).
See Isabelle of Lorraine (1410–1453).
See Ippolita (1446–1484).
See Joanna of Aragon (1454–1517).
See Isabel de Clermont (d. 1465).
See Joanna of Naples (1478–1518).
See Foix, Germaine de (1488–1538).
See Isabella del Balzo (d. 1533).
See Maria Carolina (1752–1814).
See Bonaparte, Carolina (1782–1839).

NAPLES, regent of. *See Margaret of Navarre (fl. 1154–1172).*

NAPOLETANO, Pasqualina (1949—). Italian politician. Born Sept 28, 1949, in Molfetta (Bari). ❖ Member of the party executive (1979—) and chair of national party executive (1998—); elected to 4th and 5th European Parliament (1994–99, 1999–2004); named vice-chair of the European Socialists.

NAPOLITANO, Johnette (1957—). American musician. Name variations: Concrete Blonde; Pretty & Twisted; Dreamers; Dream 6. Born Sept 22, 1957, in Hollywood, CA. ❖ Became vocalist and bass player for rock band Concrete Blonde (1981), releasing hit "Joey" (1990) and albums *Concrete Blonde* (1986), *Bloodletting* (1990), *Walking in London* (1992), *Mexican Moon* (1993) and *Concrete Blonde y Los Illegals* (1997); after leaving Concrete Blonde (1994), recorded *Vowel Movement* with Holly Vincent; formed band Pretty & Twisted and produced their self-titled album; produced album for band Maria Fatal.

NAPOLSKI, Nancy (1974—). American shooter. Name variations: Nancy Napolski-Johnson or Nancy Johnson. Born Nancy Napolski, Jan 14, 1974, in Hinsdale, ID; graduate of University of Kentucky, 1995. ❖ Won a gold medal for 10m air rifle at Sydney Olympics (2000).

NARANJO, Carmen (1928—). Costa Rican author and government administrator. Born Jan 30, 1928, in Cartago, Costa Rica. ❖ One of Central America's most important female political and cultural figures, who criticized the political and economic elite and government bureaucracy, in her novel *Diario de una multitud* (1965), but also made significant contributions as Costa Rican government official; joined Welfare Department (1954), becoming the highest-ranking female civil servant as undersecretary of social security system (1961) and 1st female top administrative officer (1971); appointed ambassador to Israel (1972); published numerous articles to promote better understanding between the 2 nations, collected in *Por Israel y las páginas de la biblia* (Through Israel and the Bible's Pages, 1976); joined cabinet of president Daniel Oduber as minister of culture, youth and sports (1974) and pursued progressive agenda, emphasizing centrality of culture and its non-elitist development; founded National Theater Company, Symphonic Orchestra of Costa Rica, and Costa Rican Film Institute; faced opposition from conservatives and resigned over her attempt to air a tv documentary presenting social, economic and environmental problems of Costa Rica (1976); became director of Museum of Costa Rican Art (1982) and of EDUCA, Central American University publishing house (1984); served as technical assistant for social security planning at Organization of American States and presided over Central American commission of aid to families of "disappeared" students and teachers; won acclaim for *Responso por el niño Juan Manuel* (Response for the Child Juan Manuel, 1971), said to be one of most important novels of contemporary Central American literature, which received Premio Educa (1974); received National Prize Aquileo Echeverría for novel *Los perros no ladraron* (The Dogs Didn't Bark, 1966), Editorial Costa Rica Prize for short story "Hoy es un largo día" (Today is a Long Day, 1974), as well as National Magón Prize (1986) and Chile's Gabriela Mistral Medal (1996). ❖ See also Luz Ivette Martínez, *Carmen Naranjo y la narrativa femenina en Costa Rica* (Editorial Universitaria Centroamericana, 1987).

NARIMAN (1934–2005). Queen of Egypt. Name variations: Nariman Sadeq or Sadiq; Narriman Sadek; Nariman Fahmi. Born Oct 31, 1934, in Cairo, Egypt; died Feb 16, 2005, in Cairo; dau. of Husain Fahmi Sadiq (secretary-general of the ministry of communications, died 1965) and Asila Kamil; became 2nd wife of King Farouk I, May 1951 (div. 1954); m. Dr Adham al-Nakib, 1954 (div. 1961); m. Dr. Ismail Fahmi, 1967 (div.); children: (1st m.) Ahmed Fouad (b. Jan 1952), king of Egypt in absentia under a regency (r. 1952–53); (2nd m.) son Akram. ❖ The last queen-consort of Egypt, married the king at 16; gave birth to an heir 6 months before the military overthrew the monarchy (1952); with husband, fled to Italy; returned to Egypt (1954) and divorced the king.

NARISHKINA, Natalya (1651–1694). Russian empress and regent. Name variations: Natalia Naryshkin, Naryshkina, Narushkin or Narushkina. Born Natalya Cyrilovna Narishkina into the powerful Narishkin family of Russian nobles, Aug 22, 1651, died Jan 25, 1694; dau. of Cyril Narishkin (or Naryshkin) and Anne Leontiev Narishkina (d. 1706); sister of Ivan Narishkin (or Naryshkin); became 2nd wife of Alexis I (1629–1676), tsar of Russia (r. 1645–1676), c. 1670 or 1671; children: Peter I the Great (1672–1725), tsar of Russia (r. 1682–1725); Theodora (1673–1676); Natalya Romanov (1674–1716). ❖ Became regent for 10-year-old son Peter (1682), and the hostility between her family and the family of her husband's 1st wife, Maria Miloslavskaia, came to a head; with son, witnessed the slayings of her brother and her guardian, among others (1682); while son Peter spent his time sailing in the north, ran the country; her efforts to free women from the binding tradition of the *terem* were passed down to her son when he finally became tsar as Peter I the Great. ❖ See also *Women in World History*.

NAROZHILENKO, Ludmila (1964—). *See Engquist, Ludmila.*

NARRIMAN (1934–2005). *See Nariman.*

NASANOVA, Tatyana (1952—). *See Goyshchik-Nasanova, Tatyana.*

NASCIMENTO PINHEIRO, Graziele (1981—). Brazilian soccer player. Name variations: Graziele. Born Mar 28, 1981, in Goi, Brazil. ❖ Forward, won a team silver medal at Athens Olympics (2004).

NASH, Diane (1938—). African-American civil-rights activist. Name variations: Diane Nash Bevel. Born Diane Judith Nash, 1938, in Chicago, IL; attended Howard University, then Fisk; m. James Bevel (SNCC leader, div.). ❖ A leader in the non-violence movement, became the spokesperson for the Sit-In demonstrations at the lunch counters of Nashville (1960); became a full-time field worker for the Student Nonviolent Coordinating Committee (SNCC); was a liaison between SNCC and Martin Luther King's SCLC; also tried to build a bridge to NAACP; 4 months pregnant, was sentenced to 2 years in Jackson, Mississippi, for teaching black children the tools of nonviolent direct action (May 1962); was released on appeal; a major organizer for the Birmingham campaign, also designed the plan used by SCLC for the successful campaign in Selma (1965).

NASH, Florence (1888–1950). American stage actress. Born Florence Ryan, Oct 2, 1888, in Troy, NY; died April 2, 1950, in Hollywood, CA; sister of actress Mary Nash (1995–1976). ❖ Came to prominence in NY debut as Madge Blake in *The Boys of Company B* (1907); appeared on stage as Aggie Lynch in *Within the Law* (1912–14), followed by *Merton of the Movies*, *When Sweet Sixteen*, *The Land of the Free*, *Lady Clara*, *The Mirage* and *A Lady's Virtue*; films include *The Women* (as Nancy Blake).

NASH, Judith Ford (c. 1950—). *See Ford, Judith.*

NASH, June (1911–1979). American actress. Born Jan 26, 1911; died Oct 8, 1979, in Hampton Bays, NY. ❖ Child actress, made film debut in *Say It with Sables* (1928); other film credits include *Strange Cargo*, *Dynamite*, *Their Own Desire* and *Two Kinds of Women*; retired from film (1932).

NASH, Mary (1885–1976). American stage and screen actress. Born Mary Ryan, Aug 15, 1885, in Troy, NY; died Dec 3, 1976, in Brentwood, CA; sister of Florence Nash (1888–1950, actress); m. José Ruben (actor). ❖ Made stage debut in *The Girl from Kay's* (1904) and NY debut in *Alice-Sit-By-the-Fire* (1905); starred or featured on Broadway in *The City*, *The Man Who Came Back*, *Big Chance*, *The Lady*, *Hassan*, *Diana*, *A Woman Denied* and *Uncle Tom's Cabin*; made film debut (1936), subsequently appearing in, among others, *Come and Get It*, *Easy Living*, *Heidi*, *Wells Fargo*, *The Little Princess*, *The Philadelphia Story*, *The Human Comedy*, *Monsieur Beaucaire* and *Till the Clouds Roll By*.

NASH, Ruth (1901–1993). *See Cowan, Ruth.*

NASHAR, Beryl (1923—). Australian geologist. Born Beryl Scott, July 9, 1923, in Maryville, Newcastle, NSW, Australia; University of Sydney, BS, 1947; University of Tasmania, PhD; m. Ali Nashar (Egyptian philosopher), July 13, 1952 (died 1980); children: 1 son. ❖ The 1st woman dean of a science department at an Australian university (Newcastle University College, 1969–70), the 1st Australian PhD in geology from an Australian university, and the 1st Australian woman to win a Rotary Foundation fellowship (to study at Cambridge University, 1949–50), was hired as a researcher in Tasmania with professor S.W. Carey's assistance; lived in Cairo, Egypt, for 3 years; returned to Australia to raise her son as a single mother (husband remained in Egypt, though they were still married); at Newcastle University College, University of New South Wales, served as a geology lecturer (1955–60), senior lecturer (1960–63), geology professor (1963–80) and dean of the Faculty of Science (1969–70); wrote *The Geology of the Hunter Valley* (1964). Received University of Sydney's University Medal; named Officer of the Order of the British Empire (1972).

NASI, Gracia Mendes (1510–1569). Portuguese businesswoman and patron of the arts. Name variations: Beatrice de Luna; Beatrice Mendes; Gracia Mendes; Doña Gracia Nasi or Naci. Born Beatrice de Luna in Portugal in 1510; died 1569 in Istanbul, Turkey; m. Francisco Mendes, 1528 (died 1536); children: Reyna Mendes. ❖ Head of an underground Jewish organization who orchestrated the boycott of the port of Ancona, was born into the Nasi family, whose ancestors had been Jewish courtiers to the kingdoms of the Iberian peninsula since the 11th century, but like many Jews, became nominal Christians and changed their name to de Luna; with Inquisition established in Portugal, fled to Antwerp (1536); fled to Venice (1545), where she was denounced as a Jew and imprisoned by Venetian authorities; as a result of numerous bribes, released from prison (1549); assured of immunity from religious persecution by Duke Ercole II, relocated to Ferrara (1550) and became a declared Jew and patron of the arts; once more expelled because she was a Jew, moved to Istanbul with family (1553); as the leader of the Jewish community there, organized a trade boycott of Ancona in retaliation for the deaths of 24 Jews who were burned to death, as a result of the election of the fanatical Pope Paul IV (1556); obtained special permission from Suleiman to build a new Jewish settlement at Tiberias (1561). ❖ See also Cecil Roth, *The House of Nasi: Dona Gracia* (Greenwood, 1947); and *Women in World History.*

NASRALLA, Emily (1931—). Lebanese novelist and short-story writer. Name variations: Abi Rashed. Born Abi Rashed, July 6, 1931, in Kfeir village, South Lebanon; attended Shoueifat National College, Beirut University College (now Lebanese American University); American University of Beirut, BA in Education, 1958; m. Philip Nasrallah (chemist), 1957; children: Ramzi, Maha, Khalil, and Mona. ❖ Remained in Beirut during war (1975–82) and wrote about struggle for existence; participated as panelist and lecturer at many conferences worldwide, including PEN International Congress in Canada (1989); novels include *Birds of September* (1962), *The Oleander Tree* (1968), *Those Memories* (1980), *Flight Against Time* (1991), and *Sleeping Ember* (1995); short-story collections include *Island of Illusion* (1973), *Women in Seventeen Stories* (1983), *The Lost Mill* (1985), and *Gypsy Nights* (1998); children's books include *The Resplendent Flower* (1975) and *A Cat's Diary* (1997).

NASRIN, Taslima (1962—). Bangladeshi doctor, feminist, columnist, poet and novelist. Born Aug 1962 to a Muslim family in Mymensingh, East Pakistan (now Bangladesh); dau. of a physician; Mymensingh Medical College, MBBS, 1984. ❖ Edited literary periodical, *Senjuti* (1978–83); worked in public hospitals as an anesthesiologist for 8 years; writing in Bengali, published 1st book of poetry (1986) and a highly successful 2nd collection, *Amar kichu jay ase na* (I Couldn't Care Less, 1989); in her columns (1989–94), wrote about women's oppression, about sexual equality and sexual freedom, and called for the prosecution of Muslim clerics whose religious courts have condemned poor women to death by stoning or burning; became a rallying cry for the Hindu minority and received the Ananda award for *Nirbachito Kolam* (Selected Columns, 1992), the 1st writer from Bangladesh to be so honored; became confined to her house and had to quit her job during the 1st fatwa against her issued by Islamic fundamentalists (1990), who began staging street demonstrations; published *Lajja* (Shame, 1993), which deals with fundamentalist hatred, which sold 50,000 copies in 6 months, then was banned by the government of Bangladesh; threatened with death by Islamic extremists with the issue of 2 more fatwas, went into hiding (1994); lives in exile in Stockholm, Sweden; has written 28 books of poetry, essays, novels and short stories, and three more of her books were banned in Bangladesh, *Amar Meyebela* (My Girlhood), *Utol Hawa* (Wild Wind) and *Shei shob ondhokar* (Those Dark Days); also wrote autobiographies *Ko* (Speak Up) and *Dwikhandito* (Split in Two).

NASSAU, duchess of.
See Pauline of Wurttemberg (1810–1856).
See Charlotte (1896–1985).

NASSER, Tahia (1923—). First lady of Egypt. Name variations: Tahia Kazem. Born Tahia Mahmoud Kazem in 1923 in Cairo, Egypt; dau. of a successful merchant; attended a French preparatory school in Cairo; m. Gamal Abdel Nasser (1918–1970, military officer and later president of Egypt from 1956 to 1970), 1944; children: daughters Hoda Nasser (b. 1946) and Mona Nasser (b. 1947); sons Khaled Nasser (b. 1949), Abdel-Hamik Nasser (b. 1951), and Hakim Amer Nasser (b. 1953). ❖ Became first lady of Egypt (1956) and voted in elections regularly after Egyptian women were given the right to vote that year; seldom attended public functions and appeared in few official photographs; shopped in local stores, attended opera, and sipped coffee in cafés without being recognized, enjoying a personal freedom known by few wives of national leaders in 20th century. ❖ See also *Women in World History.*

NASSIF, Anna (1933—). American modern dancer. Born Aug 17, 1933, in Rowlesburg, VA; trained with Martha Graham, Louis Horst, and Nina Fonoroff; studied at University of Wisconsin under Louise Kloepper, and later under Nora Kiss, Anton Dolin, Felia Doubrovska, and others. ❖ Taught at University of Wisconsin in Madison where she was

considered a great influence upon the development of modern dance in the Midwest; worked in theater as well as film, and created many works of her own, including *Time Mass* (1963), *Dance for Two Figures with Red Scarf* (1964), *Meditations on Ecclesiastes* (1965), *Dance for One Figure and Two Objects* (1965), *Composition for Ten Figures in Shades of Red* (1965), *Variations* (1965), *Six Short Pieces for One Male Figure Assisted by Two Female Figures* (1967), *Krishna, Dance Drama No. 6* (1968), *Figure in Motion with Drums* (1969), *Gloria* (1971), *Prelude by Bach* (1972), *Now What is Love* (1972), *Realizations* (1974), *Shakti* (1975), *Americana Suite* (1976) and *Six Intermedia Pieces* (1976).

NASSIF, Malak Hifni (1886–1918). Egyptian feminist. Name variations: Nasif; (pseudonym) Bahithat al-Badiya, Badiyya, or Bahissat el Badia. Born in Cairo, Egypt, 1886; died 1918; married and moved to the desert. ❖ Influential writer whose 10-point program for improving Egyptian women's position became the standard for demands in the pre-WWI era; using the pen-name Bahissat el Badia ("Searcher in the Desert"), wrote articles about education, seclusion, marriage, and divorce; was one of the 1st women in the country to qualify as a teacher (1900).

NAT, Marie-José (1940—). Corsican stage, tv, and screen actress. Name variations: Marie-Jose Nat. Born April 22, 1940, in Bonifacio, Corsica, France; m. Michel Drach (director), 1961. ❖ Won a photo contest; pursued a career in Paris as a high-fashion model; made film debut in *Crime et châtiment* (1956), followed by *Arènes joyeuses, Rue des Prairies, La Vérité, Vive le duc!, La menace, Amélie ou le temps d'aimer* (title role), *Le journal d'une femme en blanc, Dacii, Le passé simple, Anna* and *Litan,* among others. Won Best Actress prize at Canne for *Les Violons du Bal* (1974).

NATALIA SHEREMETSKAIA (1880–1952). See *Sheremetskaia, Natalia.*

NATALIE, Mlle (c. 1895–1922). Russian-born American ballroom dancer. Name variations: Natalie Dumond. Born c. 1895 in Odessa, Russia; died in the polio epidemic of 1922 in New York, NY. ❖ Moved with family to US at age 2; performed as child ballerina in Buffalo, NY; moved to London with family and trained at Alhambra Theatre, where she also performed briefly; partnered with Martin Ferrari as exhibition ballroom team, toured successfully throughout US for 7 years (1914–21); appeared as solo ballerina performing specialty dances at Hippodrome Extravaganza in *Good Times* (1920), and others.

NATALIE OF HESSE-DARMSTADT (1755–1776). Russian royal. Born Natalie Wilhelmina, June 25, 1755; died in childbirth, April 26, 1776; dau. of Caroline of Birkenfeld-Zweibrucken (1721–1774) and Louis IX (b. 1719), landgrave of Hesse-Darmstadt; m. Paul I (1754–1801), tsar of Russia (r. 1796–1801), Oct 10, 1773; children: one (b. 1776). ❖ Following Natalie's death, Paul married Sophia Dorothea of Wurttemberg.

NATHALIA KESHKO (1859–1941). Queen of Serbia. Name variations: Natalya, Natalie. Born 1859; died 1941; dau. of a Russian military officer; educated in Paris; m. Milan II (I), prince of Serbia (r. 1868–1882), king of Serbia (r. 1882–1889, abdicated 1889, died 1901), around 1875 (div. c. 1889); children: Alexander (1876–1903), king of Serbia (r. 1889–1903, who m. Draga). ❖ Became princess of Serbia (c. 1875); when husband declared himself king, became queen (1882); without her consent, was divorced from husband while out of the country (c. 1889), an act seen as heartless by the public, since he also demanded she send back their son; ignored the decree by Parliament that banished her from Serbia, until forcibly ejected (1891); settled in Biarritz, where she took pity upon a Serbian widow, Draga; when son became king (1893), returned to Belgrade and reestablished herself as queen; was soon sent packing once more; would eventually go head-to-head with Draga, her son's future queen; throughout life, was acknowledged as a religious, chaste, and charitable woman; also proved herself capable of political machination, adroit manipulation of public opinion, cruelty, and a fierce stubbornness. ❖ See also *Women in World History.*

NATHALIE SHEREMETSKAIA (1880–1952). See *Sheremetskaia, Natalia.*

NATHAN, Annie Florance (1867–1951). See *Meyer, Annie Nathan.*

NATHAN, Maud (1862–1946). American social reformer and suffragist. Born Oct 20, 1862, in New York, NY; died Dec 15, 1946, in New York, NY; dau. of Robert Weeks Nathan (member of NY Stock Exchange and railroad general passenger agent) and Annie Augusta (Florance) Nathan; sister of Annie Nathan Meyer (1867–1951); m. Frederick Nathan (stockbroker), 1880; children: Annette Florance Nathan (c. 1887–1895).

❖ Formed Consumers' League of New York with Josephine Shaw Lowell and others (1890); became president of the league (1897); was probably the 1st woman to give a speech in a synagogue in place of a rabbi's sermon (1897); was 1st vice president, Equal Suffrage League of New York, and chair of the suffrage committee of the Progressive (Bull Moose) Party (1912); resigned as president of the Consumers' League and named honorary president for life (1917); writings include *The Story of an Epoch-Making Movement* (1926). ❖ See also autobiography *Once Upon a Time and To-day* (1933); and *Women in World History*.

NATHAN, Nell Rehutai (1895–1967). *See Maihi, Rehutai.*

NATHANIEL, Cathy (1949—). American murderer. Born 1949 in US.
❖ As prostitute, picked up Chicago lawyer Steven Ticho in bar and shot him to death in his apartment in John Hancock Building (May 3, 1979); with co-worker and housemate Bernice Albright, who had assisted in seducing Ticho, looted his apartment after the murder and used Ticho's credit cards the next day; was arrested, found guilty of murder (Oct 25, 1979) and sentenced to 35 years in prison.

NATHANSEN, Fritze (1925—). *See Carstensen-Nathansen, Fritze.*

NATHHORST, Louise (1955—). Swedish equestrian. Born Mar 26, 1955, in Sweden. ❖ At Los Angeles Olympics, won a bronze medal in team dressage (1984).

NATHOY, Lalu (1853–1933). Chinese-born ex-slave and entrepreneur.
Name variations: Polly Bemis. Born Sept 11, 1853, in Northern China; died Nov 6, 1933; married Charlie Bemis (saloonkeeper), 1894.
❖ Kidnapped from China when she was 18 years old, was sold to a slave trader en route to America; on her arrival (1872), was auctioned off as a slave at a public auction for $2,500, renamed Polly, and forced to work in a saloon in a mining town in Idaho; through her bravery and wit, made friends and, with their help, won her freedom; became a successful entrepreneur, had a happy marriage, and earned the respect of her fellow townspeople.

NATION, Carry (1846–1911). American temperance leader. Born Carry Amelia Moore (1st name often erroneously spelled Carrie) in Garrard Co., Kentucky, Nov 25, 1846; died in Leavenworth, Kansas, after a period of hospitalization, June 9, 1911; dau. of George Moore (Kentucky slaveowner) and Mary Campbell Moore; obtained teaching certificate from Missouri State Normal School (now Missouri State University, Warrensburg); m. Charles Gloyd (doctor), 1867 (died c. 1868); m. David Nation (journalist, lawyer, and minister), 1877 (div. 1901); children: (1st m.) Charlien. ❖ Militant temperance leader who led a campaign of saloon-smashers in Kansas and became a national celebrity; married 1st husband, an alcoholic (1867), then left him (1868); married David Nation in a loveless marriage of convenience (1877); moved with him to Medicine Lodge, KS, a prohibition state (1889); during a 3-day religious vigil, realized that her mission on Earth was to fight the menace of alcohol; began saloon smashing campaign at Medicine Lodge, Kiowa, and Wichita, KS (1900); was divorced by husband for desertion (1901); began national lecture tours; went on lecture tour of Britain (1908); contemptuous of compromise, was willing to suffer repeated arrests and imprisonments as witness to her belief that alcohol was an unmitigated evil. ❖ See also autobiography *The Use and Need of the Life of Carry A. Nation* (Steves, 1909); Herbert Asbury, *Carry Nation* (Knopf, 1929); Robert L. Taylor, *Vessel of Wrath: The Life and Times of Carry Nation* (New American Library, 1966); and *Women in World History*.

NATTRASS, Susan (1950—). Canadian trapshooter. Born Nov 5, 1950, in Medicine Hat, Alberta, Canada; dau. of Floyd Nattrass (champion trapshooter); has a PhD in philosophy. ❖ Placed 1st at World championships (1974–75 and 1977–79); was the 1st woman to compete in trapshooting at the Olympic Games (1976); as a 4-time Olympian, competed at Sydney Olympics (2000).

NATWICK, Mildred (1908–1994). American actress. Born June 19, 1908, in Baltimore, Maryland; died Oct 25, 1994, in New York, NY; dau. of Joseph Natwick and Mildred Marion (Dawes) Natwick; attended Bryn Mawr School, Baltimore, and Bennett Junior College, Millbrook, NY; never married; no children. ❖ Pegged for character roles early in her career, made Broadway debut as Mrs. Noble in *Carry Nation* (1932); made London debut as Aunt Mabel in *The Day I Forgot* (1933); a veteran of over 40 stage productions, was memorable as the secretary in Shaw's *Candida*, as Madame Arcati in Coward's *Blithe Spirit*, for which she received a Tony nomination, and the shrewish wife in *Waltz of the Toreadors* (1957); appearing in films from 1940 on, made 4 with director

John Ford: *The Long Voyage Home* (1940), *The Three Godfathers* (1949), *She Wore a Yellow Ribbon* (1949), and *The Quiet Man* (1952); repeated Broadway role as the mother in film version of *Barefoot in the Park* (1967), for which she received an Academy Award nomination as Best Supporting Actress; made singing debut on stage in *70 Girls 70* (1971), winning a 2nd Tony nomination. Awarded an Emmy for tv series "The Snoop Sisters" (1973–74). ❖ See also *Women in World History*.

NAUBERT, Christiane Benedikte (1756–1819). German novelist and translator. Name variations: Benedikte Naubert. Born Christiane Benedikte Eugenie Hebenstreit, Sept 13, 1756, in Leipzig, Germany; died Jan 12, 1819, in Leipzig; m. Lorenz Holderieder, 1797 (died 1800); m. Johann Georg Naubert. ❖ Educated in science, music, and classical languages, published over 80 works, which draw upon folktales and medieval legends, including *Heerfort und Klärchen* (1779), *Walter von Montbarry, Großmeister des Tempelordens* (1786), *Die neuen Volksmärchen der Deutschen* (The New German Folktales, 4 vols., 1789–93), and *Velleda: Ein Zauberroman* (1795).

NAUDÉ, Adèle (1910–1981). South African poet and travel writer.
Name variations: Adele Naude. Born 1910 in Pretoria, South Africa; died 1981. ❖ Wrote *Stroeihoed en Sonbril* (1965) and *Tousandale aan my Voete* (1968) about travels with husband through North America, Middle East, and Europe; published 4 vols. of poetry in English, *Pity the Spring* (1953), *No Longer at Ease* (1956), *Only a Setting Forth* (1965) and *Time and Memory* (1974); also published book of photographs of 19th-century Cape Town, *Cape Album* (1979). ❖ See also memoir *Rondebosch and Round About* (1973).

NAVARRE, queen of.
See Estefania of Barcelona (fl. 1038).
See Munia Elvira (d. 1067).
See Placencia (fl. 1068).
See Marguerite de l'Aigle (d. 1141).
See Sancha of Castile and Leon (d. 1179).
See Urraca of Castile (d. 1179).
See Constance of Toulouse.
See Margaret de Foix (fl. 1190–1210).
See Blanche of Artois (c. 1247–1302).
See Isabella Capet (fl. 1250).
See Margaret de Foix (d. 1258).
See Joan I of Navarre (1273–1305).
See Margaret of Burgundy (1290–1315).
See Jane of France (fl. 1300s).
See Joan II of Navarre (1309–1349).
See Jane of France (1343–1373).
See Blanche of Navarre (1385–1441).
See Eleanor Trastamara (d. 1415).
See Eleanor of Navarre (1425–1479).
See Joanna Enriquez (1425–1468).
See Catherine de Foix (c. 1470–1517).
See Margaret of Angoulême (1492–1549).
See Jeanne d'Albret (1528–1572).
See Margaret of Valois (1553–1615).

NAVARRO, Mary de (1859–1940). *See Anderson, Mary.*

NAVASHINA-KRANDIEVSKAYA, Natalia (1923—). *See Krandievskaya, Natalia.*

NAVRATILOVA, Martina (1956—). Czech-born tennis player. Born Martina Subertova, Oct 18, 1956, in Prague, Czechoslovakia (now Czech Republic); dau. of Jana (Semanska) Subert Navratil and Miroslav Kamil Subert; stepdaughter of Miroslav Navratil. ❖ At 13, was the youngest player on the Czech national tennis team (1969); allowed by Communist government then in power to compete on US Tennis Association circuit (1973); during another US tour, defected and sought American citizenship (1975), which was granted (1981); during years of professional play, won 167 singles events, including 9 Wimbledon titles and 4 US Open titles, 165 doubles championships, and 55 mixed-doubles championships; was one of the 1st women to use rigorous strength training to bring a highly aggressive and physically demanding style to the women's circuit; by the time of retirement from singles play (1994), had won a record-setting $20 million in prize money; made a lively comeback in singles play (2004), winning 4 out of 6 tournament matches to the delight of tennis fans; though career was complicated by her public candor about her sexuality, continues to act as a well-known speaker for gay and women's rights. Inducted into the Tennis Hall of Fame in Newport (2000). ❖ See also (autobiography) with George Vecsey, *Martina* (Knopf, 1985); Adrienne Blue, *Martina Unauthorized* (Gollancz, 1995); and *Women in World History.*

NAWAB ALIYA (c. 1592–1631). *See Mumtaz Mahal.*

NAWFAL, Hind (fl. 1890s). Syrian journalist. Fl. in 1890s. ❖ A Syrian Christian, launched the 1st women's journal published in Egypt, *al-Fatah* (also seen as *al-Fatat*), in Alexandria (Nov 20, 1892).

NAYADU, Sarojini (1879–1949). *See Naidu, Sarojini.*

NAYAR, Sushila (1914–2001). Indian physician. Born Dec 26, 1914, in Gujarat, Pakistan; died Jan 3, 2001, at her home in Sevagram, Gujarat; studied at Lady Hardinge Medical College, Delhi; Punjab University, MBBS; sister of Pyarelal Nayar. ❖ India's 1st woman minister, was initially a personal physician to Mohandas Gandhi and a practitioner of Gandhian philosophy; was imprisoned along with Mohandas and Kasturba Gandhi for participation in Independence Movement (1942–44); after the Mahatma's death, did post-graduate work at Johns Hopkins University in US (1950); returning to India, was a medical officer and started a TB sanatorium in Faridabad; served as minister of Health, Rehabilitation, and Transport in Nehru's cabinet in Delhi State (1952–55) and speaker of Delhi Legislative Assembly (1955–56); was a member of Lower House of Parliament (1957–71 and 1977–79), serving as minister of Union Health (1962–67); was founder director of Mahatma Gandhi Institute of Medical Sciences; served as secretary of Leprosy Board of Mahatma Gandhi Memorial Trust and worked at Kasturba Hospital, New Delhi; wrote *Hamari Ba, Kasturba: Wife of Gandhi* and *Karavas Ki Kahani.*

NAYLOR, Eliot (1908–1967). *See Frankau, Pamela.*

NAYLOR, Elizabeth Mary (1832–1897). *See Palmer, Elizabeth Mary.*

NAYLOR, Genevieve (1915–1989). American photographer. Born in Springfield, Massachusetts, 1915; died in Dobbs Ferry, New York, 1989; attended Vassar College; studied at Art Students League and New School for Social Research; m. Misha Reznikoff (painter), 1946; children: Michael (b. 1947); Peter (b. 1950). ❖ One of the 1st female photojournalists employed by the Associated Press, moved to NY (1935) where she studied with Berenice Abbott; spent 4 years with Associated Press (1937–41), then worked for US State Department (1941–43), photographing Brazilian life under aegis of the "Good Neighbor Policy"; held a solo exhibition of Brazilian photographs at Museum of Fine Arts, NY (1943); worked for *Harper's Bazaar* (1944–58); also freelanced for *McCall's, Vogue, Cosmopolitan, Holiday,* and *Fortune,* and produced a number of serious photojournalism stories for *Look.*

NAYLOR, Gloria (1950—). African-American novelist, playwright and short-story writer. Born Jan 25, 1950, in New York, NY; dau. of Roosevelt Naylor (transit worker, frame-shop worker) and Alberta McAlphin Naylor (telephone operator); sister of Carolyn and Fanny Bernice Naylor; attended Medgar Evers College (1975); Brooklyn College of City University of New York, BA, 1981; Yale University, MA, 1983; married, 1980 (div. 1981). ❖ Published 1st novel, *The Women of Brewster Place* (1982), which earned an American Book Award (1983) and was adapted for tv; published *Linden Hills* (1985); became scholar-in-residence at University of Pennsylvania (1986), teaching as well at New York University, Princeton, Brandeis, Cornell and Boston universities in US and University of Kent in England; published *Mama Day* (1988); established multimedia company, One Way Productions (1990); published novel *Bailey's Café* (1992) which was also adapted for the stage (1994); edited *Children of the Night: The Best Short Stories by Black Writers, 1967 to the Present* (1996); published novel *The Men of Brewster Place* (1998). Received President's Medal from Brooklyn College; Distinguished Writer Award, Mid-Atlantic Writers Association (1983); Candace Award of National Coalition of One Hundred Black Women (1986); Lillian Smith Award (1989). ❖ See also Virginia Fowler, *Gloria Naylor: In Search of Sanctuary* (Twayne, 1996).

NAYLOR, Phyllis Reynolds (1933—). American children's writer. Born Jan 4, 1933, in Anderson, Indiana; dau. of Eugene S. (salesman) and Lura (Schield) Reynolds (teacher); Joliet Junior College, diploma, 1953; American University, BA, 1963; m. 2nd husband, Rex V. Naylor (speech pathologist), May 26, 1960; children: Jeffrey Alan, Michael Scott. ❖ Began career as clinical secretary at Billings Hospital, Chicago (1953–56); was an elementary schoolteacher in Hazelcrest, Illinois (1956); editorial assistant with *NEA Journal,* Washington, DC (1959–60); became a full-time writer (1960); active in civil rights and peace organizations, was also president of Children's Book Guild

(1974–75, 1983–84); wrote over 100 books, including *Wrestle the Mountain* (1971), *How Lazy Can You Get?* (1979), *A String of Chances* (1982), *The Solomon System* (1983), *Night Cry* (1984), which won the Edgar Allan Poe Award, *The Dark of the Tunnel* (1985), *The Keeper* (1986), *The Year of the Gopher* (1987), *Maudie in the Middle* (1988), the popular Alice series, including *The Agony of Alice* (1985), and the "Witch" trilogy. Won the Newbery Medal for *Shiloh* (1992). ❖ See also autobiographies, *Crazy Love: An Autobiographical Account of Marriage and Madness* (1977) and *How I Came to Be a Writer* (1979).

NAYMUSHINA, Yelena (1964—). *See Naimushina, Elena.*

NAZAR, Krystyna (b. 1924). *See Moszumanska-Nazar, Krystyna.*

NAZARÉ, Maria Escolástica Da Conceição (1894–1986). Brazilian spiritual leader. Name variations: Mãe (means mother) Menininha do Gantois or Mother Menininha; Mãe Menininha do Gantois; Maria Escolastica Da Conceicão Nazare or Maria Escolástica da Conceição Nazareth. Born Feb 10, 1894, in Salvador, Bahia, Brazil; died Aug 13, 1986, in Salvador; dau. of Joaquim de Assunção and Maria da Glória (spiritual leader); thought to be descended from noble Nigerian lineage; m. Alvaro MacDowell de Oliveira (lawyer); children: 2 daughters, including Cleusa Millet (c. 1931–1998, spiritual leader). ❖ Beloved Afro-Brazilian spiritual leader who sought to preserve cultural identity of Afro-Bahian people, was initiated into *candomble* (term used for Afro-Brazilian religion) at 8 months; at 28, assumed leadership position of *iyalorixá* (mother-of-saint) in Alto do Gantois *terreiro* (sacred space for *candomble* ceremonies), following footsteps of mother, grandmother and great-grandmother; experienced police persecution of religious practice (1920s–30s), but managed to skirt restrictions and continue to celebrate *candomble;* opened up *terriero* and received visits from artists, intellectuals and politicians after 1945, when Brazilian society began to liberalize and democratize and repression of Afro-Brazilian religion lifted; became most famous *iyalorixá* of Bahia region of Brazil; did not permit commercialization and thus degradation of *candomble* in Alto do Gantois *terreiro,* gaining respect for fidelity to origins; was skilled at using sacred divining shells and sought out by many for advice; opposed to use of spiritual power to do evil; celebrated 50th anniversary of Alto do Gantois *terreiro* with massive gathering, attracting Brazilians and foreigners from all walks of life, including writers, musicians and artists such as Jorge Amado and Mário Cravo; died after long illness (1986); popularity was such that 3 official days of mourning were decreed by government. Honored when Brazilian Mail and Telegraph Corporation placed her image on stamp (1994). ❖ See also Caetano Veloso, et al., eds., *Memorial Mãe Menininha do Gantois* (Fundação Cultural do Estado da Bahia, 1993).

NAZARETH, Maria Escolástica da Conceição (1894–1986). *See Nazaré, Maria Escolástica Da Conceição.*

NAZÁREVA, Kapitolina Valerianovna (1847–1900). Russian novelist and playwright. Name variations: Kapitolina Valerianovna Nazareva. Born 1847 in St. Petersburg, Russia; died 1900. ❖ Published sketches and stories in magazines and journals in St. Petersburg; wrote over 20 novels, dealing with variety of themes and characters, and plays that were staged in Moscow in 1890s; also wrote crime novels, including *In the Grip of Poverty* (1885).

NAZAROVA, Natalya (1979—). Russian runner. Born May 26, 1979, in Moscow, Russia. ❖ Placed 1st for 4 x 400-meter relay at World championships (1999); placed 1st for 400 meters at World Indoor championships (2003, 2004) and 4 x 400-meter relay (1999, 2003, 2004); won a bronze medal at Sydney Olympics (2000) and a silver medal at Athens Olympics (2004), both for 4 x 400-meter relay.

NAZAROVA, Olga (1955—). Soviet runner. Born June 1, 1965, in USSR. ❖ At Seoul Olympics, won a bronze medal in the 400 meters and a gold medal in the 4 x 400-meter relay (1988); at Barcelona Olympics, won a gold medal in the 4 x 400-meter relay (1992).

NAZAROVA-BAGRYANTSEVA, Irina (1957—). Soviet runner. Name variations: Irina Bagryantseva. Born July 31, 1957, in USSR. ❖ At Moscow Olympics, won a gold medal in 4 x 400-meter relay (1980).

NAZIMOVA, Alla (1879–1945). Russian actress, silent-film star, director, and producer. Born Mariam Adelaida Leventon, June 4, 1879, in Yalta, Russia; died July 13, 1945, in Hollywood, CA; studied acting under Constantin Stanislavski; m. Paul Orlenev also seen as Orlenieff (prominent Russian actor); c. 1902 (sep. 1905); m. Charles Bryant (under common law), c. 1914 (sep. after 10 years). ❖ One of the most brilliant theater actresses of her era, entered acting school at 17;

married Paul Orlenieff (c. 1902) and embarked on joint productions of plays; after Russian officials forbade production of their early Zionist play *The Chosen People* (1904), presented it in Berlin, London, and New York, after moving there; enjoyed significant success on stage, specializing in Ibsen plays (1906–16); signed a 99-year lease for a large property on Sunset Boulevard in Hollywood which became known as The Garden of Alla, a gathering place for writers, actors, and directors who were shaping movies in 1920s; made 17 movies, becoming one of the reigning silent-film stars (1916–25); returned to stage (1925), acting, directing and taking occasional movie and radio roles until her death from heart disease at 66 (1945); films include *War Brides* (1916), *Revelation* (1918), (also executive producer) *An Eye for an Eye* (1919), (also exec. prod. and co-screenwriter) *Out of the Fog* (1919), (also exec. prod. and co-screenwriter) *The Brat* (1919), *The Red Lantern* (1919), *Madame Peacock* (1920), *Billions* (1920), (also prod. and dir.) *Camille* (1921), (also prod.) *The Doll's House* (1922), (also prod.) *Salome* (1922), *Madonna of the Streets* (1924), *My Son, My Son* (1925), *Escape* (1940), *Blood and Sand* (1941), *In Our Time* (1944); (as the Marquesa) *The Bridge of San Luis Rey* (1944) and *Since You Went Away* (1945). ❖ See also Gavin Lambert, *Nazimova* (Knopf, 1997); and *Women in World History*.

NAZLI (1894–1978). Queen of Egypt. Name variations: Nazli Sabri or Sabry, Nazli Fouad. Born at Alexandria, June 25, 1894; died in Los Angeles, CA, May 29, 1978; great granddau. of Joseph Anthelme Sève, known as Suliyman Pasha (died 1860); m. Fuad I, aka Fouad, king of Egypt, May 26, 1919; children: Prince Faruk (b. 1920, later King Farouk I, r. 1936–52), Princess Fawzia (b. 1921, who married the shah of Iran), Princess Faiza (Fevziye, b. 1923), Princess Faika (Feyke, b. 1926), Princess Fathiya (b. 1930). ❖ Was sultana of Egypt until 1922, then queen of Egypt (1922–38), queen mother of Egypt (1938–51), queen mother of Egypt and Sudan.

NDEREBA, Catherine (1972—). Kenyan long-distance runner. Born July 21, 1972, in Nyeri, Kenya; m. Anthony Maina; children: Jane (b. 1997). ❖ Won 13 out of 18 road races (1996); won the Boston Marathon (2000, 2001, 2004, 2005), the 1st women to win 4 Boston titles; won Chicago marathon (2000 and 2001), breaking the World record with a time of 2:18.47 (2001); won Avon Global championships 10k (2001); won a silver medal for marathon at Athens Olympics (2004); placed 2nd in NY marathon (2003). Named Road Racer of the Year (1996, 1998).

NEAGLE, Anna (1904–1986). British actress and dancer. Name variations: Dame Anna Neagle; also performed under the name Marjorie Robertson. Born Marjorie Robertson at Forest Gate, London, England, Oct 20, 1904; died June 3, 1986, in West Byfleet, Surrey, England; dau. of Herbert William Robertson (captain in British Maritime Service) and Florence (Neagle) Robertson; m. Herbert Wilcox (film producer and director), 1943 (died 1977); no children. ❖ Star of stage and screen, made stage debut at 13 in *The Wonder Tales*, at Ambassadors' Theatre; was in chorus of *Bubbly* (1925); spent next 5 years in choruses of some of London's top musicals, including *Rose Marie* and *The Desert Song*; went to NY with revue *Wake Up and Dream* (1929); cast in a small role for *Stand Up and Sing* (1931) and offered film role opposite Jack Buchanan by Herbert Wilcox for *Goodnight, Vienna* (1932); came to screen prominence in title role of *Nell Gwynn* (1934), followed by *Peg of Old Drury* (1935), in which she portrayed Peg Woffington; with Wilcox, launched a series of historical films, including *Victoria the Great* (1937), which brought financial success, and *Nurse Edith Cavell* (1939); during WWII, made several films at RKO in Hollywood, including updates of musicals *Irene* (1940), *No, No, Nanette* (1940), and *Sunny* (1941); back in England, portrayed English flyer Amy Johnson in *They Flew Alone* (1942); other films include *The Yellow Canary* (1943), *Piccadilly Incident* (1946), *The Courtneys of Curzon Street* (1947), and *Odette* (1950); frequently returned to the stage, portraying Rosalind in *As You Like It* and Olivia in *Twelfth Night* (1934), Peter Pan at London Palladium (1937); also appeared in *The Glorious Days* (1953) and *Charlie Girl* (1965), which ran for 2,000 performances. Named Dame of the British Empire (1969). ❖ See also *Women in World History*.

NEAL, Alice (1827–1863). See Haven, Emily Bradley Neal.

NEAL, Jean (1871–1927). See Brown, Abbie Farwell.

NEAL, Patricia (1926—). American actress. Born Patsy Louise Neal, Jan 20, 1926, in Packard, KY; dau. of William Burdette Neal (transportation manager) and Eura Mildred (Petty) Neal; attended Northwestern University, 1943–45; m. Roald Dahl (writer), July 2, 1953 (div. Nov 1983); children: Olivia (1955–1962); Tessa (b. 1957); Theo (b. 1960); Ophelia (b. 1964); Lucy (b. 1965). ❖ Distinguished actress, made Broadway debut as Regina Giddens in *Another Part of the Forest* (1946), for which she won Donaldson Award, Drama Critics Circle Award, and 1st Tony Award ever conferred; other stage appearances include an acclaimed performance as Martha Dobie in *The Children's Hour* (1952); made London debut as Catherine Holly in *Suddenly Last Summer* (1958); made film debut opposite Ronald Reagan in *John Loves Mary* (1949), a comedy for which she was ill-suited; son endured a brain-damaging injury (1960), young daughter died (1962), and had a nearly fatal series of strokes (1965); struggled to reclaim life, then reestablished career (1968), winning Oscar nomination for Best Actress for *The Subject Was Roses*; other films include *The Fountainhead* (1949), *The Hasty Heart* (1950), *Bright Leaf* (1950); *Three Secrets* (1950), *The Day the Earth Stood Still* (1951), *A Face in the Crowd* (1957), *Breakfast at Tiffany's* (1961), *In Harm's Way* (1965), *A Mother's Right: The Elizabeth Morgan Story* (1992), *Heidi* (1993) and *Cookie's Fortune* (1999). Won an Academy Award for Best Supporting Actress for *Hud* (1963); won an Emmy for portrayal of Olivia Walton in tv movie "The Homecoming," which inspired "The Waltons." ❖ See also autobiography (with Richard DeNeut) *As I Am* (Simon & Schuster, 1988); Barry Farrell, *Pat and Roald* (Random, 1969); (tv movie) *The Patricia Neal Story*, starring Glenda Jackson (1981); and *Women in World History*.

NEALL, Gail (1955—). Australian swimmer. Born Aug 2, 1955, in Australia; trained in Sydney under Forbes Carlile; m. Ross Yeo; children: 4. ❖ At Munich Olympics, won a gold medal in 400-meter indiv. medley (1972); won 3 Australian national championships. Inducted into International Swimming Hall of Fame (1996).

NEALY, Frances (1918–1997). African-American tap dancer. Name variations: Frances E. Nealy. Born Oct 14, 1918, in San Diego, CA; died May 23, 1997, in Hollywood, CA. ❖ Danced in the chorus of numerous shows in Los Angeles (late 1930s–40s); worked for Leonard Reed at Shep's Playhouse, the leading L.A. club for black shows (1940s); performed with Bill Robinson in his show *Born Happy* in San Francisco (1940s) and later again in Philadelphia at the Shangri-la club; worked with Count Basie at Orpheum Theater in Los Angeles where she performed a 15-minute act with Ike Parrish as Parrish and Nealy; had small roles in films, including *The Manchurian Candidate* (1962), *My Brother's Wedding* (1983) and *Ghostbusters* (1984).

NEAR, Holly (1949—). American singer, songwriter, feminist, pacifist and social justice advocate. Born June 6, 1949, in Ukiah, CA; sister of Laurel and Timothy Near. ❖ Songwriter and folksinger, began career on Broadway in *Hair*; formed her own recording label, Redwood Records (1972), and used her music for political activism; recorded over 20 albums, including *Early Warnings, And Still We Sing, Edge, Harp* and *Simply Love*; with Ronnie Gilbert, released 3 albums, including *This Train Still Runs!* (1996); also performed with Pete Seeger, Arlo Guthrie, Mercedes Sosa, Bonnie Raitt, Cris Williamson and Linda Tillery, among others; wrote "We Are a Gentle, Angry People"; films include *The Magic Garden of Stanley Sweetheart* (1970), *Minnie and Moskowitz* (1971), *Slaughterhouse Five* (1972) and *Heartwood* (1998). Named Woman of the Year by *Ms* magazine (1985). ❖ See also autobiography, *Fire in the Rain: Singer in the Storm*.

NEARING, Helen (1904–1995). American writer and environmentalist. Born Helen Knothe in Ridgewood, New Jersey (some sources indicate New York, NY), Feb 23, 1904; died in auto accident near her home in Harborside, Maine, Sept 17, 1995; dau. of Frank Knothe and Maria Obreen Knothe; sister of Alice Knothe; m. Scott Nearing (1883–1983, writer, educator and activist), Dec 1947; no children. ❖ Pioneer of simple living, regarded as a "great-grandparent" of the American back-to-the-land movement and a major personality of modern environmentalism, abandoned New York City with husband for a Vermont homestead (1932), where, through hard work and simple living, they turned their backs on American materialism and became 75% self-sufficient; with husband, published *Living the Good Life* (1954) which became a virtual bible of homesteaders, and bought a 140-acre abandoned farm in Harborside, Maine, where they built an impressive stone house with their own hands (1973–76); other writings include *Loving and Leaving the Good Life* (Chelsea Green, 1995), *Wise Words for the Good Life* (Chelsea Green, 1999) and with husband, *Continuing the Good Life: Half a Century of Homesteading* (Schocken, 1979), *The Good Life: Helen and Scott Nearing's Sixty Years of Self-Sufficient Living* (Schocken, 1989) and *The Good Life Album of Helen and Scott Nearing* (Dutton, 1974). ❖ See also *Women in World History*.

NEARY, Colleen (1952—). American ballet dancer. Born May 23, 1952, in Miami, FL; sister of Patricia Neary; trained in NY at School of American Ballet. ❖ Danced with New York City Ballet (1970s), performing solo roles in numerous Balanchine works, including *Tchaikovsky Piano Concerto, Brahms-Schoenberg Quartet,* and *Jewels;* created roles for Balanchine's *Cortège Hongrois* (1973), *Coppélia* (1974), *Gaspard de la Nuit* (1975), and *Kammermusik II* (1978), as well as for Tanner's *Concerto for Two Solo Pianos* (1971), Massine's *Ode* (1972), and D'Amboise's *Sinfonietta* (1975) and *Sarabande et Danse II* (1975); began to dance and teach at sister's Geneva Ballet (1979).

NEARY, Patricia (1942—). American ballet dancer. Born Oct 27, 1942, in Miami, FL. ❖ Danced a season with National Ballet of Canada; danced with New York City Ballet (1960–68), where she created solo role for Balanchine's *Jewels* (1967) and performed in numerous works of his, including *Apollo, Concerto Barocco, Don Quixote* and *Divertimento No. 15;* moved to Europe (1968) where she staged numerous works by Balanchine, served as ballet master of German Opera Ballet (1971–73) and became director of Geneva Ballet (1973).

NECKER, Anne Louise Germain (1766–1817). See *Staël, Germaine de.*

NECKER, Suzanne (1739–1794). French-Swiss essayist and salonnière. Name variations: Suzanne Curchod; Mme Necker. Born Suzanne Curchod in France, 1739; died 1794; dau. of Louis Curchod (pastor); grew up near Lausanne; m. Jacques Necker (Swiss banker and French finance minister), 1764; children: Germaine de Staël (1766–1817). ❖ Hosted a successful salon for philosophers and encyclopaedists and was prized for her honesty and intelligence; left behind some miscellaneous writings, published as *Mélanges extraits des manuscrits* (Various Extracts from Manuscripts, 1798) and *Nouveaux Mélanges* (Further Extracts, 1801); promoted the education of women and also advocated a court of women to adjudicate petitions for legal separations. ❖ See also *Women in World History.*

NECKER DE SAUSSURE, Albertine (1766–1841). Swiss writer. Born 1766; died 1841; dau. of Horace-Bénédict de Saussure (1740–1799, Swiss physicist and geologist); cousin of Germaine de Staël (1766–1817); married into the Necker family. ❖ Cousin to Germaine de Staël and an intimate friend, was a writer whose chief works were *Notice sur le caractère et les écrits de Mme de Staël* (1820) and her treatise on children's education, *L'Éducation progressive, étude du cours de la vie* (1828–32, 3 vols.); also translated Schlegel's lectures on theater. ❖ See also *Women in World History.*

NECULA, Veronica (1967—). Romanian rower. Born May 15, 1967, in Romania. ❖ At Seoul Olympics, won a bronze medal in coxed fours and a silver medal in coxed eights (1988).

NECULAI, Viorica (1967—). Romanian rower. Born Feb 6, 1967, in Romania. ❖ At Barcelona Olympics, won a silver medal in coxed eights (1992).

NECULITA, Daisy (1974—). See *Neculita, Maria.*

NECULITA, Maria (1974—). Romanian gymnast. Name variations: Daisy Neculita. Born Mar 31, 1974, in Hunedoara, Romania. ❖ Won Romanian International (1990, 1992); at World championships, won a silver medal for balance beam and bronze medals for team all-around and floor exercises (1991) and a silver for beam and bronze for floor exercises (1992); at Barcelona Olympics, won a silver medal in team all-around (1992); won Trophee Massilia, South African Cup, and Balkan championships (1992).

NEDELCU, Elena (1964—). See *Georgescu, Elena.*

NEDREAAS, Torborg (1906–1987). Norwegian short-story writer and literary critic. Born Nov 13, 1906, in Bergen, Norway; died June 30, 1987; married a wealthy man (div. 1939); children: 2 sons. ❖ Lived in Paris for a year; during WWII, married a Norwegian communist leader; adopted anti-fascist and feminist approach in writing; works include *Før det ringer tredje gang* (1945), *Bak skapet står øksen* (1945), *Av måneskinn gror det ingenting* (1947, trans. as *Nothing Grows by Moonlight*), *Trylleglasset* (1950), *Stoppested* (1953), *Musikk fra en blå bronn* (1960, trans. as *Music from a Blue Well*), *Den siste polka* (1965), *Det dumme hjertet* (1976), *Vintervår* (1982) and *Gjennom et prisme* (1983).

NEEDHAM, Dorothy (1896–1987). English biochemist. Name variations: Dorothy Mary Needham. Born Dorothy Mary Moyle, Sept 22, 1896, in London, England; died Dec 22, 1987; Girton College, Cambridge, MA, 1923, PhD, 1926, DSc, 1945; m. Joseph Needham (Chinese science & technology history expert), 1924. ❖ Taught and researched at University of Cambridge's Biochemical Laboratory (1920–40, 1946–63); while at Cambridge, taught sporadically in Belgium, US, Germany and France (1928–40); was a research worker for Ministry of Supply (1940–43); in China, served as chemical advisor and acting director of Sino-British Science Co-operation Office (1944–45); elected a Lucy Cavendish College fellow (1965 and 1966); was the 1st woman fellow of Gonville and Caius College (1979); wrote *Machina carnis: The Biochemistry of Muscular Contraction in Its Historical Development* (1971) and (with M. Teich) *Sourcebook in the History of Biochemistry, 1740 to 1940.*

NEEDHAM, Elizabeth (d. 1731). English procuress. Name variations: Mother Needham. Born Elizabeth Needham in UK; died in London, England, 1731. ❖ Drugged young girls to supply London bordellos; convicted for keeping a disorderly house, was placed in a pillory where she was pelted with stones by mobs; died of her injuries.

NEEL, Alexandra (1868–1969). See *David-Neel, Alexandra.*

NEEL, Alice (1900–1984). American painter. Born Jan 28, 1900, in Merion Square, Pennsylvania; died Oct 13, 1984, in New York, NY; dau. of George Neel (railroad clerk) and Alice Concross (Hartley) Neel; graduate of Philadelphia School of Design for Women (now Moore College of Art), 1925; m. Carlos Enríquez (artist), June 1, 1925 (sep. 1930); lived with Kenneth Doolittle (sailor), 1931–33; lived with José Santiago (musician), 1935–39; children: Santillana Enríquez (1926–1927); Isabella Lillian Enríquez (b. 1928); Richard Neel (b. 1939); Hartley Stockton Neel (b. 1941). ❖ Artist who often referred to herself as "a collector of souls," alluding to the expressionist portraits that comprise the bulk of her work, though she also painted landscapes, cityscapes, interiors, and still lifes; consigned to canvas her family, friends, and lovers, as well as celebrities and derelicts, in an effort to record the human comedy—much the way Balzac did in literature—revealing through them a unique and poignant insight into 20th-century life; went unrecognized by her peers and the public for years; did not begin to capture the attention of the art world until 1960s; saw long-overdue retrospective exhibition of her work at Whitney Museum in NY (1974), 10 years before her death. ❖ See also Patricia Hills, *Alice Neel* (Abrams, 1983); and *Women in World History.*

NEELISSEN, Catharina (1961—). Dutch rower. Born Nov 4, 1961, in Netherlands. ❖ At Los Angeles Olympics, won a bronze medal in coxed eights (1984).

NEERA (1846–1918). See *Zuccari, Anna.*

NEF, Sonja (1972—). Swiss Alpine skier. Born April 19, 1972, in Urnäsch, Switzerland; sister of Willi and Susan Nef (both skiers). ❖ Won 1st World Cup giant slalom (1999); won 6 of 8 World Cup giant slaloms (2000–01) to take the World title; won a bronze medal for giant slalom at Salt Lake City Olympics (2002).

NEFERTARI (c. 1295–1256 BCE). Egyptian queen. Name variations: Nefertary; Nefertari-Merymut. Born c. 1295 BCE; died 1256 BCE (some sources cite 1255); m. Ramses II, king of Egypt (r. 1304–1236 BCE), c. 1280; children: 1 daughter; 1 son Amem-hir-khopshef (died young). ❖ Chief queen of Pharaoh Ramses the Great of ancient Egypt and a great beauty, judging from contemporary paintings; was apparently favored over Ramses other "chief wife" Esenofer (Istnofret), because she appears prominently on Ramses' monuments; was buried in her magnificent tomb, discovered in 1904, which is hewn into a mountain in the Valley of the Queens near modern Luxor. ❖ See also *Women in World History.*

NEFERTITI (c. 1375–1336 BCE). Egyptian queen. Name variations: Nefertiit, Nefretiti, Nofretete or Nofretiti. Born c. 1375 BCE; died 1336 BCE; probably dau. of the sun-king Amenhotep III (known as The Magnificent) and one of his many wives; sister of Mutnedjnet (c. 1360–1326 BCE); m. Amenhotep IV, later known as Akhenaten (c. 1385–1350 BCE), pharaoh of Egypt; children: 6 daughters, Meritaten, Meketaten, Ankhesenpaaten (Ankhesenpaten), Neferneferuaten minor, Neferneferure, and Satepenre. ❖ Ancient Egyptian queen who appears to have ruled with her husband (and if so was the only queen of the pharaonic period known to have done this) and may have even ruled independently for a short time following husband's death. Whether the period of her greatest power and influence was early in husband's reign (c. 1348 BCE) or at its end (c. 1338 BCE) is debatable. What *is* known is that she was extraordinarily beautiful and enjoyed great prominence and power during her adulthood and, after her death, her memory was hated and the object of a systematic persecution. During winter of 1912–13, German archaeologists working at the site of ancient city at Tell el-Amarna discovered Queen Nefertiti's now-famous painted portrait bust toppled over on the floor in the ruins of the studio of an ancient sculptor named Thutmose. Ever since its display and publication in 1923, this image of Nefertiti has been universally adored, and the sculpture—the long graceful neck supporting the lovely and serene face under the soaring conical crown (which was hers alone)—has been constantly reproduced around the world on everything from jewelry to postage stamps. ❖ See also C. Aldred, *Akhenaten and Nefertiti* (Viking, 1973); J. Samson, *Nefertiti and Cleopatra: Queen-Monarchs of Ancient Egypt* (Rubicon, 1985); Joyce Tyldesley, *Nefertiti: Egypt's Sun Queen* (Viking, 1999); and *Women in World History*.

NEFF, Hildegarde (b. 1925). *See Knef, Hildegarde.*

NEFRUSOBEK (fl. c. 1787–1783 BCE). *See Sobek-neferu.*

NEGRI, Ada (1870–1945). Italian poet. Born in Lodi, Feb 3, 1870; died in Milan, Jan 11, 1945; dau. of Giuseppe Negri and Vittoria Cornalba Negri; married Giovanni Garlanda, 1896; children: Bianca and Vittoria. ❖ Poet whose literary reputation suffered due to Mussolini's enthusiasm for her works, was the 1st Italian woman writer to spring from the lower classes; became famous overnight as a voice of working-class protest with publication of verse, *Fatalita* (1892); was awarded the Milli Prize for poetry (1894) and became a hero to the growing Italian Socialist movement; book was banned by Roman Catholic Church; continued to explore the themes that had aroused so much public interest in next book of poems, *Tempeste* (Tempests, 1896); published *Maternita* (Maternity, 1904), *Esilio* (Exile, 1914), a book of poems prompted by the final collapse of her marriage in 1913, and *Le solitarie* (Solitary Women, 1917), a collection of short stories relating the lives of unhappy women, artistically powerful statements that were autobiographical in nature; published *Il libro di Mara* (Mara's Book, 1919), a work many critics hold to be her most personal; published bestselling autobiographical novel, *Stella mattutina* (Evening Star, 1921); also wrote (short stories) *Finestre alte* (High Windows, 1923), (poetry) *I canti dell'isola* (Songs of the Island, 1925), (prose) *Le strade* (Roads, 1926) and *Sorelle* (Sisters, 1929), (verse) *Vespertina* (Evening Star, 1930) and *Di giorno in giorno* (From Day to Day, 1932) and (poetry) *Il dono* (The Gift, 1936), which earned the Firenze Prize; received Gold Medal of the Ministry of Education for her poetry (1938); was chosen, at Mussolini's insistence, as a full member of the Royal Academy of Italy (1940), the 1st, and only, woman member of this Fascist-blessed body; after the war, was considered by critics to be either a passé writer or an intellectual tainted by association with Mussolini; her work is now in the process of being reevaluated by scholars. ❖ See also *Women in World History*.

NEGRI, Pola (1894–1987). Polish-born actress. Born Barbara Apollonia (or Appolonia) Chalupec or Chalupiec in Lipno or Janowa, Poland, Dec 31, 1894; died in San Antonio, Texas, Aug 1, 1987; dau. of Jerzy Chalupec (tin master) and Eleanora (de Kielczeska) Chalupec; attended Warsaw Imperial Academy of Dramatic Arts; m. Count Eugene Dambski (diplomat), 1920 (div. 1922); m. Prince Serge Mdivani, 1927 (div. 1931); no children. ❖ In Warsaw, made film debut as a dancer in *Niewonica Zmyslow* (*Love and Passion*), a movie she financed and wrote herself; made a series of films in Germany for Ernst Lubitsch, including *Madame Dubarry* (1919), which brought her international attention and was released in US as *Passion;* came to US (1922); though most of her memorable work was done in Poland and Germany, her mysterious persona and colorful love life made her one of the most enticing personalities of the American silent era; had highly publicized liaisons with Charlie Chaplin and Rudolph Valentino; films include *Bella Donna* (1923), *The Cheat* (1923), *The Spanish Dancer* (1923), *A Woman of the World* (1925), *Barbed Wire* (1927), *Hotel Imperial* (1927), *The Woman from Moscow* (1928), *Mazurka* (1935), *Hi Diddle Diddle* (1943) and *The Moonspinners* (1964). ❖ See also *Memoirs of a Star* (Doubleday, 1970); and *Women in World History*.

NEGRON MUÑOZ, Mercedes (1895–1973). Puerto Rican poet. Name variations: Mercedes Munoz; Clara Lair. Born 1895 in Barranquitas, Puerto Rico; died Aug 26, 1973, in San Juan, Puerto Rico; dau. of Quintín Negron. ❖ Works include *Arras de Cristal* (1937) and *Trópico amargo* (1950); collection of poems published by Instituto de Literatura Puertorriqueña (1961) and fragments of memoir published in magazine of Institute.

NEGRONE, Carina (1911—). Italian aviator. Name variations: Marchesa Carina Negrone; Carina Negrone di Cambiaso. Born Carina Massone,

June 4, 1911, in Bogliasco, Italy; m. Marquis Ambrogio V. Negrone (b. 1906); children: 2. ❖ Pioneering aviator, presided over Genoa's Aeroclub for 30 years; taught by fighter pilot Giorgio Parodi, earned her pilot's license at 22 (1933); began entering international competitions (1935); set the world altitude record (June 1935) and earned instant fame; broke 7 records (1935–54).

NEHER, Carola (1900–1942). German actress. Name variations: Karoline Josefovna Henschke. Born Karoline Neher in Munich, Germany, Nov 2, 1900; died of typhus in Sol-Ilezk transit camp, near Orenburg, USSR, June 26, 1942; dau. of Josef Neher (performed with Munich Philharmonic Orchestra) and Katerina Ziegler Neher; m. Alfred Henschke (expressionist author known as Klabund), 1925; m. Anatol Becker; children: son Georg Anatol Becker. ❖ Acclaimed actress of Weimar Republic, began appearing on stage in Munich and was soon dancing in Baden-Baden; by 1922, was regularly employed at Munich's Kammerspiele; began relationship with Bertolt Brecht; made film debut in *Mysterien eines Frisiersalons* (Mysteries of a Barber Shop); could be seen regularly on stage in several German cities, including Breslau (now Wroclaw, Poland), where she secured a contract at Vereinigtes Theater; became one of the best-known actresses on German stage; appeared in several of 1st husband's stage works, including *Der Kreidekreis* (The Chalk Circle), *Brennende Erde* (Burning Earth) and *XYZ*; appeared as Polly Peachum in *Die Dreigroschenoper* (The Threepenny Opera) on stage (1929) and in film (1931); appeared as Eliza in *Pygmalion* (Deutsches Theater, Berlin, 1928), Magdalena in *Ehen werden im Himmel geschlossen* (Marriages are Made in Heaven) and Marianne in *Geschichten aus dem Wiener Wald* (Tales from the Vienna Woods, 1931); seeking refuge from Nazism (1933), fled to Soviet Union, where she spent the last 6 years of her life wrongly imprisoned. ❖ See also *Women in World History*.

NEHRU, Kamala (1899–1936). Indian leader. Born Kamala Kaul, 1899; died Feb 28, 1936; dau. of prosperous entrepreneurs in Delhi; m. Jawaharlal Nehru (1889–1964, 1st prime minister of independent India), Feb 1916; children: Indira Gandhi (1917–1984). ❖ At 17, entered into an arranged marriage with 26-year-old Jawaharlal Nehru; encouraged him to join the Nationalist movement; though diagnosed with tuberculosis (1925), worked tirelessly as president of Allahabad Congress Committee and later as a substitute member of Congress Working Committee, the high command of the Nationalist movement; spent 6 months in Lucknow Central Jail (1931); died of TB at 37. ❖ See also *Women in World History*.

NEHRU, Vijaya Lakshmi (1900–1990). *See Pandit, Vijaya Lakshmi.*

NEHUA, Katerina (1903–1948). New Zealand swimmer. Name variations: Katerina Waetford. Born Feb 6, 1903, at Whakapara in Bay of Islands, New Zealand; died June 15, 1948, in Sydney, Australia; dau. of Hare Paerau Waetford (bushman) and Mereana Teruhi Nehua; m. Joseph Darley (farmer), 1923; children: 4. ❖ Participated in endurance swimming contests popularized during depression years and eventually broke world record with swim of 72 hours 9 minutes (1931); broke own record 2 months later with swim of 72 hours 21 minutes. ❖ See also *Dictionary of New Zealand Biography* (Vol. 4).

NEHUSHTA (fl. 610 BCE). Biblical woman. Dau. of Elnathan of Jerusalem; m. Jehoiakim, king of Judah; children: Jehoiachin, successor to the throne of Judah.

NEIL, Mrs. James (1863–1948). *See Chapman, Edythe.*

NEILL, Elizabeth Grace (1846–1926). New Zealand nurse, hospital administrator, journalist, government official, and social reformer. Name variations: Elizabeth Grace Campbell. Born Elizabeth Grace Campbell, on May 25, 1846, in Edinburgh, Scotland; died Aug 18, 1926, in Wellington, New Zealand; dau. of James Archibald Campbell and Maria Grace (Cameron) Campbell; m. Channing Neill (physician), 1879 (died c. 1890); children: 1 son. ❖ Prevented by father from entering University of Cambridge to become physician, trained as nurse at King's College and Charing Cross Hospital in London (1875–76); appointed superintendent of children's hospital at Pendlebury (1876–79); joined husband on Isle of Wight until his ill health forced family to relocate to Australia (1885); after husband's death, turned to journalism and wrote for Brisbane's *Boomerang* and *Telegraph;* moved to New Zealand and helped to establish union for women workers; was Department of Labor's 1st woman inspector of hospitals (1894–1907); named deputy inspector of mental health facilities (1895); became active in nursing reform, promoting uniform system of training and national examination, and was instrumental in drafting of Nurses Registration Act of 1901, and Midwives Act of 1904; during WWII, was in charge of children's ward at Wellington Hospital. ❖ See also *Dictionary of New Zealand Biography* (Vol. 2).

NEILSON, Adelaide (1846–1880). English actress. Name variations: Lilian Adelaide Neilson. Born Elizabeth Ann Brown in Leeds, England, 1846; died in Paris, France, Aug 15, 1880; dau. of an actress named Brown or Browne; m. Philip Henry Lee (div. 1877). ❖ Played for a number of years in various stock and traveling companies; appeared in Margate as Julia in *The Hunchback* (1865), a character with which her name would long to be associated; also gained notable success as Amy Robsart in adaptation of Scott's *Kenilworth;* made US debut as Juliet (1872); became a great favorite in America, touring in 1874, 1876, and 1879. ❖ See also *Women in World History.*

NEILSON, Edith Alma Eileen (1883–1970). *See Savell, Edith Alma Eileen.*

NEILSON, Julia Emilie (1868–1957). English actress and theater manager. Born June 12, 1868, in London, England; died May 27, 1957, in London; educated in Wiesbaden and at Royal Academy of Music; m. Fred Terry (actor-manager and brother of Ellen Terry), 1891 (died 1933); children: Phyllis Neilson-Terry and Dennis Neilson-Terry (both actors). ❖ Made acting debut at Lyceum Theater (1888); for next 12 years, acted in plays opposite such luminaries as Sir Herbert Beerbohm Tree, Sir John Hare, and Sir George Alexander; in collaboration with husband, was actor-manager on a series of successful productions (1900–30), including *Sweet Nell of Old Drury* (1900), *The Scarlet Pimpernel* (1905), and *Henry of Navarre* (1909); made last stage appearance in *The Widow of Forty* (1944). ❖ See also *Women in World History.*

NEILSON, Lilian Adelaide (1846–1880). *See Neilson, Adelaide.*

NEILSON, Nellie (1873–1947). American historian. Born April 5, 1873, in Philadelphia, Pennsylvania; died May 26, 1947, in South Hadley, Massachusetts; dau. of William George Neilson (metallurgical engineer) and Mary Louise (Cunningham) Neilson; Bryn Mawr College, AB, 1893, MA, 1894, PhD, 1899. ❖ The 1st woman president of the American Historical Association (1943), taught at Mt. Holyoke College (1902–39) and chaired history department (1903–39); awarded honorary doctorates from Smith College (1938) and Russell Sage (1940); was the 1st woman to publish a volume in "Oxford Studies in Social and Legal History" series (*Customary Rents,* 1910), and to edit a yearbook of Selden Society; was also 1st woman to publish an article in *Harvard Law Review* and to be elected as a fellow of Mediaeval Academy of America; writings include *Economic Conditions on the Manors of Ramsey Abbey* (1898), *A Terrier of Fleet, Lincolnshire, from a Manuscript in the British Museum* (1920), *The Cartulary and Terrier of the Priory of Bilsington, Kent* (1928), *Year Books of Edward IV* (1931) and *Medieval Agrarian Economy* (1936), designed for use as a college text. ❖ See also *Women in World History.*

NEILSON, Sandy (1956—). American swimmer. Name variations: Sandra Neilson; Sandy Neilson-Bell. Born Sandra Neilson, Mar 20, 1956, in El Monte, CA; m. Keith Bell (sports psychologist); children: 4. ❖ Won Olympic gold medals in the 100-meter freestyle, 4 x 100-meter freestyle relay, and 4 x 100-meter medley relay in Munich (1972). Inducted into International Swimming Hall of Fame (1986).

NEILSON-TERRY, Hazel (1918–1974). *See Terry, Hazel.*

NEILSON-TERRY, Mary (1895–1954). *See Glynne, Mary.*

NEILSON-TERRY, Phyllis (1892–1977). English actress. Name variations: Phyllis Terson. Born in London, England, Oct 15, 1892; died Sept 25, 1977, in London; dau. of Fred Terry (actor-manager) and Julia Neilson (1868–1957, actress); niece of Ellen Terry (1847–1928); aunt of Hazel Terry (actress); educated at Westgate-on-Seas, Paris, and Royal Academy of Music; m. Cecil King (died); m. Heron Carvic. ❖ Made debut at Opera House, Blackpool, as Marie de Belleforet in *Henry of Navarre* (1909), under stage name Phyllis Terson; made London debut in same part (1910); played Viola in *Twelfth Night* at His Majesty's Theater, while father played Sebastian; went on to play many of Shakespeare's women, including Juliet, Lady Macbeth, Desdemona, Rosalind, Katherine and Portia; made 1st New York appearance, as Viola (1914); after she played the title role in *Trilby,* went on tour in US and Canada, returning to England (1919), following the war; took up management of Apollo Theater (1922) and continued to act; over the years, was seen in numerous plays, including *Bella Donna, Craig's Wife, Sweet Nell of Old Drury,* and *Candida;* also portrayed Elizabeth in *Elizabeth of England* and

appeared in *Separate Tables;* films include *Doctor in the House, Look Back in Anger* and *Conspiracy of Hearts.* ❖ See also *Women in World History.*

NEIMKE, Kathrin (1966—). German track-and-field athlete. Born July 18, 1966, in Germany. ❖ Won a silver medal at Seoul Olympics (1988) and a bronze medal at Barcelona Olympics (1992), both in the shot put.

NEIN, Jo (1873–1942). *See Anker, Nini Roll.*

NEISSER, Kersten (1956—). East German rower. Born May 4, 1956, in East Germany. ❖ At Moscow Olympics, won a gold medal in coxed eights (1980).

NEITHOTEP (fl. c. 3100 BCE). Egyptian queen. Name variations: Neith-hotep or Neith-hetep. Probably wife of King Aha (Ahamenes); aunt of King Djer. ❖ Queen of ancient Egypt's 1st Dynasty, is believed to have served as regent for her nephew, King Djer; was buried in an enormous tomb of 21 chambers at the site of Nagada, in Upper Egypt. ❖ See also *Women in World History.*

NELIDOVA, Lydia (1863–1929). Russian ballet dancer and teacher. Born 1863 in Moscow, Russia; died 1929 in Moscow. ❖ Trained at Bolshoi Ballet in Moscow and remained there throughout most of performance career; danced in numerous works by Petipa, including *La Esmeralda* (1893); was guest artist in Katti Lanner's *Faust* in London (1895); opened private studio in Moscow after resigning from Bolshoi and trained numerous acclaimed ballet dancers, including Vera Nemchinova.

NELIS, Mary (1935—). Northern Ireland politician. Born Mary Elliott, Aug 27, 1935, in Northern Ireland; children: 9. ❖ Was active in the civil-rights movement; joined SDLP and stood in district council elections (1973); campaigned across Northern Ireland in support of prisoners' rights after her son was sentenced to 16-years' imprisonment for IRA membership, then joined the protest in Maze Prison; left SDLP (1977); joined Sinn Féin (1980); representing Sinn Féin, elected to the Northern Ireland Assembly for Foyle (1998).

NELKEN, Margarita (1896–1968). Spanish art critic, feminist, and politician. Name variations: Margarita Nelken Mansberger; Margarita Nelkin; Margarita Nelken de Paul. Born in Spain, 1896; died in Mexico, 1968. ❖ Had exhibitions of her paintings in the major continental cities and wrote for the principal art journals of Europe and South America; became involved in leftist politics, partly from determination to improve the condition of Spanish women; during Second Republic, stood as a candidate from Badajoz for the Constituent Cortes (national assembly) and was elected (1931); representing the Spanish Socialist Workers' Party, was re-elected (1933, 1936); during Civil War, joined Spanish Communist Party and adopted an unexpectedly extremist position; fleeing Spain (1939), went to Mexico, where she became a leading figure in artistic circles; writings include *La condición social de la mujer en España* (1922), *Tres tipos de vírgenes* (1929), *Las escritoras españolas* (1930), *Por qué hicimos la revolución* (1936) and *El expresionismo en la plástica mexicana de hoy* (1964).

NELKIN, Margarita (1896–1968). *See Nelken, Margarita.*

NELLY (1899–1998). Greek photographer. Name variations: Elly Seraidari or Seraïdari. Born Elly Souyoultzoylou (also seen as Souyioultzoglou) in Aydin, Asia Minor (now Turkey), in 1899; died in 1998; m. Angelos Seraidari, also seen as Seraidaris (pianist), 1929. ❖ Shot a series of photographs of French ballerina Mona Paiva dancing nude on the Acropolis (1927), an exercise in creativity that caused a scandal in the Greek press but introduced a new movement and expressiveness into the art of photography; known later for her portraits, documentations, and landscapes, as well as her nudes, was also the 1st Greek photographer to use color, beginning with autochrome plates. ❖ See also film *Nelly, the Asia Minor Photographer* (1983); and *Women in World History.*

NELSON, Alice Dunbar (1875–1935). *See Dunbar-Nelson, Alice.*

NELSON, Ann. *See America³ Team.*

NELSON, Beryce Ann (1947—). Australian politician. Born Jan 10, 1947, in Brisbane, Australia. ❖ Radiographer; as a Liberal, was a member of Queensland Parliament for Aspley (1980–83); resigned the Liberal Party (1984); representing the National Party, returned to Queensland Parliament for Aspley (1986–89).

NELSON, Cindy (1955—). American Alpine skier. Born Cindy Nelson, Aug 19, 1955, in Lutsen, MN. ❖ Won 4 World Cup titles; won US downhill titles (1973, 1978), US slalom titles (1975, 1976), and US combined title (1978); won a bronze Olympic medal in downhill at Innsbruck Olympics (1976). ❖ See also Linda Jacobs, *Cindy Nelson: North Country Skier* (EMC, 1976); and *Women in World History.*

NELSON, Clara Meleka (1901–1979). Hawaiian singer, musician, and dancer. Name variations: Hilo Hattie. Born Clara Meleka Haili in Honolulu, Hawaii, Oct 28, 1901; died in Kaaawa, Oahu, Dec 12, 1979; graduate of Territorial Normal School; m. John Baxter, 1920 (div.); m. Milton Douglas, 1926 (div.); m. Theodore Inter, 1930 (div.); m. Carlyle Nelson (violinist), 1949. ❖ As Hilo Hattie, became well known for her comic hula; repertoire also included a group of English and Hawaiian songs, among them "The Cockeyed Mayor of Kaunakakai," "Princess Pupule," "Manuela Boy," and "Holoholo Ka'a"; appeared in 1st film *Song of the Islands*, in which she danced to "Hawaiian War Chant," followed by *Miss Tatlock's Millions* (1948), *Ma and Pa Kettle at Waikiki* (1955), and *Blue Hawaii* (1960), with Elvis Presley; was a headliner at Hawaii's Village Hotel's Tapa Room for many years. ❖ See also *Women in World History.*

NELSON, Diane (1958—). Canadian curler. Name variations: Diane Dezura. Born July 1, 1958, in Burnaby, British Columbia, Canada. ❖ Won a World championship (2000) and a team bronze medal at Salt Lake City Olympics (2002).

NELSON, Frances Herbert (1761–1831). Viscountess Nelson. Name variations: Frances Nisbet. Born Frances Woodward in 1761; died 1831; m. Josiah Nisbet (died); m. Lord Horatio Nelson, Mar 12, 1787 (sep. 1801). ❖ While Nelson was intermittently away at sea, corresponded affectionately with him, until she learned of his liaison with Lady Emma Hamilton (1798). ❖ See also *Women in World History.*

NELSON, Harriet. (c. 1909–1984). See Hilliard, Harriet.

NELSON, Jane (c. 1801–1896). See Williams, Jane.

NELSON, Jodie (1976—). American surfer. Born Jodie Rebecca Nelson, May 5, 1976, in Long Beach, CA. ❖ Competed in local surf meets while in middle school; had back-to-back wins in West Coast Pro/Am Tour (1996, 1997); qualified for World Qualifying Series (1998); began tow-in surfing; was PSTA Women's Overall champion (2002) and O'Neill Coldwater Classic champion (2002); serves as tv host for sporting events, including on-site hosting of X-Games; worked as stunt double.

NELSON, Lady (1761–1831). See Nelson, Frances Herbert.

NELSON, Lianne (1972—). See Bennion, Lianne.

NELSON, Marjorie (b. 1931). See Jackson, Marjorie.

NELSON, Marjorie (1937—). Australian softball player. Name variations: Midge Nelson. Born 1937 in Australia. ❖ One of Australia's greatest softball players, began 18-year career (1960) that included a record 4 World Series appearances with the Australia team (1965, 1970, 1974, and 1978); played in 23 consecutive national title games, mostly with the Victoria team; retired (1978); awarded British Empire Medal (BEM, 1978); inducted into International Hall of Fame (1983) and Sport Australia Hall of Fame (1985). The Midge Nelson medal was created to honor the most valuable player in Australian national championships. ❖ See also *Women in World History.*

NELSON, Maud (1881–1944). Austrian-born American baseball player. Name variations: Maud Brida; Maud Nielson; Maud Olson; Maud Dellacqua. Born Clementina Brida, Nov 17, 1881, in Tyrol, Austria; died Feb 15, 1944, in Chicago, IL; m. John B. Olson Jr. (baseball owner-manager), c. 1911 (died 1917); m. Constante Dellacqua (chef), 1922 or 1923. ❖ Immigrated to US at young age; dominated early years of women's baseball, as player, scout, manager, and owner of some of the top female teams of the day; was starring pitcher and played third base for barnstorming Boston Bloomer Girls (1897–1908); joined husband as owner-manager of Western Bloomer Girls (1911); following his death (1917), managed a women's team for Chicago Athletic Club, then the All Star Ranger Girls. ❖ See also *Women in World History.*

NELSON, Midge (b. 1937). See Nelson, Marjorie.

NELSON, Ruth (1905–1992). American actress. Born Aug 2, 1905, in Saginaw, Michigan; died Sept 12, 1992, in New York, NY; m. John Cromwell (director), 1946 (died 1979). ❖ Films include *Abe Lincoln in Illinois*, *Humoresque*, *Of Human Bondage*, *Three Women*, *The Late Show* and *Awakenings*.

NELSON, Sara (b. 1918). See Nelsova, Zara.

NELSON, Tracy (1944—). American musician. Born Dec 27, 1944, in Madison, WI; attended University of Wisconsin. ❖ Began to play piano at 5 and guitar at 13; sang in church choir; while at university, formed 1st band, Fabulous Imitations; recorded 1st solo LP, *Deep Are the Roots* (1965); moved to San Francisco and formed new band, Mother Earth (1966, later called Tracy Nelson/Mother Earth); with band, released critically acclaimed debut album, *Living With the Animals* (1968); with group, moved near Nashville, TN, and music began to reflect country influence (1969); other albums include *Satisfied* (1970), *A Poor Man's Paradise* (1973), *Homemade Songs* (1978), *I Feel So Good* (1995), and *Ebony and Irony* (2001); released solo album, *Tracy Nelson* (1974), which included Grammy-nominated "After the Fire Is Gone," and *In the Here and Now* (1993).

NELSON, Viscountess (1761–1831). See Nelson, Frances Herbert.

NELSON-CARR, Lindy (1952—). Australian politician. Name variations: Lindel Helena Nelson-Carr. Born July 15, 1952, in Sydney, Australia. ❖ Began career as a teacher; as a member of the Australian Labor Party, elected to the Queensland Parliament for Mundingburra (1998).

NELSOVA, Zara (1917–2002). Canadian-American cellist. Name variations: Sara Nelson. Born Sara Nelson in Winnipeg, Canada, Dec 24, 1917; died Oct 10, 2002, in New York, NY; dau. of Gregor Nelsov (flautist); studied with father, as well as Dezsö Mahalek, Herbert Walenn, Pablo Casals, Emanuel Feuermann, and Gregor Piatigorsky; m. Grant Johannesen (American pianist). ❖ One of the preeminent cellists of her time, known for her close collaboration with composer Ernest Bloch, played with sisters in a musical trio when young, 1st in Canada, then England, notably at Royal College of Music and with London Symphony Orchestra, conducted by Sir Malcolm Sargent; debuted as soloist at Wigmore Hall to rave reviews (1936); with advent of WWII, returned to Canada (1939); engaged by Arthur Fiedler to play with Boston Pops, then soloed with Boston Symphony; became principal cellist with Toronto Symphony and formed a 2nd Canadian Trio with Kathleen Parlow and Sir Ernest MacMillan; with Pablo Casals, made recital debut at NY's Town Hall (1942); began artistic relationship with Bloch, playing his *Shelomo* at a festival of his music in London (1949), later recording it under his baton; began teaching at Juilliard (1962); continued to tour widely in Europe, and North and South America, and was the 1st North American cellist to tour Soviet Union (1966); appeared as soloist with more than 30 orchestras throughout world; after marriage, often performed with husband; also recorded frequently. ❖ See also *Women in World History.*

NEMASHKALO, Yelena (1963—). Soviet handball player. Born Dec 25, 1963, in USSR. ❖ At Seoul Olympics, won a bronze medal in team competition (1988).

NEMCHINOVA, Vera (1899–1984). Russian ballerina. Name variations: Nemtchinova. Born Vera Nicolayevna Nemchinova in Moscow, Russia, 1899; died 1984; studied with Lydia Nelidova in Moscow, then Elizabeth Anderson-Ivantzova; m. Anatole Oboukhov or Obouhkoff (died 1962). ❖ Engaged by Diaghilev's Ballets Russes (1915), made 1st appearance in corps de ballets, rising soon to soloist, then ballerina; created roles in *Les Biches* (1924), *Les Tentations de la Bergère* (1924), and *Les Matelots* (1925); partnering with Anton Dolin, formed Nemchinova-Dolin Ballet company, which appeared in London and then toured England; was prima ballerina with Lithuanian State Ballet (1931–35), then joined Ballets Russe de Monte Carlo (1936), creating lead role in *L'Epreuve d'Amour*; danced title role of Princess Aurora with American Ballet Theatre (1943); opened a well-known studio at Ansonia Hotel in NY on stage retirement.

NEMCOVÁ, Bozena (c. 1817–1862). Czech writer. Name variations: Bozena Nemcova; Barbora Nemcová; Bozhena Nemtsova; Barbara Pankl; Betty Pankl. Born Barbara Nowotny, most likely in Vienna, 1817 (though Feb 1820 has traditionally been accepted as her birth date); died in Prague, Czechoslovakia, Jan 21, 1862; illeg. dau. of Maria Magdalena Theresia Nowotny, later known as Theresia Pankl (1797–1863) and Johann Pankl (1794–1850); became legitimized as Barbara Pankl due to her mother's marriage to Pankl; m. Josef Nemec (customs official), Sept 1837; children: daughter, Theodora "Dora" Nemec; sons, Hynek, Jaroslav (Jarous), and Karel Nemec. ❖ The 1st woman to occupy a major place in Czech literature, was largely brought up by her grandmother, Magdalena Cuda Novotná, a woman rooted in the traditional culture of Czech peasantry, who would serve as the model for her masterpiece *Babicka* (*The Grandmother*, 1855); earlier, had become a committed Czech nationalist; her poem, "Zenam ceskym" ("To Czech Women"), which appeared in the magazine *Kvety* (1843), began to establish her reputation; published a series of fairy tales in 7 successive parts (1845–48); published the autobiographical *Babicka*, recounting one year of rural life, which has been the most revered volume in the Czech language for more than a century; other writings include *The Disobedient Kids and Other Czecho-Slovak Fairy Tales* (trans. by Tolman and Smetánka, 1921), *The Shepherd and the Dragon: Fairy Tales from the Czech of Bozena Nemcová* (trans. by Ledbetter and Siegel, 1930). Her portrait was on the 500-Crown banknote issued by the newly established Czech Republic (1993). ❖ See also *Women in World History.*

NEMENOFF, Genia (1905–1989). French pianist. Born in Paris, France, Oct 23, 1905; died in New York, NY, Sept 19, 1989; studied at Paris Conservatoire with Isidor Philipp; m. Pierre Luboshutz (1891–1971), a pianist. ❖ After a successful Paris debut and tours throughout Europe, married and established a duo-piano team with husband; settling in US, made a successful NY debut as "Luboshutz & Nemenoff" (1937); with husband, served as joint head of the piano department at Michigan State University (1962–68).

NEMEROV, Diane (1923–1971). *See Arbus, Diane.*

NEMES NAGY, Agnes (1922–1991). Hungarian poet. Born 1922 in Budapest, Hungary; died in Budapest, 1991; studied Hungarian and Latin at Pázmány Péter University; m. Bálázs Lengyel (critic). ❖ Was in the resistance during WWII (1944–45); worked as magazine editor and secondary schoolteacher; published collection of poetry, *Kettös Világban* (1946); silenced for political reasons (1948–57); writings include *Szárazvillám* (Dry Lightning, 1957), and *A Lovák és az angyalok* (The Horses and the Angels, 1969). Won Joszef Attila Prize (1969) and Kossuth Prize (1983).

NEMETH, Angela (1946—). Hungarian track-and-field athlete. Born Feb 18, 1946, in Hungary. ❖ At Mexico City Olympics, won a gold medal in the javelin throw (1968).

NEMETH, Erzsebet (1953—). Hungarian handball player. Born Feb 10, 1953, in Hungary. ❖ At Montreal Olympics, won a bronze medal in team competition (1976).

NEMETH, Helga (1973—). Hungarian handball player. Born Aug 7, 1973, in Hungary. ❖ Won a team bronze medal at Atlanta Olympics (1996).

NEMETH-HUNYADY, Emise (1966—). *See Hunyady, Emese.*

NEMOURS, duchess of.
See *Philiberta of Savoy (c. 1498–1524).*
See *Nemours, Marie d'Orleans, duchess de (c. 1625–1707).*
See *Victoria of Saxe-Coburg (1822–1857).*

NEMOURS, Marie d'Orleans, duchess de (c. 1625–1707). French memoir writer. Name variations: Mlle. de Longueville; Marie de Longueville. Born Marie de Longueville c. 1625; died 1707; dau. of Henry, the duc de Longueville, and Louise de Bourbon-Soissons; stepdau. of Anne Geneviève, Duchesse de Longueville (1619–1679). ❖ Regretted her father's involvement in the Fronde during 1648–53 and wrote of it in her well-known memoirs; was a good friend and patron of Mme de Villedieu; was also proposed to by future English king, James II, then the duke of York, but France's regent Anne of Austria would not agree to the marriage.

NEMTCHINOVA, Vera (1899–1984). *See Nemchinova, Vera.*

NENADOVICH, Persida (1813–1873). Princess of Serbia. Name variations: Persida Nenadsowitsch. Born Feb 13, 1813; died Mar 29, 1873; dau. of Jevrem Nenadovich; m. Alexander (1806–1885), prince of Serbia (r. 1842–1858), on May 20, 1830; children: Peter I (1844–1921), king of Serbia (r. 1903–1921); Arsen or Arsène Karadjordjevic or Karageorgevitch (b. 1859, who m. Aurora of San Donato).

NENA EN SOCIEDAD (1899–1991). *See Cabrera, Lydia.*

NENENIENE-CASAITITE, Aldona (1949—). Soviet handball player. Name variations: Aldona Casaitite. Born Oct 13, 1949, in USSR. ❖ Won a gold medal at Montreal Olympics (1976) and a gold medal at Moscow Olympics (1980), both in team competition.

NERINA, Nadia (1927—). South African ballet dancer. Born Oct 21, 1946, in Capetown, South Africa; trained with Dorothea McNair and Eileen Keegan in Capetown. ❖ Moved to England where she studied at Sadler's Wells ballet school before joining the company (1947); performed in numerous works by Frederick Ashton, including *Cinderella* (1948), *Homage to the Queen* (1953), *Variations of a Theme by Purcell* (1955), *Birthday Offering* (1956) and as Lise in *La Fille Mal Gardée* (1960); had title role in Robert Helpmann's *Elektra* (1963) and danced in his *Miracle in the Gorbals*; retired (1966).

NERIS, Salomeja (1904–1945). Lithuanian poet. Name variations: Salomeja Bacinskaite-Buciene or S. Bacinskaite-Buciene. Born Salomeja Bacinskaite in Kirsai, Vilkaviskis-Vilkavishky Raion, Russia (now Lithuania), Nov 17, 1904; died in Moscow, July 7, 1945; graduate of University of Vytautas the Great, 1928; m. Bernardas Bucas (sculptor); children: 1. ❖ The most popular poet of the Lithuanian language, grew up with a love of the rural landscape and the rich folklore and fairy tales of the peasantry; was a teacher of Lithuanian literature in Kaunas; published 1st collection of verses, *Anksti ryta* (Early in the Morning, 1927), influenced by Romanticism and a conservative Roman Catholic Weltanschauung, followed by the popular *Pedos smely* (Prints in the Sand, 1931); also translated the writings of Goethe, Pushkin, Baudelaire, Verlaine, Rilke and Anna Akhmatova into Lithuanian; joined a left-wing artists' organization, The Third Front (1931), and published poetry of social criticism in its journal *Trecias frontas*; her verses often appeared in the illegal newspapers and journals of the banned Lithuanian Communist Party (1931–34); was a deputy to the Supreme Soviet of USSR, at the session in which Lithuania was admitted to the Soviet Union (1940); during WWII, her verse was circulated in Lithuanian units of Red Army and also dropped by air into Nazi-occupied Lithuania; wrote "Yasnaya Polyana"; best known for *Dainuok, sirdie, gyvenima* (Sing to Life, My Heart). Received Order of the Great Patriotic War, 1st Class; posthumously awarded title of People's Poet of the Lithuanian Soviet Socialist Republic (1954). ❖ See also *Women in World History.*

NERIUS, Steffi (1972—). German javelin thrower. Born July 1, 1972, in Bergen auf Rüger, Germany. ❖ Won Grand Prix in Helsinki (2003) and Super Grand Prix at Lausanne (2003); won a silver medal at Athens Olympics (2004).

NERUDA, Wilma (c. 1838–1911). Czech violinist. Name variations: Wilma Maria Franziska Neruda; Norman-Neruda; Lady Hallé. Born Vilemína Maria Franziska Neruda in Brünn, Moravia, Mar 21, probably 1838 (some sources cite 1839); died in Berlin, Germany, April 15, 1911; dau. of Josef Neruda (organist, teacher); sister of Amálie Nerudová (pianist) and Viktor Neruda (cellist); studied with Leopold Jansa and father; m. Ludwig Norman (Swedish conductor-composer), 1864 (sep. 1869, died 1885); m. Sir Charles Hallé (German-born pianist and conductor), 1888 (died 1895). ❖ Well-known concert violinist and teacher, often played with her sister and brother; by age 25, was dubbed "The Queen of Violinists" in Paris, considered the female counterpart of Joseph Joachim (1864); played 1st violin with London Philharmonic Quartet and with Joachim Quartet; was professor of violin at Stockholm Royal Academy of Music (1864–69); in London, began appearing in concerts with Philharmonic Society and Monday "Popular" series (1869); was a pioneer at a time when women violinists were still a rare commodity.

NESBIT, Edith (1858–1924). British novelist, poet, short-story writer and children's author. Name variations: E. Nesbit; (pseudonyms) Mrs. Hubert Bland, Edith Bland. Born Aug 15 or 19, 1858, in London, England; died May 4, 1924, New Romney, Kent; dau. of John Collis Nesbit and Sarah Nesbit; m. Hubert Bland (journalist), 1880 (died 1914); m. Thomas Terry Tucker (marine engineer), 1917; children: (1st m.) Paul, Iris, Fabian; (adopted) Rosamund (Mrs. Clifford Sharp) and John. ❖ Prolific writer whose most popular and enduring children's books detail the adventures of the Bastable family based roughly on her memories of the big brood in which she had blossomed as a child as well as the large family she later had; a socialist, formed the Fabian Society with husband and friends; writings for children, which sought to entertain rather than moralize or educate, include *The Story of the Treasure Seekers* (1899), *The Five Children and It* (1902), *The Railway Children* (1906, adapted to film, 1972), *The Story of The Amulet* (1906), *The Enchanted Castle* (1907), *The House of Arden* (1908), *Wet Magic* (1913) and *Long Ago When I Was Young* (1966); writings for adults include (with Hubert Bland and others) *The Prophet's Mantle* (1885), (poetry) *Lays and Legends* (1886–92), *Grim Tales* (1893), *The Secret of the Kyriels* (1899), *Thirteen Ways Home* (1901), *The Red House* (1902), *Fear* (1910), *Dormant* (1911), *The Lark* (1922) and *Many Voices* (1922).

❖ See also Julia Briggs, *A Woman of Passion: The Life of Edith Nesbit, 1858–1924* (New Amsterdam, 1991); Dorothy Langley Moore, *E. Nesbit*; and *Women in World History*.

NESBIT, Evelyn (1884–1967). American model-actress and ballroom dancer. Name variations: Evelyn Nesbit Thaw; Mrs. Harry Thaw; Florence Evelyn Nesbit. Born Florence Evelyn Nesbit, Dec 25, 1884, in Tarentum, PA; died Jan 17 (some sources cite Jan 18), 1967, in Santa Monica, CA; dau. of Winfield Scott (lawyer) and Elizabeth Nesbit; m. Harry Kendall Thaw (heir to a Pennsylvania railroad fortune), 1905 (div. 1916); m. performer Jack Clifford (div. 1919); children: (1st m.) Russell Thaw. ❖ Became part of a sensational scandal when her ex-lover, nationally renowned architect Stanford White, was murdered by her husband—a killing that dominated newspapers for weeks and resulted in two sensational trials at which she was a star witness. ❖ See also autobiographies *The Story of My Life* (1914) and *Prodigal Days* (1934); (film) *The Girl in the Red Velvet Swing* (1955); and *Women in World History*.

NESBITT, Cathleen (1888–1982). British-born actress. Born Cathleen Mary Nesbitt, Nov 24, 1888, in Cheshire, England; died Aug 2, 1982, at home in London; dau. of Thomas Nesbitt (captain in Royal Navy) and Mary Catherine (Parry) Nesbitt; sister of actor Thomas Nesbitt; Queen's University, Belfast, BA; also studied at Lisieux and Sorbonne; m. Cecil Beresford Ramage (lawyer), Nov 1922; children: Mark and Jennifer. ❖ In a career that spanned 7 decades, appeared in hundreds of plays, both serious and comic; made London debut in *The Cabinet Minister* (1910); joined Irish Players and made NY debut as Molly Byrne in *The Well of the Saints* (1911); appeared in US première of *The Playboy of the Western World* (1911); on London stage, appeared as Deirdre in *Deirdre of the Sorrows* and Phoebe Throssell in *Quality Street* (1913); back on Broadway, starred opposite John Barrymore in *Justice* (1916), one of her most successful roles, and later appeared in *The Cocktail Party* (1950), *Gigi* and *Sabrina Fair* (1951), *Portrait of a Lady* (1954) and *My Fair Lady* (1956); reprised role as Mrs. Higgins in a revival of *My Fair Lady* when she was in her 90s; films include *The Passing of the Third Floor Back* (1935), *Gaslight (Angel Street,* 1940), *Nicholas Nickleby* (1947), *So Long at the Fair* (1950), *Three Coins in the Fountain* (1954), *Desiree* (1954), *An Affair to Remember* (1957), *Separate Tables* (1958), *Family Plot* (1976) and *Julia* (1977). ❖ See also autobiography, *A Little Love and Good Companions* (1973); and *Women in World History*.

NESBITT, Louisa Cranstoun (1812–1858). *See Nisbett, Louisa Cranstoun.*

NESBITT, Miriam (1873–1954). American actress. Born Miriam Anne Skancke, Sept 14, 1873, in Chicago, IL; died Aug 11, 1954, in Hollywood, CA. ❖ Made NY stage debut in *The Cup of Betrothal* (1897) and London debut as Tiger Lily in *Peter Pan*; starred for the Edison Company in US and England (1911 on); films include *The Passer-By, Children Who Labor, Mary Stuart, The Way Back* and *Infidelity*.

NESBITT, Stephanie (1985—). Canadian-born American synchronized swimmer. Born Aug 10, 1985, in Toronto, Ontario, Canada. ❖ Won a team bronze medal at Athens Olympics (2004).

NESMITH, Bette (1924–1980). *See Graham, Bette Nesmith.*

NESSIM, Barbara (1939—). American painter and illustrator. Born Mar 30, 1939, in New York, NY; dau. of a clothing-designer; graduate of High School of Industrial Arts (later High School of Art and Design), 1956; Pratt Institute, BFA, 1960, studied under Fritz Eichenberg, Jacob Landau, Richard Lindner, Bob Weaver and Michel Ponce de Leon; studied painting at Art Students League; married 1980. ❖ Began recording on canvas the same themes of female imagery and women's relationship to the world that had earlier driven her drawings and prints; by early 1970s, was working for *New York* magazine; success accelerated throughout decade, partly due to advent of *Ms.* magazine and the women's movement; taught at School for Visual Arts, Pratt Institute, and Parsons School of Design. ❖ See also *Women in World History*.

NESSINA, Valentyna (1969—). *See Tserbe-Nessina, Valentyna.*

NESTA. *Variant of Agnes.*

NESTA TEWDR (fl. 1090). Mistress of Henry I. Name variations: Nesta Tewdwr. Dau. of Gladys and Rhys ap Tewdr or Tewdwr (Tudor), king of Deheubarth; mistress of Henry I, king of England (r. 1068–1135); children: Robert (c. 1090–1147), 1st earl of Gloucester.

NESTERENKO, Yuliya (1979—). Belarusian runner. Born June 15, 1979, in Belarus. ❖ Won a gold medal for 100 meters at Athens Olympics (2004).

NESTEROVA, Klara (1937—). *See Guseva, Klara.*

NESTLE, Joan (1940—). American essayist and historian. Born May 12, 1940, in Bronx, NY. ❖ Worked as activist for several causes in New York and co-founded Lesbian Herstory Archives of New York City to preserve Lesbian writing and artifacts; writings include *A Restricted Country* (1987) and *The Fragile Union* (1998); (with Naomi Holoch) edited *Women on Women: An Anthology of American Lesbian Short Fiction,* vols 1 and 2 (1991, 1993), *The Persistent Desire: A Femme-Butch Reader* (1992), and (with John Preston) *Sister and Brother: Lesbians and Gay Men Write About Their Lives* (1995).

NESTOR, Agnes (1880–1948). American trade unionist and labor reformer. Born Agnes McEwen Nestor in Grand Rapids, Michigan, June 24, 1880; died in Chicago, Illinois, Dec 28, 1948; dau. of Thomas Nestor and Anna (McEwen) Nestor; never married; no children. ❖ Served as vice-president, International Glove Workers Union (IGWU, 1903–06, 1915–38); served as secretary-treasurer, IGWU (1906–13); was general president, IGWU (1913–15); was director of research and education, IGWU (1938–48); was a member of the National Women's Trade Union League (WTUL) executive board (1907–48); served as president, Chicago WTUL (1913–48); was a member, National Committee on Federal Aid to Education (1914), Woman's Committee of US Council of National Defense (1918), Illinois Commission on Unemployment and Relief (early 1930s), and Illinois Minimum Wage Law Advisory Board (1935). ❖ See also autobiography, *Woman's Labor Leader* (1954); and *Women in World History*.

NETANA, Rehutai (1895–1967). *See Maihi, Rehutai.*

NETESOVA, Maria (1983—). *See Netessova, Maria.*

NETESSOVA, Maria (1983—). Russian rhythmic gymnast. Name variations: Netesova. Born 1983 in USSR. ❖ Won a team World championship (1998, 1999) and a team gold medal at Sydney Olympics (2000); won 2 team European championships.

NETHERLANDS, governor-general of the.
See Margaret of Parma (1522–1586).
See Maria Christina (1742–1798).

NETHERLANDS, queen of the.
See Frederica Wilhelmina of Prussia (1774–1837).
See Anna Pavlovna (1795–1865).
See Sophia of Wurttemberg (1818–1877).
See Emma of Waldeck (1858–1934).
See Wilhelmina (1880–1962).
See Juliana (1909–2004).
See Beatrix (b. 1938).

NETHERLANDS, regent of the.
See Margaret of Austria (1480–1530).
See Mary of Hungary (1505–1558).

NETHERLANDS, stadholder of the. *See Maria Elisabeth (1680–1741).*

NETHERSOLE, Olga (1863–1951). English actress. Name variations: Olga Isabel Nethersole. Born in Kensington, England, Jan 18, 1863, of Spanish descent; died Jan 9, 1951; dau. of Henry Nethersole (solicitor). ❖ Made stage debut at Brighton (1887) in *Harvest;* played important parts at the Garrick, London (1888–94), successfully opening as Janet Preece in Pinero's *The Profligate;* joined management of Court Theatre (1894); toured in Australia and US, playing leading parts in modern plays, notably as Fanny Legrand in *Sapho,* which sparked an uproar when she brought it to New York City (1900); hauled into court and charged with "violating public decency," was acquitted; a powerful actress, was best known for her *Carmen*. Created a Commander of the British Empire (CBE). ❖ See also *Women in World History*.

NETTER, Mildrette (1948—). African-American runner. Born June 16, 1948, in Gunnison, MS. ❖ At Mexico City Olympics, won a gold medal in the 4 x 100-meter relay (1968).

NETTLETON, Lois (1929—). American stage, tv and screen actress. Born Aug 16, 1929, in Oak Park, IL; m. Jean Shepherd (disk jockey and writer), 1961 (div. 1967). ❖ Made film debut in *Period of Adjustment* (1962), followed by *Come Fly With Me, Dirty Dingus*

Magee, Pigeons, The Man in the Glass Booth, Echoes of a Summer and *The Best Little Whorehouse in Texas,* among others; on tv, appeared in the mini-series "Washington: Behind Closed Doors" (1977), "All That Glitters" (1977) and "Centennial" (1978), and as Patsy Dennis on "The Brighter Day" (1954–57), Joanne St. John on "In the Heat of the Night" (1988), and Virginia Benson on "General Hospital" (1996–98). Won 2 Emmys (1977 and 1983).

NEUBAUER-RUEBSAM, Dagmar (1962—). East German runner. Name variations: Dagmar Ruebsam or Rübsam. Born June 1962 in East Germany. ❖ At Seoul Olympics, won a bronze medal in the 4 x 400-meter relay (1988).

NEUBER, Caroline (1697–1760). German actress and theater manager. Name variations: Frederika Neuber; Friederike Caroline Neuber; Friedericke Karoline Neuber; Carolina Neuber; "die Neuberin." Born Friederike Caroline Weissenborn, Mar 9, 1697, in Reichenbach, Vogtland, Saxony; died destitute in Laubegast near Dresden the night of Nov 29–30, 1760; dau. of Daniel Weissenborn (judge and lawyer) and Anna Rosina Weissenborn; m. Johann Neuber (1697–1759, actor), 1718; no children. ❖ A crucial player in initiating sweeping reforms on the German stage, was the leader (*Prinzipalin*) of the most important troupe of traveling players in Germany (1720s–30s); raised the standards of theater by abolishing improvisation and introducing tragic drama into the repertory; though initially successful, spent final years in obscurity. Today "die Neuberin" is universally honored as a towering figure in the history of the German theater. In 1995, a Neuber Museum was inaugurated in Reichenbach in the house where she had been born almost 3 centuries earlier. ❖ See also *Women in World History.*

NEUBER, Frederika or Friederike (1697–1760). *See Neuber, Caroline.*

NEUBERGER, Maurine B. (1906–2000). American politician. Born Maurine Brown, Jan 9, 1906, in Cloverdale, Oregon; died Feb 22, 2000, in Portland, Oregon; dau. of Walter T. Brown (physician) and Ethel Kelty Brown (teacher); earned teacher's certificate from Oregon College of Education, 1925; University of Oregon, BA, 1929; m. Richard L. Neuberger (journalist and later US senator), 1945 (died Mar 1960); m. Philip Solomon (psychiatrist), 1964 (div. 1967). ❖ Democrat, served in Oregon state House of Representatives (1951–55); after husband died while serving in US Senate (1960), ran unopposed to fill his seat for the short-term special election and triumphed in the general election, the 3rd woman in US history to win a full Senate term; as a senator (Nov 8, 1960–Jan 3, 1967), served on Agriculture Committee, Banking and Currency Committee, Committee on Commerce, Special Committee on Aging, and Committee on a Parliamentary Conference with Canada; supported bills to cap campaign expenditures, give tax deductions for child care, end the use of "national origins quotas" in the immigration system, and fund the establishment of President's Commission on the Status of Women. ❖ See also *Women in World History.*

NEUFELD, Elizabeth F. (1928—). American molecular biologist. Name variations: Elizabeth Fondal Neufeld. Born Sept 27, 1928, in Paris, France; Queen's College, BS, 1948; University of California, Berkeley, PhD in comparative biochemistry, 1956). ❖ International expert on human genetic diseases, began career as a plant biologist; worked as a research biochemist at National Institutes of Health's (NIH) National Institute of Arthritis, Metabolism, and Digestive Diseases (1963–73); served as chief of NIH Section on Human Biochemical Genetics (1973–79) and chief of National Institute of Arthritis, Diabetes, and Digestive and Kidney Diseases' (NIADDK) Genetics and Biochemistry Branch (1979–84); served as NIADDK deputy director (1981–83) for Division of Intramural Research; became chair of biological chemistry department at University of California, Los Angeles, School of Medicine (1984), the 1st woman department head there; served as a president of American Society for Biochemistry and Molecular Biology (1992–93); elected to National Academy of Sciences (1977), American Academy of Arts and Sciences (1977) and American Association for Advancement in Science (1988). Jointly with Roscoe O. Brady, received Albert Lasker Clinical Medicine Research Award (1982); received Wolf Prize in Medicine (1988) and National Medal of Science (1994), presented by President Bill Clinton.

NEUFFER, Elizabeth (1956–2003). American journalist. Born June 15, 1956, in Quincy, MA; killed near Samarra, Iraq, May 9, 2003; graduate of Cornell University; London School of Economics, MA in political philosophy. ❖ Became European correspondent for the Boston Globe, based in Berlin (1994), reporting on the fighting in Yugoslavia, Rwanda, Kuwait and Afghanistan; as foreign correspondent, was sent to Iraq

(2003); wrote *The Key to My Neighbor's House: Seeking Justice in Bosnia and Rwanda* (2002), which won the Novartis Prize (1997). Won a Courage in Journalism Award from International Women's Media Foundation (1998).

NEUFFER, Judy (1949—). American US Navy pilot. Born 1949 in US. ❖ Was the 1st woman assigned to US pilot training (1973); while measuring wind speeds and plotting location of eye of Hurricane Carmen, became the 1st person in US Navy to fly into eye of a hurricane (1974).

NEUFVIC, Madame de (fl. 17th c.). French translator. Born in France. ❖ Made verse translation of Jorge Montemayor's Spanish novel *Diana.*

NEULÄNDER-SIMON, Else (1900–1942). *See Yva.*

NEUMAN, Theresa (1898–1962). *See Neumann, Theresa.*

NEUMANN, Annett (1970—). German cyclist. Born Jan 31, 1970, in Germany. ❖ At Barcelona Olympics, won a silver medal in the 1,000-meter sprint (1992).

NEUMANN, Hanna (1914–1971). German mathematician and educator. Name variations: Hanna von Caemmerer. Born Hanna von Caemmerer, Feb 12, 1914, in Berlin, Germany; died Nov 14, 1971, in Canada; dau. of Hermann Conrad von Caemmerer (historian and archivist) and Katharina von Caemmerer; graduate of University of Berlin, c. 1936; Oxford University, PhD, 1944, DSc, 1955; m. Bernhard Neumann (Jewish mathematician), 1938; children: Irene (b. 1939), Peter, Barbara (b. 1943), Walter (b. 1946) and Daniel (b. 1951). ❖ Studied with Ludwig Bieberbach, Erhard Schmidt and Issai Schur; outspoken about opposition to the Nazis, lost job at Mathematical Institute; moved to England (1938); after WWII (1945), moved with husband to Hull, where she taught at University College (1945–57), eventually becoming senior lecturer; appointed to a lectureship in the faculty of technology at Manchester University (1958); with husband, moved to NY (1961), where they held positions at Courant Institute of Mathematical Sciences; moved to Australia with family (1963), where she became the newly created chair of Pure Mathematics in National University's School of General Studies, Australia's 1st woman professor of mathematics; lectured throughout Australia, Europe, US, and Canada. ❖ See also *Women in World History.*

NEUMANN, Katerina (1973—). *See Neumannova, Katerina.*

NEUMANN, Liselotte (1966—). Swedish golfer. Born May 20, 1966, in Finspang, Sweden. ❖ Swedish national champion (1982–83); Swedish Match Play champion (1983); member of World team (1982, 1984) and European team (1984); won US Women's Open (1988) and named Rookie of the Year; won Mazda Japan Classic (1991); won LPGA Classic and Women's British Open (1994); named Swedish golfer of the year (1994); won Chrysler-Plymouth, PING Welch's championship, and Edina Realty Classic (1996); won Welch's championship and Toray Japan Queens Cup (1997); won Standard Register PING (1998); member of European Solheim Cup team (2000).

NEUMANN, Margarete Buber (1901–1989). *See Buber-Neumann, Margarete.*

NEUMANN, Theresa (1898–1962). German religious figure. Name variations: often spelled erroneously Theresa Neuman. Born April 8, 1898, on Good Friday, in Konnersreuth, Bavaria; died Sept 18, 1962 in Konnersreuth; dau. of Anna (Grillmeier) Neumann and Ferdinand Neumann (tailor). ❖ Suffered paralysis, blindness, and convulsions after injury as child; began to recover after praying devoutly to St. Thérèse of Lisieux and developed a stigmata following the vision of Christ's passion (1926); during the periods of the stigmata's recurrences over 32 years, apparently ate no solid food but subsisted on water and daily communion wafer, eventually dying of malnutrition. Konnersreuth became site of religious pilgrimages.

NEUMANN, Vera (1907–1993). American painter and designer. Name variations: Vera. Born July 24, 1907, in Stamford, CT; died June 15, 1993, in Ossining, NY; attended Cooper Union; m. George Neumann (died 1960). ❖ Began career designing children's furniture and murals; with husband, launched Vera designs (1946), eventually emblazoning the name Vera on printed scarves, bed and table linens, draperies and sportswear; her paintings were exhibited in many countries.

NEUMANNOVA, Katerina (1973—). Czech cross-country skier and mountain biker. Name variations: Katerina Neumann; Katerina Neumannová. Born Feb 15, 1973, in Pisek, Czechoslovakia (now

Czech Republic); children: daughter Lucia (b. 2003). ❖ Competed as a mountain biker in the Atlanta Summer Olympics (1996); won a silver medal in 5 km classical cross-country race at Nagano Winter Olympics with a time of 17:42.7, and took a bronze for 10 km pursuit (1998); at World Championships, placed 3rd in 15 km freestyle (1997) and 3rd at 5 km classic (1999); won a bronze medal in 15 km freestyle at Salt Lake City Olympics (2002); had 3 World Cup wins (2004); won a gold medal for 30 km free and a silver medal for 15 km pursuit at Torino Olympics (2006).

NEUNAST, Daniela (1966—). German rower. Born Sept 19, 1966, in Germany. ❖ Won a gold medal at Seoul Olympics (1988) and a bronze medal at Barcelona Olympics (1992), both in coxed eights.

NEUNER, Angelika (1969—). Austrian luge athlete. Born Dec 23, 1969, in Innsbruck, Austria; sister of Doris Neuner (luge athlete). ❖ For singles luge, won a silver medal at Albertville Olympics (1992), finishing 73/1000s of a second behind her younger sister, placed 4th at Lillehammer Olympics (1994) and won the bronze medal at Nagano Olympics (1998); at World championships, won a bronze medal (1997); won a silver overall at World Cup (1997).

NEUNER, Doris (1970—). Austrian luge athlete. Born 1970 in Innsbruck, Austria; sister of Angelika Neuner (luge athlete). ❖ Won a silver medal for singles luge at Albertville Olympics (1992); placed 10th for singles luge at Lillehammer Olympics (1994); retired (1996).

NEUREUTHER, Rosi (1950—). See *Mittermaier, Rosi.*

NEVADA, Emma (1859–1940). American opera singer. Name variations: Mrs. Raymond Palmer. Born Emma Wixom, Feb 7, 1859 (some sources cite 1852 or 1861), in Alpha, CA; died June 20, 1940, in Liverpool, England; graduate of Mills Seminary (later Mills College), 1876; studied in Vienna with Mathilde Marchesi; m. Raymond Spooner Palmer (physician), 1885; children: Mignon Nevada (1885–1970). ❖ Debuted at Her Majesty's Theater in London as Amina in *La Sonnambula* (1880); debuted in Milan (1881) and at Opéra Comique in Paris as Zora in *La Perle du Brésil* (1883); appeared in *The Rose of Sharon* at London's Covent Garden (1884), a role written especially for her; made American debut in *La Sonnambula* at NY Academy of Music (1884); returned to Europe (1885); gave command performances for Queen Victoria and Edward VII; counted among her friends Sarah Bernhardt and Maria Christina of Austria, queen of Spain; most popular roles included those in *Faust, Lakmé, The Tales of Hoffman, Mireille, The Barber of Seville, Mignon* and *Lucia di Lammermoor*; returned to US to give a concert series at the Metropolitan Opera House (1899); performed in America again (1901–02, 1907); retired (1910) after singing *Lakmé* in Berlin; for several years, taught voice in England. ❖ See also *Women in World History.*

NEVADA, Mignon (1885–1970). English opera singer. Name variations: Mignon Palmer. Born Mignon Palmer in Paris, France, Mar 18, 1885 (some sources cite Aug 14, 1886, but likely incorrect); died in Redwood City, CA, Sept 1970; dau. of Emma (Wixom) Nevada (1859–1940, opera singer) and Raymond S. Palmer (physician); studied with mother. ❖ Made debut in Rome (1907), followed by Covent Garden (1910), Paris (1920), and Milan (1923); was particularly praised for her interpretations of Desdemona, Mimi, Lakmé, Zerlina, and Marguerite. ❖ See also *Women in World History.*

NEVEJEAN, Yvonne (1900–1987). Belgian child-welfare advocate and Holocaust rescuer. Name variations: Yvonne Feyerick-Nevejean. Born 1900; died 1987. ❖ Belgian director of the l'Oeuvre National de l'Enfance (National Child Welfare Organization or ONE) who supervised children's homes throughout Belgium; defied Nazis by saving the lives of over 3,000 Jewish children during the Holocaust; honored by Israel's Yad Vashem Holocaust Martyrs' and Heroes' Remembrance Authority, which named her one of the Righteous Among the Nations (1965). ❖ See also Eric Silver, *The Book of the Just: The Unsung Heroes Who Rescued Jews from Hitler* (Grove, 1992); and *Women in World History.*

NEVELSON, Louise (1899–1988). American sculptor. Born Leah Berliawsky, Sept 23, 1899, in Pereyaslav, near Kiev, Ukraine; died of cancer, April 17, 1988; dau. of Isaac Berliawsky (wood and junk dealer) and Zeisel "Minna" Smoleranki; studied at Art Students League with Kenneth Hayes Miller and Kimon Nicolaides, 1929; studied in Munich with Hans Hofmann, 1931; apprenticed with Diego Rivera and studied modern dance with Ellen Kearns, 1932; studied at Atelier 17 under Peter Grippi and Leo Katz, 1953–55; m. Charles S. Nevelson, June 12, 1920 (sep. 1931, div. 1941); children: Myron (Mike, b. Feb 23, 1922). ❖ One of the greatest 20th-century US sculptors, struggled

through 1930s and 1940s, then made a fortune after age 60 by recycling junk found on NY streets into assemblages and by designing environmental sculptures; moved with family to US (1905); worked for WPA (1935–39); had 1st solo show, at Nierendorf Gallery (1941); traveled to Europe (1948), Mexico (1950); works acquired by Whitney Museum, Brooklyn Museum, and MoMA (1956–58); teamed with dealer Arnold Glimcher (1961); work included in US Pavilion, at the XXXI Biennale Internazionale D'Arte, Venice (1962); completed 26 editions of lithographs at Tamarind Lithography Workshop, Los Angeles, and became president of Artists' Equity (1963); her sculptural wall, *Homage to 6,000,000 II,* purchased by Israel Museum, Jerusalem; gave a gold wall, *An American Tribute to the British People,* to Tate Gallery, London; elected president of National Artists' Equity (1966); had 1st retrospective exhibition at Whitney Museum and elected vice-president of International Association of Artists and head of Advisory Council on Art of National Historic Sites Foundation (1967); typically worked in studio wearing long, fake black eyelashes to emphasize her dark eyes, a sable coat over jeans and a plaid shirt, with an exotic scarf hiding her hair like a turban. Received American Academy of Arts and Letters Gold Medal (1983) and National Medal of the Arts from President Ronald Reagan (1985). ❖ See also Arnold Glimcher, *Louise Nevelson* (Dutton, 1976); John Gordon, *Louise Nevelson* (Whitney Museum of Art, 1967); Laurie Lisle, *Louise Nevelson: A Passionate Life* (Summit, 1990); and *Women in World History.*

NEVERS, countess of.
See *Agnes de Nevers (r. 1181–1192).*
See *Yolande of Burgundy (1248–1280).*
See *Margaret of Flanders (1350–1405).*

NEVERS, duchess of.
See *Henrietta of Cleves (r. 1564–1601).*
See *Charlotte of Vendôme.*
See *Margaret of Vendôme.*
See *Catherine of Lorraine.*

NEVERS, princess of. See *Louise Marie de Gonzague (1611–1667).*

NEVES, Claudia (1975—). Brazilian basketball player. Name variations: Cláudia Maria das Neves; known as Claudinha. Born Feb 17, 1975, in Guarujá, Brazil. ❖ Won a team bronze medal at Sydney Olympics (2000); played for Detroit Shock (1999–2001), then Miami Sol of the WNBA.

NEVEU, Ginette (1919–1949). French violinist. Born in France, 1919; died in plane crash, 1949; studied at Paris Conservatory with Carl Flesch. ❖ A child prodigy, made debut in Paris (1926), at age 7; a close friend of John Barbirolli, often played at his concerts and recorded with him; was particularly acclaimed for her performances of the concerti of Jean Sibelius. ❖ See also *Women in World History.*

NEVILL, Dorothy Fanny (1826–1913). English horticulturist. Name variations: Lady Dorothy Fanny Nevill; Lady Dorothy Fanny Walpole. Born Dorothy Fanny Walpole, April 1, 1826, in Berkeley Square, London, England; died Mar 24, 1913; dau. of Mary Fawkener and Horatio Walpole (1783–1858), 3rd earl of Orford of Wolterton (a descendent of Sir Robert Walpole's brother, Horatio Walpole, 1st baron Walpole of Wolterton, 1678–1757); m. Reginald Henry Nevill, 1847; children: Meresia Nevill (1849–1918); Edward Nevill (1851–1915); Horace Nevill (1855–1924); Ralph Nevill (1865–1930). ❖ The owner of what was once considered the world's best plant collection, specialized in orchids and tropical plants; moved to Reginald Nevill's estate, Dangstein, near Midhurst in Sussex after marriage, while concurrently maintaining a London home; enjoyed friendships with Benjamin Disraeli and Joseph Chamberlain; regularly attended Royal Horticultural Society meetings; maintained her plant collection at Dangstein; enjoyed a social life, often mingling with socialites, artists and politicians. Plant collection was dispersed when Dangstein was dismantled (1976).

NEVILL, Mary (1961—). English field-hockey player. Born Mar 12, 1961, in UK. ❖ At Barcelona Olympics, won a bronze medal in team competition (1992).

NEVILLE, Alice (c. 1406–1463). See *Montacute, Alice.*

NEVILLE, Alice (fl. 1480s). Sister of the Kingmaker. Dau. of Richard Neville (b. 1400), 1st earl of Salisbury, and Alice Montacute (c. 1406–1463); sister of Richard Neville, earl of Warwick (1428–1471, known as Warwick the Kingmaker); m. Henry Fitzhugh, 5th Lord of Fitzhugh of Ravensworth; children: Anne Fitzhugh; Richard Fitzhugh.

NEVILLE, Anne (fl. 1440–1462). See *Holland, Anne.*

NEVILLE, Anne (1456–1485). *See Anne of Warwick.*

NEVILLE, Anne (d. 1480). Duchess of Buckingham. Died 1480; dau. of Joan Beaufort (1379–1440) and Sir Ralph Neville of Raby, 1st earl of Westmoreland; m. Humphrey Stafford (1402–1460), 1st duke of Buckingham, 1st earl of Stafford; m. Walter Blount, 1st baron Mountjoy; children: (1st marriage) Humphrey Stafford (d. 1455), 7th earl of Stafford; Henry Stafford (d. 1471), who m. Margaret Beaufort (1443–1509); twins William and George Stafford; Edward Stafford; John Stafford, 9th earl of Wiltshire (r. 1469–1473); Anne Stafford (d. 1472); Joan Stafford (who m. Sir William Knyvet); Catherine Stafford (d. 1476).

NEVILLE, Catherine (c. 1397–1483). Duchess of Norfolk. Name variations: Katherine Neville. Born c. 1397; died in 1483; dau. of Joan Beaufort (1379–1440) and Sir Ralph Neville of Raby, 1st earl of Westmoreland; 2nd wife of John Mowbray (1415–1461), 3rd duke of Norfolk; m. Sir Thomas Strangeways; m. John, viscount Beaumont; m. Sir John Wydeville. John Mowbray's 1st wife was Anne Bourchier (c. 1417–1474).

NEVILLE, Catherine (fl. 1460). English aristocrat. Name variations: Katherine Neville. Flourished around 1460; dau. of Richard Neville (b. 1400), earl of Salisbury, and Alice Montacute; sister of Richard Neville, earl of Warwick (1428–1471, known as Warwick the Kingmaker); m. William Bonville, Lord Harrington, also seen as Lord Haryngton; m. William Hastings, 1st Lord Hastings; children: (1st marriage) Cecily Bonville (1460–1530), Baroness Harrington; Anne Hastings (d. after 1506).

NEVILLE, Catherine (d. 1476). *See Stafford, Catherine.*

NEVILLE, Cecily (1415–1495). Duchess of York. Name variations: Cecily, duchess of York; Lady Cecily Neville; Cecily of York; Rose of Raby. Born May 3, 1415, in Raby Castle, Durham, England; died May 31, 1495, at Hertfordshire, England; dau. of Joan Beaufort (1379–1440) and Sir Ralph Neville of Raby; m. Richard, 3rd duke of York, Lord Protector, in 1424 (died 1460); children: Joan (1438–1438); Anne Plantagenet (1439–1476); Henry (b. 1441, died young); Edward IV (1442–1483), king of England (r. 1461–1483); Edmund (1443–1460), earl of Rutland; Elizabeth de la Pole (1444–1503), duchess of Suffolk; Margaret of York (1446–1503); William (b. 1447, died young); John (b. 1448, died young); George (1449–1478), duke of Clarence; Thomas (born c. 1451, died young); Richard III (1452–1485), king of England (r. 1483–1485); Ursula (born c. 1454, died young). ❖ Important figure in England's Wars of the Roses, was as ambitious as her husband and an active participant in the political struggles which emerged between him and King Henry VI; taken into custody with her 3 youngest children by Queen Margaret of Anjou's army at Ludlow after husband was defeated in battle (1459); pleaded successfully with Henry VI to spare the lives of captured Yorkists; after husband and son were killed in battle (1460), was still determined that the House of York should rule and supported the claim of her eldest son Edward (IV); helped found the House of York. ❖ See also *Women in World History.*

NEVILLE, Cecily (fl. 1480s). Countess of Warwick. Name variations: Cecily Beauchamp; Cecily Tiptoft. Dau. of Richard Neville, 1st earl of Salisbury, and Alice Montacute (c. 1406–1463); sister of Richard Neville, earl of Warwick (1428–1471, known as Warwick the Kingmaker); m. Henry Beauchamp, duke and 6th earl of Warwick, c. 1433; m. John Tiptoft, 1st earl of Worcester; children: (1st m.) Anne Beauchamp (c. 1443–1449, died at age 6).

NEVILLE, Eleanor (c. 1413–1472). Countess of Northumberland. Name variations: Eleanor Percy. Born c. 1413; died in 1472; dau. of Joan Beaufort (1379–1440) and Sir Ralph Neville of Raby; m. Richard Despenser, Lord Despenser; m. Henry Percy (1392–1455), 2nd earl of Northumberland, in 1414; children: Henry Percy (b. 1421), earl of Northumberland; Thomas Percy (b. 1422), 1st lord Egremont; Katherine Percy (who m. Edmund Grey, 1st earl of Kent).

NEVILLE, Eleanor (fl. 1480s). Countess of Derby. Dau. of Richard Neville, 1st earl of Salisbury, and Alice Montacute (c. 1406–1463); sister of Richard Neville, earl of Warwick (1428–1471, known as Warwick the Kingmaker); m. Thomas Stanley, earl of Derby; children: George Stanley, Lord Strange (d. 1497); Edward Stanley, Lord Monteagle (d. 1523).

NEVILLE, Elizabeth (c. 1383–?). *See Holland, Elizabeth.*

NEVILLE, Isabel. *See Ingoldsthorp, Isabel.*

NEVILLE, Isabel (1451–1476). Duchess of Clarence. Born Sept 5, 1451, in Warwick Castle, Warwickshire, England; died Dec 14, 1476, in Warwick Castle; dau. of Richard Neville, earl of Warwick, and Anne Beauchamp (1426–1492); m. George, duke of Clarence, July 4, 1469; children: Anne (b. 1470, died in infancy); Margaret Pole (1473–1541), countess of Salisbury; Edward, earl of Warwick and Surrey (1475–1499); Richard (1476–1477).

NEVILLE, Jane (d. 1538). Baroness Montagu. Name variations: Jane Pole. Died 1538; dau. of George Neville, 4th Lord Bergavenny, and Margaret Fenne; m. Henry Pole (son of Margaret Pole 1538), baron Montagu (died 1538); children: at least one son. ❖ May have died in the Tower along with husband.

NEVILLE, Jane (d. 1593). *See Howard, Jane.*

NEVILLE, Joan (fl. 1468). English noblewoman. Name variations: Joan Bourchier. Probably born in 1450; dau. of John Bourchier, 1st baron Berners, and Catherine Howard (fl. 1450); m. Henry Neville (died in battle in 1469); children: Richard Neville, 2nd baron Latimer (1468–1530).

NEVILLE, Joan (fl. 1480s). Countess of Arundel. Name variations: Joan Fitzalan. Flourished in the 1480s; dau. of Alice Montacute (c. 1406–1463) and Richard Neville, 1st earl of Salisbury; sister of Richard Neville, earl of Warwick (1428–1471, known as the Kingmaker); m. William Fitzalan, 13th earl of Arundel; children: Thomas Fitzalan, 14th earl of Arundel (1450–1524).

NEVILLE, Joanna (c. 1379–1440). *See Beaufort, Joan.*

NEVILLE, Lucy (fl. 15th c.). English noblewoman. Dau. of John Neville, marquess of Montagu and earl of Northumberland, and Isabel Ingoldsthorp; sister of Margaret Neville (b. 1466); m. Sir Anthony Browne; children: Anne Browne (d. 1511, who m. Charles Brandon [1484–1545], duke of Suffolk).

NEVILLE, Margaret (d. 1372). Countess of Northumberland. Name variations: Margaret Percy. Died May 12, 1372; dau. of Ralph Neville, 2nd baron Neville of Raby, and Alice Audley (d. 1374); m. William Roos, 4th baron Ros; m. Henry Percy (1341–1408), 1st earl of Northumberland, on July 12, 1358; children: Henry Percy (Hotspur); Ralph Percy. ❖ Portrayed in William Shakespeare's *Henry IV, Part 2.*

NEVILLE, Margaret (d. 1396). *See Stafford, Margaret.*

NEVILLE, Margaret (c. 1377–c. 1424). Duchess of Exeter. Born c. 1377; died c. 1424; interred at Bury St. Edmunds Abbey, Suffolk; dau. of Sir Thomas Neville of Hornby, and Joan Furnivall; m. Thomas Beaufort, duke of Exeter, before Feb 15, 1403; children: Henry Beaufort.

NEVILLE, Margaret (b. 1466). Duchess of Suffolk. Name variations: Margaret Mortimer; Margaret Brandon. Born 1466; death date unknown; dau. of John Neville, marquess of Montagu and earl of Northumberland, and Isabel Ingoldsthorp; m. John Mortimer; m. Charles Brandon (1484–1545), 1st duke of Suffolk (r. 1514–1545), before Feb 7, 1506 (annulled in 1507). ❖ Charles Brandon was also married to Mary Tudor (1496–1533), Anne Browne (d. 1511), and Catharine Bertie (1519–1580).

NEVILLE, Margaret (d. 1506). Sister of the Kingmaker. Born before 1460; died after Nov 20, 1506; dau. of Alice Montacute (c. 1406–1463) and Richard Neville (b. 1400), 1st earl of Salisbury; sister of Richard Neville, earl of Warwick (1428–1471, known as Warwick the Kingmaker); m. John de Vere, 13th earl of Oxford; m. William Hastings, Lord Hastings; children: (2nd m.) Edward Hastings, Lord Hastings.

NEVILLE, Phoebe (1941—). American postmodern dancer and choreographer. Born Sept 28, 1941, in Philadelphia, PA; trained with Joyce Trisler and Daniel Nagrin. ❖ Worked with Clark Center for the Performing Arts, Studio Nine, and Judson Dance Theater; performed in works of Meredith Monk, Kenneth King, and Carolee Schneemann; created *Of the Dark Air* (1962), *Mask Dance* (1967), and *Night Garden* (1972). Also choreographed *Ragaroni* (1966), *Dance for Mandolins* (1966), (with Philip Hipwell) *Light Rain* (1968), *Caryatid* (1969), *Cartouche* (1974), *Mosaic* (1976) and *Dodona* (1980), among others.

NEVILLE-JONES, Pauline (1939—). English diplomat. Name variations: Dame Pauline Neville-Jones. Born Lilian Pauline Neville-Jones, Nov 2, 1939, in England; dau. of doctors; graduate of Lady Margaret Hall, Oxford University. ❖ Was Harkness fellow of Commonwealth

Fund in US (1961–63); entered British Foreign Service (1963), becoming career diplomat; served in British Mission in Rhodesia (now Zimbabwe, 1964–65), Singapore (1965–68) and Washington, DC (1971–75); worked in Foreign Commonwealth Office (FCO, 1968–71, 1975–77); was seconded to European Commission during tenure at Foreign Service, working as deputy and then *chef du cabinet* to Budget and Financial Institutions Commissioner, Christopher Tugendhat (1977–82); went on to work at Royal Institute for International Affairs (1982–83), before becoming head of planning staff at FCO (1987); served as head of Defense and Overseas Secretariat in Cabinet Office and deputy secretary to Cabinet (1991–94); was chair of the Joint Intelligence Committee (1993–94) and then became 2nd highest official in FCO as political director and deputy under-secretary, playing key role as leader of British delegation to Dayton negotiations on Bosnia peace settlement (1994–96); retired from Foreign Service (1996); also served as international governor of BBC with responsibility for external broadcasting (1998–2005). Made Commander of Order of St. Michael and St. George (1987) and Dame Commander of British Empire (1992).

NEVILLE OF RABY, Baroness (d. 1374). *See Audley, Alice.*

NEVILLES, Sis (c. 1893–1987). *See Cotten, Elizabeth.*

NEWALL, Bertha Surtees (1877–1932). *See Phillpotts, Bertha Surtees.*

NEWALL, Sybil (1854–1929). English archer. Born Oct 17, 1854; died June 24, 1929. ❖ At London Olympics, won a gold medal in the national round (1908), was the oldest female Olympic champion in history; went by the name of Queenie; won British championship (1911, 1912, and 1914), and competed for the final time in 1928 at age 74.

NEWBERRY, Barbara (1910—). American theatrical dancer and choreographer. Born April 12, 1910, in Boston, MA. ❖ Made professional debut in NY in *Penrod* (1918); had featured dance roles in *Ziegfeld's American Revue* (1926), *Betsy* (1926), and *Golden Dawn* (1927), among others; choreographed numerous Prologs for Balaban and Katz chain of Midwest theaters (1927–28) and *Take a Chance* (1932) for Broadway; co-choreographed *The Gay Divorcée* in NY (1932) and later London (1933); co-directed *Monte Carlo Follies* (1933), also in London.

NEWBERY, Chantelle (1977—). Australian diver. Name variations: Tilly Newbery. Born May 6, 1977, in Melbourne, Australia. ❖ Competed in World championships for tumbling (1992); placed 3rd for 3-meter springboard at World championships (1998) and for 10-meter platform at Grand Prix Super Final (2004); placed 1st in Grand Prix ranking for 3-meter springboard (2003); won gold medal for 10-meter platform at Athens Olympics (2004); won a bronze medal for 3-meter sychronized springboard with Irina Lashko at Athens Olympics (2004). Named Australia's Diver of the Year (1997–99).

NEWBIGIN, Marion I. (1869–1934). Scottish biologist, geographer and writer. Name variations: Marion Isobel Newbigin. Born 1869 in Alnwick, Northumberland, England; died July 20, 1934; dau. of James Leslie Newbigin (pharmacist). ❖ Longtime editor of the *Scottish Geographical Magazine* (1902–34), studied at the Edinburgh Association for the University Education of Women, at University College (Aberystwyth) and at School of Medicine for Women in Edinburgh; earned a DSc (1898); served as a School of Medicine for Women lecturer in Edinburgh; appointed president of Geographical Section of British Association for Advancement of Science (1922); was a member of Royal Scottish Geographical Society. Published 17 books, including *Life by the Sea Shore–An Introduction to Natural History* (1901), *An Introduction to Physical Geography* (1912), *Animal Geography* (1913), *Geographical Aspects of Balkan Problems* (1915), *Southern Europe* (1932) and *Commercial Geography* (1923).

NEWBURGH, countess of. *See Radcliffe, Charlotte Maria (d. 1755).*

NEWBY-FRASER, Paula (1962—). Zimbabwean-born American triathlete. Born Paula Newby-Fraser, 1962, in Harare, Zimbabwe. ❖ Won the national Ironman Triathlon in the women's division, South Africa (1985); finished 3rd in her 1st world-class Ironman race (1985); finished 2nd in the Hawaii Ironman Triathlon, but later named winner after 1st-place finisher was disqualified (1986); was 8-time Ironman Triathlon world champion (1986, 1988, 1989, 1991–94, 1996); finished 3rd in the Hawaii Ironman and the Ironman world championships (1987); was 4-time Ironman Japan champion (1988, 1990–92) and 4-time Nice International Triathlon champion (1989–92); was 3-time Ironman Europe champion (1992, 1994, 1995), 3-time Ironman

Lanzarote champion (1994, 1995, 1997), Ironman Canada champion (1996), 2-time Ironman Australia champion (1996, 1997) and Ironman South Africa champion (2000). Named Greatest All-Around Female Athlete in the World by "Wide World of Sports" and *Los Angeles Times* (1989); named Professional Athlete of the Year by Women's Sports Foundation and Female Pro Athlete of the Decade by *Los Angeles Times* (1990); inducted into Breitbard Hall of Fame at Hall of Champions Sports Museum (2000). ❖ See also *Women in World History.*

NEWCASTLE, duchess of. *See Cavendish, Margaret (1623–1673).*

NEWCOMB, Ethel (1875–1959). American pianist. Born in Whitney Point, New York, 1875; died in Whitney Point, July 3, 1959; studied in Vienna with Leschetizky, 1895–1903. ❖ Performed concertos with Vienna Symphony Orchestra; was assistant to Theodor Leschetizky (1904–08); in London debut (1904), performed concertos by Schumann, Chopin, and Saint-Saëns under baton of Richard Strauss; wrote *Leschetizky as I Knew Him* (Appleton, 1921).

NEWCOMB, Josephine L. (1816–1901). American philanthropist. Name variations: Josephine Le Monnier Newcomb. Born Josephine Louise Le Monnier, Oct 31, 1816, in Baltimore, Maryland; died April 7, 1901, in New York, NY; dau. of Alexander Le Monnier and Mary Sophia (Waters) Le Monnier; m. Warren Newcomb (merchant), 1845; children: son (died young); H(arriott) Sophie Newcomb (1855–1870). ❖ Established, through $100,000 donation, H. Sophie Newcomb Memorial College for women at Tulane University, New Orleans (1887); also donated sizable sums to Washington and Lee University and to the Confederate Orphan Home in Charleston, South Carolina; gave funds to help establish schools for poor girls and for the deaf. ❖ See also *Women in World History.*

NEWCOMB, Mary (1893–1966). American-born actress. Born Aug 21 (some sources cite Aug 24), 1893, in North Adams, MA; died Dec 26, 1966, in Dorchester, England; m. Robert Edeson (div.); m. Alexander Henry Higginson. ❖ Star of both NY and London stages, made NY debut in *Sick-a-bed* (1918) and subsequently appeared in *The Woman on the Jury, Easy Street, The Night Hawk* and *The Bridge of Distances*; made hugely successful London bow in *Jealousy* (1928) and subsequently appeared there in *Emma Hamilton, The Merchant of Venice* and *When Ladies Meet*; joined the Old Vic (1934), playing title roles in *St. Joan* and *Major Barbara*; founded Mary Newcomb Players Mobile Theatre to entertain English soldiers during WWII; served as president of the Dorset Drama League.

NEWELL, Emily Jane (1877–1951). *See Blair, Emily Newell.*

NEWELL, Harriet Atwood (1793–1812). American missionary. Born Harriet Atwood, Oct 10, 1793, in Haverhill, Massachusetts; died Nov 30, 1812, on Isle of France (now Mauritius); dau. of Moses Atwood (merchant) and Mary (Tenny) Atwood; attended Bradford Academy in Massachusetts, 1806–07, and a private academy, 1810; m. Samuel Newell (later a missionary), Feb 9, 1812; children: Harriet (born prematurely, 1812, died 5 days later). ❖ One of the 1st two American women to travel overseas as a missionary, along with Ann Hasseltine Judson, was the 1st American missionary to die on foreign soil (1812); her brief career, perceived by some as almost martyr-like, became for years an inspiration to aspiring overseas missionaries. ❖ See also *Women in World History.*

NEWELL, Susan (1893–1923). Scottish murderer. Born 1893 in Scotland; hanged at Duke Street Prison, Glasgow, Oct 10, 1923; m. John Newell; children: (by a previous marriage) Janet McLeod. ❖ With 8-year-old daughter, was seen pushing a handcart containing a bundle in Glasgow suburb of Coatbridge (June 1923); left bundle, which contained body of 13-year-old newsboy John Johnstone (or Johnston), at a tenement entrance; was arrested as she then tried to escape over a wall; at trial for murder (Sept 1923) received death sentence in a case noteworthy for its lack of motive; was 1st woman to be hanged in Scotland in 50 years.

NEWHOUSE, Alice (1924–2004). American philanthropist. Born Alice Gross, July 21, 1924, in New York, NY; died Mar 28, 2004, in New Orleans, LA; attended Wellesley College and New York University; m. Norman Newhouse (publishing executive, 1988); children: Peter, Mark, Jonathan and David Newhouse. ❖ Well-known philanthropist and socialite in New Orleans, moved there in 1968; established Odyssey House, a residential facility for substance-abuse treatment.

NEWHOUSE, Caroline H. (1910–2003). American artist and philanthropist. Born Caroline Herz, Mar 20, 1910, near Koblenz, Germany; died April 26, 2003, in Roxbury, CT; attended Art Students League;

m. Theodore Newhouse (co-founder of Newhouse communications co.), 1956 (died 1998). ❧ An artist and sculptor, immigrated to US with her widowed Jewish mother (1934); was active in fund-raising for the arts; helped found and served on the board of Career Transition for Dancers.

NEWHOUSE, Jean (1911–1998). *See Shiley, Jean.*

NEWLIN, Dika (1923—). American composer, pianist, critic, musicologist, and professor. Born in Portland, Oregon, Nov 22, 1923; Michigan State University, BA, 1939, University of California at Los Angeles, MA, 1951; awarded the 1st PhD in musicology granted by Columbia University, 1945; studied with Arnold Schoenberg, Artur Schnabel, Rudolf Serkin and Roger Sessions. ❧ Established music department at Drew University (1952–65); was professor of musicology at North Texas State University, Denton (1965–73); appointed director of Montclair State College's electronic music library (1973); developed doctoral program in music for Virginia Commonwealth University (1978); in addition to numerous compositions in the 12-tone idiom, wrote about Arnold Schoenberg and translated his works.

NEWMAN, Angelia L. (1837–1910). American church worker and reformer. Name variations: Angie Newman. Born Angelia Louise French Thurston, Dec 4, 1837, in Montpelier, Vermont; died April 15, 1910, in Lincoln, Nebraska; dau. of Daniel Sylvester Thurston and Matilda Benjamin Thurston; half-sister of US senator, John Mellen Thurston; attended Lawrence University, 1857–58; m. Frank Kilgore (died c. 1856); m. David Newman (merchant), Aug 25, 1859 (died 1893); children: (2nd m.) Cora Fanny (b. 1860); Henry Byron (b. 1863). ❧ Joined Women's Foreign Missionary Society (1875) and soon became secretary of its western branch; organized missionary trips into western Nebraska, raised funds to aid missionary work in India, and wrote numerous articles for *Heathen Woman's Friend*; argued that Mormonism was not a religion and advanced campaign of Ann Eliza Young, 27th wife of Brigham Young; sustained offensive against Mormons, becoming secretary of Mormon Bureau of the Woman's Home Missionary Society and superintendent of Mormon Department of Woman's Christian Temperance Union (WCTU); became the 1st woman appointed as a lay delegate to the General Conference, the Methodist legislative body, though she was not seated due to her "female ineligibility" (1887); was much admired for her oratory and her dedication to reform. ❧ See also *Women in World History.*

NEWMAN, Frances (1883–1928). American writer and librarian. Born Sept 13, 1883 (some sources cite 1888), in Atlanta, Georgia; died Oct 22 (or 28), 1928, in New York, NY; dau. of William Truslow Newman (judge) and Frances Percy (Alexander) Newman; attended Agnes Scott College, 1900–01, and Library School of Atlanta Carnegie Library; studied at Sorbonne, 1923; never married. ❧ Began career as a librarian at Florida State College for Women (1913); wrote book reviews for NY newspapers, where their acerbic criticism caught the attention of H.L. Mencken; her short story "Rachel and Her Children" appeared in his *American Mercury* and won an O. Henry Award (1924); writings include *The Short Story's Mutations: From Petronius to Paul Morand* (1924), *The Hard-Boiled Virgin* (1926) and *Dead Lovers Are Faithful Lovers* (1928); also translated *Six Moral Tales from Jules Laforgue* (1928). ❧ See also *Women in World History.*

NEWMAN, Julia St. Clair (1818–?). Creole swindler. Born in 1818; educated in France. ❧ Earning her livelihood through a series of scams and thefts, landed in prison in London at 19 and became one of the most incorrigible prisoners in British history; was sent on the convict ship *Nautilus* to penal colony in Australia, where she vanished from history. ❧ See also *Women in World History.*

NEWMAN, Mehetabel (c. 1822–1908). New Zealand missionary, letter writer, and teacher. Name variations: Mehetabel Buttle, Mehetabel Warren. Born Mehetabel Newman, c. 1822 (baptized, Dec 22, 1822), in Lincolnshire, England; died Jan 8, 1908, in Yorkshire, England; dau. of Joseph Newman (farmer) and Eleanor Dawson; m. George Buttle (brother-in-law), 1873 (died 1874); m. John Warren, 1878 (died 1883). ❧ Immigrated to New Zealand to join other family members (1844); lived with sister and brother-in-law, Methodist missionaries, south of Auckland, where she taught Maori girls to read, write, and sew; for decades, wrote letters home in which she described life on an inland mission and the experience of an unmarried woman in middle-class colonial society. ❧ See also *Dictionary of New Zealand Biography* (Vol. 1).

NEWMAN, Nanette (1934—). English actress and writer. Born May 29, 1934, in Northampton, England; m. Bryan Forbes (writer, producer), 1954; children: Emma Forbes (tv personality) and Sarah Forbes (actress). ❧ Began career as a child, making film debut in *Here We Come Gathering* (1945), followed by *Personal Affair, The L-Shaped Room, The Wrong Arm of the Law, Of Human Bondage, Seance on a Wet Afternoon, The Wrong Box, The Whisperers, The Madwoman of Chaillot, Captain Nemo and the Underwater City, The Stepford Wives, Man at the Top, International Velvet* and *The Mystery of Edwin Drood,* among others; famous in England for a series of tv ads for Fairy Liquid (dish detergent); author of cookbooks and children's stories.

NEWMAN, Pauline (1887–1986). American labor activist. Born in Russia, Oct 18, 1887; died April 1986 in NY; lifelong friend of Rose Schneiderman and Clara Lemlich; lived with Frieda S. Miller (1889–1973). ❧ Worked at the Triangle Shirtwaist Factory; quit job to become a labor organizer; wrote about the miserable working conditions of the factory following the Triangle fire; was the 1st full-time woman organizer for International Ladies' Garment Workers Union (ILGWU); founded the ILGWU's Health Center and was director of health education (1918–80); was also an advisor to US Department of Labor (1930s–40s.

NEWMAR, Julie (1935—). American actress and dancer. Born Julia Chalane Newmeyer, Aug 16, 1935, in Los Angeles, CA; dau. of Donald Newmeyer (professor and professional football player) and Helen Jesmar (actress); studied at University of California, Los Angeles; trained in ballet by Bonislava Nijinska and Carmelita Maracci. ❧ Worked as a dance coach at Universal Studios (1950s); made film debut in *Seven Brides for Seven Brothers* (1954), then appeared on Broadway in *Silk Stockings*; won Tony Award as Best Supporting Actress in *Marriage-Go-Round* and reprised role on screen (1960); also appeared on Broadway (1956) and film (1959) as Stupefyin' Jones in *Li'l Abner*; on tv, portrayed Catwoman on "Batman" and starred on "My Living Doll"; made cameo appearance in film *To Wong Foo, Thanks for Everything, Julie Newmar* (1995). ❧ See also *Women in World History.*

NEWPORT, Matilda (c. 1795–1837). Liberian hero. Born, perhaps in Philadelphia, c. 1795; died in Monrovia, Liberia, 1837; m. Thomas Spencer; m. Ralph Newport. ❧ Her courage during an attack by indigenous people on pioneer free black settlers (1822) came to represent the ideals of the Americo-Liberian elite in the West African republic. In 1916, the Liberian Legislature declared Dec 1 to be Matilda Newport Day, a permanent national holiday. ❧ See also *Women in World History.*

NEWSOM, Carol (1946–2003). American photographer. Born Carol Lee Natelson, 1946, in Boston, MA; died Mar 13, 2003, in Framingham, MA; attended Boston University. ❧ Began career as a math teacher; became a photographer, specializing in tennis (1974); gained international recognition (1980) as the 1st female photographer issued a pass to work in Wimbledon's Centre Court; became official photographer of the women's tour, sponsored by Virginia Slims. Inducted into New England Tennis Hall of Fame (2003).

NEWSOM, Ella King (1838–1919). American hospital administrator. Name variations: Ella King Newsom Trader. Born Ella King, June 1838, in Brandon, MS; died Jan 20, 1919, in Washington, DC; dau. of Thomas S.N. King (pastor) and Julia King; m. William Frank Newsom (physician), Feb 6, 1854 (died); William H. Trader, 1867 (died 1885); children: (2nd m.) several, but only 1 daughter survived childhood. ❧ Dubbed "Florence Nightingale of the South," named matron of Overton Hospital in Memphis, TN (1861), during Civil War; assumed control of Confederate military hospital in Bowling Green, KY (1861–62); ran Foard Hospital and was official chief matron at Academy Hospital, both in Chattanooga, TN (1862); organized hospitals in Georgia as Tennessee army retreated south; worked in various government posts in US General Land Office, Patent Office, and Pension Office (1886–1916); as part of a group of women who fought contemporary attitudes against women in military hospitals, helped set the stage for the trained nursing profession. ❧ See also Jacob Fraise Richard, *The Florence Nightingale of the Southern Army: Experiences of Mrs. Ella K. Newsom, Confederate Nurse in the Great War of 1861–65* (Broadway, 1914).

NEWTON, Joy (1913–1996). English ballet dancer and teacher. Born May 1913 in Wimbledon, England; died April 4, 1996. ❧ Trained with Ninette de Valois early on and began performing with Vic-Wells and Sadler's Wells Ballets (1930s); held principal roles in *The Nutcracker, Coppélia,* and de Valois' *The Rake's Progress* (1935), among others; served as ballet master of Sadler's Wells Ballet; acted as founding director of

Turkish Ballet School in Istanbul after WWII; taught at Royal Ballet School in London.

NEWTON, Juice (1952—). American singer and guitarist. Born Judy Kay Newton, Feb 18, 1952, in NJ; m. Tom Goodspeed, 1985; children: Jessica and Tyler. ❖ At 13, taught herself acoustic guitar; with Otha Young, formed the band Dixie Peach (late 1960s), which, adding bassist Tom Kealey, became Silver Spur (1972); with RCA Records, released unsuccessful albums, *Juice Newton and Silver Spur* (1975) and *After the Dust Settles* (1976); with band, signed with Capitol and released *Come to Me* (1976); after Silver Spur disbanded, released solo debut album, *Well Kept Secret* (1978), followed by *Take Heart* (1979), which included 1st country hit, "Sunshine"; released platinum LP, *Juice* (1981), which included hits "Angel of the Morning," "Queen of Hearts," and "The Sweetest Thing"; other albums include *Dirty Looks* (1983), *Emotion* (1987), and *American Girl* (1999); also had hit singles with "A Little Love" (1984), "I'm So Hurt" (1985), "Cheap Love" (1986), "Tell Me True" (1987) and "Break It to Me Gently."

NEWTON, Lily (1893–1981). English botanist and educator. Name variations: Lily Batten Newton. Born Lily Batten, Jan 26, 1893; died Mar 25, 1981; University of Bristol, PhD, 1922, DSc, 1950; m. Dr. W.C.F. Newton (cytologist), 1925 (died 1927). ❖ A seaweed expert, lectured at Bristol University (1919–20) and Birkbeck College, University of London (1920–23); researched at University of London's Imperial College (1923–25); was a research worker at John Innes Horticultural Institute (1927–28); at University College of Wales, Aberystwyth, served as lecturer (1928–30), botany professor (1930–58), vice principal (1951–52) and acting principal (1952–53); during WWII, helped to ensure the successful growth of seaweed for agar production; at British Association for the Advancement of Science's annual meeting (1949), served as president of its Botany Section; appointed president of the British Phycological Society (1955–56); wrote *Handbook of British Seaweeds* (1931).

NEWTON, Wharetutu Anne (fl. 1827–1870). New Zealand settlement founder. Name variations: Wharetutu. Born Wharetutu, in North Otago, New Zealand (baptized, Feb 6, 1844); died after 1870, in New Zealand; dau. of Tahuna and Tahupare; m. George Newton, 1844 (died 1853); children: 13. ❖ One of the earliest Ngai Tahu founders of a settlement of Maori-Pakeha families, produced first generations of mixed descent children in southern New Zealand. ❖ See also *Dictionary of New Zealand Biography* (Vol. 1).

NEWTON-JOHN, Olivia (1948—). English singer. Born Sept 26, 1948, in Cambridge, England; m. Matt Lattanzi (actor), 1984 (sep. 1995); children: Chloe (b. 1986). ❖ Grew up in Australia; started 1st band, Sol Four, while in high school; joined band Tomorrow; toured with Cliff Richard and appeared on his series, "It's Cliff Richard"; released 1st single, "If Not For You" (1971), which was UK and US hit; released 1st US album, *Let Me Be There* (1973), which went gold, along with title-track single; moved to LA and had hit with "Have You Never Been Mellow" (1975); won Best Female Singer Award from Country Music Association (1976); starred in *Grease* (1978), which produced 3 singles, "You're the One That I Want," "Summer Nights" and "Hopelessly Devoted to You"; appeared in unsuccessful film, *Xanadu* (1980), but had hit with soundtrack, which went double platinum; released platinum LPs *Totally Hot* (1978) and *Physical* (1981), whose title track was #1; appeared in films *Two of a Kind* (1983) and *Sordid Lives* (1999); released children's album, *Warm and Tender* (1989); treated for breast cancer (early 1990s), made documentary on experience, *Gaia: One Woman's Journey* (1994). Received Order of the British Empire (OBE).

NEWTON TURNER, Helen (1908–1995). Australian geneticist and mathematician. Name variations: Helen Newton-Turner; Helen Turner. Born Helen Alma Newton Turner, May 15, 1908, in Sydney, NSW, Australia; died Nov 26, 1995; mother was a university medalist and father worked for the State Children's Relief Department; University of Sydney, DSc, 1970. ❖ A pioneer in sheep breeding and genetics, led a research team on a merino fleece improvement project; at the Commonwealth Scientific and Industrial Research Organisation (CSIRO), worked as secretary to Dr. Ian Clunies Ross (1931–34), as a statistician (1934–36), as a technical officer (1936–38), as a consulting statistician (1939–41), as a consultant statistician for Division of Animal Health and Production (1945–56) and as a senior principal research scientist for Division of Animal Genetics (1956–76), leading a team of 8 scientists; investigated European and American sheep-breeding programs (1954); introduced population genetics to Australia; during WWII, established the University Women's Land Army with Isobel Bennett (1940), and worked as a Department of Home Security statistician in Canberra (1942) and as a Department of Manpower statistician in Sydney (1943–44); elected to Australian Academy of Technological Sciences (1973) and Australasian Association of Animal Breeding and Genetics (1990). Received Order of the British Empire (OBE, 1977), Order of Australia (1987), Farber Memorial Medal for distinguished services to agriculture.

NEY, Anna (1900–1993). *See Pasternak, Josephine.*

NEY, Elisabet (1833–1907). German sculptor. Name variations: Elise or Elisabeth Ney. Born Franzisca Bernadina Wilhelmina Elisabeth Ney, Jan 26, 1833, in Münster, Westphalia; died June 29, 1907, in Austin, Texas; dau. of Johann Adam Ney (stonemason) and Anna Elisabeth (Wernze) Ney; graduate of Bavarian Art Academy, 1853, and Berlin Art Academy, 1854; m. Edmund Duncan Montgomery (physician), Nov 7, 1863; children: Arthur (1871–1873); Lorne (b. 1872). ❖ Flamboyant artist who sculpted major European figures of the day, spent 2nd half of career in Texas, where she contributed to the development of an arts community; exhibited at Paris Salon (1861); sculpted *Sursum* (1863–65); traveled to Caprera to sculpt Garibaldi (1865); sculpted King Ludwig II of Bavaria and abruptly left Germany (1870); arrived in NY, moved to Georgia (1871), then Texas (1873); exhibited German works in San Antonio (1890); established studio in Austin and contracted for the 1893 World's Columbian Exposition in Chicago (1892); became president of Association of the Texas Academy of Liberal Arts (1894); completed self-portrait and gathered works in Europe for 1904 St. Louis World's Fair (1903); completed *Lady Macbeth* (1905); other works include *William Jennings Bryan* (1901), *Sam Houston* (1892), *Stephen F. Austin* (1893), *Oran Roberts* (1882), *Albert Sidney Johnston Memorial* (1902) and angel marker for grave of Elisabeth Emma Schnerr (1906). Studio purchased to create Elisabet Ney Museum (1908); works and personal papers donated by husband to University of Texas (1910). ❖ See also Emily Fourmy Cutrer, *The Art of the Woman: The Life and Work of Elisabet Ney* (U. of Nebraska Press, 1988); Fortune and Burton, *Elisabet Ney* (Knopf, 1943); and *Women in World History*.

NEY, Elly (1882–1968). German pianist. Born in Düsseldorf, Germany, Sept 27, 1882; died Mar 31, 1968, at Tutzing, Bavaria; descendant of France's Marshal Ney; studied at Cologne Conservatory under Isidor Seiss and Karl Bottcher, then with Theodor Leschetizky and Emil von Sauer; m. Willem van Hoogstraten (conductor), 1911 (div. 1927); m. P. F. Allais. ❖ Debuted in Vienna (1905); won the Mendelssohn and Ibach prizes; made the 1st recording of Richard Strauss' *Burleske* for Piano and Orchestra; a master of the German repertoire, taught for many years at the Cologne Conservatory and enthusiastically supported the Third Reich; widely known for her performances of Beethoven.

NEY, Marie (1895–1981). English actress. Born July 18, 1895, in Chelsea, London, England; died April 11, 1981, in London; dau. of William Fix; m. Thomas H. Menzies (div. then remarried). ❖ Made stage debut in Melbourne, Australia, as the Widow in *The Taming of the Shrew* (1916), with Allan Wilkie's Shakespearean Co.; made London debut with Old Vic as Desdemona in *Othello* (1924), followed by such roles as Lady Macbeth, Ophelia, Viola, Beatrice, and Rose Trelawny in *Trelawny of the Wells*; other plays include *The Madras House, Beyond the Horizon, The Constant Nymph, She Stoops to Conquer, The Three Musketeers, Arms and the Man* and *Ghosts*; during WWII, did broadcasts in Malaya, toured for ENSA and in her solo show *Shakespeare's Women*; made film debut in *Escape* (1930), followed by *Scrooge, Jamaica Inn, The Lavender Hill Mob, Simba* and *Witchcraft*, among others.

NEYKOVA, Rumyana (1973—). Bulgarian rower. Born April 6, 1973, in Sofia, Bulgaria. ❖ Won a silver medal for single sculls at Sydney Olympics (2000) and a gold medal at World championships (2002, 2003); won a bronze medal for single sculls at Athens Olympics (2004).

NEZHDANOVA, Antonina (1873–1950). Russian soprano. Name variations: Antonia Vasilievna Nezhdanova. Born 1873 in Krivaya Balka, near Odessa, Russia; died 1950; attended Moscow Conservatory, where she studied under Umberto Masetti; m. Nikolai Golovanov (conductor), 1920s. ❖ One of the great singers of imperial Russia, made debut in Moscow in Glinka's *A Life for the Tsar* (1902) and was immediately engaged by the Bolshoi; throughout 30-year career, mostly in Russia, sang much of the high repertoire: Gilda, Lakmé, Juliette, Frau Fluth in *The Merry Wives of Windsor*, The Queen of the Night, Queen Marguerite in *Les Huguenots*, Ophélie, and Zerlina in *Fra Diavolo*; also sang the Russian repertoire, as well as such dramatic roles as Desdemona and

Tosca; had Ukrainian roots and a sizable repertory of folksongs from Ukraine. ❖ See also *Women in World History*.

NGA HOTA (1840/42–1909). *See Matenga, Huria.*

NGA-KAHU-WHERO (fl. 1800–1836). New Zealand tribal leader. Born Nga-kahu-whero, in late 18th century, at Waihou, New Zealand; dau. of Kahi and Kaimanu; m. Muriwhenua; children: 3. ❖ Inherited tribal authority over land and people of Papanui, which entitled her to a share of all land sales, including royalties from felling of trees. ❖ See also *Dictionary of New Zealand Biography* (Vol. 1).

NGARONGOA KATENE (1840/42–1909). *See Matenga, Huria.*

NGATA, Arihia Kane (1879–1929). New Zealand tribal leader. Name variations: Arihia Kane Tamati. Born Arihia Kane Tamati, in 1879, at Whareponga on East Coast of North Island, New Zealand; died April 18, 1929, at Waiomatatini, New Zealand; dau. of Tuta Tamati and Mere arihi Kakano; m. Apirana Turupa Ngata (lawyer), 1895; children: 7 daughters, 8 sons. ❖ After husband elected to Parliament, became highly regarded for her successful work with Ngati Porou young people; during WWI, helped organize fund-raising events and provided hospitality to Maori tribesmen who enlisted. Member of British Empire (1918). ❖ See also *Dictionary of New Zealand Biography* (Vol. 3).

NGCOBO, Lauretta (1932—). South African novelist. Born 1932 in Ixopo, South Africa; m. Abednego Ngcobo (prominent founder member of Pan African Congress, died 1997); children: daughter Kethiwe Ngcobo (filmmaker), among others. ❖ KwaZulu-Natal writer, fled South Africa with husband and children to escape detention (1963); settled in London, where she taught for 25 years; returned to South Africa (1994) and became a member of the KwaZulu-Natal Provincial legislature; novels, which focus on life under apartheid, include *Cross of Gold* (1981) and *And They Didn't Die* (1990); also edited collection of essays by Black women writers in Britain, *Let it Be Told* (1987), and wrote essays on South African literature.

NGO DINH NHU, Madame (b. 1924). *See Nhu, Madame.*

NGOYI, Lilian (1911–1980). South African anti-apartheid activist. Name variations: Lilian Masediba Ngoyi; Lilie; Masediba. Born Lilian Masediba Ngoyi, 1911, at Pretoria, South Africa; died Mar 11, 1980, in Orlando Township, Johannesburg; m. John Ngoyi, 1936; children: 3. ❖ Leader in the struggle against apartheid, was president of the African National Congress Women's League (ANCWL) and of the Federation of South African Women (FSAW); was banned for her activism and held under government restriction for almost 20 years; was an effective, energetic, and courageous politician, and a brilliant public speaker. ❖ See also *Women in World History*.

NGUYEN THI DINH (1920–1992). Vietnamese revolutionary. Name variations: Madam Dinh. Pronunciation: Wen Tee Dingh. Born Nguyen Thi Dinh, Mar 15, 1920, in Luong Hoa village, Giong Taom District, Ben Tre Province, Vietnam; died Aug 26, 1992, in Ho Chi Minh City, Vietnam; dau. of Nguyen Van Tien (father) and Truong Thi Dinh (mother); m. Nguyen Van Bich, 1938 (died July 12, 1942); m. Nguyen Huu Tri (referred to as Hai Tri in Dinh's memoir *No Other Road to Take*), 1945 (died 1990); children: (1st m.) son, Nguyen Ngoc Minh (referred to as On in memoir). ❖ The most renowned woman in modern Vietnamese history, known as the "general of the long-haired army," led the insurrection against the French colonial regime in Ben Tre Province (1945), as well as the Ben Tre uprising against the US-backed Diem regime (1960), and became deputy commander of the South Vietnam Liberation Forces; married revolutionary intellectual Nguyen Van Bich (1938), who was arrested 3 days after the birth of their son (1940) and died in French prison (July 12, 1942); arrested by the French (July 19, 1940) and spent 3 years in prison; released to house arrest (1943); led Viet Minh takeover of the provincial capital of Ben Tre (Aug 1945) and elected to executive committee of the province; served on a delegation to Hanoi and transported a large shipment of arms to the South, running through a French naval blockade (1946); led the uprising in Ben Tre Province against Diem regime (Jan 1960) and appointed to leadership committee of National Liberation Front (NLF) in Ben Tre; became a member of presidium of the NLF Central Association (1964); elected chair of South Vietnam Women's Liberation Association (1965) and appointed deputy commander of the South Vietnam Liberation Armed Forces; elected president of Vietnam Women's Union (May 1982), where she served until retirement (April 1992). ❖ See also Mai

V. Elliott, trans. *No Other Road to Take: Memoir of Mrs. Nguyen Thi Dinh* (Cornell U., 1976); and *Women in World History*.

NHIWATIWA, Naomi (1940—). Zimbabwean politician. Name variations: Naomi Pasiharigutwi Nhiwatiwa. Born 1940 in Zimbabwe. ❖ Participated in campaign for creation of Zimbabwe and later became deputy minister for Posts and Telegraphs in Mugabe government; campaigned for women's rights and abolition of bride-price; retired as senior advisor to the United Nation's World Health Organization's Africa region (2000).

NHONGO, Teurai Ropa (1955—). *See Mujuru, Joyce.*

NHU, Madame (1924—). Vietnamese political hostess. Name variations: Madame Ngo Dinh Nhu; Tran Le Xuan. Born Tran Le Xuan (pronounced Trahn Lay Shuen); dau. of Tran Van Chuong (large landowner in central Vietnam and ambassador to US) and Nam Tran Tran van Chuong also known as Madame Tran van Chuong (Vietnamese councilor of the French Union); attended Lycee Albert Sarraut in Hanoi; m. Ngo Dinh Nhu, 1944; children: daughter Tran Le Thuy. ❖ Official hostess of President Ngo Dinh Diem of Republic of Vietnam, the wife of his powerful brother Ngo Dinh Nhu, and a fiery actor in the politics of US-Vietnamese relations, was at the epicenter of Vietnamese politics (1955–63); earned a reputation as an extremist supporter of brother-in-law's regime, but also fought to modernize her country, and in particular to liberate its women from traditional Confucian feudalism; as sister-in-law of the unmarried Ngo Dinh Diem, became acting first lady of the Republic of South Vietnam and attained a worldwide reputation as "Madame Nhu" (1955); became founding president of the paramilitary Women's Solidarity Movement (1961); lost power and went into exile in France upon the assassination of husband (1963). ❖ See also *Women in World History*.

NI GUIZHEN (c. 1869–1931). Chinese matriarch. Name variations: Song Guizhen; Mrs. Charles Jones Song; Mme Charlie Song or Soong; Ni Kwei-tsent or Ni Kweitseng; Ni Kwei-tseng Song or Soong; Mammy Soong. Born Ni Guizhen (Ni Kwei-tseng or Ni Kweitseng) around 1869; died of cancer, 1931; dau. of Yuin San; m. Charlie Jones Song (business leader and philanthropist born Hon Chao-Shun or Jia-shu Song), in 1886; children: 6, including Song Ailing (1890–1973); Song Qingling (1893–1981); Song Meiling (b. 1897); T.V. Song (diplomat, finance and foreign minister, who m. Anna Chang); T.L. Song (Song Zeliang or Tse-liang); and T.A. Song (Song Ze-an or Tse-an). ❖ Matriarch of the influential Song family, was instrumental in sending her daughters to Wesleyan College in Macon, Georgia. ❖ See also *Women in World History*.

NIAN YUN (c. 1983—). Chinese swimmer. Born c. 1983 in China. ❖ Won a silver medal for 4 x 100-meter relay at Atlanta Olympics (1996); age 15, tested positive for *dihydrotestosterone* (1998) and banned from international swimming for 4 years.

NIANG, Idah (1957—). *See Sithole-Niang, Idah.*

NI BHRAONÁIN, Enya (1961—). *See Enya.*

NI BHRAONÁIN, Maire (1952—). *See Brennan, Maire.*

NIBLO, Josephine (1876–1916). *See Cohan, Josephine.*

NIBOYET, Eugénie (1797–1883). French journalist, novelist, and advocate for women's rights. Name variations: Eugenie Niboyet. Born 1797 in Montpellier, France; died 1883; m. Paul-Louis Niboyet (lawyer in Lyon), 1822; children: son. ❖ Began literary career by translating English novels into French; published a number of her own works, then founded socialist journal *La Paix des deux mondes* (Peace in Both Worlds, 1844); committed pacifist and champion of the poor, was aligned for a period with Saint-Simonians; founded *La Voix des Femmes* (Women's Voice), the 1st feminist socialist daily newspaper in France (1848); memoirs of 1848 were published as *Le Vrai Livre des femmes* (The True Book of Women, 1862). ❖ See also *Women in World History*.

NICAEA (fl. 300 BCE). Queen of Macedonia, Thrace, and Anatolia. Dau. of Antipater (a great Macedonian general); sister of Eurydice (fl. 321 BCE); 1st wife of Lysimachus, king of Macedonia, Thrace, and Anatolia (his third acknowledged wife was Arsinoe II Philadelphus); children: son Agathocles and daughter Arsinoe I (fl. 280 BCE).

NICAEA, empress of.
See Anna Angelina (d. 1210?).
See Philippa of Lesser Armenia.
See Marie de Courtenay (fl. 1215).

See Constance-Anna of Hohenstaufen.
See Helen Asen of Bulgaria (d. 1255?).
See Theodora Ducas (fl. 1200s).
See Anna of Hungary (d. around 1284).
See Irene of Montferrat (fl. 1300).
See Irene of Brunswick (fl. 1300s).
See Anne of Savoy (c. 1320–1353).
See Irene Asen.
See Helena Cantacuzene (fl. 1340s).
See Maria-Kyratza Asen.
See Gattilusi, Eugenia.
See Helena Dragas (fl. 1400).
See Anna of Moscow (1393–1417).
See Sophie of Montferrat.
See Maria of Trebizond (d. 1439).
See Magdalena-Theodora Tocco.
See Gattilusi, Caterina.

NICARETE OF MEGARA (fl. 300 BCE). Greek philosopher. Lived in Megara, Greece. ❖ Studied with the philosopher Stilpo who was allayed with the Cynics; sided more with Socrates; may have been a hetaerae and Stilpo's mistress, but there are stronger indications that she was a noble. ❖ See also *Women in World History.*

NICAULA (fl. 10th c. BCE). *See Sheba, Queen of.*

NICE, Margaret Morse (1883–1974). American ornithologist. Born Dec 6, 1883, in Amherst, Massachusetts; died June 26, 1974, in Chicago, Illinois; dau. of Anson Morse (history professor) and Margaret (Ely) Morse; Mt. Holyoke College, BA, 1906; Clark University, MA, 1915; m. Leonard Blaine Nice (medical professor), 1909; children: Constance (b. 1910), Marjorie (b. 1912), Barbara (b. 1915), Eleanor (1918–1928) and Janet Nice (b. 1923). ❖ One of the world's best-known ornithologists and bird behaviorists, was the 1st to accomplish a longterm study of an individual bird in its natural habitat and the 1st woman to be elected president of a prominent American ornithological society; served as president of Wilson Ornithological Society (1938–39); awarded Brewster Medal of American Ornithological Union (1942); writings include (with husband) *The Birds of Oklahoma* (1924), *Studies in the Life History of the Song Sparrow* (2 vols., 1937, 1943) and *The Watcher at the Nest* (1939). ❖ See also autobiography, *Research Is a Passion With Me* (1979); and *Women in World History.*

NICESIPOLIS (d. around 345 BCE). Thessalian noblewoman. Died c. 345 BCE, 20 days after birth of daughter Thessalonike; niece of Jason of Pherae, a tyrant and prominent player in Thessalian politics; became one of the many wives of Philip II of Macedon, in 340s; children: Thessalonike (c. 345–297 BCE).

NICHIFOROV, Maria (1951—). Romanian kayaker. Born April 9, 1951, in Romania. ❖ At Munich Olympics, won a bronze medal in K2 500 meters (1972).

NICHOLAS, Alison (1962—). British golfer. Born Mar 6, 1962, in Gibraltar; lives in Birmingham, England. ❖ Won Yorkshire Ladies County championship (1983), British Open (1987), Western Australian Open (1992), Irish Open (1996) and 11 other titles in Europe and 1 in Asia; won LPGA Corning Classic and PING–AT&T LPGA championship (1995), US Open (1997) and Sunrise Hawaiian Open (1999). Named a Member of the British Empire (MBE, 1998).

NICHOLAS, Charlotte (fl. 1915). English inventor. Fl. 1915 in England. ❖ Developed a minesweeping apparatus (patent no. 22625 granted on July 15, 1915); was a fellow of the Institute of Inventors; patented "disintegrators" (patent no. 22552 granted on Feb 17, 1915); claimed to have thought of using tanks during WWI before Winston Churchill launched the idea.

NICHOLAS, Cindy (1957—). Canadian marathon runner. Born Aug 20, 1957, in Toronto, Ontario, Canada. ❖ Crossed Lake Ontario in record time 15:10 (1974); was the 1st and only woman to swim from Jabbul to Katakia in Syria (1975); was women's world marathon swimming champion (1976); made two-way cross of English Channel in record time 19:45 (1977); made 6th English Channel crossing (1978), the most by a woman; eventually crossed the English Channel 10 times.

NICHOLAS, Princess (1882–1957). *See Helena of Russia.*

NICHOLL, Kahe (?–c. 1871). *See Te Rau-o-te-rangi, Kahe.*

NICHOLL, Peti (?–c. 1871). *See Te Rau-o-te-rangi, Kahe.*

NICHOLLS, Helen (b. 1907). *See Varcoe, Helen.*

NICHOLLS, Mandy (1968—). English field-hockey player. Born Feb 28, 1968, in UK. ❖ At Barcelona Olympics, won a bronze medal in team competition (1992).

NICHOLLS, Marjory Lydia (1890–1930). New Zealand drama producer, drama teacher, debater, and poet. Name variations: Marjory Lydia Hannah. Born July 29, 1890, at Wellington, New Zealand; died Oct 1, 1930, at Wellington; dau. of Harry Edgar Nicholls (accountant) and Susan (Sampson) Nicholls; m. John Hannah, 1920. ❖ Active in Women's Debating Society; gave drama lessons at Chilton St James School, Lower Hutt; studied elocution and stage production in England under Edith Craig, at Pasadena Playhouse in California, and at Greenleaf Theatre in NY; member of National Repertory Theatre Society in Wellington, and of British Drama League; produced plays and lectured on drama and literature for Workers' Educational Association; published 3 vols. of poetry: *A Venture in Verse* (1917), *Gathered Leaves* (1922) and *Thirdly* (1930); also active in Wellington Society for Prevention of Cruelty to Animals. Plunket Medal for oratory (1913). ❖ See also *Dictionary of New Zealand Biography* (Vol. 3).

NICHOLLS, Rhoda Holmes (1854–1930). English-born watercolor painter. Born Rhoda Carleton Marion Holmes in Coventry, England, Mar 28, 1854; died in Stamford, Connecticut, Sept 7, 1930; dau. of a vicar; studied in London at Bloomsbury School of Art; studied in Rome as a member of Circello Artistico; m. Burr H. Nicholls (American painter), 1884. ❖ Had a brilliant and individual style, as represented in her Venetian watercolors and illustrations for William Dean Howells' *Venetian Life*; taught art classes at William Chase School in Shinnecock, LI; also taught at Art Students League in NY.

NICHOLS, Anne (1891–1966). American playwright. Born Nov 26, 1891, in Dales Mill, Georgia; died in Englewood Cliffs, New Jersey, Sept 15, 1966, after long illness; m. Henry Duffy (actor), 1915 (div. 1924); children: Henry. ❖ Wrote *Abie's Irish Rose*, a theatrical phenomenon that ran from 1922 to 1927; also wrote *The Gilded Cage* (1920), *Love Dreams* (1921) and (with Adelaide Matthews) *Just Married* (1921). ❖ See also *Women in World History.*

NICHOLS, Barbara (1929–1976). American actress. Born Barbara Nickerauer, Dec 30, 1929, in Jamaica, Queens, NY; died Oct 5, 1976, in Hollywood, CA. ❖ Began career as model, chorine, and stripper; made 28 films, including *River of No Return, Miracle in the Rain, Sweet Smell of Success, Pal Joey, Pajama Game, The Naked and the Dead* and *The Disorderly Orderly.*

NICHOLS, Clarina (1810–1885). American journalist and women's rights leader. Name variations: Mrs. C.I.H. Nichols; Clarina Irene Howard Nichols. Born Clarina Irene Howard, Jan 25, 1810, in West Townshend, Vermont; died Jan 11, 1885, in Potter Valley, California; dau. of Chapin Howard (landowner and businessman) and Birsha (Smith) Howard; m. Justin Carpenter (Baptist preacher), 1830 (div. 1843); m. George W. Nichols (newspaper publisher), 1843 (died 1855); children: (1st m.) Birsha, Chapin and Aurelius O. Carpenter; (2nd m.) George B. Nichols (b. 1844). ❖ Opened girls' seminary in Herkimer, NY (1835); began writing for Brattleboro newspaper (1840); married publisher of Brattleboro's *Windham County Democrat* and assumed editorial duties at the paper (1843); wrote series of editorials on married women's property rights which led to passage of legislation by Vermont legislature (1847); led failed campaign to secure the vote for women in district school elections (1852); lectured extensively, mainly on women's rights (1850s); settled in Kansas Territory (1855), where she wrote articles and lectured on women's rights; addressed Kansas legislature on need for married women's property law (1860); unsuccessfully campaigned with Susan B. Anthony toward full women's suffrage in the state (1867). ❖ See also *Women in World History.*

NICHOLS, Dandy (1907–1986). English stage, tv, and screen actress. Born May 21, 1907, in Hammersmith, England; died Feb 6, 1986, in London. ❖ Probably best remembered for recurring British tv role of Else Garnett in "Till Death Us Do Part" (forerunner of "All in the Family" in US); films include *Help!, Georgy Girl, Nicholas Nickleby, Fallen Angel, The Winslow Boy, The Birthday Party* and *Hue and Cry.*

NICHOLS, Etta Grigsby (1897–1994). American midwife. Name variations: Margaret Etta Grigsby Nichols; Etta Grigsby. Born Margaret Carrie Etta Grigsby, May 19, 1897, in Del Rio, TN; died Nov 25, 1994; dau. of Nova (Turner) Grigsby and John L. Grigsby ("country" medicine practitioner); granddau. of John B. Grigsby (physician);

m. James Harrison Nichols, Oct 15, 1916; children: 4. ❖ Famed midwife who worked in Tennessee's southern Appalachian mountains, delivered her 1st baby (1930) and her last in May 1989; added a birthing room to her home; originally charged a delivery fee of $2 ($15 by 1989), but often delivered babies for free for poor women; delivered more than 2,000 babies during her career.

NICHOLS, Gladys (1924–1999). *See Milton, Gladys.*

NICHOLS, Maria Longworth (1849–1932). *See Storer, Maria.*

NICHOLS, Mary Gove (1810–1884). American author, lecturer, and physician. Name variations: as author, nonfiction works up to 1848 are by Mary Gove; most of her fiction under pseudonym Mary Orme. Born Mary Sargeant Neal, Aug 10, 1810, in Goffstown, New Hampshire; died May 30, 1884, in London, England, of breast cancer; dau. of William A. Neal and Rebecca R. Neal; had little formal education; m. Hiram Gove, Mar 5, 1831 (div. 1848); m. Thomas Low Nichols, July 29, 1848; children: (1st m.) Elma Penn Gove (b. Mar 1, 1832); (2nd m.) Mary Wilhelmina Nichols (b. Nov 5, 1850). ❖ Practicing physician who advocated proper health practices for women and led the early free-love movement in demanding radical changes in marriage, converted to Presbyterianism and then Quakerism (c. 1825); took up study of principles of health; toured northeastern states lecturing on health for women (1838–41); studied water-cure methods in New England and NY (1842–45); operated a water-cure boarding house in NYC (1845–50); operated health schools in NY state and embraced the free-love movement (1851–53); lived at Modern Times, on Long Island, then the center of free love (1853–55); became a spiritualist medium (1854); opened Memnonia, school of life and health, in Yellow Springs, Ohio (July 1856); converted to Roman Catholicism (Mar 29, 1857); operated water-cure establishment in Malvern, England (1867–72); writings include *Lectures to Ladies on Anatomy and Physiology* (1842), *Experience in Water-Cure* (1849), *Agnes Morris* (1849), *The Two Loves* (1849), *Mary Lyndon* (1855) and *A Woman's Work in Water Cure and Sanitary Education* (1874). ❖ See also *Women in World History.*

NICHOLS, Minerva Parker (1861–1949). American architect. Name variations: Minerva Parker. Born May 14, 1861, in Chicago, Illinois; died Nov 17, 1949, in Westport, Connecticut; dau. of John Wesley Parker (schoolteacher) and Amanda Melvina (Doane) Parker (seamstress); graduate of Philadelphia Normal Art School, 1882; completed architectural course at Franklin Institute, 1886; m. William Ichabod Nichols (Unitarian minister), Dec 22, 1891; children: Adelaide Nichols (b. 1894); Caroline Tucker Nichols (b. 1897); John Doane Nichols (b. 1899); William Ichabod Nichols (b. 1905). ❖ One of the 1st American women to become a successful working architect, took over employer's architectural practice (1888); taught architectural and historical ornament at Philadelphia School of Design for Women (1880s–90s); won 1st place for her design of a pavilion in honor of Isabella II at World's Columbian Exposition at Chicago (1893); her 2 most noted buildings were for women's clubs, both named the New Century Club: one in Philadelphia (1892), the other in Wilmington, Delaware (1893); retired (1896). ❖ See also *Women in World History.*

NICHOLS, Ruth (1901–1960). American aviator. Born Ruth Rowland Nichols, Feb 23, 1901, in New York, NY; died Sept 25, 1960, in New York, NY, an apparent suicide; dau. of Erickson Nichols and Edith Corlies Nichols; educated at Wellesley College; never married; no children. ❖ Pioneering aviator, pursued a career as a pilot when air travel was a risky and highly competitive sport; despite several serious crashes and resulting injuries, set world records for speed, altitude and distance, becoming the 1st woman licensed to fly a seaplane, the 1st woman to fly non-stop between NY and Miami, the 1st woman to attempt a solo transatlantic crossing, and the 1st woman licensed as a commercial airline pilot; used her skills during WWII to organize an airborne ambulance corps and to fly around the world for UNESCO's Children's Relief Fund; spent last years working for Civil Air Patrol; became the 1st woman to pilot a twin-engine jet (1955), and set new speed and altitude records by flying a jet aircraft at more than 1,000 miles per hour at 51,000 feet (1958); inducted into the National Aviation Hall of Fame (1992). ❖ See also autobiography, *Wings For Life* (Lippincott, 1957); and *Women in World History.*

NICHOLSON, Dorothy Wrinch (1894–1976). *See Wrinch, Dorothy.*

NICHOLSON, Eliza Jane (1849–1896). American newspaper publisher, journalist and poet. Name variations: Eliza Jane Poitevent; Eliza Jane Holbrook; (pseudonym) Pearl Rivers. Born Eliza Jane Poitevent, Mar 11,

1849, in Hancock Co., Mississippi; died Feb 15, 1896, in New Orleans, Louisiana; dau. of William James Poitevent (lumberman and shipbuilder) and Mary Amelia (Russ) Poitevent; graduate of Female Seminary of Amite, Louisiana, 1867; m. Alva M. Holbrook (editor and newspaper publisher), May 18, 1872 (died 1876); m. George Nicholson (newspaper business manager), June 27, 1878 (died 1896); children: (2nd m.) Leonard Kimball (b. 1881); Yorke Poitevent Tucker (b. 1883). ❖ Published poetry in writing anthology (1869); became literary editor of *New Orleans Picayune* (1870); became publisher of *Picayune* after husband's death (1876), the 1st woman in Deep South to be publisher of a major newspaper; used the paper to champion such causes as Society for Prevention of Cruelty to Animals and the free night school run by Sophie B. Wright; elected president of Women's National Press Association (1884); became 1st honorary member of New York Woman's Press Club. ❖ See also *Women in World History.*

NICHOLSON, Emma (1941—). English politician. Name variations: Baroness Nicholson of Winterbourne. Born Oct 16, 1941, in Oxford, England; attended Royal Academy of Music. ❖ Served as vice-chair of the Conservative Party (1983–87); was a Conservative (1987–95), then Liberal Democrat (1995–97) member of Parliament; made life peer and member of the House of Lords (1997); as a member of the European Liberal, Democrat and Reform Party, elected to 5th European Parliament (1999–2004); named vice-chair of Committee on Foreign Affairs, Human Rights, Common Security, and Defense Policy. Wrote *Why Does the West Forget?* (1993) and *Secret Society* (1996).

NICHOLSON, Margaret (c. 1750–c. 1828). English assassin. Born c. 1750; died in Bethlehem Hospital, May 28, 1826 or 1828. ❖ A housemaid suffering from mental instability, attempted to take the life of King George III of England as he alighted from his coach at St. James's Palace (Aug 2, 1876); judged insane by the court, was confined to Bethlehem Hospital. ❖ See also *Women in World History.*

NICHOLSON, Nora (1889–1973). English actress. Born Dec 7, 1889, in Leamington, Warwickshire, England; died Sept 18, 1973, in London. ❖ Made stage debut at Stratford Memorial Theater as Dolly Clandon in *You Never Can Tell* (1912), then appeared with Benson Company and at Old Vic; during WWI, served with WRNS (1918–19); made West End debut in *Once Upon a Time* (1919), followed by *Two Kingdoms, An Enemy of the People, Dark Summer, The Lady's Not for Burning, Rosmersholm, The Millionairess* and *Forty Years On,* among others; on tv, appeared as Juley Forsyte on "The Forsyte Saga" (1967); was also seen in "A Town Like Alice" (as Mrs. Frith), "Upstairs, Downstairs" and "Diamonds for Breakfast."

NICHOLSON, Winifred (1893–1981). British painter. Name variations: painted under name Winifred Dacre, early 1930s until 1945. Born Winifred Roberts, 1893, in England; died 1981; eldest dau. of Charles Roberts (politician) and Cecilia (Howard) Roberts; studied at Byam Shaw School of Art, London; m. Ben Nicholson (painter), 1920 (div.): children: Jake, Andrew and Kate Nicholson (artist). ❖ Classified as a painter of flowers and acclaimed for the color and luminosity of her works, was well known in London art circles from mid-1920s until start of WWII; in that period, had 4 large solo exhibitions in commercial London galleries and sold the greatest number of her works, but it was not until 1987, 6 years after her death, that the Tate Gallery in London mounted a major retrospective of her work; paintings include *Mughetti* (1921), *Cyclamen and Primula* (c. 1922), *Ben and Jake* (1927), *Paris Light* (c. 1933–34), *Honeysuckle and Sweetpeas* (1950), *Mrs. Campbell's Room of 1951* (1951), *Live Pewter* (1959), *Accord* (1978) and *The Gate to the Isles* (1980). ❖ See also *Women in World History.*

NICHOLSON OF WINTERBOURNE, Baroness (1941—). *See Nicholson, Emma.*

NI CHONAILL, Eibhlin Dubh (c. 1743–c. 1800). *See O'Connell, Eileen.*

NICHTERN, Claire (c. 1921–1994). American theatrical producer. Born c. 1921; died Mar 26, 1994, age 73, in NYC; children: David Nichtern (composer) and Nicky Nichtern. ❖ Served as president of Warner Theatre Productions; produced *The Typists, The Tiger, The Banker's Daughter, Jimmy Shine, Crimes of the Heart, Cold Storage, God Bless You Mr. Rosewater, Beyond Therapy, Mass Appeal, Piaf* and *The Dresser.* Awarded a Tony for *Luv.*

NI CHUILLEANÁIN, Eiléan (1942—). Irish poet. Name variations: Eilean Ni Chuilleanain. Born Nov 28, 1942, in Cork, Ireland; dau. of Cormac (university professor) and Eilis (Dillon) O'Cuilleanain (writer); University College, National University of Ireland, BA, 1962, MA, 1964;

Lady Margaret Hall, Oxford, BLitt, 1968; m. Macdara Woods (poet and editor), 1978; children: Niall. ❖ Worked as literary magazine editor and teacher in English Literature at Trinity College, Dublin; was co-founder of literary review *Cyphers;* writings include *Acts and Monuments* (1972), *Site of Ambush* (1975), *Cork* (1977), *The Second Voyage* (1977), *The Rose Geranium* (1981), *The Magdalene Sermon* (1989), *The Brazen Serpent* (1994) and *The Girl Who Married the Reindeer* (2001). Received Patrick Kavanagh Award (1973) and O'Shaughnessy Prize (1992).

NICKERSON, Camille (1884–1982). African-American composer, musician, and educator. Name variations: Camille Lucie Nickerson; The Louisiana Lady. Born Mar 30, 1884, in New Orleans, Louisiana; died April 27, 1982, in Washington, DC; dau. of William Joseph Nickerson (bandleader and violinist) and Julia Ellen Nickerson (music teacher); Oberlin Conservatory, BMU; never married. ❖ At 9, was pianist for Nickerson Ladies' Orchestra, conducted by father; composed her own Creole arrangements; taught at Nickerson School of Music, and was a concert musician with stage name "The Louisiana Lady," dressing in Creole costume to lend an air of authenticity to performances; was on the music faculty at Howard University (1926–62), where she documented a wealth of Creole music; wrote "Go to Sleep, Dear," "Mister Banjo," "Mam'selle Zi Zi," "Suzanne," "When Love Is Done" and "Lizette." ❖ See also *Women in World History.*

NICKS, Stevie (1948—). American rock singer and composer. Born Stephanie Lynn Nicks, May 26, 1948, in Phoenix, AZ; m. Kim Anderson (div.). ❖ With Lindsay Buckingham and 2 others, formed the Fritz Raybyne Memorial Band in high school, then began performing professionally with the band in college, opening in San Francisco rock clubs for such acts as Janis Joplin and Jimi Hendrix (mid-1960s); with Buckingham, signed a deal with Polydor Records (1973) and released what came to be known as The Buckingham-Nicks Album; with Buckingham, asked to join Fleetwood Mac (Mick Fleetwood, Peter Green, John McVie, Christie McVie); along with Christie, was one of the band's two lead singers, helping to form the distinctive sound that became one of rock's most influential groups for 2 decades; wrote the bands only song to reach #1 in US, "Dreams," as well as one of its most durable hits, "Rhiannon" (1975); released 1st solo album, *Bella Donna,* while continuing to tour with band; broke with Fleetwood Mac (1991); pursued a solo career as songwriter and performer, her work noted for its mystical overtones and complex lyrics (1991–97); reunited with Fleetwood Mac (1997–98) for *Rumours* tour. With band, inducted into Rock and Roll Hall of Fame (1998). ❖ See also Edward Wincenstein, *Stevie Nicks, Rock's Mystical Lady* (Momentary Pleasures, 1993); and *Women in World History.*

NICO (1938–1988). German singer. Name variations: Christa Paffgen or Paeffgen or Päffgen. Born Christa Päffgen, Oct 16, 1938, in Cologne, Germany; died of cerebral hemorrhage after bicycle accident during holiday with son, July 18, 1988, in Ibiza, Spain; children: (with actor Alain Delon) son Ari. ❖ Worked as model in Paris; had small part in film, *La Dolce Vita* (1960); recorded British single "The Last Mile" (1965); met Andy Warhol in NY and appeared in his film, *The Chelsea Girls* (1966); through Warhol, met Lou Reed and John Cale and joined their Velvet Underground; left group after 1 album, *Velvet Underground and Nico* (1967); recorded solo album, *Chelsea Girl* (1968), which included songs by Reed and Cale; released albums *The Marble Index* (1969) and *Desertshore* (1971); performed at London's Rainbow Theatre with Kevin Ayers, Cale, and Brian Eno (June 1, 1974), resulting in album *June 1st, 1974;* released solo album, *The End* (1974); career suffered due to dependency on heroin and methadone; dropped by Island (1975), performed solo on club circuit (1970s–80s); released *Drama of Exile* (1981) and last album, *Camera Obscura* (1985). ❖ See also James Young, *Nico: The End* (1993).

NICOL, Helen Lyster (1854–1932). New Zealand suffragist and temperance reformer. Born May 29, 1854, in Edinburgh, Scotland; died Nov 22, 1932, in Dunedin, New Zealand; dau. of David Nicol and Margaret Cairns (Smith) Nicol. ❖ Active in several temperance unions, including New Zealand Women's Christian Temperance Union; also argued for women's rights, pioneering suffrage efforts in Dunedin; helped to found Women's Franchise League (1892); affiliated with National Council of Women of New Zealand. ❖ See also *Dictionary of New Zealand Biography* (Vol. 2).

NICOLA. *Variant of Nicole.*

NICOLAEVA-LEGAT, Nadine (b. 1895). *See Legat, Nadine.*

NICOLE. *Variant of Nicola.*

NICOLE, Mylène (1936—). *See Demongeot, Mylène.*

NICOLE OF LORRAINE (c. 1608–1657). Duchess of Lorraine. Name variations: Nicola of Lorraine. Reigned from 1624 to 1625; born c. 1608; died 1657 in Lorraine; dau. of Henry II, duke of Lorraine (r. 1608–1624), and Margherita Gonzaga (1591–1632); m. Charles III also seen as Charles IV (d. 1675), duke of Lorraine (r. 1625–1675), in 1624; no children. ❖ Succeeded father as ruler (1624), but had little chance to establish a regime; through the machinations of others, was deposed within a year by paternal uncle, Francis of Vaudémont. ❖ See also *Women in World History.*

NICOLL, Ashley (1963—). Canadian equestrian. Name variations: Ashley Nicoll-Holzer; Ashley Holzer. Born Oct 10, 1963, in Toronto, Ontario, Canada; m. Rusty Holzer (show jumping rider), 1996; children: Emma and Harrison. ❖ At Seoul Olympics, won a bronze medal in team dressage (1988); with husband, established the Riverdale Equestrian Center in the Bronx, NY (1994).

NICOLL, Kahe (?–c. 1871). *See Te Rau-o-te-rangi, Kahe.*

NICOLL, Peti (?–c. 1871). *See Te Rau-o-te-rangi, Kahe.*

NICOLSON, Adela Florence (1865–1904). British poet. Name variations: Adela Florence Cory or Adela Nicholson Cory; (pseudonym) Laurence Hope. Born Violet Adela Florence Cory, April 9, 1865, in Stoke Bishop, Gloucestershire, England; died from self-administered poison, Oct 4, 1904, in Madras, India; dau. of Colonel Arthur Cory and Elizabeth Fanny (Griffin) Cory; sister of Isabell and Annie Sophie Cory (1868–1952, novelist under pseudony Victoria Cross); m. Malcolm Hassels Nicolson, 1889 (died 1904); children: son. ❖ Extremely popular in Edwardian period; poems reflect experiences in India, North Africa, and Far East; committed suicide after death of husband; wrote *The Garden of Káma, and Other Love Lyrics from India, Arranged in Verse by Laurence Hope* (1901), *Stars of the Desert* (1903), *Indian Love* (1905) and *Laurence Hope's Poems* (1907).

NICOLSON, Victoria Mary, Lady (1892–1962). *See Sackville-West, Vita.*

NIC SHIUBHLAIGH, Maire (1884–1958). *See Shiubhlaigh, Maire Nic.*

NICULESCU-MARGARIT, Elena (1936—). Romanian gymnast. Name variations: Elena Margarit. Born Oct 25, 1936, in Romania. ❖ Won a bronze medal at Melbourne Olympics (1956) and a bronze medal at Rome Olympics (1960), both in team all-around.

NIDETCH, Jean (1923—). American entrepreneur. Born Jean Slutsky, Oct 12, 1923, in Brooklyn, NY; dau. of David Slutsky (cabdriver) and Mac (Fried) Slutsky (manicurist); briefly attended City College of New York; m. Martin Nidetch, April 20, 1947 (div. c. 1973); children: David (b. 1952), Richard (b. 1956). ❖ With 3 others, founded Weight Watchers, a weight-loss business (1963); within 5 years, when the corporation went public, had 81 franchises in 43 states and 10 franchises abroad; served as public relations director, made regular appearances on radio and tv, and wrote *The Story of Weight Watchers* (1970) and 2 cookbooks; sold company to H.J. Heinz for $71.2 million (1973), negotiating a consulting contract for herself in the process. ❖ See also *Women in World History.*

NI DHOMHNAILL, Nuala (1952—). Irish poet. Born 1952 in Lancashire, England; dau. of Irish physicians; graduate of University College Cork; m. Dogan Leflef (Turkish geologist), 1973; children: 4. ❖ With family, moved to Kerry (1957); moved to Holland with husband, then Turkey; returned to Ireland (1980); one of Ireland's foremost women poets writing in Irish, focuses on Irish folklore, myth and culture in such works as *Astrakhan Cloak, Pharaoh's Daughter, Selected Poems and Spionain is Roiseanna;* is a regular broadcaster on Irish radio and tv. Received American Fund Literary Award (1991).

NIEBLER, Angelika (1963—). German lawyer and politician. Born Feb 18, 1963, in Munich, Germany. ❖ As a member of the European People's Party (Christian Democrats) and European Democrats, elected to 5th European Parliament (1999–2004).

NIEDECKER, Lorine (1903–1970). American poet. Name variations: Lorine Niedecker. Pronunciation: Knee-deck-er. Born Lorine Faith Neidecker (later changed to N*ie* decker), May 12, 1903, on Blackhawk Island, near Fort Atkinson, Wisconsin; died in Madison, Wisconsin, Dec 31, 1970, of a cerebral hemorrhage; dau. of Henry Neidecker (fisherman) and Theresa "Daisy" (Kunz) Neidecker; attended Beloit College,

1922–24; m. Frank Hartwig, Nov 29, 1928 (div. 1942); m. Albert Millen, May 26, 1963. ❧ Lived in poverty and rural isolation in southern Wisconsin, publishing little during lifetime, but was well known in experimental poetry circles in US, UK, and Japan; began correspondence with Louis Zukofsky (1931); lived in NY (1933–34); after return to family in Wisconsin, moved to Madison, where she began 4 years of work on Federal Writers' Project (1938); had 5 poems published in avant-garde *New Directions* (1936); published in *Il Furioso* (1939); published 1st poetry collection, *New Goose* (1946); began correspondence with poet Cid Corman (1960); after 2nd marriage and move to Milwaukee, began most vital and creative phase (1964); featured in Corman's journal *Origin* (1966); published last book, *My Life By Water* (1969); complete works, *From This Condensery*, published (1985); collections of poetry include *My Friend Tree* (1961), *North Central* (1968), and *T&G* (1969). Posthumous collections: *Blue Chicory* (1976) and *This Granite Pail* (1985). ❧ See also Jenny Penberthy, *Niedecker and the Correspondence with Zukofsky, 1931–1970* (Cambridge U. Press, 1993); and *Women in World History*.

NIEDERKIRCHNER, Käte (1909–1944). German resistance leader. Name variations: Käthe Niederkirchner; Katja Niederkirchner. Born in Berlin, Germany, Oct 7, 1909; executed Sept 27, 1944; dau. of Michael Niederkirchner (1882–1949) and Helene Niederkirchner. ❧ Was involved in anti-Nazi activities before Hitler came to power; moved to Soviet Union (1933); during WWII, made broadcasts to Germany over Moscow Radio and was involved in educational work among German prisoners of war; captured after parachuting into Nazi-occupied Poland (Oct 1943); after interrogations and torture, taken to Ravensbrück concentration camp and executed there (1944). In East Germany, enjoyed the status of a revered martyr of the resistance movement; became a highly controversial figure after East and West Germany were unified in Oct 1990. ❧ See also *Women in World History*.

NIEDERNHUBER, Barbara (1974—). German luge athlete. Born June 6, 1974, in Germany. ❧ Won German nationals (1998, 2000, 2001); won a silver medal at Nagano Olympics (1998) and a silver medal at Salt Lake City Olympics (2002), both for singles luge.

NIEH HUALING (1925—). Chinese-born novelist and short-story writer. Name variations: Hualing Engle. Born 1925 in Hupei, China; m. Paul Hamilton Engle (poet), 1971 (died 1991). ❧ After Communist takeover of China, moved to Taiwan (1949), where she became literary editor of *Free China*; taught creative writing at National Taiwan University; settled in US (1964); founded International Writers' Project with Paul Engle at University of Iowa (1967); with husband, was nominated for Nobel Peace Prize (1975); wrote 22 nonfiction books and novels, including *Emerald Cat* (1959), *The Lost Golden Bell* (1961), *A Little White Flower* (1963), and *Mulberry and Peach: Two Women of China* (1976) and *Three Lives* (2004), a collection of her memoirs.

NIEHAUS, Jutta (1964—). West German cyclist. Born Oct 1, 1964, in Germany. ❧ At Seoul Olympics, won a silver medal in indiv. road race (1988).

NIELSEN, Alice (c. 1870–1943). American singer of light and grand opera. Born June 7, c. 1870 (some sources cite c. 1868), in Nashville, TN; died Mar 8, 1943, in New York, NY; educated at St. Teresa's Academy; m. Benjamin Nentwig (church organist), 1889 (div. 1898); m. LeRoy R. Stoddard (plastic surgeon), 1917 (div.). ❧ Became a star with The Bostonians, America's best light opera company (1896); starred in premiere of *The Serenade*; founded Alice Nielsen Comic Opera Co. (1898), enjoying successful runs in NY and London of her production of *The Fortune Teller*; was the leading US female star in light opera (late 1890s); studied grand opera in Italy and made operatic debut in Naples (1903); sang several important roles with Royal Opera at Covent Garden beginning 1904, including Zerlina in Mozart's *Don Giovanni*, Susanna in *Le Nozze di Figaro*, and Mimi in *La Bohème*; played Rosina in *Il Barbiere di Siviglia* and Norina in *Don Pasquale* for New Waldorf Theater in London; joined Boston Opera Co. (1909); played Lia in 1st US production of Debussy's *L'Enfant Prodigue* (1910) and created role of Chonita for Converse's *The Sacrifice* (1911); also made occasional appearances with Metropolitan Opera; returned to operetta in Friml's *Kitty Darlin'* (1917); gave series of concert recitals with Boston Symphony (1921–23). ❧ See also *Women in World History*.

NIELSEN, Anja (1975—). Danish handball player. Born April 12, 1975, in Denmark. ❧ Won a team gold medal at Sydney Olympics (2000).

NIELSEN, Asta (1881–1972). Danish-born actress. Born Asta Sofie Amalie Nielsen in Vesterbro, Copenhagen, Denmark, Sept 11, 1881; died May 24, 1972, in Copenhagen; attended children's school of Copenhagen's Royal Theater; m. Fred Wingard (div.); m. Sven Gade (div.); m. Peter Urban Gad (who directed her in 30 films), 1912 (div. 1915); married Grigori Chmara, c. 1921 (div.); m. Christian Theede, 1970; children: 1 daughter. ❧ One of the earliest and greatest stars of silent movies, made stage debut at Royal Theater of Copenhagen; made film debut in hit silent *The Abyss* (1910), a breakthrough for her and the Danish film industry; by 1911, was Germany's leading movie star, known as the "Duse of the Screen"; formed her own company and made *Hamlet* with herself in title role (1920); returned to stage (1932) where she played the lead in *Romantik* and appeared as Alphonsine Plessis in *The Lady of the Camelias*; appeared in 70 films, including 1 sound film, *Impossible Love* (1932). ❧ See also autobiography *The Tenth Muse* (1966); and *Women in World History*.

NIELSEN, Augusta (1822–1902). Danish ballet dancer. Born Feb 20, 1822, in Copenhagen, Denmark; died Mar 29, 1902, in Copenhagen. ❧ Trained at school of Royal Danish Ballet and later performed with that company, replacing Lucille Grahn in many principal roles, including *La Sylphide* (1839); created roles for Bournonville's *Toréadoren* (1840) and Lefebre's *Nymphen Cloris ved Dianas Hof* (1846), among others; appeared at Paris Opéra for short period and at Her Majesty's Theatre in London, before retiring from performance career (1848).

NIELSEN, Inger Kathrine (1867–1939). See Jacobsen, Inger Kathrine.

NIELSEN, Jerri (1953—). American physician. Name variations: Dr. Jerri Nielsen. Born 1953 near Canfield, Ohio; dau. of Phil and Lorine Cahill; m. Dr. Jay Nielsen (div.); children: 3. ❧ Worked as family practice and emergency room physician for 23 years in Youngstown, Ohio; joined research team sponsored by National Science Foundation at Admunsen-Scott South Pole Station on Antarctica; was solely responsible for physical and mental health of team of scientists, construction workers and support staff; found lump in breast shortly after station closed for winter, with no way in or out for 8.5 months; performed 2 biopsies and aspiration on self and confirmed diagnosis through rigging elaborate system to transmit pictures of tissue samples; received daring mid-winter drop of chemotherapy supplies and self-administered medication; was evacuated several months later and underwent mastectomy. Portrayed by Susan Sarandon in CBS tv movie, *Icebound: A Woman's Survival at the South Pole* (2003). ❧ See also Jerri Nielsen, *Ice Bound: A Doctor's Incredible Battle for Survival at the South Pole* (Miramax, 2001).

NIELSEN, Laila (1919–1998). See Schou Nilsen, Laila.

NIELSEN, Lone Smidt (1961—). Danish soccer player. Name variations: Lone Smidt Hansen. Born Lone Smidt Hansen, 1961 in Vejle, Denmark. ❧ Considered one of Denmark's most renowned strikers, played in 53 consecutive matches for the national team (1977–86); played for B1909 (1978–85) which claimed the Danish championship twice in 7 years; led Sanitas Trani team (of Italy) to 2 consecutive Italian championships.

NIELSEN, Nielsine (1858–1932). See Paget, Nielsine.

NIELSEN, Tina (1971—). See Bottzau, Tina.

NIELSON, Maud (1881–1944). See Nelson, Maud.

NIELSSON, Greta. See Malinovska, Valentina.

NIELSSON, Susanne (1960—). Danish swimmer. Name variations: Susanne Schultz Nielsson. Born July 8, 1960, in Århus, Denmark; dau. of Preben Nielsson and Birgit Schultz Nielsson; m. Sten Felsgård-Hansen, 1984; children: Sophie (b. 1997). ❧ At Moscow Olympics, won a bronze medal in 100-meter breaststroke (1980).

NIEMAN, Nancy (1933—). American cyclist. Name variations: Nancy Baranet. Born 1933 in Detroit, Michigan. ❧ Won US national women's road championship (1953, 1954, 1956, 1957); was the only woman officer of the American Bicycle League (1956–83). ❧ See also memoir *The Turned Down Bar*.

NIEMANN, Gunda (1966—). German speedskater. Name variations: Gunda Niemann Kleemann; Gunda Niemann-Stirnemann or Gunda Niemann Stirnemann. Born Sept 9, 1966, in Sondershausen, Germany. ❧ Won the European championships (1989–92, 1994–96) and came in 2nd (1997); won the World championships in the 5,000 meters by 5.30 seconds (1991) and by 6.55 seconds (1993); won gold medals in the 3,000 and 5,000 meters and a silver in the 1,500 meters at Albertville Olympics (1992); won a silver medal in the 5,000 meters and a bronze in the 1,500 meters at Lillehammer Olympics (1994); placed 1st at World championships in the 1,500, 3,000, and 5,000 meters (1997); won a gold medal for 3,000 meters and silver medals for the 1,500 and 5,000 meters (the 1st woman to skate under the 7-minute mark) at Nagano Olympics (1998). Named "German Athlete of the Year" (1995).

NIEMCZYKOWA, Barbara (1943—). Polish volleyball player. Born Nov 13, 1943, in Poland. ❖ At Mexico City Olympics, won a bronze medal in team competition (1968).

NIENHUYS, Janna. Dutch nurse. Born in the Netherlands; attended high school in the town of Haarlem; attended Sorbonne in Paris for 1 year; received R.N from Binnen Gasthuis, Amsterdam; m. Hendrick Nienhuys (agricultural consultant), c. 1937; children: Marieke and Caroline. ❖ "Dutch Nurse of Sumatra" who was captured during WWII and interned in a Japanese concentration camp; saved the lives of many women and children in the Sumatran internment camps, where she and her 2 young daughters were also prisoners for 3 years. ❖ See also *Women in World History.*

NIEPCE, Janine (1921—). French photographer. Born in Meudon, France, 1921; degree in art and archaeology, Sorbonne, 1945; distant relative of pioneering French photographer Nicéphore Niepce. ❖ One of France's 1st women photojournalists, opened Prix Niepce (1950); joined Rapho, a photo agency in Paris (1955); participated in 5 traveling exhibitions organized by the minister of foreign affairs (1960–68); photographed in India (1963), Brazil (1968), and Cambodia and Japan (1970), and contributed photographs to a book on Simone de Beauvoir (1978); created photographic documentaries (1981–85); had 2 solo exhibitions at Musée Nicéphore Niepce, Chalon-sur-Saône (1979) and at Centre Georges Pompidou in Paris (1983). Retrospective of her work, "Janine Niepce, France 1947–1992," was mounted at the Espace Electra in Paris (1992). ❖ See also *Women in World History.*

NIESE, Charlotte (1854–1935). German writer. Name variations: (pseudonym) Lucian Bürger. Born in Burg, on island of Fehmarn, June 7, 1854; died in Altona-Ottensen, near Hamburg, Dec 8, 1935; dau. of Emil August Niese; sister of Benedictus Niese (1849–1910, professor of ancient history). ❖ Prolific author whose historical novels, set mostly in Northern Germany, were once immensely popular, selling hundreds of thousands of copies over a period of nearly half a century; published 1st novel, *Cajus Rungholt* (1886), followed by *Auf halbverwischten Spuren* (On Half-Obliterated Tracks, 1888); also published memoir of trip to US, *Bilder und Skizzen aus Amerika* (Pictures and Sketches from America, 1891). ❖ See also autobiography, *Von Gestern und Vorgestern* (From Yesterday and the Day before Yesterday, 1924); and *Women in World History.*

NIESE, Hansi (1875–1934). Austrian actress and singer. Name variations: Johanna Niese; Hansi Niese-Jarno. Born Johanna Niese in Vienna, Austria, Nov 10, 1875; died in Vienna, April 4, 1934; m. Josef Jarno (1865–1932, actor and theater director), 1899; children: daughter, Hansi Jarno (1901–1933, actress). ❖ Considered the darling of Viennese stage for more than 4 decades, made stage debut at age 10 as Franzi in *Hasemanns Töchter* in a Viennese suburb tavern; became a seasoned actress, appearing in a number of provincial theaters, including those in Abbazia, Gmunden, and Karlsbad; also appeared in operettas in ingenue roles; returned to Vienna and appeared at Raimundtheater (1893–99); performed at Neues Theater in Berlin (1898); appeared at Vienna's Theater in der Josefstadt (1900), earning acclaim for her performance in title role of Radler's farce *Unsere Gusti* (Our Little Augusta); starred with husband in German-language premiere of Molnár's *Liliom* (1913); appeared in 300 performances in *Die Försterchristl*; performed in traditional Viennese operettas and farces, and by 1910 had mastered the art of dramatic acting as well; starred in plays of Gerhart Hauptmann; appeared at the Lustspieltheater, where she was a major drawing card (1923–27), the Renaissancebuhne (1923–31), and the Carltheater (1928–29); made a number of phonograph recordings; appeared in several silent films, followed by such talkies as *Kaiserwalzer* (Emperor Waltz) and *Purpur und Waschblau* (Purple and Wash Blue), among the best of her career. ❖ See also *Women in World History.*

NIESEN, Gertrude (1910–1975). American actress, comedian, and singer. Born July 8, 1910, at sea; died Mar 27, 1975, in Glendale, CA; m. Albert Greenfield (nightclub owner). ❖ Musical-comedy star of Broadway, film and nightclubs, trained for an opera career; appeared in vaudeville with Lou Holtz; had greatest stage success as Bubbles La Marr in *Follow the Girls* (1944); films include *Top of the Town, Start Cheering, Rookies on Parade, He's My Guy, This Is the Army* and *The Babe Ruth Story.*

NIETZSCHE, Elisabeth (1846–1935). *See Förster-Nietzsche, Elisabeth.*

NIEUWENHUIZEN, Anneloes (1963—). Dutch field-hockey player. Born Oct 16, 1963, in Netherlands. ❖ Won a gold medal at Los Angeles Olympics (1984) and a bronze medal at Seoul Olympics (1988), both in team competition.

NIGÂR (1862–1918). *See Hanim, Nigar.*

NIGGLI, Josefina (1910–1983). American playwright and poet. Born July 13, 1910, in Monterrey, Nuevo Leon, Mexico; died Dec 17, 1983, in NC; dau. of Frederick Ferdinand and Goldie Morgan Niggli; University of North Carolina, MA, 1937. ❖ During WWII, taught at University of North Carolina; worked in Hollywood as scriptwriter and taught English and drama at Western Carolina University (1956–75); works include *Mexican Silhouettes* (1931), *Singing Valley* (M.A. thesis, 1936), *The Red Velvet Goat* (1936), and *Sunday Cost Five Pesos* (1939); several plays published in *The Best One-Act Plays of 1937* and *The Best One-Act Plays of 1938*; wrote novels *Mexican Village* (1945) and *Step Down, Elder Brother* (1947); also published *Pointers on Playwriting* (1945).

NIGH, Jane (1925–1993). American actress. Name variations: June Nigh. Born Bonnie Lenora Nigh, Feb 25, 1925, in Hollywood, CA; died Oct 5, 1993. ❖ Made film debut in *Something for the Boys* (1944), followed by *Laura, State Fair, Dragonwyck, Give My Regards to Broadway, Red Hot and Blue, Blue Grass of Kentucky, Captain Carey U.S.A., Rodeo* and *Hold That Hypnotist*; on tv, co-starred in series "Big Town" (1952–53).

NIGHTINGALE, Florence (1820–1910). English pioneer nurse and public-health advocate. Born in Florence, Italy, May 12, 1820; died in London, England, Aug 13, 1910; dau. of William Edward Nightingale and Fanny (Smith) Nightingale; sister of Parthenope Nightingale; educated by governesses, by father at home, and by extensive European travel; never married; no children. ❖ Considered one of the great heroines of Victorian England for her nursing work in the Crimean War, learned the elements of nursing in Kaiserwerth, Germany; became superintendent of Institution for the Care of Sick Gentlewomen in London's Harley Street and nursed the dying in one of London's worst cholera epidemics (1853); having learned that British casualties of the Crimean war were being ill-treated at inadequate hospitals in Turkish town of Scutari, set out for Constantinople with 38 volunteers (1854); confronted military obstructionism and red tape, improved sanitation, spent money on suitable food, stoves, linens, and other supplies, remedied the worst abuses of the system, and walked the rounds of the hospital every evening, carrying a lamp, which gave rise to the sobriquet "Lady of the Lamp"; collapsed with a fever at Balaklava and was in imminent danger of death (1855), an illness that set off a wave of grieving in England; once recovered, turned to other reforms, trying to reduce drunkenness among the soldiers and to offer convalescents the chance to read or, for the many illiterates in the ranks, to learn reading for 1st time; returned home and helped organize a Parliamentary Royal Commission on military medicine, submitting a 1,000-page account of her experiences which served as basis of the commission's deliberations; outlined her plans for reforming both civil and military hospitals in *Notes on Hospitals* (1859); also wrote the influential *Notes on Nursing* (1859) and a book of philosophy and theology, *Suggestions for Thought to the Searchers after Truth Among the Artisans of England* (1860); had no subsequent official appointments but was a perpetual political lobbyist on health-reform issues, including the alleviation of puerperal fever in childbirth wards, the relief of the sick poor in workhouse wards, and constant attention to the suffering of both civil and military populations in India. ❖ See also Bullough, Bullough, and Stanton, *Florence Nightingale and Her Era* (Garland, 1990); Elspeth Huxley, *Florence Nightingale* (Putnam, 1975); Sue M. Goldie, *I Have Done My Duty: Florence Nightingale in the Crimean War* (U. of Iowa Press, 1987); Lytton Strachey, *Eminent Victorians* (1918), Vicinus and Nergaard, *Ever Yours, Florence Nightingale: Selected Letters* (Harvard U. Press, 1990); C.B. Woodham-Smith, *Florence Nightingale: 1820–1910* (Constable, 1950); and *Women in World History.*

NIHELL, Elizabeth (1723–after 1772). English midwife. Born 1723 in London, England; died after 1772; m. Edward Nihell (surgeon); children: at least 1. ❖ Studied at Hôtel Dieu in Paris (late 1740s), with the duke of Orleans's help; began working as a midwife in London (early 1750s); criticized Dr. William Smellie, a midwife trainer, which sparked the protest of Smellie's former student, Tobias Smollet; wrote *A Treatise on the Art of Midwifery* (1760), which criticized the higher pay rates for male midwives and the proclivity of male midwives to overuse instruments during childbirth (many at the time assumed her husband had written the book).

NIIHAU, queen of. See *Kapule, Deborah (c. 1798–1853)*.

NIJINSKA, Bronislava (1891–1972). Russian-born ballet dancer, choreographer and teacher. Name variations: Bronislawa Nijinskaya or Nijinskaia; (nickname) Bronia. Born Bronislava Fominichna Nijinskaia in Minsk, Russia, Jan 8, 1891; died of a heart attack in Pacific Palisades, California, Feb 22, 1972; dau. of Foma Nijinsky and Eleonora Nikolaevna Bereda Nijinskaia, both ballet dancers; sister of Vaslav Nijinsky (ballet dancer); sister-in-law of Romola Nijinska (1891–1978); attended Imperial Ballet School (St. Petersburg), 1900–08; m. Alexander Kotchetovsky (ballet dancer), 1912; m. Nicolas Singaevsky (ballet dancer); children (1st m.): Irina (b. 1913); Leon. ❖ One of the formative choreographers of 20th century, joined the famed Maryinsky Theater (1908) and began the 1st of her 3 careers, that of a classical ballerina; with brother, danced with Diaghilev's Ballets Russes in Paris, where she was given major roles in *Carnaval, Petrushka,* and other modern ballets; helped brother form his own company (1914); moved to Kiev (1915), where she opened a ballet school, served as ballet mistress for the Kiev Opera, and started to develop her modernist theories concerning choreography; fled Russia for Europe (1921), where she started her 2nd and most notable career, that of a choreographer for Ballets Russes in Paris and Monte Carlo, the 1st woman to gain prominence as a choreographer; choreographed 8 ballets for Diaghilev (1921–24), including 2 masterpieces, Stravinsky's *Les Noces* (1923) and Poulenc's *Les Biches* (1924); worked for at least 8 different ballet companies in Europe and South America, sometimes as a choreographer, but increasingly as a ballet mistress or director (1925–33); ran her own company, the Théâtre de la Danse, in Paris (1932–34); moved to California (1938) where she opened a ballet school in Los Angeles and started her 3rd career as a highly respected teacher of dance; also served as ballet mistress for the Grand Ballet du Marquis de Cuevas and director of the Buffalo Ballet. ❖ See also autobiography, *Early Memories* (Trans. by Irina Nijinska and Jean Rawlinson, Holt, 1981); and *Women in World History.*

NIJINSKA, Romola (1891–1978). Hungarian-born writer. Name variations: Romola Nijinsky, Nijinskaia, or Nijinskaya; Romola de Pulski. Born Romola de Pulszky in Budapest, Hungary, 1891; died in Paris, June 8, 1978; dau. of Károly de Pulszky (director of National Gallery of Hungary), and Emilia Markus (actress); attended Lycée Fénelon (Paris); m. Vaslav Nijinsky (Russian ballet dancer), Sept 10, 1913; sister-in-law of Bronislava Nijinska (1891–1972); children: Kyra Nijinsky (1914–1998, a dancer); Tamara Nijinsky (b. 1920). ❖ Wife of the great ballet dancer Vaslav Nijinsky, was also his caretaker after he was diagnosed as suffering from schizophrenia; raised funds by writing his biography (1933) and by editing his diary (1936); 2 years after his death (1950), published *The Last Days of Nijinsky.* ❖ See also *Women in World History.*

NIKAMBE, Shevantibai M. (b. 1865). Indian novelist. Born 1865 in India. ❖ Founded school for high-caste wives, widows, and grown-up Hindu girls; wrote novel *Ratanbai: A Sketch of a Bombay High-Caste Hindu Wife* (1895), advocating reform in education of women.

NIKISHINA, Svetlana (1958—). Soviet volleyball player. Born Oct 20, 1958, in USSR. ❖ At Moscow Olympics, won a gold medal in team competition (1980).

NIKITINA, Alice (1909–1978). Russian ballet dancer. Born 1909 in St. Petersburg, Russia; died 1978. ❖ Appeared in French revue *Oh! Que! Nu!!* at early age in Vienna, Austria (1919); joined Diaghilev Ballet Russe (1923) where she danced with Serge Lifar in numerous works, including Massine's *Zéphyr et Flore* (1925), Bronislava Nijinska's *Romeo et Juliette* 1926), and Balanchine's *La Chatte* (1927) and *Le Bal* (1929); performed in C.B. Cochran's London revues—also opposite Lifar—in *Night* and *Luna Park* (c. 1930); appeared with Ballet Russe de Monte Carlo in Diaghilev revivals (mid-1930s); performed in *Rigoletto* in Palermo (1938); taught dance in Paris towards end of WWII. ❖ See also memoir, *Nikitina, by Herself* (1959).

NIKOLA, Helene Knez (1765–1842). Serbian wife of Karageorge, the founder of Serbian independence. Born 1765; died Feb 8, 1842; dau. of Odor Knez Nikola; m. George Petrovich Hospodar or Gospodar, known as Karageorge (Kara George or KaraGjorgje, 1752–1817), founder of Serbia independence and ruler of Serbia (r. 1804–1813); children: Alexander (1806–1858), prince of Serbia (r. 1842–1885).

NIKOLAEVA, Klavdiia (1893–1944). Russian women's rights activist. Name variations: Klavdiya or Klavdia Ivanovna Nikolaeva; also seen as

Nikolaevna. Born 1893 in St. Petersburg, Russia; died 1944 in Soviet Union. ❖ Russian revolutionary activist and post-revolutionary campaigner for women's rights in Soviet Union, was involved in revolutionary activities from early age and arrested several times by tsarist authorities (1908–14); organized women's groups in Petrograd after Russian Revolution (1914–24); appointed head of *zhenotdel,* women's section of Communist Party of Soviet Union (1924); served as editor of journal *Rabotnitsa* (The Working Woman) which played crucial role in organizing women and rallying them to Bolshevik Party; dismissed from post for supporting Grigori Zinoviev (1926); survived political fall from grace to hold various lower-rank appointments for remainder of life.

NIKOLAEVA, Olga (1972—). Russian volleyball player. Name variations: Olga Nikolayeva. Born May 14, 1972, in USSR. ❖ Won a team silver medal at Athens Olympics (2004).

NIKOLAYEVA, Margarita (1935—). Soviet gymnast. Born Sept 23, 1935, in USSR. ❖ At Rome Olympics, won a gold medal in vault and a gold medal in team all-around (1960).

NIKOLAYEVA, Olga (1972—). See *Nikolaeva, Olga.*

NIKOLAYEVA, Tatiana (1924–1993). Russian pianist. Name variations: Tatiana Nikolaeva Petrovna; Tatyana Nikolaeva. Born in Bezhitz (near Bryansk), USSR, May 4, 1924; died in San Francisco, California, Nov 22, 1993; studied with Alexander Goldenweiser at Moscow Conservatory. ❖ After winning 1st prize in piano at Bach Bicentennial Festival in Leipzig (1950), launched a significant career in Soviet Union and Eastern Europe; began teaching at Moscow Conservatory (1959), achieving rank of professor (1965); played many premieres, including the Twenty-four Preludes and Fugues of Dmitri Shostakovich (1952); was also a prolific composer, producing symphonies, piano concertos, chamber music and solo piano pieces. Named Honored Artist of Russian Soviet Federated Socialist Republic (1955). ❖ See also *Women in World History.*

NIKOLAYEVA, Yelena (1966—). Soviet track-and-field athlete. Name variations: Elena Nikolaeva. Born Feb 1, 1966, in Cheboksary, Russia. ❖ Won a silver medal at Barcelona Olympics (1992) and a gold medal at Atlanta Olympics (1996), both for 10-km walk; won European Race Walking Cup (2003).

NIKONOVA, Valentina (1952—). Soviet fencer. Born Mar 1952 in USSR. ❖ At Montreal Olympics, won a gold medal in team foil (1976).

NIKOULTCHINA, Irina (1974—). Bulgarian biathlete. Born Dec 8, 1974, in Razlog, Bulgaria. ❖ Won a bronze medal for 10 km pursuit at Salt Lake City Olympics (2002).

NIKULINA, Marina (1963—). Soviet volleyball player. Born Mar 3, 1963, in USSR. ❖ Won a gold medal at Seoul Olympics (1988) and a silver medal at Barcelona Olympics (1992), both in team competition.

NILES, Blair (1880–1959). American travel writer and novelist. Name variations: Blair Rice Niles. Born Mary Blair Rice, 1880, in Coles Ferry, Virginia; died 1959; dau. of Henry Crenshaw Rice and Gordon (Pryor) Rice; m. William Beebe (naturalist, later div.); m. Robert Niles Jr. (architect). ❖ At young age, married naturalist William Beebe and accompanied him on scientific explorations around the globe; upon return from South Pacific and South America, wrote *Our Search for a Wilderness* (1910); later married Robert Niles, avid explorer-photographer with whom she made expeditions to Central and South America; on trip to French Guiana, collected material for her immensely popular *Condemned to Devil's Island* (1928); also wrote *Strange Brother* (1931), *The Biography of an Unknown Convict* (1928), *Free* (1930), *Light Again* (1933), *Maria Paluna* (1934), *Day of Immense Sun* (1936), *Peruvian Pageant* (1937) and *East by Day* (1940). Awarded Constance Lindsay Skinner Medal. ❖ See also *Women in World History.*

NILES, Mary Ann (1938–1987). American actress, dancer, singer, comedian and choreographer. Born May 2, 1938, in New York, NY; died Oct 4, 1987, in NY, NY; m. Bob Fosse (director and choreographer), 1949 (div. 1951). ❖ Known as "the queen of the gypsies," appeared in nightclubs with husband Bob Fosse as a dance team; made Broadway debut in *Girl from Nantucket* (1945), followed by *Dance Me a Song, Call Me Mister, Make Mine Manhattan, Carnival, Flora the Red Menace, No No Nanette, Sweet Charity* and *Irene,* among others.

NILLSON, Carlotta (c. 1878–1951). Swedish-born stage actress. Born c. 1878 in Stockholm, Sweden; died Dec 31, 1951, in New York, NY. ❖ Came to US at age 10; made stage debut with Modjeska's company; spent a few years in England studying and acting (1895–99); had a substantial NY success as Mrs. Elvsted in *Hedda Gabler* (1903); starred in many Broadway productions, with greatest triumphs as Rhy Macchesney in *The Three of Us* (1906) and in title role in Pinero's *Letty;* other appearances include *Love's Pilgrimage, This Woman and This Man,* and title role in *Deborah,* a play of some notoriety which was closed down by local authorities and which she also produced; retired for 27 years before making a final appearance in *A Delicate Story* (1940). Appeared in title role of the film *Leah Kleschna* (1913).

NILSEN, Elin (1968—). Norwegian cross-country skier. Born Aug 12, 1968, in Norway. ❖ Won silver medals at Albertville Olympics (1992), Lillehammer Olympics (1994) and Nagano Olympics (1998), all for 4 x 5 km relay.

NILSEN, Jeanette (1972—). Norwegian handball player. Born June 27, 1972, in Skien, Norway. ❖ Won a team bronze medal at Sydney Olympics (2000).

NILSEN, Laila (1919–1998). *See Schou Nilsen, Laila.*

NILSMARK, Catrin (1967—). Swedish golfer. Born Aug 30, 1967, in Goteborg, Sweden; attended University of South Florida. ❖ Won Swedish Junior championship (1984); member of Swedish national team (1983–87); won Ford Golf Classic (1994); joined LPGA tour (1994); member of European Solheim Cup team (1992, 1994, 1996, 1998).

NILSSON, Anna Q. (1889–1974). Swedish-born actress of the silent era. Born Anna Querentia Nilsson, in Ystad, Sweden, Mar 30, 1889; died in Hemet, California, Feb 11, 1974; m. Guy Coombs (actor), 1916 (div.); m. John Gunnerson (shoe manufacturer), 1923 (div. 1925). ❖ Moved to NY (1907); gained some prominence as the Stanlow Poster Girl, which led to work as a photographer's model; signed with Kalem Film Co. in NY and made debut in *Molly Pitcher* (1911); career remained in high gear until 1925, when she shattered her hip in horseback-riding accident; films include *The Siege of Petersburg* (1912), *Shenandoah* (1913), *Uncle Tom's Cabin* (1913), *Retribution* (1913), *Barbara Fritchie* (1915), *Seven Keys to Baldpate* (1917), *Over There* (1917), *Soldiers of Fortune* (1919), *Broadway After Dark* (1924), *The Masked Woman* (1927), *Sorrell and Son* (1927), *The Little Minister* (1934) and *Seven Brides for Seven Brothers* (1954). ❖ See also *Women in World History.*

NILSSON, Birgit (1918–2005). Swedish soprano. Born in Vastra Karup, Sweden, May 17, 1918; died Dec 25, 2005, in Vastra Karup; studied with Joseph Hislop; m. Bertil Niklasson, 1948. ❖ World-class Wagnerian soprano whose powerful voice was legendary, was accepted at Stockholm Royal Academy of Music (1941), earning 1st place over 47 applicants; made informal debut as Agatha in *Der Freischütz* (1946); made formal debut with Stockholm Opera as Lady Macbeth (1947); appeared at Glyndebourne as Elektra in *Idomeneo* (1951); appeared as Elsa in Bayreuth (1954), singing there for 16 years; made American debut in San Francisco (1956), as Brünnhilde in *Die Walkürie;* debuted at Covent Garden as Brünnhilde in the *Ring* (1957) and at Teatro alla Scala as Turandot during the Puccini centenary celebration (1958); debuted at Metropolitan Opera (1959), singing there until her retirement (1982); was best known for her major Wagnerian roles—all 3 Brünnhildes in the *Ring* cycle, Isolde in *Tristan,* Elsa in *Lohengrin,* Elisabeth and Venus in *Tannhäuser;* also sang Mozart and Strauss, Donna Anna in *Don Giovanni* and Elektra; made many fine recordings, including an especially distinguished *Ring* cycle in collaboration with conductor Sir Georg Solti; retired (1984). ❖ See also autobiography *My Memoirs in Pictures* (Doubleday, 1981); and *Women in World History.*

NILSSON, Christine (1843–1921). Swedish soprano. Name variations: Kristina Nilsson; Countess of Miranda. Born Aug 20, 1843, in Sjöabol, Sweden; died Nov 22, 1921, in Stockholm; studied in Stockholm with Franz Berward; and with Wartel, Masse, and Delle Sedie in Paris; m. Auguste Rouzaud, 1872 (died 1882); m. Count A. de Casa Miranda, 1887 (died 1902). ❖ Appeared in concert halls of Stockholm and Uppsala (1860), then went to Paris; after 4 years' study, debuted at Théâtre-Lyrique as Violetta in Verdi's *La Traviata* (1864) and was leading prima donna there (1864–72); debuted in same role in London (1867); created Ophélie in *Hamlet* for Paris Opéra and debuted at Covent Garden (1868); appeared in many European capitals, becoming especially known for her Queen of the Night in Mozart's *Die Zauberflöte* (*The Magic Flute*); made US debut at NY's Academy of Music (1871); sang in St. Petersburg (1872), in US (1873–74), in Germany and Austria (1876–77), as well as in Spain and Scandinavia; sang for the opening of Metropolitan Opera (1883) as Marguerite in *Faust;* retired at time of

marriage to a Spanish count (1887). ❖ See also T. Headland, *Christine Nilsson: the Songbird of the North* (Rock Island, IL: 1943); and *Women in World History.*

NILSSON, Karin (b. 1904). Swedish swimmer. Born Dec 10, 1904, in Sweden. ❖ At Antwerp Olympics, won a bronze medal in the 4 x 100-meter freestyle relay (1920).

NIMMANHEMIN, M.L. Bupha Kunjara (1905–1963). Thai novelist. Name variations: (pseudonym) Sod Dok Mai. Born M.L. Bupha Kunjara in 1905 in Thailand; died 1963; half-sister of Boonlua Kunjara Debyasuvan (Boonlua). ❖ One of pioneers of Thai modernism; novels reflect conflict between Western and Thai values and customs, and often focus on female protagonists from elite class; works include *Sattru Khong Chao Long* (1929), *Nit* (1929–30), *Khwam Phit Khrang Raek* (1930), *Karma Kao* (1932), *Ubattihet* (1934), *Chai Chana Khong Luang Naruban* (1935), *Phu Di* (1937), and *Ki Lae Lok* (1940); also published 2 collections of short stories.

NIMMO, Mary (1842–1899). *See Moran, Mary Nimmo.*

NIN, Anais (1903–1977). French-born diarist. Name variations: Anaïs Nin. Pronunciation: ANNA-ees Nin. Born Feb 21, 1903, in Nuilly (near Paris), France; died of cancer, Jan 14, 1977, in Los Angeles, California; dau. of Rosa Culmel Nin (singer of French and Danish extraction) and Joaquin Nin (Spanish composer and concert pianist); left school at 15; studied psychoanalysis in France under Otto Rank, 1930s–40s; m. Hugh P. Guiler, also known as Ian Hugo, Mar 1923; m. Rupert Pole (claimed she married him while still married to Guiler). ❖ Avant-garde writer and poet, self-mythologized by the publication of her diaries, and famed for her unconventional lifestyle, moved from France to NY and began writing her extensive diary as a letter-collection to her estranged father (1914), which would grow to over 50 volumes' of personal chronology; returned to France (1930); published 1st book, *D.H. Lawrence: An Unprofessional Study* in Paris (1932); returned to NY after WWII and settled in Greenwich Village; bought a printing press and released her own books; received 1st recognition in US (1944) for *Under a Glass Bell,* illustrated with engravings by husband Guiler; published 1st vol. of *The Diary of Anais Nin: 1931–1934* (1966); later practiced psychoanalysis, lectured at Harvard, and taught or tutored writing at the International College in Los Angeles. ❖ See also Robert Snyder, *Anais Nin Observed: From a Film Portrait of a Woman as Artist* (Swallow, 1976); Robert Zaller, *A Casebook on Anais Nin* (Meridian, 1974); Deirdre Bair, *Anaïs Nin* (Putnam, 1995); *Henry and June* (film), based on her diaries (1991); and *Women in World History.*

NINGHU, Empress (52 BCE–18 CE). *See Wang Zhaojun.*

NINIWA HEREMAIA (1854–1929). *See Niniwa-i-te-rangi.*

NINIWA-I-TE-RANGI (1854–1929). New Zealand tribal leader and editor. Name variations: Niniwa Heremaia. Born probably on April 6, 1854, at Oroi, on east coast of Wairarapa, New Zealand; died Mar 23, 1929, at Greytown, New Zealand; dau. of Heremaia Tamaihotua and Ani Kanara; m. in early 1870s (ended c. 1874); m. Kawana Ropiha, c. 1874; m. Tamaihotua Aporo, c. 1900. ❖ After father's death, controlled vast parcels of land, much of which was adjudicated in land courts; recognized for her knowledge of genealogy and tradition, and her ability to speak publicly, was recognized as rightful leader of her people; was editor for women's affairs for Maori-language newspapers, *Te Tiupiri* and *Te Puke ki Hikurangi,* the latter coming under her ownership in 1904; sponsored production of *Maori Record,* an English-language newspaper dedicated to advancing the Maori people. ❖ See also *Dictionary of New Zealand Biography* (Vol. 2).

NINNOC (fl. 6th c.). British saint and abbess. Fl. in Brittany; dau. of Brochan, king of north Britain; never married; no children. ❖ Refused to marry and gained permission to move to Brittany; was given a settlement near the town of Blemur, where she founded a monastery and became its abbess; her fame spread across Brittany, and the abbey soon became known as Lannennoc after its founder; canonized some years after her death. ❖ See also *Women in World History.*

NINON DE LENCLOS (1623–1705). *See Lenclos, Ninon de.*

NINOVA, Violeta (1963—). Bulgarian rower. Born Aug 19, 1963, in Bulgaria. ❖ At Seoul Olympics, won a bronze medal in double sculls (1988).

NIOGRET, Corinne (1972—). French biathlete. Born Nov 20, 1972, in Nantua, France. ❖ Won a gold medal for 3 x 7.5 km relay at Albertville

Olympics (1992); won a bronze medal for 4×7.5 km relay at Lillehammer Olympics (1994); won gold medals for indiv. at World championships (1995, 2000).

NISBET, Frances (1761–1831). *See Nelson, Frances.*

NISBET, Mary (1778–1855). Countess of Elgin. Name variations: Mary Elgin; Countess of Elgin. Born Mary Nisbet in 1778; died July 9, 1855; dau. of William Hamilton Nisbet; m. General Thomas Bruce (Lord Elgin), 11th earl of Kincardine and 7th earl of Elgin (ambassador to Ottoman Empire), 1799 (div. 1808); children: Lucy Bruce (d. 1881). ❖ While husband was ambassador-extraordinary in Turkey, helped finance the removal of friezes from the Parthenon which now reside in the British Museum and are known as the Elgin Marbles. ❖ See also Susan Nagel, *Mistress of the Elgin Marbles: A Biography of Mary Nisbet, Countess of Elgin* (2004).

NISBETT, Louisa Cranstoun (1812–1858). English actress. Name variations: Miss Mordaunt. Born 1812; died Jan 15, 1858; dau. of Frederick Hayes Macnamara (an actor whose stage name was Mordaunt); m. Captain John Alexander Nisbett, 1831 (killed 1831); m. Sir William Boothby, Bart., 1844 (died 1846). ❖ Had considerable experience, especially in Shakespearean leading roles, before her 1st London appearance at Drury Lane as Widow Cheerly in *Soldier's Daughter* (1829); was the original Lady Gay Spanker of *London Assurance* (1841); also appeared as Portia, Lady Teazle in *School for Scandal*, Constantine in *The Love Chase*, and Helen and Julia in *The Hunchback*, among others. ❖ See also *Women in World History.*

NI SHIUBHLAIGH, Maire (1884–1958). *See Shiubhlaigh, Maire Nic.*

NISIMA, Maureen (1981—). French fencer. Born July 30, 1981, in Bondy, France. ❖ Placed 2nd in indiv. épée at World championships (2003); won bronze medals for indiv. épée and team épée at Athens Olympics (2004).

NISSEN, Constanze von (1762–1842). *See Mozart, Constanze.*

NISSEN, Erika (1845–1903). Norwegian pianist. Born in Kongsvinger, Norway, 1845; died 1903; children: Karl Nissen (1879–1920), the composer. ❖ Gave recitals in London and eventually throughout Europe; specializing in contemporary Scandinavian music, gave premiere performances of Christian Sinding's Piano Quintet (1888) and his Piano Concerto (1890); performed Edvard Grieg's Piano Concerto on many occasions with the composer conducting; became a popular teacher in Oslo. ❖ See also *Women in World History.*

NISSEN, Greta (1906–1988). Norwegian actress. Born Grethe Ruzt-Nissen, Jan 30, 1906, in Oslo, Norway; died of Parkinson's disease in Montecito, California, May 15, 1988. ❖ Ballerina and stage actress before turning to films, was under contract to Paramount (1925–28), where she starred in a number of popular silent films, including *The Lucky Lady* (1926), *The Butter and Egg Man* (1928), *Transatlantic* (1931), *The Circus Queen Murder* (1933), *Melody Cruise* (1933) and *Best of Enemies* (1933); with advent of talkies, returned to the stage and made a few British films, the last of which was *Honors Easy* (1935). ❖ See also *Women in World History.*

NITHSDALE, countess of. *See Maxwell, Winifred (1672–1749).*

NITOCRIS (c. 660–584 BCE). Theban high priestess. Born c. 660 BCE; died 584 BCE; dau. of Nabu-Shezibanni, known as Psammetichus or Psametik; adopted by Shepenupet II, in 656. ❖ Reigned as Thebes' high-priestess for 70 years, linking upper Egypt with lower Egypt. ❖ See also *Women in World History.*

NITOCRIS (fl. 6th c. BCE). Legendary Babylonian queen. Said to have flourished in early 6th century BCE; said to have married Labynetus; children: Labynetus. ❖ Called a woman of great intelligence, was credited with planning a strategic defence of Babylonia against the encroachment of her enemy, the Medes (from modern Iran). ❖ See also *Women in World History.*

NIU JIANFENG (1981—). Chinese table tennis player. Born April 3, 1981, in Baoding, Hebei Province, China. ❖ Won a bronze medal for doubles at Athens Olympics (2004); won team World championship (2004); ranked 1st on ITTF Pro Tour (2002, 2003, 2004).

NIVEDITA, Sister (1867–1911). Irish-born activist. Name variations: Margaret Noble. Born Margaret Elizabeth Noble at Dungannon, Co. Tyrone, Ireland, Oct 28, 1867; died in Darjeeling in eastern India, Oct 12, 1911; dau. of Samuel Noble and Mary (Hamilton) Noble; never

married. ❖ Leader in the cause of Indian nationalism and independence, was known in India as Sister Nivedita (meaning "the dedicated soul"); became a schoolteacher at 18 (1884), teaching in English Lake District school; opened a school at Wimbledon with a broad conception of education for girls; became a disciple of Hindu monk Swami Vivekananda; went to Calcutta (1898), where she became involved in India's struggle for independence; was also instrumental in helping to assert the spiritual import of Indian fine arts; traveled widely to raise funds for a girls' school; left for Europe and US (1899) and organized the "Ramakrishna Guild of Help" while in the West; opened the Nivedita School in Bagh Bazar in north Calcutta (1903); consoled the weak, addressed women's meetings, and preached the use of Swadeshi goods and the boycott of British ones; placed high honor on the status of women, advocating that where women are honored gods are pleased; like Vivekananda, believed that India should borrow relevant aspects of education and science from the West but remain committed to its ancient ethical and religious values; wrote an account and study of Vivekananda's life, *The Master As I Saw Him.* ❖ See also Lizelle Raymond, *The Dedicated: A Biography of Nivedita* (Day, 1953); and *Women in World History.*

NIXON, Agnes (1927—). American tv writer. Born Agnes Eckhardt in Chicago, Illinois, Dec 27, 1927; attended Northwestern University; m. Robert Nixon (died 1997); children: 4. ❖ Creator of 2 of the longest-running afternoon dramas on tv: "One Life to Live" and "All My Children"; also created "Loving" (1983). ❖ See also Dan Wakefield, *All Her Children* (Doubleday, 1976); and *Women in World History.*

NIXON, Joan Lowery (1927–2003). American children's writer. Born Feb 3, 1927, in Los Angeles, California; died July 5, 2003, in Houston, TX; dau. of Joseph Michael (accountant) and Margaret (Meyer) Lowery; University of Southern California, BA, 1947; California State College, certificate in elementary education, 1949; m. Hershell H. Nixon (petroleum geologist), Aug 6, 1949; children: Kathleen Nixon Brush, Maureen Nixon Quinlan, Joseph Michael Nixon, Eileen Marie McGowan. ❖ Was an elementary schoolteacher in Los Angeles (1947–50); instructor in creative writing at Midland College in Texas (1971–73) and University of Houston (1974–78); wrote more than 140 books, mostly mysteries, for children and young adults; won Edgar Allan Poe and Mystery Writers of America awards for *The Mysterious Red Tape Gang* (1975), *The Kidnapping of Christina Lattimore* (1980), *The Seance* (1981), *The Ghosts of Now: A Novel of Psychological Suspense* (1985), *The Other Side of Dark* (1987) and *The Name of the Game Was Murder* (1993); won Steck-Vaughn Award for *The Alligator under the Bed* (1975); also wrote the "Holiday Mystery" series.

NIXON, Julie (1948—). American first daughter and author. Name variations: Julie Nixon Eisenhower. Born July 5, 1948, in Whittier, California; 2nd dau. of Richard M. Nixon (1913–1994, US president, 1969–74) and Pat Nixon (1912–1993); graduate of Smith College, 1970; Catholic University of America, MA in elementary education; m. David Eisenhower (lawyer), Dec 22, 1968; children: Jennie Eisenhower; Alex Eisenhower; Melanie Eisenhower. ❖ From earliest days of Watergate, became the family spokesperson in her father's defense; by the time of the president's resignation, had given over 125 interviews; wrote *Pat Nixon, The Untold Story* (1986), which, in addition to shedding light on the enigmatic first lady, provides an insider's look at some of the extraordinary events that shaped the country's history. ❖ See also *Women in World History.*

NIXON, Marion (1904–1983). American actress. Name variations: Marian Nixon. Born Maria Nissinen, Oct 20, 1904, in Superior, WI; died Feb 13, 1983, in Los Angeles, CA; m. Joe Benjamin, 1925 (div. 1926); m. Edward Hillman Jr., 1929 (div. 1933); m. William A. Seiter (director), 1934 (died 1964); m. Ben Lyon (actor), 1972 (died 1979). ❖ Made debut in Tom Mix film *Riders of the Purple Sage* (1925); appeared in over 50 films, including *What Happened to Jones, Devil's Island, Geraldine, Say It with Songs, Show of Shows, Women Go On Forever, Charlie Chan's Chance, Rebecca of Sunnybrook Farm, Winner Take All, Madison Square Garden, The Line Up, Tango, Captain Calamity* and *The Dragnet.*

NIXON, Marni (1929—). American actress and singer. Born Marni McEathron, Feb 22, 1929, in Altadena, CA; m. Ernest Gold (composer), 1950 (div. 1969); m. Dr. F. Frederick Fenster (div.); m. Albert Block, 1983; children: Martha, Melani, and Andrew Gold. ❖ Began career as a child actress and soloist with Roger Wagner Chorale; provided singing voice (dubbed) for Natalie Wood in *West Side Story*, Deborah Kerr in

An Affair to Remember and *The King and I*, and Audrey Hepburn in *My Fair Lady*; appeared as Sister Sophia in *The Sound of Music* and as Heidi Schiller in Broadway revival of *Follies* (2001).

NIXON, Pat (1912–1993). America first lady. Born Thelma Catherine Patricia Ryan on Mar 16, 1912, in Ely, Nevada; died June 23, 1993; dau. of William Ryan (copper miner) and Katharina (Halberstadt) Bender Ryan; attended Fullerton Junior College, 1931; University of Southern California, BS in merchandising (cum laude), 1934; m. Richard M. Nixon (1913–1994, US president, 1969–74), June 21, 1940; children: Tricia Nixon (b. 1946); Julie Nixon (b. 1948). ❖ During a goodwill tour of South America (1958), when an anti-American mob of 500 attacked the motorcade in which she rode with her vice-presidential husband, remained calm throughout the ordeal, even restraining and comforting the frantic wife of the foreign minister, but her strength and composure under siege, probably her greatest asset, was frequently viewed as aloofness by the public; though she would have preferred a life out of politics and out of the spotlight, was fiercely loyal to her husband; during years as first lady (1969–74), divided her time between several causes, including education, community self-help, volunteerism, and refurbishing 14 of the 36 rooms of the White House, for which she raised the money herself from private sources; traveled extensively, visiting US troops in Vietnam (the 1st first lady to visit a war zone since Eleanor Roosevelt), and serving as a foreign emissary. ❖ See also Julie Nixon Eisenhower, *Pat Nixon: The Untold Story* (Simon & Schuster, 1986); Lester David, *The Lonely Lady of San Clemente: The Story of Pat Nixon* (Crowell, 1978); and *Women in World History*.

NIXON, Tricia (1946—). American first daughter. Name variations: Patricia Nixon; Tricia Nixon Cox. Born Patricia Nixon, Feb 21, 1946, in Whittier, California; eldest dau. of Richard M. Nixon (1913–1994, president of US, 1969–74) and Pat Nixon (1912–1993); graduate of Finch College, 1968; m. Edward Cox (lawyer), June 12, 1971: children: Christopher Cox (b. Mar 14, 1979). ❖ Of the 2 Nixon daughters, was dubbed "The Thinker," while younger sister Julie was known as "The Talker"; in White House years (1969–74), became "assistant first lady," presiding over a number of events in her mother's absence and uncharacteristically hosting a tv tour of the family quarters of the White House with Mike Wallace; had a White House wedding in the Rose Garden (June 12, 1971). ❖ See also *Women in World History*.

NJAU, Rebeka (1932—). Kenyan novelist, playwright and short-story writer. Name variations: (pseudonym) Marina Gashe. Born 1932 in Kanyariri, Kenya; children: 2. ❖ Kenya's first female playwright, was educated in Kenya and Uganda and worked as teacher, textile artist, and editor; writings include *The Scar* (1965), *Ripples in the Pool* (1975), *The Hypocrite and Other Stories* (1977) and *Kenyan Women Heroes and Their Mystical Powers* (1984).

NJINGA (c. 1580s–1663). Angolan queen. Name variations: Jinga; Llinga; Nzinga; Singa; Zinga or Zhinga; Nzingha Mbande or Mbandi. Pronunciation: Oon-ZHIN-ga. Born Njinga Mbandi in 1580s in Angola; died in Angola, 1663; married many men, as she had her own harem. ❖ Warrior queen and proto-nationalist who ruled for 40 years, alternately defeating and allying herself with the Portuguese, Dutch, and local tribes, was baptized a Christian and allied herself with the Portuguese (1622); took the throne after brother died under mysterious circumstances (1624); began fighting the Portuguese after their failure to honor their treaty (1624); forced to flee her kingdom (1629), established a new kingdom in Matamba; closed the main slave trail, blocking Portuguese access to slave-producing areas (1630s); expanded Matamba into the largest state in the area and shifted alliance to the Dutch (1640s); forced the Portuguese from the area (1648); shifted alliance back to the Portuguese (1650); signed a formal treaty with the Portuguese (1656); ruled in peace until her death (1663); established a dynasty of female leaders which ruled after her death for 100 years. ❖ See also Antonia Fraser, *Boadicea's Chariot: The Warrior Queens* (Weidenfeld & Nicolson, 1988); and *Women in World History*.

NKRUMAH, Fathia (c. 1931—). Egyptian-born first lady of Ghana. Name variations: Helen Ritz Fattiah; Fathia Halim Ritzk; Madam Fathia Nkrumah. Born in Zeitoun, Egypt, around 1931; father was a clerk in the Egyptian telephone company; educated primarily by Sisters of Our Lady of the Apostles; also studied Arabic at University of Cairo; m. Kwame Nkrumah (prime minister and then life-president of Ghana), in Dec 1957 (died 1972); children: sons Gamal (b. 1959) and Sékou (b. 1963); daughter Samia Nkrumah (b. 1960). ❖ Married husband in a private civil ceremony at Christianborg Castle in Accra (the wedding may have been the 1st time they met); spoke no English, and her English-speaking groom spoke no Arabic; shy by nature, unable to speak the language, and living in a totally foreign culture, found it hard to make a good impression; by 1960s, while Nkrumah was increasingly isolated from the public for his own safety, began appearing at more public functions, and served as the chief patron of the National Council of Ghana Women and honorary chief of the Ghana Girl Guides; in later years, often lived in exile. ❖ See also *Women in World History*.

NOACH, Ilse (1908–1998). Austrian psychoanalyst. Name variations: Ilse Hellman (also seen as Hellmann); (pseudonym) Ursula. Born Ilse Hellman, Sept 28, 1908, in Vienna, Austria; died Dec 3, 1998; during WWII, mother and brother died in German concentration camps; m. Arnold "Nol" Noach (Dutch art historian, died 1976). ❖ A child development expert, studied with Charlotte Bühler at University of Vienna (1935–37); also studied at Institute of PsychoAnalysis in London (1942–45), then trained analysts (1952–78); in Paris, worked in a home for young offenders (1931–32) and took psychology courses at the Sorbonne (1931); later worked at a child assessment center in Paris (1933–35); lectured in psychology at University of Vienna (1935–37); employed at Parents' Association Institute in London (1937–39); at the Home Office, worked with child evacuees (1939–41); worked at Anna Freud's war nurseries (1941–45); was a psychologist at Anna Freud and Dorothy Burlingham's Hampstead Clinic (1945–92); published *From War Babies to Grandmothers: Forty-eight Years in Psychoanalysis* (1990); was interested in the practice of simultaneous analysis of mother and child, entailing 2 different analysts for each and 1 coordinator to synthesize the information.

NOACK, Angelika (1952—). East German rower. Born Oct 20, 1952, in East Germany. ❖ At Montreal Olympics, won a silver medal in coxless pairs (1976); at Moscow Olympics, won a gold medal in coxed fours (1980).

NOACK, Marianne (1951—). East German gymnast. Born Oct 5, 1951, in East Germany. ❖ At Mexico City Olympics, won a bronze medal in team all-around (1968).

NOADIAH. Biblical woman. ❖ A false prophet, was an agent of Tobiah and Sanballat who bribed her to stir up discontent among the people of Jerusalem, and in doing so, to hinder Nehemiah's efforts to rebuild the ruined walls of the city.

NOAH. Biblical woman. One of the five daughters of Zelophehad, of the tribe of Manasseh; sister of Mahlah, Hoglah, Milcah, and Tirzah. ❖ With her 4 sisters, was granted special permission by Moses to inherit their father's property after he died leaving no male heirs, a judgment that eventually became the general law of the land.

NOAILLES, Adrienne de (1760–1807). See Lafayette, Marie Adrienne de.

NOAILLES, Anna de (1876–1933). French poet and novelist. Name variations: Anna Elisabeth, Comtesse Mathieu de Noailles; Princesse de Brancovan. Pronunciation: noh-I. Born Anna-Elisabeth de Brançovan, Nov 15, 1876, in Paris, France; died April 30, 1933, in Paris; dau. of the Cretan-Greek Ralouka (Rachel) Musurus and Romanian Prince Grégoire Bassaraba de Brancovan; educated at home by a succession of mostly German governesses; m. Count Mathieu-Fernand-Frédérick-Pascal de Noailles, also known as Mathieu de Noailles (French soldier, b. April 13, 1873), in 1897 (sep. 1912); children: son, Anne-Jules-Emmanuel-Grégoire (1900–1979). ❖ Leading poet of early 1900s, whose themes ranged from love, nature, and patriotism to death and oblivion, published 24 books and scores of individual poems, articles, prefaces, and contributions to collective works over a 32-year period (1901–33); wrote 3 novels, but the bulk of literary output was poetry; was a member of Academy of Belgium and recipient of both the Archon Désperouses Prize and the Grand Prix of Literature of the French Academy; was the 1st woman awarded the red cravate of a Commander of the Legion of Honor; writings include *Le Coeur innombrable* (1901), *L'Ombre des jours* (1902), *La Nouvelle Espérance* (1903), *Le Visage émerveillé* (1904), *La Domination* (1905), *Les Eblouissements* (1907), *Les Vivants et les Morts* (1913), *De la rive d'Europe à la rive d'Asie* (1913), *Les Forces éternelles* (1920), *Les Innocentes ou la sagesse des femmes* (1923), *L'Honneur de Souffrir* (1927), *Poèmes d'Enfance* (1928), *Exactitudes* (1930) *Le Livre de ma Vie* (1932) and *Derniers Vers* (1933). ❖ See also autobiography *Le livre de ma vie* (1976); and *Women in World History*.

NOAILLES, Anne Claude Laurence, duchesse de (d. 1793). French duchess. Died by guillotine in 1793. ❖ While on staff at Versailles, was put in charge of training the young Marie Antoinette on her arrival in

France; rigid and punctilious, was dubbed "Madame Etiquette" by Marie. ❖ See also *Women in World History*.

NOAILLES, Marie-Laure de (1902–1970). French patron of the arts and salonnière. Name variations: Marie Laure de Noailles; Viscountess de Noailles; Marie-Laure Bischoffsheim. Born Marie-Laure Henriette Anne Bischoffsheim, Oct 31, 1902, in Paris, France; died in Paris, Jan 29, 1970; dau. of Maurice Bischoffsheim and Marie-Thérèse de Chevigné; granddau. of Laure de Chevigné (1860–1936); m. Vicomte or Viscount Charles de Noailles, 1922; children: 2 daughters, Laure de Noailles and Nathalie de Noailles. ❖ One of the most important influences in the artistic and intellectual life of Paris for many decades, funded the classic film, *L'Age d'or*, by Luis Buñuel and Salvador Dali; with husband, supported the musical composers known as Les Six (Georges Auric, Louis Durey, Arthur Honegger, Darius Milhaud, Francis Poulenc and Germaine Tailleferre), as well as Kurt Weill and Ned Rorem, among others; a talented artist, showed her pictures at the prestigious Salon de Mai; also wrote 3 novels, including *La chambre des écureuils* (The Squirrels' Room), and a book of poems, *Cires Perdues*; presided with style over Paris' outstanding center of intellectual and artistic energy, her palace on the Place des États-Unis, for more than 40 years, and set the tone for future decades of French—and Western—intellectual development. ❖ See also James Lord, *Six Exceptional Women* (Farrar, 1994); and *Women in World History*.

NOAILLES, viscountess de. *See Noailles, Marie-Laure de (1902–1970).*

NOALL, Patricia (1970—). Canadian swimmer. Name variations: Patricia Noall-Lauzon. Born June 2, 1970; trained with the Beaconsfield Bluefins in Quebec. ❖ At Seoul Olympics, won a bronze medal in the 4 x 100-meter relay (1988).

NOBILE, Giuseppina Guacci (1807–1848). *See Guacci, Giuseppina.*

NOBLE, Cheryl (1956—). Canadian curler. Born Sept 29, 1956, in Victoria, British Columbia, Canada. ❖ As alternate, won a team bronze medal at Salt Lake City Olympics (2002).

NOBLE, Cindy (1958—). American basketball player. Name variations: Cindy Noble-Hauserman. Born Nov 14, 1958, in Frankfort, Ohio. ❖ At Los Angeles Olympics, won a gold medal in team competition (1984); was an All-American player at University of Tennessee (1981); played in Italy and Japan.

NOBLE, Margaret (1867–1911). *See Nivedita.*

NOBLE, Mary (1911–2002). Scottish plant pathologist. Born Feb 23, 1911, in Leith, Scotland; died July 2002; dau. of a pharmacist; University of Edinburgh, BS, 1933, PhD, 1935. ❖ Plant pathology expert who researched potato wart disease, helping eliminate it from Scotland, studied seed pathology, the mycology of Scotland from 1970 and flax field diseases in western Scotland; studied the papers of the Perthshire naturalist Charles McIntosh and made an amazing find of letters written by Beatrix Potter to McIntosh about fungi, mosses and lichens; worked to publicize Potter's knowledge and research; employed at the Department of Agriculture and Fisheries for Scotland in East Craigs (1935–71); wrote (with E. Jay and A. S. Hobbs) *A Victorian Naturalist* (1992). Received the Benefactors' Medal of the British Mycological Association.

NOBLET, Lise (1801–1852). French ballet dancer. Born Nov 24, 1801, in Paris, France; died Sept 1852 in Paris. ❖ Made debut at Paris Opéra (1818), remaining there for 23 years; created numerous roles, including Effie in Taglioni's *La Sylphide* (1832), and the mime role of Fenella in Aumer's *La Muette di Portici* (1828), among others.

NOBLETTE, Irene (1902–1973). *See Ryan, Irene.*

NÓBREGA, Isabel da (1925—). Portuguese novelist and playwright. Name variations: Isabel da Nobrega. Born 1925 in Portugal; had a relationship with José Saramago (Nobel-Prize winning writer), 1970–86. ❖ Published *Viver com os Outros* (1965), for which she won the Camilo Castelo Branco prize; also wrote *Já Não Há Salomão* (1966), and *Solo Para Gravador* (1973); frequently contributes to newspapers in Lisbon.

NOCE, Teresa (1900–1980). Italian activist, labor leader, journalist and feminist. Name variations: "Estella" (underground name used during her years as a political émigré in France). Born in Turin, Italy, July 29, 1900; died Jan 1980; m. Luigi Longo. ❖ Parliamentary deputy who advocated sweeping social legislation on behalf of mothers, 1st worked as a turner for Fiat Brevetti and later became a journalist, writing for *Il grido del popolo* and *Ordine nuove* (1914–17); joined the Socialist Party (1919); became a member of the founding generation of the Italian Communist

Party (1921); oversaw the Communist Youth Federation and their periodical *La voce della gioventù* (1920s); helped instigate the anti-fascist strikes of female workers in the rice fields (1934); organized movements in both Italy and France, becoming a leader of the women's Communist Party in France; edited a number of periodicals, including *La voce della donne*, an anti-fascist periodical founded by women (1934); escaped from a concentration camp and aided the French Resistance; captured by the Gestapo and interred in Ravensbrück concentration camp; returned to a liberated Italy (1945); as a member of the central committee of Communist Party, worked to form the Italian Republic; had a long and successful career in public life, including election to Italian Parliament, selection as general secretary of textile workers union, and election to Central Committee of the PCI; was a driving force in achieving passage of a comprehensive maternity law (1950); writings include *Nuestros hermanos, los internacionales* (1937), *Tra gli eroi ed i martiri della liberta* (1937), *Gioventù senza sole* (1938), *Teruel martirio e liberazione di un popolo!* (1939), *Ma domani fara giorno* (1952), *Rivoluzionaria professional* (1974) and *Vivere in piedi* (1978). ❖ See also (in Italian) *Estella: Autobiographie einer italienischen Revolutionärin* (1981); and *Women in World History*.

NODDACK, Ida (1896–1978). German chemist. Pronunciation: NOD-ack. Born Ida Eva Tacke in Lackhausen-Wesel am Rhein, Germany, Feb 25, 1896; died 1978; dau. of Adelbert Tacke and Hedwig Danner Tacke; received a diploma from Technical University of Berlin-Charlottenburg, 1919, then a doctorate, 1921; m. Walter Noddack (chemist), May 20, 1926 (died Dec 7, 1960). ❖ Co-discoverer of the element Rhenium, who was one of the 1st to see that the work of the physicist Enrico Fermi might prove that atomic fission was possible, gained little public acclaim during her lifetime; worked in the laboratories of German General Electric Society (1921–24), Siemen and Haisle Co. (1924–25), then German Research Institute in Berlin (1925–35), where, with husband, concentrated on investigating 2 of the "missing elements" in the Periodic Table compiled by Dmitri Mendeleev, elements number 75 and 43; discovered an element so rare that only about 1 milligram of it could be found in 1 ton of the earth's crust; chose to name it Rhenium; with husband, published *Das Rhenium* (1933); with husband, worked in Department of Physical Chemistry at University of Freiburg (1935–41), physical chemistry department of University of Strasbourg (1947–55), then Philosophical-Technological High School of Bamberg, where they remained for the rest of their professional careers. Received Liebig Commemorative Medal of Society of German Chemists (1931); awarded Scheele Medal of Swedish Chemical Society (1934), and Grand Cross of Merit of Federal Republic of Germany (1966). ❖ See also *Women in World History*.

NÖEL, Magali (1932—). Turkish actress. Name variations: Magali Noel; Magali Guiffrais. Born Magali Giuffrai (also seen as Giuffra), June 27, 1932, in Izmir, Turkey. ❖ Star of French and Italian films; appeared in many Fellini productions, including *Amarcord* (1973).

NOEMI (fl. 1100 BCE). *See Naomi.*

NOEMI, Lea (1883–1973). Yiddish actress. Name variations: Lea Eisenberg. Born Nov 10, 1883; died Nov 6, 1973, in New York, NY; m. Abraham Eisenberg (sculptor). ❖ Played the title role in *Mirele Efros* on stage and film.

NOERGAARD, Louise Bager (1982—). Danish handball player. Name variations: Louise Bager; Louise Nørgaard. Born April 23, 1982, in Denmark. ❖ Goalkeeper, won a team gold medal at Athens Olympics (2004).

NOETHER, Emmy (1882–1935). German theoretical mathematician. Name variations: Amalie Emmy Noether. Born in Erlangen, Germany, Mar 23, 1882; died in Bryn Mawr, Pennsylvania, April 14, 1935; dau. of Ida (Kaufman) Noether and Max Noether (mathematician known as "Father of Algebraic Geometry"); sister of Alfred Noether, chemist, and Fritz Noether, physicist; studied at University of Göttingen, 1903–04; University of Erlangen, PhD, 1907; never married. ❖ Pioneer in the study of cross product and abstract algebra, who contributed to the discovery of the theory of relativity, was one of only 2 female students enrolled at University of Erlangen (1900); attended University of Göttingen, where her doctoral thesis "On the Complete Systems of Invariants for Ternary Biquadratic Forms" was widely applied by physicists, who dubbed it "Noether's theorem"; invited to teach at Göttingen (1915), was not allowed a professorship because of gender; instead, awarded honorary position of "Associate Professor without Tenure" (1919), which required no teaching and did not include a salary; granted a lectureship in algebra, which provided a tiny income (1923); while at

Göttingen, began to work on the general theory of ideals, which owed much to her father's Residual theorem; her research into ideals formed the basis for the application of axiomatic methodology to mathematical research; was a visiting professor, University of Moscow (1928) and University of Frankfurt (1930); awarded Alfred Achermann-Teubner Memorial Prize for Advancement of Mathematical Studies (1932), when the quality of her research was finally acknowledged; attended International Mathematical Congress, Zurich (Sept 1932), where she was the only woman to be given a plenary session; as a Jew, was dismissed from University of Göttingen by Nazi decree (April 7, 1933); became a visiting professor at Bryn Mawr College (1933); lectured regularly at Institute for Advanced Study, Princeton University (1934); joined American Mathematical Society (1934); among the most distinguished mathematicians of the 20th century, contributed to the discovery of the theory of relativity and to the advancement of particle physics. "Noether's theorem" is still used by physicists today. ❖ See also J.W. Brewer, and Martha K. Smith, eds. *Emmy Noether: A Tribute to Her Life and Work* (Dekker, 1981); and *Women in World History*.

NOFRETETE (c. 1375–1336 BCE). *See Nefertiti.*

NOGAMI, Yaeko (1885–1985). Japanese novelist, playwright and essayist. Born May 6, 1885, in Usuki, Oita prefecture, Japan; died Mar 30, 1985; m. Toyoichiro Nogami (translator and English literature scholar). ❖ One of the most famous of modern woman novelists in Japan, had extensive knowledge of English and Japanese literature; was made member of Japan Academy of Arts (1948) and received Cultural Medal (1971); works include *The Neptune* (1922), *Machiko* (1928), *A Maze* (1958), *Hideyoshi and Rikyu* (1963), from which the film *Rikyu* was based (2000), and *The Complete Works of Yaeko Nogami* (26 vols); also wrote essays, translations, and plays.

NOGAROLA, Isotta (c. 1416–1466). Italian scholar and writer. Born c. 1416 in Verona, Italy; died 1466; buried in Santa Maria Antica in Verona; dau. of Bianca (Borromeo) Nogarola and Leonardo Nogarola; sister of Angela and Ginevra Nogarola; niece of poet Angela Nogarola; educated by tutors. ❖ Early on, renowned for her intellect and beauty, wrote poetry, oration, and dialogue; chose to become a virgin scholar of religion, attached to no particular order; befriended Ludovico Foscarini and ran a salon for intellectual discussion; corresponded with, and was visited by, the intellectuals of the region, especially Foscarini; her letters were distributed widely, even outside Italy; wrote a philosophical dialogue on Adam and Eve (1451) and an oration on life of St. Jerome (1453), as well as *Opera quae Supersunt Omnia* (1886). ❖ See also *Women in World History*.

NOGUCHI, Constance Tom (1948—). American medical researcher. Name variations: Connie Noguchi; Constance or Connie Tom. Born Constance Tom, Dec 8, 1948, in Kuangchou, Canton, China; grew up in San Francisco, CA; dau. of James Tom (Chinese-American engineer) and Irene Cheung (Chinese); graduate in physics at University of California, Berkeley, 1970; George Washington University, PhD in theoretical nuclear physics, 1975; m. Phil Noguchi; children: 2 sons. ❖ Known for research in sickle cell disease, worked at National Institutes of Health (NIH) in Bethesda, MD, then as chief of NIH's National Institute of Diabetes, Digestive, and Kidney Diseases' (NIDDK) chemical biology laboratory; served as dean of NIH's Foundation for Advanced Education in the Sciences (FAES); studied hydroxyurea, which increases amount of healthy red blood cells; studied production of hemoglobin and red blood cell chemicals through gene interaction in both healthy and sickle cell disease patients. Received NIH EEO Recognition Award (1995).

NOGUCHI, Mizuki (1978—). Japanese marathon runner. Born July 3, 1978, in Japan. ❖ Placed 2nd for World Half Marathon championships (1999); won marathon debut in Nagoya (2002), then the Osaka Media Guide (2003); placed 2nd at World championships for marathon (2003); won gold medal for women's marathon at Athens Olympics (2004).

NOLAN, Jeanette (1911–1998). American actress. Born Dec 30, 1911, in Los Angeles, CA; died June 5, 1998, in Los Angeles; m. John McIntire (actor), 1935 (died 1991); children: Tim McIntire (actor, died 1986). ❖ Appeared as Lady Macbeth in Orson Welles' *Macbeth* (1948); other films include *The Happy Time*, *The Big Heat*, *The Man Who Shot Liberty Valance*, *Cloak and Dagger* and *The Horse Whisperer*; on tv, was a regular on "The Richard Boone Show" (1963–64) and "The Virginian" (1968–70).

NOLAN, Kathleen (1933—). American actress. Born Jocelyn Schrum, Sept 27, 1933, in St. Louis, Missouri; studied with Sanford Meisner at Neighborhood Playhouse and was an early member of Actors Studio. ❖ Best known for her role as Kate, the farm wife on the popular tv series "The Real McCoys" (1957–63), was also the 1st woman president of Screen Actors Guild (1975–80); appeared on Broadway as Wendy in the musical version of *Peter Pan*, starring Mary Martin (1954), and starred in the series "Broadside." ❖ See also *Women in World History*.

NOLAN, Mae Ella (1886–1973). American politician. Born Mae Ella Hunt, Sept 20, 1886, in San Francisco, California; died July 9, 1973, in Sacramento; attended Ayres Business College in San Francisco; m. John I. Nolan (politician), 1913 (died 1922). ❖ After husband died, was elected to US House of Representatives (1923), the 1st woman elected to serve a husband's unexpired term (Jan 23, 1923–Mar 3, 1925); a Republican, served on the Labor Committee and Woman Suffrage Committee, then took over as chair of the Committee on Expenditure in Post Office Department (Dec 1923), the 1st woman to head a congressional committee; did not seek reelection. ❖ See also *Women in World History*.

NOLAN, Rachel (1974—). Australian politician. Born Mar 13, 1974, in Ipswich, Queensland, Australia. ❖ Member of the University of Queensland Senate (2001); as a member of the Australian Labor Party, became the youngest woman elected to the Queensland Parliament, for Ipswich (2001).

NOLAN, Shirley O'Hara (1924–2002). *See O'Hara, Shirley.*

NOLLEN, Maike (1977—). German kayaker. Born Nov 15, 1977, in Berlin, Germany. ❖ Placed 1st in K4 500 at World Cup in Poznan (2002); won a gold medal for K4 500 at Athens Olympics (2004).

NONA (c. 305–c. 374). *See Nonna.*

NONG QUNHUA (1966—). Chinese badminton player. Born Mar 16, 1966, in China. ❖ At Barcelona Olympics, won a silver medal in doubles (1992).

NONGQAUSE (c. 1840–c. 1900). Xhosa visionary. Name variations: Nongqawuse. Born c. 1840 in what is now South Africa; died c. 1900. ❖ At a time when the Boers and British were pushing into the territory the Xhosa, had a vision in which her ancestors promised the Xhosa a millennium of freedom from European intruders in exchange for the sacrifice of their material wealth, which resulted in the great cattle sacrifice of 1856–57 and the destruction of crops and grain reserves; after tens of thousands of Xhosa perished in the ensuing famine, escaped by fleeing to British colonial authorities, who took her into "protective custody." ❖ See also *Women in World History*.

NONNA (c. 305–c. 374). Cappadocian spiritual leader. Name variations: Nona. Born c. 305 CE; died c. 374; dau. of Christian parents from Anatolian province of Cappadocia; m. Gregory (bishop of Nazianzus), c. 320; children: daughter Gorgonia; sons, Caesarius and Gregory Nazianzus, also seen as Gregory Nazianzen (329–389). ❖ Married a pagan named Gregory (c. 320), then convinced him to convert to Christianity (326), after which his piety became so famous that he was ordained and then made the bishop of Nazianzus; produced 3 children, all of whom were eventually recognized as saints by the Eastern Church. ❖ See also *Women in World History*.

NONSUCH, Baroness (c. 1641–1709). *See Villiers, Barbara.*

NONTETA BUNGU (c. 1875–1935). South African religious founder. Born into the Xhosa tribe in Mnqaba, in what is now South Africa, c. 1875; died of stomach and liver cancer in Pretoria, South Africa, May 1935. ❖ When the worldwide influenza epidemic of 1918–19 struck the Xhosa, began to have visions during her bouts of fever, dreaming that God was punishing the earth for the sins of the people; on her recovery, began preaching against alcohol, adultery, and the eating of pork; eventually founded the Church of the Prophetess Nonteta; though she did not expressly preach against the white government, became a victim of the government crackdown on dissident, black-led religious sects; was arrested and imprisoned in an insane asylum (1921), where she died in 1935. ❖ See also *Women in World History*.

NOONAN, Peggy (1950—). American journalist, nonfiction writer and speechwriter. Born Sept 7, 1950, in Brooklyn, NY; dau. of James (furniture salesman) and Mary Jane (Byrne) Noonan; Fairleigh Dickinson University, BA, 1974; m. Richard Rahn (economist), 1985 (div. 1990); children: Will. ❖ Began career as a producer for CBS News in NY, where she wrote and produced Dan Rather's daily radio commentary; was special assistant to President Ronald Reagan (1984–86) and chief speechwriter for George Bush when he ran for the presidency (1988); became a columnist for *Wall Street Journal*; wrote *What I Saw at the Revolution* (1990), *Life, Liberty and the Pursuit of Happiness* (1994), *The Case Against Hillary Clinton* (2000) and *When Character Was King: A Story of Ronald Reagan* (2001); served as advisor to tv series "The West Wing."

NOONUCCAL, Oodgeroo (1920–1993). *See Walker, Kath.*

NOOR AL-HUSSEIN (1951—). Queen of Jordan. Name variations: Lisa Halaby. Born Elizabeth Najeeb Halaby, Aug 23, 1951, in Washington, DC; dau. of Najeeb Elias Halaby (lawyer and pilot) and Doris (Carlquist) Halaby; graduate of Princeton University, 1974; m. Hussein Ibn Talal also seen as Hussein bin Talal, known as Hussein (1935–1999), king of Jordan (r. 1952–1999), June 15, 1978; children: Prince Hamzah (b. 1980); Prince Hashim (b. 1981); Princess Iman (b. 1983); and Princess Raiyah (b. 1986); stepchildren: 8 from the king's 3 previous marriages, including Abdullah, king of Jordan (r. 1999——). ❖ At 25, wed 42-year-old King Hussein of Jordan, thus becoming the 1st American-born queen of an Arab Muslim nation; converted to Islam and took the Arabic name Noor al-Hussein (Light of Hussein); focused much of her energy on educational development within her country, helping to found the Royal Endowment for Culture and Education and the Jubilee School, a high school for gifted students; also worked to preserve and celebrate Jordan's cultural heritage and pursued the delicate issues of women's rights and opportunities. King Hussein's 1st marriage, to a distant Egyptian cousin, ended in divorce (1956); he was then wed to Britain's Antoinette Gardiner (1961–72); his 3rd wife, Queen Alia, was killed in a helicopter crash (1977). ❖ See also *Women in World History.*

NOOR INAYAT KHAN (1914–1944). *See Khan, Noor Inayat.*

NOOR JAHAN (1577–1645). *See Nur Jahan.*

NOOR JAHAN or NOOR JEHAN (1926–2000). *See Jehan, Noor.*

NORD, Kathleen (1965—). East German swimmer. Born Dec 26, 1965, in East Germany. ❖ At Seoul Olympics, won a gold medal in the 200-meter butterfly (1988).

NORDBY, Bente (1974—). Norwegian soccer player. Born July 23, 1974, in Norway. ❖ Goalkeeper; won a team bronze medal at Atlanta Olympics (1996) and a team gold medal at Sydney Olympics (2000); played for WUSA's Carolina Courage.

NORDEN, Christine (1924–1988). English singer, dancer, and actress. Born Mary Lydia Thornton, Dec 25, 1924, in Sunderland, England; died Sept 21, 1988, in London, England; m. 5 times. ❖ Protege of Alexander Korda, was regarded as England's 1st postwar sex symbol; films include *Night Beat, Mine Own Executioner, The Interrupted Journey, Black Widow* and *An Ideal Husband.*

NORDERN, Helen Brown (b. 1907). *See Lawrenson, Helen.*

NORDHEIM, Helena (1903–1943). Dutch-Jewish gymnast. Name variations: Lea Kloot-Nordheim. Born Aug 1, 1903, in the Netherlands; killed in the gas chamber at Sobibor concentration camp, July 2, 1943, with husband and 10-year-old daughter Rebecca. ❖ At Amsterdam Olympics, won a gold medal for team all-around (1928), the 1st time women's gymnastics was on the Olympic program (no indiv. medals were awarded).

NORDI, Cleo (b. 1899). Finnish ballet dancer and teacher. Born 1899 in Kronstadt, Russia. ❖ Trained in St. Peterburg by Nicholai Legat and in Helsingford by George Gé and others; worked with Anna Pavlova, appearing both as interpretive dance specialist as well as in Pavlova company repertory such as *Chopiniana, Mazurka,* and *Autumn Leaves*; became highly regarded teacher in London, teaching at Sadler's Wells Ballet School and at her own studio.

NORDICA, Lillian (1857–1914). American mezzo-soprano. Born Lillian Norton in Farmington, Maine, Dec 12, 1857; died of pneumonia from exposure after a shipwreck in Batavia, Java, May 10, 1914; dau. of Norton (photographer) and Amanda Elizabeth (Allen) Norton; graduate of New England Conservatory of Music, 1876; m. 2nd cousin Frederick A. Gower, 1882 (disappeared after a balloon ascension, presumably drowned in English Channel, 1885); m. Zoltan Döme (tenor), 1896 (div. 1904); m. George Washington Young (NJ banker), 1909. ❖ Studied with James O'Neill at New England Conservatory for 4 years before debuting at Madison Square Garden; attended Milan Conservatory under Antonio Sangiovanni; debuted as Donna Elvira at Teatro Manzoni in Milan (1879); debuted at Paris Opéra (1882), Covent Garden (1887), and

Metropolitan Opera (1891); performed throughout Europe, where she became known as the "Lily of the North"; coached extensively by Cosima Wagner for role of Elsa in *Lohengrin* given at Bayreuth (1892); sang with Metropolitan Opera (1893–1909), becoming best known for Wagnerian roles. ❖ See also I. Glackens, *Yankee Diva: Lillian Nordica and the Golden Days of Opera* (1963); and *Women in World History.*

NORDIN, Hjoerdis (1932—). Swedish gymnast. Name variations: Hjördis Nordin. Born Aug 1932 in Sweden. ❖ At Helsinki Olympics, won a gold medal in teams all-around, portable apparatus (1952).

NORDSTROM, Bernice (1912–1975). *See Walters, Bernice R.*

NORDSTROM, Ursula (1910–1988). American editor and author. Born Feb 1, 1910, in New York, NY; died of ovarian cancer on Oct 11, 1988, in New Milford, Connecticut; dau. of William and Marie (Nordstrom) Litchfield; attended Northfield School for Girls and Scudder Preparatory School. ❖ Editor and innovator for Harper and Row, was responsible for publications of E.B. White's *Stuart Little* and *Charlotte's Web*, Maurice Sendak's *Where the Wild Things Are*, and books by Ruth Krauss, Shel Silverstein, Tomi Ungerer, Laura Ingalls Wilder, M.E. Kerr (Marijane Meaker), Louise Fitzhugh and others; her own book, *The Secret Language*, is believed to have been based on her own experiences at boarding school.

NORELIUS, Kristine (1956—). American rower. Name variations: Kristi Norelius. Born Dec 26, 1956, in Bellevue, WA; attended Washington State University. ❖ At Los Angeles Olympics, won a gold medal in coxed eights (1984).

NORELIUS, Martha (1908–1955). Swedish-born swimmer. Born Jan 29, 1908, in Stockholm, Sweden; died Sept 23, 1955. ❖ Grew up in US; won a gold medal in the 400-meter freestyle at Paris Olympics (1924); won gold medals in the 400-meter freestyle and the 4 x 100-meter relay at Amsterdam Olympics (1928), the 1st woman to win gold medals in the same event in two consecutive Games; set more than 30 world records in swimming events ranging from 50-meter races to marathons; won the 10-mile William Wrigley Marathon in Toronto, Canada. Inducted into the International Swimming Hall of Fame (1967). ❖ See also *Women in World History.*

NOREN, Svea (1895–1985). Swedish figure skater. Name variations: Svea Norén. Born Oct 1895 in Sweden; died May 1985. ❖ At Antwerp Olympics, won a silver medal for singles (1920).

NORFOLK, countess of.
See Isabel (*fl.* 1225).
See Hayles, Alice (*d. after 1326*).

NORFOLK, duchess of.
See Isabel (*fl.* 1225).
See Bourchier, Anne (*c. 1417–1474*).
See Margaret (*c. 1320–1400*).
See Fitzalan, Elizabeth (*d. 1425*).
See Howard, Margaret (*fl. 1450*).
See Howard, Anne (*1475–1511*).
See Tylney, Agnes (*1476–1545*).
See Howard, Elizabeth (*1494–1558*).
See Audley, Margaret (*d. 1564*).
See Leyburne, Elizabeth (*d. 1567*).

NORGAARD, Louise (1982—). *See Noergaard, Louise Bager.*

NORGATE, Jane (1839–1926). *See Preshaw, Jane.*

NORGATE, Kate (1853–1935). British historian. Born in St. Pancras, London, England, Dec 8, 1853; died at Gorleston-on-Sea, England, April 17, 1935; dau. of Frederick Norgate (bookseller) and Fanny Norgate. ❖ Published the 2-volume *England under the Angevin Kings* (1887), which established her as a solid historian who showed a knack for understanding original sources and expressing them in a clear, spirited narrative; helped undermine the notion that women were not as capable as men in the field of history; also wrote *John Lackland* (1902), *The Minority of Henry the Third* (1912) and *Richard the Lion Heart* (1924). ❖ See also *Women in World History.*

NORIS, Assia (1912–1998). Russian-born actress. Name variations: Assia. Born Anastasia von Gerzfeld, Feb 26, 1912, in Petrograd (St. Petersburg), Russia; died Jan 27, 1998, in San Remo, Liguria, Italy; dau. of a Ukrainian woman and a German officer; m. 3 times: 2nd husband was director Mario Camerini. ❖ Rose to prominence in Italian films (1930s–early 1940s), which were often directed by 2nd husband, Mario

Camerini; also often co-starred with Vittorio De Sica; films include *Tre Uomini in Frak* (1932), *La Signorina dell'Autobus* (1933), *Giallo* (1933), *Una Donna fra Due Mondi* (*Between Two Worlds,* 1937), *Il Signor Max* (1937), *Grandi Magazzini* (1939), *Dora Nelson* (1939), *Una Romantica Avventura* (1940), *Un Colpo di Pistola* (1941), *Una Storia d'Amore* (1942), *I Dieci Comandamenti* (*The Ten Commandments,* 1945), *Che Distinta Famiglia!* (1945), *Amina* (Egypt, 1949) and *La Celestina* (1964). ❖ See also *Women in World History.*

NORMAN, Decima (1909–1983). Australian track-and-field athlete. Name variations: Clara Decima Hamilton. Born Clara Decima, Sept 9, 1909, in Tammin, Western Australia; died Aug 29, 1983; m. Eric Hamilton (former rugby player). ❖ At age 29, at the Empire Games (now Commonwealth Games), won 5 gold medals: in the individual 100 yards, 220 yards, and broad (long) jump, and as a team member on the 440- and 660-yard medley relays (1938). Awarded MBE; appointed official custodian of the baton of the Royal Commonwealth Games (1982); inducted into Western Australian Institute of Sport Hall of Champions (1986). ❖ See also *Women in World History.*

NORMAN, Dorothy (1905–1997). American photographer, writer, and civil-rights activist. Born Dorothy Stecker, Mar 28, 1905, in Philadelphia, Pennsylvania; died April 12, 1997, in East Hampton, NY; dau. of Louis Stecker and Ester Stecker; attended Smith College, 1922–23, and University of Pennsylvania, 1924–25; m. Edward Norman (heir to Sears, Roebuck fortune), June 10, 1925 (div. 1953); children: Nancy (b. 1927); Andrew (b. 1930). ❖ An intimate and biographer of photographer Alfred Stieglitz, was also a commanding photographer in her own right, her small black-and-white images likened to the poems of Emily Dickinson; was also a poet, the editor of her own intellectual journal, a columnist for *New York Post,* and an activist for civil liberties and Indian independence; works include *Dualities* (1933), (co-editor) *America and Alfred Stieglitz* (1934), (editor-publisher) *Twice a Year: A Semi-Annual Journal of Literature, the Arts and Civil Liberties* (1938–48), (editor-publisher) *Stieglitz Memorial Portfolio* (1947), (editor) *Selected Writings of John Marin* (1949), *The Heroic Encounter* (1958), *Alfred Stieglitz: Introduction to an American Seer* (1960), (editor) *Jawaharlal Nehru, The First Sixty Years* (Vol I & II, 1965), *The Hero: Myth/Image/Symbol* (1969), *Alfred Stieglitz: An American Seer* (1973) and (editor) *Indira Gandhi: Letters to an American Friend* (1985). ❖ See also *Encounters—A Memoir* (1987); Miles Barth, ed. *Intimate Visions: The Photographs of Dorothy Norman* (Chronicle, 1993); and *Women in World History.*

NORMAN, Goodwife (fl. mid-17th c.). American colonial woman tried for lesbianism. Born in MA. ❖ In 1649, as a citizen of Plymouth in the Massachusetts Bay Colony, was charged with "lude behavior upon a bed."; was found guilty and sentenced to "public acknowledgment" of her crime, civic humiliation being a favorite punishment of Puritan authorities; is thought to be the 1st woman in America convicted of lesbianism.

NORMAN, Jessye (1945—). African-American soprano. Born Sept 15, 1945, in Augusta, GA; studied at Howard University, Peabody Conservatory, and University of Michigan. ❖ Renowned for her mastery of tragic roles, expressive power, and rich vocal ability, began singing in a nearby Baptist church; won a scholarship to International Music Competition, Munich, where she earned first prize; signed a 3-year contract at the Deutsche Oper in Berlin and made operatic debut as Elisabeth in *Tannhäuser* (1969); began radio recordings; made debuts at La Scala in Milan, Royal Opera House in Covent Garden, and Hollywood Bowl (1972); 1st sang at New York Metropolitan Opera (1983); sang at many festivals, touring US, South America, Europe, Middle East, and Australia; premiered a song cycle "woman.life.song" by composer Judith Weir; released a jazz CD, "Jessye Norman Sings Michel Legrand." Was the youngest recipient of the Kennedy Center Honor (1997).

NORMAN, Maidie (1912–1998). African-American film and tv actress. Born Oct 16, 1912, in Villa Rica, GA; died May 2, 1998, in San Jose, CA; m. McHenry Norman, 1937. ❖ Appeared as the maid in *Whatever Happened to Baby Jane?*; other films include *The Well, Torch Song, Bright Road, Susan Slept Here, Written on the Wind* and *Airport '77*; appeared as Sister Scrap Scott on "Roots" (1979). Inducted into the Black Filmmakers Hall of Fame (1977).

NORMAN, Marsha (1947—). American writer. Born Sept 21, 1947, in Louisville, Kentucky; Agnes Scott College, BA; University of Louisville, MA. ❖ Worked for 2 years with emotionally disturbed adolescents at Kentucky State Hospital; began work as journalist, writing articles and reviews for *Louisville Times;* had great success with 1st play, *Getting Out,* which she wrote for Actors' Theater of Louisville (1977), drawing on experiences at mental hospital; moved to New York; scored biggest hit with *'night, Mother* (1982), which won the Pulitzer Prize and received 4 Tony Award nominations; wrote 1st novel, *The Fortune Teller* (1987), followed by *Four Plays* (1988) and Broadway musical *The Secret Garden* (1991), for which she won a Tony; began serving on faculty of playwrights program at Juilliard (1994); also wrote teleplays.

NORMAN-NERUDA, Wilma (c. 1838–1911). See *Neruda, Wilma.*

NORMAND, Kirstin (1974—). Canadian synchronized swimmer. Born June 10, 1974, in North York, Ontario, Canada. ❖ Captain, won a team bronze medal at Sydney Olympics (2000).

NORMAND, Mabel (1892–1930). American actress and comedian of the silent screen. Name variations: early in career, worked under name Mabel Fortescue. Born Nov 16, 1892, in New Brighton, Staten Island, NY; died of TB in Monrovia, California, Feb 22, 1930; dau. of Claude G. Normand (stage carpenter and pit pianist) and Mary J. (Drury) Normand; m. Lew Cody (screen actor), Sept 17, 1926; no children. ❖ One of the greatest comedians of the silent screen, was also one of the film industry's early woman directors, taking the helm in many of the early Keystone comedies she made for Mack Sennett, and co-directing some of her later films with Charlie Chaplin, Eddie Dillon, and Fatty Arbuckle; credited with establishing a classic slapstick gesture when she impulsively threw a custard pie at actor Ben Turpin; films include *Over the Garden Wall* (1910), *Mabel's Adventures* (1912), *Mabel's Stratagem* (1912), *The Speed Queen* (1913), *For Love of Mabel* (1913), (also co-dir. with Sennett) *Mabel at the Wheel* (1914), (also co-dir. with Chaplin) *Caught in a Cabaret* (1914), *Tillie's Punctured Romance* (1914), (also co-dir. with Eddie Dillon) *Mabel's and Fatty's Wash Day* (1915), *Peck's Bad Girl* (1918), *Sis Hopkins* (1919), *The Pest* (1919), *Oh Mabel Behave* (1922), *Suzanna* (1923) and *Raggedy Rose* (1926). ❖ See also Betty Harper Fussell, *Mabel* (1984); and *Women in World History.*

NORMANDY, duchess of.
  See *Poppa of Normandy.*
  See *Gisela Martel (d. 919).*
  See *Emma of Paris (d. 968).*
  See *Judith of Rennes (c. 982–1018).*
  See *Papia of Envermeu (fl. 1020).*
  See *Gunnor of Denmark (d. 1031).*
  See *Sybil of Conversano (d. 1103).*
  See *Matilda of Anjou (1107–1154).*

NORMANTON, Helena (1883–1957). British lawyer. Born in London, England, 1883; died 1957; graduate of London University; studied at Dijon, France, obtaining qualifications in French language, literature and history; m. Gavin Clark, 1921. ❖ The 1st woman to be accepted by the Inns of Court, England (1919), was also the 2nd woman to be called to the Bar in England (1922); practiced primarily in the Central Criminal Court, earning a reputation for "earnestness and learned quotations"; was one of the 1st women to be named King's Counsel (1949) and the 1st woman to be elected to General Council of the Bar; influential in the International Society of Women Lawyers and the International Federation of Business and Professional Women, also wrote several books, including *Sex Differentiation in Salary* and *Everyday Law for Women.* ❖ See also *Women in World History.*

NORODOM MONINEATH SIHANOUK (1936—). Queen of Cambodia. Name variations: given the title Neak Moneang Monique. Born Paule Monique Izzi, June 18, 1936; dau. of Pomme Peang (1904–1991) and Jean-François Izzi (director of Crédit Foncier); sister of Anne-Marie Izzi, known as Princess Sisowath Methavi (who married Prince Sisowath Mathavi and was killed by Pol Pot in 1978), m. Norodom Sihanouk (b. 1922), king of Cambodia (r. 1941–55, 1960–1970), president of Cambodia (1991-), April 1952; children: Prince Norodom Sihamon (b. 1953) and Prince Norodom Narindrapong (b. 1954). ❖ Served as president of the Red Cross; speaks Khmer, French and English.

NORONHA, Joana de (fl. c. 1850). Argentinean-Brazilian feminist, journalist, and literary critic. Name variations: Joana Paula Manso de Noronha. Born in Argentina; flourished c. 1850; m. a Portuguese violinist-composer (sep.). ❖ After separating from husband, relocated to Rio de Janeiro, Brazil, where she became a journalist and literary critic; started a progressive feminist paper, *O journal das senhoras* (1852), a watershed publication which influenced later radical feminist journals, such as *O sexo femminiso* (1873) and *A familia* (1888). ❖ See also *Women in World History.*

NORRELL, Catherine Dorris (1901–1981). American politician. Born Mar 30, 1901, in Camden, Arkansas; died August 26, 1981, in Warren, Arkansas; dau. of William and Rose Dorris; attended Ouachita Baptist College, Arkadelphia; graduate of University of Arkansas; m. William Norrell (1896–1961, US congressional representative), 1922; children: Julia Norrell. ❖ Taught music in public schools, Arkansas; was director of music department at Arkansas A&M College; elected as a Democrat to 87th Congress (1961), taking husband's seat after his death; served until Jan 3, 1963; was deputy assistant secretary of state for Educational and Cultural Affairs (1963–65); served as director, US Department of State Reception Center, Honolulu, Hawaii (1965–69). ❖ See also *Women in World History.*

NORRIS, Kathleen (1880–1966). American novelist and short-story writer. Born Kathleen Thompson in San Francisco, California, July 16, 1880; died Jan 18, 1966, in San Francisco; dau. of James Alden Thompson (bank manager) and Josephine (Moroney) Thompson; studied briefly at University of California, Berkeley; m. Charles Norris (editor and writer), 1909 (died 1954); children: Frank (b. 1910); Josephine and Gertrude (twins, b. 1912, died in infancy); adopted 4 others, including her sister's 3 orphaned children. ❖ One of the most popular and commercially successful authors of her time, began career as society editor of the *Evening Bulletin,* then worked as a reporter on San Francisco *Examiner;* on marriage, moved to NY, where she published 1st novel, *Mother* (1911), which drew from her family and Irish-American background and was an instant success; stuck closely to formula of ordinary folk with ordinary problems and dreams, focusing primarily on family and love stories; wrote 2 novels per year and frequently contributed short stories to popular magazines; produced over 80 novels, 2 autobiographies, a play, short stories, poems and even a 1940s radio serial; writings include *Undertow* (1917), *The Callahans and the Murphys* (1924), *Margaret Yorke* (1930), *Second Hand Wife* (1932), *Heartbroken Melody* (1938), *The Runaway* (1939), *The Venables* (1941), *Dina Cashman* (1942), *The Secret of Hillyard House* (1947), *Shadow Marriage* (1952) and *Miss Harriet Townshend* (1955). ❖ See also autobiographies, *Noon* (1925) and *Family Gathering* (1959); and *Women in World History.*

NORTH, Andrew (1912–2005). See Norton, Andre.

NORTH, Iris (1905–2004). *See Morgan, Joan.*

NORTH, Marianne (1830–1890). English naturalist and flower painter. Born at Hastings, England, Oct 24, 1830; died at Alderly, Gloucestershire, Aug 30, 1890; eldest dau. of a Norfolk landowner; descendant of Roger North (1653–1734). ❖ Intent on painting the flora of distant countries, went to Canada, US, and Jamaica, then spent a year in Brazil, where she did much of her work at a hut in the depths of a forest (1871–72); after a few months at Tenerife (1875), began a journey round the world, and for 2 years was occupied in painting the flora of California, Japan, Borneo, Java and Ceylon; also painted in India, Australia and South Africa; opened a gallery at Kew (1882). ❖ See also *Women in World History.*

NORTH, Sheree (1933–2005). American stage, tv and screen actress and dancer. Born Dawn Bethel, Jan 17, 1933, in Los Angeles, CA; died Nov 4, 2005, in Los Angeles, California; dau. of June Bethel (seamstress); m. Fred Bessire, 1948 (div. 1952); m. John M. Freeman, 1955. ❖ Came to prominence on Broadway with a wild dance number in *Hazel Flagg* (1953), reprised in the Martin-Lewis film adaptation, *Living It Up* (1954); other films include *How to Be Very Very Popular, The Lieutenant Wore Skirts, The Best Things in Life Are Free, No Down Payment, Madigan, Charley Varrick, The Shootist, Telefon, The Gypsy Moths, Breakout* and *Maniac Cop;* on tv, appeared as Ed Asner's girlfriend on "The Mary Tyler Moore Show" and Kramer's mother on "Seinfeld"; co-starred in the series "Big Eddie" (1975), "I'm a Big Girl Now" (1980–81) and "Our Family Honor" (1985–86).

NORTHAMPTON, countess of.
See Judith of Normandy (c. 1054–after 1086).
See Badlesmere, Elizabeth (fl. 1315–1342).
See Fitzalan, Joan (d. 1419).

NORTHCROFT, Hilda Margaret (1882–1951). New Zealand doctor. Born April 22, 1882, in Hamilton, New Zealand; died June 14, 1951, in Auckland; dau. of Henry William Northcroft and Margaret (Henderson) Northcroft; Medical College for Women, University of Edinburgh, MB,

ChB, 1908; Rotunda Hospital, Dublin, LM, 1911. ❖ Practiced medicine in England during WWI and returned to New Zealand as medical officer on *Ayrshire* (1918); specialized in diseases of women and children and practiced obstetrics; served on committee of Auckland branch of Royal New Zealand Society for Health of Women and Children (the Plunket Society, 1919), and was member of advisory board (1920–32); member of Auckland Hospital Board (1938–47); active in Auckland district committee of Women's War Service Auxiliary during WWII; executive member of Auckland branch of New Zealand Obstetrical Society (1927), and active in New Zealand Medical Women's Association (from 1920s); president of International Federation of University Women in Auckland (1921–25); executive member of National Council of Women of New Zealand (1925–29); also active in Auckland women's section of New Zealand National Party (1930s–40s). ❖ See also *Dictionary of New Zealand Biography* (Vol. 4).

NORTHUMBERLAND, countess of.
See Ingoldsthorp, Isabel.
See Elfgifu (c. 997–?).
See Neville, Margaret (d. 1372).
See Neville, Eleanor (c. 1413–1472).
See Poynings, Eleanor (d. 1483).
See Percy, Elizabeth (d. 1704).

NORTHUMBERLAND, duchess of. *See Percy, Elizabeth (d. 1776).*

NORTON, Alice Mary (1912–2005). *See Norton, Andre.*

NORTON, Alice Peloubet (1860–1928). American teacher. Born Mary Alice Peloubet, Feb 25, 1860, in Lanesville, MA; died Feb 23, 1928, in Northampton, MA; dau. of Francis Nathan Peloubet (minister) and Mary Abby (Thaxter) Peloubet; m. Lewis Mills Norton (teacher), June 6, 1883 (died 1893); children: 3 daughters, 2 sons. ❖ Helped compile *Home Sanitation: A Manual for Housekeepers* (1887); lectured at Lasell Seminary to 1899; lectured at Hartford School of Sociology (1894), Boston Young Women's Christian Association school of domestic science (1895–1900), and Boston Cooking School (1898–1900); joined faculty of Chicago Institute (1900), then promoted to assistant professor of teaching home economics when Institute merged with University of Chicago as School of Education (1901); co-headed Chautauqua (NY) School of Domestic Science (1899–1905, 1915–17, 1920); published *Food and Dietetics* (1904); edited American Home Economics Association's publication, *Journal of Home Economics* (1915–21); oversaw home economics department at Constantinople Woman's College in Turkey (1921–23).

NORTON, Andre (1912–2005). American science-fiction writer. Name variations: Alice Mary Norton; (pseudonyms) Andrew North; Allen Weston. Born Alice Mary Norton, Feb 17, 1912, in Cleveland, Ohio; legally changed name to Andre Norton in 1934; died Mar 17, 2005, in Murfreesboro, TN; dau. of Adalbert Freely Norton (rug salesman) and Bertha Stemm Norton; attended Western Reserve University (now Case Western Reserve); never married. ❖ Author of more than 140 novels for children and young adults, as well as short-story collections, anthologies, poetry, and essays, wrote her 1st novel while in high school (later published as *Ralestone Luck,* 1938); worked in children's book section of Cleveland Public Library (1932–50); at 22, published *The Prince Commands* (1934); was a reader at Gnome Press (1950–58) and editor of science fiction at World Publishing; noted for drawing young women to the genre of science fiction, wrote such novels as *Star Man's Son, 2250 A.D.* (1952), *Sargasso of Space* (1955), *Star Guard* (1955), *The Time Traders* (1958), *The Beast Master* (1959), *Storm Over Warlock* (1960), *Catseye* (1961), *The Defiant Agents* (1962), *Witch World* (1963), *The X Factor* (1965), *Moon of the Three Rings* (1966), *Android at Arms* (1971), *The Crystal Gryphon* (1972), *Outside* (1975), *Star Ka'at* (with Dorothy Madlee, 1976), *Trey of Swords* (1977), *Wheel of Stars* (1983), *Iron Cage* (1986), *Moon Called* (1991), and *Janus* (2002); works for children include *Rogue Reynard* (1947) and *Bertie and May* (1971). Received most major science-fiction awards, including Gandalf (1st woman to win), Hugo and Nebula. ❖ See also Roger C. Schlobin, *Andre Norton: A Primary and Secondary Bibliography* (Hall, 1980).

NORTON, Caroline (1808–1877). English writer. Name variations: Caroline Sheridan, Lady Stirling-Maxwell; (pseudonym) Pearce Stevenson. Born Caroline Elizabeth Sarah Sheridan, Mar 22, 1808, in London, England; died in London, June 15, 1877; dau. of Thomas Sheridan (public official) and Caroline Henrietta (Callander) Sheridan; granddau. of Richard Brinsley Sheridan and Elizabeth Linley; sister of British poet Helen Selina Blackwood (Lady Dufferin, 1807–1867);

m. George Chapple Norton, 1827; m. William Stirling-Maxwell, 1877; children: (1st m.) Fletcher Norton (b. 1829); Thomas Brinsley Norton (b. 1831); William Norton (b. 1833). ❖ Writer who, through personal experience, became an authority on, and campaigner for the reform of, the law relating to women; moved among fashionable society in London and shared close friendship with Lord Melbourne which led to her husband bringing a court case alleging adultery (1836); subsequently was separated from children and campaigned for access to them; influenced passage of Infant Custody Bill (1839); further disputes with husband contributed to case for reforming divorce and married women's property laws (1857); continued successful writing career until her death; writings include *A Voice from the Factories: A Poem* (1836), *The Separation of Mother and Child by the Law of Custody of Infants Considered* (1837), (as "Pearce Stevenson") *A Plain Letter to the Lord Chancellor on the Infant Custody Bill* (1839), *The Child of the Islands* (1845), *English Laws for Women in the Nineteenth Century* (1854), *A Letter to the Queen on Lord Cranworth's Marriage and Divorce Bill* (1855) and *The Lady of la Garaye* (1862). ❖ See also Alice Acland, *Caroline Norton* (Constable, 1948); Alan Chedzoy, *A Scandalous Woman: The Story of Caroline Norton* (Allison & Busby, 1996); Hoge and Olney, eds. *Letters of Caroline Norton to Lord Melbourne* (Ohio State U. Press, 1974); and *Women in World History*.

NORTON, Eleanor Holmes (1937—). African-American politician and activist. Born June 13, 1937, in Washington, DC; Antioch College, BA, 1960; Yale University, MA in American studies, 1963, JD, 1964; m. Edward Norton, 1965 (div. 1993); children: John Holmes Norton and Katherine Felicia Norton. ❖ Among the few black women in US legal profession during 1960s, served as assistant legal director of American Civil Liberties Union (ACLU), specializing in First Amendment rights; appointed chair of NYC Commission on Human Rights (1970); co-founded Black Feminist Organization (1973); became 1st woman chair of Equal Employment Opportunities Commission (EEOC) when appointed by President Jimmy Carter (1977); serves as tenured law professor at Georgetown University Law Center, Washington, DC; served as board member of 3 Fortune 500 companies; as Democrat, elected to represent District of Columbia in US House of Representatives (1990); reelected (1992, 1994, 1996, 1998, 2000, 2002, 2004); served as Congresswoman for District of Columbia on House Committee on Government Reform, House Select Committee on Homeland Security, and was a ranking member of Emergency Management.

NORTON, Frances (1640–1731). British devotional poet. Name variations: Lady Frances Norton. Born Frances Freke, 1640, in Hannington, Wiltshire, England; died Feb 20, 1731, in Somerset, England; buried in Westminster Abbey; dau. of Ralph Freke and Cecili (Colepepper or Culpepper) Freke; m. Sir George Norton (knight of Abbots Leigh, Somerset), c. 1672 (died 1715); m. Colonel Ambrose Norton, 1718 (died 1723); m. William Jones, 1724; children: 3. ❖ Wrote *The Applause of Virtue. In four parts. Consisting of several divine and moral essays towards the obtaining of true virtue* (1705), *Memento Mori, or Meditations on Death* (1705), and *Miscellany of Poems* (1714).

NORTON, Katherine LaFarge (1874–1911). *See Reed, Myrtle.*

NORTON, Lillian (1857–1914). *See Nordica, Lillian.*

NORTON, Mary (1903–1992). English children's writer. Born Mary Pearson, Dec 10, 1903, in London, England; died Aug 29, 1992; dau. of Reginald Spenser Pearson (physician) and Mary Savile (Hughes) Pearson; m. Robert Charles Norton (shipping magnate), Sept 4, 1926 (died); m. Lionel Bonsey, April 24, 1970; children: Ann Mary, Robert George, Guy, Caroline. ❖ One of the major children's authors in the 1st half of the 20th century, combined elements of her own experiences, transformed to meet the needs of her fantasies, with recognizable aspects of genres popular in British children's fiction; began career as an actress with the Old Vic (1925–26); published *The Magic Bed-Knob* (1945); published *The Borrowers* (1952), which quickly assumed status as a classic; wrote 7 more books in the "Borrowers" series which present a picture of English country life at the time of her childhood; also wrote *Bonfires and Broomsticks* (1947), *Bed-Knob and Broomstick* (rev. ed. of *The Magic Bed-Knob* and *Bonfires and Broomsticks*, 1957) and *Are All the Giants Dead?* (1975). Won Carnegie Medal (1952) and Lewis Carroll Shelf Award (1960), both for *The Borrowers*. ❖ See also *Women in World History*.

NORTON, Mary T. (1875–1959). American politician. Name variations: Mary T. Hopkins Norton. Born Mary Teresa Hopkins, Mar 7, 1875, in Jersey City, New Jersey; died Aug 2, 1959, in Greenwich, Connecticut;

attended Packard Business College in New York City; m. Robert Francis Norton, 1909 (died 1934); children: 1 (died in infancy, 1910). ❖ Following the death of her only child, opened a day nursery in association with a local church (1910); became 1st woman to serve on the Democratic State Committee (1921–44); served on Board of Freeholders (1923); won election to the House of Representatives from New Jersey's 12th District, the 1st woman elected from the East and the 1st Democratic woman elected to Congress without being preceded by her husband (1924); served in 69th–81st Congresses (Mar 4, 1925–Jan 3, 1951); chaired the District of Columbia Committee (1932–37); served as chair of the House Labor Committee (1932–47); credited with the enactment of the Fair Labor Standards Act (1938); was the 1st woman to head the Democratic Party in New Jersey (1932); became a member of the Democratic National Committee (1944); retired from Congress (1951). ❖ See also *Women in World History*.

NORWAY, queen of.
See Asa (c. 800–c. 850).
See Thyra of Denmark (d. 1000).
See Elizabeth of Kiev (fl. 1045).
See Ingirid (fl. 1067).
See Thora (fl. 1100s).
See Frithpoll, Margaret (d. 1130).
See Richiza (fl. 1200s).
See Inga (fl. 1204).
See Margaret (d. 1209).
See Kanga (fl. 1220).
See Margaret of Norway (1261–1283).
See Margaret (d. 1270).
See Ingeborg of Denmark (d. 1287).
See Bruce, Isabel (c. 1278–1358).
See Euphemia of Rugen (d. 1312).
See Margaret I of Denmark (1353–1412).
See Blanche of Namur (d. 1363).
See Dorothea of Brandenburg (1430–1495).
See Christina of Saxony (1461–1521).
See Dorothea of Saxe-Lauenburg (1511–1571).
See Charlotte Amalia of Hesse (1650–1714).
See Louise of Mecklenburg-Gustrow (1667–1721).
See Anne Sophie Reventlow (1693–1743).
See Louise of England (1724–1751).
See Maria Juliana of Brunswick (1729–1796).
See Maud (1869–1938).
See Sonja (1937—).

NORWOOD, Lily (1921—). *See Charisse, Cyd.*

NORWOOD, Rayana (1979—). *See Brandy.*

NOSKOVA, Luiza (1968—). Russian biathlete. Name variations: Louiza Noskova. Born July 7, 1968, in USSR. ❖ Won a gold medal for 4 x 7.5 km relay at Lillehammer Olympics (1994).

NOSKOWIAK, Sonya (1900–1975). German-born photographer. Born in Leipzig, Germany, Nov 25, 1900; died in Greenbrae, California, April 1975. ❖ Spent early years in Valparaiso, Chile, then immigrated with family to Sacramento, California (c. 1915); had personal and professional relationship with Edward Weston; was a founding member of his Group f/64, and also contributed to its 1st exhibition (1932); opened a studio in San Francisco (1935) where she specialized in portraits and fashion layouts; worked for Works Projects Administration (WPA), photographing historical architecture in various locations and identifying and recording geometric forms in the industrial landscape (1930s). ❖ See also *Women in World History*.

NOSSIS OF LOCRI (fl. 300 BCE). Greek writer. Born in Greek colony in southern Italy. ❖ Wrote epigrams, 12 extant about worship of deities, Hera and Aphrodite; refers to her mother Theophilis and grandmother Cleocha in epigram, and compares herself to Sappho.

NÖSTLINGER, Christine (1936—). Austrian novelist and children's writer. Name variations: Christine Noestlinger or Nostlinger. Born Oct 13, 1936, in Vienna, Austria; children: 2. ❖ Author of more than 100 books for children and young adults, wrote and illustrated her 1st book, *Die feuerrote Friederike* (1970, trans. as *Fiery Frederica*, 1978); also wrote the autobiographical *Maikäfer flieg!* (1973, trans. as *Fly Away Home*, 1975) and its sequel, *Zwei Wochen im Mai* (trans as *Two Weeks in May*, 1981); other works include *Der Spatz in der Hand und die Taube auf dem Dach* (A Bird in the Bush, 1974), *Konrad* (1976), *Die unteren* *sieben Achtel des Eisbergs* (1978), *De wraak van de kelderclub* (1980), *Twee weken in mei* (1984), *Echt Sanne* (1990), *Jasper speurneus* (1993), and *Mini is de beste* (1999). Received Deutsche Jugendbuchpreis (1973), Hans Christian Andersen Medal (1984), and Astrid Lindgren Memorial Award (2003).

NOTARI, Elvira (1875–1946). Italian director and producer. Born Elvira Coda, Feb 10, 1875, in Salerno, Italy; died Dec 17, 1946, in Cava De Tirreni, Italy; m. Nicola Notari, 1902; children: Eduardo Notari (actor). ❖ Pioneer in Italian cinema, formed Dora Film production company with husband in Naples (1905); films include *Bufera d'anime* (1911), *Medea di Portamedina* (1919), *Gabriele il lampionaio del porto* (1919), *'A Legge* (1920), *A piedigrotta* (1920), *E piccerella* (1922), *A Santanotte* (1922), *'Nfama!* (1924), *Fantasia e surdato* (1927) and *Napule, terra d'ammore* (1928). ❖ See also *Off Screen: Women & Film in Italy.*

NOTESTEIN, Ada (1876–1973). *See Comstock, Ada Louise.*

NOTHNAGEL, Anke (1966—). East German kayaker. Born Sept 10, 1966, in East Germany. ❖ At Seoul Olympics, won a gold medal in K4 500 meters and a gold medal in the K2 500 meters (1988).

NOTT, Andrea (1982—). American synchronized swimmer. Born April 15, 1982, in San Jose, CA. ❖ Won a team bronze medal at Athens Olympics (2004).

NOTT, Kathleen (1909–1999). British poet, novelist and philosopher. Born Kathleen Cecilia Nott, 1909, in London, England; died 1999; dau. of Phillip Nott and Ellen Nott; m. Christopher Bailey, 1927. ❖ Wrote novels, poetry, criticism, and works of philosophy; works include *Mile End* (1938), *The Emperor's Clothes: An Attack on the Dogmatic Orthodoxy of T.S. Eliot, Graham Greene, Dorothy Sayers, C.S. Lewis and Others* (1953), *Private Fires* (1960), *An Elderly Retired Man* (1963), *Philosophy and Human Nature* (1970), *The Good Want Power: An Essay in the Psychological Possibilities of Liberalism* (1977), and *Elegies and Other Poems* (1981).

NOTT, Tara (1972—). American weightlifter. Born Tara Lee Nott, May 10, 1972, in Stilwell, Kansas. ❖ Won a gold medal for -48kg at Sydney Olympics (2000); 4-time national champion.

NOURMAHAL (1577–1645). *See Nur Jahan.*

NOURSE, Elizabeth (1859–1938). American-born artist. Born in Cincinnati, Ohio, 1859; died Oct 1938; twin sister of Louise Nourse Pitman, painter; graduate of Cincinnati School of Design; studied at Académie Julian, Paris; trained with Émile Carolus-Duran; never married. ❖ Spent most of her career living in Paris and became well known for her depictions of European peasant women and children, though she also painted portraits, still lifes, and landscapes; within a year of her arrival, submitted a painting to Paris Salon, which hung at eye-level, an honor almost unheard of for a newcomer; throughout career, traveled through Europe, even as far as Russia, researching peasant life and recording it through detailed realistic paintings; had triumphant solo exhibition at Cincinnati Art Museum (1891); exhibited at Chicago Exposition (1893), where she won a gold medal for *The Family Meal*; elected an associate of Société Nationale des Beaux-Arts (1895), one of the 1st women to be so honored; paintings include *Fisher Girl of Picardy* (1889) and *Peasant Women of Borst* (1891). ❖ See also Mary Alice Heekin Burke, *Elizabeth Nourse, 1859–1938: A Salon Career* (Smithsonian, 1983); and *Women in World History.*

NOURSE, Rebecca (1621–1692). *See Nurse, Rebecca.*

NOVAËS, Guiomar (1895–1979). Brazilian pianist. Name variations: Guiomar Novaes; "Paderewska of the Pampas." Born into a family of 19 children in Sao Joao da Boa Vista, Brazil, Feb 28, 1895; died in Sao Paulo, Mar 7, 1979; dau. of Manoel da Cruz and Anna (De Menezes) Novaës; studied at Paris Conservatoire under Isidor Philipp; m. Octavio Pinto (1890–1950, Brazilian composer and architectural engineer), Dec 1922; children: Anna Maria Pinto (vocalist); Luiz Octavio Pinto (engineer). ❖ Pianist who dominated the US and European concert stage with her Romantic performances, gave Paris debut recital 6 months before graduating from the Conservatoire (July 1911) and received a *premier prix* award; made triumphant London debut (1912); arrived in New York (1915) and took the town by storm; for decades, was identified with the works of Chopin and Schumann, and with the more lyrical works of Beethoven; made many recordings, including the works of Beethoven, Chopin Mazurkas, the Debussy Preludes, and selections from Mendelssohn's Songs without Words. ❖ See also *Women in World History.*

NOVAK, Eva (1898–1988). American film actress. Born Barbara Eva Novak, Feb 14, 1898, in St. Louis, Missouri; died of pneumonia in Woodland Hills, California, April 17, 1988; younger sister of silent star Jane Novak (1896–1990); niece of Vitagraph star Anne Schafer; married William Reed; children: 2 daughters. ❖ Began career as Mack Sennett Bathing Beauty; made her mark in Westerns and action movies, frequently playing opposite Tom Mix and performing her own stunts; career dwindled as sound came in, but she made a comeback (1940s) and continued playing occasional character roles through mid-1960s; films include *The Speed Maniac* (1919), *The Daredevil* (1920), *The Torrent* (1921), *Boston Blackie* (1923), *Sally* (1925), *Irene* (1926), *The Medicine Man* (1930), *The Bells of St. Mary's* (1945), *Sunset Boulevard* (1950), *Sergeant Rutledge* (1960) and *The Man Who Shot Liberty Valance* (1962).

NOVAK, Eva (1930—). Hungarian swimmer. Born Jan 1930 in Hungary. ❖ At London Olympics, won a bronze medal in the 200-meter breaststroke (1948); at Helsinki Olympics, won a silver medal in the 200-meter breaststroke, a silver medal in the 400-meter freestyle, and a gold medal in the 4 x 100-meter freestyle relay (1952).

NOVAK, Helga (1935—). German poet and novelist. Name variations: Helga M. Novak. Born Helga Maria Karlsdottir, Sept 8, 1935, in Berlin, Germany; studied journalism and philosophy at University of Leipzig. ❖ Lived in East Germany, Iceland, France, Spain, and US before returning to East Germany; after writing of her nation's repressive politics in *Die Ballade von der reisenden Anna* (Ballad of Wandering Anna, 1958), was expelled from East Germany (1966) and settled in West Germany and later Poland; works, which are satirical and feminist in nature, include *Margarete met dem Schrank* (1978), *Markische Feemorgana* (1989), *Silvatica* (1998) and 2-vol. autobiography, *Die Eisheiligen* (Saints of Ice, 1979) and *Vogel Federlos* (Featherless Bird, 1982), which chronicles Germany through the war years and after. Received Bremer Literature award and Brandenburg Literature award.

NOVAK, Ilona (1925—). Hungarian swimmer. Born May 16, 1925, in Hungary. ❖ At Helsinki Olympics, won a gold medal in the 4 x 100-meter freestyle relay (1952).

NOVAK, Jane (1896–1990). American actress of the silent era. Born in St. Louis, Missouri, on Jan 12, 1896; died in Woodland Hills, California, on Feb 6, 1990; elder sister of Eva Novak (1898–1988, actress); niece of Vitagraph star Anne Schafer; m. Frank Newburg (actor, div.); children: 1 daughter. ❖ Was still a teenager when she began film career (1913); made over 100 features and shorts, playing opposite such stars as Harold Lloyd, Edmund Low, Richard Dix, Buck Jones and William Hart; did not survive the advent of sound, though she had small roles in a handful of talkies; films include *The Sign of Angels* (1913), *The Kiss* (1914), *The Spirit of '76* (1917), *Man's Desire* (1919), *The Wolf* (1919), *Belle of Alaska* (1922), *Thelma* (1922), *The Man Life Passed By* (1923), *Lost at Sea* (1926), *Hollywood Boulevard* (1936), *The Yanks Are Coming* (1942), *The File on Thelma Jordan* (1950) and *Paid in Full* (1950). ❖ See also *Women in World History.*

NOVAK, Kim (1933—). American actress. Born Marilyn Pauline Novak, Feb 13, 1933, in Chicago, Illinois; dau. of Joseph Novak (railroad employee), and Blanche Novak; attended Wright Junior College, Chicago; m. Richard Johnson (British actor), 1965 (div. 1966); m. Robert Malloy (veterinarian), 1976; no children. ❖ With a combination of classic beauty and earthy sexuality, was one of Hollywood's most popular stars (1950s), particularly after her performance as the dreamy young ingenue in *Picnic* (1956); just as she was beginning to emerge as a capable dramatic actress (1962), purchased a ranch in Carmel, California, and cut back on her movie work; made film debut with bit part in *The French Line* (1954); came to prominence in *The Man with the Golden Arm* (1955), *Picnic* (1956), and *The Eddy Duchin Story* (1956); also starred in *Jeanne Eagels* (1957), *Pal Joey* (1957), Hitchcock's *Vertigo* (1958) and *The Amorous Adventures of Moll Flanders* (1965), among others. ❖ See also *Women in World History.*

NOVAK, Luba (1910–1975). *See Lesik, Vera.*

NOVAK, Nina (1927—). Polish ballet dancer. Born in Warsaw, Poland, in 1927; trained at ballet school of Warsaw Opera; studied with Bronislava Nijinska, Leon Woizikowski, and others; m. Roman Rojas Cabot (Venezuelan diplomat), 1962; settled in Caracas, Venezuela. ❖ Came to US to perform with Polish Representative Ballet at NY World's Fair (1939); remained in US (1939–48); began dancing solo with Ballets Russe de Monte Carlo (1948); promoted to ballerina (1952), continued working with the Ballets Russe for next 9 years, creating a role in *Birthday* (1949) and winning acclaim for featured roles in *The Nutcracker, Le Beau Danube, Coppélia* and *Ballet Imperial*; had her own company, Academia de Ballet Clásico Venezolano (Venezuelan Classical Ballet Co.), in Caracas (1964–84); became director of the classical repertoire at the Teresa Carreno Complex (1985).

NOVÁKOVÁ, Teréza (1853–1912). Czech regionalist writer and ethnographer. Name variations: Tereza Novakova; Theresa Lanhaus. Born Teréza Lanhausová in Prague, Czechoslovakia, July 31, 1853; died in Prague on Nov 13, 1912; married; children: at least 4. ❖ One of the masters of the realist novel in Czech literature, grew up in an atmosphere permeated by cultural nationalism; published a biography of Caroline Svetla (1890); heavily influenced by the countryside of easternmost Bohemia, made extensive field trips to this region, studying folk culture there not only from the view of a writer and artist, but also from an ethnographic perspective, resulting in *Kroj llidovy a národni vysiváni na Litomyslku* (Folk Costume and Embroidery in Litomysl, 1890) and *Z nejvychodnejsich Cech* (From Easternmost Bohemia, 1898); her collection of stories set in Eastern Bohemia, *Ulomky 'uly* (Chunks of Granite, 1902), pleased critics and readers alike, and set the stage for a successful series of regional works that have become classics; novels include *Jan Jilek, Jiri Smatlán, Na Librove grunte* (On the Libra Estate) and *Drasar;* as a feminist, edited the journal *Zensky svet* (Women's World, 1897–1907); also wrote *The Hall of Fame of Czech Women* (1894) and *From the Women's Movement* (1912); was an indispensable writer of a classic period of the Czech nation's cultural renaissance. ❖ See also *Women in World History.*

NOVALIS, Laura de (1308–1348). See Noves, Laure de.

NOVARRA-REBER, Sue (1955—). American cyclist. Name variations: Sue Novarra. Born Sue Novarra, Nov 22, 1955, in Flint, Michigan. ❖ A 7-time national track champion, was the youngest woman to win the world sprint championship (1975); won the title again (1980); won the US sprint championships (1972, 1974, 1975); became national champion in the road race (1982). ❖ See also *Women in World History.*

NOVELLA (d. 1333). Italian educator. Born in Bologna, early 1300s; died 1333. ❖ Daughter—and most promising student—of a Bolognese law professor, caused an uproar when she lectured in her father's place on the few occasions he was not able to attend class; lectured from behind a curtain to shield her students from her feminine body. ❖ See also *Women in World History.*

NOVELLO, Antonia (1944—). American physician and government official. Born Antonia Coello, Aug 23, 1944, in Fajardo, Puerto Rico; dau. of Antonio Coello and Ana Delia Coello (school principal); University of Puerto Rico, BS, 1965, MD, 1970; pediatric training at University of Michigan; training and residency in pediatric nephrology at University of Michigan Medical Center (1973–74), and Georgetown University Hospital (1974–75); Johns Hopkins University School of Public Health, MA, 1982; m. Joseph Novello (psychiatrist), 1970; no children. ❖ As the 1st woman and the 1st Hispanic surgeon general of the US (1990–93), pursued her own special interests, which included providing health care for minorities, women, and children, and protecting the nation's youth from the dangers of tobacco and alcohol; went on to serve as a special representative to UNICEF; initially had a private practice in pediatrics and nephrology in Springfield, Virginia (1976–77); served as a project officer in the artificial kidney and chronic uremia programs at National Institutes of Health (NIH); named deputy director of National Institute of Child Health and Human Development (1986); served as a legislation fellow with the Senate Committee on Labor and Human Resources; became a clinical professor of pediatrics at the Georgetown University School of Medicine (1986). ❖ See also *Women in World History.*

NOVELLO, Clara (1818–1908). English soprano. Name variations: Countess Gigliucci. Born Clara Anastasia Novello, June 10, 1818, in England; died 1908; dau. of Vincent Novello (pianist and composer); sister of Cecilia Novello (singer), Mary Sabilla Novello (soprano), and Joseph Alfred Novello (bass singer); m. Count Gigliucci, 1843. ❖ Made successful debut (1833) at a concert in Windsor and was immediately engaged for the Ancient and Philharmonic Concerts, Worcester Festival, and Westminster Abbey Festival; invited by Mendelssohn to appear at Gewandhaus concerts in Leipzig (1837), then went to Berlin, Vienna, St. Petersburg, and Dusseldorf; journeyed to Italy to study for the stage (1839), becoming a pupil of Micheroux in Milan; made opera debut at Padua in Rossini's *Semiramide* (1841), followed by appearances in Rome, Milan, Bologna and Modena; returned to England (1843) and appeared

at Drury Lane; following marriage (1843), retired from public life for 7 years; met with greatest success appearing in oratorio in England (1851) and made one last opera appearance on stage there, in the *Puritani* at Drury Lane (1853); enjoyed greatest triumphs at the opening of Crystal Palace (1854) and at Handel festivals (1857, 1859), then moved to Italy. ❖ See also *Women in World History.*

NOVELLO-DAVIES, Clara (1861–1943). Welsh choral conductor and singing teacher. Name variations: Clara Davies; Clara Novello Davies. Born Clara Novello Davies in Cardiff, Wales, 1861; died 1943; dau. of Jacob Davies (choral conductor); m. David Davies, 1882; children: David Ivor Novello Davies (1893–1951, who composed musicals and popular songs as Ivor Novello). ❖ Appeared publicly as an accompanist at age 12; assembled 1st Ladies' Choir in Wales, with 100 voices (1885), while continuing to run a music school in her home; founded and conducted a Welsh Ladies' Choir (1893), which she took to compete at the World's Fair in Chicago, returning home with the gold medal; trained singers for Metropolitan Opera in NY and also toured US, Britain, France, and South Africa with her choir; led choir in concert for Queen Victoria at Osborne House (1894), after which she could add the adjective "royal" to her choir's title; gave 70 concerts in US (1895) and at Paris Expositions (1900, 1937). ❖ See also autobiography, *The Life I Have Loved* (1940); and *Women in World History.*

NOVES, Laure de (1308–1348). French literary influence. Born Laure de Noves; Laura de Novalis; Laura de Noyes; Madame de Sale. Born 1308; died of the plague in Avignon, France, April 6, 1348; dau. of Audibert de Noves of Avignon; m. Hugues de Sale of Avignon; children: 11. ❖ Beloved by Petrarch and celebrated in his poems, was detailed in over 300 sonnets and canzoni. ❖ See also *Women in World History.*

NOVITIA (1906–1939). See Hyde, Robin.

NOVOKSHCHENOVA, Olga (1974—). Russian synchronized swimmer. Born Nov 29, 1974, in Moscow, USSR. ❖ At World championships, won a team gold medal (1998); won a team gold medal at Sydney Olympics (2000) and a team gold medal at Athens Olympics (2004).

NOVOTNA, Jana (1968—). Czech tennis player. Born Oct 2, 1968, in Brno, Czechoslovakia (now Czech Republic). ❖ Turned professional (1987); won 24 career singles and 72 doubles titles; won a silver medal for doubles and a bronze medal for singles at Atlanta Olympics (1996); was unsuccessful in the finals at Wimbledon (1993, 1997), but finally won (1998); retired from competition (1999). ❖ See also *Women in World History.*

NOVOTNA, Jarmila (1907–1994). Czech soprano. Born Jarmila Novotna, Sept 23, 1907, in Prague, Czechoslovakia; died Feb 10, 1994, in NY, NY; studied in Prague with Emmy Destinn; m. Baron George Daubek, 1931 (died 1981). ❖ Famed throughout the world, made debut at National Theater in Prague as Marenka in *La Traviata* at age 17 (1926); appointed soprano of Berlin State Opera (1928); sang at Vienna Staatsoper (1933–38), also appearing regularly at Salzburg as Octavian, Euridice, Countess Almaviva, Pamina, and Frasquita; created title role in Lehár's *Giuditta* in Vienna (1934); after Hitler's troops entered Czechoslovakia (1938), managed to get husband and children to Vienna, then US; appeared 193 times with Metropolitan Opera (1939–45); a talented actress, also appeared in such films as *The Great Caruso* and *The Search* and sang Smetana's *The Bartered Bride* for a European movie; made many recordings, including *Songs of Lidice* in memory of the victims of the Nazi massacre in her homeland; made last appearance (1957), in Vienna, then moved permanently to NY following death of husband. ❖ See also *Women in World History.*

NOWAK, Cecile (1967—). French judoka. Born 1967 in France. ❖ At Barcelona Olympics, won a gold medal in extra-lightweight 48 kg (1992).

NOWICKA, Joanna (1966—). Polish archer. Born 1966 in Poland. ❖ Won a bronze medal for teams at Atlanta Olympics (1996).

NOWLAND, Catherine Elizabeth (1863–1935). See Nowland, Mary Josepha.

NOWLAND, Mary Josepha (1863–1935). New Zealand nun and teacher. Name variations: Catherine Elizabeth Nowland; Sister Mary Josepha. Born Catherine Elizabeth Nowland, June 16, 1863, at Gunnedah, New South Wales, Australia; died Dec 14, 1935, at Westport, New Zealand; dau. of Robert Nowland (butcher) and Julia (Leary) Nowland. ❖ Joined Sisters of Mercy and became nun (1887); sent to New Zealand (1891); helped run boys' infant and girls' primary schools, and opened girls' high school at Reefton; assumed control of convent when Westport branch of order opened (1894), was appointed reverend mother (1914), then served as superior (1917–21); established O'Connor Home for aged at Westport (1920s); purchased land with own income to provide meat and milk for home; elected superior of Westport and Reefton convents when West Coast and Wellington foundations of order merged (1927–35). ❖ See also *Dictionary of New Zealand Biography* (Vol. 3).

NOYES, Blanche (1900–1981). American aviator. Born June 23, 1900, in Cleveland, Ohio; died Oct 1981 in Washington, DC; m. Dewey Noyes (airmail pilot, killed in an air crash, 1935). ❖ Soloed (Feb 15, 1929); became a demonstration pilot for Standard Oil (1931); worked for Air Marking Group of the Bureau of Air Commerce (1936–71); with co-pilot Louise Thaden, became 1st woman to enter and win the Bendix Cup Race, flying from NY to Los Angeles in a record-setting 14 hours, 54 minutes (1936); was the 1st woman to receive a gold medal from the Commerce Department. Inducted into Aviation Hall of Fame (1970).

NOYES, Clara Dutton (1869–1936). American nurse and educator. Pronunciation: noise. Born Oct 3, 1869, in Port Deposit, Maryland; died June 3, 1936, in Washington, DC; dau. of Enoch Dutton Noyes and Laura Lay (Banning) Noyes; graduate of Johns Hopkins School for Nursing, 1896. ❖ One of the most prominent professional nurses of the early 20th century, instituted many standardized procedures, maintained the Red Cross' reserve of trained nurses for emergency service, and founded the 1st school for midwives in America (1911); received Florence Nightingale Medal of the International Red Cross (1923); received French Medal of Honor (1929); inducted into the Hall of Fame of the American Nurses Association (1998). ❖ See also *Women in World History.*

NOYES, Laura de (1308–1348). *See Noves, Laure de.*

NOZIERE, Violette (1915–1966). French murderer. Born Jan 11, 1915, in Neuvy-sur-Loire, France; died 1966. ❖ At age 18, poisoned both parents with Veronal tablets, then turned on gas in the stove to make it look like they'd been overcome when a gas pipe burst (Aug 23, 1934); father died but mother survived; fled, and public hunt to find her caused national furor; once caught, faced quick trial and was found guilty (Oct 13, 1934); sentenced to be beheaded in a public place, saw sentence commuted to life. Her motive was apparently the more than 180,000 francs her father had saved which would pass to her upon the deaths of her parents. ❖ See also (film) *Violette Noziere,* directed by Claude Chabrol (1978).

NUGENT, Andrea (1968—). Canadian swimmer. Born Nov 1, 1968; attended McGill University. ❖ At Seoul Olympics, won a bronze medal in 4 x 100-meter medley relay (1988).

NUGENT, Luci Baines (b. 1947). *See Johnson, Luci Baines.*

NUGENT WOOD, Mrs. (1836–1880). *See Wood, Susan.*

NUN ENSIGN, The (1592–1635). *See Erauso, Catalina de.*

NUNES, Natália (1921—). Portuguese novelist. Name variations: Maria Natalia Nunes. Born 1921 in Portugal. ❖ Served as curator of National Archives of Torre de Tombo, Lisbon (1957–68); writings, which generally have female protagonists and deal with romantic love, include *Autobiografica duma Mulher Romântica* (1955), *Assembléia de Mulheres* (1964), and *O Caso de Zulmira* (1967).

NUNN, Glynis (1960—). Australian heptathlete. Born Glynis Saunders, Dec 4, 1960, in Toowoomba, Queensland, Australia; m. Chris Nunn (decathlete). ❖ At Los Angeles Olympics, won a gold medal in heptathlon (1984); won a bronze medal in the high hurdles at the Commonwealth Games (1986); retired from competition (1990).

NUNNELEY, Kathleen Mary (1872–1956). New Zealand tennis player and librarian. Born Sept 16, 1872, at Little Bowden, Leicestershire, England; died Sept 28, 1956, in Wellington, New Zealand; dau. of John Alexander Nunneley (grocer) and Kate (Young) Nunneley. ❖ Began tennis career early, winning numerous championships before age 15; immigrated to New Zealand with mother and siblings (1894); represented New Zealand in many tournaments; won 13 national singles titles (more than any other man or woman in New Zealand tennis history, 1895–1907); also won 10 national doubles titles and 9 national mixed doubles titles; was a librarian at Wellington Public Library until retirement (1935). ❖ See also *Dictionary of New Zealand Biography* (Vol. 3).

NUOLIKIVI, Senja (1941—). *See Pusula, Senja.*

NURBANU (1525–1583). Ottoman valide sultana. Name variations: Nurbanu Sultan; Nurubanu Sultana; Cecelia Venier Baffo. Born Cecelia Venier-Baffo in Venice, 1525; died in Constantinople, 1583; illeg. dau. of 2 Venetian noble families; m. Selim II the Drunkard (also known as Selim the Sot), sultan of the Ottoman Empire (r. 1566–1574); children: 3 daughters (names unknown), and Murad III (1546–1595), Ottoman sultan (r. 1574–1595). ❖ Captured as a slave (1537), entered the imperial harem and eventually married Selim II, son of Suleiman the Magnificent and Roxelana; became valide sultan (mother of the sultan), the most powerful woman in the empire, when her son Murad III ascended the throne (1574); was the empire's true ruler until her death.

NUR JAHAN (1577–1645). Empress of Mughal India. Name variations: Noor Jahan or Jehan; Nur Mahal or Nourmahal; Mehr-on-Nesa, Mehrunnisa, Mehr-un-nisa, Mihm-un-Nisa, Mehrunissa, Mehrunnissa or Mihr-ur-Nisa. Born Mehr-un-nisa in 1577 in Qandahar, Persia (Iran); died 1645 in Lahore, India (now in Pakistan); dau. of Mirza Ghiyas Beg (literary artist in Tehran) and Asmat Begum; studied Persian culture and language as well as tradition and languages of adopted country, India; m. Ali Quli (Sher Afghan or Afkun), 1594 (died 1607); m. Prince Salim (1569–1627), later Jahangir, 4th Mughal emperor of India (r. 1605–1627), in 1611; children: (1st m.) Ladili Begum or Ladli Begum. ❖ Brilliant political and military strategist, architect, and diplomat, who had absolute control in the Mughal court, married Emperor Jahangir (1611) and was a loving stepmother to his children from other wives, especially Prince Khurram, later the builder of the Taj Mahal as Emperor Shah Jahan; within 1st 6 months of her marriage, assumed the reins of the empire, made easy by the emperor's excessive love of drinking and opium, and by her perceptiveness and charm; quelled several revolts by planning and executing military campaigns; left an indelible mark on art, architecture, fashion, poetry, and cooking—an imprint so memorable that after 4 centuries Indians still recognize their debt to her; her legacy can be seen in the spectacular mausoleums, gardens, and mosques, or in the current fashion of women's clothing, or even in the menus of Mughalai restaurants in India and US; her name is attached to 2 magnificent buildings: her father's mausoleum in Agra and her husband's tomb in Lahore; a prolific garden designer, designed the Noor Afshan (Light Scattering), the Noor Manzil (Abode of Light) and Moti Bagh (Garden of Pearls), all in Agra, and the Shah Dara (Royal Threshold) in Lahore, which surrounds her husband's tomb; ordered the construction of inns or *sarais;* had mosques constructed, the most outstanding of which is the Shahee Masjid (Imperial Mosque) in Srinagar, Kashmir; left some of her favorite embroidery patterns in the trellis and lattice work on the buildings; a poet, was a patron of other women poets whose works survive; collected a vast number of paintings from European merchants; buried in a tomb of her own design; her legend has reached mythological proportions. ❖ See also Ellison Banks Findly, *Nur Jahan: Empress of Mughal India* (Oxford U. Press, 1993); and *Women in World History.*

NUR JEHAN (1926–2000). *See Jehan, Noor.*

NUR MAHAL (1577–1645). *See Nur Jahan.*

NURPEISSOVA, Dina (1861–1955). Kazakh composer and dombrist. Born in Beketai-Kum, Kazakhstan, 1861; died in Alma-Ata, Kazakhstan, Jan 31, 1955. ❖ Became a virtuoso on the dombra; received a prize in Moscow when her compositions were performed by the mixed National Kazakh Kolkhoz Choir (1936); was made a National Artist of the Kazakh SSR (1944); preserved many Kazakh traditions.

NURSE, Rebecca (1621–1692). English-born witchcraft-trial victim. Name variations: Rebecca Nourse. Born Feb 1621 in Great Yarmouth, England; died July 19, 1692, in Salem, MA; dau. of William Towne and Joanna (Blessing) Towne; m. Francis Nurse (woodworker); children: 4 sons, 4 daughters. ❖ Accused of witchcraft by group of young women (1692); arrested by local authorities (Mar 24, 1692) and examined by magistrates (Mar 25, 1692); insisted on innocence throughout imprisonment and during trial (June 30, 1692); hung with 4 others on "Gallows Hill" in Salem (July 14, 1692). ❖ See also Works Progress Administration, *Salem Witchcraft, 1692* (Essex Co. Court House, Salem).

NURUBANU (1525–1583). *See Nurbanu.*

NURUTDINOVA, Liliya (1963—). Soviet runner. Born Dec 15, 1963, in USSR. ❖ At Barcelona Olympics, won a silver medal in 800 meters (1992).

NUSSBAUM, Karen (1950—). American labor activist. Born April 25, 1950, in Chicago, Illinois; attended University of Chicago; married; children: 3. ❖ Was co-founder and executive director of 9to5, the National Association of Working Women (1973–93); elected president of Union District 925, Service Employees International Union (1981); served as director of the Women's Bureau at the US Department of Labor (1993–96); became the 1st director of the Working Women's Department, AFL-CIO (1996); co-wrote *9 to 5: The Working Woman's Guide to Office Survival* (1983). ❖ See also *Women in World History*.

NÜSSLEIN-VOLHARD, Christiane (1942—). German biologist. Pronunciation: noos-line. Name variations: Nusslein-Volhard; Nuesslein-Volhard. Born Christiane Volhard, Oct 20, 1942, in Magdeburg, Germany; dau. of Rolf Volhard (architect) and Brigitte (Haas) Volhard (musician and painter); received degrees in biology, physics, and chemistry, Johann-Wolfgang-Goethe-University, 1964; received diploma in biochemistry, Eberhard-Karls University, 1968; University of Tübingen, PhD, 1973; postdoctoral work at Biozentrum Basel, 1975–76, and University of Freiburg, 1977; m. a man named Nüsslein (div.). ❖ The 10th woman to win the Nobel Prize for Medicine as well as the 1st German woman to win a Nobel Prize for science (1995), initially became affiliated with the European Molecular Biology Laboratory (EMBL, 1978), where she teamed up with Eric Wieschaus, another developmental biologist; became director of the Max-Planck-Institut for Developmental Biology (1985); with Wieschaus, received the Albert Lasker Medical Research Award (1991); with Wieschaus and Edward B. Lewis, awarded the Nobel Prize for genetic research on the fruit fly; her contributions to the field of genetics may help to explain why certain birth defects occur. ❖ See also *Women in World History*.

NUTHALL, Betty (1911–1983). English tennis player. Name variations: Betty Nuthall Shoemaker. Born May 23, 1911, in England; died Nov 8, 1983; dau. of Stuart Nuthall. ❖ Won British Junior championship (1924); won 7 more titles in this event (1925, 1926, 1927); won women's singles in Westgate-on-Sea tournament (1925); won US singles championship at Forest Hills (1930), the 1st player from overseas and the only English woman to do so before Virginia Wade; also won US doubles with Sarah Palfrey (1930), Eileen Whittingstall (1931), and Freda James (1933); won US mixed-doubles championship with George Lott (1929, 1931).

NUTHEAD, Dinah (fl. 1696). Maryland printer. Name variations: Dinah Devoran; Dinah Oley. Born in Anne Arundel County, MD; m. William Nuthead (died 1695); m. Manus Devoran, c. 1700 (died Dec 1700); m. Sebastian Oley (died 1707); children: (1st m.) William and Susannah Nuthead; (3rd m.) Sebastian Oley. ❖ Took over husband's printing business, The Nuthead Press, in St. Mary's City, MD, after his death; when license was granted by Maryland House of Representatives, became 1st woman in US officially licensed to operate printing press (1696); primarily printed forms for government; considered one of 1st important printers in MD.

NUTT, Emma M. (c. 1849–1926). American telephone operator. Born c. 1849 in US; died June 4, 1926. ❖ Served as 1st woman telephone operator (1878–1911) in US, at Telephone Despatch Company in Boston, MA.

NUTTALL, Zelia (1857–1933). American archaeologist. Name variations: Mrs. Z. Nuttall. Born Zelia Maria Magdalena Nuttall in San Francisco, California, Sept 6, 1857; died at Casa Alvarado, Mexico, April 12, 1933; dau. of Robert Kennedy Nuttall (physician) and Magdalena Parrott Nuttall; m. Alphonse Louis Pinart (French ethnologist), 1880 (sep. 1884, div. 1888); children: Nadine Pinart (b. 1882). ❖ Leading authority on Mexican archaeology and ancient picture writing, who made extensive studies in antiquities, history, and languages, 1st came to prominence with publication of her work on "The Terra Cotta Heads of Teotibuacan" in the *American Journal of Archaeology* (1886); also published *The Fundamental Principles of Old and New World Civilization* and *Book of the Life of Ancient Mexicans*; named honorary professor of the National Museum of Mexico (1908).

NUTTING, Mary Adelaide (1858–1948). Canadian-born American nurse and educator. Name variations: Adelaide Nutting. Born Nov 1, 1858, in Quebec, Canada; died Oct 3, 1948, in White Plains, New York; dau. of Vespasian Nutting (county clerk for circuit court) and Harriet Sophia (Peasley) Nutting (seamstress); never married. ❖ Leader in professional nursing and nursing education, entered Johns Hopkins Hospital School for Nurses in Baltimore (1889) and graduated with the 1st class (1891); stayed on at Johns Hopkins and became superintendent of nurses and principal of the training school (1894); served as president, National League of Nursing Education (1896, 1909); helped to establish and served as director of a nursing education program at Teachers College of Columbia University (1899); co-authored 4-vol. *History of Nursing* (1907–12); awarded the 1st Mary Adelaide Nutting Medal by the National League of Nursing Education (1944). ❖ See also *Women in World History*.

NUVEMAN, Stacey (1978—). American softball player. Born April 26, 1978, in LaVerne, CA; attended University of California, Los Angeles. ❖ Catcher, won team World championship (2002); won a team gold medal at Sydney Olympics (2000) and Athens Olympics (2004).

NUYEN, France (1939—). French-Vietnamese actress. Born France Nguyen Vannga, July 31, 1939, in Marseille, France, of Vietnamese-French ancestry; earned MA in clinical psychology, 1986; m. Robert Culp (actor), 1967 (died 1970). ❖ Starred on Broadway in *The World of Suzie Wong* (1958); films include *South Pacific, In Love and War, Satan Never Sleeps, Diamond Head, A Girl Name Tamiko, Battle for the Planet of the Apes, The Joy Luck Club* and *Passion to Kill* among others; on tv, was a regular on "St. Elsewhere"; having been a victim of child abuse, works with abused children, abused and battered women, and women in prison in Los Angeles.

NWAKUCHE-NWAPA, Flora (1931–1993). *See Nwapa, Flora.*

NWAPA, Flora (1931–1993). Nigerian novelist and publisher. Name variations: Flora Nwakuche-Nwapa. Pronunciation: N-WOP-pa. Born Flora Nwanzuruahu Nwapa, Jan 13, 1931, in Oguta, Nigeria; died at University of Nigeria Teaching Hospital, Enugu, Nigeria, Oct 16, 1993; dau. of Christopher Ijoma Nwapa (managing director of British palm oil exporting co.) and Martha Onyenma Onumonu Nwapa (schoolteacher); attended Queens College, Lagos; University College, Ibadan, BA, 1957; University of Edinburgh, Scotland, Dip. in Education, 1958; m. Chief Gogo Nwakuche, 1967; children: daughter Ejine (b. 1959); son Uzoma (b. 1969); daughter Amede. ❖ The 1st African woman to write and publish a novel in English, changed African literary traditions regarding the portrayal of women; published 1st book *Efuru* (1966), with a female protagonist new to Nigerian literature—intelligent, independent, creative, and industrious; also wrote *Idu* (1971), *This Is Lagos, and Other Stories* (1971), *Never Again* (1975), *Wives at War, and Other Stories* (1980), *One Is Enough* (1981), *Women Are Different* (1986), *Cassava Song* and *Rice Song* (1986); children's books include *Emeka: The Driver's Guard* (1972), *Mammywater* (1979), *My Animal Number Book* (1979), *The Miracle Kittens* (1980), *Journey to Space* (1980) and *The Adventures of Deke* (1980); also served as minister for Health and Social Welfare, and minister for Lands, Survey and Urban Development, and was responsible for the Oguta Lake project; founded Tana Press, Ltd. (1976), followed by Flora Nwapa Books, Ltd. to publish children's books which would teach children "to value their own rich culture, and to encourage more women to write books"; received citations for Officer of the Niger (Oon, 1982); granted University of Ife merit award for authorship and publishing (1985); appointed visiting professor in creative writing at University of Maidururi (1989) and became a member of University of Harin Governing Council; appointed to Commission on the Review of Higher Education (1990); was visiting professor at East Carolina University in Greenville, North Carolina (1993–94). ❖ See also *Women in World History*.

NYAD, Diana (1949—). American marathon swimmer. Born Aug 22, 1949, in New York City; studied at Lake Forest College and New York University. ❖ Became the 1st person to swim Lake Ontario from north to south; set record for the fastest swim around the island of Manhattan at 7 hours and 57 minutes (1975); completed the longest open-water swim in history, 102.5 miles (1979); was the world's top female distance swimmer (1969–77). Inducted into Women's Sports Foundation International Sports Hall of Fame (1986). ❖ See also memoir *Other Shores* (1978); and *Women in World History*.

NYANKOMA, Efua (1924–1996). *See Sutherland, Efua.*

NYBERG, Katarina (1965—). Swedish curler. Born Nov 16, 1965, in Sweden. ❖ Four-time World champion (1992, 1995, 1998, 1999); won a bronze medal for curling at Nagano Olympics (1998); placed 6th at Salt Lake City Olympics (2002); retired (2002).

NYBRAATEN, Inger-Helene (1960—). Norwegian cross-country skier. Name variations: Inger Helene Nybräten or Nybraten. Born Aug 12, 1960, in Fagernes, Norway. ❖ Won a gold medal for 4 x 5 km relay at

Sarajevo Olympics (1984); won silver medals at Albertville Olympics (1992) and Lillehammer Olympics (1994), both for 4.5 km relay.

NYBRATEN, Inger-Helene (1960—). *See Nybraaten, Inger-Helene.*

NYEMBE, Dorothy (1930–1998). South African anti-apartheid leader. Name variations: Dorothy Nomzansi Nyembe; Mam D. Born in Thalane, KwaZulu-Natal, South Africa, Dec 31, 1930 (some sources cite 1931); died Dec 17, 1998, in KwaZulu-Natal; children: at least 1 daughter. ❖ Joined African National Congress (ANC), eventually becoming deputy chair of local ANC Women's League—and was jailed for 2 years as a result of her participation in 1952 Defiance Campaign; led a Natal women's protest against the pass laws (1956); endorsed out of Durban (1959), and was detained for 5 months during the State of Emergency (1960); represented Women's Federation in South African Congress of Trade Unions (1962); sentenced to 3 years' for her work with ANC (1963); upon release (1966), was placed under strict banning orders, but continued working clandestinely against apartheid; arrested again (1968), tortured, and charged with violating the Terrorism Act and the Suppression of Communism Act, was sentenced to 15 years in the infamous Barberton Prison; released (1984), resumed working in the ANC; elected a member of Parliament (1994). ❖ See also *Women in World History.*

NYMARK ANDERSEN, Nina (1972—). Norwegian soccer player. Name variations: Nina Nymark-Andersen; Nina Andersen; Nina Nymark Jakobsen. Born Nina Nymark Andersen, Sept 28, 1972, in Norway; twin sister of Anne Nymark Andersen (soccer player). ❖ Won a team bronze medal at Atlanta Olympics (1996); played for Sandviken (1989–96).

NYRO, Laura (1947–1997). American singer and songwriter. Born Laura Nigro, Oct 18, 1947, in the Bronx, NY; died of ovarian cancer, April 8, 1997, in Danbury, CT; dau. of Louis Nigro (piano tuner and jazz trumpeter) and Gilda (Mirsky) Nigro (bookkeeper); attended High School of Music and Art, Manhattan; m. David Bianchini (carpenter), 1971 (div.); lived with partner Maria Desiderio (painter). ❖ A singer with a 3-octave range who synthesized elements of soul, jazz, rock, and blues, relished her freedom as a songwriter to express social and political leanings; at 19, sold 1st song, "And When I Die," a hit for Peter, Paul and Mary, then Blood, Sweat and Tears; wrote numerous hits for other performers, including "Stoney End" (Barbra Streisand), "Eli's Coming" (Three Dog Night), as well as "Wedding Bell Blues," "Stoned Soul Picnic," and "Sweet Blindness" (all recorded by Fifth Dimension); as a performer, released 12 albums in 30-year career, including *Stoned Soul Picnic: The Best of Laura Nyro* (1997); dedicted US tour to animal-rights movement (1988), resulting in the album *Laura—Live at The Bottom Line*; appeared at the Newport Folk Festival (1989) and toured Japan (1994); released 1st studio album in 9 years and what would be her last original album, *Walk the Dog and Light the Light* (1993). Won Academy Award for title song for *Broken Rainbow*, a documentary about the forced relocation of the Navajo (1985). ❖ See also *Women in World History.*

NYSTROM, Karen (1969—). Canadian ice-hockey player. Born June 17, 1969, in Scarborough, Ontario, Canada. ❖ Won team gold medals at World championships (1992, 1994, 1997); won a team silver medal at Nagano (1998), the 1st Olympics to feature women's ice hockey.

NZIMIRO, Mary (1898–1993). Nigerian merchant and philanthropist. Name variations: Lady Nzimiro. Born Mary Nwametu Onumonu, Oct 16, 1898, in Oguta, Igboland, Nigeria; died Jan 16, 1993, in Oguta; dau. of Chief Onumonu Uzaru (one of 1st two warrant chiefs for Oguta appointed by Britain's Queen Victoria), and Madam Ruth Onumonu (trading magnate in palm produce); graduate of a convent school in Asaba, 1920; married Richard Okwosha Nzimiro (1st mayor of Port Harcourt), 1920; children: Priscilla Nzimiro (doctor); (stepchildren) Richard, Ifediora, and Nnamdi. ❖ One of the women Igbo traders who distinguished themselves during Nigeria's colonial period under British rule, was active in the commercial, educational and political development of her country; started trading in palm oil, salt and European manufactured goods (1921); built William Wilberforce Academy (later renamed Priscilla Memorial Grammar School), 1st of 2 secondary schools she established at Oguta (1945); became the principal factor for United African Co. (UAC) for their eastern zone (1948); was a member of the National Council of Nigeria Citizens (NCNC, 1950s); earned husband the position of 1st mayor of Port Harcourt (1956); was agent for UAC, hosted twice by Queen Elizabeth II of England (early 1960s); was a founding member of Nigeria's YWCA at Port Harcourt, and built Nzimiro Memorial Girls' Secondary School in honor of husband (1966); organized Igbo women in support of Biafran soldiers during Nigerian civil war (1967–70). ❖ See also *Women in World History.*

NZINGA (c. 1580s–1663). *See Njinga.*

O

O., Anna (1859–1936). *See Pappenheim, Bertha.*

OAKAR, Mary Rose (1940—). American politician. Born Mar 5, 1940, in Cleveland, Ohio; dau. of Joseph Oakar and Margaret Oakar; Ursuline College, Cleveland, BA, 1962; John Carroll University, Cleveland, MA (1966); graduate studies at Royal Academy of Dramatic Arts, London (1964), Westham Adult College in Warwickshire (1968), and Columbia University (1963). ❖ Eight-term Democratic US congressional representative from Ohio, taught English, drama and speech at a high school and community college (1963–75), both in Cleveland; was a member of Cleveland City Council (1973–76); served as Democratic State Central committeewoman (1973–75) and as alternate delegate to Democratic National Convention (1976); from Ohio's 20th Congressional District, elected to 95th US Congress (1976) and 7 succeeding Congresses (Jan 3, 1977–Jan 3, 1993); worked her way up to position of vice chair of Democratic Caucus in 99th and 100th Congresses; also chaired the Subcommittee on Personnel and Police and Subcommittee on Economic Stabilization of the Committee on Banking, Finance and Urban Affairs, and worked on the Committee on Post Office and Civil Service and Select Committee on Aging; was unsuccessful in her reelection bid to the 103rd Congress (1992).

OAKES, Heather (1959—). *See Hunte, Heather.*

OAKLEY, Ann (1944—). English sociologist, writer and feminist. Born Ann Titmuss, 1944, in England; dau. of Richard Titmuss (professor of social administration at London School of Economics, among founders of modern British welfare state) and Kathleen Miller (social worker); Somerville College, Oxford, BA, MA and PhD; m. Robin Oakley, 1964 (div.). ❖ Known as "mother of contemporary feminists," helped define modern feminism with such influential texts as *Subject Women* (1981); wrote many books of feminist theory and scholarship, including *Sex, Gender and Society* (1972), *The Sociology of Housework* (1974), *Scenes Originating in the Garden of Eden* (1993), *Essays on Women, Medicine and Health* (1994) and *Gender on Planet Earth* (2002); collaborated with Juliet Mitchell on *The Rights and Wrongs of Women* (1976) and *What Is Feminism?* (1986); became professor of sociology and head of Thomas Coram Research Unit at Institute of Education, University of London (1991); wrote several feminist-themed novels as well, including *Men's Room* (1988), which was serialized by BBC; also wrote *Man and Wife: Richard and Kay Titmuss* (1996), *Welfare and Wellbeing: Richard Titmuss' Contribution to Social Policy* (2002) and *Private Complaints and Public Health: Richard Titmuss on the National Health Service* (2004); served on editorial board of journal *Women and Health*. ❖ See also memoir, *Taking It Like a Woman* (Random House, 1984).

OAKLEY, Annie (1860–1926). American sharpshooter and equestrian. Name variations: Annie Oakley (stage name from 1882); Annie Butler in private life after marriage. Born Phoebe Anne Mosey (sometimes given in records as Moses and Mozee), Aug 13, 1860, near Woodland (now Willowdell), Darke Co., Ohio; died in Greenville, Ohio, Nov 3, 1926; dau. of Jacob Mosey and Susan Mosey (both farmers); mainly self-taught; m. Frank Butler (professional marksman), June 20, 1876 or 1882 (died Nov 21, 1926); children: 2 stepdaughters. ❖ A crack shot and skilled rider, was one of the most celebrated entertainers in America in late 19th and early 20th centuries and did more than anyone else to create the popular image of the self-reliant American frontierswoman; from humble beginnings, learned how to shoot ducks in the head so that pieces of shot would not be embedded in the meat; entered a Cincinnati shooting contest against Frank Butler, a well-known marksman, and defeated him, then married him; became a celebrity in traveling variety shows and circuses; joined Buffalo Bill Wild West Exposition, run by "Buffalo Bill" Cody (1885); became its star attraction during a Paris exhibition; though she had never been farther west than Kansas, came to epitomize in appearance and manner the women of the West, or at least the popular idea of such women; was reintroduced to later generations of young Americans in 1946 in the musical *Annie Get Your Gun,* starring Ethel Merman on Broadway and Betty Hutton on film, and in the ABC-TV series starring Gail Davis, which ran for 4 seasons (1953–56). ❖ See also Shirl Kasper, *Annie Oakley* (U. of Oklahoma Press, 1992); Glenda Riley, *The Life and Legacy of Annie Oakley* (U. of Oklahoma Press, 1994); and *Women in World History.*

OAKLEY, Laura (1880–1957). American silent-film actress. Born July 10, 1879, in Oakland, CA; died Jan 30, 1957, in Altadena, CA. ❖ Comedic actress with Universal, appeared in Nestor, then Powers comedies; films include *Lord John in New York, The Dumb Girl of Portici* and *Two-Gun Betty.*

OAKLEY, Violet (1874–1961). American artist. Born in Bergen Heights, New Jersey (some sources cite New York City), 1874; died 1961; dau. of Arthur Edmund Oakley and Cornelia (Swain) Oakley; studied at Art Students League in New York; studied with E. Amanlean and Raphael Colin at Académie Montparnasse in Paris; attended Pennsylvania Academy; studied with Howard Pyle at Drexel Institute; never married. ❖ Specialist in murals, mosaics, stained glass, and portraits, is known particularly for her murals at the Pennsylvania state capitol in Harrisburg; at Drexel, met and befriended Jessie Wilcox Smith and Elizabeth Shippen Green, forming a triumvirate of sorts, taking a studio together in Philadelphia; received her most extensive commission—to produce 18 murals for the governor's room at the new Pennsylvania state capitol which was to be built in Harrisburg (1902), the 1st woman to receive such a large mural assignment; when Edward Austin Abbey died, also completed all the murals for the capitol (1911–27). Awarded gold medal of honor from Pennsylvania Academy (1906). ❖ See also memoir *The Holy Experiment* (1922); Alice A. Carter, *The Red Rose Girls: An Uncommon Story of Art and Love* (2000); and *Women in World History.*

OANCIA, Ecaterina (1954—). Romanian rower. Born Mar 25, 1954, in Romania. ❖ At Los Angeles Olympics, won a gold medal in quadruple sculls with coxswain (1984); at Seoul Olympics, won a bronze medal in coxed fours and a silver medal in coxed eights (1988).

OATES, Joyce Carol (1938—). American novelist, essayist, poet and short-story writer. Name variations: (pseudonym) Rosamond Smith. Born June 16, 1938, in Millersport, NY; dau. of Frederic Oates and Caroline Oates; Syracuse University, BA, 1960; University of Wisconsin, MA, 1961; m. Raymond Smith, 1961. ❖ Preeminent fiction writer, began teaching at University of Detroit (1961–67); was a professor of English at University of Windsor, Ontario (1968–78); was writer-in-residence at Princeton University (1978); published 1st novel, *With Shuddering Fall* (1964); with husband, founded press and literary magazine *The Ontario Quarterly*; fiction includes *A Garden of Earthly Delights* (1967), *Expensive People* (1968), *Wonderland* (1971), *Marriages and Infidelities* (1972), *The Seduction and Other Stories* (1975), *Childwold* (1976), *Unholy Loves* (1979), *Bellefleur* (1980), *A Bloodsmoor Romance* (1982), *Marya: A Life* (1986), *On Boxing* (1987), *Lives of the Twins* (1987), *You Must Remember This* (1989), *Nemesis* (1990), *Blackwater* (1992), *Haunted: Tales of the Grotesque* (1994), *First Love* (1996), *Blonde* (2000), *Take Me, Take Me With You* (2004), and *I Am No One You Know: Stories* (2004); nonfiction includes *New Heaven, New Earth: The Visionary Experience in Literature* (1974), *The Profane Art: Essays and Reviews* (1983), and *The Faith of a Writer: Life, Craft, Art* (2003); writes suspense novels under pseudonym Rosamond Smith. Received National Book Award for *them* (1970).

OATMAN, Olive Ann (c. 1838–1903). American Indian captive. Born c. 1838, in Whiteside Co., IL; died Mar 20, 1903, in Sherman, TX; dau. of Royse Oatman and Mary Ann (Sperry) Oatman; m. John B. Fairchild, Nov 1865; children: 1 adopted daughter. ❖ While on wagon train with family, attacked and captured by Yavapai or Mohave Apache Indians in New Mexico Territory (Mar 18, 1851); along with sister Mary Ann (died c. 1853), forced to work by Yavapai Indians and year later sold to

Mohaves; through efforts of sole surviving brother Lorenzo, was returned to Fort Yuma by Yuma Indians (1856); had story told by Rev. Royal B. Stratton in *Life Among the Indians; Being an Interesting Narrative of the Captivity of the Oatman Girls* (1857); lectured with Stratton on captivity and Indian life (from 1859).

OBA, Minako (1930—). Japanese novelist, poet, playwright and essayist. Born 1930 in Tokyo, Japan; father was a physician; mother was a teacher; majored in English literature; married an engineer. ❖ During WWII, was sent to Hiroshima immediately after the bombing as a member of a rescue party; lived with husband in Alaska for 11 years (1959–70); published 1st book, *The Three Crabs* (1968), which received the Akutagawa Prize; other works, which explore gender stereotypes and relationships between men and women, include *Funakuimushi* (1969), *Sabita kotoba* (1971), *Urashimaso* (1977, also pub. in English and related to her experience in Hiroshima), *Stereotype* (1980), *A Theory on Man from the Standpoint of a Woman. Tsuda Umeko* (1990), and *Once There Was a Woman* (1994). ❖ See also Michiko N. Wilson, *Gender is Fair Game: Rethinking the Female in the Works of Oba Minako* (Sharpe, 1999).

OBERG, Margo (1953—). American surfer. Name variations: Margo Godfrey. Born Margo Godfrey, 1953, in La Jolla, CA; m. Steve Oberg. ❖ At age 13, ranked 4th in the World among women surfers (1966); at 15, won the Western Surfing Association amateur title and World championship (1968); moved to Kauai and became a pioneer of women's big-wave riding at Hawaii's Sunset Beach; turned pro (1975); won the Hang Ten championships at Malibu; officially crowned women's World champion (1976, 1977), then won her 4th and 5th world titles (1980–81); career spanned more than 30 years. ❖ See also film "Greats of Women's Surfing."

OBERHEUSER, Herta (1911–1978). German physician and criminal. Name variations: Hertha Oberheuser. Born in Cologne, May 15, 1911; died Jan 24, 1978, in Linz; University of Bonn, MD, 1937. ❖ Physician whose complicity in the medical experiments at the Ravensbrück concentration camp for women led to her sentence of 20 years' imprisonment at the Nuremberg Medical Trial of 1946–1947. ❖ See also *Women in World History*.

OBERHOFFNER, Ute. East German luge athlete. Born Ute Weiss in East Germany. ❖ Won a bronze medal at Sarajevo Olympics (1984) and a silver medal at Calgary Olympics (1988), both for singles; at World championships, won bronze medals (1983, 1987, 1989); was European champion (1988).

OBERON, Merle (1911–1979). Indian-born actress. Name variations: Queenie Thompson; acted briefly as Estelle Thompson. Born Estelle Merle O'Brien Thompson, Feb 19, 1911, in Bombay, India; died Nov 23, 1979, in Los Angeles, California; dau. of Arthur Terrence O'Brien Thompson (mechanical engineer for British railways) and Charlotte Constance (Selby) Thompson (nurse's assistant); attended La Martinière school in Calcutta; m. Alexander Korda (director), 1939 (div. 1945); m. Lucien Ballard (cinematographer), 1945 (div. 1949); m. Bruno Pagliai (Italian industrialist), 1957 (div. 1973); m. Robert Wolders (actor), 1975; children: Francesca Pagliai and Bruno Pagliai Jr. (both adopted, 1959). ❖ Popular actress (1930s–40s), best remembered for her portrayal of Cathy in *Wuthering Heights* (1939), moved to London at 17, where she initially worked as a dance-hall girl under name Queenie Thompson; offered 5-year contract by Alexander Korda, was cast in small role of Anne Boleyn in *The Private Life of Henry VIII* (1933), the 1st British talkie to attract an international audience; went on to play leads with Korda's company, including a Japanese woman in *The Battle* (1934) and Lady Blakeney in *The Scarlet Pimpernel* (1935); following an inauspicious debut in *Folies Bergère* (1935), gained credibility in Hollywood in *The Dark Angel* (1935), for which she was nominated for an Academy Award; came to international prominence in *Wuthering Heights* but career began to decline with 2 successive comedies, *That Uncertain Feeling* (1941) and *Affectionately Yours* (1941); by mid-1950s, was playing supporting roles, notably in *Desiree* (1954) and *Deep in My Heart* (1954); other films include *These Three* (1936), *Beloved Enemy* (1936), *Over the Moon* (1937), *'Til We Meet Again* (1940), *Lydia* (1941), *The Lodger* (1944), *Dark Waters* (1944), *A Song to Remember* (1945), *This Love of Ours* (1945), *Berlin Express* (1948), *The Oscar* (1966) and *Hotel* (1967). ❖ See also Charles Higham and Roy Moseley, *Princess Merle: The Romantic Life of Merle Oberon* (Coward, 1983); and *Women in World History*.

OBLATE SISTERS OF PROVIDENCE. *See Lange, Elizabeth Clovis.*

OBRENOVIC, Maria (fl. 1850s). *See Catargi, Marie.*

O'BRIEN, Catherine (1881–1963). Irish artist. Name variations: Kitty O'Brien. Born in Ennis, Co. Clare, Ireland, 1881; died 1963; studied at Metropolitan School of Art, Dublin, and the Tower of Glass. ❖ Joined the Tower of Glass (An Túr Gloine), a Dublin workshop dedicated to creating fine stained glass, a few years after Sarah Purser founded it in 1903; continued running the workshop after Purser's death (1943); her windows can be seen throughout Ireland, including St. Brendan's Cathedral at Loughrea, Killoughter Church at Ballyhaise, St. Nicholas' Church at Carrickfergus, Downpatrick Church at Co. Down, and St. John the Baptist's Church at Clontarf.

O'BRIEN, Edna (1930—). Irish writer. Born Edna O'Brien in Tuamgraney, Co. Clare, Ireland, Dec 15, 1930; dau. of Michael O'Brien and Lena Cleary O'Brien; attended Convent of Mercy, Loughrea, Galway, and Pharmaceutical College of Ireland; m. Ernest Gebler (novelist), 1951 (div. 1964); children: Carlos and Sasha. ❖ Published 1st novel, *The Country Girls* (1960) and its two sequels *The Lonely Girl* (1962) and *Girls in Their Married Bliss* (1964), giving voice to Irish female sexuality in her exploration of the emotional and erotic experiences of Caithleen Brady and her friend Baba (the books were banned in Ireland); wrote 5 plays for tv, as well as screenplays of some of her novels and short stories; also contributed to Kenneth Tynan's erotic revue *Oh! Calcutta!*; other books include *Mother Ireland* (1976), *The House of Splendid Isolation* (1994) and *Down by the River* (1996). Won Kingsley Amis Award (1962) and Yorkshire Post Award (1971). ❖ See also Grace Eckley, *Edna O'Brien* (Bucknell U. Press, 1974); and *Women in World History*.

O'BRIEN, Florence Roma Muir (1891–1930). *See Wilson, Romer.*

O'BRIEN, Kate (1897–1974). Irish writer. Born Catherine O'Brien in Limerick, Ireland, Dec 3, 1897; died in Canterbury, England, Aug 13, 1974; dau. of Thomas O'Brien (horse dealer) and Catherine (Thornhill) O'Brien; University College, Dublin, BA in modern literature, 1919; m. Gustaaf Renier (Dutch journalist), May 17, 1923 (div. 1925). ❖ Writer whose 5 of 9 novels deal with the period from the Famine to WWII, from the arrival of her grandparents in Limerick, escaping an impoverished countryside, to the time when her own links with the city were diminishing: *Without My Cloak* (1931), *The Ante-Room* (1934), *Pray for the Wanderer* (1938), *The Land of Spices* (1941) and *The Last of Summer* (1943); wrote 2 books which were banned under Irish censorship legislation: *Mary Lavelle* (1936) and *The Land of Spices* (1941), the latter because of a single sentence referring to homosexuality; was also banned from Spain for 20 years, because her Republican sympathies were evident in *Farewell Spain* (1937); published most financially successful book, *That Lady* (1946), a novel based on the life of the 16th-century princess of Eboli, Ana de Mendoza; published biography of St. Teresa of Avila (1951); dismissed as a romantic novelist, in part because she wrote about a feminine, provincial world, has been reprinted by Arlen House and by Virago, the London women's press. Won Hawthornden Prize (1932). ❖ See also John Logan, ed. *With Warmest Love: Lectures for Kate O'Brien 1984–93* (Mellick, 1994); Lorna Reynolds, *Kate O'Brien: A Literary Portrait* (Colin Smythe, 1987); and *Women in World History*.

O'BRIEN, Kitty (1881–1963). *See O'Brien, Catherine.*

O'BRIEN, Leah (1974—). *See Amico, Leah.*

O'BRIEN, Maire (b. 1922). *See Mhac An tSaoi, Máire.*

O'BRIEN, Margaret (1937—). American actress. Born Angela Maxine O'Brien, Jan 15, 1937, in San Diego, California; dau. of Gladys Flores (dancer); m. Harold Robert Allen Jr. (commercial artist), 1959 (div. 1968); m. Roy Thorsen, 1974 (sep.); children: 1 daughter. ❖ One of the most talented child stars to appear in film, began modeling at 3 and made movie debut at 4 in *Babes on Broadway* (1941); other films include *Journey for Margaret* (1942), *Thousands Cheer* (1943), *Madame Curie* (1943), *Jane Eyre* (1944), *The Canterville Ghost* (1944), as Tootie in *Meet Me in St. Louis* (1944), *Our Vines Have Tender Grapes* (1945), *Little Women* (1949), *The Secret Garden* (1949), *Glory* (1956), and *Heller in Pink Tights* (1960); as a child, became a charming radio personality, guesting on popular variety shows, and trading barbs with such seasoned comedians as Edgar Bergen and Bob Hope; suspended from MGM when she refused to appear in *Alice in Wonderland* (1951); resurfaced at Columbia in an unsuccessful debut as an adolescent in *Her First Romance* (1951); went on to appear in a few foreign films, in stock, and on tv, where a reprise of her role as Beth in a musical version of "Little

Women" and a role in a "Studio One" production were notable; was an active fund raiser for AIDS charities (1990s). Won special Academy Award as Outstanding Child Actress (1944). ❖ See also Allan R. Ellenberger, *Margaret O'Brien: A Career Chronicle and Biography* (2000); and *Women in World History.*

O'BRIEN, Miriam (1898–1976). American mountaineer. Name variations: Miriam Underhill. Born in Forest Glen, Maryland, 1898; died in Lancaster, New Hampshire, Jan 7, 1976; dau. of a Boston newspaperman; m. Robert Underhill, 1932; children: 2 sons. ❖ Once considered the greatest woman climber in America, traversed the Wellenkuppe and Obergabelhorn (1924); climbed the Dolomites and Aiguilles of Chamonix (1926); climbed the Via Miriam (named after her) on the Torre Grande in the Dolomites with her friend Margaret Helburn (1927); made 1st complete ascent of Les Aiguilles du Diable and was 1st female lead of the Grépon (1928); made 1st all-women's ascent of the Mer de Glace face of the Grépon (1929); made 1st all-women's ascent of the Matterhorn with Alice Damesme (1932). ❖ See also autobiography *Give Me the Hills* (Methuen, 1956); and *Women in World History.*

O'BRIEN, Nora Connolly (1893–1981). *See Connolly-O'Brien, Nora.*

O'BRIEN, Tanya (c. 1973—). *See Garcia-O'Brien, Tanya.*

O'BRIEN, Virginia (1896–1987). American stage actress and singer. Born Dec 14, 1896, in Trenton, NJ; died May 2, 1987, in Weymouth, MA; m. Donald Brian (actor). ❖ Made Broadway debut in *Her Regiment* (1917), followed by *The Chocolate Soldier, The Merry Widow, Buddies, The Girl behind the Gun, Jack and Jill, The Rise of Rosie O'Reilly, Princess Ida* and *Sabrina Fair,* among others; appeared in vaudeville with husband Donald Brian and on tv series "I Remember Mama" (1949–57).

O'BRIEN, Virginia (1919–2001). American comedic actress. Born Virginia Lee O'Brien, April 8, 1919, in Los Angeles, CA; died Jan 16, 2001, in Woodland Hills, CA; sister of Mary O'Brien (actress); niece of film director Lloyd Bacon; m. Kirk Alyn (actor), 1942 (div. 1955); m. Harry B. White. ❖ Deadpan comedic singer whose films include *Hullabaloo, Lady Be Good, Panama Hattie, Du Barry Was a Lady, Thousands Cheer, The Harvey Girls, Ziegfeld Follies* and *Till the Clouds Roll By.*

O'BRIEN-MOORE, Erin (1902–1979). American stage, tv, and screen actress. Name variations: Erin O'Brien Moore. Born May 2, 1902, in Los Angeles, CA; died May 3, 1979, in Los Angeles; m. Mark Barron (critic, div.). ❖ Made NY debut in *Makropoulis Secret* (1926), followed by *My Country, Street Scene, Yoshe Kalb* and *Tortilla Flat;* absent from stage for 2 years after suffering burns in a restaurant fire (1939–40); toured overseas in combat zones during WWII; films include *Dangerous Corner, Little Men, Seven Keys to Baldpate, Ring Around the Moon, The Plough and the Stars, Black Legion, Life of Emile Zola, Long Gray Line, Peyton Place* and *How to Succeed in Business.*

OBSCHERNITZKI, Helga (1934–1989). *See Haase, Helga.*

OBUCINA, Svetlana (1961—). *See Anastasovski, Svetlana.*

O'CALLAGHAN, Kathleen (1888–1961). Irish politician and professor. Born Kathleen Murphy, 1888, in Lissarda, Co. Cork, Ireland; died 1961; sister of Mairéad O'Donovan and Eilis Murphy (both professors); m. Michael O'Callaghan (former mayor of Limerick, killed by British forces, 1921). ❖ Republican and lifelong friend of Mary MacSwiney, was a member of the 2nd Dáil for Limerick (1921–22) and, as anti-Treaty Cumann na Poblachta candidate, refused to take seat in 3rd Dáil (1922–23); was a professor at Mary Immaculate Teacher Training College, Limerick.

OCAMPO, Roseli (1937—). *See Ocampo-Friedmann, Roseli.*

OCAMPO, Silvina (1903–1993). Argentinean poet and short-story writer. Born 1903 (some sources cite 1906) in Buenos Aires, Argentina; died in Buenos Aires, 1993; dau. of Manuel Ocampo (architectural engineer) and Ramona Máxima Aguirre; sister of writer Victoria Ocampo (1890–1979); studied painting in Paris; m. Adolfo Bioy Casares (writer), in 1934 or 1940; children: daughter Marta. ❖ Published 1st book of prose, *Viaje olvidado* (Forgotten Journey, 1937), then 1st book of poetry, *Enumeración de la patria y otros poemas* (Enumeration of the Mother Country and Other Poems, 1942); won the National Poetry Award with *Lo amargo por dulce* (Bitterness Through Sweetness, 1962); published short stories in several collections, including *La furia y otros cuentos* (The Storm and Other Stories, 1959) and *El pecado mortal* (The Mortal Sin, 1966); also wrote a number of books for children;

probably best known to English-language readers for her collaboration with Bioy Casares and Borges as an editor of *The Book of Fantasy* (1988). ❖ See also Patricia Nisbet Klingenberg, *Fantasies of the Feminine: The Short Stories of Silvina Ocampo* (Bucknell U. Press, 1999); and *Women in World History.*

OCAMPO, Victoria (1890–1979). Argentinean essayist, editor, publisher, and patron of the arts. Pronunciation: Vik-TOH-reah O-CAM-po. Born Ramona Victoria Epifanía Rufina Ocampo, April 7, 1890, in Buenos Aires, Argentina; died Jan 27, 1979, at Villa Ocampo, San Isidro, Argentina; dau. of Manuel Ocampo (architectural engineer) and Ramona Máxima Aguirre; sister of writer Silvina Ocampo (1903–1993); taught by private tutors at home; took classes at the Sorbonne with French philosopher Henri Bergson; m. Luis Bernardo de ("Monaco") Estrada; no children. ❖ Well-known and respected essayist and publisher, who also advanced the cause of women's rights in Argentina, pursued self-definition and mildly rebelled (1900s–29); cultivated great literary figures such as Ortega y Gasset and Tagore; established literary magazine *Sur* (1931) and Editorial SUR, a publishing house (1933); helped found the Union of Argentine Women (1936); arrested by the Perón regime and released after nearly a month of captivity, following an international furor (1953); was the 1st woman named to Argentine Academy of Letters (1977); writings include *Testimonios* (Testimony, 10 vols., 1935–77), *Autobiografía* (Autobiography, 4 vols., 1979–82), *De Francesca a Beatriz* (From Francesca to Beatrice, 1924), and *338171 T.E.* (biography of T.E. Lawrence, 1942, 1963); was affectionately known as *Señora Cultura* ("Mother Culture"), the 1st lady of Argentine culture and letters. Won Maria Moors-Cabot prize and was made a Commander of the British Empire (CBE, 1965). ❖ See also Doris Meyer, *Victoria Ocampo: Against the Wind and the Tide* (U. of Texas Press, 1990); and *Women in World History.*

OCAMPO-FRIEDMANN, Roseli (1937—). American botanist. Name variations: Roseli Ocampo-Friedmann; Roseli Ocampo; Roseli Friedmann. Born Roseli Ocampo, Nov 23, 1937, in Manila, Philippines; University of the Philippines, BS in botany, 1958; Hebrew University in Jerusalem, MA, 1966; Florida State University in Tallahassee, PhD, 1973; m. Imre Friedmann (research partner), 1974. ❖ Studied and grew microscopic algae and cyanobacteria (blue-green algae discovered by future husband) at Hebrew University in Jerusalem; after brief stay at National Institute of Science and Technology in Manila, returned with husband to work at Florida State University in Tallahassee (1968); traveled world with him in search of algae and microorganisms; successfully grew samples of microorganisms found inside rocks in Antarctica (mid-1970s); studied bacteria from Siberia's permanently frozen ground; became full professor of biology and microbiology at Florida A&M University (1987), and researcher with husband at Florida State; attracted media interest since scientists think microorganisms inside frozen rocks might be similar to microorganisms that could have lived on Mars (1996); researched extremeophiles as a Mars Specialist in the Search for Extraterrestrial Intelligence's (SETI) Carl Sagan Center for the Study of Life in the Universe; received National Science Foundation US Congressional Antarctic Service Medal (1981).

O'CARROLL, Maureen (1913–1984). Irish politician. Born Maureen McHugh, Mar 29, 1913, in Galway, Ireland; died May 9, 1984; dau. of Micheál McHugh (Republican prisoner in UK); m. Gerard O'Carroll (cabinetmaker); children: 5 daughters, 5 sons. ❖ Began career as a secondary schoolteacher; elected to 15th Dáil for Dublin North Central (1954–57), the 1st female Labour deputy and 1st woman Labour Party chief whip (1954); defeated for reelection (1957); was a founding member and secretary of the Lower Prices Council (1947–54); helped form Ban Gardai and campaigned to have the word "bastard" omitted from birth certificates for children born to unmarried parents.

O'CASEY, Eileen (1900–1995). Irish actress and author. Name variations: Eileen Reynolds Carey. Born Eileen Carey, 1900, in Dublin, Ireland; died at a London home for retired actors, April 1995; dau. of Edward Reynolds and Kathleen Carey; attended Ursuline Convent in Brentford, Essex; m. Sean O'Casey (Irish playwright), Sept 23, 1927 (died 1964); children: sons Breon (artist) and Niall (died 1956); daughter Shivaun (actress). ❖ Joined D'Oyly Carte Opera and toured England and US; met husband (1926) when she was auditioning for his controversial play, *The Plough and the Stars;* published 3 books about their life together: *Sean, Cheerio, Titan,* and *Eileen.* ❖ See also *Women in World History.*

OCCIDENTE, Maria del (c. 1794–1845). *See Brooks, Maria Gowen.*

OCCOMY, Marita Bonner (1899–1971). *See Bonner, Marita.*

OCHICHI, Isabella (1979—). Kenyan runner. Born Oct 28, 1979, in Kisii, Kenya. ❖ At World Cross Country championships, placed 1st for team short distance (2003); at Golden League, placed 1st for 3,000 meters at Saint-Denis (2004); won 2 Grand Prix events for 5,000 meters (2004) and 1 event (2003); won a silver medal for 5,000 meters at Athens Olympics (2004).

OCHOA, Blanca Fernández (1963—). *See Fernández Ochoa, Blanca.*

OCHOA, Elisa. Filipino politician. Born in the Philippines. ❖ Representing the province of Agusan, was elected to Lower House of Congress (1941), the country's 1st congresswoman.

OCHOA, Ellen (1958—). American astronaut. Pronunciation: O-cho-AH. Born Ellen Lauri Ochoa, May 10, 1958, at Los Angeles, California; dau. of Joseph L. Ochoa and Rosanne Ochoa; San Diego State University, BS, 1980, Stanford University, MS, 1980, PhD, 1985; m. Coe Fulmer Miles. ❖ The 1st female Hispanic astronaut, was an optical researcher (1985–90); was selected by NASA (1990); flew mission (1993), retrieving a solar observation satellite and studying the Earth's atmosphere; served as payload commmander on 2nd flight (1994); logged more than 484 hours in space. Won Hispanic Engineering National Achievement Award (1989). ❖ See also *Women in World History.*

OCHOWICZ, Sheila (1950—). *See Young, Sheila.*

OCHS, Debra (1966—). American archer. Born Jan 30, 1966, in Texas; attended Arizona State University. ❖ At Seoul Olympics, won a bronze medal in team round (1988).

OCHS, Iphigene (1892–1990). *See Sulzberger, I.O.*

OCLLO-MAMA. *See Mama-Ocllo.*

OCLOO, Esther (1919–2002). Ghanaian entrepreneur and social reformer. Born Esther Afua Nkulenu, April 18, 1919, in the Volta region of Ghana; died Feb 8, 2002, in Accra, Ghana; dau. of poor farmers; attended school in Accra; m. Stephen Ocloo; children: Vincentia Canacco, Vincent Malm, Christian Biassey and Stephen Jr. ❖ Began career selling marmalade jam; built her business into Nkulenu Industries, producing such products as canned tomatoes and soup bases; went to Britain to study food technology; intent on improving women's economic situation, trained women in agriculture and handicrafts, taught business management skills, and pioneered in microloans to help women become entrepreneurs; was the 1st chairwoman of Women's World Banking.

O'CONNELL, Sister Anthony (1814–1897). *See O'Connell, Mary.*

O'CONNELL, Eileen (c. 1743–c. 1800). Irish poet. Name variations: Eibhlin Dubh Ni Chonaill; Eileen O'Leary. Born c. 1743 in Derrynane, Co. Kerry, Munster, Ireland; died c. 1800; dau. of Maire Ni Dhonnchadha and Domhnall Mor O'Connell; m. O'Connor of Firies, Co. Kerry, 1758; m. Caoineadh Airt Ui Laoghaire (Art O'Leary), 1767 (died 1773); children: 3. ❖ Wrote lament for murdered 2nd husband *Caoineadh Airt Ui Laoghaire* (1773), printed in Mrs. Morgan John O'Connell's *The Last Colonel of the Irish Brigade: Count O'Connell and the Old Ireland at Home and Abroad* (1892), which is considered by many to be the finest lament in the English language.

O'CONNELL, Helen (1920–1993). American big-band singer. Name variations: Helen DeVol. Born in Lima, Ohio, May 23, 1920; died of cancer, Sept 9, 1993, in San Juan Capistrano, CA; m. Clifford Smith Jr. (Navy aviator and heir to Boston investment fortune), 1941 (div. 1951); m. Thomas T. Chamales (author), 1957 (died 1960); m. Bob Paris (musician), 1964 (annulled 1965); m. Frank DeVol (composer and conductor), 1991. ❖ Noted as the sunniest of the big-band singers, made a name for herself with the Jimmy Dorsey band in early 1940s, teaming with Bob Eberly on such hits as "Green Eyes" and "Tangerine," often following his romantic interpretation of the song with an upbeat, bouncy 2nd chorus; other songs include "Amapola," "Six Lessons from Madame La Zonga" and "The Jumpin' Jive"; also appeared in 2 movies: *The Fleet's In* (1942) and *I Dood It* (1943); after a career timeout, joined Dave Garroway on the early morning "Today Show" (1957), where she covered the weather and features; also appeared on the twice-weekly, 15-minute "The Helen O'Connell Show" for NBC; reignited career a 3rd time (1980s), touring in *4 Girls 4*, with singers Rosemary Clooney, Margaret Whiting, Rose Marie, and sometimes Kay Starr. ❖ See also *Women in World History.*

O'CONNELL, Mary (1814–1897). Irish-born American nun, nurse, and administrator. Name variations: Sister Anthony; Sister Anthony O'Connell. Born in Co. Limerick, Ireland, Aug 15, 1814; died in Cincinnati, Ohio, Dec 8, 1897; dau. of William O'Connell and Catherine (Murphy) O'Connell; educated at Ursuline Academy in Charlestown, Massachusetts. ❖ A key figure in the establishment and operation of hospitals and orphanages in and around Cincinnati, became a member of the community of American Sisters of Charity in Emmitsburg, MD (1835); took final vows (1837), becoming Sister Anthony, and was sent to work at St. Peter's Orphanage in Cincinnati; with 6 associates, asked to be severed from the order, and obtained permission to establish the Sisters of Charity of Cincinnati (1852); was elected procuratrix (financial officer), a position she would hold for a number of years; was also named superior of St. John's Hotel for Invalids (later St. John's Hospital), which the order founded shortly thereafter; led effort to acquire a new orphanage, St. Joseph's, in Cumminsville (1854) and was appointed its superior; during Civil War, gained renown as a field nurse, which included searching for wounded, assisting in surgery, and caring for patients in the floating hospitals; opened and supervised Good Samaritan Hospital (1866) and St. Joseph's Foundling and Maternity Hospital (1873). ❖ See also *Women in World History.*

O'CONNELL, Patricia (d. 1975). American actress and singer. Born in Alabama; died Dec 24, 1975, age 73, in New Haven, CT; m. Angus Shaw McCabe (journalist). ❖ Appeared in the original companies of *The Student Prince, The Desert Song, The Great Waltz,* and *Rosalie;* also sang with the Chicago Opera and New York Opera Comique.

O'CONNELL, Sarah (c. 1822–1870). New Zealand landholder. Name variations: Sarah Russell. Born Sarah Russell, c. 1822 (baptized, Aug 21, 1822), in Cork, Ireland; died 1870 in Canterbury, New Zealand; dau. of William Russell (army officer) and Mary (Tarrant) Russell; m. Edward Maurice O'Connell (army officer), 1844 (died 1853); children: 5. ❖ Immigrated with family to Australia (1838); arrived in New Zealand (c. 1848); husband purchased 20,000-acre run in Canterbury, which she managed after his death; ran successful dairy and raised prized sheep. ❖ See also *Dictionary of New Zealand Biography* (Vol. 1).

O'CONNOR, Colleen. American ice dancer. Born in US. ❖ With partner James Millns, won a bronze medal at Innsbruck Olympics (1976). Inducted into World Figure Skating Hall of Fame (1993).

O'CONNOR, Ellen (1857–1933). Irish politician and countess of Desart. Name variations: Countess of Desart; countess dowager; Ellen Desart. Born Ellen Odette Bischoffsheim, 1857, in London, England; died June 29, 1933; dau. of Henry Bischoffsheim (Jewish banker); m. Ulick (William) O'Connor, 4th earl of Desart, 1881 (died 1898). ❖ Held strong anti-suffragist views; protested the National Health Insurance bill (1911); became involved in the movement to revive Irish industries, establishing Kilkenny Woollen Mills and building 30 villas for the workers; made a senator of the Irish Free State (1922); was pro-divorce in Seanad divorce debate (1925); served on Seanad until death (1933).

O'CONNOR, Flannery (1925–1964). American writer. Name variations: Mary Flannery O'Connor. Born Mary Flannery O'Connor, Mar 25, 1925, in Savannah, Georgia; died of complications of disseminated lupus, Aug 3, 1964, in Milledgeville, Georgia; dau. of Edward Francis O'Connor and Regina (Cline) O'Connor; Georgia State College for Women, AB, 1945; State University of Iowa, MFA, 1947; never married; no children. ❖ Major 20th-century writer, whose work is celebrated for its unflinching, grotesquely comic, moral vision, lived in Savannah from birth until 1938, when family moved to Milledgeville; father died of lupus (1941); published 1st story, "The Geranium" (1946); was a resident at Yaddo writers' colony near Saratoga Springs, NY (1948–49); lived briefly in New York City before going to live with Robert and Sally Fitzgerald in Connecticut (1949); after 1st attack of lupus (1950), moved with mother to Andalusia, a farm near Milledgeville, where she spent the rest of her life under treatment to control her disease; published 1st novel, *Wise Blood* (1952); published 1st collection of short stories, *A Good Man Is Hard to Find* (1955); won 1st prize in O. Henry awards for short stories for "Greenleaf" (1957); traveled to Lourdes and Rome with mother (1958); published 2nd novel, *The Violent Bear It Away* (1960); lupus reactivated in severe form after hospitalization for abdominal surgery (Feb 1964); published posthumously, *Everything That Rises Must Converge* (short stories, 1965). *The Complete Stories of Flannery O'Connor* won National Book Award (1971). ❖ See also (letters) *The Habit of Being* (Farrar, 1979); Preston M. Browning Jr., *Flannery*

O'Connor (Southern Illinois U. Press, 1974); Lorine M. Getz, *Flannery O'Connor: Her Life, Library and Book Reviews* (Edward Mellen, 1980); Dorothy Walters, *Flannery O'Connor* (Twayne, 1973); and *Women in World History.*

O'CONNOR, Julia (1890–1972). *See Parker, Julia O'Connor.*

O'CONNOR, Karen (1958—). American equestrian. Name variations: Karen Lende. Born Karen Lende, Feb 17, 1958, in Bolton, MA; m. David O'Connor (equestrian), 1993. ❖ On The Optimist, was the 1st American to win the Boekelo CCI in Holland (1984); won the Chesterland CCI on Casstlewellan (1985); won the Rolex Kentucky International on Mr. Maxwell (1991), Worth the Trust (1997), and Prince Panache (1999); won a team silver medal for eventing at Atlanta Olympics (1996), on Biko; won a team bronze medal for eventing at Sydney Olympics (2000), on Prince Panache. Named US Female Equestrian Athlete of the Year 8 times.

O'CONNOR, Kathleen (1935—). Irish politician. Born 1935 in Ireland; dau. of John O'Connor (TD, Clann na Poblachta). ❖ Began career as a primary schoolteacher; following father's death, elected to 15th Dáil for North Kerry representing Clann na Poblachta in a by-election (1956–57), having just turned 21 (was the youngest member of the Dáil and the 1st single woman).

O'CONNOR, Mary Anne (1953—). American basketball player. Born Oct 1, 1953; attended Southern Connecticut State University. ❖ At Montreal Olympics, won a silver medal in team competition (1976).

O'CONNOR, Sandra Day (1930—). American Supreme Court judge. Born Sandra Day, Mar 26, 1930, in El Paso, Texas; dau. of Harry A. Day (rancher) and Ada May (Wilkey) Day; graduated magna cum laude from Stanford University, 1950; Stanford Law School, LLB, 1952; m. John Jay O'Connor III (lawyer), Dec 20, 1952; children: Scott, Brian, and Jay. ❖ The 1st woman appointed to the US Supreme Court, was admitted to California bar (1952); served as deputy county attorney in San Mateo, California (1952–53); moved to Frankfurt, Germany (1953) and served as a civilian lawyer for the Quartermaster Corps; admitted to Arizona bar (1957); practiced law in Maryvale, Arizona (1958–60); served as Arizona's assistant attorney general (1965–69); served as a member of the Arizona state senate (1969–75); elected senate majority leader (1972); elected and served as Maricopa Co. judge (1975–79); served as Arizona Court of Appeals judge (1979–81); confirmed as the 102nd US Supreme Court justice (1981); along with two other moderately conservative justices (Anthony Kennedy and David Souter), exerted "effective control" over the direction of the Supreme Court, especially in cases concerning religion, affirmative action, and abortion; resigned from the Court (July 2005). ❖ See also memoirs, *Lazy B: Growing Up on a Cattle Ranch in the American Southwest* (2002) and *The Majesty of the Law: Reflections of a Supreme Court Justice* (2003); and *Women in World History.*

O'CONNOR, Sinéad (1966—). Irish pop singer. Name variations: Sinead O'Connor. Born Dec 8, 1966, in Dublin, Ireland; attended College of Music, Dublin; m. John Reynolds (drummer), 1988 (div. 1990); m. Nick Sommerlad, July 7, 2001; children: (with Reynolds) Jake (b. 1987); (with John Waters) Roison (b. 1996); (with Sommerlad) Shane (b. 2004). ❖ Known for her trademark shaved head and outspokenness, co-wrote In Tua Nua band's 1st single, "Take My Hand," at 15; worked with U2 guitarist, the Edge, on soundtrack for film, *The Captive* (1986); released successful album, *The Lion and the Cobra* (1987); appeared in film, *Hush-a-Bye Baby* (1989), and as Virgin Mary in *The Butcher Boy* (1997); released *I Do Not Want What I Haven't Got* (1990), which went to #1 and included hit single written by Prince, "Nothing Compares 2 U"; involved in number of controversies, including tearing up photograph of the pope on "Saturday Night Live" (1992); other albums include *Am I Not Your Girl?* (1992), *Gospel Oak* (1997) and *Faith and Courage* (2000).

O'CONNOR, Una (1880–1959). Irish-born stage and screen actress. Born Agnes Teresa McGlade, Oct 23, 1880, in Belfast, Ireland (now Northern Ireland); died Feb 4, 1959, in New York, NY. ❖ Began career with Abbey Theater, Dublin, in *The Shewing-up of Blanco Posnet* (1911), made NY stage debut in same part; made film debut in *Dark Red Roses* (1929); other films include *Cavalcade, David Copperfield, Of Human Bondage, The Invisible Man, Little Lord Fauntleroy, The Canterville Ghost, Bride of Frankenstein, How Green Was My Valley, The Bells of St. Mary's, Cluny Brown, Christmas in Connecticut* and *Witness for the Prosecution.*

OCTAVIA (c. 69–11 BCE). Roman noblewoman. Name variations: sometimes designated "Minor" or "the Younger." Born c. 69 BCE; died in 11 BCE, probably in or near Rome; dau. of G. Octavius (Roman senator and governor of Macedonia) and Atia the Elder (niece of Julius Caesar); sister of Octavius (later designated Octavian and finally Augustus [there is some scholarly difference as to whether the Octavia in question is actually Octavian's older half-sister, also named Octavia, whose mother was Ancharia]); m. Gaius Claudius Marcellus (Roman consul) sometime before 54 BCE (died 40 BCE); m. M. Antonius (Marc Antony), in 40 BCE (div. 32 BCE); children: (1st m.) Marcus Claudius Marcellus, Marcella the Elder, and Marcella the Younger; (2nd m.) Antonia Major (b. 39 BCE) and Antonia Minor (36 BCE–37 CE). ❖ Link and mediator between two great Roman antagonists—her brother Octavian (Augustus) and her husband Marc Antony—who helped to avert Roman civil war for nearly a decade; married Marc Antony to seal the "Treaty of Brundisium," capping an agreement for peace between him and Octavian (40 BCE); because of her warm, personal relationship with Octavian, exerted an indirect but vital influence on the empire in her own right; mediated between the two men (37 BCE), helping to negotiate the Treaty of Tarentum; received protections of Tribunician office and other legal privileges (35 BCE). ❖ See also *Women in World History.*

OCTAVIA (39–62 CE). Roman empress. Name variations: Olympia. Born c. 39 CE; executed in 62 CE; dau. of Claudius, emperor of Rome (r. 10 BCE–54 CE) and his 3rd wife Valeria Messalina (c. 23–48 CE); became 1st wife of Nero (37–68), emperor of Rome (r. 54–68), in 53 CE (div. 62 CE). ❖ At 11, married 16-year-old Nero who would desert her for Acte, then Poppaea Sabina; falsely accused of adultery, was sent to the island of Pandataria, where she was executed by order of Nero when she was 22; is the heroine of *Octavia,* the only extant Roman historical play, or *fabula praetexta.* ❖ See also *Women in World History.*

ODA (806–913). Countess of Saxony. Born 806; died May 913; dau. of Billung I and Aeda; m. Liudolf (c. 806–866), count of Saxony, c. 836; was great-grandparent of Otto I the Great (912–973), king of Germany (r. 936–973), Holy Roman emperor (r. 962–973); children: Duke Bruno (killed in 880); Otto (c. 836–912), duke of Saxony; Liutgard (d. 885); Hathumoda (d. 874); Gerberga (d. 896); Christine of Gandersheim (d. 919).

ODA (fl. 1000). Queen of Poland. Fourth wife of Boleslav Chrobry (967–1025), king of Poland (r. 992–1025).

ODA, Cheko. Japanese gymnast. Name variations: Cheko Tsukahara. Born in Nagasaki, Japan; attended Nippon College of Physical Education; m. Mitsuo Tsukahara (gymnast); children: Naoya Tsukahara (gymnast). ❖ Placed 4th team all-around at Mexico City Olympics (1968) and 4th team all-around at World championships (1970); won Japan nationals (1969).

ODAGA, Asenath (1938—). Kenyan novelist, playwright and children's writer. Name variations: Asenath Bole Odaga. Born 1938 in Kenya; earned degrees in history and children's literature at Nairobi University. ❖ Established publishing house in Kenya and served as chair of Children's Literature Association there; writing both in English and Luo, published such fiction as *Jande's Ambition* (1966), *The Villager's Son* (1971), *The Angry Flames* (1978), *Thu Tinda* (1980), *The Storm* (1985), and *A Bridge in Time* (1987); also wrote *Yesterday's Today: The Study of Oral Literature* (1984) and (with K. Akivaga) *Oral Literature: A School Certificate Course* (1982); edited *Why the Hyena has a Crooked Neck and Other Stories: Anthology of short stories by Kenyan Grassroots Women Writers and Storytellers* (1993).

ODAKA, Emiko (1962—). Japanese volleyball player. Born Dec 14, 1962, in Japan. ❖ At Los Angeles Olympics, won a bronze medal in team competition (1984).

ODALDI, Annalena (1572–1638). Italian playwright. Name variations: Suor (Sister) Annalena Odaldi. Born Lessandra Odaldi, 1572, in Pistoia, Italy; died 1638. ❖ Entered Franciscan convent of Santa Chiara and took her religious name; wrote satirical verse comedies for novices to perform, *Commedia di Nannuccio e quindici figliastre* (1600), *Commedia di mastro Paoluccio medico* (1604), and *Commedia di tre malandrini* (1604).

ODAM, Dorothy (b. 1920). *See Tyler, Dorothy J.*

ODA OF BAVARIA (fl. 890s). Holy Roman empress. Married Arnulf of Carinthia (b. around 863), king of Germany (r. 887–899), king of the

East Franks, Holy Roman emperor (r. 896–899); children: Louis III the Child (b. 893), king of Germany (r. 899–911).

ODA OF GERMANY AND NORTH MARCK (fl. 900s). Duchess of Poland. Second wife of Mieszko I, prince of the Polanians (d. 992); his 1st wife was Dobravy of Bohemia.

ODA OF LORRAINE (fl. mid-1000). Countess of Brabant and Lorraine. Died Oct 23, year unknown; dau. of Gozelo I, duke of Lower Lorraine (r. 1023–1044); m. Lambert II, count of Brabant and Louvain (d. after Sept 21, 1062); children: Henry II, count of Brabant and Louvain (d. 1078).

O'DAY, Anita (1919—). American jazz singer. Name variations: Anita Colton. Born Anita Belle Colton, Oct 18, 1919, in Kansas City, MO (some sources cite Chicago, IL); m. Don Carter (drummer, div.); m. Carl Hoff (professional golfer, div.). ❖ Known for brilliant jazz improvisations, had 1st professional singing job with Max Miller combo at Chicago's Three Deuces club; hired by Gene Krupa, with whom she recorded her biggest hit, "Let Me Off Uptown" (1941); often shared other successful vocals with trumpeter Roy Eldridge, including "That's What You Think," "Thanks for the Boogie Ride" and "Boogie Blues"; did a stint with Stan Kenton (1944), recording the million-selling "And Her Tears Flowed Like Wine," among others; embarked on a successful solo career (1946); released 1st full-length solo album, *Anita* (1956), followed by 14 more albums on Verve label; appeared at Newport Jazz Festival and was featured in highly regarded documentary *Jazz on a Summer's Day* (1958); nearly died of drug overdose (1966); finally quit heroin (1969); reached a career milestone with a concert at Carnegie Hall celebrating 50th year in jazz (1985). ❖ See also autobiography (with George Eells) *High Times, Hard Times* (1981); and *Women in World History.*

O'DAY, Caroline (1869–1943). American politician. Born Caroline Love Goodwin, June 22, 1869, in Perry, Georgia; died Jan 4, 1943, in Rye, New York; dau. of Sidney Prior Goodwin (Confederate veteran and businessman) and Elia (Warren) Goodwin; graduate of Lucy Cobb Institute, Athens, Georgia, 1886; m. Daniel O'Day (oil contractor), April 30, 1901 (died 1916); children: Elia Warren (b. 1904); Daniel (b. 1906); Charles (b. 1908). ❖ Champion for women's rights and human rights, became active in New York Consumers' League, Women's Trade Union League, and Lillian Wald's Henry Street Settlement, for which she served on board of directors; was a member of NY State Board of Charities, later State Board of Social Welfare (1923–35); served as 1st vice-chair of NY Democratic State Committee (1926–34); as a 4-term US congressional representative from NY (Jan 3, 1935–Jan 3, 1943), helped attach child labor amendments to 1936 Walsh-Healy Act, which set employment standards for government contractors, and to 1938 Fair Labor Standards Act, which fixed minimum ages for employment; served on Committee on Insular Affairs and Committee on Immigration and Naturalization; chaired Committee on Election of President, Vice President, and Representatives in Congress (1937–43); chaired the committee that sponsored Marian Anderson's historic concert at the Lincoln Memorial (1939); as a pacifist, voted against repeal of arms embargo portion of the 1939 Neutrality Act; retired from Congress (Jan 3, 1943) and died of a cerebral hemorrhage the following day. ❖ See also *Women in World History.*

O'DAY, Dawn (1917–1993). *See Shirley, Anne.*

O'DAY, Molly (1911–1998). American actress. Name variations: Sue O'Neil. Born Suzanne Dobson Noonan, Oct 16, 1911, in Bayonne, NJ; died Oct 22, 1998, in Avila Beach, CA; dau. of a judge and Hannah Kelly (Metropolitan opera singer); sister of Sally O'Neil (actress); m. Jack Durant, 1934 (div. 1951); m. James Kenaston, 1952 (div. 1956); children: 4. ❖ Had leads in Hal Roach comedies (1920s), including "Our Gang" series; films include *The Patent Leather Kid, The Shepherd of the Hills* and *The Little Shepherd of Kingdom Come.*

ODDON, Yvonne (1902–1982). French librarian and resistance leader. Born 1902 in France; died 1982; graduate of American School in Paris, 1924; studied under Margaret Mann at Paris Library School. ❖ One of the most celebrated heroines of the French Resistance, was a key member of Musée de l'Homme network, the 1st important resistance organization to actively oppose German occupation of France; served on University of Michigan library staff (1926–28); worked at Musée d'Ethnographie du Trocadéro (1929–37), then appointed its director when it became the library in the Musée de l'Homme (1937); classified the sizable collection according to Library of Congress method, the 1st time this approach was used in France; worked with Vigilance Committee of Anti-Fascist

Intellectuals, trying to halt the spread of racist doctrines; began to harbor fugitives from the Germans, directing them to friends who could assist them in crossing the border to the unoccupied zone; made contact with Free French forces in London; arrested (1941), was tried with others (1942); found guilty of espionage, was sentenced to be executed; when sentence was commuted, was deported to Germany, where she spent the next 3 years in concentration camps; returned home to Paris (1945), and resumed career as chief librarian at Musée de l'Homme; also appointed 1st director of UNESCO/ICOM Documentation Centre (1946); retired (1964). ❖ See also *Women in World History.*

ODEBRECHT, Viola (1983—). German soccer player. Born Feb 11, 1983, in Brandenburg, Germany. ❖ Won FIFA World Cup (2003); midfielder, won a team bronze medal at Athens Olympics (2004).

ODEN, Elaina (1967—). American volleyball player. Born Mar 21, 1967, in Orange, CA; dau. of Abe Oden (volleyball player); sister of Beverly and Kimberley Oden (both volleyball players); attended University of the Pacific. ❖ Joined US team (1986); was 1st-team college All-American (1985, 1986); at Barcelona Olympics, won a bronze medal in team competition (1992); starred in the Italian Club League.

ODEN, Kimberley (1964—). American volleyball player. Born May 1964 in Orange, CA; dau. of Abe Oden (volleyball player); sister of Beverly and Elaina Oden (both volleyball players); attended Stanford University. ❖ Won the Honda/Broderick Award (1985); as team captain at Barcelona Olympics, won a bronze medal in team competition (1992); played professionally in Italy (1992), China (1993), Brazil (1994) and Turkey (1995).

ODENA, Lina (1911–1936). Spanish politician. Name variations: Catalina Odena. Born Catalina Odena in Barcelona, Spain, 1911; died 1936. ❖ Spanish Communist whose suicide when captured by the Nationalists made her a Spanish Republican martyr during the Civil War. ❖ See also *Women in World History.*

ODE OF HERISTAL (b. 586). *See Dode.*

ODETTA (1930—). African-American folksinger. Born Odetta Holmes, Dec 31, 1930, in Birmingham, Alabama; dau. of Reuben Holmes and Flora (Sanders) Holmes; graduate of Los Angeles City College; m. Don Gordon, 1959 (div.); m. Iversen Minter, 1977. ❖ Internationally famous, with a career that spanned over 5 decades, made professional debut in chorus of musical *Finian's Rainbow* in Los Angeles, at 19; drawn to folk music, taught herself to play the guitar and began singing at fundraisers; performed folk music at clubs in Los Angeles and San Francisco (1952), including the Hungry i; appeared at NYC's Blue Angel nightclub (1953) and returned to NY frequently, becoming a leader in the rebirth of folk music; with powerful, soulful voice, expanded repertoire into a number of genres, including spirituals, blues, jazz, and social protest songs (1950s); released 1st album, *The Tin Angel* (1954); acted in theater productions, as well as in several films, including *The Last Time I Saw Paris* (1954); performed at folk festivals and in solo concerts across US, in addition to releasing 16 albums (1960s); influenced the musical development of many prominent folk and rock musicians, including Bob Dylan and Janis Joplin; performed in England and toured in Soviet Union and Eastern Europe (1970s); appeared in "The Autobiography of Miss Jane Pittman" (1974); after a dormant period, made comeback at age 69 with album for Vanguard, *Blues Everywhere I Go,* which was nominated for a Grammy Award; also released *Odetta: Best of the Vanguard Years* (1999). Awarded National Endowment for the Arts Medal by Bill Clinton (1999). ❖ See also *Women in World History.*

ODETTE DE POUGY (fl. 1266). French abbess. Flourished c. 1266 in France; never married; no children. ❖ Bold abbess of France at convent of Notre-Dame-aux-Nonnains, became involved in a conflict with Pope Urban IV over his infringement on abbey land (1266), which lasted until her death. ❖ See also *Women in World History.*

ODGIVE D'ANGLETERRE (902–951). *See Edgifu.*

ODHNOFF, Camilla (1923—). Swedish politician. Born 1923 in Sweden; holds a doctorate in plant physiology. ❖ As a member of Social Democrat Party, served as minister without Portfolio of Family Affairs of Swedish parliament (1967–73); served as governor of Blekinge County (1974–92) and as chair of KASAM (National Council for Nuclear Waste).

ODILE (1905–2004). *See Villameur, Lise.*

ODILIA (fl. 620). Frankish abbess. Flourished c. 620 in Alsace; dau. of Adalric, a noble of Alsace; never married. ❖ Though blind, founded a nunnery on father's lands in the Vosges Mountains above Hohenburg in Alsace and became its abbess; while there, regained her sight, a miracle she felt was a reward from God for her deep devotion, and her convent soon became a destination for many pilgrims who were blind or afflicted with eye diseases. ❖ See also *Women in World History.*

ODINOKOVA-BEREZHNAYA, Lyubov (1955—). Soviet handball player. Name variations: Lyubov Berezhnaya. Born July 24, 1955, in USSR. ❖ Won a gold medal at Montreal Olympics (1976) and a gold medal at Moscow Olympics (1980), both in team competition.

ODIO BENITO, Elizabeth (1939—). Costa Rican lawyer, judge and political figure. Born Sept 15, 1939, in Puntarenas, Costa Rica; dau. of Emiliano Odio Madrigal (teacher, scientist and founder of 1st high school in Puntarenas, Costa Rica) and Esperanza Benito Ibañez. ❖ Forceful lawyer, judge, educator and human rights advocate, established law practice (1970); served as 1st woman professor at University of Costa Rica Law School (1986–95), while also conducting research as director of the university's Institute for Judicial Research and Institute for Social Law and eventually serving as university administrator; taught at numerous universities in US (including Fletcher School of Law) as well as in Spain, Netherlands and France; served in numerous governmental positions, including 1st woman minister of justice and attorney general (1978–82), minister of justice (1990–94) and 2nd vice president and minister of environment and energy (1998–2002); began to focus on human rights in international context (1980s–90s), working extensively with UN organizations and holding many posts, including rapporteur with Human Rights Subcommission (1984–87) and head of Costa Rican delegation to International Conference for Human Rights in Vienna (1993); elected as judge on International Criminal Tribunal for Yugoslavia (1993, 1998) and International Criminal Court (2003); taught human-rights related courses at Inter-American Institute of Human Rights and University for Peace. Received Monseñor Leónidas Proaño Award.

ODLE, Mrs. Alan (1873–1957). *See Richardson, Dorothy M.*

ODLOZIL, Vera (1942—). *See Caslavska, Vera.*

ODOEVTSEVA, Irina (c. 1895–1990). Russian novelist and poet. Name variations: Iraida Gustavovna Heinecke (also seen as Geinike); Iraida Gustavovna Ivanova; Irina Odóevtseva or Irina Vladimorovna Odoyevtseva. Born Iraida Gustavovna Heinecke (also seen as Geinike) in 1895 (some sources cite 1901, but 1895 is considered more likely) in Riga, Latvia; died Oct 1990; father was a lawyer and landlord; m. Georgii Vladimirovich Ivanov (poet), Sept 1921 (died 1958); m. Iakov Nikolaevich Gorbov (novelist), Mar 1978 (died 1982). ❖ Published 1st volume of poetry, *Dvor chudes* (Court of Wonders), in St. Petersburg (1922), after which she settled in Paris with 1st husband, where they were active in émigré literary circles; during this period, concentrated on prose, publishing several light-reading novels including *Angel smerti* (Angel of Death, 1927), *Izolda* (1931), and *Zerkalo* (Mirror, 1939); following WWII, turned to poetry once more, though it was the money she obtained for novel *Ostav nadezhdu navsegda* (All Hope Abandon, 1954) which brought much-needed funds; among later collections of poetry were *Kontrapunkt* (1951), *Stikhi napisannye vo vremya bolezni* (1952), *Stikhi* (1960), *Desyat'et* (1961), and *Odinochestvo* (1965); following 1st husband's death (1958), moved to Gagny, near Paris, and joined staff of the journal *Russkaia mysl'*; returned to St. Petersburg (1987). ❖ See also literary memoirs, *Na beregakh Nevy* (On the Banks of the Neva, 1967) and *Na beregakh Seny* (On the Banks of the Seine); and *Women in World History.*

O'DOHERTY, Eileen (b. 1891). Irish actress. Born Anna Walker in Dublin, Ireland, in Sept 1891; dau. of Marian (Doherty) Walker and Matthew Walker; sister of Maire Nic Shiubhlaigh; educated in Dublin and studied for the stage under W.G. and F.J. Fay. ❖ Made stage debut with Irish National Theatre Society at Abbey Theatre (1905), as the child in *The Hour Glass*; during career, worked regularly at the Abbey and at the Court Theatre in London, appearing as Babsy in *The Shrewing-up of Blanco Posnet,* Old Woman in *Deirdre,* Bridget Twomey in *Harvest,* Mrs. Desmond in *The Cross Roads,* Mrs. Pender in *The Casting Out of Martin Whelan,* Maura Morrissey in *Birthright,* Margaret in *The Piedish,* Nerine in *The Rogueries of Scapin,* Miss Joyce in *Hyacinth Halvey,* Mary Brien in *The Mineral Workers,* Maria Donnelly in *Family Failing,* Mrs. Keegan in *The Supplanter,* Kate Moran in *Crusaders* and Mrs.

Geoghegan in *The White Headed Boy;* also toured in England, Scotland, and US.

O'DOHERTY, Eva (1826–1910). *See O'Doherty, Mary Anne.*

O'DOHERTY, Mary Anne (1826–1910). Irish-born poet. Name variations: Eva O'Doherty; Eva Mary Kelly; Mary Anne Kelly; Mrs. Kevin Izod O'Doherty of Ireland. Born Mary Eva Kelly in Ireland, 1826; died in Brisbane, Australia, 1910; m. Kevin Izod O'Doherty (medical practitioner and political activist), 1854. ❖ As Eva Kelly, began writing career in Ireland as a contributor of patriotic verse to the *Nation,* becoming known as "Eva of the *Nation*"; settled in Brisbane, Australia, following marriage; published 2 collections of verse, both entitled *Poems* (1877 and 1880); returned to Ireland (1886), where husband served briefly as member of House of Commons; went back to Brisbane, where she published *Selections* (1908); though popular during her time, is now read mainly for her historical significance. ❖ See also *Women in World History.*

O'DOHERTY, Mignon (1890–1961). Australian-born actress. Born Jan 30, 1890, in Brisbane, Queensland, Australia; died Mar 12, 1961, in London, England; m. Tom Nesbitt. ❖ Made stage debut in London as Angélique in *Lady Frederick* (1913), followed by *Damaged Goods, The Government Inspector, The Green Hat, Marry at Leisure, The Last Trump, The Nutmeg Tree, Irene* and *The Pink Room,* among others; appeared as Mrs. Boyle in *The Mousetrap* (1952–55); made film debut in *The Faithful Heart;* other films include *Dandy Dick, The Lamp Still Burns, Ghost Ship* and *Never Let Go.*

O'DONNELL, Ann (c. 1857–1934). New Zealand farmer, grocer, and innkeeper. Name variations: Ann McNamara. Born Ann McNamara, between 1857 and 1860, in Co. Clare, Ireland; died May 5, 1934, at Waiuta, New Zealand; dau. of Patrick McNamara and Kathy (Curry) McNamara; m. Edward O'Donnell (miner), 1881 (died 1894); children: 5 daughters, 1 son. ❖ Immigrated to New Zealand to escape an arranged marriage (1879); established grocery store at Woodstock (c. 1899); granted lease of Rose and Thistle hotel at Blackwater (c. 1908); opened popular Empire hotel (1915). ❖ See also *Dictionary of New Zealand Biography* (Vol. 2).

O'DONNELL, Cathy (1923–1970). American actress. Born Ann Steely, July 6, 1923, in Siluria, Alabama; died April 11, 1970, in Los Angeles, CA; m. Robert Wyler, 1948. ❖ Best known for performance as the girlfriend of amputee Harold Russell in debut film *The Best Years of Our Lives* (1946); other films include *The Miniver Story, They Live by Night, Detective Story, The Man from Laramie* and *Ben-Hur.*

O'DONNELL, Finula (fl. 1569–1592). *See Macdonald, Finula.*

O'DONNELL, Lawrence (1911–1987). *See Moore, C. L.*

O'DONNELL, Liz (1956—). Irish politician. Born July 1956 in Dublin, Ireland; m. Michael T. Carson. ❖ Representing Progressive Democrats, elected to 27th Dáil (1992–97) for Dublin South; returned to 28th Dáil (1997–2002) and 29th Dáil (2002); named minister of State at Dept. of Foreign Affairs with responsibility for Overseas Development Assistance and Human Rights (1997).

O'DONNELL, Mary Stuart (fl. early 1600s). Irish aristocrat and adventurer. Born in England in early 17th century; dau. of Rory also known as Ruaidhrí O'Donnell (1575–1608), 1st earl of Tirconnell (Tyrconnel and Tir Chonaill), and Brigid Fitzgerald; granddau. of Finula MacDonald; m. Dudley O'Gallagher (killed 1635); remarried, 1639. ❖ A daughter of the O'Donnell clan (Irish dissenters), was placed in the care of her grandmother in England at 12; rebelled against grandmother's matchmaking plans by leaving her household (1626); dressed as a man, traveled with friends to the port of Bristol, and sailed for Brussels while still in disguise; continued to present herself as a man for some time in Europe. ❖ See also *Women in World History.*

O'DONNELL, Phyllis (1937—). Australian surfer. Born 1937 in New South Wales, Australia. ❖ Won her 1st women's title at Australian invitational held at Bondi (1963); won Australian championship (1964, 1965); won 1st Women's World championship, held at Manly Beach (1964); between 1964 and 1973, won Queensland women's championship 8 times and also represented Australia and defended her title in California and Hawaii. ❖ See also "Heart of the Sea" (documentary, PBS); and *Women in World History.*

O'DONNELL, May (1906–2004). American modern dancer, teacher and choreographer. Born May 1, 1906, in Sacramento, CA; died Feb 1,

2004, in New York, NY; m. Ray Green (composer). ❖ Was a principal dancer with Martha Graham company (1932–38) and guest artist (1944–53), creating the Pioneer woman in *Appalachian Spring* (1944) and the Earth in *Dark Meadow* and the Chorus in *Cave of the Heart* (both 1946); choreographed the classic *Suspension* (1943); was a choreographer (1937–88) and taught for many years.

O'DONNELL, Rosie (1962—). American actress and talk-show host. Born Roseann O'Donnell, Mar 21, 1962, in Commack, Long Island, NY; married longtime partner, Kelli Carpenter (2004); children: (adopted) Parker (b. 1995), Chelsea (b. 1997), Blake (b. 1999), and Vivienne (b. 2002, born to Kelli Carpenter). ❖ Began career as a standup comic; appeared as Maggie O'Brien on "Gimme a Break!" (1986–87); made film debut in *A League of Their Own* (1992), followed by *Sleepless in Seattle* (1993), *The Flintstones* (1994), *Harriet the Spy* (1996) and *Wide Awake (1998),* among others; was outspoken host of the popular "Rosie O'Donnell Show" (1998–2001); starred in tv movie "Riding the Bus with My Sister" (2005).

ODOYEVTSEVA, Irina Vladimirovna (c. 1895–1990). *See Odoevtseva, Irina.*

ODOZI OBODO, Madam (1909–1995). Igbo religious leader. Name variations: Ngozi Okoh; Madam Okoh; Prophetess Odozi Obodo. Born Ngozi Ozoemena, 1909, in Onitsha, Igboland, Nigeria; died in Ndoni, Rivers state, Nigeria, Nov 1995; dau. of petty traders from Onitsha; married D.C. Okoh (civil servant), 1925; children: D.C. Okoh, Sr. (1935–1980), who ran the affairs of the church with his mother until his death); grandchildren: D.C. Okoh Jr. (who took over affairs of the church). ❖ Igbo woman who founded one of the leading indigenous independent churches in Igboland, the Christ Holy Church of Nigeria, was an illiterate housewife and petty trader; believed to be called by God to carry out God's ministerial work (1948), became a church minister, a preacher, a prophet, a spiritual healer, and head of a famous church in Nigeria; was recognized for her spiritual powers by many, including the government of Rivers state of Nigeria which honored her twice (1988, 1992). ❖ See also *Women in World History.*

O'DRISCOLL, Margaret Collins (1878–1945). *See Collins-O'Driscoll, Margaret.*

O'DRISCOLL, Martha (1922–1998). American actress. Name variations: Martha O'Driscoll Appleton. Born Mar 4, 1922, in Tulsa, OK; died Nov 3, 1998, in Ocala, FL; m. R.D. Adams, 1943 (div. 1945); m. Arthur Appleton, 1947. ❖ Portrayed Daisy Mae in *Li'l Abner* (1940); other films include *The Lady Eve, Henry Aldrich for President, Reap the Wild Wind, House of Dracula, Down Missouri Way* and *Carnegie Hall.*

OELKERS-CARAGIOFF, Olga (1887–1969). German fencer. Name variations: Olga Caragioff. Born May 21, 1887, in Germany; died Jan 10, 1969. ❖ At Amsterdam Olympics, won a bronze medal in indiv. foil (1928).

OELRICHS, Blanche (1890–1950). *See Strange, Michael.*

OELSCHLAGEL, Charlotte (c. 1899–after 1948). German ice dancer. Name variations: Charlotte Ölschlagel; danced as Charlotte. Born Charlotte Oelschlagel, c. 1899, in Berlin, Germany; m. Anselm Goetzl (composer and Fokine Ballet conductor), c. 1916 (died Jan 9, 1923). ❖ The 1st great show skater, began career performing at Berlin Admiralspalast and Wintergarten in Berlin; discovered by Charles Dillingham, went to US to perform on ice at the Hippodrome in New York City, where she skated in numerous productions, including *Hip, Hip, Hooray* (1915), *The Big Show* (1916), and worked with the Fokine Ballet skating a sequence from *Les Sylphides* in *Get Together* (1922); performed at dinner clubs and cabarets such as Terrace Garden of New Hotel Morrison in Chicago (1917); toured with Fokine troupe after marrying; made a 5-part serial film, *Charlotte,* for Commonwealth Pictures (1919–20); returned to Europe after husband's death (1923) and appeared in cabarets and winter gardens with Irving Brokaw; went into hiding in or around Prague when Germany invaded at start of WWII; was discovered in a refugee camp by American media during Nuremburg Trials (late 1940s). Inducted into World Figure Skating Hall of Fame (1985).

OELSNER, Marlies (1958—). *See Göhr, Marlies.*

OERTLI, Brigitte (1962—). Swiss Alpine skier. Born June 10, 1962, in Egg, Switzerland. ❖ Won silver medals for combined and downhill at Calgary Olympics (1988); at World Cup, won a bronze medal (1987) and a silver medal (1988), both for overall; won a bronze medal at World championships for combined (1988).

OESTREICH, Nancy (1924—). *See Lurie, Nancy O.*

OESTVOLD, Line (1978—). Norwegian snowboarder. Born Nov 7, 1978, in Ringerike, Norway. ❖ Received 1st-place year-end ranking, VTC of Snowboarding in Boardercross (2001); was overall female rider in Vans Triple Crown Series (2000–01 series); won gold in at X Games in Snowboarder X (2001); received 1st-place season-end ISF World Ranking in Boardercross (2001); other 1st-place finishes in Boardercross include: Swatch Boardercross, Aspen, CO (2001) and Red Bull Ultracross, Northstar at Tahoe, CA (2002).

O'FAOLAIN, Julia (1932—). Irish novelist and short-story writer. Name variations: Julia Martines. Born June 6, 1932, in London, England; dau. of Sean O'Faolain and Eileen Gould O'Faolain (both authors); m. Lauro Martines. ❖ Works, which often focus on the position of women in society, include *We Might See Sights and Other Stories* (1968), *Godded and Codded* (1970), *Man in the Cellar* (1974), *Women in the Wall* (1975), *Melancholy Baby and Other Stories* (1978), *No Country for Young Men* (1980), *The Obedient Wife* (1982), the critically acclaimed *Daughters of Passion* (1982), *The Irish Signorina* (1984), and *The Judas Cloth* (1992); with husband edited *Not in God's Image: Women in History from the Greeks to the Victorians* (1973).

O'FAOLAIN, Nuala (1940—). Irish memoirist. Born Nuala O'Faolain, 1940, in Dublin, Ireland; attended Oxford and University College Dublin. ❖ Was a producer and on-air personality for Ireland's Radio Telefis Éireannl; for 10 years, wrote a column for the *Irish Times*; published the bestselling *Are You Somebody? The Accidental Memoir of a Dublin Woman* (1996); also wrote *Almost There: The Onward Journey of a Dublin Woman* and the novel, *My Dream of You.*

O'FARRELL, Bernadette (1924–1999). Irish actress. Born Jan 30, 1924, in Birr, Co. Offaly, Ireland; died Sept 26, 1999, in Monaco; m. Frank Launder (director), 1950 (died 1997). ❖ Portrayed Maid Marian on tv series "The Adventures of Robin Hood" (1955–57); appeared in such films as *The Happiest Days of Your Life, Lady Godiva Rides Again, The Story of Gilbert and Sullivan* and *The Bridal Path*, and in her husband's "St. Trinian" series; retired (1959).

O'FARRILL, Raisa (1972—). Cuban volleyball player. Name variations: Raisa O'Farrill Bolanos. Born April 17, 1972, in Cuba. ❖ Won a team gold medal at Atlanta Olympics (1996).

OFELIA (1851–1906). *See Matamoros, Mercedes.*

OFFALEY, Baroness (c. 1588–1658). *See Digby, Lettice.*

OGBEIFO, Ruth (1967—). Nigerian weightlifter. Born 1967 in Nigeria. ❖ Won a silver medal for 69–75kg at Sydney Olympics (2000).

OGIER, Bulle (1939—). French actress. Born in Boulogne-sur-Seine, France, Aug 9, 1939; married; children: one daughter, Pascale Ogier (1960–1984), also an actress. ❖ Stage star and a pioneer of the café-theatre movement, made film debut in *L'Amour fou* (1968) and subsequently found a niche interpreting unconventional roles in the films of the French New Wave; appeared in Buñuel's surreal fable *La Charme discret de la Bourgeoisie (The Discreet Charm of the Bourgeoisie, 1972)* and was notable as the compassionate dominatrix in Schroeder's *Mistress* (1976); other films include *Pauline s'en va* (1969), *Pierre et Paul* (1969), *Piège* (1969), *La Salamandre* (1971), *Rendez-vous à Bray* (1971), *La Vallée (The Valley,* 1972), *La Paloma* (1974), *Un Divorce Heureux* (1975), *Jamais plus toujours* (1976), *Duelle* (1976), *La Mémoire courte* (1979), *Agatha et les Lectures limitées* (1981), *Le Pont du Nord* (1982), *La Derelitta* (1983), *La Bande des Quatre* (1989), *North* (1991), *Regarde les Hommes Tomber* (1994) and *Irma Vep* (1996). ❖ See also *Women in World History.*

OGIER, Louisa (1729–1807). *See Courtauld, Louisa.*

OGILVIE, Catherine (1746–?). Scottish murderer. Name variations: Katharine Ogilvie. Born Catherine Nairn in Dusinan, Scotland, 1746; m. Thomas Ogilvie, Jan 31, 1765; children: (with Patrick Ogilvie) 1. ❖ Began affair with Patrick Ogilvie, her husband's brother and heir; asked Patrick to mail her arsenic which she used to kill her husband; with Patrick, was tried for murder and found guilty; though Patrick was hanged (Nov 13, 1768), was spared until she could deliver his baby; with help of servant, made prison break, boarded a boat bound for Calais, and disappeared.

OGILVIE, Maria Matilda (1864–1939). *See Ogilvie Gordon, Maria M.*

OGILVIE FARQUHARSON, Marian (1846–1912). English botanist. Name variations: Marian Ogilvie-Farquharson; Marian Ridley. Born

Marian Sarah Ridley, July 2, 1846; died April 20, 1912; m. Robert F. Ogilvie Farquharson, 1883 (died 1890). ❖ Was a member of Epping Forest and Essex Naturalists' Field Club, East of Scotland Union Naturalists' Society, and Alford Field Club Society; wrote *A Pocket Guide to British Ferns* (1881); was the 1st female elected a fellow of Royal Microscopical Society (April 8, 1885), though she was excluded from meetings and had no voting privileges; began petitioning Linnean Society to grant women eligibility for fellowship and, as members, to be permitted to attend meetings (April 1900); finally won battle when 16 women became Linnean Society fellows (Nov 17, 1904); elected Linnean Society fellow (Mar 1908), but was unable to sign its register due to illness.

OGILVIE GORDON, Maria M. (1864–1939). Scottish geologist. Name variations: Maria Matilda Gordon; Maria Matilda Ogilvie; Maria Ogilvie-Gordon; Dame Maria Ogilvie Gordon. Born Maria Matilda Ogilvie, 1864, in Scotland; died June 24, 1939; was 1st woman to earn doctor of science degree from London University, 1893; at Munich University, was the 1st woman PhD, 1900; m. Dr. John Gordon (died 1919); children: 3. ❖ At London University, researched the geology of the Wengen and St. Cassian strata (South Tyrol); conducted research in the Dolomites (South Tyrol) and discovered that the area had experienced faulting, which contradicted common beliefs about the region; wrote a geological guide to the western Dolomites; translated Zittel's *History of Geology*; chaired the Marylebone Court of Justices and served as one of the 1st women justices of peace; created the Council for the Representation of Women in the League of Nations (1919); was an honorary life president of National Women Citizens Association. Made a Dame Commander of the Order of the British Empire (1935); received the Geological Society of London's Lyell Medal (1932).

OGIVA. *Variant of Ogive.*

OGIVE (902–951). *See Edgifu.*

OGIVE OF LUXEMBURG (d. 1030). Countess of Flanders. Name variations: Ogiva; possibly Orgina. Died 1030; dau. of Frederick (c. 965–1019), count of Luxemburg; sister of Imagi of Luxemburg (c. 1000–1057); was 1st wife of Baldwin IV (c. 980–1035), count of Flanders (r. 988–1035); children: Baldwin V the Pious (b. around 1012), count of Flanders.

OGIYENKO, Valentina (1965—). Soviet volleyball player. Born May 26, 1965, in USSR. ❖ Won a gold medal at Seoul Olympics (1988) and a silver medal at Barcelona Olympics (1992), both in team competition.

OGNJENOVIC, Mirjana (1953—). Yugoslavian handball player. Born Sept 17, 1953, in Yugoslavia. ❖ Won a silver medal at Moscow Olympics (1980) and a gold medal at Los Angeles Olympics (1984), both in team competition.

OGOT, Grace (1930—). Kenyan author and politician. Born Grace Emily Akinyi, May 15, 1930, at Butere, near Kisumu, Central Nyanza, Kenya; received nursing degree at training hospital at Mengo, near Kampala, Uganda, 1953; completed 3-year course at British Hospital for Mothers and Babies (1955–58); m. Bethwell Allan Ogot (noted Kenyan historian), 1959; children: daughter, Wasonga Grace; sons, Odera-Akongo, Otieno Mudhune, Onyuna. ❖ One of Kenya's most distinguished writers, 1st worked as a broadcaster, scriptwriter, and editor for BBC Africa Service in London; returned to Nairobi; published short story, "A Year of Sacrifice," in journal *Black Orpheus* (1963); initially wrote short stories in her 1st language, Luo; would also write in Kiswahili and English; published *The Promised Land*, the 1st novel by a Kenyan woman writer and a work of lasting substance (1966); published *Land Without Thunder* (1968), (short stories) *The Other Woman* (1976), *The Graduate* (1980), *The Island of Tears* (1980), and *The Strange Bride* (1989); wrote a column for the *East African Standard*, as well, worked for a period for the "Voice of Kenya," broadcasting a weekly radio magazine in both Luo and Kaswahili; served as founding chair of Writer's Association of Kenya; served as a Kenyan delegate to UN General Assembly (1975); appointed a member of the nation's Parliament (1983), then was elected in a by-election (1985); in novels and short stories, has attempted to relate the rich traditions of Luo history and folklore to younger generation of Kenyans. ❖ See also *Women in World History.*

O'GRADY, Diane (1967—). Canadian rower. Born Nov 23, 1967, in North Bay, Ontario, Canada. ❖ Won a bronze medal for quadruple sculls at Atlanta Olympics (1996).

OGUNKOYA, Falilat (1969—). Nigerian runner. Name variations: Fali Ogunkoya-Osheku. Born Dec 5, 1969 in Nigeria. ❖ Won World Jr. championship for the 200 meters (1986); won a silver medal for the 4 x 400-meter relay and a bronze medal for the 400 meters at Atlanta Olympics (1996).

OH KYO-MOON. South Korean archer. Born in South Korea. ❖ Won a gold medal for teams at Atlanta Olympics (1996).

OH SEONG-OK (1972—). *See Oh Sung-Ok.*

OH SEUNG-SHIN. South Korean field-hockey player. Born in South Korea. ❖ Won a team silver medal at Atlanta Olympics (1996) and a team gold at Asian Games (1998).

OH SUNG-OK (1972—). South Korean handball player. Name variations: Seong-Ok Oh. Born Oct 10, 1972, in South Korea. ❖ Won a team gold medal at Barcelona Olympics (1992), a team silver at Atlanta Olympics (1996) and a team silver at Athens Olympics (2004); won World championship (1995).

OH YONG-RAN (1972—). South Korean handball player. Born Sept 6, 1972, in South Korea. ❖ Won a team World championship (1995); won a team silver medal at Atlanta Olympics (1996) and a team silver at Athens Olympics (2004).

O'HAGAN, Dara (1964—). Northern Ireland politician. Born Aug 29, 1964, in Northern Ireland. ❖ Began career as an economic researcher; representing Sinn Féin, elected to the Northern Ireland Assembly for Upper Bann (1998); contested Upper Bann (2001).

O'HAGAN, Mary (1823–1876). Religious leader. Born in Belfast, Ireland, 1823; died in Kenmare, Ireland, 1876. ❖ Devoting her life to the Sisters of Poor Clares, entered the convent in Newry (1844), becoming abbess there (1853); established another convent of Poor Clares in Kenmare (1861), where she also served as abbess until her death.

O'HAIR, Madalyn Murray (1919–1995). American lawyer, atheist philosopher, and social activist. Born Madalyn Mays on April 13, 1919, in Pittsburgh, Pennsylvania; murdered in 1995; dau. of John Irvin Mays (civil engineer) and Lena C. (Scholle) Mays; attended University of Toledo, 1936–37, University of Pittsburgh, 1938–39; Ashland College, BA, 1948; graduate study at Western Reserve University (now Case Western Reserve University), 1948–49, and Ohio Northern University, 1949–51; South Texas College of Law, LLB, 1953; South Texas College of Law, JD, 1954; Howard University, MPSW, 1954–55; Minnesota Institute of Philosophy, PhD, 1971; m. J. Roths, 1941 (div.); m. William J. Murray (div. 1950s); m. Richard Franklin O'Hair (intelligence agent), Oct 18, 1965 (div. 1976); children: (2nd m.) William J. Murray III; Jon Garth Murray; (3rd m.) legally adopted her granddaughter Robin Murray-O'Hair. ❖ Served in Women's Army Corps during WWII, achieving rank of second lieutenant; worked as psychiatric social worker (1948–64); was an attorney for the Department of Health, Education and Welfare (HEW), Washington, DC (1956–59); with son, successfully sued the Baltimore Public Schools in protest of mandatory school prayer and Bible reading, one of the major Supreme Court cases of the 2nd half of the 20th century (1963); served as director of American Atheist Center (1965–77); served as director, American Atheist Radio Series (1968–77); became editor-in-chief, *American Atheist Magazine* (1965); co-founded, with Richard O'Hair, American Atheists, Inc. (formerly Society of Separatists) and served as secretary (1965–75) and president (1975–86); writings include *Why I Am an Atheist* (1965), *The American Atheist* (1967), *What on Earth is an Atheist!* (1969), *Let Us Prey; an Atheist Looks at Church Wealth* (1970), and (ed.) *The Atheist Viewpoint* (1972); disappeared, along with son and granddaughter (Sept 1995). Bones dug up on a west Texas ranch were identified as her remains and that of her relatives (Mar 2001). ❖ See also *Women in World History.*

O'HANLON, Virginia (c. 1899–1971). American literary inspiration. Name variations: Virginia O'Hanlon Douglas. Born Virginia O'Hanlon, c. 1889, in New York, NY; died May 13, 1971, age 81, in Valatie, NY; dau. of Philip O'Hanlon, a physician for NY police department; Hunter College, BA, 1910; Columbia University, MA, 1911; married with children. ❖ Was 8 years old and lived at 115 West 95th St. when she wrote to the editor of the *New York Sun* to inquire if there really was a Santa Claus (Sept 1897), and a writer named Francis Church responded with the oft-quoted editorial that began, "Yes, Virginia, there is a Santa Claus"; taught school in New York City for 47 years (1912–59), becoming a school principal

O'HARA, Anne (1875–1951). *See Martin, Anne Henrietta.*

O'HARA, Mary (1885–1980). American author. Name variations: Mary O'Hara Alsop; Mary Sture-Vasa; Mary O'Hara Alsop Sture-Vasa. Born Mary Alsop, July 10, 1885, in Cape May Point, New Jersey; died of arteriosclerosis, Oct 14, 1980, in Chevy Chase, Maryland; dau. of Reese Fell Alsop (Episcopal cleric) and Mary Lee (Spring) Alsop; educated at Ingleside in New Milford, CT, and at Packer Institute in Brooklyn; m. Kent Parrot, 1905 (div.); m. Helge Sture-Vasa, 1922 (div. 1947); children (1st m.): Mary O'Hara; Kent Jr. ❖ In Hollywood, was a staff writer for director Rex Ingram; wrote adaptations and continuities for such films as *Toilers of the Sea* (1923), *Black Oxen* (1924) and *Turn to the Right* (1927); with 2nd husband, moved to Wyoming (1930), where they ran a dairy ranch which became the setting for her classic, *My Friend Flicka* (1941), followed by *Thunderhead* (1943); moved back to East Coast after 2nd divorce (1947), where she continued to write stories of ranch life, though they did not achieve the stunning success of 1st two novels; later works include *Green Grass of Wyoming* (1946), *The Son of Adam Wyngate* (1952) and *Wyoming Summer* (1963). ❖ See also *Flicka's Friend: The Autobiography of Mary O'Hara* (1982); and *Women in World History.*

O'HARA, Maureen (1920—). Irish-born actress. Born Maureen FitzSimons, Aug 17, 1920, at Milltown (also seen as Millwall), near Dublin, Ireland; dau. of Charles FitzSimons (clothing manufacturer) and Marguerite (Lilburn) FitzSimons (actress and singer); graduate of Guildhall School of Music, Trinity College; received a degree and associateship from London College of Music; graduate of Abbey Theatre School; m. George Hanley Brown (film director), in 1939 (div. 1941); m. Will Price (film director), Dec 29, 1941 (div. 1953); m. Charles Blair (retired brigadier general), 1968 (died in plane crash, 1978); children: Bronwyn Bridget Price (b. 1944). ❖ Film star, best known for her portrayals of feisty women, played bits in 2 films before starring in British film *Jamaica Inn* (1939), then going to Hollywood to appear as Esmeralda in *The Hunchback of Notre Dame* (1939); came to the attention of John Ford, who cast her as Angharad in *How Green Was My Valley* (1941); went on to play leads in several films directed by Ford, including *The Quiet Man* (1952); also appeared in *A Bill of Divorcement* (1940), *Dance Girl Dance* (1940), *To the Shores of Tripoli* (1942), *The Fallen Sparrow* (1943), *Buffalo Bill* (1944), *Sentimental Journey* (1946), *Miracle on 34th Street* (1947), *The Foxes of Harrow* (1947), *The Forbidden Street* (*Britannia Mews,* 1949), *Tripoli* (1950), *Rio Grande* (1950), *Against All Flags* (1952), *The Redhead from Wyoming* (1953), *The Long Gray Line* (1955), *Lady Godiva* (1955), *Everything but the Truth* (1956), *Our Man in Havana* (1959), *The Parent Trap* (1961), *Mr. Hobbs Takes a Vacation* (1962), *Spencer's Mountain* (1963), *McLintock!* (1963), *The Battle of the Villa Fiorita* (1965), *The Rare Breed* (1966), and *Big Jake* (1971); left Hollywood following marriage to Charles Blair (1968) to live in St. Croix, where she assisted husband in managing Antilles Airboats, an airline which sent seaplanes around the world; after he died in a plane crash (1978), took over his job, becoming the 1st woman president of a commercial airline; came out of retirement (1991) for film *Only the Lonely* and appeared in CBS special "The Christmas Box" (1995). ❖ See also *Women in World History.*

O'HARA, Shirley (1910–1979). American actress. Born May 23, 1910, in New York, NY; died May 5, 1979, in Hollywood, CA. ❖ Made film debut in *Backstage* (1927), followed by *A Gentleman in Paris,* and *The Wild Party,* among others; retired from film (1929).

O'HARA, Shirley (1924–2002). American stage, tv, and screen actress. Name variations: Shirley O'Hara Nolan. Born Aug 15, 1924, in Rochester, MN; died Dec 13, 2002, in Calabasas, CA. ❖ Made film debut in *Step Lively* (1943), followed by *Tarzan and the Amazons, The Little Shepherd of Kingdom Come, The Chase* and *Rocky,* among others.

OHARA, Tomie (b. 1912). Japanese novelist. Born 1912 in Kochi prefecture, Japan. ❖ Works include *A Cold Rain* (1935), *Soldier Going to the Front* (1938), *Deafness from Streptomycin* (1956), *A Woman Called En* (1960), which won the Noma Prize for Literature and Mainichi Prize, *A Woman Traveling on the Earth,* and *The Camp of Abraham.*

O'HARE, Anne (1880–1954). See McCormick, Anne O'Hare.

O'HARE, Kate Richards (1876–1948). American politician. Name variations: Kate Cunningham. Born Carrie Kathleen Richards, Mar 26, 1876, in Ottawa Co., Kansas; died in Benicia, California, Jan 10, 1948; dau. of Andrew Richards and Lucy (Sullivan) Richards, both homesteaders; Pawnee City (Nebraska) Academy, teaching certificate, 1893; m. Francis P. O'Hare, Jan 1, 1902 (div. 1928); m. Charles C. Cunningham, Nov 1928; children: (1st m.) Richard (b. 1903); Kathleen O'Hare; twins

Victor and Eugene. ❖ Prominent leader of Socialist Party of America, working on behalf of social democratic reforms, workers' rights, women's issues, and prisoners' rights, moved with family to Kansas City, Missouri (1887); taught for 1 year at a rural school; worked for Florence Crittenton Mission (1896); became a machinist in father's shop and joined International Order of Machinists; became interested in labor issues and joined Socialist Party of America; trained at a school for socialist organizers (1901), where she met and married fellow student Frank P. O'Hare; traveled cross country speaking on behalf of Socialist Party; lived in Kansas City, Kansas, and homesteaded in Oklahoma (1904–08); became a columnist for various socialist newspapers and toured constantly as a socialist lecturer; held national offices in Socialist Party, including its representative to international socialist movement in London (1913); ran unsuccessfully on Socialist ticket for US House of Representatives in Kansas (1910); moved to St. Louis (1911) as columnist and associate editor of the *National Rip-Saw;* ran unsuccessfully for US Senate from Missouri (1916); opposed US intervention in World War I; indicted in Bowman, North Dakota, and convicted under Espionage Act for antiwar speeches; served 14 months of a 5-year sentence in Missouri State Penitentiary (1919–20) before sentence was commuted by President Woodrow Wilson, and her political and civil rights were restored by presidential action soon after; toured on behalf of amnesty for political prisoners and the abolition of prison contract labor; founded Commonwealth College of New Llano, Louisiana (1923), and, later, of Mena, Arizona; by now a well-respected public figure, served on the staff of Upton Sinclair's End Poverty in California movement (1934–35); appointed to staff of Progressive Congressman Thomas R. Amlie of Wisconsin (1937); worked on staff of the California Director of Penology (1939–40). ❖ See also *Kate O'Hare's Prison Letters* (Appeal to Reason, 1919); Foner and Miller, eds. *Kate Richards O'Hare: Selected Writings and Speeches* (Louisiana State U. Press, 1982); Sally M. Miller, *From Prairie to Prison: The Life of Social Activist Kate Richards O'Hare* (U. of Missouri Press, 1993); and *Women in World History.*

O'HIGGINS, Brigid (1932—). See Hogan, Brigid.

OHLSON, Agnes K. (1902–1991). American nurse. Born Feb 20, 1902, in New Britain, CT; died 1991 in FL; dau. of Karolina (Nelson) Ohlson and Johannes Ohlson (Swedish immigrants). ❖ Leader in US nursing education and licensure, graduated from Boston's Peter Bent Brigham School of Nursing (1926) and Columbia University Teachers College (1931); served as Waterbury Hospital's director of Nurse Training and as superintendent of the nurse training school in Waterbury, CT (1931–36); was on board of directors of Connecticut Nurses Association; elected to board of directors of Connecticut State Board of Nursing Examiners (1935); served as secretary, then chief examiner of the CT state board for 27 years; lobbied for a legal definition of nursing; played a key role in the creation of University of Connecticut's school of nursing in Storrs (opened 1942), the 1st baccalaureate nursing program at a public university in CT; served as secretary (1950–54) and president (1954–58) of American Nurses Association.

OHR, Martine (1964—). Dutch field-hockey player. Born June 11, 1964, in Netherlands. ❖ Won a gold medal at Los Angeles Olympics (1984) and a bronze medal at Seoul Olympics (1988), both in team competition.

OHSAKO, Tatsuko (1952—). Japanese golfer. Born Jan 8, 1952, in Miyazeki, Japan. ❖ Won Mazda Japan Classic and Japan LPGA (1980).

OHTA, Tomoko (1933—). Japanese geneticist. Born Sept 7, 1933, in Aichi Prefecture, near Nagoya, Japan; University of Tokyo, BS in agriculture, 1956; North Carolina State University, PhD, 1967. ❖ Among the 1st women to attend University of Tokyo, worked for population geneticist Motoo Kimura at National Institute of Genetics in Mishima; helped Kimura support his theory of the way in which certain body chemicals evolved; adhered to controversial "neutral mutation-random drift" hypothesis, which maintains that most evolution at the molecular level is not caused by Darwinian natural selection but rather by random processes; best known as originator and major proponent of "nearly neutral theory" of molecular evolution; at National Institute of Genetics, served as head of the 1st laboratory of the department of population genetics (1977–84), as professor (1984–97), then professor emerita, and as vice director (1990–91); was 1st winner of Saruhashi Prize for women and Japan Academy Prize (1985). Writings include (with Motoo Kimura) *Theoretical Aspects of Population Genetics* (1971), *Evolution and Varation of Multigene Families* (1980), and (with Kenichi Aoki) *Population Genetics and Molecular Evolution* (1985).

OIGNIES, Marie d' (1177–1213). See Mary of Oignies.

OIGNT, Marguerite d' (d. 1310). French mystic and writer. Name variations: Marguerite de Duyn. Died 1310 at priory of Poletins, near Lyons, France; never married; no children. ❖ Famed holy woman of France in the Middle Ages, joined the new Carthusian order of nuns as a young woman, and was highly educated at the priory of Poletins where she gained renown for her piety and mystical visions; in a few years, elected prioress; began publishing her revelations and meditations, in which she stressed the need for total self-abnegation in order to find God; wrote *Life of St. Beatrice*, a book of meditations.

OIKONOMOPOULOU, Aikaterini (1978—). Greek water-polo player. Born Feb 16, 1978, in Athens, Greece. ❖ Won team silver medal at Athens Olympics (2004).

OINUMA, Sumie (1946—). Japanese volleyball player. Born Oct 8, 1946, in Japan. ❖ Won a silver medal at Mexico City Olympics (1968) and a silver medal at Munich Olympics (1972), both in team competition.

OKAMOTO, Ayako (1951—). Japanese golfer. Born April 2, 1951, in Hiroshima, Japan. ❖ Enormously popular in Japan, won Japan LPGA (1979); won Arizona Copper Classic (1982), Rochester International (1983), Hitachi British Open, Mayflower, and J&B (1984); won Elizabeth Arden Classic and Cellular One-PING (1986), Kyocera Inamori Classic, Chrysler-Plymouth, Lady Keystone, Nestle World, and named player of the year (1987); won Orient Leasing Hawaiian Open, San Diego Inamori, and Greater Washington Open (1988); won Corning Classic (1989), Sara Lee Classic (1990), and McDonald's (1992); compiled 28 top-20 finishes in 51 major championship starts. Recipient of Japanese Prime Minister's Award (1987).

OKAMOTO, Mariko (1951—). Japanese volleyball player. Born Dec 28, 1951, in Japan. ❖ Won a silver medal at Munich Olympics (1972) and a gold medal at Montreal Olympics (1976), both in team competition.

OKAMOTO, Yoriko (1971—). Japanese taekwondo player. Born 1971 in Japan. ❖ Won a bronze medal for 57–67kg at Sydney Olympics (2000).

OKAYO, Margaret (1976—). Kenyan marathon runner. Born 1976 in Kisii, Kenya. ❖ Won NY City Marathon (2001), then broke her own record-breaking time with a 2:22.31 to win again (2003); won Boston Marathon (2002), setting an unofficial course record of 2:20:42; won San Diego Rock 'n' Roll Marathon (2000, 2001).

OKAZAKI, Tomomi (1971—). Japanese speedskater. Born Sept 7, 1971, in Kiyosato, Shari, Hokkaido, Japan. ❖ Won a bronze medal for the 500 meters at Nagano Olympics (1998); won bronze medals for 500 meters at World Single Distance championships (1996, 1998, 1999).

O'KEEFFE, Adelaide (1776–c. 1855). Irish poet and novelist. Name variations: Adelaide O'Keefe. Born Nov 5, 1776, in Dublin, Ireland; died probably in 1855; dau. of John O'Keeffe (actor turned playwright, died 1833); never married; no children. ❖ Moved to London with family (1780); somewhat overshadowed by famous father, emerged as a writer in her own right; contributed 34 poems to *Original Poems for Infant Minds* (1804), compiled by Ann and Jane Taylor, perhaps her best-known work; continued to write poetry for children, including *Original Poems Calculated to Improve the Mind of Youth* (1808), *National Characters Exhibited in 40 Geographical Poems* (1808) and *Poems for Young Children* (1849); also wrote a number of books for adult readers, including *Patriarchal Times; or The Land of Canaan* (1811), *Zenobia, Queen of Palmyra* (1814), and the 3-vol. novel *Dudley* (1819); published last novel, *The Broken Sword: A Tale* (1854).

O'KEEFFE, Georgia (1887–1986). American artist. Born Georgia Totto O'Keeffe in Sun Prairie, Wisconsin, Nov 15, 1887; died in Santa Fe, New Mexico, Mar 6, 1986; dau. of Francis Calixtus O'Keeffe and Ida Wyckoff (Totto) O'Keeffe; m. Alfred Stieglitz, Dec 1924 (died 1946); no children. ❖ One of the foremost artists of the 20th century, whose distinctive paintings of flowers, skulls, and abstracted Western landscapes are instantly recognizable and whose long, stormy relationship with photographer Alfred Stieglitz was one of the principal art legends of the century; moved to Williamsburg, Virginia, with family (1902); attended Art Institute of Chicago (1905); attended Art Students League in New York (1907); worked as a commercial artist in Chicago (1910); 1st visited the American west (Aug 1912), supervising drawing teachers in Amarillo, Texas (1912–14); met avant-garde photographer Alfred Stieglitz (1914); taught art in a small South Carolina Methodist junior college (1915); returned to Texas (1916) to teach at West Texas Normal College in

Canyon; taught at University of Virginia (1916); began affair with Stieglitz who was married (1918); married him (1924); had career as independent artist (1919–86); bought a house in Abiquiu, New Mexico (early 1930s); made 1st visit to Europe (1953); visited Peruvian Andes (1956); spent 3 months traveling around the world (1959). Selected works among the over 2,300 she created: *Tent Door at Night* (1913), *Pink and Green Mountains III* (1917), *From the Plains* (1919), *Blue and Green Music* (1919), *Lake George* (1923), *Red Canna* (c. 1923), *Pattern of Leaves* (1924), *Large Dark Red Leaves on White* (1925), *East River No. 1* (1926), *Morning Glory with Black* (1926), *Shelton Hotel, New York, No. 1* (1926), *Black Iris* (1926), *Red Hills and Sun, Lake George* (1927), *Poppy* (1927), *Shell 1* (1927), *White Flower* (1929), *Black Hollyhock with Blue Larkspur* (1929, sold for $1.98 million in 1987), *Ranchos Church Taos, New Mexico* (1930), *Jawbone and Fungus* (1930), *White Trumpet Flower* (1932), *Barn with Snow* (1933), *Purple Hills near Abiquiu* (1935), *Three Shells* (1937), *Pink Sweet Peas* (1937), *From the Faraway Nearby* (1937), *White Camelia* (1938), *Beauford Delaney* (c. 1940), *Black Place No. 1* (1944), the Pelvis series (1944), *Winter Trees III* (1953), *Patio with Cloud* (1956), *White Patio with Red Door I* (1960), *Sky Above Clouds IV* (1965), and Black Rock series (1970). ❖ See also Jan Garden Castro, *The Art & Life of Georgia O'Keeffe* (Crown, 1985); Benita Eisler, *O'Keeffe and Stieglitz* (Doubleday, 1991); Charles C. Eldredge, *Georgia O'Keeffe* (Abrams, 1991); Jeffrey Hogrefe, *O'Keeffe* (Bantam, 1992); Sarah W. Peters, *Becoming O'Keeffe* (Abbeville, 1991); Anita Pollitzer, *A Woman on Paper* (Simon & Schuster, 1988); Roxana Robinson, *Georgia O'Keeffe* (Harper & Row, 1989); and *Women in World History*.

O'KELLEY, Mattie Lou (c. 1908–1997). American folk artist. Born in Georgia, c. 1908; died in Decatur, Georgia, July 1997. ❖ Self-taught folk artist, took up her paint brush at age 60 and created a memoir of canvases depicting rural Southern life in early part of 20th century; produced autobiographical paintings with such titles as *Papa Feeding the Stock at 4 a.m., Bringing in the Night Water* and *Mattie in the Morning Glories,* which document the hard work and simple pleasures of her youthful days in Georgia countryside; work is included in a number of museum collections, including American Museum of Folk Art. ❖ See also *Mattie Lou O'Kelley: Folk Artist* (Bulfinch, 1989); and *Women in World History*.

OKIN, Susan Moller (1946–2004). New Zealand-born feminist, educator and philosopher. Born Susan Moller, July 19, 1946, in New Zealand; died Mar 3, 2004, in Cambridge, MA; graduated in history at Auckland University, 1966; Oxford University, MPhil in politics, 1970; Harvard University, PhD in government, 1975; m. Robert Okin (div.); children: Laura and Justin. ❖ Taught at Brandeis University (1975–90), then became a professor of ethics at Stanford University (1990); said to have invented the study of feminist political theory with her book *Women in Western Political Thought* (1979), in which she argued that gender issues belong at the core of political philosophy; also wrote *Justice, Gender and the Family* (1989).

OKINO, Betty (1975—). American gymnast. Name variations: Elizabeth Okino. Born June 4, 1975, in Uganda, Africa; dau. of Ugandan father and Romanian mother. ❖ Placed 2nd all-around at US nationals and Arthur Gander Memorial (1990); won Recontre Beaucaire (1990) and American Cup (1991); at World championships, won a bronze medal for balance beam and silver for team all-around (1991) and silver for uneven bars (1992); at Barcelona Olympics, won a bronze medal in team all-around (1992); began hosting the tv show "Z-Games" for the Disney channel (2000).

OKOH, Ngozi (1909–1995). See Odozi Obodo, Madam.

OKOROKOVA, Antonina (1941—). Soviet track-and-field athlete. Born Mar 27, 1941, in USSR. ❖ At Mexico City Olympics, won a silver medal in the high jump (1968).

OKOYE, Ifeoma. Nigerian novelist, educator and children's writer. Born Anambra State, Eastern Nigeria; studied at University of Nigeria, Nsukka, 1974–77, and Aston University in UK, 1986–87; m. Mokwugo Okoye. ❖ Taught English and mass communications at Nnamdi Azikiwe University in Nigeria; novels for adults include *Behind the Clouds* (1982), *Men Without Ears* (1984), and *Chimere* (1992); children's books include *No School for Eze* (1980) and *The Village Boy* (1981).

OKUNO, Fumiko (1972—). Japanese synchronized swimmer. Born April 14, 1972, in Japan. ❖ At Barcelona Olympics, won a bronze medal in duet and a bronze medal in solo (1992).

OKWEI OF OSOMARI (1872–1943). **Nigerian entrepreneur.** Name variations: Omu Okwei, queen of Osomari or Ossomari; Felicia Ifeoma Ekejiuba or Ekejuba. Pronunciation: Oak-way. Born Felicia Ifeoma Ekejiuba in 1872; died in Onitsha, Nigeria, in 1943; dau. of Prince Osuna Afubeho, of the Ibo tribe, and one of his several wives; never formally educated; m. Joseph Allagoa, 1889 (div. 1890); m. Opene of Abo, 1895; children: (1st m.) Joseph; (2nd m.) Peter. ❖ Trader who created an extensive business network throughout Nigeria and was crowned *omu* (1935), a tribute to her leadership and success; began building a trading network by age 15; was in partnership with mother-in-law, Okwenu Ezewene (1896–1904); became an agent of the Royal Niger Co. (1904); was one of Nigeria's wealthiest women (1920s); crowned Omu (Queen) Okwei of Osomari (1935), a title bestowed on no one else after her death. ❖ See also *Women in World History*.

OLAH, Susanna (d. around 1929). **Hungarian murderer.** Name variations: Aunt Susi. Born in Hungary; executed c. 1929; sister of Lydia Olah. ❖ Chief accomplice of poison merchant Mrs. Julius Fazekas in small village of Nagyrev, was known as Aunt Susi; distributed arsenic obtained by boiling flypaper to women clients who wished to murder their husbands, lovers, and family members (the Fazekas murder ring came to include an estimated 50 poisoners who may have been responsible for as many as 300 murders, 1914–29); was 1 of 26 women tried in Szolnok, and among the 8 who received the death penalty; her sister was also sentenced to death.

OLANDER, Joan (1931—). *See Van Doren, Mamie.*

OLARU, Maria (1982—). **Romanian gymnast.** Born June 4, 1982, in Falticeni, Suceava county, Romania. ❖ At European championships, won a gold medal in team all-around and a silver in vault (1998); won Romanian nationals and Trophee Massilia (1999) and Hungarian International (2000); won gold medal for all-around indiv. at World championships in Tianjin, China (1999), only the 2nd Romanian woman to do so; at Sydney Olympics, won a gold medal for team all-around and a silver medal for indiv. all-around (2000).

OLBERG, Oda (1872–1955). **German-born journalist, feminist, socialist, and political activist.** Name variations: Oda Olberg-Lerda; Gracchus. Born Oda Olberg in Lehe bei Bremerhaven, Germany, Oct 2, 1872; died in Buenos Aires, Argentina, April 11, 1955; married Giovanni Lerda (Italian Socialist), 1897 (died 1927); children: Marcella, Renata, Edgardo, and 1 other son. ❖ One of the 1st professional female journalists in German-speaking Central Europe, contributed to important newspapers and journals of German and Austrian Social Democratic movements, earning a reputation as one of its most talented writers; moved to Italy (1896); became foreign affairs editor of Italian Socialist Party's main organ, *Avanti!*; also contributed to Vienna's *Arbeiter-Zeitung* and Berlin's *Vorwärts*, as well as *Der Kampf, Die Neue Zeit* and *Sozialistische Monatshefte*; published a comprehensive study on Italian Fascism (1923); settled in Vienna (1928), becoming a full-time correspondent for *Arbeiter-Zeitung*; published a study of Nazism (1932); fled to Buenos Aires when Hitler came to power (1934); published in a number of Argentinean journals, including *Critica* and the German-language *Argentinisches Tageblatt*; published articles in influential exile journals abroad, including *Neuer Vorwärts* and *Pariser Tageszeitung* (Paris), *Neue Volks-Zeitung* (NY), *Deutsche Blätter* (Chile), and the scholarly *Zeitschrift für Sozialforschung*; was a founding member of exile organization "Das Andere Deutschland" (The Other Germany, 1937), which became one of the most effective anti-Nazi groups in Latin America, and published articles in its journal (1944–48). ❖ See also *Women in World History*.

OLDENBURG, Alexandra (1844–1925). *See Alexandra of Denmark.*

OLDENBURG, Alexandra (1870–1891). *See Alexandra Oldenburg.*

OLDENBURG, Alexandra (1921–1993). *See Alexandra, Queen of Yugoslavia.*

OLDENBURG, Astrid (1932—). **Norwegian princess.** Name variations: Astrid Ferner. Born Feb 12, 1932, in Oslo, Norway; dau. of Olav V, king of Norway (r. 1957–1991), and Martha of Sweden (1901–1954); sister of Harold or Harald V, king of Norway (r. 1991—); m. John Ferner, Jan 12, 1961; children: Katherine Ferner; Benedikte Ferner; Alexander Ferner; Elizabeth Ferner; Charles Ferner.

OLDENBURG, Cecily (1911–1937). **Sister of England's Prince Philip.** Born June 22, 1911, in Tatoi, near Athens, Greece; died Nov 16, 1937, in Steene, Belgium; dau. of Alice of Battenberg and Prince Andrew of Greece; sister of Prince Philip, duke of Edinburgh (who m. Elizabeth II, queen of England); m. George Donatus of Hesse (1906–1937), Feb 2, 1931; children: Louis of Hesse-Darmstadt (1931–1937); Alexander of Hesse (1933–1937); Joanna of Hesse-Darmstadt (1936–1939). ❖ Was killed in a plane crash while on a flight to England to attend wedding of brother, Prince Philip, to Princess Elizabeth (future Elizabeth II); husband, mother-in-law (Eleanor of Solms-Hohensolms-Lich), and 2 sons were also killed.

OLDENBURG, countess of. *See Hedvig (d. 1436).*

OLDENBURG, duchess of.
See Friederike of Hesse-Cassel (1722–1787).
See Elisabeth of Saxe-Altenburg (1826–1896).
See Sophie Charlotte of Oldenburg (1879–1964).
See Olga Alexandrovna (1882–1960).
See Eilika of Oldenburg (1928—).
See Eilika of Oldenburg (1972—).

OLDENBURG, Ingeborg (1878–1958). *See Ingeborg of Denmark.*

OLDENBURG, Margaret (1895–1992). **Princess of Bourbon-Parma.** Name variations: Margrethe of Denmark; Margrethe Valdemarsdatter. Born Margrethe Françoise on Sept 17, 1895; died 1992; dau. of Valdemar or Waldemar Oldenburg (1858–1939, son of Christian IX of Denmark and admiral of the navy) and Mary Oldenburg (1865–1909); m. René Charles Marie, prince of Bourbon-Parma, June 9, 1921 (died 1962); children: Jacques (b. 1922); Anne of Bourbon-Parma (b. 1923); Michel Marie (b. 1926); Andre (b. 1928).

OLDENBURG, Margaret (1905–1981). **Sister-in-law of Queen Elizabeth II.** Name variations: Princess of Hohenlohe-Langenburg. Born April 18, 1905, in Athens, Greece; died April 24, 1981, in Bad Wiesse, Germany; dau. of Prince Andrew of Greece and Alice of Battenberg (1885–1969); sister of Cicely Oldenburg (1911–1937) and Prince Philip, duke of Edinburgh (who m. Elizabeth II, queen of England); m. Godfrey, 8th prince of Hohenlohe-Langenburg, on April 20, 1931; children: Kraft, 9th prince of Hohenlohe-Langenburg; Beatrice von Hohenlohe-Langenburg (b. 1936); and 4 others.

OLDENBURG, Marina (1906–1968). *See Marina of Greece.*

OLDENBURG, Martha (1971—). **Norwegian princess.** Name variations: Märtha Louise. Born Martha Louise on Sept 22, 1971, in Oslo, Norway; dau. of Harold or Harald V, king of Norway (r. 1991—), and Sonja (b. 1937), queen of Norway; married a commoner, Ari Behn (controversial writer), May 24, 2002; children: Maud Angelica Behn (b. 2003). ❖ Requested the dropping of "royal highness" from her title and cessation of royal allowance so that she might have a more normal life.

OLDENBURG, Mary (1847–1928). *See Marie Feodorovna.*

OLDENBURG, Mary (1865–1909). **Danish princess.** Name variations: Mary d'Orleans; Princess Marie d'Orleans. Born Marie Amelie Francoise Helene, Jan 13, 1865; died Dec 4, 1909, in Copenhagen; dau. of Robert (1840–1910), duke of Chartres, and Françoise d'Orleans (1844–1925); m. Valdemar or Waldemar (son of Christian IX of Denmark and admiral of the navy), on Oct 22, 1885 (died 1939); children: Aage Christian Alexander (b. 1887), count of Rosenborg; Axel Christian George (b. 1888); Erik Frederick (b. 1890), duke of Rosenborg; Viggo Christian (b. 1893); Margaret Oldenburg (1895–1992).

OLDENBURG, Mary (1876–1940). *See Marie.*

OLDENBURG, princess of. *See Amalie (1818–1875).*

OLDENBURG, Olga (1851–1926). *See Olga Constantinovna.*

OLDENBURG, Ragnhild (1930—). **Norwegian princess.** Name variations: Princess Ragnhild; Ragnhild Lorentzen. Born Ragnhild Alexandra Oldenburg on June 9, 1930, in Oslo, Norway; dau. of Olav V, king of Norway (r. 1957–1991), and Martha of Sweden (1901–1954); sister of Harold or Harald V, king of Norway (r. 1991—); m. Erling Lorentzen, on May 15, 1953; children: Haakon (b. 1954); Ingeborg Lorentzen (b. 1959, who m. Paolo Ribeiro); Ragnhild Lorentzen (b. 1968).

OLDENBURG, Sophia (b. 1914). *See Sophia of Greece.*

OLDENBURG, Theodora (1906–1969). *See Theodora Oldenburg.*

OLDENBURG, Thyra (1853–1933). *See Thyra Oldenburg.*

OLDFATHER, Irene (1954—). **Scottish politician.** Born 1954 in Glasgow, Scotland; attended Irvine Academy; married with 2 children.

❖ Elected to North Ayrshire Council (1995); as a Labour candidate, elected to the Scottish Parliment for Cunninghame South (1999).

OLDFIELD, Anne (1683–1730). English actress. Name variations: Mrs. Oldfield; Ann Oldfield. Born in London, England, 1683; died Oct 23, 1730; dau. of a soldier; m. Arthur Mainwaring (1668–1712); m. Charles Churchill, a lieutenant general (died 1745); children: (1st m.) 1 son; (2nd m.) 1 son. ❖ One of the most celebrated actresses of the English stage, appeared at Drury Lane for several years before she was finally recognized for her talent rather than her beauty and elegance; following creation of Lady Betty Modish in Colley Cibber's *Careless Husband* (1704), was generally acknowledged as the best actress of her time; was also lauded for her Lady Townley in Cibber's *Provoked Husband*; excelled as Cleopatra (VII), and also played Calista in Nicholas Rowe's *Fair Penitent* and created title role in his *Tragedy of Jane Shore* (1714). ❖ See also *Memoirs of Mrs. Anne Oldfield* (1741).

OLDFIELD, Pearl Peden (1876–1962). American politician. Born Dec 2, 1876, in Cotton Plant, Arkansas; died April 12, 1962, in Washington, DC; attended Arkansas College in Batesville; m. William Allan Oldfield (10-term US congressional representative, died Nov 19, 1928). ❖ US congressional representative from Arkansas (Jan 9, 1929–Mar 3, 1931), was elected as a Democrat to fill the vacancy, after husband died while in office (1929); represented Arkansas during a period of natural disaster and economic depression, caused in part by the flooding of the Mississippi River (1927); was responsible for sponsoring legislation that maintained federal aid for rehabilitation of farmlands damaged by floods, and worked for approval of a $15 million food appropriation to help reduce malnutrition in drought-stricken areas; chose not to run for reelection.

OLDS, Elizabeth (1896–1991). American artist. Born Dec 1896 in Minneapolis, Minnesota; died Mar 4, 1991; studied at Minneapolis School of Art (1918–20), and under George Luks at Art Students League, NY (1920–23); never married. ❖ The 1st woman awarded a Guggenheim fellowship (1926), studied painting in Europe; returned to US at onset of Depression (1929); settled in Omaha, Nebraska, where she began producing socially conscious works for which she would become known; won critical acclaim for "Stockyard Series" of lithographs; returned to NY (1935), where she worked for the graphics division of Federal Art Project and continued to create lithographs extolling laborers, including *1939 A.D.* and *Scrap Steel* (1935–39); had 1st of many solo exhibitions (1937) at American Contemporary Artists Gallery in NY; became a founding member of Silk Screen Unit of Federal Art Project (1938), a group of artists who transformed the silk-screen process to produce large editions at reasonable prices; created political illustration for *The New Masses* and became a frequent contributor to *The New Republic* and *Fortune* magazines; also wrote and illustrated 6 children's books. ❖ See also *Women in World History*.

O'LEARY, Eileen (c. 1743–c. 1800). See O'Connell, Eileen.

OLENEWA, Maria (1893–1965). Russian ballet dancer and teacher. Born Mar 28, 1893, in Moscow, Russia; died May 15, 1965, in Sao Paulo, Brazil. ❖ Because of Russian Revolution, moved to Paris (1917), where she performed at Théâtre des Champs-Elysées with Maria Kuznetsova's company; toured US and South America with company of Anna Pavlova (1921); danced with Vienna Opera Ballet in Austria; served as director for Leonid Massine's corps de ballet in Buenos Aires, Argentina (1922–24); founded ballet school Teatro Pincipale in Rio de Janeiro and served as ballet master there (1927); worked as head of ballet school in Sao Paolo (c. 1943–57), where she opened her own school (c. 1957); was considered a major influence upon development of ballet training in South America; choreographed numerous works presenting unique style of Spanish dance.

OLENIUC, Elisabeta (1964—). See Lipa, Elisabeta.

OLENKA (1933—). See Savary, Olga.

OLEY, Dinah (fl. 1696). See Nuthead, Dinah.

OLGA. See Variant of Helga.

OLGA (c. 890–969). Russian saint and regent. Name variations: Saint Olga, Ol'ga, or Olha; Helga (Scandinavian); Helen or Helena (baptismal name); Vesheii (wise). Born to a Slavic family c. 890 in Pskov, Russia; died in Kiev, Russia, 969; traditionally believed to be the dau. of a prince from Pskov; m. Igor, grand prince of Kiev (r. 912–945); children: Svyatoslav also known as Sviatoslav I, grand prince of Kiev (r. 962–972); grandchildren: Vladimir, grand prince of Kiev (r. 980–1015).

❖ Earliest female ruler of Russia who became the 1st Russian canonized by the Orthodox Christian Church; following death of husband (945), was elevated to the regency for son Sviatoslav (I), then a minor (945); became the most powerful ruler over the most extensive lands in 10th-century Russia; much wiser than husband, would use the regency to exact vengeance on his murderers, improve revenue collections, strengthen law, convert to Christianity and prepare her son for his eventual inheritance; called *vesheii* (wise) by the Russians, out of admiration for her skillful and shrewd policies, was given a prominent historical place as the 1st famous woman in Russian history. ❖ See also *Women in World History*.

OLGA (1884–1958). Danish royal. Name variations: Olga Guelph. Born Olga Adelaide Louise Mary Alexandrina Agnes on July 11, 1884, in Gmunden, Austria; died Sept 21, 1958, in Gmunden; dau. of Ernest Augustus, 3rd duke of Cumberland and Teviotdale, and Thyra Oldenburg (1853–1933, dau. of Louise of Hesse-Cassel and Christian IX, king of Denmark).

OLGA (1895–1918). Russian grand duchess. Name variations: Olga Nicholaevna. Born Olga Nicholaevna Romanov (Romanoff or Romanovna) on Nov 15, 1895, in St. Petersburg, Russia; executed by the Bolsheviks on July 16–17, 1918, at Ekaterinburg, in Central Russia; dau. of Alexandra Feodorovna (1872–1918) and Nicholas II (tsar of Russia). ❖ See also *Women in World History*.

OLGA, Princess Paley (1865–1929). Russian princess. Name variations: Olga Karnovicova or Karnovich; Princess Paleij. Born Dec 2, 1865; died Sept 2, 1929; dau. of Valerian Karnovich and Olga Meszaros; became morganatic wife of Paul (son of Alexander III, tsar of Russia), on Sept 27, 1902; children: Vladimir Pavlovitch (1897–1918); Natalie Pavlovna (1905–1981), princess Paley; Irene Pavlovna (1908–1990, who m. Theodore Romanov and Hubert de Monbrison), countess Paley. ❖ Paul's 1st wife was Alexandra Oldenburg (1870–1891).

OLGA ALEXANDROVNA (1882–1960). Russian princess and grand duchess. Name variations: Grand Duchess Olga; Olga Romanov or Romanof; duchess of Oldenburg; Olga Koulikovsky. Born June 13, 1882; died Nov 24, 1960; interred in York Cemetery, Toronto, Ontario, Canada; dau. of Marie Feodorovna (1847–1928) and Alexander III (1845–1894), tsar of Russia (r. 1881–1894); sister of Nicholas II, tsar of Russia (r. 1894–1917); m. Peter, duke of Oldenburg, on July 27, 1901 (div. 1916); m. Major Nicholas Alexandrovitch Koulikovsky, on Nov 1, 1916; children: (2nd m.) Tikhon Koulikovsky (b. 1917); Goury Koulikovsky (b. 1919). ❖ See also Ian Vorres, *The Last Grand Duchess: Her Imperial Highness Grand Duchess Olga Alexandrovna* (Scribner, 1965).

OLGA CONSTANTINOVNA (1851–1926). Queen and regent of Greece. Name variations: Konstantinovna; Olga Romanov; Olga of Russia. Born Sept 3, 1851; died June 18, 1926, in Florence, Italy; buried in Tatoi, near Athens, Greece; dau. of Constantine Nicholaevitch (son of Nicholas I, tsar of Russia) and Alexandra of Saxe-Altenburg (1830–1911); m. William of Denmark also known as George I (1845–1913), king of the Hellenes (r. 1863–1913), on Oct 27, 1867; children: Constantine I (1868–1923), king of the Hellenes (r. 1913–1917, 1920–1922); George (1869–1957, who m. Marie Bonaparte); Alexandra Oldenburg (1870–1891); Nicholas (1872–1938); Marie (1876–1940); Olga (1880–1880); Andrew (1882–1944); Christopher (1888–1940).

OLGA FEODOROVNA (1839–1891). See Cecilia of Baden.

OLGA IUREVSKAYA (1873–1925). Countess of Merenberg. Name variations: Olga Yourievsky. Born in 1873 (some sources cite 1874); died Aug 15, 1925; dau. of Ekaterina Dolgorukova (1847–1922) and Alexander II (1818–1881), tsar of Russia (r. 1855–1881); m. George, count of Merenberg, on May 12, 1895; children: George (b. 1897), count of Merenberg; Olga von Merenberg (b. 1898, who m. Michael Tarielovitch, count Loris-Melikoff).

OLGA N (1828–1894). See Engelgardt, Sofia Vladimirovna.

OLGA OF RUSSIA (1822–1892). Queen of Wurttemberg. Name variations: Grand duchess Olga; Olga Romanov. Born August 30, 1822; died Oct 30, 1892; dau. of Nicholas I (1796–1855), tsar of Russia (r. 1825–1855), and Charlotte of Prussia (1798–1860); m. Charles I (1823–1891), king of Wurttemberg (r. 1864–1891), on July 13, 1846.

OLGA OF RUSSIA (1851–1926). See Olga Constantinovna.

OLGA OLDENBURG (1903–1981). Greek princess. Name variations: Princess Olga; Olga of Greece. Born June 11, 1903; dau. of Nicholas of Greece and Helena of Russia (1882–1957); m. Paul Karadjordjevic (Prince Paul, regent of Yugoslavia), on Oct 22, 1923: children: Alexander, crown prince (b. 1924); Nicholas (b. 1928); Elizabeth of Yugoslavia (b. 1936).

OLIN, Lena (1955—). Swedish actress. Born Lena Maria Jonna Olin, Mar 22, 1955, in Stockholm, Sweden; dau. of Stig Olin (actor) and Britta Holmberg (actress); sister of singer Mats Olin; m. Orjan Ramberg (div.); m. Lasse Hallström (film director), 1994; children: (1st m.) August (b. 1986); (2nd m.) Tora (b. 1995). ❖ Began career at the Royal Theatre in Stockholm; made film debut in *Efter repetitionen* (1984, *After the Rehearsal*), directed by Ingmar Bergman; also appeared in *The Unbearable Lightness of Being* (1988), *Out of Africa* (1985), *Havana* (1990) and *Chocolat* (2000), among others; on tv, had recurring role on "Alias" (2001), for which she received an Emmy. Nominated for Academy Award for Best Supporting Actress for *Enemies: A Love Story* (1989).

OLINDA (d. 1708). *See Taylor, Elizabeth.*

OLIPHANT, Betty (1918–2004). English ballet dancer and teacher. Born Nancy Elizabeth Oliphant, Aug 5, 1918, in London, England; died July 12, 2004, in St. Catharines, Ontario, Canada; married and div.; married a Canadian soldier, Frank Grover, 1945; children: Gail Sadova and Carol Roach. ❖ Danced with Ballet Rambert and appeared in numerous West End musicals and Christmas pantomimes; at 18, opened her own studio on Wigmore Street (1936); moved with husband and children to Canada (1947), settling in Toronto; began serving as ballet master of the National Ballet of Canada (1951) and served as its associate artistic director (1969–75); with Celia Franca, also founded the National Ballet School, serving as its director (1959–89); helped reorganize the Royal Danish Ballet School (1978); was a major producer of renowned ballet dancers from Canada, including Veronica Tennant, Martine van Hamel, Karen Kain, Frank Augustyn, Kevin Pugh and Rex Harrington, and such choreographers as James Kudelka and John Alleyne. Made Officer (1973) and Companion (1985) of the Order of Canada. ❖ See also autobiography, *Miss O: My Life in Dance* (1996).

OLIPHANT, Carolina (1766–1845). *See Nairne, Carolina.*

OLIPHANT, Margaret (1828–1897). British novelist and biographer. Name variations: Mrs. Oliphant; Margaret Oliphant Wilson. Born Margaret Oliphant Wilson, April 4, 1828, in Wallyford, Scotland; died June 25, 1897, in Windsor, Berkshire, England; dau. of Francis Wilson (minor customs official) and Margaret (Oliphant) Wilson; m. her cousin Francis Oliphant (artist), 1852 (died 1859); children: Maggie (died 1864); Cyril; Frank; 2 who died in infancy. ❖ Queen Victoria's favorite novelist, authored more than 100 novels, numerous travel books, histories, and biographies, over 50 short stories, and at least 400 periodical essays over span of some 50 years; published 1st novel, *Passages in the Life of Mrs. Margaret Maitland* (1849), at 21; with serial publication of novel *Katie Stewart* (1852), began a long association with *Blackwood's Edinburgh Magazine*; published most successful series, *The Chronicles of Carlingford* in *Blackwood's* (1861–76), and subsequently in novel form as *Salem Chapel* (1863), *The Perpetual Curate* (1864), *Miss Marjoribanks* (1866), and *Phoebe Junior: A Last Chronicle of Carlingford* (1876), a series that focused on the intertwined relationships of English Dissenters in a small town; was praised for her biography, *Life of Edward Irving* (1862), and had a huge success with *The Athelings* (1857), considered the best of her domestic romances; other noted titles were *The Greatest Heiress in England* (1879), *Hester* (1883), *The Ladies Lindores* (1883), *Kirsteen* (1890) and *Sir Robert's Fortune* (1895). ❖ See also *The Days of My Life: An Autobiography* (1857) and *Autobiography and Letters* (1899); and *Women in World History.*

OLIVA, Hortencia Marcari (1959—). *See Marcari Oliva, Hortencia.*

OLIVE, Princess (1772–1834). *See Serres, Olive.*

OLIVE VANCELLS, Nuria (1968—). Spanish field-hockey player. Born Aug 20, 1968, in Spain. ❖ At Barcelona Olympics, won a gold medal in team competition (1992).

OLIVEIRA, Alessandra (1973—). Brazilian basketball player. Name variations: Alessandra Santos de Oliveira. Born Dec 2, 1973, in São Paulo, Brazil. ❖ Center; won a team silver medal at Atlanta Olympics (1996) and a team bronze medal at Sydney Olympics (2000); played for Seattle Storm of the WNBA (2000), then Indiana Fever.

OLIVEIRA, Elisangela (1978—). Brazilian volleyball player. Name variations: Elisangela Almeida de Oliveira. Born Oct 30, 1978, in Londrina, Brazil. ❖ Won a team bronze medal at Sydney Olympics (2000).

OLIVEIRA, Marli de (1935—). Brazilian poet. Born 1935 in Brazil. ❖ Traveled widely in Europe; works include *Cerco da primavera* (1957), *A suave pantera* (1962), *A vida natural/O Sangue na veia* (1967), *Aliança* (1979), and *Retrato/Vertigem/Viagem a Portugal* (1986).

OLIVEIRA, Walewska (1979—). Brazilian volleyball player. Born Oct 1, 1979, in Belo Horizonte, Minas Gerais, Brazil. ❖ Won a team gold medal at Pan American Games (1999); won a team bronze medal at Sydney Olympics (2000).

OLIVEIRA CAMPOS, Narcisa Amalia de (1852–1924). *See Amália, Narcisa.*

OLIVER, Edith (1913–1998). American drama critic. Born in New York, NY, Aug 11, 1913; died at her home in Manhattan, Feb 23, 1998; dau. of Samuel Goldsmith and Maude (Biow) Goldsmith; attended Smith College, 1931–33; never married. ❖ Influential drama critic at *The New Yorker* for over 30 years, began career as a radio actress, working on such shows as "Philip Morris Playhouse" and "Gangbusters"; also wrote radio quiz show "True or False," and wrote and produced "Take It or Leave It: The $64 Question" (1940–52); began contributing to *The New Yorker* (1947) and joined its staff (1961) as a movie and off-Broadway theater critic; spent summers serving as a dramaturg at Eugene O'Neill Theater Center in Waterford, CT; retired from *The New Yorker* (1992). ❖ See also *Women in World History.*

OLIVER, Edna May (1883–1942). American actress. Born Edna May Nutter, Sept 1883, in Malden, Massachusetts; died Nov 9, 1942; educated in Boston; m. D.W. Pratt (div.). ❖ Made a career out of supporting character roles, though she snagged the lead in an occasional low-budget comedy or mystery; on stage, appeared as Parthy Ann in *Showboat* (1927); on film, was particularly adroit with acerbic spinster roles, such as Aunt March in *Little Women* (1933), Aunt Betsey in *David Copperfield* (1935), the Nurse in *Romeo and Juliet*, and the Widow McKlennar in *Drums Along the Mohawk* (1939), for which she received a Best Supporting Actress Academy Award nomination; made last film *Lydia* (1941) just a year before her death; other films include *Manhattan* (1924), *Cimarron* (1931), *Ann Vickers* (1933), *Alice in Wonderland* (1933), *A Tale of Two Cities* (1935), *Parnell* (1937), *Rosalie* (1937), *Little Miss Broadway* (1938), *The Story of Vernon and Irene Castle* (1939), *Nurse Edith Cavell* (1939) and *Pride and Prejudice* (1940).

OLIVER, Mary (1935—). American poet. Born Mary Jane Oliver, 1935, in Cleveland, Ohio; dau. of Edward William Oliver (teacher) and Helen M.V. Oliver; attended Ohio State University; graduate of Vassar College; m. Molly Malone Cook (partner). ❖ Published 1st collection, *No Voyage and Other Poems* (1963); drew on Ohio heritage for *The River Styx and Other Poems* (1972); awarded Pulitzer Prize for *American Primitive* (1983); wrote chapbooks as well, including *Night Traveler* (1978) and *Sleeping in the Forest* (1978); taught at Case Western Reserve (1980s), was poet-in-residence at Bucknell (1986) and Sweet Briar College (1991), and held Catharine Osgood Foster chair at Bennington; won National Book Award for *New and Selected Poems* (1992) and Christopher Award for *House of Light* (1990); published book-length poem, *The Leaf and the Cloud* (2000); additional writings include *Dream Work* (1986), *White Pine* (1994), *West Wind* (1997), *Winter Hours* (1999), *Owls and Other Fantasies: Poems and Essays* (2003), *Why I Wake Early* (2004) and *Long Life: Essays and Other Writings* (2004).

OLIVER, Minnie (1868–1946). *See Fuller, Minnie Rutherford.*

OLIVER, Ruth Law (1887–1970). *See Law, Ruth.*

OLIVER, Susan (1937–1990). American stage, tv and screen actress. Born Charlotte Gercke, Feb 13, 1937, in New York, NY; died May 10, 1990, in Woodland Hills, CA. ❖ Made NY stage debut off-Broadway in *La Ronde*; films include *Up Periscope, The Disorderly Orderly, Butterfield 8, The Gene Krupa Story* and *Change of Mind*; had recurring role on "Peyton Place" and was in original pilot for "Star Trek" (1966); wrote, produced and directed film short *Cowboy-San!*, as well as a 50-minute video, and episodes of "M*A*S*H" and "Trapper John, M.D." As an aviator, won Powder Puff Derby (1970) and attempted to become 1st woman to fly a single-engine plane solo from New York to Moscow (made it to Denmark but was denied permission to cross into Soviet airspace).

OLIVER, Thelma (1941—). American dancer and actress. Born 1941 in Los Angeles, CA; dau. of Cappy Oliver (musician with Lionel Hampton's orchestra). ❖ Trained with Lavinia Williams' folklore school in Haiti; hired by Yma Sumac to tour Soviet Union and South America (1960); upon return to US, moved to New York and appeared as an actress in *The Blacks* (1961), *Fly Blackbird, The Tempest,* and the original production of *Sweet Charity* (1966); appeared in films *The Pawnbroker* (1964) and *Black Like Me* (1964); performed with The Living Premise company, and had a major role in Donald McKayle's *District Storyville.*

OLIVERO, Magda (b. 1910). Italian soprano. Born Mar 25, 1910, in Saluzzo, Piedmont, Italy; studied with Luigi Gerussi, Simonetto and Ghedini; married, June 19, 1941. ❖ A formidable advocate of the verismo style, made debut in Turin (1933), in London at Stoll Theater (1952), and in US (Dallas) as Medea (1967); appeared for 40 years on international opera stages, before making Metropolitan Opera debut at age 60 (1975); made many recordings. ❖ See also *Women in World History.*

OLIVEROS, Pauline (1932—). American composer. Born in Houston, Texas, May 30, 1932; dau. of Edith Gutierrez; studied with Paul Koepke, Robert Erickson and William Palmer. ❖ Received grants to develop a voltage-controlled audio mixer for use in electronic music composition and performance, as well as an electronic environment which also included design sound and light control devices; received a Guggenheim fellowship (1973–74), resulting in the composition of *Crow Two: A Ceremonial Opera;* received the prestigious Beethoven Prize (1977) for her piece *Bonn Feier;* established reputation in avant-garde, electronic, theatrical, and meditation music. ❖ See also *Women in World History.*

OLIVETTE, Nina (c. 1908–1971). American dancer, actress and singer. Born Elizabeth Margaret Veronica Lachmann, c. 1908, in New York, NY; died Feb 21, 1971, in New York, NY; m. Harry Stockwell (singer, 1902–1984); children: stepsons, actors Guy Stockwell (b. 1934) and Dean Stockwell (b. 1936). ❖ Grew up in family of vaudeville and theatrical performers; made theatrical debut at young age in tandem act with Violet Carlsman as Lachmann Sisters; danced in *Frank Fay's Fables* (1922) and appeared in musicals *Sweet Little Devil* (1924) and *Captain Jinks* (1925); later performed as vocalist.

OLIVIA (1830–1910). See *Briggs, Emily Edson.*

OLIVIER, Edith (c. 1879–1948). English novelist and biographer. Born Edith Maud Olivier, c. 1879, in the rectory at Wilton, Wiltshire, England; died May 10, 1948, at home on the earl of Pembroke's estate in Wilton, England; dau. of Dacres Olivier (rector of Wilton and chaplain to earls of Pembroke) and Emma (Eden) Olivier; sister of Henry Eden Olivier (b. 1866, Anglican priest and writer); attended St. Hugh's Hall, Oxford University; never married. ❖ Published 1st novel *The Love Child* (1927), followed by *As Far as Jane's Grandmother's* (1928); during WWI, was an officer in Women's Land Army; also served as mayor of Wilton for several terms; other books include *The Triumphant Footman* (1930), *Dwarf's Blood* (1931) and *Moonrakings* (1930), and 2 biographies: *Mary Magdalen* (1935) and *The Eccentric Life of Alexander Cruden* (1934). ❖ See also autobiography, *Without Knowing Mr. Walkley* (1938).

OLIVIER, Fernande (1884–1966). French artist's model. Name variations: Madame de la Baume. Born Amélie Lang out of wedlock in 1884; died 1966; raised by her mother's half-sister; m. Paul Percheron, c. 1899. ❖ Earned a respectable living as a model, calling herself Madame de la Baume; lived with Pablo Picasso (1905–12), a 7-year relationship that spanned one of Picasso's most creative periods, culminating with his experimentation in Cubism; ran off with an Italian painter named Ubaldo Oppi (1912). ❖ See also memoirs *Picasso and His Friends* (1933) and *Souvenirs Intimes* (1955); and *Loving Picasso: The Private Journal of Fernande Olivier* (2001); and *Women in World History.*

OLIVIER, Lady.
See *Leigh, Vivien (1913–1967).*
See *Plowright, Joan (b. 1929).*

OLIZARENKO, Nadezhda (1953—). Soviet runner. Name variations: Nadyezhda Olizarenko. Born Nov 28, 1953, in USSR. ❖ At Moscow Olympics, won a gold medal in the 800 meters and a bronze medal in the 1,500 meters (1980).

OLKYRN, Iris (1866–1953). See *Milligan, Alice.*

OLLIWIER, Eva (1904–1955). Swedish diver. Born Jan 13, 1904, in Sweden; died Aug 7, 1955. ❖ At Antwerp Olympics, won a bronze medal in platform (1920).

OLMSTEAD, Gertrude (1897–1975). See *Olmsted, Gertrude.*

OLMSTED, Barbara (1959—). Canadian kayaker. Born Aug 17, 1959; Queen's University, BA, BPhe, and BEd; University of Western Ontario, MA. ❖ At Los Angeles Olympics, won a bronze medal in K4 500 meters (1984).

OLMSTED, Gertrude (1897–1975). American actress. Name variations: Gertrude Olmstead. Born Nov 13, 1897 in Chicago, IL; died Jan 18, 1975, in Beverly Hills, CA; m. Robert Z. Leonard (director), 1926 (died 1968). ❖ Won Chicago beauty contest for Hollywood contract (1920); starred opposite Hoot Gibson in 5 westerns; other films include *Ben-Hur, Babbitt, The Torrent, The Callahans and the Murphys, Bringing Up Father* and *Show of Shows;* retired (1927).

OLMSTED, Mildred Scott (1890–1990). American peace activist. Born Mildred Scott, Dec 5, 1890, in Glenolden, PA; died July 2, 1990; attended Friends' Central School; graduate of Smith College, 1912; m. Allen Olmsted, 1921; children: 1; (adopted) 2. ❖ Went to France with YMCA to organize recreation for soldiers at the Sorbonne (1913); joined the German Unit of the American Friends Service Committee in Berlin (1920); became executive secretary of the PA branch of Women's International League for Peace and Freedom (WILPF, 1922), then national secretary (1934–64), with title changed to national executive director (1964–66); was also an early leader in the birth-control movement. ❖ See also Margaret Hope Bacon, *One Woman's Passion for Peace and Freedom* (Syracuse U. Press, 1992).

OLNEY, Violet (1911—). English runner. Born May 22, 1911, in UK. ❖ At Berlin Olympics, won a silver medal in 4 x 100-meter relay (1936).

O'LOUGHLIN, Alice May (1889–1949). See *Parkinson, Alice May.*

OLRICH, April (1931—). English ballet dancer and actress. Born April Penrick, 1931, in Zanzibar, East Africa (now Tanzania); dau. of an English diplomat; studied ballet in Paris with Lubov Tchernicheva and in Buenos Aires with Irina Borowska. ❖ At 13, joined Ballet Russe and danced in *Aurora's Wedding,* and Edward Caton's *Sebastien* and *Cain and Abel;* danced with Sadler's Wells Ballet (1950–54) where she was featured in *Giselle, Swan Lake,* and *The Sleeping Beauty;* danced in West End in Alfred Rodrigues' *Pay the Piper* (1954) and appeared in Shakespearean productions; performed in London (1964) and New York City (1966) with the South African revue *Wait a Minim;* films include *Women without Men* (1956), *Room at the Top* (1959), *The Intelligence Men* (1965), *Hussy* (1980), and *Riding High* (1981); on tv, was in "Princess Daisy" (1983), among others.

OLSEN, Tillie (c. 1912—). American writer. Name variations: Tillie Lerner. Born Tillie Lerner in 1912 or 1913 in Nebraska (neither the date nor the town is documented); dau. of Samuel Lerner (laborer and political activist) and Ida (Beber) Lerner; studied creative writing at San Francisco State College, 1953–54, and Stanford, 1955–56; m. Jack Olsen, 1943 (died 1989); children: Karla (b. 1932); Julie (b. 1938); Katherine Jo (b. 1943); Laurie (b. 1948). ❖ Writer whose fiction and nonfiction speaks for those who are least represented in Western literature and who has, through her writing and life, brought to the reading public hundreds of writers who would otherwise have remained silent or unknown; with family, settled in Omaha (c. 1917); joined Young Communist League (YCL) and was jailed in Kansas City, Kansas, for organizing packinghouse workers (1932); moved to Faribault, Minnesota, to recover from 1st stages of TB; began *Yonnondio* (1932); settled permanently in San Francisco (1933); arrested for taking part in San Francisco Maritime Strike, wrote poetry and reportage for YCL (1934); attended American Writers Congress in NY (1935); spent next 20 years raising 4 daughters, working at a succession of low-paying jobs to help support family, participating in community, union, and political activity, and writing; won O. Henry award for year's best American short story for "Tell Me a Riddle" (1961); worked on recovered manuscript of *Yonnondio* and biographical interpretation of *Life in the Iron Mills* by Rebecca Harding Davis (1972); published *Silences* (1978); was international visiting scholar, Norway; visited Soviet Union and China (1984); also wrote *Mother to Daughter, Daughter to Mother: A Daybook and Reader* (1984). May 18 declared Tillie Olsen Day in San Francisco (1981). ❖ See also Mara Faulkner, *Protest and Possibility in the Writing of Tillie Olsen* (U. Press of Virginia, 1993); Pearlman and Werlock, *Tillie Olsen* (Twayne, 1991); Constance Coiner, *Better Red: The Writing and*

Resistance of Tillie Olsen and Meridel Le Sueur (Oxford U. Press, 1995); Elaine Neil Orr, *Tillie Olsen and a Feminist Spiritual Vision* (U. Press of Mississippi, 1987); and *Women in World History*.

OLSEN, Zoe Ann (1931—). American diver. Name variations: Zoe Ann Olsen-Jensen; Zoe Ann Jensen. Born Feb 11, 1931, in Council Bluffs, IA; m. Jackie Jensen (football player, div. 1963, remarried 1964, div. 1970); children: 3. ❖ Won a silver medal at London Olympics (1948) and a bronze medal at Helsinki Olympics (1952), both in springboard; won AAU indoor 1-meter springboard (1945, 1946, 1947, 1949) and 3-meter springboard (1945, 1948, 1949); won AAU outdoor 3-meter springboard (1946–49) and 1-meter (1948–49).

OLSON, Heather (1975—). *See Pease, Heather.*

OLSON, Leslee (1978—). American snowboarder. Born Mar 14, 1978, in Bend, OR. ❖ Ranked Junior Rider of the Year, Overall (1996); received 2nd-place ISF World Ranking, Overall (1997); placed 2nd at Mt. Baker Banked Slalom, Mt. Baker, WA, in Banked Slalom (1999) and at US Open, Stratton, VT, in Boardercross (2000); won gold in Snowboarder X (Winter 2000) and silver in Boarder X (Winter 1999) at X Games.

OLSON, Maud (1881–1944). *See Nelson, Maud.*

OLSON, Nancy (1928—). American tv and screen actress. Born July 14, 1928, in Milwaukee, WI; m. Alan J. Lerner (songwriter), 1950 (div. 1957); m. Alan Livingston (pres. of Capitol Records); children: (1st m.) Liza and Jennifer Lerner; (2nd m.) Christopher Livinston (director-writer). ❖ Made film debut in *Canadian Pacific*, followed by *Union Station, Force of Arms, Submarine Command, Big Jim McLain, So Big, Battle Cry, Pollyanna, The Absent-Minded Professor, Son of Flubber, Airport* and *Making Love,* among others; on tv, co-starred in "Paper Dolls" (1984). Nominated for Oscar for Best Supporting Actress for *Sunset Boulevard* (1950).

OLSSON, Ann-Margret (1941—). *See Ann-Margret.*

OLSSON, Anna (1964—). Swedish kayaker. Born Mar 14, 1964, in Karlstad, Sweden. ❖ At Los Angeles Olympics, won a gold medal in K2 500 meters and a silver medal in K4 500 meters (1984); at Barcelona Olympics, won a bronze medal in K4 500 meters (1992); won a bronze medal for K4 500 meters at Atlanta Olympics (1996).

OLSSON, Hagar (1893–1978). Finnish poet, essayist and novelist. Born 1893 in Gustavs (Kustavi), Finland; died Feb 21, 1978, in Helsinki; dau. of a Protestant minister; attended Swedish School of Economics, 1913–14, and University of Helsinki; never married. ❖ Introduced modernism and Expressionist drama into Finnish and Swedish literature and theater; works, which focus on young female protagonists and are often heavily experimental, include *Lars Thormann och döden* (Lars Thormann and Death, 1916), *Själarnas ansikten* (The Faces of the Souls, 1917), *Kvinnan och nåden* (Woman and Grace, 1919), the partly autographical novel *Chitambo* (1933), which is now considered a classic, (essays) *Ny generation* (1925), *Lumisota* (1939), *Hurskaat Herjaajat* (1946), *Hemkost* (1961) and *Riddaren och andra berättelser* (1968); was a close friend of Edith Sodergran.

OLTEANU, Ioana (1966—). Romanian rower. Born Feb 25, 1966, in Bucharest, Romania. ❖ At Barcelona Olympics, won a silver medal in coxed eights (1992); won a gold medal at Atlanta Olympics (1996) and a gold medal at Sydney Olympics (2000), both for coxed eights; won World Rowing championships for coxed eights (1993, 1997, 1998, 1999).

OLUKOJU, Fatima. *See Yusuf, Fatima.*

OLUNINA, Alevtina (1930—). Russian cross-country skier. Name variations: Alevtina Olyunina; Alewtina Oljunina; Alevtina Olyunina-Kolchina; Aleftina or Alevtina Kolchina; Alewtina Koltschina or Koltshina or Koltsjina. Born Nov 11, 1930, in USSR. ❖ Won a silver medal for 3 x 5 km at Corina Olympics (1956); won a gold medal for 3 x 5 km relay and a bronze medal for 5 km at Innsbruck Olympics (1964); won bronze medals for 3 x 5 km and 5 km at Grenoble Olympics (1968); won a silver medal for 10 km and a gold medal for 3 x 5 km at Sapporo Olympics (1972).

OLYMPE (c. 1544–c. 1596). *See Estienne, Nicole d'.*

OLYMPIA (39–62 CE). *See Octavia.*

OLYMPIAS (c. 371–316 BCE). Macedonian royal. Name variations: Myrtale; Polyxena; Stratonike. Pronunciation: Oh-LIM-pee-as. Born Polyxena in (or about) 371 BCE, probably at Dodona in Epirus; died at

Pydna in Macedonia in 316 BCE; dau. of King Neoptolemus of Epirus, who died when she was young; raised by his brother, Arybbas; educated as befit a princess: she was literate, versed in politics and economic management, and devoted to esoteric religious rites; married Philip II, king of Macedon, in 357 BCE; children: Alexander III the Great (356–323 BCE), king of Macedon; Cleopatra (b. 354 BCE). ❖ Wife of Philip II of Macedon and mother of Alexander the Great, who pursued dynastic interests through her son and grandson until the struggle to establish the latter as the sole king of an enormous empire prompted enemies to orchestrate her execution; honored with the name "Olympias" by her husband after the twin good fortunes of Alexander's birth and Philip's chariot victory in the Olympic Games (356 BCE); saw relationship with Philip cool (late 330s); suspected of complicity when Philip was assassinated (336 BCE); during son's Asian sojourn (334–323 BCE), helped look after his interests in Europe (where she feuded with Antipater, also appointed by Alexander); after Alexander's death (June 323 BCE), and the posthumous birth of his son, Alexander IV (autumn 323 BCE), championed her grandson's dynastic interests against the rival claims of Philip III (Philip II's son by a different wife); because of resulting conflict, murdered Philip III and his wife, Eurydice (317 BCE); captured by Cassander, son of Antipater and a supporter of Philip III, was judicially executed (316 BCE). ❖ See also *Women in World History*.

OLYMPIAS (c. 365–408). Deaconess in Constantinople. Born c. 365; died 408 in Nicomedia; buried at a monastery on shore of the Bosporus; in early 7th century, remains removed from the original site to the convent she had founded; m. Nebridius (prefect of Constantinople), in 386 (died 386). ❖ Had extensive estates in Thrace, Galacia, Cappadocia, and Bithynia, as well as her property in Constantinople; used her wealth to underwrite a host of Christian causes; was ordained a deaconess and founded a convent in Constantinople (situated near Hagia Sophia) to promote the religiosity of others; when John Chrysostom was exiled from Constantinople for opposing the imperial will, refused to recognize the religious authority of his appointed successor; exiled from the capital to Nicomedia where she eventually died; was later recognized as a saint and her convent in Constantinople continued to flourish until it was physically destroyed during the "Nika" riots of 532. ❖ See also *Women in World History*.

OLYMPIAS (fl. 1st c.). Ancient Greek painter. Would have flourished long before the birth of Pliny the Elder in 23 CE. ❖ Is mentioned at the end of Pliny the Elder's list of women painters in his *Natural History*. ❖ See also *Women in World History*.

O'MALLEY, Grace (c. 1530–1603). Irish shipowner, sea captain and pirate. Name variations: Grainne Ui Mhaille or Mhaol; Grany Imallye; Grana O'Malley; Grany O'Maly; Granuaile or Grania Uaile or Grana Wale; queen of Connaught. Born Grace O'Malley, c. 1530; died, probably at Rockfleet Castle, Co. Mayo, c. 1603; dau. of Owen O'Malley (chieftain of Umhall Uachtarach) and Margaret (dau. of Conchobhar Og Mac Conchobhair mic Maoilseachloinn); m. Donal O'Flaherty, c. 1546 (died c. 1565); m. Richard Burke, c. 1566 (died 1583); children: (1st m.) Owen, Murrough, Margaret; (2nd m.) Tibbot. ❖ As wife of Donal O'Flaherty, was involved in the government of the O'Flaherty territories and commanded the clan's vessels on missions of trade and piracy (c. 1546–65); on O'Flaherty's death, established her headquarters on Clare Island, from which she continued her activities; repulsed an attack on her fortress of Rockfleet (or Carrickahowley) by government forces (1574); met the viceroy, Sir Henry Sidney, to offer her services (1577); captured during a raid on the earl of Desmond's lands, and imprisoned in Limerick and Dublin (c. 1577–78); with 2nd husband, Richard Burke, attended a meeting between Gaelic chiefs and the president of Connaught in Galway (1582); on Burke's death, took possession of Rockfleet, from where she continued her operations (1583); implicated in rebellion on a number of occasions (1586–90); reported to have been involved in piracy off the west coast (1590–91); traveled to London, where she had an audience with, and obtained a pardon from, Queen Elizabeth I (1593); involved in rebellion, but subsequently came to terms with the government (1596–97); her ships intercepted on a raiding mission off the Mayo coast (1601). ❖ See also Anne Chambers, *Granuaile: The Life and Times of Grace O'Malley* (Wolfhound, 1979); and *Women in World History*.

O'MALLEY, Grania (1885–1973). Irish-born actress. Born June 21, 1885, in Ireland; died June 14, 1973, in New York, NY; m. William Dunham. ❖ Performed with husband in vaudeville; made Broadway debut in *Juno and the Paycock* (1940); other plays include *Lily of the Valley, The Snark was a Boojum, Playboy of the Western World, Shadow and Substance* and *Hogan's Goat* (off-Broadway).

O'MALLEY, Mary Dolling (1889–1974). British novelist. Name variations: (pseudonyms) G. Allenby; Ann Bridge. Born Mary Dolling Sanders, Sept 11, 1889, in Hertfordshire, England; died Mar 9, 1974, in Oxford, England; dau. of James Harris Sanders and Mary Louise (Day) Sanders; m. Sir Owen St. Clair O'Malley, 1913; children: 3. ❖ Drew upon travels with diplomat husband for themes and settings of novels, which include *Peking Picnic* (1932), *Enchanter's Nightshade* (1937), *A Place to Stand* (1953), *The Dark Moment* (1961), *The Episode at Toledo* (1966) and *Julia in Ireland* (1973); also wrote account of husband's diplomatic service, *Permission to Resign: Goings On in the Corridors of Power* (1973).

OMAGBEMI, Mary (1968—). *See Onyali, Mary.*

OMAN, Elizabeth (c. 1844–1918). *See Yates, Elizabeth.*

OMAN, Julia Trevelyan (1930–2003). English designer. Name variations: Lady Strong. Born July Trevelyan Oman, July 11, 1930, in Kensington, London, England; died of cancer, Oct 10, 2003, in Herefordshire, England; dau. of Joan Trevelyan and Charles Chichele Oman; attended Royal College of Art; m. Sir Roy Strong (writer, historian and director of Victoria & Albert Museum who was knighted in 1982), 1971. ❖ One of the great theater, tv and film designers, began career as a set designer for BBC-TV (1955–67); came to prominence with her designs for Jonathan Miller's *Alice in Wonderland* (1966) and Frederick Ashton's *Enigma Variations* (1968); a stickler for detail, continued to design for the theater, including *Brief Lives* (1967) and *Merchant of Venice*, for the ballet, including *Swan Lake*, and for the opera at Covent Garden, including *La Bohème* (1974), *Die Fledermaus* and *The Nutcracker* (1984); films include *Charge of the Light Brigade* (1968) and *Straw Dogs* (1971). Made a Commander of the British Empire (1986).

OMBRES, Rossana (1931—). Italian poet and novelist. Born 1931 in Turin, Piedmont, Italy. ❖ Draws on childhood in Piedmont in novels and poetry and often focuses on women's lives; works include *Principessa anche tu* (1956), *Le ciminiere di Casale* (1962), *L'ipotesi di Agar* (1968), *Bestiario d'amore* (1974), *Le belle statuine* (1975), *Memorie di una dilettante* (1977), and *Serenata* (1980).

O'MEARA, Kathleen (1839–1888). Irish novelist and biographer. Name variations: (pseudonym) Grace Ramsay. Born Kathleen O'Meara, 1839, in Dublin, Ireland; died Nov 10, 1888, in Paris, France; dau. of Dennis O'Meara; granddau. of Barry Edward O'Meara (surgeon in the British navy and medical attendant to Napoleon at St. Helena). ❖ At 5, moved to Paris with parents, where she would continue to live; under pseudonym Grace Ramsey, published 1st novel, *A Woman's Trials* (1867); probably best known for novel *Narka: A Story of Russian Life*, as well as *The Bells of the Sanctuary*, which contain sketches of Catholic men and women; was a Paris correspondent to *The Tablet* and frequent contributor to the *Atlantic Monthly*.

O'MEARA, Kathleen (1960—). Irish politician. Born 1960 in Roscrea, Ireland; one of triplet daughters from a family of 6 children; married with 2 children. ❖ Was a freelance journalist, press officer for Labour Party, and worked in the RTE newsroom for 5 years; became special advisor to Eithne Fitzgerald, minister of State (1994); representing the Labour Party for North Tipperary, successfully contested the general election (1997).

OMELENCHUK, Jeanne (1931—). American speedskater and cyclist. Born Jeanne Robinson, Mar 25, 1931, in Detroit, Michigan; graduate of Wayne State University; m. George Omelenchuk (skater and cyclist, div., died 1994); children: Kristin. ❖ Won 10 US and North American speed-skating championships (1957–65); was also a USCF Masters cycling champion. Inducted into Michigan Sports Hall of Fame (1984).

OMELIANCHIK, Oksana (1970—). Soviet gymnast. Born Jan 2, 1970, in Kiev, Ukraine, USSR; m. Boz Mofid (div.). ❖ At European championships, won a gold in beam, silver in floor, and bronze in all-around and uneven bars (1985); won Rome Grand Prix, USSR nationals and World championships (1985); won the World Sports Fair (1986).

OMENS, Estelle (1928–1983). American stage, tv, and screen actress. Born Oct 11, 1928, in Chicago, IL; died Dec 4 (also seen as Dec 5), 1983, in North Hollywood, CA; m. Frank Gregory (writer). ❖ Made NY stage debut in *Summer and Smoke* (1952), followed by *The Grass Harp, Plays for Bleecker Street, Gandhi, Shadow of a Gunman* and *The Watering Place*; made film debut in *The Secret Cinema* (1968); also appeared in *Dog Day Afternoon, Law and Disorder* and *Stir Crazy*.

OMILADE, Navina (1981—). German soccer player. Born Nov 3, 1981, in Germany. ❖ Midfielder, won a team bronze medal at Athens Olympics (2004).

OMLIE, Phoebe Fairgrave (1902–1975). American aviation pioneer. Born Phoebe Jane Fairgrave, Nov 21, 1902, in Des Moines, Iowa; died of lung cancer, July 17, 1975, in Indianapolis, Indiana; dau. of Andrew Fairgrave (saloon keeper) and Madge (Traister) Fairgrave; attended Guy Durrel Dramatic School (St. Paul, Minnesota); m. Vernon Omlie (pilot and flight instructor), Jan 22, 1922 (died 1936). ❖ Set 15,200-foot parachute-jumping record while a member of the Glenn Messer Flying Circus (1921); with husband, opened airport in Memphis, Tennessee (c. 1923); was the 1st woman to be issued a federal pilot's license and 1st woman to receive aircraft and mechanic's licenses (1920s); was the 1st woman to be granted a transport pilot's license by US Department of Commerce (1927); was the 1st woman to complete a Ford National Air Reliability Tour (1928); appointed 1st woman government official in aviation (1933); worked for the Civil Aeronautics Administration (1941–52). ❖ See also *Women in World History*.

OMM SETI or OMM SETY (1904–1981). *See Eady, Dorothy Louise.*

O'MORPHI, Louise (1737–1814). *See O'Murphy, Marie-Louise.*

OMU OKWEI (1872–1943). *See Okwei of Osomari.*

O'MURPHY, Marie-Louise (1737–1814). Mistress of Louis XV. Name variations: Marie Louise Murphy; Louise O'Murphy; Mlle O'Morphi; Morphise. Born in Rouen in 1737; died 1814; dau. of Irish shoemaker; m. Major Beaufranchet d'Ayat, 1755; m. François-Nicolas Le Normant, 1757; m. Louis Philippe Dumont (div. 1799). ❖ Became mistress of Louis XV (1753); was ousted for scheming to supplant Madame de Pompadour. ❖ See also *Women in World History*.

ONASSIS, Christina (1950–1988). Greek heiress. Name variations: Cristina Onassis. Born Dec 11, 1950, in New York, NY; died of an apparent heart attack, Nov 19, 1988, in Buenos Aires, Argentina; dau. of Aristotle Onassis (billionaire shipping tycoon) and Athina (Livanos) Onassis; attended St. George's College, Lausanne, and Queen's College in London; m. Joseph Bolker (realtor), July 26, 1971 (div. 1972); m. Alexander Andreadis (mechanical engineer), July 22, 1975 (div. 1976); m. Sergei Kauzov, Aug 1, 1978 (div. c. 1980); m. Thierry Roussell (businessman), Mar 17, 1984 (div. c. 1987); children: (4th m.) Athina Roussell (b. Jan 29, 1985). ❖ Upon death of father (1975), inherited a large share of the vast Onassis fortune, becoming the richest woman in the world at age 24; quickly showed a good understanding of finance, but lived a life marred by failed marriages, family deaths, and problems with self-image. ❖ See also Nigel Dempster, *Heiress: The Story of Christina Onassis* (Charnwood, 1990); and *Women in World History*.

ONASSIS, Jacqueline (1929–1994). *See Kennedy, Jacqueline.*

ONDIEKI, Lisa (1960—). Australian long-distance runner. Name variations: Lisa Martin. Born Lisa O'Dea, May 12, 1960, in Australia; m. Ken Martin (runner, div.); m. 2nd husband Yobes Ondieki (Kenyan distance runner, div.). ❖ One of Australia's greatest female distance runners, won back-to-back marathon gold medals at Commonwealth Games (1986, 1990); broke the Australian marathon record with a time of 2:23:51 at Osaka (1988); at Seoul Olympics, won a silver medal in the marathon (1988); won NY Marathon (1992) with a time of 2:24.

ONDRA, Anny (1902–1987). Polish-born film actress. Name variations: Ondrakova. Born Anna Sophie Ondrakowa, May 15, 1902, in Tarnow, Poland; died Feb 28, 1987, in Hollenstedt, Germany; m. director Karel Lamac (div. 1933); m. Max Schmeling (boxer), July 6, 1933. ❖ Trained as a dancer, began career in Czech film *Woman with Small Feet* (1919) and quickly gained popularity in both comic and serious roles; during 1920s, formed a production company with director-producer Karel Lamac, whom she also married; made a number of films under his direction, and also gave a memorable performance in Hitchcock's early talkie *Blackmail* (1929), though her heavily accented voice had to be dubbed; made over 35 films. ❖ See also *Women in World History*.

O'NEAL. *Variant of O'Neill.*

O'NEAL, Christine (1949—). American ballet dancer. Born Christine Knoblauch, Feb 25, 1949, in St. Louis, Missouri; ❖ Trained and worked with St. Louis Municipal Theater; joined the National Ballet in Washington, DC, performing in numerous revivals of 19th-century classics; performed with American Ballet Theater in classical works, as well as numerous works by Tudor, creating a role in his *Leaves are Fading*

(1974) and appearing as Hagar in his *Pillar of Fire*; joined touring chamber company—Dancers—where she was featured in Bolender's *The Still Point* and Anderson's *The Entertainers*.

O'NEAL, Peggy (c. 1799–1879). *See Eaton, Peggy.*

O'NEAL, Rose (c. 1817–1864). *See Greenhow, Rose O'Neal.*

O'NEAL, Tatum (1963—). **American actress.** Born Tatum Beatrice O'Neal, Nov 5, 1963, in Los Angeles, CA; dau. of Ryan O'Neal and Joanna Moore (both actors); sister of actor Griffin O'Neal; m. John McEnroe (tennis player), 1986 (div. 1994); children: Kevin, Sean, and Emily. ❖ At 11, won Academy Award for Best Supporting Actress for *Paper Moon* (1974), the youngest person to win in a competitive category; also starred in *The Bad News Bears* (1976), *Nickelodeon* (1976), *International Velvet* (1978), *Little Darlings* (1980), *Prisoners* (1981) and *Woman on the Run: The Lawrencia Bembenek Story* (1993). ❖ See also autobiography, *A Paper Life* (2005).

O'NEAL, Zelma (1903–1989). **American comedic actress, singer and dancer.** Born Zelma Ferne Schrader (also seen as Schroeder), May 28, 1903, in Rock Falls, IL; died Nov 3, 1989, in Largo, FL; m. Raymond Buffington (div.); m. Henry Burns (div.); m. Anthony Bushell (actor, div.); m. Patrick O'Moore. ❖ Made vaudeville debut in a popular sister act with Bernice O'Neal and kept the surname; as Flo in *Good News*, gained fame introducing the Varsity Drag in NY and London (1927); also appeared in *Follow Through* (1929), originating the songs "Button Up Your Overcoat" and *The Gang's All Here* (1931); films include *Give Her a Ring*, *Freedom of the Seas* and *Mister Cinders*.

O'NEALE. *Variant of O'Neill.*

O'NEALE, Lila M. (1886–1948). **American anthropologist.** Name variations: Lila Morris O'Neale; (nickname) Pat O'Neale. Born Lila Morris O'Neale, Nov 2, 1886, in Buxton, ND; died 1948; dau. of Carrie Margery Higgins O'Neale (English teacher) and George Lester O'Neale; attended Leland Stanford Junior University in Palo Alto and State Normal School at San José; Stanford University, AB, 1910; Columbia University Teachers College, BS in household arts; University of California, Berkeley, AM, 1927, PhD, 1930. ❖ Considered the leading expert on prehistoric textiles of Indian Americans during her lifetime, 1st collaborated with Alfred Kroeber at University of California, Berkeley; with Kroeber, began research on pre-Columbian textiles with *Textile Periods in Ancient Peru: 1* (1930); performed fieldwork among basket weavers in northern CA; published dissertation *Yurok-Karok Basket Weavers* (1932); performed fieldwork in Guatemala (1936) and published *Textiles of Highland Guatemala* (1945); served as chair of Decorative Art Department at Berkeley; served as acting curator, and as assistant curator with special responsibilities for textiles, at Museum of Anthropology; had 38-year teaching career.

O'NEALE, Margaret (c. 1799–1879). *See Eaton, Peggy.*

O'NEALE, Pat (1886–1948). *See O'Neale, Lila M.*

O'NEALE, Peggy (c. 1799–1879). *See Eaton, Peggy.*

O'NEIL. *Variant of O'Neill.*

O'NEIL, Barbara (1909–1980). **American stage and screen actress.** Born July 10, 1909, in St. Louis, Missouri; died Sept 3, 1980, in Cos Cob, CT; graduate of Sarah Lawrence College; m. Joshua Logan (playwright-director, 1930s, div.). ❖ Made Broadway debut in *Saint's Parade* (1930), then appeared in *Carry Nation*, *Forsaking All Others*, *Mother Lode*, *Affairs of State*, *Portrait of a Lady*, *The Seagull* and *Little Moon of Alban*, among others; made film debut in *Stella Dallas* (1937), followed by *When Tomorrow Comes*, *Tower of London*, *Shining Victory*, *I Remember Mama*, *Whirlpool*, *Angel Face* and *The Nun's Story*; at age 28, portrayed Ellen O'Hara, Scarlett O'Hara's mother, in *Gone with the Wind*. Nominated for Academy Award for *All This and Heaven Too* (1940).

O'NEIL, Kitty (1947—). **American athlete and stunt performer.** Born 1947 in Corpus Christi, TX; m. Duffy Hambleton (stunt performer). ❖ Held official waterskiing speed record at 104.85 miles per hour (1970); held women's world land speed record (1976); was the only woman in the world deemed qualified for international motorcycle competition (1977); was the 1st woman accepted into Stunts Unlimited, an assemblage of Hollywood's top stunt performers; set records for the longest fall and the highest fall accomplished by a woman while set ablaze (1977); was the only woman to perform the "cannon car rollover" stunt. ❖ See also *Women in World History.*

O'NEIL, Nance (1874–1965). **American stage and screen actress.** Name variations: Nance O'Neill. Born Gertrude Lamson, Oct 8, 1874, in Oakland, CA; died Feb 7, 1965, in Englewood, NJ; m. Alfred Hickman (British actor, died 1931). ❖ Had enormously successful international stage career as a tragedian, most notably in *The Lily* and *The Passion Flower*; other plays include *Hedda Gabler*, *The Jewess*, *Monna Vanna*, *Judith of Bethulia*, *Camille* and *Macbeth*; made film debut (1929); films include *Ladies of Leisure*, *Cimarron*, *The Lady of Scandal*, *Call of the Flesh*, *Westward Passage*, *The Rogue Song* and *Resurrection*.

O'NEIL, Nancy (1911–1995). **Australian actress.** Born Nancy Smith, Aug 25, 1911, in Sydney, Australia; died Mar 5, 1995, in London, England; m. Dermot George Crosbie Trench. ❖ Made stage debut in Salisbury, England, as Sadie in *The Chinese Bungalow* (1931); returned to Australia to tour (1932); made London debut on the variety stage with Donald Calthrop in *The Man in the Street* (1932); also appeared in *Man Proposes*, *Vintage Wine* and *Someone at the Door*; films include *Brewster's Millions*, *Fifty-Shilling Boxer*, *Darts Are Trumps*, *Convoy* and *Solo for Sparrow*.

O'NEIL, Peggy (1898–1960). **Irish actress.** Born June 16, 1898, in Gneeveguilla, Co. Kerry, Ireland; died Jan 7, 1960, in London, England. ❖ Came to America as a child; made stage debut in Chicago in *The Sweetest Girl in Paris* (1910); also appeared there in *Top o' the Morning*, *Mavourneen*, and had enormous success in title role in *Peg o' My Heart*; made NY debut as Maya in *The Flame*, and subsequently appeared in *By Pigeon Post* and *Tumble Inn*; debuted in London as Paddy in *Paddy the Next Best Thing* (1920), which ran over 800 performances; remained in England for rest of career, appearing in numerous productions, including *What Every Woman Knows*, *The Sea Urchin*, *Mercenary Mary* and *First Episode*.

O'NEIL, Sally (1908–1968). **American actress.** Name variations: Sally O'Neill. Born Virginia Louise Concepta Noonan, Oct 23, 1908, in Bayonne, NJ; died June 18, 1968, in Galesburg, IL; dau. of a judge and Hannah Kelly (Metropolitan opera singer); sister of Molly O'Day (1911–1998, actress); m. Stewart S. Battles. ❖ Made film debut at 17 in *Sally, Irene and Mary*; starred in 2nd film *Mike*; appeared in *On with the Show*, the 1st dialogue movie in color; other films include *The Callahans and the Murphys*, *Hardboiled*, *The Battle of the Sexes*, *The Brat*; and title role in *Kathleen Mavourneen*.

O'NEIL, Sue (1911–1998). *See O'Day, Molly.*

O'NEILL, Agnes Boulton (1893–1968). *See Boulton, Agnes.*

O'NEILL, Carlotta (1888–1970). **American actress.** Name variations: acted under Carlotta Monterey. Born Hazel Neilson Tharsing in Oakland, California, Dec 1888; died in New Jersey in 1970; dau. of Christian Neilson Tharsing (fruit farmer) and Nellie (Gotchett) Tharsing; studied at Academy of Dramatic Arts under Sir Herbert Beerbohm Tree; m. John Moffat (lawyer), 1911 (div.); m. Melvin C. Chapman Jr. (law student), 1916 (div. 1923); m. Ralph Barton (caricaturist), 1923 (div. 1926); m. Eugene O'Neill (1885–1953, playwright), July 22, 1929; children: (2nd m.) Cynthia Jane Chapman. ❖ Third wife of Eugene O'Neill who became his secretary and executor, met him when she agreed to take over a role in his play *The Hairy Ape* (1922); had strong influence over the playwright; at time of his death, had full ownership and command of all his work; faded from public scrutiny until her controversial release of the play *Long Day's Journey into Night* (1955), giving the publication rights to Yale University Press. ❖ See also Barbara Gelb (play) *My Gene* (1987); and *Women in World History.*

O'NEILL, Eliza (1791–1872). **Irish actress.** Name variations: Lady Eliza Becher. Born 1791; died Oct 29, 1872; dau. of an actor in Drogheda, Ireland; m. an Irish member of Parliament, William Wrixon (afterwards Baron Becher), in 1819. ❖ Made 1st appearance on stage as a child; later, played in the theaters of Belfast and Dublin; debuted at Covent Garden as Juliet to William Conway's Romeo (1814); was a reigning favorite for 5 years, delighting audiences with comedic portrayals, including Lady Teazle, and causing a sensation when she took on the tragic roles of Belvidera, Mrs. Haller, Mrs. Beverley, and Monimia; had short but brilliant career, retiring at time of marriage. ❖ See also Charles Inigo Jones, *Memoirs of Miss O'Neill; containing her public character, private life and dramatic progress* (1816); and *Women in World History.*

O'NEILL, Jan (1941—). *See Lehane, Jan.*

O'NEILL, Lidia Falcón (1935—). *See Falcón, Lidia.*

O'NEILL, Maire (1885–1952). **Irish actress.** Name variations: Mary Allgood; Molly Allgood or Molly O'Neill. Born Mary Allgood in

Dublin, Ireland, Jan 12, 1885 (some sources cite 1887); died in Basingstoke, Hampshire, England, Nov 2, 1952; dau. of George Allgood (printing compositor) and Margaret Harold Allgood; sister of actress Sara Allgood (1883–1950); m. G.H. Mair (journalist for *Manchester Guardian*), 1911 (died Jan 1926); m. Arthur Sinclair (actor), June 1926 (div.); children: (1st m.) Pegeen and John. ❖ Joined the 1st Abbey Theatre company (1904); as Maire O'Neill, debuted on stage (1905) as a walk-on in Synge's *The Well of the Saints*; created the roles of Cathleen in his *Riders to the Sea*, Nora in his *The Shadow of the Glen*, Pegeen Mike in his *The Playboy of the Western World* (1907), and title part in his *Deirdre of the Sorrows* (1909); remained at Abbey until 1911 and appeared as the Woman in *The Shewing-Up of Blanco Posnet*; on marriage, joined Liverpool Repertory and appeared in *The Shadow of the Glen*, *Hannele* and *Candida*; appeared as Nerissa in Beerbohm Tree's production of *The Merchant of Venice* (1913); made NY debut in *General John Regan* (1914), then returned to Abbey (1916) to play in *Whiteheaded Boy*; with 2nd husband and sister Sara, toured Britain and US regularly in O'Casey's plays. ❖ See also Ann Saddlemyer, ed. *Letters to Molly: John Millington Synge to Maire O'Neill* (Harvard U. Press, 1971); and *Women in World History*.

O'NEILL, Margaret (c. 1799–1879). *See Eaton, Peggy.*

O'NEILL, Moira (c. 1865–1955). *See Skrine, Agnes.*

O'NEILL, Nance (1874–1965). *See O'Neil, Nance.*

O'NEILL, Oona (1925–1991). *See Chaplin, Oona O'Neill.*

O'NEILL, Peggy (c. 1799–1879). *See Eaton, Peggy.*

O'NEILL, Rose Cecil (1874–1944). American artist, illustrator, poet, and novelist. Name variations: Rose O'Neill Latham; Rose O'Neill Wilson; Rosie O'Neill. Born Rose Cecil O'Neill, June 25, 1874, in Wilkes-Barre, Pennsylvania; died April 6, 1944, in Springfield, Missouri; dau. of Alice Asenath Cecelia (Smith) O'Neill and William Patrick O'Neill (book merchant); enrolled at Convent of the Sisters of St. Regis, NY, 1889–96, but followed no formal curriculum; m. Gray Latham, 1892 (div., though some accounts say she was widowed, 1901); m. Harry Leon Wilson, 1902 (div. 1907); children: none. ❖ Best known for her Kewpie dolls, began publishing drawings in such major magazines as *Puck*, *Life* and *Harper's* before age 15; after securing a reputation as an illustrator, wrote 1st novel, *The Loves of Edwy* (1904); created 1st Kewpies (1909), plump cupid figures with small wings, which were an instant hit with Americans just emerging from Victorian Age; obtained a patent on Kewpies (1913) and oversaw the manufacturing of 9 Kewpie dolls in Germany; drew her famed Kewpies as a comic strip for over a quarter of a century, and the dolls she created were a marketing phenomenon that circled the globe; active within the artistic community of New York, also worked avidly in women's suffrage movement, producing posters and drawings for the cause; exhibited a group of drawings at the Galerie Devambez in Paris (1921) and was elected to Société des Beaux Arts. ❖ See also Miriam Formanek-Brunell, *The Story of Rosie O'Neill: An Autobiography* (U. of Missouri Press, 1997); and *Women in World History*.

O'NEILL, Sally (1908–1968). *See O'Neil, Sally.*

O'NEILL, Susie (1973—). Australian swimmer. Name variations: Susan O'Neill. Born Aug 2, 1973, in Mackay, Queensland, Australia. ❖ At Barcelona Olympics, won a bronze medal for 200-meter butterfly (1992); at Commonwealth Games, placed 1st in the 200-meter butterfly (1994, 1998) and 400-meter freestyle (1998); won a gold medal for 200-meter butterfly, silver medal for 4 x 100-meter medley, and bronze medal for 800-meter freestyle relay at Atlanta Olympics (1996); won a gold medal for 200-meter butterfly at World championships (1998); won a gold medal for 200-meter freestyle and silver medals for 200-meter butterfly, 4 x 100 meter medley relay, and 800-meter freestyle relay at Sydney Olympics (2000).

ONETO, Vanina (1973—). Argentinean field-hockey player. Born Vanina Paula Oneto, June 15, 1973, in San Fernando, Argentina; married; children: Maia. ❖ Forward, won a team silver medal at Sydney Olympics (2000) and a team bronze medal at Athens Olympics (2004); won Champions Trophy (2001), World Cup (2002), and Pan American Games (2003); played for the Hertogenbosch Club in the Netherlands.

ONIANS, Edith (1866–1955). Australian social reformer. Born Edith Charlotte Onians, Feb 2, 1866, in Lancefield, Victoria, Australia; died Aug 16, 1955, in Highbury, Australia; dau. of Richard Onians and Charlotte Onians; was boarding student at Fontainebleau Ladies'

College in St. Kilda, Australia; never married. ❖ Devoted to saving teenage boys from poverty and delinquency, began the City Newsboys' Club (1897); studied boys' clubs and children's courts overseas (1901–02, 1911–12); participated in the Imperial Health Conference held in London (1914); wrote a memoir of her work with the Newsboys' Club, *Read All About It* (1914); appointed to board which enforced the Street Trading Act (1926). ❖ See also *Women in World History*.

ONIONS, Mrs. Oliver (1878–1978). *See Ruck, Berta.*

ONISHI, Junko (1974—). Japanese swimmer. Born Oct 18, 1974, in Hyogo, Japan. ❖ Won a bronze medal for 4 x 100-meter medley relay at Sydney Olympics (2000).

ONO, Kiyoko (1936—). Japanese gymnast. Born Feb 4, 1936, in Miyagi, Japan; m. Takashi Ono. ❖ At World championships, won a bronze medal for team all-around (1962); at Tokyo Olympics, won a bronze medal in team all-around (1964).

ONO, Yoko (1933—). Japanese artist and musician. Name variations: Yoko Ono Lennon. Born Feb 18, 1933, in Tokyo, Japan; dau. of Eisuke Ono (banker) and Isoko Yasuda Ono; attended Gakushuin University, 1952–53, 1st woman to be admitted to study philosophy, and Sarah Lawrence College, 1953; m. Toshi Ichiyangi (musician, artist), 1956 (div. 1963); m. Tony Cox (filmmaker), 1963 (div. 1969); m. John Lennon (musician), 1969 (murdered 1980); children: (2nd m.) Kyoko Chan Cox; (3rd. m.) Sean Lennon (musician). ❖ Avant-garde artist, received training in classical music, German lieder and Italian opera and spent some of childhood in US; moved to US (1953); became part of movement that mixed poetry, music and visual art in installations and "happenings"; staged series of concerts and performance events with Toshi Ichiyangi at venues throughout NY, including Carnegie Recital Hall (1961); collaborated and toured with John Cage (1962); married Ichiyangi (1956) and moved back to Tokyo (1962); as marriage disintegrated, attempted suicide, and returned to NY with filmmaker Tony Cox; developed and collected conceptual art projects in book *Grapefruit* (1964); joined colleagues in movement Fluxus; gave 2nd performance at Carnegie Recital Hall, *Cut Piece* (1965); with Cox, opened conceptual art gallery, IsReal Gallery (1965); received raves for work presented in London's Destruction in Art Symposium (1966), leading to show at Indica Gallery which featured *Box of Smile*; met John Lennon (1967) and recorded controversial *Two Virgins* with him (1968); blamed for break-up of Beatles, married Lennon (1969), became involved in peace movement, engaged in series of "Bed-ins," and recorded with Lennon *Give Peace a Chance* (1969); formed Plastic Ono Band and produced recordings, solo and with Lennon, including *Life with the Lions* (1969), *Wedding Album* (1969), *Live Peace in Toronto* (1969), *Some Time in New York City* (1972), *Yoko Ono/Plastic Ono Band* (1970), *Fly* (1971), *Approximately Infinite Universe* (1973), and *Double Fantasy* (1980), which won Grammy for Album of the Year (1981); following assassination of Lennon (1980), recorded *Season of Glass* (1981); had retrospective at Whitney Museum (1989) and release of *Onobox* (1992); other albums include *Milk and Honey* (1984), *Live in New York City* (1986), *Starpeace* (1985), *Walking on Thin Ice* (1992) and *Rising* (1996). ❖ See also Clayson, Jungr, Johnson, *Woman: The Incredible Life of Yoko Ono* (Chrome Dreams, 2004).

ONODI, Henrietta (1974—). Hungarian gymnast. Name variations: Henrietta Ónodi. Born May 22, 1974, in Bekescsaba, Hungary. ❖ Won Catania Cup (1988), DTB Cup and Hungarian nationals (1989), Grand Prix (1990), Chunichi Cup (1991), and Cottbus and Hungarian International (1992); at European championships, won a gold medal in uneven bars and bronze in floor exercises (1989) and a bronze in all-around and floor exercises (1990); at World championships, won a silver for vault (1991) and a gold for vault and silver for floor exercises (1992); at Barcelona Olympics, won a gold medal in vault and a silver medal in floor exercises (1992); moved to US.

ONO NO KOMACHI (c. 830–?). Japanese poet. Pronunciation: Owe-noh noh Koe-ma-chee. Born probably between 830 and 835; location not known. ❖ One of her nation's most celebrated poets, was a lady-in-waiting in the imperial capital (850–59); wrote love poems, more than 100 of which were preserved in imperial anthologies. ❖ See also Jane Hirshfield with Mariko Aratani, trans. *The Ink Dark Moon: Love Poems by Ono no Komachi and Izumi Shikibu* (Scribner, 1988), and *Women in World History*.

ONOPRIENKO, Galina (1963—). Soviet handball player. Born Feb 2, 1963, in USSR. ❖ At Barcelona Olympics, won a bronze medal in team competition (1992).

ONSHI (872–907). Empress of Japan. Born 872; died 907; consort of Emperor Uda (867–945); sister of Fujiwara no Nakahira (875–945).

ONYALI, Mary (1968—). Nigerian runner. Name variations: Mary Onyali-Omagbemi. Born Feb 3, 1968, in Nigeria; attended Texas Southern University (1985–90). ❖ Known as the "Queen of Nigerian Sprints," won silver medals in both 100 and 200 meters at World Cup (1990); at African Games, won the 100 meters (1987, 1991, 1998) and 200 meters (1987); won a bronze medal in 4 x 100-meter relay at Barcelona Olympics (1992) and a bronze medal for the 200 meters at Atlanta Olympics (1996).

ONYANGO, Grace (1934—). Kenyan politician. Name variations: Grace Aktech Onyango. Born 1934 in Gobei, Kenya; married. ❖ Elected chair of the education committee of Kisumu; served as mayor of Kisumu (1961–69), Kenya's first African woman mayor; was the 1st woman to be elected to the Kenyan Parliament (1969), serving as deputy speaker of the National Assembly (1979–84).

OOMEN-RUIJTEN, Ria G. H. C. (1950—). Dutch politician. Born Sept 6, 1950, in Echt, Netherlands. ❖ Member of the CDA (Christian Democrats) Parliamentary Party Executive (1981–89); as a member of the European People's Party (Christian Democrats) and European Democrats (EPP), elected to 4th and 5th European Parliament (1994–99, 1999–2004); named vice-chair for relations with South Africa. Awarded Knight of the Order of the Netherlands Lion (1994).

OOSTERWYCK, Maria van (1630–1693). Dutch painter. Name variations: Oosterwijk. Born Aug 20, 1630, in Nootdorp, near Delft, Holland, the Netherlands; died in Dec 1693, near Uitdam; dau. of a Dutch Protestant minister; never married. ❖ Painter of flower pieces and still lifes, had an international reputation and the patronage of France's Louis XIV, Holy Roman Emperor Leopold I, Stadholder William III (later king of England), and the king of Poland; at 38, painted *Vanitas*, considered her masterpiece; other works include *Vase of Tulips, Roses, and Other Flowers with Insects* (1669); though only 2 dozen extant works are credited to her, possibly did other misattributed paintings. ❖ See also *Women in World History*.

OPAL. See Smith, Kendra.

OPALS (1874–1944). See Custance, Olive.

OPARA, Charity (1972—). Nigerian runner. Born May 20, 1972, in Lagos, Nigeria. ❖ Won a silver medal for the 4 x 400-meter relay at Atlanta Olympics (1996).

OPARA-THOMPSON, Christy (1971—). Nigerian runner. Name variations: Christy Opara. Born Dec 24, 1971, in Nigeria. ❖ At Barcelona Olympics, won a bronze medal in the 4 x 100-meter relay (1992).

OPDYKE, Irene (1918–2003). Polish hero. Born Irene Gut, May 5, 1918, in Kozienice, Poland, into a Catholic family; died May 17, 2003, in Los Angeles, CA; m. William Opdyke (United Nations worker), 1956; children: Jean Smith. ❖ Was a nursing student when Germany invaded Poland (1939); joined a Polish army unit, was captured and forced to work at a munitions factory in Ternopol; at 25, became a housekeeper for a German major there; on hearing about an intended Gestapo sweep through a local Jewish ghetto, smuggled some Jews to a nearby forest and hid 12 Jews in a cellar beneath the major's villa; when he discovered them, became his mistress to protect them further (all the Jews survived); after the war, moved to US (1948), then married an American; became a well-known speaker. ❖ See also memoir, *In My Hands: Memories of a Holocaust Rescuer.*

OPIE, Amelia (1769–1853). English writer. Born Amelia Alderson, Nov 12, 1769, in Norwich, England; died Dec 2, 1853, in Norwich; dau. of James Alderson (physician) and Amelia (Briggs) Alderson; m. John Opie (painter), May 8, 1798 (died 1807); no children. ❖ Popular and prolific writer, who numbered among her friends Thomas Holcroft, William Godwin, Mary Wollstonecraft, Germaine de Staël, William Wordsworth, Walter Scott, Elizabeth Inchbald, Richard Brinsley Sheridan, and Sarah Siddons, anonymously published 1st novel, *The Dangers of Coquetry* (1790); established reputation as a writer with *The Father and Daughter* (1801), which achieved significant popularity; released a volume of poetry (1802); published the immensely successful *Adeline Mowbray; or, The Mother and Daughter* (1805) and the short

stories, *Tales of Real Life* (1813); began to show an increasing interest in Quakerism (1814), which seems to have precipitated a decline in the quality of her work, including the short-story collections *New Tales* (1818) and *Tales of the Heart* (1820), though her final novel, *Madeline* (1822), received good notices; formally joined Society of Friends (1825), and gave up writing fiction; focused energies on philanthropy and instructive tracts, including *Illustrations of Lying, in All Its Branches* (1825) and *Detraction Displayed* (1828), as well as pamphlets and essays decrying the evils of slavery. ❖ See also *Women in World History.*

OPIE, Iona (1923—). British author and authority on children's literature and lore. Born Iona Archibald, Oct 13, 1923, in Colchester, England; dau. of Sir Robert George Archibald (pathologist) and Olive (Cant) Archibald; m. Peter Opie (author and folklorist), Sept 2, 1943 (died Feb 5, 1982); children: James, Robert and Letitia Opie. ❖ With husband, began a collaborative project on origins of nursery rhymes that would occupy them for next 40 years (1943); published *Oxford Dictionary of Nursery Rhymes* (1951), followed by *The Oxford Nursery Rhyme Book* (1955) and *The Lore and Language of Schoolchildren* (1959); served as author and host of a series, *The Lore and Language of Schoolchildren*, on the BBC; also collected children's books, comics, toys, games and educational aids; following husband's death (1982), donated more than 20,000 vols. of children's books to Bodleian Library; published *The Treasures of Childhood: Books, Toys and Games from the Opie Collection* (1989). Joint winner with husband of Coote Lake Research Medal (1960), European Prize of City of Caorle (Italy, 1964), and Chicago Folklore Prize (1970); was May Hill Arbuthnot Lecturer (1991). ❖ See also *Women in World History.*

OPITZ, Martina (1960—). See Hellmann-Opitz, Martina.

OPORTO, duchess of. See Hayes, Nevada (1885–1941).

OPPELT, Britta (1978—). German rower. Born July 5, 1978, in Berlin, Germany. ❖ At World championships, placed 2nd for double sculls (2003); won a silver medal for double sculls at Athens Olympics (2004).

OPPENHEIM, Méret (1913–1985). Swiss-German painter and sculptor. Name variations: Meret Oppenheim. Born in Berlin-Charlottenburg in 1913; died in Switzerland, 1985 (some sources cite 1986); studied briefly at Académie de la Grande Chaumière. ❖ Grew up in Switzerland; at 19, moved to Paris, where she participated in Surrealist meetings and group exhibitions and for a time was romantically linked to Max Ernst; also modeled nude for photographer Man Ray; displayed a series of woodcuts and paintings at Surrealist Exhibition and had 1st solo show, at Galerie Schulthess in Basle (1933); best known for creating household objects out of unexpected materials, including *Fur-Covered Cup, Saucer, and Spoon* which caused a sensation at International Surrealist Exhibit in London (1936), and is still considered a quintessential symbol of Surrealism (now owned by MoMA); saw a major retrospective of her work at Moderna Museet in Stockholm (1967), by which time her reputation in Europe was again secure. The 1st major museum exhibition of her work in US was held at Guggenheim Museum in NY (1996). ❖ See also *Women in World History.*

OPPENHEIMER, Jane Marion (1911–1996). American biologist and educator. Born Jane Marion Oppenheimer, Sept 19, 1911, in Philadelphia, Pennsylvania; died Mar 19, 1996, in Philadelphia; dau. of James Harry Oppenheimer and Sylvia (Stern) Oppenheimer; Bryn Mawr, BA, 1932; Yale University, PhD in zoology, 1936. ❖ Best known for her experiments studying the effects of weightlessness on fish embryos, also had a keen interest in the historical aspects of biology and wrote several articles and books on the subject; began teaching at Bryn Mawr (1942), as professor and researcher, and would remain there for her entire career, retiring as the Kenan Professor Emeritus of Biology and History of Science (1980); elected to American Academy of Arts and Sciences (1992). Won several awards for her research, including, among others, the Wilbur Cross Medal from Yale Graduate Alumni Association; also given the National Aeronautics and Space Administration's Achievement Award and Soviet Kosmos Award (both 1975). ❖ See also *Women in World History.*

OPPENS, Ursula (1944—). American pianist. Born 1944 in New York, NY; dau. of Kurt Oppens (writer) and Edith Oppens (classical pianist); received undergraduate degree from Radcliffe College and graduate degree from Juilliard School of Music; studied under Rosina Lhévinne, Leonard Shure and Guido Agosti; lived with Julius Hemphill (jazz musician and composer, died 1995). ❖ Champion of modern composers and accomplished classical pianist, won Busoni International Piano

Competition (1969), launching professional career; was a founder, with cellist Fred Sherry and percussionist Richard Fitz, of Speculum Musicae (early 1970s); premiered or commissioned works by Elliott Carter (joint commission for *Night Fantasies*), Tobias Picker (*Old and Lost Rivers*), Frederic Rzewski (premiere of *The People United Will Never Be Defeated*, which she also recorded), Joan Tower, Julius Hemphill, Wuorinen (*The Blue Bamboula*), Anthony Davis (*Middle Passage*), Conlon Nancarrow (*Two Canons for Ursula*), Lois Vierk, and John Harbison (Piano Sonata No. 1); with Arditti String Quartet, premiered Elliott Carter's Piano Quintet (1998–99). ❖ See also *Women in World History*.

ORAIB (797–890). Arabian singer. Name variations: Oreib; Uraib; Arib. Born in Baghdad (present-day Iraq), 797; died in July or Aug, 890; illeg. dau. of Garaf ibn Yahya al-Barmaki, also seen as Jafar ibn Yahya al-Barmaki (husband of Abassa). ❖ One of the Arab world's greatest singers, was born into an influential family but later sold into slavery; came into the hands of Abdallah ibn Ismail al-Marakibi, who took her to Basra (now Iraq) to be educated; learned calligraphy, grammar, poetry, singing, and playing the lute; brought to court of al-Amin, remaining there until his murder (812); forcefully reclaimed by al-Marakibi but escaped; confined to the royal harem by the new caliph, al-Mamun (r. 813–833); eventually freed, established a singing school and became a wealthy woman; had great influence over al-Mutawakki who succeeded to the throne (847); became the foremost singer of classical music, a school of Arabian music led by Ibrahim al-Mausuli (d. 804) and his son Ishaq (d. 850); continued to sing at court of al-Mutazz, who ordered music theoretician Yahya Ibn Ali to make a collection of her songs; lived into her 90s, surviving 10 caliphs; following her death, her songs were performed for centuries. ❖ See also *Women in World History*.

O'RANE, Patricia (1901–1985). *See Dark, Eleanor.*

ORANGE, princess of.
See Catherine of Brittany (1428–c. 1476).
See Jeanne of Bourbon (d. 1493).
See Anna of Saxony (1544–1577).
See Coligny, Louise de (1555–1620).
See Amelia of Solms (1602–1675).
See Mary of Orange (1631–1660).
See Albertina Agnes (d. 1696).
See Anne (1709–1759).
See Wilhelmina of Prussia (1751–1820).

ORANTES, Ana (c. 1937–1997). Spanish housewife. Born c. 1937; died in Granada, Spain, Dec 17, 1997; m. Jose Parejo (div.). ❖ At 60, discussed on a tv talk show the physical abuse she had suffered for 20 years at the hands of then ex-husband (Dec 4, 1997); was set on fire by him and killed (Dec 17), causing a review and revision of domestic-violence laws in Spain which at that time favored abusers. ❖ See also *Women in World History*.

ORBAN, Olga (1938—). *See Szabo-Orban, Olga.*

ORBELL, Margaret (1934—). New Zealand translator. Born 1934 in Auckland, New Zealand; m. Gordon Walters, 1963. ❖ Trained as anthropologist but began translating Maori folktales, songs, and poetry; became leading proponent of development of Maori literature, teaching at Auckland and University of Canterbury; edited *Maori: Folktales* (1968), *Contemporary Maori Writing* (1970), *Traditional Songs of the Maori* (1975), *Maori Poetry: An Introductory Anthology* (1978), and *Traditional Maori Stories* (1992); wrote *Birds of Aotearoa: A Natural and Cultural History* (2003).

ORCHARD, Sadie (c. 1853–1943). English-born stage-coach driver. Name variations: Sadie Creek Orchard; Cockney Sadie Orchard. Born c. 1853 in London, England; died 1943 in Hillsboro, NM. ❖ Moved to Kingston, a mining town in Black Range District in Sierra County, NM (1886); with husband, operated the Kingston State and Express line for 14 years; was also said to have run a brothel on Virtue Avenue and used the profits to build the 1st church in Kingston; became owner of the Orchard Hotel in Hillsboro, NM.

ORCOYEN TORMO, Cristina (1948—). *See García-Orcoyen Tormo, Cristina.*

ORCUTT, Edith (c. 1918–1973). American modern dancer. Born c. 1918; died Mar 25, 1973, in New York, NY. ❖ Trained at studio of Doris Humphrey and Charles Weidman; joined Humphrey/Weidman concert group, creating roles for Humphrey's *New Dance* (1935), *With My Red Fires* (1936), *Theater Piece* (1936) and *Race of Life*

(1938), and for Weidman's *Quest* (1937) and *The Happy Hypocrite* (1938); remained with Humphrey/Weidman until she retired (1940s).

ORCUTT, Maureen (b. 1907). American golfer and writer. Name variations: Mrs. J.D. Crews. Born April 1, 1907, in New York, NY; dau. of a journalist; sister of William and Sinclair Orcutt, both golfers; m. J.D. Crews. ❖ Won over 65 championships during long career, though the National Golf championship continually eluded her; won Metropolitan Junior (1922, 1924); won 3 North and South championships, 7 Women's Easterns, 10 New Jersey Women's 54-Hole Medal titles, and 6 New Jersey State championships; beat Helen Hicks on 19th hole to win Flagler gold trophy in Florida East Coast championship (1934); won Canadian Women's Amateur; came in 2nd in USGA Women's Amateur (1927); was a member of Curtis Cup team (1922, 1934, 1936, and 1938); won 2 USGA Women's Senior championships (1962, 1966, 2002), 3 North and South Seniors, and 6 Metropolitan Women's Seniors; was on sports staff for *The New York Times* (1927–72). Elected to the Ladies' PGA Hall of Fame (1966); received Tanqueray Award (1969), honoring her 50 years in golf. ❖ See also *Women in World History*.

ORCZY, Emma (1865–1947). Hungarian-born English author. Name variations: Emmuska Orczy; Baroness Orczy. Born Emmuska Magdalena Rosalia Maria Josefa Barbara Orczy, Sept 23, 1865, in Tarna-Örs, Hungary; died Nov 12, 1947, in London, England; dau. of Baron Felix Orczy (gifted amateur composer) and Countess Emmuska Wass; studied music at schools in Brussels and Paris and painting at West London School of Art and at Heatherley's; m. Montagu Barstow (illustrator), 1894 (died 1943); children: John Montagu Orczy Barstow (b. 1899). ❖ Settled in London with family (1880s); in collaboration with husband, translated and illustrated fairy tales; published 1st novel, *The Emperor's Candlesticks* (1899), to little fanfare, followed by the widely successful *The Scarlet Pimpernel* (1905), which inspired 5 films and would be translated into at least 20 languages; from that point on, wrote prolifically, including sequels to her most famous book, as well as other adventure stories and romances; also created Irish lawyer Patrick Mulligan for a collection of detective stories, *Skin o' My Tooth* (1928) and the 1st fictional woman detective in *Lady Molly of Scotland Yard* (1910), a series of 12 tales. ❖ See also *Women in World History*.

ORDONÓWNA, Hanka (1904–1950). Polish actress and singer. Name variations: Hanka Ordonka; Hanka Ordonowna; Maria Anna Tyszkiewiczowa; Marysia Pietruszynska; Maria Anna Pietruszkich. Born Maria Anna Pietruszynska in Warsaw, Russian Poland, Aug 11, 1904; died in Beirut, Lebanon, Sept 2, 1950; m. Count Michael Tyszkiewicz. ❖ Enormously popular cabaret and film star of interwar Poland, starred at Warsaw's Qui Pro Quo (1926–31), a 500-seat cabaret that showcased the nation's most talented performers; made film debut in *Orle* (*The Eaglet*, 1926); made 1st solo tour of Europe, giving acclaimed performances in Berlin, Vienna and Paris; starred in film *Szpieg w Masce* (The Masked Spy), singing her trademark tune, "Love Forgives Everything" (1933); made stage debut in a play directed by Juliusz Osterwa, *Wieczór Trzech Króli* (Night of the Three Kings), and then played opposite him in the comedy *Teoria Einsteina* (Einstein's Theory); starred in revue *Frontem do Radosci* (A Smiling Face, 1936); made a month-long tour of US (1938), appearing in NY and other cities with large Polish-speaking populations; with German occupation of Poland (1939), fled to husband's family estate outside Wilno; invited to perform in Moscow (1940), attempted to establish contact with husband who had been arrested by Soviet NKVD; was arrested and sent to a labor camp in Uzbekistan; became part of an exodus of Poles from Soviet Union to Middle East (1942) and was reunited with husband; settled in Beirut; contracted typhus and died. ❖ See also *Women in World History*.

ORDWAY, Katharine (1899–1979). American biologist, art collector and conservationist. Born April 3, 1899; died June 27, 1979, in Weston, CT. ❖ Heiress to the 3M fortune, set out to preserve tallgrass prairies; established the Goodhill foundation (1959); was benefactor to 54,000 acres of grassland in 5 midwestern states, the largest private prairie-sanctuary system in the world; donated $64 million to conservation causes; her contributions to the Nature Conservancy served to make the group a major force in land preservation.

O'REGAN, Katherine (1946—). New Zealand politician. Born Katherine Newton, May 24, 1946; m. Neil O'Regan, 1968 (div.); m. Michael Cox (MP), 1992; children: (1st m.) two. ❖ Served as Marilyn Waring's electorate assistant; elected National MP for Waipa (1984), becoming minister of Consumer Affairs and associate minister of Women's Affairs and of Health, outside Cabinet (1990); was an MP for 15 years, stepping down from party politics (2000).

OREIB (797–890). *See Oraib.*

O'REILLY, Heather (1985—). American soccer player. Born Jan 2, 1985, in New Brunswick, NJ; attended University of North Carolina. ❖ Forward, headed Soccer America's College Women's All-American team (2003); won a team gold medal at Athens Olympics (2004).

O'REILLY, Leonora (1870–1927). American labor leader and suffragist. Name variations: Nora. Born Feb 16, 1870, in New Yorkm NY; died at home in Brooklyn, NY, April 3, 1927; dau. of John O'Reilly (printer and grocer) and Winifred (Rooney) O'Reilly (garment worker); graduate of Pratt Institute, 1900; never married; children: Alice (adopted 1907, died 1911). ❖ Advocate of vocational training for women and an early leader of the Women's Trade Union League, who struggled for many years, seeking a balance between feminism and labor politics; started work at 11 in a collar factory (1881); inducted into Knights of Labor (1886); formed Working Women's Society (1886); joined Synthetic Circle (1888) and Social Reform Club (1894); organized a women's local for United Garment Workers Union (1897); was a founder of National Women's Trade Union League (1903) and a member of its executive committee (1903–15); was a founding member of New York Women's Trade Union League (1904); was a founder of the group that became the National Association for the Advancement of Colored People (1909); joined Socialist Party (1910); appointed chair of industrial committee of NYC Woman Suffrage party (1912); was a trade union delegate to International Congress of Women (1915) and International Congress of Working Women (1919); a powerful orator, could move an audience with plain talk about the conditions women faced as industrial workers. ❖ See also *Women in World History.*

ORELLI, Susanna (1845–1939). Swiss social reformer. Name variations: Susanna Orelli-Rinderknecht. Born Susanna Rinderknecht, Dec 27, 1845, in Oberstrass, Canton Zurich, Switzerland; died in Zurich, Jan 12, 1939; sister of Caroline Rinderknecht; m. Johannes Orelli; no children. ❖ Founder-leader of the Frauenverein für Mässigkeit und Volkswohl (Women's Union for Temperance and Social Advancement), who emphasized the creation of alternatives to taverns and restaurants that served alcoholic beverages; when public drunkenness became a major problem in Zurich, inaugurated a non-alcoholic restaurant, Karl der Grosse, universally called "der Karli" (1898), which was a success from the 1st day; opened the Frauenverein spa hotel (Kurhaus, 1900), another resounding success; as president of the Zürcher Frauenverein (1918–21), could point to 13 successful restaurants that the organization ran in Zurich. A number of the non-alcoholic restaurants are still in existence, including the Rütli on the Zähringerstrasse, the venerable Karl der Grosse, the Seidenhof and Olivenbaum, and the Kurhaus Zürichberg overlooking the city. ❖ See also *Women in World History.*

OREMANS, Miriam (1972—). Dutch tennis player. Born Sept 9, 1972, in Bercilum, Netherlands. ❖ Turned pro (1989); won a silver medal for singles at Sydney Olympics (2000).

ORENBURGSKAIA, Gloria Guseva- (c. 1870–1942). *See Mamoshina, Glafira Adolfovna.*

ORGAN, Diana (1952—). English politician. Born Diana Mary Pugh, Feb 21, 1952; m. Richard Thomas Organ, 1975. ❖ Contested Somerset and Dorset West (1989) for European Parliament election; representing Labour, elected to House of Commons for Forest of Dean (1997, 2001), left Parliament (2005).

ORGENI, Aglaja (1841–1926). Hungarian coloratura opera singer and teacher. Name variations: Anna Maria Aglaia Orgeni or Orgenyi. Born Dec 17, 1841, in Tismenice, Galicia; died in Vienna, Austria, Mar 15, 1926; pupil of Pauline Viardot. ❖ Made debut at Berlin Opera (1865); became teacher in Dresden Conservatory (1886).

ORIEL (1920–2003). *See Gray, Oriel.*

ORINDA (1631–1664). *See Philips, Katherine.*

ORKIN, Ruth (1921–1985). American photojournalist and filmmaker. Born Ruth Orkin in Boston, Massachusetts, Sept 3, 1921; died of cancer in New York, NY, Jan 18, 1985; dau. of Sam Orkin (businessman) and Mary Ruby Orkin (actress); m. Morris Engel, 1945; children: Andy Engel (b. 1959); Mary Engel (b. 1961). ❖ One of the most successful photojournalists of her time, photographed a wide variety of subjects— from Hollywood starlets to classical musicians to people on the street;

moved to California with family (1924); received 1st camera, a 39c Univex (1931); had 1st photo exhibit, at Eagle Rock camera store (1939); moved to NY and purchased 1st 35mm camera (1943); photographed classical musicians at Tanglewood Music Festival (1946–50); photographed her famous 6-picture sequence, "The Cardplayers" (1947); traveled with Israeli Philharmonic during its 1st American tour (1951); collaborated with husband on award-winning feature film *Little Fugitive* (1953) and on a 2nd feature, *Lovers and Lollipops* (1955); saw "The Cardplayers" included in "Family of Man" exhibition at MoMA (1955); photographs included in Photography in the Fine Arts exhibition at Metropolitan Museum of Art (1965); had 1st retrospective exhibit, Nikon House (1974); was an instructor at School of Visual Arts (1976–78) and at International Center for Photography (1980); posthumous retrospective exhibit at International Center of Photography, NY (1995). Won Silver Lion Award at Venice Film Festival and nominated for Academy Award for Best Motion Picture Story (1953); voted one of Top Ten Women Photographers in US by Professional Photographers of America (1959); Manhattan Cultural Award for Photography (1980). ❖ See also *A World Through My Window* (Harper and Row, 1978), *More Pictures from My Window* (Rizzoli, 1983) and *A Photo Journal* (Viking, 1981); and *Women in World History.*

ORKNEY, countess of.
See Douglas, Elizabeth (d. before 1451).
See Villiers, Elizabeth (c. 1657–1733).

ORLANDO, Mariane (1934—). Swedish ballet dancer. Born June 1, 1934, in Stockholm, Sweden. ❖ Trained at Royal Swedish Ballet School under Vallborg Franck; studied in Paris with Mme Roussane; joined Royal Swedish Ballet (late 1940s), performing in classical as well as contemporary works, including *Miss Julie, Medea* and *Sisyphus.*

ORLEANS, duchess of.
See Blanche of France (1328–1392).
See Visconti, Valentina (1366–1408).
See Bonne of Armagnac (d. 1415).
See Marie of Cleves (1426–1486).
See Jeanne de France (c. 1464–1505).
See Marguerite of Lorraine (fl. 1632).
See Henrietta Anne (1644–1670).
See Charlotte Elizabeth of Bavaria (1652–1722).
See Françoise-Marie de Bourbon (1677–1749).
See Augusta Maria of Baden-Baden (1704–1726).
See Louisa Henrietta de Conti (1726–1759).
See Montesson, Charlotte Jeanne Béraud de la Haye de Riou, marquise de (1737–1805).
See Louise Marie de Bourbon (1753–1821).
See Maria Dorothea of Austria (1867–1932).

ORLEANS, Maid of. *See Joan of Arc (c. 1412–1431).*

ORLOFF, Fadia (1943–2002). *See Fadia.*

ORLOVA, Liubov (1902–1975). Russian actress and singer. Name variations: Liubov'; Lyubov or Lubov Orlova; Luba Orlova. Born Liubov Petrovna Orlova, Feb 11, 1902, in Zvenigorod (now part of Greater Moscow); died in Moscow, Jan 26, 1975; was distantly related to Leo Tolstoy; m. Grigorii or Gregori Alexandrov. ❖ The most popular Soviet film star of her day, who reigned for more than 4 decades, was often cast in roles as a "woman of the people," though she reflected a certain amount of elegance; studied music at Moscow Conservatory (1919–22) and dance at Theatrical Technicum (1922–25); made singing debut at Moscow's V.I. Nemirovich-Danchenko Musical Theater (1926), then starred in many of its productions, including operettas *La Périchole* and *Les Cloches de Corneville;* had supporting role in 1st film, *Petersburg Nights* (1933), then starred in *Jazz Comedy* (1933); in breakthrough role, appeared as Aniuta in Gregori Alexandrov's musical-comedy *Veselye Rebiata* (The Happy Guys), released in US as *Moscow Laughs* (1934); followed that with Alexandrov's *Tsirk* (The Circus, 1936), the greatest box-office success in the history of Soviet cinema; starred in another Alexandrov-directed musical comedy, *Volga-Volga* (1938), Stalin's favorite film, then *Bright Path* (1940), also known as *The Radiant Road* but released in US as *Tanya;* played lead in film *Meeting on the Elbe* (1949), a glorification of Stalin; appeared as Tatiana in *Mussorgsky* (1950) and Ludmilla Glinka in *Glinka: Man of Music* (1952); in last important role, appeared as Varvara Komarova in *Russian Memory* (1960); also became a permanent member of Moscow's Mossovet Theater (1955), where she appeared in a broad range of roles, including Jessie in *The Russian Question* and Mrs. Patrick Campbell in *Dear Liar.* Awarded

Order of Lenin (1939) and 2 USSR State Prizes (1941, 1950); honored as People's Artist of the USSR (1950). ❖ See also Ivan Frolov, *Liubov' Orlova: V Grime i Bez Grima* (Moscow: Panorama, 1997); *Liubov' Orlova* (video of Soviet film biography of Orlova), directed by Gregori Alexandrov (San Francisco: Ark's Intervideo); and *Women in World History.*

ORMANI, Maria (fl. 1453). Florentine manuscript artist and nun. Flourished 1453 in Florence, Italy; never married; no children. ❖ Entered a convent as a young woman; became a prominent illustrator of manuscripts at her convent's scriptorium. ❖ See also *Women in World History.*

ORME, Mary (1810–1884). *See Nichols, Mary Gove.*

ORMEROD, Eleanor A. (1828–1901). English entomologist. Born at Sedbury Park, Gloucestershire, England, May 11, 1828; died at St. Albans, July 19, 1901; dau. of George Ormerod, FRS (author of *The History of Cheshire*). ❖ When Royal Horticultural Society began collecting insect pests for practical purposes, contributed largely to it (1868) and was awarded Flora medal of the society; distributed a pamphlet, *Notes for Observations on Injurious Insects* (1877), to those interested in this field, and when recipients readily sent her results of their researches, the well-known *Annual Series of Reports on Injurious Insects and Farm Pests* was launched; served as consulting entomologist to Royal Agricultural Society (1882–92); was also a lecturer on scientific entomology at Royal Agricultural College, Cirencester, and wrote *Cobden Journals, Manual of Injurious Insects,* and *Handbook of Insects Injurious to Orchard and Bush Fruits.* Received silver and gold medals from University of Moscow and silver medal from Société Nationale d'Acclimatation de France (1899); granted honorary LLD from Edinburgh University (1901), the 1st woman upon whom the university had conferred this degree. ❖ See also *Women in World History.*

ORMISTON, Elizabeth (c. 1845–1897). *See Mackay, Elizabeth.*

ORMONDE, countess of.
See Bohun, Eleanor (fl. 1327–1340).
See Fitzalan, Amy (fl. 1440).
See Hankford, Anne (1431–1485).
See Beaufort, Eleanor (d. 1501).

OROS, Rozalia (1963—). Romanian fencer. Born Jan 28, 1963, in Romania. ❖ At Los Angeles Olympics, won a silver medal in team foil (1984).

O'ROURKE, Heather (1975–1988). American actress. Born Heather Michele O'Rourke, Dec 27, 1975, in San Diego, CA; died Feb 1, 1988, in San Diego of cardiopulmonary arrest. ❖ Child star of "They're baack!" fame, who appeared in *Poltergeist, Poltergeist II* and *Poltergeist III;* later made tv guest appearances on "Happy Days," "Chips" and "The New Leave It to Beaver."

O'ROURKE, Mary (1937—). Irish politician. Born Mary Lenihan, May 1937, in Athlone, Ireland; dau. of P.J. Lenihan (TD, Longford Westmeath, 1965–70); sister of Brian Lenihan (TD, Roscommon Leitrim); m. Enda O'Rourke. ❖ Began career as secondary schoolteacher; representing Fianna Fáil, elected to the 24th Dáil (1982–87) for Longford Westmeath; returned to 25th–26th Dáil (1987–1992) for Longford Westmeath and 27th–28th Dáil (1992–2002) for Westmeath; appointed deputy leader of Fianna Fáil (1994); served as minister for Education (1987–91), minister for Health (1991–92), and minister for Public Enterprise (1997–2002); was one of the Taoiseach's nominees to the Seanad (2002).

ORPAH (fl. 1100 BCE). Biblical woman. Born a Moabite; m. Chilion (younger son of Elimelech and Naomi). ❖ Following death of husband, set out for Bethlehem with mother-in-law Naomi and sister-in-law Ruth, both of whom had also lost their husbands; made only part of the journey, then decided to return to Moab to be with her people and her gods.

ORPHEE, Elvira (1930—). Argentinean novelist and short-story writer. Born May 29, 1930, in San Miguel de Tucumán, Argentina; m. Miguel Ocampo; children: 3. ❖ A neo-realist, studied literature at University of Buenos Aires and Sorbonne; lived in France, Italy, Spain, Venezuela and Argentina; writings include *Dos veranos* (1956), *Uno* (1962), *Aire tan dulce* (1966), *En el fondo* (1969), *Su demonio preferido* (1973), *La última conquista de El Angel* (1977), *Las viejas fantasiosas* (1981), *Ciego del cielo* (1991), *Basura y luna* (1996), and *La muerte y los desencuentros* (1999).

ORR, Alice Greenough (1902–1995). American rodeo champion. Name variations: Alice Greenough. Born Alice Greenough in Montana in 1902;

died Aug 31, 1995, in Tucson, Arizona; grew up on a ranch near Red Lodge, Montana; m. Ray Cahill; m. Joe Orr; children: (1st m.) 2, including Jay Cahill. ❖ For 20 years, under maiden name Alice Greenough, was the reigning queen of rodeo bronc riders; named to both the Cowboy and Cowgirl halls of fame, won 4 world saddle bronc championships and was a star attraction on rodeo tours of US, Australia, and Europe; also did occasional stunt work for motion pictures and was a member of the Riding Greenoughs, a team which included her sister Marge Henderson and brothers Bill and Turk; with others, founded what is now known as Professional Rodeo Cowboys Association (1936); began to run her own rodeo with 2nd husband Joe Orr (1946). ❖ See also *Women in World History.*

ORR, Kay (1939—). American politician. Name variations: Kay A. Orr. Born Jan 2, 1939, in Burlington, Iowa; moved to Lincoln, Nebraska, 1963. ❖ Republican, was Nebraska state treasurer (1981–86); defeated Democrat Helen Boosalis to become governor of Nebraska (1986), in the 1st woman-versus-woman gubernatorial race in US; was also the 1st Republican woman elected governor of a state; served until 1991.

ORR, Lucinda Lee (fl. 1787). *See Lee, Lucinda.*

ORR, Vickie (1967—). American basketball player. Name variations: Vickie Orr-Wiley. Born April 4, 1967; attended Auburn University. ❖ At World championships, won team gold medal (1990); at Barcelona Olympics, won a bronze medal in team competition (1992).

ORRERY, countess of. *See Monckton, Mary (1746–1840).*

ORRIS (1820–1897). *See Ingelow, Jean.*

ORSINI, Adriana (fl. 1469–1502). *See Mila, Adriana.*

ORSINI, Alfonsina (d. 1520). *See Medici, Alfonsina de.*

ORSINI, Belleza (d. 1528). Italian condemned to death for sorcery. Committed suicide in 1528. ❖ A semi-educated widow, practiced general medicine and phytotherapy and perhaps procured abortions, reaping the mistrust and hate of the little rural community of Collevecchio; was called to defend herself against the charge of sorcery in court in Fiano, with no success. ❖ See also (Italian) Ileana Tozzi, *Bellezza Orsini, cronaca di un processo per stregoneria* (Nova Italica, 1990); and *Women in World History.*

ORSINI, Clarice (c. 1453–1487). *See Medici, Clarice de.*

ORSINI, Isabella (1542–1576). *See Medici, Isabella de.*

ORSINI, Marie-Anne de la Tremouille (c. 1642–1722). *See Marie-Anne de la Trémouille, princess of the Ursins.*

ORTA, Teresa M. da Silve e (c. 1711–1793). *See Silve e Orta, Teresa M. da.*

ORTENBERG, Elizabeth (b. 1929). *See Claiborne, Liz.*

ORTESE, Anna Maria (1914–1998). Italian novelist, journalist and short-story writer. Born June 13, 1914, in Rome, Italy; died Mar 9, 1998, in Rapallo, Italy. ❖ Works, which combine fabulism and realism, include *Angelici dolori* (1937), *Il mare non bagna Napoli* (1953), *I giorno del cielo* (1958), *Poveri e semplici* (1967), *L'alone grigio* (1969), *Il porto di Toledo* (1975), *Il treno russo* (1983), *In sonno en in veglia* (1987), *Il cardillo addolorato* (1993), and *Corpo celeste* (1997).

ORTHRYTH OF MERCIA (fl. 7th c.). Queen of Mercia. Name variations: she is possibly Ostrith. Born in late 7th century in Northumbria, England; died in Mercia. ❖ A Saxon princess of Northumbria, was married to the king of Mercia as part of a political liaison between the 2 small kingdoms; soon found herself warring, unwillingly, for Mercia against her native people; after husband died, effected a truce and was killed for it. ❖ See also *Women in World History.*

ORTIZ, Cristina (1950—). Brazilian pianist. Born in Bahia, Brazil, April 17, 1950; studied 1st in Brazil and then in Paris with Magda Tagliaferro; later studied with Rudolf Serkin. ❖ Won the Van Cliburn Competition (1969); made successful New York recital debut (1971); by mid-1970s, had launched an international touring career; specializing in the works of French composers, also made highly acclaimed recordings of the compositions of Heitor Villa-Lobos and other Brazilian composers.

ORTIZ, Letizia (1972—). Spanish tv journalist and crown princess. Name variations: Princess of Asturias. Born Letizia Ortiz Rocasolano, Sept 15, 1972, in Oviedo, Asturia, Spain; eldest dau. of Jesus Ortiz Alvarez (founder of tv channel, Antena 3) and Paloma Rocasolano (nurse and union official); attended Instituto Alfonso II and Centre

Ramiro de Maeztu; Universidad Complutense de Madrid, degree in information sciences, MA in audiovisual journalism; m. Alonso Guerrero (college professor), Aug 7, 1998, in a civil ceremony (div. 1 year later); m. Felipe, crown prince of Spain, prince of Asturias, and son of Juan Carlos I and Sophia of Greece, May 22, 2004. ❖ Worked for the newspaper *Siglo XXI* in Mexico City, then the Asturian daily *La Nueva España* and the international desk of Agencia EFE, Spain's news agency; joined CNN Plus (Jan 1999); moved to Televisión Española (TVE, 2000), working as a daily newscaster at "Telediario 2"; was also a presenter on "Informe Semanal" (morning newscast); retired at time of engagement (2003). Received Larra prize for journalism (2001).

ORTIZ CALVO, Tania (1965—). Cuban volleyball player. Born Oct 30, 1965, in Cuba. ❖ At Barcelona Olympics, won a gold medal in team competition (1992).

ORTIZ CHARRO, Yahima (1981—). Cuban volleyball player. Born Nov 9, 1981, in Cuba. ❖ Won a team bronze medal at Athens Olympics (2004).

ORTÍZ DE DOMINGUEZ, Josefa (c. 1768–1829). Mexican revolutionary and political activist. Name variations: Josefa Ortiz de Dominguez; La Corregidora. Born María Josefa Ortíz Girón in 1768 (some historians cite 1775), in either Valladolid or Mexico City; died at home in Mexico City, May 3, 1829; dau. of Captain Juan José Ortíz and Manuela Girón; attended Colegio de las Vizcaínas in Mexico City; m. the distinguished government official, Miguel Dominguez, regularized in 1793; children: María Ignacia (b. 1792); J.M. Florencio (b. 1793); Mariano (b. 1794); M. Dolores (b. 1796); Miguel (b. 1797); M. Juana (b. 1799); M. Micaela (b. 1800); Remigio (b. 1801); M. Teresa (b. 1803); M. Manuela (b. 1804); M. Ana (b. 1806); J.M. Hilarion (b. 1807); M. Magdalena (b. 1811); M. del Carmen (b. 1812). ❖ Known as "the mother of Mexico's nationhood," was one of a handful of women of the elite class to actively support Mexico's independence from Spain (1810–21); despite numerous children and husband's high position in the royalist bureaucracy, participated with him in a conspiracy in Querétaro to overthrow Spanish rule (1810); warned Father Miguel Hidalgo and militia Captain Ignacio Allende, co-conspirators in neighboring Guanajuato, that their plans to overthrow the viceregal government had been betrayed (Sept 14, 1810); arrested and imprisoned the day Hidalgo commenced the revolt against Spanish rule (Sept 16, 1810); released for lack of evidence of sedition (Oct 22, 1810); secretly continued to support independence movement until arrested and taken to Mexico City (Dec 29, 1813); imprisoned in Convent of St. Teresa (Jan 6, 1814); released due to serious illness (April 1814); resumed contacts with insurgents and rearrested (Dec 22, 1815); imprisoned in Convent of St. Catherine of Siena until her release (June 17, 1817); after Mexico gained independence, deplored the seizure of power by ex-royalist Agustín Iturbide, who was crowned emperor (1822); refused to serve as "dame of honor" in the empress' court; vindicated after Iturbide's overthrow (1823); lived to see husband's elevation to highest ranks of the executive and judiciary in early Republic of Mexico; a legendary heroine, has been admired, extolled and praised by Mexicans for close to 200 years. ❖ See also *Women in World History*.

ORTON, Beth (1970—). English singer. Born Dec 14, 1970, in East Dereham, Norfolk, England. ❖ Studied acting in London; joined William Orbit to form duo, Spill, and record *SuperPinkyMandy* (1993), which was released in Japan and included cover of John Martyn's "Don't Wanna Know About Evil"; was guest artist on numerous albums, including Chemical Brothers' *Exit Planet Dust* (1995); released successful solo debut album, *Trailer Park* (1996), and folk-music-flavored *Central Reservation* (1999).

ORTRUD OF SCHLESWIG-HOLSTEIN-SONDERBURG-GLUCKSBURG (1925—). Princess of Schleswig-Holstein-Sonderburg-Glucksburg. Born 1925; dau. of Albert, prince of Schleswig-Holstein-Sonderburg-Glucksburg, and Hertha of Ysenburg and Budingen (1883–1972); m. Ernest Augustus Guelph, in 1951; children: 6, including Ernest Augustus and Alexandra.

ORVIETO, Laura (1876–1953). Italian children's writer. Born Laura Cantoni, Mar 7, 1876, in Milan, Italy, of Jewish parentage; died May 9, 1953, in Florence, Italy; m. Angiolo Orvieto (Florentine poet). ❖ Works collected as *Storia della Storia del mondo* (1953, 1955); also wrote *Storia di Angiolo e Laura*.

ORWIG, Bernice (1976—). American water-polo player. Born Feb 24, 1976, in Anaheim, CA; attended Cyprus College; graduate of University of South California. ❖ Goalkeeper, won a team silver medal at Sydney Olympics (2000). Won the Pete Cutino Award (1999); named National College Player of the Year (1999).

ORZESZKOWA, Eliza (1841–1910). Polish advocate for women's rights and novelist. Name variations: Eliza Orzeszko or Orszeszko or Orzeskowa. Born Eliza Pawlowska in 1841 in Milkowszczyzna, Lithuania; died 1910 in Grodno, Poland; m. Pietr Orzeszko (Polish noble), 1857; no children. ❖ One of the best-known Polish writers of 19th century, was forced to flee during Polish revolt against Russian rule (1863); after husband was exiled to Siberia, never saw him again; settled in Grodno (present-day Byelorussia, 1866) and turned to writing as a means of supporting herself, publishing novels and short stories that are at once patriotic, feminist, and humanitarian; wrote most powerful novel, *Marta* (1872); by 1870s, had become a well-known and outspoken proponent of women's rights, a role she maintained both in her fiction and politically throughout her life; wrote of the Polish peasantry and their struggles against oppressive landowners in *Cham* (1889) and addressed the widespread religious and racial intolerance faced by Polish Jews in *Eli Makower* (1874) and *Meir Ezofowicz* (1878); was perhaps the major influence on the later development of the Polish women's movement. ❖ See also *Women in World History*.

OSADCHAYA, Liliya (1953—). Soviet volleyball player. Born Feb 1953 in USSR. ❖ At Montreal Olympics, won a silver medal in team competition (1976).

OSATO, Sono (1919–1953). Japanese-American ballet and theatrical dancer. Born Aug 29, 1919, in Omaha, Nebraska. ❖ Danced with Ballet Russe de Monte Carlo (1930s), appearing in numerous classical productions by Balanchine, Massine, Lichine, and others; danced with Ballet Theater (1941–43) where she created roles for Antony Tudor, including Lover in Experience in *Pillar of Fire* (1943); on Broadway, was featured in de Mille's *One Touch of Venus* (1943) and Robbins' *On the Town* (1944); also appeared in *Ballet Ballads* (1948), Valerie Bettis' *Peer Gynt* (1950), *One Over Lightly* (1955) and in film *The Kissing Bandit* (1947). ❖ See also memoir, *Distant Dances* (1980).

OSBORN, Daisy (1888–1957). New Zealand painter and art teacher. Born Daisy Frances Christina Osborn, April 27, 1888, in Christchurch, New Zealand; died May 3, 1957, in Christchurch; dau. of Alfred Patterson Osborn (engraver) and Emily Jane (Turvey) Osborn. ❖ Exhibited at Canterbury Society of Arts (1913–56) and at New Zealand Academy of Fine Arts (1909–53); taught art at School of Art (1921–27); illustrated Esther Glen's *Twinkles on the Mountain* (1920) and Edith Howe's *The Dream-girl's Garden* (1923); best known for small studies of flowers, portraits, and for religious paintings (1930s). ❖ See also *Dictionary of New Zealand Biography* (Vol. 4).

OSBORN, Emily Mary (1834–c. 1885). British artist. Born in Essex, England, 1834; died c. 1885; eldest child of a cleric; attended art classes at Mr. Dickinson's Academy, London; continued studies with John Mogford and James Matthew Leigh; never married. ❖ Though she earned the bulk of her living from genre paintings and portraits, is best known for her narrative paintings, particularly those dealing with the plight of women; at 17, had some of her genre and landscape paintings accepted at Royal Academy (1851); continued to exhibit there through 1884, and later had exhibitions at Society of British Artists, as well as in such commercial establishments as Grosvenor Gallery and the New Gallery, London; early in career, was honored by patronage of Queen Victoria who purchased *My Cottage Door* (1855) and *The Governess*, the latter of which won acclaim at Royal Academy show (1860); narrative works include *Nameless and Friendless* (1857), *For the Last Time* (1864), *God's Acre* (1868), and the prize-winning *Half the World Knows Not How the Other Half Lives* (1864); portraits include *Philip Gosse, Jr., Madame Bodichon*, and *Mrs Sturgis and Children*. ❖ See also *Women in World History*.

OSBORN, Sarah (1714–1796). American diarist. Name variations: Sarah Haggar Wheaten Osborn. Born Feb 22, 1714, in London, England; died Aug 2, 1796, in Newport, RI. ❖ Devout Puritan Congregationalist, who led a revival (1760s) and whose concern for women's roles led her to integrate men's and women's religious services, was also an abolitionist and held religious meetings for African-Americans; works include *The Nature, Certainty, and Evidence of True Christianity* (1755), *The Memoirs of the Life of Mrs Sarah Osborn* (1799), and *Familiar Letters Written by Mrs Sarah Osborn, and Miss Susanna Anthony* (1807).

OSBORNE, Baby Helen Marie (b. 1911). See Osborne, Marie.

OSBORNE, Dorothy (1627–1695). English letter writer. Born in 1627 in Chicksands Priory, Bedfordshire, England; died in 1695 in Moor Park, near Farnham, Surrey, England; dau. of Sir Peter Osborne (eminent Royalist) and Lady Dorothy Danvers; m. Sir William Temple (diplomat, statesman, and writer), in 1654 or 1655; children: Diana Temple; John Temple; several who died in infancy. ❖ Met Sir William Temple when she was 21; for next 7 years, was courted, mostly through correspondence; during 40-year marriage, was a diplomat and hostess while husband served as ambassador in Brussels, The Hague, Ireland, and London; her published letters, known for their wit and acerbic tone, were extremely useful to historians for the detail they provide about the lives of young English women of the time. ❖ See also *Women in World History*.

OSBORNE, Estelle Massey (1901–1981). African-American nurse. Name variations: Geneva Estelle Massey Riddle Osborne; Estelle Massey Riddle Osborne; Estelle Massey and Estelle Massey Riddle. Born Geneva Estelle Massey, May 3, 1901, in Palestine, TX; died Dec 12, 1981, in Oakland, CA; dau. of Bettye and Hall Massey; graduate of school of nursing at St. Louis City Hospital (later Homer G. Phillips Hospital), 1923; Columbia University Teachers College, BS, 1930, MA, 1931; m. Bedford N. Riddle, c. 1935; Herman Osborne, c. 1945. ❖ Was the 1st African-American nurse to earn an MA, the 1st African-American to receive a Julius Rosenwald Fund scholarship at Columbia University, the 1st African-American instructor at Harlem Hospital School of Nursing, the 1st director of nursing education at Freedmen's Hospital School of Nursing (Washington, DC), the 1st African-American superintendent of nurses and director of Homer G. Phillips Hospital nursing school (1940), the 1st African-American professor at New York University (1945–54) and the 1st African-American member of board of directors of the American Nurses Association (ANA, 1948–52); as an advocate for the National Nursing Council for War Service (later National Nursing Council), influenced the admitting policies of the navy (which accepted its 1st African-American nurses), of the army (which increased its acceptance rate of African-American nurses) and of nurse training schools; held an executive position at National League for Nursing (1954–66). Inducted into ANA Hall of Fame; Nurses' Education Fund established the Estelle Massey Osborne Memorial Scholarship (1982).

OSBORNE, Fanny (1852–1934). New Zealand painter. Name variations: Fanny Malcolm. Born Fanny Malcolm, Jan 29, 1852, at Auckland, New Zealand; died on Mar 12, 1934, at Auckland; dau. of Neill Malcolm (barrister) and Emilie Monson (Wilton) Malcolm; m. Alfred Joe Osborne, 1874; children: 8 sons, 5 daughters. ❖ Formally untrained, gained renown for her excellent watercolors of flora on Great Barrier Island. The largest collection of her work is housed at Auckland Institute and Museum. ❖ See also *Dictionary of New Zealand Biography* (Vol. 2).

OSBORNE, Joan (1962—). American singer. Born July 8, 1962, in Anchorage, KY; attended film school at New York University. ❖ Raised near Louisville, KY, moved to NY to study film (mid-1980s); formed own band and released *Soul Show* (1991) and *Blue Million Miles* (1993) on own label, Womanly Hips; with producer Rick Chertoff and ex-Hooters members, Eric Bazilian and Rob Hyman, wrote songs for triple platinum *Relish* (1995), which was nominated for 7 Grammys, and included hit song, "One of Us"; released compilation, *Early Recordings* (1996); toured with Lilith Fair; sang title song for tv series, *Joan of Arcadia* (2003).

OSBORNE, Margaret (1918—). American tennis player. Name variations: Margaret Osborne duPont; Mrs. W. duPont. Born Margaret Evelyn Osborne, Mar 4, 1918, in Joseph, Oregon; married William duPont, in 1947 (div. 1964); children: 1 son. ❖ Won 1st national title (1936); won French Open singles titles (1946, 1949); won Wimbledon singles title (1947); won US championship singles titles (1948, 1949, 1950); with Louise Brough, won French Open doubles titles 3 times, Wimbledon doubles titles 5 times, US doubles championship 12 times, and US mixed doubles championship 9 times. Inducted into the Tennis Hall of Fame (1967). ❖ See also *Women in World History*.

OSBORNE, Marie (1911—). American actress. Name variations: Baby Marie, Baby Helen Marie Osborne. Born Helen Alice Myres, Nov 5, 1911, in Denver, CO; m. Frank J. Dempsey, 1931 (div. 1936); m. Murray F. Yates, 1945 (died 1975). ❖ Considered the most prominent child star in early silents, made film debut in *Little Mary Sunshine* (1916); formed own company (1918); later was stand-in and costumer; films include *Twin Kiddies*, *The Child of M'sieu* and *The Little Diplomat*.

OSBORNE, Mary (1921–1992). American jazz guitarist. Born July 17, 1921, in Minot, North Dakota; died in Bakersfield, California, Mar 4, 1992; m. Ralph Scaffidi (trumpet player). ❖ As a singer-guitarist, played for Dick Stabile, then joined Buddy Rogers' band; in New York, formed her own trio; with husband, moved to Bakersfield, where they formed the Osborne Guitar Co. (later Osborne Sound Laboratories), which manufactured amplifiers for guitars, then branched out into public-address systems; well known in the jazz world, recorded 9 albums, backed recordings for Mary Lou Williams, Coleman Hawkins, and Ethel Waters, and continued to give concerts. ❖ See also *Women in World History*.

OSBORNE, Mary D. (1875–1946). American nurse. Born April 27, 1875 in Ohio; died July 7, 1946 in Ohio; graduate of Akron City Hospital School of Nursing, 1902; conducted postgraduate work at Woman's Hospital in NY. ❖ Elected supervisor of nurses for the Association for Improving the Condition of the Poor in NY (1912); appointed supervisor (1921), then associate director (1933) at Mississippi State Board of Health's Division of Maternal and Child Health; during Depression, ensured that every Mississippi county (82 total) had at least 1 public health nurse; increased educational standards and opportunities for nurses and required all nurses to become members of the Mississippi State Nurses Association; dedicated to the education and empowerment of "granny" midwives who delivered roughly 85% of the African-American babies born in MS state; created the *Manual for Midwives* and provided educational opportunities for state midwives.

OSBORNE, Penelope (1932—). *See Gilliatt, Penelope.*

OSBORNE, Sandra (1956—). Scottish politician and member of Parliament. Born Sandra Clark, Feb 23, 1956; m. Alastair Osborne, 1982; children: 2. ❖ Representing Labour, elected to House of Commons for Ayr, Carrick and Cumnock (1997, 2001, 2005).

OSBORNE, Susan M. (1858–1918). American philanthropist. Born 1858; died 1918. ❖ At 19, founded the Home for Friendless Women and Girls in New York City, and later established a refuge shelter there; for 41 years, continued as the active head of these institutions, which were supported by voluntary subscriptions.

OSBORNE, Vivian (1896–1961). *See Osborne, Vivienne.*

OSBORNE, Vivienne (1896–1961). American stage and screen actress. Name variations: Vivian Osborne. Born Dec 10, 1896, in Des Moines, IA; died Ju 10, 1961, in Malibu, CA; m. Francis Worthington Hine (div.). ❖ Made stage debut as a dancer at age 5; made NY debut in *The Whirlwind* (1919), followed by *The Bonehead, The Silver Fox, The Love Child, Scaramouche, Aloma of the South Seas* (title role), *Fog, Week-end* and *The Royal Virgin*, among others; films include *In Walked Mary, Week-End Marriage, Sailor Be Good, Tomorrow at Seven, Sinner Take All* and *Dragonwyck.*

OSBURGA (?–c. 855). Queen of Wessex and the English. Name variations: Osburh; Osburgha; she is often confused with a St. Osburga who founded Coventry Abbey. Date of birth unknown; died c. 855; dau. of Oslac the Thane of the Isle of Wight, grand butler of England; became 1st wife of Æthelwulf also known as Ethelwolf or Ethelwulf (c. 800–858), king of Wessex and the English (r. 839–856, abdicated), about 835 (div. 853); children: Ethelstan, king of Kent; Ethelbald (c. 834–860), king of Wessex and the English (r. 855–860); Ethelbert (c. 836–865), king of Kent and the English (r. 860–865); Ethelred I (c. 840–871), king of the English (r. 865–871); Alfred the Great (c. 848–c. 900), king of the English (r. 871–899); Ethelswyth (c. 843–889). Ethelwulf's 2nd wife was Judith Martel. ❖ Thought to be noble by birth and nature, could also read, a rare accomplishment for a woman of her day. ❖ See also *Women in World History*.

OSBURN, Lucy (1835–1891). British nurse. Name variations: Sister Osburn. Born in Leeds, England, May 10, 1835; died of diabetes in Harrogate, England, Dec 22, 1891; dau. of William Osburn (respected Egyptologist) and Ann (Rimington) Osburn; studied at Nightingale Training School of Nursing attached to London's St. Thomas' Hospital, graduating in Sept 1867; studied midwifery at King's College Hospital; never married. ❖ Universally admired as "Australia's Florence Nightingale," studied nursing in London against family's wishes; chosen by Nightingale to introduce her nursing principles to Australia (1868); as Lady Superintendent, despite her own poor health, transformed the Sydney Infirmary and Dispensary into a model institution; resigned position because of declining health (1884) and returned to England where she continued to minister to the indigent sick. ❖ See also Freda

MacDonnell, *Miss Nightingale's Young Ladies: The Story of Lucy Osburn and Sydney Hospital* (Angus & Robertson, 1970); and *Women in World History*.

OSBURN, Ruth (1912–1994). American track-and-field athlete. Born April 24, 1912; died Jan 8, 1994, in Tucson, Arizona. ❖ At Los Angeles Olympics, won a silver medal in the discus throw (1932).

OSCEOLA. *See Dinesen, Isak.*

OSGERBY, Ann (1963—). English swimmer. Born Jan 20, 1963, in England. ❖ At Moscow Olympics, won a silver medal in the 4 x 100-meter medley relay (1980).

OSGITH (d. around 700). *See Osith.*

OSGOOD, Frances (1811–1850). American writer. Name variations: Fanny Osgood; (pseudonyms) Florence, Ellen, Kate Carol. Born Frances Sargent Locke, June 18, 1811, in Boston, Massachusetts; died May 12, 1850, in New York, NY; dau. of Joseph Locke (merchant) and Mary (Ingersoll) Foster Locke; sister of writer Andrew Aitchison Locke, and half-sister of writer Anna Maria Wells; m. Samuel Stillman Osgood (portrait painter), Oct 7, 1835; children: Ellen Frances Osgood (b. 1836); May Vincent Osgood (b. 1839); Fanny Fay Osgood (1846–1847). ❖ By 14, was publishing in the *Juvenile Miscellany* under pseudonym Florence; on marriage, moved to London (1836); mingled with London literary circles, contributed to reputable periodicals, and published 2 collections of verse; moved to New York City (1839) where she contributed to prominent journals and newspapers of the day, and became a prominent member of NY's literary community; also published several collections of poetry and prose; was estranged from husband and living in separate residences, when she met Edgar Allan Poe (1845), shortly after he had lauded her talent. While many Poe biographers consider their relationship innocent, John Evangelist Walsh contends that she not only had an affair with Poe but a child, daughter Fanny Fay, who died before she was 2; whatever happened, rumors at the time all but ruined Poe in NY literary society (though not Osgood), and quite probably contributed to the many dark stories and stains on his character that have come down through the years. ❖ See also John Evangelist Walsh, *Plumes in the Dust: The Love Affair of Edgar Allan Poe and Fanny Osgood* (Nelson-Hall, 1980); and *Women in World History*.

O'SHAY, Constance (1891–1959). *See Emerald, Connie.*

O'SHEA, Katherine (1845–1921). English paramour. Name variations: Kitty O'Shea; Katherine O'Shea Parnell. Born Katherine Wood, Jan 30, 1845, at Bradwell, Essex, England; died Feb 5, 1921, at 39 East Ham Road, Littlehampton, Sussex, England; dau. of Sir John Page Wood; m. Captain William H. O'Shea (1840–1905, politician and adventurer), Jan 24, 1867 (div. 1891); m. Charles Stewart Parnell (1846–1891, politician), June 1891; sister-in-law of Anna Parnell (1852–1911); children: (with Parnell) 3, including daughters Clare and Katie (born between 1882 and 1884). ❖ After living apart from husband for 5 years, met Charles Stewart Parnell (1880) and began an illicit liaison, a poorly kept secret from the start; eventually had 3 children with him; her divorce from 1st husband (1891) created an enormous scandal which eventually destroyed his career and her reputation; married Parnell (June 25, 1891), but he died in her arms a few months later (Oct 6). ❖ See also memoir *Charles Stewart Parnell: His Love Story and Political Life* (London, 1914); and *Women in World History*.

O'SHEA, Kitty (1845–1921). *See O'Shea, Katherine.*

O'SHEA, Marlene (1934—). *See Mathews, Marlene.*

O'SHEA, Tessie (1913–1995). Welsh-born singer and actress. Born Teresa O'Shea, Mar 13, 1913, in Cardiff, Wales; died April 21, 1995, in Leesburg, FL. ❖ A music-hall performer who cheerfully capitalized on her wide girth, made 1st tour at age 7; was a veteran headliner of the Bristol Hippodrome by 15; appeared in a Blackpool revue singing "Two-Ton Tessie from Tennessee," the song that ultimately became her anthem; headlined British revues *On With the Show* and *High Time*; made NY debut in *The Girl Who Came to Supper* (1963), a Tony-winning performance; appeared on CBS variety series "The Entertainers" (1964) and on Broadway in *A Time for Singing* (1966), *Something's Afoot* (1976) and *Broadway Follies* (1981); films include *The Russians Are Coming, the Russians Are Coming* (1966) and *Bedknobs and Broomsticks* (1971). ❖ See also *Women in World History*.

OSHEKU, Fali (1969—). *See Ogunkoya, Falilat.*

OSIIER, Ellen (1890–1962). Danish fencer. Name variations: Ellen Ottilia Osiier; Ellen Osiier-Thomsen. Born Aug 13, 1890; died Sept 1962; m. Dr. Ivan Osiier (1888–1965, Olympic fencer who won a gold medal for indiv. epee in Stockholm in 1912). ❖ Became the 1st female Olympic fencing champion, winning the gold medal for individual foil in Paris (1924). ❖ See also *Women in World History*.

OSIPENKO, Alla (1932—). Soviet dancer. Born June 16, 1932, in Leningrad, USSR. ❖ Trained with Agrippina Vaganova at Leningrad Choreographic School; danced with Kirov Ballet (1954–71), where she created the role of Mistress of the Copper Mountain in Yuri Grigorovitch's *The Stone Flower* (1959) and was Nureyev's partner until he defected; danced lead roles in Leonid Iakobsen's *Fantasia*, Igor Belsky's *Coast of Hope*, and Chabukiani's *Othello*, among others; began teaching at the Vaganova School (1966).

OSIPENKO, Polina (1907–1939). Russian aviator. Name variations: Paulina Ossipenko. Born Polina Denisovna Osipenko, Oct 8, 1907, in Osipenko, Berdansk; died in air crash on military duty, May 11, 1939; buried near Kremlin Wall in Red Square; graduate of Kacha Aviation School, 1932. ❖ Set 5 world flight records for women; with Valentina Grizodubova and Marina Raskova, flew 3,717 miles nonstop from Moscow to the Soviet east coast near Japan (1938), a journey one-third longer than Amelia Earhart's solo flight, and crash landed, spending 10 days in the Siberian *taiga* until rescued. Awarded Two Orders of Lenin and Order of the Red Banner of Labor. ❖ See also Bruce Myles, *Night Witches: The Untold Story of Soviet Women in Combat* (Presidio, 1981); and *Women in World History*.

OSIPOVA, Irina (1981—). Russian basketball player. Born June 25, 1981, in Moscow, Russia. ❖ Center, won a team bronze medal at Athens Olympics (2004); placed 2nd at World championships (2002) and 1st at European championships (2003).

OSIPOWICH, Albina (1911–1964). American swimmer. Born Feb 26, 1911; died June 6, 1964; graduate of Brown University, 1933; m. Harrison Van Aken (basketball player). ❖ At Amsterdam Olympics, won a gold medal in the 4 x 100-meter freestyle relay and a gold medal in the 100-meter freestyle (1928).

OSITH (died c. 700). English saint and nun. Name variations: Saint Osith, Osyth or Osgith. Born at Quarendon, near Aylesbury, Buckinghamsire, England; died c. 700; dau. of Frithuwold, Mercian sub-king of Surrey, and Wilburga (dau. of Penda of Mercia and Cynewise); niece of Edburga of Bicester and Edith of Aylesbury. ❖ Spent childhood in the care of her maternal aunts; was engaged to Sighere, king of Essex, but opted to become a nun; parents built her a church and monastery (St. Osiths) in Essex; was beheaded during a Dane raid, for not renouncing her religion.

OSLIN, K.T. (1941—). American country singer. Name variations: Kay Toinette Oslin. Born May 15, 1941, in Crossitt, Arkansas; moved to Mobile, Alabama. ❖ At 5, father died, and she moved with family to Houston; sang in chorus of Broadway musicals and in commercials; released 1st singles, "Clean Your Own Tables" and "Younger Men" (1981), to little notice; had initial success as a songwriter, writing "Round the Clock Lovin'" for Gail Davies (1982), "Old Pictures" for the Judds, and others songs for Davies, Dottie West and Judy Rodman; recorded country single "80's Ladies" which hit Top 10; went on to release album of *80's Ladies* (1986), winning Grammy for best country female vocal performance (1987); won 2 Grammys for album *Hold Me* and declared top female vocalist of year by Academy of Country Music (1988); released 3rd album *Love in a Small Town* (1990) to continued success; took several years off, then returned with moderately successful *Live Close By, Visit Often* (2001); films include *This Thing Called Love* (1993) and *Murder So Sweet* (1994).

OSMANOGLU, Gevheri (1904–1980). Turkish composer and musician. Name variations: Princess Fatma Gevheri Osmanoglu. Born in Constantinople (now Istanbul) in 1904; died in 1980; granddau. of sultan Abdul-Aziz (r. 1861–76). ❖ Player of the oud, tanbur, and lavta, wrote a number of compositions, many of them folksongs; work is preserved in recordings made by Turkish radio and tv. ❖ See also *Women in World History*.

OSMOND, Marie (1959—). American musician. Born Oct 13, 1959, in Ogden, UT; dau. of George Osmond and Olive Osmond (died 2004); sister of Alan, Wayne, Merrill, Jay, Donny and Jimmy Osmond; m. Steve Craig, 1982 (div. 1985); m. Brian Blosil, Oct 28, 1986; children: 8 (5 adopted): Stephen (b. 1983), Jessica (b. 1987), Rachael (b. 1989), Michael (b. 1991), Brandon (b. 1996), Brianna (b. 1997), Matthew

(b. 1999), Abigail (2002). ❖ At 4, began performing with brothers as part of the Osmonds; released debut solo album, *Paper Roses* (1973), with hit title track, followed by *Who's Sorry Now* (1975), *There's No Stopping Your Heart* (1985), with hit title track, and *Steppin' Stone* (1989); with brother, hosted tv musical variety series, "The Donny and Marie Show" (1975), and released several albums, including *Goin' Coconuts* (1978); with actor John Schneider, co-founded Children's Miracle Network Telethon to raise money for children's hospitals; toured in *The Sound of Music* and made Broadway debut in *The King and I* (1990s); co-hosted syndicated tv talk show, "Donny and Marie" (1998). Received Roy Acuff Award from Country Music Foundation in recognition of work for children (1989). ❖ See also autobiography, *Behind the Smile* (2001).

OSOMARI, queen of. *See Okwei of Osomari (1872–1943).*

OSÓRIO, Ana de Castro (1872–1935). Portuguese essayist and children's writer. Born 1872 in Portugal; died 1935. ❖ Was concerned with welfare of children and participated in feminist movement; co-founded Republican League of Portuguese Women and started National Crusade of Portuguese Women (1917), published children's books in series *Para as Crianças* and wrote pamphlets on education published as *O Bem da Pátria*.

OSSERMAN, Wendy (1942—). American modern dancer and choreographer. Born 1942 in New York, NY; graduate of Smith College, 1964. ❖ Trained at Martha Graham school with Muriel Manning and Bonnie Bird, and with Betty Jones and José Limón; studied at Ballet Russe School and Ballet Arts school; performed professionally with Hellenic Chorograma in Athens (1964); danced with Alice Condolina troupe in NY and Europe (c. 1965–70) and for other choreographers, including Kai Takei, Valerie Bettis, Frances Alenikoff; began choreographing own works (1968), performing mainly in NY and Greece, then formed the Wendy Osserman Dance Company (1976); won acclaim for *I Never Saw Another Butterfly* (1977), based on writings of children in Theresienstadt Concentration Camp.

OSSIPENKO, Paulina (1907–1939). *See Osipenko, Polina.*

OSSOLI, Margaret Fuller (1810–1850). *See Fuller, Margaret.*

O'STEEN, Shyril (1960—). American rower. Born Oct 5, 1960, in Seattle, Washington; attended University of Washington. ❖ At Los Angeles Olympics, won a gold medal in coxed eights (1984).

OSTEN, Maria (1908–1942). German journalist. Name variations: Maria Gresshöner or Gresshoener. Born Maria Emilie Alwine Gresshöner in Muckum bei Bünde, Westphalia, Germany, Mar 20, 1908; executed in Moscow, Aug 8, 1942; dau. of Heinrich Gresshöner and Anna Maria (Pohlmann) Gresshöner; m. Yevgenii Cherbiakov (Russian director, div. c. 1931); companion of Mikhail Yefimovich Koltsov (1898–1940, Russian writer and an editor of *Pravda*); children: (adopted) Hubert L'Hoste; José. ❖ Frontline reporter for Moscow's *Deutsche Zentral-Zeitung* during the Spanish Civil War, who was later executed by the Soviets. ❖ See also (in German) Ursula El-Akramy, *Transit Moskau: Margarete Steffin und Maria Osten* (Hamburg: Europäische Verlagsanstalt, 1998); and *Women in World History*.

OSTENSO, Martha (1900–1963). Canadian-American writer. Born Sept 17, 1900, in Bergen, Norway; reared in Minnesota, South Dakota, and Canada; died Nov 24, 1963, in Seattle (one source cites Tacoma), Washington; dau. of Sigurd Brigt Ostenso and Lena (Tungleland) Ostenso; m. Douglas Leader Durkin (writer), Dec 16, 1944 (or 1945); attended University of Manitoba, beginning 1918; attended Columbia University, 1921–22. ❖ Immigrated to US at 2, living in small towns in Minnesota and South Dakota (1902); contributed to junior page of *Minneapolis Journal* as a child; immigrated to Manitoba, Canada (1915); taught one semester of school in Manitoba (1918) and worked as a reporter for *Winnipeg Free Press*; worked as a social worker with Bureau of Charities in Brooklyn, NY (1920–23); published 1st book, *A Far Land: Poems by Martha Ostenso* (1924); won 1st prize in a competition for best 1st novel by North American writer for *Wild Geese* (1925), set in the Canadian west; other novels set in Canada are *The Young May Moon* (1929) and *Prologue to Love* (1932), though in 1929 she settled in US, living 1st in New Jersey and finally in Brainerd, Minnesota; published *And They Shall Walk: The Life Story of Sister Elizabeth* (1943). ❖ See also *Women in World History*.

OSTERGAARD, Solveig (1939—). Danish ballet dancer. Born Jan 7, 1939, in Skjern, Denmark. ❖ Trained in Denmark at school of Royal Danish Ballet, then performed with company throughout career;

appeared in wide range of works, including in *Coppélia* (as Swanilda), in Ashton's *Romeo and Juliet* (as Rosalind), in Macmillan's *Solitaire*, Lander's *Etude*, Fokine's *Spectre de la Rose*, Bruce Marks' *Dicterliebe* and Eliot Feld's *Winter's Court*.

OSTERMAN, Catherine (1983—). American softball player. Born April 16, 1983, in Houston, TX; attended University of Texas. ❖ Pitcher, won team gold medal at Athens Olympics (2004).

OSTERMEYER, Micheline (1922–2001). French track-and-field athlete and concert pianist. Born Dec 23, 1922, in Rang-du-Fliers, France; grew up in North Africa; died Oct 17, 2001, in Rouen; married 1952. ❖ Moved to Tunisia with family (1929); at 14, moved back to France to study music at Paris Conservatory (1936); returned to Tunisia with advent of World War II (1940) and joined French Athletic Association, competing in several track-and-field events; at war's end, returned to France (1945); won gold medals for discus and shot put and a bronze medal for high jump at London Olympics (1948); retired from athletic competition (1951); moved to Lebanon with husband (1952); following his death (1960), returned to France and began to perform in concerts, then taught music at a conservatory just outside Paris; also made recordings. ❖ See also *Women in World History*.

OSTLER, Emma Brignell (c. 1848–1922). New Zealand teacher, temperance reformer, suffragist, and landowner. Name variations: Emma Brignell Roberts. Born Emma Brignell Roberts, in 1848 or 1849, in Essex, England; died April 14, 1922, in Remuera, Auckland, New Zealand; dau. of Thomas Roberts (cleric) and Mary (Griffith) Ostler; m. William Henry Ostler (runholder), 1868 (died 1879). ❖ Immigrated to Australia with parents (1852); relocated with husband to New Zealand, where they purchased Ben Ohau station (1874); lost everything when husband died and moved to Waitohi Flat to pursue position as teacher (1887); began to secure and clear land, making fortune in land leases and real estate; actively supported women's suffrage; held office with New Zealand Women's Christian Temperance Union, and was vice president of New Zealand Alliance (1898–1918). ❖ See also *Dictionary of New Zealand Biography* (Vol. 2).

OSTLER, Helen Mary (1869–1957). *See Wilson, Helen Mary.*

OSTRICHE, Muriel (1896–1989). American silent-film actress. Name variations: The Moxie Girl. Born May 24, 1896, in New York, NY; died May 3, 1989, in St. Petersburg, FL. ❖ Starred in films (1912–21); became the face for Moxie, a popular soft drink, and was known as the "Moxie Girl" (1915–20); films include *A Tale of the Wilderness, Lobster Salad and Milk, All's Well That Ends Well, Journey's End, The Shadow* and *The Sacred Flame*; retired (1921).

OSTRITH (d. 697). Queen of Mercia. Name variations: Osthryth; she is possibly Orthryth. Died in 697; dau. of Eanfleda (626–?) and Oswy (Oswin, Oswio), king of Northumbria; m. Ethelred, king of Mercia.

OSTROMECKA, Krystyna (1948—). Polish volleyball player. Born Mar 12, 1948, in Poland. ❖ At Mexico City Olympics, won a bronze medal in team competition (1968).

O'SULLIVAN, Jan (1950—). Irish politician. Born Jan Gale, Dec 6, 1950, in Clonlara, Co. Clare, Ireland; m. Paul O'Sullivan. ❖ Was mayor of Limerick (1993–94); elected to Seanad from Administrative Panel (1993–97); representing Labour, elected to the 28th Dáil in a by-election (1998–2002) for Limerick East; returned to 29th Dáil (2002).

O'SULLIVAN, Keala (1950—). American diver. Name variations: Keala O'Sullivan Watson. Born Rachel Kealaonapua O'Sullivan, Nov 3, 1950, in Hawaii. ❖ At Mexico City Olympics, won a bronze medal in springboard (1968).

O'SULLIVAN, Mairan D. (1919–1987). Irish-born stage, radio, and tv actress. Born Jan 1, 1919, in Ireland; died Oct 27, 1987, in Dublin. ❖ Character actress at Abbey Theater (1940s); appeared on Broadway in *Lovers* and *Borstal Boy*. Nominated for Tony Award for *Philadelphia, Here I Come* (1986).

O'SULLIVAN, Mary Kenney (1864–1943). American labor organizer. Name variations: Mary Kenney. Born Mary Kenney in Hannibal, Missouri, Jan 8, 1864; died in West Medford, Massachusetts, Jan 18, 1943; dau. of Michael Kenney and Mary (Kelly) Kenney; m. John (Jack) F. O'Sullivan, Oct 10, 1894; children: 4. ❖ Founded Chicago Women's Bindery Union No. 1 (1891); lived at Hull House for a time and became friends with its founder, Jane Addams; appointed 1st woman organizer for American Federation of Labor (AFL, 1892); co-founded Union for

Industrial Progress, part of the Women's Educational and Industrial Union of Boston (1894); was executive secretary, Union for Industrial Progress (1894–1903); co-founded National Women's Trade Union League (WTUL, 1903); served as WTUL national secretary (1903–06), treasurer (1907), and vice-president (1909–11); served as factory inspector, Massachusetts State Board of Labor and Industries (1914–34); was also an advocate of women's suffrage and an active pacifist. ❖ See also *Women in World History*.

O'SULLIVAN, Maureen (1911–1998). Irish-born actress. Born May 17, 1911, in Boyle, Co. Roscommon, Ireland; died June 22, 1998, in Phoenix, Arizona; dau. of a British army major; m. John Farrow (screenwriter), 1936 (died 1963); m. James E. Cushing (real-estate contractor), 1983; children: (1st m.) 7, including Michael Farrow (1940–1958) and actress Mia Farrow (b. 1945). ❖ At 18, with no acting experience, made film debut in *Song O' My Heart* (1930), with Irish tenor John McCormack; subsequently starred as Jane in 6 Tarzan films; had more serious roles in such films as *Strange Interlude* (1932), *Payment Deferred* (1932), *Tugboat Annie* (1933), *The Thin Man* (1934), *David Copperfield* (1935), *The Barretts of Wimpole Street* (1934), *Cardinal Richelieu* (1935), *Anna Karenina* (1935), *Pride and Prejudice* (1940), and *The Big Clock* (1948); hosted tv series "Irish Heritage" (1950s); appeared in several Broadway and touring productions and was briefly a regular on "Today" show (1960s); played opposite Paul Ford in Broadway production of *Never Too Late* (1962), a role she reprised in 1965 film; played daughter Mia's mother in Woody Allen's *Hannah and Her Sisters* (1985); filmed last movies, *Peggy Sue Got Married* (1986) and *Stranded* (1987). ❖ See also *Women in World History*.

O'SULLIVAN, Sonia (1969—). Irish runner. Born Nov 28, 1969, in Cobh, Co. Cork, Ireland; attended Villanova University; lives with Nick Bideau; children: daughter Ciara (b. 1999). ❖ Won a silver medal for 5,000 meters at Sydney Olympics (2000); at World championships, won a silver medal for the 1,500 meters (1993) and a gold medal for the 5,000 meters (1995); at European championships, won a gold medal for the 3,000 meters (1994), gold medals for the 5,000 and 10,000 meters (1998), and silver medals for the 5,000 and 10,000 (2002).

OSWALD, Marina (1941—). Russian-American. Name variations: Marina Alexandrovna Medvedeva; (erroneously) Marina Pruskova; Marina Oswald Porter. Born Marina Nikolayevna Prusakova, July 17, 1941, in Molotovsk, Russia; dau. of Klavdia Prusakova (an unmarried laboratory worker); received diploma from Pharmacy Institute, 1959; m. Lee Harvey Oswald, April 30, 1961 (died Nov 24, 1963); m. Kenneth Porter, 1965 (div. 1974); children: (1st m.) June Lee Oswald (b. Feb 1962); Audrey Marina Rachel Oswald (b. Oct 1963); (2nd m.) Mark Porter (b. 1966). ❖ Russian-born wife of presidential assassin Lee Harvey Oswald, immigrated to US (1962); became a US citizen (1990). ❖ See also Priscilla Johnson McMillan, *Marina and Lee* (Harper & Row, 1977); and *Women in World History*.

OSWALDA, Ossi (1897–1948). German silent-film star. Born Oswalda Stäglich in Berlin, Germany, Feb 2, 1897; died Jan 1, 1948, in Prague, Czechoslovakia. ❖ One of Germany's most popular silent stars during 1920s, was a model and chorus dancer before making film debut in *Nacht des Grauens* (1916); a protégé of Ernst Lubitsch, appeared in such films as *The Oyster Princess* and *The Doll* (both 1919); did not survive the advent of sound and retired (1933). ❖ See also *Women in World History*.

OSYGUS, Simone (1968—). German swimmer. Born Sept 30, 1968, in Wuppertal, Germany. ❖ At Barcelona Olympics, won a bronze medal in 4 x 100-meter freestyle relay and a silver medal in the 4 x 100-meter medley relay (1992); won a bronze medal for 4 x 100-meter freestyle relay at Atlanta Olympics (1996).

OSYPENKO, Inna (1982—). Ukrainian kayaker. Born Sept 20, 1982, in USSR. ❖ Won a bronze medal for K4 500 at Athens Olympics (2004).

OSYTH (d. around 700). See Osith.

OTAKE, Eiko (1952—). Japanese dancer and choreographer. Name variations: Eiko. Born Feb 14, 1952, in Tokyo, Japan; studied law and political science at Waseda University; m. Koma Otake (dancer); children: son, Yuta Otake. ❖ Joined Tatsumi Hijikata dance company, Tokyo (1971); established 1st partnership with Koma and soon began working as Eiko and Koma (1972); with husband, studied with Manja Chmiel in Germany (1972–73), then toured Germany, Netherlands, Switzerland and Tunisia (1973–75); with husband, took up residency in NY and presented 1st collaborative work, *White Dance* (1976); also choreographed works for CoDanceCo and Dance Alloy, Pittsburgh;

received 2 New York Dance and Performance (Bessie) awards (1984, 1990) and a MacArthur fellowship, known as a "genius" award (1996). Further works of choreography—all in collaboration with Koma—include *Fur Seal* (1976), *New Moon Stories* (1986, comprising the 4 works *Night Tide, Beam, Shadows,* and *Elegy*), *Passage* (1989), *Wind* (1993), and an outdoor collaboration *River* (1995).

OTANI, Sachiko (1965—). Japanese volleyball player. Born Aug 3, 1965, in Japan. ❖ At Los Angeles Olympics, won a bronze medal in team competition (1984).

OTERO, Caroline (1868–1965). Spanish-born dancer and courtesan. Name variations: La Belle Otero; Augustina Otero; billed in New York as Countess Carolina de Otero; (nickname) Lina. Born Augustina Iglesias Otero (but took name Caroline Otero after older sister Carolina died as a child) in village of Valga or Balga, in Galicia, Spain, Nov 4 (or 24), 1868; died in Nice, France, April 10, 1965; dau. of a Spanish Gypsy (Roma) prostitute and an unknown father, possibly a Greek noble; did not attend school, but spoke French and English; married at 15 (div.). ❖ Flourished in *Belle Époque* as one of Paris' "grand horizontals," ostensibly making her living as a Spanish dancer, though it appears she had a lucrative side business in the boudoir; toured in cabarets in eastern Spain and southern France (1882–89); made debut on legitimate stage at Eden Musée in New York City (Oct 1, 1890); went on 1st European tour (1891–92); appeared in Paris at Cirque d'Été (1892); went on world tour (1894); appeared in Paris, including Folies Bergère (1894–95); went on Italian tour (1896–97); returned to NY (1897); gave last performance in London, in the revue *Come Over Here* (Nov 1913); retired from stage (June 1914). ❖ See also Arthur H. Lewis, *La Belle Otero* (Trident, 1967); film *La Belle Otéro,* starring Maria Felix (1954); and *Women in World History*.

OTERO, Katherine Stinson (1891–1977). *See Stinson, Katherine.*

O'TOOLE, Barbara (1960—). English politician. Born Feb 24, 1960, in Kendal, England. ❖ Member of the Newcastle City Council; lecturer and researcher in government and public policy at the School for Advanced Urban Studies, University of Bristol (1991–94) and University of Newcastle (1994–97); worked on the Northern Ireland peace and reconciliation process for Unison; as a European Socialist, elected to 5th European Parliament (1999–2004) from UK.

O'TOOLE, Maureen (1961—). American water-polo player. Name variations: Queen of Water Polo. Born Feb 24, 1961, in Piedmont, CA. ❖ Regarded as the greatest female water-polo player ever, played for 23 years; won a team silver medal at Sydney Olympics (2000). Named World MVP 6 times and US Water Polo Female Athlete of the Year 5 times.

OTSETOVA, Svetlana (1950—). Bulgarian rower. Born Nov 23, 1950, in Bulgaria. ❖ At Montreal Olympics, won a gold medal in double sculls (1976).

OTT, Mirjam (1972—). Swiss curler. Born Jan 27, 1972, in Switzerland. ❖ Won a silver medal for curling at Salt Lake City Olympics (2002) and Torino Olympics (2006).

OTT, Patricia (1960—). West German field-hockey player. Born May 15, 1960, in West Germany. ❖ At Los Angeles Olympics, won a silver medal in team competition (1984).

OTTENBERG, Nettie Podell (1887–1982). American social worker. Born Nettie Podell in Ukraine, Russia, April 5, 1887; died in Washington, DC, May 11, 1982; dau. of Mordecai "Max" Podell (bookkeeper) and Mannie Podell; attended New York School of Philanthropy and graduated in 1st class, 1905; m. Louis Ottenberg, April 10, 1912 (died May 10, 1960); children: Regina, Miriam, and Louis Ottenberg Jr. ❖ One the 1st formally trained social workers in US, worked for more than 60 years to improve laws and social policies affecting women and children; immigrated to America (1893); spent childhood in New York City; moved to Washington, DC (1912); worked as juvenile probation officer, Philadelphia (1906–09); examined newly arrived immigrant girls, Brooklyn Council of Jewish Women (1909–11); organized and ran 1st political settlement house for suffrage workers, Harlem, NY (1909–11); was state organizer and speaker, NY State Suffrage Association (1912); was a founding member of a Voteless DC chapter of League of Women Voters (1920), and served as president (1937–39); served as president for Washington, DC Section, National Council of Jewish Women (1937–39) and representative to its Women's Joint Congressional Committee (1928–77); appointed to Public Welfare Advisory Committee on day care (1963); won 1st federal funding for day care (1964); was a board member, National Child Day Care Association, Washington, DC (1964–70s); advocated use of federal Medicaid money for early and periodic screening, diagnosis and treatment for underprivileged children (1971). ❖ See also *Women in World History.*

OTTENBRITE, Anne (1966—). Canadian swimmer. Born May 12, 1966, in Whitby, Ontario, Canada; attended University of Southern California, 1984–86, and Wilfrid Laurier University, 1987–90; m. Marlin Maylaert; children: Cameron. ❖ Won the silver and bronze medals in the 100-meter and 200-meter breaststroke at World championships (1982) and the gold and silver medals in the 100-meter and 200-meter breaststroke at Commonwealth Games (1982); won 5 Canadian national titles in breaststroke; at Los Angeles Olympics, won a gold medal in the 200-meter breaststroke (Canada's 1st gold medal in women's swimming), a silver medal in the 100-meter breaststroke, and a bronze medal in the 4 x 100-meter medley relay (1984).

OTTENDORFER, Anna Uhl (1815–1884). German-born American newspaper publisher and philanthropist. Born Anna Sartorius, Feb 13, 1815, in Wurzburg, Bavaria (now part of Germany); died April 1, 1884, in New York, NY; dau. of Eduard Sartorius (by some accounts Eduard Behr, a shopkeeper); m. Jacob Uhl (printer, died 1852); m. Oswald Ottendorfer (editor), July 23, 1859; children: (1st m.) 6, including Edward Uhl; Mathilde Uhl von Riedl; Emma Uhl Schalk; and Anna Uhl Woerishoffer. ❖ Immigrated to New York City from Bavaria (c. 1836); with 1st husband, bought a print shop and began printing German weekly *New-Yorker Staats-Zeitung* (1844); bought newspaper outright and with husband shared responsibilities of printing and publishing it (1845); took over paper's leadership after 1st husband died (1852); married Oswald Ottendorfer, who had become editor of her newspaper (1859); contributed $100,000 to build the Isabella Home for aged German-American women in Astoria (1875); contributed another $100,000 to establish Hermann Uhl Memorial Fund to support the study of German in American schools (1881); gave funds for women's pavilion and a German dispensary and reading room to New York's German Hospital (1882 and 1884, respectively). Awarded gold medal by Augusta of Saxe-Weimar. ❖ See also *Women in World History.*

OTTESEN-JENSEN, Elise (1886–1973). Norwegian-born feminist and author. Name variations: (pseudonym) Ottar. Born in Jaaren [Jaeren], Hojland, Sweden (now Norway), Jan 2, 1886; died in Stockholm, Sweden, Sept 4, 1973; 17th of 18 children of Immanuel Ottesen (Lutheran cleric) and Karen Ursula (Essendrop) Ottesen; m. Albert Jensen (well-known Swedish syndicalist), 1931; children: 1 son (died two days after birth, 1917). ❖ One of the major personalities in European family planning and sex education, began career as a respected journalist, using pen name "Ottar"; articles on need for reform of Sweden's abortion laws, as well as her spirited advocacy of women's rights, including suffrage, made her well known in working-class circles; began to write and lecture on need for sex education, even traveling to remote outposts (1923); spread the message through pamphlets, including *Unwanted Children* (1926) and *Tell Your Child the Truth* (1945); also published a periodical devoted to these social problems and maintained that masturbation in a healthy adolescent was a normal activity and that homosexuality was a biological phenomenon and should not be stigmatized; played a key role in founding Sweden's National League for Sexual Education (RFSU, 1932); saw the opening of "Ottar House," for unwed mothers and their children (1942); during WWII, provided assistance to Jewish refugees who had fled Nazi-occupied Norway and Denmark; convened an international conference in Stockholm that resulted in the founding of International Committee on Planned Parenthood (1945) and was elected its 2nd president (1959). Received Lasker Award (1945) and Illis Quorum gold medal from Swedish Medical Board (1951). ❖ See also *Women in World History.*

OTTEY, Merlene (1960—). Jamaican runner. Name variations: Merlene Ottey-Page. Born Merlene Ottey, May 10, 1960, in Pondside (Cold Springs), Jamaica; graduate of University of Nebraska, 1984; m. Nat Page (American high jumper and hurdler), 1984. ❖ Won more World championship medals (outdoors 14, indoors 6) than any other athlete at the time, male or female; won 34 medals in major championships, including the NCAA championship in the 100-meter sprint (1982); at the Commonwealth Games, won a gold medal in the 200 meters (1982 and 1991), and gold medal in the 60 meters (1995); won a bronze medal in the 200 meters at the Moscow Olympics (1980) and bronze medals in the 100 and 200 meters at Los Angeles Olympics (1984); won a bronze medal in the 200 meters at Barcelona Olympics (1992); won silver

medals for the 100 meters and 200 meters and a bronze for the 4 x 100-meter relay at Atlanta Olympics (1996); won a silver medal in the 4 x 100-meter relay at Sydney Olympics (2000), the oldest female Olympian ever at 40 years and 143 days. ❖ See also Claire Forrester and Alvin Campbell, *Unyielding Spirit;* and *Women in World History.*

OTTO, Kristin (1966—). East German swimmer. Born Feb 7, 1966, in Leipzig, East Germany. ❖ At World championships, won gold medals for the 100-meter backstroke, 4 x 100-meter medley relay and 4 x 100-meter free relay (1982) and gold medals for the 100-meter freestyle, 200-meter indiv. medley, 4 x 100-meter medley relay and 4 x 100-meter free relay (1986); won Olympic gold medals at Seoul in the 50-meter freestyle, 100-meter freestyle, 100-meter backstroke, 100-meter butterfly, 4 x 100-meter freestyle relay and 4 x 100-meter medley relay (1988); set the world record in the 100-meter with a time of 54.73 (1986), which stood for years. After German reunification, Stasi (secret police) documents revealed that most of the GDR woman swimmers, including Otto, had been forced to take performance-enhancing drugs. ❖ See also *Women in World History.*

OTTO, Louise (1896—). German swimmer. Born Aug 30, 1896, in Germany. ❖ At Stockholm Olympics, won a silver medal in the 4 x 100-meter freestyle relay (1912).

OTTO, Sylke (1969—). German luge champion. Born July 7, 1969, in Germany. ❖ Won World championship for luge (2000, 2001, 2003, and 2005); won a gold medal for single luge at Salt Lake City Olympics (2002), breaking the track record twice; won a gold medal for single luge at Torino Olympics (2006).

OTTO-CREPIN, Margit (1945—). French equestrian. Name variations: Margit Crepin. Born Feb 9, 1945, in France. ❖ At Seoul Olympics, won a silver medal in indiv. dressage (1988).

OTTO-PETERS, Luise (1819–1895). German women's-rights activist. Name variations: Louise Otto; Louise Otto-Peters; Luise Otto; Luise Peters; Louise Peters; Luise Otto Peters; (pseudonym) Otto Stern. Born Luise Otto, Mar 26, 1819, in Meissen, Germany; died Mar 13, 1895, at Leipzig; dau. of Wilhelm Otto (court assessor) and Charlotte Matthäi Otto (dau. of a porcelain painter); m. August Peters (poet and revolutionary), July 8, 1858 (died July 4, 1864); no children. ❖ Co-founder of the General German Women's Association and editor of the 1st German women's political newspaper, the *Frauen-Zeitung,* who was the most important figure in the early German women's movement; published 1st poem (1842); published 1st book, *Songs of a Young German Woman* (*Lieder eines deutschen Mädchens,* 1847); published the social novel *Schloss und Fabrik* (*Castle and Factory,* 1845); edited the *Women's Newspaper* (*Frauen-Zeitung,* 1849–52); was a co-founder of the General German Women's Association, the 1st major women's organization in Germany, and elected its 1st president (1865); co-edited the association's journal, *New Paths* (*Neue Bahnen,* 1866–95); co-founded the Leipzig Women's Educational Association (1865) and the Leipzig Women's Writers Association (1890); came to believe that organizations, by providing education and vocational training for women, would achieve the equality of men and women in everyday life and thus "emancipate" the German middle class. ❖ See also *The Path of My Life* (*Mein Lebensgang,* 1893); (in German) Cordula Koepcke, *Louise Otto-Peters: Die rote Demokratin* (Herderbücherei, 1981); and *Women in World History.*

OTWAY-RUTHVEN, Jocelyn (1909–1989). Irish historian. Name variations: J. A. Otway-Ruthven. Born Jocelyn Annette Otway-Ruthven in Dublin, Ireland, Nov 7, 1909; died in Dublin, Mar 18, 1989; dau. of Captain Robert Mervyn Birmingham Otway-Ruthven and Margaret Casement Otway-Ruthven; Trinity College, Dublin, BA, 1931; Girton College, Cambridge, PhD, 1937. ❖ One of the legendary figures at Trinity, won the Thirlwall prize (1937), and her prize-winning essay on the "King's Secretary and the Signet Office" in the 15th century was published by Cambridge University Press (1939); was a lecturer, Trinity College, Dublin (1938–51); appointed Lecky Professor of History (1951); named a fellow of Trinity College, one of the 1st women fellows there (1968) and built up the Medieval History Department into one of the finest departments in the college; served as dean of Faculty of Humanities (1969–73); was a member of the Irish Manuscripts Commission; was a member of International Commission for the History of Representative and Parliamentary Institutions; retired (1980); also wrote *A History of Medieval Ireland* (1968). ❖ See also *Women in World History.*

OU JINGBAI. Chinese softball player. Born in China. ❖ Won a silver medal at Atlanta Olympics (1996).

OUDEN, Willemijntje den (1918–1997). Dutch swimmer. Name variations: Willie den Ouden; Willy de Ouden. Born Jan 1918 (some sources cite 1919) in Rotterdam, Netherlands; died 1997. ❖ Won silver medals for 4 x 100-meter freestyle relay and 100-meter freestyle at Los Angeles Olympics (1932); won a gold medal for 4 x 100-meter freestyle relay at Berlin Olympics (1936); was the 1st woman to break a minute for 100-yard freestyle, and held the record for 20 years. Inducted into International Swimming Hall of Fame (1970). ❖ See also *Women in World History*.

OUDH, begum of (c. 1820–1879). *See Hazrat Mahal.*

OUELLETTE, Caroline (1979—). Canadian ice-hockey player. Born May 25, 1979, in Montreal, Quebec, Canada. ❖ Won a team gold medal at Salt Lake City Olympics (2002) and a team gold medal at Torino Olympics (2006).

OUGHTON, Diana (1942–1970). American radical terrorist. Born Jan 26, 1942, in Dwight, IL; died Mar 6, 1970, in Greenwich Village, NY; dau. of James Oughton (served in Illinois State legislature) and Jane Oughton; attended Bryn Mawr College. ❖ Radicalized while witnessing poverty during work for American Friends Service Committee in Guatemala; taught children in a radical, free children's school in Michigan (1966); joined Students for a Democratic Society (SDS); joined Weather Underground (WU), a militant split-off group from SDS; died with 2 other members of WU (Ted Gold and Terry Robins) in an accidental explosion at a Greenwich Village home that had been turned into a bomb-making factory (1970). ❖ See also Thomas Powers, *Diana: The Making of a Terrorist* (1971); Bill Ayers, *Fugitive Days* (2001); (film) *The Weather Underground* (2004).

OUGHTON, Winifred (1890–1964). English actress and acting teacher. Born 1890 in London, England; died Dec 26, 1964, in England. ❖ Made stage debut as a walk-on in *The Merchant of Venice* at the Old Vic (1915), then played over 70 men's parts at the same theater during WWI (1915–20); appeared with Sybil Thorndike and Lewis Casson (1924–30); taught at Royal Academy of Dramatic Art (RADA, 1935–58).

OUIDA (1839–1908). *See Ramée, Louise de la.*

OULEHLOVA, Lenka (1973—). Czech rhythmic gymnast. Born June 14, 1973, in Czechoslovakia. ❖ Was Czech National champion; competed in 3 Olympics.

OUMANSOFF or OUMANSOV, Raïssa (1883–1960). *See Maritain, Raïssa.*

OURY, Anna Caroline de Belleville (1808–1880). *See Belleville-Oury, Anna Caroline de.*

OUSPENSKAYA, Maria (1876–1949). Russian stage and screen actress. Name variations: Marie Ouspenskaya. Born in Tula, Russia, July 29, 1876; died in a fire that also destroyed her home in Hollywood, California, Dec 3, 1949. ❖ Legendary actress who was nominated for Academy Awards for *Dodsworth* (1936) and *Love Affair* (1939), gained early fame with Moscow Art Theater (1876); made US stage debut in *Tsar Fyodor Ivanovitch* (1923); appeared on Broadway in *The Saint, The Witch, Dodsworth, Abide with Me, Daughters of Atreus, Outrageous Fortune,* a revival of *The Jest,* and an updated *Taming of the Shrew*; for a number of years, also ran a New York acting school; a dominant Hollywood character actress (1936–40s), is probably best remembered as fortuneteller Maleva in *The Wolf Man* (1941); other films include *The Cricket on the Hearth* (Russian, 1915), *Dr. Torpokov* (Russian, 1917), *Conquest* (1937), *The Rains Came* (1939), *Judge Hardy and Son* (1939), *Dr. Ehrlich's Magic Bullet* (1940), *Waterloo Bridge* (1940), *Dance Girl Dance* (1940), *Kings Row* (1942), *The Mystery of Marie Roget* (1942), *Frankenstein Meets the Wolf Man* (1943) and *Wyoming* (1947). ❖ See also *Women in World History*.

OUSSET, Cécile (1936—). French pianist. Name variations: Cecile Ousset. Born in Tarbes, France, Mar 3, 1936; studied with Marcel Ciampi at Paris Conservatoire. ❖ At 5, made debut; at 14, graduated from Paris Conservatoire (1950); won many major piano competitions (1953–62), including the Pagès, the Marguerite Long–Jacques Thibaud, the Geneva, the Queen Elisabeth of Belgium (in honor of Elizabeth of Bavaria), the Busoni, and the Van Cliburn prizes; enjoyed a world virtuoso career, performing almost all of the great concertos; acclaimed for her Chopin and Schumann interpretations and some of her solo pieces of Saint-Saëns, is also well known for championing such lesser-known scores as Camille Saint-Saëns' *Allegro appassionato*.

OUTHWAITE, Ida Rentoul (1888–1960). Australian illustrator. Signed work: I.S. Rentoul, I.S.R. Pronunciation: OOTH-wait. Born Ida Sherbourne Rentoul, June 9, 1888, in Melbourne, Victoria, Australia; died in Melbourne, June 25, 1960; dau. of John Laurence Rentoul (Presbyterian moderator-general and professor of theology) and Annie Isobel (Rattray) Rentoul (amateur watercolorist); sister of Annie Rattray Rentoul (1882–1978); attended Presbyterian Ladies' College; m. (Arthur) Grenbry Outhwaite, Dec 9, 1909; children: Robert Rentoul (1910–1941); Anne Isobel Rentoul (b. 1911); Wendy Laurence Rentoul (b. 1914); William Grenbry Rentoul (1919–1945). ❖ Highly popular children's fantasy illustrator who assisted in raising the status of illustration in her country and the quality of publishing for children; published 1st illustrated stories (1903); began illustrating for magazines (1903); illustrated 1st book, *Mollie's Bunyip,* by A.R. and I.S. Rentoul (Melbourne 1904); began exhibiting in Australia (1907); with pictures and verse depicting an Australian landscape, published the costly 4-color-process edition of *Elves and Fairies* (1916), from which reproductions decorated the walls of kindergartens, schools and homes for decades afterwards; exhibited in Paris and London (1920); wrote and illustrated *Blossom: a Fairy Story* (1928), *Bunny and Brownie* (1930), *A Bunch of Wildflowers* (1933) and *Sixpence to Spend* (1935); earned last substantial commission for *Legends From the Outback* by P.M. Power (1958); also illustrated Tarella Quin's *Gum Tree Brownie and Other Faerie Folk of the Never Never* (1907), Annie R. Rentoul's *The Lady of the Blue Beads* (1908), Quin's *Before the Lamps are Lit* (1911), A.R. Rentoul's *The Little Green Road to Fairyland* (1922), *The Fairyland of Ida Rentoul Outhwaite* (1926), "Benjamin Bear" comic strip, *Weekly Times* (Sydney, 1933–39), and Tarella Quin Daskein's *Chimney Town* (1934). ❖ See also Marcie Muir and Robert Holden, *The Fairy World of Ida Rentoul Outhwaite* (Craftsman, 1985); and *Women in World History*.

OUTLAND, Kit (1910–1985). *See Klein, Kit.*

OVARI, Eva (1961—). Hungarian gymnast. Born April 28, 1961, in Hungary. ❖ Won Hungarian International (1979); competed in 2 Olympics (1976, 1980).

OVCHINNIKOVA, Elena (1982—). Russian synchronized swimmer. Name variations: Yelena Ovchinnikova. Born June 17, 1982, in USSR. ❖ At World championships, won team gold medals (2001, 2003); won a team gold medal at Athens Olympics (2004).

OVCHINNIKOVA, Yelena.
See Chebukina, Yelena (1965—).
See Ovtchinnikova, Elena (1965—).

OVECHKINA, Nadezhda (1958—). Soviet field-hockey player. Born Sept 30, 1958, in USSR. ❖ At Moscow Olympics, won a bronze medal in team competition (1980).

OVECHKINA, Tatyana (1950—). Soviet basketball player. Born Mar 19, 1950, in USSR. ❖ Won a gold medal at Montreal Olympics (1976) and a gold medal at Moscow Olympics (1980), both in team competition.

OVERBECK, Carla (1969—). American soccer player. Born Carla Werden, May 9, 1969, in Pasadena, CA; attended University of North Carolina; m. Greg Overbeck (restaurateur). ❖ Defender and midfielder; at World Cup, won a team gold medal (1991, 1999) and a bronze medal (1995); won a team gold medal at Atlanta Olympics (1996) and a team silver at Sydney Olympics (2000); was a founding member of the Women's United Soccer Association (WUSA); signed with the Carolina Courage (2001). ❖ See also Jere Longman *The Girls of Summer* (HarperCollins, 2000).

OVERESCH, Bettina (1962—). *See Hoy, Bettina.*

OVERLACH, Helene (1894–1983). German politician. Name variations: Lene Overlach; (underground names) Frieda, Klara, Frau Teschmer. Born in Greiz, Thuringia, Germany, July 7, 1894; died in East Berlin, Aug 7, 1983; dau. of Martin Overlach (physician); never married; children: daughter, Hanna. ❖ German Communist leader, moved to Munich (1919); joined Freie Sozialistische Jugend (Free Socialist Youth); became a Communist (1920); worked as secretary to Wilhelm Pieck (1921–25), a top KPD leader; was a member of editorial staff of Essen's KPD newspaper, *Ruhr-Echo* (1923–25); became closely identified with KPD faction led by Ernst Thälmann; chosen de facto leader of KPD women's organization, the Roter Frauen- und Mädchenbund (Red Girls' and Women's League, RFMB, 1925); though Clara Zetkin was nominal RFMB leader, headed the day-to-day work of the organization; at 11th Party Congress of KPD, elected a member of national Central Committee (1927) and put in charge of women's affairs; elected to Reichstag (1928), representing a working-class district in Düsseldorf; re-elected to Central Committee (1929) and was a candidate member of policy-making KPD Politburo; became increasingly involved in Soviet and international Communist activities, traveling to Moscow, France and Britain (1931–32); addressed 1,500 women at a Congress of Working Women and a mass rally of 10,000 women in Sportpalast (both Berlin, 1931); with Hitler's rise to power, was arrested in Essen (1933) and imprisoned in concentration camps (1934–38) for the Nazi-concocted charge of "preparation for high treason"; again arrested after failed assassination attempt on Hitler (1944), sent to Ravensbrück; with help of friends, was put on a list to be sent to Sweden (1945); returned to Berlin (1946); joined Socialist Unity Party; became a professor at Pedagogical Academy in East Berlin (1950). Awarded Clara Zetkin Medal (1955). ❖ See also *Women in World History*.

OVERSLOOT, Maria (1914—). Dutch swimmer. Name variations: Puck Oversloot. Born May 22, 1914, in Netherlands. ❖ At Los Angeles Olympics, won a silver medal in the 4 x 100-meter freestyle relay (1932).

OVERTON, Harriet Maria (1818–1907). *See Ritchie, Harriet Maria.*

OVINGTON, Mary White (1865–1951). American social reformer. Born Mary White Ovington, April 11, 1865, in Brooklyn, NY; died July 15, 1951, in Newton Highlands, Massachusetts; dau. of Theodore Tweedy Ovington (china and glass importer) and Ann Louise (Ketcham) Ovington; attended Packer Collegiate Institute, 1888–91, and Radcliffe College, 1891–93. ❖ A white feminist and civil-rights activist who was one of the founders of NAACP, worked as registrar of Pratt Institute in Brooklyn; was head worker at Greenpoint Settlement (1895–1903); served as vice-president of Brooklyn Consumers' League; was assistant secretary of Social Reform Club; joined Socialist Party of America (c. 1905); was a social worker at Greenwich House; helped to found the National Negro Committee, later to become the National Association for the Advancement of Colored People (NAACP, c. 1909); published *Half a Man: The Status of the Negro in New York* (1911); served as chair of the board of NAACP (1919–32); wrote a number of books and articles, including a profile of black leaders, *Portraits in Color* (1927). ❖ See also autobiography, *The Walls Came Tumbling Down* (1947); Carolyn Wedin, *Inheritors of the Spirit: Mary White Ovington and the Founding of the NAACP* (Wiley, 1997); and *Women in World History*.

OVTCHINNIKOVA, Elena (1965—). Russian-American climber. Name variations: Elena, Lena or Yelena Ovchinnikova. Born June 29, 1965, in Selenginsk, Siberia, Russia; married; children: 2. ❖ Among the top speed climbers in the world, began competing on World Cup circuit for Russia (1988); began competing for US (1996); won gold in Speed Climbing at X Games (1995, 1997, and 1998) and silver in Bouldering and Difficulty (1995). Other 1st-place finishes include: National, San Francisco, CA (in Difficulty, 1997); National, Boulder, CO (in Difficulty, 1997); Sony Xtreme Games, Gold Coast, Australia (in Speed and in Difficulty, 1998); Phoenix Bouldering, Phoenix, AZ (in Rock, 1998); and National, NY, NY (in Speed, 1998).

OVTCHINNIKOVA, Yelena (1965—). *See Chebukina, Yelena.*

OWEN, Catherine Dale (1900–1965). American stage and screen actress. Born July 28, 1900, in Louisville, KY; died Sept 7, 1965, in New York, NY. ❖ Made NY stage debut in *Little Women* (1920); had successful Broadway career in such plays as *Happy Go Lucky, The Mountain Man, Trelawny of the Wells* and *The Play's the Thing*; films include *His Glorious Night* (with John Gilbert), *The Rogue Song, Born Reckless, Forbidden Woman, Behind Office Doors* and *Such Men Are Dangerous*.

OWEN, Jane (fl. 1617–1634). British devotional writer. Fl. between 1617 and 1634 in England. ❖ Wrote *Antidote Against Purgatory* (1634), which gives practical and spiritual advice to English Catholic recusants.

OWEN, Laurence (1945–1961). American figure skater. Born 1945 in Massachusetts; died in plane crash near Berg, Belgium, Feb 15, 1961, on way to Prague, Czechoslovakia, to compete in World championships; daughter of Maribel Vinson Owen (1911–1961, skater and coach) and Guy Owen (top-ranked skater who died in 1952); sister of Maribel Owen (1941–1961, figure skater). ❖ Placed 3rd at US nationals and 6th at Squaw Valley Olympics (1960); placed 1st at US nationals senior singles and 1st at North American championships (1961).

OWEN, Margaret (d. 1941). *See Lloyd George, Margaret.*

OWEN, Maribel (1941–1961). American pairs skater. Born Maribel Owen Jr., 1941, in MA; died in a plane crash near Berg, Belgium, Feb 15, 1961, on way to Prague, Czechoslovakia, to compete in World championships; dau. of Maribel Vinson Owen (1911–1961, skater and coach) and Guy Owen (skater); sister of Laurence Owen (1945–1961, figure skater). ❖ Participated at Squaw Valley Olympics (1960); placed 1st at US National senior pairs competition and 2nd at North American championships (1961).

OWEN, Maribel Vinson (1911–1961). American figure skater and coach. Name variations: Maribel Vinson or Maribel Y. Vinson; Maribel Vinson-Owen. Born Maribel Y. Vinson, 1911, in Winchester, MA; died in plane crash near Berg, Belgium, Feb 15, 1961, on way to Prague, Czechoslovakia, for World championships; dau. of Thomas Vinson (renowned skater) and Gertrude Vinson; graduate of Radcliffe College; married Guy Owen (skater, died 1952); children: Maribel Owen (1941–1961, figure skater); Laurence Owen (1945–1961, figure skater). ❖ Finished 4th at St. Moritz Olympics (1928); won a bronze medal at Lake Placid Olympics (1932); won US National figure skating championships 9 times (1928–33, 1936–37); won US pairs title 6 times.

OWEN, Nora (1945—). Irish politician. Born Nora O'Mahony, June 1945, in Dublin, Ireland; grandniece of Michael Collins (1890–1922, Irish nationalist) and Margaret Collins-O'Driscoll (1878–1945, TD); sister of Mary Banotti (Member of the European Parliament, MEP); m. Brian Owen. ❖ Began career as an industrial chemist; representing Fine Gael, elected to 22nd Dáil (1981–82) for Dublin North; returned to 23rd–24th (1982–87) and 26th–28th Dáil (1989–2002); served as minister for Justice (1994–97).

OWEN, Ruth Bryan (1885–1954). *See Rohde, Ruth Bryan Owen.*

OWEN, Seena (1894–1966). American actress. Name variations: Signe Auen. Born Signe Auen, Nov 14, 1894, in Spokane, WA; died Aug 15, 1966, in Hollywood, CA; m. George Walsh (actor), 1916 (div. 1924). ❖ Leading player during silent era, appeared in such films as *The Blue Danube, Lavender and Old Lace, The Rush Hour, Sinners in Love, Marriage Playground, Queen Kelly*, and as Princess Beloved in *Intolerance*, having used her real name in early credits; retired from acting (1933), then collaborated on many screenplays (1934–47).

OWENS, Claire Myers (1896–1983). American writer. Name variations: (pseudonym) Claire Myers Spotswood. Born Clairene Lenora Allen Myers in Denton, Texas, 1896; died in Rochester, New York, 1983; dau. of Coren Lee Myers (schoolteacher and principal) and Susan (Allen) Myers; College of Industrial Arts (now Texas Woman's University), BS in Domestic Science, 1916; m. 1st husband, reporter George Wanders (div.); m. 3rd husband, H. Thurston Owens III, 1937 (died 1969). ❖ Published 1st book, *The Unpredictable Adventure: A Comedy of Woman's Independence* (1935), which explored the double standard by which she felt women were judged and was banned by New York Public Library because of its explicit treatment of female sexuality; experienced a spiritual transformation (1949) and undertook the study of the humanistic and transpersonal psychology of Abraham Maslow and Anthony Sutich, as well as the philosophy of Aldous Huxley, who became a close friend; met and interviewed psychologist Carl Jung (1954) and later wrote a prizewinning article about their encounter; at age 70, took up Zen and published *Zen and the Lady* (1979). ❖ See also autobiography *Discovery of Self* (1963) and the autobiographical *Awakening to the Good: Psychological Or Religious?* (1958); and *Women in World History*.

OWENS, Dana (1970—). *See Queen Latifah.*

OWENS, Evelyn P. (1931—). Irish politician. Born Jan 22, 1931, in Dublin, Ireland. ❖ Elected to the Seanad from the Labour Panel: Nominating Bodies Sub-Panel (1969–77); was the 1st woman appointed deputy chair of the Labour Court (1984), then the 1st woman chair (1994–98).

OWENS, Patricia (1925–2000). Canadian actress. Born Jan 17, 1925, in Golden, British Columbia, Canada; died Aug 31, 2000, in Lancaster, CA; m. Sy Bartlett (screenwriter and producer); m. twice more. ❖ Lead player in English and American films, including *Miss London Ltd.* (1943), *The Good Die Young* (1954), *Sayonara* (1957), *No Down Payment* (1957), *Black Spurs* (1966) and *The Destructors* (1968); portrayed the heroine in sci-fi classic *The Fly* (1958).

OWENS, Shirley (1941—). African-American singer. Name variations: Shirley Owens Alston; The Shirelles. Born Shirley Owens, June 10, 1941, in Passaic, NJ. ❖ With Doris Coley, Addie "Micki" Harris and Beverly Lee, formed the Shirelles in Passaic, NJ (1958), among the 1st all-girl groups of rock era; with group, had hit singles "I Met Him on a Sunday," "Tonight's the Night" (1960), "Will You Love Me Tomorrow?" (1961), "Baby It's You" (1963), "Mama Said," "Soldier Boy," and "Foolish Little Girl"; sang with group's surviving members, Coley and Lee, at Rhythm and Blues Foundation awards ceremony (1994), and on Dionne Warwick album. Shirelles were inducted into Rock and Roll Hall of Fame (1996).

OWENS-ADAIR, Bethenia (1840–1926). American physician and eugenics advocate. Born Bethenia Angelina Owens, Feb 7, 1840, in Van Buren Co., Missouri; died Sept 11, 1926, in Portland, Oregon; dau. of Thomas Owens (farmer) and Sarah Damron Owens; Eclectic Medical College, MD, 1874; University of Michigan, MD, 1880; m. Legrand Hall, May 4, 1854 (div. 1859); m. Colonel John Adair, 1884 (died 1915); children: (1st m.) George (b. April 17, 1856); Mattie Belle Palmer (adopted 1875); (2nd m.) daughter (1887–1887); (adopted) Victor Adair Hill and John Adair Jr. ❖ At 3, moved with family to Oregon; married at 14; opened a dressmaking shop (1867); obtained MD from University of Michigan; set up successful medical practice in Portland (1881), one of the 1st women doctors in Oregon; also became active in Oregon State Medical Society and supported suffrage and eugenics; like many educated and influential people of her day, became a champion of sterilization for, among others, the mentally retarded, epileptics, and those who were "feebleminded" or "insane"; joined with several other physicians (1907) to lobby the legislatures in both Washington State and Oregon for passage of a bill mandating sterilization of people committed to state mental institutions; published *Human Sterilization* (1910), *Human Sterilization: Its Social and Legislative Aspects* (1922), and *The Eugenic Marriage Law and Human Sterilization* (1922). ❖ See also memoir *Dr. Owens-Adair: Some of Her Life Experiences* (1906); Helen Markely Miller, *Woman Doctor of the West: Bethenia Owens-Adair* (1960); and *Women in World History*.

OWENSON, Miss Sydney (1780–1859). See Morgan, Sydney.

OWINGS, Margaret Wentworth (1913–1999). American conservationist. Born Margaret Wentworth, April 29, 1913, in Berkeley, CA; died at home in Big Sur, CA, Jan 21, 1999; dau. of Jean and Frank Wentworth (trustee of Mills College); graduate of Mills College, 1934; completed graduate studies in art at Fogg Museum at Harvard University, 1935; m. Malcolm Millard (div.); m. Nathaniel Owings (architect and founding partner in Skidmore, Owings & Merrill, died 1984); children: (1st m.) Wendy Millard Benjamin. ❖ Served as commissioner of California Parks (1963–69); chaired the California Mountain Lion Preservation Fund; founded Friends of the Sea Otter, to save the threatened California sea otters (1968), and served as its president (1968–90s); campaigned to keep Big Sur coast in its undeveloped state; founded the Rachel Carson Council; wrote *Voice from the Sea: Reflections on Wildlife and Wilderness* (1999).

OXFORD, countess of.
See Mortimer, Margaret (d. around 1296).
See Vere, Maud de (fl. 1360s).
See Badlesmere, Maud (d. 1366).
See Howard, Elizabeth (c. 1410–1475).
See Trussel, Elizabeth (1496–1527).
See Howard, Anne (d. 1559).
See Cecil, Anne (1556–1589).

OXFORD AND ASQUITH, countess of. See Asquith, Margot (1864–1945).

OZEGOVIC, Sanja (1959—). Yugoslavian basketball player. Born June 15, 1959, in Yugoslavia. ❖ At Moscow Olympics, won a bronze medal in team competition (1980).

OZICK, Cynthia (1928—). Jewish-American novelist, essayist, playwright, short-story writer, and poet. Born Cynthia Ozick, April 17, 1928, in New York, NY; raised in the Bronx; dau. of William Ozick (pharmacy owner) and Celia (Regelson) Ozick (both Russian immigrants); attended Hunter College High School, New York University; Ohio State University, MA; m. Bernard Hallote (lawyer), 1952; children: Rachel Hallotte (PhD in biblical archaeology). ❖ One of most important of 20th-century Jewish-American writers, translated Yiddish poetry and published many reviews; writings, suffused with central European culture, include *Trust* (1966), *The Pagan Rabbi and Other Stories* (1971), *Bloodshed and Three Novellas* (1976), *Levitation: Five Fictions* (1982), *Art and Ardor Essays* (1983), *The Messiah of Stockholm* (1987), *Metaphor and Memory* (1989, *Fame and Folly* (1996), *The Puttermesser Papers* (1997), and *Quarrel and Quandary: Essays* (2000); also wrote the play *The Shawl*, 1st produced off-Broadway (1996). Thrice won O. Henry Prize for short stories; was the 1st recipient of the Michael Rea Award (1986).

OZOLINA, Elvira (1939—). Soviet track-and-field athlete. Born Oct 1939 in USSR. ❖ At Rome Olympics, won a gold medal in the javelin throw (1960); set world records (1960, 1963, 1964).

P-Q

❖

P., Kaare (1873–1942). *See Anker, Nini Roll.*

PAALEN, Alice (1904–1987). *See Rahon, Alice.*

PAALZOW, Henriette (1788–1847). German novelist and salonnière.
Name variations: Henriette von Paalzow or Palzow. Born Henriette
Wach, Feb 22, 1788, in Berlin, Germany; died Oct 30, 1847, in
Berlin; sister of Wilhelm Wach (1787–1845, painter); m. Major Carl
Philipp Paalzow, 1816 (div. 1822). ❖ Following brief marriage, set up a
house with mother and brother in Berlin, which became a meeting place
for artists and intellectuals; became well known for historical novels such
as *Godwie Castle* (1836) and *Sainte Roche* (1939).

PAASCHE, Maria (1909–2000). Anti-Nazi activist in the 1930s. Name
variations: Maria Therese von Hammerstein. Born Maria Therese von
Hammerstein, 1909, in Magdeburg, Germany; died Jan 21, 2000, in San
Francisco, California; dau. of General Kurt von Hammerstein (comman-
der-in-chief of German army, 1930–34, and anti-Hitler conspirator);
granddau. of General Walther von Lüttwitz; sister of anti-Hitler conspirators Ludwig von Hammerstein and Kunrat von Hammerstein;
attended University of Berlin; m. John H. Paasche, 1935 (died 1994);
children: Gottfried Paasche; Joan Briegleb; Michaela Grudin; Virginia
Dakin. ❖ Transported Jews to Prague (1930s); smuggled information to
anti-Nazi community; exiled in Japan during WWII; immigrated to US
(1948); worked as literary researcher; subject of documentary *Silent
Courage: Maria Therese von Hammerstein and Her Battle Against Nazism*
(1999). ❖ See also *Women in World History.*

PACA (1825–1860). Duchess of Alba. Name variations: Francisca Teresa;
Paquita. Born Maria Francisca in 1825; died of breast cancer in 1860;
dau. of Cipriano Guzman y Porto Carrero, count of Teba (subsequently
count of Montijo and grandee of Spain) and Manuela Kirkpatrick,
countess of Montijo (dau. of William Kirkpatrick, US consul at
Malaga); sister of Eugénie (1826–1920), empress of France; married
the duke of Alba and Berwick. ❖ See also *Women in World History.*

**PACARI, Nina (1961—). Ecuadorian politician and indigenous rights
activist.** Born Maria Estela Vega Conejo, Oct 9, 1961, in Cotacachi,
Imbabura, Ecuador; dau. of José Manuel Vega (tradesman) and Rosa
Elena Conejo. ❖ Advocate for indigenous self-determination, land
rights, preservation of cultural identity, values and language, was one of
1st indigenous persons in Cotacachi to attain higher education and 1st
indigenous woman in Ecuador to earn a university degree in jurisprudence; became involved with student movement embracing indigenous
roots; changed name to Nina Pacari, which in *Quichua* (indigenous
language) means "light dawn" or dawning of new consciousness; worked
with Federation of Indigenous and Country Peoples of Imbabura (FICI);
used legal training to work with indigenous communities on land and
labor rights as well as social problems; began to press for legal reforms that
would recognize indigenous nationalities, officially recognize *Quichua*
language, democratize access to political power and provide indigenous
people with land; worked on national level (1989–93), as legal advisor
with pan-indigenous Confederation of Indigenous Nationalities of
Ecuador (CONAIE), helped coordinate CONAIE-led peasant uprisings
(1990, 1994), which paralyzed nation and yielded substantive government concessions for reforms; appointed national executive secretary for
planning and development of indigenous and Afro-Ecuadorian groups
(1997); served 1-year term as representative from province of
Chimborazo in National Constituent Assembly, which wrote new constitution that recognizes multicultural and multiethnic nature of
Ecuadorian state; was 1st woman elected to Ecuador's National
Assembly and served as its vice president (1998–2000); enacted numerous reforms for women, children, adolescents, indigenous peoples,
Afro-Ecuadorians, the elderly and disabled; served as national judge
(1998–2003); named minister of external relations for Ecuador (2003).

PACHECO, Maria de (c. 1496–1531). *See Padilla, Maria Pacheco.*

PACHEN DOLMA (c. 1933–2002). *See Dolma, Pachen.*

PACHLER-KOSCHAK, Marie (1792–1855). Austrian pianist. Born in
Graz, capital of the Austrian province of Styria, Oct 2, 1792; died in
Graz, April 10, 1855. ❖ One of Beethoven's favorite performers, had a
distinguished career.

PACIOTTI, Elena Ornella (1941—). Italian judge and politician. Born
Jan 9, 1941, in Rome, Italy. ❖ Became a magistrate (1967), spending
much of career at the Milan Court as a civil judge and criminal judge;
elected member of the Supreme Court of the Magistrature, the 1st
woman to hold this office; served as president of National Magistrates'
Association (1994–95, 1997–98); as a European Socialist, elected to 5th
European Parliament (1999–2004).

PACK, Doris (1942—). German politician. Born Mar 18, 1942, in
Schiffweiler/Saar, Germany. ❖ Member of the Bundestag (1974–83,
1985–89); named Federal vice-chair of the CDU (Christian Democrats
Union) women's organization (1989); as a member of the European
People's Party (Christian Democrats) and European Democrats, elected
to 4th and 5th European Parliament (1994–99, 1999–2004); chaired
delegation for relations with countries of southeast Europe. Awarded
Order of Zvonimir (Croatia, 1995), Federal Order of Merit, first class
(1996), and Ordre internationale de mérite (France, 1996).

PACK, Betty or Elizabeth (1910–1963). *See Brousse, Amy.*

PACKARD, Clarissa (1794–1888). *See Gilman, Caroline.*

**PACKARD, Elizabeth (1816–1897). American mental health and legal
reformer.** Born Elizabeth Parsons Ware, Dec 28, 1816, in Ware,
Massachusetts; died of paralysis, July 25, 1897, in Chicago, Illinois;
dau. of Samuel Ware (Congregational minister) and Lucy (Parsons)
Ware; m. Theophilus Packard Jr. (Calvinist minister), 1839; children:
Theophilus (b. 1842); Isaac Ware (b. 1844); Samuel (b. 1847); Elizabeth
Ware (b. 1850); George Hastings (b. 1853); Arthur Dwight (b. 1858).
❖ Was the principal teacher in a girls' school at age of 19 (c. 1835);
spent 5 weeks in the state hospital for mental illness (1836); married and
moved to Illinois (1839); committed to an insane asylum by husband
(1860) for voicing her religious beliefs; released (1863); acquitted of
insanity in a jury trial in Kankakee, Illinois (1864); published books
supporting the rights of married women and mental health patients,
and lobbied for legislative reform in both areas (1860s–70s). ❖ See
also Barbara Sapinsley, *The Private War of Mrs. Packard* (Paragon, 1995);
and *Women in World History.*

PACKARD, Sophia B. (1824–1891). American educator. Born Jan 3,
1824, in New Salem, Massachusetts; died June 21, 1891, in
Washington, DC; dau. of Winslow Packard (farmer) and Rachel
(Freeman) Packard; received diploma from Charlestown
(Massachusetts) Female Seminary, 1850; never married; lifelong compa-
nion of Harriet E. Giles; no children. ❖ Founder of Spelman College,
taught for several years in Massachusetts schools; became preceptress and
a teacher in the New Salem (Massachusetts) Academy (1855); with
Harriet E. Giles, taught at Connecticut Literary Institution, Suffield
(1859–64); was co-principal of the Oread Collegiate Institute in
Worcester, Massachusetts (1864–67); became pastor's assistant under
Rev. George C. Lorimer (1870); presided over organizing meeting of
Woman's American Baptist Home Mission Society, and played active
role in organization (1877); toured South to determine what type of aid
should be given to African-American population (1880); moved to
Atlanta, Georgia, and with Giles opened the Atlanta Baptist Female
Seminary (1881), which relocated and was renamed Spelman
Seminary, with a hall erected and named after Packard (1888); became
treasurer of board of trustees and president of Spelman Seminary (1888).
❖ See also *Women in World History.*

PACKER, Ann E. (1942—). English runner. Name variations: (married name) Ann Brightwell. Born Ann E. Packer in Moulsford, Berkshire, England, Mar 8, 1942. ❖ Won English Schools 100 yards (1959); won WAAA long jump (1960); was a finalist in the 200 meters at European championships (1962) and a finalist in the 80-meter hurdles at Commonwealth Games; won a silver medal for the 400 meters and a gold medal for the 800 meters at Tokyo Olympics (1964). ❖ See also *Women in World History.*

PACKER, Joy (1905–1977). South African novelist and travel writer. Name variations: Lady Packer. Born Joy Petersen, Feb 11, 1905, in Cape Town, South Africa; died 1977; dau. of Julius (doctor) and Ellen (Marais) Petersen; m. Sir Herbert Packer (admiral in Royal Navy), 1925 (died); children: Peter. ❖ Traveled widely with husband and wrote of experiences in *Pack and Follow: One Person's Adventures in Four Different Worlds* (1945), *Grey Mistress* (1949), and *Home from the Sea* (1963); wrote about husband's naval career in *Deep as the Sea* (1975); probably best known for novels *Valley of the Vines* (1955), which became a tv series, and *Nor the Moon By Night* (1957); other novels include *The High Roof* (1959), *The Glass Barrier* (1961), *The Man in the Mews* (1964), *The Blind Spot* (1967), *Leopard in the Fold* (1969) and *Veronica* (1970); was broadcaster to South Africa for BBC in London (1939–43).

PACKER, Vin (1927—). *See Meaker, Marijane.*

PACSAI, Marta (1952—). *See Megyerine-Pacsai, Marta.*

PADAR, Ildiko (1970—). Hungarian handball player. Name variations: Ildikó Pádár. Born April 19, 1970, in Hungary. ❖ Won a team bronze medal at Atlanta Olympics (1996) and a team silver medal at Sydney Olympics (2000).

PADDLEFORD, Clementine (1900–1967). American food editor and columnist. Born Clementine Haskin Paddleford in Stockdale, Kansas, Sept 27, 1900; died Nov 13, 1967; dau. of Solon Marian Paddleford (prosperous farmer) and Jennie (Romick) Paddleford; Kansas State College School of Journalism, BA, 1921; graduate work at New York University; m. Lloyd D. Zimmerman (engineer), July 10, 1923 (sep. 1923, div. 1932); children: (ward) Clare Duffe. ❖ One of the best-known food editors in US, was women's editor of *Farm and Fireside* (1924–29), before turning to freelance writing; joined NY *Herald Tribune* (1936); wrote for the *Tribune,* the monthly magazine *Gourmet,* and *This Week,* the syndicated Sunday magazine.

PADGETT, Lewis (1911–1987). *See Moore, C.L.*

PADILLA, Juana Azurduy de (1781–1862). *See Azurduy de Padilla, Juana.*

PADILLA, Maria Pacheco (c. 1496–1531). Castilian patriot. Name variations: Doña María de Pacheco; Maria Pacheco; Marie Pacheco de Padilla. Born c. 1496 in Granada; died Mar 1531 in Oporto, Portugal; dau. of Iñigo López de Mendoza, marquis of Mondéjar and 2nd count of Tendilla, known as el Gran Tendilla) and Francisca Pacheco (dau. of Juan de Pacheco, 1st marquis of Villena); m. Juan López de Padilla (Spanish revolutionary general and caudillo of Toledo, 1490–1521), Aug 18, 1511; children: 1 son. ❖ With husband, led the rebels during the Comunero revolt against Charles V and absolutism; after he was captured and executed, assumed command of the troops and defended Toledo for 9 months (1520–21); took refuge in Portugal after the fall of Toledo, where she lived in exile until her death.

PADILLA, Marie de (1335–1365). *See Marie de Padilla.*

PADOVANI, Lea (1920–1991). Italian actress. Name variations: Léa Padovani. Born July 28, 1920, in Montalto di Castro, Italy; died June 23, 1991, in Rome. ❖ Lead and featured actress in European films including *L'Innocente Casimiro, Il sole sorge ancora, Il diavolo bianco, Che tempi!, Call of the Blood, Give Us this Day, Three Steps North, Atto d'accusa, Roma ore 11, Una di quelle, Tempi nostri, Il seduttore, La Contessa di Castiglione, Le dossier noir, Chéri-Bibi, L'Intrusa, Montparnese 19, El Alamein, The Naked Maja, La Princesse de Clèves, The Reluctant Saint, Germinal, Candy, Ciao Gulliver* and *La putain du roi.*

PADUA, Maria Tereza Jorge (1943—). *See Jorge Pádua, Maria Tereza.*

PADURARU, Maria (1970—). Romanian rower. Born Oct 1970 in Romania. ❖ At Barcelona Olympics, won a silver medal in coxed eights (1992).

PAEFFGEN, Christa (1938–1988). *See Nico.*

PAEK MYONG-SUK (1954—). North Korean volleyball player. Born Feb 24, 1954, in North Korea. ❖ At Munich Olympics, won a bronze medal in team competition (1972).

PAEMEL, Monika van (1945—). Flemish novelist. Name variations: Baroness van Paemel. Born May 4, 1945, in Poesele, Belgium; m. Theo Butzen. ❖ Works, which are experimental and often structured cyclically, include *Amazone met het blauwe voorhoofd* (The Blue-Crested Amazonian Parrot, 1971), *De Confratatie* (The Confrontation, 1974), *Marguerite* (1976), *Die Vermaledijde vaders* (The Cursed Fathers, 1985), *Het wedervaren* (1993), and *Het verschil* (2000).

PAERSON, Anja (1981—). Swedish Alpine skier. Name variations: Anja Pärson. Born April 25, 1981, in Taernaby, Sweden; sister of Frida Paerson (skier). ❖ Placed 3rd in the giant slalom and 1st in slalom at the World championships (2001); won a bronze medal for slalom and silver medal for giant slalom at Salt Lake City Olympics (2002); at World championships, won a gold medal for giant slalom (2003) and was overall World Cup champion (2004); won bronze medals for combined and downhill at Torino Olympics (2006).

PAETINA (fl. 30 CE). Roman noblewoman. Name variations: Aelia Paetina. Became 2nd wife of Claudius (10 BCE–54 CE), Roman emperor (r. 41–54 CE), before 27 CE (div. 38 CE); children: Claudia Antonia (27–66 CE). ❖ Claudius' first wife was Plautia Urgulanilla; after his divorce from Paetina, he married Valeria Messalina, then Agrippina the Younger.

PAETZ, Sabine (1957—). *See John-Paetz-Moebius, Sabine.*

PÄFFGEN, Christa (1938–1988). *See Nico.*

PAGAN, Isobel (c. 1742–1821). Scottish lyricist. Born c. 1742 in Scotland; died 1821 in Scotland. ❖ Wrote two well-known folk lyrics, "Ca' the Yowes to the Knowes" and "The Crooked and the Plaid" (found in various anthologies); also published *A Collection of Songs and Poems on Several Occasions* (1803).

PAGAVA, Ethery (1932—). French ballet dancer. Born Nov 13, 1932, in Paris, France; trained with Lyubov Egorova. ❖ Appeared with Ballets de la Jeunesse (1937); danced in Roland Petit's Ballets des Champs-Elysées, creating roles in his *Les Forains* (1945), *Les Amours de Jupiter* (1946), and *Le Déjeuner sur l'Herbe* (c. 1947); danced with Grand Ballet du Marquis de Cuevas (1950s), where she was highly acclaimed for performances in Balanchine's *La Somnambule,* Lifar's *Noir et Blanc,* Massine's *Le Beau Danube,* and others; performed mainly as a guest artist (1960s), dancing with companies in Europe.

PAGE, Annette (1952—). English ballet dancer. Born Dec 18, 1952, in Manchester, England; m. Ronald Hynd (ballet dancer and choreographer). ❖ Trained with Sadler's Wells Ballet and later joined the company; danced with Sadler's Wells—later Royal Ballet—throughout career, with principal roles in *Giselle, Coppélia, Swan Lake, Cinderella,* and *La Fille Mal Gardée;* created roles in Alfred Rodrigues' *Ile Sirenes* (1952) and *Café des Sports* (1954), and Macmillan's *Danses Concertantes* (1955); retired from performance (1986).

PAGE, Dorothy G. (1921–1989). American mayor, considered the "Mother of the Iditarod." Born Jan 23, 1921, in Bessemer, Michigan; died Nov 16, 1989, in Wasilla, AK; married Vondolee Page. ❖ Moved to Alaska (1960); served on Wasilla City Council for 10 years, then elected mayor (1986); created the Sled Dog Mushers Hall of Fame in the Knik museum (1964); proposed a sled-dog race over part of the Iditarod trail (1965). Wasilla Museum was renamed the Dorothy G. Page Museum. ❖ See also *Women in World History.*

PAGE, Estelle Lawson (1907–1983). American golfer. Name variations: Estelle Lawson, Mrs. E.L. Page. Born Estelle Lawson on Mar 22, 1907, in East Orange, NJ; married; died May 1983 in Chapel Hill, NC; dau. of R.B. Lawson (athletic director of University of North Carolina). ❖ Won USGA Amateur (1937) and was runner-up (1938) and semifinalist (1941, 1947); was a member of the Curtis Cup team (1938, 1948); won many national championships, including the North and South (1933, 1936, 1940, 1941, 1946, 1947, and 1949); held the world record score of 66 in medal-play competition.

PAGE, Ethel (c. 1875–1958). Australian prime-ministerial wife. Born Ethel Esther Blunt, c. 1875; died May 26, 1958, in Grafton, New South Wales, Australia; m. Earle Page (prime minister of Australia, 1939), Sept 18, 1906; children: 5. ❖ With husband, helped found the Country Party and was on the party executive for over 7 years; was also an executive member of Australian Red Cross, YWCA, and National Council of Women; began career as a trained nurse.

PAGE, Evelyn (1899–1987). New Zealand painter. Born Evelyn Margaret Polson, 1899, in Christchurch, New Zealand; died 1987 in Wellington; trained at Canterbury College of Art, 1915–22; m. Frederick Page (composer). ❖ Influenced by French Impressionists, painted portraits, the female nude, still life, landscape and cityscapes; set up The Group (1927), to exhibit the work of emerging artists; traveled to Europe where she was particularly impressed with work of Pierre Bonnard (1937); moved to Wellington with husband (1947), where she exhibited regularly with New Zealand Academy of Fine Arts, Otago Arts Society and Canterbury Society of Arts; awarded a Queen Elizabeth II Arts Council grant to travel and study overseas (1956); was said to have introduced a vitality to New Zealand contemporary art with her handling of color and light.

PAGE, Gale (1913–1983). American actress. Born Sally Rutter, July 23, 1913, in Spokane, WA; died Jan 8, 1983, in Santa Monica, CA. ❖ Made film debut in *Crime School* (1938); other films include *The Amazing Dr. Clitterhouse, Four Daughters, Daughters Courageous, Naughty but Nice, Four Wives, They Drive By Night, Knute Rockne, Four Mothers, The Time of Your Life, Anna Lucasta* and *About Mrs. Leslie*.

PAGE, Geneviève (1930—). French stage and screen actress. Name variations: Genevieve Page. Born Geneviève Bronjean, Dec 13, 1930, in Paris, France. ❖ Lead and featured actress on Paris stage, also appeared in French and international films, including *Ce siècle a cinquante ans, Pas de pitié pour les femmes, Fanfan la Tulipe, Les plaisirs de Paris, Lettre ouverte, Noches andaluzas, Cherchez la femme, Michel Strogoff, The Silken Affair, Some without End, El Cid, Le jour et l'heure, Youngblood Hawke, Grand Prix, Tendre voyou, Belle du jour, Mayerling, The Private Life of Sherlock Holmes, Beyond Therapy, Les bois noirs* and *Lovers*.

PAGE, Geraldine (1924–1987). American actress. Born Nov 22, 1924, in Kirksville, Missouri; died June 13, 1987, in New York, NY; dau. of Leon Page (osteopathic doctor) and Pearl (Maize) Page; attended University of Chicago and Herbert Berghof School, NY; graduate of Goodman Theater Dramatic School, Chicago, 1945; m. Alexander Schneider (violinist), 1954 (div. 1957); m. Rip Torn (actor and director), 1958; children: (2nd m.) Angelica Torn; (twins) Anthony and Jonathan Torn. ❖ Made New York debut as the Sophomore in *Seven Mirrors* (Blackfriars Guild, 1945); achieved stardom for portrayal of Alma Winemiller in off-Broadway production of Tennessee Williams' *Summer and Smoke* (1953), for which she won her 1st New York Drama Critics award; became one of the icons of stage, screen, and tv, winning particular acclaim for her performance in another Williams play, *Sweet Bird of Youth* (1959), a role for which she received her 2nd New York Drama Critics Award; made Broadway debut as Lily in *Midsummer* (1953), then had successful run as Lizzie Curry in *The Rainmaker* (1954); other Broadway roles include Nina Leeds in *Strange Interlude* (1963) and Olga in *The Three Sisters* (1964). Nominated for Academy Awards as Best Actress for *Summer and Smoke* (1961), *Sweet Bird of Youth* (1962) and *Interiors* (1978), and as Best Supporting Actress for *Hondo* (1953), *You're a Big Boy Now* (1967), *Pete 'n' Tillie* (1972) and *The Pope of Greenwich Village* (1984); won Academy Award for *The Trip to Bountiful* (1985); won Emmy Awards for performances in teleplays of Truman Capote's "A Christmas Memory" (1967) and "The Thanksgiving Visitor" (1969). ❖ See also *Women in World History*.

PAGE, Gertrude (1873–1922). Zimbabwean novelist. Name variations: Mrs G.A. Dobbin. Born 1873 in England; died April 1, 1922; dau. of John E. Page; m. George Alexander Dobbin. ❖ Moved to Rhodesia (c. 1900); works, which reflect experiences of colonial life and were popular during her lifetime, include *Love in the Wilderness: A Story of Another African Farm* (1907), *Paddy the Next Best Thing* (1908), *Jill's Rhodesian Philosophy* (1910), *The Pathway* (1914), *The Supreme Desire* (1916), and *The Veldt Trail* (1919); with R.A. Foster-Melliar, wrote *The Course of My Ship* (1918).

PAGE, Gilbert H. (c. 1856–1937). See D'Arcy, Ella.

PAGE, LaWanda (1920–2002). African-American actress. Born Oct 19, 1920, in Cleveland, Ohio; died Sept 14, 2002, in Los Angeles, CA; children: Clara Johnson. ❖ Comedic character actress, probably best known as Aunt Ester in tv's "Sanford and Sons" (1973–77), began career as a dancer; films include *Zapped!* (1982) and *Friday* (1995).

PAGE, Mary Caroline (1845–1931). See Fillmore, Myrtle Page.

PAGE, Merlene (1960—). See Ottey, Merlene.

PAGE, Myrtle (1845–1931). See Fillmore, Myrtle Page.

PAGE, P.K. (1916—). Canadian poet and painter. Name variations: P. K. Irwin; Pat Irwin; Mrs. W.A. Irwin; (pseudonym) Judith Cape. Born Patricia Kathleen Page, Nov 23, 1916, in Swanage, Dorset, England; m. (William) Arthur Irwin (diplomat), 1950. ❖ Immigrated to Canada with parents (1919); was active in Montreal writing community and helped found *Preview*; worked as scriptwriter for National Film Board (1946–50); after husband became Canadian high commissioner, traveled with him to Brazil, Mexico, and Guatemala; under name P. K. Irwin, began painting and exhibiting widely; returned to Victoria, British Columbia (1964); writings include *As Ten, As Twenty* (1946), *The Metal and the Flower* (1954), which won the Governor General's Award, *Cry Ararat!* (1967), *P.K. Page, Poems Selected and New* (1974), *Evening Dance of the Grey Flies* (1981), *The Glass Air* (1985), *Brazilian Journal* (1987), *A Flask of Sea Water* (1989), and *Planet Earth* (2003).

PAGE, Patti (1927—). American pop singer. Born Clara Ann Fowler, Nov 8, 1927, in Claremore, OK; briefly attended Tulsa University; m. Charles O'Curran, 1956 (div.); m. Jerry Filiciotto (aerospace executive), 1990. ❖ One of only 5 singers (and the only woman) whose hits spanned 5 decades on Billboard country charts; sold more than 100-million records during career, among them 13 gold singles, including "Tennessee Waltz," "Old Cape Cod," "Allegheny Moon," "That Doggie in the Window," "With My Eyes Wide Open I'm Dreaming," "Mockin' Bird Hill," "Mr. and Mississippi," "Detour," "You Belong to Me," "Changing Partners," and "Cross Over the Bridge"; had her own show on CBS; appeared in film *Elmer Gantry* (1960). Received Pioneer Award by Academy of Country Music (ACM, 1980), in recognition of her groundbreaking, multiple-voice technique and successful cross-over into country music; inducted into Oklahoma Hall of Fame. ❖ See also autobiography *Once Upon a Dream* (1966); and *Women in World History*.

PAGE, Ruth (1899–1991). American dancer and choreographer. Name variations: Ruth Fisher. Born Mar 22, 1899, in Indianapolis, Indiana; died in Chicago, Illinois, Aug 15, 1991; dau. of Lafayette Page (brain surgeon) and Marian (Heinly) Page (professional pianist); studied ballet with Anna Pavlova, Adolph Bolm, and Enrico Cecchetti; m. Thomas Hart Fisher (Chicago lawyer), 1925. ❖ Made Chicago debut (1919), creating lead role in *The Birthday of the Infanta*; with Adolph Bolm, went on several tours with his Ballet Intime; was *première danseuse* in Broadway hit *Music Box Revue* (1921–23); joined experimental Chicago Allied Arts (1924), as prima ballerina, where she choreographed *The Flapper and the Quarterback* and *Oak Street Beach*; was guest soloist with Metropolitan Opera, NY (1926–28); created *La Guiablesse* for Chicago Symphony, which featured Katherine Dunham (1933); was *première danseuse* and ballet director of Chicago Opera Co. (1934–37, 1942–43, 1945), where she choreographed *Hear Ye! Hear Ye!, An American Pattern*, and a revival of her ballet of Ravel's *Bolero*; co-ran the Page-Stone Ballet Co. with Bentley Stone (1938–41), which presented *Frankie and Johnny*, the longest-running ballet in Chicago's history; was 1st choreographer to turn a full-length opera into full-length ballet, remaking *Carmen* in *Guns and Castanets* (1939); restaged 3 of Page-Stone works for Ballet Russe de Monte Carlo: *Frankie and Johnny* (1945), *The Bells* (1946), and *Billy Sunday* (1948); in connection with Chicago Lyric Opera, organized Chicago Opera ballet (1956), subsequently renamed Ruth Page's International Ballet (1966), and remained its director for a number of years; founded Ruth Page School of Dance (1970). ❖ See also autobiography *Page by Page* (Dance Horizons, 1978); John Martin, *Ruth Page* (Dekker, 1977); and *Women in World History*.

PAGET, Lady Arthur (1865–1919). See Paget, Mary.

PAGET, Debra (1933—). American screen actress. Born Debralee Griffin, Aug 19, 1933, in Denver, CO; sister of Teala Loring and Lisa Gaye (actresses); m. David Street (actor-singer), 1958 (annulled 1958); m. Budd Boetticher (director), 1960 (div. 1961); m. Louis (Ling-Chieh) C. Kung (Chinese-American oilman and nephew of Song Meiling [Mme Chiang Kai-Shek]), 1964 (div. 1980). ❖ Made film debut in *Cry of the City* (1948), followed by *Broken Arrow, Belles on Their Toes, Les Miserables* (as Cosette), *Stars and Stripes Forever, Prince Valiant, Demetrius and the Gladiators, Princess of the Nile, White Feather, Seven Angry Men, The Ten Commandments, Love Me Tender* and *Tales of Terror*, among others; in Germany, starred in Fritz Lang's *The Tiger of Eschnapur* and *The Indian Tomb* (released together in US as *Journey to the Lost City*).

PAGET, Dorothy (1905–1960). English racehorse owner. Born Dorothy Wyndham Paget, Feb 21, 1905, in England; died Feb 9, 1960; dau. of Sir Almeric Hugh Paget, 1st and last Lord Queensborough and Pauline Whitney (American dau. of William Whitney and Flora Payne, died 1916); never married; children: Anthony Paul Paget (b. 1942). ❖ Famous racehorse owner, 1st registered her colors (1930) and became involved in Northolt Park; spent huge sums on horses and was the most successful owner of the late 1930s; her brilliant steeplechaser, Golden Miller, won 5 consecutive Cheltenham Gold Cups (1932–36) and the Grand National at Aintree (1934).

PAGET, Mary (1865–1919). English-American social leader, philanthropist and war nurse. Name variations: Minnie Paget; Minnie Stevens; Mrs. Arthur Paget; Lady Arthur Paget. Born Mary Stevens, 1865; died May 1919; dau. of Paran Stevens (wealthy Boston socialite); m. Sir Arthur H. Paget (British envoy to Belgrade), July 27, 1878 (died 1928); children: Louise (d. 1958), Albert (1879–1917), and twins Arthur (1888–1966) and Reginald (1888–1931). ❖ One of the foremost leaders of London society during reign of Edward VII, equipped a hospital ship and named it the *Maine* during Boer War; when husband was minister at Belgrade, became well known for her services in relieving distress and suffering during the 1st and 2nd Balkan wars; during WWI, maintained a hospital in Serbia and worked in cooperation with the American Red Cross. ❖ See also *Women in World History.*

PAGET, Muriel (1876–1938). British philanthropist. Name variations: Lady Muriel Paget; Muriel Evelyn Vernon Paget. Born Muriel Evelyn Vernon Finch-Hatton, Aug 19, 1876; died June 16, 1938; dau. of Murray Edward Gordon Finch-Hatton, 12th earl of Winchilsea, and Edith Harcourt (died 1944); m. Sir Richard Arthur Surtees Paget (1869–1955), 2nd baronet, of Cranmore (barrister and physicist), 1897; children: Richard (1898–1898), Sylvia Mary Paget (1901–1996), Pamela Paget (1903–1989), Angela Paget (b. 1906) and John Starr Paget (1914–1992). ❖ Supported a number of local and worldwide efforts to aid the sick and underprivileged; founded the Invalid Kitchens of London (1905), of which she served as honorary secretary until her death; organized the Anglo-Russian Hospital in Russia (1915–17); inaugurated and administered hospital and child-welfare organizations in Czechoslovakia, Latvia, Estonia, Lithuania and Romania; began conducting relief work for British subjects in Russia (1924). Received OBE (1918) and CBE (1938).

PAGET, Nielsine (1858–1932). New Zealand homemaker and community nurse and midwife. Name variations: Nielsine Nielsen. Born Nielsine Nielsen, July 21, 1858, in Jelling, Vejle, Denmark; died on July 13, 1932, in Napier, New Zealand; dau. of Lauritz Nielsen (dairy farmer) and Mette Marie (Simans) Nielsen; m. Thomas (Tom) Paget, 1875 (died 1923); children: 15. ❖ Immigrated with family to New Zealand (1873); was in domestic service before marriage, then farmed 200 acres in Hawkes' Bay area with husband (1882); served as nurse and midwife to community. ❖ See also *Dictionary of New Zealand Biography* (Vol. 2).

PAGET, Rosalind (1855–1948). English social reformer, nurse, and midwife. Name variations: Dame Rosalind Paget. Born Mary Rosalind Paget in 1855; died 1948; dau. of John Paget (1811–1898, police magistrate and author); cousin of Eleanor Rathbone (1872–1946). ❖ A nurse at London Hospital, helped found Midwives' Institute (Royal College of Midwives, 1881), and also worked to obtain the registration of midwives, which was granted (1902). Awarded DBE (1935).

PAGET, Violet (1856–1935). English writer. Name variations: (pseudonym) Vernon Lee. Born Oct 14, 1856, in Boulogne-sur-Mer, France; died Feb 13, 1935, in San Gervasio, Italy; dau. of Henry Ferguson Paget (who was involved in the Warsaw insurrection of 1848) and Matilda (Abadam) Lee-Hamilton; never married; no children. ❖ Prolific and wide-ranging writer, published 1st essay at 13 (1869); published 1st and best-known book, *Studies of the Eighteenth Century in Italy* (1880); also won wide acclaim for another travel guide, *Genius Loci* (1899); her 40-plus publications included travel books, short stories, novels, historical fiction, satire, international politics, women's rights, psychology, and aesthetic critiques of the arts; other works include a biography of Louise of Stolberg-Gedern, *The Countess of Albany* (1884), a satirical attack on the London art scene, *Miss Brown* (1884), as well as *Euphorian* (1884), *Hauntings* (1890), *Vanitas* (1892), *Limbo and Other Essays* (1897), *Ariadne in Mantua: A Drama in Five Acts* (1903), *Penelope Brandling* (1903), *Pope Jacynth* (1904), *Horus Vitae* (1904), *The Enchanted Woods*

(1905), *The Spirit of Rome: Leaves from a Diary* (1906) and *The Sentimental Traveller* (1908). ❖ See also Peter Gunn, *Vernon Lee: Violet Paget, 1856–1935* (Oxford U. Press, 1964); and *Women in World History.*

PAGLIA, Camille (1947—). American academic. Born Camille Anna Paglia, April 2, 1947, in Endicott, New York; dau. of Pasquale Paglia (professor of romance languages) and Lydia Anne (Colapietro) Paglia (dressmaker and bank teller); sister of Lenora Paglia; Harpur College of State University of New York at Binghamton, BA, 1968; Yale University, PhD, 1974; m. Alison Maddex (artist and curator), 1993. ❖ Controversial and pugnacious essayist, taught at Bennington College (1972–80), then Wesleyan, Yale and University of New Haven; joined faculty of Philadelphia College of Performing Arts (1984), which later merged with Philadelphia College of Art to form University of the Arts; published *Sexual Personae* (1990), *Sex, Art, and American Culture* (1992) and *Vamps and Tramps* (1994); wrote for Salon.com (1996–2002); was frequent contributor to journals and magazines, including *Interview.*

PAGLIERO, Camilia (1859–1925). Italian mime. Born Mar 13, 1859, in Castel Rosso, Italy; died May 12, 1925, in Lovrano; m. Nicola Guerra (ballet master). ❖ As mime, created title role in Josef Hassreiter's ballet *Die Puppenfee* (1888); performed with Vienna Court Opera Ballet in Austria, where she appeared in numerous ballets by Hassreiter and Nicola Guerra; taught at Magyar Kiralfy Opera Ballet in Budapest.

PAGLIUGHI, Lina (1907–1980). American soprano. Born May 27, 1907, in Brooklyn, NY; died Oct 2, 1980, in Ruicone, Italy; studied with Manlio Bavagnoli in Milan; m. Primo Montanari (tenor). ❖ When young, returned to Italy for singing career; at 8, began giving public recitals; debuted at Teatro Nazionale in Milan (1927); sang at Teatro alla Scala (1930–47); debuted in Monte Carlo (1931) and Covent Garden (1938); gave up the stage (1948) and began singing on Italian radio until retirement (1956); became a popular recording and radio star. ❖ See also *Women in World History.*

PAGU (1910–1962). *See Galvão, Patricia.*

PAHLAVI, Ashraf (1919—). Princess of Persia and women's rights activist. Name variations: Princess Ashraf Pahlevi. Born Oct 26, 1919, in Tehran, Iran; dau. of Tajolmolouk and Reza Shah Pahlavi, shah of Iran (r. 1925–1941 abdicated); sister of Shams Pahlavi (1917–1996); twin sister of Muhammad Reza Pahlavi, also known as Riza I Pahlavi, shah of Iran (r. 1941–1979, deposed); m. Ali Ghavam (prime minister), in 1936 or 1937 (div. 1941); m. Ahmed Chafik or Shafiq Bey (b. 1911, director general of civil aviation), in 1944 (div. 1960); m. Dr. Mehdi Boushehri (b. 1916); children: (1st m.) Prince Shahram Ghavam (b. 1939); (2nd m.) Prince Chahriar Chafik, also seen as Shahriar or Shahryar Chafik (b. 1945, killed in Paris on Dec 7, 1979); Princess Azadeh Chafik (b. 1951, who m. Farshad Vahid). ❖ Twin sister of the shah of Iran, served as president of the Women's Organization of Iran (WOI), which provided women with family welfare centers where childcare, vocational training, family planning and legal issues were addressed; at UN Conference on Women's Rights (1975), proposed the formation of a permanent research and training institute for women's affairs, which was established in Tehran; also served as chair of Iranian Human Rights Committee and presided over several important international conferences, including UN Commission on the Status of Women, UN Commission on Human Rights, and International Human Rights Conference held in Tehran (1988); writings include *Faces in a Mirror* (1980) and *Time for Truth.* ❖ See also *Women in World History.*

PAHLAVI, Farah (1938—). Empress of Iran. Name variations: Farah Diba. Crowned empress on Oct 26, 1967. Born in Tehran, Iran, Oct 14, 1938; dau. of Sohrab Diba (captain in imperial Iranian army) and Farideh Ghotbi; attended Tehran's Jeanne d'Arc and Razi schools; attended École d'Architecture in Paris; became 3rd wife of Muhammad Reza Pahlavi, also known as Riza I Pahlavi, shah of Iran (r. 1941–1979, deposed), on Dec 20, 1959; children: Prince Reza (crown prince) also known as Reza II Pahlavi (b. 1960); Princess Farahnaz (b. 1963); Prince Ali Reza (b. 1966); Princess Leila (1970–2001). ❖ Champion of women's broader roles in Iranian society, was also a highly visible patron of numerous charitable, cultural, medical and educational organizations; became the 1st woman in 2,500 years to be crowned empress of Iran (1967); deposed with husband (1979). ❖ See also memoir, *An Enduring Love* (Miramax, 2004); and *Women in World History.*

PAHLAVI, Soraya (1932–2001). Iranian princess. Name variations: Princess Soraya Esfandiari Bakhtiari; Princess Soraya; HM Empress Soraya; Queen of Persia. Born Soraya Esfandiari Bakhtiari on June 22, 1932, in Isfahan, Iran; died in Paris in Oct 2001; dau. of Khalil Esfandiari Bakhtiari and Eva Karl; educated in Isfahan, England and Switzerland; became 2nd wife of Muhammad Reza Pahlavi, also known as Riza I Pahlavi, shah of Iran (r. 1941–1979, deposed), on Feb 12, 1951 (div. Mar 14, 1958); never remarried; no children. Muhammad Reza Pahlavi was also married to Fawzia and to Farah Pahlavi. ❖ Spent 7 years at the royal court in Iran, but failed to give birth to any children (specifically, a male heir). ❖ See also *Soraya: The Autobiography of Her Imperial Highness Princess Soraya*; and *Women in World History*.

PAIGE, Elaine (1948—). English actress and singer. Born Elaine Bickerstaff, Mar 5, 1948, in Barnet, Hertfordshire, England; attended Aida Foster Drama School. ❖ First lady of British musical theater, made professional debut in *The Roar of the Greasepaint*, followed by *Roar Like a Dove* at Alexandra Theater and *Rock Carmen* at The Roundhouse; made West End debut in *Hair* (1969); created role of Evita Peron in original production of *Evita* (1978), winning Society of West End Theater Award for Best Actress; performed extensively in West End theaters in such shows as *Jesus Christ Superstar*, *Grease* and *Billy*; starred as Grizabella in original production of *Cats* (1981) and had hit recording of "Memory"; starred as Carabosse in *Abbacadabra* (1983) and in original production of *Chess* (1986), from which she recorded the hit single "I Know Him So Well" with Barbara Dickson; starred in and co-produced *Anything Goes* (1989); received critical acclaim for performance as Edith Piaf in musical play *Piaf* by Pam Gems (1993); made Broadway debut as Norma Desmond in *Sunset Boulevard* (1996); appeared as Mrs. Lovett in *Sweeney Todd* at New York City Opera to great reviews (2004); hosted weekly BBC radio show "Elaine Paige on Sunday," BBC-TV specials and starred in several BBC tv films, most notably in "A View of Harry Clark" and "Unexplained Laughter"; had 8 consecutive gold and 4 multi-platinum albums. Received Order of the British Empire (OBE, 1995).

PAIGE, Janis (1922—). American stage, tv and screen actress and singer. Born Donna Mae Tjaden, Sept 16, 1922, in Tacoma, WA; m. Frank Martinelli, 1947 (div. 1950); m. Arthur Stander, 1956 (div. 1957); m. Ray Gilbert (composer), 1962 (died 1976). ❖ Made film debut in *Hollywood Canteen* (1944), followed by *Of Human Bondage*, *Two Guys from Milwaukee*, *Love and Learn*, *Romance on the High Seas*, *Two Gals and a Guy*, *Silk Stockings*, *Please Don't Eat the Daisies*, *Bachelor in Paradise*, *Follow the Boys* and *Welcome to Hard Times*, among others; co-starred on Broadway in original production of *The Pajama Game* (1954); on tv, starred in her own series "It's Always Jan" (1955–56) and as a regular on "Trapper John, M.D." (1985–86).

PAIGE, Jean (1895–1990). American actress. Born July 3, 1895, in Paris, IL; died Dec 15, 1990, in Los Angeles, CA; m. Albert E. Smith (co-founder of Vitagraph), 1920. ❖ Appeared with Vitagraph (1917–24); films include *The Discounters of Money*, *Tangled Lives* and *Captain Blood*.

PAIGE, Mabel (1879–1954). American screen actress. Born Mabel Paige Roberts, Dec 19, 1879, in New York, NY; died Feb 9, 1954, in Van Nuys, CA; m. Charles Ritchie (actor, died 1931). ❖ Made stage debut at age 4; made film debut in silent comedy short *Mixed Flats* (1915) and appeared in many more, sometimes with husband; graduated to matronly comedy parts in talkies; probably best known for the lead in *Someone to Remember* (1943); other films include *Murder He Says*, *Nocturne*, *Johnny O'Clock*, *If You Knew Susie*, *Johnny Belinda*, *Roseanna McCoy*, *The Sniper* and *Houdini*.

PAINTER, Eleanor (1890–1947). American actress and singer. Born 1890 in Walkerville, IA; died Nov 4, 1947, in Cleveland, Ohio; m. Louis Graveure (Wilfred Douthitt, div.). ❖ Made stage debut at Deutsches Opera House, Charlottenberg as Fatima in *Oberon;* made London debut at Covent Garden (1915); abandoning grand opera, starred in Vincent Herbert's *Princess Pat* (1915); also appeared in *Glorianna*, *The Last Waltz*, *The Lilac Domino*, *Floradora*, *The Chiffon Girl*, and as Jennie Lind in *The Nightingale;* toured Germany in leading operatic roles; retired from the stage (1931).

PAISLEY, Eileen (1934—). Northern Ireland politician. Born Eileen Emily Cassels, 1934, in Belfast, Northern Ireland; m. Rev. Ian Paisley (leader of Democratic Unionist Party); children: 3 daughters; twin sons, Kyle and Ian Paisley Jr. ❖ Representing Democratic Unionist Party for Belfast East, sat in Northern Ireland Assembly (1973–74); stood in for husband, who had been refused a visa, as a member of a joint UUP-DUP publicity group visiting US (1982).

PAISLEY, Sylvia (1955—). See Hermon, Sylvia.

PAIVA, La (1819–1884). See Lachman, Thérèse.

PAK, Se Ri (1977—). Korean golfer. Born Sept 28, 1977, in Daejun, South Korea; dau. of Joon Chul (building contractor) and Jeong Suk Kim; coached by her father. ❖ Began athletic career as a hurdler and shotputter; became a national celebrity in Korea, winning 30 amateur events in 4 years; during rookie year on LPGA tour, won US Open (1998), then shot the best round in LPGA history, a 61, at the Jamie Farr Kroger Classic, and won 4 more tournaments, including 2 major titles; became the youngest woman in history to win 4 majors when she won the LPGA championship (2002); won the Vare Trophy (2003); became the 1st woman in 58 years to make the cut in a men's golf tournament, when she played the SBS Super Tournament in the Korean PGA tour, finishing 10th (2003); won Michelob Open (2004), for 22nd LPGA win.

PAKENHAM, Antonia (1932—). See Fraser, Antonia.

PAKENHAM, Elizabeth (1906–2002). See Longford, Elizabeth.

PAKENHAM-WALSH, Patricia (1923–2000). See Moyes, Patricia.

PAKHALINA, Yulia (1977—). Russian diver. Name variations: Ioulia Pakhalina; Julia Pakhalina. Born Sept 12, 1977, in Penza, USSR; dau. of Vladimir Pakhalin (her coach); attended University of Houston in TX. ❖ Won European championship for 3-meter springboard (1997); at World championships, won gold medals for 3-meter springboard and 3-meter synchronized springboard (1998); won 8 Grand Prix events (2001–04); with Vera Ilyina, won a gold medal for 3-meter synchronized springboard diving at Sydney Olympics (2000); won a bronze medal for 3-meter springboard at Athens Olympics (2004), as well as a silver medal for 3-meter synchronized springboard with Ilyina.

PAKHOVSKAYA, Tatyana (1954—). See Skachko-Pakhovskaya, Tatyana.

PAKHMUTOVA, Alexandra (1929—). Russian composer. Name variations: Alexandra Nikolaievna Pakhmutova. Born in Beketovka, near Stalingrad, USSR (now Volgograd, Russia), Nov 9, 1929; graduate of Moscow Conservatory, 1953; continued post-graduate work at the conservatory, concentrating on composition studies with Vladimir Shebalin. ❖ Premiered her bouncy Trumpet Concerto in Moscow (1955), a work that became immensely popular in USSR; wrote popular urban ballads, songs alluding to pressing Soviet problems but which praised Soviet achievements (1960s–70s); wrote *Lenin is in Our Hearts*, a suite for narrator, children's chorus and orchestra (1957). Named "Artist of the USSR" (1977). ❖ See also *Women in World History*.

PAKHOLCHIK, Olena (1964—). Ukrainian sailor. Name variations: Panholchyk. Born Nov 2, 1964, in Maykain, Ukraine; m. Dmytro Tsalik. ❖ Won European championship for 470 (1993, 1995); won bronze medals for double-handed dinghy (470) at Atlanta Olympics (1996) and Sydney Olympics (2000).

PAKHOMOVA, Ludmila (d. 1986). Russian ice dancer. Name variations: Liudmila. Born in USSR; died of cancer in 1986; m. Alexandr Gorshkov, 1970. ❖ With partner Alexandr Gorshkov, won 6 World championships (1970–74, 1976), 6 European championships (1970–76), and a gold medal at Innsbruck Olympics (1976). Inducted into World Figure Skating Hall of Fame (1988).

PAKINGTON, Dorothy (d. 1679). English author and moralist. Died May 10, 1679; dau. of Thomas Coventry, 1st baron of Coventry; m. Sir John Pakington (1620–1680). ❖ Recognized for her intellect as well as her piety, reputedly wrote a series of theological volumes, including *The Gentlemen's Calling, The Ladies' Calling, The Government of the Tongue, The Christian's Birthright* and *The Causes of the Decay of Christian Piety*. ❖ See also *Women in World History*.

PALACIOS, Lucila (1902–1994). Venezuelan novelist, playwright, short-story writer and diplomat. Name variations: Mercedes Carvajal de Arocha; was known as Lucila Palacios from 1931 on. Born Mercedes Carvajal de Arocha, Nov 8, 1902, in Trinidad; died Aug 31, 1994, in Caracas, Venezuela; dau. of Francisco Carvajal and Anita Montes. ❖ Served in National Assembly and as senator; appointed ambassador to Uruguay (1963); works include *Desatemos el nudo* (1935), *Rebeldía* (1940), *La gran serpiente* (1943), *El córcel de las crines albas* (1950), *El mundo en miniatura* (1955), *El día de Caín* (1958), *Poemas de noche y de silencio* (1964), and *La piedra en el vacío* (1970).

PALATINATE, electress of.
See Marie of Brandenburg-Kulmbach (1519–1567).
See Anna Constancia (1619–1651).
See Elizabeth Amalia of Hesse (1635–1709).
See Medici, Anna Maria Luisa de (1667–1743).

PALATINE, Charlotte-Elisabeth de Baviere, princesse (1652–1722). *See Charlotte Elizabeth of Bavaria.*

PALATINE, countess.
See Matilda of Saxony (978–1025).
See Richesa of Lorraine (d. 1067).
See Gertrude of Swabia (c. 1104–1191).
See Agnes of Saxony (fl. 1200s).
See Matilda of Nassau (fl. 1285–1310).
See Irmengard of Oettingen.
See Magdalena (fl. late 1500s).
See Catherine (1584–1638).
See Gonzaga, Anne de (1616–1684).
See Charlotte (1896–1985).

PALATINE, electress.
See Dorothea of Denmark (1520–1580).
See Louisa Juliana (1576–1644).
See Elizabeth of Bohemia (1596–1662).
See Maria Leopoldina (1776–1848).

PALATINE, Madame. *See Charlotte Elizabeth of Bavaria (1652–1722).*

PALATINE, Princess.
See Elizabeth of Bohemia (1618–1680).
See Louisa (1622–1709).
See Charlotte Elizabeth of Bavaria (1652–1722).

PALCHIKOVA, Irina (1959—). Soviet handball player. Born Mar 22, 1959, in USSR. ❖ At Moscow Olympics, won a gold medal in team competition (1980).

PALCY, Euzhan (1957—). French film director. Born Jan 13, 1958, in Martinique, France; earned a degree in French literature from the Sorbonne and a film degree from Vaugirard. ❖ Moved to Paris (1975); made film debut with *Sugar Cane Alley* (1984); became the 1st black woman filmmaker of a feature-length movie with *A Dry White Season* (1989), a film about apartheid starring Zakes Mokae, Marlon Brando and Donald Sutherland; other films include *Comment vont les enfants* (1990), *Siméon* (1992) and *Aimé Césaire: A Voice for History* (1994); for tv, directed "Ruby Bridges" (1998) and "The Killing Yard" (2001).

PALECKOVA, Dagmar. *See Svubova, Dagmar.*

PALEIJ, princess (1865–1929). *See Olga, Princess Paley.*

PALENCIA, Isabel de (1878–c. 1950). Spanish author and diplomat. Name variations: Isabel Oyarzábal de Palencia. Born Isabel Oyarzábal, June 12, 1878 (some sources cite 1881) in Málaga, Spain; died c. 1950; dau. of Juan Oyarzábal and Anne Guthrie (a Scot); m. Ceferino Palencia Tubau (artist), July 8, 1909; children: Ceferino; Marissa. ❖ The 1st Spanish woman to hold an ambassadorial post, was employed as a foreign correspondent for several English-language publications and for 2 years published Spain's 1st woman's magazine, *La Dama*; worked with Spanish women's organizations to fight for female suffrage and education and began associating with Spanish socialists; traveled to US under auspices of the Institute of International Education, lecturing on gender conditions in Spain (1920s); after the Spanish Civil War began (July 1936), served as the Republican government's ambassador to Sweden (1936–39); immigrated to Mexico with family; wrote a biography of Alexandra Kollontai; lectured in US against the fascist powers during WWII and remained a vocal critic of the Franco regime in Spain. ❖ See also autobiography *I Must Have Liberty* (Longmans, 1940); and *Women in World History*.

PALEOLOGA, Sophia (1448–1503). *See Sophia of Byzantium.*

PALETZI, Juliane (d. 1569). Princess of Uglitsch. Died 1569; dau. of Dimitri Paletski; m. Yuri (1533–1563), prince of Uglitsch, Nov 3, 1548; children: Vassili of Uglitsch (b. 1559).

PALEY, Babe (1915–1978). American socialite. Name variations: Barbara Cushing; Barbara Mortimer. Born Barbara Cushing, July 5, 1915; died July 6, 1978; dau. of Henry Cushing (prominent neurosurgeon) and Katherine "Kate" (Crowell) Cushing, sister of Betsey Cushing Roosevelt Whitney (1908–1998) and Minnie Astor Fosburgh (1906–1978); m. Stanley Grafton Mortimer Jr. (Standard Oil heir), Sept 21, 1940

(div. 1946); m. William Paley (chair of board of CBS-TV); children: Stanley Grafton Mortimer III (b. 1942); Amanda Joy Mortimer (b. 1943); William Cushing Paley (b. 1948); Kate Paley (b. 1950); (stepchild by 2nd marriage) Hilary Paley; (stepchild by 2nd marriage) Jeffrey Paley. ❖ Popular socialite with an abundance of intelligence and charm, was a fashion editor for *Glamour* magazine, then *Vogue*. ❖ See also David Grafton, *The Sisters: The Lives and Times of the Fabulous Cushing Sisters* (Villard, 1992); and *Women in World History*.

PALEY, Grace (1922). American short-story writer, poet, professor, and peace activist. Born Grace Goodside, Dec 11, 1922, in New York, NY; dau. of Isaac Goodside (physician) and Manya (Ridnyik) Goodside (photographer and medical assistant); attended Hunter College, 1938–39; m. Jess Paley (cinematographer), June 20, 1942 (div. 1972); m. Bob Nichols, 1972; children: (1st m.) Nora Paley (b. 1949); Danny Paley (b. 1951). ❖ Major voice in 20th-century American literature and prominent peace activist, studied poetry with W.H. Auden (early 1940s); published 1st collection of short stories, *The Little Disturbances of Man* (1959), to critical acclaim; was founder of Greenwich Village Peace Center (1961); engaged in demonstrations and civil disobedience protesting the Vietnam War; taught at Columbia and Syracuse universities (1960s); taught at Sarah Lawrence College (1966–88); traveled to Vietnam (1969), representing the antiwar movement, as well as to Chile (1972), Moscow (1973) and China (1974); elected to American Academy of Letters (1980); writings include *Enormous Changes at the Last Minute* (1975), *Later the Same Day* (1985), *Leaning Forward* (1985), *Long Walks and Intimate Talks* (1991), *New and Collected Poems* (1992), *Grace Paley: The Collected Stories* (1994) and *Just As I Thought* (1998). Was 1st recipient of Edith Wharton Citation of Merit and was named 1st state author of New York (1986); received REA Award for Short Stories (1992); given Vermont Award for Excellence in the Arts (1993). ❖ See also Judith Arcana, *Grace Paley's Life Stories* (U. of Illinois Press, 1993); and *Women in World History*.

PALEY, princess (1865–1929). *See Olga, Princess Paley.*

PALFI, Marion (1907–1978). German-born photographer. Name variations: Marion Magner. Born in Berlin, Germany, Oct 21, 1907; died in Los Angeles, California, Nov 1978; dau. of Victor Palfi (theater producer); m. Erich Abraham, mid-1930s (div.); m. Benjamin Weiss, 1940 (div. 1944); m. Martin Magner (Danish-born producer-director), 1955. ❖ Acted in several German films before taking up photography (1932); operated her own portrait studio in Berlin (1934–36), while freelancing for magazines; moved to Amsterdam (1936), then NY (1940); traveled US on a Rosenwald fellowship (1944), which led to photo-essay, "There Is No More Time," documenting segregation in the South; also published *Suffer Little Children*, on child neglect and juvenile delinquency, and documented conditions among the elderly; work was represented in a number of major museum exhibitions, including Steichen's *Family of Man* (1955). ❖ See also *Women in World History*.

PALFREY, Sarah (1912–1996). American tennis player. Name variations: Sarah Palfrey Fabyan; Sarah Fabyan Cooke; Sarah Palfrey Cooke; Sarah Palfrey Danzig. Born Sarah Palfrey, Sept 18, 1912, in Sharon, MA; m. a man named Fabyan, 1934 (div.); m. Elwood Cooke (tennis player, div.), c. 1940; m. Jerome Danzig. ❖ Won 3 national jr. championships (1928–30); with Alice Marble, won Wimbledon women's doubles (1938, 1939) and US doubles (1938, 1940); also won US doubles with Betty Nuthall (1930), and with Helen Hull Jacobs (1932, 1935); won US mixed doubles (1932, 1935, 1937, 1941); won US singles championship (1941, 1945).

PALFYOVA, Matylda (1912–1944). Czech gymnast. Name variations: Matilda Palfyova; Matilda Palfyova-Marekova. Born Mar 11, 1912, in Czechoslovakia; died Sept 23, 1944. ❖ At Berlin Olympics, won a silver medal in team all-around (1936).

PALINGER, Katalin (1978—). Hungarian handball player. Name variations: Pálinger. Born Dec 6, 1978, in Hungary. ❖ Goalkeeper, won a team silver medal at Sydney Olympics (2000).

PALIYSKA, Diana (1966—). Bulgarian kayaker. Born Aug 20, 1966, in Bulgaria. ❖ At Seoul Olympics, won a bronze medal in K4 500 meters and a silver medal in K2 500 meters (1988).

PALL, Olga (1947—). Austrian Alpine skier. Born Dec 3, 1947, in Austria. ❖ Won a gold medal for downhill at Grenoble Olympics (1968).

PALLADINO, Emma (c. 1860–1922). Italian ballet dancer. Born c. 1860, in Milan, Italy; died April 13, 1922, in London, England; dau. of dancer Andrea Palladino. ❖ Trained at Teatro alla Scala's ballet school in

Milan; performed with Mapleson Opera Troupe in New York City (c. 1878) and at Her Majesty's Theatre in London; danced with Alhambra Theater for 7 years, while she continued to perform in opera ballet; joined Empire Theatre's Ballet in London, where she danced in Katti Lanner's *Diana* (1888), *A Dream of Wealth* (1889) and *Dolly* (1890); retired (1899).

PALLADINO, Eusapia (1854–1918). Italian spiritualistic medium. Born Jan 21, 1854, at Minervo-Murge, near Bari, Italy; died 1918; mother died just after her birth; father was assassinated by brigands (1866). ❖ Became a nursemaid in Naples, working in a household where séances were held; began to attract attention as a powerful medium (1872), known for her presentation of movements of physical phenomena without contact and spectral appearances; over a course of 20 years (1890–1910), traveled to US, Cambridge, Paris, Warsaw and other cities to submit to tests by investigators and skeptics; for a time, deceived many noted scientists, and many of her presentations are still being explained. ❖ See also Carrington, *Eusapia Palladino and Her Phenomena.*

PALLERINI, Antonia (1790–1870). Italian ballet dancer. Born June 25, 1790, in Pesaro, Italy; died Jan 11, 1870, in Milan, Italy. ❖ Trained at Teatro alla Scala's ballet school in Milan, and remained with that company throughout professional career; created major roles for Salvatore Vigano's *Prometeo* (1813), *Otello* (1818), *I Titani* (1819), and *Didone* (1821).

PALLI, Angelica (1798–1875). Greek-Italian poet, novelist and short-story writer. Name variations: Angeliki Palli; Angelica Palli Bartolomei or Bartolommei. Born Angeliki Palli, 1798, in Greek community in Livorno, Italy; died in Livorno, 1875; m. Giampaolo Bartolomei (politician). ❖ Though she never lived in Greece, often wrote of Greek struggle for independence; works include *Discorso di una donna alle giovani maritote del suo paese* (1851) and *Epiro e Thessalia*; also wrote tragedies, dramas, short stories, and poetry, and translated various works into Italian.

PALLI, Anne-Marie (1955—). French golfer. Born April 19, 1955, in Ciboure, France. ❖ Won 26 tournaments in Europe as an amateur; joined tour (1979); won Samaritan Tourquoise Classic (1983) and ShopRite Classic (1992); founding member of the Women's Senior Golf Tour. Received French Academy of Sport Gold medal.

PALM, Etta Aelders (1743–1799). French secret agent and feminist. Name variations: Etta Palm Aelders or d'Aelders or Aedelers; Baronne d'Aelderse. Born Etta Lubina Johanna Derista Aelders in Groningen, Netherlands, April 1743; died in The Hague, Mar 28, 1799; dau. of Johan Aelders van Nieuwenhuys (d. 1749) and his 2nd wife, Agatha Pierteronella de Sitten; well educated at home by mother; m. Christiaan Ferdinand Loderwijk Palm (humanities student), 1762 (div. or sep., 1763); children: Agatha (b. 1763, died in infancy). ❖ Secret agent of the Dutch, Prussian, and French governments, was also one of the three most prominent advocates of women's rights during early years of the French Revolution; after husband divorced her, became an adventurer, left for Dutch East Indies, and disappeared (1763); moved to Paris and set up a salon (1773); frequented by philosopher Condorcet and politicians Pierre Choudieu, Claude Basire, François Buzot, François Chabot, Jean-François de Menou, Théodore de Lameth, Emmanuel Fréteau, Jérôme Pétion, Jean-Louis Carra, and even Maximilien de Robespierre; became an agent for France (1778), and possibly for Prussia (1780s); opposed the Patriot movement in Dutch Republic (1784–87); became an agent for the stadholder (1788); joined the Social Circle during the French Revolution and spoke out on women's rights (1790–91); founded and directed the Patriotic and Charitable Society of the Women Friends of Truth (1791–92), the only club involved seriously in women's issues up to 1793; was briefly arrested on suspicion of spying (1791); presented a radical petition on women's rights (1792); went to Dutch Republic and served as a diplomatic intermediary (1792–93); was imprisoned by Dutch Patriots of the Batavian Republic (1795–98). ❖ See also (in Dutch) Koppins, W.J. *Etta Palm: Nederland's eerste feministe tijdens de Franch revolutie te Parijs* (Ploegsma, 1929); and *Women in World History.*

PALMA, Felip (1862–1917). *See Ventós i Cullell, Palmira.*

PALMER, Alice Freeman (1855–1902). American educator. Name variations: Alice E. Freeman. Born Feb 21, 1855, in Colesville, New York; died Dec 6, 1902, in Paris, France; dau. of James Freeman (farmer and physician) and Elizabeth (Higley) Freeman (teacher and social reformer); sister of Ella Freeman (teacher); University of Michigan, BA, 1876; m. George Herbert Palmer (Harvard philosophy professor), Dec 23, 1887;

no children. ❖ The most celebrated woman educator of her time, was nationally and internationally known for her success in integrating women into US system of higher education; became principal at a high school in Saginaw, MI (1877); accepted a faculty position in history at newly established Wellesley College (1879); served as president of Wellesley (1881–87), overseeing its progress from a fledgling institution to a leader among American women's colleges; on marriage, remained officially only on the board of trustees at Wellesley, though in essence became a co-president with successor Helen Shafer; awarded doctorate by University of Michigan (1881); went on annual speaking tours (1889–92); served as dean of the women's college of University of Chicago (1892–94); published *Why Go to College?* (1897); was a leading voice in US educational reform. ❖ See also Ruth Bordin, *Alice Freeman Palmer: The Evolution of the New Woman* (U. of Michigan Press, 1993); George H. Palmer, *The Life of Alice Freeman Palmer* (Houghton Mifflin, 1915); Caroline Hazard, ed. *An Academic Courtship: Letters of Alice Freeman Palmer and George Herbert Palmer* (Harvard U. Press, 1940); and *Women in World History.*

PALMER, Alice May (1886–1977). New Zealand labor activist, feminist, editor, and public official. Born Aug 6, 1886, at Gordon, near Gore, New Zealand; died on June 26, 1977, in Silverstream, New Zealand; dau. of Walter Henry Palmer (court clerk), and Alice (Shepard) Palmer; Victoria College, BA, 1912. ❖ As result of Public Service Act of 1912, became one of 1st women to be hired by New Zealand Public Service Association (PSA, 1914); fought for equal pay and was elected 1st woman executive vice president of PSA (1934); edited *New Zealand School Journal* and *New Zealand Education Gazette* (late 1930s). ❖ See also *Dictionary of New Zealand Biography* (Vol. 3).

PALMER, Anne (1661–1722). Countess of Sussex. Name variations: Lady Dacre; Anne Lennard. Born in Feb 1661; died in 1722; dau. of Barbara Villiers (c. 1641–1709) and probably Charles II, king of England; m. Thomas Lennard, Lord Dacre, in 1674, who was created earl of Sussex in 1684 (died 1715). ❖ See also *Women in World History.*

PALMER, Barbara (1672–1737). Daughter of Barbara Villiers. Born 1672; died 1737; dau. of Barbara Villiers (c. 1641–1709) and possibly John Churchill, duke of Marlborough; children: (with James Douglas, afterwards 4th duke of Hamilton) Charles Hamilton. ❖ Entered a nunnery in France, before having illegitimate son. ❖ See also *Women in World History.*

PALMER, Bertha Honoré (1849–1918). American socialite and philanthropist. Name variations: Mrs. Potter Palmer; Bertha Honore Palmer. Born Bertha Honoré in Louisville, Kentucky, May 22, 1849; died in Chicago, Illinois, May 5, 1918; dau. of Henry H. Honoré (businessman) and Eliza J. (Carr) Honoré; graduate of Convent of Visitation in Georgetown, Washington, DC, 1867; m. Potter Palmer (entrepreneur), July 28, 1870; children: Honoré (b. 1874) and Potter II (b. 1875). ❖ Leading figure in Chicago society, organized benefits, held receptions, and hosted dinners to fete scions of US business and government, European nobility, labor leaders, and welfare reformers; was also a supporter of Jane Addams' welfare work at Hull House, and was concerned with the issues of women in the workplace; served as chair of board of "Lady Managers" (1890–93) for Columbian Exposition held in Chicago (1893); was directly responsible for its Woman's Building, one of the most popular buildings of the Fair, which was a sort of museum exhibit illustrating the progress of women through the previous 400 years and included murals by Mary Cassatt; also was responsible for the Children's Building and a dormitory for women visitors; appointed the only woman member of the national commission representing US at Paris Exposition. Presented with France's Legion of Honor. ❖ See also Ishbel Ross, *Silhouette in Diamonds: The Life of Mrs. Potter Palmer* (Harper, 1960); and *Women in World History.*

PALMER, Caroline Harriet (1809–1877). *See Abraham, Caroline Harriet.*

PALMER, Eliza (c. 1812–1891). *See Wohlers, Eliza.*

PALMER, Elizabeth (1778–1853). *See Peabody, Elizabeth Palmer.*

PALMER, Elizabeth Mary (1832–1897). New Zealand music and singing teacher, performer, composer, and theatrical promoter. Name variations: Elizabeth Mary Naylor. Born Elizabeth Mary Naylor, Nov 3, 1832, in Suffolk, England; died May 31, 1897, in Wellington, New Zealand; dau. of George Naylor and Elizabeth Caroline (Smith) Naylor; m. George Palmer (gardener), 1853 (died 1896); children: 8 sons, 4 daughters. ❖ Immigrated with husband to New Zealand (1856); taught music and voice from her Nelson home, and began performing in and promoting theatrical events (1871); continued when family relocated to Wellington (1876) and to Wairarapa (1878), where she also taught at Clareville School; composed words and lyrics to popular ballad, "Twas Only a Dream" (1884). ❖ See also *Dictionary of New Zealand Biography* (Vol. 2).

PALMER, Frances Flora (1812–1876). English-born American lithographer. Name variations: Fanny Palmer; Frances Flora Bond Palmer; occasionally signed work "F.F. Palmer." Born Frances Flora Bond, June 26, 1812, in Leicester, England; died of TB, Aug 20, 1876, in Brooklyn, NY; dau. of Robert Bond (attorney) and Elizabeth Bond; m. Edmund Seymour Palmer, early 1830s (died 1859); children: Flora E. and Edmund Seymour (possibly twins, b. about 1834). ❖ Noted American artist, immigrated to US (early 1840s); joined the prestigious Nathaniel Currier lithograph firm as a staff artist (1849); drew praise for 2 lithographic views of Manhattan (1849), as well as a watercolor painting that many would later consider her most significant original artwork, *The High Bridge at Harlem New York* (1849); also collaborated with Charles Currier in improving the lithographic crayon; better works during this time included *American Farm Scenes* (1853), *American Winter Scenes* (1854), and *American Country Life* (1855); after James M. Ives joined the firm (1857), her work became more varied and dramatic, as exhibited by *A Midnight Race on the Mississippi* (1860), *The 'Lightning Express' Train, Leaving the Junction* (1863), and *American Express Train* (1864), lithographs which captured the public's imagination regarding western expansion and manifest destiny (late 1860s). ❖ See also *Women in World History*.

PALMER, Helen (1917–1979). Australian writer and teacher. Born Helen Gwynneth Palmer, May 9, 1917, in Emerald, Victoria, Australia; died May 6, 1979, in Australia; dau. of Vance Palmer (writer) and Nettie Palmer (1885–1964, writer and literary critic); attended Presbyterian Ladies' College in Melbourne, 1934; Melbourne University, BA, DipEd, 1939. ❖ Began career as a teacher (1939); joined the Women's Australian Auxiliary Air Force as director of educational services (1942); traveled to China (1952); founded (1957) and edited *Outlook*, a journal dedicated to progressive socialist issues (1957–70); writings include *An Australian Teacher in China* (1953), *Beneath the Southern Cross* (1954), *Australia: The First Hundred Years* (with Jessie MacLeod, 1956), *After the First Hundred Years* (with MacLeod, 1961), *Fencing Australia* (1961) and *'Banjo' Paterson* (1966). ❖ See also Doreen Bridges, ed. *Helen Palmer's Outlook* (1982); and *Women in World History*.

PALMER, Henrietta (1856–1911). See Winter, John Strange.

PALMER, Janet Gertrude (1885–1964). See Palmer, Nettie.

PALMER, Leland (1940—). American dancer and choreographer. Born June 16, 1940, in New York, NY. ❖ Trained with Eugene Loring, Bella Lewitsky, John Butler, and others at American School of Dance in Los Angeles, and with Jaime Rogers and Alvin Ailey in New York City; worked as assignment choreographer for Michael Bennett, Grover Dale, Ron Field, and Bob Fosse, for whom she worked on *Pippin* and *All That Jazz*; performed with Loring's Dance Players in Los Angeles, NY, and on tour; appeared in Bennett's *A Joyful Noise* (1967), *Your Own Thing* (1968), *Hello Dolly* (1968), and others; on tv, made numerous appearances as dancer, including "Glen Campbell's Goodtime Hour" (1970) and "Dinah Shore Summer Series" (1976); films include *Valentino* (1977) and *All That Jazz* (1979). Nominated for Tony Awards for Best Supporting Actress for *A Joyful Noise* (1967) and Best Actress for *Pippin* (1973).

PALMER, Lilli (1914–1986). German-born actress. Name variations: Lilli Peiser; Maria Lilli Peiser. Born Maria Lilli Peiser, May 24, 1914, in German city of Posen (now Poznan, Poland); died of cancer, Jan 27, 1986, in Los Angeles; dau. of Dr. Alfred Peiser (surgeon) and Rose (Lissman) Peiser; attended Ilka Gruning School of Acting, Berlin, 1930–32; m. Rex Harrison (actor), Jan 1943 (div. 1957); m. Carlos Thompson (actor), 1957; children: (1st m.) Carey Harrison. ❖ Jewish refugee from Nazi Germany who became a noted film and stage actress, writer, and painter, made 1st stage appearance in an operetta at Darmstadt State Theater (1932); exiled in France (1933), then Britain (1934); made 1st film appearance, *Crime Unlimited* (1935); immigrated to US (1945); made American film debut in *Cloak and Dagger* (1946) and Broadway debut in *Bell, Book and Candle* (1950); launched NY tv program, "Lilli Palmer Presents" (1951); made 1st German film, *Feuerwerk* (1954); held 1st art exhibit, London (1965); wrote 1st novel, *The Red Raven* (1978); other films include *Secret Agent* (1936), *English Without Tears* (1944), *The Rake's Progress* (1945), *Body and Soul* (1947),

The Four-Poster (1952), *Madchen in Uniform* (1958), *Conspiracy of Hearts* (1960), *The Pleasure of His Company* (1961), *Le Rendezvous de Minuit* (1961), *The Counterfeit Traitor* (1962), *Amorous Adventures of Moll Flanders* (1965), *Oedipus the King* (1968), *Lotte in Weimar* (1968), *The Boys from Brazil* (1978) and *The Holcroft Covenant* (1985). ❖ See also autobiography *Change Lobsters—and Dance* (1975); and *Women in World History*.

PALMER, Lillian (b. 1913). Canadian runner. Born June 23, 1913, in Canada. ❖ At Los Angeles Olympics, won a silver medal in the 4 x 100-meter relay (1932).

PALMER, Lizzie Merrill (1838–1916). American philanthropist. Name variations: Lizzie Merrill-Palmer. Born Lizzie Pitts Merrill in Portland, Maine, Oct 8, 1838; died at Great Neck, Long Island, NY, July 28, 1916; only child of Charles Merrill (lumber baron) and Frances (Pitts) Merrill; m. Thomas Witherell Palmer (businessman and US Senator), Oct 16, 1855 (died 1913); raised and educated several homeless children. ❖ Philanthropist whose bequest founded the Palmer Motherhood and Home Training School in Detroit, later known as the Merrill-Palmer Institute; moved to central Michigan with family (1850s); with husband, supported Detroit Institute of Art, YMCA, University of Michigan, and a number of hospitals in Detroit area; also founded the Michigan branch of Society for the Prevention of Cruelty to Animals; gave a parcel of land to the city (1893), which became known as Palmer Park. ❖ See also *Women in World History*.

PALMER, Maria (1917–1981). Austrian stage, screen and tv actress. Born Sept 5, 1917, in Vienna, Austria; died Sept 6, 1981, in Los Angeles, CA. ❖ First appeared on Broadway (1938); films include *Mission to Moscow, Days of Glory, Lady on a Train, The Web, Surrender, Strictly Dishonorable, By the Light of the Silvery Moon, Flight Nurse* and *The Evil of Frankenstein*; appeared as Mady Stevens on tv series "The Young Marrieds" (1964–65).

PALMER, Mary (1716–1794). English author. Born Mary Reynolds, 1716; died 1794; sister of painter Sir Joshua Reynolds (1723–1792); m. John Palmer, 1740. ❖ The older sister of Sir Joshua Reynolds, was the author of *Devonshire Dialogue* (1st complete edition, 1839), which is frequently reprinted.

PALMER, Mignon (1885–1970). See Nevada, Mignon.

PALMER, Nettie (1885–1964). Australian critic, poet, and journalist. Name variations: Janet Gertrude Palmer. Born Janet Gertrude Higgins, Aug 18, 1885, in Bendigo, Victoria, Australia; died Oct 19, 1964; dau. of John Higgins (accountant) and Catherine (MacDonald) Higgins; University of Melbourne, BA, 1909, MA, 1912; m. Vance Palmer (writer), May 23, 1914; children: Aileen Palmer (b. 1915); Helen Palmer (1917–1979, writer). ❖ Credited with raising the prestige of Australian literature in general, and Australian women's literature in particular, published 2 vols. of poetry, *The South Wind* (1914) and *Shadowy Paths* (1915), while living in London; moved with family to Emerald, Victoria, and with husband became an important contributor to Australia's literary circles; an outspoken foe of mandatory military enlistment during WWI, wrote a regular column for *Argus;* published the widely praised *Modern Australian Literature 1900–1923* (1924), followed by *Australian Story-Book* (1928); wrote a personal column, "A Reader's Notebook," for *All About Books* (1928–38) and contributed longer pieces to *Illustrated Tasmanian Mail* (1927–33); moved with family to Melbourne (1929), where she published *Henry Bourne Higgins* (1931) and *Talking It Over* (1932), as well as co-edited a collection of women's writings in *The Centenary Gift Book* (1934); was the 1st to recognize the importance of novelist Henry Handel Richardson, and wrote critical studies of the works of several others, including Barbara Baynton and Katharine Susannah Prichard; became involved in international political issues as she opposed the rise of fascism and promoted world peace; published what many regard as her best work, *Fourteen Years: Extracts from a Private Journal 1925–1939,* in journal *Meanjin* (1948), followed by *The Dandemongs* (1952) and *Bernard O'Dowd* (1954); was a frequent broadcaster over ABC radio. ❖ See also *Women in World History*.

PALMER, Olive E. (1902–1976). See Diefenbaker, Olive.

PALMER, Phoebe Worrall (1807–1874). American evangelist and author. Born Dec 18, 1807, in New York, NY; died Nov 2, 1874, in NY, NY; dau. of Henry Worrall (owner of a machine shop and iron foundry) and Dorothea Wade; m. Walter Clark Palmer (physician), Sept 28, 1827; children: Alexander and Samuel (both died in infancy). ❖ Began conducting popular Methodist revival meetings in NYC

(c. 1835); published the highly successful *The Way of Holiness*, the 1st of 8 books promoting the perfectionist movement (1845); founded Five Points Mission to care for the indigent in an inner-city section of NY (1850); edited the movement's principal journal, *Guide to Holiness* (1862–74). ❖ See also *Women in World History.*

PALMER, Mrs. Potter (1849–1918). *See Palmer, Bertha Honoré.*

PALMER, Sandra (1941—). American golfer. Name variations: Sandra Jean Palmer. Born Mar 10, 1941, in Fort Worth, TX; North Texas State University, degree in physical education. ❖ Had 21 professional career wins, including Sealy Classic (1973), Titleholders (1973), Burdine's Invitational (1974), US Open (1975), Bloomington Classic (1976), Kathryn Crosby/Honda Classic (1977), Boston Five Classic (1982) and Mayflower Classic (1986). Named LPGA Player of the Year (1975); inducted into Texas State Golf Hall of Fame (1985) and National Collegiate Hall of Fame (1988).

PALMER, Sophia French (1853–1920). American nurse and administrator. Born May 26, 1853, in Milton, Massachusetts; died April 27, 1920, at Forest Lawn, New York; dau. of Simeon Palmer (physician) and Maria Burdell (Spencer) Palmer; graduate of Boston Training School for Nurses (now Massachusetts General Hospital School of Nursing), 1878; never married; children: adopted 8-year-old daughter (1906). ❖ In Washington, DC (1889), founded and then served as the administrator of the training school for nurses at Garfield Memorial Hospital (1889–96); was superintendent of Rochester (NY) City Hospital and Training school (1896–1900); was instrumental in the development of professional nursing organizations, and established and edited several professional nursing journals; was a founding member of American Society of Superintendents of Training Schools for Nurses (1893) and served as its representative in organizing the national Nurses' Associated Alumnae of US and Canada (later American Nurses' Association); served as 1st editor-in-chief of *American Journal of Nursing* (1900–20); was appointed a member of NY Board of Nurse Examiners and elected its 1st chair (1903). ❖ See also *Women in World History.*

PALMER, Victorine (1844–1935). *See Goddard, Victorine.*

PALMERSTON, Viscountess (d. 1869). *See Lamb, Emily.*

PALMOLIVE (1955—). Spanish-English musician. Name variations: Paloma Romero; The Slits. Born Paloma Romero, 1955, in Spain. ❖ Drummer, made stage debut with The Slits in London (1977); joined punk group, the Raincoats (1979); with Raincoats, released 1st single, "Fairytale in the Supermarket" and album *The Raincoats* (1979); quit Raincoats, traveled to India, and settled in Massachusetts as a born-again Christian.

PALMYRA, queen of. *See Zenobia (r. 267–272).*

PALTROW, Gwyneth (1972—). American actress. Born Gwyneth Kate Paltrow, Sept 28, 1972, in Los Angeles, CA; dau. of Blythe Danner (actress) and Bruce Paltrow (producer); sister of Jake Paltrow; m. Chris Martin (lead singer with Coldplay), Dec 5, 2003; children: daughter Apple Martin (b. 2004) and son Moses Martin (b. 2006). ❖ Received early acting training at Williamstown Theater in the Berkshires; made film debut in *Shout* (1991); appeared in *Flesh and Bone* (1993), *Mrs. Parker and the Vicious Circle* (1994), *Jefferson in Paris* (1995), and *Emma* (1996) among others; won Academy Award for Best Actress for *Shakespeare in Love* (1998); other films include *The Talented Mr. Ripley* (1999), *Duets* (2000), *The Royal Tenenbaums* (2001), *Shallow Hal* (2001), *Sylvia* (2003) and *Running with Scissors* (2006).

PALUCCA, Gret (1902–1993). German dancer and dance teacher. Born in Munich, Germany, Jan 8, 1902; died in Dresden, Mar 22, 1993; studied with Mary Wigman, 1920–25. ❖ For almost 7 decades was one of Germany's most famous and influential modern dancers, whose choreography, inspired by music and linked to German expressionist culture, was rooted in improvisation, a key element in her pedagogy; managed her own school of dance in Dresden (1925–39); by late 1920s, had included in her repertory the popular *Technical Improvisations* (1927); performed at Berlin Dance Festival (1934); played a role in the pageantry that accompanied the staging of Olympic Games in Berlin (1936), then the Nazis closed her school (1939); served as director of Dresden Academy of Dance (1945–93); was a founding member of GDR's German Academy of the Arts; students include Ruth Berghaus, Hannelore Bey, Arila Siegert, and Hanne Wandtke. ❖ See also (in German) Edith Krull and Werner Gommlich, *Palucca* (3rd ed., 1967); and *Women in World History.*

PÀMIES, Teresa (1919—). Spanish memoirist. Name variations: Teresa Pamies. Born 1919 in Balaguer, Spain; dau. of Tomás Pàmies (peasant farmer). ❖ Left-wing militant whose works tend toward the autobiographical and sociological, wrote *La filla del pres* (The Prisoner's Daughter, 1967), (with Tomás Pàmies) *Testament a Praga* (Testament in Prague, 1971), *Quan érem capitans* (When We Were Captains, 1974), and *Rosalia no hi era* (Rosalia Wasn't There, 1982), among others.

PAMPANINI, Silvana (1925—). Italian actress. Born Sept 25, 1925, in Rome, Italy. ❖ Named Miss Italy (1947); made film debut in *L'Apocalisse* (1947), followed by *When Love Calls, Snow White and the Seven Thieves, Antonio di Padova, O.K. Nerone, Una Bruna indiavolata, Le avventure di Mandrin, Viva il cinema, Processo alla città, La Presidentessa, The Woman Who Invented Love, Bufere, Koenigsmark, Vortice, La tratta delle bianche, Noi cannibali, Orient Express, La tour de Nesle* and *La bella di Roma,* among others.

PAMPHILA (fl. 1st c.). Greek historian. Born in Epidaurus, of Egyptian family; married Soteridas or Socratidas. ❖ Historian of considerable reputation in her day, was a scholar in Rome during the reign of Nero (r. 54–68), but wrote in Greek; only a summary of her *Miscellaneous History* (33 books), which was provided by Byzantine writer Photius, survives; also wrote epitomes of historical works.

PAN CHAO (c. 45–c. 120). *See Ban Zhao.*

PAN WENLI (1969—). Chinese volleyball player. Name variations: Pan Wen Li. Born Mar 8, 1969, in China. ❖ Won a team silver medal at Atlanta Olympics (1996).

PANA, Tini (c. 1846–1934). *See Taiaroa, Tini Kerei.*

PANAEVA, Avdotia (c. 1819–1893). Russian memoirist and short-story writer. Name variations: Avdot'ia Iakovlevna Panáeva; (pseudonym) N. Stanitskii. Born c. 1819 in Russia; died 1893; m. Ivan Panaev (writer); m. Apollon Golovachev; children: (with Golovachev) Evdokiia Nagrodskaia (1866–1930, novelist). ❖ Lived in an apartment with husband and his partner poet Nikolai Nekrasov, where they held Monday gatherings, which included Tolstoy, Dostoevsky, Turgenev, and others; helped edit liberal journal *The Contemporary* (1848–63); wrote *Reminiscences* (1899), about literary gatherings at home; with Nekrasov, under pseudonym N. Stanitskii, published popular novels, *Three Countries of the World* (1948–49) and *The Dead Lake* (1951); other works include stories, sketches, and autobiographical novella *The Talnikov Family* (1848).

PANAGIOTATOU, Angeliki (1878–1954). Greek scientist. Name variations: Angeliki Panajiotatou. Born 1878 (some sources cite 1875); died 1954; attended Medical School of National University of Athens; advanced studies in Germany. ❖ Specialist in tropical diseases, whose research halted the spread of a number of lethal epidemics of cholera and typhus, was the 1st woman to become physician, microbiologist, and professor of hygiene at National University of Athens (1938). ❖ See also *Women in World History.*

PANCHUK, Lyudmila (1956—). Soviet handball player. Born Jan 18, 1956, in USSR. ❖ At Montreal Olympics, won a gold medal in team competition (1976).

PANDIT, Nayantara (b. 1927). *See Sahgal, Nayantara.*

PANDIT, Vijaya Lakshmi (1900–1990). Indian diplomat and politician. Name variations: Nan; Vijayalaxmi Pandit; Vijay Laksmi Pandit; Mrs. Ranjit Pandit; Swarup Kumari Nehru. Pronunciation: Pun-dit. Born Swarup Kumari Nehru, Aug 18, 1900, at Anan Bhavan, Allahabad, India; died Dec 1, 1990, in India; dau. of Motilal Nehru (1861–1931, prominent lawyer dedicated to Mohandas Gandhi's nonviolent campaign) and a mother, full name unknown, who was a Swarup from the Punjab; sister of Jawaharlal Nehru (1889–1964, prime minister of India); m. Ranjit Sitaram Pandit (lawyer and activist for independence), May 10, 1921; children: 3 daughters, Chandralekha Mehta (journalist), Nayantara Sahgal (novelist), Rita Dar (director of public relations). ❖ Leading figure in one of Asia's most important political dynasties, was often called the "Lamp of India"; became active in Indian National Congress Party and the national movement to obtain India's freedom from British rule by nonviolent methods; imprisoned by the British (1932–33) for defying the Crown by publicly observing Indian Independence Day; elected to Allahabad Municipal Board (1934); elected to Assembly of the United Provinces (Uttar Pradesh, 1936); was the 1st Indian woman to become a Cabinet minister as minister of Local Self-Government and Public Health (1937); imprisoned by the British (1940); imprisoned again (1942–43), for issuing a "Quit India" resolution; elected to India's Constituent Assembly (1946); was leader of Indian Delegation to United Nations (1946–48, 1952–53, 1963); was India's 1st ambassador to Soviet Union (1947–49); served as ambassador to US (1949–52) and concurrently to Mexico (1949–51); was 1st woman and 1st Asian to serve as president of UN General Assembly (1953–54); served as Indian high commissioner (ambassador) to United Kingdom (1954–61); served as governor of the state of Maharashtra (1962–63); decried Indira Gandhi's takeover of the Indian government and the imprisonment of thousands of opposition members (1975–77). ❖ See also memoir *The Scope of Happiness* (Crown, 1979); and *Women in World History*.

PANDITA RAMABAI (1858–1922). *See Ramabai, Pandita.*

PANFIL, Wanda (1959—). Polish marathon runner. Name variations: Wanda Panfil-Gonzalez; Wanda González. Born Jan 26, 1959, in Poland. ❖ Won NY City Marathon (1990) and Boston Marathon (1991); won World championship (1991).

PANG JIAYING (1985—). Chinese swimmer. Born Jan 6, 1985, in China. ❖ At World championships SC, won 200-meter freestyle (2002); won a silver medal for 4 x 200-meter freestyle relay at Athens Olympics (2004).

PANHOLCHYK, Olena (1964—). *See Pakholchik, Olena.*

PANKHURST, Adela (1885–1961). English suffragist. Name variations: Adela Walsh. Born Adela Constantia Mary Pankhurst in Manchester, England, June 19, 1885; died May 23, 1961, in Australia; youngest dau. of Richard Marsden Pankhurst and Emmeline Goulden Pankhurst (1858–1928); sister of Christabel (1880–1958), Sylvia (1882–1960), Frank, and Harry Pankhurst; m. Tom Walsh (socialist labor leader), 1919 (died 1943); children: Richard Walsh (b. 1919), and daughters Sylvia Walsh (b. 1920), Christian Walsh (b. 1921), and Ursula Walsh (b. 1923). ❖ Participant with her mother and sisters in the prewar militant British women's suffrage movement, who immigrated to Australia (1914) where she helped found, at different times, 2 ideologically opposed organizations, the Australian Communist Party and the Australian Women's Guild of Empire; published influential pacifist booklet, *Put up the Sword!* (1915); joined Victoria Socialist Party (1917); founded Australian Women's Guild of Empire (1929); served as editor, *The Empire Gazette* (c. 1930–39); as an anti-Bolshevik campaigner, flirted with fascism, joined the isolationist "Australia First" movement, and visited Japan (1940) as a guest of the Japanese government; was interned (1942); was the most politically radical, ideologically inconsistent, and personally humane of the 3 sisters. ❖ See also *Women in World History*.

PANKHURST, Christabel (1880–1958). English suffragist. Name variations: Dame Christabel Pankhurst. Born Christabel Harriette Pankhurst in Manchester, England, Sept 22, 1880; died in Los Angeles, California, Feb 13, 1958; eldest of 4 children of Richard Marsden Pankhurst, LLD (died 1898), and Emmeline Goulden Pankhurst (1858–1928, suffragist); sister of Sylvia (1882–1960), Adela (1885–1961), Henry Francis (Frank), and Francis Henry (Harry) Pankhurst; attended Victoria University in Manchester and received a first class degree in law, LLB (1906); children: adopted daughter Betty, in 1930. ❖ English co-founder of the Women's Social and Political Union and the strategist behind its increasingly militant policy and violent tactics; joined Manchester Women's Trade Union Council and began working behind the scenes on behalf of women's causes; joined and was made a member of executive committee of North of England Society for Women's Suffrage (1901); joined with mother to co-found a more radical independent women's suffrage organization, the Women's Social and Political Union (WSPU, 1903); served as editor of *The Suffragette* (1908–15); sent to prison for resisting arrest (1906), a significant event, because it was covered by a newspaper, thus breaking the unofficial boycott against women's suffrage press coverage; unsuccessfully stood for Parliament as a coalition candidate for Smethwick (1918); became increasingly interested in Second Adventism, a movement which proclaimed the Second Coming of Christ (1921); moved to US (1940); writings include *The Commons Debate on Woman Suffrage with a reply by Christabel Pankhurst* (1908), *The Militant Methods of the NWSPU* (1908), *The Great Scourge and How to End It* (1913), *International Militancy* (1915), *No Peace without Victory* (1917), *The Lord Commeth!* (1922), *Some Modern Problems in the Light of Biblical Prophecy* (1922), *The World Unrest or Visions of the Dawn* (1926), *The Uncurtained Future* (1940), *Unshackled: The Story of How We Won the Vote* (1959). Made Dame Commander of British Empire (DBE, 1936). ❖ See also Barbara Castle, *Sylvia and Christabel Pankhurst* (Penguin, 1987); David Mitchell, *The Fighting Pankhursts* (Macmillan, 1967) and *Queen Christabel: A Biography of*

Christabel Pankhurst (Macdonald & Jane's, 1977); and *Women in World History*.

PANKHURST, E. Sylvia (1882–1960). *See Pankhurst, Sylvia.*

PANKHURST, Emmeline (1858–1928). English suffragist. Born Emmeline Goulden in Manchester, England, July 14, 1858; died June 14, 1928, in London, England; dau. of Robert Goulden (owner of a calico-printing and bleach works who helped found the original Women's Suffrage Committee) and Sophia Jane Craine (Crane) Goulden (suffragist); attended École Normale in Paris; m. Richard Marsden Pankhurst (barrister and suffragist), 1879 (died 1898); children: Christabel Harriet Pankhurst (1880–1958); Estelle Sylvia Pankhurst (1882–1960); Francis Henry (Frank) Pankhurst (1884–1888); Adela Constantia Mary Pankhurst (1885–1961); Henry Francis (Harry) Pankhurst (1889–1910). ❖ Matriarch of radical feminism in Britain who, along with daughter Christabel, founded the Women's Social and Political Union (1903), the organization which represented the most militant wing of the British women's suffrage movement; with husband, co-founded the Women's Franchise League to obtain the right for women to vote in local elections (1889); became involved with work of the Manchester Suffrage Society; joined the new Independent Labour Party (1894) for which husband stood twice, unsuccessfully, as a candidate for Parliament; after husband's death (1898), broke with Labour Party and founded Women's Social and Political Union (WSPU, 1903), an organization which was from its inception independent of all political parties and committed to direct and immediate radical political action to achieve its only goal—women's suffrage; severed all ties with the moderate National Union of Women's Suffrage Societies (NUWSS); endured many episodes of imprisonment and forcible feeding which left her weak, bruised, and battered but still defiant; was arrested and released 12 times (Jan–June 1914), the final time in such a debilitated condition that she was not recognized by some of her colleagues; with Christabel, co-founded British Women's Party (1917), a party which supposedly combined conservative politics with feminist and suffrage activity; moved to Canada (1918) and made a living there and in US by lecturing on behalf of social hygiene; returned to England (1926); writings include *The Trial of the Suffragette Leaders* (190?) and *The Importance of the Vote* (1908). ❖ See also *My Own Story* (1914); Josephine Kamm, *The Story of Emmeline Pankhurst* (Meredith, 1968); David Mitchell, *The Fighting Pankhursts* (Macmillan, 1967); and *Women in World History*.

PANKHURST, Estelle Sylvia (1882–1960). *See Pankhurst, Sylvia.*

PANKHURST, Sylvia (1882–1960). English suffragist, writer, and politician. Name variations: E. Sylvia Pankhurst; Estelle Sylvia Pankhurst. Born Estelle Sylvia Pankhurst in Manchester, England, May 5, 1882; died in Addis Ababa, Sept 27, 1960; 2nd dau. of Richard Marsden Pankhurst (died 1898) and Emmeline Goulden Pankhurst (1858–1928, suffragist); sister of Christabel (1880–1958), Adela (1885–1961), Frank, and Harry Pankhurst; attended the Accademia, Venice, and Royal Academy of Art in London; lived with Italian radical socialist Silvio Corio; children: (with Corio) Richard Kier Pethick Pankhurst (b. 1928). ❖ Activist, primarily for socialist, anti-fascist and feminist causes, was one of the original members who began the Women's Social and Political Union (WSPU, 1903); joined Labour Party (1904); founded East London Federation of Suffragettes (ELFS, 1912); joined pacifist movement during the Great War (1914–18) and British Communist Party in postwar era; continued to work on art sporadically, but was dedicated primarily to socialist-feminist causes; after mother died (1928), became more deeply involved in anti-fascist politics; edited *Ethiopian News* (1936–56) and *Ethiopian Observer*; in later life, adopted cause of Abyssinian independence and helped found Abyssinian Association; moved to Ethiopia (1956), where she died (1960); well known for her paintings and drawings of working-class women, designed many of the logos, posters, and murals for the causes which she championed; writings include *The Suffragette: The History of the Women's Militant Suffrage Movement 1905–1910* (1911), *Rebel Ireland: Thoughts on Easter Week 1916* (1920), *Lloyd George takes the Mask Off* (1920), *Soviet Russia as I Saw It* (1921), *India and the Earthly Paradise* (1926), *The Suffragette Movement: An Intimate Account of Persons and Ideals* (1932), *The Home Front* (1932), *The Life of Emmeline Pankhurst* (1936), *The Ethiopian People* (1946) and *Ethiopia: A Cultural History* (1955); founded and edited *The Women's Dreadnought, The Worker's Dreadnought,* and *New Times*. ❖ See also Barbara Castle, *Sylvia and Christabel Pankhurst* (Penguin, 1987); Richard Pankhurst, *Sylvia Pankhurst: Artist and Crusader* (Paddington, 1979); Patricia

Romero, *E. Sylvia Pankhurst: Portrait of a Radical* (University Press, 1987); and *Women in World History.*

PANKINA, Aleksandra. Belarusian rower. Born in Belarus. ❖ Won a bronze medal for coxed eights at Atlanta Olympics (1996).

PANOV, Galina (1949—). Soviet ballet dancer. Born Galina Ragozina, 1949, in Archangel, USSR; studied with Galina Ulanova; m. Valery Panov (ballet dancer and choreographer). ❖ Danced with Kirov Ballet (1970–74), in classical repertory works, including *The Nutcracker* and *Sleeping Beauty,* and numerous Soviet works, such as *Creation of the World* (1971); with husband, defected to Israel (1974), then made guest appearances in US, Canada, Australia and England; danced with Berlin Opera Ballet in such works as *Cinderella* (1978) and *The Idiot* (1979).

PANOVA, Bianca (1970—). Bulgarian rhythmic gymnast. Born May 27, 1970, in Sofia, Bulgaria; m. Tchavdar Ninor (physician). ❖ Was 3-time Bulgarian champion; won European championship (1986); at World championships, won a gold medal for ribbon (1985) and all 5 gold medals (1987); coaches in Belgium.

PANOVA, Vera (1905–1973). Russian writer. Name variations: Vera Fyodorovna (or Feodorovna or Fëdorovna) Panova; (pseudonyms) Vera Veltman; V. V-an; V V; V. Starosel'skaiia; V.S. Born Vera Fedorovna Panova, Mar 20, 1905, in Rostov-on-Don, Russia; died in Leningrad, Mar 3, 1973; dau. of a bank clerk; m. Arseny Staroselsky, 1925 (div.); m. Boris Vakhtin (died in the Gulag); m. David Yakovlevich Rivkin (writer under pseudonym David Dar); children: 1 daughter, 2 sons. ❖ Novelist, short-story writer and dramatist, one of the most beloved writers in USSR starting mid-1940s, who won the Stalin Prize 3 times but did not bend to the dictates of political expediency; was a journalist with a Rostov newspaper, *Trudovoi Don* (The Working Don, 1922), then worked on newspaper *Sovetskii iug* (The Soviet South); won prizes for 2 plays, *Ilya Kosgor* (1939) and *V staroi Moskve* (In Old Moscow, 1940); published *Sputniki* (The Train also seen as The Travelling Companions, 1946), an innovative work that did not criticize the Soviet system but also did not create false heroes, turning her into a major star in Soviet literary firmament; published *Kruzhilikha* (The Factory, 1947), based on her wartime observations in a Urals factory; released *Vremena goda* (Seasons of the Year, 1953), a look at the realities of Soviet life which was lauded by critics and attacked by conservatives; after 1953, was able to maintain a secure place in top ranks of Soviet writers; published largely autobiographical work, *Sentimental'nyi Roman* (A Sentimental Novel, 1958); also wrote *Seryozha: Several Stories from the Life of a Very Small Boy,* a classic in children's literature; her books were read by millions. Awarded Order of Red Banner of Labor (1955, 1965). ❖ See also *Women in World History.*

PANSY (1841–1930). *See Alden, Isabella.*

PANTAZI, Charikleia (1985—). Greek rhythmic gymnast. Name variations: Charoklia or Chariklia. Born Mar 18, 1985, in Greece. ❖ Won a bronze medal for team all-around at Sydney Olympics (2000).

PANTELIMON, Oana (1972—). Romanian high jumper. Born Oana Manuela Musunoi, Sept 27, 1972, in Tecuci, Romania. ❖ Tied with Kajsa Bergqvist for a bronze medal at Sydney Olympics (2000).

PANTER-DOWNES, Mollie (1906–1997). Anglo-Irish novelist and journalist. Born Aug 25, 1906, in London, England; died Jan 22, 1997, in Haslemere, Surrey, England; m. Clare Robinson, 1927; children: Virginia and Diana. ❖ Correspondent, whose fortnightly "Letter from London," describing British life, appeared in *The New Yorker* for 47 years (1939–84) and resulted in *Good Evening, Mrs. Craven: The Wartime Stories of Mollie Panter-Downes,* among other collections; also wrote several novels, including *The Shoreless Sea* (1923) and *One Fine Day* (1947).

PANTHEA (?–c. 545 BCE). Noblewoman of Susa. Died c. 545 BCE; m. Abradatas or Abradatus. ❖ Noblewoman of Susa whose virtue and loyalty, as recorded by Xenophon, won the respect of Cyrus II the Great. ❖ See also *Women in World History.*

PANTOJA, Antonia (1922–2002). Puerto Rican-born educator and reformer. Born 1922 in San Juan, Puerto Rico; died May 24, 2002, in New York, NY; earned teaching certificate from University of Puerto Rico, 1942; Hunter College, BA in sociology, 1952; Columbia University's New York School of Social Work, MA, 1954; Union Graduate School, PhD; lived with partner, Dr. Wilhelmina Perry. ❖ An advocate for New Yorkers of Puerto Rican origin, moved to NY (1944); founded the Puerto Rican Forum (1957), to promote self-sufficiency; established Aspira (1961), to help improve the performance of Puerto Rican children in New York City public schools; with Aspira, won a landmark lawsuit that brought bilingual education to NY schools (1974); established the Universidad Boricua and the Puerto Rican Research and Resource Center in Washington, DC, becoming its chancellor (1973); joined the faculty of San Diego State University's School of Social Work (1978). Received the Presidential Medal of Freedom from Bill Clinton (1996). ❖ See also autobiography, *Memoir of a Visionary* (2002).

PANTON, Catherine (1955—). Scottish golfer. Name variations: Catherine Panton-Lewis or Panton Lewis. Born June 14, 1955, in Stirlingshire, Scotland; dau. of John Panton (of Ryder Cup fame); graduate of Edinburgh University. ❖ Won Scottish Girls' championship (1969); won British championship (1976); member British World Amateur team (1977); turned pro (1983).

PAOLA (1937—). Queen of the Belgians. Name variations: Paola Ruffo de Calabria or di Calabria; Paolo Ruffo di Calabria. Born Paola Ruffo di Calabria in Italy on Sept 11, 1937; m. Albert (b. 1934), prince of Liège, later Albert II, king of the Belgians (r. 1993—); children: Crown Prince Philippe (b. 1960); Princess Astrid (b. 1962, who m. Archduke Lorenz of Austria); Prince Laurent (b. 1963).

PAOLI, Betty (1814–1894). Austrian poet, novelist and journalist. Name variations: Barbara Grund; Barbara Elisabeth Glück; (pseudonym) Branitz. Born Babette Barbara Elisabeth Glück in Vienna, Dec 30, 1814; died in Baden bei Wien, July 5, 1894; illeg. dau. of Hungarian noble and Belgian-born Theresia Glück; never married. ❖ The 1st woman journalist in Austria, began supporting herself by working as a governess (1830), then as a language tutor and translator; adopted nom de plume Betty Paoli with publication of short story "Clary" in *Wiener Zeitschrift;* published 1st book, *Gedichte* (Poems, 1841), causing a sensation in Austrian literary circles; won fame and access to the salon of Henriette Wertheimer; enjoyed a large circle of friends including writers Marie Ebner-Eschenbach, Franz Grillparzer, and Adalbert Stifter; soon after publication of 2nd collection of poems, *Nach dem Gewitter* (After the Storm, 1843), became reader and companion to Princess Marie Anna von Schwarzenberg; after a brief stay in Berlin, published *Romancero* (1845), a work she dedicated to Bettine von Arnim; employed as a companion to Countess Bünau, who lived in Dahlen near Dresden (1849–54); became a successful theater and art critic, publishing in *Österreichische Zeitung,* then in a number of other respected Viennese newspapers including *Wiener Allgemeine Zeitung* and *Neue Freie Presse.* ❖ See also Annie A. Scott, *Betty Paoli* (Routledge, 1926); and *Women in World History.*

PAOLINI MASSIMI, Petronilla (1663–1726). *See Massimi, Petronilla Paolini.*

PAPADAT-BENGESCU, Hortensia (1876–1955). Romanian novelist. Born Dec 8, 1876 in Galati, Romania; died Mar 5, 1955, in Bucharest; m. Nicolae Papadat. ❖ Works, which analyze urban and suburban life, include *Ape adinci* (1919), *Femeia în fata oglinzii* (1921), *Romantă provinciala* (1925), *Desenuri tragice* (1927), *Drumul ascuns* (1933), *Logodnicul* (1933), and *Radacini* (1938).

PAPADOPOULOU, Alexandra (1867–1906). Greek novelist and short-story writer. Born 1867 in Constantinople, of Greek parents; died 1906. ❖ Published *Miss Lesviou's Diary* (1894), the 1st novel written by a Greek woman; favoring use of modern Greek, wrote over 200 articles and short stories for Greek journals about social and political problems; with others, published journal *Literary Echoes* (1896).

PAPAKURA, Maggie (1873–1930). *See Papakura, Makereti.*

PAPAKURA, Makereti (1873–1930). New Zealand tribal leader, guide, writer, and ethnographer. Name variations: Margaret Pattison Thom, Maggie Papakura, Makereti Dennan, Makereti Staples-Browne. Born Margaret Pattison Thom, Oct 20, 1873, at Matata, in Bay of Plenty, New Zealand; died April 16, 1930, at Oxford, England; dau. of William Arthur Thom (shopkeeper) and Pia Ngarotu Te Rihi; m. Francis (Frank) Joseph Dennan (surveyor, div. 1900), 1891; m. Richard Charles Staples-Browne, 1912 (div. 1924); children: (1st m.) 1 son. ❖ Following eruption of Mt. Tarawera (1885), became well-known guide under name of Maggie Papakura (late 1880s); dressed in Pakeha or Maori costume, was a popular subject for photographers; published *Guide to the Hot Lakes District* (1905); accompanied group of singers and performers on successful tour of London (1911–12); enrolled at University of Oxford to study for BSc in anthropology (1926), but died before final examination. *The Old-time Maori,* first extensive ethnographic work by

Maori scholar, was published (1938). ❖ See also *Dictionary of New Zealand Biography* (Vol. 3).

PAPARIGA, Alexandra (1945—). Greek politician. Name variations: Aleka Papariga. Born in Athens, Greece, 1945; studied history and archaeology at University of Athens; married; children: 1 daughter. ❖ The first woman to be elected secretary general of the Communist Party of Greece, trained as an archaeologist but was barred from pursuing a teaching post in archaeology during the right-wing military dictatorship (1967–74); became active in Communist Party of Greece (KKE, 1968); founded Women's Federation of Greece (OGE) and participated in various international women's fora, including the UN; was elected a member of the Central Committee of the Communist Party (1978) and advanced to executive branch as a member of the KKE Political Bureau (1986); with support of orthodox wing, was elected secretary general (1991); was elected to Parliament for 2nd electoral district of Athens (1993) and reelected (1996).

PAPAS, Irene (1926—). Greek actress. Born Irene Lelekou, Sept 3, 1926, in Chiliomodion, Corinth, Greece. ❖ International actress, acclaimed for her portrayals of some the most famous heroines of classical Greek drama, began career as a teenager, singing and dancing in variety shows and only playing an occasional straight role; made 1st film, *Lost Angels* (1950), in Greece, and also appeared in several Italian films before signing a contract with MGM; made US debut in *Tribute to a Bad Man* (1956), followed by *The Guns of Navarone* (1961), but it was her appearance in *Electra* (1962) and *Zorba the Greek* (1964), both of which were directed by Michael Cacoyannis, that established her as an international star; went on to play leading roles in international productions and on US stage and screen; collaborated with Vangelis on *Odes* (1979) and *Rhapsodies* (1986); other films include *Antigone* (1960), *The Moon-Spinners* (1964), *The Brotherhood* (1968), *Z* (1969), *Anne of the Thousand Days* (1969), *The Trojan Women* (1971), *Moses* (1976), *Iphigenia* (1977), *Bloodline* (1979), *Erendira* (1983), *Into the Night* (1985), *The Assisi Underground* (1985), *Cronica de una Muerte anunciada* (*Chronicle of a Death Foretold*, 1987), *Island* (1989) and *Zoe* (1992). Honored for lifetime achievement by the European Cinema Panorama (2000).

PAPIA OF ENVERMEU (fl. 1020). Duchess of Normandy. Name variations: Popa. Became 2nd wife of Richard II the Good (d. 1027), duke of Normandy (r. 996–1027); children: William, count of Arques and Toulouse; Mauger, archbishop of Rouen (d. 1055); Popa of Normandy. ❖ Richard II's 1st wife was Judith of Rennes (c. 982–1018).

PAPPENHEIM, Bertha (1859–1936). German feminist, social worker and famous patient. Name variations: "Anna O."; (pseudonym) Paul Berthold. Born Feb 27, 1859, in Vienna, Austria; died at Isenburg, Germany, May 18, 1936; dau. of Sigmund Pappenheim (grain dealer) and Recha (Goldschmidt) Pappenheim; educated by governesses and at a Catholic school in Vienna; never married. ❖ Founder of several pioneering Jewish social organizations in Germany and Austria, who was later revealed to be "Anna O.," the subject of a famous case in the early history of psychoanalysis; was treated by Dr. Josef Breuer in Vienna (1880–82); moved to Frankfurt with family (1889); was described as patient "Anna O." in *Studies in Hysteria*, by Breuer and Sigmund Freud (1895); became director of the Jewish Orphanage for Girls (1895); translated into German and published the English feminist Mary Wollstonecraft's *A Vindication of the Rights of Women* (1899); wrote a play entitled *Women's Rights* (1899); raised the issue of the "white slavery" of young Jewish women in Eastern Europe (1900); traveled to Eastern Europe and Middle East (1903–05); spoke at International Congress to Fight White Slave Traffic in London (1910); founded home for Wayward Girls and Illegitimate Children in Neu-Isenburg, Germany (1907); founded Care by Women, an organization seeking to apply the goals of feminism to Jewish social work (1902); founded Federation of Jewish Women's Associations (1904), and served on its board of directors (1914–24); translated into German and published the *Memoirs of Glückel von Hameln* (1910); wrote newspaper article advocating a national Jewish welfare association for Germany (1916); participated in founding of the Central Welfare Office of German Jews (1917); honored with a stamp by West Germany as a pioneer in German social work (1954). ❖ See also Dora Edinger, *Bertha Pappenheim: Freud's Anna O.* (Congregation Solel, 1968); Lucy Freeman, *Anna O.* (Walker, 1972); and *Women in World History*.

PAPUC, Ioana (1984—). Romanian rower. Born Jan 4, 1984, in Romania. ❖ Won a gold medal for coxed eight at Athens Olympics (2004).

PARADIS, Maria Theresia von (1759–1824). Austrian composer. Born in Vienna, Austria, May 15, 1759; died in Vienna, Feb 1, 1824; dau. of the imperial secretary in the court of Empress Maria Theresa of Austria (1719–1780); goddau. of Empress Maria Theresa of Austria; studied piano with Leopold Kuzeluch and Vincenzo Righini. ❖ By age 3, was completely blind; sang the soprano part in *Stabat Mater* (1779) at a concert for the empress; became friendly with Mozart and Salieri, who dedicated works to her; a virtuoso pianist, began touring Europe as well as composing pieces for her own concerts; composed several piano sonatas, 3 cantatas, 2 operas and many songs as well as other works; also founded and headed a music school in Vienna, whose express purpose was improving women's musical education.

PARADIS, Marie (fl. 1808). French mountaineer. Born in Chamonix, France; dau. of peasants. ❖ At 18, made the 1st female ascent of Mt. Blanc (1808).

PARAIN-VIAL, Jeanne (b. 1912). French philosopher. Born 1912 in France; University of Lyon, agrégée in philosophy, 1938; Sorbonne, PhD, 1951; teacher at Aix-en-Provence; teacher at University of Dijon. ❖ Writings include *Le sens du Présent: Essai sur la rupture de l'unité originelle* (1952), *De l'être musical* (1952), *Gabriel Marcel ou les niveau de l'experience* (1966), *La nature du fait dans les sciences humaines* (1967), *Analyses structurales et idéologies structuralistes* (1969), and *Tendances nouvelles de la philosophie* (1978). ❖ See also *Women in World History*.

PARAMYGINA, Svetlana (1965—). Belarusian biathlete. Name variations: Svetlana Paramyguina. Born April 5, 1965, in Sverdlovsk, Belarus. ❖ At World championships, won team gold medals (1990, 1991); won a silver medal for 7.5 km at Lillehammer Olympics (1994).

PARASKEVIN-YOUNG, Connie (1961—). American cyclist and speedskater. Name variations: Connie Paraskevin; Connie Anne Young. Born Constance Anne Paraskevin, July 4, 1961, in Detroit, MI; m. Roger Young (cycling coach). ❖ At Seoul Olympics, won a bronze medal in the 1,000-meter sprint (1988); was 4-time World champion; was US national speedskating champion. Inducted into Bicycling Hall of Fame (2003).

PARATA, Mrs. C. (1873–1939). See Parata, Katherine Te Rongokahira.

PARATA, Katherine Te Rongokahira (1873–1939). New Zealand tribal leader. Name variations: Katherine Te Rongokahira Asher, Mrs. C. Parata, Katherine Te Rongokahira Robertshaw. Born Katherine Te Rongokahira Asher, on Nov 21, 1873, at Tauranga, New Zealand; died on June 7, 1939, in Wellington; dau. of David Asher and Katerina Te Atirau; m. Charles Rere Parata (Taare Rakatauhake Parata), 1896 (died 1918); m. Leonard Robertshaw (clerk), 1920 (died 1934); children: (1st m.) 2 sons. ❖ Active in Young Maori Party (early 1900s); during South African War (1899–1902) and World War I, helped raise funds for soldiers; was executive member of Maori Red Cross. ❖ See also *Dictionary of New Zealand Biography* (Vol. 3).

PARDO BAZÁN, Emilia (1852–1921). Spanish writer. Name variations: Emilia Pardo-Bazán or Pardo-Bazan. Born Sept 16, 1852, in La Coruña, Spain; died in Madrid, May 12, 1921; only child of the count (elected in 1869 to Constitutent Cortes of Spain's 1st Republic) and countess of Pardo Bazán; m. José Quiroga (lawyer), July 10, 1868; children: Jaime, Carmen, Blanca. ❖ Leading Spanish writer of 19th century, known for her novels, essays, and short stories, published 1st novel, *Pascual López* (1879), followed by *Un viaje de novios* (1881); wrote a series of essays explaining Naturalism to Spanish readers (published as *La cuestión palpitante*), which progressives extolled and conservatives condemned; also wrote a religious study of St. Francis of Assisi that was warmly received; published *Los pazos de Ulloa*, one of her most important novels (1886); championed feminism in Spain and published a number of important essays advocating equal rights and better education for women; campaigned for membership in Spanish Royal Academy (1891), but was denied because of gender; had hereditary title of countess conferred on her by Alphonso XIII (1907). ❖ See also Francisca González-Arias, *Portrait of a Woman as Artist: Emilia Pardo Bazán and the Modern Novel in France and Spain* (Garland, 1992); Maurice Hemingway, *Emilia Pardo Bazán: The Making of a Novelist* (Cambridge U. Press, 1983); Walter T. Pattison, *Emilia Pardo Bazán* (Twayne, 1971); and *Women in World History*.

PARDOE, Julia (1804–1862). British novelist and historical writer. Born 1804 (some sources cite 1806) in Beverley, Yorkshire, England; died Nov 26, 1862, in London, England; dau. of Thomas Pardoe (British army major) and Elizabeth Pardoe; never married. ❖ Popular writer of travel literature and historical works in 19th century, published a book of poetry at 13 (1818), which went through several printings; issued 1st novel, the historical romance *Lord Morcar of Hereward* (1829); because of ill health, traveled with father to Portugal for warmer climate (1835) where she kept a journal, the basis of her 1st travelogue, *Traits and Traditions of Portugal*; with father, undertook extended stays in Turkey, France, and Hungary (1836–37), then settled in London, where she published 2 travelogues on Turkey (1837–38), and one book each on southern France and Hungary; turned back to novels and short stories (late 1830s), often using foreign cities she had lived in as her settings; her romances had a wide readership in England and US; also wrote historical works on royalty, such as *Louis XIV and the Court of France in the Seventeenth Century* (1846) and *The Court and Reign of Francis the First.* ❖ See also *Women in World History.*

PAREK, Lagle (1941—). Estonian architect and politician. Born 1941 in Estonia. ❖ Employed by the Estonian Architectural Memorials Institute for 11 years (1972–83), was charged with "anti-Soviet agitation" (1983) and imprisoned for 4 years; following release, was leader of the center-right Estonian National Independence Party (ERSP, 1989–93); ran for president of Estonia (1992), finishing 4th with 4.3% of the vote; appointed interior minister (Oct 1992), remained in office until Nov 1993, at which time she resigned amid allegations of friction between the police and the army.

PAREPA-ROSA, Euphrosyne (1836–1874). Scottish-born soprano. Name variations: Euphrosyne Parepa Rosa. Born Euphrosyne Parepa de Boyesku, May 7, 1836 (one source cites 1839), in Edinburgh, Scotland; died Jan 21, 1874, in London, England; dau. of Baron Georgiades de Boyesku of Bucharest (noble) and a mother whose last name was Seguin (lyric stage actress); niece of Arthur Edward Sheldon Seguin; m. Captain Henry de Wolfe Carvell, 1864 (died 1865); m. Carl August Nicholas Rosa (violinist), 1867. ❖ At 16, made debut in Malta; performed throughout Europe (1850s); debuted in London in *Il Puritani* (1857), receiving high praise; appeared in America for 1st time (1866); with husband, established an English opera company which toured cities throughout the US (1869–72); performed in Egypt at court of the khedive (1872–73); major roles included Amina in *La Sonnambula* (Malta, 1855) and Rosina in *The Barber of Seville* (US, 1860s). ❖ See also *Women in World History.*

PARETSKY, Sara (1947—). American detective-fiction writer. Born Sept 21, 1947, in Ames, Iowa; University of Kansas, BA; University of Chicago, MBA and PhD; m. Courtenay Wright (naval officer and physicist). ❖ Had immediate success with 1st novel, *Indemnity Only* (1982), which introduced the feisty detective V.I. Warshawski, and went on to publish more in the series, *Killing Orders* (1983), *Deadlock* (1984), *Blood Shot* (1988), *Guardian Angel* (1992), *Hard Time* (1999), and *Blacklist* (2003), among others; was a founding member of Sisters in Crime (1986), to raise the profile of women crime writers; strayed from Warshawski with novel, *Ghost Country* (1998), which features Mara and Harriet Stonds; also edited several anthologies of crime fiction, including *A Woman's Eye* (1991) and *Women on the Case* (1996). Received Crime Writers' Association Silver Dagger (1988) and Gold Dagger (2004).

PARGETER, Edith (c. 1913–1995). British author. Name variations: (pseudonym) Ellis Peters, Peter Benedict, Jolyon Carr, John Redfern. Born Sept 29, 1913, in Horschay, Shropshire, England; died in Madeley, England, Oct 14, 1995; dau. of Edmund Valentine Pargeter and Edith Hordley Pargeter. ❖ Though she wrote some 60 books under the name Ellis Peters, including historical novels and a wartime trilogy, is remembered primarily as the creator of the popular Cadfael Chronicles, a series of murder mysteries about a crime-solving 12th-century monk; began writing crime stories (1959), turning out a series of Inspector Felse novels; published 1st book featuring the Benedictine monk Brother Cadfael (1977); also wrote *The Heaven Tree Trilogy, Brothers of Gwynedd Quartet,* and *The Eighth Champion of Christendom,* a wartime trilogy. ❖ See also *Women in World History.*

PARIS, countess of.
See Hedwig (c. 915–965).
See Maria Isabella (1848–1919).
See Isabella of Orleans (b. 1911).

PARIS, queen of.
See Ingoberge (519–589).
See Vultrogotha (fl. 558).
See Maria Isabella (1848–1919).

PARIS, Widow (1801–1881). See Laveau, Marie.

PARISEAU, Esther (1823–1902). See Joseph, Mother.

PARISIEN, Julie (1971—). American skier. Born Aug 2, 1971, in Quebec, Canada; raised in Auburn and Sugarloaf, Maine. ❖ Won the silver medal at World championships (1993); won 3 World Cups; consistently placed in the top 5 in the Nor Am and Europa Cup level; joined the pro tour (1994), and named Rookie of the Year; came in 13th in slalom in Nagano Olympics (1998).

PARISH, Mrs. Henry II (1910–1994). See Parish, Sister.

PARISH, Sister (1910–1994). American interior designer and entrepreneur. Name variations: Mrs. Henry Parish II. Born Dorothy May Kinnicutt in 1910; died in Dark Harbor, Maine, Sept 1994; dau. of Gustav Hermann Kinnicutt (wealthy financier) and May Appleton (Tuckerman) Kinnicutt; m. Harry Parish, Feb 14, 1930 (died 1977); children: 2 daughters, including Apple Parish Bartlett, and 1 son. ❖ The driving force behind the Parish-Hadley firm and the creator of the "American Country" look, which graced the homes of the nation's socially elite for 6 decades, gained renown (late 1950s), when Jacqueline Kennedy hired her to assist with various White House renovations; founded firm (1962); clientele included Bill and Babe Paley, Jock and Betsey Whitney, and Gordon and Ann Getty. ❖ See also Apple Parish Bartlett and Susan Bartlett Crater, *Sister: The Life of Legendary American Decorator, Mrs. Henry Parish II* (St. Martin, 2000); and *Women in World History.*

PARK CHAN-SOOK (1959—). Korean basketball player. Born June 3, 1959, in South Korea. ❖ At Los Angeles Olympics, won a silver medal in team competition (1984).

PARK, Grace (1979—). South Korean golfer. Born Mar 6, 1979, in Seoul, Korea; grew up in Arizona; attended Arizona State University. ❖ Came to US at age 12; was the 1st player since Patty Berg in 1983 to sweep all major amateur championships, winning the Trans-Am, Western, and US Women's Amateur (1998); won Kathy Ireland Greens.com LPGA Classic (2000), Office Depot (2001), and CISCO World Match Play championship (2002).

PARK HAE-JUNG. South Korean table tennis player. Born in South Korea. ❖ Won a bronze medal for doubles at Atlanta Olympics (1996).

PARK HYE-WON (1983—). Korean short-track speedskater. Born Aug 15, 1983, in South Korea. ❖ Won a gold medal for the 3,000-meter relay at Salt Lake City Olympics (2002).

PARK, Ida May (1879–1954). American film director. Born Dec 28, 1879, in Los Angeles, CA; died June 13, 1954, in Los Angeles Co., CA; m. Joseph De Grasse (actor). ❖ One of only a handful of women directors at Universal Studios (early 1900s), was initially a stage actress and writer; began directing husband's projects, making 12 features with him before going solo (1917); made a series of films (1917–20), including *Bondage* (1917), *Fires of Rebellion* (1917), *Bread* (1918), *Broadway Love* (1918), *Risky Road* (1918), *Boss of Powderville* (1918?), *Amazing Wife* (1919) and *The Butterfly Man* (1920). ❖ See also *Women in World History.*

PARK JEONG-LIM (1970—). South Korean handball player. Born Sept 25, 1970, in South Korea. ❖ Won a team gold medal at Barcelona Olympics (1992) and a team silver at Atlanta Olympics (1996).

PARK KAP-SOOK (1970—). Korean handball player. Born Nov 25, 1970, in South Korea. ❖ At Barcelona Olympics, won a gold medal in team competition (1992).

PARK, Maud Wood (1871–1955). American suffragist. Born Maud May Wood in Boston, Massachusetts, Jan 25, 1871; died in Reading, Massachusetts, May 8, 1955; dau. of James Rodney Wood and Mary Russell (Collins) Wood; graduated summa cum laude from Radcliffe, 1898; m. Charles Edward Park, 1898 (died 1904); m. Robert Hunter, 1908 (died 1928); children: none. ❖ Served as chair of Massachusetts Woman Suffrage Association (1901–08); adept at lobbying, was also a member of the Congressional Committee of National American Woman Suffrage Association and served as 1st president of League of Women Voters (1919–24); with Alice McLellan Birney, helped organize the 1st Parent-Teacher Association in Boston; authored play *Lucy Stone* (1936) and co-authored *Victory, How Women Won It: A Centennial Symposium, 1840–1940.* ❖ See also *Front Door Lobbying;* and *Women in World History.*

PARK, Merle (1937—). Rhodesian ballet dancer, teacher and director. Name variations: Dame Merle Park. Born Oct 8, 1937, in Salisbury,

Rhodesia (now Zimbabwe); trained with Betty Lamb in Rhodesia; m. James Monahan, 1965 (div. 1970); m. Sidney Bloch, 1970 (died 2000); children: (1st m.) 1. ❖ Moved to England (1951); joined Royal Ballet (1954) and performed with that company throughout career; promoted to principal (1959), danced in classical repertory works, including *La Fille Mal Gardée, Coppélia, Cinderella* and *La Bayadère*; created role of Celestial for Tudor's *Shadowplay* (1967), Countess Marie Larish for Macmillan's *Mayerling* (1978) and title role for his *Isadora* (1981); opened her own school (1977); while still senior ballerina of the Royal Ballet, became a director there (1983), serving until 1998. Named Commander of Order of British Empire (1974) and Dame Commander of Order of British Empire (1986); received Queen Elizabeth Award (1982).

PARK MI-KUM (1955—). Korean volleyball player. Born Oct 6, 1955, in South Korea. ❖ At Montreal Olympics, won a bronze medal in team competition (1976).

PARK, Rosemary (1907–2004). American educator. Name variations: Rosemary Park Anastos. Born 1907 in Andover, MA; died April 17, 2004, in Los Angeles, CA; dau. of J. Edgar Park (German scholar and president of Wheaton College) and Grace Park (taught Greek and mathematics); sister of William E. Park (president of Simmons College); Radcliffe College, MA, 1929; University of Cologne, PhD, 1934; m. Milton Anastos (professor of Byzantine Greek at UCLA), 1965 (died 1997); children: 1 stepson. ❖ Nationally known for her leadership as an administrator, began career teaching German at Connecticut College (1935); became academic dean there, then served as president (1947–62); was president of Barnard College (1962–67), and the 1st woman vice chancellor at University of California, Los Angeles (1967–70); remained on UCLA faculty as professor emeritus of education until 1974.

PARK, Ruth (1923—). New Zealand-born Australian author. Born 1923 in Auckland, New Zealand; attended St. Benedict's College, Auckland University, and University of New Zealand; m. D'Arcy Niland (writer), 1942 (died 1967); children: Anne, Rory, Patrick, Deborah, Kilmeny. ❖ One of the most prolific writers of Australian literature in the 20th century, began career as an editor of the children's page for *Auckland Star*, followed by a position as editor of children's page for *Zealandia*, in Auckland; with husband, moved to Sydney (1943), where the only housing available was in the slums of Surry Hills, which provided the environment for *The Harp in the South* (1948), one of her most beloved books; her sequel, *Poor Man's Orange* (1949), was also successful, as was a prequel, *Missus* (1985); wrote 2 novels that drew on her early memories of New Zealand, *The Witch's Thorn* (1951), another bestseller, and *Pink Flannel* (1955); with husband, also wrote several plays for radio and tv, including *No Decision* (1961); wrote for ABC Children's Session for decades, creating "The Muddle-Headed Wombat" series, which resulted in 14 books published (1962–81); also wrote *Playing Beatie Bow* (1980), which won the Children's Book of the Year Award for 1981, and *When the Wind Changed* (1980), winner of the 1981 New South Wales Premier's Award, among many others. Won *The Sydney Morning Herald* prize for *The Harp in the South* (1948); won Miles Franklin Award for *Swords and Crowns and Rings* (1977); received Order of Australia (1987) and Australian Book Industry's Lloyd O'Neill Magpie Award (1993). ❖ See also autobiographies *The Drums Go Bang!* (1956, with husband), *A Fence around the Cuckoo* (1992), and *Fishing in the Styx* (1993); and *Women in World History*.

PARK SOON-JA (1966—). Korean field-hockey player. Born Jan 3, 1966, in South Korea. ❖ At Seoul Olympics, won a silver medal in team competition (1988).

PARK SUNG-HYUN (1983—). South Korean archer. Born Jan 1, 1983, in South Korea. ❖ At Athens Olympics, won a gold medal for team round and a gold medal for indiv. (2004); at World championships, placed 1st in indiv. (2001) and team (2003).

PARKE, Mary (1908–1989). English marine biologist. Born Mary Winifred Parke, Mar 23, 1908, in Liverpool, England; died July 17, 1989; University of Liverpool, BS, 1929, PhD, 1932, DSc in botany, 1950; attended Glasgow School of Art. ❖ Marine algae expert, discovered that *Isochrysis galbana* (a flagellate) is ideal for feeding oyster larvae; as a phycologist (seaweed expert) at Marine Biological Station at Port Erin, Isle of Man, studied the food of oyster larvae and algal cultures (1930–40); studied marine algae distribution on Britain's coasts for Development Commission and the Ministry of Supply (1941–46); employing a light microscope, created algae drawings; collaborated with

professor Irene Manton of Leeds University to study algal structure using an electron microscope (1950s); was a founding member of British Phycological Society; became a fellow of Royal Society (1972).

PARKER, Agnes Miller (1895–1980). Scottish artist. Born Mar 25, 1895, in Irvine, Ayrshire, Scotland; died 1980, on Island of Arran, Scotland; attended Glasgow School of Art; m. William McCance (sculptor, typographer). ❖ Wood engraver, printmaker and illustrator, taught at Glasgow School for 2 years and also in London (1920s); worked with husband and former tutors, Gertrude Hermes and Blair Hughes-Stanton, at Gregynog Press, where she produced one of the finest pieces in the history of British book design, *Fables of Aesop* (1931); created most praised works after leaving Gregynog, illustrating Gray's *Elegy Written in a Country Churchyard* and 2 commercially successful books for H.E. Bates, *Through the Woods* (1936) and *Down the River* (1937); illustrated many works for Limited Edition Club in New York; later retired to Island of Arran, becoming increasingly reclusive. ❖ See also Ian Rogerson and John Dreyfus, *Agnes Miller Parker, Wood-Engraver and Book Illustrator, 1895–1980* (Fleece, 1990).

PARKER, Bonnie (1910–1934). American criminal. Born Oct 1, 1910, in Rowena, Texas; shot to death, May 23, 1934; dau. of Emma Parker; m. Roy Thornton, but was known for her long relationship with Clyde Barrow; no children. ❖ Bank robber and folk legend who became Public Enemy Number One with Clyde Barrow during the hard times of the Great Depression; met Clyde Barrow (1930); as one of the Barrow gang, went on a robbery and killing spree (1932–34); though the gang took over a dozen lives indiscriminately, became a symbol of defiance against the established societal order. ❖ See also Ted Hinton, *Ambush: The Real Story of Bonnie and Clyde* (Shoal Creek, 1979); John Treherne, *The Strange History of Bonnie and Clyde* (Stein & Day, 1985); (film) *Bonnie and Clyde* (1967); and *Women in World History*.

PARKER, Bridget (1939—). English equestrian. Born Jan 1939 in UK. ❖ At Munich Olympics, won a gold medal in team 3-day event (1972).

PARKER, Catherine Langloh (c. 1856–1940). Australian writer. Name variations: Katie Langloh Parker or K. Langloh Parker; Catherine Stow. Born Catherine Field, May 1, 1856 (some sources cite 1855), in Encounter Bay, South Australia; died Mar 27, 1940, in Adelaide, South Australia; dau. of Henry Field (overlander and pastoralist) and Sophia Field; m. Langloh Parker (pastoralist), Jan 12, 1875 (died 1903); m. Percy Randolph Stow (lawyer), Nov 7, 1905; no children. ❖ Published the 1st systematic description of Aborigine legends and indigenous folkways (1896); posthumously accorded a Children's Book of the Year Award for published collection of her studies (1954); writings include *Australian Legendary Tales: Folklore of the Noongahburrahs* (1896), *More Australian Legendary Tales* (1898), *The Euhlayi Tribe: A Study of Aboriginal Life in Australia* (1905), *The Walkabouts of the Wur-Run-Nah* (1918), *Woggheeguy: Australian Aboriginal Legends* (1930) and a previously unpublished manuscript, *My Bush Book: K. Langloh Parker's 1890s Story of Outback Station Life* (1982), with a background and biography of Parker by Marcie Muir. ❖ See also *Women in World History*.

PARKER, Cecilia (1905–1993). Canadian-born actress. Born April 26, 1905, in Fort William, Ontario, Canada; died July 25, 1993, in Ventura, CA; m. Dick Baldwin, 1938. ❖ Appeared as Mickey Rooney's sister Marian in the "Andy Hardy" film series; other films include *The Painted Veil, Naughty Marietta* and *You're Only Young Once*; became US citizen (1940).

PARKER, Claire (1906–1981). American film animator. Born Aug 31, 1906, in Boston, Massachusetts; died Oct 3, 1981, in Paris, France; attended Bryn Mawr College; also studied in Austria and France; m. Alexander Alexeieff (Russian-born animator), 1941; children: 1. ❖ Pioneer film animator who, with husband Alexander Alexeieff, co-invented the "pin screen" method, involving the illumination of thousands of pinheads to produce a printlike effect in animated films; films include *Une nuit sur le mont chauve* (*Night on Bald Mountain*, 1933), *Étude sur L'Harmonie des Lignes* (1934), *Rubens* (1935), *En Passant* (1942), *The Nose* (1963), *Pictures at an Exhibition* (1972) and *Three Moods* (*Trois Thèmes*, 1980). ❖ See also *Women in World History*.

PARKER, Cynthia Ann (c. 1827–c. 1864). Indian captive. Born c. 1827 in either Clark Co. or Crawford Co., Illinois; died c. 1864 (some sources cite 1870); dau. of Silas M. Parker (farmer) and Lucy (Duty) Parker; m. Peta Nocoma (Quahadi Comanche chief), 1845; children: sons Quanah and Pecos; daughter Topsannah. ❖ Taken captive by Native

Americans after attack on Texas settlement where she lived (1836); married a Comanche chief and had 3 children, including future Chief Quanah Parker; refused attempt to ransom her (1840s); captured with her daughter during attack on Nocoma's camp by Texas Rangers and reunited with her white family (1860); died of self-inflicted starvation after learning of son's death from smallpox and daughter's death from influenza. ❖ See also Margaret Schmidt Hacker, *Cynthia Ann Parker: The Life and the Legend* (Texas Western, 1990); Grace Jackson, *Cynthia Ann Parker* (1959); Margaret Waldraven-Johnson, *White Comanche: The Story of Cynthia Ann Parker and Her Son, Quanah* (Comet, 1956); and *Women in World History*.

PARKER, Dehra (1882–1963). Northern Ireland politician. Name variations: Dame Dehra Parker, Dehra Chichester, Dehra Kerr-Fisher. Born Dehra Kerr-Fisher, 1882, in Kilrea, Co. Derry, Northern Ireland; died Nov 28, 1963; dau. of James Kerr-Fisher; m. Lt. Col. Robert Spencer Chichester, 1901 (died 1921); m. Admiral W.H. Parker, 1928 (died 1940). ❖ Representing the Unionist Party for Londonderry, was the 1st woman to sit in the Northern Ireland Cabinet (1921–29); was the 1st woman in Britain selected to present the annual address on behalf of the House of Commons (1924); was reelected (1933) for South Londonderry, serving in the Northern Ireland House, all told, for 35 years; introduced Education Act (1938) which reformed Northern Ireland's education system; served as minister of Health and Local Government (1949–57); resigned from Parliament (1960). Named Officer of the British Empire (OBE, 1949).

PARKER, Denise (1973—). American archer. Born Dec 12, 1973, in South Jordan, Utah. ❖ At Seoul Olympics, won a bronze medal in team round (1988), the youngest American competitor there; won 4 gold medals and 1 silver medal at Pan American Games (1995); won US national title (1990–91, 1993, 1999).

PARKER, Dorothy (1893–1967). American writer and critic. Born Dorothy Rothschild, August 22, 1893, in West End, NJ; died June 7, 1967, in New York, NY; dau. of Eliza Rothschild and Henry Rothschild; attended private and parochial schools in New York City; m. Edward Parker, 1917 (div. 1928); m. Alan Campbell, 1933 (div. 1942, remarried 1950); no children. ❖ Writer whose collections of short stories and verse, along with well-publicized acerbic wit, made her one of America's most famous and widely quoted women of the 20th century; began literary career at age 24 as caption writer for *Vogue* (1916); transferred to *Vogue's* sister publication, *Vanity Fair* (1917); eventually promoted to literary and dramatic criticism and began publishing short stories; joined staff of Harold Ross' new humor magazine, *The New Yorker* (1926); became a fixture of New York's literary smart set and a member of Algonquin Round Table; was plagued throughout life by depression and alcoholism, which were exacerbated by ruinous love affairs and two ultimately unhappy marriages. Poetry collections include *Enough Rope* (1926), *Sunset Gun* (1928), and "Excuse My Dust,"; also published short stories in *Laments for the Living*, which included "Big Blonde" (1930), and wrote the play *Ladies of the Corridor* (1953). ❖ See also Marion Meade, *Dorothy Parker: What Fresh Hell Is This?* (Villard, 1988); *Mrs. Parker and the Vicious Circle* (film), starring Jennifer Jason Leigh as Dorothy Parker (1994); and *Women in World History*.

PARKER, Eleanor (1922—). American actress. Born Eleanor Jean Parker in Cedarville, Ohio, June 26, 1922; m. Fred Losee, 1943 (div. 1944); m. Bert Friedlob, 1946 (div. 1953); m. Paul Clemens, 1954 (div. 1965); m. Raymond Hirsch, 1966; children: (2nd m.) 3, including Paul Clemens (actor); (3rd m.) 1. ❖ Received early acting experience at Cleveland Playhouse, as well as in stock and at Pasadena Playhouse; made film debut in bit part in *They Died with Their Boots On* (1941); played a variety of roles, from vixens to long-suffering wives, and won Academy Award nominations as Best Actress for performances in *Caged* (1950), *Detective Story* (1951), and *Interrupted Melody* (1955), in which she portrayed opera singer Marjorie Lawrence; after 1960, made few films, among them *The Sound of Music* (1965); other films include *Pride of the Marines* (1945), *Of Human Bondage* (1946), *Escape Me Never* (1947), *The Voice of the Turtle* (1948), *The Woman in White* (1948), *Three Secrets* (1950), *Valentino* (1951), *Scaramouche* (1952), *Above and Beyond* (1953), *Escape from Fort Bravo* (1954), *The Naked Jungle* (1954), *Valley of the Kings* (1954), *Many Rivers to Cross* (1955), *The Man with the Golden Arm* (1955), *The King and Four Queens* (1956), *Lizzie* (1957), *A Hole in the Head* (1959), *Home from the Hill* (1960), *Return to Peyton Place* (1961) and *The Oscar* (1966).

PARKER, Elizabeth (1814–1870). *See Guard, Elizabeth.*

PARKER, Flora (1883–1950). *See DeHaven, Flora.*

PARKER, Jane (d. 1542?). English royal. Name variations: Jane Boleyn. Executed around 1542; dau. of Henry, Lord Morley; sister-in-law of Anne Boleyn; m. George Boleyn, 2nd viscount Rochford and brother of Anne Boleyn (George was beheaded and burned at Tyburn in 1536); children: George Boleyn, dean of Lichfield. ❖ Portrayed by Judy Kelley in film *The Private Life of Henry VIII* (1933).

PARKER, Jean (1915–2005). American stage and screen actress. Born Lois Mae Green, Aug 11, 1915, in Deer Lodge, Powell Co., Montana; dau. of Louis Green (gunsmith and hunter) and Melvina Burch; died Nov 30, 2005, in Los Angeles, California; m. George McDonald (actor), 1936 (div. 1940); m. Douglas Dawson (asst. director), 1941 (div. 1943); m. Curtis Grotter, 1944 (div. 1949); m. Robert Lowery (actor), 1951 (div. 1957). ❖ Made film debut in *Divorce in the Family* (1932), followed by *Gabriel Over the White House, The Ghost Goes West, Sequoia, Little Women, Operator 13, Limehouse Blues, Deerslayer, Bluebeard, The Gunfighter, Those Redheads from Seattle* and *Stigma,* among others, starred on Broadway in *Loco* (1946).

PARKER, Julia O'Connor (1890–1972). American labor leader. Name variations: Julia Sarsfield O'Connor, Julia O'Connor, Julia Sarsfield O'Connor Parker, Julia Parker. Born Julia Sarsfield O'Connor, Sept 9, 1890, in Woburn, MA; died Aug 27, 1972, in Wayland, MA; dau. of John O'Connor (leather currier) and Sarah (Conneally) O'Connor; m. Charles Austin Parker (journalist), 1925 (died 1960); children: Sarah (b. 1926), Carol (b. 1928). ❖ Joined Boston Telephone Operators' Union (1912); began work with Women's Trade Union League (1912), serving as 1st working woman president of Boston chapter (1915–18), member of national executive board (1917–26), and delegate to First International Congress of Working Women (1919); served as only labor representative on Ryan Commission (WWI), but resigned protesting postmaster general's opposition to labor unions (Jan 1919), and led successful New England Telephone Operators' Union strike (April 1919); served as president of telephone operators division in International Brotherhood of Electrical Workers (1918–38); strongly supported Franklin Roosevelt, and worked with labor division of Democratic National Committee in presidential elections (1932, 1936, 1940); worked as organizer for American Federation of Labor in northeast, south, and southwest US (1939–57); visited industries in Britain as part of 4-woman delegation studying war production and labor conditions for US Office of War Information (1945).

PARKER, K. Langloh (c. 1856–1940). *See Parker, Catherine Langloh.*

PARKER, Leslie (1890–1961). *See Thirkell, Angela.*

PARKER, Lottie Blair (c. 1858–1937). American actress and playwright. Name variations: Lottie May Blair. Born c. 1858 in Oswego, NY; died Jan 5, 1937, in Great Neck, LI, NY; m. Harry Doel Parker. ❖ Began career as an actress; wrote such plays as *White Roses, Way Down East* (later filmed by D.W. Griffith and starred Lillian Gish), *Under Southern Skies, The Lights of Home* and *The Redemption of David Corson.*

PARKER, Madeleine (c. 1909–1936). American theatrical and ballet dancer. Name variations: Mira Dimina. Born c. 1909 in New York, NY; died Dec 1936, while on tour in Australia. ❖ Trained in NY with Mikhail Fokine, Theodore Kosloff, Ivan Tarasoff, and others; joined Fokine Ballet (c. 1925); in theater, replaced Mary Eaton in *The Five O'Clock Girl,* in London; danced in Max Reinhardt's film *A Midsummer Night's Dream* (1934); joined Ballet Russe de Monte Carlo in Los Angeles, CA, where she performed in Massine's *Choreartium* and *Symphonie Fantastique,* and Nijinska's *Les Cents Baiser.*

PARKER, Mary Ann (fl. 1795). British travel writer. Born in UK; m. Captain John Parker; children. ❖ After husband died, wrote about her travels with him, *A Voyage Round the World in the "Gorgon" Man of War: Performed and Written by Captain John Parker, His Widow, for the Advantage of a Numerous Family* (1795), in which she visited Australian penal settlements.

PARKER, Mary Ann (1817–1884). *See Martin, Mary Ann.*

PARKER, Minerva (1861–1949). *See Nichols, Minerva.*

PARKER, Pat (1944–1989). African-American poet, essayist and feminist. Name variations: Patricia Parker. Born Jan 20, 1944, in Houston, TX; died of breast cancer, June 17, 1989; m. Ed Bullins (playwright, div.). ❖ Outspoken lesbian activist, moved to Oakland, California, and worked as medical coordinator at Oakland Feminist Women's Health

Center (1978–87); political activist, had early involvement with Black Panther Party and Black Women's Revolutionary Council, and helped form Women's Press Collective; called attention to problems in women's health issues, especially concerning domestic and sexual violence; poetry collections include *Child of Myself* (1971), *Pit Stop* (1974), *Womanslaughter* (1978), *Jonestown and Other Madness* (1985), and *Movement in Black: The Collected Poetry of Pat Parker, 1961–1978* (1990); essays published in *This Bridge Called My Back* (1983) and *Politics of the Heart: A Lesbian Parenting Anthology* (1987).

PARKER, Pauline Yvonne (1938—). New Zealand murderer. Name variations: Pauline Yvonne Rieper; Hilary Nathan. Born May 26, 1938, in New Zealand; dau. of Honora Mary Parker. ❖ At 16, had intensely bonded relationship with 15-year-old Juliet Hulme and wanted to accompany her to South Africa; knowing she would not be allowed to go, murdered her mother with the help of Juliet by beating the 45-year-old Honora Mary Parker in the head with a brick (June 22, 1954); with Juliet, tried in Christchurch and found guilty; imprisoned until 1958; was discovered (1990s) living under name of Hilary Nathan near Rochester, Kent, England, where she runs a children's riding school. ❖ See also Glamuzina and Laurie, *Parker and Hulme: A Lesbian View* (Firebrand, 1995); (film) *Heavenly Creatures*, starring Kate Winslet and Melanie Lynskey.

PARKER, Suzy (1932–1932). American model and actress. Born Cecilia Parker, Oct 28, 1932, in Long Island City, NY; died May 3, 2003, in Montecito, CA; sister of Dorian Leigh (model); m. Charles Staton, c. 1949 (div.); m. Pierre de la Salle, 1958 (div.); m. Bradford Dillman (actor), 1963; children: (2nd m.) Georgia (b. 1959); (3nd m.) Dinah, Charles and Christopher Dillman. ❖ Highly successful fashion model, known as one of the "Revlon girls," made film debut in *Funny Face* (1957); also appeared in *Kiss Them for Me* (1957), *Ten North Frederick* (1958), *The Best of Everything* (1959), *Circle of Deception* (1961), *The Interns* (1962), *Flight from Ashiya* (1964) and *Chamber of Horrors* (1966); retired to raise a family.

PARKER, Valeria Hopkins (1879–1959). American physician. Born Valeria Hopkins, Feb 11, 1879, in Chicago, IL; died Oct 25, 1959; dau. of Martha (Leath) Hopkins and Anson Jones Hopkins; studied at Augusta Hospital in Berlin, 1892, then in Switzerland until 1895; graduate of Oxford (OH) College, 1895; Hering Homeopathic Medical College in Chicago, MD, 1902; m. Dr. Edward O. Parker, 1905; children: 2. ❖ Pioneering physician who played an important role in the social hygiene movement, practiced medicine before marriage; became a social hygiene activist (fought prostitution and venereal diseases and supported sex education); worked at Connecticut Social Hygiene Association (1914–19), then at Dr. Rachelle Yarros' American Social Hygiene Association; began lecturing on venereal disease and social hygiene for US Public Health Service (1920); was executive secretary of board of US Interdepartmental Social Hygiene, social hygiene committee chair of National League of Women Voters (1919–21) and member of advisory committee for General Federation of Women's Clubs; became 1st woman probation officer of Greenwich, CT (1913) and the 1st woman officer in the police force of state of CT.

PARKER-BOWLES, Camilla (1947—). English paramour. Name variations: Camilla Parker Bowles; Duchess of Cornwall. Born Camilla Shand, July 17, 1947, at King's College Hospital in London, England; eldest of 3 children of Bruce Shand (army officer turned educational film representative) and Rosalind (Cubitt) Shand; sister of Annabel Elliott (antique dealer) and Mark Shand (explorer); great-granddau. of Alice Keppel (mistress of King Edward VII); attended Queen's Gate, London; m. Andrew Parker-Bowles (a cavalry officer), July 1973 (div. 1995); m. Charles Windsor, prince of Wales, April 9, 2005 children: Thomas Parker-Bowles; Laura Parker-Bowles. ❖ Socialite romantically linked to Charles, prince of Wales, for over 30 years, even during his marriage to Princess Diana; married her prince and became duchess of Cornwall (2005). ❖ See also Christopher Wilson, *A Greater Love* (Morrow, 1994); Caroline Graham, *Camilla: The King's Mistress* (Contemporary, 1997); and *Women in World History*.

PARKES, Bessie Rayner (1829–1925). English feminist, poet, and essayist. Name variations: Bessie Belloc. Born 1829; died 1925; dau. of Joseph Parkes (Birmingham solicitor) and Elizabeth (Priestley) Parkes (dau. of Unitarian scientist Joseph Priestley); m. Louis Belloc (Irish-French writer), 1867 (died 1872); children: Hilaire Belloc (1870–1953); Marie Belloc-Lowndes (1868–1947). ❖ With Barbara Bodichon, established and edited the *English Woman's Journal* (1858), which served as a magnet

to a circle of women known as the Langham Place Group; writings include *Remarks Upon the Education of Girls* (1854), *Essays on Women's Work* (1865) and *In a Walled Garden* (1895). ❖ See also *Women in World History*.

PARKHOMCHUK, Irina (1965—). Soviet volleyball player. Born May 15, 1965, in USSR. ❖ At Seoul Olympics, won a gold medal in team competition (1988).

PARKHOUSE, Hannah (1743–1809). *See Cowley, Hannah.*

PARKHURST, Charlotte (d. 1879). American legend. Name variations: Charley (also seen as Charlie) Parkhurst; "One-Eyed" Charley; Charley Darkey Parkhurst. Born probably in New Hampshire; died near Watsonville, California, Dec 29, 1879; children: may have had at least one. ❖ Dressed in men's clothes, became a stagecoach driver, sometimes controlling a 6-horse team pulling a 20-passenger coach; from the mid-1850s, drove the mountain route between Santa Cruz and San Jose; ran a saloon and way station between Santa Cruz and Watsonville; successfully hid gender from others until her death. ❖ See also *Women in World History*.

PARKHURST, Helen (1887–1973). American educator. Born Helen Parkhurst on Mar 7, 1887, in Durand, WI; died June 1, 1973, in New Milford, CT; dau. of James Henry Parkhurst (hotel keeper and civic leader) and Ida (Underwood) Parkhurst (teacher); Wisconsin State College, BS, 1907; Yale University, MA, 1943. ❖ Taught in Wisconsin and Washington (1900s); drafted Laboratory Plan (later renamed Dalton Plan), to reorganize structure of schooling (1910); participated in International Montessori Teachers Training in Rome, Italy (1914); became 1st authorized trainer of Montessori teachers in US, as head of teacher training department at Montessori training college in NY (1917–18); in NYC, founded (1918) and directed (1918–42) renowned Children's University School (renamed Dalton School, 1920); wrote numerous books, including *Education on the Dalton Plan* (1922), *And They Found Jimmy* (1947) and *Undertow* (1963); was 1st Yale Fellow in Education (1943); produced radio and tv programs, "Child's World," "Growing Pains," and "The World of Sound" (1947–50); taught at College of the City of New York (1952–54).

PARKIN, Sheila (1945—). *See Sherwood, Sheila.*

PARKINSON, Alice May (1889–1949). New Zealand murderer. Name variations: Alice May O'Loughlin. Born Dec 29, 1889, at Hampden in Hawke's Bay, New Zealand; died on July 21, 1949, in Auckland; dau. of George Parkinson (farm laborer) and Rosina (Beazley) Parkinson; m. Charles Henry O'Laughlin (carpenter), 1923 (died 1942); children: 4 sons, 2 daughters. ❖ Worked as domestic before becoming maid at hotels in Napier (early 1900s); was impregnated by Walter Albert West, who had promised marriage; when baby was stillborn and West reneged, shot and killed him (1915); tried and convicted of manslaughter, was sent to prison; after case drew wide attention in *New Zealand Truth* newspaper and was championed by labor movement and feminists of socialist movement, was released (mid-1921). The case focused on issues of unequal social and economic condition of women and stirred debate on judicial reform. ❖ See also *Dictionary of New Zealand Biography* (Vol. 3).

PARKINSON, Georgina (1938—). English ballet dancer. Born Aug 20, 1938, in Brighton, England. ❖ Trained locally at Audrey Kepp's school, and later with Royal Ballet; joined Royal Ballet (1954), becoming a soloist (1959), then principal dancer; created roles in Ashton's *Monotones II* (1966) and *Enigma Variations* (1968) and title role in Howard's *La Belle Dame Sans Merci*; danced with Royal Ballet in Ashton's *La Fille Mal Gardée*, Nijinska's *Les Biches*, and Macmillan's *Romeo and Juliet, The Invitation* and *Mayerling*; appointed ballet master of American Ballet Theatre (1978), where she also created the role of Mrs. Harriman in Twyla Tharp's *Everlast*.

PARKINSON, Mary (1823–1889). *See Cuddie, Mary.*

PARKS, Mrs. George (1862–1952). *See Robins, Elizabeth.*

PARKS, Hildy (1926–2004). American producer, actress, and writer. Name variations: Hildy Parks Cohen. Born Mar 12, 1926, in Washington, DC; died Oct 7, 2004, in Englewood, NJ; graduate of University of Virginia; m. Jackie Cooper (actor), 1950 (div. 1951); m. Alexander H. Cohen (theatrical producer, died 2000); children: 1 daughter, 2 sons. ❖ Made Broadway debut in *Bathsheba* (1947), followed by *Summer and Smoke*, among others; appeared in early tv dramas, on the soap "Love of Life" and in films; with husband, created Tony Awards programs (1967–86), scripting all 20; also wrote and produced

2 Emmy-winning specials: "Placido Domingo: Steppin' Out with the Ladies" and "The Night of 100 Stars."

PARKS, Rosa (1913–2005). African-American civil-rights activist. Born Rosa Louise McCauley, Feb 4, 1913, in Tuskegee, Alabama died Oct 24, 2005, in Detroit, Michigan; dau. of James McCauley (carpenter) and Leona (Edwards) McCauley (schoolteacher); received high school diploma, 1933; m. Raymond Parks, 1932 (died 1977); no children. ❖ Veteran activist whose arrest for refusing to give up her seat to a white man on a segregated bus in Montgomery, Alabama, triggered a black boycott of the bus line and helped launch the civil-rights movement in US; was sent to Montgomery to live with relatives and attend Montgomery Industrial School for Girls (1924); became secretary of the local NAACP and was forced from city bus for using "white" door (Dec 1943); after repeated efforts, was registered to vote (1945); became adviser to NAACP Youth Council (1949); arrested and convicted of refusing, in violation of Alabama law, to surrender a bus seat to a white man (Dec 1955); participated in the Montgomery Bus Boycott (1955–56), resulting in US Supreme Court affirmation of lower court decision declaring bus segregation to be unconstitutional (Nov 13, 1956); moved to Detroit (1957); participated in March on Washington (1963); participated in Selma-to-Montgomery march for voting rights (Mar 1965); worked in Detroit office of Congressman John Conyers (1965–88), known as "first lady of civil rights" or "mother of the civil rights movement." Received Spingarn Medal from NAACP (1979), Martin Luther King Jr., Nonviolent Peace Prize (1980), Presidential Medal of Freedom (1996), Congressional gold medal (1999), and 1st Governor's Medal of Honor for Extraordinary Courage from state of Alabama (Dec 1, 2000). Rosa Parks Library and Museum at Troy State University opened (Dec 1, 2000). After she died, was 1st woman to lie in state at the nation's Capitol Rotunda. ❖ See also (with Jim Haskins) *Rosa Parks: My Story* (Dial, 1992) and (with Gregory Reed) *Quiet Strength* (Zondervan, 1994); Jo Ann Robinson, *The Montgomery Bus Boycott and the Women Who Started It* (U. of Tennessee Press, 1987); Douglas Brinkley, *Rosa Parks* (Lipper-Viking, 2000); and *Women in World History*.

PARKS, Suzan-Lori (1963—). African-American playwright. Born May 10, 1963, in Kentucky; spent part of childhood in Germany; dau. of an army colonel; graduate of Mount Holyoke College, 1985; studied acting in London; m. Paul Oscher (musician), 2001. ❖ Became the 1st black woman to win the Pulitzer Prize for Drama (April 2002), with her play *Topdog/Underdog*, which was also nominated for a Tony Award; also wrote the teleplay "Their Eyes Were Watching God" (2005); directs the theatre program at California Institute of the Arts.

PARLBY, Irene (1868–1965). Canadian politician, feminist and advocate of social reform. Born Mary Irene Marryat, Jan 9, 1868, in London, England; died July 12, 1965, in Red Deer, Alberta; dau. of Colonel Ernest Lindsay Marryat (civil engineer) and Elizabeth Lynch Marryat; closely related to author Captain Frederick Marryat; had no formal education; m. Walter Parlby (rancher), 1897; children: Humphrey Parlby (b. 1899). ❖ Grew up in India (1868–71, 1881–84) and England; moved to Alberta, Canada (1896); married and ran a ranch with husband; was a delegate to United Farmers of Alberta (UFA) convention in Calgary (1916); served as president of United Farm Women of Alberta (UFWA, 1917–20); as an articulate advocate of the rights of farm women, quickly gained a national reputation; was invited by Canadian government to attend the Dominion conference in Ottawa (1918); sat on board of governors at University of Alberta (1919–21); as a Liberal, won a seat in Alberta legislature for riding (district) of Lacombe (1921); was appointed minister without portfolio in new government, only the 2nd woman in Canadian politics to be nominated to a Cabinet post; was the official government observer to 1st conference of International Council of Women held in Washington, DC (1924); sent on a tour of Denmark and Sweden by Alberta government in order to study the organization and impact of rural cooperatives (1928); was one of 5 women involved in the famous "Persons" case, which led to the appointment of the 1st female senator in Canadian history, Cairine Wilson; was a delegate to Assembly of the League of Nations in Geneva (1930); retired to the family ranch (1934). ❖ See also Claire Mary McKinlay, *The Honorable Irene Parlby* (West Canada Graphic Industries, 1978); and *Women in World History*.

PARLO, Dita (1906–1971). German-born actress. Born Grethe Gerda Kornstadt (or Kornwald), Sept 4, 1906, in Stettin, Pomerania, Germany (now Szczecin, Poland); died Dec 13, 1971, in Paris, France; m. Frank Guetal, 1949. ❖ Made highly successful film debut in Germany in *Die Dame mit der Maske* (*The Lady with the Mask*, 1928); then appeared in *Geheimnisse des Orients* (*Secrets of the Orient*, 1928), *Heimkehr* (*Homecoming*, 1928), *Ungarische Rhapsodie* (*Hungarian Rhapsody*, 1928), *Manolescu* (1929) and *Melodie des Herzens* (*Melody of the Heart*, 1929); made a few US films, including *The Hollywood Revue of 1929*, then moved to France where she enjoyed popularity in such films as *L'Affaire du Courrier de Lyon* (*The Courier of Lyons*, 1937), *La Grande Illusion* (*Grand Illusion*, 1937), *Ultimatum* (1938), *Paix sur le Rhin* (1938), and *L'Inconnue de Monte-Carlo* (1939); shortly after outbreak of WWII, was arrested as an alien by French authorities and deported to Germany; reemerged (1950s), appearing in 3 more films before her death.

PARLOA, Maria (1843–1909). American domestic economist and author. Born Maria Parloa, Sept 25, 1843, in Massachusetts; died of acute nephritis, Aug 21, 1909, in Bethel, Connecticut; nothing is known of her parents or early years; attended Maine Central Institute, in Pittsfield. ❖ An authority on household management and proper preparation of food, lectured and wrote on these subjects extensively; gave courses of lessons in sickroom cookery to Harvard medical students (1877); after visiting Paris for study, opened a cooking school in New York City; writings include *Miss Parloa's New Cook Book and Marketing Guide*, *The Young Housekeeper* and *Home Economics*.

PARLOW, Cindy (1978—). American soccer player. Born Cynthia Marie Parlow, May 8, 1978, in Memphis, TN; attended University of North Carolina. ❖ Won a team gold medal at Atlanta Olympics (1996) and a team silver medal at Sydney Olympics (2000); won a team gold at World Cup (1999); was a founding member of the Women's United Soccer Association (WUSA); signed with Atlanta Beat (2001); won a team gold medal at Athens Olympics (2004). Awarded the Hermann Trophy. ❖ See also Jere Longman *The Girls of Summer* (HarperCollins, 2000).

PARLOW, Kathleen (1890–1963). Canadian violinist. Born Kathleen Mary Parlow in Calgary, Canada, 1890; died 1963; studied with Henry Holmes, an English violinist, in San Francisco, and with Leopold Auer in St. Petersburg. ❖ At 15, had a command performance before England's queen, Alexandra of Denmark (1905); made successful Russian debut (1908); after touring extensively until 1941, retired in Toronto to teach and lead her own string quartet.

PARMA, duchess of.
See Margaret of Parma (1522–1586).
See Maria of Portugal (1538–1577).
See Margaret of Parma (1612–?).
See Farnese, Elizabeth (1692–1766).
See Louise Elizabeth (1727–1759).
See Maria Amalia (1746–1804).
See Marie Louise of Austria (1791–1847).
See Theresa of Savoy (1803–1879).
See Louise of Bourbon-Berry (1819–1864).

PARMENTER, Ruella (1951–1998). See Sunn, Rell.

PARNELL, Anna (1852–1911). Irish activist. Born Catherine Maria Anna Mercer Parnell, May 13, 1852, at Avondale, near Rathdrum, Co. Wicklow; drowned while swimming off Ilfracombe, Devon, 1911; dau. of John Henry Parnell (landowner) and Delia (Stewart) Parnell; sister of Charles Stewart Parnell (1846–1891, Irish reformer and politician) and younger sister of Fanny Parnell; sister-in-law of Katherine O'Shea (1845–1921); educated at Royal Dublin Society Art School and South Kensington School of Design; never married; no children. ❖ Co-founder and leader of the Ladies' Land League, the 1st women's political organization in Ireland, which was suppressed by her brother; following father's death (1859), lived with family in Dublin, Paris and London; while studying in London, attended parliamentary sittings and wrote accounts of them for an Irish-American journal; helped to organize an American fund for relief of famine in Ireland (1879–80); established Central Land League of the Ladies of Ireland (LLL), of which she became organizing secretary and effective leader (Jan 1881); co-ordinated and took part in the League's activities throughout Ireland (1881–82); after LLL was dissolved by brother (Aug 1882), retired from public life and broke off all relations with him, an estrangement which lasted until his death; moved to England (1886), where she lived for the remainder of her years; with publication of Michael Davitt's *The Fall of Feudalism in Ireland*, which contained criticism of the LLL (1904), produced her own account, *The Tale of a Great Sham*, but was unable to find a publisher. Lost manuscript of *Tale* was discovered (1959) and published (1986). ❖ See also Jane McL. Cote, *Fanny and Anna Parnell: Ireland's Patriot Sisters* (Macmillan, 1991); and *Women in World History*.

PARNELL, Katherine O'Shea (1845–1921). *See O'Shea, Katherine.*

PARNIS, Mollie (1905–1992). American fashion designer, philanthropist, and socialite. Name variations: Mollie Parnis Livingston. Born Mar 18, 1905, in New York, NY; died July 18, 1992, in New York, NY; dau. of Abraham Parnis and Sara (Rosen) Parnis; graduate of Wadleigh High School, 1923; m. Leon Livingston (textile specialist), June 26, 1930; children: Robert. ❖ One of New York's leading couturières for 5 decades, created dresses that were understated, comfortable and versatile; with husband, started 7th Avenue fashion house, Parnis-Livingston (1933); introduced the sheath dress (1955); clientele included Mamie Eisenhower, Margaret Truman, and Sarah Churchill, as well as a number of stage and screen stars; also presided over a salon for actors, journalists, and Democratic politicians; closed her design enterprise (1984) and formed the Mollie Parnis Livingston Foundation, through which she channeled a number of philanthropic ventures. ❖ See also *Women in World History.*

PARNOK, Sophia (1885–1933). Russian poet. Name variations: Sonya Parnokh; (pseudonym) Andrey Polyanin. Born July 30, 1885, in Taganrog, Russia; died Aug 1933, in Kirinsky, USSR; dau. of Yakov Solomonovich Parnokh (Jewish pharmacist and apothecary owner) and Alexandra Parnokh (doctor); studied music in Geneva, Switzerland, and history, philosophy, and law in St. Petersburg; m. briefly to Vladimir Volkenshtein, 1907; no children. ❖ Published 1st book of poetry (1916); published final book of poetry, *In a Hushed Voice* (1928), which was later considered by critics a major work; wrote successful libretto, *Almast,* for an opera staged at Moscow's Bolshoi Theater (1930); celebrated her lesbianism, frequently invoking mythological goddesses and the poet Sappho in her work; maintained intimate relationships with several women, including Nadezhda Polyakova, poet Marina Tsvetayeva, physicist Nina Vedneyeva, and wrote freely about her experiences; also wrote *Roses of Pieria* (1922), *The Vine* (1923) and *Music* (1926). ❖ See also Diana Lewis Burgin, *Sophia Parnok: The Life and Work of Russia's Sappho* (New York U. Press, 1994); Sophia Polyakova, *The Sunset Days of Yore: Tsvetayeta and Parnok* (Ardis, 1983); and *Women in World History.*

PARR, Anne (d. 1552). Countess of Pembroke. Died Feb 20, 1552; sister of Catherine Parr (1512–1548, last queen of Henry VIII); dau. of Thomas Parr and Maud Greene Parr; m. William Herbert, 1st earl of Pembroke, before 1534; children: Henry Herbert, 2nd earl of Pembroke (d. 1601, who m. Mary Herbert [1561–1621]). ❖ Was appointed a lady-in-waiting by her sister Catherine.

PARR, Catherine (1512–1548). Queen of England. Name variations: Katherine Parr. Born 1512 in England; died of puerperal fever, Sept 5, 1548, after giving birth to a girl; dau. of Sir Thomas Parr of Kendal and Maud Greene Parr (1495–1529); m. Edward Borough, 1529 (died 1532); m. John Neville (1493–1543), 3rd Lord Latimer, 1533; m. Henry VIII (1491–1547), king of England (r. 1509–1547), in 1543 (died 1547); m. Thomas Seymour (brother of Jane Seymour), Lord Admiral of England, Mar 1547; children (4th m.) Mary Seymour (Aug 29 or 30, 1548–Sept 5, 1548; an 18th-century historian claimed that she grew to adulthood and m. Sir Edward Bushell). ❖ Sixth wife of Henry VIII, whose tact and intelligence enabled her to act as regent and nursemaid for the ailing king, was widowed twice before marrying him (1543); acted as regent (1544); wrote and published religious treatise (1545); argued with Henry over religious issues and was almost convicted of heresy (1546); after Henry VIII died (Jan 1547), published 2nd religious treatise (1547); writings include *Prayers and Meditations* (1545) and *Lamentations of a Sinner* (1547).

PARR, Harriet (1828–1900). British writer. Name variations: (pseudonym) Holme Lee. Born Jan 31, 1828, in York, England; died Feb 18, 1900, in Shanklin, Isle of Wight; dau. of William Parr (salesman of luxury goods) and Mary (Grandage) Parr; educated in York; never married. ❖ Author of over 30 novels as well as a substantial work on the life of Joan of Arc (1866), also wrote a number of children's stories and published a collection called *Legends from Fairyland* (1860). ❖ See also *Women in World History.*

PARR, Katherine (1512–1548). *See Parr, Catherine.*

PARR, Maud Greene (1495–1529). English noblewoman. Name variations: Maud Greene or Green; Maude. Born Maud Green or Greene in 1495; died in 1529; dau. of Sir Thomas Green or Greene of Northamptonshire; m. Sir Thomas Parr of Kendal; children: Catherine

Parr (1512–1548, last queen of Henry VIII): William Parr, marquess of Northampton; Anne Parr (d. 1552).

PARR, Susanna (fl. 1659). British writer. Born in England. ❖ Had religious dispute with minister Lewis Stuckley who excommunicated her (1658); wrote account of dispute in *Susanna's Apology Against the Elders* (1659).

PARRA, Teresa de la (1889–1936). Venezuelan novelist and short-story writer. Name variations: Ana Teresa Parr Sanojo; (pseudonym) Fru-fru. Born to wealthy parents in 1889 (some sources cite 1891 or 1895) in Paris, France; died of TB in 1936; longtime companion of Lydia Cabrera (1899–1991, Cuban-born American scholar of Afro-Cuban culture, particularly santeria); no children. ❖ One of Venezuela's best-known writers, lived on her family's plantation in Tazón, near Cúa, as a child; following father's death, moved with family to Valencia, Spain (1906), returning to Caracas as an adolescent; published 1st book, *Diario de una señorita que se fastidiaba* (Diary of a Lady Who Was Bored, 1922), a *succès de scandale,* which used the format of a young woman's journal to explore the limited options available to women in Caracas; republished the book as *Ifigenía* (1924); published 2nd novel, *Las memórias de Mamá Blanca* (1929), which is considered her masterpiece (published in English as *Mama Blanca's Souvenirs* [1959], and as *Mama Blanca's Memoirs* [1993]); formed a group of French and South American writers (1926); began lecturing on role of women in South America (1927), which she continued doing throughout life. ❖ See also *Women in World History.*

PARRA, Violeta (1917–1967). Chilean poet, painter and singer. Born Oct 4, 1917, in San Carlos, Chile; committed suicide, April 5, 1967; dau. of Nicanor Parra and Clarisa Sandoval Navarrete; sister of Nicanor Parra; m. Luis Cereceda, 1937 (div. 1948); m. Luis Arce; children: 4. ❖ International folklorist, who inspired the New Chilean song movement, wrote songs and set them to traditional rhythms; studied musical folklore and founded Museum of Popular Art at University of Concerción; works include *Poésie populaire des Andes, Violeta* (1965), *Décimas* (1970), *Toda Violeta Parra* (1974), and *Violeta del pueblo* (1976); also composed "Gracias a La Vida," which was recorded by Joan Baez.

PARREN, Kalliroe (1861–1940). Greek feminist, journalist, novelist, and educator. Name variations: Kallirroi Parren. Born 1861 in Crete; died 1940; married a French journalist. ❖ Was founding editor of *The Ladies' Newspaper* (1887); founded the Union for the Emancipation of Women (1894), the Union of Greek Women (1896), and the Lyceum of Greek Women (1911); also wrote novels with feminist themes, a feminist play (which was never staged), and 2 studies: *The History of Women* and *The History of Greek Women from 1650–1860.* Awarded Golden Cross of the Saviour by Greek Academy for advancing the status of women. ❖ See also *Women in World History.*

PARRISH, Anne (1760–1800). American philanthropist. Born Oct 17, 1760, in Philadelphia, Pennsylvania; died Dec 26, 1800, in Philadelphia. ❖ Founded the House of Industry (1795), the 1st charitable organization for women in America, which would provide employment opportunities to poor women in Philadelphia for over 125 years; also established a school for needy girls (1796), later known as the Aimwell School. ❖ See also *Women in World History.*

PARRISH, Anne (1888–1957). American writer and illustrator. Name variations: Mrs. Charles Albert Corliss. Born Nov 12, 1888, in Colorado Springs, Colorado; died of cerebral hemorrhage, Sept 5, 1957, in Danbury, Connecticut; dau. of Maxfield Parrish (famed illustrator) and Anne Lodge Parrish (portrait painter); sister-in-law of M.F.K. Fisher; studied art at Philadelphia School of Design for Women; m. Charles Albert Corliss, 1915 (died 1936); m. Josiah Titzell (poet who wrote novels as Frederick Lambeck), 1938. ❖ Wrote and illustrated *The Dream Coach* (1924), which was nominated for Newbery Medal, as were 2 more of her books for children, *Floating Island* (1930) and *The Story of Appleby Capple* (1950); also wrote more than a dozen novels for adults, many of which featured protagonists who have been described as "poseurs" (the title of one of her earliest books was *A Pocketful of Poses*). ❖ See also *Women in World History.*

PARRISH, Celestia (1853–1918). American educator. Name variations: Celeste Parrish. Born Celestia Susannah Parrish on Sept 12, 1853, on a plantation near Swansonville, Pittsylvania Co., Virginia; died Sept 7, 1918, in Clayton, Georgia; dau. of William Perkins Parrish (plantation owner) and Lucinda Jane Walker; graduate of Roanoke Female Institute (later Averett College), 1876, and Virginia State Normal School (later

Longwood College), 1886; studied mathematics and astronomy at University of Michigan, 1891–92; Cornell University, PhB, 1896; studied under John Dewey at University of Chicago; never married; children: 1 adopted daughter. ❖ Taught in Danville Public Schools (1874–83), at Roanoke Female Institute (1884), Virginia State Normal School (1886–91), and Randolph-Macon Woman's College (1892–1902); founded an alumnae association at Randolph-Macon; served as professor of pedagogic psychology and head of department of pedagogy at Georgia State Normal School (1902–11); served as Virginia state president and national vice-president of Association of Collegiate Alumnae; founded and served as 1st president of Southern Association of College Women (1903); served as 1st president of Georgia's Mothers and Teachers Cooperative Club; worked on behalf of public schools as state supervisor of rural schools for the North Georgia District (1911–18). ❖ See also *Women in World History.*

PARRISH, Mrs. Dillwyn (1908–1992). *See Fisher, M.F.K.*

PARRISH, Helen (1922–1959). American tv and screen actress. Born Mar 12, 1922, in Columbus, GA; died Feb 22, 1959, in Hollywood, CA; dau. of Laura Parrish (actress); sister of Robert Parrish (director) and Beverly Parrish (actress, 1919–1930); m. Charles Lang (screenwriter), 1942 (div. 1954); m. John Guedel (tv producer), 1956. ❖ Made film debut playing Babe Ruth's daughter in *When Babe Comes Home*; appeared in *Our Gang* comedies; other films include *The First Command, Mad About Music, Little Tough Guy* and *Little Tough Guys in Society.*

PARRITT, Barbara (1944—). African-American singer. Name variations: Barbara Parritt Toomer; The Toys. Born Oct 1, 1944, in Wilmington, NC. ❖ Vocalist formed R&B girl group, The Toys, in Jamaica, NY, with June Montiero and Barbara Harris; with trio, had huge hit with single, "A Lover's Concert," based on Bach's "Minuet in G" (1964), followed by another hit, "Attack" (1966); appeared in film *It's a Bikini World* (1967); with trio, released last hit single, "Sealed With a Kiss" (1968); after group disbanded (1968), went on to do session work.

PARSLEY, Lea Ann (1968—). American skeleton athlete. Born June 12, 1968, in Granville, Ohio. ❖ Won a silver medal at Lillehammer World Cup (2000); won US National Trials (2000); won a silver medal for indiv. skeleton at Salt Lake City Olympics (2002); became firefighter (1994). Named Ohio Firefighter of the Year (1999).

PÄRSON, Anja (1981—). *See Paerson, Anja.*

PARSONS, Betty Pierson (1900–1982). American artist and art promoter. Born in New York, NY, Jan 31, 1900; died 1982; dau. of J. Fred Pierson and Suzanne (Miles) Pierson; m. Schuyler Livingston Parsons, May 8, 1919 (div. 1923); no children. ❖ Dubbed the "midwife of the New York School," opened the Parsons Gallery (1946); gained renown as a promoter of the New York abstractionists of 1940s, and was instrumental in the careers of well-known artists such as Lee Krasner, Perle Fine, Jackson Pollock, Anne Ryan, Mark Rothko, and Irene Rice Pereira; also enjoyed some success as a painter and sculptor in her own right. ❖ See also Lee Hall, *Betty Parsons: Artist, Dealer, Collector* (Abrams, 1991); and *Women in World History.*

PARSONS, Eliza (c. 1748–1811). British novelist and dramatist. Born Eliza Phelps c. 1748; died in Leytonstone, Essex, England, Feb 5, 1811; only dau. of a wine merchant; married a turpentine merchant who died in 1790; children: 8. ❖ Popular writer of Gothic fiction, produced more than 19 works; also translated Molière's 2-act farce *The Intrigues of a Morning*, which was produced at Covent Garden (1792), and published 6 tales of Jean de La Fontaine as *Love and Gratitude* (1804); writings include *The History of Miss Meridith* (1790), *The Errors of Education* (1791), *Woman as She Should Be* (1793), *The Castle of Wolfenbach* (1793), *Lucy* (1794), *The Girl of the Mountains* (1794) and *The Mysterious Warning* (1794). ❖ See also *Women in World History.*

PARSONS, Elizabeth (1846–1924). New Zealand singer. Name variations: Elizabeth Widdop. Born Elizabeth Widdop, Feb 10, 1846, in London, England; died Mar 1, 1924, in New Zealand; dau. of William Widdop (coachman) and Hannah (Byatt) Widdop; m. William Frederick Parsons (builder), 1864; children: 13. ❖ Immigrated with family to New Zealand (1855); a soprano, joined Wellington Choral Society (1860), and St. Paul's choir (1861), and performed regularly at Theatre Royal. ❖ See also *Dictionary of New Zealand Biography* (Vol. 1).

PARSONS, Elsie Clews (1875–1941). American anthropologist and sociologist. Name variations: Elsie Worthington Parsons; Elsie Worthington Parsons Clews; (pseudonym) John Main. Born Nov 27, 1875, in New York, NY; died Dec 19, 1941, in New York, NY; dau. of Henry Clews (founder of a New York City banking firm) and Lucy Madison (Worthington) Clews; Barnard College, AB, 1896; Columbia University, AM, 1897, PhD, 1899; m. Herbert Parsons (lawyer and US congressional representative), Sept 1, 1900; children: Elsie (b. 1901); John Edward (b. 1903); Herbert (b. 1909); McIlvaine (b. 1911); 2 who died in childhood. ❖ Taught history at Columbia's Horace Mann High School (1897) and graduate courses in sociology at Columbia University (1902–05); published 1st book, *The Family* (1906); made 1st visit to Southwest (1915); studied Native American tribes in a series of annual field trips (1916–36); lectured on anthropology at New School for Social Research (1919); served as president of American Folklore Society (1918–20); was associate editor of *Journal of American Folklore* (1918–41); served as president of American Ethnological Association (1923–25); was 1st female president of American Anthropological Association (1940–41). Writings include (under pseudonym John Main) *Religious Chastity* (1913), *Fear and Conventionality* (1914), *Folk-Tales of Andros Island, Bahamas* (1918), *Folk-Lore of the Cape Verde Islands* (1923), *Folk-Lore of the Sea Islands, South Carolina* (1923), *The Social Organization of the Tewa of New Mexico* (1929), *Hopi and Zuñi Ceremonialism* (1933), *Folk-Lore of the Antilles, French and English* (3 vols., 1933–43), *Mitla: Town of the Souls* (1936), *Pueblo Indian Religion* (2 vols., 1939), and *Peguche, Canton of Otavalo* (1945). ❖ See also Desley Deacon, *Elsie Clews Parsons: Inventing Modern Life* (U. of Chicago Press, 1997); and *Women in World History.*

PARSONS, Emily Elizabeth (1824–1880). Civil War nurse. Born in Taunton, Massachusetts, Mar 8, 1824; died in Cambridge, Massachusetts, May 19, 1880; dau. of Theophilus Parsons (lawyer and later Dane Professor of Law at Harvard University) and Catherine Amory (Chandler) Parsons; student and volunteer nurse at the Massachusetts General Hospital; never married. ❖ During Civil War, was assigned as a nurse to Fort Schuyler military hospital on Long Island Sound; appointed head nurse of *City of Alton,* a hospital transport ship which steamed down the Mississippi carrying sick and wounded soldiers to hospitals in Memphis (1863); made supervisor of nurses at the newly established Benton Barracks Hospital in St. Louis, a 2,500-bed facility and largest military hospital in the West (1864), one of the most important appointments given to a woman during Civil War; following the war, opened a general hospital in Cambridge (later named the Mount Auburn Hospital) where she lived and treated destitute women and children. ❖ See also *Women in World History.*

PARSONS, Estelle (1927—). American stage, tv, and screen actress. Born Nov 20, 1927, in Lynn, MA; m. Richard Gehman (div.). ❖ Began career as a writer and feature producer on tv's "Today" Show; made NY acting debut in *Happy Hunting* (1956), followed by *Beg Borrow or Steal, The Automobile Graveyard, Mrs. Dally Has a Lover, Next Time I'll Sing to You, Ready When You Are C.B.!, Malcolm, The East Wind* and *Galileo*; made film debut in *Ladybug Ladybug* (1964); other films include *Don't Drink the Water, Watermelon Man, I Never Sang for My Father, For Pete's Sake, The Lemon Sisters, Dick Tracy* and *That Darn Cat*; on tv, appeared regularly as Roseanne's mother on "Roseanne"; serves as artistic director of the Actors' Studio. Nominated for Best Actress Tony's for *The Seven Descents of Myrtle* (1968), *And Miss Reardon Drinks a Little* (1971), *Miss Margarida's Way* (1978), and as Featured Actress for *Mornings at 7* (2002); received Oscar for Best Supporting Actress for *Bonnie and Clyde* (1967) and nominated for another for *Rachel Rachel* (1968).

PARSONS, Harriet (1906–1983). American producer. Born in Burlington, Iowa, Aug 23, 1906; only child of Louella Parsons (Hollywood gossip columnist) and John Dement Parsons (real-estate salesman); Wellesley College, BA, 1928; m. King Kennedy (writer and publicist), Sept 28, 1939 (div. April 1946). ❖ At 6, appeared as "Baby Parsons" in 2 Essanay movies, *Margaret's Awakening* and *The Magic Wand*; wrote for *Modern Screen, Silver Screen* and *Photoplay*; became radio commentator ("Harriet Parsons' Hollywood Highlights" on NBC), and columnist for *Liberty* and Hearst Syndicate; produced over 100 short subjects called *Screen Snapshots* for Columbia (1933–40); produced another series, *Meet the Stars,* for Republic; followed 1st full-length film, *Joan of the Ozarks* (1942), with many highly successful films, including *The Enchanted Cottage* (1945), *Night Song* (1947), *I Remember Mama* (1947), *Never a Dull Moment* (1950), *Clash by Night* (1951) and *Susan Slept Here* (1954). ❖ See also *Women in World History.*

PARSONS, Juanita (1895–1961). *See Hansen, Juanita.*

PARSONS, Louella (1881–1972). American gossip columnist. Name variations: Louella Oettinger; Louella O. Parsons. Born Aug 6, 1881, in Freeport, IL; died of a stroke, after a lengthy illness, in Santa Monica, CA, Dec 9, 1972; dau. of Joshua Oettinger (clothing store owner) and Helen (Stine) Oettinger; attended Dixon College and Normal School; m. John Dement Parsons, Oct 31, 1905 (div., died 1919); m. Jack McCaffrey, c. 1915 (div.); m. Harry Martin, c. 1942 (died 1951); children: (1st m.) Harriet Oettinger Parsons (b. Aug 23, 1906). ❖ Driven, sometimes ruthless, Hollywood gossip columnist who wielded considerable power in the entertainment industry (1940s–50s); wrote one of 1st US movie columns, for the *Chicago Record-Herald* (1914–18); wrote a movie gossip column for Hearst Publications, syndicated in 400 newspapers (1922–65); also wrote *The Gay Illiterate* (1944) and *Tell It to Louella* (1961), and appeared in films *Hollywood Hotel* (1937), *Without Reservations* (1946) and *Starlift* (1951). ❖ See also George Eells, *Hedda and Louella* (Putnam, 1972); and *Women in World History*.

PARSONS, Mary (1813–1885). Irish photographer. Name variations: Mary Field; Mary, Countess of Rosse. Born Mary Field, July 21, 1813, at Heaton Hall, Yorkshire, England; died July 22, 1885; dau. of John Wilmer Field; sister of Delia Field (1821–1873, who married Admiral Arthur Duncombe); m. William Parsons, 3rd earl of Rosse (astronomer), July 14, 1836 (died Oct 31, 1867); children: (11, only 4 of who survived to adulthood) Laurence Parsons, 4th earl of Rosse (1840–1929), Rev. Randal Parsons (1848–1936), Hon. Richard Clere Parsons (1851–1923); Sir Charles Algernon Parsons (1954–1931, inventor of the steam turbine engine). ❖ The 1st recipient of the Photographic Society of Ireland's Silver Medal (1859), for best paper negative, joined the Dublin Photographic Society as one of its 1st women members (1856); established the world's earliest known darkroom in her house, Birr Castle, Co. Offaly (June 1842); financed the construction of "the Leviathan of Parsonstown," which was the world's largest reflecting telescope from 1845 to 1917; exhibited photographs of the telescope at Photographic Society's 1st show (1854); after husband's death, moved to London (1870). University College, London, fully restored her telescope (1999).

PARSONS, Nancie (1904–1968). English actress. Born Lady Mercy Greville, April 3, 1904, in England; died 1968; dau. of Charles Greville (1853–1924), 5th earl of Warwick, and Frances Evelyn Greville (1861–1938, philanthropist and social leader); m. Basil Dean (div. 1933); m. Patrick Gamble, 1933 (div. 1936); m. Richard Marter, 1936. ❖ Made stage debut in London as the Maid in *The Lilies of the Field* (1923), followed by *The Little Minister, London Life, Spring Cleaning* and *The Constant Nymph,* among others.

PARTANNA, Lucia (1770–1826). *See Migliaccio, Lucia.*

PARTENIDE, Fidalma (1663–1726). *See Massimi, Petronilla Paolini.*

PARTENIDE, Irminda (1703–1779). *See Bergalli, Luisa.*

PARTHENAY, Anne de (fl. 16th c.). French poet. Aunt of Catherine de Parthenay. ❖ Studied classical languages and theology and wrote poems and songs; praised by Clément Marot and Théodore de Bèze.

PARTHENAY, Catherine de (1554–1631). French poet, translator and playwright. Name variations: Catherine de Rohan; duchesse de Rohan. Born Catherine de Parthenay, 1554, into a family of Huguenots named Parthenay-Levêque; died 1631; dau. of the seigneur of Soubise; niece of Anne de Parthenay; m. Charles de Quelennec, baron of Pont-l'Abbe (killed 1572); m. René de Rohan, viscount of Rohan and Prince of Léon, 1575 (killed 1586); children: 5, including Henri de Rohan (1579–1638, famed general). ❖ First husband was killed in the Saint Bartholomew's Day massacre (1572); wrote elegies about Calvinist cause, death of Protestants in religious conflicts, and a poem in honor of Henry IV after his assassination (1610); was imprisoned after siege of La Rochelle by the forces of Cardinal Richelieu (1628) and died in captivity in Poitou; her tragedy, *Judith et Holopherne,* was performed in 1573; a satire, *Apologie de Henri IV,* was also attributed to her.

PARTHENIS (fl. 2nd c. BCE). Greek poet. Epigrammatist. ❖ Mentioned only once, by Meleager, in a poem on Greek women poets; probably wrote epigrams.

PARTHIA, queen of.
See Laodice *(fl. 129 BCE).*
See Rhodogune *(fl. 2nd c. BCE).*

PARTON, Dolly (1946—). American musician. Born Dolly Rebecca Parton, Jan 19, 1946, in Sevierville, TN; dau. of Robert Lee Parton

(tobacco farmer) and Avie Lee (Owens) Parton; sister of Rachel Dennison (actress), Stella Parton (actress), and Randy Parton (actor); m. Carl Dean (businessman), 1966. ❖ Appeared on Cass Walker tv show at 10, Grand Ole Opry at 12, and was regular on Walker's radio show until 18; joined Porter Wagoner's country-music tv show and became popular as "Miss Dolly"; sang hit duets with Wagoner, including "Just Someone I Used to Know" (1969) and "Daddy Was an Old Time Preacher Man" (1970); had many solo country hits, including "Joshua" (1970) and "Coat of Many Colors" (1971); left Wagoner and released album, *Jolene* (1974), which included #1 country hit title track; had hit with her own song, "I Will Always Love You" (1974), which was also a blockbuster for Whitney Houston (1992); hosted tv music show, "Dolly" (1976); released platinum pop LP, *Here You Come Again* (1977), whose title track went gold (1978); other hits include "You're the Only One" (1979), "Islands in the Stream" (1983) and "Yellow Roses" (1989); nominated for Oscar for film debut, *9 to 5* (1980); other films include *The Best Little Whorehouse in Texas* (1982) and *Steel Magnolias* (1989); opened theme park, Dollywood (1986); with Emmylou Harris and Linda Ronstadt, released Grammy Award-winning *Trio* (1987); other albums include *White Limozeen* (1989), *Straight Talk* (1992) and *Little Sparrow* (2001); with debut bluegrass album, *The Grass Is Blue* (1994), won Album of Year at International Bluegrass Music Awards; established Dolly Parton Wellness and Rehabilitation Center. Received numerous Country Music Association Awards and Grammy Awards; inducted into Country Music Hall of Fame (1994). ❖ See also autobiography, *Dolly: My Life and Unfinished Business* (1994).

PARTON, Mabel (b. 1881). English tennis player. Born July 22, 1881, in UK. ❖ At Stockholm Olympics, won a bronze medal in singles–indoor courts (1912).

PARTON, Sara Willis (1811–1872). *See Fern, Fanny.*

PARTRIDGE, Dora (1893–1932). *See Carrington, Dora.*

PARTRIDGE, Frances (1900–2004). English memoirist. Name variations: Frances Marshall. Born Frances Catherine Marshall, Mar 28, 1900, in London, England; died Feb 5, 2004; dau. of Eleanor and William Marshall (architect); graduate of Newnham College; m. Ralph Partridge, 1932 (died 1960); children: Burgo (died 1963). ❖ Taken in by the Bloomsbury group, became an intimate of Lytton Strachey, Dora Carrington and Ralph Partridge at Ham Spray; after Strachey and Carrington died, married Partridge and continued to live at Ham Spray; at 78, began publishing her diaries, the 1st being *A Pacificst's War* (1978), followed by *Memories* (1981), *Everything to Lose* (1986) and *Ups and Downs* (2001), among others; also wrote *Julia* (1983), about the life of Julia Strachey. ❖ See also (film) *Carrington* (1995).

PARTRIDGE, Kathleen (1963—). Australian field-hockey player. Born Dec 1963 in Australia. ❖ At Seoul Olympics, as goalkeeper, won a gold medal in team competition (1988); became a coach and wrote book *The Rebound Revolution.*

PARTRIDGE, Margaret (b. 1891). English electrical engineer and contractor. Born Margaret Mary Partridge, April 8, 1891; studied math at Bedford College, London, 1911–14. ❖ Lectured for Electrical Association for Women (EAW); with Caroline Haslett, founded the journal, *Electrical Age for Women* (1926); wired electricity for 4 English villages by 1921; established Electrical Enterprise Inc. with Haslett (1921), to help rural communities gain access to electricity.

PARTURIER, Françoise (1919—). French novelist, journalist, and playwright. Name variations: (pseudonym) Nicole. Born in Paris, France, Oct 12, 1919; attended Paris University; m. Jean Gatichon, in 1947. ❖ Feminist whose popular writings challenge sexual and racial inequality, taught briefly in US (1950–51), before becoming a professional journalist and writer; work appeared in a number of popular French journals, including *Literary News* and *Le Figaro*; collaborated with Josette Raoul-Duval on 3 novels (published under pseudonym Nicole), before writing under own name (1959); subsequent work includes novels, feminist essays, and a 3-act play, *This Crazy Life* (1977).

PARUN, Vesna (1922—). Croatian poet. Born April 10, 1922, on the island of Zlarin, near Sibenik; attended University of Zagreb. ❖ One of her country's most controversial and influential poets, published 1st collection of poems, *Zore i vihori* (Dawns and Gales, 1947), considered by some to be her best work, though it was attacked for being out of step with the prevailing school of Socialist Realism; silenced for a time, did not publish another collection until *Crna maslina* (The Black Olive Tree, 1955); over next decade, published several more volumes, focusing on personal rather than political issues and detailing a number of blissful but short-lived romantic relationships. ❖ See also *Women in World History.*

PARUZZI, Gabriella (1969—). Italian cross-country skier. Born June 21, 1969, in Udine, Italy; m. Alfredo Baron. ❖ Won bronze medals at Albertville Olympics (1992), Lillehammer Olympics (1994), and Nagano Olympics (1998), all for the 4 x 5 km relay; won a gold medal for 30 km at Salt Lake City Olympics (2002) and a bronze medal for 4 x 5 km relay at Torino Olympics (2006).

PARVIAINEN, Katri (1914–2002). Finnish javelin thrower. Name variations: Kaisa Parviainen; K.V. Parviainen; Katri Vellamo. Born Dec 3, 1914 in Finland; died Oct 21, 2002. ❖ Won a silver medal at London Olympics (1948) with a javelin throw of 43.79 meters (143′8), the 1st Finnish woman to win an Olympic medal.

PARYSATIS I (fl. 440–385 BCE). Queen of Persia. Dau. of Artaxerxes I, king of Persia, and Andia, a Babylonian; m. half-brother Darius II Ochus, king of Persia (r. 424–404 BCE), in 424 BCE (died 404 BCE); children: daughter, Amestris; 2 sons, Arsaces, also known as Artaxerxes II, king of Persia (r. 404–358 BCE), and Cyrus (d. 401 BCE). ❖ With her political savvy, abetted husband's ascendance to his father's throne and remained influential during his entire reign; apparently maintained a kind of intelligence network both at court and throughout the empire for the purpose of uncovering any whiff of disloyalty. ❖ See also *Women in World History.*

PARYSATIS II (c. 350–323 BCE). Persian princess. Born c. 350 BCE; died 323 BCE; youngest dau. of Artaxerxes III Ochus, king of Persia (r. 359/8–338 BCE) and sister of Artaxerxes IV, king of Persia (r. 338–336 BCE); m. Alexander III the Great (356–323 BCE), king of Macedonia (r. 335–323 BCE). ❖ As a Persian hostage from the Achaemenid royal house, became one of 3 wives of Alexander the Great (324), receiving all of the honor such an exalted status endowed; was murdered by Roxane, another wife. ❖ See also *Women in World History.*

PASCA, Mirela (1975—). Romanian gymnast. Born Mirela Ana Pasca, Feb 19, 1975, in Baia-Mare, Romania. ❖ Won Romanian nationals (1989); placed 1st for uneven bars at Europeans (1990) and International of Romania (1990); at Barcelona Olympics, won a silver medal in team all-around (1992).

PASCAL, Amy (1959—). American film executive. Name variations: Amy B. Pascal. Born 1959; raised in Los Angeles, CA; graduate of University of California, Los Angeles, with a degree in international relations; m. Bernard Weinraub (*New York Times* reporter), 1997; children: (adopted) Anthony. ❖ Was vice-president of production at 20th Century-Fox (1986–87) and president of production for Turner Pictures (1994–96); was a studio executive at Columbia Pictures (1997–94); then served as president of Columbia (2000–03); became chair of Motion Picture Group of Sony Pictures Entertainment (2003).

PASCAL, Christine (1953–1996). French actress and director. Born Nov 29, 1953, in Lyon, France; died Aug 30 or 31, 1996, apparently a suicide, in Garches, Paris, France; m. Robert Boner, 1982. ❖ As actress, appeared in over 30 films, including *The Clockmaker, Black Thursday, Spoiled Children,* and *Round Midnight*; directed *Le Petit prince a dit (The Little Prince Said)* and *Adultery: A User's Guide.* Won Louis Dellec Prize for directing *Le Petit prince a dit* (1992).

PASCAL, Gilberte (1620–1687). French biographer. Name variations: Gilberte Pascal Périer. Born 1620 at Clermont-Ferrand, France; died April 25, 1687, in Paris; sister of Jacqueline Pascal and Blaise Pascal; m. Florin Périer, June 1641; children: at least 4, including Etienne (b. 1642) and Marguerite Périer (c. 1645–?, writer). ❖ With husband converted to Jansenism and sent children to school at Port Royal; frequented Parisian intellectual gatherings and was known for eloquent conversation; wrote biographies of brother and sister, *Vie de la Soeur Saint-Eustache* and *Vie de Monsieur Pascal*; helped in preparation of Blaise Pascal's *Apologie de la religion chrétienne* and posthumous publication of fragments of *Apologie* as *Pensées* (1670).

PASCAL, Jacqueline (1625–1661). French nun. Born at Clermont-Ferrand, France, Oct 4, 1625; died in Paris, Oct 4, 1661; sister of scientist and philosopher Blaise Pascal (1623–1662) and biographer Gilberte Pascal (1620–1687); aunt of Marguerite Périer (writer). ❖ A child prodigy, composed verses at 8 and a 5-act comedy at 11; under influence of brother, converted to Jansenism (1646), though he strongly objected when she became a nun at Port Royal (1652); later had a hand in converting him. ❖ See also *Women in World History.*

PASCAL-TROUILLOT, Ertha (1943—). Haitian lawyer and politician. Born Ertha Pascal, 1943, in Haiti. ❖ Was Haiti's 1st female member of the bar; was the 1st female judge in the Haitian Civil Court, and the Court of Appeals, and the 1st woman judge on the Supreme Court; served as provisional president of Haiti (Mar 13 1990–Feb 7, 1991), helping to stabilize the country and prepare it for the democratic election that brought Aristide to power.

PASCALINA, Sister (1894–1983). German nun. Name variations: Josefine Lehnert; La Popessa. Born Aug 25, 1894, in Ebersberg, Bavaria, Germany; died of a brain hemorrhage, 1983, in Vienna, Austria; dau. of farmers George and Maria Lehnert. ❖ A powerful confidante of Pope Pius XII, who came to rely heavily on her advice, joined the Teaching Sisters of the Holy Cross (a Catholic convent) at age 15 (1910); took final vows at 19 and adopted the name Sister Pascalina (1914); met Eugenio Pacelli, the future Pope Pius XII (1917); moved to Munich to head Pacelli's household (1917); moved to Berlin with Pacelli (1925); moved to the Vatican and worked in the press relations office (1930); transferred to the secretariat of the Vatican (1932); traveled with Pacelli to US (1936); served Pacelli during his term as Pope Pius XII (1939–58); following his death, was forced out of the Vatican and went into exile in Switzerland (1958); built a home in Italy for herself and other retired nuns (1960s). ❖ See also Paul I. Murphy, *La Popessa: Biography of Sister Pascalina, the Most Powerful Woman in Vatican History* (Warner, 1983); and *Women in World History.*

PASCU-ENE-DERSIDAN, Ana (1944—). Romanian fencer. Born Sept 22, 1944, in Romania. ❖ Won a bronze medal at Mexico City Olympics (1968) and a bronze medal at Munich Olympics (1972), both in team foil.

PASCUAL, Carolina (1976—). Spanish rhythmic gymnast. Name variations: Carolina Pascual Gracia. Born June 17, 1976, in Orihuela, Spain. ❖ At European championships, won a team bronze medal (1990); at Barcelona Olympics, won a silver medal in rhythmic gymnastics, all-around (1992); won a bronze medal at the European Cup (1993).

PASHLEY, Anne (1935—). English runner and soprano. Born June 5, 1935, in Skegness, England; studied at Guildhall School of Music and Drama. ❖ At Melbourne Olympics, won a silver medal in the 4 x 100-meter relay (1956); made stage debut (1959) with Handel Opera Society in *Semele*; appeared at Glyndebourne (1963) and Covent Garden (1965); sang with English National Opera, Welsh National Opera, Scottish Opera, and at Aldeburgh.

PASINI, Claudia (1939—). Italian fencer. Born Mar 2, 1939, in Italy. ❖ At Rome Olympics, won a bronze medal in team foil (1960).

PASIONARIA, La (1895–1989). See *Ibárruri, Dolores.*

PASKUY, Eva (1948—). East German handball player. Born Nov 14, 1948, in East Germany. ❖ At Montreal Olympics, won a silver medal in team competition (1976).

PASOKHA, Anna (1949—). Soviet rower. Born Dec 1949 in USSR. ❖ At Montreal Olympics, won a bronze medal in coxed fours (1976).

PASSFIELD, Lady (1858–1943). See *Webb, Beatrice.*

PASTA, Giuditta (1797–1865). Italian soprano. Born Giuditta Maria Costanza Negri in Saronno, near Milan, Italy, Oct 26, 1797; died in Blevio, Lake Como, Italy, April 1, 1865; studied at Conservatory of Milan with Bartolomeo Lotto and Giuseppe Scappa. ❖ One of 19th-century Europe's greatest sopranos, influenced Italy's romantic composers, Gaetano Donizetti (1797–1848), Vincenzo Bellini (1801–1835), and Gioacchino Rossini (1792–1868), all of whom wrote operas for her; made debut in première of Scappa's opera *Le tre Eleonore* (1816), followed by performances at Théâtre Italien in Paris in Paer's *Il principe di Taranto* (1816), and at King's Theater in London, where she appeared as Telemachus in Cimarosa's *Penelope* (1817); embarked on another year of study, returning to the stage in Pacini's *Adelaide Comingo* (1819), in Venice; toured all major opera centers in Italy, culminating in her performance as Desdemona in Rossini's *Otello,* at Théâtre Italien (1821), a triumphant appearance that established her as a major talent; saw career hit its zenith (1821–31); returned to London as Desdemona (1824), and also performed Zerlina and Semiramide; was acclaimed for her portrayals of Amina in Bellini's *La sonnambula* (1831), and title role in his *Norma* (1831), which she sang for her debut at Milan's La Scala (1831); repertoire also included title roles in Donizetti's *Anna Bolena* (1830), Pacini's *Niobe* (1826) and Bellini's *Beatrice di Tenda*; an accomplished natural actress, excelled as Strauss' Electra, Salome, and the Dyer's

Wife, as well as Marie in *Wozzek*, all intense roles; retired from stage (1835), though she continued to make occasional appearances, performing in London (1837) and in Berlin and Russia (1840–41). ❖ See also *Women in World History.*

PASTERNAK, Josephine (1900–1993). Russian-born British philosopher, poet, and intellectual. Name variations: Anna Ney or Anna Nei; Josephina Pasternak; Josephine Leonidovna Pasternak; Zhosefina Pasternak; Zozefina Pasternak; Zhozefina Leonidovna Pasternak. Born Zhosefina Leonidovna Pasternak in Moscow, Russia, Feb 19, 1900; died in Oxford, England, Feb 16, 1993; dau. of Leonid Osipovich Pasternak (1862–1945, Impressionist painter) and Rosalia (Rozalia) Isidorovna Kaufman Pasternak (1867–1939, pianist); sister of Aleksandr Pasternak (1893–1982), Boris Pasternak (1890–1960, writer), and Lydia Leonidovna Pasternak-Slater (1902–1989); awarded doctorate in philosophy by University of Munich, 1931; m. 2nd cousin Fyodor Pasternak. ❖ Leaving behind brother Boris, immigrated with family to Germany (1921); published 1st vol. of collected poems, *Koordinaty* (Coordinates, 1938); fled Nazi Germany for Oxford, England (1938); edited and published father's memoirs, which appeared in a full edition in Moscow (1975), as well as in abridged form in England (1982); organized exhibitions of his work in UK, Germany, Soviet Union, and US; assisted by sister Lydia, worked in cooperation with Oxford's Ashmolean Museum to create Leonid Pasternak Memorial Exhibition of Paintings and Drawings (1958), the 1st major retrospective of his work in the West; published 2nd and last collection of verse, *Pamyati Pedro* (Memories of Pedro, 1981); worked on an informal study in epistemology entitled *Indefinability*, which would appear in print (1999), 6 years after her death. ❖ See also *Women in World History.*

PASTON, Agnes (c. 1405–1479). English aristocrat. Name variations: Agnes Berry. Born c. 1405 in Norfolk, England; died Aug 17, 1479, in London; dau. of Edmund Berry, lord of Hertfordshire; m. William Paston (lawyer and judge), 1420 (died 1444); mother-in-law of Margaret Paston (1423–1484); children: John Paston (b. 1421, lawyer who married Margaret Mauteby Paston); Edmund Paston (b. 1425); Elizabeth Paston (b. 1429); William Paston (b. 1436); Clement Paston (b. 1442). ❖ As her father's only heir, was greatly enriched by inheritance of lands in Norfolk and Hertfordshire (1433); when husband died (1444), gained control of over half of his estates, since he willed her a considerable amount of property, and her own dower lands. ❖ See also Roger Virgoe, ed. *Private Life in the Fifteenth Century: Illustrated Letters of the Paston Family* (Weidenfeld & Nicolson, 1989); and *Women in World History.*

PASTON, Margaret (1423–1484). English gentlewoman and warrior. Name variations: Margaret Mauteby. Born 1423; died 1484; dau. of Margery Berney and John Mauteby; daughter-in-law of Agnes Paston (c. 1405–1479); m. John Paston, c. 1440; children: 8, including Margery Paston Calle. ❖ Over the years, with husband frequently absent on business, had to defend hearth and home against at least 3 attacks. ❖ See also H.S. Bennett, *The Pastons and their England* (Cambridge U. Press, 1932); and *Women in World History.*

PASTOR, Claudia (1971—). Brazilian basketball player. Born Claudia Maria Pastor, July 15, 1971, in Barão de Cocais, Brazil. ❖ Won a team silver medal at Atlanta Olympics (1996).

PASTOR, Hebe Maria (1928—). *See Bonafini, Hebe de.*

PASTOR, Kika (1928—). *See Bonafini, Hebe de.*

PASTURE, Elizabeth M. de la (1890–1943). *See Dashwood, Elizabeth Monica.*

PASTURE, Mrs. Henry de la (d. 1945). *See de la Pasture, Mrs. Henry.*

PASTUSZKA, Aneta (1978—). Polish kayaker. Born May 11, 1978, in Krosno Odrzanskie, Poland. ❖ Placed 1st at World championships for K2 500 (1999) and K4 1000 (2002); won a bronze medal for K2 500 meters at Sydney Olympics (2000) and a silver medal for K2 500 at Athens Olympics (2004).

PATCH, Edith (1876–1954). American entomologist. Born Edith Marion Patch, 1876, in Worcester, Massachusetts; died 1954; University of Minnesota, BS, 1901; University of Maine, MS, 1910; Cornell University, PhD, 1911; never married. ❖ Leading entomologist who had a genus and several species of insects named in her honor, served as head of the department of entomology, University of Maine Agricultural Experiment Station (1904–37); was also head of University of Maine Agricultural Experiment Station (1924–37); appointed president of the Entomological Society of America (1930). ❖ See also *Women in World History.*

PATERSON, Ada Gertrude (1880–1937). New Zealand physician and child health administrator. Born June 6, 1880, at Caversham, Dunedin, New Zealand; died Aug 26, 1937, in Wellington; dau. of James Paterson (librarian) and Margaret Smith (Ayton) Paterson; University of Otago School of Medicine, 1906; post-graduate study at Dublin University. ❖ Joined medical service under Education Department (1912); traveled to Australia, Britain, and North America to study health programs (1920s); served on Committee of Inquiry into Mental Defectives and Sexual Offenders in New Zealand (1924); was director of Health Department's Division of School Hygiene (1923); promoted children's health camps movement and founded Wellington Children's Health Camp Association and Raukawa Children's Health Camp at Otaki (1932); member of New Zealand Federation of University Women. ❖ See also *Dictionary of New Zealand Biography* (Vol. 3).

PATERSON, Emma (1848–1886). English labor organizer. Born Emma Ann Smith, April 5, 1848, in London, England; died Dec 1, 1886, in Westminster; dau. of Henry Smith (schoolmaster) and Emma Dockerill Smith; m. Thomas Paterson, July 24, 1873. ❖ Founded Women's Protective and Provident League (1874), known as Women's Trade Union League after 1891, which would organize working women, advocate vocational training, and seek protective labor legislation in both Great Britain and US; was the 1st woman to attend the annual Trades Union Congress (1875); edited *The Women's Union Journal* (1876–86); founded the Women's Printing Society (1876) and published several articles. ❖ See also Harold Goldman, *Emma Paterson: She Led Woman Into a Man's World* (Lawrence & Wishart, 1974); and *Women in World History.*

PATERSON, Isabel (c. 1886–1961). Canadian-born literary critic and novelist. Born Isabel Bowler on Manitoulon Island, Lake Huron, Canada, c. 1886; died 1961; dau. of Francis Bowler and Margaret (Batty) Bowler; attended public schools in Mountain View and Cardston, Alberta, Canada; m. Kenneth Birrell Paterson. ❖ Served as literary critic for New York *Herald Tribune* for many years, writing the popular column, "Turns With a Bookworm"; also wrote a number of novels, including *If It Prove Fair Weather* (1940). ❖ See also *Women in World History.*

PATERSON, Jennifer (1928–1999). English cook. Born April 3, 1928, in London, England; died Aug 10, 1999, in London. ❖ Television personality and cook who, with Clarissa Dickson Wright, was one of the "Two Fat Ladies," a popular cooking show; was also the owner and driver of the old Triumph motorcycle that ferried them around.

PATERSON, Pat (1911–1978). English actress. Name variations: Pat Boyer. Born Patricia Paterson, April 7, 1911, in Bradford, Yorkshire, England; died Aug 24, 1978, in Scottsdale, AZ; m. Charles Boyer (actor), 1934 (committed suicide 2 days after Paterson died); children: Michael (committed suicide 1965). ❖ Films include *Night Shadows, Murder on the Second Floor, Bitter Sweet, Bottoms Up, Charlie Chan in Egypt, 52nd Street* and *Idiot's Delight*; retired (1936).

PATEY, Janet Monach (1842–1894). English vocalist. Name variations: Janet Whytock. Born Janet Whytock in London, England, May 1, 1842; died in Sheffield, Feb 28, 1894; studied singing under J. Wass, Pinsuti and Mrs. Sims Reeves; m. John Patey (bass singer), 1866. ❖ Recognized as one of the leading contraltos, without rival both in oratorio and in ballad music, had 1st regular engagement (1865), in the provinces; sang at Worcester festival (1866); toured US (1871), and sang in Paris (1875) and Australia (1890). ❖ See also *Women in World History.*

PATIL, Smita (1955–1986). Indian actress. Name variations: sometimes credited as Smita. Born 1955 in Poona, India; died from complications in childbirth, Dec 13, 1986; children: (with Raj Babbar) Smit Prateek (b. 1986). ❖ One of the finest actresses of her generation, began career acting with a theater group in Poona; worked as tv newscaster in Bombay; at 17, cast in Shyam Benegal's *Charandos Chor* and *Nishaant* (both 1975), became an instant star of the New Indian Cinema; appeared in over 70 films, including *Bhumika* (1977) and *Chakra* (1981), for which she won National Best Actress awards, *Namak Halaal* (1982), *Shakti* (1982), *Mandi* (1983), *Ardh Satya* (1983), *Raowan* (1984), *Mirch Masala* (1985), *Amrit* (1986) and *Dilwala* (1986). Awarded the Padmashri from the president of India (1985).

PATINIERE, Agnes (fl. 1286). Flemish artisan. Flourished 1286 in Douai, Flanders; m. Jehanne Dou Hoc. ❖ Her life and involvement in a civil lawsuit (1286) provides clues about the realities of labor in a medieval town for a woman, of the inequities she faced and the resources she had for redress. ❖ See also *Women in World History.*

PATMORE, Sharon (1963—). Australian field-hockey player. Born Mar 12, 1963, in Australia. ❖ At Seoul Olympics, won a gold medal in team competition (1988).

PATON WALSH, Jill (1937—). British children's writer and novelist. Name variations: Gillian Paton Walsh. Born Gillian Honoinne Mary Bliss, April 29, 1937, in London, England; dau. of John Llewellyn Bliss and Patricia Dubern Bliss; attended St. Michael's Convent, North Finchley, and St. Anne's College, Oxford; m. Antony Edmund Paton Walsh, 1961 (sep.); children: 1 son, 2 daughters. ❖ Best-known for her children's books, taught English at Enfield Girls' Grammar School in Middlesex (1959–62); was a visiting faculty member of the Center for Children's Literature, Simmons College, Boston (1978–86); served as Gertrude Clarke Whittall lecturer at Library of Congress (1978) and as a Whitbread Prize judge (1984); with John Rowe Townsend, founded Green Bay Publications, a small specialist imprint in Cambridge (1986); works include *Hengest's Tale* (1966), *Goldengrove* (1972), *The Island Sunrise: Prehistoric Britain* (1975), *Persian Gold* (1978), *Babylon* (1981), *A Parcel of Patterns* (1983), *Torch* (1987), *Can I Play Jenny Jones* (1990), *The Wyndham Case* (1993), *A Piece of Justice* (1995), and *A Desert in Bohemia* (2000). Won Book World Festival Award for *Fireweed* (1970), Whitbread Prize for *The Emperor's Winding Sheet* (1974), Boston Globe-Horn Book Award for *Unleaving* (1976), and Universe Prize for *A Parcel of Patterns* (1984); her novel *Knowledge of Angels* was shortlisted for Booker Prize (1994); made CBE (1996); elected fellow of Royal Society of Literature.

PATOULIDOU, Paraskevi (1965—). Greek runner. Name variations: Voula Patoulidou. Born Mar 29, 1965, at Tripotamon, Florina, Greece. ❖ At Barcelona Olympics, won a gold medal in the 100-meter hurdles (1992), the 1st woman in Greece to win an Olympic medal in track and field; competed in the long jump at Atlanta Olympics.

PATRASCOIU, Aneta (1957—). Romanian swimmer. Name variations: also seen as Anke and Anca Patrascoiu. Born Oct 17, 1957, in Romania. ❖ At Los Angeles Olympics, won a bronze medal in the 200-meter backstroke (1984).

PATRICK, Dorothy (1921–1987). Canadian actress. Born June 3, 1921, in St.-Boniface, Manitoba, Canada; died May 31, 1987, in Los Angeles, CA. ❖ Made over 30 films, including *Boy's Ranch, The Mighty McGurk, 711 Ocean Drive, Till the Clouds Roll By, Come to the Stable, Torch Song* and *The View from Pompey's Head.*

PATRICK, Gail (1911–1980). American actress and tv producer. Name variations: Gail Patrick Jackson. Born Margaret LaVelle Fitzpatrick, June 20, 1911, in Birmingham, Alabama; died July 6, 1980, in Hollywood, CA; m. Robert Howard Cobb, 1936 (div. 1940); m. Arnold Dean White, 1944 (div. 1945); m. Thomas Cornwall Jackson (literary agent), 1947 (div. 1969); m. John E. Welde Jr., 1974; children: (3rd m., adopted) daughter and son. ❖ Appeared in over 50 films, including *Cradle Song, Death Takes a Holiday, Murder in the Vanities, Artists and Models, Stage Door, My Favorite Wife, The Doctor Takes a Wife, Tales of Manhattan, Hit Parade of 1943, Up in Mabel's Room, Brewster's Millions, Claudia and David,* and *The Plainsman and the Lady*; was executive producer on the CBS-TV series "Perry Mason."

PATRICK, Mary Mills (1850–1940). American educator and missionary. Born Mar 10, 1850, in Canterbury, New Hampshire; died Feb 25, 1940, in Palo Alto, California; dau. of John Patrick (farmer) and Harriet (White) Patrick; graduate of Lyons Collegiate Institute, 1869; University of Iowa, MA, 1890; University of Bern, PhD, 1897. ❖ Appointed as a teacher at a mission school in Erzurum, in what is now eastern Turkey (1871); transferred to American High School for Girls in Constantinople (1875); became co-principal (1883) and then sole principal of the American High School (1889); converted the school into American College for Girls and served as its 1st president until her retirement (1890–1924); wrote *Sappho and the Island of Lesbos* (1912), *The Greek Skeptics* (1929) and *A Bosporus Adventure* (1934). ❖ See also memoir *Under Five Sultans* (1929); and *Women in World History.*

PATRICK, Ruth (1907—). American botanist and ecologist. Born Ruth Patrick, Nov 26, 1907, in Topeka, Kansas; dau. of Frank Patrick (lawyer) and Myrtle (Jetmore) Patrick; graduate of Coker College in SC, 1929; University of Virginia, MS in botany, 1931, PhD, 1934; m. Charles Hodge IV, 1931; Lewis H. Van Dusen Jr., 1995; children: (1st m.) 1. ❖ Cofounder of field of limnology, founded Estuarine Laboratory on Chesapeake Bay, MD, to study coastal ecosystems (1947); created (1947), directed (1947–73), and became curator of the limnology department, formerly Environmental Research Division, called The Patrick Center for Environmental Research (1983); served as board of trustees chair (1973–76) and later honorary chair of Academy of Natural Sciences in Philadelphia; took post of adjunct professor at University of Pennsylvania (1970); wrote *Diatoms of the United States* (1966) with Charles Reimer; proved that diatoms indicate freshwater pollution levels, and invented diatometer; advocated study of ecological communities rather than focusing on individual species to evaluate pollution levels; became 1st woman and 1st environmentalist to serve on board of du Pont; elected to National Academy of Sciences (1970); served as president of American Society of Naturalists (1975–77); created *Rivers of the United States,* a multivolume series (1994). Received Botanical Society of America's Award of Merit (1971), American Philosophical Society's Benjamin Franklin Award (1993), American Society of Limnology and Oceanography's Lifetime Achievement Award (1996) and National Medal of Science (1996).

PATRICK, Sandra (1962—). *See Farmer-Patrick, Sandra.*

PATRIE, Béatrice (1957—). French judge and politician. Name variations: Beatrice Patrie. Born May 12, 1957, in Lorient, France. ❖ Served as judicial officer at the Ministry of Justice (1983), judge at the Paris Regional Court (1989), president of the Saint-Quentin regional court (1997), secretary-general of the Association of Judicial Officers (1990), then its president (1992); as a European Socialist, elected to 5th European Parliament (1999–2004).

PATTEN, Dorothy (1905–1975). American stage, tv, and film actress. Born 1905; died April 11, 1975, in Westhampton, NY; lived with Cheryl Crawford (producer-director). ❖ Best remembered for role in the film *Botany Bay.*

PATTEN, Luana (1938–1996). American actress. Born July 6, 1938, in Long Beach, CA; died May 1, 1996, in Long Beach; m. John Smith (actor), 1960 (div. 1964). ❖ Made film debut as a child in a featured role in Disney's *Song of the South* (1947); other films include *So Dear to My Heart, The Little Shepherd of Kingdom Come* and *Home from the Hill.*

PATTEN, Marguerite (1915—). English home economist and cookery writer. Name variations: (stage name) Marguerite Eve. Born Marguerite Brown, Nov 4, 1915, in England; m. Bob Patten, 1943 (died 1997); children: Judith. ❖ Known throughout Britain for her books and tv cooking shows, began career as a senior food advisor for the Ministry of Food, demonstrating how families could survive during WWII when food was limited (1942–43); was featured on BBC's "Kitchen Front" (1944); led an advice bureau at London's Harrods for the Ministry of Food (1947–51); was a frequent visitor to Radio 4's "Woman's Hour" (1946–2005) and BBC TV's "Designed for Women" (1947–60); tested and made recipes sent by viewers for BBC's "Cookery Club" (1956–61); sold more than 17 million books and 500 million cookery cards; published over 165 books and cookbooks, including *The Victory Cookbook* (1995), *What's Cooking* (1999), *Marguerite Patten's Century of British Cooking* (1999) and (with Jeannette Ewin) *Eat to Beat Arthritis* (2001). Named Officer of the Order of the British Empire (1991).

PATTEN, Mary Ann (1837–1861). American clipper ship commander. Born 1837 in Boston, MA; died Mar 17, 1861; m. Joshua Adams Patten, April 1, 1853; children: 1 son. ❖ Learned to navigate on her 1st clipper voyage aboard *Neptune's Car* (1855); with husband, embarked from NY in *Neptune's Car* for voyage around Cape Horn to San Francisco (1856); when he fell into coma en route, became 1st woman to navigate a clipper ship (1856). Mary Patten Infirmary at US Merchant Marine Academy, King's Point, NY, was named in her honor, and the Captain Mary Ann Patten Memorial was established at Piers Park, East Boston, MA. ❖ See also (novel) Deborah Mcroff, *Captain My Captain* (Inheritance, 1992).

PATTERSON, Alicia (1906–1963). American newspaper editor and publisher. Born Alicia Patterson in Chicago, Illinois, Oct 15, 1906; died of bleeding ulcers, July 2, 1963; dau. of Joseph Medill Patterson (founder of *New York Daily News*) and Alice (Higinbotham) Patterson; sister of Josephine Patterson Albright (who wrote a column for *Newsday*) and Elinor Patterson Baker; niece of Eleanor Medill Patterson (1881–1948); m. James Simpson Jr. (director of Marshall Field & Co.), 1920s (div. 1 year later); m. Joseph W. Brooks, 1931 (div. 1939); m. Harry F.

Guggenheim, 1939. ❖ Worked as a cub reporter on father's newspaper, *New York Daily News* (1927–28); joined the staff of family-owned *Liberty* magazine; became a transport pilot (1931), setting the women's New York to Philadelphia air record; served as literary critic for *Daily News* (1932–43); came to prominence as founder, editor, and publisher of Long Island's successful tabloid *Newsday*. ❖ See also *Women in World History*.

PATTERSON, Audrey (1926–1996). African-American runner. Name variations: Mickey Patterson; Audrey Patterson-Tyler. Born Sept 27, 1926, in New Orleans, LA; died Sept 1996 after a heart attack in San Diego, CA; attended Tennessee State. ❖ Won a bronze medal in the 200 meters at London Olympics (1948), the 1st African-American woman medalist in the history of the Games; coached more than 5,000 youths in track and field in Southern California.

PATTERSON, Carly (1988—). American gymnast. Born Feb 4, 1988, in Baton Rouge, LA. ❖ Won US Jr. championships (2002); won team World championship (2003); won World Cup in Hawaii for beam and floor exercise (2004); won a gold medal for indiv. all-around and silver medals for beam and team all-around at Athens Olympics (2004).

PATTERSON, Catherine (1842–1935). *See Carran, Catherine.*

PATTERSON, Cissy (1881–1948). *See Patterson, Eleanor Medill.*

PATTERSON, Eleanor Medill (1881–1948). American editor and publisher. Name variations: Cissy Patterson; Eleanor M. Gizycka. Born Elinor Josephine Patterson, Nov 7, 1881, in Chicago, Illinois; changed name early to Eleanor Medill Patterson; died July 24, 1948, in Washington, DC; dau. of Robert Wilson Patterson Jr. (newspaper editor and publisher of *Chicago Tribune*) and Elinor Medill (heiress and socialite and dau. of Joseph Medill, owner of *Chicago Tribune*); sister of Joseph (Joe) Medill Patterson (founder of *New York Daily News*); aunt of Alicia Patterson (1906–1963, founder of *Newsday*); attended Miss (Sarah) Porter's school; m. Count Josef Gizycki (cavalry officer and playboy), April 14, 1904 (div. June 1917); m. Elmer Schlesinger (corporation lawyer), April 11, 1925 (died Feb 1929); children: (1st m.) Leonora Felicia Gizycka (b. 1905, who was married to Drew Pearson, 1925–28). ❖ Controversial editor and publisher of *Washington Times-Herald* who was one of America's leading press magnates, the 1st woman to possess such status; published 1st novel, *Glass Houses* (1926), followed by *Fall Flight* (1928), a fictionalized account of her youth and 1st marriage; assumed editorship of *Washington Herald* (1930) and revamped the entire operation; purchased the morning *Washington Herald* and the evening *Washington Times* (1939), then combined the papers into the round-the-clock *Washington Times-Herald*, making it the 1st multiple-edition daily newspaper in US. ❖ See also Paul F. Healy, *Cissy: The Biography of Eleanor M. "Cissy" Patterson* (Doubleday, 1966); Alice Albright Hoge, *Cissy Patterson* (Random House, 1966); Ralph G. Martin, *Cissy* (Simon & Schuster, 1979); John Tebbel, *An American Dynasty* (Doubleday, 1947); and *Women in World History*.

PATTERSON, Elizabeth (1785–1879). *See Bonaparte, Elizabeth Patterson.*

PATTERSON, Elizabeth (1874–1966). American actress. Born Mary Elizabeth Patterson, Nov 22, 1874, in Savannah, TN; died Jan 31, 1966, in Los Angeles, CA. ❖ Character actress on stage, screen and tv, made Broadway debut in *A Midsummer Night's Dream* (1910); other plays include *The Intimate Strangers, Peer Gynt, An Ideal Husband, Candida, Rope* and *His and Hers*; appeared in over 100 films, generally as the mother, including *Tobacco Road, Kiss the Boys Goodbye, Her Cardboard Lover, My Sister Eileen, Lady on a Train, Little Women, Pal Joey, Intruder in the Dust, Bright Leaf* and *The Oregon Trail*.

PATTERSON, Elizabeth J. (1939—). American politician. Born Elizabeth Johnston, Nov 18, 1939, in Columbia, South Carolina; dau. of Olin D. Johnston (1896–1965, former governor of South Carolina as well as US senator, 1945–65) and Gladys Atkinson Johnston; Columbia College, Columbia, South Carolina, BA in political science, 1961; graduate study at University of South Carolina, 1961–62; m. Dwight Fleming Patterson Jr., 1967; children: Dwight Fleming DeWitt Patterson; Catherine Leigh Patterson. ❖ Served as recruiting officer for Peace Corps (1962–64) and VISTA (1965–67); was director of a Head Start program (1967–68) and staff assistant for Representative James R. Mann (1969–70); served on Spartanburg Co. Council (1975–76); was a member of South Carolina senate (1979–86); elected as a Democrat to 100th and to 2 succeeding Congresses (Jan 3, 1987–Jan 3, 1993); sat on Committee on Veterans' Affairs, the Committee on Banking, Finance and Urban Affairs, and the Select Committee on Hunger. ❖ See also *Women in World History*.

PATTERSON, Francine (1947—). American psychologist. Name variations: Penny Patterson. Born Francine Patterson, 1947, in Chicago, IL; dau. of C.H. Patterson (professor of educationalpsychology at University of Illinois); University of Illinois, BA in psychology, 1970; Stanford University, PhD in developmental psychology, 1979; lived with Ronald Cohn. ❖ Known for teaching American Sign Language (ASL or Ameslan) to captive-born lowland gorillas Michael and Koko (who acquired a vocabulary of over 1,000 words), began teaching ASL to Koko at San Francisco Zoo (1972); with Ronald Cohn, established The Gorilla Foundation (1976), serving as its president and research director, as well as editor-in-chief of journal, *Gorilla*; raised funds for The Maui Ape Preserve in Hawaii; was adjunct psychology professor at Santa Clara University. ❖ See also Emily Hahn, *Eve and the Apes* (Weidenfeld & Nicholson, 1988).

PATTERSON, Hannah (1879–1937). American suffragist. Born Hannah Jane Patterson, Nov 5, 1879, in Smithton, PA; died Aug 21, 1937, in Pittsburgh, PA; dau. of John Gilfillan Patterson (banker) and Harriet (McCune) Patterson. ❖ Worked with Consumers' League of Western Pennsylvania and the Allegheny Co. Committee on School Legislation; lobbied for suffrage amendment to the Pennsylvania constitution (1915); headed a state Woman Suffrage Party (PA); elected as corresponding secretary to National American Woman Suffrage Association (1915); appointed member (1917), then associate director of the field division (1918), of Woman's Committee of the Council of National Defense by President Woodrow Wilson; headed women's department of J.Y. Holmes & Co., a Pittsburgh brokerage firm (1920s); served as 1st woman director of bank in West Newton; was an active member of Pennsylvania Federation of Republican Women; managed successful election campaign of friend Sara Soffel to local judgeship (1931); was asked, but declined, to run for Congress.

PATTERSON, Mrs. Jefferson (1905–2002). *See Breckinridge, Mary Marvin.*

PATTERSON, Louise (1901–1999). *See Thompson, Louise.*

PATTERSON, Mickey (1926–1996). *See Patterson, Audrey.*

PATTERSON, Marie (1934—). British labor activist. Born Constance Marie Abraham, 1934, in UK; m. Thomas Patterson, 1960 (died 1976). ❖ Became member of Transport and General Workers' Union (1957) and woman's officer of union (1963–76); became member of General Council of Trades Union Congress and served as chair (1974–75, 1977); was president of Confederation of Shipbuilding and Engineering Unions (1977–78) and member of various industrial training boards; served as director of Remploy (1966–87). Awarded OBE (1973) and CBE (1978).

PATTERSON, Martha Johnson (1828–1901). White House hostess. Born Martha Johnson, 1828; died 1901; dau. of Eliza McCardle Johnson (1810–1876) and Andrew Johnson (1808–1875, 17th president of US, 1865–69); sister of Mary Johnson Stover (1832–1883); m. David Trotter Patterson (1818–1891, a judge of the circuit court of Tennessee and later US senator), in 1885; children: 2. ❖ Acted as White House hostess for her ailing mother, refurbishing the mansion after the wear and tear of the Civil War years. ❖ See also *Women in World History*.

PATTERSON, Mary Jane (1840–1894). African-American educator. Born 1840 near Raleigh, North Carolina; died 1894; dau. of Henry Patterson (mason and former slave) and Emeline Patterson; graduate of Oberlin College, 1862, the 1st African-American woman to graduate from college in US. ❖ Taught in Philadelphia (1862–69); appointed to Washington, DC, school system (1869); served as principal of Washington Colored High School (1871–72, 1873–84). ❖ See also *Women in World History*.

PATTERSON, Mary Marvin (1905–2002). *See Breckinridge, Mary Marvin.*

PATTERSON, Nan (c. 1882—). American dancer and actress tried for murder. Name variations: Nan Randolph Patterson. Born c. 1882; married. ❖ Was a young dancer-actress in popular musical *Floradora*; though married, began an affair with Caesar Young, a wealthy book-maker, who was also married; divorced her husband and was bankrolled by Young; was traveling in a hansom cab with Young on the day he was to leave for an overseas tour with his wife (June 4, 1904), but Young never left the cab alive (he died of a gunshot wound); claimed Caesar had shot himself, but was charged with murder; saw 1st trial result in mistrial, the 2nd in hung jury (Dec 1904); released after jury was deadlocked in 3rd trial (April 1905). Patterson's case generated enormous press; because of a sympathetic press, public support was in Patterson's favor and thousands cheered her eventual release.

PATTERSON, Penny (1947—). *See Patterson, Francine.*

PATTI, Adelina (1843–1919). Spanish-born soprano. Name variations: Marchioness de Caux; Baroness Cederström or Cederstrom. Born Adelina Juana Maria Patti, Feb 19, 1843, in Madrid, Spain; died Sept 27, 1919, at Craig-y-Nos Castle, Brecknockshire, Wales; dau. of Salvatore Patti (Italian singer) and Caterina Chiesa Barili-Patti (Spanish singer known before her marriage as Signora Barili); younger sister of Carlotta Patti (1835–1889), singer, and Amelia Patti, who married Maurice Strakosch; m. Louis de Cahuzac, marquis de Caux, 1868 (div. 1885); m. Ernesto Nicolini (tenor), 1885 (died 1898); m. Baron Rolf Cederström, 1899. ❖ The most renowned singer in Europe and US for over 30 years, moved to NY at age 4; was recognized as a child prodigy at 7; gave debut concert at NYC's Tripler Hall at 8; went on a 3-year tour of US cities (1851–54); at 16, made a critically praised debut in title role of *Lucia di Lammermoor* at New York Academy of Music (1859); toured eastern US and West Indies (1859–61); went abroad to perform in *La sonnambula* at Covent Garden in London (1861), performing there every autumn for next 25 years; remained on tour in Europe continuously for 20 years, playing to crowded houses in Berlin, Brussels, Amsterdam, Vienna, Paris, and across Italy, choosing operatic roles from light comedy, which she preferred, to tragedy; did a concert tour on return to NY (1881), followed by 2 operatic tours of US; gave farewell performance at Metropolitan Opera (1887); went into semi-retirement on estate in Wales; began last operatic tour at Carnegie Hall (1903); made formal farewell appearance at Albert Hall in London (1906); also made numerous recordings. ❖ See also John F. Cone, *Adelina Patti: Queen of Hearts* (Amadeus, 1993); Herman Klein, *The Reign of Patti* (Century, 1920); L. Lauw, *Fourteen Years with Adelina Patti* (1884); and *Women in World History.*

PATTISON, Dorothy W. (1832–1878). English surgical nurse. Name variations: Sister Dora. Born Dorothy Wyndlow Pattison, 1832; died 1878; sister of Mark Pattison, scholar and writer who was once married to Emily Dilke (1840–1904). ❖ Entered a Church of England Sisterhood of the Good Samaritan (1864), adopting the name Sister Dora; was a surgical nurse and had sole charge of a new hospital in Walsall (1867–77).

PATTON, Abigail Jemima (1829–1892). *See Hutchinson, Abigail.*

PATTON, Frances Gray (1906–2000). American writer. Born Frances Gray Lilly, Mar 19, 1906, in Raleigh, North Carolina; died Mar 28, 2000, in Durham, NC; dau. of Robert Lilly (newspaper editor) and Mary S. MacRae (Gray) Lilly; attended Trinity College (now Duke University); graduate of University of North Carolina; m. Lewis Patton (English professor), 1927; children: Robert, Mary, and Susannah. ❖ Earned a place in American letters through her single novel, *Good Morning, Miss Dove* (1954), and her numerous short stories, which appeared in *The New Yorker* and other major magazines (1940s–50s) and were collected in several volumes; taught creative writing at Duke and University of North Carolina. ❖ See also *Women in World History.*

PAUAHI, Princess (1831–1884). *See Bishop, Bernice Pauahi.*

PAUCA, Simona (1969—). Romanian gymnast. Born Sept 19, 1969, in Azuga, Romania; m. Gheorghe Rus (chair of Castrum Corp.). ❖ Placed 1st all-around at Balkan championships (1983) and Arthur Gander (1984); at Los Angeles Olympics, won a bronze medal in indiv. all-around and gold medals in the balance beam and team all-around (1984).

PAUKER, Ana (c. 1893–1960). Romanian politician. Pronunciation: POW-ker. Born Ana Rabinovici in Moldavia in northern Romania, 1893 or 1894; died in Bucharest, June 1960; dau. of a Jewish butcher who held the status of rabbi in his community; attended medical school in Switzerland for a period beginning 1915; m. Marcel Pauker, fellow Romanian student (died, probably 1937); children: 3. ❖ Foreign minister of Romania and a leading Communist official, who played a crucial role in Eastern Europe in the period after WWII; studied for a period in Switzerland (1915–21); joined Communist Party (1921); elected to Central Committee (1922); imprisoned (late 1920s); in exile in Moscow (1931–34); imprisoned in Romania (1935); husband executed in Soviet Union (c. 1937); released from prison at request of Soviet Union (1940); reentered Romania with the Red Army and led the way in establishing a Communist government in Romania (1944); led Communist demonstrations in Bucharest (1944–45); appointed foreign minister of Romania, the 1st woman to serve as Cabinet minister in charge of a European country's international relations, became a key figure in her country's government and helped to organize the Warsaw Pact (1947); attacked the heretical leadership of the Yugoslav Communist Party (1948); named vice-premier (1949); treated in the Soviet Union for breast cancer (1950); lost her position in the Politburo, the top-ranking body of the Communist Party (1952); vanished from the spotlight. ❖ See also Robert Levy, *Ana Pauker: The Rise and Fall of a Jewish Communist* (U. of California Press, 2001); and *Women in World History.*

PAUL, Alice (1885–1977). American suffragist. Born Alice Paul, Jan 11, 1885, in Moorestown, New Jersey; died in Moorestown, July 9, 1977; dau. of William Mickle Paul (banker and businessman) and Tacie Parry Paul; Swarthmore College, BS in biology, 1905; University of Pennsylvania, MA in sociology, 1907; University of Pennsylvania, PhD in sociology, 1912; Washington College, LLB, 1922; American University, LLM, 1927; American University, DCL, 1928; never married. ❖ Relentless women's rights activist who led the final push for suffrage and wrote the Equal Rights Amendment; studied and served as a social worker in England (1906–10), where she joined the Women's Social and Political Union (WSPU) and was thrice jailed; returned to US to found the Congressional Union (CU), an auxiliary of National American Woman Suffrage Association (NAWSA, 1913); at odds over strategy, broke with NAWSA to found National Woman's Party (NWP, 1914) which utilized militant, flamboyant civil disobedience tactics to dramatize the suffrage cause; after picketing the White House daily for months, was arrested, force fed, and ultimately put in a psychopathic ward in an effort to portray her as insane (1917); health suffered considerably from her prison experiences, especially the hunger strikes; wrote the Equal Rights Amendment (1923); returned to Europe as chair of Woman's Research Federation (1927–37), where she founded World Women's Party; lobbied League of Nations on women's rights issues (1930s); worked the rest of her life to remove all legal restrictions on women's rights; protested at rallies for women's rights and against the Vietnam War while in her 80s. ❖ See also Christine A. Lunardini, *From Equal Suffrage to Equal Rights: Alice Paul and the National Woman's Party, 1910–1928* (New York U. Press, 1986); and *Women in World History.*

PAUL, Annette (1863–1952). New Zealand Salvation Army officer and social worker. Born Nov 4, 1863, in Auckland, New Zealand; died April 19, 1952, in Auckland; dau. of James Paul (military officer) and Annette (McKellar) Paul. ❖ Attended early meetings of Salvation Army movement in Wellington (1883); became secretary for Rescue Affairs for Salvation Army (1890), then the 1st woman in New Zealand to hold staff rank (1894); rose through ranks to brigadier by 1902; helped establish many services provided to women and families in rescue missions, and was appointed to administer women's social work in South Australia (1902); resigned from Salvation Army (1911). ❖ See also *Dictionary of New Zealand Biography* (Vol. 2).

PAUL, Annette (1944—). *See Av-Paul, Annette.*

PAUL, Christina Allan (1863–1932). *See Massey, Christina Allan.*

PAUL, Joanna (1945–2003). New Zealand poet, playwright and painter. Born Dec 14, 1945, in Hamilton, New Zealand; died May 29, 2003; dau. of Blackwood Paul and Janet Paul; m. Jeffrey Harris, 1979 (div. 1984); m. Peter Harrison, 2003. ❖ Works include *Imogen* (1978) and *Unwrapping the Body* (1980); had two shows of art work, *A Chronology* and *Resisting Foreclosure* (1983); also made experimental films, practiced photography, and wrote criticism.

PAUL, Josephine Bay (1900–1962). *See Bay, Josephine Perfect.*

PAUL-FOULDS, June (1934—). English runner. Name variations: June Paul. Born May 13, 1934, in UK. ❖ Won a bronze medal at Helsinki Olympics (1952) and a silver medal at Melbourne Olympics (1956), both in 4 x 100-meter relay.

PAULA (347–404). Roman founder. Born 347; died in 404; dau. of patricians, Rogatus and Blesilla; through her Hellenic father, traced her roots back to Agamemnon, while through her mother, was related to the great Scipios and Gracchi of Republican fame; m. Toxotius; children: 4 daughters, Blesilla (d. 384), Paula the Younger (d. 395), Eustochium (c. 368–c. 419), and Rufina; 1 son, Toxotius. ❖ Roman widow and associate of Jerome who founded 2 influential religious communities in Bethlehem; was raised a Christian; though married at 15 to a pagan, nevertheless knew a happy marriage; after husband died (378), embraced a life of chastity, kept in close contact with the Christian community of Marcella (325–410), and allowed her daughter, Eustochium, to take up residence within that community; also began to distribute largesse among the poor, and personally began to eschew outward manifestations of wealth, coming to prefer to dress in sackcloth; met Jerome, whose devout disciple she became; began withdrawal from the secular world—a process which was accelerated by the visit to Rome of the eastern bishops, Paulinus and Epiphanius (382); acted as host for Epiphanius during his stay; with Jerome and Eustochium as companions, toured Cyprus, Antioch, Jerusalem, Bethlehem and Alexandria (385); returned to Bethlehem (late 386) where she established 2 religious communities near the site of Jesus' nativity (389); based community rules upon those of Pachomius: poverty and mortification of the flesh were embraced, as was a life divided among physical labor, study and prayer, though isolation was neither attempted nor realized her foundations flourished and her fame grew in association with that of Jerome, for it was there that he produced his famous edition of the Bible, a work destined to have profound impact upon the medieval church. ❖ See also *Women in World History.*

PAULA, Ana (1972—). See Connelly, Ana Paula.

PAULEY, Jane (1950—). American tv newscaster. Born Margaret Jane Pauley, Oct 31, 1950, in Indianapolis, IN; dau. of Richard and Mary Pauley; attended Indiana University; m. Garry Trudeau (creator of Doonesbury), 1980; children: twins Ross and Rachel (b. 1983); Thomas (b. 1986). ❖ In tv broadcasting for over 30 years, began career as a news anchor in Chicago; came to prominence and popularity as co-host on the "Today" show (1976–89), followed by "Dateline NBC" (1992–2003); launched "The Jane Pauley Show" (2004).

PAULI, Hertha (1909–1973). Austrian-born writer. Born Hertha Ernestine Pauli in Vienna, Austria, Sept 4, 1909; died in Bay Shore, Long Island, New York, Feb 9, 1973; dau. of Wolfgang Pauli (Jewish physician and biochemist) and Bertha Schütz Pauli (Jewish writer); sister of Wolfgang Pauli (who won the Nobel Prize in physics, 1945); studied drama and acting at Vienna's Academy of Arts; m. Ernest B. Ashton (Ernst Basch), 1951. ❖ Became a member of Lobetheater in Breslau, Germany (today Wroclaw, Poland), then joined Max Reinhardt's Deutsches Theater until the anti-Semitism of the Third Reich ended her German career and she was forced to return to Vienna (1933); worked as a freelance writer and established a literary agency, Österreichische Korrespondenz; published *Toni: Ein Frauenleben für Ferdinand Raimund* (Toni: A Woman's Life for Ferdinand Raimund, 1936), a historical novel set in 19th century, followed by a biography of Bertha von Suttner, *Nur eine Frau* (Only a Woman, 1937), which was banned in Nazi Germany; at the time of the anschluss, fled to Paris (1938), then escaped to NY with the help of Varian Fry (1940); published *Alfred Nobel: Dynamite King, Architect of Peace* (1942) and a book for young readers, *Silent Night: The Story of a Song* (1943); went on to produce a large number of children's books, including *The Most Beautiful House and Other Stories* (1949), *The Golden Door* (1949), *Lincoln's Little Correspondent* (1952), *Three Is a Family* (1955), *Bernadette and the Lady* (1956), *The First Easter Rabbit* (1961), *The Two Trumpeters of Vienna* (1961), *Handel and the Messiah Story* (1968) and *Pietro and Brother Francis* (1971); also wrote *I Lift My Lamp: The Way of a Symbol* (1948), *Cry of the Heart* (1957), *Jugend nachher* (Youth Afterwards, 1959) and *The Secret of Sarajevo* (1965). Awarded Silver Medal of Honor by Republic of Austria (1967). ❖ See also autobiography *Break of Time* (1972); and *Women in World History.*

PAULINA. Variant of Paula.

PAULINE OF SAXE-WEIMAR (1852–1904). Grand duchess of Saxe-Weimar. Born July 25, 1852; died May 17, 1904; dau. of Augusta of Wurttemberg (1826–1898) and Hermann Henry, prince of Saxe-Weimar; m. Charles Augustus, grand duke of Saxe-Weimar, Aug 26, 1873; children: William Ernest (b. 1876), grand duke of Saxe-Weimar; Bernard Charles (b. 1878).

PAULINE OF WURTTEMBERG (1800–1873). Queen of Wurttemberg. Born Sept 4, 1800; died Mar 10, 1873; dau. of Louis Frederick Alexander, duke of Wurttemberg, and Henrietta of Nassau-Weilburg (1780–1857); became 3rd wife of William I (1781–1864), king of Wurttemberg (r. 1816–1864), on April 15, 1820; children: Catherine Frederica of Wurttemberg (1821–1898), who m. her cousin Frederick); Charles I (1823–1891), king of Wurttemberg (r. 1864–1891); Augusta of Wurttemberg (1826–1898), who m. Hermann of Saxe-Weimar).

PAULINE OF WURTTEMBERG (1810–1856). Duchess of Nassau. Born Pauline Frederica Marie, Feb 25, 1810; died July 7, 1856; dau. of Catherine Charlotte of Hildburghausen (1787–1847) and Paul of Wurttemberg; m. William George (1792–1839), duke of Nassau, on April 23, 1829; children: Helen of Nassau (1831–1888); Nicholas

of Nassau (1832–1905), who m. Natalia Alexandrovna Pushkin, countess Merenberg); Sophia of Nassau (1836–1913).

PAULINE OF WURTTEMBERG (1877–1965). Princess of Wied. Born Pauline Olga Helene Emma, Dec 19, 1877; died in 1965; dau. of Maria of Waldeck (1857–1882) and William II (1848–1921), king of Wurttemberg (r. 1891–1918, abdicated); m. Frederick William, 6th prince of Wied, on Oct 29, 1898; children: Herman William (b. 1899); Dietrich William (b. 1901).

PAULL, Stephanie (1916–2006). See Massen, Osa.

PAULO, Blanka. See Paulu, Blanka.

PAULSEN, Marit (1939—). Swedish writer and politician. Born Nov 24, 1939, in Oslo, Norway. ❖ Was a columnist and leader-writer for 29 years; member of the People's Party Executive; as a member of the European Liberal, Democrat and Reform Party, elected to 5th European Parliament (1999–2004); also wrote 23 books, films, and plays. Awarded the National Order of Merit (France, 1998), His Majesty's Medal, blue ribbon (1993), and the highest distinction of the Royal Academy of Agriculture and Forestry (1997).

PAULU, Blanka (1954—). Czech cross-country skier. Name variations: Blanka Paulo. Born 1954 in Czechoslovakia. ❖ Won a silver medal for 4 x 5 km relay at Sarajevo Olympics (1984).

PAULZE, Marie Anne Pierrette (1758–1836). See Lavoisier, Marie.

PAUSIN, Ilse (1919—). Austrian pairs skater. Born Feb 7, 1919, in Austria. ❖ With brother Erich Pausin, won 5 silver medals at World championships (1935–39) and a silver medal at Garmisch-Partenkirchen Olympics (1936).

PAVAN, Marisa (1932—). Italian actress. Born Marisa Pierangeli, June 19, 1932, in Cagliari, Sardinia, Italy; sister of Pier Angeli (actress); m. Jean-Pierre Aumont (actor). ❖ Made film debut in *What Price Glory* (1952), followed by *Down Three Dark Streets, Diane, The Man in the Gray Flannel Suit, The Midnight Story, Solomon and Sheba* and *Antoine et Sébastian,* among others; on tv, appeared as Chantal DuBujak on "Ryan's Hope" (1985–89). Nominated for Oscar for Best Supporting Actress for *The Rose Tattoo* (1955).

PAVICEVIC, Zorica (1956—). Yugoslavian handball player. Born May 1956 in Yugoslavia. ❖ At Los Angeles Olympics, won a gold medal in team competition (1984).

PAVLINA, Yevgenia (1979—). Belarusian rhythmic gymnast. Born July 20, 1979, in Minsk, Belarus. ❖ Placed 3rd in all-around at Medico Cup (1993); won International of Ljubljana (1995), San Francisco Invitational (1996), and Schmiden International (1998); at European championships, won a silver medal for all-around, bronze with ribbon, and team gold (1998); placed 3rd at Goodwill Games.

PAVLOVA, Anna (1881–1931). Russian ballerina. Born Anna Matveevna Pavlova, Jan 31, 1881 (o.s.), in St. Petersburg; died of pneumonia in The Hague, Netherlands, Jan 23, 1931; illeg. dau. of Lazar Jacovlevich Poliakov (aristocratic Jewish banker) and Liubov Fedorovna Pavlova (laundress); attended Imperial Ballet School, 1891–99; reputedly married Victor Dandré, in 1914; no children. ❖ One of the greatest classical Russian ballerinas of the 20th century, was responsible for popularizing ballet throughout the world; was a member of the Maryinsky Theater company (1899–1913) becoming 2nd soloist (1902), 1st soloist (1903), ballerina (1905), prima ballerina (1906); danced with Diaghilev's Ballets Russes in Paris (1909) and London (1911); formed her own company, Les Ballets d'Anna Pavlova (1912), which toured throughout the world until her death; lived in London (1912–31); best known for her roles in *La Bayadère, Giselle, Bacchanale* and *The Dying Swan*; also appeared in the film *The Dumb Girl of Portici* (1915). ❖ See also autobiography *Pages from My Life* (1912); Oleg Kerensky, *Anna Pavlova* (Hamish Hamilton, 1973); Keith Money, *Anna Pavlova: Her Life and Art* (Knopf, 1982); John and Roberta Lazzarini, *Pavlova: Repertoire of a Legend* (Schirmer, 1980); and *Women in World History.*

PAVLOVA, Anna (1987—). Russian gymnast. Born Sept 6, 1987, in Orekhovo-Zuevo, Russia; dau. of Natalia Pavlova (gymnast and her coach). ❖ At World Cups, had 3 1st place finishes in beam, 1 in floor exercise and 1 in vault (2003); won bronze medals for vault and team all-around at Athens Olympics (2004).

PAVLOVA, Irina (1940—). See Yegorova, Irina.

PAVLOVA, Karolina (1807–1893). Russian poet, translator, and 19th-century belletrist. Born Karolina Karlovna Jaenisch in Russian city of Yaroslavl, 1807; died in Dresden, 1893; dau. of Karl Jaenisch (served at School of Medicine and Surgery in Moscow); m. Nikolai Pavlov (writer), Dec 1836. ❖ Talented poet and translator, who composed verse in Russian, French, and German and translated freely between these languages, and whose influential literary translations generally move from Russian into French or German, also had a certain knowledge of Spanish, Italian, Swedish and Polish; wrote original works, translations, and maintained a literary salon; issued 1st collection of poetry, *Nordlicht* (1833), containing the translations of numerous Russian poets into German; composed the largest of her works, the multigenre piece *A Double Life* (1844–48), which combined both a prose narrative and abundant lyric verse; concurrently, was also actively engaged in lyric poetry, composing some of her most memorable and valued pieces; wrote another work of substantial length, the narrative poem *Quadrille;* after husband squandered her wealth, moved to Dresden (1858), and lived there for remainder of her life; released a collection *Poems* (1863); began a long professional relationship with writer Alexei K. Tolstoy, translating large portions of his work into French and German; was considered the preeminent Russian woman poet until the emergence of Symbolism in the 1890s. ❖ See also *Women in World History.*

PAVLOVA, Nadezhda (1956—). Soviet ballet dancer. Name variations: Nadeshda Pavlova; Nadezhda Vasilyevna Pavlova. Born 1956 in Tsheboksari, Russia. ❖ Trained at Perm State Ballet and performed with that company until 1975; joined Bolshoi Ballet (1975), where she performed as a soloist in *Giselle, Romeo and Juliet, The Stone Flower,* and others; toured over 40 countries; appeared in Soviet-American film *The Blue Bird* (1976); was artistic director of Nadezhada Pavlova's Ballet Company (1992–94), and Renaissance Ballet Company (1995); became a teacher at the Bolshoi. Awarded People's Artist of USSR (1984).

PAVLOVICH, Yaroslava. Belarusian rower. Born in Belarus. ❖ Won a bronze medal for coxed eights at Atlanta Olympics (1996).

PAVLOW, Muriel (1921—). English stage and screen actress. Born June 27, 1921, in Lee, Kent, England; m. Derek Farr. ❖ Made London stage debut as a child in *Oedipus Rex* (1936), followed by *Victoria Regina, April Clouds, Dear Octopus, Dear Brutus, Old Acquaintance, There Shall Be No Night, The Gainsborough Girls, Odd Man In, Critic's Choice,* and a season at Shakespeare Memorial Theatre; made screen debut in *A Romance in Flanders* (1936); other films include *Doctor in the House, Simon and Laura, Doctor at Large, Rooney, Meet Miss Marple, Whirlpool* and *Murder, She Said.*

PAWLIK, Eva (1927–1983). Austrian figure skater. Born 1927 in Vienna, Austria; died 1983; earned doctorate in German and English at University of Vienna, 1954; married. ❖ Won a silver medal at St. Moritz Olympics and silver medals at the World and European championships (1948); won gold medal at European championship (1949); turned pro (1950) and joined the Vienna Ice Revue; retired from skating (1961); became the 1st female sportscaster of Austrian Broadcasting Corp (ORF); died 4 months after husband's death.

PAWLIKOWSKA, Maria (1891–1945). Polish poet and playwright. Name variations: Maria Kossak; Maria Pawlikowska-Jasnorzewska; Marii Pawlikowskiej-Jasnorzewskiej; Maria Jasnorzewska Pawlikowska. Born Maria Kossak in Cracow, Austrian Poland, Nov 24, 1891; died in exile in Manchester, England, July 9, 1945; dau. of Wojciech Kossak and granddau. of Juliusz Kossak (both celebrated painters); cousin of Zofia Kossak (1890–1968, writer); attended Cracow's Academy of Fine Arts; married 3 times; last husband was aviator Stefan Jasnorzewski. ❖ Now regarded one of Poland's most original modern poets, a highly controversial artist in her own lifetime, whose verse was considered infantile by some, while she was hailed as a major voice by others; published 1st volume of verse, *Niebieskie migdaly* (Blue Haze, 1922); published 11 more books of poetry, as well as one volume of lyrical prose (1922–39); major themes remained the same throughout her career: her preoccupation with youth, aging and the onset of old age, as well as her fears in the realms of love, death, and nature; also wrote a number of controversial plays (1930s); with pilot husband, fled Poland to escape the Nazis (Sept 1939); settled in Blackpool, England, where Polish aviators had their headquarters. ❖ See also *Women in World History.*

PAX (1859–1925). *See Cholmondeley, Mary.*

PAXINOU, Katina (1900–1973). Greek stage and film actress. Born Katina Konstantopoulou (also seen as Constantopoulos) in Piraeus,
Greece, Dec 17, 1900; died of cancer, Feb 22, 1973, in Athens; dau. of Basil Konstantopoulou; studied voice at Geneva Conservatoire; m. Ivannis Paxinou (div.); m. Alexis Minotis (actor and director), 1940; children: 1 daughter. ❖ Originally appeared in opera in Athens; made acting debut there in *La Femme Nue* (1924); joined Greek National Theatre, becoming leading actress in such roles as Clytemnestra in *Agamemnon* (1932), title role in *Anna Christie* (1932), Mrs. Alving in *Ghosts* (1934), Phaedra in *Hippolytus* (1937), Lady Windermere in *Lady Windermere's Fan* (1937), Goneril in *King Lear* (1938), and Mrs. Chevely in *An Ideal Husband* (1938); as Clytemnestra in *Electra,* made New York debut (1930) and London debut (1939); unable to return to Greece during WWII, appeared on Broadway in title role of *Hedda Gabler* (1942), and later as Bernarda in *The House of Bernarda Alba* (1951); films include *Hostages* (1943), *Confidential Agent* (1945), *Mourning Becomes Electra* (1947), *Prince of Foxes* (1949), *The Miracle* (1959), *Rocco e i suoi Fratelli (Rocco and His Brothers,* 1960), *Tante Zita (Zita,* 1968), and *Un Eté sauvage* (1972); with husband, established the Royal Theatre in Athens. Won Academy Award for performance in *For Whom the Bell Tolls* (1943). ❖ See also *Women in World History.*

PAYNE, Doris (1937–2004). *See Troy, Doris.*

PAYNE, Ethel (1911–1991). African-American journalist. Name variations: Ethel Lois Payne. Born Aug 14, 1911, in Chicago, Illinois; died May 4, 1991; dau. of William Payne (Pullman porter) and Bessie (Austin) Payne (Latin teacher); educated at Crane Junior College in Chicago and Garrett Institute; awarded degree from Medill School of Journalism at Northwestern University. ❖ An investigative reporter for some 40 years whom many of her peers called "The First Lady of the Black Press," was also the 1st African-American woman radio and tv commentator employed by a national network (CBS) and a passionate advocate of civil rights; was on the staff of *Chicago Defender* for 27 years; also wrote a nationally syndicated newspaper column. Professorship in journalism was established in her name at Fisk University. ❖ See also *Women in World History.*

PAYNE, Freda (1945—). American singer and actress. Born Freda Charcelia Payne, Sept 19, 1945, in Detroit, MI; sister of Scherrie Payne (singer with the Supremes); m. Gregory Abbott (music producer, div.); children: Gregory Abbott Jr. ❖ As child, studied voice and piano at Detroit Institute of Musical Arts, and later studied ballet; moved to NYC at 18; was understudy for Leslie Uggams in Broadway musical, *Hallelujah, Baby* (1965) and toured with Quincy Jones; was jazz singer with top bands, including Duke Ellington's (1960s); joined Eddie Holland in his new label, Holland-Dozier-Holland Records; released single, "Band of Gold" (1970) and Vietnam War protest song, "Bring the Boys Home" (1971), both of which went gold; other records include "Deeper and Deeper" (1970), "Cherish What Is Dear to You (While It's Near to You)" (1971) and "You Brought the Joy" (1971); films include *Book of Numbers* (1973), *Ragdoll* (1999), and *Deadly Rhapsody* (2001); recorded with ABC and Capitol records; hosted tv talk show, *For You Black Woman* (1980s).

PAYNE, Katy (1937—). American zoologist. Name variations: Katharine Boynton; Katharine Boynton Payne. Born Katharine Boynton, 1937 in Ithaca, NY; dau. of a professor at Cornell University; m. Roger Payne, 1960; children: 4. ❖ Developer in the field of bioacoustics, the study of animal sounds and communication, particularly whales and elephants, 1st studied music at Cornell University, where she met Roger Payne, who would discover repetitive and melodic communication patterns of humpback and right whales (1966); revealed that whales pass on learned traits of communication which evolve over time like human languages; became research associate and visiting fellow at Cornell (1984); discovered that elephants use infrasonic vocalizations (too-low pitched for humans to hear) to communicate; collaborated with Joyce Poole at Kenya's Amboseli National Park (1985, 1986) to record and study sounds made by elephant group also studied by Cynthia Moss; worked with many meteorologists to evaluate how atmosphere affects infrasound communication used by lions, elephants, and other animals (1998). Writings include *Elephants Calling* (1992) and *Silent Thunder: In the Presence of Elephants* (1998).

PAYNE, Marita (1960—). Canadian runner. Born Oct 7, 1960, in Barbados; attended Florida State University. ❖ At Los Angeles Olympics, won silver medals in the 4 x 400-meter relay and the 4 x 100-meter relay (1984).

PAYNE, Nicola (1960—). New Zealand rower. Name variations: Nikki Mills Payne; Nikki Mills. Born July 26, 1960, in Hong Kong; m. Peter

Mills (rowing club coach). ❖ At Seoul Olympics, won a bronze medal in coxless pairs (1988); won 14 New Zealand titles.

PAYNE, Nicolle (1976—). American water-polo player. Born July 15, 1976, in Paramount, CA; attended University of California, Los Angeles. ❖ Goalkeeper, won a team silver medal at Sydney Olympics (2000) and a team bronze at Athens Olympics (2004); won World championship (2003).

PAYNE, Sylvia (1880–1974). English psychoanalyst. Born Sylvia Moore, 1880; died 1974; dau. of a cleric; graduate of London Hospital School of Medicine (now Royal Free Hospital School of Medicine), 1906; m. J.E. Payne (surgeon); children: 3. ❖ A pioneer in psychoanalysis, served as commandant and medical officer at Torquay Red Cross Hospital during WWI; subsequently became a psychiatrist at London Clinic of Psychoanalysis; later served variously as chair of the board of directors of the Institute of Psychoanalysis, president of the British Psychoanalytical Society, and a fellow of the British Psychological Society. Created CBE (1918).

PAYNE, Thelma (1896–1988). American diver. Name variations: Thelma Payne Sanborn. Born July 18, 1896; died Aug 1988 in Laguna Niguel, CA. ❖ At Antwerp Olympics, won a bronze medal in springboard (1920).

PAYNE, Virginia (1908–1977). American actress. Name variations: Ma Perkins. Born June 19, 1908, probably in Cincinnati, Ohio; died Feb 10, 1977, in Cincinnati. ❖ Portrayed the title role on the popular daytime radio serial "Ma Perkins" for 27 years (Dec 4, 1933–1960); was also an active member of American Federation of Television and Radio Artists (AFTRA) and served a term as its national president. ❖ See also *Women in World History.*

PAYNE-GAPOSCHKIN, Cecilia (1900–1979). American astrophysicist. Name variations: Cecelia Gaposhkin; Cecilia Gaposchkin. Born Cecilia Helena Payne, Mar 10, 1900, in Wendover, England; died Dec 7, 1978, in Cambridge, Massachusetts; dau. of Edward John Payne (lawyer and historian) and Emma (Pertz) Payne (artist); Newnham College, Cambridge University, BA, 1923; Radcliffe College, PhD in astronomy, 1925; m. Sergei I. Gaposchkin (astronomer), Mar 6, 1934; children: Edward Michael Gaposchkin; Katherine Leonora Gaposchkin; Peter John Arthur Gaposchkin. ❖ One of the 20th century's most renowned women scientists, conducted pioneering research into the composition and classification of stars, contributing greatly to our knowledge of the structure of the Galaxy; was the 1st to receive a PhD in astronomy from Radcliffe (1925), submitting a doctoral thesis in which she determined temperature scale for stellar atmospheres and also concluded that stars are made up primarily of hydrogen and helium, with traces of other elements, a theory still held; became a permanent member of Harvard College observatory staff, serving in a somewhat ill-defined position (1927); was appointed Phillips Astronomer and a lecturer at the observatory (1938); was the 1st woman to achieve the rank of professor at Harvard and the 1st to be appointed chair of the astronomy department (1956); retired from Harvard (1966); wrote *Stars of High Luminosity* (1930), *Stars in the Making* (1952), *Introduction to Astronomy* (1954), *Variable Stars and Galactic Structure* (1954) and *Galactic Novae* (1957). Awarded the 1st Annie Jump Cannon Medal of American Astronomical Society (1934); received Henry Norris Russell Prize from American Astronomical Society (1976). ❖ See also Katherine Haramundanis, ed. *Cecilia Payne-Gaposchkin: An Autobiography and Other Recollections* (1984); and *Women in World History.*

PAYNE-SCOTT, Ruby (1912–1981). *See Scott, Ruby Payne.*

PAYSON, Joan Whitney (1903–1975). American philanthropist. Born Joan Whitney, Feb 5, 1903, in New York, NY; died Oct 4, 1975, in New York, NY; dau. of Payne Whitney (investor) and Helen (Hay) Whitney (dau. of John Hay, US secretary of state); granddau. of W. C. Whitney; sister of Jock Whitney; attended Barnard College for a year; m. Charles Shipman Payson (industrialist and Wall Street investor), July 5, 1924; children: Sandra Payson (arts patron), Payne Whitney Middleton, Lorinda Payson deRoulet and John Whitney Payson (another son was killed in WWII). ❖ One of the world's wealthiest women, backed a number of successful plays and movies, including *A Streetcar Named Desire, Rebecca* and *Gone With the Wind*; put up 85% of the funds to establish New York Mets (1962), and then urged Casey Stengel to come out of retirement to manage the team; philanthropic projects encompassed medical, art, and civic institutions, among them New York Hospital, St. Mary's Hospital in Palm Beach, Florida, United Hospital Fund, Lighthouse in Manhattan, and North Shore Hospital in Manhasset, Long Island, which she also founded; served as president of Helen Hay Whitney Foundation, which financed research in rheumatic fever, rheumatic heart disease, and diseases of the connective tissues; supported New York Metropolitan Museum of Art and MoMA and established Country Art Gallery in Westbury, Long Island; active politically, donated regularly to Republican Party. ❖ See also *Women in World History.*

PAYSON, Sandra (c. 1926–2004). American arts patron. Born Sandra Helen Payson, in Manhasset, NY; died July 15, in New York, NY; dau. of Joan Whitney Payson (philanthropist) and Charles Shipman Payson; m. William Blair Meyer (div.); m. George (later Lord) Weidenfeld of London (div.); children: William Blair Meyer Jr, Joan Curci Meyer and Averil Payson Meyer. ❖ Founded the Manhasset Stable for thoroughbred racing; was on the board of Lincoln Center for Arts, Whitney Museum, and Madeira School, among others; was active in Women's Leadership Forum of Democratic National Committee in Washington, DC.

PAYTON, Barbara (1927–1967). American screen actress. Born Barbara Lee Redfield, Nov 16, 1927, in Cloquet, MN; died May 8, 1967, in San Diego, CA; m. John Payton, 1945 (div. 1948); m. George A. Provas, 1957 (div, 1958); m. two more times, including 1-month marriage to Franchot Tone (actor). ❖ Leading lady of 1950s, appeared in a number of films, including *Kiss Tomorrow Goodbye, Once More My Darling, Dallas, Bad Blonde, Murder is My Beat, Only the Valiant* and *The Great Jesse James Raid*; received negative publicity when actors Franchot Tone and Tom Neal got into a serious bar brawl while competing for her affections. ❖ See also autobiography *I Am Not Ashamed* (1963).

PAYTON, Carolyn Robertson (1925–2001). African-American psychologist, educator and administrator. Born May 13, 1925, in Norfolk, VA; died April 11, 2001, at her home in Washington, DC; graduate of Bennett College; University of Wisconsin, MA in psychology; Columbia University Teachers College, PhD in counseling and school administration. ❖ Was a professor of psychology at Livingstone College (Salisbury, NC), Virginia State University, and Elizabeth City State University (NC); was head of counseling services at Howard University (1970–78), then dean of counseling (1980–95); became a field assessment officer in the Peace Corps (1964), then director of the Peace Corps (1977–78), the 1st black and 1st woman; also worked as an overseas country director, supervising 130 volunteers on projects in the Caribbean.

PAZ PAREDES, Margarita (1922–1980). Mexican poet. Name variations: (real name) Margarita Camacho Baquedano. Born Margarita Camacho Baquedano, Mar 30, 1922, in San Felipe Torresmochas, Guanajuato, Mexico; died May 22, 1980, in Mexico City, Mexico; studied journalism at Universidad Obrera of Mexico and literature at the Independent National University of Mexico. ❖ Works include *Sonaja* (1942), *Voz de la tierra* (1946), *Andamios de sombra* (1950), *Dimensión del siléncio* (1953), *Casa en la niebla* (1956), *Los amantes y el sueño* (1960), *Elegia a César Garizurieta* (1962), and *Adám en sombra y noche final y siete oraciones* (1964).

PAZYUN, Mariya (1953—). Soviet rower. Born July 17, 1953, in USSR. ❖ At Moscow Olympics, won a silver medal in coxed eights (1980).

PEABODY, Elizabeth Palmer (1778–1853). American author and teacher. Name variations: Elizabeth Palmer. Born Elizabeth Palmer in 1778; died in 1853; m. Nathaniel Peabody; children: Elizabeth Palmer Peabody (1804–1894); Sophia Peabody Hawthorne (1809–1871); Mary Peabody Mann. ❖ Ran a girls' boarding school in Billerica, Massachusetts. ❖ See also *Women in World History.*

PEABODY, Elizabeth Palmer (1804–1894). American author, educator and social reformer. Born Elizabeth Palmer Peabody in Billerica, Massachusetts, May 16, 1804; died in Boston, Jan 3, 1894; dau. of Nathaniel Peabody (doctor and dentist) and Elizabeth Palmer Peabody (1778–1853, author and teacher); sister of Mary Peabody Mann (1806–1887) and Sophia Peabody Hawthorne (1809–1871); aunt of Rose Hawthorne Lathrop (1851–1926); never married. ❖ Started a school (1825) and gave a series of history lectures to women audiences (1827), making her the nation's 1st female lecturer; ran a bookshop on West Street in Boston (1840–50), which was a hub for such Boston intellectuals as Ralph Waldo Emerson, Bronson Alcott, William Ellery Channing and Margaret Fuller, and an incubator for the literary movement known as the "American Renaissance"; the 1st female publisher in US, issued some of Nathaniel Hawthorne's earliest works and became publisher of the *Dial,* the Transcendentalists' journal (1841), a major landmark in American literary history; was active in abolitionist, Native American rights and women's suffrage movements; founded 1st kindergarten in America (1860); wrote numerous books and articles on philosophy, theology and education, including *First Steps to the Study of History* (1832), *A Record of a School* (1835), *Moral Culture of Infancy, and Kindergarten Guide* (1863), and *Reminiscences of the Rev. William E. Channing* (1880); for over 70 years, championed new, and sometimes controversial, reforms in the education of women and young children. ❖ See also Louise Hall Tharp, *The Peabody Sisters of Salem* (Little, Brown, 1950); Bruce A. Ronda, ed. *Letters of Elizabeth Palmer Peabody: American Renaissance Woman* (Wesleyan U. Press, 1984); and *Women in World History*.

PEABODY, Josephine Preston (1874–1922). American poet and dramatist. Name variations: Josephine Marks. Born in Brooklyn, New York, May 30, 1874; died in Cambridge, Massachusetts, Dec 4, 1922; dau. of Charles Kilham Peabody (merchant, died 1884) and Susan Josephine (Morrill) Peabody; attended Radcliffe College as a special student, 1894–96; m. Lionel Simeon Marks (professor of mechanical engineering at Harvard), June 21, 1906; children: Alison Marks (b. 1908); Lionel Marks (b. 1910). ❖ Published 1st volume of poetry, *The Wayfarers* (1898), followed by *Fortune and Men's Eyes*, a one-act play built around Shakespeare's sonnets, and *Marlowe*, a play in verse; held a lectureship in poetry and literature at Wellesley College (1901–03); published another collection of poems, *The Singing Leaves* (1903), and a choric idyl, *Pan*, which was performed in Ottawa (1904); wrote *The Book of Little Past*, for children (1908), followed by *The Piper*, a poetic play on Pied Piper legend, produced in England and US (1910–11); during later years, embraced a number of liberal and radical reform movements, joining Fabian Society (1909) and publishing *The Singing Man*, a poetry collection dealing with human rights (1911); later works included another volume of poems, *Harvest Moon* (1916), and 3 more plays: *The Wolf of Gubbio* (1913), a drama about St. Francis of Assisi, *The Chameleon* (1917), a comedy, and *Portrait of Mrs. W.* (1922), a prose play about Mary Wollstonecraft. ❖ See also *Women in World History*.

PEABODY, Kate Nichols Trask (1853–1922). *See Trask, Kate Nichols.*

PEABODY, Lucy (1861–1949). American missionary. Name variations: Lucy McGill Waterbury. Born Lucy Whitehead McGill in Belmont, Kansas, Mar 2, 1861; died in Danvers, Massachusetts, Feb 26, 1949; dau. of John McGill (merchant) and Sarah Jane (Hart) McGill; attended University of Rochester; m. Norman Mather Waterbury (Baptist minister), Aug 18, 1881 (died 1886); m. Henry W. Peabody (businessman), June 16, 1906 (died 1908); children: (1st m.) 3, of whom 2 survived to adulthood. ❖ Sailed with husband to India (1882), working among the Telugus people of Madras until his death (1886); took a position as corresponding secretary of Woman's Baptist Foreign Missionary Society (1890); with Helen Barrett Montgomery, promoted an annual day for united prayer for missions, known today as World Day of Prayer; served as chair of Central Committee on United Study of Foreign Missions (1902–29); founded *Everyland* (1908), a missionary journal for children which she edited until 1920; became a founding member of Committee on Christian Literature for Women and Children (1912); became vice-president for foreign department of newly unified Woman's American Baptist Foreign Mission Society, an organization through which she transformed the Interdenominational Conference into the more effective Federation of Women's Board of Foreign Missions (1916); made 2 world tours (1913, 1919), inspecting various missions; led drive to establish 7 women's colleges in Far East (1920–23); successful in her efforts, later served on board of 3 of the colleges: Woman's Christian College (Madras, India), Women's Christian Medical College (Vellore, India), and Shanghai Medical College; formed Association of Baptists for World Evangelism, serving as president (1927–34). ❖ See also *Women in World History*.

PEABODY, Mary (1806–1887). *See Mann, Mary Peabody.*

PEABODY, Sophia (1809–1871). *See Hawthorne, Sophia Peabody.*

PEACHES AND HERB. *See Barker, Francine.*

PEACOCK, Lucy (fl. 1785–1816). English bookseller and author. Probably born c. 1770 in London; not much is known about her personal history. ❖ Ran a bookshop on Oxford Street, London; wrote children's stories, for the most part anonymously, including *The Adventures of the Six Princesses of Babylon*, also edited *The Juvenile Magazine.*

PEACOCK, Miriam (1836–1914). *See Leslie, Miriam Folline Squier.*

PEACOCKE, Isabel Maud (1881–1973). New Zealand novelist and children's writer. Name variations: Inez Isabel Maud Cluett; Mrs. Cluett. Born Inez Isabel Maud Peacocke, Jan 31, 1881, in Devonport, Auckland, New Zealand; died Oct 12, 1973, in Roskill Masonic Village, Onehunga, New Zealand; dau. of Emily Frances (Mitchell) Peacocke and Gerald Loftus Torin Peacocke (Madeira-born English barrister and editor of *New Zealand Farmer*); educated privately; m. George Edward Cluett (engineer), June 1920 (died 1936); no children. ❖ Taught at the Dilworth Ulster Institute for disadvantaged boys, where she quickly established a reputation as a storyteller; published 1st children's novel, *My Friend Phil* (1915) and went on to publish 24 more, including *Quicksilver* (1922) and *Marjolaine* (1936); was a founding member of New Zealand League of Penwomen; following husband's death, wrote 16 adult novels under married name; became popular as radio broadcaster presenting local history of Auckland; also wrote for magazines and newspapers in New Zealand and elsewhere. ❖ See also autobiographical *When I Was Seven* (1927); *Dictionary of New Zealand Biography* (Vol. 4).

PEAKE, Felicity (1913–2002). English aviator and military leader. Name variations: Dame Felicity Peake; Felicity Hanbury. Born Felicity Hyde Watts, May 1, 1913, in Cheadle Hulme, Cheshire, England; died Nov 2, 2002; dau. of Colonel Humphrey Watts; Jock Hanbury (pilot), 1935 (killed Oct 3, 1939); m. Sir Harald Peake, 1952 (died 1978); children: 1 son. ❖ Air commodore, joined Women's Auxiliary Air Force (WAAF, 1939); became 2nd in command at Biggin Hill (May 1940), the most heavily attacked RAF base during Battle of Britain; became the 1st woman in the war to be appointed MBE (military, 1941) and the WAAF's 1st public relations officer; became staff officer at Bomber Command headquarters (1943); served as director of Women's Auxiliary Air Force (WAAF, 1946–49) and 1st director of Women's Royal Air Force (WRAF, 1949–50). Appointed DBE (1949). ❖ See also memoir, *Pure Chance* (1993).

PEAKE, Mary S. (1823–1862). African-American educator. Born in Norfolk, Virginia, 1823; died in Hampton, Virginia, Feb 22, 1862; dau. of a free mulatto woman and a prominent Englishman; attended private school for free blacks in Alexandria, Virginia, for several years; m. Thomas D. Peake, 1851; children: Hattie ("Daisy") Peake. ❖ The 1st teacher in the American Missionary Association schools, was enlisted to begin a school for the children at Fort Monroe, VA (1861), during Civil War. ❖ See also *Women in World History*.

PEALE, Anna Claypoole (1791–1878). American painter. Name variations: Anna Peale; Anna Staughton; Anna Duncan. Born Anna Claypoole Peale, Mar 6, 1791, in Philadelphia, Pennsylvania; died in Philadelphia, Dec 25, 1878; 1st dau. of James Peale (1749–1831, painter) and Mary Claypoole Peale (1753–1829); sister of Margaretta Angelica Peale (1795–1882) and Sarah Miriam Peale (1800–1885); learned painting from father and encouraged by her famous uncle, Charles Willson Peale; m. Reverend Dr. William Staughton, 1829; m. General William Duncan, 1841 (died 1864); no children. ❖ Painter of miniature portraits and still lifes, who pioneered in establishing a niche in professional life for American women; learned how to paint miniatures of watercolor on ivory from cousin Raphaelle Peale; probably did much of the work on father's paintings; exhibited at Pennsylvania Academy of the Fine Arts (PAFA, 1811–42); elected to membership (Academician) in PAFA (1842); was a popular miniature painter whose work was in much demand (1820–41); did work in Baltimore, Boston, Washington, DC, but primarily in Philadelphia; paintings include *Self-Portrait* (1818), *Marianne Beckett* (1829), *Gen. Andrew Jackson* (1819), *James Peale, Mrs. James Peale, Rembrandt Peale*, and *Nathaniel Kinsman* (1820–24), *Rosalba Peale* (1820), *Mrs. Andrew Jackson* (1819), *Edgar Allan Poe* (1834) and *Miss Susannah Williams* (1825). ❖ See also Charles H. Elam, *The Peale Family: Three Generations of American Artists* (Wayne State U. Press, 1967); and *Women in World History*.

PEALE, Margaretta Angelica (1795–1882). American painter. Born Margaretta Angelica Peale, Oct 1, 1795, in Philadelphia, Pennsylvania; died in Philadelphia, Jan 17, 1882; 2nd dau. of James Peale (1749–1831, painter) and Mary Claypoole Peale (1753–1829); sister of Anna Claypoole Peale (1791–1878) and Sarah Miriam Peale (1800–1885); never married; no children. ❖ Still life and portrait painter, who was the least accomplished or prolific of the 3 artist sisters; exhibited at Artists' Fund Society and Pennsylvania Academy of the Fine Arts (1828–31); paintings include *Catalog Deception* (1813), *Still Life: Grapes and Pomegranates, Still Life: Strawberries and Cherries* and *Still Life* (1828). ❖ See also Charles H. Elam, *The Peale Family: Three Generations of*

American Artists (Wayne State U. Press, 1967); and *Women in World History.*

PEALE, Ruth Stafford (b. 1906). American church leader. Born Ruth Stafford, Sept 10, 1906, in Fonda, IA; dau. of a Methodist minister in Detroit; attended Syracuse University; m. Norman Vincent Peale (1898–1993, minister); children: John Stafford Peale, Elizabeth Peale Allen, Margaret Peale Everett. ❖ Served as national president of women's board of domestic missions of Reformed Church of America (1936–46, 1955–56), national president of Home Missions Council (1942–44), and in various capacities at Foundation for Christian Linguistics (1940); served as 1st woman president of National Board of North American Missions (NBNAM, 1967–69) and 1st woman chair of program and planning committee of National Council of Churches General Assembly (1966); with husband, became founder and publisher of *Guideposts* (interfaith monthly magazine, 1940s) and served as its chair (1992–2003); with husband, founded Peale Center for Christian Living.

PEALE, Sarah Miriam (1800–1885). American painter. Name variations: known as Sally. Born Sarah Miriam Peale, May 19, 1800, in Philadelphia, Pennsylvania; died in Philadelphia, Feb 4, 1885; 3rd dau. of James Peale (1749–1831, painter) and Mary Claypoole Peale (1753–1829); sister of Margaretta Angelica Peale (1795–1882) and Anna Claypoole Peale (1791–1878); never married; no children. ❖ Painter of canvas portraits and still lifes (ranging in size from 8 x 10 to 17 x 22, both in rectangles and ovals), who widened the opportunities for American women as professional artists; the most successful of the 3 sisters, rendered earliest known work, self-portrait *Portrait of a Lady* (1818); exhibited annually at Pennsylvania Academy of the Fine Arts (1824–31); elected a member of that institution (1824); moved to Baltimore (1825); in competition with more noted artists, such as Thomas Sully, executed some 100 portraits during the Baltimore years, including that of Marquis de Lafayette; made portraits of prominent statesmen in Washington, DC (1841–43), many of them closely associated with President John Tyler's administration, including Daniel Webster and other Cabinet members and various senators and congressional representatives; lived in St. Louis as a painter of portraits and still lifes (1847–78); returned to Philadelphia (1877); other portraits include *Mrs. Theodore Denny, Sarah Jane Armstrong, John Montgomery,* and *Mrs. George Henry Keerl* (1826–35), *Edward Johnson Cole, Anthony Thompson, Mrs. George Michael Krebs, Children of Commodore John Daniel Danels* and *William Hollingsworth* (1824–36), *Henry A. Wise* (1842), *Thomas Hart Benton* (1842); still life paintings include *Still Life: Watermelon and Grapes* (1820), *Peaches, Plums & Grapes, A Slice of Watermelon* (1825), and *Still Life* (1880). ❖ See also Wilbur H. Hunter and John Mahey, *Miss Sarah Miriam Peale, 1800–1885: Portraits and Still Life* (1967); Charles H. Elam, *The Peale Family: Three Generations of American Artists* (Wayne State U. Press, 1967); and *Women in World History.*

PEARCE, Alice (1913–1966). American comedian of stage, screen, tv and nightclubs. Born Oct 16, 1913, in New York, NY; died Mar 3, 1966, in Hollywood, CA; m. John J. Rox (died); m. Paul Davis. ❖ Made Broadway debut in *New Faces of 1943*; other NY stage appearances include *On the Town* (1944), *Gentlemen Prefer Blondes, The Grass Harp, John Murray Anderson's Almanac, Bells Are Ringing* and *Sail Away*; films include *Kiss Me, Stupid, On the Town, Dear Heart, Tammy and the Doctors* and *The Glass Bottom Boat*. Won an Emmy award for on-going role of Gladys Kravitz on "Bewitched" (1964–66).

PEARCE, Caroline (1925—). Australian field-hockey player. Name variations: Caroline Ash. Born 1925 in Moulyinning, Australia; sister of Jean, Morna and May Pearce (field-hockey players). ❖ With sisters May and Jean, played on the unbeaten Australian team which toured New Zealand (1948). ❖ See also *Women in World History.*

PEARCE, Christie (1975—). American soccer player. Name variations: Christie Rampone. Born June 24, 1975, in Fort Lauderdale, FL; grew up in Pt. Pleasant, NJ; attended Monmouth University; m. Chris Rampone. ❖ Defender; won a silver medal at Sydney Olympics (2000); signed with New York Power (2001); won a team gold medal at Athens Olympics (2004).

PEARCE, Jean (1921—). Australian field-hockey player. Name variations: Jean Wynne. Born 1921 in Moulyinning, Australia; sister of Caroline, Morna and May Pearce (field-hockey players). ❖ Second oldest of the Pearce sisters, who dominated Australian women's field hockey (1936–56), played center half-back and was also a captain; led Australia to its 1st victory over England (1953), then retired. ❖ See also *Women in World History.*

PEARCE, Louise (1885–1959). American physician and pathologist. Born Louise Pearce in Winchester, Massachusetts, Mar 5, 1885; died in New York, NY, Aug 10, 1959; dau. of Susan Elizabeth Hoyt and Charles Ellis Pearce; Stanford University, AB, 1907; attended Boston University; Johns Hopkins University, MD, 1912; lived with Ida A.R. Wylie (1885–1959, novelist); never married; no children. ❖ One of the central participants in the development and testing of tryparsamide to treat sleeping sickness, moved to California (c. 1890); interned at Johns Hopkins Hospital (1912), the 1st woman on the staff of the psychiatry department; named fellow of Rockefeller Institute (1913), the 1st woman to be appointed assistant to Dr. Simon Flexner; worked with pathologist Wade Hampton Brown, testing arsenic-based compounds on the parasite which causes African trypanosomiasis or sleeping sickness (1913–19); traveled alone to Belgian Congo to test tryparsamide (1920) and her monograph, "The Treatment of Human Trypanosomiasis with Tryparsamide," became a formative work in the field; investigated syphilis in rabbits (1920–28); appointed trustee, New York Infirmary for Women and Children (1921); appointed associate member of Rockefeller Institute (1923); discovered the Brown-Pearce Carcinoma (1924); appointed to General Advisory Council of American Social Hygiene Association (1925); appointed visiting professor of syphilology at Peiping Union Medical College, China (1931); appointed to National Research Council (1931); isolated the rabbit pox virus (1932); named member of board of Corporation of Philadelphia Women's Medical College (1941), then president (1946); was director of Association of University Women (1945); retired (1951). Received Order of the Belgian Crown (1921), Elizabeth Blackwell Award (1951), King Leopold II Prize (1953); made officer of the Royal Order of the Lion (1953). ❖ See also *Women in World History.*

PEARCE, May (1915–1981). Australian field-hockey player. Name variations: May Campbell. Born 1915 in Moulyinning, Australia; died 1981; sister of Jean, Morna and Caroline Pearce (field-hockey players). ❖ Oldest of the legendary Pearce sisters (no relation to the famous hockey-playing Pearce brothers) who dominated Australian women's field hockey (1936–56), played left-inner and captained for both state and national teams; was regarded as a scoring phenomenon, making 100 goals in 1936 alone; left the field of play to become a coach and administrator (1948). ❖ See also *Women in World History.*

PEARCE, Morna (1932—). Australian field-hockey player. Name variations: Morna Hyde. Born 1932 in Moulyinning, Australia; sister of Jean, Caroline and May Pearce (field-hockey players). ❖ Youngest of the legendary Pearce sisters, who dominated Australian women's field hockey (1936–56), captained in the international tournament at Sydney (1956). Won the WA's first Sportsman of the Year award (1956). ❖ See also *Women in World History.*

PEARCE, Philippa (1920—). English children's novelist and short-story writer. Name variations: Philippa Christie. Born Ann Philippa Pearce, 1920, in Great Shelford, Cambridgeshire, England; dau. of Ernest and Gertrude (Ramsden) Pearce; attended Cambridge University; m. Martin Christie, 1963 (died 1965); children: Sarah. ❖ Worked for 13 years as scriptwriter and producer for BBC's schools broadcasting department (1945–58), then as editor at Clarendon Press (1959–60) and editor of children's books for Andre Deutsch Ltd. (1960–67); wrote 1st children's novel, *Minnow on the Say* (1954), during long stay in hospital with tuberculosis, drawing on childhood memories of village life on banks of River Cam; published Carnegie Medal-winning classic *Tom's Midnight Garden* (1958); wrote *The Battle of Bubble and Squeak* (1979), winning Whitbread Award; won Kate Greenaway Medal for *Mrs. Cockle's Cat* (1988); also wrote *Still Jim and Silent Jim* (1960), *The Children of the House* (1968), *Lion at School* (1973), *The Shadow-Cage: And Other Tales of the Supernatural* (1985), *The Children of Charlecote* (1997), *The Ghost in Annie's Room* (2001) and *Amy's Three Best Things* (2004); became fellow of Royal Society of Literature. Awarded Order of British Empire (OBE) for services to children's literature.

PEARCE, Vera (1896–1966). Australian actress and singer. Born 1896 in Australia; died Jan 21, 1966, in London, England. ❖ At 4, made 1st stage appearance, then toured in England prior to WWI; appeared in *The Tivoli Follies* in Sydney (1915), followed by *The Beauty Shop, The Officers' Mess* and *Chu Chin Chow,* among others; made London debut in *Love's Awakening* (1922); other plays include *Leap Year, The New Moon, Dear Love, Stand Up and Sing, Wild Oats, Sitting Pretty, High Time* and *Liberty Bill*; films include *Just My Luck, Nicholas Nickleby* (as Mrs, Crummles), *Men of Sherwood Forest* and *Nothing Barred*.

PEARCEY, Mary Eleanor (1866–1890). English murderer. Born 1866; hanged Dec 23, 1890, in England. ❖ Fell in love with a married furniture mover named Frank Hogg; murdered his wife Phoebe and his 18-month-old daughter (Oct 1890); as police searched her house for evidence—finding broken glass, bloodstains, 2 bloody knives and a chopper—played the piano while maintaining that blood had come from mice she had killed; tried at Old Bailey and condemned to death (Dec 1890); maintained innocence until the very end.

PEARL, Cora (c. 1837–1886). English-born courtesan. Name variations: Eliza Crouch. Born Eliza Emma Crouch near Plymouth, England, c. 1837; died in Paris, France, 1886; dau. of a musician father and a singer mother. ❖ One of the most notorious courtesans of France's 2nd Empire, amassed wealth and earned a spot in *Dictionary of National Biography*; at height of career, was said to have received her clientele in a reception salon carpeted in violet petals; died penniless in a Paris garret at age 50. ❖ See also *Grand Horizontal: The Erotic Memoirs of a Passionate Lady* (Stein & Day, 1983); and *Women in World History*.

PEARL, Minnie (1912–1996). American comedian. Name variations: Ophelia Colley Cannon; Sarah Ophelia Colley. Born Sarah Ophelia Colley in Centerville, Tennessee, 1912; died in Nashville, Mar 4, 1996; dau. of Thomas K. Colley (lumber merchant) and Fannie Tate (House) Colley; attended Ward-Belmont College; m. Henry Cannon (her manager), 1947. ❖ The 1st humorist in country music to achieve worldwide recognition, joined the Grand Ole Opry (1940); with her trademark price tag dangling from a dime-store hat and her greeting of "Howdyyyyy! I'm just so proud to be here," worked at the Grand Ole Opry for 56 years. Inducted into Country Music Association's Hall of Fame (1975); received Brotherhood Award from National Conference of Christians and Jews (1975). ❖ See also (with Joan Dew) *Minnie Pearl: An Autobiography* (Simon & Schuster, 1980); and *Women in World History*.

PEARL OF YORK (1556–1586). *See Clitherow, St. Margaret.*

PEARSALL, Phyllis (1906–1996). English artist, writer and mapmaker. Born Phyllis Gross in London, England, 1906; died in Shoreham, England, Aug 28, 1996; dau. of Alexander Gross (1880–1958, Hungarian-born map publisher of Jewish descent) and Isabelle Crowley (1886–1938, playwright and suffragist); sister of Anthony Gross (1905–1995, painter); m. Richard Pearsall, 1928. ❖ Catalogued 23,000 streets for the 1st edition of her *Geographer's A–Z Street Atlas* (1936) and published it herself. ❖ See also autobiography *From Bedsitter to Household Name: The Personal Story of A–Z Maps* (1990); and *Women in World History*.

PEARSE, Margaret (1857–1932). Irish politician. Born Margaret Brady, 1857, in Ireland; died 1932; dau. of Patrick Brady (coal factor); m. James Pearse (stone carver and sculptor), c. 1876; children: Margaret Mary Pearse (1878–1968, TD and senator), Mary Brigid Pearse, William Pearse, and Patrick Pearse (1879–1916, writer and revolutionary who was executed along with brother William after 1916 Rising). ❖ Served as matron and housekeeper at St. Enda's School; was a committee member, Irish Volunteers' Dependants' Fund (1916), and honorary member of Cumann na mBan (1917–18); elected to 2nd Dáil as a Sinn Féin deputy for Dublin Co. (1921–22); was anti-Treaty.

PEARSE, Margaret Mary (1878–1968). Irish politician. Born 1878 in Great Brunswick Street (later Pearse Street), Dublin, Ireland; dau. of James Pearse (stone carver and sculptor) and Margaret Pearse (1857–1932, TD for Dublin Co.); sister of Mary Brigid Pearse, William Pearse, and Patrick Pearse (1879–1916, writer and revolutionary). ❖ Founded, with brothers, St. Enda's College, Rathfarnham (later bequeathing it to the nation); elected to 8th Dáil as Fianna Fáil deputy for Co. Dublin (1933–37); elected to Seanad from the Administrative Panel, retaining the seat until her death (1938–68).

PEARSON, Issette (fl. 1893). English golfer. Name variations: Isette or Issette Pearson Miller. Born in London, England, into the well-known Pearson publishing family; m. the son of a Lancashire cotton baron, 1912. ❖ Led in the formation of the Ladies Golf Union (LGU) in London (April 19, 1893), which developed a handicapping system and held the 1st Women's British Amateur championship.

PEARSON, Landon Carter (1930—). Canadian senator. Name variations: Lucy Pearson. Born Nov 16, 1930; m. Geoffrey A.H. Pearson (son of Lester and Maryon Pearson). ❖ Liberal representing Ontario, called to Senate (Sept 15, 1994); prominent advocate for children.

PEARSON, Lucy (1930—). *See Pearson, Landon Carter.*

PEARSON, Maryon (1901–1989). Canadian first lady. Born Maryon Elspeth Moody, 1901, in Winnipeg, Manitoba, Canada; died Dec 26, 1989; m. Lester Bowles Pearson (prime minister of Canada, 1963–68), Aug 22, 1925 (div. Dec 27, 1972); children: Geoffrey A.H. Pearson (b. 1927, who m. Landon Carter Pearson, Canadian senator), Patricia Lillian Pearson (b. 1929). ❖ Honorary chair of the board of trustees of Lester B. Pearson College (1973–89); once said, "Behind every successful man is a surprised woman."

PEARSON, Michele (1962—). Australian swimmer. Born April 22, 1962, in Australia. ❖ At Los Angeles Olympics, won a bronze medal in the 200-meter indiv. medley (1984).

PEARSON, Molly (d. 1959). Scottish-born stage actress. Born in Edinburgh, Scotland; died Jan 26, 1959, age 83, in Newton, CT; m. Ethelbert Hales. ❖ Made stage debut in England in *The Little Minister*; came to prominence in the title role in *Lady Babbie*; made NY debut as Dolores in *Carmen* with Olga Nethersole (1906); Broadway appearances include *The Passing of the Third Floor Back, Hobson's Choice, The Dover Road, Mr. Pim Passes By, Housewarming, Laburnum Grove, Young Mr. Disraeli* and *Save Me the Waltz*; greatest success was as Bunty Biggar in *Bunty Pulls the Strings* (1911).

PEARSON, Virginia (1886–1958). American silent-screen actress. Born Mar 7, 1886, in Anchorage, KY; died June 6, 1958, of uremic poisoning, in Los Angeles, CA; m. Sheldon Lewis (actor, died 1958). ❖ Appeared on Broadway; known for exotic or vamp roles; films include *A Fool There Was* and *The Hawk*; films include *A Royal Romance, The Bishop's Emeralds, Blazing Love, The Vital Question, The Hunchback of Notre Dame, What Price Beauty, The Big City, The Actress* and *The Phantom of the Opera*.

PEARY, Josephine (1863–1955). American author and explorer. Name variations: Jo Peary; Josephine Diebitsch Peary. Born Josephine Diebitsch in Washington, DC, May 22, 1863; died in Portland, Maine, Dec 19, 1955; dau. of Herman Henry Diebitsch and Magdalena Augusta (Schmid) Diebitsch; m. Robert Edwin Peary (Arctic explorer), 1888 (died 1920); children: Marie Ahnighito Peary Stafford (b. 1893); Francine (d. 1899 in infancy); Robert Peary Jr. (b. 1903). ❖ The 1st Caucasian woman to live in the world's high Arctic regions, played a significant role in advancing the career of her husband, whom she accompanied on expeditions to the far North (1891 and 1893) and for whom she would raise funds to successfully effect his rescue (1895); spent 3 winters and 8 summers in the high Arctic region; wrote *Children of the Arctic* (1903). ❖ See also memoir *My Arctic Journal* (Contemporary, 1893); and *Women in World History*.

PEASE, Heather (1975—). American synchronized swimmer. Name variations: Heather Pease-Olson. Born Sept 29, 1975, in Monterey, CA. ❖ Won a team gold medal at Atlanta Olympics (1996); was 7-time member of US National team.

PEATTIE, Cathy (c. 1956—). Scottish politician. Born c. 1956 in Grangemouth, Scotland; married; children: Cara and Emma. ❖ Served as chair of Scottish Labour's Women's Committee; as a Labour candidate, elected to the Scottish Parliament for Falkirk East (1999, 2003).

PECHENKINA, Natalya (1946—). Soviet runner. Born July 15, 1946, in USSR. ❖ At Mexico City Olympics, won a bronze medal in the 400 meters (1968).

PECHERSKAYA, Svetlana (1968—). Russian biathlete. Name variations: Pecherskaia, Petcherskaia or Petcherskaya. Born Nov 14, 1968, in Russia. ❖ Won a silver medal for 15 km at Albertville Olympics (1992).

PECHEY-PHIPSON, Edith (1845–1908). British physician. Born Mary Edith Pechey in Langham, Essex, England, Oct 7, 1845; died in Folkestone, England, April 14, 1908; dau. of William Pechey (Baptist minister) and Sarah Rotton Pechey; m. Herbert Phipson (wine merchant and social reformer), Mar 1889; no children. ❖ As one of the "Edinburgh Seven," was in the 1st class of women allowed into University of Edinburgh (1869); when Edinburgh balked, had to complete studies at University of Berne; after the English College of Physicians remained adamant in its refusal to license women, was admitted to Royal College of Physicians of Ireland for final examinations (1877); upon receiving license, established a successful private practice at Leeds and Birmingham; also studied surgery at University of Vienna; became an advocate for women's suffrage; served as senior medical officer of Cama Hospital in Bombay (modern-day Mumbai), India, the 1st hospital not only specifically built for women but also staffed entirely by women (1886–94); was the 1st woman appointed to the Senate of University of Bombay; was also elected a member of the Royal Asiatic Society. ❖ See also *Women in World History*.

PECHSTEIN, Claudia (1972—). East German speedskater. Born Feb 22, 1972, in Berlin, Germany. ❖ Won a bronze medal for the 3,000 at Albertville Olympics (1992); won a gold medal for the 5,000 meters and a bronze for the 3,000 meters at Lillehammer Olympics (1994); won a silver medal at Nagano Olympics for the 3,000 meters and a gold medal for the 5,000, the 2nd woman to skate under 7 minutes with a time of 6:59.61 (1998); at World Cup (2001), was the 1st woman to skate the 3,000 meters in under 4 minutes; at Salt Lake City, won her 3rd consecutive gold medal in the 5,000 meters and a gold medal in the 3,000 meters, breaking her own world record (2002); won a gold medal for Team Pursuit and a silver medal for 5,000 meters at Torino Olympics (2006). ❖ See also *Women in World History*.

PECHSTEIN, Heidi (1944—). East German swimmer. Born July 4, 1944, in Germany. ❖ At Rome Olympics, won a bronze medal in 4 x 100-meter freestyle relay (1960).

PECK, Annie Smith (1850–1935). American mountaineer and explorer. Born Oct 19, 1850, in Providence, Rhode Island; died July 18, 1935, in New York, NY; dau. of George Peck (lawyer and state legislator) and Anna Smith Peck; graduate of Rhode Island State Normal School, 1872; University of Michigan, degree in Greek, 1878, MA, 1881; never married; no children. ❖ Captivated by her 1st sight of the Swiss Alps during a Continental tour (1885), climbed 1st major mountain, California's Mount Shasta (1888), and went on to lead expeditions up important European heights before discovering the Andes of South America; gained international fame after 6 attempts by becoming the 1st to reach the top of Peru's highest mountain, Huascarán (1908); when not climbing mountains, explored the headwaters of the Amazon River, traversed Peru's vast inland desert on horseback, and lectured widely on her experiences; at age 80, embarked on a 7-month air tour of South America encompassing 20,000 miles (1930), after which she became an enthusiastic proponent of air travel. ❖ See also memoir, *A Search for the Apex of America* (Dodd, 1911); and *Women in World History*.

PECK, Ellen (1829–1915). American con artist. Born Ellen Crosby (known as Nellie), 1829, in Woodville, New Hampshire; died 1915. ❖ Con artist who used her wiles to swindle a series of lovers out of at least $1 million, earned a reputation as the "Queen of Confidence Women," an accolade all the more astonishing in light of her late start in criminal activities at age 51. ❖ See also *Women in World History*.

PECKA (1901–1944). *See Heikel, Karin Alice.*

PECKOVA, Kvetoslava (1956—). *See Jeriova, Kvetoslava.*

PEDEN, Irene (1925—). American engineer. Born 1925 in Topeka, Kansas. ❖ Participated in Antarctic program at University of Washington but, as a woman, could not get permission from Navy to travel on-site until after Lois Jones' all-women team of geochemists reached the Pole; became 1st American woman to journey into interior of Antarctica (1970) and provided important information about subjects, including electromagnetic properties of the ice sheet as well as radio propagation and the polar ionosphere; retired from University of Washington as professor emerita of electrical engineering (1994); received National Science Foundation's Engineer of the Year (1993).

PEDERSEN, Elaine (1936–2000). American marathon runner. Born Dec 27, 1936; died Mar 6, 2000, in Mill Valley, CA; m. Gary Loverman. ❖ After being rejected by Boston Marathon because of gender, helped smash the men-only barrier in long-distance running by integrating the Dipsea Race in Marin County (1966) and the San Francisco's Bay to Breakers (1967); also ran in the 1st race open to women in Boston Marathon (1972).

PEDERSEN, Helga (1911–1980). Danish lawyer and politician. Born Inger Helga Pedersen, June 24, 1911, in Hulby Møllegård, Tårnborg, Denmark; died Jan 27, 1980, in Korsør, Denmark; dau. of Jens Peder Nicolaj Pedersen (1877–1955) and Vilhelmine Sofie Kolding (1884–1973). ❖ A member of the Danish Parliament (1950–71), distinguished herself as an advocate of prison and penal reform and the advancement of women's legal status; was appointed the 1st woman judge at the European Court of Human Rights (1971); also served as a supreme court justice and as a delegate to UNESCO (1949–74). Received the gold medal from Association of World Peace Through Law.

PEDERSEN, Hilde G. (1964—). Norwegian cross-country skier. Born Aug 11, 1964, in Brumunddal, Norway. ❖ Won a silver medal for the 4 x 5 km relay at Salt Lake City Olympics (2002) and a bronze medal for 10 km at Torino Olympics (2006).

PEDERSEN, Lena (1940—). Canadian-Inuit politician. Name variations: Elizabeth Magdalena Pedersen. Born 1940 in Greenland; moved to Northwest Territories, 1959. ❖ Representing the constituency of Central Arctic, was the 1st woman and the 1st Inuit woman elected to the Northwest Territories Council (Dec 21, 1970); served until Mar 10, 1975; also recorded radio programs for the CBC in Inuktitut.

PEDERSEN, Share (1963—). American musician. Name variations: Sharon Pedersen, Share Ross (married name), Vixen. Born Sharon Pedersen; Mar 21, 1963, in Glencoe, MN; m. Bam (musician). ❖ Was bassist and backup singer for all-girl pop-metal band, Vixen, which was formed in Los Angeles, CA (c. 1980); with band, signed with EMI and released debut album, *Vixen* (1988), which went gold and included Top-40 hits "Cryin'" and "Edge of a Broken Heart"; with group, also released *Rev It Up* (1990), which included hit, "How Much Love"; after band split up (early 1990s), performed on *Contraband* (1991), with several other musicians.

PEDERSEN, Solveig. Norwegian cross-country skier. Born in Norway. ❖ Won a silver medal for 4 x 5 km relay at Albertville Olympics (1992).

PEDERSEN, Susan (1953—). American swimmer. Name variations: Sue Pedersen. Born Oct 16, 1953, in Sacramento, CA; children: Trish (equestrian). ❖ At Mexico City Olympics, won a silver medal in the 200-meter indiv. medley, a silver medal in the 100-meter freestyle, and gold medals in the 4 x 100-meter medley relay and the 4 x 100-meter freestyle relay (1968); won 6 US national championships; set 3 world records and 9 American records.

PEDRETTI, Erica (1930—). Swiss novelist and sculptor. Born 1930 in ternberk, Czechoslovakia; m. Gian Pedretti (sculptor), 1952; children: 5. ❖ Immigrated to Switzerland (1945) and lived in New York (early 50s); works include *Harmloses, bitte* (1970), *Heiliger Sebastian* (1973), and *Valerie oder Das unerzogene Auge* (1986). Received several awards including Ingeborg Bachmann Prize and Berliner Prize.

PEEBLES, Ann (1947—). American singer. Born April 27, 1947, in East St. Louis, Missouri; m. Don Bryant. ❖ At 8, began performing with gospel group, Peebles Choir; signed with Hi Records (1969) and released successful 1st single, "Walk Away"; other hits include "Part Time Love," "I Pity the Fool" and "Breaking Up Somebody's Home"; albums include *Straight From the Heart* (1972), *Tellin' It* (1976), and *If This Is Heaven* (1978); with husband, co-wrote the hit "I Can't Stand the Rain" (1973); went on hiatus to raise family (late 1970s); released *Full Time Love* (1992) and *Fill This World With Love* (1996).

PEEBLES, Florence (1874–1956). American biologist and teacher. Born in Pewee Valley, Kentucky, 1874; died in Pasadena, California, 1956; dau. of Thomas Peebles and Elizabeth (Cummins) Peebles; Woman's College of Baltimore (later Goucher College), BA, 1895; Bryn Mawr College, PhD, 1900; never married. ❖ Creative research biologist and influential teacher, studied biology under Thomas Hunt Morgan, with whom she shared an interest in regeneration; conducted research on marine specimens (1894–24), working much of the time out of Marine Biological Laboratory at Woods Hole; taught biology for 30 years, beginning in 1897 as a demonstrator at Bryn Mawr, where she later became an associate professor; also held teaching and administrative posts at Goucher College, Miss Wright's School (Bryn Mawr, PA), and Sophie Newcomb College at Tulane University; established a bacteriology department at Chapman College in California (1928), where she also served as professor of biology until 1942; then founded the biology laboratory at Lewis and Clark College in Portland, Oregon. ❖ See also *Women in World History*.

PEEK, Alison (1969—). Australian field-hockey player. Born Alison Louise Peek, Oct 12, 1969, in Adelaide, SA, Australia. ❖ Halfback/midfielder; won a team gold medal at Sydney Olympics (2000).

PEEL, Lady (1894–1989). *See Lillie, Beatrice.*

PEETE, Louise (1883–1947). American murderer. Born Lofie Louise Preslar in LA, 1883; executed April 11, 1947; m. Richard C. Peete, 1915, and others; children: at least 1. ❖ After being acquitted for murder in Waco, Texas, found guilty in California for murder of her employer and lover, Jacob Charles Denton; served 19 years before being paroled (1943) to an elderly couple, Margaret and Arthur Logan, who had offered her a home with them; murdered Margaret Logan (1944) and had Arthur Logan placed in an asylum; convicted for Margaret's murder, became 2nd woman in California history to be executed in gas chamber.

PEETERS, Clara (1594–after 1657). Flemish painter. Baptized May 15, 1594, in Antwerp, Belgium; died after 1657; dau. of Jan Peeters; m. Hendrick Joossen, May 31, 1639. ❖ During early career, specialized in breakfast or banquet pieces: tabletop arrangements of goblets, coins, flowers, and shells, and expensive food and drink; earliest signed work was painted in 1608, predating all known dated examples of Flemish still-life painting of its type. Though art scholars have credited some 26 still lifes to her, including *Still Life* (1612), *Flowers in a Glass Vase* (1615), *Still Life with Cheese, Bread, and Pretzels* (c. 1630), details of her life are based on conjecture. ❖ See also *Women in World History.*

PEGGE, Catherine (fl. 1657). English paramour. Name variations: Katherine Pegg. Dau. of Thomas Pegge, a Derbyshire squire; mistress of Charles II (1630–1685), king of England (r. 1661–1685); children: (with Charles II) Charles Fitzcharles, earl of Plymouth (b. 1657); Catherine Fitzcharles (1658–1759, a nun at Dunkirk), possibly had another daughter who died in infancy.

PEGGY. *Variant of Margaret.*

PEIJS, Karla M.H. (1944—). Dutch politician. Born Sept 1, 1944, in Tilburg, Netherlands. ❖ Was a member of the Utrecht Provincial Council (1982–89); as a member of the European People's Party (Christian Democrats) and European Democrats (EPP), elected to 4th and 5th European Parliament (1994–99, 1999–2004).

PEIRCE, Mary (1896–1939). *See Heath, Sophie.*

PEIRCE, Sophie (1896–1939). *See Heath, Sophie.*

PEIXOTTO, Jessica (1864–1941). American professor and social economist. Born Jessica Blanche Peixotto, Oct 9, 1864, in New York, NY; died Oct 19, 1941, in Berkeley, CA; dau. of Raphael Peixotto (merchant) and Myrtilla Jessica (Davis) Peixotto; sister of Ernest Clifford Peixotto (author and artist, 1869–40). ❖ Second woman to earn a doctorate from University of California, studied English, economics, and political science at Berkeley (1891–1900); published doctoral dissertation, *The French Revolution and Modern French Socialism* (1901); lectured in Berkeley's sociology department (1904), later earned full professorship (1918), and briefly served as chair, working predominantly in economics department until retirement (1935); developed renowned graduate seminar in history of economic thought; initiated special economics department program (1917–18) for welfare work that led to establishment of separate social work school at Berkeley; was a founder of Heller Committee for Research in Social Economics; served as executive chair of child welfare department of Woman's Committee of Council of National Defense and then as chief of its child conservation section, working with Julia Lathrop; elected vice-president of American Economic Association (1928); served briefly as member of Consumers' Advisory Board of federal National Recovery Administration; wrote *Getting and Spending at the Professional Standard of Living: A Study of the Costs of Living an Academic Life* (1927), among others.

PEJACEVIC, Dora (1885–1923). Croatian composer and violinist. Name variations: Countess Dora Pejacevic or Pejacsevich. Born in Bucharest, Romania, Sept 10, 1885; died in Munich, Germany, Mar 5, 1923. ❖ In Zagreb, studied violin with V. Huml, theory with C. Junek, and instrumentation with D. Kaiser; studied composition and violin with P. Sherwood and H. Petri in Dresden and W. Courvoisier in Munich; strongly influenced by Schumann, Brahms, Grieg, and Tchaikovsky, composed 2 Piano Sonatas, 2 Piano Quintets (the 1st one published in Dresden, 1909), 2 String Quartets, and Sonatas for both violin and cello; orchestral works include an Overture, a Piano Concerto, a Concert Fantasy for Piano and Orchestra, and a Symphony (1916); is credited with founding modern Croatian chamber and concert music.

PEKIC, Sofija (1953—). Yugoslavian basketball player. Born Feb 15, 1953, in Yugoslavia. ❖ At Moscow Olympics, won a bronze medal in team competition (1980).

PEKLI, Maria (1972—). Australian-Hungarian judoka. Born June 12, 1972, in Baja, Hungary. ❖ Competed for Hungary at Barcelona (1992) and Atlanta (1996) Olympics; moved to Melbourne; representing Australia, won a bronze medal for 52–57kg lightweight at Sydney Olympics (2000); won gold medal at Commonwealth Games (2002); placed 1st in 57kg at US Open (2003) and 1st at Oceanic championships (2002, 2003).

PELAGIA Saint. Born in Antioch. ❖ Determined to remain a virgin, at age 15 turned away the many who admired her beauty; seized by the soldiers of a magistrate intent upon claiming her, jumped off the roof of a house so as not to allow dishonor. ❖ See also *Women in World History.*

PELEN, Perrine (1960—). French Alpine skier. Born July 3, 1960, in Grenoble, France. ❖ Won a bronze medal for giant slalom at Lake Placid Olympics and a World Cup title for slalom (1980); won a bronze medal for giant slalom and a silver medal for slalom at Sarajevo Olympics (1984); at World championships, won a bronze medal for combined (1982) and a gold medal for slalom (1985).

PELESHENKO, Larisa (1964—). Russian shot putter. Born Feb 29, 1964, in Slantsy, Leningrad Region, USSR. ❖ Won a silver medal at Sydney Olympics (2000).

PELHAM, Mary Singleton Copley (c. 1710–1789). Colonial shopkeeper. Name variations: Mary Singleton Copley. Born Mary Singleton in Ireland, c. 1710; died in Boston, Massachusetts, April 29, 1789; dau. of John Singleton and Jane (Bruffe) Singleton; m. tobacconist Richard Copley (died c. 1741); m. Peter Pelham (engraver, portrait painter, and schoolmaster), May 22, 1748 (died Dec 1751); children: (1st m.) John Singleton Copley (1738–1815, artist); (2nd m.) Henry Pelham. ❖ Mother of the celebrated portrait painter John Singleton Copley, immigrated to Boston (c. 1738); ran a tobacco shop, which, according to the *Boston News-Letter,* sold "the best Virginia Tobacco, cut, Pigtail and spun, of all sorts, by Wholesale, or Retail, at the cheapest Rates." ❖ See also *Women in World History.*

PELIKAN, Lillian (1892–1931). *See Leitzel, Lillian.*

PELISH, Thelma (1926–1983). American actress. Born Dec 24, 1926, in NYC; died Mar 6, 1983, in Woodland Hills, CA. ❖ Appeared on stage and tv; film credits include *The Pajama Game, Splendor in the Grass, Sweet Charity, Every Which Way but Loose* and *Flicks.*

PELL, Anna Johnson (1883–1966). *See Wheeler, Anna Johnson Pell.*

PELLEGRINI, Federica (1988—). Italian swimmer. Born Aug 5, 1988, in Mirano, Italy. ❖ Won a silver medal for 200-meter freestyle at Athens Olympics (2004).

PELLEGRINO, Aline (1982—). Brazilian soccer player. Name variations: Aline (Brazilian soccer players use only their first name). Born July 6, 1982, in Brazil. ❖ Defender, won a team silver medal at Athens Olympics (2004).

PELLETIER, Annie (1973—). Canadian diver. Born Dec 22, 1973, in Montreal, Canada. ❖ At World championships, placed 3rd for 1-meter springboard (1994), the 1st Canadian diver to medal at the World championships; won 2 gold medals at Commonwealth Games (1994); won 11 Canadian National diving championships; won a gold medal for 1-meter springboard at Pan American Games (1995) and a bronze medal for springboard at Atlanta Olympics (1996); does tv commentary. Inducted into Canadian Olympic Hall of Fame (2003).

PELLETIER, Henriette (c. 1864–1961). Canadian midwife. Name variations: Henriette Blier Pelletier; Henriette Blier. Born Henriette Blier, c. 1864, probably in Sainte Alexandre, Quebec, Canada; died Mar 31, 1961, in Fort Kent, Maine; dau. of Salomee and Mathias Blier; m. Damase Pelletier (folk healer), Jan 9, 1882; children: 13. ❖ Successful midwife in the state of Maine, began to deliver babies (1880s); employed herbal medicines and also served as a healer; delivered more than 500 babies in her career and never lost a child, though 2 mothers died; retired around age 74.

PELLETIER, Madeleine (1874–1939). French physician, psychiatrist, feminist, and journalist. Born Anne Pelletier (later adopted name Madeleine) in Paris, France, May 18, 1874; died in Perray-Vaucluse asylum near Paris, Dec 29, 1939, and was buried in the asylum's cemetery; dau. of Louis Pelletier (b. 1831) and Anne de Passavy (b. 1836); educated at University of Paris Faculty of Medicine; never married; no children. ❖ The 1st woman in France admitted to an internship in psychiatry who became a highly controversial socialist journalist and "integral" feminist, left school (1886); passed the baccalaureate examinations after intensive self-study (1896–97); studied and published in anthropology and medicine (1898–1906); admitted as a psychiatric intern (1903); failed examination to enter the state psychiatric service (1906); was active in freemasonry (1904–46); led Women's Solidarity (1906–12); founded and directed *La Suffragiste* (1907–14); fined for breaking a window at a polling place (1908); wrote 7 books on feminist and political topics (1908–14); was a member of Socialist Party's Permanent Administrative Council (1909–11); ran for public offices (1910, 1912); was a member of Communist Party (1920–26); went to Moscow to view the Russian Communist regime (1921); was a leading advocate of birth control (1920s–30s); published 2 autobiographical novels (1932–33); was investigated as a possible abortionist (1933); published *La Rationalisation sexuelle* and participated in the Poldès pornography trial (1935); suffered a stroke (1937); arrested for directing an abortion (a case that resulted from incest between a teenaged sister and brother), was committed to an asylum (1939); has come to be ranked as one of the earliest and most important theorists of the 20th century's feminist movement. Writings include *La Femme en lutte pour ses droits* (1908), *Idéologie d'hier: Dieu, la morale, la patrie* (1910), *L'Emancipation sexuelle de la Femme* (1911), *Philosophie sociale: les opinions, les partis, les classes* (1912), *Justice sociale?* (1913), *Le Droit à l'avortement* (1913), *L'Éducation féministe des filles* (1914), *In anima vila, ou un crime scientifique: Pièce en trois actes* (1920), *Mon voyage aventureux en Russie communiste* (1922), *Supérieur! Drame des classes sociales en cinq actes* (1923), *L'Amour et la maternité* (1923), *Une Vie nouvelle: roman* (1932), *La Femme vierge: roman* (1933) and *La Rationalisation sexuelle* (1935). ❖ See also Felicia Gordon, *The Integral Feminist: Madeleine Pelletier, 1874–1939. Feminism, Socialism, and Medicine* (University of Minnesota Press, 1990); and *Women in World History*.

PELLETIER, Rose (b. 1907). *See Bampton, Rose.*

PELLICER, Pina (1935–1964). Mexican actress. Born April 3, 1935, in Mexico City, Mexico; died Dec 10, 1964, an apparent suicide, in Mexico City. ❖ Received critical praise for her performance as Louisa in *One-Eyed Jacks* (1961); other films include *Rogelia, Macario* and *Autumn Days.*

PELOSI, Nancy (1940—). American politician. Born Nancy Patricia D'Alesandro, Mar 26, 1940, in Baltimore, Maryland; dau. of Thomas J. D'Alesandro Jr. (5-term member of US House of Representatives and later mayor of Baltimore) and Annunciata D'Alesandro; Trinity College, BA, 1962; sister of Tom D'Alesandro (mayor of Baltimore); married Paul F. Pelosi (San Francisco investment banker); children: Nancy Corinne Prowada; Christine Pelosi (chief of staff for a Massachusetts congressman); Jacqueline Kenneally; Paul Pelosi Jr; Alexandra Pelosi (tv producer who made HBO documentary about George W. Bush presidential campaign, *Journeys with George*). ❖ Served as chair of the California State Democratic Party (1981–83); served as finance chair of Democratic Senatorial Campaign Committee (1986); as Democratic representative of San Francisco, elected to US House of Representatives to replace Sala Burton after Burton's death (1987); in early years in the House, served on the Banking, Finance and Urban Affairs Committee and the Government Operations Committee, while sponsoring a wide variety of legislation; served for 6 years on Committee on Standards of Official Conduct (Ethics); also served as senior member on the House Appropriations Committee and the Permanent Select Committee on Intelligence; served as co-chair of Democratic Platform Committee of Democratic National Committee (1992) and vice-chair of the Democratic National Convention (1996); served as House Democratic Whip (2001), the highest position any woman had held in either house of Congress; became minority leader (2002), the 1st woman in US history to lead a major party in Congress.

PELS, Auguste van (1900–1945). Dutch-Jewish woman. Name variations: Petronella van Daan in diary. Born Sept 9, 1900; died in concentration camp, 1945; m. Hermann van Pels; children: Peter. ❖ Known as Petronella van Daan in Anne Frank's original diary, was caught in the Secret Annex, transported to Auschwitz, then Bergen-Belsen, Buchenwald, and Theresienstadt. ❖ See also *Women in World History*.

PEMBER, Phoebe Yates (1823–1913). Confederate hospital administrator. Born Phoebe Yates Levy, Aug 18, 1823, in Charleston, South Carolina; died Mar 4, 1913, in Pittsburgh, Pennsylvania; dau. of Jacob Clavius Levy (businessman) and Fanny (Yates) Levy; m. Thomas Pember (died July 1861); no children. ❖ As matron at Chimborazo, a large Confederate Army hospital near Richmond (1862–65), was in charge of housekeeping and food service for 31 wards, and it is estimated that she and her staff cared for 15,000 soldiers during course of Civil War; published a wartime remembrance, *A Southern Woman's Story* (1879). ❖ See also *Women in World History*.

PEMBROKE, countess of.
See Clare, Isabel de (c. 1174–1220).
See Bohun, Maud (fl. 1240s).
See Marjory (d. 1244).

See Marie de St. Pol (1304–1377).
See Mortimer, Agnes (fl. 1347).
See Manny, Anne (b. 1355).
See Herbert, Katherine (c. 1471–?).
See Grey, Catherine (c. 1540–1568).
See Parr, Anne (d. 1552).
See Herbert, Mary (1561–1621).
See Clifford, Anne (1590–1676).

PEÑA, Tonita (1893–1949). Puebloan artist. Name variations: Tonita Pena; Quah Ah (Little Bead or Pink Shell). Born Quah Ah, May 10, 1893, in the Tewa pueblo called San Ildefonso in what is now New Mexico; baptized as Maria Antonia Peña; died Sept 1949; dau. of Ascencion Vigil Peña and her husband Natividad Peña; attended San Ildefonso Day School and St. Catherine's, Santa Fe; m. Juan Rosario Chavez, Mar 2, 1908 (died May 17, 1912); m. Felipe Herrera, July 14, 1913 (died July 16, 1920); m. Epitacio Arquero (governor of the Pueblo), June 12, 1922; children: (1st m.) Helia Chavez (b. 1909); Richard Chavez (b. 1912); (2nd m.): Hilario J. (b. 1920, became the noted artist Joseph H. Herrara); (3rd m.) Maria Cyrella Arquero (b. 1923); Virginia Arquero (1924–1926); Margaretta Arquero (b. 1927); Sam Arquero (b. 1929); Victoria Arquero (b. 1935). ❖ Using traditional Tewan motifs as the source of her paintings, was the only woman in a group of painters known as the "San Ildefonso Self-taught group"; was the 1st Pueblo woman easel painter and the 1st Puebloan to work in watercolor; probably influenced and advanced Pueblo painting more than any other artist, male or female, leading her to be nicknamed the Grand Old Lady of Pueblo Art. ❖ See also Samuel Gray, ed. *Tonita Peña* (Avanyu, 1990); and *Women in World History*.

PENDARVES, Mary (1700–1788). *See Delany, Mary Granville.*

PENDLETON, Ellen Fitz (1864–1936). American educator. Born Ellen Fitz Pendleton in Westerly, Rhode Island, Aug 7, 1864; died in Newton, Massachusetts, July 26, 1936; dau. of Enoch Burrows Pendleton (merchant and postmaster) and Mary Ette (Chapman) Pendleton; Wellesley College, BA, 1886, MA, 1891; attended Newnham College, Cambridge, 1889–90; never married; no children. ❖ Tutored in mathematics at Wellesley College (1886–88), then served as instructor (1888–97), secretary (1897–1901), dean and associate professor of mathematics (1901–11), and president (1911–36), the 1st alumna appointed to the post; oversaw a remarkable increase in the college's endowment, to nearly $10 million, as well as a complete rebuilding of the physical plant, most of which was destroyed by a fire in Mar 1914; elected president of New England Association of Colleges and Secondary Schools (1917); also served as president of College Entrance Examination Board and vice-president of Associated Boards for Christian Colleges in China. ❖ See also *Women in World History*.

PENDZIKI, Hrisoula (1901–1998). *See Argiriadou, Chryssoula.*

PENES, Mihaela (1947—). Romanian track-and-field athlete. Born July 22, 1947, in Romania. ❖ Won a gold medal at Tokyo Olympics (1964) and a silver medal at Munich Olympics (1972), both in javelin throw.

PENFOLD, Merimeri (1924—). New Zealand poet and translator. Name variations: Ngati Kuri Ki Te Aupouri. Born 1924 at Te Hapua, Northland, New Zealand. ❖ Lectured in Maori Studies in Auckland and worked on behalf of Maori language; poetry, which makes use of traditional forms and themes, has been published in major New Zealand anthologies; also published works on Maori women artists and collaborated on bilingual children's books.

PENG PING (1967—). Chinese basketball player. Born Jan 14, 1967, in China. ❖ At Barcelona Olympics, won a silver medal in team competition (1992).

PENGELLY, Edna (1874–1959). New Zealand teacher, nurse, school and hospital matron, and diarist. Born July 5, 1874, in Canada; died Aug 20, 1959, in Wellington, New Zealand; dau. of William and Laura Ann (Brown) Pengelly. ❖ Taught at small private school (early 1900s); trained as nurse (1907); supervised wards at Wellington District hospital and was in charge of nurses' home (1900–15); joined New Zealand Army Nursing Service and worked in military hospitals in Egypt (1915–19); was matron of Queen Mary Military Hospital (1919–21); managed private hospital in Wellington (1921–28); was executive member of Wellington branch of New Zealand Trained Nurses' Association; became matron of Wanganui Collegiate School (1929); retired from nursing (1941); assisted at clearing hospital in Wellington during WWII;

published diaries, *Nursing in Peace and War* (1956). ❖ See also *Dictionary of New Zealand Biography* (Vol. 3).

PENICHEIRO, Ticha (1974—). Portuguese-American basketball player. Pronounced Pen-a-chair-o. Born Patricia Nunes Penicheiro, Sept 18, 1974, in Portugal; dau. of Joao Penicheiro (basketball player and coach); sister of Paulo Penicheiro (basketball player); attended Old Dominion. ❖ Guard, was 2-time 1st team All-American; represented the Portuguese national team from age 14; signed with the Sacramento Monarchs, led the WNBA in assists (1998, 1999, 2000, 2001, 2002).

PENINNAH. Biblical woman. Name variations: Penina. Pronunciation: pih-NIN-uh. ❖ One of two wives of Elkanah of Ephraim, a Levite and a man of wealth and position, gave birth to many children; taunted Elkanah's other wife, Hannah, because she remained barren, until Hannah's continual prayers for a child were finally answered with the birth of the prophet Samuel.

PENKINSON, Sophie (fl. late 1890s). Russian-American blacksmith. Born in Russia. ❖ Possibly the 1st woman blacksmith, assisted husband in blacksmithing in Odessa; immigrated to US and lived in New York City; after husband's death (1919), continued work as a blacksmith at Pike Street shop until 1933.

PENN, Gulielma Springett (1644–1694). English Quaker. Name variations: Guli or Guly. Pronunciation: Goo-lee-EL-ma. Born Gulielma Maria Springett, Feb 1644, probably in London (exact date and place undocumented); died in Warminghurst, Sussex, Feb 23, 1694; dau. of Sir William Springett (lawyer who was killed while fighting for Cromwell, 1644) and Mary (Proude) Springett Penington; stepdau. of Sir Isaac Penington, son of the mayor of London; m. William Penn (Quaker and founder of Pennsylvania), April 4, 1672; children: Gulielma Maria (b. 1673); William and Mary (twins, b. 1674); Springett (b. 1676); Laetitia (b. 1678); William (b. 1681); Gulielma Maria (b. 1685). ❖ The 1st wife of William Penn, who was a leading figure of early Quaker women's meetings in England, joined Quakers at age 15, when the family estate in Buckinghamshire served as a gathering place; was active in Quaker women's meetings in London, Buckinghamshire, and Sussex. ❖ See also L.V. Hodgkin, *Gulielma: Wife of William Penn* (Longmans, 1947); and *Women in World History*.

PENN, Hannah (1671–1726). English-born Quaker. Name variations: HP. Born Hannah Callowhill in 1671 in Bristol, England; died in London, Dec 1726; dau. of Quakers Thomas Callowhill (linendraper) and Hannah (Hollister) Callowhill; m. William Penn (Quaker and founder of Pennsylvania), 1696; children: John (b. 1700), Thomas (b. 1702), Hannah Margarita (b. 1703), Margaret (b. 1704), Richard (b. 1706), Dennis (b. 1707), Hannah (b. 1708). ❖ Acting proprietor of Pennsylvania (1713–26) who successfully balanced competing interests of creditors, colonists, and crown to insure that her sons would inherit the proprietorship and that Quaker interests would be preserved in the colony; from England, traveled to Pennsylvania with husband (1699–1701); was active in Quaker women's meetings in Bristol, Berkshire, Sussex, and London; became the virtual proprietor of Pennsylvania, managing affairs in secret for nearly 6 years after husband suffered a stroke (1712), and openly for 8 more years following his death (1718). ❖ See also Sophie Drinker, *Hannah Penn and the Proprietorship of Pennsylvania* (Society of Colonial Dames, 1958); and *Women in World History*.

PENNELL, Elizabeth Robins (1855–1936). American writer. Name variations: Elizabeth Robins. Born Feb 21, 1855, in Philadelphia, Pennsylvania; died of chronic myocarditis, Feb 7, 1936, in New York, NY; dau. of Edward Robins (bank president) and Margaret (Holmes) Robins; educated at Sacred Hearts convents near Paris and in Torresdale, Pennsylvania; m. Joseph Pennell (artist), June 1884; no children. ❖ First published in the *Atlantic Monthly* (1881); published "A Ramble in Old Philadelphia," the 1st of many collaborations with husband (1882); served as art critic for US and English newspapers; wrote *Life of Mary Wollstonecraft* (1884); traveled through Europe with husband for 33 years (1884–1917), resulting in 9 books written by her and illustrated by him, including *An Italian Pilgrimage* (1886), *Our Sentimental Journey through France and Italy* (1888), *Our Journey to the Hebrides* (1889), and *Over the Alps on a Bicycle* (1898); with husband, wrote biography of James McNeill Whistler (1908); also wrote the 2-vol. *Life and Letters of Joseph Pennell* (1929). ❖ See also *Women in World History*.

PENNEY, Jennifer (1946—). Canadian ballet dancer. Born April 5, 1946, in Vancouver, British Columbia, Canada. ❖ Joined Royal Ballet in

London (1963), where she created roles for Macmillan's *Anastasia* (1971), *Elite Syncopations* (1974), *The Four Seasons* (1975) and *Manon* (1982); danced in company's classical repertory, including *Swan Lake* and *Sleeping Beauty*; appeared in Ashton's *A Wedding Bouquet* and Robbins' *Dances at a Gathering* and *Afternoon of a Faun*.

PENNINGTON, Ann (1892–1971). American actress and dancer. Born Anna Pennington, Dec 23, 1892, in Camden, NJ (some sources cite Wilmington, Delaware); died Nov 4, 1971, in New York, NY; trained by Ned Wayburn and Jack Blue. ❖ Made Broadway stage debut in *The Red Widow* (1911); appeared with *Ziegfield Follies* (1913–18, 1923–24); also appeared in *Jack and Jill, The New Yorkers, Everybody's Welcome, The Student Prince,* and in George White's *Scandals* through 5 editions, in one of which she introduced "The Black Bottom" which swept the nation (1926); made film debut in *Susie's Snowflake* (1916), and subsequently appeared in numerous movies.

PENNINGTON, Mary Engle (1872–1952). American chemist. Name variations: M.E. Pennington; Polly. Born Mary Engle Pennington, Oct 8, 1872, in Nashville, Tennessee; died in New York, NY, Dec 27, 1952; dau. of Henry Pennington (businessman) and Sarah B. Molony Pennington; University of Pennsylvania, certificate of proficiency, 1892, PhD, 1895. ❖ Considered the greatest refrigeration authority in the early 20th century, focused on preserving poultry products; her methods to refrigerate perishable foods drastically changed consumer behavior; was a fellow in botany at University of Pennsylvania (1895–97) and physiological chemistry at Yale (1897–98); was a researcher, department of hygiene, University of Pennsylvania (1898–1901); worked as consultant, Philadelphia Clinical Laboratory (1898–1907); was a lecturer, Woman's Medical College of Pennsylvania (1898–1906); served as director of Philadelphia Department of Health and Charities' bacteriological laboratory (1901–07); was 1st chief and bacteriological chemist, US Department of Agriculture's Food Research Laboratory, Philadelphia (1905–19); developed refrigeration techniques to prevent food spoilage and devised standards for refrigerated railroad cars (1907–17); was director of research and development, American Balsa Co., NY (1919–23); was 1st female member of American Society of Refrigerating Engineers (1920), then fellow (1947); was a private chemical consultant to food industry and developed techniques to freeze food and design commercial and household refrigerators (1922–52); co-authored *Eggs* (1933); was 1st female member of Poultry Historical Society's Hall of Fame; was vice-president American Institute of Refrigeration at time of death (1952). Won Francis P. Garvan Medal for women in chemistry presented by American Chemical Society (1940). ❖ See also *Women in World History*.

PENNINGTON, Patience (1845–1921). *See Pringle, Elizabeth Allston.*

PENNINGTON, Winifred (1915—). English freshwater biologist. Name variations: Winifred Anne Pennington; Winifred Tutin; Mrs. T. G. Tutin. Born Oct 8, 1915, in UK; Reading University, BS, 1938, PhD, 1941; m. Dr. Thomas Gaskell Tutin, 1942. ❖ Pioneer in the examination of lake bottom deposit cores, studied algae as a research student at the Freshwater Biological Association (BFA), Windermere (1940–45) and later worked there (1956–67); researched the ecology of freshwater algae and the process of sedimentation; held a great interest in paleobotany; studied with professor Harry Godwin at Cambridge University; at the University of Leicester, served as a lecturer (1947), special lecturer (1961) and honorary professor (1980); was a principal scientific officer at National Environmental Research Council's (NERC) Quaternary Research Unit (1965); wrote *The History of British Vegetation* (1969) and *The Lake District, a Landscape History* (1973); became a member of Royal Danish Academy (1974) and a fellow of Royal Society (1978).

PENNINX, Nelleke (1971—). Dutch rower. Born Sept 14, 1971, in Netherlands. ❖ Won a silver medal for coxed eight at Sydney Olympics (2000).

PENNISON, Marleen (1951—). American modern dancer and choreographer. Born Aug 26, 1951, in New Orleans, LA; trained at University of Southern Louisiana. ❖ Performed for choreographers Barbara Roan in *Blue Mountain Paper Parade* (1974) and Ping Chong in *Fear and Loathing in Gotham* (1980); began teaching movement for actors, and became director of Stella Adler Studio movement program in NY (1977); wrote and directed the play *Busy Signal* (1980).

PENSON, Lillian Margery (1896–1963). British historian and educator. Name variations: Dame Lillian Penson. Born 1896; died 1963; received undergraduate degree at Birkbeck College; University College, London, PhD, 1921. ❖ Began teaching career at Birkbeck College (1921);

became professor of modern history at Bedford College (1930), then served as dean of faculty of arts (1938–44), chair of Academic Council (1945), and vice chancellor (1948–51), the 1st woman to hold such a position; was acting chair of US Educational Commission in United Kingdom (1953–54); writings include *The Colonial Agents of the British West Indies* (1924) and *British Documents on the Origins of the War, 1898–1914* (11 vols., 1926–38), which she co-authored with G.P. Gooch and H.W.V. Temperley. Named Dame of the British Empire (DBE, 1951).

PENTHIÈRRE, Jeanne de (c. 1320–1384). *See Jeanne de Penthièrre.*

PENTHIEVRE, countess of. *See Hawise (d. after 1135).*

PENTHIÈVRE, Jeanne de (c. 1320–1384). *See Jeanne de Penthièrre.*

PENTLAND, Barbara (1912–2000). Canadian composer. Name variations: Lally Pentland. Born in Winnipeg, Manitoba, Canada, Jan 2, 1912; died in 2000; studied at Juilliard School of Music with Frederick Jacobi and Bernard Wagenaar, and with Aaron Copland; also studied in Darmstadt (1955). ❖ Using dissonant linear counterpoint and dodecaphonic melodic structures within a classical structure, composed over 60 works, including *Disasters in the Sun*; was an instructor at Royal Conservatory of Music of Toronto, then University of British Columbia (1949–63).

PENTREATH, Dolly (1685–1777). English fishmonger. Name variations: Dorothy Pentreath; Dorothy Jeffery. Born in Mousehole, on Mounti Bay, Cornwall, England, 1685; died in Mousehole, 1777; married to a man named Jeffery. ❖ Reputed to have been the last person to speak native Cornish, was an itinerant fishmonger and fortuneteller by trade. A monument in her honor was erected by Prince Louis Lucien Bonaparte (1860).

PEPA, Mari (1913–2004). Spanish aviator. Name variations: Mari Pepa Colomer. Born Mar 31, 1913, in Barcelona, Spain; died May 24, 2004; dau. of a textile wholesaler who was a friend of Picasso and Dali; m. Josep Carreras (pilot). ❖ At 17, was the 1st woman in Spain to qualify as a pilot (1930); worked as an instructor at El Prat; during Civil War, trained fliers, tested aerial bomb fuses, piloted airborne ambulances, helped civilians escape to France, then escaped to France herself (1939); with husband, moved to Surrey, England, at start of WWII.

PEPLAU, Hildegard E. (1909–1999). American nurse. Born Hildegard Elizabeth Peplau, Sept 1, 1909, in Reading, PA; died Mar 17, 1999, in Sherman Oaks, CA; dau. of Ottylie and Gustav Peplau (Polish immigrants from Germany); graduated from Pottstown (PA) Hospital School of Nursing (1931); Bennington College, BA in interpersonal psychology, 1943; Columbia University Teachers College, MA in psychiatric nursing, 1947. ❖ Called the "mother of psychiatric nursing" and "nurse of the century" for playing a major role in developing the theory and practice of psychiatric and mental health nursing, was a faculty member of Rutgers University College of Nursing (1954–74); served as American Nurses Association executive director (1969–70) and president (1970–72); was a visiting professor in Europe, Latin America and Africa; wrote *Interpersonal Relations in Nursing* (1952), introducing the concept of patient-nurse relationships, an interpersonal approach.

PEPPER, Beverly (1924—). American sculptor and painter. Born Beverly Stoll, Dec 20, 1924, in Brooklyn, NY; Pratt Institute, BA in industrial and advertising design, 1941; attended Art Students League, 1946, and Atelier André Lhote, 1948, and Atelier Fernand Léger, 1949, both in Paris; m. Lawrence Gussin, 1941 (div. 1948); m. Bill Pepper (author and journalist), 1949; children: (1st m.) son; (2nd m.) daughter. ❖ Known for her monumental abstract sculptures and sprawling environmental forms, evolved as a sculptor in her late 30s, after a successful career in advertising and several years as a painter; took up wood sculpture (1960), then welded sculpture (1962); exhibited early welded sculptures in "Sculpture in Metallo" show in Turin (1965) and was selected for Venice Biennale (1972); produced polished stainless steel structures (late 1960s), then triangular forms (1970s); did 1st large environmental project, *Land Canal Hillside* (1971–74), along center-strip divider of a highway in Dallas, Texas; conceived *Amphisculpture* (1974–75), an outdoor concrete amphitheater set in grass at AT&T in Bedminister, NJ; exhibited in Houston's "Monumental Sculpture of the Seventies" (1975) and at André Emmerich Gallery in NY; rendered *Thel* at Dartmouth College (1977); at New Smyrna Beach, Florida, created *Sand Dunes* (1985); began to create monumental steel columns (late 1980s), which she 1st exhibited in the piazza at Todi, Italy. ❖ See also *Women in World History.*

PEPPER, Dottie D. (1965—). American golfer. Born Aug 17, 1965, in Saratoga Springs, NY; attended Furman University. ❖ Was a 3-time All-American; was the 1st amateur to win a tournamet on the LPGA Futures Tour (1985); joined LPGA tour (1988); won 4 tournaments (1992), including the Dinah Shore, which she won again in 1999; retired (2004). Won Vare Trophy (1992).

PEPPER, Reginald (1931–2003). *See Carrington, Joanna.*

PEPPLER, Mary Jo (1944—). American volleyball player. Born Oct 17, 1944, in Rockford, IL; attended Los Angeles State College and Sul Ross State University, Alpine, Texas. ❖ Recognized as one of the best woman volleyball players in the world (1970s), was also one of the most controversial; played with the women's national championship team, the Long Beach Shamrocks, while in high school; selected for US Olympic team (1964 and 1968) but quit the 1968 team, claiming disappointment with the coaching and quality of US athletes; with Marilyn McReavy, organized the E Pluribus Unum team of Houston, which won back-to-back national championships (1972 and 1973); seemingly destined for an Olympic bid (1976), was passed over as a player or a coach by the US Volleyball Association because "she couldn't be handled"; turned professional (1974), signing on as a player-coach with El Paso-Juarez Sols of the newly formed International Volleyball Association; won the 1st Women's Superstar Competition, against such athletes as Billy Jean King, Micki King, and Diane Hollum (1975). ❖ See also Pat Jordan, *Broken Patterns* (Dodd, 1977).

PEPYS, Elizabeth (1640–1669). English gentlewoman. Name variations: Elizabeth de St. Michel; Elizabeth Saint-Michel; Mrs. Pepys. Born Elizabeth de St. Michel, 1640, in Devon, England; died Nov 10, 1669, in London; dau. of Alexandre le Marchant, French knight and sire of St. Michel, and Dorothea Kingsmill; m. Samuel Pepys (diarist and naval secretary), Dec 1655; no children. ❖ Her life, which has survived in the famous diary of husband Samuel Pepys, demonstrates the constraints and possibilities available to a 17th-century European woman. ❖ See also Patrick Delaforce, *Pepys in Love: Elizabeth's Story* (Bishopsgate, 1985); and *Women in World History.*

PEQUEGNOT, Laure (1975—). French Alpine skier. Born Sept 30, 1975, in Echirolles, France. ❖ Won a silver medal in the slalom at Salt Lake City Olympics (2002); placed 7th in slalom at World championships (2003).

PERATROVICH, Elizabeth Wanamaker (1911–1958). Tlingit activist. Born Kaaxgal.aat in Petersburg, Alaska, July 4, 1911; died after a long battle with cancer, Dec 1, 1958; a Tlingit, she was born into the Lukaax.adi clan of the Raven moiety; attended Western College of Education in Bellingham, Washington; m. Roy Peratrovich, Dec 15, 1931; children. ❖ Grand Camp President of the Alaska Native Sisterhood, was in the forefront of the fight to end discrimination against the indigenous peoples in Alaska; with husband and others, was instrumental in the eventual passing of an Anti-Discrimination Bill (1945). Alaska formally recognized her contribution to the battle for human rights by setting aside Feb 16 as "Elizabeth Peratrovich Day" (1989). ❖ See also *Women in World History.*

PERAZIC, Jasmina (1960—). Yugoslavian basketball player. Born Dec 1960 in Yugoslavia. ❖ At Moscow Olympics, won a bronze medal in team competition (1980).

PERCHINA, Irina (1978—). Russian synchronized swimmer. Born Sept 13, 1978, in USSR. ❖ Won a team gold medal at Sydney Olympics (2000).

PERCOTO, Caterina (1812–1887). Italian short-story writer. Born 1812 in Soleschiano sul Natisone, Friuli, Italy; died 1887 in Rome, Italy. ❖ Never married but looked after family land and was involved with local community; wrote realist works and often in dialect, including *Racconti* (1958), *Ventisei racconti vecchi e nuovi* (1878), *Novelle scelte* (1880), *La matrigna* (1881), and *Novelle popolari edite e inedite* (1883); also wrote preface to Giovanni Verga's *Storia di una capinera* (1871); work republished as *Scritti friulani: L'inno della fame ed altri racconti* (1945).

PERCY, Agnes (fl. 1120s). Sister-in-law of King Henry I. Dau. of William Percy, 3rd baron Percy, and Alice Tunbridge (dau. of Richard Tunbridge, earl of Clare); m. Josceline Louvain (brother of Adelicia of Louvain and brother-in-law of King Henry I); children: Henry Percy; Richard Percy (died c. 1244).

PERCY, Anne (fl. 1470s). Countess of Arundel. Name variations: Anne Fitzalan. Married William Fitzalan, 15th earl of Arundel; children: Henry Fitzalan (c. 1476–1544), 16th earl of Arundel, and Katherine Fitzalan (fl. 1530s).

PERCY, Charles Henry. *See Smith, Dodie.*

PERCY, Eileen (1899–1973). Irish-born silent-film star. Name variations: Eileen Persey. Born Aug 21, 1899, in Belfast, Ireland (now Northern Ireland); died July 29, 1973, in Beverly Hills, CA; sister of Thelma Percy (actress, 1903–1970); m. Ulric Busch; m. Harry Ruby (songwriter), 1936. ❖ Raised in Brooklyn; modeled and appeared on stage; came to prominence as Douglas Fairbanks' leading lady in 4 films (1917); other films include *Backstage, Maid of the West, The Tomboy, East Side West Side, Souls for Sables, Cobra, Burnt Fingers* and *The Cohens and Kellys in Hollywood*; retired from the screen (1927) and wrote a society column for the Los Angeles *Examiner*. Portrayed by Arlene Dahl in *Three Little Words*, a film bio of her husband (1950).

PERCY, Eleanor (c. 1250–?). *See Eleanor de Warrenne.*

PERCY, Eleanor (c. 1413–1472). *See Neville, Eleanor.*

PERCY, Eleanor (d. 1530). Duchess of Buckingham. Name variations: Eleanor Stafford; Alianore Percy. Died in 1530; dau. of Henry Percy (1421–1461), earl of Northumberland (r. 1455–1461), and Eleanor Poynings (d. 1483); m. Edward Stafford (1478–1521), 3rd duke of Buckingham (executed on May 17, 1521); children: Henry Stafford (b. 1501); Elizabeth Stafford (1494–1558); Lady Mary Stafford (who m. George Nevill, 5th Lord Abergavenny); Catherine Stafford (who m. Ralph Neville, 4th earl of Westmoreland).

PERCY, Elizabeth (1371–1417). English noblewoman. Name variations: Elizabeth Mortimer. Born Feb 12, 1371, in Usk, Gwent, Wales; died in April 1417 at Trotton, West Sussex, England; buried in Trotton; dau. of Edmund Mortimer (1352–1381), 3rd earl of March, and Philippa Mortimer (1355–1382); sister of Edmund Mortimer (1376–1438); great-granddau. of King Edward III; m. Henry Percy (1364–1403), also known as Harry Percy or Hotspur (son of the 1st earl of Northumberland); m. Thomas, 1st baron Camoys; children: (first marriage) Henry Percy (1392–1455), 2nd earl of Northumberland (r. 1415–1455); Elizabeth Percy (d. 1437). ❖ A rebel immortalized by Shakespeare as "Kate Percy" in *Henry IV,* could claim royal descent on mother's side; married the important military leader Sir Henry Percy, called Harry "Hotspur" because of his boldness in battle; supported husband in a massive rebellion against Henry IV (1402), which sought to put her brother Edmund Mortimer on the throne; after husband was killed at Battle of Shrewsbury (1403), was arrested as a traitor to the king; though eventually released, was stripped of all rights to Hotspur's properties. ❖ See also *Women in World History.*

PERCY, Elizabeth (d. 1437). Countess of Westmoreland. Name variations: Elizabeth Neville; Elizabeth Clifford. Died Oct 26, 1437, at Staindrop Church; dau. of Henry Percy (1364–1403), also known as Harry Percy or Hotspur (son of the 1st earl of Northumberland), and Elizabeth Percy (1371–1417); m. John Clifford, 7th Lord Clifford, in May 1404; m. Ralph Neville, 2nd earl of Westmoreland, in 1426; children: (1st m.) Thomas Clifford, 8th Lord Clifford (b. 1414); (2nd m.) John Neville.

PERCY, Elizabeth (1667–1722). Duchess of Somerset. Name variations: Lady Elizabeth Percy; countess of Ogle. Born Jan 26, 1667, in Petworth, Sussex; died of breast cancer, Nov 23, 1722, at Northumberland House; only surviving daughter and sole heir of Josceline also known as Jocelyn Percy (1644–1670), 11th and last earl of Northumberland, and Elizabeth Wriothesly; m. Henry Cavendish, earl of Ogle, Mar 27, 1679; m. Thomas Thynne (1648–1682), Nov 15, 1681 (marriage never consummated because he was murdered by Königsmark, one of her suitors); m. Sir Charles Seymour, 6th duke of Somerset, May 30, 1682; children: Charles Seymour, earl of Herford; Elizabeth Seymour (1685–1734, who m. Henry O'Brien, 8th earl of Thomond); Lady Catherine Seymour (d. 1731, who m. Sir William Wyndham); Algernon Seymour (b. 1684), 7th duke of Somerset; Anne Seymour (d. 1722, who m. Peregrine Hyde Osborne, 3rd duke of Leeds). ❖ Was mistress of the robes to Queen Anne.

PERCY, Elizabeth (d. 1704). Countess of Northumberland. Name variations: Elizabeth Howard. Died Mar 11, 1704; dau. of Theophilus Howard (1584–1640), 2nd earl of Suffolk (r. 1584–1640), and Elizabeth Hume (c. 1599–1633); m. Algernon Percy (1602–1668,

admiral), 10th earl of Northumberland (r. 1632–1668), on Oct 1, 1642; children: Josceline also known as Jocelyn Percy (1644–1670), 11th and last earl of Northumberland. Algernon Percy's 1st wife was Anne Cecil. ❖ With husband, became guardians of the youngest children of King Charles I: Elizabeth Stuart (1635–1650) and Henry, duke of Gloucester, in 1645.

PERCY, Elizabeth (1716–1776). Duchess of Northumberland. Name variations: Lady Elizabeth Seymour; Baroness Percy. Born Nov 26, 1716; died Dec 5, 1776, at Alnwick Castle; dau. of Frances Thynne (1699–1754) and Algernon Seymour (b. 1684), Baron Percy, 7th duke of Somerset; m. Sir Hugh Smithson (1714–1786, a wealthy Yorkshire baronet who assumed the name Percy), 1st duke of Northumberland (r. 1766–1786), on July 16, 1740; children: Hugh Percy (b. 1742), 2nd duke of Northumberland; Algernon Percy (b. 1750), 1st earl of Beverley.

PERCY, Florence (1832–1911). *See Allen, Elizabeth Chase.*

PERCY, Karen (1966—). Canadian Alpine skier. Born Oct 10, 1966, in Banff, Canada. ❖ Won bronze medals for downhill and super-G at Calgary Olympics (1988); at World championships, won a silver medal for downhill (1989).

PERCY, Katherine (b. 1423). Countess of Kent. Born May 28, 1423, in Leconfield, Yorkshire; dau. of Henry Percy (1392–1455), 2nd earl of Northumberland (r. 1415–1455), and Eleanor Neville (c. 1413–1472); m. Edmund Grey (b. 1416), 1st earl of Kent, before 1440; children: Anthony Grey, Baron de Ruthin; George Grey, 2nd earl of Kent; John Grey, Lord Grey of Ruthin; Edmund Grey; Elizabeth Grey (who m. Sir Robert Greystoke); Anne Grey (who m. John Grey, Lord Grey of Wilton).

PERCY, Mary (1320–1362). Baroness Percy. Name variations: Mary Plantagenet. Born in 1320 (some sources cite 1321); died Sept 2, 1362; interred at Alnwick, Northumberland; dau. of Henry (b. 1281), 3rd earl of Lancaster, and Maud Chaworth (1282–c. 1322); m. Henry Percy, 3rd baron Percy, in Sept 1341 (some sources cite 1334); children: Henry Percy (1341–1408), 1st earl of Northumberland (r. 1377–1408); Maud Percy, also seen as Mary Percy (1360–1395, who m. John, Lord Ros).

PERCY, Mary (1904–2000). *See Jackson, Mary Percy.*

PERDITA.
See Lennox, Charlotte (1720–1804).
See Robinson, Mary (1758–1800).

PEREC, Marie-Jose (1968—). French track-and-field athlete. Born May 9, 1968, in Basse Terre, Guadeloupe. ❖ Hugely popular in France, won a gold medal in the 400 meters at Barcelona Olympics (1992); at European championships, won a bronze medal in the 400 meters (1990) and gold medals in the 400 meters and 4 x 400 meter relay (1994); at World championships, won a gold medal in the 400 meters (1991, 1995); won gold medals for the 200 meters as well as the 400 meters at Atlanta Olympics (1996), the 1st athlete to win a gold medal in that event at 2 successive Olympics; at the last minute, pulled out of the Sydney Olympics amid much controversy (2000).

PEREGRINA, La.
See Gómez de Avellaneda, Gertrudis (1814–1873).
See Reed, Alma (1889–1966).

PEREIRA, Irene Rice (1902–1971). American painter, poet, and essayist. Name variations: I. Rice Pereira. Born Irene Rice in Chelsea, Massachusetts, Aug 5, 1902; died in Marbella, Spain, Jan 11, 1971; dau. of Emanuel (known as Emery) Rice (baker and businessman) and Hilda Vanderbilt Rice; m. Humberto Pereira, 1929 (div. 1938); m. George Wellington Brown, 1942 (div. 1950); m. George Reavey, 1950 (div. 1959). ❖ Until recently, one of the forgotten women of 20th-century American art, was a cutting-edge figure in abstract art whose work was widely praised and regularly exhibited in major galleries (1933–53); enrolled in art classes at Art Students League, NY (1929); traveled through Europe (1931) and North Africa (1932); gave 1st solo art show, American Contemporary Arts Gallery, NY (1933); was a member of the fine arts faculty, Federal Arts Project Design Laboratory (1936); painted on glass (1939–52); was a sponsor of Cultural and Scientific Conference for World Peace held at Waldorf-Astoria (1949); published philosophy, "Light and the New Reality," in *Palette* (1952); was the subject of a Whitney Museum retrospective exhibit (1953), the crowning moment of her career; her abstract compositions integrated her intellectual interests in psychology, physics, alchemy, and occult philosophy. ❖ See also

Karen A. Bearor, *Irene Rice Pereira: Her Paintings and Philosophy* (U. of Texas Press, 1993); and *Women in World History*.

PEREIRA, Jacqueline (1964—). Australian field-hockey player. Name variations: Jackie Pereira. Born Jacqueline Margaret Pereira, Oct 29, 1964, in Willetton, Western Australia. ❖ Was a member of the national team (1986–96); won team gold medals at Seoul Olympics (1988) and Atlanta Olympics (1996); was the 1st Australian woman to total 100 career goals; turned to coaching. Named to the World Eleven Team (1988, 1989); inducted into Australian Hall of Fame (1998) and received the Order of Australia Medal from Queen Elizabeth II.

PEREIRA DA SILVA, Kelly (1985—). Brazilian soccer player. Name variations: Kelly. Born May 8, 1985, in Rio de Janeiro, Brazil. ❖ Forward, won a team silver medal at Athens Olympics (2004).

PEREIRA RIBEIRO, Tania (1974—). Brazilian soccer player. Name variations: Tania. Born Oct 3, 1974, in Brazil. ❖ Defender, won a team silver medal at Athens Olympics (2004).

PERENA, Natalia Via Dufresne (1973—). *See Via Dufresne, Natalia.*

PERESTRELLO-MONIZ, Filippa (d. 1483). Portuguese wife of Christopher Columbus. Name variations: Filippa Columbus or Columbo; Filippa Colón; Felipa Perestrello e Moniz. Died in 1483; dau. of a Portuguese officer (governor of an island near Madeira); m. Christopher Columbus (1451–1506, the explorer), also seen as Cristóbal Colón (Spanish) and Cristoforo Columbo (Italian); children: Diego (later governor of Hispaniola). Christopher Columbus also had an illegitimate son Ferdinand. ❖ Was married to Columbus during a portion of the 10 years he spent chartmaking in Portugal (1476–86). ❖ See also *Women in World History*.

PERESZTEGINE MARKUS, Erzsebet (1969—). *See Markus, Erzsebet.*

PEREVOZCHIKOVA, Maria. *See Stanislavski, Maria.*

PEREY, Marguerite (1909–1975). French nuclear chemist and physicist. Born Marguerite Catherine Perey, Oct 19, 1909, in Villemomble, France; died in Louveciennes, France, May 14, 1975; youngest of 5 children of an industrialist; educated at École d'Enseignement Technique Féminine; awarded Diplôme d'Etat de Chimiste (1929); during WWII, attended the Sorbonne and received her secondary school *licence* diploma, becoming qualified to defend a thesis there for a Docteur ès Sciences Physiques degree, which she successfully accomplished (Mar 2, 1946); never married. ❖ Began scientific career as assistant and confidante of Marie Curie at Paris Institut du Radium; discovered Francium, the long-sought 87th element in the periodic table (1938); worked closely with France's National Center of Scientific Research (CNRS), as well as with the International Union of Pure and Applied Chemistry; named chair of nuclear chemistry at University of Strasbourg (1949); became director of a research facility at Strasbourg-Cronenbourg (1958); was the 1st woman admitted to the French Academy of Sciences (1962). Received Grand Prix de la Ville de Paris, Lavoisier Prize of the Académie des Sciences, Silver Medal of the Société Chimique de France, Officier of the Légion d'Honneur, and Commandeur of the Ordre Nationale du Mérite and of the Order of Palmes Académiques; twice awarded the lauréat of France's Académie des Sciences (1950 and 1960). ❖ See also *Women in World History*.

PEREYASLAVEC, Valentina (1907–1998). Soviet ballet dancer and teacher. Born Feb 10, 1907, in Ukraine; died Jan 4, 1998, in Woodside, NY; studied at the Bolshoi Ballet School in Moscow. ❖ Joined Asaf Messerer and Vladimir Ryabster's troupe in Kharkov, where she performed Swanilda and Kitri, among others; danced with State Ballet in Sverdlovsk, appearing in premiere of Iakobson's *Lost Illusions* (1936); studied with Agrippina Vaganova in Leningrad; joined State Ballet of Lvov (1940); during WWII, deported and sentenced to work in factories in Leipzig; moved to New York and began teaching at Ballet Theater School (1951).

PÉREZ, Eulalia Arrila de (c. 1773–c. 1878). Chicana oral historian. Name variations: Eulalia Arrila de Perez. Born Eulalia Arrila de Pérez in Loreto, California, c. 1773; died in California, c. 1878; dau. of Diego Pérez (US Navy employee) and Antonia Rosalía Cota; m. Miguel Antonio Guillér, c. 1788 (died c. 1818); m. Juan Marín, 1833; children: at least 6, daughters Petra, Rita, and María, son Indoro, and 2 sons who died in infancy. ❖ Was nearly 100 years old when she participated in one of the first oral histories of the settlement of California, detailing the growth of what was in the late 18th century a Spanish-held territory; was

housekeeper at the Mission San Gabriel (c. 1818–35). ❖ See also *Women in World History*.

PEREZ, Gontrada (fl. 1100s). Mistress of Alphonso VII. Name variations: Pérez. Had liaison with Alphonso VII (1105–1157), king of León and Castile (r. 1126–1157); children: Urraca of Castile (d. 1179). ❖ Alphonso VII was married to Berengaria of Provence and Ryksa of Poland.

PEREZ, Inez (fl. 1400). Mistress of John I of Portugal. Name variations: Pérez. Dau. of Pedro Esteves and Maria Annes; had liaison with João I also known as John I (1385–1433), king of Portugal (r. 1385–1433); children: (with John I) Alfonso, duke of Braganza (b. around 1377); Beatrice of Portugal (d. 1439, who m. Thomas Fitzalan and John Holland). ❖ John I was married to Philippa of Lancaster.

PEREZ, Maria (fl. 13th c.). Spanish composer and singer. Name variations: Maria Perez Balteira; La Balteira. ❖ Medieval composer and singer who wrote sacred plainsong, performed in the courts of Europe, and was somewhat of an adventurer. ❖ See also *Women in World History*.

PEREZ DEL SOLAR, Gabriela (1968—). Peruvian volleyball player. Born July 10, 1968, in Peru. ❖ At Seoul Olympics, won a silver medal in team competition (1988).

PERHAM, Linda (1947—). English politician and member of Parliament. Born Linda Conroy, June 29, 1947; m. Raymond Perham, 1972. ❖ Representing Labour, served in House of Commons for Ilford North (1997–2005); lost bid for reelection (2005).

PERHAM, Margery (1895–1982). British scholar, writer and lecturer on African affairs. Name variations: Dame Margery Freda Perham. Born 1895; died 1982; gained an Open Scholarship to St. Hugh's College, Oxford, 1914, and left with a first class honors degree in modern history, 1917. ❖ Appointed assistant lecturer at Sheffield University (1917); returned to St. Hugh's College, Oxford, as tutor and fellow, then reader in colonial administration, then fellow of Nuffield College (1939); was also associated with Institute of Colonial (now Commonwealth) Affairs at Oxford; became the 1st woman invited to give the BBC annual Reith lecture (1961); wrote *African Apprenticeship* (1929), *Native Administration in Nigeria* (1937), *Africans and British Rule* (1941), *The Life of Lord Lugard* (2 vols., 1956, 1960), *The Colonial Reckoning* (1963) and *The Colonial Sequence* (2 vols., 1967, 1970). ❖ See also *Women in World History*.

PÉRICHOLE, La (1748–1819). *See Villegas, Micaela.*

PERICTIONE (fl. 400 BCE). Greek mother. Name variations: Petone. Descendant of Solon; lived in Athens; dau. of Glaucon; sister of Charmides; m. Ariston; children: sons Adimantus, Glaucon, and Plato (philosopher, born c. 428 BCE); daughter Petone (who was the mother of Speusippus).

PÉRIER, Gilberte Pascal (1620–1687). *See Pascal, Gilberte.*

PÉRIER, Marguerite (c. 1645–?). French writer. Name variations: Margot Perier. Born in 1645 or 1646; death date unknown; dau. of Florin Périer and Gilberte Pascal (biographer, 1620–1687); had at least two sisters and one brother; educated at Port Royal; had miraculous recovery from an ulcerated eye on Mar 24, 1656. ❖ Niece of Jacqueline Pascal and Blaise Pascal, whose miraculous cure inspired his religious conversion; wrote *Life of Pascal*. ❖ See also *Women in World History*.

PERI ROSSI, Cristina (1941—). Uruguayan author, feminist and political activist. Born Nov 12, 1941, in Montevideo, Uruguay; dau. of Ambrosio Peri (textile worker) and Julieta Rossi (schoolteacher). ❖ One of the best-known foes of military dictatorship in Uruguay (1973–85), published 1st book, a collection of short stories *Viviendo* (Living, 1963), at 22; caused scandal with her book of Sapphic erotic poems, *Evohé* (1971); joined leftist Frente Amplio (Broad Front); wrote for progressive publication *Marcha* (March) and Communist party newspaper *El Popular* (The People's Paper), and harbored students associated with Tupamaro guerrilla movement; forced into exile (1972), fled to Barcelona, which became permanent residence; had 10-year romantic relationship with Ana Basualdo, Argentinean exile; wrote many novels, including best-known *La nave de los locos* (The Ship of Fools, 1984) and *El amor es una droga dura* (Love Is a Hard Drug, 1999); earned acclaim for short stories and books of poetry, including *Europa después de la lluvia* (Europe after the Rain, 1980), and essays, including *Fantasías eróticas* (Erotic Fantasies, 1993); worked as translator for such writers as Clarice

Lispector and Monique Wittig and as journalist for such leftist publications as *Triunfo*. Received Youth Prize of *Arca* (Treasure Chest) magazine for collection of short stories *Los museos abandonados* (Abandoned Museums, 1968), Marcha Prize for 1st novel *El libro de mis primos* (My Cousins' Book, 1969), Grand Prize of City of Barcelona for novel *Babel bárbara* (Barbarous Babel, 1991), and International Rafael Alberti Prize for Poetry (2003).

PERIS-KNEEBONE, Nova (1971—). Australian-Aboriginal field-hockey player and runner. Name variations: Nova Peris. Born Nova Peris, Feb 15, 1971, in Darwin, Australia, a member of the Muran Clan, traditional owners of Kakadu and Arnhem Land regions; m. Sean Kneebone. ❖ Won a team gold medal for field hockey at Atlanta Olympics (1996), the 1st Aboriginal to win a gold medal; as a runner, won the 200 meters at the Commonwealth Games (1998); attended the Constitutional Convention at the request of the prime minister (1998); also an accomplished artist. Named Young Australian of the Year (1997). ❖ See also autobiography *Nova: My Story*.

PERKINS, Betty Williams (b. 1943). See *Williams, Betty*.

PERKINS, Charlotte (1860–1935). See *Gilman, Charlotte Perkins*.

PERKINS, Elizabeth Peck (c. 1735–1807). American businesswoman. Born Elizabeth Peck, Feb 14, 1735 or 1736, in Boston, MA; died May 24, 1807, in Boston, MA; dau. of Elizabeth (Spurrier?) Peck and Thomas Handasyd Peck (fur trader and hatter); m. James Perkins (general-store merchant and friend of Paul Revere), Dec 24, 1754 (died 1773); children: 9, including Thomas Handasyd Perkins (major China trade merchant, b. 1764). ❖ Admired for her ability to support her large family after husband's death, established "grossary shop" business (1773), selling chinaware, glass, wine, and other imported goods; inherited real estate from parents' deaths (late 1770s); during war years, subscribed $1,000 for the Continental Army (1780); focused energies on civic and philanthropic endeavors after children married; was a friend of many religious leaders, including Jean de Cheverus, Boston's 1st Roman Catholic bishop; helped found and finance the 1st Boston female-founded charitable institution, the Boston Female Asylum (1800), of which she served as director and treasurer; owned a good deal of Boston real estate; esteemed as a great lady of character and a mother of prominent children who made significant civic and philanthropic contributions.

PERKINS, Frances (1880–1965). American Cabinet official. Born Fannie Coralie Perkins in Boston, Massachusetts, April 10, 1880; died May 14, 1965, in New York, NY; dau. of Frederick W. Perkins and Susan E. (Bean) Perkins; graduated, with a major in chemistry and physics, from Mt. Holyoke College, 1902; m. Paul C. Wilson (economist), 1913; children: Susanna Winslow Perkins (b. 1916). ❖ Skillful administrator and politician, patient negotiator and conciliator, was the 1st American woman to hold a Cabinet office in the federal government; moved to Chicago as a teacher at Ferry Hall School (1904); became secretary of Philadelphia Research and Protective Association (1907); worked for New York Consumers' League (1910); as an observer of the Triangle Shirtwaist fire (1911), became an influential witness, then executive secretary, for NY Committee of Safety; appointed to Industrial Commission by NY governor Al Smith (1918), reappointed (1922, 1924, 1926); promoted to NY Labor Commissioner with election of Franklin D. Roosevelt as NY governor (1928); at onset of Depression, frequently challenged Hoover's claims that the depression was not very serious; appointed secretary of labor with election of FDR as US president (1932), becoming one of the longest-serving and most trusted members of the New Deal government; created the Bureau of Immigration and Naturalization, the Bureau of Labor Statistics, a new US Employment Service (1932) and the Division of Labor Standards (1933); also played a key role in the planning stages of the Civilian Conservation Corps, the Federal Emergency Relief Act, the National Labor Relations Act, and the Social Security Act of 1935; nearly underwent impeachment action instituted by a conservative member of the House Committee on Un-American Activities, but the judiciary committee found no grounds for proceeding (1935); resigned as secretary of labor (1945); appointed by President Truman to Civil Service Commission (1947); wrote *The Roosevelt I Knew* (Viking, 1946). ❖ See also George Martin, *Madam Secretary: Frances Perkins* (Houghton, 1976); Lillian Holmen Mohr, *Frances Perkins: "That Woman in FDR's Cabinet!"* (North River, 1979); Elisabeth Myers, *Madam Secretary: Frances Perkins* (Messner, 1972); Bill Severn, *Frances Perkins; A Member of the Cabinet* (Hawthorn, 1976); and *Women in World History*.

PERKINS, Lucy Fitch (1865–1937). American author of children's books. Born July 12, 1865, in Maples, Indiana; died Mar 18, 1937, in Pasadena, California; dau. of Appleton Howe Fitch (factory owner) and Elizabeth (Bennett) Fitch (teacher); graduate of Museum of Fine Arts School, Boston, 1886; m. Dwight Heald Perkins (architect), Aug 18, 1891; children: Eleanor Ellis Perkins (b. 1893, writer); Lawrence Bradford Perkins (b. 1908). ❖ Illustrated and wrote 1st book, *The Goose Girl* (1906); began popular and profitable 26-vol. "Twins of the World" series with publication of *The Dutch Twins* (1911), engaging young readers with whimsical drawings, humor, simple language, and glimpses into the lives of children from various nations. ❖ See also Eleanor Ellis Perkins, *Eve among the Puritans: A Biography of Lucy Fitch Perkins* (1956); and *Women in World History*.

PERKINS, Ma. See *Payne, Virginia*.

PERKINS, Millie (1938—). American actress. Born May 12, 1938, in Passaic, New Jersey; dau. of a sea captain; m. Dean Stockwell (actor), 1960 (div. 1964); m. Robert Thom (writer-director). ❖ Had just launched a successful modeling career when she was cast in the coveted role of Anne Frank in film version of *The Diary of Anne Frank* (1959); other films include *Wild in the Country* (1961), *Ensign Pulver* (1964), *Wild in the Streets* (1968), *Table for Five* (1983), *At Close Range* (1986), *Jake Speed* (1986), *Slamdance* (1987), *Wall Street* (1987), *Two Moon Junction* (1988), *The Birth of a Legend* (1991) and *Sharkskin* (1991).

PERKINS, Susan (c. 1954—). Miss America. Name variations: Susan Botsford. Born Susan Yvonne Perkins, c. 1954, in Columbus, Ohio; m. Alan Botsford; children: 2. ❖ Named Miss America (1978), representing Ohio; became a professional singer and tv reporter.

PERKUCIN, Gordana (1962—). Yugoslavian table-tennis player. Born May 1962 in Yugoslavia. ❖ At Seoul Olympics, won a bronze medal in doubles (1988); won European championship in doubles (1992).

PERMON, Laure (1784–1838). See *Abrantès, Laure d'*.

PERÓN, Eva (1919–1952). Argentine social activist and first lady. Name variations: Eva María Ibarguren; Eva María Duarte de Perón; Evita. Pronunciation: A-vah Pay-RONE. Born Eva María Ibarguren, May 7, 1919, in Los Toldos, Buenos Aires, Argentina; died July 26, 1952, of cancer in Buenos Aires; illeg. dau. of Juan Duarte (landowner) and Juana Ibarguren, his mistress; m. Juan Domingo Perón (president of Argentina, 1946–55, 1973–74), Oct 22, 1945 (died 1974); no children. ❖ Social activist and wife of Juan Domingo Perón who represented the revolutionary potential of Peronism and pushed the involvement of women in the nation's politics; left her family in Junín and made her way to the capital of Buenos Aires intent on a career in the theater (1934); became a radio personality and actress; married Juan Domingo Perón (1945) and was catapulted into the forefront of Argentine politics; campaigned over the radio for women's suffrage and began to make her 1st appearances before labor groups (1946); to mend international fences, went on "Rainbow Tour" (1947), representing Argentina to Europe's heads of state; pushed a social agenda for Argentine workers and the disadvantaged; created the María Eva Duarte de Perón Foundation, which dispensed money and largesse to the poor (1948); named president of the women's branch of Peronist Party (1949) which initiated a widespread membership drive and asserted its demand that women appear on Peronist slates for office; failed in bid to run for office of vice-president (1951); as death neared, her speeches grew more impassioned, violent, and apocalyptic. ❖ See also ghostwritten autobiography, *La Razón de mi Vida* (trans. in English as *My Mission in Life*, 1952); Fraser and Navarro, *Eva Peron* (Norton, 1987); J.M. Taylor, *Eva Perón: The Myths of a Woman* (U. of Chicago Press, 1979); Alicia Dujovne Ortiz, *Eva Péron* (trans. by Shawn Fields, St. Martin's, 1996); film *Eva Peron*, starring Esther Goris (1997); musical and film of *Evita* by Andrew Lloyd Webber and Tim Rice; and *Women in World History*.

PERÓN, Evita (1919–1952). See *Perón, Eva*.

PERÓN, Isabel (1931—). Argentine president. Name variations: María Estela Martínez de Perón; Isabelita. Pronunciation: Pay-rone. Born María Estela Martínez Cartas, Feb 4, 1931, in the province of La Rioja, Argentina; dau. of Marcelo Martínez Rosales (branch manager of National Mortgage Bank) and María Josefa Cartas; left school after 6th grade to study ballet, Spanish dancing, French and piano; became 3rd wife of Juan Domingo Perón (president of Argentina, 1946–55, 1973–74), in Madrid, Spain, Nov 15, 1961; no children. ❖ President of Argentina (1974–76) and head of Argentina's largest political party, the Peronist Party (1974–85), who was the 1st woman chief executive of a

Latin American nation and the 1st female head of state in the Western Hemisphere; joined Cervantes dance troupe (1955); while dancing with Joe Herald's ballet in Panama City, met Juan Perón during his exile from Argentina (1956); became his private secretary; followed him in exile to Venezuela, Dominican Republic, and finally Spain; married him (1961) and assumed role as his political representative; traveled to Argentina to promote Peronist candidates in provincial elections (1964); spent 9 months in Argentina promoting husband's cause (1965) and supervising provincial election campaigns that the Peronists swept; returned to Argentina (Dec 1971–Mar 1972) to prepare for national elections and head off challenges to husband's leadership; traveled to Argentina with husband, who had spent 17 years in exile (Nov 1972); nominated for vice-president at Peronist Party convention where husband was nominated for president (Aug 1973); with Peronists' victory, became husband's vice-president; appeared at state functions when husband became ill (late 1973); spoke to the International Labor Organization in Geneva and met with Pope Paul (June 1974); called home to Argentina to assume the presidency after husband's death (July 1, 1974); declared state of siege to combat economic and political chaos (Nov 1974); took leave from presidency for health reasons (Sept 1975); despite increasing opposition, determined to complete her term; succumbed to a military coup and placed under house arrest (Mar 1976); returned to Spain (1981); was official head of Peronist Party (until 1985); lives in Madrid, Spain, but makes frequent visits to Argentina. ❖ See also *Women in World History*.

PEROVSKAYA, Sonia (1853–1881). Russian revolutionary. Name variations: Sofya or Sofia Perovskaia. Pronunciation: Sown-ya Pair-ov-SKY-ya. Born Sophia Lvovna Perovskaya, Sept 13, 1853; executed, April 3, 1881; dau. of a general who served briefly as governor-general of St. Petersburg, and a mother who was a member of the nobility; never married; lived with Andrei Ivanovich Zhelyabov (revolutionary); no children. ❖ Member of the Russian aristocracy who turned to terrorism and was executed for engineering the assassination of Tsar Alexander II; joined the Chaikovski Circle and took part in the Going to the People movement (1870s); arrested for political activities (1874); met Andrei Ivanovich Zhelyabov during the Trial of 193 and acquitted (1878), but under a clause which allowed the police to prescribe "administrative exile"; was soon picked up again, acquired false papers and went underground; joined Land and Liberty, the 1st full-fledged political opposition party in Russian history; joined the extremist group Will of the People (Narodnaya Volya) and made several attempts on the life of Alexander II; led group in the assassination of Alexander II (1881); following her execution for murder of the tsar, was recognized as a martyr to the cause of revolution in Russia and the Soviet Union. ❖ See also Engel and Rosenthal, eds. *Five Sisters: Women Against the Tsar* (Knopf, 1975); and *Women in World History*.

PERPETUA (181–203). Christian saint and martyr. Name variations: Vibia Perpetua. Born in Thuburbo, a small town in northern Africa, in 181; executed Mar 7, 203, in the amphitheater at Carthage; probably married; children: at least one. ❖ Found guilty of treason, having publicly professed her Christianity; ordered put to death by Hilarianus (then governor of Africa) during the games; wrote a diary of her last days, now known as "The Martyrdom of Saints Perpetua and Felicitas," a vivid recollection of a tragic encounter between 2 very different religious perspectives. ❖ See also Joyce E. Salisbury, *Perpetua's Passion: The Death and Memory of a Young Roman Woman* (Routledge, 1997); and *Women in World History*.

PERRAULT-HARRY, Mme (1869–1958). See Harry, Myriam.

PERREAU, Gigi (1941—). American screen actress. Born Ghislaine Elizabeth Marie Thérèse Perreau-Saussine, Feb 6, 1941, in Los Angeles, CA; dau. of French fugitives from Nazi-occupied Paris; sister of Gerald Perreau (aka Peter Miles), Lauren Perreau, Janine Perreau (all child actors). ❖ At 2, made film debut in *Madame Curie* (1943), followed by *Green Dolphin Street, Enchantment, Roseanna McCoy, My Foolish Heart, Reunion in Reno, Weekend with Father, Has Anybody Seen My Gal?, Bonzo Goes to College, The Man in the Gray Flannel Suit, Tammy Tell Me True* and *Journey to the Center of the Earth*.

PERREAULT, Annie (1971—). Canadian short-track speedskater. Born July 28, 1971, in Windsor, Quebec, Canada; sister of Maryse Perreault (World champion short-track speedskater, 1982). ❖ Won a gold medal for the 3,000-meter relay at Albertville Olympics (1998); won a gold medal for the 500 meters and a bronze medal for the 3,000-meter relay at Nagano Olympics (1998).

PERRERS, Alice (d. 1400). Mistress of the English king Edward III. Name variations: Alice de Windsor; Lady of the Sun. Died 1400; m. Sir William de Windsor, deputy of Ireland (died 1384). ❖ Entered royal service as a woman of the bedchamber to Queen Philippa of Hainault sometime before 1366; intimacy with the king began around that time; during next few years, received several grants of land and gifts of jewels from him; after Philippa's death (1369), became more powerful; interfered in the proceedings of the courts of law to secure sentences in favor of friends, which induced the Parliament of 1376 to forbid all women from practicing in the law courts. ❖ See also *Women in World History*.

PERRIAND, Charlotte (1903–1999). French furniture and interior designer. Born Oct 24, 1903, in Paris, France; died Oct 27, 1999, in Paris; attended École de l'Union Central des Arts Décoratifs; married 1926 (div.); m. Jacques Martin (government official), 1943 (died 1986); children: (2nd m.) daughter Pernette Perriand. ❖ In a career that spanned 8 decades, became a legend of the modernist movement; designed tubular "equipment for living" with Le Corbusier and Pierre Jeanneret, furniture in Japan, lobbies for Air France, workers' housing in the Sahara desert, and the interiors of ski resorts in the French Alps; subscribed to the modernist notion that furnishings and architecture should be considered a single entity; also favored flexible space, free-form shapes, natural materials, and functional design with a humanistic touch. ❖ See also *Women in World History*.

PERRICHOLI, La (1748–1819). See Villegas, Micaela.

PERRIER, Glorianne (1929—). American kayaker. Born Mar 21, 1929; lived in Washington, DC. ❖ At Tokyo Olympics, won a silver medal in K2 500 meters (1964).

PERRIN, Ethel (1871–1962). American physical education expert. Born Ethel Perrin, Feb 7, 1871, in Needham, MA; died May 15, 1962, in Brewster, NY; dau. of David Perrin (merchant) and Ellen (Hooper) Perrin. ❖ Physical education specialist who believed that women's health was weakened by strenuous sports, which should be modified to suit women's physical and social limitations; taught at Boston Normal School of Gymnastics (1892–1906); was girls' physical education director in Central High School in Detroit (1908); became supervisor of physical education for Detroit Public Schools (1909); co-developed State of Michigan Course of Study in Physical Education, which became model for public school physical education programs across US (1914); was appointed 1st female vice president of American Physical Education Association (1920); served as assistant director of health education in Detroit (1920–23); became executive officer of National Amateur Athletic Federation (1923); served as associate director of Health Education Division of American Child Health Association (1923–36); was dairy farmer at Rocky Dell Farm in Brewster, NY (1936–62). Became 2nd woman to receive Luther Halsey Gulick Award for distinguished service in physical education (1946).

PERRIN, Gillian (1959—). See Gilks, Gillian.

PERRON, Lycette (1912–1996). See Darsonval, Lycette.

PERRONE, Elisabetta (1968—). Italian track-and-field athlete. Born July 9, 1968, in Camburzano, Italy. ❖ Won a silver medal for 10 km walk at Atlanta Olympics (1996); won National Indoor championship 3000m walk and National championship 5000m walk (both 2003).

PERROT, Kim (c. 1967–1999). African-American basketball player. Born c. 1967; died Aug 19, 1999, in Houston, TX; attended University of Southwestern Louisiana. ❖ During college career, held 26 school records; as a senior, led the nation in scoring, averaging 30.1 points a game; played professionally in Sweden, Germany, Israel and France; led the Houston Comets to a WNBA championship (1997).

PERRY, Agnes (1843–1910). See Booth, Agnes.

PERRY, Anne (1938—). See Hulme, Juliet Marion.

PERRY, Antoinette (1888–1946). American actress, producer, director, and activist. Born Antoinette Mary Perry, June 27, 1888, in Denver, Colorado; died June 28, 1946, in New York, NY; only child of William Russell Perry (attorney) and Minnie Betsy (Hall) Perry (Christian Science activist); m. Frank Wheatcroft Frueauff (businessman), Nov 30, 1909 (died July 1922); children: Margaret Perry (b. 1913, actress); Virginia (b. 1917, died in infancy); Elaine Perry (1921–1986, actress and producer). ❖ One of the most enduring figures in the American theater, made acting debut in Chicago in *Mrs. Temple's Telegram*; in NY, co-starred with David Warfield in *The Music Master* (1906), appearing with him again in *A Grand Army Man* (1907); appeared in Zona Gale's *Mr. Pitt* (1924); subsequently performed in *Minick* (1924), *The Dunce Boy* (1925), *Engaged* (1925), *The Masque of Venice* (1926), *The Ladder* (1926), and *Electra* (1927); took up directing (1928); after a moderate success with *Goin' Home*, directed *Strictly Dishonorable* (1928), a comedy by Preston Sturges, which ran for 557 performances; over the next 18 years, directed some 30 plays, many of them in collaboration with producer Brock Pemberton; most memorable productions included *Christopher Comes Across* (1932), *Red Harvest* (1937), *Kiss the Boys Goodbye* (1938), *Lady in Waiting* (1940), *Cuckoos on the Hearth* (1941), *Janie* (1942), and *Harvey* (1944); was chair of the committee of Apprentice Theater of the American Theater Council (1937–39), president of the Experimental Theater of the Actors' Equity Association (1941), and helped establish the American Theater Wing during WWII; honored posthumously when the Antoinette Perry Awards, known as the "Tonys," were introduced in her name (1947). ❖ See also *Women in World History*.

PERRY, Elaine (1921–1986). American stage actress and producer. Born Elaine Frueauff in 1921; died Jan 30, 1986, in Buena Vista, CO; dau. of Antoinette Perry (actress and producer, 1888–1946); sister of Margaret Perry (b. 1913, actress). ❖ Began career as understudy to Ingrid Bergman in *Liliom*; Broadway credits include *Glamour Preferred, The Trojan Women* and *Pillar to Post*, among others; produced and directed such plays as *A Race of Hairy Men!*; also produced *Touchstone, King of Hearts, Anastasia, How's the World Treating You?* and *The Late Christopher Bean*.

PERRY, Eleanor (1915–1981). American screenwriter and feminist. Name variations: Eleanor Bayer; (joint pseudonym with 1st husband) Oliver Weld Bayer. Born Eleanor Rosenfeld in Cleveland, Ohio, in 1915; died of cancer, Mar 14, 1981; briefly attended Sarah Lawrence College; Case Western Reserve, MA; m. Leo G. Bayer (lawyer and writer, div.); m. Frank Perry (director and producer), c. 1960 (sep. 1970, div. 1971); children: (1st m.) William Bayer; Anne Bayer. ❖ Entered the movie business when she was well into her 40s; within a decade, had written the screenplays for 9 films, *David and Lisa* (1962), *Ladybug, Ladybug* (1963), *The Swimmer* (1968), *Last Summer* (1969), *Trilogy* (1969), *Diary of a Mad Housewife* (1970), *Lady in the Car with Glasses and a Gun* (1970), *The Deadly Trap* (1971), and *The Man Who Loved Cat Dancing* (1973); often spoke out against the shabby treatment of women within the movie industry. ❖ See also *Women in World History*.

PERRY, Frances (1907–1993). English horticulturist. Name variations: Frances Mary Perry. Born Frances Mary Everett, Feb 19, 1907; died Oct 11, 1993; m. Gerald Perry (fern specialist), 1930 (died 1964); Robert Hay, 1977 (died 1989). ❖ The 1st woman council member of Royal Horticultural Society (1968), was elected its vice president (1978); appeared on early gardening tv programs; visited more than 70 countries, often as a horticulture lecturer; served as a horticultural adviser (1943) and as a chief educational adviser (1951–53) to Middlesex Co. Council; was the principal of Norwood Hall College of Horticulture and Agricultural Education (1953–67); writings include *Water Gardening* (1938), *Herbaceous Borders* (1949), *The Collins Guide to Border Plants* (1957); was also a gardening correspondent for the *Observer* for 26 years. Made a Member of the Order of the British Empire (1962); received Royal Horticultural Society's Veitch Memorial Medal (1964) and Victoria Medal of Honor (1971).

PERRY, Julia (1924–1979). African-American composer. Born Julia Amanda Perry in Lexington, Kentucky, Mar 25, 1924; died in Akron, Ohio, April 29, 1979; studied at Westminster Choir College in Princeton and Tanglewood; studied with Nadia Boulanger in Paris and Luigi Dallapiccola in Italy. ❖ Organized and gave a series of concerts in Europe sponsored by US Information Service (1957); awarded the Boulanger Grand Prix for her *Violin Sonata* (1952); in her *Homunculus C.F.*, wrote a composition for harp, celesta-piano and an ensemble of 8 percussionists; also wrote 2 operas and an opera ballet as well as 12 symphonies, meshing the neoclassic European tradition with music from her African-American heritage. Received American Academy and National Institute of Arts and Letters fellowship and Fontainebleau award. ❖ See also *Women in World History*.

PERRY, Katherine (1897–1983). American actress. Name variations: Kathryn Perry; Mrs. Owen Moore. Born Jan 5, 1897, in New York, NY; died Oct 14, 1983, Woodland Hills, CA; m. Owen Moore (actor), 1921 (died 1939). ❖ Once a Ziegfeld Follies beauty, starred in a series of Selznick comedies with husband; films include *Way Down East, The Chicken in the Case, Main Street, The First Year* and *Is Zat So?*

PERRY, Lilla Cabot (c. 1848–1933). American poet and painter. Born in Boston, Massachusetts, c. 1848; died in Hancock, New Hampshire, Feb 1933; studied art at Cowles School, Boston; attended Julian and Colarossi academies in Paris, France; m. Thomas Sargeant Perry (scholar and professor of 18th-century English literature), 1874; children: 3 daughters. ❖ Best remembered for her association with artist Claude Monet (1840–1926), and for her efforts in promoting French Impressionism in US during early years of 20th century, was also a respected artist in her own right, however, as a retrospective of her work at the Hirschl and Adler Galleries in New York (1969) helped reestablish; published the 1st of her 4 volumes of poetry, *Heart of Weed* (1886); founded Guild of Boston Artists (1914), of which she also served as the 1st secretary; frequently exhibited with the Guild, as well as with museums and art societies along East Coast; published *Reminiscences of Claude Monet from 1889 to 1909* (1927). ❖ See also *Women in World History*

PERRY, Margaret (1913—). American actress. Born Margaret Frueauff, Feb 23, 1913, in Denver, CO; dau. of Antoinette Perry (actress and producer, 1888–1946); sister of Elaine Perry (actress and producer, 1921–1986); m. Winsor Brown French (div.); m. Burgess Meredith (actor); m. Paul Fanning. ❖ Made stage debut succeeding Muriel Kirkland in *Strictly Dishonorable* (1929) to great success; other plays include *After All, Ceiling Zero, Now You've Done It* and *The Greatest Show on Earth*; films include *New Morals for Old* (1932).

PERRY, Mary (?–1906). *See Tautari, Mary.*

PERRY, Nanceen (1977—). African-American runner. Born April 19, 1977, in Fairfield, TX; dau. of Czar E. Perry and Goldie Hill; graduate of University of Texas, 1999. ❖ Won a bronze medal for 4 x 100-meter relay at Sydney Olympics (2000); was US indoor champion in the 200 meters (2000) and a 12-time All-American at Texas.

PERRY, Ruth (1939—). Liberian politician. Name variations: Ruth Sando Perry. Born in Grand Cape Mount, Liberia, July 16, 1939, into a family of Vai Muslims; dau. of Marjon and Al-Haji Semila Fahnbulleh; m. McDonald Perry (circuit court judge and senator); children: 4 sons, 3 daughters. ❖ The 1st female head of state in modern Africa, who served as interim president of her war-torn West African nation (Aug 1996–July 1997), 1st trained as a teacher at the Teachers College of the University of Liberia; taught elementary classes in hometown of Grand Cape Mount; when husband died, finished his term as senator; won a Senate seat representing United Party (UP, 1980); when UP officeholders and other opposition members boycotted the Senate to protest a fraudulent election, argued that "one cannot resolve problems by staying away" and became the lone member of the opposition in the chamber; when full-scale civil war broke out in Liberia (1989), returned home; named chair of Council of State by Economic Community of West African States (ECOWAS, 1996), the 1st woman in contemporary Africa to become a head of state (1996); wielded little in the way of real power, but helped nudge Liberians toward national elections (1997). ❖ See also *Women in World History*.

PERRY, Wanda (1917–1985). American actress. Born July 24, 1917, in Brooklyn, NY; died Feb 17, 1985, in Hollywood, CA; children: 1 daughter, 2 sons. ❖ Began career as a child model in NY; made film debut at 16 in *Murder at the Vanities*; other films include *Kid Millions, Roberta, Rosalie, Born to Dance, The Great Ziegfeld, Follow the Sun* and *Mame*.

PERSEY, Eileen (1899–1973). *See Percy, Eileen.*

PERSIA, princess of. *See Pahlavi, Ashraf (b. 1919).*

PERSIA, queen of.
See Atossa (c. 545–470s BCE).
See Cassandane (fl. 500s BCE).
See Statira I (c. 425–? BCE).
See Parysatis I (fl. 440–385 BCE).
See Statira II (c. 360–331 BCE).
See Sati Beg (c. 1300–after 1342).
See Soraya, Princess (b. 1932).

PERSIDA. *See Nenadovich, Persida (1813–1873).*

PERSIS. Biblical woman. A Christian woman of Rome. ❖ Was acknowledged by the apostle Paul, who spoke of her as "beloved" and as having "labored much in the Lord."

PERSSON, Elisabeth (1964—). Swedish curler. Born Feb 21, 1964, in Sweden. ❖ Four-time World champion (1992, 1995, 1998, 1999), won a bronze medal for curling at Nagano Olympics (1998); placed 6th at Salt Lake City Olympics (2002); retired (2002).

PERT, Camille (1865–1952). See Grillet, Louise.

PERT, Candace B. (1946—). American medical researcher. Name variations: Candace Beebe; Candace Beebe Pert; Candace Ruff. Born Candace Dorinda Beebe, June 26, 1946, in New York, NY; dau. of Robert and Mildred Beebe (court clerk); studied English at Hofstra University; Bryn Mawr, BS in chemistry and psychology; Johns Hopkins University, PhD, 1974; m. Agu Pert (Estonian scientist), 1966 (div. 1982); m. Michael Ruff (research partner), 1986; children: (1st m.) 3. ❖ Began looking for opiate receptor while studying with brain chemistry expert Solomon Snyder at Johns Hopkins (1970); proved that opiate receptors exist (Sept 1972); joined National Institute of Mental Health (NIMH) in Bethesda, MD (1975), where she headed her own laboratory, then became chief of brain biochemistry within the clinical neuroscience branch (1983), the only female chief; studied peptides; left NIMH to start own research company (1987); discovered that CD-4 receptor on immune system cells appear in brain; with Michael Ruff, researched and published results (1986) on Peptide T; was research professor at Georgetown University Medical Center; received Arthur S. Fleming Award for outstanding government service (1978) and Kilby Award (1993).

PERVERSI, Luigina (1914–1983). Italian gymnast. Born Feb 3, 1914, in Italy; died Oct 26, 1983. ❖ At Amsterdam Olympics, won a silver medal in the team all-around (1928).

PERY, Angela Olivia (1897–1981). Countess of Limerick and humanitarian activist. Born Angela Olivia Trotter, 1897; died 1981; dau. of Lieutenant-Colonel Sir Henry Trotter; awarded diploma in social science and administration from London School of Economics; m. Edmund Colquhoun Pery ("Mark"), 5th earl of Limerick, 1926; children: Anne Pery (b. 1928); Sir Patrick Edmund Pery, 6th earl of Limerick (b. 1930), and Michael Pery (b. 1937). ❖ Leader of the British and International Red Cross movements, began her long career with the Red Cross during WWI, serving as an ambulance driver (1914–18); started serving in the London branch of British Red Cross Society (1928), working her way to president (1939); was deputy chair of Joint War Organization, Red Cross, and St. John (1941–47), and vice-chair of executive committee of British Red Cross Society (1946–63); also served variously as vice chair of League of Red Cross Societies (1957–73) and chair of supreme coordinating committee of International Red Cross (1965–73). Awarded CBE (1942), DBE (1946), GBE (1954), and CH (1974). ❖ See also Women in World History.

PERY, Sylvia (1935—). English public health worker. Name variations: Sylvia Rosalind Lush; Countess of Limerick. Born Sylvia Rosalind Lush, 1935, in England; dau. of Brigadier Maurice Stanley Lush; graduate of Lady Margaret Hall, Oxford University; m. Patrick Edmund Pery, 6th earl of Limerick (Baron Glentworth of Mallow, Baron Foxford of Stackpole Court), 1961; daughter-in-law of Angela Olivia Pery; children: 2 sons, 1 daughter. ❖ Public health worker who earned acclaim for campaign against Sudden Infant Death Syndrome (SIDS), served as research assistant at Foreign Office (1959–62); worked on staff of British Red Cross Society (1962–66) and trained as medical officer before embarking on 1962 botanical expedition to Nepal with husband; had distinguished career in health field, serving on several hospital governing boards, area health authorities, community health councils and numerous other health-care organizations; began serving as vice-chair of Foundation for Study of Infant Deaths (1971); served as vice-president of Community Practitioners' and Health Visitors Association (1978–84), then president (1984–2002); appointed chair of British Red Cross (1985–95), chairing Chief Medical Officer's expert group to investigate SIDS (1994–98) and co-writing report Sudden Infant Death. Named Commander of British Empire (CBE, 1991).

PESCARA, marchioness of. See Colonna, Vittoria (c. 1490–1547).

PESOTTA, Rose (1896–1965). Russian-born American labor organizer and union official. Name variations: Rose Peisoty. Born Rose Peisotaya in Derazhnya, Russia (now Ukraine), Nov 20, 1896; died in Miami, Florida, Dec 7, 1965; dau. of Itsaak Peisoty and Masya Peisotaya;

attended Brookwood Labor College at Katonah, NY; possibly married twice (one source claims she lived with 3 men, but the relationships were never formalized); no children. ❖ A lifelong anarchist and major force in American labor movement in 1st half of 20th century, immigrated to America (1913); began working as a waistmaker in one of Manhattan's garment factories; joined International Ladies' Garment Workers' Union (ILGWU), becoming active in Local 25; also became involved in anarchist politics among NY's Jewish workers (1914); by early 1920s, was serving as a member of Local 25 executive board; served as general secretary of anarchist publication The Road to Freedom (1925–29); echoed Emma Goldman in her denunciation not only of capitalism, but also of the Communist dictatorship in the Soviet Union; became only woman member on ILGWU's General Executive Board (1934); also became an ILGWU vice president; spent 1930s conducting organizing campaigns in Atlantic City, Buffalo, Milwaukee, San Francisco and Seattle; in Puerto Rico and Los Angeles, conducted effective campaigns among female Latino workers; played a leading role in United Auto Workers' organizing campaign in Flint, Michigan (1936–37); determining that ILGWU women leaders had been kept in a subordinate role, quit her staff position and returned to a job sewing in a Manhattan clothing factory (1942); writings include Bread Upon the Waters and Days of Our Lives. ❖ See also Elaine Leeder, The Gentle General: Rose Pesotta, Anarchist and Labor Organizer (State U. of New York Press, 1993); and Women in World History.

PESTANA, Alice (1860–1929). Portuguese feminist activist, novelist and playwright. Name variations: Alice Pestana de Blanco; (pseudonym) Caiel or Caïel. Born 1860 in Portugal; died 1929 in Madrid, Spain. ❖ Wrote treatises and essays on women's education, including O Que Deve Ser a Ecucação Secundária da Mulher? (1892); wrote on Spanish life for Lisbon newspaper, Diário de Notícias; moved to Spain after marriage to Spanish-born husband (1901); translated Spanish authors into Portuguese; also wrote fiction, including Desgarrada (1902).

PETACCI, Clara (1912–1945). Italian paramour. Born Claretta Petacci, Feb 28, 1912, in Rome, Italy; died near Como, Italy, on April 28, 1945. ❖ Italian mistress of Benito Mussolini, was machine-gunned to death with Mussolini by partisans late in WWII; had been offered the chance to escape, but instead tried to protect Mussolini with her body. ❖ See also Women in World History.

PETCHERSKAYA, Svetlana (1968—). See Pecherskaya, Svetlana.

PETER, Birgit (1964—). East German rower. Born Jan 27, 1964, in East Germany. ❖ At Seoul Olympics, won a gold medal in double sculls (1988); at Barcelona Olympics, won a gold medal in quadruple sculls without coxswain (1992).

PETER, Paul and Mary. See Travers, Mary.

PETER, Sarah Worthington (1800–1877). American charity worker and philanthropist. Born Sarah Anne Worthington, May 10, 1800, near Chillicothe, Ohio; died of a coronary thrombosis, Feb 6, 1877, in Cincinnati; dau. of Thomas Worthington (governor and senator) and Eleanor (Van Swearingen) Worthington; m. Edward King, May 15, 1816 (died Feb 1836); m. William Peter (British consul in Philadelphia), Oct 21, 1844 (died 1853); children: (1st m.) Rufus (b. 1817); Thomas Worthington (b. 1820); Mary Alsop (b. 1821, died young); Edward (b. 1822, died young); James (b. 1828, died young). ❖ Helped to found the Cincinnati Protestant Orphan Asylum (1833); organized an association to provide assistance to seamstresses; raised funds for a shelter for reformed prostitutes, the Rosine House for Magdalens; established Philadelphia School of Design (1848), where women learned commercial design as well as wood engraving and lithography; founded (1853) and was the 1st president of Ladies' Gallery of Fine Arts (now Cincinnati Academy of Fine Arts); was responsible for founding of several local charitable organizations and convents belonging to various orders, including Sisters of the Good Shepherd (1857), which helped female prisoners, Sisters of Mercy (1858), which participated in social work and educational efforts, Order of the Poor of St. Francis (1858), and Little Sisters of the Poor (1868); also helped to establish the Cincinnati convent and school of Order of the Sacred Heart (1869). ❖ See also Margaret R. King, Memoirs of the Life of Mrs. Sarah Peter (1889); Anna Shannon McAllister, In Winter We Flourish: Life and Letters of Sarah Worthington King Peter (1939); and Women in World History.

PETERBOROUGH, countess of. See Robinson, Anastasia (c. 1692–1755).

PETERKIN, Julia (1880–1961). American novelist. Born Julia Mood, Oct 31, 1880, in Laurence Co., South Carolina; died Aug 10, 1961;

dau. of Julius Andrew Mood (physician) and Alma (Archer) Mood (died 1880); Converse College, BA, 1896, MA, 1897; m. William George Peterkin, June 3, 1903; children: William George. ❖ Raised largely by a Gullah nurse; assuming managerial duties on husband's large estate, supervised approximately 450 Gullah employees; wrote often of Gullah life and culture in her fiction; published 1st book, *Green Thursday*, a collection of sketches about the struggles of an African-American plantation family (1924); published 1st novel, *Black April* (1927); won Pulitzer Prize for *Scarlet Sister Mary* (1929), which was barred from several Southern public libraries and eventually sold more than 1 million copies; also wrote *Bright Skin* (1932), *Roll, Jordan, Roll* (1933) and *A Plantation Christmas* (1934). ❖ See also Susan Millar Williams, *A Devil and a Good Woman, Too* (U. of Georgia, 1997); and *Women in World History*.

PETERS, Alice Mary (1887–1963). *See Cassie, Alice Mary.*

PETERS, Bernadette (1948—). American singer and actress. Born Bernadette Lazzara, Feb 28, 1944, in Ozone Park, NY; m. Michael Wittenberg, 1996 (died 2005). ❖ Star of Broadway musicals, 1st appeared in *The Most Happy Fella* (1958), *Gypsy* (1961) and *Curly McDimple* (1967); came to prominence in *Dames at Sea* (1968); starred in *George M!* (1968), *La Strada* (1969), *W.C.* (1970), *Mack and Mabel* (1975), *Sunday in the Park with George* (1983), *Into the Woods* (1987) and *The Goodbye Girl* (1993); won Tony Award for *Song and Dance* (1984) and *Annie Get Your Gun* (1999); won a Golden Globe award for film *Pennies from Heaven*; other films include *The Longest Yard* (1974), *Silent Movie* (1976), *W.C. Fields and Me* (1976), *The Jerk* (1979), *Annie* (1982) and *Alice* (1990).

PETERS, Ellis (c. 1913–1995). *See Pargeter, Edith.*

PETERS, Jean (1926–2000). American actress. Born Elizabeth Jean Peters, Oct 15, 1926, in Canton, Ohio; died Oct 13, 2000, in Carlsbad, California; m. Stuart Cramer III, c. 1954 (div.); m. Howard Hughes (film producer and millionaire), 1957 (div. 1971); m. Stanley Hough (film producer), 1971 (died 1990). ❖ Named Miss Ohio State (1946); made film debut starring opposite Tyrone Power in *Captain from Castile* (1947); other films include *A Man Called Peter, Viva Zapata!, Three Coins in the Fountain, It Happens Every Spring, Wait Till the Sun Shines Nellie!, Niagara, Apache* and *Broken Lance.*

PETERS, Kristina (1968—). German field-hockey player. Born Mar 24, 1968, in Germany. ❖ At Barcelona Olympics, won a silver medal in team competition (1992).

PETERS, Linda (1948—). *See Thompson, Linda.*

PETERS, Luise (1819–1895). *See Otto-Peters, Luise.*

PETERS, Mary (1939—). English-born Irish pentathlete. Name variations: Dame Mary Peters. Born Mary Elizabeth Peters, July 6, 1939, in Halewood, Lancashire, England. ❖ At age 11, moved to Northern Ireland; represented Northern Ireland at Commonwealth Games (1958–74), winning a silver medal in shot put (1966), gold medal in shot put (1970), and gold in pentathlon (1974); represented Britain internationally (1961–74); won a gold medal in pentathlon at Munich Olympics (1972); set 25 British records (1962–72); campaigned for more sports facilities in Northern Ireland. Named Member of the British Empire (MBE, 1973), Commander of British Empire (CBE, 1994) and Dame Commander of the British Empire (DBE, 2001).

PETERS, Phillis (c. 1752–1784). *See Wheatley, Phillis.*

PETERS, Roberta (1930—). American soprano. Born Roberta Peterman, May 4, 1930, in NY, NY; Elmira College, LittD, 1967; Ithaca College, MusD, 1968; m. Robert Merrill (opera singer), 1952 (div.); m. Bertram Fields, 1955. ❖ Studied with William Pierce Hermann; made Metropolitan debut as Zerlina in *Don Giovanni* (1950) and was an overnight sensation; remained at Met for 35 seasons, singing most frequently *Il Barbiere di Siviglia, Don Pasquale, Lucia di Lammermoor, Die Zauberflöte* (as Queen of the Night) and *Rigoletto;* also performed beside Marian Anderson in Anderson's historic debut at the Met (1954) and created the role of Kitty in US premiere of Menotti's *The Last Savage;* debuted at Salzburg (1963) and Kirov Opera, Leningrad, and Bolshoi Opera, Moscow (1972); appeared frequently on tv (including commercials and some 65 visits to "The Ed Sullivan Show") and in film and musical comedy; retired from Met (1987). Awarded the Handel Medallion (2000). ❖ See also autobiography (with Louis Biancolli) *Debut at the Met* (1967); and *Women in World History.*

PETERS, Roumania (1917–2003). African-American tennis player. Name variations: Matilda Roumania Peters Walker. Born Matilda Roumania Peters, July 21, 1917, in Washington, DC; died May 16, 2003, in Maryland; sister of Margaret Peters (tennis player); graduate of Tuskegee Institute, 1941; New York University, MA in physical education; m. James Walker (mathematics professor), c. 1957 (died 1992); children: daughter and son. ❖ One of America's top-ranked tennis players at a time when segregation kept her off the world's mainstream courts, won the national title of the American Tennis Association (ATA, 1944 and 1946), the nation's oldest black organization; with sister, won 14 ATA doubles titles; taught at Howard University and in DC public schools.

PETERS, Susan (1921–1952). American actress. Name variations: Suzanne Carnahan. Born Suzanne Carnahan, July 3, 1921, in Spokane, WA; died Oct 23, 1952, in Visalia, CA; m. Richard Quine (director), 1943 (div. 1948). ❖ Films include *Santa Fe Trail, Susan and God, Meet John Doe, Random Harvest, Andy Hardy's Double Life, Song of Russia* and *Keep Your Powder Dry;* paralyzed from the waist down in a hunting accident (1944). Nominated for Academy Award for Best Supporting Actress for *Random Harvest* (1942).

PETERSEN, Alicia O'Shea (1862–1923). Australian reformer and political candidate. Born Alicia Teresa Jane McShane, July 2, 1862, in Broadmarsh, Tasmania, Australia; died Jan 22, 1923, in Hobart, Australia; dau. of Hugh McShane and Jane (Wood) McShane (both farmers); m. Patrick O'Shea, 1884 (died 1886); m. Hjalma Petersen (mining investor), 1891 (died 1912); children: (1st m.) stepson Francis Patrick. ❖ Influenced by her work experiences, was a prominent speaker for Citizens' Social and Moral Reform League (1906); founded and served as life president of Australian Women's Association; became 1st woman political candidate in Tasmania when she ran unsuccessfully for the federal seat of Denison (1913); established the Bush Nurses and Child Health Associations; campaigned for social reform; was also thwarted in a run for Tasmanian House of Assembly (1922). ❖ See also *Women in World History.*

PETERSEN, Rikke (1975—). *See Schmidt, Rikke.*

PETERSEN-KALLENSEE, Marga (1919—). West German runner. Born Sept 18, 1919, in Germany. ❖ At Helsinki Olympics, won a silver medal in the 4 x 100-meter relay (1952).

PETERSMANN, Cerstin (1964—). German rower. Born Nov 27, 1964, in Germany. ❖ At Barcelona Olympics, won a bronze medal in coxed eights (1992).

PETERSON, Amy (1971—). American short-track speedskater. Born Nov 29, 1971, in Maplewood, MN. ❖ The 9-time US short-track champion (1993–96, 1998–2000, 2002), won a silver medal in the 3,000-meter relay at Albertville Olympics (1992); won bronze medals for the 500 meters and the 3,000-meter relay at Lillehammer Olympics (1994).

PETERSON, Ann (1947—). American diver. Born June 16, 1947, in US. ❖ At Mexico City Olympics, won a bronze medal in platform (1968).

PETERSON, Esther (1906–1997). American labor activist and US government official. Born Esther Eggertsen in Provo, Utah, Dec 9, 1906; died Dec 21, 1997; dau. of Lars Eggertsen and Annie (Nielsen) Eggertsen; Brigham Young University, BA, 1927; Columbia University Teachers College, MA, 1930; m. Oliver A. Peterson, 1932; children: Eric, Iver, Lars, and Karen. ❖ Was assistant director of education for Amalgamated Clothing Workers of America (1939–44) and served as their Washington legislative representative (1945–48); also worked with Swedish Confederation of Trade Unions while living with husband abroad (1948–52); when husband was transferred to Brussels (1952–57), worked with International Confederation of Free Trade Unions and helped organize their 1st international school for working women at LaBrevière; lobbied for AFL-CIO (1958–61); was invited to join John F. Kennedy's "little cabinet" as assistant secretary of labor and director of Women's Bureau in US Department of Labor (1961), which then made her the highest-ranking woman in US government. ❖ See also *Women in World History.*

PETERSON, Lauri (1960—). *See Merten, Lauri.*

PETERSON, Marjorie (1906–1974). American dancer. Born Feb 9, 1906, in Houston, TX; died Aug 19, 1974, in New York, NY. ❖ Made New York debut as a featured dancer in *Greenwich Village Follies* (1923); danced in *Annie Dear* (1924) and Earl Carroll's *Vanities* (1925); in Broadway operettas, performed in *Countess Maritz* (1926) and *The Red*

Robe (1928); appeared for Shubert Brothers in numerous musical comedies as well as dramatic plays.

PETERSON, Mary (1927—). Native Alaskan midwife. Born Mary Peterson, Sept 18, 1927, in Akhiok, on Kodiak Island, Alaska; dau. of Ephrezenea Peterson and Teacon Peterson; m. Willy Eluska (died); Walter Simeonoff; children: (1st m.) 5; (2nd m.) 13. ❖ Native Alaskan midwife, practiced midwifery in the Alutiiq village of Akhiok on Kodiak Island; elected Akhiok's midwife (1947) after having delivered roughly 25 children; respected traditional Native practices of midwifery (e.g., keeping mothers warm and relaxed); also served as a community nurse.

PETERSON, Sylvia (1946—). American vocalist. Name variations: The Chiffons. Born Sept 30, 1946, in Bronx, NY. ❖ Joined Judy Craig, Patricia Bennett, and Barbara Lee as member of the Chiffons (1962), all-girl vocal group which had international hits in early 1960s; with Chiffons, released such hits as "He's So Fine" (1963), "One Fine Day" (with Carole King on piano, 1963), "Nobody Knows What's Going On" (1965) and "Sweet Talkin' Guy" (1966).

PETHERICK, Mary (fl. 1887). British mountaineer. Flourished in 1887; m. A.F. (Fred) Mummery (mountaineer), 1883. ❖ With husband and Alexander Burgener, climbed the Jungfrau, Zinal Rothorn, Drieckhorn, and the Taschorn, making the 1st ascent of the Teufelsgrat (Devil's Ridge) in the process (1887).

PETHICK-LAWRENCE, Emmeline (1867–1954). English suffragist and social worker. Name variations: Emmeline Pethick; Emmeline Pethick Lawrence. Born 1867 in Bristol, England; died 1954; dau. of Henry Pethick; educated at private schools in England, France, and Germany; m. Frederick Lawrence (newspaper editor, Labour politician and suffragist) who took the name Frederick Pethick-Lawrence (later Baron Pethick-Lawrence of Peaslake), in 1901; no children. ❖ A major force in the suffragist movement, worked for improvement of conditions for women (early 1900s); served as co-leader and treasurer of the Women's Social and Political Union (1906–12); created and edited periodical *Votes for Women* with husband (1907–14); participated in the Women's Peace Congress at The Hague (1915); served as treasurer of the Women's International League for Peace (1915–22); became president of Women's Freedom League (1918); named president of honor of Women's Freedom League (1953). ❖ See also memoir *My Part in a Changing World* (1938); Vera Brittain, *Pethick-Lawrence: A Portrait* Allen & Unwin, 1963 (biography of Frederick Pethick-Lawrence); and *Women in World History*.

PETHOE, Zsuzsanna (1945—). See *Kezine-Pethoe, Zsuzsanna*.

PETIPA, Marie (1836–1882). Russian ballet dancer. Born Marie Surovschikova (also seen as Sourvshikova), 1836, in Russia; died Mar 1882 in Pytigorsk, in the Caucasus; studied at St. Petersburg Imperial Ballet academy; m. Marius Petipa (1818–1910), ballet master and choreographer), 1854 (div. 1869); children: Marie Petipa (1857–1930). ❖ Performed with Maryinsky Theater (under Marius Petipa, her husband) throughout career, creating roles for him in *Le Marché des Innocents* (1859), *La Belle de Lebanon* (1860), and *La Danseuse Ambulate* (1865), among others; danced opposite brother-in-law Lucien Petipa at Paris Opéra in numerous works (1861–62).

PETIPA, Marie (1857–1930). Russian ballet dancer. Born Marie Mariusovna Petipa, 1857, in Russia; died 1930; dau. of Marie Petipa (1836–1882, ballet dancer) and Marius Petipa (1818–1910, ballet master and choreographer); studied with her father. ❖ A character dancer, created many national dances in ballets and operas; was the first Lilac Fairy in her father's *Sleeping Beauty*.

PETIT, Magdalena (1900–1968). Chilean novelist, essayist and short-story writer. Name variations: Magdalena Petit Marfán. Born 1900 in Santiago, Chile; died 1968 in Chile; dau. of a physician. ❖ As part of Chile's literary "Generation of 1927," was best known for *La Quintrala* (1930), the historical novel of Doña Catalina de los Ríos, for which she won the La Nación prize; also wrote *Don Diego Portales* (1937), *Los Pincheira* (1939), *Caleuche* (1946), *Un hombre en el universo* (1951) and *El patriota Manuel Rodríguez* (1951).

PETIT, Margaret (b. 1904). See *Caron, Margaret Pettibone*.

PETIT, Wanda (1895–1963). See *Hawley, Wanda*.

PETIT, Zizi (b. 1924). See *Jeanmaire, Zizi*.

PETIT-VANHOVE, Madame (1771–1860). See *Talma, Madame*.

PETITE ADELAIDE, La (c. 1884–1959). See *Adelaide*.

PETKOVA, Ognyana (1964—). Bulgarian kayaker. Born Dec 20, 1964, in Bulgaria. ❖ At Seoul Olympics, won a bronze medal in K4 500 meters (1988).

PETKOVA-VERGOVA, Mariya (1950—). Bulgarian track-and-field athlete. Name variations: Mariya Vergova. Born Nov 3, 1950, in Bulgaria. ❖ Won a silver medal at Montreal Olympics (1976) and a silver medal at Moscow Olympics (1980), both in the discus throw.

PETO, Mechtild (1879–1958). See *Lichnowsky, Mechthilde*.

PETONE. See *Perictione*.

PETRASS, Sari (1890–1930). Hungarian-born actress. Born Nov 5, 1890, in Budapest, Hungary; died Sept 7, 1930; m. F.A. Sommerhoff (div.); m. Gordon Crocker. ❖ Made stage debut in Budapest as Hippolit in *The Two Hippolits* (1906); came to prominence in Hungary as a singer in light opera; made triumphant London debut as Ilona in *Gipsy Love* (1912), followed by *The Marriage Market*, among others; made NY debut as Rosika Wenzel in *Miss Springtime* (1916).

PETRE, Maude (1863–1942). English writer and activist. Born in Coptfold Hall, Essex, England, 1863; died in London, England, Dec 1942; dau. of Arthur Petre and Lady Catherine Howard Petre, a Catholic convert; never married. ❖ Catholic modernist writer-activist and champion of the excommunicated Jesuit George Tyrrell, joined the Society of the Daughters of the Heart of Mary, the Filles de Marie (1890); took vow of perpetual celibacy (1901); after Pius X prohibited Catholics from reading, writing, and speculating on a broad range of "modernist" issues, and required of all priests an oath of loyalty (1907), published *Catholicism and Independence*, urging the priority of the individual conscience over the authority of priests and bishops; also left her leadership position in the Filles de Marie (1907); when Tyrrell was excommunicated (1907), offered him a refuge and refused to evict him when her bishop said she should not be harboring a condemned modernist; following death of Tyrrell (1909), published *Autobiography and Life of George Tyrrell* (1912); also published *Modernism: Its Failure and its Fruits* (1918) and her spiritual autobiography, *My Way of Truth* (1937). ❖ See also Clyde F. Crews, *English Catholicism: Maude Petre's Way of Faith* (Notre Dame U. Press, 1984); and *Women in World History*.

PETRENKO, Tatyana (1938—). See *Samusenko-Petrenko, Tatyana*.

PETRI, Heather (1978—). American water-polo player. Born June 13, 1978, in Orinda, CA; attended University of California, Berkeley. ❖ Won a team silver medal at Sydney Olympics (2000) and a team bronze at Athens Olympics (2004); won World championship (2003).

PETRICKOVA, Kvetoslava (1952—). Czech field-hockey player. Born July 17, 1952, in Czechoslovakia. ❖ At Moscow Olympics, won a silver medal in team competition (1980).

PETRIE, Haylea (1969—). Australian softball player. Born Aug 5, 1969, in Queensland, Australia. ❖ Won a bronze medal at Atlanta Olympics (1996).

PETRIE, Hilda (1871–1957). English archaeologist. Name variations: Hilda Mary Isobel Petrie. Born Hilda Mary Isobel Urlin, 1871, in Dublin, Ireland; died after a stroke, 1957, at London's University College Hospital; moved with family to Sussex, England (1875); dau. of Denny Urlin (lawyer in Dublin); m. Sir Flinders Petrie (Egyptology professor), Nov 26, 1897 (died 1942); children: at least 1. ❖ Assisted husband on Egyptian digs, prepared his research for publication, and lectured to raise funds; after his death (1942), served as director of British School of Archaeology in Egypt (1942–47) and organized his books and research; wrote *Seven Memphite Tomb Chapels* (1952).

PETRIK, Larissa (1949—). Soviet gymnast. Name variations: Larisa Petrik. Born Aug 28, 1949, in Belarus; m. Viktor Klimenko (gymnast). ❖ Won USSR nationals (1964), Yerevan Invitational (1966), and University Games (1970); at European championships, won a bronze medal in balance beam (1965); at World championships, won silver medal in team all-around and bronze medal for balance beam (1966) and gold medal for team all-around and bronze medal for balance beam (1970); at Mexico City Olympics, won gold medals in team all-around and floor exercises and a bronze medal in balance beam (1968); worked as commentator for Soviet tv.

PETRONILLA (1135–1174). Queen of Aragon. Born in 1135; died Oct 17, 1174, in Barcelona, Spain; dau. of Ramiro II, king of Aragon (r.

1134–1137), and Agnes de Poitiers; m. Ramon Berenguer also known as Raymond Berengar IV, count of Provence and king of Aragon (r. 1150–1162), on Aug 11, 1137; children: Douce of Aragon (1160–1198); Pere; Sancho of Provence, count of Provence (r. 1181–1185); Fernando; Alphonso II the Chaste (b. 1152), king of Aragon (r. 1162–1196).

PETROVA, Elena (1972—). *See Petrova, Olena.*

PETROVA, Ioulia (1979—). Russian water-polo player. Born May 24, 1979, in USSR. ❖ Won a team bronze medal at Sydney Olympics (2000).

PETROVA, Ludmila (1968—). Russian marathon runner. Name variations: Lyudmila. Born Oct 7, 1968, in Novo Cheboksary, Russia. ❖ Won New York City Marathon (2000) with a time of 2:25:45, the 1st Russian to win the event.

PETROVA, Maria (1975—). Bulgarian rhythmic gymnast. Born Nov 13, 1975, in Plovdiv, Bulgaria; m. Borislav Mihailov (soccer player), 1998. ❖ At World championships, won the silver medal in all-around (1992) and gold medals in all-around (1993, 1994, 1995); won Medico Cup (1992, 1993), European championship (1992, 1994), European Cup (1993), Gymnastics Masters (1994), Chichmanova Prize (1994, 1996), Universiade (1995), and Hungarian International Cup (1996).

PETROVA, Olena (1972—). Ukrainian biathlete. Name variations: Elena Petrova. Born Sept 24, 1972, in Moscow, Russia. ❖ Won a silver medal for 15 km at Nagano Olympics (1998).

PETROVA, Olga (1886–1977). English actress. Born Muriel Harding in England, 1886 (some sources cite 1884); died 1977. ❖ Billed by studio publicists as the daughter of a Russian noble from Poland, played femmes fatales in Hollywood silents for Metro, including *The Tigress* (1914), *The Soul Market* (1916), *The Undying Flame* (1917), *The Soul of a Magdalene* (1917), *Daughter of Destiny* (1918) and *Panther Woman* (1918); produced and wrote several of her own films; after retiring from the screen (1918), returned to the stage, starring in many plays, including 3 that she had also written. ❖ See also autobiography *Butter with My Bread* (1942).

PETROVA, Tatiana (1973—). Russian water-polo player. Born May 22, 1973, in USSR. ❖ Won a team bronze medal at Sydney Olympics (2000).

PETROVA, Yelena (1966—). Soviet judoka. Name variations: Elena Petrova. Born Oct 13, 1966, in USSR. ❖ At Barcelona Olympics, won a bronze medal in half-middleweight 61 kg (1992).

PETROVNA, Anne (1708–1728). *See Anne Petrovna.*

PETROVNA, Elizabeth (1709–1762). *See Elizabeth Petrovna.*

PETROVNA, Tatiana Nikolayeva (1924–1993). *See Nikolayeva, Tatiana.*

PETROVSCHI, Oana (1986—). Romanian gymnast. Born Feb 5, 1986, in Voiteg, Romania. ❖ At European championships, won a bronze medal for vault (2002).

PETROVÝKH, Mariia (1908–1979). Russian poet and translator. Name variations: Maria, Mariia or Mariya Sergeevna Petrovykh. Born 1908 in Russia; died 1979. ❖ Friend and editor to Anna Akhmátova, was highly regarded by Osip Mandelshtám and Boris Pasternak; translated from Armenian, Polish, and Yiddish; published book of original poems and translations, *A Distant Tree* (1968). Two works were published posthumously: *Predestination* (1983) and *The Line on the Horizon: Poems and Translations, Reminiscences of Mariia Petrovýkh* (1986).

PETRUCCI, Roxy (1962—). American drummer and singer. Name variations: Vixen. Born Mar 17, 1962, in Detroit, MI; sister of Maxine Petrucci (musician). ❖ Drummer and backup singer for all-girl pop-metal band Vixen, which was formed in Los Angeles (c. 1980); with group, signed with EMI (1988) and released debut album *Vixen* (1988), which went gold and included Top-40 hits, "Cryin'" and "Edge of a Broken Heart"; with group, released *Rev It Up* (1990), which included hit "How Much Love"; after band split up (1990s), joined Janet Gardner and Jan Kuehnemund to reform Vixen with original lineup (2001).

PETRUNOVA, Silva (1956—). Bulgarian volleyball player. Born Feb 13, 1956, in Bulgaria. ❖ At Moscow Olympics, won a bronze medal in team competition (1980).

PETRUSEVA, Natalia (1955—). Russian speedskater. Name variations: Natalya Petrusyova. Born Sept 2, 1955, in USSR. ❖ Won a gold medal for the 1,000 meters and a bronze for 500 meters at Lake Placid Olympics

(1980); won bronze medals for 1,000 and 1,500 meters at Sarajevo Olympics (1984); at World championships, won a gold medal for small allround (1980, 1981); at European championships, placed 1st in small allround (1981, 1982); won World sprint title (1982).

PETRUSHEVSKAYA, Ludmilla (1938—). Russian playwright, novelist and short-story writer. Name variations: Liudmila Stepanovna Petrushévskaia. Born 1938 in USSR. ❖ Pioneer of new Russian literature after *glasnost*, whose plays were 1st performed by avant-garde troupes but later became popular in mainstream theaters, appeared on the literary scene in 1970s; works, which are noted for sardonic humor and gritty presentations of daily life, include *Balancing Acts* (1973), *Images . . .* (1974), *Three Girls in Blue* (1980), *Our Crowd* (1988, trans. into English, 1990) and (novel) *The Time: Night* (1992, trans. into English, 1994).

PETRY, Ann (1908–1997). African-American writer. Name variations: Ann Lane Petry. Born Ann Lane, Oct 12, 1908, in Old Saybrook, Connecticut; died April 28, 1997, in Old Saybrook; dau. of Peter C. Lane (pharmacist) and Bertha (James) Lane (chiropodist); University of Connecticut, PhG, 1931; attended Columbia University, 1943–44; m. George D. Petry, 1938; children: Elisabeth Ann "Liz" Petry. ❖ Published 1st novel, *The Street* (1946), about a single black woman and her 8-year-old son in Harlem, which sold over 1.5 million copies, making her one of the few bestselling African-American women of the time; also wrote *Country Place* (1947), *The Narrows* (1953), *Miss Muriel and Other Stories* (1971), as well as books for young people, including *Harriet Tubman: Conductor on the Underground Railroad* (1955), *The Drugstore Cat* (1949), *The Common Ground* (1964), *Legends of the Saints* (1970) and *Tituba of Salem Village* (1964). ❖ See also *Women in World History*.

PETRY, Lucile (1902–1999). American founding director of the US Cadet Nurse Corps. Name variations: Lucile Petry Leone. Born Jan 23, 1902, in Frog Heaven, Ohio; died Nov 25, 1999, in San Francisco, California; dau. of Dora (Murray) Petry and David Petry (high school principal); University of Delaware, BA, 1924); graduate of Johns Hopkins School of Nursing, 1928, Columbia University Teachers College, MA, 1929; m. Nicholas Leone (US Public Health Service researcher), 1952 (div. 1967). ❖ Initiated US Public Health Service (USPHS) program to attract women into nursing to cope with expected casualties of war (1941); founded and became director of Cadet Nurse Corps, a more formal effort to attract women to nursing field (1943); became the 1st female assistant surgeon general at USPHS, the 1st woman to direct a division of the US Public Health Service (1949); retired from government service (1966); retired as teacher and associate dean at Texas Women's University (1971). ❖ See also *Women in World History*.

PETTER, Simone (1967—). *See Greiner-Petter-Memm, Simone.*

PETTERSEN, Brit. Norwegian cross-country skier. Name variations: Brit Pettersen Tofte. Born in Norway. ❖ Won a bronze medal for 4 x 5 km relay at Lake Placid Olympics (1980); won a bronze medal for 10 km and a gold medal for 4 x 5 km relay at Sarajevo Olympics (1984).

PETTERSEN, Karin (1964—). Norwegian handball player. Born Nov 21, 1964, in Norway. ❖ Won a silver medal at Seoul Olympics (1988) and a silver medal at Barcelona Olympics (1992), both in team competition.

PETTERSEN, Marianne (1975—). Norwegian soccer player. Born April 12, 1975, in Norway. ❖ Won a team bronze medal at Atlanta Olympics (1996) and a team gold medal at Sydney Olympics (2000).

PETTERSSON, Ann-Sofi (1932—). Swedish gymnast. Name variations: Ann-Sofi Colling. Born Jan 1, 1932, in Sweden. ❖ At Helsinki Olympics, won a gold medal in teams all-around, portable apparatus (1952); at Melbourne Olympics, won a bronze medal in vault and a silver medal in teams all-around, portable apparatus (1956).

PETTERSSON, Goeta (1926—). Swedish gymnast. Born Dec 18, 1926, in Sweden. ❖ At Helsinki Olympics, won a gold medal in teams all-around, portable apparatus (1952).

PETTERSSON, Wivan (1904–1976). Swedish swimmer. Born Jan 24, 1904, in Sweden; died Nov 7, 1976. ❖ At Paris Olympics, won a bronze medal in 4 x 100-meter freestyle relay (1924).

PETTIBONE, Margaret. *See Caron, Margaret Pettibone.*

PETTIS, Bridget (1971—). African-American basketball player. Born Jan 1, 1971; attended University of Florida. ❖ Averaging more than

25 points per game throughout career, was selected in the 1st round by the WNBA Phoenix Mercury (1997).

PETTIS, Shirley Neil (1924—). American politician. Name variations: Shirley Pettis-Robe; Shirley Neil Pettis-Robe; Shirley McCumber Pettis-Robe. Born Shirley Neil McCumber, July 12, 1924, in Mountain View, Santa Clara Co., California; dau. of Harold Oliver McCumber and Dorothy Susan (O'Neil) McCumber; attended Andrews University, Berrien Springs, Michigan, 1942–43, and University of California, Berkeley, 1944–45; m. Jerry Lyle Pettis (politician and congressional representative, died 1975); m. Ben Robe, 1988; children: Peter Dwight Pettis; Deborah Neil Pettis. ❖ US Republican congressional representative, 94th–95th Congresses (April 29, 1975–Jan 3, 1979), 1st co-founded and managed the Audio-Digest Foundation (1950–53); was a newspaper columnist for the *Sun-Telegram,* San Bernardino, California (1967–70); served as vice president of Republican Congressional Wives Club (1975); elected as a Republican to the 94th Congress by special election (April 29, 1975); reelected to 95th Congress; as a member of Committee on Interior and Insular Affairs, gained legislation protecting the deserts in her district; secured wilderness status for nearly half a million acres in Joshua Tree National Monument, establishing the California Desert Conservation area; was vice president, Women's Research and Education Institute, Washington, DC (1980–81); was a member of the Arms Control and Disarmament Commission (1981–83), and Commission on Presidential Scholars (1990–92). ❖ See also *Women in World History.*

PETTIT, Katherine (1868–1936). American settlement worker. Born Feb 23, 1868, near Lexington, Kentucky; died Sept 3, 1936, in Lexington; dau. of Benjamin F. Pettit (farmer) and Clara Mason (Barbee) Pettit; educated in Lexington and Louisville, Kentucky, and at Sayre Female Institute of Lexington; never married. ❖ Worked to improve the lives of rural residents in Kentucky; was instrumental in founding (1902) and running the Hindman Settlement School in Knott Co. (1902–13) and the Pine Mountain Settlement School in Harlan Co. (1913–30). ❖ See also *Women in World History.*

PETTY, Mary (1899–1976). American illustrator. Born in Hampton, New Jersey, 1899; died in Paramus, New Jersey, 1976; m. Alan Dunn (cartoonist), 1927. ❖ Employed by *The New Yorker* (1927–66), created 38 satirical cover illustrations; artwork was exhibited at Cincinnati Art Museum (1940) and at Syracuse University (1979).

PETUSHKOVA, Yelena (1940—). Soviet equestrian. Born Nov 17, 1940, in USSR. ❖ At Mexico City Olympics, won a silver medal in team dressage (1968); at Munich Olympics, won a silver medal in indiv. dressage and a gold medal in team dressage (1972).

PETZOLD, Barbara (1955—). East German cross-country skier. Born Aug 8, 1955, in East Germany. ❖ Won a bronze medal for 4 x 5 km relay at Innsbruck Olympics (1976); won gold medals for 10 km and 4 x 5 km relay at Lake Placid Olympics (1980).

PEYTON, Kim (1957–1986). American swimmer. Name variations: Kim Peyton McDonald. Born Kimberly Peyton, Jan 26, 1957, in Portland, Oregon; attended Stanford University; died Dec 13, 1986, in Pacifica, CA. ❖ At Montreal Olympics, won a gold medal in 4 x 100-meter freestyle relay (1976).

PEZZO, Paola (1969—). Italian mountain biker. Born Jan 8, 1969, in Boscochiesanuova, Italy. ❖ Won World championship (1993, 1997); won Grundig World Cup (1997); won gold medals for cross-country mountain bike at Atlanta Olympics (1996) and Sydney Olympics (2000). Inducted into Mountain Bike Hall of Fame (1999).

PFEFFER, Anna (1945—). Hungarian kayaker. Born Aug 31, 1945, in Hungary. ❖ At Mexico City Olympics, won a silver medal in K2 500 meters (1968); at Munich Olympics, won a bronze medal in K1 500 meters (1972); at Montreal Olympics, won a silver medal in K2 500 meters (1976).

PFEIFFER, Anna Ursula (1813–1863). German thief. Born 1813 in Germany; died 1863. ❖ Lived in Nuremberg, supporting herself as a burglar, pickpocket, and the like; was imprisoned 41 times (1838–63).

PFEIFFER, Emily Jane (1827–1890). British poet and essayist. Born Nov 26, 1827, in Oxfordshire, England; died Jan 1890 in Putney, London; dau. of R. Davis (army officer); m. Jurgen Edward Pfeiffer (German banker), 1853. ❖ Published 1st book of poetry, *Valesneria; or A Midsummer's Night's Dream* (1857), followed by the long poem *Margaret; or The Motherless* (1861); after 12-year hiatus, published a

number of books of poetry, including *Gerard's Monument and Other Poems* (1873), *Glan-Alarch: His Silence and Song* (1877), *Sonnets and Songs* (1880), *The Wynnes of Wynhavod* (1881), *Under the Aspens* (1882), *The Rhyme of the Lady of the Rock and How It Grew* (1884) and *Flowers of the Night* (1889); sympathetic to women's problems, wrote numerous essays about dress reform, rape, education, sexuality, marriage, and women in the workplace; also wrote the travel book *Flying Leaves from East and West* (1885). ❖ See also *Women in World History.*

PFEIFFER, Ida (1797–1858). Austrian travel writer. Born Ida Laura Reyer in Vienna, Austria, Oct 14, 1797; died in Vienna, Oct 27–28, 1858, of an illness she had contracted in Madagascar; dau. of Aloys Reyer (manufacturer, died 1806) and Anna Rosina Reyer (died 1831); m. Mark Anton Pfeiffer (lawyer of Lemberg), 1820 (sep 1833); children: 1 sons; 1 daughter who died soon after birth. ❖ Intrepid traveler, set out on a 10-month trip to Middle East at 45 (Mar 22, 1842), the 1st of 5 major journeys; published *Die Reise einer Wienerin in das Heilige Land* (Travels of a Viennese Lady in the Holy Land, 1844), which became a bestseller; journeyed to Scandinavia and Iceland (1845), which resulted in another popular volume; after a trip around the world (May 1, 1846–Nov 1848), published 3-vol. account, *Eine Frauenfahrt um die Welt* (A Lady's Journey around the World, 1850); encircled the globe once more (1851–55), then released the 4-vol. *Meine zweite Weltreise* (My Second Voyage around the World, 1856); visited the then little-known island of Madagascar, off coast of southeastern Africa (1857), where she developed a tropical fever; her outrage at injustice runs like a thread throughout all of her travelogues, as does her sympathy for women of the lower classes; respected by scientists and geographers, was the 1st woman admitted as an honorary member to geographical societies of Berlin and Paris. ❖ See also Margo McLoone, *Women Explorers in Polar Regions* (Capstone, 1997); and *Women in World History.*

PFEIFFER, Jane Cahill (1932—). American businesswoman. Born Jane Cahill, Sept 29, 1932, in Washington, DC; m. Ralph A. Pfeiffer Jr. (business executive). ❖ Joined IBM (1955) and eventually became Bermuda site manager for NASA's computer complex; was the 1st woman White House fellow (1966); at White House, worked with undersecretary of Department of Housing and Urban Development to upgrade House and Home Finance Agency; served as vice president of communications and government relations at IBM (1972–76); hired as consultant for RCA (1977), then served as 1st woman chair of board for National Broadcasting Company (NBC, 1978–80); became consultant in management organization, communications, and government relations (1980). Received Eleanor Roosevelt Humanitarian Award (1980).

PFEIFFER, Michelle (1957—). American actress. Born April 29, 1958, in Santa Ana, CA; dau. of Dick and Donna Pfeiffer; sister of De Dee Pfeiffer and Lori Pfeiffer (former actresses); studied at Beverly Hills Playhouse; m. Peter Horton (actor), 1981 (div. 1988); m. David E. Kelley (producer and writer), 1993; children: (adopted) Claudia Rose (1993); (2nd m.) John Henry (b. 1994). ❖ Came to prominence in *Grease 2* (1982); received 6 Golden Globe nominations, including for *Married to the Mob* (1988); nominated for Academy Awards for Best Actress for *Love Field* (1993), *The Fabulous Baker Boys* (1989) and *Dangerous Liaisons* (1988); other films include *Scarface* (1983), *The Witches of Eastwick* (1987), *The Russian House* (1990), *Frankie and Johnny* (1991), *Batman Returns* (1992), *The Age of Innocence* (1993), *Dangerous Minds* (1995), *What Lies Beneath* (2000), *I Am Sean* (2001) and *White Oleander* (2002).

PFLUEGER, Joan (1931—). American trapshooter. Born 1931 in Miami, FL. ❖ At 18, broke 100 straight and 74 x 75 shootoff targets to become the 1st woman to win the Champion of Champions event at the Grand American (1950), against an all-male field; won Florida women's title 7 times (1947–70); named to 10 All-American teams (1949–71). Inducted into the Florida Trapshooting Hall of Fame (1980) and National Trapshooting Hall of Fame (2004).

PFLUG, Monika (1954—). Germany speedskater. Name variations: Monika Holzner-Gawenus; Gawenus-Pflug; Holzner-Pflug. Born Mar 1, 1954, in West Germany. ❖ Won a gold medal for 1,000 meters at Sapporo Olympics (1972); at World Sprint championships, won a gold medal (1972) and bronze medals (1973–74, 1982).

PFOHL, Cornelia (1971—). German archer. Born Feb 23, 1971, in Erlabrunn, Germany. ❖ Won a silver medal for teams at Atlanta Olympics (1996) and a bronze medal for teams at Sydney Olympics (2000).

PFOST, Gracie (1906–1965). American politician. Pronunciation: Post. Born Grace Bowers, Mar 12, 1906, in Harrison, Arkansas; died Aug 11, 1965, in Baltimore, Maryland; dau. of William Lafayette Bowers and Lily Elizabeth (Wood) Bowers; educated at Links Business University, Boise, Idaho; m. John Walter Pfost (master mechanic), Aug 4, 1923. ❖ Was deputy county clerk, auditor and recorder for Canyon Co., Idaho (1929–39), then county treasurer (1939–49); made unsuccessful bid for US House of Representatives (1950); was Democratic US congressional representative from Idaho for 5 terms (Jan 3, 1953–Jan 3, 1963), Idaho's 1st female member of Congress, serving on the Committee on Public Works, the Committee on Post Office and Civil Service, and the Committee on Interior and Insular Affairs, where she chaired the public lands subcommittee; as a member of the House, supported Fair Deal legislation, repeal of Taft-Hartley act, increase in minimum wage, better Social Security benefits, federal aid to education, and an Equal Rights Amendment; best remembered for support of a federal dam project and her opposition to the private Snake River dam projects in Idaho (1950s); also worked as a special assistant for Elderly Housing in Federal Housing Administration. ❖ See also *Women in World History*.

PHAGAN, Mary (c. 1899–1913). American murder victim. Born c. 1899 in Georgia; killed, April 27, 1913, in Atlanta, GA. ❖ At age 13, was working at the National Pencil Co. in Atlanta, GA, when she was found dead in the basement (April 27, 1913). The company's Jewish superintendent, Leo Frank, was tried and found guilty of the murder (July 1913); after Frank's death sentence was commuted to life by Governor John M. Slaton, a group known as the Knights of Mary Phagan abducted Frank from prison and lynched him outside Marietta (Aug 17, 1915). Frank's trial and lynching—called by many a gross miscarriage of justice due to anti-Semitism—prompted formation of Jewish Anti-defamation League and was responsible for several US Supreme Court rulings which altered American trial standards. Frank was considered by many to be vindicated in 1982 when Alonzo Mann admitted to seeing company employee Jim Conley dragging Phagan's body (Conley had testified against Frank). ❖ See also Steve Oney, *And the Dead Shall Rise: The Murder of Mary Phagan and the Lynching of Leo Frank* (2003); tv miniseries, "The Murder of Mary Phagan" (1987).

PHAIR, Liz (1967—). American musician. Born Elizabeth Clark Phair, April 17, 1967, in New Haven, CT; adopted dau. of John and Nancy Phair; studied art at Oberlin College; m. Jim Staskauskas (film editor), 1995 (div. 2001); children: James Nicholas Staskauskas (b. Dec 21, 1996). ❖ Alternative-music performer who broke into music industry with bold lyrics and in-your-face style; signed with Matador Records and released *Exile in Guyville* (1993), a response to Rolling Stones' album, *Exile on Main Street*; released more introspective *Whip-Smart* (1994), followed by *Juvenalia* (1995), which included "Girlytapes" material; released albums *Whitechocolatespaceegg* (1998) and *Liz Phair* (2003); toured with band and with Lilith Fair festival (1998); appeared in films *Cherish* (2002) and *Seeing Other People* (2004).

PHALLE, Niki de Saint (1930–2002). French sculptor, painter and filmmaker. Born Catherine Marie-Agnes Fal de Saint Phalle, Oct 29, 1930, in Neuilly-sur-Seine, France; died May 21, 2002; dau. of Jeanne Jacqueline (Harper) and Andre Marie-Fal de Saint Phalle; m. Harry Mathews (div. 1960); m. Jean Tinguely (Swiss artist), 1971; children: 2. ❖ Moved to US with family (1933); lived in New York (1933–51), where she began career as a fashion model; married young and had 2 children; returned to Paris and took up painting; held 1st exhibition in Switzerland (1956); introduced shooting paintings (1961); became known for her oversize figures of women (earth-mother sculptures, or Nanas) found in gardens and parks; returned to NY (1960s), where she was prominent in the development of Happenings, an effort to integrate art and life; famed for her monumental mosaics, Cyclops, in the Fontainbleu forest near Paris, and Tarot Garden (Giardino del Tarocchi), near Tuscany, Italy.

PHANTASIA. Egyptian poet. Lived in Egyptian Memphis or Naucratis; dau. of Nicarchus. ❖ Mentioned by Byzantine writer Photius as having written epic poems, *A Trojan War* and *Adventures of Odysseus*, works allegedly used by Homer for his poems.

PHARANDZEM (c. 320–c. 364). Queen of Armenia. Name variations: P'arandzem; (maiden name) Pharandzem Siuni; the name Pharandzem is of Iranian origin, the attested Middle Persian form being Khorandzem. Pronunciation: p'ar an-DZEM, with a slight hesitation between the *p* and the *a*. Born c. 320; killed in late 364; dau. of Antiochus Siuni; m. Prince Gnel, nephew of King Arsaces II; m. Arsaces II, king of

Armenia, c. 338 (marriage repudiated by Arsaces so he could marry Olympias); children: (2nd m.) Prince Tiridates, possibly eldest son (b. around 340, possibly died young); Prince Pap (b. around 342). ❖ One of the most remarkable women to appear in Armenian history before the modern era, who, after the capture of her husband, assumed the responsibility for the defense of Armenia during a massive Persian invasion; according to *Epic Histories*, husband Gnel executed by King Arsaces II; married Arsaces, but never forgave him for executing her 1st husband; when Arsaces repudiated her marriage to wed Olympias, had a priest mix poison in the Holy Eucharist so that Olympias was murdered while taking communion (c. 361); was sole queen, once again; when summoned to Persia by King Sapor who had captured Arsaces, ignored the order; during the Persian invasion of Armenia (363–64), assumed defense of Armenia, taking refuge in the great castle of Artagers; finally surrendered after a courageous and resourceful defense of 14 months; was thrown to the Persian troops, who were allowed to rape her to death. ❖ See also *The Epic Histories* (English trans. by Nina G. Garsoian, Harvard University, 1989); and *Women in World History*.

PHEBE. *Variant of Phoebe.*

PHELAN, Mrs. (1790–1846). *See Tonna, Charlotte Elizabeth.*

PHELPS, Almira Lincoln (1793–1884). American educator and textbook writer. Name variations: Alma Hart; Almira Hart Lincoln. Born Almira Hart, July 15, 1793, in Berlin, Connecticut; died July 15, 1884, in Baltimore, Maryland; dau. of Samuel Hart and Lydia (Hinsdale) Hart; sister of educator Emma Hart Willard (1787–1870); educated at Berlin Academy; m. Simeon Lincoln (editor of *Connecticut Mirror* in Hartford), Oct 4, 1817 (died 1823); m. John Phelps (attorney), Aug 17, 1831 (died 1849); children: (1st m.) James (died in infancy); Emma Lincoln; Jane Lincoln (d. 1856); (2nd m.) Charles Phelps; Almira Phelps. ❖ Joined staff of her sister's Troy Female Seminary (1823), serving for a time as principal in Emma's absence, and became interested in natural sciences; published her 1st science textbook aimed at women, *Familiar Lectures on Botany* (1829), defying common beliefs that women were incapable of comprehending such things as scientific methods, ancient languages, and higher mathematics (the book would go through 9 editions by 1872); produced a novel, *Caroline Westerley* (1833); headed several boarding schools and seminaries for girls, most notably Patapsco Female Institute in Maryland (1841–56); wrote many more science textbooks which became standard works in schools of her day. Was the 2nd woman (following astronomer Maria Mitchell) elected to American Association for the Advancement of Science. ❖ See also *Women in World History*.

PHELPS, Caroline (1854–1909). *See Stokes, Caroline Phelps.*

PHELPS, Elizabeth (1815–1852). *See Phelps, Elizabeth Wooster Stuart.*

PHELPS, Elizabeth Porter (1747–1817). American diarist. Born 1747; lived in Hadley, MA; died 1817. ❖ Recorded personal experiences during American Revolution; her diary was included in a collection of colonial writings, *Under a Colonial Roof-Tree* (1891). ❖ See also Elizabeth Pendergast Carlisle, *Earthbound and Heavenbent: Elizabeth Porter Phelps and Life at Forty Cares (1747–1817)* (Scribner, 2004).

PHELPS, Elizabeth Stuart (1844–1911). *See Ward, Elizabeth Stuart Phelps.*

PHELPS, Elizabeth Wooster Stuart (1815–1852). American novelist. Name variations: Elizabeth Phelps; (pseudonym) H. Trusta. Born Elizabeth Stuart, Aug 13, 1815, in Andover, MA; died in Boston, MA, Nov 30, 1852, from "cerebral disease," from which she had suffered since she was 19; dau. of Moses Stuart (minister and professor) and Abigail (Clark) Stuart; m. Reverend Austin Phelps, Sept 1842; children: Elizabeth Stuart Phelps Ward (1844–1911, novelist); Moses Stuart Phelps (b. 1849); Amos Lawrence Phelps (b. 1852). ❖ Author of the popular religious novel *The Sunny Side; or, The Country Minister's Wife* (1851); also wrote *A Peep at "Number Five"; or, A Chapter in the Life of a City Pastor* (1852), *The Angel over the Right Shoulder, or the Beginning of a New Year* (1852), *The Tell-tale; or, Home Secrets Told by Old Travellers* (1853), *The Last Leaf from Sunny Side* (1853) and *Little Mary; or, Talks and Tales for Children* (1854).

PHELPS, Jaycie (1979—). American gymnast. Born Sept 26, 1979, in Indianapolis, IN. ❖ Won US Classic (1995) and American Classic (1996); at World championships, won a bronze medal for team all-around (1995); at Atlanta Olympics, won a gold medal for team all-around (1996).

PHELPS, Olivia Egleston (1847–1927). *See Stokes, Olivia Phelps.*

PHELPS, Susanna Stewart (1857–1915). *See Gage, Susanna Phelps.*

PHERETIMA (fl. 6th c. BCE). Queen of Cyrene. Flourished in 6th century BCE in Cyrene or Cyrenaica (present-day northern Libya); m. Battus III the Lame, king of Cyrene; children: Arcesilaus III, king of Cyrene. ❖ Known from the 4th book of Herodotus' *Histories,* was a member of the Battid dynasty which ruled over Cyrene, that part of north Africa where Libya thrusts northward towards Greece; after husband Battus III was reduced to a figurehead and son failed in attempt to regain powers of office, fled to Salamis on island of Cyrene; later returned with son who reclaimed his heritage in Cyrene; while son was exiled once more, this time in Barca, remained in Cyrene to manage its government; learning of son's assassination in Barca, fled Cyrene for Egypt and sought help from Aryandes; returned to her native land at the head of a powerful force and laid siege to Barca for 9 months; had those guilty of her son's assassination crucified. ❖ See also *Women in World History.*

PHILA I (fl. c. 320 BCE). Macedonian noblewoman. Flourished around 320 BCE; dau. of Antipater (general, died 319); m. Demetrius Poliorcetes (a Macedonian general-king); sister of Cassander, Eurydice (fl. 321 BCE) and Nicaea; children: Antigonus II Gonatus (who m. his niece Phila II); Stratonice I (c. 319–254 BCE). ❖ See also *Women in World History.*

PHILA II (c. 300 BCE–?). Seleucid princess and queen of Macedonia. Born c. 300 BCE; dau. of Stratonice I (c. 319–254 BCE) and Seleucus I Nicator, Seleucid king; granddau. of Phila I; m. her uncle Antigonus II Gonatus (son of Demetrius Poliorcetes and Phila I, and brother of Stratonice), king of Macedonia; children: Demetrius II of Macedonia (who m. Stratonice II). ❖ See also *Women in World History.*

PHILAENIS (fl. 2nd c.). Greek writer. Fl. in 2nd century in Samos; dau. of Okymenes. ❖ Wrote *The Art of Love,* prose erotica of which some papyrus fragments survive (one of them is headed, "On the Art of Making Passes").

PHILBIN, Eva (1914—). Irish organic chemist. Name variations: Eva Maria Philbin. Born Eva Maria Ryder, Jan 4, 1914, in Ballina, Co. Mayo, Ireland; m. John Madden Philbin (secretary), 1943. ❖ Was a chief chemist at Cold Chon Ltd. (1939–43) and Hygeia Ltd. (1940–43), both Galway; at University College, Dublin, joined the staff (1945), became organic chemistry professor (1962), then head of chemistry department (1963); was a member of Council of Royal Irish Academy and Natural Science Council; was a fellow of Royal Institute of Chemistry and Institute of Chemistry of Ireland; published roughly 90 papers on flavanoids.

PHILBIN, Mary (1903–1993). American actress. Born July 16, 1903, in Chicago, IL; died May 7, 1993, in Huntington Beach, CA. ❖ Starred opposite Lon Chaney in *Phantom of the Opera* (1925); other films include *Penrod and Sam, Fifth Avenue Models, Stella Maris, Merry-Go-Round, Drums of Love, Surrender, The Man Who Laughs, Girl Overboard* and *The Shannons of Broadway.*

PHILIBERTA OF SAVOY (c. 1498–1524). Duchess of Nemours. Name variations: Philiberta de Medici; Philiberte of Savoy. Born c. 1498; died in 1524; aunt of Francis I, king of France (r. 1515–1547); m. Giuliano de Medici (1479–1516), duke of Nemours, in 1515; no children. ❖ Giuliano de Medici's son, the cardinal Ippolito (1511–1535), was illegitimate. ❖ See also *Women in World History.*

PHILINNA (c. 380–after c. 356 BCE). Thessalian noblewoman. Born c. 380 BCE in Larissa in Thessaly; died after 356 BCE; one of 7 wives of Philip II, king of Macedon; children: (with an unnamed man) Amphimachus; (with Philip) Arrhidaeus, king of Macedon. ❖ Philip's six other wives were Audata, Olympias, Meda, Nicesipolis, Roxane and Cleopatra of Macedon. ❖ See also *Women in World History.*

PHILIPPA. *Variant of Philippine.*

PHILIPPA (1394–1430). Queen of Denmark, Norway, and Sweden. Name variations: Philippa Plantagenet. Born July 4, 1394, in Peterborough Castle, Cambridgeshire, England; died Jan 5, 1430, at the convent of Valdstena also known as Wadstena, Linkoping, Sweden; interred at the convent of Wadstena; dau. of Mary de Bohun (1369–1394) and Henry IV (1366–1413), king of England (r. 1399–1413); m. Erik or Eric VII (or XIII) of Pomerania (1382–1459), king of Denmark (r. 1396–1439), Norway (r. 1389–1442), and Sweden, on Oct 26, 1406. ❖ When husband was away at war and Copenhagen was besieged, saved the city. ❖ See also *Women in World History.*

PHILIPPA DE COUCY (fl. 1300s). Countess of Oxford. Name variations: Philippa di Couci; Philippa de Vere. Born Philippa de Coucy in mid-1300s; dau. of Enguerrand VII, lord of Coucy and earl of Bedford, and Isabella (1332–1382, dau. of Philippa of Hainault and King Edward III); m. Robert de Vere, 9th earl of Oxford, in 1378 (div. 1387).

PHILIPPA DE DREUX (d. 1240). Countess of Bar. Died Mar 17, 1240; dau. of Robert II, count of Dreux, and Yolande de Coucy (d. 1222); sister of Yolande de Dreux (d. 1238); m. Henry II, count of Bar, in 1219; children: Margaret (d. 1275), countess of Bar.

PHILIPPA DE ROUERGUE (c. 1074–1118). Queen of Aragon and duchess of Aquitaine. Name variations: Philippa of Toulouse. Born c. 1074; died Nov 28, 1118, in Fontevraud, Anjou, France; dau. of William IV, count of Toulouse; became 2nd wife of Sancho Ramirez, king of Aragon (r. 1063–1094) and Navarre (r. 1076–1094), in 1086; m. William IX, duke of Aquitaine, around 1094 following the death of her first husband; children: (2nd m.) William X, duke of Aquitaine (1099–1137); Agnes de Poitiers (who m. Ramiro II); Raymond I of Poitiers (1115–1149), prince of Antioch. ❖ Sancho Ramirez was first married to Isabel of Urgel.

PHILIPPA-ELIZABETH (1714–1734). Princess of Orléans. Name variations: Philippine-Elizabeth d'Orleans. Born Nov 18, 1714; died May 21, 1734; dau. of Philip Bourbon-Orléans (1674–1723), 2nd duke of Orléans (r. 1701–1723) and Françoise-Marie de Bourbon (1677–1749).

PHILIPPA MARERIA (c. 1190–1236). *See Mareri, Filippa.*

PHILIPPA OF ANTIOCH (fl. 1100s). Princess of Antioch. Flourished in the 1100s; dau. of Constance of Antioch (1128–1164) and Raymond I of Poitiers, prince of Antioch (d. 1149, son of William IX of Aquitaine); sister of Bohemund III and Marie of Antioch (d. 1183); half-sister of Anne of Chatillon-Antioche (c. 1155–c. 1185, who m. Bela III, king of Hungary); m. Andronicus I Comnenus, Byzantine emperor (r. 1183–1185); children: 1 son. ❖ Andronicus married his 2nd wife, Agnes-Anne of France, in 1183.

PHILIPPA OF CLARENCE (1355–1382). *See Mortimer, Philippa.*

PHILIPPA OF FOIX (fl. 13th c.). French religious reformer. Flourished in 13th century in Foix; born into lower nobility of France. ❖ Was an active participant in the heretical religious sect called Catharism (also known as Albigensianism) which swept southern France, rejecting materialism and the rituals of the Catholic Church and believing that women, through study, could become men's equals and then preach themselves. ❖ See also *Women in World History.*

PHILIPPA OF GUELDERS (d. 1547). Duchess of Lorraine. Name variations: Philippa of Gelderland; Philippine von Geldern. Died Feb 25, 1547; dau. of Adolf (b. 1438), duke of Guelders, and Catherine of Bourbon (d. 1469); became second wife of Rene II (1451–1508), duke of Lorraine (r. 1480–1508), on Sept 1, 1485; children: Anthony or Antoine (1489–1544), duke of Lorraine (r. 1508–1544); Claude (d. 1550), 1st duke of Guise (r. 1527–1550, who m. Antoinette of Bourbon); John, 1st cardinal of Lorraine; Ferri (killed at Marignano); Louis (killed at Naples); Francis (killed at Pavia); 4 daughters who never married (names unknown); and 2 sons who died in infancy; grandmother of Mary of Guise (1515–1560). ❖ Rene II's first wife was Johanna Harcourt (d. 1488).

PHILIPPA OF HAINAULT (1314–1369). Queen of England, regent and founder. Name variations: Phillipa. Pronunciation: HAN-olt. Born 1314 in Valenciennes, Hainault; died of dropsy on Aug 14, 1369, at Windsor, England; dau. of William III the Good, count of Hainault and Holland, and Countess Jeanne of Valois (c. 1294–1342); m. Edward III (1312–1377), king of England (r. 1327–1377), on Jan 28, 1328; children: Edward "the Black Prince" (1330–1376), prince of Wales; Isabella (1332–1382); Joanna (1333–1348); William (b. 1336 and died in infancy); Lionel of Antwerp (1338–1368), duke of Clarence; John of Gaunt (1340–1399), duke of Lancaster; Edmund of Langley (1341–1402), duke of York; Blanche (b. 1343 and died in infancy); Mary (1344–1362); William (b. 1345); Margaret (1346–1361); Thomas of Woodstock (1355–1397), duke of Gloucester. ❖ One of England's most popular queens, was in many ways responsible for the establishment of both the coal industry and the textile industry of England, the two primary sources of England's national wealth for many centuries; also raised 12 children, including 5 sons who were renowned warriors and 3 who were also intellectuals, and daughters who were reputedly well educated and beautiful; provided a necessary contrast to her husband

Edward III, a great king but one whose impulsiveness and tendency toward violence and vengefulness needed her calm, rational influence; married Edward (1328); crowned queen (1330); gave birth to Edward the Black Prince (1330); went on military campaigns with Edward (1333–45); established textile industry at Norwich (1335); appointed regent when Edward invaded France (1346); quickly assembled an army which repelled invasion of Scottish army and captured King David of Scotland (1346); established coal industry at Tynedale (1348); became ill with dropsy (1367). ❖ See also *Women in World History*.

PHILIPPA OF LANCASTER (c. 1359–1415). Queen of Portugal. Name variations: Filipa de Lencastre; Philippa Plantagenet. Born Mar 31, 1359 or 1360, in Leicester, Leicestershire, England; died of the plague, July 19, 1415, in Odivelas, Lisbon, Portugal; interred in Batalla Abbey, Portugal; reigned from 1387 to 1415; 1st child of John of Gaunt (son of Edward III of England) and his 1st wife Blanche of Lancaster (1341–1369); sister of Henry Bolingbroke (1366–1413, later Henry IV, king of England, r. 1399–1413) and Elizabeth of Lancaster (1364–1425, who m. John Holland, duke of Exeter); m. João I of Aviz also known as John I (1385–1433), king of Portugal (r. 1385–1433), on Feb 2, 1387, at Oporto Cathedral, Portugal; children: Branca (1388–1388); Affonso (1390–1400); Duarte I (1391–1438), king of Portugal (r. 1433–1438); Pedro or Peter, regent of Portugal (b. 1392); Henry the Navigator (Henrique, the Navigator, 1394–1460); Isabella of Portugal (1397–1471, who m. Philip the Good of Burgundy); João or John (1400–1442), grand master of Santiago; Fernando or Ferdinand the Constant (1402–1443), grand master of Aviz. John I also had 2 children with Inez Perez. ❖ After mother died from the Black Death (1369), was raised by Catherine Swynford, her father's mistress; received an exceptional education, with Geoffrey Chaucer among her tutors; because of it, valued *noblesse oblige*, courtly love, and Christian charity; wed John I (1387); as queen, conducted herself with the utmost decorum throughout her marriage and helped restore respect for the monarchy; wielded great influence through her piety, generosity, and refinement. ❖ See also T.W.E. Roche, *Philippa: Dona Filipa of Portugal* (Phillimore, 1971); and *Women in World History*.

PHILIPPA OF LESSER ARMENIA (fl. 1200s). Nicaean empress. Name variations: Philippa of Little Armenia. Flourished in the 1200s; second wife of Theodore I Lascaris, emperor of Nicaea (r. 1204–1222); briefly married; no children.

PHILIPPA OF TOULOUSE (c. 1074–1118). *See Philippa de Rouergue.*

PHILIPPART, Nathalie (c. 1926—). French ballet dancer. Born c. 1926, in Bordeaux, France; m. Jean Babilée (ballet dancer). ❖ Made professional debut in Irene Lidova's *Soirée de Danse* (1944); with Ballets de Paris and Ballets des Champs-Elysées, performed in Roland Petit's *Le Rendez-vous, Les Forains*, and *Le Jeune Homme et la Mort*; danced principal parts in *La Sylphide, Pas de Quatre, L'Amour et Son Amour*, and others; often partnered husband Jean Babilée on tour.

PHILIPPINE. *Variant of Philippa.*

PHILIPPINE CHARLOTTE (1716–1801). Duchess of Brunswick-Wolfenbuttel. Born Mar 13, 1716; died Feb 17, 1801; dau. of Sophia Dorothea of Brunswick-Lüneburg-Hanover (1687–1757) and Frederick William I (1688–1740), king of Prussia (r. 1713–1740); m. Charles, duke of Brunswick-Wolfenbuttel; children: Charles II (1716–1801), duke of Brunswick-Wolfenbuttel; George (b. 1736); Sophie Caroline (1737–1817); Christian Ludwig (b. 1738); Anne Amelia of Saxe-Weimar (1739–1807); Lt. General Frederick Augustus (b. 1740); Albert Henry (b. 1742); Louise (1743–1744); Elizabeth of Brunswick (1746–1840); Friederike (1748–1758); Augusta Dorothea (1749–1803), abbess of Gandersheim; Maximilian (b. 1752).

PHILIPPINE OF LUXEMBURG (d. 1311). Countess of Hainault and Holland. Name variations: Phillipine. Died April 6, 1311; dau. of Henry V the Blond, count of Luxemburg, and Margaret, countess of Bar (d. 1275); m. John II, count of Hainault and Holland; children: William II the Good, count of Hainault and Holland; Margaret of Hainault (d. 1342, who m. Robert II, count of Artois).

PHILIPS, Katherine (1631–1664). English poet. Name variations: Catherine or Katharine; (pseudonym) Orinda. Born Katherine Fowler, Jan 1, 1631 (some sources cite 1632), in London; died of smallpox, June 22, 1664; dau. of John Fowler (merchant) and Katherine Oxenbridge (whose father was a fellow of Royal College of Physicians in London); m. stepbrother James Philips (54-year-old Welsh royalist), in 1647; children: son who died in infancy; daughter Katherine (who m. Lewis

Wogan of Boulston, Pembrokeshire). ❖ At her home at the Priory, Cardigan, instituted a Society of Friendship, a salon where literary companions were known by fanciful names: Philips became "Orinda," dubbed the "matchless Orinda" by contemporaries; husband James was Antenor; Mary Aubrey was Rosania; Anne Owen was Lucasia; Lady Margaret Cavendish was Policrite; and Sir Charles Cotterel, a master of ceremonies at the court of Charles II, was Poliarchus; began circulating her poetry, which often celebrated or concerned her intense friendships and used the same poetic monikers; within cultivated London, became a literary darling; translated and adapted Corneille's *Pompey* (*La Mort du Pompée*) for the stage (1662); poems were released posthumously. ❖ See also *Letters of Orinda to Poliarchus* (1705 and 1709); P.W. Souers' *The Matchless Orinda* (1931); and *Women in World History*.

PHILIPS, Mary (1901–1975). American stage and screen actress. Born Jan 23, 1901, in New London, CT; died April 22, 1975, in Santa Monica, CA; m. Humphrey Bogart (actor, div.); m. Kenneth MacKenna (actor and story editor, died 1964). ❖ Made NY stage debut in chorus of *Apple Blossoms* (1919), subsequently appearing over next 33 years in such plays as *The Old Soak, The Tavern, The Song and Dance Man, Merrily We Roll Along, Spring Thaw* and *Chicken Every Sunday*; films include *Farewell to Arms, Lady in the Dark, The Bride Wore Red, Leave Her to Heaven, Dear Ruth, I Can Get It for You Wholesale* and *Prince Valiant*.

PHILIPSE, Margaret Hardenbrook (d. 1690). Colonial merchant and shipowner. Born in Elberfeld, in Rhine Valley, Prussia; died c. 1690; dau. of Adolph Hardenbrook (also seen as Hardenbroeck); married Peter Rudolphus (de Vries), Oct 10, 1659 (died 1661); m. Frederick Philipse (businessman and later a politician), Oct 1662; children: (1st m.) Maria (later adopted by Frederick Philipse and renamed Eve); (2nd m.) daughter Annetje; 3 sons, Philip, Adolph, and Rombout. ❖ Quite possibly the 1st female business agent in the colonies, accompanied brother Abel to Dutch colony of New Netherland (now part of New York State, c. 1659); began serving as a business agent for Dutch merchants trading with New Netherland (1660), and by some accounts, became a shipowner as well; following husband's death (1661), took over his business as a merchant and trader, shipping furs to Holland in exchange for Dutch goods which she sold in New Amsterdam. ❖ See also *Women in World History*.

PHILLIDA (1900–1989). *See Soper, Eileen Louise.*

PHILLIPA. *Variant of Philippa.*

PHILLIPINE OF LUXEMBURG (d. 1311). *See Philippine of Luxemburg (d. 1311).*

PHILLIPOT, Alice (1904–1987). *See Rahon, Alice.*

PHILLIPPS, Adelaide (1833–1882). English-born actress and opera singer. Born in Stratford-on-Avon, England, Oct 26, 1833; died at Karlsbad, Germany, Oct 3, 1882; never married. ❖ Immigrated to America (1840); began a career on Boston stage at age 10; was sent to London, then Italy to study (1850); returned to America an accomplished vocalist (1855); for many years, was the leading American contralto, equally successful in oratorio and on concert platform. ❖ See also *Women in World History*.

PHILLIPS, Anita Frances. Australian politician. Born in Melbourne, Australia. ❖ Was a social worker; as a member of the Australian Labor Party, elected to the Queensland Parliament for Thuringowa (2001).

PHILLIPS, Brenda (1958—). Zimbabwean field-hockey player. Born Jan 18, 1958, in Zimbabwe. ❖ At Moscow Olympics, won a gold medal in team competition (1980).

PHILLIPS, Chynna (1968—). American singer. Name variations: Wilson Phillips. Born Feb 12, 1968, in Los Angeles, CA; dau. of John Phillips and Michelle Phillips (both singers with The Mamas and the Papas); m. William Baldwin (actor), Sept 9, 1995; children: 2 daughters: Jamison Baldwin (b. Feb 27, 2000) and Brooke Michelle Baldwin (b. Dec 6, 2004); 1 son: Vance Alexander Baldwin (b. Oct 23, 2001). ❖ Appeared in numerous films, including *Little Boy Blue* (1975), *Some Kind of Wonderful* (1987), *The Invisible Kid* (1988), and *Say Anything* (1989), and on tv; with Carnie Wilson and Wendy Wilson, formed the vocal trio Wilson Phillips in Los Angeles (1989) and released eponymous debut album (1990), which went to #2, sold 10 million copies worldwide, and had #1 hit singles "Hold On," "Release Me" and "You're in Love"; with group, released darker album, *Shadows and Light* (1992), which, despite going platinum and reaching #4 on charts, failed to deliver any hit singles; after Wilson Phillips disbanded (1993), pursued solo career, releasing album, *Naked and Sacred* (1995); reunited with group to perform televised tribute to Brian Wilson (2001) and to record *California* (2004).

PHILLIPS, Clara (1899—). American murderer. Born 1899; m. Armour Phillips. ❖ Murdered husband's mistress, 22-year-old widow Alberta Meadows, with hammer (July 6, 1922); confessed to husband, who turned her in; because she had stalked Meadows for days before the killing, was dubbed the "Tiger Woman" by the press during sensational trial; sentenced to 10 years to life (Nov 16, 1922); released from Tehachapi (June 21, 1935).

PHILLIPS, Dorothy (1889–1980). American silent-film actress. Born Oct 30, 1889, in Baltimore, MD; died Mar 1, 1980, in Woodland Hills, CA; m. Allen Holubar (director). ❖ Star of Universal films in early silents; later worked as an extra for over 30 years; films include *The Mark of Cain, A Doll's House, Bondage, The Right to Happiness* and *The Cradle Snatchers.*

PHILLIPS, Esther (1935–1984). American rhythm and blues singer. Name variations: Little Esther Phillips. Born Esther Mae Jones in Galveston, TX, Dec 23, 1935; died in Carson, CA, Aug 7, 1984. ❖ Recorded "Double Crossing Blues" on Savoy label with Johnny Otis' Orchestra (1950) and became the youngest female vocalist to land a #1 record on R&B charts; sang a duet with Mel Walker, "Mistrustin' Blues," which went to #1, as did "Cupid's Boogie," "Misery," "Deceivin' Blues," "Wedding Boogie" and "Faraway Blues" (all 1950); left Otis (1950); signed with Federal and had only one hit out of 30 sides, "Ring-a-Ding-Doo" (1952); age 20, became addicted to heroin and career was dormant for 10 years; recorded "Release Me," a country tune that went to #1 (1962); lost battle with heroin a second time; recorded "Home Is Where the Hatred Is" (1972), a haunting account of drug use; died age 49. ❖ See also *Women in World History.*

PHILLIPS, Frances L. (1896–1986). American publisher. Born 1896 in Walla Walla, Washington; niece of Cornelia Phillips Spencer (writer and reformer); died June 15, 1986, in Chapel Hill, NC. ❖ Joined the staff of William Morrow and Co. (1926); was editor-in-chief of Morrow (1931–67), and the 1st editor for Margaret Mead.

PHILLIPS, Harriet Newton (1819–1901). American nurse. Born Dec 29, 1819 in PA; died Aug 29, 1901, in Gladwyne, PA. ❖ One of the 1st trained nurses in America, volunteered as a Western Sanitary Commission nurse at General Hospital Jefferson Barracks (1862–63) and at General Hospital Benton Barracks (1863–64), both near St. Louis, MO; worked for the Nineteenth General Hospital (Nashville, TN, Feb 1864); discharged (Mar 23, 1864); attended a nurse training class at Woman's Hospital of Philadelphia (later Woman's Medical College of Pennsylvania) and was probably trained by Dr. Emeline Cleveland; completed nurse training (before 1870) ahead of Linda Richards, who is often mistakenly credited as the 1st trained nurse in America; served as a head nurse (1870–71) and as an instructor at Woman's Hospital; conducted missionary work with the Ojibway and Sioux tribes in Wisconsin (1872–75); employed as a matron at a San Francisco Presbyterian mission; pursued advanced training (1878) at Woman's Hospital in Philadelphia.

PHILLIPS, Irna (1901–1973). American radio and tv writer. Born July 1, 1901, in Chicago, Illinois; died of cancer, Dec 22, 1973, in Chicago; dau. of William S. Phillips (businessman) and Betty (Buxbaum) Phillips; University of Illinois, BA, 1923; University of Wisconsin, MA; never married; children: (adopted) Thomas Dirk Phillips and Katherine Louise Phillips. ❖ Once heralded as Queen of the Soap Opera, created family drama "Painted Dreams" for Chicago radio station WGN (1930), which ran for 2 years and is considered by some to have been the 1st soap opera; moved to NBC (1932), collaborating with Walter Wicker on another version of "Painted Dreams," retitled "Today's Children," which ran until 1938; in the meantime, launched 2 additional soap operas, "The Road of Life" and "The Guiding Light" (created with Emmons Carlson); turned out a series of popular serials, including "Woman in White" (1938), "The Right to Happiness" (1939), "Lonely Women" (1942), and "The Brighter Day" (1948); with advent of tv, created 7 shows over 20 years: "The Brighter Day" (1954), "The Road of Life" (1954), "As The World Turns" (1956), "Another World" (1964), "Days of Our Lives" (1965), "Love Is a Many-Splendour'd Thing" (1967) and "The Guiding Light" (which transferred to tv in 1952 and went on to become one of the longest-running soap operas in broadcast history). ❖ See also *Women in World History.*

PHILLIPS, Julia (1944–2002). American film producer. Name variations: Julia Miller Phillips. Born Julia Miller, April 7, 1944, in New York, NY; died Jan 1, 2002, in West Hollywood, CA; dau. of a scientist who worked on the Los Alamos project that developed the atomic bomb; attended Mount Holyoke College; m. Michael Phillips (producer), 1966 (div. 1974); children: Kate Phillips. ❖ Served as editorial assistant at *Ladies Home Journal* (1965–69), associate editor and East coast story editor for Paramount Pictures, NY (1969), head of Mirisch Productions, NY, and creative executive for First Artists Productions, NY (1971); cofounded Bill/Phillips productions (1971); worked as producer for Ruthless Productions, Los Angeles; with husband and Tony Bill, produced such 1970s hits as *The Sting, Taxi Driver,* and *Close Encounters of the Third Kind*; became 1st woman to win Academy Award for Best Picture, as producer of *The Sting* (1974). ❖ See also autobiographies *You'll Never Eat Lunch in This Town Again* (1990) and *Driving Under the Influence* (1995).

PHILLIPS, Karen (1966—). Australian swimmer. Born May 4, 1966, in Australia. ❖ At Los Angeles Olympics, won a silver medal in the 200-meter butterfly (1984).

PHILLIPS, Kristie (1972—). American gymnast. Born Mar 23, 1972, in Baton Rouge, LA; m. Horatio Bannister (singer, songwriter). ❖ Won American Cup (1986, 1987), Canadian Classic, Jr. American Classic, and Jr. US nationals (1986), US Classic and US nationals (1987), and Reese's Cup (1996).

PHILLIPS, Lena Madesin (1881–1955). American lawyer, women's rights advocate, and writer. Born Anna Lena Phillips, Sept 15, 1881, in Nicholasville, Kentucky; died May 21, 1955, in Marseilles, France; dau. of William Henry Phillips (judge) and Alice (Shook) Phillips; educated at Jessamine Female Institute, Woman's College of Baltimore (later Goucher College), and Peabody Conservatory of Music; graduate of University of Kentucky Law School, 1917; New York University Law School, LLM, 1923; lived with Marjory Lacey-Baker (actress). ❖ The first female graduate of University of Kentucky Law School (1917), founded and presided over both the National and the International Federation of Business and Professional Women's Clubs; also founded its official journal, *Independent Woman*; practiced law, contributed to publications, championed women's rights, and was one of the main organizers of the International Congress of Women, held at Chicago Century of Progress Exposition (1933); gave up practice of law to become an associate editor of *Pictorial Review,* for which she wrote a regular column (1935). ❖ See also *Women in World History.*

PHILLIPS, Margaret (1923–1984). Welsh-born actress. Born July 6, 1923, in Cwmgwrach, South Wales; died Sept 9, 1984, in New York, NY. ❖ Arrived in US (1939); made NY debut in *Proof Through the Night* (later titled *Cry Havoc,* 1942), followed by *The Late George Apley, Summer and Smoke, The Heiress, The Cocktail Party, The Merchant of Venice, Dial M for Murder, Fallen Angels, The Lady's Not for Burning* and *The Ginger Man*; films include *A Life of Her Own* and *The Nun's Story.* Won Clarence Derwent award for Best Supporting Actress for *Another Part of the Forest* (1946).

PHILLIPS, Marion (1881–1932). British labor activist and feminist. Born 1881 in Melbourne, Australia; died 1932; dau. of a lawyer; attended Melbourne Presbyterian Ladies' College, Ormond College, University of Melbourne; London School of Economics, PhD. ❖ Moved to England (1904), where she participated in the suffrage movement; served as secretary of National Union of Women's Suffrage Societies (1913–18); worked for Labour Party (1911), becoming its chief woman officer (1918); was one of the 1st women justices of the peace; during General Strike (1926), organized Women's Committee for Relief of Miners' Wives and Children; won parliamentary seat for Sunderland (1929). ❖ See also *A Woman of Vision—A Life of Marion Phillips.*

PHILLIPS, Michelle (1944—). American singer and actress. Born Holly Michelle Gilliam, June 4, 1944, in Long Beach, CA; m. John Phillips (singer), 1962 (div. 1968); m. Dennis Hopper (actor), 1970 (div. 1970); m. Grainger Hines; m. Robert Burch (radio executive; marriage ended); children: Gilliam Chynna Phillips (b. 1968, singer known as Chynna Phillips); Austin Devereux Hines (b. 1982); Aron Wilson (adopted 1988); (stepdaughter) Mackenzie Phillips (actress). ❖ Filled in as a singer with John Phillips' band, the Journeymen, then married him; with John and Marshall Brickman, formed New Journeymen folk group, performing at folk clubs in NYC; was joined by Denny Doherty and Cass Elliot to become The Mamas and the Papas; signed with Dunhill Records (1965) and released 1st single, "California Dreamin'," an instant hit (1966); followed with a string of hits, "Monday Monday," "I Saw Her Again," "Creeque Alley," "Words of Love," and "Dedicated to the One I Love"; performed at Monterey Pop Festival and can be seen in documentary *Monterey Pop*; when group dissolved (1968), pursued an acting career, appearing in tv series and such films as *Dillinger* (1973), *Shampoo* (1975), *American Anthem* (1986) and *Star Trek: The Next Generation* (1988). Inducted into Rock and Roll Hall of Fame (1998). ❖ See also autobiography *California Dreamin'* (Warner, 1986); and *Women in World History*.

PHILLIPS, Mrs. Morton (b. 1918). *See Friedman, Pauline Esther.*

PHILLIPS, Siân (1934—). Welsh actress. Name variations: Sian Phillips. Born Jane Elizabeth Ailwen Phillips, May 14, 1934, in Bettws, Carmarthenshire, Wales; m. Peter O'Toole (actor), 1959 (div. 1979); m. Robin Sachs (actor), 1979. ❖ At 11, broadcast for the BBC in Wales; made London debut at a special charity matinee as Hedda in *Hedda Gabler* (1957), followed by *The Taming of the Shrew, The Duchess of Malfi, Ondine, Gentle Jack, Night of the Iguana, Ride a Cock Horse, Man and Superman* and *The Burglar*; films include *Becket, Laughter in the Dark, Goodbye Mr. Chips, Murphy's War, Under Milk Wood, Dune, Clash of the Titans* and *Valmont*; on tv, appeared as Emmeline Pankhurst in "Shoulder to Shoulder" (1974), Beth Morgan in "How Green Was My Valley" (1975), Livia in "I Claudius" (1976), Boudica in "Warrior Queen" (1978), Ann Smiley in "Tailor Tinker Soldier Spy" (1980) and "Smiley's People" (1982), and Matilda Crawley on "Vanity Fair" (1987). Named Commander of the British Empire (CBE).

PHILLIPS, Zara (1981—). English royal. Born Zara Anne Elizabeth Phillips, May 15, 1981, in Paddington, London, England; dau. of Anne (b. 1950), princess royal, and Mark Phillips; attended Exeter University. ❖ Became a qualified physiotherapist.

PHILLPOTTS, Adelaide (1896–c. 1995). American actress. Name variations: Adelaide Eden Phillpotts; Eden Ross. Born April 23, 1896, in England; died c. 1995; dau. of Eden Phillpotts (playwright and novelist) and Emily (Topham) Phillpotts; m. Nicholas Ross. ❖ With father, wrote *Yellow Sands, My Lady's Mill* and *The Good Old Days*; other plays include *Akhnatou, The Wasp's Nest, Laugh with Me* and *A Song of Man*; also wrote over 20 novels.

PHILLPOTTS, Bertha Surtees (1877–1932). British scholar. Name variations: Dame Bertha Surtees Newall; Dame Bertha Phillpotts. Born 1877; died 1932; graduated from Girton College in Cambridge with first class honors, 1901; m. H.F. Newall (1857–1944, astrophysicist whose father constructed the Newall telescope), 1931. ❖ For 12 years (1901–13), devoted herself to the study of Scandinavian culture and eventually became the first Lady Carlisle fellow of Somerville College at Oxford; served as principal of Westfield College (1919–22), and as mistress of her alma mater (1922–25); became a university lecturer (1926), a post she would hold until her death; published her notable work *Edda and Saga* (1931). Created Dame of the British Empire (DBE, 1929).

PHILOCLEA (1658–1708). *See Masham, Damaris.*

PHILOMENA Saint. Name variations: Filomena or Filumena. ❖ Was noted for her miraculous powers of healing the sick through prayer. Feast day is Aug 10.

PHILOMENA (1854–1935). *See Miller, Florence Fenwick.*

PHILPORT, Mary Elizabeth (1812/13–1908). *See Small, Mary Elizabeth.*

PHINTYS OF SPARTA (fl. c. 400 BCE). Greek philosopher. Flourished around 400 BCE; dau. of Kallikratides (Kallicrates, or Kallikratidas), a Greek admiral who died in the 406 BCE battle of Arginusae. ❖ Wrote *On the Moderation of Women*.

PHIPPS, Mary Elizabeth (1812/13–1908). *See Small, Mary Elizabeth.*

PHIPPS, Sally (1909–1978). American actress. Born Byrnece Beutler, May 24, 1909, in San Francisco, CA; died Mar 17, 1978, in New York, NY; children: Robert Harned. ❖ Made film debut in *Broncho Billy and the Baby* (1915); starred in other films, including *Bertha, the Sewing Machine Girl, Why Sailors Go Wrong, The News Parade, None but the Brave* and *Joy Street*.

PHIPSON, Edith Pechey (1845–1908). *See Pechey-Phipson, Edith.*

PHIPSON, Joan (1912–2003). Australian children's writer. Name variations: Joan Phipson-Fitzhardinge, Joan Fitzhardinge. Born Joan Margaret Phipson, Nov 16, 1912, in Warrawee, NSW, Australia, only child of English parents; died April 2, 2003, in Australia; m. Colin Hardinge Fitzhardinge (sheep and cattle farmer), 1944 (died 1998); children: Guy and Anna Fitzhardinge. ❖ Traveled widely with family, receiving education in Mittagong, Bombay and Birmingham; taught at Frensham School under Winifred West and later served as printer and librarian, going on to establish small private Frensham Press; worked for Reuters in London, studying journalism there, and later was copy and scriptwriter for a radio station in Sydney; served as telegraphist for Women's Auxiliary Air force during WWII; published 1st story with Angus and Robertson (early 1950s); had great success with 1st novel, *Good Luck to the Rider*, which won Australian Children's Book of the Year award (1953); lived most of married life on farm in Central Tablelands of NSW and frequently evoked outback life in writing; began tackling social and environmental issues in such novels as *The Bird Smugglers* (1977), *A Tide Flowing* (1981), *The Watcher in the Garden* (1982) and *Dinko* (1985); wrote 30 books before retiring (1994). Won Children's Book of the Year award for *The Family Conspiracy* (1963); received Dromkeen Medal (1987); member of Order of Australia in (1994).

PHLEGER, Audrey (1943—). *See McElmury, Audrey.*

PHLIPON, Manon (1754–1793). *See Roland, Madame.*

PHOEBE OF CENCHREAE (fl. 1st c.). Christian religous leader. Name variations: Phebe; Phoebe of Cenchrea; Phoebe of Cenchreæ. Flourished in the 1st century; lived in the Greek port city of Cenchreae. ❖ Early Christian patron and leader who delivered St. Paul's Epistle to the church at Rome (c. 57), in which he commends that they treat her as a saint: "I commend to you our sister Phoebe, a deaconess [*diakonos*] of the church at Cenchreae, so that you may welcome her in the Lord as befits the saints, and help her in whatever she may require from you, for she has been a benefactor [*prostasis*] of many and of myself as well" (Romans 16: 1–2); is increasingly seen by scholars as having played a crucial role in creating the position of deaconess in the early church. Feast day is Sept 3. ❖ See also *Women in World History*.

PHOOLAN DEVI (1963–2001). Bandit queen and politician of India. Born Phoolan Devi (Goddess of Flowers) in Upper Predash, India, Aug 10, 1963; gunned down in July 25, 2001, by 4 men in front of her house in New Delhi; dau. of Devidin Kewat and Moola; learned to read and write in prison; m. Puttilal (farmer), c. 1967; married Ummed Singh. ❖ Highly spirited, was married off at 11, but returned to parents by husband a couple years later because she was often sick; as a discarded woman with no future, was urged by mother to commit suicide; captured and raped by a gang of *dacoits* (July 1979), was protected by gang member Vikram Mullah, became his mistress, and learned to fire a gun; was sleeping next to Vikram when he was shot and killed by Thakur gang members (Aug 13, 1980); formed a gang with Man Singh, the Phoolan Devi–Man Singh gang (Oct 1980); determined to avenge Vikram's death, raided 90 homes in Baijamau (Dec 1980), the town that housed the upper-caste Thakurs; became a national legend, her exploits celebrated in song; with a reward of 50,000 rupees on her head, dead or alive, went on a crime spree: robbing Thakur villages, hijacking lorries, robbing tourists; was involved with the Behmai massacre (Feb 14, 1981), where 22 Thakur men were shot in the back, causing a furor in the national and international press; tried and condemned in the press, went from heroine to ruthless killer; surrendered on her terms (Feb 12, 1983); admitted to raiding the village, but long claimed that she was not at the massacre site, and members of her gang backed her up; spent 11 years in prison; two years after her release, was elected to federal Parliament on a Samajwadi Party ticket (1996). ❖ See also Mala Sen, *India's Bandit Queen: The True Story of Phoolan Devi* (Harvill, 1991); films *Outlaw, Phoolan Devi* and *The One with Courage*; and *Women in World History*.

PHRANC (1957—). American musician. Name variations: Susan Gottlieb. Born Susan Gottlieb, Aug 28, 1957, in Santa Monica, CA. ❖ Joined local lesbian-feminist community and changed name to Phranc (1975); performed with 3 punk bands, including Catholic Discipline, but, disenchanted with music's misogyny and Nazi iconography, wrote "Take Off Your Swastika"; switched to folk music and performed with such bands as Dead Kennedys and Morrissey; released critically acclaimed cult album, *Folksinger* (1985); signed with Island Records and released *I Enjoy Being a Girl* (1989) and *Positively Phranc* (1991); released *Goofyfoot* (1995) and *Milkman* (1998).

PHRYNE (c. 365–c. 295 BCE). Greek artist's model. Pronunciation: FRIN-ih. Born Phryne near Thebes around 365 BCE; died in Athens, at nearly 70 years of age, around 295 BCE; mother was an unknown worker on a Theban chicken farm; father was a passing army officer. ❖ One of the most beautiful women in Greece, became a model for the best artists and sculptors in 4th-century Athens; was sold as a slave to the hetaerae (courtesans) in Athens by the time she was 15; modeled for Appeles, the most famous painter of the day, for his masterpiece, *Aphrodite Emerging*, which has been lost since antiquity; next posed for Praxiteles, the foremost Athenian sculptor, who fell in love with her; formed a relationship with the sculptor that furthered both their careers (he became famous, she became rich); posed nude for his famed *Aphrodite of Cnidus*; often portrayed as Aphrodite arising from the sea by Praxiteles, went on to become a cult figure; was the only woman ever granted permission to dedicate a golden statue of herself in the Temple of Delphi (the inscription read, "To Phryne who inspired all artists and lovers"); accused of impiety for making derogatory comments about Athenian matrons who participated in the Eleusian rites, went on trial for her life before an all-male jury in the court of the Areopagus (May 10, 318 BCE), but was acquitted; lived for several more years, a wealthy and successful hetaera. ❖ See also *Women in World History.*

PHUC, Kim (c. 1963——). Vietnamese icon and activist. Name variations: Phan Thi Kim Phuc. Born c. 1963; attended college in Cuba; married in 1992; children: 2. ❖ At age 9 (1972), with her clothes burned off her body by napalm, ran naked from her village, her arms outstretched, screaming in agony (the Pulitzer Prize-winning photograph of that moment, taken by Nick Ut before he hurried her to a hospital, is perhaps the best-known image of the Vietnam War); received treatment for burns covering much of her body well into adulthood; sought political asylum in Canada (1992); founded the Kim Foundation to assist noncombatants victimized by war and was named a Goodwill Ambassador for a Culture of Peace by the United Nations Educational, Scientific and Cultural Organization (UNESCO, 1997). ❖ See also Denise Chong, *The Girl in the Picture: The Story of Kim Phuc, the Photograph, and the Vietnam War* (Viking, 2000); and *Women in World History.*

PHULE, Savitribai (1831–1897). Indian reformer and educator. Name variations: Savitribai Jotirao Phule. Born Jan 3, 1831, in Satara, India; died Mar 10, 1897, in Pune; dau. of Laxmi and Khandoji Nevse; m. Jyotirao or Jotirao Phule (social reformer), 1840 (died 1890). ❖ With husband, opened the 1st girls' school in India (1848), in Pune; became its head mistress; started a night school for farmers and laborers (1855); opened the well to untouchables (1868); supported the remarriage of widows; died while serving plague victims during an epidemic.

PI HONGYAN (1979——). Chinese badminton player. Born Jan 25, 1979, in Chong Qing, China; lives in Copenhagen, Denmark. ❖ Won US Open (1999), Swiss Open, German Open, and Portuguese International (2001).

PIAF, Edith (1915–1963). French singer. Born Edith Giovanna Gassion, Dec 19, 1915, in Paris, France; died at Plascassier (Alpes-Maritimes) of cirrhosis and hepatitis, Oct 10, 1963 (some sources erroneously cite the 11th); dau. of Louis-Alphonse Gassion (1881–1944, contortionist) and Anette Giovanna Maillard (1895–1945, singer under the name Line Marsa); m. Jacques Pills, 1952 (div. 1957); m. Théo Sarapo, 1962. ❖ France's greatest popular singer of the 20th century, whose tragic life made her an interpreter of the lives and loves of ordinary people and whose ability to perform despite near-fatal bouts of illness became legendary; sang in the streets of Paris (1930–35); discovered by Louis Leplée, proprietor of Gerny's, a club which was then popular with the smart set (1935); questioned in Leplée's murder but recovered career (1936); taken in tow by Raymond Asso, lyricist who wrote her hit *Mon Légionnaire*; appeared at A.B.C., the top music hall in Paris, and became a star (1937); had a sensational run at the Bobino (1939); starred in Cocteau's *Le Bel Indifférent* (1940); sang for French POWs in Germany (1942–43); appeared in film *Montmartre-sur-Seine* (1941) and *Étoile sans lumière*, with Yves Montand (1945); wrote words and refrain to her greatest international hit, "La vie en rose" (1945); made NY debut (1947); had affair with middleweight-boxing champion Marcel Cerdan which ended with his death in a plane crash (1947–49); began addiction to morphine and other drugs after 2 auto accidents (1951); continued to record, appeared in a musical, *La P'tite Lili* (1951), and in 5 films—*Paris chante toujours* (1951), *Si Versailles n'était conté* (1953), *Boum sur Paris* (1954), *French-Cancan* (1954) and *Les Amants de demain* (1958); starred at the Olympia (1956, 1958); collapsed in NY, and at Dreux after a "suicide tour" (1959); had a sensational run at Olympia after long illnesses (1961); made another triumphal return to Olympia (1962); made last Paris appearance, at Bobino, and last performance, at Lille (1963). ❖ See also autobiographies *Au bal de la chance* (Éditions Jeheber, 1958, trans. as *The Wheel of Fortune*, Chilton, 1965)

and (with Jean Noli) *Ma Vie* (1964, trans. by Crosland as *My Life*, 1990); Simone Berteaut, *Piaf* (Harper & Row, 1972); Margaret Crosland, *Piaf* (Putnam, 1985); and *Women in World History.*

PIA OF SICILY (1849–1882). Duchess of Bourbon-Parma. Name variations: Maria Pia of Sicily. Born Aug 2, 1849; died Sept 29, 1882; dau. of Ferdinand II, king of the Two Sicilies (r. 1830–1859) and Theresa of Austria (1816–1867); m. Robert, duke of Bourbon-Parma, on April 5, 1869; children: Marie Louise of Parma (1870–1899); Ferdinand (b. 1871); Louise of Parma (b. 1872); Henry (b. 1873); Maria Imaculata (1874–1914); Joseph (b. 1875); Maria Theresa (b. 1876); Maria Pia (1877–1915); Beatrix of Parma (1879, who m. Count Pietro Lucchesi); Elias (b. 1880); Anastasia (1881–1881); Auguste (b. 1882).

PICASSO, Jacqueline (d. 1986). *See Roque, Jacqueline.*

PICASSO, Paloma (1949——). French designer. Born in Paris, France, Aug 19, 1949; 2nd child and only dau. of Pablo Picasso (1881–1973, artist) and Françoise Gilot (b. 1922, artist); studied jewelry design and fabrication at a school in Nanterre, France; m. Rafael López-Sanchez (playwright-director, div. 1999); m. Eric Thevennet (gynecologist), Feb 1999. ❖ A top jewelry designer for the prestigious Tiffany and Co. as well as an arbiter of fashion among the international set, was 1st commissioned by St. Laurent to design a line of fashion jewelry (1969); also designed furs for Jacques Kaplan and gold jewelry for Zolotas, a Greek firm, and dabbled in the cinema, appearing in Walerian Borowczyk's *Immoral Tales* (1974); branched out into perfume (1984), creating a 10-product line bearing her name. ❖ See also *Women in World History.*

PICCININI, Amelia (1917–1979). Italian track-and-field athlete. Born Jan 17, 1917, in Italy; died April 3, 1979. ❖ At London Olympics, won a silver medal in the shot put (1948).

PICHLER, Karoline (1769–1843). Austrian writer and salonnière. Name variations: Caroline Pichler. Born Karoline von Greiner in Vienna, Austria, Sept 7, 1769; died in Vienna, July 9, 1843; dau. of Franz Sales von Greiner (court advisor and *hofrat* [privy counselor], died 1798) and Charlotte Hieronymus von Greiner (orphan adopted by Empress Maria Theresa of Austria); had one brother; m. Andreas Pichler (official in Habsburg court chancellery), 1796 (died 1837); children: Elisabeth Pichler. ❖ One of the most influential personalities in the intellectual life of pre-1848 Vienna for 40 years, was the center of a literary salon frequented by Germaine de Staël, Dorothea Mendelssohn (Schlegel), Franz Grillparzer, Nikolaus Lenau, Franz Schubert, Adalbert Stifter and Wilhelm von Humboldt; published *Gleichnisse* (Parables, 1800) to considerable critical acclaim; over next decades, would write a number of highly popular novels, including *Leonore* (1803), *Agathokles* (1808), and *Frauenwürde* (The Dignity of Woman, 1818), as well as the novella *Stille Liebe* (Quiet Love, 1808); also wrote verse, ballads, essays, and historical and patriotic dramas, and several Roman Catholic devotional books based on Fénelon's model; her posthumously published memoirs, *Denkwürdigkeiten aus meinem Leben* (Memorable Events of My Life), remain an important source of information on the Romantic era in Austria. ❖ See also *Women in World History.*

PICHLER, Magdalena (1881–1920). German novelist. Name variations: (pseudonym) Lena Christ. Born Magdalena Pichler, Oct 30, 1881, in Glonn, Oberbayern, Bavaria; committed suicide by cyanide after being accused of forgery, June 30, 1920, in Munich, Germany; illeg. dau. of a cook; grew up with grandparents in Bavaria; m. Anton Lex (accountant), 1901 (sep. 1909); married Peter Benedix (writer under Peter Jerusalem); children: (1st m.) 6. ❖ At 8, was brought to Munich to work in the inn of her stepfather and was exploited; at 19, married an alcoholic and had 6 children; came down with TB which brought on economic difficulties; tried to make money by forgery and was threatened with imprisonment; wrote the semi-autobiographical *Erinnerungen einer Überflüssigen* (Memoirs of a Superflous Woman, 1912); other writings include *Mathias Bichler* (1914), *Die Runplhanni* (1916), and *Madam Bäuerin* (1919). *Die Rumplhanni* was made into a successful film.

PICHOT, Sophie (1962——). *See Moressee-Pichot, Sophie.*

PICK, Lady (1832–1899). *See Pickens, Lucy.*

PICK-GOSLAR, Hannah (b. 1928). *See Goslar, Hannah.*

PICKELL, Ellen Liddy (1861–1889). *See Watson, Ellen.*

PICKENS, Helen (1910——). American singer. Name variations: Pickens Sisters. Born July 10, 1910, in Macon, GA; dau. of E. Monte Pickens Jr.; sister of Jane and Patti Pickens. ❖ Performed with the Pickens Sisters, a popular radio and recording trio (1932–35); with sisters, appeared in the film *Sitting Pretty* (1933).

PICKENS, Jane (1908–1992). American actress and singer. Name variations: Jane Pickens-Hoving; Jane Hoving; Pickens Sisters. Born Georgia Pickens, Aug 10, 1908, in Macon, GA; died Feb 21, 1992, in Newport, RI; dau. of E. Monte Pickens Jr.; sister of Helen and Patti Pickens; m. Russell Clark (div.); m. William C. Langley (died); m. Walter Hoving (head of Tiffany & Co. and Bonwit Teller). ❖ Performed with the Pickens Sisters, a popular radio and recording trio (1932–35); group disbanded (1935); appeared on Broadway in *Thumbs Up, Boys and Girls Together,* and in the title role in *Regina;* in Manhattan, ran unsuccessfully for US House of Representatives against Ed Koch (1972).

PICKENS, Lucy (1832–1899). American confederate hostess. Name variations: Lady Pick. Born Lucy Petway Holcombe, June 11, 1832, in La Grange, Fayette Co., TN; died Aug 8, 1899, in Edgefield, SC; dau. of Eugenia Dorothea (Hunt) Holcombe and Beverly Lafayette Holcombe (distinguished plantation owner); m. Francis Wilkinson Pickens (US Congressional representative and political leader), April 26, 1858 (died 1869); children: 1 daughter. ❖ Celebrated as a beautiful southern belle, was groomed from a young age for society life; moved to Russia soon after marriage to Francis Pickens, who was newly appointed by President James Buchanan as American minister there; had instant social success and gave birth to only child in Russia; returned to SC (1860), where husband was elected secession state governor; entertained well during Confederate salad days and her image was engraved upon the Confederate $100 bill; inherited and entertained at family mansion, Edgewood at Edgefield (SC), after husband's death (1869); served as vice-regent for South Carolina of Ann Pamela Cunningham's Mount Vernon Ladies' Association and raised funds for Confederate monument at Edgefield.

PICKENS, Patti (1914–1995). American singer. Name variations: Pickens Sisters. Born Dec 20, 1914, in Macon, GA; died Nov 16, 1995, in Bethlehem, PA; dau. of E. Monte Pickens Jr. ❖ Performed with the Pickens Sisters, a popular radio and recording trio (1932–35).

PICKENS SISTERS.
See Pickens, Helen.
See Pickens, Jane.
See Pickens, Patti.

PICKERILL, Cecily Mary Wise (1903–1988). New Zealand plastic surgeon. Name variations: Cecily Mary Wise Clarkson. Born on Feb 9, 1903, in Taihape, New Zealand; died on July 21, 1988, in Wellington; dau. of Percy Wise Clarkson (clergyman) and Margaret Ann (Hunter) Clarkson; University of Otago, MB, ChB, 1925; m. Henry Percy Pickerill (surgeon), 1934 (died 1956). ❖ Served as house surgeon at Dunedin Hospital (1926); worked with husband at North Shore Hospital in Sydney, Australia, and at Lewisham Hospital in Wellington (1930s); with husband, established Bassam Hospital in Wellington (1939), where she worked (1939–67); specialized in plastic surgery for children with congenital problems, and later in injuries sustained by soldiers in WWII; published in *New Zealand Medical Journal* and *British Journal of Plastic Surgery.* OBE (1958); DBE (1977). ❖ See also *Dictionary of New Zealand Biography* (Vol. 4).

PICKERING, Evelyn (1850–1919). *See DeMorgan, Evelyn.*

PICKERING, Jean Desforges (1929—). *See Desforges, Jean Catherine.*

PICKERSGILL, Mary (1776–1857). American flagmaker and reformer. Name variations: Mary Young Pickersgill. Born Mary Young, 1776, in Philadelphia, PA; died 1857 in Baltimore, MD; dau. of Rebecca Young (a flagmaker); m. John Pickersgill, 1795 (died 1807); children: Caroline. ❖ Moved to Baltimore, MD, as a child; on marriage, lived in Philadelphia (1795–1807); returned to Baltimore and established a flag-making business in her home at 44 Queen St. (now 844 E. Pratt St.); created the 30 x 42 foot American flag that flew over Fort McHenry during the 1814 Battle of Baltimore and inspired our national anthem (it is now housed in the Smithsonian); as a philanthropist and reformer, addressed such issues as housing and financial aid for disadvantaged women; was president of the Impartial Female Humane Society (1828–51) and established a home for elderly women, then men.

PICKETT, Fuchsia T. (1918–2004). American evangelical, scholar and writer. Born Dec 29, 1918; died Jan 30, 2004, in Kingsport, Tennessee; attended John Wesley College; m. Leroy Pickett (died May 27, 2004). ❖ Ordained minister in the Methodist Church for 17 years and former

pastor of Fountain Gate church in Plano, TX, had a 50-year ministry that impacted many Christian leaders; after being dramatically healed of Hodgkin's disease, became a teacher in the Pentecostal movement (1959); renowned Bible teacher, wrote such books as *Cultivating the Gifts and Fruit of the Holy Spirit, Understanding the Personality of the Holy Spirit, Receiving Divine Revelation, Possess Your Promised Land* and *Stones of Remembrance.*

PICKFORD, Lillian Mary (1902–2002). *See Pickford, Mary.*

PICKFORD, Lottie (1895–1936). American actress. Name variations: Lottie Pickford Forrest. Born Charlotte Smith, June 9, 1895, in Toronto, Ontario, Canada; died Dec 9, 1936, in Los Angeles, CA; sister of Jack Pickford (actor-director) and Mary Pickford (actress); m. George Rupp, 1920; m. Allan Forrest (actor), 1922 (div. 1928). ❖ Began career with American Biograph (1909); films include *The Two Paths, The House of Bondage, Fanchon the Cricket* and *They Shall Pay.*

PICKFORD, Mary (1893–1979). Canadian-born film actress. Born Gladys Louise Smith, April 8, 1893, in Toronto, Canada; died May 29, 1979, in California; eldest of 3 children of Charlotte and John Smith; m. Owen Moore, 1911 (div. 1920); m. Douglas Fairbanks (actor), 1920 (div. 1933); m. Charles "Buddy" Rogers (actor), 1937; children: (2nd m.) 1 stepson. ❖ Actress and 1st female studio executive, whose ingenue screen persona captivated film audiences in a long series of Cinderella-style stories, many of which she wrote and/or produced; began touring with a vaudeville company at age 5, appeared on Broadway by the time she was 14, and in her 1st film at 16; became the highest-paid film actress up to that time, exercising nearly total control over her career; was among the 4 partners who formed United Artists Corporation (UA), a film distributor (1919); found her acting career languishing (mid-1920s), when she could no longer play ingenues and had turned to more mature dramatic roles; retired from the screen (1933) but remained actively involved in the business of film making into 1950s; received a special Academy Award (1976); films include *The Unwelcome Guest* (1913), *Tess of the Storm Country* (1914), *Cinderella* (1914), *Mistress Nell* (1915), *Fanchon the Cricket* (1915), *Esmeralda* (1915), *Madame Butterfly* (1915), *The Pride of the Clan* (1917), *The Poor Little Rich Girl* (1917), *Rebecca of Sunnybrook Farm* (1917), *The Little Princess* (1917), *Stella Maris* (1918), *M'Liss* (1918), *Johanna Enlists* (1918), *Daddy Long Legs* (1919), *Pollyanna* (1920), *Suds* (1920), *Little Lord Fauntleroy* (1920), *Tess of the Storm Country* (remake, 1922), *Rosita* (1923), *Dorothy Verdon of Haddon Hall* (1924), *Little Annie Rooney* (1925), *My Best Girl* (1927), *Coquette* (first sound film, 1929), *The Taming of the Shrew* (1929) and *Secrets* (1933). ❖ See also memoir *Sunshine and Shadow* (Doubleday, 1955); Scott Eyman, *Mary Pickford: America's Sweetheart* (Fine, 1990); Eileen Whitfield, *Pickford: The Woman Who Made Hollywood* (U. of Kentucky Press, 1997); and *Women in World History.*

PICKFORD, Mary (1902–2002). English physiologist. Name variations: Lillian Mary Pickford. Born Lillian Mary Pickford, Aug 14, 1902, in India; died on her 100th birthday, Aug 14, 2002, in Edinburgh, Scotland; degree in physiology at Bedford College, 1925; University College, London, MSc, 1926. ❖ Pioneer of endocrinology, was the 1st woman to be elected to the Pharmacological Society; trained as a doctor at University College Hospital; served as a house physician and as a casualty officer at Stafford General Infirmary (1935); at University of Edinburgh's Department of Physiology, worked as a lecturer (1939–42), reader (1952–66) and professor (1966–72), the 1st woman to be appointed to a professorship in the faculty of medicine there; served as a special professor of endocrinology at University of Nottingham (1973–83); elected a fellow of University College, London (1968); elected a Royal Society fellow (1966).

PICKING, Anne (1958—). Scottish politician and member of Parliament. Born Anne Moffat, Mar 30, 1958; m. David Adair Harold Picking, 1984; children: 1 son. ❖ Began career as a nurse; representing Labour, elected to House of Commons at Westminster (2001, 2005), for East Lothian.

PICKLES, Edith Carrie. English gymnast. Born in UK. ❖ At Amsterdam Olympics, won a bronze medal in the team all-around (1928).

PICKTHALL, Marjorie (1883–1922). Canadian poet and novelist. Born Marjorie Lowry Christie Pickthall, Sept 14, 1883, near Middlesex, England; died April 19, 1922, in Vancouver, Canada; dau. of Arthur C. Pickthall and Lizzie Helen Mary (Mallard) Pickthall; never married. ❖ A praised poet in her time, immigrated to Canada with family (1899); sold 1st story at 15; while in early 20s, published 3 juvenile adventure novels; published many of her early poems and stories in *Atlantic Monthly, Century, Scribner's, McClure's,* and *Harper's,* as well as in Canadian newspapers; worked as a librarian at Victoria College, Toronto, during which she assisted in compilation of annual bibliography of Canadian poetry; achieved some success as a novelist, though she is best known as a premodernist poet of such collections as *The Drift of Pinions* (1913) and *The Lamp of Poor Souls, and Other Poems* (1916); also wrote a verse drama, *The Wood Carver's Wife* (1922).

PICO, Caterina (d. 1501). Noblewoman of Mantua. Name variations: Caterina Gonzaga. Died in 1501; m. Rodolfo Gonzaga (1451–1495); children: Luigi Gonzaga of Castelgoffredo and Castiglione della Stiviere.

PICON, Molly (1898–1992). Jewish-American actress, comedian, and singer. Born June 1, 1898, in New York, NY; died April 6, 1992, in Lancaster, PA; m. Jacob Kalich (theater manager), 1919. ❖ One of the most beloved figures of the Yiddish theater, perfected singing and comedic skills on vaudeville circuit (1918–19); on European tour, appeared in operetta *Yankele,* the 1st of 40 vehicles written for her by her husband, actor-manager Jacob Kalich (1921); appeared at NY's Second Avenue Theater (1923–30), starring in *Tzipke* and *Shmendrik* (1924), *Gypsy Girl* (1925), *Rabbi's Melody* (1926), *Raizele* (1927), *Mazel Broche* (1928), and *Hello Molly* (1929), as well as in *Abi Gezunt* ("So Long as You're Healthy"), which had the largest advance sale in the history of Yiddish theater (1949); followed that with *Saidie Is a Lady* (1950) and *Mazel Tov Molly* (1950), a show based on her life that was also written by husband; interspersed theater appearances with vaudeville and singing tours in US and abroad; during WWII, toured Army camps (1944–45); appeared in 1st English-speaking dramatic role on Broadway, performing the lead in the disappointing *Morning Star* (1940); had more success with *For Heaven's Sake Mother, The Front Page, Paris Is Out, Something Old, Something New,* and *Milk and Honey,* which ran for 2 seasons; wrote and appeared in the revue *Those Were the Days* (1979). ❖ See also autobiography (with Eth Clifford Rosenberg) *So Laugh a Little* (Messner, 1962); and *Women in World History.*

PICOTTE, Susan La Flesche (1865–1915). *See La Flesche, Susan.*

PIELEN, Silke (1955—). West German swimmer. Born Aug 29, 1955, in West Germany. ❖ At Munich Olympics, won a bronze medal in the 4 x 100-meter medley relay (1972).

PIELKE, Christiane (1963—). West German swimmer. Born May 12, 1963, in West Germany. ❖ At Los Angeles Olympics, won a bronze medal in the 4 x 100-meter freestyle relay (1984).

PIELOTH, Kerstin (1965—). *See Forster-Pieloth, Kerstin.*

PIENKOWSKA, Alina (1952–2002). Polish labor leader and politician. Born Jan 12, 1952, in Gdansk, Poland; died of cancer, Oct 17, 2002, in Gdansk; dau. of a Gdansk shipyard worker; married and widowed; m. Bogdan Borusiewicz (labor activist), 1983; children: (1st m.) 1 daughter Kinga; (2nd m.) 1 son Sebastian. ❖ A crucial figure in the Gdansk shipyard strike, joined the underground anti-Communist workers' organization, Free Trade Unions (1970s); was working as a nurse in the shipyard clinic when Gdansk workers went on strike (Aug 14, 1980); managed to get news of the strike to the outside world, causing strikes across Poland; convinced Lech Walesa and fellow strikers not to accept the government's offer of improved pay and conditions, but to continue to protest for political reforms; was one of the authors of the 21 Points agreement that legalized Solidarity (Aug 31, 1980); was one of Solidarity's regional leaders in Gdansk for a decade (1980–90); during the period of martial law, was imprisoned for more than a year; after the fall of Polish communism, served as a member of Poland's senate on the Solidarity ticket (1991–93); became a member of Gdansk City Council (1998).

PIER, Florida (1883–1979). *See Scott-Maxwell, Florida.*

PIERANGELI, Rina Faccio (1876–1960). Italian novelist, poet, and essayist. Name variations: Rina Faccio; (pseudonym) Sibilla Aleramo. Born Rina Faccio in Alessandria, Italy, in 1876; died in Rome, Jan 13, 1960; dau. of Ambrogio Faccio (science teacher) and Ernesta Faccio; attended elementary school, only formal education; m. Ulderico Pierangeli, 1892 (sep 1902); children: 1 son (b. 1895). ❖ At 12, moved with family to Marches, a small town in southern Italy; soon after, was raped by one of her father's employees; shamed, married her attacker Ulderico Pierangeli when she was 16; attempted suicide (1897); in Milan, began to edit feminist journal *L'Italia Feminile* (1899); under pseudonym Sibilla Aleramo, published autobiographical *Una donna* (A

Woman, 1906) to great success; prose collection *Gioie d'occasione* (Joys on Sale, 1930) won the Prix de la Latinité in Paris (1933), and poetry collection *Selva d'amore* (Forest of Love, 1947) took the Versilia Prize (1948); also wrote 2 dramas—*Endimione* (1923) and the unpublished "Francesca Diamante"—and translated works by Marie-Madeleine de La Fayette and Charles Vildrac, in addition to her translations of the love letters of George Sand and Alfred de Musset; was an active member of the Italian Communist Party from 1946 until her death.

PIERANTOZZI, Emanuela (1968—). Italian judoka. Born Aug 22, 1968, in Bologna, Italy. ❖ Won World titles (1989, 1990) and European titles (1989, 1992), all for 66 kg; won a silver medal in middleweight 66 kg at Barcelona Olympics (1992) and a bronze medal for 70–78 kg half-heavyweight at Sydney Olympics (2000); won 66 kg title at World University Games (1996).

PIERCE, Mrs. Franklin (1806–1863). *See Pierce, Jane Means.*

PIERCE, Jane Means (1806–1863). American first lady. Name variations: Mrs. Franklin Pierce; Jeanie Pierce. Born Jane Means Appleton, Mar 12, 1806, in Hampton, New Hampshire; died Dec 2, 1863, in Andover, Massachusetts; dau. of Elizabeth (Means) Appleton and Rev. Jesse Appleton (president of Bowdoin College); m. Franklin Pierce (president of US, 1853–1857), Nov 19, 1834, in Amherst, New Hampshire; children: Franklin Jr. (died 3 days after birth); Frank Robert (1840–1844); Benjamin (1841–1853). ❖ First lady (1853–57) who never functioned in that capacity due to the loss of her 3rd son in a train accident just weeks before her husband's inauguration; ill with consumption and anguished by the previous loss of 2 other sons, could not get past this final blow. ❖ See also *Women in World History.*

PIERCE, Joanne E. (c. 1941—). American FBI special agent. Born c. 1941 in US. ❖ A former Roman Catholic nun, served as secretary at Federal Bureau of Investigation (FBI); after J. Edgar Hoover died and acting director L Patrick Gray III changed policy to allow women agents, became one of two (with Susan Lynn Roley) of the 1st women special agents for FBI (1972).

PIERCE, Judith (1930–2003). English opera singer. Born Nov 21, 1930, in Lancashire, England; died Oct 9, 2003, in Canterbury; attended Royal Manchester College of Music and Royal College of Music's Opera School; m. Theo Barker, 1955 (died 2001). ❖ Stalwart of Scottish Opera who had a special feeling for works of Benjamin Britten, made debut as Helmwige in Wagner's *Die Walküre* (1958); had relatively brief career with several major British companies, including Royal Opera, Sadler's Wells, Scottish Opera and English Opera Group; played many *comprimario* (minor) roles, such as Marianne in *Der Rosenkavalier,* 2nd lady in *The Magic Flute* and flower maiden in *Parsifal;* progressed to more challenging parts, such as Hecuba in Michael Tippett's *King Priam,* and Donna Anna in *Don Giovanni* and Elisabeth in *Tannhäuser,* both for Sadler's Wells; exhumed neglected pieces, portraying Euryanthe in Weber's opera (1962) and title role in *Queen of Cornwall,* Boughton's Celtic version of *Tristan and Isolde;* scored huge successes with Britten's English Opera Group and later performed his works with Scottish Opera; played Mrs. Grose in *Turn of the Screw* at Aldeburgh Festival (1959, 1960) and Lady Billows in *Albert Herring* with Scottish Opera (1967); continued working with Scottish Opera until 1976, gradually reverting to *comprimario* status.

PIERCE, Mary (1975—). Canadian tennis player. Born Jan 15, 1975, in Montreal, Canada. ❖ Representing France, won singles championship at Australian Open (1995); won singles and doubles championship at Roland Garros (2000), but beaten in singles finals by Henin-Hardenne (2005).

PIERCE, Sarah (1767–1852). American educator. Born June 26, 1767, in Litchfield, Connecticut; died Jan 19, 1852, in Litchfield; dau. of John Pierce (potter and farmer) and Mary (Paterson) Pierce; never married. ❖ Head of Litchfield Female Academy, began teaching career with just a few students in her dining room in Litchfield (1792); her school, which would be incorporated as the Litchfield Female Academy (1827), became nationally known for its excellent academics and the training it offered in conduct and manners. ❖ See also *Women in World History.*

PIERCY, Marge (1936—). American novelist and poet. Born Mar 31, 1936, in Detroit, MI; dau. of Robert Douglas Piercy and Bert Bunnin Piercy; attended University of Michigan; m. Ira Wood, 1982. ❖ Belonged to Students for a Democratic Society (1965–69); lectured and conducted workshops at many universities from late 1960s; novels include *Going Down Fast* (1969), *Dance the Eagle to Sleep* (1970), *Woman on the Edge of Time* (1976), *Vida* (1980), *Fly Away Home* (1984), *Summer People* (1987), *The Longings of Women* (1994), and *Three Women* (1999); poetry collections include *Breaking Camp* (1968), *To Be of Use* (1973), *Circles on the Water: Selected Poems of Marge Piercy* (1982), *My Mother's Body* (1985), *Available Light* (1985), and *Early Grrrl* (1999). Received Carolyn Kizer Poetry prize (1986, 1990) and Arthur C. Clarke award (1992).

PIERONNE OF BRITTANY (d. 1430). French peasant soldier. Name variations: Pierrone; Pierronne. Burned at the stake in Paris in 1430. ❖ Contemporary of Joan of Arc, suffered the same fate; saw visions of God appearing to her and urging her to fight for her nation; joined the army, fought boldly and gained some renown among her fellow soldiers; was eventually arrested and condemned to die at the pyre for practicing witchcraft. ❖ See also *Women in World History.*

PIERRA, Dr. (b. 1909). *See Vejjabul, Pierra.*

PIERRE, Eugénie Potonié (1844–1898). *See Potonié-Pierre, Eugénie.*

PIERREPONT, Elizabeth Chudleigh (1720–1788). *See Chudleigh, Elizabeth.*

PIESTEWA, Lori Ann (1980–2003). Hopi soldier. Born Lori Ann Piestewa, Dec 1980, in Winslow, Arizona; grew up in Tuba City; killed in an ambush near Nasiriyah, Iraq, Mar 23, 2003; dau. of Hopi father Terry Piestewa and Hispanic mother Priscilla Baca Piestewa; m. Bill Whiterock, a Navajo, 1997 (div. 2002); children: Brandon (b. 1998) and Carla (b. 1999). ❖ Assigned to the 507th Maintenance Company, was the 1st US female soldier killed in the Iraq war and the 1st Native American woman to die in combat on foreign soil.

PIETERSE, Zola (1966—). *See Budd, Zola.*

PIGEON, Anna (fl. 1860s). English mountaineer. Sister of Ellen Pigeon (mountaineer). ❖ With sister, crossed the Sesia Joch between Zermatt and Alagna (1869), made the 1st female traverse of the Matterhorn up the Breuil side and down the Zermatt, and eventually ascended the mountain from all 4 approaches: the North East (or Hörnli Ridge), the Zmutt Ridge, the West Face (the Italian Ridge), and the Furggengrat.

PIGEON, Ellen (fl. 1860s). English mountaineer. Sister of Anna Pigeon (mountaineer). ❖ With sister, crossed the Sesia Joch between Zermatt and Alagna (1869), made the 1st female traverse of the Matterhorn up the Breuil side and down the Zermatt, and eventually ascended the mountain from all 4 approaches.

PIGNICZKI, Krisztina (1975—). Hungarian handball player. Born Sept 18, 1975, in Hungary. ❖ Won a team silver medal at Sydney Olympics (2000).

PIGOTT, Mimi Forde (d. 1966). *See Crawford, Mimi.*

PIKE, Ada (1863–1933). *See Wells, Ada.*

PIKE, Mary (1824–1908). American author. Name variations: (pseudonyms) Mary Langdon and Sydney A. Story, Jr. Born Mary Hayden Green, Nov 30, 1824, in Eastport, Maine; died Jan 15, 1908, in Baltimore, Maryland; dau. of Elijah Dix Green (bank director and colonel of militia) and Hannah Claflin (Hayden) Green; attended Female Seminary, Charlestown, Massachusetts; m. Frederick Augustus Pike (lawyer and politician), Sept 28, 1845 (died 1886); children: 1 adopted daughter. ❖ Under pseudonym Mary Langdon, published antislavery novel, *Ida May* (1854), a melodramatic story of a white child kidnapped into slavery, which enjoyed immediate success, selling 60,000 copies in less than 2 years and generating several British editions; under pseudonym Sydney A. Story, Jr., published 2nd novel, *Caste: A Story of Republican Equality,* concerning a quadroon forbidden to marry a white man (1856), also well received by critics and readers. ❖ See also *Women in World History.*

PIKE, Mervyn (1918–2004). English politician. Name variations: Baroness Pike of Melton. Born Irene Mervyn Parnicott Pike, Sept 16, 1918, in Castleford, West Yorkshire, England; died Jan 11, 2004; dau. of I.S. Pike (chair of a family pottery company); attended Hunmanby Hall and Reading University; never married. ❖ Known as a Tory with a social conscience, served in the Women's Auxiliary Air Force (1941–46); was managing director of the family pottery firm, Clokie and Co. (1946–59); became the Yorkshire representative on the Conservative Party's national executive; served as MP for Melton (1956–74), stressing the needs of widows, deserted mothers and the elderly; was assistant postmaster

general (1959–63); served as chair of the Women's Royal Voluntary Reserve (WRVS, 1974–81); appointed chair of the Broadcasting Complaints Commission (1981); named a life peeress (1974). Appointed DBE (1981).

PILCHER, Rosamunde (1924—). English novelist. Name variations: often wrongly spelled Rosamund; Jane Fraser. Born Rosamunde Scott, Sept 22, 1924, in Lelant, Cornwall, England; attended Miss Kerr-Sanders' Secretarial College; m. Graham Hope Pilcher, 1946; children: Robin, Fiona, Philippa and Mark Pilcher. ❖ Served with Women's Royal Naval Service (1943–46); married and moved to Dundee, Scotland; under pseudonym Jane Fraser, published romances for Mills & Boon, including *Half-way to the Moon* (1949), *The Brown Fields* (1951), *Dear Tom* (1954), *Bridge of Corvie* (1956), *A Family Affair* (1958), *The Keeper's House* (1963) and *A Long Way From Home* (1963); under her own name, published novel *A Secret to Tell* (1955), but came to prominence with *The Shell Seekers* (1987); also wrote the bestselling *September* (1989) and *Coming Home* (1995), which took 5 years to write and includes her own experiences of the war years (adapted for tv miniseries, 1998); as Rosamunde Pilcher, also wrote *April* (1957), *On My Own* (1965), *Another View* (1969), *Snow in April* (1972), *The Day of the Storm* (1975), *Wild Mountain Thyme* (1978), *The Carousel* (1982), *The Blue Bedroom and Other Stories* (1985), *The Blackberry Day* (1991), *Winter Solstice* (2000) and the plays *The Dashing White Sergeant* (1955) and *The Tulip Major* (1957). ❖ See also book of photography, *The World of Rosamunde Pilcher* (St. Martin, 1996).

PILECKA-LEWICKA, Daniela (1935—). *See Walkowiak, Daniela.*

PILEJCZYK, Helena (1931—). Polish speedskater. Born April 1, 1931, in Poland. ❖ Won a bronze medal for 1,500 meters at Squaw Valley Olympics (1960).

PILGRIM (1839/40–1900). *See Innes, Catherine Lucy.*

PILGRIM, Ada (1867–1965). New Zealand healer. Name variations: Ada Chadwick. Born Ada Chadwick, Sept 13, 1867, at Paparoa, North Auckland, New Zealand; died on July 7, 1965, at Auckland; dau. of John Chadwick (farmer) and Hannah Mary (Blakeley) Chadwick; m. Richard Edward Pilgrim (miller), 1888 (died 1926). ❖ Established successful therapy practice based on massage and physical activity (early 1900s), maintaining it until the late 1940s. ❖ See also *Dictionary of New Zealand Biography* (Vol. 3).

PILKINGTON, Laetitia (c. 1708–1750). British writer and memoirist. Born Laetitia Lewen, c. 1708 (some sources cite 1712), in Dublin, Ireland; died Aug 29, 1750 (some sources cite 1759), in Dublin; dau. of John Lewen (physician); mother's maiden name was Meade; m. Matthew Pilkington (vicar and poet), 1725 (div. 1738); children: 3, including John Carteret Pilkington. ❖ Introduced into the literary circle around Jonathan Swift, published *The Statues* and *An Excursory View on the Present State of Men and Things* (1739); after being imprisoned for debt, opened a bookshop and printshop, producing letters and pamphlets to order; for a time, was befriended by writer Samuel Richardson; produced 1st volume of her *Memoirs* (1748), the work for which she is best known; wrote 2 additional volumes of memoirs, the last of which was published after her death with additions by son; also thought to have been the author of a comedy, *The Turkish Court.* After her death, her witty sayings were collected in a book, *The Celebrated Mrs. Pilkington's Jests,* and her poems were included in *Poems by Eminent Ladies* (1755). ❖ See also *Women in World History.*

PILKINGTON, Mary (1766–1839). British writer. Born Mary Hopkins, 1766, in Cambridge, England; died in 1839; dau. of man named Hopkins (surgeon); married a man named Pilkington (surgeon), in 1786. ❖ Turned out an astonishing number of educational works, moral tracts, and novels, some of which were translated into French; was particularly interested in improving the moral character of the young; writings include *Obedience Rewarded and Prejudice Conquered* (1797), *Edward Barnard* (1797), *Historical Beauties for Young Ladies* (1798), *Marvellous Adventures* (1802), *The Disgraceful Effects of Falsehood* (1807), *Original Poems* (1811), and *Celebrity* (1825).

PILLAR, Cathy (1948—). *See Ferguson, Cathy Jean.*

PILLEY, Dorothy (1893–1986). British mountaineer. Name variations: Dorothy Pilley Richards. Born Dorothy Eleanor Pilley, 1893; died 1986; m. I(vor) A(rmstrong) Richards (1893–1979, British literary critic, theorist and climber). ❖ Probably the best-known English woman climber (1920s–30s), made the first ascent of the North Ridge of the Dent

Blanche with others (1928); was secretary of the British Women's Patriotic League. ❖ See also autobiography, *Climbing Days* (Secker & Warburg, 1953); and *Women in World History*.

PIMENTEL, Eleonora (c. 1768–1799). Italian patriot. Name variations: Marchesa de Fonseca; Marquesa of Fonseca. Born Eleonora Pimentel in Rome around 1768 or possibly 1758; raised in Naples; executed in Naples, July 20, 1799; married the marquis of Fonseca, in 1784. ❖ A liberal elite, founded and edited the anti-royalist newspaper *Monitore Napoletano* (1798) and was a heroine of the Neapolitan uprising (1799); upon restoration of the Neapolitan monarchy, was executed along with other revolutionaries, signaling the end of liberalism in southern Italy; has long been revered by Italian leftists and feminists. ❖ See also Maria Macciocchi, *Cara Eleonora* (1993); opera *Eleonora* (1999); and *Women in World History*.

PIMIKO or PIMIKU (fl. 3rd c.). *See Himiko.*

PIMNACOVA, Bohumila (1947—). Czech gymnast. Born Sept 1947 in Czechoslovakia. ❖ At Mexico City Olympics, won a silver medal in team all-around (1968).

PINAYEVA-KHVEDOSYUK, Lyudmila (1936—). Soviet kayaker. Name variations: Lyudmila Khvedosyuk. Born Jan 14, 1936, in USSR. ❖ At Tokyo Olympics, won a gold medal in K1 500 meters (1964); at Mexico City Olympics, won a bronze medal in K2 500-meters and a gold medal in K1 500 meters (1968); at Munich Olympics, won a gold medal in K2 500 meters (1972).

PINCHOT, Cornelia (1881–1960). American politician and suffragist. Name variations: Cornelia Elizabeth Bryce, Leila Bryce, Cornelia Bryce Pinchot, Mrs. Gifford Pinchot. Born Cornelia Elizabeth Bryce, Aug 26, 1881, in Newport, RI; died Sept 9, 1960, in Washington, DC; dau. of Lloyd Stevens Bryce (congressman, novelist, editor of *North American Review*, political adviser to Theodore Roosevelt, and US minister to Netherlands) and Edith (Cooper) Bryce; m. Gifford Pinchot (governor of PA), Aug 15, 1914 (died 1946); children: Gifford Bryce Pinchot (b. 1915). ❖ Campaigned for women's suffrage (early 1900s); served as secretary of Pennsylvania Woman Suffrage Association (1918–19), and successfully campaigned for ratification of 19th amendment by state legislature; was 1st woman representative from county to state committee of Republican Party, and served as treasurer of Pennsylvania Republican Women's Committee; as first lady of Pennsylvania, worked for women's rights (1923–27), and for organized labor and women and child workers (1931–35); unsuccessfully ran from PA's 15th Congressional District (1928); championed minimum wage laws for women and children, and publicly supported workers on strike (early 1930s); when husband was hospitalized, gained national attention by taking over running of state (1935); was US representative at International Women's Conference in Paris (1945); was elected to board of Americans for Democratic Action (1947); advocated disarmament, and control of atomic research by United Nations.

PINCKNEY, Eliza Lucas (1722–1793). American botanist and patriot. Name variations: Elizabeth or Eliza Lucas. Born Elizabeth Lucas on island of Antigua, British West Indies, Dec 28, 1722; died of cancer in Philadelphia, Pennsylvania, May 26, 1793; dau. of Major (later Colonel) George Lucas of the British Army and Ann Lucas; m. Charles Pinckney (South Carolina's 1st native attorney, colonel in the militia, and planter), 1744 (died 1758); children: Charles Cotesworth Pinckney (b. 1746, helped to write US Constitution); George Lucas Pinckney (died in infancy, 1747); Harriott Pinckney Horry (b. 1749); Thomas Pinckney (b. 1750). ❖ South Carolina plantation owner, botanist, and Revolutionary War patriot, who introduced commercial-grade indigo as a North American crop, moved with family from Antigua to England (1735); moved to a plantation near Charleston, South Carolina (1738); after father was recalled to active military duty, managed his 3 plantations and was soon experimenting with indigo and other exotic crops including silk (1739); proved to be an almost revolutionary innovator in colonial agriculture; after marriage to neighboring widower Charles Pinckney, helped to manage a total of 5 plantations (1744); lived with husband and children in England for 5 years (1753–58); helped to finance the cause of the colonies during Revolution (1776–81); entertained President Washington on one of her plantations (1791). ❖ See also *The Letterbook of Eliza Lucas Pinckney, 1739–1762* (U. of North Carolina Press, 1972); Harriet Horry Ravenel, *Eliza Pinckney* (Adams, 1896); George C. Rogers, *Charleston in the Age of the Pinckneys* (U. of Oklahoma Press, 1969); and *Women in World History*.

PINEPINE TE RIKA (1857/58–1954). New Zealand tribal leader. Born probably in 1857 or 1858, at Rahitiroa, east of Te Waiiti in Bay of Plenty, New Zealand; died Aug 9, 1954, at Tuapou, Matahi, New Zealand; dau. of Te Rika Te Wheura and Tuhiwai Taheke; m. Rua Kenana (religious prophet), 1880s; children: 17. ❖ Became spiritual wife of religious leader who took 6 other wives; was keeper of sacred covenant, large English-language Bible, and lived most of her life in imposed isolation and purity; upon husband's arrest, as religious followers dwindled, began to live more ordinary life. ❖ See also *Dictionary of New Zealand Biography* (Vol. 3).

PING HSIN (1900–1999). *See Xie, Wanying.*

PINIGINA-KULCHUNOVA, Mariya (1958—). Soviet runner. Name variations: Mariya Kulchunova. Born Feb 9, 1958, in USSR. ❖ At Seoul Olympics, won a gold medal in 4 x 100-meter relay (1988).

PINKERTON, Rachel Selina (1838–1928). *See Reynolds, Rachel Selina.*

PINKHAM, Lydia E. (1819–1883). American entrepreneur. Born Feb 9, 1819, in Lynn, Massachusetts; died May 17, 1883; dau. of William and Rebecca Estes Quakers (both Quakers active in the anti-slavery cause); m. Isaac Pinkham; children: 5, including Daniel, William, and Aroline Pinkham. ❖ Founder of the Lydia E. Pinkham Medicine Co., was also an early feminist; while raising children, often resorted to home remedies which she kept in a notebook; obtained a formula for a medicine to cure female complaints (which contained 20% alcohol); with 2 sons, manufactured the medicine, naming it "Lydia E. Pinkham's Vegetable Compound"; within a few years, her compound had become a national medicine. ❖ See also Jean Burton, *Lydia Pinkham Is Her Name* (Farrar, 1949); Sarah Stage, *Female Complaints: Lydia Pinkham and the Business of Women's Medicine* (Norton, 1979); and *Women in World History*.

PINK LADY, The (1891–1988). *See Dawn, Hazel.*

PINKSTON-BECKER, Elizabeth (1903–1989). *See Becker-Pinkston, Elizabeth.*

PINNEY, Eunice Griswold (1770–1849). American folk artist. Born Eunice Griswold in Simsbury, Connecticut, Feb 9, 1770; died in Simsbury, 1849; dau. of Elisha Griswold (farmer) and Eunice (Viets) Griswold; m. Oliver Holcombe, late 1700s (drowned); m. Butler Pinney, 1797; children: (1st m.) Hector and Sophia Holcombe; (2nd m.) Norman, Viets, and (Minerva) Emeline Pinney. ❖ Taking up her paintbrush around the age of 40, created some of America's earliest primitive watercolors, which, unlike the stereotypical watercolors of the period, are striking in their boldness and vigor; amazingly prolific, turned out more than 50 signed works which today are dispersed among her descendants, museums, and private collections. ❖ See also *Women in World History*.

PINO, Rosario (d. 1933). Spanish actress. Born in Spain; died July 15, 1933. ❖ Made stage debut with Maria Tubau (1897); came to prominence appearing in ingenue parts in plays by Jacinto Benaventa and the Brothers Quinteros; other plays include *Los Conejos, Casa de Banos, El Marido de la Tellez, Fédora, Zaza* and *Madame Flirt*; appeared with the Teatro Lara, Madrid, then the Teatro de la Comedia.

PIÑON, Nélida (1937—). Brazilian novelist and short-story writer. Name variations: Nelida Pinon. Born May 3, 1937, in Rio de Janeiro, Brazil. ❖ Traveled widely and taught at University of Miami, Universidad Complutense da Madrid, Johns Hopkins University, and Columbia University; writings, many of which have been translated into several languages, include *Guia-mapa de Gabriel Arcanjo* (1961), *Madeira feita cruz* (1963), *Fundador* (1969), *A casa da paixão* (1972), *Tebas do meu coração* (1974), *A força do destino* (1978), *O calor das coisas* (1980), *A república dos sonhos* (1984), *O Pão de cada dia* (1994), and *A casa da Paixao* (1999). Won José Geraldo Vieira Prize and PEN Fiction Prize.

PINTASILGO, Maria de Lurdes (1930–2004). Portuguese politician, social activist, and author. Name variations: Maria de Lourdes Pintasilgo or Pintassilgo. Born Jan 18, 1930, in Abrantes, Portugal; died July 11, 2004, in Lisbon, Portugal; first child of Jaime de Matos Pintasilgo (textile merchant) and Amélia Ruivo da Silva; graduate of Superior Technical Institute, 1953. ❖ As a scientist, was part of Portugal's Nuclear Energy Commission's 1st research team; worked for the Companhia União Fabril (CUF, 1954–60), the 1st woman employed there in research and development; served as president of Catholic Feminine University Youth (1952–56) and then headed Pax Romana, the International Movement of Catholic Students (1956–58); lived in France (1964–69), where she was international vice-president of a

Catholic organization (Graal) intended to modernize the Church in keeping with Vatican II; returned to Portugal (1969); served as *procuradora* (attorney) for the Corporative Chamber (1969–74); also headed a governmental committee that evolved into the Commission of the Feminine Condition; after the overthrow of the Salazar dictatorship (1974), held offices in the 1st three provisional governments, at one point serving as secretary of state for social security; represented Portugal at UNESCO and was elected to its executive council (1975–79); named prime minister of a caretaker government until new elections were held (1979); following the election, served as adviser to President Eanes (1981–85); thereafter, occupied a post on the University Council of the UN and founded the Movement for the Deepening of Democracy (1983); was an unsuccessful candidate for the presidency of Portugal; represented her country in the European Parliament (1986–89); writings include *Sulcos do Nosso Querer Comum* (1980), *Imaginar a Igreja* (1980), *Les Nouveaux Féminismes: Question pour le Chrétiens* (1980), *Dimensões da mudança* (1985) and *As Minhas Respostas* (1985). ❖ See also *Women in World History.*

PINTER, Lady Antonia (1932—). See Fraser, Antonia.

PINTO, Adriana (1978—). Brazilian basketball player. Name variations: Adriana Moisés Pinto. Born Dec 16, 1978, in Franca, Brazil. ❖ Won a team bronze medal at Sydney Olympics (2000); signed with Phoenix Mercury of the WNBA (2001).

PIO, Margherita (d. 1452). See Este, Margherita d'.

PIOMBINO, princess of. See Bonaparte, Elisa (1777–1820).

PIOTROWSKA, Gabriela (1857–1921). See Zapolska, Gabriela.

PIOUS, Minerva (1903–1979). Russian-born actress. Born Mar 5, 1903, in Russia; died Mar 16, 1979, in New York, NY. ❖ Succeeded Fanny Brice in *Ziegfeld Follies*; other credits include *The World of Sholom Aleichem, Dear Me, the Sky is Falling* and *The Last Analysis*; best remembered for portrayal of Mrs. (Pansy) Nussbaum on radio's "Fred Allen Show" in the segment know as "Allen's Alley," where she frequently referred to "mine husband, Pierre" (1945–49).

PIOZZI, Hester Lynch (1741–1821). English-Welsh writer. Name variations: Hester Lynch Thrale; Hester Lynch Thrale Piozzi; Hester Salusbury; Mrs. Thrale; Mrs. Piozzi. Born Jan 1741 in Carnarvonshire, Wales; died May 1821 in Clifton, England; dau. of John Salusbury (died 1762) and Hester Maria Cotton; m. Henry Thrale (wealthy landowner and Conservative member of Parliament), Oct 1763 (died 1781); m. Gabriel Piozzi (Italian musician), July 1784 (died 1809); children: (1st m.) Hester Maria Elphinstone (1764–1857, known as Queeney); Frances (1765–1765); Henry (1767–1776); Anna Maria (b. 1768); Lucy (1769–1773); Susanna (b. 1770); Sophia (b. 1771); Penelope (b. 1772); Ralph (1773–1775); Frances Anna (b. 1775, died at 7 months); Cecilia (b. 1777); Henrietta (b. 1778); grandmother of Margaret Mercer Elphinstone (1788–1867). ❖ Intellectual, who was second only to Boswell in fame among writers on Dr. Samuel Johnson, began a family journal at the encouragement of Johnson (1766), which now stands as a unique record of daily life in 18th-century England, especially since it was written by a woman; composed her compelling *Three Dialogues on the Death of Hester Lynch Thrale* (1781); published *Anecdotes of the Late Samuel Johnson during the Last Twenty Years of his Life* (1786); having married an Italian musician thought to be beneath her, was coldly received by daughters and London society on return to England (1787); began work on an edition of the letters of Samuel Johnson which was published to considerable success (1788); also wrote *Journey Through France, Italy, and Germany* (1789), *British Synonymy, or an Attempt at Regulating the Choice of Words in Familiar Conversation* (1794), *Three Warnings to John Bull Before He Dies* (1798), on the state of British politics, and *Retrospection* (1801), a multi-volume narrative of world history. ❖ See also Katherine Balderston, ed. *Thraliana: The Diary of Mrs. Hester Lynch Thrale, 1776–1809* (Clarendon, 1951); Mary Hyde, *The Thrales of Streatham Park* (Harvard U. Press, 1977); and *Women in World History.*

PIPELET, Madame (1767–1845). See Salm-Dyck, Constance de.

PIPER, Carly (1983—). American swimmer. Born Sept 23, 1983, in Grosse Pointe, Michigan. ❖ Won a gold medal for 4 x 200-meter free-style relay at Athens Olympics (2004).

PIPER, Cherie (1981—). Canadian ice-hockey player. Born June 29, 1981, in Scarborough, Ontario, Canada; dau. of Alan and Christine Piper; attended Dartmouth College. ❖ Forward, won a team gold medal at Salt Lake City Olympics (2002) and a team gold medal at Torino Olympics (2006).

PIPER, Leonora E. (1859–1950). American medium. Name variations: Leonore Piper. Born Leonora Evelina Simonds on June 27, 1859, in Nashua, New Hampshire; died July 3, 1950, in Brookline, Massachusetts; dau. of Stillman Simonds and Hannah (Stevens) Simonds; m. William R. Piper (manufacturer, salesman, and clerk), Oct 6, 1881 (died 1904); children: Alta Laurette Piper (b. 1884); Minerva Leonora Piper (b. 1885). ❖ One of the world's most celebrated psychic mediums, and certainly one of the most scrutinized, not only possessed extraordinary gifts, but used them for the good of humanity rather than personal gain; had 1st experiences with "supernormal" powers in childhood, suffering occasional episodes where she lost consciousness and had visions portending future events; as an adult, invoking trances at will, delivered to her sitters many personal messages from deceased relatives, receiving her information from a number of controlling figures, including a French physician by the name of Phinuit and later George Pelham, a young man who had recently died; visited England under the auspices of the British Society for Psychical Research (1889), passing their many tests. ❖ See also *Women in World History.*

PIPER, Myfanwy (1911–1997). English art critic, editor and librettist. Pronunciation: mih-VAHN-wih. Born Mary Myfanwy Evans, 1911, in London, England; died near Henley, England, Jan 18, 1997; attended St. Hugh's College, Oxford; m. John Piper (artist and set designer), 1937; children: 4. ❖ Founded and edited *Axis,* an English review of abstract art (1935–37); was librettist for 3 of the operas of Benjamin Britten: *The Turn of the Screw* (1954), *Owen Wingrave* and *Death in Venice.*

PIPOTA, Constanta (1971—). Romanian rower. Born Mar 15, 1971, in Romania. ❖ At Barcelona Olympics, won a silver medal in quadruple sculls without coxswain (1992).

PIPPA (1894–1972). See Duggan, Eileen May.

PIPPIG, Uta (1965—). German marathon runner. Born Sept 7, 1965, in Leipzig, then East Germany; grew up outside Berlin. ❖ Moved to Stuttgart (1989), then won the Unification Marathon in Berlin (1990); became the 1st woman to win 3 consecutive Boston Marathons (1994, 1995, 1996); won New York Marathon (1993), Berlin Marathon (1990, 1992, 1995), and Tokyo Marathon (1994–95); Voted Runner of the Year (1995, 1996). ❖ See also *Women in World History.*

PIRCKHEIMER, Caritas (1467–1532). German nun and writer. Born 1467 in Germany; died 1532. ❖ Descended from a long line of German scholars, joined the order of Poor Clares (Convent of St. Klara) at Nuremberg, at 16, and eventually became abbess; was able to correspond in Latin with the notables of her day, and in doing so became an important voice in the German intelligentsia; wrote a history of her convent, as well as *Denkwürdigkeiten* (1524–28), a documentation of the intellectual, political, and religious arguments of the Reformation in Nuremberg.

PIRES, Maria-Joao (1944—). Portuguese pianist. Born in Lisbon, Portugal, July 23, 1944; studied at Lisbon Conservatory and in Munich with Karl Engel. ❖ Famous Portuguese pianist who dominated the concert stages (1970s–80s), made recital debut at 5 and performed a Mozart concerto in public by 7; won 1st prize at Beethoven Competition in Brussels (1970); appeared throughout Europe, then with the Montreal Symphony (1986); made 1st US tour (1988); was a superb Mozart performer, particularly of the sonatas, which she recorded.

PIRES TAVARES, Sandra (1973—). Brazilian beach volleyball player. Name variations: Sandra Pires. Born June 16, 1973, in Rio de Janeiro, Brazil. ❖ With Jackie Silva, won a gold medal at Atlanta Olympics (1996) and was FIVB Tour champion (1995, 1996); with Adriana Samuel, won a bronze medal at Sydney Olympics (2000). Was AVP Rookie of the Year (1994).

PIRIE, Antoinette (1905–1991). English ophthalmologist. Name variations: Tony Pirie. Born Antoinette Patey, Oct 4, 1905, in UK; died Oct 11, 1991; Cambridge University, PhD, 1933; m. Norman Wingate Pirie (university demonstrator), Mar 11, 1931 (died Mar 29, 1997); children: son and daughter. ❖ Combining interests in ophthalmology and biochemistry, was committed to the prevention of blinding eye disease; researched vitamins; during WWII, worked with Ida Mann to study the effects of gases on eyes as well as eye development and metabolism; invited international scientists to symposium, "Lens Metabolism in Relation to Cataract," which led to the establishment of the

International Society for Eye Research; was its committee chair (1968–72); invited by Royal Commonwealth Society for the Blind (later Sightsavers International) to help prevent nutritional blindness (xerophthalmia) as a consultant in Tamil Nadu (southern India); taught Indian women to grow and use vegetables to support eye health; was Oxford University Margaret Ogilvie Reader in Ophthalmology (1947–73); writings include (with Ida Mann) *The Science of Seeing* (1946), (with Ruth van Heyningen) *The Biochemistry of the Eye* (1956). Was 1st woman recipient of Proctor Award (1968).

PIROCCHI, Livia (1909–1985). *See Tonolli, Livia.*

PIROSKA (c. 1085–1133). *See Priska-Irene of Hungary.*

PIRRICHOLI, La (1748–1819). *See Villegas, Micaela.*

PIRRIE, Margaret Montgomery (1857–1935). Irish activist. Born Margaret Montgomery Carlile, 1857; died in London, England, 1935; m. William Pirrie (partner and later chair of Harland & Wolff's shipbuilding firm), 1879 (died 1924). ❖ Became Belfast's 1st woman justice of the peace and was the 1st woman to receive the freedom of the city; active in charity work, served as president of Royal Victoria Hospital; also served on the Senate of Queen's University, Belfast, and as president of Harland & Wolff's, the Belfast shipbuilding firm of which her husband was chair.

PISAN, Christine de (c. 1363–c. 1431). *See Christine de Pizan.*

PISANI, Sandra (1959—). Australian field-hockey player. Born Jan 23, 1959, in South Australia. ❖ At Seoul Olympics, won a gold medal in team competition (1988); represented Australia in 3 World Cups, 2 Olympics (1981–88) and numerous international matches; was Australian captain (1985 and 1986). Awarded OAM (1989).

PISANO, Nicola (fl. 1278). Italian sculptor. Flourished 1278 in Perugia, Italy; m. Giovanni Pisano (sculptor). ❖ Worked with husband on a carved fountain, still in existence, which was commissioned by the town.

PISAREVA, Mariya (1934—). Soviet track-and-field athlete. Name variations: Maria Pissaryeva. Born April 1934 in USSR. ❖ At Melbourne Olympics, tied for a silver medal in the high jump with Thelma Hopkins of Great Britain (1956).

PISCATOR, Maria Ley (1899–1999). Austrian actress, teacher and director. Born Aug 1, 1899, in Vienna, Austria; died Oct 14, 1999, in New York, NY; m. 3rd husband, Erwin Piscator (theatrical director), 1936. ❖ Began career as a dancer in Berlin and Paris and later turned to choreography; helped stage several productions with Max Reinhardt, including *A Midsummer Night's Dream*; immigrated with Erwin Piscator to US, where they founded the Dramatic Workshop at New School for Social Research in NYC; directed stage productions off-Broadway and in Europe; became honorary director of Elysium Theater in Munich (1993); wrote *The Piscator Experiment* (1967); was the subject of *Dolly, Lotte, und Maria*, a West German documentary by Rosa von Praunheim concerning Piscator, Lotte Goslar, Dolly Haas (1987). ❖ See also autobiography, *Mirror People* (1989).

PISCOPIA, Elena Lucrezia Cornaro (1646–1684). *See Cornaro Piscopia, Elena Lucrezia.*

PISERCHIA, Doris (1928—). American science-fiction writer. Name variations: (pseudonym) Curt Selby. Born Doris Elaine Summers, Oct 11, 1928, in Fairmont, WV; dau. of Dewey Summers and Viola Summers; m. Joseph John Piserchia, 1953; children: 5. ❖ Served in navy (1950–54); novels include *Mister Justice* (1973), *Earthchild* (1977), *The Spinner* (1980), *Earth in Twilight* (1981), and *The Deadly Sky* (1983); also published short stories in *Worlds of If, Galaxy,* and *Orbit* magazines.

PISETH PILIKA (1965–1999). Cambodian actress, traditional dancer and singer. Name variations: Piseth Pelika or Peaklica. Born Oak Eap Pili, 1965, in Phnom Penh, Cambodia; died of her wounds, July 13, 1999; dau. of Oak Harl (professor at University of Korokosol) and Meng Mony (both parents were killed during the regime of the Khmer Rouge); raised by uncle and aunt, Sao Piseth and Meng Sonali, and changed name to Sao Pili; trained in the Cambodian cultural dance at School of Fine Arts (1980–88); m. Khai Praseth, also seen as Kie Vaseth (actor), 1990 (div. 1998); children: Kai Seth Lesak. ❖ Popular entertainer, revered in Cambodia, came to prominence with her performance in King Norodom Sihanouk film *Sromorl Anthakal* (*Shadow of Darkness,* 1988); changed her name to Piseth Pilika (1980); appeared with husband in many films and music videos; starred in more than 60 films and appeared on stage; was

also a dancing star of the royal ballet of Cambodia; was gunned down execution-style in broad daylight on a Phnom Penh street (July 6, 1999); mourned by the nation, as Cambodians blared her music from their homes and crowded the grounds of Phnom Penh University's School of Fine Arts where she was lying in state. It was later reported that her diary related her relationship with Prime Minister Hun Sen and her fears that his wife, Bun Rany, was planning to kill her.

PISIER, Marie-France (1944—). French actress, screenwriter and director. Born May 10, 1944, in Dalat, Vietnam (then French Indochina); dau. of a colonial governor. ❖ At 12, moved to Paris with family; made film debut in *Les saintes nitouches* (1962); starred as Colette in a segment of *L'Amour à vingt ans* (Love at Twenty, 1962); made screenwriting debut with *Celine et Julie vont en bateau* (Celine and Julie Go Boating, 1973); as an actress, came to prominence in *Cousin, Cousine* (1975); made 1st US feature, *The Other Side of Midnight* (1977); wrote and directed *La bal du gouveneur* (The Governor's Party, 1990); featured in *Le temps retrouve* (Time Regained, 1999). Won a Cesar award (1976 and 1977).

PISKUN, Elena (1978—). Belarusian gymnast. Born Feb 1, 1978, in Bobruisk, Belarus. ❖ Won Cottbus Cup (1991, 1996), Arthur Gander Memorial (1993, 1996), South African Cup (1995), and Australian Cup (1996); at World championships, won gold medals for vault (1993) and uneven bars (1996).

PISSARYEVA, Maria (1934—). *See Pisareva, Mariya.*

PISSAVINI, Diana (1911–1989). *See Pizzavini, Diana.*

PISZCZEK, Renata (1969—). Polish climber. Born Aug 6, 1969, in Krakow, Poland. ❖ Earned #1 ranking in Poland for Speed Climbing and #2 ranking in Difficulty; won gold at X Games in Speed Climbing (1999); finished 1st in Speed at Polish Cup, Krakow, Poland (2000).

PITCHER, Molly (1754–1832). *See McCauley, Mary Ludwig Hays.*

PITINI-MORERA, Hariata Whakatau (1871/72?–1938). New Zealand tribal leader, genealogist, historian, conservationist, and weaver. Name variations: Hariata Whakatau Hampstead. Born Hariata Whakatau Hampstead, probably in 1871 or 1872, at Little River, Banks Peninsula, New Zealand; died on April 2, 1938, at Kaikoura, New Zealand; dau. of John Hampstead (farmer) and Hariata Whakatau; m. Hoani Pitini-Morera (John Beaton-Morel), c. 1890; children: 3 daughters, 3 sons. ❖ Raised to care for traditional sites and to learn tribal legends of Kaikoura district, was responsible for reserving many sites and in recording traditional place names; was also skilled in traditional weaving; fought to preserve plant species, which renewed scholarly interest in traditional Maori use of microclimates in southern regions. ❖ See also *Dictionary of New Zealand Biography* (Vol. 3).

PITMAN, Jenny (1946—). English horse trainer. Name variations: Jennifer Susan Pitman. Born June 11, 1946, in Hoby, Leicestershire, England; m. Richard Pitman (jockey, horse trainer and tv commentator), 1965 (div. 1978); m. David Stait, 1997; children: Mark (jockey and horse trainer), Paul. ❖ The 1st woman to train Grand National and Gold Cup winners, set up training stables with 1st husband (1965); with Biretta, won 1st race at Fakenham (1975) and went on to have numerous successes, including Gold Cup won by son Mark on her horse; won Grand National with Corbieire (1983) and Royal Athlete (1995), as well as King George VI Cup, Hennessey Gold Cup and Cheltenham Gold Cup with Burrough Hill Lad (all 1984); other winnings include Welsh National (3 times), Scottish Grand National, Irish Grand National, Whitbread Trophy, Anthony Mildmay/Peter Cazalet (2 times), Gainsborough Chase, Welsh Champion Hurdle (2 times) and Ladbroke Hurdle (1975–1999). Awarded Order of British Empire (OBE, 1998); named Piper Heidsieck Trainer of the Year (1983–84, 1989–90) and Golden Spurs Best National Hunt Trainer (1984). ❖ See also autobiographies, *Glorious Uncertainty* (1984) and *Jenny Pitman* (1994).

PITNEY, Patricia Spurgin (1965—). *See Spurgin, Patricia.*

PITOËFF, Ludmilla (1896–1951). Russian actress. Name variations: Elisabeth Ludmilla Pitoëff, Elisabeth Pitoëff, Milla Pitoëff. Born Dec 25, 1896, in Tiflis, Russia; died Sept 15, 1951; m. Georges Pitoëff (died 1939). ❖ Began to appear with husband Georges Pitoëff's company (1917) at such Paris theaters as Théatre des Arts, Comédie des Champs-Elysées, Vieux Colombier, and Mathurins; made London debut as Jeanne in *Saint Jeanne* (1930), followed by Marguerite Gautier in *La Dame aux Camélias*; after death of husband (1939), went to US, later appearing there as Madame Fisher in *The House in Paris* (1944); films include *La danseus rouge, Mollenard* and *Les eaux troubles*.

PITOT, Genevieve (c. 1920—). American pianist, composer and arranger. Born c. 1920, in New Orleans, LA. ❖ Composed numerous works for Helen Tamiris, including *Adelante, As in a Dream*, and *Liberty Song*; worked for Donald Saddler, Agnes de Mille, Charles Weidman, and others, accompanying their works at recital performances (1930s–40s); worked for numerous choreographers on Broadway musicals, where she arranged and adapted musical components to fit their choreography (1939–89), among them Jerome Robbins, Michael Kidd, and Hanya Holm.

PITOU, Penny (1938—). American Alpine skier. Born Penelope Pitou, Oct 8, 1938, in NY; grew up in Center Harbor, NH; m. Egon Zimmermann (Austrian skier). ❖ Won silver medals for downhill and giant slalom at Squaw Valley (1960), the 1st American to win an Olympic downhill medal. Inducted into New England Sports Hall of Fame (2003).

PITSEOLAK (c. 1900–1983). Inuit printmaker. Name variations: Pitseolak means sea pigeon in Inuit. Born c. 1900 on Nottingham Island, Hudson Bay, in Arctic Canada; died May 28, 1983, in Canada; dau. of Timungiak (mother) and Ottochie (father); m. Ashoona; children: 17, most of whom died (4 of her sons, Ottochie, Kumwartok, Kaka and Kiawak, are sculptors, and daughter Nawpachee is a printmaker). ❖ Was discovered by an administrator for Department of Northern Affairs and National Resources on Baffin Island, who promoted the works of a group of Inuits who eventually became internationally recognized as Cape Dorset artists; rendered over 7,000 drawings with felt pen or colored pencil, which depict the world of her ancestors; designs have been exhibited internationally and several are displayed in Canada's National Gallery. Elected to Royal Canadian Academy of Arts (1974); awarded Order of Canada (1977). ❖ See also Dorothy Eber, ed. *Pitseolak: Pictures Out of My Life* (Oxford U. Press, 1971); and *Women in World History*.

PITT, Marie E.J. (1869–1948). Australian radical poet, socialist, feminist, ecologist and anarchist. Name variations: Marie Elizabeth Josephine Pitt. Born 1869 in Bullumwaal, Australia; died 1948; lived with poet Bernard O'Dowd, 1920–48. ❖ Married a miner (1893) and lived in mining communities in Tasmania before moving to Melbourne (1905); was member of Victorian Socialist Party and edited party magazine, *The Socialist*; an anarchist and ecologist, was also a strong supporter of Unitarian church; works include *The Horses of the Hills and Other Verses* (1911), *Bairnsdale and Other Poems* (1922), *The Poems of Marie E.J. Pitt* (1928), and *Selected Poems* (1944). ❖ See also Colleen Burke, *Doherty's Corner: The Life and Work of Australian Poet Marie E.J. Pitt* (1985).

PITT-RIVERS, Rosalind (1907–1990). English physiologist. Name variations: Rosalind Venetia Pitt-Rivers; Rosalind Venetia Henley. Born Rosalind Venetia Henley, Mar 4, 1907, in London, England; died Jan 14, 1990; Bedford College, London, BS, 1930, MS, 1931; University College Hospital Medical School, PhD, 1939; m. Captain George Henry Lane-Fox Pitt-Rivers, 1931 (div. 1937, died 1966); children: at least 1. ❖ As a research student at University College Hospital Medical School in London, studied methyl glucosaminides under Sir Charles Harington; in his lab, researched the biosynthesis of L-thyroxine (thyroid hormone) and iodinated peptides; with Dame Janet Vaughan and Dr. Charles Dent, conducted a nutritional study of force-marched prisoners of war at Bergen-Belson concentration camp; began working on a thyroid hormone with Canadian Dr. Jack Gross (1950); discovered triiodothyronine (a thyroid hormone); was made a Royal Society fellow (1954); worked at the Medical Research Council's National Institute for Medical Research (1942–72), serving as Chemical Division head (1969–72); elected honorary fellow of Royal Society of Medicine (1983) and Royal College of Physicians (1986).

PITTER, Ruth (1897–1992). British poet. Born Nov 7, 1897, in Ilford, Essex, England; died Feb 29, 1992, in Aylesbury, England; dau. of George and Louisa (Murrell) Pitter (both teachers); educated at Coburn School, Bow, London; never married; lived with Kathleen O'Hara. ❖ One of the most respected English poets of the 20th century, published 1st poem at 14; worked for an arts and crafts firm, developing skills that would bring her income throughout life; published 1st collection of poetry, *First Poems* (1920), to unenthusiastic reviews; finally captured the interest of British critics with *A Mad Lady's Garland* (1934), and reaped even loftier praise with *A Trophy of Arms: Poems 1926–1935* (1936); over next several years, published *The Spirit Watches* (1939) and *The Rude Potato* (1941), which celebrated such earthy subjects as potatoes and weeds; released wartime poems in *The Bridge, Poems 1939–1944* (1945); also wrote weekly column on country life for magazine *Woman*, and appeared regularly on tv show "Brain Trusts"; last collections were *Poems 1926–1966* (1968), *The End of Drought* (1975), *A Heaven to Find* (1987) and *Collected Poems* (1990). Won Hawthornden Prize for *A Trophy of Arms* (1937); won William E. Heinemann Award for *The Ermine, Poems 1942–1952* (1954); became 1st woman to receive the Queen's Gold Medal for Poetry (1955); named a Companion of Literature (1974) and Commander of the British Empire (1979). ❖ See also *Women in World History*.

PITTS, ZaSu (1898–1963). American actress. Born Jan 3, 1898, in Parsons, Kansas; died June 7, 1963; dau. of Rulandus Pitts and Nellie (Shea) Pitts; m. Thomas S. Gallery (boxing promoter), July 24, 1920 (div. 1932); m. John Edward Woodall (tennis champion and real estate broker), Oct 8, 1933; children: (1st m.) Ann Gallery; (adopted) Donald Gallery. ❖ Acclaimed for her dramatic turns in the silent films *Greed* (1924) and *The Wedding March* (1928), was also noted for her scatter-brained comedic performances during 1930s, having perfected a woebe-gone persona that she said was patterned after one of her schoolteachers; made a series of 13 highly successful shorts with Thelma Todd, and several features with Slim Summerville; also played memorable characters in *The Guardsman* (1931) and *Ruggles of Red Gap* (1935); appeared in tv series "Oh! Susanna," which later became "The Gale Storm Show"; made over 150 movies in a career that spanned close to 50 years, including *The Little Princess* (1917), *Rebecca of Sunnybrook Farm* (1917), *No No, Nanette* (1930), *All Quiet on the Western Front* (silent version, 1930), *Back Street* (1932), *Once in a Lifetime* (1932), *Dames* (1934), *Mrs. Wiggs of the Cabbage Patch* (1934), *Nurse Edith Cavell* (1939), *Eternally Yours* (1939), *No No, Nanette* (remake, 1940), *Life with Father* (1947), *Francis* (1950), *The Thrill of It All* (1963) and *It's a Mad Mad Mad Mad World* (1963). ❖ See also *Women in World History*.

PIVOVAROVA, Olga (1956—). Soviet rower. Born Jan 29, 1956, in USSR. ❖ At Moscow Olympics, won a silver medal in coxed eights (1980).

PIX, Mary Griffith (1666–1709). English playwright. Born Mary Griffith in 1666, in Nettlebed, Oxfordshire, England; died May 1709 (some sources cite 1720), in London, England; dau. of Roger Griffith (vicar) and Lucy (Berriman) Griffith; m. George Pix (merchant-tailor), July 25, 1684; children: at least one (d. 1690). ❖ Of the 3 women playwrights—the others being Mary de la Rivière Manley and Catherine Trotter Cockburn—whose works premiered during London theatrical season of 1695–96, was the only one to sustain an active career in the theater; during next 10 years, wrote 6 comedies and 7 tragedies that were produced in London; writings include *Ibrahim, the Thirteenth Emperour of the Turks* (1696), *The Spanish Wives* (1696), *The Deceiver Deceived* (1697), *Queen Catherine, or, The Ruins of Love* (1698), *The False Friend, or, The Fate of Disobedience* (1699), *The Beau Defeated, or, The Lucky Younger Brother* (1700), *The Double Distress* (1701), *The Czar of Muscovy* (1701), *The Different Widows, or, Intrigue à la Mode* (1703), *Zelmane, or, The Corinthian Queen* (1704) and *The Adventures in Madrid* (1705). ❖ See also *Women in World History*.

PIZAN, Christine de (c. 1363–c. 1431). See *Christine de Pizan*.

PIZARNIK, Alejandra (1936–1972). Argentinean poet and translator. Name variations: Flora Alejandra Pizarnik. Born Flora Alejandra Pizarnik, April 29, 1936, in Avellaneda, Buenos Aires, Argentina; committed suicide, Sept 26, 1972, in Argentina; dau. of Elías I. Pizarnik (jewelry vendor) and Rejzla (Rosa) Bromiker. ❖ Daughter of Russian-Jewish immigrants who lost extended families in Holocaust, published 1st book of poems, *La tierra más ajena* (The Most Alien Land, 1955); became part of avant-garde group, Poesía de Buenos Aires, and published *La última inocencia* (The Last Innocence, 1956) and *Las aventuras perdidas* (The Lost Adventures, 1958); lived in Paris (1960–64), where she wrote *Arbol de Diana* (Diana's Tree, 1962) and *Los trabajos y las noches* (The Labors and the Nights, 1965); contributed to literary reviews and journals in France, Spain and Latin America, and translated works of André Breton, Aimé Cesaire, Leopold S. Senghor and Antonin Artaud, among others; returned to Argentina (1965), having established reputation as important lyric voice in Latin America; published last 2 books of poems, *Extracción de la piedra de la locura* (Extraction of the Madness Stone, 1968) and *El infierno musical* (Musical Hell, 1971); feeling marginalized as a lesbian, woman and Jew, was tormented by depression; killed herself while on leave from psychiatric clinic. Received Buenos

Aires Prize for Poetry (1966). ❖ See also Cristina Piña, *Alejandra Pizarnik* (Planeta, 1991).

PIZZAVINI, Diana (1911–1989). Italian gymnast. Name variations: Diana Pissavini. Born Aug 6, 1911, in Italy; died Jan 23, 1989. ❖ At Amsterdam Olympics, won a silver medal in team all-around (1928).

PIZZEY, Erin (1939—). British social reformer and novelist. Name variations: Erin Shapiro; Erin Patria Pizzey. Born Erin Patricia Margaret Carney, 1939, in China; dau. of Cyril Carney (diplomat) and Ruth Patricia Last; had a twin sister; m. John Pizzey (broadcaster), 1961 (div. 1979); m. Jeffrey Shapiro (psychologist, div.). ❖ Worked at community center in Chiswick, where she founded the 1st refuge for battered women (1971); campaigned on behalf of battered women, often clashing with other activists; writings include *Scream Quietly or the Neighbours will Hear* (1974) and (with Jeffrey Shapiro) *Prone to Violence* (1982); novels include *The Watershed* (1983), *Morningstar* (1992), *Swimming with Dolphins* (1993) and *The Wicked World of Women* (1996). Received San Valentino d'Oro prize for literature (1994). ❖ See also memoir *Infernal Child* (1978).

PLÁ, Josefina (1909–1999). Paraguayan poet, journalist, ceramic artist and art critic. Name variations: Josefina Pla. Born María Josefina Plá Guerra Galvany, Jan 9, 1909, in Fuerteventura, Canary Islands, Spain; died Jan 11, 1999, in Paraguay; dau. of Leopoldo Plá (government employee) and Rafaela Guerra Galvani; m. Andrés Campos Cervera (ceramic artist also known as Julián de la Herrería), 1926 (died 1937). ❖ Spent childhood in Spain; at 14, published poems in magazine *Domostia* (1923); at 18, moved to Paraguay with husband; became Paraguayan correspondent for Argentinean magazine *Orientación* (Orientation, 1928); was 1st female radio reporter in Paraguay; displayed ceramic works in Madrid exposition (1931); became editorial secretary of Paraguayan newspaper *El Liberal* (The Liberal, 1934); published 1st poetry collection, *El precio de los sueños* (The Price of Dreams, 1934); as a leading ceramic artist, exhibited work in Latin America and Europe; wrote (with João Rossi) *Arte Nuevo* (New Art, 1952), followed by such poetry collections as *La raíz Y la aurora* (The Root and the Dawn, 1960) and *El polvo enamorado* (Enamored Dust, 1968); was editor of *Suplemento cultural* (Cultural Supplement) and appeared on radio's "Cinco minutos de cultura" (Five Minutes of Culture); wrote prolifically (1980s), producing poetry, such as *Tiempo y tiniebla* (Time and Shadow, 1982), short stories, such as *La muralla robada* (The Stolen Wall, 1989), and literary criticism, such as *En la piel de la mujer* (In Women's Skin, 1987); opened Julián de Herrería Museum (1988). Josefina Plá Hall was dedicated in Paraguay's Center of Visual Arts.

PLÁ, Mirta (1940–2003). Cuban ballet dancer. Born July 23, 1940, in Havana, Cuba; died of cancer, Sept 21, 2003, in Barcelona, Spain. ❖ Trained with Fernando and Alicia Alonso, Mary Skeaping, and others; made professional debut in Ballet Alicia Alonso (1953); danced with Ballet Nacional de Cuba where she served as understudy to Alonso in such works as *Les Sylphides* and *Giselle;* performed in contemporary works, including Alberto Mendez's *Plasmosis* (1970); served as company teacher at Ballet Nacional; became a dance instructor in Barcelona. Received Cuba's National Dance Prize (2003).

PLACE, Emma (fl. 1896–1905). See Place, Etta.

PLACE, Etta (fl. 1896–1905). American bandit. Name variations: Emma Place; Eva Place. Flourished around 1896–1905; dates and locations for her birth and death are unknown, as are parents' names, marriages, and children; thought to have been educated in the East as a teacher. ❖ Joined the Wild Bunch, an outlaw gang whose 2 most notable members were Butch Cassidy and the Sundance Kid; accompanied them to Argentina in an attempt to "go straight"; for a time, lived anonymously and ran a ranch with them; returned to formerly successful life as a bandit, when her identity, along with theirs, was discovered; with her accomplices, caused a sensation with daring robberies; later parted paths with others, each to face an unknown fate. ❖ See also Edward M. Kirby, *The Saga of Butch Cassidy and the Wild Bunch* (Filter Press, 1977); F. Bruce Lamb, *The Wild Bunch* (High Plains, 1993); film *Butch Cassidy and the Sundance Kid,* starring Paul Newman, Robert Redford, and Katharine Ross as Etta Place (1969); and *Women in World History.*

PLACE, Marcella (1959—). American field-hockey player. Born April 23, 1959; lived in Long Beach, CA. ❖ At Los Angeles Olympics, won a bronze medal in team competition (1984).

PLACE, Martha (1848–1899). American murderer. Born 1848; executed at Auburn Prison, New York, Mar 20, 1899; m. William Place. ❖ The

1st woman to be executed in the electric chair, had wounded her husband and killed her stepdaughter Ida with an axe on Feb 7, 1898.

PLACENCIA (fl. 1068). Queen of Navarre. Born in France; m. Sancho IV (1039–1076), king of Navarre (r. 1054–1076), after 1068; children: Garcia, titular king of Navarre; Urraca (a nun). ❖ Following the murder of Sancho IV, king of Navarre, Navarre was united with Aragon until 1134.

PLACHYNE-KORONDI, Margit (1932—). Hungarian gymnast. Name variations: Margit Korondi. Born June 24, 1932, in Hungary. ❖ At Helsinki Olympics, won a bronze medal in teams all-around, portable apparatus, bronze medal in balance beam, bronze medal in floor exercises, bronze medal in indiv. all-around, silver medal in team all-around, and gold medal in uneven bars (1952); at Melbourne Olympics, won a silver medal in team all-around and a gold medal in teams all-around, portable apparatus (1956).

PLACIDE, Suzanne (1778–1826). See Douvillier, Suzanne.

PLACIDIA (fl. 440s). Roman noblewoman. Flourished in 440s; dau. of Licinia Eudoxia (422–before 490) and Valentinian III, West Roman emperor.

PLACIDIA, Galla (c. 390–450). Roman empress. Name variations: (full name) Aelia Galla Placidia, sometimes called Placidia or Galla Placidia Augusta (though Augusta is only a title accorded to women of the Late Roman imperial family); born c. 390 CE; died while on a visit to Rome, 450; dau. of Theodosius I, Roman emperor, and Galla (c. 365–394, dau. of Valentinian I); sister of Emperor Arcadius (r. 395–408) and Emperor Honorius (r. 395–423); m. Athaulf (Adolf), chieftain of the Visigoths (West Goths), in 414 (assassinated 415); m. Constantius III (ruler of the Western Empire, r. 411–422), in 417 (died 422); children: (1st m.) Theodosius (died in infancy); (2nd m.) Valentinian III (b. around 419, assassinated 455); Honoria (b. around 420), an *augusta.* ❖ Empress who, as one of a triumvirate of remarkable women in the waning days of the Roman Empire, reached a position of power and influence; was captured by the Goths and taken to Gaul (modern France); was married to Athaulf (414), who was assassinated (415); restored to the Romans (416); married Constantius (417), who died (422); as regent, ascended throne with son Valentinian III (425); for the first 8 years of Valentinian's reign, was the actual ruler of the West; was forced by the general Aetius to utilize his services (425); guided the Western Roman Empire through many of its most perilous later years with far more character than the emperor whom she served; fearing the growing power of Aetius, appointed Boniface to be Master of Soldiers (430), who defeated Aetius in battle in Italy (432); when Aetius returned with an army of Huns (433), was forced to restore him to his former offices and grant him the title of patrician, so that he became virtual ruler of the empire for Valentinian III (433). ❖ See also Stewart Irwin Oost, *Galla Placidia Augusta* (U. of Chicago, 1968); and *Women in World History.*

PLAETZER, Kjersti (1972—). Norwegian track-and-field athlete. Name variations: Kjersti Platzer; Kjersti Tysse-Plätzer or Tysse Plätzer. Born Kjersti Tysse, Jan 18, 1972, in Bergen, Norway; m. Stephan Plätzer (her trainer). ❖ Won a silver medal for 20 km road walk at Sydney Olympics (2000).

PLAIDY, Jean (1906–1993). See Hibbert, Eleanor.

PLAISANCE OF ANTIOCH (d. 1261). Queen and regent of Cyprus and Jerusalem. Died in 1261; dau. of Bohemund V, prince of Antioch and count of Tripoli (r. 1233–1252), and his second wife Lucienne of Segni (r. around 1252–1258); m. Henry I, king of Cyprus (r. 1218–1253); children: Hugh II, king of Cyprus (r. 1253–1267); Isabella of Cyprus (who m. Hugh III).

PLAMINKOVA, Franziska (1875–1942). Czech feminist and politician. Name variations: sometimes erroneously spelled Franciska Plamnikova. Born 1875 in Czechoslovakia; executed by the Nazis in 1942. ❖ Founded Women's Club of Prague (1901) and Committee for Women's Suffrage (1905); elected to Municipal Council of Prague (1918), and to Legislative Assembly (1925) and Senate of Czechoslovia (1929); became the 1st chair of Czech Council of Women and vice-chair of International Council of Women (ICW, 1923); campaigned on behalf of Czech women in UK (1939); arrested upon return to Czechoslovakia in retaliation for the death of Heydrich, was sent to a concentration camp (1942).

PLAMNIKOVA, Franciska (1875–1942). See Plaminkova, Frantiska.

PLANCK-SZABÓ, Herma (1902–1986). Austrian figure skater. Name variations: Herma Szabo; Herma Planck-Szabo or Herma Planck Szabo; also seen as Herma Szabo Planck or Herm Szabo-Plank; Herma Jaross-Szabo. Born Feb 22, 1902, in Vienna, Austria; died May 7, 1986, in Rottenmann, Styria. ❖ Won 5 indiv. World Skating championships (1922–26); with Ludwig Wrede, won 2 Austrian National championships for pairs and 2 World championships (1925 and 1927); won a gold medal in singles at Chamonix Olympics (1924); dominated the international skating world until rise of Sonja Henie. ❖ See also *Women in World History.*

PLANINC, Milka (1924—). Yugoslav politician. Born Milka Malada, 1924, in Croatia. ❖ The 1st woman to serve as prime minister of a Communist country (Croatia), joined Marshal Tito's Liberation Army during WWII; began political career after the war as a member of League of Yugoslav Communists; eventually became head of the League and a member of the National Parliament, where she earned a reputation as a tough politician; became prime minister of Croatia (May 1982), following the inauguration of a new policy to rotate senior government posts to nationals within the various Yugoslavian provinces; served until May 15, 1986.

PLANT, Mary Meagher (1964—). *See Meagher, Mary T.*

PLASMATICS, The. *See Williams, Wendy O.*

PLATER, Emilja (1806–1831). Lithuanian patriot. Name variations: Emilija, Emilia or Emily Plater. Born 1806 in Vilnius, Lithuania; died in Justinava (near Kapčiamiestis) in 1831 of an unspecified illness; dau. of Count Ksawery and Countess Anna Plater. ❖ From an early age, studied military strategy and weaponry, intent on the forceful liberation of Lithuania from the Russians; when a number of Lithuanians staged an insurrection, organized an insurgent unit with her cousin, and participated in the capture of Ukmerge; received an appointment as commander, and was given rank of captain. ❖ See also *Women in World History.*

PLATH, Sylvia (1932–1963). American poet, novelist, short-story writer, and essayist. Name variations: (pseudonym) Victoria Lucas. Born in Boston, Massachusetts, Oct 27, 1932; committed suicide in London, England, Feb 11, 1963; dau. of Otto Plath and Aurelia Schober Plath, both professors at Boston University; graduate of Smith College, 1955; m. Edward James Hughes, known as Ted Hughes (poet), June 16, 1956, in London (sep. Oct 1962, died 1998); children: Frieda Rebecca Hughes (b. April 1, 1960, poet who wrote *Wooroloo* and married Hungarian-born painter Laszlo Lukacs); Nicholas Farrar Hughes (b. Jan 17, 1962). ❖ Entered Smith College (1950); attempted suicide (Aug 1953); graduated summa cum laude (June 1955); received Fulbright fellowship to Cambridge University, England (1955); taught at Smith College (1957–58); returned to England (Dec 1959); published *The Colossus and Other Poems* (autumn 1960); bought house (Green Court) in Devonshire, England (1961); separated from husband and moved to London (Dec 1962); published *The Bell Jar* (Jan 1963); at age 30, put her head in the open oven in her kitchen and turned on the gas, ending her struggle between her "warring selves": the outwardly articulate, energetic, intelligent, and talented young woman and the woman who endured an inner hell. *Ariel*, edited by Ted Hughes, published posthumously (1966); *Collected Poems* awarded Pulitzer Prize (1982). ❖ See also Anne Stevenson, *Bitter Fame: A Life of Sylvia Plath* (Houghton, 1989); Linda Wagner-Martin, *Sylvia Plath* (Simon & Schuster, 1987); Paul Alexander, *Rough Magic: A Biography of Sylvia Plath* (Viking, 1991); Karen V. Kukil, ed. *The Unabridged Journals of Sylvia Plath, 1950–1962: Transcripts from the Original Manuscripts at Smith College* (Anchor, 2000); Aurelia Plath, ed. *Letters Home by Sylvia Plath, Correspondence, 1950–1963* (Harper & Row, 1975); Jacqueline Rose, *The Haunting of Sylvia Plath* (Harvard U. Press, 1993); and *Women in World History.*

PLATIÈRE, Marie-Jeanne Roland de la (1754–1793). *See Roland, Madame.*

PLATO, Ann (c. 1820–?). African-American writer and poet. Born c. 1820 in Hartford, Connecticut; date of death unknown. ❖ Believed to be only the 2nd African-American woman to publish a book (the 1st was Phillis Wheatley), as well as the 1st African-American to publish a book of essays, self-published her only known book, *Essays; Including Biographies and Miscellaneous Pieces in Prose and Poetry* (1841) in Hartford. ❖ See also *Women in World History.*

PLATT, Beryl (1923—). *See Platt of Writtle, Baroness.*

PLATT, Louise (1915–2003). American stage and screen actress. Born Aug 3, 1915, in Stamford, CT; died Sept 6, 2003, in Greenport, NY; m. Jed Harris (theatrical producer). ❖ Appeared in several Broadway shows before making the 1st of her 7 films, *I Met My Love Again* (1938); probably best remembered as Lucy Mallory in *Stagecoach* (1939); appeared as Ruth Jannings Holden on "The Guiding Light" (1958–59).

PLATT, Martha (1862–1941). *See Falconer, Martha Platt.*

PLATT, Sarah Sophia Chase (1852–1912). *See Decker, Sarah Platt.*

PLATT OF WRITTLE, Baroness (1923—). English aeronautical engineer. Name variations: Beryl Catherine Myatt; Beryl Platt. Born Beryl Catherine Myatt, April 18, 1923; grew up at Leigh-on-Sea in Essex, England; dau. of Ernest and Dorothy Myatt; sister of Lt. Col. James Myatt, noted sailing trainer; Girton College, Cambridge, BA in mechanical sciences, 1943, MA; m. Stewart Sidney Platt, 1949 (died 2003); children: 1 son, 1 daughter. ❖ Worked as a technical assistant in Hawker Aircraft's Experimental Flight Test Department, Langley (1943–46); employed in Project and Development Department of British Airways Corp. (1946–49), but was forced to give up position after she married, then a standard policy for female employees; served on council of Chelmsford Rural District (1958–74) and Essex County (1965–85); raised to the life peerage as Baroness Platt of Writtle (1981), became a Conservative in the House of Lords; appointed chair of Equal Opportunities Commission (1983–88); encouraged girls to enter science and engineering; elected nonexecutive director of British Gas (1988–94); was president of Association of Science Education (1988); was a member of the House of Lords Select Committee for Science and Technology. Named freeman of the City of London, a liveryman of the Worshipful Company of Engineers (1988); made CBE (1978).

PLATTS, Elizabeth (1868–1956). *See Platts-Mills, Daisy Elizabeth*

PLATTS-MILLS, Daisy Elizabeth (1868–1956). New Zealand physician. Name variations: Elizabeth Platts. Born Elizabeth Platts, July 13, 1868, at Sandridge, Victoria, Australia; died Aug 1, 1956, in Auckland, New Zealand; dau. of Frederick Charles Platts (cleric) and Emma (Walton) Platts; University of Otago Medical School, MB, ChB, 1900; m. John Fortescue Wright Mills (merchant), 1902 (died 1944); children: 3. ❖ First woman doctor in private practice in Wellington, was a house physician to children's ward at Wellington Hospital (1912–18); served 2 successive terms on Wellington Hospital and Charitable Aid Board; was 1st president of Plunket Society in Wellington; was also the 1st woman medical officer to Public Service Commission (1915). ❖ See also *Dictionary of New Zealand Biography* (Vol. 3).

PLATZ, Elizabeth. American Lutheran pastor. Name variations: Elizabeth Alvina Platz; graduate of Gettysburg Seminary, 1965; m. Reverend Canon Wofford K. Smith, Episcopal priest and chaplain at University of Missippi, then University of Maryland; children: Robert F. Smith. ❖ The 1st woman to be ordained in the Lutheran Church in America, served at the University of Maryland, College Park, as associate in Ministry (beginning in 1965) and then became campus pastor after her ordination (Nov 22, 1970); named the University of Maryland's Outstanding Woman of the Year (1995).

PLÄTZER, Kjersti (1972—). *See Plaetzer, Kjersti.*

PLAUTIA URGULANILLA (fl. 25). Roman noblewoman. Flourished around 25 CE; 1st wife of Claudius (10 BCE–54 CE), Roman emperor (r. 41–54 CE), div.; children: Drusus. Claudius then m. Paetina, Valeria Messalina, and Agrippina the Younger.

PLAVSIC, Biljana (1930—). Serbian politician, president and war criminal. Born July 7, 1930, in Tuzla, Bosnia and Herzegovina. ❖ Once known as Bosnia's "Iron Lady," was a leading member of the Serbian Democratic Party (SDS) of Bosnia and Herzegovina and a close associate of Radovan Karadzic; was a member of the collective presidency of Serbian republic (Nov 1990–April 1992), then a member of the 3-member presidency (May 1992); served as Bosnian Serb president (1996–98); sentenced to 11 years in prison by the World Court at The Hague, for promoting a campaign of murder, rape and torture during the Bosnian war (Feb 2003); then the highest-ranking politician from the former Yugoslavia to be sentenced by the court, had pled guilty on one count of crimes against humanity; her sentence was mitigated by her remorse and her efforts to seek reconciliation after the war; was moved to a Swedish prison (June 2003).

PLAYER, Mary Josephine (c. 1857–1924). New Zealand midwife, social-welfare worker and reformer, and feminist. Name variations:

Mary Josephine Crampton. Born Mary Josephine Crampton, c. 1857 or 1858, in Co. Kilkenny, Ireland; died Jan 5, 1924, in Atawhai, Nelson, New Zealand; dau. of Patrick Crampton and Mary (O'Brien) Crampton; m. Edward Player (shopkeeper), 1877 (died 1905); children: 7. ❖ Immigrated to New Zealand (1874); served as midwife to local disadvantaged women; founded Women's Social and Political League (WSPL, 1894), and served as its 1st president; lobbied for Women's Branch of Department of Labor, which was established in 1895; to support family after death of husband, nursed incurable patients and provided home for their families. ❖ See also *Dictionary of New Zealand Biography* (Vol. 2).

PLAYER, Willa B. (1909–2003). African-American educator. Born Aug 9, 1909, in Jackson, Mississippi; died Aug 27, 2003, in Greensboro, NC; Ohio Wesleyan University, BA; Oberlin College, MA; Columbia University, PhD. ❖ The 1st black woman in US to head a 4-year college, began career at Bennett, a small liberal arts school for women, as a Latin and French instructor (1930), then served as its president (1955–66); became director of division of college support for US Department of Health, Education and Welfare (1966); retired (1986); was also an activist during the civil-rights movement.

PLAYFAIR, Judy (1953—). Australian swimmer. Born Sept 14, 1953, in Australia. ❖ At Mexico City Olympics, won a silver medal in the 4 x 100-meter medley relay (1968).

PLEASANT, Mammy (c. 1814–1904). *See Pleasant, Mary Ellen.*

PLEASANT, Mary Ellen (c. 1814–1904). African-American civil-rights activist and entrepreneur. Name variations: Mammy Pleasant; some sources indicate surname as Pleasants or Plaissance. Born Aug 19, 1814 (according to her own account), in Philadelphia, Pennsylvania; died Jan 11, 1904, in San Francisco, California; m. Alexander Smith (Cuban tobacco planter and abolitionist, died 1848); m. John Pleasant (or Pleasants), c. 1848 (sep.). ❖ Reportedly was involved in the Underground Railroad and was so successful in assisting escaping slaves that she had "a price on her head in the South"; moved to California (1849), where she owned a boarding house and lent money to businessmen and miners at an interest rate of 10%, while also investing wisely; gained a reputation as "The Fabulous Negro Madam," acting as a procurer for her male associates; sought out and rescued slaves being held illegally in the California countryside; was integral in winning African-Americans the right to testify in court in California (1863); also fought to win the right of African-Americans to use San Francisco's streetcars. ❖ See also *Women in World History.*

PLECTRUDIS (fl. 665–717). Queen and regent of Austrasia and Neustria. Name variations: Plectrud or Plectrude. Dau. of Hugobert and Irmina, both founders of Echternach; 1st and senior wife of Pepin II of Herstol or Heristal, mayor of Austrasia and Neustria (r. 687–714); children: Grimoald II, mayor of Austrasia and Neustria (d. 714); Drogo, also known as Drogon, duke of Champagne. ❖ Became a factor in the political conflicts of the Frankish kingdoms when Pepin fell ill (714), the same year that her only surviving son Grimoald II was assassinated in Liège; in accordance to husband's wishes, placed her 6-year-old grandson Theudoald on the throne; imprisoned stepson Charles Martel and established herself at Cologne, assuming the guardianship of Theudoald; after Martel escaped, was persuaded to surrender Pepin II's possessions and to accept him as head of the family. ❖ See also *Women in World History.*

PLEDGE, Sarah (d. 1752). English murderer. Hanged at Horsham, Sussex (Aug 14, 1752); widowed; children: at least 1. ❖ Rented rooms in Horsham to Ann Whale and her husband James; with Ann, laced James pudding with arsenic; convicted of murder and sentenced to death, was hanged in a double execution with Ann Whale.

PLEIJEL, Agneta (1940—). Swedish poet, novelist and playwright. Born 1940 in Stockholm, Sweden. ❖ Taught at University of Gothenburg and wrote literature reviews; appointed chair at Institute of Drama, Stockholm (1992); works, which focus on conditions of Swedish society, include *Ordning härskar i Berlin* (with Ronny Ambjörnsson, 1969), *Lycko-Lisa* (1979), *Änglar, dvärgar* (1981), *Ögon ur en dröm* (1984), *Vindspejare* (1987), *Hundstjärnan* (1989) and *Fungi* (1993).

PLESCA, Aurora (1963—). Romanian rower. Born Sept 1963 in Romania. ❖ At Los Angeles Olympics, won a silver medal in coxed eights (1984).

PLESHETTE, Suzanne (1937—). American stage, tv, and screen actress. Born Jan 31, 1937, in New York, NY; dau. of Eugene Pleshette

(tv production exec) and Geraldine Rivers (ballet dancer); cousin of John Pleshette (actor); m. Troy Donahue (actor), 1964 (div. 1964); m. Tom Gallagher, 1968 (died 2000); m. Tom Poston (actor), 2001. ❖ Appeared on Broadway in *The Cold Wind and the Warm* and replaced Anne Bancroft in *The Miracle Worker* to excellent reviews; made film debut in *The Geisha Boy* (1958), followed by *Rome Adventure, 40 Pounds of Trouble, The Birds, A Distant Trumpet, Fate Is the Hunter, Youngblood Hawke, Mister Buddwing, Blackbeard's Ghost, Support Your Local Gunfighter, The Shaggy D.A.* and *Oh God! Book II,* among others; on tv, appeared as Emily Hartley on "The Bob Newhart Show" (1972–78) and in title role in "Leona Helmsley: The Queen of Mean" (1990).

PLESMAN, Suzanne. Dutch field-hockey player. Born in Netherlands. ❖ Won a team bronze medal at Atlanta Olympics (1996).

PLESS, princess of (1873–1943). *See Daisy, Princess.*

PLESSIS, Alphonsine (1824–1847). French courtesan and literary inspiration. Name variations: "The Lady of the Camellias"; (pseudonym) Marie Duplessis; (fictional names) Margaret Gautier or Gauthier; Marguerite Gautier or Gauthier; Rita Gauthier; Camille; La Dame aux camélias or La Dame aux camelias; Violetta Valéry. Pronunciation: AHL-FON-SEEN play-SEE. Born Rose Alphonsine Plessis in Nonant-le-Pin (Orne), Jan 15, 1824; died in Paris, Feb 3, 1847; dau. of Jean-Martin (called Marin) Plessis (1790–1841) and Marie-Louise-Michelle Deshayes (1794–1834); m. Viscount Édouard de Perrégaux, Feb 21, 1846; children: (with Count Agénor de Guiche) possibly a son (b. 1841). ❖ Parisian courtesan whose brief, brilliant, tragic life inspired the novel and play *La Dame aux camélias* ("Camille") by Alexandre Dumas *fils* and the opera *La Traviata* by Guiseppe Verdi; was abandoned by mother, along with siblings (1832); extraordinarily beautiful, became a restaurant owner's mistress after her father left her in Paris (1839); was the mistress of Count de Guiche, the future duke de Gramont (1819–1880), and may have given birth to a child (1840–41); also changed her name to the more distinguished-sounding Duplessis and soon after dropped the plebeian Alphonsine for Marie; was mistress of Viscount Perrégaux (1842–43), often called the "great love" of her life; also held soirées at her apartment which attracted the likes of Eugène Sue, Théophile Gautier, Alfred de Musset and Honoré de Balzac; during this period, exhibited unmistakable symptoms of tuberculosis; became Count Stackelberg's mistress (1844–45); decked her person and apartment with wild flowers and camellias; had affair with Dumas *fils* (1844–45) and Franz Liszt (1845); married Perrégaux, appeared triumphantly at the Brussels ball opening the Paris-Brussels railway, then went into seclusion because of illness (1846), arguably the most famous case of tuberculosis in history. ❖ See also Charles Dolph, *The Real "Lady of the Camellias" and Other Women of Quality* (T. Werner Laurie, 1927); Edith Saunders, *The Prodigal Father: Dumas Père et Fils and "the Lady of the Camellias"* (Longmans, 1951); and *Women in World History.*

PLEWINSKI, Catherine (1968—). French swimmer. Born July 12, 1968, in Courrieres, France. ❖ At Seoul Olympics, won a bronze medal in 100-meter freestyle (1988); at Barcelona Olympics, won a bronze medal in 100-meter butterfly (1992).

PLEYEL, Maria Felicite (1811–1875). French pianist. Born Maria Felicite Moke in Paris, France, July 4, 1811; died at Saint-Josse-Ten-Noode near Brussels, Belgium, Mar 30, 1875; studied with Moscheles, Herz and Friedrich Kalkbrenner, and later with Thalberg; m. Camille Pleyel (piano builder). ❖ Had an impressive career as a pianist and was admired by Chopin and Liszt who both dedicated pieces to her— Chopin, his Nocturnes Op. 9, and Liszt, his *Norma* paraphrase; was the best-known teacher at the Brussels Conservatory (1848–72).

PLISETSKAYA, Maya (1925—). Russian ballerina. Name variations: Maia Plisetskaia or Plisvetskaia; Mayechka (pronounced MY-echka). Pronunciation: MY-ya Plee-SYET-skaya. Born Maya Mikhailovna Plisetskaya, Nov 20, 1925, in Moscow; dau. of Mikhail Borisovich Plisetsky (noted engineer) and Raissa (Rachel) Mikhailovna Plisetskaya (actress who starred in silent films); niece of Asaf and Sulamith Messerer, prominent dancers and teachers with Bolshoi Ballet; attended Bolshoi Ballet School; m. Rodion Shchedrin (composer), 1958; children: none (in Dec 2000, Plisetskaya won a libel suit against a Moscow newspaper, *Moskovskiye Vedomosti,* which had earlier reported that she had secretly given birth to a daughter in 1978; the newspaper printed a retraction). ❖ Prima ballerina of the Bolshoi Ballet, who challenged the traditional artistic standards of the Russian dancing establishment, entered ballet school (1934); gave 1st performance with Bolshoi (1936); father arrested and killed during the purges of 1930s (1937); returned to wartime

Moscow (1942); entered Bolshoi Ballet Co. (1943); soon began to dance leading roles in such ballets as *The Dying Swan, Raymonda, Don Qixote, Sleeping Beauty,* and, starting in late 1940s, *Swan Lake,* in which she danced her greatest role, Odette-Odile, a role she would portray more than 500 times; made 1st trip abroad (1959); became prima ballerina at Bolshoi (1960); awarded Lenin Prize (1964); used her prestige as her country's leading ballerina to develop and perform a different kind of dance, as seen in her portrayal of Carmen in the *Carmen Suite,* with music arranged by husband (1967); also danced title role in *Isadora* (1977); as she grew older, became a choreographer at Bolshoi while continuing career as a dancer, creating the ballets *Anna Karenina* (1972) and *The Sea Gull* (1980); served as director, Spanish National Ballet (1987–90); celebrated 50th anniversary of her debut as member of Bolshoi (1993); appeared in such films as *Stars of the Russian Ballet* (1953), *Swan Lake* (1957), *The Little Humpbacked Horse* (1962), *Plisetskaya Dances* (1966) and *Anna Karenina* (1972). Awarded People's Artist of the USSR (1959); named Hero of Socialist Labor (1985). ❖ See also *Women in World History.*

PLISSON, Marie-Prudence (1727–1788). French poet and short-story writer. Born 1727 in Chartres, France; died 1788. ❖ Worked as midwife and devised project to help rural poor; was considered authority on late births; writings include *La Promenade de Province* (1783), *Ode sur la vie champêtre* (1750), *Stances à une amie* (1753), and *Les Voyages d'Oromasis*; also wrote collection of moral maxims.

PLOCH, Jutta (1960—). East German rower. Born Jan 13, 1960, in East Germany. ❖ At Moscow Olympics, won a gold medal in quadruple sculls with coxswain (1980).

PLOENNIES, Luise von (1803–1872). German poet. Name variations: Plönnies. Born in Hanau, Germany, Nov 7, 1803; died in Darmstadt, Jan 22, 1872; dau. of Philipp Achilles Leisler (naturalist); m. August von Ploennies (physician), 1824 (died 1847). ❖ Published several volumes of verse (1844–70); wrote 2 Biblical dramas, *Maria Magdalena* (1870) and *David* (1873); translated into German 2 collections of English poems, *Britannia* (1843) and *Englische Lyriker des 19ten Jahrhunderts* (1863).

PLOOIJ-VAN GORSEL, Elly (1947—). Dutch politician. Born Mar 20, 1947, in Tholen, Netherlands; State University of Leiden, PhD in psychology, 1980. ❖ Served as chief scientific adviser, State University of Leiden (1972–87) and head of conference and seminars for NIVE (Netherlands Management Association, 1987–91); as a member of the European Liberal, Democrat and Reform Party, elected to 4th and 5th European Parliament (1994–99, 1999–2004); chaired the Delegation for relations with the People's Republic of China.

PLOTINA (d. 122). Roman empress. Name variations: Pompeia Plotina. Born Pompeia Plotina, a Roman of Nemausus (Nimes) in Gallia Narbonensis (southern France); m. Trajan (Marcus Ulpius Traianus, c. 53–117), Roman emperor (r. 98–117); children: none, but eventually adopted Publius Aelius Hadrianus, also known as Hadrian, Roman emperor (r. 117–138), as heir to Trajan. ❖ A formidable and intellectual woman whose interests included literature, mathematics, music, and works of charity, enjoyed as good a reputation as her husband; noted for her modesty, refused to be made augusta (empress) until 105, seven years after Trajan had become Roman emperor; was devoted to religion and philosophical pursuits, especially epicurianism, and was highly respected in Rome; on death of husband, became Hadrian's friend and advocate and arranged his marriage to Sabina, Trajan's grandniece; was deified at time of death. ❖ See also *Women in World History.*

PLOTNIKOVA, Elena (1978—). Russian volleyball player. Born July 26, 1978, in USSR. ❖ Placed 3rd at World championships (1998, 2002); won a team silver medal at Athens Olympics (2004).

PLOWRIGHT, Joan (1929—). English actress. Name variations: Lady Olivier. Born Joan Anne Plowright, Oct 28, 1929, in Brigg, Lincolnshire, England; dau. of Ernest Plowright (newspaper editor) and Daisy Margaret (Burton) Plowright; graduate of Old Vic drama school; m. Roger Gage (actor), 1953 (div. 1960); m. Laurence Olivier (actor), Mar 17, 1961 (died 1989); children: (with Olivier) daughters Tamsin Olivier and Julie-Kate Olivier; son Richard Olivier. ❖ One of Britain's most acclaimed actresses, made stage debut at Grand Theatre in Croydon (1951), in *If Four Walls Told;* joined Bristol Old Vic and toured South Africa; made London debut as Donna Clara in musical version of Sheridan's *The Duenna* (1954); received 1st critical notice as the cabin boy in Orson Welles' film of *Moby Dick* (1955); came to prominence as

Margery Pinchwife in revival of *The Country Wife* (1956); replaced Dorothy Tutin in *The Entertainer,* opposite Laurence Olivier (1957); made a stunning NY debut in double bill of Ionesco's *The Chairs* and *The Lesson* (1958); back in England, was notable in title role of *Major Barbara* and as Beatie Bryant in *Roots;* also appeared with Olivier in *Rhinoceros* (1960); created some of her most memorable roles with National Theatre at the Old Vic, including title role in *Saint Joan* (1963), Beatrice in *Much Ado* (1967), Masha in *Three Sisters* (1967), Portia in *The Merchant of Venice* (1970), and Rosa in *Saturday, Sunday, Monday* (1973); with Lyric Theatre, alternated role of Irena Arkadina in *The Seagull* with that of Alma in *The Bed Before Yesterday* (1975); also appeared in *Filumena;* reprised several of her best stage roles in films, notably Jean Rice in *The Entertainer* (1960), Sonya in *Uncle Vanya* (1963), and Masha in *Three Sisters* (1970); other films include *Equus* (1977), *Brimstone and Treacle* (1982), *Enchanted April* (1992), *The Summer House* (1993), *101 Dalmations* (1996) and *Tea with Mussolini* (1998). Received Tony Award as the Best Dramatic Actress for *A Taste of Honey* (1961). ❖ See also *Women in World History.*

PLUM, Polly (1836–1885). See Colclough, Mary Ann.

PLUMMER, Edith. See Yevonde (1893–1975).

PLUMMER, Mary Wright (1856–1916). American librarian, educator, and writer. Born Mar 8, 1856, in Richmond, Indiana; died Sept 21, 1916, in Dixon, Illinois; dau. of Jonathan Wright Plummer (wholesale druggist) and Hannah Ann (Ballard) Plummer; educated at Wellesley College; graduate of Columbia College Library School, 1888. ❖ Was a member of 1st class of Columbia College's library school (1887); organized a training program for librarians at Pratt Institute Free Library (1890); became director of Pratt's Free Library and its library school (1895); at Pratt, oversaw creation of 1st children's library section (1896); as principal, helped establish and direct the New York Public Library's library school (1911); elected the 2nd woman president of American Library Association (1915); writings include *Roy and Ray in Mexico* (1907), *Roy and Ray in Canada* (1908) and *Stories from the Chronicle of the Cid* (1910). ❖ See also *Women in World History.*

PLUNKETT, Elizabeth (1769–1823). See Gunning, Elizabeth.

POATA, Fanny Rose (1868–1916). See Howie, Fanny Rose.

POCAHONTAS (c. 1596–1617). Algonquin heroine. Name variations: Matoaka (or Matowka, Matoka, Matoaks, Matoax [meaning "Little Snow Feather"]); Pocahantes or Pokahantesu (meaning "playful" or "little wanton"); Rebecca or Lady Rebecca Rolfe. Born Matoaka in 1595 or 1596 in James River region of what became Virginia; died in Gravesend, England, Mar 1617; dau. of Powhatan (headman of the Powhatan nation) and Winganuske (meaning "lovely woman") or another of Powhatan's wives; m. Kocoum (Powhatan or Potomac man), c. 1609–13; m. John Rolfe, 1614; children: Thomas (b. 1615). ❖ Young Algonquian woman of the Powhatan nation who became famous for allegedly saving Captain John Smith's life in the early days of the Jamestown colony (1608); was captured by the English (1613), adopted European dress and customs, and studied the Book of Common Prayer and other Christian texts; an apt student, possessed of high intelligence and curiosity, absorbed the teachings quickly; during captivity, fell in love with, then married, John Rolfe, the Englishman partly responsible for the development of tobacco as a cash crop in Virginia; sailed for England (1616); moved in the higher social circles in full lady's costume and became a favorite at the Stuart court; fell ill in London, boarded a ship, the *George,* bound for Virginia, and died about 25 miles from the London point of embarkation; child of the wilds and yet comfortable in court, became the best of all symbolic bridges in a drastic cultural confrontation and exchange. ❖ See also Philip L. Barbour, *Pocahontas and Her World* (Houghton, 1970); Mary V. Dearborn, *Pocahontas's Daughters: Gender and Ethnicity in American Culture* (Oxford U. Press, 1986 [especially Chapter 5]); J.A. Leo Lemay, *Did Pocahontas Save Captain John Smith?* (U. of Georgia Press, 1992); Frances Mossiker, *Pocahontas: The Life and the Legend* (Knopf, 1976); Grace Steele Woodward, *Pocahontas* (U. of Oklahoma Press, 1969); and *Women in World History.*

POCKELS, Agnes (1862–1935). Austrian chemist. Born Feb 14, 1862, in Venice, Italy; dau. of a Royal Austrian Army officer stationed there; died 1935. ❖ An amateur chemist and namesake of "Pockels point" (scientific term regarding surface molecules), researched the properties of water surfaces; communicated scientific findings for 1st time (1891); corresponded with British physicist Lord Rayleigh, who submitted her 1st paper to *Nature* (1891); reported that substances (water-insoluble layers) dissolved in benzene could be added to the surface of water (1892), a method used a century later; invited to professional gatherings in Germany; conducted less research after 1902, in large part due to responsibilities as a caregiver to ill family members and her own poor health.

PODESTÀ, Rossana (1934—). Italian-Argentine actress. Name variations: Rossanna Podesta, Rossana Podesta. Born Carla Podestà, June 20, 1934, in Tripoli, Libya, to Italian-Argentine parents. ❖ Star of Italian and international films, made debut in *Strano appuntamento* (1950), and came to prominence in title role of *Helen of Troy* (1956); other films include *Santiago, La Bigorne, Raw Wind in Eden, La furia dei barbari, Sodom and Gomorrah, Solo contro Roma, La vergine di Norimberga, Sette uomini d'oro, Homo Eroticus, Il gatto mammone, Siete chicas peligrosas, Sunday Lovers* and *Hercules.*

PODGORSKY, Desha (1892–1965). *See Desha.*

PODHANYIOVA, Viera (1960—). Czech field-hockey player. Born Sept 19, 1960, in Czechoslovakia. ❖ At Moscow Olympics, won a silver medal in team competition (1980).

PODKOPAYEVA, Lilia (1978—). Ukrainian gymnast. Born Aug 15, 1978, in Donetsk, Ukraine. ❖ At European championships, won a gold medal in floor exercises, a silver in balance beam and bronze medals in team all-around and vault (1994) and a gold medal in all-around (1996); at World championships, won a silver medal in balance beam (1994) and a gold medal in all-around (1995); won Gymnix International, Kosice International, and Subway Challenge (1995), and Grand Prix of Rome (1996); at Atlanta Olympics, won gold medals for all-around and floor exercises and a silver medal for balance beam (1996).

POE, Elizabeth (c. 1787–1811). American actress. Born in London, England, c. 1787; died in Richmond, Virginia, Dec 8, 1811; probably dau. of Henry Arnold and Elizabeth Smith (both actors); m. Charles D. Hopkins (actor), 1802 (died 1805); m. David Poe (actor), 1806; children: William Henry Poe (b. 1807); Edgar Allan Poe (1809–1849, poet and short-story writer); Rosalie Poe (b. 1810?). ❖ The mother of Edgar Allan Poe, sailed for US with her mother (late 1795); at 9, made stage debut in Boston in *The Mysteries of the Castle* (1796); after mother died (1798), joined a theatrical company in Philadelphia; worked as an actress in theaters along East Coast, performing in comedy, drama, and musicals, and enjoying minor popularity; toured with husband David Poe in Richmond, Philadelphia, and NY, then spent 3 years at Federal Street Theater in Boston; husband seems to have dropped from picture (c. 1809); with 3 children, endured a period of severe financial hardship; joined a troupe in Richmond, VA (fall 1811), where she died the following December of pneumonia (her orphaned children were brought up by 3 different families). ❖ See also *Women in World History.*

POE, Virginia Clemm (1822–1847). American literary inspiration. Born Virginia Eliza Clemm, Aug 22, 1822; dau. of Maria (Poe) Clemm (sister of Edgar Allan Poe's father, David Poe) and William Clemm Jr. (1779–1826); died Jan 30, 1847, in NY; m. her cousin Edgar Allan Poe (the writer), May 16, 1836. ❖ Married at 13; showed 1st sign of onset of TB at 20 (Jan 20, 1842); became an invalid; had a powerful effect on the writings of Poe, including the poem "Annabel Lee."

POEHLSEN, Paula (1913—). German gymnast. Born Sept 11, 1913, in Germany. ❖ At Berlin Olympics, won a gold medal in team all-around (1936).

POELVOORDE, Rita (1951—). Belgian ballet dancer. Born Feb 23, 1951, in Anvers, Belgium. ❖ As a child, starred in Flemish films; performed in Jeanne Brabands' Ballet du Koninklijke Vlaamse and with Netherlands Dance Theater; joined Ballet du XXième Siècle (1971) where she created roles for Maurice Béjart's *Le Marteau sans Maitre* (1973) and *Dichterliebe* (1979); was also featured in his *Romeo et Juliette, Farah, I Trionfi di Petracha, Pli Selon Pli,* and others.

POERTNER, Margit (c. 1973—). *See Pörtner, Margit.*

POETZL, Ine (1976—). Austrian snowboarder. Name variations: Catherine Ine Poetzl or Pötzl; Ine Maierhofer; Ine Maierhofer-Pötzl. Born Catherine Pötzl, Sept 10, 1976, in Graz, Austria; m. Christopher Maierhofer (snowboarder), June 2003. ❖ Placed 1st overall in ISF world ranking (1998 and 2002); won gold in Boarder X at X Games (2002); placed 2nd at the Austrian Open (2002).

POEWE, Sarah (1983—). German swimmer. Name variations: Sarah Powe. Born Mar 3, 1983, in Cape Town, South Africa; attended University of Georgia. ❖ At World championships SC, placed 1st in the 100-meter breaststroke (2000); won a bronze medal for 4 x 100-meter medley relay at Athens Olympics (2004).

POGOSHEVA-SAFONOVA, Tamara (1946—). Soviet diver. Name variations: Tamara Safonova. Born June 24, 1946, in USSR. ❖ At Mexico City Olympics, won a silver medal in springboard (1968).

POHL, Sabine Bergmann (b. 1946). *See Bergmann-Pohl, Sabine.*

POHLERS, Conny (1978—). German soccer player. Born Nov 16, 1978, in Halle, East Germany. ❖ Striker, won a team bronze medal at Athens Olympics (2004).

POHORYLLE, Gerda (1910–1937). *See Taro, Gerda.*

POH'VE'KA (1887–1980). *See Martinez, Maria Montoya.*

POINSO-CHAPUIS, Germaine (1901–1981). French government official. Born Germaine Chapuis, March 6, 1901, in Marseilles, France; died 1981; dau. of Sophie (Chamontin) Chapuis and Léon Chapuis; University of Aix-en-Provence, licentiate in law, 1921, PhD, 1923; m. Henri Poinso (jurist), Nov 18, 1930. ❖ Joined the syndicalist movement and the Popular Democratic Party; advocated suffrage for women and worked to improve working conditions for female employees; organized a municipal social agency in Marseilles; during WWII, joined the resistance and helped Jewish refugees escape; elected to the National Constituent Assembly (Oct 1946), to represent the Bouches-du-Rhône district for the Popular Republican Movement (MRP); appointed minister of Public Health and Population, the 1st woman to achieve rank of Cabinet minister in France (Nov 24, 1947).

POINTER, Anita (1948—). African-American pop singer. Born Jan 23, 1948, in Oakland, CA; dau. of ministers; sister of Bonnie, Ruth and June Pointer. ❖ With Bonnie and June, sang background vocals for such performers as Elvin Bishop, Taj Mahal, Dave Mason, Boz Scaggs, and Esther Phillips, then released 1st single on Atlantic to little success (1972); with Ruth joining them, became the Pointer Sisters, recording "Yes We Can Can" and "Wang Dang Doodle" for ABC's Blue Thumb label, which hit both the pop and R&B charts and brought them national recognition (1973); made guest appearances on tv variety shows; with sisters, became the 1st African-American women to perform at Nashville's Grand Ole Opry and the 1st pop act to play San Francisco Opera House; minus Bonnie, signed with Planet Records and had a steady string of hits (1980s), including "Fire," "He's So Shy," "Slow Hand," "I'm So Excited," and "Neutron Dance"; also had 2 platinum albums, *Break Out* and *Contact;* made solo album: *Love for What It Is* (1987); with sisters, released album *Only Sisters Can Do That* (1994). ❖ See also *Women in World History.*

POINTER, Bonnie (1950—). African-American pop singer. Born July 11, 1950, in Oakland, CA; dau. of ministers; sister of Anita, Ruth and June Pointer. ❖ With June, began performing in clubs around San Francisco, calling themselves Pointers, a Pair (1969); with Anita and June, sang background vocals on several albums; with Ruth joining them, became the Pointer Sisters, recording "Yes We Can Can" and "Wang Dang Doodle," which hit both the pop and R&B charts and brought national recognition (1973); went solo (1977), signing with Motown; made solo albums: *Bonnie Pointer* (1978), *Bonnie Pointer II* (1979), and *The Price Is Right* (1984); with sisters, released album *Only Sisters Can Do That* (1994). ❖ See also *Women in World History.*

POINTER, June (1954–2006). African-American pop singer. Born Nov 30, 1954, in Oakland, CA; died Apr 11, 2006, in Santa Monica, CA; dau. of ministers; sister of Bonnie, Ruth and Anita Pointer. ❖ With Bonnie, began performing in clubs around San Francisco, calling themselves Pointers, a Pair (1969); with Anita and Bonnie, sang background vocals on several albums; with Ruth joining them, became the Pointer Sisters, recording the hits "Yes We Can Can" and "Wang Dang Doodle" (1973); minus Bonnie, signed with Planet Records and had a steady string of hits (1980s), including "Fire," "He's So Shy," "Slow Hand," "I'm So Excited," and "Neutron Dance"; also had 2 platinum albums, *Break Out* and *Contact;* with sisters, released album *Only Sisters Can Do That* (1994). ❖ See also *Women in World History.*

POINTER, Ruth (1946—). African-American pop singer. Born Mar 19, 1946, in Oakland, CA; dau. of ministers; sister of Bonnie, Anita and June Pointer. ❖ Joined June, Bonnie and Anita as the Pointer Sisters (1972), recording "Yes We Can Can" and "Wang Dang Doodle" for ABC's Blue Thumb label, which hit both the pop and R&B charts (1973); minus Bonnie, signed with Planet Records and had a string of hits (1980s), including "Fire," "He's So Shy," "Slow Hand," "I'm So Excited," and "Neutron Dance"; also had 2 platinum albums, *Break Out* and *Contact*; with sisters, released album *Only Sisters Can Do That* (1994). ❖ See also *Women in World History.*

POINTON, Robert (b. 1914). *See Rooke, Daphne.*

POIREE, Liv Grete (1974—). Norwegian biathlete. Name variations: Liv Grete Skjelbreid; Liv Grete Skjelbreid-Poiree or Poirée. Born July 7, 1974, in Bergen, Norway; sister of Ann-Elen Skjelbreid (biathlete); m. Raphael Poiree (French biathlete), 2000. ❖ Won a bronze medal for the 4 x 7.5 km relay at Nagano Olympics (1998); won World championship sprint (2000); won 4 out of 5 medals at World championships (2001), coming in 2nd overall; won silver medals for the 4 x 7.5 km relay and 15 km indiv. at Salt Lake City (2002).

POIROT, Catherine (1963—). French swimmer. Born April 9, 1963, in France. ❖ At Los Angeles Olympics, won a bronze medal in 100-meter breaststroke (1984).

POISSON, Jeanne-Antoinette (1721–1764). *See Pompadour, Jeanne-Antoinette Poisson, Duchesse de.*

POISSON, Madeleine-Angelique (1684–1770). French playwright. Name variations: Madeleine-Angélique, Gabriel de Gomez; Madeleine Angelique Poisson de Gomez; Madame de Gomez. Born Madeleine-Angelique Poisson in 1684 in Paris, France; died 1770; dau. of Paul Poisson (actor). ❖ One of few women to have plays performed at Comédie Française, wrote *Habis* (1714), one of most successful plays of 1700–15; other plays include *Semiramis* (1704), *Cléarque, tyran d'Héraclée* (1717), and *Marsidie, reine des Cimbres* (1735); volumes of short prose include *Journées amusantes* (1722–31), *La Belle Assemblée* (1750), and *Cent Nouvelles* (1811); her collections of short fiction also enjoyed popular success.

POISSY, prioress of.
See Marie de Bourbon (fl. 1350s).
See Marie (1393–1438).

POITEVENT, Eliza Jane (1849–1896). *See Nicholson, Eliza Jane.*

POITIERS, Diane de (1499–1566). *See Diane de Poitiers.*

POITOU, countess of. *See Adele of Normandy (c. 917–c. 962).*

POKER ALICE (1851–1930). *See Tubbs, Alice.*

POKOU (c. 1700–c. 1760). African ruler. Name variations: Abla Pokou; Aura Pokou; Awura Pokou; Queen of the Ashanti. Born Pokou sometime between 1700 and 1720; dau. of an unrecorded father (as a member of Ashanti royalty her status was inherited through her mother) and Nyakou Kosiamoa; married Tano (warrior); children: 1 son. ❖ Ruler of 1st rank, who led the Baule people, a subgroup of the Ashanti tribe, across the Comoé River near the Ivory Coast of West Africa to establish a new state (c. 1750), which became powerful in trade during the 19th century; during the journey, when faced with a raging torrent with no shallow fords to cross the banks of the Comoé, decided that a major sacrifice must be made to the river spirits and threw her only child into the swirling waters; to claim her new homeland, led her meager troops against the local ruler Agpatu and his forces, and ultimately gained the upper hand; died not long after the establishment of new kingdom; became legendary for her willingness to sacrifice her own happiness and well being for the sake of her people. ❖ See also (in French) Jean Noel Loucou and Françoise Ligier, *La Reine Pokou: Fondatrice du Royaume Baoulé* (Paris: ABC, 1978); and *Women in World History.*

POLAIRE (1879–1939). Algerian-born actress. Name variations: Mdlle Polaire; Mlle Polaire. Born Emilie Zouzé, May 13, 1879, in Agha, Algiers, Algeria; died Oct 14, 1939. ❖ Appeared at the Bouffes-Parisiens in the title role in Colette's *Claudine à Paris* (1902); other plays include *Le Friquet*, *Les Hannetons*, *La revue de centenaire*, *La Glu*, *La maison de Danses*, *Montmartre*, *Le Visiteur*, *Mioche* (title role), and *Les Yeux ouverts*; films include *Le Visiteur*, *Le Friquet*, *Le dernier pardon*, *La dame de Montsoreau* and *Monsieur Lecoq.*

POLAK, Anna (1906–1943). Dutch-Jewish gymnast. Name variations: Ans Polak; Anna Dresden-Polak. Born Nov 25, 1906, in Netherlands; killed at Sobibor concentration camp, July 23, 1943, with her 6-year-old daughter Eva; m. Barend Dresden (killed at Auschwitz, 1944). ❖ At Amsterdam Olympics, won a gold medal for team all-around (1928), the 1st time women's gymnastics was on the Olympic program (no indiv. medals were awarded).

POLAND, duchess of.
See Oda of Germany and North Marck (fl. 900s).
See Dobravy of Bohemia (d. 977).

POLAND, queen of.
See Wanda of Poland (fl. 730).
See Gorka (fl. 920s).
See Judith of Hungary (fl. late 900s).
See Oda (fl. 1000).
See Richesa of Lorraine (d. 1067).
See Maria of Kiev (d. 1087).
See Salomea (d. 1144).
See Lucia of Rugia (fl. 1220s).
See Cunegunde (1234–1292).
See Ryksa (fl. 1288).
See Malgorzata (fl. 1290s).
See Krystyna Rokiczanska (fl. 1300s).
See Elizabeth of Bosnia (d. 1339).
See Jadwiga of Glogow (fl. late 1300s)
See Jadwiga (1374–1399).
See Elizabeth of Hungary (c. 1430–1505).
See Helene of Moscow (1474–1513).
See Sforza, Bona (1493–1557).
See Barbara Zapolya (fl. 1500).
See Elizabeth of Habsburg (d. 1545).
See Barbara Radziwell (1520–1551).
See Anna Jagello (1523–1596).
See Catherine of Habsburg (1533–1572).
See Anna of Styria (1573–1598).
See Constance of Styria (1588–1631).
See Cecilia Renata of Austria (1611–1644).
See Louise Marie de Gonzague (1611–1667).
See Marie Casimir (1641–1716).
See Eleanor Habsburg (1653–1697).
See Marie Josepha (1699–1757).

POLAND, regent of. *See Elizabeth of Poland (1305–1380).*

POLÁNYI, Ilona (1897–1978). *See Duczynska, Ilona.*

POLASTRON, Yolande Martine Gabrielle de (1749–1793). *See Polignac, Yolande Martine Gabrielle de.*

POLCZ, Alaine (1921—). Hungarian psychologist and novelist. Born Oct 7, 1921, in Kolozs, Hungary; m. Miklós Mészöly. ❖ Psychologist and founder of the hospice movement in Hungary, wrote autobiographical novel about her life during WWII, *Asszony a Fronton* (1991), trans. by Albert Tezla as *One Woman in the War: Hungary 1944–1945* (2002).

POLDOWSKI, Mme (1880–1932). *See Wieniawska, Irene Regine.*

POLE, Catherine de la (d. 1419). *See Stafford, Catherine.*

POLE, Elizabeth de la (1444–1503). Duchess of Suffolk. Born April 22, 1444, in Rouen, Normandy, France; died after Jan 1503; buried in Wingfield, Suffolk, England; dau. of Richard, 3rd duke of York, and Cecily Neville; sister of Margaret of York (1446–1503); m. John de la Pole, 1st duke of Suffolk, in 1460; children: 8, including John de la Pole, earl of Lincoln (c. 1462–1487); Edmund de la Pole, 2nd duke of Suffolk (1471–1513); Richard de la Pole (d. 1525); Anne de la Pole.

POLE, Margaret (1473–1541). Countess of Salisbury. Name variations: Margaret, Countess of Salisbury; Margaret Plantagenet; Lady Salisbury. Born c. Aug 14, 1473, at Farley Castle, Somerset, England; executed on May 27, 1541, in the Tower of London; dau. of George, duke of Clarence (brother of Richard III), and Isabel Neville (1451–1476); sister of Edward (1475–1499), earl of Warwick and Salisbury; m. Richard Pole, Sept 22, 1491 (died 1505); children: Henry Pole, baron Montagu (executed 1538); Geoffrey Pole (d. 1558); Ursula Pole (d. 1570); Arthur Pole (d. 1570); Reginald Pole (1500–1558), archbishop of Canterbury. ❖ The last of the Plantagenets, was granted the family lands of the earldom of Salisbury and the title countess of Salisbury by Henry VIII (1513); became custodian of 3-year-old Princess Mary, later Mary I (c. 1519), and, in time, the young princess grew to love her like a grandmother; when her son Reginald Pole, a cardinal in Padua, published *Pro Ecclesiasticae Unitatis Defensione*, severely criticizing Henry VIII's conduct in divorcing his 1st wife Catherine, was arrested for treason and sent to the Tower of London, along with sons Geoffrey and Henry (1538); beheaded (1541). ❖ See also *Women in World History.*

POLE, Ursula (d. 1570). English baroness. Name variations: Lady Stafford. Died in 1570; dau. of Richard Pole and Margaret Pole (1473–1541), countess of Salisbury; sister of Reginald Pole, archbishop of Canterbury; m. Henry Stafford (d. 1563), Lord Stafford; children: Richard Stafford.

POLESKA, Anne (1980—). German swimmer. Born Feb 20, 1980, in Krefeld, Germany. ❖ Won a bronze medal for 200-meter breaststroke at Athens Olympics (2004).

POLETTI, Syria (1919–1991). Argentinean novelist and short-story writer. Born Feb 10, 1919, in Pieve di Cadore, Italy; died April 11, 1991, in Buenos Aires, Argentina. ❖ Lived in Italy, Argentina, and US, and was deeply interested in immigration and national identity; worked as radio and newspaper journalist and became professor at University of Los Angeles; was one of the 1st Hispanic-American women to write detective fiction; works include *Veinte cuentos infantiles* (1955), *Gente commigo* (1962), *Línea del fuego* (1964), *Rojo en la salina* (1964), *Extraño oficio* (1971), *Reportajes supersónicos* (1972), *El juguete misterioso* (1977), and *El rey que prohibió los globos* (1987). Received Donzel Prize in Spain and Losada International Prize.

POLEY, Viola (1955—). East German rower. Born April 13, 1955, in East Germany. ❖ At Montreal Olympics, won a gold medal in quadruple sculls with coxswain (1976).

POLGAR, Judit (1976—). Hungarian chess player. Name variations: Judith Polgar. Born Judit Polgár, July 23, 1976, in Hungary; youngest dau. of Laszlo (psychologist) and Klara Polgar (teacher); sister of Sofia (Sophia) and Zsuzsa (Susan) Polgar (both chess players); m. Gustav Fonts (veterinarian). ❖ A grandmaster at 15 years, 4 months (breaking a record owned by Bobby Fischer), beat Boris Spassky at 16 (1994); won US Open (1998), the only woman to ever win it; won Hoogeveen (1999); won the Japfa Classic (Category 16), the greatest chess tournament victory ever recorded by a woman (2000).

POLI, Barbara (1972—). *See Fusar-Poli, Barbara.*

POLIAKOFF, Olga (c. 1935—). French actress. Name variations: Olga Baïdar-Poliakoff; Olga Ken; Olga De Poliakoff. Born Olga de Poliakoff-Baidaroff (also seen as Baidarov), c. 1935, in France; sister of Marina Vlady, Hélène Vallier, and Odile Versois (all actresses). ❖ Made film debut in *Orage d'eté* (1949), followed by *Grand gala, Giorni d'amore, Sophie el le crime, The Unbearable Lightness of Being, Bonjour l'angoisse, La joie de vivre* and *Cible émouvante.*

POLIAKOVA, Elena (1884–1972). Russian ballet dancer and teacher. Name variations: Jelena Poliakova. Born 1884 in St. Petersburg, Russia; died July 25, 1972, in Santiago, Chile. ❖ Trained at Imperial Ballet school in St. Petersburg; joined Maryinsky Ballet (1902), where she performed primarily in works by Marius Petipa, including *The Sleeping Beauty, La Esmeralda,* and *Paquita;* danced with Diaghilev Ballet Russe during its premiere season; danced with and taught for Yugoslavia's 1st independent ballet company, now part of the Belgrade National Opera; immigrated to Chile (c. 1940), where she taught at National Ballet of Chile in Santiago.

POLI BORTONE, Adriana (1943—). Italian politician. Born Aug 25, 1943, in Lecce, Italy. ❖ Was a member of Italian Parliament (1983–99), becoming deputy speaker (1994) and agriculture minister (1994–95), and a member of Alleanza nazionale (AN) political executive (1994–99); elected mayor of Lecce (1998); representing Union for Europe of the Nations Group (UEN), elected to 5th European Parliament (1999–2004).

POLIDOURI, Maria (1902–1930). Greek poet. Born 1902 in Kalamata, Greece; died 1930. ❖ Studied law in Athens and moved to Paris after disappointed love affair with poet Kostas Kariotakis; returned to Greece suffering from tuberculosis; intense poems reflect loss and disappointment; published *Margerites* (1917), *Dying Trills* (1928), and *Echo and Chaos* (1929).

POLIER, Marie-Elizabeth (1742–1817). Swiss journalist and translator. Name variations: Chanoinesse de Heiliggraben; chanoinesse de Polier; canoness of Heiliggraben. Born 1742 in Lausanne, Switzerland; died 1817. ❖ Translations from German include Sophie de La Roche's *Eugénie, ou la résignation* (1795); edited literary periodical *Journal littéraire de Lausanne* (1794–98); other works include *Recueil d'histoirettes* (1792), *Le Club des Jacobins, comédie* (1792), *La Sylphide ou l'ange gardien* (1795), and *Mythologie des Indous* (1809); with J. de Maimieux, produced

Bibliothèque germanique (1800–01), *Midi industrieux,* and *Gazette brittanique.*

POLIER DE BOTTENS, Madame (1751–1832). *See Montolieu, Pauline.*

POLIGNAC, Princess Edmond de (1865–1943). *See Singer, Winnaretta.*

POLIGNAC, Yolande Martine Gabrielle de (1749–1793). French royal. Name variations: Yolande Martine Gabrielle de Polastron; Duchess or Countess of Polignac; Comtesse de Polignac; Duchesse de Polignac. Born Yolande Martine Gabrielle de Polastron in Paris in 1749; died 1793; m. Armand Jule François Polignac, Duc de Polignac, 1767; children: Armand, who took part in the conspiracy against Napoleon. ❖ Became Marie Antoinette's favorite (1775) and appointed governess to the king and queen's children; said to be non-ambitious for herself, was pressured by the Polignac family to seek favors from the queen, arousing popular hatred; beheaded during French Revolution.

POLIMITA, D. (b. 1910). *See Alonso, Dora.*

POLIS, Carol. American boxing judge. Married a boxing referee, 1971. ❖ Became 1st woman to be licensed as boxing judge (1974); went on to judge over 30 title bouts over a span of 30 years.

POLIT, Cornelia (1963—). East German swimmer. Born Feb 18, 1963, in East Germany. ❖ At Moscow Olympics, won a silver medal in the 200-meter backstroke (1980).

POLITE, Carlene Hatcher (1932—). African-American novelist. Born Carlene Hatcher, Aug 28, 1932, in Detroit, Michigan; dau. of John Hatcher and Lillian (Cook) Hatcher. ❖ Studied dance under Martha Graham before moving to Paris (1964); returned to US (1971) and became associate professor of English at State University of New York, Buffalo; works include *Les Flagellants* (1966) and *Sister X and the Victims of Foul Play* (1975).

POLK, Sarah Childress (1803–1891). American first lady. Born Sarah Childress, Sept 4, 1803, in Murfreesboro, Tennessee; died Aug 14, 1891, in Nashville; dau. of Elizabeth (Whitsitt) Childress and Captain Joel Childress (wealthy Tennessee plantation owner); attended Moravian Seminary in Salem, North Carolina; m. James Knox Polk (president of US, 1845–49), Jan 1, 1824 (died 1849). ❖ First lady of US, admired for her intelligence and resolve, held a unique position in the White House as husband's official confidential secretary (1845–49); following marriage, was husband's most valuable political asset during his 14-year tenure in Congress and his term as governor of Tennessee; charming and witty in conversation, also supplied the social graces he lacked; while in the White House, instituted a strict Sabbath observance, forbade alcohol, card playing, and dancing, and had neither the time nor inclination for entertaining. ❖ See also *Women in World History.*

POLKUNEN, Sirkka (1927—). Finnish cross-country skier. Name variations: Sirkka Vilander. Born Nov 6, 1927, in Jyväskylä, Finland. ❖ Won a gold medal for 3 x 5 km relay at Cortina Olympics (1956).

POLL, Claudia (1972—). Costa Rican swimmer. Born Dec 21, 1972, in Managua; sister of Sylvia Poll (swimmer). ❖ Won a gold medal with a time of 1:58.16 in 200-meter freestyle at Atlanta Olympics (1996); won bronze medals for 200- and 400-meter freestyle at Sydney Olympics (2000); won a silver medal for 400-meter freestyle at World championships (2001); banned from international swimming for 4 years and cancelled all swimming results (Sept 26, 2001–Mar 26, 2002), when a drug test turned up *norandrosterone* (2002).

POLL, Sylvia (1970—). Costa Rican swimmer. Born Sept 24, 1970, in Managua; sister of Claudia Poll (swimmer). ❖ At Seoul Olympics, won a silver medal in the 200-meter freestyle (1988).

POLLACK, Andrea (1961—). East German swimmer. Born May 8, 1961, in Schwerin, Mecklenburg, East Germany. ❖ Won silver medals for 100-meter butterfly and 4 x 100-meter freestyle and gold medals for 200-meter butterfly and 4 x 100 medley relay at Montreal Olympics (1976); won a silver medal for 100-meter butterfly at Moscow Olympics (1980); set 2 world records for butterfly within a day of each other, with a time of 59.46 in the 100 meters (July 3, 1978) and a time of 2:09.87 for 200 meters (July 4, 1978).

POLLAK, Anna (1912–1996). English mezzo-soprano. Born May 1, 1912, in Manchester, England; died Nov 28, 1996, in Hythe, Kent, England; studied with Hyslop and, in London, with Cross. ❖ A leading singer at Sadler's Wells Opera in London (1940s–1950s), appeared 1st with provincial repertory troupes, performing in revues and musicals;

debuted at Sadler's Wells (1945), as Dorabella in Mozart's *Cosi fan Tutte,* the 1st time she had ever sung an operatic role; became the company's leading soprano, appearing as Cherubino, Fatima, Orlovsky, and Siebel, and creating the roles of Bianca in *Rape of Lucretia,* Lady Nelson in Berkeley's *Nelson* and title role in his *Ruth.* ❖ See also *Women in World History.*

POLLAK, Burglinde (1951—). East German pentathlete. Born June 10, 1951, in East Germany. ❖ Won a bronze medal at Munich Olympics (1972) and a bronze medal at Montreal Olympics (1976), both in pentathlon.

POLLARD, Marjorie (1899–1982). English hockey player and sports journalist. Born 1899 in Great Britain; died 1982. ❖ Played for Midlands, Northants, and Peterborough teams and was recognized as a top goal maker (1921–36); scored 13 goals against Wales in a 20–0 win (1926); scored all 8 goals in another shutout against Germany, as well as 5 against Scotland, 7 against Ireland, and 5 against South Africa; served as acting president of All-England Women's Hockey Association; also played cricket and was a founding member of the England Women's Cricket Association; employed as a sports journalist, writing for such leading newspapers as *The Times, The Guardian,* and the *Morning Press;* served as editor of journal *Hockey Field* (1946–70).

POLLARD, Velma (1937—). Jamaican poet, literary critic and short-story writer. Born 1937 in Jamaica; sister of Erna Brodber (writer, b. 1936); McGill University, MA in Education; Columbia University, MA. ❖ Appointed senior lecturer in education at University of West Indies; works include *Crown Point* (1988), *Considering Women* (1989), *Shame Trees Don't Grow Here* (1992), *From Jamaican Creole to Standard English: A Handbook for Teachers* (1994), and *The Best Philosophers I Know Can't Read or Write* (2001); contributed to *Jamaica Journal, Arts Review,* and *Caribbean Quarterly.*

POLLATOU, Anna (1983—). Greek rhythmic gymnast. Born Oct 8, 1983, on the island of Kefalonia, Greece. ❖ At world championships, won a gold and silver medal (1999); won a bronze medal for team all-around at Sydney Olympics (2000).

POLLITZER, Anita (1894–1975). American feminist and suffragist. Born Anita Lily Pollitzer, Oct 31, 1894, in Charleston, South Carolina; died in Queens, New York, July 3, 1975; dau. of Clara Pollitzer (German teacher) and Gusta Morris Pollitzer (cotton exporter and civic activist); sister of Mabel and Carrie Pollitzer; studied at Winthrop College, and Art Students League, NY, 1914; Teachers College, Columbia University, BS in art and education, 1916, AM in international law, 1933; m. Elie Charlier Edson (press agent), 1928. ❖ Equal-rights advocate, became a close friend of classmate Georgia O'Keeffe while at Columbia (1915) and would correspond with O'Keeffe until 1965, the longest association O'Keeffe ever maintained; met Alice Paul, with whom she was to be closely associated for decades as a member of the National Woman's Party (NWP); had dinner with Tennessee state legislator Henry Burn (Aug 1920) and convinced him to cast the deciding vote the following day, as his state became the 36th and last to ratify the 19th Amendment; for next 40 years, fought for Equal Rights Amendment (ERA); succeeded Paul as chair of NWP; writings include a biography of O'Keeffe, *A Woman on Paper* (1988). ❖ See also *Women in World History.*

POLLOCK, Jessie. American archer. Born in US. ❖ At St. Louis Olympics, won bronze medals in double national round and double Columbia round (1904).

POLLOCK, Judy (1940—). *See Amoore, Judith Pollock.*

POLLOCK, Karen (b. 1962). *See Brancourt, Karen.*

POLLOCK, Lady (1869–1921). *See Yavorska, Lydia.*

POLLOCK, Nancy (1905–1979). American stage and screen actress. Born Nancy Reiben, Feb 10, 1905, in Brooklyn, NY; died June 2, 1979, in New York, NY; m. Herbert H. Pollock. ❖ Made Broadway debut in *Diamond Lil* (1950), followed by *One Bright Day, In the Summer House, Middle of the Night, Period of Adjustment, Come Blow Your Horn, Ceremony of Innocence, A Day in the Death of Joe Egg* and *Wrong Way Light Bulb;* films include *The Last Angry Man, The Pawnbroker* and *The Best of Friends;* also appeared on radio and tv.

POLLOCK, Sharon (1936—). Canadian playwright, director and actress. Born April 19, 1936, in Fredericton, New Brunswick, Canada. ❖ Taught at University of Alberta in Edmonton and at Banff School of Fine Arts; writings, which reflect concern with racism and patriarchy, include *Walsh* (1973), *The Komagata Maru Incident* (1976), *One Tiger to a Hill* (1979), *Blood Relations* (1981), *Whiskey Six Cadenza* (1983), *Doc* (1984), *Getting it Straight* (1992), *Saucy Jack* (1994), and *Sharon Pollock: Three Plays* (2003).

POLOKOVA, Iveta (1970—). Czech gymnast. Born Aug 17, 1970, in Frydek-Nistek, Czechoslovakia. ❖ Won Bohemian championships (1985) and Czech nationals (1987).

POLOZKOVA, Alëna (1979—). Belarusian gymnast. Born Aug 11, 1979, in Mogilev, Belarus. ❖ Won the bronze medal for floor exercises at the World Cup (1998).

POLSAK, Udomporn (1981—). Thai weightlifter. Born Oct 6, 1981, in Nakhon Ratchasima, Thailand. ❖ At World championships, won a gold medal for 53kg and 53kg snatch (2003); won a gold medal for 53kg at Athens Olympics (2004).

POLSON, Florence Ada Mary Lamb (1877–1941). New Zealand rural women's advocate and writer. Name variations: Florence Ada Mary Lamb Wilson; (pseudonyms) Martha, Columbine. Born Oct 4, 1877, at Aberfeldy, Victoria, Australia; died May 14, 1941, at Wanganui, New Zealand; dau. of John Alfred Wilson (merchant) and Martha Brown (Lamb) Wilson; m. William John Polson, 1910; children: 4. ❖ Contributed to *New Zealand Farmers' Advocate* under pseudonyms, Martha and Columbine (1920s); wrote column, "Wives in Council," for *Farmers' Weekly* (1924); helped found women's division of New Zealand Farmers' Union, and advocated for rural women's rights, including establishing market system, Women's Exchange, in which women could sell farm produce; became justice of peace at Stratford (1931). ❖ See also *Dictionary of New Zealand Biography* (Vol. 4).

POLSON, Lady (1897–1971). *Grigg, Mary.*

POLSON, Mary (1897–1971). *Grigg, Mary.*

POLUSKI, Bino (1908–1987). *See Ward, Polly.*

POLWHELE, Elizabeth (fl. mid-to-late 17th c.). English playwright and author. Name variations: Mistress E.P., Mrs. E.P., E. Polewheele. Pronunciation: Pol-wheel. Flourished in mid-to-late 1600s; nothing is known of her date of birth, parents, possible marriage(s), children or date of death; extent of her education and her familiarity with the London theater can only be inferred from the manuscripts of her plays. ❖ May well have been one of the 1st women to write for the professional stage in England; plays include *The Faithful Virgins,* a tragedy (c. 1661–63, or 1667–71), *Elysium* (before 1671), and *The Frolicks, or the Lawyer Cheated* (1671). ❖ See also Judith Milhous and Robert D. Hume, eds. *The Frolicks, or The Lawyer Cheated (1671) Elizabeth Polwhele* (Cornell U. Press, 1977); and *Women in World History.*

POLYBLANK, Ellen Albertina (1840–1930). British-born missionary and educator. Name variations: Sister Albertina. Born Sept 30, 1840, in St. Saviour, Dartmouth, Devon, England; died July 20, 1930, in Honolulu, Hawaii; dau. of Joseph Polyblank (linen draper) and Selina (Stocker) Polyblank. ❖ Joined the novitiate as Sister Albertina in First Order of Congregation of the Society of the Most Holy Trinity (Jan 1867); traveled with Sister Beatrice (Elizabeth Ann Rogers) to Hawaii at request of Hawaii's Queen Emma to open 2nd Anglican school; taught at St. Andrew's Priory with Sister Beatrice for 35 years.

POLYXENA (c. 371–316 BCE). *See Olympias.*

POLYXENA-CHRISTINA OF HESSE (fl. 1726). *See Louisa Christina of Bavaria.*

POMALES, Catherine. *See Scott-Pomales, Catherine.*

POMARE, Hariata (fl. 1863–1864). New Zealand tribal representative. Born Hariata, in Te Ahuahu, near Ohaeawai, New Zealand; died late 1860s; dau. of Pikimana; m. Hare Pomare (died 1864); m. Ngati Huia; children: 1. ❖ Was a member of a tour party of Maori, organized by William Jenkins, to accompany him on lecture tour of England, performing songs and dances (1863); presented to Queen Victoria, who asked to be named godmother to Hariata's son, Albert Victor, born while in England; with group, treated badly during voyage, exploited and abandoned by Jenkins; returned to New Zealand (1864). ❖ See also *Dictionary of New Zealand Biography* (Vol. 1).

POMERANIA, duchess of.
See Elizabeth of Poland (d. 1361).
See Margaret of Brandenburg (c. 1450–1489).

POMFRET, countess of (d. 1761). *See Fermor, Henrietta Louisa.*

POMOSHCHNIKOVA, Natalya (1965—). Soviet runner. Name variations: Natalia or Natalya Pomoshchnikova-Voronova; Natalya Voronova. Born Natalya Pomoshchnikova, July 9, 1965, in USSR. ❖ At Seoul Olympics, won a bronze medal in the 4 x 100-meter relay (1988); under name Voronova, won Russian nationals for 100 meters (1992, 1993, 1994) and 200 meters (1992); participated at Sydney Olympics (2000).

POMPADOUR, Jeanne-Antoinette Poisson, Duchesse de (1721–1764). French royal mistress. Name variations: Jeanne-Antoinette Poisson; Marquise de Pompadour; Madame Lenormand d'Étiolles or d'Étioles. Born Dec 30, 1721, in Paris; died at Palace of Versailles, April 15, 1764; dau. of François Poisson (1684–1754, supply agent for Pâris brothers) and Louise-Madeleine de la Motte Poisson (c. 1699–1745); m. Charles-Guillaume Lenormand d'Étiolles (or Le Normand, Lenormant, Le Normant, and Étioles), in 1741; mistress of Louis XV (1710–1774), king of France (r. 1715–1774); children: son Charles-Guillaume-Louis (1741–1742); daughter Alexandrine d'Étiolles (1744–1754). ❖ Mistress of Louis XV who, for almost 2 decades, exercised great political influence; father lived in exile because of fraud charges (1726–36); married and became socially prominent (1741–45); became the king's acknowledged mistress, causing a great scandal (1745), since no king of France had ever made a commoner his officially recognized mistress (*maîtresse en titre*); remained the Favorite for 19 years, with death alone ending her reign; opened an intimate theater at Versailles (1747); her life became entwined with the general history of France; made her voice heard in foreign affairs from the start when she helped get Marie Josèphe of Saxony chosen as the new wife of the dauphin; also weighed in on the side of establishing contacts with Austria in order to end the War of the Austrian Succession, which resulted in the Peace of Aix-la-Chapelle (1748); had ceased sexual relations with the king and moved to a downstairs apartment (1751); was made duchess (1752); survived some threats to her position and probably exerted her most important political influence (1752–58); daughter and father died (1754); became a lady-of-honor to the queen (1756); played a role in the famous Diplomatic Revolution on the eve of the Seven Years' War, when the France-Prussia vs. England-Austria alignment of the War of the Austrian Succession changed to a France-Austria vs. England-Prussia scheme; died after a long decline in her health (1764); was the epitome of exquisite taste in arguably the most visually opulent of ages, while her easy grace introduced a gaiety and intimacy to the court which it had never known; exemplified the best of 18th-century high culture; in the sphere of government, however, her backstage influence, lavish spending, and promotion of the power and social standing of the rich, tax-collecting *fermiers-généraux* drew criticism down on the king. ❖ See also Jacques Levron, *Pompadour* (trans. by C.E. Engel, McKay, 1960); Nancy Mitford, *Madame de Pompadour* (Harper & Row, 1968); H. Noël Williams, *Madame de Pompadour* (Harper, 1912); Margaret Crosland, *Madame de Pompadour: Sex, Culture, and Power* (Sutton, 2000); and *Women in World History.*

POMPEIA (c. 87 BCE–?). Roman noblewoman. Born c. 87 BCE; death date unknown; dau. of Quintus Pompeius Rufus and Cornelia; granddau. of Quintus Pompeius Rufus (consul in 88) and Lucius Cornelius Sulla Felix; 2nd wife of Julius Caesar (100–44 BCE); children: none. Julius Caesar was 1st married to Cornelia (c. 100–68 BCE); his 3rd wife was Calpurnia (c. 70 BCE–?). ❖ Became the 2nd wife of Julius Caesar in marriage of political convenience (67 BCE); under cover of the annual religious ritual dedicated to the Bona Dea (Good Goddess), arranged a tryst with Publius Clodius through a maidservant Abra (62 BCE); was divorced by Caesar during the ensuing scandal. ❖ See also *Women in World History.*

POMPEIA (fl. 60 BCE). Roman noblewoman. Born between 80 and 63 BCE; dau. of Mucia and Gnaeus Pompeius Strabo, also known as Gnaeus Pompeius Magnus or Pompey the Great (106–48 BCE, a Roman general and consul).

POMPEIA, Núria (1938—). Spanish novelist, cartoonist and short-story writer. Name variations: Nuria Pompeia. Born Nuria Vila, 1938, in Barcelona, Spain. ❖ Catalan feminist and newspaper cartoonist, who uses her syndicated comic-strip, Palmira, to depict the stultifying position of women in society (collected in *Mujercitas and Maternasis*); also published the short stories, *Cinc cèntims* (1981), and the novel, *Inventari de l'últim dia* (1986).

POMPEIA PLOTINA (d. 122 CE). *See Plotina.*

POMPILJ, Vittoria Aganoor (1855–1910). Italian poet. Name variations: Vittoria Pompili. Born Vittoria Aganoor in Padua, Italy, 1855; died in Umbria, April 9, 1910; dau. of Count Edoardo Aganoor (Armenian noble) and Giuseppina Pacini; sister of Elena Aganoor; tutored by the poet Giacomo Zanella, 1863–72; m. Guido Pompilj (secretary of foreign affairs for Umbria), in 1901 (killed himself, 1910); no children. ❖ Published 1st vol. of poetry, *Leggenda eterna* (Eternal Legend, 1900), to critical praise; moved to Umbria with husband (1901); published 2nd collection, *Nuovo liriche* (New Lyrics, 1908). ❖ See also *Women in World History.*

POMPONIA (fl. 25 BCE). Roman noblewoman. Dau. of Atticus; 1st wife of Marcus Vipsanius Agrippa, known as Marcus Agrippa (died 12 BCE); children: Vipsania Agrippina (?–20 CE, who married the Roman emperor Tiberius). ❖ Marcus Agrippa's 2nd wife was Marcella the Elder; his 3rd was Julia (39 BCE–14 CE, dau. of Augustus Caesar).

PONIATOWSKA, Elena (1932—). Mexican feminist, journalist, novelist and short-story writer. Born May 19, 1932, in Paris, France; dau. of Juan Evremont Sperry Poniatowski and Paula Amor de Poniatowska; m. Guillermo Haro, 1968 (astronomer, died 1988); children: 3. ❖ Moved with family to Mexico (1942); began career in journalism (1954), conducting and publishing daily interviews for Mexico City newspaper *Excélsior*, went on to write for newspaper *Novedades* (News) and several other publications, including *Vuelta* (Return) and *La Jornada* (The Journey); known for her commitment to marginalized sectors of society, as evidenced in the compilation of her *Excélsior* and *Novedades* interviews in *Palabras cruzadas* (Crossed Words, 1961), won international acclaim with *Hasta no verte, Jesús mío* (Here's to You, Sweet Jesus, 1969), based on her interviews with a resident of Mexico City's slums; served as founding editor of influential feminist magazine *fem* (1976); blending fiction and nonfiction, chronicled 1968 student movement through montage of oral histories in *La noche de Tlatelolco* (Massacre in Mexico, 1971) and returned to topic of popular resistance in *Fuerte es el silencio* (Silence is Strong, 1980); contributed to founding of publishing house, Editorial Siglo Veintiuno, and National Film Library; often collaborated on photographic essays on Mexican culture, such as *Juchitán de las Mujeres* (The Women of Juchitán, 1989). Was the 1st woman to win the Mexican National Journalism Prize (1978); received Mazatlán Prize for novel *Tinísima* (1992) and Alfaguara Prize for novel *La Piel del Cielo* (The Skin of the Sky, 2001). ❖ See also Beth Jörgensen, *The Writing of Elena Poniatowska: Engaging Dialogues* (U. of Texas Press, 1994).

PONOMAREVA-ROMASHKOVA, Nina (1929—). Ukrainian-born discus thrower. Name variations: Nina Ponomareva or Ponomaryeva; Nina Romachkova or Romashkova. Born Nina Romachkova, April 27, 1929, in Kiev, Ukraine. ❖ Won a gold medal at Helsinki Olympics (1952) with a throw of 51.42, the 1st gold-medal winner for the Soviet Union; at Melbourne Games, won a bronze medal (1956); won a gold medal with a throw of 55.10 at Rome Olympics (1960).

PONOR, Catalina (1987—). Romanian gymnast. Born Aug 20, 1987, in Constanta, Romania. ❖ Won gold medals for beam, floor exercise, and team all-around at Athens Olympics (2004); won 4 World Cup events (2003–04).

PONS, Lily (1898–1976). French-born soprano. Born Alice Joséphine Draguigan, April 12, 1898, near Cannes, France; died Feb 13, 1976, in Dallas, TX; dau. of Auguste Pons and Maria Naso Pons; studied piano at Paris Conservatoire before vocal training with Alberti di Gorostiaga; m. August Mesritz, 1923 (div.); m. André Kostelanetz (orchestra conductor), 1938; became US citizen (1940). ❖ Debuted at Mulhouse Municipal Opera in Alsace as Lakmé (1928); debuted at NY's Metropolitan in title role of *Lucia di Lammermoor* (1931), causing a sensation; remained with the Met for 27 seasons, appearing triumphantly as Gilda in *Rigoletto*, Rosina in *The Barber of Seville*, Amina in *La sonnambula*, Shemakhan in *Le Coq d'Or*, Marie in *La fille du régiment* (*Daughter of the Regiment*), Philine in *Mignon*, and above all in *Lakmé*; was also a member of the San Francisco Opera and Chicago City Opera and made guest appearances throughout the world; appeared in such films as *I Dream Too Much* (1935), *That Girl From Paris* (1936), *Hitting a New High* (1938); during WWII, entertained US troops in China, Burma (now Myanmar), India, Russia, Germany, Italy, Africa, and Persian Gulf; stood on a balcony at Paris Opéra before a quarter of a million people, many of them soldiers whom she had entertained, singing the "Marseillaise" when France was liberated (1945). Awarded Asiatic-Pacific campaign service ribbon, India-Burma Theater; made honorary consul of France (1934); received gold medal of City of Paris (1937);

given Chevalier, Legion of Honor (France); bestowed Order of the Cross of Lorraine by Charles de Gaulle. ❖ See also *Women in World History.*

PONSELLE, Carmela (1892–1977). American mezzo-soprano. Born Carmela Ponzillo, June 7, 1892, in Schenectady, NY; died in 1977; sister of Rosa Ponselle (1897–1981, singer). ❖ Made debut as Amneris in *Aïda* at Metropolitan Opera (1925); other principle roles included that of Aldalgisa in *Norma* and Laura in *La Gioconda*; also concertized throughout US and was often heard on radio. ❖ See also *Women in World History.*

PONSELLE, Rosa (1897–1981). American operatic soprano. Name variations: Rosa Melba Ponzillo. Born Rosa Melba Ponzillo in Meriden, CT, Jan 22, 1897; died in Baltimore, MD, May 25, 1981; sister of Carmela Ponselle (1892–1977, singer); briefly studied voice with William Thorner; studied opera with Romano Romani; m. Carle A. Jackson, 1936 (div. 1946 or 1950). ❖ Considered by many to be one of the greatest prima donnas of all time, was so dominant that future divas were compared with her for decades; with older sister Carmela, opened at Star Theater in the Bronx as the Ponzillo Sisters and toured for 3 seasons on vaudeville circuit; debuted at Metropolitan Opera as Leonora in *La Forza del Destino* opposite Caruso, the 1st American-born singer to perform there without having 1st performed in Europe; remained at the Met through 19 seasons, giving 465 performances and singing a varied repertory of at least 22 different roles; had greatest successes with *Il Trovatore, Andrea Chenier, Ernani, La Traviata, L'Africaine, Cavalleria Rusticana, La Gioconda, Luisa Miller,* and *Don Giovanni* (as Donna Ana); sang the role of Giulia in the Met's 1st production of Spontini's *La Vestale* (1925), a role she repeated for her Italian debut at the Florence May Festival (1933); appeared in title role of *Norma* at Met (1927), which became her most celebrated interpretation; made hundreds of recordings for Victor; left the Met over an altercation and never returned (1936); stayed in retirement for 13 years, refusing even to make recordings; became artistic director of Baltimore Civic Opera (1950), revitalizing the company and reversing its financially downward trend. ❖ See also autobiography (with James A. Drake) *Ponselle* (1982); Mary Jane Phillips-Matz, *Rosa Ponselle: American Diva* (Northeastern U. Press, 1997); and *Women in World History.*

PONSONBY, Caroline (1785–1828). See Lamb, Caroline.

PONSONBY, Henrietta Frances (1761–1821). See Spencer, Henrietta.

PONSONBY, Sarah (1755–1831). Irish diarist and letter writer. Name variations: Ladies of Llangollen. Born in Ireland in 1755; died in Llangollen, Wales, Dec 8, 1831; dau. of Chambre Barbazon Ponsonby and Louise (Lyons) Ponsonby (both of whom died when Sarah was a child); in 1768 adopted by father's 1st cousin Lady Betty Fownes and her husband Sir William Fownes, who lived in a mansion at Woodstock, near Kilkenny; attended Miss Parke's School for Young Ladies in Kilkenny, 1768–73, where Eleanor Butler acted as Sarah's guardian during the Fownes' frequent absences from Woodstock. ❖ One of the celebrated women of Llangollen who lived with Eleanor Butler for 50 years in rural Wales in an age when romantic friendship between women and retirement to the countryside were fashionable; left Ireland forever (early May 1778), to avoid the unwanted sexual advances of her supposed guardian Sir William; after six weeks of wandering in Wales and England, settled with Eleanor Butler in rural Llangollen in northern Wales, residing in a cottage they called Plas Newydd (New Place); read and studied the classics as well as contemporary literature in English, French, Italian and Spanish; tended a large garden; took frequent walks around Llangollen; kept up a voluminous correspondence with the greatest minds of the day; frequently entertained genteel neighbors as well as distinguished persons who went out of their way to visit Llangollen, "the vale of friendship." Tourists still stream to Llangollen to visit Plas Newydd. ❖ See also Elizabeth Mavor, *The Ladies of Llangollen: A Study in Romantic Friendship* (Michael Joseph, 1971); and *Women in World History.*

PONTEN, Clare van der (fl. 14th c.). Flemish wool merchant. Flourished in 14th century in Ghent, Flanders; married. ❖ With husband, built up a solid business importing and selling wool. ❖ See also *Women in World History.*

PONTES, Sister Dulce Lopes (1914–1992). Brazilian nun. Name variations: Sister Dulce; Maria Rita Lopes Pontes; Dulce Souza Brito Lopes Pontes. Born Maria Rita Lopes Pontes in Salvador de Bahia, Brazil, May 26, 1914; died Mar 13, 1992, in the convent of Santo Antonio; dau. of Augusto Lopes Pontes (professor) and Dulce Souza Brito Lopes Pontes;

graduate of Bahia Normal School. ❖ Joined Sisters of the Immaculate Conception, an order devoted to service to the poor; began setting up migratory hospitals in condemned buildings to nurse those sick with tuberculosis, cancer, anemia, infection and malnutrition, many near death; eventually was allowed to transform a large chicken coop on the convent property into a facility, then raised enough money to build the Albergue Santo Antonio (Shelter of Saint Anthony), which was erected on donated land in back of the convent and opened its door in Feb 1960; also sponsored two medical centers, took in juvenile delinquents, and organized a food distribution hub. The process for beatification was begun (Jan 2000). ❖ See also Nathan A. Haverstock, *Give Us This Day: The Story of Sister Dulce, the Angel of Bahia* (Appleton, 1965); and *Women in World History.*

PONTHIEU, countess of.
See Joanna of Ponthieu (d. 1251).
See Joanna of Ponthieu (d. 1279).

PONTHIEY, Adelaide (fl. 1248). French crusader. Born in France into a lower noble family; flourished in 1248. ❖ Joined the army of King Louis IX (St. Louis) when he led the 7th Crusade to the Middle East; gained considerable fame for her skill with a sword and for her bravery.

PONTHON, Louise de (d. 1821). Countess of Ponthon. Died 1821; m. Henry Seymour (1729–1805), Groom of the Bedchamber (nephew of the 8th duke of Somerset), on Oct 5, 1775; children: Henry Seymour, MP, JP (b. 1776). ❖ Henry Seymour's 1st wife was Caroline Cowper.

PONTOIS, Noëlla (1943—). French ballet dancer. Name variations: Noella Pontois. Born Dec 24, 1943, in Vendôme, France. ❖ Entered Paris Opéra school (1953), before joining its professional company (1961); promoted to principal (1966) and étoile (1968), performed there in numerous classics including the lead in premiere of Lacotte's *La Sylphide* (1972), and in productions of *Giselle, The Sleeping Beauty,* and others; created roles in Petit's *Adage et variations* (1965), *Extase* (1968), and *Mouvances* (1976), Descombey's *Jazz Suite* and *Zuklus* (both 1966), Flindt's *Jeux* (1973), Alonso's *Pas de quatre* (1973) and Robbins' *Scherzo fantastique* (1974); was often partnered with Rudolf Nureyev; was guest artist in US with Boston Ballet and American Ballet Theater, and in Austria with Vienna State Opera; retired from Paris Opera Ballet (1983). Awarded Chevalier de la Légion d'Honneur (1984).

PONTOPPIDAN, Clara (1883–1975). Danish actress. Name variations: Clara Wieth; Clara Wieth Pontoppidan. Born Clara Rasmussen, April 23, 1883, in Copenhagen, Denmark; died Jan 22, 1975; dau. of Eduard Heinrich Rasmussen (1857–1901) and Sara Vilhelmine Caroline Brammer (1859–1935); m. Carlo Rossini Wieth (actor), Oct 20, 1906 (div. 1917); m. Povl Vilhelm Pontoppidan, Feb 2, 1920 (died 1953); children: (adopted) Flemming and Richard. ❖ Famed Danish actress of stage and screen, made film debut as a ballet dancer in *Pas de deux* (1902); as Clara Wieth, made over 25 silent films (1910–20), and was the 1st screen vampire in *Vampyrdanserinden* (1912), directed by August Blom; became an international star; began using name Clara Pontoppidan (1921); known for her naturalistic style, was one of the Danish theater's leading tragediennes, working well into her 80s; often appeared in the works of Shakespeare; other films include *Häxan* (1922) and Carl Theodore Dreyer's *Blade of Satans Bog* (Leaves from Satan's Book, 1921).

PONTUS, queen of. See Laodice II (fl. 250 BCE).

PONYAEVA, Tatyana (1946—). Soviet volleyball player. Born Dec 13, 1946, in USSR. ❖ Won a gold medal at Mexico City Olympics (1968) and a gold medal at Munich Olympics (1972), both in team competition.

POOL, Judith Graham (1919–1975). American physiologist. Born June 1, 1919, in Queens, New York; died July 13, 1975, in Stanford, California; dau. of Leon Wilfred Graham (stockbroker) and Nellie (Baron) Graham (schoolteacher); University of Chicago, BS, 1939, PhD, 1946; m. Ithiel de Sola Pool (political scientist), 1938 (div. 1953); m. Maurice D. Sokolow (professor of hematology and medicine), 1972 (div. 1975); children: (1st m.) Jonathan Robert (b. 1942) and Jeremy David (b. 1945); Lorna (b. 1964). ❖ Employed as a research associate at Stanford Research Institute (1949); received a grant to study hemophilia (1953), and worked at Stanford University School of Medicine as a research fellow and trainee; promoted to senior research associate (1957); lived and worked in Oslo, Norway, on a Fulbright (1958–59), then returned to Stanford, where she was made a senior scientist (1970); was so well known in her field that by 1972 she was promoted to a full professor, skipping lower professorial ranks; along with 2 colleagues, isolated blood's antihemophilic factor (AHF), also called Factor VIII, which led to the successful treatment of hemophilia A (1964); became a member of the national scientific advisory committees for American Red Cross Blood Program and National Institutes of Health; elected co-president of Association of Women in Science (1971), and served as 1st chair of Professional Women of Stanford University Medical Center. Received National Hemophilia Foundation's Murray Thelin Award (1968), Elizabeth Blackwell Award from Hobart and William Smith Colleges (1973), and Professional Achievement Award from University of Chicago (1975). ❖ See also *Women in World History.*

POOL, Maria Louise (1841–1898). American author. Born Aug 20, 1841, in Rockland, Massachusetts; died May 21, 1898, in Rockland; never married. ❖ Became a regular contributor to *New York Tribune* and *Evening Post*, submitting humorous home-spun essays about her native New England and her travels in Florida and the Carolinas; published 1st novel, *A Vacation in a Buggy* (1887), which was well received, as were those that followed at a rate of about 1 a year; writings include *Tenting at Stony Beach* (1888), *Dally* (1891), *Katharine North* (1893), *The Two Salomes* (1893), *Mrs. Gerald* (1896), *In Buncombe County* (1896), *Boss and Other Dogs* (1898) and *The Melon Farm* (1900). ❖ See also *Women in World History.*

POOLE, Elizabeth (fl. 1648). British devotional writer. Born before 1640 in England; died after 1668; m. possibly Robert Poole. ❖ Wrote the prophetic works *A Vision: Wherein is Manifested the Disease and Cure of the Kingdome* (1648), *An Alarum of War Given to the Army* (1649), and *A Prophecie Touching the Death of King Charles* (1649).

POOLE, Monica (1921–2003). English wood engraver. Born May 20, 1921, in Canterbury, England; died Aug 3, 2003; attended Thanet School of Art; studied under John Farleigh at Central School of Arts and Crafts; m. Alistair Small (engineer), 1952 (died 1969). ❖ Celebrated for her intense images of organic form, converted roots, vegetation and stones into surreal wood engravings; illustrated her only book, Reginald Turner's *Kent* (1950); elected to Royal Society of Painter-Etchers and Engravers (1967). The Ashmolean Museum held a major retrospective of her work (1993). ❖ See also *Monica Poole: Wood Engraver* (Florin, 1984).

POOLEY, Violet (1886–1965). Canadian golfer. Name variations: Violet Pooley Sweeny. Born 1886 in Victoria, British Columbia, Canada; died 1965; m. Campbell Sweeny (rower), 1919. ❖ Was 9-time British Columbia champion and 7-time Pacific Northwest champion (1905–29); was Oregon state champion (1909) and a semifinalist in the British ladies' championship (1913), the 1st overseas player to reach the semi-finals; founded Canadian Ladies' Golf Union (1924). Inducted into Canadian Golf Hall of Fame (1998).

POOR, Anne (1918–2002). American painter. Name variations: Anne B. Poor. Born Jan 2, 1918, in New York, NY; died Jan 12, 2002, in Nyack, NY; stepdau. of Henry Varnum Poor (artist); attended Art Students League. ❖ Began career helping stepfather paint murals for US Justice Department and Department of the Interior in Washington, DC; while in Women's Army Corp during WWII, painted combat scenes which were exhibited at Metropolitan Museum of Art and National Gallery; later concentrated on dreamlike landscapes.

POPA, Celestina (1970—). Romanian gymnast. Name variations: Celestina Popa-Toma. Born July 12, 1970, in Ploiesti, Romania; m. Flaviu Toma (gymnastic coach). ❖ Came in 1st all-around at Chunichi Cup (1985) and Catania Cup (1987); at World championships, won team all-around (1987); at Seoul Olympics, won a silver medal in team all-around (1988); her skill (the "Popa"), a full twisting straddle jump used in floor exercises, was named for her; retired with knee injury (1989); moved to Canada to coach.

POPA, Eugenia (1973—). Romanian gymnast. Born Sept 10, 1973, in Bucharest, Romania. ❖ Won a gold medal in uneven bars at Romanian International (1991); at World championships, won a bronze medal for team all-around (1991); placed 2nd all-around at World Sports Fair (1991) and Hungarian International (1992); began coaching in Ireland.

POPA OF BAYEUX (fl. 880). See Poppa of Normandy.

POPE, Jane (1742–1818). English actress. Born 1742; died July 30, 1818; dau. of a London theatrical wigmaker. ❖ Began career in a Lilliputian company for David Garrick (1756), at age 14, then quickly shifted into ingenue roles; originated the part of Mrs. Candour in *The School*

for Scandal (1777) and thereafter tackled many other important parts. ❖ See also *Women in World History.*

POPE, Maria Sophia (1818–1909). New Zealand shopkeeper. Name variations: Maria Sophia Bloor. Born Maria Sophia Bloor, Aug 20, 1818, in London, England; died Nov 18, 1909, in Timaru, New Zealand; dau. of John Wesley Bloor (timber merchant) and Ann (Banson) Bloor; m. Thomas Pope (dyer), 1835 (died 1850); children: 2. ❖ Immigrated to New Zealand (c. 1858–1860); opened the 1st variety shop in Christchurch (1862), a venture that expanded to include several branches. ❖ See also *Dictionary of New Zealand Biography* (Vol. 1).

POPE, Paula Jean (1934—). See Myers, Paula Jean.

POPE JOAN (fl. 850s). See Joan.

POPESCU, Marioara (1962—). Romanian rower. Name variations: Marioara Ciobana or Popescu-Ciobana. Born Nov 9, 1962, in Bucharest, Romania. ❖ At Los Angeles Olympics, won a gold medal in double sculls (1984); won a gold medal for coxed eights at Atlanta Olympics (1996); at World championships, won a silver medal for W4x (1996) a gold medal for coxed eights (1999), and a bronze for W4-(2000).

POPKOVA, Vera (1943—). Soviet runner. Born April 1943 in USSR. ❖ At Mexico City Olympics, won a bronze medal in the 4 x 100-meter relay (1968).

POPLAVSKAJA, Kristina (1972—). Lithuanian rower. Born 1972 in Lithuania. ❖ Won a bronze medal for double sculls at Sydney Olympics (2000).

POPOTA, Constanta (1971—). See Burcica, Constanta.

POPOVA, Diana (1976—). Bulgarian rhythmic gymnast. Born Oct 12, 1976, in Polvdiv, Bulgaria; married the son of Bulgarian coach Julieta Shishmanova. ❖ Finished 7th all-around at Barcelona Olympics (1992); at World University Games, took bronze medal (1995).

POPOVA, Liubov (1889–1924). Russian artist. Name variations: Lyubov. Pronunciation: Lyoo-BOFF Pa-POE-va. Born April 24, 1889, in Ivanovskoe, near Moscow; died of scarlet fever in Moscow, May 25, 1924; dau. of Sergei Maksimovich Popov (Moscow merchant) and Liubov Vasilievna Zubova Popova; studied art formally under private teachers, 1907–11; m. Boris Nikolaevich von Eding (Russian art historian); children: 1 son. ❖ Talented Russian artist of the 1st decades of 20th century who absorbed the currents of Impressionism, Cubism, Futurism, Suprematism, and Constructivism, and turned her energies to practical forms of art to further the goals of the Bolshevik Revolution; moved to Moscow (1906); 1st visited Italy (1910); toured ancient Russian cities (1911); set up studio in Moscow (1912); visited Paris and rendered 1st purely Cubist painting (1913); exhibited painting in Moscow (1914); began association with Malevich (1915); exhibited her 1st non-objective paintings (1916); husband died, contracted typhus, joined Council of Masters (1919); taught at Higher State Artistic and Technical Studio (1920); shifted interests to utilitarian art (stage design, textiles, 1921); posthumous exhibit of her work in Moscow (1924–25); played a major role within the lively Russian artistic world of the early 20th century. Works include *Still Life: Milk Pitcher, Plein Air* (1908), *Italian Still Life* (1914), *Birsk* (1916), *Painterly Architectonics* (1916–17), Work uniform design for Actor No. 5 (1921), set design for *The Magnanimous Cuckold* (1922). ❖ See also Magdalena Dambrowski, *Liubov Popova* (MoMA, 1991); Dmitri V. Sarabianov and Natalia L. Adaskina, *Popova* (trans. by Marian Schwartz, Abrams, 1989); and *Women in World History.*

POPOVA, Nina (1922—). Soviet ballet dancer and teacher. Name variations: Nina Popova-Orloff. Born Nina Alekseyevna Popova, Oct 20, 1922, in Novorossisk, USSR; m. Nicholas Orloff (1914–2001), 1940 (div. 1950); children: Alex Orloff. ❖ Grew up in Paris where she performed as a child in Lyubov Egorova's Ballet de la Jeunesse; immigrated to New York (1939), where she joined Original Ballet Russe; performed with numerous NY companies, including Ballet Theater, Ballet Russe de Monte Carlo, and touring company of Alicia Alonso, and was often associated with the works of David Lichine and Leonid Massine; danced on tv's "Your Show of Shows" (1949–54); taught at High School of Performing Arts in New York City (1954–67); was original artistic director and principal teacher of Houston Ballet and Ballet Academy (1966–75).

POPOVA, Valentina (1972—). Russian weightlifter. Born Sept 25, 1972, in Voronezh, USSR; m. Sergei Popov (her coach). ❖ Won European championships (1999–2003); won a silver medal for 58–63kg at Sydney Olympics (2000); won World championship for 69kg (2001), 69kg snatch (2001, 2002), and 69kg clean & jerk (2001); won a bronze medal for 75kg at Athens Olympics (2004).

POPOVA-ALEKSANDROVA, Larisa (1957—). Soviet rower. Born April 1957 in USSR. ❖ At Montreal Olympics, won a silver medal in quadruple sculls with coxswain (1976); at Moscow Olympics, won a gold medal in double sculls (1980).

POPOVICI, Elise (1921—). Romanian composer, concert pianist, conductor, and lecturer. Born in Suceava, Romania, May 11, 1921; studied with August Karnet in Suceava, 1928–40; studied piano with Elisa Ciolan and orchestral and choral conducting with Antonin Ciolan at Iasi Conservatory; also studied with Constantin Georgescu and George Pascu until her graduation from Iasi in 1947. ❖ Began career on the concert stage (1944), became a research worker at the Folklore Institute in Bucharest (1949) before returning to Iasi, where she lectured in harmony, counterpoint, and piano at George Enescu Conservatory; was also music mistress and pianist for Romanian State Opera, and conducted; wrote 2 symphonies, numerous vocal, piano, and chamber works, as well as pieces for marionette theater; compositions were greatly influenced by the traditions of Romanian folk music.

POPP, Adelheid (1869–1939). Austrian labor leader. Name variations: Adelheid Dvorak, Dworak or Dworschak. Born Adelheid Dworschak in Vienna-Inzersdorf, Feb 2, 1869; died in Vienna, Mar 7, 1939; dau. of Adalbert Dworschak and Anna (Kubeschka) Dworschak; m. Julius Popp (Social Democrat editor and journalist, 1849–1902), 1893; children: Felix (died 1924) and Julius "Jultschi" Popp (reporting missing in action during WWI, 1916). ❖ By 10, was working as a seamstress (12-hour days, 6-day weeks) for low wages; by 14, collapsed of ill health caused by soldering work in bronze factory; declared "an incurable case" was sent to the municipal Poor House for aged and infirm women; at 17, was one of the 1st women to join ranks of Austrian Social Democratic Party; as a militant trade unionist, organized a strike of 600 women in a clothing factory near Vienna; became editor-in-chief of newly founded *Arbeiterinnen-Zeitung* (Working Women's Newspaper, 1892); within a few years, was one of Central Europe's most respected labor leaders; agitated for reduced work hours and improved working conditions, and began to demand suffrage for all Austrian women (1890s); appointed to a seat on the Social Democratic Frauenreichskomitee (National Women's Committee, 1898); served as elected member to the party's policy-making Parteivorstand (executive committee, 1904–33); attended the 1st International Conference of Socialist Women (1907); elected to Vienna City Council (1918); elected to the constituent national assembly (1919), then to the Nationalrat (Parliament); as a member of Nationalrat, helped reform the working conditions of domestic employees; also played an active role in attempts to reduce the legal restrictions against abortion and to restore the pre-1914 unity of the international working-class movement; was the women's representative on executive board of Socialist International (1926). ❖ See also *The Autobiography of a Working Woman* (trans. by F.C. Harvey, Unwin, 1912); and *Women in World History*.

POPP, Lucia (1939–1993). Czech lyric soprano. Born in Uhorská Ves, Czechoslovakia, Nov 12, 1939; died in Munich, Germany, Nov 16, 1993; studied with Anna Hrusovska-Prosenková. ❖ Debuted at Bratislava Opera (1963); debuted in Vienna as Barbariana in *The Marriage of Figaro* at Theater an der Wien (1963); asked to join Vienna State Opera by Herbert von Karajan (1963); debuted at Covent Garden (1966) and Metropolitan (1967); at first, won considerable acclaim for such roles as the Queen of the Night in *Magic Flute,* then began to perform most of Mozart's soubrette parts and much of the traditional lyric soprano repertoire; moved into Wagnerian roles for more powerful spinto voices; made over 75 recordings, including her interpretations of Handel, Mahler, Janacek and Puccini. Made an Austrian *Kammersängerin* (court singer, 1979). ❖ See also *Women in World History*.

POPPA OF NORMANDY (fl. 880). Duchess of Normandy. Name variations: Papie; Popa of Bayeux; Poppa of Valois. Flourished around 880; dau. of Berenger, count of Bayeux; became 1st wife of Rollo or Rolf or Hrolf also known as Robert (870–932), Norse conqueror of Normandy and 1st duke of Normandy (r. 911–932), in 886; children: William I Longsword, 2nd duke of Normandy (r. 932–942); Robert, count of Corbeil; Crespina; Gerloc (d. 963); possibly Kathlin (who m. Biolan, king of Scotland).

POPPAEA SABINA (d. 47 CE). Roman matron. Birth date unknown; committed suicide in 47 CE; dau. of Poppaeus Sabinus, governor of Moesia for 24 years; married; mistress of Valerius Asiaticus; children: Poppaea Sabina (d. 65), Roman empress and wife of Nero. ❖ See also *Women in World History.*

POPPAEA SABINA (d. 65 CE). Roman empress. Died in 65 or 66 CE; dau. of Poppaea Sabina (d. 47); granddau. of Poppaeus Sabinus, governor of Moesia; m. Rufius Crispinus; m. Marcus Salvius Otho, Roman emperor (r. 68); m. Nero, Roman emperor (r. 37–68), in 63. ❖ Of senatorial background and married to Marcus Salvius Otho, who would briefly reign as emperor after Nero's death, began affair with Nero (58); was killed when he kicked her in the stomach while she was pregnant. ❖ See also *Women in World History.*

POPPLER, Jericho (1951—). American surfer. Name variations: Jericho Poppler Bartlow. Born Dec 13, 1951; raised in Long Beach, CA; children: Raquel and Sophia Bartlow (surfers). ❖ Surfing pioneer, became US champion (1970); co-founded the Women's International Surfing Association (WISA); won the 1st woman's World pro tour (1976). Inducted into Surfers Hall of Fame (2004). ❖ See also "Heart of the Sea" (documentary, PBS).

PORADNIK-BOBRUS, Lyudmila (1946—). Soviet handball player. Born Jan 11, 1946, in USSR. ❖ Won a gold medal at Montreal Olympics (1976) and a gold medal at Moscow Olympics (1980), both in team competition.

PORCIA (c. 70–43 BCE). *See Portia.*

PORDEN, Eleanor Anne (1795–1825). *See Franklin, Eleanor.*

PORE, Heni (1840–1933). *See Te Kiri Karamu, Heni.*

PORECEANU, Uta (1936—). Romanian gymnast. Born Nov 13, 1936, in Romania. ❖ At Rome Olympics, won a bronze medal in team all-around (1960).

PORETE, Marguerite (d. 1310). French mystic. Name variations: Poiret or Porret, or Marguerite of Hainault. Died 1310. ❖ A beguine, wrote the book, *Mirror of Simple Souls,* which espoused the doctrine of the pure love of God and was in tune with a conception of personal spirituality shared by many others; was forbidden to spread her ideas by the bishop of Cambrai, and the book was burned on the public square in Valenciennes (1306); despite his warnings, disseminated both her ideas and her book; was brought before the Inquisitor of Haute Lorraine (1308); imprisoned for 2 years, was again interrogated in Paris where articles from her book had been examined by 21 theologians of University of Paris and declared heretical; refusing to retract, was burned in the Place de Grève. ❖ See also *Women in World History.*

PORN, Hanna (1860–1913). Finnish midwife. Born Hanna Kuniholm, Nov 11, 1860, in Mustari, Finland; died July 8, 1913; dau. of Eva and Adam Kuniholm; m. Edward Porn (died before 1895). ❖ Joined brother in Gardner, Massachusetts (1895); received a midwifery diploma from Chicago Midwife Institute (1896); worked almost entirely with immigrant mothers from Sweden, Finland and Russia; registered 642 births in 11 years of practice; though the physician-guided births in Gardner exhibited a higher infant mortality rate than those she delivered, was repeatedly convicted of illegally practicing medicine (since the Medical Practice Act of 1901 in Massachusetts had no clause that officially permitted midwives to perform births); was imprisoned for 3 months for continuing to deliver babies.

POROU, Ngati (1932—). *See Hineira, Arapera.*

PORRINA, Tarquinia Molza (1542–1617). *See Molza, Tarquinia.*

PORTAL, Magda (1903–1989). Peruvian activist, feminist and poet. Born May 27, 1903 (some sources cite 1900), in Lima, Peru; died July 11, 1989, in Lima; m. Federico Bolaños (div.); children: with poet Serafin Delmar [pen name], brother of her ex-husband) Gloria del Mar (committed suicide, 1947). ❖ Hailed as "Poet of the Poor" for lifelong push for social justice, was involved in student activism at University of San Marcos and a founding member of American Popular Revolutionary Alliance (APRA) movement; with encouragement of José Carlos Mariátegui, began publishing poetry and essays in influential journal *Amauta;* deported to Mexico with Serafin Delmar, Mariátegui and others (1927), helped found Mexican cell of APRA movement; after overthrow of repressive Leguía regime, returned to Peru (1930) and helped develop Peruvian APRA Party, PAP, serving as leader of women's section of national executive committee; moved to Chile with daughter because of renewed political persecution (1939), then returned to Peru and organized National Congress of Aprista Women in Lima (1946); after PAP colleagues denied women active membership in party (1948), broke all ties with accusatory essay *¿Quienes traicionaron al pueblo?* (Who Betrayed the People?, 1950); served as director of Mexico's Fondo de Cultura Económica publishing house (1958–71); published poetry collection *Constancia del ser* (Constancy of Being, 1965); joined one of Lima's 1st feminist groups, Action for the Liberation of Peruvian Women (now Flora Tristán Peruvian Women's Center); served as president of Peru's National Association of Writers and Artists (1982–86). Honored by Inter-American Congress of Women Writers (1981). ❖ See also Kathleen Weaver, *Magda Portal, Peruvian Rebel: A Life and Poems* (Teachers College Press).

PORTAL, Marta (1930—). Spanish journalist and writer. Name variations: Marta Portal Nicolás. Born Marta Portal Nicolás on Aug 10, 1930, in Nava, Asturias, Spain; earned BA in journalism and doctorate in information science. ❖ Acclaimed Spanish writer and journalist, earned the Planeta prize for novel *A tientas y a ciegas* (Groping Blindly, 1966); received scholarships from March Foundation to study abroad (1966) and chose Colombia; worked as journalist and professor of literature with faculty of information sciences at Complutense University in Madrid; wrote numerous literary studies and essays; works of fiction and nonfiction focus on women and lesbians, and explore the Latin American boom in literature; published semi-autobiographical *Tu y yo, nosotros tres* (2002); honored by the naming of cultural center, Casa de la Cultura Marta Portal, in native Asturias; won Adelaida Ristori Prize (1975), Hucha Prize (1991) and Horizonte prize (1992). Selected works: (novels) *El malmuerto* (He Who Died Badly, 1967), *A ras de las sombras* (Level with the Shadows, 1968), *Ladridos a la luna* (Howls at the Moon, 1970), *El buen camino* (The Good Road, 1975), *Un espacio erótico* (An Erotic Space, 1982), *Pago de traición* (Payback for Betrayal, 1983), *El ángel caído* (The Fallen Angel, 1994); (short stories) *La veintena* (The Twentieth, 1973); (literary studies) *Proceso narrativo de la revolución mexicana* (The Narrative Process of the Mexiacn Revolution, 1977), *Análisis semiológico de Pedro Páramo* (Semiologic Analysis of Pedro Páramo, 1981), and *Rufo: Dinámica de la violencia* (Rufo: The Dynamic of Violence, 1984).

PORTAPOVITCH, Anna Knapton (1890–1974). Russian ballet dancer and teacher. Name variations: Anna Povitch. Born Anna Knapton, Jan 16, 1890; died Dec 11, 1974, in West Roxbury, MA; m. Stanislaw Portapovitch (1895–1964, Polish ballet dancer whose name was originally Potopowicz, then changed to Povitch). ❖ Trained at the Imperial Ballet in St. Petersburg; performed with Anna Pavlova's company; with husband, appeared in featured roles in the Fokine repertory of Diaghilev Ballet Russe (1914–20); moved to New York City with husband (1919), where they opened a dance studio; taught there for many years.

PORTEN, Henny (1888–1960). German actress. Born Frieda Ulricke Porten, Jan 7, 1888, in Magdeburg, Germany; died Oct 15, 1960, in Berlin; dau. of Franz Porten (opera singer); sister of Rosa Porten; m. Kurt Stark (director, died at the front, 1916); m. Wilhelm von Kaufmann (physician), July 24, 1921. ❖ Began working for film pioneer Oskar Messter and became Germany's 1st screen superstar; made debut in *Apachentanz* (1906); films include *The Marriage of Luise Rohrbach* and *Rose Bernd* (both with Emil Jannings), *Fairy Hands, Kohlhiesel's Daughters, Anna Boleyn, Queen Luise, Mother and Child* and *Family Buchholz*; formed her own production company (1924); worked in silents and talkies, though career stalled during Third Reich (her 2nd husband was, according to racial laws, a "complete Jew").

PORTER, Anna Maria (1780–1832). English novelist. Born 1780 in Durham, England; died of typhus, Sept 21, 1832, in Bristol, England; dau. of William Porter (army surgeon, died c. 1780) and Jane Blenkinsop Porter; younger sister of Jane Porter (1776–1850) and Robert Ker Porter; attended school in Edinburgh; never married; no children. ❖ Shortly after her birth, moved to Edinburgh with family; became enchanted by fairy tales and accounts of Scottish history; moved back to London; by 16, had published a 2-vol. collection of stories, *Artless Tales* (1793, 1795), which, though not well written, captured the fancy of readers; published 1st novel, *Walsh Colville* (1797); published most popular novel, *The Hungarian Brothers* (1807), a historical romance set against the French Revolution that went through more than 15 printings and was translated into French; also wrote a number of other historical romances, including *Don Sebastian, or The House of Braganza* (1809), *The Knight of St. John*

(1817), *The Village of Mariendorpt* (1821), and *The Barony* (1830), her last novel; with sister Jane, who achieved much more lasting recognition as a novelist, collaborated on *Tales Round a Winter Hearth* (1826) and *Coming Out* (1828). ❖ See also *Women in World History.*

PORTER, Annie (1880–1963). English parasitologist. Name variations: Mrs. H.B. Fantham. Born Anne Porter, Feb 20, 1880, in Sussex, England; died May 9, 1963; dau. of Samuel Porter; University College, London, DSc, 1910; m. Dr. Harold Benjamin Fantham, Nov 24, 1915 (died Oct 1937). ❖ Was head of department of parasitology at South African Institute for Medical Research in Johannesburg (1917–33), then senior parasitology lecturer at University of Witwatersrand in Johannesburg (1921–33); often published with husband; served as president of South African Association for the Advancement of Science (1922) and South African Geographical Society (1924); became a fellow of Linnean Society (1911) and Royal Society of South Africa; was research associate in department of zoology at McGill University in Montreal (1933–37); returned to England after husband's death (1937).

PORTER, Carla. *See Boyd, Carla.*

PORTER, Charlotte Endymion (1857–1942). American writer and publisher. Name variations: (joint pseudonym) H.A.C. Born Helen Charlotte Porter on Jan 6, 1857, in Towanda, Pennsylvania; died Jan 16, 1942, in Melrose, Massachusetts; dau. of Henry Clinton Porter (physician) and Elisa Eleanor (Betts) Porter; graduate of Wells College, Aurora, NY; studied briefly at the Sorbonne in Paris; never married; lived with Helen Archibald Clarke. ❖ With Helen Archibald Clarke, founded the literary magazine *Poet Lore*; also edited *First Folio Edition of Shakespeare* (40 vols., 1903–13). ❖ See also *Women in World History.*

PORTER, Dorothy Germain (1924—). American golfer. Name variations: Dorothy V. Germain; Mrs. Mark Porter. Born Dorothy Germain, May 3, 1924, in Atlantic, IA; m. Mark Porter; children: 3, including Nancy Porter (golfer with city, state, and amateur titles); grandchildren: Kelsey Engman (Philadelphia Under-18 Girls' Amateur champion). ❖ Won Philadelphia City championship seven times; won Women's Western (1943, 1944, 1967); won USGA Women's Amateur (1949); member of Curtis Cup team (1950), captain (1966); won USGA Senior Women's championship (1974); coached field hockey and refereed field hockey and basketball.

PORTER, Eleanor H. (1868–1920). American writer. Name variations: (pseudonym) Eleanor Stewart. Born Eleanor Emily Hodgman, Dec 19, 1868, in Littleton, New Hampshire; died of TB, May 21, 1920, in Cambridge, Massachusetts; dau. of Francis Fletcher Hodgman (pharmacist) and Llewella French (Woolson) Hodgman; studied at New England Conservatory of Music; m. John Lyman Porter (businessman), May 3, 1892. ❖ Bestselling author of the hugely successful *Pollyanna*, had more than 200 of her short stories published by 1915, many of which appeared under pseudonym Eleanor Stewart; published 1st novel, *Cross Currents* (1907), but 1st achieved real success with *Miss Billy* (1911); published *Pollyanna* (1913), the story of an orphan so dauntless in her optimism that she turns those around her into believers; other writings include *Miss Billy's Decision* (1912), *Pollyanna Grows Up* (1915), *Just David* (1916), *The Road to Understanding* (1917), *Dawn* (1919), *Across the Years* (stories, 1919), *Mary-Marie* (1920) and *Money, Love and Kate* (stories, 1925). ❖ See also *Women in World History.*

PORTER, Eliza Chappell (1807–1888). American educator and relief worker. Born Eliza Emily Chappell, Nov 5, 1807, in Geneseo, New York; died Jan 1, 1888, in Santa Barbara, California; dau. of Robert Chappell (farmer, died 1811) and Elizabeth (Kneeland) Chappell (died 1831); m. Jeremiah Porter (missionary), June 15, 1835; children: 9, 6 of whom survived infancy. ❖ Opened a school modeled after the infant schools, designed to bring religious-oriented education to poor children (1828); opened and staffed a school in the French and Indian settlement of St. Ignace, near Mackinac (1833), then another in Chicago; married (1835) and settled in Green Bay, Wisconsin (1840), where husband served for 18 years as pastor of local Presbyterian church; returned to Chicago (1858); with outbreak of Civil War, became office manager of Chicago Sanitary Commission (later Northwest Sanitary Commission), a volunteer organization established to distribute supplies to Union army and military hospitals; escorted women volunteers to Cairo, Illinois (1862), where they helped establish hospitals to care for casualties from battle of Shiloh; later assisted in hospitals in Tennessee towns of Savannah and Memphis, where she also established a school for black children; joined Mary Ann Bickerdyke in ministering to Sherman's army during its march toward Atlanta (1863). ❖ See also *Women in World History.*

PORTER, Elizabeth Kerr (1894–1989). American nurse. Born Elizabeth Kerr, May 21, 1894, in Pittsburgh, PA; died 1989; dau. of Catherine (Anderson) Kerr and Richard Kerr; graduate of Western Pennsylvania Hospital School of Nursing, 1930; Columbia University Teachers College, BS, 1935; University of Pennsylvania, MA, 1936, PhD in nursing education, 1946; m. Eugene Vandergrift Porter, 1914 (died 1921). ❖ Was a teaching supervisor at Western Pennsylvania School of Nursing (1930–35); lectured at Margaret Morrison Carnegie College in Pittsburgh (1933–35); was full professor at University of Pennsylvania School of Nursing (1935–49); began serving as professor, director and dean of Advanced Programs in Nursing Education at Case Western Reserve University's Frances Payne Bolton School of Nursing (1953); elected president of American Nurses Association (ANA, 1950), and instituted a 40-hour work week and improved nurse employment conditions; served as president of Ohio Nurses Association (1958–60).

PORTER, Fanny Rose (1868–1916). *See Howie, Fanny Rose.*

PORTER, Gene Stratton (1863–1924). *See Stratton-Porter, Gene.*

PORTER, Gladys M. (1894–1967). Canadian politician. Name variations: Gladys Muriel Porter. Born Aug 1894 in Sydney, Nova Scotia, Canada; died April 30, 1967, in Kentville, Nova Scotia; dau. of the mayor of Sydney; married. ❖ Was the 1st woman elected mayor in Kentville (1946), and the 1st woman in the Maritimes to hold a mayoral position; remained mayor until 1960; as a Progressive Conservative, was the 1st woman elected to the Nova Scotia Legislative Assembly (1960); was still a sitting member of the legislature at time of death. Named a Member of the Order of the British Empire (1946).

PORTER, Gwendoline (c. 1909—). English runner. Born c. 1909 in UK. ❖ At Los Angeles Olympics, won a bronze medal in 4 x 100-meter relay (1932).

PORTER, Helen Kemp (1899–1987). English plant physiologist. Name variations: Helen Kemp Archbold; Helen Kemp Huggett. Born Helen Kemp Archbold, Nov 10, 1899, in Farnham, Surrey, England; died Dec 3, 1987; Bedford College, London, BS, 1921, DSc, 1932; m. Dr. William George Porter (physician), 1937 (died); m. Arthur St. George Huggett (professor and physiologist), 1962. ❖ One of Britain's 1st scientists to use radioactive tracers, studied plant photosynthesis; at Imperial College, London, studied barbiturate derivatives (1921–22), was a member of the plant physiology team (1931–39), had her own research unit (1953–57), and was named the 1st woman professor (1959); also researched carbohydrate metabolism at Department of Scientific and Industrial Research (1922–31); pioneered techniques of chromatography; elected fellow of Royal Society (1956).

PORTER, Helen Tracy (1876–1963). *See Lowe-Porter, Helen.*

PORTER, Jane (1776–1850). English novelist. Born Dec 3, 1776, in Durham, England; died May 24, 1850, in Bristol, England; dau. of William Porter (army surgeon, died c. 1780) and Jane (Blenkinsop) Porter (died 1831); sister of writer Anna Maria Porter (1780–1832) and Robert Ker Porter (painter and writer); educated at George Fulton's School in Edinburgh; never married; no children. ❖ At 4, moved with family to Edinburgh, Scotland, where she was introduced to the heroic tales of early Scottish history; wrote *Thaddeus of Warsaw* (1803), her 1st romance novel, which was an immediate popular success, followed by *Sketch of the Campaign of Count A. Suwarrow Ryminski* (1804); published *The Scottish Chiefs* (1810), which celebrated (without strict regard to historical accuracy) the heroic exploits of Scotland's William Wallace, another hugely popular book, praised by such writers as Joanna Baillie, Thomas Campbell, and Mary Russell Mitford; after writing a few unsuccessful plays, wrote a well-received historical novel, *The Pastor's Fire-Side* (1817); collaborated with sister Anna on a collection of short fiction, *Tales round a Winter Hearth* (1826); also wrote *The Two Princes of Persia, Addressed to Youth* (1801), *Owen, Prince of Powys* (play, 1822), *Duke Christian of Luneberg* (1824), and *Sir Edward Seward's Narrative of His Shipwreck and Consequent Discovery of Certain Islands in the Caribbean Sea* (1831). ❖ See also *Women in World History.*

PORTER, Jean (1924—). American dancer and actress. Born Dec 8, 1924, in Cisco, TX; m. Edward Dmytryk (director), 1948 (died 1999); children: Richard, Victoria and Rebecca. ❖ Performed in vaudeville as a child; during adolescence, joined MGM stock company as a tap dancer; generally featured as second lead, danced and acted in numerous shows, including *Bathing Beauty* (1944), *Andy Hardy's Blonde Trouble* (1944), *Betty Co-Ed* (1946), *Till the End of Time* (1946) and *Little Miss Broadway*

(1947); when husband was blacklisted (1949), her career suffered as well; made last appearance in his *The Left Hand of God* (1955).

PORTER, Katherine Anne (1890–1980). American writer. Name variations: (pseudonym) M.T.F. Born Callie Russell Porter, May 15, 1890, in Indian Creek, Texas; died Sept 18, 1980, in Silver Spring, Maryland; dau. of Mary Alice (Jones) Porter and Harrison Boone Porter; m. John Koontz, 1906 (div. 1915); m. Ernest Stock, 1925 (div. c. 1928); m. Eugene Pressly, 1930 (div. c. 1936); m. Albert Erskine, 1938 (div. c. 1942); no children. ❖ Pulitzer Prize-winning author, known for her novel *Ship of Fools,* who was a brilliant practitioner of the art of the short story; worked as a newspaper reporter in Fort Worth; was a journalist in Mexico (1921); published 1st short story, "Maria Concepción," (1922), based on her experiences; published 3 short-story collections to considerable acclaim for their meticulous crafting and subtle irony (by 1944); was brought to public attention and wide readership with novel *Ship of Fools* (1962); won O. Henry Prize for short fiction (1962); awarded National Book Award and Pulitzer Prize (1965) for *Collected Short Stories*; suffered a debilitating stroke (1970) just as she finished her last published work, *The Never-Ending Wrong,* about the Sacco-Vanzetti case. Writings include *Flowering Judas* (1930), *Hacienda* (1934), *Noon Wine* (1937), *Pale Horse, Pale Rider: Three Short Novels* (1939), *The Leaning Tower and Other Stories* (1943), *The Days Before* (1952), *The Old Order: Stories of the South* (1955) and *A Christmas Story* (1967). ❖ See also Harold Bloom, ed. *Katherine Anne Porter* (Chelsea, 1986); Virginia Spencer Carr, *Flowering Judas: A Casebook* (Rutgers U. Press, 1993); Joan Givner, *Katherine Anne Porter* (Simon & Schuster, 1982); Janis P. Stout, *Katherine Anne Porter* (U. of Virginia Press, 1995); Ray B. West Jr. *Katherine Anne Porter* (U. of Minnesota Press, 1963); and *Women in World History.*

PORTER, Marguerite (c. 1956—). English ballet dancer. Born c. 1956 in Doncaster, England. ❖ Danced professionally with Royal Ballet where she appeared in productions of classics, such as *Swan Lake, Giselle* and *Sleeping Beauty,* as well as such contemporary works as Ashton's *The Dream* and *The Two Pigeons,* and Macmillan's *Mayerling* and *Manon;* featured in *On Your Toes* (2003).

PORTER, Mrs. Mark (1924—). *See Porter, Dorothy Germain.*

PORTER, Mary (d. 1765). English actress. Died Feb 24, 1765. ❖ Made 1st appearance with Thomas Betterton's company in a tragedy, in which she specialized (1709), but she would also be seen in a long string of comedies; after friends Elizabeth Barry, Anne Bracegirdle and Anne Oldfield retired from the stage, was left its undisputed queen.

PORTER, Mary Bea (1949—). American golfer. Name variations: Mary Bea Porter-King; Mary Bea King. Born Dec 4, 1949, in Everett, WA; m. Charles King; children: son. ❖ Was Collegiate All-American, while attending Arizona State University (1972); joined LPGA tour (1973); won Golf Inns of America Classic (1975); co-founded the Hawaii State Junior Golf Association (1998).

PORTER, Mary Winearls (1886–1980). English crystallographer. Born Mary "Polly" Winearls Porter, July 26, 1886; died Nov 25, 1980; dau. of a *Times* correspondent; Somerville College, Oxford, BS, 1918, and DSc, 1932. ❖ Worked as a cataloguer at Oxford's University Museum (1905–07), National Museum in Washington, DC (1911–12) and Bryn Mawr College (1913–14); served as crystallographer researcher in Heidelberg (1914–15) and Oxford's University Museum (1916–59); was a fellow of Mineralogical Society of America (1921–27) and council member of Mineralogical Society of Great Britain (1918–21, 1929–32); co-edited *The Barker Index of Crystals* (1951, 1956 and 1963).

PORTER, Natalia (1980—). Australian basketball player. Born Dec 16, 1980, in Melbourne, Australia. ❖ Forward, placed 1st at Oceania championships (2001, 2003); won a team silver medal at Athens Olympics (2004); played for Townsville Fire. Won the WNBL Defensive Player of the Year award (2003).

PORTER, Nyree Dawn (1936–2001). New Zealand actress. Born with the Maori name Ngaire (heart-shaped flower) which became NY-ree, Jan 22, 1936, in Napier, New Zealand; died April 10, 2001, in London, England; m. Bryon O'Leary (died of drug overdose, 1970); m. Robin Halstead (div. 1987); children: (2nd m.) daughter Talya (b. 1975). ❖ Had a long, successful stage career; made film debut in *Sentenced for Life* (1960), followed by *Identity Unknown, The Cracksman, Jane Eyre, The House That Dripped Blood* and *Hilary and Jackie* (as Dame Margot Fonteyn), among others; appeared in a number of tv series, including title role in "Madame Bovary" (1964), "The Liars" (1966),

"The Protectors" (1972), and "The Martian Chronicles" (1980), but probably best known for her role as Irene Forsyte in 26-part BBC "Forsyte Saga" (1967). Awarded OBE (1971).

PORTER, Sarah (1791–1862). English writer. Name variations: Sarah Ricardo Porter. Born Sarah Ricardo in 1791; died Sept 13, 1862, at West Hill, Wandsworth, England; dau. of Abraham Ricardo; sister of David Ricardo (principal founder of the classical school of political economy); m. George Richardson Porter (1792–1852). ❖ Writer on education, published *Conversations on Arithmetic* (1830), *On Infant Schools for the Upper and Middle Classes* (1838), among others; also wrote the children's book, *Alfred Dudley, or, the Australian Settlers* (1830).

PORTER, Sarah (fl. 1791). American poet. May have been resident of Plymouth, MA. ❖ Only one book extant, *The Royal Penitent* (1791).

PORTER, Sarah (1813–1900). American educator. Born Sarah Porter, Aug 16, 1813, in Farmington, Connecticut; died Feb 17, 1900, in Farmington; dau. of Noah Porter (pastor) and Mehetabel Meigs Porter; sister of Noah Porter (1811–1892, Congregational cleric and president of Yale) and Samuel Porter (teacher of the deaf); educated at Farmington Academy, and under the informal tutelage of several Yale professors in New Haven, Connecticut; never married; no children. ❖ The founder of Miss Porter's School for Girls, taught at schools in Springfield (MA), Philadelphia (PA), and Buffalo (NY), in the 1st decade after completing her studies in New Haven; founded Miss Porter's School (1843), which in time grew into one of the most famous girls' boarding schools in the world, and remained active there as a teacher and administrator until her death. ❖ See also *Women in World History*.

PORTER, Stacey (1982—). Australian softball player. Born Mar 29, 1982, in Tamworth, Australia; attended University of Hawaii. ❖ Playing third and first base, won a team silver medal at Athens Olympics (2004).

PORTER, Sylvia (1913–1991). American financial writer. Name variations: S.F. Porter; Sylvia Field Porter. Born Sylvia Field Feldman, June 18, 1913, in Patchogue, Long Island, New York; died June 5, 1991, in Pound Ridge, NY; dau. of Louis Feldman (doctor) and Rose (Maisel) Feldman; Hunter College, BA, 1932; graduate work in economics at New York University's School of Business Administration; m. Reed R. Porter (banker), 1931 (div.); m. G. Summer Collins, 1943 (died Jan 1977); m. James F. Fox, 1979; children: Cris Sarah. ❖ Through her syndicated financial columns and numerous books, was able to make the most complex economic concepts accessible to the average reader; began writing a financial column for *New York Post* (1935), under byline "S.F. Porter" to prevent gender bias in what had been a male-dominated field; column was later syndicated nationwide to over 400 newspapers; writings include *How to Make Money in Government Bonds* (1939), *The Nazi Chemical Trust in the US* (1942), (with Jacob Kay Lasser) *How to Live Within Your Income* (1948), *Sylvia Porter's Money Book* (1975); also author of *Sylvia Porter's Income Tax Guide*, published annually from 1961; was contributing editor, *Ladies' Home Journal*. Received National Headliner's Club medal (1943) and New York Newspaper Women's Club award (1945, 1947, 1957, and 1962). ❖ See also *Women in World History*.

PORTER-KING, Mary Bea (1949—). See *Porter, Mary Bea.*

PORTIA (fl. 80 BCE). Roman patrician. Dau. of Livia (fl. 100 BCE) and M. Portius Cato; sister of Cato the Younger; half-sister of Servilia I and Servilia II.

PORTIA (c. 70–43 BCE). Roman patrician. Name variations: Porcia. Born c. 70 BCE; died in 43 BCE (some sources cite 42 BCE); dau. of Marcus Porcius Cato Uticensus (Cato of Utica), known as Cato the Younger, and Atilia; m. Marcus Calpurnius Bibulus (died 48 BCE); m. Marcus Junius Brutus (one of the assassins of Julius Caesar); children: (1st m.) 3 sons, only one of whom (also named Bibulus) outlived her. ❖ Zealously embraced the political ideals of her father, an ardent opponent of Julius Caesar, and seems to have had no objection to her arranged marriage with Bibulus, another lifelong adversary of Caesar; took as her 2nd husband her cousin, Marcus Junius Brutus 45 BCE; seems to have had a decisive influence on Brutus; when he joined the conspiracy to murder Caesar (Mar 15, 44 BCE), insisted on being told of the assassination plot prior to the fact, demonstrating her toughness by taking a knife and making a deep cut in her thigh; after the assassination of Caesar, was a vocal presence at the conference of Republicans which met at Antium (in June); beset by the deteriorating position of Brutus and suffering physically, committed suicide by inhaling the poisonous fumes wafting from a brazier, or by swallowing live coals. ❖ See also *Women in World History*.

PORTILLO, Lourdes. Mexican-born filmmaker. Born in Chihuahua, Mexico; graduate of San Francisco Art Institute, 1978. ❖ Came to US (1960); founded her own film company, Xochitl Productions (1976); released 1st short film, *Después del terremoto* (*After the Earthquake,* 1979); focused on the mothers who disappeared in Argentina in *Las Madres: The Mothers of Plaza de Mayo* (1985) and Tejano singer Selena in *Corpus: A Home Movie for Selena* (1999); also filmed *Columbus on Trial* (1993), *La Ofrenda: The Days of the Dead* (1989), and *Señorita Extraviada* (*Missing Young Women,* 2001), about the unsolved sex murders of hundreds of young women and girls in Juárez.

PORTILLO-TRAMBLEY, Estela (1936–1999). American playwright, educator and short-story writer. Name variations: Estela Portillo; Estela Trambley; Estela Portillo Trambley. Born Estela Portillo, 1936, in El Paso, TX; died spring 1999; children: 6. ❖ Taught high school, hosted tv show, and worked as director of Fine Arts in El Paso schools; writings include *Day of the Swallows* (1971), *Impressions by a Chicana* (1974), *Rain of Scorpions* (1975), *Sun Images* (1979), *Sor Juana and Other Plays* (1983), and *Trini* (1986); edited special edition of *El Grito* (1973). Awarded Quinto Sol Literary Prize (1972).

PORTINARI, Beatrice (c. 1265–1290). See *Beatrice Portinari.*

PORTLAND, countess of. See *Villiers, Anne (d. 1688).*

PORTLAND, duchess of. See *Bentinck, Margaret (1714–1785).*

PÖRTNER, Margit (c. 1973—). Danish curler. Name variations: Margit Poertner or Portner. Born c. 1973 in Denmark. ❖ Won a silver medal for curling at Nagano Olympics (1998), the 1st-ever Danish medal in any sport at Winter Olympics.

PORTNOY, Ethel (1927–2004). Dutch essayist and playwright. Born Mar 8, 1927, in Philadelphia, PA; grew up in New York; died May 25, 2004 in The Hague; m. Rudy Kousbroek (Dutch writer), 1951; children: 2. ❖ Entered University of Lyon on a Fulbright (1950); lived in Paris and worked at UNESCO; moved to the Hague, Netherlands (1970); works in Dutch include *Steen en been* (1971), *Broodje Aap* (1978), *Vliegende vellen* (1983), *Vluchten* (1984), and *Rook over Rusland* (1990); with Hannes Meinkema and Hanneke van Buuren, founded literary magazine *Chrysallis* (1978–81).

PORTSMOUTH, duchess of. See *Kéroüalle, Louise de (1649–1734).*

PORTUGAL, queen of.
See *Matilda of Maurienne (c. 1125–1157).*
See *Douce of Aragon (1160–1198).*
See *Urraca of Castile (c. 1186–1220).*
See *Beatrice of Castile and Leon (1242–1303).*
See *Mencia de Haro (d. 1270).*
See *Elizabeth of Portugal (1271–1336).*
See *Beatrice of Castile and Leon (1293–1359).*
See *Constance of Castile (1323–1345).*
See *Leonora Telles (c. 1350–1386).*
See *Philippa of Lancaster (c. 1359–1415).*
See *Leonora of Aragon (1405–1445).*
See *Isabel la Paloma (d. 1455).*
See *Eleanor of Portugal (1458–1525).*
See *Isabella of Asturias (1471–1498).*
See *Maria of Castile (1482–1517).*
See *Eleanor of Portugal (1498–1558).*
See *Catherine (1507–1578).*
See *Mary of Portugal (d. 1545).*
See *Luisa de Guzman (1613–1666).*
See *Marie Françoise of Savoy (1646–1683).*
See *Maria Sophia of Neuberg (1666–1699).*
See *Maria Antonia of Austria (1683–1754).*
See *Maria Ana Victoria (1718–1781).*
See *Maria I of Braganza (1734–1816).*
See *Carlota Joaquina (1775–1830).*
See *Maria II da Gloria (1819–1853).*
See *Adelheid (1831–1909).*
See *Stephanie (1837–1859).*
See *Maria Pia (1847–1911).*
See *Marie-Amelie of Orleans (1865–1951).*

PORTWICH, Ramona (1967—). German kayaker. Born Jan 5, 1967, in Germany. ❖ At Seoul Olympics, won a gold medal in K4 500 meters (1988); at Barcelona Olympics, won a silver medal in K4 500 meters and a gold medal in K2 500 meters (1992); won a gold medal for K4 500 meters and a silver medal for K2 500 meters at Atlanta Olympics (1996).

PORZECOWNA, Elzbieta (1945—). Polish volleyball player. Born Jan 27, 1945, in Poland. ❖ At Mexico City Olympics, won a bronze medal in team competition (1968).

POS, Alette (1962—). Dutch field-hockey player. Born Mar 30, 1962, in the Netherlands. ❖ At Los Angeles Olympics, won a gold medal in team competition (1984).

POSEVINA, Elena (1986—). Russian rhythmic gymnast. Born Feb 13, 1986, in USSR. ❖ Won 3 group competition events at World championships (2003); won team all-around gold medal at Athens Olympics (2004).

POSNEROVA, Jana (1945—). See Kubickova-Posnerova, Jana.

POSSEKEL, Elvira (1953—). West German runner. Born April 11, 1953, in West Germany. ❖ At Montreal Olympics, won a silver medal in the 4 x 100-meter relay (1976).

POST, Emily (1872–1960). American writer and etiquette expert. Name variations: Emily Price Post. Born Emily Price, Oct 27, 1872 (some sources cite Oct 3, 1873), in Baltimore, Maryland; died Sept 25, 1960, in New York, NY; dau. of Bruce Price (architect who designed Quebec City's Chateau Frontenac) and Josephine (Lee) Price; educated by governesses and at private schools in New York; m. Edwin M. Post (banker and investor), in 1892 (div. c. 1905); children: Edwin M. Jr. (b. 1893), Bruce Price (b. 1895). ❖ Published 1st book, *The Flight of the Moth* (1904); produced 1st etiquette guide *Etiquette in Society, in Business, in Politics, and at Home* (1922, later republished as *Etiquette: The Blue Book of Social Usage*) which became immensely popular, despite the rapidly changing social mores in America after WWI, and went through 90 printings and about 10 editions in her lifetime; started a daily column on "good taste" (1932) that was syndicated in 160 newspapers; was an expert on etiquette and home decoration on radio; founded the Emily Post Institute for the Study of Gracious Living (1946). ❖ See also *Women in World History.*

POST, Lydia Minturn (fl. 1776–1783). American diarist. Lived on Long Island, NY. ❖ Excerpts from journal collected in *Personal Recollections of the American Revolution: A Private Journal. Prepared from Authentic Domestic Records by Lydia Minturn Post* (1859).

POST, Marion (1910–1990). See Wolcott, Marion Post.

POST, Marjorie Merriweather (1887–1973). American businesswoman and philanthropist. Born in Springfield, Illinois, Mar 15, 1887; died Sept 12, 1973; dau. of Charles William Post, known as C.W. Post (started Postum Cereal Co.) and Ella Letitia (Merriweather) Post; m. Edward B. Close, Dec 3, 1905; m. Edward F. Hutton (stockbroker and founder of Wall Street firm), July 7, 1920; m. Joseph E. Davies (Washington lobbyist and ambassador to USSR), Dec 15, 1935 (div. 1955); m. Herbert May (Pittsburgh executive), June 18, 1958 (div. 1964); children: (1st m.) Adelaide Close (m. Augustus Riggs IV), Eleanor Close (m. Leon Barzin); (2nd m.) Nedenia Hutton (b. 1925, who as an actress adopted the stage name Dina Merrill). ❖ Following father's suicide (1914), became sole heir of Postum Cereal of Battle Creek; ran the company as owner and operator for next 8 years; with help from 2nd husband, E.F. Hutton, acquired Birdseye frozen foods, creating the food empire, General Foods; was a member of its board of directors (1936–58) and director emeritus (1958–73); was also director of National Savings and Trust, Washington, DC (1959–73); her philanthropies included NY's Emergency Unemployment Drive (1929–33), Good Samaritan Hospital (Palm Beach), and Long Island University. ❖ See also Nancy Rubin, *American Empress: The Life and Times of Marjorie Merriweather Post* (Villard, 1995).

POST, Sandra (1948—). Canadian golfer. Name variations: Sanda Post-McDermid. Born June 4, 1948, in Oakville, Ontario, Canada. ❖ Won Canadian Jr. championship (1964–66); became the 1st Canadian woman to join the LPGA tour (1968); beat Kathy Whitworth in an 18-hole playoff for LPGA championship (1968); won 9 LPGA tour events, including Colgate Far East Open (1974) and Colgate-Dinah Shore Open (1978, 1979). Named LPGA Rookie of the Year (1968); named Canadian Athlete of the Year (1979); won Lou Marsh Trophy (1979); inducted into Canada Sports Hall of Fame (1988), Canadian Golf Hall of Fame (1988), and Ontario Golf Hall of Fame (2000).

POSTAN, Eileen (1889–1940). See Power, Eileen.

POSTEL-VINAY, Anise (1928—). French resistance fighter. Name variations: Anise Girard; called Danielle. Born Anise Girard, 1928, in Paris, France; m. André Postel-Vinay. ❖ Mother began to take in Catholic and Jewish refugees fleeing Germany (1933); with family, left Paris to live in Rennes; studied for MA in German; was 18 when Germans invaded Paris (1940); joined resistance (1942); arrested same day as her father (1943); imprisoned at La Santé in Paris, then Fresnes; traveled in same passenger car to Ravensbrück as Germaine Tillion (Oct 21, 1943), becoming close friends; managed to hide from transports to Auschwitz (1945); testified as a key witness to some of the medical horrors perpetrated on concentration camp inmates. ❖ See also (film) *Sisters in Resistance.*

POSTELL, Ashley (1986—). American gymnast. Born June 6, 1986, in Cheverly, MD. ❖ Placed 2nd all-around at US nationals (1998); won a gold medal at International Team championships (1999); won World championship on beam (2002).

POSTLEWAIT, Kathy (1949—). American golfer. Born Nov 11, 1949, in Norfolk, VA; graduate of East Carolina University, 1971. ❖ Joined LPGA (1974); won San Jose Classic (1983); won Mazda Classic (1987); won McDonald's championship and had 8 top-10 finishes (1988); won Sara Lee Classic (1989).

POSTMA, Joan (1943—). See Spillane, Joan.

POSTON, Elizabeth (1905–1987). English pianist and composer. Born Oct 24, 1905, in Highfield, Hertfordshire, England; died Mar 18, 1987, in Highfield; studied at Royal College of Music; never married. ❖ A student of Harold Samuel, published 1st composition (1925), and shortly thereafter heard her violin sonata broadcast by the BBC; during WWII, was the director of music in the Foreign Service of BBC in London, and later served as president of Society of Women Musicians (1955–61); wide range of compositions includes choral music, hymns, Christmas carols, and music for radio dramas and films; compositions include: *The Holy Child* (1950), *Concertino da Camera on a Theme of Martin Peerson* (1950), *Peter Halfpenny's Tunes* (1959), *Harlow Concertante* (1969) and *An English Day Book* (1971).

POTACHOVA, Olga (1976—). Russian volleyball player. Name variations: Potashova. Born June 26, 1976, in Potsdam, Germany. ❖ Made national team debut (1999); won a team silver medal at Sydney Olympics (2000); won European team championship (2001).

POTATAU, Kahupake (1868/69?–1947). See Rongonui, Kahupake.

POTEC, Camelia Alina (1982—). Romanian swimmer. Born Feb 19, 1982, in Braila, Romania. ❖ Won a gold medal for 200-meter freestyle at Athens Olympics (2004); placed 1st in 9 World Cup events (2003–04).

POTO, Alicia (1978—). Australian basketball player. Born Mar 28, 1978, in Sydney, Australia. ❖ Guard, placed 1st at Oceania championships (2003); won a team silver medal at Athens Olympics (2004).

POTONIÉ-PIERRE, Eugénie (1844–1898). French feminist and socialist. Name variations: Eugenie Potonie Pierre. Pronunciation: yew-JAY-nee po-TOE-nee-ay pee-AIR. Born Eugénie Pierre, Nov 5, 1844; died June 12, 1898; sister of Dr. Marie Pierre; m. Edmond Potonié (historian and pacifist), 1881; no children. ❖ Reformer who worked to make the women's movement more socially conscious, helping middle-class women come to understand that their plight was, like it or not, linked to that of the humblest reaches of society; emerged as an important figure when she served as secretary of the organizing committee of the 1st French International Congress for Women's Rights (1878); helped found Union of Socialist Women (1880); with Auclert and others, tried to register to vote (Feb 2, 1880) but was denied; helped to run *La Citoyenne* (1886?–91); helped found Women's Solidarity Group and French Federation of Feminist Societies (1891); helped sponsor French Congress for Women's Rights (1892, 1896); wrote for Argyriadès' *La Question sociale* (1894–97); served as delegate to Brussels World Congress of Women (1897). ❖ See also *Women in World History.*

POTORAC, Gabriela (1973—). Romanian gymnast. Born Feb 6, 1973, in Bacau, Romania. ❖ Placed 1st all-around at Catania Cup (1986) and Balkan Junior championships and Cottbus Cup (1987); at Seoul Olympics, won a bronze medal in the balance beam and silver medals in team all-around and vault (1988); placed 1st all-around at Balkan championships, Arthur Gander Memorial, and Swiss Cup (1988); at World championships, won a silver in team all-around and bronze in balance beam (1989); had to retire at age 16, when gym closed during Romanian revolution; moved to Japan.

POTTER, Beatrice (1858–1943). *See Webb, Beatrice.*

POTTER, Beatrix (1866–1943). British author. Name variations: Beatrix Heelis. Born Helen Beatrix Potter, July 28, 1866, in South Kensington, London; died Dec 22, 1943, at Sawrey, Cumbria; dau. of Rupert Potter (barrister) and Helen (Leech) Potter; m. William Heelis, Oct 14, 1913; no children. ❖ Best remembered not only as a brilliant writer of books for children but also as the champion of Herdwicks, a breed of sheep then in danger of disappearing, and as a supporter and benefactor of The National Trust in the Lake District of England; sold some drawings to Hildersheimer and Faulkner, publishers (1890); wrote a letter to young Noël Moore, telling him a story about 4 rabbits which she illustrated with pen-and-ink drawings (Sept 4, 1893); her research paper "On the Germination of the Spores of Agaricineae" read to Linnean Society of London (April 1, 1897); privately published *The Tale of Peter Rabbit* (1901), which was then published by Frederick Warne (1902); bought Hill Top Farm, near Sawrey (summer 1905); went to live at Castle Cottage Farm, Sawrey (1913); 1st became involved with National Trust (1914); bought Troutbeck Park (1923) and began sheepbreeding; became president of Herdwick Sheep-breeders Association (1930); writings include *The Tailor of Gloucester* (1902), *The Tale of Squirrel Nutkin* (1903), *The Tale of Benjamin Bunny* (1904), *The Tale of Mrs. Tiggy-Winkle* (1905), *The Tale of Mrs. Jeremy Fisher* (1906), *The Tale of Jemima Puddle-Duck* (1908), *Ginger and Pickles* (1909), *The Tale of Pigling Bland* (1913), *Appley Dapply's Nursery Rhymes* (1917) and *The Fairy-Caravan* (1929). ❖ See also Margaret Lane, *The Tale of Beatrix Potter* (Warne, 1946); Judy Taylor, *Beatrix Potter: Artist, Storyteller and Countrywoman* (Warne, 1986); Elizabeth Buchan, *Beatrix Potter* (Hamilton, 1987); and *Women in World History.*

POTTER, Bessie (1872–1955). *See Vonnoh, Bessie Potter.*

POTTER, Mrs. Brown (1857–1936). *See Potter, Cora.*

POTTER, Cora (1857–1936). American actress. Name variations: Cora Urquhart, Mrs. Brown Potter, Mrs. Brown-Potter. Born Cora Urquhart, May 15, 1857, in New Orleans, LA; died Feb 12, 1936; m. James Brown-Potter (div. 1903). ❖ Made stage debut in Brighton as Faustine de Bressier in *Civil War*, London debut in *Man and Wife*, and NY debut in *Civil War* (all 1887); other plays include *Hero and Leander, Charlotte Corday* (title role), *The Lady of Lyons, The Musketeers, Ulysses, Cavalleria Rusticana* and *Du Barri* (title role); assumed management of the Savoy (1904). ❖ See also memoir *The Age of Innocence and I* (1933).

POTTER, Cynthia (1950—). American diver. Name variations: Cynthia Potter McIngvale; Cynthia McIngvale. Born Cynthia Potter, Aug 27, 1950, in Houston, TX; graduate of Indiana University; m. James Franklin McIngvale (div.). ❖ At Montreal Olympics, won a bronze medal in springboard (1976); won silver medal for springboard at World championships (1978); won 28 national championships, voted World Diver of the Year three times, and was on 4 Olympic teams. Inducted into International Swimming Hall of Fame (1989).

POTTER, Electa (1790–1854). American philanthropist. Name variations: Mrs. H.B. Potter. Born Electa Miller, Mar 16, 1790; died Oct 13, 1854; 2nd dau. of Frederick and Elizabeth (Babcock) Miller; m. Heman B. Potter (judge), July 12, 1812 (died Oct 7, 1854); children: Mary Eliza Potter (1813–1814); Mary Bradley Babcock (1815–1877, who m. George Reed Babcock); Frederick Miller Potter (1817–1818); Elizabeth Miller Potter (1819–1854); Heman Bradley Potter (1824–1859). ❖ Was a prominent philanthropist in Buffalo, NY.

POTTER, Mrs. H.B. (1790–1854). *See Potter, Electa.*

POTTER, Jenny (1979—). *See Schmidgall, Jenny.*

POTTER, Lela (1908—). *See Brooks, Lela.*

POTTER, Maureen (1925–2004). Irish actress and variety performer. Born Maria Philomena Potter in Fairview, Dublin, Ireland, Jan 3, 1925; died April 7, 2004; dau. of James Benedict Potter and Elizabeth (Carr) Potter; m. Jack O'Leary (army officer), 1959; children: 2 sons. ❖ At 7, made professional stage debut in Dublin, singing *Broadway's Gone Hillbilly*; began to make regular appearances with Jimmy Campbell band at Theatre Royal, Dublin's premier variety venue; sang with Jack Hylton Band in London for 2 years, billed as "Maureen Potter Child Impressionist, Dancer and Burlesque Actress"; when war broke out (1939), returned to Ireland and went straight into pantomime with Jimmy O'Dea, with whom she formed a legendary comic partnership that lasted until O'Dea's death in 1965; formed a new stage partnership with Danny Cummins; in film, appeared as Josie Breen in *Ulysses* (1967)

and as Mrs. Riordan *Portrait of the Artist* (1977); portrayed Maisie Madigan in the celebrated Gate Theatre production of Sean O'Casey's *Juno and the Paycock* (1984) and the mother in Hugh Leonard's *Da.* ❖ See also *Women in World History.*

POTTER, Sally (1949—). British director and screenwriter. Born Sept 19, 1949, in London, England. ❖ Directed 1st film, *Thriller* (1979); also directed *The Gold Diggers,* starring Julie Christie (1984); came to international prominence with an adaptation of Virginia Woolf's *Orlando* (1992), followed by *The Tango Lesson* (1997), *The Man Who Cried* (2000) and *Yes* (2004); for tv, directed "Tears, Laughter, Fear and Rage" (1986) and a documentary on Soviet women (1988).

POTTHARST, Kerri-Ann (1965—). Australian beach volleyball player. Born June 25, 1965, in Adelaide, Australia. ❖ With Natalie Cook, won a bronze medal at Atlanta Olympics (1966) and a gold medal at Sydney Olympics (2000).

POTTINGER, Judith (1956—). New Zealand equestrian. Born April 26, 1956, in New Zealand. ❖ At Seoul Olympics, won a bronze medal in team 3-day event (1988).

POTTS, Mary Florence (c. 1853–?). American inventor. Born Mary Florence Webber c. 1853; dau. of a plasterer in Ottumwa, IA; m. Joseph Potts; children: 6. ❖ Granted 3 patents for improvements in sad irons, invented the most popular iron ever used, a double pointed iron with detachable handle that was cast hollow rather than solid; her irons were manufactured from 1871 until 1951; also jointly held one patent for a medical device with husband, an early version of a heating pad. ❖ See also *Women in World History.*

PÖTZSCH, Anett (1961—). East German figure skater. Name variations: Anett Potzsch or Poetzsch; Anett Poetzsch-Rauschenbach; frequently misspelled Annet or Annett. Born Karl-Marx-Stadt (now Chemnitz), East Germany, in 1961; m. Axel Witt (brother of skater Katerina Witt). ❖ Won a gold medal at Lake Placid (1980), the 1st East German to win a gold medal in Olympic figure skating; won the World championship (1978, 1980); won the European championship (1980). ❖ See also *Women in World History.*

POUGHT, Emma (1942—). American singer. Name variations: The Bobbettes. Born April 28, 1942, in New York, NY; sister of Jannie Pought (singer). ❖ Was second lead singer of The Bobbettes, the 1st female vocal group with #1 R&B hit and Top-10 hit on pop charts: "Mr. Lee" (1957); with The Bobbettes, toured with Clyde McPhatter and Ruth Brown. Other singles by The Bobbettes include "Have Mercy, Baby" (1960), "Dance With Me, Georgie" (1960), and "I Don't Like It Like That, Part 1" (1961).

POUGHT, Jannie (1944–1980). American singer. Name variations: Janice Pought; The Bobbettes. Born Janice Pought, Jan 11, 1944, in New York, NY; died Sept 1980 in New Jersey; sister of Emma Pought (singer). ❖ Sang with The Bobbettes, the 1st female vocal group with Top-10 hit on pop charts: "Mr. Lee" (1957); with group, had other hit singles "Have Mercy, Baby" (1960), "Dance With Me, Georgie" (1960) and "I Don't Like It Like That, Part 1" (1961).

POUGY, Liane de (1866–c. 1940). French courtesan. Name variations: Princess Ghika. Born Anne de Chassaigne c. 1866; died after 1936; dau. of an army officer; educated at the Sacred Heart in Rennes; married a naval officer at age 19 (div. soon after); m. Prince Georges Ghika of Moldavia (penniless Romanian aristocrat and nephew of the queen of Greece). ❖ One of the most important *grande horizontals* of the Belle Epoque, had beauty, style, poise, and class, not to mention her skill at the guitar and piano; admirers included Pierre de Nolhac, curator of the Versailles museum, Henri Meilhac, a book writer for operettas, Jean Lorrain, a columnist, and poets Catulle Mendès and Robert de Montesquiou. Eighty small volumes written by de Pougy, which contain her memoirs, reside at the Bibliothèque Nationale. ❖ See also *Women in World History.*

POUGY, Odette de. *See Odette de Pougy.*

POULAIN, Mme (c. 1750–c. 1800). French poet and essayist. Name variations: Mademoiselle Poulain de Nogent. Born c. 1750; died c. 1800. ❖ Works include *Lettre de Mme la comtesse de la Rivière* (1776), *Tableau de la parole* (1783), *Anecdotes intéressantes* (1786), and *Poésies diverses* (1787); also wrote short history of Port Royal (1786).

POULOS, Leah (b. 1951). *See Mueller, Leah Poulos.*

POUND, Ginger (1918—). *See Booth, Adrian.*

POUND, Louise (1872–1958). American scholar. Born June 30, 1872, in Lincoln, Nebraska; died June 28, 1958, in Lincoln; dau. of Stephen Bosworth Pound (state senator) and Laura (Biddlecombe) Pound; University of Nebraska, BL, 1892, AM, 1895; awarded PhD in Heidelberg, Germany, 1900. ❖ An expert on American speech and folklore, founded and served as senior editor of *American Speech*; taught at University of Nebraska; was the 1st woman president of Modern Language Association (1955); published *Folk-Song of Nebraska and the Central West: A Syllabus* (1915) and *Nebraska Folklore* (1959). ❖ See also *Women in World History*.

POUNDER, Cheryl (1976—). Canadian ice-hockey player. Born June 21, 1976, in Mississauga, Ontario, Canada; graddau. of Phil Wimmer (general manager of Montreal Junior Canadiens); graduate of Wilfrid Laurier University in kinesiology. ❖ Won a gold medal at World championships (2001), a gold medal at Salt Lake City Olympics (2002), and a gold medal at Torino Olympics (2006), won 3 World titles with Canadian national team.

POUNDS, Louie (1872—). English actress and singer. Born 1872 in Kensington, England; sister of Courtice Pounds (tenor), Lily, Nancy and Rosy Pounds (all appeared with D'Oyly Carte). ❖ Made stage debut in provinces under George Edwardes' management (1890) and London debut at the Opéra Comique; created role of Heart's Desire in *The Rose of Persia* (1899), Molly O'Grady in *The Emerald Isle* (1901), Christina in *Ib and Little Christina* (1901), Jill-all-Alone in *Merrie England* (1902), Joy Jellicoe in *A Princess of Kensington* (1903), all for the Savoy theater.

POVITCH, Anna (1890–1974). *See Portapovitch, Anna Knapton.*

POWDERMAKER, Hortense (1896–1970). American anthropologist, ethnologist, and educator. Born Dec 24, 1896, in Philadelphia, Pennsylvania; died June 15, 1970; dau. of Louis Powdermaker (businessman) and Minnie (Jacoby) Powdermaker; younger sister of Florence Powdermaker, psychiatrist; Goucher College, BA, 1919; London School of Economics, PhD, 1928; studied with anthropologist Bronislaw Malinowski; children: foster son, Won Mo Kim. ❖ The 1st woman ethnologist to live alone among the Melanesians of New Ireland, an island belonging to the Bismarck Archipelago in Southwest Pacific, published her study, *Life in Lesu* (1933); worked at Yale University's Institute of Human Relations with National Research Council (1930–32); conducted a study of rural Indianola, Mississippi, the 1st community study to be conducted by an anthropologist in US (1932); also helped psychologist John Dollard survey Indianola, then published *After Freedom* (1939) a survey of the social structure of the black and white communities of that town; joined teaching staff at Queens College in NYC (1938), where she became a full professor (1954) and taught anthropology until her retirement (1968); offered a course on cultural anthropology at William Alanson White Institute (1944–52) and in psychiatry department at New York College of Medicine (1958); published *Hollywood, The Dream Factory* (1950); spent a year in Northern Rhodesia (later Zambia), studying relationship between mass media and social change (1953–54), which resulted in *Copper Town* (1962); served as president of American Ethnological Society (1946–47). ❖ See also memoir *Stranger and Friend: The Way of an Anthropologist* (Norton, 1966); and *Women in World History*.

POWE, Sarah (1983—). *See Poewe, Sarah.*

POWELL, Dawn (1897–1965). American writer. Born Nov 28, 1897, in Mount Gilead, Ohio; died Nov 15, 1965, in New York, NY; dau. of Roy K. Powell and Hattie B. (Sherman) Powell; Lake Erie College, BA, 1918; m. Joseph Roebuck Gousha (advertising executive), Nov 20, 1920 (died 1962); children: Joseph Jr. (b. 1921). ❖ A brilliant satirist, whose work began receiving renewed attention at end of 20th century, ran away from home at 12, after her stepmother incinerated the stories she had been writing; moved in with an aunt in Shelby, Ohio; moved to NY (1918); published 1st novel, *Whither* (1925), followed by *She Walks in Beauty* (1928), after collecting more than 35 rejection slips; followed this with *The Bride's House* (1929), *Dance Night* (1930), *The Tenth Moon* (1932), *The Story of a Country Boy* (1934), *Turn, Magic Wheel* (1936), *Angels on Toast* (1940) and *My Home Is Far Away: An Autobiographical Novel* (1944), among others; in all, wrote 15 novels, more than 100 short stories and a half-dozen plays, including 1933's *Big Night*, which was produced by Theater Guild. ❖ See also Tim Page, *Dawn Powell* (Holt, 1998); Tim Page, ed. *The Diaries of Dawn Powell, 1931–1965* (Steerforth, 1995); and *Women in World History*.

POWELL, Dilys (1901–1995). English film critic. Born Dilys Elizabeth Powell, July 20, 1901, in London, England; died June 3, 1995, in London; attended Somerville College, Oxford; m. Humfry Payne (classical archeologist, director of British School of Athens), 1926 (died 1936); m. Leonard Russell (literary editor for *The Sunday Times*), 1943. ❖ Outspoken and powerful film critic, began work at *The Sunday Times* (1928) and remained with newspaper for 40 years; also wrote reviews for *Punch* (1979–92); compilations include *The Golden Screen* (1989) and *The Dilys Powell Film Reader* (1991); wrote *The Traveler's Journey Is Done* (1943), after 1st husband's sudden death, and published *The Villa Ariadne* (1973). Awarded Commander of British Empire (CBE, 1974).

POWELL, Eleanor (1910–1982). American dancer and actress. Born Nov 21, 1910, in Springfield, Massachusetts; died of cancer, Feb 11, 1982; m. Glenn Ford (actor), 1943 (div. 1959); children: Peter. ❖ Star of MGM musicals (1930s–40s), made only 13 movies during Hollywood career but her dancing talent and exuberance have never been duplicated; on Broadway, landed a part in *Follow Thru* (1929), after which she did a string of shows, including *George White's Music Hall Varieties* (1932); made MGM debut in *Broadway Melody of 1936* (1935), executing a couple of dazzling tap numbers that catapulted her into stardom; other films include *Born to Dance* (1936), *Broadway Melody of 1938* (1937), *Rosalie* (1937), *Broadway Melody of 1940* (1940), *Lady Be Good* (1941) and *Thousands Cheer* (1943); retired (1950); became an ordained minister of the Unity Church (1964). ❖ See also *Women in World History*.

POWELL, Jane (1929—). American singer and actress. Born Suzanne Burce, April 1, 1929, in Portland, OR; m. Geary Anthony Steffen Jr. (professional ice skater), 1949 (div.); m. Patrick Nerney (writer), 1954 (div. 1963); m. James Fitzgerald (later her manager), 1965 (div. 1976); m. David Parlour (producer-director), 1978 (div. 1981); m. Dickie Moore (former child star), 1988; children: (1st m.) Geary Anthony Steffen (b. 1951), Suzanne Irene Steffen (b. 1952); (2nd m.) daughter, Lindsay Averille Nerney (b. 1956). ❖ At 5, made singing debut on a Portland children's radio show; at 11, landed her own Sunday evening radio program; made film debut in *Song of the Open Road* (1944), with W. C. Fields (1944); appeared in *Holiday in Mexico* (1946), singing "Ave Maria"; lit up a series of MGM musicals (1946–54), including *A Date with Judy* (1948), *Royal Wedding* (1951), and *Seven Brides for Seven Brothers* (1954), her last 1st-rate screen role; on stage, replaced Debbie Reynolds in a revival of *Irene* (1974); on tv, had a recurring role in soap opera "Loving" and made an occasional guest appearance on such shows as "Murder, She Wrote" and "Growing Pains." ❖ See also autobiography *The Girl Next Door and How She Grew* (1988); and *Women in World History*.

POWELL, Katrina (1972—). Australian field-hockey player. Born April 18, 1972, in Canberra, ACT, Australia. ❖ Forward; won team gold medals at Atlanta Olympics (1996) and Sydney Olympics (2000).

POWELL, Kristy (1980—). American gymnast. Born Feb 13, 1980, in FL. ❖ Won American Cup (1995); won a gold medal for team all-around at Pan American Games (1995); tied for 1st at US nationals (1997).

POWELL, Lisa (1970—). Australian field-hockey player. Name variations: Lisa Carruthers. Born Lisa Josephine Powell, July 8, 1970, in Sydney, NSW, Australia; moved to Canberra at age 2. ❖ Forward, won team gold medals at Atlanta Olympics (1996) and Sydney Olympics (2000).

POWELL, Lois Harris (1940—). *See Harris, Lois.*

POWELL, Louise Mathilde (1871–1943). American nursing educator. Born Mar 12, 1871, in Staunton, VA; died Oct 6, 1943, near Brownsburg, VA; dau. of Hugh Lee Powell and Ella (Stribling) Powell. ❖ Served as superintendent of nurses at St. Luke's Hospital in Richmond, VA (1899–1904); enrolled in graduate nursing program of Columbia University Teachers College (1908); was superintendent of University of Minnesota School of Nursing (1910–24) and acting superintendent of University of Minnesota hospital (1918–19); was dean of Western Reserve University School of Nursing (1924–27).

POWELL, Mary Sadler (1854/55?–1946). New Zealand temperance reformer, suffragist, and writer. Name variations: Aunt Kate. Born probably in 1854 or 1855, in Gloucestershire, England; died Mar 8, 1946, in Dunedin, New Zealand; dau. of William Powell (cleric) and Mary (Sadler) Powell. ❖ Immigrated to New Zealand (1885); active in New Zealand Women's Christian Temperance Union (WCTU), from 1885, and organized for New Zealand Alliance; under pen name Aunt

Kate, wrote column "Our Girls" for *New Zealand Methodist*; involved in WCTU's campaign for women's suffrage. ❖ See also *Dictionary of New Zealand Biography* (Vol. 3).

POWELL, Maud (1867–1920). American violinist. Born Aug 22, 1867, in Peru, Illinois; died Jan 8, 1920, in Uniontown, Pennsylvania; dau. of Wilhelmina (Minnie) Bengelstraeter (Paul) Powell (amateur composer and pianist) and (William) Bramwell Powell (nationally known educator and textbook author); began piano lessons with mother at age 4; subsequent piano teachers included Emma Fickensher and Agnes Ingersoll; violin teachers included G. William Fickensher, William Lewis, Henry Schradieck, Charles Dancla, and Joseph Joachim; m. H. Godfrey "Sunny" Turner (concert manager), Sept 21, 1904; no children. ❖ Concert artist, the 1st American violinist to win international critical acclaim, made debut (1876); studied at Leipzig Conservatory (1881–82), then Paris Conservatory (1882–83); toured UK (1883–84); studied at Berlin Hochschule (1884–85); performed as a soloist with Joseph Joachim conducting the Berlin Philharmonic (1885); made NY debut with Theodore Thomas conducting New York Philharmonic (1885); toured western US (1887–88); gave US premiere of Tchaikovsky Violin Concerto (1889) and Dvorak Violin Concerto (1894); made European tour with Arion Society (1892); chosen as representative American violinist for Theodore Thomas' Exposition Orchestra concerts at World's Columbian Exposition in Chicago (1893); delivered a paper on "Women and the Violin" and premiered Amy Beach's "Romance" with Beach at the piano at Women's Musical Congress (1893); formed Maud Powell String Quartet (1894); toured Europe (1898–1905), twice as soloist with John Philip Sousa and his band (1903, 1905); was the 1st solo instrumentalist to record for Victor's Celebrity Artist series (Red Seal label, 1904–19); led her own concert company on tour of South Africa (1905); gave US premiere of Sibelius Violin Concerto (1906); formed Maud Powell Trio (1908–09); performed for US soldiers during WWI (1917–18); easily ranked among the supreme violinists of her time, was also a popular favorite, winning the affection of US public with her unabashed enthusiasm for the violin. ❖ See also Karen A. Shaffer and Neva Garner Greenwood. *Maud Powell, Pioneer American Violinist* (Iowa State U. Press, 1988); and *Women in World History*.

POWELL, Olave Baden- (1889–1977). *See Baden-Powell, Olave.*

POWELL, Sandy (1960—). English costume designer. Born April 7, 1960, in London, England; attended Central Saint Martin's College of Art & Design. ❖ Began career as an assistant designer in theater; costumed over 25 films beginning with *Caravaggio* (1986); other films include *Edward II* (1991), *The Crying Game* (1992), *Interview with the Vampire* (1994), *Rob Roy* (1995), *Michael Collins* (1996) and *Hilary and Jackie* (1998); nominated for Academy Awards for *Orlando* (1992), *The Wings of the Dove* (1997), *Velvet Goldmine* (1999), *Shakespeare in Love* (1999) and *Gangs of New York* (2002); won an Oscar for *The Aviator* (2004).

POWELL, Susan (c. 1959—). Miss America. Born Susan Powell c. 1959 in Elk City, Oklahoma; graduate of Oklahoma City University. ❖ Named Miss America (1981), representing Oklahoma; hosts "Home Matters" for the Discovery Channel.

POWER, Eileen (1889–1940). English historian. Name variations: Eileen Postan. Born Eileen Edna le Poer in Altrincham, Cheshire, England, 1889; died 1940; dau. of a London stockbroker; obtained a 1st in history at Girton College, Cambridge, 1910; studied in Paris and Chartres, 1910; attended London School of Economics, 1911–13; m. Michael Postan. ❖ Carried out her groundbreaking work in women's history as director in history studies at Girton College, Cambridge (1913–20), lecturer and reader in economic history at the University of London (1924–31), and professor of economic history at London School of Economics (1931–40); writings include a study of community life in *Medieval English Nunneries c. 1275–1535* (1922), *Medieval People* (1924), a translation of *Le ménagier de Paris* (*The Goodman of Paris*, 1928) and Michael Postan, ed. *Medieval Women* (1975); also helped to found *Economic History Review* (1927).

POWER, Jennie Wyse (1858–1941). *See Wyse Power, Jennie.*

POWER, Laurel Jean (1953—). Australian politician. Born Dec 7, 1953, in Augathella, Queensland, Australia. ❖ As a member of the Australian Labor Party, served in the Queensland Parliament for Mansfield (1989–95).

POWER, Marguerite (1789–1849). *See Blessington, Marguerite, Countess of.*

POWERS, Georgia Davis (1923—). African-American politician. Name variations: Mrs. James L. Powers. Born Georgia Montgomery, Oct 29, 1923, in Springfield, Kentucky; dau. of Ben Montgomery and Frances (Walker) Montgomery; attended Louisville Municipal College, 1940–42; m. Norman F. Davis, 1943 (div. 1968); m. James L. Powers, 1973 (div.); m. a 3rd time; children: (1st m.) William Davis. ❖ Served as the 1st African-American and 1st woman elected to Kentucky State Senate (1967–88); marched with Dr. Martin Luther King Jr. on the Kentucky state capital of Frankfort and elsewhere (1960s); chaired Jesse Jackson's presidential campaigns in Kentucky (1984, 1988). Awarded Anderson Laureate from state of Kentucky (1991); was also among the 1st 21 inductees of Kentucky Commission on Human Rights Hall of Fame. ❖ See also memoir *I Shared the Dream: The Pride, Passion, and Politics of the First Black Woman Senator from Kentucky* (New Horizon, 1995); and *Women in World History*.

POWERS, Harriet (1837–1911). African-American quilter. Born Harriet, last name unknown, into slavery in Clarke Co., Georgia, 1837; died 1911; m. Armstead Powers (farmhand); children: 2 born in slavery—Amanda (b. 1855) and LeonJoe (b. 1860)—and Nancy (born free, 1866). ❖ One of America's finest quilters, completed a quilt consisting of 11 squares depicting Biblical scenes (1886), which was eventually displayed at the Smithsonian. ❖ See also *Women in World History*.

POWERS, Leona (1896–1970). American stage, radio, and tv actress. Born Mar 13, 1896, in Salida, CO; died Jan 7, 1970, in New York, NY; m. Howard Miller (actor). ❖ At 5, made stage debut in Chicago; made NY debut as Ruth in *The Charity Nurse* (1903); on Broadway, appeared in *Mary of Scotland, End of Summer, The Moon is Down, Dear Ruth, The Big Knife, Wallflower* and *My Father and Me*; made film debut in *Sweet September* (1935); had her own theatrical company in New Orleans; on radio, appeared on "The Aldrich Family."

POWERS, Mala (1931—). American stage, radio and screen actress. Born Mary Ellen Powers, Dec 29, 1931, in San Francisco, CA. ❖ At 11, made film debut in *Tough as They Come* (1942), followed by *Outrage, Cyrano de Bergerac* (as Roxane), *Rose of Cimarron, City Beneath the Sea, City That Never Sleeps, Tammy and the Batchelor* and *Six Tickets to Hell*; appeared regularly on radio in "Cisco Kid," "Red Ryder," "This is Your FBI" and "Lux Radio Theater"; teaches the Michael Chekhov acting technique.

POWERS, Marie (1902–1973). American contralto. Born June 20, 1902, in Mount Carmel, PA; died Dec 28 (or 29), 1973, in New York, NY; m. Count Luigi Crescenti (died 1938). ❖ First appeared in a Wagnerian cycle at La Scala; had enormous success in Menotti's *The Medium* (1947), singing 2,341 performances, starring in a film adaptation in Europe and recording it for Decca; other NY appearances include *Noye's Fludde, The Old Maid and the Thief, Becket* and Menotti's *The Consul*; could sing 50 operatic roles in 10 languages, favored roles being Dalila, Messalina, and Orpheus; also appeared on radio and tv.

POWYS, queen of. *See Susan of Powys (fl. 1100).*

POYNINGS, Eleanor (d. 1483). Countess of Northumberland. Died 1483; dau. of Richard de Poynings; m. Henry Percy (1421–1461), earl of Northumberland (r. 1455–1461), killed at the battle of Towton), on June 25, 1435; children: Eleanor Percy (d. 1530); Henry Percy (b. around 1449), earl of Northumberland; Elizabeth Percy (who m. Henry, Lord Scrope of Bolton); Anne Percy (who m. Sir Thomas Hungerford and Sir Laurence Rainsford); Margaret Percy (who m. Sir William Gascoigne).

POYNINGS, Philippa (1375–1401). *See Mortimer, Philippa.*

POYNTON, Dorothy (1915—). American diver. Name variations: Dorothy Poynton-Hill or Dorothy Poynton Hill. Born Dorothy Poynton, July 17, 1915, in Portland, OR. ❖ At 13, was the youngest American to win an Olympic medal, taking the silver in springboard diving at Amsterdam (1928); won a gold medal in platform at Los Angeles Olympics (1932); won a gold medal in platform and a bronze medal in springboard at the Berlin Olympics (1936); ran the Dorothy Poynton Swim Club in Los Angeles.

POYNTZ, Juliet Stuart (1886–c. 1937). American spy for Soviet secret police. Name variations: Juliet Poyntz; Juliet Stuart Points. Born Juliet Stuart Points (changed name to Poyntz, c. 1913), Nov 25, 1886, in Omaha, Nebraska; disappeared early June 1937; valedictorian at Barnard College, 1907; m. Friedrich Franz Ludwig Glaser (attaché at German consulate in NY), 1913. ❖ Socialist, feminist, and trade unionist, married a Communist (1913) and became a founding member of American Communist Party (1919); listed as 1 of 10 principal Communist leaders of the US in NY Police files, went to work for Soviet secret police (OGPU) as spy (c. 1934); after she witnessed Stalin's purges on a trip to Moscow (1936), broke ties with Communism and was unwilling to continue work for OGPU; left her room at the American Woman's Association Clubhouse in NY one evening in early June 1937 and was never seen again; thought to have been murdered by OGPU.

POYSTI, Toini K. Finnish cross-country skier. Name variations: Poeysti, Pöysti or Püysti. Born in Finland. ❖ Won a bronze medal at Squaw Valley Olympics (1960) and at Innsbruck Olympics (1964), both for 3 x 5 km relay.

POZZI, Antonia (1912–1938). Italian poet. Born 1912 in Milan, Italy; committed suicide at 26 in 1938; dau. of Lina Cavagna Sangiuliani and Roberto Pozzi (lawyer); attended University of Milan. ❖ Work praised by Elsa Morante, published *Parole* (1939) and *Flaubert: la formazione letteraria* (1940); upset with the winds of war beginning to swirl around her, took her life.

POZZO, Modesta (1555–1592). Italian poet. Name variations: (pseudonym) Moderata Fonte. Born 1555 in Venice, Italy; died in childbirth in 1592; m. Giovanni Nicolò Doglioni. ❖ Well educated, was encouraged by husband to continue studies; writings include *Tredici canti del Floridoro* (1581), *Le feste: Rappresentazione avanti il Serenissimo Principe di Venezia Nicolò da Ponte* (1581), and *Il Merito delle Donne* (1600), her best known work, which contributed to the debate over the relationship between the sexes.

PRAAGH, Margaret van (1910–1990). See Van Praagh, Peggy.

PRACHT, Eva-Maria (1937—). Canadian equestrian. Born June 29, 1937, in Ontario, Canada; children: Martina Pracht (equestrian). ❖ At Seoul Olympics, won a bronze medal in team dressage (1988).

PRADO, Adélia (1936—). Brazilian poet and short-story writer. Name variations: Adelia Luzia Prado de Freitas. Born Dec 13, 1936, in Divinópolis, Brazil. ❖ Works, which often focus on life in Brazil from a woman's perspective, include *Bagagem* (1976), *O coraçao disparado* (1978), *Solte os cachorros* (1979), *Cacos para um vitral* (1980), *Os componentes da banda* (1984) and *A faca no peito* (1988).

PRAED, Rosa (1851–1935). Australian-born writer. Name variations: Rosa Caroline Praed; (pseudonym) Mrs. Campbell Praed. Born Rosa Murray-Prior, Mar 27, 1851, near Beaudesert, southern Queensland, Australia; died April 13, 1935, in Torquay, England; dau. of Thomas Lodge Murray-Prior (pastoralist and later postmaster-general of Queensland); m. Arthur Campbell Praed, 1872 (sep. 1880s); children: 1 daughter, 3 sons. ❖ Born in the Australian Outback, spent early childhood on stations in Burnett River district of Queensland; with husband, owned a station at Port Curtis, near Gladstone; sailed for England with family (1875), where she would spend rest of her days, but conditions of life in the bush had made a strong impression, and would provide fodder for a number of her novels; published 1st book, *An Australian Heroine* (1880), which drew heavily on the early years of her marriage; wrote some 40 novels, including *Policy and Passion* (1881), *Nadine* (1882), *The Head Station* (1885), *Australian Life: Black and White* (1885), *Miss Jacobsen's Chance* (1886), *The Romance of a Station* (1889), *Nulma* (1897), *As a Watch in the Night* (1900), *My Australian Girlhood* (1902), *Dwellers by the River* (1902), *The Ghost* (1903), *Nyria* (1904), *The Luck of Leura* (1907), *Lady Bridget in the Never-Never Land* (1915) and *Soul of Nyria* (1931). ❖ See also Colin Roderick, *In Mortal Bondage: The Strange Life of Rosa Praed* (1948); and *Women in World History*.

PRAEGER, Sophia Rosamund (1867–1954). Irish sculptor, author, and illustrator of children's books. Born in Holywood, Co. Down, Ireland, 1867; died 1954; studied art at Belfast School of Art and Slade School, London; also studied in Paris. ❖ Achieved fame with sculpture *The Philosopher*, now displayed in the Colorado Springs Museum and Art Gallery; other works, executed mostly in plaster, and including relief panels and memorial plaques and stones, have been exhibited in London, Paris, and at Irish Decorative Art Association; also wrote and illustrated children's books, including 3 in collaboration with brother Robert Praeger; served as president of Royal Ulster Academy. Awarded MBE (1939).

PRANG, Mary D. Hicks (1836–1927). American arts educator. Name variations: Mary Dana Hicks; Mrs. Louis Prang. Born Mary Amelia Dana, Oct 7, 1836, in Syracuse, NY; died Nov 7, 1927, in Stoneham, MA; dau. of Major Dana (merchant) and Agnes Amelia Livington (Johnson) Dana; m. Charles Spencer Hicks (lawyer), Oct 7, 1856 (died 1858); Louis Prang (lithographer and arts-supplies manufacturer), April 15, 1900 (died June 14, 1909); children: (1st m.) 1 daughter. ❖ Became supervisor of drawing for schools in Syracuse (1868); worked for Prang Educational Co. (1879–1900), including as director of correspondence normal school (from 1884); served as president of Civic Club of Ward 19 in Boston, MA (1909–12). Through collaboration on Prang's correspondence-school manuals, helped disseminate principles of German educator Friedrich Froebel.

PRASKOVYA SALTYKOVA (1664–1723). See Saltykova, Praskovya.

PRATT, Adelaide Minola (1895–1994). See Luxford, Nola.

PRATT, Anna Beach (1867–1932). American social worker. Born June 5, 1867, in Elmira, NY; died Jan 3, 1932, in Philadelphia, PA; dau. of Timothy Smith Pratt (dry-goods merchant) and Catherine Elizabeth (Beach) Pratt; University of Pennsylvania, MA, 1916. ❖ Established Alpha Club to provide relaxation and recreation for female workers in knitting mills in Elmira area; served as secretary and overseer of Bureau of Associated Relief to 1916; appointed executive of Magdalen Society of Philadelphia (1916); selected for seat on Philadelphia Board of Education (1929); established casework and counseling services in Philadelphia public schools, and was influential interpreter of social-work theory, training, and practice (1920s).

PRATT, Anne (1806–1893). British botanist and author. Born in Strood, Kent, England, 1806; died in London, July 1893; dau. of Robert Pratt (grocer) and Sarah Pratt; m. John Peerless, 1866. ❖ As a child, created an herbarium which became quite valuable; published 1st book, *The Field, The Garden and The Woodland*, at 20, and wrote 16 additional botanical volumes during lifetime; began best-known and most extensive work, *The Flowering Plants and Ferns of Great Britain* (1849), which included 5 vols. at time of publication (1855); also wrote *Flowers and their Associations, Pratt's Catechism of Botany* and *Common Things of the Seashore*. ❖ See also *Women in World History*.

PRATT, Daria (1861–1938). American golfer. Born 1861 in US; died June 26, 1938. ❖ At Paris Olympics, won a bronze medal in singles (1900).

PRATT, Dolly (1955—). Australian politician. Born Mar 11, 1955, in Coffs Harbour, Queensland, Australia. ❖ Was a member of Pauline Hanson's One Nation Party (1998–99); as an Independent, elected to the Queensland Parliament for Nanango (2001).

PRATT, Eliza Jane (1902–1981). American politician. Born Mar 5, 1902, in Morven, Anson Co., North Carolina; died May 13, 1981, in Charlotte, NC. ❖ Was a newspaper editor at Troy, NC (1923–24); elected as Democrat to 79th Congress to fill vacancy, serving from May 25, 1946, to Jan 3, 1947; employed with Office of Alien Property in Washington (1947–51), Department of Agriculture (1951–54) and Library of Congress (1954–56).

PRATT, Ruth (1877–1965). American politician. Name variations: Ruth Sears Baker Pratt. Born Aug 24, 1877, in Ware, Massachusetts; died Aug 23, 1965, in Glen Cove, New York; dau. of a manufacturer; educated at Wellesley College; m. John T. Pratt. ❖ A staunch Republican, was appointed vice-chair of Republican National Ways and Means Committee (1918); elected to NY Board of Aldermen (1925 and 1927), the 1st woman to serve in that post; was responsible for legislation to construct tunnels under the East River to connect Manhattan with the city's outer boroughs; won NY's 17th District (known as the "Silk Stocking" district) seat in US House of Representatives (1929); during term, served on Committee on Banking and Currency, Committee on the Library, and Committee on Education; supported repeal of Prohibition, and (1930) sought legislation that would appropriate funds to publish books for the blind; was also in favor of Hoover's refusal to provide federal funds for relief of the unemployed as the Great Depression took hold; as the Depression deepened, was defeated in bid for a 3rd term (1933); was a member of Republican National Committee (1929–43); served as president of Woman's National Republican Club (1943–46), and also served as chair of Fine Arts Foundation, a predecessor to National Endowment for the Humanities.

PRAXILLA (fl. 450 BCE). Greek musician and poet. Born in Sicyon. ❖ One of the nine "lyric" Muses, composed poetry from the Dorian school, poems that were considered equal to those of Alcaeus and

Anacreon; her songs, known as drinking songs (*skolias* or *scolias*), were often sung at banquets; was also the author of epic poem *Adonia* as well as dithyrambs and hymns, chiefly on mystic and mythological subjects, genealogies, and the love stories of the gods and heroes.

PRAY, Anna (1830–1906). *See Florence, Malvina Pray.*

PREBBLE, Mary Elizabeth (1833–1924). *See Dawson, Mary Elizabeth.*

PREDESLAVA OF HUNGARY (fl. 960). Princess of Kiev. Dau. of Taskany also seen as Taksony (931–972), prince of Hungary, also known as prince of the Magyars; m. Svyatoslav I, prince of Kiev; children: Yaropolk I (b. around 958), prince of Kiev; Oleg (b. around 959). ❖ See also *Women in World History.*

PREIS, Ellen (1912—). German-Jewish fencer. Name variations: Ellen Müller-Preis; Ellen Mueller or Muller-Preis. Born Ellen Preis, May 6, 1912, in Berlin-Charlottenburg, Germany; niece of Wilhelmine Werdnik (fencing master). ❖ Became Austrian fencing champion at age 12; considered one of the greatest female fencers in history, participated in 5 Olympics representing Austria (1932, 1936, 1948, 1952, 1956), winning a gold medal in indiv. foil in Los Angeles (1932), a bronze medal in Berlin (1936), and, as Ellen Müller-Preis, a bronze medal in London (1948); won gold medal at World championships (1947, 1949, 1950).

PREISS, Julia (1902–1980). *See Brystygierowa, Julia.*

PREISSER, Cherry (1918–1964). American acrobatic dancer. Born 1918 in New Orleans, LA; died July 12, 1964, in Sydney, Australia; sister of June Preisser (1920–1984, dancer); m. David J. Hopkins, 1937. ❖ With sister June, won international fame with an acrobatic dance act, the Preisser Sisters, in vaudeville and revues (1920s–30s); also appeared with her in *Ziegfeld Follies* (1934, 1936); retired (1937).

PREISSER, June (1920–1984). American actress and dancer. Name variations: June Terry; Preisser Sisters. Born June 26, 1920, in New Orleans, LA; died Sept 19, 1984, along with her son, in auto accident in Boca Raton, FL; sister of Cherry Preisser (d. 1964, dancer); children: J. Moss Terry IV. ❖ With sister Cherry, had international vaudeville acrobatic dance act (The Preisser Sisters) and made Broadway debut at 17 in *Ziegfeld Follies* (1934); with sister's retirement (1937), went solo, making film debut in *Babes in Arms* (1939); often appeared as the ingenue girlfriend in such films as *Judge Hardy and Son, Strike Up the Band, Henry Aldrich for President, Merrily We Sing, Junior Prom* and *The Music Man*; opened a string of dance studios in Los Angeles area.

PREISSER SISTERS.
See Preisser, Cherry.
See Preisser, June.

PREISSOVA, Gabriela (1862–1946). Czech short-story writer and playwright. Name variations: Gabriela Preissová; Gabriela Pressova or Pressová. Born Gabriela Sekerová in Kuttenberg, Austrian Moravia (modern-day Kutná Hora, Czech Republic), Mar 23, 1862; died in Prague, Mar 27, 1946; married twice. ❖ Her naturalistic drama *Gazdina roba* (*The Farm Mistress* or *The Farmer's Maidservant*) was produced at Prague National Theater to great success (1889); wrote a less successful 2nd play, *Její pastorkyna* (Her Stepdaughter, 1890). Both plays were turned into operas: *Gazdina Roba* was the basis for Josef Bohuslav Foerster's *Eva* (1899) and *Její pastorkyna* was the basis for Leos Janacek's *Jenufa* (1904). ❖ See also *Women in World History.*

PREJEAN, Helen (1939—). American nun and death-penalty opponent. Name variations: Sister Helen Prejean C.S.J. Born April 21, 1939, in Baton Rouge, LA; dau. of a lawyer and a nurse; St. Mary's Dominican College, BA, 1962; St. Paul's University in Ottawa, MA in religious education, 1973. ❖ Joined the Sisters of St. Joseph of Medaille in New Orleans (1957); began her prison ministry (1981); wrote *Dead Man Walking: An Eyewitness Account of the Death Penalty in the United States* (1993); served as chair of the board of the National Coalition to Abolish the Death Penalty (1993–95). Received the Peace Prize of the City of Ypres (2005).

PRELLE, Micheline (b. 1922). *See Presle, Micheline.*

PREMICE, Josephine (1926–2001). Haitian-American actress. Born Josephine Premice, July 21, 1926, in Brooklyn, NY, to Haitian parents; died April 13, 2001, in New York, NY; studied dance with Martha Graham and Katherine Dunham; m. Capt. Timity Fales, 1960; children: Susan Fales-Hill (producer) and Enrico Fales (actor). ❖ Nominated for Tony Awards for performances in the musical *Jamaica* (1957) and *A Hand Is on the Gate* (1967), also starred in *Bubbling Brown Sugar* (1976–77); was a frequent guest on tv's "Merv Griffin Show" and appeared as Louise Jefferson's sister on "The Jeffersons."

PREMONT, Marie-Hélène (1977—). Canadian cyclist. Name variations: Marie-Helene Premont. Born Oct 24, 1977, in Quebec City, Quebec, Canada. ❖ Won a silver medal for cross country at Athens Olympics (2004); placed 3rd overall in World Cup ranking for cross country (2004).

PRENDERGAST, Sharon Marley (1964—). Jamaican singer. Name variations: Ziggy Marley and the Melody Makers; Sharon Marley. Born Nov 23, 1964, in Kingston, Jamaica; dau. of Bob Marley (reggae singer); half-sister of Cedella, David "Ziggy" Marley and Stephen Marley. ❖ With Marley siblings, formed Ziggy Marley and the Melody Makers in Kingston and recorded single, "Children Playing in the Streets" (1979); with group, signed with EMI America and released pop-reggae albums, *Play the Game Right* (1985) and *Hey World!* (1986); with group, moved to Virgin Records and released successful album, *Conscious Party* (1988), which included hit, "Tomorrow People"; appeared in film, *The Mighty Quinn* (1989). Other albums include *One Bright Day* (1989), *Free Like We Want* (1995), and *Fallen Is Babylon* (1997).

PRENTICE, Bridget (1952—). Scottish politician and member of Parliament. Born Bridget Corr, Dec 28, 1952, in Glasgow, Scotland; dau. of James (a joiner) and Bridget Corr (clerical worker); University of Glasgow, MA; South Bank University, LLB; m. Gordon Prentice (MP), 1975 (div. 2000). ❖ Representing Labour, elected to House of Commons for Lewisham East (1992); reelected (1997, 2001, 2005); appointed government whip (1997).

PRENTICE, Jo Ann (1933—). American golfer. Name variations: JoAnn Prentice; (nickname) Fry. Born Feb 9, 1933, in Birmingham, Alabama. ❖ Won Jackson Open (1965), Dallas Civitan (1967), Corpus Christi (in 10-hole play-off with Sandra Palmer, 1972), the Burdines (1973), Colgate-Dinah Shore (1974), and LPGA American Defender-Raleigh Classic (1974); had 20 finishes in top 20 (1974).

PRENTISS, Adella (1869–1950). *See Hughes, Adella Prentiss.*

PRENTISS, Elizabeth Payson (1818–1878). American writer. Born Oct 26, 1818, in Portland, Maine; died Aug 13, 1878, in Dorset, Vermont; dau. of Edward Payson (Congregational minister) and Ann Louisa (Shipman) Payson; sister of Louisa Payson (teacher and writer); m. George Lewis Prentiss (Presbyterian minister), April 16, 1845; children: Anna Louise; Mary Williams; George Lewis; Henry Smith; 2 who died in infancy. ❖ Published the 1st of her "Little Susy" series, *Little Susy's Six Birthdays* (1853), to notable success; most popular book, the bestselling *Stepping Heavenward* (1869), had been serialized in *Chicago Advance*; also wrote *The Flower of the Family* (1853), *Henry and Bessie, or, What They Did in the Country* (1855), *Peterchen and Gretchen* (1860), *The Little Preacher* (1867), *Fred, and Maria, and Me* (1867), *The Old Brown Pitcher* (1868), *Nulworth* (1869), *The Percys* (1870), *Six Little Princesses* (1871), *Golden Hours* (1874) and *Avis Benson* (1879); her autobiographical tales of Christian family life included *The Story Lizzie Told* (1870), *The Home at Greylock* (1876), *Pemaquid* (1877) and *Gentleman Jim* (1878), among others; also wrote the hymn, "More Love to Thee, O Christ." ❖ See also *Women in World History.*

PRENTISS, Paula (1939—). American tv and screen actress. Born Paula Ragusa, Mar 4, 1939, in San Antonio, TX; sister of Ann Prentiss (actress); m. Richard Benjamin (actor), 1961. ❖ Made auspicious film debut in *Where the Boys Are* (1960), followed by *Bachelor in Paradise, The Horizontal Lieutenant, Follow the Boys, The World of Henry Orient, In Harm's Way, What's New Pussycat?, Catch-22, Last of the Red Hot Lovers* and *The Stepford Wives*, among others; co-starred with husband on tv series "He and She" (1967–68).

PREOBRAJENSKA, Nina (1956—). *See Preobrazhenskaya, Nina.*

PREOBRAJENSKA, Olga (1871–1962). *See Preobrazhenskaya, Olga.*

PREOBRAZHENSKA, Olga (1871–1962). Russian ballet dancer. Name variations: Ol'ga Iosifovna (or Ossipovna) Preobrazhenskaia; Preobrazhenskaya; Preobrajenska; known to her students as Madame Préo. Born Ol'ga Iosifovna (or Ossipovna) Preobrazhenska, Jan 21 (Feb 2, old style), 1871, in St. Petersburg, Russia; died in Sainte-Mande, France, Dec 27, 1962; at St. Petersburg theater school, studied under Lev Ivanov, Christian Johansson, and Marius Petipa; never married. ❖ Foremost Russian dancer who devoted the last 40 years of her career to teaching in Paris, where she left a profound mark upon ballet in the

Western World; graduated from St. Petersburg theater school (1889); joined Maryinsky Co. and was a leading dancer there for nearly 30 years (1889–1917), becoming a soloist (1896), then prima ballerina (1900); as one of the most important dancers at the Maryinsky, performed a broad and varied range of roles, including almost all the ballets choreographed by Petipa, Ivanov, and Legat, and a number of parts that she was the 1st to perform: Anne in Petipa's *Barbe-Bleu* (*Blue Beard*), Henriette in his *Raymonda* (1898), Pierette in his *Les Millions d'Arlequin* (*Harlequinade*, 1900), the title role in Gerdt's *Javotte* (1902), and Cleopatra's slave in Fokine's *Une Nuit d'Egypte* (*A Night in Egypt*, 1908); also danced in Fokine's *Chopiniana* (1908, 1909), and Tchaikovsky's *Romance*, when she was 44; as she matured, danced Isaure in *Barbe-Bleu* (after 1900), the title role in *Raymonda* (after 1903), and Bérénice in *Une Nuit d'Égypt* (after 1910); also appeared in Petipa's *Esmerelda, Paquita* and *The Talisman*, and in Lev Ivanov's *Acis et Galathée* (*Acis and Galathea*), *Camargo* and *La Fille du Mikado* (*The Mikado's Daughter*); taught at St. Petersburg theater school (1901–02) and Akim Volynsky's School of Russian Ballet (1917–21); immigrated to Berlin (1921); danced there and at La Scala in Milan, Covent Garden in London, and Theatro Colon in Buenos Aires (1922); settled in Paris, where she opened a prominent school of ballet (1923); retired (1960). ❖ See also Elvira Roné, *Olga Preobrazhenskaya* (trans. and adapted by Fernau Hall, 1978); and *Women in World History*.

PREOBRAZHENSKAYA, Nina (1956—). Soviet rower. Name variations: Preobrazhenska, Preobrazhenskaia, or Preobrajenska. Born Feb 16, 1956, in USSR. ❖ At Moscow Olympics, won a silver medal in coxed eights (1980).

PRERADOVIC, Paula von (1887–1951). Austrian writer. Name variations: Paula Preradovic; Paula Molden. Born in Vienna, Austria, Oct 12, 1887; died in Vienna, May 25, 1951; dau. of Dusan von Preradovic (career officer in Austro-Hungarian navy); mother's maiden name was Falke; granddau. of Petar Preradovic (1818–1872), poet of the Croatian National Revival and general in Austrian army; niece of Amalie Falke, author and advocate of women's rights, and Croatian painter Zora von Preradovic (1867–1927); m. Ernst Molden (1886–1953), historian and journalist who became chief of anti-Nazi resistance group), April 1916; children: Fritz and Otto. ❖ Writer whose literary legacy bridged the Slavic and Germanic cultures of Austria and the Balkans, published 1st book of poems *Südlicher Sommer* (Southern Summer, 1929), followed by *Dalmatinische Sonnette* (Dalmatian Sonnets, 1933) and *Lob Gottes im Gebirge* (Praising God in the Mountains, 1936); as a conservative traditionalist linked to the multinational culture of the Habsburgs, writings were anathema to the political Left and even more so to Austria's Nazis; published what would become one of her most impressive literary legacies, her only novel *Pave und Pero* (1940), which received excellent reviews in Austria and enjoyed bestseller status; after the failure of the German resistance plot to assassinate Hitler (July 1944), was arrested, along with husband and many other anti-Nazis, but eventually released; continued to publish after Austria regained its sovereignty (April 1945); her lyric "Land der Berge, Land am Strome" ("Land of Mountains, Land of Streams") was officially adopted as the text of Austria's new national anthem (1947); wrote the novellas *Nach dem Tode* (After Death, 1949), *Königslegende* (Royal Legends, 1950) and *Die Verschwörung des Columba* (The Conspiracy of Columba, 1951). ❖ See also *Women in World History*.

PRESACAN, Claudia (1979—). Romanian gymnast. Name variations: Maria Claudia Presacan. Born Dec 28, 1979, in Sibiu, Romania. ❖ Won Balkan Games (1995), Romanian International (1997); at World championships, won a gold medal in team all-around (1994, 1995, 1997); at Sydney Olympics, won a gold medal for team all-around and placed 4th on beam (2000); retired (2000).

PRESHAW, Jane (1839–1926). New Zealand nurse, midwife, and hospital matron. Name variations: Jane Norgate. Born Jane Norgate, May 30, 1839, in Norfolk, England; died Dec 12, 1926, at Reefton, New Zealand; dau. of Henry Norgate (agricultural laborer) and Jane (Lidle) Norgate; m. Mr. O'Brien, c. 1868; m. David Ogilvy Preshaw (hospital chemist), 1879 (died 1903); children: 1 daughter. ❖ Immigrated to Australia (1856); worked as servant before securing a position as domestic midwife and nurse in Melbourne; sailed for New Zealand with daughter (c. 1868); continued work as midwife and nurse until her appointment as matron of cottage hospital at Reefton (1876–1901). ❖ See also *Dictionary of New Zealand Biography* (Vol. 2).

PRESLAVA OF RUSSIA (fl. 1100). Queen of Hungary. Name variations: Predeslava. 1st wife of Koloman also known as Coloman the Booklover (1070–1114), king of Hungary (r. 1095–1114); children: Stephen II (1100–1131), king of Hungary (r. 1116–1131). ❖ Coloman was also married to Euphemia of Kiev.

PRESLE, Micheline (1922—). French actress. Name variations: Micheline Michel; Micheline Prelle. Born Micheline Chassagne, Aug 22, 1922, in Paris, France; m. William Marshall (American actor), 1950 (div. 1954); children: Tonie Marshall (actess and director). ❖ Made screen debut at 16 in *Je chante* (1938), under name Micheline Michel; attained almost instant success; career peaked (late 1940s), following her role opposite French actor Gérard Philipe in *Le Diable au Corps* (*Devil in the Flesh*, 1947); films include *Jeunes Filles en Détresse* (1939), *Paradis perdu* (*Four Flights to Love*, 1940), *La Comédie du Bonheur* (1942), *Félicie Nanteuil* (1945), *Boule de Suif* (*Angel and Sinner*, 1945), *Les Derniers Jours de Pompéi* (*Sins of Pompeii*, 1948), *Under My Skin* (1950), *An American Guerilla in the Philippines* (1950), *Adventures of Captain Fabian* (1951), *La Dame aux Camélias* (1953), *L'Amour d'une Femme* (1954), *Napoléon* (1955), *Beatrice Cenci* (1956), *If a Man Answers* (1962), *Vénus Impériale* (1962), *The Prize* (1963), *La Religieuse* (*The Nun*, 1965), *Le Roi de Coeur* (*King of Hearts*, 1966), *Le Bal du Comte d'Orgel* (1970), *Nea* (1976), *Le Chien* (1986), *La Fête des Pères* (1990, and *Après Après-Demain* (1990).

PRESS, Irina (1939—). Soviet track-and-field athlete. Born Irina Natanova Press, Mar 10, 1939, in Kharkov, Ukraine; younger sister of Tamara Press; graduate of Leningrad Institute of Railway Engineers, 1962. ❖ At Rome Olympics, won a gold medal in the 80-meter hurdles (1960); at Tokyo Olympics, won a gold medal in the pentathlon (1964); set 6 World records for 80-meter hurdles and 8 for pentathlon.

PRESS, Tamara (1939—). Soviet track-and-field athlete. Born Tamara Natanovna Press, May 10, 1937, in Kharkov, Ukraine; older sister of Irina Press. ❖ At Rome Olympics, won a silver medal for the discus throw and a gold medal for the shot put (1960); at Tokyo Olympics, won gold medals for the discus throw and the shot put (1964); broke 12 World records for shot and discus (1959–65); won 3 European titles; retired (1965) and worked for All-Union Council of Trade Unions.

PRESSOVÁ or PRESSOVA, Gabriela (1862–1946). *See Preissova, Gabriela.*

PRESTES, Olga Benario (1908–1942). *See Benario, Olga.*

PRESTI, Ida (1924–1967). French classical guitarist. Born Yvette Ida Montagnon at Suresnes, France, May 31, 1924; died in Rochester, New York, April 24, 1967; dau. of Italian mother Olga Lo-Presti and French father Claude Montagnon (musician and teacher, died 1939); married, mid-1940s (div.); m. Alexandre Lagoya (guitarist), 1955; children: (1st m.) Elisabeth Rigaud Lagoya; (2nd m.) son, Sylvain. ❖ One of the greatest classical guitarists in musical history, had no other teacher but her father; played for the 1st time in public at 8, and gave her 1st concert in Paris at 10; by 11, had already recorded works such as Federico Moreno-Torroba's *Sonatina* and Manuel Ponce's *Mexican Songs*; often performed with husband Alexandre Lagoya. ❖ See also *Women in World History*.

PRESTON, Ann (1813–1872). American physician and educator. Born Dec 1, 1813, in West Grove, Pennsylvania; died April 18, 1872, in Philadelphia, Pennsylvania; dau. of Amos Preston (Quaker minister) and Margaret (Smith) Preston; Female Medical College (later Woman's Medical College of Philadelphia), MD, 1851; never married. ❖ With support of her Quaker community, was encouraged to obtain a medical education; received degree with 1st graduating class of Female Medical College of Pennsylvania (1851), which aroused much ire and the commencement was mobbed by over 500 male medical students; appointed professor of physiology and hygiene at Female Medical College (1853); after Pennsylvania State Medical Society declared that patients of women doctors could not be admitted to local hospitals (1859), founded Woman's Hospital in Philadelphia (1861); started a nursing school (1863); appointed dean of Woman's Medical College (1866), the 1st woman so appointed both at that school and at any medical school in US. ❖ See also *Women in World History*.

PRESTON, Frances F. (1864–1947). *See Cleveland, Frances Folsom.*

PRESTON, Margaret Junkin (1820–1897). American poet. Born Margaret Junkin, May 19, 1820, in Milton, Pennsylvania; died Mar 28, 1897, in Baltimore, Maryland; dau. of George Junkin (minister and educator) and Julia Rush (Miller) Junkin; sister of Eleanor Junkin

(d. 1854, 1st wife of General Thomas "Stonewall" Jackson); m. John T.L. Preston (professor of Latin), Aug 3, 1857; children: George Junkin and Herbert Rush. ❖ A Northerner who made her reputation as a Southern poet, moved south with family (1848), when father became president of Washington College in Lexington, VA; wrote 1st and only novel, *Silverwood*, a story of Southern life, which was published anonymously (1856); produced 2nd book, *Beechenbrook: A Rhyme of the War* (1865), solidifying her literary reputation throughout the South; produced 4 additional collections: *Old Song and New* (1870), *Cartoons* (1875), *For Love's Sake* (1886) and *Colonial Ballads, Sonnets, and Other Verse* (1887). ❖ See also Coulling, Mary Price, *Margaret Junkin Preston* (Blair, 1993); and *Women in World History*.

PRESTON, Margaret Rose (c. 1875–1963). Australian painter and graphic artist. Born Margaret Rose McPherson in Adelaide, Australia, April 29, 1875; died 1963; dau. of David McPherson (marine engineer) and Prudence (Lyle) McPherson; studied art at National Gallery of Victoria Art School and Adelaide School of Design; m. William George Preston, 1919; no children. ❖ Celebrated painter and one of the 1st Australians to recognize the beauty and value of Aboriginal art, embarked on 1st trip to Europe (1904) and had a 2nd extended visit (1912–19), where she began to move away from her traditional training to explore alternative modes of expression; settling in Sydney with husband (1919), pursued painting and printmaking, interior decoration, fabric design, and flower arrangement; challenged the 19th-century traditionalism of Australian art with a series of decorative and technically adventurous still lifes. ❖ See also *Women in World History*.

PRESTON, May Wilson (1873–1949). American illustrator. Born May Wilson, Aug 11, 1873, in New York, NY; died May 18, 1949, in East Hampton, NY; dau. of John J. Wilson and Ann (Taylor) Wilson; attended Oberlin College; attended Art Students League, 1892–1897, studying with Robert Henri, John H. Twachtman, and William M. Chase; in Paris, studied with James McNeill Whistler (1899); m. Thomas Henry Watkins, 1898 (died 1900); m. James Moore Preston (painter), Dec 19, 1903; no children. ❖ By 16, was an accomplished self-taught artist and founding member of the Women's Art Club (later National Association of Women Artists); illustrated 1st story (1901), for *Harper's Bazaar*; with Edith Dimock and Lou Seyme, moved into quarters at Sherwood Studios on West 57th St., which became a meeting ground for young artists and writers; helped establish Society of Illustrators (1901), and was the 1st and only woman member for many years; became increasingly successful, her commercial illustrations appearing regularly in *McClure's*, *Woman's Home Companion*, *Saturday Evening Post*, *Metropolitan*, and *Harper's Bazaar*, where they accompanied stories by Mary Roberts Rinehart, F. Scott Fitzgerald, Ring Lardner and P.G. Wodehouse, among others; was also active in the National Woman's Party. Awarded bronze medal at San Francisco Panama-Pacific Exposition (1915). ❖ See also *Women in World History*.

PRETINHA (1975—). Brazilian soccer player. Name variations: Delma Gonçalves. Born Delma Gonçalves, May 19, 1975, in Rio de Janeiro, Brazil. ❖ At 16, was added to the National team; played in 3 World Cups for Brazil; signed with Washington Freedom (2000); traded to San Jose CyberRays; won a team silver medal at Athens Olympics (2004).

PRETS, Christa (1947—). Austrian sports teacher, coach, and politician. Born Oct 2, 1947, in Diez an der Lahn, Germany. ❖ Coached various sporting groups (1969–94); member of the Land government (1994–99); as a European Socialist, elected to 5th European Parliament (1999–2004).

PRETTY, Arline (1885–1978). American silent-film actress. Born Sept 5, 1885, in Washington, DC; died April 14, 1978, in Hollywood, CA. ❖ Made screen debut (1913); starred for Vitagraph (1915–19); films include *The Thirteenth Girl*, *The Secret Kingdom* (serial), *A Woman in Grey*, *Rouged Lips* and *The Primrose Path*; was later an extra.

PRETTY, Violet (1932—). See Heywood, Anne.

PRETTY & TWISTED. See Napolitano, Johnette.

PRETTY MARY (c. 1908–1938). See Bonita, Maria.

PRETTYMAN, Kathleen Collins (1942–1988). See Collins, Kathleen.

PREUSS, Phyllis (1939—). American golfer. Name variations: Tish Preuss. Born Feb 9, 1939, in Detroit, Michigan. ❖ Was runner-up in USGA Women's Amateur (1961); won Eastern Amateur (1963), Southern Amateur (1965, 1968), and North and South Amateur (1964, 1967); member Curtis Cup team (1962, 1964, 1966, 1968,

1970), captain (1984); won USGA Senior Women's Amateur (1991). Inducted into the Colorado Golf Hall of Fame (1970).

PREUSS, Tish (1939—). See Preuss, Phyllis.

PRÉVOST, Françoise (1680–1741). French ballerina. Name variations: Francoise Prevost. Born in France, possibly in Paris, 1680; died 1741 in Paris. ❖ Made debut in a revival of Jean-Baptiste Lully's *Atys* (1699); within 6 years, replaced Marie-Thérèse Subligny at Opéra de France; a gifted actress, moved the audience to tears while dancing the final scene of Corneille's *Horace* in a small theater at the Château de Sceaux (1714); created *Les Caractères de la danse*, which would later become a showpiece for Marie-Anne Cupis de Camargo and Marie Sallé; retired at 50 and began to teach at the Opéra's School of Dance.

PREVOST, Hélène. French tennis player. Name variations: Helene Prevost. Born in France. ❖ At Paris Olympics, won a silver medal in singles and a silver medal in mixed doubles–outdoors (1900).

PREVOST, Marie (1895–1937). Canadian actress. Born Mary Bickford Dunn, Nov 8, 1895, in Sarnia, Ontario, Canada; died Jan 23, 1937, in Hollywood, CA; sister of Marjorie Prevost (actress); m. 2nd husband Kenneth Harlan (screen star), 1924 (div. 1927). ❖ Launched film career as a Mack Sennett bathing beauty (1916), then became a leading lady; joined Universal (1921); specializing in romantic comedy, appeared in 3 Ernst Lubitsch films, *The Marriage Circle*, *Three Women* and *Kiss Me Again*; made over 70 films, including *Up in Mabel's Room*, *Getting Gertie's Garter* and *The Godless Girl*; when career waned because of weight gain, went on a radical diet and was found dead of extreme malnutrition.

PREWITT, Cheryl (c. 1957—). Miss America and writer. Name variations: Cheryl Salem. Born Cheryl Prewitt c. 1957 in Choctaw Co., MS; graduate of Mississippi State University; m. Harry Salem (vice president of operations and production, Oral Roberts Ministry); children: 3. ❖ Named Miss America (1980), representing Mississippi; with husband Harry, runs Salem Family Ministries; wrote over 16 books focusing on family. ❖ See also Cheryl Salem *A Bright Shining Place* and, with husband, *Mourning to Morning*, about daughter Gabrielle's losing battle with cancer (d. 1999).

PRIBYSLAVA (fl. 10th c.). Bohemian princess. Only dau. of Drahomira of Bohemia and Ratislav also known as Vratislav I (887–920), duke of Bohemia (r. 912–920).

PRICE, Ellen (1814–1887). See Wood, Ellen Price.

PRICE, Ellen (1878–1968). Danish ballet dancer. Born 1878 in Copenhagen, Denmark; died 1968 in Copenhagen; dau. of Carl Price and granddau. of James Price (English theatrical family working in Denmark); great-niece of Juliette Price (ballet dancer). ❖ Performed with Royal Danish Ballet where she danced numerous roles originally created by her great-aunt, including in *La Silfiden*, *Konservatoriet*, *Flower Festival in Genzano*, and *Kermesse in Bruges*; was featured to great acclaim in Hans Beck's *The Little Mermaid* (1909), which inspired the statue that sits on a rock in Copenhagen harbor.

PRICE, Eugenia (1916–1996). American author. Born in Charleston, West Virginia, June 22, 1916; died in Brunswick, Georgia, May 28, 1996; attended Ohio University; studied dentistry at Northwestern University; never married; lived with Joyce Blackburn (editor). ❖ The author of numerous inspirational books and popular antebellum romantic novels, broke into the profession by writing soap operas, 1st in Chicago, then NY and Cincinnati; following a conversion to Christianity (late 1940s), began writing inspirational books, among them *Beloved World* and *The Eugenia Price Treasury of Faith*; turned out some 2 dozen books of this nature and won a wide following before turning to novels; moved to St. Simons in Georgia (1960); using this Southern locale as a backdrop, began a series of romantic novels, the 1st three of which—*Lighthouse*, *New Moon Rising* and *Beloved Invader*—focused on an actual St. Simons cleric and his 2 wives; experiencing instant success, wrote a Florida trilogy and a Savannah quartet before returning to the St. Simons setting for a Georgia trilogy, which included the bestsellers *Bright Captivity* (1991) and *Beauty from Ashes* (1995).

PRICE, Florence B. (1888–1953). African-American composer and symphonist. Born Florence Beatrice Smith, April 9, 1888, in Little Rock, Arkansas; died June 3, 1953, in Chicago, Illinois; dau. of Florence Irene Smith (schoolteacher and musician) and James H. Smith (dentist and musician); graduate of New England Conservatory of Music, 1907; m. Thomas Price (attorney); children: Tommy, Florence, and Edith. ❖ The 1st black woman to win fame as a symphonist, studied under composer George Whitefield Chadwick who used African-American musical idioms in his compositions and likely encouraged her to do the same; taught at Clark College in Atlanta (1910–12); moved to Chicago (1927), where she began to publish her work, including "At the Cotton Gin," a piano piece (1928), and "Songs to a Dark Virgin" (1941); her Symphony in A Minor was 1st performed with Chicago Symphony Orchestra (1933); conducted the Women's Symphony of Chicago with Margaret Bonds at the piano (1934); was named a member of American Society of Composers, Authors, and Publishers (1940). Won Wanamaker awards for Symphony in A Minor and a piano sonata (1930). ❖ See also *Women in World History.*

PRICE, Hayley. British gymnast. Born in West Midlands, England. ❖ Won GBR championships (1983 and 1985); on the British team at the Olympics (1984).

PRICE, Juliette (1831–1906). Danish ballet dancer. Born Aug 13, 1831, in Copenhagen, Denmark, into an English theatrical family working in Denmark; died April 4, 1906, in Copenhagen; dau. of Adolph Price; great aunt of Ellen Price (ballet dancer). ❖ Made professional debut in Auguste Bournonville's *Konservatoriet* with Royal Danish Ballet (1849); created numerous roles for Bournonville, including in his *Valdemar* (1953), *Flower Festival in Genzano* (1858), and *Far from Denmark* (1860); retired (1866).

PRICE, Kate (1872–1943). Irish-born comedic actress. Born Katherine Duffy, Feb 13, 1872, in Cork, Ireland; died Jan 4, 1943, in Woodland Hills, CA; aunt of actress Mary Charleson; sister of Jack Duffy; m. Joseph Ludwig Price. ❖ Starred opposite Oliver Hardy in "Vim" comedies (1917); went on to specialize in Irish landlady types; made over 170 films, including *Little Lord Fauntleroy, The Spoilers, The Sea Hawk, The Cohens and the Kellys* and *Show Girl.*

PRICE, Leontyne (1927—). African-American soprano. Born Mary Violet Leontine Price in Laurel, MS, Feb 10, 1927; graduate of Wilberforce College (later Central State University); attended Juilliard School of Music; studied with Florence Page Kimball; m. William Warfield (baritone), Aug 31, 1952 (div. 1967). ❖ Gave 1st public recital (1943); enrolled at Juilliard (1948), even though opportunities for African-Americans in classical opera were extremely limited; with William Warfield, toured with *Porgy and Bess* (1952), to great reviews; sang *Tosca* for NBC-TV's Opera Theater (1955), though 11 NBC affiliates in the South refused to carry the show; appeared in 3 other NBC Opera Theaters, Mozart's *The Magic Flute* and *Don Giovanni* and as Madame Lidoine in Poulenc's *Dialogue of the Carmelites*, over next 5 years; made American opera debut as Madame Lidoine in San Francisco (1957), and remained with San Francisco Opera for next 10 years, singing the title role in *Aïda*, Doña Anna in *Don Giovanni*, Leonora in *Il Trovatore*, Cio-Cio-San in *Madame Butterfly*, Amelia in *Un Ballo in Maschera* and Doña Elvira in *Ernani*; made European debut in *Aïda* at Vienna Staatsoper (1958), followed by productions in Paris, London and, finally, at La Scala (1960); debuted at the Met, only the 5th black artist to sing a leading role there, when she appeared as Leonora in *Il Trovatore* to great acclaim (1961); became especially known for her interpretations of many of Verdi's heroines during 24-year tenure with the Met; performed in *Ariadne auf Naxos* at San Francisco Opera (1977), considered by many to be her finest work; retired from opera stage (1985), concentrating on more intimate concert settings, and on teaching and recording; raised money for NAACP, Martin Luther King Jr. Center for Non-Violent Social Change, and National Urban League. Won 19 Grammys and 3 Emmys; received the Kennedy Center award and President's Medal of Freedom. ❖ See also *Women in World History.*

PRICE, Margaret (1941—). Welsh soprano. Name variations: Dame Margaret Berenice Price. Born April 13, 1941, in Blackwood, Wales, to musical family; attended Trinity College of Music (1956). ❖ Opera and concert star, made debut with Welsh National Opera as Cherubino in *Marriage of Figaro* (1962); debuted in Royal Opera House at Covent Garden in same role (1963), while understudy to Teresa Berganza who fell ill, becoming overnight sensation; became regular performer at Glyndebourne (from 1968), notably as Constanze and Fiordiligi; internationally renowned for opera and lieder, particularly of Mozart and Verdi, gave acclaimed performances of Pamina in San Francisco (1969), and Donna Anna in Cologne (1971); praised for her Desdemona during US tour with Paris Opera (1976), made debut at NY's Metropolitan Opera in the same role (1985); performed as recitalist as well, frequently accompanied by conductor James Lockhart; lived for many years in Germany, but returned to Wales following retirement (1999); recordings

include *Tristan and Isolde* (1990), *The Magic Flute* (1994) and *Otello* (2001). Awarded Commander of British Empire (CBE, 1982) and Dame of British Empire (DBE, 1993).

PRICE, Nancy (1880–1970). English actress-manager and writer. Born Lillian Price, Feb 3, 1880, in Kinver, Worcestershire, England; died Mar 31, 1970, in Worthing, Sussex, England; m. Charles Maude (died); children: Joan Maude (actress, 1908–1998). ❖ Made stage debut with F.R. Benson's co. in Birmingham (1899); made London debut in *Henry V* (1900); came to prominence as Calypso in *Ulysses* (1902); other plays include *Letty, The Lady of Leeds* (title role), *Julius Caesar* (as Calpurnia), *Toddles, Mr. Sheridan, The Gay Lord Quex, The Borstal Boy, Richard III* (as Queen Elizabeth), *Macbeth* (as Lady Macbeth), *Nurse Cavell* (title role), and *Thérèse Raquin*; during WWI, worked with the blind and for war charities; founded People's National Theatre (1930), producing over 80 plays at many London theaters; was actress-manager of The Little Theatre in the Adelphi off the Strand, London; wrote such books as *Behind the Nightlight, Shadows on the Hills, Hurdy Gurdy, Tamera, Feathered Outlaw* and *Winged Builders.* Named Commander of the British Empire (CBE, 1950).

PRICE, Roberta MacAdams (1881–1959). Canadian politician. Name variations: Roberta MacAdams. Born Roberta Catherine MacAdams, July 21, 1881, in Sarnia, Ontario, Canada; died Dec 16, 1959, in Calgary, Alberta, Canada; graduate of Macdonald Institute, 1911; m. Harvey Stinson Price, Sept 21, 1920; children: Robert. ❖ Elected to the Alberta Legislature (1917), the 2nd woman elected to a legislature in Canada and in the British Empire; was the 1st woman to introduce legislation in the British Empire (1918); served in the legislature until 1921, choosing not to seek reelection after her marriage. ❖ See also *Women in World History.*

PRICHARD, Katharine Susannah (1883–1969). Australian writer. Name variations: KSP. Born Dec 4, 1883, in Fiji; died 1969 in Perth, Western Australia; dau. of Tom Prichard (journalist) and Edith Isabel Fraser (painter); attended South Melbourne College; m. Hugo Throssell (soldier), 1919; children: Ric Throssell (b. 1922). ❖ Author, pacifist, and founder member of the Communist Party of Australia, recognized as one of Australia's foremost writers, whose initiatives made a profound impact upon the lives of many West Australians, spent childhood in Fiji and Australia (1st in Launceston, Tasmania, and later in Melbourne, Victoria); at age 21, went to South Gippsland to governess (1904); father committed suicide (1907); made 1st visit to London as a journalist (1908); returned to London (1912), where she wrote 1st prizewinning novel, *The Pioneers*, which won the Hodder & Stoughton All-Empire novel competition, enabling her to return to Australia as a radical writer of some promise; published 2nd novel, *Windlestraws* (1916); brother Alan killed on the battlefields of northern France (1917); moved with new husband to Perth, Western Australia, to the hillside suburb of Greenmount (1919); published novels *Working Bullocks, Coonardoo* and *Haxby's Circus* (1920s); was a founding member of Communist Party of Australia (early 1920s); went to Russia (1933) and, while she was gone, husband Hugo Throssell committed suicide; returning to Australia, threw herself into political work, becoming a founder member of the Movement against War and Fascism; at outbreak of Spanish Civil War, organized the Spanish Relief Committee in Western Australia; became a member of Communist Party's Central Committee (1943); awarded the World Council's Silver Medallion for services to peace (1959); on her death (1969), her coffin was draped with the Red Flag and she was given a Communist funeral. Other writings include *Intimate Strangers* (1937), *Moon of Desire* (1941), *The Roaring Nineties* (1946), *Golden Miles* (1948), *Winged Seeds* (1950) and *Subtle Flame* (1967). ❖ See also (autobiography) *Child of the Hurricane* (1964); Ric Throssell, ed. *Straight Left: The Articles and Addresses of Katharine Susannah Prichard* (1982) and *Wild Weeds and Wind Flowers: The Life and Letters of Katharine Susannah Prichard* (Angus & Robertson, 1975); and *Women in World History.*

PRICKETT, Maudie (1914–1976). American character actress. Name variations: Maude Prickett. Born Oct 25, 1914; died April 14, 1976, in Pasadena, CA. ❖ Made over 400 films, including *Song of Idaho, Her First Romance, Stars and Stripes Forever, A Man Called Peter, Legend of Tom Dooley, North by Northwest* and *Rascal.*

PRIE, Jeanne Agnes Berthelot de Pléneuf, Marquise de (1698–1727). French marquise. Name variations: Madame de Prie. Born Jeanne Agnes Berthelot de Pléneuf in 1698; died 1727; dau. of rich but unscrupulous parents; m. Louis, marquis de Prie, in 1713. ❖ At 15, was married to Louis, marquis de Prie, and moved to the court of Savoy at Turin, where he was ambassador; at 21, returned to France and was soon mistress of Louis Henry, duke of Bourbon; during the duke's ministry (1723–25), was in many respects the true ruler of France, but when she tried to have Bourbon's rival Cardinal Fleury exiled (1725), her influence came to an end; was exiled to Courbépine, where she committed suicide.

PRIEMER, Petra (1961—). East German swimmer. Born Feb 6, 1961, in East Germany. ❖ At Montreal Olympics, won a silver medal in the 4 x 100-meter freestyle relay and a silver medal in the 100-meter freestyle (1976).

PRIESAND, Sally Jane (1946—). Jewish-American rabbi. Born June 27, 1946, in Cleveland, Ohio; dau. of Irving Theodore Priesand and Rosetta Elizabeth (Welch) Priesand; graduate of University of Cincinnati, 1968; attended Hebrew Union College–Jewish Institute of Religion. ❖ The 1st woman in the history of Judaism to be ordained a rabbi, was admitted to the HUC–JIR rabbinic school (1968); ordained in Cincinnati's Plum Street Temple, became the 1st female ordained rabbi in the world (June 3, 1972), the only other claimant being Regina Jonas, who died in the Holocaust and had never been ordained by a seminary; found 1st job as an assistant in Manhattan's Stephen Wise Free Synagogue, eventually advancing to associate rabbi; took a position at Monmouth Reform Temple in Tinton Falls, New Jersey (1981); writings include *Judaism and the New Woman* (1975). ❖ See also *Women in World History.*

PRIEST, Ivy Baker (1905–1975). American political organizer and US treasurer. Born Ivy Maude Baker, Sept 7, 1905, in Kimberly, Piute Co., Utah; died June 1975, in Santa Monica, California; dau. of Orange Decatur Baker (miner) and Clara (Fearnley) Baker; attended University of Utah; m. Harry Howard Hicks (traveling salesman), 1924 (div. 1929); m. Roy Fletcher Priest (furniture dealer), Dec 7, 1935 (died 1959); m. Sidney William Stevens (real-estate agent), 1961 (died 1972); children: (2nd m.) Patricia (b. 1936); Peggy (b. 1938, died young); Nancy (b. 1941); Roy (b. 1942). ❖ Became active in Utah state Republican organizations (1930s); ran unsuccessfully for US House of Representatives (1950); named treasurer of US (1953), only the 2nd woman to hold that post, serving until 1961; served as California state treasurer (1967–74); was the 1st woman to nominate a presidential candidate when she put forth Ronald Reagan's name at the convention of 1968, during his 1st failed bid to head the Republican ticket. ❖ See also autobiography *Green Grows Ivy* (McGraw-Hill, 1958); and *Women in World History.*

PRIESTLY, L. A. M. (c. 1865–1944). See McCracken, Elizabeth.

PRIESTNER, Cathy (1958—). Canadian speedskater. Name variations: Cathy Priestner Faminow; Cathy Priestner-Allinger. Born 1958 in Windsor, Ontario, Canada; m. Todd Allinger, 1986. ❖ Placed 14th in the 500 meters at Sapporo Olympics (1972); won a silver medal for the 500 meters at Innsbruck Olympics (1976); coached speedskating, most especially Bonnie Blair; was an Olympic tv commentator for CBC and CTV.

PRIMAROLO, Dawn (1954—). English politician and member of Parliament. Born May 2, 1954; m. 2nd husband Thomas Ian Ducat, 1990; children: 1 son. ❖ Member of Avon County Council (1985–87); representing Labour, elected to House of Commons for Bristol South (1987); in opposition, was a front bench spokesperson on health (1992–94) and Treasury and economic affairs (1994–97); appointed financial secretary to the Treasury (1997); named paymaster general, HM Treasury (1999).

PRIME, Alberta (1895–1984). See Hunter, Alberta.

PRIMETTES, The. See Supremes, The.

PRIMO DE RIVERA, Pilar (1913–1991). Spanish political activist. Born in Madrid, Spain, Nov 5, 1913; died 1991; dau. of Miguel Primo de Rivera (Spanish general who ruled as dictator of Spain from 1923 to 1930 and whose fall led to the 2nd Republic and the Spanish Civil War) and Casilda Sáenz de Heredia. ❖ Founder and leader of the Sección Feminina of the Spanish Falange, became involved in the political activities of her brother, José Antonio Primo de Rivera; when he founded the Falange Española, a quasi-fascist movement (1933), established the Sección Feminina, a female appendage of the Falange (1934); played an active role in the political tumult that led up to the Spanish Civil War; when war began (July 1936), sided with Franco's Nationalists, who sought to overthrow the leftist Republic; helped organize the Woman's Social Service (1937), which obligated all able-bodied single women between 17 and 35 to provide 6 months of public service; after the war,

continued to play an active political role, generally in favor of the Falange's social agenda; served in Spanish Cortes (Parliament) and was a member of the National Council of Education; also spoke and wrote about women's role in Spanish society. Awarded the Great Cross of Isabella the Catholic (Isabella I). ❖ See also (in Spanish) *Recuerdos de una vida* (Madrid: Ediciones DYRSA, 1983); and *Women in World History.*

PRIMROSE, Lady Mary (c. 1780–1847). See Shepherd, Mary.

PRIMROSE-SMITH, Elizabeth (c. 1948—). American athlete and sports manager. Name variations: Elizabeth Smith. Born c. 1948 in US. ❖ Won gold medal in swimming at Pan American Games, Sao Paulo, Brazil (1963); began sports management career as assistant director of World Games in Santa Clara, CA (1981); served as associate vice president of Los Angeles Olympic Organizing Committee (1981–84) and as member of consulting team at McKinsey & Co., Los Angeles; was executive director of 1st World Games (1981); became 1st woman and 1st athlete to be president of US Olympic Festival, Los Angeles (1991); served as managing director and chief administrative officer of World Cup USA (1994); joined IBM to manage their Olympic and sports sponsorships (1994).

PRIMUS, Pearl (1919–1994). African-American dancer and choreographer. Born Pearl Primus, Nov 29, 1919, in Trinidad, British West Indies; died in New Rochelle, New York, Oct 29, 1994; dau. of Edward Primus and Emily Primus; Hunter College, BA, 1940; New York University, PhD, 1977; m. Percival Borde (Trinidadian dancer), 1954; children: Onwin Babajide Primus Borde (b. 1955). ❖ Choreographer, dancer, and ethnographer, whose anthropological work opened up pathways to the origins of African dance movements that have helped to unify the African-American identity through dance, moved with family to US (1921); while performing at 92nd Street YMHA, was catapulted into forefront of concert dance by glowing reviews (1943), which focused on her high, airborne leaps; found a creative home at Café Society Downtown (1943), a politically active club in Manhattan with an integrated audience, performing her variety of dances, often to blues accompaniment of Josh White; danced on Broadway and in nightclubs, the bulk of her repertory often dealing with social protest in such dances as "Strange Fruit" (1943), "The Negro Speaks of Rivers" (1943), "Hard Time Blues" (1943), "Slave Market" (1944) and "Sometimes I Feel Like a Motherless Child" (1945); traveled to Georgia, Alabama, and South Carolina (1944) where she began to recognize the integral role of spirituality in African-American culture; was soon headed for the Gold Coast, Angola, Liberia, Senegal, and the Belgian Congo (1948); promoted African dance in both US and Africa (1950s); established Liberian Cultural Center in Monrovia, Liberia (1959) and appointed director; returned to US and the burgeoning civil-rights movement (1962); with husband, opened the African-Caribbean-American Institute of Dance in NY; premiered "The Wedding" (1961); held various college positions, including professor of ethnic studies at Amherst College (1980s); continued to restage her works for performance groups, most notably the Alvin Ailey Dance Theater; other works include "Fanga" (1949), "The Initiation" (1950), "Impinyuza" (1951), "Mr. Johnson" (1955), "Fertility Dance" (1967) and "Michael, Row Your Boat Ashore" (1979). Received National Medal of Arts (1991). ❖ See also *Women in World History.*

PRINCE, Celia (1930—). See Rosser, Celia.

PRINCE, Lucy Terry (c. 1730–1821). African-American poet and orator. Name variations: Lucy Terry. Born c. 1730, somewhere in West Africa (real name unknown); died 1821 in Sunderland, Vermont; m. Abijah or Bijah Prince, May 16, 1756; children: Caesar (b. 1757); Durexa (b. 1758); Drucella (b. 1760); Festus (b. 1763); Tatnai (b. 1765); Abijah (b. 1769). ❖ Kidnapped, sold into slavery, and brought to Rhode Island as an infant (early 1730s); worked as a household slave in Deerfield, Massachusetts (1735–56); wrote only surviving poem "Bars Fight," which was based on an ambush of white settlers by Native Americans that she witnessed in Deerfield in 1746; freed from slavery by her husband, who purchased her freedom (1756); moved to Guilford, Vermont, where he owned land; when a dispute arose with a neighbor over property boundaries, successfully argued a case before US Supreme Court (1797). ❖ See also *Women in World History.*

PRINCE, Mary (c. 1788–after 1833). Caribbean writer. Born at Brackish-Pond in Bermuda, c. 1788; died after 1833. ❖ After purchasing her freedom from slavery (1831), published her autobiography *The History of Mary Prince, a West Indian Slave, Related by Herself,* a powerful document that inflamed public opinion and created political upheaval between pro- and anti-slavery factions; worked for the editor of *Anti-Slavery Reporter* and was an outspoken campaigner against slavery. ❖ See also *The History of Mary Prince, A West Indian Slave, Related by Herself* in *Six Women's Slave Narratives* (Schomburg Library of 19th Century Black Women Writers); and *Women in World History.*

PRINCE, Nancy Gardner (1799–?). African-Amerindian domestic servant, humanitarian, and writer. Born Sept 15, 1799, in Newburyport, Massachusetts; death date unknown; dau. of Thomas Gardner (mother's 1st name unknown, though her maiden name was presumably Wornton); married a Mr. Prince (a freeborn), Feb 15, 1824 (died c. 1833). ❖ In her single volume *A Narrative of the Life and Travels of Mrs. Nancy Prince,* recorded her life, from her poverty-stricken childhood in Massachusetts, though her teenage years as a domestic, her marriage, and her travels with husband to the Russian courts of Alexander I and Nicholas I and the newly emancipated Jamaica. ❖ See also *Women in World History.*

PRINCEN, baronne de (1736–1812). *See Montanclos, Marie-Emilie Maryon de.*

PRINCESS SOPHIA (1820s?–1875). *See Te Paea Tiaho.*

PRINGLE, Aileen (1895–1989). American star of silent screen and early talkies. Name variations: Aileen Savage. Born Aileen Bisbee, July 23, 1895, in San Francisco, CA; died Dec 16, 1989, in New York, NY; m. Sir Charles MacKenzie Pringle (governor of Bahamas), 1912 (div. 1933); m. James M. Cain (novelist), 1944 (div. 1947). ❖ Made acting debut on London stage (1915), Broadway debut (1917), and screen debut as Aileen Savage (1919); made more than 60 films, including *Three Weeks, Souls for Sale, His Hour, Wife of the Centaur, Adam and Evil, Puttin' on the Ritz, Piccadilly Jim, Nothing Sacred, Since You Went Away* and *Laura.*

PRINGLE, Elizabeth Allston (1845–1921). American planter and author. Name variations: (pseudonym) Patience Pennington. Born Elizabeth Waties Allston, May 29, 1845, in Canaan Seashore, South Carolina; died Dec 5, 1921, near Georgetown, South Carolina; dau. of Robert Francis Withers Allston (rice planter who served as governor and state legislator) and Adele Petigru Allston (sister to Unionist leader James Louis Petigru); m. John Julius Pringle (plantation owner), April 26, 1870 (died 1876); children: 1 (died in infancy). ❖ Moved to Chicora Wood (1868), the last of her father's plantations; acquired White House, late husband's plantation, from his heirs (1880) and took on its management (1885); showed an interest in finding new ways to run the plantation more efficiently; bought Chicora Wood (1896) and struggled for the following years to operate the 2 plantations; when a majority of the plantations in the Carolinas were forced to fold, was financially ruined (1906); entries from her diary were printed in a series in *New York Sun* (1905); using pseudonym Patience Pennington, published these entries along with further commentary, and illustrations by Alice R. Huger Smith, under title *Woman Rice Planter* (1913). A 2nd book, *Chronicles of Chicora Wood,* was posthumously published (1922). ❖ See also *Women in World History.*

PRINGLE, Mia Lilly (1920–1983). Austrian-born psychologist. Born Mia Lilly Kellmer in Vienna, Austria, 1920; died 1983; dau. of Samuel Kellmer; Birkbeck College, London, BA in psychology, with 1st-class honors, 1944; awarded PhD, 1950; m. William Joseph Somerville Pringle, 1946 (div. 1962). ❖ The 1st director of the National Children's Bureau, immigrated to Britain as a refugee (1938); worked for a year as an educational and clinical psychologist at London Child Guidance Training Center; served as an educational psychologist in Hertfordshire (1945–50); taught at Birmingham University (1950–63), while also serving as head of Remedial Education Center; served as director of National Bureau for Co-operation in Child Care (later National Children's Bureau, 1963–81); following retirement, served as consultant to UNICEF; published numerous articles and books on child care, including *The Needs of Children* (1974), *Adoption, Facts and Fallacies* (1967) and *Foster Home Care, Facts and Fallacies* (1967); made frequent appearances on radio and tv. Awarded CBE (1975).

PRINSLOO, Christine (1952—). Zimbabwean field-hockey player. Born May 3, 1952, in Zimbabwe. ❖ At Moscow Olympics, won a gold medal in team competition (1980).

PRINTEMPS, Yvonne (1894–1977). French actress. Name variations: Yvonne Wignolle. Born Yvonne Wignolle, July 25, 1894, in Ermont, France; died Jan 19, 1977, in Paris, France; dau. of Leon Wignolle and Palmire Wignolle; m. Sacha Guitry (playwright), 1919 (div. 1934), no children. ❖ Famed actress of stage and screen, joined a local theater troupe at 11; supported family by working in Paris vaudeville as a dancer (1907); when vocal talent was discovered, became a performer at Folies-Bergère, where she remained for 4 years and earned nickname Printemps (springtime) for her beauty and cheerful disposition; performed in comedies, dramas, and operas across Paris, becoming its most celebrated female performer (1912–19); marriage to Sacha Guitry truly made her a star; performed as the lead in dozens of plays and musicals which he wrote, produced, and often co-starred in, especially his production of *Mozart* (1926), which they toured in London, US, and Canada (1927); left husband (1934) and starred in Coward's *Conversation Piece* in London and on Broadway; returning to France, had 1st starring role in a major film, *Les Trois Valses* (*Three Waltzes,* 1938); with lover Pierre Fresnay, served as business and artistic manager of Michodière Theater (1938–73), even during WWII; made *Le Valse de Paris* (*The Paris Waltz,* 1948) and dominated Paris stage for another 10 years; retired from acting at 65 (1959). ❖ See also *Women in World History.*

PRINZ, Birgit (1977—). German soccer player. Born Oct 25, 1977, in Frankfurt, Germany. ❖ Won a team bronze medal at Sydney Olympics (2000) and Athens Olympics (2004); led Germany to European championships (1995, 1997, 2001); played for FFC Frankfurt; signed with Carolina Courage (2002); won FIFA World Cup (2003). Named German Player of the Year (2001 and 2002).

PRINZEN, baronne de (1736–1812). *See Montanclos, Marie-Emilie Maryon de.*

PRIOR, Maddy (1947—). English folksinger. Name variations: Steeleye Span. Born Aug 14, 1947, in Blackpool, England; m. Rick Kemp (bass player); children: 2. ❖ Lead singer for band Steeleye Span (formed 1969), which attempted to combine traditional British folk songs with electric instruments; initially performed and recorded traditional music with Tim Hart (late 1960s), before they both joined Steeleye Span; with band, found success with 3rd album, *Below the Salt* (1972), had hit single "Thomas the Rhymer" and made 1st US chart appearance with title track from *All Around My Hat* (1975); with traditional singer June Tabor, recorded album *Silly Sisters* (1976); with Steeleye Span, gave live performance, recorded as *Live at Last* (1978), before disbanding; reunited with group (1980) and released several albums, including *Sails of Silver* (1980), *Back in Line* (1986), and *Tonight's the Night, Live* (1992); left band (1999) and went solo, releasing numerous albums, including *Flesh and Blood* (1998), *Ravenchild* (2000) and *Bib and Tuck* (2002).

PRIOR, Margaret (1773–1842). American social-welfare worker. Name variations: Margaret Barrett Allen Prior. Born Margaret Barrett, 1773, in Fredericksburg, VA; died April 7, 1842, in New York, NY; dau. of William Barrett (farmer); m. William Allen (linen merchant), c. 1789 (died c. 1808); William Prior (merchant), 1814 (died 1829); children: (1st m.), several, but only 1 son survived infancy; (2nd m.) several who died young and 2 adopted daughters. ❖ Operated soup kitchen for poor in Ninth Ward in New York (1819–19) and opened school for children of poor in NY (1822); served as member of board of managers of New York Orphan Asylum; was 1st female missionary for New York Female Moral Reform Society (1834–42). ❖ See also Sarah R. Ingraham, *Walks of Usefulness, or Reminiscences of Mrs. Margaret Prior* (American Female Guardian Society, 1843).

PRISCA. *Variant for Priscilla.*

PRISCA OF HUNGARY (c. 1085–1133). *See Priska-Irene of Hungary.*

PRISCILLA (fl. 1st c.). Christian missionary. Name variations: St. Prisca; St. Priscilla. Flourished in 1st century, around 54 CE; date and place of death unknown; m. Aquila (Jewish-Christian tentmaker). ❖ Early Christian evangelist, missionary and teacher, was designated by St. Paul as being one of his "fellow workers" (Romans 16:3–5); with the passage of time, became known as an apostle; has frequently been confused with another woman named Priscilla, who founded a cemetery on Rome's Via Salaria and was a noblewoman of the Roman senatorial family of Acilii Glabriones. Feast day is Jan 18. ❖ See also Ruth Hoppin, *Priscilla's Letter: Finding the Author of the Epistle to the Hebrews* (Christian Universities Press, 1997); and *Women in World History.*

PRISCILLA (c. 1602–c. 1685). *See Alden, Priscilla.*

PRISHCHEPA, Nadezhda (1956—). Soviet rower. Born June 28, 1956, in USSR. ❖ At Moscow Olympics, won a silver medal in coxed eights (1980).

PRISKA-IRENE OF HUNGARY (c. 1085–1133). Byzantine empress. Name variations: Princess Prisca of Hungary; Irene of Hungary. Born

c. 1085; died August 13, 1133; dau. of St. Ladislaus also known as Ladislav or Ladislas, king of Hungary (r. 1077–1095) and Adelheid of Rheinfelden (c. 1065–?); m. John II Comnenus (brother of Anna Comnena), emperor of Byzantium (r. 1118–1143), in 1103 (died as the result of a poisoned arrow on April 8, 1143); children: 4 sons and 4 daughters, including twin sons Alexius (1104–1142) and Andronicus (1104–1142), and Manuel I Comnenus (1120?–1180), emperor of Byzantium (r. 1143–1180). ❖ See also *Women in World History.*

PRISKA OF HUNGARY (c. 1085–1133). *See Priska-Irene of Hungary.*

PRITAM, Amrita (1919–2005). Indian poet, novelist and short-story writer. Born Aug 31, 1919, into a Sikh family in Gujranwala, India (now Pakistan); died Oct 31, 2005; dau. of a schoolteacher and poet; married an editor (div. 1960). ❖ The 1st prominent woman Punjabi poet and fiction writer, moved to New Delhi after Partition (1947) and worked for All India Radio until 1961; works include *Amrit Lehran* (1936), *Trel Dhote Phul* (1942), *Pagthar Glite* (1946), *Sunehray* (1955), *Kasturi* (1957), *Ik Si Anita* (1964), *Cham Nambar Chatti* (1964, trans. into English as *A Line in Water*), *Uninja Din* (1979), *Kagaz Te Kanvas* (1981), *The Skeleton* (1987) and (short stories) *Teesri Aurat*; edited monthly magazine in Punjabi, *Nagmani.* Was the 1st woman to receive the Sahitya Akademi Award and the 1st Punjabi woman to receive the Padma Shree from the president of India (1969); also received the Jananpeeth award (1982) for lifetime contribution to Punjabi literature. ❖ See also autobiography *Shadows of Words.*

PRITCHARD, Hannah (1711–1768). English actress. Name variations: Mrs. Pritchard. Born Hannah Vaughan in 1711; died in 1768. ❖ A member of David Garrick's company for 20 years, was considered the best Lady Macbeth (Gruoch) until Sarah Siddons; a renowned actress, eminent in both comedy and tragedy, excelled in playing characters of intrigue, including Lady Betty Modish and Lady Townly in *The Provoked Husband*; was also seen as Gertrude in *Hamlet*, Cleopatra in Dryden's *All for Love* and Zara in *The Mourning Bride.*

PRIVALOVA, Irina (1968—). Russian runner. Born Nov 12 (some sources cite the 22nd), 1968, in Malakhovka, Russia. ❖ At Barcelona Olympics, won a bronze medal in the 100 meters and a silver medal in the 4 x 100-meter relay (1992); at age 31, attempting a new event, won a gold medal for 400-meter hurdles as well as a bronze for the 4 x 400-meter relay at Sydney Olympics (2000); at European championships, won gold medals for 100 and 200 meters (1994) and gold for 200 meters (1998).

PROBA (fl. 4th c.). Roman poet and aristocrat. Name variations: Faltonia Betitia Proba. Manuscripts call the author only Proba; name Faltonia Betitia is doubtful; dau. of Petronius Probianius (consul in 322); grand-dau. of Probus (consul in 310); m. Claudius Celcinus Adalphius (prefect of Rome in 351); children: C. Clodius Hermogenianus Olybrius (consul in 379) and Faltonius Alypius. ❖ Born a pagan, converted to Christianity; wrote one poem that is extant, relating the life of Christ in terms borrowed from Virgil, in 694 hexameter lines.

PRÖBER, Martina (1963—). *See Proeber, Martina.*

PROBERT, Michelle (1960—). English runner. Name variations: Michelle Probert Scutt. Born June 17, 1960, in UK. ❖ At Moscow Olympics, won a bronze medal in 4 x 400-meter relay (1980).

PROCOPÉ, Ulla (1921–1968). Finnish designer of ceramics. Name variations: Ulla Procope. Born in Finland, 1921; died 1968; graduate of Helsinki Institute of Industrial Arts, 1948. ❖ Worked for the firm of Arabia, a producer of ceramic tableware, creating her own designs, which included the Liekki pattern (1957) and the popular Ruska (1960), distinguished by its rich brown glaze. Honored at Milan Triennale (1957); won numerous awards and medals at exhibitions in Holland and the US.

PROCOPIA. *Variant of Prokopia.*

PROCTER, Adelaide (1825–1864). English poet and feminist. Name variations: (pseudonym) Mary Berwick. Born Adelaide Anne Procter, Oct 30, 1825, in London, England; died in London, Feb 3 (some sources cite 2), 1864; dau. of Bryan Waller Procter (1787–1874, English poet who wrote under pseudonym Barry Cornwall) and Anne Skepper Procter; studied at Queen's College, London; never married. ❖ Under pseudonym Mary Berwick, contributed verse to Charles Dickens' periodical *Household Words*; published poems in 2 vols. under title *Legends and Lyrics* (1858), which went through 9 editions in 7 years; had similar success with a 2nd series (1861); best known for poems "The Angel's Story" and "The Lost Chord" (set to music by Sir Arthur Sullivan); a dedicated feminist, helped Bodichon and Boucherett to found the Society

for Promoting the Employment of Women; also contributed the proceeds of a volume of poems to a night shelter for homeless women, and had her anthology *Victoria Regina* published by Emily Faithfull's Victoria Press (1861). Dickens supplied the foreword to her *Complete Works.*

PRODANOVA, Diana (1942—). *See Yorgova, Diana.*

PRODUNOVA, Elena (1980—). Russian gymnast. Born Feb 15, 1980, in Rostov-on-Don, Russia. ❖ At World championships, won a silver medal in team all-around and bronze medals in all-around and floor exercises (1997) and a silver medal in team all-around (1999); won Russian nationals (1999, 2000), Russian Cup (1999), World Stars (1999, 2000), and American Cup (2000); at European championships, won a gold medal in team all-around, silver in floor, and bronze in bars (2000).

PROEBER, Martina (1963—). East German diver. Name variations: Martina Pröber. Born Jan 4, 1963, in East Germany. ❖ At Moscow Olympics, won a silver medal in springboard (1980).

PROELL-MOSER, Annemarie (1953—). Austrian Alpine skier. Name variations: Annemarie Proell or Ann-Marie Pröll or Moser-Pröll; Annemarie Moser-Proell; Annemarie Moser. Born Annemarie Proell in Kleinarl, Austria, on Mar 27, 1953; m. Herbert Moser (salesman), 1975; sister of Cornelia Proell (b. 1961, Alpine skier). ❖ Won 6 World Cup overall titles; won silver medals in the downhill and giant slalom at Sapporo Olympics (1972); won World championship in downhill (1974, 1978) and combined (1978); won the World Cup (1971–75, 1979); completed a record of 11 consecutive downhill wins (1973); in 10 seasons, won a total of 59 individual events (1970–79); won a gold medal in the downhill at Lake Placid Olympics (1980). ❖ See also *Women in World History.*

PROENSA, Comtesse de (1170–1257). *See Garsenda.*

PROKASHEVA, Lyudmila (1969—). Kazakhstan speedskater. Born Jan 23, 1969, in Pavlodar, USSR. ❖ Won a silver medal for all-around at World championships (1995); won a bronze medal for 5,000 meters at Nagano Olympics (1998).

PROKHOROVA, Yelena (1978—). Russian heptathlete. Born April 16, 1978, in Kemerovo, Russia. ❖ Won a silver medal at Sydney Olympics (2000) and a gold medal at World championships (2001).

PROKOFF, Sandra (1975—). German bobsledder. Born Jan 4, 1975, in Germany. ❖ With Ulrike Holzner, won a gold medal for the two-man bobsleigh at the World Cup (2002) and a silver medal for the two-man bobsleigh at Salt Lake City Olympics (2002), the 1st women's bobsleigh competition in Winter Games history; with Anja Schneiderheinze, won a gold medal for bobsleigh at Torino Olympics (2006).

PROKOP, Liese (1941—). Austrian pentathlete and politician. Name variations: Elisabeth Prokop. Born Mar 27, 1941, in Vienna, Austria; attended University of Vienna. ❖ At Mexico City Olympics, won a silver medal in the pentathlon (1968); was a member of the Landtag (1981–92); served as deputy governor of Lower Austria (1992–2004); served as president of the Assembly of European Regions and as president of Austria's sport union; became minister of the Interior (2004).

PROKOPIA (fl. 800s). Byzantine empress. Name variations: Procopia. Dau. of Nicephorus I; sister of Stauracius, Byzantine emperor (r. 811); m. Michael Rangabe also seen as Michael I Rhangabé, Byzantine emperor (r. 811–813, died c. 845).

PRÖLL, Annemarie (b. 1953). *See Proell-Moser, Annemarie.*

PROPHET, Elizabeth (1890–1960). African-American sculptor. Born Nancy Elizabeth Prophet, Mar 19, 1890, in Warwick, Rhode Island; died Dec 1960, in Providence, Rhode Island; dau. of William H. Prophet (laborer) and Rosa E. (Walker) Prophet; graduate of Rhode Island School of Design, 1918; m. Francis Ford, Jan 30, 1915 (legally sep., 1932); no children. ❖ Enjoyed brief periods of success (1920s–1930s), but fell victim to prejudice and struggled with poverty throughout life; in Paris, completed 2 busts (1923), one of which was included in "Salon d'Automne" (1924); exhibited 2 works, *Violence* and *Buste ébène*, at Société des Artistes Française; returned to US (1932), at which time the Whitney Museum purchased her best-known work, *Congolaise* (c. 1930), the cherry wood head of a Masai warrior; taught at Spelman College in Atlanta (1934–44); continued to exhibit, at Whitney Sculpture Biennials (1935, 1937) and Philadelphia Museum of Art's Sculpture International (1940); returned to Rhode Island, where she worked as a domestic in the years preceding her death. Less than 10 of her sculptures are presently accounted for in collections; the rest have disappeared, their existence verified only through archival photographs and publications. ❖ See also *Women in World History*.

PROPHET, Elizabeth Clare (1940—). American religious founder. Born Elizabeth Clare Wulf, 1940, in Red Bank, NJ; Boston University, BA in political science; m. Dag Ytreburg (div.); m. Mark L. Prophet, 1963 (died 1973); m. Randall King (div.); m. Ed Francis (div.); children: (2nd m.) Sean, Erin, Moira, Tatiana; (4th m.) Seth. ❖ A follower of Saint Germain, became the leader of The Summit Lighthouse after the death of its founder, her husband Mark L. Prophet (1973); founded the Church Universal and Triumphant (1974), which is headquartered in Corwin Springs, Montana; known as Guru Ma by her followers, taught thousands of students, established centers throughout the world, and wrote dozens of books; announced she was suffering from Alzheimer's disease (1999).

PROROCHENKO-BURAKOVA, Tatyana (1952—). Soviet runner. Name variations: Tatyana Burakova. Born Mar 15, 1952, in USSR. ❖ Won a bronze medal in the 4 x 100-meter relay at Montreal Olympics (1976) and a gold medal in the 4 x 400-meter relay at Moscow Olympics (1980).

PROSKOURIAKOFF, Tatiana (1909–1985). Russian-American archaeologist and epigrapher. Born Jan 23, 1909, in Tomsk, Siberia, Russia; came to US in 1916; died 1985; dau. of Avenir Proskouriakoff (chemist) and Alla Nekrassova (physician); Pennsylvania State University, BS in architecture, 1930. ❖ Began work at Museum of University of Pennsylvania; participated in Museum's expedition to Piedras Negras (1936) and made drawings of archaeological reconstructions of sites, including Chichén Itzá, Tikal, and Yaxchilán; made major discovery regarding dynastic sequence of political reigns of Piedras Negras rulers and published pioneering work "Historical Implications of a Pattern of Dates at Piedras Negras, Guatemala" (1960); for her discovery that ancient Mayans were recording their own history, received Alfred V. Kidder Medal (1962); served as honorary curator of maya art at Peabody Museum; awarded Order of Quetzal by Guatemala (1984). Other major works include *An Album of Maya Architecture* (1946), *A Study of Classic Maya Sculpture* (1950).

PROSPERI, Carola (1883–1975). Italian feminist, novelist and short-story writer. Born 1883 in Turin, Italy; died 1975. ❖ Contributed to *La Stampa* newspaper and published stories in magazines; works, which often focus on socially confined, middle-class women, include *La paura d'amare* (1911), *L'estranea* (1915), *La felicità in gabbia* (1922), *Agnese, amante ingenua* (1934), *Fiamme burgiarde* (1951), and *Raconti del Piemonte* (1954).

PROTOPOPOV, Ludmila (1935—). Russian pairs skater. Name variations: Lyudmilla, Ljudmilla, or Ludmilla Belovsova (also Belousova or Beloussova). Born Ludmila Belovsova, Nov 22, 1935, in Ulyanovsk, USSR; m. Oleg Protopopov (pairs skater), c. 1966. ❖ With partner and husband, dominated pairs competition (1960s), winning gold medals at Innsbruck Olympics (1964) and Grenoble Olympics (1968) and 4 World championships (1965–68). Known for their artistic innovation, became Swiss citizens.

PROTT, Dagmar. *See Lurz, Dagmar.*

PROU, Suzanne (1920–1995). French novelist. Born in 1920; died in Paris, France, night of Dec 29–30, 1995. ❖ Wrote 2 dozen novels, including her best known *La Terrasse des Bernardini (The Bernardini Terrace,* 1973), which won the Prix Renaudot; during French occupation in WWII, helped produce an underground paper that condemned anti-Semitism; was also a human-rights activist and ardent feminist.

PROULX, E. Annie (1935—). American novelist. Pronunciation: Proulx rhymes with true. Born Edna Annie Proulx, 1935, in Norwich, CT; University of Vermont, BA, 1969; Sir George Williams (now Concordia) University, MA, 1973. ❖ Began career as a journalist; started writing fiction in her 50s, with *Heart Songs and Other Stories* (1988) and *Postcards* (1992); won the Pulitzer Prize and National Book Award for *The Shipping News* (1993); also wrote *Accordion Crimes* (1996), *Close Range* (1999) and *That Old Ace in the Hole* (2002).

PROUT, Mary Ann (1801–1884). African-American school founder and educator. Name variations: Aunt Mary Prout. Born, possibly in Baltimore, Maryland, Feb 14, 1801 (some sources cite 1800, while another source maintains that she was born a slave in South River, Maryland); died in Baltimore, 1884; dau. of mixed-African parentage.

❖ Founded a day school in Baltimore (c. 1830), where she taught for over 30 years; after the school closed (1867), continued to pursue humanitarian work, becoming one of two black trustees of the Gregory Aged Women's Home, also in Baltimore; additionally served as president of the association in charge of the home, the National Reform Educational Association; founded a secret order (1867) which evolved into the Independent Order of St. Luke, a black organization which provided financial aid to the sick and funds for burial of the dead. ❖ See also *Women in World History*.

PROUTY, Olive Higgins (1882–1974). American novelist. Born Olive Higgins in Worcester, Massachusetts, on Jan 10, 1882; died in Brookline, Massachusetts, Mar 24, 1974; dau. of Milton Higgins (head of Mechanical Department of the Worcester Polytechnic Institute) and Katharine Elizabeth (Chapin) Higgins; Smith College, BL, 1904; m. Lewis Isaac Prouty, 1907; children: 3 daughters, 1 son. ❖ Published 1st story "When Elsie Came" in *American Magazine* (1909), a family chronicle narrated by a young girl named Bobbie; wrote a series of additional stories focusing on the same family, and later turned them into her 1st and 3rd novels, *Bobbie, General Manager* (1913) and *The Fifth Wheel* (1916); published best-known novel, *Stella Dallas* (1923), about a mother who sacrifices her own life to assure her daughter's social position, which spawned a successful play (1924), 3 films (1925, 1937, 1990), and became one of the longest-running soap operas in radio history; later works included a series of novels about a wealthy Boston family named Vale, including the highly successful *Now, Voyager* (1941) and *Home Port* (1947). ❖ See also memoir *Pencil Shavings* (1961); and *Women in World History*.

PROVENCE, countess of.
See Douce I (d. 1190).
See Garsenda (1170–c. 1257).
See Beatrice of Savoy (d. 1268).
See Jeanne of Lorraine (1458–1480).
See Marie Josephine of Savoy (d. 1810).

PROVENCE, duchess of. *See Jeanne de Laval (d. 1498).*

PROVIDOKHINA-FYODORENKO, Tatyana (1953—). Soviet runner. Name variations: Tatyana Fyodorenko. Born Mar 26, 1953, in USSR. ❖ At Moscow Olympics, won a bronze medal in 800 meters (1980).

PROVINE, Dorothy (1937—). American actress, singer and dancer. Born Jan 20, 1937, in Deadwood, SD; m. Robert Day (cinematographer), 1969. ❖ Made film debut in *Live Fast Die Young* (1958), followed by *It's a Mad Mad Mad World, Good Neighbor Sam, The Great Race, That Darn Cat* and *Never a Dull Moment,* among others; probably best remembered on film for title role in *The Bonnie Parker Story* (1958); on tv, starred on "The Alaskans" (1959–60) and as Pinky Pinkham in "The Roaring Twenties" (1960–62); retired (1969).

PROVIS, Nicole (1969—). Australian tennis player. Name variations: Nicole Bradkte. Born Nicole Provis, Sept 22, 1969, in Melbourne, Australia; sister of Natasha Woodbridge (who married Todd Woodbridge); m. Mark Bradtke (Australian basketball star). ❖ At 18, made it to the semifinals of French Open (1988); at Barcelona Olympics, won a bronze medal in doubles (1992); with Todd Woodbridge, won mixed doubles at US Open (1992).

PROVOOST, Mary Spratt (1693–1760). *See Alexander, Mary.*

PROWSE, Anne (c. 1530–c. 1590). *See Locke, Anne Vaughan.*

PROWSE, Juliet (1936–1996). South African dancer and actress. Born Sept 25, 1936, in Bombay, India; died of pancreatic cancer, Sept 14, 1996, in Holmby Hills, California; m. Eddie Frazier, 1969 (div. 1970); m. actor John McCook (div.); children: son, Seth. ❖ Raised in Durban, South Africa; studied for the ballet from an early age, performing with Johannesburg Festival Ballet at 14; made film debut in *Gentlemen Marry Brunettes* (1955), followed by *Can-Can* (1960) and *G.I Blues* (1960); also appeared in *The Fiercest Heart* (1961), *The Right Approach* (1961), *The Second Time Around* (1961), *Who Killed Teddy Bear?* (1965), *Dingaka* (1965), *Run for Your Wife* (1966) and *Spree* (1967); went on to star in tv specials, stage musicals, and nightclubs; starred in her own tv sitcom, "Mona McCluskey" (1965).

PROZUMENSHCHYKOVA, Galina (1948—). Soviet swimmer. Name variations: Galyna. Born Nov 26, 1948, in Sevastopol, Ukraine. ❖ At Tokyo Olympics, won a gold medal in the 200-meter breaststroke (1964); at Mexico City Olympics, won a bronze medal in the 200-meter breaststroke and a silver medal in the 100-meter breaststroke

(1968); at Munich Olympics, won a bronze medal in the 200-meter breaststroke and a silver medal in the 100-meter breaststroke (1972).

PRUDSKOVA, Valentina (1938—). Soviet fencer. Born Dec 27, 1938, in USSR. ❖ Won a gold medal at Rome Olympics (1960) and a silver medal at Tokyo Olympics (1964), in team foil.

PRUNSKIENE, Kazimiera (1943—). Lithuanian political leader. Name variations: Kazimiera Danutë Prunskienë. Born Kazimiera Danute Stankeviciute in Vasiuliskiai, Lithuania, Feb 26, 1943; dau. of Pranas Stankevicius (killed during WWII); University of Vilnius, degree in economics, 1965; m. 2nd husband Algimantis Tarvidas; children: daughters, Dayvita and Raisa; son, Vaidotos. ❖ With the onset of *perestroika* advocated by Gorbachev, became one of the founding members of Sajudis (1988), the grass-roots Lithuanian movement that hoped to turn his ideas into reality within the republic; became deputy chair for economic affairs in Council of Ministers of the Lithuanian Soviet Socialist Republic (1989), as well as being elected to Supreme Soviet of USSR; served as the 1st prime minister of the self-proclaimed independent Republic of Lithuania (Mar 1990–Jan 1991) during a time of turbulence; went on to found the Lithuanian-European Institute; was elected leader of Lithuanian Women's Party (1995); published 15 books. ❖ See also *Women in World History.*

PRUSSIA, queen of.
See Sophie Charlotte of Hanover (1668–1705).
See Sophie Louise of Mecklenburg (1685–1735).
See Sophia Dorothea of Brunswick-Lüneburg-Hanover (1687–1757).
See Elizabeth Christina of Brunswick-Wolfenbuttel (1715–1797).
See Frederica of Hesse (1751–1805).
See Louise of Prussia (1776–1810).
See Elizabeth of Bavaria (1801–1873).
See Augusta of Saxe-Weimar (1811–1890).

PRYAKHINA, Svetlana (1970—). Soviet handball player. Born July 29, 1970, in USSR. ❖ At Barcelona Olympics, won a bronze medal in team competition (1992).

PRYOR, Mrs. Roger (1830–1912). *See Pryor, Sara Agnes.*

PRYOR, Sara Agnes (1830–1912). American author and social leader. Name variations: Mrs. Roger Pryor. Born Feb 19, 1830, in Halifax Co., Virginia; died 1912; attended a female seminary in Charlottesville, Virginia; m. Roger Atkinson Pryor (lawyer, member of New York Supreme Court, and US congressional representative); children: 7. ❖ Founded the National Society of the Daughters of the American Revolution and was a charter member of the Colonial Dames of America; frequently contributed articles to magazines. ❖ See also memoir *My Day: Reminiscences of a Long Life;* and *Women in World History.*

PRYOR, Vanessa (1942—). *See Yarbro, Chelsea Quinn.*

PRZYBYSZEWSKA, Dagny Juel (1867–1901). Norwegian-born writer. Pronunciation: Pshi-bi-shef-ska. Name variations: changed the spelling of surname from Juell to Juel. Born in Kongsvinger, Norway, June 8, 1867; killed by her lover Wladyslaw Emeryk, June 5, 1901; dau. of Hans Lemmich Juell (doctor and attendant physician to king of Sweden) and Minda (Blehr) Juell (sister of Otto Blehr, a Norwegian prime minister); sister of Ragnhild Juell; m. Stanislaw Przybyszewski (1868–1927, well-known Polish playwright and father of playwright Stanislawa Przybyszewska whose mother was Aniela Pajakowna), late summer 1893; children: son Zenon P. Westrup (b. Sept 1895); daughter Iwa Dahlin (b. Oct 1897). ❖ A central figure in Berlin's avant-garde movement of the 1890s and the muse of the city's *Schwarze Ferkel* artist's circle, served as the model for several of Strindberg's destructive women characters: Aspasia in *Inferno* and *Svarta fanor* (Black Banners), Laïs in *The Cloister* and *Karantänmästaarns andra berättelse* (The Quarantine Officer's Second Story), and Henriette in *Crimes and Crimes;* was painted by Edvard Munch; a talent in her own right, wrote 4 plays, a short story, and a collection each of prose and lyric poems, and was an agent for a number of Scandinavian artists; writings include short story "Rediviva" (1893), play *Den sterkere* (The Stronger, 1896) and prose-poem cycle *Sing mir das Lied vom Leben und vom Tode* (Sing Me the Song of Life and Death, 1900). ❖ See also Mary Kay Norseng, *Dagny: Dagny Juel Przybyszewska: The Woman and the Myth* (U. of Washington Press, 1991); and *Women in World History.*

PRZYBYSZEWSKA, Stanislawa (1901–1935). Polish playwright. Pronunciation: Pshi-bi-shef-ska. Born Stanislawa Pajak in 1901; died of malnutrition and TB in Gdansk (formerly Danzig), Aug 15, 1935; illeg. dau. of Aniela Pajakowna (d. 1912, professional artist) and Stanislaw Przybyszewski (1868–1927, well-known Polish playwright who was married to Dagny Juel Przybyszewska); m. Jan Panienski (painter and teacher), 1923 (died 1925); no children. ❖ One of the great talents of modern European literature, produced several novels and other works of lesser significance; work was rediscovered (1960s–70s); gained posthumous fame for her powerful dramatic trilogy on the French Revolution—*Thermidor,1793,* and *The Danton Case*—which is now firmly established in the repertory of the Polish theater. ❖ See also Jadwiga Kosicka and Daniel Gerould, *A Life of Solitude–Stanislawa Przybyszewska: A Biographical Study with Selected Letters* (Northwestern U. Press, 1989); and *Women in World History.*

PSAPPHA or PSAPPHO (c. 612–c. 557 BCE). *See Sappho.*

PTASCHKINA, Nelly (1903–1920). Russian diarist. Born in Russia, 1903; died at age 17 while climbing in Chamonix, France, July 2, 1920; never married; no children. ❖ Kept a series of notebooks from age 10, several of which were published by her mother following her death (1920); during Russian Revolution (1917), fled with family from Moscow to Kiev, then on to Paris, surviving harassment by the Bolsheviks and threats of shooting and pillaging by both the Red and White armies. ❖ See also *Women in World History.*

PTOLEMAIS (c. 315 BCE–?). Egyptian princess. Born c. 315 BCE; dau. of Ptolemy I Soter, king of Egypt (r. 305–285 BCE), and Eurydice (fl. 321 BCE); cousin of Magas and Ptolemy II; m. Demetrius Poliorcetes ("the City Besieger"); children: Demetrius the Fair (who m. Berenice II of Cyrene [c. 273–221 BCE]).

PTUJEC, Jasna (1959—). Yugoslavian handball player. Born Jan 19, 1959, in Yugoslavia. ❖ At Los Angeles Olympics, won a gold medal in team competition (1984).

PUCELLE, La. *See Joan of Arc (c. 1412–1431).*

PUCK, Eva (1892–1979). American vaudeville and musical-comedy star. Name variations: Eve Puck. Born 1892 in Brooklyn, NY; died Oct 24, 1979, in Grenada Hills, CA; m. Sammy White (entertainer). ❖ At 3, began career with brother Harry in vaudeville; following marriage, became a vaudeville headliner with husband and also performed in numerous Broadway shows; came to prominence in *The Greenwich Follies of 1923,* followed by *Irene* (1924), *Melody Man* (1924) and *The Girl Friend* (written for her by Rodgers and Hart); created the role of Ellie in *Show Boat.*

PUDNEY, Daisy (1894–1976). *See Pudney, Elizabeth Allen.*

PUDNEY, Elizabeth Allen (1894–1976). New Zealand religious leader and nurse. Name variations: Daisy Pudney, Elizabeth Allen Storey. Born Dec 5, 1894, at Colyton, near Feilding, New Zealand; died May 21, 1976, in Oratia, Auckland, New Zealand; dau. of Robert Leaper Pudney (professor) and Elizabeth Jane Pudney; m. Harry Frank Storey, 1956. ❖ Trained as nurse (1920); worked in private hospital in Wanganui (1922); set out to become medical missionary in west China, but illness en route forced her return to New Zealand (1924); became active in Society of Friends, and helped to produce its newsletter; also promoted mission work of Friends' Foreign Mission Association. ❖ See also *Dictionary of New Zealand Biography* (Vol. 3).

PUDNEY, Elizabeth Jane (1862–1938). New Zealand religious leader. Name variations: Eliza Jane Matthews. Born Eliza Jane Matthews, Aug 15, 1862, at Earls Colne, Essex, England; died on Mar 1, 1938, in Auckland, New Zealand; dau. of William Matthews (farmer) and Rebecca (Allen) Matthews; m. Robert Leaper Pudney (professor), 1892; children: 2 daughters, including Elizabeth Allen Pudney, and 1 son. ❖ Immigrated to New Zealand (c. 1893); settled on 600-acre farm, which became regular meeting house for Quakers; was a founding executive member of New Zealand Women's Christian Temperance Union (1897); moved to England to educate children at Society of Friends' Sidcot School (1905); returned to New Zealand (1909) and became founding member of New Zealand Freedom League (1913); active in Auckland Women's Peace Committee. ❖ See also *Dictionary of New Zealand Biography* (Vol. 3).

PUESCHEL, Karin (1958—). East German volleyball player. Name variations: Karin Püschel. Born Jan 1958 in East Germany. ❖ At Moscow Olympics, won a silver medal in team competition (1980).

PUFE, Margitta (1952—). East German track-and-field athlete. Born Sept 10, 1952, in East Germany. ❖ At Moscow Olympics, won a bronze medal in the shot put (1980).

PUGACHEVA, Alla (1949—). Russian pop singer. Name variations: Alla Borisovna Pugacheva, Pugachova or Pugachyova. Born April 15, 1949, in Moscow, USSR; attended Ippolitov-Ivanov School of Music and Lunacharsky School of Theatrical Arts; m. Mikolas Edmundas Orbakas, 1969 (div.); m. 3 more times, lastly to singer Philipp Kirkorov, 1995; children: (with Orbakas) Kristina Orbakaite (singer and actress). ❖ Made 1st recordings for radio station at age 16; toured USSR and Far East with Russian bands, including New Electron, Moscovites and Happy Fellows; won 3rd prize at All Union competition of pop artists, receiving national attention (1974); won Grand Prix at Golden Orpheus competition in Bulgaria with song "Arkelino" (Harlequin, 1975); won 1st prize at International Sopot Song Festival, becoming a musical superstar of concerts, films and tv shows throughout Russia and Eastern Europe (1978); recorded over 20 albums—a mix of pop, rock, folk and torch songs—which have sold between 140 and 200 million copies; appeared in several popular films, including *The Woman Who Sings* (1977) and *Came to Say* (1985). Was the last singer to win National Artist of the USSR award; awarded medal for "service to the fatherland," Russia's highest civilian award (1999). ❖ See also *Women in World History*.

PUGH, Madelyn (c. 1921—). American comedy writer. Name variations: Madelyn Martin; Madelyn Pugh Davis. Born Madelyn Pugh, c. 1921, in Indianapolis, IN; Indiana University, BA, 1942; married twice. ❖ With Bob Carroll Jr., wrote the pilot episode of "I Love Lucy" (1951), then helped shape the characters of Lucy and Ricky Ricardo and Fred and Ethel Mertz for years afterward; also wrote for and created "Those Whiting Girls" (1955), "The Mothers-in-Law" (1967) and "Alice" (1976); wrote over 400 scripts. Received the Women in Film Award (1996).

PUGH, Sarah (1800–1884). American teacher, abolitionist, and suffragist. Born in Alexandria, Virginia, Oct 6, 1800; died in Germantown, Pennsylvania, Aug 1, 1884; dau. of Jesse Pugh and Catharine (Jackson) Pugh (Quakers); attended Quaker-run Westtown (PA) Boarding School for 2 years; never married. ❖ Best remembered for her intelligent, dedicated support of both the anti-slavery and the woman's suffrage movements, established her own elementary school in Philadelphia (1829), where she taught for more than a decade; joined both the Female Anti-Slavery Society, of which she served as an officer for many years, and the American Anti-Slavery Society (1835); was a US delegate to the London meeting of British and Foreign Anti-Slavery Society; often worked with Lucretia Mott. ❖ See also *Women in World History*.

PUGOVSKAYA, Olga (1942—). Soviet rower. Born Nov 1942 in USSR. ❖ At Montreal Olympics, won a silver medal in coxed eights (1976).

PUHIWAHINE TE RANGI-HIRAWEA, Rihi (d. 1906). New Zealand tribal leader and composer. Name variations: Elizabeth Gotty. Born possibly about 1816, near Taumarunui, New Zealand; died Feb 18, 1906, at Ongarue, New Zealand; dau. of Rawiri Te Rangi-hirawea and Hinekiore; m. John Gotty (Johann Maximilian Goethe), mid-1840s (died 1893); children: 2 sons. ❖ Schooled in tribal traditions and songs by her mother, and well-traveled, composed numerous songs, including a love song that remains currently popular at weddings. ❖ See also *Dictionary of New Zealand Biography* (Vol. 2).

PÜHRINGER, Uta Barbara (1943—). Austrian politician. Name variations: Uta Puhringer or Puehringer. Born April 27, 1943, in Linz, Austria. ❖ Conservative, was a member of the Landtag (1996–96); became a member of the Bundesrat (Austrian Parliament, 1996); served as president of the Bundesrat (Jan 1, 2002–June 30, 2002).

PUICA, Maricica (1950—). Romanian runner. Born July 29, 1950, in Romania. ❖ At Los Angeles Olympics, won a gold medal in the 3,000 meters and a bronze medal in the 1,500 meters (1984).

PUIHI (?–1855). See Faulkner, Ruawahine Irihapeti.

PUISIEUX, Madeleine de (1720–1798). French novelist. Name variations: Madeleine d'Arsant de Puisieux; Marie Madeleine D'arsant. Born 1720 in Paris, France; died 1798. ❖ Held reformist and anti-clerical ideas about education, religious intolerance, individual rights, and position of women; best known for *Les caractères* (1750–51), written while she was having an affair with Denis Diderot; other works include *Conseils à une amie* (1749), *Le Plaisir et la volupté* (1752), *L'Education du Marquis de **** (1753), *Alzarac* (1762), *Le marquis à la mode* (1763), and *Histoire de Mlle de Terville* (1768); also may have written feminist essay attributed to her husband, *Le Femme n'est pas inférieure à l'homme* (1750); collection of poems, *Une suite de poèmes* (1746) remains in manuscript form in Bibliothèque Nationale.

PUKUI, Mary Kawena (1895–1986). Hawaiian musician. Born Mary Abigail Kawena-'ula-o-ka-lani-a-hi'jaka-i-ka-poli-o-pepe-ka-wahine-l'ai-hou na Pukui in Ka'u, Hawaii, April 20, 1895; died May 1986 in Honolulu. ❖ Composer, chanter, teacher, translator and writer, composed over 50 Hawaiian songs ranging from hula music to Christmas carols, blending Hawaiian and European cultures, but remained a proponent of, and authority on, Hawaiian language and culture. Received honorary LLDs from University of Hawaii (1960) and Brigham Young University, Hawaii (1974).

PULCHERIA (c. 376–385). Roman noblewoman. Born c. 376; died in 385; dau. of Flaccilla (c. 355–386) and Theodosius I the Great, emperor of Rome (r. 379–395); sister of Arcadius, emperor of Rome in the East (r. 395–408), and Honorius, emperor of Rome in the West (r. 395–423).

PULCHERIA (c. 398–453). Roman-Byzantine empress. Name variations: Aelia Pulcheria or Aelia Pulcheria Augusta; Pulcheria means "beautiful woman" from the Latin word *pulcher* (beautiful). Reigned 408–450; born Jan 19, 398 or 399; died in 453; dau. of Emperor Arcadius (r. 395–408); mother's name unknown; sister of Arcadia and Marina, half-sister of Emperor Theodosius II; great-granddau. of Emperor Valentinian I (r. 364–375), granddau. of Theodosius I (r. 379–395) and his wife Flaccilla (c. 355–386), grandniece of Valentinian II (r. 375–392), niece of Emperor Honorius (r. 395–423), and 1st cousin of Valentinian III (r. 425–455); stepdau. of Eudocia of Byzantium (d. 404); m. Marcian (a general). ❖ Romano-Byzantine empress who shaped a decisive period in the history of an empire in which few women reached such positions of power and influence; brother Theodosius born (c. 400); father Arcadius died (408); granted title "Augusta" (414); served as regent for brother Emperor Theodosius II (July 4, 414–416) and assumed responsibility for his rearing; arranged brother's marriage to Athenais (renamed Eudocia, 421); led affairs of state throughout brother's 42-year reign (408–450); had a hand in founding of the University of Constantinople (Feb 25, 425), the convocation of the Council of Ephesus (431), and possibly the promulgation of the Code of Theodosius (438); quarreled with sister-in-law Eudocia, who moved permanently to Jerusalem (c. 440); retired from court life (443); brother Theodosius died (450); became 1st woman to hold the Roman throne, marrying General Marcian, whom she made her co-ruler (450); called for the Council of Chalcedon (451); in guiding the Eastern Roman Empire through so many of its most perilous early years, as well as the important role she played in generating the councils of Ephesus and Chalcedon, two of the most significant events in the annals of the Christian Church, was one of the most important women in history. ❖ See also *Women in World History*.

PULCHERIA (fl. 800s). Roman noblewoman. Flourished in the 800s; dau. of Theophilus I (r. 829–842) and Theodora the Blessed, empress and regent of Eastern Roman Empire (r. 842–856).

PULITZER, Mrs. Ralph (1893–1974). See Leech, Margaret.

PULLING, Mary Etheldred (1871–1951). New Zealand headmistress and religious writer. Born July 26, 1871, at Belchamp St Paul, Essex, England; died Mar 24, 1951, at Te Awamutu, New Zealand; dau. of James (cleric) and Elizabeth Mary (Hodgson) Pulling. ❖ Immigrated to New Zealand to establish church school for girls, Diocesan School (1904); served as headmistress until retirement (1926); wrote religious treatises and book of Lenten meditations; lived reclusive life from 1930. ❖ See also *Dictionary of New Zealand Biography* (Vol. 3).

PULMAN, Elizabeth (1836–1900). New Zealand photographer. Name variations: Elizabeth Chadd, Elizabeth Blackman. Born Elizabeth Chadd, Aug 1, 1836, at Lymm, Cheshire, England; died Feb 3, 1900, at Auckland, New Zealand; dau. of William Chadd (bricksetter) and Mary (Clayton) Chadd; m. George Pulman (photographer), 1861 (died 1871); m. John Blackman (reporter), 1875 (died 1893); children: (1st m.) 3 sons, 2 daughters, and 2 stepsons; (2nd m.) 1 son. ❖ Immigrated with husband to New Zealand (1861); assumed management of husband's photographic studio after his death (1871); specialized in portrait and scenic subjects. ❖ See also *Dictionary of New Zealand Biography* (Vol. 2).

PULSKI, Romola de (1891–1978). See Nijinska, Romola.

PULVER, Lilo (1929—). Swiss-born actress. Name variations: Lilo Pulver. Born Liselotte Pulver. Born Oct 11, 1929, in Berne, Switzerland. ❖ Trained for the stage; starred in German films and in European co-productions (1950s–60s); portrayed a number of notable characters on screen, among them Antonie Buddenbrook in Thomas Mann's *Buddenbrooks* (1959), Queen Anne in *Das Glas Wasser* (*A Glass of Water,* 1960), and Marie Antoinette in *Lafayette* (1962); appeared in such US films as *A Time to Love and a Time to Die* (1958), *One Two Three* (1961) and *A Global Affair* (1964).

PULZ, Penny (1953—). Australian golfer. Born Feb 2, 1953, in Melbourne, Australia. ❖ Won Corning Classic (1979) and Circle K Tucson Open (1986); commentator for ESPN.

PUNG, Jackie (1921—). American golfer. Name variations: Jacqueline Pung. Born Dec 13, 1921, in Honolulu, Hawaii. ❖ Won the Hawaiian Women's Amateur (1937–39, 1948); won USGA Women's Amateur (1952); clearly won USGA Women's Open (1957), but had to forfeit because her marker, Betty Jameson, had inadvertently noted a 5 instead of a 6 at the 4th hole on Pung's scorecard; named LPGA Teacher of the Year (1967); LPGA Master Professional, ran her own golf academy in Waikoloa, Hawaii. Received Ben Hogan Award (1974).

PURCELL, Irene (1902–1972). American stage and screen actress. Born Aug 7, 1902, in Hammond, IN; died July 9, 1972, in Racine, WI; m. Herbert Fisk Johnson Jr., 1941. ❖ Made stage debut with Otis Skinner's company and Broadway debut in *The New Poor* (1924); appeared in other plays such as *Cross Roads, The Ladder, Dancing Partner, Accent on Youth* and *The First Apple;* films include *Just a Gigolo, Man in Possession* and *The Passionate Plumber;* retired (1941).

PURCELL, Samuelene (1898–1982). New Zealand trade unionist. Born July 25, 1898, in Auckland, New Zealand; died Dec 20, 1982, in Auckland; dau. of Michael Joseph Purcell and Jane (Galbraith) Purcell. ❖ Active at executive level in several trade unions in Auckland, including Retail Shop Assistants' Union, Retail Chemists' Employees' Union, Grocers' Assistants' Union, and Trade Union Secretaries' Association (1920s–71). ❖ See also *Dictionary of New Zealand Biography* (Vol. 4).

PURSER, Sarah (1848–1943). Irish artist, patron, and salonnière. Born Sarah Henrietta Purser in Kingstown (Dun Laoghaire), Co. Dublin, Ireland, Mar 22, 1848; died in Dublin, Aug 7, 1943; dau. of Benjamin Purser and Anne (Mallet) Purser; educated at Moravian school in Switzerland; never married. ❖ Studied in Paris (1878); returned to Dublin where she secured important commissions, among them a portrait of sisters Constance Markievicz and Eva Gore-Booth; with J.B. Yeats and Walter Osborne, was a founder member of Dublin Art Club (1886); helped to organize a major exhibition in Dublin of works by Corot, Courbet, Degas, Manet, Monet and others, which made a considerable impact (1899); founded An Túr Gloine (Thoor Glinna), The Tower of Glass (1903), which would become one of the finest stained-glass workshops in the world and produce generations of gifted artists, among them Michael Healy, Catherine O'Brien, Wilhelmina Geddes, Ethel Rhind and Hubert MacGoldrick; held her famous "Second Tuesdays," the most notable salon in Dublin, where artists, politicians, writers, academics and professional people gathered and conversed; founded Friends of the National Collections of Ireland (1924). ❖ See also John O'Grady, *The Life and Work of Sarah Purser* (Four Courts, 1996); and *Women in World History.*

PURSLEY, Barbara. *See Roles, Barbara.*

PURVIANCE, Edna (1894–1958). American actress. Pronunciation: per-VY-unce. Born in Loeclock, Paradise Valley, Nevada, Oct 21, 1894; died Jan 11, 1958, in Hollywood, CA; m. John P. Squires. ❖ Made film debut opposite Charlie Chaplin in *The Champion* (1915); appeared in other silent films opposite Chaplin (1915–23), including *The Tramp* (1915), *By the Sea* (1915), *Work* (1915), *A Woman* (1915), *The Bank* (1915), *The Fireman* (1916), *The Vagabond* (1916), *The Pawnshop* (1916), *The Rink* (1916), *The Immigrant* (1917), *A Dog's Life* (1918), *Shoulder Arms* (1918), *Sunnyside* (1919), *The Kid* (1921), *The Pilgrim* (1923) and *A Woman of Paris* (1923). ❖ See also *Women in World History.*

PURVIS, Harriet Forten (1810–1875). African-American abolitionist. Name variations: Harriet Forten; Hattie Purvis. Born Harriet Davy Forten, 1810, in Philadelphia, Pennsylvania; died of TB, June 11, 1875, in Philadelphia; dau. of James Forten (b. 1766, wealthy businessman) and his 2nd wife Charlotte (Vandine) Forten; sister of Sarah Forten Purvis (c. 1811–c. 1898) and Margaretta Forten (1808–1875); aunt of Charlotte Forten Grimké (1837–1914); attended a private black academy in Philadelphia; m. Robert Purvis (abolitionist), Sept 13, 1831; children: William Purvis (b. 1832); Joseph Parrish Purvis (b. 1837); Harriet Purvis (b. 1839, abolitionist and suffragist); Charles Burleigh Purvis (b. 1840 or 1841); Henry Purvis (b. 1843 or 1844); Robert Purvis (b. 1844 or 1845); Granville Sharp Purvis (b. 1845 or 1846); Georgianna Purvis (b. 1848 or 1849). ❖ Longtime member of the Philadelphia Female Anti-Slavery Society, opened home with husband to escaped slaves whom they fed, clothed, and financed, while arranging for them to make their way north to Canada; household served as an intellectual meeting place for some of the more progressive members of Philadelphia society, and the family's dedication to the abolition of slavery attracted visits from some of the most outspoken abolitionists in the country. ❖ See also *Women in World History.*

PURVIS, Sarah Forten (c. 1811–c. 1898). African-American poet and abolitionist. Name variations: Sarah Forten; (pseudonyms) Ada, Magawisca, Sarah Louisa. Born Sarah Louisa Forten sometime between 1811 and 1814 in Philadelphia, Pennsylvania; died c. 1898 (though some sources indicate as early as 1883) in Philadelphia; dau. of James Forten (b. 1766, wealthy businessman) and his 2nd wife Charlotte (Vandine) Forten; sister of Harriet Forten Purvis (1810–1875) and Margaretta Forten (1808–1875); aunt of Charlotte Forten Grimké (1837–1914); educated in a private black academy in Philadelphia; m. Joseph Purvis, Jan 7, 1838 (died 1857); children: Joseph Purvis (b. 1838 or 1839); James Purvis (c. 1839–1870); William Purvis (b. 1841 or 1842); Sarah Purvis (b. 1842 or 1843); Emily Purvis (1844–1870s); Alfred Purvis (c. 1845–1865); Harriet Purvis (b. 1847 or 1848); Alexander Purvis (b. 1850). ❖ Dedicated abolitionist, began submitting poems under the name "Ada" to *Liberator,* an abolitionist journal published by William Lloyd Garrison; along with mother and older sisters Harriet and Margaretta, joined in the founding of the Philadelphia Female Anti-Slavery Society (1833), an organization she would later serve as a member of its board of managers; published "An Appeal to Woman" (1834), likely her most well-known poem, in the *Liberator.* ❖ See also *Women in World History.*

PUSCATU, Rodica (1962—). *See Arba-Puscatu, Rodica.*

PÜSCHEL, Karin (1958—). *See Pueschel, Karin.*

PUSCHEVICH, Olga (1983—). *See Puzhevich, Olga.*

PUSICH, Antónia Gertrudes (1805–1883). Portuguese poet, playwright, and editor. Name variations: Antonia Pusich. Born 1805 in Portugal; died 1883. ❖ Founded and edited several reviews, including *A Assembléia Literária* (1849–51).

PUSTOVIT, Antonina (1955—). Soviet rower. Born Oct 16, 1955, in USSR. ❖ At Moscow Olympics, won a silver medal in the quadruple sculls with coxswain (1980).

PUSULA, Senja (1941—). Finnish cross-country skier. Name variations: Senja Nuolikivi. Born Mar 26, 1941, in Pieksämäki, Finland. ❖ Won a bronze medal for 3 x 5 km relay at Innsbruck Olympics (1964).

PUTLI BAI (1929–1958). Indian bandit queen. Born c. 1929 into a Muslim family of prostitutes in Agra, India; dau. of (mother) Ashgari (who ran a brothel); shot and killed while crossing the Kunwari River, trying to escape an ambush, 1958; children: daughter Tanno. ❖ One of the most well-known and revered bandit queens in India (1950s); 1st came to public attention as a willowy dancer in mother's traditional *Nauchghar* (brothel of dancing girls) in town of Agra; kidnapped by the leader of a *dacoit* gang, eventually chose to stay with him; when he was killed, teamed with another gang leader, Kalyan Singh, known as Kalla; injured in a police gun battle, lost left arm at the elbow but could still hold a gun. ❖ See also *Women in World History.*

PUTNAM, Alice Whiting (1841–1919). American educator. Born Alice Harvey Whiting, Jan 18, 1841, in Chicago, Illinois; died Jan 19, 1919, in Chicago; dau. of William Loring Whiting (commission merchant and a founder of Chicago Board of Trade) and Mary (Starr) Whiting; attended a private school run by mother and sister and then schooled at Dearborn Seminary; m. Joseph Robie Putnam (in real estate), May 20, 1868; children: Charlotte, Alice, Helen and Henry Sibley Putnam. ❖ Using the theories of Friedrich Froebel, supervised the training of kindergarten teachers for the Chicago Froebel Association for 30 years (1880–1910), helping establish the kindergarten movement in Chicago. ❖ See also *Women in World History.*

PUTNAM, Bertha Haven (1872–1960). American historian. Born Mar 1, 1872, in New York, NY; died Feb 26, 1960, in South Hadley, Massachusetts; dau. of George Haven Putnam (died 1930, head of publishing firm G.P. Putnam) and Rebecca Kettel (Shepard) Putnam (died 1895); stepdau. of Emily James Putnam (1865–1944); Bryn Mawr College, AB, 1893; Columbia University, PhD, 1908; never married. ❖ Expert on medieval English legal and economic history who was a professor at Mt. Holyoke College for 29 years; became an instructor in history at Mt. Holyoke (1908), then full professor (1924); was 1st woman and nonlawyer to receive a research grant from Harvard Law School (1938); elected a fellow of Mediaeval Academy (1949); retired from Mt. Holyoke (1937), after which she served as a lecturer at Bryn Mawr for 1 year. Received 1st Haskins Medal awarded from Mediaeval Academy of America. ❖ See also *Women in World History*.

PUTNAM, Eleanor (1856–1886). *See Bates, Harriet Leonora.*

PUTNAM, Emily James (1865–1944). American author and educator. Born Emily James Smith in Canandaigua, New York, April 15, 1865; died in Kingston, Jamaica, Sept 7, 1944; dau. of Judge James Cosslett Smith and Emily Ward (Adams) Smith; Bryn Mawr, AB, 1889; attended Girton College, Cambridge, 1889–90 (one of the 1st American women to do so); became 2nd wife of George Haven Putnam (head of the publishing firm G.P. Putnam), April 27, 1899 (died 1930); children: Palmer Cosslett Putnam (b. 1900, author of scientific and technical works); (stepdaughter) Bertha Haven Putnam (1872–1960). ❖ Was a teacher of Greek at Packer Collegiate Institute in Brooklyn (1891–93), a fellow in Greek at University of Chicago (1893–94), and served as 1st dean and associate in history at the 5-year-old Barnard College, at Columbia University (1894–1900); was president of League for Political Education (1901–04) and vice president and manager of Women's University Club, NY; besides translations from the Greek, wrote *The Lady: Studies of Certain Significant Phases of Her History* (1913); also helped establish the New School for Social Research (1919) and was a regular lecturer there.

PUTNAM, Helen (1857–1951). American physician. Born Sept 14, 1857, in Stockton, MN; died Feb 3, 1951; dau. of Celintha T. (Gates) Putnam and Herbert Asa Putnam; graduate of Vassar College, 1878, and Woman's Medical College of Pennsylvania 1889, and Hahnemann University School of Medicine; attended Harvard University's Sargent School of Physical Training. ❖ Suffragist leader and nationally recognized children's health advocate, began career as director of physical education at Vassar College (1883–90); served as vice president of American Association for the Advancement of Physical Education (1885–88); practiced gynecology in Rhode Island; as president of American Academy of Medicine (1908), organized a Conference on the Prevention of Infant Mortality, an event which led to the establishment of American Association for the Study and Prevention of Infant Mortality; with Dr. Abraham Jacobi, founded American Child Health Organization, which merged with American Association for the Study and Prevention of Infant Mortality to become the American Academy of Pediatrics (1923); retired (1935) in Providence, RI.

PUTNAM, Mary (1842–1906). *See Jacobi, Mary Putnam.*

PUTNAM, Mary T.S. (1810–1898). American author. Name variations: Mary Lowell. Born Mary Traill Spence Lowell, Dec 3, 1810; died in Boston, June 1, 1898; dau. of Charles Lowell (minister of the West Church in Boston) and Harriet Brackett (Spence) Lowell (d. 1850); m. Samuel R. Putnam (merchant), April 25, 1832; sister of James Russell Lowell (poet, 1819–1891) and Robert Traill Spence Lowell (writer and Episcopal priest, 1816–1891); sister-in-law of Maria White Lowell (1821–1853). ❖ After having lived abroad collecting material, especially in Poland and Hungary, published anonymously a *History of the Constitution of Hungary in Its Relations to Austria* (1850); resided in France and Germany (1851–57), perfecting linguistic abilities; returning to US, played a prominent role in the abolitionist movement, which she supported with her writings; besides numerous contributions to magazines on literature and history, wrote 2 dramas on slavery and translated Fredrika Bremer's *The Neighbors* from the Swedish.

PUTZER, Karen (1978—). Italian Alpine skier. Born Sept 29, 1978, in Bolzano, Italy. ❖ Was two-time World Jr. champion in the giant slalom (1996–97); won a silver medal for giant slalom and a bronze in the combined at the World championships (2001); won a bronze medal for super-G at Salt Lake City Olympics (2002).

PÜYSTI, Toini K. *See Poysti, Toini K.*

PUZHEVICH, Olga (1983—). Belarusian rhythmic gymnast. Name variations: Olga Puschevich. Born May 17, 1983, in Belarus. ❖ Won a silver medal for team all-around at Sydney Olympics (2000).

PYE, Edith (1876–1965). British nurse and pacifist. Name variations: Edith M. Pye. Born Edith Mary Pye, 1876, in London, England; died 1965; life companion of Hilda Clark (1881–1955, physician and relief worker). ❖ Trained as nurse and midwife and became superintendent of District Nurses, London; joined Society of Friends (1908) and began relief work; with Hilda Clark, helped women and children war victims in France; traveled to Vienna (1919), Ruhr region (1923), and China (1927) to do relief work; served as chair of Friends' Service Council France and Switzerland Committee and vice-chair of German Emergency Committee; organized Friends' work in Spain during Civil War, working for International Commission for the Assistance of Child Refugees and Women's International League for Peace and Freedom; campaigned for lifting of blockade during WWII to prevent starvation in Europe; after war, continued work in Europe into old age.

PYKE, Margaret (1893–1966). English birth-control activist. Born Aug 1, 1893, in Hampshire, England; died 1966; dau. of a physician; Somerville College, Oxford, degree in history; m. Geoffrey Pyke (educator), 1918 (died 1929); children: 1 son. ❖ Became 1st general secretary of Britain's National Birth Control Association (1929), renamed the Family Planning Association (1938); became chair of the organization (1954). ❖ See also *Women in World History*.

PYLEVA, Olga (1975—). Russian biathlete. Born July 7, 1975, in Borodino, near Krasnoyarsk, Russia. ❖ Competed at Nagano Olympics with the Russian cross country team (1998); won a gold medal for 10 km pursuit and a bronze medal for 4 x 7.5 km relay at Salt Lake City Olympics (2002); at World Cup, placed 1st as Startskier (2002).

PYLON (1955—). *See Hay, Vanessa Briscoe.*

PYM, Barbara (1913–1980). English novelist. Name variations: Mary Crampton. Born Barbara Mary Crampton Pym, June 2, 1913, in Oswestry, Shropshire, England; died Jan 11, 1980, in Oxford, England; dau. of Frederic Crampton Pym (solicitor) and Irena Spenser Pym; sister of Hilary Pym; St. Hilda's College, Oxford, BA in English literature. ❖ Was employed with the International African Institute (1946–74), working as a research assistant and later as assistant editor of the institute's journal *Africa;* published 1st novel, *Some Tame Gazelle* (1950), followed by *Excellent Women* (1952), *Jane and Prudence* (1953), *Less Than Angels* (1955), *A Glass of Blessings* (1958) and *No Fond Return of Love* (1961); discouraged by a series of rejections, stopped writing; when *Times Literary Supplement* published a list of writers whom contemporary critics felt were the most underrated (1977), was the only writer to be named twice, setting off a rebirth of interest in her work; other books include *Quartet in Autumn* (1977), *The Sweet Dove Died* (1978), *A Few Green Leaves* (1980), *An Unsuitable Attachment* (1982), *Crampton Hodnet* (1985), *An Academic Question* (1986) and *Civil to Strangers and Other Writings* (1988). ❖ See also Hazel Holt and Hilary Pym, eds. *A Very Private Eye: An Autobiography in Diaries and Letters* (Dutton, 1984); and *Women in World History*.

PYM, Catherine Ann (1896–1990). *See Cook, Freda Mary.*

PYRISCA (c. 1085–1133). *See Priska-Irene of Hungary.*

PYRITZ, Dana (1970—). German rower. Born Aug 31, 1970, in Germany. ❖ At Barcelona Olympics, won a bronze medal in coxed eights (1992).

QIAN HONG (1971—). Chinese swimmer. Born Jan 30, 1971, in China. ❖ Won a bronze medal at Seoul Olympics (1988) and a gold medal at Barcelona Olympics (1992), both in the 100-meter butterfly.

QIAN ZHENGYING (1923—). Chinese engineer and politician. Born of Han nationality in Jiaxing, Zhejiang Province, China, July 1923 (one source cites birth place as US); dau. of a civil engineer who studied water conservancy at Cornell University; graduate of Department of Civil Engineering of Datong University, Shanghai; m. Huang Xinbai (former vice minister of education); children: 3. ❖ One of China's 1st women engineers, became active in revolutionary politics in Shanghai as early as 1937; became secretary of an underground Communist group there (1941); as the Huaibei River rose suddenly and broke its dykes (1944), began working in flood relief; spent the rest of her life harnessing rivers throughout China and tackling technical problems at sites of all major hydropower projects; served as section chief of Bureau of Water Conservancy under Jiangsu-Anhui Regional government, director of the Front Engineering Division of Department of Army Service Station of East China Ministry Command (1945–48), party secretary and deputy director of Bureau of Shadong Yellow River Management (1948–50), deputy head of the Department of Water Conservancy under East China Military Administrative Committee and concurrently deputy head of Engineering Department under the Committee for Harnessing Huai River (1950–52); after 35 years as an engineer, served as vice minister and then minister of Water Conservancy (1952–88), a top position in her field, particularly for a woman; was elected and reelected vice chair of 7th to 9th CPPCC National Committees (1988, 1993, 1998); was also a member of the 10th through 14th CPC Central Committees. Awarded China Engineering Science and Technology prize (2000).

QIAO HONG (1968—). Chinese table tennis player. Born Nov 21, 1968, in Wuhan, Hubei, China. ❖ At World Table Tennis championships, won singles and doubles titles (1989); at Barcelona Olympics, won a silver medal for singles and a gold medal for doubles (1992); at Atlanta Olympics, won a bronze medal for singles and a gold medal, with partner Deng Yaping, for doubles (1996).

QIAO YUNPING. Chinese table tennis player. Born in China. ❖ Won a silver medal for doubles at Atlanta Olympics (1996).

QIN DONGYA (1978—). Chinese judoka. Born July 8, 1978, in China. ❖ Won a bronze medal for 70 kg at Athens Olympics (2004).

QIN YIYUAN. Chinese badminton player. Born in China. ❖ Won a bronze medal for doubles at Atlanta Olympics (1996) and at Sydney Olympics (2000).

QIONG YAO (1938—). Chinese novelist. Born 1938 in Taiwan. ❖ Wrote romances popular in Taiwan and mainland China, including *Lucky Blade, I Am a Cloud,* and *The Heart's Knots.*

QIU CHEN (1963—). Chinese basketball player. Born June 11, 1963, in China. ❖ At Los Angeles Olympics, won a bronze medal in team competition (1984).

QIU JIN (c. 1875–1907). Chinese revolutionary, poet, and feminist. Name variations: Ch'iu Chin (romanized version) or incorrectly Chiu Chin; Qiu Xuanqing; Qiu Jingxiong. Pronunciation: Chee-o Jean. Born Qiu Jin, Nov 8, 1875 (some sources cite 1877, 1878, and 1879), in Xiamen, Fujian, China; executed in Shaoxing, Zhejiang, China, July 15, 1907; dau. of Qiu Shounan (government bureaucrat) and Shan; educated in the family school and Japanese Language School, Tokyo (1904); took Special Training Course for Chinese Women at Aoyama Women's Vocational School, Tokyo (July–Dec 1905); m. Wang Tingjun, 1896; children: son Wang Yuande (b. 1897); daughter Wang (Qiu) Canzhi (b. 1901, also seen as Wang Guifen), edited her mother's poetry, which was continually reprinted and widely read. ❖ Champion of women's rights, who was executed for her role in an attempt to overthrow the Qing Dynasty, returned with family to native home of Shaoxing (1891); moved with family to Hunan province (early 1890s); accompanied husband to live in Beijing (c. 1902); left husband and family to study in Japan (1904); became active in Chinese revolutionary societies and in writing and lecturing in Japan (1904–05); joined the Restoration Society in Shaoxing (1905); joined the Revolutionary Alliance (Tongmenghui), which had been organized by the revolutionary leader Sun Yat-sen in Tokyo (1905); returned to China (1905 or 1906); taught for a few months in a girls' school in Zhejiang province (1906); founded the popular *Chinese Women's Journal* in Shanghai to promote women's liberation (summer 1906); headed the Datong School in Shaoxing, a front for revolutionary activity in Zhejiang province (Feb–July 1907); organized the failed Restoration Army uprising in Zhejiang (1907); hailed by the Communist government in China and the Nationalist government in Taiwan as a martyred hero who offered her life to the revolutionary cause. ❖ See also *Qiu Jin ji* (Collected works of Qiu Jin, Shanghai: New China Publishing House, 1960); Lionel Giles, *Ch'iu Chin: A Chinese Heroine* (East & West, 1917); and *Women in World History.*

QIU JINGXIONG (c. 1875–1907). *See Qiu Jin.*

QIU XUANQING (c. 1875–1907). *See Qiu Jin.*

QU YUNXIA (1972—). Chinese runner. Born Dec 25, 1972, in China. ❖ At Barcelona Olympics, won a bronze medal in the 1,500 meters (1992).

QUAH AH (1893–1949). *See Peña, Tonita.*

QUAIAPAN (d. 1676). *See Magnus.*

QUALTER, Tot (1894–1974). American theatrical dancer. Name variations: Marguerite Qualters. Born Marguerite Qualters, Mar 28, 1894, in Detroit, Michigan; died Mar 27, 1974, in New York, NY; sister of Fritzie (Gertrude) Qualter and Cassie Qualter (dancers); sister-in-law Stella Qualter. ❖ Raised in family of theatrical performers, made Broadway debut as adolescent in *The Winsome Widow* (1912); worked for Florenz Ziegfeld under contract, as did her sisters Cassie and Fritzie (1916–21), appearing in several *Follies,* as well as *The Century Girl* (1916), and *Miss 1917;* danced for Shubert Brothers in numerous productions, including *Move On* (1919) and *Passing Show of 1921.*

QUANCE, Kristine (1975—). American swimmer. Born April 1, 1975, in Northridge, CA. ❖ Won a gold medal at Pan Pacific championships for 200-meter breaststroke (1991), 400-meter indiv. medley (1993, 1997), and 200-meter indiv. medley (1997); was on the gold-medal team that won the 4 x 100-meter medley relay at Atlanta Olympics (1996).

QUANN, Megan (1984—). American swimmer. Born Jan 15, 1984, in Tacoma, WA. ❖ Won gold medals for 100-meter breaststroke and 4 x 100-meter medley relay at Sydney Olympics (2000).

QUANT, Mary (1934—). English designer and entrepreneur. Born Mary Quant, Feb 11, 1934, in Blackheath, London; dau. of Jack and Mildred Quant; attended Goldsmiths College of Art; m. Alexander Plunkett Greene, 1957 (div. 1990); children: Orlando (b. 1970). ❖ Entrepreneur whose perception, business acumen, and interpretation of fashion and design repeatedly revolutionized conventional ideas of style, promotion, and manufacture in several branches of the industrial arts; left school at 16 on winning a scholarship to art school (1950), where she met Alexander Plunkett Greene who would be her life and business partner for over 40 years; ran Bazaar (with Greene and Archie McNair) in King's Road, Chelsea (1955–68); began to design clothes for Bazaar (1956); opened and oversaw 2nd branch in Knightsbridge (1957–69); signed with J. C. Penney (US) to design fashions for their US stores (1962–71); started the Ginger Group (wholesale company) and pioneered use of PVC (oil-skin) in fashion rainwear (1963); created exclusive designs for Puritan Fashion and Butterick paper-patterns for home dressmakers (1964); launched Quant hosiery and lingerie line (1965); launched "Mary Quant Cosmetics" (1966); elected Royal Designer for Industry by Royal Society of Arts (1969); her coordinated range of household furnishings and domestic textile designs promoted by ICI (Imperial Chemical Industries, 1970); was a member of Design Council (1971–74) and British-American Liaison Committee (1973); exhibition "Mary Quant's London" at London Museum (1973–74); opened 1st Tokyo "Mary Quant Color Shop" (1983); published *Color by Quant* (1984) and *Quant on Makeup* (1986); became co-chair of Mary Quant Group (1991); opened Mary Quant Color Shops in Chelsea and Knightsbridge (both London), as well as Paris (1994–97). Received Order of the British Empire (OBE, 1966); elected to the Hall of Fame British Fashion Council (1990). ❖ See also autobiography *Quant on Quant* (1966); and *Women in World History.*

QUARANTA, Isabella (1892–1975). Italian silent-screen actress. Born Dec 30, 1892, in Turin, Italy; died April 3, 1975, in Milan; twin sister of Letizia Quaranta and sister of Lidia Quaranta (both actresses). ❖ Appeared in *Romanticismo* (1915).

QUARANTA, Lidia (1891–1928). Italian silent-screen actress. Name variations: Lydia Quaranta. Born Mar 6, 1891, in Turin, Italy; died Mar 5, 1928, in Turin; sister of Isabella Quaranta (actress) and Letizia Quaranta (actress). ❖ Starred in the film spectacular *Cabiria* (1914) and other extravaganzas; films include *I Cavalieri della Morte, Padre, Nel Votice del Peccato, Gioiello sinistro, Notte di Nozze, Fiamma, I Tre Sentimentali* and *Una Marito.*

QUARANTA, Letizia (1892–1974). Italian silent-screen actress. Born Dec 30, 1892, in Turin, Italy; died Jan 9, 1974 (some sources cite 1977), in Rome, Italy; sister of Lidia Quaranta (actress); twin sister of Isabella Quaranta (actress); m. Carlo Campogalliani (director), 1921. ❖ Made film debut in *Addio giovinezza!* (1913), followed by *Nerone e Agrippina, L'Eterno Romanzo, L'Isola tenebrosa, La Casa della Paura, La Nave dei Morti, La Signora delle Miniere, La Mujer de Medianoche, Musica proibita* and *L'Orfana del Ghetto.*

QUARETTI, Lea (1912–1981). Italian novelist. Born 1912 in Rigoso, Italy; died 1981. ❖ Studied in Parma and settled in Venice where she contributed regularly to newspapers, including *La Stampa* and *Gazzettino;* works include *Il faggio* (1946), *La voce del fiume* (1947), *La donna sbagliata* (1950) and *L'estate di Anna* (1955).

QUASS, Margaret (1926–2003). English educator. Born April 6, 1926, in England; died Dec 9, 2003, in England; attended Cambridge University and London School of Economics. ❖ Served as director of Council for Education in World Citizenship (CEWC, 1974–86), set up after WWII to keep international ideals alive and to encourage schoolchildren to study world problems. Awarded OBE.

QUAST, Anne Decker (1937—). See Sander, Anne Quast.

QUATRO, Suzi (1950—). American musician. Name variations: Susan Kay Quatro, Suzi Soul (early stage name). Born Suzi Quatrocchio, June 3, 1950, in Detroit, Michigan; dau. of Helen and Art Quatro (jazz bandleader); m. Len Tuckey (guitarist), 1978 (div. 1992); m. Rainer Haas (German tour promoter), 1993; children: (1st m.) Laura (b. Sept 23, 1982), Richard Leonard (b. Oct 1984). ❖ Bass-playing singer-songwriter, quit high-school and formed band, Suzi Soul and the Pleasure Seekers (called Cradle by late 1960s), with sisters Patti, Nancy, and Arlene (1965); after Cradle broke up (1970), went to England and signed with RAK Records; wrote unsuccessful debut single, "Rolling Stone" (1972); came to prominence in England as a "glitter rocker" with her leather-clad look (1973); had numerous UK hits, including "Can the Can" (1973), "48 Crash" (1973), "The Wild One" (1974) and "Devil's Gate Drive"; albums included *Your Mama Won't Like Me* (1975), *Aggro Phobia* (1977), *The Wild One* (1996), and *If You Can't Give Me Love* (2004); was a regular on US tv show, "Happy Days," as Leather Tuscadero (1977); signed with RSO Records, released *If You Knew Suzi* (1978), and had hit with "Stumblin' In," a duet with Chris Norman; hosted British tv show, "Gas" (1983); portrayed Tallulah Bankhead in UK musical, *Tallulah Who?* (1991); hosted "Rockin' With Suzi Q" on BBC Radio 2 (1999).

QUEDLINBURG, abbess of.
See Matilda of Quedlinburg (c. 953–999).
See Adelaide of Quedlinburg (977–1045).
See Agnes of Quedlinburg (1184–1203).
See Königsmark, Aurora von (1662–1728).

QUEEN LATIFAH (1970—). African-American musician. Name variations: Dana Owens, D. Owens. Born Dana Elaine Owens, Mar 18, 1970, in East Orange, NJ; dau. of Rita and Lance Owens (police officer). ❖ The first lady of Hip-hop, was a high-school basketball star; released debut single, "The Wrath of My Madness" (1988); released album *All Hail the Queen* (1989), with hit "Ladies First," in answer to the prevailing misogynist scene, and was nominated for a Grammy and named Best Female Rapper of the Year by *Rolling Stone* magazine (1990); gained wider audience by appearing on David Bowie's remake of "Fame," and singing "For the Love of Money" on soundtrack of film *New Jack City* (1991); released gold-selling album, *Black Reign* (1993), with hit, "U.N.I.T.Y.," which won Grammy for Best Rap Performance (1994); starred in tv sitcom, "Living Single" (1993); released *Order in the Court* and toured with Lilith Fair festival (1998); began hosting tv talk show, *Queen Latifah* (1999); appeared in such films as *Set It Off* (1996), *The Bone Collector* (1999), *Taxi* (2004) and *Chicago* (2002), for which she was nominated for an Academy Award. ❖ See also autobiographical *Ladies First: Revelations of a Strong Woman* (1999).

QUEENSBURY, duchess of. See Hyde, Catherine (1701–1777).

QUEENY, Mary (1913–2003). Egyptian actress and producer. Born Mary Boutros Younis, 1913, to a Christian family in Lebanon; died Nov 23, 2003, in Cairo, Egypt; m. Ahmad Galal (film producer), 1940 (died 1947); children: son Nadar Galal (film producer). ❖ Influential force in the development of the Egyptian film industry, was among the 1st woman in Egypt to appear on screen without a veil; moved to Cairo with her actor-producer aunt, Assia Dagher (1923); appeared in 20 films, often as a femme fatale, including *Pangs of Conscience* (1931), *When a Woman Loves* (1933), *Rebellious Girl* (1940), *Prisoner No. 17* (1949), *The Seventh Wife* (1950), *Sacrificing My Love* (1951) and *Women Without Men* (1953); with husband, founded Galal Films (1942), which became Galal Studios (1944); following husband's death (1947), continued as a producer, producing more than 20 movies; retired (1967).

QUEIROS, Dina Silveira de (1911–1983). See Castro Alves, Diná Silveira de.

QUEIRÓS, Raquel de (1910–2003). Brazilian novelist, playwright and short-story writer. Name variations: Raquel de Queiros; Rachel de Queiroz; (pseudonym) Rita de Queluz. Born 1910 in Ceará, Brazil; died Nov 4, 2003, in Rio de Janeiro, Brazil. ❖ Published works in magazines and newspapers and was the 1st woman elected to Brazilian

Academy of Letters (1977); works, which are critically acclaimed and explore independent women, include *O Quince* (The Fifteenth, 1930), *As três Marias* (1963) and *Dora Doralina* (1974).

QUEIZÁN, María Xosé (1938—). Spanish novelist and literary critic. Name variations: Maria Xose Queizan. Born 1938 in Vigo, Galicia. ❖ Works include *A orella no buraco* (1965), *Amantia* (1984), and *O segredo da Pedra Figueira* (1985); served as president of FIGA (Feministas Independentes Galegas).

QUELER, Eve (1936—). American orchestra conductor. Name variations: Eve Rabin Queler. Born Eve Rabin, Jan 1, 1936, in New York, NY; attended City College of New York, Mannes College of Music, and Hebrew Union School of Education and Sacred Music; married Stanley N. Queler (lawyer), Dec 1956. ❖ Made operatic conducting debut in Fair Lawn, NJ, at outdoor performance of Mascagni's *Cavalleria Rusticana* (1966); known for championing little-known works, founded her own group, the Opera Orchestra, based at Carnegie Hall (1967), and served as its 1st director; was conductor of Fort Wayne Philharmonic Orchestra (1970–71), the 1st woman to hold a full-time position; conducted Verdi's *I Vespri Siciliani* at Teatro del Liceo, Barcelona, the 1st woman to conduct at a major European opera house (1974); staged performances for the Orchestre Lyrique of Paris, the Prague National Theater, the Puerto Rico Symphony Orchestra, and the New Philharmonia of London, and conducted for the Mostly Mozart festival at Lincoln Center.

QUELUZ, Rita de (1910–2003). See Queirós, Raquel de.

QUEROUAILLE or QUEROUILLE, Louise de (1649–1734). See Kéroüalle, Louise de.

QUESADA, Violetta (1947—). Cuban runner. Name variations: Violeta Quesada. Born July 11, 1947, in Santa Clara, Cuba. ❖ At Mexico City Olympics, won a silver medal in the 4 x 100-meter relay (1968).

QUESTEL, Mae (1908–1998). American actress. Born Sept 13, 1908, in The Bronx, NY; died Jan 4, 1998, in New York, NY. ❖ The 2nd actress to take on the voice of Betty Boop, a popular cartoon character of the 1930s, made over 1,900 short films; also vocalized for Popeye's girlfriend Olive Oyl, Casper the Friendly Ghost, Winky Dink, and Swee'Pea; appeared as Woody Allen's mother in his *New York Stories* (1989).

QUESTIAUX, Nicole (1931—). French politician. Born Nicole Françoise Valayer in Nantes, France, in 1931 (one source cites 1930); graduate of University of Paris; studied at École Nationale d'Administration, 1953–55; m. Paul Questiaux, 1951; children: 2. ❖ Served on France's Council of State as full member (1963–74); was prominent in the launching of the new French Socialist Party (1971), becoming a member of its executive committee (1979); was also a member of the left-wing Comité d'Etudes Regionales, Économiques et Sociales (CERES); served as minister of state for national solidarity under Prime Minister François Mitterand (1981–82); became president of the 4th Subsection of the Council of State (1983); served on the board of the European Human Rights Foundation, and as its president (1998); also became a member of France's Commission Nationale Consultative des Droits de l'Homme, a human-rights organization; wrote *Traité du social*.

QUICK, Evelyn (1897–1984). See Carmen, Jewel.

QUICK SILVER (1891–1994). See Harsant, Florence Marie.

QUIK, Martijntje (1973—). Dutch rower. Born Oct 24, 1973, in Netherlands. ❖ Won a silver medal for coxed eight at Sydney Olympics (2000).

QUILL, Máirin (1940—). Irish politician. Name variations: Mairin Quill. Born Sept 15, 1940, in Kilgarvan, Co. Kerry, Ireland; dau. of Danny Quill (founder member of Fianna Fáil). ❖ Was a founder member of the Progressive Democrats (1985); representing Progressive Democrats, elected to the 25th Dáil (1987–89) for Cork North Central; returned to 26th–27th Dáil (1989–1997); was one of the Taoiseach's nominees to the Seanad (1997).

QUIMBY, Edith (1891–1982). American physicist. Born Edith Hinkley, July 10, 1891, in Rockford, Illinois; died Oct 11, 1982; dau. of Arthur S. Hinkley (architect and farmer) and Harriet H. Hinkley; Whitman College, BS, 1912; University of California, MA, 1915; m. Shirley L. Quimby (physicist), 1915. ❖ One of the 20th century's most prominent researchers in radiation physics, who focused primarily on the biological effects of radiation on humans, obtained employment at New York City Memorial Hospital for Cancer and Allied Diseases (1919); spent hours measuring the penetrability of various sources of radiation, and in particular studied the medical application of X-radiation and radioactive nuclides in the treatment of tumors; was the only woman in America working in this then little-researched area of physics (1920s–30s); created standards of radiation measurement, developed safe-handling techniques for radioactive materials, and essentially devised methods of diagnosis and treatment; taught radiology courses at Cornell University Medical College (1941–42); named associate professor of radiology at Columbia University's College of Physicians and Surgeons (1943); retired as professor emeritus of radiology (1960); writings include *Physical Foundations of Radiology* (Harper, 1970). Awarded Janeway Medal of the American Radium Society (1940); awarded honorary Doctor of Science, Whitman College (1940). ❖ See also *Women in World History*.

QUIMBY, Harriet (1875–1912). American aviator and journalist. Born Harriet Quimby, May 11, 1875, near Coldwater, Michigan; died in a plane accident at the Boston Air Meet, July 1, 1912; dau. of William Quimby (itinerant salesman) and Ursula (Cook) Quimby; never married; no children. ❖ One of the most famous and celebrated pilots at the dawn of aviation, was the 1st American woman to earn a pilot's license and the 1st woman to pilot a plane across the English Channel; moved with family to California (1884); worked in family business packaging herbal remedies; at 26, began career as a reporter for various San Francisco periodicals and newspapers (1901); moved to New York City (1903), where she worked as the drama critic and feature writer at *Leslie's Illustrated Weekly*; became 1st American woman to earn her pilot's license (Aug 1, 1911); was 1st woman to fly at night (Sept 4, 1912); was 1st woman to pilot a plane across the English Channel (April 16, 1912); was also about to become the 1st woman to carry the US mail by airplane when she was killed at a Boston Air Meet, age 37. ❖ See also Ed. Y. Hall, ed. *Harriet Quimby: America's First Lady of the Air* (Honoribus, 1990); Henry M. Holden, *Her Mentor Was an Albatross: The Autobiography of Pioneer Pilot Harriet Quimby* (Black Hawk, 1993); and *Women in World History*.

QUIN, Ann (1936–1973). British novelist. Born 1936 in Brighton, Sussex, England; committed suicide, 1973; dau. of Ann Reid Quin. ❖ Struggled with mental illness and was hospitalized for depression throughout her adult life; wrote experimental novels about death and mental illness: *Berg* (1964), *Three* (1966), *Tripticks* (1972), and *Passages* (1973); novel, *The Unmapped Country*, was unfinished at time of her suicide drowning.

QUIN, Joyce (1944—). English politician and member of Parliament. Born Joyce Quin, Nov 26, 1944. ❖ Lecturer in French; served as Member of European Parliament for Tyne and Wear (1979–89); representing Labour, elected to House of Commons for Gateshead East and Washington West (1992, 1997, 2001); left Parliament (2005).

QUINDLEN, Anna (1953—). American journalist and novelist. Born July 8, 1953, in Philadelphia, PA; dau. of Robert and Prudence Quindlen; Barnard College, BA, 1974; m. Gerald Krovatin (lawyer), 1978; children: Quindlen, Christopher and Maria. ❖ Was a reporter for *New York Post* (1974–77), then *New York Times* (1977–81); became a columnist (1981); won the Pulitzer Prize for her *New York Times* op-ed column, "Public and Private" (1992); began writing a back-page column for *Newsweek* (1999); nonfiction includes *Living Out Loud,* a collection of her "Life in the 30s" columns (1988), *Thinking Out Loud, and How Reading Changed My Life* (1993), *A Short Guide to a Happy Life* (2000), *Loud and Clear* (2004) and *Being Perfect* (2005); novels include *Object Lessons* (1991), *One True Thing* (1994), *Black and Blue* (1998) and *Blessings* (2002).

QUINLAN, Karen Ann (1954–1985). American woman. Born Mar 29, 1954, in Scranton, Pennsylvania; died of respiratory failure due to acute pneumonia, June 11, 1985, in Morris Plains, New Jersey; adopted dau. of Joseph Quinlan (employee in the accounting department of a pharmaceutical firm) and Julia Quinlan (church secretary); graduated from high school, 1972; never married. ❖ Comatose patient whose removal from a ventilator set a precedent for future legislation governing an individual's right to die; at 21, collapsed and stopped breathing during a party (April 14, 1975); in a coma, was placed on a respirator and doctors concluded that she would never achieve a "cognitive state"; after parents' petition to take her off life support was granted by State Supreme Court (Mar 31, 1976), continued to breath without ventilator for 10 more years, but never regained consciousness. ❖ See also Joseph and Julia Quinlan (with Phyllis Battelle) *Karen Ann: The Quinlans Tell Their Story* (Doubleday, 1977); Julia Quinlan's *My Joy, My Sorrow* (2005); and *Women in World History*.

QUINN, Helen (1943—). Australian-American physicist. Name variations: Helen R. Quinn; Helen Arnold. Born Helen Rhoda Arnold, May 19, 1943, in Melbourne, Australia; studied at University of Melbourne; Stanford University, BS in physics, 1963, MA, 1964, PhD, 1967; m. Daniel Quinn, 1966; children: 2. ❖ Moved to US (c. 1960); researched Standard Model of Fundamental Particles and Interactions with Joel Primack and Thomas Applequist; later studied electromagnetism with Howard Georgi and Steven Weinberg at Harvard University (1970s); began work at Stanford University's atom-smasher research facility (1978) and the Stanford Linear Accelerator Center (SLAC), as both researcher and as education and public outreach manager (1988); researched and explained laws of physics called CP symmetry and proposed Peccei- Quinn symmetry with Roberto Peccei at Stanford; founded and worked as president of Contemporary Physics Education, a nonprofit organization that creates materials for college and high school teachers. Elected to American Academy of Arts and Sciences (1998) and made a fellow of American Physical Society; appointed 4th female president of American Physical Society (APS, 2004).

QUINN, Jane Bryant (1939—). American journalist and financial expert. Born Jane Bryant, Feb 5, 1939, in Niagara Falls, NY; graduate of Middlebury College, 1960; m. David Conrad Quinn (attorney), June 10, 1967; children: 2, including stepdaughter Martha Quinn (host on MTV). ❖ Was a financial columnist for *Woman's Day* (1974–95); wrote a column for the *Washington Post* (1974–2001); began writing a column for *Newsweek* (1978) and *Good Housekeeping* (1995).

QUINN, Katherine DeMille (1911–1995). See DeMille, Katherine.

QUINN, Maire (1950—). See Geoghegan-Quinn, Máire.

QUINN, Mary Ann (c. 1928—). American steeplejack. Born c. 1928. ❖ Likely the 1st woman to be licensed as a steeplejack (1946), was employed at Aerial Engineering, Los Gatos, CA, which had been started by her late husband; assignments included painting a National Broadcasting Company (NBC) tower which required a 300-foot climb; responsible for painting in excess of 2,000 school and municipal flagpoles yearly.

QUINQUET, Madame Bertrand (1770–?). See Morency, Barbe-Suzanne-Aimable Giroux de.

QUINTANAL, Maria (1969—). Spanish trapshooter. Born Dec 17, 1969, in Spain. ❖ Won World championship in double trap (2003); won a silver medal for trap at Athens Olympics (2004).

QUINTANILLA-PEREZ, Selena (1971–1995). See Selena.

QUINTASKET, Christal or Christine (c. 1888–1936). See Mourning Dove.

QUINTERO ALVAREZ, Ioamnet (1972—). Cuban track-and-field athlete. Born Sept 8, 1972, in Cuba. ❖ At Barcelona Olympics, won a bronze medal in the high jump (1992).

QUINTON, Amelia S. (1833–1926). American advocate for Native American land rights. Name variations: Mrs. James Franklin Swanson. Born Amelia Stone in Jamesville, near Syracuse, New York, July 31, 1833; died in Ridgefield Park, New Jersey, June 23, 1926; dau. of Jacob Thompson Stone and Mary (Bennett) Stone; m. Rev. James F. Swanson; m. Rev. Richard L. Quinton (lecturer in history and astronomy from London). ❖ Appalled by US government's behavior toward Native Americans, helped organize the Women's National Indian Association; was president for over 6 years, preparing its pamphlets and editing its paper. ❖ See also *Women in World History*.

QUINTON, Carol (1936—). English runner. Born July 11, 1936, in UK. ❖ At Rome Olympics, won a silver medal in 80-meter hurdles (1960).

QUINTON, Cornelia B. Sage (1876–1936). American museum director. Name variations: Cornelia Bentley Sage. Born Cornelia Bentley Sage in 1876 (some sources cite 1879 and 1880) in Buffalo, NY; died 1936 (some sources cite 1938) in Hollywood, CA; dau. of William Sparkes Sage and Josephine (Bentley) Sage; attended Art Students League; m. William Warren Quinton (retired major), Oct 31, 1917. ❖ Served as assistant to director of Albright Art Museum/Gallery (later known as Albright-Knox Art Gallery), Buffalo, NY (1905–09); with appointment to position of director at Albright (1910), became the 1st woman to head an art museum; became 1st secretary-treasurer of Association of Art Museum Directors (1916); served as art director of Buffalo Fine Arts Academy (1905–1924); organized traveling exhibitions of French art during WWI and received Cross of the Legion of Honor from France (1920); left Albright (1924) and became director of California Palace of the Legion of

Honor (merged with M.H. de Young Memorial Museum in 1972 to later become The Fine Arts Museum of San Francisco).

QUIROGA, Elena (1919–1995). Spanish novelist. Born Elena Quiroga de Abarca in Santander, Spain, Oct 26, 1919; died Oct 3, 1995 in La Coruña, Spain; dau. of Count San Martin de Quiroga (minor noble) and Isabel Abarca Fornés; m. Dalmiro de la Valgoma y Díaz-Varela (genealogist and historian, later secretary of Royal Academy of History), in 1950. ❖ Published *La soledad sonora* (*Sonorous Solitude* 1949), followed by breakthrough novel *Viento del norte* (*North Wind*, 1950), which won the Nadal Prize; moved from northern Spain to Madrid (1950); over next decade, produced 6 more novels; eschewing the social realism then in vogue in Spain, explored the psyches of her characters and experimented with narrative techniques; renown in Spain grew when her novel *Escribo tu nombre* (*I Write Your Name*) was nominated for the international Rómulo Gallegos Prize (1967). ❖ See also Phyllis Zatlin Boring, *Elena Quiroga* (Twayne, 1977); and *Women in World History*.

QUIROT, Ana (1963—). Cuban track-and-field athlete. Name variations: Ana Quirot Moret. Pronunciation: KEE-rote. Born Ana Fidelia Quirot Moret, Mar 23, 1963, in Cuba. ❖ Won the bronze medal in the 800 meters at Barcelona Olympics (1992); suffered 3rd-degree burns over 40% of body while lighting a kerosene stove (1993); won the World championship (1995); won a silver medal in the 800 meters at Atlanta Olympics (1996).

QUIST, Anne Marie (1957—). Dutch rower. Born Dec 26, 1957, in Netherlands. ❖ At Los Angeles Olympics, won a bronze medal in coxed eights (1984).

QUISTHOUDT-ROWOHL, Godelieve (1947—). German politician. Born June 18, 1947, in Etterbeek, Belgium; Qualified chemist (1969), Doctor of Science (1973). ❖ As a member of the European People's Party (Christian Democrats) and European Democrats, elected to 4th and 5th European Parliament (EP, 1994–99, 1999–2004); named quaestor of the EP (1999). Awarded Federal Order of Merit (1997).

QUIVOGNE, Mrs. (1848–1912). *See Chartroule, Marie-Amélie.*

QUOIREZ, Françoise (1935–2004). *See Sagan, Françoise.*

QVIST, Trine (c. 1967—). Danish curler. Born c. 1967 in Denmark. ❖ Won a silver medal for curling at Nagano Olympics (1998), the first-ever Danish medal in any sport at Winter Olympics.

R

RA KYUNG-MIN (1976—). South Korean badminton player. Born Nov 25, 1976, in Hwasun, Korea; attended Korean National University. ❖ At World championships, won doubles (1999, 2003); won a bronze medal for doubles at Athens Olympics (2004).

RAAB, Esther (1894–1981). Israeli poet. Born 1894 in Petah Tikva, Israel; died 1981; dau. of Judah Raab; married in Cairo. ❖ Born into one of the founding families of one of the 1st agricultural settlements in Eretz Israel; joined the group that founded Kibbutz Degania (1913); settled in Tel Aviv, where her home became a center for writers and artists; works in Hebrew include *Kimshonim* (Thistles, 1930) and *Shirei Esther Raab* (1963); books in translation include *Selected Poems* (1996).

RABASOVA, Jana (1933—). Czech gymnast. Born July 22, 1933, in Czechoslovakia. ❖ At Helsinki Olympics, won a bronze medal in team all-around (1952).

RABBANI, Ruhiyyih (1910–2000). American-born religious leader. Name variations: Mary Sutherland Maxwell. Born Mary Sutherland Maxwell, 1910, in New York, NY; died in Haifa, Israel, Jan 19, 2000; only child of William Sutherland (architect) and May (Bolles) Maxwell (both prominent Bahais); m. Shoghi Effendi Rabbani (known as Shoghi Effendi), the last official leader of the Bahai faith (died 1957); no children. ❖ Following death of husband, became the preeminent member of the governing legislature of the Bahais, who number more than 5 million and believe in the spiritual unity of all mankind; worked to promote the Bahai faith around the world and was always available to meet with pilgrims to Haifa, where she made her home; wrote biography about husband, *The Priceless Pearl*, and authored a small volume of poetry about the loneliness she endured after his death. ❖ See also *Women in World History*.

RABI'A (c. 714–801). Islamic mystic and saint. Name variations: Rabia; Rabi'a the Mystic; Rabiah of Basra; Rabiah al-Adawiyah or Adawiyya; Rabi'ah, Rabe'a. Pronunciation: ra-be-a. Born Rabi'a al-Adawiya al-Kaisiya in Basra (modern-day Iraq) in 714 or 717 (some sources cite 712); died 801; the 4th dau. of Isma'il; mother's name unknown. ❖ Renowned holy woman and mystic of Islam, known for her asceticism, miracles, and focus on God as love, who played a pivotal role in the development of Islamic transcendentalism; born to penurious parents, turned to begging when older (and, according to some sources, prostitution) to sustain herself; seized in the street and sold into slavery; was released when her master awoke and saw her praying while a lantern was suspended over her head which put out a brilliant light; retired to a life of seclusion and celibacy in the deserts near Basra, where she lived out the rest of her days committed to chastity and the adoration of Allah; furthered and deepened Islamic spiritualism by her development of the doctrine of Pure Love and fellowship with God; expressed her feeling in poems and prayers, and had long intimate conversations with her Beloved, the Lord; rejected the common belief that she was capable of performing miracles and thought that miracles were Satanic temptations to pride and vainglory; her reputation attracted disciples to her, including many of the most notable Sufis of the next generation (such as Adham of Balkh [d. 770?]). The historical events of Rabi'a's life are recorded principally in *Memoir of the Saints* by Attar. ❖ See also Margaret Smith, *Rabi'ah the Mystic, and Her Fellow Saints in Islam* (Cambridge U. Press, 1984); and *Women in World History*.

RABIA OF BASRA (c. 714–801). See Rabi'a.

RABIA THE MYSTIC (c. 714–801). See Rabi'a.

RABIN, Leah (1928–2000). First lady of Israel. Born Leah Schlossberg, April 8, 1928, in Koenigsberg, Germany (now Kaliningrad, Russia); died of cancer, Nov 12, 2000, near Tel Aviv, Israel; father was a textile manufacturer and real-estate investor; received a teaching degree; m. Yitzhak Rabin (1922–1995, prime minister of Israel [1974–77,

1992–95]), Aug 23, 1948; children: daughter Dalia Rabin-Pelossof (lawyer and member of Israeli parliament); son Yuval Rabin. ❖ First lady of Israel, was warmly admired in US and Europe during and after husband's career, less so in Israel; moved with family to Palestine when Hitler came to power (1933); met Yitzhak Rabin; joined the Palmach, the top force in the underground Jewish militia; lived in Washington while husband was Israel's ambassador to US (1968); was first lady of Israel (1974–77); stood trial and was fined for having kept open a bank account in US, albeit with only a small amount of money, and husband resigned as prime minister (1977); was widely blamed for husband's political downfall; with husband prime minister once more (1992–95), accompanied him to Oslo where he signed a historic peace accord with Yasser Arafat; strong willed, intelligent, and outspoken, became an untiring advocate of peace between Israel and the Palestinians after husband's assassination (Nov 4, 1995), carrying on the cause he had championed. ❖ See also memoirs (with husband) *Wife by His Side* (1991) and *Rabin: Our Life, His Legacy* (1997); and *Women in World History*.

RABLEN, Eva (1905—). American murderer. Born 1905; m. Carroll Rablen. ❖ Attended a weekly dance at Tuttletown, CA, while her deaf husband waited for her in car (April 26, 1929); around midnight, brought coffee out to him (he died in agony after complaining of bitter taste); after strychnine bottle was traced to her, was tried outdoors to accommodate enormous public interest in the killing; sentenced to life imprisonment.

RABOUTOU, Robyn (1963—). See Erbesfield, Robyn.

RABUTIN-CHANTAL, Jeanne Françoise de (1572–1641). See Chantal, Jeanne de.

RABUTIN-CHANTAL, Marie de (1626–1696). See Sévigné, Marie de.

RABY, Mary (1777–1855). See Reibey, Mary.

RACHEL (fl. c. 1500 BCE). Matriarch of Israel. Fourth matriarch of Israel. Flourished around 1500 BCE; died in childbirth; grave near Bethlehem (called *kever* Rachel) is a site of pilgrimage; dau. of Laban; sister of Leah; favorite wife of Jacob and one of the four mothers of the 12 tribes of Israel; children: Joseph and Benjamin. ❖ Throughout Jewish history, the tomb of Rachel has been a symbol and place of solace and miracles; she has become a metaphor for compassion—for motherhood. ❖ See also Samuel H. Dresner, *Rachel* (Fortress, 1994); and *Women in World History*.

RACHEL (1821–1858). French actress. Name variations: Rachel Félix or Felix. Born Elisabeth-Rachel Félix near Aargau, Switzerland, probably Feb 1821; died Jan 3, 1858, in Le Cannet, France, of TB; 2nd child of poor Jewish peddlers, Jacques and Thérèse Félix; sister of Lia Félix; never married, but her numerous affairs among the European aristocracy produced at least one child. ❖ French tragedian whose talent in the classical French tradition brought her a lifetime post with Comédie-Française, during which she was credited with reviving respect in post-revolutionary France for the great dramatists of the *ancien règime*; at 14, appeared in Théâtre Molière and was soon attracting attention (1834); offered a position at Comédie's acting school, the Conservatoire (1836); made professional début in a play written especially for her, *La Vendéene*, at Théâtre Gymnase (1837); signed year's contract as a *pensionnaire* (apprentice) with Comédie (1838); debuted at Théâtre Française (June 1838), playing Camille in Corneille's *Horace*; during next 4 months, played every one of the classic *jeunes princesses*—Hermione in *Andromaque*, Aménaïde in *Tancrède*, Eriphile in *Iphegénie in Aulide*, Roxane in *Bajazet*; by end of 2nd season with Comédie-Française (1839), was given permanent rank of *sociètaire*; singlehandedly saved the moribund Comédie-Française with her electrifying interpretations of French classics; made London debut (May 1841) and was granted a private audience with Queen Victoria; her portrayal of title role in

Racine's *Phèdre,* was considered the greatest triumph of her career (1843); made NY debut (1855), but the TB that had 1st appeared 10 years earlier began to take its toll; on advice of US doctors, sailed to Cuba for a "sun cure"; was then sent to Egypt, where it was thought the drier air would help clear her congested lungs; died on the journey home. ❖ See also Madame Barrera, *Memoirs of Rachel* (Harper, 1858); Rachel M. Brownstein, *Tragic Muse: Rachel of the Comédie-Française* (Knopf, 1993); and *Women in World History.*

RACHEL (1890–1931). *See Bluwstein, Rachel.*

RACHILDE (1860–1953). *See Vallette, Marguerite.*

RACILA, Valeria (1957—). *See Rosca-Racila, Valeria.*

RACINE, Jean (1978—). American bobsledder. Born Sept 20, 1978, in Pontiac, MI. ❖ Spent early career in luge (1992–96); with Jen Davidson, won the World Cup (1999–2000 and 2000–2001) and a silver medals at World championships (2000, 2001), all in bobsleigh.

RACINET, Delphine (1973—). French shooter. Born Sept 19, 1973, in Melun, France. ❖ Won a silver medal for trap at Sydney Olympics (2000).

RADAGUNDA. *See Radegund.*

RADANOVA, Evgenia (1977—). Bulgarian short-track speedskater. Born Nov 4, 1977, in Bulgaria. ❖ Won a bronze medal for the 1,500 meters and a silver medal for the 500 meters at Salt Lake City Olympics (2002); won a silver medal for 500 meters at Torino Olympics (2006).

RADCHENKO, Olena (1973—). Ukrainian handball player. Born May 21, 1973, in Ukraine. ❖ Won a team bronze medal at Athens Olympics (2004).

RADCLIFFE, Ann (1764–1823). English writer. Name variations: her books were always attributed to Ann Radcliffe, never Mrs. Radcliffe, but she was subsequently referred to by husband and literary critics as Mrs. Radcliffe. Born Ann Ward, July 9, 1764, in London, England; died Feb 7, 1823, in London; only dau. of William Ward (haberdasher) and Ann (Oates) Ward; m. William Radcliffe, 1787; no children. ❖ Hugely popular and prolific 18th-century English writer who developed the Gothic novel as a distinctive genre and whose works continued to have a considerable influence on major writers for 20 years after her death; lived in London until age 8, when her parents moved to Bath; after marriage at St. Michael's Church in Bath (1787), settled in London and began writing novels; visited Holland and Germany with husband (1794); published last novel during her lifetime (1797); spent next 25 years living quietly at home, writing for pleasure and traveling widely in England; in later years, suffered from ill health and traveled less; last novel and extracts from her journals published posthumously. Writings include *The Castles of Athlin and Dunbayne: A Highland Story* (1789), *A Sicilian Romance* (2 vols. 1790), *The Romance of the Forest: Interspersed with Some Pieces of Poetry* (3 vols. 1791), *The Mysteries of Udolpho* (4 vols. 1792), *A Journey made in the Summer of 1794, through Holland and the Western frontier of Germany, with a return down the Rhine . . .* (1795), *The Italian, or The Confessional of the Black Penitents* (3 vols. 1797) and *Gaston de Blondeville, or, The Court of Henry III* (4 vols. 1826). ❖ See also Aline Grant, *Ann Radcliffe* (Swallow, 1951); Clara McIntyre, *Ann Radcliffe in Relation to Her Time* (Yale U. Press, 1920); Robert Miles, *Ann Radcliffe: The Great Enchantress* (Manchester U. Press, 1995); and *Women in World History.*

RADCLIFFE, Charlotte (b. 1903). English swimmer. Born Aug 1903 in UK. ❖ At Antwerp Olympics, won a silver medal in the 4 x 100-meter freestyle relay (1920).

RADCLIFFE, Charlotte Maria (d. 1755). Countess of Newburgh. Name variations: Charlotte Maria Radclyffe. Died 1755; dau. of Charles Livingstone, 2nd earl of Newburgh; granddau. of Sir James Livingstone, 1st earl of Newburgh; m. Thomas Clifford (died 1718); m. Charles Radcliffe (later titular earl of Derwentwater), in 1724. ❖ Succeeded father, becoming countess of Newburgh (1694); spurned the matrimonial advances of Charles Radcliffe who responded by sneaking into her private room via the chimney; had no choice but to marry him.

RADCLIFFE, Margaret. *See Stanley, Margaret.*

RADCLIFFE, Mary Ann (c. 1746–after 1810). Scottish-born writer. Name variations: Mrs. Radcliffe; Mary Anne Radcliffe. Born c. 1746 in Scotland; died after 1810; m. Joseph Radcliffe, c. 1760; children: 8.

At 2, became heir to a sizeable fortune, which husband eventually squandered; when their marriage collapsed, was left to support her children and found low paying work; published *Radzivil* and *The Fate of Velina de Guidova* (1790), followed by *Manfrone; or The One-Handed Monk* (1809), which was so successful it had a 2nd edition (1819); also wrote *The Female Advocate; or An Attempt to Recover the Rights of Women from Male Usurpation* (1799), which later formed part of *The Memoirs of Mrs. Mary Ann Radcliffe in Familiar Letters to her Female Friend* (1810). Use of "Mrs. Radcliffe," as well as the Gothic-tinged flavor of her fiction, led to some contemporary confusion between her works and those of Ann Radcliffe. ❖ See also *Women in World History.*

RADCLIFFE, Nora (1946—). Scottish politician. Born Mar 4, 1946, in Aberdeen, Scotland; attended Aberdeen University; married with 2 children. ❖ As a Liberal Democrat, elected to the Scottish Parliment for Gordon (1999).

RADCLIFFE, Paula (1973—). English long-distance runner. Born Paula Jane Radcliffe, Dec 17, 1973, in Northwich, Cheshire, England; dau. of Peter and Pat Radcliffe; great niece of Charlotte Radcliffe (English swimmer); m. Gary Lough (English runner). ❖ Won the World jr. cross-country title (1992); at the European 10,000-meter challenge, placed 2nd (1998) and 1st (1999); at World championships, won a silver medal (1999); set 5 United Kingdom records at 5,000 meters and 10,000 meters (1998–2004); won the World half-marathon title (2000, 2001, 2003) and World cross-country titles (2001, 2002); placed 1st in the 5,000 meters at Commonwealth Games (2002); placed 1st in London marathon (2002, 2003) and Chicago (2002); won the tightest race in New York marathon history (2004). Awarded MBE (2002); named British Female Athlete of the Year (1999, 2001, 2002) and IAAF World Female Athlete of the Year (2002). ❖ See also autobiography *My Story So Far.*

RADCLYFFE-HALL, Marguerite. *See Hall, Radclyffe.*

RADEGONDA OR RADEGONDE. *Variant of Radegund.*

RADEGONDE (d. 1445). French princess. Died in 1445; dau. of Charles VII (1403–1461), king of France (r. 1422–1461), and Marie of Anjou (1404–1463); sister of Louis XI (1423–1483), later king of France (r. 1461–1483).

RADEGUND OF POITIERS (518–587). Queen of the Franks and saint. Name variations: Radegond; Radegonde; Radegonda; Radagunda. Born in 518 (some sources cite 519) in Thuringia; died Aug 13, 587, at abbey of Sainte Croixe, Poitiers, France; dau. of Berthair, Berthaire, or Berthar, king of Thuringia; m. Clothar also known as Lothair I (497–561), king of Soissons and the Franks (r. 558–561), in 534; no children. ❖ One of the most famous of medieval saints, was taken prisoner at 12 and brought to the Frankish royal court to later become the wife of King Lothair I, who already had 4 wives; at 18, was forced to marry Lothair, whom she despised; after several years, her intense devotion to God and the fact that she remained childless weakened Lothair's interest in her; had the courage to escape from him when she learned that he had murdered her brother; found refuge with a bishop who agreed to consecrate her as a deaconess; founded a monastery at Poitiers (c. 557), which became known as Ste. Croixe; was a poet and corresponded with religious leaders across Europe. ❖ See also *Women in World History.*

RADI, Nuha al- (1941–2004). Iraqi artist and diarist. Born Jan 27, 1941, in Baghdad, Iraq; died of leukemia, Aug 31, 2004, in Beirut, Lebanon; dau. of an Iraqi diplomat who was ambassador to Iran, India and Suad Munir Abbas; sister of Selma al-Radi (archaeologist); studied at Byam Shaw School of Art and Chelsea Pottery in London. ❖ Taught at American University of Beirut (1961–63); produced ceramic wall reliefs (1971–75); began painting, etching and making sculpture from found objects (1990); had many solo exhibitions; published *Baghdad Diaries* about her experiences during the 1991 Gulf War (1998); returned to Beirut (1995); died of the leukemia that she thought might be connected to the hundreds of tons of depleted uranium the allies fired at Iraqi tanks in 1991.

RADKE, Lina (1903–1983). German runner. Name variations: Karoline Radke; Lina Batschauer. Born Karoline Batschauer, Oct 8 (some sources cite Oct 18), 1903, in Baden-Baden, Germany; died Feb 14, 1983, in Karlsruhe, Germany; m. George Radke (her coach). ❖ At Amsterdam Olympics, won a gold medal in the inaugural 800 meters event, with a time of 2:16.8 (1928), a time that was not bested until 1944; won several regional and national titles.

RADKOVA, Kostadinka (1962—). Bulgarian basketball player. Born June 26, 1962, in Bulgaria. ❖ At Moscow Olympics, won a silver medal in team competition (1980).

RADNER, Gilda (1946–1989). American actress and comedian. Born June 28, 1946, in Detroit, Michigan; died of ovarian cancer, May 20, 1989, in Los Angeles, California; dau. of Herman Radner (prominent Detroit businessman) and Henrietta (Dworkin) Radner; attended University of Michigan, 1964–69; m. G.E. Smith (musician), 1980 (div. 1982); m. Gene Wilder (actor), Sept 18, 1984; no children. ❖ Popular comic actress, appeared on NBC's "Saturday Night Live" (1975–80), creating such characters as Babwa Wawa, Roseanne Roseanadanna, and Emily Litella, known for the catch phrase "Never mind"; on Broadway, appeared in *Gilda Radner Live From New York* (1979); films include *First Family* (1980), *Gilda Live* (1980), *Hanky Panky* (1982) and *The Woman in Red* (1984). Received Emmy for "Saturday Night Live" (1977–78) and Tony nomination for *Lunch Hour* (1980). ❖ See also memoir *It's Always Something* (1989); Alan Zweibel, *Bunny, Bunny: Gilda Radner: A Sort of Love Story* (Villard, 1994); and *Women in World History*.

RADOCHLA, Birgit (1945—). East German gymnast. Born Jan 31, 1945, in Germany. ❖ At Tokyo Olympics, won a silver medal in the vault (1964).

RADOVIC, Vesna (1950—). Yugoslavian handball player. Born Sept 1950 in Yugoslavia. ❖ At Moscow Olympics, won a silver medal in team competition (1980).

RADU, Elena (1975—). Romanian kayaker. Born 1975 in Romania. ❖ Won a bronze medal for K4 500 meters at Sydney Olympics (2000).

RADUCAN, Andreea (1983—). Romanian gymnast. Name variations: Andreea Madalina Raducan. Born Sept 30, 1983, in Birlad, Romania. ❖ At Sydney Olympics, won a gold medal for team all-around and a silver for vault but was stripped of a gold medal for indiv. all-around after failing a drug test, having taken an over-the-counter cold medicine (2000); at World championships, won a gold medal for team all-around (1999) and 3 gold medals (2001); retired (2003).

RADULOVIC, Bojana (c. 1973—). Hungarian handball player. Born c. 1973 in Hungary. ❖ Won a team silver medal at Sydney Olympics (2000).

RADVANYI, Netty (1900–1983). *See Seghers, Anna.*

RADYONSKA, Tanya (1924—). Soviet spy. Name variations: Tanya Markovna Radyonska; Eileen Jenkins. Born 1924 in Murmansk, Russia. ❖ Passed qualifying exams for Secret Service at 21 and entered Gaczyna spy school as Eileen Jenkins; perfected cover, as English spinster, in London; arrived in Canada (1959), where she became established as a master spy, working as a clerk in a bakery, then lingerie shop, then opening her own lingerie shop; maintained an espionage squad that used kidnapping and murder as tactics; when Moscow became concerned with the number of deaths and disappearances she organized, was ordered to use less violent means; left Canada for another, unknown country of operation.

RADZEVICH, Nadezhda (1953—). Soviet volleyball player. Born Mar 10, 1953, in USSR. ❖ At Moscow Olympics, won a gold medal in team competition (1980).

RADZIWELL, Barbara (1520–1551). *See Barbara Radziwell.*

RADZIWILL, Francisca (1705–1753). Polish playwright. Name variations: Princess Franciszka Radzwill. Born Ursula Francisca Wisniowiecka, Feb 13, 1705, in Czartorysk; died May 23, 1753, in Pucewicze; dau. of Janusz, Prince Wisniowiecki, and Countess Theophila Leszczynska; m. Michael Casimir, Prince Radziwill (1702–1762), duke of Nieswiez, April 23, 1725. ❖ Wrote plays for a theater founded at Nieswiez by her husband; was the 1st Pole to translate and adapt comedies of Molière; works published posthumously as *Komedie i tragedie* (1754).

RAE, Edna (1932—). *See Burstyn, Ellen.*

RAEBURN, Agnes Middleton (1872–1955). Scottish watercolor artist. Born 1872 in Glasgow, Scotland; died 1955 in Glasgow; entered Glasgow School of Art, 1887. ❖ A close friend of Margaret Macdonald and associate of Charles Rennie Mackintosh and "The Immortals," was also an active member of Glasgow Society of Lady Artists and served as its president (1940–43); was influenced by Glasgow Style and symbolism and work of Katherine Cameron; began

contributing to *The Magazine* (1893), most notably with a series of fairy drawings; went on to paint landscapes of France and Holland as well as flower studies with free, fluid style; became teacher in later years, serving as head of Laurel Bank School in Glasgow; exhibited many works at Royal Scottish Academy. Elected to Royal Scottish Watercolor Society (1901).

RAEVA, Iliana (1963—). Bulgarian rhythmic gymnast. Born Mar 15, 1963, in Sofia, Bulgaria; m. Nasko Sirakov (soccer player). ❖ At World championships, came in 4th all-around (1979) and 2nd all-around (1981); won the Julieta Shishmanova Cup and the European championship (1980).

RAFAEL, Sylvia (1938–2005). Israeli intelligence agent. Name variations: also seen as Raphael; used cover name of Patricia Roxburgh. Born April 1, 1938, near Cape Town, South Africa; died of leukemia, Feb 9, 2005 in South Africa; dau. of a Jewish father and non-Jewish mother; m. Anneaus Schjodt (her Norwegian lawyer). ❖ Immigrated to Israel (1963); became a member of Mossad and attained the highest rank for an agent; was sent with a group of Mossad agents to Lillehammer, Norway, to kill Ali Hassan Salameh (1973), who had orchestrated the killing of 11 Israeli athletes at the Munich Olympics (Sept 5, 1972); with her colleagues, mistakenly identified a Moroccan waiter and shot him dead; received the modest sentence of 5½ years in prison, and served only 22 months before being pardoned and released. ❖ See also *Women in World History*.

RAFAEL MARÉS, Carmen de (1911–1999). *See Kurtz, Carmen.*

RAFANELLI, Leda (1880–1971). Italian novelist and short-story writer. Born 1880 in Tuscany, Italy; died 1971; m. Luigi Polli (publisher); lifelong companion of Giuseppe Monanni; children: Marsilio Monanni (b. 1910). ❖ Went to Alexandria, Egypt (1900), where she converted to Islam and became an anarchist; with husband and Giuseppe Monanni, founded publishing house of Rafanelli-Polli; settled in Milan with Monanni (1908); with Ettore Molinari and Nella Giacomelli, formed the group Protesta umana; founded Casa Editrice Sociale to disseminate anarchist ideas; works, which denounced fascism, colonialism, clericalism, militarism, and the oppression of women, include *Un sogno d'amore* (1905), *Seme nuove* (1905–08), *L'eroe della folla* (1920), *Incantesimo* (1921), *Donne e femmine* (1922), *L'oasi. Romanzo Arabo* (1929), and *Una donna e Mussolini* (1946).

RAFFERTY, Frances (1922–2004). American tv and screen actress. Born June 16, 1922, in Sioux City, IA; died April 18, 2004, in Paso Robles, CA. ❖ On tv, was a regular on "December Bride" (1954–59) and "Pete and Gladys" (1961–62); films include *Thousands Cheer, Girl Crazy, Dragon Seed, Mrs. Parkington, Abbott and Costello in Hollywood, Curley* and *Wings of Chance*.

RAFIRA-LOVIN, Fita (1951—). *See Lovin, Fita.*

RAFKO, Kaye Lani (c. 1963—). Miss America and nurse. Name variations: Kaye Lani Wilson. Born Kaye Lani Rae Rafko c. 1963 in Monroe, Michigan; m. Charles (Chuck) Wilson; children: 3. ❖ Became a registered nurse; named Miss America (1988), representing Michigan; became a motivational speaker and an advocate for nursing and hospice programs; opened a hospice in Monroe, Michigan.

RAFSANJANI, Faezeh (1963—). *See Hashemi, Faezeh.*

RAFTOR, Kitty (1711–1785). *See Clive, Kitty.*

RAGGHIANTI, Marie (1942—). American whistleblower and prison reformer. Born Marie Fajardo, June 13, 1942; Vanderbilt University, BS, 1975, MS, 1978; Harvard University, MPA, 1992; divorced, 1968; children: 3. ❖ Single mother of three who, as chair of the Pardons & Parole Board in Tennessee (1976–77), exposed the widespread sale of pardons and paroles to convicted rapists, armed robbers, and murderers by the office of the governor (1977); served as chief of staff of the US Parole Commission (1997–99). ❖ See also Peter Maas, *Marie: A True Story* (1997); (film) *Marie,* starring Sissy Spacek.

RAGNETRUDE (fl. 630). Queen of Austrasia and the Franks. Name variations: Rainetrude. Married Dagobert I (c. 606–639), king of Austrasia (r. 623–628), king of the Franks (r. 629–639); children: Sigibert III (630–656), king of Austrasia (r. 634–656).

RAGNHILD. Queen of the Isles. Married Olva the Red, king of the Isles; m. Somerled, 1st lord of Argyll; children: Dugall, king of the Isles and founder of the clan Dougall; Reginald or Ranald, king of the Isles; Angus, king of the Isles.

RAGNHILD (fl. 1100s). Danish royal. Married Hagen Sunnevason (son of Erik Egode, king of Denmark); children: Erik Lam or Lamb, king of Denmark (r. 1137–1146).

RAGNO, Antonella (1940—). See Lonzi-Ragno, Antonella.

RAGUSA, Cinzia (1977—). Italian water-polo player. Born May 24, 1977, in Italy. ❖ Center back, won a team gold medal at Athens Olympics (2004).

RAHAB (fl. 1100 BCE). Biblical woman. Name variations: Rahab comes from Rehabiah (meaning wide or broad). Pronunciation: RAY-hab. Flourished around 1100 BCE; m. Salmon, a prince of the tribe of Judah; children: Boaz (who married Ruth). ❖ Harbored Hebrew spies sent by Joshua and helped them escape. ❖ See also Women in World History.

RAHEL. Variant of Rachel.

RAHEL (1771–1833). See Varnhagen, Rahel.

RAHMAN, Aisha 'Abd al- (1913–1998). See Abdel Rahman, Aisha.

RAHN, Muriel (1911–1961). African-American singer and actress. Born Muriel Ellen Rahn, 1911, in Boston, MA; died of cancer in New York, NY, Aug 8, 1961; attended Tuskegee Institute and Atlanta University; graduate of Music Conservatory of the University of Nebraska, at Lincoln; attended Teachers College, Columbia University; studied voice at Juilliard School of Music; m. Charles Rountree, 1932 (div.); m. Richard Campbell, 1934. ❖ Launched professional career in NY (1929), with Eva Jessye's Jubilee Singers; cast in Broadway musicals Blackbirds of 1929 and Hot Chocolates (1929–30); sang at Chez La DuBarry in Paris (1933), before returning to Broadway in Come of Age (1934); appeared as Carmen in Carmen Jones, which ran for 231 performances, then embarked on an extensive concert tour through US; was the only black member of the opera division of NYC's National Orchestral Association, singing in a number of productions, including Abduction from the Seraglio, Suor Angelica and Gianni Schicchi; performed title role in Aïda with Salmaggi Opera (1948) and was the lead in Salome (1954); appeared in 2 US operas by Harry Freeman: The Martyr (1947) and The Barrier, which premiered at Columbia University, then opened on Broadway (1950), her last Broadway appearance. ❖ See also Women in World History.

RAHON, Alice (1904–1987). French Surrealist painter and poet. Name variations: Alice Paalen; Alice Phillipot. Born Alice Marie Yvonne Phillipot, 1904, in Doubs, France; died 1987 in San Angel, Mexico; mother's maiden name was Rahon; m. Wolfgang Paalen (Austrian Surrealist painter), 1934 (div. 1947); m. Edward Fitzgerald (American decorator), 1950 (div. 1960); no children. ❖ Important member of Surrealist art movement, published 1st book of poems, On the Same Ground, followed by 2nd collection, Hourglass Lying Down, illustrated by Pablo Picasso (both 1936); immigrated to Mexico with husband (1940), where they organized the International Surrealist Exhibition in Mexico City; published 3rd book of poetry, Animal Black (1941); with husband, produced Surrealist journal Dyn (1942–45); after separating from 1st husband, became a full-time painter and assumed mother's maiden name of Rahon as her professional name; adopted Mexico and its culture to a large degree, using its landscape and symbolism as inspiration for her colorful, abstract, and vibrant paintings, which were exhibited widely in Mexico, US and Europe until late 1960s. ❖ See also Women in World History.

RAI, Pamela (1966—). Canadian swimmer. Born Mar 29, 1966, in New Westminster, British Columbia, Canada; attended University of Victoria. ❖ Began career with Hyack Swim Club; by age 14, held 16 Canadian age-group records; was on the national team (1980–87); in 4 x 100-meter medley relay, won a bronze medal at Los Angeles Olympics (1984) and a gold medal at Commonwealth Games (1986); became a coach. Named Canadian University Swimmer of the Year (1985).

RAIBY, Mary (1777–1855). See Reiby, Mary.

RAICHE, Bessica (c. 1874–1932). American aviator. Born Bessica Medlar, c. 1874, in Beloit, Wisconsin; died in Balboa, California, April 10, 1932; studied music in Paris; married François Raiche. ❖ Became the 1st American woman to fly solo (Sept 16, 1910); went on to make as many as 25 flights in a single week, and with husband formed the French-American Aeroplane Company, using piano wire to construct the lightest possible planes. ❖ See also Women in World History.

RAICHO HIRATSUKA (1886–1971). See Hiratsuka, Raicho.

'RAIHANAH BINT ZAID (fl. 7th c.). Wife of Muhammad. Widow of Jewish origin; m. Muhammad around 628 CE. ❖ See also Women in World History.

RAIKH, Zinaida (1894–1939). Russian actress. Born 1894 in Russia; murdered in Moscow, July 14, 1939; dau. of Nikolai Andreevich Raikh (German-born railway worker) and Anna Ivanovna Viktorova; m. Sergei Esenin (poet); m. Vsevolod Meyerhold (theater director); children: (1st m.) Tatiana Esenin; Konstantin "Kostia" Esenin. ❖ Actress whose murder remains one of the mysteries of the Stalin era, was working as a secretary for the Socialist Revolutionary newspaper Delo Naroda when she met 1st husband, the brilliant but unstable poet Sergei Esenin; later met and married theater director Vsevolod Meyerhold and became one of his leading actresses; soon after husband was arrested and taken to Moscow's infamous Lubianka prison, resisted police officers who came to search their apartment; several weeks later, was stabbed to death (1939), and, even though she was one of the most famous actresses in the Soviet Union, the press carried no mention of the slaying. ❖ See also Women in World History.

RAIMANN, Ingrid. See Haralamow, Ingrid.

RAIMOND, C.E. (1862–1952). See Robins, Elizabeth.

RAINCOATS, The.
See Birch, Gina.
See Da Silva, Ana.

RAINE, Kathleen (1908–2003). English poet. Born Kathleen Jessie Raine in Ilford, Essex, England, June 14, 1908; died July 7, 2003, in London; dau. of George Raine (schoolteacher and Methodist preacher) and Jessie (Wilkie) Raine; Girton College, Cambridge University, MA, 1929; m. Hugh Sykes Davies (professor at Cambridge), c. 1930 (div.); m. Charles Madge (prominent sociologist, div.); children: (2nd m.) Anna and James. ❖ Romantic poet who also produced major works of criticism on William Blake, Samuel Taylor Coleridge and W.B. Yeats, received a scholarship to study science at Cambridge (1926); settled in Penrith, Northumberland (1939); returned to wartime London and published 1st vol. of poems, Stone and Flower (1943); converted to Catholicism (c. 1944); had a long and unhappy relationship with the travel writer and naturalist Gavin Maxwell (1952–69); held post as research fellow, Girton College, Cambridge University (1955–61); was Andrew Mellon Lecturer, National Gallery of Art, Washington, DC (1962); founded literary journal Temenos (1980); also achieved a reputation as a translator of Honoré de Balzac. Poetry includes The Pythoness (1949), The Hollow Hill (1965), Six Dreams (1968), and Living with Mystery, Poems 1987–1991 (1992). Won W.H. Smith Award (1972); received Queen's Gold Medal for Poetry (1993). ❖ See also autobiographies Farewell Happy Fields: Memories of Childhood (1973), The Lands Unknown (1975), and The Lion's Mouth: Concluding Chapters of Autobiography (1977); and Women in World History.

RAINE, Nancy Greene (1943—). See Greene, Nancy.

RAINER, Luise (1910—). Austrian actress. Born Jan 12, 1910, in Vienna, Austria (some sources cite Dusseldorf, Germany), to Jewish parents; studied with Max Reinhardt; m. Clifford Odets (playwright), 1937 (div. 1940); m. Robert Knittel (English publisher), 1953 (died 1989); no children. ❖ At 16, made stage debut in Austria; after establishing herself on stage and in films in Austria and Germany, arrived in Hollywood (1935) and immediately distinguished herself by winning back-to-back Academy Awards as Best Actress for her work in The Great Ziegfeld (1936) and The Good Earth (1937); by 1939, her US film career was pretty much over; other films include Escapade (1935), The Emperor's Candlesticks (1937), The Big City (1937) and The Toy Wife (1938); made a less-than-memorable Broadway debut in A Kiss for Cinderella (1940), followed by a tour in Joan of Lorraine by Maxwell Anderson; married an English publisher and settled in London (1951); later filmed The Best of Everything (1983) and The Gambler (1997). ❖ See also Women in World History.

RAINER, Yvonne (1934—). American filmmaker, dancer and choreographer. Born in San Francisco, California, 1934; studied dance with Martha Graham and Merce Cunningham. ❖ Co-founded Judson Dance Theater (1962); invented the minimalist style of modern dance, resolutely unartificial and unemotional; soon gained a name as a daring choreographer and dancer; by mid-1960s, also began using slides, recorded and live voices, short films and narrative within her pieces, creating what have been likened to performance "collages"; made 1st feature-length film, Lives of Performers (1972), followed by Film about a

Woman Who . . . (1974); later films include *Journeys from Berlin/1971* (1980), which won Los Angeles Film Critics' 1st prize for independent film, *The Man Who Envied Women* (1985) and *Privilege* (1990); taught at a number of universities and institutes; published *The Films of Yvonne Rainer* (1989). Received American Film Institute's Maya Deren Award (1988); awarded MacArthur Foundation grant (1990). ❖ See also *Women in World History.*

RAINES, Ella (1920–1988). American actress. Born Ella Wallace Raubes, Aug 6, 1920, in Snoqualmie Falls, WA; died May 30, 1988, in Sherman Oaks, CA; m. Kenneth Trout, 1942 (div. 1945); m. Robin Olds, 1947; children: 2 daughters. ❖ Films include *Hail the Conquering Hero, The Suspect, Cry Havoc, Time Out of Mind, The Web, Enter Arsene Lupin, The Walking Hills, A Dangerous Profession, A Man in the Road,* and most memorably, *Phantom Lady;* starred in NBC-TV series "Janet Dean, Registered Nurse" (1953–54).

RAINETRUDE. *Variant of Ragnetrude.*

RAINEY, Barbara Allen (1948–1982). American military aviator. Born Aug 20, 1948, in Bethesda, Maryland; died in plane crash near Evergreen, Alabama, July 13, 1982; father was an officer in the Navy; Whittier College, BA; m. John C. Rainey (Navy pilot); children: 2 daughters. ❖ Joined Naval Reserves as an officer (late 1970); received "wings of gold," becoming 1st female pilot in history of US Navy (Feb 1974); served with Pacific Fleet Squadron; left active duty (Nov 1977) but remained in Naval Reserves and became qualified to fly a C-118 (DC-6); recalled to active duty as a flight instructor (1981), was assigned to air station at Whiting Field in Milton, Florida; was training another pilot in touch-and-go landings at Middleton Field in Alabama when her plane crashed.

RAINEY, Gertrude (1886–1939). *See Rainey, Ma.*

RAINEY, Ma (1886–1939). African-American blues singer. Name variations: Gertrude Rainey; Madame Rainey. Born Gertrude Malissa Nix Pridgett, April 26, 1886, in Columbus, GA; died Dec 22, 1939, in Rome, GA; m. William "Pa" Rainey, 1904. ❖ At 14, made 1st stage appearance in a musical revue in Columbus, GA (1900); began touring with traveling tent shows and vaudeville acts; introduced blues numbers into act (1902); adopted professional name Ma Rainey after marrying William "Pa" Rainey (1904), with whom she performed a comedy-and-dance routine throughout South with the Rabbit Foot Minstrels; joined Tolliver's Circus and Musical Extravaganza (1914), billed as "Rainey and Rainey, Assassinators of the Blues"; signed to a recording contract (1923), released "Moonshine Blues"; for next 5 years, recorded over 90 other blues numbers, including such classics as "See See Rider," "Cell Bound Blues," "I Ain't Got Nobody," "Bo-Weevil Blues," "Jelly Bean Blues" and, with Louis Armstrong, "Counting the Blues," in addition to performing them live before packed houses in Chicago, Detroit, Philadelphia, Newark, and NY, where she recorded with Fletcher Henderson's band (1923–28); known as "Mother of the Blues," greatly influenced blues singers who would become better known than herself, such as Bessie Smith and Ethel Waters; touring with her own band, variously called The Harmony Boys, The Jazz Hounds, or the Jazz Wildcats, was a leading star of the so-called "Toby tours," playing black theaters throughout the South run by Theatre Owners' Booking Association (TOBA); released the wildly popular "Ma Rainey's Black Bottom" (1928); watched career decline during Depression, leading to her retirement from show business (1935). ❖ See also Sandra Lieb, *Mother of the Blues: A Study of Ma Rainey* (U. of Massachusetts Press, 1981); Derrick Stewart-Baxter, *Ma Rainey and the Classic Blues Singers* (Stein and Day, 1970); Angela Y. Davis, *Blues Legacies and Black Feminism: Gertrude "Ma" Rainey, Bessie Smith, and Billie Holiday* (Pantheon, 1998); and August Wilson's *Ma Rainey's Black Bottom* (play in 2 acts, 1984); and *Women in World History.*

RAINIER, Priaulx (1903–1986). South African-born composer. Born Feb 3, 1903, at Howick, Natal, South Africa; died in Besse-en-Chandesse (Auvergne), France, Oct 10, 1986; dau. of Ellen (Howard) Rainier and William Gregory Rainier of English-Huguenot descent; studied at South African College of Music Cape Zaon, and at Royal Academy of Music (London) with Rowsby Woof; studied with Nadia Boulanger, 1937. ❖ Her String Quartet was 1st performed by the Gertler Quartet in London (1939) and later recorded by the Amadeus Quartet; appointed professor at Royal Academy of Music (1942), teaching composition there until 1961; elected fellow of Royal Academy (1952); received many commissions from BBC; awarded honorary doctorate of music from University of Cape Town (1982); was the 1st

woman initiated into the Liveryman of the Worshipful Company of Musicians, a guild which dates back to 1500 (1983).

RAINSBERGER, Lisa (c. 1962—). *See Weidenbach, Lisa Larsen.*

RAISA, Rosa (1893–1963). Polish-born soprano. Born Rose Burchstein, May 30, 1893, in Bialystock, Poland; died Sept 28, 1963, in Los Angeles, CA; m. Giacomo Rimini (1887–1952, baritone); studied with Eva Tetrazzini and Barbara Marchisio. ❖ Debuted as Leonora in *Oberto* in Parma (1913); debuted at Chicago Opera (1913) and Covent Garden (1914); spent 3 seasons at Teatro alla Scala (1916–18), where she appeared in the world premieres of *Turandot* and Boito's *Nerone*; was primarily associated with Chicago Opera (1913–37), working for 9 of those seasons with Claudia Muzio. ❖ See also *Women in World History.*

RAISIN, Catherine (1855–1945). English geologist. Name variations: Catherine Alice Raisin. Born April 24, 1855, in London, England; died July 12, 1945; studied zoology with T.H. Huxley and geology with T.G. Bonney at University of London, earning a BS, 1884, and becoming the 2nd woman to earn a DSc, 1898. ❖ The 1st woman to head a geology department at a university in Britain, began career as a demonstrator at Bedford College, University of London (1886–90), then served as head of the geology department (1890–1920), head of the botany department (1891–1908), resident vice principal (1898–1901), and head of the geography department (1916–20); published in many journals (1887–1905), including *Quarterly Journal of the Geological Society* and *Geological Magazine;* made a fellow of Linnaean Society (1906) and London Geographical Society (1919).

RAITT, Bonnie (1949—). American musician. Born Nov 8, 1949, in Burbank, CA; dau. of John Raitt (singer) and Marjorie Haydock; attended Radcliffe College; m. Michael O'Keefe (actor), April 1991 (div. 2000). ❖ Began playing guitar at 12; performed with blues legends Howlin' Wolf and Sippie Wallace; signed with Warner Bros. and released albums *Give It Up* (1972) and *Home Plate* (1975); had gold album, *Sweet Forgiveness* (1977); founded M.U.S.E. (Musicians United for Safe Energy); after album *Nine Lives* flopped (1986), dropped by Warner's; bounced back with *Nick of Time* (1989), which topped the charts and won 4 Grammys, including Album of the Year (1990); released *Luck of the Draw* (1991), which included hit singles, "Something to Talk About" and "I Can't Make You Love Me," and won 3 Grammys; followed that with platinum album, *Longing In Their Hearts* (1994); speaks out on such issues as nuclear power and environment; other albums include *Green Light* (1982), *Road Tested* (1995) and *Fundamental* (1998). Inducted into Rock and Roll Hall of Fame (2000).

RAJALAKSHMI, R. (1926—). Indian biochemist. Born Lakshmi Ramaswami Iyer (added Raja to given name), 1926, in Quilon, Kerala, India; dau. of G.S. Ramaswami Iyer (postal audit officer); graduate in mathematics from Wadia College in Poona, 1945; earned teaching certificate from Lady Willingdon Training College, 1949; Banaras Hindu University, MA in philosophy, 1953; McGill University, PhD in psychology, 1958; m. C.V. Ramakrishnan (professor), 1951; children: 2. ❖ Worked in foods and nutrition department at University of Baroda (1964–67), then biochemistry department, rising to full professorship (1976) and serving as department head (1984–86); developed economical and accessible nutrition programs for people of India that utilized readily available plants; after retirement (1986), moved to US with husband (1990s).

RAJNAI, Klara (1953—). Hungarian kayaker. Born Nov 1953, in Hungary. ❖ At Montreal Olympics, won a bronze medal in K1 500 meters and a silver medal in K2 500 meters (1976).

RAKELS, Heidi (1968—). Belgian judoka. Born June 22, 1968, in Leuven, Belgium. ❖ At Barcelona Olympics, won a bronze medal in middleweight 66 kg (1992).

RAKHMATULINA, Oxana (1976—). Russian basketball player. Name variations: Oksana Anufrieva. Born Dec 7, 1976, in Alma Ata, USSR. ❖ Guard, won a team bronze medal at Athens Olympics (2004); placed 2nd at World championships (2002) and 1st at European championships (2003).

RAKOCZY, Helena (1921—). Polish gymnast. Born Helena Krzynowkowna, Dec 23, 1921, in Poland. ❖ At Melbourne Olympics, won a bronze medal in teams all-around, portable apparatus (1956).

RAKUSZ, Eva (1961—). Hungarian kayaker. Born May 13, 1961, in Hungary. ❖ At Moscow Olympics, won a bronze medal in K2 500 meters (1980); at Seoul Olympics, won a silver medal in K4 500 meters (1988).

RALENKOVA, Anelia (1963—). Bulgarian rhythmic gymnast. Born Dec 25, 1963, in Sofia, Bulgaria. ❖ Won World championship (1981) and European championship (1982, 1984), winning 10 gold medals in World and European competition.

RALFE, Catherine Hester (c. 1831–1912). New Zealand dressmaker, teacher, shopkeeper, and diarist. Born c. 1831 or 1832, at Bantry Bay, Co. Cork, Ireland; died April 5, 1912, in Ashhurst, New Zealand; dau. of Pilcher (naval officer) and Ann Susannah (Lamothe) Ralfe. ❖ Immigrated to New Zealand (1866); taught at isolated settlement (early 1870s), then at private school established by her brother (1873); briefly ran unsuccessful shop in Hokitika before serving as housekeeper and supporting herself through teaching and needlework; recorded her early experiences in diary and documented domestic life for colonial women (c. 1896). ❖ See also *Dictionary of New Zealand Biography* (Vol. 2).

RALOV, Kirsten (1922–1999). Danish ballet dancer and choreographer. Born Kirsten Laura Gnatt, Mar 26, 1922, in Baden, Austria; died May 30, 1999, in Copenhagen; dau. of Kai Gnatt and Kaja Olsen; sister of Poul Gnatt (dancer); m. Borge Ralov (ballet dancer and choreographer), Mar 15, 1944 (div. 1951, died 1981); lived with Fredbjørn Bjørnsson (1926–1993, ballet dancer and mime), 1954–93; children: Helge (b. 1946) and Bjørn (b. 1955). ❖ Performed with Royal Danish Ballet (1940–62), where she danced principal roles in the Bournonville repertory, including in *Napoli, A Folk Tale,* and *Kermesse in Bruges*; performed in Massine's *Le Beau Danube,* Fokine's *Petrouchka,* and created role of Rosalind in Frederick Ashton's *Romeo and Juliet* (1955); choreographed works for company, including *Kameliadamen* (1960) and *Doren* (1962).

RALPH, Jessie (1864–1944). American stage and screen character actress. Born Jessie Ralph Chambers, Nov 5, 1864, in Gloucester, MA; died May 30, 1944, in Gloucester. ❖ Often appeared on Broadway; made film debut in *The Galloper* (1915), followed by *Mary's Lamb, Elmer the Great, Cocktail Hour, Nana, Murder at the Vanities, Evelyn Prentice, Jalna, Little Lord Fauntleroy, San Francisco, Camille, The Good Earth, The Last of Mrs. Cheyney, Drums Along the Mohawk, The Bank Dick* and *They Met in Bombay,* among others.

RALPH, Margaret (c. 1822–1913). New Zealand landowner, innkeeper, mining entrepreneur. Name variations: Margaret Riley, Margaret Schlinker. Born Margaret Riley, in 1822 or 1823, at Strabane, Co. Tyrone, Ireland; died Mar 6, 1913, at Auckland, New Zealand; dau. of John Reilly and Esther (Yates or Gates) Reilling; m. Anthony Ralph, 1837 (died 1873); m. Albert Schlinker (farmer), 1876 (died 1913); children: (1st m.) 12. ❖ Immigrated with husband to New Zealand (1849); established hotel in Rahuipokeka (Huntly, late 1860s); discovered coal on their property and began coal mining business with sons (1876); acquired considerable landholdings and personal wealth. ❖ See also *Dictionary of New Zealand Biography* (Vol. 2).

RALSTON, Esther (1902–1994). American actress. Name variations: The American Venus. Born Esther Ralston in Bar Harbor, Maine, Sept 17, 1902; died in Ventura, California, Jan 14, 1994; dau. of vaudevillians, billed as "The Ralston Family"; m. George Webb (director-actor), 1925 (div. 1933); m. Will Morgan (singer), 1934 (div. 1938); m. Ted Lloyd (journalist), 1939 (div. 1954). ❖ At 2, billed as Baby Esther, joined parents on stage in vaudeville with "The Ralston Family"; at 14, made screen debut in Hoot Gibson western, while 1st sizeable role was in Lon Chaney's *Oliver Twist* (1922); became silent-screen star; appeared as Mrs. Darling in silent version of *Peter Pan* (1925) and shared lead with Clara Bow in *Children of Divorce* (1927); made 1st talkie, *The Wheel of Life* (1931); other films include *Beggar on Horseback* (1925), *A Kiss for Cinderella* (1925), *Old Ironsides* (1926), *Ten Modern Commandments* (1927), *The Case of Lena Smith* (1931), *Black Beauty* (1933), *The Marines Are Coming* (1934), *Reunion* (1936) and *Tin Pan Alley*; retired from films (1941); played title role in radio soap opera, "Woman of Courage" (1941–42), and had running part on "Our Five Daughters" for NBC-TV (1961–62). ❖ See also autobiography *Some Day We'll Laugh* (1985); and *Women in World History.*

RALSTON, Jobyna (1900–1967). American stage and screen actress. Born Jobyna Lancaster Raulston, Nov 21, 1900, in South Pittsburgh, TN; died Jan 22, 1967, in Woodland Hills, CA; m. Richard Arlen (actor), 1927 (div. 1945); children: Richard Arlen Jr. (actor). ❖ Made Broadway debut in *Two Little Girls in Blue* and film debut (both 1921); subsequently starred opposite Max Linder in *The Three Must-Get-Theres* (1922) and Harold Lloyd in 6 films (1923–27); other films include *The Night Flyer, Wings, Little Mickey Grogan, Gigolo, Kid Brother, The Toilers* and *Rough Waters.*

RALSTON, Vera Hruba (1921–2003). Czech-born actress and figure skater. Name variations: Vera Hruba. Born Vera Hruba, June 12, 1921, in Prague, Czechoslovakia (now Czech Republic); died Feb 9, 2003, in Santa Barbara, CA; m. Herbert J. Yates (head of Republic Pictures), 1952 (died 1966); m. Charles de Alva, 1973. ❖ At 10, took up figure skating, eventually winning local championships, then competed against Sonja Henie in Olympics (1936); brought to US by Herbert Yates, head of Republic Pictures, was featured in *Ice Capades* (1941), then *Ice Capades Revue* (1942); other Republic films include *The Lady and the Monster, Lake Placid Serenade, Storm over Lisbon, I Jane Doe, Dakota, The Fighting Kentuckian, The Plainsman and the Lady* and *Fair Wind to Java*; retired from the screen at the demise of Republic (1958).

RAMABAI, Pandita (1858–1922). Indian scholar and social reformer. Name variations: Ramabai Medhavi; Saraswati or Sarasvati. Born Ramabai Dongre, April 23, 1858, in Mysore State, India; died in Kedgaon, Bombay Presidency, India, April 5, 1922; dau. of Anant Sastri Dongre and Lakshmibai (both Sanskrit scholars); educated by parents in Sanskrit and Hindu sacred texts; attended Cheltenham Ladies College in England, 1884–86; m. Bipin Beharidas Medhavi (lawyer), 1880 (died 1882); children: Manoramabai (b. 1881). ❖ Reformer who drew international attention to the plight of Hindu widows and whose school offered shelter and education to thousands of these young women, adopted family's peripatetic lifestyle, traveling to Hindu holy places and earning money by reciting sacred Sanskrit texts; after deaths of father, mother and sister, continued travels with brother, arriving in Calcutta (1878), where her remarkable learning brought fame and entrée to educated Calcutta society; after brother died, married one of his friends, a low-caste but educated lawyer (1880); widowed (1882) and, with young daughter, moved to Poona; founded Arya Mahila Samaj, a reform organization working for the improvement of women's condition; traveled to England (1883); baptized a Christian (Sept 29, 1883); lectured and studied in US (1886–89); published *The High-Caste Hindu Woman* (1887), which led to the founding of the Ramabai Association to fund education for high-caste child-widows; returned to Bombay (1889) and opened Sarada Sadan, an institution for the education of widows; moved school to Poona (1890); during famine in Central India, saved hundreds of starving girls and young women (1896); after outbreak of plague in Poona, moved school to Kedgaon on the outskirts of the city; her institution, now called the Mukti Mission, expanded to include a "rescue home" for "fallen women" and an orphanage; during famine (1900), took in more starving girls, including those of lower castes. Awarded Kaiser-i-Hind Medal (1919). ❖ See also Helen S. Dyer, *Pandita Ramabai*; Nicol Macnicol, *Pandita Ramabai* (1930); and *Women in World History.*

RAMA RAU, Dhanvanthi (1893–1987). Indian social-welfare worker. Name variations: Lady Dhanvanthi Rama Rau. Born Dhanvanthi Handoo, 1893, into an aristocratic Indian family; died 1987; m. Sir Benegal Rama Rau (1889–1969, diplomat, ambassador to Tokyo, 1947–48); children: Santha Rama Rau (b. 1923, writer). ❖ One of 1st Indian women to attend college, taught English at Queen Mary's College in Madras (1917–21); began social-welfare work after marriage; served as secretary of All-India Child Marriage Abolition League (1927–28), member of International Alliance for Suffrage and Equal Citizenship (1932–38), and president of All-India Women's Conference (1946–47); worked for Family Planning Association of India (1949–63) and was president of International Planned Parenthood Association (1963–71). ❖ See also *An Inheritance: The Memoirs of Dhanvanthi Rama Rau.*

RAMA RAU, Santha (1923—). Indian travel writer and novelist. Name variations: Santha Rama Rau Wattles. Born Vasanthi Rama Rau, Jan 24, 1923, in Madras, India; dau. of Benegal Rama Rau (diplomat) and Dhanvanthi Rama Rau (social worker and women's rights advocate); educated at St. Paul's Girls' School in London; Wellesley College, BA, 1944; m. Faubion Bowers, 1951 (div.); m. Gurdon W. Wattles, 1970; children: (1st m.) Jai Peter. ❖ Published 1st book, *Home to India* (1945); when father was named India's 1st ambassador to Japan (1947), traveled with him to Tokyo to serve as his hostess; her travels with husband Faubion Bowers became the basis for such books as *East of Home* (1950), *This Is India* (1954), *View to the Southeast* (1957) and *My Russian Journey* (1959), which were praised for their vivid portrayals of each country's people; published 1st novel, *Remember the House,* an examination of the upper class in Bombay (1956), followed by 2nd novel, *The Adventuress* (1971); adapted Forster's *A Passage to India* for the stage (1960); with Gayatri Devi, co-authored *A Princess Remembers: The Memoirs of the Maharani of Jaipur.* Won Mademoiselle Award (1947); received National Association of Independent Schools Award for *My Russian Journey* (1960). ❖ See also *Women in World History.*

RAMAVO (1792–1861). See *Ranavalona I.*

RAMBAUT, Mary Lucinda (1816–1900). See *Bonney, Mary Lucinda.*

RAMBEAU, Marjorie (1889–1970). American stage, tv, and screen actress. Born July 15, 1889, in San Francisco, CA; died July 7, 1970, in Palm Springs, CA; m. Willard Mack (actor-writer), 1913 (div. 1917); m. Hugh Dillman, 1919 (div. 1923); m. Francis A. Gudger, 1931 (died 1967). ❖ Made NY stage debut (1913) and subsequently appeared in *Kick In, Sadie Love, Eye of Youth, Where Poppies Bloom, As You Like It* and *Valley of Content,* among others; made movie debut (1916) and appeared in numerous films, including *Min and Bill, Tugboat Annie Sails Again* (title role), *Tobacco Road, A Man Called Peter, The View from Pompey's Head* and *Man of a Thousand Faces.* Nominated for Academy Awards for Best Supporting Actress for performances in *The Primrose Path* (1940) and *Torch Song* (1953).

RAMBERG, Cyvia Myriam (1888–1982). See *Rambert, Marie.*

RAMBERT, Marie (1888–1982). Polish-born ballet dancer, director, and teacher. Name variations: Cyvia Rambam; Cesia Rambam; Miriam Ramberg; Miriam Rambert; Dame Marie Rambert. Born Cyvia Ramberg (or Rambam), Feb 20, 1888, in Warsaw, Poland; died June 12, 1982, in London, England; 3rd dau. of a Warsaw bookseller who was registered as Ramberg, though his father's surname was Rambam; attended gymnasia in Warsaw until 1904; 1-year course at Sorbonne, 1906 (Certificat d'Etudes Françaises); attended Jacques Dalcroze Institute, 1910; m. Ashley Dukes (playwright), Mar 7, 1918; children: Angela Dukes Ellis; Helen (Lulu) Dukes. ❖ Dance pioneer, especially remembered for her ability to recognize and develop brilliant choreographers, whose Ballet Rambert was a significant influence on British ballet; saw Isadora Duncan dance in Warsaw which had a profound effect on her future (1904); moved to Paris (1906); attended Jacques Dalcroze Institute (1910–12); joined Ballets Russes to work with Diaghilev and Nijinsky (1912); with outbreak of WWI, went to London where she taught the technique of movement at London School of Eurythmics and studied ballet with Serafima Astafieva (1914); gave 1st public performance of *La Pomme d'Or,* a ballet created for her by Vera Donnet (1917); opened a dancing school (1920); launched Frederick Ashton as a choreographer (1926); with husband, bought the freehold of a large church hall in Notting Hill Gate (1927), opened the Ballet Club there (1931), then adopted the name Ballet Rambert (1934); toured Australia with company (1947–48); toured China (1957); made 1st American tour (1959), achieving greatest success there with *Two Brothers,* choreographed by Norman Morrice; continued to be involved with Ballet Rambert until her death. Named CBE (1953); awarded Chevalier de la Legion d'Honneur (1957); named DBE (1962). ❖ See also *Quicksilver: The Autobiography of Marie Rambert* (Macmillan, 1972); Crisp, Sainsbury, and Williams, eds. *Ballet Rambert: 50 Years On and On* (Scolar, 1976); and *Women in World History.*

RAMBOUILLET, Catherine de Vivonne, Marquise de (1588–1665). French salonnière. Name variations: Marquise de Rambouillet. Born in Rome, 1588; died in Dec 1665; dau. of Jean Vivonne, marquis de Pisani, and Julia (or Giulia) Savelli, a Roman woman of noble family; m. Charles d'Angennes, marquis de Rambouillet, 1600; children: Julie d'Angennes, duchesse de Montausier; Angélique d'Angennes (who was the 1st wife of the marquis de Grignan). ❖ Known as the founder of preciosity, presided over the 1st of the salons which were to dominate French intellectual and literary life during 17th and 18th centuries; founded a salon in a mansion located near the Louvre, known as the Hôtel Rambouillet (1618), remodeling the structure so as to arrange a suite of large reception rooms for the purpose of gathering intellectuals, nobility, and literary greats for discussion; her salon served as the center of France's social and literary currents for 30 years. ❖ See also *Women in World History.*

RAMBOVA, Natacha (1897–1966). American dancer, playwright, actress, costume and set designer, spiritualist, couturier, and Egyptologist. Name variations: Natasha Rambova; Natacha Valentino. Born Winifred Kimball Shaughnessy, Jan 27, 1897, in Salt Lake City, Utah; died June 5, 1966, in Los Angeles, California; dau. of Michael

Shaughnessy (federal marshal, died 1910) and his 2nd wife Winifred (Kimball) Shaughnessy (interior decorator), later Winifred de Wolfe (having married the brother of Elsie de Wolfe), later Winifred Hudnut (having married the cosmetics magnate Richard Hudnut); studied with Russian dancer Theodore Kosloff; m. Rudolph Valentino (actor), May 13, 1922 (div. Jan 1926, died Aug 1926); m. Alvaro de Urzáiz (Spanish tour guide), Aug 6, 1934 (div. 1939); no children. ❖ Remembered primarily as the 2nd wife of Rudolph Valentino and credited with transforming him into Hollywood's 1st great screen idol, was also the creator of her own exotic persona and reinvented herself many times; at 17, toured as a dancer and costume and set designer for Theodore Kosloff's Imperial Russian Ballet; designed costumes for Cecil B. De Mille film *The Woman God Forgot* (1917); met Valentino (1920); designed costumes for Alla Nazimova for a series of films, including *Camille* (1921), *A Doll's House* (1922) and *Salome* (1923); exercised almost total control over Valentino's career, designing his costumes, handling his publicity, negotiating his fees; produced film, *What Price Beauty?* (1928); starred in film *When Love Grows Cold* (1926); appeared on Broadway in *The Purple Vial*; became a theosophist; wrote play "All That Glitters"; opened an exclusive dress-designing studio in NY (1927); married once more (1934), settled on island of Mallorca; with onset of Spanish Civil War (1936), fled to France where she embraced the philosophy of George Gurdjieff; returned to US (1939); with James H. Smith, wrote *Technique for Living*; receiving a grant (1946), sailed for Egypt to explore Ramses' tomb and the vaults of the 9 pyramids at Sakkara (1947); returned to NY (1951) and taught classes in symbolism, mythology, and comparative religion; published *The Tomb of Ramesses VI* (1954), followed by *The Shrines of Tut-Ankh-Amon* (1955) and *Mythological Papyri* (1957) for the Bollingen Series. ❖ See also *Rudy: An Intimate Portrait of Rudolph Valentino by His Wife Natacha Rambova*; Michael Morris, *Madam Valentino: The Many Lives of Natacha Rambova* (Abbeville, 1991); and *Women in World History.*

RAME, Franca (1929—). Italian playwright and actress. Born July 18, 1929, in Parabiago, Italy; dau. of Domenico Rame and Emilia Baldini (professional comedians); m. Dario Fo (playwright). ❖ Born into theatrical family, grew up on the stage; co-founded a theater with husband (1956); began campaigning for rights of women and political prisoners; most works, produced in collaboration with husband, often attack patriarchy, including *Tutto casa, letto e chiesa* (1978, trans. as *Female Parts: One-Woman Plays,* 1981).

RAMÉE, Louise de la (1839–1908). English novelist. Name variations: Louise de la Ramee; (pseudonym) Ouida. Born Marie Louise Ramé, Jan 1, 1839, at Bury St. Edmunds, Suffolk, England; died Jan 25, 1908, in Viareggio, Italy; dau. of Louis Ramé (French instructor) and Susan (Sutton) Ramé. ❖ Published 1st story in *Bentley's Miscellany* (1859); in *New Monthly Magazine,* published 1st full-length novel, *Granville de Vigne,* which was then published in 3 vols. as *Held in Bondage* (1863) and attributed to "Ouida"; continued to use this pseudonym for subsequent books, and soon began using it in personal life as well; published 45 novels, including *Chandos* (1866), the hugely popular *Under Two Flags* (1867), *Folle-Farine* (1871), *Two Little Wooden Shoes* (1874), *Signa* (1875) and *Moths* (1880); also published the popular children's books, *A Dog of Flanders and Other Tales* (1872) and *Bimbi: Stories for Children* (1882); abandoned fiction and wrote for the *Fortnightly Review, Nineteenth Century,* and *North American Review* both on literature and on causes dear to her heart, which included the campaign against women's suffrage, support for the Boers in South Africa, and the antivivisection campaign. ❖ See also *Women in World History.*

RAMENOFSKY, Marilyn (1946—). American swimmer. Born Aug 20, 1946, in Phoenix, Arizona. ❖ At Maccabiah Games, won a gold medal in 400-meter freestyle relay and a bronze medal in 400-meter freestyle (1961) and gold medals for the 220-meter and 400-meter freestyle (1965); won a silver medal in the 400-meter freestyle at Tokyo Olympics and set World records for that event 3 times (all 1964). Inducted into International Jewish Sports Hall of Fame (1988).

RAMEY, Nancy (1940—). American swimmer. Born June 29, 1940; trained with Ray Daughters at the Washington Athletic Club, Seattle. ❖ At Melbourne Olympics, won a silver medal in the 100-meter butterfly (1956).

RAMEY, Venus (c. 1925—). Miss America and politican. Born c. 1925 in Ashland, Kentucky; children: 2 sons. ❖ Named Miss Washington, DC (1944); named Miss America (1944); ran for a seat in the Kentucky House of Representatives; hosted radio show and published a political newspaper; served on the Cincinnati City Council (1970s). ❖ *See also* Frank Deford, *There She Is* (Viking, 1971).

RAMIREZ, Maria Teresa (1953—). Mexican swimmer. Born Aug 15, 1953, in Mexico. ❖ At Mexico City Olympics, won a bronze medal in the 800-meter freestyle (1968).

RAMIREZ, Sara Estela (1881–1910). Mexican poet, teacher, journalist, political activist and feminist. Name variations: Sarita Ramirez. Born Sara Estela Ramirez, 1881, in Coahuila, Mexico; died in Laredo, Texas, Aug 21, 1910; parents undocumented; graduate of Teachers' College, ateneo Fuentes, at Saltillo, Coahuila; never married; no children. ❖ At 17, moved to Laredo, Texas, and began publishing poems, essays, and literary articles in local newspapers, *La Crónica* and *El Demócrata Fronterizo*, and was hired to teach Mexican children at Seminary of Laredo (1898); joined Partido Liberal Mexicano (PLM), the party working for the overthrow of Mexican dictator Porfirio Díaz (1901); founded radical daily newspaper *La Corregidora* (1904); was a journalist for *Vésper*, and prominent member of Regeneracion y Concordia and Club Redención; acted in play *Noema* in Laredo; founded literary periodical *Aurora* in Laredo (1910); through her poetry, journalism, and political activities, helped to sow the seeds of the Mexican Revolution of 1910, which would erupt only 3 months after her early death; also helped to establish a firm basis for the emergence of the contemporary Chicana feminist movement, and thus is considered one of the founders of Mexican feminism. ❖ *See also* Inés Hernandez Tovar, *Sara Estela Ramirez: The Early Twentieth Century Texas-Mexican Poet* (Houston U. Press, 1984); and *Women in World History*.

RAMIREZ HECHEVARRIA, Daymi (1983—). Cuban volleyball player. Born Oct 8, 1983, in Cuba. ❖ Won a team bronze medal at Athens Olympics (2004).

RAMIREZ MERINO, Virginia (1964—). Spanish field-hockey player. Born May 22, 1964, in Spain. ❖ At Barcelona Olympics, won a gold medal in team competition (1992).

RAMLAH (fl. 7th c.). One of the wives of Muhammad. Name variations: Umm Habibah. Dau. of Abu Sufyan, a distant cousin of Muhammad; m. Muhammad in 629 CE. ❖ *See also Women in World History*.

RAMO, Roberta Cooper (1942—). American lawyer. Born Aug 8, 1942, in Denver, CO; dau. of David and Martha L. (Rosenblum) Cooper; University of Colorado, BA, 1964; University of Chicago, JD, 1967; m. Barry W. Ramo, June 17, 1964. ❖ Admitted to the Bar in New Mexico (1967), Texas (1971); opened a law office in Alburquerque; became the 1st woman president of the American Bar Association (ABA, 1995).

RAMOLINO, Letizia (1750–1836). *See Bonaparte, Letizia.*

RAMOMA (1829–1883). *See Ranavalona II.*

RAMONDINO, Fabrizia (1936—). Italian novelist and short-story writer. Born Aug 30, 1936, in Naples, Italy. ❖ Published *Althénopis* (1981), about her family; other works, which focus on social issues, include *Napoli* (1977, *Storie di patio* (1983), *Taccuino tedesco* (1987), *Un giorno e mezzo* (1988), *In viaggio* (1995), and *Per un sentiero chiaro* (2004); tends to publish with feminist houses.

RAMOS, Tina S. (1921—). *See Hills, Tina S.*

RAMOSKIENE, Genovaite (1945—). Soviet rower. Born May 12, 1945, in USSR. ❖ At Montreal Olympics, won a bronze medal in double sculls (1976).

RAMPHELE, Mamphela (1947—). South African doctor, anthropologist, educator, and activist. Born Dec 28, 1947, near Pietersburg, South Africa, to rural schoolteachers; qualified in medicine at University of Natal in 1972; University of Cape Town, Ph.D. in social anthropology, 1991; University of South Africa, BCom in administration; married and div.; children: (with Steven Biko) son Hlumelo; and later son Malusi. ❖ While in medical school, joined Steven Biko's Black Consciousness Movement; founded Zanempilo Health Clinic at King William's Town through auspices of Black Community Programmes (1975); was arrested and, without trial, banned to a far corner of the Transvaal (1977), where she continued to work as a doctor; founded another health clinic, the Ithuseng Community Health Program, while still in detention at Trichardsdal; wrote about Biko and their relationship in *Mamphela Ramphele—A Life* (published in US as *Across Boundaries*); with banning order lifted (1983), became a research fellow at University of Cape Town (1986), then deputy vice-chancellor (1991) and

vice-chancellor (1996), the 1st black woman to be appointed to such a post in South Africa; left University of Cape Town to become the 2nd woman managing director at the World Bank (2000). ❖ *See also* autobiography *Across Boundaries: The Journey of a South African Woman Leader* (Feminist Press, 1997); and *Women in World History*.

RAMPLING, Anne (1941—). *See Rice, Anne.*

RAMPLING, Charlotte (1945—). English actress. Born Feb 5, 1945, in Sturmer, England; dau. of a NATO commander; m. Brian Southcombe, 1972 (div. 1976); m. Jean-Michel Jarre (musician), 1977 (sep. 1997); children: (1st m.) Barnaby Southcombe (director); (2nd m.) David Jarre (magician). ❖ Began career as a model; came to prominence as the callous friend in film *Georgy Girl* (1966), played the wife in a decadent German family in *The Damned* (1969), explored sado-mashochism in *The Night Porter* (1974) and seduced and betrayed Paul Newman in *The Verdict* (1982); acclaimed for her performance in *Under the Sand* (2001); other films include *The Knack* (1965), *Zardoz* (1974), *Farewell, My Lovely* (1975), *Orca* (1977), *Stardust Memories* (1980), *The Wings of the Dove* (1997) and *The Cherry Orchard* (2000). Awarded an OBE (2003); won Best Actress Award from European Film Academy for *Swimming Pool* (2003); received French Legion of Honor (2004).

RAMPONE, Christie (1975—). *See Pearce, Christie.*

RAMSAY, Alison (1959—). Scottish field-hockey player. Born April 16, 1959, in Scotland. ❖ At Barcelona Olympics, won a bronze medal in team competition (1992).

RAMSAY, Katharine (1874–1960). *See Stewart-Murray, Katharine.*

RAMSAY, Martha Laurens (1759–1811). American diarist. Born Nov 3, 1759, in Charleston, South Carolina; died June 10, 1811, in Charleston; dau. of Henry Laurens (plantation owner, patriot, and later president of the Continental Congress) and Eleanor (Ball) Laurens; m. David Ramsay (physician and member of Continental Congress), Jan 23, 1787; children: Eleanor (b. 1787); Martha (b. 1789); Frances (b. 1790); Katharine (b. 1792); Sabine Elliot (b. 1794); David (b. 1795); Jane Montgomery (b. 1796); James (b. 1797); a 2nd Jane Montgomery (b. 1799); Nathaniel (b. 1801); William (b. 1802). ❖ Following her death, husband published her diary as *Memoirs of the Life of Martha Laurens Ramsay* which became quite popular, and she was seen as the essence of a proper woman, devoted to her religion and her family, well educated but not spoiled from it, and content with her subordinate place as a woman. ❖ *See also Women in World History*.

RAMSAY, Patricia (1886–1974). English princess and granddaughter of Queen Victoria. Name variations: Lady Patricia Ramsay; Patricia Saxe-Coburg. Born Victoria Patricia Helena Elizabeth on Mar 17, 1886, at Buckingham Palace, London, England; died Jan 12, 1974, in Windlesham, Surrey, England; dau. of Louise Margaret of Prussia (1860–1917) and Arthur, duke of Connaught (son of Queen Victoria); m. Alexander Ramsay, on Feb 27, 1919; children: Alexander Ramsay (b. 1919). ❖ When father was governor-general of Canada (1911–16), stayed with him in Canada to serve as his hostess, rather than her mother; proved so popular with Canadians that "Princess Patricia's Canadian Light Infantry" was named in her honor, and she was made the colonel-in-chief of the regiment.

RAMSEIER, Doris (1939—). Swiss equestrian. Born May 18, 1939, in Switzerland. ❖ At Montreal Olympics, won a silver medal in team dressage (1976).

RAMSEY, Alice (1864–1933). *See Ramsey, Alicia.*

RAMSEY, Alice Huyler (1886–1983). American pioneer. Born in Hackensack, New Jersey, Nov 11, 1886; died in Covina, California, Sept 10, 1983; graduate of Vassar College, 1907; m. John Rathbone Ramsey (lawyer); children: at least 1 son and 1 daughter, Alice Ramsey Bruns. ❖ The 1st woman to drive across US, set off from New York City in a Maxwell touring car (June 6, 1909), reaching San Francisco (Aug 8). Was also 1st woman inducted into Automotive Hall of Fame (2000). ❖ *See also Women in World History*.

RAMSEY, Alicia (1864–1933). English playwright. Name variations: Alice Ramsey. Born 1864 in London, England; died May 7, 1933; dau. of William Royston and Isabel Morgan (Harris) Royston; m. Cecil Ramsey (died); m. Rudolph de Cordova (writer). ❖ Wrote such plays as *Only a Model* (1892), *Gaffer Jarge* (1896), *Bridge* (1917), *Eve's Daughter* (1917) and *Byron* (1929); co-wrote, with husband de Cordova, *Monsieur de Paris, As a Man Sows, The Mandarin, Honor* and

Edmund Kean, among others; wrote several spectacles for the Hippodrome starting 1902, including *The Bandits, The Redskins, The Golden Princess, The Typhoon* and *The Silver Candlestick;* also wrote novels, short stories, and provided scenarios for the screen.

RAMSEY, Anne (1929–1988). American actress. Born Anne Mobley, Sept 1, 1929, in Omaha, NE; died Aug 11, 1988, in Los Angeles, CA; m. Logan Ramsey (actor), 1954. ❖ After 37-year stage and screen career, achieved prominence for her performance as Momma in *Throw Momma from the Train* and was nominated for an Academy Award (1988); other films include *The Sporting Club, Up the Sandbox, For Pete's Sake, The New Centurions, National Lampoon's Class Reunion, The Goonies, Scrooged* and *Any Which Way You Can.*

RAMSEY, Elizabeth M. (1906–1993). American physician and placentologist. Name variations: Elizabeth M. Klagsbrunn; Mrs. Hans A. Klagsbrunn. Born in New York, NY, Feb 17, 1906; died in Washington, DC, July 2, 1993; dau. of Charles Cyrus Ramsey and Grace (Keys) Ramsey; Mills College, BA, 1928; Yale Medical School, MD, 1932; Medical College of Pennsylvania, DSc, 1965; also studied in Hamburg, Germany; m. Hans Alexander Klagsbrunn (lawyer), Jan 27, 1934 (died 1993). ❖ Graduated from Yale Medical School as 1 of 2 women in her class (1932); while conducting a routine autopsy, discovered a 14-day-old embryo, at the time the youngest ever seen (1930s); extensively studied the anatomy of human embryos and published her findings; later used radioactive dyes and X-rays to conclude that the human embryo and placenta have a similar circulation system; wrote *The Placenta of Laboratory Animals and Man* (1975) and, with Martin Donner, *Placental Vasculature and Circulation* (1982); spent 36 years working in the Carnegie Institute's embryology department at Johns Hopkins University, where she also taught and lectured. Inducted into American College of Obstetricians and Gynecologists Hall of Fame; named distinguished scientist by Society for Gynecologic Investigation (1987). ❖ See also *Women in World History.*

RAMSEY, Grace (1839–1888). See O'Meara, Kathleen.

RAMSEY, Sue (1970—). Northern Ireland politician. Born Sept 13, 1970, in Springhill, Ballymurphy, Northern Ireland. ❖ Attended Portrush Catering College, then worked as a chef (1988–94); representing Sinn Féin, elected to the Northern Ireland Assembly for West Belfast (1998); named deputy chair, public accounts (2000) and chief whip (2002).

RAMSLAND, Sarah Katherine (1882–1964). Canadian legislator. Name variations: Sarah Katherine McEwen; Sarah Katherine McEwen Ramsland. Born July 19, 1882, in Buffalo Lake, Minnesota; died April 4, 1964, in Prince Albert, Saskatchewan, Canada; married 1906; children: 3. ❖ Married and moved to Saskatchewan, Canada (1906); husband elected to Saskatchewan legislature as a member of the Liberal Party (1917), then died (1918); gained the Liberal Party's nomination for Pelly riding (district) and won by-election (1919), the 1st woman elected to Saskatchewan Legislative Assembly; was reelected in the provincial election (1921); stressed the need for rural high schools and libraries. ❖ See also *Women in World History.*

RAN, Shulamit (1949—). American composer. Born Oct 21, 1949, in Tel Aviv, Israel. ❖ Came to US at 14 on scholarship to Mannes College of Music, NY (1963); performed original work *Capriccio* with New York Philharmonic conducted by Leonard Bernstein (1963); premiered *Concert Piece* for piano and orchestra with Zubin Mehta and Israel Philharmonic (1971); became professor of composition at University of Chicago, IL (1973); became 1st woman composer-in-residence at major US orchestra, at Chicago Symphony (1991); has received all prestigious awards for composers, including the Pulitzer Prize (1991) for her *Symphony.* Other works include *Between Two World (The Dybbuk), Hyperbolae, East Wind, Voices, Legends,* and *Vessels of Courage and Hope.*

RANAVALONA I (1792–1861). Monarch of Madagascar. Name variations: Ramavo. Pronunciation: rah-nah-VAH-loo-nah. Born Ramavo in Madagascar, 1792; died in Madagascar, 1861; member of the Hova royal family; m. King Radama I (died 1828); children: Rakoto. ❖ Opponent of European imperialism, assumed power at age 36 upon death of husband-cousin King Radama I (1828) and proved herself to be a formidable political strategist and a ruler of iron will; refused to grant an interview to the British ambassador and repudiated the Anglo-Malagasy treaty of friendship; attempted to expand her kingdom at the expense of the Sakalava tribe (1829), but her aggression drove the Sakalavas to seek French protection; when a punitive French force landed

on Madagascar, sent an army of 14,000 conscripts to meet them, but they were defeated (1829); enjoined all missionaries to respect the cultural traditions of the nation and to cease baptizing its subjects (1835); when this proved ineffective, began persecution of Malagasy Christians (1836); deprived Europeans of trading privileges (1845); had all Europeans expelled from Madagascar (1857); is alternately characterized as a bloodthirsty despot or an anti-imperialist heroine, though the truth of her reign probably lies somewhere in between. ❖ See also *Women in World History.*

RANAVALONA II (1829–1883). Queen of Madagascar. Name variations: Ranavalomanjaka; Princess Ramoma. Pronunciation: rah-nah-VAH-loo-nah. Born 1829 into the royal family of the Imerina, rulers of the largest kingdom on African island of Madagascar; died July 13, 1883, in Tananarive, Madagascar; dau. of Prince Ramasindrazana of Madagascar; m. Radama II, king of Madagascar (assassinated 1863); m. Rainilaiarivony, prime minister of Madagascar, 1869; no children. ❖ When husband Radama II married Rasoherina, was relegated to status of 2nd wife; when Rasoherina, who had succeeded Radama II, died (1868), was chosen queen and took the name Ranavalona II; had a significant impact on Madagascar's history; during reign of 15 years, implemented Protestant Christianity as the state religion, rejecting the traditional gods of the Imerina; with husband, issued new legal codes, which borrowed heavily from European liberal political ideology while preserving royal authority (1873 and 1881); followed an "open-door" strategy towards European missionaries and traders, which ultimately led to French demands that she accept the establishment of a French protectorate over the island and allow the sale of land to French nationals; rejected these demands, which resulted in the French-Malagasy war (1883). ❖ See also *Women in World History.*

RANAVALONA III (1861–1917). Last queen of Madagascar. Name variations: Razafindrahety. Pronunciation: rah-nah-VAH-loo-nah. Born 1861 into ruling family of Imerina, in Madagascar; died 1917 in Algiers; dau. of Princess Raketaka of Madagascar; m. Rainilaiarivony, prime minister of Madagascar, Aug 1883; no children. ❖ Chosen by the nobility of the Malagasy people of Madagascar to succeed Queen Ranavalona II (July 1883), took the name Ranavalona III; on accession, faced a war with the French, who wanted to establish Madagascar as a colony in order to control its rich natural resources and strategic geographical location; forced to surrender Tananarive to French troops (1895); was exiled to Réunion to prevent her from becoming a focus for uprisings among her former subjects (1897). ❖ See also *Women in World History.*

RAND, Ayn (1905–1982). Russian-born writer and philosopher. Name variations: Alissa Rosenbaum (1905–1926); Ayn Rand (1926–1929 and in professional life throughout); Ayn O'Connor (1929–1982). Pronunciation: *Ayn* rhymes with *pine.* Born Alissa Rosenbaum in St. Petersburg, Russia, Feb 2, 1905; died in New York, NY, Mar 6, 1982; dau. of Fronz Rosenbaum (chemist) and Anna Rosenbaum; University of Petrograd, BA in history, 1924; m. Charles Francis "Frank" O'Connor (actor and painter), April 15, 1929; no children. ❖ Pro-capitalist, antireligious novelist and philosopher, and founder of philosophical "Objectivism," immigrated to US (1926); became naturalized citizen (1931); was a movie extra and screenwriter in Hollywood, then wardrobe chief for RKO pictures (1926–32); was a screenwriter, playwright, and novelist (1932–44); published huge didactic novels *The Fountainhead* (1943) and *Atlas Shrugged* (1957) which developed a cult following; was a freelance writer and Objectivist leader (1950–82); served as co-editor and contributor to *The Objectivist Newsletter* (1962–65) and its successor *The Objectivist* (1966–71); wrote and published *The Ayn Rand Letter* (1971–76); was a columnist for *Los Angeles Times;* one of the most outspoken anti-Communists of the 20th century, glorified capitalism, hated all forms of socialism, and thought of selfishness as a positive virtue. Other writings include *We, the Living* (1936), *Anthem* (1946), *For the New Intellectual: The Philosophy of Ayn Rand* (1961), *The Virtue of Selfishness: A New Concept of Egoism* (1964), *Capitalism: The Unknown Ideal* (1966), *The Romantic Manifesto: A Philosophy of Literature* (1969), *Philosophy: Who Needs It?* (1971), *The New Left: The Anti-Industrial Revolution* (1982) and *The Ayn Rand Lexicon: Objectivism from A to Z* (1984). ❖ See also Barbara Branden, *The Passion of Ayn Rand* (Doubleday, 1986); David Harriman, ed. *Journals of Ayn Rand* (Dutton, 1997); Ronald E. Merrill, *The Ideas of Ayn Rand* (Open Court, 1991); and *Women in World History.*

RAND, Caroline Amanda (1828–1905). American socialist philanthropist. Born Caroline Amanda Sherfey, Feb 4, 1828, in Hagerstown, MD; died July 23, 1905, in Florence, Italy; dau. of

Solomon Sherfey (merchant, sawmill operator, and farmer) and Catherine (McNeil) Sherfey; m. J.W. Roberts (died 1851); Elbridge Dexter Rand (businessman), June 13, 1852 (died 1887); children: (2nd m.) 3 sons and daughter Carrie Rand Herron (1867–1914). ❖ Gave $35,000 to establish Department of Applied Christianity at Iowa College in Grinnell, IA (later Grinnell College) for socialist-oriented Rev. George Davis Herron (1893); was longterm supporter of school to become center for social gospel and Christian socialist movement; provided financial support to Social Apostolate, ministers' group in Chicago.

RAND, Ellen (1875–1941). American portrait painter. Name variations: Bay Rand; Ellen "Bay" Emmet. Born Ellen Gertrude Emmet, Mar 4, 1875, in San Francisco, California; died Dec 18, 1941, in New York, NY; dau. of Christopher Temple Emmet (lawyer) and Ellen James (Temple) Emmet; cousin of writer Henry James; studied art under Dennis Bunker, with William Merritt Chase at Art Students League, 1889–93, and with sculptor Frederick MacMonnies; m. William Blanchard Rand (gentleman farmer and legislator), May 6, 1911; children: Christopher Temple Emmet (b. 1912); William Blanchard Jr. (b. 1913); John Alsop (b. 1914). ❖ Set up a studio in Washington Square South in New York City (1900); had a solo show at Durand-Ruel Galleries on Fifth Avenue (1902); had one-woman exhibition of 90 paintings at Copley Hall in Boston, where the only previous solo shows had been dedicated to Sargent, Monet and Whistler (1906); worked on commissioned portraits for a wealthy clientele, including public officials, heads of industry, society women and admired intellectuals, but was more than a society portraitist; portraits of Augustus Saint-Gaudens and Benjamin Altman are in Metropolitan Museum of Art (NY); also painted official portraits of Elihu Root and Franklin Delano Roosevelt; elected an Associate of the National Academy of Design (1926) and an Academician (1934). Won many awards, including a gold medal at Panama-Pacific Exposition (1915) and Beck Gold Medal from Pennsylvania Academy of the Fine Arts (1922). ❖ See also *Women in World History*.

RAND, Gertrude (1886–1970). American scientist. Name variations: Marie Gertrude Rand; Gertrude Ferree. Born Marie Gertrude Rand in Brooklyn, New York, Oct 29, 1886; died in Stony Brook, Long Island, NY, June 30, 1970; dau. of Lyman Fiske Rand (president of a manufacturing company) and Mary Catherine (Moench) Rand; Cornell University, AB, 1908; Bryn Mawr, AM, PhD, 1911; post-doctoral fellow (1911–12) and Sarah Berliner research fellow (1912–13), Bryn Mawr; m. Clarence Ferree (professor and scientist), Dec 28, 1918 (died 1942). ❖ With husband, researched the effects of illumination on color perception, conducted research which led to the development of the Ferree-Rand perimeter, a tool for diagnosing vision problems which maps the perceptual abilities of the retina, and developed glare-control lighting for public places; became an associate professor of research ophthalmology and then of physiological optics at Wilmer Ophthalmological Institute of Johns Hopkins University School of Medicine (1928); became associate director of Research Laboratory of Physiological Optics in Baltimore (1935); also worked as a research associate at Knapp Foundation of Columbia University College of Physicians and Surgeons, concentrating on detection and measurement of color blindness. Was the 1st woman fellow of Illuminating Engineering Society of North America (1952); was the 1st woman to win Edgar D. Tillyer Medal of Optical Society of America (1959); received gold medal from Illuminating Engineering Society of North America (1963). ❖ See also *Women in World History*.

RAND, Marie Gertrude (1886–1970). See Rand, Gertrude.

RAND, Mary (1940—). English track-and-field athlete. Name variations: Mary Toomey. Born Mary Denise Bignal, Feb 10, 1940, in Wells, Somerset, England; married, 1960; m. Bill Toomey (American decathlon champion), 1969; children: Alison (b. 1962). ❖ Broke the British national record in the pentathlon with 4,046 points (1957); won a silver medal (1958) and a gold medal (1966), both for long jump at Commonwealth Games; won a bronze medal for long jump at European championships (1962); shared the world record in the 4 x 100 relay (1963); won a gold medal for long jump, a silver for pentathlon, and a team bronze for the 4 x 100-meter relay at Tokyo Olympics (1964); retired (1968). Named MBE. ❖ See also *Women in World History*.

RAND, Sally (1904–1979). American dancer and burlesque star. Born Helen Gould Beck, Jan 2, 1904, in Elkton, Hickory County, Missouri; died Aug 31, 1979, in Glendora, California; m. and div. several times; children: 1 son. ❖ During early years, performed in clubs, with carnivals, and Ringling Brothers Circus, before making way to Hollywood; as Sally Rand, appeared in a number of silent movies (1920s), notably Cecil

B. De Mille's *King of Kings* (1927), but was forced out with advent of sound; after initially performing her fan dance in a speakeasy in Chicago, made her way to Chicago World's Fair (1933–34), riding a white horse to the fairgrounds à la Lady Godiva; organized a dance troupe and toured US; appeared at San Diego World's Fair (1936) and San Francisco Exposition (1939), then found steady employment as the headliner at various burlesque houses across the country; continued to perform for 40 years and replaced Ann Corio as emcee for Broadway revue *This Was Burlesque* (1965). ❖ See also *Women in World History*.

RANDALL, Amelia Mary (1844–1930). New Zealand landowner and benefactor. Name variations: Amelia Mary Davenport. Born Jan 23, 1844, at Boulogne-sur-Mer, France; died Oct 17, 1930, at Greenmeadows, New Zealand; dau. of Theodore Alfred Davenport (scholar) and Charlotte (Tiffen) Davenport; m. Joseph Randall (merchant), 1869. ❖ Immigrated to New Zealand with parents; inherited vast amounts of land, including Greenmeadows Vineyard and Fruit Farm, upon death of uncle (1875); managed farm with staff and helped found Hawke's Bay Children's Home (1892); upon her own death, bequeathed half her estate to charities. ❖ See also *Dictionary of New Zealand Biography* (Vol. 3).

RANDALL, Claire (1919—). American religious pioneer. Born in Dallas, Texas, Oct 15, 1919; Scarritt College for Christian Workers, BA, 1950. ❖ Served as director of the Christian World Mission, then as program director and associate director of Church Women United (1962–73); became secretary of National Council of the Churches of Christ (1974), the 1st woman in America to hold such a high-ranking religious post; worked toward ecumenism and better ties between the council and Roman Catholic Church; also served on National Commission on International Women's Year (1975–77), and on the Martin Luther King Jr. Federal Holiday Commission (1985); served as national president of Church Women United (1988–92). ❖ See also *Women in World History*.

RANDALL, Marta (1948—). American science-fiction and short-story writer. Name variations: Martha Conley. Born April 26, 1948, in Mexico City, Mexico; m. Robert H. Bergstresser, 1966 (div. 1973); m. Christopher E. Conley, 1983. ❖ Served as president of Science Fiction Writers of America (1982–84); works include *Islands* (1976), *A City in the North* (1976), *Journey* (1978), *Dangerous Games* (1980), *The Sword of Winter* (1983), *Those Who Favor Fire* (1984), and *Growing Light* (1993); published short fiction in such magazines as *New Dimensions, New Worlds,* and *Isaac Asimov's Science Fiction Magazine.*

RANDALL, Martha (1948—). American swimmer. Born June 12, 1948, in US. ❖ At Tokyo Olympics, won a bronze medal in the 400-meter indiv. medley (1964).

RANDE, Mary (c. 1621–after 1653). See Cary, Mary.

RANDOLPH, Agnes (1312–1369). See Dunbar, Agnes.

RANDOLPH, Amanda (1896–1967). African-American actress and singer. Name variations: Mandy Randolph. Born Sept 2, 1896, in Louisville, KY; died Aug 24, 1967, in Duarte, CA; sister of Lillian Randolph (1898–1980, actress); aunt of Barbara Randolph (singer, member of The Platters). ❖ Appeared in nightclubs and musical comedies; on radio and tv, was the meddling mother-in-law on "Amos 'n Andy"; on tv, was the maid Louise on "Make Room for Daddy" (1955–64) and starred briefly on "Beulah" (1950); films include *The Black Network, Swing!* and *Mister Scoutmaster.*

RANDOLPH, Angie Brooks (1928—). See Brooks, Angie.

RANDOLPH, Barbara (d. 2002). African-American singer and actress. Born in Detroit, MI; died July 15, 2002, in South Africa; dau. of Lillian Randolph (actress); m. Eddie Singleton. ❖ Was a Motown recording artist and member of The Platters (1964); appeared in film *Guess Who's Coming to Dinner.*

RANDOLPH, Elsie (1904–1982). English dancer and comedian. Born Dec 9, 1904, in London, England; died Oct 15, 1982, in London. ❖ Performed in musical shows as an adolescent, including *The Girl for the Boy* (1919); with Jack Buchanan, performed to great success in numerous shows, including *Sunny* (1926), *Wake Up and Dream* (1929) and *Stand Up and Sing* (1931); danced solo roles in popular musicals like *The Co-Optimist* (1930) and *The Wonder Bar* (1930); films include *That's a Good Girl* and *This'll Make You Whistle*; also appeared in Hitchcock's *Frenzy.*

RANDOLPH, Isabel (1889–1973). American stage, radio, tv, and screen actress. Name variations: Mrs. Uppington. Born Dec 4, 1889, in Illinois; died Jan 11, 1973, in Burbank, CA. ❖ Appeared on Broadway in *The Noose* and *Bird of Paradise*; films include *On their Own, Yesterday's Heroes* and *Look Who's Laughing*; also appeared in westerns with Gene Autry and Roy Rogers, was a regular on radio's "Fibber McGee and Molly," and portrayed Dick Van Dyke's tv mother in "The Dick Van Dyke Show."

RANDOLPH, Lillian (1898–1980). African-American screen, radio, and tv actress. Born Dec 14, 1898, in Louisville, KY; died Sept 12, 1980, in Arcadia, CA; sister of Amanda Randolph (1896–1967, actress); children: Barbara Randolph (d. 2002, member of The Platters). ❖ Films include *Little Men, The Great Gildersleeve, The Bachelor and the Bobby-Soxer, Hush Hush Sweet Charlotte, The Onion Field* and *Magic*; portrayed the Bailey family housekeeper in *It's a Wonderful Life*; also had recurring role as the maid Birdie on radio and tv's "The Great Gildersleeve," Madame Queen on tv's "Amos 'n' Andy," and the title role in "Beulah," having replaced Hattie McDaniel.

RANDOLPH, Mandy (1896–1967). See Randolph, Amanda.

RANDOLPH, Martha Jefferson (1775–1836). American first daughter. Name variations: Patsy Randolph. Born at Monticello, Albemarle Co., Virginia, Sept 27, 1775; died Oct 10, 1836, and was buried at Monticello; eldest dau. of Thomas Jefferson (president of US, 1801–09) and Martha (Wayles) Jefferson (1748–1782); m. cousin Thomas Mann Randolph Jr. (congressional representative and governor of Virginia), Feb 23, 1790 (died 1828); children: 12, including Anne Carey Randolph (b. 1791); Thomas Jefferson Randolph (b. 1792); Ellen (1794–1795); Ellen Wayles Randolph Coolidge (b. 1796, who m. Joseph Coolidge Jr.); Cornelia Jefferson Randolph (b. 1799); Virginia Jefferson Randolph (b. 1801); Mary Jefferson Randolph (b. 1803); James Madison Randolph (b. 1806); Benjamin Franklin Randolph (b. 1808); Meriwether Lewis Randolph (b. 1810); Septimia Anne Randolph (b. 1814); George Wythe Randolph (b. 1818). ❖ Known as Patsy, not only resembled her father but was apparently the most devoted to him of all the 6 Jefferson children; accompanied him to Philadelphia, where he attended the Continental Congress, and then sojourned with him on a 5-year diplomatic mission to Paris, beginning 1784; though she visited father only twice during his presidency (1801–09), spent most of her time with him at Monticello after he left the White House. ❖ See also *Women in World History*.

RANDOLPH, Patsy (1775–1836). See Randolph, Martha Jefferson.

RANDOLPH, Virginia (1874–1958). African-American educator and social worker. Name variations: Virginia E. Randolph. Born Virginia Estelle Randolph in Richmond, Virginia, June 6, 1874 (some sources erroneously cite 1870); died Mar 16, 1958; dau. of former slaves Nelson and Sarah Elizabeth Randolph; attended City Normal School in Richmond, Virginia; never married; no children. ❖ Innovative educator and social worker who spent nearly 60 years trying to improve the lives of both African-American children and their parents in poverty-stricken Henrico County, Virginia; was a pioneer of vocational education whose teaching methods were widely adopted, both in US and internationally; named the 1st "Jeanes Teacher," charged with spreading her educational methods through black schools in the state (1908); as a Jeanes Teacher, oversaw 23 rural schools, visiting them regularly to plan improvements and teaching methods; built the Virginia Randolph Training School, the 1st high school for black students in Henrico Co. (1915). The Virginia Randolph High School is now known as the Virginia Randolph Education Centers, the campus of which includes both Randolph's gravesite and a museum dedicated to her life and achievements. Inducted into Virginia Women's Hall of Fame (1993). ❖ See also *Women in World History*.

RANDZIO-PLATH, Christa (1940—). German lawyer and politician. Born Oct 29, 1940, in Ratibor, Germany. ❖ As a European Socialist, elected to 4th and 5th European Parliament (1994–99, 1999–2004); named chair of the Committee on Economic and Monetary Affairs.

RANFAING, Élizabeth of (d. 1649). French zealot. Name variations: Elizabeth de Ranfaing. Died in Nancy, France, 1649. ❖ During a famous episode of diabolic possession (1618–25), denounced, among others, her doctor, who was burned at the stake (1622); founded a congregation for repentant prostitutes (1631), which was condemned by the pope as a sect.

RANGONI, Alda. See Este, Alda d'.

RANGUELOVA, Kristina (1985—). Bulgarian rhythmic gymnast. Born Jan 24, 1985, in Sofia, Bulgaria. ❖ Won team all-around bronze medal at Athens Olympics (2004).

RANIA (1970—). Queen of Jordan. Name variations: Queen Rania Al-Abdullah. Born Rania Al-Yasin, Aug 31, 1970, in Kuwait, to Palestinian refugee parents; father a physician; graduated with honors in business administration from American University in Cairo, 1991; m. Abdullah II, king of Jordan (r. 1999—), June 10, 1993; children: Prince Hussein (b. 1994) and Princess Iman (b. 1996), Princess Salma (b. 2000) and Prince Hashem (b. 2005). ❖ Once worked for Citibank, then for Apple Computer in Amman; became queen (1999); developed an agenda of charity and change; became head of a foundation that combats child abuse; works with husband to promote Jordan's exports; focuses on women's and children's rights, and has campaigned against honor killings.

RANI OF GONDWANA. See Durgawati (d. 1564).

RANI OF GURRAH. See Durgawati (d. 1564).

RANI OF JAIPUR. See Gayatra Devi (b. 1919).

RANI OF JHANSI. See Lakshmibai (c. 1835–1858).

RANKIN, Annabelle (1908–1986). Australian politician and diplomat. Name variations: Dame Annabelle Rankin. Born Annabelle Jane Mary Rankin in Brisbane, Queensland, Australia, July 28, 1908; died Aug 30, 1986; dau. of Annabelle (Davidson) Rankin and Colin Dunlop Wilson Rankin (cane grower and member of the Queensland Legislative Assembly); never married. ❖ Achieved a number of 1sts: 1st woman whip; 1st Australian woman to hold a federal ministerial portfolio; and 1st Australian woman to hold ambassadorial rank; as a Liberal-Country Party representative, elected to the Senate for Queensland (1946); during long tenure, which lasted until 1971, was concerned with a wide range of issues, particularly those connected with housing, health, and communications; participation in parliamentary committees included the Senate Standing Committee on Regulations and Ordinances; served as Opposition Whip in the Senate (1947–49), the 1st woman to hold such a position in the British Commonwealth; was also elected vice president of the Queensland Liberal Party (1949); served as Government Whip (1951–66); served as Minister of Housing (1966–71); after retiring from Senate (1971), was appointed High Commissioner (ambassador) to New Zealand, the 1st Australian woman named to a top-level diplomatic post. Created Dame of the British Empire (1957). ❖ See also Waveney Browne, *A Woman of Distinction: The Honourable Dame Annabelle Rankin D.B.E.* (Boolarong, 1981); and *Women in World History*.

RANKIN, Janice (1972—). Scottish curler. Born Feb 8, 1972, in Scotland. ❖ Won a the World Jr. championship (1992); won a silver medal at European championships (1998); won a team gold medal for curling at Salt Lake City Olympics (2002).

RANKIN, Jeannette (1880–1973). American suffragist, pacifist, and politician. Born Jeannette Pickering, June 11, 1880, at Grant Creek Ranch, near Missoula, Montana Territory; died in Carmel, California, May 18, 1973; dau. of Olive Pickering Rankin (schoolteacher and home-maker) and John Rankin (rancher and building contractor); University of Montana, BSc in biology, 1902; enrolled in New York School of Philanthropy, 1908; also attended University of Washington; never married; no children. ❖ The 1st woman to be elected to US House of Representatives, spent a lifetime speaking her mind, even if her opinions were unpopular, and accepting the consequences; joined the state of Washington's campaign for women's suffrage (1910); spoke before Montana state legislature on behalf of woman suffrage (1911); became field secretary for National American Woman Suffrage Association (1913); ran a successful campaign for US House of Representatives (1916); during WWI, voted against declaration of war, which would cost her a seat in Congress (1917); appointed delegate to 2nd International Congress of Women (1919); became field secretary for National Consumers' League (1920) and Women's International League for Peace and Freedom (1925); founded Georgia Peace Society (1928); elected to 2nd term in US House of Representatives (1940); in Congress, was the only person to vote against a declaration of war against Japan after Pearl Harbor (1941); during Vietnam war, marched in Washington at the front of the Jeannette Rankin Brigade in protest (1967). ❖ See also Judy R. Block, *The First Woman in Congress: Jeannette Rankin* (Silver Burdett, 1978); Ted Harris, *Jeannette Rankin: Suffragist, First Woman in Congress, and Pacifist* (Arno, 1982); Florence

White, *First Woman in Congress: Jeannette Rankin* (Messner, 1980); and *Women in World History.*

RANKIN, Judy (1945—). American golfer. Name variations: Judy Torluemke. Born Judith Torluemke in St. Louis, MO, on Feb 18, 1945; m. Yippy Rankin, 1967. ❖ Was 3-time winner of Vare trophy, also held 26 LPGA victories; won Corpus Christi Open (1968); won 4 LPGA events (1973); won the Colgate-Dinah Shore Open (1976); won Bent Tree Classic (1976) and Colgate European Open (1974, 1977); won Colgate Hong Kong Open and 5 other tournaments (1976); won Peter Jackson Classic and 5 other tournaments (1977). Named Player of the Year (1976, 1977). ❖ See also *Women in World History.*

RANKIN, Nell (1924–2005). American mezzo-soprano. Born Jan 3, 1924, in Birmingham, Alabama; died Jan 13, 2005, in New York, NY; sister of Ruth Rankin (soprano); studied with Jeanne Lorraine at Birmingham Conservatory, then with Karin Branzell; m. Dr. Hugh Clark Davidson. ❖ Sang at the Metropolitan Opera for 25 years (1951–76); best known for her portrayals of Amneris in *Aida* and title role in *Carmen*, also sang Eboli in *Don Carlo*, Azucena in *Il Trovatore*, Ulrica in *Un Ballo en Maschera*, Ortrud in *Lohengrin*, Santuzza in *Cavalleria Rusticana*, Herodias in *Salome* and Laura in *Gioconda*; sang at the Zurich Opera (1948–49); was the 1st American singer to win the International Music Competition in Geneva (1950), and sang at major houses throughout the world.

RANSOME-KUTI, Funmilayo (1900–1978). Nigerian teacher and feminist. Name variations: Olufunmilayo Ransome-Kuti; Lioness of Lisabiland. Born Frances Abigail Olufunmilayo Thomas in Abeokuta, Nigeria, Oct 25, 1900; died in Abeokuta, April 12, 1978; dau. of Daniel Olumoyewa Thomas (farmer and trader) and Phyllis Moyeni Dese (dressmaker); studied in Great Britain, 1919–22; m. Reverend Israel Oludotun Ransome-Kuti, 1925; children: Dolupo; Olikoye; Fela Anikulapo-Kuti (singer and musician, known as the king of Afrobeat who died from AIDS in 1997); Beko. ❖ As a teacher of literacy classes, became concerned with issues surrounding the status of women (1930–40s); led thousands in a protest against a special flat tax on women imposed by the British, leading to the resignation of the government and institutional reforms (1947–48); as a member of the Abeokuta Provincial Conference, worked on a new constitution (1948–51); ran unsuccessfully for the House of Assembly in the Egba Division (1951); made 2nd run for a legislative seat (1959); elected a world vice-president of the Women's International Democratic Federation (1952); was a political force of international stature. Awarded Order of Niger for her contributions to the nation (1965); received honorary doctorate of laws from University of Ibadan (1968). ❖ See also *Women in World History.*

RANSON, Ernita (1890–1972). See Lascelles, Ernita.

RANTALA, Lene (1968—). Danish handball player. Born Aug 10, 1968, in Denmark. ❖ Goalkeeper; played for Larvik (Norway); won a team gold medal at Atlanta Olympics (1996) and at Sydney Olympics (2000); won team European championships (1994, 1996) and World championships (1997).

RANTANEN, Heli Orvokki (1970—). Finnish javelin thrower. Born Feb 26, 1970, in Lammi, Finland. ❖ Won a gold medal at Atlanta Olympics (1996).

RANTANEN, Siiri (1924—). Finnish cross-country skier. Born Dec 14, 1924, in Finland. ❖ Won a bronze medal for the 10 km at Oslo Olympics (1952); won a gold medal at Cortina Olympics (1956) and a bronze medal at Squaw Valley Olympics (1960), both for 3 x 5 km relay.

RAPHAEL, Sylvia (1938–2005). See Rafael, Sylvia.

RAPONI, Ana (1907–1953). See Hato, Ana Matawhaura.

RAPOPORT, Lydia (1923–1971). Austrian-born American social-work educator. Name variations: Lydia Rappoport. Born Lydia Rappoport (later changed spelling of last name) in Vienna, Austria, Mar 8, 1923; died in New York, NY, Sept 6, 1971; dau. of Eugenia (Margulies) Rappoport and Samuel Rappoport (businessman and later translator); Hunter College, BA, 1943; Smith College School for Social Work, MSW, 1944; received certificate in child therapy from Chicago Institute for Psychoanalysis; studied at London School of Economics; studied with Erich Lindemann at Harvard School of Public Health (1959–60). ❖ Moved with family to US (1932); became an assistant professor at School of Social Welfare, University of California, Berkeley (1955), then full professor (1969); was a visiting professor at Baerwald School of Social Work of the Hebrew University in Jerusalem (1963);

became the 1st United Nations inter-regional adviser on family welfare and family planning (1971). ❖ See also *Women in World History.*

RAPP, Anita (1977—). Norwegian soccer player. Born July 24, 1977, in Lillehammer, Norway. ❖ Midfielder; played 54 games for the Norwegian National team; won a team gold medal at Sydney Olympics (2000); signed with the New York Power (2002).

RAPP, Susan (1965—). American swimmer. Name variations: Susan Rapp von der Lippe. Born July 5, 1965; graduate of Stanford University, 1987. ❖ At Los Angeles Olympics, won a silver medal in the 200-meter breaststroke and a gold medal in the 4 x 100-meter medley relay (1984).

RASCH, Albertina (1896–1967). Austrian-born ballerina and choreographer. Name variations: Albertina Tiomkin; Madame Albertina Rasch. Born Jan 19, 1896, in Vienna, Austria; died Oct 2, 1967, in Woodland Hills, CA; trained in ballet at School of the Royal Opera House, Vienna; m. Dmitri Tiomkin (composer), 1927. ❖ At 7, made professional debut with Royal Opera House Ballet in Vienna; moved to US (1911); was *première danseuse* at NY Hippodrome for some years; toured in vaudeville; danced and choreographed for NY Century Opera (1913–14), Chicago Opera (1914–15), American Opera Co. in Los Angeles (1915–16), and Geraldine Farrar's All-Star Ellis Opera (1916–18); back in Austria, worked in silent films (1921–23); opened a school of dance in NY (1923), training troupes known as The Albertina Rasch Dancers; choreographed many plays, including *Rio Rita, Three Musketeers, The Band Wagon, The Great Waltz, Jubilee* and *Lady in the Dark,* and such films as *Naughty Marietta, The New Moon, Hell's Angels, Rosalie, Sweethearts, The Great Waltz, Idiot's Delight* and *Broadway Melody of 1940.*

RASCHHOFER, Daniela (1960—). Austrian politician. Born June 19, 1960, in Braunau am Inn, Austria. ❖ Vocational schoolteacher (1984–91); member of the Landtag of Upper Austria (1991–1996); as an Independent or Non-attached (NI), elected to 4th and 5th European Parliament (1994–99, 1999–2004).

RASHAD, Phylicia (1948—). African-American actress. Name variations: Phylicia Allen; Phylicia Ayers-Allen; credited as Phylicia Ayres Allen in film *The Wiz*. Born Phylicia Ayers Allen, June 19, 1948, in Houston, TX; dau. of Andrew Allen (dentist) and Vivian Ayers-Allen (poet); sister of Debbie Allen (dancer); magna cum laude graduate of Howard University; m. William Lancelot Bowles Jr. (dentist), 1972 (div. 1975); m. Victor Willis (lead singer for Village People), 1978 (div. 1980); m. Ahmad Rashad (sportscaster), 1985 (div. 2001); children: (1st m.) 1; (3rd m.) 1. ❖ Made film debut under name Phylicia Ayers-Allen in *The Broad Coalition* (1972); appeared as Courtney Wright on tv soap opera "One Life to Live" (1983–84); also appeared on "Santa Barbara" (1984); came to prominence as Claire Huxtable on "The Cosby Show" (1984–92); won Tony for Best Leading Actress for performance as Lena Younger in *A Raisin in the Sun* (2004), the 1st African-American to win in that category.

RASHED, Abi (b. 1931). See Nasralla, Emily.

RASHID, Saleha Abdul (1939—). Malaysian novelist, poet and short-story writer. Name variations: (pseudonym) Salmi Manja. Born 1939 in Singapore; m. A. Samad Said (writer and journalist). ❖ Novels include *Hari Mana Bulan Mana* (1960), *Dari Mana Punai Melayang* (1961), *Hendal Hujan, Hujan Sekali* (1967), *Sayang Ustazah Sayang* (1968), and *Entah Mengapa Hatiku Duka* (1968); with husband, published short-story collection *Daun-daun Beguguran* (1962). Some of her poems appeared in English in *Modern Malay Verse 1946–61* (1963).

RASK, Gertrud (fl. 1721). Danish missionary. Name variations: Gertrud Rask Egede. Flourished around 1721; died in Greenland; m. Hans Egede (1686–1758, Danish missionary known as the "Apostle of Greenland"); children: Paul Egede (1708–1789, missionary in Greenland). ❖ Sailed with husband to Greenland (1721) and took up residence among the Inuit population, embarking on a mission to convert the Greenlanders to Christianity; in the process, befriended and assisted the Inuits, overcoming the language barrier and the unfamiliar living conditions.

RASKIN, Judith (1928–1984). American soprano. Born Judith Raskin, June 21, 1928, in New York, NY; died Dec 21, 1984; Smith College, BA, 1949; studied with Anna Hamlin in NY; m. Raymond Raskin (physician), 1948. ❖ Debuted in Central City, CO (1956); made tv debut as Susanna in Mozart's *Le nozze di Figaro* with NBC Opera (1957); made NYC Opera debut in *Cosi Fan Tutte* (1959); made Metropolitan Opera debut (1962) and continued to sing at Met (1962–72); debuted at

Glyndebourne (1963); established herself as an international star but was forced to retire early because of ill health; taught at Manhattan School of Music and Mannes College of Music. ❖ See also *Women in World History*.

RASKINA, Yulia (1982—). Belarusian gymnast. Born April 9, 1982, in Minsk, Belarus. ❖ At World championships, won silver medals in team all-around, all-around, hoop and ball (1999); at European championships, won silver medals in all-around and hoop and a bronze medal in ribbon (1999); won a silver medal for indiv. all-around at Sydney Olympics (2000).

RASKOVA, Marina (1912–1943). Russian aviator. Born Marina Mikhailovna Raskova, Mar 28, 1912, in Moscow, Russia; died Jan 4, 1943, in military combat, near Saratov; buried in the Kremlin Wall in Red Square; dau. of teachers; married with children. ❖ Began work at air navigation laboratory of N.E. Zhukovski Air Force Academy (1932); graduated from Central Training Center of the Civil Air Fleet (1934); joined Red Army (1938); wrote *Notes of a Navigator* (1939); commanded an air detachment for the formation of air regiments and was made commander of a women's bombardment aviation regiment (1942); with Valentina Grizodubova and Polina Osipenko, flew 3,717 miles nonstop from Moscow to Soviet east coast near Japan (1938), a journey one-third longer than Amelia Earhart's solo flight, and crash landed, spending 10 days in the Siberian *taiga* until rescued. Awarded 2 Orders of Lenin and Order of the Patriotic War 1st Class (posthumously). ❖ See also Bruce Myles, *Night Witches: The Untold Story of Soviet Women in Combat* (Presidio, 1981); and *Women in World History*.

RASMUSSEN, Bodil Steen (1957—). Danish rower. Born Dec 12, 1957, in Denmark. ❖ At Los Angeles Olympics, won a bronze medal in quadruple sculls with coxswain (1984).

RASMUSSEN, Louise Christine (1815–1874). Danish countess and paramour. Name variations: Louisa Rasmussen; Countess Danner; Countess von Danner. Born Louise Christine (also seen as Christiana) Rasmussen, April 21, 1815 (some sources cite 1814 and 1818), in Copenhagen, Denmark; died Mar 6, 1874, at Cannes, Nice, France; was an illeg. child; trained as a ballet dancer at Royal Theatre; m. Frederick VII (1808–1863), king of Denmark (r. 1848–63), Aug 7, 1850; children: (with printer Carl Berling) 1 child. ❖ Retired as a dancer and opened a fashion store; became mistress, then 3rd wife of Frederick VII in a morganatic marriage; said to have had a stabilizing effect on the king; was created Countess Danner; bequeathed her assets to a foundation in Copenhagen for poor working-class women and established several orphanages for poor girls.

RASP, Renate (1935—). German novelist and poet. Born 1935 in Berlin. ❖ Emerged as important new voice in 1960s West Germany; works include the novel *Ein ungeratener Sohn* (1967), and poetry collections, *Eine Rennstrecke* (1969) and *Junges Deutschland* (1978).

RASTVOROVA, Valentina (1933—). Soviet fencer. Born June 17, 1933, in USSR. ❖ At Rome Olympics, won a silver medal in indiv. foil and a gold medal in team foil (1960); at Tokyo Olympics, won a silver medal in team foil (1964).

RATA (1893–1972). *See Burns, Violet Alberta Jessie.*

RATANA, Iriaka (1905–1981). New Zealand politician. Born Iriaka Te Rio, Feb 25, 1905, in Jerusalem, NZ; died Dec 22, 1981; m. Matiu Ratana (MP), 1940 (died 1949); children: 6. ❖ Representing Labour Party, became MP for Western Maori (1949), replacing her husband following his death; won election (1949) and remained an MP for the next 20 years; resigned because of poor health (1969). Concentrated on land issues and living conditions for Maori people; made Member of the Order of the British Empire.

RATAZZI, Maria (1830–1902). *See Rute, Mme de.*

RATCLIFFE, Jane (1917–1999). English naturalist and writer. Name variations: Edna Jane Ratcliffe. Born June 2, 1917, in Dewsbury, West Yorkshire, England; died Dec 3, 1999; m. Teddy Ratcliffe, 1940. ❖ Writer and wildlife campaigner, especially for badgers, initially worked as a home economics teacher; assisted Lord Arran with the passage of the Badgers Act, Parliament's 1st passage of a protective animal act (1973); counted and rescued badgers; retired to the Lake District with husband (1980), where she lectured at the Lake District Visitor Centre at Brockhole; wrote *Through the Badger Gate* (1974), *Fly High, Run Free* (1979) and *Wildlife in My Garden* (1986).

RĀTEB, Aisha (1928—). Egyptian politician, diplomat and professor of law. Name variations: Aisha Rāteb; Aisha Rateb Soad. Born 1928 in Egypt; studied at the Faculty of Law in Cairo. ❖ Studied in Cairo and Paris and became first Professor of International Law at Cairo University; was 2nd woman elected to Egyptian cabinet (1971) and served as minister of Social Affairs and Social Insurance (1971–77); became chair of Legislative Affairs Committee (1973) and Minister of Foreign Affairs (1978); was 1st woman appointed ambassador for Egypt and served in Denmark (1979–81) and Germany (1981–84).

RATEBZAD, Anahita (1931—). Afghan physician and political leader. Born in 1931 in Guldara, Kabul province, Afghanistan; attended Chicago School of Nursing; Kabul University, MD, 1963; m. Dr. Qamaruddin Kakar (div.). ❖ Was the 1st woman physician in the history of Afghanistan; was one of three successful female candidates for the Afghan Parliament (1965); founded the Democratic Women's Organization (1965), a branch of the Marxist-inspired People's Democratic Party of Afghanistan (PDPA), and was the highest-ranking woman member within the PDPA; for a brief period, was minister of Social Affairs and Tourism, but was purged when another faction took power; under regime of Babrak Karmal, served as minister of Education (1980–81) and was elected to the ruling PDPA Politburo; also was caretaker of the Ministries of Information and Culture, Higher and Vocational Education, and Public Health; was a member of the Revolutionary Council's Presidium (1981–88); after 1990, with emergence of the Taliban movement, withdrew from public life. ❖ See also *Women in World History*.

RATHBONE, Eleanor (1872–1946). British feminist, social reformer, and member of Parliament. Born in Liverpool, England, 1872; died 1946; dau. of William Rathbone (social reformer and Liberal MP); cousin of Rosalind Paget (1855–1948); educated at Somerville College, Oxford; never married; no children; lived with Elizabeth Macadam. ❖ Prominent in the British feminist movement between WWI and WWII, joined the "non-militant" National Union of Women's Suffrage Societies (NUWSS), which led to a seat in the union's executive committee (1900); remained active in NUWSS until 1919, when it was transformed into the National Union of Societies for Equal Citizenship (NUSEC), of which she became president; ran unsuccessfully as an Independent for a parliamentary seat in East Toxteth (1922); again as an Independent, won a seat representing the 2-member Combined English Universities (1929), which she would hold for the rest of her life; published *Disinherited Family*, a milestone in social reform, prompting enactment of Inheritance (Family Provision) Act (1938); also published *The Case for Family Allowances* (1940); one of only three women MPs to endorse birth control between the world wars, contributed financially to the predecessor of the Family Planning Association; was a strong proponent of rights for Indian women and an end to the traditional practices (such as suttee and the proscription against the remarriage of widows) that oppressed them, and spoke out against female circumcision in the British colonies in Africa. ❖ See also Johanna Alberti, *Eleanor Rathbone* (Sage, 1996); Mary D. Stocks, *Eleanor Rathbone* (Gollancz, 1949); Brian Harrison, *Prudent Revolutionaries: Portraits of British Feminists between the Wars* (Clarendon, 1987); and *Women in World History*.

RATHBONE, Hannah Mary (1798–1878). British novelist. Born near Wellington in Shropshire, England, July 5, 1798; died in Liverpool, England, Mar 26, 1878; granddau. of Quaker philanthropist Richard Reynolds; m. half-cousin Richard Rathbone, in 1817; children: 6. ❖ Anonymously introduced the autobiographic type of historical novel with her popular *Diary of Lady Willoughby* (1844), which purported to be a journal written during the civil war that erupted under King Charles I; became instantly famous when the 3rd edition was published with her name; published a 2nd vol., bringing Lady Willoughby's journal up to the Restoration (1847). ❖ See also *Women in World History*.

RATHBONE, Josephine Adams (1864–1941). American librarian and educator. Born in Jamestown, New York, Sept 10, 1864; died in Augusta, Georgia, May 17, 1941; dau. of Joshua Henry Rathbone (physician) and Elizabeth Bacon Adams; attended Wellesley College and University of Michigan; New York State Library School, BLS, 1893; never married. ❖ Joined the staff of the Pratt Institute Free Library in Brooklyn as an assistant cataloguer (1893); also taught in the Institute's library school, becoming chief instructor (1895); left to join the New York Public Library School (1911); was a member of American Library Institute, served as secretary of New York State Library Club Association (1908), and served New York Library Club as secretary

(1895–97, 1909–10) and as president (1918–19); served as a member of American Library Association council (1912–29) and as president (1931–32). ❖ See also *Women in World History.*

RATHBONE, Ouida (1885–1974). *See Bergere, Ouida.*

RATHBUN, Mary Jane (1860–1943). American marine zoologist. Born in Buffalo, New York, June 11, 1860; died in Washington, DC, April 4, 1943; dau. of Charles Howland Rathbun (stonemason) and Jane (Furey) Rathbun (died 1861); sister of Richard Rathbun (curator and head of department of marine invertebrates in the National Museum); George Washington University, PhD, 1917; never married. ❖ Self-taught zoologist, began to spend summers with brother at Marine Biological Station at Woods Hole (1881), assisting him as he catalogued specimens; assigned to the National Museum, helped to organize, catalogue, and preserve the museum's collections (1884); was transferred from the commission staff to the museum staff (1886), where she would work as a clerk and copyist in the department of marine invertebrates for next 53 years; published some 158 scientific papers; as assistant curator (1907–14), focused research on classifying and describing contemporary and fossil decapod crustaceans (shrimps, crabs and their near relatives). ❖ See also *Women in World History.*

RATHEBE, Dolly (1928–2004). South African singer and actress. Born Josephine Kedibone, April 2, 1928, in Randfontein, near Johannesburg, South Africa; died Sept 16, 2004, near Pretoria, South Africa; dau. of a migrant laborer; married twice; children: 2 daughters and 1 son. ❖ Became Africa's 1st acknowledged international female actor when she starred in *Jim Comes to Jo'burg* (1949), the 1st film to portray urban Africans in a positive light; was lead singer with 2 popular township bands: Harlem Swingsters and Inkspots; also led the Elite Swingsters, an Afro-Jazz group; when other singers that she had mentored, such as Miriam Makeba, left South Africa because of apartheid, remained behind but found it increasingly difficult to perform; with the advent of democracy, rejoined the Elite Swingsters and sang at the inauguration of Nelson Mandela; also had a role in the film *Cry, The Beloved Country.*

RATHGEBER, Lisa (1961—). American bowler. Name variations: Lisa Rathgeber Wagner. Born May 19, 1961, in Hillsboro, IL. ❖ Won the Robby's Midwest Classic, then the Greater Milwaukee Open, becoming the 1st bowler in 5 years to take back-to-back titles, leading the tour in match play winning percentage, average, and competition points (1983); won the Roto Grip Classic (1984). Named Rookie of the Year (1980).

RATIA, Armi (1912–1979). Finnish entrepreneur. Born in Karelia, Finland, 1912; died 1979; graduated from Art Industry Central School, 1935; m. Viljo Ratia (sep. 1969); children: Ristomatti Ratia. ❖ Co-founder and managing director of the Marimekko fashion firm, which drew worldwide attention to Finnish design (1960s); founded Marimekko with husband (1951), to build on the recovering fashion industry after the devastation of WWII; intending Marimekko's designs to reflect purity and simplicity, hired a woman designer, Vuokko Eskolin-Nurmesniemia (1953); with fresh ideas, brought the company to international prominence; retired from Marimekko (1976). Received Nieman Marcus Award; granted Order of the Rose, Finland's highest honor. ❖ See also *Women in World History.*

RATNER, Anna (c. 1892–1967). American theatrical dancer. Born c. 1892 in Los Angeles area, CA; died July 2, 1967, in Chicago, IL. ❖ Worked as stock dancer for Essenay Studio, performing Spanish solos, Chinese dances, chorus kicks, and ballet divertissements; appeared in numerous Charlie Chaplin films as tango, one-step, or fox-trot dancer; performed as band dancer for Paul Ash, in Balaban and Katz theaters around Chicago (early 1920s).

RATNER, Letitia Ide (1909–1993). *See Ide, Letitia.*

RATTAZZI, Countess (b. 1922). *See Agnelli, Susanna.*

RATTAZZI, Madame (1831–1902). *See Rute, Mme de.*

RATTENBURY, Alma (c. 1904–1935). English murderer (accused). Born c. 1904 in England; stabbed herself to death, June 4, 1935, in Bournemouth, England; m. Caledon Dolling, 1914 (died Aug 1916); m. Captian Compton Pakenham, 1921; m. Francis Mawson Rattenbury (British architect), 1925 (murdered 1935); children: (2nd m.) Christopher (b. July 8, 1921); (3rd m.) John (b. 1928). ❖ Found husband Francis Rattenbury with fractured skull at their home in Bournemouth (Mar 24, 1935) and he later died; drunk while talking to authorities, claimed to have beaten him with a mallet, while her lover, 18-year-old George Stoner, also confessed to the murder, claiming she was

not involved; tried at Old Bailey with Stoner (May 1935), was acquitted, though Stoner received the death sentence, then was later reprieved.

RATTRAY, Lizzie Frost (1855–1931). New Zealand journalist and suffragist. Name variations: Lizzie Frost Fenton. Born Lizzie Frost Fenton, Mar 22, 1855, in Dunedin, New Zealand; died on Aug 12, 1931, in Auckland; dau. of John Albert Fenton (cleric) and Mary (Lister) Fenton; m. William Rattray, 1883; children: 2 sons. ❖ Educated in England and France before settling in Auckland and assuming control of Young Women's Institute (1880); was one of New Zealand's first women journalists, working as correspondent for *Gentlewoman* magazine, and as social editor for *New Zealand Graphic* (1892); elected to committee of Auckland branch of Women's Franchise League (1892). ❖ See also *Dictionary of New Zealand Biography* (Vol. 2).

RATUSHINSKAYA, Irina (1954—). Russian poet and memoirist. Name variations: Irina Borisovna Ratushínskaia. Born 1954 in USSR; m. Igor Gerashchenko. ❖ Participated in Soviet human-rights movement in Kiev and was arrested (1982); at 28, sentenced to 7 years' hard labor and 5 years internal exile (1983); was detained for 3 years in a labor camp, though her poems were smuggled out and published as *No, I'm Not Afraid* (1986), which led to an international outcry over her case; released, emigrated with husband (1986); works in translation include *A Tale of Three Heads* (1986), *Beyond the Limit* (1987), and prison memoir, *Grey is the Color of Hope* (1988).

RAU, Dhanvanthi Rama (1893–1987). *See Rau, Dhanvanthi Rama.*

RAU, Santha Rama (b. 1923). *See Rama Rau, Santha.*

RAUBAL, Geli (c. 1908–1931). German niece of Adolf Hitler. Born c. 1908; died of a gunshot wound in Munich, Germany, on Sept 18, 1931; dau. of Angela Raubal (half-sister of Adolf Hitler). ❖ Died from a gunshot wound in her chest at the Munich apartment she shared with Hitler (1931), causing rumors of sexual perversion and talk of murder. Hitler would later declare that she was the only woman he had ever loved. ❖ See also (novel) Ron Hansen, *Hitler's Niece* (HarperCollins, 1999); Ronald Hayman, *Hitler & Geli* (Bloomsbury, 1998); and *Women in World History.*

RAUCOURT, Mlle (1756–1815). French actress. Born Françoise Marie Antoinette Saucerotte in Nancy, France, Mar 3, 1756; died Jan 15, 1815; buried at Père Lachaise; dau. of a provincial actor. ❖ Daughter of an actor who took her to Spain, where she began appearing in dramatic parts at 12; by 1770, was back in France at Rouen, and her success as Euphémie in Belloy's *Gaston et Bayard* led to a stint at the Comédie Française, where she made her debut as Dido (1772); played all the classical tragedy parts to crowded houses, until her extravagance and personal scandals ended her popularity; suddenly disappeared from France (1776); under protection of French queen Marie Antoinette, reappeared at Théatre Français (1779) and was again triumphant, reprising her former roles which included Phèdre and Cleopatra. ❖ See also *Women in World History.*

RAUKAWA, Ngati (1937—). *See Grace, Patricia.*

RAVAN, Genya (1942—). Polish-American musician. Name variations: Goldie Zelkowitz; The Escorts; Goldie and the Gingerbreads. Born Goldie Zelkowitz, 1942, in Lodz, Poland. ❖ Grew up in New York's Lower East Side; began music career as lead singer with the Escorts; led the 1st all-female band, Goldie and the Gingerbreads (1962–67); with Gingerbreads, moved to England, where they were extremely successful, touring with Rolling Stones, Yardbirds, and Kinks; changed name to Genya Ravan and formed jazz-blues band, Ten Wheel Drive (1969); formed band Baby (1971), which toured with Sly and the Family Stone; albums include *They Love Me/They Love Me Not* (1973), *Urban Desire* (1978), and *And I Mean It* (1979); founded Polish Records (1980); performed with Gingerbreads in 30-year reunion show.

RAVENSCROFT, Gladys (1888–1960). English golfer. Name variations: Mrs. Temple Dobell. Born in Rock Ferry, England, in 1888; died in Wirral, England, in 1960; m. Temple Dobell. ❖ Won British Women's Amateur (1912); placed 1st at USGA Women's Amateur (1913), the 3rd non-American woman to win the championship.

RAVENSDALE, Baroness (1896–1966). *See Curzon, Irene.*

RAVERA, Camilla (1889–1988). Italian feminist and social reformer. Name variations: resistance names, Silvia and Micheli. Born 1889 in Acqui Terme, in province of Alessandria, Italy; died 1988 in Rome, Italy. ❖ Worked as teacher in Turin before joining Socialist Party and becoming active in group Ordine nuovo; joined Communist Party at its inception and had a feminist column in the newspaper *Ordine nuove*; became editor of periodical *La compagna*; after meeting Zetkin and Lenin, became secretary of Communist Party and traveled with Togliatti to Moscow to work in Comintern; arrested upon return to Italy (1930), was imprisoned until 1935, then held under house arrest (1943); resumed political work (1945) and was elected to the Chamber of Deputies; nominated senator for life for work in politics and on behalf of women. Writings include *La donna italiana dal primo al secondo Risorgimento* (1951), *Diario de trenti anni, 1913–43* (1974), and *Breve storia del movimento femminile in Italia* (1978).

RAVERAT, Gwen (1885–1957). British wood engraver and book illustrator. Name variations: Gwen Reverat. Born Gwendolen Mary Darwin in Cambridge, England, 1885; died 1957; dau. of Sir George Howard Darwin (1845–1912, scientist and professor) and Maud Du Puy (1861–1947, an American); granddau. of Charles Darwin (1809–1882); studied at Slade School, 1908–11; m. Jacques Pierre Raverat (mathematician who became a painter), 1911 (died 1925); children: 2 daughters. ❖ Painted, designed for theater, and also did illustration (including drawings for *Spring Morning*, a vol. of poetry by Frances Cornford, 1915), but is best known for her wood engravings; taught herself the art, a rare feat, and was a founding member of the Society of Wood Engravers; among the enormously successful works which featured her engravings was the *Cambridge Book of Poetry for Children* (1932); also designed the sets for Ralph Vaughan Williams' ballet *Job*, which remained in use for 20 years; wrote art criticism for the periodical *Time and Tide* (1928–39), and worked for naval intelligence during WWII; also translated Perrault's fairy tales, which were published posthumously. ❖ See also memoir *Period Piece: A Cambridge Childhood* (Faber, 1952).

RAVESKAYA, Maria (1805–1863). *See Volkonskaya, Maria.*

RAVIKOVITCH, Dahlia (1936—). Israeli poet, short-story and children's writer. Name variations: Dalia Ravikovitch. Born 1936 in Ramat Gan, Tel Aviv, Israel. ❖ Sent to Kibbutz after father's death; studied at Hebrew University and worked as journalist and high school teacher; poetry collections include *Ahavat Tapuach Ha'Zahav* (The Love of an Orange, 1959), *Horef Kasheh* (Hard Winter, 1964), *Ha'Sefer Ha'Shlishi* (The Third Book, 1969), *Col Mashberaich Ve'Galaich* (All Thy Breakers and Waves, 1972), *Tehom Koreh* (Calleth Unto Deep, 1976), *Ahavah Amitit* (True Love, 1987), *Col Ha'Shirim Ad Co* (All the Poems Till Now, 1995), and *Hatzi Sh'ah Lifnei Ha'Monsoon* (Half an Hour Before the Monsoon, 1998); children's books include *Mechonit Ha'Playim* (The Magic Car, 1959), *Micha Ve'Mechabei Ha'Esh* (Micha and the Fire Squad, 1962) and *Alilot Deddy Ha'Muflah* (Wonder Deddy's Adventures, 1978); also wrote stories, *Kvutzat Ha'Caduregel Shel Winnie Mandela* (Winnie Mandela's Football Team, 1997). Won Bialik Prize (1987) and Israel Prize (1998).

RAWCLIFFE, Constance Alice (1898–1994). *See Birchfield, Constance Alice.*

RAWINIA (LAVINIA) (?–1868). *See Rere-o-maki.*

RAWLE, Anna (c. 1757–1828). American diarist. Name variations: Anna Rawle Clifford. Born c. 1757 into Quaker family in Philadelphia, PA; died 1828; dau. of Rebecca Warner and Francis Rawle; stepdau. of Samuel Shoemaker (prominent Loyalist); m. John Clifford; children: Rebecca. ❖ A Loyalist who kept a diary during the American Revolution, also recorded her outrage over the persecution of Loyalists in Philadelphia after Cornwallis' surrender (Oct 1781) in letters to her mother and stepfather.

RAWLINGS, Marjorie Kinnan (1896–1953). American writer. Name variations: Marjorie Kinnan; (pseudonym) Lady Alicia Thwaite. Born Marjorie Kinnan, Aug 8, 1896, in Washington, DC; died Dec 14, 1953; dau. of Arthur Frank Kinnan (employee of US Patent Office, died 1913) and Ida May (Traphagen) Kinnan; graduate of University of Wisconsin, 1918; m. Charles Rawlings (journalist), 1919 (div. 1933); m. Norton Baskin (hotel manager), 1941; no children. ❖ Champion of nature and its caretakers, is best known for Florida-based works, especially for the transcendental essays in *Cross Creek* and the realistic novel *The Yearling*; published 1st story at age 13, in Washington *Post* (1909); was editor of high school newspaper; moved with mother and brother to Madison, Wisconsin (1914); contributed to *Wisconsin Literary Magazine*; worked for YWCA in New York City (1918); was a feature reporter for the Louisville, Kentucky, *Courier-Journal* (1920–21); was a reporter for Rochester, NY, *Journal-American* (1922); wrote daily feature column, "Songs of a Housewife" (1926–28), for Rochester *Times-Union*; moved

to Cross Creek, Florida (1928); published "Cracker Chidlings" in *Scribner's Magazine* (1931); received Pulitzer Prize for *The Yearling* (1939); wrote numerous short stories for *Saturday Evening Post, The New Yorker* and *Scribner's Magazine*; other writings include *South Moon Under* (1933), *Golden Apples* (1935), *When the Whippoorwill* (1940), *Cross Creek Cookery* (1942), *The Sojourner* (1953) and *The Secret River* (posthumous, 1955). ❖ See also Elizabeth Silverthorne, *Marjorie Kinnan Rawlings; Sojourner at Cross Creek* (Overlook, 1988); Rodger L. Tarr, ed. *Max and Marjorie: The Correspondence Between Maxwell E. Perkins and Marjorie Kinnan Rawlings* (U. of Florida Press, 1999); and *Women in World History*.

RAWLINSON, Gloria (1918–1995). New Zealand poet, novelist, and short-story writer. Name variations: Gloria Jasmine Rawlinson. Born Oct 1, 1918, in Ha'apai, Tonga; died on July 25, 1995, at Auckland, New Zealand; dau. of Alexander John Rawlinson (photographic artist) and Ethel Rose (Jennings) Rawlinson. ❖ Confined to wheelchair due to contracting poliomyelitis soon after migrating to New Zealand in 1924; published popular volumes of poetry, *Gloria's Book* (1933) and *The Perfume Vendor* (1935); wrote novel, *Music in the Listening-place* (1938); frequent contributor of short fiction to Australian *Bulletin* and to anthology, *Coast to Coast* (1940s–50s); also published *Houses by the Sea: The Later Poems of Robin Hyde* (1952), *The Islands Where I Was Born* (1955), *Of Clouds and Pebbles* (1963), *New Zealand Best Poems* and *New Zealand Poetry Yearbook*; co-edited *Jindyworobak Anthology* (1951); with Derek Challis, wrote *The Book of Iris: A Life of Robin Hyde.* ❖ See also *Dictionary of New Zealand Biography* (Vol. 4).

RAWLS, Betsy (1928—). American golfer. Born Elizabeth Earle Rawls, May 4, 1928, in Spartanburg, SC; graduate of University of Texas. ❖ Won the Vare trophy; was the 1st woman to serve on the Rules Committee for US Men's Open; won 4 US Open titles (1951, 1953, 1957, 1960); won her namesake tournament, Betsy Rawls Open (1956); won 10 tournaments, including Mount Prospect Women's Open (1959); all told, won 55 LPGA tournaments. ❖ See also *Women in World History*.

RAWLS, Elizabeth (b. 1928). *See Rawls, Betsy.*

RAWLS, Katherine (1918–1982). American swimmer, diver and aviator. Born June 14, 1918, in Fort Lauderdale, FL; died April 1982. ❖ Dominant female swimmer of the 1930s; at Los Angeles Olympics, won a silver medal in springboard diving (1932); at Berlin Olympics, won a bronze medal in the 4 x 100-meter freestyle relay and a silver medal in springboard diving (1936); won record number of national titles in swimming and diving, including 14 national outdoor, 11 national indoor, and 5 national diving; was possibly the 1st to flip turn in swimming competition; retired (1939); during WWII, was one of the original 25 women pilots selected for US Squadron of Women's Army Ferry Service.

RAWSON, Gertrude Helen (1886–1964). *See Benson, Gertrude Helen.*

RAY, Charlotte E. (1850–1911). African-American lawyer. Born in New York, NY, Jan 13, 1850; died in Long Island, NY, Jan 4, 1911; dau. of Charles Bennett Ray (Congregational minister and abolitionist) and Charlotte Augusta Burroughs Ray; sister of H. Cordelia Ray (c. 1849–1916); graduate of Howard University Law School, 1872; married a man named Fraim after 1886. ❖ Became the 1st African-American woman lawyer in US and the 1st woman admitted to the bar in District of Columbia (April 23, 1872); when she opened a law office, was only the 3rd woman in the nation to do so, but because of double bias (against women and blacks), was unable to sustain her Washington practice; attended National Women's Suffrage Association convention in NY (1876); became an active member of National Association of Colored Women (1895); worked as a teacher in the Brooklyn public school system. ❖ See also *Women in World History*.

RAY, Cordelia (c. 1849–1916). *See Ray, H. Cordelia.*

RAY, Dixy Lee (1914–1994). American scientist. Born Margaret Ray in Tacoma, Washington, Sept 3, 1914; died Fox Island, Washington, Jan 2, 1994; Mills College, degree in zoology, 1937, MA, 1938; Stanford University, PhD, 1945; never married; no children. ❖ Became an instructor in zoology at University of Washington (1945), where she would remain for 25 years, becoming assistant professor (1947) and associate professor (1957); often traveled internationally to conduct research, which focused primarily on certain marine crustaceans, especially *Limnoria*, and organisms that attack submerged wood; produced "Animals of the Seashore," a popular 15-part series of half-hour tv shows about various marine animals (1958); long before the rise of the environmental movement, was vocal about the contamination of oceans by radioactive materials and dangerous pesticides; was special consultant in biological oceanography to National Science Foundation (1960–62), which led to appointment as director of Pacific Science Center in Seattle (1963); after serving as a member of the President's Task Force on Oceanography (1969), was nominated for a seat on Atomic Energy Commission (1972); became chair of the commission (1973), a post that brought her arguably more power than that held by any other woman in the federal government; worked to improve opportunities for minority job applicants in the field, and championed broader research into the safety of nuclear reactors; after Atomic Energy Commission was reorganized (1974), became assistant secretary for oceans and international environmental scientific affairs at Department of State; elected 1st woman governor of the state of Washington (1977); co-authored *Trashing the Planet* (1990) and *Environmental Overkill* (1993). ❖ See also *Women in World History.*

RAY, Elise (1982—). American gymnast. Born Feb 6, 1982, in Tallahassee, FL. ❖ Won a silver medal for uneven bars at Goodwill Games (1998); won Aussie Invitational, Pacific Alliance, and US nationals (2000); placed 4th for team all-around at Sydney Olympics (2000).

RAY, Emily Patricia (1863/64?–1947). *See Gibson, Emily Patricia.*

RAY, H. Cordelia (c. 1849–1916). African-American poet and scholar. Name variations: Henrietta Cordelia Ray; Cordelia Ray. Born Henrietta Cordelia Ray in New York, NY, c. 1849; died 1916; dau. of Charles B. Ray (Congregational minister and abolitionist) and Charlotte Augusta (Burroughs) Ray; sister of Florence Ray and Charlotte E. Ray (1850–1911); University of the City of New York, master of pedagogy degree, 1891; attended Sauveneur School of Languages; never married; no children. ❖ With sister Florence, produced a 79-page biography of father's life and work, *Sketches of Life of Rev. Charles E. Ray* (1887); published poems in journal of African Methodist Episcopal Church, the *AME Review*; at unveiling ceremony for the Freedman's Monument in Washington, DC (April 14, 1876), heard her 81-line poem "Lincoln" read; published a collection of poetry entitled *Sonnets* (1893), followed by *Poems* (1910); wrote mainly philosophical poems, as well as verses lamenting disappointed love and tributes to those who fought for freedom; works are included in the series *Collected Black Women's Poetry* (1988). ❖ See also *Women in World History.*

RAY, Ina (1916–1984). *See Hutton, Ina Ray.*

RAY, Martha (d. 1779). Mistress of the earl of Sandwich. Dau. of a London stay-maker; murdered outside the Covent Garden Theatre, London, in 1779; mistress of John Montagu (1718–1792), 4th earl of Sandwich (1st Lord of the Admiralty); never married; no children. ❖ A talented singer, became the mistress of John Montagu at age 18 and reportedly had some input into his naval appointments; also became the obsession of James Hackman, a lieutenant in the army and later incumbent of Wiveton, Norfolk; when she spurned Hackman's marriage proposal, was shot dead by him as she left the Covent Garden theater.

RAY, René (1911–1993). English actress and writer. Name variations: Renee Ray. Born René Creese, Sept 22, 1911, in London, England; died Aug 28, 1993, in Jersey, Channel Islands. ❖ Made London debut in *Wonder Bar* (1930), followed by *The Dominant Sex, Yes and No, Three Blind Mice, They Walk Alone, Other People's Houses, Night of the Garter,* title role in *Claudia, Summer at Nohant, John Keats Lived Here, Arms and the Man* and *Women of Twilight*; made only Broadway appearance, as Sheila Birling in *An Inspector Calls* (1993); wrote and appeared in *The Tree Surgeon* (1961); films include *The Passing of the Third Floor Back, The Rat, If Winter Comes, Women of Twilight* and *Farewell, Again*; wrote novels *Wraxton Marne, Emma Conquest, A Man Named Seraphin, This Man is Mine* and *The Strange World of Planet X.*

RAY, Rita (1914–1989). *See Drake, Dona.*

RAY, Terry (1915—). *See Drew, Ellen.*

RAYE, Martha (1916–1994). American comedian, actress, and singer. Born Margaret Theresa Yvonne Reed, Aug 27, 1916, in Butte, MT; died Oct 19, 1994, in Los Angeles, CA; dau. of Pete Reed and Maybelle (Hooper) Reed (vaudeville performers); m. Hamilton (Buddy) Westmore (Hollywood make-up artist), 1937 (div. 1937); m. David Rose (orchestra leader), 1938 (div. 1941); m. Neal Lang (hotel manager), 1941 (div. 1944); m. Nick Condos (dancer and her personal manager), 1944 (div. 1953); m. Edward Begley (dancer), 1954 (div. 1956); m.

Robert O'Shea (her bodyguard), 1958 (div. 1962); m. Mark Harris (ex-hairdresser), 1991; children: (4th m.) Melodye Raye Condos. ❖ Joined family song-and-dance act at age 3; as a teenager, went out on her own, playing burlesque houses, musical revues, and nightclubs; had stints with Benny Davis Revue, Ben Blue Co., and Will Morrissey Co.; known for her booming voice, elastic mouth, and raucous humor, made Broadway debut in *Calling All Stars* (1934); made film debut opposite Bing Crosby in *Rhythm on the Range* (1936), her show-stopping rendition of "Mr. Paganini" rocketing her to stardom; subsequently made over 30 films, most notably *The Big Broadcast of 1937* (1936), *Artists and Models* (1937), *The Big Broadcast of 1938* (1938), *The Boys from Syracuse* (1940), *Hellzapoppin* (1941), *Four Jills in a Jeep* (1944) and *Monsieur Verdoux* (1947), with Charlie Chaplin; co-starred with Al Jolson in stage revue *Hold On to Your Hats* (1940), then appeared on Jolson's radio show for 2 years; on tv, hosted her own show on NBC (1953–54); for several years, starred at her nightclub in Miami. Received Jean Hersholt Humanitarian Award (1969) for her tireless work for USO; received Presidential Medal of Freedom from Bill Clinton (1993). ❖ See also Noonie Fortin, *Memories of Maggie* (Langmarc, 1995); Jean Maddern Pitrone, *Take It from the Big Mouth: The Life of Martha Raye* (U. Press of Kentucky, 1999); and *Women in World History.*

RAYET, Jacqueline (1932—). French ballet dancer. Born June 26, 1932, in Paris, France. ❖ Joined Paris Opéra (1946), where she became a principal dancer and performed in Lifar's *Blanche-Neige* and *Daphnis et Chloe,* Balanchine's *Palais de Cristal,* and Petit's *Turnagalila,* among others; was guest artist with Hamburg State Opera in Germany, creating roles in numerous works by Peter van Djik, most notably in his pas de deux *Unfinished Symphony* (1957); established the Festival International de Danse Classique (1958).

RAYHEL, Oxana (1977—). Ukrainian handball player. Born Feb 24, 1977, in Ukraine. ❖ Won a team bronze medal at Athens Olympics (2004).

RAYMOND, Eleanor (1887–1989). American architect. Born in Cambridge, Massachusetts, 1887; died 1989; graduate of Wellesley College, 1909; Cambridge School of Architecture and Landscape Architecture, MA in architecture, 1919; never married; longtime companion of Ethel Power (architectural journalist and writer). ❖ A residential architect in the Boston area for over half a century, opened an office with Henry Atherton Frost and received her 1st commission (1919); became known for the graceful simplicity of her designs and gave careful consideration to environment and to meshing her buildings with their surroundings; opened solo office in Boston (1928), working exclusively on homes; wrote *Early Domestic Architecture of Pennsylvania* (1931); among her buildings were a Plywood House (1940) and a Masonite House (1944), both created for Boston sculptor Amelia Peabody; also designed and built a Sun House in Dover, Massachusetts, for Peabody (1948); elected fellow of American Institute of Architects (1961). ❖ See also *Women in World History.*

RAYMOND, Helen (c. 1885–1965). American comedic actress. Born c. 1885 in Philadelphia, PA; died Nov 26, 1965, in New York, NY; m. Ira J. Perry. ❖ Made NY debut in *Mrs. Wiggs of the Cabbage Patch* (1909); other plays include *Very Good Eddie, Stepping Sisters, Peacock, Broadway, The DuBarry, Shady Lady, Anything Goes, A Private Affair, One Touch of Venus* and *The Music Man* (for 3 years); appeared in several silent films, including *Dangerous to Men, Wild Honey* and *The Huntress.*

RAYMOND, Lisa (1973—). American tennis player. Born Aug 10, 1973, in Norristown, PA. ❖ Won doubles titles at Australian Open (2000), Wimbledon (2001), and US Open (2001).

RAYMOND, Paula (1923–2003). American stage, tv and screen actress. Name variations: Paula Rae Wright. Born Paula Ramona Wright, Nov 23, 1923, in San Francisco, CA; died Dec 31, 2003, in West Hollywood, CA; m. Floyd Leroy Patterson (Marine captain), 1944 (div. 1946). ❖ Began career as a model and stage actress; made film debut in *Keep Smiling* (1938), followed by *Rusty Leads the Way, Crisis, Duchess of Idaho, The Tall Target, The Sellout, The Bandits of Corsica, The Beast from 20,000 Fathoms, City That Never Sleeps, Blood of Dracula's Castle* and *Mind Twister,* among others; made dozens of guest appearances on early tv.

RAYNER, Elizabeth (1868–1947). *See Belloc-Lowndes, Marie.*

RAYNER, M.C. (c. 1894–1948). English botanist. Name variations: Mabel Cheveley Rayner. Born Mabel Mary Cheveley Rayner, 1894, in UK; died Dec 17, 1948; London University, BS, 1908, DSc, 1915;

m. Dr. William Neilson Jones, 1912. ❖ Plant expert (especially on mycotrophy), researched the ecology of *Calluna vulgaris* or common healer on the Wiltshire and Berkshire Downs (1910); studied mycorrhiza (a plant and fungus relationship); collaborated on scientific projects with husband; researched mycorrhiza and conifers in Wareham Heath, Dorset; while with the Forestry Commission, researched the cultivation of conifers and published in *Problems in Tree Nutrition* (1944); pursued further research on conifers at Bedford College, University of London; also wrote *Trees and Toadstools* (1915), (with F. Keebel) *Practical Plant Physiology* (1911) and (with husband) *A Text Book of Plant Biology* (1920).

RAZAFINDRAHETY (1861–1917). *See Ranavalona III.*

RAZIA (1211–1240). Queen of India. Name variations: Razia Sultana or Sultana Razia; Raziya or Raziyya Sultana; Raziyyatuddin or Raziyat-ud-din; Razia Iltutmish (or Altamsh). Pronunciation: Ra-ZEE-ya. Born Raziyat-ud-din ("Devoted to the Faith") in 1211 in Delhi, India; died Oct 13, 1240, outside of Delhi; dau. of Emperor Shams-ud-din Iltutmish of the Mamluk dynasty; mother's name unknown; had private tutors for reading and writing; military training; m. Altuniya (governor of Bhatinda), in 1240; no children. ❖ The only queen to be crowned at the Delhi court, defied the norms of the time to reign as sovereign, and her courage, intelligence and pragmatism remain unparalleled in medieval Indian history; had 1st experience governing when father went on the Gwalior expedition, leaving her in charge of affairs of state; upon his return (1228), was named his successor; following father's death, proclaimed queen (1236); discarded the *purdah* system, threw off the veil, rode out in combat dressed like any other soldier, and was committed to enhancing the power and benevolence of the kingdom her father had established; set a governing structure in place that would continue to be the system of choice not only for the Sultanate but, with some changes, for early Mughal rule in India; suppressed revolts by Turkish nobles quickly and effectively; led armies against rebelling Hindu princes, who attempted several times to regain control of their territory from the Muslim rulers; made peace with the marauding hordes of the Mongols (1238); declared a policy of religious tolerance towards the Hindus and ordered that the *jaziya* (a tax placed by Muslim rulers on "infidel" subjects) be discontinued; reformed the penal code, making crimes punishable on the basis of evidence and abolishing trial by ordeal; developed a uniform system of currency, transport, and communication; established several schools and employed important literary figures as teachers; established libraries which were made available to the public; after Turkish nobles staged a coup and took control of the throne in Delhi, died in battle when an arrow pierced her left breast. ❖ See also Rafiq Zakaria, *Razia: Queen of India* (Bombay: India Printing Works, 1966); and *Women in World History.*

RAZUMOVA, Natalya (1961—). Soviet volleyball player. Born Nov 21, 1961, in USSR. ❖ At Moscow Olympics, won a gold medal in team competition (1980).

READ, Annie (1867–1962). *See Elsom, Sarah Ann.*

READ, Cari (1970—). Canadian synchronized swimmer. Born Sept 4, 1970, in Edmonton, Alberta, Canada. ❖ Won a team silver medal at Atlanta Olympics (1996).

READ, Deborah (1707–1774). American colonial. Name variations: Deborah Read Rogers, Deborah Franklin. Born Deborah Read in 1707; died of a stroke, Dec 1774; m. a man named Rogers; common-law wife of Benjamin Franklin from 1730 to 1774; children: Francis Folger (b. 1732, died of smallpox) and Sarah Bache (1743–1808). ❖ Unable to divorce her deserting husband, could not wed Benjamin Franklin legally, but when her daughter Sarah Bache was born 13 years later, the baby was deemed legitimate by Philadelphia society. ❖ See also *Women in World History.*

READ, Imelda Mary (1939—). English politician. Born Jan 8, 1939, in Hillingdon, Middlesex, England. ❖ Served as chair of the European Parliamentary Labour Party (1990–92, 1998–99); as a European Socialist, elected to 4th and 5th European Parliament (1994–99, 1999–2004) from UK.

READ, Mary (1680–1721). English pirate. Born 1680 in England; died in Jamaica, April 28, 1721; husband died c. 1712–13; children: none. ❖ Moved with mother to London (1684); ran away to sea, signing on as a cabin boy aboard a British man-of-war (1694); joined British army, serving as an infantryman and dragoon in Flanders during War of the Spanish Succession (somewhere between 1702–12); donned female clothing and married a former comrade-in-arms, much to the delight

and amusement of her fellow soldiers; after husband died, signed on as a crew member aboard a Dutch merchantship bound for the West Indies; when the vessel was attacked at sea and plundered by pirates, was invited to join them and met Anne Bonney (1719); captured by Royal Navy while pregnant, was sentenced to death (1720); died in prison, just before she was to deliver her child (1721). ❖ See also *Women in World History.*

READ, Miss (1913—). *See Saint, Dora Jessie.*

READ, Sarah Ann (1867–1962). *See Elsom, Sarah Ann.*

READING, Stella (1894–1971). *See Isaacs, Stella.*

REAGAN, Maureen (1941–2001). American activist and first daughter. Born Jan 4, 1941, in Los Angeles, California; died Aug 8, 2001, in Sacramento, California; dau. of Ronald Reagan (president of US) and Jane Wyman (b. 1914, actress); stepdau. of Nancy Reagan (b. 1921); briefly attended Marymount Junior College; married and div. twice; m. 3rd husband Dennis Revell (lobbyist and public relations firm owner), 1991; children: (adopted) Rita Revell. ❖ Outspoken feminist who disagreed with father on abortion rights and Equal Rights Amendment, chaired the US delegation to World Conference of UN Decade for Women (1985) and served as US representative to UN Commission on the Status of Women; served as co-chair of Republican National Committee (1987–89) and created a political action committee that supported over 100 women candidates; ran unsuccessfully for US Senate seat (1982); was also a political analyst and radio and tv talkshow host. Received Alzheimer's Association's Distinguished Service Award (2000). ❖ See also *First Father, First Daughter: A Memoir* (1989); and *Women in World History.*

REAGAN, Nancy (1921—). American actress and first lady. Born Anne Frances Robbins, July 6, 1921, in New York, NY; dau. of Kenneth Robbins (insurance salesman) and Edith (Luckett) Robbins Davis (actress); Smith College, BA, 1943; m. Ronald Reagan (actor and later president of US), Mar 4, 1952; children: Patricia Anne Reagan, known as Patti (b. 1952), and Ronald Prescott Reagan (b. 1958); (stepchildren) Maureen Reagan (1941–2001) and Michael Reagan. ❖ Signed 7-year contract with MGM (1949); starred in *The Next Voice You Hear* (1950), but failed to garner much attention; made 11 films (1950s), including *Night into Morning* (1951) and *Hellcats of the Navy* (1957), in which she co-starred with husband; when he served as governor of California (1966–74), became active in Foster Grandparents Program; after moving into White House (1981), endured a constant stream of criticism and controversy ranging from her clothes, wealthy friends, extravagance, and plans to redecorate the White House; was also accused of usurping husband's power, of taking control of the actions and appointments of the executive branch; after husband was shot by would-be assassin John Hinckley (Mar 30, 1981), admitted that the psychological effects of the shooting lasted throughout the 8 years she spent as first lady (1981–89); launched drug-abuse program, "Just Say No," which remained her cause for next 7 years; out of the White House, began to reap far more respect from the public; enjoyed a few good years before the former president was diagnosed with Alzheimer's disease (1994); remains active in causes, including Alzheimer's research, her anti-drug campaign, and speaking out for stem-cell research. ❖ See also (with William Novak) *My Turn: The Memoirs of Nancy Reagan* (Random House, 1989) and *I Love You, Ronnie: The Letters of Ronald Reagan to Nancy Reagan* (Random House, 2000); Kitty Kelley, *Nancy Reagan: The Unauthorized Biography* (Simon & Schuster, 1991); Frances Spatz Leighton, *The Search for the Real Nancy Reagan* (Macmillan, 1987); Chris Wallace, *First Lady: A Portrait of Nancy Reagan* (St. Martin, 1986); and *Women in World History.*

RÉAGE, Pauline (1907–1998). *See Aury, Dominique.*

REALS, Gail (c. 1937—). American marine. Born c. 1937 near Syracuse, NY. ❖ Commissioned second lieutenant (1961); became personnel officer in marine security guard battalion, Beirut, Lebanon (1968); was commanding officer of Woman Recruit Training Battalion, Parris Island, SC (1970s); became 1st woman brigadier general in Marine Corps (1985); served as commanding general of Marine Corps Base at Quantico, VA, the 1st woman to command a marine base; retired from Marine Corps (1990).

REAM, Vinnie (1847–1914). American sculptor. Name variations: Vinnie Ream Hoxie. Born Vinnie Ream, Sept 25, 1847, in Madison, Territory of Wisconsin; died in Washington, DC, Nov 21, 1914; dau. of Robert Lee Ream (surveyor, recorder of deeds, and employee of US Treasury, died 1885) and Lavinia (McDonald) Ream (died 1893); studied sculpture privately with Clark Mills in Washington, DC, 1863; studied art abroad, 1869–71; m. Lieutenant Richard Leveridge Hoxie (brigidier general of US Army), May 28, 1878; children: Richard Ream Hoxie (b. 1883). ❖ Known as "the girl who sculpted Lincoln," spent childhood in Wisconsin, Missouri and Arkansas; during Civil War (1861–65), moved with family to Washington, DC; at 15, became a postal clerk-copyist and church vocalist (1862); allowed to sketch President Abraham Lincoln at White House; after his assassination (April 14, 1865), won a Congressional competition for the Lincoln statue for the Capitol—the 1st woman to sculpt for US government (Aug 30, 1866); signed a $20,000 contract for bronze statue of Admiral Farragut (Jan 28, 1875); after marrying into a wealthy family, gave up sculpting, except as a hobby, to become a Washington society hostess; after a lapse of 18 years, returned to professional sculpting (1906); while working on a statue of Civil War governor Samuel Jordan Kirkwood, was stricken ill at her summer home in Iowa City; returned by private train to Washington for treatment, where she died. Sculptures include *Bust of Lincoln* (Cornell University, 1865), *Thaddeus Stevens* (1865), *Sappho, Typifying the Muse of Poetry* (replica on her grave, 1865–70), *Lincoln* (Rotunda, US Capitol, 1865–69), *Franz Liszt* (1869), *Giacomo Cardinal Antonelli* (1870), *Gustave Doré* (1870), *Albert Pike* (1872), *Chief Justice Morrison R. Waite* (1877), *Admiral Farragut* (Farragut Square, Washington, DC, 1873–80), *Miriam* (shown 1876 Exposition), *The West* (1866–68), *The Spirit of Carnaval* (1866) as well as *Governor Samuel Kirkwood* (1906) and *Sequoyah* (1914, both in Statuary Hall, US Capitol). ❖ See also Gordon Langley Hall, *Vinnie Ream: The Story of the Girl Who Sculpted Lincoln* (Holt, 1963); O.B. Campbell, *The Story of Vinnie Ream* (Eastern Trails Historical Society); and *Women in World History*.

REBAC, Anica Savić- (1892–1935). See *Savić-Rebac, Anica*.

REBAY, Hilla (1890–1967). German-born artist and museum director. Name variations: Baroness Hilla Rebay von Ehrenweisen. Born Hildegard Anna Augusta Elisabeth Rebay, May 31, 1890, in Strasbourg, Alsace, Bavaria; died Sept 27, 1967, in Green Farms, Connecticut; dau. of Baron Franz Joseph Rebay (career army officer) and Antonie von Eicken Rebay; studied at Dusseldorf Academy, and in Paris and Munich. ❖ Director of New York's Guggenheim Museum, was a successful painter before arriving in US (1927), having exhibited with such avant-garde groups as the Secession (Munich), Salon des Indépendents (Paris), November Gruppe (Berlin), and Krater (1914–20); also exhibited in Berlin at Herwarth Walden's gallery, Der Sterm (1917); was commissioned to render a portrait of Solomon R. Guggenheim, who, with wife Irene Guggenheim, was an avid collector of old-master art; convinced the Guggenheims to take a look at the modern-art movement in Germany, then convinced them to share their private collection with the public; became the moving spirit behind Solomon Guggenheim Museum and was instrumental in establishing a base for non-objective art; over the years, introduced modern artists like Piet Mondrian, Theo van Doesburg, Georges Vantongerloo, Laszló Moholy-Nagy, Klee, Chagall and Kandinsky to American audiences; retired as director of museum (1951). ❖ See also Joan M. Lukach, *Hilla Rebay: In Search of the Spirit of Art* (Brazillier, 1983); and *Women in World History*.

REBECCA. Variant of *Rebekah*.

REBEKAH (fl. around 18th c. BCE). Jewish matriarch. Name variations: Rebecca; Rebecah. Born in Mesopotamia; buried in Hebron; dau. of Bethuel (nephew of the Jewish patriarch Abraham); sister of Laban (the father of Rachel and Leah); m. Isaac, son of Abraham; children: Esau and Jacob. ❖ By chance, met a servant at the well outside her city of Nahor, who was looking for a wife for Abraham's son Isaac; when the servant asked for a drink, readily assented and offered to water his camels as well, thereby fulfilling the sign that she was the one; during marriage, was infertile for 20 years; after 60-year-old Isaac pleaded with God for a child, delivered twin boys Esau and Jacob. ❖ See also *Women in World History*.

REBER, Sue (1955—). See *Novarra-Reber, Sue*.

REBUCK, Gail (1950—). English businesswoman. Born Gail Denise Rebuck, Feb 10, 1950, in London, England; attended Lycée Français; graduate of University of Sussex; m. Philip Gould (advisor to Tony Blair). ❖ One of the most powerful women in UK publishing, began career as production assistant with Grisewood & Dempsey (1975–76); progressed through editorial ranks at Robert Nicholson Publications to become publisher (1976–78); joined Hamlyn Group (1979) and helped establish mass-market paperbacks division; co-founded Century Publishing (1982–85); merged company with Century Hutchinson, serving as publisher (1985–89), until company was bought by Random

House; became chair of Random House Division (1989); appointed chair and chief executive of Random House UK Ltd. (1991), taking on responsibility for group and subsidiaries in South Africa, New Zealand and Australia; remained in position when company was bought by international media group, Bertelsman (1999), overseeing operations of Jonathan Cape, Chatto & Windus, Heinemann, Doubleday, Arrow, Vintage, and Corgi paperbacks.

RÉCAMIER, Juliette (1777–1849). French salonnière. Name variations: Madame Récamier or Madame Recamier; Jeanne Françoise Julie Adelaïde Récamier; de Récamier. Born Jeanne Françoise Julie Adelaïde Bernard in Lyons, France, Dec 4, 1777; died in Paris, May 11, 1849; dau. of Jean Bernard (notary of Lyons and later collector of customs in Paris) and Juliette Matton Bernard; m. Jacques Rose Récamier (wealthy banker), April 24, 1793; no children. ❖ Parisian woman, one of the most beautiful of her day, who attracted the devotion of many of the leading politicians, writers, and social leaders in Europe; met and established a lasting friendship with Germaine de Staël (1798); presided over one of the wealthiest and most popular salons in Paris (1795–1806); with Napoleon's rise to power, lived in exile in Europe (1806–07, 1811–14); returned to Paris and continued to attract the cream of Parisian society to her gatherings (1814–49); was widely praised for her tact, which allowed her to bring together men of contrary ideas or competing political factions in apparent harmony under her roof. ❖ See also Isaphene M. Luyster, *Memoirs and Correspondence of Madame Recamier* (Knight and Millet, 1867); Joseph Turquan, *A Great Coquette: Madame Recamier and Her Salon* (Brentano's, 1913); Maurice Levaillant, *The Passionate Exiles: Madame de Stael and Madame Recamier* (Farrar, 1958); and *Women in World History*.

RECKE, Elisa von der (1754–1833). German poet, diarist and salonnière. Name variations: Elisabeth von der Recke; Baroness von der Recke. Born Charlotte Elisabeth Konstantia von Médem, May 20, 1754, in Schönberg, Kurland; died April 13, 1833, in Dresden; dau. of Friedrich von Médem; sister of Duchess Anna Dorothea von Kurland (1761–1821), who married Duke Petr Biron; m. Georg von der Recke (div.); lived with writer Christoph August Tiedge. ❖ After death of only child, divorced husband and traveled among European courts meeting many writers, among them Goethe, Schiller, Kant and Tischbein; exchanged poems with friend Sophie Becker-Schwarz which were published as *Elisens und Sophiens* (1790); moved to Dresden (1818), where she maintained a salon; diaries (1789–1804), which incorporate essays on various topics, including French Revolution, emerging German middle class, and repression of women, were republished as *Tagebücher und Selbstzeugnisse* (1984).

RED BIRD (1876–1938). See *Bonnin, Gertrude*.

REDBURGA (fl. 825). Queen of Wessex, Kent, and the English. Said to be a sister of the king of the Franks, possibly Louis I the Pious, which would make her a dau. of Charlemagne; m. Ecgbert also known as Egbert III (c. 775–839), king of Wessex, Kent, and the English (r. 802–839), before 825; children: Edith (d. 871); Æthelwulf or Ethelwulf (b. around 800), king of Wessex and England (r. 839–858); Ethelstan, king of Kent (d. around 851). Her husband Egbert had a long and glorious reign.

REDDICK, Cat (1982—). American soccer player. Born Feb 10, 1982, in Birmingham, AL; dau. of Anne and Phil Reddick; attended University of North Carolina. ❖ Defender, won a team gold medal at Athens Olympics (2004).

REDDON, Lesley (1970—). Canadian ice-hockey player. Born Nov 15, 1970, in Fredericton, New Brunswick, Canada. ❖ Goaltender, won four OWIAA championships at University of Toronto; was the 1st female to play men's CIAU hockey (with University of New Brunswick Reds, 1994–96); won gold medals at World championships (1994, 1997); won a team silver medal at Nagano (1998), the 1st Olympics to feature women's ice hockey; was also a silver medalist at World Roller Hockey championships (1994).

RED DUCHESS, The.
See *Elizabeth von Habsburg (1883–1963)*.
See *Alvarez de Toledo, Luisa Isabel (1936—)*.

REDDY, Helen (1941—). Australian-born singer and actress. Born in Melbourne, Australia, Oct 25, 1941; dau. of Max Reddy (comedian) and Stella Lamond (actress); half-sister of actress Toni Lamond; m. 2nd husband Jeff Wald (div. 1982); m. Milton Ruth, 1983 (div. 1996); children: (1st m.) Traci Wald; (2nd m.) Jordan Ruth. ❖ Made professional debut on parents' radio show at age 2; in early 20s, had a twice-weekly radio program on Australian Broadcasting Commission, "Helen

Reddy Sings"; moved to NY (1966), then Los Angeles (1968); landed a spot on "The Tonight Show," (1970) which opened doors to a contract with Capitol Records; recording of "I Don't Know How to Love Him," from rock opera *Jesus Christ Superstar,* went to #13 on the charts (1971); became involved in growing feminist movement and co-wrote, with Ray Burton, 'I Am Woman,' which languished without radio play for over a year until makers of a feminist documentary, *Stand Up and Be Counted,* included the song in their film and it hit #1 on the charts; released 7 albums that made Top 20, had 2 more #1 hits, "Delta Dawn" and "Angie Baby," and others that made the Top 10 (1972–76): "Leave Me Alone (Ruby Red Dress)," "You and Me Against the World" and "Ain't No Way to Treat a Lady"; hosted variety program "The Midnight Special" (1973), becoming its regular host (1975); made film debut in *Pete's Dragon* (1977); appeared frequently on stage, in revivals of *Call Me Madame* and *Anything Goes,* among others, as well as starring roles in both West End and Broadway productions of *Shirley Valentine* and *Blood Brothers.* Won Grammy for Best Contemporary Female Pop Vocal Performance for "I Am Woman." ❖ See also *Women in World History.*

REDETZKY, Heike (1964—). See Henkel-Redetzky, Heike.

REDGRAVE, Lynn (1943—). English-born actress. Born Mar 8, 1943, in London, England; dau. of Sir Michael Redgrave and Rachel Kempson (both actors); sister of Corin Redgrave (actor) and Vanessa Redgrave (actress); granddau. of Margaret Scudamore (actress); aunt of Natasha Richardson, Joely Richardson, and Jemma Redgrave (all actresses); m. John Clark, 1967 (div. 2000); children: Ben, Annabel, and Kelly Clark (actress). ❖ Made stage debut at the Royal Court as Helena in *A Midsummer Night's Dream* (1962); made film debut in *Tom Jones* (1967), followed by *The Deadly Affair, Every Little Crook and Nanny, The National Health, The Big Bus, The Happy Hooker, Getting It Right* and *Midnight*; on tv, co-hosted talk show "Not For Women Only," starred on "House Calls" (1979–81), "Teachers Only" (1982–83), and "Chicken Soup" (1989–90), and co-starred with sister Vanessa in *Whatever Happened to Baby Jane?* (1991); became a US citizen. Nominated for an Oscar for performance in *Georgy Girl* (1966); nominated for Tony Award for *Mrs. Warren's Profession* (1976) and *Shakespeare for My Father* (1993), her autobiographical one-woman show; made Officer of the British Empire (OBE, 2001).

REDGRAVE, Vanessa (1937—). English star of stage, tv, and screen and political activist. Born Jan 30, 1937, in London, England; dau. of Sir Michael Redgrave and Rachel Kempson (both actors); sister of Corin Redgrave (actor) and Lynn Redgrave (actress); granddau. of Margaret Scudamore (actress); aunt of Jemma Redgrave (actress); m. Tony Richardson (director), 1962 (div. 1967); m. Franco Nero (actor); children: Natasha Richardson and Joely Richardson (both actresses). ❖ Made London stage debut as Caroline Lester in *A Touch of the Sun* (1958), followed by *Major Barbara, The Tiger and the Horse, The Lady from the Sea, The Seagull, The Threepenny Opera* and *As You Like It* (Rosalind), among others; made film debut with her father in *Behind the Mask* (1958) and came to prominence with *Blow-Up* (1966); other films include *A Man for All Seasons, Camelot, Isadora, Mary Queen of Scots, Murder on the Orient Express, The Trojan Women, Wetherby, Consuming Passions, The Ballad of the Sad Cafe, Little Odessa, A Month by the Lake, The Devils, Agatha, Prick Up Your Ears* and *Howards End.* Received *Evening Standard* award as Actress of the Year (1961 and 1967); named Commander of the British Empire (CBE, 1967); won Best Actress prize at Cannes for *Morgan!* (1966); nominated for Oscars as Best Actress for *Morgan!* (1966), *Isadora* (1968), *Mary Queen of Scots* (1971) and *The Bostonians* (1984); won an Oscar for Best Supporting Actress for *Julia* (1977) and an Emmy for "Playing for Time" (1980). ❖ See also autobiography *Vanessa Redgrave* (Random House, 1994).

REDMOND, Bridget Mary (1905–1952). Irish politician. Born Bridget Mary Mallick, 1905, in Ireland; died May 3, 1952; m. Captain William Archer Redmond (TD). ❖ Following the death of deputy husband (April 1932), elected to 8th Dáil as a Cumann na nGaedheal representative for Waterford, then returned to the 9th–14th Dáil (1933–52), serving until her death.

REDONDO JIMÉNEZ, Encarnación (1944—). Spanish agricultural engineer and politician. Name variations: Encarnacion Redondo Jimenez. Born April 18, 1944, in Molinos de Razón (Soria). ❖ As a member of the European People's Party (Christian Democrats) and European Democrats, elected to 4th and 5th European Parliament (1994–99, 1999–2004).

REDPATH, Anne (1895–1965). Scottish painter. Born in Galashiels, Selkirkshire, Scotland, Mar 29, 1895; died 1965; dau. of Thomas Brown Redpath (designer of tweed) and Agnes Frier (Milne) Redpath; graduate of Edinburgh College of Art, 1918; received formal art instruction from John Gray; earned teaching certificate from Moray House, 1918; m. James Beattie Michie (architect), Sept 20, 1920; children: sons Alastair Milne, Lindsay, David. ❖ Made a name for herself as a painter in many parts of Europe, including Scotland, France, and England; her paintings and watercolors, belonging to no defined school of art, either traditional or modern, were praised for their "clarity and freshness" and sense of cheerful beauty, and her use of color was judged remarkable; considered among her best works were her interiors of European churches and townscapes, though she was also noted for her still-lifes and paintings of flowers; served as president of Scottish Society of Women Artists (1944–47), and sat on board of management of Edinburgh College of Art for 6 years. Elected to full membership in Royal Scottish Academy (1951), the 1st woman so honored; received Order of the British Empire. ❖ See also *Women in World History.*

REDPATH, Christine (1951—). American ballet dancer. Born Jan 19, 1951, in St. Louis, MO. ❖ Danced with New York City Ballet where she created roles in Robbins' *An Evening's Waltzes* (1973) and the Balanchine Danilova revival of *Coppélia* (1974) and appeared in numerous premieres, including Richard Tanner's *Concerto for Two Solo Pianos* (1971) and *Octandre* (1971), Lorca Massine's *Printemps* (1972), and Jacques D'Amboise's *Saltarelli* (1974); also danced in Balanchine's *Western Symphony, Symphony in C, Brahms-Schoenberg Quartet,* and most notably in *Symphony in Three Movements* (1972).

REDPATH, Jean (1937—). Scottish folksinger. Born April 28, 1937, in Edinburgh (Scotland); graduate of Edinburgh University; attended School of Scottish Studies. ❖ Famed for interpretations of Scottish ballads and songs of Robert Burns, moved to US (1961), performing in coffeehouses in San Francisco, then New York City; performed at Gerde's Folk City (1961), earning raves; began touring extensively throughout US, Canada and Australia (1962); performed at Edinburgh Festival, Avery Fisher Hall at Lincoln Center, Sydney Opera House and many other venues; was artist-in-residence at Wesleyan University (1972–76) and 1st artist-in-residence at Stirling University (1979–89); made more than 40 recordings, ranging from songs of Robert Burns and traditional ballads to legendary performance of "Song of the Seals" and contemporary favorite "Sonny's Dream"; appeared frequently on radio, including "Morning Pro Musica" on WGBH and Garrison Keillor's "A Prairie Home Companion." Made Member of the British Empire (MBE, 1987).

RED SONIA or SONJA (1907–2000). See Kuczinski, Ruth.

REDVERS, Isabella de (1237–1293). See Isabella de Redvers.

REECE, Gabrielle (1970—). American volleyball player. Born Jan 6, 1970, in La Jolla, CA; attended Florida State University; m. Laird Hamilton (extreme surfer). ❖ At Florida State, set school records for solo and total blocks; ranked 5th in NCAA in career blocks; was the Bud Light Pro Beach Volleyball League leader in kills (1994–96) and Offensive Player of the Year (1994–95); earned $23,400 for 1st full season on the 2-person pro beach circuit (1999); modeled and wrote a column for *Women's Sports and Fitness.* Inducted into Florida State's Athletic Hall of Fame. ❖ See also memoir (with Karen Karbo) *Big Girl in the Middle* (1997).

REECE, Louise Goff (1898–1970). American politician. Name variations: Mrs. Carroll Reece. Born Louise Goff in Milwaukee, Wisconsin, Nov 6, 1898; died in Johnson City, Tennessee, May 14, 1970; dau. of Guy Despard Goff (US senator from West Virginia) and Louise (Van Nortwick) Goff; granddau. of Nathan Goff (US senator and congressional representative); married B. Carroll Reece (12-term US congressional representative from Tennessee), Oct 30, 1923 (died 1961); children: Louise Goff Reece (who m. George W. Marthens II). ❖ When husband died in the midst of his 12th term in office (1961), was endorsed by the 1st District Republican Committee as a candidate for his House seat and won the special election (May 16, 1961); declined the opportunity to seek a full term (1962). ❖ See also *Women in World History.*

REED, Alma (1889–1966). American journalist. Name variations: (pseudonym) Mrs. Goodfellow; "La Peregrina" (the Pilgrim). Born Alma Marie Sullivan in San Francisco, California, June 17, 1889; died Nov 20, 1966, in Mexico City, Mexico; dau. of Eugene J. Sullivan and Adelaide Frances (Murphy) Sullivan; m. Samuel Payne Reed, Aug 8,

1915 (div. c. 1916); no children. ❖ Began career as a reporter at *San Francisco Call*, where she was assigned to write tales of woe as "Mrs. Goodfellow"; nonetheless, succeeded in using her articles to challenge public thinking on such critical issues as capital punishment; campaigned to prevent the state execution of a young Mexican who, because of her efforts, became the 1st beneficiary of a law that made it illegal to hang prisoners who were under 18 years of age; now something of a celebrity, became a columnist for *San Francisco Bulletin*; when *The New York Times* offered her a job, took it with the stipulation that she be assigned stories in Mexico; while covering an archaeological team from Carnegie Institute that was surveying the Mayan ruins in Mexico's Yucatán (1923), reported on the thefts from the ruins of artifacts which were subsequently smuggled to Boston's Peabody Museum; became passionate about archaeology, which would take her to the excavation of Carthage in North Africa and the exploration of Cozumel, the Mayan equivalent of Jerusalem; set up a dazzling salon in Greenwich Village where US and foreign intellectuals and artists gathered (1928); returned to Mexico to work at the English-language *Mexico City News* (1950); published *Ancient Past of Mexico* (1966). Received the Aztec Eagle, the highest decoration the Mexican government can bestow on a foreigner. ❖ See also Antoinette May, *Passionate Pilgrim: The Extraordinary Life of Alma Reed* (Paragon, 1993); and *Women in World History*.

REED, Belle (1848–1889). See Starr, Belle.

REED, Corinne (1877–1947). See Rider-Kelsey, Corinne.

REED, Donna (1921–1986). American actress. Name variations: Donna Adams; Donna Asmus. Born Donna Belle Mullenger, Jan 27, 1921, in Denison, Iowa; died Jan 14, 1986, in Beverly Hills, California; dau. of William R. Mullenger and Hazel Mullenger; attended Los Angeles City College, 1938–40; m. William Tuttle (make-up artist), Jan 30, 1943 (div. 1944); m. producer Anthony I. Owen, known as Tony Owen, June 15, 1945 (div. 1971); m. Grover Asmus (retired army officer), 1974; children: Penny Jane, Anthony R., Timothy G., and Mary Anne. ❖ Best known for tv series, "The Donna Reed Show" (1958–66) and performance in *It's a Wonderful Life* (1946), 1st signed with MGM (1941), and made a series of films under the name of Donna Adams before graduating to starring roles (mid-1940s); films include *The Shadow of the Thin Man* (1941), *Babes on Broadway* (1942), *The Courtship of Andy Hardy* (1942), *Calling Dr. Gillespie* (1942), *The Human Comedy* (1943), *Thousands Cheer* (1943), *See Here, Private Hargrove* (1944), *Mrs. Parkington* (1944), *The Picture of Dorian Gray* (1945), *They Were Expendable* (1945), *Green Dolphin Street* (1947), *The Last Time I Saw Paris* (1954), *The Benny Goodman Story* (1956), *The Whole Truth* (1958), and *Pepe* (1960). Won Academy Award for Best Supporting Actress for *From Here to Eternity* (1953). ❖ See also Jay Fultz, *In Search of Donna Reed* (U. of Iowa, 1998); and *Women in World History*.

REED, Dorothy (1874–1964). See Mendenhall, Dorothy Reed.

REED, E. (1923—). See Evans, Mari.

REED, Elizabeth Armstrong (1874–1911). See Reed, Myrtle.

REED, Esther De Berdt (1746–1780). American colonial. Born Esther De Berdt, Oct 22, 1746, in London, England; died Sept 18, 1780, in Philadelphia, Pennsylvania; dau. of Dennys De Berdt (agent for colonies of Delaware and Massachusetts who helped win revocation of the Stamp Act) and Martha (Symons) De Berdt; m. Joseph Reed (lawyer and patriot), May 31, 1770; children: Martha, Joseph, Esther, Theodosia (d. 1778), Dennis De Berdt, George Washington. ❖ Co-founder of the 1st relief organization during the American Revolution, 1st moved to America (1771); as a supporter of the American cause, was hostess to many delegates to the 1st Continental Congress (1774); published the broadside *The Sentiments of an American Woman* (1780); co-founded the Philadelphia Ladies Association and led a fund-raising campaign to support the Continental Army (1780). ❖ See also *Women in World History*.

REED, Florence (1883–1967). American stage and screen actress. Born Jan 10, 1883, in Philadelphia, PA; died Nov 21, 1967, in East Islip, LI, NY; m. Malcolm Williams (actor, died 1937). ❖ Made Broadway debut in a monologue (1901); toured with E.H. Sothern company as Ophelia in *Hamlet* (1907–08); starred or was featured in *If I Were King, Don Quixote, Seven Days, The Typhoon, Chu Chin Chow, East of Suez, Macbeth* (as Lady Macbeth), *Mourning Becomes Electra, Madame X, Rebecca* (as Mrs. Danvers), and *Outward Bound*; films include *The Woman under Oath, The Code of Honor, Great Expectations, Frankie and*

Johnnie, The Typhoon, The Yellow Ticket and *Chu Chin Chow*; elected to Actor's Equity council board (1918).

REED, Frances Elliott (1882–1965). See Davis, Frances Elliott.

REED, Janet (1916–2000). American ballet dancer. Born Sept 15, 1916, in Central Point, Oregon; died Feb 28, 2000, in Seattle, WA; m. Branson Erskng (interior designer); children: Reed Erskine. ❖ Was leading ballerina at San Francisco Ballet (1927–41); in NY, danced with Ballet Theater (1942–47), in such productions as Tudor's *Dim Luster* (1943) and *Undertow* (1945), Robbins' *Fancy Free* (1944), and Kidd's *On Stage* (1945); appeared on Broadway in Robbins' *Look Ma, I'm Dancing* (1948); joined New York City Ballet (1948), where she performed in further works by Robbins, such as *The Pied Piper* (1951) and *Ballade* (1952), and in numerous Balanchine works, then served as ballet mistress (1958–64); helped found Pacific Northwest Ballet in Seattle (1974), remaining for 2 years as its 1st artistic director; had a gift for comedy and characterization.

REED, Jasna (1970—). See Fazlic, Jasna.

REED, Kit (1932—). American science-fiction and short-story writer. Name variations: named legally changed to Kit; (pseudonym) Shelley Hyde. Born Lillian Craig, 1932, in San Diego, CA; dau. of John Rich (lt. commander in US Navy) and Lillian (Hyde) Craig; College of Notre Dame of Maryland, BA, 1954; m. Joseph Wayne Reed Jr. (professor), 1955; children: 3. ❖ Worked as reporter and book reviewer for newspapers in Florida and Connecticut; novels include *Mother Isn't Dead She's Only Sleeping* (1961), *Armed Camps* (1969), *Fat* (1974), *Magic Time* (1980), *Fort Privilege* (1985), *Catholic Girls* (1987), *Little Sister of the Apocalypse* (1994), and *@expectations* [sic] (2000); short-story collections include *Mister da V. and Other Stories* (1967), *The Killer Mice* (1976), *The Revenge of the Senior Citizens* (1986), *Thief of Lives* (1992), and *Seven for the Apocalypse* (1999); nonfiction includes *Story First: The Writer as Insider* (1982), *Revision: Elements of Fiction Writing* (1989), and *Mastering Fiction Writing* (1991). Received New England Newspaperwoman of the Year award (1958, 1959).

REED, Margaret Adaline (1881–1970). See Lewis, Margaret Reed.

REED, Mary (1854–1943). American Methodist missionary. Born Mary Reed, Dec 4, 1854, in Lowell, Ohio; died April 8, 1943, in Chandag, India; dau. of Wesley W. Reed and Sarah Ann (Henderson) Reed; graduate of Ohio Central Normal School in Worthington, 1878. ❖ Taught school (1879–84); joined the Cincinnati branch of the Methodist Women's Foreign Missionary Society and sailed to India (1884); returned to US due to ill health (1890); went back to India after being diagnosed with leprosy (1891); appointed superintendent of a leper asylum near Pithoragarh (1892); awarded the Kaisar-i-Hind Medal by government of India (1917); supervised the asylum and local schools (1892–1938); honored by the American Mission to Lepers (1941). ❖ See also *Women in World History*.

REED, Myrtle (1874–1911). American novelist. Name variations: Myrtle Reed McCullough; (pseudonyms) Katherine LaFarge Norton, Olive Green. Born Myrtle Reed, Sept 27, 1874, in Norwood Park, Illinois; died of a sedative overdose, Aug 17, 1911, in Chicago, Illinois; dau. of Hiram Von Reed (preacher who established Chicago's 1st literary periodical, the *Lakeside Monthly*) and Elizabeth (Armstrong) Reed (writer); m. James Sydney McCullough (businessman), Oct 22, 1906. ❖ Published 1st story in juvenile periodical at age 10; published 1st novel, *Love Letters of a Musician* (1899), which was so popular that it was in its 15th printing by 1904; continued to write highly popular works (1899–1911), including *The Spinster Book* (1901), *Lavender and Old Lace* (1902), *What to Have for Breakfast* (cookbook, 1905), and *Weaver of Dreams* (1911). ❖ See also *Women in World History*.

REED, Rowena (1900–1988). American sculptor and design educator. Name variations: Rowena Kostellow. Born July 6, 1900; died Sept 1988 in New York, NY; graduate of University of Missouri in Kansas City; studied sculpture at Kansas City Art Institute; studied with sculptor Alexander Archipenko, and with Josef Hoffmann; attended Carnegie Institute of Technology; m. Alexander Kostellow (art teacher). ❖ Joined staff of Pratt Institute in Brooklyn (1938) and became industrial design chair there (1962); retired from that position (1966), but continued teaching until 1987; was an important influence on her students and Pratt's industrial design curriculum. ❖ See also *Women in World History*.

REEL, Chi Cheng (1944—). Taiwanese-American track-and-field star. Name variations: Chi Cheng; Mrs. Vincent Reel. Born Mar 15, 1944, in Isinchu, Taiwan; m. Vince Reel (track coach). ❖ Broke world records at 100 yards, 100 meters, 220 yards, and 200 meters; won a bronze medal for hurdles at Mexico City Olympics (1968); due to injuries, had to retire from competition; became a coach at Redlands University in California. Named Woman Athlete of the Year (1970). ❖ See also *Women in World History*.

REEL, Mrs. Vincent (b. 1944). *See Reel, Chi Cheng.*

REES, Annie Lee (1864–1949). New Zealand writer, teacher, and lawyer. Name variations: Lily Rees. Born April 24, 1864, at Beechworth, Victoria, Australia; died Aug 20, 1949, at Gisborne, New Zealand; dau. of William Lee Rees (cleric) and Hannah Elizabeth (Staite) Rees; University of Otago, BA, 1901, MA, 1902, LLB, 1910. ❖ Helped father write political pamphlets and published articles on historical and current topics (1890s); taught in Boer concentration camps of South Africa (1902); founded Cook County College in Gisborne. Received Coronation Medal (1937). ❖ See also *Dictionary of New Zealand Biography* (Vol. 3).

REES, Florence Gwendolen (1906–1994). *See Rees, Gwendolen.*

REES, Gwendolen (1906–1994). Welsh Zoologist. Name variations: Florence Gwendolen Rees. Born July 3, 1906, in Aberdare, Wales; died Oct 4, 1994; University College, Cardiff, BS, 1928, PhD, 1930. ❖ The 1st Welsh woman elected a Royal Society fellow (1971) and one of the 1st parasitologists to research the larval stages of parasites in vertebrates and invertebrates (especially parasitic worms and helminths in fish), worked as assistant zoology lecturer at University College of Wales, Aberystwyth (1930–37), then lecturer (1937–46), senior lecturer (1946–66), reader (1966–71) and professor (1971–74); served as an editorial board member (1960–70) and as board chair (1970–81) of *Parasitology*; was vice president (1970–72) and president (1972–74) of British Society for Parasitology; featured in *Vogue* (1975) as one of Britain's most interesting and influential women.

REES, Lily (1864–1949). *See Rees, Annie Lee.*

REES, Rosemary (c, 1876–1963). New Zealand actress, theater producer, and novelist. Born Rosemary Frances Rees, 1875 or 1876, at Auckland, New Zealand; died Aug 19, 1963, in Gisborne, New Zealand; dau. of William Lee Rees (lawyer and politician) and Hannah Elizabeth (Staite) Rees. ❖ Entertained troops and organized theatrical performances for Allied forces in France during WWI; formed theater company (early 1920s); wrote 24 romantic novels, which enjoyed wide readership during lifetime, including *April's Sowing* (1924), *Wild, Wild Heart* (1928), *Home's Where the Heart Is* (1935), *Little Miss Independent* (1940), and *The Mended Citadel* (1949); published well-received travel book, *New Zealand Holiday*, 1933; served as volunteer fire warden during WWII. ❖ See also *Dictionary of New Zealand Biography* (Vol. 4).

REESE, Della (1931—). African-American singer and actress. Born Delloreese Patricia Early, July 6, 1931, in Detroit, MI; m. Leroy Gray (div.); m. Vermont Taliaferro (div.); m. Franklin Lett, 1983; children: Delloreese, James, Franklin and Dominique. ❖ Began career as a singer, recording dozens of albums; had biggest hit with "Don't You Know," a redo of "Musetta's Waltz" from *La Boheme* (1959); other hits include "In the Still of the Night," "And Now" and "And That Reminds Me"; starred on tv series "Touched by an Angel" (1994–2003); also appeared on "Chico and the Man" (1976–78), "It Takes Two" (1982), "Charlie & Co." (1985), and "The Moving of Sophia Myles" (2000); is an ordained minister.

REESE, Gail (1946—). American modern dancer. Born Aug 13, 1946, in Queens, NY. ❖ Made professional debut in Cleo Quitman's concert troupe, then danced with Talley Beatty's company where she was acclaimed for *The Road of the Phoebe Snow* and *Come and Get the Beauty of It Hot*; danced with Alvin Ailey Dance Theater in New York City, performing in his *A Lark Ascending* (1972), *Mary Lou's Mass,* and *Blues Suite,* among others.

REESE, Lizette Woodworth (1856–1935). American poet. Born Lizette Woodworth Reese, Jan 9, 1856, in Huntingdon (later Waverly), Maryland; died Dec 17, 1935, in Baltimore; dau. of David Reese (who served with Confederates during Civil War and was later a prisoner of war) and Louise Sophia (Gabler) Reese; had a twin sister. ❖ Taught at various Baltimore schools (1873–1921); published 1st poem, "The Deserted House" (1874); her most famous sonnet "Tears" 1st appeared in *Scribner's Magazine* (1899); other works include *A Branch of May* (1887), *A Quiet Road* (1896), "Tears" (sonnet, 1899), *A Wayside Lute* (1909), *Spicewood* (1920), *Wild Cherry* (1923), *Little Henrietta* (1927) and *A Victorian Village* (1929). ❖ See also *Women in World History*.

REESE, Sarah (1814–1893). *See Bolton, Sarah T.*

REEVE, Alice Elsie (1885–1927). *See Reeve, Elsie.*

REEVE, Clara (1729–1807). English novelist and poet. Born 1729 at Ipswich, England; died Dec 3, 1807, at Ipswich; dau. of William Reeve (Suffolk cleric) and Hannah Smithies. ❖ Translated the 1621 Latin novel *Argenis* as *The Phoenix* (1772), before achieving great success with her Gothic novel *The Champion of Virtue: A Gothic Story* (1777); changed the title of the novel to the better-known *The Old English Baron,* for 2nd and subsequent editions; published *Progress of Romance* (1785), a critical examination of the history of romance and fiction; also wrote *The Two Mentors* (1780), *The School for Widows* (1791), *Plans of Education* (1792), *Memoirs of Sir Roger de Clarendon* (1793) and *Destination; or Memoirs of a Private Family* (1799). ❖ See also *Women in World History*.

REEVE, Ella (1862–1951). *See Bloor, Ella Reeve.*

REEVE, Elsie (1885–1927). New Zealand jeweler. Born Alice Elsie Reeve, Mar 23, 1885, in Ascot Vale, Melbourne, Australia; died April 6, 1927, in Wellington, New Zealand; dau. of Alfred Reeve (chemist) and Cornelia (Petty) Reeve. ❖ Studied jewelry design at School of Art in London; immigrated with parents and sisters to New Zealand (1909); returned to England during WWI to work in office of Admiralty; opened studio in Auckland (1922); was an active member of craft community; member of Auckland Lyceum and Auckland Society of Arts; exhibited widely and promoted work in advertisements in *Ladies' Mirror* magazine. ❖ See also *Dictionary of New Zealand Biography* (Vol. 3).

REEVE, Lady (1910–1990). *See Browne, Marjorie.*

REEVE, Marjorie (1910–1990). *See Browne, Marjorie.*

REEVES, Connie (1901–2003). American cowgirl. Born Constance Douglas, Sept 26, 1901, in Eagle Pass, TX; died Aug 17, 2003, in San Antonio, TX, age 101, 12 days after being thrown from her horse; graduate of Texas Women's University; was one of the 1st women to study law at University of Texas; m. Jack Reeves (rodeo star), 1942 (died 1985); no children. ❖ Managed a ranch and taught riding for 67 years. Inducted into National Cowgirl Museum and Hall of Fame (1997).

REEVES, Helen (1980—). English kayaker. Born Helen Joy Reeves, Sept 6, 1980, in Fleet, Hampshire, England. ❖ Won World Cup for K1 in La Seu d'Urgell, Spain (2004); won a bronze medal in K1 singles at Athens Olympics (2004).

REEVES, Helen Buckingham (1853–1920). *See Mathers, Helen.*

REEVES, Magdalene Stuart (1865–1953). New Zealand suffragist, social reformer, government official, literary inspiration, and writer. Name variations: Maud Robison, Mrs. Pember Reeves. Born Dec 24, 1865, at Mudgee, New South Wales, Australia; died Sept 13, 1953, in London, England; dau. of William Smoult Robison (bank manager) and Mary Magdalene (Saunders) Robison; m. William Pember Reeves (politician), 1885; children: 5. ❖ Moved to New Zealand with family (1868); became lady editor of weekly *Canterbury Times* (1889); was founding executive member of Canterbury Liberal Association (1890) and active in Canterbury Women's Institute's petition for women's suffrage (1893); moved to London with family (1896); joined Fabian Society (1904); was instrumental in establishing Fabian Women's Group (1907); published *Round About a Pound a Week* as Mrs. Pember Reeves (1913); friendship with H.G. Wells developed into affair and pregnancy, which inspired Wells' *Ann Veronica*; joined Board of Trade inquiry into food costs during WWI, which resulted in an appointment to Ministry of Food as director of women's services (1917). ❖ See also *Dictionary of New Zealand Biography* (Vol. 3).

REEVES, Martha (1941—). African-American Motown singer. Born July 18, 1941, in Eufala, AL; m. "Wiley," 1967 (div.); m. Willie Dee (div.); sister of Lois Reeves (singer). ❖ Migrated with family to Detroit (1942); joined Rosalind Ashford, Annette Beard, and Gloria Williams in girl-group, the Del-Phis (1960); sang backup at Motown; signed with Motown, along with 2 of the Del-Phis (Beard and Ashford), and became lead singer of Martha and the Vandellas (1962); joined by Betty Kelly (1964); had 1st Top-10 hit with "Heat Wave" (1963); churned out other popular hits, such as "Dancing in the Street" and "Nowhere to Run"; toured successfully in England (1965–66); had last Top-10 hit for

Motown, "Honey Chile" (1967); because of strained relationship with Betty Kelly (1968), replaced her with sister Lois Reeves; acquired a reputation for being difficult and relationship with Motown began to deteriorate (1968); released last album with Vandellas (1972); went solo, touring and producing several fruitless albums with various labels (mid-1970s); recorded disco album *Gotta Keep Moving* (1980). Awarded Dinah Washington Award from Detroit's Ballentine Belles; won Dionne Warwick's Soul Award; won Heroes and Legends Award; received Pioneer Award with the Vandellas (1993). ❖ See also autobiography (with Mark Bego) *Dancing in the Street: Confessions of a Motown Diva* (Hyperion, 1994); and *Women in World History.*

REEVES, Mrs. Pember (1865–1953). *See Reeves, Magdalene Stuart.*

REGAN, Agnes (1869–1943). American social worker and educator. Born Agnes Gertrude Regan, Mar 26, 1869, in San Francisco, CA; died Sept 30, 1943, in Washington, DC; dau. of James Regan and Mary Ann Morrison. ❖ Worked for 3 decades in San Francisco school system as teacher, principal, and member and president of Board of Education; helped bring about 1st teachers' pension law in CA; was 1st executive secretary of National Council of Catholic Women in Washington, DC (1920–41); became instructor in community organization for National Catholic Service School for Women in Washington, DC (later National Catholic School of Social Service), then served as assistant director (1925–43) and acting director (1935–37); played a crucial role during the national expansion of Catholic social work and fostered leadership among Catholic women. ❖ See also Loretto R. Lawler, *Full Circle: The Story of the National Catholic School of Social Service, 1918–1947* (1951).

REGAN, Sylvia (1908–2003). American actress and playwright. Name variations: Sylvia Hoffman; Sylvia Ellstein. Born Sylvia Hoffenberg, April 15, 1908, in New York, NY; died Jan 8, 2003, in New York, NY; m. James J. Regan (lawyer, div.); m. Abraham Ellstein, 1940 (died 1963). ❖ Began career as an actress under the name Sylvia Hoffman; wrote the 2-act hit, *The Fifth Season* (1953), a comedy about the dress trade; also wrote *Morning Star* (1940) and (with 2nd husband) the musical *Great to be Alive!* (1950).

REGER, Janet (1935–2005). English lingerie designer. Born Janet Phillips, Sept 30, 1935, in London, England; grew up in Reading; died Mar 14, 2005; dau. of Hyman Phillips (in the textile industry); attended Leicester College of Art and Technology; m. Peter Reger (German chemist), 1961 (div., committed suicide 1985); children: Aliza Reger (took control of the Reger firm, 1998). ❖ Began career in the corsetry industry; moved to Israel and lived on a kibbutz; with husband, formed the label, Janet Reger Creations Ltd., and opened a luxury lingerie shop in Paddington (1968); became a huge success with her "wisps of silk," opening shops in Bond Street, then in Paris and NY. ❖ See also autobiography, *Janet Reger: Her Story* (1991).

REGIER, Gladys (d. 1987). *See Vaughan, Gladys.*

REGINA (d. around 251). Saint. Martyred in Alesia around 251 when tormenters cut her throat. ❖ Baptized a Christian by her wet nurse and subsequently disowned by parents for her conversion, refused to marry Olybrius, prefect of Gaul, or deny her faith; imprisoned, was whipped and burned with heated iron plates and pincers but still held firm to her faith and her vow of virginity. Feast day is Sept 7. ❖ See also *Women in World History.*

REGINA (fl. 9th c.). Mistress of Charlemagne. Associated with Charles I also known as Charlemagne (742–814), king of the Franks (r. 768–814): children: (with Charlemagne) Drogo (b. 801), bishop of Metz; Hugh (b. 802), abbot of St. Quentin.

REGINA, Elis (1945–1982). Brazilian pop singer. Born Elis Regina Carvalho Costa, Mar 17, 1945, in Porto Alegre, Brazil; died of cocaine and alcohol overdose, Jan 19, 1982, in São Paulo, Brazil; m. Ronaldo Boscoli (composer and producer), 1967 (div. 1973); m. César Camargo Mariano (pianist, div. 8 years later). ❖ One of Brazil's best-loved performers, could sing in both Spanish and Portuguese at a young age; at 12, began singing on children's radio show "Clube do Guri"; at 13, signed with Radio Gaucha; at 15, recorded 1st album (1961); snared tv contract and rocketed to fame by age 20, interpreting classic bossa nova tunes in a passionate style; after singing a controversial song at a music festival that had been frowned on by the government in power (1965), began a lifelong career as Brazil's reigning diva; at 21, was country's highest-paid vocalist (1966); enjoyed a popular 3-year collaboration with singer Jair Rodrigues; toured Europe and recorded in Sweden with Toots Thielemans and in London with Peter Knight; recorded celebrated

album *Elis & Tom* in Los Angeles with Antonio Carlos Jobim (1974); had huge triumphs with her dance, music, and mime stage shows, *Falso Brilhante, Essa Mulher, Saudade do Brasil* and *Trem Azul.* Won Queen of the Disco Club award (1961); awarded Best Singer of Year (1962). ❖ See also *Women in World History.*

REGINA OF OSTREVANT. Saint. Name variations: Saint Regina. Married Albert, count of Ostrevant; children: daughter St. Renfroie. ❖ Feast day is July 1.

REGINTRUD (fl. 8th c.). Duchess of Bavaria. Dau. of Dagobert II, Merovingian king of Austrasia (r. 674–678), and possibly Matilda (fl. 680s); m. Theodo II, duke of Bavaria (died 716); children: Lantpert of Haimhram, bishop of Haimhram; Oda of Bavaria (fl. 680); Theodebert, duke of Bavaria; Grimoald (d. 725), duke of Bavaria; Theodebald, duke of Bavaria; Tassilo II of Bavaria. ❖ See also *Women in World History.*

REGITZE. *Variant of Richeza.*

REGNELL, Lisa (1887–1979). Swedish diver. Born Feb 3, 1887, in Sweden; died Nov 5, 1979. ❖ At Stockholm Olympics, won a silver medal in platform (1912).

REGNIER, Jeanne-Marie (1914–1944). *See Khan, Noor Inayat.*

REGO, Paula (1935—). Portuguese artist. Born 1935 in Lisbon, Portugal; studied at Slade School of Art, 1952–56; m. Victor Willing (painter). ❖ Moved to London (1952); lived in Portugal with husband (1957–63), where she became established as narrative artist, holding 1st solo exhibition at SNBA in Lisbon (1965); was strongly influenced in early work by Dubuffet, creating abstract, surreal collages, sometimes with political themes, but eventually moved on to more figurative work; settled permanently in London (1976); became visiting lecturer in painting at Slade School; held retrospective exhibition at Gulbenkian Foundation, Lisbon, and Serpentine Gallery, London (1988), confirming international reputation; appointed 1st associate artist at National Gallery in London (1990) and produced mural in Sainsbury Wing of gallery (1991); held retrospective at Tate Gallery, London, and Centro Cultural de Belém, Lisbon (1997); uses printmaking, collage, painting, sketching and etching. ❖ See also *Paula Rego–The Complete Graphic Work* (2003); John McEwen, *Paula Rego* (1993); Fiona Bradley, *Paula Rego* (Tate, 2002).

REGOCZY, Krisztina. Hungarian ice dancer. Born in Hungary. ❖ With partner Andras Sallay, won Hungarian nationals 9 times, a World championship (1980) and a silver medal at Lake Placid Olympics (1980).

REHAN, Ada (1857–1916). Irish-American actress. Born Ada Crehan, April 22, 1857, in Limerick, Ireland; died Jan 8, 1916, in New York, NY; dau. of Thomas Crehan and Harriett (Ryan) Crehan; sister of actresses Hattie and Kate (known professionally as Kate O'Neil and married to playwright Oliver Doud Byron). ❖ At 8, immigrated to US with family (1865); made stage debut in Newark with a minor role in *Across the Continent* at 14; stayed 2 seasons with Louisa Lane Drew's Philadelphia theatrical company, then apprenticed at Macaulay's Theater in Louisville and stock companies in Baltimore and Albany, where she played some 90 characters, among them Ophelia to Booth's Hamlet and Lady Anne to McCullough's Richard III; debuted in NY at Wood's Museum in *Thoroughbred* (1875); began a 20-year professional and personal association with producer Augustin Daly (1879), playing Fanny Adrianse in his production of *Divorce*, then becoming his leading lady; drew accolades after her London debut (1884); played more than 200 parts in 26 years, but her best work surfaced in Shakespearean comedies, 17th- and 18th-century "Old Comedies," and American adaptations of German farces; was extremely successful with her Lady Teazle in *The School for Scandal,* but her most legendary role was that of Katherine in *The Taming of the Shrew,* which she 1st played in NY (1887); her characterizations of Rosalind in *As You Like It* and Viola in *Twelfth Night* were also favorites; brought Maid Marian to life in Tennyson's *The Foresters* (1892). ❖ See also William Winter, *Ada Rehan: A Study* (1898); and *Women in World History.*

REHN, Elisabeth (1935—). Finnish administrator and politician. Born April 16, 1935, in Helsinki, Finland; BSc (Economics), Helsinki, 1957; DSc (Economics), Helsinki, 1994; DSc (Politics), Turku, 1998; m. Ove Rehn, 1955; children: Veronica, Joakiam, Charlotta, and Johan. ❖ Worked as an office manager for Renecta Ltd. (1960–79) and Rehn Trading Ltd. (1978–79); also taught vocational guidance and was a member of the Kauniainen City Council (1973–79); as a member of Swedish People's Party (SFP), was elected to Finnish Parliament (1979) and would remain there until 1995; served as leader of SFP parliamentary group (1987–90); appointed defense minister (1990), the 1st woman in Europe to hold a defense portfolio, and the 2nd woman in the world to do so; came in 2nd in Finland's presidential election of Jan–Feb 1994; was a member of the European Parliament (1995–96), and spent 4 years working in the Balkans: 1st as Special Rapporteur for Human Rights in Bosnia-Herzegovina, the Republic of Croatia, and the Federal Republic of Yugoslavia, then as UN undersecretary general, Special Representative of Secretary-General in Bosnia-Herzegovina (Jan 16, 1998–July 15, 1999).

REHOR, Grete (1910–1987). Austrian politician. Born Grete Daurer in Vienna, Austria, June 30, 1910; died in Vienna, Jan 28, 1987; father (a state official) was declared missing in action in 1918 during WWI; mother was a registered nurse; m. Karl Rehor (activist), 1935 (declared missing on Russian front [1943], probably having been killed during battle of Stalingrad); children: Marielies Rehor. ❖ Politician and trade union official who was the 1st woman to hold a Cabinet post in her nation's history, became active in the Christian (i.e., non-Socialist) trade union movement; advanced to post of general secretary of the central organization of Christian textile workers (1933); during WWII, joined a conservative resistance circle, becoming a member of the "hard core" of anti-Nazi Catholic trade unionists within the Austrian resistance movement; began serving as an ÖVP member of Austrian National Assembly (1949); was reelected several times and served until her retirement (1970); served as minister of Social Administration (1966–70) and created a new division for women's issues within the ministry. ❖ See also *Women in World History.*

REIBEY, Mary (1777–1855). Australian entrepreneur. Name variations: Mary Raby or Raiby; Mary Haydock. Born Molly Haydock, May 12, 1777, at Bury, Lancashire, England; died at Newtown, a suburb of Sydney, Australia, May 30, 1855; dau. of James Haydock and Jane (Law) Haydock; m. Thomas Reibey (Raby, or Raiby), Sept 1794; children: 3 sons, 4 daughters. ❖ Orphaned when young, was sent into service but ran away; at 13, while in male disguise and using name James Burrow, was arrested for trying to sell a horse that had been stolen (1791); was sentenced to 7 years transportation (1792); in New South Wales (Sydney, Australia), married a junior officer for East India Co. (1794); with husband, took up farming and prospered; in husband's frequent absences, ran a hotel as well as the business; on death of husband (April 1811), having inherited substantial property, opened new warehouses, bought more ships, and purchased 2,000 acres in Van Diemen's Land; became a noted philanthropist and religious worker. ❖ See also Nance Irvine, *Mary Reibey: Molly Incognita* (1982); and *Women in World History.*

REICH, Lilly (1885–1947). German designer and architect. Born in Berlin, Germany, June 16, 1885; died in Berlin, Dec 11, 1947; studied with Joseph Hoffmann in Vienna. ❖ Collaborated with the renowned Mies van der Rohe and was a significant creative force in her own right; began career as a designer of textiles and women's apparel; directed exhibitions of the influential Deutscher Werkbund, becoming the 1st woman member of its board of directors; extensively influenced the work of Mies van der Rohe (1920s–30s), playing a crucial role in designing furniture (the Barcelona Chair) and the interiors of the German pavilion at the Barcelona Exposition (1929); has begun to emerge from his shadow. ❖ See also Matilda McQuaid, *Lilly Reich: Designer and Architect* (Abrams, 1996); and *Women in World History.*

REICHARD, Gladys (1893–1955). American anthropologist. Born Gladys Amanda Reichard, July 17, 1893, in Bangor, Pennsylvania; died July 25, 1955, in Flagstaff, Arizona; dau. of Dr. Noah W. Reichard and Minerva Ann (Jordan) Reichard; graduate of Swarthmore College, 1919; Columbia University, AM, 1920, PhD, 1925; never married; no children. ❖ Taught in country and elementary schools (1909–15); earned Lucretia Mott fellowship for graduate study (1919); moved to NY to study anthropology under Franz Boas at Columbia University (1919); assisted Boas in classes at Barnard College (1920–21); taught at Barnard (1923–55), becoming assistant professor (1928) and professor of anthropology (1951); 1st visited Navajo reservation (1923); spent 4 summers living with a Navajo family (1930 on); ran the successful Navajo reservation Hogan School (1934); writings include *Social Life of the Navajo Indians* (1928), *Spider Woman* (1934), *Navajo Shepherd and Weaver* (1936), *Dezba, Woman of the Desert* (1939), *Navajo Religion: A Study of Symbolism* (1950), and *Navajo Grammar* (1951). Awarded A. Cressy Morrison Prize in Natural Science by New York Academy of Sciences (1932). ❖ See also *Women in World History.*

REICHARDT, Louise (1779–1826). German composer. Born April 11, 1779, in Paris, France; died Nov 17, 1826, in Hamburg, Germany; dau. of Johann Friedrich Reichardt (composer at court of Frederick II the Great) and Juliane Benda (singer, pianist, and composer); studied with her father and with Johann Friedrich Clasing. ❖ Organized and conducted several women's choruses (1817); mainly composed songs; prepared singers for Hamburg's musical festival (1818) but was not allowed to conduct as that was considered inappropriate for a woman. ❖ See also *Women in World History.*

REICHE, Maria (1903–1998). German mathematician. Born May 15, 1903, in Dresden, Germany; died of cancer, June 8, 1998, in Lima, Peru; graduated from a local university in Dresden, 1928; studied with Long Island University scholar Paul Kosok. ❖ Guardian of Peru's Nazca Lines petroglyphs, shallow lines etched into the Peruvian desert floor about 250 miles south of Lima, left Germany for Peru (1932); 1st visited Nazca lines with mentor Kosok (1941); began scientific work in Nazca desert (1946); when Kosok left Peru (1948), took over his work and shortly thereafter discovered and mapped 18 animal images; spent next 50 years dwelling in a small house near the puzzling drawings, measuring, charting, studying and protecting them; awarded Peruvian government's highest honor, the Order of the Sun (1993); became Peruvian citizen (1994). ❖ See also *Women in World History.*

REICHERT, Ossi. German Alpine skier. Name variations: Rosa Reichert. Born Rosa Reichert in West Germany. ❖ Won a silver medal for slalom at Oslo Olympics (1952) and a gold medal for giant slalom at Cortina Olympics (1956).

REICHERT, Rosa. See Reichert, Ossi.

REICHMANN, Frieda (1889–1957). See Fromm-Reichmann, Frieda.

REICHOVA, Alena (1933—). Czech gymnast. Born July 27, 1933, in Czechoslovakia. ❖ At Helsinki Olympics, won a bronze medal in team all-around (1952).

REID, Beryl (1918–1996). British actress. Born June 17, 1918, in Hereford, England; died of pneumonia after a knee operation, Oct 13, 1996, in Slough, England; m. Derek Franklin (div.); m. Bill Worsley (div.). ❖ Versatile character actress who was equally adept at comedy and drama, began career as a music-hall performer, then graduated to stage and screen; won wide acclaim in US for Broadway portrayal of the caustic lesbian radio soap-opera star in *The Killing of Sister George* (1966), a role she reprised in the 1968 film; also appeared in such films as *The Bells of St. Trinian's* (1954), *Inspector Clouseau* (1968), *Star!* (1968), *The Assassination Bureau* (1969), *Entertaining Mr. Sloane* (1970), *The Beast in the Cellar* (1971), *Dr. Phibes Rises Again* (1972), *The Death Wheelers* (1973), *Joseph Andrews* (1977) and *Carry on Emannuelle* (1978). Awarded Order of British Empire (1986).

REID, Beth Heiden (1959—). See Heiden, Beth.

REID, Charlotte Thompson (b. 1913). American politician. Name variations: Mrs. Frank R. Reid; (stage name) Annette King. Born Charlotte Leota Thompson, Sept 27, 1913, in Kankakee, Illinois; dau. of Edward Charles Thompson and Ethel (Stith) Thompson; attended Illinois College in Jacksonville, 1930–32; m. Frank R. Reid Jr. (attorney), Jan 1, 1938 (died Aug 1962); children: Patricia Reid (who m. George Lindner); Frank R. Reid III; Edward Thompson Reid; Susan Reid. ❖ Began career singing on radio under name Annette King on NBC's *Don McNeill's Breakfast Club* (1936); after husband died while campaigning for Republican seat in US House of Representatives (1962), ran in his place and won; as Republican congressional representative (1963–71), served on Committee on Interior and Insular Affairs, Committee on Public Works, and Committee on Standards of Official Conduct; introduced a constitutional amendment to allow public school students to engage in noncompulsory prayer, and opposed many of President Lyndon Johnson's social programs; supported improvements to auto safety standards, a measure to outlaw certain types of rifle sales, a "Truth In Lending Law," and the proposed Equal Rights Amendment; resigned from House (1971) to serve a 5-year term on the Federal Communications Commission; also served on the President's Task Force on International Private Enterprise (1983–85). ❖ See also *Women in World History.*

REID, Christian (1846–1920). See Tiernan, Frances Fisher.

REID, Clarice D. (1931—). African-American physician and researcher. Born in Birmingham, Alabama, 1931; graduate of University of Cincinnati Medical School, 1959. ❖ Was Cincinnati's 1st African-

American with a private practice in pediatrics; served as deputy director of the Sickle Cell Program of the Health Service Administration in Washington DC; received US Public Health Service's highest honor, the Superior Service Award. ❖ See also *Women in World History.*

REID, Dorothy Davenport (1895–1977). American actress, producer, director, and screenwriter. Name variations: Dorothy Davenport; Mrs. Wallace Reid. Born Mar 13, 1895, in Boston, Massachusetts; died Oct 12, 1977, in Woodland Hills, CA; dau. of Harry Davenport (character actor) and Alice Davenport (silent-screen comedian); niece of Fanny Davenport (actress); m. Wallace Reid (actor), in 1913 (died from drug addiction, 1923); children: Betty and Wallace Reid Jr. ❖ Began acting career at Biograph (1909); starred in numerous silent films, often with husband Wallace Reid; produced and starred in *Human Wreckage* (1923), a biographical account of husband's death from drugs; turned attention to producing, directing, and screenwriting, forming her own production company to produce *The Red Kimono* (1926); though she also directed many of her own movies, did not take screen credit until *Linda* (1929); directed 2 features, *The Road to Ruin* and *The Woman Condemned* (1934); established the Wallace Reid Foundation Sanitarium, a drug-addiction center. ❖ See also *Women in World History.*

REID, Elisabeth Mills (1858–1931). American philanthropist. Born in New York, NY, Jan 6, 1858; died in Cap Ferrat, Nice, France, April 29, 1931; dau. of Darius Ogden Mills (California financier) and Jane Templeton (Cunningham) Mills (dau. of a prominent shipowner and shipbuilder); sister of Ogden Mills who was father of Ogden L. Mills, secretary of treasury; educated by governesses, at Mlle Vallette's School in Paris, and at Anna C. Brackett School in NY; m. Whitelaw Reid (editor and chief owner of *New York Tribune* and minister to France, 1889–92), April 26, 1881 (died 1912); children: Ogden Mills Reid (b. 1882, publisher of *New York Tribune*); Jean Reid (who m. Sir John Hubert Ward, equerry to England's Queen Alexandra of Denmark). ❖ During Spanish-American War, was the acting head of the nursing division of American Red Cross; was also chair of American Red Cross in London during WWII; as a philanthropist, helped establish Dr. Trudeau's T.B. sanitarium and the D.O. Mills training school for nurses, both at Saranac Lake, New York.

REID, Florence (c. 1870–1950). Australian prime-ministerial wife. Born Flora Ann Brumbry, c. 1870, in Australia; died Sept 1, 1950, in Rose Bay, Sydney; m. George Reid (prime minister of Australia, 1904–05), Nov 5, 1891 (died 1918); children: Thelma (b. 1893), Douglas (b. 1895), and Clive (b. 1899). ❖ Served as vice-president of the Sydney Women's Electoral League (1899); was particularly active at Australia House in London when husband was High Commissioner (1910–16); after WWI, was closely involved with work for returned service personnel in England, then Australia. Was the 1st Australian woman to be awarded the Dame Grand Cross of the British Empire (GBE, 1917).

REID, Frances (b. 1913). American actress. Born Dec 9, 1913, in Wichita Falls, TX; raised in Berkeley, CA; trained at Pasadena Playhouse; m. Philip Bourneuf (div.). ❖ Made NY debut as Juliette Lecourtois in *Where There's a Will* (1939); played Ophelia to Maurice Evans' Hamlet and Roxane to Jose Ferrer's Cyrano; on tv, appeared as Alice Horton on "Days of Our Lives" for over 37 years, since its debut (1965). Nominated for Emmy for Outstanding Lead Actress in a Drama Series (1986–87).

REID, Helen Rogers (1882–1970). American publisher. Name variations: Mrs. Ogden Mills Reid. Born Helen Miles Rogers, Nov 23, 1882, in Appleton, Wisconsin; died in New York, NY, July 27, 1970; dau. of Benjamin Talbot Rogers (hotel operator) and Sarah Louise (Johnson) Rogers; Barnard College, AB, 1903; m. Ogden Mills Reid (editor of *New York Herald Tribune*), Mar 14, 1911; children: Whitelaw Reid (newspaper executive); Elisabeth Reid (1916–1924); Ogden Rogers Reid (newspaper executive). ❖ For many years, was the dominant figure of one of the 10 best newspapers of the world; as advertising director, joined staff of *New York Tribune* (1918), which became *New York Herald Tribune* (1924); served as vice president and became its driving spirit (1922–47), turning the paper into the 2nd-best daily in US, one that in many areas even outdid its arch-rival, *The New York Times*; served as president (1947–52); designated board chair (1953–68); lost the magic touch and the paper went into decline. ❖ See also *Women in World History.*

REID, Kate (1930–1993). English-born stage, tv, and screen actress. Born Daphne Katherine Reid, Nov 4, 1930, in London, England; died Mar 27, 1993, in Stratford, Ontario, Canada; m. Austin Willis (div.).

❖ Made stage debut in London as Lizzie in *The Rainmaker*; joined the Stratford (Ontario) Shakespearean Festival (1959), becoming one of its leading mainstays; films include *This Property is Condemned, The Andromeda Strain, A Delicate Balance, Equus, Death Ship* and *Circle of Two*; appeared as the ex-moll, Grace, in *Atlantic City.* Made Officer of the Order of Canada (1976); nominated for Tony awards for *Dylan* (1964) and *Slapstick Tragedy* (1966).

REID, Liz Allan (1947—). *See Allan-Shetter, Liz.*

REID, Margaret (1935—). Australian politician. Name variations: Margaret Elizabeth Reid. Born May 28, 1935, in Crystal Brook, South Australia, Australia; Adelaide University, LLB; married; children: 2 sons, 2 daughters. ❖ The 1st woman to be elected president of the Australian Senate, held that position for 6 years (Aug 20, 1996–Aug 18, 2002); began career as a barrister and solicitor; was deputy government whip in Senate (1982–83), deputy opposition whip (1983–87) and opposition whip (1987–95); became deputy president of the Senate, chair of Committees, and president of the Senate (1996). Awarded Queen Elizabeth II Silver Jubilee Medal (1977) and Order of Polonia Restituta (1987).

REID, Maria (1895–1979). Gibraltar-born actress. Name variations: Marita Reid. Born Aug 29, 1895, in Gibraltar; died July 18, 1979, in New York, NY; m. José Tavira (bullfighter). ❖ Pioneered Spanish theater in New York City.

REID, Mrs. Ogden Mills (1882–1970). *See Reid, Helen.*

REID, Rose Marie (1906–1978). Canadian-born designer. Born Rose Marie Yancey, Sept 12, 1906, in Cardston, Alberta, Canada; died Dec 19, 1978, in Provo, Utah; dau. of Marie Hyde Yancey (designer and seamstress) and William Elvie Yancey; m. Garreth Rhynhart (div. 1935); m. Jack C. Reid (swimming pool manager and instructor), Nov 30, 1935 (div. 1946); children: (2nd m.) Bruce (b. 1937); Sharon Reid Alden (b. 1938); Carole Reid Burr (b. 1940). ❖ Swimsuit designer and businesswoman whose innovative styling put her at the top of the swimwear industry, moved with family to Weiser, Idaho (1916); after marriage, designed a swim suit that led to orders from a Vancouver department store and launched Holiday Togs, Ltd., later changed to Rose Marie Reid, Ltd.; saw business sales top $1 million a year (1946); entered partnership with Jack Kessler and relocated to California (1947–49); her company became the leading fashion house and manufacturer of swimsuit industry (1950s); saw company sales reach $18.4 million, almost 10% of women's bathing suit sales in nation (1960); refusing to design bikinis, left the company (1960); sold the rights to her name (1964); shifted to the design and manufacture of synthetic-fiber wigs for women; moved to Provo, Utah, to be with family; continued civic service involvement, especially as a speaker at university and business meetings, and remained active in the Mormon Church. ❖ See also Burr and Petersen, *Rose Marie Reid: An Extraordinary Life Story* (Covenant, 1995); and *Women in World History.*

REID, Virginia (1909–1955). *See Carver, Lynne.*

REID, Mrs. Whitelaw (1858–1931). *See Reid, Elisabeth Mills.*

REID-BANKS, Lynne (1929—). *See Banks, Lynne Reid.*

REIGNOLDS, Catherine Mary (1836–1911). English-born American actress, dramatic reader, and teacher. Name variations: Kate Reignolds; Kate Winslow. Born Catherine Mary Reignolds, May 16, 1836, near London, England; died July 11, 1911, in Concord, Massachusetts; dau. of Robert Gregory Taylor Reignolds and Emma (Absolon) Reignolds (actress); sister of Georgie and Jane Reignolds (actresses); m. Henry Farren (actor), Dec 1857 (died Jan 8, 1860); m. Alfred Erving Winslow (merchant), June 28, 1861; children: Charles-Edward Amory Winslow (b. 1877). ❖ Came to US with family (1850); at 14, made stage debut with mother in Chicago in *Cinderella*; made NY debut (1855); joined Ben De Bar's Opera House co. in St. Louis, Missouri (1857), where she associated with some of the most prominent stars of the day, including Charlotte Cushman; became leading lady of the stock company of Boston Museum (1860), where she was quite popular; after 1865, traveled abroad as a celebrated actress, appearing in London's Princess Theatre (1868) and other major English venues, but Boston would be home for rest of her life; toured in US as head of her own company; retired (1877), but some years later began giving dramatic readings. ❖ See also memoirs *Yesterdays with Actors* (1887); and *Women in World History.*

REIK, Haviva (1914–1944). Jewish resistance fighter. Name variations: Havivah. Born Haviva Emma Reik in Slovakia (now

Czechoslovakia), 1914; executed by German military during WWII, 1944. ❖ Immigrated to Palestine (late 1930s) and joined kibbutz Ma'anit; during Nazi occupation of Slovakia, parachuted into former homeland with 3 other volunteers to assist the Jewish resistance and to spy for Allied forces (1944); was eventually captured by German military and executed; regarded as a national hero in present-day Israel (both the kibbutz Lehavot Haviva and the Givat Havivah research center bear her name).

REILLY, Dianne (1969—). Australian politician. Born Jan 29, 1969, in Brisbane, Australia. ❖ As a member of the Australian Labor Party, elected to the Queensland Parliament for Mudgeeraba (2001).

REIMAN, Elise (c. 1910—). American ballet dancer and teacher. Born c. 1910 in Terre Haute, IN. ❖ Performed with companies of Adolf Bolm in Chicago (c. 1927–32), including in his *Ballet Mécanique* and *Apollon Musagète* (1928); joined American Ballet, where she performed in the premiere of *Serenade* (1934), among others; with Ballet Society, created roles for Balanchine's *Four Temperaments* and *Divertimento*; served as teacher at School of American Ballet; on Broadway, appeared in *Alma Mater* (1935), *Liberty Jones* (1941) and *Rosalinda* (1942–44).

REIMANN, Brigitte (1933–1973). East German novelist. Born July 21, 1933, in Burg, East Germany; died of cancer, Feb 20, 1973, in Berlin, Germany; dau. of Willi Reimann and Elisabeth Reimann; m. 2nd husband Siegfried Pitschmann (writer). ❖ Worked as teacher, bookseller, and reporter; came to prominence with *Die Geschwister,* for which she received the Heinrich Mann Prize (1965); spent 10 years on the novel, *Franziska Linkerhand,* which was published the year after her death (1974); her diaries, *Ich bedaure nichts* (I Regret Nothing, 1997) and *Alles schmeckt nach Abschied* (Everything Tastes of Goodbye, 1998), were bestsellers.

REIMER, Daniela (1982—). German rower. Born Sept 26, 1982, in Potsdam, Germany. ❖ Won a silver for lightweight double sculls at Athens Olympics (2004); placed 1st at 2 World Cups (2004).

REINDERS, Agnes (1913–1993). American nun and nurse-midwife. Name variations: Agnes Shoemaker; Sister M. Theophane. Born Agnes Shoemaker, Aug 27, 1913, near Owensboro, KY; died Sept 28, 1993; Catholic University of America, BS in nursing, 1941, MA in administration, 1946; Maternity Center Association in NYC, nurse-midwifery certificate, 1943; m. Henry Reinders, 1970. ❖ Developed nurse-midwifery services in Santa Fe, NM; joined the Medical Mission Sisters (Roman Catholic order); directed and helped found the Catholic Maternity Institute (CMI), which opened the 1st freestanding birth center in America at La Casita (1951), offered the 1st school of nurse-midwifery associated with a university (Catholic University), and was the 1st to offer a nurse-midwifery MA program; advocated and later chaired a committee for establishment of American College of Nurse-Midwifery (ACNM, 1955, renamed American College of Nurse-Midwives, 1969); served as ACNM's 2nd president (1957–59); served as the 1st editor of *Bulletin of American College of Nurse-Midwifery,* an ACNM publication; taught at Marquette University College of Nursing.

REINECK, Heidemarie (1952—). West German swimmer. Born Feb 15, 1952, in West Germany. ❖ At Mexico City Olympics, won a bronze medal in the 4 x 100-meter medley relay (1968); at Munich Olympics, won a bronze medal in the 4 x 100-meter medley relay and a bronze medal in the 4 x 100-meter freestyle relay (1972).

REINER, Ethel Linder (d. 1971). American theatrical producer. Died Feb 8, 1971, in Barbados. ❖ Co-produced such plays as *Four Saints in Three Acts, Masterpieces of the 20th Century, Camino Real, The Rainmaker* and *Candide;* moved to London.

REINHARD, Anna (1487–c. 1538). See Zwingli, Anna Reinhard.

REINHARDT, Aurelia Henry (1877–1948). American educator. Born Aurelia Isabel Henry, April 1, 1877, in San Francisco, California; died Jan 28, 1948, in Palo Alto, California; dau. of William Warner Henry and Mollie (Merritt) Henry; graduate of University of California at Berkeley, 1898; Yale, PhD, 1905; m. Dr. George Frederick Reinhardt (founder and director of University Health Service in Berkeley), Dec 4, 1909 (died June 1914); children: George Frederick (b. 1911); Paul Henry (b. 1913, physician). ❖ Lectured in English at University of California extension (1914–16), before accepting a position as president of Mills College in Oakland, CA; her dynamic 27-year administration transformed Mills from an unstable establishment into an important, internationally known institution; was also national president of American

Association of University Women (1923–27) and department of education chair for General Federation of Women's Clubs (1928–30); became American Unitarian Association's 1st female moderator (1940). ❖ See also *Women in World History.*

REINHARDT, Helene (1889–1974). See Thimig, Helene.

REINHARDT, Sybille (1957—). East German rower. Born Oct 20, 1957, in East Germany. ❖ At Moscow Olympics, won a gold medal in quadruple sculls with coxswain (1980).

REINHILD (fl. 8th c.). Flemish nun and artist. Flourished in 8th century at convent of Maasryck in modern-day Flanders, in the region north of France then called the Low Countries. ❖ Became famous for her learning and for her artistic abilities, primarily as a painter but also for her beautiful cloth designs; was also reported to be highly skilled in copying and illuminating manuscripts.

REINIG, Christa (1926—). German feminist writer. Born in Berlin, Germany, Aug 6, 1926; studied 4 years at Humboldt University. ❖ Published one of her 1st poetry collections, *Der Abend–der Morgen* (Evening–Morning, 1951), followed by *Die Steine von Finisterre* (The Stones of Finisterre, 1960), and *Die Schwalbe von Olevano* (The Swallow from Olevano, 1969); served as curator at Märkisches Museum (1957–64); moved from East Germany to West Germany (1964); wrote several radio plays, among them the award-winning *Aquarium* (1968); also wrote for children, including a book of verse, *Hantipanti* (1972), and a story, *Der Hund mit dem Schlüssel* (The Dog with the Key, 1976); published feminist novel, *Die Entmannung* (Emasculation or Castration, 1976); other works include *Die himmlische und die irdische Geometrie* (Heavenly and Earthly Geometry, 1975), *Orion trat aus dem Haus* (Orion Has Left the House, 1969), *Die Ballade vom blutigen Bomme* (The Ballad of Bloody Bomme, 1972), *Mädchen ohne Uniform* (Girl Without Uniform, 1981), *Feuergefährlich: Gedichte und Erzählungen für Frauen und Männer* (Inflammatory: Poems and Stories for Men and Women, 1982), and *Idleness is the Root of All Love* (poems, published in English, 1991).

REINIGER, Lotte (1899–1981). German film animator. Born in Berlin, Germany, June 2, 1899; died in Dettenhausen, West Germany, June 19, 1981; dau. of Karl Reiniger (banker) and Eleonore Reiniger; studied with Max Reinhardt, 1916–17; studied with Paul Wegener at Berlin Institut für Kulturforschung, 1918–19; m. Carl Koch (art historian and filmmaker), 1921 (died Dec 1, 1963). ❖ Talented animator, who produced pioneering works in the early 1920s and continued production for next 50 years, began career as animator, employing handcut silhouettes and a stand she herself had designed, thereby anticipating the work that Disney's studio would do a decade later (1918); completed her 1st silhouette film short, *The Ornament of the Loving Heart* (1919); released *The Adventures of Prince Achmed* (1926), considered by most historians to be the 1st full-length animated film; left Germany for England (1935 or 1936); worked on films in Italy (1939–45); returned to Berlin (1944 or 1945); settled in England (1949), where she spent most of the next 3 decades making films for BBC; received 1st prize, Venice Film Festival (1955); produced final silhouette films in Canada (1974–78), including *Aucassin and Nicolette;* settled in Dettenhausen, West Germany, and was made the subject of special program and symposium, American Film Festival (1980); honored by Museum of Modern Art, NY (1986); wrote *Shadow Theatres and Shadow Films* (1970). Films include *Dr. Doolittle and His Animals* (1927–28), *Carmen* (1933), *Papageno* (1935), *Snow White and Rose Red* (1955), *Jack and the Beanstalk* (1955), *Thumbelina* (1955) and *The Rose and the Ring* (1979). ❖ See also Eric Walter White, *Walking Shadows: An Essay on Lotte Reiniger's Silhouette Films* (Hogarth, 1931); and *Women in World History.*

REINISCH, Rica (1965—). East German swimmer. Born April 6, 1965, in East Germany. ❖ At Moscow Olympics, won gold medals in the 200-meter backstroke, 100-meter backstroke, and 4 x 100-meter medley relay (1980).

REINKING, Ann (1949—). American dancer and choreographer. Born Nov 10, 1949, in Seattle, WA; m. Peter Talbert, 1991; children: 1. ❖ Trained at Robert Joffrey's American Ballet Center, made Broadway debut in *Coco* (1969); began professional and personal relationship with Bob Fosse when she appeared in his *Pippin* (1972); also worked with Fosse in *Chicago* (1975), *Dancin'* (1978), and in his film *All That Jazz* (1980); appeared in *Goodtime Charley* (1975) and replaced Donna McKechnie in *A Chorus Line;* on film, appeared in *Movie Movie* (1978), *Annie* (1982), and *Micki and Maude* (1984), among others; on tv, performed for "Lights, Camera, Annie" (1982), "A Night on the Town" (1983), and as guest on "The Cosby Show" (1984). Won Tony Award as Best Choreographer for revival of *Chicago* (1997).

REINSBURG-DURINGSFELD, Ida von (1815–1876). *See Düringsfeld, Ida von.*

REINSHAGEN, Gerlind (1926—). German novelist and playwright. Born May 4, 1926, in Königsberg, Germany; attended Hochschule der Küntse in Berlin, 1953–56. ❖ Wrote numerous novels, plays and radio plays, including *Doppelkopf* (1967), *Himmel und Erde* (1974), *Sonntagskinder* (1981), and *Die flüchtige Braut* (1984). English translations include *Twelve Nights* and *The Life and Death of Marilyn Monroe*.

REIS, Maria Firmina dos (1825–1917). Brazilian novelist and poet. Name variations: (pseudonym) Uma Brasileira. Born 1825 in São Luís, Brazil; died 1917; never married but adopted several children. ❖ Worked as teacher in Guimarães, Maranhão; wrote *Úrsula* (1859), the 2nd novel by a woman and 1st abolitionist novel in Brazil; also wrote *Maria Firmina, fragmentos de uma vida* (1975); contributed to *Semanário Maranhense*, wrote hymns and abolitionist songs in *Cantos à beira-mar* (1871), and contributed 2 stories to *Moraes Filho* (1975).

REISCHAUER, Haru (c. 1915–1998). Japanese-born American journalist. Name variations: Haru Matsukata. Born Haru Matsukata in Japan, c 1915; died in La Jolla, California, Sept 23, 1998; granddau. of Prince Masayoshi Matsukata, former prime minister of Japan; attended American School in Japan; graduate of Principia College, Illinois, 1937; m. Edwin O. Reischauer (scholar and diplomat), 1956; children: (stepchildren) Robert, Ann, and Joan. ❖ Began career as a journalist in Tokyo; following marriage and a move to Belmont, MA (1956), reported on Japan for *Saturday Evening Post* and *Christian Science Monitor*; while husband was ambassador to Japan (1961–66), became extremely popular there; served as honorary chair of policy advisory committee on US-Japan relations at Harvard (1990–98) and honorary chair of Center for East Asian Studies at Johns Hopkins University's School of Advanced International Studies (1993–98). ❖ See also memoir *Samurai and Silk: A Japanese and American Heritage* (1986); and *Women in World History*.

REISENBERG, Clara (1910–1998). *See Rockmore, Clara.*

REISENBERG, Nadia (1904–1983). Lithuanian-American pianist. Born Nina Reisenberg in Vilna (now Vilnius), Russian Lithuania, July 14, 1904; died in New York, NY, June 10, 1983; sister of Clara Rockmore (1910–1998); studied with Leonid Nicolaiev at St. Petersburg Conservatory; children: Robert Sherman (pianist). ❖ Immigrated with family to New York as a refugee from Soviet Russia (1922); made NY debut at Aeolian Hall (1924), playing Paderewski's *Polish Fantasy*; recorded several neglected works, including Tchaikovsky's Piano Sonata and Paderewski's *Polish Fantasy*; had a long career as a teacher at Mannes College of Music, Juilliard School, Queens College of City University of New York, and Rubin Academy in Jerusalem. ❖ See also *Women in World History*.

REISNER, Larissa (1895–1926). Russian poet, journalist, revolutionary, and diplomat. Name variations: Larisa Reisner. Born Larissa Mikhailovna Reisner near Vilnius, Lithuania, May 1, 1895; died of typhus, Feb 9, 1926, in Moscow; dau. of Mikhail Andreevich Reisner (aristocrat, lawyer, and socialist of German descent) and Ekaterina Alexandrovna Khitrova (aristocrat with socialist leanings); attended St. Petersburg University; m. Fyodor Raskolnikov (Bolshevik deputy commissar for Naval Affairs), 1918 (div. 1924); children: 1 adopted son. ❖ Fled with family to Germany at age 8 because of father's political activities as a Marxist (1903); returned to Russia to live in St. Petersburg (1907); became chief editor of *Rudin* (1913); following overthrow of Nicholas II, became involved in Bolshevik government (1917); married Raskolnikov (1918); during Civil War, became a legend and a symbol of hope for the fledgling Soviet Union, running an espionage operation with Raskolnikov and commanding members of the Russian navy; wrote of her exploits in the popular *Letters from the Front*; traveled with Raskolnikov as ambassadors of the Soviet Republic to Afghanistan, where they carried out diplomatic negotiations (1921); returned to Moscow (1923); went to Germany, became romantically involved with Polish Communist Karl Radek, and wrote journalistic accounts of life in Weimar Republic (1923), later issued as *Hamburg at the Barricades*; returned to Russia, and wrote about mining conditions in the Urals (1924). ❖ See also Cathy Porter, *Larissa Reisner* (Virago, 1988); and *Women in World History*.

REITER, Frances (1904–1977). American nurse. Name variations: Frances Ursula Reiter. Born June 13, 1904, in Smithton, PA; graduate of Johns Hopkins Hospital Training School for Nurses, 1931; Columbia University Teachers College, BA in nursing education, 1941, MA, 1942; m. Harry Kreuter, 1951. ❖ One of the 1st nurses to become a researcher, coined the term "nurse-clinician"; worked as a nurse at Johns Hopkins Hospital (1931–34); taught at Columbia University Teachers College (1945–60); became 1st dean of New York Medical College Graduate School of Nursing (1960); chaired American Nurses Association Committee on Education; was on the 1st editorial board of *Nursing Research*.

REITSCH, Hanna (1912–1979). German flier and test pilot. Born Hanna Reitsch, Mar 29, 1912, in Hirschberg, German Silesia; died Aug 24, 1979, in Frankfurt, Germany; dau. of Dr. Willy Reitsch (eye specialist) and Emy Reitsch (member of Austrian aristocracy); briefly attended medical school; never married; no children. ❖ One of the foremost aviators of the 20th century, broke 1st world record for gliding (1931); gave up medical school for job with Germany's top research establishment for motorless flight, Deutsche Forschungsanstalt für Segelflug (DFS), gaining renown as one of the world's best pilots; tested all the newest planes, including the Stuka and the Dornier bomber; joined Ernst Udet's elite band of military test pilots (1937) and was promoted to rank of Flugkapitän; flew the FW 61, the world's 1st viable helicopter (1937); after managing to escape from a crash in a Dornier, became the 1st woman to be awarded Germany's Iron Cross, 2nd Class (1940); crashed again when the controls jammed in an unpowered Me 163B, and was again awarded the Iron Cross (1942); recovery took months; was one of the last to visit Hitler in his bunker (April 1945); was imprisoned for 18 months after WWII as a Nazi sympathizer until her name was cleared; wrote numerous books; sent to India where she became friends with Jawaharlal Nehru, premier of India, and his daughter Indira Gandhi (1959); at request of President Kwame Nkrumah, founded a gliding school in Ghana (1961); was a founding member of the German Association of Women Pilots and of the 99s, an international women pilots' organization 1st established in US. ❖ See also memoirs *Fliegen mein Leben* (Flying My Life, 1951) and *The Sky My Kingdom* (Greenhill, 1991); Judy Lomax, *Hanna Reitsch: Flying for the Fatherland* (Murray, 1988); Dennis Piszkiewicz, *From Nazi Test Pilot to Hitler's Bunker: The Fantastic Flights of Hanna Reitsch* (Praeger, 1997); and *Women in World History*.

REITZ, Dana (1948—). American dancer and choreographer. Born Oct 19, 1948, in Rochester, NY; graduate of University of Michigan, 1970. ❖ Trained in range of styles and techniques with Elaine Summers, Maggie Black, Andre Bernard, and at Alwin Nikolais and Cunningham studios in NY; joined Twyla Tharp and Dancers Co.; toured with Laura Dean and Dance; had a major role in the premiere of Wilson-Glass *Einstein on the Beach* (1976); choreographed numerous works, often incorporating film or video footage.

RÉJANE, Gabrielle (1857–1920). French actress. Name variations: Gabrielle Rejane; Gabrielle Charlotte Reju. Born Gabrielle-Charlotte Réju in Paris, France, in 1857 (some sources cite 1856); died 1920; dau. of an actor; studied at Conservatoire, Paris; m. M. Porel (theater director), 1892 (div. 1905); children: daughter, G. Réjane. ❖ Made stage debut at Théâtre du Vaudeville (1875), after which her reputation as a player of light comedy grew steadily; had 1st great success in *Ma camarade* (1883), and soon became known as a dramatic actress as well, notably in *Divorçons, Sapho, La Dame aux Camélias, Germinie Lacerteux, Ma cousine, Amoureuse, Lysistrata,* and Ibsen's *A Doll's House*; made London debut (1894); appeared in title role of *Madame Sans-Gêne* in NY (1895), believed to be her most notable part; was also famed for performances in *La Parisienne, Zaza* and *La Passerelle*; in Paris, opened her own theater, the Théâtre Réjane (1906), and continued acting until the year of her death. ❖ See also *Women in World History*.

REJCKA. *Variant of Ryksa.*

REJTO, Ildiko (1937—). *See Sagine-Ujlakine-Rejto, Ildiko.*

REJU, Gabrielle (1857–1920). *See Réjane, Gabrielle.*

REKHA (1954—). Indian actress. Name variations: Baby Bhanurekha or Bhanurekha; Rekhaji. Born Bhanurekha Ganesan, Oct 10, 1954, in Madras, India; dau. of Gemini Ganesan and Pushpavalli; m. Vinod Mehra (div.); m. Mukesh Aggarwal, 1990 (died 1991). ❖ Cast by director Mohan Segal in *Sawan Bhadon* (1970), became instant star; went on to become highest paid actress in Indian film and win

National Award for role in *Umrao Jaan*; stopped acting for music and dance tour of US (1985); returned to cinema with *Aurat* (1987); appeared in 9 films opposite Amitabh Bachchan, including *Silsila* (1982), as well as over 170 other films, among them *Dharam Karam* (1975), *Ghar* (1978), *Geetanjali* (1993), *Kama Sutra: A Tale of Love* (1996), and *Mother 98* (1998).

RELJIN, Milena (1967—). Yugoslavian rhythmic gymnast. Born May 25, 1967, in Belgrade, Yugoslavia; m. Nenad Tatic. ❖ Won Jr. Yugoslavian nationals (1980), Balkan championships (1981), and 9 Yugoslavian nationals (1981–89); placed 5th in all-around at Los Angeles Olympics (1984) and 9th at Seoul Olympics (1988); won Medico Cup (1985).

REMEY, Ethel (1895–1979). American stage and tv actress. Born Jan 22, 1895; died Feb 28, 1979, in Neptune, NJ. ❖ Made Broadway debut in *Rose Briar* (1922), followed by *Connie Goes Home, Such is Life, Forsaking All Others, Our Town, Chicken Every Sunday* and *The Women*; probably best remembered as Alma Miller, Lisa Miller's mother, on tv series "As the World Turns" (1961–79).

REMICK, Lee (1935–1991). American stage and screen actress. Born Dec 14, 1935, in Quincy, MA; died July 2, 1991, in Brentwood, CA; m. William Colleran (tv director-producer), 1957 (div. 1968); m. William "Kip" Gowans (British producer), 1970. ❖ Appeared on Broadway in *Be Your Age, Anyone Can Whistle* and *Wait Until Dark*, for which she received a Tony award nomination; made film debut in *A Face in the Crowd* (1957) and starred in such films as *The Long Hot Summer, These Thousand Hills, Anatomy of a Murder, Wild River, Sanctuary, Experiment in Terror, Baby the Rain Must Fall, No Way to Treat a Lady, The Detective, Sometimes a Great Notion, A Delicate Balance, The Omen, Loot* and *Tribute*. Nominated for Academy Award for Best Actress for performance in *Days of Wine and Roses* (1962).

REMINGTON, Barbara (1936—). Canadian ballet dancer. Born 1936 in Windsor, Ontario, Canada. ❖ Performed 1 year with the corps de ballet of American Ballet Theater in NY (1958); moved to London, where she danced with the Royal Ballet in such works as *The Sleeping Beauty, Les Sylphides* and *Cinderella* (1959–62); joined City Center Joffrey Ballet (1966) and was featured in Balanchine's *Scotch Symphony* and Bournonville's *Konservatoriet* and as Venus in Ruthanna Boris' *Cakewalk*.

REMLER, Emily (1957–1990). American jazz guitarist. Born Sept 18, 1957, in New York, NY; grew up in Englewood, New Jersey; died of a drug overdose (some say heart attack), May 4, 1990, in Sydney, Australia; studied at Berklee College, 1974–76. ❖ Influenced by Wes Montgomery, Charlie Christian and George Benson, recorded 1st album, *Firefly* (1980); as a result, was invited to jazz festivals around the world; bebopper and composer, also had her own band and accompanied Astrud Gilberto; listed as one of 100 greatest guitarists of the 20th century in *Musician* (Feb 1993); released a string of fine recordings with Concord (1981–88); albums include *East to West* and *Catwalk*.

REMOND, Sarah Parker (1826–1894). African-American abolitionist. Born in Salem, Massachusetts, June 6, 1826; died in Rome, Italy, Dec 13, 1894; dau. of John Remond and Nancy (Lenox) Remond (both abolitionists); sister of Charles Lenox Remond, well-known anti-slavery lecturer in both US and Great Britain; educated at Bedford College for Ladies in London; studied medicine at Santa Maria Nuova Hospital in Florence, Italy, 1866–68; m. Lazzaro Pinto (an Italian), April 1877. ❖ At 16, gave 1st lecture against slavery (1842); came to prominence among abolitionists, when she refused to sit in the segregated section of the Howard Athenaeum in Boston (1853); became an agent of the American Anti-Slavery Society (1856), lecturing widely with brother in New York State and eastern half of US; appeared on platform of Women's Rights Convention in New York City (1858); arrived in England (1859), where she began a lecture tour; spent nearly the rest of her life abroad; through involvement with the London Emancipation Society and the Freedmen's Aid Association, helped raise funds to support former slaves and their families; moved to Florence, Italy (1866). ❖ See also *Women in World History*.

RÉMUSAT, Claire, comtesse de (1780–1821). French writer and countess. Name variations: Claire de Rémusat or Claire de Remusat; countess of Remusat. Pronunciation: Ray-MU-zah. Born Clair Élisabeth Gravier de Vergennes in 1780; died 1821; m. Comte de Rémusat (court chamberlain); children: François Marie Charles de Rémusat, known as Charles, comte de Rémusat (1797–1875, politician and writer). ❖ A noted beauty in the court of Napoleon, was a lady-in-waiting and intimate friend of Empress Josephine; her *Mémoirs* are particularly valuable for the light they throw on the court of the First Empire. ❖ See also *Women in World History*.

RÉMY, Caroline (1855–1929). *See Séverine.*

RENARD, Rosita (1894–1949). Chilean pianist. Born in Santiago, Chile, 1894; died of encephalitis in Santiago, May 24, 1949; studied in Berlin with Martin Krause. ❖ Made American debut (1917) and was immediately hailed as one of the greatest living pianists; after WWI, returned to Chile where she played an important role in reorganizing the Santiago Conservatory; recorded *Rosita Renard at Carnegie Hall: Jan 19, 1949,* which includes stunning performances of works by Bach, Chopin, Mendelssohn and Ravel. ❖ See also *Women in World History*.

RENATA. *Variant of Renée.*

RENATO (1833–1913). *See Acosta de Samper, Soledad.*

RENAUD, Madeleine (1903–1994). French actress. Born in Paris, France, Feb 21, 1903; died in Neuilly, Sept 23, 1994; educated at Conservatoire of Dramatic Art in Paris; m. Charles Grandval; m. Jean-Louis Barrault (actor and director), 1940. ❖ Made stage debut as Agnes in *L'École des Femmes* at Comédie Française (1923), beginning a professional relationship there that would endure for next 26 years; performing in productions by Molière, Marivaux and Musset, acted with the company in Paris and on tour; had 1st sizeable film role in *Jean de la Lune* (1931), followed by *La Belle Marinière, La Couturière de Lunéville* and *Mistigri* (all 1932); also appeared as Ophelia in Grandval's stage production of *Hamlet* (1932); received Grand Prize of French Cinema for performance in *Maria Chapdelaine* (1934); appeared at Comédie Française in *Le Chandelier* and *Les Fausses Confidences* (1935); starred opposite Jean-Louis Barrault in film *Hélène* (1936); appeared in several films of Jean Grémillon, including *L'Etrange M. Victor* (1938), *Remorques* (1940), *Lumière d'Été* (1942) and *Le Ciel est à Vous* (1943); at Comédie Française, starred in husband's productions of *Les Mal Aimés* and *Le Soulier de Satin*; also appeared with him in Salacrou's *Les Fiancés du Havre*; formed Madeleine Renaud–Jean-Louis Barrault Co. (1946), taking over management of the Marigny Theatre and quickly gaining a reputation for showcasing both classics by Molière and Shakespeare as well as adaptations and/or premieres of works by modern writers, including Kafka, Camus, Beckett, Genet, Ionesco, and Anouilh. ❖ See also *Women in World History*.

RENAULT, Mary (1905–1983). English-born writer. Name variations: Mary Challans; (pseudonym) Mary Martin. Pronunciation: Rehn-OHLT. Born Mary Challans, Sept 4, 1905, in London, England; died Dec 13, 1983, at Cape Town, South Africa; dau. of Dr. Frank Challans (physician) and Mary Clementine Newsome Baxter Challans; attended St. Hugh's College, Oxford, and Radliffe infirmary, Oxford; never married; lived with Julie Mullard (a nurse), for approximately 50 years; no children. ❖ Bestselling author whose historical novels, set in ancient Greece, drew both an international following and the admiration of classical scholars, 1st worked as a nurse (1938–45); published 1st novel, *Purposes of Love* (1939); won the annual Metro-Goldwyn-Mayer prize for the best novel of the year for *Return to Night* (1947); moved to South Africa (1948); published *The Last of the Wine,* the 1st of a series of novels set in ancient Greece (1956); became active in Women's Defence of the Constitution League (1956); elected fellow of Royal Society of Literature (1959); helped reorganize the PEN Clubs in South Africa (1961); was the 1st writer to acquire a worldwide reading audience for novels dealing predominantly with homosexual characters. Writings include *The Charioteer* (1953), *The King Must Die* (1958), *The Bull from the Sea* (1962), *The Mask of Apollo* (1966), *The Persian Boy* (1972) and *Funeral Games* (1981). ❖ See also Bernard F. Dick, *The Hellenism of Mary Renault* (Southern Illinois Press, 1972); David Sweetman, *Mary Renault* (Harcourt, 1993); Peter Wolfe, *Mary Renault* (Twayne, 1969); and *Women in World History*.

RENDALL, Martha (d. 1909). Western Australian serial killer. Hanged in Fremantle Jail in western Australia, Oct 6, 1909; m. Thomas Morris. ❖ Using a throat swab to administer hydrochloric acid, murdered 3 of her stepchildren (1909); condemned to death, was the last woman hanged in western Australia.

RENDELL, Ruth (1930—). British mystery novelist and short-story writer. Name variations: (pseudonym) Barbara Vine. Born Ruth Barbara Grasemann, Feb 17, 1930, in London, England; dau. of Arthur Grasemann and Ebba Elise (Kruse) Grasemann (teachers); m. Donald John Rendell (journalist), 1950 (div. 1959, remarried him, 1977); children: Simon Rendell. ❖ Published 1st novel, *From Doon with Death* (1964), in which she introduced the character of Chief Inspector

Wexford; after a slow start, began to win prizes and sell well; admired by critics for characterization and ability to build suspense, wrote over 50 crime novels and collections of short stories; works include *Wolf to the Slaughter* (1967), *Murder Being Once Done* (1972), *A Demon in My View* (1976), *The Lake of Darkness* (1980), *The Tree of Hands* (1984), *The House of Stairs* (1989), *Anna's Book* (1993), *Road Rage* (1997), *Piranha to Scurfy* (2000) and *The Bridesmaid*. Awarded Crime Writers' Association Cartier Diamond Dagger (1977) and Sunday Times Literary Award (1990); made CBE (1996).

RENDLE, Sharon (1966—). English judoka. Born June 18, 1966, in UK. ❖ At Barcelona Olympics, won a bronze medal in half-lightweight 52 kg (1992).

RENDSCHMIDT, Elsa (1886–1969). German figure skater. Name variations: Else Rendschmidt. Born Jan 11, 1886, in Germany; died Oct 9, 1969. ❖ At London Olympics, won a silver medal for singles (1908); placed 2nd at World championships (1908, 1910) and won German nationals (1911).

RENÉE (1926—). New Zealand novelist and playwright. Name variations: Renée Taylor (married name). Born Renée Gertrude Jones in 1926 in Napier, New Zealand; dau. of Maori mother; attended Massey University; married (div. 1981). ❖ Worked as journalist and teacher and published in feminist publication *Broadsheet*; works are realist, with feminist, lesbian sensibility; plays include *Setting the Table* (1982), *Dancing* (1983), *Wednesday to Come* (1985), *Pass it On* (1986), *Born to Clean* (1987), *Touch of the Sun* (1990), and *Jeannie Once* (1991); fiction includes *Finding Ruth* (1987), *Willy Nilly* (1990), *Daisy and Lily* (1993), and *Does This Make Sense to You?* (1995).

RENÉE DE BOURBON (fl. 1477). Abbess of Fontevrault. Name variations: Renee of Bourbon. Flourished in 1477 in central France. ❖ Spent most of her life trying to rid France's monasteries of corruption. ❖ See also *Women in World History*.

RENÉE OF FRANCE (1510–1575). Duchess of Ferrara. Name variations: Renata of France; Renee of France; Renée of Ferrara; Renée, duchess of Ferraro; Renee, duchess of Italy; (Ital.) Renata di Francia. Born at Blois on Oct 25, 1510; died in 1575; 2nd dau. of Louis XII, king of France (r. 1498–1515), and Anne of Brittany (1477–1514); sister of Claude de France (1499–1524); m. Hercules II also known as Ercole II (1508–1559, future duke of Ferrara and son of Lucrezia Borgia), in 1528; children: Alfonso II (1533–1597), 5th duke of Ferrara and Modena; Cardinal Luigi d'Este (1538–1586); Anne of Ferrara (1531–1607, who m. Francis of Lorraine, 2nd duke of Guise); Lucrezia d'Este (1535–1598, duchess of Urbino, who m. Francesco Maria II della Rovere); Eleonora d'Este (1537–1581). ❖ After being betrothed successively to Gaston de Foix, Charles of Austria (future emperor Charles V), his brother Ferdinand, Henry VIII of England, and elector Joachim II of Brandenburg, was married at 18 to Ercole II d'Este; her court became a rendezvous for men and women of letters and her closest friends were Vittoria Colonna and Margaret of Angoulême, queen of Navarre; her court was also a refuge for the persecuted French Calvinists, much to the displeasure of husband who eventually banished her friends, took her children from her, and threw her into prison; was released when she recanted; after husband's death (1559), returned to France and turned her duchy of Montargis into a center for Protestantism. ❖ See also *Women in World History*.

RENÉE OF MONTPENSIER (fl. 1500s). Duchess of Lorraine. Name variations: Renee of Montpensier. Flourished in early 1500s; m. Antoine or Anthony, duke of Lorraine (r. 1508–1544); children: Francis I, duke of Lorraine (r. 1544–1545).

RENGER, Annemarie (1919—). German politician. Name variations: Annemarie Renger-Loncarevic. Born Annemarie Wildung in Leipzig, Oct 7, 1919; dau. of Fritz Wildung (one of the founders of German socialist workers' sports movement) and Martha (Scholz) Wildung; had 4 brothers (3 of whom were killed on battlefields as German soldiers during WWII) and 1 sister; attended a lyceum in Berlin; m. Emil Renger (advertising manager), 1938 (killed fighting near Chartres, France, 1944); m. Aleksandar Loncarevic; children: (1st m.) Rolf Renger (b. 1938). ❖ One of the best-known women in public office in West Germany, began working as personal assistant to Social Democratic leader Kurt Schumacher (1945); successfully ran as a Social Democratic candidate for a seat representing Schleswig-Holstein in the Bundestag (1953); would retain her parliamentary seat without interruption until 1990; was a member of SPD Parteivorstand (managing committee,

1961–73) and a member of SPD Parteipräsidium (party council, 1970–73); was 1 of the 4 members of SPD parliamentary office responsible for the financial, personnel, and organizational affairs of the party within the Bundestag (1969–72); elected president of the Bundestag (1972), the 1st woman to hold that office; relinquished the Bundestag presidency to run unsuccessfully for presidency of the Federal Republic (1976), then became the Bundestag's vice-president, a post she retained until the 1st national elections of newly unified Germany were held in Dec 1990; retired from politics (1990); was chair of the Bundestag delegates working for better German-Israeli relations and chaired German Helsinki Human Rights Committee; was also a leading personality of German Council for the European Movement, serving as its president for many years. ❖ See also *Women in World History*.

RENIE. *Variant of Renée.*

RENK, Silke (1967—). German track-and-field athlete. Born June 30, 1967, in Erfurt, Germany. ❖ At Barcelona Olympics, won a gold medal in javelin throw (1992).

RENNEVILLE, Sophie de (1772–1822). French novelist. Name variations: Sophie de Senneterre. Born Sophie de Senneterre, 1772, in Caen, France; died 1822. ❖ Highly educated, began writing to support family after Revolution; was regarded as a pioneering feminist writer, though she held traditional views about a woman's relationship to her husband; works include *Lettres d'Octavie, une pensionnaire* (1806), *Contes à ma petite fille et à mon petit garçon* (1811), *La Mère gouvernante* (1811), *Le Conteur moraliste* (1816), and *Les Secrets du coeur* (1816); helped run the women's journal *Athénée des Dames*.

RENNIE, Rhoda. South African swimmer. Born in South Africa. ❖ At Amsterdam Olympics, won a bronze medal in 4 x 100-meter freestyle relay (1928).

RENO, Janet (1938—). American lawyer and attorney general. Born in Miami, Florida, July 21, 1938; dau. of Henry Reno (police reporter for *The Miami Herald*) and Jane (Wood) Reno (investigative reporter for *Miami News*); Cornell University, AB in chemistry, 1960; Harvard University Law School, law degree, 1963; never married; no children. ❖ One of 16 women in class of 500 at Harvard Law School, was elected state attorney for Dade County, the 1st woman to head a county prosecutor's office in Florida (1978); despite being a Democrat in a heavily Republican county, won 4 reelections; reformed the juvenile justice system, aggressively prosecuting child-abuse cases and pursuing delinquent fathers for child support; also established an innovative drug court in which non-violent offenders without records were not automatically sent to jail; though she became widely respected for her tough fair-mindedness and approachability, her tenure as chief prosecutor was seldom smooth; became 1st woman appointed attorney general of the US (1993) and served through 2 administrations (1993–2001); made her mark as a pioneer in law enforcement, gaining both admirers and detractors during an often volatile tenure as the nation's "top cop" in the Clinton administration; stood firm in her belief that prison is not necessarily the best response to criminal acts, strongly supported the strict principles of due process and protection of the innocent, advocated for reformation and community reintegration of youthful offenders, and demonstrated concern about the elimination of sexual and racial discrimination and about protection of the environment; unsuccessfully ran for governor of Florida (2001). Inducted into Women's Hall of Fame at Seneca Falls, New York (autumn 2000). ❖ See also *Women in World History*.

RENOIR, Catherine (1899–1979). *See Hessling, Catherine.*

RENOTH, Heidi Maria (1978—). German giant-slalom snowboarder. Born Feb 28, 1978, in Berchtesgaden, Germany. ❖ Won a gold medal for slalom at World championships (1997); at Nagano, won the 1st silver medal ever awarded for women's giant-slalom snowboarding at Winter Olympics (1998); retired (2003).

RENSCH, Katharina (1964—). East German gymnast. Born Oct 7, 1964, in East Germany. ❖ At Moscow Olympics, won a bronze medal in team all-around (1980).

RENTOUL, Annie Isobel (c. 1855–1928). Australian artist. Born Anne Isoble Rattray in South America, c. 1855; died in Hawthorne, Melbourne, 1928; m. John Laurence Rentoul (Presbyterian moderator-general and professor of theology); children: 6, including artist Ida Rentoul Outhwaite (1888–1960) and writer Annie Rattray Rentoul (1882–1978). ❖ An artist in her own right, collaborated with daughter

Ida in creating *Mollie's Staircase* (1906). ❖ See also *Women in World History*.

RENTOUL, Annie Rattray (1882–1978). Australian educator and writer. Born Annie Rattray Rentoul, Sept 22, 1882; died 1978; dau. of John Laurence Rentoul (Presbyterian moderator-general and professor of theology) and Annie Isobel Rentoul (amateur watercolorist); elder sister of artist Ida Rentoul Outhwaite (1888–1960). ❖ Became the 1st student at Presbyterian Ladies' College (PLC) to take the classics exhibition (1902); went on to earn a 1st-class honors degree at University of Melbourne (1905), as well as winning the Wyselaskie Scholarship in Classics and Logic and sharing the Higgins prize for poetry; her many published fairy stories proved lastingly popular. ❖ See also *Women in World History*.

RENZI, Anna (c. 1620–1660). Italian mezzo-soprano. Born c. 1620 in Rome, Italy; died 1660. ❖ Began singing in teens and trained under Filiberto Laurenzi with whom she remained associated until 1644; moved to Venice and became well known for important roles in operas by Sacrati, Monteverdi, and others.

REPKO, Elena (1975—). Ukrainian climber. Born Aug 1, 1975, in Kharkov, Ukraine. ❖ Dominated speed climbing in 2000–01 season, winning every event except X Games; won 1st place in Speed at competitions including UKR National championship, Sevastopol, Ukraine (1999), UIAA World Cup-Speed, Nantes, France (2000), European championship, Munich, Germany (2000), X Games (2001), UIAA World championship, Winterthur, Switzerland (2001), UIAA World Cup, Lecco, Italy (2002), and UIAA Worldcup, Singapore (2002); won silver at X Games in Speed Climbing (2000); received 1st-place year-end ranking (2001).

REPPLIER, Agnes (1855–1950). American essayist and short-story writer. Pronunciation: Rep-LEER. Born in Philadelphia, Pennsylvania, April 1, 1855; died in Philadelphia, Dec 15, 1950; dau. of John George Repplier and Agnes (Mathias) Repplier; never married; no children. ❖ Published 1st short stories and sketches (1871); received 1st national attention for a short story appearing in *Catholic World* (1881); turned to writing essays, a form she would never abandon, and work appeared often in *Atlantic Monthly*; traveled and lectured extensively, primarily in Europe (from 1890s); writings include *Books and Men* (1888), *Points of View* (1891), *Essays in Miniature* (1892), *In the Dozy Hours and Other Papers* (1894), *Varia* (1897), *Philadelphia: The Place and the People* (1898), *Compromises* (1904), *A Happy Half-Century and Other Essays* (1908), *The Cat* (1912), *Counter-Currents* (1916), *Points of Friction* (1920), *Time and Tendencies* (1931), *In Pursuit of Laughter* (1936), and *Eight Decades: Essays and Episodes* (1937); also wrote biographies *J. William White, M.D.* (1919), *Père Marquette* (1929), *Mère Marie of the Ursulines* (1931), *Junípero Serra* (1933) and *Agnes Irwin* (1934). ❖ See also autobiography *In Our Convent Days* (1905); and *Women in World History*.

RERE-O-MAKI (d. 1868). New Zealand tribal leader. Name variations: Rawinia (Lavinia). Born Rere-o-maki, c. late 1780s, near Wanganui River (baptismal name was Rawinia); died 1868 (about 85 years old); buried Mar 24, 1868, near Putiki; dau. of Te Aewa (warrior) and Titia; m. Mahuera Paki Tanguru-o-te-rangi (Muaupoko leader, died 1868); children: 2. ❖ Of Te Arawa and Ngati Tupoho ancestry, was one of 5 women to sign Treaty of Waitangi (1840); carving of her likeness held at Wanganui Regional Museum and portion of Wanganui River named in her honor. ❖ See also *Dictionary of New Zealand Biography* (Vol. 1).

RESCHKE, Karin (1940—). German novelist. Born 1940 in Krakow, Poland. ❖ Works include autobiographical *Memoiren eines Kindes* (Memoirs of a Child, 1980), *Verfolgte des Glücks. Findebuch der Henriette Vogel* (1982), *Dieser Tage über Nacht* (1984), *Margarete* (1984), *Das Lachen im Wald* (1993), *Von Schleswig nach Holstein: Skizzen vom Ostseestrand* (1999), *Spiel ende* (2000), and *Birnbaums Bilder* (2001).

RESINO, Carmen (1941—). Spanish playwright. Born 1941 in Spain. ❖ Was first president of Asociación de Dramaturgas Españolas founded in Madrid (1987); works include *El presidente* (1969).

RESNIK, Judith (1949–1986). American astronaut. Born Judith Arlene Resnik, April 5, 1949, at Akron, Ohio; killed in space, Jan 28, 1986; dau. of Dr. Marvin Resnik (optometrist) and Sarah Polensky Resnik (secretary); m. Michael D. Oldak, July 14, 1970 (div. 1976); Carnegie-Mellon University, BS, 1970, University of Maryland, PhD, 1977. ❖ The 1st Jewish astronaut to fly in space, was selected for 1st group of women

astronauts (1978); on the shuttle "Discovery," completed one mission as 2nd American woman in space (1984); killed on *Challenger* space mission (1986). ❖ See also *Women in World History*.

RESNIK, Muriel (c. 1917–1995). American novelist and playwright. Born c. 1917 in New Haven, CT; died Mar 6, 1995, age 78, in NYC; m. Wallace Litwin. ❖ Wrote many novels, including *The Girl in the Turquoise Bikini* (later filmed as *How Sweet It Is!*), and the long-running play *Any Wednesday* (1964–66), also adapted for the screen.

RESNIK, Regina (1922—). American soprano, mezzo-soprano, and opera director. Born Aug 30, 1922, in the Bronx, NY; dau. of Ukrainian immigrants; Hunter College, BA, 1942; studied with Rosalie Miller and Giuseppe Danise; m. Harry W. Davis (attorney), 1946. ❖ Made concert debut at Brooklyn Academy of Music (1942); made operatic debut at New Opera Company (1942); debuted at Metropolitan Opera as Leonora in *Il Trovatore* (1944), then sang Leonore in *Fidelio*, in Met's 1st English-language version of that Beethoven opera (1945); over the next years, sang such roles as Tosca, Aïda, Butterfly, Donna Anna, and Donna Elvira; also sang in US premieres of Benjamin Britten's *Rape of Lucretia* (as the Chorus, 1947) and *Peter Grimes* (1948); debuted as Sieglinde in *Die Walküre* at Bayreuth (1953); switched from soprano to mezzo-soprano roles (1955), among them: Marina in *Boris Godunoff*, Amneris in *Aïda*, Ortrud in *Lohengrin*, Giulietta in *Tales of Hoffmann*, and Lucretia in *Rape of Lucretia*; retired from opera and achieved success as a director of opera, with productions of *Carmen* in Hamburg, *Elektra* in Venice, and *Falstaff* in Warsaw. ❖ See also *Women in World History*.

RESPIGHI, Elsa (1894–1996). Italian composer, organist, pianist, singer, and writer. Born Olivieri Sangiacomo in Rome, Italy, Mar 24, 1894; died at age 101, April or May 1996; m. Ottorino Respighi (1879–1936, composer). ❖ Studied piano with Clotide Poce and Giovanni Sgambati; attended Accademia de Santa Cecilia, studying advanced harmony and counterpoint under Remigio Renzi and fugue and composition under Ottorino Respighi whom she later married; with husband, toured the world and often sang their compositions; devoted latter part of her life to husband's music, completing the orchestration of his opera *Lucrezia* and producing *Belfagor*, *Fiamma*, *Campana Sommersa*, and *Maria Egiziaca*; founded the *Respighi Fondo* in Venice (1969); wrote 2 operas, *Alcesti* (1941) and *Samurai* (1945), composed 4 orchestral works as well as a ballet and many vocal works, and also wrote the text for 2 ballets by her husband as well as his biography. ❖ See also *Women in World History*.

RESTELL, Madame (1812–1878). *See Lohman, Ann Trow.*

RESTITUTA, Sister (1894–1943). Austrian nun and nurse. Name variations: Helene Kafka. Born Helene Kafka, May 1, 1894, in Husowitz near Brünn, Moravia (now Brno, Czech Republic); executed by decapitation in Vienna, Austria, Mar 30, 1943. ❖ Worked for years as an operating-room nurse at Vienna's Mödling Hospital; critical of Nazi regime in Austria from its inception, wrote 2 pamphlets disparaging the war and Hitler's rule and placed them in the pockets of her patients, all of whom were wounded soldiers (1941); arrested (Feb 18, 1942), was found guilty by the Nazi People's Court in Vienna on charges of "preparation for high treason" (Oct 29, 1942). ❖ See also *Women in World History*.

RESTOUX, Marie-Claire (1968—). French judoka. Name variations: Restoux-Gasset. Born April 9, 1968, in La Rochefoucauld, France. ❖ Won a gold medal for 48–52 kg half-lightweight at Atlanta Olympics (1996); won World championships (1995, 1997).

RESTREPO, Ximena (1969—). Colombian track-and-field athlete. Name variations: Ximena Restrepo Gaviria; Ximena Restrepo-Gaviria. Born Mar 10, 1969, in Medellin, Colombia; attended University of Nebraska-Lincoln; m. Gert Weil; children: son. ❖ Won NCAA 400 meters (1991); at Barcelona Olympics, won a bronze medal in 400 meters (1992).

RESTZOVA, Anfisa (1964—). *See Reztsova, Anfisa.*

RESVOLD, Hanna (1873–1943). *See Resvoll-Holmsen, Hanna.*

RESVOLD, Thekla (1871–1948). *See Resvoll, Thekla.*

RESVOLD-DIESET, Hanna (1873–1943). *See Resvoll-Holmsen, Hanna.*

RESVOLL, Thekla (1871–1948). Norwegian botanist. Name variations: Thekla Ragnhild Holmsen; Thekla Resvold. Born Thekla Susanne Ragnhild Resvoll, May 22, 1871, in the Vågå valley of southern Norway; died June 14, 1948; dau. of Hans and Julie Marie (Deichman) Resvoll; sister of Hanna Resvoll-Holmsen (1873–1943),

Norwegian explorer; married Andreas Holmsen, 1895; children: son Dag Resvoll Holmsen (b. 1905). ❖ An expert on Norway's mountain flora, attended University of Christiana (Oslo, 1892–99), University of Copenhagen (1899–1900), University of Zurich and University of Munich (1903–04); earned PhD (1917) and wrote a thesis on the adaptations of mountain plants (germane to cold and short summers); elected a Norwegian Academy of Sciences member (1923); worked as an assistant professor and lecturer at University of Christiana (1902–36); took a sabbatical year at Botanical Garden in Buitenzog (Bogor), Java (1923–24).

RESVOLL-HOLMSEN, Hanna (1873–1943). Norwegian explorer, photographer and botanist. Name variations: Hanna Resvoll-Dieset; Hanna Resvold. Born Hanna Marie Resvoll, Sept 11, 1873, in the Vågå valley of southern Norway; died Mar 13, 1943, in Oslo, Norway; dau. of Hans and Julie Marie (Deichman) Resvoll; sister of Thekla Resvoll, botanist; m. a man named Dieset; m. Gunnar Holmsen (1880–1976), 1909; children: Per Holmsen (b. 1911). ❖ Was a member of a small Norwegian scientific expedition to Svalbard (Spitsbergen archipelago, 1907); photographed plant life.

RETHBERG, Elisabeth (1894–1976). German-born soprano. Name variations: Lisabeth Sättler or Sattler. Born Elisabeth Sättler, Sept 22, 1894, in Schwarzenberg, Saxony, Germany; died June 6, 1976, in Yorktown Heights, NY; studied piano and voice with Otto Watrin at Dresden Conservatory; became US citizen (1939); m. George Cehanovsky (baritone), 1957. ❖ Made debut in Strauss' *Der Zigeunerbaron* (1911); appeared as Agatha in *Der Freischütz* at Dresden Hofoper (1915); debuted at Salzburg (1922); made Metropolitan Opera debut in title role of *Aïda* (1922); starred at the Met (1922–42), in 30 roles and performed Aïda 51 times; also sang with Ravinia Park Opera in Chicago (1926–27); debuted at Covent Garden (1925); created title role in Strauss' *Ægyptische Helena* (*The Egyptian Helen*); was made an honorary member of State Theaters of Saxony (1930); often appeared on radio and made many recordings. ❖ See also *Women in World History*.

RETKVICKA, Solimna (1847–1926). See *Krasnohorska, Eliska*.

RETTER, Hannah (1839–1940). New Zealand midwife. Name variations: Hannah Stickle. Born Dec 12, 1839, probably in Sydney, Australia; died Aug 2, 1940, at Levin, New Zealand; dau. of Thomas Stickle (trader) and Turikatuku; m. Joseph Chapman Retter, 1861; children: 3 daughters, 5 sons. ❖ Served as midwife in small practice in village settlement of Levin (1900–26). ❖ See also *Dictionary of New Zealand Biography* (Vol. 3).

RETTON, Mary Lou (1968—). American gymnast. Born Jan 24, 1968, in Fairmont, West Virginia; m. Shannon Kelley (financial analyst), Dec 29, 1990; children: 4 daughters, Shayla (b. 1995), McKenna (b. 1997), Skyla (b. 2000) and Emma (b. 2002). ❖ Won Sanlam Cup (1982), American Cup, Chunichi Cup and Emerald Empire Cup (1983), American Classic, American Cup, Mardi Gras Invitational, Caesar's Palace Invitational, and US nationals (1984), and American Cup (1985); at Los Angeles Olympics, won a gold medal in all-around, silver medals in team all-around and vault, and bronze medals in uneven bars and floor exercises (1984); was the 1st woman in the world to complete a variation of the Tsukahara vault, the 1st American woman to win an individual Olympic medal in gymnastics, and the 1st official female spokesperson for Wheaties. ❖ See also Mary Lou Retton and Bela Karolyi *Mary Lou: Creating an Olympic Champion* (McGraw-Hill, 1986); Herman Silverstein *Mary Lou Retton and the New Gymnasts* (Watts, 1985); Rosemary G. Washington *Mary Lou Retton, Power Gymnast* (Lerner, 1985).

RETZ, duchesse de (1545–1603). See *Clermont, Claude-Catherine de*.

REUSS, Eleanor (1860–1917). See *Eleanora of Reuss*.

REUSS, princess of.
See *Hermine of Reuss (1887–1947)*.
See *Ida of Schaumburg-Lippe (1852–1891)*.

REUTELER, Fabienne (1979—). Swiss snowboarder. Born Sept 2, 1979, in Uster, Switzerland. ❖ At X Games, won a bronze medal for Superpipe (2000–01); won a bronze medal for halfpipe at Salt Lake City (2002) and a bronze medal for halfpipe at World championships (2003).

REUTER, Gabriele (1859–1941). German novelist. Born in Alexandria, Egypt, Feb 8, 1859; died in Weimar, Germany, Nov 16, 1941; dau. of Karl Reuter (businessman) and Johanne (Behmer) Reuter; granddau. of Magdalene Philippine Engelhard; some schooling in Wolfenbüttel and Neuhaldensleben, Germany; never married; no children. ❖ Began

writing after father's death (1872); published 1st novel *Glück und Geld* (Happiness and Money, 1888); published *Aus guter Familie* (From a Good Family, 1895), which was a phenomenal success and inspired extensive commentary and public debate about women's education and their role in modern society; writing about ordinary, middle-class German women at turn of 20th century, described the psychological bondage imposed on women by the expectations of society and the resulting frustration and anguish of their lives; writings include *Der Lebenskünstler* (The Artist of Life, 1897), *Frau Bürgelin und ihre Söhne* (Mrs. Bürgelin and Her Sons, 1899), *Ellen von der Weiden* (1900), which proved popular enough to merit 65 editions, *Frauenseelen* (Women's Souls, 1902), *Liselotte von Reckling* (1904), and *Das Tränenhaus* (The House of Tears, 1909), a picture of a maternity house for unmarried, pregnant women scorned by society; also wrote topical essays, including *Die Probleme der Ehe* (The Problems of Marriage, 1907) and *Liebe und Stimmrecht* (Love and Suffrage, 1914), and biographies of Marie Ebner-Eschenbach (1904) and Annette von Droste-Hülshoff (1905). ❖ See also autobiography (in German), *Vom Kinde zum Menschen* (From the Child to the Person, 1922); and *Women in World History*.

REVE JIMENEZ, Odalis (1970—). Cuban judoka. Born 1970 in Cuba. ❖ At Barcelona Olympics, won a gold medal in middleweight 66 kg (1992).

REVELL, Elizabeth Henrietta (1835/36–1922). See *Torlesse, Elizabeth Henrietta*.

REVENTLOV. See *Reventlow*.

REVENTLOW, Anne Sophie (1693–1743). Queen of Norway and Denmark. Name variations: Anna Sophie von Reventlow; Anna Sofie von Reventlow. Born April 16, 1693; died Jan 7, 1743, in Klausholm; became 3rd wife of Frederick IV, king of Norway and Denmark (r. 1699–1730), on April 4, 1721; children: Christiane Amalie (1723–1724); Frederick Christian (b. 1726); Charles (b. 1728).

REVENTLOW, Franziska von (1871–1918). German novelist and diarist. Name variations: Franziska Gräfin zuReventlow; Franziska gräfin von Reventlow; Franziska zu Reventlov. Born Fanny Liane Wilhelmine Sophie Adrienne Auguste Comtesse zu Reventlow, May 18, 1871, in Husumer Castle, Germany; died July 26, 1918, in Ascona, Italy; dau. of Detlev F. Count zu Reventlow, and Emilie Julia Anna Luise zu Reventlow; m. Walter Lübke, May 22, 1894 (div. 1897); children: Rolf (b. 1897). ❖ Daughter of aristocratic family who lived a bohemian life with son after marriage ended; scandalized Germany with countless affairs; lived in various places, including the Greenwich Village of Germany, Munich's Schwabing; her writing is essentially autobiographical and retains its value as a mirror to its time; her humor is sharp and still effective; works include *Ellen Olestjerne* (1903), *Herrn Dames Aufzeichnungen* (1913), and *Von Paul zu Pedro* (1912); also trans. works of Maupassant, Prévost and Anatole France into German.

REVERE, Anne (1903–1990). American actress. Born June 25, 1903, in New York, NY; died Dec 18, 1990, in Locust Valley, New York; studied acting at American Laboratory Theater; attended Wellesley College; m. Samuel Roser (stage director), 1935. ❖ Prominent character actress, made Broadway debut in *The Great Barrington* (1931) and reprised role in film version (1934); returning to New York, was cast as Martha Dobie in *The Children's Hour* (1934), which ran for 691 performances; worked in Hollywood (1940–51), appearing in such films as *The Howards of Virginia* (1940), *Men of Boys Town* (1941), *Old Acquaintance* (1943), *The Keys of the Kingdom* (1945), *The Thin Man Goes Home* (1945), *Dragonwyck* (1946), *The Shocking Miss Pilgrim* (1947), *Forever Amber* (1947), *Scudda-Hoo! Scudda-Hay!* (1948), *You're My Everything* (1949) and *A Place in the Sun* (1951); film career came to a crashing halt during McCarthy era (1951), when she was blacklisted for refusing to testify before House Un-American Activities Committee; returned to the stage and won a Tony for her performance in *Toys in the Attic* (1960); had a running part on ABC-tv soap opera "A Time for Us." Won Academy Award for Best Supporting Actress for *National Velvet* (1945); nominated for Best Supporting roles in *The Song of Bernadette* (1943) and *Gentleman's Agreement* (1947). ❖ See also *Women in World History*.

REVIER, Dorothy (1904–1993). American actress. Name variations: Dorothy Valegra. Born Doris Velegra, April 18, 1904, in San Francisco, CA; died Nov 19, 1993, in Hollywood, CA; m. Harry J. Revier (director). ❖ Began career as a cabaret dancer; made film debut in *The Broadway Madonna* (1922), followed by *The Wild Party, The Rose of Paris, Dangerous Pleasure, The Tigress, Sinner's Parade, Submarine, The*

Donovan Affair, Father and Son, Call of the West, Arm of the Law, By Candlelight, Unknown Blonde and *The Cowboy and the Kid*; probably best remembered as Milady de Winter in Allan Dwan's *The Iron Mask* (1929).

REVILLE, Alma (1899–1982). English screenwriter and screen editor. Name variations: Alma Hitchcock. Born Aug 14, 1899, in England; died July 6, 1982, in Bel Air, CA; m. Alfred Hitchcock (film director), Dec 1926; children: Patricia Hitchcock O'Connell (b. 1928, actress who appeared in *Strangers on a Train*). ❖ Broke into films (early 1920s), working as editor's assistant; was "script girl" for Alfred Hitchcock on 2 of his early directing projects: *The Pleasure Garden* (1925) and *The Lodger* (1926); subsequently edited many of his films; also collaborated as a screenwriter with him, earning story credits on 16 of his films, and collaborated with other directors as well. ❖ See also *Women in World History*.

REVSIN, Leslie (1944–2004). American chef. Born Leslie Kim Revsin, Oct 19, 1944, in Chicago, IL; died Aug 9, 2004, Shoreline, WA; attended University of California, Berkeley; graduate of Macalester College, 1966; graduate of New York Technical College; m. Bill Arp (tv producer, div.); m. Philip Carlson (talent agent), 1980; children: Rachel Arp Ramstead. ❖ Became the 1st woman to work as a chef in the kitchen of the Waldorf-Astoria Hotel in NY (1973); had her own place, Restaurant Leslie, in Greenwich Village (1977–81); became a tv cook and cookbook author; was chef at the Inn at Pound Ridge (1990–95).

REXACH, Lucienne Benitez (1905–1968). *See Benitez-Rexach, Lucienne.*

REXACH, Sylvia (1922–1961). Puerto Rican composer. Born in Santurce, Puerto Rico, Jan 20, 1922; died in Santurce, Oct 20, 1961; children: Sharon. ❖ Worked to lend dignity to pop music with such songs as "Y Entonces" ("And Then"), "Alma Adrentro" ("Deep in the Soul"), "Quisiera Ser" ("I Wish to Be"), "Anochecer" ("Dusk") and "Ola y Arena" ("Surf and Sand"), which became popular after her death; was a founding member and secretary general of the Puerto Rican Society of Writers, Composers, and Musical Editors. ❖ See also *Women in World History*.

REY, Margret (1906–1996). German-born American author. Name variations: Margret Elizabeth Rey. Born Margret Elizabeth Waldstein in Hamburg, Germany, May 16, 1906; died in Cambridge, Massachusetts, Dec 21, 1996; dau. of Felix Waldstein (member of the German Parliament) and Gertrude (Rosenfeld) Waldstein; attended Bauhaus in Dessau, 1927, Dusseldorf Academy of Art, 1928–29, University of Munich, 1930–31; m. H(ans) A(ugusto) Rey (1898–1977, writer and illustrator), in 1935; no children; became naturalized US citizen, 1946. ❖ Fled France with husband (1940), just hours before Nazis invaded Paris; took up residence in Greenwich Village, NY; immediately found a publisher for *Curious George*, illustrated by husband, which was destined to become a children's classic; published 7 books in the "Curious George" series which sold more than 20 million copies worldwide in 12 different languages; taught creative writing at Brandeis University (1978–84). ❖ See also Louise Borden, *The Journey That Saved Curious George: The True Wartime Escape of Margret and H. A. Rey* (2005); and *Women in World History*.

REYBAUD, Fanny (1802–1871). French novelist. Name variations: Henriette Arnaud or H. Pierre Arnaud; Henriette Reybaud; Fanny-Henriette Reybaud; Madame Reybaud; (pseudonym) Mme Charles Reybaud. Born Henriette Étienette Fanny Arnaud, 1802, in Aix, France; died Jan 1, 1871; m. M(arie) R(och) L(ouis) Reybaud (1799–1879, writer and politician). ❖ Writings include *Clémentine et Félise, Edouard Mongeron, Gabrielle, L'oncle César, La dernière bohémienne, Lazarilla, Le cabaret de Gaubert, Le Moine de Chaalis, Mademoiselle de Malepeire, Mémoires d'un garde de Paris,* and *Sans dot*; also wrote *Les Épaves* (1838), a story that influenced Hans Christian Andersen's play *Mulatten* (The Mulatto).

REYES, Dana Schoenfield (1953—). *See Schoenfield, Dana.*

REYES, Deborah Elizabeth (1952—). *See Meyer, Debbie.*

REYMOND, Claire (c. 1868—). French murderer (accused). Born c. 1868; m. Paul Reymond, 1888. ❖ Discovering husband's affair with Yvonne Lassimone, murdered Lassimone; turned herself into police; was tried for murder, but acquitted by a jury after only a few minutes of deliberation.

REYNOLDS, Adeline DeWalt (1862–1961). American actress. Name variations: Adeline De Walt Reynolds. Born Sept 19, 1862, in Benton County, IA; died Aug 13, 1961, in Hollywood, CA. ❖ Began career at age 78; made film debut in *Come Live with Me* (1941); other films

include *Going My Way, A Tree Grows in Brooklyn, The Corn is Green* and *Pony Express*; died, age 98, having just appeared on tv's "Have Gun, Will Travel."

REYNOLDS, Belle (fl. 1860s). American Civil War nurse and diarist. Born in Shelburne Falls, Massachusetts; m. William Reynolds from Peoria, Illinois, 1861. ❖ Began traveling with husband, a lieutenant in the Union Army who was serving in the 17th Infantry of Illinois (Aug 1861); survived battles and nursed wounded Union soldiers; awarded commission of major by governor of Illinois for her bravery and work during Battle of Shiloh (April 1862); with husband, left the army (1864). ❖ See also *Women in World History*.

REYNOLDS, Debbie (1932—). American actress and singer. Born Mary Frances Reynolds, April 1, 1932, in El Paso, TX; m. Eddie Fisher (singer), 1955 (div. 1959); m. Harry Karl (shoe magnate), 1960 (div. 1975); m. Richard Hamlett (real estate developer), 1984 (div.); children: Todd Fisher (tv director); Carrie Fisher (actress and writer). ❖ Named Miss Burbank (CA, 1948); made film debut in *June Bride* (1948), followed by *Three Little Words, Two Weeks with Love, Singin' in the Rain, Susan Slept Here, The Tender Trap, Bundle of Joy, Tammy and the Bachelor, This Happy Feeling, The Mating Game, The Pleasure of His Company, My Six Loves, Mary Mary, Goodbye Charlie, The Singing Nun* and *Mother,* among others; starred on Broadway in a revival of *Irene,* on tv in "The Debbie Reynolds Show" (1969–70), and frequently in nightclubs; opened her own Las Vegas museum for her enormous collection of Hollywood memorabilia. Nominated for Oscar for performance in *The Unsinkable Molly Brown* (1964). ❖ See also autobiography *Debbie: My Life* (1988).

REYNOLDS, Jane (c. 1897—). Irish murderer. Born c. 1897; children: 1 (b. July 1915). ❖ At 17, worked in Sligo at ice-cream shop of the married Angelo di Lucia, who began an affair with her; at Angelo's suggestion, helped him murder his wife Rosa di Lucia (Dec 9, 1914); was arrested shortly thereafter; trial was delayed a year, during which time, she gave birth to a child by Angelo (July 1915); found guilty of murder in Dublin, was sentenced to be hanged, but sentence was commuted to life imprisonment due to her age at time of crime; served 3 years then released with stipulation that she enter a convent. Di Lucia received the death sentence but his sentence was also commuted to life imprisonment.

REYNOLDS, Malvina (1900–1978). American folksinger and songwriter. Born Malvina Milder, Aug 23, 1900, in San Francisco, California; died Mar 17, 1978, in Berkeley, California; dau. of David Milder and Lizzie (Shenson) Milder; sister of Eleanor Milder Lawrence (b. 1910); University of California at Berkeley, BA in English language and literature, 1925, MA, 1927, PhD, 1939; m. Ben Goodman; m. Bud Reynolds (musician and labor organizer), 1935 (died 1971); children: Nancy Reynolds Schimmel (b. 1935). ❖ Prolific lyricist, musician, and muse of American folk and protest music, became a member of the Communist Party (1930s), having inherited parents' socialist philosophy and conscience; began to record thoughts and observations on social justice, world peace, and women's rights in poetry and song; started to perform her music publicly (1940s); was blacklisted for her Communist sympathies because of appearance before House Un-American Activities Committee (early 1950s); was "discovered" by the socially conscious folk-music world (early 1960s); wrote scores of songs, some of them classics which became major hits for well-known folk artists (mid-1970s); produced several collections of children's songs, as well as establishing her own music publishing company and recording company. Songs include "If I Had a Hammer" (co-written with Pete Seeger and Lee Hays), "Magic Penny," "Pied Piper," "Don't Talk to Me of Love," "We Hate to See Them Go," "Turn Around" (co-written with Harry Belafonte), "What Have They Done to the Rain?," "Morningtown Ride" and "Little Boxes," a sly swipe at the conformist ethic that so dominated the late 1950s and early 1960s. ❖ See also *Women in World History*.

REYNOLDS, Marjorie (1917–1997). American actress and dancer. Name variations: Marjorie Moore, Marjorie Goodspeed. Born Marjorie Goodspeed, Aug 12, 1917, in Buhl, ID; raised in Los Angeles; died Feb 1, 1997, in Manhattan Beach, CA; m. Jack Reynolds, 1936 (div. 1952); m. Jon M. Haffen (film editor), 1953 (died 1985). ❖ As a child, danced in a score of silent films, including the Ramon Navarro version of *Scaramouche*; made adult film debut as Marjorie Moore in *Wine, Woman and Song* (1939), followed by over 40 Westerns; starred with Crosby and Astaire in *Holiday Inn* (1942); other films include *Up in Mabel's Room, Ministry of Fear, Duffy's Tavern, The Great Swindle,*

Monsieur Beaucaire, The Time of Their Lives and *Heaven Only Knows*; starred as William Bendix's wife on tv series "The Life of Riley" (1953–58).

REYNOLDS, Mary (c. 1890–1974). Irish politician. Born c. 1890 in Drumcowra, Ballinamore, Co. Leitrim, Ireland; died Aug 29, 1974; m. Patrick Reynolds (Fine Gael TD, Sligo, died 1932); children: 7, including Patrick Joseph Reynolds (TD, later senator); grandchildren: Gerry Reynolds (TD). ❖ Following the death of deputy husband who was fatally shot during the election campaign, was returned to the 7th Dáil for Sligo/Leitrim (1932); though defeated in the following election, was returned to the 9th–16th Dáil (1937–61), holding the record for the woman winning the most elections; did not contest the election when Leitrim was divided between Sligo and Roscommon (1961).

REYNOLDS, Myra (1853–1936). American scholar and educator. Born in Troupsburg, New York, Mar 18, 1853; died in Los Angeles, California, Aug 20, 1936; dau. of Newell Lent Reynolds (school principal turned Baptist minister) and Emily (Knox) Reynolds; graduate of State Normal School, Mansfield, Pennsylvania, 1870; Vassar College, AB, 1880; University of Chicago, PhD, 1895. ❖ Acted as head of the English department at Wells College in Aurora, NY (1880–82); taught at Corning (NY) Free Academy (1882–84); taught English at Vassar (1884–92); named one of the 1st four fellows in English at University of Chicago (1892), becoming an assistant in English (1894), instructor, then assistant professor (1897), associate professor (1903), and full professor (1911); also became chair of a committee that founded the University of Chicago Settlement (1894); beginning in 1893, served as head of one of the university's earliest women's residence halls, Nancy Foster Hall, a position she held for next 30 years; published *The Treatment of Nature in English Poetry between Pope and Wordsworth* (1909), among others. ❖ See also *Women in World History*.

REYNOLDS, Rachel Selina (1838–1928). New Zealand social worker, suffragist, community leader, and memoirist. Name variations: Rachel Selina Pinkerton. Born Rachel Selina Pinkerton, Dec 19, 1838, in South Australia; died Aug 21, 1928, in Dunedin, New Zealand; dau. of William Pinkerton and Eleanor (Smith) Pinkerton; m. William Hunter Reynolds (merchant), 1856; children: 5 daughters, 4 sons. ❖ Active in numerous social-welfare organizations, helped found St Andrew's Church and established groups to assist the disadvantaged (late 1880s); served as president of Dunedin Free Kindergarten Association (1889); elected vice president of women's franchise league (1892). ❖ See also memoir, *Pioneering in Australia and New Zealand* (1929) and *Dictionary of New Zealand Biography* (Vol. 2).

REYNOLDS, Vera (1899–1962). American actress. Born Nov 25, 1899, in Richmond, VA; died April 22, 1962, in Beverly Hills, CA; m. Robert Ellis, 1926. ❖ Began career in Mack Sennett films (1918); also appeared in several Cecil B. DeMille productions; films include *The Golden Bed, The Road to Yesterday, Corporal Kate* and *Golf Widows*.

REZA, Yasmina (1959—). French playwright, novelist and screenwriter. Born 1959 in Paris, of Hungarian, Russian and Iranian descent; attended Paris X University and Jacques Lecoq Drama School; married a filmmaker; children: 1. ❖ Began career as an actress; wrote *Conversations after a Burial* (1987) and *Winter Crossing* (1990), both of which won the Molière Award; her 3rd play, *Art*, won the Molière Award (1994), became a smash hit in London (1996), and won a US Tony Award (1998); nominated for BBC Awards for Best New Play for *The Unexpected Man* (1999) and *Life x 3* (2001); wrote screenplays for *See You Tomorrow* and *Lulu Kreutz's Picnic*; wrote novel *Hammerklavier* (1997).

REZKOVA, Miloslava (1950—). Czech track-and-field athlete. Born July 22, 1950, in Czechoslovakia. ❖ At Mexico City Olympics, won a gold medal in high jump (1968).

REZTSOVA, Anfisa (1964—). Russian biathlete. Name variations: Anfisa Restzova. Born Dec 16, 1964, in Russia. ❖ Won a gold medal for 4 x 5 km relay and a silver medal for 20 km at Calgary Olympics (1988); won a gold medal for 7.5 km and a bronze medal for 3 x 7.5 km relay at Albertville Olympics (1992); won a gold medal for 4 x 7.5 km relay at Lillehammer Olympics (1994).

RHEAUME, Manon (1972—). Canadian ice-hockey player. Pronounciation: MAY-nohn RAY-ohm. Born Feb 24, 1972, in Lac Beauport, Quebec, Canada; sister of Pascal Rheaume (hockey player); m. Gerry St. Cyr (Canadian roller-hockey player). ❖ Won a gold medal at World championships (1992, 1994); became the 1st woman to play in the National Hockey League (NHL), as goaltender for the Tampa Bay Lightning (1992); won a team silver medal at Nagano (1998), the 1st Olympics to feature women's ice hockey; retired from Canadian national team (2000) but continued to play professionally in the National Women's Hockey League.

RHIND, Ethel (c. 1879–1952). Irish artist. Born c. 1879 in Bengal, India; died 1952; educated at Londonderry High School, School of Art, Belfast, and Dublin Metropolitan School of Art. ❖ Awarded a scholarship to study mosaic at the Dublin Metropolitan School of Art (1902); her window in Old Court Chapel in Strangford, Co. Down, won 1st prize at Royal Dublin Society (1908); worked at An Túr Gloine (Tower of Glass) and also designed pieces for Grangegorman Church in Dublin, Magheralin Church in Co. Down, and Edna's Church in Spiddal, Co. Galway; was a member of the Guild of Irish Artworkers and exhibited at the Arts and Crafts Society of Ireland (1910, 1917, and 1921). ❖ See also *Women in World History*.

RHODA. Biblical woman. Servant in the house of Mary of Jerusalem.

RHODE, Kim (1979—). American shooter. Born Kimberly Rhode, July 16, 1979, in Whittier, CA; dau. of Richard Rhode (her coach); attended California State Polytechnic University. ❖ Won a gold medal at Atlanta Olympics (1996) and a bronze medal at Sydney Olympics (2000), both for double trap (120 targets); won a gold medal at Pan American Games (1998) and a World Cup in Perth (2003); won a gold medal for double trap at Athens Olympics (2004).

RHODES, Betty (c. 1935–1987). American actress and singer. Born c. 1935 in WA; died Dec 30, 1987, in New York, NY. ❖ Appeared in the original (1968) and 2 revivals (1981 and 1983) of *Jacques Brel is Alive and Well . . .*; also performed in cabarets and at Carnegie Hall; released album *No Regrets*.

RHODES, Billie (1894–1988). American comedic star of stage, vaudeville, and silent-screen. Born Aug 15, 1894, in San Francisco, CA; died Mar 12, 1988, in Los Angeles, CA. ❖ Made film debut with Kalem Company in *Perils of the Sea* (1913); made over 200 other films, including *The Big Horn Massacre, Putting Her Foot in It, Hoop-La, Almost a King, And the Best Man Won, Beware of Blondes, The Lion and the Lamb, The Love Call* and *Leave it to Gerry*.

RHODES, Izora. (1942–2004). See Armstead, Izora.

RHODES, Mary (c. 1782–1853). American nun and religious founder. Born c. 1782 in Maryland; died at Loretto, Kentucky, Feb 27, 1853; dau. of Abraham Rhodes (planter and slave owner) and Elizabeth Rhodes; sister of Ann Rhodes (1st mother superior of Sisters of Loretto, died 1812); educated by Nuns of the Visitation in Georgetown (now Washington, DC); never married; no children. ❖ Roman Catholic nun and co-founder of the Sisters of Loretto, moved to Kentucky and opened a school for girls (1811); with Reverend Charles Nerinckx, founded the Sisters of Loretto, one of the 1st orders of Roman Catholic nuns on the frontier, and took the veil (1812); served as mother superior (1812–22). ❖ See also *Women in World History*.

RHODES, Zandra (1940—). English fashion designer. Name variations: Zandra Lindsey Rhodes. Born 1940 in Chatham, Kent, England; attended Medway College of Art, 1959–61, and Royal College of Art, School of Textile and Design, 1961–64; lived with Salah Hassanein (former president of Warner Bros. International Theaters). ❖ Was introduced to the world of fashion by her mother who was a fitter in Paris fashion house and teacher at Medway College of Art; became part of the new wave of British designers who put London at forefront of international fashion scene (1970s), opening The Fulham Road Clothes Shop with others; took cues from street-punk fashion for "Conceptual Chic" collection (1977), employing safety pins, exposed seams and torn fabrics in designs; known for screen prints and hand-decorated textiles adorned with flowers, lips, rock landscapes and zigzag patterns, designed for everyone from Princess Diana to Freddie Mercury; established studio in California (1995), to develop interior design business; worked with David Humphries to produce terrazzo floors for The Fashion and Textile Museum Grand Entrance in London (2000); commissioned by San Diego Opera to design costumes for *The Magic Flute* (2001). Named British Royal Designer of the Year (1972); won Emmy Award for costumes for *Romeo and Juliet on Ice* (1984); made Commander of the British Empire (CBE, 1997). ❖ See also Zandra Rhodes and Anne Knight, *The Art of Zandra Rhodes* (Jonathan Cape, 1984).

RHODOGUNE (fl. 2nd c. BCE). Queen of ancient Parthia. Name variations: Rodogune. Dau. of Mithradates I, king of Parthia (died 138 BCE); sister of Phraates II; m. Demetrius II Nicator of Syria (former Seleucid king who was already married to Cleopatra Thea), 140 BCE. ❖ Was married to her father's captive, Demetrius. ❖ See also *Women in World History.*

RHODOPIS (fl. 6th c. BCE). Thracian courtesan. Name variations: Rhadopis; Rhodope; (real name) Doricha. Flourished in the 6th century BCE. ❖ Legendary beauty, was owned by Iadmon from the Greek island of Samos, who also owned Aesop, the fabulist; was relocated to Naucratis where she met Charaxus of Mytilene, who purchased her freedom and set her up in business; made a fortune at Naucratis, but not enough to finance the great pyramid at Giza which some of Herodotus' contemporaries (5th century BCE) believed she had erected as a monument to herself. ❖ See also *Women in World History.*

RHONDDA, Margaret (1883–1958). Welsh publisher. Name variations: Lady Margaret Rhondda; Margaret Haig, Viscountess Rhondda; Margaret Haig Thomas; Margaret Mackworth. Born Margaret Haig Thomas in South Wales, 1883; died 1958; only dau. of David Alfred Thomas (industrialist) and Sybil (Haig) Thomas; educated at St. Andrews; spent 1 year at Somerville College, Oxford; m. Humphrey Mackworth, 1908 (div. 1923). ❖ As a business associate of her father's, was sent to America on *Lusitania* (1916), but rescued from the sinking ship; went on to a viscountcy (1918); after becoming a successful businesswoman, at one time serving as director of 33 companies, was granted royal permission to attend the House of Lords; founded the weekly *Time and Tide* (1920) and served as its editor (1926–58), shifting the journal's emphasis to politics. ❖ See also memoirs *This Was My World* (1933) and *Notes on the Way* (1937); Shirley M. Eoff, *Viscountess Rhondda: Equalitarian Feminist* (Ohio State U. Press, 1991); and *Women in World History.*

RHYS, Jean (1890–1979). English novelist and short-story writer. Name variations: Gwen Williams; Ella Williams; Ella or Emma Gray. Born Ella Gwendolen Rees Williams in Roseau, Dominica (West Indies), Aug 24, 1890; died in Exeter, England, May 14, 1979; dau. of William Rees Williams (Welsh doctor, died 1909) and Minna Lockhart (3rd-generation Dominican Creole); m. Jean Lenglet (who fought with French Foreign Legion and served as French secret agent), 1919 (div. 1932); m. Leslie Tilden-Smith (literary agent), 1934 (died 1945); m. Max Hamer (solicitor), 1947; children: (1st m.) William Owen (1919–1919); Maryvonne Lenglet (b. 1922). ❖ At 16, left Dominica for England (1907); attended Perse School, Cambridge (1907–08) and Academy of Dramatic Art, London (1909); had affair with Ford Madox Ford (1924); husband Jean Lenglet in prison for selling *objects d'art* "of dubious origin" (1923–24); published *The Left Bank* (1927), *Quartet* (1928), *After Leaving Mr. Mackenzie* (1930), *Voyage in the Dark* (1934) and *Good Morning, Midnight* (1939); having slapped the face of a neighbor man whom she claimed was rude to her, was convicted of assault (1949); husband Max Hamer in prison for illegal financial dealings (1950–52); won W.H. Smith & Son Annual Literary Award for *Wide Sargasso Sea* (1967), considered by many to be her best novel. ❖ See also autobiography *Smile Please* (1979); Carole Angier, *Jean Rhys* (Viking, 1985); Coral Ann Howells, *Jean Rhys* (St. Martin, 1991); Francis Wyndham and Diana Melly, eds. *Jean Rhys: Letters 1931–1966* (Deutsch, 1984); and *Women in World History.*

RHYS-JONES, Sophie (1965—). English countess. Name variations: Sophie, Countess of Wessex; Princess Sophie. Born Sophie Helen Rhys-Jones, Jan 20, 1965, in Oxford, Oxfordshire, England; dau. of Christopher Bournes Rhys-Jones and Mary O'Sullivan; m. Prince Edward, 1st earl of Wessex (and son of Elizabeth II), June 19, 1999; children: Louise Alice Elizabeth Mary Windsor (b. Nov 8, 2003).

RI CHUN-OK (1947—). North Korean volleyball player. Born May 25, 1947, in North Korea. ❖ At Munich Olympics, won a bronze medal in team competition (1972).

RI SONG HUI (1978—). North Korean weightlifter. Born 1978 in Taesong district, Pyongyang, North Korea. ❖ Won a silver medal for 53–58 kg at Sydney Olympics (2000); won Asian championship (2000) and Asian Games (2002); at World championships, won for 58 kg clean and jerk (1999), 53 kg and 53 kg snatch (2002) and 53 kg clean and jerk (2003); won a silver medal for 58 kg at Athens Olympics (2004).

RIABOUCHINSKA, Tatiana (1917–2000). Russian ballerina. Name variations: Riabouchinskaia; Riabouchinskaya; Riabuchinskaya. Born in Petrograd, Russia, May 23, 1917; died Aug 24, 2000, in Los Angeles, California; father was a banker to Tsar Nicholas II; studied dance with Olga Preobrazhenska and Mathilda Kshesinskaia; m. David Lichine (choreographer, dancer and teacher), 1943; children: Tania Lichine Crawford. ❖ A member of the "baby ballerina" triumvirate, debuted at 15 with Nikita Balieff's *Chauve-Souris* revue in Paris; danced with Ballet Russe de Monte Carlo (1932–41), creating Frivolity in *Les Présages,* the Daughter in *Le Beau Danube,* the Child in *Jeux d'Enfants,* Florentine Beauty in *Paganini,* Junior Girl in *Graduation Ball,* and the title roles in *Coq d'Or* and *Cinderella;* was best known for performances in *Les Sylphides* and *Le Spectre de la Rose;* provided the model for the dancing hippopotamus in Disney's classic *Fantasia;* taught dance in Beverly Hills (1950–2000). ❖ See also *Women in World History.*

RIALE, Karen (c. 1949—). American clarinetist. Name variations: Karen Riale Erler. Born c. 1949 in US. ❖ While serving in rank of airman, became 1st female instrumentalist with US Air Force Band (1973).

RIANO, Renie (1899–1971). English-born stage, tv, and screen actress. Born Aug 7, 1899, in London, England; died July 3, 1971, in Woodland Hills, CA; dau. of Irene Riano (stage actress). ❖ Broadway credits include *Honey Girl, Music Box Revue* and *The Man Who Came to Dinner;* made film debut (1937); appeared in over 150 films, including *Tovarich, Spring Madness, Blondie for Victory, None But the Lonely Heart, Take It or Leave It, The Time of Your Life* and *Maggie and Jiggs;* tv credits include "The Partridge Family" and "Mayberry R.F.D."

RIARIO, Caterina Sforza (1462–1509). See *Sforza, Caterina.*

RIBEIRO, Fernanda (1969—). Portuguese runner. Born Maria Fernanda Moreira Ribeiro, June 23, 1969, in Penafiel, Portugal. ❖ Won European indoor championship for 3,000 meters (1993) and outdoor championship for 10,000 meters (1994); won World championship for 10,000 meters and silver for the 5,000 meters (1995) and silver for the 10,000 meters and bronze for the 5,000 (1997); won a gold medal at Atlanta Olympics (1996) and a bronze medal at Sydney Olympics (2000), both for the 10,000 meters; at World Cross Country championships, placed 2nd for 6 km (1995–97) and 1st for 6 km (2003).

RIBEIRO, Ingeborg (b. 1957). See *Lorentzen, Ingeborg.*

RIBEIRO CABRAL, Juliana (1981—). Brazilian soccer player. Name variations: Juliana. Born Oct 3, 1981, in Brazil. ❖ Defender, won a team silver medal at Athens Olympics (2004).

RIBERIO DA SILVA, Ana Maria de Jésus (c. 1821–1849). See *Garibaldi, Anita.*

RIBOUD, Barbara Chase- (1936—). See *Chase-Riboud, Barbara.*

RICARD, Marthe (1889–1982). French spy, reformer, and feminist. Born Marthe Betenfeld in German-occupied eastern France in 1889; died 1982; m. Henri Richer (grocer, killed in battle of Verdun during WWI); m. Thomas Crompton (died); m. a man named Ricard. ❖ Qualified as a pilot (1911); served as a spy in WWI for the French secret service; served in French resistance in WWII; elected a city councilor in Paris (c. 1945). Awarded Cross of the Légion d'Honneur (c. 1918). ❖ See also *Women in World History.*

RICARDA, Ana (c. 1925—). American Spanish dancer and choreographer. Born c. 1925 in San Francisco, CA; trained with La Argentina and La Argentinita. ❖ Trained in ballet as well as Spanish dance technique; performed with Markova-Dolin concert troupe in NY; appeared at Metropolitan Opera in *Carmen;* performed numerous Fanny Elssler Spanish dance specialties, including *La Cachucha* and *Pas Espagnol;* joined Grand Ballet du Marquis de Cuevas (1949), where she served as dancer and choreographer, and created such well-known works as *Del Amor y de la Muerte* (1953), *La Tertulia* (1952), and *Bolero 1830* (1953); taught in London at Royal Ballet and staged numerous dances for that company. Works of choreography include *Dona Ines de Castro* (1952), *Bolero 1830* (1953), *Serenade* (1955), *La Chanson de l'Eternelle Tristesse* (1957) and *La Esponta* (1971).

RICCI, Nina (1883–1970). Italian-born Paris fashion designer. Born Maria Nielli in Turin, Italy, 1883; died 1970; m. Louis Ricci (jeweler); children: Robert. ❖ Moved with family to France (1890); having learned the fashion industry as an apprentice dressmaker in Paris, soon became a head designer; with husband Louis, opened her own store (1932); her elegant and feminine styles would remain the trademarks of her label. ❖ See also *Women in World History.*

RICCOBONI, Marie-Jeanne (1713–1792). French novelist. Name variations: Jeanne Riccoboni. Born Marie-Jeanne Laboras de Mézières in Paris, France, 1713 (some sources cite 1714); died Dec 6, 1792; m. Antoine François Riccoboni (Italian actor), 1734 or 1735 (sep.); companion to Marie-Thérèse Biancolleli (actress), from 1753 to 1792. ❖ Launched literary career with a continuation of Marivaux's unfinished novel *La vie de Marianne* (The Life of Marianne, 1745); had further success with *Lettres de Mistriss Fanni Butlerd* (Letters from Mistress Fanny Butlerd, 1757), *Histoire de M. lemarquis de Cressy* (The History of the Marquis de Cressy, 1758), and *Lettres de Milady Juliette Catesby* (Letters from Juliette Catesby, 1759); also wrote *Lettres de Milord Rives* (Letters of Lord Rivers, 1776), which recounts the relationship between two Frenchwomen who prefer their union to love between men and women, and the play, *Les Caquets* (The Gossipers, 1761); last novel, *Ernestine,* which appeared posthumously (1798), was considered by some to be her masterpiece.

RICE, Alice Hegan (1870–1942). American novelist. Name variations: Alice Caldwell Rice. Born Alice Caldwell Hegan in Shelbyville, Kentucky, Jan 11, 1870; died in Louisville, Kentucky, Feb 10, 1942; dau. of Samuel Watson Hegan and Sallie P. (Caldwell) Hegan; m. Cale Young Rice (poet and playwright), Dec 18, 1902 (died Jan 24, 1943); no children. ❖ Known for her wildly popular *Mrs. Wiggs of the Cabbage Patch* (1901), the story of an indomitably cheery though poverty-stricken widow with 5 children, also wrote *Lovey Mary* (1903), the sequel to *Mrs. Wiggs, Sandy* (1905), *Mr. Opp* (1909), *A Romance of Billy-Goat Hill* (1912) and *Calvary Alley* (1917), among others. ❖ See also *Women in World History.*

RICE, Anne (1941—). American novelist. Name variations: (pseudonym) A.N. Roquelaure; Anne Rampling. Born Howard Allen O'Brien, Oct 4, 1941, in New Orleans, LA; sister of Alice Borchardt; San Francisco State University, MA, 1971; m. Stan Rice (poet and painter), 1961; children: Michele (b. 1966, died of leukemia at age 5); Christopher (b. 1978, novelist). ❖ Published her 1st novel, *Interview with the Vampire* (1976), which launched her bestselling "Vampire Chronicles," followed by *The Vampire Lestat* (1985), *Queen of the Damned* (1988), *The Tale of the Body Thief* (1992), *The Vampire Armand* (1998), *Blackwood Farm* (2002) and *Blood Canticle* (2003); wrote the "Lives of the Mayfair Witches" series, including *The Witching Hour* and *Taltos* (1994); also wrote *The Feast of All Saints* (1980), *Cry to Heaven* (1982), *The Mummy, or Ramses the Damned* (1989) and *Servant of the Bones* (1996); as A.N. Roquelaure, published the Beauty Series; as Anne Rampling, published such works as *Exit to Eden* (1985) and *Belinda* (1986).

RICE, Bridget Mary (1885–1967). Irish politician. Born Bridget Mary Henaghan, 1885, in Louisburgh, Co. Mayo, Ireland; died Dec 7, 1967; m. Eamon Rice (Fianna Fáil TD for Monaghan, 1932–33, 1937–38); children: 2 daughters, 2 sons. ❖ Following husband's death (1938), elected as a Fianna Fáil representative to the 10th Dáil (1938–43), the 1st woman TD for Monaghan; returned to the 11th–14th Dáil (1943–54), focusing primarily on issues concerning agriculture, education, tourism and culture.

RICE, Condoleezza (1954—). African-American politician and Cabinet official. Born Nov 14, 1954, in Birmingham, Alabama; dau. of Rev. John Rice (pastor, university professor) and Angelena Rice (music teacher, university professor); University of Denver, BA, 1974; University of Notre Dame, MA, 1975; Graduate School of International Studies at University of Denver, PhD, 1981; never married. ❖ Joined faculty at Stanford University (1981), serving initially as fellow in arms control and disarmament program and going on to become tenured professor of political science; served as provost of Stanford (1993–99); was member of Center for International Security and Arms Control and fellow of both Institute for International Studies and Hoover Institution; specializing in Communism and Cold War policies, wrote (with Philip Zelikow) *Germany Unified and Europe Transformed* (1995), (with Alexander Dallin) *The Gorbachev Era* (1986), and *Uncertain Allegiance: The Soviet Union and the Czechoslovak Army* (1984); served in the 1st Bush Administration as director, then senior director, of Soviet and East European Affairs in the National Security Council, and special assistant to the president for National Security Affairs (1989–91); served as national security advisor to President George W. Bush (2001–05); became secretary of state (2005), the most powerful woman in Washington.

RICE, Florence (1907–1974). American stage and screen actress. Born Feb 14, 1907, in Cleveland, OH; died Feb 23, 1974, in Honolulu, HI; dau. of Grantland Rice (sportscaster and columnist); m. 2nd husband Robert Wilcox (actor); m. Fred Butler. ❖ Broadway appearances include *June Moon, She Loves Me Not* and *Voice of the Turtle;* often starring opposite Robert Young, appeared in over 25 films, including *Carnival, Escape from Devil's Island, Pride of the Marines, Double Wedding, Sweethearts, Broadway Melody of 1940, Girl in 313, Mr. District Attorney* and in *Thin Man* series.

RICE, Joan (1930–1997). English screen actress. Born Feb 3, 1930, in Derby, England; died Jan 1, 1997. ❖ Made film debut in *Blackmailed* (1950), followed by *The Story of Robin Hood and His Merry Men* (Maid Marian), *The Gift Horse, A Day to Remember, Curtain Up, His Majesty O'Keefe, One Good Turn, The Long Knife, Payroll* and *The Horror of Frankenstein,* among others.

RICE-DAVIES, Mandy (1944—). British call girl. Born in Birmingham, England, in 1944; m. Rafael Shaul (Israeli airline pilot), 1966; children: 1 daughter. ❖ Quit school at 15 and worked as a shopgirl; moved to London where she befriended Christine Keeler; became embroiled in the Profumo scandal which brought the Tory Party to the brink of disaster (1963); converted to Judaism (1966), married and settled in Tel Aviv. ❖ See also *Women in World History.*

RICE-PEREIRA, Irene (1902–1971). See Pereira, Irene Rice.

RICH, Adrienne (1929—). American poet and feminist. Born Adrienne Cecile Rich in Baltimore, Maryland, May 16, 1929; dau. of Dr. Arnold Rice Rich (professor of pathology) and Helen Jones Rich (composer and pianist); graduated cum laude from Radcliffe College, 1951; m. Alfred Haskell Conrad (economist at Harvard), 1953 (committed suicide 1970); lived with Michelle Cliff (1976—); children: David (b. 1955); Paul (b. 1957); Jacob (b. 1959). ❖ One of modern-day America's most distinguished and influential poets and feminist theorists, published 1st vol. of verse, *A Change of World,* in Yale Younger Poets Series (1951); published 2nd vol. of poetry, *The Diamond Cutters* (1955), followed by *Snapshots of a Daughter-in-Law* (1963); began to change both style and content of work, revealing her conversion to an increasingly radical feminism; published 2 subsequent vols. of poetry (1960s), reflecting the social and political turmoil engendered by both the civil-rights movement and the war in Vietnam; moved to NY (1966); while teaching part-time at several colleges and universities and raising sons alone, continued to write poetry, receiving National Book Award (1974) for *Diving into the Wreck;* came out as a lesbian in *Twenty-One Love Poems* (1976); published 1st prose work *Of Woman Born: Motherhood as Experience and Institution* (1976); entered a long-term relationship with Jamaican-born writer and editor Michelle Cliff (1976); moved to Santa Cruz, California, with Cliff (1984), where both women continue to write about, and in support of, the outsiders and the oppressed; has long sought, in her writings and in her life, alternatives to patriarchal capitalism, which system she believes is not just anti-woman, but anti-human at its core, and destructive of the environment. Writings include *Ariadne: A Play in Three Acts and Poems* (1939), *Not I, But Death, A Play in One Act* (1941), *Necessities of Life: Poems, 1962–1965* (1966), *The Will to Change* (1971), *The Dream of a Common Language: Poems, 1974–1977* (1978), *On Lies, Secrets, and Silence* (1979), *A Wild Patience Has Taken Me This Far: Poems, 1978–1981* (1981), *The Fact of a Doorframe: Poems Selected and New, 1950–1984* (1984), *Blood, Bread, and Poetry* (1986), *Time's Power: Poems 1985–1988* (1989), *What Is Found There: Notebooks on Poetry and Politics* (1993), *Dark Fields of the Republic: Poems, 1991–1995* (1995), *Midnight Salvage: Poems, 1995–1998* (1999), and (essays) *Arts of the Possible: Essays and Conversations* (2001). ❖ See also *Women in World History.*

RICH, Edith Juliet (1878–1956). See Isaacs, Edith.

RICH, Elizabeth (fl. 1710). English baroness. Name variations: Lady Rich. Born Elizabeth Griffith, probably in the 1680s; death date unknown; m. Sir Robert Rich (1685–1768), 4th baronet and field marshal, around 1710; children: 3 sons, 1 daughter. ❖ Known to history as one of the correspondents of Lady Mary Wortley Montagu. ❖ See also *Women in World History.*

RICH, Irene (1891–1988). American stage and screen actress. Born Irene Luther, Oct 13, 1891, in Buffalo, NY; died April 22, 1988, in Hope Ranch, CA; m. Charles Rich (div.); m. Elvo Deffenbaugh (div.); m. David Blankenthorn, 1926 (div.); m. George Henry Clifford, 1950; children: (1st m.) 2 daughters. ❖ Gave over 5,000 performances in vaudeville; played the hectoring wife opposite Will Rogers in 7 films; other movies include *Lady Windermere's Fan, Craig's Wife, They Had to*

See Paris, That Certain Age, The Lady in Question, Fort Apache and *Joan of Arc*; went on to star on stage in *Seven Keys to Baldpate* and on radio's long-running "Dear John" (beginning 1933).

RICH, Louise Dickinson (1903–1991). American author. Born Louise Dickinson in Huntington, Massachusetts, June 14, 1903; died in Mattapoisett, Massachusetts, April 9, 1991; dau. of James Henry Dickinson (newspaper editor) and Florence Myrtie (Stewart) Dickinson; Massachusetts State Teachers' College, BSc, 1924; m. Ralph Eugene Rich (businessman), Aug 27, 1934 (died 1945); children: Rufus and Dinah. ❖ Naturalist whose 2 autobiographical books, the bestselling *We Took to the Woods* (1942) and *My Neck of the Woods* (1950), are accounts of her family's isolated life in the wilderness; also wrote young adult novels *Trail to the North* (1952), *Start of the Trail* (1949) and *Summer at High Kingdom* (1975), as well as many history books for children. ❖ See also *Women in World History.*

RICH, Mary (1625–1678). Irish diarist, memoirist, and countess of Warwick. Name variations: Mary Boyle. Born at Youghal near Cork, Ireland, in 1625 (some sources cite 1624); died in Essex, England, in 1678; 7th daughter and 13th child of Richard Boyle, 1st earl of Cork; m. Charles Rich, 4th earl of Warwick, in 1641 (died 1673); children: 1 son (died at 21). ❖ Became a convert to Puritanism in the middle of the English Civil War between the Puritans and the Royalists; made her home in Essex a refuge and hiding place for Puritan ministers and bishops who had escaped from London, and helped to hide armaments from the Royalist soldiers during siege of Colchester; when husband died (1673), inherited his estate; used her fortune to help those in need and was renowned for both her devotion and charity; began a religious diary (1666) and maintained it through the rest of her life; diaries are preserved in the British Museum. ❖ See also *Women in World History.*

RICH, Penelope (c. 1562–1607). English baroness and literary inspiration. Name variations: Lady Penelope Rich; Penelope Blount; Penelope Devereux; Stella. Born Penelope Devereux around 1562 (some sources cite 1560); died July 7, 1607, in Westminster, London, England; dau. of Walter Devereux, 1st earl of Essex, and Lettice Knollys (c. 1541–1634, a cousin of Elizabeth I); great-grandniece of Anne Boleyn; sister of Robert Devereux, 2nd earl of Essex (beheaded, Feb 25, 1601); m. Robert Rich, 3rd Baron Rich, later earl of Warwick, in 1581 (div. 1605); m. Charles Blount, 8th Lord Mountjoy, earl of Devonshire, in 1605 (died 1606); children: (1st m.) 6, including Robert Rich (1587–1658), 2nd earl of Warwick, and Henry Rich (1590–1649, beheaded for his part in the civil war during reign of Charles I), earl of Holland; (2nd m.) 5, including eldest son Mountjoy Blount (c. 1597–1665), Baron Mountjoy and earl of Newport. ❖ The inspiration for *Astrophel and Stella*, one of the most famous sonnet sequences in English literature, caught the eye of the celebrated poet and soldier Sir Philip Sidney when only 14. ❖ See also *Women in World History.*

RICHARDIS. *Variant of Richilde.*

RICHARDIS VON STADE (d. 1152). *See Stade, Richardis von.*

RICHARDS, Ann (1917—). Australian actress and poet. Name variations: Sally Ann Richards, Shirley Ann Richards. Born Shirley Ann Richards, Dec 13, 1917, in Sydney, Australia; dau. of American father and New Zealander mother; m. Paul Krammer (div.); m. Edmond Angelo (died). ❖ Made film debut in Australia in *It Isn't Done* (1937), followed by *Tall Timber, Lovers and Luggers, Come Up Smiling* and *Don't Call Me Girlie*, among others; made US debut in *Random Harvest* (1942), followed by *Dr. Gillespie's New Assistant, An American Romance, Love Letters, The Searching Wind, Love from a Stranger, Sorry Wrong Number* and *Ann Richards in the USSR* (documentary); published 2 vols. of poetry, *The Grieving Senses* (1971) and *Odyssey for Edmond* (1991), and the verse play *Helen of Troy.*

RICHARDS, Ann Willis (1933—). American politician. Name variations: Ann Willis; Ann Richards. Born Dorothy Ann Willis in Lakeview, Texas, Sept 1, 1933; dau. of Robert Cecil Willis (pharmaceutical salesman) and Iona (Warren) Willis (dressmaker); Baylor University, BA, 1954; University of Texas, Austin, teaching certificate, 1955; m. David Read Richards (lawyer), 1953 (div. 1984); children: Cecile, Dan, Clark, and Ellen. ❖ Managed the campaign of Wilhelmina Delco, who became the 1st black woman ever elected to Texas House of Representatives (1974); served as county commissioner, Travis County, Texas (1976–82); served as state treasurer of Texas (1982–90), the 1st woman in 50 years to hold state office in Texas; gave keynote speech at Democratic National Convention (1988); as a famously blunt-spoken politician, served as

governor of Texas (1990–94), only the 2nd woman governor in the state's history; advanced women's causes and women in political life. ❖ See also Mike Shropshire and Frank Schaefer, *The Thorny Rose of Texas: An Intimate Portrait of Governor Ann Richards* (Birch Lane, 1994); and *Women in World History.*

RICHARDS, Audrey Isabel (1899–1984). English social anthropologist. Born in London, England, July 8, 1899; died June 29, 1984; dau. of Sir Henry Erle Richards (diplomat and law professor) and Isabel (Butler) Richards; Newnham College, Cambridge University, MS, 1922; London School of Economics and Political Science, PhD, 1929. ❖ Spent childhood in India, returning to England (1911); studied functional anthropology under Bronislaw Malinowski at London School of Economics; spent 30 months in Africa studying the Bemba tribe in Zambia (1930–34), while also lecturing in social anthropology at London School of Economics; lectured in social anthropology at University of Witwatersrand in Johannesburg, South Africa (1938–40) and at University of London (1946–50); was director of East African Institute of Social Research at Makerere University College in Kampala, Uganda (1950–56); published a number of books, including *Hunger and Work in a Savage Tribe* (1932), *Land, Labour and Diet in Northern Rhodesia* (1939), *Chisungu: A Girl's Initiation Ceremony among the Bemba of Northern Rhodesia* (1956) and *The Multicultural States of East Africa* (1969); served as president of Royal Anthropological Institute (1960–62) and president of African Studies Association (1963–66). Named Commander of the Order of the British Empire (1955); named fellow of the British Academy (1967). ❖ See also *Women in World History.*

RICHARDS, Beah (1920–2000). African-American actress, poet, and playwright. Born Beah Richardson in Vicksburg, Mississippi, on July 12, 1920; died of emphysema in Vicksburg, Sept 14, 2000; dau. of Wesley Richardson (Baptist minister) and Beulah Richardson (seamstress); attended Dillard University in New Orleans; m. artist Hugh Harrell (div.). ❖ Made professional stage debut at Old Globe Theater in San Diego (1948); had 1st major NY role (1954), as the grandmother in Off Broadway revival of *Take a Giant Step* and played same role in film version (1960); co-founded Harlem Community Theater (1958); made Broadway debut in *The Miracle Worker* (1959), followed by *Purlie Victorious*; starred on Broadway in *The Amen Corner* (1965), receiving the *Theatre World* Award and New York Drama Critics Circle Award; also wrote poetry and plays, including *All's Well That Ends* and *One Is a Crowd* (1971), and published collection of poems, *A Black Woman Speaks* (1974); frequently directed tv shows and plays as well; other films include *In the Heat of the Night* (1967), *Hurry Sundown* (1967), *The Great White Hope* (1970), *Mahogany* (1975), *Drugstore Cowboy* (1989) and *Beloved* (1998). Nominated for Academy Award for Best Supporting Actress for *Guess Who's Coming to Dinner* (1967); inducted into Black Filmmakers Hall of Fame (1974); won Emmy awards for *A Black Woman Speaks* and for guest roles on "Frank's Place" (1980s) and "The Practice" (2000). ❖ See also *Women in World History.*

RICHARDS, Cornelia Wells Walter (1813–1898). *See Walter, Cornelia Wells.*

RICHARDS, Dorothy Pilley (1893–1986). *See Pilley, Dorothy.*

RICHARDS, Ellen Swallow (1842–1911). American chemist and founder. Name variations: Ellen Swallow; Ellen Henrietta Richards. Born Ellen Henrietta Swallow in Dunstable, Massachusetts, Dec 3, 1842; died at her Boston home, Mar 30, 1911; dau. of Mary (Taylor) Swallow and Peter Swallow (farmer); graduate of Vassar, 1870; Massachusetts Institute of Technology (MIT), science degree, 1873; m. Robert Hallowell Richards (MIT professor of geology and mining), 1875; no children. ❖ Founder of the American domestic-science movement, food-reform advocate, and early environmentalist who was the 1st woman faculty member at MIT, was also the 1st woman to obtain a science degree from MIT (1873); began women's classes in Women's Laboratory, MIT (1876), teaching the chemical makeup of domestic food products and how to trace unwanted additives; published *The Chemistry of Cooking and Cleaning* (1882); was an instructor in sanitary chemistry, MIT (1884–1911); created the New England Kitchen (1890); became, in effect, an early consumer advocate, gaining influential legislators' support, warning other women against inferior products in magazine articles, and pressuring fraudulent manufacturers and wholesalers to reform their ways; organized and was elected 1st president of American Home Economics Association (1908); published *Euthenics: The Science of Controllable Environment* (1910); throughout career, her aim was not so much to take women out into the wider world but to bring one aspect of that world, science, into every home. ❖ See also Robert Clarke, *Ellen Swallow: The Woman Who Founded Ecology* (Follett, 1973); Caroline Hunt, *The Life of Ellen H. Richards* (Whitcomb & Barrows, 1912); and *Women in World History*.

RICHARDS, Julie Burns (1970—). American equestrian. Name variations: Julie Burns; Julie Burns Black. Born Julie Burns, Sept 26, 1970, in Newnan, Georgia. ❖ On Jacob Two Two, won a bronze medal for team eventing at Athens Olympics (2004).

RICHARDS, Laura E. (1850–1943). American novelist, poet, and short-story writer. Born Laura Elizabeth Howe in Boston, Massachusetts, Feb 27, 1850; died Jan 14, 1943; dau. of Samuel Gridley Howe (Boston reformer and educator who founded Perkins Institute for the Blind) and Julia (Ward) Howe (1819–1910); sister of Maud Howe Elliott (1854–1948); m. Henry Richards (architect and illustrator), June 17, 1871; children: Alice Maude Richards; Rosalind Richards; Henry Howe Richards; Julia Ward Richards; Maud Richards (died in childhood, 1885); John Richards; Laura Elizabeth Richards. ❖ Published 80 books in her lifetime, including many juveniles; wrote the highly popular *Captain January* (1891) and biographies on Elizabeth Fry (1916), Abigail Adams (1917), Joan of Arc (1919), Laura Bridgman (1928), and Samuel Gridley Howe (1935); with sister Maud Howe Elliott, also wrote the Pulitzer Prize-winning book *Julia Ward Howe, 1819–1910* (1916). ❖ See also autobiography *Stepping Westward* (1931); and *Women in World History*.

RICHARDS, Linda (1841–1930). American nurse and educator. Born Melinda Ann Judson Richards, July 27, 1841, in Potsdam, New York; died April 16, 1930, in Boston, Massachusetts; dau. of Sanford Richards and Betsy (Sinclair) Richards; graduate of New England Hospital for Women and Children nursing school, 1873, the 1st of 5 women to graduate from the 1st nursing school in US history; never married; no children. ❖ Began work at Boston Training School (later Massachusetts General Hospital School of Nursing) and was subsequently named supervisor of nursing staff, a position she held until her resignation in 1877; traveled to England to observe training schools set up by Florence Nightingale (1877); opened a training school for nurses at Boston City Hospital (1878), serving as matron of the hospital and superintendent of the school; volunteered at American Board of Commissioners for Foreign Missions, which sent her to Japan (1886), where she established the 1st Japanese nursing school, at Doshisha Hospital in Kyoto; founded a school at Methodist Episcopal Hospital in Philadelphia (1892); headed nurses' training schools at New England Hospital for Women and Children, Taunton Insane Hospital in Massachusetts, and Michigan Insane Asylum in Kalamazoo (1893–1911); also worked at Brooklyn Homeopathic Hospital, Hartford Hospital, and University of Pennsylvania Hospital in Philadelphia, and established a training school at Worcester Hospital for the Insane; became the 1st president of American Society of Superintendents of Training Schools (1894). ❖ See also memoir, *Reminiscences of Linda Richards*; and *Women in World History*.

RICHARDS, Renée (1934—). American doctor, tennis player and transsexual. Name variations: Renee Richards. Born Richard Raskind, Aug 19, 1934, in New York, NY; graduate of Yale University; married and div.; children: 1 son, Nicholas. ❖ Began life as Richard Raskind; served as captain of Yale's tennis team, competing at Wimbledon, before becoming a leading ophthalmologist; underwent transsexual surgery (1975) and took name Renée Richards at age of 43; found herself barred from competing on the Women's tennis circuit; went to court, won, and made the finals of US Open doubles (1977); played on the tour and worked as tennis coach for such athletes as Martina Navratilova; continued to practice medicine in New York and served on editorial board of *Journal of Pediatric Ophthalmology & Strabismus*; published novel, *Remembering to Forget* (2003). ❖ See also autobiography (John Ames), *Second Serve: The Renée Richards Story* (Random House, 1985), which was a tv-movie starring Vanessa Redgrave.

RICHARDS, Sally Ann (1917—). *See Richards, Ann.*

RICHARDS, Sandie (1968—). Jamaican runner. Name variations: Sandie Angela Richards. Born Nov 6, 1968, in Clarendon Park, Jamaica; attended University of Texas. ❖ At Commonwealth Games, won a gold medal for the 400 meters (1998); at World Indoor championships, won gold medals for 400 meters (1993, 2001); won a silver medal for 4 x 400-meter relay at Sydney Olympics (2000); at World championships, won a gold medal for 4 x 400-meter relay (2001); won a bronze medal for 4 x 400-meter relay at Athens Olympics (2004).

RICHARDS, Sanya (1985—). Jamaican-American runner. Born Feb 26, 1985, in Kingston, Jamaica; attended University of Texas. ❖ Moved to US at age 12; became US citizen (2002); won gold medal for 4 x 400-meter relay at World championships (2003) and at Athens Olympics (2004).

RICHARDS, Shelah (1903–1985). Irish actress, manager and producer. Born Sheila Geraldine Richards in Dublin, Ireland, May 23, 1903; died at Ballybrack, Co. Dublin, Ireland, Jan 19, 1985; dau. of John William Richards and Adelaide Roper Richards; educated at Alexandra College, Dublin, and at finishing school in Paris; m. Denis Johnston (playwright), Dec 28, 1928 (div. 1945); children: Jennifer Johnston (b. 1930, novelist); Michael Johnston. ❖ One of the most prominent Irish actresses of her time, began performing with Dublin Drama League, then was asked to replace Eileen Crowe as Mary Boyle in *Juno and the Paycock* at Abbey Theatre; created role of Nora Clitheroe in *The Plough and the Stars* (1926); was also the 1st actress to tackle the lead in *The Player Queen* since Maire O'Neill; played other leading roles at the Abbey; appeared on Broadway in *Spring Meeting* (1938); during war years, ran her own company with Nigel Heseltine at Olympia Theatre in Dublin, scoring particular successes with *The Strings are False* and *Red Roses for Me*; took over Abbey School of Acting; produced *The Playboy of the Western World* in Edinburgh, London and Dublin with Siobhan McKenna (1950s); became one of the 1st producers for the Irish tv service, RTE (1961) and directed the 1st Irish play during RTE's opening week; though she specialized in drama, produced and directed a wide range of other programs: documentaries, religious telecasts, and soap operas, including the 1st two important soaps ever screened by RTE, *Tolka Row* and *The Riordans*. Nominated for Best Actress award for RTE production "Trial at Lisieux." ❖ See also *Women in World History*.

RICHARDS, Shirley Ann (1917—). *See Richards, Ann.*

RICHARDSON, Dorothy (1873–1957). English writer. Name variations: Dorothy M. Richardson; Mrs. Alan Odle. Born Dorothy Miller Richardson, May 17, 1873, in Abington, Berkshire, England; died June 17, 1957, in Beckenham, Kent; dau. of Charles Richardson and Mary Miller (Taylor) Richardson; attended Southwest London College; m. Alan Odle (artist), 1917 (died 1948). ❖ Writer associated with the development of modern psychological fiction who wrote *Pilgrimage*, a work of autobiographical fiction consisting of 13 novels, or "chapter-volumes"; educated by a governess and in private schools until reversals in family fortunes resulted in her teaching position in Germany (1891); after father's bankruptcy (1893), took a position as governess in London's West End; had career as dental assistant in London (1896–1908); began association with H.G. Wells that developed into a brief affair and remained a longterm friendship; at his suggestion, wrote essays and reviews for journals; published 1st book, *The Quakers Past and Present*, and an anthology, *Gleanings from the Works of George Fox* (1914); published *Pointed Roofs*, her 1st novel and the beginning of the extended work that would become *Pilgrimage* (1915); continued writing individual novels or "chapter-volumes" in ongoing series, along with other writing and translations (1916–38), culminating in the publication of *Pilgrimage* in 4 vols. (1938); began a 13th part of *Pilgrimage* entitled *March Moonlight* (1944); though originally praised for her innovation in rendering interior states of mind and feeling, lost critical esteem when her technique was surpassed by James Joyce and Virginia Woolf; her work has recently been revalued for its significance as a historical and cultural document. ❖ See also Gloria G. Fromm, *Dorothy Richardson: A Biography* (U. of Georgia Press, 1994); and *Women in World History*.

RICHARDSON, Dorothy (1961—). *See Richardson, Dot.*

RICHARDSON, Dot (1961—). American softball player and orthopedic surgeon. Name variations: Dorothy Richardson. Born Dorothy Richardson, Sept 22, 1961, in Orlando, FL; attended Western Illinois University; graduate of University of California, Los Angeles; University of Louisville, MD; Adelphi University, MA in exercise and physical health. ❖ Won 3 World championships with national team, achieving a record of 110 wins and a single loss between 1986 and 1996; won gold medals at Pan American Games (1979, 1987, 1995, 1999); won a team gold medal at Atlanta Olympics (1996) and Sydney Olympics (2000). Named NCAA (National Collegiate Athletic Association) player of the decade (1989); inducted into Florida Hall of Fame (1999). ❖ See also *Women in World History*.

RICHARDSON, Effie Newbigging (1849/50?–1928). New Zealand landowner. Name variations: Euphemia Johnstone. Born probably in 1849 or 1850, in Kilmeny parish on island of Islay, Argyllshire,

Scotland; died Dec 27, 1928, in Nelson, New Zealand; dau. of Robert Johnstone (farmer) and Susanna (Newbigging) Johnstone; m. Ralph Richardson (lawyer and landowner), 1884 (died 1889); children: 2 daughters. ❖ Immigrated to New Zealand with mother and family (1860s); upon death of husband, began to consolidate land holdings and was involved in lengthy legal battles in which she often represented herself (Nelson City Council eventually won right to purchase large tract of her land, which became Maitai recreational area). ❖ See also *Dictionary of New Zealand Biography* (Vol. 3).

RICHARDSON, Ethel Florence Lindesay (1870–1946). *See Richardson, Henry Handel.*

RICHARDSON, Gloria (1922—). African-American civil-rights activist. Name variations: Gloria St. Clair Hayes Richardson; Gloria Richardson Dandridge. Born Gloria St. Clair Hayes, May 6, 1922, in Baltimore, Maryland; dau. of John Edwards Hayes and Mabel Pauline (St. Clair) Hayes; granddau. of Herbert Maynadier St. Clair; graduate of Howard University, 1942; married and div.; m. Frank Dandridge, mid-1960s; children: (1st m.) Donna. ❖ Spearheaded the Cambridge Movement in Cambridge, Maryland (1961–63), which is now recognized as the 1st grassroots civil-rights movement to erupt beyond the Deep South. ❖ See also *Women in World History.*

RICHARDSON, Henrietta (1870–1946). *See Richardson, Henry Handel.*

RICHARDSON, Henry Handel (1870–1946). Australian author. Name variations: Henrietta Richardson; Ethel Florence Lindesay Richardson. Born Ethel Florence Lindesay Richardson near Melbourne, Australia, Jan 3, 1870; died in Hastings, England, Mar 30, 1946; dau. of Walter Lindesay Richardson (medical doctor) and Mary Bailey Richardson; attended Ladies Presbyterian College in Melbourne, 1883–88, and studied piano at Music Conservatorium in Leipzig, Germany, 1889–92; m. John G. Robertson, Dec 20, 1895; no children. ❖ Best known for *The Getting of Wisdom* (1910) and her trilogy *The Fortunes of Richard Mahony* (1915–1929), did not achieve fame until she was almost 60; gave up a musical career (1892) after becoming engaged to John G. Robertson; lived in Strasbourg, France (1897–1903), where husband taught German literature and where she translated 2 works by Scandinavian authors and began writing 1st novel, *Maurice Guest*; lived in London, where husband served as chair of German and Scandinavian literature at University of London while she, working under pen name Henry Handel Richardson, completed *Maurice Guest, The Getting of Wisdom* and *The Fortunes of Richard Mahony* (1903–33); with publication of *Ultima Thule* (1929), the 3rd and final volume in the Mahony series, finally won universal praise in English-speaking world; following husband's death, moved to "Green Ridges" in Sussex (1934), where she continued to write until her death 12 years later; wrote slowly, completing only 6 novels (the last was *The Young Cosima,* 1939) over a period of 41 years; her novels are among the most important yet produced by an Australian writer. Awarded Australian Literature Society's Gold Medal (1930); nominated for Nobel Prize (1932). ❖ See also Dorothy Green, *Ulysses Bound: Henry Handel Richardson and Her Fiction* (Australian National U. Press, 1973); Nettie Palmer, *Henry Handel Richardson: A Study* (Angus & Robertson, 1950); Louis Triebel, *Henry Handel Richardson: Australian Novelist and Lover of Wisdom* (Cat & Fiddle, 1976); and *Women in World History.*

RICHARDSON, Jillian (1965—). Canadian runner. Born Mar 10, 1965, in Trinidad; attended University of Toronto. ❖ At Los Angeles Olympics, won a silver medal in 4 x 400-meter relay (1984).

RICHARDSON, Katy (1864–1927). English mountaineer. Born Kathleen Richardson, 1864; died 1927; lived and climbed with French mountaineer Mary Paillon at Oullins, near Lyons, France. ❖ Made 6 1st ascents and 14 1st ascents by a woman; climbed the Aiguille de Bionnassay and traversed the Eastern Ridge to the Dôme du Goûter (1888). ❖ See also *Women in World History.*

RICHARDSON, LaTasha (1976—). *See Colander-Richardson, LaTasha.*

RICHARDSON, Luba Lyons (1949—). American midwife and nurse. Born Luba Eisenberg, Mar 15, 1949, in New York, NY; dau. of Florence Eisenberg and Jules Eisenberg; attended Nassau Community College; studied psychology at State University of New York at Stonybrook, 1969–70; m. Jim Richardson, 1971; children: 3, including raising Max, her grandson. ❖ Completed a midwifery preceptorship with midwife Raven Lang in Nanaimo, British Columbia, Canada; practiced midwifery in Parksville, British Columbia (1976–79), served as chair of the 1st regulatory body to develop midwife regulations of College of Midwives of British Columbia (CMBC); committed to keeping home birthing as an option for women, served as CMBC president; appointed chief of department of midwifery for the Capital Health Region in Victoria; contributed to *Island Parent Magazine.*

RICHARDSON, Margaret (1844–1905). *See Sievwright, Margaret Home.*

RICHARDSON, Mary Elizabeth (1870–1939). *See Tripe, Mary Elizabeth.*

RICHARDSON, Michelle (1969—). American swimmer. Born April 28, 1969, in Managua, Nicaragua; dau. of Frank and Dolores Armengol de Richardson; attended Clemson University. ❖ Moved to US (1979); at Los Angeles Olympics, won a silver medal in 800-meter freestyle (1984).

RICHARDSON, Miranda (1958—). English actress. Born Miranda Jane Richardson, Mar 3, 1958, in Southport, Lancashire, England; dau. of William (marketing executive) and Marian Richardson; trained at Bristol Old Vic; never married. ❖ Made London stage debut (1981); had breakthrough role portraying Ruth Ellis in film *Dance with a Stranger* (1985); other films include *The Innocent* (1985), *Empire of the Sun* (1987), *Enchanted April* (1991), *The Crying Game* (1992), *Damage* (1992), *The Apostle* (1997), *Get Carter* (2000), *The Hours* (2002), *Spider* (2003), *The Phantom of the Opera* (2004) and *Harry Potter and the Goblet of Fire* (2005); on tv, appeared in "A Woman of Substance" (1984) and "Dance to the Music of Time" (1997), among others; on stage, was seen in *Etta Jenks* (1990) and *Aunt Dan and Lemon* (1999). Nominated for Oscar for *Tom & Viv* (1994).

RICHARDSON, Nicole (1970—). Australian softball and netball player. Born June 25, 1970, in Victoria, Australia. ❖ Member of the Australian softball team (1992–98), won a bronze medal at Atlanta Olympics (1996); member of the Australian netball team (1999–2002), won a gold medal at Commonwealth Games (2002); retired (2002). Voted Victoria's 3rd Greatest Sportswoman in History (2002).

RICHARDSON, Ruth (1950—). New Zealand politician. Born Ruth Richardson, Dec 13, 1950, in Waitotara, NZ. ❖ Worked for Justice Department and Federated Farmers; elected National MP for Selwyn (1981); was 1st woman minister of Finance (1990–93); left Parliament (1994).

RICHENSIA OF NORDHEIM (1095–1141). Holy Roman empress. Name variations: Richenza of Northeim. Born 1095; died June 10, 1141; dau. of Henry the Fat, duke of Saxony, and Gertrude of Meissen (d. 1117); m. Lothair II (b. 1075), Holy Roman emperor (r. 1125–1137), around 1100; children: Gertrude of Saxony (1115–1143).

RICHEPIN, Jeanne (1868–1943). *See Avril, Jane.*

RICHESA OF LORRAINE (d. 1067). Queen of Poland. Name variations: Rycheza; Richeza of Palatine, countess Palatine. Born c. 1000 in Lorraine, France; died Mar 31, 1067 (some sources cite 1063); dau. of Ezzo, count Palatine, and Matilda of Saxony (978–1025); niece of Otto III; m. Mieszko II (990–1034), king of Poland (r. 1025–1034), around 1013; children: Richesa of Poland (fl. 1030–1040); Gertrude of Poland (d. 1107); Casimir I the Restorer (1015–1058), king of Poland (r. 1038–1058).

RICHESA OF POLAND (fl. 1030–1040). Queen of Hungary. Name variations: Richesa or Rycheza. Flourished between 1030 and 1040; dau. of Mieszko II (990–1034), king of Poland (r. 1025–1034) and Richesa of Lorraine (d. 1067); m. Bela I, king of Hungary (r. 1060–1063); children: St. Ladislas I (1040–1095), king of Hungary (r. 1077–1095); Geza I, king of Hungary (r. 1074–1077); Helen of Hungary (who m. Zwoinimir, king of Croatia); Sophie of Hungary (d. 1095); Lanka of Hungary (who m. Rstislav, prince of Tmutarakan).

RICHEY, Helen (1910–1947). American aviator. Born in 1910 in Pennsylvania; died from an apparent overdose of sleeping pills, Jan 7, 1947. ❖ Was the 1st woman to fly airmail transport (Dec 31, 1934); was the 1st woman to become a licensed instructor (1940); was a flight instructor with rank of major, US Army; discharged (1944); established world record for continuous flight: 9 days, 21 hours, 42 minutes (1933); hired by Central Airlines (1934), had to resign 10 months later when the male pilots' union refused to accept her; established world record for Class C plane speed of 55 minutes across 100 kilometers at Langley Field in Virginia (1936); held world altitude record for a midget plane—18,448 feet (1936); died nearly penniless. ❖ See also *Women in World History.*

RICHEZA. *Variant of Ryksa.*

RICHEZA ERIKSDOTTIR (fl. 1200s). Scandinavian princess. Name variations: Regitze. Dau. of Agnes of Brandenburg (d. 1304) and Erik

V Klipping or Clipping, king of Denmark (r. 1259–1286); m. Niels of Werle also known as Nicholas II von Werle; children: Sophie (who m. Gerhard).

RICHIER, Germaine (1904–1959). French sculptor. Born 1904 in Grans, Bouches-de-Rhîne, near Arles, France; died 1959 in Juan-Les-Pins; attended Montpelier École des Beaux Arts, 1922–25; studied with Emile-Antoine Bourdelle (1925–29); m. Otto Baenninger (sculptor), 1929. ❖ Held 1st solo show, at Galerie Max Kaganovitch in Paris (1934); sculpted *The Toad* (1942); won the sculpture prize at Sâo Paolo Biennale (1951); also rendered *Don Quichotte de la Forêt* (Walker Art Center, Minneapolis). "Hommage Germaine Richier" was held at the Musée Rodin, in Paris (1968); other retrospectives followed in London (1973) and Paris (1992).

RICHILDA. *See Richilde.*

RICHILDE (d. 894). Saint, queen of France, and Holy Roman empress. Name variations: Richardis or Richilda, princesse d'Ecosse; Saint Richardis or Saint Richilda. Died 894; dau. of Erchingen (powerful lord of the Nordgrau); m. Charles III the Fat (839–888), king of Germany (r. 876–887), king of France (r. 884–887), and known as Charles II, Holy Roman emperor (r. 881–887), in 877. ❖ Shortly before husband's death (Jan 13, 888), was accused of adultery; claiming that the marriage had not been consummated and that she remained a virgin, retired to the abbey of Andlau and died there; was venerated by Pope Leo IX (1049). Feast day is Sept 18.

RICHILDE (1034–1086). Countess of Hainault and Flanders. Name variations: Richildis, Richilda; countess of Namur. Born about 1034 in Hainault (Belgium); died Mar 15, 1086, in Flanders; dau. of Renier or Rainier V, count of Hainault; m. Herman, count of Hainault (died c. 1054); m. Baldwin VI the Peaceable, count of Flanders (r. 1067–1070), in 1055 (killed in battle against his brother Robert the Frisian, 1070); m. William FitzOsbern, 1st earl of Hereford; children: (2nd m.) Arnulf III the Unlucky (1055–1071), count of Flanders; Baldwin II (b. 1056), count of Hainault; Gilbert de Gant. ❖ Daughter of Rainier V, ruler of Hainault, an important medieval province of northwestern Europe, inherited the county on his death; married Baldwin VI, count of Flanders, temporarily uniting Flanders and Hainault under joint rule; following 2nd husband's death, became regent of Flanders for eldest son Arnulf III, but ruled only a few months; when Baldwin's brother Robert the Frisian tried to seize control, led her troops to meet his army at the battle of Ravenshoven, near Cassel in Prussia (1071); defeated, was taken prisoner, and her son was killed; later released, was allowed to return to Hainault where she ruled jointly with son Baldwin II. ❖ See also *Women in World History.*

RICHILDE (d. 1100). Saint. Name variations: Blessed Richilde. Died in 1100. ❖ Lived as a recluse with the Benedictines at Hohenwart (Bavaria). Feast day is Aug 23.

RICHILDE (fl. 1300s). Danish royal. Name variations: Richardis. Flourished in 1300s; m. Valdemar also known was Waldemar III (1314–1364), king of Denmark (r. 1326–1330, deposed), duke of Schleswig (acceded 1325); children: Henry; Valdemar or Waldemar.

RICHILDE OF AUTUN (d. around 910). Queen of France. Name variations: Richild; Richilda; Richildis. Born into a noble Frankish family; died c. 910 in France; dau. of Count Beuves (Biwin or Buwin) and Richilde of Lotharingia; became 2nd wife of Charles I the Bald, king of France (r. 840–877), known also as Charles II, Holy Roman emperor (r. 875–877), in 870; children: Rothild (c. 871–c. 928); Charles (b. 876); stepchildren: Judith Martel and Louis II the Stammerer (846–879), king of France (r. 877–879). ❖ Was the mistress of Charles I the Bald for several years before they married (870), one year after the death of his 1st wife Ermentrude; crowned queen in a special ceremony, went on to become a crucial member of Charles' administration; ruled as an equal authority with husband, in the established tradition of Frankish queens. ❖ See also *Women in World History.*

RICHIZA (fl. 1251). Queen of Norway. Name variations: Richiza Birgersdottir. Dau. of Birger of Bjälbo, regent of Sweden, and Ingeborg (d. 1254); m. Haakon the Younger (1232–1257), king of Norway (r. 1240–1257), in 1251; m. Henry I, prince of Werle, in 1262; children: (1st m.) Sverker Magnus.

RICHIZZA OF DENMARK (d. 1220). Queen of Sweden. Name variations: Rikisa of Denmark; Rikisa Valdimarsdottir or Waldimarsdottir. Died May 8, 1220; dau. of Sophie of Russia (c. 1140–1198) and

Waldemar or Valdemar I the Great (b. 1131), king of Denmark (r. 1157–1182); sister of Ingeborg (c. 1176–1237/38), queen of France; sister of Canute VI (1163–1202), king of Denmark (r. 1182–1202), and Waldemar II the Victorious (1170–1241), king of Denmark (r. 1202–1241); m. Eric X, king of Sweden (r. 1208–1216), in 1210; children: Ingeborg (d. 1254); Erik XI (b. 1216), king of Sweden (r. 1222–1250); Helen (who m. Knut Johnsson); Margaret, also known as Marta (who m. Niels Sixtenson).

RICHIZZA OF POLAND (1116–1185). Polish princess. Name variations: Richza; Ryksa. Born April 12, 1116, in Poland; died June 16, 1185; dau. of Boleslaus III (b. 1084), king of Poland, and Salomea (d. 1144); m. Magnus, in 1129; m. Sverker also known as Swerker I the Elder, king of Sweden (r. 1133–1156); m. Vladimir, Prince of Novgorod; children: (1st m.) Knud or Canute III, king of Denmark (r. 1146–1157); Neils; (2nd m.) Boleslaw; Sune Sverkersson (b. around 1132); (3rd m.) Sophie of Russia (c. 1140–1198).

RICHMAN, Julia (1855–1912). American educator and children's rights activist. Born in New York, NY, Oct 12, 1855; died in Paris, France, June 24, 1912; dau. of Moses Richman (painter and glazier) and Theresa (Melis) Richman; graduate of New York Normal College (later Hunter College), 1872; graduate work in school of pedagogy at New York University, 1897–98; never married; no children. ❖ Served as principal of girls' department at P.S. 77 in NY (1884–1903); was 1st president of Young Women's Hebrew Association (1886–90), a member of Jewish Chautauqua Society's educational council (1889–98), and chair of committee on religious school work for Council of Jewish Women (1895–99); promoted to district superintendent of city schools (1903), chose to work on the city's Lower East Side, which at the time was a crowded, poor neighborhood inhabited primarily by Jewish immigrants; retired (1912), leaving behind her a vastly improved school environment. Julia Richman High School in New York City was named in her honor. ❖ See also *Women in World History.*

RICHMOND, countess of. *See Beaufort, Margaret (1443–1509).*

RICHMOND, Dorothy Kate (1861–1935). New Zealand artist and art teacher. Born Sept 12, 1861, at Parnell, Auckland, New Zealand; died on April 16, 1935, in Wellington; dau. of James Crowe Richmond (politician) and Mary (Smith) Richmond. ❖ Attended Bedford College for women in London and Slade School of Fine Art (late 1870s); gained Slade scholarship (1880); appointed art mistress at Nelson College for Girls (1883); became artist member of New Zealand Academy of Fine Arts (1890); leased studio with Frances Hodgkins in Wellington, and taught private pupils (early 1900s); held classes at Fitzherbert Terrace School (1920). ❖ See also *Dictionary of New Zealand Biography* (Vol. 3).

RICHMOND, duchess of.
See Alice (1201–1221).
See Fitzroy, Mary (c. 1519–1557).
See Villiers, Frances (c. 1633–1677).
See Stuart, Frances Teresa (1647–1702).
See Cadogan, Sarah (1706–1751).

RICHMOND, Jane Maria (1824–1914). *See Atkinson, Jane Maria.*

RICHMOND, Lynne (1948–2003). *See Thigpen, Lynne.*

RICHMOND, Mary E. (1861–1928). American social worker and founder. Born Mary Ellen Richmond, Aug 5, 1861, in Belleville, Illinois; died Sept 12, 1928, in New York, NY; dau. of Henry Richmond (carriage blacksmith) and Lavinia (Harris) Richmond; never married; no children. ❖ Founder of professional social work, in essence creating a new profession, who pioneered the casework methodology and helped to establish training programs for social workers, dramatically improving the level of assistance provided to the troubled and poor; served as assistant treasurer, Baltimore Charity Organization Society (BCOS, 1889); volunteered as a friendly visitor; promoted to general secretary of BCOS (1891); moved to Philadelphia to become general secretary of Society for Organizing Charity; named director of Charity Organization Department of Russell Sage Foundation in NY (1909); led Charity Organization Institute, a summer training program for social workers (1910–22); writings include *Friendly Visiting Among the Poor* (1899), *Social Diagnosis* (1917), *What is Social Case Work* (1922), *Child Marriages* (1925) and *The Long View* (published posthumously, 1930). ❖ See also *Women in World History.*

RICHMOND, Mary Elizabeth (1853–1949). New Zealand teacher and writer. Born Aug 30, 1853, at New Plymouth, New Zealand; died on July 3, 1949, in Wellington; dau. of Christopher William Richmond (lawyer) and Emily Elizabeth (Atkinson) Richmond. ❖ Active in Forward Movement, which tried to match contemporary societal conditions with Christianity; taught at Wellington Girls' High School (1884–90); trained at Froebel Institute in London, and opened private school in Wellington for children from kindergarten to preparatory level (1886); founded free kindergarten movement in Wellington (1905); also active in League of Mothers, New Zealand Society for Protection of Women and Children, and Women's Social Progress Movement; returned to England and joined Kensington Society for Female Suffrage (c. 1913); published articles and sermons, and vol. of children's songs and stories, *Bindy Ballads* (1924). Commander of the British Empire (1949). ❖ See also *Dictionary of New Zealand Biography* (Vol. 3).

RICHSA. *Variant of Ryksa.*

RICHTER, Annegret (1950—). West German runner. Born Annegret Irrgang, Oct 13, 1950, in Dortmund, West Germany; m. Manfred Richter (hurdler). ❖ At Munich Olympics, won a gold medal in 4 x 100-meter relay (1972); at Montreal Olympics, won a silver medal in 4 x 100-meter relay, silver medal in the 200 meters, and gold medal in the 100 meters (1976).

RICHTER, Elise (1865–1943). Austrian Romance language scholar. Born Mar 2, 1865; died in Theresienstadt concentration camp in 1943. ❖ Became the 1st woman to hold a faculty position in an Austrian university (1907); became an associate professor at the University of Vienna (1921); founded the Verband der akademischen Frauen Österreichs (1922), which she headed until 1930.

RICHTER, Emma (1888–1956). German paleontologist. Born Emma Hüther, Mar 4, 1888; died Nov 15, 1956; m. Rudolf Richter (paleontologist). ❖ Prominent paleontologist, was considered a trilobites expert; based with husband at the University of Frankfurt, was also associated with the Senckenberg Museum in Frankfurt; appointed an honorary member of the Palaeontological Society of America (1934); awarded a University of Tübingen doctorate (1949).

RICHTER, Gisela (1882–1972). English-born American archaeologist. Born Gisela Marie Augusta Richter in London, England, Aug 15, 1882; died in Rome, Italy, Dec 24, 1972; dau. of Jean Paul Richter (art historian) and Luise Marie (Schwaab) Richter; sister of Irma Richter (painter); received bachelor's degree from Girton College, Cambridge, 1905; studied at British School of Archaeology, 1904–05; Trinity College, Dublin, LittD, 1913; Cambridge University, AM, 1933, LittD; never married; no children; became US citizen (1917). ❖ Took a temporary job helping to organize an exhibit on Greek vases at Metropolitan Museum of Art in NY (1905), then named assistant curator of classical art (1910), curator (1925), and purchasing agent (1928); augmented collections of Greek, Roman, and Etruscan art into world-class collections; was soon an acknowledged expert in all facets of archaic art aside from architecture; remained at the Metropolitan until retirement (1948); published a number of highly regarded studies, including *The Craft of Athenian Pottery* (1923), *Sculpture and Sculptors of the Greeks* (1929), *Kouroi* (1942), and the popular *Handbook of Greek Art* (1959). Received gold medal of Archaeological Institute of America (1968). ❖ See also *My Memoirs, Recollections of an Archaeologist's Life* (1972); and *Women in World History.*

RICHTER, Ilona (1953—). East German rower. Born Mar 11, 1953, in East Germany. ❖ Won a gold medal at Montreal Olympics (1976) and a gold medal at Moscow Olympics (1980), both in coxed eights.

RICHTER, Kristina (1946—). East German handball player. Born Oct 24, 1946, in East Germany. ❖ Won a silver medal at Montreal Olympics (1976) and a bronze medal at Moscow Olympics (1980), both in team competition.

RICHTER, Marga (1926—). American composer. Born in Reedsburg, Wisconsin, Oct 21, 1926; dau. of Paul Richter and Inez (Chandler) Richter (soprano); studied piano at Juilliard School under Rosalyn Tureck and composition with William Bergsma and Vincent Persichetti; m. Alan Skelly (professor of philosophy), 1953; children: Michael and Maureen. ❖ Was one of the youngest composers to have her compositions programmed on the Composers Forum series in NY; began to compose *Landscapes of the Mind I* (1968) and produced 6 other major works in a 10-year period, which were increasingly performed internationally.

RICHTER, Simona Marcela (1972—). Romanian judoka. Born 1972 in Romania. ❖ Won a bronze medal for 70–78 kg half-heavyweight at Sydney Olympics (2000).

RICHTER, Ulrike (1959—). East German swimmer. Born June 17, 1959, in East Germany. ❖ Won gold medals for the 100-meter backstroke, 200-meter backstroke, and 4 x 100-meter medley relay at Montreal Olympics (1976); held World record for 100-meter backstroke at 1:01.51 (1976); held World record for 4 x 100-meter relay at 4:07.95 (1976); won World championship for 100-meter backstroke (1973, 1975). ❖ See also *Women in World History.*

RICHTEROWNA, Halina (1938—). *See Gorecka, Halina.*

RICHTHOFEN, Else von. *See von Richthofen, Else.*

RICHTHOFEN, Frieda von (1879–1956). *See Lawrence, Frieda.*

RICKER, Elswyth (1900–1984). *See Thane, Elswyth.*

RICKER, Maelle (1978—). Canadian snowboarder. Born Dec 2, 1978, in North Vancouver, British Columbia, Canada. ❖ Won gold at X Games in Boarder X (Winter 1999); also placed 1st at Swatch World championships, Val Di Sol, Italy, in Boardercross (1999), 2nd at Vans Triple Crown, Breckenridge, CO, in Boardercross (1999), 2nd at Swatch Boardercross, Aspen, CO (2001), and 1st at season-opening World Cup, Valle Nevado, Chile, in Halfpipe (2002).

RICKER, Marilla (1840–1920). American lawyer and suffragist. Name variations: Marilla Young Ricker. Born Marilla Marks Young in New Durham, New Hampshire, Mar 18, 1840; died Nov 12, 1920 in Dover, New Hampshire; dau. of Jonathan Young and Hannah (Stevens) Young; attended Colby Academy; m. John Ricker (farmer), May 19, 1863 (died 1868); no children. ❖ Protested conditions in New Hampshire state prison to the governor of that state (1879); also set in motion legislation to grant prisoners the right to send sealed letters to the governor without interference of prison wardens; passed District of Columbia bar (May 12, 1882); appointed notary public in District of Columbia by President Chester A. Arthur; appointed US commissioner by District's Supreme Court judges, becoming the 1st woman in the District of Columbia to secure such a position; was admitted to the bar of the Supreme Court of US (1891); played a pivotal role in ending District of Columbia's "poor convict's law," which allowed indigent criminals to be held indefinitely if they were unable to pay fines; dubbed the "Prisoner's Friend" by area newspapers (1890s). ❖ See also *Women in World History.*

RICKERT, Edith (1871–1938). American educator and writer. Born Martha Edith Rickert in Dover, Ohio, July 11, 1871; died in Chicago, Illinois, May 23, 1938; dau. of Francis and Josephine (Newburg) Rickert; Vassar College, AB, 1891; University of Chicago, PhD, 1899. ❖ Lived in England (1900–09); while researching and editing medieval texts, published 5 novels: *Out of Cypress Swamp* (1902), *The Reaper* (1904), *Folly* (1906), *The Golden Hawk* (1907) and *The Beggar in the Heart* (1909); in addition, published over 50 short stories and produced numerous translations of medieval literature; collaborated with John M. Manly on *The Writing of English* (1919), *Contemporary British Literature* (1921), *Contemporary American Literature* (1922), and *The Text of the Canterbury Tales, Studied on the Basis of All Known Manuscripts* (1940); accepted an associate professorship at University of Chicago (1924), becoming full professor (1930); produced 3 vols. of children's tales, *The Bojabi Tree* (1923), *The Blacksmith and the Blackbirds* (1928) and *The Greedy Goroo* (1929), as well as her last novel, *Severn Woods* (1930). ❖ See also *Women in World History.*

RICKETSON, Gail (1953—). American rower. Name variations: Gail Ricketson Helfer. Born Sept 12, 1953; graduate of University of New Hampshire, 1975. ❖ At Montreal Olympics, won a bronze medal in coxed eights (1976).

RICKETT, Mary Ellen (1861–1925). English mathematician and educator. Born Mar 4, 1861, in UK; died Mar 20, 1925; Bedford College, University of London, BA, 1881, graduate of Newnham College, 1886. ❖ Long-time faculty member of Newnham College, Cambridge, served as a mathematics lecturer (1886–1908) and as a vice-principal of Old Hall (1889–1908); retired (1908); was the 1st woman recipient of University of London's Gold Medal and the 1st Wrangler of Newnham College (highest award possible for Cambridge math students).

RICKON, Kelly (1959—). American rower. Name variations: Kelly Rickon Mitchell. Born Oct 27, 1959, in US. ❖ At Los Angeles Olympics, won a silver medal in quadruple sculls with coxswain (1984).

RICNA, Hana (1968—). Czech gymnast. Born Dec 20, 1968, in Brno, Czechoslovakia; m. Lorin Jessen (gymnastics coach). ❖ Won a gold medal in uneven bars at Riga (1983); placed 1st all-around at TCH championships (1983); at World championships, won a silver medal for balance beam (1983) and a bronze for uneven bars (1985); at European championships, won a bronze medal for balance beam (1985); won the Chunichi Cup (1985) and Kosice International (1986).

RIDDELL, Charlotte (1832–1906). Irish-born British novelist and short-story writer. Pronunciation: Riddle. Name variations: (pseudonyms) Mrs. J.H. Riddell; F.G. Trafford; R.V. Sparling; Rainey Hawthorne. Born Charlotte Eliza Cowan in Carrickfergus, Co. Antrim, Ireland, Sept 30, 1832; died in London, England, Sept 24, 1906; dau. of James Cowan (high sheriff) and Ellen (Kilshaw) Cowan; m. Joseph Hadley Riddell (civil engineer), 1857 (died 1880); no children. ❖ Known in Victorian England as the "Novelist of the City" for her books about the financial and business worlds, and best known to modern readers as an exemplar of the Victorian-era ghost story, published 3rd novel, *The Moors and the Fens* (1858), under pseudonym F.G. Trafford, which finally brought some success; continued to publish under this pseudonym until 1866; wrote most successful novel, *George Geith of Fen Court* (1864); began publishing as Mrs. J.H. Riddell (1866); wrote some 46 novels, including *City and Suburb* (1861), *Home, Sweet Home* (1873), *Above Suspicion* (1876), *Berna Boyle* (1882), *A Struggle for Fame* (1883), *Mitre Court* (1885), *Miss Gascoyne* (1887), *The Nun's Curse* (1888) and *The Head of the Firm* (1892); primarily remembered for her ghost stories, including "The Old House in Vauxhall Walk," "Nut Bush Farm," "Diarmid Chittock's Story," "Walnut-Tree House," "Hertford O'Donnell's Warning" and "Forewarned, Forearmed." ❖ See also *Women in World History*.

RIDDLE, Estelle (1901–1981). See Osborne, Estelle Massey.

RIDDLES, Libby (1956—). American sled-dog racer. Born April 1, 1956, in St. Cloud, MN. ❖ Was the 1st woman to win the Iditarod (1985). ❖ See also autobiography *Race Across Alaska: First Woman to Win the Iditarod Tells Her Story* (Stackpole, 1988); and *Women in World History*.

RIDE, Sally (1951—). American astronaut. Born Sally Kristen Ride, May 26, 1951, at Los Angeles, California; dau. of Dr. Dale Ride (educator) and Joyce (Anderson) Ride (counselor); attended Swarthmore College, 1968–1970; Stanford University, BS and BA, 1973, MS, 1975, PhD, 1978; m. Dr. Steven Hawley, July 26, 1982 (div. 1987). ❖ Selected for 1st group of women astronauts (1978), was the 1st American woman in space (June 18, 1983); after 2nd flight in 1984, served on the Rogers Commission to investigate the Challenger disaster and was a special assistant to the NASA administrator; resigned from NASA (1987); became director of the Space Science Institute at University of California at San Diego; published *To Space and Back* (1986), *Voyager: An Adventure to the Edge of the Solar System* (1992) and *The Third Planet: Exploring the Earth From Space* (1994). Inducted into Women's Hall of Fame (1988). ❖ See also *Women in World History*.

RIDER-KELSEY, Corinne (1877–1947). American oratorio and concert singer. Name variations: Mme. Rider-Reed; Corinne Rider Kelsey; Corinne Reed. Born Corinne Rider, Feb 24, 1877, near Bergen, NY; died July 10, 1947, in Toledo, OH; dau. of Fannie Rider; m. George Russel Kelsey, Jan 1, 1900 (div.); m. Lynnel Reed (violinist and composer), Aug 25, 1926. ❖ One of America's top musical artists before WWI, became a soloist at First Presbyterian Church in Brooklyn, NY (1903); maintained heavy concert schedule on East Coast, including appearances in *The Messiah* with New York Oratorio Society (1904) and *St. Matthew Passion* at Bach Festival in Bethlehem, PA (1905); toured with New York Symphony (1908–09); was 1st American-trained singer to perform major role with Royal Opera, as Micaëla in *Carmen* (1908), but abandoned opera after 3 performances; gave 1st solo recital in New York (1913). ❖ See also Lynnel Reed, *Be Not Afraid: Biography of Madame Rider-Kelsey* (1955).

RIDER-REED, Mme (1877–1947). See Rider-Kelsey, Corinne.

RIDGE, Lola (1873–1941). Irish-born American poet. Name variations: Rosa Delores Ridge. Born Rose Emily Ridge, Dec 12, 1873, in Dublin, Ireland; died in Brooklyn, NY, May 19, 1941; dau. of Joseph Henry Ridge and Emma (Reilly) Ridge; attended Trinity College in Australia; studied art under Julian Ashton at Academie Julienne; m. David Lawson, Oct 22, 1919; no children. ❖ While still a child, moved with mother to New Zealand and later to Sydney, Australia; immigrated to America (1907); received critical acclaim when poem "The Ghetto" appeared in *New Republic* (1918) and was the title poem of her 1st vol. of poetry released that same year; published *Sun-Up and Other Poems* (1920) and *Red Flag and Other Poems* (1927); after WWI, revived magazine *Others*, while also serving as an editor of *Broom* and contributing to *The Left* and *New Masses*; most successful poem, "Three Men Die," from her last volume, *Dance of Fire* (1935), linked the deaths of Sacco and Vanzetti to Christ's crucifixion. Won *Poetry* magazine's Guarantor's Prize (1923) and Shelly Memorial Award (1934 and 1935). ❖ See also *Women in World History*.

RIDGE, Therese (1941—). Irish politician. Born Mar 1941 in Dublin, Ireland; m. James Ridge. ❖ Representing Fine Gael, elected to the Seanad from the Labour Panel: Nominating Bodies Sub-Panel (1997–2002).

RIDGLEY, Cleo (1893–1962). American actress. Born May 12, 1893, in New York, NY; died Aug 18, 1962, in Glendale, CA; m. James Horne (director). ❖ Began career (1912); often co-starred with Wallace Reid.

RIDGWAY, Rozanne Lejeanne (1935—). American diplomat and ambassador. Name variations: Roz Ridgway. Born Aug 22, 1935, in St. Paul, Minnesota; dau. of H. Clay Ridgway and Ethel Rozanne (Cote) Ridgway; Hamline University in Minnesota, BA, 1957; m. Theodore (Ted) Deming (officer in the Coast Guard), 1983. ❖ Entered Foreign Service (1957); landed a position as a class 4 political officer in Oslo, Norway (1967), working for Ambassador Margaret Tibbetts, then became a desk officer for Ecuador; named deputy assistant secretary in Bahamas and, within a year, had helped rewrite postwar international fisheries laws as they applied to US; also negotiated bilateral fishing treaties with 14 nations, earning her informal title, "Lobster Lady of the Bahamas"; became ambassador to Finland; returned to US as a counselor in the State Department (1980), then became ambassador to East Germany; named assistant secretary for European and Canadian Affairs (1985), which led to her becoming the 1st woman to actively participate in a presidential summit when she took part in Geneva conference between Reagan and Gorbachev (Nov 1985); retired (1989); became president of Atlantic Council (1995). ❖ See also *Women in World History*.

RIDING, Laura (1901–1991). American poet. Name variations: Laura Reichenthal; Laura Riding Gottschalk; Laura Riding Jackson. Born Jan 16, 1901, in New York, NY; died Sept 2, 1991, in Sebastien, Florida; dau. of Nathan Reichenthal (garment worker and labor activist) and Sarah (Sadie) Edersheim Reichenthal (garment worker); attended Cornell University, 1918–21; m. Louis R. Gottschalk, 1920 (div. 1925); m. Schuyler Jackson (critic), June 20, 1941 (died 1968). ❖ Major poet of 1st half of 20th century and contributor to literary modernism, stressed the unique ability of poetry to penetrate a reality beyond that of the senses; moved with husband to Urbana, Illinois (1921), then Louisville, Kentucky, where she submitted 1st work to *Fugitive* (1923); won Nashville Poetry Prize (1924); joined Robert and Nancy Graves in England and published 1st book of poetry, *The Close Chaplet* (1926); as an editor and critic, had a particularly strong influence on Robert Graves, with whom she also maintained a personal relationship for 13 years (1926–39); assumed the name "Laura Riding" (1927); founded Seizin Press with Graves (1928); attempted suicide, moved to Spanish island of Mallorca (1929); left Spain for Brittany (1938), then settled in Pennsylvania (1939); abandoned writing poetry and settled in Florida (1941); participated in BBC broadcast explaining her long literary silence (1962); was also an important literary critic, who played a crucial role in promoting the work of Gertrude Stein; poetry includes *Love as Love, Death as Death* (1928), *Selected Poems: In Five Sets* (1970); prose includes *A Survey of Modernist Poetry* (with Robert Graves, 1927), *The Telling* (with Schuyler Jackson, 1972), and *Rational Meaning: A New Foundation for the Definition of Words* (1997). Awarded Bollingen Prize for poetry (1991). ❖ See also Deborah Baker, *In Extremis: The Life of Laura Riding* (Grove, 1993); Joyce Piell Wexler, *Laura Riding's Pursuit of Truth* (Ohio U. Press, 1979); Richard Perceval Graves, *Robert Graves: The Years with Laura, 1926–1940* (Weidenfeld & Nicolson, 1990); and *Women in World History*.

RIDLER, Anne (1912–2001). English poet and dramatist. Born Anne Bradby in Rugby, Warwickshire, England, July 30, 1912; died Oct 15, 2001; dau. of Henry Christopher Bradby (housemaster of Rugby School) and Violet (Milford) Bradby; attended Downe House School in Berkshire; King's College in London, degree in journalism, 1932; m. Vivian Ridler (printer at University of Oxford), in 1938; children: 4. ❖ Worked as secretary to T.S. Eliot at Faber & Faber (1935–40); published 1st collection, *Poems* (1939), followed by *The Nine Bright Shiners* (1943); her *The Golden Bird* (1951), focuses on the pain and anxiety of separation, and *A Matter of Life and Death* (1959) highlights the sadness of children growing to adulthood; also wrote plays, translated opera libretti, and edited works of Charles Williams, James Thomson, Walter de la Mare, Thomas Traherne, George Darley, and William Austin; wrote plays *Cain* (1943), *Henry Bly* (1947), and *The Trial of Thomas Cranmer* (1956); other poetry collections include *Dies Natalis* (1980) and *New and Selected Poems* (1988); collaborated with E.J. Scovell on *Ten Poems* (1984).

RIDLEY, Marian (1846–1912). See Ogilvie Farquharson, Marian.

RIDRUEJO, Mónica (1963—). Spanish politician. Name variations: Monica Ridruejo. Born April 25, 1963, in San Francisco, CA; Mount Holyoke College, BA in Economics, magna cum laude. ❖ Served as director-general of Radio Televisión Española (1996–97); as a member of the European People's Party (Christian Democrats) and European Democrats, elected to 5th European Parliament (1999–2004).

RIE, Lucie (1902–1995). Austrian-born British potter. Name variations: Dame Lucie Rie. Born Lucie Gomperz, 1902, in Vienna, Austria; died 1995; studied at Vienna Kunstgewerbeschule; m. Hans Rie, 1926 (div. 1940). ❖ Fled Nazism (1938); shared a workshop with Hans Coper, producing ceramic jewelry and buttons; started working in stoneware and porcelain (1948), creating a style rooted in modernism; became the most famous potter in the United Kingdom; was also internationally acclaimed, and had solo exhibition at New York Metropolitan Museum of Art (1994). BBC film by Sir David Attenborough documented her life and work (1982); made OBE (1968), CBE (1981) and DBE (1991). ❖ See also *Women in World History*.

RIEDEL, Petra (1964—). East German swimmer. Born Sept 17, 1964, in East Germany. ❖ At Moscow Olympics, won a bronze medal in the 100-meter backstroke (1980).

RIEFENSTAHL, Leni (1902–2003). German film director. Pronunciation: LANE-ee REEF-in-shtall. Born Helene Berta Amalie Riefenstahl in Berlin, Germany, Aug 22, 1902; died Sept 8, 2003, in Pöcking, Germany; dau. of Alfred Riefenstahl (owner of a plumbing business) and Berta (Scherlach) Riefenstahl; attended Realgymnasium and Kunstakademie in Berlin; began studying classical ballet, 1919; m. Peter Jacob, 1944 (div. 1946); no children. ❖ One of the most innovative, influential film directors of the 20th century, who made *Triumph of the Will* for the Nazi Party and *Olympia* for the IOC, both considered classics, and whose work for the Nazis virtually blocked her from directing after WWII, began career as a dancer (1923), until she injured her knee (1924); made 1st film appearance, in *Der Heilige Berg* (The Holy Mountain, 1926); after founding her own film company, directed *Das Blaue Licht* (The Blue Light, 1932), *Sieg des Glaubens* (Victory of Faith, 1933), *Triumph des Willens* (Triumph of the Will, 1935), *Olympia* (1938), *Tiefland* (Lowland, 1944); appointed "film expert" to Germany's National Socialist Party by Adolf Hitler (1933); received the Staatspreis (1935); won the gold Venice Biennale medal (1936); won the Grand Prix of the Exposition Internationale des Art et des Techniques for *Triumph of the Will* (1937); briefly held prisoner after WWII for supposed pro-Nazi activities but released and her name cleared; received a gold medal from International Olympic Committee for *Olympia* (1948); traveled extensively in Africa and produced book *The Last of the Nuba* (1973); continued into her 90s to work in photography and film. A Hollywood panel of judges named *Olympia* one of the 10 finest motion pictures of all time (1955). ❖ See also *Leni Riefenstahl: A Memoir* (St. Martin, 1993); David B. Hinton, *The Films of Leni Riefenstahl* (Scarecrow, 1978); Glenn B. Infield, *Leni Riefenstahl: The Fallen Film Goddess* (Crowell, 1976); *The Wonderful, Horrible Life of Leni Riefenstahl* (documentary, 1995); and *Women in World History*.

RIEPP, Mother Benedicta (1825–1862). Swabian-born nun and founder. Name variations: Mother Benedicta. Born Maria Sybilla Riepp, June 28, 1825, in Waal, Swabia; died Mar 15, 1862, in St. Cloud, Minnesota; dau. of Johann Riepp (glassblower) and Katharina (Mayr) Riepp. ❖ Founder of the 1st Benedictine convent in US, entered the Benedictine Convent of Saint Walburga in Eichstätt at 19; took her final vows (1849) and became a teacher and mistress of novices; sailed for America with 2 companions (1852); settled in German colony of St. Marys, Elk County, Pennsylvania, the site of an existing Benedictine

monastery, and established St. Joseph's Convent and School, of which she became superior. ❖ See also *Women in World History*.

RIES, Frédérique (1959—). Belgian tv journalist and politician. Name variations: Frederique Ries. Born May 14, 1959, in Balen. ❖ Managed FM 56, a radio station in Liège (1982–84); served as chief editor and presenter of tv news and current affairs programs for RTL-TVI (Belgium) and presented documentaries for Télévie (1984–98); as a member of the European Liberal, Democrat and Reform Party, elected to 5th European Parliament (1999–2004).

RIFAAT, Alifa (1930–1996). Egyptian short-story writer. Name variations: Alifa Rif'at. Born Fatma Abdalla Rifaat, June 5, 1930, in Cairo, Egypt; died Jan 1996 in Cairo; married; widowed (1978); children: 3. ❖ Wrote about difficulties faced by Muslim women; works include *Eve Returns with Adam* (1981), *Who Can Be The Man* (1981), *Distant View of a Minaret* (1984), and *A Long Winter Night*; stories also appeared in collection *Opening the Gates: A Century of Arab Feminist Writing* (1990).

RIGBY, Cathy (1952—). American gymnast. Born Dec 12, 1952, in Long Beach, CA; m. Tommy Mason, Jan 1973; m. Tom McCoy (producer). ❖ Earned highest US scores in gymnastics at Mexico City Olympics (1968); at World championships, was the 1st American woman to win a medal (silver for balance beam) in international competition (1970); won World Cup (1971); holds 12 international medals, 8 of them gold; made theatrical debut as Dorothy in *The Wizard of Oz* (1981); returned to Broadway with *Peter Pan* (1998), earning a Tony nomination; toured with *Annie Get Your Gun* (1999) and *Peter Pan*. ❖ See also Linda Jacobs *Cathy Rigby: On the Beam* (EMC, 1975); and *Women in World History*.

RIGBY, Elizabeth (1809–1893). See Eastlake, Elizabeth.

RIGELSFORD, Sarah Ann (c. 1821–1892). See Cripps, Sarah Ann.

RIGG, Diana (1938—). English actress. Name variations: Dame Diana Rigg. Born July 20, 1938, in Doncaster, Yorkshire, England; m. Menachem Gueffen, 1973 (div. 1976); m. Archie Stirling, 1982 (div. 1990); children: Rachael Stirling (b. 1977, actress). ❖ Joined the Royal Shakespeare Company (1959); made London debut in *Ondine* (1961), followed by *A Midsummer Night's Dream, The Comedy of Errors, The Physicists, King Lear, Jumpers* and *Macbeth*, among others; films include *A Midsummer Night's Dream* (as Helena), *On Her Majesty's Secret Service, Julius Caesar* (as Portia), *The Hospital, Theatre of Blood, A Little Night Music, The Great Muppet Caper, Evil Under the Sun* and *A Good Man in Africa*; on tv, starred as Emma Peel on "The Avengers" (1965–67) and in title role of "Diana" (1973–74); hosts the PBS series "Mystery!"; compiled *No Turn Unstoned* (a collection of nasty theatrical reviews through history, 1982); serves as chancellor of Stirling University in Scotland. Nominated for Tony awards for *Abelard and Heloise* (1972) and *The Misanthrope* (1975); won a Tony for *Medea* (1994); named Dame Commander of the Order of the British Empire (DBE, 1994).

RIGG, Kathleen Maisey (1892–1994). See Curtis, Kathleen Maisey.

RIGG, Lady (1892–1994). See Curtis, Kathleen Maisey.

RIGGIN, Aileen (1906–2002). American diver and swimmer. Name variations: Aileen Riggin Soule. Born Aileen Riggin, May 2, 1906, in Newport, RI; died Oct 17, 2002, in Honolulu, Hawaii; m. Dwight D. Young (doctor injured in WWII), 1924 (died); m. Howard Soule; children: Yvonne May. ❖ Shortly after 14th birthday, won a gold medal in springboard diving at Antwerp Olympics (1920), the youngest to win a gold medal in springboard until 13-year-old Marjorie Gestring of the US (1936); won bronze medal in 100-meter backstroke and silver medal in springboard in Paris Olympics (1924); set 6 world records in freestyle and backstroke sprints in the World Masters for those swimmers in the 85 to 89-year-old age group (1991).

RIGGS, Betty (1899–1975). See Brent, Evelyn.

RIGGS, Katherine Witchie (d. 1967). American dancer and vaudeville star. Died April 19, 1967, in Babylon, LI, NY; m. Ralph Riggs (dancer, died). ❖ With husband, headlined vaudeville in a dance and acrobatic act for many years, and appeared on Broadway in *The Enchantress, Louisiana Purchase, Oklahoma!* and Gilbert & Sullivan operettas.

RIGGS MILLER, Anna (1741–1781). See Miller, Anna Riggs.

RIGUNTHA (fl. 580s). Frankish princess. Dau. of Fredegund (c. 547–597) and Chilperic I, king of Soissons (r. 561–584), king of the Franks (r. 561–584); betrothed to the Visigothic prince Reccared.

RIIHIVUORI, Hilkka (1952—). Finnish cross-country skier. Name variations: Hilkka Kuntola. Born Dec 24, 1952, in Jurva, Finland. ❖ Won a silver medal for 3 x 5 km relay at Sapporo Olympics (1972) and a silver medal for 4 x 5 km relay at Innsbruck Olympics (1976); won silver medals for 10 km and 5 km at Lake Placid Olympics (1980).

RIIS-JORGENSEN, Karin (1952—). Danish lawyer and politician. Name variations: Karin Riis-Jørgensen or Riis Jorgensen. Born Nov 7, 1952, in Odense, Denmark. ❖ Awarded law degree (1978); member of the Venstre (Liberal) Party Executive (1994—); as a member of the European Liberal, Democrat and Reform Party, elected to 4th and 5th European Parliament (1994–99, 1999–2004).

RIISE, Hege (1969—). Norwegian soccer player. Born July 18, 1969, in Lorenskog, Norway. ❖ Midfielder; was captain of the Norwegian National team, scoring 58 goals in 175 matches; won team gold medal at FIFA World Cup (1995); won a team bronze medal at Atlanta Olympics (1996) and a team gold medal at Sydney Olympics (2000); played for Setskog/Holand (1989–99), Nikko in Japan (1995–97) and Asker in Norway (2000); signed with WUSA's Carolina Courage (2002).

RIISE-ARNDT, Eva (1919—). Danish swimmer. Name variations: Eva Arndt. Born Nov 27, 1919, in Denmark. ❖ At London Olympics, won a silver medal in the 4 x 100-meter freestyle relay (1948).

RIJKER, Lucia (1967—). Dutch boxer. Born Dec 7, 1967, in Amsterdam, Netherlands. ❖ Won the Amsterdam fencing championships at 13, then took up kickboxing, amassing a 36–0 record, winning 4 World titles; began boxing (1988); in US debut, knocked out Melinda Robinson (1996); captured the WIBF European championship (1997); won the WIBF super lightweight title (1997) and IBO Women's junior welterweight title (1998); was the subject of documentary *Shadow Boxers* (2000).

RIKIRIKI, Atareta Kawana Ropiha Mere (c. 1855–1926). New Zealand tribal prophet. Name variations: Mere Rikiriki. Born probably in 1855 or 1856, at Parewanui, Rangitikei, New Zealand; died Mar 13, 1926, at Parewanui; dau. of Kawana Ropiha and Mere Rikiriki; m. Inia Te Rangi. ❖ Only woman prophet in 19th-century tradition of healers, practiced faith healing and herbal remedies; inaugurated Church of the Holy Spirit (early 1900s); was instrumental in spreading Maramatanga movement, a blend of Maori custom and Catholic beliefs. Anniversary of date that she baptized herself in special ritual (July 27, 1910), still commemorated at Parewanui. ❖ See also *Dictionary of New Zealand Biography* (Vol. 3).

RIKIRIKI, Mere (1855/56?–1926). See Rikiriki, Atareta Kawana Ropiha Mere.

RIKISA. *Variant of Richizza.*

RILEY, Betsy Snite. See Snite, Betsy.

RILEY, Bridget (1931—). British painter. Name variations: Bridget Louise Riley. Born 1931 in London, England; studied at Goldsmiths College of Art in London, 1949–52, and Royal College of Art; never married. ❖ Taught art and traveled in Europe before gaining recognition for exhibition at Gallery One (1962); became associated with Op Art movement of 1960s; work has appeared in several retrospectives and is held in major collections; had an exhibition at Serpentine Gallery which drew long lines (2000).

RILEY, Corinne Boyd (1893–1979). American politician. Born Corinne Boyd, July 4, 1893, in Piedmont, Greenville County, South Carolina; died April 12, 1979, in Sumter, South Carolina; graduate of Converse College, Spartanburg, 1915; m. John Jacob Riley (1895–1962, US congressional representative). ❖ Taught in secondary schools in South Carolina (1915–37); served as field representative, South Carolina State Text Book Commission (1938–42); was associated with Civilian Personnel Office, Shaw Air Force Base, Sumter, South Carolina (1942–44); elected as a Democrat to the 87th Congress by special election (1962); served from April 1962 until Jan 1963, and did not seek reelection to the 88th Congress. ❖ See also *Women in World History.*

RILEY, Dawn (1964—). American sailor. Born 1964 in Detroit, MI; graduate of Michigan State University. ❖ Sailed with 1st all-women's Whitbread Round the World Race team (1989); became 1st woman invited to try out for an America's Cup team (1991); won 1st place in Santa Maria Cup, Baltimore, Maryland, and Women's Cup, Portofino, Italy (1992); was team captain of the 1st all-women's crew in America's Cup (1995); set a record in 153-mile Newport-to-New-York Race (1997); named Rolex Yachtswoman of the Year (1999); became 1st woman to manage and captain an America's Cup team (2000); served as president of the Women's Sports Foundation board of trustees (2003–04). ❖ See also autobiography (with Cynthia Flanagan Goss) *Taking the Helm* (Little, Brown, 1995) and Christina Lessa, *Women Who Win* (Universe, 1998).

RILEY, Jeannie C. (1945—). American singer. Born Jeanne Carolyn Stephenson, Oct 19, 1945, in Anson, TX; m. Mickey Riley (div. remarried, 1976). ❖ Worked as secretary in Nashville, TN; released *Harper Valley PTA* (1968), winning Grammy for Best Female Country Vocal Performance, and becoming 1st female artist to hit #1 on both country and pop charts with album's title track, which inspired film and tv series; other C&W hit singles include "The Girl Most Likely," "There Never Was a Time" and "Good Enough to Be Your Wife"; albums include *Yearbooks and Yesterdays* (1969), *Here's Jeannie C.* (1991) and *Praise Him* (1995).

RILEY, Margaret (c. 1822–1913). *See Ralph, Margaret.*

RILEY, Mary Velasquez (1908–1987). Native American tribal leader. Born 1908 in Arizona; died in 1987. ❖ Raised in Arizona on the White Mountain Apache Reservation, became the 1st woman elected to the tribal council (1958) and remained in a leadership role for the next 20 years, promoting economic development and independence. ❖ See also *Women in World History.*

RILEY, Polly Ann (1926–2002). American golfer. Born Aug 27, 1926, in San Antonio, TX; died Mar 13, 2002, in Fort Worth, TX; never married; no children. ❖ Won Southern Amateur (1948, 1950–51, 1953–54, 1961), Western (1950, 1952), Trans-Mississippi (1947–48, 1955); won the Tampa Open (1950), the LPGA Tour's inaugural event, by five strokes; member of Curtis Cup team (1948, 1950, 1952, 1954, 1956, 1958), and non-playing captain (1962); director of the Women's Western Golf Association and Women's Southern Golf Association. Inducted into Texas Golf Hall of Fame and Texas Sports Hall of Fame.

RILEY, Ruth (1979—). American basketball player. Born Aug 28, 1979, in Macy, IN; attended University of Notre Dame. ❖ Center, led Notre Dame to NCAA championship (2001); played for Miami Sol (2001–03); as 1st overall pick for WNBA, signed with Detroit Shock (2003); named MVP of the WNBA finals (2003); won a team gold medal at Athens Olympics (2004). Won Naismith Award and named AP College Player of the Year (2001).

RILEY, Samantha (1972—). Australian swimmer. Born Samantha Linette Riley, Nov 13, 1972, in Brisbane, Queensland, Australia. ❖ At Barcelona Olympics, won a bronze medal for 100-meter breaststroke (1992); at Commonwealth Games, won gold medals for 100-meter breaststroke (1994) and 200-meter breaststroke (1994, 1998); at LC World championships, won gold medal for 100- and 200-meter breaststroke (1994); at SC World championships, won gold medal for 100- and 200-meter breaststroke (1995); at Atlanta Olympics, won a silver medal for 4 x 100-meter medley relay and a bronze medal for 100-meter breaststroke (1996).

RILEY, Sara (1979—). *See Hildebrand, Sara.*

RIMINGTON, Stella (1935—). English secret service director. Name variations: Dame Stella Rimington. Born May 1935 in London, England; Edinburgh University, BA; Liverpool University, post-graduate diploma; m. John Rimington (government official, secretary of Department of Health and Social Services, div.); children: 2 daughters. ❖ The 1st female director of the British secret service, traveled to New Delhi, India, where husband was posted to British High Commission (1965); worked part time for Security Service while there; returned to UK (1969) and joined Security Service (MI5), becoming director of counter-subversion (F2), director of counter-espionage, and then director of counter-terrorism; appointed director general of MI5 (1992), the 1st director general to be publicly named; led Service's counter-espionage work in closing days of Cold War, as well as campaign against International and Irish terrorism; pursued policy of openness for Security Service, seeking to explain the nature of MI5 to the public (1994); retired (1996); wrote thriller novel, *At Risk* (2004). Made Dame Commander of Order of Bath (1996). ❖ See also *Open Secret: The Autobiography of the Former Director-General of MI5* (Arrow, 2002).

RIMINI, Francesca da (d. 1285?). *See Francesca da Rimini.*

RIMOLDI, Jorgelina (1972—). Argentinean field-hockey player. Name variations: Jorgelina Rimoldi Puig. Born July 9, 1972, in Argentina. ❖ Won a team silver medal at Sydney Olympics (2000).

RIMSKAYA-KORSAKOVA, Yulia (1878–1942). *See Veysberg, Yuliya Lazarevna.*

RINA. *Variant of Catherine or Katherine.*

RINALDI, Angela (c. 1916—). Soviet spy. Name variations: Angela Maria Rinaldi; (nickname) The Tsarina. Born c. 1916; m. Giorgio Rinaldi (parachutist and spy). ❖ Became Resident Network Operator of spy ring in Italy (1954), which successfully supplied information, including NATO secrets, to Moscow for 13 years; arrested by counter-intelligence in Turin with husband (1967), who was one of her agents; charged with espionage and received a long jail sentence. After her network was exposed, numerous arrests followed.

RINCÓN DE GAUTIER, Felisa (1897–1994). *See Gautier, Felisa Rincón de.*

RIND, Clementina (c. 1740–1774). American newspaper publisher and editor. Name variations: Clementine Bird Rind. Born c. 1740, possibly in Maryland; died in 1774 in Williamsburg, Virginia; m. William Rind (printer), between 1758 and 1765 (died 1773); children: 4 sons, 1 daughter. ❖ When husband died (Aug 1773), assumed the role of editor and publisher of the *Virginia Gazette*; maintained the integrity of the newspaper, which covered both national and international events as well as shipping news; was appointed public printer by the House of Burgesses. ❖ See also *Women in World History.*

RINEHART, Mary Roberts (1876–1958). American novelist and war correspondent. Born Mary Roberts, Aug 12, 1876, in Pittsburgh, Pennsylvania; died Sept 22, 1958, in Brooklyn, NY; dau. of Thomas Beveridge Roberts (sewing machine salesman, committed suicide 1895) and Cornelia (Grilleland) Roberts; graduate of Pittsburgh Training School for Nurses, 1896; m. Stanley M. Rinehart (surgeon), April 1896 (died 1932); children: Stanley Jr., Alan, and Frederick Rinehart. ❖ Famed for her mystery novels, published 1st full-length book, *The Circular Staircase* (1908), which fused the detective story with the humorous novel, the prototype of nearly all the mysteries she would later write; published 2nd novel, *The Man in Lower Ten,* the 1st detective novel by an American writer to make the bestseller list; introduced character Letitia Carberry, a middle-aged amateur detective otherwise known as Tish, as part of a series of short stories in *Saturday Evening Post* (later collected in *The Amazing Adventures of Letitia Carberry,* 1911); also wrote numerous romance novels, which constituted 8 of her 11 bestsellers, and several plays with Avery Hopwood, including *Seven Days* (1909) and *The Bat* (1920), a dramatization of *The Circular Staircase*; achieved fame during WWI as the 1st American correspondent to report from front lines; was also 1st reporter to interview England's Queen Mary of Teck (1915); produced over 60 books, many for the publishing house Farrar & Rinehart, which was established by her sons; books include *When a Man Marries* (1909), *The Window at the White Cat* (1910), *Kings, Queens and Pawns* (1915), *Bab: A Sub-Deb* (1917), *The Amazing Interlude* (1918), *The Red Lamp* (1925), *The Door* (1930), *Miss Pinkerton* (1932), *The Yellow Room* (1945) and *Episode of the Wandering Knife* (1950). ❖ See also autobiography *My Story* (1931); Charlotte MacLeod, *Had She But Known: A Biography of Mary Roberts Rinehart* (Mysterious Press, 1994); and *Women in World History.*

RING, Blanche (1877–1961). American musical-comedy star. Born April 24, 1877, in Boston, MA; died Jan 13, 1961, in Santa Monica, CA; sister of Frances Ring (actress, 1882–1951); m. James Walker Jr.; m. Edward Wentworth; m. Frederick E. McKay; m. Charles Winninger (div.). ❖ Had 1st success singing "In the Good Old Summertime" (1902); appeared in numerous musicals and plays, including *Tommy Rot, The Jewel of Asia, The Blonde in Black, The Jersey Lily, The Pink Hussars, The Great White Way, The Wall Street Girl, The Passing Show of 1919, No No Nanette, Strike Up the Band* and *Right This Way*; popularized such songs as "I've Got Rings on My Fingers," "Bedelia," and "Come, Josephine, in My Flying Machine."

RING, Frances (1882–1951). American actress. Born July 4, 1882; died Jan 15, 1951; sister of Blanche Ring (1877–1961, actress); m. Thomas Meighan (actor). ❖ Made stage debut in *Lost in Siberia* (1900); was a member of Julia Marlowe's company; plays include *Man and His Angel, The Boys of Company B, The College Widow, The Master Key* and *Get-Rich-Quick Wallingford.*

RINGART (fl. 822–825). Queen of Aquitaine. Dau. of Theutbert, count of Madric; m. Pepin I (797–838), king of Aquitaine (r. 814–838), in 822; children: Pepin II (b. 823), king of Aquitaine; Charles (b. around 825), archbishop of Mainz.

RINGGOLD, Faith (1934—). African-American painter and sculptor. Born 1934 in Harlem, NY; m. Robert Wallace, 1950 (div. 1954); City College of New York, MA; m. Burdelle Ringgold, 1962. ❖ Became full-time artist; lectured and taught throughout US; works, which address social and political themes, include murals, such as *Die* (1967), *The Flag is Bleeding* (1967) and *Postage to Commemorate the Advent of Black Power,* as well as sculptures, masks and the story quilt, *Who's Afraid of Aunt Jemima?* (1983); was professor of art at University of California, San Diego; also wrote and illustrated children's books, receiving Caldecott Honor Award for *Tar Beach* and Jane Addams Award for *Aunt Harriet's Underground Railroad in the Sky.* ❖ See also memoir, *We Flew Over the Bridge* (1995).

RINGWOOD, Gwen Pharis (1910–1984). Canadian playwright. Born Aug 13, 1910, in Anatone, Washington; died of cancer, May 27, 1984; dau. of Leslie and Mary (Bowerstock) Pharis; University of Alberta, BA, 1934; attended Banff School of Fine Arts (1935) and Carolina Playmakers School at University of North Carolina; m. John Brian Ringwood. ❖ Important influence on contemporary Canadian drama, became known as the voice of prairie regionalism; moved with family to Canada (1913), farming first near Barons (1913–17), then Magrath (1917–25), in southern Alberta; lived in Montana (1926–29); produced and wrote over 60 plays, including *The Dragons of Kent* (1935), *Still Stands the House* (1939), *Dark Harvest* (1945), *The Rainmaker, Widgers Way,* and *The Collected Plays of Gwen Pharis Ringwood* (1982); also wrote novel *Younger Brother* (1959).

RINKER, Laurie (1962—). American golfer. Name variations: Laurie Rinker-Graham. Born Sept 28, 1962, in Stuart, FL; m. Rob Graham, 1991; children: 2 sons. ❖ Won Doherty Challenge Cup (1982); won Boston Five Classic and Bridgestone Ladies Open on JLPGA tour (1984); won Corning Classic (1986).

RINNE, Fanny (1980—). German field-hockey player. Born April 15, 1980, in Mannheim, Germany. ❖ Won a team gold medal at Athens Olympics (2004).

RINSER, Luise (1911–2002). German novelist, short-story writer, diarist and essayist. Born 1911 in Pitzling, Bavaria; died Mar 17, 2002, in Upper Bavaria; dau. of devout Catholics; studied psychology at University of Munich and became a teacher. ❖ Published 1st book, *Die gläsernen Ringe* (The Glass Rings, 1940), about a woman growing up under National Socialism, to great success, though it was banned from a 2nd edition; arrested by Nazis on charges of high treason and disruption of the military (Oct 1944), survived only because the documentary evidence against her was burned in an air raid; spent last months of WWII in prison; after the war, became one of the best-known German writers of the postwar period, publishing such works as *Gefangnis-Tagebuch* (Prison Diary, 1946), *Hochebene* (High Plateau, 1948), *Die Stärkeren* (Those Who Are Stronger, 1948), and the highly acclaimed *Jan Lobel aus Warschau* (Jan Lobel from Warsaw) and *Mite des Lebens* (Middle of Life, 1950); lived for many years in Rome. ❖ See also autobiography, *Wolf umarmen* (Embracing the Wolf, 1981).

RINSHI (fl. 900s). Japanese royal. Dau. of a high-ranking court official; became principal wife of Fujiwara no Michinaga (966–1028, head of the famous Fujiwara family during their period of greatest power and influence), in 987; children: daughters Shoshi (fl. 990–1010), Kenshi, Ishi, and Kishi, and son Yorimichi (who became emperor).

RIO, Rita (1914–1989). *See Drake, Dona.*

RIPERTON, Minnie (1947–1979). African-American pop singer. Name variations: (pseudonym) Andrea Davis; Minnie Riperton Rudolph. Born in Chicago, IL, Nov 8, 1947; died July 12, 1979, in Los Angeles, CA; m. Richard (Dicky) Rudolph (musician and producer). ❖ Gifted with a 5-octave voice, joined all-girl group, the Gems (1961); was a backup singer for such artists as Etta James and Johnny Nash; became lead singer of soul group, Rotary Connection (1960s), which released a number of albums and opened for such acts as Sly and the Family Stone, Janis Joplin, and Rolling Stones; recorded as a solo artist under name Andrea Davis; released 1st album under own name, *Come to My Garden* (1970); toured as a backup singer for Roberta Flack and Quincy Jones; signed with Epic (1973); found fame with album *Perfect Angel* (1974), which became an instant smash, propelled by international hit single "Loving You," co-written by Riperton and husband Dicky Rudolph; released 2 more albums for Epic, *Adventures in Paradise* (1975), which reached Top 20, and *Stay in Love* (1977); career slowed significantly when diagnosed with breast cancer at age 29; did not hide fight with cancer, at the time considered an improper subject for discussion, but toured the talk-show circuit and told other women about her surgery and treatment; signed with Capitol Records and released album *Minnie,* which included hit singles "Memory Lane" and "Lovers and Friends" (1979); her album *Love Lives Forever* was released posthumously by Capitol (1980); has been credited with influencing the next generation of women singers (such as Whitney Houston and Mariah Carey) who use their wide-ranging voices instrumentally. Received award for courage and public service from President Jimmy Carter (1977); became 1st African-American woman named national educational chair of the American Cancer Society (1978). ❖ See also *Women in World History.*

RIPLEY, Martha Rogers (1843–1912). American physician and suffragist. Born Martha George Rogers in Lowell, Vermont, Nov 30, 1843; died April 18, 1912, in Minneapolis, Minnesota; dau. of Francis and Esther Ann (George) Rogers; graduate of Boston University Medical School, 1883; m. William Warren Ripley (operated a sawmill), June 25, 1867; children: Abigail Louise; Clara Esther; Edna May. ❖ Elected president of Minnesota Woman Suffrage Association (mid-1880s); founded the Maternity Hospital, a home for unwed mothers, in Minneapolis (1887). ❖ See also *Women in World History.*

RIPLEY, Sarah Alden (1793–1867). American scholar and teacher. Name variations: Sarah Alden Bradford Ripley. Born Sarah Alden Bradford in Boston, Massachusetts, July 31, 1793; died in Concord, Massachusetts, July 26, 1867; dau. of Gamaliel Bradford III (prison warden and reformer) and Elizabeth (Hickling) Bradford; m. Samuel Ripley (minister and half-brother of Mary Moody Emerson), Oct 6, 1818 (died 1847); children: Elizabeth; Mary Emerson; Christopher Gore; Phebe Bliss; Ezra; Ann Dunkin; Sophia Bradford; one who died young. ❖ Was a teacher of Latin and Greek and a friend of Ralph Waldo Emerson. ❖ See also *Women in World History.*

RIPLEY, Sophia (1803–1861). American educator and Transcendentalist. Born Sophia Willard Dana, July 6, 1803, in Cambridge, MA; died Feb 4, 1861; dau. of Francis and Sophia (Willard) Dana; cousin of Richard Henry Dana, author of *Two Years Before the Mast;* m. George Ripley (1802–1880, leading Transcendentalist), Aug 1827; no children. ❖ A close friend of Margaret Fuller, was the 1st to touch on the "women's question" in her article "Woman," in the *Dial* (1841), complaining that women lose themselves in marriage; was a leading spirit in developing with husband their utopian Brook Farm, a model community based on the ideals of Christianity and Transcendentalism.

RIPPIN, Jane Deeter (1882–1953). American social worker. Born Jane Parker Deeter in Harrisburg, Pennsylvania, May 30, 1882; died in Tarrytown, New York, June 2, 1953; dau. of Sarah Emely (Mather) Deeter and Jasper Newton Deeter; Irving College, BS, 1902, AM, 1914; m. James Yardley Rippin (architect and contractor), Oct 13, 1913. ❖ As an advocate for women and children, played an important role in developing court systems geared to women, and in organizing programs aimed at steering them away from delinquency; served as assistant superintendent of Meadowbrook's Children's Village (1908–10), a Pennsylvania foster home and orphanage; became a caseworker in Philadelphia for Society for the Prevention of Cruelty to Children (1910); founded the Coop, a cooperative boardinghouse, with 5 other women (1911), a forerunner of modern cooperative living; appointed Philadelphia's chief probation officer (1915), supervised probation work for 5 courts: domestic relations, women's court for sex offenders, petty criminal court for unmarried mothers, and the courts for juveniles and miscreants; became director of War Department's Commission on Training Camp Activities for women and girls (1918); appointed national director of Girl Scouts of America (GSA, 1919), serving for 11 years and transforming the Scouts into a well-run, up-to-date organization. ❖ See also *Women in World History.*

RIQUETTI, Gabrielle-Marie-Antoinette de, Comtesse de Martel de Janville. *See Martel de Janville, Comtesse de (1850–1932).*

RISDON, Elisabeth (1887–1958). English-born stage and screen actress. Name variations: Elizabeth Risdon; Elizabeth Evans. Born April 26, 1887, in Wandsworth, London, England; died Dec 20, 1958, in Santa Monica, CA; dau. of John Jenkins Risdon and Martha (Harrop) Risdon; m. George Loane Tucker (died); m. Brandon Evans. ❖ Made London debut as a walk-on in *Lady Patricia* (1911) and NY debut in *Fanny's First Play* (1912); appeared on Broadway in *Misalliance, Footloose, The Green Goddess, The Silver Cord* and *Ned McCobb's Daughter;* film credits include *The Unseen, Mama Loves Papa, Tall in the Saddle, They Made Me a Killer,*

The Egg and I, Shocking Miss Pilgrim, High Wall, Life with Father, Mourning Becomes Electra and *Scaramouche.*

RISSON, Robyn (1945—). *See Thorn, Robyn.*

RISTORI, Adelaide (1822–1906). Italian actress. Born Adelaide Ristori in Cividale del Friuli, Jan 30, 1822 (some sources cite 1821); died Oct 9, 1906, in Rome, Italy; dau. of strolling players; m. Giuliano Capranica del Grillo (Italian marquis), 1847 (died 1861); children: Georgio Capranica del Grillo, a marquis. ❖ One of the leading actresses of the European theater, took to the stage at 4 while parents were members of a touring theatrical company; at 14, enjoyed 1st success in title role in *Francesca da Rimini;* was 18 when she played Mary Stuart in an Italian version of Schiller's play, which would become one of her most famous roles; as a member of the Sardinian company and the Ducal company at Parma, starred in *La Locandiera, Adrienne Lecouvreur, Antigone* and *Romeo and Juliet;* following a short retirement after marriage, appeared regularly in Turin and the provinces; made Parisian debut (1855), taking the city by storm in title roles in *Myrrha* and *Medea;* paid 1st of 4 visits to US (1866), where she won acclaim, particularly in Paolo Giacometti's *Elizabeth;* retired (1885). ❖ See also (in Italian) *Ricordi e studi artistici* (*Studies and Memoirs,* 1888); Kate Field, *Adelaide Ristori: A Biography* (1867); and *Women in World History.*

RITA. *Variant of Margaret.*

RITA OF CASCIA (1381–1457). Italian saint. Name variations: Margarita of Cascia; Rita La Abogada de Imposibles. Born in Roccabornena (also seen as Roccaparena), Umbria, Italy, in 1381 (some sources cite 1377 or 1386); died of TB, May 22, 1457 (some sources cite 1447), at Augustinian convent at Cascia; married a noble at age 12; children: 2 sons. ❖ Patron saint of parenthood and the impossible, endured physical and emotional abuse from ill-tempered husband, who was also unfaithful, for 18 years; following his death and death of her sons, joined the Augustinian convent (1413); worked tirelessly to aid the ill and to convert negligent Christians; experienced extreme pain in her forehead, and an open wound appeared, possibly from a thorn (1441); canonized (May 24, 1900). Feast day is May 22. ❖ See also *Women in World History.*

RITCHARD, Madge (1896–1955). *See Elliott, Madge.*

RITCHIE, Anna Cora Mowatt (1819–1870). *See Mowatt, Anna Cora.*

RITCHIE, Anne Isabella (1837–1919). British novelist and essayist. Name variations: Anne Thackeray; Lady Ritchie; Anna Isabella Ritchie; Lady Anne Thackeray Ritchie; Mrs. Richmond Ritchie. Born Anne Isabella Thackeray, 1837, in England; died Feb 1919 on Isle of Wight; eldest dau. of William Makepeace Thackeray (1811–1863, novelist) and Isabella Gethin Shawe; aunt of Virginia Woolf; m. 2nd cousin Richmond Thackeray Willoughby Ritchie, also seen as Sir Richard Ritchie (worked in Indian civil service and was knighted, 1907), in 1877; children: 2. ❖ Grew up surrounded by many of the leading literary figures of the Victorian era, several of whom became the subjects of her biographical studies; published 1st novel, *The Story of Elizabeth* (1863), based upon her childhood in Paris; became known for novels with domestic settings and themes, in particular *The Village on the Green* (1867) and *Old Kensington* (1873); based 4th novel, *Miss Angel* (1875), on life of Angelica Kauffmann; set 5th novel, *Mrs. Dymond* (1885), often considered one of her best, during Franco-Prussian War (1870–71); nonfiction titles include *Toilers and Spinners* (1874), which exposed the difficulties of unmarried, unemployed women, and *A Book of Sibyls* (1883), a collection of essays about women writers; also wrote *Madame de Sévigné* (1881), *Records of Tennyson, Ruskin and Browning* (1892), *Alfred Tennyson and His Friends* (1893), and the essay collections *Blackstick Papers* (1908) and *From the Porch* (1913); was the model for the character of Mrs. Hilbery in Virginia Woolf's *Night and Day.* ❖ See also *Women in World History.*

RITCHIE, Harriet Maria (1818–1907). New Zealand hospital matron, servants' home matron, and dressmaker. Name variations: Harriet Maria Overton, Harriet Maria Simpson. Born Harriet Maria Overton, Dec 1, 1818, in London, England; died Sept 30, 1907, in New Zealand; dau. of Thomas Overton (laborer) and Mary Overton; m. Joseph Simpson, 1839; m. David Ritchie, 1862; children: (1st m.) 1. ❖ Immigrated to New Zealand (1850); 1st husband left and presumably died in Australia; appointed matron of Lyttleton hospital (1856–62); appointed matron of servants' home and registry office (1864–67); worked as dressmaker from her home (c. 1870s). ❖ See also *Dictionary of New Zealand Biography* (Vol. 1).

RITCHIE, Jean (1922—). American folksinger and folklorist. Born in Viper, KY, Dec 8, 1922; attended Cumberland College in Williamsburg, KY; University of Kentucky in Lexington, AB, 1946; m. George Pickow (photographer), 1950. ❖ Dedicated to preserving traditional songs of the Cumberland Mountain region of Appalachia, served briefly as a teacher in KY before moving to NY to work as a music counselor in Henry St. Settlement; began to sing and play the dulcimer; made 1st solo appearance at Greenwich Mews Playhouse (1950) and could be heard on radio; received Fulbright grant to travel throughout England, Scotland, and Ireland to trace origins of Appalachian folksongs (1952); published *The Swapping Song Book* (1952) and a portrait of her family, *Singing Family of the Cumberlands* (1955), which received favorable reviews; sang to great acclaim at 1st annual Newport (RI) Folk Festival (1959), of which she was one of the original directors; was central in inspiring the American folk music renaissance (1960s); issued 2-vol. album *British Traditional Ballads in the Southern Mountains* (1960), *The Appalachian Dulcimer* (1964), *High Hills and Mountains* (1979), and *None But One* (1981), which received the *Rolling Stone* Critics Award as best folk album of the year; also wrote original material, "The L&N Don't Stop Here Anymore," "Black Waters," and "Blue Diamond Mine," among others; recorded and performed with a number of notable folk musicians, including Doc Watson, Odetta, Sonny Terry, and Brownie McGhee, and was joined on later albums by her sons; performed "Amazing Grace" on PBS video of that name. ❖ See also *Women in World History.*

RITCHIE, Mrs. Richmond. *See Ritchie, Anne Isabella (1837–1919).*

RITCHIE, Sharon Kay (c. 1937—). Miss America. Name variations: Sharon Ritchie Mullin. Born c. 1937; m. Don Cherry (singer); m. Terry Mullin; children: (1st m.) Sean Cherry; Stephen Patrick Cherry who died in the collapse of the World Trade Center. ❖ Named Miss America (1956), representing Colorado; continued career as an actress in theater and tv. ❖ See also Frank Deford, *There She Is* (Viking, 1971).

RITTENHOUSE, Jessie Belle (1869–1948). American poet and critic. Born Jessie Bell Rittenhouse in Mount Morris, New York, Dec 8, 1869; died in Detroit, Michigan, Sept 28, 1948; dau. of John E. Rittenhouse (farmer) and Mary J. (MacArthur) Rittenhouse; graduate of Genesee Wesleyan Seminary, Lima, NY, 1890; m. Clinton Scollard (poet and professor), 1924 (died 1932); no children. ❖ Best known for such works as *The Younger American Poets* (1904), considered a groundbreaking study, and *The Little Book of Modern American Verse* (1913), an anthology that sold over 1,000 copies and was instrumental in creating a receptive audience for new poetry, reviewed regularly for *The New York Times Review of Books* (1905–15); co-founded the Poetry Society of America (1910), serving for 10 years as the organization's 1st secretary; also compiled *The Little Book of American Poets* (1915), *The Second Book of Modern Verse* (1919), *The Little Book of Modern British Verse* (1924), and *The Third Book of Modern Verse* (1927), all of which were both commercially successful and influential; published several volumes of her own poems, including *The Door of Dreams* (1918), *The Lifted Cup* (1921), *The Secret Bird* (1930), and *Moving Tide* (1939), which was awarded a gold medal from National Poetry Center; advanced the cause of modern American poetry in early 20th century. ❖ See also *Women in World History.*

RITTENHOUSE, Sharon (1946—). *See Finneran, Sharon.*

RITTER, Erika (1948—). Canadian writer and comedian. Born 1948 in Regina, Saskatchewan, Canada; McGill University, BA, 1968; University of Toronto, Drama Center, MA, 1970. ❖ Taught at Loyola College (1970–73), then embarked on writing career; had great success with autobiographical play *Automatic Pilot* (1980), about a female stand-up comic; published 2 collections of humor, *Urban Scrawl* (1984) and *Ritter in Residence* (1987), as well as 2 novels, *The Hidden Life of Humans* (1997) and *The Great Big Book of Guys* (2004); hosted regular weekday radio show "The Arts Report" on CBC. Won ACTRA Award for Best Radio Drama (1981) and for Best Host (1986).

RITTER, Louise (1958—). American high jumper. Born Dorothy Louise Ritter, Feb 18, 1958, in Dallas, TX; graduate of Texas Women's University. ❖ Won a gold medal for high jump at Seoul Olympics (1988); won 10 National championships, indoors and outdoors (1979–89). Inducted into USA Track & Field (1995).

RITTER, Thelma (1905–1969). American actress. Born in Brooklyn, New York, Feb 14, 1905; died Feb 5, 1969; graduate of Manual Training High School, Brooklyn, and American Academy of Dramatic Arts; dau. of a singer father; m. Joseph Moran (actor), April 21, 1927; children:

Joseph; Monica Ann. ❖ One of the few character actresses to receive star billing, began career in radio (1944), featured on such programs as "Mr. District Attorney," "Big Town" and "The Aldrich Family"; landed a small part in film *Miracle on 34th Street* (1946); had breakthrough role as wisecracking maid in *All About Eve* (1950), for which she was nominated for Academy Award for Best Supporting Actress; was also nominated for *The Mating Game* (1951), *With a Song in My Heart* (1952), *Pickup on South Street* (1953), *Pillow Talk* (1959) and *Birdman of Alcatraz* (1962); made tv debut in "The Catered Affair" (1955), for which she won an Emmy; won Tony Award for performance in musical *New Girl In Town* (1957); other films include *A Letter to Three Wives* (1949), *Rear Window* (1954), *The Proud and the Profane* (1956), *The Misfits* (1961), *Move Over, Darling* (1963), and *What's So Bad About Feeling Good?* (1968). ❖ See also *Women in World History.*

RIVA, Emmanuelle (1927—). French actress. Born Feb 24, 1927, in Chénimenil, France. ❖ Began career as a dressmaker; made Paris stage debut (1954); made screen debut as Elle in Alain Resnais' *Hiroshima Mon Amour* (1958), followed by *The Eighth Day, Kapò, Climats, Adua e le compagne, Thérèse Desqueyroux* (title role), *Le Coup de Grâce, Thomas the Impostor, Fruits amers, Les risques du Métier, L'Homme de désir, Les portes de feu, Le diable au Coeur, Un home à mataille, Liberté la nuit, Pour Sacha, Blue* and *C'est la vie,* among others.

RIVA, Maria (1924—). American writer and actress. Born Maria Sieber, Dec 23, 1924, in Berlin, Germany; dau. of Marlene Dietrich (1901–1992, actress) and Rudolph Sieber; married; children: 3 sons. ❖ Appeared in the film *The Scarlet Empress*; under name Maria Riva, made frequent appearances on many top shows in the early years of tv, including "Hallmark Hall of Fame," "Philco Playhouse," "Armstrong Circle Theater," "Omnibus," "Studio One" and "Robert Montgomery Presents"; published *Marlene Dietrich* to critical acclaim (1993). ❖ See also *Women in World History.*

RIVÉ-KING, Julie (1854–1937). American pianist and composer. Name variations: Julie Rive-King. Born Oct 30, 1854, in Cincinnati, Ohio; died July 24, 1937, in Indianapolis, Indiana; dau. of Leon Rivé (painter) and Caroline (Staub) Rivé; studied with mother, a musician and alumna of Paris Conservatory; also studied piano in US with Henry Andres, William Mason, and Sebastian Bach Mills, and abroad with Carl Reinecke, Adolf J.M. Blassmann, Wilhelm Albert Rischpieter, and Franz Liszt; m. Frank H. King (businessman who became her manager), 1878 (died 1900); no children. ❖ The 1st great American woman pianist, made public debut at 8; made European debut at Euterpe Musical Association of Leipzig (1874), performing Beethoven's Third Concerto and Liszt's Second Hungarian Rhapsody; for American debut (April 24, 1875), played Liszt's Concerto in E flat and Schumann's "Faschingsschwank aus Wien" with New York Philharmonic Society; by 1936, had given over 4,000 concerts and recitals in US and Canada, 500 of which were with orchestras, and had appeared with Theodore Thomas' Chicago orchestra more than 200 times; frequently played her own compositions, including *Polonaise héroique, On Blooming Meadow, Bubbling Spring* and *Impromptu in A Flat.* ❖ See also *Women in World History.*

RIVERA, Chita (1933—). American dancer, singer and actress. Born Delores Conchita Figueroa del Rivero, Jan 23, 1933, in Washington, DC; dau. of Katherine and Pedro del Rivero (Puerto Rican musician); m. Tony Mordente (dancer), 1957 (div.); children: Lisa Mordente (actress). ❖ Trained on scholarship at School of American Ballet in New York City, but interrupted studies to perform on tour in the chorus of *Call Me Madam* (c. 1952); on Broadway, performed in *The Shoestring Revue* (1955), *Seventh Heaven* (1955), and *Mr. Wonderful*; came to prominence as Anita in *West Side Story* (1957); appeared in Gower Champion's *Bye Bye Birdie* (1960), *Zenda* (1963) and *Zorba* (1968), and Bob Fosse's *Sweet Charity* (1967) and *Chicago* (1975); also starred in *Jerry's Girls, Bring Back Birdie* and *Nine*; appeared on tv and film. Received 8 Tony award nominations and won Tonys for *The Rink* (1984) and *Kiss of the Spiderwoman* (1993); was among those feted at the Kennedy Center Honors (2002).

RIVERA, Frida (1907–1954). *See Kahlo, Frida.*

RIVERA, Magaly Esther Carvajal (1968—). *See Carvajal Rivera, Magaly Esther.*

RIVERA, Pilar Primo de (1913–1991). *See Primo de Rivera, Pilar.*

RIVERO, Lorraine (1924–1974). *See Gaughin, Lorraine.*

RIVERS, Pearl (1849–1896). *See Nicholson, Eliza Jane.*

RIVES, Amélie (1863–1945). American author. Name variations: Amelie Louise Rives; Amélie Rives Troubetzkoy; Princess Troubetzkoy. Born Amélie Louise Rives in Richmond, Virginia, Aug 23, 1863; died in Charlottesville, Virginia, June 15, 1945; dau. of Alfred Landon Rives (civil engineer) and Sarah (MacMurdo) Rives; granddau. of William Cabell Rives (diplomat and writer) and Judith Page Walker Rives (writer); m. John Armstrong Chanler (lawyer), June 14, 1888 (div. 1895); m. Prince Pierre Troubetzkoy (Russian portrait painter), Feb 18, 1896; no children. ❖ Published 1st story, "A Brother to Dragons," anonymously in *Atlantic Monthly* (1886); established literary reputation with bestseller *The Quick or the Dead?* (1888); was active in movements promoting Southern writing; best-known works include the novels *Shadows of Flames* (1915), one of the 1st realistic presentations in American literature of the experience of drug addiction, and *Firedamp* (1930); also wrote several plays and championed educational reform and women's suffrage; works have been associated with the Southern literary renaissance. ❖ See also *Women in World History.*

RIVOYRE, Christine de (1921—). *See De Rivoyre, Christine.*

RIWAI, Kiti Karaka (1870–1927). New Zealand tribal leader. Name variations: Kiti Karaka, Catherine Clark, Kate Clark, Kitty Clark, Kiti Karaka Te Ao Ahitana, Kiti Ashton. Born Sept 12, 1870, on Ruapuke Island in Foveaux Strait, New Zealand; died on Jan 21, 1927, at Greytown, New Zealand; dau. of Arapetere Karaka (Albert Clark) and Mary (Owen) Karaka; m. Riwai Te Ropiha, late 1880s (div. early 1900s); m. Te Ao Ahitana Matenga (Joseph Ashton), 1906; children: (1st m.) 9; (2nd m.) 1. ❖ After 1st marriage ended in bitter family dispute, petitioned for return of inherited land, claiming she and another Maori woman were sole surviving relatives of then ruler; though awarded more than 600 acres, abandoned the land and her children from that marriage when residents demanded succession order be overturned. ❖ See also *Dictionary of New Zealand Biography* (Vol. 3).

RIZEA, Elisabeta (1912–2003). Romanian resistance hero and Gulag survivor. Name variations: Elizabeth Rizea. Born July 28, 1912, in Domnesti, in the southern Carpathians; died Oct 6, 2003, in Pitesti, Romania; married young. ❖ Anti-Communist resistance fighter and Romanian peasant, became a symbol in the battle against tyranny; after their land was expropriated by the Communists, husband joined a resistance group in the Fagaras mountains and she supplied them with food and money (1945); captured by Romanian militia (summer 1949), was tortured and sentenced to 7 years for aiding criminals; after arrest of anti-Communist leader Gheorghe Arsenescu, was sentenced to another 25 years (1961), but pardoned 3 years later under a general amnesty; placed under constant surveillance, was pressured to become an informer; after the collapse of the Ceausescu regime, came to national attention when her story emerged in Romanian newspapers and film (1989).

RIZK, Amina (1910–2003). Egyptian actress. Name variations: Amina Rizq. Born April 13, 1910, in Tanta, Egypt; died Aug 24, 2002, in Cairo, Egypt; never married. ❖ Pioneer in the Egyptian movie industry, began acting (1924) and appeared in 1st stage play, *Soad the Gypsy* (1928); appeared in over 30 films, including *Land of Dreams, I Want a Solution* and *A Beginning and an End*; appointed to the Egyptian Parliament's Upper House, a mostly ceremonial role, by Hosni Mubarak (1997).

RIZPAH. Biblical woman. Dau. of Aiah; concubine of King Saul; children: (with Saul) sons, Armoni and Mephibosheth. ❖ After sons were killed by hanging as retribution for Saul's wrongdoing, kept vigil over their suspended bodies for 5 months, protecting them from wild beasts and birds of prey. ❖ See also *Women in World History.*

RIZZO, Patti (1960—). American golfer. Born June 19, 1960, in Hollywood, FL; attended University of Miami. ❖ Won Trans-National, World Amateur, Eastern and Mexican Amateur (1980); won North and South, South Atlantic, and Harder Hall (1981); joined LPGA and named Rookie of the Year (1982); won Boston Five (1983); won Red Robin Kyocera Inamori Classic (1989). Was *Golf Digest's* #1 ranked amateur (1980).

RIZZOTTI, Jennifer (1974—). American basketball player and coach. Born May 15, 1974, in New Fairfield, CT; attended University of Connecticut; m. William Sullivan, July 17, 1999; children: Holden. ❖ Guard, led University of Connecticut women's basketball team to NCAA championship (1995); was the top pick of the New England Blizzard in American Basketball League (ABL); was twice named to ABL all-star team; joined Houston Comets of WNBA after ABL folded

(1999); traded to Detroit Shock (2001), then Cleveland Rockers (2002); began coaching at University of Hartford, becoming the youngest women's basketball coach in Division I (1999). Named First Team All-America by Kodak, Associated Press (AP) and United Press International (1995–96); named AP Player of the Year (1995–96); named outstanding woman college athlete (1997). ❖ See also *Women in World History.*

ROACHE, Viola (1885–1961). English stage actress. Born Oct 3, 1885, in Norfolk, England; died May 17, 1961, in Hollywood, CA; attended RADA; m. Lionel Bevans (actor-director, div.); children: Phillipa Bevans (actress, d. 1968). ❖ Made London stage debut as Ruth Aiken in *The College Widow* (1908); toured South Africa and Canada (1912–13); made Broadway debut as Elsa in *Panthea* (1914); other NY credits include *Hobson's Choice, The Distaff Side, Pride and Prejudice, Call It a Day, Craig's Wife* and *Angel in the Wings*; was in original cast of *My Fair Lady* as Mrs. Eynsford-Hill (1956), then took over the part of Mrs. Higgins.

ROBA, Fatuma (1973—). Ethiopian marathon runner. Born Dec 18, 1973, in Ethiopia. ❖ Won a gold medal for the marathon at Atlanta (1996), the 1st African woman to win an Olympic marathon; won 3 consecutive Boston Marathons (1997–99).

ROBARDS, Rachel (1767–1828). *See Jackson, Rachel Donelson.*

ROBB, Isabel Hampton (1860–1910). Canadian-born nursing educator. Name variations: Isabel Adams Hampton. Born Isabel Adams Hampton in Welland, Ontario, Canada, 1860; died in Cleveland, Ohio, crushed to death between two streetcars, April 15, 1910; dau. of Samuel James Hampton and Sarah Mary (Lay) Hampton; earned teaching certificate from Collegiate Institute in St. Catherines, Ontario; graduate of Bellevue Hospital Training School for Nurses in NY, 1883; m. Hunter Robb (physician and professor of gynecology), 1894; children: Hampton; Philip Hunter. ❖ Began nursing career in Rome, caring for ill English and American tourists (1883); became superintendent of nurses at Illinois Training School for Nurses at Cook County Hospital in Chicago (1886); appointed superintendent of nurses and principal of the nurses' training school at newly opened Johns Hopkins Hospital in Baltimore (1889); was a founding member of American Society of Superintendents of Training Schools for Nurses of US and Canada (later National League of Nursing Education); played a central role in founding Nurses' Associated Alumnae of the US and Canada (later American Nurses' Association), presiding as its 1st president (1897–1901). ❖ See also *Women in World History.*

ROBB, Mrs. John (1829–1912). *See Robb, Mary Anne.*

ROBB, Lynda Bird (b. 1944). *See Johnson, Lynda Bird.*

ROBB, Mary Anne (1829–1912). English plant collector and botanist. Name variations: Mary Anne Boulton; Mrs. John Robb. Born Mary Anne Boulton, 1829; grew up in Oxfordshire, England; died 1912; dau. of Matthew Robinson Boulton (landowner); granddau. of Matthew Boulton (noted Birmingham coinmaker, manufacturer and engineer); m. Captain John Robb, 1856 (died 1858); children: 2 sons. ❖ Plant collector who introduced an evergreen spurge species, *Euphorbia robbiae*, known as Mrs. Robb's Bonnet, to Britain (1891); nurtured her 150-acre garden in Liphook, Hampshire; donated plant seeds to Royal Botanic Gardens (1890).

ROBBIANI, Heidi (1950—). Swiss equestrian. Born Oct 27, 1950, in Switzerland. ❖ At Los Angeles Olympics, won a bronze medal in indiv. jumping (1984).

ROBBINS, Amy Catherine (d. 1927). *See Wells, Catherine.*

ROBBINS, Frieda Robscheit- (1893–1973). *See Robscheit-Robbins, Frieda.*

ROBBINS, Gale (1921–1980). American actress and singer. Born May 7, 1921, in Chicago, IL; died Feb 12, 1980, in Tarzana, CA; children: 2 daughters. ❖ WWII "pin-up girl," films include *In the Meantime, Darling, My Girl Tisa, Oh, You Beautiful Doll, Three Little Words, The Fuller Brush Girl, Strictly Dishonorable, Belle of New York, Calamity Jane, Double Jeopardy, Girl in the Red Velvet Swing* and *Gunsmoke in Tucson.*

ROBBINS, Jane Elizabeth (1860–1946). American social worker and physician. Born Dec 28, 1860, in Wethersfield, CT; died Aug 16, 1946, in Hartford, CT; dau. of Richard Austin Robbins (seed merchant) and Harriet (Welles) Robbins. ❖ Helped organize and was early resident of New York College Settlement on Lower East Side of NY (1889); opened medical practice in Little Italy section of NY (c. 1891); served as head worker at New York College Settlement (1894–97) and used settlement to advocate for labor, public parks, tenement and educational causes; was head worker at Normal College Alumnae House in NY (1901), Alta House in Cleveland, OH (1902), Little Italy Settlement in Brooklyn (1911), and Jacob A. Riis Neighborhood Settlement in NY (1914); helped organize temporary hospitals in Greece after WWI; returned to Greece to assist refugees of uprising against Turkey (1927–29).

ROBBINS, Kelly (1969—). American golfer. Born Sept 29, 1969, in Mt. Pleasant, MI; dau. of Steve and Margie Robbins; attended University of Tulsa. ❖ Had Rookie year in LPGA (1992); won LPGA Corning Classic (1993); won Jamie Farr Toledo Classic (1994); won McDonald's LPGA championship (1995); won Twelve Bridges LPGA Classic (1996); won Diet Dr. Pepper National Pro-Am, as well as the Jamie Farr Kroger Classic (1997), with the lowest 4-round score in LPGA history; won Healthsouth Inaugural (1998, 1999); was a member of the victorious Solheim Cup Team (1994, 1996, 1998, 2002).

ROBBINS, Pauline Frederick (1908–1990). See Frederick, Pauline.

ROBE, Shirley Pettis (b. 1924). See Pettis, Shirley Neil.

ROBERSON, LaTavia (1981—). American singer. Name variations: Destiny's Child. Born Nov 1, 1981, in Houston, TX. ❖ With Beyonce Knowles, Kelly Rowland and LeToya Luckett, formed the girl-group Destiny's Child (1989) and had hit singles "No, No, No," "The Writing's on the Wall," "Bills, Bills, Bills" and "Say My Name"; replaced, along with LeToya Luckett, formed group Angel with Nadi (early 2000). Albums with Destiny's Child include *Destiny's Child* (1998) and *The Writing's on the Wall* (1999).

ROBERT, Enif Angelini (1886–1976). See Robert-Angelini, Enif.

ROBERT, Louise (1758–1821). See Robert-Kéralio, Louise.

ROBERT, Marie-Anne de Roumier (1705–1771). French novelist. Born 1705 in Paris, France; died 1771. ❖ Works, which focus on injustices done to women and lower classes, include *La Paysanne philosophe* (The Peasant Woman Philosopher, 1762), *La Voix de la nature* (The Voice of Nature, 1763) and *Nicole de Beauvais* (1766); also wrote 2 novels of fantasy, *Voyage de milord Céton dans les sept planètes* (Journey of Lord Seton in the Seven Planets, 1765–66) and *Lesondins* (1768).

ROBERT-ANGELINI, Enif (1886–1976). Italian novelist and actress. Name variations: Enif Angelini; Enif Robert; Enif Angelini Robert. Born 1886 in Italy; died 1976. ❖ Friend of Eleonora Duse, participated in the futurist movement and wrote for futurist journals; established a deep, intimate relationship with F.T. Marinetti; with him, wrote *Un Ventre di donna* (A Woman's Womb: A Surgical Novel, 1919), an autobiographical novel about the futurist women's manifesto and her fight to overcome cancer of the uterus, though Marinetti's voice dominates.

ROBERT-KÉRALIO, Louise (1758–1821). French novelist, translator and historian. Name variations: Louise Félicité de Kéralio; Louise Felicite de Keralio; Louise Félicité Robert; Madame Robert. Born Louise-Félicité Guinement de Kéralio, Aug 25, 1758, in Paris, France, into a noble Breton family; died 1821 in Brussels, Belgium; dau. of Chevalier de Kéralio (professor at the Military Academy) and Françoise (Abeille) Kéralio (writer); m. François Robert (whose father Pierre was député to the Paris Convention). ❖ At 18, wrote 1st novel *Adélaïde* (1782); became a printer and publisher (1786), serving as director of *Journal de l'État et du citoyen* and working for *Mercure national* and *Censeur universel*; with husband, was member of Société fraternelle des deux sexes; worked for 10 years on *Histoire d'Elisabeth, reine d'Angleterre* (History of Elizabeth of England, 1786–88); other writings include *Amélie et Caroline* (1808), *Alphonse et Matilde, ou la famille espagnole* (1809), and *Rose et Albert ou le tombeau d'Emma* (1810); historical and political works include *Observations sur quelques articles du projet de constitutions de M. Monnier* (1789), *Adresse aux femmes de Montauban* (1790), and *Les Crimes des reines de France* (1830); completed 14 vols. of *Collection des meilleurs ouvrages français composés par des femmes* (1786–88); trans. works from Italian and English; went into exile in Belgium with husband after the return of the Bourbons.

ROBERTI, Lyda (1906–1938). Polish-born actress and singer. Born May 20, 1906, in Warsaw, Poland; died Mar 12, 1938, in Los Angeles, CA, of a heart attack; dau. of Roberti (German clown) and a Polish trick rider; sister of Manyi Roberti (actress); m. R.A. Golden (div.); m. Hugh "Bud" Ernst, 1935. ❖ Born into a circus, toured Europe and Asia with father as a child trapeze artist, then abandoned the circus (and reputedly her abusive father) in Shanghai while still quite young; became a child café entertainer; immigrated to US (1927), appeared in

vaudeville, and made a triumphant debut on Broadway in *You Said It!*; made screen debut in *Dancers in the Dark* (1932), followed by *Million Dollar Legs, The Kid from Spain, Torch Singer, College Rhythm, George White's Scandals, The Big Broadcast of 1936, Nobody's Baby* and *Wide Open Faces*, among others; briefly starred with Patsy Kelly in Hal Roach comedy shorts, replacing Thelma Todd.

ROBERTS, Caroline Alice (1848–1920). See Elgar, Alice.

ROBERTS, Cokie (1943—). American television journalist. Born Mary Martha Corinne Morrison Clairborne Boggs, Dec 27, 1943, in New Orleans, LA; dau. of Hale Boggs and Lindy Boggs (both US congressional representatives); Wellesley College, graduate in political science, 1964; m. Steve Roberts (professor and journalist); children: Lee and Rebecca. ❖ Was a contributor to PBS-TV's "MacNeil/Lehrer Newshour"; co-hosted "The Lawmakers" (1981–84); served as congressional correspondent for NPR for 10 years and as a political commentator for ABC News; co-anchored "This Week with Sam Donaldson and Cokie Roberts" (1996–2002); wrote *We Are Our Mother's Daughters* (1998) and *Founding Mothers: The Women Who Raised Our Nation* (2004). Received Edward R. Murrow Award and Everett McKinley Dirksen Award. ❖ See also memoir, *From This Day Forward* (2000).

ROBERTS, Doris (1929—). American actress. Born Doris May Roberts, Nov 4, 1929, in St. Louis, MO; grew up in the Bronx and Manhattan; studied at Neighborhood Playhouse; m. Michael Cannata, 1950 (div. 1962); m. William Goyen, 1963 (died 1983); children: (1st. m) Michael. ❖ Character actress, appeared on Broadway in *The Time of Your Life* (1955), *Last of the Red Hot Lovers* (1969) and *Bad Habits* (1974), among others; tv appearances include "The Mary Tyler Moore Show," "Soap," "Maggie," and "Remington Steele"; had best role as Marie Barone in "Everybody Loves Raymond" (1996–2005); films include *Something Wild* (1961), *Little Murders* (1971), *A New Leaf* (1971), *The Taking of Pelham One Two Three* (1974), *Hester Street* (1975), *The Rose* (1979) and *Dickie Roberts: Former Child Star* (2003).

ROBERTS, Dorothea Klumpke (1861–1942). See Klumpke, Dorothea.

ROBERTS, Edith (1899–1935). American actress. Born Edith Josephine Roberts, Sept 17, 1899, in NYC; died in childbirth, Aug 20, 1935, in Los Angeles, CA; sister of Leona Roberts (actress); aunt of Josephine Hutchinson (actress); m. Kenneth Snoke. ❖ Began work for Universal (1914), specializing in comedies; appeared on Broadway in Ziegfeld's *Midnight Frolic*; films include *Beans, Lasca, The Adorable Savage, Seven Keys to Baldpate* and *The Jazz Girl*.

ROBERTS, Eirlys (b. 1911). English consumer activist. Born in London, England, Jan 3, 1911; dau. of a doctor; attended Clapham High School in London; earned a Classics degree from Girton College, Cambridge; m. John Cullen, in 1941. ❖ Founded the Consumers' Association (1957), heading up the research and editorial division; created the pioneer publication *Which?* (1961), advocating greater safety and efficiency standards for products as well as public accountability; served as part-time director of Bureau of European Consumer Organizations, based in Brussels (1973–78); was chair of the Research Institute for Consumer Affairs and chair of the Environment and Consumer Protection subcommittee of European Economic Community. Awarded Order of the British Empire (OBE, 1971) and made Dame Commander of the British Empire (DBE, 1977). ❖ See also *Women in World History*.

ROBERTS, Elisa Mary (1970—). Australian politician. Born Sept 3, 1970, in Sydney, Australia. ❖ Served as a soldier with the Australian Defence Force at Victoria Barracks, Sydney (1989–93); was a member of Pauline Hanson's One Nation Party (2001–02); as an Independent, elected to the Queensland Parliament for Gympie (2001).

ROBERTS, Elizabeth (1864–1922). See MacDonald, Elizabeth Roberts.

ROBERTS, Elizabeth Madox (1881–1941). American novelist and poet. Born in Perryville, Kentucky, Oct 30, 1881; died in Orlando, Florida, Mar 13, 1941; dau. of Simpson Roberts and Mary Elizabeth (Brent) Roberts; attended State College (later University) of Kentucky; University of Chicago, PhB, 1921; never married; no children. ❖ Taught school in hometown and nearby villages for 10 years; published 1st poems, *In the Great Steep's Garden* (1915); won Fiske Prize from University of Chicago for poems later published in *Under the Tree* (1922); published 1st novel, *The Time of Man* (1926), which reworked *The Odyssey* into the epic story of a pioneer woman's life, and was translated into several languages; published 2nd novel, *My Heart and My Flesh* (1927), followed by *Jingling in the Wind* (1928); returned to historical novel genre for 4th book *The Great Meadow* (1930); also a gifted short-story writer, wrote such collections as *The Haunted Mirror* (1932) and *Not by Strange Gods* (1941); wrote last novel, *Black Is My Truelove's Hair* (1938). Won John Reed Memorial Prize of Poetry (1928) and Poetry Society of South Carolina's prize (1931); won O. Henry short story award (1930). ❖ See also *Women in World History.*

ROBERTS, Emma Brignell (c. 1848–1922). *See Ostler, Emma Brignell.*

ROBERTS, Flora (c. 1921–1998). American theatrical agent. Born c. 1921; died Dec 13, 1998, in New York, NY. ❖ Represented many theatrical clients for over 40 years, including Ira Levin, Stephen Sondheim, Tina Howe, Alfred Uhry, Maury Yeston, Susan Stroman, and Jennifer Tipton.

ROBERTS, Florence (1861–1940). American stage and screen actress. Born Mar 16, 1861, in Frederick, MD; died June 6, 1940, in Hollywood, CA. ❖ Made film debut in *A Wife's Suspicion* (1917); appeared in Mack Sennett's *Grandma's Girl* and *Dance Hall Marge*; played Granny Jones in "The Jones Family" series of films (1936–40).

ROBERTS, Florence (1871–1927). American stage and screen actress. Born Feb 14, 1871, in New York, NY; died July 17, 1927, in Los Angeles, CA; cousin of Theodore Roberts (actor); m. Lewis Morrison (died 1906); m. Frederik Vogednig. ❖ Made stage debut in San Francisco in *Arrah-Na-Pogue* (1888); for many years, played leads in her 1st husband's repertory company; toured Pacific Coast as Sylvia in *Giaconda*, Zaza, Sapho, Magda, Lady Ursula in *The Adventure of Lady Ursula*, Nora in *A Doll's House*, and Tess in *Tess of the D'Urbervilles* (1903–04); made NY debut in *The Strength of the Weak* (1906); other plays include *Jim the Penman, Diplomacy* and *The Claim*; starred in the film *Sapho* (1913).

ROBERTS, Jane Elizabeth (c. 1852–1942). *See Harris, Jane Elizabeth.*

ROBERTS, Jane Elizabeth Gostwycke (1864–1922). *See Macdonald, Jane Elizabeth Gostwycke.*

ROBERTS, Julia (1967—). American actress. Born Julie Fiona Roberts, Oct 28, 1967, in Smyrna, GA; sister of Lisa Roberts Gillan (actress) and Eric Roberts (actor); m. Lyle Lovett (singer and musician), 1993 (div. 1995); m. Daniel Moder (cameraman), July 4, 2002; children: (twins) Phinnaeus and Hazel (b. 2004). ❖ Came to prominence in *Mystic Pizza* (1988) and had a smash hit with *Pretty Woman* (1990), becoming the highest-paid actress in film history; won Academy Award for Best Actress for performance in *Erin Brockovich* (2000); other films include *Steel Magnolias* (1989), *The Pelican Brief* (1993), *Michael Collins* (1996), *My Best Friend's Wedding* (1997), *Notting Hill* (1999), *Runaway Bride* (1999), *Ocean's Eleven* (2001) and *Mona Lisa Smile* (2003).

ROBERTS, Kate (1891–1985). Welsh nationalist, writer, publisher and journalist. Born in North Wales, 1891; died 1985; dau. of a quarryman; attended University College of North Wales, Bangor; m. Morris T. Williams (publisher), 1928. ❖ Began career as a teacher of Welsh in South Wales during Depression; with husband, bought publishing firm of Gwasg Gee in Denbigh and its Welsh-language paper, *Y Faner* (The Banner); joined Welsh Nationalist Party (Plaid Cymru), whose aim is self-government for Wales, and wrote for its newspaper *Y Ddraig Goch* (The Red Dragon); her short stories are reminiscent of those of Chekhov and Maupassant; also wrote books for children. ❖ See also *Women in World History.*

ROBERTS, Lydia (1879–1965). American nutritionist and educator. Born Lydia Jane Roberts, June 30, 1879, in Hope Township, Barry Co., MI; died May 28, 1965, in Rio Piedras, Puerto Rico; dau. of Warren Roberts (carpenter) and Mary (McKibbin) Roberts; graduate of Mt. Pleasant Normal School (later Central Michigan University), 1899, Life Certificate, 1909; University of Chicago, BS, 1919, MS, 1919, PhD, 1928. ❖ American nutritionist and educator who believed in relation between diet and health, taught at schools in Michigan, Missouri, and Virginia (1899–1915); was assistant professor in home economics department at University of Chicago (1919–28), then associate professor (1928–30), full professor and chair of department (1930–44); served on Committee on Nutrition of White House Conference on Child Health and Protection (1929); during WWII, recommended enrichment of flour and bread with vitamins and minerals to improve nutrition; conducted nutrition survey of Puerto Rico for US Department of Agriculture (1943); worked for University of Puerto Rico (1946–52), serving as chair of home economics department; led nutrition education project which increased economic assistance to isolated communities in PR, and became model for island.

ROBERTS, Lynne (1919–1978). American actress. Name variations: Lynn Roberts, Mary Hart. Born Theda Mae Roberts, Nov 22, 1919, in El Paso, TX; died April 1, 1978, in Sherman Oaks, CA; m. William Englebert Jr., 1941 (div. 1944); m. Louis John Gardella, 1944 (div. 1952); m. Hyman B. Samuels, 1953 (div. 1961); m. Don Sebastian, 1971. ❖ Star of numerous B pictures and serials, made film debut as Lynne Roberts in *Dangerous Holiday*, followed by *The Lone Ranger, Dick Tracy Returns, Hi-Yo Silver, High School, Romance of the Rio Grande, Yank in the RAF, Call of the Klondike,* among many others (1937–53); appeared under name Mary Hart in *Love Is on the Air* (1938), followed by *Billy the Kid Returns, Come on Rangers, Shine on Harvest Moon,* and 7 other films (1938–39); appeared under Lynn Roberts in *Hollywood Stadium Mystery* (1938).

ROBERTS, Margaret (b. 1925). *See Thatcher, Margaret.*

ROBERTS, Marguerite (1905–1989). American screenwriter. Name variations: Maggie Roberts; Marguerite Sanford. Born in Clarks, Nebraska, Nov 26, 1905; died Feb 17, 1989, in Santa Barbara, California; attended Colorado State Teaching College; m. 2nd husband, John Sanford (writer). ❖ Screenwriter for Fox and MGM (1930s–40s), wrote several box-office hits for Clark Gable, including *Honky Tonk* (1941) and *Somewhere I'll Find You* (1942); took a job at Fox as secretary to studio head Winfield Sheehan (1927); later apprenticed in script department; wrote screenplay for *Peck's Bad Boy* (1934), a vehicle for Jackie Cooper, as well as *Hollywood Boulevard* (1936); went on to become one of MGM's most respected and highly paid screenwriters, with such films as *Escape* (1940), *Ziegfeld Girl* (1941), *Dragonseed* (1944) *Desire Me* (1947), *The Sea of Grass* (1947), *Ambush* (1949) and *Soldiers Three* (1951); accused of being a Communist by House Un-American Activities Committee (1951), was blacklisted and did not work for over a decade; reemerged to write her most celebrated screenplay, *True Grit* (1969); later screenplays include *Diamond Head* (1962), *Five Card Stud* (1968), *Norwood* (1970), *Red Sky at Morning* (1971) and *Shoot Out* (1971). ❖ See also John Sanford, *Maggie: A Love Story* (Barricade, 1993); and *Women in World History.*

ROBERTS, Mary (1788–1864). English natural history writer. Born Mar 18, 1788, in Gloucestershire, England; died Jan 13, 1864; granddau. of Reverend Thomas Lawson (Quaker herbalist and botanist). ❖ Until father's death, lived at Painswick in Gloucestershire; moved to London with mother; wrote 15 books about natural history, including *The Conchologist's Companion* (1824 and 1834) and *Annals of My Village, Being a Calender of Nature for Every Month in the Year* (1831).

ROBERTS, Mary Louise (1886–1968). New Zealand masseuse, physiotherapist, and mountaineer. Born Feb 17, 1886, in Dunedin, New Zealand; died May 27, 1968, in Dunedin; dau. of Edward Roberts (mechanical engineer) and Elizabeth (Fletcher) Roberts. ❖ Trained as physiotherapist and entered private practice with orthopedic surgeon; appointed masseuse and instructor at Dunedin Hospital Training School of Massage and Physiotherapy (1922), and was principal of Dunedin Hospital school of Massage (1925–46); member of Otago Hospital Board (1947–53); founding member of New Zealand Alpine Club's Otago section; a climber, made ascents of Mt. Sybil (1931), Mt. La Perouse and Mt. Copland (1932), Price Peak (1934) and Eros (1935). Awarded OBE (1946). ❖ See also *Dictionary of New Zealand Biography* (Vol. 4).

ROBERTS, Mary May (1877–1959). American nurse. Born Jan 30, 1877, in Duncan City (now part of Cheboygan), MI; died Jan 11, 1959; graduate of Jewish Hospital School of Nursing in Cincinnati, OH, 1899. ❖ An editor of the *American Journal of Nursing* (*AJN*) for 30 years, 1st worked as superintendent of nurses at Savannah Hospital (1900–03); served as a director of American Red Cross' Lake Division Bureau of Nursing (1917); was chief nurse and director at Army School of Nursing at Camp Sherman, OH (1918–19); succeeded Sophia Palmer as editor of *American Journal of Nursing*; as *AJN* editor, moved its headquarters from Rochester to NY and improved the journal's quality and circulation; directed American Nurses Association's (ANA) Nursing Information Bureau (1934–48); retired from *AJN* (1949).

ROBERTS, Patricia (1955—). African-American basketball player. Born June 14, 1955, in Monroe, GA; attended Kansas State University. ❖ At Montreal Olympics, won a silver medal in team competition (1976).

ROBERTS, Rachel (1927–1980). Welsh actress. Born Sept 20, 1927, in Llanelly, Wales; committed suicide, Nov 26, 1980, in Los Angeles, California; dau. of Richard Roberts (Baptist minister) and Rachel Ann

(Jones) Roberts; graduate of University of Wales; attended Royal Academy of Dramatic Art; m. Alan Dobie (actor), 1955 (div. 1961); m. Rex Harrison (actor), in Mar 21, 1962 (div. 1971); no children. ❖ Had breakthrough part of the blowsy, unfaithful wife in *Saturday Night and Sunday Morning* (1960), for which she won the British Film Academy's Best Actress award; went on to play a similar role in *This Sporting Life* (1963), earning a nomination for Academy Award as Best Supporting Actress; allowed career to lapse while married to Rex Harrison; appeared in *A Flea in Her Ear* (1968), opposite Harrison, and in *The Reckoning* (1969); appeared at London's Royal Court in *Alpha Beta* (1972), for which she won *Evening Standard* Best Actress award; starred in 2 plays, *The Visit* and *Chemin de Fer*, staged "back to back" by New Phoenix Company, receiving a Tony nomination for each of the characterizations, the 1st "double" in the history of the award (1973); after roles in films *Murder on the Orient Express* (1974) and *Picnic at Hanging Rock* (1976), and a tour in the British play *Habeas Corpus,* had running part as Mrs. McClelland on tv sit-com "The Tony Randall Show" (1976–77); appeared in British tv film "The Old Crowd" and made several features, including *Yanks* (1979); had last feature film role in *Charlie Chan and the Curse of the Dragon Queen* (1980). ❖ See also Alexander Walker, ed. *No Bells on Sunday: The Rachel Roberts Journals* (Harper & Row, 1984); and *Women in World History.*

ROBERTS, Robin (1960—). African-American television sportscaster. Born Nov 23, 1960, in Tuskegee, Alabama; dau. of Lawrence Roberts (one of the Tuskegee Airmen); graduate of Southeastern Louisiana University, 1983. ❖ Was a tennis player, then basketball player in college; was sports director at WHMD/WFPR radio in Hammond, LA (1980–83); served as sports anchor and reporter at WDAM-TV in Hattiesburg, MS (1983–84), WLOX-TV in Biloxi (1984–86), WSMV-TV in Nashville, TN (1986–88) and WAGA-TV in Atlanta (1988–89); became correspondent, then anchor, of ESPN's "Sportscenter" (1990); became co-host on ABC's "Good Morning America" (1998) and host of ABC's "Wide World of Sports" (1998).

ROBERTS, Sally (1884–1955). *See Martin, Sara.*

ROBERTS, Sheila (1937—). South African novelist and short-story writer. Born 1937 in Johannesburg, South Africa. ❖ Settled in US (1970s) and became professor of English at University of Wisconsin, Milwaukee; short stories explore lives of underclass in South Africa; fiction includes *Outside Life's Feast* (1975), *He's My Brother* (1977), *The Weekenders* (1981), *This Time of Year and Other Stories* (1983), *Jacks in Corners* (1987), and *Coming In and Other Stories* (1993); poetry includes *Lou's Life and Other Poems* (1977) and *Dialogues and Divertimenti* (1985); published criticism on South African writers, including Dan Jacobson, and book of essays on women writers, *Still the Frame Holds* (1986). Received Thomas Pringle Prize.

ROBERTS, Sue (1948—). American golfer. Name variations: Susan Roberts. Born June 22, 1948, in Oak Park, IL. ❖ Joined the LPGA tour (1969); won the Niagara Frontier, was co-winner of Southgate Open, and had 12 top-10 finishes (1974); won San Isidro Open (1975) and American Defender (1976).

ROBERTS, Susan (1939—). South African swimmer. Born April 21, 1939, in South Africa. ❖ At Melbourne Olympics, won a bronze medal in the 4 x 100-meter freestyle relay (1956).

ROBERTS, Tiffany (1977—). American soccer player. Born May 5, 1977, in Petaluma, CA. ❖ Midfielder; won a gold medal at Atlanta Olympics (1996); won a team gold at World Cup (1999); was a founding member of the Women's United Soccer Association (WUSA); signed with the Carolina Courage (2002), becoming captain. ❖ See also Jere Longman *The Girls of Summer* (HarperCollins, 2000).

ROBERTSHAW, Katherine Te Rongokahira (1873–1939). *See Parata, Katherine Te Rongokahira.*

ROBERTSON, Agnes (1833–1916). Scottish actress. Name variations: Agnes Kelly Robertson; Mrs. Dion Boucicault. Born in Edinburgh, Scotland, Dec 25, 1833; died in London, England, Nov 6, 1916; dau. of Thomas Robertson; m. Dionysius Lardner (Dion) Boucicault, also known as Dion Boucicault the Elder (1822–1890, actor and dramatist), in 1853 (div. 1889); children: Dion William; Eva (or Eve) Boucicault; Darley George ("Dot") Boucicault, later known as Dion Boucicault the Younger (1859–1929, actor, manager and stage director who m. actress Irene Vanbrugh; Patrice Boucicault; Nina Boucicault (1867–1950, actress); Aubrey Boucicault (actor and writer). ❖ Began acting career at 10, with an appearance at Theatre Royal in Aberdeen; appeared at

Princess' Theatre in London in several plays (1850–53), including *The Vampire* and *The Prima Donna* by Irish playwright Dion Boucicault the Elder; with husband, left for US (1853); made NY debut at Burton's Theater (1853), playing multiple roles in *The Young Actress,* a musical farce adapted by Boucicault; quickly became one of the most popular actresses in US, often starring in husband's plays, such as *Jessie Brown, or The Relief of Lucknow* (1858) and the enduringly popular *The Colleen Bawn* (1860); also starred in successful productions of *Dot and Smike* (1859), *The Octoroon* (1859) and *Jeanie Dreams* (also called *The Heart of Midlothian,* 1860); reappeared in England (1860–72), in Boucicault's *Arrah-na-Pogue* (1865) and *The Long Strike* (1866); gave final performance, at the Princess' Theatre (1896). ❖ See also *Women in World History.*

ROBERTSON, Alice Mary (1854–1931). American educator and politician. Born Mary Alice Robertson at Tullahassee Mission, Indian Territory (now Tullahassee, Oklahoma), Jan 2, 1854; died in Muskogee, Oklahoma, July 1, 1931; dau. of William Schenck Robertson and Ann Eliza (Worcester) Robertson (both missionary teachers); granddau. of Congregational minister Samuel A. Worcester; attended Elmira College in NY, 1871–73; never married; children: adopted Native American daughter, Suzanne Barnett. ❖ Ran a Presbyterian mission girls' boarding school at Muskogee which was expanded (1894) into a coeducational college (it would later be moved to Tulsa and renamed University of Tulsa); became federal supervisor of Creek schools (1899); also served as postmistress of Muskogee (1905–13); though she had opposed women's suffrage, ran for Congress on a Republican ticket after ratification of 19th amendment (1920); as the only woman member of Congress, garnered much public attention, though career was fairly unremarkable; was assigned to the House Committee on Indian Affairs, the Committee on Expenditures in the Interior Department, and the Committee on Woman Suffrage; became the 1st woman to preside over a session of House of Representatives, when she announced the vote for the funding of a US delegation to Peru for the centennial celebration of Peru's independence (1921); lost election (1922). ❖ See also *Women in World History.*

ROBERTSON, Ann (1825–1922). New Zealand hotel and landowner. Name variations: Ann West. Born May 17, 1825, at New Scone, Perthshire, Scotland; died Dec 14, 1922, at Rotorua, New Zealand; dau. of John West (weaver) and Mary (Brough) West; m. James Robertson (soldier), 1853 (died 1897); children: 4. ❖ Immigrated when husband enlisted for military service in New Zealand (1864); purchased Ohinemuru Hotel in Rotorua, but was ejected when ownership challenged by prominent businessman (1880); later lost property on which she had established bakery, resulting in her bankruptcy; petitioned Parliament to receive compensation for losses resulting from Thermal-Springs District Act (1884); reportedly the 1st woman to address House of Representatives. Initially denied, her claim was eventually successful and she awarded a 40-acre estate and land leases in Rotorua. ❖ See also *Dictionary of New Zealand Biography* (Vol. 2).

ROBERTSON, Ann Worcester (1826–1905). American missionary and teacher. Born Ann Eliza Worcester, Nov 7, 1826, at Brainerd Mission, in Cherokee Nation, TN; died Nov 19, 1905, in Muskogee, OK; dau. of Samuel Austin Worcester (linguist and missionary) and Ann (Orr) Worcester; m. William Schenck Robertson (principal of Tullahassee Manual Labor Boarding School), April 16, 1850 (died June 1881); children: 1 son, 3 daughters, including Alice Mary Robertson (2nd woman elected to US Congress). ❖ Named teacher at new Tullahassee Manual Labor Boarding School in OK (1849); forced to leave area due to closure of school and mission after outbreak of Civil War (1861); returned to OK and rebuilt school (1866); finished Creek translation of New Testament (1887); published translations of Psalms and Genesis, as well as Creek hymnal.

ROBERTSON, Annie (1844–1928). *See Rudman, Annie.*

ROBERTSON, Brenda May (1929—). Canadian politician. Born May 23, 1929, near Sussex, New Brunswick, Canada; Mount Allison University, BSc (Home Econ.), 1950; m. Wilmont Waldon Robertson; children: 3. ❖ Served as president of the New Brunswick Women's Progressive Conservative Association, as well as president of the New Brunswick Association of Home Economists; elected as a Progressive Conservative to New Brunswick Legislative Assembly (Oct 23, 1967), the 1st woman member of the assembly; worked to reduce unemployment and improve social programs, health care and conditions for underprivileged children, as youth minister (1970–74), minister of social welfare (1971–72), minister of social services (1972–74), minister of health (1976, 1978–82), and minister for social program reform (1982–84); appointed to Canadian Senate (Dec 21, 1984); co-wrote with Solange Chaput-Rolland, *Chère Sénateur* (Dear Senator, 1992). ❖ See also *Women in World History.*

ROBERTSON, Carol (d. 1963). One of the Birmingham Four. Murdered Sept 15, 1963, age 14. ❖ With Denise McNair (11), Cynthia Wesley (14), and Addie Mae Collins (14), was in the Sixteenth Street Baptist church basement in Birmingham, Alabama, preparing to attend Sunday school and the monthly Youth Day service, when a bomb went off, killing her and the others (Sept 15, 1963). ❖ See also Spike Lee documentary *4 Little Girls* (1998).

ROBERTSON, E. Arnot (1903–1961). British novelist and film critic. Name variations: Eileen Arnot Robertson; Eileen Arbuthnot Robertson; Mrs. Henry Ernest Turner. Born Eileen Arbuthnot Robertson in Holmwood, Surrey, England, 1903; committed suicide in London, England, Sept 21, 1961; dau. of G.A. Robertson (doctor); m. Henry Turner (general secretary of Empire Press Union), 1927 (drowned in a boating accident, spring 1961); children: 1 son. ❖ Published 1st novel, *Cullum,* followed by *Three Came Unarmed* (both 1928); gained recognition with novel *Four Frightened People* (1931) and her bestseller, *Ordinary Families* (1933); subsequent novels, including *Thames Portrait* (1937), *Summer's Lease* (1940), *The Signpost* (1943), *Devices and Desires* (1954), *Justice of the Heart* (1958) and *Strangers on my Roof* (1964), were never as notable as early writings; after WWII, began working as a film critic. ❖ See also *Women in World History.*

ROBERTSON, Florence (1870–1946). See Richardson, Henry Handel.

ROBERTSON, Grace (1930—). English photographer and photojournalist. Name variations: (pseudonym) Dick Muir. Born 1930 in Manchester, England; dau. of Fyfe Robertson (Scottish journalist); m. Godfrey Thurston Hopkins (journalist and photographer), 1954; children: Joanna and Robert Hopkins. ❖ Publishing all early work under the male pseudonym Dick Muir, became a regular contributor to *Picture Post* (1950–57), documenting postwar life in England; worked in advertising and produced stories for such periodicals as *Life*; for 12 years, was primary schoolteacher while raising children; returned to photojournalism, working frequently for BBC and Channel 4; was subject of retrospective exhibition held at Royal National Theater in London (1993) and a show at Leica Gallery in NY (2000). Received Order of British Empire (OBE, 1999). ❖ See also *Grace Robertson: Photojournalist of the Fifties* (1989) and *A Sympathetic Eye* (2002).

ROBERTSON, Heather (1942—). Canadian novelist and journalist. Born 1942 in Winnipeg, Canada. ❖ Attended universities of Manitoba and Columbia and worked as journalist for *Winnipeg Tribune,* Canadian Broadcasting Corporation, and *Maclean's* magazine; nonfiction includes *Reservations Are for Indians* (1970), *Grass Roots* (1973), *Salt of the Earth* (1974), *The Flying Bandit* (1981), and *More Than a Rose: Prime Ministers, Wives, and Other Women* (1991); novels include *Willie: a Romance* (1983) and *Lily: A Rhapsody in Red* (1986).

ROBERTSON, Jean Forbes- (1905–1962). See Forbes-Robertson, Jean.

ROBERTSON, Jeannie (1908–1975). Scottish folksinger. Born 1908 in Aberdeen, Scotland; died Mar 13, 1975, in Aberdeen; children: Lizzie Higgins (folksinger). ❖ Folksinger who had a profound influence on folk music revival, was one of the "traveling people" who went to Blairgowrie to pick raspberries once a year and whose music was passed down orally from generation to generation; was virtually unknown beyond northeast Scotland until discovered by Scottish folklorist Hamish Henderson (1953); met Alan Lomax; began recording extensively (1950s), mostly on Lomax label; made the earliest known recording of "The Battle of Harlow"; also recorded the celebrated "I'm a Man You Don't Meet Every Day" (also known as "Jock Stewart"); albums include *The Queen Among the Heather: The Alan Lomax Portrait Series* (1998). Awarded MBE (1968).

ROBERTSON, Kelly McCormick (b. 1960). See McCormick, Kelly.

ROBERTSON, Kim Mulkey- (1962—). See Mulkey, Kim.

ROBERTSON, Madge (1849–1935). See Kendal, Madge.

ROBERTSON, Margaret Brunton (1849–1935). See Kendal, Madge.

ROBERTSON, Margaret Murray (1823–1897). Canadian children's writer. Born Aug 22, 1823, in Aberdeenshire, Scotland; died Feb 14, 1897; dau. of James Robertson (minister) and Elizabeth Murray; aunt of

Charles William Gordon (novelist who wrote under name Ralph Connor). ❖ Came to Quebec with family via US; wrote sentimental novels, including *Christie Redfern's Troubles* (1866) and *Shenac's Work at Home: The Story of Canadian Life* (1868).

ROBERTSON, Marjorie (1904–1986). See Neagle, Anna.

ROBERTSON, Muriel (1883–1973). Scottish protozoologist. Born April 8, 1883, in Glasgow, Scotland; died June 14, 1973; Glasgow University, MA, 1905, DSc, 1922. ❖ Studied reptile blood parasites, especially trypanosomes, in Ceylon (now Sri Lanka, 1907–08); assisted professor E.A. Minchin at Lister Institute of Preventive Medicine in London, then served as a full-time staff member (1909–11) and protozoologist (1914–61); while with the Colonial Office for the Protectorate of Uganda (1911–14), studied Uganda's sleeping sickness epidemic (200,000 victims by 1900) and made an outstanding contribution to the control of the disease; during WWI, investigated and helped to create an antitoxin to tetanus; during WWII, studied bacteria-causing gas gangrene; worked on immunopathology of trichomoniasis in cattle with Dr. W.P. Kerr; became a fellow of Royal Society (1947); was a founding member of the Society for General Microbiology.

ROBERTSON, Noel (1915—). See MacDonald, Noel.

ROBERTSON, Selina (1849–1929). See Cossgrove, Selina.

ROBERTSON, Shirley (1968—). Scottish sailor. Born Shirley Ann Robertson, July 15, 1968, in Dundee, Scotland; attended Herriott Watt University. ❖ Won a gold medal for single-handed dinghy (Europe) at Sydney Olympics (2000), the 1st British woman to win an Olympic sailing gold medal; won a gold medal for Yngling class at Athens Olympics (2004), a debut event. Awarded MBE (2000); named International Female Sailor of the Year (2000).

ROBERTSON, Sonia (1947—). Zimbabwean field-hockey player. Born June 2, 1947, in Zimbabwe; identical twin sister of Sandra Chick (field-hockey player). ❖ At Moscow Olympics, won a gold medal in team competition (1980).

ROBERTSON, Mrs. Wybrow (1847–1884). See Litton, Marie.

ROBESON, Eslanda Goode (1896–1965). African-American activist. Born Eslanda Cardoza Goode Robeson; Essie Goode; Essie Robeson. Born Eslanda Cardoza Goode in Washington, DC, 1896; died Dec 13, 1965, New York, NY; dau. of John Goode (former slave and a clerk in War Department) and Eslanda (Cardoza) Goode (osteopath); attended University of Illinois, 1912–14; Columbia University, 1920; studied anthropology at London University, 1935–37; studied at London School of Economics, 1938; enrolled in doctoral course at Hartford Seminary, c. 1939; m. Paul Robeson (activist and actor), Aug 17, 1921 (died 1976); children: son Paul (Pauli) Robeson Jr. (b. 1927). ❖ Advocated racial equality and withstood considerable political and social pressure in the course of her long activist career; began work as an analytical chemist at Columbia Presbyterian Medical Center—probably the 1st black woman to do so; resigned position to accompany husband to London (1925); became his full-time manager (1926); wrote *Paul Robeson, Negro* (1930); was separated from husband (1930–33); with husband, was intensely sympathetic to British Labour's views on social equality, a leftist affiliation they would stretch even further when they traveled in Soviet Union (1935); also traveled to Spain during Civil War to support antifascists; returned with husband to US (1939); joined with other influential blacks to found Council on African Affairs (1941); published *African Journey* (1945), the 1st work by an American to show the need for reform among the colonial powers; represented the Council on African Affairs at founding convention of United Nations; ran as a Progressive candidate for secretary of state of Connecticut (1948), then made a bid for Connecticut's at-large congressional seat (1950), both unsuccessful; with Pearl S. Buck, wrote *An American Argument* (1949), which argued that US failed to be a complete democracy, particularly in its treatment of its black citizens; called before House Un-American Activities Committee, had passport revoked along with husband, effectively ending his career as a concert singer for next 10 years. ❖ See also *Women in World History.*

ROBESPIERRE, Charlotte (1760–1840). French author. Name variations: Marie-Marguerite-Charlotte Robespierre; Charlotte de Robespierre; Charlotte Carrault. Born Charlotte Robespierre, Feb 5, 1760, in Arras, France; died Aug 1, 1840, in Paris; dau. of François Robespierre and Jacqueline-Marguerite (Carrault, also seen as Carraut) Robespierre; sister of Maximilien Robespierre (1758–1794, lawyer and diplomat who served on Committee of Public Safety during Reign of Terror); never married; no children. ❖ Best known for the memoirs she composed on her famous brother Maximilien Robespierre, perhaps the central figure of the French Revolution, and on her own experiences during the Revolution; lived with and kept house for brother Maximilien, and, later, for their younger brother Augustin; was a devoted follower of her brothers' increasingly radical ideas of liberty and democracy; after Augustin was elected to the National Convention (1792), joined him and Maximilien in Paris, where they set up a household together; as the sister of the de facto ruler of France, was a witness to the politics of the innermost circle of the Jacobin leadership; was eventually suspected of opposing the Revolution by both brothers; apparently opposed on moral grounds the widespread violence and bloodshed for which Maximilien was responsible. ❖ See also *Women in World History.*

ROBILANT, Daisy di (fl. 1922–1933). *See Di Robilant, Daisy.*

ROBIN, Dany (1927–1995). French actress. Born April 14, 1927, Clamart, France; died May 25, 1995, in Paris; m. Georges Marchal (actor), m. Michael Sullivan (British producer), 1969. ❖ Began career as a ballet dancer with the Paris Opera; made film debut in *Lunegarde* (1946), followed by *Les portes de la nuit, L'Éventail, Une Histoire d'amour, Jupiter, Elle et moi, Holiday for Henrietta* (title role), *Les amants de minuit, Julietta* (title role), *The Anatomy of Love, Act of Love, Frou-Frou* (title role), *Napoléon* (as Désirée Clary), *Mimi Pinson* (title role), *The Chasers, Waltz of the Toreadors, Tales of Paris, Follow the Boys, The Best House in London* and *Topaz,* among others.

ROBIN, Mado (1918–1960). French soprano. Born in Yseures-sur-Creuse near Tours, France, Dec 29, 1918; died in Paris, Dec 10, 1960; studied with Giuseppe Podestà. ❖ Began career as a concert artist before moving on to opera; was well known in French regional theaters as well as in Brussels and Monte Carlo; sang Gilda from *Rigoletto* and Queen of the Night at Paris Opéra (1945), followed by Constanze from Mozart's *Die Entführung* (1953); also sang at Opéra-Comique and appeared in Brussels, Liège, and San Francisco; was best known for roles of Lakmé and Lucia, though some felt her facility for coloratura were displayed to greatest advantage in such roles as Stravinsky's *The Nightingale.* ❖ See also *Women in World History.*

ROBINE, Marie (d. 1399). French prophet. Name variations: Marie of Gascony; Marie of Avignon. Died 1399. ❖ Peasant woman, arrived at Avignon on a pilgrimage (1387), in the hope of being cured of an illness; miraculously healed at the tomb of the cardinal Pierre of Luxembourg, settled at the cemetery of St. Michael, where she lived as a recluse; visions compelled her to advise her king, Charles VI, and particularly his queen, Isabeau of Bavaria, whom she reproached for her misconduct; was in Paris (June 2, 1398), where the French prelates were holding a council, when she tried in vain to speak before them in favor of the French pope of Avignon; warned the monarchy in apocalyptic tones that if the instructions coming from her voices were not followed, France and Paris would be destroyed by the Antichrist (1399).

ROBINS, Denise Naomi (1897–1985). British romance novelist. Name variations: (pseudonyms) Denise Chesterton; Ashley French; Harriet Gray; Hervey Hamilton; Julia Kane; Francesca Wright. Born Denise Naomi Klein, Feb 1, 1897, in London, England; died May 1, 1985, in Haywards Heath, Sussex, England; dau. of Herman Klein and Denise Clarice (Cornwell) Klein; m. Arthur Robins, 1918; m. O'Neill Pearson, 1939; children: 3. ❖ Works include *The Marriage Bond* (1924), *And All Because* (1930), *Love Game* (1936), *Winged Love* (1941), *The Uncertain Heart* (1949), *The Price of Folly* (1955), *Dance in the Dust* (1959), *The Crash* (1966), *Dark Corridor* (1974), and *Fauna* (1978). ❖ See also autobiography *Stranger Than Fiction* (1965).

ROBINS, Elizabeth (1855–1936). *See Pennell, Elizabeth Robins.*

ROBINS, Elizabeth (1862–1952). American actress, novelist, playwright and author. Name variations: Claire, Clara or C.E. Raimond; Mrs. George Parks; Bessie; Lisa. Born Elizabeth Robins, Aug 6, 1862, in Louisville, Kentucky; died in Brighton, Sussex, England, May 8, 1952; dau. of Charles Ephraim Robins (banker and metallurgist) and Hannah Maria Crow; attended Putnam Female Seminary, Zanesville, Ohio; m. George Richmond Parks, Jan 12, 1885 (committed suicide, 1887); no children. ❖ Hailed as England's 1st great intellectual actress, made her home in Britain, became a suffragist, and promoted women's causes; left home for New York stage in her teens, toured in various companies, and worked for Boston Museum Company where she met her actor husband; in repertory and on tour in America (1881–88), starred in

The Count of Monte Cristo, A Celebrated Case, Forgiven, Julius Caesar and *The Merchant of Venice;* following husband's death (1887), toured with Barrett and Booth; visited Norway (1888) and settled in England; popularized Ibsen on British stage, playing the 1st Hedda Gabler in English (1891) and creating the role of Hilde in *The Master Builder* (1893); managed, produced and wrote plays and co-founded The New Century Theatre; also appeared as Rebecca West in *Rosmersholm* (1893), Princess Zicka in *Diplomacy* (1893), Asta in *Little Eyolf* (1896), Ella in *John Gabriel Borkman* (1896–97), title role in *Mariana* (1897), and Alice (final role) in *Eleanor* (1902); retired from stage (1902); published 1st of 14 novels pseudonymously (under name C.E. Raimond, 1894), also wrote plays, several vols. of short stories and nonfiction; wrote bestselling Klondike tale *The Magnetic North* (1904), after a trip to Alaska to visit brother Raymond; launched suffrage drama in Britain with her play *Votes for Women!* (1907); sat on executive committee of the suffragist Women's Social and Political Union (1907–12); helped convert Dr. Octavia Wilberforce's Sussex house into a women's convalescent home (1920s). ❖ See also Angela V. John, *Elizabeth Robins: Staging a New Life* (Routledge, 1995); Joanne E. Gates, *Elizabeth Robins: Actress, Novelist, Feminist* (U. of Alabama Press, 1994); and *Women in World History.*

ROBINS, Margaret Dreier (1868–1945). American labor and women's rights activist. Pronunciation: DRY-er. Name variations: Gretchen; frequently misspelled as Drier. Born Sept 6, 1868, in Brooklyn, NY; died at Chinsegut Hill, Brooksville, FL, Feb 21, 1945; dau. of Dorothea Adelheid Dreier and her cousin Theodor Dreier (iron merchant); sister of Mary Elisabeth Dreier and Katherine Sophie Dreier; m. Raymond Robins (1873–1954, brother of Elizabeth Robins), June 21, 1905; no children. ❖ Served as chair, legislative committee, the Women's Municipal League (1903–04); was a member of the WTUL (1904–44), president of Chicago WTUL (1907–13), president of National Women's Trade Union League (1907–22); served as executive board member of Chicago Federation of Labor (1908–17); was a member of Illinois state committee of Progressive Party (1912); was a member of the women's division of Republican Party National Committee (1919–20); served as president of International Federation of Working Women (1921–23); was an active member of League of Women Voters (1920s); was a member of the White House Conference on Child Health and Protection planning committee (1929); was reelected to NWTUL executive board (1934); was chair of the League's committee on Southern work (1937). ❖ See also Mary E. Dreier, *Margaret Dreier Robins: Her Life, Letters, and Work* (NY: Island Cooperative, 1950); and *Women in World History.*

ROBINS, Mrs. Raymond (1868–1945). *See Robins, Margaret Dreier.*

ROBINSON, Agnes Mary F. (1856–1944). *See Duclaux, Agnes Mary F.*

ROBINSON, Anastasia (c. 1692–1755). English opera singer. Name variations: Countess of Peterborough. Born c. 1692 in Italy; died in Southampton, England, April 1755; dau. of Thomas Robinson (portrait painter); studied under Dr. Croft, Sandoni, and Baroness Lindelheim; m. Charles Mordaunt, 3rd earl of Peterborough, c. 1722 (died 1735). ❖ Made operatic debut in London in the pasticcio *Creso* (1714) and went on to sing the soprano roles of Almirena in *Rinaldo* and Oriana in *Amadigi,* and in A. Scarlatti's *Pirro e Demetrio;* because of illness, began singing as a contralto (1719), including such roles as Matilda in *Ottone,* Teodata in *Flavio,* and Cornelia in *Giulio Cesare;* also sang in operas by Porta and Bononcini; upon retiring (1724), maintained a musical salon highlighting the works of Greene, Bononcini, and Tosi, among others. ❖ See also *Women in World History.*

ROBINSON, Anna Johnstone (1913–1992). *See Johnstone, Anna Hill.*

ROBINSON, Betty (1911–1997). American runner. Name variations: Elizabeth Robinson; Betty Robinson Schwartz. Born Aug 23, 1911, Riverdale, IL; died May 17, 1997, in CO; m. Richard S. Schwartz (upholsterer), 1939. ❖ At Amsterdam Games, won a silver medal for relay and a gold medal for the 100-meter dash, becoming the 1st woman to win an Olympic gold medal in track and field (1928); seriously injured in a plane crash (1932); won a gold medal for 4 x 100-meter relay at Berlin Olympics (1936). Inducted into National Track-and-Field Hall of Fame, US Track-and-Field Hall of Fame, and Helms Hall of Fame. ❖ See also *Women in World History.*

ROBINSON, Cynthia (1946—). African-American musician. Name variations: Sly and the Family Stone. Born Jan 12, 1946, in Sacramento, CA; children: (with Sly whose real name is Sylvester

Stewart) Sylvettha Phunne Robinson. ❖ Considered the 1st black female trumpet player in pop music, started short-lived group, the Stoners, with Sly Stone (1966), before forming Sly and the Family Stone in San Francisco (1967) and releasing debut single, "I Ain't Got Nobody," backed with "I Can't Turn You Loose"; with group, had hits with "Dance to the Music" (1968) and "Everyday People," which went to #1 on both pop and R&B charts; also released hit album, *Stand* (1969), which stayed on charts for over 80 weeks, and included songs "Don't Call Me Nigger Whitey," "Somebody's Watching You," and "I Want to Take You Higher"; other hit singles include "Hot Fun in the Summertime" and "Thank You (Falettinme Be Mice Elf Agin)"; released *There's a Riot Goin' On* (1971), which contained darker material, went to #1 and included hit, "Family Affair"; saw group disband (1975); other albums include *Fresh* (1973), *Small Talk* (1974), *Back on the Right Track* (1979), and *Ain't But the One Way* (1983). Sly and the Family Stone was inducted into Rock and Roll Hall of Fame (1993).

ROBINSON, Dawn (1968—). American singer. Name variations: Dawn Tshombe; Dawn Tshombe-Robinson; En Vogue; Vogue. Born Nov 28, 1968, in New London, CT; m. Andre Allen, May 2003. ❖ Member of En Vogue, R&B girl group known for 4-part harmonies, which enjoyed great R&B and pop success with such hits as "Hold On" (1990), "My Lovin' (You're Never Gonna Get It)" (1992) and "Free Your Mind" (1992); left En Vogue and joined trio Lucy Pearl, releasing *Lucy Pearl* (2000); embarked on solo career. En Vogue albums include *Born to Sing* (1990) and *Funky Divas* (1992, multiplatinum).

ROBINSON, Dot (1912–1999). Australian-born motorcyclist. Born Dorothy Goulding, April 22, 1912, in Melbourne, Australia; died Oct 8, 1999; dau. of Jim Goulding; m. Earl Robinson (d. 1996), 1931; children: Betty Robinson Fauls. ❖ Known for promoting motorcycling for women, moved to US; raced competitively (1930–61); earned 1st trophy at Flint 100 Endurance race (1930); competed in other off-road enduros including Michigan State championship Enduro, Thanksgiving Day Enduro and Jack Pine Enduro; with husband, set transcontinental sidecar record from Los Angeles to NY in 89 hours and 58 minutes (1935); also road as duo with daughter; traveled the country searching for women who owned and rode their own motorcycles, so as to form Motor Maids of America (now Motor Maids, Inc.), of which she served as co-founder and as 1st president for 25 years; became 1st woman to win Jack Pine Enduro in sidecar division (1940) and won again in 1946; ran successful Harley-Davidson dealership with husband (until 1971); inducted into Motorcycle Hall of Fame Museum (1998).

ROBINSON, Elizabeth (1911–1997). *See Robinson, Betty.*

ROBINSON, Emma (1971—). Canadian rower. Born Nov 26, 1971, in Montreal, Quebec, Canada. ❖ Won a silver medal at Atlanta Olympics (1996) and a bronze medal at Sydney Olympics (2000), both for coxed eights.

ROBINSON, Fiona (1969—). Australian basketball player. Born Feb 7, 1979, in Collie, Western Australia. ❖ Won a team bronze medal at Atlanta Olympics (1996).

ROBINSON, Gertrude (1890–1962). American actress. Born Oct 7, 1890, in New York, NY; died Mar 19, 1962, in Hollywood, CA; sister of Daisy Jefferson (costumer, who also acted under name Daisy Robinson); m. James Kirkwood, Sr. (1875–1963, actor, div.). ❖ Featured with the American Biograph Co. (1908–13), later worked as a bit player or extra until 1957; in later years, was taken care of by Mary Pickford; films include *Pippa Passes, A Corner in Wheat, Willful Peggy* and *Strongheart.*

ROBINSON, Harriet Hanson (1825–1911). American mill girl and suffragist. Born Harriet Jane Hanson in Boston, Massachusetts, Feb 8, 1825; died in Malden, Massachusetts, Dec 22, 1911; dau. of William Hanson (carpenter) and Harriet (Browne) Hanson; m. William Stevens Robinson (newspaper editor and abolitionist), 1848 (died 1876); children: Harriette Lucy Robinson (later Harriette R. Shattuck); Elizabeth Osborne Robinson; William Elbridge Robinson (died at age 5); Edward Warrington Robinson. ❖ At 10, began working in the mill as a bobbin doffer; a year later, led young workers in protest over a wage cut; became husband's editorial assistant on *Lowell Offering,* the monthly literary magazine of the Lowell mill girls, and joined in his efforts on behalf of abolition; after Civil War, shifted concerns to women's suffrage; founded New England Women's Club with Julia Ward Howe (1868); following husband's death (1876), continued activist work with oldest daughter, Harriette Lucy Robinson, organizing a chapter of NWSA in

Massachusetts, speaking before a special Senate committee in Washington (1882); served on 1st board of directors of General Federation of Women's Clubs (1890s); wrote a number of books, including *Massachusetts in the Woman Suffrage Movement* (1881), *"Warrington" Pen Portraits* (1877) and *Loom and Spindle* (1898); other works include the novel *Captain Mary Miller* (1887) and a verse play, *The New Pandora* (1889). ❖ See also *Women in World History.*

ROBINSON, Henrietta (1816–1905). American poisoner. Name variations: The Veiled Murderess. Born 1816; died May 14, 1905. ❖ Mysterious resident of Troy, NY, told various stories as to her origins; was charged with the murders of Timothy Lanagan, grocery-store owner, and Catherine Lubee, whose beer she had laced with arsenic (May 1853); became famous in press as the Veiled Murderess for wearing heavy blue lace veils over her face throughout trial; found guilty, condemned to death, but had sentence commuted to life imprisonment; relocated from Sing Sing to Auburn Prison (1873) and finally to Matteawan State Hospital for the Criminally Insane, where she died in her cell after 52 years of incarceration. ❖ See also D. Wilson, *Henrietta Robinson* (1855).

ROBINSON, Iris (1949—). Northern Ireland politician and member of Parliament. Born Iris Collins, Sept 6, 1949, in Belfast, Northern Ireland; m. Peter Robinson (MP for East Belfast), 1970; children: 3. ❖ Along with husband, served a prison sentence (1988) for refusal to pay fines arising out of protests against the Anglo-Irish Agreement and the public order laws; representing Democratic Unionist Party (DUP), elected to the Northern Ireland Assembly for Strangford (1998); elected to House of Commons at Westminister (2001).

ROBINSON, Jane Bancroft (1847–1932). American Methodist deaconess leader. Name variations: Jane Marie Bancroft; Jane Marie Bancroft Robinson. Born Jane Marie Bancroft in West Stockbridge, Massachusetts, Dec 24, 1847; died in Pasadena, California, May 29, 1932; dau. of George C. Bancroft (Methodist minister) and Caroline J. Orton; half-sister of Henrietta Ash Bancroft; Syracuse University, PhB, 1877, PhM, 1880, PhD, 1884; attended University of Zurich, 1886–87; m. George Orville Robinson (lawyer), 1891 (died 1915). ❖ Was dean of Woman's College and professor of French language and literature at Northwestern University (1876–84) and founded the Western Association of Collegiate Alumnae, an early model of American Association of University Women; was the 1st woman to be admitted to École Pratique des Hautes Études; in Europe, conducted a study of European Protestant laywomen organized in social service—otherwise known as deaconesses—which sparked a desire to see a similar movement among American Methodist women; released findings upon return to US in report *Deaconesses in Europe and Their Lessons for America* (1889), and took control of the newly formed Deaconess Bureau; by end of the century, had charge of 32 deaconess homes, schools and hospitals; served as president of Woman's Home Missionary Society (1908–13). ❖ See also *Women in World History.*

ROBINSON, Jo Ann (1911–1992). African-American civil-rights activist. Name variations: Jo Ann Gibson Robinson. Born Jo Ann Gibson, April 17, 1911, near Culloden, Georgia; died Aug 29, 1992, in Los Angeles, California; Fort Valley State College, teaching degree; Atlanta University, MA in English; married briefly to Wilbur Robinson; children: 1 who died in infancy. ❖ Was a chief participant in the historic bus boycott (1955–56) that led to the desegregation of the bus system in Montgomery, Alabama, and sparked the civil-rights movement nationwide; took a position as a professor of English at Alabama State College in Montgomery (1949); quickly became involved with the Dexter Avenue Baptist Church and Women's Political Council (WPC), assuming its presidency (1950s); after Rosa Parks was arrested, was chief advocate of the bus boycott (1955) and at the heart of activities throughout the 381-day protest; moved to Los Angeles, where she worked as an English teacher in the public school system until retirement (1976). ❖ See also memoir, *The Montgomery Bus Boycott and the Women Who Started It* (U. of Tennessee Press, 1987); and *Women in World History.*

ROBINSON, Joan Violet (1903–1983). British economist. Born Joan Violet Maurice, Oct 31, 1903, in Camberley, England; died Aug 5, 1983, in Cambridge, England; dau. of Helen (Marsh) Maurice and Major-General Sir Frederick Maurice; attended Girton College, Cambridge; m. E.A.G. Robinson (economist), 1926; children: 2 daughters. ❖ Post-Keynesian economist who developed the theory of imperfect competition and linked neoclassical economic theory to that of Karl Marx, was admitted to Cambridge (Oct 1922) and passed the

Economics Tripos (1925); taught in India (1926–28); returned to Cambridge (1928); appointed junior assistant lecturer (1931), full lecturer (1937), reader (1949); after husband retired (1965), appointed full professor; became chair of the Economics Faculty (1965); retired from Cambridge University (Sept 30, 1971); suffered a stroke (Feb 1983); one of the leading unorthodox economists of the 20th century, was the only woman of her generation to achieve prominence in the field of economic theory. Writings include *The Economics of Imperfect Competition* (1933), *Essays in the Theory of Employment* (1937), *An Essay on Marxian Economics* (1942), *The Accumulation of Capital* (1956), *Essays in the Theory of Economic Growth* (1962), *Economic Philosophy* (1962), *Freedom and Necessity* (1970), *The Cultural Revolution in China* (1970), *Economic Heresies: Some Old-fashioned Questions in Economic Theory* (1971), *An Introduction to Modern Economics* (1973), *Aspects of Development and Underdevelopment* (1979) and *Further Contributions to Modern Economics* (1980). ❖ See also Mark Blaug, ed. *Joan Robinson (1903–1983) and George Shackle (1903–1992)* (Elgar, 1992); George R. Feiwel, *Joan Robinson and Modern Economic Theory* (New York U. Press, 1989); and *Women in World History*.

ROBINSON, Julia B. (1919–1985). American mathematician. Name variations: Julia Bowman Robinson. Born Julia Bowman, Dec 8, 1919, in St. Louis, Missouri; died July 30, 1985, in Oakland, California; dau. of Ralph Bowers Bowman and Helen Hall Bowman; attended San Diego State College; University of California at Berkeley, PhD, 1948; m. Raphael Robinson (assistant professor of mathematics), Dec 1941; no children. ❖ Was the 1st woman mathematician elected to National Academy of Science (1976); named full professor at University of California at Berkeley (1976); became the 1st woman officer of the American Mathematical Society (1978) and named its 1st woman president (1982); demonstrated that there is no automatic method of deciding which equations have integer solutions (1961). Awarded fellowship from MacArthur Foundation. ❖ See also Solomon Feferman, ed. *The Collected Works of Julia Robinson* (American Mathematical Society, 1996); and *Women in World History*.

ROBINSON, Kathleen (1901–1983). Australian theatrical producer. Born 1901 in Melbourne, Australia; died Dec 28, 1983; dau. of Mary Louise (McKay) Robinson (niece of millionaire pastoralist Sir Samuel McCaughey) and Matthew John McWilliams Robinson; attended Frensham School in Mittagong, Australia; studied in London at Royal Academy of Dramatic Art. ❖ In London, joined an Australian tour with Lewis Casson and Dame Sybil Thorndike and played minor roles in *St. Joan, Madame Plays Nap* and *Macbeth*; after father's death (1929), moved back to London with mother, where she studied theatrical production; ran Westminster Theatre with Osmond Daltry (1932–35); on return to Sydney (1940), leased the Minerva Theater at Kings Cross with co-director Alex Coppel and formed Whitehall Productions; established an academy for dramatic art (1944). ❖ See also *Women in World History*.

ROBINSON, Madeleine (b. 1908). English child actress. Born Mar 21, 1908, in Pinner, Middlesex, England; dau. of Thomas Heath Robinson and Edith (Barnett) Robinson. ❖ Popular child actress, made stage debut at Covent Garden in *Madame Butterfly* (1919), followed by Lorraine in *Daddies*, Mimsey in *Peter Ibbetson*, Emmeline in *The Blue Lagoon* and Betty in *Where the Rainbow Ends*.

ROBINSON, Madeleine (1916–2004). French stage and screen actress. Born Madeleine Svoboda, Nov 5, 1916, in Paris, France, of Czech parents; died Aug 1, 2004, in Lausanne, Switzerland. ❖ Made film debut in *Soldats sans uniformes* (1934), followed by *Promesses* (1935); other films include *Le Mioche, Les beaux jours, L'Innocent, Nuits de feu, Lumière d'été, Douce, Sortilèges, La Grande Maguet, Entre onze heures et minuit, L'Invité du mardi, L'Homme de ma vie, Leur dernière nuit, Les Louves, On ne triche pas avec la vie, L'Affaire Maurizius, Seuls au monde, Leda, Un monde nouveau, À double tour, Leviathan, Le Procès, Le Petit matin, L'Amant de poche* and *Camille Claudel*; also appeared as Mme Weber in tv miniseries "Mozart" (1982), among others.

ROBINSON, Mary (1758–1800). English actress, author, and mistress. Name variations: Perdita Robinson; Mrs. Robinson; (pseudonym) Anne Frances Randall. Born Mary Darby of Irish descent in Bristol, England, Nov 27, 1758; died in Windsor Park, Berkshire, Dec 26, 1800; dau. of a whaling captain named Darby; mother's maiden name was Seys; m. Thomas Robinson (clerk in London), 1774; children: Mary Elizabeth Robinson (b. around 1775); another daughter who died in infancy. ❖ Completed collection *Poems*, while in King's Bench prison with husband for debt, which was published in 2 vols. (1775); made successful debut as Juliet at Drury Lane (1776) and continued to act there for several years; opened in role of Perdita in Garrick's version of *The Winter's Tale* (1779); was mistress of George, prince of Wales (later King George IV), for 2 years; published several collections of poetry, among them *Sight: The Cavern of Woe and Solitude* (1793) and *The Sicilian Lover: A Tragedy* (1796), and was a member of the Della Cruscan poets' circle; also published a number of novels, including *Vancenza* (1792), *The Widow* (1794), *Hubert de Sevrac* (1796), *Walsingham* (1796), and *The Natural Daughter* (1799), which the public bought eagerly because of the scandal attached to her name; under pseudonym Anne Frances Randall, published a book on marriage, *A Letter to the Women of England on the Injustice of Mental Subordination* (1799). ❖ See also *Memoirs of Mrs. Robinson* (4 vols., Richard Phillips, 1801, new edition, edited by Martin J. Levy, published as *Perdita: The Memoirs of Mary Robinson*, Dufour, 1995); and *Women in World History*.

ROBINSON, Mary (d. 1837). English literary inspiration. Name variations: Mary of Buttermere; Maid of Buttermere; the Buttermere Beauty. Died 1837; unwittingly married infamous forger and imposter John Hatfield, 1802 (convicted of forgery and hanged); m. Richard Harrison; children: 4. ❖ English beauty known as the Buttermere Beauty, achieved such fame for her looks that Samuel Taylor Coleridge, William and Dorothy Wordsworth, and Charles and Mary Lamb all found her to be the most beautiful woman in England; inspired poets to write verses extolling her virtue and grieving over her marriage to a scoundrel and bigamist. ❖ See also Melvyn Bragg, *The Maid of Buttermere* (Putnam, 1987); and *Women in World History*.

ROBINSON, Mary (1944—). Irish lawyer, feminist, and politician. Name variations: Mary Bourke. Born Marie Terese Winifred Bourke, May 21, 1944, in Ballina, Co. Mayo, Ireland; dau. of Aubrey de Vere Bourke and Tess O'Donnell Bourke (both doctors); Trinity College Dublin, BL, 1968; Harvard Law School, LLM, 1969; m. Nicholas Robinson, Dec 12, 1970, children: Tessa (b. 1972); William (b. 1974); Aubrey (b. 1981). ❖ Human-rights lawyer and feminist who helped to advance the legal rights of Irish women and was elected the 1st woman president of Ireland, was 1st elected to Irish Senate (1969) and remained there until 1989; was Reid Professor of Constitutional and Criminal Law at Trinity College (1969–75) and lecturer in European Community Law (1975–90); introduced in senate 1st bill to legalize sale of contraceptives (1971); joined Irish Labour Party (1976); stood unsuccessfully for the Dail (1977, 1981); was a member of Dublin City Council (1979–83); introduced 1st bill to provide for divorce (1980); was a member of the New Ireland Forum (1983–84) and Advisory Commission of Inter-Rights (1984–90); resigned from Labour Party (1985); was a member of International Commission of Jurists (1987–90); was founder and director of Irish Centre for European Law (1989); was a member of Euro Avocats (1989–90); elected president of Ireland (Nov 7, 1990); became the 1st Irish president to meet a British monarch, Queen Elizabeth II (1993); was the 1st head of state to go to Rwanda after the genocide there (1994) and the 1st head of state to visit the International Criminal Tribunal for the Former Yugoslavia; decided not to seek reelection (Mar 12, 1997); served as UN High Commissioner for Human Rights (1997–2002). Received European Media Prize (1991); Special Humanitarian CARE Award (1993) and International Human Rights Award (1993). ❖ See also Fergus Finlay, *Mary Robinson: A President with a Purpose* (O'Brien, 1990); John Horgan, *Mary Robinson: An Independent Voice* (O'Brien, 1997); O'Leary & Burke, *Mary Robinson: An Authorised Biography* (Hodder & Stoughton, 1998); Michael O'Sullivan, *Mary Robinson: The Life and Times of an Irish Liberal* (Blackwater, 1993); Lorna Siggins, *Mary Robinson: The Woman Who Took Power in the Park* (Mainstream, 1997); and *Women in World History*.

ROBINSON, Mary F. (1856–1944). See Duclaux, Agnes.

ROBINSON, Moushaumi (1981—). American runner. Born April 13, 1981, in Hattiesburg, MS; attended University of Texas. ❖ Won a gold medal for 4 x 400-meter relay at Athens Olympics (2004).

ROBINSON, Mrs. Perdita (1758–1800). See Robinson, Mary.

ROBINSON, Ruby Doris Smith (1942–1967). African-American civil-rights activist. Name variations: Rubye. Born Ruby Doris Smith in Atlanta, Georgia, April 25, 1942; died in Atlanta, Oct 9, 1967; dau. of J.T. Smith and Alice Smith; Spelman College, BA in physical education, 1964; m. Clifford Robinson, 1963; children: Kenneth Toure Robinson

(b. 1965). ❖ Civil-rights activist, founding member of the Atlanta Student Movement and the Student Non-Violent Coordinating Committee (SNCC), and outstanding organizer who urged those in the movement for racial justice not only to work for goals which would benefit poor- and middle-class African-Americans but to risk their lives in the process; joined Atlanta Student Movement and Atlanta Committee on Appeal for Human Rights (1960); attended founding meeting of SNCC (1960), elected to executive committee (1962), executive secretary (1966); quickly achieved legendary status within the ranks of SNCC; her ability to merge the passion of a field activist with the careful attention to detail of an effective administrator, made her, in James Forman's words, "one of the true revolutionaries of the civil rights movement." ❖ See also Cynthia Griggs Fleming, *Soon We Will Not Cry: The Liberation of Ruby Doris Smith Robinson* (Rowman & Littlefield, 1998); and *Women in World History.*

ROBINSON, Sarah Jane (d. 1905). Irish-American serial killer. Born in Ireland; died in prison, 1905; married a man named Robinson (murdered 1882); children: William and Lizzie. ❖ While living in Cambridge, MA, indicted for 6 murders by arsenic poisoning (1886), though she may have been suspected in even more cases; killed her husband, sister, and at least 1, if not both, of her children; convicted for murder of her brother-in-law.

ROBINSON, Shawna (1964—). Ameriacn stock car racer. Born Nov 30, 1964, in Des Moines, Iowa; married; children: 1 son, 1 daughter. ❖ Made racing debut on Great American Truck Racing tour (1980); moved to NASCAR stock cars (1988), finishing 3rd in debut race in Goody's Dash Series at Daytona; became the 1st woman to win a NASCAR touring event when she won the Dash race at New Asheville (NC) Speedway (1988); became 1st woman to win a NASCAR Touring pole position in a Dash race at I-95 Speedway in Florence, SC (1989); also won the pole for Busch Light 300 at Atlanta, with a record lap (1994); became the 1st woman to finish in the top-6 of a national motorsports oval series (2000) and the 1st female to run a full season in a national stock car racing series; made Winston Cup debut (2001); had 7 Winston Cup starts (2002) and finished 24th at Daytona 500.

ROBINSON, Sylvia (1936—). *See Vanderpool, Sylvia.*

ROBINSON, Therese Albertine Louise von Jakob (1797–1870). German novelist and translator. Name variations: (pseudonyms) Ernst Berthold; Talvj. Born Jan 26, 1797, in Halle, Saxony; died April 13, 1870, in Hamburg, Germany; m. Edward Robinson, 1828 (died 1863). ❖ Mastered classical languages, Anglo-Saxon, several Slavic and Scandinavian languages, English, French and Spanish; moved with husband to US (1830) and lived in Boston and NY; returned to Germany after husband's death; translations include Sir Walter Scott's *Old Mortality* and *The Black Dwarf* (1821) and John Pickering's *Essay . . . the Indian Languages of North America* (1834); fiction includes *Psyche* (1821), *Heloise* (1850), and *Die Auswander* (1852); nonfiction includes *Volkslieder der Serben* (1825), *Historical View of the Slavic Languages* (1834), *Die Unächteit der Lieder Ossians und des Mcpherson'schen Ossians insbesondere* (1840) and *Fifteen Years, a Picture from the Last Century* (1870).

ROBINSON, Vicki Sue (1954–2000). African-American pop-gospel singer. Born May 31, 1954, in Harlem, NY; died of cancer, April 27, 2000, in Wilton, CT; dau. of Bill Robinson (black Shakespearean actor) and Marian Robinson (white radical folksinger who performed under name Jolly Robinson); m. Bill Good, 1990. ❖ Made public singing debut at 6; signed with RCA, made 4 albums and was nominated for Grammy for Best Pop Female Vocalist; had a huge hit with "Turn the Beat Around," a signature anthem of the disco era (1976); had hit single in UK, "House of Joy"; had off-Broadway show, *Vicki Sue Robinson: Behind the Beat* (1999).

ROBISON, Emily (1972—). American musician. Name variations: Dixie Chicks. Born Emily Burns Erwin, Aug 16, 1972, in Pittsfield, MA; sister of Martie Seidel (fellow Dixie Chicks member); m. Charlie Robison (singer and songwriter). ❖ Vocalist, guitarist, banjoist, and Dobro player, was an original member of country-music group Dixie Chicks, which was formed in Dallas (1989); with group, released back-to-back multiplatinum and Grammy-winning country albums, *Wide Open Spaces* (1998) and *Fly* (1999). Additional albums with Dixie Chicks include *Thank Heavens for Dale Evans* (1990), *Little Ol' Cowgirl* (1992), and *Shouldn't a Told You That* (1993).

ROBISON, Mary (1858–1942). *See Robson, May.*

ROBISON, Maud (1865–1953). *See Reeves, Magdalene Stuart.*

ROBISON, Paula (1941—). American flutist. Born Paula Judith Robison in Nashville, Tennessee, June 8, 1941; m. Scott Nickrenz (violist); studied flute with Julius Baker at Juilliard School of Music and with Marcel Moyse. ❖ Took 1st prize in the Munich Competition (1964); was the 1st American to win 1st prize for flute in Geneva International Competition (1966); with husband, served as artistic co-director of Spoleto Festival of Two Worlds in Italy and Charleston, South Carolina (1977) and Spoleto-Melbourne, Australia Festival of Three Worlds (1986). ❖ See also *Women in World History.*

ROBISON, Shona (1966—). Scottish politician. Born 1966 in Redcar, Scotland; Glasgow University, MA; married. ❖ Began serving on the SNP National Executive Committee; elected to the Scottish Parliment for North East Scotland (1997) and for Dundee East (2003); lost election (1999); became shadow health minister.

ROBSART, Amy (c. 1532–1560). English noblewoman. Name variations: Lady Amy Dudley; Lady Amye Dudley. Born Amye Robsart around 1532 (some sources cite 1535) in Norfolk, England; died Sept 8, 1560, at Cumnor Hall, North Berkshire, England; dau. of Sir John Robsart; m. Robert Dudley (c. 1532–1588), earl of Leicester (r. 1563–1588), June 4, 1550; no children. ❖ Noblewoman whose mysterious death has been the subject of fiction by many writers, including Sir Walter Scott; with her beauty and large inheritance, married into one of England's most prominent families, the Dudleys, hereditary dukes of Northumberland (1550); husband rose to position of prominence at court of Elizabeth I (1558), which led to widespread rumors of a love affair between the queen and courtier; at husband's bidding (1560), set up residence at Cumnor Hall, a house near Oxford; was found dead at the foot of the staircase (Sept 8), causing a major scandal, especially when the queen and Dudley cut short the inquiry into her death. ❖ See also *Women in World History.*

ROBSCHEIT-ROBBINS, Frieda (1888–1973). American pathologist. Name variations: Frieda Sprague. Born June 8, 1888, in Germany; died Dec 1973 in Tucson, Arizona; University of Chicago, BS; University of California, MS; University of Rochester, PhD; married O.V. Sprague. ❖ Moved to US when young; began working with George Whipple at University of Rochester (1917) and remained his research partner for 18 years; with Whipple, conducted research on iron metabolism, discovering factors which cause pernicious anemia, and the usefulness of liver therapy in treatment of the disease; published 21 papers with Whipple (1925–30); was passed over for Nobel Prize (1934), which was awarded to Whipple, though he did share prize money; after Whipple's death, continued research until retirement (1955), still only an associate professor.

ROBSON, Eleanor (1879–1979). *See Belmont, Eleanor Robson.*

ROBSON, Flora (1902–1984). English actress. Name variations: Dame Flora Robson. Born Mar 28, 1902, in South Shields, Durham, England; died July 7, 1984, in Brighton, East Sussex, England; attended Royal Academy of Dramatic Art; never married; no children. ❖ Made stage debut in *Will Shakespeare* (1921); spent 18 months with Tyrone Guthrie at Cambridge Festival Theatre, playing leads and maids; cast as Abbie in *Desire Under the Elms,* followed by Mary Paterson in *The Anatomist,* her breakthrough role (1931); joined Old Vic-Sadler's Wells (1933); appeared in title role of *Mary Read* (1934); was in numerous films, including *Catherine the Great* (1934), *Fire Over England* (1937), *Wuthering Heights* (1939), *The Sea Hawk* (US, 1940), *Caesar and Cleopatra* (1945), *Saratoga Trunk* (1946), for which she was nominated for Academy Award for Best Supporting Actress, *Black Narcissus* (1947), *55 Days at Peking* (1963), *Young Cassidy* (1965), *Those Magnificent Men in Their Flying Machines* (1965), *Alice's Adventures in Wonderland* (1972) and *Clash of the Titans* (1981); made NY stage debut as Ellen Creed in *Ladies in Retirement* (1940); stayed in US for several years, playing in *Anne of England* and touring; returned to NY to play Lady Macbeth opposite Michael Redgrave (1948); was particularly masterful in highly charged roles, as was evident in portrayal of Thérèse Raquin in *Guilty* (1944); was also memorable in *Black Chiffon* (1949); won *Evening Standard* Award as Best Actress for *The Aspern Papers* (1960); made last West End appearance in *The Old Ladies* (1969). Named Dame Commander of the British Empire (1960). ❖ See also *Women in World History.*

ROBSON, Madge (1856–1933). *See Carr-Cook, Madge.*

ROBSON, May (1858–1942). Australian-born actress. Name variations: Mary Robison. Born Mary Jeannette Robison, April 19, 1858, in Wagga

Wagga, NSW, Australia; died Oct 20, 1942, in Los Angeles, California; dau. of Henry Robison (retired sea captain) and Julia Robison; m. Charles Livingston Gore (rancher), 1874 (died 1884); m. Augustus Homer Brown (police surgeon), May 29, 1889 (died 1920); children: (1st m.) 3 (2 died young). ❖ In a 60-year career, was one of America's most enduring and beloved character actresses; moved to US with 1st husband (1874); made debut at Brooklyn Grand Opera House in *Hoop of Gold* (1883); performed with a number of different theater companies during early career, including Daniel and Charles Frohman's; began acting under own management (1889); over next several years, obtained a greater variety of roles, notably in *Dorothy Vernon of Haddon Hall* (1904) and *Cousin Billy* (1905); received particular acclaim for *The Mountain Climber* (1906) and *The Rejuvenation of Aunt Mary* (1907), her 1st starring role; began appearing in silent films for Vitagraph and other companies (1914); moved to Hollywood to make the film version of *The Rejuvenation of Aunt Mary* (1927), then went on to play a series of character roles; best remembered for portrayal of Apple Annie in *Lady for a Day* (1933), for which she was nominated for Academy Award as Best Actress; also appeared in *Dinner at Eight* (1933), *Reunion in Vienna* (1933), *Wife vs. Secretary* (1936), *A Star Is Born* (1937), *The Adventures of Tom Sawyer* (1938), *Bringing Up Baby* (1938), *Nurse Edith Cavell* (1939), *Irene* (1940) and *Joan of Paris* (1942). ❖ See also *Women in World History*.

ROBU, Doina (1967—). Romanian rower. Born July 22, 1967, in Romania. ❖ At Barcelona Olympics, won a silver medal in coxed eights (1992).

ROC, Patricia (1915–2003). English actress. Born Felicia Miriam Ursula Herold, June 7, 1915, in St. Pancras, London, England; died Dec 30, 2003, in Locarno, Switzerland; adopted as infant by Andre Riese, wealthy Dutch-Belgian stockbroker, and named Felicia Riese (was unaware of adoption until age 34); m. Dr. Murray Laing (Canadian osteopath), 1939 (div. 1944); m. André Thomas (French cinematographer), 1949 (died 1954); m. Walter Reiss or Reif (Viennese import-exporter), 1962 (died 1986); children: (with actor Anthony Steel) Michael Thomas. ❖ Popular British star (1940s–50s), made stage debut in *Nuts in May* (1937); made film debut in *The Rebel Son* (1938), followed by *The Gaunt Stranger, Pack Up Your Troubles, Millions Like Us, We'll Meet Again, Love Story, Madonna of the Seven Moons, 2,000 Women, The Wicked Lady, Canyon Passage, Jassy, The Brothers, When the Bough Breaks* and *So Well Remembered*, among others; moved to Paris (1949) on 2nd marriage and worked in European cinema; retired (1963).

ROCH, Madeleine (1884–1930). French actress. Born 1884 in France; died Dec 9, 1930. ❖ Made 1st appearance at Comédie Française as Hermione in *Andromache* (1903) and subsequently appeared there as Chorus in *Electre*, Madame Armières in *La Maison d'Argile*, La Comtesse de la Molinière in *Chacun sa Vie*, Phèdre, Divonne in *Sapho*, Dona Sol in *Hernani*, Dona Clorinde in *L'Aventurière*, Berthe in *La Fille de Roland*, Iphégénie in *Iphégenie en Aulide*, Princess d'Aurec in *Le Prince d'Aurec*, among others; elected sociétaire (1910); films include *Antony and Cleopatra* (title role, 1910).

ROCHA, Alicia de la (b. 1923). See Larrocha, Alicia de.

ROCHA, Michelle (1962—). See Mitchell, Michelle.

ROCHAT, Laurence (1979—). Swiss cross-country skier. Born Aug 1, 1979, in Switzerland. ❖ Won a bronze medal for the 4 x 5 km relay at Salt Lake City Olympics (2002).

ROCHAT-MOSER, Franziska (1966–2002). Swiss marathon runner. Name variations: Franziska Moser. Born Franziska Moser, Aug 17, 1966, in Crissier, Switzerland; died of injuries, Mar 7, 2002, when a snow ledge collapsed while she was climbing in Swiss Alps, near Lausanne; m. Philippe Rochat (chef). ❖ Began athletic career in orienteering; won Swiss marathon championship (1989) and Frankfurt Marathon (1994); won New York City Marathon (1997); placed 2nd in Boston Marathon (1999); retired from competition following hip operation (2001); gave up law career to run the three-star gourmet restaurant Girardet at L'Hotel de Ville in hometown of Crissier with husband.

ROCHE, Adela Mary (1878–1969). See Younghusband, Adela Mary.

ROCHE, Barbara (1954—). English politician and member of Parliament. Born Barbara Margolis, April 13, 1954; m. Patrick Roche, 1977. ❖ Called to the bar (1977); representing Labour, elected to House of Commons for Hornsey and Wood Green (1992, 1997,

2001); named minister of state, Office of the Deputy Prime Minister; lost election (2005).

ROCHE, Baroness de la (1886–1919). See Deroche, Elise-Raymonde.

ROCHE, Danni (1970—). Australian field-hockey player. Born Danielle Roche, May 25, 1970, in Melbourne, Victoria, Australia. ❖ Midfielder, won a team gold medal at Atlanta Olympics (1996).

ROCHE, Josephine (1886–1976). American labor leader and US Treasury official. Born Josephine Aspinwall Roche in Neligh, Nebraska, Dec 2, 1886; died in Bethesda, Maryland, July 13, 1976; dau. of John J. Roche (mine owner) and Ella (Aspinwall) Roche; Vassar College, BA, 1908; Columbia University, MSW, 1910; m. Edward Hale Bierstadt (broadcast writer), July 2, 1920 (div. 1922); no children. ❖ Became 1st woman police officer in Denver, Colorado (1912); operated the Rocky Mountain Fuel Co., the 2nd largest coal mining company in Colorado (1927–39); was the 1st woman to serve as assistant secretary of the Treasury of the US, under President Franklin Roosevelt (1934–37); organized and ran the United Mine Workers' welfare and retirement fund (1947–71). ❖ See also *Women in World History*.

ROCHE, Maggie (1951—). American singer and songwriter. Name variations: The Roches. Born Oct 26, 1951, in Detroit, MI; sister of Terre Roche (singer) and Suzzy Roche (singer); attended Bard College. ❖ Began singing professionally with sister Terre (late 1960s); sang backup harmonies on Paul Simon's album, *There Goes Rhymin' Simon* (1972); with Terre, signed with Columbia and released unsuccessful album, *Seductive Reasoning* (1975); with the addition of sister Suzzy, formed the band, The Roches, in NY (1976) and released albums *The Roches* (1979), *Another World* (1985) and *A Dove* (1992); with the Roches, also appeared on albums by Indigo Girls and Kathy Mattea; disbanded after release of album, *Can We Go Home Now?* (1995).

ROCHE, Mazo de la (1879–1961). See de la Roche, Mazo.

ROCHE, Melanie (1970—). Australian softball player. Born Nov 9, 1970, in Bankstown, NSW, Australia. ❖ Pitcher, won team bronze medals at Atlanta Olympics (1996) and Sydney Olympics (2000) and a team silver medal at Athens Olympics (2004).

ROCHE, Regina Maria (c. 1764–1845). Irish novelist. Name variations: Regina Maria Dalton. Born Regina Maria Dalton in Co. Wexford, Ireland, c. 1764; died in Waterford, Ireland, May 17, 1845; dau. of Captain Blundel Dalton; m. Ambrose Roche, in 1793 or 1794 (died 1829). ❖ Gained prominence with 3rd novel, *The Children of the Abbey*, which rivaled the success of Ann Radcliffe's *Mysteries of Udolpho*; other writings include *The Vicar of Lansdowne* (1789), *The Maid of the Hamlet* (1793), *Clermont* (1798), *The Nocturnal Visit* (1800), *The Discarded Son, or, The Haunt of the Banditti* (1807), *The Houses of Osma and Almeria, or, The Convent of St. Ildefonso* (1810), *The Monastery of St. Colomb* (1812), *Trecothiek Bower* (1813), *London Tales* (1814), *The Munster Cottage Boy* (1819), *The Tradition of the Castle* (1824), *The Castle Chapel* (1825), *Contrast* (1828) and *The Nun's Picture* (1834). ❖ See also *Women in World History*.

ROCHE, Suzzy (1956—). American singer. Name variations: The Roches. Born Sept 29, 1956, in Bronxville, NY; sister of Maggie Roche and Terre Roche (singers); attended State University of New York in Purchase. ❖ Known for deadpan stage humor, formed critically acclaimed band, The Roches, in NY (1976), with sisters Maggie and Terre; appeared in several films, including *Crossing Delancey* (1988), for which she also sang, and *Me and Veronica* (1992); pursued solo career (1995), releasing albums *Holy Smokes* (1997) and *Songs From an Unmarried Housewife and Mother, Greenwich Village, USA* (2000).

ROCHE, Terre (1953—). American singer. Name variations: The Roches. Born April 10, 1953, in New York, NY; sister of Maggie Roche and Suzzy Roche (singers); Empire State College, BA in music. ❖ Toured with sister Maggie; sang backup harmonies on Paul Simon's album, *There Goes Rhymin' Simon* (1972); with Maggie, signed with Columbia Records and released unsuccessful album, *Seductive Reasoning* (1975); with sisters Maggie and Suzzy, formed band The Roches, performed in folk-music clubs in Greenwich Village (1976), and released albums *Keep On Doing* (1982), *No Trespassing* (1987), and *Speak* (1989); with sisters, provided voices for animated cockroach sisters in Steven Spielberg's tv cartoon series, *Tiny Toons* (mid-1990s); pursued solo career (1995), forming 12-piece band, Terre Roche and Her Mood Swings; released debut solo album, *The Sound of a Tree Falling* (1998).

ROCHECHOUART, Gabrielle de (1645–1704). French abbess. Name variations: Marie-Madeleine-Gabrielle de Mortemarte. Born Marie-Madeleine-Gabrielle de Rochechouart de Mortemarte, 1645; died 1704; dau. of Gabriel de Rochechouart, marquis (later duke) de Mortemart, and Diane de Grandseigne (d. 1666); sister of Françoise, Marquise de Montespan (1640–1707). ❖ Served as abbess of the famous abbey of Fontevrault (1670–1704); won universal esteem for her wisdom, piety, and administrative skill; was said to have translated all the works of Plato from the Latin version of Ficino.

ROCHEFORT, Christiane (1917–1998). French writer and feminist. Born July 17, 1917, in Paris, France; died April 24, 1998, at Le Pradet, France; studied for several years at Sorbonne; married for 4 years. ❖ Writer of novels and nonfiction who harshly condemned the abuse of women in what she considered a brutalized, patriarchal society; returned to Paris after spending several childhood years in Limousin (1922); became successful author with publication of 1st book *Le Repos du guerrier* (*Warrior's Rest*, 1958), which was adapted for film and released as *Love on a Pillow* in US and *Le Repos du Guerrier* in France (1962); won Roman Populiste award (1961); fired as press attaché at Cannes Film Festival (1968); participated in Mouvement de Libération des Femmes (MLF) demonstration at the Tomb of the Unknown Soldier (1970); participated in MLF campaign publicizing prominent women who had undergone abortions (1971); joined pro-abortion group Choisir (1972); her works, which incorporate large doses of black humor, present a scathing picture of women's constricted life and subordination in modern French society; other writings include *Les Petits enfants du siècle* (*Children of the Century,* 1961), *Une Rose pour Morrisson* (*A Rose for Morrisson,* 1966), *Printemps au parking* (*Blossom on the Tarmac,* 1969), *Archaos ou le jardin étincelant* (*Archaos or the Glittering Garden,* 1972), *Encore heureux qu'on va ver l'été* (*Luckily Summer Will Come Soon,* 1975), *Les Enfants d'abord* (*Children First,* 1976), *Quand tu vas chez les femmes* (*Now It's Time for the Girls,* 1982), *Le Monde est comme deux chevaux* (*The World Is Like Two Horses,* 1984) and *Conversations sans paroles* (*Conversations without Words,* 1997). Won Prix Mèdici for *La Porte du Fond* (1988). ❖ See also *Women in World History.*

ROCHEFOUCAULD, Edmée de la (1895–1991). See La Rochefoucauld, Edmée, Duchesse de.

ROCHES, Catherine des (1542–1587). French poet, playwright and salonnière. Name variations: Catherine Fradonnet des Roches; Les Dames des Roches or Les Demoiselles des Roches. Born 1542 in Poitiers, France; died of the plague in 1587 in Poitiers; dau. of Madeleine des Roches (1520–1587, writer); never married. ❖ Lived in Poitiers and became famous for weekly salon in parish of Saint-Michel which rivaled Paris salons; with mother, wrote prose and poetry, translated works from Latin, published 2 sets of dialogues (*Placide et Sévère* and *Iris et Pasithaé*) and often corresponded, resulting in the 1st correspondence between women to be published in France, *Les Missives de Mes Dames Des Roches* (1586); also wrote Biblical tragicomedy, *La Tragédie de Tobie et Sarra.*

ROCHES, Madeleine des (1520–1587). French poet, playwright and salonnière. Name variations: Madeleine Neveu; Madeleine Neveu des Roches; Les Dames des Roches or Les Demoiselles des Roches (the surname comes from landholdings). Born 1520 in Poitiers, France; died of the plague in 1587 in Poitiers; married and widowed; m. 2nd husband François Eboissard (died 1578); children: (1st m.) Catherine des Roches (1542–1587, writer). ❖ Lived in Poitiers and became famous for a weekly salon in the parish of Saint-Michel; lived an unconventional life with daughter and insisted on a woman's right to culture and learning; with daughter, also wrote prose and poetry, translated works from Latin, published 2 sets of dialogues (*Placide et Sévère* and *Iris et Pasithaé*) and frequently corresponded, resulting in *Les Missives de Mes Dames Des Roches* (1586), the 1st correspondence between women published in France.

ROCHES, The.
See Roche, Maggie (1951—).
See Roche, Suzzy (1956—).
See Roche, Terre (1953—).

ROCHESTER, Anna (1880–1966). American economist and historian. Born Anna Rochester, Mar 30, 1880; grew up in Englewood, NJ; died May 11, 1966, in New York, NY; dau. of Roswell Hart Rochester and Louise Agatha (Bamman) Rochester; attended Bryn Mawr College, 1897–99; lived with Grace Hutchins. ❖ Marxist economist and historian who was lifelong partner and professional collaborator of social reformer Grace Hutchins, worked in Boston settlement house (1909); was member of New Jersey Consumers' League (1911–12); researched child-labor conditions (1912–15); was analyst with US Children's Bureau (1915); worked for Christian pacifist organization, Fellowship of Reconciliation, as editor-in-chief of monthly publication, *The World Tomorrow* (1922–26); co-authored, with Hutchins, *Jesus Christ and the World of Today* (1922); also wrote *Rulers of America: A Study of Finance Capital* (1936) and *Why Farmers Are Poor: The Agricultural Crisis in the United States* (1949); with Hutchins, traveled across Asia and Europe, meeting social reformers, including Gandhi, and writing for several US publications (1926–27); left Church and joined Communist Party (1927); with Hutchins and Robert W. Dunn, co-founded Labor Research Association, which provided information to labor organizations and publications (1927).

ROCHESTER, countess of. See Hyde, Jane (d. 1725).

ROCHESTER, J.W. (1861–1924). See Kryzhanovskaia, Vera.

ROCHEVA, Nina. Russian cross-country skier. Name variations: Nina Rotschewa. Born in USSR. ❖ Won a silver medal for 4 x 5 km relay at Lake Placid Olympics (1980).

ROCK, Blossom (1895–1978). See MacDonald, Blossom.

ROCKEFELLER, Abby Aldrich (1874–1948). American philanthropist. Born Abby Greene Aldrich, Oct 26, 1874, in Providence, Rhode Island; died April 5, 1948, in New York; dau. of Nelson Wilmarth Aldrich (US senator from Rhode Island) and Abby Pearce (Chapman) Aldrich; became 1st wife of John D. Rockefeller Jr. (b. 1874, only son of the founder of Standard Oil Trust who would later marry Martha Baird Rockefeller), Oct 9, 1901; children: Abby Rockefeller (b. 1903); John Davison Rockefeller III (1906–1978); Nelson Aldrich Rockefeller (b. 1908, politician); Laurance Spelman Rockefeller (b. 1910); Winthrop Rockefeller (1912–1973); David Rockefeller (b. 1915). ❖ With Lillie Bliss and Mary Sullivan, founded the Museum of Modern Art (1929); throughout life, took a profound interest in the museum's collection and in the works of living American artists, whom she supported; by 1940, had given most of her private collection to the museum, including works by Picasso, Modigliani, and Matisse, as well as 1,600 etchings, lithographs, and woodcuts that comprised her print collection. ❖ See also Mary Ellen Chase, *Abby Aldrich Rockefeller* (Macmillan, 1950); Bernice Kert, *Abby Aldrich Rockefeller: The Woman in the Family* (Random, 1993); Clarice Stasz, *The Rockefeller Women: Dynasty of Piety, Privacy, and Service* (St. Martin, 1995); and *Women in World History.*

ROCKEFELLER, Blanchette Hooker (1909–1992). American philanthropist. Born Blanchette Ferry Hooker, Oct 2, 1909, in New York, NY; died in Briarcliff Manor, New York, Dec 2, 1992; dau. of Elon Huntington Hooker (owned Hooker Chemical Co.) and Blanche (Ferry) Hooker; m. John D. Rockefeller III (1906–1978, millionaire heir), Nov 11, 1932; children: Sandra Ferry Rockefeller (b. 1935); John (Jay) Davison Rockefeller IV (b. 1937, US Senator of West Virginia); Hope Aldrich Rockefeller (b. 1938); Alida Davison Rockefeller (b. 1949). ❖ Renowned for her varied roles in philanthropy, art, and politics, served as president of Museum of Modern Art. ❖ See also Clarice Stasz, *The Rockefeller Women: Dynasty of Piety, Privacy, and Service* (St. Martin, 1995).

ROCKEFELLER, Cettie (1839–1915). See Rockefeller, Laura Spelman.

ROCKEFELLER, Edith (1872–1932). See McCormick, Edith Rockefeller.

ROCKEFELLER, Happy (b. 1926). See Rockefeller, Margaretta "Happy."

ROCKEFELLER, Mrs. John D.
See Rockefeller, Laura Spelman (1839–1915).
See Rockefeller, Abby Aldrich (1874–1948).
See Rockefeller, Martha Baird (1895–1971).
See Rockefeller, Blanchette Hooker (1909–1992).

ROCKEFELLER, Laura Spelman (1839–1915). American socialite. Name variations: Cettie Spelman Rockefeller. Born Laura Celestia Spelman in 1839; died 1915; m. John D. Rockefeller (1839–1937, founder of Standard Oil and philanthropist), Sept 8, 1864; children: Elizabeth or Bessie Rockefeller (1866–1906); Alice Rockefeller (1869–1870); Alta Rockefeller (1871–1962); Edith Rockefeller McCormick (1872–1932); John D. Rockefeller Jr. (1874–1960). ❖ Indifferent to the social whirl to which her position entitled her, believed strongly that life was for duty, not enjoyment. ❖ See also Clarice Stasz, *The Rockefeller*

Women: Dynasty of Piety, Privacy, and Service (St. Martin, 1995); and Women in World History.

ROCKEFELLER, Margaret (1915–1996). American conservationist. Name variations: Peggy Rockefeller; Peggy McGrath. Born Margaret McGrath, Sept 28, 1915; died in New York, Mar 26, 1996; m. David Rockefeller (b. 1915, son of Abby Aldrich Rockefeller and chair of the Chase Manhattan Bank); children: David Rockefeller Jr. (b. 1941); Abby Aldrich Rockefeller (b. 1943); Neva Goodwin Rockefeller (b. 1944); Margaret Dulany Rockefeller (b. 1947); Richard Gilder Rockefeller (b. 1949); Eileen McGrath Rockefeller (b. 1952). ❖ Was a founding board member of American Farmland Trust, a national land-preservation group; was sole founding member of the Maine Coast Heritage Trust (1970); was also a trustee of New York Philharmonic Orchestra and served on the board of New York Botanical Garden. ❖ See also Clarice Stasz, The Rockefeller Women: Dynasty of Piety, Privacy, and Service (St. Martin, 1995); and Women in World History.

ROCKEFELLER, Margaretta (1926—). American socialite. Name variations: Margarite. Born Margaretta Fitler Murphy in 1926; m. Dr. James Murphy (div. 1963); m. Nelson Aldrich Rockefeller (1908–1979, governor of New York and vice-president of US whose 1st wife was Mary Todhunter Rockefeller), in May 1963; children: (1st m.) 4; (2nd m.) Nelson Aldrich Jr. (b. 1964); Mark Fitler Rockefeller (b. 1967). ❖ Served as first lady of New York State for 2 of husband's terms (1966 and 1970); having undergone a radical mastectomy (1974), used her position as a public figure to advocate for early breast-cancer detection; served as an alternate representative to the UN General Assembly (1991–92). ❖ See also Women in World History.

ROCKEFELLER, Martha Baird (1895–1971). American philanthropist and pianist. Born Martha Baird Allen in 1895; died 1971; became 2nd wife of John D. Rockefeller Jr. (1874–1960, whose 1st wife was Abby Aldrich Rockefeller, 1874–1948). ❖ Studied piano with Artur Schnabel and performed in recitals and as a solo pianist before retiring (1931); following husband's death (1960), used inheritance to set up the Martha Baird Rockefeller Fund, which distributed study grants to numerous young musicians, many of whom later became prominent. ❖ See also Women in World History.

ROCKEFELLER, Mary Todhunter (1907–1999). American socialite. Born Mary Todhunter Clark, June 17, 1907; died April 21, 1999, in New York, NY; became 1st wife of Nelson Aldrich Rockefeller (1908–1979, governor of New York and vice-president of US, whose 2nd wife was Margaretta "Happy" Rockefeller), on June 23, 1930 (div. 1962); children: Rodman Clark Rockefeller (b. 1932); Ann Clark (b. 1934); Steven Clark Rockefeller (b. 1936); (twins) Michael Clark Rockefeller (1938–1961, disappeared while traveling in Papua New Guinea) and Mary Clark Rockefeller (b. 1938). ❖ Longtime advocate of nurses' education, served on the National Advisory Health Council and the Defense Advisory Committee on Women in the Services (1950s), and on the board of the National League of Nursing for many years; served as 1st lady of New York State during husband's 1st gubernatorial term. ❖ See also Women in World History.

ROCKEFELLER, Peggy (1915–1996). See Rockefeller, Margaret.

ROCKFORD ROSIE (1915–2004). See Gacioch, Rose.

ROCKMORE, Clara (1911–1998). Lithuanian musician. Name variations: Clara Reisenberg. Born Clara Reisenberg in Vilna (now Vilnius), Lithuania, Feb 24, 1911; died in New York, NY, May 10, 1998; sister of Nadia Reisenberg (1904–1983). ❖ Admitted to St. Petersburg Conservatory as a violinist at age 5, the youngest musician to enroll at the time; took up the theremin, an electronic musical instrument, and became its recognized master; appeared in the film Theremin: An Electronic Odyssey (1994). ❖ See also video documentary, Clara Rockmore, the Greatest Theremin Virtuosa (1998); and Women in World History.

RODD, Kylie Tennant (1912–1988). See Tennant, Kylie.

RODDICK, Anita (1942—). English retail entrepreneur. Born Anita Lucia Perella, Oct 23, 1942, in Littlehampton, England; dau. of Italian immigrants; graduate of Bath College of Education; m. Thomas Gordon Roddick, 1970; children: Justine and Samantha Roddick. ❖ Opened her 1st upscale Body Shop to sell cosmetics "stripped of hype" and made from natural materials (1976), ushering in progressive business philosophy of "caring capitalism" and green marketing boom; experienced immediate success and soon began to franchise stores, opening shops throughout UK and eventually worldwide, beginning in Belgium (1978); promoted environmental and human-rights causes; served as managing director of Body Shop until becoming CEO (1994); had over 1,200 stores worldwide in 45 countries; founded Anita Roddick Publications, issuing 1st book, Brave Hearts, Rebel Spirits: A Spiritual Activists Handbook (2003). Made Order of the British Empire (OBE, 1988) and Dame Commander of the British Empire (DBE, 2003). ❖ See also autobiography, Business Unusual (Thorsons, 2001).

RODE, Lizzie (1933—). Danish ballet dancer. Name variations: Lizzie Schmidt Pedersen. Born Sept 12, 1933, in Copenhagen, Denmark; dau. of Mogens Ferdinand Philipson and Gerda Rode Osterberg; m. Ernst Bülow, 1953 (div. (1960); m. Ole Schmidt Pedersen, 1960; children: (2nd m.) Henriette (b. 1962) and Tine (b. 1964). ❖ Trained at Royal Danish Ballet and performed with that company for most of performance career; danced in Birgit Cullberg's Miss Julie and Medea, and Lichine's Graduation Ball, as well as in most of company's Bournonville repertory, including La Sylphide and Kermesse; became ballet master there.

RODEWALD, Marion (1976—). German field-hockey player. Born Dec 24, 1976, in Mülheim an der Ruhr, Germany. ❖ Won a team gold medal at Athens Olympics (2004).

RODGERS, Brid (1935—). Irish politician. Born Brid Stratford, Feb 20, 1935 (some sources cite 1931), in Gweedore, Co. Donegal, Ireland; m. Antoin Rodgers; children: 6. ❖ Became involved in civil-rights movement in Northern Ireland (1965), while living in mid-Ulster; as an Independent, nominated to the Seanad by Taoiseach Garret FitzGerald (1983–87); elected to the Northern Ireland Assembly for Upper Bann (1998); named minister for Agriculture and Rural Development (1999); was a founder member of the Social Democratic and Labour Party (SDLP, Northern Ireland), chair (1978–80), general secretary (1981–83), deputy leader (2001).

RODGERS, Elizabeth Flynn (1847–1939). Irish-born American labor leader. Born Elizabeth Flynn in Woodford, Ireland, Aug 25, 1847; died in Wauwatosa, Wisconsin, Aug 27, 1939; dau. of Robert Flynn and Bridget (Campbell) Flynn; m. George Rodgers (iron worker active involvement in labor movement, died 1920); children: 10. ❖ Immigrated with family to London, Ontario, early in life; after marriage, moved to Chicago (c. 1876); joined Knights of Labor, reputedly the 1st woman in Chicago to do so, and became head of an all-woman local assembly (1881); appointed Master Workman (president) of her district, including all the Knights of Labor assemblies in Chicago and its suburbs except for the stockyard area (1886); left labor movement for a role as a partner in a printing firm (c. 1887); with 12 others, formed the fraternal life insurance agency Women's Catholic Order of Foresters, serving as High Chief Ranger (chief executive officer) until 1908. ❖ See also Women in World History.

RODIANI, Onorata (d. 1452). Italian artist and military leader. Name variations: Honorata Rodiana. Died in 1452 in Cremona; never married; no children. ❖ Trained as a professional painter, began a successful career in that field; while working on commission at palace of Gabrino Fondolo, was attacked by one of Fondolo's courtiers and stabbed him to death; fled and eventually joined a troop of mercenary soldiers; received a pardon from city authorities and returned to Cremona; reportedly died in battle leading a troop of soldiers in the defense of Cremona from its Venetian enemies.

RODIN, Judith (1944—). American psychologist and educator. Born Judith Seitz, Sept 9, 1944, in Philadelphia, PA; dau. of Morris and Sally R. (Winson) Seitz; University of Pennsylvania, AB, 1966; Columbia University, PhD, 1970; m. Nicholas Niejelow, 1978 (div.). ❖ Began career as assistant professor of psychology at New York University (1970); moved to Yale University (1972), where she became associate professor (1975), full professor of psychology (1979), professor of medicine and psychiatry (1985), and served as provost (1992–94); served as president of University of Pennsylvania (1994–2004), the 1st woman president of an Ivy League school; held faculty appointments there as professor of psychology in the School of Arts and Sciences and professor of medicine and psychiatry in the School of Medicine.

RODNINA, Irina (1949—). Russian pairs skater. Born Sept 12, 1949, in USSR; married her pairs partner Alexsandr Zaitsev (also seen as Zaytsev, Zaitzev), 1975. ❖ Won 10 World, 11 European titles (1969–78, 1980), and 3 Olympic gold medals: with Alexei Ulanov, won 4 World championship titles (1969–72) and a gold medal at Sapporo Olympics (1972); with Alexsandr Zaitsev, won 6 World championships (1973–78) and Olympic gold medals at Innsbruck (1976) and Lake Placid (1980). ❖ See also *Women in World History.*

RODOGUNE. *Variant of Rhodogune.*

RODOREDA, Mercè (1909–1983). Spanish author. Name variations: Merce Rodoreda. Born in Barcelona, Spain, Oct 10, 1909 (some sources cite 1908); died 1983; as a teenager, married her mother's brother (separated); was mistress and housekeeper of Joan Armand Obiols, another Catalan writer; children: 1. ❖ After separating from husband, began writing, using Catalan rather than Spanish; finished 5 novels (she later disowned 4 of them, retaining only the Crexells prize-winning *Aloma* [1938]) and a number of short stories (mid-1930s); a supporter of the Republic, fled to France during Spanish Civil War (1939); after the war, remained in exile, 1st in Paris and later Geneva; won Victor Català prize for short stories, *Vint-i-dos contes* (1957); published *La plaça del Diamant* (*The Time of the Doves,* 1962), a masterpiece of Iberian literature; later publications include another collection of short stories *La meva Cristina i altres contes* (1984), and the novels *Jardí vora el mar* (1967), *Mirall trencat* (1974), and *Quanta, quanta guerra* (1980); at her death (1983), left several drafts of another major novel, *La Mort e la Primavera.*

RODRIGUES, Amalia (1921–1999). Portuguese fado singer. Born Amalia Rodrigues, 1921 (she was never sure of month and day), in Lisbon, Portugal; died Oct 6, 1999; m. Francisco Cruz (div. in less than a year); m. Cesar Seabra (engineer), 1961. ❖ Known as "the soul of the nation," had a career that spanned more than 50 years and made her Portugal's best-loved performer; began performing at various festivals in her district, particularly the one known as the "March of Lisbon"; was soon performing at Retiro da Severa, one of the best fado clubs in Lisbon; enjoyed sudden ascent to fame (1940s); expanded performances into larger theaters, began to star in movies and was booked into the country's best theaters, while Portuguese poets vied to write lyrics for her to sing; had 1st international triumph at Olympia in Paris (1953), followed by successful engagements at La Vie en Rose and Mocambo in US; appeared at Lincoln Center with New York Philharmonic, under direction of Andre Kostelanetz (1966); recordings helped establish her reputation worldwide, including "Grandola Vila Morena." Awarded Order of Santiago, her nation's highest honor. ❖ See also *Women in World History.*

RODRIGUES, Karin (1971—). Brazilian volleyball player. Born Nov 8, 1971, in Brazil. ❖ Won a team bronze medal at Sydney Olympics (2000).

RODRIGUES, Monica (1967—). Brazilian beach volleyball player. Name variations: Mônica Rodrigues. Born Sept 20, 1967, in Rio de Janeiro, Brazil. ❖ With Adriana Samuel, was FIVB Tour champion (1994) and won a silver medal at Atlanta Olympics (1996); with Sandra Pires, won a bronze medal at Sydney Olympics (2000).

RODRÍGUEZ, Ana (1938—). Cuban political activist and writer. Born April 17, 1938, in Cuba; dau. of Filiberto Rodríguez and Juana Hernandez Rodríguez; attended University of Havana and Cetec University. ❖ Participated in the pro-democratic Cuban underground; confined in Cuba as a political prisoner (1961–79); immigrated to US (1980); wrote *Diary of a Survivor,* inspired by her 19-year prison term, to bring attention to the human-rights abuses occurring in Cuban women's prisons (1995). ❖ See also *Women in World History.*

RODRIGUEZ, Estelita (1928–1966). Cuban actress. Name variations: Estelita. Born July 2, 1928, in Guanajay, Cuba; died Mar 12, 1966, in Van Nuys, CA; m. Grant Withers (actor); m. 4 more times; children: daughter. ❖ Known professionally as Estelita, began career in Cuba at age 9; came to Hollywood (1945) and appeared in a number of films, mostly B-Westerns, including *Cuban Fireball, In Old Amarillo, The Golden Stallion, Parade of 1951, Federal Agent at Large, California Passage, The Fabulous Senorita* and *Rio Bravo;* retired (1958), returning for *Jesse James Meets Frankenstein's Daughter* (1966).

RODRÍGUEZ, Evangelina (1879–1947). Dominican Republic physician. Name variations: Evangelina Rodriquez; Andrea Evangelina Rodríguez Perozo. Born Andrea Evangelina Rodríguez Perozo out of wedlock of part-African descent in Higuey, Dominican Republic, 1879; died in San Pedro de Macoris, Dominican Republic, Jan 11, 1947; University of the Dominican Republic, medical degree, 1909; graduate of University of Paris, 1925; never married; children: 1 adopted daughter, Selisete. ❖ Family planning advocate, educator, and social reformer, became the 1st Dominican woman physician (1909); studied

in France (1921–25); after returning home, worked to improve the lives of the poor, particularly women; was an outspoken opponent of the Trujillo dictatorship (late 1930s). Honored on a commemorative postage stamp (Sept 26, 1985). ❖ See also *Women in World History.*

RODRIGUEZ, Jennifer (1976—). American speedskater and roller skater. Born June 8, 1976, in Miami, FL; dau. of a Cuban father and American mother; m. K.C. Boutiette (speedskater), 2002. ❖ As a roller skater, won 12 World championships, including gold medals for artistic roller skating and speed roller skating, won silver medal at Pan American Games (1995), became 2-time USOC Athlete of the Year for Roller Sports, and inducted into USA Roller Sports Hall of Fame (2002); as a speedskater, placed 4th in the 3,000 meters at Nagano Olympics (1998), thought to be the 1st athlete of Hispanic descent to compete at Winter Games; won overall at US Allround championships (1999–2001); won bronze medals for the 1,000 and 1,500 meters at Salt Lake City Olympics (2002); became American record holder in 1,500-meter and 3,000-meter for ice; as ice skater, became one of few skaters in history to medal at World championships in both figure and speedskating (gold and silver at Rome World Speed championships and silver at Figure Skating World championships, Tampa, FL, both 1995); as inline skater, became 3-time World champion. Named US Roller Skating Athlete of the Year (1991–92).

RODRIGUEZ, Judith (1936—). Australian poet and short-story writer. Born 1936 in Perth, Australia; m. Thomas Shapcott. ❖ Worked as poetry editor for *Meanjin* magazine, poetry reviewer for *Sydney Morning Herald,* and lecturer at Macarthur Institute, Sydney; writings include *Nu-Plastik Fanfare Red* (1973), *Shadow on Glass* (1978), *Water Life* (1978), *Mudcrab at Gambaro's* (1980), *Witch Heart* (1982), *New and Selected Poems* (1988), *The Cold* (1992), and libretto for Opera, *Lindy* (2002). Received F.A.W. Christopher Brennan Award for Poetry, and PEN/Stuyvesant Prize for Literature.

RODRIGUEZ, Zhandra (1947—). Venezuelan ballet dancer. Born Mar 17, 1947, in Caracas, Venezuela. ❖ Performed with National Ballet of Venezuela, dancing in numerous works by William Dollar, including *Constantia, The Combat,* and *Divertimento;* was member of American Ballet Theater in NY (1968–74), where she danced in *Coppélia* and *The Sleeping Beauty* and created roles in Dennis Nahat's *Mendelssohn Symphony* (1971) and *Some Times* (1972); danced for numerous choreographers, such as Michael Smuin and Eliot Feld, and in Alvin Ailey's *The River* (1969–74); moved to Germany where she danced with Hamburg State Opera in works by Neumeier, among them *Third Symphony* (1975) and *A Midsummer Night's Dream* (1977); returned to Venezuela where she danced in newly established International Ballet de Caracas.

RODRÍGUEZ DE TIÓ, Lola (1843–1924). Puerto Rican writer and political activist. Name variations: Lola Rodriguez de Tio. Born in San Germán, Puerto Rico, Sept 14, 1843; died in Havana, Cuba, Nov 10, 1924; dau. of Sebastián Rodríguez de Astudillo (dean of judiciary in Puerto Rico) and Carmen Ponce de León (who counted among her ancestors Ponce de León, the explorer and 1st governor of the colony); m. Bonocio Tió Segarra (journalist and poet), in 1863; children: Patria (b. 1865) and Mercedes (1870–1873). ❖ Revered in both Cuba and Puerto Rico, used talents as a writer and poet to promote Puerto Rican liberty and democracy at a time of Spanish dominance; composed "La Borinqueña," a fiery lyric for a traditional melody (1868), which became Puerto Rico's national anthem, causing her to be deported with husband; allowed to return with family (1885); published "Nochebuena," a tribute to political prisoners (1887); exiled to Cuba (1889); continued to seek independence for both her homeland and Cuba; expelled from Havana (1892), joined a group of Cuban exiles in New York City; returned to Cuba (1899) after the Spanish-American War, where she worked for social justice and the betterment of the condition of women, as one of Latin America's most influential early feminists; became a member of Cuban Academy of Arts and Letters (1910); named Patron of the Galician Beneficent Society (1911); served as inspector general of the private schools in Havana and in the Ministry of Education; chief among her works are *Mis Cantares* (My Songs, 1876). *Claros y Nieblas* (Fair Weather and Fog, 1885), *Mi Libro de Cuba* (My Book on Cuba, 1893) and *Claros de Sol* (Sunshine). ❖ See also *Women in World History.*

RODRÍGUEZ RAMOS, María (1963—). Spanish lawyer and politician. Name variations: Maria Rodriguez Ramos. Born Dec 1, 1963, in Valladolid, Spain. ❖ Served as lawyer for Valladolid battered women's shelter (1988–90) and director of the Municipal Women's Rights Information Center (1994–97); as a European Socialist, elected to 5th European Parliament (1999–2004).

RODRIGUEZ SUAREZ, Maria (1957—). Spanish field-hockey player. Born April 12, 1957, in Spain. ❖ At Barcelona Olympics, won a gold medal in team competition (1992).

RODRIGUEZ VILLANUEVA, Estela (1967—). Cuban judoka. Name variations: Estela Rodriquez. Born Nov 17, 1967, in Cuba. ❖ Won World championship (1989); won a silver medal at Barcelona Olympics (1992) and a silver medal at Atlanta Olympics (1996), both for + 72 kg heavyweight.

ROE, Allison (1957—). New Zealand marathon runner. Born May 30, 1957, in Auckland, New Zealand. ❖ Won New Zealand Cross-Country championship at age 18; won Boston Marathon and NY City Marathon (1981); also won the Peachtree 10k Race; won New Zealand championships in cycle and triathlon. Named Member of the British Empire (MBE); won the Abebe Bakila Award (2002).

ROE, Marion (1936—). English politician and member of Parliament. Born Marion Keyte, July 15, 1936; m. James Kenneth Roe, 1958. ❖ As a Conservative, elected to House of Commons for Broxbourne (1992, 1997, 2001); served as chair of the Health committee (1992–97); named chair of Administration committee (1997); retired (2005).

ROEBLING, Emily (1844–1903). American engineer. Name variations: Emily Warren Roebling; Mrs. Washington Roebling. Born Emily Warren, 1844, in Cold Spring, New York; died in Trenton, New Jersey, 1903; dau. of Phebe (Lickley) Warren and Sylvanus Warren; m. Washington Roebling (chief engineer), Jan 18, 1865; children: John A. Roebling II (b. 1867). ❖ Met Washington Roebling (1864); when father-in-law died, husband became chief engineer of the Brooklyn Bridge project, an engineering feat of monumental proportions (1869); when husband became ill, took crash course in engineering (1872); began to act as unofficial chief engineer (1872), supervising the construction for 11 of the 13 years it took to build the Brooklyn Bridge; escorted Ferdinand de Lesseps on his visit to NY (Feb 1880); crossed Brooklyn Bridge for 1st time (spring 1880); when Trustees of Brooklyn Bridge attempted to dismiss Washington Roebling, defended husband before American Society of Civil Engineers (1882); played the role of emissary, diplomat, secretary, purchasing agent, spokesperson, and engineer until the Brooklyn Bridge opened (May 24, 1883); moved to Trenton, New Jersey (1884). ❖ See also Hamilton Schuyler, *The Roeblings: A Century of Engineers, Bridge Builders and Industrialists* (Princeton U. Press, 1931); and *Women in World History*.

ROEBLING, Mary G. (1906–1994). American financier. Born Mary Gindhart in West Collingswood, New Jersey, July 29, 1906; died in Trenton, New Jersey, Oct 25, 1994; dau. of Isaac Gindhart Jr. (telephone company employee) and Mary W. (Simon) Gindhart (music teacher); attended finance classes at University of Pennsylvania; attended banking and finance courses at New York University; m. Arthur Herbert (died); m. Siegfried Roebling (banking and steel-cable magnate who was the grandson of Washington and Emily Roebling, died 1936); children: (1st m.) Elizabeth Herbert (Mrs. E.H. Dutch); (2nd m.) Paul Roebling. ❖ Was 1st woman to head a major bank when she became president of the Trenton Trust Co. (1937); named governor of the American Stock Exchange (1958), the 1st woman to hold a policy-making position on any major stock exchange; was involved in organizing the Women's Bank N.A. of Denver (1978), the 1st federally chartered bank organized by women; founded the American Women's Council, of which she was a director; was a delegate to the Atlantic Congress of NATO, and a trustee of the US Council of the International Chamber of Commerce. ❖ See also *Women in World History*.

ROEBLING, Mrs. Washington (1844–1903). *See Roebling, Emily.*

ROENNLUND, Toini (1938—). *See Gustafsson, Toini.*

ROENSTROEM, Eva (1932—). Swedish gymnast. Born Dec 29, 1932, in Sweden. ❖ At Melbourne Olympics, won a silver medal in teams all-around, portable apparatus (1956).

ROERING, Gun (1930—). Swedish gymnast. Born June 17, 1930, in Sweden. ❖ At Helsinki Olympics, won a gold medal in teams all-around, portable apparatus (1952).

ROETHER, Sabine (1957—). East German handball player. Name variations: Sabine Röther. Born June 17, 1957, in East Germany. ❖ At Moscow Olympics, won a bronze medal in team competition (1980).

ROETHLISBERGER, Nadia (1972—). Swiss curler. Name variations: Nadia Röthlisberger. Born June 30, 1972, in Switzerland. ❖ Won a silver medal for curling at Salt Lake City Olympics (2002).

ROFFE, Diann (1967—). American Alpine skier. Name variations: Dian Roffe-Steinrotter; Dian Steinrotter. Born Mar 24, 1967, in Potsdam, NY. ❖ At World Alpine Ski championships, was the 1st American woman to win a gold medal in giant slalom (1985); tied for a silver medal (with Anita Wachter) at Albertville Olympics (1992); won a gold medal for super-G at Lillehammer Olympics (1994).

ROFFEIS, Karla (1958—). East German volleyball player. Born July 4, 1958, in East Germany. ❖ At Moscow Olympics, won a silver medal in team competition (1980).

ROGACHYOVA, Lyudmila (1966—). Soviet runner. Born Oct 10, 1966, in USSR. ❖ At Barcelona Olympics, won a silver medal in the 1,500 meters (1992).

ROGATIS, Teresa de (1893–1979). Italian composer, guitarist, pianist, and lecturer. Name variations: Teresa Feninger. Born in Naples, Italy, Oct 15, 1893; died in Naples, Jan 8, 1979; studied piano, composition, counterpoint, harmony, conducting and voice at Conservatorio San Pietro at Majella in Naples; married; children: Mario Feninger (concert pianist). ❖ A child prodigy, gave 1st recital at 7; while in Egypt on a concert tour, married and settled in Cairo; helped found the National Conservatory of Egypt (late 1950s), where she also taught piano and guitar; returned to Italy (1963) and continued to teach and compose; wrote over 60 works, half for piano. ❖ See also *Women in World History*.

ROGÉ, Charlotte Fiske (1838–1916). *See Bates, Charlotte Fiske.*

ROGERS, Adela (1894–1988). *See St. Johns, Adela Rogers.*

ROGERS, Annette (b. 1913). American runner. Born Oct 22, 1913. ❖ Won a gold medal at Los Angeles Olympics (1932) and a gold medal at Berlin Olympics (1936), both in the 4 x 100-meter relay.

ROGERS, Clara Kathleen (1844–1931). English-born composer, singer and teacher. Name variations: Clara Doria. Born Clara Kathleen Barnett in Cheltenham, England, Jan 14, 1844; died in Boston, MA, Mar 8, 1931; dau. of John Barnett (composer); m. Henry Munroe Rogers (Boston attorney), 1878. ❖ Showed an early interest in composition; at 12, was the youngest student ever accepted by Leipzig Conservatory, where she studied singing and piano but not composition, an area then closed to women; graduated from Leipzig (1860) with honors; continued studies with Hans von Bülow in Berlin and began a singing career; debuted under name Clara Doria in Milan, and enjoyed a successful career in Italy and England; made NY debut (1871); ceased performing 7 years later at time of marriage, then concentrated on composing, though she occasionally appeared as a performer to play her own works; appointed a professor at New England Conservatory of Music (1902); wrote several books on the art of singing as well as a 3-vol. autobiography. ❖ See also *Women in World History*.

ROGERS, Dale Evans (1912–2001). American actress, singer and writer. Name variations: Dale Evans; Frances Fox. Born Frances Octavia Smith in Uvalde, TX, Oct 31, 1912; died in Apple Valley, CA, Feb 7, 2001; m. Thomas Frederick Fox, 1928 (div. 1930); m. Dale Butts (div.); m. Roy Rogers (actor and singer), 1947 (died 1998); children: (1st m.) Tom Fox Jr. (b. 1929); (3rd m.) Robin (1950–1952); (adopted) Sandy, Dodie, and Debbie. ❖ One of the most popular Western film heroines of her generation, sang on radio programs in Memphis, Louisville, and Dallas early in career before starring on Chicago airwaves; with songwriter husband Dale Butts, collaborated on a number of songs, including "Will You Marry Me, Mr. Laramie?"; signed with Republic Studios, making film debut in *The Cowboy and the Senorita*, starring Roy Rogers (1944); with Rogers and her horse Buttermilk, made another 19 Westerns in next 3 years, though much of her success was driven by her gutsy heroines; all told, appeared with Rogers in over 30 Western-themed movies, including *Sunset in El Dorado* (1945), *My Pal Trigger* (1946), *Under Nevada Skies* (1946), *Song of Arizona* (1946), *The Golden Stallion* (1949) and *Pals of the Golden West* (1951); collaborated with Rogers on radio to create "The Roy Rogers Show," (1948), writing the show's theme song, "Happy Trails to You," then moved show to tv (1951–57); made brief comeback with hour-long tv variety program, "The Roy Rogers and Dale Evans Show" (1962); recorded several albums for children which included some of her own compositions such as "Aha, San Antone," which sold in excess of 200,000 copies; with Roy, debuted the 1st of their Christian albums with release of *Hymns of Faith* (1950); wrote the well-known children's song "The Bible Tells Me So" and worked closely with Billy Graham and Norman Vincent Peale; wrote the bestselling *Angel Unaware*, about her child Robin who died shortly before her 2nd birthday (1953); followed that with *My Spiritual Diary* (1955) and *Dear Debbie* (1964); published 25 inspirational works by 1988, including *Time Out Ladies!* (1966), *Where He Leads* (1974), and *Let Freedom Ring* (1975); hosted "The Dale Evans Show," on Trinity Christian broadcasting station. ❖ See also autobiography, *The Woman at the Well* (1970); and *Women in World History.*

ROGERS, Deborah Read (1707–1774). *See Read, Deborah.*

ROGERS, Edith MacTavish (1876–1947). Canadian politician. Born 1876 in Norway House, Rupert's Land; died 1947 in Colborne, Ontario, Canada; dau. of an officer of Hudson's Bay Co.; educated in Montreal; married with children. ❖ Liberal, was the 1st woman elected to the Manitoba Legislative Assembly (1920), as a member for Winnipeg riding; served until 1932; was the only woman board member of the Winnipeg General Hospital.

ROGERS, Edith Nourse (1881–1960). American politician. Born Edith Francis Nourse, Mar 19, 1881, in Saco, Maine; died Sept 10, 1960, in Boston, Massachusetts; dau. of Franklin D. Nourse (mill manufacturer) and Edith Frances (Riversmith) Nourse; attended Rogers Hall, Lowell, Massachusetts, and Madame Julien's, Neuilly, France; m. John Jacob Rogers (lawyer and 6-term US congressional representative), in 1907 (died 1925). ❖ US Republican congressional representative (1925–60) who gained a national reputation advancing the cause of the American veteran, was 1st named personal representative to President Harding in charge of assistance for disabled veterans (1922), an appointment renewed by presidents Calvin Coolidge and Herbert Hoover; after husband died, was elected to US Congress from 5th Congressional District of Massachusetts (1925), only the 6th woman elected to the US House; remained some 35 years, establishing a record for the longest span of service ever held by a woman; became extremely influential behind the scenes, playing the leading role in creation of both the Women's Army Corps, commonly known as the WACs, and GI Bill of Rights; also was one of the 1st in Congress to speak against Hitler's treatment of the Jews (1933); became chair of House Veterans' Affairs Committee (1947); sponsored Korean Veterans Benefits bill, a permanent Nurse Corps in Veterans Administration, and legislation to support the development of prosthetic appliances and automobiles for amputees; introduced 1,242 bills during her career, over half of which dealt with military matters. ❖ See also *Women in World History.*

ROGERS, Elizabeth Ann (1829–1921). British-born missionary and educator. Name variations: Sister Beatrice. Born Nov 2, 1829, in St. Erth, Hayle, Cornwall, England; died Feb 20, 1921, in Honolulu, HI; dau. of James (carpenter) and Ann (Ellis) Rogers. ❖ Became Sister Beatrice in First Order of Congregation of Religious of the Society of the Most Holy Trinity (Jan 1867); with Sister Albertina, opened Anglican school, St. Andrew's Priory, in Honolulu (Mar 1867); after closing of mission, was permitted to remain in Hawaii to serve as guardian for several local children and to continue teaching at St. Andrew's (1892–1902).

ROGERS, Emily Louisa Merielina (1839–1936). *See White, Emily Louisa Merielina.*

ROGERS, Ginger (1911–1995). American actress and dancer. Born Virginia Katherine McMath in Independence, Missouri, July 16, 1911; died April 25, 1995, in Rancho Mirage, California; dau. of Lela Owens McMath (managed daughter's career) and William Eddins McMath (electrical engineer); m. Edward Jackson Culpepper, 1929 (div. 1931); m. Lew Ayres (actor), 1934 (div. 1940); m. John Calving Briggs II, 1943 (div. 1948); m. Jacques Bergerac (actor), 1953 (div. 1957); m. G. William Marshall (producer), 1961 (div. 1967); no children. ❖ Film star, dancer and actress who through verve, grace and hard work captured the public's imagination, particularly when she danced with Fred Astaire; toured with "Ginger and The Redheads" at 14; made Broadway musical debut in *Top Speed* (1929); was ingenue star of *Girl Crazy* (1930); made film debut in *Young Man of Manhattan* (1930); made 14 films over next 2 years (1932–33), including *42nd Street* (1933), *Gold Diggers of 1933*, in which she sang "We're in the Money," and *Flying Down to Rio* (1933), in which she danced "The Carioca" with Astaire, launching the remarkable dancing partnership; teamed again in *Roberta* (1935), partnering for

"I Won't Dance" and "Smoke Gets in Your Eyes" which became classics; danced with Astaire in *The Gay Divorcee* (1934), *Top Hat* (1935), *Follow the Fleet* (1936), *Swing Time* (1936), *Shall We Dance* (1937) and *Carefree* (1938); had 1st opportunity to show acting ability in *Stage Door* (1937); other films include *Roxie Hart* (1942), *Tales of Manhattan* (1942), *The Major and the Minor* (1942), *Lady in the Dark* (1944), *I'll Be Seeing You* (1944), *Weekend at the Waldorf* (1945), *It Had to Be You* (1947), *The Barkleys of Broadway* (1949), *Storm Warning* (1950), *Forever Female* (1953), *Oh Men! Oh Women!* (1957) and *Harlow* (1965). Won Academy Award for Best Actress for *Kitty Foyle* (1940); granted Lifetime Achievement award at Kennedy Center Honors (1992). ❖ See also autobiography *Ginger: My Story* (1991); and *Women in World History.*

ROGERS, Grace Rainey (1867–1943). American art collector and philanthropist. Born in Cleveland, Ohio, June 28, 1867; died in Greenwich, Connecticut, May 9, 1943; dau. of William J. Rainey and Eleanor B. (Mitchell) Rainey (art collector and philanthropist); m. Henry Welsh Rogers (NY businessman), Sept 28, 1907 (div. 1918); no children. ❖ One of the 20th century's greatest patrons of the arts, spent much of her life supporting various art museums; was a fellow of Metropolitan Museum of Art and an original trustee of the Museum of Modern Art; also supported the Cleveland Museum of Art, as a member of the advisory council, as well as through one of her most noteworthy gifts, the Rousseau de la Rottière Room. ❖ See also *Women in World History.*

ROGERS, Harriet B. (1834–1919). American educator of the deaf. Born Harriet Burbank Rogers in North Billerica, Massachusetts, April 12, 1834; died in North Billerica, Dec 12, 1919; dau. of Calvin Rogers (farmer) and Ann (Faulkner) Rogers (dau. of a woolen manufacturer); graduate of Massachusetts State Normal School, 1851; never married; no children. ❖ Began privately instructing a young deaf girl (1863); opened her own school for deaf children (June 1866), the 1st American woman to teach deaf children solely through the use of the German oral method of speaking and lip reading; appointed director of Clarke Institution for Deaf Mutes (later Clarke School for the Deaf, 1867); resigned due to ill health (1886). ❖ See also *Women in World History.*

ROGERS, Jean (1916–1991). American actress. Born Eleanor Lovegren, Mar 25, 1916, in Belmont, MA; died Feb 24, 1991, in Sherman Oaks, CA; m. Dan Winkler, 1943 (died 1970). ❖ Played Dale Arden in the "Flash Gordon" series; other films include *My Man Godfrey, Whistling in Brooklyn* and *Speed to Spare.*

ROGERS, Marilyn (1916–2001). *See Meseke, Marilyn.*

ROGERS, Martha E. (1914–1994). American nurse. Born Martha Elizabeth Rogers, May 12, 1914, in Dallas, TX; died of pulmonary failure, Mar 13, 1994, in Phoenix, AZ; dau. of Lucy Mulholland Keener Rogers and Bruce Taylor Rogers; graduate of Knoxville General Hospital School of Nursing, 1936; George Peabody College. BS in public health nursing, 1937; Johns Hopkins University, DSc, 1954. ❖ Worked as a rural health nurse in Clare, Michigan (1937–39); was acting director of education at Visiting Nurse Association (1940–45); as head of New York University's nursing division (1954–75), established a 5-year undergraduate nursing program; helped establish Society for Advancement in Nursing (SAIN, 1974); wrote *Education Revolution in Nursing* (1961), *Reveille in Nursing* (1964) and *Introduction to the Theoretical Basis of Nursing* (1970).

ROGERS, Mother Mary Joseph (1882–1955). American nun and religious founder. Name variations: Mary Josephine Rogers; Mollie Rogers. Born Mary Josephine Rogers, Oct 27, 1882, in Roxbury, Massachusetts; died Oct 9, 1955, in New York, NY; dau. of Abraham Rogers and Mary Josephine (Plummer) Rogers; Smith College, BA, 1905; Boston Normal School, teacher's certificate, 1909. ❖ Returned to Smith to work and organize a mission-study class for Catholic undergraduates (1906); went to Boston to help Reverend James Anthony Walsh propagate the Catholic faith (1908); moved to Maryknoll Seminary to assist Walsh and became intent on forming a women's religious community (1912); with others, founded the Maryknoll Sisters of St. Dominic, a missionary congregation (1921); elected superior general of order (1925); established 1st contemplative branch of community of religious women (1933); after years of service, declined reelection as superior general (1947). ❖ See also *Women in World History.*

ROGERS, Victorine (1844–1935). *See Goddard, Victorine.*

ROGERS, Wanda. *See Young, Wanda.*

ROGGE, Florence (b. 1904). American choreographer. Born 1904 in Detroit, MI. ❖ Trained with Luigi Albertieri, Michio Ito, Theodore Kosloff and Ella Dagnova; performed as soloist at Roxy Theater under Gae Foster for 4 years; served as ballet choreographer at Radio City Music Hall in New York City (1932–52), working in close collaboration with Rockettes director Russell Markert and general producer Leon Leonidoff; choreographed large number of ballet sequences throughout career including best known *Snowflakes* and *Undersea Ballets*.

ROGNONI, Cecilia (1976—). Argentinean field-hockey player. Name variations: Ceci Rognoni. Born Maria Cecilia Rognoni, Dec 1, 1976, in Buenos Aires, Argentina. ❖ Defender, won a team silver medal at Sydney Olympics (2000) and a team bronze medal at Athens Olympics (2004); won Champions Trophy (2001) and was named Player of the Tournament; also placed 1st at World Cup (2002) and Pan American Games (2003); also played for the Dutch club, HC Rotterdam, and for Cologne in Germany. Awarded the Olimpa de Oro as the top sportsperson in Argentina (2002); named FIH Player of the Year (2002).

ROGOWSKA, Anna (1981—). Polish pole vaulter. Born May 21, 1981, in Gdynia, Poland. ❖ Won a bronze medal at Athens Olympics (2004).

ROGOZHINA, Lyudmila (1959—). Soviet basketball player. Born May 27, 1959, in USSR. ❖ At Moscow Olympics, won a gold medal in team competition (1980).

ROHAN, duchess de (1554–1631). See Parthenay, Catherine de.

ROHAN, Jacqueline de (c. 1520–1587). See Rothelin, Jacqueline de Rohan, Marquise de.

ROHAN-CHABOT, Marie Charlotte de (1729–1807). See Beauvau, Marie Charlotte.

ROHAN-MONTBAZON, Marie de (1600–1679). Duchesse de Chevreuse. Name variations: Marie de Rohan; Marie de Rohan-Montbazon, duchesse de Luynes. Born Marie de Rohan-Montbazon in Dec 1600; died at Gagny, near Paris, Aug 12, 1679; dau. of Hercule de Rohan, duke of Montbazon; m. Charles d'Albert, duke of Luynes, in 1617 (died 1621); m. Claude de Lorraine, duke of Chevreuse (son of Catherine of Cleves and Henry I of Lorraine, 3rd duke of Guise), in 1622. ❖ French intriguer at the royal court, was considered one of the most engaging women of her day; was a good friend of Anne of Austria, queen of Louis XIII; in what is known as the *Conspiration des Dames*, was caught, in cahoots with Queen Anne and Princesse de Condé, conspiring to thwart Cardinal Richelieu's royal matchmaking in respect to the king's brother; was forced to leave France. ❖ See also *Women in World History*.

ROHDE, Brigitte (1954—). East German runner. Born Oct 8, 1954, in East Germany. ❖ At Montreal Olympics, won a gold medal in the 4 x 400-meter relay (1976).

ROHDE, Lisa (1955—). American rower. Born Aug 12, 1955. ❖ At Los Angeles Olympics, won a silver medal in quadruple sculls with coxswain (1984).

ROHDE, Ruth Bryan Owen (1885–1954). American politician and diplomat. Name variations: Ruth Bryan Owen; Ruth Bryan Leavitt. Pronunciation: Rohde rhymes with soda. Born Ruth Baird Bryan, Oct 2, 1885, in Jacksonville, Illinois; died July 26, 1954, in Copenhagen, Denmark; dau. of Mary Baird Bryan (lawyer) and William Jennings Bryan (well-known politician); attended Monticello Seminary, 1899–1901, and University of Nebraska, 1901–03; m. William Homer Leavitt, Oct 3, 1903 (div. 1909); m. Reginald Altham Owen, May 3, 1910 (died 1927); m. Borge Rohde (captain of the Danish King's Life Guards), July 11, 1936; children: (1st m.) Ruth "Kitty" Leavitt (b. 1904), John Baird Leavitt (b. 1905); (2nd m.) Reginald Bryan Owen, Helen Rudd Owen. ❖ Speaker, author, US congressional representative, diplomat, and 1st woman envoy, served as father's presidential campaign secretary and manager (1908); was a spellbinding speaker on Chautauqua circuit (1919–28); served as a nurse in WWI; elected US congressional representative from Florida (1928–32), the 1st woman elected to Congress from the Old South; worked all 4 years for economic development in Florida as well as for feminist goals like a Cabinet-level Department of Home and Child; appointed US minister to Denmark (1933–36), the 1st woman to head an embassy overseas; named presidential appointee to San Francisco Conference to create the United Nations (1945); named alternate delegate to 4th United Nations General Assembly (1949–50); served as acting president of Institute for International Government (1952–53); writings include *Leaves from a Greenland Diary* (1935), *Denmark Caravan* (1936), *The Castle in the*

Silver Wood and Other Scandinavian Fairy Tales (1939), *Picture Tales From Scandinavia* (1939), *Look Forward, Warrior* (1942) and *Caribbean Caravel* (1949). Danish Order of Merit conferred by King Frederick IX (1954); inducted into Florida Women's Hall of Fame (1992). ❖ See also *Women in World History*.

RÖHL, Ulrike (1934–1972). See Meinhof, Ulrike.

ROHLÄNDER, Linda (1969—). See Kisabaka, Linda.

ROHLÄNDER, Uta (1969—). German runner. Name variations: Rohlander or Rohlaender; Uta Rohlander-Fromm. Born June 30, 1969, in Merseburg, Germany. ❖ Won a bronze medal for the 4 x 400-meter relay at Atlanta Olympics (1996).

ROHLFS, Anna Katharine Green (1846–1935). See Green, Anna Katharine.

ROJCEWICZ, Susan (1953—). American basketball player. Name variations: Sue Rojcewicz. Born May 29, 1953; graduate of Southern Connecticut State, 1975. ❖ At Montreal Olympics, won a silver medal in team competition (1976); coached at Stanford. Inducted into Women's Basketball Hall of Fame (2000).

ROJF, Ana (1909—). Yugoslavian ballet dancer. Born 1909 in Split, Yugoslavia. ❖ Performed for Nicholai Legat in Yugoslav State Ballet in Zagreb and later served as his assistant; moved to US where she joined Ballet Russe de Monte Carlo (1938); during WWII, returned to Yugoslavia and continued to dance in Zagreb and Split, in *Giselle*, *Romeo and Juliet*, and Oskar Harmos' *Fifth Symphony*; taught classes in Yugoslavia and abroad at Monte Carlo School (as of 1954), Bermuda Ballet Festival (as of 1959), and in England where she also served as president of Society of Russian-style Ballet Schools; considered among best known teachers of Legat system.

ROKEYA, Begum (1880–1932). See Hossain, Rokeya Sakhawat.

RÖKK, Marika (1913–2004). German actress, dancer and singer. Name variations: Marika Rokk or Roekk. Born Maria Korrer, Nov 3, 1913, in Cairo, Egypt; died May 16, 2004, in Baden, Lower Austria, Austria; m. Georg Jacoby (film director); children: Gabriele Jacoby. ❖ Began career as a dancer at the Moulin Rouge in Paris; appeared in English films (1930s); became one of the biggest film stars of Nazi Germany; made some of her best-known films after the war, including *Maske in Blau* (1953) and *Nachts im Grünen Kakadu* (1957); retired from films (1960s) but continued to perform on the stage.

ROKNE, Marianne (1978—). Norwegian handball player. Born Mar 9, 1978, in Bergen, Norway. ❖ Won a team bronze medal at Sydney Olympics (2000).

ROLAND, Betty (1903–1996). Australian dramatist and writer. Name variations: Elizabeth Maclean. Born Elizabeth Maclean in Kaniva, Victoria, Australia, July 22, 1903; died 1996; dau. of Roland Maclean (physician) and Matilda (Blayney) Maclean; m. Ellis H. Davies, 1923 (div. 1934); m. Guido Baracchi (journalist), 1930s (died 1975); children: (1st m.) Peter Ellis Davies; (2nd m.) Gilda Baracchi. ❖ Began career as a journalist for *Table Talk* and *Sun News-Pictorial*; wrote 1st full-length play, *The Touch of Silk* (1928), followed by *Morning* (1932); eloped to Russia with Guido Baracchi, a journalist and well-known Australian Communist (1933), where she worked as a journalist for 15 months; returned to Australia (1935) and wrote full-length political play, *Are You Ready, Comrade?*, which won Western Australian Drama Competition (1938); disillusioned with Communism by 1939, began to write radio plays, including "Daddy Was Asleep," (1945) and the serial "A Woman Scorned," which was later the basis for the popular tv series "Return to Eden" (1983); wrote several books for children as well as 3 novels, *The Other Side of Sunset* (1972), *No Ordinary Man* (1974) and *Beyond Capricorn* (1976). ❖ See also memoir *Caviar for Breakfast* (1979); and *Women in World History*.

ROLAND, Eudora (1781–1858). See Champagneux, Madame.

ROLAND, Madame (1754–1793). French writer. Name variations: Marie-Jeanne Roland de la Platière; Manon Roland; Manon Phlipon. Pronunciation: RO-lun or ro-LAH. Born Marie-Jeanne Phlipon, Mar 17, 1754; guillotined, Nov 9, 1793; only child of Pierre-Gatien Phlipon (d. 1788), master engraver aided by his wife, Marie-Marguerite (Bimont) Phlipon (d. 1775); m. Jean-Marie Roland de la Platière (inspector of manufactures and writer), 1780 (committed suicide Nov 10, 1793); children: Marie-Thérèse-Eudora (Madame Champagneux, 1781–1858). ❖ Intellectual, who was among the 1st women to have a marked impact as a journalistic correspondent, focused on her education and constant reading (1758–75) until the death of her mother; by 14, was fascinated by the banned Enlightenment movement and its *philosophes*; began to question the absolute validity of any dogmatic interpretation and developed an aversion to the traditions of a French society built on rank, privilege and limited opportunities; taught herself algebra, geometry, physics and natural history; helped to manage father's shop, wrote an essay on the education of girls and met husband (1775–80); served as husband's editor, researcher and coauthor (1780–89); became integral to the completion of his *Dictionary of Manufactures, Arts, and Trades* (1784, 1785, 1790); catapulted into the public arena by French Revolution (1789), as the Lyons correspondent for a revolutionary newspaper, *Patriote français* (1789–80); husband named minister of the interior by Legislative Assembly (Mar 1792); like husband, demonstrated marked Girondin tendencies, favoring limited, decentralized government; wrote of her increasing awareness that many of the people's representatives were far more interested in promoting their own careers than in promoting the common welfare; became a bitter enemy of Robespierre, writing that he was the puppet of the Parisian mobs and their demagogues; called before the legislature which was now known as the National Convention and charged with having been a moving force behind the royalist conspiracy (1792), but she so eloquently defended herself that the Convention rose in a standing ovation after her presentation; arrested as part of the "Girondin conspiracy against the republic" (1793); wrote *Memoirs* while in prison which contain numerous sketches of some of the leading figures of the French Revolution, including Robespierre; went to trial (Nov 8); was condemned to death as one of the participants in a conspiracy against the "indivisibility of the Republic, and the liberty and safety of the French people"; last words were, "O Liberty, what crimes are committed in thy name!" ❖ See also *Mémoires de Madame Roland* (ed. by Paul de Roux, Paris: Mercure de France, 1986); Madeleine Clemenceau-Jacquemaire, *The Life of Madame Roland* (trans. by Laurence Vail, Longmans, 1930); Gita May, *Madame Roland and the Age of Revolution* (Columbia U. Press, 1970); and *Women in World History*.

ROLAND, Pauline (1805–1852). French journalist and activist. Pronunciation: paw-LEEN ro-LAH. Born Marie-Désirée-Pauline Roland, June 6, 1805, at Falaise (Calvados); died at Lyons, Dec 16, 1852; dau. of Joseph-Jouachine Roland (d. 1806, postmaster) and Françoise-Marie-Adélaide Lesne (d. 1833); tutored by Desprèz (1827–31); never married; children: (with Adolphe Guéroult) son, Jean-François Roland (b. 1835); (with Jean-François Aicard) Maria (1837–1839), Moïse (1839–c. 1852), and Irma (c. 1841–1923); also took in Aline-Marie Chazal, dau. of the deceased social reformer Flora Tristan (1803–1844) and later mother of the painter Paul Gauguin. ❖ Socialist journalist and activist whose agitated, tragic life reflected typical features of the Romantic movement; went to Paris to join Enfantin's Saint-Simonians, a new secular religion (1832), having identified sacrifice with virtue, a theme that would remain powerful throughout her life; had liaison with Jean-François Aicard (1834–47); published histories of France and England (1835, 1838, 1844); probably wrote for *La Femme libre* (c. 1832) and certainly its successor, the 1st French feminist review, *La Femme nouvelle/La Tribune des femmes*, followed in its turn by *Le Journal des femmes*—all short-lived Saint-Simonian gazettes (mid-1830s); wrote for Pierre Leroux's journals (1841–48); was named joint director of *L'Éclaireur* (1847); lived at Leroux's socialist commune at Boussac (1847–48); founded a teachers' association and, with Jeanne Deroin, a union of associations (1849); arrested, tried, and imprisoned as an unwed mother, a communist socialist, and "an enemy of marriage" (1850–51); arrested and deported to Algeria for life, for having participated in charity lotteries for prisoners' families (false), for belonging to women's clubs (false), and for being a notorious socialist propagandist, which she was (1852); became an icon of the Left in Europe, enshrined in Victor Hugo's poem in *Les Châtiments* (The Punishments). ❖ See also *Women in World History*.

ROLAND, Ruth (1892–1937). American actress. Name variations: Baby Ruth. Born Aug 26, 1892, in San Francisco, CA; died Sept 22, 1937, in Hollywood, CA; m. Lionel T. Kent, 1917 (div. 1919); m. Ben Bard, 1929. ❖ Began career on stage billed as Baby Ruth; appeared in films (1911–35), debuting in Kalem western comedies; considered 2nd only to Pearl White in popularity and athletic ability as a serial star; serials include *The Red Circle, The Neglected Wife, Hands Up!, The Adventures of Ruth* and *Ruth of the Rockies*.

ROLAND DE LA PLATIERE, Marie-Jeanne Phlipon (1754–1793). *See Roland, Madame.*

ROLAND HOLST, Henriëtte (1869–1952). Dutch writer and militant. Name variations: Henriette Roland Holst; Henriëtte Roland Holst-van der Schalk or Henriëtte Roland Holst van der Schalk. Born Henriëtte Goverdina Anna van der Schalk, Dec 24, 1869, in Noordwijk, the Netherlands; died Nov 21, 1952, in Amsterdam; dau. of a wealthy family of Dutch bourgeoisie; married Richard Nicolaüs Roland Holst (artist and writer), 1896 (died 1938); no children. ❖ Socialist militant, poet, and essayist, held in high regard for her contributions to her country's modern literature, whose anti-Nazi stance was vital to the morale of the Dutch resistance movement during WWII; published 1st vol. of poetry, *Sonnets and Poems Written in Terzinas* (1895); with husband, joined Dutch Social Democratic Labor Party (1897); published *Capital and Labor in the Nineteenth Century* (1902); withdrew from politics (1912); returned to politics in opposition to WWI (1914); was a founding member of Dutch Communist Party (1918); disillusioned with the Soviet system on visit to Russia (1921); quit the Dutch Communist Party (1927); became the voice of the Dutch resistance movement through her poetry published by the underground (1940–45); resistance poems were collected and published as *From the Very Depths* (1946); also wrote *The New Birth* (1903), (poetry) *Upward Roads* (1907), *The Rebels* (1910), *The Woman in the Woods* (1912), *Thomas More* (1912), *Michael* (1916), *Between Two Worlds* (1923), *Children of this Time* (1931), *The Mother* (1932), *Between Time and Eternity* (1934), *Friends of India* (1935), and biography of Gandhi (1947). ❖ See also autobiography, *The Fire Burned On* (1949); and *Women in World History*.

ROLDÁN, Luisa (1656–1704). Spanish sculptor. Name variations: Luisa Roldán; La Roldana; Luisa de los Arcos. Born Luisa Ignacia Roldán in Sevilla, Spain, 1656; died in Madrid, 1704; dau. of Pedro Roldán (sculptor) and Teresa de Mena y Villavicencio; sister of Maria Roldán, who also helped their father produce sculpture; m. Luis de los Arcos (sculptor), 1671; children: 2. ❖ Appointed sculptor to the court by the crown (June 21, 1695), produced a number of religious pieces and achieved particular renown for small polychrome clay (terra-cotta) grouped figures for Nativity scenes, a technique virtually unknown before this time; most important pieces include *The Death of Saint Mary Magdalene, The Annunciation* and *The Mystical Marriage of St. Catherine*. ❖ See also *Women in World History*.

ROLDAN REYNA, Pilar (1944—). Mexican fencer. Born June 27, 1944, in Mexico. ❖ At Mexico City Olympics, won a silver medal in indiv. foil (1968).

ROLES, Barbara. American figure skater. Name variations: Barbara Roles Pursley; Barbara Roles-Williams; Barbara Roles Williams. ❖ Placed 3rd at US nationals (1959), 2nd (1960), and 1st (1962); won a bronze medal at Squaw Valley Olympics (1960); turned to coaching. Inducted into US Figure Skating Hall of Fame (1997).

ROLEY, Susan Lynn (c. 1947—). American special agent. Born c. 1947. ❖ Served as first lieutenant in Marine Corps; became one of two (with Joanne E. Pierce) of the 1st women special agents for Federal Bureau of Investigation (FBI, 1972), after J. Edgar Hoover died and acting director L Patrick Gray III changed policy to allow women agents. The Bureau of Investigation, which preceded the FBI, had hired the 1st woman, Emma R.H. Jentzer, in 1911.

ROLFE, Lady Rebecca (c. 1596–1617). *See Pocahontas.*

ROLIG, Marjut. *See Lukkarinen, Marjut.*

ROLLE, Esther (1920–1998). African-American actress. Born Nov 8, 1920, in Pompano Beach, FL; died Nov 17, 1998, in Los Angeles, CA; sister of Rosanna Carter (actress) and Estelle Evans (1906–1985, actress). ❖ Had recurring role of Florida Evans on "Maude" (1972–74) and "Good Times" (1974); films include *The Mighty Quinn, Driving Miss Daisy, Rosewood* and *Down in the Delta*.

ROLLESTON, Elizabeth Mary (1845–1940). New Zealand political hostess and salonnière. Name variations: Elizabeth Mary Brittan, Mary Brittan. Born Elizabeth Mary Brittan, Mar 30, 1845, in Dorset, England; died June 4, 1940, in Christchurch, New Zealand; dau. of Joseph Brittan (physician) and Elizabeth Mary (Chandler) Brittan; m. William Rolleston (politician), 1865 (died 1903); children: 9. ❖ Immigrated with family to New Zealand (1852); served as hostess to Wellington's elite, and established a popular salon. ❖ See also *Dictionary of New Zealand Biography* (Vol. 1).

ROLLETT, Hilda (1873–1970). New Zealand teacher, journalist, art critic, and writer. Name variations: Emma Hilda Keane. Born Emma

Hilda Keane, May 18, 1873, in Auckland New Zealand; died on April 2, 1970, in Auckland; dau. of Henry Keane (innkeeper) and Elizabeth (Hancock) Keane; m. Frederick Carr Rollett (editor), 1902 (died 1931); children: 2 daughters. ❖ Taught at St Hilda's Collegiate School in Dunedin; contributor and editor, *New Zealand Illustrated Magazine* (1902–05); New Zealand correspondent, New York *Sun* and *Sphere*; contributor of articles on politics and economics to *Britannia* for 10 years; contributor to *National Review, Empire Review,* and *Macmillan's Magazine*; fiction published in English periodicals, New York *Sun*, and Australian *Bulletin*; art critic for *New Zealand Herald* and *Auckland Weekly News* (1920s); member of Lyceum Club of London (1904); one of founding executives of League of New Zealand Penwomen (1925); published collected articles, *A Pleasant Land* (1925). ❖ See also *Dictionary of New Zealand Biography* (Vol. 3).

ROLLINS, Charlemae Hill (1897–1979). African-American librarian and author. Born in Yazoo City, Mississippi, June 20, 1897; died Feb 3, 1979; dau. of Allen G. Hill (farmer) and Birdie (Tucker) Hill (teacher); attended graduate library school at University of Chicago, 1934–36; m. Joseph Walter Rollins, April 8, 1918; children: Joseph Walter Rollins Jr. (b. 1920). ❖ As head of the children's department at George Cleveland Hall branch of Chicago Public Library, sought to increase the visibility of African-Americans in books for children; after retirement, made her own contribution through her publications *Christmas Gif', an Anthology of Christmas Poems, Songs, and Stories Written by and about Negroes* (1963), *They Showed the Way* (1964), *Famous American Negro Poets for Children* (1965), *Famous Negro Entertainers of Stage and Screen* (1967) and *Black Troubadour, Langston Hughes* (1971); was a distinguished librarian and authority on black literature. ❖ See also *Women in World History.*

ROLTON, Gillian (1956—). Australian equestrian. Name variations: Gill Rolton. Born May 3, 1956, in South Australia. ❖ Began eventing on Saville Row (1981); won a team gold medal in 3-day event at Barcelona Olympics (1992), Australian 3-day eventing championship (1995), a team gold medal for eventing at Atlanta Olympics, finishing with a broken collarbone and ribs (1996), and a team gold medal for eventing at Sydney Olympics (2000), all on Peppermint Grove. Named South Australian Sports Woman of the Year (1992); given Order of Australia (1993); inducted into Australian Sport Hall of Fame (2000).

ROM, Dagmar (1928—). Austrian Alpine skier. Born June 16, 1928, in Innsbruck, Austria; married; children: 3. ❖ Won 2 gold medals at the World championships in Aspen (1950); won a silver medal for giant slalom at Oslo Olympics (1952). Starred in the film "Nacht am Montblanc" (1951).

ROMACHKOVA, Nina (1929—). *See Ponomareva-Romashkova, Nina.*

ROMACK, Barbara (1932—). American golfer. Born Nov 16, 1932, in Sacramento, CA. ❖ Won Canadian Women's Amateur (1953); won USGA Women's Amateur (1954), was runner-up (1958); member of Curtis Cup team (1954, 1956, 1958); was four-time California state champion; joined the pro tour (1958); won Rock City Open (1963); LPGA Master Professional.

ROMAGNOLI, Diana (1977—). Swiss fencer. Name variations: Romagnoli-Takouk or Diana Romagnoli Takouk. Born Feb 14, 1977, in Männedorf, Switzerland. ❖ Won a silver medal for team épée at Sydney Olympics (2000).

ROMAN, Ruth (1922–1999). American actress. Born Norma Roman, Dec 22, 1922, in Lynn, MA; died Sept 9, 1999, in Laguna Beach, CA; m. Mortimer Hall, 1950 (div. 1955); m. Budd Burton Moss, 1956 (div. 1964); m. Bill Wilson, 1974 (div. 1999). ❖ Leading lady, made film debut in *Stage Door Canteen* (1943), followed by *Belle Starr's Daughter* (title role), *Since You Went Away, The Affairs of Susan, Colt .45, Three Secrets, The Big Clock, The Window, Champion, Beyond the Forest, Strangers on a Train, The Far Country* and *The Killing Kind,* among others. With 3-year-old son, survived the sinking of the *Andrea Doria* cruise ship (1956).

ROMAN, Susan (1927–1986). *See Cabot, Susan.*

ROMANCE, Viviane (1909–1991). French actress. Born Pauline Ronacher Ortmanns (also seen as Ortmans) on July 4, 1909, in Roubaix, France; died Sept 25, 1991, in Nice, France. ❖ Named Miss Paris (1930); entered films as an extra and within a year had star billing; appeared in such films as Fritz Lang's *Lilliom* (1934), Abel Gance's *Vénus aveugle* (1941), and Julien Duvivier's *Panique* (1946); in addition

to acting, produced several movies, including *Maya* (1950), *Passion* (1950), *Le Chair et le Diable (Flesh and Desire,* 1953), and *Pitié pour les vamps* (1956); appeared in last film, Chabrol's *Nada* (1973); other films include *La Maison du Maltais (Sirocco,* 1938), *Gibraltar (It Happened in Gibraltar,* 1938), *La Tradition de Minuit* (1939), *Une Femme dans la Nuit* (1941), *Carmen* (1943), *L'Affaire du Collier de la Reine (The Queen's Necklace,* 1946), *L'affaire des poisons* (1955) and *Mélodie en sous-sol (Any Number Can Win,* 1963).

ROMAN EMPRESS. *See Rome, empress of.*

ROMANIA, queen of.
See *Elizabeth of Wied (1843–1916).*
See *Marie of Rumania (1875–1938).*

ROMANO, Francesca (fl. 1321). Italian physician. Name variations: Francesca Romana. Flourished 1321 in Calabria; m. Matteo de Romano; was a licensed surgeon. ❖ One of the few medieval women allowed to study medicine at a university, received permission to enter the medical school at the University of Salerno to take a degree in surgery. ❖ See also *Women in World History.*

ROMANO, Lalla (1906–2001). Italian novelist and short-story writer. Born Graziella Romano, Nov 11, 1906, in Demonte, Cuneo, Italy; died June 26, 2001, in Milan, Italy; dau. of Roberto Romano and Giuseppina Peano; attended Turin University; m. Innocenzo Monti, 1932 (died); children: son Pietro. ❖ Was a librarian and teacher in Turin; after the war, moved to Milan; began career as a poet with the collection *Fiore* (1941); published many autobiographical narratives, including *La penumbra che abbiamo attraversato* (The Shadows through Which We Have Passed, 1964, trans. as *The Penumbra*), *Le parole tra noi leggere* (The Gentle Words Between Us, 1969), which won the Strega Prize, *L'ospite* (1973), *Inseparabile* (1981), *Nei mari estremi* (In Heavy Seas, 1987) and *Un caso di coscienza* (1992); also wrote *Le metamorfosi* (1951), *Maria* (1953), *Tetto murato* (1957), *L'uomo che parlava solo* (1961), and *Opere* (1991); translated works of Flaubert, Delacroix and Beck into Italian.

ROMANOV, Alexandra (1825–1844). *See Alexandra Nikolaevna.*

ROMANOV, Anastasia (1901–1918). *See Anastasia.*

ROMANOV, Anna (fl. 1550). Russian aristocrat. Name variations: Romanova. Dau. of Eudoxia Jaroslavovna (1534–1581) and Nikita Romanov (1530–1586); m. Ivan Troiekurow.

ROMANOV, Anna (1632–1692). Russian princess. Born Anna Mikhailovna Romanov on July 14, 1632; died Oct 26, 1692; dau. of Eudoxia Streshnev (1608–1645) and Michael (1596–1645), tsar of Russia (r. 1613–1645); m. Boris Morozov.

ROMANOV, Anna or Anne (1795–1865). *See Anna Pavlovna (1795–1865).*

ROMANOV, Catherine.
See *Catherine of Mecklenburg-Schwerin (1692–1733).*
See *Catherine of Russia (1788–1819).*

ROMANOV, Catherine (1827–1894). Duchess of Mecklenburg-Strelitz. Born Catherine Michailovna Romanov, Aug 28, 1827; died May 12, 1894; dau. of Helene of Wurttemberg (1807–1873) and Grand Duke Michael of Russia (1798–1849); m. George (1824–1876), duke of Mecklenburg-Strelitz, Feb 16, 1851; children: Nickolas (b. 1854); Helena Marie of Mecklenburg-Strelitz (1857–1936); George Alexander (b. 1859); Charles Michael (b. 1863).

ROMANOV, Catherine (1878–1959). *See Catherine Romanov.*

ROMANOV, Elizabeth (1826–1845). Grand duchess of Luxemburg. Born Elizabeth Michailovna Romanov, May 26, 1826; died Jan 28, 1845; dau. of Helene of Wurttemberg (1807–1873) and Grand Duke Michael of Russia (1798–1849); m. Adolphe, grand duke of Luxemburg, on Jan 31, 1844.

ROMANOV, Euphamia (fl. 1550). Russian aristocrat. Name variations: Romanova. Dau. of Eudoxia Jaroslavovna (1534–1581) and Nikita Romanov (1530–1586); m. Ivan Sitzki.

ROMANOV, Hélène.
See *Helena Pavlovna (1784–1803).*
See *Helena of Russia (1882–1957).*

ROMANOV, Irina (fl. 1601). Russian aristocrat. Name variations: Romanova. Dau. of Eudoxia Jaroslavovna (1534–1581) and Nikita Romanov (1530–1586); m. Ivan Godunov (d. 1610), in 1601.

ROMANOV, Irina (1627–1679). Russian princess. Name variations: Irinia. Born Irina Mikhailovna Romanov, 1627; died in 1679; dau. of Eudoxia Streshnev (1608–1645) and Michael (1596–1645), tsar of Russia (r. 1613–1645); sister of Alexis I, tsar of Russia.

ROMANOV, Irina (1895–1970). *See Irina.*

ROMANOV, Marie.
See Maria Nikolaevna (1819–1876).
See Marie Alexandrovna (1853–1920).

ROMANOV, Martha (fl. 1550). Russian aristocrat. Name variations: Martha Romanova. Dau. of Eudoxia Jaroslavovna (1534–1581, matriarch of the House of Romanov) and Nikita Romanov (1530–1586, patriarch of the House of Romanov); m. Boris Tscherkaski.

ROMANOV, Martha (1560–1631). *See Martha the Nun.*

ROMANOV, Mary.
See Marie Alexandrovna (1853–1920).
See Marie Pavlovna (1890–1958).

ROMANOV, Natalya (1674–1716). Grand duchess of Russia. Name variations: Natalie Alexinov Romanov. Born Natalya Alexinova Romanov on Sept 4, 1674; died June 29, 1716; dau. of Natalya Narishkina (1651–1694) and Alexis I (1629–1676), tsar of Russia (r. 1645–1676); sister of Peter I the Great (1672–1725), tsar of Russia (r. 1682–1725).

ROMANOV, Olga.
See Olga of Russia (1822–1892).
See Olga Constantinovna (1851–1926).
See Olga Alexandrovna (1882–1960).

ROMANOV, Sophie (1634–1676). Russian princess. Born Sept 14, 1634; died in 1676; dau. of Eudoxia Streshnev (1608–1645) and Michael (1596–1645), tsar of Russia (r. 1613–1645).

ROMANOV, Vera (1854–1912). *See Vera Constantinovna.*

ROMANOV, Xenia (1876–1960). *See Xenia Alexandrovna.*

ROMANOV, Yekaterina Ivanova (1692–1733). *See Catherine of Mecklenburg-Schwerin.*

ROMANOVA, Anastasia.
See Anastasia Romanova (d. 1560).
See Anastasia Romanova (1860–1922).

ROMANOVA, Maria (1886–1954). Russian ballerina. Name variations: Maria Ulanova. Born Maria Fedorovna Romanova in 1886; died 1954; m. Sergei Nikolaevich Ulanov (1881–1950, ballet dancer and regisseur of the Kirov ballet); children: Galina Ulanova (1910–1998, ballerina). ❖ Graduated from her theater school's corps de ballet (1903); toured abroad with Anna Pavlova's company (1911) and was a soloist with Maryinsky Ballet, then known as the State Theater of Opera and Ballet; taught at Leningrad Ballet School and School of Russian Ballet. ❖ See also *Women in World History.*

ROMANOVA, Yelena (1963—). Soviet runner. Born Mar 20, 1963, in USSR. ❖ At Barcelona Olympics, won a gold medal in the 3,000 meters (1992).

ROMANOVSKY-KRASSINSKY, Princess (1872–1971). *See Kshesinskaia, Matilda.*

ROMANS, queen of the.
See Matilda of Saxony (c. 892–968).
See Marshall, Isabel (1200–1240).
See Sancha of Provence (c. 1225–1261).
See Falkestein, Beatrice von (c. 1253–1277).

ROMANZINI, Maria (1769–1838). *See Bland, Maria Theresa.*

ROMARY, Janice-Lee (1927—). American fencer. Name variations: Janice-Lee York. Born Janice-Lee York, Aug 6, 1927, in San Mateo, CA; University of Southern California, AB, 1949; m. Charles Gerald Romary, Nov 26, 1953. ❖ Won 10 national championships (1950, 1951, 1956, 1957, 1960, 1961, 1964, 1965, 1966, 1968); was a member of 6 Olympic teams (1948, 1952, 1956, 1960, 1964, 1968); was the 1st woman chosen to carry the American flag during the parade of

champions at Montreal Olympics (1968). ❖ See also *Women in World History.*

ROMASHKOVA, Nina (1929—). *See Ponomareva-Romashkova, Nina.*

ROMASKO, Olga (1968—). Russian biathlete. Born April 18, 1968, in Borodino, Russia. ❖ Won a silver medal for 4 x 7.5 km relay at Nagano Olympics (1998); at World championships, won gold medals for sprint (1996, 1997), bronze medals for pursuit and relay (1997) and a silver medal for relay (1999).

ROMAY, Fulgencia (1944—). Cuban runner. Born Jan 16, 1944, in Havana, Cuba. ❖ Won a silver medal at Mexico City Olympics (1968) and a bronze medal at Munich Olympics (1972), both in the 4 x 100-meter relay.

ROMBAUER, Irma S. (1877–1962). American cookbook writer. Born Irma von Starkloff in St. Louis, Missouri, Oct 30, 1877; died in St. Louis, Oct 14, 1962; dau. of Hugo von Starkloff (physician and surgeon) and Clara (Kuhlman) von Starkloff (assisted Susan Blow in founding 1st public-school kindergarten in US); briefly attended Washington University; m. Edgar Roderick Rombauer (lawyer), Oct 14, 1899 (committed suicide Feb 1930); children: Marion Rombauer Becker (1903–1976, author); Edgar Rombauer. ❖ Author of America's classic cookbook, *The Joy of Cooking*, privately published the 1st slim edition (1931); after selling 3,000 copies, revised and enlarged the volume, adding additional recipes and the step-by-step method which, along with its chatty style, became one of the book's unique features. ❖ See also Anne Mendelson, *Stand Facing the Stove: The Story of the Women Who Gave America The Joy of Cooking* (Holt, 1996); and *Women in World History.*

ROME, empress of.
See Livia Drusilla (58 BCE–29 CE).
See Messalina, Valeria (c. 23–48).
See Lollia Paulina (fl. 38–39).
See Poppaea Sabina (d. 47).
See Octavia (39–62).
See Messalina, Statilia (fl. 66–68).
See Faustina I (c. 90–141).
See Plotina (d. 122).
See Faustina II (130–175).
See Bruttia Crispina (d. 185).
See Julia Domna (c. 170–217).
See Julia Maesa (c. 170–224).
See Julia Mamaea (c. 190–235).
See Julia Paula.
See Julia Soaemias (d. 222).
See Helena (c. 255–329).
See Eutropia (fl. 270–300).
See Charito (fl. 300s).
See Constance (d. 305).
See Galla (fl. 320).
See Fausta (d. 324).
See Constantina (c. 321–c. 354).
See Justina (fl. 350–370).
See Flaccilla (c. 355–386).
See Galla (c. 365–394).
See Eudocia (c. 400–460).
See Licinia Eudoxia (422–before 490).
See Ariadne (fl. 457–515).

ROME, Esther (1945–1995). American writer and advocate for women's health. Name variations: Esther Seidman. Born Esther Seidman, Sept 8, 1945, in Norwich, Connecticut; died June 24, 1995, in Somerville, Massachusetts; graduate of Brandeis University, 1966; Harvard Graduate School of Education, MA, 1968; m. Nathan Rome; children: Judah and Micah. ❖ Was a founder of the Boston Women's Health Book Collective which produced the pioneering *Our Bodies, Ourselves* (early 1970s); served as an advocate for a variety of women's health issues, particularly breast cancer, body image, nutrition, and eating disorders; served as a consumer representative for US Food and Drug Administration committee that investigated the potential hazards of silicone breast implants and ran a support group for women with silicone implant difficulties (early 1990s). ❖ See also *Women in World History.*

ROMEIN-VERSCHOOR, Annie (1895–1978). Dutch novelist, historian and literary critic. Name variations: Anna Helena Margaretha Romein-Verschoor. Born Anna Helena Margaretha Verschoor, Feb 4,

1895, in Hatert, Netherlands; died Feb 5, 1978, in Amsterdam, Netherlands; grew up in Java (Dutch East Indies); m. Jan Romein (historian). ❖ Studied Dutch, history, and Russian; with husband, was involved with the left-wing intellectual journal, *De Nieuwe Stem*, in which the 1st extracts of the diary of Anne Frank was published; pushed for publication and provided a foreword for the 1st editions of the *Diary*; works include *Aan de Oedjoeng* (1928), *Vrouwenspiegel* (1935), *Slib en wolken* (1947), *Met eigen ogen* (1953), a historical novel about Hugo de Groot, *Zedelijkheid en schijnheiligheid* (1962), *Ja vader, nee vader* (1974) and *Spelen met de tijd* (1979).

ROMERO, Pilar Miro (1940–1997). *See Miró, Pilar.*

ROMERO, Rebecca (1980—). English rower. Born Jan 24, 1980, in Carshalton, Surrey, England; attended St. Mary's College. ❖ Won a silver medal for quadruple sculls at Athens Olympics (2004).

ROMIEU, Marie de (c. 1545–c. 1590). French poet. Born c. 1545, possibly in Viviers, France; died c. 1590; thought to have been born into the nobility; sister of Jacques de Romieu. ❖ Wrote *Bref discours de l'excellence des femmes* in response to brother's invective against women; translated Alessandro Piccolomini's *Dialogo della bella creanza delle donne* as *Instruction pour les jeunes dames* (1573); her brother published her *Premières ouevres poétiques de Mademoiselle de Romieu* (1581).

ROMSEY, abbess of.
See Ethelflaeda (fl. 900s).
See Ethelflaeda (c. 963–c. 1016).
See Marie of Boulogne (d. 1182).

RONETTES, The.
See Spector, Ronnie (1943—).
See Bennett, Estelle (1944—).
See Talley, Nedra (1946—).

RONGONUI, Kahupake (1868/69?–1947). New Zealand tribal leader. Name variations: Hariata Whareiti, Kahupake Potatau. Born probably in 1868 or 1869, in Tamaki-makau-rau (Auckland isthmus), New Zealand; died Jan 17, 1947, at Pukaki, New Zealand; dau. of Te Rongonui Reihana Te Haupatahi Te Aroha and Te Tahuri; m. Tautahi Paraihe; children: adopted several. ❖ Principal tribal leader, traditional healer, seer, and expert on her people's history, hosted tribal gatherings over land disputes; was the last woman of Te Wai-o-Hua to be traditionally tattooed. ❖ See also *Dictionary of New Zealand Biography* (Vol. 3).

RONGOWHAKAATA (1932—). *See Hineira, Arapera.*

RONNE, Edith (1919—). American explorer. Name variations: Edith "Jackie" Ronne; Jackie Ronne. Born 1919 in US; dau.-in-law of Martin Ronne (Antarctic explorer); m. Finn Ronne (Norwegian-born Antarctic explorer), Mar 18, 1941 (died Jan 12, 1980); children: at least 1 daughter, Karen Ronne. ❖ Accompanied husband to Antarctica on *Port of Beaumont* and became one of 1st two women (with Jenny Darlington) to set foot there (1947); with Darlington, became one of 1st two women to overwinter in Antarctica; on expedition, served as historian and correspondent for North American Newspaper Alliance, sending articles describing progress; after expedition left South Pole (1948), area discovered by husband was named Edith Ronne Land by US Board of Geographic Names. The Ronne Ice Shelf was named in honor of Edith, her husband Finn, and his father Martin Ronne.

RONNER-KNIP, Henriette (1821–1909). Dutch painter. Name variations: Henriëtte Ronner. Born 1821 in Amsterdam, Holland; died 1909; dau. of Joseph Knip (painter); m. Feico Ronner, c. 1850. ❖ A member of the Belgian School of Art, was one of the best known female European artists of the 19th century; her speciality was cats, though she painted other animals; married and moved to Brussels (c. 1850), where she painted stray dogs of the Flemish streets; began painting cats (c. 1870); work was displayed at Chicago World's Fair. Received the Order of Leopold (1887).

RONNLUND, Toini (1938—). *See Gustafsson, Toini.*

RONSTADT, Linda (1946—). American singer. Born July 15, 1946, in Tucson, AZ, to a German-Mexican father and a Dutch English mother; attended University of Arizona; children: (adopted) 2. ❖ One of America's 1st rock superstars, began career with folk-rock group, Stone Poneys (1964), and had hit single "Different Drum"; had 1st solo hit with country rock crossover, "Long Long Time" (1970); released chart-topping album, *Heart Like a Wheel* (1974), with hit songs, "You're No Good," "When Will I Be Loved," "That'll Be the Day" and

"It's So Easy"; was the 1st to record songs by such performers as Karla Bonoff, Emmylou Harris, and Dolly Parton; released #1 hit albums, *Simple Dreams* (1977) and *Living in the U.S.A.* (1978); outspoken and political, appeared on cover of *Time* magazine with then-companion, California governor Jerry Brown; starred on Broadway in *Pirates of Penzance* (1983); released triple-platinum album *What's New* (1983) and gold *Sentimental Reasons* (1986); released platinum Spanish-language album, *Canciones de Mi Padre* (*Songs of My Father*), and platinum *Trio*, recorded with Dolly Parton and Emmylou Harris (1987), which won Grammy for Best Country Vocal Duo/Group (1988); released double platinum *Cry Like a Rainstorm, Howl Like the Wind* (1989), with Grammy-winning songs, "Don't Know Much" and "All My Life"; toured with Emmylou Harris (1995). Won 11 Grammy Awards and recorded 17 gold or platinum albums.

RONZHINA, Olena (1970—). Ukrainian rower. Name variations: Elena Ronzina, Ronzhyna or Rouzina. Born Nov 18, 1970, in Ukraine. ❖ Won a silver medal for quadruple sculls at Atlanta Olympics (1996).

ROOD, Florence (1873–1944). American teacher and labor activist. Born 1873 in St. Paul, Minnesota; died 1944. ❖ Served as kindergarten teacher; became demonstration teacher and critic teacher at St. Paul Normal School, MN (1913); appointed assistant supervisor in charge of kindergartens in St. Paul school system (1916); helped form Grade Teachers Organization; elected leader of Department of Classroom Teachers of National Education Association (NEA, 1910); managed pension system for St. Paul teachers (until 1939); served as 1st woman president of American Federation of Teachers (1924–26).

ROOKE, Daphne (1914—). South African novelist, journalist and children's writer. Name variations: (pseudonym) Robert Pointon. Born Daphne Marie Pizzey, 1914, in Boksburg, Transvaal, South Africa; grew up in Durban; dau. of an English father and Afrikaans mother (writer); granddau. of Siegfried Mare, founder of Pietersburg; niece of Leon Mare (Afrikaans short-story writer); m. Irvin Rooke (an Australian). ❖ Moved to Zululand, where she worked as a journalist and set her 1st novel, *A Grove of Fever Trees* (1950), which was 1st published as *The Sea Hath Bounds* (1946); on marriage, moved to Australia; published the international bestseller, *Mittee* (1951); other works include *Ratoons* (1953), set in the cane fields of Natal, *Beti* (1959), *A Lover for Estelle* (1961), *Diamond Jo* (1965), *Double Ex!* (1971), and *Margaretha de la Porte* (1974); children's books include *The South African Twins* (1953), *The Australian Twins* (1955), and *The New Zealand Twins* (1957).

ROOKE, Emma. *See Emma (1836–1885).*

ROOKE, Irene (c. 1878–1958). English actress. Born c. 1878 in Bridgeport, Dorset, England; died June 14, 1958, in Chesham, Buckinghamshire, England; dau. of George Rooke (journalist); m. Francis Greppo; m. Milton Rosmer. ❖ Made London stage debut as Ophelia to Gordon Craig's Hamlet (1897); subsequently appeared as Mary Gale in *For Auld Lang Syne*, Fanny in *Quality Street*, Nan in *The Tragedy of Nan*, Mrs. Dowey in *The Old Lady Shows Her Medals*, Mrs. Cromwell in *Oliver Cromwell*, and Mrs. Alving in *Ghosts*, among others; often worked with Annie Horniman's company; films include *Pillars of Society*, *The Loves of Mary Queen of Scots* (as Catherine de Medici), and *The Woman in White*.

ROOKE, Katerina (1939—). *See Anghelaki-Rooke, Katerina.*

ROOKH, Lalla.
See Lalla Rookh (fl. 1600s).
See Truganani (1812–1876).

ROONEY, Giaan (1982—). Australian swimmer. Born Nov 15, 1982, in Brisbane, Australia. ❖ Won the 100-meter backstroke at Commonwealth Games (1998); won a silver medal for 800-meter freestyle relay at Sydney Olympics (2000); won 200-meter freestyle World championship (2001); won a gold medal for 4 x 100-meter medley relay at Athens Olympics (2004).

ROONEY, Josie (b. 1892). American dancer. Born 1892 in New York, NY; dau. of Pat Rooney and Josie Granger; sister of Pat, Katherine, Mathilda, Julia Rooney. ❖ Made debut as a child in her parents' vaudeville troupe; formed duet act with sister Julia as Rooney Sisters (1905), performing cake-walk on Orpheum circuit and at European cabarets (1906–13).

ROONEY, Julia (b. 1893). American dancer. Born 1893 in New York, NY; dau. of Pat Rooney and Josie Granger; sister of Pat, Katherine, Mathilda, Julia Rooney. ❖ Made debut as a child in her parents' vaudeville troupe;

formed duet act with sister Josie as Rooney Sisters (1905), performing cake-walk on Orpheum circuit and at European cabarets (1906–13); performed on tour with Walter Clinton in exhibition ballroom act (1913–c. 1925).

ROOPE, Clover (1937—). English ballet dancer and choreographer. Born 1937 in Bristol, England. ❖ Joined Royal Ballet (1957), where she appeared in 19th-century classics as well as works by Ashton and Howard; became member of Western Ballet Theatre (1960), where she danced in Walter Gore's *Street Games,* Ray Powell's *One in Five,* and Kenneth Macmillan's *Valse Eccentrique,* and choreographed numerous works; trained in US for 2 years at studios of Martha Graham, Margaret Craske, and Antony Tudor; appeared in Helen McGehee's *After Possession* (1965) and at Jacob's Pillow opposite Christopher Lyall.

ROOS, Margaret (b. around 1388). *See Fitzalan, Margaret.*

ROOS, Margaret (fl. 1420). English aristocrat. Name variations: Lady Grey of Ruthin. Dau. of William Roos, 7th baron Roos, and Margaret Fitzalan (b. around 1388); m. Reginald Grey, 3rd Baron Grey of Ruthin; children: John Grey.

ROOSCHÜTZ, Ottilie (1817–1877). *See Wildermuth, Ottilie.*

ROOSEVELT, Alice (1884–1980). *See Longworth, Alice Roosevelt.*

ROOSEVELT, Alice Lee (1861–1884). American socialite. Name variations: Alice Hathaway Lee; Alice Hathaway Lee Roosevelt; Mrs. Theodore Roosevelt. Born Alice Hathaway Lee, July 29, 1861, in Boston, Massachusetts; died Feb 14, 1884, in New York, NY; 2nd dau. of George Cabot Lee (banker) and Caroline Watts (Haskell) Lee; became 1st wife of Theodore Roosevelt (future president of US), Oct 27, 1880, in Brookline, Massachusetts; children: Alice Roosevelt Longworth (1884–1980). ❖ Soon after giving birth to daughter Alice (Feb 12, 1884), became very ill; died two days later, age 22, the same day Theodore Roosevelt's mother Martha Bulloch Roosevelt died of typhoid fever, one floor away in their 57th Street house. ❖ See also *Women in World History.*

ROOSEVELT, Anna (1855–1931). *See Cowles, Anna Roosevelt.*

ROOSEVELT, Anna Hall (1863–1892). American socialite. Name variations: Mrs. Elliott Roosevelt. Born Anna Livingston Ludlow Hall in 1863; died of diphtheria, Dec 7, 1892; dau. of Valentine G. Hall and Mary Livingston Ludlow Hall; sister of Elizabeth Livingston "Tissie" Hall Mortimer, Edith Livingston Ludlow "Pussie" Hall Morgan, and Maude Hall Waterbury Gray; m. Elliott Roosevelt (brother of US president Theodore Roosevelt), Dec 2, 1883; children: (Anna) Eleanor Roosevelt (1884–1962, first lady of US); and sons Elliott Roosevelt Jr. (1889–1893) and Gracie Hall Roosevelt (b. 1891).

ROOSEVELT, Betsey (1908–1998). *See Whitney, Betsey Cushing.*

ROOSEVELT, Edith Kermit Carow (1861–1948). American first lady. Name variations: Mrs. Theodore Roosevelt; Mrs. Theodore Roosevelt, Sr. Born Aug 6, 1861, in Norwich, Connecticut; died Sept 30, 1948, in Oyster Bay, NY; eldest dau. of Charles Carow and Gertrude Elizabeth (Tyler) Carow; became 2nd wife of Theodore Roosevelt (US president, 1901–09), Dec 2, 1886; children: Theodore Roosevelt Jr. (1887–1944), Kermit Roosevelt (1889–1943), and Quentin Roosevelt (1897–1918), all killed while in service to their country; Archie Roosevelt (1894–1979), who served in both world wars; Ethel Carow Roosevelt (1891–1977); (stepdaughter) Alice Roosevelt Longworth (1884–1980). ❖ As a youngster, shared a love of outdoor activities with neighborhood pal Theodore Roosevelt; after his 1st wife died (1884), married him (1886); opposed his attempts to win public office and did not widely participate in his campaign for vice presidency (1900); as first lady of US (1901–09), brought renewed energy and vibrancy to the White House with help of her children; oversaw extensive renovations of the mansion, creating a distinct division between official and family quarters; hired a social secretary and employed professional caterers; presided over an abundance of social occasions, renowned for their interesting mixes of distinguished men and women from all walks of life; initiated a portrait gallery to memorialize all the presidents' wives; throughout later years, remained active in the Republican Party and campaigned for Herbert Hoover (1932). ❖ See also *Women in World History.*

ROOSEVELT, Eleanor (1884–1962). American first lady, diplomat, writer, and social reformer. Name variations: ER. Born Anna Eleanor Roosevelt, Oct 11, 1884, in New York, NY; died Nov 7, 1962 in

New York, NY; dau. of Elliott Roosevelt and Anna Ludlow Hall Roosevelt (socialites); m. Franklin Delano Roosevelt (1882–1945, governor of NY as well as US president, 1932–45), Mar 17, 1905 (died April 12, 1945); children: Anna Eleanor Roosevelt Dall Boettiger (b. 1906); James Roosevelt (b. 1907, US congressional representative); Franklin Delano Roosevelt Jr. (1909–1909); Elliott Roosevelt (b. 1910); Franklin Delano Roosevelt Jr. (b. 1914, US congressional representative); John Aspinwall Roosevelt (b. 1916). ❖ Reformer, humanitarian, UN diplomat, and the most effective woman ever in American politics, who was frequently called "First Lady of the World," served as director, national legislation committee, League of Women Voters (1920); was chair, finance committee, women's division, New York State Democratic Committee (1924–28); was co-chair, bureau of women's activities, Democratic National Campaign Committee (1928); was editor, *Women's Democratic News* (1925–28); as first lady (1932–45), broke precedent in several significant ways; was the 1st president's wife to hold weekly press conferences, limited to women reporters and often centering on women's issues; wrote newspaper column "My Day" (1935–62), which, for its 1st 3 years, centered on domestic matters but soon addressed general political topics; wrote monthly columns for *Women's Home Companion, Ladies' Home Journal* and *McCall's*; launched radio program (1934) which became enormously popular; instead of holding with the tradition that the first lady was primarily the social leader of Washington, was forever on the road; was a delegate to UN General Assembly (1945–53); served as permanent chair of UN Commission on Human Rights (1947–48); served as chair of John F. Kennedy's Commission on the Status of Women (1961). ❖ See also *This is My Story* (Harper, 1937), *This I Remember* (Harper, 1949), *On My Own* (Harper, 1958) and *The Autobiography of Eleanor Roosevelt* (Harper, 1961); Allida M. Black, *Casting Her Own Shadow: Eleanor Roosevelt and the Shaping of Postwar Liberalism* (Columbia U. Press, 1996); Blanche Wiesen Cook, *Eleanor Roosevelt: Vol. I, 1884–1933* (Viking, 1992) and *Eleanor Roosevelt: Vol. II, 1933–1938* (Viking, 1999); Doris Kearns Goodwin, *No Ordinary Time; Franklin and Eleanor Roosevelt* (Simon & Schuster, 1994); Joseph P. Lash, *Eleanor and Franklin* (Norton, 1971), *Eleanor: The Years Alone* (Norton, 1972), and *Love, Eleanor: Eleanor Roosevelt and Her Friends, 1943–1962* (Doubleday, 1982); and *Women in World History.*

ROOSEVELT, Mrs. Elliott.
See Roosevelt, Anna Hall (1863–1892).
See Emerson, Faye (1917–1983).

ROOSEVELT, Ethel Carow (1891–1977). American first daughter. Name variations: Mrs. Richard Derby. Born 1891; died 1977; dau. of Theodore Roosevelt (US president, 1901–08) and Edith Kermit Carow Roosevelt (1861–1948); half-sister of Alice Roosevelt Longworth (1884–1980); m. Richard Derby.

ROOSEVELT, Mrs. James (1908–1998). *See Whitney, Betsey Cushing.*

ROOSEVELT, Sara Delano (1854–1941). American socialite. Born Sara Delano in Sept 21, 1854; died at Hyde Park, New York, Sept 7, 1941; dau. of Catherine Lyman Delano and Warren Delano (business associate of James Roosevelt); m. James Roosevelt of Hyde Park (known as Squire James who was 1st married to Rebecca Howland Roosevelt [d. 1876] and had a son, James Roosevelt (Rosy) Roosevelt), in Oct 1880; children: Franklin Delano Roosevelt (1882–1945), president of US (1932–1945).

ROOSEVELT, Mrs. Theodore.
See Roosevelt, Alice Lee (1861–1884).
See Roosevelt, Edith Kermit Carow (1861–1948).

ROPER, Margaret More (1505–1544). English scholar. Born 1505; died Dec 25, 1544; eldest dau. of Sir Thomas More (1478–1535, English scholar and statesman who was slain for his opposition to detaching England from the spiritual authority of the Roman Catholic Church) and Jane Colt More (c. 1488–1511); had one brother John More (who m. Anne Cresacre in 1529), and 2 sisters, Elizabeth More Daunce or Dancy (b. around 1506, who m. William Daunce on Sept 29, 1521, the same day Margaret married), and Cecily More Heron (b. around 1507, who m. Giles Heron in 1522); tutored by her father and other scholars; m. William Roper, in 1521; children: 5, including Mary Roper Basset, English writer and translator (fl. 1544–1572). ❖ Won great praise from Erasmus for her intelligence; devoted a great deal of time to study, particularly to philosophy, but all that remains of her work are letters to her father and a translation of Erasmus' *A Devout Treatise upon the Paternoster* (1523); was greatly distressed by execution of father (1535);

saved his books and papers; also rescued his head from a stake on London Bridge. ❖ See also *Women in World History*.

ROPER, Marion. American diver. Name variations: Marion Dale Roper. Attended University of California at Los Angeles. ❖ At Los Angeles Olympics, won a bronze medal in platform (1932).

ROPER, Mary (fl. 1544–1562). *See Basset, Mary Roper.*

ROQUE, Jacqueline (d. 1986). French wife of Picasso. Name variations: Jacqueline Hutin; Jacqueline Picasso; Madame Z. Died from a self-inflicted gunshot wound, Oct 19, 1986; married an engineer or civil servant by name of Hutin (div.); m. Pablo Picasso (1881–1973, the artist, whose 1st wife was Olga Khoklova), Mar 2, 1961; children: (1st m.) Catherine Hutin. ❖ Became 2nd wife of Picasso (1961), when he was 80 and she was 35; by all accounts, was obsessively devoted to him; posed for several paintings, including *Portrait de Jacqueline aux mains croisées* and *Portrait of Madame Z*; survived Picasso by 13 years and arranged for a number of exhibits of his work from her large collection. ❖ See also *Women in World History*.

ROQUELAURE, A.N. (1941—). *See Rice, Anne.*

RORER, Sarah Tyson (1849–1937). American cookbook writer and dietitian. Born Sarah Tyson Heston, Oct 18, 1849, in Richboro, Bucks County, PA; died Dec 27, 1937, in Colebrook, PA; dau. of Charles Tyson Heston (pharmacist) and Elizabeth (Sagers) Heston; m. William Albert Rorer (bookkeeper), Feb 23, 1871 (sep. 1890s); children: 2 sons, 1 daughter. ❖ Served as director of New Century Club Cooking School in Philadelphia, PA (1880–83); established Philadelphia Cooking School (1883); expanded school to train teachers for domestic arts and teach cooking and hygiene to girls at Bedford Street Mission; launched monthly periodical *Table Talk* (1885) and published *The Philadelphia Cook Book* (1886); became editor and part owner of *Household News* (1893); assumed position of domestic editor at *Ladies' Home Journal* after it absorbed *Household News* (1897); published a number of cookbooks, including *Mrs. Rorer's New Cook Book* (1902); served as head of culinary department of *Good Housekeeping* (1914); helped establish cooking as science in US.

RORK, Ann (1908–1988). American actress. Born June 12, 1908, in Darien, CT; died Jan 23, 1988, in Nashville, TN; dau. of Sam Rork (producer) and Helen Welch (actress); m. J. Paul Getty (oil tycoon). ❖ Supporting player in such films as *Old Loves and New, The Blond Saint, The Notorious Lady* and *A Texas Steer*.

RORKE, Kate (1866–1945). English actress. Born Feb 22, 1866, in London, England; died July 31, 1945, in Little Hadham, Hertfordshire, England; dau. of John and Lucy (Whithall) Rorke; sister of Mary Rorke (actress); m. E.W. Gardiner (died 1899); m. Dr. Douglas Cree. ❖ Made stage debut in London as one of the schoolchildren in *Olivia* (1878); under the management of Charles Wyndham, appeared at the Criterion for a number of years; came to prominence as Lucy Preston in *The Silver Shield* (1885); other plays include *The Profligate, Lady Bountiful, A Fool's Paradise, Diplomacy, Dr. and Mrs. Neill, The Sin of St. Hulda* (title role), *Moths, Honor* (title role), *Candida* (title role), and *A Pair of Spectacles*; toured England and US with Beerbohm Tree.

RORKE, Mary (1858–1938). English actress. Born Feb 14, 1858, in London, England; died Oct 12, 1938, in London; dau. of John and Lucy (Whithall) Rorke; sister of Kate Rorke (actress); m. Frank W. St. Aubyn (architect). ❖ Made stage debut in London in *Little Puss in Boots* (1873); subsequently appeared as Mrs. Erroll in *Little Lord Fauntleroy*, Elizabeth of York in *Richard III* (with Richard Mansfield), title role in *Duchess of Malfi*, Morgan Le Fay in *King Arthur*, and Madame de Rovigo in *Madame Sans-Gêne*; films include *Caste, The Second Mrs. Tanqueray, The Marriage of William Ashe, Merely Mrs. Stubbs, Tinker Tailor, The Bridal Chair* and *Testimony*.

ROS, Amanda (1860–1939). Irish writer. Name variations: Anna Margaret M'Kittrick; Amanda M'Kittrick Ros; Amanda McKittrick Ros; Amanda Malvina Fitzalan Anna Margaret McLelland Ros; (pseudonym) Monica Moyland. Born Anna Margaret M'Kittrick in Drumaness, Co. Down, Ireland, Dec 8, 1860; died Feb 3, 1939; dau. of Edward Amlane M'Kittrick (school principal); educated at Marlborough Teacher Training College, Dublin; m. Andy Ross, 1887 (died 1917); m. Thomas Rodgers (farmer), 1922 (died 1933). ❖ Eccentric author of *Irene Iddesleigh* (1897), *Delina Delaney* (1898), and *Helen Huddleson* (posthumous, 1969), whose works inspired one critic to call her the "worst novelist in the world" for her artificial plots and florid narratives;

used her writing to take revenge on enemies in bald-faced attacks not even remotely masked as satire; did have a group of admirers at St. John's College in Cambridge, England, who helped elevate her to the level of cult status; published collections of poetry *Poems of Puncture* (1913) and *Fumes of Formation* (1933); wrote ballads during WWI that were printed in broadsheets under the pseudonym Monica Moyland. ❖ See also Jack Loudan, *O Rare Amanda: The Life of Amanda McKittrick Ros* (1954); and *Women in World History*.

ROS-LEHTINEN, Ileana (1952—). American politician. Born Ileana Ros in Havana, Cuba, July 15, 1952; Miami-Dade Community College, AA, 1972; Florida International University, BA, 1975, MS, 1987; married Dexter Lehtinen (lawyer); children: Amanda, Patricia. ❖ The 1st Cuban-American elected to US Congress (1989) and the first Hispanic woman to chair a Congressional subcommittee, fled Cuba with family when she was 7; became a teacher, later founding and becoming the 1st administrator of a private elementary school called Eastern Academy; a Republican, began political career in Florida House of Representatives (1982); elected to Florida State Senate (1986); defeated 10 opponents in a special election for US House of Representatives (August 29, 1989); won reelection numerous times, representing a large Cuban-American population in Florida's 18th Congressional District; initially assigned to the Committee on Foreign Affairs and the Committee on Government Operations, assumed further responsibilities on the Committee on Government Reform and Oversight; known as a defender of international human rights and democracy, was selected as a member of the Committee on International Relations and served as chair of the Subcommittee on International Economic Policy and Trade, the first Hispanic woman to achieve such a post.

ROSA (1800–1841). *See Schoolcraft, Jane Johnston.*

ROSA (1906–1983). Duchess of Wurttemberg. Born Sept 22, 1906, in Parsh near Salzburg; died Sept 17, 1983, in Friedrichshafen; dau. of Maria Cristina of Sicily (1877–1947) and Peter Ferdinand (1874–1948), archduke of Austria.

ROSA, Anella de (1613–1649). Neapolitan painter. Name variations: Anna di Rosa or Aniella Beltrano. Born in Naples, 1613; possibly murdered in 1649; pupil of Francesco di Rosa; niece of Massimo Stanzioni; m. Agostino Beltrano (painter). ❖ A historical artist, whose paintings were highly praised, especially that of the *Birth and Death of the Virgin* in the church of Santa Maria de' Turchini; according to a Neapolitan named De' Dominici, was stabbed to death by husband in a fit of jealous rivalry, over favoritism shown by their master Stanzioni (1649); survived her wounds only long enough to pardon him. Entire murder theory is debunked by Germaine Greer who claims that the true scandal was that she did most of Stanzioni's work. ❖ See also *Women in World History*.

ROSA, Anna di (1613–1649). *See Rosa, Anella de.*

ROSA, Euphrosyne Parepa (1836–1874). *See Parepa-Rosa, Euphrosyne.*

ROSA, Rosa (1894–1978). *See von Haynau, Edith.*

ROSA DI VITERBO (1235–1252). *See Rose of Viterbo.*

ROSAMALIN (b. 1911). *See Kiengsiri, Kanha.*

ROSA MATILDA (c. 1772–1825). *See Dacre, Charlotte.*

ROSAMOND THE FAIR (c. 1145–1176). *See Clifford, Rosamund.*

ROSANA.
See Humilitas of Faenza (1226–1310).
See dos Santos Augusto, Rosana (1982—).

ROSANOVA, Olga (1886–1918). *See Rozanova, Olga.*

ROSA OF LIMA (1586–1617). *See Rose of Lima.*

ROSAS, Encarnación de (1795–1838). Argentinean first lady. Name variations: Encarnacion de Rosas; Encarnación Ezcurra de Rosas. Born Encarnación Ezcurra y Arguibel, Mar 25, 1795; died Oct 19, 1838; came from an upper-class Buenos Aires family; m. Juan Manuel de Rosas (1793–1877, whose dictatorship was one of the harshest in 19th-century Latin American history), in 1813; children: daughter Manuela; sons Juan Bautista and Juan Manuel. Juan Manuel de Rosas also had five illeg. offspring with his mistress María Eugenia Castro (2 sons, Joaquín and Adrian, and 3 daughters, Nicanora, Angela, and Justina). ❖ Had a forceful personality, much like husband's, and shared his political and cultural views (his opposition to liberalism, democracy, and disorder);

worked to rally support for husband among the lower classes through extra-official patronage. ❖ See also *Women in World History.*

ROSATI, Carolina (1826–1905). Italian ballet dancer. Born Carolina Galletti, Dec 13, 1826, in Bologna, Italy; died May 1905 in Cannes, France. ❖ Made performance debut at Teatro alla Scala in Milan (1846) and danced there for 6 years in such works as Casati's *Abd-el-Kadar* (1846) and Borri's *Zoloë* (1952); performed at Her Majesty's Theatre in London for 3 seasons in *Pas de Quatre* and Paul Taglioni's *Fiorita* (1848) and *La prima ballerina* (1849); danced at Paris Opéra (after 1853) where she held principal roles in several works by Mazilier, among them *Jovita, Le Corsaire,* and *Marco Spada*; created role of Aspacia for Marius Petipa's *La Fille du Pharon* (1862) while performing in St. Petersburg.

ROSAY, Françoise (1891–1974). French actress. Name variations: Françoise Rosay. Born Françoise Bandy de Nalèche in Paris, France, April 19, 1891; died in Paris, Mar 28, 1974; graduate of Conservatoire National de Déclamation, Paris; m. Jacques Feyder (film director), 1917 (died 1948); children: 3 sons. ❖ One of the greatest actresses of the French cinema, whose career spanned more than 6 decades, made stage debut in *Fantaisies Parisiennes* (1908), then joined a French theatrical troupe that was performing in St. Petersburg, Russia (1912); made film debut in *Falstaff* (1913); also sang as a member of Paris Opera (1916–18); appeared in Jacques Feyder's film *Têtes de femmes, femme de têtes* (1916); accompanied husband to Hollywood (1928), surfacing the next year in *The One Woman Idea*; starred with Fernandel in *Le Rosier de Madame Husson* (The Virtuous Isidore, 1931); now a star, was featured in such films as *Le Grand Jeu* (1934), *La Kermesse héroïque* (*Carnival in Flanders,* 1935), *Un Carnet de Bal* (1937), *Jenny* (1936) and the surrealist film, *Drôle de drame* (1937); when France was defeated (summer 1940), fled with husband; worked as broadcaster for Free French in London, then as a director of Radio Algiers in charge of cultural broadcasting (1944–47); made NY stage debut as Catherine II the Great in *Once There Was a Russian* (1961); other films include *La Reine Margot* (1954), *The Sound and the Fury* (1959), *The Longest Day* (1962) and *The Pedestrian* (1973). ❖ See also *Women in World History.*

ROSAZZA, Joan (1935—). American swimmer. Name variations: Joan Alderson; Joan Alderson-Rosazza. Born Mar 5, 1935 (some sources cite May 19, 1937) in US. ❖ As Joan Alderson, won a bronze medal in the 4 x 100-meter freestyle relay at Helsinki Olympics (1952); at Melbourne Olympics as Joan Rosazza, won a silver medal in 4 x 100-meter freestyle relay (1956).

ROSCA, Ninotchka (1941—). Filipino-American novelist and short-story writer. Born 1941 in Philippines. ❖ Jailed for speaking out against Marcos' declaration of martial law in Philippines (1972); fled to US (1976) and taught Tagalog at University of Hawaii; novels and journalism reflect experiences of political suppression; works include *Bitter Country and Other Stories* (1970), *Monsoon Collection* (1983), *Endgame: The Fall of Marcos* (1987), *State of War* (1988) and *Twice Blessed* (1992), which won the American Book Award.

ROSCA-RACILA, Valeria (1957—). Romanian rower. Name variations: Valeria Racila. Born June 1957 in Romania. ❖ Won a bronze medal in double sculls at Moscow Olympics (1980) and a gold medal in single sculls at Los Angeles Olympics (1984).

ROSÉ, Alma (1906–1944). Austrian-Jewish violinist and conductor. Name variations: Alma Rose. Born Alma Maria Rosé in 1906 in Vienna, Austria; died in Auschwitz, April 4, 1944; dau. of Arnold Rosé (concertmaster of Vienna Philharmonic Orchestra and Court Opera Orchestra) and Justine Mahler (sister of Gustav Mahler); sister of Alfred Rosé (1902–1975), noted conductor who escaped to US and Canada). ❖ Violinist and conductor of the women's orchestra at the Auschwitz-Birkenau concentration camp, portrayed in the book and film *Playing for Time,* whose efforts saved countless musicians condemned to the camps; following in father's footsteps, studied the violin and was a virtuoso performer by her teens; with father, recorded Concerto for Two Violins and Orchestra of Johann Sebastian Bach (1931); struck out on her own and established a solid career in Austria and other European nations (mid-1930s); following the Nazi annexation of Austria (Mar 1938), did not follow father into exile but remained in Europe; arrested in the Netherlands and sent to Westerbork (1942); transported to Auschwitz, where she became conductor of that concentration camp's women's orchestra (1943). ❖ See also Fania Fénelon, *Playing for Time* (Atheneum, 1977); Richard Newman with Karen Kirtley, *Alma Rosé: Vienna to Auschwitz* (Timer-Amadeus, 2000); and *Women in World History.*

ROSE, Christine Brooke (1923—). *See Brooke-Rose, Christine.*

ROSE, Ernestine (1810–1892). Polish-born feminist and reformer. Born Ernestine Louise Siismondi Potowski, Jan 13, 1810, at Piotrków, Russian Poland; died Aug 4, 1892, in Brighton, England; only child of Isaac Potowski (rabbi); m. William Rose (jeweler and follower of Robert Owen), in 1835 (died 1882); no children. ❖ Early advocate of women's rights and abolition of slavery; moved to London, England (1832), where she met several of that country's most famous social reformers, including Elizabeth Fry and Robert Owen; with husband, immigrated to New York (1836), where they established a small business (a combined jewelry and perfumery store); for next 12 years, traveled the state to prod the legislature to recognize a woman's right to keep her own property; also kept an increasingly busy schedule of speaking engagements at which she addressed various issues of social reform, particularly the abolition of slavery; became a popular speaker, known as the "Queen of the Platform"; was a featured speaker at 1st National Woman's Rights Convention (1850), where she was elected to the central executive committee; remained active in the movement for next 19 years; joined the executive committee of the markedly more radical National Woman's Suffrage Association (1869); retired in London (1869). ❖ See also Carol A. Kolmerten, *The American Life of Ernestine L. Rose* (Syracuse U., 1998); and *Women in World History.*

ROSE, Helen (1904–1985). American costume designer. Born Feb 2, 1904, in Chicago, Illinois; died in Palm Springs, California, Nov 1985; dau. of William Bromberg and Ray (Bobbs) Bromberg; attended Chicago Institute of Fine Arts; m. Harry Rose, Dec 28, 1929; children: Judy Rose. ❖ One of Hollywood's most renowned costume designers, moved to Los Angeles (1929); designed costumes for nightclubs and for Fanchon and Marco's Ice Follies for many years; made 1st film designs for 3 Fox musicals: *Hello Frisco Hello, Coney Island* and *Stormy Weather* (all 1943); moved to MGM, where she remained for next 3 decades; nominated for 10 Academy Awards and won the statue for *The Bad and the Beautiful* (1952) and *I'll Cry Tomorrow* (1955); other films include *Ziegfeld Follies* (1945), *The Harvey Girls* (1946), *Till the Clouds Roll By* (1947), *Good News* (1947), *Take Me Out to the Ball Game* (1949), *Father of the Bride* (1950), *Annie Get Your Gun* (1950), *Three Little Words* (1950), *Summer Stock* (1950), *The Great Caruso* (1951), *The Merry Widow* (1952), *Mogambo* (1953), *Rose Marie* (1954), *Interrupted Melody* (1955), *Love Me or Leave Me* (1955), *The Tender Trap* (1955), *High Society* (1956), *Tea and Sympathy* (1956), *Designing Woman* (1957), *Silk Stockings* (1957) and *Cat on a Hot Tin Roof* (1958); established successful fashion business after retirement from films (late 1960s). ❖ See also *Women in World History.*

ROSE, Kay (1922–2002). American sound editor. Born Feb 12, 1922, in New York, NY; died Dec 11, 2002, in Burbank, CA; m. Sherman Rose (film editor), 1951 (div.); children: Victoria Rose Sampson (director and sound editor). ❖ Was the 1st woman to win an Academy Award for sound editing, for work on *The River* (1984); other sound editing credits include *Comes a Horseman, The Rose, Ordinary People, On Golden Pond, The Prince of Tides* and *Speed*; with husband, produced the sci-fi classic *Target Earth.* Granted career achievement awards from Motion Picture Sound Editors (1993) and Cinema Audio Society (2002); at USC, directors Spielberg and Lucas endowed the Kay Rose chair in the Art of Sound and Dialogue Editing.

ROSE, Margo (1903–1997). American puppeteer. Born Margaret Skewis in Inway, Iowa, Jan 31, 1903; died in Waterford, Connecticut, Sept 13, 1997; dau. of Charles Skewis and Myrtle Skewis; graduate of Cornell College, Iowa, 1924; m. Rufus Rose (puppeteer), 1930 (died 1975); children: Christopher, James, Rufus. ❖ Noted pioneer in American puppetry, was one of the founders of Puppeteers of America (1937); with husband, made the 1st full-length film using marionettes, *Jerry Pulls the Strings* (1938); animated the puppet Howdy Doody for the tv show (1952). Received President's Award for Artistic Achievement and Connecticut Commission on the Arts' Excellence in the Arts Award; inducted into Connecticut Women's Hall of Fame (1997). ❖ See also *Women in World History.*

ROSE, Merri (1955—). Australian politician. Name variations: Hon. Merri Rose. Born Jan 24, 1955, in Kilcoy, Australia. ❖ As a member of Australian Labor Party, elected to the Queensland Parliament for Currumbin (1992); named minister for Tourism and Racing (1999) and minister for Fair Trading (2001).

ROSE, Saint.
See Rose of Viterbo (1235–1252).
See Rose of Lima (1586–1617).

ROSE, Sylvia (1962—). East German rower. Born Dec 23, 1962, in East Germany. ❖ At Seoul Olympics, won a gold medal in coxed fours (1988).

ROSEANNE (1952—). American actress. Name variations: Roseanne Barr, Roseanne Arnold. Born Roseanne Cherie Barr, Nov 3, 1952, in Salt Lake City, Utah; m. Bill Pentland, 1974 (div. 1990); m. Tom Arnold (actor), 1990 (div. 1994); m. Ben Thomas (body guard), 1995 (div. 2002); children: Brandi Brown (given up for adoption); James, Jessica and Jennifer Pentland; Buck Thomas. ❖ Brash and brassy comedic actress with working-class persona, began career doing standup in Denver; toured nationally on comedy circuit, moved to Hollywood (1983), appeared at Mitzi Shore's Comedy Store, then on "The Tonight Show" (1985); starred on sitcom "Roseanne" (1988–1997), the #1 show for many years; films include She-Devil (1989) and Even Cowgirls Get the Blues (1994); hosted daytime talk show "The Roseanne Show" (1999); set-up The Roseanne Foundation, non-profit organization focusing on child abuse. Received 4 American Comedy Awards (1988, 1989, 1993, 1997), 2 Emmys, 2 Golden Globes, Lucy Award from Women in Film, and Peabody Award. ❖ See also autobiography, My Life as a Woman (HarperCollins, 1989).

ROSELI (1969—). See de Belo, Roseli.

ROSEMEYER, Elly (b. 1907). See Beinhorn, Elly.

ROSENBAUM, Hedwig. Bohemian tennis player. Born in Bohemia. ❖ At Paris Olympics, won a bronze medal in singles and a bronze medal in mixed doubles–outdoors (1900).

ROSENBAUM, Katharine (1903–1987). See Sturgis, Katharine Boucot.

ROSENBERG, Anna M. (1902–1983). American public official, businesswoman, and labor relations consultant. Name variations: Anna Marie Rosenberg. Born Anna Maria Lederer in Budapest, Hungary, June 19, 1902; died in New York, NY, 1983; dau. of Albert Lederer (furniture manufacturer) and Charlotte (Bacskai) Lederer (author and illustrator of children's books); m. Julius Rosenberg (rug merchant), Oct 12, 1919 (died); m. Paul Gray Hoffman (administrator of Marshall Plan, 1948–50), in 1962; children: (1st m.) Thomas Rosenberg. ❖ Immigrated with family to US (1912); became naturalized citizen (1919); became regional director of National Recovery Administration (NRA) for NY area (1935); served as NY regional director of Social Security Board (1936–37); became a member of New York City Industrial Relations Board (1937); served as a director of Office of Defense and regional director of Health and Welfare Services (1941–42), consultant to Retraining and Re-employment Administration (1941–42), and director of Region 2, New York State, of the War Manpower Commission (1942–45), the only woman to hold such a position; concurrently, held membership in New York City and State War Councils and in the policy committee of Office of Coordinator of Inter-American Affairs, and the secretaryship of the President's Combined War Labor Board; while with War Manpower Commission, forced the union of Henry J. Kaiser Pacific Coast plants to accept African-American labor; during war, was sent to European Theater of Operations as personal observer of both President Roosevelt and successor Harry Truman, for which she was awarded Medal of Freedom (Oct 20, 1945); served as assistant secretary of defense (1950–53). Was 1st woman decorated with US Medal for Merit (May 28, 1947); received Horatio Alger Award (1949). ❖ See also Women in World History.

ROSENBERG, Carroll Smith-. See Smith-Rosenberg, Carroll.

ROSENBERG, Ethel (1915–1953). American political activist. Born Esther Ethel Greenglass, Sept 28, 1915, in New York, NY; died in electric chair at Sing Sing Prison, NY, June 19, 1953; dau. of Barnet Greenglass (sewing-machine repairer) and Tessie (Fiet) Greenglass; sister of Bernard and David Greenglass; half-sister of Samuel Greenglass; m. Julius Rosenberg, June 18, 1939; children: Michael Allen Rosenberg Meeropol (b. 1943) and Robert Harry Rosenberg Meeropol (b. 1947). ❖ Activist sentenced to death for espionage, went to the electric chair resolutely proclaiming her innocence; was a union activist with Ladies Apparel Shipping Clerks Union (1935–38), Workers Alliance of America (1935–38), and Ladies Auxiliary, Federation of Architects, Engineers, Chemists, and Technicians (1936–40); hired as clerk, Census Bureau (1940); served on East Side Defense Council to Defend America and

Crush Hitler (1941–43); with husband, indicted and imprisoned for conspiracy to commit espionage by passing atomic secrets to the Soviets (Aug 11, 1950); convicted (Mar 29, 1951); sentenced to death by Judge Irving Kaufman (April 5, 1951), which sparked international protests; transferred to Sing Sing where she was the only woman in the Condemned Cells; appeal denied by US Court of Appeals (Feb 25, 1952); continued to proclaim innocence as Supreme Court refused a certiorari (Oct 13, 1952), Judge Kaufman refused to reduce sentence (Jan 2, 1953), Supreme Court again refused certiorari (May 25, 1953), Judge Kaufman denied motion to hear new evidence (June 8, 1953), and Supreme Court refused to grant new trial (July 19, 1953); executed after Eisenhower refused clemency for a 2nd time (June 19, 1953). In 1997, a retired KGB officer confirmed that he had been the spy handler for Julius Rosenberg; he also stated that Ethel Rosenberg had been aware of husband's spying, but had not been a spy herself, had played no part in his network, and "wasn't doing anything for" the Soviets. ❖ See also Michael Meeropol, The Rosenberg Letters: The Complete Edition of the Prison Correspondence of Julius and Ethel Rosenberg (Garland, 1994); Michael and Robert Meeropol, We Are Your Sons: The Legacy of Ethel and Julius Rosenberg (U. of Illinois Press, 1975); Ilene Philipson, Ethel Rosenberg: Beyond the Myths (Watts, 1988); and Women in World History.

ROSENBERG, Grete (1896–1979). German swimmer. Born Oct 7, 1896, in Germany; died Feb 5, 1979. ❖ At Stockholm Olympics, won a silver medal in 4 x 100-meter freestyle relay (1912).

ROSENDAHL, Heidemarie (1947—). West German track-and-field athlete. Name variations: Heide Rosendahl; Heidemarie Ecker; Heide Ecker-Rosendahl. Born Feb 14, 1947, in Hückeswagen, West Germany; dau. of a national discus-thrower. ❖ Won a silver medal for pentathlon at European championships (1967) and a gold medal (1971); won a gold medal in the long jump, team gold in 4 x 100-meter relay, and silver for pentathlon at Munich Olympics (1972). ❖ See also Women in World History.

ROSENFELD, Bobbie (1905–1969). See Rosenfeld, Fanny.

ROSENFELD, Fanny (1905–1969). Russian-born Canadian runner and sportswriter. Name variations: Bobbie Rosenfeld. Born Dec 28, 1905, in Katrinaslov, Russia; died Nov 13, 1969, in Toronto, Ontario, Canada. ❖ Grew up in Canada; tied the world record of 11.0 for the 100-yard dash (1925); won a gold medal in the 4 x 100-meter relay and a silver medal in the 100 meters in the Amsterdam Olympics (1928); wrote the column "Feminine Sports Reel" for the Toronto Globe and Mail (1937–57). Named Canadian woman athlete of the half-century (1949).

ROSENQVIST, Susanne (1967—). Swedish kayaker. Born Nov 26, 1967, in Sweden. ❖ Won a bronze medal at Barcelona Olympics (1992) and a bronze medal at Atlanta Olympics, both for K4 500 meters.

ROSENTHAL, Hedwig Kanner (1882–1959). See Kanner-Rosenthal, Hedwig.

ROSENTHAL, Ida Cohen (1886–1973). Russian-born American manufacturing executive. Born Ida Kaganovitch in Rakov, Russia, Jan 9, 1886; died in New York, NY, Mar 29, 1973; dau. of Abraham Kaganovitch (Hebrew scholar) and Sarah (Shapiro) Kaganovitch, who changed the family name to Cohen after immigrating to US; m. William Rosenthal (manufacturer and designer), June 10, 1906 (died 1958); children: Lewis Rosenthal (1907–1930); Beatrice Rosenthal Coleman (b. 1916, who took over Maidenform). ❖ Founder of Maidenform, Inc., moved to Warsaw, Poland, at 16, then immigrated to US (1904), where she opened a small seamstress shop in Hoboken, NJ; with husband, moved shop to Washington Heights, NY (1918); became a partner in a dress shop in Manhattan (early 1920s), then incorporated the Maiden Form Brassiere Co. (1923); assumed presidency after husband died (1958); was an important contributor to the establishment of Yeshiva University's Albert Einstein College of Medicine in New York City. ❖ See also Women in World History.

ROSENTHAL, Jean (1912–1969). American designer of architectural and theater lighting. Born Eugenie Rosenthal, Mar 16, 1912, in New York, NY; died May 1, 1969, in New York, NY; dau. of Morris and Pauline (Scharfmann) Rosenthal (physicians); attended Neighborhood Playhouse, 1928–30, and Yale University Drama School, 1931–33; never married; no children. ❖ Pioneer in the craft of lighting design and originator of many techniques still in use, was considered by some to have been a genius at evoking mood and creating special effects; one of only a handful of women in technical theater during her time, fought constantly against discrimination, but was eventually accepted and even sought after; designed over 4,000 theatrical productions, including dance, opera, plays and musicals (including *West Side Story* and *Hello, Dolly*), and also consulted on dozens of architectural lighting projects; had a 37-year association with Martha Graham and an 18-year association with Lincoln Kirstein and his Ballet Society; also designed for New York City Ballet and American Ballet Theater, among others; with Lael Wertenbaker, wrote *The Magic of Light* (1972). ❖ See also *Women in World History*.

ROSENTHAL, Jody (1962—). American golfer. Name variations: Jody Rosenthal Anschutz. Born Jody Rosenthal, Oct 18, 1962, in Minneapolis, MN; attended University of Tulsa; m. Fred Anschutz, 1989. ❖ Won British Amateur championship (1984); won du Maurier Classic at age 24 (1987), the youngest American to win a major. Named LPGA Rookie of the Year (1986).

ROSENTHAL, Lyova (1927—). *See Grant, Lee.*

ROSENWALD, Edith (1895–1980). *See Stern, Edith Rosenwald.*

ROSE OF BURFORD (fl. 15th c.). Wool merchant of England. Probably born into a merchant or gentry family. ❖ Became a wholesaler, exporting raw English wool to Calais and selling it to textile manufacturers there; by running her own business, qualified as a *femme sole* ("woman alone"), a phrase signifying a woman who could conduct transactions independently and in her own name, making her an equal with male merchants. ❖ See also *Women in World History*.

ROSE OF LIMA (1586–1617). Peruvian mystic, ascetic and saint. Name variations: Rosa de Lima; Rosa de Santa María; Rosa of Lima. Born Isabel Flores de Oliva, April 20 or 30, 1586, in Lima, Peru; died Aug 24, 1617, in Lima; dau. of Gaspar de Flores (soldier) and María de Oliva; never married; no children. ❖ The 1st person born in the Americas to be canonized by the Roman Catholic Church, was confirmed at Quives by the famous archbishop of Lima, Toribio Alfonso de Mogrovejo (1597); took habit as Dominican tertiary, which permitted her to become betrothed to Jesus Christ, while continuing to live at home (1606); subjected herself for years to painful acts of self-torture, which include wearing a pewter crown of thorns, often with the reluctant assistance of her devoted servant Mariana, who had cared for her as an infant; became known for her visions and other mystical experiences; established an infirmary in her parents' home for the treatment of the poor; as a result of her growing fame, was visited by representatives of the Lima tribunal of the Holy Office of the Inquisition who declared their finding that her gifts were of the Holy Spirit; said to have saved Lima from pirates (1615); formally sanctified her spiritual marriage (Palm Sunday, 1617); foretold the date of her own demise; one year after death, canonization proceedings began (1618); was beatified (1668) and canonized (1671); though she is remembered as a gifted mystic, wrote no books of devotion, and, unlike other religious women of her time, never penned a spiritual autobiography. ❖ See also Frances Parkinson Keyes, *The Rose and the Lily: The Lives and Times of Two South American Saints* (Hawthorn, 1961); and *Women in World History*.

ROSE OF VITERBO (1235–1252). Italian saint. Name variations: Rosa di Viterbo. Born 1235 in Viterbo, Italy; died in 1252 (some sources cite 1253 or 1261) in Viterbo; never married; no children. ❖ Franciscan preacher, joined the informal tertiary order of Franciscans, a group who traveled constantly to preach in the streets; became a well-known figure in Viterbo, giving sermons on various sins, urging residents to oppose heretical movements and making political speeches as well; gained a considerable following. ❖ See also *Women in World History*.

ROSHANARA (1849–1926). Indian dancer. Name variations: Olive Craddock. Born Olive Craddock, Jan 1894, in Calcutta, India; died July 14, 1926, in New York, NY; dau. of an Irish officer in the British Army in India. ❖ Trained in Indian dance forms as a child in India; moved to London where she soon performed as specialty dancer in Oscar Ash's staging of *Kismet*; moved to US (1916), where she performed solo specialty dance act on the Keith circuit; created and performed numerous Indian and Oriental dances, including *Harvest Dance* (1917) and *A Moon Flower* (1918); appeared in non-ethnic productions—theatrical in nature—such as *The Field of Honor* and *After the War* (1917); serving as an expert on India, collaborated on many theatrical works in NY, including Winthrop Ames' *The Green Goddess* (1920); was a major contributor to the introduction of Indian dance forms in US, while writing and teaching in New York City. Works of choreography include *Dagger Dance* (1911), *Incense Dance* (1911), *The Snake Dance* (1911),

A Hindu Fantasy (1917), *East Indian Folk Dances* (1917), *On the Way to the Temple* (1917) and *A Burmese Boat* (1918).

ROSHCHINA, Nadezhda (1954—). Soviet rower. Born June 30, 1954, in USSR. ❖ At Montreal Olympics, won a silver medal in coxed eights (1976).

ROSHCHINA, Tatyana (1941—). Soviet volleyball player. Born June 23, 1941, in USSR. ❖ At Tokyo Olympics, won a silver medal in team competition (1964).

ROSHER, Dorothy (1913–2000). *See Marsh, Joan.*

ROSIAK, Aneta (1972—). *See Szczepanska, Aneta.*

ROSLAVLEVA, Natalia (1907–1977). Ukrainian dance critic. Name variations: Natalia Petrovna Roslavleva. Born Natalia Rene, 1907, in Kiev, Ukraine; died of cancer, Jan 3, 1977, in Moscow, Russia; attended Lunacharski Institute of Theatre Art in Moscow. ❖ Wrote critiques of Russian dance and dancers; published *Era of the Russian Ballet, 1770–1965*, the most widely used English-language history of Russian ballet (1966).

ROSLYNG, Christina (1978—). *See Hansen, Christina Roslyng.*

ROSMAN, Alice Grant (1887–1961). Australian novelist. Name variations: (pseudonym) Rosna. Born in Dreamthorpe, Kapunda, South Australia, in 1887; died 1961; dau. of Alice Mary (Bowyer) Rosman (poet); attended Dominican Convent in Cabra, South Australia. ❖ Quickly earned international acclaim for novels, *The Window* (1928) and *Visitors to Hugo* (1929), which became the standard by which her subsequent works were judged; wrote over 15 novels, including *Jock the Scot* (1930), *The Sixth Journey* (1931), *Mother of the Bride* (1936), *Unfamiliar Faces* (1938) and *William's Room* (1939), the best of which have been described as "domestic romances in comfortable households." ❖ See also *Women in World History*.

ROSNA (1887–1961). *See Rosman, Alice Grant.*

ROSS, Araminta "Minty" (1821–1913). *See Tubman, Harriet.*

ROSS, Annie (1930—). English jazz singer and actress. Name variations: Annabelle Logan. Born Annabelle Short, July 25, 1930, in Mitcham, Surrey, England, into a Scottish showbusiness family; raised in Los Angeles, CA; sister of Jimmy Logan (entertainer); niece of Ella Logan (actress). ❖ Began career as a child actess; sang "Loch Lomond" in the film *Our Gang Follies of 1938* and played Judy Garland's sister in *Presenting Lily Mars* (1942); was a member of the jazz vocal group, Lambert, Hendricks & Ross (1957–62); quit the act and moved to London; released album *Annie Ross Sings a Handful of Songs* (1963); appeared in *Superman III* (1983).

ROSS, Betsy (1752–1836). American Quaker. Name variations: Elizabeth Ross; Elizabeth Ashburn; Elizabeth Claypoole; Elizabeth Griscom Ross Ashburn Claypoole. Born Elizabeth Griscom in Philadelphia, Pennsylvania, Jan 1, 1752; died in Philadelphia, Jan 30, 1836; dau. of Samuel Griscom (builder who allegedly worked on construction of Independence Hall in Philadelphia) and Rebecca (James) Griscom; m. John Ross (upholsterer), Nov 4, 1773 (killed 1776); m. Joseph Ashburn (sailor), June 1777 (died in a British prison, 1782); m. John Claypoole, May 8, 1783 (died 1817); children: (2nd m.) Zillah Ashburn (b. 1779, died young); Eliza Ashburn (b. 1781); (3rd m.) Clarissa Sidney Claypoole Wilson (b. 1785); Susan Claypoole (b. 1786); Rachel Claypoole (b. 1789); Jane Claypoole (b. 1792); Harriet Claypoole (b. 1795, died as infant). ❖ Provided "ship's colours, etc." (a flag) for Pennsylvania's navy (1777); became legendary, however, for her disputable involvement in creation of the nation's 1st flag; according to legend, was visited by George Ross, George Washington, and Robert Morris, as members of a secret committee of the Continental Congress seeking a flag for the nascent nation (1776 or 1777); though there is no known documentation, was 1st connected publicly with the flag almost 100 years after the American Revolution, when her grandson William Canby presented a history of the family, including the popularly known tale that his great-aunt had created the flag (Mar 1870). ❖ See also *Women in World History*.

ROSS, Betty Clark (1896–1947). *See Clarke, Betty Ross.*

ROSS, Charlotte Whitehead (1843–1916). English-Canadian physician. Name variations: Charlotte Whitehead. Born Charlotte Whitehead, July 15, 1843, in Darlington, England; died of arteriosclerosis, Feb 21, 1916, in Winnipeg, Canada; dau. of Isabella Whitehead and Joseph

Whitehead (railroad engineer); grandmother of Edith Ross (1st female anesthesiologist at Winnipeg General Hospital, Canada); graduate of Woman's Medical College of Pennsylvania (later Medical College of Pennsylvania and Hahnemann University School of Medicine), 1875; m. David Ross (Scottish railroad engineer, died 1912); children: 8, including Minnie (Ross) Ross. ❖ The 1st practicing woman physician in the Canadian West and in Montreal, immigrated with family to a farm in Huron Co., Canada (1848); after completing a medical education, moved to Whitemouth, Manitoba, with family and practiced medicine in the Whitemouth community, mostly treating male workers' injuries in the beginning of her career; was an active member of the Manitoba Medical Association; after husband's death (1912), moved to Winnipeg to live with her daughter, Minnie.

ROSS, countess of.
See Bruce, Matilda (c. 1285–c. 1326).
See Ross, Euphemia (d. after 1394).
See Leslie, Euphemia (d. after 1424).
See Leslie, Mary (d. 1429).

ROSS, Diana (1944—). African-American singer and actress. Name variations: The Supremes. Born Diane Ross, Mar 26, 1944, in Detroit, MI; dau. of Fred Earl Ross and Ernestine (Moten) Ross (d. 1984); m. Robert Silberstein Jr., 1971 (div. 1976); m. Arne Naess (shipping magnate), 1985 (div. 1999). ❖ With Mary Wilson and Florence Ballard, recorded 1st song for Motown (1964) as one of "The Supremes"; saw recording of "Where Did Our Love Go" reach *Billboard*'s Top 100; had 7 #1 hits and was rarely out of Top 10 (1965–69) with such songs as "Your Heart Belongs to Me" (1964), "Baby Love" (1964), "Come See about Me" (1964), "Stop! In the Name of Love" (1965), "Back in My Arms Again" (1965), "Nothing But Heartaches" (1965), "I Hear a Symphony" (1965), "My World Is Empty Without You" (1966), "You Can't Hurry Love" (1966), "You Keep Me Hangin' On" (1966), "Love Is Here and Now You're Gone" (1967), "Love Child" (1968) and "Someday We'll Be Together" (1969); left the group to pursue solo career (1970), appearing in films *Lady Sings the Blues* (1972), *Mahogany* (1975), and *The Wiz* (1978); on tv, starred in "Double Platinum" (1999). Inducted into Rock and Roll Hall of Fame (1988). ❖ See also J. Randy Taborrelli, *Call Me Miss Ross* (Carol, 1989); *Dreamgirls*, loosely based on The Supremes, opened on Broadway (1981); and *Women in World History.*

ROSS, Eden (1896–c. 1995). *See Phillpotts, Adelaide.*

ROSS, Elisabeth Kübler (b. 1926). *See Kübler-Ross, Elisabeth.*

ROSS, Elizabeth (1883–1953). *See Haynes, Elizabeth Ross.*

ROSS, Euphemia (d. 1387). Queen of Scotland. Name variations: Euphemia of Ross; countess of Moray. Died in 1387; dau. of Hugh Ross, 4th earl of Ross, and Matilda Bruce (c. 1285–c. 1326, sister of Robert I the Bruce); m. John Randolph, 3rd earl of Moray; became 2nd wife of Robert II Stewart or Stuart (1316–1390, his 1st wife was Elizabeth Muir), king of Scots (r. 1371–1390), c. May 2, 1355; children: David Stewart, earl of Strathearn (c. 1356–c. 1382); Walter Stewart, earl of Atholl and Caithness (c. 1360–1437); Egidia Stewart (who m. William Douglas of Nithsdale in 1387); Katherine Stewart (who m. David Lindsay, 1st earl of Crawford). ❖ See also Elizabeth Sutherland, *Five Euphemias: Women in Medieval Scotland, 1200–1420* (St. Martin, 1999).

ROSS, Euphemia (d. after 1394). Countess of Ross. Died after Sept 5, 1394; interred at Fortrose Cathedral, Ross and Cromarty; dau. of William Ross, 3rd earl of Ross, and Mary Og (dau. of Angus Og, lord of the Isles); m. Walter de Lesly, earl of Ross (some sources cite Andrew Leslie), around 1361; m. Alexander Stewart (c. 1343–1394), 1st earl of Buchan (r. 1382–1394), known as the Wolf of Badenach (some sources cite a 1405 death date), around July 22, 1382; children: (1st m.) Alexander Leslie, 7th earl of Ross; Mary Leslie (d. 1429, who m. Donald MacDonald, lord of the Isles). ❖ See also *Women in World History.*

ROSS, Forrestina Elizabeth (1860–1936). New Zealand teacher, mountaineer, journalist, and writer. Name variations: Forrestina (Forrest) Elizabeth Grant. Born Forrestina (Forrest) Elizabeth Grant, June 23, 1860, at Brixton, Surrey, England; died Mar 29, 1936, at Wellington, New Zealand; dau. of George Grant and Forrestina (Hay) Grant; University of Otago, c. 1881; m. Malcolm Ross (journalist and mountaineer), 1890 (died 1930); children: 1 son. ❖ Immigrated with family to New Zealand (1870); appointed mistress at Forbury School (1881); taught English at Otago Girls' High School until 1890; became 1st

woman member of New Zealand Alpine Club and, with husband, promoted sport of mountaineering (Forrest Ross Glacier named after her); became parliamentary reporter for several newspapers and was named 1st lady editor of *Evening Post* (c. 1897); published *Round the World with a Fountain Pen* (1913) and *Mixed Grill* (1934); also wrote short stories. ❖ See also *Dictionary of New Zealand Biography* (Vol. 2).

ROSS, Frances Adams (1919–1995). *See Le Sueur, Frances.*

ROSS, Frances Jane (1869–1950). New Zealand school principal and teacher. Born April 26, 1869, at Otepopo, North Otago, New Zealand; died July 13, 1950, at Dunedin, New Zealand; dau. of Angus Ross and Dorathea (Mee) Ross; University of Otago, BA, 1890, MA, 1900. ❖ Served as co-principal and then principal of Girton College (1890s–1914); served as principal of Columba College, Dunedin (1914–30), acting warden of St Margaret's College (1939), and principal of Presbyterian Women's Training Institute (1943, 1944); active in New Zealand Federation of University Women. ❖ See also *Dictionary of New Zealand Biography* (Vol. 3).

ROSS, Granny (1762–1860). *See Ross, Marie-Henriette LeJeune.*

ROSS, Harriet (1821–1913). *See Tubman, Harriet.*

ROSS, Hilda (1883–1959). New Zealand politician. Name variations: Dame Hilda Ross. Born Grace Nixon (adopted name Hilda Cuthbertha at time of marriage), July 6, 1883, in Whangarei, NZ; died Mar 6, 1959; m. Harry C. Ross, 1904 (died 1940); children: 2 sons. ❖ Heavily involved with the health camp movement; standing for Hamilton, became the 2nd woman to represent the National Party in Parliament (1945); appointed minister of Health and Child Welfare (1949), the 1st and last woman of her party to be named a minister until 1990; appointed minister of Social Security (1957); died while in office (1959). Made Dame Commander of the British Empire (CBE, 1956).

ROSS, Ishbel (1895–1975). Scottish-born American journalist and writer. Name variations: Isabel Rae; Ishbella Rae. Born Ishbella Margaret Ross in Sutherlandshire, Scotland, Dec 15, 1895; died Sept 21, 1975, in New York, NY; dau. of David Ross and Grace (McCrone) Ross; educated at Tain Royal Academy in Ross-Shire, Scotland; m. Bruce Rae (journalist and editor), 1922; children: Catriona. ❖ At 20, immigrated to Toronto, Ontario; moved to New York City (1919), where she became a general assignment reporter and member of editorial staff for *New York Tribune* (later *Herald-Tribune*); covered sensational crimes, fires, explosions, prize fights, and sought out high-profile interviews; was held in high esteem by colleagues; published 1st novel, *Promenade Deck*, which became a bestseller and later filmed; continued to write prodigiously, focusing on nonfiction books, especially biographies, including *Ladies of the Press* (1936), *Margaret Fell: Mother of Quakerism* (1949), *Rebel Rose: Life of Rose O'Neal Greenhow, Confederate Spy* (1954), *First Lady of the South: The Life of Mrs. Jefferson Davis* (1958), *The General's Wife: The Life of Mrs. Ulysses S. Grant* (1959), *Silhouette in Diamonds: The Life of Mrs. Potter Palmer* (1960), *Power with Grace: The Life of Mrs. Woodrow Wilson* (1975) and *The President's Wife: Mary Todd Lincoln* (1973). ❖ See also *Women in World History.*

ROSS, Ishobel (1890–1965). Scottish nurse. Born on the Isle of Skye, Feb 18, 1890; died 1965; dau. of James Ross (who is credited with the development of the famous liquor, Drambuie); attended Edinburgh Ladies College; married; children: daughter Jess Dixon. ❖ During WWI, volunteered to accompany Elsie Inglis to Serbia, where a hospital unit was being established, arriving in nearby Salonika, Greece (Aug 1916); remained on Balkan front until July 1917 and kept a diary of her experiences. ❖ See also *Little Grey Partridge: First World War Diary of Ishobel Ross Who Served with the Scottish Women's Hospitals in Serbia* (1988); and *Women in World History.*

ROSS, Lillian (1926—). American journalist and writer. Born June 8, 1926, in Syracuse, New York; dau. of Louis Ross and Edna (Rosenson) Ross; children: Erik Jeremy Ross (adopted). ❖ Wrote for *The New Yorker* for more than 50 years, beginning in 1945, when she was not yet 20; became well known for her laudatory portraits of movie stars, famous writers, and other celebrity subjects, including John Huston and Ernest Hemingway. ❖ See also memoir *Here But Not Here: A Love Story* (1998); and *Women in World History.*

ROSS, Marie-Henriette LeJeune (1762–1860). Canadian midwife. Name variations: Marie-Henriette LeJeune-Ross; Marie-Henriette LeJeune; Granny Ross. Born Maria Tharsile LeJeune, Aug 13, 1762, in Rochefort, France; died May 1860 in Margaree, Nova Scotia, Canada;

dau. of Martine Roy and Joseph LeJeune (Acadian farmers); m. Joseph Comeau, Feb 17, 1780 (died 1785); Lamaud Briard LeJeune (a cousin) 1786 (died); James Ross (disbanded Irish soldier of Scottish parents), Mar 18, 1793 (died 1825); children: (3rd m.) 4 (2 lived to adulthood). ❖ Noted midwife, known for homeopathic techniques, settled on Cape Breton Island (Bras d'Or region) with 3rd husband James Ross; gained community recognition after skillfully employing an inoculation practice from Turkey during a smallpox epidemic (early 1800s); saved a sample of the vaccine, which was later used by a grandson during another outbreak 70 years later; moved to Northeast Margaree River (1802) and was the 1st Caucasian and the only medically skilled resident in the area.

ROSS, Martin (1862–1915). *See Martin, Violet.*

ROSS, Mother (1667–1739). *See Cavanagh, Kit.*

ROSS, Nellie Tayloe (1876–1977). American politician. Born Nellie Tayloe, Nov 29, 1876, near St. Joseph, Missouri; died in Washington, DC, Dec 20, 1977; dau. of James Wynns Tayloe (merchant and farmer) and Elizabeth (Blair) Tayloe; had 2 years training in Omaha, Nebraska, as kindergarten teacher; m. William Bradford Ross (later governor of Wyoming), Sept 11, 1902 (died 1924); children: (twins) George and Ambrose (b. 1903); Alfred (b. 1905, died young); William Bradford II (b. 1912). ❖ Director of the US Mint and 1st woman governor, worked for Cheyenne, Wyoming, community activities, including Cheyenne Woman's Club, Boy Scouts and Episcopal Church (1902–22); was wife of governor (1922–24); served as governor of Wyoming (1925–27); served as vice-chair, Democratic National Committee (1928–33) and seconded the nomination of Alfred E. Smith at the national convention (1928); served as director of US Mint for 20 years (1933–53); was the 1st woman to have her likeness on a Mint medal, and the 1st to have her name on the cornerstone of a government building. ❖ See also *Women in World History.*

ROSS, Shirley (1909–1975). American singer, dancer and actress. Born Bernice Gaunt, Jan 7, 1909, in Omaha, NE; died Mar 9, 1975, in Menlo Park, CA; children: 1 daughter, 2 sons. ❖ Began career as singer with Phil Harris band, then Gus Arnheim orchestra; in films, often starred opposite Bob Hope to whom he first sang "Thanks for the Memories"; sang and danced in such films as *Big Broadcast of 1937, What Price Jazz, 100% Pure, Blossoms on Broadway, Waikiki Wedding, Thanks for the Memory, A Song for Miss Julie* and *Some Like It Hot* (1939); also appeared in *Cafe Society, Devil's Squadron* and *San Francisco*; introduced Rogers and Hart ballad, "It Never Entered My Mind" on Broadway in *Higher and Higher.*

ROSS, Violet Florence (1862–1915). *See Martin, Violet.*

ROSS-CRAIG, Stella (1906—). Botanical artist. Born 1906 in UK; m. J.R. Sealy; studied at the Art School, Thanet Chelsea Polytechnic in London. ❖ Known for artistic and scientifically accurate drawings, worked as a Royal Botanical Gardens (Kew) botanical artist; was a Linnean Society fellow (1948–74). Publications include *Drawings of British Plants* (published in 31 parts, 1948–74) and botanical illustrations for *Botanical Magazine,* among others; a large collection of her drawings (3,000 total) are in the Kew collection.

ROSSE, countess of (1813–1885). *See Parsons, Mary.*

ROSSELLI, Amelia (1930–1996). Italian poet. Born 1930 in Paris, France; died Feb 11, 1996, in Rome, Italy; dau. of Carlo Rosselli (died 1937) and Marion Cave (an English woman); granddau. of Amelia Pincherle Rosselli (Jewish-Italian playwright, 1870–1954); studied in France, England, and US. ❖ Born in France because her Italian father, an anti-fascist, had escaped from an Italian prison in 1929 and was living in exile while forming a resistance movement; after father and father's brother Nello Rosselli were assassinated in Normandy (1937), moved with mother and grandmother to England (1940), then US; moved to Italy (1948), where she worked in publishing houses; wrote in English and Italian; works include *Variazioni belliche* (1964), *Serie ospedaliera* (1969), *Documento* (1976), *Primi scritti 1952–63* (1981), *Impromptu* (1981), *La libellula* (1985), *Antologia poetica* (1987) and *Diario Ottuso* (1990).

ROSSER, Celia E. (1930—). Australian botanical artist. Name variations: Celia Elizabeth Rosser; Celia Elizabeth Prince. Born Celia Elizabeth Prince, 1930, in Australia. ❖ Noted botanical artist, began career in fashion illustration at a Melbourne advertising agency; at Monash University, served as science faculty artist (1970–74), before becoming a university botanical artist (1974); set out to paint all of the Australian

Banksia species; published *Wild Flowers of Victoria* (1967) and *The Banksias* (1st vol., 1981, 2nd vol., 1988, and 3rd vol., 2000). Received the Linnean Society of London's Jill Smythies Award for Botanical Illustration (1977) and the Medal of the Order of Australia (1966).

ROSSETTI, Christina (1830–1894). English poet. Name variations: (pseudonym) Ellen Alleyne. Born Christina Rossetti in London, England, Dec 5, 1830; died in London, Dec 29, 1894; dau. of Gabriele Rossetti (professor of Italian at King's College, London) and Lavinia Polidori Rossetti; sister of Maria Francesca Rossetti (1827–1876), Dante Gabriel Rossetti (1828–1882), the painter and poet, and William Michael Rossetti (1829–1906); never married; no children. ❖ Celebrated Victorian poet who 1st drew public attention to the Pre-Raphaelite movement, enjoyed the same educational advantages as her siblings; at an early age, was encouraged to mix freely with adults—a rarity in Victorian families of the time; remained unmarried, despite 2 engagements: James Collinson (1848) and Charles Bagot Cayley (1866); suffered from a mysterious malady, exophthalmic bronchocele (1871–73), and remained an invalid the rest of her life; though her reputation rests on the fact that her verse contributed significantly to the direction in which the poetry of the 20th century was to move, will perhaps be best remembered and appreciated for the searing directness, integrity, and lyricism of her poetry; poetic works include *Goblin Market and other poems* (1862), *The Prince's Progress* (1866), *Sing-Song* (nursery rhymes, 1872), *A Pageant* (1881) and *New Poems* (unpublished poems collected by brother William and printed after her death in 1896). ❖ See also C.H. Sisson, *Christina Rossetti* (Carcanet, 1984); Frances Thomas, *Christina Rossetti: A Biography* (Virago, 1994); and *Women in World History.*

ROSSETTI, Mrs. Dante Gabriel (1829–1862). *See Siddal, Elizabeth.*

ROSSETTI, Elizabeth (1829–1862). *See Siddal, Elizabeth.*

ROSSETTI, Maria Francesca (1827–1876). English author. Born 1827; died 1876; dau. of Gabriele Rossetti (professor of Italian at King's College, London) and Lavinia Polidori; sister of Christina Rossetti (1830–1894), Dante Gabriel Rossetti (1828–1882), and William Michael Rossetti (1829–1906). ❖ Wrote *A Shadow of Dante* (1870); became an Anglican nun (1874).

ROSSI, Countess de or di. *See Sontag, Henriette (c. 1803–1854).*

ROSSI, Eleonora (1925—). *See Rossi Drago, Eleonora.*

ROSSI, Properzia de (c. 1490–1530). Italian sculptor. Name variations: Properzia de' Rossi; Properzia di Rossi. Born c. 1490 in Bologna, Italy; died 1530 in Bologna. ❖ Famous Italian sculptor, was instructed in drawing and painting by Marc Antonio Raimondi, but showed the most aptitude and love for sculpture and carving; created works praised widely for their beauty; began accepting public commissions (c. 1520); modeled the bust of Count Guido Pepoli now in the sacristy of basilica of St. Petronius; employed to assist in finishing reliefs about the portal, which Giacomo della Quercia had left unfinished; also executed 2 bas-reliefs now in St. Petronius sacristy, which represent *Joseph and Potiphar's Wife* and *Solomon receiving the Queen of Sheba.* ❖ See also *Women in World History.*

ROSSIANKA (1744–1810). *See Dashkova, Ekaterina.*

ROSSI DRAGO, Eleonora (1925—). Italian actress. Name variations: Eleonora Rossi; Eleanor Rossi-Drago. Born Palmira Omiccioli, Sept 23, 1925, in Quinto, Italy. ❖ Made film debut in *Altura* (1949), followed by *Persiane chiuse, Tre storie proibite, Verginità, Sensualità, La Fiammata, L'Esclave, La tratta delle bianche, Destinées, L'Affaire Maurizius, Napoléon, Donne sole, Kean, Le fric, Vacanze d'inverno, L'Estate violenta, David e Golia, Under Ten Flags, Anima nera, Rosmunda e Alboino, L'amour à vingt ans, Hipnosis* and *La Bibbia,* among others.

ROSSNER, Petra (1966—). German cyclist. Born Nov 14, 1966, in Germany. ❖ At Barcelona Olympics, won a gold medal in 3,000-meter indiv. pursuit (1992).

ROST, Christina (1952—). East German handball player. Born Aug 14, 1952, in East Germany. ❖ Won a silver medal at Montreal Olympics (1976) and a bronze medal at Moscow Olympics (1980), both in team competition.

ROSTOCK, Marlies East German cross-country skier. Born in East Germany. ❖ Won a gold medal for 4 x 5 km relay at Lake Placid Olympics (1980).

ROSTOPCHINA, Evdokiya (1811–1858). Russian poet, writer, and salonnière. Name variations: Evdokia or Evdokiia Rostopchina; Countess Rostopchina. Born Evdokiya Petrovna Sushkova in Moscow, Dec 23, 1811; died Dec 3, 1858; her mother died while Evdokiya was still young, and her father, due to his civil service, was frequently absent; m. Count Andrei Rostopchin (conservative aristocrat), in 1833. ❖ Host to one of Russia's most active 19th-century literary salons, gained renown throughout Russia because of her intellect, her well-respected poetry, and her salon which was visited by all of the major literary personages of the era, including Aleksander Pushkin, Mikhail Lermontov, and Nikolai Gogol; remains a significant component of the intellectual and literary history of Russian Romanticism of the 1830s and 1840s. ❖ See also *Women in World History.*

ROSTOPCHINE, Sophie (1799–1874). See Ségur, Sophie Rostopchine, Comtesse de.

ROSTOVA, Anna (1950—). Soviet volleyball player. Born Dec 17, 1950, in USSR. ❖ At Montreal Olympics, won a silver medal in team competition (1976).

ROSTOVTEVA, Olga (1969—). See Slyusareva, Olga.

ROSTROPOVICH, Galina (b. 1926). See Vishnevskaya, Galina.

ROSU, Monica (1987—). Romanian gymnast. Name variations: Mona Rosu. Born May 11, 1987, in Bacau, Romania. ❖ At World championships, placed 2nd for team and 4th for vault (2003); won a gold medal for the vault and a team gold medal for all-around at Athens Olympics (2004).

ROSWITHA (c. 935–1001). See Hrotsvitha of Gandersheim.

ROTCH, Elizabeth (1791–1870). See Farrar, Eliza Rotch.

ROTH, Ann (1931—). American stage and film costume designer. Born Oct 30, 1931, in Hanover, PA. ❖ Costumer for many Broadway plays, began film career as an assistant to Irene Sharaff; made film debut with *The World of Henry Orient* (1964), followed by over 90 films, including *Midnight Cowboy, The Owl and the Pussycat, Klute, Mandingo, The Happy Hooker, Murder by Death, The Goodbye Girl, Coming Home, Only When I Laugh, The World According to Garp, Silkwood, Maxie, Sweet Dreams, The Unbearable Lightness of Being, Working Girl, Sabrina, The Birdcage, The Talented Mr. Ripley, Finding Forrester, Adaptation, The Hours* and *Cold Mountain.* Won an Oscar for *The English Patient* (1996).

ROTH, Hella (1963—). West German field-hockey player. Born Sept 21, 1963, in West Germany. ❖ At Los Angeles Olympics, won a silver medal in team competition (1984).

ROTH, Lillian (1910–1980). American actress and singer. Born Lillian Rutstein, Dec 13, 1910, in Boston, Massachusetts; died May 10, 1980, in New York, NY; dau. of Arthur Rutstein and Katie (Silverman) Rutstein (later changed to Roth); attended Professional Children's School, NY; m. David Lyons (died); m. William Scott (div.); m. Judge Benjamin Shalleck (div.); m. Eugene Weiner (div.); m. Edward Goldman (div.); m. Mark Harris (div.); m. Thomas Burt McGuire (div. 1963); no children. ❖ At 7, made Broadway debut in *The Inner Man* (1917); went on to appear in *Penrod* and *The Betrothed* (both 1918), then toured in vaudeville with sister Ann; during this period, introduced the songs "When the Red, Red Robin Comes Bob Bob Bobbin' Along" and "Ain't She Sweet," both of which became standards; as an adult, became a popular attraction in *Earl Carroll's Vanities* (1928, 1931, and 1932), and in Ziegfeld's *Midnight Frolics* (1929), among other shows; made film debut in musical short *Lillian Roth and Piano Boys* (1929), singing "Ain't She Sweet," then signed with Paramount; made 1st feature film *Illusion* (1929); also appeared in *The Love Parade* (1929) and *Animal Crackers* (1930); starred on CBS radio's "The Lillian Roth Show" (1934); bout with alcohol seriously began to undermine career (1930s); comeback was aided by Ralph Edwards tv program "This Is Your Life" (1953); wrote autobiography (with Mike Connolly and Gerold Frank), *I'll Cry Tomorrow,* which sold over 1 million copies; published a 2nd, less-successful autobiography, *Beyond My Worth* (1958), and returned to Broadway in musical *I Can Get It for You Wholesale* (1962). ❖ See also *Women in World History.*

ROTH-BEHRENDT, Dagmar (1953—). German lawyer and politician. Born Feb 21, 1953, in Frankfurt am Main, Germany. ❖ Served as adviser in the chancellery of the governing mayor of Berlin; as a European Socialist, elected to 4th and 5th European Parliament (1994–99, 1999–2004).

ROTHE, Mechtild (1947—). German politician. Born Aug 10, 1947, in Paderborn, Germany. ❖ Schoolteacher (1978–84); as a European Socialist, elected to 4th and 5th European Parliament (1994–99, 1999–2004).

ROTHELIN, Jacqueline de Rohan, Marquise de (c. 1520–1587). French aristocrat. Born c. 1520; died 1587; dau. of Charles de Rohan and Jeanne de Saint-Séverin; m. François of Orleans-Longueville, marquis de Rothelin (died 1548); children: 1 son. ❖ Was brought into contact with religious reformers in Switzerland; turned her château at Blandy, in Brie, into a refuge for Huguenots; was imprisoned for harboring Protestants (1567).

ROTHENBERGER, Anneliese (1924—). German soprano. Born in Mannheim, Germany, June 19, 1924; studied with Erika Müller at Mannheim Conservatory; m. Gerd W. Dieberitz (journalist), 1954. ❖ Debuted in Koblenz (1943); appeared at Hamburg State Opera (1946–56); debuted at Salzburg (1954); made Metropolitan Opera debut (1960); created the title role in Sutermeister's *Madame Bovary* and Telemachus in Liebermann's *Penelope*; a skilled actress, sang in other operas, including Hindemith's *Mathis der Maler,* Liebermann's *Die Schule der Frauen,* and Berg's atonal *Lulu;* was also a specialist in Mozart and Strauss; made numerous recordings. ❖ See also *Women in World History.*

ROTHENBERGER, Gonnelien. Dutch equestrian. Name variations: Gonnelien Rothenberger-Gordijn. Born in Netherlands; m. Sven Rothenberger (equestrian). ❖ Won a team silver medal at Atlanta Olympics (1996), on Weyden.

ROTHENBURGER-LUDING, Christa (1959—). East German cyclist and speedskater. Name variations: Christa Luding; Christa Luding-Rothenburger; Christa Rothenburger. Born Christa Rothenburger, Dec 4, 1959, in Weisswasser, German Democratic Republic; m. Ernst Luding (her skating coach), 1988. ❖ Won a gold medal for the 500-meter speedskating race at Sarajevo Olympics (1984); was World sprint-skating champion (1984, 1988); became World champion for the 1,000-meter speedskating race (1986); won a silver medal for the 500-meter speedskating race and a gold medal for the 1,000-meter at Calgary Olympics (1988); won a silver medal for the 1,000-meter cycling race at Seoul Olympics (1988), becoming the 1st athlete to win medals in both the Summer and Winter Olympic games in the same year; won a bronze medal for the 500-meter speedskating race at Albertville Olympics (1992). ❖ See also *Women in World History.*

RÖTHER, Sabine (1957—). See Roether, Sabine.

ROTHHAMMER, Keena (1957—). American swimmer. Name variations: Keena Rothhammer Weisbly. Born Feb 26, 1957, in Santa Clara, CA. ❖ Won a gold medal for the 800-meter freestyle and a bronze medal for 200-meter freestyle at Munich Olympics (1972); set 2 World records and 10 indiv. American records. Named North American Athlete of the Year (1973); inducted into Jewish Sports Hall of Fame (1980).

ROTHILD (c. 871–c. 928). Countess of Maine. Born c. 871; died c. 928; dau. of Richilde of Autun (d. around 910) and Charles I the Bald, king of France (r. 840–877), also known as Charles II, Holy Roman emperor (r. 875–877); m. Rotger also known as Roger, count of Maine; children: Hugh I, count of Maine.

ROTHILDE (fl. 840). German princess. Dau. of Lothair I, Holy Roman emperor (r. 840–855) and Irmengard (c. 800–851); sister of Louis II (c. 822–875), Holy Roman emperor (r. 855–875), and Lothair II, king of Lorraine (r. 855–869); m. Guido of Spoleto; children: Guido of Spoleto, Holy Roman emperor (r. 891–894).

ROTHLEIN, Arlene (1939–1976). American dancer, choreographer and actress. Born 1939 in Brooklyn, NY; died Nov 20, 1976, in Brooklyn; studied dance at Merce Cunningham studios. ❖ Appeared in several off-Broadway productions. Was associated with the dance and theater productions of James Waring; won an Obie for her performance in *The Little Match Girl* (1968).

RÖTHLISBERGER, Nadia (1972—). See Roethlisberger, Nadia.

ROTHMAN, Stephanie (1936—). American director and screenwriter. Name variations: Dallas Meredith. Born Nov 9, 1936, in Paterson, NJ. ❖ Wrote and directed many films for Roger Corman's studio, including *It's a Bikini World, Blood Bath, The Student Nurses, The Velvet Vampire,*

Group Marriage, Terminal Island and *The Working Girls*; wrote *Beyond Atlantis* and *Sweet Sugar*.

ROTHMANN, Maria Elisabeth (1875–1975). South African novelist and essayist. Name variations: M.E.R. Born 1875 in Swellendam, South Africa; died 1975 in Swellendam; children: Anna. ❖ Worked as teacher and social worker; edited 1st Afrikaans women's magazine *Die Boerevrou,* and 1st women's page of *Die Burger* newspaper; appointed secretary of Afrikaans Christian Women's Organization and published its history (1954); was the only woman appointed to the Carnegie Commission; works include *Kinders van die Voortrek* (1920), *Omweekrshoogte* (1927), *Jong Dae* (1933), *Na Vaste Gange* (1944), *Uit en Tuis* (1946), *Die Gevers* (1950), *So is Onse Maniere* (1965), and *Hanne en die Bessiekinders* (1972); also translated works from Dutch into Afrikaans and wrote 3 vols. of essays; published autobiography *My Beskeie Deel* (1972); with daughter, wrote *The Drostdy at Swellendam* (1960); letters to daughter published posthumously as *Familigesprek* (1976) and *'n Kosbare Erfenis* (1977).

ROTHRUDE (d. 724). See *Chrotrud.*

ROTHSCHILD, Constance de (1843–1931). English baroness. Name variations: Constance Flower; Lady Battersea. Born Constance de Rothschild, April 29, 1843; died Nov 22, 1931; dau. of Baron Sir Anthony de Rothschild, 1st Baronet (1810–1876), and Louise Montefiore Rothschild (1821–1910); sister of Baroness Annie de Rothschild (1844–1926, who m. Eliot Yorke); m. Cyril Flower, MP and 1st Lord Battersea, 1877 (he was made Baron Battersea in 1892). ❖ See also *The Memoirs of Lady Battersea* (1922).

ROTHSCHILD, Baroness Eugene de (1908–2003). See *Rothschild, Jeanne de.*

ROTHSCHILD, Baroness Henri de (1874–1926). See *Rothschild, Mathilde de.*

ROTHSCHILD, Jeanne de (1908–2003). English actress and baroness. Name variations: Jeanne Stuart; Baroness Eugene de Rothschild; Lady Docker. Born Ivy Sweet, Aug 13, 1908, in Hampstead, London, England; died Feb 12, 2003, in Monte Carlo, Monaco; m. Bernard Dudley Docker (industrialist), 1933 (div. 1935); m. Baron Eugene de Rothschild, Dec 1952 (died April 1976). ❖ As Jeanne Stuart, made stage debut in NY as Judy in *Nine Till Six* (1930) and London debut as Greta in *After All* (1931); also appeared in *It's a Girl, Roadhouse, Afterwards, Espionage, The Two Mrs. Carrolls* and *Quiet Weekend*; films include *Life Goes On, The Shadow, The King of Paris, Bella Donna, Forget Me Not, The Great Defender, Death on the Set, Kathleen Mavourneen* and *Bonnie Prince Charlie.*

ROTHSCHILD, Judith (1921–1993). American painter and philanthropist. Born Sept 4, 1921, in New York, NY; died Mar 6, 1993, in New York, NY; dau. of Herbert Rothschild (owner of a furniture manufacturing company); Wellesley College, BA; studied with Reginald Marsh of Art Students League in NY; attended Cranbrook Academy of Art in Bloomfield Hills, MI; studied with Hans Hofmann and Karl Knaths; studied with Stanley William Hayter at Atelier 17 in NY; married for 23 years to Anton Myrer (novelist, div.). ❖ During 55-year career, moved from abstract, geometric style to landscape and figurative painting (1950s–60s); paintings were shown internationally and are in the collections of the Metropolitan Museum of Art, Guggenheim Museum, Whitney Museum of American Art, National Gallery in Washington, DC, and Fogg Art Museum in Cambridge, Massachusetts, as well as many other museums and private collections; was founder and president of the American Abstract Artists Association. ❖ See also *Women in World History.*

ROTHSCHILD, Mathilde de (1874–1926). Baroness. Name variations: Baroness or Baronne Henri de Rothschild; Baroness or Baronne de Rothschild. Born Mathilde Weissweiler on May 17, 1874; died Aug 12, 1926; m. Henri de Rothschild, May 22, 1895; children: James Nathaniel de Rothschild (b. 1896, who m. Claude Dupont); Nadine Charlotte de Rothschild (1898–1958, who m. Adrien Thierry); Philippe de Rothschild (1902–1935, who m. Elisabeth de Chambure [d. 1945] and Pauline Fairfax Potter). ❖ Known for her charity events in turn-of-the-century Paris. ❖ See also *Women in World History.*

ROTHSCHILD, Miriam (1908–2005). British entomologist and naturalist. Born Miriam Louisa Rothschild, Aug 5, 1908, in Ashton Wold, England; died Jan 20, 2005; dau. of Charles Rothschild (banker and naturalist) and Rozsika von Wertheimstein Rothschild; granddau. of Nathan Mayer Rothschild, Baron Rothschild (the British financier); niece of Walter Rothschild; educated privately; m. George Lane, 1943 (div. 1957); children: 6. ❖ Despite the virtual absence of any formal education, became a highly regarded scientist and naturalist, specializing in the study of fleas and other insects; made a fellow of the Royal Society (1985); published numerous books on insects and gardens, including the 6-vol. *Catalogue of the Rothschild Collection of Fleas,* which was published over a period of 30 years; also wrote biography *Dear Lord Rothschild* (1983). Named Commander of the British Empire (CBE). ❖ See also *Women in World History.*

ROTHWELL, Evelyn (b. 1911). English oboist. Name variations: Lady Evelyn Barbirolli. Born in Wallingford, England, Jan 24, 1911; studied under Leon Goossens at Royal College of Music; m. Sir John Barbirolli (the conductor), 1939 (died 1970). ❖ Joined Covent Garden Opera touring orchestra (1931); played with Scottish Orchestra (1933–36), Glyndebourne Festival Orchestra (1934–39), and London Symphony Orchestra (1935–39); following marriage, began a solo career; gave 1st performance of the rediscovered Mozart Oboe Concerto (1934); was appointed a professor at Royal Academy of Music, London (1971). ❖ See also memoir, *Life with Glorious John: A Portrait of Sir John Barbirolli* (2003).

ROTI, Anna (c. 1862–1914). See *Lipperini, Guendalina.*

ROTI, Guendalina (c. 1862–1914). See *Lipperini, Guendalina.*

ROTOVÁ, Johanna (1830–1899). See *Svetla, Caroline.*

ROTROU. Variant of *Chrotrud* and *Rotrud.*

ROTROU OF BELGIUM (d. 724). See *Chrotrud.*

ROTRUD (800–841). French princess. Born 800; died 841; dau. of Ermengarde (c. 778–818) and Louis I the Pious (778–840), king of Aquitaine (r. 781–814), king of France (r. 814–840), and Holy Roman Emperor (r. 814–840).

ROTRUDE (c. 778–after 839). Frankish princess. Name variations: Hrotrud or Hrotrude; (Greek) Erythro. Born c. 778; died after 839; dau. of Charles I also known as Charlemagne (742–814), king of the Franks (r. 768–814), Holy Roman emperor (r. 800–814), and Hildegarde of Swabia (c. 757–783); sister of Gisella of Chelles (781–814); m. Count Rorico, c. 800; children: Louis (b. around 800), abbott of St. Denis. ❖ See also *Women in World History.*

ROTSCHEWA, Nina. See *Rocheva, Nina.*

ROTTENBERG, Silke (1972—). German soccer player. Born Jan 25, 1972, in Euskirchen, Germany. ❖ Goalkeeper, won a team bronze medal at Sydney Olympics (2000) and Athens Olympics (2004); signed with Brauweiler-Pulheim (2000); won team European championships (1997, 2001); won FIFA World Cup (2003) and named Player of the Match. Named Female Football Player of the Year (1998).

ROTTER, Emilia. Jewish-Hungarian pairs skater. Name variations: Emilie Rotter. Born in Hungary. ❖ With partner László Szollás, won 4 World championships (1931, 1933, 1934, 1935), 1 European championship (1934), and bronze medals at Lake Placid Olympics (1932) and Garmisch-Partenkirchen Olympics (1936).

ROUDENKO, Lubov (1915—). Bulgarian ballet dancer. Born 1915 in Sofia, Bulgaria. ❖ Moved to US with Ballet Russe de Monte Carlo (1936), and created roles in Massine's *Gaité Parisienne* (1938), *The New Yorkers* (1940), and *Vienna–1814* (1940); performed in Agnes de Mille's *Rodeo* (1942); danced on Broadway in *Nellie Bly* (1945) and *Annie Get Your Gun* (1946).

ROUDY, Yvette (1929—). French politician and feminist. Born 1929 in Bordeaux, France; attended Collège de Jeune Filles; m. Pierre Roudy, 1951. ❖ Became secretary of Mouvement Démocratique Féminin (1964) and was elected to European Parliament (1979); was named secretary of state for Women's Rights (1981), then minister (1985); elected Socialist Deputy for Calvados (1986); was founder and editor in chief of *La femme du 20ème siecle*; writings include *La réussite de la femme* (1969), *La femme en marge* (1975), *Les metiers et les cajoints* (1981), and *A cause d'elles* (1985); translated Betty Friedan's *The Feminine Mystique* (1963).

ROUET, Catherine or Katherine (c. 1350–1403). See *Swynford, Catherine.*

ROUET, Philippa (c. 1348–c. 1387). French-born wife of Geoffrey Chaucer. Name variations: Philippa Chaucer; Philippa de Ruet or

Philippa de Roet. Born c. 1348; died c. 1387; dau. of Sir Payne Roelt (knight from Hainault, France, who arrived in England with the train of Edward III's queen Philippa of Hainault); sister of Catherine Swynford (c. 1350–1403); m. Geoffrey Chaucer (the poet); children: Thomas Chaucer; grandchildren: Alice Chaucer. ❖ Probably met Geoffrey Chaucer while at court attending Philippa of Hainault.

ROUG, Kristine (1975—). Danish sailor. Born Mar 12, 1975, in Horsholm, Denmark. ❖ Won World championships in the Europe class (1994, 1995) and Laser Radial class (1994); won a gold medal for single-handed dinghy (Europe) at Atlanta Olympics (1996). Named Danish Sailor of the Year (1994).

ROUILLARD, Nancy. *See Ludington, Nancy.*

ROUKEMA, Margaret (1929—). American politician. Name variations: Margaret Scafati Roukema; Margaret S. Roukema. Born Margaret "Marge" Scafati, Sept 19, 1929, in Newark, New Jersey; Montclair State University, BA, 1951; graduate work at Montclair State University; graduate work in city and regional planning at Rutgers University, 1975; m. Richard W. Roukema (psychiatrist); children: Greg, Meg, and Todd (died at age 17). ❖ A moderate Republican, began career as a high school history teacher; ran unsuccessfully for a seat in US House of Representatives for New Jersey (1978), but won (1980); served from 1980 to 2002; one of the most respected fiscal conservatives in the House, was chair of the House Banking Committee's Subcommittee on Financial Institutions; sponsored legislation to update financial services laws dating back to the Depression; strongly supportive of health insurance reform, believed that insurance company profit considerations unfairly affected decisions about treatment, and that patients and their doctors should maintain sole discretion about patient care; fought to restore $38 million that had been cut from the Women, Infants and Children (WIC) food program and, at the same time, contributed to legislation that would require parents to support their children financially; was a member of the Congressional Task Force on Immigration Reform.

ROULSTONE, Elizabeth (fl. 1804). American printer. Lived in Tennessee. ❖ Like a number of other early women printers in America, was the widow of a printer; became Public Printer for state of TN (1804); was responsible for publishing *The Knoxville Gazette*; received chickens, butter, corn and additional farm products as payment for subscriptions.

ROUMPESI, Antigoni (1983—). Greek water-polo player. Born July 19, 1983, in Greece. ❖ Won team silver medal at Athens Olympics (2004).

ROUND, Dorothy (1908–1982). English tennis player. Name variations: Dorothy Round Little; Mrs. Douglas Little. Born Dorothy Edith Round, July 13, 1908, in Dudley, Worcestershire, England; died Nov 12, 1982, in Kidderminster, England. ❖ Was the only British player (besides Kitty McKane) to win Wimbledon twice after WWI (1934 and 1937); also won Wimbledon mixed doubles (1934–36); was the only woman from overseas to win the Australian championship (1935); was a member of the British Wightman Cup team (1931–36).

ROUNTREE, Martha (1911–1999). American radio and tv producer. Name variations: Martha Presbrey. Born in Gainesville, Florida, Oct 23, 1911; died Aug 23, 1999, in Washington, DC; sister of Ann Rountree Forsberg; attended University of South Carolina; m. Albert N. Williams Jr. (magazine and radio writer), 1941 (div. 1948); m. Oliver M. Presbrey (tv producer and advertising executive), June 18, 1952 (died 1988); children: Martha Presbrey Wiethorn; Mary Presbrey Greene. ❖ Pioneer radio and tv producer, was co-creator of "Meet the Press," the newsmaker series that began as a radio program (1945), moved to tv (1948), and became that medium's longest-running series. ❖ See also *Women in World History*.

ROURE, Martine (1948—). French educator and politician. Born Sept 28, 1948, in Lyon, France. ❖ Secondary teacher, then head of a college of secondary education; member of the Socialist Party Executive Committee and National Council (1992–96); as a European Socialist, elected to 5th European Parliament (1999–2004). Named Knight (1992) and Officer (1999) of the Order of Academic Palms.

ROURKE, Constance (1885–1941). American scholar and writer. Born Constance Mayfield Rourke, Nov 14, 1885, in Cleveland, Ohio; died Mar 23, 1941, in Grand Rapids, Michigan; dau. of Henry Rourke (designer of hardware specialties) and Elizabeth Constance (Davis) Rourke (schoolteacher and proponent of the kindergarten movement);

Vassar College, BA, 1907; attended Sorbonne, 1908–09; never married; no children. ❖ Scholar of American folklore and culture who sought to recover and revalue American traditions, 1st served as English instructor at Vassar (1910–15); published 1st article, "The Rationale of Punctuation" (1915); began writing for various journals (1918); was introduced to Van Wyck Brooks, and it was in opposing his conclusion that America lacked a worthy cultural tradition that she found new subject matter (1920); set out to rediscover the lost and undervalued cultural life of America; published 1st book, *Trumpets of Jubilee* (1927), followed by *Troupers of the Gold Coast, or The Rise of Lotta Crabtree* (1928) and *American Humor: A Study of the National Character* (1931), considered her finest work and the one for which she is most remembered; produced a biography of naturalist John James Audubon (1936) and also wrote *Charles Sheeler: Artist in the American Tradition* (1938); following her death, her *The Roots of American Culture*, edited and introduced by Van Wyck Brooks, was issued. ❖ See also Joan Shelley Rubin, *Constance Rourke and American Culture* (U. of North Carolina Press, 1980); and *Women in World History*.

ROUSANNE, Mme (1894–1958). Russian ballet teacher. Name variations: Rousanne Sarkissian. Born Rousanne Sarkissian, 1894, in Baku, Azerbaijan; died Mar 19, 1958, in Paris, France. ❖ Began studying ballet at a late age, having completed a law degree in Russia; moved to Paris (mid-1920s) to train with Vera Trefilova, Ivan Clustine, and Alexandre Volinine; taught ballet in Paris (1928–58), where her classes were highly popular.

ROUSSEL, Nelly (1878–1922). French activist. Pronunciation: roo-SELL. Born in Paris, France, Jan 5, 1878; died in Paris of TB, Dec 18, 1922; m. Henri Godet (b. 1863), in 1898; children: daughter Mireille Godet and son Marcel Godet; another son died in infancy. ❖ One of France's finest orators of her time, who was a leading advocate of birth control and "integral" feminism, converted to left-wing causes following marriage to Henri Godet (1898); experienced 3 exceptionally difficult childbirths (1899–1904); met Paul Robin, leading advocate of birth control ("neo-Malthusianism," 1900); went on tours lecturing on birth control and women's rights (1901–13); testified at the trial of Hervé and other anti-militarists (1905); opposed the war (1914–18); testified at Hélène Brion's trial for antiwar activities (1918); wrote and spoke against the advocates of large families (neo-natalists) and for women's suffrage (1919–22); started a school to train women speakers (1920); wrote some 200 articles for 46 newspapers and periodicals; across the spectrum of women's issues, took positions most of which by the end of the 20th century would seem all but self-evident. ❖ See also *Women in World History*.

ROUT, Ettie Annie (1877–1936). New Zealand stenographer, journalist, medical-health educator, social activist, and writer. Name variations: Ettie Annie Hornibrook. Born Feb 24, 1877, in Launceston, Tasmania, Australia; died Sept 17, 1936, in Rarotonga, New Zealand; dau. of William John Rout (ironmonger) and Catherine Frances (McKay) Rout; m. Frederick Hornibrook (physiotherapist), 1920. ❖ One of first stenographers for Supreme Court (1902), established own typing business (1904); became involved in labor movement (1907); established New Zealand Volunteer Sisterhood during WWI, and accompanied volunteers to Egypt to care for New Zealand soldiers (1916); when confronted with high rate of venereal disease, developed and sold prophylactic kits to soldiers (a program eventually adopted by New Zealand Expeditionary Force); wrote several books, including *Sex and Exercise, Safe Marriage* which was banned in New Zealand (1923). ❖ See also *Dictionary of New Zealand Biography* (Vol. 3).

ROUTLEDGE, Patricia (1929—). English actress. Born Katherine Patricia Routledge, Feb 17, 1929, in Birkenhead, Cheshire, England; dau. of Catherine and Isaac Routledge (haberdasher); attended Liverpool University; studied at Old Vic Theatre School in Bristol; never married; no children. ❖ Made stage debut at Liverpool Playhouse (1952), then had a long stage and tv career; won a Tony Award for Best Actress in a Musical for *Darling of the Day* (1967); appeared in title role in *The Duchess of Gerolstein* (1978) and as Queen Margaret in *Richard III* (1984); won an Olivier Award for Best Actress in a Musical for *Candide* (1988); probably best known for comedic turn as Hyacinth Bucket on tv series "Keeping Up Appearances" (1990–95); also appeared as Hetty Wainthropp in "Hetty Wainthropp Investigates" (1996–98). Awarded OBE (1993).

ROUX, Aline (1935—). French ballet dancer. Born Aug 22, 1935, in Brest, France; studied at University of Kansas. ❖ Trained at École

Normale Supérieure d'Education Physiques and with Karin Waehner, among others; formed her own troupe, Rythme et Structure (1969), for which she created several works; taught traditional American modern dance in Paris.

ROUX, Maria de (c. 1821–1849). *See Manning, Maria.*

ROUZINA, Olena. *See Ronzhina, Olena.*

ROVER, Constance (1910–2005). English historian. Born Dec 15, 1910, in Cumbria, England; died Feb 16, 2005; m. Frederick Rover (solicitor); children: Helen Self (historian). ❖ Originated the 1st university course in women's studies in England (1960s), at Northwestern Polytechnic, Kentish Town (now part of London Metropolitan University); also wrote *Women's Suffrage and Party Politics 1866–1914* (1967), a pioneering study, and *Love, Morals and the Feminists* (1970).

ROVERE, Claude della (1604–1648). *See Medici, Claudia de.*

ROVERE, Giulia della (fl. 16th c.). Duchess of Ferrara. Name variations: Giulia d'Este. Married Alfonso d'Este (1527–1587), duke of Ferrara; children: Alfonsino (1560–1578, who m. Marfisa d'Este); Cesare (1562–1628), duke of Ferrara (r. 1597), duke of Modena (r. 1597–1628). Cesare m. Virginia de Medici (Virginia d'Este).

ROVERE, Lucrezia della (1535–1598). *See Este, Lucrezia d'.*

ROVERE, Vittoria della (d. 1694). *See Medici, Vittoria de.*

ROWAN, Ellis (1848–1922). Australian botanical artist. Name variations: Marian Ellis Rowan. Born Marian Ellis Ryan, July 30, 1848, in Melbourne, Australia; died Oct 4, 1922; eldest of 7 children of Charles and Marian Ryan; paternal granddau. of Ellis Agar Hartley, illeg. dau. of King George IV and Ellis Agar, countess of Brandon (died 1789); tutored in oil painting by Marianne North (1880); m. Frederic Charles Rowan, Oct 23, 1873 (died 1892); children: 1 son. ❖ Illustrated many plants and animals found during explorations in New Guinea and Australia; traveled, painted, and exhibited (1873–93); exhibited at the London International Exhibition at Crystal Palace (1884) and at Melbourne's 1888 Centennial International Exhibition (awarded highest honors); met and collaborated with American botanist, Alice Lounsberry, on *A Guide to the Wild Flowers* (1899), *A Guide to the Trees* (1900) and *Southern Wild Flowers and Trees* (1901); returned to Australia (1905–06); exhibited more than 1,000 paintings at the Fine Arts Gallery in Sydney (Mar 1920); published *Flower Hunter in Queensland and New Zealand* (1898). Clients included Queen Victoria, who chose 3 paintings to be made into a screen (1895); over 900 paintings were purchased by the Australian federal government (1923) and are held at National Library of Australia, Canberra.

ROWAN, Marian Ellis (1848–1922). *See Rowan, Ellis.*

ROWBOTHAM, Sheila (1943—). British social historian and feminist. Born 1943 in Leeds, England; attended universities of Oxford and London. ❖ An important figure in British feminist politics, worked as a teacher in schools and tertiary institutions; became involved in Women's Liberation movement and socialist politics and was on editorial board of radical paper *Black Dwarf*; writings include *A New World for Women* (1971), *Woman, Resistance and Revolution* (1973), *Woman's Consciousness, Man's World* (1973), *Hidden from History: 300 Years of Women's Oppression and the Fight against it* (1973), (with Segal and Wainwright) *Beyond the Fragments: Feminism and the Making of Socialism* (1979), *Dreams and Dilemmas* (1983), *Women in Movement* (1993), *Women Encounter Technology: Changing Patterns of Employment in the Third World* (1995) and *Promise of a Dream: Remembering the Sixties* (2000).

ROWE, Elizabeth (c. 1814–1902). *See George, Elizabeth.*

ROWE, Elizabeth Singer (1674–1737). English poet and writer. Name variations: Elizabeth Singer. Born Elizabeth Singer, Sept 11, 1674, in Ilchester, Somerset; died in Frome, Somerset, England, Feb 20, 1737; dau. of Walter Singer (Nonconformist minister) and Elizabeth Portnell; m. Thomas Rowe (classical scholar and Nonconformist), 1710 (died 1715). ❖ Began writing poetry at early age; contributed some poems to *Athenian Mercury* (1694–95); published *Poems on Several Occasions: Written by Philomela* (1696), then 2 Latin translations in Tonson's *Poetic Miscellanies V* (1704); published most well-known and popular work, *Friendship in Death in Twenty Letters from the Dead to the Living* (1728), followed by another moralistic tome, *Letters Moral and Entertaining*, which appeared in 3 parts (1729–33); published a long poem in 8 books, *The History of Joseph*, which was based on the Biblical

story (1736); asked Isaac Watts to edit a collection of her prayers, *Devout Exercises of the Heart*, which merited several editions, one of which was published in US (1792); credited with being the 1st English poet to combine the qualities of romantic and religious verse. ❖ See also *Women in World History.*

ROWE, Marilyn (1946—). Australian ballet dancer. Name variations: Marilyn Rowe Cowden. Born Aug 20, 1946, in Sydney, NSW, Australia; attended Australian Ballet School; married an Australian Ballet stage director who was killed in plane crash, 1980; m. Peter Cowden (died); children: 2 sons. ❖ At 17, joined the company of the Australian Ballet (1964), where she performed for most of career; was promoted to principal (1969); was most acclaimed for performances in *Giselle, Don Quixote*, with Rudolph Nureyev (1973), *Romeo and Juliet*, with John Meehan, *Raymonda, Cinderella*, Balanchine's *Ballet Imperial*, and Prokovsky's *Anna Karenina*; also danced with Kelvin Coe and Gary Norman; had to cut short dancing career after husband died and she awaited birth of her first-born, Christopher; served as director of the Dancers Company at Australian Ballet School (1984–90), became director of Australian Ballet School (1999). Made OBE.

ROWE, Natalie (1904–1994). *See Hall, Natalie.*

ROWELL, Mary (1958—). American violinist. Name variations: The Silos. Born Sept 6, 1958, in Newport, VT. ❖ With Walter Salas-Humara and Bob Rupe, formed core of folk-rock band, the Silos (1985), considered trailblazers for alternative music. Silos' albums include *About Her Steps* (1985), *Hasta La Victoria* (1992) and *Susan Across the Ocean* (1994).

ROWLAND, Kelly (1981—). American singer. Name variations: Destiny's Child. Born Kelendria Rowland, Feb 11, 1981, in Houston, TX. ❖ As an original member of girl-group Destiny's Child (formed 1989), released hit singles "No, No, No," "The Writing's on the Wall," "Bills, Bills, Bills," "Say My Name," "Jumpin', Jumpin'," and "Independent Women, Part 1" (from film *Charlie's Angels* soundtrack). Albums with Destiny's Child include *Destiny's Child* (1998), *The Writing's on the Wall* (1999), and *Survivor* (2001).

ROWLANDS, Gena (1934—). American stage, tv, and screen actress. Born Virginia Cathryn Rowlands, June 19, 1934, in Cambria, WI; dau. of E.M. Rowlands (state assemblyman); m. John Cassavetes (actor-director), 1954 (died 1989); children: Nick Cassavetes (b. 1959, actor). ❖ Made Broadway debut as understudy for the lead in *The Seven Year Itch* (1952), eventually assuming the role; also starred in *Middle of the Night* (1956–57), among others; made screen debut in *The High Cost of Living* (1958), followed by *Lonely are the Brave, The Spiral Road, A Child is Waiting, Tony Rome, The Brink's Job, Tempest, Light of Day, Another Woman* and *Once Around*, among others; often appeared in films written and directed by husband, including *Faces, Minnie and Moskowitz* and *Love Streams*. Nominated for Oscars as Best Actress for *A Woman Under the Influence* (1974) and *Gloria* (1980); named Best Actress at Berlin Film Festival for *Opening Night* (1978); won Emmys for title role in "The Betty Ford Story" (1987) and "Face of a Stranger" (1991).

ROWLANDSON, Mary (c. 1635–after 1682). American colonial and captive. Born Mary White Rowlandson, c. 1635, in Somersetshire, England; died after 1682 in Wethersfield, Connecticut; dau. of John White and Joane West White; m. Reverend Joseph Rowlandson, in 1656; children: Joseph (b. 1661); Mary (b. 1665); Sarah (1669–1676). ❖ Colonial American whose memoirs of her years in captivity with the Narragansett tribe were published in 1682; as a child, traveled with Puritan family to the colony of Massachusetts; was wounded and taken captive with daughter by a party of Narragansett Indians during Native American uprising against the English colonists known as King Philip's War (1676); held for 3 months; daughter died. ❖ See also *The Captive: The True Story of the Captivity of Mrs. Mary Rowlandson* (American Eagle, 1987); and *Women in World History.*

ROWLING, J.K. (1965—). English children's writer. Name variations: Joanne Kathleen Rowling. Born Joanne Rowling (since she had only one given name, added Kathleen, her grandmother's name, when the publisher asked her to use initials on the first book), July 31, 1965, in Yate, near Bristol, England; dau. of Anne and Peter Rowling (engineer for Rolls Royce); read French and Classics at Exeter University; married Jorge Arantes (Portuguese tv journalist), Oct 16, 1992 (div. 1993); m. Neil Murray (anesthesiologist), Dec 26, 2001; children: (1st m.) Jessica Rowling Arantes (b. 1993); (2nd m.) David (b. 2003), Mackenzie (b. 2005). ❖ Author of the "Harry Potter" series, a publishing phenomenon, 1st worked for Amnesty International, researching human-rights abuses in French-speaking Africa, then taught English as a Foreign Language in Portugal; returned to UK, settling in Edinburgh (1994); began making notes for Harry Potter while on public assistance as a single mother; spent 6 years writing the 1st book and received 9 publishers' rejections before she introduced the Hogwarts School of Witchcraft and Wizardry in *Harry Potter and the Philosopher's Stone* (1997), published in US as *Harry Potter and the Sorcerer's Stone* (1998); followed this with *Harry Potter and the Chamber of Secrets* (1998) and *Harry Potter and the Prisoner of Azkaban* (1999); her *Harry Potter and the Goblin of Fire* (2000) had the biggest 1st printing in the history of trade publishing; *Harry Potter and the Half-Blood Prince* sold 6.9 million copies in US in 1st 24 hours on sale (2005). Awarded OBE.

ROWSON, Susanna (1762–1824). English-born novelist, essayist, poet, dramatist, lyricist, actress, and educator. Born Susanna Haswell on or about Feb 5, 1762, in Portsmouth, England; died in Boston, Massachusetts, Mar 2, 1824; dau. of William Haswell (British naval officer) and Susanna (Musgrave) Haswell; m. William Rowson, in 1786; no children. ❖ Bestselling novelist, was brought to America by father (1767); returned to England (1778); served as governess until publication of her 1st novel *Victoria* (1786); was author of the 1st bestselling novel in US history, *Charlotte Temple: A Tale of Truth* (London, 1791, Philadelphia, 1794); continued writing novels and joined a theatrical touring company with husband (1792); joined Philadelphia New Theater Co. (1793) and then Federal Street Theater in Boston (1796); retired from stage (1797); established a Young Ladies' Academy in Boston where she served as headmistress until her retirement (1822); also wrote 8 other didactic novels, 5 plays on patriotic themes, 2 vols. of poetry, and 6 pedagogical works on geography, history, religion and spelling. ❖ See also Elias Nason, *Memoir of Mrs. Susanna Rowson* (Munsell, 1876); Dorothy Weil, *In Defense of Women: Susanna Rowson (1762–1824)* (Pennsylvania U. Press, 1976); and *Women in World History.*

ROXANA. *Variant of Roxane.*

ROXANA (fl. 350 BCE). Macedonian noblewoman. One of seven wives of Philip II, king of Macedonia (r. 359–336 BCE); his other wives were Audata, Olympias, Meda, Nicesipolis, Philinna, and Cleopatra of Macedon.

ROXANE (c. 345–310 BCE). Bactrian warrior-princess. Name variations: Roxana; Roxané. Born c. 345 BCE; murdered in 310 BCE (some sources cite 311); dau. of Oxyartes, a Bactrian noble; m. Alexander III the Great (356–323 BCE), king of Macedonia (r. 336–323 BCE), in 327 BCE; children: Alexander IV, king of Macedonia. ❖ Was captured by Alexander III the Great, king of Macedonia, along with mother and father Oxyartes, who had been a participant in an uprising against Alexander (327 BCE); married Alexander and accompanied him to India where she delivered a child which died soon after its birth (326); her status was threatened when Alexander married (324) two additional wives (Statira III and Parysatis II); when Alexander died near Babylon (June 323), was again pregnant; to protect her child, connived with the Macedonian general, Perdiccas, to secretly murder both Statira and Parysatis; gave birth to Alexander IV (Sept 323), who would be championed by his grandmother Olympias; was murdered by Cassander, along with her son. ❖ See also *Women in World History.*

ROXELANA (c. 1504–1558). Ottoman empress. Name variations: Hurrem or Khurrem (Joyful or The Laughing One); Hurrem Sultana; Roxalana, Roxalena, Rossa, Roksoliana. Pronunciation: ROCKS-uh-LAN-ah. Born (probably) Aleksandra Lisowska c. 1504 in Rogatin, near Lvov; died April 15, 1558, in Constantinople; daughter (probably) of a Ruthenian priest; mother unknown; m. Suleiman or Suleyman the Magnificent, Ottoman sultan (r. 1520–1566), in 1530; children: sons Mehmed; Selim II, Ottoman sultan (r. 1566–1574); Beyazit or Beyazid or Bayezid (d. 1561), Jehangir; and daughter Mihrimah (1522–1575). ❖ Captured slave who became wife and consort of the sultan Suleiman, reinstated marriage among the Ottoman rulers, influenced husband's foreign and domestic policies, consolidated her power by wiping out rivals, and initiated a period of Ottoman history known as the "reign of women"; remained Suleiman's domestic and foreign advisor and closest confidante, while eliminating her eldest son Mustafa as heir to the throne, and paving the way for the ultimate succession of her own son, Selim. ❖ See also *Women in World History.*

ROXETTE. *See Fredriksson, Marie (1958—).*

ROXON, Lillian (1932–1973). Australian journalist and rock critic. Born Lillian Ropschitz, 1932, in Savona, Italy; died of a severe asthma attack in her New York apartment, Aug 10, 1973; attended University of Queensland and University of Sydney; never married; no children. ❖ With the rise of fascism, migrated to Australia with her Jewish family (1937), settling in Brisbane; family anglicized name to Roxon; began career writing for Sydney newspapers and contributed to tabloid magazine, *Weekend*; moved to NY (1959); was New York correspondent for *Sydney Morning Herald* (1962–72); began writing on pop music and the hippie movement (1960s) and is now considered one of the 1st journalists to write seriously about the rock scene; wrote rock's 1st encyclopedia (1969); a feminist, also wrote about the women's rights march in NY (1970); hosted a rock radio show (1971).

ROY, Arundhati (1961—). Indian novelist and screenwriter. Born Nov 24, 1961, in Shillong, Meghalaya, India; grew up in Aymanam, near Kerala; dau. of Mary Roy (Christian from Kerala and social activist) and Rajib Roy (Bengali Hindu tea planter); graduate of Delhi School of Architecture, 1981; m. Gerard Da Cunha (architect, div.); m. Pradip Krishen (filmmaker), 1993. ❖ Began career as an actress, starring in the film *Massey Sahib*; came to prominence with her 1st semi-autobiographical novel, the international bestseller *The God of Small Things* (1997), and was the 1st Indian citizen to win the Booker Prize; wrote screenplays for 2 Indian films directed by her husband: *In Which Annie Gives It Those Ones* and *Electric Moon*; an anti-nuclear activist, also wrote "The End of Imagination" which was published in her essay collection, *The Cost of Living.* Awarded Sydney Peace Prize (2004).

ROY, Gabrielle (1909–1983). French-Canadian writer. Born Mar 22, 1909, in St. Boniface, Manitoba; died July 13, 1983; dau. of Léon Roy and Mélina Roy; sister of Bernadette "Dédette" Roy (nun, died 1970); attended Winnipeg Normal Institute; m. Marcel Carbotte (physician), 1945. ❖ Traveled to Europe where she published several articles in a French magazine (1937); with war imminent, returned to Canada (1939), settling in Montreal; published 1st novel, *Bonheur d'occasion* (1945), which marked the beginning of a new era in French-Canadian literature, winning the French Prix Fémina (1947), as well as Canada's Governor-General's Award for its English translation *The Tin Flute*; published 2nd novel, *La Petite Poule d'Eau* (1950, *Where Nests the Water Hen*, 1951), followed by *Rue Deschambault* (1955), whose English translation *Street of Riches* also won Governor-General's Award (1957), as did final novel, *Ces enfants de ma vie* (*Children of My Heart*, 1978). ❖ See also *Enchantment and Sorrow: The Autobiography of Gabrielle Roy* (trans. by Patricia Claxton, Lester & Orpen Dennys, c. 1987); and *Women in World History.*

ROY, Julie (c. 1938—). American activist. Born c. 1938 in Port Huron, MI. ❖ Became 1st woman to successfully sue psychiatrist for inveigling her into sexual relationship under guise of therapy (1971); awarded compensatory damages of $250,000 and punitive damages of $100,000 in case against Dr. Renatus Hartogs in NY (1975), and Hartogs's appeal was turned down (1976); wrote with Lucy Freeman, *Betrayal* (1976). ❖ See also (tv movie) "Betrayal" (1978), starring Lesley Ann Warren and Rip Torn.

ROYALL, Anne (1769–1854). Colonial writer. Name variations: Anne Newport Royall. Born Anne Newport, June 11, 1769, near Baltimore, Maryland; died Oct 1, 1854, in Washington, DC; dau. of William Newport (farmer) and Mary Newport; m. William Royall (farmer who served in American Revolution), 1797 (died 1813); no children. ❖ One of the 1st women journalists in US, began traveling throughout the country and writing accounts of her trips in order to make a living; produced 5 books in 10 vols. about her travels, which are still considered important sources of information about America in that era: *Sketches of History, Life and Manners in the US* (1826), *The Black Book; or, A Continuation of Travels in the United States* (3 vols., 1828–29), *Mrs. Royall's Pennsylvania* (2 vols., 1829), *Mrs. Royall's Southern Tour* (3 vols., 1830–31), and *Letters from Alabama* (1830); also wrote a novel, *The Tennessean* (1827), and a play, *The Cabinet*; published *Paul Pry*, a weekly Washington, DC, paper featuring political gossip and her sharp-tongued comments (1831–36), followed by *The Huntress*, which she edited for nearly 20 years (1836–54). ❖ See also *Women in World History.*

ROYCE, Sarah (1819–1891). American pioneer and writer. Name variations: Sarah Eleanor Bayliss Royce. Born Sarah Eleanor Bayliss in Stratford-on-Avon, England, Mar 2, 1819; died in San Jose, California, 1891; dau. of Benjamin Bayliss (businessman) and Mary T. Bayliss;

educated at Albion Female Seminary in Rochester, NY; m. Josiah Royce, 1847 (died 1889); children: Mary, Hattie, Ruth and Josiah Royce. ❖ Wrote *A Frontier Lady: Recollections of the Gold Rush and Early California* (1932), an autobiographical account of her family's westward trek to California during the gold rush. ❖ See also *Women in World History*.

ROY DE CLOTTE LE BARILLIER, Berthe (1868–1927). French poet and novelist. Name variations: Berthe Le Barillier or Berthe-Corinne Le Barillier; (pseudonym) Jean Bertheroy. Born July 4, 1868 in Bordeaux, France; died 1927. ❖ Wrote about 50 novels, some gothic, some historical, some salacious, some modern; works include *Vibrations* (1888), *Cléopatre* (1891), *Ximénès* (1893), *La Danseuse de Pompéi* (1899), *Les Délices de Mantoue* (1906), and *Sybaris* (1907). Received 3 awards from Académie Française.

ROYDE-SMITH, Naomi Gwladys (c. 1880–1964). English writer. Name variations: Naomi Gwladys Royde Smith; Mrs. Ernest Milton. Born Naomi Gwladys Smith in Llanwrst, Wales, c. 1880 (some sources cite 1875 but birth date unknown); died July 28, 1964, in a London hospital; eldest dau. of Ann Daisy (Williams) Smith and Michael Holroyd Smith; educated at private school in Geneva, Switzerland; m. Ernest Milton (British actor), 1926. ❖ As the successful literary editor of the *Westminister Gazette* (1912–22) and a dashing host of literary gatherings, was enormously influential; adopted novelist Rose Macaulay as her protégée; wrote over 40 books, including many well-received novels which gently satirized class and gender, such as *The Tortoiseshell Cat* (1925) and *The Delicate Situation* (1931), a historical novel set in the Victorian 1840s; detailed her childhood in novel *In the Wood,* published in US as *Children in the Wood*. ❖ See also *Women in World History*.

ROYDEN, A. Maude (1876–1956). English preacher. Name variations: Agnes Maude Royden. Born 1876; died July 30, 1956; dau. of Sir Thomas Royden, 1st baronet of Frankby Hall; educated at Cheltenham Ladies' College and Lady Margaret Hall, Oxford; Glasgow University, Doctor of Divinity, 1931; m. George W.H. Shaw (cleric). ❖ Was the 1st woman to become a pastor of the Church of England (late 1910s), though she was never officially ordained; was assistant preacher at City Temple in London (1917–20); with Dr. Percy Dearmer, founded a nondenominational church called the Fellowship Services (1920); during 16-year association with this church, became Britain's 1st female Doctor of Divinity (1931); as a member of National Union of Women's Suffrage Societies, served as editor of the organization's journal, *Common Cause*; wrote a number of inspirational books, among them *The House and the Church* (1922), *The Church and Woman* (1924), *Here–and Hereafter* (1933), and the most well known, *A Threefold Cord* (1947), in which she wrote about her marriage. ❖ See also *Women in World History*.

ROYER, Clémence (1830–1902). French writer and activist. Name variations: Clemence Royer; Clémence-Auguste Royer; Lux. Pronunciation: Clay-MONCE Raw-yeah. Born Clémence-Auguste Royer, April 21, 1830, in Nantes, France; died in Paris, Feb 5, 1902; dau. of Augustin-René Royer (commissioned officer in the French army and entrepreneur) and Josephine-Gabrielle Andouard; partner of Pascal Duprat; children: son, René Duprat (b. 1866). ❖ Autodidact, philosopher, scientist, feminist, translator, and social critic whose works were alternately scorned, praised, and ignored; translated Charles Darwin's *Origin of Species,* with extensive introduction and footnotes (1862, 1866, 1870); wrote 5 books: *Théorie de l'impôt, ou la dîme sociale* (Theory of Taxation, or the Social Tithe, 1862), (novel) *Les Jumeaux d'Hellas* (The Twins of Hellas, 1864), *Origine de l'homme et des sociétés* (Origin of Man and Societies, 1869), *Le Bien et la loi morale: ethique et téléologie* (Goodness and Moral Law: Ethics and Teleology, 1881), and *Natura Rerum: la Constitution du monde, dynamique des atomes, nouveaux principes de philosophie naturelle* (The Nature of Things: the Constitution of the World, Energy of Atoms, and New Principles of Natural Philosophy, 1900); wrote for the feminist newspaper *La Fronde*; also wrote over 150 articles, reviews, and monographs ranging in subject matter from anthropology to economics to ethics to feminism to politics to various natural and social scientific disciplines; was the 1st woman member of the Société d'Anthropologie de Paris. Received Legion of Honor because of her services as a *"femme de lettres, écrivain scientifique"* (woman of letters and scientific writer, 1900). ❖ See also Joy Harvey, *"Almost a Man of Genius:" Clémence Royer, Feminism, and Nineteenth-Century Science* (Rutgers U. Press, 1996); Sara Miles, *Evolution and Natural Law in the Synthetic Science of Clémence Royer* (PhD dissertation, U. of Chicago, 1988); and *Women in World History*.

ROYLE, Selena (1904–1983). American actress. Born Nov 6, 1904, in New York, NY; died April 23, 1983, in Guadalajara, Mexico; dau. of Edwin Milton Royle (playwright) and Selena (Fetter) Royle; sister of Josephine Royle (actress); m. Earle Larrimore, 1932 (div. 1942); m. George Renavent (actor), 1948 (died 1969). ❖ On Broadway, appeared in *Lancelot and Elaine, Golden Days, Peer Gynt, She Stoops to Conquer, Merchant of Venice, When Ladies Meet* and *Young Mr. Disraeli,* among others; films include *Stage Door Canteen, The Sullivans, 30 Seconds over Tokyo, Mrs. Parkington, The Harvey Girls, Night and Day, Till the End of Time, The Courage of Lassie, Cass Timberlane, Joan of Arc, A Date with Judy, The Heiress, Come Fill the Cup* and *Murder Is My Beat*; during depression, founded the Actors Free Dinner Club with Elizabeth Beatty in Union Church.

ROYS, Elmina M. (1828–1898). See Roys-Gavitt, Elmina M.

ROYS-GAVITT, Elmina M. (1828–1898). American physician and magazine founder. Name variations: Elmina M. Roys Gavitt; Elmina M. Roys. Born Elmina M. Roys, Sept 8, 1828, in Fletcher, VT; died Aug 25, 1898; m. Rev. F.C. Gavitt, 1876. ❖ The 1st known woman physician of Toledo, Ohio, began career assisting her military surgeon brother, who was head of Maryland hospitals during the Civil War; graduated from the Woman's Medical College of Pennsylvania (1867); interned 2 years at the Clifton Springs Sanitarium in NY; established a Rochester, Minnesota, practice; moved to Toledo (1871); was the founder and 1st editor of the *Woman's Medical Journal* (1893–98), which became the *Medical Woman's Journal* and was published until 1952.

ROZANOVA, Olga (1886–1918). Russian artist. Name variations: Rosanova. Pronunciation: Roe-ZAHN-ova. Born Olga Vladimirovna Rozanova at Malenki, Vladimir Province, in 1886; died of diphtheria in Moscow, Nov 8, 1918; dau. of Vladimir Rozanov; attended Stroganov Institute, Moscow, 1904–10, Zvantseva School of Art, St. Petersburg, 1912–13; m. Alexei Kruchenykh (poet), 1916. ❖ Prominent Russian avant-garde painter who devoted final years to developing a form of art appropriate to the society created by the Bolshevik Revolution of 1917; moved to Moscow to study art (1904); exhibited works in St. Petersburg with Union of Youth (1910); moved from Moscow to St. Petersburg (1911); began to illustrate future husband's books (1912); wrote major manifesto on her artistic principles, "The Bases of the New Creation and the Reasons Why It is Misunderstood" (1913); exhibited paintings at "Free Futurist Exhibition" in Rome (1914); exhibited 1st non-objective painting (1915); helped organize Supremus group, adopted Suprematism, used collage technique for *Universal War* (1916); joined IZO and Proletkult (1918); posthumous exhibition of her work in Moscow (1919). Major works include *The Poet* (1912), *Factory and Bridge* (1912), *Dissonance, Man in the Street* (1913), *Nonobjective Composition* (1914), *Workbox* (1915) and *Green Stripe* (1917). ❖ See also *Women in World History*.

ROZANSKA, Renata (1969—). See Mauer, Renata.

ROZEANU, Angelica (1921–2006). Romanian table tennis player. Name variations: Angelica Adelstein-Rozeanu. Born Angelica Adelstein, Oct 15, 1921, in Bucharest, Romania; died Feb 21, 2006, in Haifa, Israel; married. ❖ One of the greatest female table-tennis players in history, won her 1st Hungarian national championship in 1936 and went on to win every year until 1957, excluding the war years (1940–45); won the Hungarian Open (1938); was denied passport to take part in World championships in London (1938), by strongly anti-Semitic government; won 17 World titles, including 6 successive World singles championships (1950–55), 3 World women's doubles titles (1953–55), 3 World mixed doubles crowns (1951–53) and helped win the Corbillon Cup; served as president of Romanian Table Tennis Commission (1950–60); moved to Israel (1960) and won Maccabiah Games Table Tennis championship (1961); was ranked #1 in the world for several years. Named Merited Master of Sport, Romania's highest sports distinction; inducted into International Jewish Hall of Fame (1981).

ROZEIRA DE SOUZA SILVA, Cristiane (1985—). Brazilian soccer player. Name variations: Cristiane. Born May 15, 1985, in Brazil. ❖ Forward, won a team silver medal at Athens Olympics (2004).

ROZENGOLTS-LEVINA, Eva (1898–1975). Russian artist. Name variations: Eva Levina-Rozengolts; Eva Rozengolts. Born Eva Rozengolts in Vitebsk, Russia, 1898; died in Moscow, 1975; dau. of Klara Frumkin Rozengolts (artist); studied with sculptor Anna Golubkina and painter Robert Falk; married a man named Levine; children: Elena Levina (b. around 1928, geologist). ❖ Became a hospital nurse, and later studied at School of Dentistry at Tomsk University; during Russian Revolution, nursed dying Red Army soldiers on the front during a typhus epidemic; completed art training (1925) and received permission from Soviet authorities to travel abroad; began working on smaller canvases with pastels (1930s); as she became more introspective throughout this decade, worked more on cityscapes, such as *Chimneys* and *Moscow River at Twilight*; was exiled to Siberia (1949–55), for being Jewish and the half-sister of Arkady Rozengolts, who had been executed during a Stalinist purge (1938); spent the rest of her life distilling into art her sufferings in Siberia and the suffering she had seen around her, creating 227 drawings in 7 series. Following the collapse of the Soviet Union, the 1st exhibit devoted to her art opened at State Tretiakov Gallery (1996). ❖ See also *Women in World History.*

ROZGON, Nadezhda (1952—). Soviet rower. Born Nov 15, 1952, in USSR. ❖ At Montreal Olympics, won a silver medal in coxed eights (1976).

ROZHANSKAYA, Mariam (1928—). Russian historian of mathematics and mechanics. Name variations: Mariam Mikhaylovna Rozhanskaia. Born July 28, 1928, in Shigry, near Kursk, Russia; moved to Moscow with mother when young; m. Vladimir Nikolaevich Rozhansky (professor and physicist). ❖ Noted math historian, was hired by S.P. Tolstov, director of Institute of Ethnography of the Academy of Sciences, to research the ancient astronomer and mathematician al-Biruni; with B.A. Rosenfeld and P.G. Bulgakov, published an annotated translation of al-Biruni's astronomical encyclopaedia, *Canon of Mas'ud* (1973–76); joined (1967) and later served as a senior fellow of Institute for History of Science and Technology at USSR's Academy of Sciences; with Rosenfeld and Z.K. Sokolovskaya, published an al-Biruni biography (1973); published an annotated translation of medieval Muslim scholar al-Khazani's *The Book of the Balance of Wisdom* (1983); became a corresponding member of Académie Internationale d'Histoire des Sciences (1991) and full member (1997).

ROZSNYOI, Katalin (1942—). Hungarian kayaker. Born Nov 20, 1942, in Hungary. ❖ At Mexico City Olympics, won a silver medal in K2 500 meters (1968).

RU ZHIJUAN (1925—). Chinese short-story writer. Born 1925; lived in Shanghai, China. ❖ Joined the drama troupe of the Communist army (1940s) and drew on experiences for many of her stories, which have been collected into 10 volumes; best known for "Lilies."

RUANO PASCUAL, Virginia (1973—). Spanish tennis player. Name variations: Virginia Ruano. Born Sept 21, 1973, in Madrid, Spain; sister of Juan Ramon Ruano (tennis player and coach). ❖ With Conchita Martinez, won the silver medal for doubles at Athens Olympics (2004); turned professional (1992).

RUAWAHINE (?–1855). *See Faulkner, Ruawahine Irihapeti.*

RUBASHOV, Rachel (1888–1975). *See Katznelson-Shazar, Rachel.*

RUBENS, Alma (1897–1931). American actress. Name variations: billed as Alma Reuben or Reubens during early career. Born Alma Smith in San Francisco, California, Feb 19, 1897; died Jan 22, 1931, in Los Angeles, CA; m. Franklyn Farnum (actor), 1918 (div.); m. Daniel Carson Goodman (director, producer, author and physician), 1923 (div. 1925); m. Ricardo Cortez (actor), 1926. ❖ A stunning star of over 40 silent pictures, made film debut in *The Half-Breed* (1916) and became a screen regular soon after; appeared in such well-known films as *Intolerance* (1916), *Humoresque* (1920), and an adaptation of Edna Ferber's *Show Boat* (1929), in which she played Julie; died, age 34, from complications arising from an addiction to heroin. ❖ See also *Women in World History.*

RUBENS, Bernice (1928–2004). Welsh novelist and short-story writer. Born Bernice Ruth Rubens, July 26, 1928, in Cardiff, Wales; died Oct 13, 2004; dau. of Eli Rubens and Dorothy Cohen; attended University of Wales; m. Rudi Nassbauer (wine merchant), 1947 (div., died 1997); children: Sharon and Rebecca. ❖ Taught English; traveled widely making documentary films for organizations, including the UN, and won American Blue Ribbon for documentary film *Stress* (1968); began writing at age 30; won Booker Prize for novel *The Elected Member* (1970), pub. in US as *Chosen People,* and was Booker runner-up for *A Five Year Sentence* (1978); saw 2 of her novels filmed: *Madame Sousatzka* (1962), with Shirley MacLaine, and *I Sent a Letter to My Love* (1975), with Simone Signoret; her *Mr. Wakefield's Crusade* became a BBC-TV miniseries; also wrote *Set on Edge* (1960), *Go Tell the Lemming* (1973),

The Ponsonby Post (1977), *Spring Sonata* (1979), *Brothers* (1983), *Our Father* (1987), *Kingdom Come* (1990), *Mother Russia* (1992), *The Waiting Game* (1997), *I, Dreyfus* (1999), *Nine Lives* (2002), and *The Sergeant's Tale* (2003), among others.

RUBENSTEIN, Blanche (c. 1897–1969). American entrepreneur and resistance fighter. Name variations: Blanche Rubenstein Auzello; acted briefly as Blanche Ross. Born in New York, NY, c. 1897; killed by husband in Paris, France, May 29, 1969 (he then killed himself); dau. of Isaac Rubenstein and Sara Rubenstein (German-Jewish émigrés); m. Claude Auzello (hotel manager), c. 1924; no children. ❖ Ran the famed Ritz Hotel in Paris with husband (1924–69); assisted the French Resistance during the Nazi occupation; was caught and imprisoned several times. ❖ See also Samuel Marx, *Queen of the Ritz* (Bobbs-Merrill, 1978); and *Women in World History.*

RUBENSTEIN, Ida (1880–1960). *See Rubinstein, Ida.*

RUBIN, Barbara Jo (1949—). American jockey. Born Nov 21, 1949, in Highland, IL. ❖ Was the 1st female jockey to defeat male riders in a major race in Florida (1969); won many races and was a media star for 4 years before injury forced retirement. ❖ See also *Women in World History.*

RUBIN, Chandra (1976—). African-American tennis player. Born Feb 18, 1976, in Lafayette, LA. ❖ Won doubles championship at Australian Open (1996) and was runner-up at US Open (1999).

RUBIN, Vera (1911–1985). American cultural anthropologist. Name variations: Vera Dourmashkin Rubin. Born Vera Dourmashkin, Aug 6, 1911, in Moscow, Russia; came to US at age 1; died 1985; dau. of Jennie Frankel Dourmashkin (died 1911) and Elias Dourmashkin (journalist); graduate of New York University in French literature, 1930; Columbia University, PhD, 1952; m. Samuel Rubin (businessman); children: Cora and Reed Rubin. ❖ Studied with Ruth Benedict, Margaret Mead and Julian Steward at Columbia University; founded Research Institute for the Study of Man (RISM, 1955), of which she served as director for 30 years; developed anthropological study of English-speaking Caribbean; helped to make fieldwork by women possible through RISM scholarships.

RUBIN, Vera Cooper (1928—). American astronomer. Name variations: Vera Cooper; Vera C. Rubin. Born Vera Cooper, July 23, 1928, in Philadelphia, PA; dau. of Philip and Rose Cooper; Vassar College, BS, 1948; Cornell University, MA, 1951; Georgetown University, PhD, 1954; m. Robert Rubin (physicist), 1948; children: 4. ❖ Studied astronomy at Vassar, the motion of galaxies at Cornell, and used mathematics to research the distribution of galaxies at Georgetown; presented motion of galaxies theories at an American Astronomical Society meeting where ideas were dismissed, only to be recognized later; was on the faculty at Georgetown University for 11 years; joined the Carnegie Institution of Washington for the Department of Terrestrial Magnetism; contributed research leading to the discovery of "dark matter" or invisible mass in the universe; elected to National Academy of Science, presented National Medal of Science (1993), was 1st woman awarded Gold Medal of London's Royal Astronomical Society (1996) since Caroline Herschel, and received Bruce medal (2003).

RUBINSTEIN, Helena (1870–1965). Polish-born American entrepreneur. Born Dec 25, 1870, in Cracow, Poland; died April 1, 1965, in New York, NY; dau. of Horace Rubinstein (egg merchant) and Augusta (Silberfeld) Rubinstein; sister of Ceska Rubinstein; aunt of Mala Rubinstein; attended University of Cracow and briefly studied medicine in Switzerland; studied dermatology in Paris, Vienna and London (1908); m. Edward Titus (journalist and founder of Black Mannequin Press), 1908 (div. 1937 or 1938); m. Artchil Gourielli-Tchkonia (Russian prince), 1938 (died 1956); children: (1st m.) Roy (b. 1909), Horace (1912–1958). ❖ Founder of the Helena Rubinstein cosmetics empire, moved to Australia where she opened a small beauty shop in Melbourne; set up a successful beauty salon in London with her "Creme Valaze" as the founding product (1908); married and moved to Greenwich, CT (1914); built salons in San Francisco, Boston and Philadelphia, in addition to selling her wares in department stores; returned to Paris (1918) and became enmeshed in the art world; beyond innovations in the marketing of cosmetics and beauty treatments, also initiated changes in the development of cosmetics themselves; championed the use of silk in cosmetics and sold the 1st tinted face powder and foundation; also developed various medicated creams and waterproof mascara; founded Helena Rubinstein Pavilion of Contemporary Art in

Tel Aviv and Helena Rubinstein Foundation to provide funds to health organizations, medical research, and rehabilitation. ❖ See also autobiography, *My Life for Beauty* (1964); Patrick O'Higgins, *Madame: An Intimate Biography of Helena Rubinstein* (Viking, 1971); and *Women in World History.*

RUBINSTEIN, Ida (1880–1960). Russian ballerina. Name variations: Ida Rubenstein. Born of Russian-Jewish parentage in St. Petersburg, Russia, Sept 21, 1880 (some sources cite 1875, 1883 and 1885) in St. Petersburg, Russia; died Sept 20, 1960, in Venice; of Russian-Jewish parentage; studied with Michel Fokine. ❖ Made debut (1907), in a private performance of *Salomé,* choreographed by Fokine; made Paris debut in premiere season of Diaghilev's Ballets Russes, dancing title role in Fokine's *Cléopâtre* (1909); danced Queen Zobeide to Bronislava Nijinska's Golden Slave in Fokine's *Schéhérazade* (1910) and became the rage of Paris; stayed with Ballets Russes, while also financially supporting the world of ballet and other principal artists; commissioned Ravel to write "Bolero" for a Fokine ballet; also commissioned Debussy to write the score for d'Annunzio's *Le Martyre de Saint Sébastien* (*The Martyrdom of Saint Sebastian*), and played the title role; after leaving Ballets Russes (1915), formed her own company and hired Vaslav Nijinsky and Leonide Massine to direct and choreograph; made final appearance in title role of *Orphée* in Paris (1928). ❖ See also Vicki Woolf, *Dancing in the Vortex: The Story of Ida Rubinstein* (2001).

RUBINSTEIN, Mala (1905–1999). Polish-born cosmetics executive. Name variations: Mala Kolin; Mala Rubinstein Silson. Born Mala Kolin in Cracow, Poland, Dec 31, 1905; died July 1999 in New York, NY; niece of Helena Rubinstein (1870–1965); sister of Oscar Kolin (chair of Helena Rubinstein, Inc.); m. Victor Silson. ❖ At 18, moved to Paris to learn the cosmetics business from her aunt Helena Rubinstein; worked at the company (1920s–70s) until its sale to L'Oréal; as vice president in charge of creative services, wrote several books on beauty. ❖ See also *Women in World History.*

RUBINSTEIN, Renate (1929–1990). Dutch columnist, essayist and travel writer. Name variations: Renate Ida Rubenstein; (pseudonym) Tamar. Born Nov 16, 1929, in Berlin, Germany; died Nov 23, 1990, in Amsterdam, Netherlands. ❖ Fled Germany with family (1935), but Jewish father was arrested in Netherlands at start of German occupation; spent some years in Israel; known for taking bold stands on issues, including nuclear power and feminism, began writing a weekly magazine column in Amsterdam (1962); works include *Namens Tamar* (1964), *Tamarkolommen en andere berichten* (1973), *Was getekend Tamar* (1977), *Niks te verliezen en toch bang* (1978), *Twee eendjes en wat brood* (1981), *Liefst verliefd* (1983), *Toekomstmuziek* (1986) and *Wat vliegt tijd* (1992). ❖ See also memoir (in Dutch) *Mijn beter ik* (My Better Self, 1991), about her secret liaison with Dutch writer Simon Carmiggelt.

RUBLEVSKA, Jelena (1976—). Latvian pentathlete. Born Mar 23, 1976, in Riga, Latvia. ❖ Placed 1st in over World Cup indiv. ranking (2002); won silver medal at Athens Olympics (2004).

RUBY, Karine (1978—). French snowboarder. Born April 1, 1978, in Chamonix, France. ❖ Won 6 giant slalom races in succession (1998); at Nagano, won the 1st gold medal ever awarded for women's giant slalom snowboarding at Winter Olympics (1998), with a 2-run time of 2:17.34; won a silver medal for giant parallel slalom at Salt Lake City (2002); in 7 World Cup seasons, won 27 giant slalom and parallel giant slalom races; retired from competition (2002).

RUCK, Berta (1878–1978). British novelist and illustrator. Name variations: Amy Roberta Ruck; Mrs. Oliver Onions. Born Amy Roberta Ruck in Murree, India, in 1878; died in Aberdovey, Merioneth, Wales, Aug 11, 1978; dau. of Arthur Ashley Ruck (British army officer and later chief constable) and Elizabeth Eleanor D'Arcy; attended Lambeth School of Art, Slade School of Art, and art college in Paris; m. George Oliver (who wrote as Oliver Onions), in 1909; children: 2 sons. ❖ At 2, moved with family to Wales; began career illustrating stories in *Idler* and *Jabberwock;* contributed stories to such magazines as *Home Chat;* published *His Official Fiancée* (1914), which was successful in Britain and US and set the stage for her long career as a novelist; published up to 3 books a year over next 50-odd years; also wrote several autobiographical books, including *A Story-Teller Tells the Truth* (1935), *A Smile for the Past* (1959), *A Trickle of Welsh Blood* (1967), *An Asset to Wales* (1970) and *Ancestral Voices* (1972). ❖ See also *Women in World History.*

RÜCKER, Anja (1972—). German runner. Name variations: Rucker or Ruecker. Born Dec 20, 1972, in Lobenstein, Germany. ❖ Won a bronze medal for the 4 x 400-meter relay at Atlanta Olympics (1996).

RUCKER, Elizabeth (1911–1964). See Barkley, Jane Hadley.

RÜCKES, Anette (1951—). See Rueckes, Anette.

RUDASNE-ANTAL, Marta (1937—). Hungarian track-and-field athlete. Name variations: Marta Antal. Born Feb 14, 1937, in Hungary. ❖ At Tokyo Olympics, won a silver medal in the javelin throw (1964).

RUDDINS, Kimberly (1963—). American volleyball player. Name variations: Kim Ruddins. Born Sept 1963; University of Southern California, BS, 1987. ❖ At Los Angeles Olympics, won a silver medal in team competition (1984).

RUDDOCK, Joan (1943—). Welsh anti-nuclear activist, politician and member of Parliament. Born Joan Mary Anthony, Dec 28, 1943, in Pontypool, Wales; attended Imperial College; m. Keith Ruddock, 1963 (sep 1990, died 1996). ❖ Worked for Shelter, the national campaign for the homeless (1968–73); was director for an Oxford housing aid center; joined the Manpower Services Commission (1977); chaired the Campaign for Nuclear Disarmament (CND, 1981–87); representing Labour, was elected to House of Commons for Lewisham Deptford (1987) and quickly became a member of the Opposition Front Bench; appointed the 1st full-time minister for Women (1997); reelected (1992, 1997, 2001, 2005); wrote *The CND Story* (1983) and *Voices for One World* (1988).

RUDEL-ZEYNEK, Olga (1871–1948). Austrian politician and journalist. Name variations: Zeynick or Zeyneck. Born Olga von Zeynek, Jan 28, 1871, in Olmütz, Czechoslovakia, into a family of authors; died Aug 25, 1948, in Graz. ❖ Moved to Graz (1911); was a suffragist; wrote for women's newspapers and the Catholic press; as a member of the Christian Socialist Party, was elected to the Landtag (1919), then the Upper House (1927); was a presiding officer of the Bundesrat (Austrian Parliament, Dec 1, 1927–May 31, 1928 and June 1, 1932–Nov 30, 1932).

RUDISHAUSER, Corrie (1973—). American snowboarder. Born May 25, 1973, in Ashland, OR. ❖ Competed in Halfpipe, Boardercross, and Big Air events; received silver medal in Snowboarder X at X Games (Winter 1998); 1st-place finishes include Vegetate, Mt. Hood, OR, in Slopestyle (1998), ESPN/Airwalk Freeride, Sierra at Tahoe, Lake Tahoe, in Freeride (1998), and AST, Big Bear Lake, CA, in Big Air (2001).

RUDKIN, Margaret (1897–1967). American entrepreneur. Born Margaret Fogarty, Sept 14, 1897, in New York, NY; died June 1, 1967, in New Haven, Connecticut; dau. of Joseph I. Fogarty and Margaret (Healy) Fogarty; m. Henry Albert Rudkin (stockbroker), April 8, 1923 (died 1966); children: Henry Jr. (b. 1924); William (b. 1926); Mark (b. 1929). ❖ With husband, bought 125 acres near Fairfield, Connecticut, built a mansion in the Tudor style, and called it Pepperidge Farm (1920s); during Depression, began devising ways to make money at home and baked bread to provide additive-free slices for son Mark, who suffered from asthma; perfecting a recipe for stone-ground whole wheat bread, sold 1st batch of loaves to a grocer in Fairfield (Aug 1937); turned Pepperidge Farm into a major firm (1940s–50s); oversaw the daily operations of the bakery as president, while husband handled finances and marketing; sold the business to Campbell Soup Co. (1960); continued to run Pepperidge Farm, and was also a director of Campbell Soup; wrote the bestselling *The Margaret Rudkin Pepperidge Farm Cookbook* (1963). ❖ See also *Women in World History.*

RUDKO, Galina (1931—). See Shamray-Rudko, Galina.

RUDKOVSKAYA, Yelena (1973—). Soviet swimmer. Born April 21, 1973, in USSR. ❖ At Barcelona Olympics, won a bronze medal in the 4 x 100-meter medley relay and a gold medal in the 100-meter breaststroke (1992).

RUDMAN, Annie (1844–1928). New Zealand Salvation Army officer and social worker. Name variations: Annie Robertson. Born Annie Robertson, Mar 23, 1844, in Hertfordshire, England; died Aug 15, 1928, in New Zealand; dau. of David and Ann Robertson; m. Henry Rudman (tanner), 1865; children: 7. ❖ Immigrated to New Zealand with family (1857); became one of 1st converts when Salvation Army met in Wellington (1883); pioneered Salvation Army's social work by opening her home to reformed prostitutes and aiding unmarried expectant mothers. ❖ See also *Dictionary of New Zealand Biography* (Vol. 2).

RUDNER, Sara (1944—). American postmodern dancer. Born 1944 in Brooklyn, NY; Barnard College, BA, 1964. ❧ Trained in ballet as well as modern-dance technique; joined company of Paul Sanasardo, where she created roles in his *Excursions, The Animal's Eye,* and *Fatal Birds* (1964–66); danced with Twyla Tharp Dance Co., creating roles in most of Tharp's works, among them *Re-moves, One Two Three* (1966), *Generation* (1968), *The Bix Pieces* (1971), *Deuce Coupe I* (1973), and in the film *Hair* (1979); danced for short period with Pilobolus and Lar Lubovitch (1975–76); choreographed numerous works for own company, the Sara Rudner Performance Ensemble (1976–82), as well as for Lubovitch's troupe; became chair of dance department at Sarah Lawrence College (1999).

RUDOLPH, Renate (1949—). East German handball player. Born Nov 24, 1949, in East Germany. ❧ At Moscow Olympics, won a bronze medal in team competition (1980).

RUDOLPH, Wilma (1940–1994). African-American track-and-field champion. Name variations: (nickname) Skeeter. Born Wilma Glodean Rudolph, June 23, 1940, in St. Bethlehem, TN; died Nov 12, 1994, at home in Brentwood, TN, of brain cancer; Tennessee State University, BA, 1963; m. William Ward, Oct 14, 1961 (div. 1962); m. Robert Eldrige, 1963 (div. 1976). ❧ As a member of the famed Tennessee Tigerbelles, became youngest member of US women's track-and-field team (1956); won a bronze medal in 400-meter relay at Melbourne Olympics (1956); at Rome, won gold medals in the 100 meters, 200 meters, and 400-meter relay (1960), the 1st American woman to win 3 gold medals at 1 Olympics; retired (1962), becoming a teacher and speaker. Named Associated Press' Athlete of the Year (1960, 1961); won European Sportswriters' Association award for Most Outstanding Athlete of the Year (1960); received Babe Didrickson Zaharias Trophy (1960) and James E. Sullivan Award (1961); won Women's Sports Foundation's America's Greatest Women Athletes' award (1984); received National Collegiate Athletic Association's Silver Anniversary Award (1990); inducted into Black Sports Hall of Fame (1973), National Track and Field Hall of Fame (1974), and US Olympics Hall of Fame (1978); received the 1st National Sports Award (presented by President Bill Clinton, 1993); following her death, US Olympics Committee established the Wilma Rudolph Scholarship Fund (1994). ❧ See also autobiography *Wilma: The Story of Wilma Rudolph* (Signet, 1977), Linda Jacobs, *Wilma Rudolph: Run for Glory* (EMC, 1975), and "Wilma: The Story of Wilma Rudolph" (tv movie), starring Cicely Tyson and Shirley Jo Finney (1977); and *Women in World History.*

RUDOVSKAYA, Lyubov (1950—). Soviet volleyball player. Born Nov 1950 in USSR. ❧ At Montreal Olympics, won a silver medal in team competition (1976).

RUE, Rosemary (1928–2004). English physician. Name variations: Dame Rosemary Rue. Born Elsie Rosemary Laurence, June 14, 1928, in Hutton, Essex, England; died Dec 24, 2004; attended Oxford University Medical School; London University, bachelor of medicine and bachelor of surgery, 1951; m. Roger Rue (RAF pilot), 1950 (div.); children: Randalph and Rolf. ❧ Overcame paralytic polio to help other women balance their careers in medicine with their family lives; as regional medical officer for Oxford health authority (1973–84), then regional general manager (1984–88), opened career opportunities for women doctors by allowing them to work part-time while training to be specialists, an idea that evolved into the flexible training scheme now in use throughout Britain; was president of the Women's Medical Federation (1982–83). Awarded DBE (1989).

RUEBSAM, Dagmar (1962—). See *Neubauer-Ruebsam, Dagmar.*

RUECKER, Anja (1972—). See *Rücker, Anja.*

RUECKES, Anette (1951—). West German runner. Name variations: Anette Rückes. Born Dec 19, 1951, in West Germany. ❧ At Munich Olympics, won a bronze medal in 4 x 400-meter relay (1972).

RUEDA, Eva (1971—). Spanish gymnast. Born Sept 13, 1971, in Madrid, Spain. ❧ Won Blume Memorial and Ibero-American championships (1988), Spanish championships (1989); won a bronze medal for vault at European championships (1990) and a silver for vault at World championships (1990).

RÜEGG, Annelise (1879–1934). Swiss pacifist and travel writer. Name variations: Annelise Ruegg or Rueegg. Born 1879 in Switzerland; died 1934; married Alexander Alekhine (1892–1946, world chess champion), Mar 15, 1921 (he left her soon after). ❧ Traveled widely and worked in many countries, including Russia, working as a maid, waitress and nurse; was a pacifist and an activist in the women's movement; wrote the autobiographical *Erlebnisse einer Serviertochter* (Experiences of a Waitress, 1914) and *Im Kriege durch die Welt* (Through the World in Wartime, 1918).

RUEGG, Yvonne. Swiss Alpine skier. Name variations: Yvonne Rüegg. Born in Switzerland. ❧ Won a gold medal for giant slalom at Squaw Valley Olympics (1960).

RUEHLE, Heide (1948—). See *Rühle, Heide.*

RUEHN, Melita (1965—). Romanian gymnast. Name variations: Melita Ruhn or Rühn. Born April 19, 1965, in Romania. ❧ at World championships, won a gold medal in team all-around and bronze medals in all-around and floor exercises (1979); at Moscow Olympics, won bronze medals in vault and uneven bars and a silver medal in team all-around (1980).

RUEHROLD, Ute. See *Rührold, Ute.*

RUETHER, Rosemary (1936—). American theologian. Born Rosemary Radford, 1935, in Minneapolis, Minnesota; Scripps College, BA in philosophy, 1958; Claremont Graduate School, MA, 1960, PhD, 1965; m. Herman J. Ruether (political scientist and cultural historian); children: Rebecca, David and Mimi. ❧ Pioneer Christian feminist theologian, taught at Garrett-Evangelical Theological Seminary (1976–2000), focusing on the interrelation between Christian theology and history and social justice issues, including sexism, racism, poverty, militarism, ecology and interfaith relations; joined staff at Pacific School of Religion (2000); wrote extensively on women and theological issues in such books as *Sexism and God-Talk: Toward a Feminist Theology* (1983), *Woman-Church: Theology and Practice of Feminist Liturgical Communities* (1986), *Contemporary Catholicism* (1987), *The Wrath of Jonah: The Crisis of Religious Nationalism in the Israeli-Palestinian Conflict* (1989), *Gaia and God: An Ecofeminist Theology of Earth Healing* (1992), *Women Healing Earth* (1996), *Gender and Redemption* (1997), *Christianity and Ecology* (2000), *Visionary Women: Three Medieval Mystics* (2001) and *Goddesses and the Divine Feminine* (2005); frequent contributor to *National Catholic Reporter* and *Sojourners*; on the board of Friends of Sabeel and Catholics for Free Choice.

RUFF, Candace (1946—). See *Pert, Candace B.*

RUFFIN, Josephine St. Pierre (1842–1924). African-American civic leader and reformer. Born Josephine St. Pierre in Boston, Massachusetts, Aug 31, 1842; died in Boston, Mar 13, 1924; dau. of John St. Pierre (founder of the Zion Church in Boston) and Elizabeth (Menhenick) St. Pierre; educated at Bowdoin School; m. George Lewis Ruffin (1st black municipal judge in Boston), 1858 (died 1886); children: Hubert St. Pierre Ruffin; Florida Yates Ridley; Stanley Ruffin; George Lewis Ruffin; Robert Ruffin (died in infancy). ❧ Edited a black newspaper, the weekly *Boston Courant,* and was a member of New England Women's Press Association; served on executive board of Massachusetts Moral Education Association; with daughter Florida, co-founded the Woman's Era Club (1893) and the club's monthly illustrated magazine, *Woman's Era,* the 1st periodical owned, published and managed by black women in the US; was also a co-founder of National Federation of Afro-American Women (NFAAW); was one of the 56 charter members of the NAACP. ❧ See also *Women in World History.*

RUGGIERO, Angela (1980—). American ice-hockey player. Born Jan 3, 1980, in Simi Valley, CA; attended Harvard University. ❧ Won a team gold medal at Nagano (1998), the 1st Olympics to feature women's ice hockey; won team silver medals at World championships (1997, 1999, 2000, 2001); won a team silver medal at Salt Lake City Olympics (2002) and a team bronze medal at Torino Olympics (2006). ❧ See also Mary Turco, *Crashing the Net* (HarperCollins, 1999); and *Women in World History.*

RÜHLE, Heide (1948—). German politician. Name variations: Heide Ruehle. Born Nov 5, 1948, in Heilbronn, Germany. ❧ Served as chair of the Greens in Baden–Württemberg (1987–90), speaker of the Federal Executive (1990–91), and political affairs officer (1991–98); representing Group of the Greens/European Free Alliance, elected to 5th European Parliament (1999–2004).

RÜHROLD, Ute. East German luge athlete. Name variations: Ruhrold or Ruehrold. Born in East Germany. ❧ Won a silver medal for singles at Sapporo Olympics (1972) and Innsbruck Olympics (1976).

RÜHN, Melita (1965—). *See Ruehn, Melita.*

RUICK, Barbara (1930–1974). American actress. Born Dec 23, 1930, in Pasadena, CA; died Mar 3, 1974, in Reno, Nevada; dau. of Lurene Tuttle (actress); m. Robert Horton (actor), 1953 (div. 1956); m. John Williams (composer); children: Joseph Williams (lead singer of Toto and voice of Simba in Disney's *The Lion King*), Mark Towner Williams (music producer and drummer for Air Supply), and a daughter. ❖ Actress and singer on radio, tv and in films, including *Invitation, You for Me, Above and Beyond* and *Carousel.*

RUICK, Lurene (1906–1986). *See Tuttle, Lurene.*

RUILLY, Macette de (d. 1391). French woman. Married Hennequin de Ruilly; burned at the stake, 1391. ❖ Tried as an accomplice of Jehenne de Brigue for witchcraft (1390). ❖ See also *Women in World History.*

RUIZ, Brunhilda (1936—). American ballet dancer. Born 1936 in Puerto Rico. ❖ Danced as charter member of Robert Joffrey Ballet (1955), later New York City Opera Ballet (1957–61) and City Center Joffrey Ballet (1968–72); created roles for Joffrey's *Le Bal Masque* (1954), *Harpsichord Concerto in D Minor* (1955), *Pierrot Lunaire* (1955) and *Gamelan* (1962); danced with Harkness Ballet (1964–68) where she was featured in Butler's *A Season in Hell* and *Sebastian*; appeared on PBS in "El Banquiné de Angeliton Negros" (1977).

RUIZ, Rosie (c. 1954—). Cuban hoaxer. Name variations: Rosie M. Vivas. Born c. 1954 in Havana, Cuba; grew up in Florida; attended University of Nebraska; lived in NY. ❖ Faked running the Boston Marathon by starting the race, taking a subway shortcut, then reentering the race at the last half-mile (1980). Following Boston, evidence began to surface that she had also faked running the earlier NY marathon (Susan Morrow, a *New York Times* photographer, recalled having ridden the subway with Ruiz to the finish line).

RUIZ, Tracie (1963—). American synchronized swimmer. Name variations: Tracie Ruiz-Conforto. Born Feb 4, 1963, in Honolulu, HI. ❖ Won more than two-dozen international and national gold medals in synchronized swimming; at Los Angeles Olympics, won a gold medal in duet and a gold medal in solo (1984); at Seoul Olympics, won a silver medal in solo (1988); also won World solo championship (1982); served as announcer for Olympic synchronized swimming events. Named Synchronized Swimmer of the Century by International Swimming Hall of Fame (2001).

RUIZ, Yumilka (1978—). Cuban volleyball player. Name variations: Yumilka Daisy Ruiz Luaces. Born May 8, 1978, in Camagüey, Cuba. ❖ Placed 1st at World championship (1998); won team gold medals at Atlanta Olympics (1996) and Sydney Olympics (2000) and a team bronze medal at Athens Olympics (2004).

RUIZ DE BURTON, Maria Amparo (1832–1895). *See Amparo Ruiz de Burton, Maria.*

RUKAVISHNIKOVA, Olga (1955—). Soviet pentathlete. Born Mar 13, 1955, in USSR. ❖ At Moscow Olympics, won a silver medal in pentathlon (1980).

RUKEYSER, Muriel (1913–1980). American poet and political activist. Pronunciation: ROO-kaiser. Born in New York, NY, Dec 15, 1913; died Feb 12, 1980, in New York, NY; dau. of Lawrence B. Rukeyser (engineer and businessman) and Myra Lyons Rukeyser; attended Vassar College, 1930–32, Columbia University, 1931–32; m. Glynn Collins (painter), 1945 (annulled 1945); children: William Laurie Rukeyser (b. 1947). ❖ Significant and often controversial writer, who turned much of her attention to political and social injustices in US and abroad but also produced a body of verse that explored such issues as her experiences as a woman; as a journalist, was arrested while covering Scottsboro trial in Alabama (1933); won Yale Series of Younger Poets competition with *Theory of Flight* (1935); worked as investigative reporter in West Virginia, studying effects of lung disease on local miners (1936); witnessed early stage of Spanish Civil War (1936); published *U.S. 1* (1938), a documentary in poetic form on the suffering from silica poisoning of the miners in West Virginia; taught at Sarah Lawrence (1954–67); active in the anti-Vietnam War movement, made trip to Hanoi (1972); as president of PEN, journeyed to South Korea to protest the imprisonment of poet Kim Chi-Ha (1975); other poetry includes *A Turning Wind* (1939), *Wake Island* (1942), *The Green Wave* (1948), *Body of Waking* (1958), *Breaking Open* (1973), *The Gates* (1976); prose includes *Willard Gibbs* (1942), *The Life of Poetry* (1949), *One Life* (1957), *The Orgy* (1966), *The Traces of Thomas Hariot* (1971); (trans.) *Selected*

Poems of Octavio Paz (1963). Won Copernicus Prize (1977). ❖ See also *Women in World History.*

RULE, Jane (1931—). Canadian-American novelist and short-story writer. Born Mar 28, 1931, in Plainfield, NJ; dau. of Arthur Rule and Carlotta Jane Rule; lived with Helen Sonthoff on Galiano Island, British Columbia, Canada. ❖ Taught English at Concord Academy in MA (1954–56); moved to Vancouver, Canada (1957), where she adopted Canadian citizenship and taught English and creative writing at University of British Columbia; published *The Desert of the Heart* (1964), which was filmed as *Desert Hearts* (1985); other writings include *This Is Not For You* (1970), *Lesbian Images* (1975), *Themes for Diverse Instruments* (1975), *The Young in One Another's Arms* (1977), *Contract with the World* (1980), *Outlander* (1981), *A Hot-Eyed Moderate* (1985), *Inland Passage* (1985), *Memory Board* (1987) and *After the Fire* (1989). Received Canadian Authors' Association Award for Best Novel (1978) and Benson and Hedges Award for Best Short Stories (1978).

RULE, Janice (1931–2003). American stage, tv and screen actress and dancer. Born Mary Janice Rule, Aug 15, 1931, in Norwood, OH; died Oct 17, 2003, in New York, NY; m. N. Richard Nash, 1956 (div. 1956); m. Robert Thom, 1960 (div. 1961); m. Ben Gazzara (actor), 1961 (div. 1979); children: Kate Thom Fitzgerald and Elizabeth Gazzara. ❖ Made NY stage debut as a dancer in *Miss Liberty* (1949) and starred on Broadway as Madge in original production of *Picnic* (1953); other plays include *The Flowering Peach, Night Circus, The Happiest Girl in the World* and *The Homecoming*; made film debut in *Goodbye My Fancy* (1951), followed by *Bell Book and Candle, The Subterraneans, Invitation to a Gunfighter, The Chase, Alvarez Kelly, The Ambushers, The Swimmer, Doctors' Wives, Three Women, Missing* and *Rainy Day Friends*, among others; frequently appeared in such episodic tv shows as "Twilight Zone"; became a psychoanalyst.

RULE, Margaret (1928—). English archaeologist. Name variations: Margaret Helen Rule. Born Margaret Helen Martin, Sept 27, 1928; m. Arthur Walter Rule, 1949. ❖ Organized and directed the raising of Henry VIII's flagship, the *Mary Rose* (1982); published *The Mary Rose: The Excavation and Raising of Henry VIII's Flagship* (1982) and *Life at Sea: Tudors and Stuarts* (1994), among others; elected honorary fellow of Portsmouth Polytechnic (1982); served as chair of Council for Nautical Archaeology. Made Commander of the Order of the British Empire (1983).

RULON, Kelly (1984—). American water-polo player. Born Kelly Kristen Rulon, Aug 16, 1984, in Point Loma, CA; attended University of California, Los Angeles. ❖ Won a team bronze medal at Athens Olympics (2004).

RUMANIA, queen of.
See Elizabeth of Wied (1843–1916).
See Marie of Rumania (1875–1938).

RUMBEWAS, Raema Lisa (1980—). Indonesian weightlifter. Born Sept 10, 1980, in Jayapura, Papua, Indonesia. ❖ Won a silver medal for - 48 kg at Sydney Olympics (2000) and a silver medal for 53 kg at Athens Olympics (2004).

RUMBOLD, Freda (1913—). English murderer. Born 1913; m. Albert Rumbold; children: at least 1 daughter. ❖ After using husband's name to forge checks and take out loans, shot him dead in his bed (Aug 25, 1956); once body was discovered by police, claimed he had been shot when they both struggled for the shotgun during an argument, but the bullet wounds in his head suggested otherwise; received life sentence.

RUMFORD, countess of.
See Lavoisier, Marie (1758–1836).
See Thompson, Sarah (1774–1852).

RUMSEY, Elida Barker (1842–1919). *See Fowle, Elida Rumsey.*

RUMSEY, Mary Harriman (1881–1934). American social-welfare leader. Name variations: Mary Harriman. Born Mary Harriman, Nov 17, 1881, in New York, NY; died Dec 18, 1934, in Washington, DC; dau. of Edward Henry Harriman (financier and railroad magnate) and Mary Williamson (Averell) Harriman; sister of W. Averell Harriman (governor of New York); graduate of Barnard College, 1905; m. Charles Cary Rumsey (sculptor), May 26, 1910 (died 1922); children: Charles Cary Jr. (b. 1911); Mary Averell Harriman (b. 1913); Bronson Harriman (b. 1917). ❖ Founded the Junior League for the Promotion of Settlement Movements (1901), later renamed the Junior League of New York, which launched the Junior League movement to encourage wealthy girls and women to devote more time and resources to the community; became lifelong trustee of Barnard College (1905); named trustee of United Hospital Fund of New York (1925) and played a leading role in the Women's Auxiliary there; appointed chair of Consumers' Advisory Board of National Recovery Administration (NRA, 1933). ❖ See also *Women in World History*.

RUNAWAYS, The.
See Currie, Cherie (1960—).
See Ford, Lita (1958—).
See Fox, Jackie (1960—).
See Jett, Joan (1960—).
See Steele, Micki (1954—).
See West, Sandy (1960—).

RUNCIE, Constance Faunt Le Roy (1836–1911). American composer and pianist. Born Constance Faunt Le Roy in Indianapolis, Indiana, Jan 15, 1836; died in St. Joseph, Missouri, May 17, 1911; dau. of Robert Henry Faunt Le Roy (astronomer and amateur composer) and Jane Dale (Owen) Faunt Le Roy (dau. of social reformer Robert Owen); studied piano and composition in Stuttgart, Germany (1852–57); m. James Runcie (Episcopal cleric); children: 2 sons, 2 daughters. ❖ Spent childhood in New Harmony, Indiana; composed songs and chamber music; may have been the 1st American woman to compose a symphony, but it was never published and the manuscript remains lost; her music was enormously popular in 19th century, but seldom played after her death. ❖ See also autobiography, *Divinely Led* (1895).

RUNCIMAN, Jane Elizabeth (1873–1950). New Zealand tailor, union official, and social reformer. Born June 4, 1873, at Waterford, Co. Waterford, Ireland; died Nov 13, 1950, at Dunedin, New Zealand; dau. of William Edward Runciman (grocer) and Susan Propert (Williams) Runciman. ❖ Worked as a tailor at New Zealand Clothing Factory and became active in Dunedin Tailoresses' Union (DTU, 1897), one of few women active in trade unionist activity; elected to New Zealand Labor Party's national executive (1918); her membership in Otago and Southland Women's Patriotic Association during WWI, distanced her from political left and she withdrew from national politics; involved in several social-welfare organizations, including Dunedin branch of New Zealand Society for the Protection of Women and Children; appointed justice of peace (1926). ❖ See also *Dictionary of New Zealand Biography* (Vol. 3).

RUND, Cathleen (1977—). German swimmer. Born Nov 3, 1977, in Berlin, Germany. ❖ Won a bronze medal for 200-meter backstroke at Atlanta Olympics (1996); at European championships, won a gold medal for 200-meter backstroke (1997).

RUNDLE, Elizabeth (1828–1896). *See Charles, Elizabeth.*

RUNEBERG, Fredrika (1807–1879). Finnish writer and feminist. Born Fredrika Charlotta Tengström, Sept 2, 1807, in Jakobstad (Pietarsaari), Finland; died May 27, 1879, in Helsinki; attended University of Turku; m. J(ohan) L(udvig) Runeberg (national poet of Finland), 1828 (died 1877); children: Anna (died 1833) and 7 sons, including the sculptor Walter Runeberg (1838–1920). ❖ The 1st important woman writer in Finland and a pioneer in the feminist movement, wrote sketches and stories for a literary magazine and *Helsingfors Morgonblad*, which were published as *Teckningar och drömmar* (1861); also pubished Finland's 1st historical novel, *Fru Catharina Boije och hennes döttar* (1858), followed by *Sigrid Liljeholm* (1862); wrote in Swedish.

RUNGE, Erika (1939—). East German writer. Born Jan 22, 1939, in Halle an der Saale, Germany. ❖ Studied art and literature in East and West Germany, earning PhD (1962); published interviews with coal-mine workers in *Bottroper Protokolle* (1968) and interviews with women in *Frauen: Versuche zur Emnzipation* (1974); for tv, wrote "Warum is Frau B. glücklich?" (1968), "Ich heiße Erwin und bin 17 Jahre" (1971), "Lias Traum vom Glück" (1988), among others.

RUOLAN (fl. 4th c.). *See Su Hui.*

RUOPPA, Eeva (1932—). Finnish cross-country skier. Name variations: Eeva Saarainen. Born May 2, 1932, in Miehikkälä, Finland. ❖ Won a bronze medal for 3 x 5 km relay at Squaw Valley Olympics (1960).

RUPILIA FAUSTINA (fl. 90 CE). Roman noblewoman. Married M. Annius Verus; children: Faustina I (c. 90–141 CE); M. Annius Verus; M. Annius Libo.

RUPSHIENE, Angele (1952—). Soviet basketball player. Born June 27, 1952, in USSR. ❖ Won a gold medal at Montreal Olympics (1976) and a gold medal at Moscow Olympics (1980), both in team competition.

RUSAN, Otilia Valeria Coman (1942—). *See Coman, Otilia.*

RUSANOVA, Lyubov (1954—). Soviet swimmer. Born Feb 1954 in USSR. ❖ At Montreal Olympics, won a silver medal in 100-meter breaststroke and a bronze medal in 200-meter breaststroke (1976).

RUSH, Barbara (1927—). American stage, tv and screen actress. Born Jan 4, 1927, in Denver, CO; m. Jeffrey Hunter (actor), 1950 (div. 1955); m. Warren Cowan, 1959 (div.); children: (1st m.) Christopher Hunter; (2nd m.) Claudia Cowan (journalist for Fox News); aunt of actress Carolyn Hennesy. ❖ Made film debut in *The Goldbergs* (1950), followed by *When Worlds Collide, Prince of Pirates, It Came from Outer Space, Magnificent Obsession, Captain Lightfoot, No Down Payment, The Young Lions, Harry Black and the Tiger, The Young Philadelphians, Strangers When We Meet, Come Blow Your Horn, Robin and the 7 Hoods* and *Hombre*, among others; on tv, appeared as a regular on "Peyton Place" (1968–69), "Flamingo Road" (1981–82), and as Nola Orsini on "All My Children" (1992–93).

RUSH, Cathy. American basketball coach. Born in West Atlantic City, NJ; West Chester University, BS, 1968, MA, 1972. ❖ Head coach at Immaculata College for 7 seasons who created the 1st basketball dynasty; compiled 149 wins and 15 losses at Immaculata, winning 3 consecutive National AIAW championship titles (1972–74), and making 6 consecutive AIAW Final Fours (1972–77); also coached the women's national team at Pan Am Games (1975), winning a gold medal; founded Future Stars Camps. Inducted into Pennsylvania Hall of Fame; nominated for inclusion in Basketball Hall of Fame (2003).

RUSH, Rebecca (1779–1850). American novelist. Born 1779 in Philadelphia, PA; died in 1850; dau. of Jacob Rush (jurist) and Mary Rench (or Wrench) Rush (painter of miniatures); niece of Benjamin Rush (physician and essayist). ❖ Wrote *Kelroy, A Novel* (1812).

RUSNACHENKO, Natalya (1969—). Soviet handball player. Born June 13, 1969, in USSR. ❖ At Seoul Olympics, won a bronze medal in team competition (1988).

RUSS, Joanna (1937—). American science-fiction writer. Born Feb 22, 1937, in New York, NY; m. Albert Amateau, 1963 (div. 1967). ❖ Worked as instructor, lecturer, and professor in speech and in English at several universities, including State University of New York at Binghampton, Cornell University, and University of Washington, Seattle; writings include *Picnic on Paradise* (1968), *The Female Man* (1975), *We Who Are About To . . .* (1977), *On Strike Against God* (1980), *Magic Mommas, Trembling Sisters, Puritans and Perverts* (1985), and *Souls* (1989); also wrote feminist nonfiction, including *What Are We Fighting For?: Sex, Race, Class, and the Future of Feminism* (1997); published short stories in anthologies and magazines. Received Nebula Award (1972, 1983), Hugo Award (1983) and Locus Award (1983).

RUSSELL, Ada Dwyer (1863–1952). *See Dwyer, Ada.*

RUSSELL, Alys Smith (1866–1951). American wife of Bertrand Russell. Name variations: Alys Pearsall Smith; Alys Pearsall-Smith. Born Alys Pearsall Smith, 1866, in Philadelphia, Pennsylvania; died 1951; dau. of Hannah (Whitall) and Robert Smith (preacher); sister of Mary Berenson; aunt of Ray Strachey; graduate of Bryn Mawr; became 1st wife of Bertrand Russell (pacifist, philosopher and author), Dec 1894 (div. 1921). ❖ See also *Women in World History.*

RUSSELL, Anna (b. 1911). English-born contralto and comedian. Name variations: Claudia Anna Russell-Brown. Born Claudia Anna Russell-Brown, Dec 27, 1911, in London, England; dau. of Claude Russell-Brown and Beatrice Russell-Brown; m. John L. Denison, 1934 (div. 1946); m. Charles Goldhammer, 1948 (div. 1954); became US citizen (1957). ❖ Studied cello, composition, piano and voice at Royal College of Music, London; was a contralto on Britain's concert circuit with moderate success; performed in Canadian troop show during WWII; while performing with Toronto Symphony Orchestra (1935), rendered humorous material professionally at conductor's suggestion; switched from traditional performances to her own comic compositions, satirizing excesses of classical music and operatic styles; turning a failed career into international fame as a musical satirist, debuted at NY's Town Hall to great success; was soon performing her own material in concerts across Canada, Europe, US and Japan; appeared with New York City Center

Opera as the Witch in *Hansel and Gretel,* and reprised the role in the film version; also starred in a musical version of *The Importance of Being Earnest* (1957); recorded 3 albums for Columbia (1953, 1972), which included such famed routines as an analysis of Wagner's "Ring of the Nibelung" cycle and "How To Write Your Own Gilbert and Sullivan Opera"; lived and worked in Australia for about 9 years, returning to US (1983); at 74, gave a televised farewell performance in Baltimore, released an album, published autobiography, and retired to Unionville, Ontario (all 1985). ❖ See also autobiography *I'm Not Making This Up, You Know* (Continuum, 1985); and *Women in World History.*

RUSSELL, Annie (1864–1936). English-born actress. Born Jan 12, 1864, in Liverpool, England; died Jan 16, 1936, in Winter Park, Florida; dau. of Joseph Russell (civil engineer) and Jane (Mount) Russell; m. Eugene Wiley Presbrey (stage manager), Nov 2, 1884 (div. 1897); m. Oswald Yorke (English actor), Mar 27, 1904 (died 1931). ❖ At 5, immigrated with family to Canada; made professional stage debut in *Miss Moulton* at Montreal Academy of Music (1872); with a Gilbert and Sullivan company, made 1st NY appearance in *H.M.S. Pinafore* (1879); came to prominence in title role of *Esmeralda,* which ran for 350 performances; toured in *Hazel Kirke,* before joining A.M. Palmer's co. in Madison Square; appeared in several plays throughout 1880s, including *Broken Hearts* (1885), *Engaged* (1886), *Elaine* (1887) and *Captain Swift* (1888), but personal problems with an abusive husband aggravated her poor health and she spent 2 years in Italy, recovering; in NY, appeared in *The New Woman, Sue, A Royal Family, Miss Hobbs, The Girl and the Judge* and *The Younger Mrs. Parling;* in London, starred in premiere of Shaw's *Major Barbara* (1905), which the playwright directed; back in NY (1906), gave highly regarded performance as Puck in *A Midsummer Night's Dream;* formed Annie Russell Old English Comedy Co. (1912); became a professor of theater arts at Rollins College. ❖ See also *Women in World History.*

RUSSELL, Annie (1868–1947). *See Maunder, Annie Russell.*

RUSSELL, Mrs. Bertrand.
See Russell, Alys Smith (1866–1951).
See Russell, Dora (1884–1986).

RUSSELL, Christine (1945—). English politician and member of Parliament. Born Christine Carr, Mar 25, 1945; m. Dr. James Russell, 1971 (div. 1991). ❖ Representing Labour, elected to House of Commons for City of Chester (1997, 2001, 2005).

RUSSELL, Dora (1894–1986). English feminist, educator, writer and peace activist. Name variations: Dora Black; Countess Russell; Mrs. Bertrand Russell. Born Dora Winifred Black in London, England, April 3, 1894; died in Porthcurno, Cornwall, England, May 31, 1986; dau. of Frederick William Black (later Sir Frederick Black, civil servant) and Sarah Isabella Davisson; became 2nd wife of Bertrand Russell (pacifist, philosopher and author), later 3rd earl Russell, Sept 27, 1921 (div. 1935); m. Patrick Grace, 1940 (died 1948); children: (1st m.) John (b. 1921) and Kate (b. 1923); (with Griffin Barry) Harriet (b. 1930) and Roderick (1932–1983). ❖ Intellectual activist whose accomplishments have often been overshadowed by her marriage to Bertrand Russell, won a scholarship to Cambridge University (1912); traveled with father to US (1917) and was awarded MBE for her contribution to the war effort; traveled alone to Russia at height of the post-revolutionary civil war and accompanied Bertrand to China (1920); ran unsuccessfully for Parliament as a Labour Party candidate (1924); helped establish Workers' Birth Control Group to function within Labour Party for reform of the law regarding contraception; published 3 important books, *Hypatia or Woman and Knowledge, The Right to be Happy* and *In Defense of Children* (1925–32); founded and ran a primary school based on advanced educational concepts (1927–43); worked for women's rights, nuclear disarmament and international understanding as an active member of the Six Points Group, the Married Women's Association, and the Women's International Democratic Federation; organized and led Women's Caravan of Peace (1958); published *The Religion of the Machine Age,* a summation of her views on industrialization, 1st drafted in 1920s (1983). ❖ See also autobiographies *The Tamarisk Tree: My Quest For Liberty and Love* (Virago, 1977), *The Tamarisk Tree 2: My School and the Years of the War* (Virago, 1980), and *The Tamarisk Tree 3: Challenge to the Cold War* (Virago, 1985); and *Women in World History.*

RUSSELL, Dora Isella (1925—). Uruguayan poet and essayist. Born 1925 in Argentina. ❖ Moved to Montevideo at 8; worked as teacher and journalist and specialized in work of poet Juana de Ibarbourou; works include *Sonetos* (1943), *Oleaje* (1949), *El otro olvido* (1952), *Los barcos de la noche* (1954), *Elegía de juinio* (1963), *El tiempo de regreso* (1967), *Los sonetos de Simbad* (1970), *Memorial para Don Bruno Mauricio de Zavala* (1977) and *Los sonetos de Carass Cort* (1983).

RUSSELL, Dorothy Stuart (1895–1983). English pathologist. Born June 27, 1895, in Sydney, Australia; died Oct 19, 1983; graduate of Girton College in Cambridge, 1918; London Hospital Medical College, MB, BS, 1923, MD, 1930. ❖ Well-known pathologist and professor of pathology, wrote highly regarded treatises on various aspects of pathology, including "A Classification of Bright's Disease" (1929) and "Observations on the Pathology of Hydrocephalus" (1940); worked at Nuffield Department of Surgery in Oxford (1940–44); while serving as director of the Bernhard Baron Institute of Pathology (1946–60), also taught morbid anatomy; was the 1st female member of the Medical Research Society. ❖ See also *Women in World History.*

RUSSELL, Elizabeth (1540–1609). English writer. Name variations: Lady Elizabeth Russell; Lady Elizabeth Cooke; Lady Elizabeth Hoby. Born Elizabeth Cooke, 1540, in Essex, England; died 1609; dau. of Sir Anthony Cooke (tutor to young English king Edward VI) and Anne Fitzwilliam Cooke; sister of Anne Cooke Bacon (1528–1610), Mildred Cooke Cecil and Catherine Killigrew; m. Sir Thomas Hoby (scholar, Calvinist, and English ambassador to Paris), 1558 (died 1566); m. John, Lord Russell, heir to the earl of Bedford, 1574 (died 1584); children: (1st m.) Elizabeth Hoby (died young), Anne Hoby (died young), Edward Hoby, Thomas Hoby; (2nd m.) Francis Russell (died young), Elizabeth Russell (died young), and Anne Russell, Lady Herbert. ❖ Poet, translator and Calvinist, went into exile in Germany (1552) when the Catholic Mary I succeeded as queen of England; returned after Mary's death (1558); after 1st husband died (1566), composed touching elegies in Latin for his monument at Bisham Abbey in Berkshire; wrote epitaphs to honor the memory of her 2 young daughters who died a week apart at ages 7 and 9 (1570); when 2nd husband died (1584), composed a cycle of Greek and Latin verses in his memory which adorn his tomb in Westminster Abbey; published translation of Bishop John Ponet's Latin treatise on the Eucharist (1605) as *A Way of Reconciliation of a good and learned man, touching the Truth, Nature, and Substance of the Body and Blood of Christ in the Sacrament.* ❖ See also *Women in World History.*

RUSSELL, Elizabeth (1832–1912). *See Caradus, Elizabeth.*

RUSSELL, Elizabeth Mary, Countess (1866–1941). *See Arnim, Elizabeth von.*

RUSSELL, Elizabeth S. (1913—). American geneticist. Name variations: Elizabeth Shull Russell; Elizabeth Shull. Born Elizabeth Shull, May 13, 1913; University of Michigan, AB, 1933; Columbia University, MA, 1934; University of Chicago. PhD in zoology, 1937; m. William Lawson Russell, 1936; children: 4. ❖ Worked as a University of Chicago assistant zoologist (1935–37); served as an independent investigator at the Jackson Laboratory (Bar Harbor, ME, 1939–40), then as resident associate (1946–57) and senior staff scientist (1957–82), becoming emerita senior scientist (1982); investigated how genes cause cancers and pioneered muscular dystrophy research; became a member of National Academy of Sciences (1963).

RUSSELL, Elizabeth Watts (1827/31–1881). *See Watts Russell, Elizabeth Rose Rebecca.*

RUSSELL, Ernestine (1938—). Canadian gymnast. Name variations: Ernestine Russell Weaver; Ernie Russell. Born June 10, 1938, in Windsor, Ontario, Canada; m. Jim Weaver (football coach). ❖ Won 9 Canadian championships; as a participant at Melbourne, became Canada's 1st female gymnast to compete in the Olympics (1956); also competed in Rome Olympics (1960); won gold medals for floor exercise, balance beam, vault, uneven bars and overall at Pan American games (1959); became a gymnastics coach and named head coach for US gymnastic team (1977). Awarded Velma Springstead Trophy as the outstanding woman athlete in Canada (1955, 1956, 1957); inducted into Canadian Sports Hall of Fame.

RUSSELL, Francia (1938—). American ballet dancer. Born Jan 10, 1938, in Los Angeles, CA; m. Kent Stowell. ❖ Performed throughout most of career with New York City Ballet where she was featured in Balanchine works, including *Figure in the Carpet* (1960); with husband Kent Stowell, was co-director of Frankfurt Opera Ballet in Germany (1975–77), where she staged numerous Balanchine revivals; became director at Pacific Northwest Ballet in Seattle, WA (1977); known especially for her staging of works by Balanchine.

RUSSELL, Gail (1924–1961). American actress. Name variations: Mrs. Robert Moseley. Born Sept 21, 1924, in Chicago, Illinois; died Aug 27, 1961, in Los Angeles, California; dau. of George Russell (auto bond salesman) and Gladys (Barnet) Russell; m. Guy Madison (actor), Aug 31, 1949 (div. 1954); no children. ❖ Made film debut in *Henry Aldrich Gets Glamour* (1943), followed by *Lady in the Dark* (1944); from the first, suffered debilitating attacks of stage fright and would later turn to alcohol to numb the terror; came to prominence in the hit *The Uninvited* (1944); also scored a success portraying Cornelia Otis Skinner in *Our Hearts Were Young and Gay* (1944) and *Our Hearts Were Growing Up* (1946); received best reviews for sleeper *The Lawless* (1950); entered a sanitarium in Seattle for treatment for alcoholism (1953); other films include *Duffy's Tavern* (1945), *Night Has a Thousand Eyes* (1948), *The Angel and the Badman* (1947), *Wake of the Red Witch* (1948), *Song of India* (1949), *No Place to Land* (1958) and *The Silent Call* (1961). ❖ See also *Women in World History*.

RUSSELL, Lady Hamilton (1875–1938). *See Scott, Margaret.*

RUSSELL, Jane (1840–1933). *See Te Kiri Karamu, Heni.*

RUSSELL, Jane (1921—). American actress. Born Ernestine Jane Geraldine Russell, June 21, 1921, in Bemidji, Minnesota; dau. of an actress; studied acting at Max Reinhardt's Theatrical Workshop and with Maria Ouspenskaya; m. Bob Waterfield (football player and coach), 1943 (div. 1968); m. Roger Barrett (actor), 1968 (died months later); m. John Calvin Peoples (real-estate agent), 1974 (died 1999); children: (1st m.) adopted 3. ❖ Tall, voluptuous brunette, spent most of acting career attempting to overcome her initial image as a sex symbol; made film debut in Howard Hughes' *The Outlaw* (1943), causing a furor with her sultry pose in a haystack; had best film role opposite Marilyn Monroe in *Gentlemen Prefer Blondes* (1953); replaced Elaine Stritch in Broadway musical *Company* (1971); other films include *The Paleface* (1948), *The Las Vegas Story* (1952), *Montana Belle* (1952), *Son of Paleface* (1952), *The French Line* (1954), *Foxfire* (1955), *Gentlemen Marry Brunettes* (1955), *The Revolt of Mamie Stover* (1956), *Fate Is the Hunter* (1964), *Johnny Reno* (1966) and *Darker Than Amber* (1971). ❖ See also autobiography, *My Path and Detours* (1985); and *Women in World History*.

RUSSELL, Jane Anne (1911–1967). American biochemist and endocrinologist. Name variations: Jane A. Russell; Jane Russell Wilhelmi. Born Feb 9, 1911, in Los Angeles County (now Watts), California; died Mar 12, 1967, in Atlanta, Georgia; dau. of Josiah Howard Russell (rancher and deputy sheriff) and Mary Ann (Phillips) Russell; University of California at Berkeley, BS, 1932; Institute of Experimental Biology, PhD, 1937; m. Alfred Ellis Wilhelmi (scientist and professor), Aug 26, 1940. ❖ As a PhD candidate, worked in the Institute of Experimental Biology, researching the role of pituitary hormones in carbohydrate metabolism; also collaborated with Carl and Gerty T. Cori on carbohydrate research at Washington University; considered an international expert in the field of carbohydrate metabolism, began work as a National Research Council fellow at Yale University (1938) and served as an instructor (1941–50); despite the fact that she was a worldrenowned authority in her field, was never formally recognized by Yale through academic promotions, an omission that would later be cited as an example of discrimination against women in academia; moved to Emory University in Atlanta (1950), where she became an assistant professor; continued to earn recognition for her research by expanding her focus to include nitrogen metabolism; was finally promoted to associate professor at Emory (1953), but was not named full professor until 1965, 3 years into her battle with breast cancer. Won Ciba Award (1946); with husband, shared Upjohn Award of the Endocrine Society (1961). ❖ See also *Women in World History*.

RUSSELL, Katherine (1829–1898). *See Russell, Mother Mary Baptist.*

RUSSELL, Kathleen. South African swimmer. Born in South Africa. ❖ At Amsterdam Olympics, won a bronze medal in the 4 x 100-meter freestyle relay (1928).

RUSSELL, Lady (1636–1723). *See Russell, Rachel.*

RUSSELL, Lillian (1861–1922). American actress, singer and political activist. Name variations: Nellie; Diamond Lil. Born Helen Louise Leonard, Dec 4, 1861, in Clinton, Iowa; died June 6, 1922, in Pittsburgh, PA; dau. of Charles Egbert Leonard (newspaper and book publisher) and Cynthia Leonard (women's rights advocate); studied voice privately with Leopold Damrosch; m. Harry Braham (orchestra conductor), 1880 (div.); m. Edward Solomon (musician), 1883 (div.); m. John

Haley (actor), 1894 (div.); m. Alexander Pollock Moore (newspaper publisher), 1912; children: (1st m.) son, died in infancy; (2nd m.) Dorothy Solomon. ❖ Tall and blonde, with a fair complexion and the ample, hour-glass curves that late 19th-century Americans loved, was widely hailed as the embodiment of American Beauty; moved with family to Chicago (c. 1863–65); moved to New York City with mother to study for opera career (1878); made 1st stage appearance as a chorus girl in *H.M.S. Pinafore* (1879); made professional debut at Tony Pastor's, billed as "The English Ballad singer" (1880); appeared in 1st comic opera "The Pie Rats of Penn Yann" (1881); sang in genuine Gilbert and Sullivan productions, such as *Patience* and *The Sorcerer,* as well as other musicals; lived and worked in England (1883–85); returned to NY to play at the Casino where she enjoyed some of her greatest successes, including *Princess Nicotine* and *An American Beauty*; at the peak of her singing career, met and befriended Diamond Jim Brady (1890) who showered her with so many diamonds that the press dubbed her "Diamond Lil"; shifted from comic opera to burlesque, working with the famous comedy team of Weber and Fields (1899); endured voice problems (1906), making a shift from singing to acting a necessity; joined Weber and Fields again in *Hokey-Pokey* (1912); appeared in only film, *Wildfire* (1914); during last few years, concentrated on political and personal concerns, campaigning actively for Theodore Roosevelt (1912) and Warren G. Harding (1920), and wrote a column for 2 Chicago papers; sold war bonds during WWI; though not a union officer, helped negotiate a settlement for the 1st Actors Equity strike (1919); worked for women's suffrage. ❖ See also Lois Banner, *American Beauty* (Knopf, 1983); Parker Morell, *Lillian Russell: The Era of Plush* (Random House, 1940); John Burke, *Duet In Diamonds: The Flamboyant Saga of Lillian Russell and Diamond Jim Brady in America's Gilded Age* (Putnam, 1972); and *Women in World History*.

RUSSELL, Lucy (c. 1581–1627). English patron of poets. Name variations: Lucy, Countess of Bedford; Lucy Harington. Born c. 1581; died 1627; dau. of John Harington, 1st Baron Harington of Exton, and Anne Harington; m. Edward Russell, 3rd earl of Bedford, in 1594. ❖ Received large inheritance from father; was a patron of some of the foremost English poets of her day, including Ben Jonson and John Donne; apparently wrote verse herself, though none of her writings survive. ❖ See also *Women in World History*.

RUSSELL, Margery (d. around 1380). English merchant. Died c. 1380 in Coventry, England. ❖ Traded internationally in a variety of goods; though married to another merchant, ran her business as a *femme sole*, or "woman alone," from the town of Coventry. ❖ See also *Women in World History*.

RUSSELL, Mary Annette, Countess (1866–1941). *See Arnim, Elizabeth von.*

RUSSELL, Mother Mary Baptist (1829–1898). Irish-born nun and founder. Name variations: Katherine Russell; Sister Mary Baptist; Mary Baptist Russell. Born in Newry, Co. Down, Ireland, April 18, 1829; died in San Francisco, California Aug 6, 1898; dau. of Arthur Russell (sea captain and brewer) and Margaret (Hamill) Russell; sister of Matthew Russell; never married; no children. ❖ Roman Catholic nun, established the House of Mercy, a shelter for unemployed women (1855); founded St. Mary's Hospital, the 1st Catholic hospital on the West Coast (1857); established the Magdalen Asylum for reformed prostitutes (1861). ❖ See also Matthew Russell, *The Life of Mother Mary Baptist Russell, Sister of Mercy* (1901); and *Women in World History*.

RUSSELL, Mary du Caurroy (1865–1937). English aviator. Name variations: Duchess of Bedford. Born Mary Tribe, Sept 26, 1865, in England; died 1937; 2nd dau. of Walter Harry Tribe, archdeacon of Lahore; attended Cheltenham Ladies College; m. Lord Herbrand Arthur Russell (1858–1937), 1888, became 11th duke of Bedford, 1893. ❖ Funded a cottage hospital in Woburn (1898), then founded the larger Woburn Hospital (1903), to accomodate the latest scientific advances in nursing and medicine (it would later be renamed Marylands); devoted herself to nursing, becoming surgeon's assistant (1917); took 1st flight (1926), age 61; made record flight to India and back (1929) and to the Cape and back (1930); opened the world's 1st All Women's Flying Meeting (1931); obtained pilot's "A" license (1933); was a member of the Society of Radiographers; at 71, took off on a solo flight to view the extensive flooding in the fens and was never seen again (Mar 22, 1937), though four struts from the wings of her plane washed ashore on the East Coast. Made DBE (1928).

RUSSELL, Rachel (1636–1723). English aristocrat. Name variations: Rachel Wriothesley; Rachel Vaughan; Lady Russell. Born Sept 1636 in Hampshire, England; died Sept 29, 1723, in Southampton; dau. of Thomas Wriothesley (1607–1667, moderate Royalist leader in House of Lords), 5th earl of Southampton (r. 1624–1667), and Rachel Massuy de Ruvigny also seen as Rachel de Massue (b. 1603); sister of Elizabeth and Magdalene Wriothesley; m. Francis Vaughan, Lord Vaughan, Oct 1654 (died of the plague 1667); m. William Russell, Lord Russell (leader of the House of Commons), Aug 1669 (beheaded 1683); children: (1st m.) 2 who died young; (2nd m.) Rachel Russell (1674–1725, who m. William Cavendish, 2nd duke of Devonshire), Catherine Russell (1676–1711, who m. John Manners, 2nd duke of Rutland), Wriothesley Russell (b. 1680), duke of Bedford. ❖ Husband William was arrested and tried for treason for conspiring to dethrone Charles II (1683); did everything in her power before and during trial to get him released, but he was executed as a traitor (July 21); successfully petitioned James II to have husband's conviction overturned posthumously and to reverse the attainder that had denied the Russells their legal and property rights (1688); her life is preserved in hundreds of her letters and in the numerous treatises she composed. ❖ See also Lois G. Schwoerer, *Lady Rachel Russell* (Johns Hopkins U. Press, 1988); and *Women in World History*.

RUSSELL, Rosalind (1908–1976). American actress. Born June 4, 1908, in Waterbury, Connecticut; died Nov 28, 1976, in Los Angeles, California; dau. of Clara Russell and James Russell (trial lawyer); graduate of American Academy of Dramatic Arts; m. Frederick Brisson (producer); children: Lance. ❖ Famed for performances in *Auntie Mame* and *Gypsy,* won several parts on the stage before making film debut in *Evelyn Prentice* (1934); enjoyed success in a string of comedies in which she often played witty career women, including *The Women* (1939), *His Girl Friday* (1940), *No Time for Comedy* (1940), *The Feminine Touch* (1941) and *Design for Scandal* (1941); appeared in her most famous role as Auntie Mame both on Broadway (1956) and in the film adaptation (1958); was given a specially created award for the charity work which marked much of her later life (1972); other films include *Craig's Wife* (1936), *Night Must Fall* (1937), *The Citadel* (1938), *Flight for Freedom* (1943), *Roughly Speaking* (1945), *The Guilt of Janet Ames* (1947), *Mourning Becomes Electra* (1947), *The Velvet Touch* (1948), *A Woman of Distinction* (1950), *Never Wave at a Wac* (1953), *A Majority of One* (1962), *Five Finger Exercise* (1962), *The Trouble with Angels* (1966) and *Mrs. Pollifax—Spy* (1971). Nominated 4 times for Academy Awards for performances in *My Sister Eileen* (1942), *Sister Kenny* (1946), *Picnic* (1956) and *Auntie Mame* (1958). ❖ See also autobiography (with Chris Chase) *Life Is a Banquet* (Random House, 1977); Nicholas Yanni, *Rosalind Russell* (Pyramid, 1975); and *Women in World History*.

RUSSELL, Sarah.
   See O'Connell, Sarah (c. 1822–1870).
   See Laski, Marghanita (1915–1988).

RUSSIA, empress of.
   See Vassiltschikov, Anna.
   See Sophia of Byzantium (1448–1503).
   See Anastasia Romanova (d. 1560).
   See Maria of Circassia (d. 1569).
   See Sobakin, Marta (d. 1571).
   See Godunova, Irene (d. 1603).
   See Maria Skuratova (d. 1605).
   See Mniszek, Marina (c. 1588–1614).
   See Dolgorukova, Marie (d. 1625).
   See Miloslavskaia, Maria (1626–1669).
   See Narishkina, Natalya (1651–1694).
   See Grushevski, Agraphia (1662–1681).
   See Marpha (1664–1716).
   See Saltykova, Praskovya (1664–1723).
   See Eudoxia Lopukhina (1669–1731).
   See Catherine I of Russia (1684–1727).
   See Anna Ivanovna (1693–1740).
   See Elizabeth Petrovna (1709–1762).
   See Catherine II the Great (1729–1796).
   See Sophia Dorothea of Wurttemberg (1759–1828).
   See Elizabeth of Baden (1779–1826).
   See Marie of Hesse-Darmstadt (1824–1880).
   See Marie Feodorovna (1847–1928).
   See Alexandra Feodorovna (1872–1918).

RUSSIA, grand duchess of.
   See Anna Pavlovna (1795–1865).
   See Helene of Wurttemberg (1807–1873).
   See Olga of Russia (1822–1892).
   See Marie Alexandrovna (1853–1920).
   See Maria of Mecklenburg-Schwerin (1854–1920).
   See Ella (1864–1918).
   See Helena of Russia (1882–1957).
   See Olga Alexandrovna (1882–1960).
   See Karadjordjevic, Helen (1884–1962).
   See Olga (1895–1918).
   See Tatiana (1897–1918).
   See Anastasia (1901–1918).

RUSSO, Marine (1980—). Argentine field-hockey player. Born Marine Russo, Jan 9, 1980, in Quilmes, Argentina. ❖ Midfielder, won a team bronze medal at Athens Olympics (2004); won Champions Trophy (2001) and World Cup (2002).

RUSTAMOVA, Zebinisso (1955—). Soviet archer. Born Jan 29, 1955, in USSR. ❖ At Montreal Olympics, won a bronze medal in double FITA round (1976).

RUSUDANI (b. 1195). Queen of Georgia. Name variations: Russudan or Rusudan. Born 1195 in Georgia (Russia); dau. of Queen Tamara (1160–1212) and David Soslan or Sosland; sister of Giorgi (b. 1194), later George IV, king of Georgia; children: son David Narin. ❖ Inherited the throne of Georgia (1223); from 1225, battled off and on for years with a prince of the Khwarizmians, whose armies had claimed part of southern Georgia and occupied and sacked the capital city of Tiflis; ruled from the city of Kutais until the Khwarizmian prince beat a retreat from the approach of a Mongol army; reoccupied Tiflis; was forced to flee again (1236) as the Mongols returned. ❖ See also *Women in World History.*

RUTE, marchesa de (1830–1902). See Rute, Mme de.

RUTE, Mme de (1831–1902). French novelist. Name variations: Comtesse Rattazzi; Marie Rattazzi; Madame Ratazzi or Rattazzi; Marie Wyse; Marie-Laetitia-Studolmine Wyse; Marie Wyse Bonaparte; Marie Wyse Bonaparte Rattazzi; Marie de Solms; Princesse de Solms; Maria Rattazzi de Rute; marchesa de Rute. Born Marie-Laetitia-Studolmine Wyse in Co. Cork, Ireland, in 1831; grew up in France; died 1902; dau. of Sir Thomas Wyse (English noble) and Laetitia Bonaparte (dau. of Lucien Bonaparte); great-granddau. of Napoleon I; m. Comte de Solms; m. Urbano Rattazzi (1808–1873), Italian statesman, 1861 (died 1873); m. Marquis de Rute. ❖ Abandoned by 1st husband, lived as Mme de Solms in France, until forced to leave by Napoleon III (1853); later returned to France as Comtesse Rattazzi, where her novel *Bicheville* (1865), which was set in Florence, was published; wrote a number of plays, travelogues and novels, including *Si j'étais reine* (If I Were Queen) and *Les Mariages de la Créole* (The Marriages of a Creole Woman, 1866).

RUTH (fl. 1100 BCE). Biblical woman. Born in Moab; possibly the dau. of King Eglon of Moab; m. Mahlon (son of Naomi and Elimelech); m. Boaz; children: (2nd m.) son Obed (grandfather of King David). ❖ Moabite widow of the Old Testament, model of unwavering devotion, who moved with Naomi, her mother-in-law, to Judah where she met and married Boaz and became the great-grandmother of King David. The Book of Ruth is one of only two canonical Biblical texts named after a woman; its simple, symmetrical structure, its length (4 chapters), and its modest narrative style belie the ideological and literary complexity of this masterful tale. ❖ See also Athalya Brenner, ed. *A Feminist Companion to Ruth* (Sheffield, 1993); Edward F. Campbell, *Ruth* (Doubleday, 1975); Katrina J.A. Larkin, *Ruth and Esther* (Sheffield, 1996); Ellen van Wolde, *Ruth and Naomi* (trans. by John Bowden, Smyth and Helwys, 1998; M.D. Gow, *The Book of Ruth: Its Structure, Theme and Purpose* (Apollos, 1994); and *Women in World History.*

RUTH-ROLLAND, J.M. (1937–1995). Central African official. Name variations: Jeanne-Marie Ruth-Rolland. Born in 1937; died in Paris, France, on June 4, 1995. ❖ Trained as a teacher, became director of social services in army of the Central African Republic; was also an adviser to the prime minister on women's issues and a campaigner on behalf of the homeless children of the republic's capital, Bangui; because of her candor, which was anathema to the republic's military ruler General Andre Kolingba, was imprisoned for 5 years (1986–91); upon release, served in the Cabinet as minister of social affairs (1992–93).

RUTHERFORD, Ann (1917—). Canadian-born actress. Born Therese Ann Rutherford, Nov 2, 1917, in Vancouver, British Columbia, Canada; dau. of John Guilberty ([Rutherford], tenor at Metropolitan Opera) and Lucille Mansfield (actress who played 2nd lead in the Pearl White serials); m. David May (department-store heir), 1942 (div. 1953); m. William Dozier (tv producer), 1953 (died 1991); children: Gloria May (b. 1943). ❖ Moved to San Francisco, then Los Angeles when young; began career on radio; made film debut in *Waterfront Lady* (1935), then appeared opposite Gene Autry and John Wayne in several movies; other films include *Dancing Coed, A Christmas Carol, Pride and Prejudice, Happy Land, Whistling in Brooklyn, The Secret Life of Walter Mitty, The Adventures of Don Juan, Orchestra Wives* and *Gone with the Wind* (Careen O'Hara); probably best remembered as Andy Hardy's girlfriend Polly Benedict in 12 Hardy films.

RUTHERFORD, Frances Armstrong (1842–1922). American physician. Born Oct 8, 1842, in Bath, NY; died May 24, 1922; attended Elmira College in NY, 1855–56; studied medicine with Dr. Rachel Gleason in Elmira (from 1863); graduate of Woman's Medical College of Pennsylvania (later Medical College of Pennsylvania and Hahnemann University School of Medicine), 1868; briefly married to a lawyer. ❖ Interned with Elizabeth and Emily Blackwell at New York Infirmary for Women and Children; had further training at New York Woman's Hospital (1873) and at London and Berlin clinics and hospitals (1882–83); established a Grand Rapids, Michigan, practice (1868); appointed the 1st female city physician in America; was the 1st elected woman member of the Michigan State Medical Society (1872) and served as its vice president; established and organized the 1st training school for nurses in Grand Rapids, at Union Benevolent Association Hospital, later Blodgett Memorial Hospital.

RUTHERFORD, Margaret (1892–1972). English actress. Born Margaret Taylor Rutherford, May 11, 1892, at 15 Dornton Road, Balham, England; died May 22, 1972, at Chalfont St. Peter, England; dau. of William Rutherford Benn (who killed his father and was remanded to Broadmoor) and Florence (Nicholson) Benn (hanged herself); m. (James Buckley) Stringer Davis (actor), Mar 26, 1945 (Aug 7, 1973); children: adopted 4, including writer Dawn Langley Hall Simmons (d. Sept 18, 2000, who before her sex-correction operation, 1968, was known as Gordon Langley Hall). ❖ Character actress who rose to stardom in middle age and created an ensemble of eccentrics for film and stage, including Agatha Christie's Miss Marple; had 1st professional job, as an understudy for Mabel Terry-Lewis in *A Hundred Years Old* at the Lyric, Hammersmith (1928); at Croydon, appeared opposite Donald Wolfit as Mrs. Solness in *The Master Builder*; made West End debut in *Wild Justice* (1933); reaped glowing reviews for *Hervey House*; made film debut in *Dusty Ermine* (1936); came to prominence as Aunt Bijou Furze in *The Spring Meeting* (1938), then appeared as Miss Prism in *The Importance of Being Earnest*, with Edith Evans as Lady Bracknell (1939); played Mrs. Danvers to Celia Johnson's Mrs. de Winter in *Rebecca* (1940), followed by Madame Arcati in *Blithe Spirit*, which ran for 1,997 performances; also appeared as Lady Wishfort in *The Way of the World*; films include *The Yellow Canary* (1943), *English Without Tears* (1944), *Blithe Spirit* (1945), *Passport to Pimlico* (1949), *Curtain Up* (1952), *The Importance of Being Earnest* (1952), *The Runaway Bus* (1954), *Aunt Clara* (1954), *I'm All Right Jack* (1959), *Murder She Said* (1961), *Murder at the Gallop* (1963), *Murder Ahoy* (1964), *Murder Most Foul* (1964), *Chimes at Midnight* (1966), *A Countess from Hong Kong* (1967) and *Arabella* (1968). Named Officer of the Order of the British Empire (1962) and Dame of the British Empire (1967); won Academy Award for Best Supporting Actress for *The VIPs* (1963). ❖ See also Dawn Langley Simmons, *Margaret Rutherford: A Blithe Spirit* (McGraw-Hill, 1983); and *Women in World History.*

RUTHERFORD, Mildred (1851–1928). American educator and Confederate apologist. Name variations: Miss Millie. Born Mildred Lewis Rutherford in Athens, Georgia, July 16, 1851; died in Athens, Aug 15, 1928; dau. of Williams R. Rutherford (professor of mathematics at University of Georgia) and Laura Battaille Rootes (Cobb) Rutherford (sister of Thomas Reade Rootes Cobb who established the Lucy Cobb Institute for Girls); graduate of Lucy Cobb Institute for Girls, 1868; never married; no children. ❖ Spent several years teaching in public schools in Atlanta before returning to Lucy Cobb Institute as principal (1880); remained there for next 46 years, working to educate young women in the traditions and manners of antebellum South; wrote textbooks for her literature classes, including *English Authors* (1890), *French Authors* (1906), and *The South in Literature and History* (1907), placing greater emphasis on morality of writers than on artistic merit; took stands

against women's suffrage, child-labor laws, and national prohibition, arguing that they violated states' rights. ❖ See also *Women in World History.*

RUTHERFORD, Minnie (1868–1946). *See Fuller, Minnie Rutherford.*

RUTHSTRÖM, Sonja. *See Edstrom, Sonja.*

RUTH THE GLEANER (fl. 1100 BCE). *See Ruth.*

RUTHVEN, Jocelyn Otway (1909–1989). *See Otway-Ruthven, Jocelyn.*

RUTKIEWICZ, Wanda (1943—). Polish mountain climber. Born Feb 4, 1943, in Lithuania; acquired a Master of Science in computer science; married 1970 (div. 1973); m. Helmut Scharfetter, 1982 (div. 1984). ❖ Made the 1st all-women's ascent of the North Face of Matterhorn (1978); was the 1st European woman and 1st Pole to climb Mount Everest (1978); made the 1st all-female ascent of Nanga Parbat, without oxygen or high altitude porters; ascended K2 (1986). ❖ See also *Women in World History.*

RUTKOWSKA, Jadwiga (1934—). Polish volleyball player. Born Feb 2, 1934, in Poland. ❖ At Tokyo Olympics, won a bronze medal in team competition (1964).

RUTLEDGE, Ann (1813–1835). American woman. Born Ann Mayes Rutledge, Jan 7, 1813, in Kentucky; died in Illinois, Aug 25, 1835; 1 of 10 children of James Rutledge (mill-owner and tavernkeeper) and Mary Ann (Miller) Rutledge; never married; no children. ❖ Reputedly, became the beloved of Abraham Lincoln when he boarded at her father's tavern (c. 1833); died of typhoid (or "milk fever" or "brain fever"), causing Lincoln extreme grief. ❖ See also *Women in World History.*

RUTLEDGE, Margaret Fane (1914–2004). Canadian aviator. Name variations: Margaret Fane. Born April 15, 1914, in Edmonton, Alberta, Canada; died Dec 2, 2004; m. Keith Rutledge, 1956. ❖ Pioneering aviator who helped open up the Canadian wilderness (1930s–40s); obtained private license (1933); gained professional qualifications (1935); was the 1st woman to fly a radio-equipped plane over the Rocky mountains; moved to Vancouver (1936) and set up the Canadian chapter of the 99s Club; later worked for Bridge River & Cariboo Airways, then Canadian Pacific Airways.

RUTSCHOW, Katrin (1975—). German rower. Name variations: Rutschow-Stomporowski. Born April 2, 1975, in Berlin, Germany. ❖ Won a gold medal for quadruple sculls at Atlanta Olympics (1996); at World championships, won gold medals for quadruple sculls (1994, 1995) and single sculls (2001); won a bronze medal for single sculls at Sydney Olympics (2000) and a gold medal for single sculls at Athens Olympics (2004).

RUTTNER-KOLISKO, Agnes (1911–1991). Freshwater biologist. Name variations: Agnes Kolisko. Born Agnes Kolisko, July 14, 1911; died Nov 22, 1991; m. W.A. Ruttner (geologist), 1938; children: 5. ❖ The 1st deputy director of the Lünz Biological Station of the Austrian Academy of Sciences' Institute of Limnology (1972–76), was the 1st to apply genetic concepts to rotifers (planktonic spinning microscopic organisms); maintained algae cultures successfully for years.

RUUSKA, Sylvia (1942—). American swimmer. Born July 1942, in Berkeley, CA; sister of swimmer Pat Ruuska. ❖ Won a bronze medal in the 400-meter freestyle and a silver medal in the 4 x 100-meter freestyle relay at the Melbourne Olympics (1956); won 20 national championships. Inducted into International Swimming Hall of Fame (1976).

RUYSCH, Rachel (1664–1750). Dutch painter. Born in Amsterdam, Holland, 1664; died in Amsterdam in 1750; dau. of Anthony Frederick Ruysch (professor of anatomy and botany) and Maria (Post) Ruysch (dau. of architect Pieter Post); elder sister of Anna Elisabeth Ruysch (c. 1680–1741, painter); apprenticed to Willem van Aelst; m. Juriaen Pool (portrait painter), 1693; children: 10. ❖ Major international artist, created detailed and exquisitely colored flower arrangements, often with outdoor settings and including small mammals, reptiles, and insects; became a member of The Hague guild (1701); was court painter to Elector Palatine, Johann Wilhelm von Pfalz (1708–16); in lifetime, rendered about 200 paintings. ❖ See also *Women in World History.*

RUZICKA, Marla (1976–2005). American activist. Born Dec 31, 1976, in Lakeport, CA; killed by a car bomber in Iraq, April 16, 2005; dau. of Nancy and Clifford Ruzicka (civil engineer); attended Long Island University. ❖ Aid worker, sought to get compensation for victims of the wars in Afghanistan and Iraq (2001–05); persuaded US Senator

Patrick Leahy to put an amendment into a foreign aid bill to give $2.5 million for Afghan victims; got $20 million for victims in Iraq.

RUZICKOVA, Hana (1941–1981). Czech gymnast. Born Feb 18, 1941, in Czechoslovakia; died May 29, 1981. ❖ Won a silver medal at Rome Olympics (1960) and a silver medal at Tokyo Olympics (1964), both in team all-around.

RUZICKOVA, Vera (1928—). Czech gymnast. Born Aug 10, 1928, in Czechoslovakia. ❖ At London Olympics, won a gold medal in team all-around (1948).

RUZINA, Yelena (1964—). Soviet runner. Born April 3, 1964, in USSR. ❖ At Barcelona Olympics, won a gold medal in the 4 x 400-meter relay (1992).

RYABCHINSKAYA, Yuliya (1947–1973). Soviet kayaker. Name variations: Yulia, Julia, or Yuliya Petrovna Ryabchinskaya. Born Jan 21, 1947; lived in Odessa; died Jan 13, 1973. ❖ At Munich Olympics, won a gold medal in K1 500 meters (1972).

RYAN, Anne (1889–1954). American artist. Born July 20, 1889, in Hoboken, New Jersey; died April 18, 1954, in Morristown, New Jersey; dau. of John Ryan (banker) and Elizabeth (Soran) Ryan; attended St. Elizabeth's College; m. William J. McFadden (lawyer), 1911 (sep. 1923); children: (twins) William and Elizabeth McFadden; Thomas McFadden. ❖ Finding her metier at age 50, enjoyed a short but intense art career, 1st painting and then creating the abstract collages of paper and fabric for which she became known; published vol. of poetry, *Lost Hills* (1925); lived on island of Majorca, writing poetry, stories and articles, some of which were published in *The Literary Digest* and *Commonweal* (1931–33); discovered painting and had 1st solo exhibition of oils (1941); joined Atelier 17 to study printmaking, producing a number of woodblock prints and engravings (1941); began to experiment with collages (1948) and had 1st public showing at Betty Parson's Gallery (1950); work included in exhibition "Abstract Painting and Sculpture in America" at MoMA (1951). Major exhibition, "Anne Ryan Collages," was held at Brooklyn Museum (1974). ❖ See also *Women in World History.*

RYAN, Catherine O'Connell (1865–1936). American inventor. Born Catherine O'Connell, May 26, 1865, in Mayo, Ireland; immigrated to US, 1870; m. Thomas J. Ryan (operator of a hay and grain business), May 22, 1882; children: 6, youngest of whom was attorney Kingsley Ryan who assembled her papers. ❖ Invented the self-locking nut and bolt and held 6 patents which revolutionized joining of tracks for railroads and trolleys; when US Steel, Carnegie Steel, and Illinois Steel infringed on her patent, sued unsuccessfully to protect her patent rights. ❖ See also *Women in World History.*

RYAN, Elizabeth (1891–1979). American tennis player. Name variations: Bunny Ryan. Born Feb 5, 1891, in Los Angeles, CA; died of a stroke while at Wimbledon, England, July 1979; dau. of a British immigrant. ❖ Won Russian championship (1914); won 19 doubles titles and 7 mixed-doubles titles at Wimbledon; won 4 mixed-doubles titles in France and 2 in US. ❖ See also *Women in World History.*

RYAN, Fran (1916–2000). American screen and tv actress. Born Nov 29, 1916, in Los Angeles, CA; died Jan 15, 2000, in Burbank, CA. ❖ Films include *Scandalous John, The Apple Dumpling Gang, Straight Time, The Long Riders, Pale Rider* and *The Sure Thing.*

RYAN, Irene (1902–1973). American stage, radio, tv and screen actress. Name variations: Irene Noblette. Born Oct 17, 1902, in El Paso, TX; died April 26, 1973, in Santa Monica, CA; m. Tim Ryan, 1922 (div. 1942); m. Harold E. Knox, 1946 (div. 1961). ❖ Began career at 10 as Irene Noblette in vaudeville; best remembered as Granny on tv series "The Beverly Hillbillies" (1962–71); made Broadway debut in *Pippin* (1972).

RYAN, Joan (1955—). English politician and member of Parliament. Born Joan Ryan, Sept 8, 1955; m. 2nd husband Martin Hegarty. ❖ Was a teacher; elected deputy leader of Barnet Council (1994); representing Labour, elected to House of Commons for Enfield North (1997, 2001, 2005); named assistant government whip (2003), then senior government whip.

RYAN, Mrs. John (1857–1934). See Cline, Maggie.

RYAN, Kathleen (1922–1985). Irish actress. Born Sept 8, 1922, in Dublin, Ireland; died Dec 11, 1985, in Dublin. ❖ Came to prominence in film debut as Kathleen Sullivan in *Odd Man Out* (1947), followed by *Captain*

Boycott, Esther Waters (title role), *Christopher Columbus, Give Us This Day, Laxdale Hall, Captain Lightfoot, Jacqueline* and *The Tree,* among others.

RYAN, Mary (1885–1948). American actress. Name variations: Mary E. Ryan. Born Nov 11, 1885, in NY; died Oct 2, 1948, in Cranford, NJ; m. Samuel Forrest. ❖ Made Broadway debut as Margaret Gray in *Brewster's Millions* (1906); starred opposite John Barrymore as Betty Graham in *The Fortune Hunter*; other credits include *Stop Thief, On Trial, The Little Teacher, Only 38* and *Red Light Annie*; made film debut under name Mary E. Ryan in *The Uprising* (1912), followed by 15 more films.

RYAN, Mary Bridget (1898–1981). Irish politician. Born Mary Bridget Carey, 1898, in Coonmore, Rear Cross, Co. Tipperary, Ireland; died Feb 8, 1981; m. Martin Ryan (TD, Tipperary, 1933–43), 1923; children: 4 daughters, 5 sons. ❖ Served as a despatch rider for Cumann na mBan after the Rising (1916); was a founder member of Fianna Fáil (1926); following death of husband, elected as a Fianna Fáil representative to the 12th Dáil for Tipperary (1944–48); returned to 13th (for North Tipperary), 14th (for South Tipperary), 15th and 16th (for North Tipperary) Dáil (1948–61).

RYAN, Meg (1961—). American actress. Born Margaret Mary Emily Ann Hyra, Nov 19, 1961, in Fairfield, CT; majored in journalism at New York University; m. Dennis Quaid (actor), 1991 (div. 2001); children: Jack (b. 1992). ❖ Made screen debut in *Rich and Famous* (1981); on tv, appeared as Betsy on soap opera "As the World Turns" (1982–84) and on "Wildside" (1985); came to prominence in film *Top Gun* (1986); co-starred with Dennis Quaid in *Innerspace* (1987) and *D.O.A.* (1988); had blockbuster hits with light comedies, *When Harry Met Sally . . .* (1989), *Sleepless in Seattle* (1993) and *You've Got Mail* (1998); other films include *When a Man Loves a Woman* (1994), *Courage Under Fire* (1996), *Proof of Life* (2000) and *Against the Ropes* (2004).

RYAN, Melissa (1972—). See Schwen, Missy.

RYAN, Pam (1939—). See Kilborn, Pam.

RYAN, Peggy (1924–2004). American actress, singer and dancer. Born Margaret O'Rene Ryan, Aug 28, 1924, in Long Beach, CA; dau. of vaudeville dancers; died Oct 30, 2004, in Las Vegas, Nevada; m. James Cross (actor), 1945 (div. 1952); m. Ray McDonald (dancer), 1953 (div. 1957); Eddie Sherman (novelist and columnist for *Honolulu Advertiser*) 1958; children: (1st m.) James "Spike" Cross (songwriter, died 1987); (2nd m.) dau. Kerry McDonald English; (3rd m.) Sean Sherman (adopted). ❖ At 3, made theatrical debut in parents' vaudeville act, The Dancing Ryans; made film debut at 6 in *The Wedding of Jack and Jill* (1930); was a song-and-dance ingenue in a score of movies, including *Follow the Boys, Mister Big, When Johnny Comes Marching Home, Patrick the Great, The Merry Monahans, Bowery to Broadway,* and *All Ashore,* among others; also appeared in *The Grapes of Wrath* (1940); retired and ran a dancing school; in later years, appeared on tv as Jack Lord's secretary Jenny on "Hawaii Five-O."

RYAN, Sarah (1977—). Australian swimmer. Born Feb 20, 1977, in Canberra, Australia. ❖ Won a silver medal for 4 x 100-meter medley relay at Atlanta Olympics (1996).

RYAN, Sheila (1921–1975). American actress. Name variations: Betty McLaughlin. Born Katherine Elizabeth McLaughlin, June 8, 1921, in Topeka, KS; died Nov 4, 1975, in Los Angeles, CA; m. Pat Buttram; children: daughter. ❖ Lead actress, appeared in over 60 B films, including *Dead Men Tell, Sun Valley Serenade, Dressed to Kill, Something for the Boys, Western Pacific Agent, The Gang's All Here, The Big Fix* and *Street of Darkness.*

RYBICKA, Anna (1977—). Polish fencer. Born Mar 28, 1977, in Poland. ❖ Won a silver medal for team foil at Sydney Olympics (2000).

RYCHEZA. *Variant of Richesa.*

RYDER, Sue (1923–2000). British social worker and philanthropist. Name variations: Baroness Ryder of Warsaw; Lady Ryder. Born Margaret Susan Ryder in England in 1923; died in Bury St. Edmunds, England, Nov 2, 2000; married a naval officer (killed in WWII); m. Leonard Cheshire (social worker, war hero and founder of Cheshire Homes for the disabled), 1959 (died 1992); children: (2nd m.) Jeremy Cheshire; Elizabeth Cheshire. ❖ During WWII, was assigned to Special Operations Executive (SOE), a unit involved in organizing sabotage and supporting resistance movements in occupied countries; attached to the Polish section, endured extreme danger; served in North Africa and Italy, and at war's end performed relief work in France and Poland; established 1st Sue Ryder Home in Suffolk, England (1953), a refuge for concentration camp survivors, as well as the mentally and physically ill; with husband, founded 24 Sue Ryder Houses in Britain and 80 other centers in 20 nations, including Eastern Europe and India; also set up 500 Sue Ryder charity shops; took name Warsaw as part of her title when she was elevated to House of Lords as a life peer (1979). ❖ See also autobiographies *And the Morrow Is Theirs* and *Child of My Love*; and *Women in World History.*

RYE, Daphne (1916—). English producer. Born April 17, 1916, in London, England; m. Roland Culver (actor, div.); m. John Janvrin (div.); m. Henry Ainley. ❖ Began career as an actress; was assistant stage manager at the Everyman (1930), stage manager at "Q" (1932–33), and assistant producer for *The Skin of Our Teeth* (1945); produced *Private Lives, Deep Are the Roots, Honour and Obey, Castle Anna, Present Laughter, The Damask Cheek, Royal Highness, Edward My Son, Surfeit of Lampreys, The Same Sky* and *The Little Hut*; was also casting director with H.M. Tennent.

RYE, Maria Susan (1829–1903). English social reformer and feminist. Born in London, England, Mar 31, 1829; dau. of Edward Rye (solicitor and bibliophile) and Maria Tuppen Rye (Quaker); died Nov 12, 1903 in Hempstead, Hertfordshire, England. ❖ Became secretary of a committee supporting the Married Women's Property Bill (1856); as a member of Society for Promoting the Employment of Women, opened a law stationers' business with express intent of hiring middle-class women to work for her (1859); assisted in the establishment of the Female Middle Class Emigration Society (1861), which for nearly a decade helped educated women pursue opportunities in Canada, Australia and New Zealand; established homes for impoverished children in both London and Canada (1868); was also influential in the creation of the Church of England Waifs and Strays Society (1891), with which she remained closely involved during remainder of her life. ❖ See also C. Macdonald, *A Woman of Good Character* (1989); and *Women in World History.*

RYGIER-NALKOWSKA, Zofia (1884–1954). *See Nalkowska, Zofia.*

RYKSA (1116–1185). *See Richizza of Poland.*

RYKSA (fl. 1288). Queen of Poland. Name variations: Richeza, Richizza, or Rycheza; Richiza Valdemarsdottir. Dau. of Waldemar or Valdemar I (b. 1243), king of Sweden (r. 1250–1275), and Sophie of Denmark (d. 1286); m. Przemysl II (1257–1296), duke of Cracow (r. 1290–1291), king of Poland (r. 1290–1296), in 1285; children: Ryksa of Poland (1288–1335, who m. Vaclav, king of Bohemia and Poland, r. 1300–1305).

RYKSA OF POLAND (d. 1185). Queen of Castile and Leon. Name variations: Richeza of Poland. Died June 16, 1185 (some sources cite 1166); dau. of Wladyslaw also known as Ladislas II the Exile (1105–1159), king of Hungary (r. 1162); became 2nd wife of Alphonso VII, king of Castile and Leon (r. 1126–1157), in July 1152 or 1153; children: Fernando (b. 1154); Sancha of Castile and Leon (1164–1208). ❖ Alphonso VII was also married to Berengaria of Provence.

RYKSA OF POLAND (1288–1335). Queen of Bohemia, Hungary, and Poland. Name variations: Richeza or Rycheza; Richsa; Rejcka; Ryksa Elizabeth; Elisabeth or Elizabeth-Ryksa; Elizabeth of Poland. Born in 1288 (some sources cite 1286); died Oct 19, 1335, in Koniggratz; dau. of Przemysl II (1257–1296), king of Poland (r. 1290–1296) and Ryksa (fl. 1288); 2nd wife of Vaclav or Waclaw or Wraclaw II also known as Wenceslas II (1271–1305), king of Bohemia (r. 1278–1305), and Poland (r. 1300–1305); 2nd wife of Rudolph or Rudolf III (1281–1307), king of Bohemia and Poland (r. 1306–1307). ❖ Wenceslas II's 1st wife was Judith (1271–1297); his 3rd was Elizabeth of Poland (fl. 1298–1305).

RYLOVA, Tamara (1931—). Russian speedskater. Born Tamara Nikolayevna Rylova, Oct 1, 1931, in Vologda, USSR. ❖ Won a bronze medal for the 1,000 meters at Squaw Valley Olympics (1960); at World championships, won silver medals for allround (1955) and small allround (1957, 1958, 1960) and gold medals for small allround (1959).

RYMAN, Brenda (1922–1983). English biochemist. Name variations: Brenda Edith Ryman. Born Dec 6, 1922, in UK; died Nov 20, 1983; m. Dr. Harry Barkley, 1948 (died 1978). ❖ Served as assistant lecturer in Biochemistry department at Royal Free Hospital Medical School (1948–51), then lecturer (1952–61), senior lecturer (1961–69), reader (1970–72) and biochemistry professor (1972–83); became the 1st married mistress of Girton College, Cambridge (1976).

RYMILL, Mary Ann (c. 1817–1897). New Zealand missionary, teacher, and nurse. Born Mary Ann Rymill, c. 1817, in Oxfordshire, England; died Dec 18, 1897, at Rangiora, New Zealand; dau. of William and Mary (Herbert) Rymill. ❖ Orphaned when young, was raised by aunt in London; immigrated with Robert and Susan Maunsell to New Zealand (1842); learned Maori language and taught in native school; assumed other teaching positions until health failed; became nurse and companion to several women and was active in Anglican church at Christchurch. ❖ See also *Dictionary of New Zealand Biography* (Vol. 1).

RYOM CHUN-JA (1942—). North Korean volleyball player. Born Nov 19, 1942, in North Korea. ❖ At Munich Olympics, won a bronze medal in team competition (1972).

RYON, Luann (1953—). American archer. Born Jan 13, 1953, in Long Beach, CA. ❖ At Montreal Olympics, won a gold medal in double FITA round (1976); won World championship (1977), shooting 2,515 for a women's world record; won US national championships (1976–77).

RYSANEK, Leonie (1926–1998). Austrian soprano. Born Nov 14, 1926, in Vienna, Austria; died Mar 7, 1998, in Austria; studied with Alfred Jerger, Rudolf Grossman, and Clothide Radony von Ottean at Vienna Conservatory; m. E.L. Gaussmann (musicologist). ❖ Made debut in Innsbruck (1949); appeared as Sieglinde in *Die Walkuere* in the 1st postwar Bayreuth Festival, to great success (1951); debuted at Covent Garden (1953) and Vienna State Opera (1954); made American debut in San Francisco (1956); debuted at Metropolitan Opera as Verdi's Lady Macbeth (1959); sang at Met for next 25 years, performing 20 roles in a total of 298 performances, especially that of Senta in Wagner's *The Flying Dutchman*; gave last performance at the Met (1996); over 4 decades, appeared on international opera stages over 2,100 times, in the process gaining an ardent following; made many recordings. ❖ See also *Women in World History.*

RYSKAL, Inna (1944—). Soviet volleyball player. Born June 15, 1944, in USSR. ❖ Won a silver medal at Tokyo Olympics (1964), gold medal at Mexico City Olympics (1968), gold medal at Munich Olympics (1972), and silver medal at Montreal Olympics (1976), all in team competition.

RYTOVA, Galina (1975—). Russian water-polo player. Born Sept 10, 1975, in USSR. ❖ Won a team bronze medal at Sydney Olympics (2000).

RYU JI-HAE (1976—). South Korean table tennis player. Name variations: Ryu Ji Hae or Ryu Ji-Hye or Ryu Ji Hye. Born Feb 10, 1976, in Busan-si, South Korea. ❖ Won a bronze medal for doubles at Atlanta Olympics (1996) and bronze medal for doubles at Sydney Olympics (2000).

RYUM, Ulla (1937—). Danish novelist, playwright and short-story writer. Born May 4, 1937, in Fredriksborg, Denmark; dau. of Steen Ryum and Elise Kirstine Hammer; children: Rasmus (b. 1968), Martin (b. 1973). ❖ Works include *Spejl* (Mirror, 1962), *Natsangersken* (Night Singer, 1963), *Latterfuglen* (1965), *Tusindskove* (1969), and *Noter om idag og igår* (1971). Published in English, *Two Plays by Ulla Ryum* (2001). Received several awards.

RYZHOVA, Antonina (1934—). Soviet volleyball player. Born July 1934 in USSR. ❖ At Tokyo Olympics, won a silver medal in team competition (1964).

S

SAAD, Siti binti (c. 1880–1950). Tanzanian singer. Name variations: Siti bint Saad. Born Mtumwa binti Saad in Kisuani, near Zanzibar Town (not Tanzania), probably in 1880; died 1950. ❖ Recording star from island of Zanzibar (Tanzania) whose recordings in Swahili, Arabic, and Hindustani continue to be heard in many parts of Africa, India, and the Arab-speaking world; moved to port town of Zanzibar (1911); learned singing and Arabic; combined her booming voice and acting skills to slowly build a reputation; frequently performed at festivals of song and dance in Swahili, the *lingua franca* over large portions of the African continent; began to widen her reputation as a Taarab singer, performing in Swahili, singing to large audiences; signed contract with His Master's Voice, a recording company located in Bombay, India (1928); with her Taarab group, made a concert tour of India and learned to mimic songs sung in Hindustani; signed with Columbia Records in US; singing in Arabic for Arabs, Hindustani for Indians, and Swahili for everyone, became one of the 1st modern popular singing stars, tapping into a huge audience which was bound together by religious and economic ties. ❖ See also *Women in World History.*

SAADAWI, Nawal el (b. 1931). See El Saadawi, Nawal.

SAADI, Elvira (1952—). Soviet gymnast. Born Jan 2, 1952, in Uzbekistan. ❖ Won a gold medal at Munich Olympics (1972) and a gold medal at Montreal Olympics (1976), both in team all-around; was USSR national champion (1973); won Champions All (1973); placed 3rd at World University Games (1973), Moscow News (1974), and World Cup (1975); coached at Moscow Dynamo Club, now coaches in Canada. Named Coach of the Year by Canadian Gymnastics Federation (1996). ❖ See also Soviet film *Are You Going to the Ball?* (1987).

SAALFELD, Romy (1960—). East German rower. Born Dec 14, 1960. ❖ At Moscow Olympics, won a gold medal in coxed fours (1980).

SAARAINEN, Eeva (1932—). See Ruoppa, Eeva.

SAARIAHO, Kaija (1952—). Finnish composer. Born Kaija Anneli Laakkonen, Oct 14, 1952, in Helsinki, Finland; Sibelius Academy, BA, 1980 (studied under Paavo Heininen); Freiburg University, composition diploma, 1983; attended courses in computer music at IRCAM in Paris; m. Jean-Baptiste Barrière (French composer). ❖ With other young Finnish composers and musicians, helped found the pro-Modernist Korvat auki! (Ears open!) society; moved to Paris (1982), where she remained; came to international prominence with *Verblendungen* (orchestra and tape, 1982–84) and *Lichtbogen* (ensemble and electronics, 1985–86); awarded the Kranichsteiner Prize in Darmstadt (1986) and Prix Italia (1988), for *Stilleben*; composed the solo song cycle *Lonh* (soprano and electronics, 1996), which was awarded the Nordic Music Prize (2000); works performed at concerts worldwide, including Savonlinna Opera Festival (1986), London (1989), Jakarta (1989), Paris (1989, 1991) and Vienna (1993); served as professor of composition at Sibelius Academy (1997–98); premiered 1st opera *L'amour de loin* to great acclaim at Salzburg Festival in Austria (2000).

SAARINEN, Aline (1914–1972). American art critic and tv commentator. Name variations: Aline B. Louchheim; Mrs. Eero Saarinen. Born Aline Milton Bernstein in New Yorkm NY, Mar 25, 1914; died in New Yorkm NY, July 13, 1972; dau. of Allen M. Bernstein and Irma (Lewyn) Bernstein; Vassar College, AB, 1935; Institute of Fine Arts, New York University, AM, 1941; m. Joseph H. Louchheim (public welfare administrator), June 17, 1935 (div. 1951); m. Eero Saarinen (1910–1961, architect), Dec 26, 1953 (died Sept 1961); daughter-in-law of Loja Saarinen (1879–1968); aunt of Pipsan Saarinen Swanson (1905–1979); children: (1st m.) Donald Louchheim (b. 1937), Harry Louchheim (b. 1939); (2nd m.) Charles Eames Saarinen (b. 1954). ❖ Was an assistant at *Art News* magazine (1944–46), becoming managing editor; named associate art editor and art critic of *The New York Times* (1947), then promoted to associate art critic; began appearing as art and architecture editor for "Sunday Show" on NBC and art critic for the "Today" show (1963); became the 3rd woman correspondent for NBC News (1964), as well as the moderator of "For Women Only," a tv-panel program; named chief of NBC Paris News Bureau (1971), the 1st woman appointed to head a foreign tv division; writings include *The Proud Possessor* (1958) and *Eero Saarinen on His Work* (1962); also wrote for *Atlantic Monthly, House Beautiful,* and other magazines. Received International Award for Best Foreign Criticism at the Venice Biennale (1951) and American Federation of Arts Award for best newspaper criticism (1953). ❖ See also *Women in World History.*

SAARINEN, Mrs. Eero (1914–1972). See Saarinen, Aline.

SAARINEN, Eva Louise (1905–1979). See Swanson, Pipsan Saarinen.

SAARINEN, Loja (1879–1968). Finnish-born designer. Name variations: Loja Gesellius; Loja Gesellius Saarinen; Louise Gesellius; Louise Saarinen. Born Louise Gesellius, Mar 15, 1879, in Finland; died April 1968; sister of architect Herman Gesellius; studied art in Finland and Paris; m. (Gottlieb) Eliel Saarinen (1873–1950, architect), Mar 6, 1903; mother-in-law of Aline Saarinen (1914–1972); children: Eero Saarinen (1910–1961, architect); Eva Lisa Saarinen Swanson (1905–1979, designer known as Pipsan Saarinen Swanson). ❖ Weaver and textile designer who combined Modernist design with traditional Scandinavian weaving and Art Deco techniques of 1920s and 1930s, immigrated to US (1923); joined the creative community at Cranbrook Academy of Art, becoming director of the weaving shops (1930), and serving as department head until her retirement (1942); also opened her own textile studio (1928).

SAARINEN, Louise (1879–1968). See Saarinen, Loja.

SAARINEN, Pipsan (1905–1979). See Swanson, Pipsan Saarinen.

SABA, queen of (fl. 10th c. BCE). See Sheba, Queen of.

SABAITE, Nijole (1950—). Soviet runner. Born Aug 12, 1950. ❖ At Munich Olympics, won a silver medal in the 800 meters (1972).

SABALSAJARAY, Nibuya (1951–1974). Uruguayan labor activist. Name variations: Nibuya Sabalsagaray. Born in Uruguay, 1951; died in Uruguay, 1974. ❖ Became school teacher and joined labor union; after participating in a large demonstration opposing the dictatorship, was arrested and tortured; died, age 23, as a result of her injuries. Revered as a martyr to the government's violent opposition toward the unionization movement of the 1970s.

SABATINI, Gabriela (1970—). Argentinean tennis player. Name variations: Gaby Sabatini. Born May 16, 1970, in Buenos Aires, Argentina. ❖ Began playing tennis at age 6; moved to Florida at age 12 to continue training; joined pro tour, became youngest semifinalist in history of the French Open, and named Rookie of the Year (1985); won a silver medal at Seoul Olympics (1988); ranked #3 in the world (1989, 1991, 1992); won US Open (1990) and Australian Open (1995); retired (1996). ❖ See also *Women in World History.*

SABBA. See Sambethe.

SABBE (fl. 10th c. BCE). See Sheba, Queen of.

SABIN, Ellen (1850–1949). American educator and administrator. Born Ellen Clara Sabin in Sun Prairie, Wisconsin, Nov 29, 1850; died in Madison, Wisconsin, Feb 2, 1949; dau. of Samuel Sabin (farmer) and Adelia Sabin; attended University of Wisconsin, 1886–89; never married; no children. ❖ Innovative educator, became the 1st woman principal in Portland, Oregon (1872), then the 1st woman superintendent of schools in Portland (1887, no other large US city had a woman in such a position at the time); signed on as president of Downer College for Women in Wisconsin (1891) and orchestrated its merger with Milwaukee College for Women (1895), becoming president of

Milwaukee-Downer College (1897); retired (1921). ❖ See also *Women in World History.*

SABIN, Florence (1871–1953). American physician and medical researcher. Pronunciation: SAY-bin. Born Florence Rena Sabin, Nov 9, 1871, in Central City, Colorado; died Oct 3, 1953, in Denver; dau. of George Kimball Sabin (mining engineer) and Serena (Miner) Sabin; graduate of Vermont Academy, 1889; Smith College, BS, 1893; Johns Hopkins School of Medicine, MD, 1900; never married; no children. ❖ Preeminent woman scientist of her generation, made substantial contributions to the fields of histology, immunology, and public health and fought for women's rights within and outside her profession; was instructor in zoology, Smith College (1895–96); interned at Johns Hopkins Hospital (1900–01), where she made a major contribution to the understanding of the structure of the human brain; at Johns Hopkins School of Medicine department of anatomy, was a fellow under Franklin Paine Mall (1901–02), where she began research on the development and structure of the lymphatic system, work that would occupy her for a number of years; became an instructor, the 1st woman on Johns Hopkins medical faculty (1902–05), then associate professor (1905–17), then the 1st woman promoted to full professorship there, serving as professor of histology (1917–25); served as 1st woman president of American Association of Anatomists (1924–26); was a member of Research Committee of National Tuberculosis Committee (1926); was a member of Rockefeller Institute for Medical Research (1925–38), working on various projects on the immune system, including a groundbreaking study on the immune response to tuberculosis; served on advisory board, John Simon Guggenheim Memorial Foundation (1939–47); served on board of directors and was vice-president for 3 years of Children's Hospital, Denver (1942–46); served as chair, Sabin Committee, Governor of Colorado Post-War Planning Committee (1944), resulting in the passage of a series of public-health bills, commonly referred to as the "Sabin laws"; was manager, Denver Department of Health and Welfare (1947–51); served as president, Western Branch of American Public Health Association (1948); served as chair, Board of Health and Hospitals, Denver (1951); writings include *Atlas of the Medulla and Midbrain* (1901) and *Franklin Paine Mall: The Story of a Mind* (1934). Appointed 1st woman full member of the Rockefeller Institute for Medical Research (1925); elected 1st woman member of the National Academy of Sciences (1925); received M. Carey Thomas Prize, Bryn Mawr (1935), Jane Addams Medal (1947) and Lasker Award (1951); recognition of her life's accomplishments culminated in the installation of a bronze statue in National Statuary Hall, Washington, DC, in honor of "Florence Sabin, Teacher-Scientist-Citizen" (1956). ❖ See also Elinor Bluemel, *Florence Sabin: Colorado Woman of the Century* (U. of Colorado Press, 1959); and *Women in World History.*

SABIN, Pauline Morton (1887–1955). American political reformer. Name variations: Pauline Smith; Mrs. Charles H. Sabin. Born Pauline Morton in Chicago, Illinois, April 23, 1887; died Dec 27, 1955, in Washington, DC; dau. of Paul Morton (railroad executive and president of Equitable Life Assurance Society) and Charlotte (Goodridge) Morton; granddau. of J. Sterling Morton (US secretary of agriculture); m. James Hopkins Smith Jr., Feb 2, 1907 (div.); m. Charles Hamilton Sabin (president of Guaranty Trust Co. of NY), Dec 28, 1916 (died 1933); m. Dwight F. Davis (US secretary of war, governor-general of Philippines, and donor of Davis Cup tennis trophy), May 9, 1936; children: (1st m.) Paul Morton Smith (1908–1956); James Hopkins Smith (b. 1909), who became assistant secretary for the navy. ❖ Considered the "mother" of prohibition reform in America, resigned as a member of the Republican National Committee to organize the Women's Organization for National Prohibition Reform (1929), of which she was made national chair; though a lifelong Republican, supported Franklin D. Roosevelt for the presidency because he came out for repeal of the 18th Amendment to the Constitution (1932).

SABINA (88–136 CE). Roman empress. Name variations: Vibia Sabina. Born in 88 CE; dau. of Matidia I (d. 119 CE) and L. Vibius Sabinus; maternal granddau. of G. Salonius Matidius Patruinus and Ulpia Marciana, and grandniece of Ulpia's brother, M. Ulpius Traianus (Trajan); sister of Matidia II; m. Hadrian, Roman emperor (r. 117–138 CE). ❖ Soon as she reached puberty, was married to Hadrian (100), Trajan's military and political protégé; became an important link between the 2 men; was quickly disillusioned by Hadrian's private aloofness (he clearly harbored primarily homosexual inclinations), and her marginal (if publicly proper) role in his life; let it be known that the reason Hadrian remained childless was that she refused to have sex with

him; though she loathed Hadrian, enjoyed being the empress of Rome, with all its perquisites; accompanied husband on state visits to the provinces, so there is ample testimony to the continuation of her public status throughout the Roman world; was styled as the "Augusta" (after 128) and widely recognized as the "new Hera" (after 129), and her portrait graced many a contemporary coin. ❖ See also *Women in World History.*

SABINA (b. 166). See *Vibia Aurelia Sabina.*

SABINA, Poppaea.
See *Poppaea Sabina (d. 47).*
See *Poppaea Sabina (d. 65).*

SABINE OF BAVARIA (1492–1564). Duchess of Wurttemberg. Born April 23, 1492; died Aug 30, 1564; dau. of Albert IV the Wise (1447–1508), duke of Bavaria (r. 1465–1508); m. Ulrich VI (1487–155), duke of Wurttemberg (r. 1503–1519, 1534–1550), Mar 2, 1511; children: Christof (b. 1515), duke of Wurttemberg.

SABINE OF BRANDENBURG-ANSBACH (1529–1575). Electress of Brandenburg. Name variations: Sabine von Brandenburg-Ansbach or Anspach. Born May 12, 1529; died Nov 2, 1575; dau. of George of Ansbach (b. 1484) and Hedwig of Munsterberg (d. 1531); became 2nd wife of John George (1525–1598), elector of Brandenburg (r. 1571–1598), on Feb 12, 1548; children: Sophie of Brandenburg (1568–1622). ❖ John George's 1st wife was Sophie of Liegnitz (1525–1546); his 3rd was Elizabeth of Anhalt (1563–1607).

SABLÉ, Madeleine de Souvré, Marquise de (c. 1599–1678). French writer and salonnière. Name variations: Magdeleine, Marquise de Sable, Sablé, or Sabele; Madame de Sablé. Born c. 1599; died Jan 16, 1678; dau. of Gilles de Souvré, marquis de Courtenvaux (tutor of Louis XIII and marshal of France); m. Philippe Emmanuel de Laval, marquis de Sablé, 1614 (died 1640); children: 4. ❖ Following death of husband (1640), took rooms in the Place Royale, Paris, with the Countess of St. Maur, where she established an important literary salon frequented by Marie-Madeleine de La Fayette, Antoine Arnauld, and La Rochefoucauld; composed the *Maximes et Pensées diverse* before those of La Rochefoucauld, but it was not published until after her death; retired, with Countess of St. Maur, to Convent of Port Royal des Champs (1655). ❖ See also *Women in World History.*

SABLIÈRE, Marguerite de la (1640–1693). See *La Sablière, Marguerite de.*

SABRI, Nazli (1894–1978). See *Nazli.*

SABUCO, Oliva de Nantes Barrera (1562–1625). Spanish philosopher and medical writer. Name variations: Luisa. Born in Alcarez, Spain, in 1562; died in Alcarez, 1625; dau. of Bachiller Miguel Sabuco and Francisca de Cozar; sister of Alonso Sabuco; m. Acacio de Buedo of Alcaraz, 1580. ❖ Published the philosophical treatise, *Nueva filosof'ia de la naturaleza del hombre* (1587), though father attempted to claim authorship; in the work, she presaged Descartes in her concern over the interaction of the soul and the body, placing their nexus in the brain. The treatise is now usually published along with her colloquy on medicine, *Vera Medicine,* which includes a philosophical discussion of the human body and emotions.

SABUROVA, Irina (1907–1979). Russian novelist, poet and short-story writer. Name variations: Irina Evgenevna Sabúrova. Born 1907 in Russia; died 1979. ❖ Émigré author, immigrated with family to Finland (1917); lived in Latvia, then settled in Munich (1943); wrote the short stories *The Shadow of Blue March* (1938), the poetry collection *Conversation in Silence* (1956), and the novels, *After . . .* (1960), *Ships of the Old City* (1964), and *About Us* (1972).

SABUROVA, Salome (fl. 16th c.). See *Solomonia.*

SACAGAWEA (c. 1787–c. 1812 or 1884). See *Sacajawea.*

SACAJAWEA (c. 1787–c. 1812 or 1884). Native American guide and interpreter. Name variations: Sacagewea; Sacagawea; Sakajawea; Sakakawea; "Bird Woman." Born into a tribe of Northern Shoshonis, in what is now the Lemhi Valley of Idaho, c. 1787; died as early as 1812, in childbirth, or as late as April 9, 1884; m. Touissant Charbonneau (common-law), a fur trapper and guide; children: Jean Baptiste (b. Feb 11 or 12, 1805); Bazil (adopted, son of her deceased sister); possibly a daughter, Lizette (or Lisette). ❖ Spent 20 months as a guide and interpreter for historic Lewis and Clark Expedition as they traveled up the Missouri River and westward to the Pacific Ocean to explore the country's new holdings in the West (1805–06), then passed out of history except for a few unreliable references; a small, resilient Shoshoni woman with a newborn baby on her back, earned the respect of the explorers she led and may well have won the heart of expedition leader Captain William Clark; with her baby, was a symbol of the expedition's peaceful (or at least non-warlike) intentions to the Indian tribes they encountered and thus served as the explorers' ambassador of good will as they made their historic journey. ❖ See also Grace Raymond Hebard, *Sacajawea: Guide of the Lewis and Clark Expedition* (1932); Harold P. Howard, *Sacajawea* (U. of Oklahoma, 1971); and *Women in World History.*

SACALICI, Elena (1937—). Romanian gymnast. Born 1937 in Romania. ❖ At Melbourne Olympics, won a bronze medal in team all-around (1956).

SACCHETTO, Rita (1879–1959). Italian dancer and choreographer. Born 1879 in Monaco di Baviera; died Jan 18, 1959, in Nervi, Italy. ❖ Trained as dancer in Munich; performed as concert dancer in numerous European cities including Dresden, Vienna, Berlin, Madrid, and Amsterdam; choreographed own repertory of dance works and mime pieces, such as *Krinoline*; danced with Metropolitan Opera in NY (1909–10), where she interpolated own solos into operas; returned to Europe where she taught classes in Munich; directed and performed in numerous silent films in Italy and Denmark.

SACH, Amelia (1873–1902). English murderer. Born 1873; hanged, Feb 3, 1903. ❖ In East Finchley, London, advertised services for unwed mothers; duped mothers into thinking that, for appropriate fee, she would place their babies in foster homes when in fact she turned the infants over to Annie Walters who murdered them; with Walters, tried at Old Bailey (Jan 1903), and became 1st women to be hanged at Holloway.

SACHARISSA (1617–1684). See Sidney, Lady Dorothy.

SACHENBACHER, Evi (1980—). German cross-country skier. Name variations: Evi Sachenbacher Stehle. Born Nov 27, 1980, in Reit im Winkl, Germany. ❖ Won a gold medal for the 4x5 km relay and a silver medal for the 1.5 km sprint at Salt Lake City Olympics (2002); won a silver medal for 4x5 km relay at Torino Olympics (2006).

SACHER, Anna (1859–1930). Austrian hotel administrator. Born Anna Maria Fuchs in Vienna, Austria, Jan 2, 1859; died in Vienna, Feb 25, 1930; dau. of Johann Fuchs (butcher); m. Eduard Sacher (1843–1892, hotel owner), 1880 (died 1892); children: Anna, Fanny and Eduard Sacher. ❖ Owner of Vienna's world-famous Hotel Sacher, who was famed for the elegance of her hotel and her colorful personality; following death of husband (1892), took over management of the hotel, which was renowned for its fine cuisine, fabled Sachertorte, superb wines, excellent location (across the street from the Hofoper, today's State Opera House), and her discretion when it came to the numerous *Chambre separées,* places of assignation for many a Habsburg archduke; retired (1929). Received Goldene Verdienstkreuz (Golden Achievement Cross) from Republic of Austria. ❖ See also *Women in World History.*

SACHIKO, Hidari (b. 1930). See Hidari, Sachiko.

SACHS, Nelly (1891–1970). German-Jewish poet and playwright. Pronunciation: SAX. Born Leonie Sachs, Dec 10, 1891, in Berlin, Germany; died May 12, 1970, in Stockholm, Sweden; dau. of William Sachs (manufacturer, died 1930) and Margarete (Karger) Sachs (died 1950); attended the exclusive Aubert-Schule, a private girls' school in Berlin, 1903–08; never married; no children. ❖ Nobel Prize winner, who was celebrated as one of the greatest German-language poets, though she lived in Sweden, and became a symbol of a German-Jewish reconciliation; grew up in Berlin; published 1st poems in *Vossische Zeitung* (Berlin, 1929); published poems in *Berliner Tagblatt* (1932) and in Jewish paper *Der Morgen* (1936–38); endured Nazi Germany's policies against Jews (1933–40); fled with mother to Sweden (1940); published 1st and only prose book, *Legenden und Erzählungen* (Legends and Stories, 1921); published 1st volume of poetry, *In the Habitations of Death* (1947); trans. Swedish poetry into German and edited anthologies of Swedish poetry (1947, 1958, 1963 and 1965); journeyed to Germany, Zürich, and Paris, and met poet Paul Celan with whom she had corresponded since 1954 (1960), forming a deep bond of friendship; was hospitalized, with short interruptions, for paranoia and persecution mania (1960–63); together with S. Y. Agnon, awarded Nobel Prize for Literature (Dec 10, 1966) for her work commemorating the suffering of Holocaust victims; writings include *Eclipse of the Stars* (1949), *Eli: A Mystery Play of the Sufferings of Israel* (1951), *And No One Knows How to Go On* (1957), *Flight and Metamorphosis* (1959), *Journey into a Dustless Realm* (1961), *Death Still Celebrates Life* (1961), *Glowing Enigmas I–IV* (1963–66) and *Die Suchende* (1966). Received Droste Prize for poets (1960); named 1st winner of the newly established Nelly-Sachs-Prize (1961); given Peace Prize of the German Book Sellers Association (1965). A Nelly Sachs room at the Kungliga Library in Stockholm was opened (Dec 10, 1971). ❖ See also Barbara Wiederman, ed. *Paul Celan-Nelly Sachs: Correspondence* (trans. by Christopher Clark, Sheep Meadow, 1995); and *Women in World History.*

SACHSE, Diana (1963—). See Gansky-Sachse, Diana.

SACHSE, Sandra. See Wagner, Sandra.

SACKVILLE-WEST, Vita (1892–1962). English writer. Name variations: Lady Victoria Mary Nicolson. Born Victoria Mary Sackville-West at Knole in Kent, England, Mar 9, 1892; died at Sissinghurst Castle, Kent, June 2, 1962; dau. of Lionel Sackville-West, 3rd Lord Sackville, and his cousin Victoria Sackville-West; m. Harold Nicolson (writer), Oct 1, 1913 (knighted, 1953; died May 1, 1968); children: Benedict "Ben" Lionel Nicolson (b. Aug 6, 1914); Nigel Nicolson (b. Jan 19, 1917). ❖ Poet, novelist, short-story writer, biographer, gardener and member of the Bloomsbury group, whose unusual lifestyle was portrayed in her son's book *Portrait of a Marriage*; bought Long Barn (1915); published *Poems of West and East* (1917), followed by novel, *Heritage* (1919); had an affair with Violet Keppel Trefusis (1918–21); wrote bestseller *The Dragon in Shallow Waters* (1921); published poetry *Orchard and Vineyard* (1921) and her history *Knole and the Sackvilles* (1922); met Virginia Woolf (Dec 1922) and began affair; edited *The Diary of Lady Anne Clifford* (1923) and completed *Grey Wethers* (both 1923); published 16 of her works with Hogarth Press owned by Virginia and Leonard Woolf (1924–33); won Hawthornden Prize for *The Land* (1927); published her most commercially successful book, *The Edwardians* (1930); bought Sissinghurst Castle (1930), which would be passed to the National Trust (1969); began giving popular series of talks on gardening for BBC; with Harold, went on lecture tour of US (1932); published *Pepita* (1937); published 10 works on gardening (1939–58); won Heinemann Prize for *The Garden* (1946); all told, produced 15 books of poetry, 12 novels, 3 collections of short stories, 6 biographies, and 17 works of nonfiction, mostly on gardening and travel; statuesque, sophisticated, well traveled, and well connected, cherished her independence which she was able to maintain in her "open" marriage and her numerous love affairs. Awarded Companion of Honor (1947). ❖ See also Victoria Glendinning, *Vita: The Life of Vita Sackville-West* (Penguin, 1983); Nigel Nicholson, *Portrait of a Marriage* (Atheneum, 1980); and *Women in World History.*

SADA JACCO (d. 1946). See Yakko, Sada.

SADA YAKKO (d. 1946). See Yakko, Sada.

SADAKO (r. 976–1001). Empress of Japan. Reigned from 976 to 1001; member of the powerful and influential Fujiwara family and dau. of Fujiwara Michitaka (d. 990); niece of Fujiwara Michinaga (966–1028), a major figure in Japanese history; sister of Shigei Sha. Sei Shōnagon (c. 965–?), author of the Japanese masterpiece *Makura no sōshi (The Pillow Book)*, served as Sadako's lady-in-waiting.

SADAKO (1885–1951). Empress of Japan. Name variations: Princess Sadako; Taisho empress. Born 1885; died May 17, 1951, in Japan; dau. of Prince Kujo Michitaka; m. Yoshihito Haru-no-miya (Emperor Taisho), emperor of Japan (r. 1912–1926), May 10, 1900; children—four sons: Prince Michi (b. April 29, 1901, reigned as Emperor Hirohito, r. 1926–1989); Prince Yasuhito Chichibu (1902–1953, who m. Chichibu Setsuko); Prince Takamatsu (b. 1905); Mikasa. ❖ A member of the aristocratic Fujiwara clan that had provided royal brides for centuries, married Yoshihito Haru-no-miya when he was crown prince (1900); is credited with helping her husband to encourage the inculcation of Western ideas. ❖ See also *Women in World History.*

SADAT, Jehan (1933—). Egyptian first lady and activist. Name variations: Gehan Sadat; Jihan Sadat. Born Jehan Raouf, 1933, in Roda Island, Egypt; dau. of Safwat Raouf (physician) and Gladys Charles Cotrell (British); Cairo University, BA in Arabic literature, 1978, MA, 1980, PhD in literary criticism, 1986; m. Anwar Sadat (president of Egypt, 1970–81), May 1949 (assassinated 1981); children: Loubna, Noha, Jihan and Gamal. ❖ First lady who, unlike wives of previous Egyptian leaders, played a prominent role in Egyptian politics, particularly in advancing the cause of women's rights; aware of the subservient condition of Egyptian women, began advocating for change; to emphasize education for women, enrolled in Cairo University to study Arabic literature at age 41; was influential in the passage of a set of laws, known as

"Jehan's Laws," whereby 30 seats in the Egyptian Parliament were set aside for women, and women were granted the power to divorce their husbands for polygamy or repudiation and retain custody of their children (1979); scandalized many with her independence and activism, her Western mannerisms and her willingness to grant personal interviews to Western magazines; after husband's assassination, held lectureships in US at University of South Carolina, American University in Washington, DC, Radford University in Virginia; became a professor of international studies at University of Maryland (1993). ❖ See also autobiography *A Woman of Egypt* (Simon & Schuster, 1987); and *Women in World History*.

SADE (1959—). Nigerian-English singer and songwriter. Name variations: Helen Folasade Adu, Sade Adu (stage name). Born Helen Folasade Adu, Jan 16, 1959, in Ibadan, Nigeria; dau. of Bisi Adu (professor of economics) and Anne Hayes; educated in London; children: (with producer, Bob Morgan) daughter Ila (b. July 1996). ❖ Studied fashion design and modeled briefly before becoming backup singer with British R&B band, Pride; known for husky, soulful voice, formed group Sade in London (1983); released album, *Diamond Life* (1984), with singles "Your Love Is King" and "Smooth Operator," which became the top-selling debut album of a British female vocalist; performed for Live Aid in Wembley Stadium (1985); released US #1 album, *Promise* (1985), with hits "The Sweetest Taboo" and "Never as Good as the First Time"; sang for and appeared in the film *Absolute Beginners* (1986); released successful albums, *Love Deluxe* (1992) and *Lovers Rock* (2000); had 6 multiplatinum albums and received 4 Grammy awards. Awarded Order of the British Empire (OBE, 2002).

SADEK, Nariman (1934–2005). *See Nariman.*

SADELER, Agnes (fl. 1386). English rebel. Name variations: Sadler. Flourished in Ramsley (Romley), England. ❖ Rebellious serf, listed in court records of 1386 as being the leader of the villagers of Ramsley, when they rose against their feudal lord. ❖ See also *Women in World History*.

SADEQ, Nariman (1934–2005). *See Nariman.*

SADIQ, Nariman (1934–2005). *See Nariman.*

SADLER, Agnes. *See Sadeler, Agnes.*

SADLIER, Mary Anne (1820–1903). Irish-born author. Name variations: Mary Anne Madden; Mary Ann Sadlier; Mrs. J. Sadlier. Born Mary Anne Madden, Dec 31, 1820, in Cootehill, Co. Cavan, Ireland; died April 5, 1903, in Montreal, Canada; dau. of Francis Madden (merchant); m. James Sadlier (owned a Catholic publishing house), Nov 1846; children: 3 sons and 3 daughters, including Anna T. Sadlier (writer); 1 foster son. ❖ At 18, published 1st poems in London periodical *La Belle Assemblée*; immigrated to US (1844); lived in Montreal, Canada (1846–60); wrote nearly 60 novels, many of which originally appeared in serial form in Catholic newspapers, exploring the cultural and religious dimensions of Irish immigration in US, with a distinctively conservative Catholic perspective; used the novel as a forum for providing young Irish Catholics with models for ways to resist what she felt were the damaging effects of American liberal Protestantism; writings include *The Blakes and the Flanagans* (1855), *Willie Burke: A Tale of the Irish Orphan in America* (c. 1856), *The Confederate Chieftains* (1860), *Aunt Honor's Keepsake* (1866), *Confessions of an Apostate* (1868) and *De Fromental* (1887); also published a translation of Matthieu Orsini's *Life of the Blessed Virgin, Mother of God* (1885) and wrote *Purgatory: Doctrinal, Historical, and Poetical* (1886). Awarded Laetare Medal from University of Notre Dame (1895). ❖ See also *Women in World History*.

SADOVA, Natalya (1972—). Russian discus thrower. Born July 15, 1972, in Gorki, Russia. ❖ Won a silver medal at Atlanta Olympics (1996); won a gold medal at World championships (2001) and a silver medal at European championships (2002); won a gold medal at Athens Olympics with a throw of 219:10.58 (2004).

SADOVNYCHA, Olena (1967—). Ukrainian archer. Born Nov 4, 1967, in Ukraine. ❖ Won a bronze medal for indiv. FITA round at Atlanta Olympics (1996) and a silver medal for teams at Sydney Olympics (2000).

SADOVSKAYA, Tatyana (1966—). Soviet fencer. Born April 3, 1966, in USSR. ❖ At Barcelona Olympics, won a bronze medal in indiv. foil (1992).

SAENGER VON MOSSAU, Renata (1680–1749). German accused of witchcraft. Name variations: Maria Renata Saenger von Mossau. Born 1680; died June 1749. ❖ Joined convent at Unter-Zell and rose to

become sub-prioress (1740); after several members of convent became ill and claimed to be possessed by demons, was denounced as a Satanist; confessed to relationship with devil and gave vivid account of occult and poison arts; despite penitence, was charged with sorcery and heresy and sentenced to be beheaded and burned.

SÁENZ, Manuela (1797–1856). South American revolutionary. Name variations: Manuela Saenz. Born Manuela Sáenz, Dec 27, 1797, in Quito, Ecuador; died Nov 23, 1856, in Paita, Peru; dau. of Simón Sáenz de Vergara (well-born Spanish adventurer) and María Joaquina de Aispuro (wealthy woman in her own right); briefly attended a convent school; m. James Thorne (English merchant), 1817; no children. ❖ Companion to Simón Bolívar, the Liberator of South America, who accompanied him into combat, saved his life on 2 occasions, fought for his reputation, and guarded his papers until her death; when young, became enamored of the revolutionary politics then sweeping the continent, where many people, inspired by the recent revolutions in North America and France, longed for liberation from Spain; sent to a convent school, from which she fled with a military officer (1814); fell in love with Bolívar (1822); remained his companion in the revolutionary cause until independence from Spain was achieved (1824); was separated from Bolívar at time of his death (1830); lived to see him reinstated as a hero (1842); has become more recognized for her contributions during the struggle for independence. ❖ See also Victor W. and Christine von Hagen, *The Four Seasons of Manuela: The Love Story of Manuela Sáenz and Simón Bolvar* (Duell, 1952); and *Women in World History*.

SAENZ-ALONSO, Mercedes (1916–2000). Spanish essayist, journalist and literary critic. Name variations: Mercedes Saenz-Alonso Gorostiza. Born May 2, 1916, in San Sebastián, Spain; died in 2000. ❖ Was correspondent for Radio Nacional de España (national radio of Spain); works include *Bajos fondos* (1949), *El tiempo que se fue* (1951), and *La pequeña ciudad* (1952).

SAETTEM, Birgitte (1978—). Norwegian handball player. Born July 9, 1978, in Molde, Norway. ❖ Won a team bronze medal at Sydney Olympics (2000).

SAEWARA (fl. 630). Queen of East Anglia. Dau. of Saethryth, an abbess; m. Anna, king of East Anglia (r. 635–654); children: Saint Sexburga (d. 699?); Elthelthrith (630–679); Withburga; (stepdaughter) Ethelburga (d. 665). ❖ King Anna's 2nd wife was Hereswitha.

SÁEZ, Irene (1961—). Venezuelan politician. Name variations: Irene Saez Conde. Born Irene Layling Sáez Conde, Dec 13, 1961, in Caracas, Venezuela; dau. of Carlos and Ligia Saez; m. Humberto Briceño Leon (lawyer), 1999 (div.); children: son (b. 2000). ❖ Venezuelan governor who used her fame as beauty pageant winner to launch successful career as progressive politician; gained national attention as winner of Miss Venezuela (1981) and went on to win Miss Universe (1981) in New York City; traveled world, fulfilling duties of position, but rejected offers to model and act, opting instead for university; became envoy for Banco Consolidado (Consolidated Bank, 1989); served as Venezuela's cultural representative at UN (1989 and 1991) and as head of board of Institutional Relations and Salesian Women's Association; ran for mayor of Chacao as official candidate for 2 parties, Acción Democrática (AD) and Comité de Organización Política Electoral Independiente (COPEI), winning 96% of vote (1992); while serving as mayor (1992–98), worked to make local government more efficient and responsive to citizens, focusing on quality of life issues such as police, ambulance and sanitation services; gained national reputation for clean, effective governance, leading to presidential bid (1998) on COPEI party line; campaigned against opponent Hugo Chávez as reformist and moderate but lost popularity and ultimately the backing of COPEI during campaign; immediately after losing presidential run, launched campaign for governor of Nueve Esparta (1999) and won with 70% of vote.

SAFFORD, Mary Jane (1834–1891). American Civil War nurse, physician, and reformer. Name variations: Mary Jane Safford Blake. Born Dec 31, 1834, in Hyde Park, Vermont; died Dec 8, 1891, in Tarpon Springs, Florida; dau. of Joseph Safford (farmer) and Diantha Little Safford; sister of Anson P. K. Safford (territorial governor of Arizona); graduate of New York Medical College for Women, 1869; advanced medical training at General Hospital of Vienna, medical centers in Germany, and at University of Breslau; m. James Blake, 1872 (probably div. 1880); children: (adopted) Margarita and Gladys Safford. ❖ Was nicknamed the "Cairo Angel" for her service to wounded Union soldiers in Cairo, Illinois, during the Civil War; credited with being the 1st woman to perform an ovariotomy (early 1870s); joined the faculty of the newly formed Boston University School of Medicine as professor of women's diseases (1872); focused her activities on women's issues, writing on dress, hygiene, and exercise, and striving to improve the conditions of working-class women; was one of the 1st women elected to the Boston School Committee (1875). ❖ See also *Women in World History.*

SAFIER, Gloria (d. 1985). American theatrical and literary agent. Born in OH; died Oct 9, 1985, age 63, in New York, NY. ❖ Opened her own office on Broadway (1948); client list included Leora Dana, Liz Smith and Ethel Merman.

SAFINA, Yuliya (1950—). Soviet handball player. Born July 1950 in USSR. ❖ At Moscow Olympics, won a gold medal in team competition (1980).

SAFIYAH (fl. 7th c.). One of the wives of Muhammad. Widow of Jewish origin; m. Muhammad around 628 CE. ❖ See also *Women in World History.*

SAFIYE (d. 1603). Ottoman sultana. Name variations: sometimes referred to as Baffa Sultana. Probably born in Venice with the maiden name of Baffa, though birth date unknown; assassinated in Constantinople in 1603; favorite consort of Murad III (1546–1595), Ottoman sultan (r. 1574–1595); children: Mohammed III (1566–1603, also seen as Mahomet, Mehmed, Mehemmed, Mehmet, Mohammed, and Muhammed), Ottoman sultan (r. 1595–1603). ❖ Entered the imperial harem as a young girl after being captured as a slave; personally corresponded with Elizabeth I of England and pledged assistance to the English in affairs of state and trade; also acted as regent during the rule of Mehmed III, starting in 1595. ❖ See also *Women in World History.*

SAFONOVA, Tamara (1946—). See *Pogosheva-Safonova, Tamara.*

SAFRONOVA, Natalia (1979—). Russian volleyball player. Born Feb 6, 1979, in Krasnoyarsk, USSR. ❖ Placed 3rd at World championships (1998, 2002); won a team silver medal at Athens Olympics (2004).

SAGA, Michiko (1934—). Japanese actress. Born Mar 1 (some sources cite Mar 3), 1934, in Kyoto, Japan; dau. of Isuzu Yamada (actress). ❖ Made film debut in *Miyamoto Musashi konketsuhen* (1956), followed by *Rindo garasu, Ten no me, Kunisada Chuji, Dancing Mistress, Gamblers on the Road, Ginda jumon, Bijo komori, Tsuma-koi dochu, Edo yumin den, Ratai, Juroku-sai no senso* and *Utamaro,* among others.

SAGAN, Françoise (1935–2004). French novelist, playwright and short-story writer. Name variations: Françoise Quoirez. Born Françoise Quoirez, June 21, 1935, in Cajarc, southwestern France; died Sept 24, 2004, in Honfleur, near Normandy, France; dau. of Paul and Marie Quoirez; attended the Sorbonne; m. Guy Schoeller (publisher), 1958 (div. 1960); m. Bob Westhof (American sculptor), 1962 (div. 1963); children: (2nd m.) Denis. ❖ Using a surname taken from Proust because her father wouldn't let her publish under the family name, gained international fame with 1st book, the controversial bestseller *Bonjour tristesse* (Hello Sadness, 1954), which she wrote at 18; also wrote *Un Certain Sourire* (1956, pub. in English as *A Certain Smile,*), *Aimez-vous Brahms?* (1959, pub. in English as *Goodbye Again*), *Chateau en Suède* (1959), *La Chamade* (1965), *Les Bleus Dans L'me* (1972), *Le Chien Couchant* (1980), *Un Sang d'aquarelle* (1987), *La Laisse* (1990), *Le Chien* (1993), and *Le Miroir égaré* (1998), among others; also wrote for the theater and films, including work on Claude Chabrol's screenplay for *Landru* (1963); died in poverty. ❖ See also autobiography *Avec mon meilleur souvenir* (1984).

SAGAN, Ginetta (1923–2000). Human-rights activist. Born Ginetta Moroni, June 1, 2003, in Milan, Italy; died Aug 25, 2000, in Atherton, CA; dau. of physicians who were also in the resistance (they were arrested in 1943 and never seen again); attended the Sorbonne and University of Illinois; m. Leonard Sagan (physician, died 1997); children: sons Loring, Duncan and Pico. ❖ Fought in Italy's anti-Fascist resistance as a young girl during WWII; was arrested, interrogated and tortured; escaped (1945); came to Washington to help establish the American division of Amnesty International (1960s); served 2 terms on the national board. Received the Presidential Medal of Freedom (1994).

SAGAN, Leontine (1889–1974). Jewish actress and film director. Name variations: Leontine Fleischer; Leontine Sagan-Fleischer; Leontine Fleischer-Sagan; Leontine Schlesinger. Pronunciation: Leon-teen-AH ZAH-gahn. Born Leontine Schlesinger, Feb 13, 1889, in Budapest, Hungary; died in Pretoria, South Africa, May 20, 1974; dau. of Josef Schlesinger and Emma (Fasal) Schlesinger; attended the Acting School of the German Theater (Reinhardt School) in Berlin, 1910–12; m. Dr. Victor Fleischer (archivist, dramatist, and novelist); children:

not known. ❖ One of the great directors in pre-World War II Germany and Britain, moved from Vienna to Johannesburg with parents sometime after 1900; returned to Berlin (1910); was a member of Cooperative of German Stage Actors (Genossenschaft Deutscher Bühnen-Angehöriger, GDBA, 1912–34), acting in various cities, including Vienna, Frankfurt am Main, and Berlin; far ahead of her time, directed *Mädchen in Uniform* (1931), which brought her worldwide acclaim; directed her 2nd and only other film *Men of Tomorrow* (also titled *Young Apollo*), in UK (1932); used new photography and sound techniques and handled radical subject matter in both; remained in UK after Nazi takeover and toured South Africa (1933); produced operettas by Ivor Novello in London, Glasgow, NY, and other cities (1934–39); worked as a stage director in Johannesburg and Capetown, South Africa (1939–42); helped co-found the National Theatre in Johannesburg; produced for the theater and BBC in London after 1943; returned to South Africa (1950s), where she worked as a director and impresario there and in Rhodesia until her death. Awarded Lion of San Marco at Venice Film Festival (1932) for *Mädchen in Uniform* (variously translated as *Maidens in Uniform,Girls in Uniform,* and *Children in Uniform*). ❖ See also *Women in World History.*

SAGAN, Lynn (1938—). See *Margulis, Lynn.*

SAGE, Cornelia (1876–1936). See *Quinton, Cornelia B. Sage.*

SAGE, Juniper.
See *Brown, Margaret Wise.*
See *Hurd, Edith Thacher.*

SAGE, Kay (1898–1963). American artist. Name variations: Katherine Linn Sage; Katherine Sage Tanguy; K. di San Faustino or Kay di San Faustino; Princess di San Faustino. Born Katherine Linn Sage in Albany, NY, June 25, 1898; committed suicide, Jan 8, 1963, in Woodbury, Connecticut; dau. of Henry Manning Sage (heir to an industrial fortune) and Anne Wheeler (Ward) Sage; attended Corcoran Art School, 1919–20, and Italian art schools in Rome; m. Prince Ranieri di San Faustino, 1925 (annulled, 1935); m. Yves Tanguy (Surrealist painter), 1940 (died 1955). ❖ Painter whose works embodied an elegant and refined form of Surrealism, 1st worked as a government censor during WWI (1917–18); though she enjoyed the benefits of inherited wealth throughout life, abandoned the role of social dilettante, as well as her marriage to 1st husband, an Italian noble, to become a serious artist (1935); had 1st solo exhibit (1936); moved to Paris (1937); despite the unwillingness of most Surrealist painters to take a woman colleague seriously, managed to enter the Surrealist circle; attended International Surrealist Exhibit in Paris and held 1st exhibit there (1938); returned to US to live (1939) and had 1st solo exhibit there (1940); won Watson F. Blair Purchase Prize at Art Institute of Chicago (1945); began to produce paintings of striking originality which won her a considerable degree of recognition; created an eerie world of geometric shapes, draperies and lattices; exhibited work at Catherine Viviano Gallery, NY (1950); eyesight began to fail (1958); made 1st suicide attempt (1959); her work had 1st full-scale retrospective showing (1960). Major works include *Monolith* (1937), *Egg on Sill* (1939), *Danger, Construction Ahead* (1940), *I Saw Three Cities* (1944), *The Unicorns Came Down to the Sea* (1948), *This is Another Day* (1949) and *Tomorrow is Never* (1955). ❖ See also Judith D. Suther, *A House of Her Own: Kay Sage, Solitary Surrealist* (U. of Nebraska Press, 1997); and *Women in World History.*

SAGE, Margaret Olivia (1828–1918). American philanthropist. Name variations: Margaret Olivia Sage; Olivia Sage; Mrs. Russell Sage. Born Margaret Olivia Slocum in Syracuse, New York, Sept 8, 1828; died in New York, NY, Nov 4, 1918; dau. of Joseph Slocum (merchant) and Margaret Pierson (Jermain) Slocum; graduate of Troy Female Seminary, 1847; m. Russell B. Sage (financier and former congressional representative), Nov 24, 1869 (died July 1906); no children. ❖ One of the top public benefactors in the early 20th century, established the Russell Sage Foundation with a $10 million endowment (then the largest-ever single gift for the public good), to improve living and social conditions in US (1907); donated huge numbers of modest sums to hospitals, churches, homes for the elderly, the YWCA and YMCA, Bible tract societies, and the American Seaman's Friend Society; as philanthropic work progressed, focused on education, religion, and welfare, though she also supported such causes as fresh air funds, humane treatment for animals, milk inspection, the Women's Christian Temperance Union, and the women's suffrage movement. ❖ See also *Women in World History.*

SAGE, Mrs. Russell (1828–1918). See *Sage, Margaret Olivia.*

SAGER, Ruth (1918–1997). American geneticist. Born Feb 7, 1918, in Chicago, Illinois; died Mar 29, 1997, in Brookline, Massachusetts; graduate of University of Chicago, 1938; Rutgers University, MS in plant physiology, 1944; Columbia University, PhD in genetics, 1948; m. Arthur Pardee. ❖ Became an assistant in biochemistry at Rockefeller Institute for Medical Research (later Rockefeller University), where she began investigations into genetic theory; challenging the prevailing notion regarding the location of the genetic material in cells, examined alternative theories that suggested the possibility of a 2nd genetic system governing heredity existing outside the chromosomes; findings changed the direction of genetic research (1953); for next 20 years, held research posts at several different institutions, including Columbia University, where she was research associate in zoology from 1955 until she advanced to senior research associate (1961); became professor of biology at Hunter College of City University of New York (1966); was on the staff of Boston's Dana-Farber Cancer Institute, an affiliate of Harvard University Medical School, while also serving as professor of cellular genetics at Harvard Medical School; retired as professor emerita (1988), but continued working at Dana-Farber, eventually becoming chief of cancer genetics there. Elected to National Academy of Sciences (1977). ❖ See also *Women in World History.*

SAGINE-UJLAKINE-REJTO, Ildiko (1937—). Hungarian fencer. Name variations: Ildiko Sagine; Ildiko Ujlakine; Ildiko Sagine-Ujlaki-Rejto; Ildkio Rejlö; Ildiko Rejt. Born May 11, 1937, in Budapest, Hungary. ❖ At Rome Olympics, won a silver medal in team foil (1960); at Tokyo Olympics, won gold medals in team foil and indiv. foil (1964); at Mexico City Olympics, won a bronze medal in indiv. foil and a silver medal in team foil (1968); at Montreal Olympics, won a bronze medal in team foil (1976); won World championship (1963); she was born deaf.

SAGITTINANDA, Turiya (b. 1937). See *Coltrane, Alice.*

SAGSTUEN, Tonje (1971—). Norwegian handball player. Born Nov 17, 1971, in Norway. ❖ At Barcelona Olympics, won a silver medal in team competition (1992).

SAH (fl. 1500s). Ottoman princess. Name variations: Sah Sultana. Born c. 1490 in Trebizond, a Black Sea caravan city in Asia Minor (present-day Turkey); dau. of Selim I the Grim, Ottoman sultan (r. 1512–1520) and Hafsa (d. 1534); sister of Suleiman or Suleyman the Magnificent, Ottoman sultan (r. 1520–1566), and Hatice; aunt of Mihrimah (1522–1575); m. Lutfi Pasha (a grand vizier). ❖ According to accounts of the period, protested against husband's inhumane treatment of a prostitute; when husband asserted that he would continue to punish prostitutes in this way, lost her temper and was beaten by him; divorced husband, ending his career. ❖ See also *Women in World History.*

SAHGAL, Nayantara (1927—). Indian novelist and journalist. Name variations: Nayantara Pandit. Born Nayantara Pandit, 1927, in Allahabad, India; dau. of Vijaya Lakshmi Pandit (1900–1990, politician and diplomat) and Ranjit Pandit; niece of Jawaharlal Nehru; cousin of Indira Gandhi; sister of Chandralekha Mehta (journalist) and Rita Dar; educated in India and US; children: 3. ❖ Was writer-in-residence at Southern Methodist University, TX (1973, 1977), visiting scholar at Radcliffe Institute, Harvard University (1976), and fellow of Woodrow Wilson Center (1981–82); was member of Indian delegation to UN General Assembly (1978); works include *Prison and Chocolate Cake* (1954), *From Fear Set Free* (1962), *A Time to be Happy* (1958), *This Time of Morning* (1965), *Storm in Chandigarh* (1969), *A Voice for Freedom* (1977), *A Situation in New Delhi* (1977), *Rich Like Us* (1985), *Plans for Departure* (1985), and *Mistaken Identity* (1988); also wrote *The Freedom Movement in India* (1970) and *Indira Gandhi: Her Road to Power* (1982).

SAIKI, Patricia Fukuda (1930—). American politician. Name variations: Patricia Fukuda; Mrs. Stanley Mitsuo Saiki. Born Patricia Fukuda in Hilo, Hawaii, May 28, 1930; dau. of Kazuo Fukuda and Shizue (Inoue) Fukuda; University of Hawaii at Manoa, BS, 1952; m. Stanley Mitsuo Saiki, June 19, 1954; children: Stanley Mitsuo Saiki; Sandra S. Saiki; Margaret C. Saiki; Stuart K. Saiki; Laura H. Saiki. ❖ After serving as a delegate to Hawaii State Constitutional Convention, was elected to Hawaii House of Representatives (1968); remained in Hawaiian House until 1974; served in state senate (1974–83); served as chair of Republican Party of Hawaii (1983–85); elected to Congress from 1st Congressional District (1986), the 1st Republican to represent Hawaii in US House of Representatives since the islands achieved statehood; during 2 terms in the House (Jan 3, 1987–Jan 3, 1991), served on Committee on

Banking, Finance and Urban Affairs, Select Committee on Aging, and Committee on Merchant Marine and Fisheries; was instrumental in helping to secure authorization for additional land for the Kiluea National Wildlife Refuge, and co-sponsored the bill to provide compensation for Japanese-Americans interned during WWII; became director of the Small Business Administration under President George Bush. ❖ See also *Women in World History.*

SAIMAN, Nurfitriyana (1962—). Indonesian archer. Born Mar 7, 1962, in Jakarta, Indonesia. ❖ At Seoul Olympics, won a silver medal in team round (1988).

SAIMEI, Empress (594–661). See *Kōgyoku-Saimei.*

SAIMO, Sylvi (1914–2004). Finnish kayaker. Born Nov 12, 1914, in Finland; died Mar 12, 2004. ❖ At Helsinki Olympics, won a gold medal in K1 500 meters (1952), the 1st Finnish female to win a gold medal in the summer Olympics; was elected to the Finnish Parliament 4 times.

SAINT, Dora Jessie (1913—). British novelist. Name variations: Dora Saint; (pseudonym) Miss Read. Born Doris Jessie Shafe, April 17, 1913, in Surrey, England; dau. of Arthur Gunnis Shafe and Grace Read Shafe; m. Douglas Edward John Saint (schoolmaster), 1940; children: 1 daughter. ❖ Works, which draw on her memoirs of living and teaching in a small English village, include *Village School* (1955), *Fresh from the Country* (1960), *Chronicles of Fairacre* (1964), *The Howards of Caxley* (1967), *Battles at Thrush Green* (1975), *The White Robin* (1979), *A Fortunate Grandchild* (1982), *Time Remembered* (1986), *Miss Read's Christmas Book* (1992) and *A Peaceful Retirement* (1996).

SAINT, Eva Marie (1924—). American actress. Born July 4, 1924, in Newark, New Jersey; dau. of John Saint (businessman) and Eva Saint; Bowling Green State University, Bowling Green, Ohio, BA, 1946; studied at Actors Studio; m. Jeffrey Hayden (producer-director), Oct 27, 1951; children: 2. ❖ Began career in radio, then moved into tv, playing dramatic roles on such shows as "Robert Montgomery Presents," "Studio One" and "Philco Playhouse," and winning the 1954 Sylvania award as Best Dramatic Actress in TV; in 1st major Broadway play, appeared as the traveling companion in *A Trip to Bountiful* (1953), for which she received the Drama Critics Award; made film debut in *On the Waterfront*, for which she won an Academy Award (1954); other films include *That Certain Feeling* (1956), *A Hatful of Rain* (1957), *Raintree County* (1957), *North by Northwest* (1959), *Exodus* (1960), *All Fall Down* (1962), *36 Hours* (1964), *The Sandpiper* (1965), *The Russians Are Coming, the Russians Are Coming* (1966), *Grand Prix* (1966), *The Stalking Moon* (1969), *Loving* (1970) and *Nothing in Common* (1986).

ST. ALBANS, duchess of (c. 1777–1837). See *Mellon, Harriot.*

SAINT-CHAMOND, Claire-Marie Mazarelli, Marquise de La Vieuville de (1731—). French essayist, playwright and short-story writer. Name variations: Saint Chaumond. Born Claire Mazarelli (also seen as Mazzarelli), 1731, in Paris, France; dau. of Ange Mazarelli (of Italian descent) and Marie-Catherine Mathée; m. Charles-Louis-Auguste Vieuville (b. 1726), marquis de Saint-Chamond, count of Vienne and of Confolens, 1st baron of Lyonese (colonel for the king), June 1, 1765; children: Charles-Louis-Auguste Vieuville (b. 1766). ❖ Wrote pieces for periodicals, including self-portrait in *Mercure* (1751) and letter to Jean-Jacques Rousseau in *L'Année littéraire* (1763); published 2 eulogies, *Éloge de Sully* (1763) and *Éloge de René Descartes* (1965), and 1 play, *Les Amants sans le savoir* (1771).

ST. CLAIR, Lydia (1898–1970). Austrian-born stage, film and tv actress. Name variations: Lydia Busch. Born Dec 19, 1898, in Austria-Hungary; died Jan 1, 1970, in New Milford, CT. ❖ Was a lead player in Frankfurt before coming to US (1940); stage credits include *Flight to the West, Trio* and *Time of the Cuckoo.*

ST. CLAIR, Sallie (1842–1867). American ballet dancer. Born 1842, possibly in Philadelphia, PA; died of consumption, Jan 23, 1867, in Buffalo, NY. ❖ Performed at Bates Theater in St. Louis, MO, throughout short career in such works as *Giselle, La Vivandière* and *La Bayadère.*

ST. CLAIR, Stephanie (fl. 1920s–30s). African-American racketeer. Name variations: Madame Stephanie St. Clair; Queenie St. Clair. Born in Martinique; briefly married to Abdul Hamid. ❖ Famed Numbers Queen of Harlem who arrived in US from Martinique (1912) and started banking numbers 10 years later with a bankroll of $10,000; ran an extortion gang known as The Forty Thieves; sentenced to 3 years on Welfare Island (1929), was paroled 1 month later; questioned by the

Seabury investigators, named names of those involved in graft, most specifically the name of the district attorney, a score of policemen, and two judges. ❖ See also (film) *Hoodlum* (1997), in which she's portrayed by Cicely Tyson.

ST. CLAIR, Yvonne (1914–1971). American actress and dancer. Born 1914 in Seattle, WA (or possibly in Vancouver, British Columbia, Canada); died Sept 22, 1971, in Seattle; dau. of Jessie Hall (costumes and stage designer); sister of Irma St. Clair (dancer); children: Mark Dempsey (actor). ❖ Dancer in vaudeville, nightclubs (including Ciro's), and such films as *The Great Ziegfeld, Anna Karenina, A Night at the Opera* and *A Midsummer Night's Dream*; became an aeronautical engineer.

SAINT-CYR, Renée (1904–2004). French actress and producer. Name variations: Renee St.-Cyr, Renee Saint Cyr. Born Marie-Louise Eugénie Vittore (also seen as Raymonde-Renée Vittoré), Nov 16, 1904, in Beausoleil, France; died July 11, 2004, in Neuilly-sur-Seine, France; children: Georges Lautner (film director). ❖ Made film debut in *Les deux orphelines* (1933), followed by *D'amour et d'eau fraiche, Les perles de la couronne, 27 Rue de la Paix, Strange Boarders, Nuit de décembre, La symphonie fantastique, Madame et la mort, Pierre et Jean, Le beau voyage, Fusillé à l'aube* (also producer), *Capitaine Ardant, Le chevalier de la nuit* (also producer), *Lafayette*, among others. ❖ See also memoir *Les temps de vivre*.

ST. DENIS, Ruth (1877–1968). American dancer. Name variations: Mrs. Edwin Shawn. Born Ruth Dennis, Jan 20, 1877, in Newark, New Jersey; died July 21, 1968; dau. of Thomas L. Dennis (inventor) and Ruth Emma (Hull) Dennis (one of the 1st licensed woman doctors in US); m. Ted Shawn (dancer), Aug 13, 1914 (sep., 1928). ❖ One of the greatest figures in the dance world in 1st half of 20th century and a founder of modern dance, began theatrical career in 1893; danced in productions of David Belasco (1899–04); began to steep herself in the cultures of the East, eventually coming under the influence of Hindu dance; made successful NY debut performing several "oriental" dances, set to the music from *Lakmé*, including *Incense, The Cobra* and *Radha* (1906); went on triumphant European tour (1906–09) and devised the cycle of Indian dances that were to make her famous; went on US tour (1909–11); staged 1st full-length dance, *Egypta* (1910); created several dances on Japanese themes, especially *O-mika*; advertising for a partner, met future husband Ted Shawn (1914); with Shawn, ran Ruth St. Denis School of Dancing and the Related Arts, soon called Denishawn (1915–31), which became the most important, most original, and most interesting dance company in America and schooled some 75 dancers, including Doris Humphrey, Charles Weidman and Martha Graham; went on Denishawn concert and vaudeville tours (1915–19), performing several new dances—*Soaring, Valse Caprice*; had her dancers attempt virtually every type of dance known, from American Indian to East Indian, from Japanese to Javanese, from Spanish to Russian to Greek, though not necessarily authentic; set off on the now-famous tour of the Orient (1925); toured with Ziegfeld Follies (1927); after dissolving Denishawn (1931), found it difficult to secure bookings and saw her life's work suddenly pass out of style; published *Lotus Light*, a book of poetry (1932); revived career when she appeared as part of *Dance International* at Radio City Music Hall (1937); ran School of Natya with La Meri (1940–42); gave last public performance, at Jacob's Pillow (Aug 1964); spent final years teaching at colleges and traveling about the country giving lectures. ❖ See also autobiography *An Unfinished Life* (1939); Walter Terry, *Miss Ruth: The "More Living" Life of Ruth St. Denis* (Dodd, 1969); Ted Shawn, *Ruth St. Denis: Pioneer and Prophet* (2 vols., 1920); and *Women in World History*.

ST. DENIS, Teddie (b. 1909). Scottish actress and singer. Born June Catherine Church Denham, 1909, in Bearsden, Glasgow, Scotland; m. Jack Eggar (div.); m. R. A. C. Holme. ❖ Made stage debut in variety in Glasgow (1924); toured in South Africa (1927, 1929); made London debut as Jean in *Jill Darling* (1934), followed by Dolly Jordan in *Over She Goes* (1936); appeared as Sally opposite Lupino Lane at the Victoria Palace in *Me and My Girl*, which ran for 1,646 performances and introduced the Lambeth Walk (1937–39).

ST. GEORGE, Katharine (1894–1983). American politician. Born Katharine Delano Price Collier in Bridgnorth, England, July 12, 1894; died in Tuxedo Park, New York, May 2, 1983; dau. of Price Collier (Iowa-born writer, Unitarian minister and European editor of *Forum* magazine) and Katharine Delano (sister of Sara Delano Roosevelt, the mother of Franklin Delano Roosevelt); cousin of President Franklin D.

Roosevelt; m. George St. George (broker), April 1917; children: Priscilla St. George. ❖ Became executive vice-president and treasurer of the St. George Coal Co. (1947); was 1st woman to become chair of a Republican campaign committee in New York State, aligning herself with Thomas E. Dewey in his unsuccessful attempt to unseat her cousin Franklin for the presidency (1940); won election to US House of Representatives from NY (1946), serving 9 terms (Jan 3, 1947–Jan 3, 1965); appointed to Committee on Post Office and Civil Service, Committee on Government Operations, Committee on Armed Services, and Rules Committee; presented legislation to include the Women's Army Auxiliary Corps under the provisions of the Veteran's Administration law; pressed for the establishment of a federal safety division in the Labor Department. ❖ See also *Women in World History*.

ST. JAMES, Lyn (1947—). American race-car driver. Name variations: Evelyn Cornwall. Born Evelyn Cornwall, Mar 13, 1947, in Willoughby, Ohio; dau. of Alfred Cornwall and Maxine (Rawson) Cornwall; m. John Carusso, 1970 (div. 1979); m. Roger Lessman, Feb 1993. ❖ The 1st woman to average more than 200 miles per hour on an oval track, at Alabama's Talladega Superspeedway, was also the 1st woman to win a solo North American professional road race, at Watkins Glen, NY (both 1985); won the SCCA (Sports Car Club of America) Florida Regional championship (1976 and 1977); won, along with male teammates, the GTO class of the Daytona 24 Hours marathon (1987 and 1990); finished in 11th place in the Indianapolis 500, becoming the 2nd woman to participate in that race, and won Rookie of the Year honors (1992). ❖ See also *Women in World History*.

SAINT JEAN, Anne (1927—). See *Cloutier, Suzanne*.

ST. JOHN, Florence (1854–1912). English actress and singer. Name variations: Florence Leslie. Born Margaret Florence Grieg, Mar 8, 1854, in Tavistock, Devonshire, England; died Jan 30, 1912, in London, England; married a naval officer surnamed St. John (died); m. Lithgow James (singer, div.); m. Claude Marius (actor), 1882. ❖ At 14, made stage debut as a vocalist with a touring diorama; made London debut in title role of *Madame Favart* (1879), followed by *Olivette, Nell Gwynne* (title role), *Faust Up to Date* and *La Mascotte*, among others; appeared with D'Oyly Carte (1894–95, 1897–98), creating the role of Rita in *The Chieftain* and appearing in title roles in *Mirette* and *The Grand Duchess of Gerolstein*; also appeared in *Florodora* and recorded "He Loves Me; He Loves Me Not" from that show.

ST. JOHNS, Adela Rogers (1894–1988). American journalist, author, and educator. Born Adela Nora Rogers in Los Angeles, California, May 20, 1894; died Aug 10, 1988, in Arroyo Grande, California; dau. of Earl Rogers (prominent trial lawyer) and Harriet (Greene) Rogers; m. William Ivan St. Johns (journalist), Dec 24, 1914 (div. 1929); m. Richard Hyland (div.); m. Francis Patrick O'Toole (div.); children: (1st m.) William Ivan St. Johns II; Elaine St. Johns; McCullah St. Johns; Richard Rogers St. Johns. ❖ Worked as a reporter for *San Francisco Examiner* (1913), *Los Angeles Herald* (1914–18), *International News Service* (1925–49), *Chicago American* (1928) and *New York American* (1929); earned sobriquet of world's greatest "girl" reporter with her controversial 16-part exposé on the treatment of LA's indigent for the *Herald*; covered all beats, encompassing crime, local politics, sports, and society stories, but was noted for inside scoops on Hollywood film community; also considered the 1st woman sportswriter in US; conducted daily radio program "Woman's Viewpoint of the News"; wrote 15 books and 13 screenplays; her numerous films were based on her early novels and short stories, chief among them *Pretty Ladies* (1925), *The Single Standard* (1929), *Scandal* (1929), *A Woman's Man* (1934), *I Want A Divorce* (1940), and *Government Girl* (1943); published a biography of her father, *Final Verdict* (1962), and recounted facets of her life in *The Honeycomb* (1969) and *Some Are Born Great* (1974); also wrote bestseller *Tell No Man* (1966); was the 1st woman faculty member of the graduate school of journalism at University of California at Los Angeles (1950–52). Awarded a Medal of Freedom by President Richard Nixon (1970). ❖ See also *Women in World History*.

SAINT-LAURENT, Jeanne (1887–1966). Canadian first lady. Name variations: Jeanne St. Laurent. Born Jeanne Renault, 1887, in Beauceville, Quebec, Canada; died Nov 14, 1966; m. Louis Saint-Laurent (prime minister of Canada, 1948–57), May 19, 1908; children: Marthe (b. 1909), Renault (b. 1910), Jean-Paul (b. 1912, MP 1955–58), Thérèse (b. 1915), and Madeleine (b. 1917).

SAINT-LÉGER DE COLLEVILLE, Anne-Hyacinthe de (1761–1824). See *Colleville, Anne-Hyacinthe de Saint-Léger de*.

ST. LÉON, Fanny (1817–1909). *See Cerrito, Fanny.*

ST. LOUIS, France (1959—). Canadian ice-hockey player. Born Oct 17, 1958, in St. Hubert, Quebec, Canada. ❖ Won a gold medal at World championships (1990, 1992, 1994, 1997); at age 39, the oldest Canadian hockey player at Nagano, won a team silver medal (1998), the 1st Olympics to feature women's ice hockey; was also a member of the Canadian Women's Lacrosse Team, participating at World championships (1986, 1989). Named MVP at National championships (1988, 1990, 1991, 1997); named Quebec's Athlete of the Decade (1980–90).

SAINTE-MARIE, Buffy (1941—). Cree folksinger, songwriter, and activist. Name variations: Beverly Sainte-Marie. Born Feb 20, 1941, on Cree Piapot reservation in Craven, Saskatchewan, Canada; adopted dau. of Albert C. Sainte-Marie and Winifred Kendrick Sainte-Marie (part Micmac Indian); graduate of University of Massachusetts, 1963; m. Dewain Kamaikalani Bugbee, 1967; children: (with actor Sheldon Wolfchild) Dakota Starblanket Wolfchild (b. 1977). ❖ Orphaned in 1st months of life, was adopted by a Massachusetts couple; while in college, sang in local coffee shops; moved to NY (1963) and joined Greenwich Village's folk movement, performing in such nightclubs as the Bitter End, Gaslight Cafe, and Gerde's Folk City; released 1st album *It's My Way* on Vanguard Records (1964); rose to international prominence as a folk singer and songwriter and produced a number of gold records (1960s); singing reflected a range of musical styles, including contemporary folk songs, American folk standards, popular love songs, antiwar ballads, and songs celebrating her Indian heritage; also recorded songs protesting injustices, such as "My Country 'Tis of Thy People You're Dying," "Universal Soldier," and "Now That the Buffalo's Gone"; during height of antiwar era, her outspoken views on Vietnam War and treatment of Native Americans resulted in an FBI dossier and the banning of some of her releases from radio and tv; appeared with son on "Sesame Street" (1976–81); songs have been recorded by more than 100 artists in 7 languages and performed by Elvis Presley, Janis Joplin, Barbra Streisand, and Tracy Chapman, among others. Won Academy Award for "Up Where We Belong," theme song for the film *An Officer and a Gentleman*, co-written with Jack Nitzsche. ❖ See also *Women in World History.*

SAINT MARS, Gabrielle de (1804–1872). French novelist. Name variations: Gabrielle de Saint-Mars; Gabrielle-Anne Cisterne; Vicomtesse de Saint-Mars; Marquise de Poilow or du Poilloüe; (pseudonyms) Marie Michon, Jacques Reynaud, and Countess Dash or Comtesse Dash. Born Gabrielle-Anne Cisterne de Courtiras, Aug 2, 1804, in Poitiers, France; died Sept 11, 1872, in Paris; m. E.-J. du Poilloüe de Saint Mars (cavalry officer and viscount), in 1824 (sep. 1834); children: 1 son. ❖ Popular fiction writer for nearly 40 years, began to write to support herself and son, finding benefactors among friends in the Parisian elite, including Alexander Dumas *père*; became a journalist for *Revue de Paris* (late 1830s); published 1st novel, *Le jeu de la reine* (*The Queen's Game*), which met with moderate success; published new works, mostly formulaic historical romance novels, regularly for next 3 decades; is believed to have ghost-written several of Dumas' shorter fictional works, and is known to have written for his *Mousquetaire* (The Musketeer), under name Marie Michon; contributed literary "portraits" to *Le Figaro*; composed a 6-vol. set of memoirs, *Memoires des Autres* (*Memories of Others*), a nostalgic look at her life and friendships. ❖ See also *Women in World History.*

ST. MARTIN-PERMON, Laurette de (1784–1838). *See Abrantès, Laure d'.*

ST. MICHEL, Elizabeth de (1640–1669). *See Pepys, Elizabeth.*

SAINT-PHALLE, Niki de (1930–2002). *See Phalle, Niki de Saint.*

ST. PIERRE, Kim (1978—). Canadian ice-hockey player. Born Dec 14, 1978, in Chateauguay, Quebec, Canada. ❖ Goaltender, played for McGill University; won a gold medal at World championships (2001); won a gold medal at Salt Lake City Olympics (2002) and a gold medal at Torino Olympics (2006).

ST. POL, Marie de (1303–1377). *See Marie de St. Pol.*

SAINT SIMON, countess of (1773–1860). *See Bawr, Alexandrine de.*

SAIS, Marin (1890–1971). American actress. Born Aug 2, 1890, in San Rafael, CA; died Dec 31, 1971, in Woodland Hills, CA; m. Jack Hoxie (cowboy actor), 1920 (div. 1925). ❖ Leading lady with the Kalem Co. (1911–17); films include *Shannon of the Sixth, The Pitfall, The Vanity*

Pool, Riders of the Law, The Measure of a Man and *The Wild Horse Stampede*; continued to appear in smaller roles and bits until 1950.

SAITO, Haruka (1970—). Japanese softball player. Born Mar 14, 1970, in Hirosaki, Japan. ❖ Outfielder, won a team silver medal at Sydney Olympics (2000) and a team bronze at Athens Olympics (2004).

SAKAI, Hiroko (1978—). Japanese softball player. Born Nov 3, 1978, in Fukui, Japan. ❖ Pitcher, won a team bronze at Athens Olympics (2004).

SAKAJAWEA OR SAKAKAWEA (c. 1787–c. 1812 or 1884). *See Sacajawea.*

SAKAMOTO, Naoko (1985—). Japanese softball player. Born May 11, 1985, in Japan. ❖ Pitcher, won a team bronze at Athens Olympics (2004).

SAKAUE, Yoko (1968—). Japanese judoka. Born Aug 29, 1968, in Japan. ❖ At Barcelona Olympics, won a bronze medal in + 72 kg heavyweight (1992).

SAKHAROFF, Clotilde (1892–1974). German concert dancer. Name variations: Clothilde von Derp Sakharoff or von Derp-Sakharoff. Born Clothilde von der Planitz, 1892, in Berlin, Germany; died Jan 11, 1974, in Rome, Italy; m. Alexandre Sakharoff (1886–1963, dancer). ❖ Performed debut solo recital at age 15, to works by Chopin, Strauss, and Schubert; danced in Max Reinhardt's *Sumurun* and *Songe d'une Nuit d'Eté* in Germany and London; appeared in numerous concert recitals on tour with Alexandre Sakharoff, whom she later married; with husband, opened dance studio in Rome (early 1950s) and choreographed *Visions du Moyen Age* (1920), *May Day Danse* (1920), *Humoresque* (1922), *Chanson Negre* (1922), *Valses Rouges* (1923), *Plein Bonheur* (1926), *Prelude et Fugue* (1930), *Papillon* (1933) and *Danse de Destin* (1937).

SAKHAROV, Elena (b. 1923). *See Bonner, Elena.*

SAKICKIENE, Birute (1968—). Lithuanian rower. Born Nov 26, 1968, in Lithuania. ❖ Won a bronze medal for double sculls at Sydney Olympics (2000).

SAKOVITSNE-DOMOLKY, Lidia (1936—). Hungarian fencer. Name variations: Lidia Domolky. Born Mar 1936 in Hungary. ❖ At Rome Olympics, won a silver medal in team foil (1960); at Tokyo Olympics, won a gold medal in team foil (1964); at Mexico City Olympics, won a silver medal in team foil (1968).

SALABERGA OF LAON (d. around 665). Sainted abbess of Laon. Born in France; died c. 665; m. Blandinus Boson (Frankish noble); children: at least 6, including Anstrude of Laon (abbess). ❖ Though always drawn to a religious life, was pressured by parents to marry; widowed, became an abbess, using her own resources to found 7 churches; was one of the numerous holy women of the 7th century who had more authority than women were supposed to, taking on the duties of a priest, and managing the spiritual and material lives of more than 300 nuns; daughter Anstrude succeeded her. Feast day is Sept 22. ❖ See also *Women in World History.*

SALAPATYSKA, Stella (1979—). Bulgarian rhythmic gymnast. Born April 25, 1979, in Bulgaria. ❖ Won Happy Rhythmic Days (1996) and Chichmanovav Cup (1996, 1997); placed 2nd all-around at International Tournament (1995), Coupe d'Opale (1998), and Julieta Shishmanova Cup (2000).

SALAVARRIETA, Pola (1795–1817). Colombian revolutionary. Name variations: La Pola; Policarpa Salavarrieta. Born Policarpa Salavarrieta in Guaduas, Colombia, Feb 22, 1795; executed in Bogotá, Colombia, Nov 14, 1817; dau. of José Joaquin Salavarrieta and Mariana (Rios) Salavarrieta. ❖ Rebel in the fight for independence, played a key role in the patriot underground, 1st in Guaduas, then in Bogotá; captured and imprisoned by Royalists, was accused of espionage and subversion against the Spanish crown and condemned to death; as she walked to her execution, shouted a tirade against Spanish oppression and urged her people to avenge her death; was the 1st Latin American woman commemorated on a postage stamp, her image appearing on a 1910 independence-centennial issue.

SALAZAR BLANCO, Iridia (1982—). Mexican taekwondo player. Born June 14, 1982, in Mexico. ❖ Placed 2nd for featherweight 55–59 kg at World championships (1999, 2001, 2003); won a bronze medal for -57 kg at Athens Olympics (2004).

SALE, Florentia (c. 1790–1853). British diarist. Name variations: Lady Sale. Born Florentia Wynch, c. 1790; died in Cape Town, South Africa, in 1853; married Sir Robert Henry Sale, in 1809. ❖ In the Anglo-Afghan Wars, was taken captive during the British retreat from Kabul (1842); was ultimately rescued, and her journal was published (1843).

SALE, Jamie (1977—). Canadian pairs skater. Name variations: Jamie Salé. Born April 21, 1977, in Calgary, Alberta, Canada; grew up in Red Deer; m. David Pelletier. ❖ With pairs partner Jason Turner, placed 12th at Lillehammer Olympics (1994); with partner David Pelletier, won a gold medal at World championships (2001); came in 2nd at Salt Lake City Olympics to Russian pairs Elena Berezhnaya and Anton Sikharulidze, until a judging scandal caused an IOC decision to have the Canadian team share the gold medal (2002); skated for Stars on Ice.

SALE, Madame de (1308–1348). See Noves, Laure de.

SALE, Virginia (1899–1992). American stage, tv and screen actress. Born May 20, 1899, in Urbana, IL; died Aug 23, 1992, in Woodland Hills, CA; sister of Charles "Chic" Sale (actor); m. Sam Wren (died 1962). ❖ Appeared on Broadway in *Montmartre* (1922) and *Play, Genius, Play* (1935); made over 200 films, including *Moby Dick, Badman's Territory, Trail Street, Strike Up the Band* and *Slither*.

SALEM, Cheryl (c. 1957—). See Prewitt, Cheryl.

SALERNO-SONNENBERG, Nadja (1961—). Italian-born violinist. Born 1961 in Rome, Italy; studied with Dorothy DeLay at Juilliard School. ❖ Immigrated to US at age 8, to study at Curtis Institute; professional career began when she won the Walter W. Naumberg International Violin Competition (1980); recognized with an Avery Fisher Career Grant (1983); was Ovation's Debut Recording Artist of the Year (1988); has recorded over 15 albums and gives recitals worldwide. ❖ See also autobiography for children, *Nadja: On My Way*; (documentary) *Speaking in Strings* (1999).

SALETE, Mme de (fl. 1600). French poet. Name variations: Mademoiselle de Salete. Born in France. ❖ Only 2 poetic pieces extant, written in response to court poet Bertaut; probably maid of honor at the court of Henry IV of France (r. 1589–1610).

SALHIAS DE TOURNEMIRE, Elizaveta (1815–1892). Russian novelist, editor and literary critic. Name variations: Countess Elizaveta Vasilevna Salias (also seen as Salhas) de Tournemire; Countess Salias de Turnemir; (pseudonym) Evgeniya or Evgeniia Tur. Born Elizaveta Vasilyevna Sukhovo-Kobylina in 1815 in Russia; died 1892; m. Henry Salhias de Tournmire (French aristocrat); children: several, including Count Eugene Andreevich Salhias de Tournemire, also known as Yevgeny Salias (1841–1908, author of historical novels); Olga Andreevna (who m. K. Zhukov, a governor); and a daughter who m. Field Marshal Josef Vladimirovich Gurko, the liberator of Bulgaria. ❖ Moved abroad after coming under government surveillance for sympathy for Polish nationalists (1860s); articles helped introduce French and English writers to Russian readers; hosted salon frequented by prominent intellectuals, including Ivan Turgenev and Timofei Granovsky; used pseudonym Evgeniia Tur for all her writings; novels include *Three Stages of Life* (1854), *The Shalonskii Family* (1880), *Princess Dubrovina* (1886), and *Sergei Bor-Ramenskii* (1888); also wrote critical articles on French and English literature for the journal *Russian Messenger* and founded the journal *Russian Discourse* (1861); wrote children's books as well. ❖ See also *Finding the Middle Ground: Krestovskii, Tur, and the Power of Ambivalence in Nineteenth-Century Russian Women's Prose* (2003).

SALIH, Halide (c. 1884–1964). See Adivar, Halide Edib.

SALIKHOVA, Roza (1944—). Soviet volleyball player. Born Sept 24, 1944, in USSR. ❖ Won a gold medal at Mexico City Olympics (1968) and a gold medal at Munich Olympics (1972), both in team competition.

SALIS-MARSCHLINS, Meta (1855–1929). Swiss feminist and essayist. Name variations: Meta von Salis. Born Barbara Margaretha von Salis-Marschlins, 1855, in Switzerland; died 1929. ❖ Born into wealthy family but left home to travel; worked as governess; was the 1st Swiss woman to obtain a doctorate from University of Zurich (in history); wrote thesis on Agnes of Poitou (1024–1077); advocated equal rights and especially rights of women; met Friedrich Nietzsche (1894); purchased Villa Silberblick in Weimar for use by the Nietzsche Archive and as a residence for Elisabeth Förster-Nietzsche and Friedrich Nietzsche (1897); wrote *Die Zukunft der Frau* (1886), *Die Schutzengel* (3 vols, 1889–91), a series of portraits of women in *Auserwählte Frauen unserer Zeit, I und II* (1900, 1916), and an account of her friendship with Nietzsche, *Philosoph under Edelmann* (1897).

SALISACHS, Mercedes (1916—). Spanish novelist. Born Sept 18, 1916, in Barcelona, Spain. ❖ Works include *Los que se quedan* (1942), *Primera mañana, última mañana* (1955), *Carretera intermedia* (1956), *Una mujer llega al pueblo* (1956), *Vendimia interrumpida* (1960), *Adagio confidencial* (1973), *La gangrena* (1975), *Derribos: crónicas intimas de un tiempo soldado* (1981), *El volumen de la ausencia* (1983), *Sea breve, por favor* (1983), *Feliz Navidad, señor Ballesteros* (1983), *La danza de los salmones* (1985), *Los clamores del silencio* (2000), and *El ultimo laberinto* (2004). Won several awards, including City of Barcelona Prize (1956), Ateneo de Sevilla Prize (1983), and Planeta Prize (1975, 1985).

SALISBURY, countess of.
See Mohun, Elizabeth.
See Grandison, Katharine (fl. 1305–1340).
See Montacute, Maud (fl. 1380s).
See Holland, Eleanor (c. 1385–?).
See Chaucer, Alice (fl. 1400s).
See Pole, Margaret (1473–1541).
See Howard, Catherine (d. 1672).
See Cecil, Georgiana (1827/–1899).

SALISBURY, duchess of. See Montacute, Alice (c. 1406–1463).

SALLÉ, Marie (1707–1756). French ballerina and choreographer. Name variations: Marie Salle. Born 1707, probably in France; died July 27, 1756, in Paris; dau. of an acrobat and theatrical performer; studied with Françoise Prévost, Jean Balon, and Blondy; lived with Rebecca Wick. ❖ Born into a large theatrical family who toured the small towns of France, made center-stage debut at Lincoln's Inn Fields in London at 9 (1716); made Opéra de Paris debut (1727) and had greatest success that season in Prévost's *Les Caractères de la danse,* arranged as a *pas de deux* with Antoine Laval; ill prepared for backstage intrigues and the press' eagerness to promote a rivalry with Marie-Anne Cupis de Camargo, fled to London to dance with her brother, where she was a huge success; opened in *Pygmalion* at Covent Garden and made ballet history (1734), by creating her own ballet, letting her hair flow freely, choosing her own costumes, and trying to communicate inner feelings rather than settle for technical effect; shortly thereafter, appeared in another ballet of her own creation, *Bacchus and Ariadne*; became rage of London, acclaimed as a dancer, choreographer, and innovator; as rumors surfaced in London about her amorous preferences, was the subject of crude verses and scornful lampoons, including those by Voltaire; during last Paris Opéra engagement (1735), was allowed to impose some choreography on the season's opener, Rameau's *Les Indes galantes*; danced at Versailles with David Dumoulin in 20 ballets (1745–47); named Rebecca Wick "*amiable amie*" as her sole heir (1756). ❖ See also *Women in World History.*

SALLY FORTH (1892–1959). See Tracy, Mona Innis.

SALM-DYCK, Constance de (1767–1845). French poet, novelist and playwright. Name variations: Madame Pipelet; Princess of Salm-Dyck. Born Constance Marie de Theis, Nov 17, 1767, in Nantes, France; died April 13, 1845, in Paris, France; m. Jean-Baptiste Pipelet; m. Prince of Salm-Dyck, 1803; children: 1. ❖ Well-known intellectual during the Napoleonic Empire whose writings were feminist in tone; countered Ecouchard-Lebrun's misogynist discourses with her "Epistle on Women"; works include *Sapho* (1794), *Vingt-quatre heures d'une femme sensible* (1924), and *Souvenirs politiques et littéraires* (1833); also wrote series of letters in verse (collected 1811).

SALMINEN, Sally (1906–1976). Finnish author. Born April 25, 1906, in Vargata on Åland Islands, an archipelago in the Gulf of Bothnia, forming part of Finland; died in Copenhagen, Denmark, July 19, 1976; dau. of Erika Norrgaard and Hindrik Salminen; m. Johannes Dührkop (Danish painter), 1940. ❖ At 18, moved to Stockholm and later to Linköping; with a sister, set out for New York (1930), where she worked as a maid and wrote *Katrina,* the novel which would bring her world fame; won 1st prize for the book in a literary competition (1936), which enabled her to return to Åland and start a life as a full-time writer; moved to Denmark with husband and actively participated in Danish Resistance movement during WWII; published 2 novels (1939, 1941), after which she wrote a series about an Åland emigrant: *Lars Laurila* (1943), *New Land* (1945), *Small Worlds* (1949) and *The Star and the Chasm* (1951); published *Prince Efflam* (1953), arguably her best novel; also wrote 2 travel books: *Jerusalem* (1970) and *Journeys in Israel* (1971); wrote 4 autobiographical works detailing her stays in US and Denmark (1966–74); published last major work, *On the Ocean* (1963); was deeply engaged in social and cultural issues. ❖ See also *Women in World History.*

SALMON, Lucy Maynard (1853–1927). American historian and educator. Born July 27, 1853, in Fulton, New York; died in Poughkeepsie, New York, Feb 14, 1927; dau. of George Salmon (banker and manufacturer) and Maria Clara (Maynard) Salmon (principal of Fulton Female Seminary, died 1860); University of Michigan, BA, 1876, AM, 1883; lived with Adelaide Underhill (Vassar librarian). ❖ Became 1st history teacher at Vassar College (1887), then promoted to full professor (1889) and remained at Vassar until end of career; proved to be an influential member of the college faculty, not only in the construction of Vassar's fledgling history department, but also in the greater administration of the college; writings include *Domestic Service* (1897), *Progress in the Household* (1906), *The Newspaper and the Historian* (1923), *Why Is History Rewritten?* (1929) and *Historical Material* (1933); served on executive committee of American Historical Association (1915–19); was instrumental in the founding of Association of History Teachers of the Middle States and Maryland, serving as its 1st president; was a pacifist and suffragist. ❖ See also *Women in World History.*

SALMOND, Sarah (1864–1956). New Zealand governess and astronomer. Name variations: Sarah Cockburn. Born Sarah Cockburn, Aug 7, 1864, in Berwickshire, Scotland; died Oct 18, 1956, in Dunedin, New Zealand; dau. of John Cockburn (farm worker) and Elizabeth (Liddle) Cockburn; m. John Salmond (carpenter), 1886 (died 1940); children: 8. ❖ Immigrated with family to New Zealand (1873); settled in remote wilderness of Rees valley by Lake Wakatipu, to keep house for her brothers, and was first woman to live there (c. 1879); developed profound interest in astronomy and later lobbied for and dedicated local monument to mark gathering of scientists at Queenstown to observe Venus travel between Sun and Earth (1874). ❖ See also *Dictionary of New Zealand Biography* (Vol. 2).

SALMONOVA, Lyda (1889–1968). Czech silent-screen actress. Born July 14, 1889, in Prague, Czechoslovakia; died Nov 18, 1968, in Prague; m. Paul Wegener (actor, died 1948). ❖ Films include *Die Loewenbraut, Der Student von Prag, Evintrude, Der Golem, Rubenzahls Hochzeit, Der Yoghi, Der Golem und die Tanzerin, Der Galeerenstrafling, Wie er in die Welt Kam, Steuermann Holck, Der Verlorene Schatten, Irrende Seelen, Herzog Ferrantes Ende, Lucrezia Borgia, Monna Vanna* and *The Lost Shadow.*

SALMONS, Josephine (b. 1904). South African anthropologist. Born Josephine Edna Salmons, 1904, in South Africa. ❖ Discovered a hominid skull at Taung that contributed to the theory of human geographical origins; shared the skull with professor Raymond Dart (Nov 1924), who published an article on it titled "*Australopithecus africanus*: The Man-Ape of South Africa" (*Nature,* 1925); received little credit for the discovery of the "Missing Link," which supported the theory that humans originated from Africa, not Asia.

SALM-SALM, Agnes, Princess (1840–1912). American war-relief worker. Name variations: Agnes Leclercq; Agnes, princess Salm Salm. Born Agnes Elisabeth Winona Leclercq Joy, Dec 25, 1840, in Vermont (some sources cite Quebec or Baltimore); died in Karlsruhe, Germany, Dec 21, 1912; dau. of William L. Joy and Julia (Willard) Joy; m. Felix Constantin Alexander Johann Nepomuk, Prince Salm-Salm (German mercenary), Aug 30, 1862 (died in battle, Aug 18, 1870); m. Charles Heneage, 1876. ❖ While following husband, a German soldier of fortune, from one battleground to another, brought relief to wounded and imprisoned soldiers in US, Mexico, and Prussia; served as a federal hospital worker during American Civil War; accompanied husband to Mexico (1866), where she became a trusted member of the court of Emperor Maximilian and Carlota; pled for life of husband and Maximilian (1867), which became the subject of a well-known painting by Manuel Ocaranza; was a relief worker during Franco-Prussian War (1870). Received Prussian Medal of Honor and recommended for the Iron Cross. ❖ See also *Zehn Jahre aus meinem Leben* (Ten Years of My Life, 1875); and *Women in World History.*

SALOME (c. 65 BCE–10 CE). Biblical woman. Born c. 65 BCE; died c. 10 CE; dau. of Antipater (wealthy Idumaean) and Cyprus (c. 90 BCE–?); sister of Herod the Great; m. Joseph (executed in 28 BCE); m. Costobar (div.); m. Alexas; children: (2nd m.) Alexander; Herod; Antipater; Berenice (c. 35 BCE–?); and another unnamed daughter. ❖ Influential sister of Herod the Great who, angered by the slights received by her sister-in-law Mariamne the Hasmonian, sought opportunities to turn Herod against her; accused Mariamne of having sent a portrait of herself to Antony in Egypt; also convinced brother that Mariamne had seduced her husband Joseph, resulting in the executions of Mariamne and Joseph (29); briefly came into conflict with brother (14), after another brother, Pheroras, revealed that she had fallen in love with one Syllaeus (son of Obadas, one of Herod's regional enemies); also played a role in nephew Antipater's ruin; most positive contribution came in immediate aftermath of Herod's death at Jericho, having been ordered to murder a large number of Jewish leaders whom Herod had already rounded up and incarcerated in Jericho's hippodrome; disobeyed, telling the guard that Herod had changed his mind. ❖ See also *Women in World History.*

SALOME II (fl. 1st c.). Biblical saint. Flourished in 1st century in Galilee; m. Zebedee (prosperous fisherman); children: John the Evangelist; James the Greater. ❖ Mentioned in the books of Mark and Matthew in New Testament, was the wife of Zebedee and lived on the Sea of Galilee, probably at Capernaum; mother of apostles John the Evangelist and James the Greater, was herself a devoted follower of Jesus; ambitious for the prestige of her sons, is said to have asked Jesus to allow them to sit on either side of him in his kingdom; is also recorded in Mark as being a witness, along with Mary Magdalene and Mary of Cleophas, to Jesus' crucifixion and the resurrection. Some scholars have identified Salome as the sister of Mary the Virgin, the mother of Jesus.

SALOME III (c. 15 CE–?). Biblical woman. Flourished around 15 CE; dau. of Herodias (dau. of Aristobulus I and Berenice) and Herod Philip I; granddau. of Herod the Great; married her father's half-brother Herod Philip II, the Jewish tetrarch of Batanea, Trachonitis, and Auranitis (died 34 CE); married her cousin Aristobulus IV (son of Herod IV, the full brother of Salome's mother Herodias); children: (2nd m.) at least 3 sons, Herod VI, Agrippa III, and Aristobulus V. ❖ The Jezebel of the New Testament, whose lasting fame was earned when she was probably around 15 years old; after her mother had divorced and married Herod Antipas (then tetrarch of Galilee and of Peraea), caused a scandal and was censured by John the Baptist; during a birthday celebration for Herod Antipas, performed a dance which was so well received as to induce a promise from Herod that she could have anything from him which she desired; is reported to have consulted with her mother and requested the head of John the Baptist. ❖ See also *Women in World History.*

SALOMÉ, Lou or Louise von (1861–1937). *See Andreas-Salomé, Lou.*

SALOMEA. *Variant of Salome.*

SALOMEA (d. 1144). Queen of Poland. Name variations: Salome of Berg-Schelklingen. Died July 27, 1144; dau. of Henry, count of Berg; 2nd wife of Boleslaw III Krzywousty also known as Boleslaus III the Wrymouthed (1085–1138), king of Poland (r. 1102–1138); children: Richizza of Poland (1116–1185); Boleslaus or Boleslaw IV the Curly (1125–1173), king of Poland (r. 1146–1173); Mieszko III Stary (1126–1202), king of Poland; Henryk (1132–1166); Dobronega Ludgarda; Judyta (who m. Otto I, margrave of Brandenburg); Agnes of Poland (b. 1137); Casimir II (1138–1194), king of Poland (r. 1177–1194). ❖ Boleslaus III's 1st wife was Zbyslawa.

SALOMEA (1201–c. 1270). *See Salome of Hungary.*

SALOME ALEXANDRA. *See Alexandra (r. 76–67 BCE).*

SALOME OF BERG-SCHELKLINGEN (d. 1144). *See Salomea.*

SALOME OF HUNGARY (1201–c. 1270). Saint and queen of Hungary. Name variations: Saint Salomea. Born c. 1201; died c. 1270; dau. of the duke of Cracow; 2nd wife of Bela IV, king of Hungary (r. 1235–1270; he had been married to Maria Lascaris); children: Elizabeth of Hungary (who m. Henry I, duke of Lower Bavaria); Anna of Hungary (who m. Rastislav, ex-prince of Novgorod); and possibly Yolanda of Gnesen. ❖ Upon death of husband (1270), entered the order of the Poor Clares; died soon after. Feast day is Nov 17.

SALOMON, Alice (1872–1948). German reformer. Born in Berlin, Germany, April 19, 1872; died in New York City on Aug 29 or 30, 1948; dau. of Albert Salomon (leather merchant) and Anna Potocky-Nelken Salomon (died 1914); attended University of Berlin; never married. ❖ Reformer who played a key role in the establishment of social work as a profession in Germany and was a leader in the new field of social work education, joined Mädchen- und Frauengruppen für soziale Hilfsarbeit (Girls' and Women's Group for Social Assistance, 1893) and became chair (1899); established 1st full one-year course in social work education in Berlin (1899); though she had not been awarded an Abitur (school-leaving certificate), began auditing courses at University of Berlin (1902); was awarded a doctorate for dissertation, "The Causes of Unequal Payment for Men's and Women's Work," from University of Berlin (1906); founded Soziale Frauenschule (Social Work School for

Women) in Berlin-Schöneberg (1908), the 1st modern interdenominational institution teaching social work skills in Germany, and remained director until 1925; over next half century, wrote 28 books and approximately 250 articles, advocating the emerging profession of social work, which she distinguished from the religiously grounded charitable activities of the past; established German Conference of Schools of Social Work (1917); initiated and headed the Women's Academy of Germany (Deutsche Akademie für soziale und pädagogische Frauenarbeit, 1925); was also active in the women's and peace movements; as a result of the Nazi purge of Jews and anti-Nazis from public jobs (1933), lost her state positions; because of her worldwide fame, was offered the choice to leave Germany within 3 weeks or be taken to a concentration camp (1937); immigrated to US; became a citizen (1944). ❖ See also *Women in World History*.

SALOMON, Charlotte (1917–1943). German-Jewish artist. Name variations: Lotte Nagler. Born Charlotte Salomon, April 16, 1917, in Berlin, Germany; died in Auschwitz, Oct 10, 1943; dau. of Albert Salomon (1883–1976, surgeon who achieved success at University of Berlin) and Franziska (Fränze) Grünwald Salomon (who committed suicide, 1926); stepdaughter of singer Paula Lindberg; m. Alexander Nagler (Jewish refugee), June 17, 1943. ❖ Artist whose *Life? or Theater?*, a documentation of her life under Nazi rule, is considered to be one of the greatest artistic works of the Holocaust, was admitted to the Art Academy of Berlin as one of that institution's few "non-Aryan" students (1935); expelled from the Academy because she was Jewish (1938); fled to live with friends in Nice, France (early 1939); with grandfather, was deported to the infamous Gurs detention camp in the Pyrenees but released after several weeks' incarceration (1940); while in France, created an extraordinary autobiography in art entitled *Leben? oder Theater? Ein Singespiel* (Life? or Theater? An Operetta), consisting of 1,325 paintings, which was saved from destruction and became recognized as the visual equivalent of the diary of Anne Frank (1941–42); arrested with husband by Gestapo (Sept 21, 1943); five months pregnant, arrived on Transport 60 at Auschwitz (Oct 10) and was dead before the end of that day. ❖ See also *Charlotte: A Diary in Pictures* (Harcourt, 1963); Mary Lowenthal Felstiner, *To Paint Her Life: Charlotte Salomon in the Nazi Era* (HarperCollins, 1994); and *Women in World History*.

SALONINA (r. 254–268). Roman empress. Reigned from 254 to 268; born Cornelia Salonina Chrysogone; m. Gallienus (c. 218–268), emperor of Rome (r. 253–268). ❖ Thought to be a cultivated woman, was probably a Greek, possibly from Bithynia; with husband, was a friend of Plotinus and other intellectuals (husband also had a concubine named Pipa).

SALOTE TOPOU III (1900–1965). Queen of Tonga. Name variations: Salote Tupou III; Queen Salote. Born Mar 13, 1900; died 1965; dau. of King George Topou (or Tupou) II; educated at Diocesan Ladies' College of the Church of England (Auckland) and University of Sydney; m. Sione (John) Fe'iloakitau Kaho (Prince Viliami Tungi or Tugi), in 1917 (prime minister of Tonga, died 1941); children: sons Taufa or Tung (b. 1918, later known as King Taufa'ahou Topou IV), and Jione Gu Manumataogo. ❖ Ruled Tonga (1918–65); was a benevolent and enlightened monarch, among whose many accomplishments was the institution of free and compulsory education. Created an Honorary Dame Commander of the Order of the British Empire (1932), and Honorary Grand Commander of the Order of the British Empire (1945). ❖ See also *Women in World History*.

SALSBERG, Germain Merle (1950—). Canadian-born dancer, teacher and choreographer. Born July 22, 1950, in Toronto, Ontario, Canada; trained in modern dance, jazz and tap styles. ❖ Began peforming with Toronto Dance Theater (1970), appearing in works of Peter Randazzo, David Earle, and Patricia Beatty; danced in Barry Smith's *Coronation* (1969), *Lady Fox* (1969), *Lacemakers* (1970), and others; moved to New York City where she continued to perform in works by Smith, among them *Filligree* (1977) and *Meadow Ring* (1978); choreographed numerous works of her own, integrating ballroom, jazz and tap; also choreographed for such productions as *Anything Goes, 42nd Street* and *Dames at Sea*; joined the faculty of the Broadway Dance Center (c. 1985). Choreography includes *Between Two Waves and the Sea* (1970), *Funeral for Nellie Runie* (1971), (with Barry Smith) *Hey Girl* (1977), *Album* (1978) and *Trouble in Paradise* (1980).

SALT, Barbara (1904–1975). American-born British diplomat. Name variations: Dame Barbara Salt. Born in Oreville, California, Sept 30, 1904; died in London, England, Dec 28, 1975; dau. of Reginald John Salt (banker) and Maud Fanny (Wigram) Salt; granddau. of Sir Thomas Salt, chair of Lloyds Bank and a member of Parliament for Stafford; attended universities in Munich and Cologne; never married. ❖ The 1st woman to receive a British ambassadorial appointment, was taken back to England with family soon after birth; during WWII, began work as a secretary for Special Operations Executive (SOE, 1940); posted as vice-consul to SOE office in Tangier, Morocco (1942); promoted head, remained in Tangier until 1946; began work at British Foreign Office (1946); appointed 1st secretary at British embassy in Washington, DC, serving as counsellor *sur place* (1955–57); started serving as counsellor and consul-general, and occasionally acting as chargé d'affaires in Tel Aviv (1957); became 1st woman diplomat to be named a minister, as deputy head of UK delegation to UN disarmament negotiations in Geneva (1960); was transferred to New York as UK representative on Economic and Social Council of UN (1961); named UK ambassador to Israel but could not take post because of illness; after having both legs amputated (1962), resumed work in a wheelchair, heading SOE section of the Foreign and Commonwealth Office (1967–73); retired (1973). Named MBE (1946), CBE (1959), and Dame Commander of the Order of the British Empire (DBE, 1963). ❖ See also *Women in World History*.

SALTER, Susanna Medora (1860–1961). American politician. Name variations: Suzanna Madora Salter. Born Mar 1, 1860, in Kansas; died Mar 17, 1961, in Norman, Oklahoma. ❖ Though she had not campaigned for the post of mayor of Argonia, Kansas (population 500), or even knew she had been nominated, was elected by a two-thirds majority, making her the 1st woman in US to be elected mayor of any city (1887). ❖ See also *Women in World History*.

SALT-N-PEPA.
See Denton, Sandy.
See James, Cheryl.

SALTYKOVA, Praskovya (1664–1723). Russian empress. Name variations: Dowager Empress Praskovya; Praskovia Saltykova; Proscovia or Proskuvia Soltykov. Born Praskovya Fedorovna Saltykova on Oct 21, 1664; died Oct 24, 1723; dau. of Feodor Soltykov; m. Ivan V Romanov (1666–1696), tsar of Russia (r. 1682–1689), on Jan 9, 1684; children: Marie (died young); Theodosia (1690–1691); Catherine of Mecklenburg-Schwerin (1692–1733); Anna Ivanovna (1693–1740); Proskovia Romanov (1694–1731, who m. Ivan Momonov).

SALÚCIO, Ida (1876–1901). *See Souza, Auta de.*

SALUKVADZE, Nino (1969—). Soviet shooter. Born Feb 1, 1969, in USSR. ❖ At Seoul Olympics, won a silver medal in air pistol and a gold medal in sport pistol (1988).

SALUMAE, Erika (1962—). Soviet cyclist. Born June 11, 1962, in USSR. ❖ Won a gold medal at Seoul Olympics (1988) and a gold medal at Barcelona Olympics (1992), both in the 1,000-meter sprint.

SALVERSON, Laura Goodman (1890–1970). Canadian novelist. Born 1890 in Winnipeg, Manitoba, Canada; died 1970; m. George Salverson (Norwegian immigrant), 1913; children: George Salverson Jr. (b. 1914). ❖ Daughter of Icelandic immigrants, lived in almost every region in Canada; popular in the 1920s and 1930s, was one of the 1st Canadian writers to address problems of immigrants; probably best known for 1st novel *The Viking Heart* (1923), also wrote *When Sparrows Fall* (1925), *The Dark Weaver* (1937) and *Immortal Rock* (1954); edited *Icelandic Canadian*. Won 2 Governor General's Awards. ❖ See also autobiography, *Confessions of an Immigrant Daughter* (1939).

SALVIATI, Elena (fl. early 1500s). Florentine noblewoman. Name variations: Elena Appiani. Flourished in the early 1500s; dau. of Lucrezia de Medici (b. around 1480) and Jacopo or Giacomo Salviati; sister of Maria Salviati (1499–1543); m. Jacopo V. Appiani.

SALVIATI, Lucrezia (b. around 1480). *See Medici, Lucrezia de.*

SALVIATI, Maria (1499–1543). Florentine noblewoman. Name variations: Maria de Medici. Born Maria de Medici in 1499; died in 1543; dau. of Lucrezia de Medici (b. around 1480) and Jacopo or Giacomo Salviati; sister of Elena Salviati; granddau. of Florentine ruler Lorenzo "the Magnificent" de Medici; m. Giovanni (delle Bande Nere) de Medici (1498–1526, son of Caterina Sforza who became a renowned commander of the pope's army), in 1516 (killed in battle, 1526); children: Cosimo I (1519–1574), ruler of Florence (r. 1537), grand duke of Tuscany (r. 1569–1574, who m. Eleonora de Medici) ❖ A courageous woman, intelligent, and devoted, whose husband relied heavily on her, despite the fact that she remained in her parents' palace in Florence while he was on campaign; administered their lands and offered him advice on maintaining his professional and political alliances; when he was wounded in battle (1525) and the pope withheld pay for his troops, traveled to Rome and successfully demanded that the pope pay the soldiers; widowed (1526); once son was grown, joined the Third Order of St. Dominic and devoted herself to working with the poor and sick of the Tuscan countryside. ❖ See also *Women in World History*.

SALVINI-DONATELLI, Fanny (c. 1815–1891). Italian soprano. Name variations: Francesca Lucchi. Born c. 1815 in Florence, Italy; died June 1891 in Milan. ❖ Probably best remembered as the soprano who created the role of Violetta in the disastrous 1st performance of Verdi's opera *La Traviata* (1853); a plump singer, was given the role of the dying consumptive over Verdi's objections, but managed to salvage the opera with her reputation and voice after audience burst into laughter when she 1st appeared on stage; had debuted in Venice (1839); went abroad to perform in Vienna (1842), moved on to Paris, and closed her career singing in London (late 1850s). ❖ See also *Women in World History*.

SALVIONI, Guglierma (1842—). Italian ballet dancer. Born 1842 in Milan, Italy. ❖ Performed at Teatro alla Scala in Milan, Italy, in Rafaele Rossi's *La Capricciosa* (c. 1862), among others; danced at Paris Opéra as exquisite point dancer in such works as Artur Saint-Leon's *La Source* (1866); also created role of Naila for Saint-Leon's *The Little Goldfish* (1867); danced at Vienna Court Opera Ballet in Austria (1870s).

SALZGEBER, Ulla (1958—). German equestrian. Name variations: Ulla Helbing. Born Ulla Helbing, Aug 5, 1958, in Oberhausen, Germany. ❖ At World Equestrian games, placed 1st for team dressage (1998, 2002) and 3rd for indiv. dressage (1998, 2002); on Rusty, won a bronze medal for indiv. dressage and a gold medal for team dressage at Sydney Olympics (2000); won 3rd consecutive World Cup title at the World Cup finals in Sweden (2003); on Rusty, won a silver medal for indiv. dressage and a gold medal for team dressage at Athens Olympics (2004). Named Rider of the Year (2001 and 2002).

SAMAN, Mme de (1801–1879). *See Allart, Hortense.*

SAMAROFF, Olga (1882–1948). American pianist and music teacher. Name variations: Olga Samaroff Stokowski; Olga Stokowski. Born Lucie Mary Olga Agnes Hickenlooper, Aug 8, 1882, in San Antonio, TX; died in New York, NY, May 17, 1948; attended Paris Conservatoire de Musique, graduated with honors, 1898; m. Boris Loutzky (civil engineer), 1900 (div. 1904); m. Leopold Stokowski (1882–1977, musical conductor), 1911 (div. 1923); children: Sonya Stokowski. ❖ Virtuoso concert pianist and advocate for American-born performing artists, exerted considerable influence on musical life in US during 1st half of 20th century; at age 12, departed for France to study with Charles Marie Widor and François Marmontel; won 2-year scholarship, the 1st awarded to an American girl for piano classes, at Paris Conservatoire de Musique; studied with Elie Delaborde; went to Berlin to study with Ernst Jedliczka, Ernest Hutcheson, and Otis Bardwell Boise (1898); married (1900) and stopped giving concerts; obtained a papal annulment and returned to US (1904); made professional concert debut with NY Symphony Orchestra at Carnegie Hall, playing Schumann's *A Minor Concerto,* Liszt's *E-Flat Concerto* and some solo pieces by Chopin (1905); made records for Welte-Mignon Co. in Germany, the 1st American woman pianist to record (1908); toured as concert artist in US and performed extensively in London until 2nd marriage (1911); resumed concert touring (1914); played a series of 8 concerts (1920), performing all 32 Beethoven piano sonatas, the 1st American woman pianist to achieve this feat; made more than 20 recordings for Victory Talking Machine Co. (1921–31); divorced (1923) and moved to NY, accepting a post at Juilliard (1924); after an injury ended performing career (1925), lectured extensively on music appreciation and wrote several books, including *The Magic World of Music* (1936); appointed head of piano department at Philadelphia Conservatory (1928), and held the post concurrently with her Juilliard position for next 20 years. ❖ See also autobiography *An American Musician's Story* (Norton, 1939); and *Women in World History*.

SAMBETHE. The Jewish Sibyl. Name variations: Sabba; Sambathe. Dau. of Berosos and Erymanthe. ❖ Believed to have been a sibyl (female prophet), plied her trade in the general vicinity of Judea. ❖ See also *Women in World History*.

SAMMAN, Ghada al- (1942—). Syrian novelist and poet. Name variations: Ghada as-Samman; Ghada Samman. Born Ghada al-Samman in 1942 in Beirut, Lebanon (some sources cite al-Shamiya, Syria); dau. of the University of Damascus rector and minister of Education for Syria;

graduate of University of Damascus; University of London, MA; also studied at American University in Beirut. ❖ The best known woman writer in Arabic, worked as journalist, broadcaster and translator; began writing fiction (early 1960s); in order to prevent censorship, established Ghada al-Samman Publications to publish her own works; published short-story collection *Your Eyes Are My Destiny* (1962); moved to Paris after events in Beirut; wrote over 25 volumes of stories, verse, essays, drama and novels, including *Beirut 1975* (1975), *Beirut Nightmares* (1976), *The Incomplete Works of Gada al-Samman* (1978), *Love in the Veins* (1980), and *The Square Moon: Supernatural Tales* (1999); poetry includes *I Declare Love on You!* (1976–83) and *I Testify Against the Wind* (1987); an outspoken woman in a culture where women are not heard often, challenged the oppression of women in Arabic society.

SAMMURAMAT (fl. 8th c. BCE). Queen of Assyria. Name variations: (Assyrian) Sammuramat; (Greek) Semiramis or Sémiramis, also Semiramide; (Armenian) Shamiram. Pronunciation: sam-mu-RA-mat; semi-RAM-is; Sem-EE-rham-i-day; shah-mi-RAM. Flourished around 8th century BCE; either the wife or mother of King Adadnirari III (r. 811–783 BCE). ❖ The historical figure behind the legends of an Assyrian queen known to the Greeks and Romans as Semiramis and to the Armenians as Shamiram. While only generalities may be inferred about Sammuramat from stories of the legendary Semiramis, the latter served as an important player on the pages of ancient accounts which ascribed to her no end of accomplishments; led warriors in battle, went out on the hunt, and undertook extraordinary building projects normally considered the province of kings. The Greek historian of the 2nd century BCE Diodorus of Sicily calls Semiramis "the most renowned woman of whom we have any record." ❖ See also *Women in World History*.

SAMOILOVA, Konkordiya (1876–1921). Russian political activist. Name variations: Konkordiia Samoilova; K.N. Samoilova; K. N. Samoilova-Gromova; (party pseudonyms) Natasha, Vera, and Bol'shevikova; (literary pseudonym) N. Sibirskii. Pronunciation: Sam-OY-lo-va. Born Konkordiya Nikolaevna Gromova in Irkutsk in 1876; died June 2, 1921, near Astrakhan of cholera; dau. of Nikolai Gromov (priest); attended gymnasium in Irkutsk, 1884–94, Bestuzhev-Riumin Courses (St. Petersburg), 1896–1901, and Free Russian School of Social Sciences (Paris), 1902–03; m. Arkadii Aleksandrovich Samoilov, in 1906; no children. ❖ Social Democrat who was a leading Communist organizer of working women, was 1st active in Russian student movement (1897–1901); joined Russian Social Democratic Labor Party (1903) and became a Bolshevik (1906); was an underground party propagandist (1903–12); was secretary of the editorial board of *Pravda* (1912–14) and member of the editorial board of *Rabotnitsa* (1914, 1917); was a party organizer among working women (1917–21); helped organize 1st Conference of Women Workers (Nov 1917) and 1st All-Russian Congress of Working Women (Nov 1918); was instrumental in laying the groundwork for Zhenotdel (the Women's Section of the Central Committee, 1919); served as head of Zhenotdel operations in Ukraine (1919–20); was a member of the editorial board of *Kommunistka* (1920–21); headed the political department on the agitational steamship *Krasnaia Zvezda* (1920–21); wrote numerous articles and brochures in Russian on topics relating to working women. ❖ See also *Women in World History*.

SAMOILOVA, Tatania (1934—). American actress. Name variations: Tatyana Samoylova; Tatyana Samojlova. Born May 4, 1934, in Leningrad (now St. Petersburg), USSR; dau. of Evgeny Samoilov (distinguished stage and screen actor); m. Vasili Lanovoy (actor). ❖ Joined the Mayakovsky Theater; made film debut in *Meksikanets* (*The Mexican,* 1957); came to international prominence in *Letjat zhuravli* (*The Cranes Are Flying,* 1957), followed by *The Letter That Was Never Sent, Alba Regia, Italiani Brava Gente, Anna Karenina* (title role), *No Return, Okean,* and *24 chasa,* among others.

SAMOJLOVA, Tatyana (1934—). *See Samoilova, Tatania.*

SAMOLENKO, Tatyana (1961—). Soviet runner. Born Aug 12, 1961, in USSR. ❖ At Seoul Olympics, won a bronze medal in the 1,500 meters and a gold medal in the 3,000 meters (1988); at Barcelona Olympics, won a silver medal in the 3,000 meters (1992).

SAMOTESOVA, Lyudmila (1939—). Soviet runner. Born Oct 26, 1939, in USSR. ❖ At Mexico City Olympics, won a bronze medal in 4 x 100-meter relay (1968).

SAMOYLOVA, Tatyana (1934—). *See Samoilova, Tatania.*

SAMPSON, Agnes (d. 1591). Scottish witch. Name variations: Agnis Sampson. Born in Haddington, East Lothian, Scotland; died 1591 in Edinburgh, Scotland. ❖ Lay-healer, lived during reign of King James VI of Scotland (later James I of England), an enthusiastic witch-hunter, who traveled to Denmark to bring home his new bride, Anne of Denmark, after her ships had been beset by storms while attempting to land in Scotland (1590); was accused of heading coven of North Berwick Witches who had cursed royal voyage; initially repudiating all charges, was subjected to the 1st trial in Scottish history where sustained torture was sanctioned by law to extract names and confessions; eventually caving in, she listed over 70 souls, including the earl of Bothwell, the king's cousin; executed by strangulation then burned.

SAMPSON, Deborah (1760–1827). American soldier. Name variations: Mrs. Deborah Sampson Gannett; (aliases) Timothy Thayer, Robert Shurtleff, Shurtliff, Shurtlieff, or Shirtliffe, and Ephraim Sampson. Born Deborah Sampson, Dec 17, 1760, in Plymton, Massachusetts (near Plymouth); died in Sharon, Massachusetts, April 19, 1827; dau. of Jonathan Sampson (farmer and sailor) and Deborah (Bradford) Sampson; m. Benjamin Gannett, April 7, 1785; children: Mary Gannett; Patience Gannett; Earl Bradford Gannett. ❖ Revolutionary War soldier who, disguised as a man, fought in several engagements with the enemy; lived on family farm (1760–66); became an indentured servant (1770–78); unsuccessfully enlisted as a soldier (early 1782); enlisted in the Continental Army (May 20, 1782) as "Robert Shurtleff"; served with army north of New York City and in detachments versus Tories; wounded on head (June 1782) and on thigh (July 1782); went on expedition to Fort Ticonderoga (Nov 1782); appointed orderly to Gen. John Patterson in Philadelphia (June–Sept 1783); took ill, gender discovered, and discharged (Oct 25, 1783); granted pay settlement by Massachusetts (1792); published romanticized biography (1797); joined lecture circuit (1802); granted federal pensions, as a female army veteran (1805 and 1818); is the only documented female soldier, masquerading as a man, who served in the ranks of the Continental Army; is also regarded as the 1st paid woman lecturer in America. ❖ See also William F. Norwood, *Deborah Sampson, Alias Robert Shirtliff of the Continental Line* (Johns Hopkins Press, 1957); and *Women in World History*.

SAMPSON, Edith S. (1901–1979). African-American lawyer and judge. Name variations: Edith Spurlock; Edith Clayton. Born Edith Spurlock in Pittsburgh, Pennsylvania, Oct 13, 1901; died Oct 1979; dau. of Louis Spurlock and Elizabeth (McGruder) Spurlock; attended New York School of Social Work; John Marshall Law School, LLB, 1925; Loyola University, LLM, 1927; m. Rufus Sampson (field agent, div.); m. Joseph E. Clayton (attorney), 1934 (died 1957); no children. ❖ Served as probation officer for Juvenile Court of Cook County, Illinois (1925–43); was the 1st woman to receive an LLM from Loyola University (1927); set up a private law practice in Chicago (1927), which she maintained until 1942, specializing in criminal law and domestic relations; was one of the 1st black women admitted to practice before US Supreme Court (1934); appointed assistant state's attorney of Cook County (1947); as chair of the executive committee of National Council of Negro Women (1949), began to participate in international lecture tours; was the 1st African-American appointed delegate to United Nations (1950); at UN, served on Social, Humanitarian, and Cultural Committee; reappointed (1952), and later made member-at-large of US Commission of UNESCO; served on US Citizens Commission on North Atlantic Treaty Organization (1961–62); was a member of Advisory Committee on Private Enterprise in Foreign Aid (1964–65); elected associate judge of Municipal Court of Chicago, the 1st black woman elected judge in US (1962); retired from the bench (1978). ❖ See also *Women in World History*.

SAMPSON, Kathleen (1892–1980). British mycologist and plant pathologist. Born Nov 23, 1892; died Feb 21, 1980; Royal Holloway College, University of London, BS, 1914, MSc, 1917. ❖ Pioneer in herbage crops and cereal diseases, published research on *Phylloglossum* in *Annals of Botany* (1916); served as the president of the British Mycological Society (1938); worked as an assistant agricultural botany lecturer at University of Leeds (1915–17); served as an agricultural botany senior lecturer at University College of Wales, Aberystwyth (1919–45).

SAMPSON, Teddy (1898–1970). American actress. Born Aug 8, 1898, in New York, NY; died Nov 24, 1970, in Woodland Hills, CA; m. Ford Sterling (comedian). ❖ Performed in vaudeville with Gus Edwards; appeared in Al Christie comedies and the movies of D. W. Griffith;

films include *Home Sweet Home, The Fox Woman, Cross Currents, Her American Husband, Outcast* and *The Bad Man*.

SAMPTER, Jessie (1883–1938). American poet and Zionist activist. Born Jessie Ethel Sampter, Mar 22, 1883, in New York, NY; died Nov 11, 1938, at Givat Brenner, Palestine; dau. of Rudolph Sampter (attorney) and Virginia (Kohlberg) Sampter; attended Columbia University, 1902–03; never married; children: (adopted daughter) Tamar. ❖ Early leader in the women's Zionist organization Hadassah, relocated to Palestine (1919), where she would remain; wrote *The Seekers* (1910), *The Coming of Peace* (1919), *The Emek* (1927), *In the Beginning* (1935) and *Brand Plucked from the Fire* (1937); also translated the juvenile poetry of Hayyim Nahman Bialik from Hebrew to English. ❖ See also Bertha Badt-Strauss, *With Fire: The Life and Work of Jessie Sampter* (Reconstructionist, 1956); and *Women in World History*.

SAMS, Doris (1927—). American baseball player. Born Feb 2, 1927, in Knoxville, TN. ❖ Was pitcher and outfielder for Muskegon-Kalamazoo Lassies (1946–53); threw a perfect game (1947), won batting championship (1949), and took the home-run title (1952); had a lifetime batting average of .290. Named Player of the Year (1947, 1949).

SAMUEL, Mrs. Zerelda (c. 1824–1911). See James, Zerelda.

SAMUEL RAMOS, Adriana (1966—). Brazilian beach volleyball player. Name variations: Adriana Samuel. Born April 12, 1966, in Rezende, Brazil. ❖ With Monica Rodrigues, was FIVB Tour champion (1994) and won a silver medal at Atlanta Olympics (1996); with Sandra Pires Tavares, won a bronze medal at Sydney Olympics (2000).

SAMUELSON, Joan Benoit (1957—). American long-distance runner. Name variations: Joan Benoit. Born Joan Benoit, May 16, 1957, in Cape Elizabeth, ME; Bowdoin College, BA in history and environmental studies, 1979; m. Scott Samuelson, 1984. ❖ Placed 1st in Boston Marathon, with a time of 2:35:15 (1979); placed 1st and set a world record, Boston Marathon, 2:22:43 (1983); placed 1st, Olympic Marathon Trials, 2:31:04 (1984); won a gold medal at Los Angeles Olympics (1984) in the 1st Olympic marathon for women; set world and American records, Chicago Women's Marathon, 2:21:21 (1985). Received Jessie Owens Award (1984); named Women's Sports Foundation Amateur Sportswoman of the Year (1984). ❖ See also autobiography (with Sally Baker) *Running Tide* (Knopf, 1987); and *Women in World History*.

SAMUSENKO-PETRENKO, Tatyana (1938—). Soviet fencer. Name variations: Tatyana Petrenko. Born Feb 1938. ❖ At Rome Olympics, won a gold medal in team foil (1960); at Tokyo Olympics, won a silver medal in team foil (1964); won a gold medal in team foil at Mexico City Olympics (1968), and Munich Olympics (1972).

SANBORN, Thelma Payne (1896–1988). See Payne, Thelma.

SANCHA (c. 1178–1229). Portuguese abbess. Name variations: Princess Sancha. Born c. 1178; died Mar 13, 1229, at Lorvano; dau. of Douce of Aragon (1160–1198) and Sancho I (1154–1211 or 1212), king of Portugal (r. 1185–1211 or 1212). ❖ Was the 1st abbess of Lorvano.

SANCHA DE AYBAR (fl. 11th c.). Mother of two kings. Mistress of Sancho III the Great (c. 991–1035), king of Navarre (r. 970–1035); children: (with Sancho) Ferdinand or Fernando I, king of Castile and Leon; Ramiro I, king of Aragon (r. 1035–1063).

SANCHA OF ARAGON (d. 1073). Countess of Urgel. Died 1073; dau. of Gilberga (d. 1054) and Ramiro I, king of Aragon (r. 1035–1069); m. Pons, count of Toulouse; m. Armengol III, count of Urgel; children: Isabel of Urgel.

SANCHA OF ARAGON (1478–1506). Italian noblewoman. Name variations: Sanchia of Aragon. Born in Gaeta in 1478; died in Naples in 1586; illeg. dau. of Alfonso also known as Alphonso II of Aragon (1448–1495), king of Naples (r. 1494–1495), and Trogia Gazzela; niece of Ferrante of Aragon, king of Naples; sister of Duke Alfonso di Biselli (husband of Lucrezia Borgia); betrothed to Joffré Borgia in 1493.

SANCHA OF CASTILE AND LEON (d. 1179). Queen of Navarre. Name variations: sometimes referred to as Beatrice or Beatrice of Castile. Died Aug 5, 1179 (some sources cite 1177); dau. of Alphonso VII, king of Castile and Leon (r. 1126–1157), and Berengaria of Provence (1108–1149); m. Sancho VI the Wise or el Sabio (d. 1194), king of Navarre (r. 1150–1194); children: Sancho VII (b. after 1170), king of Navarre (r. 1194–1234); Berengaria of Navarre (1163–1230); Blanche of Navarre

(d. 1229, who m. Theobald III, count of Champagne); Costanza (died young); Fernando (d. 1207); Ramiro (d. 1228), bishop of Pamplona.

SANCHA OF CASTILE AND LEON (1164–1208). Queen of Aragon. Born Sept 21, 1164; died Nov 9, 1208, in Sijena; dau. of Alphonso VII, king of Castile and Leon (r. 1126–1157), and his 2nd wife Ryksa of Poland (d. 1185); became 2nd wife of Alphonso II (1152–1196), king of Aragon (r. 1162–1196), count of Barcelona (r. 1162–1196), and count of Provence as Alphonso I (r. 1166–1196), on Jan 18, 1174; children: Alphonso II, count of Provence and Forcalquier (d. 1209); Pedro also known as Peter II the Catholic (1174–1213), king of Aragon (r. 1196–1213); Ramon Berengar, count of Ampurias; Fernando; Constance of Aragon (d. 1222). ❖ Alphonso II's 1st wife was Matilda of Portugal (c. 1149–1173).

SANCHA OF LEON (1013–1067). Queen of Leon and Castile. Born 1013; died Nov 7, 1067, in Castile; dau. of Alphonso V, king of Leon, and Elvira Gonzalez of Galicia; m. Ferdinand I (c. 1017–1065), king of Castile (r. 1038–1065), around 1032; children: Sancho II (b. around 1037), king of Castile and Leon (r. 1065–1072); Garcia of Galicia (c. 1042–1090), king of Galicia (r. 1065–1090); Alphonso VI (c. 1030–1109), king of Castile and Leon; Urraca (1033–1101); Elvira (1038–1101). ❖ Inherited the crown of Leon from father; on marriage, became queen of Castile (1037), which united the 2 kingdoms into Leon-Castile, one of the most powerful nations in Western Europe; a popular queen, was involved in the daily administration of the combined kingdoms, and was also an important figure in the *Reconquista* of Spain, the political, religious, and military movement to eliminate Muslim rulers from their strongholds on the Iberian peninsula; when husband died (1065), was chosen as regent of Leon-Castile, a position in which she served well for 2 years. ❖ See also *Women in World History.*

SANCHA OF PROVENCE (c. 1225–1261). Duchess of Cornwall. Name variations: Sanchia. Born c. 1225 in Aachen, North Rhine, Westphalia, Germany; died Nov 9, 1261, in Berkhamsted, Hertfordshire, England; dau. of Beatrice of Savoy (d. 1268) and Raymond Berengar or Berenger IV (some sources cite V), count of Provence and Forcalquier; sister of Eleanor of Provence (1222–1291), Beatrice of Provence (d. 1267), and Margaret of Provence (1221–1295); m. Richard (1209–1272), 1st earl of Cornwall and king of the Romans, on Nov 23, 1243; children: Richard (died days after birth in 1246); Edmund (1249–1300), 2nd earl of Cornwall; Richard (c. 1252–1296). ❖ Richard of Cornwall 1st married Isabel Marshall (1200–1240); his 3rd wife was Beatrice von Falkestein (c. 1253–1277).

SANCHEZ, Carol Lee (1934—). American poet, essayist and painter. Born 1934 in Albuquerque, NM, of Laguna Pueblo, Sioux, and Lebanese descent; grew up in the Laguna and Acoma Pueblo Indian communities in Cubero, NM; dau. of E. Lee Francis (Lt. Gov. of New Mexico, 1967–70) and Ethel Francis; sister of Paula Gunn Allen (writer); cousin of Leslie Marmon Silko (writer). ❖ Writings include *Conversations From the Nightmare* (1975), *Message Bringer Woman* (1977), *Excerpts from a Mountain Climber's Handbook* (1985), *She Poems* (1995) and *From Spirit to Matter: New and Selected Poems, 1969–1996* (1997); also contributed essays and poems to various magazines and journals.

SANCHEZ, Celia (1920–1980). Cuban revolutionary. Name variations: Celia Sanchez; Celia Sanchez Mandeley or Manduley; (revolutionary names) Aly and Norma. Born 1920 in Media Luna, near Manzanillo, Cuba; died in Havana, Jan 11, 1980; dau. of Dr. Manuel Sanchez Silveira. ❖ Revolutionary leader, one of the key personalities in the movement to overthrow Batista, who was a political and personal intimate of Fidel Castro's for 2 decades; met Castro (Feb 16, 1957) and joined his growing band of rebels; following the ousting of Batista (1959), held positions as secretary of both the Presidency and the Council of Ministers, as well as membership in the Central Committee of the Communist Party of Cuba (CPC) and the holding of a seat in the National Assembly; unofficially, continued to be the single most important person in Castro's life, serving as his conscience and alter ego; helped design the extensive Lenin Park complex in suburban Havana, and helped preserve museums and sites of historic interest; to the millions of Cubans who supported the revolution, became its human face. Stamps were issued in her honor (1985, 1990); was also remembered by the minting of 1 peso and 5 peso commemorative coins (1990). ❖ See also *Women in World History.*

SÁNCHEZ, Cristina (1972—). Spanish bullfighter. Name variations: Cristina Sanchez; Cristina Sánchez de Pablos. Born Feb 20, 1972, in Madrid, Spain; dau. of a bullfighter; m. Alejandro da Silva, 2000. ❖ The

1st woman bullfighter to earn the title matador, fought her 1st bull at 18; graduated from Madrid's Escuella De Tauromaquia; debuted as a bullfighter in Madrid (Feb 13, 1993); was successful in bullrings in Ecuador, Mexico and Spain; after over 100 bullfights, earned title Matador; popular with spectators, became the only woman to fight in Madrid's Las Ventas ring (1998); retired (May 1999), tired of the prejudice she continued to encounter. ❖ See also Dulce Chacón, *Matadora* (1999).

SANCHEZ, Linda T. (1969—). American politician. Name variations: Linda Sánchez. Born Jan 28, 1969, in Orange, CA; sister of Loretta Sanchez (politician); attended University of California, Berkeley; University of California, Los Angeles, law degree. ❖ Labor leader and civil-rights lawyer, was elected to the US House of Representatives (2003), as a Democrat representing the 39th district of California; served on the Judiciary and Government Reform Committees; co-founded the Congressional Labor and Working Families Caucus; reelected (2004).

SANCHEZ, Loretta (1960—). American politician. Name variations: Loretta Sánchez; Loretta Brixey. Born Jan 7, 1960, in Lynwood, CA; sister of Linda T. Sanchez (politician); graduate of Chapman University, 1982; American University, MBA, 1984; married Steve Brixey (securities trader). ❖ Began career as a financial analyst and a Republican; was 1st elected to the US House of Representatives (1996), as a Democrat representing California, defeating Robert Dornan; reelected (1998, 2000, 2002).

SANCHEZ, Munia Mayor (995–1067). See Munia Elvira.

SANCHEZ, Sonia (1934—). African-American poet and playwright. Born Wilsonia Benita Driver, Sept 9, 1934, in Birmingham, AL; dau. of Wilson L. Driver and Lena Jones Driver; m. Etheridge Knight, 1968; children: 3. ❖ Taught at several universities before becoming professor of English at Temple (1977); works include *Homecoming* (1969), *We a BadddDDD People* (1970), *It's a New Day* (1971), *Love Poems* (1973), *A Blues Book for Blue Black Magical Women* (1974), *I've Been a Woman: New and Selected Poems* (1978), *Homegirls and Handgrenades* (1984), and *Under a Soprano Sky* (1987). Won PEN Writing Award (1969), National Academy of Arts and Letters Award, and American Book Award (1985).

SANCHEZ DE CEPEDA Y AHUMADA, Teresa (1515–1582). See Teresa of Avila.

SANCHEZ SALFRAN, Marta (1973—). Cuban volleyball player. Name variations: Martha Sanchez Salfran. Born May 17, 1973, in Holguin, Cuba. ❖ Placed 1st at World championships (1998); won a team gold medal at Sydney Olympics (2000) and a team bronze medal at Athens Olympics (2004).

SANCHEZ VICARIO, Arantxa (1971—). Spanish tennis player. Born Dec 18, 1971, in Barcelona, Spain. ❖ Turned pro (1985); won Belgian Open (1988), Spanish Open (1989, 1990, 1993, 1994, 1995, 2001), Canadian Open (1992, 1994), and German Open (1995); won French Open (1989, 1994, 1998) and US Open (1994); won a silver medal for doubles and a bronze for singles at Barcelona Olympics (1992) and a silver for singles and bronze for doubles at Atlanta Olympics (1996); became the 5th woman in the Open Era to win 700 singles matches (2001). Named ESPN Best Female Tennis Player of the Year (1994); received the Principe De Asturiasi, the 1st Spanish woman and 3rd female athlete so honored (1998).

SANCHIA or SANCIA. *Variant of Sancha.*

SANCTO, Matilda (c. 1825–1907). See Meech, Matilda.

SAND, George (1804–1876). French author. Name variations: Amandine-Lucile-Aurore Dupin; Mme Dudevant. Born Amandine-Aurore-Lucile Dupin in Paris, France, July 1, 1804; died at Nohant (Berry), France, June 8, 1876; dau. of Maurice Dupin de Francueil (died 1808) and Antoinette-Sophie-Victoire Delaborde; m. Baron Casimir Dudevant, Sept 17, 1822 (died Mar 1871); children: Maurice (b. 1823); (with Stéphane Ajasson de Grandsagne) Solange Sand. ❖ One of the foremost Romantic writers of her century, who gained literary fame during her lifetime and infamy for her unconventional lifestyle; at age 18, as heiress to Nohant and an investment house in Paris, married Casimir Dudevant (1822), who would control and manage her holdings according to the dictates of French law; with husband's assent, left Nohant for Paris (Jan 4, 1831); as an independent, free-thinking woman, who dressed as a man and smoked cigars, was an anomaly, even among sophisticated, worldly Parisian society; published 2 novels, the favorably reviewed *Indiana* and *Valentine* (1832) as George Sand; assured her reputation as a writer with the publication of *Lélia* (1833), though she was accused of advocating free love and other morally dangerous ideas; often the pursuer rather than the pursued, had affair with Alfred de Musset (1833–35), which provided materials for several novels, notably *Elle et Lui* (1858); won legal separation from Dudevant and regained Nohant (1836); had affair with Frédéric Chopin (1833–1847); wrote plays, tracts, and open letters supporting social change (1848); published *Histoire de ma Vie* (1854–55); was vilified by critics as a loose woman, a political radical, and a "lioness" who devoured her numerous lovers; was praised by her admirers, including the French literary elite, for her prodigious production of novels and plays, and as the originator of the genre of rustic, regional literature in France. ❖ See also Donna Dickenson, *George Sand: A Brave Man—The Most Womanly Woman* (Berg, 1988); Ruth Jordan, *George Sand* (Constable, 1976); David A. Powell, *George Sand* (Twayne, 1990); Belinda Jack, *A Woman's Life Writ Large* (Knopf, 2000); André Maurois, *Lélia: The Life of George Sand* (trans. by Gerard Hopkins, Penguin, 1977); and *Women in World History*.

SAND, Inge (1928–1974). Danish ballet dancer. Born July 6, 1928, in Copenhagen, Denmark; died Feb 9, 1974, in Copenhagen; dau. of Ernst Vilhelm Sand Sørensen and Else Johannsen; m. Niels Juul Bondo, 1952; m. Paul Svarre, 1958; m. Hans Jørgen Christensen, 1962; children: Liselotte (b. 1958). ❖ Joined Royal Danish Ballet (1946), where she was celebrated for portrayal of "Swanilda" in *Coppélia*; was also noted for performances in Balanchine's *Night Shadow* and Lichine's *Graduation Ball*, among others, and equally adept at dancing in classical as well as contemporary works; toured US and South America with chamber concert group (1950s); created own work, *Liv i kludene* (1964); worked as ballet master of Copenhagen Ballet Theater; served as assistant director at Royal Danish Ballet.

SAND, Monique (1944—). French ballet dancer. Born June 24, 1944, in Dakar, Senegal. ❖ Made performance debut at Opera Ballet in Toulon, France; performed with numerous European companies, including Geneva Opera Ballet and Hamburg State Opera; joined Dutch National Ballet (1970), where she performed in Peter Van Dyk's *Pinocchio* (1969), Glen Tetley's *Chronochromie* (1971) and Hans Van Manen's *Adagio Hammerklavier* (1973), and others.

SANDA, Dominique (1948—). French actress. Born Dominique Varaigne, Mar 11, 1948, in Paris, France. ❖ Married at 16; divorced at 18; made film debut starring in Robert Bresson's *Un femme douce* (1969), followed by the lead in Vittorio De Sica's *Il Giardino dei Finzi-Contini* (*In the Garden of the Finzi-Continis*, 1970); appeared in Bertolucci's *Il Conformista* (1970) and *1900* (1976); won Cannes Film Festival Best Actress Prize for performance in *L'Eredità Ferramonti*; other films include *The MacKintosh Man* (1973), *Steppenwolf* (1974), *Damnation Alley* (1977) and *Une chambre en ville* (1982).

SANDAHL, Ingrid (1924—). English gymnast. Born Nov 5, 1924. ❖ At Helsinki Olympics, won a gold medal in teams all-around, portable apparatus (1952).

SANDARS, Nancy K. (1914—). English archaeologist. Name variations: Nancy Katharine Sandars. Born June 29, 1914; University of London Institute of Archaeology, diploma, 1949; attended British School at Athens, 1954–55; St. Hugh's College at Oxford University, BLitt, 1957. ❖ Conducted archaeological research in Europe (1949–69) and Middle East (1957, 1958, 1962, 1966); involved in conferences at Montreal's McGill University as well as in Sofia and Prague; became a fellow of Society of Archaeologists (1984); joined faculty of Oxford University's School of Archaeology; wrote *Prehistoric Art in Europe* (1968) and *The Sea Peoples: Warriors of the Ancient Mediterranean, 1250–1150 BC* (1978), among others; translated *The Epic of Gilgamesh*.

SANDAUNE, Brit (1972—). Norwegian soccer player. Born June 5, 1972, in Norway. ❖ Won a team bronze medal at Atlanta Olympics (1996) and a team gold medal at Sydney Olympics (2000).

SANDBAEK, Ulla Margrethe (1943—). Danish politician. Name variations: Sandbæk. Born April 1, 1943, in Viborg, Denmark; University of Copenhagen, degree in theology, 1971. ❖ Representing Group for a Europe of Democracies and Diversities (EDD), elected to 4th and 5th European Parliament (1994–99, 1999–2004).

SANDBERG-FRIES, Yvonne (1950—). Swedish politician. Born Oct 14, 1950, in Umeå, Sweden. ❖ Member of the Swedish Parliament (1982–96) and executive director of the Baltic Institute (1996–); as a European Socialist (PSE), elected to 4th and 5th European Parliament (1994–99, 1999–2004).

SANDEL, Cora (1880–1974). Norwegian author. Name variations: Sara Fabricius; Sara Jönsson. Born Sara Cecilia Margarete Gjørwel Fabricius, Dec 20, 1880, in Kristiania (now Oslo), Norway; died April 3, 1974, in Uppsala, Sweden; dau. of Anna Margareta Greger and Jens Schou Fabricius (naval captain); art training (painting) at Harriet Backer's studio, Kristiania, 1899 and 1905, and in Paris from 1906; m. Anders Jönsson (Swedish sculptor), 1913 (div. 1926); children: Erik (b. 1917). ❖ Best known for her *Alberta* trilogy, which was described by the *Christian Science Monitor* as "one of the most complete portrayals of a woman's life that exist in modern fiction"; spent 2 years in Italy with husband (1913–15); spent a period in Brittany where she began to write (1918), otherwise stayed in Paris until 1921; moved to Stockholm, Sweden; had a temporary teaching post in Tromsø (1922); published short stories under pseudonym; published volume I of the trilogy, *Alberte og Jakob* (Alberta and Jacob), her 1st novel (1926); divorced (1926), but continued to live in Sweden, except for a brief period in Norway (1936–39); published *Alberte og Friheten* (Alberta and Freedom) and *Bare Alberte* (Alberta Alone, 1931 and 1939); won 1st prize in Norwegian short-story competition for novella *Nina* (1939); awarded author's stipend for life by Norwegian government (1940); published novel *Kranes Konditori* (Krane's Café) after liberation of Norway (1945), which was adapted for the stage (1947) and filmed (1951); moved to Uppsala (1960); published final novel, *Kjøp ikke Dondi* (The Leech), which won 2nd prize in a European literary competition when she was 80 (1960); exhibited paintings (1972). *Alberta and Freedom* was filmed for tv (1972). ❖ See also stories and reminiscences *Barnet som elsket veier* (The Child Who Loved Roads, 1973); Ruth Essex, *Cora Sandel: Seeker of Truth* (Peter Lang, 1995); and *Women in World History*.

SANDELIN, Lucy Giovinco (c. 1958—). American bowler. Name variations: Luicy Giovinco; Lucy Giovinco-Sandelin. Born Lucy Giovinco, Mar 15, c. 1959, in Tampa, FL; dau. of Julio and Sue Giovinco; attended Hillsborough Community College, 1978; also attended Georgia Tech for 1 year; m. Steve Sandelin, 1997. ❖ The 1st American bowler to win Women's Bowling World Cup (1976), bowled 620 to beat Swedish contender Doris Gradin by 116 pins in Teheran, Iran; served as 7 time member of US National Team; had 2nd-place finish at World Cup (1994); became Amateur champion (1996); was twice US Olympic committee Athlete of the Year for bowling and won 2 WBIC championship Tournament doubles event titles with Cindy Coburn-Carroll. Inducted into Women's International Bowling Congress (WIBC) Hall of Fame (1999).

SANDENO, Kaitlin (1983—). American swimmer. Born Mar 13, 1983, in Lake Forest, IL; attended University of Southern California. ❖ At Pan American Games, won gold medals for 400- and 800-meter freestyle (1999); won a bronze medal for 800-meter freestyle at Sydney Olympics (2000); won a silver medal for 400-meter indiv. medley, bronze for 400-meter freestyle and a gold medal 4 x 200-meter freestyle relay at Athens Olympics (2004).

SANDER, Anne Quast (1937—). American golfer. Name variations: Anne Quast; Anne Decker Quast; Mrs. Jay D. Decker; Anne Quast Welts; Mrs. David Welts. Born Anne Quast, Aug 31, 1937, in Everett, WA; m. Jay D. Decker, 1960; m. David Welts, 1962. ❖ Won USGA Women's Amateur (1958, 1961, 1963) and was runner-up (1965, 1968, 1973); won the Western Amateur (1956, 1961); member of Curtis Cup team (1958, 1960, 1962, 1966, 1968, 1974). Inducted into the Pacific Northwest Hall of Fame (1999).

SANDER, Helke (1937—). German filmmaker. Born Jan 31, 1937, in Berlin, Germany; attended Berlin Deutsche Film- und Fernsehakademie (DFFB). ❖ Worked in tv in Finland; was the founder of *Frauen und Film*, which she edited (1974–83); produced, directed and often starred in semi-autobiographical films: *Die Allseitig reduzierte Persönlichkeit–Redupers* (The All-round Reduced Personality: Outtakes, 1977), *Der subjektive Faktor* (The Subjective Factor, 1981) and *Der Beginn aller Schrecken ist Liebe* (Love is the Beginning of all Terrors, 1984); was professor of film at Hochschule für Bildene Künste Hamburg; directed for tv.

SANDER, Jil (1943—). German fashion designer. Name variations: Heidi Sander. Born Heidemarie Jiline Sander, Nov 27, 1943, in Wesselburen, Germany; dau. of Walker and Erna-Anna Sander. ❖ Studied textile engineering in Krefeld for 2 years; began career as a editor for fashion magazines, *Constanze* and *Petra* (1963); opened her 1st boutique in Hamburg (1968); designed the 1st collection under her own label (1973), all in white; a minimalist, her sleek designs are often compared to Bauhaus architecture of the 1920s; began to dress the elite and built and empire; by 1996, had a chain of 54 boutiques worldwide.

SANDER, Maria (1924—). West German runner. Born Oct 30, 1924, in Germany. ❖ At Helsinki Olympics, won a bronze medal in the 80-meter hurdles and a silver medal in the 4 x 100-meter relay (1952).

SANDERS, Annemarie (1958—). Dutch equestrian. Born April 3, 1958, in Netherlands. ❖ At Barcelona Olympics, won a silver medal in team dressage (1992).

SANDERS, Dorothy Lucie (1903–1987). Australian writer. Name variations: (pseudonym) Lucy Walker. Born May 4, 1903 (some sources cite 1907 and 1917), in Boulder Gold Fields, Western Australia; died 1987; dau. of William Joseph McClemans (cleric and founder of a grammar school) and Ada Lucy (Walker) McClemans; attended Perth College, University of Western Australia and Claremont Teachers' College, receiving teaching certificate in 1938; m. Colsell Sanders (professor), Sept 5, 1936; children: Jonathan William; (twins) Colin Creeth and Lucyann. ❖ Chiefly known for stories of young women and love; novels, several of which are set in Perth, include *Fairies on the Doorstep* (1948), *Waterfall* (1956), *Pepper Tree Bay* (1959) and *Monday in Summer* (1961); under pseudonym Lucy Walker, also wrote *Love in a Cloud* (1960), *The Distant Hills* (1962), *The Man from Outback* (1964), *The River Is Down* (1967), *The Run Away Girl* (1975) and *So Much Love* (1977); was a contributor of short stories and articles to magazines in Australia and the UK.

SANDERS, Elizabeth Elkins (1762–1851). American social critic. Born Aug 12, 1762, in Salem, MA; died Feb 19, 1851, in Salem; dau. of Thomas Elkins and Elizabeth (White) Elkins; m. Thomas Sanders, April 18, 1782; children: 2 sons, 4 daughters. ❖ Anonymously published pamphlet "Conversations, Principally on the Aborigines of North America," critical of Andrew Jackson's actions toward American Indians and overall destruction of Indian culture and society (1828); continued outspoken support of Indians in *The First Settlers of New England* (1829); spoke out against foreign missions in pamphlet "Tract on Missions" (1844), "Second Part of a Tract on Missions" (1845), and "Remarks on the "Tour around Hawaii," by the Missionaries, Messrs. Ellis, Thurston, Bishop, and Goodrich" (1848).

SANDERS, Marlene (1931—). American journalist and tv executive. Born Jan 10, 1931, in Cleveland, Ohio; dau. of Mac Sanders and Evelyn R. (Menitoff) Sanders; attended Ohio State University, 1948–50; attended Sorbonne, 1950; m. Jerome Toobin, May 27, 1958; children: Jeffrey Toobin (tv news correspondent); Mark Toobin. ❖ A 3-time Emmy Award winner, broke barriers for women in network news throughout career; worked on Mike Wallace's "Night Beat" (1956–58); became assistant director of news and public affairs for WNEW radio in NY (1962); wrote radio documentary "The Battle of the Warsaw Ghetto" for which she received Writers Guild of America Award (1964); joined ABC-TV, where she became 1st woman to anchor a nightly tv network newscast (1964), 1st woman to report from Vietnam War (1966), and 1st woman vice president of a tv network news division (1976); produced award-winning documentaries, including "Children in Peril" (1972) and "The Right to Die" (1974); at CBS, produced the news magazine "CBS Reports" (1978); joined New York's public-tv station WNET (1989); wrote (with Marcia Rock) *Waiting for Prime Time* (1989). ❖ See also *Women in World History.*

SANDERS, Summer (1972—). American swimmer and tv commentator. Born Oct 13, 1972, in Roseville, CA; attended Stanford University; m. Mark Henderson (Olympic swimmer), 1997. ❖ Won 8 US National championships; won World championship for 200-meter butterfly (1991); won gold medals for the 200-meter butterfly and 4 x 100-meter medley relay, a silver medal for the 200-meter indiv. medley and a bronze medal for the 400-meter indiv. medley at Barcelona Olympics (1992); retired from competition (1993); co-hosted and did commentary for major tv networks, including "NBA Inside Stuff." Named NCAA Swimmer of the Year (1991 and 1992); inducted into International Swimming Hall of Fame (2002). ❖ See also *Women in World History.*

SANDERS, Tonya (1968—). American volleyball player. Name variations: Tonya Sanders Williams. Born Mar 28, 1968. ❖ At Barcelona Olympics, won a bronze medal in team competition (1992).

SANDERS-BRAHMS, Helma (1940—). German screenwriter and director. Name variations: Helma Sanders. Born Helma Sanders, Nov 20, 1940, in Emden, Germany; attended acting school in Hanover, 1960–62, and Cologne University; never married; children: Anna

Sanders. ❖ Worked at tv station WDR-3 in Cologne as an on-air introducer of film classics, then produced film shorts and documentaries; made 1st film for tv, an interview with Ulrike Meinhof; joined New German Cinema movement in constructing scripts around political left; completed 1st tv film, *Gewalt* (Violence), for WDR (1971); made *Der Angestellte* (The Employee, 1972); won Fipresci prize for hour-long documentary *Die Maschine* (The Machine, 1973); made *Die letzten Tage von Gomorrah* (The Last Days of Gomorrah, 1974) and gained international success with her portrayal of the exploitation of Germany's foreign workers in film *Shirins Hochzeit* (Shirin's Wedding, 1976); probably best known for *Deutschland bleiche Mutter* (Germany, Pale Mother, 1980), which took 1st prize at 3 film festivals; released improvisational film *Die Berührte,* which won British Film Institute Award under title *No Mercy, No Future* (1981); became associated with European art cinema with such films as *Flügel und Fesseln* (The Future of Emily, 1984) and *Laputa* (1986); hyphenated her surname to Sanders-Brahms (composer Johannes Brahms is an ancestor) to distinguish herself from the German director Helke Sander. ❖ See also *Women in World History.*

SANDERS-TEN HOLTE, Maria Johanna (1941—). Dutch politician. Born Nov 7, 1941, in Assen, Netherlands. ❖ Lecturer in English (1966–88); member of the North Holland Provincial Council (1987–99); as a member of the European Liberal, Democrat and Reform Party, elected to 5th European Parliament (1999–2004). Named Knight of the Order of Orange Nassau (1999).

SANDERSON, Julia (1887–1975). American musical-comedy star. Born Julia Sackett, Aug 20, 1887, in Springfield, MA; died Jan 27, 1975, in Springfield; dau. of Albert Sackett (actor); m. J. T. Sloan (well-known jockey, div.); m. Bradford Bennett (naval officer); m. Frank Crumit (actor, died 1943). ❖ Made 1st stage appearance as a child; made NY debut in the title role of *Winsome Winnie* (1903), and subsequently starred in *The Dairy Maid, The Arcadians, The Siren, Fantana, Sunshine Girl, Kitty Grey, The Canary, Rambler Rose, Tangerine, Moonlight, No No Nanette, Oh Kay!* and *Queen High;* on radio, sang with husband Frank Crumit for years, retiring at the time of his death; also appeared in vaudeville.

SANDERSON, Sybil (1865–1903). American soprano. Name variations: debuted under name Ada Palmer. Born Sybil Swift Sanderson, Dec 7, 1865, in Sacramento, CA; died May 15, 1903, in Paris, France; dau. of Margaret Beatty (Ormsby) Sanderson and Silas Woodruff Sanderson (CA state supreme court justice); studied with Jean-Baptiste Sbriglia and Mathilde Marchesi at Paris Conservatory, and with Jules Massenet; m. Antonio Terry (Cuban millionaire), 1897 (died 1898). ❖ Forever linked with the operas of Jules Massenet, made debut in *Manon* at The Hague (1888) and created the role of Esclarmonde at Opéra-Comique (1889) and *Thaïs;* also created Saint-Saëns' *Phryné;* had enormous success at Paris Opéra (1894), but fared less well in debuts at Metropolitan (1895) and Covent Garden, possibly because her voice simply did not fill larger houses; saw career wither at turn of century; at 37, contracted influenza and died of complications; left no recordings. ❖ See also *Women in World History.*

SANDERSON, Tessa (1956—). British track-and-field athlete. Name variations: Theresa Sanderson. Born Mar 14, 1956, in St. Elizabeth, Jamaica. ❖ Won the javelin throw at the Commonwealth Games (1978 and 1986); took 2nd place, European championships (1978); set a Commonwealth record of 6,114 points in the heptathlon (1981); came in 4th in the World championships, Helsinki (1983); won a gold medal for javelin throw at Los Angeles Olympics (1984), setting an Olympic record: 228 feet and 2 inches (69.56 meters). ❖ See also *Women in World History.*

SANDERSON, Theresa (1956—). See Sanderson, Tessa.

SANDES, Flora (1876–1956). English nurse and soldier. Born in Poppleton, outside of York, England, Jan 1876; died in Suffolk, England, Nov 1956; attended finishing school in Switzerland; m. Yuri Yudenitch (Russian colonel), 1927 (died during World War II); no children. ❖ The only British woman to fight in the trenches during WWI, was a hero of the Allied Serbian Army and as such was awarded the Kara George Star, the highest Serbian military award (equivalent to British Victoria Cross); commissioned as a 2nd lieutenant by a special act of the Serbian Parliament (June 1919), also served briefly in WWII, during which time she escaped from her Gestapo captors. ❖ See also *The Autobiography of a Woman Soldier* (H. F. & G. Witherby, 1927) and *An English Woman Sergeant in the Serbian Army* (Hodder & Stoughton,

1916); Alan Burgess, *The Lovely Sergeant* (Heinemann, 1963); and *Women in World History*.

SANDFORD, Nell Mary (1936—). See *Dunn, Nell*.

SANDIE, Shelley (1969—). Australian basketball player. Name variations: Shelley Sandie-Gorman. Born Jan 22, 1969, in Melbourne, Victoria, Australia. ❖ Guard; played for 11 years on the Australian national team; won a team bronze medal at Atlanta Olympics (1996) and a silver medal at Sydney Olympics (2000); played for San Jose Lasers of the American Basketball League (1996–98); played for WNBL's Canberra Capitals (1998–2000).

SANDIG, Marita (1958—). East German rower. Born April 4, 1958, in East Germany. ❖ At Moscow Olympics, won a gold medal in coxed eights (1980).

SANDORNE-NAGY, Margit (1921—). Hungarian gymnast. Name variations: Margit Nagy. Born May 29, 1921, in Hungary. ❖ Won a bronze medal at Berlin Olympics (1936) and a silver medal at London Olympics (1948), both in team all-around.

SANDOZ, Mari (1896–1966). American biographer and historian. Name variations: Mari Macumber. Born Marie Susette Sandoz, May 11, 1896, in Sheridan Co., Nebraska; died Mar 10, 1966, in New York, NY; dau. of Jules Ami Sandoz (trapper, horticulturalist, and locator for new settlers) and Mary Elizabeth (Fehr) Sandoz (both Swiss immigrants living as homesteaders); attended University of Nebraska, 1922–31 (non-continuous); m. Wray Macumber, 1914 (div. 1919). ❖ Following death of father (1928), set to work on 1st full-length biography, *Old Jules*, which won nonfiction prize from Atlantic Monthly Press (1935); worked for assorted state and local publications in Nebraska (1927–40); after release of 2nd novel, *Capital City* (1939), which was banned in many Nebraska libraries, left home state; taught creative writing at University of Colorado (1941), Indiana University (1946), and at University of Wisconsin for almost 10 years; moved to Greenwich Village in NY (1943); completed more than 20 books, including *Slogum House* (1937) and her "Great Plains Series"—or "Trans-Missouri Series"—considered her great opus, which contains *Crazy Horse*, *Cheyenne Autumn*, and 3 other historical studies of the Old West; also wrote stories for children, including *The Horsecatcher* and *The Story Catcher*. ❖ See also *Women in World History*.

SANDS, Diana (1934–1973). African-American actress. Born Aug 22, 1934, in New York, NY; died of cancer, Sept 21, 1973, in NY. ❖ Created the role of Beneatha in Lorraine Hansberry's *Raisin in the Sun* for Broadway stage and Hollywood screen; on Broadway, also appeared in *Blues for Mr. Charlie*, *The Owl and the Pussycat*, *We Bombed in New Haven*, *Gingham Dog*, *Ain't Supposed to Die a Natural Death* and *Tiger at the Gate*; received Theater World Award for performance in *Tiger, Tiger Burning Bright*.

SANDS, Dorothy (1893–1980). American stage, radio, and tv actress and acting teacher. Born Mar 5, 1893, in Cambridge, MA; died Sept 11, 1980, in Croton-on-Hudson, NY. ❖ Made Broadway debut in *Catskill Dutch* (1924), followed by *Little Clay Cart*, *Exiles*, *The Critic*, *Grand Street Follies*, *The Dybbuk*, *The Apothecary*, *The Seagull*, *Jeannie*, *Misalliance*, *Quadrille*, *Mary Stuart*, *My Fair Lady* and *Bell Book and Candle*; had 2 one-woman shows, *Styles in Acting* and *Our Stage and Stars*. Received Tony Award for her teaching of classic acting at the American Theatre Wing (1959).

SANDVE, Monica (1973—). Norwegian handball player. Born Dec 3, 1973, in Stavanger, Norway. ❖ Won a team bronze medal at Sydney Olympics (2000).

SANDWICH ISLANDS, princess of.
See *Nahienaena (c. 1815–1836)*.
See *Kamamalu, Victoria (1838–1866)*.
See *Kaiulani (1875–1899)*.

SANDWICH ISLANDS, queen of.
See *Kamamalu (c. 1803–1824)*.
See *Kinau (c. 1805–1839)*.
See *Kalama (c. 1820–1870)*.
See *Kapiolani (1834–1899)*.
See *Emma (1836–1885)*.
See *Liliuokalani (1838–1917)*.

SANDWICH ISLANDS, queen-regent of. See *Kaahumanu (1777–1832)*.

SANDYS, Diana (1909–1963). See *Churchill, Diana Spencer*.

SAN FÉLIX, Sor Marcela de (1605–1688). Spanish poet. Name variations: Sister Marcela de San Felix. Born 1605; died 1688; illeg. dau. of Lope de Vega (1562–1635, dramatist) and actress Micaela de Luján (also seen as Luxán). ❖ Became a nun (1621); poetry collections include *Poesías* and *Coloquios*.

SANFORD, Isabel (1917–2004). African-American actress. Born Eloise Gwendolyn Sanford, Aug 29, 1917, in New York, NY; died July 9, 2004, in Los Angeles, CA; m. William "Sonny" Richmond (div.); children: 3. ❖ The 1st black woman to win an Emmy for Best Actress in a Comedy series, co-starred as Weezie on "The Jeffersons" (1975–85); began career with the American Negro Theater in Harlem, making stage debut in *On Strivers Row* (1946); appeared on Broadway in *The Amen Corner* and made film debut in *Guess Who's Coming to Dinner* (1967).

SANFORD, Katherine (1915—). American medical researcher. Name variations: Katherine K. Sanford. Born 1915 in Wellesley, Massachusetts; Brown University, PhD. ❖ Worked at the National Cancer Institute for entire career, developing tissue-culture techniques and examining ways of promoting cancerous transformations in cultured cells; was the 1st to clone mammalian cell (1948), isolating single cell in order for it to propagate itself and creating vital tool for detailed pathological study of cancer-causing mechanisms.

SANFORD, Maria Louise (1836–1920). American educator. Born Dec 19, 1836, in Saybrook (now Old Saybrook), Connecticut; died April 21, 1920, in Washington, DC; dau. of Henry Sanford and Mary (Clark) Sanford; attended Meriden Academy; graduate of New Britain Normal School, 1855. ❖ Began innovative teaching career in Connecticut towns, earning a reputation as an instructor who cultivated a love of learning as a substitute for the harsh disciplinary tactics common at the time; taught in Parkersville and Unionville, Pennsylvania (late 1860s); became an English teacher at Swarthmore College (1869), then promoted to full professor (1870); appointed assistant professor at University of Minnesota (1880), eventually becoming a full professor of rhetoric and elocution, and made an indelible mark in her nearly 30-year career there; retired (1909), lectured on art, public affairs, and women's suffrage throughout the country. A statue was erected to her memory in Statuary Hall in the US Capitol Building in Washington, DC. ❖ See also *Women in World History*.

SANG LAN (1981—). Chinese gymnast. Born June 11, 1981, in Ningbo, Zhejiang Province, China. ❖ Won bronze medals (1995, 1996, 1998) and a gold medal at Chinese nationals (1997), all on vault; at Goodwill Games in NY, fractured neck vertebrae doing a practice vault and was paralyzed from mid-chest down (1998); took up table tennis to qualify for paralympics.

SANG XUE (1984—). Chinese diver. Born Dec 7, 1984, in Tian Jin, China. ❖ Won FINA World Cup for platform and synchronized platform (1999); won a gold medal for synchronized diving 10-meter platform at Sydney Olympics (2000); won a gold medal for synchronized platform at Sydney World Cup (2000); won synchronized platform at World championships (2001).

SANGALLI, Rita (1849–1909). Italian ballet dancer. Born Aug 20, 1849, in Antegnate, Italy; died Nov 3, 1909, in Arcellasco, Italy. ❖ Made debut at Teatro alla Scala in Paul Taglioni's *Flik e Flok* (1864) and remained there for 2 seasons; danced at Her Majesty's Theatre in London; performed at Niblo's Garden Theatre in NY and in Boston in *The Black Crook*, *Cinderella*, and *Bluebeard*; appeared on tour for many years with her own company (1868–79), in such shows as *Humpty-Dumpty*, *Hickory Dickory Dock*, and *The Tempest*; returned to Europe, dancing at Alhambra Theatre in London; made Paris Opéra debut in *La Source* (1872) and created title role in *Namouna* (1880); retired (1881).

SANGER, Alice B. American stenographer. Born in Indianapolis, Indiana; dau. of Joseph Sanger (died 1899) and Susan Webster Smith Sanger (died 1924). ❖ As stenographer for President Benjamin Harrison, was the 1st woman employed in executive offices of an American president (1889–93).

SANGER, Margaret (1879–1966). American feminist, reformer, and reproductive-rights activist. Born Margaret Louisa Higgins, Sept 14, 1879, in Corning, New York; died Sept 6, 1966, in Tucson, Arizona; dau. of Michael Hennessey Higgins (stonemason) and Anne (Purcell) Higgins; attended Claverack College and Hudson River Institute, 1896–98, and nurses' training program at White Plains Hospital, 1900–02; m. William Sanger, Aug 1902 (sep., div. Oct 1921), m. James Henry Noah Slee, Sept 18, 1922 (died 1943); children: (1st m.) Stuart (b. 1903),

Grant (b. 1908), and Margaret "Peggy" (b. 1910). ❖ Flamboyant social activist who led the modern birth-control movement, founded the International Planned Parenthood Federation, and was instrumental in distributing contraception information and opening birth-control clinics around the globe; lived a conventional life in Hastings-on-Hudson as a wife and mother of 3 (1902–10); relocated with family to NY and became involved in Socialist activities, with particular interest in issues of health and sexuality for poor women (1910–14); published *The Woman Rebel*, indicted for violating obscenity laws, and fled to Europe where she met Havelock Ellis (1914); returned to US (1915); opened the 1st birth-control clinic, was arrested, and spent 30 days in prison (1915–16); published *The Birth Control Review* (1917–28) and 1st book, *Woman and the New Race* (1920); incorporated and became president of American Birth Control League (1921); published 2nd bestseller, *The Pivot of Civilization* (1922); established the Birth Control Clinical Research Bureau (1923); sponsored the World Population Conference in Geneva, Switzerland (1928); organized the National Committee for Federal Legislation for Birth Control (1930–36); with Dr. Hannah Stone, won court battle to license physicians to dispense birth-control information through the mails (1936); traveled to Hawaii, China, and India on behalf of the birth-control movement (1935–36); served as president of Birth Control International Information Centers, London (1930–36); served as vice-president of Family Planning Organization (1939); was honorary chair of Planned Parenthood Federation of America (1942); was 1st president of International Committee on Planned Parenthood (1946); organized the Cheltenham Congress on World Population and World Resources in Relation to the Family (1948), which resulted in the formation of the International Planned Parenthood Federation (IPPF, 1952). Received Albert and Mary Lasker Foundation Award from Planned Parenthood Federation of America (1950). ❖ See also *My Fight for Birth Control* (Farrar, 1931) and *Margaret Sanger: An Autobiography* (Norton, 1938); Ellen Chesler, *Woman of Valor: Margaret Sanger and the Birth Control Movement in America* (Simon & Schuster, 1992); and *Women in World History*.

SANGER, Ruth Ann (1918–2001). Australian hematologist. Born June 6, 1918, in Southport, Queensland, Australia; died June 4, 2001, in UK; University of Sydney, BS, 1939, and University of London, PhD, 1948; m. Dr. Robert Russell Race, 1956 (died 1984). ❖ Noted for work in hematology, was a scientific staff member of Red Cross Blood Transfusion Service in Sydney (1940–46); worked for the Blood Group Unit at the Medical Research Council (MRC, 1946–73) and later served as its director (1973–83); elected fellow of Royal Society (1972); with Dr. Robert Race, wrote *Blood Groups in Man* (1950), which went through many editions and helped make transfusions safer.

SANGLARD, Ana Flavia (1970—). Brazilian volleyball player. Born June 20, 1970, in Belo Horizonte, Brazil. ❖ Middle blocker, won team World Grand Prix (1994, 1996, 1998); won South American championship (1991, 1995, 1997); won a team bronze medal at Atlanta Olympics (1996).

SANGSTER, Margaret (1838–1912). American writer. Name variations: Elizabeth Munson. Born Margaret Elizabeth Munson, Feb 22, 1838, in New Rochelle, New York; died June 3, 1912, in South Orange, New Jersey; dau. of John Munson and Margaret R. (Chisholm) Munson; grandmother of writer Margaret Elizabeth Sangster (b. 1894); graduate of Monsieur Paul Abadie (NY); m. George Sangster, Oct 1858; children: George Munson Sangster (b. 1859). ❖ Following death of husband (1871), wrote to support family; contributed to many periodicals, including *Atlantic Monthly* and *Hearth and Home*, where she secured a permanent position as editor of the children's page (1873), then assistant editor; her poems "Elizabeth Aged Nine" and "Are the Children at Home?" were known the country over; accepted editorial position at *Christian Intelligencer* (1875); later worked as a literary adviser for Harper & Brothers; was an editor at *Harper's Young People* (1882–89) and edited *Harper's Bazaar* for 10 years until it ceased publication; became a member of the editorial staff of *Woman's Home Companion* (1904); also wrote such novels as *Hours with Girls, Little Knights and Ladies, Good Manners, Radiant Motherhood* and *My Garden of Hearts*. ❖ See also *Women in World History*.

SAN JUAN, Olga (1927—). American actress. Born Mar 16, 1927, in Brooklyn, NY; m. Edmond O'Brien (actor), 1948 (div. 1976); children: Maria O'Brien (actress). ❖ Made film debut in *Caribbean Romance* (1943), followed by *Rainbow Island, Duffy's Tavern, Blue Skies, Variety Girl, One Touch of Venus, The Countess of Monte Cristo, The Beautiful Blonde from Bashful Bend* and *The Barefoot Contessa*.

SANKOVA, Galina (b. 1904). Russian photojournalist. Born 1904 in Russia. ❖ One of the finest photojournalists to document WWII, gained access to Russian front after becoming a correspondent for magazine *Frontovaya Illyustracia* (The Front Illustrated); against orders, stormed into battle in order to accurately record the western front and the Briansk and Don campaigns near Stalingrad; was present at northern offensive at Leningrad (1944), even attending to 100 wounded soldiers after a battle; suffered serious injuries in an airplane accident, but was photographing Russian children in a German concentration camp the following day; published *On the Trail of Horror*, a collection of war photographs; at war's end, joined staff of *Ogonyok* magazine.

SANKOVSKAYA, Yekaterina (c. 1816–1878). Russian ballet dancer. Name variations: Ekaterina or Ykaterina Alexandrovna Sankovskaya. Born c. 1816 in Moscow, Russia; died 1878 in Moscow. ❖ Performed at Bolshoi Ballet in Moscow for most of her professional career (1836–54); danced principal roles in numerous French repertory works, among them *La Sylphide, Giselle, Esmeralda*, and *La Fille du Danube*; called the soul of Moscow ballet, was acclaimed for her dramatic portrayals; on retiring, taught ballroom dancing.

SANSAY, Leonora (fl. 1807–1823). American novelist. Name variations: Madame D'Auvergne. Fl. between 1807 and 1823; born Leonora Mary Hassall, probably early 1780s; dau. of Philadelphia innkeeper William Hassall; m. Louis Sansay (French businessman), 1800. ❖ Began a romantic and intellectual relationship with Aaron Burr (c. 1796), which lasted around 20 years; moved with husband to St. Dominique (later Haiti, 1802), but fled because of expulsions of whites by black revolutionaries (1804); as Madame D'Auvergne, was said to be involved in Burr's alleged conspiracy; anonymously published novels *Secret History, or, The Horrors of St. Domingo, in a Series of Letters Written by a Lady of Cap Francois, to Colonel Burr* (1808) and *Laura* (1809). A revised version of *Secret History* was discovered in 20th century under title *Zelica, the Creole* (1820), containing a reference to 2 other novels not extant: *The Scarlet Handkerchief* and *The Stranger in Mexico*.

SANS-GÈNE, Madame.
See Lefebvre, Catherine (c. 1764–after 1820).
See Figueur, Thérèse (1774–1861).

SANSOM, Odette (1912–1995). French resistance leader. Name variations: Odette Hallowes; Odette Churchill; (code names) Odette Matayer, Céline, Lise. Born Odette Marie Céline Brailly, April 28, 1912, in France; died 1995 in England; dau. of Yvonne Brailly and Gaston Brailly (bank official and soldier); m. Roy Sansom, 1930; m. Captain Peter Morland Churchill, 1947; m. Geoffrey Hallowes; children: (1st m.) Françoise (b. 1932); Lily (b. 1934); Marianne (b. 1936). ❖ Hero of the French Resistance, known as Odette, who worked for the British War Department during WWII; joined the Resistance (1942); captured and brought to Fresne Prison in Paris (1943); tortured by the Gestapo (May 26, 1943), but refused to divulge classified information; transferred to Karlsruhe prison (May 12, 1944); brought to Ravensbrück concentration camp for women in Germany under sentence of death (July 18, 1944); released from Ravensbrück (April 28, 1945); received George Cross from King George VI (Nov 19, 1946), the 1st woman to be awarded the UK's highest civilian award; testified for the prosecution at the War Crimes Court in Hamburg, Germany (Dec 16, 1946). ❖ See also Jerrard Tickell, *Odette: The Story of a British Agent* (Chapman & Hall, 1949); film *Odette*, starring Anna Neagle (1951); and *Women in World History*.

SANSOME, Eva (1906–?). English mycologist. Name variations: E. Sansome. Born Eva Richardson, Sept 9, 1906, possibly in New Zealand; Manchester University, DSc; m. Dr. Frederick Whalley Sansome (university lecturer). ❖ Researched mycology and genetics; taught in West Africa; appointed a Linnean Society fellow (1928); published work in *Nature* (1937 and 1938) and in the *Transactions of the British Mycological Society* (1963); researched meiosis in the oogonium; studied the antheridium of *Pythium debaryanum*; lectured in horticulture at University of Manchester and University of Ghana; employed as a reader at Ahmadu Bello University in Zaria, Nigeria.

SANSON, Ivonne (1926—). *See Sanson, Yvonne.*

SANSON, Yvonne (1926—). Greek-born actress. Name variations: Ivonne Sanson. Born 1926 in Salonika, Greece. ❖ Lead actor, later character actor, in Italian films, made film debut in *La grande aurora* (1946); was also featured in *Aquila nera, Nerone e Messalina, L'Imperatore di Capri, Campane a martello, Nous sommes tous des assassins, Les trous mousquetairs, Quand tu liras cette lettre, Torna!, Tormento, Star of India, La bella* *mugnaia, This Angry Age, Il re di Poggioreale, I giorni dell'ira, The Biggest Bundle of Them All* and *The Conformist,* among others.

SANTAMARÍA, Haydée (1922–1980). Cuban political activist and promoter of the arts. Name variations: Haydée Santamaria Cuadrado, Haydee Santamaria; (alias) María. Born Haydée Santamaria Cuadrado, Dec 30, 1922, in Encrucijada, Cuba; died July 26, 1980, in Cuba; sister of Abel Santamaría (Cuban revolutionary, died 1953); m. Armando Hart; children: 2. ❧ As a revolutionary, helped depose Batista (1952–59); held several political posts in Castro government and traveled throughout Communist bloc for conferences and official business; became key cultural administrator, promoting Caribbean and Latin American culture and intercultural exchange, as founding director of Casa de las Américas; published the journal *Casa de las Américas,* as well as thousands of books by some of Latin America's best writers (1959–80); developed theater and music departments as well as centers of research, such as Center for Caribbean Studies (1979); committed suicide (July 26, 1980), on the anniversary of the revolutionary 26th of July Movement, a day of national celebration.

SANTHA RAMA RAU (b. 1923). *See Rama Rau, Santha.*

SANTIGLIA, Peggy (1944—). American vocalist. Name variations: Peggy Santiglia McCannon; The Angels. Born May 4, 1944, in Bellview, NJ. ❧ Sang commercial jingles; appeared on Broadway in *Do Re Mi;* replaced Linda Jansen as lead vocalist for The Angels (1962), one of most successful early 1960s girl groups; with Angels, released million-selling hit "My Boyfriend's Back" (1963). Other Angels singles include "I Adore Him" (1963), "Thank You and Goodnight" (1963), "Wow Wow Wee (He's the Boy for Me)" (1964), and "Papa's Side of the Bed" (1974).

SANT JORDI, Rosa de (b. 1910). *See Arquimbau, Rosa Maria.*

SANTOLALLA, Irene Silva de (1902–1992). Peruvian educator and politician. Born Irene Silva Linares, May 10, 1902, in Cajamarca, Peru; died July 30, 1992, in Lima, Peru; dau. of Oscar Silva Burga and Susana Linares de Silva; attended Liceo del Carmen in Cajamarca, Peru, and Colegio Sagrados Corazones in Lima; m. Fausto Santolalla Bernal (engineer), June 4, 1922; children: Irene Santolalla Silva; Maria Teresa Santolalla Silva; Javier Santollalla Silva; Nelly Santolalla Silva. ❧ Advocate of issues related to women and children in international political circles, was a regular attendee at major conferences, such as Lima Congress for the Protection of Children (1943), 1st International Congress for the Protection of Children in Rural Areas (1945), 1st Feminine Spanish-American Congress (1951), International Study Congress (1952), and World Movement of Mothers (1954); founded and was 1st president of the Peruvian Committee for Collaboration with the United Nations (1949); led movement to enfranchise Peruvian women (1955); was the 1st woman elected to the Peruvian senate (1956); named "Woman of the Americas" by the Unión de Mujeres Americana (1956); awarded Peru's highest honor, the Order of the Sun (1982). ❧ See also *Women in World History.*

SANTONI, Elisa (1987—). Italian rhythmic gymnast. Born Dec 10, 1987, in Rome, Italy. ❧ Won team all-around silver medal at Athens Olympics (2004).

SANTOS, Adriana (1971—). Brazilian basketball player. Name variations: Adriana Aparecida dos Santos; Adriana dos Santos. Born Jan 18, 1971, in Sao Bernardo do Campo, Brazil. ❧ Guard; won a team gold medal at World championships (1994), a team silver medal at Atlanta Olympics (1996), and a team bronze medal at Sydney Olympics (2000).

SANTOS, Cintia dos (1975—). *See dos Santos, Cintia.*

SANTOS, Kelly (1979—). Brazilian basketball player. Name variations: Kelly da Silva Santos. Born Nov 10, 1979, in São Paulo, Brazil. ❧ Center; won a team bronze medal at Sydney Olympics (2000); drafted for WNBA by Detroit Shock (2001).

SANTOS ARRASCAETA, Beatriz (1947—). Uruguayan performer, writer and civil-rights activist. Name variations: Beatriz Santos. Born Beatriz Santos Arrascaeta, Jan 20, 1947, in Montevideo, Uruguay; niece of Juan Julio Arrascaeta, the "Langston Hughes" of Uruguayan poetry. ❧ Championed racial and economic justice as well as appreciation of Afro-Uruguayan cultural contributions through work as performer, writer, educator and activist; worked as singer and theater performer, eventually joining Afro-Uruguayan dance group, Odín; began giving lectures on customs, history and folklore of blacks in Uruguay; founded and served as president of Cultural Center for Peace and Integration (CECUPI) to combat discrimination; starred on stage in

El desalojo de la calle de los negros (Blacks Out on the Street, 1995), written by Jorge Emilio Cardoso; ran for political office on Colorado Party ticket but lost (1996); received Lolita Rubial Foundation Morosoli Prize for contributions to Uruguayan culture (1999); writings include *Historias de vida: Negros en el Uruguay* (Life Stories: Blacks in Uruguay, 1994), *El negro en el Río de la Plata* (Blacks in the River of Silver, 1995), and *La herencia cultural africana en las Américas* (African Cultural Heritage in the Americas, 1998).

SANUTI, Nicolosa (fl. 1453). Bolognese writer. Flourished c. 1453 in Bologna, Italy. ❧ An aristocrat, was a learned writer who composed several treatises; is mostly remembered for an essay she published in response to sumptuary laws enacted in Bologna (1453), which regulated women's dress. ❧ See also *Women in World History.*

SANVITALE, Francesca (1928—). Italian novelist, journalist and short-story writer. Born 1928 in Milan, Italy; studied in Florence. ❧ Critically acclaimed novelist, moved to Rome (1961); worked for Radio-audizione italiane (RAI), for which she wrote teleplays and contributed to cultural programs; novels include *Il cuore borghese* (The Bourgeois Heart, 1972), *Madre e figlia* (Mother and Daughter, 1980), *L'uomo del parco* (The Man in the Park, 1984), *La realtà è un dono* (Reality is a Gift, 1987), and *Camera ottica* (1999); published articles in literary journals and newspapers, including *Nuovi Argomenti, Il Messagero,* and *L'Unità.*

SANZARA, Rahel (1894–1936). *See Bleschke, Johanna.*

SAPENTER, Debra (1952—). African-American runner. Born Feb 27, 1952, in Indianapolis, IN. ❧ Won AAU 440 yards (1974) and 400 meters (1975); at Montreal Olympics, won a silver medal in 4 x 400-meter relay (1976).

SAPP, Carolyn (1967—). Miss America. Born Carolyn Suzanne Sapp, 1967, in Kona, Hawaii; graduate of Hawaii Pacific University. ❧ Named Miss America (1992), representing Hawaii; served as a motivational speaker and writer and host for Fox Sports; wrote syndicated column, "Safe Places for Abused Women and Children." ❧ Starred in tv movie "Miss America: Behind the Crown" (depicting her ordeal with an abusive boyfriend).

SAPPHIRA (fl. 1st c.). Biblical woman. Married Ananias. ❧ According to Luke in the Acts of the Apostles, sold a property in or near Jerusalem to give to the apostles, but instead of turning over all of the profits, she and husband surrendered only a portion; when confronted by the apostle Peter, dropped dead (as did her husband). ❧ See also *Women in World History.*

SAPPHIRA (c. 1690–1757). *See Barber, Mary.*

SAPPHO (c. 612–c. 557 BCE). Greek poet. Name variations: Sapho; Psappho; Psappha. Born c. 612 BCE in Eresos, on island of Lesbos, Greece; died under unknown circumstances, c. 557 BCE; dau. of Scamandronymus or Scamandrus (probably a noble wine merchant) and Cleïs (probably a noblewoman of Lesbos); had 3 brothers, Charaxus, Larichus, and Eurygyius; possibly married Cercylas from Andros; children: daughter Cleïs. ❧ One of the greatest poets of Lyric Age Greece, who revolutionized Greek literature by writing about her personal thoughts and feelings and by describing her physical surroundings, moved at approximately 6 years of age from Eresos to Mytilene, the largest city on Lesbos (c. 606 BCE); founded a school or sorority for young women for the study of music and poetry; banished from Lesbos, possibly for political reasons (c. 598–c. 581 BCE); famous in her own day, honored in busts, statues and coins, and painted on Greek vases with quotes from her verses; after her death, became extremely popular among the Athenians of the 5th century BCE. Nine volumes of her poetry were said to have been published during her lifetime or shortly afterward, none of which now exist; her work is known to modern scholars only in fragments. ❧ See also Page Dubois, *Sappho is Burning* (U. of Chicago Press, 1995); Richard Jenkyns, *Three Classical Poets: Sappho, Catullus, and Juvenal* (Harvard University Press, 1982); David M. Robinson, *Sappho and Her Influence* (Cooper Square, 1963); Arthur Weigall, *Sappho of Lesbos: Her Life and Time* (Stokes, 1932); and *Women in World History.*

SAPPHO (1737–1814). *See Moody, Elizabeth.*

SAPPHO OF BRABANT (1493/94–1575). *See Bijns, Anna.*

SAPPINGTON, Margo (1947—). American ballet dancer and choreographer. Born July 30, 1947, in Baytown, TX. ❧ Charter member of

City Center Joffrey Ballet (1965–66), created roles in Loring's *These Three* (1966) and performed in works by Sokolow and Arpino; on Broadway, appeared in *Sweet Charity* and *Promises, Promises*; served as choreographer for several Broadway and off-Broadway productions, including *Oh, Calcutta!* (1969) and *Pal Joey* (1976); staged her own works with the Joffrey, Harkness Ballet, Atlanta Ballet and Pennsylvania Ballet, among others. Nominated for a Tony Award for choreography for *Where's Charley?* (1975).

SARA. *Variant of Sarah.*

SARABHAI, Anusyabehn (1885–1972). Indian labor leader. Born 1885; died 1972; attended London School of Economics. ❖ Labor organizer who founded assorted craft unions, undertook the education of the children of mill workers (1914); organized workers into a cohesive group that ultimately called for a labor strike (1917), the 1st strike in the history of India; a colleague of Mohandas Gandhi, supported him in his Ahmedabad strike (1918); was instrumental in establishing the Textile Labour Association (1920), a conglomeration of separate unions that she had organized earlier in her career.

SARACENS, queen of the. *See Mavia (c. 350–c. 430).*

SARAGOSSA, Maid of (1786–1857). *See Agostina.*

SARAH (fl. 3rd, 2nd, or 1st c. BCE). Biblical matriarch. Name variations: Sara ("princess"); was originally named Sarai ("mockery"). Flourished in 3rd, 2nd, or 1st century BCE; m. Abram, later known as Abraham or Abrahim ("father of a multitude," though his original name appears to have been Abram, "exalted father"); children: Isaac (who m. Rebekah). ❖ Fearing barrenness, offered her slave Hagar to husband Abram for child-bearing, with the understanding that if Hagar gave birth, she, Sarah, would become the acknowledged mother of the child; after Hagar gave birth and made fun of Sarah for her inability to conceive, abused Hagar who fled; 13 years later, laughed when the Lord promised that she would bear a son; at age 90, gave birth to Isaac ("he laughed"). ❖ See also *Women in World History.*

SARAH OF GÖRLITZ (fl. 1388). Jewish townswoman of Görlitz. Flourished around 1388 in Görlitz, Germany. ❖ Inherited a house from another Jew; used her money to convert the house into a school for Jewish children (who could not attend Christian schools). ❖ See also *Women in World History.*

SARAH OF ST. GILLES (fl. 1326). Jewish physician of France. Flourished in 1326 in Marseilles; m. Abraham, a physician. ❖ A Jewish doctor of Marseilles, seems to have avoided trouble with the local authorities, unlike so many medieval women, even though she had a substantial practice and was widely respected for her healing abilities. ❖ See also *Women in World History.*

SARAI (fl. 3rd, 2nd, or 1st c. BCE). *See Sarah.*

SARALEGUI, Cristina (1948—). Cuban-born journalist, editor and tv host. Name variations: Cristina. Born Jan 29, 1948, in Havana, Cuba; dau. of Christy and Francisco Saralegui (publisher); granddau. of Francisco Saralegui (publisher); attended University of Miami; m. Tony Menendez (div. 1983); m. Marcus Avila (founding member of Gloria Estefan's Miami Sound Machine), 1986; children: (1st m.) Cristina; (2nd m.) Jon. ❖ Came to US with family (1960); began career as a journalist, working for the women's magazine *Vanidades*; was editor-in-chief of *Cosmopolitan En Español* (1979–89); began hosting the Spanish-language talk show, "El Show de Cristina" on Univision (1989), which would eventually have an estimated audience of 100 million throughout Latin America; became a media mogul, publishing her own monthly magazine, hosting a daily radio show, and launching an English version of "The Cristina Show." ❖ See also autobiography, *Cristina!: My Life as a Blonde* (1997).

SARANDON, Susan (1946—). American actress and activist. Born Susan Abigail Tomalin, Oct 4, 1946, in Jackson Heights, Queens, NY; dau. of Philip Leslie Tomalin (big band singer, advertising executive) and Lenora Marie (Criscione) Tomalin; Catholic University, BA, 1968; m. Chris Sarandon (actor), 1967 (div. 1979); lived with Tim Robbins (actor); children: (with Franco Amurri) Eva Amurri; (with Tim Robbins) Jack Henry Robbins and Miles Guthrie Robbins. ❖ Outspoken social and political activist, began acting career on soap operas, such as "As the World Turns"; appeared in off-beat, low-budget musical film, *The Rocky Horror Picture Show* (1975), which eventually attracted a cult following; had 1st substantial film role in Louis Malle's *Pretty Baby* (1978), then starred in *Atlantic City* (1980), for which she earned an Oscar

nomination; co-starred with Geena Davis in *Thelma and Louise* (1991), earning a 2nd Oscar nod; nominated for *Lorenzo's Oil* (1992) and *The Client* (1994), finally won Oscar for Best Actress (1995), for *Dead Man Walking*; other films include *The Hunger* (1983), *The Witches of Eastwick* (1987), *Bull Durham* (1988), *A Dry White Season* (1989), *Stepmom* (1998), *Cradle Will Rock* (1999), *Igby Goes Down* (2002), *The Banger Sisters* (2002), *Alfie* (2004) and *Elizabethtown* (2005). ❖ See also Betty Jo Tucker, *Susan Sarandon: A True Maverick* (Hats Off, 2004).

SARANTI, Galateia (1920—). Greek novelist, short-story and children's writer. Born 1920 in Patras, Greece; studied law in Athens. ❖ Works include *The Castle* (1942), *The Book of Johannes and Maria* (1952), *Our Old House* (1959), *Colors of Trust* (1962) and *The Boundaries* (1966); also published stories for children and several plays. Named Grand Commander of the Order of the Phoenix (2004).

SARASHINA (c. 1008–1060). Japanese diarist. Born c. 1008; died 1060; dau. of Fujiwara Takasue; children: 2. ❖ Lived on fringe of court society and wrote diary *Sarashina Nikki,* describing journeys from Shimosa to Kyoto (1021).

SARDINIA, queen of.
See Anne-Marie d'Bourbon-Orleans (1669–1728).
See Marie Clotilde (1759–1802).
See Maria Teresa of Austria (1773–1832).
See Maria Theresa of Tuscany (1801–1855).
See Marie Adelaide of Austria (1822–1855).

SARFATTI, Margherita (1880–1961). Italian art critic, author, poet, and journalist. Name variations: Margherita Sarfatti-Grassini; (pseudonyms) Cidie and El Sereno. Pronunciation: Sar-FAHT-tee. Born Margherita Grassini, April 8, 1880, in Venice, Italy; died Oct 30, 1961, near Lake Como; dau. of Amedeo Grassini (heir to a large fortune) and Emma (Levi) Grassini; m. Roberto Sarfatti, May 29, 1898; children: Roberto (1900–1918); Amedeo (b. June 24, 1902); Fiammetta (b. Jan 1909). ❖ One of the most influential Italian art critics and connoisseurs of 20th century, a major figure in Italian cultural life for almost 50 years, wrote two dozen books and thousands of newspaper articles, mostly on the subject of art; was also, for almost 2 decades, Benito Mussolini's lover and influential adviser; at 15, became a socialist (1895); after marriage (1898), moved to Milan (1902); began writing for a number of feminist and socialist journals (1901); became art critic for the socialist newspaper *Avanti!* (1909); began an intermittent love affair with Mussolini (early 1913); left Socialist Party (Oct 1915); became cultural editor of Mussolini's newspaper, *The People of Italy* (Dec 1918), and managing editor of *Hierarchy: A Political Review*, co-founded with Mussolini (Jan 1922); played a key role in founding the post-World War I Novecento (Twentieth Century) art movement, which proved influential during 1920s (1922); wrote the 1st biography of Mussolini, published in English (1925), then Italian and titled *Dux* (1926); converted to Catholicism (1928); wrote articles for Hearst Press under Mussolini's name (April 1930–1934); toured Brazil and Argentina with Twentieth Century art exhibit (Dec 1930); ended affair with Mussolini (late 1931); left positions at *The People of Italy and Hierarchy* (1932); made triumphant tour of US, culminating with a visit to the White House (Mar–June 1934); fled Italy (Nov 1938); sailed to Montevideo, Uruguay (Oct 1939); lived in Montevideo and Buenos Aires (1939–47); returned to Italy (Mar 1947). ❖ See also Cannistraro and Sullivan, *Il Duce's Other Woman: The Untold Story of Margherita Sarfatti* (Morrow, 1993); and *Women in World History.*

SARGANT, Ethel (1863–1918). British botanist. Born Oct 28, 1863, in London, England; died Jan 16, 1918; dau. of Henry Sargant and Catherine (Beale) Sargant; graduate of Girton College, Cambridge, 1884. ❖ Studied research methodologies at Kew Gardens with D. H. Scott (1892–93); principal areas of study included cytology and the morphology of plants; by 1895, embarked on extensive research into monocotyledons; writings include *A Theory of the Origin of Monocotyledons Founded on the Structure of Their Seedlings, The Evolution of Monocotyledons* and *The Reconstruction of a Race of Primitive Angiosperms*; was the 1st woman to serve on the council of the Linnaean Society; served as president of Botanical Section of the British Association meeting (1913); served as president of Federation of University Women.

SARGANT, Mary (1857–1954). *See Florence, Mary Sargant.*

SARGEANT, N. C. (fl. 1895). American golfer. Fl. 1895. ❖ Runner-up at the unofficial 1st national women's golf tournament at the Meadow

Brook Club in Hempstead, NY, where she lost by two strokes to Lucy Brown (Mrs. Charles S. Brown, 1895); runner-up behind Brown at the 1st US Women's Amateur championship (Nov 9, 1895).

SARGENT, Pamela (1948—). American science-fiction writer and editor. Born Mar 20, 1948, in Ithaca, NY; State University of New York at Binghamton, BA in philosophy, 1968, MA, 1970. ❖ Master of characterization, writings address such issues as bioengineering and immortality; works include *Cloned Lives* (1976), *Watchstar* (1980), *The Alien Upstairs* (1983), *Venus of Dreams* (1986), *Heart of the Sun* (1997), and *Child of Venus* (2000); short fiction collections include *The Best of Pamela Sargent* (1987) and *The Mountain Cage and Other Stories* (2002); edited collections include *Bio-Futures* (1976) and *Women of Wonder: The Contemporary Years* (1995).

SARGSIAN, Inessa (1972—). Russian volleyball player. Name variations: Inessa Sargsyan; Inessa Emelyanova. Born Jan 17, 1972, in Saratov, USSR. ❖ Made national team debut (1989); won European team championship (1993, 1997, 1999, 2001) and World Grand Prix (1997, 1999); won a team silver medal at Sydney Olympics (2000).

SARGSYAN, Inessa (1972—). *See Sargsian, Inessa.*

SARIA. *Variant of Sarah.*

SARK, dame of. *See Hathaway, Sibyl (1884–1974).*

SARKISIAN, Cher (1946—). *See Cher.*

SAROLTA (fl. 900s). Duchess of Hungary. Name variations: Sarolt. Flourished in the late 900s; m. Prince Geysa also known as Prince or Duke Geza (r. 970–997); children: St. Stephen I (c. 975–1038), the 1st king of Hungary; Sarolta (fl. 1000s); Judith of Hungary (fl. late 900s); Maria (fl. 995–1025, who m. the doge of Venice). ❖ With husband Duke Geza, received baptism late in life from St. Adelbert; as a sign of faith, changed son's name from Vajk to Stephen and raised him as a Christian (as Stephen I, he left a remarkable imprint on the history of Europe and the world).

SAROLTA (fl. 1000s). Hungarian princess. Dau. of Prince Geza (r. 970–997) and Sarolta (fl. 900s); m. Samuel Aba, king of Hungary (r. 1041–1044).

SARRAUTE, Nathalie (1900–1999). French writer. Pronunciation: Sa-ROTE. Born Nathalie Cherniak, July 18, 1900, in Ivanovo-Voznesensk, Russia; died in Chérence, France, Oct 1999; dau. of Ilya or Elie Cherniak (chemist) and Pauline Chatunskaya Cherniak (writer); attended Sorbonne, 1914–20, Oxford University, 1920–21, University of Berlin, 1921–22, University of Paris Law School, 1922–25; m. Raymond Sarraute (lawyer), July 1923 (died 1984); children: daughters, Claude, Anne and Dominique Sarraute. ❖ One of 20th-century France's most distinguished writers, was a pioneer in the development of an experimental form of fiction known variously as the "new novel" or the "antinovel"; left Russia to live part-time in France (1902); after parents divorced (1904), began to live permanently with father in France (1908); started practice of law (1925); began to write fiction (1932); published 1st book, *Tropismes* (1939); hid from the Germans during occupation of France (1941–43); won International Literary Prize for *Les Fruits d'or* (*The Golden Fruits*, 1964); a master of dialogue, eschewed any effort to connect her work to present-day events or political positions, concentrating instead on the interior life and thoughts of the human species. Fiction includes *Portrait d'un inconnu* (*Portrait of a Man Unknown*, 1948), *Martereau* (1953), *Le Planétarium* (*The Planetarium*, 1959), *Entre la vie et la mort* (*Between Life and Death*, 1968), *Vous les entendez?* (*Do You Hear Them?*, 1972), *Tu ne t'aimes pas* (*You Don't Love Yourself*, 1989), and *Ici* (*Here*, 1995); essays include *L'Ere du soupçon* (*Age of Suspicion*, 1956). ❖ See also memoir, *Enfance* (*Childhood*, 1983); Ruth Z. Temple, *Nathalie Sarraute* (Columbia U. Press, 1968); Sarah Barbour, *Nathalie Sarraute and the Feminist Reader* (Bucknell U. Press, 1993); Valerie Minoque, *Nathalie Sarraute and the War of Words* (Edinburgh U. Press, 1981); and *Women in World History.*

SARRAZIN, Albertine (1937–1967). French writer. Name variations: Albertine Damien; Anne-Marie R. Pronunciation: Al-bear-TEEN Sarah-ZAN. Born in Algiers, French North Africa, Sept 17, 1937; died suddenly, age 30, during an operation on a diseased kidney, July 10, 1967, in Montpellier, France; m. Julien (Jules) Sarrazin (fellow criminal), Feb 7, 1959. ❖ Writer whose work was based upon her experiences as a criminal and prison inmate, was adopted by a couple in Algiers at age 2 (1939); moved from Algeria to France and was raped by member of adopted family (1947); incarcerated in reform school (1952), escaped

and rearrested following robbery of a dress store (1953); saw adoption revoked by adopted family (1956); escaped from prison and met husband (1957); freed following several additional terms in prison (1960); injured in automobile accident (1961); underwent new series of crimes and imprisonments (1961–65); had 1st autobiographical novels, *La Cavale* and *L'Astragale*, accepted for publication (1965); quickly became a public personality as her books reached the bestseller list; received Four Jury Prize for *La Cavale* (1966); published 3rd novel, *La Traversière*, likewise autobiographical (1966); saw film version of *L'Astragale* appear (1967). ❖ See also *Journal de Prison 1959* (1972) and *Le Passe-peine, 1949–1967* (1976); and *Women in World History.*

SARRE, countess of. *See Marie José of Belgium (b. 1906).*

SARRY, Christine (1946—). American ballet dancer. Born 1946 in Long Beach, CA. ❖ Performed with Robert Joffrey Ballet in New York City; danced with American Ballet Theater (1964–70, 1971–74), where she had featured roles in *Coppélia* and *Rodeo* and created roles for Feld's *A Poem Forgotten, Cortège Parisien, Early Songs, Romance, Intermezzo,* and others.

SARSTADT, Marian (1942—). Dutch ballet dancer. Born July 11, 1942, in Amsterdam, Netherlands. ❖ Made debut performance with Johanna Snoek's Scapino Ballet (1957); danced in Grand Ballet du Marquis de Cuevas (1960–61), then with Netherlands Dance Theater (1962–72), where she was celebrated for principal roles in contemporary ballets, including Tetley's *Mythical Hunters,* Harkavy's *Recital for Cello and Eight Dancers,* Van Manen's *Dualis and Metaforen,* and others; after retiring from performing (1972), served as ballet mistress at Scarpino Ballet.

SARTAIN, Emily (1841–1927). American artist and educator. Born Mar 17, 1841, in Philadelphia, Pennsylvania; died June 17, 1927; dau. of John Sartain (engraver, artist, and publisher) and Susannah (Longmate) Sartain; studied in Philadelphia at Pennsylvania Academy of the Fine Arts, 1864–70; studied in Paris under Evariste Luminais. ❖ Mezzotint artist and influential art educator, had 2 paintings accepted by Paris Salon (1878), one of which, *La Piece de Conviction* (*The Reproof*), had won a medal at the Centennial Exhibition in Philadelphia (1876); was art editor of *Our Continent* magazine (1881–83); served as principal of Philadelphia School of Design for Women (1886–1920), the 1st industrial arts school for women in US. ❖ See also *Women in World History.*

SARTON, May (1912–1995). American writer. Born Eléanore Marie Sarton at Wondelgem near Ghent, Belgium, May 3, 1912; died in York, Maine, July 16, 1995; dau. of George Sarton (historian of science) and Eleanor Mabel (Elwes) Sarton (artist and designer); fled Belgium for England (1914), then settled permanently in Cambridge, Massachusetts (1917); never married; lived with Judith Matlack, 1945–58; no children. ❖ Prolific writer of poetry, fiction, autobiography, and journals who was largely ignored by the literary establishment but always enjoyed an appreciative and discerning readership; joined Eva Le Gallienne's Civic Repertory Theater in NY as an apprentice (1929); founded and directed the Apprentice Theater (1933); when company failed (1936), left the theater to devote life to writing, supporting herself by brief stints of teaching and by yearly lecture tours to colleges and universities throughout US; published 1st volume of poetry, *Encounter in April* (1937), followed by 1st novel, *The Single Hound* (1938), both of which won high praise; completed 4 novels and 5 vols. of verse (1939–55) which were also favorably reviewed; after 1955 publication of *Faithful Are the Wounds,* was ignored by the literary establishment for years but gained an ever-widening readership with the publication of 4 autobiographies and 7 journals (1959–96); at age 53 and in her 10th novel, *Mrs. Stevens Hears the Mermaids Singing* (1965), "came out" as a lesbian, which rather than alienating her readers, enhanced her reputation for honesty and courage; wrote 15 vols. of verse, 19 novels, including *As We Are Now* (1973) and *A Reckoning* (1978), 11 memoirs and journals, including *I Knew A Phoenix* (1959), *Journal of a Solitude* (1973) and *The House by the Sea* (1977), 2 children's books, several plays and other miscellaneous writings. ❖ See also Constance Hunting, ed. *May Sarton: Woman and Poet* (U. of Maine, 1982); Earl G. Ingersoll, ed. *Conversations with May Sarton* (U. Press of Mississippi, 1991); Margot Peters, *May Sarton: A Biography* (Knopf, 1997); and *Women in World History.*

SARTORI, Amalia (1947—). Italian politician. Born Aug 2, 1947, in Valdastico, Vicenza, Italy. ❖ Elected to Veneto Regional Council (1985 and 1990), serving as its vice-chair (1995–2000); as a member of the European People's Party (Christian Democrats) and European Democrats, elected to 5th European Parliament (1999–2004).

SARTORIS, Adelaide Kemble (1814–1879). *See Kemble, Adelaide.*

SARUHASHI, Katsuko (1920—). Japanese geologist and chemist. Born Mar 22, 1920, in Tokyo, Japan; graduate of Toho University, 1943; University of Tokyo, ScD, 1957, 1st female to earn a doctorate in chemistry there. ❖ While at University of Tokyo, designed techniques to measure carbon dioxide concentration levels in seawater (c. 1950); upon request of Japanese government, directed research of widespread affects of nuclear bomb testing (1954), discovering that fallout from US bomb test site, Bikini Island, had spread to Japan's seawater 18 months after test; her research helped persuade US and Soviet Union to stop above-ground nuclear testing (1963); discovered that seawater in Pacific releases twice as much carbon dioxide as it absorbs, negating hypothesis that seawater carbon dioxide absorption would stop global warming; served as director of Geochemical Research Laboratory (1979–80) and as executive director of Tokyo-based Geochemistry Research Association (1990–98); was the 1st woman elected to Science Council of Japan (1980). Received Miyake Prize for geochemistry (1985) and Society of Sea Water Sciences' Tanaka Prize (1993).

SARYCHEVA, Tatyana (1949—). Soviet volleyball player. Born Feb 1949 in USSR. ❖ Won a gold medal at Mexico City Olympics (1968) and a gold medal at Munich Olympics (1972), both in team competition.

SAS-ADLER, Valentine (1898–1942). *See Adler, Valentine.*

SASAKI, Setsuko (1944—). Japanese volleyball player. Born Oct 16, 1944, in Japan. ❖ At Tokyo Olympics, won a gold medal in team competition (1964).

SASKATOON LILY (1910–1987). *See Catherwood, Ethel.*

SASS, Marie Constance (1834–1907). Belgian soprano. Name variations: Marie Sax. Born in Ghent, Jan 26, 1834; died in Auteuil, near Paris, Nov 8, 1907; m. the baritone Castelmary (div. 1867). ❖ As a chansonette singer in a Paris café, performed under name Marie Sax, before being discovered and taught by Mme Ugalde; made debut as a soprano at Théâtre-Lyrique (1859); appeared at Paris Opéra (1860–71), and in Italy (1864). ❖ See also *Women in World History.*

SATA, Ineko (1904–1998). Japanese novelist. Name variations: Sata Ine. Born 1904 in Nagasaki, Japan; died Oct 12, 1998, in Tokyo, Japan; m. 2nd husband Kubokawa Inejiro (div. 1945); children: (1st m.) daughter. ❖ Published *A Factory for Candy* (1928) and *A Restaurant Called Rakuyo* (1928); joined Union for Japanese Proletarian Literature and edited *Working Women*; joined Communist Party (1932), but was later expelled (1951), because she opposed its meddling in literature; after 2 failed marriages, became president of women's liberation organization, Fujin Minshu Club (1970); other writings, often autobiographical, include *Crimson, A Girl with Naked Feet, My Map of Tokyo, A Tree's Shadow,* and *Standing Still in Time,* which won the Kawabata Yasunari Prize.

SATCHELL, Elizabeth (c. 1763–1841). *See Kemble, Elizabeth.*

SATI BEG (c. 1300–after 1342). Il-Khanid queen of Persia. Reigned 1338–1339; born c. 1300; died after 1342; niece of Mahmud Ghazan (1295–1304), Il-Khan; dau. of Oljeitu, an Il-Khan; sister of Abu Said; m. Choban (a military amir, died); m. Arpa Ke'un (died 1336); m. Sulaiman; children: (1st m.) daughters Baghdad Khatun and Sorghan Shira. ❖ See also *Women in World History.*

SATO, Aiko (1923—). Japanese novelist and essayist. Born 1923 in Osaka, Japan; dau. of Sato Koroku (novelist); sister-in-law of poet Sato Hachiro; divorced; children: 2. ❖ Wrote *A Mansion in Winter* (1960), *Sunset after Battle,* which won the Naoki Prize, and a biography of her father, *A Deep Red Flower–Sato Koroku.*

SATO, Liane (1964—). American volleyball player. Born Sept 9, 1964, in Santa Monica, CA; attended San Diego State University. ❖ At Barcelona Olympics, won a bronze medal in team competition (1992).

SATO, Rie (1980—). Japanese softball player. Born Aug 14, 1980, in Japan. ❖ Third base player, won a team bronze at Athens Olympics (2004).

SATO, Yuka (1973—). Japanese figure skater. Born Feb 14, 1973, in Tokyo, Japan; dau. of figure skaters Kumiko Ohkawa (mother), who placed 8th at Grenoble Olympics, 1968, and Nobuo Sato (father), who placed 8th at Innsbruck Olympics, 1964. ❖ Won World Jr. championships (1990); placed 7th at Albertville Olympics (1992); won World championship (1994).

SATO, Yuki (1980—). Japanese softball player. Born Nov 3, 1980, in Japan. ❖ Outfielder, won a team bronze at Athens Olympics (2004).

SATOYA, Tae (c. 1977—). Japanese freestyle skier. Born c. 1977 in Sapporo, Japan. ❖ Won a gold medal for moguls at Nagano (1998), the 1st Japanese woman to win a gold medal in a Winter Olympics; won a bronze medal for moguls at Salt Lake City (2002); won a silver medal for moguls at World Cup (2003).

SATTHIANADHAN, Krupabai (1862–1894). Indian short-story writer. Name variations: Sattianathan. Born into a Brahmin family, 1862; died 1894; dau. of Christian converts; married; children: 1 (died young). ❖ First woman to study medicine at Madras Medical College, had to drop out because of poor health; published stories in *The Journal of Madras Christian College,* which were released in book form as *Kamala: A Story of a Hindu Life* (1894) and *Saguna: A Story of Native Christian Life* (1894), the 1st autobiographical novel in English written by an Indian woman; also wrote *Story of a Conversion.*

SATTIN, Rebecca (1980—). Australian rower. Born Oct 29, 1980, in Honiara, Solomon Islands. ❖ At World championships, placed 1st in four (2002) and 1st in eight (2001); won a bronze medal for quadruple sculls at Athens Olympics (2004).

SAUBERT, Jean. American Alpine skier. Born and raised in Oregon; attended Oregon State University and Brigham Young University. ❖ Won a silver medal for giant slalom and a bronze medal for slalom at Innsbruck Olympics (1964); won all 4 US National titles (slalom, giant slalom, downhill and combined, 1964); taught elementary school for 32 years. Inducted into National Ski Hall of Fame.

SAUCA, Lucia (1963—). Romanian rower. Born Sept 30, 1963, in Romania. ❖ At Los Angeles Olympics, won a silver medal in coxed eights (1984).

SAUCEROTTE, Françoise (1756–1815). *See Raucourt, Mlle.*

SAUNDERS, Cicely (1918–2005). British founder. Name variations: Cicely Saunders until 1980; Mrs. Cicely Bohusz or Dame Cicely Saunders from 1980. Born in Barnet, north London, England, June 22, 1918; died July 14, 2005, in the London hospice she had founded; dau. of Gordon Saunders (estate agent) and Chrissie (Knight) Saunders; attended St. Anne's College, Oxford, and St. Thomas's Hospital, London; m. Marian Bohusz-Szyszko (Polish artist), 1980; no children. ❖ Founder of the hospice movement for the care of terminal cancer patients and head of St. Christopher's, London, Britain's 1st modern hospice, who was ahead of her time in recognizing the close connection between a patient's physical, emotional, and spiritual condition; worked as a nurse (1939–43); served as an almoner (medical social worker, 1945–51); served as a doctor (1951—); was a research scientist (1957–59); realizing that British doctors and hospitals were dedicated to attempting cures, and that patients who had no prospect of recovery were out of place in their hands, founded and became head of St. Christopher's Hospice (1963); taught a semester at Yale School of Nursing (1965); writings include *The Management of Terminal Malignant Disease* (1984) and (with Mary Baines) *Living with Dying: The Management of Terminal Disease* (1989); also edited with Robert Kastenbaum, *Hospice Care on the International Scene* (1997). ❖ See also Shirley du Boulay, *Cicely Saunders: Founder of the Modern Hospice Movement* (Amaryllis, 1984); and *Women in World History.*

SAUNDERS, Doris (1921—). African-American publisher and journalist. Born Doris Evans, Aug 8, 1921, in Chicago, Illinois; dau. of Alvesta Stewart Evans and Thelma (Rice) Evans; attended Northwestern University, 1938–40; attended Central YMCA College, 1940–41; Roosevelt University, BA, 1951; Boston University, MS and MA, 1977; attended Vanderbilt University, 1983–84; m. Sydney S. Smith (div.); m. Vincent E. Saunders Jr., Oct 28, 1950 (div. Aug 1963); children: (2nd m.) Ann Camille Saunders; Vincent E. Saunders III. ❖ As librarian for the Johnson Publishing Co., publisher of *Ebony* (1949), created an important reference library, specializing in contemporary black history during 20th century; produced hardcover titles about African-Americans and African-American history (1960), such as *Before the Mayflower* by Lerone Bennett Jr.; established and operated Plus Factor and Information Public Relations (1966); hosted "The Doris Saunders Show," a lunchtime radio talk show on WBEE in Chicago; wrote and associate produced "Our People" on WTTW-TV (1968–70); at Chicago State University, served as director of community relations (1968), then acting director of institutional development (1970–72). ❖ See also *Women in World History.*

SAUNDERS, Edith (1865–1945). English botanist. Name variations: Edith Rebecca Saunders. Born Oct 14, 1865, in Brighton, Sussex, England; died June 6, 1945; attended Newnham College, Cambridge, 1884–89. ❖ One of the 1st female fellows of the Linnean Society (1905), worked as a demonstrator in natural sciences at Newnham College, Cambridge (1888–89), then lecturer (1892–1925), then director of studies in natural sciences (1889–1925); researched plant genetics and studied floral morphology; collaborated with William Bateson, a pioneer on inheritance in plants and animals; served as a society council member (1910–15) and as a vice president (1912–13) of Linnean Society; joined the British Association for the Advancement of Science (1903); served as head of the Genetical Society (1936). Received Royal Horticultural Society's Banksian Medal (1906).

SAUNDERS, Jackie (1892–1954). American actress. Name variations: Jacqueline Saunders. Born Oct 6, 1892, in Philadelphia, PA; died July 14, 1954, in Palm Springs, CA; m. E. D. Horkheimer. ❖ Made film debut with Vitagraph (1911); was a star with Balboa Company; films include *The Will o' the Wisp, Rose of the Alley, Shattered Reputations, Alimony* and *The People vs. Nancy Preston.*

SAUNDERS, Jennifer (1958—). English comedic actress and writer. Born Jennifer Jane Saunders, July 12, 1958, in Sleaford, Lincolnshire, England; attended Central School of Speech and Drama; m. Adrian Edmondson (comic), 1985; children: daughters Beattie, Ella and Freya Edmondson. ❖ With Dawn French, began career at The Comedy Store in London; wrote and starred on tv in "Girls on Top" (1985) and "Happy Families" (1985), before reteaming with French in hit show "French and Saunders" (1987); drew on sketch from "French and Saunders" to create the hugely successful BBC series "Absolutely Fabulous" (1991–95, 2001 and 2003); also starred on British tv in "Let Them Eat Cake" (1999), "The Magician's House" (1999) and "Pongwiffy" (2002); films include *Muppet Treasure Island* (1996), *Spice World* (1997), *Fanny and Elvis* (1999) and *Shrek 2* (2004). Won BAFTA Award for Best Comedy Series for *Absolutely Fabulous.*

SAUNDERS, Marshall (1861–1947). Canadian writer. Born Margaret Marshall Saunders, April 13, 1861, in Milton, Nova Scotia; died Feb 15, 1947; dau. of Edward Manning Saunders (minister) and Maria K. (Freeman) Saunders; never married; no children. ❖ The 1st Canadian author to sell over 1 million copies of a single book, attended finishing school in Edinburgh, Scotland, for 2 homesick years (1877–79); returning home, worked as a schoolteacher; published 1st book *My Spanish Sailor* (1889), followed by *Beautiful Joe: The Autobiography of a Dog* (1893), which gained worldwide fame; published a sequel, *Beautiful Joe's Paradise; or, The Island of Brotherly Love* (1902); also wrote *Deficient Saints* (1899), *A Tale of Maine* (1899), *Princess Sukey* (1905), *The Wandering Dog* (1914), *The Girl from Vermont: The Story of a Vacation School Teacher* (1910) and *Esther de Warren: The Story of a Mid-Victorian Maiden* (1927), among others; in her work, attacked such social issues as urbanization, child labor and inhumane treatment of animals. Created a commander of the Order of the British Empire (1934). ❖ See also *Women in World History.*

SAUNDERS, Muriel Emma (1898–1974). See Bell, Muriel Emma.

SAUNDERS, Vivien (1946—). English golfer. Name variations: Viv Saunders. Born Nov 24, 1946, in Sutton, Surrey, England; earned 3 university degrees. ❖ Founder and 1st chair of British Women's Professional Golf Association; member of the Curtis Cup (1968); was 1st European to qualify for American women's tour (1969); won 1st two titles in Australia; won British Women's Open (1977); named coach of the year twice; solicitor; owns Abbotsley G&CC in Cambridgeshire. Has written 9 books on golf; awarded OBE.

SAUNDERSON, Mary (d. 1712). English actress. Name variations: Mrs. Betterton, Mrs. Saunderson. Died 1712 (some sources cite 1711); m. Thomas Betterton (1635–1710, one of the great actors of the English stage), in 1662. ❖ A member of the Lincoln's Inn company, was the 1st female actor for hire (until then, all women had been played by men); her Lady Macbeth was lauded by actor-dramatist Colley Cibber.

SAUQUILLO PÉREZ DEL ARCO, Francisca (1943—). Spanish lawyer and politician. Born July 31, 1943, in Madrid, Spain. ❖ Was a member of the Madrid Regional Assembly (1983–94) and senator (1983–94); as a European Socialist, elected to 4th and 5th European Parliament (1994–99, 1999–2004). Author of books on divorce law and the Great Lakes region.

SAUVAGE, Louise (1973—). Australian paralympic athlete. Born Sept 18, 1973, with a severe spinal disability, a type of paraplegia, in Perth, Western Australia. ❖ In wheelchair sports, won 9 paralympic gold and 2 silver medals; also won gold medals in 800-meter demonstration events at Atlanta and Sydney Olympics; won the women's wheelchair division, Boston Marathon (1997, 1998, 1999 and 2001); holds world records in the 1,500 meters, 5,000 meters, and 4 x 100-meter and 4 x 440-meter relays. Named Paralympian of the Year (1998).

SAUVÉ, Jeanne (1922–1993). Canadian feminist and government official. Name variations: Jeanne Sauve. Pronunciation: Zhahn So-VAY. Born Jeanne Mathilde Benoît, April 26, 1922, at Prud'homme, Saskatchewan; died Jan 26, 1993, in Montreal, Quebec; dau. of Charles Benoît (building contractor) and Anna (Vaillant) Benoît; attended Notre Dame du Rosaire Convent, Ottawa, University of Ottawa, as well as University of Paris, graduating with a diploma in French civilization, 1952; m. Maurice Sauvé (MP and Cabinet member), 1948 (died 1992); children: Jean-François Sauvé (b. 1959). ❖ The 1st woman to be appointed governor-general of Canada, joined Jeunesse Étudiante Catholique (JÉC), a Catholic action organization which advocated the continuance of Quebec within the Canadian federation (1937); became president of the women's section of JÉC (1942); became a journalist for Canadian Broadcasting Corporation (CBC) and its sister French-language network Radio-Canada (1953); over next 20 years, became one of the country's most distinguished public broadcasters, widely regarded as an astute interviewer and insightful commentator on major political issues of the day; when an increasingly strident nationalist movement began to call for the recognition of Quebec as an independent, sovereign country (1970), abandoned journalism and entered politics; was elected as Liberal Party member for Quebec riding (district) of Laval des Rapides (1972); was invited to join the federal Cabinet (the 1st woman from Quebec to be awarded this distinction) as minister of science and technology; reelected (1974), was assigned to ministry of the environment before switching to the newly created department of communications a year later; served as the 1st woman speaker of the House of Commons (1980–84); served as governor-general of Canada (1984–90). ❖ See also Shirley E. Woods, *Her Excellency Jeanne Sauvé* (Macmillan, 1986); and *Women in World History.*

SAVAGE, Aileen (1895–1989). See Pringle, Aileen.

SAVAGE, Augusta (1892–1962). African-American sculptor and teacher. Born Augusta Christine Fells, Feb 29, 1892, in Green Cove Springs, Florida; died Mar 26, 1962; dau. of Reverend Edward Fells and Cornelia (Murphy) Fells; attended Cooper Union Art Program, 1921–24; studied with George Brewster, 1929–30; studied with Félix Beauneteaux, at the Grand Chaumière, France; studied with Charles Despiau, in France; m. John T. Moore, 1907 (died); m. James Savage, c. 1915 (div. early 1920s); m. Robert L. Poston, Oct 1923 (died 1924); children: (1st m.) Irene Connie Moore (b. 1908). ❖ One of the distinguished black artists of the Harlem Renaissance who helped increase opportunities for other black artists, moved to Manhattan (1920); received a commission for a portrait of NAACP founder W. E. B. Du Bois for New York Public Library (1922); was commissioned to portray other black leaders, including Marcus Garvey; refused entrance to a summer-school program at France's Palace of Fountainebleau because of her race; won Julius Rosenwald fellowship (1929 and 1931); became 1st African-American to win election to National Association of Women Painters and Sculptors (1934); won citations at Salon d'Automne and Salon de Printemps at Grand Palais, Paris; established the Savage Studio of Arts and Crafts, working with such students as William Artis, Norman Lewis and Jacob Lawrence; as the Harlem Community Art Center's 1st director (1937), developed recreational, artistic, and educational programming; was also among the main organizers of Harlem Artists Guild, of which she became its 2nd president; was awarded a medallion at Colonial Exposition in France; was influential in opening Salon of Contemporary Negro Art (1939), the country's 1st gallery dedicated to showing art of African-Americans; selected works include *Gamin,* a portrait of a Harlem boy, and *Lift Every Voice and Sing* for New York World's Fair (1939). ❖ See also *Women in World History.*

SAVARY, Olga (1933—). Brazilian journalist, poet, essayist and short-story writer. Name variations: Olga Augusta Maria Savary; (pseudonym) Olenka. Born May 21, 1933, in Belém, Pará, Brazil; dau. of a Russian immigrant. ❖ Published poems, fiction and criticism in several magazines and journals in Rio de Janeiro, which were issued by the National Library in Rio as her "Collective Work" (1998); worked for journal *O Pasquim;* trans. more than 40 Spanish authors.

SAVELL, Edith Alma Eileen (1883–1970). New Zealand farmer and nurse. Name variations: Edith Alma Eileen Neilson. Born Dec 31, 1883, in Lyttelton, New Zealand; died Aug 27, 1970, at Feilding, New Zealand; dau. of Charles Magnus Neilson (mariner) and Sarah Alma (Brown) Neilson; m. Alfred Leopold Savell, 1940 (died 1940). ❖ Volunteered to serve with New Zealand Volunteer Sisterhood to care for New Zealand soldiers in Egypt (1915); returned to New Zealand to farm property (1918). ❖ See also *Dictionary of New Zealand Biography* (Vol. 3).

SAVELYEVA, Tatyana (1947—). Soviet swimmer. Born May 22, 1947, in USSR. ❖ At Tokyo Olympics, won a bronze medal in 4 x 100-meter medley relay (1964).

SAVERY, Jill (1972—). American synchronized swimmer. Born May 2, 1972, in Ft. Lauderdale, FL. ❖ Won a team gold medal at Atlanta Olympics (1996).

SAVIC, Rada (1961—). Yugoslavian handball player. Born June 18, 1961, in Yugoslavia. ❖ At Moscow Olympics, won a silver medal in team competition (1980).

SAVIĆ-REBAC, Anica (1892–1935). Serbian poet and educator. Born 1892; died 1935. ❖ Published work on European and other southern Slavic writers, including Montenegrin poet Njegoš; taught classical philology, wrote on philosophy and painting, and translated works from Greek, Latin, German and English.

SAVIGNAC, Alida de (1790–1847). French novelist. Name variations: Madame de Savignac. Born 1790 in France; died 1847; never married. ❖ Argued for thorough education for girls; wrote educational fiction for young people, including *La Comtesse de Meley* (1823), *Les Petits Proverbes dramatiques* (1826), *Les Vacances* (1828), *La Pauvre Cécile* (1829), and *La Jeune propriétaire* (1837); also wrote for women's journals, including *Journal des Dames*.

SAVILLE, Helena (1817–1898). *See Faucit, Helena Saville.*

SAVILLE, Jane (1974—). Australian track-and-field athlete. Born Nov 5, 1974, in Sydney, Australia. ❖ Won a bronze medal for 20 km road walk at Athens Olympics (2004).

SAVILLE, Kathleen (1956—). American long-distance rower and explorer. Born Kathleen McNally, Mar 22, 1956, in New England; lived in Derby Line, Vermont; m. Curtis Saville (1946–2001, died while on a solo desert mountain expedition in the eastern desert of Egypt); children: Christopher. ❖ With husband, rowed the custom-built craft *Excalibur* from North Africa to the West Indies, the 1st woman in the world to row the Atlantic (1981); with husband, rowed icebound coast of Labrador (1982) and length of Mississippi River from Northern Minnesota to Gulf of Mexico (1983); with husband, rowed the South Pacific from Peru to Australia, and conducted scientific work, on longest rowing voyage ever recorded (about 10,000 miles, 1984); was a USIS English teaching fellow in Pakistan (1993–95), and taught in Kuwait and American University in Cairo.

SAVINA, Nina (1915–1965). Soviet kayaker. Born Sept 29, 1915, in Russia; died in 1965. ❖ At Helsinki Olympics, won a bronze medal in K1 500 meters (1952).

SAVITCH, Jessica (1947–1983). American journalist and newscaster. Born Jessica Beth Savitch in Wilmington, Delaware, Feb 1, 1947; died in New Hope, Pennsylvania, Oct 23, 1983; dau. of David (Buddy) Savitch (clothing merchant) and Florence (Spadoni) Savitch (nurse); Ithaca College, degree in communications, 1968; m. Melvin Korn (advertising executive), Jan 1980 (div. Nov 1980); m. Donald Rollie Payne (gynecologist), Mar 21, 1981 (committed suicide Aug 1981); no children. ❖ One of the 1st female tv anchors, landed a job with WBBF-AM as the weekend disc jockey (1966), the 1st female Top-40 disc jockey in the area; moved to NY (1968) and was hired as administrative assistant for CBS (1969); joined KHOU-TV in Houston, Texas, a CBS affiliate, as on-air assignment reporter (1971); 3 months later, became weekend anchor, the 1st woman tv anchor in the South; signed 5-year contract with KYW-TV, NBC affiliate in Philadelphia (1972), anchoring weekend newscast; won Clarion Award from Women in Communications (1974); became weeknight co-anchor for "Eyewitness News," at 5:30 PM (Aug 1974) and ratings soared; became part of tri-anchor team on nightly news at 11:00 PM (1976); when contract expired (1977), joined NBC and was attached to Washington news bureau covering US Senate; also anchored Sunday edition of "NBC Nightly News" and teamed with David Brinkley and John Chancellor in a 3-way broadcast; periodically

appeared as a substitute on the weekday "Nightly News"—a position never held by a woman; though she was extremely popular with the public and the press, was under constant pressure to prove herself, and the strain began to take its toll; spent career fighting health problems and abusing amphetamines and cocaine; moved to NY (1982), where she worked on documentaries, served as principal correspondent for A-News Capsules to NBC affiliates, and appeared on "Frontline" for PBS; during a 60-second, live spot for "News Digest," lost control on the air, slurring her speech in what has been described as a mini-nervous breakdown (Oct 1983); died 20 days later. Won 4 Emmy awards. ❖ See also autobiography, *Anchorwoman* (1982); Gwenda Blair, *Almost Golden: Jessica Savitch and the Selling of Television News* (Simon & Schuster, 1988); and *Women in World History*.

SAVITSKAYA, Galina (1961—). Soviet basketball player. Born July 13, 1961, in USSR. ❖ At Seoul Olympics, won a bronze medal in team competition (1988).

SAVITSKAYA, Svetlana (1948—). Soviet astronaut. Pronunciation: SVET-lawn-AH Sah-VIT-sky-AH. Born Svetlana Savitskaya, Aug 8, 1948, in Moscow, Soviet Union; dau. of Yevgeny Yakovlevich (pilot) and Lidiya Pavlovna Savitsky; graduate of Moscow Aviation Institute, 1972; m. Viktor Stanislavovich Khatkovsky; children: son Konstantin (1986). ❖ The 2nd woman in space, won the world flying aerobatics championship (1970); set world flying records for speed and altitude in supersonic aircraft (1974–81); was named a cosmonaut (1980) and flew on 2 missions (1982, 1984), becoming the 1st woman to walk in space (July 25, 1983); published *Yesterday and Always* (1988); elected to Congress of People's Deputies (1989). Honored twice as a Hero of the Soviet Union and received the Order of Lenin and numerous sports medals, including the Gold Space Medal. ❖ See also *Women in World History*.

SAVKINA, Larisa (1955—). Soviet handball player. Born Feb 1955 in USSR. ❖ At Moscow Olympics, won a gold medal in team competition (1980).

SAVOLAINEN, Jaana (1964—). Finnish cross-country skier. Born Jan 23, 1964, in Lappeenranta, Finland. ❖ Won a bronze medal for 4 x 5 km relay at Calgary Olympics (1988).

SAVON CARMENATE, Amarilys (1974—). Cuban judoka. Name variations: Amarilis Savon Carmenaty; Amarilis Savon. Born May 13, 1974, in Cuba. ❖ Won a bronze medal at Barcelona Olympics (1992) and a bronze medal at Atlanta Olympics (1996), both for extra-lightweight 48 kg; at World championships, won a gold medal for 52 kg (2003); won a bronze medal for 52 kg at Athens Olympics (2004).

SAVORGNAN, Maria (fl. 1500). Italian poet. Born in Italy. ❖ Married into aristocratic Venetian family but had passionate relationship with poet Pietro Bembo (1500–01); exchanged poems and letters with him which were collected and published (1950). Wrote poetry in Petrarchan tradition.

SAVOY, countess of.
See Matilde of Vienne (d. after 1145).
See Clementina of Zahringen (fl. 1150s).
See Margaret of Geneva (fl. late 1100s–early 1200s).

SAVOY, duchess of.
See Blanche of Burgundy (1288–1348).
See Mary of Burgundy (d. 1428).
See Anne of Lusignan (b. around 1430).
See Yolande of France (1434–1478).
See Margaret of Bourbon (d. 1483).
See Margaret of Austria (1480–1530).
See Beatrice of Portugal (1504–1538).
See Margaret of Savoy (c. 1523–1574).
See Catherine of Spain (1567–1597).
See Christine of France (1606–1663).
See Françoise d'Orleans (fl. 1650).
See Jeanne of Nemours (d. 1724).
See Louisa Christina of Bavaria (fl. 1726).
See Maria Antonia of Spain (1729–1785).
See Louise of Parma (1802–1857).

SAVOY, regent of.
See Christine of France (1606–1663).
See Jeanne of Nemours (d. 1724).

SAVOY-CARIGNAN, duchess of.
See Este, Catherine d'.
See Maria Christina of Saxony (1779–1851).

SAVOY-CARIGNAN, princess of.
See Anna Victoria of Savoy.
See Mancini, Olympia (c. 1639–1708).

SAVOY-PIEDMONT, queen of. See Maria Theresa of Tuscany (1801–1855).

SAW, Ruth (1901–1983). English philosopher. Born Ruth Lydia Saw in England, Aug 1, 1901; died in 1983; dau. of Samuel James Saw and Matilda Louisa (Horner) Saw; sister of Grace Saw (mathematician); Bedford College, University of London, BA, 1926; Smith College, PhD, 1934. ❖ Was a lecturer in philosophy, Smith College (1927–34) and Bedford College (1939–44); at Birkbeck College, was lecturer in philosophy (1939–46), reader in philosophy (1946–61), head of the department of philosophy, then professor emeritus (1964); was a member of executive committee of the Aristotelian Society (1946–49), treasurer (1950–62) and president (1965); served as professor of aesthetics, University of London (1961–64); was a founder of British Society of Aesthetics; writings include *The Vindication of Metaphysics: A Study in the Philosophy of Spinoza* (1951), *Leibniz* (1954) and *Aesthetics, an Introduction* (1971).

SAWACHI, Hisae (1930—). Japanese nonfiction writer and essayist. Born 1930 in Japan. ❖ Was deputy editor of *Fujin Koron*; works of historical nonfiction include *Wives and the Coups d'état Caused by Young Army Officers on 26th February 1936, Documents–Midway Sea War*, and *Soldiers' Rebellion at Takenishijiken in 1878*.

SAWAKO NOMA (c. 1944—). Japanese publisher. Born c. 1944 in Japan; granddau. of Seiji Noma (founder of Kodansha); attended Seisen Women's University; children: son Yoshinibu and 3 daughters, including Chikako Noma (senior editor for Kodansha America in NY). ❖ After death of husband, with no editorial experience or background in business, took over as president and CEO of Kodansha (1987), Japan's largest publishing house; handles an empire of close to 2,000 employees, 54 magazines, a newspaper, and book companies in Japan, US and Europe that publish around 2,500 new titles a year; added popular women's magazines to an already successful group, *Voce, Vivi* and *Mine*. Business analysts credit her with Kodansha's success.

SAWDAH BINT ZAMA (fl. 7th c.). Wife of Muhammad. As a 30-year-old Muslim widow, married Muhammad around 621. ❖ See also *Women in World History*.

SAWYER, Caroline M. Fisher (1812–1894). American short-story writer and poet. Born Caroline Mehitable Fisher, Dec 10, 1812, in Newton, MA; died May 19, 1894, in Somerville, MA; dau. of Jesse Fisher and Anna (Kenrick) Fisher; m. Thomas Jefferson Sawyer (pastor), Sept 21, 1831; children: 4 sons, 3 daughters. ❖ Best known among contemporaries for poetry, also wrote stories and essays for such publications as *Christian Messenger, Democratic Review*, and *Knickerbocker Magazine*; headed Youth Department for *Universalist Union* (1840–45); published 1st book, *The Merchant's Widow, and Other Tales* (1841), which sold out its 1st edition of 1,000 copies; published 4-vol. collection of stories, *The Juvenile Library* (1845).

SAWYER, Ivy (1898–1999). English-born dancer. Born Feb 13, 1898, in London, England; died Nov 16, 1999, in Irvine, CA; m. Joseph Santley (1889–1971, American actor, dancer and singer); children: Joseph and Betty. ❖ Made debut performance at Prince of Wales Theatre in *Alice in Wonderland* pantomime (1909); danced with Diaghilev Ballet Russe in London (1912); immigrated to US (1915), where she danced on Broadway with Joseph Santley in 11 musicals, including *Betty* (1916), *Oh, Boy!* (1917), *Just Fancy* (1927) and several editions of *Music Box Revue*.

SAWYER, Laura (1885–1970). American silent-screen actress. Born Feb 3, 1885; died Sept 7, 1970, in Matawan, NJ. ❖ Starred for the Edison Company; made over 30 films, including *A Woman's Triumph* and *The Lighthouse Keeper's Daughter*.

SAWYER, Ruth (1880–1970). American writer and storyteller. Born Aug 5, 1880, in Boston, Massachusetts; died June 3, 1970; dau. of Francis Milton Sawyer and Ethelinda J. (Smith) Sawyer; attended Packer Collegiate Institute in Brooklyn, 1895–96; Garland Kindergarten Training School, 1900; Columbia University Teachers College, BS, 1904; m. Albert C. Durand, June 4, 1911 (died 1967); children: David Durand (b. 1912); Margaret Durand McCloskey (b. 1916, married the illustrator Robert McCloskey). ❖ As a professional storyteller with New York Public Lecture Bureau (1904–06), also set up 1st storytelling program for children at New York Public Library; received Newbery Medal for *Roller Skates* (1937); received Caldecott Honor Medals for *The Christmas Anna Angel* (illus. by Kate Seredy, 1945) and *Journey Cake, Ho!* (illus. by Robert McCloskey, 1954); also wrote *The Way of the Storyteller* (1942); children's books include *Seven Miles to Arden* (1916), *Leerie* (1920), *The Silver Sixpence* (1921), *Gladiola Murphy* (1923), *Four Ducks on a Pond* (1928), *Gallant: The Story of Storm Veblen* (1936), *The Year of Jubilo* (1940), *The Least One* (1941), *Old Con and Patrick* (1946), *Maggie Rose* (1952), *A Cottage for Betsy* (1954), *The Enchanted Schoolhouse* (1956) and *Daddles* (1964). ❖ See also *Women in World History*.

SAX, Marie (1834–1907). See Sass, Marie Constance.

SAXE, Susan (1947—). American political terrorist. Name variations: Susan Edith Saxe. Born 1947. ❖ An honors graduate from Brandeis University and antiwar activist, joined a revolutionary group; was involved in the robbery of a bank in Brighton, Massachusetts, during which a Boston police officer was murdered; along with Katherine Ann Power, was 1 of 5 people accused of the crime; became underground fugitive until finally arrested (1975); after a deadlocked jury resulted in a mistrial, pleaded guilty to robbery and manslaughter; received 12-to-14-year sentence; after release, reportedly became gay-rights activist.

SAXE-ALTENBURG, duchess of.
See Elizabeth of Brunswick-Wolfenbuttel (1593–1650).
See Amelia of Wurttemberg (1799–1848).

SAXE-COBURG AND GOTHA, duchess of.
See Mary of Wurttemberg (1799–1860).
See Louise of Saxe-Gotha-Altenburg (1800–1831).
See Alexandrina of Baden (1820–1904).

SAXE-COBURG-SAALFELD, duchess of. See Augusta of Reuss-Ebersdorf (1757–1831).

SAXE-GOTHA, duchess of.
See Elizabeth Sophie of Saxe-Altenburg (1619–1680).
See Christine of Baden-Durlach (1645–1705).
See Madeleine of Anhalt-Zerbst (1679–1740).
See Louise Charlotte of Mecklenburg-Schwerin (1779–1801).

SAXE-HILDBURGHAUSEN, duchess of. See Charlotte (1769–1818).

SAXE-LAUENBURG, duchess of. See Dorothea of Brandenburg (1446–1519).

SAXE-LÜNEBURG, duchess of. See Catherine of Brunswick-Wolfenbuttel (1488–1563).

SAXE-MEININGEN, duchess of. See Louise of Hohenlohe-Langenburg (1763–1837).

SAXE-WEIMAR, duchess of.
See Anna Amalia of Saxe-Weimar (1739–1807).
See Marie Pavlovna (1786–1859).
See Louise of Hesse-Darmstadt (d. 1830).

SAXE-WEIMAR, grand duchess of.
See Sophia of Nassau (1824–1897).
See Pauline of Saxe-Weimar (1852–1904).

SAXON, Marie (1904–1941). American dancer. Born Marie Saxon Landry, 1904, in Lawrence, MA; died Nov 12, 1941, in Harrison, NY; parents managed theaters and vaudeville houses. ❖ After father's death, toured with mother Pauline Saxon in a sister act on the Keith circuit; made Broadway debut in chorus of *Battling Butler* (1923); featured as an ingenue in *Passing Show of 1923, My Girl* (1924), *Merry Merry* (1925), *The Ramblers* (1926), and others; appeared in several early musical films, including *The Broadway Hoofer* (1929).

SAXONY, countess of. See Oda (806–913).

SAXONY, duchess of.
See Hedwig (d. 903).
See Ulfhild of Denmark (d. before 1070).
See Sophie of Hungary (d. 1095).
See Gertrude of Saxony (1115–1143).
See Matilda of England (1156–1189).
See Helene of Brunswick-Luneburg (d. 1273).
See Cunegunde (d. after 1370).

See *Margaret of Saxony (c. 1416–1486)*.
See *Barbara of Poland (1478–1534)*.
See *Amalie of Saxony (1794–1870)*.
See *Alice Maud Mary (1843–1878)*.
See *Adelaide of Saxe-Meiningen (1891–1971)*.

SAXONY, electress of.
See *Agnes of Habsburg (c. 1257–1322)*.
See *Agnes of Saxony (c. 1416–1486)*.
See *Agnes of Hesse (1527–1555)*.
See *Anna of Denmark (1532–1585)*.
See *Elizabeth of Wittelsbach (1540–1594)*.
See *Sophie of Brandenburg (1568–1622)*.
See *Hedwig of Denmark (1581–1641)*.
See *Magdalena Sybilla (1587–1659)*.
See *Anna Sophia of Denmark (1647–1717)*.
See *Maria Antonia of Austria (1724–1780)*.

SAXONY, queen of.
See *Theresa (1767–1827)*.
See *Amalia of Bavaria (1801–1877)*.
See *Maria of Bavaria (1805–1877)*.
See *Caroline of Saxony (1833–1907)*.
See *Toselli, Louisa (1870–1947)*.

SAY, Lucy Sistare (1801–1885). American scientific illustrator. Name variations: Lucy Way Sistare. Born Lucy Way Sistare in New London, Connecticut, 1801; died in Lexington, Massachusetts, 1885 (some sources cite 1886); dau. of Nancy Sistare and Joseph Sistare; m. Thomas Say (entomologist and conchologist), 1827 (died 1834). ❖ Lived for a time at New Harmony colony in Indiana, involving herself with the free public school and free library there, the 1st such institutions in US; illustrated many of husband's scientific writings, becoming noted for her unusually fine drawings of invertebrates, and for other illustrations that she created to accompany his text; was 1st woman admitted to Philadelphia Academy of Natural Sciences (1841).

SAYAO, Bidu (1902–1999). Brazilian soprano. Name variations: Bidú Sayão. Born Balduina de Oliveira Sayao, May 11, 1902, in Niteroi near Rio de Janeiro, Brazil; died Mar 12, 1999, in Rockport, ME; studied with Elena Theodorini, Jean de Reszke, Lucien Muratore, Reynaldo Hahn, and Luigi Ricci; m. Walter Mocchi (impresario), 1927 (div. 1934); m. Giuseppe Danise (baritone), 1947 (died 1963). ❖ At 14, began studying with Romanian opera singer Elena Theodorini; debuted as a concert singer at Teatro Municipal in Rio de Janeiro (1925), a still-remembered triumph; debuted in Rome and at Opéra-Comique in Paris (1926); made Rome her base (1927) and began to make extended concert tours and to perform opera in Europe and South America; met Toscanini (1936) and was given the part as soloist for Debussy's *La damoiselle élue* at Carnegie Hall, which won critical acclaim; debuted at Metropolitan Opera (1937) and remained there for 16 seasons, during which she sang 12 roles in 226 performances, of which 38 were broadcast, so recordings of all her Metropolitan roles except Serpina exist; retired (1958). ❖ See also *Women in World History*.

SAYER, Ettie (1875–1923). English physician. Born Aug 28, 1875; died July 7, 1923. ❖ Became a house surgeon for Tunbridge Eye and Ear Hospital (1899); served as a physician to Cowley Mission to Mohammedan and Kaffer Women; provided first aid lectures as assistant medical officer for the London County Council; served as honorary medical officer to Society for Distressed Gentlefolks; worked as a consulting physician to National Society for the Welfare of the Feeble-minded; was a Cape Colonial government medical officer for plague (1901); visited concentration camps and the lepers on Robben Island, South Africa; employed as an International Safety Immigration Officer medical officer; joined the British Association for the Advancement of Science.

SAYERS, Dorothy L. (1893–1957). English writer. Born Dorothy Leigh Sayers in Oxford, England, June 13, 1893; died in Witham, Essex, Dec 17, 1957; dau. of Reverend Henry Sayers (headmaster of Christ Church Choir School, Oxford) and Helen (Leigh) Sayers; graduate of Somerville College, Oxford, 1915; m. Oswald Atherton Fleming (journalist), 1926 (died 1950); children: (illeg.) John Anthony (b. 1924). ❖ Though best remembered for a fine series of detective novels, with suave Lord Peter Wimsey and his beloved Harriet Vane leading the fight against crime, was also an outstanding scholar and linguist, one of the 1st women to be awarded a degree by Oxford University; began work at Benson's advertising agency, London (1922); published 1st novel *Whose Body?* (1923);

co-founded the Detection Club (1929); left advertising to become full-time writer-lecturer (1931); published *Gaudy Night* (1935), which many detective fans regard as her masterpiece; had 1st stage success with *Busman's Honeymoon* (1937); had Christian radio play "The Man Born to be King" on BBC (1941); when mystery writing freed her of financial anxiety, turned increasingly to the study of medieval literature and to writing in defense of her ardent Christian faith; also wrote extensively for the British press, and became a familiar figure on BBC radio during WWII, a popular moralist and a gifted lecturer; published Dante translation, Cantica I, *Hell* (1949); published Dante, Cantica II, *Purgatory* (1955); also wrote *Clouds of Witness* (1926), *Unnatural Death* (1927), *The Unpleasantness at the Bellona Club* (1928), *Strong Poison* (1930), *The Five Red Herrings* (1931), *Murder Must Advertise* (1933) and *The Nine Tailors* (1934). ❖ See also James Brabazon, *Dorothy L. Sayers: The Life of a Courageous Woman* (Gollancz, 1981); David Coomes, *Dorothy L. Sayers: A Careless Rage for Life* (Lion, 1992); Catherine Kinney, *The Remarkable Case of Dorothy L. Sayers* (1990); Barbara Reynolds, *Dorothy L. Sayers: Her Life and Soul* (St. Martin, 1993); Nancy M. Tischler, *Dorothy L. Sayers: A Pilgrim Soul* (Knox, 1980); and *Women in World History*.

SAYERS, Peig (1873–1958). Irish storyteller. Born Máiréad (Margaret) Sayers in Vicarstown, Dunquin, Co. Kerry, Ireland, Mar 1873 (exact date unknown but christened on Mar 29); died in Dingle, Co. Kerry, Dec 8, 1958; dau. of Tomás Sayers (storyteller) and Máiréad Ní Bhrosnacháin (Margaret "Peig" Brosnan) Sayers; educated at Dunquin National School; m. Pádraig Ó Guithín (Patrick Flint), Feb 1892 (died 1921); children: 2 daughters, 4 sons. ❖ Renowned storyteller, grew up on the Dingle Peninsula, one of the last bastions of the native Irish language; at 12, went to work as a servant for merchants in nearby town of Dingle; married and moved to Great Blasket Island; through English scholar Robin Flower, who visited the Blaskets and was appreciative of her stories and tales, became known to the academic world; published *Peig* (1936), followed by *Machnamh Sean-mhná* (An Old Woman's Reflections, 1939); for the Irish Folklore Commission, recorded 350 ancient legends, ghost stories, folk stories, and religious stories on an Ediphone cylinder (1938). ❖ See also *Peig: The Autobiography of Peig Sayers of the Great Blasket Island* (Talbot, 1973) and *An Old Woman's Reflections* (Oxford U. Press, 1962); and *Women in World History*.

SAYRE, Nora (1932–2001). American film critic and essayist. Born Nora Clemens Sayre, Sept 20, 1932, in Hamilton, Bermuda; died Aug 8, 2001, in New York, NY; dau. of Joel Sayre (staffwriter for *New Yorker*) and Gertrude (Lynahan) Sayre (reporter for *The New York World*; graduate of Radcliffe, cum laude, 1954; m. briefly to Robert Neild (Labour politician). ❖ Served as NY correspondent for *New Statesman* (1965–70), and as film critic for *The New York Times* (1973–75); for next 7 years, freelanced as film critic for *The Nation, The Progressive, Esquire* and *The New York Times Book Review*; wrote on cultural effects of McCarthyism and the Cold War in *Running Time: Films of the Cold War* (1982) and *Previous Convictions* (1995). ❖ See also memoir, *On the Wing: A Young American Abroad* (Counterpoint, 2001).

SAYRE, Zelda (1900–1948). See *Fitzgerald, Zelda*.

SAYRES, Aurelie (1977—). American snowboarder. Born Sept 21, 1977, in Farmington, CT. ❖ First place finishes in Halfpipe include Vans Triple Crown overall champion (1997), Vans Triple Crown, Breckenridge, CO (1998), and ESPN Freeride (1998); was a two-time bronze medalist at X Games (Boarder X in Winter 1997 and Slopestyle in Winter 1998).

SAYYIDAH (1052–1137). See *Arwā*.

SAZ, Leyla (1850–1936). See *Hanim, Leyla*.

SAZANOVICH, Natalya (1973—). Belarusian heptathlete. Name variations: Natasha Sazanovich. Born Aug 15, 1973, in Baranovich, Belarus. ❖ Won a silver medal at Atlanta Olympics (1996) and a bronze medal at Sydney Olympics (2000); won a silver medal at World championships (2001); at European championships, won bronze medals (1998, 2002).

SAZONENKOVA, Elena (1973—). Latvian gymnast. Born Oct 22, 1973, in Riga, Latvia, USSR. ❖ At World championships, won a gold medal in team all-around (1989); won Champions All and University Games (1991).

SBARBATI, Luciana (1946—). Italian politician. Born May 10, 1946, in Rome, Italy. ❖ Partito repubblicano italiano (PRI) member of Italian Parliament (1992), becoming chair of PRI Group (1993–94), vice-chair of the I Democratici mixed group (1994–96), and vice-chair of the FLDR mixed group (1996—); as a member of the European Liberal, Democrat and Reform Party, elected to 5th European Parliament (1999–2004).

SBISLAVA OF KIEV (d. 1110). *See Zbyslawa.*

SCADUTO, Matilda (1925–2003). *See Bryant, Felice.*

SCALA, Beatrice della (1340–1384). *See della Scala, Beatrice.*

SCALA, Gia (1934–1972). Italian-English actress. Born Giovanna Sgoglio, Mar 3, 1934, in Liverpool, England; died, age 38, from accidental overdose of drugs and alcohol, April 30, 1972, in Hollywood, CA; sister of Tina Scala (actress); studied with Stella Adler; m. Donald Burnett (actor), 1957 (div. 1970). ❖ Raised in Rome from age 3 on; moved with family to NY, age 16 (1951); films include *All That Heaven Allows, Never Say Goodbye, Four Girls in Town, Garment Jungle, Don't Go Near the Water, Two-Headed Spy, Battle of the Coral Sea* and *Guns of Navarone.*

SCALA, Reginna della (1340–1384). *See della Scala, Beatrice.*

SCALES, Helen Flora Victoria (1887–1875). New Zealand painter. Born on May 24, 1887, in Lower Hutt, New Zealand; died Jan 11, 1985, at Rotorua, New Zealand; dau. of George Herbert Scales (insurance agent) and Gertrude Maynard (Snow) Scales. ❖ Joined Academy Studio Club (1914); studied abroad at Académie de la Grande Chaumiére in Paris, Hans Hoffmann's school of art in Munich, and Académie Ranson (1920s–30s); worked in Europe for many years before resettling in New Zealand (1970s); known primarily for modernistic landscapes, portraits, and flower studies. ❖ See also *Dictionary of New Zealand Biography* (Vol. 4).

SCALES, Jessie Sleet (fl. 1900). African-American nurse. Born in Stratford, Ontario, Canada; graduate of Provident Hospital School of Nursing, Chicago, 1895. ❖ The 1st black public health nurse active in the US, was hired by the Charity Organization Society in NY to make home visits to black tuberculosis sufferers and convince them to seek medical treatment (1900); continued work with the society for 9 years. ❖ See also *Women in World History.*

SCALES, Prunella (1932—). English actress. Born Prunella Margaret Rumney Illingworth, June 22, 1932, in Sutton Abinger, Surrey, England; trained at the Old Vic and HB Studios in NY; m. Timothy West (actor), 1963; children: Joseph and Samuel West (actor). ❖ Appeared as Eileen Hughes on "Coronation Street" (1961); came to prominence as Sybil Fawlty on "Fawlty Towers" (1975–79), then starred on "Mapp & Lucia" (1985) and "After Henry" (1987); films include *The Lonely Passion of Judith Hearne* (1987), *Consuming Passions* (1988), *Howard's End* (1992), *An Ideal Husband* (1998) and *Mad Cows* (1999); received Patricia Rothermere Award (2001).

SCALLON, Dana Rosemary (1950—). Irish politician and singer. Born Dana Rosemary Brown, Aug 30, 1950, in London, England; m. Damien Scallon, 1979. ❖ Became the 1st Irish winner of the Eurovision Song Contest (1970) with "All Kinds of Everything"; hosted a talk show, "Say Yes," on Eternal Word Television Network (EWTN); ran unsuccessfully for the Irish presidency (1997); as an Independent, elected member of the European Parliament for Connaught-Ulster (MEP, 1999–2004).

SCANLAN, Nelle (1882–1968). New Zealand journalist, novelist, and radio commentator. Name variations: Ellen Margaret Scanlan. Born Jan 15, 1882, in Picton, New Zealand; died Oct 5, 1968, in Wellington; dau. of Michael Scanlan (gold prospector and police officer) and Ellen (Kiely) Scanlan. ❖ Became reporter and freelance journalist during WWI; published syndicated articles as *Boudoir Mirrors of Washington* (1923); was based in England until 1950s and reported on lives of wealthy and famous; wrote 15 popular novels over period of 20 years, including "Pencarrow" tetraology, *Pencarrow* (1932), *Tides of Youth* (1933), *Winds of Heaven* (1934), and *Kelly Pencarrow* (1939), which established her as most popular New Zealand novelist of her generation; became well-known radio speaker with series of 200 broadcasts, "Shoes and Ships and Sealing-wax" (1940s). ❖ See also autobiography, *Road to Pencarrow* (1963); and *Dictionary of New Zealand Biography* (Vol. 4).

SCANLON, Mary (1947—). Scottish politician. Born May 25, 1947, in Dundee, Scotland; University of Dundee, MA in economics and politics; children: 2. ❖ Was a lecturer in economics and management at Perth College (1983–88), Dundee Institute of Technology (1988–94), and Inverness College (1994–99); as a Scottish Conservative and Unionist, elected to the Scottish Parliament for Highlands and Islands (1999).

SCAPIN, Ylenia (1975—). Italian judoka. Born in Jan 8, 1975, in Bolzano, Italy. ❖ Won a bronze medal for 66–72 kg half-heavyweight at Atlanta Olympics (1996) and a bronze medal for 63–70 kg middleweight at Sydney Olympics (2000).

SCARBOROUGH, Dorothy (1878–1935). American novelist and musicologist. Born in Mount Carmel, Texas, on Jan 27, 1878; died Nov 7, 1935; dau. of John B. Scarborough (lawyer) and Mary Adelaide Scarborough; sister of Martha McDaniel Scarborough and George Moore Scarborough, both writers; received bachelor's and master's degrees from Baylor University, 1890s; studied at University of Chicago; studied at Oxford University in England, 1910–11; Columbia University, PhD, 1917; never married. ❖ Known equally well for a series of realistic novels and for pioneering investigations of American folk music, helped to pave the way for the generation of Southern women writers who came to prominence in mid-20th century; though she wrote and taught in NY for much of her professional life, drew upon Texas origins in her fiction and was perhaps that state's most important contributor to the regionalist style that gained favor between the world wars; writings include *Fugitive Verses* (1912), *The Supernatural in Modern English Fiction* (1917), *From a Southern Porch* (1919), *On the Trail of Negro Folk-Songs* (1925), *The Unfair Sex* (1925), *Impatient Griselda* (1927), *Can't Get a Red Bird* (1929), *The Stretch-berry Smile* (1932), *A Song Catcher in Southern Mountains* (1937, posthumous) and her most famous novel, *The Wind* (1925). ❖ See also *Women in World History.*

SCARLAT, Roxana (1975—). Romanian fencer. Born 1975 in Romania. ❖ Won a silver medal for team foil at Atlanta Olympics (1996).

SCARLETT, Susan (1895–1986). *See Streatfeild, Noel.*

SCARY SPICE (1975—). *See Brown, Melanie.*

SCEMIOPHRIS (fl. 1680–1674 BCE). *See Sobek-neferu.*

SCEPENS, Elizabeth (fl. 1476). Artist and bookmaker of Belgium. Name variations: Elisabeth Betkin. Flourished c. 1476 in Bruges, Flanders. ❖ Ran a successful art studio in Bruges; studied book production and illustration under illuminator William Vrelandt, and upon his death took over his studio in partnership with Vrelandt's widow; earned a membership in Bruges guild of scribes and artists (1476).

SCHAAF, Petra (1969—). *See Behle, Petra.*

SCHACHERER-ELEK, Ilona (1907–1988). Hungarian-Jewish fencer. Name variations: Ilona Elek; Ilona Elek-Schacherer. Born Ilona Elek, May 17, 1907; died July 24, 1988; sister of Margit Elek (fencer). ❖ Won a gold medal for indiv. foil at Berlin Olympics (1936); took a 2nd gold medal at London Olympics (1948) and a silver medal at Helsinki Olympics (1952); was world champion (1934, 1935, and 1951).

SCHAEFER, Laurel Lea (c. 1949—). Miss America and actress. Name variations: Laurie Lea Schaefer; Laurel Schaefer. Born Laurel Lea Schaefer, c. 1949, in Bexley, Ohio; Ohio University School of Theater, BFA. ❖ Named Miss America (1972), representing Ohio; founding chair of the Women's Leadership Foundation; serves on the Zonta International Committee for Strategies to Eliminate Violence Against Women; motivational speaker; vocalist. Was a regular on "Falcon Crest" (1986–87) and guest starred on "Matlock," "LA Law," and "Rockford Files," among other tv shows.

SCHAEFFER, Rebecca (1967–1989). American actress. Born Nov 6, 1967, in Portland, OR; died July 18, 1989, in West Hollywood, CA. ❖ At 16, began modeling; had recurring role as kid sister of Pam Dawber on "My Sister Sam" (1986); at 21, was shot to death outside her West Hollywood apartment by an obsessed fan; films include *Radio Days* and *Scenes from the Class Struggle in Beverly Hills.* ❖ See also "Rebecca Schaeffer: The E! True Hollywood Story" (1991).

SCHAEFFER, Wendy (c. 1975—). Australian equestrian. Born c. 1975 in South Australia. ❖ Won a team gold medal for eventing on Sunburst at Atlanta Olympics (1996). Inducted into Sport Australia Hall of Fame (2002).

SCHAFER, Natalie (1900–1991). American actress. Born Nov 5, 1900, in Red Bank, NJ; died April 10, 1991, in Los Angeles, CA; m. Louis Calhern (actor), 1934 (div. 1942). ❖ Made NY debut as Eleanor Stafford in *Trigger* (1927), followed by *Susan and God, Lady in the Dark* and *The Doughgirls*, among others; probably best known for role of Mrs. Howell on "Gilligan's Island"; films include *Keep Your Powder Dry, Dishonored Lady, Snake Pit, Anastasia, Forever Darling, Susan Slade, Bernadine, 40 Carats* and *The Day of the Locust.*

SCHAFFER, Ine (1923—). *Austrian track-and-field athlete.* Born Mar 28, 1923, in Austria. ❖ At London Olympics, won a bronze medal in shot put (1948).

SCHAFFNER, Anne-Marie (1945—). *French politician.* Born May 31, 1945, in Nancy, France. ❖ Served as Conseiller Général, Seine-et-Marne (1986–98) and vice-president of the Conseil Général of Seine-et-Marne (1992–94); was national secretary of the RPR (1995–97, 1998); as a member of the European People's Party (Christian Democrats) and European Democrats, elected to 4th and 5th European Parliament (1994–99, 1999–2004). Awarded Chevalier de la Légion d'honneur.

SCHAFFNER, Katherine (1944—). *See Anderson, Katherine.*

SCHAFT, Hannie (1920–1945). *Dutch resistance leader.* Name variations: Johanna Jannetje Schaft; Johanna Elderkamp. Born Jannetje Johanna Schaft in Haarlem, the Netherlands, Sept 16, 1920; executed April 17, 1945; dau. of Pieter Schaft (teacher) and Aafje Talea (Vrijer) Schaft; was a law student attending University of Amsterdam during German occupation of the Netherlands; never married; no children. ❖ During WWII, joined the small, Communist-leaning Raad van Verzet (Council of Resistance) in Haarlem, hiding and assisting Jews who were being rounded up for "resettlement" to death camps in the East (1941); with Freddie and Truus Oversteegen, carried out assassinations and became notorious in German and Dutch Nazi circles for bold effectiveness (1942–43); when German Commissioner of Occupied Netherlands, Arthur Seyss-Inquart, required students to sign a loyalty oath or relinquish the right to study, encouraged student solidarity that led to closing down of the Dutch universities (1943); arrested (Mar 1945) and executed (April 17, 1945), only 3 weeks before the collapse of Nazi Germany and the liberation of her country. ❖ See also *Women in World History.*

SCHALK, Henriëtte van der (1869–1952). *See Roland Holst, Henriëtte.*

SCHALLER, Johanna (1952—). *See Klier-Schaller, Johanna.*

SCHALLING, Heike (1966—). *See Warnicke, Heike.*

SCHANNE, Margrethe (1921—). *Danish ballet dancer.* Born Margrethe Sophie Marie Schanne, Nov 21, 1921, in Copenhagen, Denmark; dau. of Jean Baptiste Schanne and Emilie Lind Hansen; m. Kjeld Noack (ballet dancer), 1971. ❖ Performed professionally in Royal Danish Ballet (1942–66), where she was acclaimed for work in Bournonville ballets, most notably in *La Sylphide, Giselle, La Ventana, Napoli, A Folk Tale,* and others; while on leave from Royal Danish, danced with Ballet des Champs-Elysées in Petit's *Les Amours de Jupiter* and *Lac des Cygnes* (1946–47); returned to Royal Danish where she created roles in Kirsten Ralov's *La Dame aux Camilias* (1960), Bjørn Larsen's *Drift* (1964), and Hans Brenaa's *Stemninger* (1964); retired (1966) and turned to teaching.

SCHARFF-GOLDHABER, Gertrude (1911–1998). *American nuclear physicist.* Name variations: Gertrude Scharff Goldhaber; Mrs. Maurice Goldhaber. Born Gertrude Scharff in Mannheim, Germany, on July 14, 1911; died Feb 2, 1998, in Bayport, NY; dau. of Otto Scharff and Nelly (Steinharter) Scharff; attended universities of Freiburg, Zurich, and Berlin; University of Munich, PhD, 1935; m. Maurice Goldhaber (director of Brookhaven National Laboratory), May 24, 1939; sister-in-law of Sulamith Goldhaber (d. 1965, physicist); children: Alfred Scharff Goldhaber; Michael Henry Goldhaber. ❖ Was a research associate at Imperial College, London (1935–39); arrived in US (1939) and became US citizen (1944); was a research physicist at University of Illinois, Champaign (1939–48), then assistant professor (1948–50); served as associate physicist at Brookhaven National Laboratory in Upton, NY (1950–58), becoming senior physicist (1962); at Brookhaven, was immersed in both theoretical and experimental work, ascertaining the detailed properties of nuclear energy levels and magnetic moments to gain a better grasp of nuclear structure; served on Committee on Problems of Women in Physics (1971).

SCHARLIEB, Mary Ann (1845–1930). *English physician and judge.* Name variations: Dame Mary Ann Dacomb Scharlieb. Born Mary Ann Dacomb Bird, June 16, 1845 (some sources cite 1844); died Nov 21, 1930; entered Medical School of Madras in India, 1877; earned degree from Royal Free Hospital, 1882; London University, MD, 1888; m. W. M. Scharlieb (lawyer), 1865 (died 1891). ❖ Accompanied husband to India (1866), where she was motivated to seek a medical education from witnessing the dangers that Indian women experienced in childbirth; established a private practice in England; overcame Victorian prejudice against women in the medical profession and became a noted

gynecological surgeon; served as chief surgeon at New Hospital for Women (1892–1903); played an important role in establishing Royal Victoria Hospital for Caste and Gosha Women (1880s), and worked to form a Women's Medical Service for India during WWI; became one of the 1st English women named to a judgeship (1920). Created Dame Commander of the Order of the British Empire (1926).

SCHARPF, Brandy Johnson (1973—). *See Johnson, Brandy.*

SCHARRER, Berta (1906–1995). *German-born American neuroscientist.* Born Berta Vogel in Munich, Germany, Dec 1, 1906; died in the Bronx, NY, July 23, 1995; dau. of Karl Phillip Vogel (judge) and Johanna (Greis) Vogel; University of Munich, doctorate in biology, 1930; m. Ernst Albert Scharrer (1906–1965, biologist), 1934 (died 1965). ❖ With husband, discovered the ability of some nerve cells to secrete hormonal substances, which quickly became the new discipline of neuroendocrinology, and published *Neuroendocrinology* (1963), a basic textbook. Was a member of US National Academy of Sciences; received Kraepelin Medal of Max Planck Institute in Munich (1978) and US National Medal of Science (1983). ❖ See also *Women in World History.*

SCHARRER, Irene (1888–1971). *English pianist.* Born in London, England, Feb 2, 1888; died in London, Jan 11, 1971; cousin of Myra Hess (1890–1965); studied with Tobias Matthay. ❖ Made successful London debut (1904); often played 2-piano recitals with cousin, Myra Hess; made 1st tour of US (1925), performing concertos and working as a recitalist and chamber-music pianist. ❖ See also *Women in World History.*

SCHARY, Hope Skillman (1908–1981). *American business executive.* Name variations: Hope Skillman; Mrs. Saul Schary. Born Hope Skillman in Grand Rapids, Michigan, Feb 16, 1908; died in New Milford, Connecticut, May 23, 1981; dau. of Frederic Cameron Skillman and Mary (Christie) Skillman; graduate of Goucher College, 1961; m. Saul Schary (artist), Dec 15, 1934. ❖ Probably the 1st woman to own a textile-manufacturing company, was an associate editor at *Parnassus* magazine (1932–33) and *The Fine Arts* (1933–34), both in NY; as a textile designer, was assistant stylist with Ameritex division of Cohn-Hall-Marx Co. (1934–35), stylist (1935–39), and director (1939–42); founded Skillmill, Inc., a textile-manufacturing firm (1944), which employed only women for some years; remained the company's CEO until retirement (early 1960s); served as president of Fashion Group, Inc., an industry association of 5,000 women (1958–60) and as president of National Council of Women of the US (1970–72, 1976–78).

SCHAU, Virginia M. (1915–1989). *American photographer.* Born Feb 23, 1915; died May 28, 1989, in Santa Rosa, CA; m. Walter Schau. ❖ While an amateur photographer, became 2nd person and 1st woman to win Pulitzer Prize for spot news photography (1954), shooting the 2 winning pictures of husband rescuing a truck driver whose vehicle went over side of Pit River Bridge near Redding, CA (1953).

SCHAUBEL, Ruth (1906–1988). *See Malcomson, Ruth.*

SCHAUDT, Carol (1957—). *See Menken-Schaudt, Carol.*

SCHAUMANN, Ruth (1899–1975). *German poet and painter.* Born Aug 24, 1899, in Hamburg, Germany; died Mar 13, 1975, in Munich, Germany; dau. of Kurt and Elisabeth Schaumann; m. Friedrich Fuchs, 1924 (died 1948); children: 5. ❖ Published 1st poetry collection, *Die Kathedrale* (The Cathedral, 1920); converted to Catholicism (1924); later writings, which often focused on love and marriage and were banned under Nazi rule, included poems, stories, novels, and self-illustrated children's books.

SCHAURTE, Anneliese (1929—). *See Küppers, Anneliese.*

SCHAW, Janet (d. around 1801). *Scottish travel writer.* Born Janet Schaw between 1730 and 1737 in Scotland; died c. 1801 in Edinburgh, Scotland; dau. of Gideon Schaw and Anne (Rutherford) Schaw. ❖ Resided briefly in Wilmington, NC; wrote *Journal of a Lady of Quality* (1774–76), which was a series of travel letters to friends in Scotland about manners and customs of North Carolina and conditions on plantations in Antigua.

SCHEELE, Karin (1968—). *Austrian politician.* Born July 22, 1968, Baden, Austria. ❖ Member of the Land Executive of the Socialist Youth of Lower Austria (1987–99) and the Land Party committee of the SPÖ (Socialist Party of Austria) in Lower Austria (1999—); as a European Socialist, elected to 5th European Parliament (1999–2004).

SCHEEPSTRA, Maartje (1980—). Dutch field-hockey player. Born a twin, April 1, 1980, in Irian Jaya, Indonesia, to parents of the Yali tribe; adopted by a Dutch doctor. ❖ Won European championship (2003); midfielder, won a team silver medal at Athens Olympics (2004).

SCHEFF, Fritzi (1879–1954). Austro-American soprano. Born in Vienna, Austria, Aug 30, 1879; died in New York, NY, April 8, 1954; dau. of a physician and a Wagnerian soprano. ❖ Trained at Hoch Conservatory in Frankfurt; debuted in Nuremberg (1897); sang a variety of operatic roles; debuted at Metropolitan Opera (1900), but left after 3 seasons to appear in *Babette*, an operetta written for her by Victor Herbert; had greatest triumph in another operetta by Herbert, *Mlle Modiste* (1906), but had damaged her career as a classical singer; had to perform in vaudeville, Broadway shows, and nightclubs in order to survive as a singer; later became a star on radio and tv, but always lamented her choice. ❖ See also *Women in World History*.

SCHEIBLICH, Christine (1954—). East German rower. Born Dec 31, 1954, in East Germany. ❖ At Montreal Olympics, won a gold medal in single sculls (1976).

SCHEKERYK, Melanie (1947—). American rock, pop, and folksinger and songwriter. Name variations: Melanie; Melanie Safka. Born Melanie Safka, Feb 3, 1947, in Queens, NY; studied at American Academy of Dramatic Arts; m. Peter Schekeryk (music publisher), 1968; children: Beau Jarred (guitarist). ❖ Known simply as Melanie, signed with Columbia Records (1967); performed at Woodstock (1969), gaining considerable notice; released album, *Candles in the Rain,* which sold over 1 million copies and earned her *Billboard's* award as top female vocalist (1970); became well known in Western Europe, where her records were often in Top 10; with husband, started Neighborhood Records (1971) and released her biggest hit, "Brand New Key," which sold over 3 million copies and was #1 in US; other hit songs include "What Have They Done to My Song, Ma?," "Lay Down," and "Beautiful People"; became a spokeswoman for UNICEF (1972). Was the 1st female pop artist to have 3 albums on *Billboard* charts simultaneously; won an Emmy for writing song "The First Time I Loved Forever" for CBS-TV's "Beauty and the Beast: A Distant Shore" (1989). ❖ See also *Women in World History*.

SCHELL, Maria (1926–2005). Austrian actress. Name variations: acted as Gritli Schell. Born Maria Margarethe Anna Schell in Vienna, Austria, Jan 15, 1926; died April 26, 2005, in Preitenegg, Carinthia, Austria; dau. of Hermann Ferdinand Schell (Swiss playwright) and Marguerite (de Noé) Schell (actress); sister of Maximilian Schell (actor, director, producer, and screenwriter); attended School of Theatrical Arts, Zurich; m. Horst Hächler (film director), April 27, 1957 (div. 1965); m. Veit Relin (Austrian actor and director), 1966 (div. 1988); children: (1st m.) Oliver Schell; (2nd m.) Marie-Theres Relin. ❖ Internationally acclaimed actress, auditioned for a small role in Swiss film and was awarded the lead (1942); did a stint with State Theater of Bern; featured in Austrian film *Der Engel mit der Posaune* (1948), which led to 7-year contract with Alexander Korda; starred in over 20 European films, including *The Magic Box* (1951), *The Heart of the Matter* (1953), *Die letzte Brücke* (*The Last Bridge*), for which she won Best Actress at Cannes (1954), as well as *Napoléon* (1955) and *Gervaise* (1956); made US film debut as Grushenka in *The Brothers Karamazov* (1958), followed by *Hanging Tree* (1959) and *Cimarron* (1961), both westerns; also starred in 3 US tv dramas, including a 2-part dramatization of *For Whom the Bell Tolls*; all but retired from films (1963), returning occasionally for a character role; acted and served as co-producer of film *So oder so ist das Leben* (1976); made last American film, *Superman* (1978); continued to perform in theater; other films include *The Mark* (1961), *The Odessa File* (1974), *Follies Bourgeoises* (1976), *Voyage of the Damned* (1976), *La Passante du Sans-Souci* (*La Passante,* 1982) and *1919* (1985). ❖ See also (documentary) *My Sister Maria* (2002); and *Women in World History*.

SCHELLING, Caroline (1763–1809). *See Schlegel-Schelling, Caroline.*

SCHENK, Franziska (1974—). German speedskater. Born Mar 13, 1974, in Erfurt, Germany. ❖ Won a bronze medal for the 500 meters at Lillehammer Olympics (1994); placed 1st in the German distance championship and the German sprint championship (1995); placed 3rd in World sprint championship (1996); at World Cup, placed 2nd in 500 meters and 1st in 1,000 meters (1997); won the World sprint championships (1997); is also a fashion model and tv personality in Germany.

SCHENK, Lynn (1945—). American politician. Born Jan 5, 1945, in the Bronx, NY; University of California, Los Angeles, BA, 1967; University of California, San Diego, JD, 1970; attended London School of Economics, 1970–71. ❖ Was deputy attorney general in California State Attorney General's Office, Criminal Division; served as special assistant to vice presidents Nelson Rockefeller and Walter Mondale (1976–77); was deputy secretary of California State Department of Business, Transportation and Housing (1977–80), then secretary (1980–83); as a Democrat, served in US House of Representatives (1993–95), representing California.

SCHENNIKOVA, Angelika (1969—). Russian gymnast. Born 1969 in Izhevsk (Udmurt Republic), USSR. ❖ Won the China Cup and Jr. USSR nationals (1985) and Rome Grand Prix (1986); was a bronze medalist in all-around at University Games (1987).

SCHERBAK, Barb (1958—). Canadian golfer. Name variations: Barb Bunkowsky; Barb Bunkowsky-Scherbak. Born Oct 13, 1958, in Toronto, Ontario, Canada; attended Florida State University; m. Mark Scherbak, 1995; children: Alexa (b. 1998). ❖ Won Ontario Amateur and AIAW national championship (1981); Chrysler-Plymouth Charity Classic (1984).

SCHERBERGER-WEISS, Rosemarie (1935—). West German fencer. Name variations: Rosemarie Weiss. Born July 19, 1935, in Germany. ❖ At Tokyo Olympics, won a bronze medal in team foil (1964).

SCHERCHEN, Tona (1938—). Swiss-born French-Chinese composer. Name variations: Tona Scherchen-Hsiao. Born Mar 12, 1938, in Neuchatel, Switzerland; dau. of Hermann Scherchen (German conductor) and Hsiao Shusien (Chinese composer); became naturalized French citizen (1972). ❖ Spent teenage years in China and studied Chinese classical music and Chinese lute; in Europe, studied composition with Ligeti, Messiaen and Henze, and won Premier Prix du Conservatoire National Superieur de Musique de Paris (1964); lectured in Europe and US and worked as radio producer and sound engineer in New York; works include *Tzang* (1966), *Shen* (1968), *Khouang* (1966–68), *Vague-T'ao* (1974–75), *Oeil de chat* (1976), *L'illégitime* (1985–86) and *Fuite* (1987); created multimedia projects, including *Between '86* (1978–86) and *Cancer, Solstice '83* (1983–87).

SCHIAFFINO, Rosanna (1938—). Italian actress. Born Nov 25, 1938, Genoa, Italy. ❖ Made film debut in *Totò lascia o raddoppia?* (1956), followed by *La notte brava, Il vendicatore, Un ettaro di cielo, Ferdinando I re di Napoli, Teseo contro il minotauro, Il ratto delle sabine, Lafayette, I briganti italiani, The Victors, The Long Ships, La corruzione, La Mandragola, El Greco, Drop Dead Darling, Simón Bolivar* and *Trastevere,* among others.

SCHIAPARELLI, Elsa (1890–1973). French designer. Name variations: Comtesse or Countess de Kerlor. Pronunciation: Skya-pa-RELL-ee. Born Elsa Luisa Maria Schiaparelli, Sept 10, 1890, in Rome, Italy, to an aristocratic Italian family; died in Paris, France, Nov 13, 1973; dau. of Celestino Schiaparelli and Maria Luisa Domenitis Schiaparelli; m. Comte William de Wendt de Kerlor (French theosophist), 1919 (div. 1922); children: Yvonne "Gogo" de Kerlor (b. 1920). ❖ Influential couturiere whose designs changed the face of fashion in the 2 decades prior to WWII; defied parents by marrying a French theosophist and moving with him to New York (1919); divorced and moved to Paris (1922); began designing sweaters and casual wear for women; introduced 2 full collections of casual and formal wear (mid-1930s); ran her own company of several hundred employees and was the most famous purveyor of French haute couture in the world; spent most of WWII in US, lecturing and doing volunteer work to raise money for French war victims, though her company continued to operate in France; never regained her prewar popularity but her influence on contemporary fashion is still much in evidence in the bright colors, arresting patterns and unusual materials that she 1st introduced; launched last collection (1954). ❖ See also autobiography *Shocking Life* (Dutton, 1954); Palmer White, *Elsa Schiaparelli* (Rizzoli, 1986); and *Women in World History*.

SCHIEFERDECKER, Bettina (1968—). East German gymnast. Born April 30, 1968, in East Germany. ❖ At Seoul Olympics, won a bronze medal in team all-around (1988).

SCHIERHUBER, Agnes (1946—). Austrian agriculturist and politician. Born May 31, 1946, in Reith, Austria. ❖ Member of the Bundesrat (1986–95); served as vice-chair of the district farmers' chamber (1975–95), district chair of women farmers of Ottenschlag (1974–94), member of the Land committee of the farmers' social security fund (1983–98), and chair of the Austrian Association for Medicinal and Herbal Plants (1993—); as a member of the European People's Party (Christian Democrats) and European Democrats, elected to 4th and 5th European Parliament (1994–99, 1999–2004). Awarded Grand Silver Decoration of Merit of the Republic of Austria (1996) and Goldene Kammermedaille of Lower Austria (1996); awarded the title of Ökonomierat (2000).

SCHIFANO, Helen (1922—). American gymnast. Name variations: Helen Schifano Sjursen. Born April 13, 1922. ❖ At London Olympics, won a bronze medal in team all-around (1948).

SCHIFF, Dorothy (1903–1989). American newspaper publisher. Name variations: Dorothy Hall; Dorothy Backer; Dorothy Thackrey; Dolly Schiff. Born Dorothy Schiff in New York, NY, Mar 11, 1903; died in New York, NY, Aug 30, 1989; dau. of Mortimer L. Schiff (investment banker) and Adele A. (Neustadt) Schiff; granddau. of banker Jacob Schiff; attended Bryn Mawr College, 1920–21; m. Richard B.W. Hall (broker), Oct 17, 1923 (div. 1932); m. George Backer (publisher), 1932 (div. 1943); m. Theodore Olin Thackrey (editor), July 1943 (div. 1949); m. Rudolf G. Sonneborn (petroleum executive), 1953 (sep. 1965, div.); children: (1st m.) Mortimer Ball (b. 1924), Adele Ball (b. 1925); (2nd m.) Sarah Ann Backer. ❖ The 1st woman to become a newspaper publisher in New York City, gained control of the *New York Post* as majority stockholder (1939), and served as director, vice-president, and treasurer (1939–42), and as publisher, president, and owner (1942–76); championed liberal causes and changed the paper to reflect popular tastes; sold paper to Rupert Murdoch (1976); was friend, acquaintance, and occasionally lover of the influential, powerful, and glamorous personalities of the time, as well as a crusader for social justice and an adamant supporter of President Franklin Roosevelt's New Deal. ❖ See also Jeffrey Potter, *Men, Money, and Magic: The Story of Dorothy Schiff* (Coward, 1976); and *Women in World History.*

SCHIFFER, Claudia (1970—). German supermodel. Born Aug 25, 1970, in Dusseldorf, Germany; dau. of Heinze Schiffer (lawyer) and Gudrun Schiffer; m. Matthew Vaughn (producer), 2002; children: Caspar and Clementine. ❖ Made modeling debut with Guess Jeans advertising campaign (1988), which led to career with Chanel (1990); also modeled for Versace, Valentino, Revlon, Ralph Lauren, among others; graced covers of hundreds of magazines, including *Time* and *Rolling Stone*; partnered with supermodels Naomi Campbell and Elle McPherson in chain of Fashion Café restaurants.

SCHIFFMAN, Suzanne (1929–2001). French screenwriter and director. Born 1929 in Paris, France; died June 6, 2001, in Paris. ❖ Began career as a continuity clerk for Jean-Luc Godard and Francois Truffaut, becoming Truffaut's long-time associate, assistant director, and script collaborator; after Truffaut's death (1984), began directing; screenplays include *Spectre, The Story of Adele H., Small Change, The Man Who Loved Women, Love on the Run, The Last Metro, The Woman Next Door, Le pont du nord, Merry Go Round, Vivement dimanche!, Love on the Ground, Sorceress* (also director), *Front Woman* (also director), and *Corpos perdidos*; also collaborated on scripts with director Jacques Rivette. Was portrayed by Nathalie Baye in Truffaut's autobiographical film *Day for Night* (1974); nominated for Oscar for Best Screenplay for *Day for Night* (1974).

SCHILERU, Dacia W. American swimmer. Name variations: Dacia Schileru-Clark. Born in Romania; m. Alan Clark; children: 3. ❖ Immigrated to US at age 18; after passage of Title IX (1972), while a student at Wayne State University (Detroit, MI), was the 1st woman to compete in National Collegiate Athletic Association (NCAA) event (1973), as a diving competitor in college division swimming championships; became a physician.

SCHILLER, Litta (c. 1905–1945). *See Stauffenberg, Litta von.*

SCHINDLER, Emilie (1909–2001). Czech Holocaust rescuer. Born Emilie Pelze in 1909 (some sources cite 1907) in Alt-Molstein, Czechoslovakia; died Oct 6 2001, in Strausberg, Germany; dau. of a wealthy farmer; educated in an Austrian convent school; m. Oskar Schindler (industrialist); no children. ❖ Wife of Oskar Schindler who helped him protect Jewish workers in Zablocie, Poland, from the Nazi concentration camps; played an active role in the saving of the Jews (1942–45), hunting down medicine, vitamins and food on the black market to stock the factory's clinic and to increase the Jews' meager rations; immigrated to Argentina (1949). ❖ See also autobiography *Where Light and Shadow Meet* (1997); and *Women in World History.*

SCHINDLING, Liselott (1927—). *See Linsenhoff, Liselott.*

SCHIRMACHER, Käthe (1859–1930). German journalist and feminist. Born 1859 in Danzig, Germany; died 1930; studied literature in Paris and obtained doctorate from University of Zurich (1895). ❖ Participated in International Women's Congress (Chicago, 1893) and lectured around world on women's rights.

SCHJOLDAGER, Mette (1977—). Danish badminton player. Born April 21, 1977, in Viby J., Denmark. ❖ With Jens Ericksen, won a bronze medal for mixed doubles at Athens Olympics (2004).

SCHLAAK, Evelin (1956—). *See Jahl, Evelin.*

SCHLAFLY, Phyllis (1924—). American author, lecturer, and anti-feminist campaigner. Name variations: Mrs. John Fred Schlafly. Born Phyllis Stewart in Port Stewart, Missouri; grew up in St. Louis; Washington University, AB, 1944; Radcliffe, MA in government, 1945; m. John Fred Schlafly, 1949; children: 6. ❖ Worked as research librarian, 1st National Bank, St. Louis (1946–49); was research director Cardinal Mindszenty Foundation (1958–63); was a commentator for "America Wake Up" radio program (1962–66); served as a delegate to Republican National Convention, several years; was president of the Illinois Federation of Republican Women (1960–64); caused a stir with ultra-conservative book *A Choice not an Echo* in support of Barry Goldwater (1964); was 1st vice-president, National Federation of Republican Women (1965–67); crisscrossed the US to build a powerful lobby to defeat the ERA; also wrote *The Power of the Positive Woman.*

SCHLAMME, Martha (1922–1985). Austrian-born singer and actress. Born Martha Haftel, Sept 25, 1922, in Vienna, Austria; died Oct 6, 1985, in Jamestown, NY; dau. of Meier and Gisa Braten Haftel (Orthodox Jews); m. Hans Schlamme, c. 1948 (annulled 1960s); m. Mark Lane (Democratic politician). ❖ A major force in the revival of Jewish-Yiddish music (1950s), fled to England with family to escape the Nazis (1938); studied piano and voice in London; came to US (1948); sang at Town Hall and Village Gate; as an actress-singer, made off-Broadway debut in *The World of Kurt Weill* (1963), followed by *A Month of Sundays, Mata Hari, Beethoven and Karl, Aspirations, Twilight Cantata,* and *Mrs. Warren's Profession*; on Broadway, appeared in *Fiddler on the Roof, Threepenny Opera, Solitaire/Double Solitaire* and *A Kurt Weill Cabaret*; made 15 albums.

SCHLEE, Valentina (1899–1989). *See Valentina.*

SCHLEGEL, Dorothea von (1764–1839). *See Mendelssohn, Dorothea.*

SCHLEGEL, Elfi (1964—). Canadian gymnast. Born May 17, 1964, in Toronto, Ontario, Canada; m. Marc Dunn (Olympic volleyball player). ❖ Won Canadian nationals (1978, 1981) and gold medals in all-around and team all-around at the Commonwealth Games (1978); placed 2nd at Canadian nationals (1979) and 3rd in all-around and 1st in team all-around at Pan American Games (1979); won the bronze medal on the vault at the World Cup (1980); won Hunt International (1981); did commentary for NBC during Olympics (1992, 1996, 2000).

SCHLEGEL-SCHELLING, Caroline (1763–1809). German translator and critic. Name variations: Caroline Bohmer, Böhmer or Boehmer. Born Caroline Michaelis, 1763, in Göttingen, Germany; died 1809; dau. of Johann David Michaelis (1717–1791, professor of Oriental Studies); m. Dr. Böhmer (physician), 1784 (died 1788); m. August Schlegel (1767–1845), 1796 (div. 1803); m. Friedrich Schelling (philosopher); children: (1st m.) 3. ❖ Wrote unsigned reviews for August and Friedrich Schlegel's literary magazine, *Athenäum*; also worked on translation of Shakespeare with August Schlegel.

SCHLEICHER, Ursula (1933—). German politician. Born May 15, 1933, in Aschaffenburg, Germany. ❖ Member of the Bundestag (1972–80); served as president of the European Women's Union (1983–87) and vice-president of the European Movement; as a member of the European People's Party (Christian Democrats) and European Democrats, elected to European Parliament (1979); served as vice-president of EP (1994–99) and president of the Parliamentary Society in the EP (1998). Awarded the Bavarian Order of Merit, Federal Order of Merit, First Class (1990), Gold medal of the Bavarian constitution (1996), Robert Schuman Medal of the EPP Group (1998), Grand Cross of Merit of the Order of Merit of the Federal Republic of Germany (2001), and Bavarian Environment Medal (2001).

SCHLEIN, Miriam (1926–2004). American children's writer. Born Miriam Schlein, 1926, in Brooklyn, NY; died Nov 23, 2004, in New York, NY; Brooklyn College, BA, 1947; m. Harvey Weiss (illustrator, div.); children: Elizabeth S. Weiss and John M. Weiss. ❖ Wrote over

100 books, which taught very young children about animals and concepts like time and space.

SCHLEPER, Sarah (1979—). American Alpine skier. Born Feb 19, 1979, in Glenwood Springs, CO. ❖ Won US National championship for giant slalom (1998) and slalom (2001).

SCHLESINGER, Leontine (1889–1974). See Sagan, Leontine.

SCHLESINGER, Therese (1863–1940). Austrian feminist and politician. Name variations: Therese Schlesinger-Eckstein. Born Therese Eckstein in Vienna, Austria, June 6, 1863; died in Blois/Loire, France, June 5, 1940; dau. of Albert Eckstein (industrialist) and Amalie (Wehle) Eckstein; sister of Emma Eckstein (feminist and one of the 1st patients of Sigmund Freud), Gustav Eckstein (editor of *Die Neue Zeit*), and Friedrich Eckstein (scholar); m. Viktor Schlesinger (bank employee), June 24, 1888 (died 1891); children: Dr. Anna Frey (1889–1920). ❖ One of the most important women in the history of the Social Democratic Party of Austria (SPÖ), became an active member in Allgemeiner Österreichischer Frauenverein (General Austrian Women's Association or AÖF) and wrote articles for its newspaper *Die Volksstimme*; joined Austrian Social Democratic Party (1897); was one of the founding members of the Association of Social Democratic Women and Girls (1901), an organization in which she would play a significant role for next 3 decades; was an orator and journalist, publishing articles in such SPÖ organs as *Der Kampf* (The Struggle), *Die Unzufriedene* (The Dissatisfied Women) and *Arbeiter-Zeitung*; represented SPÖ at 1st International Socialist Women's Conference (1907); chaired the 1st SPÖ Women's Conference in Vienna (1911); as a pacifist, founded the antiwar circle, the Verein "Karl Marx"; after women received the vote in Austria (1918), served as a member of Austria's constituent National Assembly (1919–20), as an SPÖ delegate to the new republican National Assembly (1920–23), and as a delegate to upper house of Austrian Parliament (1923–30); fled to France (1939), after the Nazis took power. ❖ See also *Women in World History*.

SCHLESSINGER, Rose (1914–1988). See Coyle, Rose.

SCHLESWIG-HOLSTEIN, countess of. See Munk, Kristen (1598–1658).

SCHLESWIG-HOLSTEIN, duchess of. See Louise Augusta (1771–1843).

SCHLESWIG-HOLSTEIN-SONDERBURG-AUGUSTENBERG, duchess of.
See Adelaide of Hohenlohe-Langenburg (1835–1900).
See Helena (1846–1923).
See Caroline Matilda of Schleswig-Holstein (1860–1932).

SCHLESWIG-HOLSTEIN-SONDERBURG-GLUCKSBURG, duchess of.
See Louise of Hesse-Cassel (1789–1867).
See Adelaide (1821–1899).
See Marie Melita of Hohenlohe-Langenburg (1899–1967).

SCHLEY, Gabriela (1964—). West German field-hockey player. Born Feb 26, 1964, in Germany. ❖ At Los Angeles Olympics, won a silver medal in team competition (1984).

SCHLICHT, Svenja (1967—). West German swimmer. Born June 26, 1967, in Germany. ❖ At Los Angeles Olympics, won a silver medal in 4 x 100-meter medley relay (1984).

SCHLINKER, Margaret (c. 1822–1913). See Ralph, Margaret.

SCHLÖSINGER, Rose (1907–1943). German political activist. Name variations: Rose Schloesinger or Schlosinger. Born in Frankfurt am Main, Germany, Oct 5, 1907; executed in Berlin's Plötzensee prison, Aug 5, 1943; m. Bodo Schlösinger (translator at Foreign Ministry in Berlin), in 1936 (committed suicide, Feb 22, 1943); children: Marianne Schlösinger. ❖ Anti-Nazi activist, was active in the underground work of Berlin Communists who cooperated with Schulze-Boysen-Harnack group ("Red Orchestra" organization); arrested (Oct 1942); was sentenced to death by the Reich War Tribunal (Jan 20, 1943). ❖ See also *Women in World History*.

SCHLOSSBERG, Caroline Kennedy (1957—). American lawyer, author, and first daughter. Name variations: Caroline Kennedy. Born Caroline Bouvier Kennedy, Nov 27, 1957, in New York, NY; dau. of John F. Kennedy (1917–1963, president of US) and Jacqueline (Bouvier) Kennedy (1929–1994); sister of John F. Kennedy Jr. (1960–1999); graduate of Radcliffe College, 1960, and Columbia University Law School, 1988; m. Edwin Schlossberg, June 19, 1986: children: Rose Schlossberg (b. 1988); Tatiana Schlossberg (b. 1990); John Schlossberg (b. 1992). ❖ Member of one of America's most prominent political families, judiciously protected her anonymity, working quietly behind the scenes on a variety of civic, social, and cultural projects, and choosing carefully each encounter with the media; after receiving undergraduate degree (1980), worked for the Film and TV Development Office of Metropolitan Museum of Art in NY; passed bar exam (1989); with Ellen Alderman, wrote *Our Defense: The Bill of Rights in Action* and *The Right to Privacy* (1995), a scholarly work; with mother and brother, founded Profile in Courage Awards (1989); took over as president of Kennedy Library Foundation (1997). ❖ See also Laurence Leamer, *The Kennedy Women: The Saga of an American Family* (Villard, 1994); and *Women in World History*.

SCHLOTFELDT, Rozella M. (b. 1914—). American nurse. Born Rozella May Schlotfeldt, June 29, 1914, in DeWitt, IA; dau. of Clara Cecelia (Doering) Schlotfeldt (trained nurse) and John William Schlotfeldt (businessman); State University of Iowa, BS in nursing, magna cum laude (1935); University of Chicago, MS, 1947, PhD, 1956; pursued postgraduate work at New York Hospital. ❖ Worked as a maternity nurse at University of Iowa Hospital (1935–36); spent 2 years in Europe with US Army Nurse Corps (1944–46); as dean (1956–72) and professor (1956–82) of Case Western Reserve University's Frances Payne Bolton School of Nursing, developed a PhD program and recruited noted nursing specialists; served as a member of Office of the US Surgeon General's advisory committee (1961–63).

SCHLUETER-SCHMIDT, Karin (1937—). West German equestrian. Name variations: Karin Schlüter-Schmidt. Born Mar 12, 1937, in Germany. ❖ At Munich Olympics, won a silver medal in team dressage (1972).

SCHLUNEGGER, Hedy (1923–2003). Swiss Alpine skier. Born Mar 10, 1923, in Switzerland; died 2003; grandmother of Martina Schild (skier). ❖ Won a gold medal for downhill at St. Moritz (1948), the 1st women's downhill event in Olympic history.

SCHLÜTER, Karin (1937—). See Schlueter-Schmidt, Karin.

SCHMAHL, Jeanne (1846–1916). French feminist. Born Jeanne Elizabeth Archer in Great Britain, 1846, to an English father and French mother; died 1916; studied medicine in Paris; became naturalized French citizen through marriage to Henri Schmahl, 1873. ❖ One of the most influential feminists of her time, practiced as a midwife until 1893, living comfortably in a fine residence at the Parc Montsouris with husband; joined Maria Deraismes' Society for the Amelioration of Woman's Condition and the Demand of Her Rights; from 1884, began to work to change provisions of the Code Napoléon, which denied women the right to dispose of their own income; became active, too, in the Protestant women's movement for moral and social reform; founded L'Avant-courrière (The Advance Messenger, 1893), an organization focused on persuading Parliament to enact 2 specific reforms: the right of women to bear legal witness to public and private acts, and the right of women, including wives, to have full control of their own income; elected as one of the three French delegates to 1904 organizational meeting of Carrie Chapman Catt's International Women's Suffrage Alliance (IWSA); wrote a series of powerfully argued essays on the suffrage question in *La Française* (1909), which resulted in the organization of the French Union for Women's Suffrage (UFSF); was elected its president. ❖ See also *Women in World History*.

SCHMEISSER, Richarda (1954—). East German gymnast. Born Aug 20, 1954, in East Germany. ❖ At Munich Olympics, won a silver medal in team all-around (1972).

SCHMICH, Mary Teresa (1954—). American journalist and comic-strip writer. Born 1954 in Savannah, Georgia; graduated with liberal arts degree from Pomona College; studied at Stanford; never married. ❖ Writer of the comic strip "Brenda Starr," had 15 years newspaper experience when she began writing the comic strip after Dale Messick's retirement. ❖ See also *Women in World History*.

SCHMID, Adelheid (1938—). West German fencer. Born Dec 5, 1938, in Germany. ❖ At Rome Olympics, won a gold medal in indiv. foil (1960); at Tokyo Olympics, won a bronze medal in team foil (1964).

SCHMID, Susanne (1960—). West German field-hockey player. Born Aug 27, 1960, in West Germany. ❖ At Los Angeles Olympics, won a silver medal in team competition (1984).

SCHMIDGALL, Jenny (1979—). American ice-hockey player. Name variations: Jenny Potter. Born Jennifer Lynn Schmidgall, Jan 12, 1979, in Edina, Minnesota; attended University of Minnesota–Duluth; married. ❖ Won a team gold medal at Nagano (1998), the 1st Olympics to feature women's ice hockey; won team silver medals at World championships (1999–2001). won a team silver medal at Salt Lake City Olympics (2002) and a team bronze at Torino Olympics (2006). ❖ See also Mary Turco, *Crashing the Net* (HarperCollins, 1999); and *Women in World History*.

SCHMIDT, Auguste (1833–1902). German feminist and educator. Born Aug 3, 1833, in Breslau, Germany; died June 10, 1902, in Leipzig; dau. of a Prussian artillery captain. ❖ As head of Women's Teacher Training College in Leipzig, taught several who would become leaders in feminist movement; politically conservative, believed in importance of marriage, self-sacrifice and high morals, but encouraged charity work and sought to improve status of women in society, especially in the area of education; with Luise Otto-Peters and Henriette Goldschmidt, founded Leipziger Frauenbildungsverein (Leipzig Women's Educational Association, 1865); co-founded Verein Deutscher Lehrerinnen und Erzieherinnen (1869); with Helene Lange and Marie Löper-Houselle, founded Allgemeiner Deutscher Frauenverein (1888) and became its head; was chair of Bundes Deutscher Frauenverein (1894–99).

SCHMIDT, Birgit (1962—). See Fischer, Birgit.

SCHMIDT, Carmela (1962—). East German swimmer. Born May 16, 1962, in East Germany. ❖ At Moscow Olympics, won a bronze medal in the 400-meter freestyle and a bronze medal in the 200-meter freestyle (1980).

SCHMIDT, Cerstin. East German luge athlete. Born in East Germany. ❖ Won a bronze medal for singles at Calgary Olympics (1988); won World championships (1987).

SCHMIDT, Helene (1906–1985). German runner. Born Dec 28, 1906, in Germany; died Nov 11, 1985. ❖ At Amsterdam Olympics, won a bronze medal in the 4 x 100-meter relay (1928).

SCHMIDT, Ingrid (1945—). East German swimmer. Born Mar 3, 1945, in Germany. ❖ At Rome Olympics, won a bronze medal in 4 x 100-meter medley relay (1960).

SCHMIDT, Karin (1937—). See Schlueter-Schmidt, Karin.

SCHMIDT, Kathryn (1953—). American track-and-field athlete. Name variations: Kate Schmidt. Born Dec 29, 1953, in Long Beach, CA; attended California State University at Long Beach and UCLA. ❖ Won a bronze medal at Munich Olympics (1972) and a bronze medal at Montreal Olympics (1976), both in javelin throw; broke 9 US records and 1 World record, raising the javelin record from 198–8 to 227–5 (1972–77); won 7 national titles; was AIAW javelin champion (1975).

SCHMIDT, Magdalena (1949—). East German gymnast. Born June 30, 1949, in East Germany. ❖ At Mexico City Olympics, won a bronze medal in team all-around (1968).

SCHMIDT, Martina (1960—). East German volleyball player. Born Sept 1, 1960, in East Germany. ❖ At Moscow Olympics, won a silver medal in team competition (1980).

SCHMIDT, Rikke (1975—). Danish handball player. Name variations: Rikke Petersen; Rikke Poulsen Schmidt. Born Jan 14, 1975, in Denmark. ❖ Goalkeeper, won a team gold medal at Sydney Olympics (2000) and a team gold medal at Athens Olympics (2004).

SCHMIDT, Sybille (1967—). German rower. Born Aug 31, 1967, in Germany. ❖ At Barcelona Olympics, won a gold medal in quadruple sculls without coxswain (1992).

SCHMIDT, Veronika. East German cross-country skier. Name variations: Veronika Hesse-Schmidt; Veronika Schmidt Hesse; Veronika Hesse. Born Veronika Schmidt in East Germany. ❖ Won a bronze medal for the 4 x 5 km at Innsbruck Olympics (1976); won a gold medal for 4 x 5 km relay at Lake Placid Olympics (1980).

SCHMIDT-FISCHER, Birgit (1962—). See Fischer, Birgit.

SCHMIRLER, Sandra (1963–2000). Canadian curler. Born July 11, 1963, in Biggar, Saskatchewan, Canada; died Mar 3, 2000, in Regina, Saskatchewan; attended University of Regina; m. Shannon England (computer systems analyst). ❖ Represented high school in sport of curling; was a member of Caledonian Curling Club; made national debut (1987); played in Canadian Mixed championships (1992); won

6 Saskatchewan Women's championships with Marcia Gudereit, Joan McCusker and Jan Betker; won Scott Tournament of Hearts (1993); won Canadian and World titles (1993, 1994 and 1997); won 1st full-medal gold in Olympic curling history at Nagano Games (1998). Inducted into Canadian Curling Hall of Fame (1999). ❖ See also *Gold on Ice* (Coteau, 1989) and Perry Lefko, *Sandra Schmirler: Queen of Curling* (2000).

SCHMITT, Christine (1953—). East German gymnast. Born May 26, 1953, in East Germany. ❖ At Munich Olympics, won a silver medal in team all-around (1972).

SCHMITT, Julie (b. 1913). German gymnast. Born April 6, 1913, in Germany. ❖ At Berlin Olympics, won a gold medal in team all-around (1936).

SCHMITT, Nadine (1975—). See Kleinert, Nadine.

SCHMITT, Sandra (c. 1982–2000). German freestyle skier. Born c. 1982, in Germany; died along with her parents, Nov 11, 2000, in Kaprun, Austria, in the cable-car tunnel fire that killed over 150 people. ❖ Placed 9th in moguls at Nagano Olympics (1998); won a gold medal in dual moguls at the World championships (1999).

SCHMITT-FONTYN, Jacqueline (1930—). See Fontyn, Jacqueline.

SCHMITZ, Ingeborg (1922—). German swimmer. Born April 22, 1922, in Germany. ❖ At Berlin Olympics, won a silver medal in 4 x 100-meter freestyle relay (1936).

SCHMUCK, Christa. German luge athlete. Born in Germany. ❖ Won a silver medal for singles at Grenoble Olympics (1968).

SCHMUCK, Uta (1949—). East German swimmer. Born Aug 19, 1949, in East Germany. ❖ At Mexico City Olympics, won a silver medal in 4 x 100-meter freestyle relay (1968).

SCHNACKENBERG, Annie Jane (1835–1905). New Zealand missionary, temperance reformer, welfare worker, and suffragist. Name variations: Annie Jane Allen. Born Annie Jane Allen, Nov 22, 1835, in Warwickshire, England; died May 2, 1905, in Auckland, New Zealand; dau. of Edward Allen (businessman and farmer) and Elizabeth (Dodd) Allen; m. Cort Henry Schnackenberg (minister), 1864 (died 1880); children: 3 daughters, 2 sons. ❖ Immigrated with her family to New Zealand (1851); taught at Wesleyan mission school on west coast of North Island (1861); was a founding member of New Zealand's Women's Christian Temperance Union (WCTU, 1885); fluent in Maori, was appointed superintendent of Maori work and was active in welfare work; served as WCTU national president (1892–1901); active in suffrage movement and promoted further rights for women. ❖ See also *Dictionary of New Zealand Biography* (Vol. 2).

SCHNEIDER, Angela (1959—). Canadian rower. Born Oct 28, 1959, in Canada; children: 3 sons. ❖ At Los Angeles Olympics, won a silver medal in coxed fours (1984); became assistant dean of ethics and equity for the faculty of health science at University of Western Ontario; served as vice-chair of World Anti-Doping Agency's Ethics and Education Committee.

SCHNEIDER, Claudine (1947—). American politician. Born Claudine Cmarada in Clairton, Pennsylvania, Mar 25, 1947; attended University of Barcelona, Spain, and Rosemont College in Pennsylvania; Windham College, BA, 1969; attended University of Rhode Island School of Community Planning; fellow at Harvard University Institute of Politics, 1990s. ❖ US congressional representative (1981–1990), founded Rhode Island Committee on Energy (1973); became executive director of Conservation Law Foundation (1974) and was named federal coordinator of Rhode Island Coastal Management Program (1978); produced and hosted a public affairs tv program in Providence; elected to US House of Representatives (1981), the 1st Republican elected from heavily Democratic Rhode Island in more than 40 years; served on Committee on Science, Space, and Technology, on the Committee on Merchant Marine and Fisheries, and Select Committee on Aging; sometimes took progressive stands at odds with party; was a key player in the effort to stop construction of a controversial nuclear power project, the Clinch River reactor, and worked to ban ocean dumping of medical waste and industrial byproducts; introduced legislation to establish a national energy policy aimed at reduction of greenhouse gas emissions believed to contribute to global warming (1989); after losing election (1990), became a member of the faculty of Harvard's John F. Kennedy School of Government. ❖ See also *Women in World History*.

SCHNEIDER, Hortense (1833–1920). French soprano. Born in Bordeaux, France, April 30, 1833; died in Paris, May 6, 1920. ❖ Left home at 16; made operatic debut in Agen in *La Favorite,* a work by composer Inès (1853); introduced to Jacques Offenbach, quickly became the most famous operetta star in Paris, creating the lead roles in Offenbach's *La Belle Hélène, Barbe-Bleue, La Grande-Duchesse de Gérolstein, La Vie Parisienne* and *La Périchole*; also created the lead in Camille Saint-Saëns' *Samson and Delilah*; an international star, appeared in London (1867) and in St. Petersburg (1872); retired (1878); for nearly 2 decades, was the undisputed queen of the French musical stage; was also very likely the most celebrated *grande horizontale* of her day. ❖ See also *Women in World History.*

SCHNEIDER, Magda (1909–1996). German actress. Born in Augsburg, Bavaria, Germany, May 17, 1909; died in Schöenau, Germany, July 30, 1996; m. Wolf Albach-Retty (leading actor of Vienna's Volkstheater); children: Romy Schneider (1938–1982, actress); Wolf-Dieter Albach-Retty. ❖ One of the most popular prewar German actresses, made more than 70 films, including *The Story of Vicki* and *Be Mine Tonight,* and gave her most memorable performance in Max Ophüls' *Liebelei,* known in English as *Flirtation* (1933); acted in a number of supporting roles with daughter Romy Schneider, 1st in *When the White Lilacs Bloom Again* and later in popular "Sissi" films, about the Austro-Hungarian royal family, which were released in US as *Forever, My Love* (1962). ❖ See also *Women in World History.*

SCHNEIDER, Petra (1963—). East German swimmer. Born Jan 11, 1963, in East Germany. ❖ At Moscow Olympics, won a silver medal in the 400-meter freestyle and a gold medal in the 400-meter indiv. medley (1980).

SCHNEIDER, Romy (1938–1982). Austrian actress. Born Rosemarie Albach-Retty in Vienna, Austria, Sept 23, 1938; died in Paris, France, May 29, 1982; dau. of Wolf Albach-Retty (actor) and Magda Schneider (1909–1996, actress); paternal granddau. of Rosa Albach-Retty, popular actress of the Austrian theater; m. Harry Meyen-Haubenstock (German actor and director), 1966 (div. 1975, committed suicide 1979); m. Daniel Biasini (photographer), 1975 (div. 1977); children: (1st m.) David Christophe (1967–1981); (2nd m.) Sarah Magdalena Biasini (b. 1976). ❖ Actress, whose life, like that of the empress she portrayed, ended tragically; at 14, was cast as her mother's screen daughter in *Wenn der weisse Flieder wieder blüht* (When the White Lilacs Bloom Again, 1953); over next 6 years, made a score of films in Germany, including *Mädchenjahre einer Königin* (*The Story of Vickie* 1954) and *Mädchen in Uniform* (1958); became one of European cinema's most famous actresses because of portrayal of Empress Elizabeth of Bavaria (1837–1898) in 3 films: *Sissi* (1955), *Sissi, Die Junge Kaiserin* (1956), and *Sissi, Schicksalsjahre einer Kaiserin* (1957); in Paris, appeared in *Christine* (1958), a remake of the classic film *Liebelei,* one of her mother's successes; remained in France, appearing successfully on Paris stage and starring opposite Alain Delon in *'Tis Pity She's a Whore* (1961); became internationally acclaimed film star (1962), when she appeared in *Boccaccio '70*; also appeared in Foreman's *The Victors* (1962) and Preminger's *The Cardinal* (1963); starred in 1st Hollywood film, *Good Neighbor Sam* (1963); also appeared in *What's New, Pussycat?* (1965), *Les choses de la vie* (The Things of Life, 1970), *The Assassination of Trotsky* (1972), *Ludwig* (1973) and *Claire de femme* (1979); during 1970s, was twice awarded a César; made last film, *La passante du Sans-Souci* (1982); found dead in Paris apartment. ❖ See also *Women in World History.*

SCHNEIDER, Vreni (1964—). Swiss Alpine skier. Born Nov 26, 1964, in Elm, Switzerland. ❖ One of the greatest female Alpine skiers of all time, won gold medals for slalom and giant slalom at Calgary Olympics (1988); won a gold medal for slalom, silver for combined, and bronze for giant slalom at Lillehammer Olympics (1994), the 1st female alpine skier to win 3 gold medals and the 1st to win 5 medals at the Olympic Winter Games; at World championships, won gold medals for giant slalom (1987, 1989) and slalom (1991); won 5 World Cup giant slalom titles, 6 slalom titles, as well as overall titles (1989, 1994–95). ❖ See also *Women in World History.*

SCHNEIDERMAN, Rose (1882–1972). American labor leader. Born Rachel Schneiderman, April 6, 1882, in Saven, Russian Poland; died in New York, NY, Aug 11, 1972; dau. of Adolph Samuel Schneiderman (tailor) and Deborah (Rothman) Schneiderman; attended nightschool at the Rand School of Social Science; never married; no children. ❖ President of the Women's Trade Union League who struggled for workers' rights, helping to establish the 8-hour day,

minimum-wage regulations, and safer working conditions; moved with family to New York (1890); spent a year in a Jewish orphanage; began work at 13; founded 1st women's branch of United Cloth Hat and Cap Makers' Union (1903); joined Women's Trade Union League (WTUL, 1905); served as vice president of New York WTUL (1906); co-ordinated garment workers' strikes (1909–14); was national organizer for International Ladies Garment Workers' Union (ILGWU, 1915–16); was a speaker and organizer for National American Woman Suffrage Association (1913, 1915, 1917); served as president of New York WTUL (1918–49); helped found International Congress of Working Women (1919); member of WTUL delegation to Paris Peace Conference (1919); ran for US Senate (1920); organized Bryn Mawr Summer School for Women Workers (1921); served as president of the National League (1926); served in the National Recovery Administration (1933–35); was secretary of New York State Department of Labor (1937–43). ❖ See also autobiography *All for One* (1967); and *Women in World History.*

SCHNELL, Betty (1850–1939). *See Hennings, Betty.*

SCHNEYDER, Nathalie (1968—). American synchronized swimmer. Name variations: Nathalie Schneyder Bartleson. Born May 25, 1968, in Walnut Creek, CA. ❖ Won a team gold medal at Atlanta Olympics (1996).

SCHNITZER, Henriette (1891–1979). Romanian-born actress. Name variations: Henrietta Schnitzer. Born June 13, 1891, in Romania; died May 4, 1979, in Miami Beach, FL. ❖ Age 4, made stage debut in Romania; in US, appeared on the Yiddish stage and in such English-speaking plays as *One Life for Another, Alexander Pushkin, Awake and Sing, Green Fields, The Bronx Express* and *Potash and Perlmutter*; appeared on radio's "The Goldbergs" for 15 years.

SCHOENBERG, Bessie (1906–1997). German modern dancer and teacher. Born Dec 27, 1906, in Hanover, Germany; died 1997. ❖ One of the most influential and recognized teachers in modern dance choreography, trained with Martha Hill at University of Oregon, then at Martha Graham school and Neighborhood Playhouse in NY; began performing in Graham company (1931), where she danced in premieres of *Primitive Mysteries, Ceremonials,* and *Project in Movement for a Divine Comedy*; served as dance teacher at numerous institutions, including Bennington College and Sarah Lawrence College, where she was also director of the dance department for over 30 years (1941–71), then professor emeritus. ❖ See also (documentary) *Portrait of Bessie Schoenberg.*

SCHOENBRUNN, Gabi (1961—). *See Zange-Schönbrunn, Gabi.*

SCHOENFIELD, Dana (1953—). American swimmer. Name variations: Dana Schoenfield Reyes. Born Aug 13, 1953, in Anaheim, CA; attended University of California at Los Angeles. ❖ At Munich Olympics, won a silver medal in the 200-meter breaststroke (1972).

SCHOENOVA, Lydmila (1936—). *See Svedova-Schoenova, Lydmila.*

SCHOENROCK, Sybille (1964—). East German swimmer. Name variations: Schönrock. Born July 28, 1964, in East Germany. ❖ At Moscow Olympics, won a silver medal in the 200-meter butterfly (1980).

SCHOEPF, Regina. *See Schöpf, Regina.*

SCHOERLING, Inger (1946—). *See Schörling, Inger.*

SCHOFF, Hannah Kent (1853–1940). American welfare worker and reformer. Born Hannah Kent, June 3, 1853, in Upper Darby, Pennsylvania; died in Philadelphia, Pennsylvania, Dec 10, 1940; dau. of Thomas Kent and Fanny (Leonard) Kent; attended Waltham (Massachusetts) Church School; m. Frederic Schoff (engineer), 1873 (died c. 1922); children: Wilfred Harvey (b. 1874), Edith Gertrude (b. 1877), Louise (b. 1880), Leonard Hastings (b. 1884), Harold Kent (b. 1886), Eunice Margaret (b. 1890), and Albert Lawrence (b. 1894). ❖ Elected president of National Congress of Mothers (later National Congress of Parents and Teachers), a group that lobbied for reform in child labor, marriage laws, and education; lobbied for passage of legislation in Philadelphia to establish a separate juvenile court system; wrote *The Wayward Child* (1915) and *Wisdom of the Ages in Bringing Up Children* (1933). ❖ See also *Women in World History.*

SCHOFIELD, Martha (1839–1916). American educator. Born Feb 1, 1839, near Newton, Pennsylvania; died in Aiken, South Carolina, Jan 13, 1916; dau. of Oliver Schofield and Mary Jackson Schofield (Quakers); educated in private school run by uncle John Jackson in Sharon, Pennsylvania. ❖ Taught at a Quaker school in Purchase, New York, and later at a school for African-Americans in Philadelphia;

volunteering for the Pennsylvania Freedmen's Relief Association (1865), was sent to the Sea Islands of South Carolina, where she established the Garrison School; moved to Aiken, South Carolina (1868); donated land for the construction of a new schoolhouse in Aiken (1870), which was incorporated as the Schofield Normal and Industrial School (1886), becoming one of the premier black educational institutions in the South. ❖ See also *Women in World History*.

SCHOLASTICA (c. 480–543). Catholic saint. Born c. 480 in Nursia (now called Norcia) in Umbria, Italy; died 543 in Monte Cassino; dau. of Europious and Abundantia (according to 12th-century source); twin sister of St. Benedict of Nursia (c. 480–c. 547, who founded Monte Cassino, the 1st monastic order in Western Europe). ❖ Devoted her life to pious worship, participated in religious communal life, and founded a convent at Monte Cassino, near her brother's monastery. ❖ See also *Women in World History*.

SCHOLASTICA OF CHAMPAGNE (d. 1219). Countess of Macon. Name variations: Scholastica of Champaigne. Died 1219; dau. of Marie de Champagne (1145–1198) and Henry I, count of Champagne; m. William IV, count of Macon and Vienne.

SCHOLL, Inge (c. 1917–1998). Germany pacifist. Name variations: Inge Aicher-Scholl. Born c. 1917, in Forchtenberg, Germany; died Sept 4, 1998, in Frankfurt, Germany; dau. of Robert Scholl (mayor of Forchtenberg) and Magdalene (Müller) Scholl (deaconess in the local church); sister of Hans and Sophie Scholl. ❖ Inspired a generation of pacifists by writing of her brother and sister and the White Rose movement (1952); her book, *Students Against Tyranny: The Resistance of the White Rose, Munich, 1942–1943*, became a classic about the Third Reich.

SCHOLL, Sophie (1921–1943). German resistance fighter. Born Sophia Scholl, May 9, 1921, in Forchtenberg, Germany; executed with brother Hans, Feb 22, 1943, at Gestapo headquarters near Munich; dau. of Robert Scholl (mayor of Forchtenberg) and Magdalene (Müller) Scholl (deaconess in the local church); sister of Inge Scholl; attended University of Munich; never married. ❖ Student and member of the White Rose resistance movement, who was executed with brother Hans because of their opposition to Hitler's Nazi regime; was 1st arrested by the Gestapo because of brother's activities in the outlawed German Boys' League (children were supposed to join the Hitler Youth, 1937); finished high school and labor service required by Third Reich (1941); entered University of Munich (1942); shuttling between Augsburg, Stuttgart, and Ulm, served as a courier for the White Rose, a small circle of anti-Nazi activists calling for the overthrow of the Third Reich; with brother, arrested for distributing anti-Nazi leaflets at the university (Feb 18, 1943); executed by guillotine. ❖ See also Richard Hanser, *A Noble Treason: The Revolt of the Munich Students Against Hitler* (Putnam, 1979); Inge Jens, ed. *At the Heart of the White Rose: Letters and Diaries of Hans and Sophie Scholl* (Harper & Row, 1987); Alfred Neuman, *Six of Them* (Macmillan, 1946); Inge Scholl, *Students Against Tyranny: The Resistance of the White Rose, Munich, 1942–1943* (Wesleyan U. Press, 1970); Hermann Vinke, *The Short Life of Sophie Scholl* (Harper & Row, 1984); and *Women in World History*.

SCHOLLAR, Ludmilla (c. 1888–1978). Russian ballerina. Name variations: Ludmilla Shollar. Born c. 1888 in St. Petersburg, Russia; died July 10, 1978, in San Francisco, CA; m. Anatole Vilzak. ❖ Joined Maryinsky Ballet in St. Petersburg (1906); as an original member of Diaghilev Ballet Russe, performed in Paris and London; danced roles in Fokine's *Carnaval, Petrouchka, Papillon*, and Vaslav Nijinsky's *Jeux* (1913); served as an Army Red Cross nurse during WWI; performed with GATOB/Kirov (until 1921) and again with Diaghilev; also performed with Ida Rubinstein Ballet, Karsavina Vilzak troupe, and Nijinska company; immigrated to US with Vilzak (1935) and taught ballet in New York City (1935–63); joined San Francisco Ballet School with husband (1965).

SCHOLTZ, Ingrid (b. 1948). *See Winterbach, Ingrid.*

SCHOLTZ-KLINK, Gertrud (1902–1999). German Nazi leader. Born in Adelsheim, Baden, Germany, Feb 9, 1902; died Mar 24, 1999, in Bebenhausen, Germany; married 3 times; children: 11. ❖ Joined Nazi Party (1928); appointed Nazi women's leader in German state of Baden (1929), which led to a promotion to head the women's group in Hessen (1931); became prominent in Nazi national organization for women party leaders, the Nationalsozialistisches Frauenschaft (National Socialist Women's Association, or NSF), as well as in the group designed to incorporate the rank and file of Germany's women, the Deutsches Frauenwerk (German Women's Enterprise, or DFW); named head of national Women's Labor Service (Frauenarbeitsdienst, 1934); took charge of both the NSF and the DFW, becoming Reichsfrauenführerin (women's Führer) and thus exercising the same dictatorial power within these organizations as Hitler did on the national scale (1934); enjoyed considerable autonomy within the boundaries of her own bureaucratic organizations; outside this realm, wielded no power; captured by Soviet soldiers (1945), was able to escape, living under an assumed name in the French occupation zone; arrested (1948), served 18 months; remained convinced that the Third Reich had been beneficial to the German people and particularly to its women. ❖ See also *Women in World History*.

SCHOLZ, Anke (1978—). German swimmer. Born 1978 in Germany. ❖ Won a silver medal for 800-meter freestyle relay at Atlanta Olympics (1996).

SCHOLZ, Lilly. Austrian pairs skater. Name variations: Lilly Gaillard, Lilly Scholz-Gaillard; Lily Scholz. Born in Austria. ❖ With Otto Kaiser, won silver medals (1926, 1927, 1928) and a gold medal (1929) at World championships, and a silver medal at St. Moritz Olympics (1928); with Willi Petter, placed 4th at World championships (1931).

SCHÖN, Elizabeth (1921–2001). Venezuelan poet and playwright. Name variations: Elizabeth Columba Schön de Cortina; Elizabeth Schon. Born 1921 in Caracas, Venezuela; died Nov 30, 2001; dau. of Miguel Antonio Schön and Maria Luisa Ibarra; m. Alfredo Cortina (pioneer in radio, died). ❖ Studied literature, philosophy, and music history in Caracas; works include *La gruta venidera* (1953), *En el allá disparado desde ningún comienzo* (1962), *El abuelo, la cesta y el mar* (1965), *La cisterna insondable* (1971), *Incesante aparecer* (1977), *Del antiguo labrador* (1983), *Concavidad de horizontes* (1986), *Ropaje de ceniza* (1993), *La flor, el barco, el alma* (1995) and *Del río hondo aqui* (2000); helped establish theater of absurd in Venezuela with her plays, *Intervalo* (1957) and *Melisa y yo*, which were performed in Caracas (1961).

SCHÖNBRUNN, Gabi (1961—). *See Zange-Schönbrunn, Gabi.*

SCHÖNE, Andrea Mitscherlich (1961—). East German speedskater. Name variations: Andrea Schoene or Andrea Schone; Andrea Ehrig; Andrea Mitscherlich; Andrea Ehrig-Mitscherlich; competed in Olympics in 1984 as Andrea Schöne and in 1988 as Andrea Ehrig. Born Andrea Mitscherlich, Dec 1 1961, in Dresden, East Germany; m. Ingolf Schöne (rower, div.); m. Andreas Ehrig (div. 1987). ❖ Won the European and World championship for 3,000 meters (1983); won a silver medal for the 3,000 at Innsbruck Olympics (1976) and a gold medal for the 3,000 and silver medals for the 1,000 and 1,500 meters at Sarajevo Olympics (1984); won the World championships at all distances (1985); won European championships (1985–88); took silvers in the 3,000 and 5,000 meters and a bronze in the 1,500 meters at Calgary Olympics (1988).

SCHÖNOVA, Lydmila (1936—). *See Svedova-Schoenova, Lydmila.*

SCHONTHAL, Ruth (1924—). American composer, pianist and teacher. Born in Hamburg, Germany, June 27, 1924; began musical studies at age 5 at Berlin's Stern Conservatory, studying piano with Luise Lehde and music theory with Hilda Bischoff. ❖ Immigrated to Sweden with parents (1938), continuing studies at Royal Academy of Music in Stockholm; immigrated to Mexico (1941), where she studied at National Conservatory with Manuel Ponce and Rodolfo Halffter; studied at Yale University with Paul Hindemith, graduating with BA in Music (1948); taught at Westchester Conservatory (1976—), Adelphi University (1974–77), and New York University (1977–82); a modernist, composed *Sonata Breve* (1976), along with compositions that reflect her years in Mexico, including her piece for solo guitar, *Fantasia in a Nostalgic Mood* (1978), the 1942 *Concerto Romantico* for Piano and Orchestra, and *The Beautiful Days of Aranjuez* for Harp and String Orchestra (1981); active in organizations defending the interests of American women composers.

SCHOOLCRAFT, Jane Johnston (1800–1841). Ojibwe-American poet and folklorist. Name variations: (pseudonyms) Rosa, Leelinau. Born 1800 in Sault Sainte Marie, Michigan; died 1841; dau. of John Johnston (Irish fur trader) and Ozha-guscody-way-quay; maternal granddau. of Ojibwe or Ojibway leader Waub Ojeeb (White Fisher); m. Henry Rowe Schoolcraft (celebrated for his work in Indian languages), 1823. ❖ Learned Ojibwe language and folklore from mother's family and received Western education from father; with husband, published *Literary Voyager or Muzzeniegun* magazine (1826–27), containing articles, legends, and poems on American Indian themes.

SCHOOLING, Elizabeth (1919—). English ballet dancer. Born 1919 in London, England. ❖ Performed professionally with Ballet Club and Ballet Rambert, both under Marie Rambert, appearing in Antony Tudor's *Descent of Hebe* and *Judgment of Paris*, Andrée Howard's *La Fête Etrange*, and Agnes de Mille's *Three Virgins and a Devil*; retired from ballet, but continued to appear in West End musicals and operettas.

SCHOONMAKER, Thelma (1940—). American film editor. Born Jan 3, 1940, in Algeria; attended New York University; m. Michael Powell (English screenwriter and director), 1984 (died 1990). ❖ Met Martin Scorsese while studying at New York University; edited his debut film *Who's That Knocking at My Door* (1968); played a key role in helping to create his distinctive visual style and continued collaborating with him for over 4 decades; was one of the principal editors of *Woodstock* (1970), for which she was nominated for Academy Award; won Academy Award for *Raging Bull* (1980) and nominated once more for *Goodfellas* (1990); other films include *Finnegan's Wake* (1965), *The King of Comedy* (1983), *After Hours* (1985), *The Color of Money* (1986), *The Last Temptation of Christ* (1988), *New York Stories* (1989), *Cape Fear* (1991), *The Age of Innocence* (1993), *Casino* (1995), *Grace of My Heart* (1996) *Kundun* (1997), *Bringing Out the Dead* (1999), *Gangs of New York* (2002) and *The Aviator* (2004).

SCHOPENHAUER, Adele (1797–1849). German poet and novelist. Born Luise Adele Schopenhauer, June 12, 1797, in Hamburg, Germany; died 1849 in Bonn, Germany; dau. of Johanna Schopenhauer (1766–1838, writer) and Heinrich Floris Schopenhauer (d. 1805, merchant); sister of Arthur Schopenhauer (Romantic philosopher); never married; no children. ❖ Grew up in Weimar surrounded by the leading writers and artists of Germany who flocked to her mother's biweekly literary salons; wrote novels, including *Anna* (1844), but preferred poetry; also had a strong interest in folklore and composed children's fairy tales based on popular legends; edited many of her mother's works. ❖ See also *Women in World History*.

SCHOPENHAUER, Johanna (1766–1838). German writer and salonnière. Name variations: Johanna Henriette Trosiener; Henriette Trosiener or Trosina; Madame Schopenhauer. Born Johanna Henriette Trosiener (also seen as Trosina) in Danzig, West Prussia, July 9, 1766; died April 18, 1838, in Jena, Prussia; dau. of Christian Heinrich Trosiener (merchant, banker, and senator) and Elisabeth (Lehmann) Trosiener; m. Heinrich Floris Schopenhauer (merchant), May 16, 1785 (committed suicide 1805); children: Arthur Schopenhauer (philosopher, b. Feb 22, 1788); (Luise) Adele Schopenhauer (writer, b. June 12, 1797). ❖ Moved with daughter to Weimar following husband's death (1805), where she soon became part of the social elite; hosted an influential salon for writers and poets, including Johann Wolfgang von Goethe; took up writing herself and also studied painting; published a biography of writer Karl Fernow (1810); wrote and published for next 2 decades, gaining a considerable reputation; writing across genres, produced travelogues from her trips abroad, as well as biographies of artists, novellas, story collections, and several full-length novels, the best known being *Gabriele* (1819); enjoyed considerable fame across Germany. ❖ See also *A Lady Travels: Journeys in England and Scotland from the Diaries of Johanna Schopenhauer*; and *Women in World History*.

SCHÖPF, Regina. Austrian Alpine skier. Name variations: Regina Schoepf or Schopf. Born in Austria. ❖ Won a silver medal for slalom at Cortina Olympics (1956).

SCHOPMAN, Janneke (1977—). Dutch field-hockey player. Born April 26, 1977, in the Netherlands. ❖ Won European championship (2003); defender, won a team silver medal at Athens Olympics (2004).

SCHÖRLING, Inger (1946—). Swedish politician. Name variations: Schorling or Schoerling. Born Mar 7, 1946, in Al. Kalvträsk, Sweden. ❖ Member of the Riksdag and leader of the Green Party parliamentary group (1988–91); member of the Speaker's Conference (1988–91); representing Group of the Greens/European Free Alliance, elected to 4th and 5th European Parliament (1994–99, 1999–2004).

SCHOU NILSEN, Laila (1919–1998). Norwegian Alpine skier and speedskater. Name variations: Laila Schou-Nilsen or Schou-Nielsen; Laila Schou Nielsen. Born Mar 18, 1919, in Norway; died July 30, 1998. ❖ At World championships, won gold medals for speedskating allround (1935, 1937, 1938); won a bronze medal for Alpine combined skiing at Garmisch-Partenkirchen Olympics (1936).

SCHOULTZ, Solveig von (1907–1996). Finnish poet and short-story writer. Born May 8, 1907, in Porvoo, Finland; died Mar 12, 1996; dau. of Hanna Frosterous-Segerstråle (painter). ❖ Works, which she wrote in Swedish, include *Min timme* (1940), *De sju dagarna* (1942), *Eko av ett rop* (1945), *Ingenting Ovanligt* (1947), *Nätet* (1956), *Sänk ditt ljus* (1963), and *Somliga mornar* (1976); also wrote biography of her mother, *Porträtt av Hanna* (1978). Received Pro Finlandia Medal (1980); awarded honorary doctorate from Helsinki University (1986).

SCHOYEN, Alexia (1889–1983). *See Bryn, Alexia.*

SCHRADER, Catharina Geertuida (1656–1745). German-Dutch midwife. Born 1656 in Bentheim, Germany; died 1745; m. Ernst Cramer, 1683 (died 1692); m. Thomas Hight, 1713 (died 1721); children: 6. ❖ Moved with husband to Friesland; after his death, moved to Dokkum and began to practice as midwife; built up substantial practice and by retirement at 88 had attended 3,060 deliveries; wrote *Notebook* which stressed traditional skills and discouraged use of instruments and manual intervention in births.

SCHRADER, Hilde (1910–1966). German swimmer. Born Jan 4, 1910, in Germany; died Mar 26, 1966. ❖ At Amsterdam Olympics, won a gold medal in the 200-meter breaststroke (1928).

SCHRAMM, Beate (1966—). East German rower. Born June 21, 1966, in East Germany. ❖ At Seoul Olympics, won a gold medal in quadruple sculls without coxswain (1988).

SCHRAMM, Bernardina Adriana (1900–1987). New Zealand pianist and music teacher. Name variations: Bernardina Adriana Soetermeer. Born Oct 12, 1900, in Rotterdam, Germany; died April 18 or 19, 1987, in Wellington, New Zealand; dau. of Cornelis Martinus Soetermeer (lawyer) and Apolonia (de Rek) Soetermeer; m. Leo Paul Schramm (pianist and composer), 1928; children: 1 son. ❖ Formed successful piano duo with husband, performing in concert and on radio (late 1920s); immigrated to New Zealand (1937); opened studio and taught piano, singing, and chamber music; after becoming estranged from husband, began teaching performance courses at Victoria University of Wellington (late 1950s). ❖ See also *Dictionary of New Zealand Biography* (Vol. 4).

SCHRATT, Katharina (1853–1940). Austrian actress. Born Sept 11, 1853, in Baden, Austria; died April 17, 1940, in Vienna, Austria; dau. of a middle-class shopkeeper; attended convent school; studied acting in Vienna; married into the von Kiss family, 1877 (sep.); children: son Anton (b. 1878). ❖ As a member of the Stadttheater, became a popular figure on the stage; on marriage (1877), briefly retired; by 1884, was a member of the *Burgtheater*, a company supported privately by the emperor Franz Joseph I, then 53 years old and estranged from his wife Elizabeth of Bavaria (1837–1898), known as Empress Sissi; summoned to a private audience with the empress, who saw an opportunity to free herself from husband's emotional needs, agreed to become companion to the emperor (1886); eased Franz Joseph's loneliness and helped restore a degree of charm and civility to the royal palace. ❖ See also Joan Haslip, *The Emperor and the Actress: The Love Story of Emperor Franz Josef and Katharina Schratt* (Dial, 1982); and *Women in World History*.

SCHREIBER, Adele (1872–1957). Austrian feminist and politician. Name variations: Adele Schreiber-Krieger. Born in Vienna, Austria, April 29, 1872; died Feb 20, 1957, in Herrliberg, near Zurich, Switzerland; dau. of a doctor; married a doctor. ❖ Worked as a reporter for *Frankfurter Zeitung* in Berlin; helped found International Women's Suffrage Alliance (1904) and German Association for the Rights of Women and Children (1910); won a seat as a Social Democrat in the 1st Reichstag (1919); was a member of the Reichstag (1919–33), until rise of Hitler; edited women's journals and produced a number of books about mothers and children, among them *Mutterschaft* and *Das Buch von Kinde*; went into exile (1933), living in Great Britain until 1947, then moving to a town near Zurich, Switzerland; co-authored *Journey Towards Freedom* (1956), the history of the International Alliance of Women, for which she had served as vice-president.

SCHREIBER, Lady Charlotte Guest (1812–1895). *See Guest, Lady Charlotte.*

SCHREINER, Olive (1855–1920). South African novelist, socialist and feminist. Name variations: Emilie Schreiner; (pseudonym) Ralph Iron. Born Olive Emilie Albertina Schreiner, Mar 24, 1855, in Wittebergen, South Africa; died in Cape Town, South Africa, Dec 10, 1920; dau. of Gottlob Schreiner (missionary and businessman) and Rebecca (Lyndall) Schreiner; sister of William Schreiner (prime minister); m. Samuel Cron Cronwright (politician who changed his name to Samuel Cronwright-

Schreiner), Feb 24, 1894; children: daughter (died one day after birth, April 30, 1895). ❖ Important critic of British imperial policy, who also struggled to reduce the many social restrictions placed on Victorian women, worked as a governess and began writing novels (1874–81); set sail for England (1881); published *The Story of an African Farm* under pseudonym Ralph Iron (1883), which was very well received; developed her feminism and socialism as member of Men's and Women's Club in London; returned to South Africa (1889); hailed as a feminist pioneer after publication of *Dreams* (1890); became vocal opponent of Cecil Rhodes, British imperial policy, and the Boer War (1899–1902); campaigned for end to racial and gender restrictions on vote in South Africa; wrote *Women and Labor* (1911), hailed by many as the bible of early 20th-century feminist movement; defended pacifism and conscientious objectors during WWI; last unfinished work, the semi-autobiographical novel *Undine,* published posthumously (1929). Other writings include *Dream Life and Real Life* (1893), (with husband) *The Political Situation* (1896), *Trooper Peter Halkett of Mashonaland* (1897), *An English South African's View of the Situation* (1899), *Closer Union* (1909), *Thoughts on South Africa* (1923), *Stories, Dreams and Allegories* (1923) and *From Man to Man* (1926). ❖ See also Samuel Cron Cronwright-Schreiner, ed. *The Letters of Olive Schreiner* (Unwin, 1924) and *The Life of Olive Schreiner* (Unwin, 1924); Joyce Avrech Berkman, *The Healing Imagination of Olive Schreiner* (U. of Massachusetts Press, 1989) and *Olive Schreiner: Feminism on the Frontier* (Eden Press, 1979); Ruth First and Ann Scott, *Olive Schreiner* (Schocken, 1980); and *Women in World History.*

SCHRIBER, Margrit (1939—). Swiss novelist. Born Apr, 6, 1939, in Lucerne, Switzerland. ❖ Works include *Aussicht gerahmt* (1976), *Ausser Saison* (1977), *Dazwischen: Ein monologischer Dialog* (1979), *Vogel flieg* (1980), *Muschelgarten* (1984), *Tresorschatten* (1987), *Rauchrichter* (1993), *Schneefessel* (1998) and *Von Zeit zu Zeit klingelt ein Fisch* (2001).

SCHRIECK, Louise van der (1813–1886). Dutch nun. Born Josephine van der Schrieck, Nov 14, 1813, in Bergen-op-Zoom, Netherlands; died Dec 3, 1886, in Cincinnati, OH. ❖ Joined the order of Sisters of Notre Dame de Namur in Belgium (1837); moved to US to help establish an order in Cincinnati (1840) and became its superior (1845), then superior-provincial of convents east of Rocky Mountains; during her 38 years as superior-provincial, added 27 convents.

SCHROEDER, Bertha (1872–1953). New Zealand religious leader, social worker, and probation officer. Born Dec 8, 1872, in Australia; died Jan 20, 1953, at Invercargill, New Zealand; dau. of Frederick William Schroeder and Mary Ann (Hughes) Phelps. ❖ Entered Salvation Army Training Garrison in Christchurch to train as officer (1892); performed social work primarily among women and children in many appointments during her 40 years with Salvation Army; appointed court worker and probation officer for Invercargill (1934). ❖ See also *Dictionary of New Zealand Biography* (Vol. 3).

SCHROEDER, Ilka (1978—). German politician. Name variations: Ilka Schröder. Born Jan 22, 1978, in Berlin, Germany. ❖ Co-founded the Green Alternative Youth Alliance; joined Bündnis 90/Greens (1993); representing the Confederal Group of the European United Left/ Nordic Green Left (GUE/NGL), elected to 5th European Parliament (1999–2004); resigned from Bündnis 90/Greens (2001).

SCHROEDER, Louise (1887–1957). German politician. Name variations: Luise Schröder. Born Louise Dorothea Sophie Schroeder in Hamburg-Altona, Germany, April 2, 1887; died in West Berlin, June 4, 1957; educated in Hamburg; never married. ❖ Social Democratic leader who as deputy mayor of West Berlin was a symbol of defiance against Soviet and Communist pressure during Berlin blockade (1948–49), one of the tensest periods of the Cold War; served as a Reichstag deputy (1919–33); appointed acting Oberbürgermeisterin ("lord mayoress," May 8, 1947); stepped down from mayoral post (1951); remained active in politics in West Germany (1950s); was immensely popular throughout West Germany for final decade of her life. City of Berlin began to award an annual Louise Schroeder Medal (1998). ❖ See also *Women in World History.*

SCHROEDER, Patricia (1940—). American politician. Name variations: Pat Schroeder. Born Patricia Scott, July 30, 1940, in Portland, Oregon; dau. of Bernice Lemoin Scott (elementary schoolteacher) and Lee Combs Scott (pilot and aviation insurance adjuster); University of Minnesota, BA, 1961; Harvard Law School, JD, 1964; certification from Colorado Bar, 1964; m. James W. Schroeder, Aug 18, 1962; children: Scott William Schroeder (b. 1966); Jamie Christine Schroeder (b. 1970). ❖

US representative, advocate for families and women, who used her position on the House National Security Committee to challenge assumptions about spending priorities to see if money could be saved from military spending and used for other purposes; practiced law and taught law at Denver area schools (1964–72); won 2 primary and 12 general elections for Congress (1972–96); served on House National Security Committee (formerly House Armed Services Committee, 1973–96), House Judiciary Committee (1980–96), and House Post Office and Civil Service Committee (1973–94); served as co-chair, Congressional Caucus for Women's Issues (1979–95), deputy whip, Democratic Caucus (1987–96), and chair, House Select Committee on Children, Youth, and Families (1991–93); formed exploratory presidential campaign committee, raised $1 million in 3 months (1987); retired undefeated from Congress (1996); by the time of her retirement, was the longest-serving woman in Congress, widely respected not only for her efforts on behalf of women and children, but for her shrewd study of arms control and economics; became president and chief executive of Association of American Publishers (1997). Inducted into National Women's Hall of Fame (1995). ❖ See also memoirs *Champion of the Great American Family: A Personal and Political Book* (Random House, 1989) and *24 Years of House Work . . . and the Place is Still a Mess* (McMeel, 1998); and *Women in World History.*

SCHRÖDER, Ilka (1978—). *See Schroeder, Ilka.*

SCHRÖDER-DEVRIENT, Wilhelmine (1804–1860). German soprano. Name variations: Wilhelmine Schroeder-Devrient. Born Dec 6, 1804, in Hamburg, Germany; died Jan 26, 1860, in Coburg; dau. of Friedrich Schröder (singer) and Antoinette Sophie (Bürger) Schröder (1781–1868, actress known as Sophie Schröder); studied with Mozatti in Vienna; m. Karl Devrient, 1823 (div. 1828); m. Herr Van Döring (div.); m. Baron von Bock, 1850. ❖ Trained as an actress by mother, dramatic roles were her forte; at 17, made debut as Pamina in Vienna (1821); had a remarkable success as Leonore in *Fidelio*; sang at Dresden Court Opera (1823–47); during early career, sang mostly in Vienna, Berlin, Dresden, and Paris, but later appeared frequently in London; retired (1856). ❖ See also *Women in World History.*

SCHROEDTER, Elisabeth (1959—). German politician. Born Mar 11, 1959, in Dresden, Germany. ❖ Spokeswoman for ecology working party in Bündnis 90/Greens (1991–94); representing Group of the Greens/European Free Alliance, elected to 4th and 5th European Parliament (1994–99, 1999–2004).

SCHRÖER-LEHMANN, Beatrix (1963—). East German rower. Name variations: Beatrix Lehmann. Born May 1963 in East Germany. ❖ At Seoul Olympics, won a gold medal in coxed eights (1988).

SCHROETER, Martina (1960—). East German rower. Born Nov 16, 1960, in East Germany. ❖ At Moscow Olympics, won a bronze medal in single sculls (1980); at Seoul Olympics, won a gold medal in double sculls (1988).

SCHROTH, Clara (1920—). American gymnast. Name variations: Clara Schroth Lomady. Born Clara M. Schroth, Oct 5, 1920, in Philadelphia, PA; m. "Fuzz" Lomady; children: 4. ❖ At London Olympics, won a bronze medal in team all-around (1948); was AAU All-Around champion (1945–46, 1949–51); won 39 national titles during career, including 11 consecutive balance beam titles; also won the AAU standing broad jump title (1945).

SCHROTH, Frances (b. 1893). American swimmer. Born April 11, 1893. ❖ At Antwerp Olympics, won bronze medals in the 300-meter freestyle and 100-meter freestyle and a gold in the 4 x 100-meter freestyle relay (1920); at Paris Olympics, was an alternate in the 100-meter backstroke at age 31 (1924).

SCHUBA, Beatrix (1951—). Austrian figure skater. Name variations: Trixie Schuba. Born May 15, 1951, in Vienna, Austria. ❖ Won the European and World championships (1971, 1972); won a gold medal at Sapporo Olympics (1972); won Austrian nationals (1967–72).

SCHUBERT, Helga (1940—). East German short-story writer. Born 1940 in Berlin, Germany; m. Johannes Helm. ❖ Trained as psychotherapist, had 1st success with *Lauter Leben* (Nothing But Life, 1975), a collection of psychological cameos of women in postwar Germany; other works include *Das verbotene Zimmer* (1982) and *Die Welt da drinnen* (2003). Awarded honorary doctorate by Purdue University (1991).

SCHUBIN, Ossip (1854–1934). *See Kirschner, Lola.*

SCHUCH, Clara Bohm (1879–1936). *See Bohm-Schuch, Clara.*

SCHUCK, Anett (1970—). German kayaker. Born April 11, 1970, in Leipzig, Germany. ❖ Won a gold medal at Atlanta Olympics (1996) and a gold medal at Sydney Olympics (2000), both for K4 500 meters; won 12 World championships and a gold medal for K4 at European championships (2000).

SCHUESSLER, Elisabeth (1938—). *See Fiorenza, Elisabeth Schuessler.*

SCHUETZ, Birgit (1958—). *See Schütz, Birgit.*

SCHULENBURG, Ehrengard Melusina von der (1667–1743). Duchess of Kendal and paramour. Name variations: Ehrengard Melusine von der Schulemburg; Ermengarde Melusina von der Schulenburg, baroness Schulenburg; duchess of Munster; known as Melusine. Born in Germany, 1667; died in England, 1743 (some sources cite 1746); dau. of Gustavus Adolphus, Baron Schulenburg; had liaison (*maitresse en titre*) with George I, king of England; children: (with George I) 3 daughters: Anna Louise (b. 1682); Petronilla Melusina, baroness of Aldborough, countess of Walsingham (1693–1778); Margaret Gertrude of Schulenburg (b. 1703). ❖ Came to Great Britain (1714) as the paramour of its newly crowned king, George I, the 1st in a succession of Hanoverian monarchs; notoriously unpopular with the British public and an object of ridicule to courtiers; was also a necessary and useful ally to those hoping to curry favor with the king; was regarded as the unofficial queen. ❖ See also *Women in World History.*

SCHULER, Carolyn (1943—). American swimmer. Born Jan 1943 in US. ❖ At Rome Olympics, won a gold medal in the 4 x 100-meter medley relay and a gold medal in the 100-meter butterfly (1960).

SCHÜLER, Else Lasker (1869–1945). *See Lasker-Schüler, Else.*

SCHULER, Laura (1970—). Canadian ice-hockey player. Born Dec 3, 1970, in Scarborough, Ontario, Canada. ❖ Played at Northeastern University (Boston) and University of Toronto; won a gold medal at World championships (1990, 1992, 1997); won a team silver medal at Nagano (1998), the 1st Olympics to feature women's ice hockey.

SCHULTER-MATTLER, Heike (1958—). West German runner. Name variations: Heike Mattler. Born May 27, 1958, in Germany. ❖ At Los Angeles Olympics, won a bronze medal in the 4 x 400-meter relay (1984).

SCHULTZ, Annette (1957—). East German volleyball player. Born May 14, 1957, in East Germany. ❖ At Moscow Olympics, won a silver medal in team competition (1980).

SCHULTZ, Sigrid (1893–1980). American journalist and author. Name variations: (pseudonym) John Dickson. Born Sigrid Lillian Schultz in Chicago, Illinois, Jan 5, 1893; died in Westport, Connecticut, May 14, 1980; dau. of Herman Schultz (portrait painter) and Hedwig (Jaskewitz) Schultz; attended Lycée Racine in Paris; graduate of Sorbonne in Paris, 1914; studied international law at Berlin University; never married; no children. ❖ Began work at Berlin office of *Chicago Tribune* (1919); elected a member of board of directors of Berlin's Foreign Press Club (1924), the 1st woman journalist so honored; was named bureau chief of *Tribune*'s Berlin office (1925); witnessed rise of Nazi party (1920s–30s); despite threats and intimidation, remained in Berlin in early years of WWII (1939–41), reporting on Nazi regime; conducted interviews with Goering and Hitler; under an assumed name, filed stories that exposed concentration camps, the persecution of Jews, and other Nazi brutalities; wrote *Germany Will Try It Again* (1942); returned to Europe as a war correspondent with 1st and 3rd Armies and Air Power Press Camp for *Chicago Tribune* (1943). Honored by the Overseas Press Club (1969). ❖ See also *Women in World History.*

SCHULZE, Sabina (1972—). East German swimmer. Born Mar 19, 1972, in East Germany. ❖ At Seoul Olympics, won a gold medal in 4 x 100-meter freestyle relay (1988).

SCHULZE-BOYSEN, Libertas (1913–1942). German resistance leader. Name variations: Libertas Haas-Heye. Born Libertas Haas-Heye in Paris, France, Nov 20, 1913; executed along with husband, Dec 22, 1942; dau. of Professor Otto Haas-Heye (architect) and Countess Thora Eulenburg; m. Harro Schulze-Boysen (1909–1942, resistance leader), 1936. ❖ Anti-Nazi activist, author, and actress, became a freelance journalist (1935), working 1st for the *National-Zeitung* of Essen, then employed by a cultural film organization closely associated with the Ministry of Popular Enlightenment and Propaganda of Joseph Goebbels; with husband, was a leading member of the "Red Orchestra" spy organization that relayed crucial information from the Nazi Air Ministry to the Soviet Union during WWII. ❖ See also *Women in World History.*

SCHUMACHER, Elisabeth (1904–1942). German resistance leader. Born Elisabeth Hohenemser, April 28, 1904, in Darmstadt, Germany; executed along with husband, Dec 22, 1942, at Berlin's Plötzensee prison; dau. of a prominent engineer; spent childhood in Meiningen; m. Kurt Schumacher (1905–42, sculptor and resistance leader). ❖ Artist and anti-Nazi activist, worked for the Berlin Communist underground with husband; was able to provide important material from her job at Reich Center for Labor Protection for the "Red Orchestra" spy network. ❖ See also *Women in World History.*

SCHUMACHER, Sandra (1966—). German cyclist. Born Dec 25, 1966, in Germany. ❖ At Los Angeles Olympics, won a bronze medal in the indiv. road race (1984).

SCHUMANN, Clara (1819–1896). German pianist, composer, and teacher. Name variations: Clara Wieck. Born Clara Josephine Wieck in Leipzig, Germany, Sept 13, 1819; died at Frankfurt am Main, May 20, 1896; dau. of Friedrich Wieck (music teacher) and Marianne Tromlitz Wieck (well-known singer under maiden name); m. Robert Schumann (the composer), Sept 12, 1840 (died 1856); children: Marie (b. 1841); Elise (b. 1843); Julie (b. 1845); Emil (1846–1847); Ludwig (b. 1848); Ferdinand (b. 1849); Eugenie (b. 1851); Felix (b. 1854). ❖ Famed concert pianist, composer and music teacher, wife of composer Robert Schumann, whose innovations in performance during a 60-year career helped to shape the standard modern-day piano repertory; made performance debut at age 9 (1828); during an extended tour in Austria, awarded the honorary position of chamber musician (*K. k. Kammervirtuosin*), generally reserved for established performers, in Vienna (1837); after marriage to Robert Schumann and despite the births of 8 children, traveled to Russia, Denmark, France and England to perform the music of Liszt, Rubinstein, Chopin, Schumann and Brahms; dominated the concert stage, playing over 1,300 public programs in England and Europe throughout long career; for practical reasons, became one of the 1st soloists to play concerts without supporting artists and soon considered it preferable; appointed principal piano teacher at Hoch Conservatory in Frankfurt (1878); made last public appearance (1891); was a towering figure in the musical world, introducing some of the finest works of her day; off stage, her teaching influenced generations of young performers. ❖ See also Joan Chissell, *Clara Schumann: A Dedicated Spirit. A Study of her Life and Work* (Taplinger, 1983); Florence May, *The Girlhood of Clara Schumann: Clara Wieck and Her Time* (Arnold, 1912); Nancy B. Reich, *Clara Schumann: The Artist and the Woman* (Cornell U. Press, 1985); Gerd Nauhaus, ed. *Marriage Diaries of Robert and Clara Schumann* (trans. by Peter Ostwald, Northeastern U. Press, 1993); and *Women in World History.*

SCHUMANN, Elisabeth (1885–1952). German soprano. Born in Merseburg, Thuringia, Germany, June 13, 1885; died in New York, NY, April 23, 1952; studied with Natalie Hänisch in Dresden, Marie Dietrich in Berlin, and Alma Schadow in Hamburg; m. Karl Alwin (conductor); became American citizen (1944). ❖ Debuted at Hamburg Opera as the Shepherd in *Tannhäuser* (1909) and quickly became a popular singer; made Metropolitan Opera debut (1914), winning high praise for interpretation of Sophie in *Der Rosenkavalier,* which would go on to become one of her best-known roles; was a principal member of Vienna State Opera (1919–38), particularly acclaimed for appearances in Mozart's operas; also known as a supreme Lieder singer, traveled to US with Strauss to perform many of his Lieder on tour (1921); made Covent Garden debut, again as Sophie (1924); fled Vienna for America with Jewish husband and joined the faculty of the Curtis Institute of Music in Philadelphia (1938). ❖ See also *Women in World History.*

SCHUMANN, Margit (1952—). East German luge athlete. Born Sept 14, 1952, in East Germany. ❖ Won the World championship (1973, 1974, 1975, 1977); won a bronze medal for singles at Sapporo Olympics (1972); won a gold medal for singles at Innsbruck Olympics (1976). Was one of the 1st champions to be inducted into International Luge Federation Hall of Fame (2004).

SCHUMANN-HEINK, Ernestine (1861–1936). Czech-born contralto. Name variations: Tini Rössler, Rossler, or Roessler; Ernestine Heink; Madame Schumann Heink. Born Ernestine Rössler in Lieben near Prague, Bohemia (now Czechoslovakia), June 15, 1861; died Nov 17, 1936, in Hollywood, CA; studied with Marietta von Leclair in Graz, and Karl Krebs, Franz Wüllner and G. B. Lamperti; m. Ernst Heink (secretary to the Dresden Royal Opera), 1882 (div. 1893); m. Paul Schumann (actor and stage manager), 1893 (died 1904); m. William Rapp Jr. (her secretary), 1905 (div. 1914). ❖ Made debut under name Tini Rössler, in Dresden (1878); had breakthrough role as Carmen at Hamburg (1889) and appearances throughout Europe soon followed; performed in London production of *Der Ring des Nibelungen* under Gustav Mahler (1892); coached by Cosima Wagner, made Bayreuth debut in *Der Ring des Nibelungen* (1896); debuted at Covent Garden (1897), Berlin Opera (1898), Chicago Opera (1898), and Metropolitan Opera (1899); moved permanently to US (1903) and began a 40,000-mile concert tour, becoming a great favorite on opera and concert stage; created role of Klytemnestra in *Elektra* in Dresden (1909); during WWI, made endless appearances on behalf of American troops; made 1st radio appearance (1926); forced by stock-market crash (1929), entered vaudeville; appeared in film *Here's to Romance* (1935); made recordings for Victor (1903–31), the most famous of which is "Stille Nacht" ("Silent Night"). ❖ See also M. Lawton, *Schumann-Heink: The Last of the Titans* (1928); and *Women in World History*.

SCHURMANN, Anna Maria van (1607–1678). *See van Schurmann, Anna Maria.*

SCHURZ, Margarethe Meyer (1833–1876). German-born educator. Born Margarethe Meyer, Aug 27, 1833, in Hamburg, Germany; died in New York, NY, Mar 15, 1876, of complications after birth of 5th child; dau. of Heinrich Meyer (merchant-manufacturer); sister of Bertha Ronge; m. Carl Schurz (1829–1906, Civil War general [1862–65], US senator from Missouri [1869–75], and editor of New York *Evening Post*[1881–83]), July 6, 1852; children: Agathe Schurz (b. 1853); Marianne Schurz; Carl Lincoln Schurz; Herbert Schurz; daughter who died in infancy. ❖ At 16, attended lectures by founder of kindergarten philosophy, Friedrich Froebel, and became a disciple of his educational approach; moved to England to assist in administration of a kindergarten school (1852), the 1st in England, started by sister Bertha and Bertha's husband John Ronge; married and moved to US (1852); settling in Watertown, Wisconsin, opened what is often regarded as the 1st kindergarten in US in a back room of home; shared Froebel's theories with Elizabeth Palmer Peabody in Boston (1859), who would found her own kindergarten school (1860). ❖ See also *Women in World History*.

SCHÜSSLER, Elisabeth (1938—). *See Fiorenza, Elisabeth Schuessler.*

SCHUSTER, Norah (1892–1991). English pathologist. Born Norah Henriette Schuster, July 14, 1892; died Mar 14, 1991; dau. of Arthur Schuster (physics professor who contributed to the incorporation of X-ray technology in clinical practice); attended Newnham College, Cambridge, 1912–15; University of Manchester School of Medicine, ChB, 1918, MB; m. Marriott Fawchner Nicholls, July 2, 1925. ❖ The 1st woman to take a University of Cambridge preclinical science class and the 1st woman president of the Association of Clinical Pathologists (1950), worked as an unpaid assistant with professor H.R. Dean at the Manchester Royal Infirmary (1916), while pursuing studies at University of Manchester School of Medicine; served as assistant pathologist at St. George's Hospital in London and at Infants' Hospital in London; worked as pathologist at Royal Chest Hospital in London (1927–54); employed at Pinewood Hospital, Wokingham (1954–59); elected fellow of Royal Society (1981).

SCHUSTER, Susanne (1963—). West German swimmer. Born May 9, 1963, in Germany. ❖ At Los Angeles Olympics, won a bronze medal in the 4 x 100-meter freestyle relay (1984).

SCHUT, Ans (1944—). *See Schut, Johanna.*

SCHUT, Johanna (1944—). Dutch speedskater. Name variations: Ans Schut. Born Joannah Schut, Nov 26, 1944, in the Netherlands. ❖ Won a gold medal for the 3,000 meters at Grenoble Olympics (1968); at World championships, won a silver medal (1968) and a bronze (1969), both for small allround.

SCHÜTTE-LIHOTZKY, Margarete (1897–2000). Austrian architect. Name variations: Margaret Shutte-Lihotzky or Schuette-Lihotzky; Margarethe Lihotzky; Grete Lihotzky; Grete Schütte-Lihotzky. Born Margarete Lihotzky in Vienna, Austria, Jan 23, 1897; died in Vienna, Jan 18, 2000; dau. of Erwin Lihotzky and Julie (Bode) Lihotzky; studied architecture under Oskar Strnad and Heinrich Tessenow at Vienna's Akademie für angewandte Kunst; m. Wilhelm Schütte (1900–1968, architect), 1927 (div. 1950); no children. ❖ First Austrian woman to become a professional architect, known for her "Frankfurt kitchen," designed simple and affordable dwellings and interiors for working-class and white-collar families; helped design the Winarsky-Hof, a pioneering housing project comprising 840 apartments, 40 units of which she and several other architects helped plan as models for the future; working for city of Frankfurt am Main (1926), designed a modern kitchen which was immensely successful (in Frankfurt am Main alone over 10,000 would be installed in next few years); with husand, designed schools, kindergartens and public-housing developments in Soviet Union (1927–37), then taught at Turkish Academy of Fine Arts in Istanbul (1938–39); joined Austrian Communist Party (KPÖ, 1939), who sent her to Vienna to assist in rebuilding an underground network weakened by several years of Nazi infiltration and persecution (1940); betrayed by a Nazi agent, was arrested by Gestapo and sentenced to 15 years hard labor (1941); liberated (1945); in postwar decades, served as president of Austrian Federation of Democratic Women, served on board of Austrian organization of victims of Nazism and Fascism, and was active in Austrian Peace Council; carried out a number of successful kindergarten projects in Sofia, Bulgaria (1945–46), and made extended trips as a consultant and lecturer to several nations. Awarded Bronze Medal of City of Vienna (1922) and Silver Medal (1923); design for a modern kitchen won Max Mauthner Prize (1917) and Lobmeyr Prize (1919); received City of Vienna Prize for Architecture (1980); awarded Ehrenring der Stadt Wien (Ring of Honor of the City of Vienna, 1997). ❖ See also (autobiography in German) *Erinnerungen aus dem Widerstand: Das kämpferische Leben einer Architektin von 1938–1945* (ed. by Irene Nierhaus, Promedia, 1994); and *Women in World History*.

SCHUTTING, Julian (1937—). Austrian poet and short-story writer. Name variations: Jutta Schutting. Born Jutta Schutting, Oct 25, 1937, in Amstetten, Austria; attended University of Vienna. ❖ Works include *In der Sprache der Inseln* (1973), *Lichtungen* (1976), *Der Vater* (1980), *Liebesgedichte* (1982), *Liebesroman* (1983), *Reisefieber* (1988), *Katzentage* (1995), *Dem Erinnern entrissen* (2001) and *Was schön ist* (2002). Received several awards, including Culture Prize of City of Vienna (1988) and Georg Trakl Prize (1989).

SCHUTTPELZ, Barbara (1956—). West German kayaker. Born Sept 1956 in Germany. ❖ At Los Angeles Olympics, won a bronze medal in K2 500 meters and a silver medal in K1 500 meters (1984).

SCHÜTZ, Birgit (1958—). East German rower. Name variations: Birgit Schuetz. Born Oct 1958 in East Germany. ❖ At Moscow Olympics, won a gold medal in coxed eights (1980).

SCHÜTZ, Helga (1937—). East German novelist. Name variations: Helga Schutz or Schuetz. Born Oct 2, 1937, in Germany. ❖ Works, which focus on Third Reich and post-war division of Germany, include *Festbeleuchtung* (1973), *Jette in Dresden* (1977) and *Julia oder Die Erziehung zum Chorgesang* (1980).

SCHÜTZ-ZELL, Katherine (c. 1497–1562). *See Zell, Katharina Schütz.*

SCHÜTZIN, Katherina (c. 1497–1562). *See Zell, Katharina Schütz.*

SCHUYLENBURG, Helga Maria (b. 1910). *See Löwenstein, Helga Maria zu.*

SCHUYLER, Catherine Van Rensselaer (1734–1803). American patriot. Name variations: Kitty Van Rensselaer. Born Catherine Van Rensselaer, Nov 4, 1734, in Claverack, New York; died Mar 7, 1803, in Albany, NY; dau. of Johannes Van Rensselaer (officer in British Army and later defender of American struggle for independence) and Engeltie (Livingston) Van Rensselaer; m. distant cousin Philip Schuyler (Revolutionary War general), Sept 7, 1755; children: Angelica Schuyler (b. 1756); Elizabeth Schuyler Hamilton (1757–1854); Margaret Schuyler (b. 1758); John Bradstreet Schuyler (b. 1765); Philip Jeremiah Schuyler (b. 1768); Rensselaer Schuyler (b. 1773); Cornelia Schuyler (b. 1775); Catherine Van Rensselaer Schuyler (b. 1781). ❖ Wife of a Revolutionary War general, nursed the wounded when husband's army was defeated at Ticonderoga (1757); with husband, established what would become the town of Schuylerville (NY), complete with saw and grist mills, fields of flax and wheat, and a country house; as British forces threatened the area (1775), burned the extensive wheat fields to prevent the British from harvesting them. ❖ See also *Women in World History*.

SCHUYLER, Louisa Lee (1837–1926). American social reformer. Born Oct 26, 1837, in New York, NY; died Oct 10, 1926, in Highland Falls, NY; dau. of George Lee Schuyler (engineer, lawyer, and grandson of Revolutionary War general Philip Schuyler and Catherine Van Rensselaer Schuyler) and Eliza Hamilton Schuyler (great-granddau. of the same Philip Schuyler and Catherine Van Rensselaer Schuyler and granddau. of Elizabeth Schuyler Hamilton and Alexander Hamilton, the famous American statesman); educated privately; never married. ❖ Chaired a committee for Woman's Central Association of Relief (1861), which provided regional support to the Union cause during Civil War; organized prominent New York City women into a visiting committee to local jails and hospitals, then created the State Charities Aid Association (SCAA) to formalize these citizen groups (1872); established professional training school for nurses at Bellevue Hospital (1873), the 1st of its size to maintain such high standards; initiated a campaign to move the mentally ill from county poorhouses to state hospitals (1884); became a charter trustee in Russell Sage Foundation (1907); worked with several organizations to create the National Committee (later renamed Society) for Prevention of Blindness (1915); demonstrated the need for women of social standing to take on leadership roles in bringing about reform. Granted honorary doctorate of Laws from Columbia University (1915), only the 2nd woman to receive such an honor. ❖ See also *Women in World History.*

SCHUYLER, Philippa Duke (1931–1967). African-American pianist and composer. Name variations: Felipa Monterro y Schuyler; Felipa Monterro. Born in 1931 in Harlem, New York; died May 9, 1967, in a helicopter crash in Vietnam; interracial dau. of Josephine "Jody" Cogdell Schuyler (white artist and writer who used maiden name Josephine Cogdell) and George Schuyler (African-American journalist); privately educated in New York. ❖ Composer whose well-known compositions include "Manhattan Nocturne" (1943), "Rhapsody of Youth" (1948), and "Nile Fantasy" (1965), received acclaim for her music from audiences of all races when young; at 10, was invited to become a member of National Association of American Composers and Conductors, and won several prizes for her compositions and performances; made NY debut as a composer and pianist with the Philharmonic Symphony Orchestra (1946); as an adult, felt she did not fit in on either side of America's racially divided society; chose a voluntary exile of traveling and performing in more than 80 countries in Latin America, Asia, Africa and Europe; as concert schedule decreased (early 1960s), supplemented income by writing about travels, publishing more than 100 newspaper and magazine articles in US and Europe; was one of the few black writers to be syndicated by UPI; also published 4 nonfiction books: *Adventures in Black and White* (1960), *Who Killed the Congo?* (1962), *Jungle Saints* (1963), and (with mother) *Kingdom of Dreams* (1966); reinvented herself as "Felipa Monterro" in hopes of re-entering the American music community as a Spanish musician (1962); went to Vietnam as a correspondent for *Manchester Union Leader* to perform for the troops. ❖ See also Kathryn Talalay, *Composition in Black and White: The Life of Philippa Schuyler* (Oxford U. Press, 1995); and *Women in World History.*

SCHVUBOVA, Dagmar. *See Svubova, Dagmar.*

SCHWANDT, Rhonda (1963—). American gymnast. Born April 19, 1963, in US. ❖ Won World School Games (1976), KIPS Invitational (1978), Dial Selection Meet and Pacific championships (1979); at World Cup, won a silver medal for vault and a bronze for uneven bars (1978).

SCHWARCZENBERGER, Ildiko (1951—). *See Tordasi Schwarczenberger, Ildiko.*

SCHWARTZ, Anna Jacobson (1915—). American economist. Born Nov 11, 1915 in New York, NY; Barnard College, BA, 1934; Columbia University, MA, 1935, PhD, 1964; married; children: 4. ❖ Conducted research in economic history and international monetary system at Columbia University and National Bureau of Economic Research; with Milton Friedman, wrote *A Monetary History of the United States, 1867–1960* (1963) and *The Great Contraction, 1929–1933* (1965); wrote other works on international monetary system, gold standard, and international lending; was staff director of US Commission on the Role of Gold in the Domestic and International Monetary System.

SCHWARTZ, Betty Robinson (1911–1997). *See Robinson, Betty.*

SCHWARZ, Elisabeth (1936—). Austrian pairs skater. Name variations: Sissy Schwarz; Elizabeth Schwarz. Born 1936 in Austria. ❖ With partner Kurt Oppelt, won a silver medal (1955) and a gold medal (1956) at World championships, a gold medal at European championships (1956), and a gold medal at Cortina Olympics (1956).

SCHWARZ, Sissy. *See Schwarz, Elisabeth.*

SCHWARZ, Solange (1910–2000). French ballet dancer. Born 1910 in Paris, France; died in 2000; dau. of Jean Schwarz (well-known teacher in

Paris). ❖ Performed at Paris Opéra throughout most of career (1930–33, 1937–57), where best-known performances include Swanilda in *Coppélia* and roles in Lifar's *Le Chevalier et la desmoiselle* and *Les animeux modèles*; also created major roles for Lifar's *Alexandre le Grand* (1937) and *Entre Deux Rondes* (1940); danced as guest artist at Opéra-Comique, Ballet de L'Etoile, and Grand Ballet du Marquis de Cuevas; served as teacher at l'Ecole du Conservatoire Nationale de Musique et de Déclamation.

SCHWARZ, Sybilla (1621–1638). German poet. Born Feb 14, 1621, in Greifswald, Germany; died July 31, 1638. ❖ Wrote poems from early age for family occasions that treat themes of war, family, friendship, and death; work published in anthology *Deutsche Poetische Gedichte* (1650).

SCHWARZ, Vera (1888–1964). Austrian soprano. Born in Agram (now Zagreb, capital of Croatia) July 10, 1888; died in Vienna, Austria, Dec 4, 1964. ❖ Made debut at Theater an der Wien in Vienna (1908) and was soon singing Rosalinde in *Die Fledermaus*, as well as other leading roles; went to Hamburg and Berlin; sang *Der Zarewitsch* with Richard Tauber, marking the beginning of many Lehár operettas in which the couple would star (1927); because she was Jewish, left for US (1938), as the Nazi threat loomed over Europe; returned to Vienna (1948). ❖ See also *Women in World History.*

SCHWARZ-BART, Simone (1938—). French-born novelist and playwright. Born 1938 in Charente, France; returned with family to Guadaloupe, French Antilles, at age 3; studied in Pointe-à-Pitre, Paris and Dakar; m. André Schwarz-Bart (Jewish writer), 1961. ❖ Works, which show the harsh life Caribbean women endured during slavery and colonization, include *Pluie et vent sur Télumée Miracle* (1972, trans. as *The Bridge of Beyond,* 1972), *Ti Jean l'Horizon* (1979, trans. as *Between Two Worlds,* 1981), and (play) *Ton Beau Capitaine* (1987); with husband, wrote the historical novels, *Un plat de porc aux bananes vertes* (A Dish of Pork with Green Beans, 1967) and *La Mulâtresse Solitude* (A Woman Named Solitude, 1972); also published 6 vols. on black women, *Homage à la Femme Noire* (1989).

SCHWARZENBACH, Annemarie (1908–1942). Swiss-German author. Born in Zurich, Switzerland, 1908; died 1942; dau. of a wealthy industrialist. ❖ Wrote many novels, travelogues, and stories, but few have been published; often appears in the memoirs and biographies of many literati of early and mid-20th century: Klaus and Erika Mann, Roger Martin du Gard, André Malraux, Carson McCullers, and Ella Maillart, who traveled with her through Iran and Afghanistan (1939) and refers to Schwarzenbach as "Christina" in *The Cruel Way* (1947); published *Eine Frau allein* (*A Woman Alone,* 1989). ❖ See also *Women in World History.*

SCHWARZHAUPT, Elisabeth (1901–1986). German judge and politician. Born in Frankfurt am Main, Germany, Jan 7, 1901; died in Frankfurt am Main, Oct 29, 1986; dau. of Wilhelm Schwarzhaupt (educator and politician) and Frieda (Emmerich) Schwarzhaupt; never married. ❖ As a member of Christian Democratic Union, held a seat in West Germany's Bundestag (1953–69); served on the parliamentary committee on legal affairs, specializing in family law; promoted improvements in the legal position of married women as well as the entrenchment of the principle of gender equality in the Basic Law of the Federal Republic (*Grundgesetz*), through her work on drafting article 3 of the Basic Law; served as minister of Health (1962–66), the 1st woman government minister in German history. Awarded Federal Republic's Grand Cross of the Order of Merit (1966). ❖ See also *Women in World History.*

SCHWARZKOPF, Elisabeth (1915—). German soprano. Name variations: Elisabeth Legge-Schwarzkopf. Born Elisabeth Schwarzkopf, Dec 9, 1915, in Jarotschin near Posen, Germany (now Jarocin near Poznán, Poland); studied at Hochschule für Musik in Berlin, 1934–38; m. Walter Legge (1906–1979, artistic director of EMI Records), 1953. ❖ One of the great singers of the post-war era, acclaimed for performances of Mozart and Strauss, made debut as 2nd Flower Maiden at Berlin's Municipal Opera (1938) in *Parsifal*; in following season (1938–39), added 16 parts to a growing repertory, the most important being Frasquita in *Carmen* and Musetta in *La Bohème*; joined Nazi Party (1940); began studying with Maria Ivogün and graduated to starring roles, in operas and operettas, including Adele in *Die Fledermaus*; began giving recitals in Berlin's Beethoven Saal (1942), the beginning of what would become one of the great careers of Lieder singing; joined Vienna State Opera (1944) and appeared in *Entführung aus dem Serail* (Abduction from the Seraglio), *La Bohème*, and *Der Freischütz*; fled Vienna at time of Germany's surrender (1945); declared de-Nazified

(1947), was free to resume career; traveled to London with Vienna State Opera (1946); with urging of Walter Legge, began singing roles appropriate to her voice, including Agathe in *Der Freitschütz* and Countess in *Le nozze di Figaro*; joined London's Covent Garden Opera Co. (1948), remaining with it for 5 seasons; performed on a regular basis at La Scala (1948–63); originated role of Anne Trulove in Stravinsky's *The Rake's Progress*, which premiered in Venice's Teatro Fenice (1951) and participated in world premiere of Orff's *Trionfo d'Afrodite* at La Scala (1953); concentrated for next 15 years on 3 Mozart heroines (Fiordiligi, Donna Elvira, and Countess Almaviva), 2 Richard Strauss roles (Marschallin in *Der Rosenkavalier* and Countess in *Capriccio*), and Alice in Verdi's *Falstaff* (1955–70); also sang in several operetta classics, particularly *Die Fledermaus* and *Die lustige witwe* (The Merry Widow); recordings remain classics; made US debut with a Lieder recital at NY's Town Hall (1953); made US operatic debut as the Marschallin (1955) with San Francisco Opera and sang there to great success for 10 years; debuted at Metropolitan Opera (1964) as the Marschallin; at Carnegie Hall, gave last opera performance in America (1972); made farewell recital tour of US (1975) and gave last Liederabend in Zurich (1979). Awarded Federal Republic of Germany's Grosses Bundesverdienstkreuz (Large Cross of Achievement) as well as its coveted Pour le Mérite; named Dame Commander of the British Empire (DBE) by Queen Elizabeth II (1992). ❖ See also Alan Jefferson, *Elisabeth Schwarzkopf* (Northeastern U. Press, 1996); and *Women in World History*.

SCHWARZWALD, Eugenie (1872–1940). Austrian educator and philanthropist. Name variations: Eugenia Schwarzwald; Genia Schwarzwald; "Fraudoktor" Schwarzwald. Born Eugenie Nussbaum into an assimilated German-speaking Jewish family in Polupanowka, near Czernowitz, Galicia, Austria (now Chernovtsy, Ukraine), July 4, 1872; died in exile in Zurich, Switzerland, Aug 7, 1940; dau. of Leo and Esther Nussbaum; awarded doctorate from University of Zurich, 1900; married Hermann ("Hemme") Schwarzwald (economist), 1900 (died Aug 17, 1939); no children. ❖ Educational reformer, salonnière, and philanthropist whose private school for girls, which encouraged intellectual independence, started an educational revolution in Vienna; as one of the 1st women in Austria-Hungary to earn a PhD, moved to Vienna (1900), where she purchased a girls' lyceum from educational pioneer Eleonore Jeiteles (1901); moved the Schwarzwald-Schule to the Wallnerstrasse in Vienna's exclusive 1st District (1902), where she modernized the curriculum and hired 1st-class teachers; received statute of approval as a Mädchen-Reform-Gymnasium (Modern Girls' Secondary School), making graduates fully qualified to enter universities of the Habsburg Empire (1912); during WWI, actively participated in war relief, especially for the elderly of Vienna; because of her growing reputation, presided over a star-studded salon at her home, attended by such figures as Karin Michaëlis, Rainer Maria Rilke, Bertolt Brecht, Elias Canetti, Rudolf Serkin, Lotte Leonard, Greta Kraus, Dorothy Thompson, Sinclair Lewis, Adolf Loos and Oskar Kokoschka; graduates of her school included Helene Weigel and Hilde Spiel; when Hitler's troops marched into Austria (1938), was in Copenhagen for scheduled cancer surgery; with husband, went into exile in Switzerland, where they found themselves impoverished and in rapidly worsening health; her school was shut down by the Nazis (Sept 15, 1938), 37 years to the day of its opening; never returned to Vienna. ❖ See also *Women in World History*.

SCHWEDE, Bianka (1953—). East German rower. Born Jan 9, 1953, in East Germany. ❖ At Montreal Olympics, won a gold medal in coxed fours (1976).

SCHWEITZER, Lucille (1902–1999). *See Lortel, Lucille.*

SCHWEITZER, Nicole Henriot (b. 1925). *See Henriot-Schweitzer, Nicole.*

SCHWEN, Missy (1972—). American rower. Name variations: Missy Schwen-Ryan; Melissa Ryan. Born Melissa Schwen, July 17, 1972, in Bloomington, IN; graduate of Georgetown University, 1994; m. Tim Ryan (Australian rower). ❖ Won a silver medal for coxless pair at Atlanta Olympics (1996) and a bronze medal for coxed eight at Sydney Olympics (2000).

SCHWERIN, Jeanette (1852–1899). German social reformer. Born 1852 in Germany; died 1899. ❖ Was a well-known assimilated Jewish reformer in Berlin; with Minna Cauer and Professor Gustav Schmoller, founded Mädchen- und Frauengruppen für soziale Hilfsarbeit (Girls' and Women's Group for Social Assistance, 1893).

SCHWERZMANN, Ingeburg (1967—). German rower. Born June 2, 1967, in Germany. ❖ At Barcelona Olympics, won a silver medal in coxless pairs (1992).

SCHWIKERT, Tasha (1984—). American gymnast. Born Nov 21, 1984, in Las Vegas, Nevada; dau. of Joy Schwikert and Shannon Warren; sister of Jordan Schwikert (gymnast). ❖ Won American Classic (2000); won team World championship (2003).

SCHWIMMER, Rosika (1877–1948). Hungarian pacifist, feminist, writer and diplomat. Born in Budapest, Hungary, Sept 11, 1877; died in New York, NY, Aug 3, 1948; dau. of Max B. Schwimmer and Bertha (Katscher) Schwimmer; married, Jan 16, 1911 (div. Jan 4, 1913); no children. ❖ First woman diplomat and advocate of world government, who came to prominence through her successful organization of suffrage and feminist groups and her influential opposition to WWI, began work as a bookkeeper and office worker (1891); started organizing women in the struggle for improved working conditions as well as their political, educational and social rights (1892); founded the Hungarian Feminist Association (1904), which would be instrumental in winning the vote for Hungarian women (1920); during WWI, persuaded automobile magnate Henry Ford to support an unofficial neutral conference in Sweden, sending delegates from US in a "peace ship" (1915); devoted to the cause of international peace (1914–20), traveled throughout Europe and North America to promote neutral mediation and organize women in an attempt to stop the hostilities; named Hungary's ambassador to Switzerland, the 1st woman in history to be given a diplomatic post (1918); forced to flee to Vienna because of revolution and counter-revolution in Hungary (1920) and seek refuge in US (1921); unpopular with many because of her uncompromising pacifism, was denied US citizenship and spent rest of life in US as a stateless person, working for the cause of world government; nominated for the Nobel Peace Prize (1948) but died before the recipient was selected. Writings include *Tisza Tales* (1928), (with Lola Maverick Lloyd) *Chaos, War or a New World Order?* (1937) and *Union Now for Peace or War? The Danger in the Plan of Clarence Streit* (1939). ❖ See also Edith Wynner, *Rosika Schwimmer, World Patriot* (Odhams, 1947); and *Women in World History*.

SCIDMORE, Eliza Ruhamah (1856–1928). American travel writer. Born Oct 14, 1856, in Madison, WI; died Nov 3, 1928, in Geneva, Switzerland. ❖ Studied at Oberlin College; moved to Washington, DC, and began writing articles for newspapers; traveled to Alaska, Japan, India, and elsewhere; served in various positions at National Geographic Society and contributed articles to the magazine; was secretary to Oriental Congress in Rome (1897) and delegate to Oriental Congress in Hamburg (1902); works include *Alaska, Its Southern Coast and the Sitkan Archipelago* (1885), *Jinrikisha Days in Japan* (1891), *Appleton's Guide-Book to Alaska and the Northwest Coast* (1893), *Java, the Garden of the East* (1897), *China, the Long-Lived Empire* (1900), *Winter India* (1903) and *As the Hague Ordains* (1907); contributed to *Harper's Weekly* and *World Today*.

SCIERI, Antoinette (fl. 1920s). Italian-born murderer. Born in Italy; married a man named Salmon; m. Joseph Rossignol (common-law); children: (with Salmon) 2; (with Rossignol) 1. ❖ Immigrated to France at young age; at a clearing station in Doullens during WWI, nursed soldiers from whom she stole money and personal items; arrested (1915) and briefly imprisoned; settled in St. Gilles with Joseph Rossignol (1920) and offered her services as a nurse; poisoned her wards, killing at least 6 (some sources cite 12), including Rossignol; received death sentence (April 27, 1926), which was later commuted to life imprisonment.

SCIOCCHETTI, Marina (1954—). Italian equestrian. Name variations: Marina Scioccheti Campello. Born April 13, 1954, in Italy. ❖ At Moscow Olympics, won a silver medal in team 3-day event (1980).

SCIOLTI, Gabriella (1974—). Italian water-polo player. Born Dec 17, 1974, in Italy. ❖ At World championships, won team gold medal (2001); won a team gold medal at Athens Olympics (2004).

SCIUTTI, Graziella (1927–2001). Italian soprano and director. Born April 17, 1927, in Turin, Italy; died April 9, 2001, in Geneva, Switzerland; studied at Santa Cecilia Conservatory in Rome; children: Susanna. ❖ Admired for her Mozart, Puccini and Verdi roles, was a soloist in a performance of "St. Matthew Passion," conducted by Herbert von Karajan, in her student days; at Aix-en-Provence, made formal debut as Lucy in Menotti's *Telephone* (1951), and sang there for many years; signature roles included Susanna in *Nozze di Figaro*, Despina in *Cosi Fan Tutte*, Zerlina in *Don Giovanni* and Nanetta in *Falstaff*; also created title role in Henri Sauguet's *Caprices de Marianne* (1954); made Glyndebourne debut as Rosina (1954); sang Carolina in *Matrimonio Segreto* in inaugural performances of the Piccola Scala, in Milan; made Covent Garden debut (1956) and US debut at San Francisco Opera (1961); also sang with Vienna State Opera; as a director, staged productions at the Canadian Opera, New York City Opera and Juilliard School; taught at Royal College of Music, London.

SCOATES, Vonda (c. 1944—). *See Van Dyke, Vonda.*

SCOTLAND, queen of.
See Margaret (fl. 1000s).
See Gruoch (fl. 1020–1054).
See Elflaed (fl. 1030).
See Ingebiorge (fl. 1045–1068).
See Margaret, St. (c. 1046–1093).
See Matilda of Northumberland (c. 1074–1131).
See Ethelreda (fl. 1090).
See Sybilla (d. 1122).
See Matilda (d. 1130?).
See Joan (1210–1238).
See Ermengarde of Beaumont (d. 1234).
See Mary de Coucy (c. 1220–c. 1260).
See Margaret (1240–1275).
See Margaret, Maid of Norway (c. 1283–1290).
See Isabella of Mar (d. 1296).
See Yolande de Dreux (d. 1323).
See Elizabeth de Burgh (d. 1327).
See Joan of the Tower (1321–1362).
See Drummond, Margaret (d. 1375).
See Ross, Euphemia (d. 1387).
See Drummond, Annabella (1350–1401).
See Beaufort, Joan (c. 1410–1445).
See Mary of Guelders (1433–1463).
See Margaret of Denmark (1456–1486).
See Tudor, Margaret (1489–1541).
See Mary of Guise (1515–1560).
See Mary Stuart (1542–1587).
See Anne of Denmark (1574–1619).
See Mary II (1662–1694).
See Anne (1665–1714).

SCOTS, queen of. *See Scotland, queen of.*

SCOTT, Agnes Neill (1890–1970). *See Muir, Willa.*

SCOTT, Amy May (1888–1985). *See Hutchinson, Amy May.*

SCOTT, Ann London (1929–1975). American feminist. Born Claire Ann London, July 29, 1929, in Seattle, Washington; died in Baltimore, Maryland, Feb 17, 1975; dau. of Claire Chester London and Daniel Edwin London (manager of St. Francis hotel in San Francisco); attended Stanford University, 1947–49; University of Washington, BA, 1954, PhD, 1968; m. Paul de Witt Tufts (musician), 1951 (div.); m. Gerd Stern (poet), 1956 (div. 1961); m. Thomas Jefferson Scott (artist), 1969; children: (2nd m.) son Jared London (b. 1957). ❖ Elected to board of directors of National Organization for Women (NOW, 1970), and became its Federal Contract Compliance Officer; as such, lobbied to include women in affirmative-action guidelines for all firms holding federal contracts, 1st at Department of Labor and then for all radio and tv stations holding Federal Communications Commission licenses; became NOW's vice president for legislation and worked for passage of 1972 Equal Employment Opportunity Act Amendment and Equal Rights Amendment; invited to serve on national boards of Common Cause and Leadership Conference on Civil Rights. ❖ See also *Women in World History.*

SCOTT, Anne (1651–1731). Countess of Buccleuch. Name variations: also seen as Duchess of Buccleuch. Born Feb 11, 1651; died Feb 6, 1731; dau. of Francis Scott (1626–1651), 2nd earl of Buccleuch; m. James Crofts Scott, duke of Monmouth (1649–1685, illeg. son of Charles II, king of England, and Lucy Walter), on April 20, 1663 (executed); children: Charles Scott (b. 1672), earl of Doncaster; James Scott (b. 1674), earl of Dalkeith; Henry Scott, 1st earl of Deloriane. ❖ James Crofts Scott, who always claimed his parents were married, took his wife's name upon marriage.

SCOTT, Barbara Ann (1929—). Canadian figure skater and equestrian. Name variations: Barbara Ann Scott King. Born May 9, 1929, in Ottawa, Ontario, Canada; dau. of Clyde Scott (military secretary to Canada's Minister of Defense) and Mary Scott; m. Tommy King (press agent), Sept 17, 1953. ❖ Began skating at 6; was Canadian Junior Ladies' champion (1939), Canadian Senior Women's champion (1944–48), North American champion (1945–48), European and World champion (1947–48); at 19, won Figure Skating gold medal at Olympic Games, St. Moritz, Switzerland (Feb 6, 1948); was the 1st Canadian woman to win the Lou Marsh Trophy as best Canadian athlete (1945, 1947, 1948); skated professionally (1949–54); upon retirement, began training horses and was rated among the top equestrians in US. Made an Officer of the Order of Canada (1991); inducted into International Women's Sports Hall of Fame (1997). ❖ See also Cay Moore, *She Skated Into Our Hearts* (McClelland & Stewart, 1948) and autobiography *Skate With Me* (Doubleday, 1950); and *Women in World History.*

SCOTT, Beckie (1970—). Canadian cross-country skier. Born Jan 8, 1970, in Vegreville, Alberta, Canada; m. Justin Wadsworth. ❖ Won a bronze medal for 5 km pursuit at Salt Lake City Olympics (2002) and a silver medal for Team Sprint at Torino Olympics (2006).

SCOTT, Blanche (1885–1970). American aviator. Name variations: Blanche Stuart Scott. Born in Rochester, New York, April 8, 1885; died Jan 12, 1970, in Rochester; attended Fort Edward College, New York. ❖ The 1st American woman to fly an airplane, drove from New York to San Francisco in a car (1910), only the 2nd woman to do so; took 1st solo airplane flight by a woman (1910), albeit by accident when a sudden wind lifted her training plane above the runway; made her 1st flight across the country (1912), a 69-day trip; barnstormed with a flying exhibition team (1912–16); switched careers to screenwriting and radio broadcasting (1920s); invited to fly in a US Air Force Shooting Star jet fighter (1948), became the 1st woman to fly in a jet. ❖ See also *Women in World History.*

SCOTT, Caroline Lavinia (1832–1892). *See Harrison, Caroline Scott.*

SCOTT, Charlotte Angas (1858–1931). English mathematician and educator. Born Charlotte Angas Scott on June 8, 1858, in Lincoln, England; died Nov 8, 1931, in Cambridge, England; dau. of Caleb Scott (educator and minister) and Eliza Ann Exley Scott; Girton College of Cambridge University, honors degree, 1880; University of London, BS, 1882, DSc, 1885. ❖ Lectured in math at Girton (1880–84), while studying at University of London; became the only woman of 6 faculty members at newly formed Bryn Mawr College in Pennsylvania (1886); wrote *An Introductory Account of Certain Modern Ideas in Plane Analytical Geometry* (1894), which became the standard textbook for colleges in US and Europe, and *Cartesian Plane Geometry Part I: Analytical Cones* (1907); was also editor of US version of *Arithmetic for Schools*; was the only woman to serve on board of directors of American Mathematical Society and served as its vice president (1906); retired from Bryn Mawr (1924) and returned to England (1925). ❖ See also *Women in World History.*

SCOTT, Christine Margaret (1946—). Australian politician. Born Mar 17, 1946, in Broome, Western Australia. ❖ Teacher and librarian; was a member of the Premier's Council for Women; as a member of the Australian Labor Party, elected to the Queensland Parliament for Charters Towers (2001).

SCOTT, Mrs. Clement *See Clement-Scott, Margaret.*

SCOTT, Desley Carleton (1943—). Australian politician. Born June 27, 1943, in Toowoomba, Australia. ❖ Began career as a dental nurse; as a member of the Australian Labor Party, elected to the Queensland Parliament for Woodridge (2001).

SCOTT, Elizabeth Whitworth (1898–1972). British architect. Born in England, 1898; died in England, 1972; granddau. of architect Sir Gilbert Scott; attended private school in Bournemouth, England; received degree from Architectural Association School, 1924. ❖ Designed the Shakespeare Memorial Theatre at Stratford-upon-Avon (1928), which became her claim to fame, though she also worked in Welwyn Garden City, Cheltenham and London, and designed extensions to Cambridge's Newnham College. ❖ See also *Women in World History.*

SCOTT, Esther Mae (1893–1979). African-American blues singer. Name variations: Mother Scott. Born Mar 25, 1893, in Bovina, MS; died in Washington, DC, Oct 16, 1979; had occasional schooling at Clover Valley Baptist School. ❖ Learned to play guitar at 8, then mandolin, banjo and piano; left home at 14 to join a vaudeville group, W. S. Wolcott's Rabbit Foot Minstrels; was a maid and nurse for wealthy family in Vicksburg, MS, for 27 years (1911–38); through the years, met several blues artists, including Leadbelly and Bessie Smith; for next 20 years, was maid in Baltimore, MD; moved to Washington, DC (1958) and revived performing career by joining St. Stephen and the Incarnation Episcopal Church, becoming an integral part of their singing programs; expanded performances to nightclubs, as blues and folk music made a comeback (1950s–60s), as well as festivals and civil-rights demonstrations; appeared at Smithsonian Folk Festival in Washington, DC (1976); performed on the Mall at Smithsonian Festival of American Folklife (1978), at Washington's National Cathedral, at Rutgers University, and to an audience of 72,000 in Pocono Mountains; recorded her only album, *Momma Ain't Nobody's Fool* (1971). ❖ See also *Women in World History.*

SCOTT, Evelyn (1893–1963). American novelist and poet. Name variations: Evelyn Metcalfe. Born Elsie Dunn, Jan 17, 1893, in Clarksville, TN; died 1963 in New York, NY; dau. of Maude Thomas and Seely Dunn; attended Tulane University; m. John Metcalfe (novelist), 1925; children: (with Wellman) son Creighton Scott. ❖ Became a feminist as teenager; ran away to Brazil with married man, Tulane professor Frederick Creighton Wellman (1913); to protect identity, changed her name to Evelyn Scott, while Wellman became Cyril Kay Scott; while in Brazil (1914–20), published poetry in *Dial, Egoist,* and *Poetry* magazines; lived in Greenwich Village but moved frequently, living in New Mexico, Bermuda, France, New York, and England; wrote autobiographies *Escapade* (1923) and *Background in Tennessee* (1937); published poetry collections, *Precipitations* (1920) and *The Winter Alone* (1930); novels include *The Narrow House* (1921), *Narcissus* (1922), *The Golden Door* (1925), and *The Wave* (1929).

SCOTT, Hazel (1920–1981). African-American musician, singer and actress. Born June 11, 1920, in Port-of-Spain, Trinidad; died Oct 2, 1981; dau. of a college professor and Alma Long Scott (pianist and saxophonist); attended Juilliard School of Music; m. Adam Clayton Powell Jr. (Baptist pastor and US congressional representative), 1945 (div. Oct 1956); children: Adam Clayton Powell III. ❖ Child prodigy, made debut playing the piano at age 3 in Trinidad; moved to US (1924) and, at 5, made NY debut at Town Hall; at 8, granted a 6-year scholarship to Juilliard; at 14, played piano and trumpet with mother's all-women orchestra, American Creolians, and, at 16, was featured on her own national radio program (1936–37); made Broadway debut with Count Basie Orchestra (1937), followed by *Sing Out the News* (1938), *Priorities of 1942*; appeared in top NYC clubs (1938–44), developing a showy style in performing a combination of classics and jazz music; recorded more than a dozen records; starred on "The Hazel Scott Show" (seen 3 days a week, 1950), the 1st network series hosted by a black woman; blacklisted during McCarthy era, despite denying any involvement in communist activities; lived in France and Switzerland (1962–67); films include *Something to Shout About* (1943), *I Dood It* (1943), *Tropicana* (1943), *Broadway Rhythm* (1944) and *Rhapsody in Blue* (1945). Inducted into Black Filmmakers Hall of Fame (1978). ❖ See also *Women in World History.*

SCOTT, Ivy (1886–1947). Australian-born musical-comedy and operatic star. Born 1886 in Australia; died Feb 4, 1947, in New York, NY. ❖ Made stage debut at age 5; appeared in *The Merry Widow, Robin Hood, Music in the Air, Sunny River* and *The Song of Norway.*

SCOTT, Janette (1938—). English actress. Born Thora Janette Scott, Dec 14, 1938, in Morecambe, Lancashire, England; dau. of James Scott and Dame Thora Hird (actress, b. 1911); m. Jackie Rae, 1959 (div. 1965); m. Mel Torme (singer), 1966 (div. 1977); m. William Rademaekers, 1981; children: (2nd m.) James and Daisy Torme. ❖ Made film debut as a child actress in *Went the Day Well?* (1942), followed by *2,000 Women, No Place for Jennifer* (title role), *No Highway in the Sky, The Magic Box, Now and Forever, Helen of Troy* (as Cassandra), *The Devil's Disciple* (as Judith), *School for Scoundrels, Two and Two Make Six, The Day of the Triffids* (as Karen Goodwin), *The Old Dark House, Crack in the World* and *Bikini Paradise,* among others. Alluded to in *The Rocky Horror Picture Show* lyrics: "And I really got hot/ when I saw Janette Scott/ fight a triffid that spits poison and kills."

SCOTT, Jessie Ann (1883–1959). New Zealand physician, medical officer, and prisoner of war. Born Aug 9, 1883, at Brookside, Canterbury, New Zealand; died Aug 15, 1959, at Christchurch; dau. of David Scott (farmer) and Mary (Armit) Scott; University of Edinburgh, Scotland, MB, ChB, 1909, MD, 1912. ❖ After serving as medical officer at Edinburgh Hospital and Dispensary for Women and Children, and as medical officer at London County Council, established private practice in Auckland, New Zealand (1913); joined Scottish

Women's Hospitals for Foreign Service and served in Serbia, where her unit was held captive by Austrian forces (1915–16); attached to Royal Army Medical Corps in Salonika, and served in France (1919); returned to Christchurch to work as obstetrician and gynecologist at Christchurch Hospital (1924). Received Order of St Sava, third class, by Serbian government. ❖ See also *Dictionary of New Zealand Biography* (Vol. 3).

SCOTT, Lady John (1810–1900). See Spottiswoode, Alicia Ann.

SCOTT, Lizabeth (1922—). American screen actress. Born Emma Matzo, Sept 29, 1922, in Scranton, PA. ❖ Began stage career in stock, did fashion modeling for *Harper's Bazaar,* and understudied for Tallulah Bankhead (1942) in *Skin of Our Teeth;* cast in lead role of Ivy in *You Came Along* for film debut (1945); other films, many in the film-noir genre, include *The Strange Love of Martha Ivers, Dead Reckoning, Desert Fury, I Walk Alone, The Pitfall, Easy Living, Paid in Full, The Company She Keeps, The Racket, Scared Stiff, Bad for Each Other, Loving You* and *Pulp.*

SCOTT, Margaret (1809–1873). See Gatty, Margaret.

SCOTT, Margaret (1875–1938). English golfer. Name variations: Lady Margaret Scott; Lady Hamilton Russell. Born 1875 in Wiltshire, England; died 1938; daughter of earl of Eldon; m. Lord Hamilton Russell. ❖ Won British Ladies' championship during each of the union's first 3 years (1893–95), and the fact that she was a member of the aristocracy removed much of the stigma from women playing the game; retired from competition (1895). ❖ See also *Women in World History.*

SCOTT, Margaret (1922—). English ballet dancer. Name variations: Dame Margaret Scott. Born Catherine Margaret Mary Scott, April 26, 1922, in Johannesburg, South Africa; married Derek Ashworth Denton (an Australian), 1953. ❖ Trained at Sadler's Wells School and with Marie Rambert in London, England; joined Ballet Rambert (1941), where she danced Odile in the company's one-act *Swan Lake* and The Hen in Howard's *Carnival of Animals;* also performed in *La Sylphide,* and Tudor's *Gala Performance* and *Judgment of Paris;* after touring Australia with Ballet Rambert (1947), remained there, dancing with National Theatre Ballet in Melbourne; founded the Australian Ballet School (1963) and served as its director (1963–90). Received DBE (1981) and Companion of the Order of Australia (2005).

SCOTT, Margaret Clement-. See Clement-Scott, Margaret.

SCOTT, Margaret Jane (1869–1958). See Hawthorne, Margaret Jane Scott.

SCOTT, Margaretta (1912–2005). English actress. Born Feb 13, 1912, in London, England; died April 15, 2005; dau. of Bertha Eugene and Hugh Arthur Scott (music critic); attended RADA; m. John Wooldridge (composer), 1948 (killed in car accident, 1958); children: Susan Wooldridge (actress) and Hugh Wooldridge (director). ❖ Probably best known for her portrayal of Mrs. Pumphrey on tv series "All Creatures Great and Small" (1978–90), had a career that spanned 70 years; at 14, made stage debut as Mercutio's page in *Romeo and Juliet* at the Strand; appeared as Ophelia (1931) and as Gertrude to Peter O'Toole's Hamlet (1958); was the 1st woman to appear in Shakespeare on tv (as Portia); also specialized in Oscar Wilde; helped establish Equity (1934), Britain's actors union; films include *Things to Come* (1936), *The Girl in the News* (1940), *Quiet Wedding* (1930) and *Fanny by Gaslight* (1944).

SCOTT, Martha (1914–2003). American actress. Born Martha Ellen Scott, Sept 22, 1914, in Jamesport, Missouri; died May 28, 2003, in Van Nuys, CA; dau. of Walter Scott and Letha (McKinley) Scott; University of Michigan, BA, 1934; m. Carleton Alsop (radio and film producer), Sept 16, 1940 (div. 1946); m. Mel Powell (composer, pianist), 1946 (died 1998); children: (1st m.) Scott Alsop; (2nd m.) Mary Powell Harpel and Kathleen Powell. ❖ Made Broadway debut originating the role of Emily Webb in *Our Town* (1938), one of America's oft-produced classics; reprised role in film version, earning an Oscar nomination for Best Actress (1940); other films include *The Howards of Virginia* (1940), *Cheers for Miss Bishop* (1941), *So Well Remembered* (1947), *The Desperate Hours* (1955), *The Ten Commandments* (1956), *Sayonara* (1957), *Ben-Hur* (1959), *Charlotte's Web* (1973), *Airport 1975* (1974), *The Turning Point* (1977) and *Doin' Time on Planet Earth* (1988); with others, organized the Plumstead Playhouse (1969), and served as director; appeared on a number of radio serials (1930s); was narrator and host on daytime series "Modern Romances" (1954–57) and was seen on "Omnibus," "Robert Montgomery Presents," "The F.B.I." and

"Ironside"; also had recurring role as Bob Newhart's mother on "The Bob Newhart Show." ❖ See also *Women in World History*.

SCOTT, Mary (1751–1793). British poet and feminist. Name variations: Mary Scott Taylor. Born Mary Scott, June 29, 1751, in Ilminster, Somerset, England; died June 4, 1793, in Bristol, England; dau. of John Scott (linen merchant) and Mary Russell Scott; m. John Taylor (Unitarian minister), May 7, 1788 (died 1817); children: John Edward Taylor (b. Sept 11, 1791), founded the *Manchester Guardian*. ❖ Friend of Anna Seward and supporter of equal rights for women, wrote poems and hymns; as a sequel to John Duncombe's *Feminiad*, published *The Female Advocate* (1774), in which she praised specific women writers and argued in favor of women's education; also published *The Messiah* (1788).

SCOTT, Mary Edith (1888–1979). New Zealand teacher, novelist, newspaper columnist. Name variations: Mary Edith Clarke, Marten Stuart, J. Fiat. Born Sept 23, 1888, in Waimate North, Bay of Islands, New Zealand; died July 16, 1979, at Tokoroa, New Zealand; dau. of Marsden Clarke (grazier) and Frances Emily (Stuart) Clarke; Auckland University College, MA, 1910; m. Walter Scott, 1914; children: 4. ❖ Taught English at Thames High School (early 1910s); contributed articles and stories to magazines and newspapers (1920s); wrote weekly column for Dunedin *Evening Star* for 50 years; under pseudonym Marten Stuart, published novels *Where the Apple Reddens* (1934) and *And Shadows Flee* (1935); became bestselling novelist with *Breakfast at Six* (1953), writing 30 more novels under own name until 1978; also wrote 2 thrillers with Joyce West and monograph under pen-name J. Fiat. ❖ See also autobiography *Days That Have Been* (1966) and *Dictionary of New Zealand Biography* (Vol. 4).

SCOTT, Minnie (1868–1946). See Fuller, Minnie Rutherford.

SCOTT, Mother (1893–1979). See Scott, Esther Mae.

SCOTT, Rose (1847–1925). Australian feminist. Born in Glendon, near Singleton, NSW, Australia, on Oct 15, 1847; died April 21, 1925; dau. of Sarah Anne (Rusden) Scott (linguist and scholar, died 1896) and Helenus Scott (police magistrate in Maitland); never married; children: (adopted) son of her deceased sister. ❖ Founded the Womanhood Suffrage League and became its secretary (1891); lobbied heavily for protective legislation; became president of women's committee for Prisoners' Aid Association (1896) and soon called for a separate women's prison; organized League for Political Education (1901), of which she later became president (1910); elected foundation president of Women's Political and Educational League (1902), campaigning for a widow's rights to share in husband's estates and for the removal of gender barriers in the legal profession; adamantly opposed a bill to regulate prostitution; an ardent pacifist, condemned the British for Boer War (1900), was president of Peace Society for many years, and decried Australia's involvement in WWI; retired from public life (1922); bequeathed money for establishment of Rose Scott Memorial Prize in International Law at University of Sydney. ❖ See also *Women in World History*.

SCOTT, Rosie (1948—). New Zealand novelist and short-story writer. Born 1948 in Johnsonville, Wellington, New Zealand; Victoria University, MA. ❖ Works include *Glory Days* (1987), *Queen of Love and Other Stories* (1989), *Nights With Grace* (1990), *Feral City* (1992), *Lives on Fire* (1995), *Movie Dreams* (1995) and *The Red Heart* (1999); also published play, *Say Thank You to the Lady*, that was made into film *Redheads*.

SCOTT, Ruby Payne (1912–1981). Australian radiophysicist. Name variations: Ruby Payne-Scott; Ruby Violet Hall. Born Ruby Violet Hermann, May 28, 1912, in Grafton, NSW, Australia; died May 25, 1981; dau. of Amy and Cyril Hermann (accountant); University of Sydney, BS, 1933, MS, 1936, education diploma, 1938; m. W. H. Hall, 1944; children: 1 son, 1 daughter. ❖ Australia's 1st woman radioastronomer, studied the relative intensity of spectral lines in indium and gallium; researched the use of photographic film to measure gamma radiation; investigated the effects of a magnetic field on tissue cultures, and published results (with W. H. Love) in *Nature* (1936); worked as a Cancer Research Committee fellow at University of Sydney (1932–35), as an engineer at AWA Ltd. (1939–41), and as a researcher at Commonwealth Scientific Radiophysics Division (1941–51); taught at Danebrook Church of England School in Sydney (1963–75).

SCOTT, Sarah (1723–1795). English novelist. Born Sarah Robinson, 1723, in West Layton, Hutton Magna, Yorkshire; died Nov 30, 1795,

in Catton, near Norwich; dau. of Matthew Robinson (Yorkshire landowner) and Elizabeth Drake Robinson (Cambridge heiress); sister of Elizabeth Montagu (1720–1800); m. George Lewis Scott (mathematician who served as tutor to future King George III), in 1751 or 1752 (sep. soon after); lived with Lady Barbara Montagu. ❖ Wrote 6 novels, all published anonymously, which covered such topics as female independence and clandestine marriage; with Lady Barbara Montagu (to whom she was not related), ran a community for unattached women at Bath Easton (1754–56), where single women could live while teaching poor children who otherwise lacked the means to obtain education; best-known novel, the utopian *Description of Millenium Hall* (1762), uses the backdrop of the female community for its plot; also published a biography of Gustavus I Vasa (1761), a history of the House of Mecklenburg (1762), and *Life of Théodore Agrippa d'Aubigné* (1772).

SCOTT, Sheila (1927–1988). British aviator. Name variations: Sheila Christine Scott. Born Sheila Christine Hopkins, April 27, 1927, in Worcester, Worcestershire, England; died Oct 20, 1988, in London, England; m. Rupert Bellamy, 1945 (div. 1950). ❖ Became a trainee nurse at Haslar Naval Hospital (1944), where she tended the wounded during WWII; spent a year acting with a reportory company under the stage name Sheila Scott; worked as a model (1945–59); began flying (1959) and won De Havilland Trophy (1960); set over 100 records by 1971; completed longest consecutive solo flight around world (1965); flew equator to equator over North Pole in a flight monitored by NASA (1971), the 1st pilot, male or female, to fly directly over true North Pole in a light aircraft; made many public appearances to raise money for other flights and founded British section of Ninety Nines and British Balloon and Airships Club. Made an Officer of the British Empire (OBE, 1968). ❖ See also memoirs *I Must Fly* (1968), *On Top of the World* (1973) and *Barefoot in the Sky* (1974).

SCOTT, Sherry (c. 1948—). American musician. Name variations: Earth, Wind & Fire. Born c. 1948 in Chicago, IL. ❖ Served as 1st female vocalist for Earth, Wind & Fire (1970–72); wrote and sang lead vocal for group's 1st major hit "I Think About Loving You"; received Afrique "Bob Marley" Music Award for cultural music growth in greater Chicago (1999); performed concerts for Michigan Council for Arts and Cultural Affairs.

SCOTT, Shirley (1934–2002). African-American jazz organist. Born 1934 in Philadelphia, PA; died Mar 10, 2002, in Philadelphia, PA; m. Stanley Turrentine (musician), 1960; children: Everett Yancey; Thomas, Lisa, Pamela and Nicole Turrentine. ❖ Known as Queen of the Organ, merged bebop, gospel and the blues; recorded more than 50 albums for Prestige and Impulse labels, often with saxophonists Eddie Davis and Stanley Turrentine; taught jazz history at Cheyney University.

SCOTT-BROWN, Denise (1931—). American architect. Name variations: Denise Scott Brown. Born 1931 in Nkana, Zambia; m. Robert Scott-Brown; m. Robert Venturi, 1967. ❖ Studied at University of Witwatersrand, South Africa, Architectural Association, London, and University of Pennsylvania; taught urban planning at various institutions in US and developed studio classes at Yale that combined architecture, media studies, and social sciences; with Venturi and Steven Izenour, wrote *Learning from Las Vegas* (1972); joined Venturi's architectural firm (1967) and with colleagues developed plans for major urban centers and institutions; projects include Denver Civic Center Cultural Complex.

SCOTT-MAXWELL, Florida (1883–1979). American-born writer, suffragist and psychologist. Name variations: Florida Scott Maxwell; Florida Pier. Born Florida Morse, Sept 24, 1883, in Florida; died Mar 6, 1979, in Devonshire, England; dau. of Charles Morse and Beth White Pier; m. John Maxwell Scott-Maxwell, 1911 (div. 1929); children: Stephen, Peter, Denis, and Hilary Scott-Maxwell Henderson. ❖ Frequently quoted, wrote for women's magazines and newspapers; worked for women's suffrage before beginning practice in Jungian analysis; wrote *The Flash Point* (1914), (with S. Botcharsky) *The Kinsmen Knew How to Die* (1931), *Many Women* (1933), *Towards Relationship* (1939), *I Said to Myself* (1949), *Women and Sometimes Men* (1957) and *The Measure of My Days* (1968).

SCOTT-POMALES, Catherine. Jamaican runner. Name variations: Catherine Pomales; Catherine Scott. Born Catherine Pomales in Jamaica; attended Central State in Ohio, 1994–96. ❖ Won a silver medal for 4 x 400-meter relay at Sydney Olympics (2000).

SCOTTO, Renata (1933—). Italian soprano. Born Feb 24, 1933, in Savona, Italy; studied with Emilio Ghirardini, Merlini, and Mercedes

Llopart; m. Lorenzo Anselmi, June 2, 1960; children: Laura (b. 1969) and Filippo (b. 1972). ❖ As fine an actress as she was a vocalist, debuted as Violetta at the Teatro Nuovo in Milan (1952); sang at La Scala in *La Wally* (1953); successfully replaced Maria Callas as Amina in Edinburgh (1957), which brought her international fame; debuted in Chicago (1960); made Metropolitan Opera debut as Cio-Cio-San in *Madama Butterfly* (1965) and remained there as a leading soprano (1965–87); won wide recognition in a "Live from Lincoln Center" broadcast (1977); moved from lyric to dramatic roles, illuminating the characters of Gioconda, Norma, and Lady Macbeth. ❖ See also O. Roca, *Scotto: More Than a Diva* (1986).

SCOVELL, E. J. (1907–1999). British poet. Born Edith Joy Scovell, April 9, 1907, in West Yorkshire, England; died 1999; dau. of Canon F. G. Scovell; m. Charles Sutherland Elton (ecologist), 1937; children: 2. ❖ Received BA from Somerville College, Oxford, before moving to London and contributing reviews to feminist weekly, *Time and Tide*; wrote *Shades of Chrysanthemums and Other Poems* (1944), *The Midsummer Madness* (1946), *The River Steamer* (1956), *The Space Between* (1982), *Listening to Collared Doves* (1986) and *Selected Poems* (1991). Won Cholmondeley award for *Collected Poems* (1988).

SCRIABIN, Vera (1875–1920). Russian pianist. Born Vera Ivanovna Isakovich in Moscow, 1875; died 1920; studied at Moscow and St. Petersburg conservatories; married Alexander Scriabin, 1897; children. ❖ With her talent as a pianist, impressed Moscow musical circles, including the composer Alexander Scriabin; married him and championed his music, even after he abandoned her for Tatiana Schloezer, one of his former piano students; taught at the Moscow and St. Petersburg conservatories, and traveled to Paris for the premiere performance of her estranged husband's Third Symphony; refused to divorce him and continued to play all-Scriabin recitals.

SCRIBONIA (c. 75 BCE–after 16 CE). Roman noblewoman. Name variations: Sempronia. Born c. 75 BCE; died after 16 CE; younger sister of L. Scribonius Libo; m. (probably) Cn. Lentulus Marcellinus (consul), in 56 BCE; m. Cornelius Scipio; m. Octavian (63 BCE–14 CE), who after their marriage became Augustus Caesar, emperor of Rome (r. 27 BCE–14 CE), in 40 BCE; children: (2nd m.) Cornelia (who m. Paullus Aemilius Lepidus, a consul in 34 BCE); (3rd m.) Julia (39 BCE–14 CE). ❖ In a marriage that was purely political, wed 3rd husband Octavian, who long after their marriage became Augustus Caesar (40 BCE); soon after giving birth to Julia, was divorced by Octavian so he could quickly marry Livia Drusilla; also was forced to part with Julia, who would be raised with strictness by Augustus and Livia; when Julia fell into disgrace and was exiled (2 BCE), voluntarily followed her into exile, 1st to Pandateria and then to Rhegium (4 CE). ❖ See also *Women in World History*.

SCRIPPS, Ellen Browning (1836–1932). English-born American newspaper publisher and philanthropist. Born Oct 18, 1836, in London, England; died Aug 3, 1932, in La Jolla, California; dau. of James Mogg Scripps and Ellen Mary Scripps; aunt of Ellen Scripps Booth; graduate of Knox College, 1859; never married; no children. ❖ Began journalism career (1867), assisting older brother James E. Scripps in his management of a Detroit newspaper; with the founding of his *Detroit Evening News* (1873), served as proofreader, copyreader, front-page feature writer, and wrote the column, "Matters and Things"; provided financial backing for half-brother Edward Scripps to begin a newspaper, the *Penny Press*, in Cleveland, Ohio (1878); helped Edward lay the basis for what would become the Scripps-Howard conglomerate of papers; eventually, had holdings in 16 daily newspapers across the country; moved to California where her generosity made her a major philanthropic figure; with brother Edward, spearheaded the establishment of Marine Biological Association of San Diego, which later became the Scripps Institution of Oceanography; also funded the Scripps Memorial Hospital in her new hometown of La Jolla, later known as the Scripps Clinic and Research Foundation; helped to found Scripps College for Women (1926); also politically active, opposed the wave of deportations of alleged communist agitators (1919–20) and demanded freedom for political prisoners as a member of the Amnesty League; also opposed the death penalty. ❖ See also *Women in World History*.

SCRIVENER, Christiane (1925—). French economist and politician. Born Sept 1, 1925; graduate of Lycée de Grenoble and Harvard Business School; m. Pierre Scrivener, 1944; children: 1 son (died). ❖ Served as the director of various business and governmental agencies dedicated to international technical cooperation (1958–76); as a member of the Union for French Democracy (UFD), became directly involved in politics when she

started a 2-year term as junior minister for consumer affairs (1976); served as a member of the European Parliament (1979–88); named a commissioner of the European Community (EC, 1989); stepped down as commissioner (1995) and became a mediator with the Society General (1996). Named an officer of the Legion of Honor (1995).

SCRIVENS, Jean (1935—). English runner. Born Oct 15, 1935, in UK. ❖ Won a silver medal for 4 x 100-meter relay at Melbourne Olympics (1956).

SCUDAMORE, Margaret (1884–1958). English actress. Born Nov 13, 1884, in Portsmouth, England; died Oct 5, 1958, in London, England; dau. of F. A. Scudamore (playwright); m. Roy Redgrave (died); children: Michael Redgrave (actor); grandchildren: Corin, Lynn, and Vanessa Redgrave (all actors). ❖ Made West End debut as Martha Hadden in *The Fire Screen* (1912); subsequently appeared as Lady Bracknell in *The Importance of Being Earnest*, Catherine Petkoff in *Arms and the Man*, Lady Britomart Undershaft in *Major Barbara*, Mrs. Markham in *The Visitor*, and Mrs. Armitage in *Robert's Wife*, among others; films include *Arms and the Man* and *A Canterbury Tale*.

SCUDDER, Ida (1870–1960). American physician and missionary. Born Ida Sophia Scudder, Dec 9, 1870, in Ranipet, Madras Presidency, India; died in Kodaikanal, India, May 24, 1960; dau. of John Scudder II (medical missionary) and Sophia Weld Scudder (missionary); attended Northfield Seminary in Massachusetts and Woman's Medical College of Pennsylvania; Cornell Medical College, MD, 1899; never married; lived with Gertrude Dodd, from 1916 until Dodd's death in 1944. ❖ Founder of the Christian Medical College and Hospital in Vellore, South India, began a lifelong service as a medical missionary in Vellore (1900); opened the Mary Taber Schell Hospital (1902), which also provided a central locale for much-needed medical care and for the training of nurses; while continuing to make medical rounds in the outlying rural areas, would remain the only surgeon at the hospital for 22 years; with Gertrude Dodd, founded the Union Mission Medical School for Women in Vellore (1918), which provided formal and certified medical education. ❖ See also Dorothy Clarke Wilson, *Dr. Ida: The Story of Dr. Ida Scudder of Vellore* (McGraw-Hill, 1959); Mary Pauline Jeffery, *Ida S. Scudder of Vellore: The Life Story of Ida Sophia Scudder* (Wesley, 1951); and *Women in World History*.

SCUDDER, Janet (1869–1940). American sculptor. Name variations: Netta Deweze Frazee Scudder. Born Netta Deweze Frazee Scudder, Oct 27, 1869, in Terre Haute, Indiana; died June 9, 1940, in Rockport, Massachusetts; dau. of William Hollingshead Scudder (confectioner) and Mary (Sparks) Scudder; studied drawing at Rose Polytechnic Institute and Colarossi Academy; studied anatomy, drawing, and modeling at Cincinnati Academy of Art. ❖ Creator of garden sculptures and fountains that became highly popular in US, was hired by Lorado Taft to help with sculptures for a display in front of Horticulture Building for the World's Columbian Exposition of 1893; was then commissioned to create her own statues for the exposition's Illinois and Indiana buildings; traveled to Paris (1893) and became an assistant to Frederick MacMonnies; returning to NY (1894), designed the NY Bar Association's seal; decided to create decorative sculptures, lighthearted in nature; in Paris, used a street urchin as the model for one of her most famous works, *Frog Fountain* (1901); had an honorable mention in Paris Salon (1911) for her *Young Diana*; had a solo exhibition in NY (1913); concerned with women's rights, participated in the art committee of National American Woman Suffrage Association (NAWSA); exhibited 10 pieces at Panama-Pacific Exposition in San Francisco (1915), where she won a silver medal; developed an interest in painting which led to a NY exhibition (1933). Made a Chevalier of the Legion of Honor by French government (1925). ❖ See also autobiography *Modeling My Life* (1925); and *Women in World History*.

SCUDDER, Laura Clough (1881–1959). American entrepreneur. Born Laura Emma Clough, 1881; died 1959 in La Habra, CA; m. Charles Scudder. ❖ Called the Potato Chip Queen, was marketing Mayflower Potato Chips in southern California and Blue Bird Potato Chips in northern California (potato chip manufacturing was regional, as chips did not travel well and were not mass produced); developed small, sealable wax paper bags for her potato chips in Monterey Park, CA (1926) and built an empire.

SCUDDER, Vida (1861–1954). American educator and social reformer. Name variations: Vida Dutton Scudder. Born Julia Davida Scudder, Dec 15, 1861, in Madura, India; died Oct 9, 1954, in Wellesley, Massachusetts; dau. of David Coit Scudder (Congregationalist missionary) and Harriet Louisa (Dutton) Scudder; Smith College, AB, 1884; graduate work, Oxford University, 1884–85; Smith College, AM, 1889; lived with Florence Converse (1871–1967, writer), from 1919 to 1954; no children. ❖ Novelist, scholar, teacher, settlement-house pioneer, friend of labor, pacifist, and Christian Socialist, was an instructor (1887–92), assistant professor (1892–1910), full professor (1910–28), at Wellesley College; founded College Settlements Association (1889); became a member for life of Society for the Companions of the Holy Cross (1889); founded Denison House (1892); was active in Boston Women's Trade Union (1903–12); was a founding member, Episcopal Church Socialist League (1911); founded Church League for Industrial Democracy (1919); involved with Fellowship of Reconciliation and Women's International League for Peace and Freedom (1920s–30s); writings include *The Life of the Spirit in the Modern English Poets* (1895), *Social Ideals in English Letters* (1898), *A Listener in Babel* (1903), *The Disciple of a Saint* (1907), *Socialism and Character* (1912) and *The Franciscan Adventure* (1931); also contributed to *Atlantic Monthly* and several religious periodicals. ❖ See also memoir *On Journey* (Dutton, 1937); Sister Catherine Theresa Corcoran, *Vida Dutton Scudder: The Progressive Years* (UMI, 1974); and *Women in World History.*

SCUDÉRY, Madeleine de (1607–1701). French novelist and poet. Name variations: Madeleine de Scudery or Scuderi. Born Nov 15, 1607, in Le Hâvre, France; died June 2, 1701, in Paris; dau. of Georges de Scudéry (army captain) and Madeleine de Martel de Goutimesnil; sister of Georges de Scudéry (soldier and playwright who m. Marie-Madeleine du Moncel de Montinvall de Scudéry); never married; no children. ❖ Perhaps the most widely read novelist of 17th-century France, who was renowned for her classical learning and sharp wit, even though her works were usually published under her brother's name, was orphaned (1613); became a member of Hôtel de Rambouillet (1637); had 1st novel published, *Ibrahim, ou l'Illustre Bassa* (*Ibrahim, or the Illustrious Bassa*, 1641), which was an immediate success with the French reading public, as all of her novels would be; wrote 1st nonfiction piece, *Les Femmes illustres ou les harangues héroiques* (*Illustrious Women or Heroic Speeches*, 1642), her longest contribution to the ongoing intellectual debates on the nature and proper roles of women; published 1st vol. of her masterpiece, the bestseller *Artamène, ou Le Grand Cyrus* (*Artamenes, or the Grand Cyrus*, 1649), while the remaining 9 vols. appeared between 1650 and 1653; began Samedi salon (1653); as one of the leading hostesses of the French salons, was a founding member of the aristocratic movement known as preciosity; counted among her friends members of Europe's highest elite, including Louis XIV of France, his prime minister Cardinal Mazarin, and Queen Christina of Sweden; published 1st vol. of her most feminist novel, *Clélie, Histoire romaine* (*Clelia, a Romance*, 1654); suffered onset of deafness (1666); awarded prize by Académie Française (1671) for her *Discours de la Gloire* (*Discourse on Glory*); elected to Academy of the Ricovrati of Padua, Italy (1684); had last work published, *Entretiens de Morale* (*Treatise on Morality*, 1692). ❖ See also Nicole Aronson, *Mademoiselle de Scudéry* (trans. by Stuart R. Aronson, Twayne, 1978); Dorothy McDougall, *Madeleine de Scudéry, Her Romantic Life and Death* (Methuen, 1938); and *Women in World History.*

SCUDÉRY, Marie-Madeleine du Moncel de Montinvall de (1627–1711). French writer. Name variations: Marie-Madeleine de Scudéry. Born 1627; died 1711; m. Georges de Scudéry (writer and brother of Madeleine de Scudéry), in 1654. ❖ Became one of the *précieux*, and assisted husband with the novel *Almahide, ou l'esclave reine* (Almahida, or The Slave Queen, 1661–63); now considered a better writer than husband, is known primarily for her letters, many of which extolled friendship. ❖ See also *Women in World History.*

SCULLIN, Sarah (1880–1962). Australian prime-ministerial wife. Born Sarah Maria McNamara, 1880, in Ballarat, Victoria, Australia; died May 31, 1962, in Kew, Melbourne, Australia; m. James Scullin (prime minister of Australia, 1929–32), Nov 11, 1907; children: none. ❖ Strongly interested in politics, sometimes filled in for her ailing husband, in particular making arrangements for a crucial Cabinet meeting, before the two left for London for the Imperial Conference (1930).

SCURRY, Briana (1971—). African-American soccer player. Born Briana Collette Scurry, Sept 7, 1971, in Minneapolis, MN; graduate of University of Massachusetts, 1995. ❖ Goalkeeper; at World Cup, won a team gold medal (1991, 1999) and a bronze medal (1995); won a team gold medal at Atlanta Olympics (1996) and a team silver at Sydney Olympics (2000); was a founding member of the Women's United Soccer Association (WUSA); signed with the Atlanta Beat (2001); won

a team gold medal at Athens Olympics (2004); was also an All-State basketball player. ❖ See also Jere Longman *The Girls of Summer* (HarperCollins, 2000).

SCUTT, Michelle (1960—). *See Probert, Michelle.*

SEACOLE, Mary Jane (c. 1805–1881). Jamaican writer and physician. Name variations: Mrs. Seacole; Mother Seacole; Aunty Seacole. Born Mary Jane Grant sometime between 1805 and 1810 in Kingston, Jamaica; died, possibly in Jamaica, May 14, 1881; dau. of a Scottish soldier father and a free black mother; received no formal education; m. Edwin Horatio Seacole (English merchant), Nov 10, 1836; no children. ❖ Adventurer, autobiographer and doctor, whose exploits led her from a boarding house in Jamaica to the battlefields of the Crimean War, was widowed (c. 1837); inherited lodging house from mother (1840s); began to rebuild lodging house after fire (1843); assisted doctor during a cholera outbreak (1850); lived and worked in Panama (early 1850s); returned to Jamaica (1853); nursed numerous patients in the yellow fever epidemic (1853); traveled to England after outbreak of the Crimean War (1854); set up her "British Hotel" in Balaclava (winter 1855); returned to England at war's end (1856); published *Wonderful Adventures of Mrs. Seacole in Many Lands* (1857), which may be the only record of the life and character of a Jamaican woman in the 19th century; cultivated a friendship with the Princess of Wales (1870s); born black and female in the 19th century, challenged the middle-class conventions of her day, living independently while she pursued her various careers. ❖ See also Alexander and Dewjee, eds. *Wonderful Adventures of Mrs. Seacole in Many Lands* (Falling Wall, 1984); and *Women in World History.*

SEAGER, Esther (c. 1835–1911). New Zealand prison matron and asylum matron. Name variations: Esther Coster. Born Esther Coster, c. 1835 (baptized, Dec 6, 1835), in Gloucestershire, England; died Mar 16, 1911, in Christchurch, New Zealand; dau. of Thomas Coster (farmer) and Miriam (Curtis) Coster; m. Edward William Seager, 1854; children: 12. ❖ Appointed matron at Lyttelton jail (1862–1863), then Canterbury Asylum (1863–1887). ❖ See also *Dictionary of New Zealand Biography* (Vol. 1).

SEAMAN, Elizabeth Cochrane (1864–1922). American journalist. Name variations: Elizabeth Cochrane; (pseudonym) Nellie Bly. Born Elizabeth Jane Cochran (later changed to Cochrane), May 5, 1864, at Cochran's Mills, Pennsylvania; died Jan 27, 1922, in New York, NY; dau. of Michael Cochran (mill owner) and Mary Jane (Kennedy) Cummings Cochran; attended Indiana State Normal School, 1879; m. Robert Livingston Seaman, April 5, 1895. ❖ Pioneering investigative reporter who went around the world in 72 days, also managed a large manufacturing business, was an active feminist and acquainted with most of the prominent personalities of her day; worked as a reporter for the *Pittsburg Dispatch* (1885–87); was a reporter for *The New York World* (1887–96), for which she spent 10 days disguised as a patient at Blackwell's Island Insane Asylum for Women, then published her experiences in a series called "Inside the Madhouse"; assumed other disguises: a maid to investigate unethical employment agencies and an unwed mother to uncover agencies that bought and sold infants, among others; during WWI, was the 1st woman and one of the 1st foreigners to visit the war zone between Serbia and Austria-Hungary; served as reporter and columnist for *New York Journal* (1912–22); writings include *Six Months in Mexico* (1888), *The Central Park Mystery* (1888) and *Nellie Bly's Book: Around the World in Seventy-two Days* (1890). ❖ See also Brooke Kroeger, *Nellie Bly: Daredevil, Reporter, Feminist* (Times, 1994); Mignon Rittenhouse, *The Amazing Nellie Bly* (Books for Libraries, 1956); and *Women in World History.*

SEARLE, Edith (1863–1931). *See Grossmann, Edith Searle.*

SEARS, Eleanora (1881–1968). American sportswoman. Born Eleanora Randolph Sears, Sept 28, 1881, in Boston, MA; died Mar 26, 1968, in Palm Beach, FL; only daughter of Frederick Richard Sears (heir to shipping fortune) and Eleanora Randolph (Coolidge) Sears (great-granddau. of Thomas and Martha Jefferson); never married; no children. ❖ Won national doubles tennis championship 4 times (1911, 1915, 1916, 1917); was one of the founders of US Women's Squash Racquets Association (1928); sponsored US Olympic figure-skating team and equestrian team; an accomplished equestrian, shocked society by riding in a men's riding habit, instead of a skirt, and astride, instead of sidesaddle; reputedly won 240 trophies in golf, tennis, squash, field hockey, horse racing, swimming, and distance walking. ❖ See also *Women in World History.*

SEARS, Mary (1905–1997). American oceanographer. Born July 18, 1905, in Wayland, Massachusetts; died Sept 2, 1997, in Woods Hole, Massachusetts; attended the Winsor School in Boston; Radcliffe College, BS, 1927, MS, 1929; never married; no children. ❖ One of the foremost American oceanographers of 20th century, began career at a time when women were barred from sailing on research and Navy vessels; became one of the 1st staff research assistants at Woods Hole Oceanographic Institute in Cape Cod (1932); worked as a research assistant at Harvard (1933–49) and instructor at Wellesley (1938–43), spending summers working at Woods Hole before 1940, when she received a year-round position there as a staff planktonologist; during WWII, was commissioned a lieutenant j.g. in the WAVES (1943), where she organized an oceanographic unit that helped American submarines avoid detection; helped found the journals *Progress in Oceanography* and *Deep-Sea Research,* the latter of which she served as editor (1953–74); also edited *Oceanography* (1961) and, with Daniel Merriman, *Oceanography: The Past* (1980), considered benchmarks in the field; was chair of 1st International Congress on Oceanography (1959); retired from Naval Reserve as a commander and became a senior scientist in biology department at Woods Hole (1963), then scientist emeritus (1978). Honored with the 1st Navy oceanographic ship to be named after a woman, the USNS *Mary Sears.* ❖ See also *Women in World History.*

SEARS, Mary (1939—). American swimmer. Name variations: Mary Jane Sears. Born May 10, 1939, in US. ❖ Won a bronze medal at Melbourne Olympics in the 100-meter butterfly (1956).

SEARS, Zelda (1873–1935). American actress and screenwriter. Born Jan 21, 1873, in Brockway, Michigan; died Feb 19, 1935, in Hollywood, CA; dau. of Justin Paldi and Roxa (Tyler) Paldi; m. Herbert E. Sears; m. L. C. Wiswell. ❖ Made NY debut in *Woman and Wine* (1900), then had a huge success as Mrs. Brown in *Lover's Lane* (1901); also appeared in *Glad of It, The Coronet of a Duchess, Cousin Billy, The Truth, Girls, The Blue Mouse* and *Standing Pat,* among others; wrote scenarios for Cecil B. De Mille (1925–27) and MGM (1928–34), including dialogue for *Susan Lenox (Her Fall and Rise)* and the adaptation for *Tugboat Annie.*

SEASTRAND, Andrea (1941—). American politician. Born Aug 5, 1941, in Chicago, IL; DePaul University, BA, 1963; m. Eric Seastrand (California assemblyman, 1982–90), c. 1964 (died 1990); children: 2. ❖ Was an elementary school teacher; served as president of California Federation of Republican Women; was a member of California State Assembly (1990–94), and assistant minority leader; elected as a Republican for California to US House of Representatives (1995); served on the Committee on Science and the Transportation Infrastructure Committee; lost bid for reelection (1997); was executive director of California Space & Technology Alliance (1997–2001).

SEATON, Anna (1964—). American rower. Name variations: Anna Seaton Huntington. Born Feb 12, 1964; attended Harvard University; Columbia University, MA in journalism; m. Stuart Huntington (journalist). ❖ At Barcelona Olympics, won a bronze medal in coxless pairs (1992); during 9-year rowing career, won 14 national championships and 4 World championship silver medals; was a member of the crew of America3 which competed for the America's Cup (1995), resulting in her book, *Making Waves* (1996).

SEAXBURH (c. 627–673). *See Sexburga.*

SEBA (fl. 10th c. BCE). *See Sheba, queen of.*

SEBASTIAN, Dorothy (1903–1957). American actress. Born Dorothy Sabiston, April 26, 1903, in Birmingham, AL; died April 8, 1957, in Woodland Hills, CA; m. William Boyd (cowboy star as Hopalong Cassidy), 1931 (div. 1935); m. Herman Shapiro. ❖ Made film debut in *Sackcloth and Scarlet* (1925); other films include *The Single Standard, Our Dancing Daughters, Spite Marriage* and *They Never Came Back*; had long-running affair with Buster Keaton (1929–35).

SEBASTIANI, Sylvia (1916–2003). American business executive. Born Sylvia Scarafoni, May 10, 1916, in Cordelia, CA; died Nov 30, 2003, in Sonoma, CA; dau. of Italian immigrants; m. August Sebastiani (winemaker), 1936; children: Sam and Don Sebastiani; Mary Ann Cuneo. ❖ Following death of husband, inherited Sebastiani Vineyards (1980), one of America's most prominent wineries; became CEO, with son Sam as president; after Sam embarked on a costly plan to focus on higher-quality wines, replaced him with her younger son Don (1986).

SEBBAR, Leila (1941—). Algerian novelist. Born Nov 19, 1941, in Aflou, Algeria; dau. of Algerian father and French mother. ❖ Moved to Paris at 17; works, which often focus on immigrant Algerian women in France, include *J'etais enfant en Algerie* (1962), *Fatima ou les Algériennes au square* (1981), *Shérazade* (1982), *Parle, mon fils, parle à ta mère* (1984), *Les Carnets de Shérazade* (1985), and *Je ne parle pas la langue de mon père* (2003).

SEBEK-NEFERU or SEBEKNEFERU (fl. 1680–1674 BCE). *See Sobekneferu.*

SEBERG, Jean (1938–1979). American-born actress. Born Nov 13, 1938, in Marshalltown, Iowa; thought to have died Aug 31, 1979, in Paris, France, ruled a suicide; m. François Moreuil (Paris attorney and filmmaker), 1958 (div. 1960); m. Romain Gary (novelist), 1962 (div. 1970); m. Dennis Berry (film director), 1972 (sep. 1978); m. Ahmed Hasni, May 1979; no children. ❖ Star of the French New Wave, soared to fame at age 17 when Otto Preminger selected her from thousands to play title role in film *Saint Joan* (1957), which was shot in France; also appeared in his *Bonjour Tristesse* (1958); in Hollywood, had inconsequential roles in several films, including *The Mouse That Roared* (1959) and *Let No Man Write My Epitaph* (1960); returned to France to star opposite Jean-Paul Belmondo in *Breathless* (1960); was featured in a series of films in which she often recreated the same corruptible innocent that had won over audiences in *Breathless*; turned in most solid performance in *Lilith* (1964); suffered a miscarriage that led to a nervous breakdown; was also harassed by the FBI and other governmental agencies during 1960s for her support of the Black Panthers; other films include *L'Amant de Cinq Jours (The Five Day Lover,* 1961), *Les Grandes Personnes (Time Out for Love,* 1961), *In the French Style* (1963), *Moment to Moment* (1966), *A Fine Madness* (1966), *Paint Your Wagon* (1969), *Airport* (1970), *Le Chat et la Souris (Cat and Mouse,* 1974), *Le Grand Délire* (1975) and *Die Wildente (The Wild Duck,* 1976). ❖ See also *Women in World History.*

SECORD, Laura (1775–1868). Canadian patriot. Born Sept 13, 1775, in Great Barrington, Massachusetts; died Oct 17, 1868, at Chippawa (Niagara Falls), Ontario, Canada; dau. of Thomas Ingersoll and Elizabeth (Dewey) Ingersoll; m. James Secord, 1797; children: Charles, Mary, Charlotte, Harriet, Appolonia, Laura, Hannah. ❖ Canadian hero was born in US but moved to Canada with parents (1795); retrieved husband from battlefield after he was wounded at Battle of Queenston Heights; walked 20 miles to warn British and Canadian troops of impending attack (1813), which prevented American domination of the Niagara peninsula and eventually paved the way for a peace settlement in 1814; remained unrewarded and unrecognized for over 20 years after her heroic deed; received payment from Prince Edward Albert (1860) as recognition for her contribution to the war effort. Monument was erected on Queenston Heights by the federal government of Canada (1910); provincial government of Ontario commissioned a painting of her that was hung in Parliament buildings in Toronto (1905). ❖ See also Ruth McKenzie, *Laura Secord: The Legend and the Lady* (McClelland & Stewart, 1971); Emma Currie, *The Story of Laura Secord and Canadian Reminiscences* (St. Catharines, 1913); and *Women in World History.*

SEDA, Dori (1951–1988). American comic-strip artist. Born in 1951; died in 1988 of alcoholism. ❖ Was a frequent contributor to *Wimmen's Comix*; works also appeared in *Cannibal Romance, Lonely Nights, Prime Cut, Yellow Silk, Rip Off, Sexy Stories From the World's Religions, San Francisco Comic Book, Weirdo* and *Viper.*

SEDAKOVA, Olga (c. 1972—). Russian synchronized swimmer. Born c. 1972 in Moscow, Russia; lives in Switzerland. ❖ Won World Cup (1997); was triple World champion (solo, duet, and team, 1998); won 11 European titles.

SEDDON, Elizabeth May (1880–1960). *See Gilmer, Elizabeth May.*

SEDDON, Margaret (1872–1968). American stage and screen actress. Name variations: Margaret Sedden; Marguerite Sidden. Born Marguerite H. W. Sloan, Nov 18, 1872, in Washington, DC; died April 17, 1968, in Philadelphia, PA. ❖ Had vaudeville act with Margaret McWade as the Pixilated Sisters; made film debut in *The Dawn of a Tomorrow* (1915); continued in films for 60 years, including *The Bank Dick* and *The Meanest Man in Town*; best remembered for role in *Mister Deeds Goes to Town* (1939).

SEDDON, Rhea (1947—). American astronaut. Born Margaret Rhea Seddon in Murfreesboro, Tennessee, Nov 8, 1947; served a surgical internship and 3 years of general surgery residency in Memphis, Tennessee; did clinical research into the effects of radiation therapy on nutrition in cancer patients. ❖ Out of the original group of 6 women astronaut trainees, was the 1st to achieve the full rank of astronaut and the

1st to be selected for the space-shuttle program (1979); before initial space mission, worked on orbiter and payload software, functioned as launch and landing rescue helicopter physician, and as technical assistant to the director of Flight Crew Operations; boarded *Discovery* shuttle for a 168-hour mission (April 12, 1985), which, among other things, made an unscheduled attempt to repair a malfunctioning satellite; had next flight on Spacelab Life Sciences (SLS-1) mission on board *Columbia* (June 5, 1991), a 9-day mission that explored microgravitational pull on humans and animals.

SEDGWICK, Anne Douglas (1873–1935). American-born novelist. Name variations: Anne de Selincourt or Sélincourt; Anne De Sélincourt. Born Mar 28, 1873, in Englewood, New Jersey; died in Hampstead, England, July 19, 1935; dau. of George Stanley Sedgwick (attorney) and Mary (Douglas) Sedgwick; studied painting in Paris for 5 years; m. Basil De Sélincourt (essayist and biographer), Dec 11, 1908. ❖ At 9, moved with family to London; at father's urging, published *The Dull Miss Archinard* (1898), which proved to be a success; eventually produced 20 books, the vast majority of which were fictional and often contrasted the traits of the Americans, the English, and the French; published *The Little French Girl* (1924), which became a bestseller in US; other books include *The Confounding of Camelia* (1899), *Anabel Channice* (1908), *Franklin Winslow Kane* (1910), *Tante* (1911), *The Third Window* (1920), *Adrienne Toner* (1922), *The Old Countess* (1927), *Dark Hester* (1929) and *Philippa* (1930). Inducted into US National Institute of Arts and Letters (1931). ❖ See also *Portrait in Letters* (edited by Basil De Sélincourt, 1936); and *Women in World History*.

SEDGWICK, Catharine (1789–1867). American writer. Born Catharine Maria Sedgwick in Stockbridge, Massachusetts, Dec 28, 1789; died near Roxbury, Massachusetts, July 31, 1867; dau. of Theodore Sedgwick (US senator, speaker in US House of Representatives) and Pamela (Dwight) Sedgwick; never married; no children. ❖ Writer of popular works in early 19th century, was reluctantly induced by her 4 brothers to expand and publish her novel, *A New England Tale*, which she did anonymously to much success (1822); published 2-volume novel *Redwood* (1827), which was followed by *Hope Leslie* (1827), *Clarence, a Tale of our Own Times* (1830), *Le Bossu* (1832), *The Linwoods, or Sixty Years Since in America* (1835), *The Poor Rich Man, and the Rich Poor Man* (1836), *Live and Let Live* (1838) and *Letters from Abroad to Kindred at Home* (1840); also produced juvenile tales. ❖ See also *Women in World History*.

SEDGWICK, Edie (1943–1971). American screen actress. Born Edith Minturn Sedgwick, April 20, 1943, in Santa Barbara, CA; died Nov 16, 1971, apparently of barbiturate overdose, in Santa Barbara; cousin of actress Kyra Sedgwick; m. Michael B. Post, 1971. ❖ Star of Andy Warhol films (1960s), including *Vinyl, Space, Poor Little Rich Girl, Restaurant, Kitchen, Beauty II,* and the "Afternoon" segment in *Chelsea Girls*; other films include *Superartist* and *Ciao Manhattan*. ❖ See also Jean Stein, *Edie: An American Biography* (1982); (film) *Girl on Fire: The Edie Sedgwick Story* (2002).

SEDGWICK, Josie (1898–1973). American vaudevillian and silent-film actress. Name variations: Josephine Sedgwick. Born Josephine Sedgwick, Mar 13, 1898, in Galveston, TX; died April 30, 1973, in Santa Monica, CA; dau. of Edward Sedgwick and Josephine Walker (both stage actors); sister of Eileen Sedgwick (actress) and Edward Sedgwick (director); m. Justin H. McCloskey. ❖ Appeared in vaudeville with parents, brother and sister as "The Five Sedgwicks"; played the lead in many silent-films, including *The Man above the Law, Hell's End, Wild Life, The Lone Hand, Western Hearts, The Sunset Trail, The Outlaw's Daughter* and *Michael O'Halloran*.

SEDLACKOVA, Jaroslava (1946—). Czech gymnast. Born June 21, 1946. ❖ At Tokyo Olympics, won a silver medal in team all-around (1964).

SEDLEY, Catharine (1657–1717). Countess of Dorchester. Name variations: Katherine Sedley; Baroness of Darlington. Born 1657; died 1717; only child of Sir Charles Sedley (c. 1639–1701, playwright and member of Parliament); associated with James II (1633–1701), king of England (r. 1685–1689); m. Sir David Colyear, 2nd baronet, in 1696; children: (with James II) Katherine Darnley (c. 1680–1743, who m. James, earl of Anglesey, and was associated with John Sheffield, duke of Buckingham); James Darnley (b. 1684); Charles Darnley. ❖ As mistress to the duke of York (later James II), had 3 children; was created baroness of Darlington and countess of Dorchester (1686). ❖ See also *Women in World History*.

SEDOVA, Julia (1880–1969). Russian-French ballet dancer and teacher. Born Mar 21, 1880, in St. Petersburg, Russia; died 1969 in Cannes, France. ❖ Joined Maryinsky Theater's ballet (1898), where she was featured in works by Petipa and Lev Ivanov; danced in Mikhail Mordkin's touring company, All Star Imperial Russian Ballet, in US and Canada (1911); moved to Nice, France (1917), where she trained many future members of Paris Opéra.

SEDOVA-TROTSKY, Natalia (1882–1962). *See Trotsky, Natalia.*

SEEFRIED, Irmgard (1919–1988). German soprano. Born Oct 9, 1919, in Köngetried, Swabia (southwest Bavaria); died Nov 24, 1988, in Vienna, Austria; m. Wolfgang Schneiderhan (violinist and concert master), 1948; children: Barbara Maria Schneiderhan (b. Jan 1950). ❖ Spent 5 years studying at Augsburg Conservatoire under Albert Mayer, then attended State Academy of Music in Munich; joined Aachen Opera under Herbert von Karajan (1939) and debuted as a priestess in Verdi's *Aïda* (1940); joined Vienna State Opera (1943), debuting as Eva in *Die Meistersinger*; sang in London, NY, Milan, Salzburg, Edinburgh, and other cities, appearing as Micaëla in *Carmen*, Susanna in *The Marriage of Figaro*, Fiordiligi in *Così Fan Tutte*, Octavian, Cleopatra, Marie, and Blanche; also admired as a Lieder singer. ❖ See also *Women in World History*.

SEEGER, Peggy (1935—). American folksinger and songwriter. Born 1935; dau. of Ruth Crawford (1901–1953) and Charles Louis Seeger; sister of Penny Seeger (1943—); half-sister of Pete Seeger; m. Ewan MacColl (British folk artist, died). ❖ Wrote and sang folk ballads, mostly with a feminist slant, as represented by the song "I'm Gonna Be an Engineer"; collaborated with husband, or her brother and sister, on many of her albums, including *At the Present Moment* for Rounder; with brother Mike Seeger, recorded album *American Folk Songs for Children*; with Mike and sister Penny, recorded album *American Folk Songs for Christmas*. ❖ See also *Women in World History*.

SEEGER, Ruth Crawford (1901–1953). *See Crawford, Ruth.*

SEELEY, Blossom (1891–1974). American actress and singer. Name variations: Blossom Fields. Born in San Pueblo, CA, July 16, 1891; died in New York, NY, April 1974; m. Joseph Kane (div.); m. Rube Marquard (baseball player, div.); m. Benny Fields (singer), 1921 (died 1959). ❖ Began stage career singing between acts at San Francisco Repertory Theater; co-starred on Broadway with Weber and Fields in *The Hen-Pecks* (1914); subsequently appeared with Al Jolson in *Whirl of Society* and Marion Davies in Irving Berlin's musical *Stop! Look! Listen!*; had greatest success, however, on vaudeville circuit, where she received top billing and popularized such songs as "The Japanese Sandman," "Smiles," "Way Down Yonder in New Orleans" and "California, Here I Come"; performed in an act with 3rd husband, Benny Fields (1921–34); after Paramount musical film *Somebody Loves Me* (1952), based on her life with Fields, was released, enjoyed a resurgence in career, appearing on tv and in such clubs as the Coconut Grove; also cut album, *Two a Day at the Palace*. ❖ See also *Women in World History*.

SEELYE, Emma E. (1841–1898). *See Edmonds, Emma.*

SEGAL, Vivienne (1897–1992). American actress and singer. Born April 19, 1897, in Philadelphia, PA; died Dec 29, 1992, in Los Angeles, CA; m. Robert Ames, 1923 (div. 1926); m. Hubbell Robinson Jr. (died 1974). ❖ Starred in operettas and musicals from age 16; on Broadway, originated the roles of Margot Bonvalet in *Desert Song* (1928) and Vera Simpson in *Pal Joey* (1940); films include *Song of the West, Bridge of the Regiment, Viennese Nights* and *The Cat and the Fiddle*.

SÉGALAS, Anais (1814–1895). French poet and playwright. Name variations: Anaïs Ségalas or Segalas. Born Anais Menard, 1814; died 1895; dau. of Charles Menard an Anne Bonne Portier, a creole of Santo Domingo; m. Victor Ségalas (Basque barrister), c. 1829. ❖ Wrote sentimental poetry, novels, short stories, and plays which were popular in her day; poetry collections include *Les Algériennes* (1831), *Oiseaux de passage* (1836), and the didactic *La Femme* (1848), for which she is best known; joined Société de la Voix des Femmes (1848) and other Parisian feminist organizations, but stressed that a woman's sphere was in the home.

SEGHERS, Anna (1900–1983). German writer. Name variations: Netty Reiling; Netty Radvanyi or Radványi. Born Netti Reiling in Mainz, Germany, Nov 19, 1900; died in East Berlin, June 1, 1983: dau. of Isidor Reiling (art dealer); University of Heidelberg, PhD in History of Art, 1924; m. László Radványi, 1925; children: Peter (b. 1926); Ruth (b.

1928). ❖ Leading German literary figure in exile during the Nazi years and one of the most significant writers in Communist East Germany, whose career extended from the Weimar era to 1970s; published *Aufstand der Fischer von St. Barbara* (*The Revolt of the Fishermen of Santa Barbara*), which won the Kleist prize (1928); joined Communist Party (1928) and published 1st major novel, *Die Gefährten* (*The Comrades*, 1932), which expressed her political sympathies clearly for 1st time; fled Germany for Paris after Hitler came to power (1933); wrote most famous novel, *Das Siebte Kreuz* (*The Seventh Cross*, 1938–40), which was 1st published in English (1942); fled France (1940), for Mexico (1941); returned to Germany and received the prestigious West German Büchner prize in Darmstadt (1947); published *Transit* (1948); served as chair of East German Writers' Union (1950–77); published *The Dead Stay Young*, the 1st of a trilogy of novels containing an examination of Germany from the close of WWI to 1950s; published controversial 2nd and 3rd didactic volumes, *The Decision* (1959) and *Trust* (1968); a committed Communist, saw the need for writers to involve themselves in creating a new society; at the same time, sometimes found her literary interests taking her in directions that led Marxist critics to question her ideological orthodoxy; also wrote *Der Weg durch den Februar* (1935), *The Excursion of the Dead Girls* (1946), *Crossing* (1971), *Encounter While Travelling* (1972) and *Peculiar Meetings* (1973). ❖ See also Lowell A. Bangerter, *The Bourgeois Proletarian; A Study of Anna Seghers* (1980); Kathleen J. LaBahn, *Anna Segher's Exile Literature: The Mexican Years (1941–1947)* (Lang, 1986); and *Women in World History*.

SEGOVIA, duchess of. *See Dampierre, Emmanuela del (b. 1913).*

SEGRAVE, Anne (d. around 1377). Abbess of Barking. Died c. 1377; dau. of John Segrave, 3rd baron Segrave (also seen as 4th baron Segrave), and Margaret, Duchess of Norfolk (c. 1320–1400); sister of Elizabeth Segrave (1338–1399).

SEGRAVE, Christian (c. 1250–?). *See Christian de Plessetis.*

SEGRAVE, Elizabeth (1338–1399). English noblewoman. Name variations: Elizabeth Seagrave; Elizabeth Mowbray. Born in 1338; died in 1399 (Burke's Peerage says died in 1375); dau. of John Segrave, 3rd baron Segrave (also seen as 4th baron Segrave), and Margaret, Duchess of Norfolk (c. 1320–1400); sister of Anne Segrave; m. John Mowbray (1340–1368), 4th baron Mowbray, in 1353 (slain near Constantinople, on the way to the Holy Land, on Oct 9, 1368); children: John Mowbray, earl of Nottingham; Thomas Mowbray (c. 1362–1399), 1st duke of Norfolk; Margaret Mowbray (fl. 1380).

SEGRAVE, Margaret (c. 1280–?). Baroness Ferrers of Groby. Name variations: Margaret Ferrers. Born c. 1280; dau. of John Segrave (1256–1325), 2nd baron Segrave, and Christian de Plessetis; m. William Ferrers, 1st baron Ferrers of Groby (d. 1325); children: Anne Ferrers (d. 1342); Henry Ferrers, 2nd baron Ferrers of Groby (d. 1343).

SEGRAVE, Margaret (c. 1320–1400). *See Margaret, duchess of Norfolk.*

SEGUN, Mabel (1930—). Nigerian short-story and children's writer. Name variations: Mabel Dorothy Segun. Born Feb 18, 1930, in Ondo, Nigeria; attended University College of Ibadan. ❖ Worked as editor, broadcaster, teacher, and researcher; was founder and first president of Children's Literature Association of Nigeria; works include *My Father's Daughter* (1965), *Youth Day Parade* (1983), *My Mother's Daughter* (1985), *Sorry, No Vacancy* (1985), *Conflict and Other Poems* (1986), and *The Surrender and Other Stories* (1995); radio broadcasts collected as *Friends, Nigerians, Countrymen* (1977); also was the 1st Nigerian woman to become a table tennis champion and wrote about experiences in *Ping Pong* (1989).

SÉGUR, Sophie Rostopchine, Comtesse de (1799–1874). Russian-born French children's writer. Name variations: Countess of Segur or Comtesse de Segur; Sophie Rostopchine. Born Sophie Rostopchin or Rostopchine, Aug 1, 1799, in St. Petersburg, Russia, of Mongolian heritage; died Feb 9, 1874, in Paris, France; dau. of General Rostopchine (who ordered Moscow to be set ablaze after the battle of Borodine in 1812, causing Napoleon to retreat); m. Eugène Comte de Ségur (nephew of Philippe Paul de Ségur, officer and writer), July 14, 1819; children: 8. ❖ With family, lived in exile in Poland (1814), then Germany and Italy, then moved to France (1817); contributed a number of stories to *Bibliothèque Rose*, a collection of short novels for young people, including *Nouveaux Contes de fées* (1856), *Les vacances* (1858), *Un bon petit diable* (1865), *Le mauvais génie* (1867), *Pauve Blaise* and *Les malheurs de Sophie*; writings, which give insight into the lives of various social classes in France during the Second Empire, remained popular with children for several generations.

SEHMISCH, Elke (1955—). East German swimmer. Born May 4, 1955, in East Germany. ❖ At Munich Olympics, won a silver medal in the 4 x 100-meter freestyle relay (1972).

SEI SHŌNAGON (c. 965–?). Japanese writer. Name variations: Sei Shonagaon. Pronunciation: SAY SHOW-nah-gohn. Born possibly in Kiyohara, c. 965, possibly in Kyoto, Japan; circumstances of her death are not known; great-granddau. of Kiyohara Fukayabu (paternal great-grandfather, a poet of distinction); dau. of Kiyohara Motosuke (father, a noted scholar and poet of some repute); perhaps m. Tachibana no Norimitsu (minor court official); perhaps m. Fujiwara no Muneyo (minor court official); sometimes mentioned that she was married to, or had a relationship with, Fujiwara no Sanekata (minor court official); children: (with Tachibana no Norimitsu) possibly a son, Norinaga; (with Fujiwara no Muneyo) possibly a daughter, Koma no Myōbu. ❖ One of the most renowned prose writers in the history of Japanese literature, was the author of *The Pillow Book*, a masterpiece of world literature; became lady-in-waiting at court of Empress Sadako (early 990s); at court, had a measure of autonomy not permitted other Japanese women; likely served until the empress' death (1001); wrote *Makura no sōshi* (*The Pillow Book*) during that time. The book, a compilation of her tastes, insights, and prejudices, derives its immense charm from the author's own irascible and irrepressible personality; from her detailed observations, we learn much about the daily lives of members of Japan's upper class in the 10th and 11th centuries. ❖ See also *Women in World History*.

SEIBERT, Florence B. (1897–1991). American biochemist. Born Florence Barbara Seibert, Oct 6, 1897, in Easton, Pennsylvania; died Aug 23, 1991; dau. of George Peter Seibert and Barbara (Memmert) Seibert; sister of Mabel Seibert (who served as her laboratory assistant); Goucher College, AB and LLD; University of Chicago, ScD; Yale University, PhD. ❖ Among the 20th century's most eminent biochemists, developed a reliable skin test for tuberculosis, once the leading cause of death in America; was disabled from childhood experience with polio; took a position at University of Chicago as instructor in pathology and assistant to Esmond R. Long, where she began her work with tuberculosis (1924); became associate professor in biochemistry (1928), before following Long to University of Pennsylvania's Henry Phipps Institute; promoted from assistant to associate professor (1937); having become an international authority on the bacillus responsible for tuberculosis, prepared the National Standard for Tuberculins (1939), but retired 8 years before the skin test developed from her work became the standard (1966). Received Trudeau Gold Medal from National Tuberculosis Association (1938) and Garvan Gold Medal from American Chemical Society (1942); inducted into the Women's Hall of Fame (1990). ❖ See also *Women in World History*.

SEICK, Karin (1961—). West German swimmer. Born Nov 11, 1961, in Germany. ❖ At Los Angeles Olympics, won a bronze medal in the 4 x 100-meter freestyle relay, a bronze medal in the 100-meter butterfly, and a silver medal in the 4 x 100-meter medley relay (1984).

SEID, Ruth (1913–1995). American novelist and short-story writer. Name variations: (pseudonym) Jo Sinclair. Born July 1, 1913; died April 3, 1995, in Jenkintown, PA; dau. of Russian-Jewish immigrants; grew up in Cleveland, Ohio. ❖ Was a contributor to the *New Masses*; wrote novel *Wasteland* (1946), which won the Harper Prize; also wrote *The Changelings* (1955), *Sing at My Wake* and *Anna Teller*. ❖ See also memoir *The Seasons: Death and Transfiguration* (1993).

SEIDEL, Amalie (1876–1952). Austrian politician. Name variations: Amalie Rausnitz. Born Amalie Ryba in Vienna, Austria, Feb 21, 1876; died in Vienna, May 11, 1952; dau. of Jakob Ryba (locksmith) and Anna (Stach) Ryba; m. Richard Seidel (engineer), 1895 (div.); m. Sigmund Rausnitz (Jewish activist), 1934 (died 1942); children: daughters Emma and Olga; 1 son. ❖ One of the most effective orators and organizers among the leadership of Austrian Social Democratic Workers Party (Sozialdemokratische Arbeiterpartei Österreichs, or SDAP), who served as a parliamentary delegate (1919–34) and was imprisoned for her beliefs by 3 different regimes (1893, 1934, and 1944); served as chair of SDAP national women's conference (Frauenreichskonferenz, 1903–32); was also chair of SDAP's consumers' cooperative (Konsumgenossenschaft); championed the cause of women workers and demanded full political rights for women. ❖ See also *Women in World History*.

SEIDEL, Ina (1885–1974). German poet and novelist. Born 1885 in Halle an der Saale, Germany; died 1974; m. Heinrich Wolfgang Seidel (writer), 1907. ❖ Published *Gedichte* (Poems, 1914), followed by *Neben der Trommel her* (Next to the Trumpet, 1915), and *Weltinnigkeit* (World Inwardness, 1918); published 1st novel, *Das Haus zum Monde* (The House at the Moon, 1916), followed 5 years later by the powerful *Das Labyrinth* (The Labyrinth, 1921); wrote *Das Wunschkind* (The Wish Child, 1930), which was considered one of the great novels of its generation; though she did not perceive the evils of National Socialism during WWII, her works, based on a spirit of cultural conservatism and the restoration of traditional values, remained popular in postwar West Germany; published shorter prose, *Der vergrabene Schatz* (The Buried Treasure, 1955) and *Die alte Dame und der Schmetterling* (The Old Woman and the Butterfly, 1964), as well as the novels *Das unverwesliche Erbe* (The Incorruptible Inheritance, 1958) and *Michaela: Aufzeichnungen des Jürgen Brook* (Michaela: Notebooks of Jürgen Brook, 1959), which deals with the guilt of middle-class German Christians who had supported Hitler's Third Reich; also wrote a volume of essays, *Frau und Wort* (Woman and Word, 1965) and such autobiographical works as *Vor Tau und Tag: Geschicte einer Kindheit* (Before Dew and Day: Story of a Childhood, 1962) and *Lebensbericht 1885–1923* (Life Story 1885–1923, 1970). ❖ See also *Women in World History.*

SEIDEL, Martie (1969—). American musician. Name variations: Dixie Chicks. Born Martha Elenor Erwin, Oct 12, 1969, in York, PA; sister of Emily Robinson (member of Dixie Chicks). ❖ Vocalist and fiddle and mandolin player, released back-to-back multiplatinum country albums with Dixie Chicks, *Wide Open Spaces* (1998) and *Fly* (1999). Additional albums with Dixie Chicks include *Thank Heavens for Dale Evans* (1990), *Little Ol' Cowgirl* (1992) and *Shouldn't a Told You That* (1993).

SEIDELMAN, Susan (1952—). American film director. Born Dec 11, 1952, in Abington, Pennsylvania; graduate of Drexel University; attended New York University Graduate School of Film and Television (1974–77). ❖ At NYU, won student Oscar for short film *And You Act Like One, Too* (1976), and made several other feminist-oriented student films (1976–77); won acclaim for *Yours Truly, Andrea G. Stern* (1978); self-financed *Smithereens* (1982), the 1st independent US feature to be accepted in main competition at Cannes Film Festival; had hit debut in mainstream cinema with *Desperately Seeking Susan* (1985), screwball comedy starring Madonna; had less success with successive films, *Making Mr. Right* (1987), *Cookie* (1989) and *She-Devil* (1989); wrote and directed several short films, including documentary *Confessions of a Suburban Girl* (1992) and *The Dutch Master* (1994); made moderately successful feature-length film *Gaudi Afternoon* (2003) and *The Boynton Beach Bereavement Club* (2005); for tv, directed "Sex and the City" pilot episode (1998), as well as "A Cooler Climate" (1999), "Now and Again" (1999), "Power and Beauty" (2002) and "The Ranch" (2004).

SEIDL, Lea (1895–1987). Viennese actress and singer. Born Caroline Mayrseidl, Aug 22, 1895, in Vienna, Austria; died Jan 4, 1987, in London, England. ❖ Made stage debut in Vienna as Janku in *Rastelbinder* by Franz Lehar (1917); appeared in Zurich (1919–20), then Berlin (1922–26), eventually under the direction of Max Reinhardt; made London debut in title role of *Frederica* (1930), then appeared as Josepha in *The White Horse Inn,* which ran nearly a year; became a naturalized British subject; in films, appeared as Fraulein Schneider in *I Am a Camera* (1955), Countess Rostov in *War and Peace* (1956) and Baroness von Braun in *Wernher von Braun* (1959).

SEIDLER, Helga (1949—). East German runner. Born Aug 5, 1949, in East Germany. ❖ At Munich Olympics, won a gold medal in the 4 x 100-meter relay (1972).

SEIDMAN, Esther (1945–1995). See Rome, Esther.

SEIFULLINA, Lydia (1889–1954). Russian short-story writer. Name variations: Lydia, Lidia, or Lidiia Nikolaevna Seifúllina/ Lidiia Nikolaevna Seifulina. Born 1889 in western Siberia, Russia; died 1954. ❖ Worked as teacher before the Russian Revolution; began writing after the Civil War (1920); was founding editor and contributor to *Siberian Fires*; established salon for writers in Moscow (1920s); stories include "Four Chapters: A Novella in Excerpts," "The Old Woman," and "Lawbreakers."

SEIGNEURET, Michele (1934—). French ballet dancer. Born 1934 in Paris, France. ❖ Performed with the companies of Maurice Béjart: the Ballet de L'Etoile and Ballet du Théâtre de la Monnaie in Belgium;

created roles for *Symphonie pour un Homme seul* (1955), *Sonate à Trois* (1957), and *Orphée* (1959), among others.

SEITZ, Madeline (1897–1990). See Gaxton, Madeline.

SEIZINGER, Katja (1972—). German Alpine skier. Born May 10, 1972, in Datteln, West Germany. ❖ Compiled 6 medals at the World Jr. championships (1989, 1990), including a gold in super-G and a silver in the downhill (1990); won a gold medal in super-G at World championships (1993); won a bronze medal at Albertville Olympics in super-G and finished 4th in downhill and 8th in giant slalom (1992); won a gold medal for downhill at Lillehammer Olympics (1994); won downhill World Cup titles (1992, 1993); won World Cup overall title (1996, 1998); won gold medals for the downhill (the 1st skier to retain a downhill title) and the combined and a bronze medal for giant slalom at Nagano Olympics (1998); had 36 World Cup wins; retired (1999). ❖ See also *Women in World History.*

SEKAJOVA, Gabriela (1953—). See Svobodova, Gabriela.

SEKARIC, Jasna (1965—). Yugoslavian shooter. Born Dec 17, 1965, in Beograd, Serbia, Yugoslavia. ❖ Won European championship (1986) and World championship (1987), both for air pistol; at Seoul Olympics, won a bronze medal in sport pistol and a gold medal in air pistol (1988); won silver medals at Barcelona Olympics (1992) and Sydney Olympics (2000), both for air pistol; won a silver medal for 10 m air pistol at Athens Olympics (2004). Named Yugoslav Woman Athlete of the Year (2000).

SEKULIĆ, Isadora (1877–1958). Serbian short-story writer, novelist, and critic. Name variations: Isidora Sekulic. Born 1877 in Mošorin, Bačka; died 1958; trained to be a teacher; held PhD from a German university. ❖ Published her lyrical *Saputnici* (Fellow Travelers, 1913), which established her reputation as a fresh voice in Serbian literature; demonstrated identification with Serbian Orthodox tradition with 3rd book, the novella *Djakon Bogorodičinecrkve* (The Deacon of the Church of Our Lad, 1919), an affiliation that can be seen in later works as well, such as *Kronika palanačkog grohlja* (The Chronicle of a Provincial Graveyard, 1940); as a critic, was best known for *Njegošu knjiga duboke odanosti* (A Book of Deep Homage to Njegoš, 1951) and *Mir I nemir* (Peace and Unrest, 1957). ❖ See also *Women in World History.*

SELASSIE, Menen (1899–1962). See Menen.

SELASSIE, Tsahai Haile (1919–1942). See Tsahai Haile Selassie.

SELBACH, Johanna (1918—). Dutch swimmer. Name variations: Johanna Katarina Selbach. Born July 27, 1918, in the Netherlands. ❖ At Berlin Olympics, won a gold medal in 4 x 100-meter freestyle relay (1936).

SELBERT, Elisabeth (1896–1986). German politician. Born Elisabeth Rhode in Kassel, Germany, Sept 22, 1896; died in Kassel, June 9, 1986; dau. of Georg Rhode (minor civil servant) and Eva Elisabeth Rhode; graduate of University of Göttingen; m. Adam Selbert (printer and political activist), 1920; children: Gerhart and Herbert. ❖ Social Democratic Party (Sozialdemokratische Partei Deutschlands, or SPD) activist and attorney who played a crucial role in expanding and defending the legal rights of women in the German Federal Republic after WWII; ran unsuccessfully for a Reichstag seat on SPD ticket (1933); became one of the last women admitted to the bar in Nazi Germany (1934), before women were excluded from the legal profession; after WWII (1945), achieved a rapid political ascent, from city representative in Kassel, to a member of Hesse constitutional state assembly, to deputy of Hesse Parliament, in which she served continuously (1946–58); rose quickly as well in ranks of her party, serving on SPD federal executive; served on Parliamentary Council (Parlamentarischer Rat, 1948), where she championed the cause of full equality for women, a principle which was anchored in the Basic Law (*Grundgesetz*) of Federal Republic of Germany when it was born in the fall of 1949. ❖ See also *Women in World History.*

SELBIG, Elisa or Elise (1781–1849). See Ahlefeld, Charlotte von.

SELBY, Curt (1928—). See Piserchia, Doris.

SELBY, Sarah (1905–1980). American character actress. Name variations: Sara Selby. Born Aug 30, 1905, in St. Louis, MO; died Jan 7, 1980, in Los Angeles, CA. ❖ Films include *Beyond the Forest, Battle Cry, An Affair to Remember, Tower of London* and *Don't Make Waves;* on tv, appeared as Ma Smalley in "Gunsmoke."

SELCUK, Furuzan (1935—). See Füruzan.

SELENA (1971–1995). Mexican-American singer. Name variations: Selena Quintanilla-Pérez. Born Selena Quintanilla in Lake Jackson, south of Houston, TX, April 16, 1971; died of a gunshot wound in Corpus Christi, TX, Mar 31, 1995; dau. of Marcela Quintanilla and Abraham Quintanilla Jr.; m. Chris Pérez (guitar player), 1992. ❖ Known as the queen of Tejano, began performing as a child, with brother Abraham III on bass and sister Suzette on drums; at 8, recorded 1st song in Spanish; at 9, fronted the Tex-Mex band, Selena y Los Dinos; cut albums for a small regional label; won best female vocalist and performer of the year at Tejano Music Awards (1987); with band, which now included husband Chris Pérez, signed with EMI (1989); by age 19, was the center of the Tejano music industry; released 6 albums, each one growing in sales; sold more than 1.5 million records in US and Mexico, and her recording *Selena Live* won a Grammy for best Mexican-American album (1994); filmed a scene in movie *Don Juan DeMarco* with Johnny Depp; with her song "Fotos y Recuerdos" (Photographs and Memories) #4 on the Billboard Latin charts, her single from the album *Amor Prohibido* (Forbidden Love) nominated for another Grammy, and having signed a $5 million record contract with SBK Records, was on the verge of a crossover to mainstream music when she was shot to death outside a motel in Corpus Christi by Yolanda Saldivar (1995). Following her death, her album *Dreaming of You* sold 175,000 copies on the 1st day of its release, an all-time record for a female artist; the biographical film *Selena*, starring Jennifer Lopez, premiered (1997), and a tv movie *The Selena Murder Trial*, starring Lizett Padilla, aired on cable. ❖ See also *Women in World History.*

SELES, Monica (1973—). Serbian-American tennis player. Born Dec 2, 1973, in Novi Sad, Yugoslavia. ❖ At age 12, named Female Athlete of the Year in Yugoslavia (1985); moved to Florida to train (1986); at 14, played in 1st pro tournament; won Australian Open (1991, 1992, 1993, 1996), French Open (1990, 1991, 1992), and US Open (1991, 1992); at 17, named #1 in the world, the youngest player to reach that spot (Mar 11, 1991); stabbed by a deranged tennis fan during a quarterfinal match in Hamburg, Germany (April 30, 1993); won a bronze medal for singles at Sydney Olympics (2000); won Italian Open (2000), Brazil Open (2001), and Japan Open (2001); became a US citizen. ❖ See also autobiography (with Nancy Ann Richardson) *Monica Seles: From Fear to Victory* and Joseph Layden, *Return of a Champion.*

SELEZNEVA, Larisa (1963—). Russian pairs skater. Born 1963 in Leningrad (now St. Petersburg), Russia. ❖ With partner Oleg Makarov, won European championships (1987, 1989) and a bronze medal at Sarajevo Olympics (1984); turned professional (1990).

SELL, Janie (1941—). American actress. Name variations: Jane Trese. Born in Detroit, Michigan, Oct 1, 1941; attended University of Detroit; graduate of Hunter College, 1989; married in 1965 and div.; m. Patrick Trese, c. 1990; children: (1st m.) 1 son. ❖ Made debut in *Mixed Doubles* (1966); was also featured in *Dark Horses, Dames at Sea, George M, Irene, Pal Joey, Happy End, I Love My Wife* and *Over Here*, for which she received a Theater World Award.

SELLARS, Elizabeth (1923—). Scottish actress. Born May 6, 1923, in Glasgow, Scotland; m. Francis Henley. ❖ Made London debut as Grushenka in *The Brothers Karamazov* (1946), followed by *The Other Side, Angels in Love, The Remarkable Mr. Pennypacker, South Sea Bubble, The Sound of Murder, A Friend Indeed, The Prime of Miss Jean Brodie* (title role), and *The Italian Girl*, among others; appeared with Shakespeare Memorial Theatre Company (1960–61); made film debut in *Floodtide* (1948); other films include *55 Days in Peking, The Chalk Garden, The Barefoot Contessa, Desiree, Prince of Players, The Mummy's Shroud* and *The Hireling.*

SELLEN, Billie Bird (1908–2002). See Bird, Billie.

SELLERS, Kathryn (1870–1939). American attorney and judge. Born Dec 25, 1870, in Broadway, OH; died Feb 23, 1939. ❖ Served as clerk at US Weather Bureau, Washington, DC (1891–1900), assistant in Department of State Library (1900–11), and bibliographer and librarian for Carnegie Endowment for International Peace (1911–18); started law practice (1913); performed reference work for US Neutrality Board (1914–17); served as professor of law at Washington College of Law (1914–21); made law clerk at US State Department's Division of Foreign Intelligence (1917); nominated to be head judge of Washington, DC, juvenile court by President Woodrow Wilson (1918), the 1st woman to hold such a post, and served until 1934.

SELLICK, Phyllis (b. 1911). English pianist. Born in Newburg Park, Essex, England, June 16, 1911; studied at Royal Academy of Music in London and then with Isidor Philipp in Paris; m. Cyril James Smith (pianist), 1937. ❖ Often appeared with husband in works for 2 pianos written by British composers Ralph Vaughan Williams and Lennox Berkeley; gave world premiere of Michael Tippett's 1st Piano Sonata (1938); continued duo-piano partnership with husband even after he suffered a stroke that cost him use of one of his hands, performing piano music arranged—or in some instances composed—for 3 hands; began teaching at Royal College of Music (1964). Granted the Order of the British Empire (1971).

SELLWOOD, Emily (1813–1896). See Tennyson, Emily.

SELOVE, Fay (b. 1926). See Ajzenberg-Selove, Fay.

SELVA, Blanche (1884–1942). French pianist. Born in Brive, France, Jan 29, 1884; died in Saint-Armand, France, Dec 3, 1942; studied at Paris Conservatory. ❖ Made debut (1897); at 20, stunned musical Paris by performing the entire keyboard output of Johann Sebastian Bach in 17 recitals (1904); taught at Schola Cantorum in Paris (1901–22), as well as at Strasbourg and Prague and Barcelona conservatories; a highly regarded scholar, wrote several books, perhaps the most important being *La Sonate* (1913); as a pianist, brought many works of the modern French school to the public, including the premieres of Isaac Albeniz's *Iberia*, Vincent D'Indy's Sonata, Op. 63 (1908), and Albert Roussel's Suite for Piano, Op. 14.

SELZNICK, Irene Mayer (1910–1990). American theater producer. Name variations: Irene Mayer. Born Irene Gladys Mayer, April 2, 1910, in Brookline, Massachusetts; died Oct 10, 1990, in New York, NY; dau. of Louis B. Mayer (film producer) and Margaret (Shenberg) Mayer; m. David O. Selznick (film producer), April 29, 1930 (div. 1948); children: Jeffrey Selznick (b. 1932); Daniel Mayer Selznick (b. 1936). ❖ Had enormous success with 2nd produced play, Tennessee Williams' *A Streetcar Named Desire* (1947), which ran for 855 performances and won every major honor, including Pulitzer Prize, Donaldson Award, and New York Drama Critics' Award; went on to produce *Bell, Book and Candle* (1950), *Flight into Egypt* (1952), *The Chalk Garden* (1955) and *The Complaisant Lover* (1961). ❖ See also memoir *A Private View* (Knopf, 1983); and *Women in World History.*

SEMBRICH, Marcella (1858–1935). Polish-born American lyric soprano. Name variations: Marcella Sembrich-Kochanska. Born Praxede Marcelline Kochanska (also seen as Prakseda Marcelina Kochanska, while some sources cite Kadanska) in Wisniewczyk, Galicia (part of Austrian Poland), Feb 15, 1858; died in New York, NY, Jan 11, 1935; dau. of Casimir Kochanski (teacher and instrumentalist) and Juliana (Sembrich) Kochanska; studied with Wilhelm Stengel at Lemberg (Lvov) Conservatory, Viktor Rokitansky in Vienna, and G. B. Lamperti in Milan; m. Wilhelm Stengel (piano teacher and later her manager), 1877 (died 1917). ❖ Ranked with operatic sopranos Adelina Patti, Nellie Melba, and Christine Nilsson, debuted in Athens as Elvira in Bellini's *I puritani* (1877); made German debut at Saxon Royal Opera in Dresden (1878), singing the role of Lucia, then stayed in Dresden for 2 years; signed 5-year contract with Royal Italian Opera in London, making debut at Covent Garden (1880), again as Lucia; subsequently performed in Scandinavia, France, Spain, Austria and Russia; made US debut at Metropolitan Opera singing *Lucia di Lammermoor* (1883), then appeared in 55 performances there, singing 11 different roles; returned to Europe, performing in Austria, Germany, France, Russia and Scandinavia; reappeared at the Met as Rosina in *The Barber of Seville* (1898) and remained there for next 10 years; sang Susanna, Zerlina, Lucia, Rosina, Queen of the Night, Gilda, Violetta, and Mimi; sang in Columbia's Grand Opera Series of recordings (1903) and later recorded extensively for Victor; following retirement from Met, embarked on a concert career which lasted until 1917; performed a broad repertoire that included Brahms, Schumann, and the French and Italian composers, as well as Debussy and Ravel; retired (1924); became department head at Curtis Institute of Music in Philadelphia and Juilliard School in NY, teaching Sophie Braslau, Alma Gluck, and Maria Jeritza, among others. ❖ See also H. G. Owen, *A Recollection of Marcella Sembrich* (1950); and *Women in World History.*

SEMENOVA, Ekaterina (1786–1849). Russian actress. Born 1786; died 1849; studied at St. Petersburg Theater School with Russian actor Dmitrevsky; m. Prince Ivan Gagarin, 1826. ❖ At 17, made stage debut and became known for her powerful voice and impassioned acting, particularly in classics by Shakespeare, Racine, Schiller, and Ozerov; was widely praised for performance in *Phèdre* (1823); went into semiretirement, confining herself to roles in private theaters in St. Petersburg and Moscow, after marriage; was lauded in several of Pushkin's poems.

SEMENOVA, Iuliana (1952—). *See Semjonova, Uljana.*

SEMIRAMIDE (fl. 8th c. BCE). *See Sammuramat.*

SEMIRAMIS (fl. 8th c. BCE). *See Sammuramat.*

SEMIRAMIS OF THE NORTH. *See Margaret I of Denmark (1353–1412).*

SEMJONOVA, Uljana (1952—). **Latvian basketball player.** Name variations: Iuliana Semenova. Born Mar 9, 1952, in Daugavpils, Latvia; height 7 feet. ❖ Representing the Soviet Union, won a gold medal at Montreal Olympics (1976) and a gold medal at Moscow Olympics (1980), both in team competition; won team World championships (1971, 1975, 1983); in 18 seasons of international competition, never lost a game (1968–86); scored more than 15,000 points in career; named the most popular athlete in Latvia (1970–85); was the 1st international female player enshrined in Basketball Hall of Fame.

SEMPIER, Evelyn (c. 1934—). *See Ay, Evelyn.*

SEMPILL, Elizabeth Forbes- (1912–1965). *See Forbes-Sempill, Elizabeth.*

SEMPLE, Carol Keister (1948—). *See Thompson, Carol Semple.*

SEMPLE, Ellen Churchill (1863–1932). **American geographer and educator.** Born Jan 8, 1863, in Louisville, Kentucky; died May 8, 1932, in West Palm Beach, Florida; dau. of Alexander Bonner Semple (merchant) and Emerine (Price) Semple; Vassar College, BA, 1882, MA, 1891; studied under Friedrich Ratzel at University of Leipzig, 1891–92, 1895. ❖ Founded Semple Collegiate School for Girls (1893); published *Influences of Geographical Environment on the Basis of Ratzel's System of Anthropo-geography* (1911); received Cullum Medal of American Geographical Society (1914); served as president of Association of American Geographers (1921); published last book, the fruit of 20 years' research, *The Geography of the Mediterranean: Its Relation to Ancient History* (1931); taught alternate years at University of Chicago (1906–24); taught at Wellesley College (1914–15), University of Colorado (1916), Columbia University (1918); was a professor of anthropogeography at Clark University (1923–32); work was fundamental in establishing geography as a field of university study in 20th century. Received gold medal of the Geographic Society of Chicago (1932). ❖ See also *Women in World History.*

SEMPLE, Letitia Tyler (1821–1907). **White House hostess.** Name variations: Letty Tyler. Born Letitia Tyler in 1821; died 1907; dau. of John Tyler (president of US) and Letitia Tyler (1790–1842); m. James Semple, 1839; no children. ❖ Stood in for invalid mother as White House hostess (1841–42), along with her sister-in-law, Priscilla Cooper Tyler. ❖ See also *Women in World History.*

SEMPLE MCPHERSON, Aimee (1890–1944). *See McPherson, Aimee Semple.*

SEMPRONIA (c. 168 BCE–?). **Roman noblewoman.** Born c. 168 BCE; dau. of Cornelia (c. 195–c. 115 BCE) and Tiberius Sempronius Gracchus; m. Scipio Aemilianus, around 155 (died 129 BCE); no children. ❖ See also *Women in World History.*

SEMPRONIA (fl. 2nd–1st c. BCE). **Roman noblewoman.** Flourished between the 1st and 2nd centuries BCE; m. Marcus Fulvius Bambalio; children: Fulvia (c. 85/80–40 BCE). ❖ There is some confusion between this Sempronia, the mother of Fulvia, and the Sempronia who was mother or stepmother of Decimus Junius Brutus Albinus. ❖ See also *Women in World History.*

SEMPRONIA (fl. 2nd–1st c. BCE). **Roman noblewoman.** Flourished between the 2nd and 1st century BCE; dau. of Gaius Sempronius Tuditanus; granddau. of Gaius Sempronius Tuditanus (who had served as consul—the highest political office in the Roman Republic—in 129 BCE and had written one of the earliest works on Roman law); m. Decimus Junius Brutus, a Roman consul (r. 77 BCE); m. D. Junius Silanus, a Roman consul (r. 62 BCE); children: (1st m.) mother or stepmother of Decimus Junius Brutus Albinus. ❖ Thought to have been the 1st woman in history to appear in a Roman court, played a role in the political upheaval of the times when she supported the Catiline. ❖ See also *Women in World History.*

SEMPRONIA (c. 75 BCE–after 16 CE). *See Scribonia.*

SEMYKINA, Tetyana (1973—). **Ukrainian kayaker.** Born Oct 19, 1973, in USSR. ❖ Won a bronze medal for K4 500 at Athens Olympics (2004).

SEMYONOVA, Marina (b. 1908). **Soviet ballet dancer.** Born Marina Timofeyevna Semyonova, June 12, 1908, in St. Petersburg, Russia; was the 1st important protégée of Agrippina Vaganova. ❖ At 17, became a principal with the Leningrad Ballet and danced there from 1925 to 1929, a great exponent of classical ballet; made Bolshoi debut as Nikiya in *La Bayadère* (1930), which was to become a signature role; danced with Bolshoi Ballet (1930–52), as Odette/Odile, Aurora, and Raymonda, among others; danced Giselle at Paris Opéra partnered by Serge Lifar (1935); was among the 1st representatives of Soviet ballet to dance in the West (1930s), but often irritated Soviet authorities with her outspoken, independent nature; began teaching advanced company classes at Bolshoi (1952) and was still teaching at age 95.

SEMYONOVA, Olga (1964—). **Soviet handball player.** Born Jan 6, 1964, in USSR. ❖ At Seoul Olympics, won a bronze medal in team competition (1988).

SEMYONOVA, Svetlana (1958—). **Soviet rower.** Born May 11, 1958, in USSR. ❖ At Moscow Olympics, won a bronze medal in coxed fours (1980).

SENDER, Toni (1888–1964). **German-born American economist, journalist, politician and consultant.** Born Nov 29, 1888, in Biebrich, Germany; died June 26, 1964, in New York, NY; dau. of Moritz Sender and Marie Dreyfuss Sender. ❖ Began career as a journalist; as Social Democrat, was a member of the Reichstag for 14 years (1918–32); fled Nazism and came to US (1936); during WWII, was employed by US Office of Strategic Services (OSS); served as senior economist with UNRRA; as a consultant of the American Federation of Labor to the Economic and Social Council of the United Nations, was instrumental in the US investigating forced labor conditions. ❖ See also *The Autobiography of a German Rebel* (Vanguard, 1939).

SENDLER, Irena (b. 1910). **Polish social worker and hero.** Name variations: Irena Sendlerowa; (code name) Jolanta. Born 1910 in Otwock, near Warsaw, Poland; dau. of a Socialist physician; married; children: 2. ❖ As head of the children's section of Zegota, an underground organization of gentiles dedicated to assisting and aiding the Jews of Poland, helped smuggle more than 2,500 Jewish children out of the Warsaw ghetto; arrested by the Gestapo (Oct 1943), was tortured (both her feet and legs were broken) and sentenced to death, but Zegota rescued her before her execution; assumed a new identity and continued work for Zegota. Named Righteous Among the Nations by Yad Vashem (1965); awarded Order of White Eagle (2003); received Jan Karski Award for Valor and Compassion from the American Center of Polish Culture (2003).

SENENA (fl. 1200s). **Lady of Lleyn.** Married Gruffydd, Lord of Lleyn (son of Llewelyn the Great [1173–1240], Ruler of All Wales); children: 5, including Llewelyn III the Last, prince of Wales.

SENESCH, Hannah (1921–1944). *See Senesh, Hannah.*

SENESH, Hannah (1921–1944). **Jewish resistance fighter.** Name variations: Anna ("Anikó") Szenes (1921–39); Chana Szenes (1939–44); or Hannah Senesh or Senesch. Born Anna Szenes in Budapest, Hungary, July 17, 1921; executed in Budapest on Nov 7, 1944; buried in Israel's Cemetery of Heroes; dau. of Katalin, Katherine, or Kató (Salzberger) Szenes and Béla (r.n. Schlesinger) Szenes (well-known humorist); never married; no children. ❖ Israel's national hero who undertook a parachute mission to help rescue Jews in her native Hungary and was captured, tortured, and executed by the Nazis; became a Zionist (1938); moved to Eretz Israel (1939); attended Agricultural School in Nahalal (1939–41); joined Sedot Yam ([Sdot-Yam], Fields of the Sea) kibbutz (1941–44); parachuted into Yugoslavia (Mar 13, 1944); captured by Germans and Hungarians (June 1944); stood trial for treason (Oct 1944); resisting the blindfold, was executed. ❖ See also Marta Cohn, *Hannah Senesh: Her Life and Diary* (Schocken, 1973); Peter Hay, *Ordinary Heroes: The Life and Death of Chana Szenes, Israel's National Heroine* (Paragon, 1989); Antony Masters, *The Summer That Bled: A Biography of Hannah Senesh* (Michael Joseph, 1972); Marie Syrkin, *Blessed is the Match* (Jewish Publications Society of America, 1947); (film) *Hannah's War*, starring Ellen Burstyn and Maruschka Detmers (1988); and *Women in World History.*

SENESH, Katalin (b. 1899). *See Szenes, Katalin.*

SENFF, Dina (1920—). Dutch swimmer. Born April 3, 1920, in the Netherlands. ❖ Won a gold medal in the 100-meter backstroke at the Berlin Olympics (1936).

SENIOR, Olive (1941—). Jamaican novelist and short-story writer. Born 1941 in Jamaica. ❖ Worked as editor of *Jamaica Journal* and as journalist in Jamaica and Canada; poetry includes *Talking of Trees* (1986) and *Gardening in the Tropics* (1994); short-story collections include *Summer Lightning* (1986), which won the Commonwealth Writers Prize, *Arrival of the Snake-Woman* (1989) and *Discerner of Hearts* (1995); nonfiction includes *A-Z of Jamaican Heritage* (1984) and *Working Miracles: Women's Lives in the English-Speaking Caribbean* (1991); lives in Jamaica and Canada.

SENNETERRE, Sophie de (1772–1822). *See Renneville, Sophie de.*

SENSINI, Alessandra (1970—). Italian windsurfer. Born Jan 26, 1970, in Grosseto, Italy; attended Instituto Tecnico Commerciale in Grosseto. ❖ Won a bronze medal for board (Mistral) at Atlanta Olympics (1996) and Athens Olympics (2004); won World championship for Mistral (1989, 2000, 2004), and funboard (1990); won European championship for Mistral (1997, 2000); won a gold medal for board (Mistral) at Sydney Olympics (2000). Named Italian Sailor of the Year (2000).

SENYURT, Hulya (1973—). Turkish judoka. Born Nov 10, 1973. ❖ At Barcelona Olympics, won a bronze medal in extra-lightweight 48 kg (1992).

SEPTEMBER, Anna (1921–1995). *See Manner, Eeva-Liisa.*

SEPTEMBER, Dulcie (1935–1988). South African activist. Born Dulcie Evonne September, 1935, in Cape Town, South Africa; killed Mar 29, 1988, in Paris; attended public schools and then Battswood Teacher Training College; never married; no children. ❖ Educator and longtime member of African National Congress (ANC), whose murder shocked both France and South Africa; became a teacher (mid-1950s); became politically involved when she saw how poorly black and mixed-race children were being educated in comparison to white children; joined Unity Movement but left when she became dissatisfied with its passive approach to political change; became a member of National Liberation Front (NLF) of South Africa; arrested for covert political activities for NLF (Oct 1963), served a 5-year prison term for sabotage and inciting political violence, though she always denied being a supporter of any kind of violence; banned from teaching after release, left to study in London (1974), where she also worked for Anti-Apartheid Movement; returning to South Africa, joined African National Congress, serving 1st in ANC headquarters in Lusaka, then as Chief Representative to France, Luxemburg, and Switzerland (1984); established an ANC office in Paris, where she was subjected to death threats from supporters of apartheid government; was shot five times from behind as she opened the ANC office (1988). ❖ See also *Women in World History.*

SEPTIMIA ZENOBIA (r. 267–272). *See Zenobia.*

SERAÏDARI, Elly (b. 1899). *See Nelly.*

SERANUS (1859–1935). *See Harrison, Susie Frances.*

SERAO, Matilde (1856–1927). Italian journalist, novelist, and short-story writer. Name variations: (pseudonyms) Chiquita, Paolo Spada, and Gibus. Pronunciation: Ser-OW. Born Feb 26, 1856, in Patras, Greece; died July 25, 1927, in Naples, Italy; dau. of Francesco Saverio Serao (exiled Neapolitan journalist) and Paolina Bonelly Serao (Greek noblewoman); m. Edoardo Scarfoglio, Feb 1885 (sep. 1902); children: (1st m.) 4 sons; (with Giuseppe Natale, a Neapolitan lawyer) daughter Eleonora (b. 1904). ❖ Writer who commented extensively on the role of women in the newly unified Italian state, moved to Italy with mother (1860); began work as journalist (1876); published 1st short stories (1878); published 1st novel, *Cuore infermo* (*The Sick Heart*), and moved to Rome to work as a journalist (1881); became editor of Roman newspaper (1882); founded *Corriere di Roma* with husband (1885); returned to Naples (1887); published *Fantasia* (*Fantasy*, 1882), *La conquista di Roma* (*The Conquest of Rome*, 1885), *Vita e avventure di Riccardo Joanna* (*The Life and Adventures of Riccardo Joanna*, 1887), *Il paese di Cuccagna* (*The Land of Cockaigne*, 1891), *Suor Giovanna della Croce* (*Sister Joan of the Holy Cross*, 1901); having hitherto written penetrating novels about Italian society in a mainly realistic style, now shifted to what some consider Gothic, melodramatic potboilers such as *Il delitto di via Chiatamone* (*The Crime of Via Chiatamone,* 1908) and *La mano tagliatta* (*The Severed Hand,* 1912); founded literary weekly review, *La Settima*

(1902); founded her own newspaper, *Il Giorno* (1904); published *Mors tua* (*The Harvest*), which was critical of Italy's entry into WWI (1926); spent last years of career as a journalist confronting Mussolini's Fascist movement; published almost 40 volumes of fiction, including 30 novels and 100 short stories; focused on urban problems, such as those demonstrated in her home city of Naples and crusaded against the poverty in which Italian women found themselves, especially those in the South. ❖ See also Anthony M. Gisolfi, *The Essential Matilde Serao* (Las Americas, 1968); Laura A. Salsini, *Gendered Genres: Female Experiences and Narrative Patterns in the Works of Matilde Serao* (Fairleigh Dickinson U. Press, 1999); and *Women in World History.*

SERBEZOVA, Mariana (1959—). Bulgarian rower. Born Nov 15, 1959, in Bulgaria. ❖ At Moscow Olympics, won a bronze medal in quadruple sculls with coxswain (1980).

SERBIA, queen of.
See Nikola, Helene Knez (1765–1842).
See Nathalia Keshko (1859–1941).
See Draga (1867–1903).

SERDYUK, Kateryna. Ukrainian archer. Born in Ukraine. ❖ Won a silver medal for teams at Sydney Olympics (2000).

SEREBRIANSKAYA, Yekaterina (1977—). Ukrainian rhythmic gymnast. Name variations: Ekaterina Serebryanskaya. Born Oct 25, 1977, in Simferopol, Ukraine. ❖ Won the European Cup (1993); took 2nd place at World championships (1993) and tied Maria Petrova for all-around (1995); at Atlanta Olympics, won the gold medal in all-around (1996).

SEREBRYAKOVA, Zinaida (1884–1967). Russian painter. Name variations: Sinaida Serebryakova. Born Zinaida Lanceray in Neskuchnoe, near Kharkov, Russia, 1884; died in Paris, France, 1967; dau. of Yevgeny, also seen as Evgeny Lanceray (celebrated sculptor); mother's maiden name was Benois; sister of Nikolai Lanceray, architect, and Evgeny Lanceray, painter, graphic artist and leading member of World of Art group; granddau. of Nikolai Benois, architect; niece of Nikolai and Alexander Benois, both well-known artists; studied art in Italy, then under Osip Braz; studied in Paris at Académie de la Grande Chaumière, 1905–06; m. Boris Serebryakov (railroad engineer), 1905 (died 1919); children: 4. ❖ Joined World of Art group (1906), which believed in the concept of national art, encompassing not only Russian folk art traditions but also architecture and other indigenous Russian art forms; embracing the group's ideals, emphasized style over naturalistic depictions in her work, and her choice of painting Russian contemporary life and environment was unique to her; entered one of her most successful paintings, *Self-Portrait at the Dressing Table,* at Union of Russian Artists exhibition in St. Petersburg (1910); commissioned to execute a mural, moved to Paris (1924) and was exiled for remainder of life. Paintings include *Portrait of a Student* (1909), *At Dinner* (1914), *Bleaching Linen* (1917), *The House of Cards* (1919) *Ballerina in the Dressing Room* and *Snowflakes from Tchaikovsky's Ballet "The Nutcracker."* ❖ See also *Women in World History.*

SEREBRYANSKAYA, Ekaterina (1977—). *See Serebrianskaya, Yekaterina.*

SEREDINA, Antonina (1930—). Soviet kayaker. Born Dec 23, 1960, in USSR. ❖ At Rome Olympics, won gold medals in K2 500 meters and K1 500 meters (1960); at Mexico City Olympics, won a bronze medal in K2 500 meters (1968).

SERENA (d. 410). Roman woman. Executed in 410; niece of Theodosius I, Roman emperor, and Galla (c. 365–394); cousin of Galla Placidia (c. 390–450); m. Flavius Stilicho (Master of Soldiers), c. 384 (died 408); children: daughter who m. Honorius.

SERENA (1774–1831). *See Fouqué, Karoline Freifrau de la Motte.*

SERENA, Amalie (1794–1870). *See Amalie of Saxony.*

SERENO, El (1880–1961). *See Sarfatti, Margherita.*

SERGAVA, Katharine (1910–2005). Russian ballet dancer and musical performer. Name variations: also seen as Katherine or Kathryn Sergava; Katya Sergeiva. Born July 30, 1910, in Tiflis (now Tblisi), Georgia; died Nov 26, 2005, in New York, NY; studied drama and ballet in Paris and London. ❖ Began career in London theater and in such films as *Bedside* (1934), *Cock of the Air* (1934), and *Eighteen Minutes* (1935); moved to US where she danced with Mordkin Ballet (1938–39), Ballet Theater (1940–41) and Original Ballet Russe (1941); achieved acclaim as the "dream" Laurey in Agnes de Mille's long balletic fantasy sequence in

Oklahoma (1943), a role she reportedly danced over 1,000 times; also danced in Jerome Robbins' *Look Ma, I'm Dancing* (1948); joined Actor's Studio and appeared in straight plays, including *Misalliance* (1953) and *The Typewriter* (1955); was falsely reported as having died in Palm Springs (CA), Dec 4, 2003, by the *London Telegraph* and *New York Times*, when in actuality she'd been living in Manhattan, hospitalized that November, and placed in a nursing home.

SERGEANT, Adeline (1851–1904). British novelist. Born Emily Frances Adeline Sergeant, July 4, 1851, in Derbyshire, England; died Dec 4, 1904; attended Queen's College, London; never married; no children. ❖ While she is now little read or known, achieved a fair measure of success in lifetime with the more than 90 novels she wrote at a rapid clip (8 of them were produced in the same year); writings include *Dicky and His Friends* (1879), *Una's Crusade* (1880), *Jacobi's Wife* (1882), *Beyond Recall* (1883), *An Open Foe* (1884), *Seventy Times Seven* (1888), *Esther Denison* (1889), *The Story of a Penitent Soul* (1892), *The Idol Maker* (1897), *The Story of Phil Enderby* (1898) and *This Body of Death* (1901). ❖ See also *Roads to Rome* (1901); and *Women in World History.*

SERGEIVA, Katya (b. 1910). See Sergava, Katharine.

SE RI PAK (1977—). See Pak, Se Ri.

SERLENGA, Nikki (1978—). American soccer player. Born Nichole Lee Serlenga, June 20, 1978, in San Diego, CA. ❖ Midfielder; won a silver medal at Sydney Olympics (2000); signed with Atlanta Beat (2001).

SEROCZYNSKA, Elwira (1931—). Polish speedskater. Name variations: Elwira Seroczyńska. Born Elwira Potapowicz, May 1, 1931, in Vilnius, Poland. ❖ Won a silver medal for 1,500 at Squaw Valley Olympics (1960); competed at Innsbruck Olympics (1964), but did not medal.

SEROTA, Beatrice (1919–2002). English politician and baroness. Name variations: Baroness Serota. Born Beatrice Katz, Oct 15, 1919, in London, England; died Oct 21, 2002; dau. of a clothing wholesaler; attended London School of Economics; m. Stanley Serota (civil engineer), 1942; children: Judith Serota and Sir Nicholas Serota (director of the Tate Gallery). ❖ As a member of the Longford committee on crime (1964), the advisory council on the penal system (1966–68, 1974–79) and the Lately committee on the age of majority (1965–67), played a major role in the development of policies to deal with the welfare of children and the treatment of offenders; promoted to the House of Lords (1967); apppointed Baroness in Waiting (a Government whip); appointed minister of State at Department of Health and Social Security (1969); became a deputy speaker of the House of Lords (1985). Appointed DBE (1992).

SERRAHIMA, Nuria (1937—). Spanish novelist. Name variations: Núria Serrahima. Born 1937 in Barcelona, Spain. ❖ Worked as journalist; one of first women to write in Catalan, wrote such novels as *Mala guilla* (1973) and *L'olor dels nostres cossos* (1982).

SERRANO, Eugenia (1918—). Spanish jounalist, novelist and short-story writer. Born 1918 in Spain. ❖ Works include *Retorno a la tierra* (1945), *Perdimos la primavera* (1953) and *Pista de baile* (1963).

SERRANO, Lupe (1930—). Mexican ballet dancer. Born Dec 7, 1930, in Santiago, Chile; raised in Mexico City; children: Vera Lynn (ballet dancer). ❖ Trained and performed under Nelsy Dambré in Mexico City as an adolescent; danced in Fokine's *Les Sylphides* with Ballet de Palacio de Bellas Artes at age 13; performed with Ballet Alicia Alonso and Ballet Russe de Monte Carlo, where she was featured in 19th-century classics; joined American Ballet Theater in New York City (1951), where she danced as Myrthe, Giselle and Odette, and in pas de deux, and appeared in premieres of Loring's *The Capital of the World* (1957), de Mille's *Sebastien* (1957) and Cullberg's *Lady from the Sea* (1960); was a guest star with numerous companies, including Metropolitan Opera Ballet in New York City (1958–59); taught at Washington School of Ballet.

SERREAU, Coline (1947—). French director, actress and screenwriter. Born Oct 29, 1947, in Paris, France; dau. of Jean-Marie Serreau (actor and stage director) and Geneviève Serreau (writer); children: Nathanaël Serreau; (with Beno Besson) Madeleine Besson. ❖ Began career as a stage and screen actress; made first full-length film, *Mais qu'est ce qu'elles veulent* (But What Do These Women Want?, 1977), had greatest success with *3 hommes et un couffin* (Three Men and a Cradle, 1985), for which she won Cesar awards for Best Film and Best Screenplay, then served as technical advisor on the Hollywood remake, *Three Men and a Baby*; other films include *Romuald et Juliette* (1988), *3 Men and a Little Lady* (1990),

La Crise (1992), *La Belle verte* (1996) and *18 ans après* (2003). Awarded the French Legion of Honor by Jaques Chirac (2004).

SERREAU, Geneviève (1915–1981). French novelist, playwright short-story writer and theater founder. Name variations: Genevieve Serreau. Born 1915 in Oléron, France; died 1981; m. Jean-Marie Serreau (actor and stage director, died 1973); children: Coline Serreau (film director and screenwriter). ❖ Co-founded *Théâtre de Babylone,* which premiered Beckett's *Waiting for Godot* (1953); introduced Brecht to France through translations of his work; wrote *Histoire de nouveau théâtre* (1966), which championed Ionesco, Adamov, Beckett and Genet; wrote novels and short stories, including *Ricercare* (1973) and *Dix-huit mètres cubes de silence* (1976); had a hit play with *Peines de coeur d'une chatte anglaise,* which she adapted from Balzac (1977).

SERRES, Olivia (1772–1834). English painter and impostor. Name variations: Princess Olive, Olive Serres. Born Olivia Wilmot, April 3, 1772, in Warwick, England; died Nov 21, 1834, in England; dau. of Robert Wilmot (house painter); m. John Thomas Serres (Marine Painter to George III), 1791 (sep. 1804); children: 2 daughters, including Lavinia Janetta Horton de Serres (who married portrait painter Antony Ryves). ❖ Infamous impostor who claimed to be the niece of George III; studied drawing with John Thomas Serres, former marine painter to George III and married him (1791); separated from husband (1804), devoting life to painting and literature; appointed landscape painter to George, Prince of Wales (later King George IV); produced novel, poems and memoir of uncle Rev. Dr. Wilmot which endeavored to prove that her uncle wrote *Letters of Junius;* claimed to be illeg. daughter of the king's brother, Henry Frederick (b. 1745), duke of Cumberland (1817), petitioning George III and later George IV; supported claim with documents and also bore significant resemblance to Henry Frederick, thereby winning some to her cause; had herself re-christened with title Princess Olive of Cumberland, placed royal arms on carriage, dressed servants in royal liveries, and published *Memoirs of a Princess* (1812); created a public scandal with her extravagance, pretensions and claims of royalty, leading to husband's attempted suicide (1808) and his death in debtor's prison (1825); was herself arrested for debt (1821), but produced a will of George III, leaving her £15,000; found to have falsified all claims, was officially rebuffed by Sir Robert Peel, while speaking in Parliament (1823); died in King's Bench Prison (1834); daughter Lavinia pursued Olivia's cause, but a jury found the documentation to be false (1866).

SERRUYS, Jenny. See Bradley, Jenny.

SERT, Misia (1872–1950). Russian-born pianist and art patron. Name variations: Misia Godebska Sert. Born Marie Sophie Olga Zenaide Godebska, Mar 30, 1872, in St. Petersburg, Russia; died Oct 15, 1950; dau. of Cyprien Quentin Godebski (Polish sculptor) and Eugénie Sophie Léopoldine Servais Godebska (Frenchwoman); m. Thadée Natanson, April 25, 1893; m. Alfred Edwards (newspaper baron), Feb 24, 1905 (div. Feb 24, 1909); m. José-María Sert (Spanish painter), Sept 2, 1920 (div. Dec 28, 1927). ❖ Patron of the arts during Belle Époque, gave 1st public concert in Paris (1892); married Thadée Natanson (1893), who founded *La Revue Blanche,* which became one of the main journals of Belle Époque culture; befriended and patronized many of the great artists and writers of the time, including Sergei Diaghilev, Igor Stravinsky, Claude Debussey, Marcel Proust and Gabrielle "Coco" Chanel; beautiful and vivacious, modeled for Auguste Renoir, Henri Toulouse-Latrec, Edouard Vuillard and Pierre Bonnard; following 2nd marriage, became one of the chief patrons of the arts in Western Europe. ❖ See also *Misia and the Muses: The Memoirs of Misia Sert* (Day, 1953); Gold and Fizdale, *Misia: The Life of Misia Sert* (Knopf, 1980); and *Women in World History.*

SERVEN, Ida (c. 1850s–c. 1896). See Simpson-Serven, Ida.

SERVICE, Eileen Louise (1900–1989). See Soper, Eileen Louise.

SERVILIA I (fl. 100 BCE). Roman noblewoman. Name variations: Servilia the Elder. Flourished around 100 BCE; dau. of Q. Servilius Caepio (praetor) and Livia (fl. 100 BCE); sister of Servilia II (c. 100–after 42 BCE); half-sister of Portia (fl. 80 BCE) and Cato the Younger; m. L. Licinius Lucullus (a consul).

SERVILIA II (c. 100–after 42 BCE). Roman noblewoman. Name variations: Servilia the Younger. Born c. 100; died after 42 BCE; dau. of Q. Servilius Caepio (praetor in 91) and Livia (fl. 100 BCE); sister of Servilia I; half-sister of Portia (fl. 80 BCE) and Cato the Younger; married M. Junius Brutus (tribune in 83, executed 77 BCE); married D. Junius Silanus (a consul); children: (1st m.) M. Junius Brutus (the famous assassin of Julius Caesar); (2nd m.) 3 daughters (all named Junia), Junia (who m.

M. Aemilius Lepidus); Junia (who m. P. Servilius Isauricus); Junia (who m. C. Cassius Longinus, better known as Cassius, another assassin of Julius Caesar). ❖ A political creature by nature and breeding and ambitious to oversee the political rehabilitation of her paternal line, worked tirelessly behind the scenes to weave a web of influence which she intended would establish her as the arbiter of Roman politics; through daughters marriages, maintained firm contacts with the 2 factions which defined the political extremes of the last generation of the Roman Republic; during her heyday, reigned as a Roman princess in all but name; established herself as a political broker with the appropriate contacts to attempt a reconciliation of Rome's feuding factions; as Julius Caesar's mistress (66–44), seems to have been the Roman love of his life, though both knew other "acquaintances" and neither seriously contemplated marriage with the other; did not abandon son's interests after Caesar's assassination, probably because, despite what he had done, he represented the continuation of the political influence she had worked so hard to win for her line. ❖ See also *Women in World History*.

SERVOSS, Mary (1881–1968). American actress. Born June 2, 1881, in Chicago, IL; died Nov 20, 1968, in Los Angeles, CA. ❖ Made Broadway debut as Alice in *Bedford's Hope* (1906); other appearances include *The Master of the House*, *Tiger Cats*, *Consequences*, Portia in *Merchant of Venice*, Anna Maurrant in *Street Scene*, Gertrude in *Hamlet*, Cora Simon in *Counsellor-at-Law*, Ada Lester in *Tobacco Road*, Mrs. Morales in *Tortilla Flat*, Stella Hemingway in *Swan Song*, and First Woman of Corinth in *Medea*; managed summer stock companies (1911–16).

SESSIONS, Almira (1888–1974). American stage, tv, and screen actress. Born Sept 16, 1888, in Washington, DC; died Aug 3, 1974, in Los Angeles, CA. ❖ Appeared in vaudeville, radio and tv; made over 500 films, including *Little Nelly Kelly*, *Chad Hanna*, *Sullivan's Travels*, *Miracle of Morgan's Creek*, *Apartment for Peggy*, *The Fountainhead*, *Boston Strangler* and *Rosemary's Baby*.

SESSIONS, Kate O. (1857–1940). American horticulturist. Born Kate Olivia Sessions, Nov 8, 1857, in San Francisco, California; died Mar 24, 1940, in La Jolla, California; dau. of Josiah Sessions (horse breeder) and Harriet (Parker) Sessions; University of California at Berkeley, PhB in chemistry, 1881. ❖ Leased a 30-acre parcel of land from the San Diego municipal government to cultivate plants for her nursery (1892), land that would become the city's Balboa Park; became co-founder (1909), officer, and member of the board, San Diego Floral Association (1909–30s); is also credited with bringing numerous plants to Southern California, including the popular palm tree and assorted varieties of poppies, shrubs, eucalyptus, juniper, oak, and vines. Was 1st woman to receive the Meyer Medal from American Genetic Association (1939). ❖ See also *Women in World History*.

SESSIONS, Patty Bartlett (1795–1892). American midwife. Born Patty Bartlett, Feb 4, 1795, in Bethel, Oxford, ME; died Dec 14, 1892; dau. of Anna (Hall) Bartlett and Enoch Bartlett (shoemaker); m. David Sessions, June 13, 1812 (as a Mormon, he took 2 additional wives in Utah, died 1850); m. John Parry (the 1st leader of Mormon Tabernacle Choir who took a 2nd wife as well), after 1850; children: 8, including sons David Sessions Jr. and Perrigrine Sessions, who founded Bountiful, Utah, and daughter Sylvia Sessions Lyon Clark. ❖ The mother of Mormon midwives, moved to her midwife mother-in-law's home in Ketcham, ME, after marriage to David Sessions (1812); moved to Andover West Surplus, ME, with family (1814); baptized as a Mormon (July 1834), followed by husband (1835); with the Mormons, moved with family to Far West, MO (June 1837), and eventually to the valley of the Great Salt Lake, Utah (1847); delivered the 1st Mormon baby shortly after her arrival; was a charter member (1848) and a president of the Council of Health. ❖ See also Donna Toland Smart, ed. *Mormon Midwife: The 1846–1888 Diaries of Patty Bartlett Sessions* (Utah State U. Press, 1997).

SETH, Reidun (1966—). Norwegian soccer player. Born June 9, 1966, in Norway. ❖ Won a team bronze medal at Atlanta Olympics (1996).

SETON, Elizabeth Ann (1774–1821). American saint and religious founder. Name variations: Elizabeth Bayley Seton; Mother Seton; Saint Elizabeth Ann Seton. Born Elizabeth Ann Bayley in New York, NY, Aug 28, 1774; died of TB at Emmitsburg, Maryland, Jan 4, 1821; dau. of Richard Bayley (prominent physician and 1st professor of anatomy at Columbia) and Catherine (Charlton) Bayley; m. William Magee Seton, Jan 25, 1794 (died 1803); children: Anna Maria Seton (b. 1795); William Seton (b. 1796); Richard Bayley Seton (b. 1798); Catherine Josephine Seton (b. 1800); Rebecca Seton (b. 1802). ❖ Catholic convert

and founder of American Sisters of Charity who was the 1st person born in US to be canonized a saint by the Roman Catholic Church; helped found the Society for the Relief of Poor Widows with Small Children (1797); following death of husband, was received into Catholic Church (1805); moved to Baltimore to found Catholic school for girls (1808); took 1st vows as Sister of Charity, received 1st recruits into the order, and moved school and her community to Emmitsburg, Maryland (1809); had to battle male superiors for a say in the writing of the constitution and the community rule; cause for canonization introduced at the Vatican (1907), and 12 vols. of her diaries, letters, prayer books and other material were submitted for study as authenticated writings, in place of living witnesses to her sanctity; declared Saint Elizabeth Ann Seton by Pope Paul VI (1975). ❖ See also *Elizabeth Seton: Selected Writings* (ed. by Kelly and Melville, Paulist Press, 1987); Joseph I. Dirvin, *Mrs. Seton: Foundress of the American Sisters of Charity* (Farrar, 1975); William Jarvis, *Mother Seton's Sisters of Charity* (Columbia U., 1984); and *Women in World History*.

SETON, Grace Gallatin (1872–1959). American feminist, suffragist, explorer, and writer. Name variations: Grace Seton-Thompson. Born Jan 28, 1872, in Sacramento, California; died Mar 19, 1959, in Palm Beach, Florida; dau. of Albert Gallatin and Clemenzie (Rhodes) Gallatin; graduate of Packer Collegiate Institute, 1892; m. Ernest Thompson Seton (naturalist and writer), 1896 (div. 1935); children: Ann Seton, known as Anya Seton (1904–1990, writer). ❖ Participated in the organization of the Camp Fire Girls (1912); served as president of Connecticut Woman Suffrage Association (1910–20) and president of National League of American Pen Women (1926–28, 1930–32); established Biblioteca Femina, a collection of 2,000 volumes and 100 pamphlets written by women from all over the world (1930s), which was eventually donated to Northwestern University; sought out adventure and wrote about it in a series of books which provided historical perspectives on the countries she traveled in, including Egypt, Japan, China and India; writings include *A Woman Tenderfoot* (1900), *Nimrod's Wife* (1907), *A Woman Tenderfoot in Egypt* (1923), *Chinese Lanterns* (1924), *Yes, Lady Saheb* (1925), *Poison Arrows* (1938) and (poetry) *The Singing Traveler* (1947). ❖ See also *Women in World History*.

SETON, Mother (1774–1821). *See Seton, Elizabeth Ann.*

SETON-THOMPSON, Grace (1872–1959). *See Seton, Grace Gallatin.*

SETOUCHI, Harumi (1922—). *See Setouchi, Jakucho.*

SETOUCHI, Jakucho (1922—). Japanese novelist. Name variations: Setouchi Harumi. Born May 15, 1922, in Tokushima prefecture, Japan; graduate of Tokyo Women's Christian University; married and divorced. ❖ Under her secular name, Setouchi Harumi, published novel *The Core of a Flower* (1957), which was considered pornographic at the time because of her sexual candor; wrote *Tamura Toshiko* (1962), which won the 1st Tamura Toshiko Prize, as well as *The End of Summer* (1962) and *Beauty in Disarray* (1966); shaved her head, entered the Buddhist priesthood at Chusonji Temple (1973), and took the name Setouchi Jakucho; became chief priestess of Tendaiji temple in Iwate Prefecture (1987); moved to Kyoto; translated Lady Murasaki's *Tale of Genji* from classical to modern Japanese, and turned it into a huge bestseller (1999), all 10 volumes; retired as chief priestess (2005); also wrote *Feminine Virtue* (2000) and autobiographical novel, *From Which Place*. Won Tanizaki Prize for *Hana ni Toe (Ask the Flowers*, 1992).

SETSUKO CHICHIBU (1909–1995). *See Chichibu, Setsuko.*

SETZER, Marian (1918–2002). *See Bergeron, Marian.*

SEUFERT, Christina (1957—). American diver. Born Jan 13, 1957, in Sacramento, CA. ❖ At Los Angeles Olympics, won a bronze medal in springboard (1984).

SEVENS, Elizabeth (1949—). Dutch field-hockey player. Born June 29, 1949, in the Netherlands. ❖ At Los Angeles Olympics, won a gold medal in team competition (1984).

SEVERA, Marina (fl. 4th c.). Roman noblewoman. First wife of Valentinian I, Roman emperor (r. 364–375); children: Gratian. ❖ Valentinian's 2nd wife was Justina (fl. 350–370).

SEVERANCE, Caroline M. (1820–1914). American suffragist, abolitionist, and club founder. Born Caroline Maria Seymour, Jan 12, 1820, in Canandaigua, New York; died Nov 10, 1914, in Los Angeles, California; dau. of Orson Seymour (banker) and Caroline (Clark) Seymour; m. Theodoric Cordenio Severance (banker), 1840; children: Orson (1841–

1841), James (b. 1842), Julia (b. 1844), Mark (1846) and Pierre (1849). ❖ With husband, was active in liberal causes and founded the Independent Christian Church, which was against slavery; presided over the 1st meeting of Ohio Women's Right's Association (1853); spoke on abolitionism to audiences in Massachusetts and Rhode Island (1856–61); founded American Equal Rights Association with Susan B. Anthony (1866); founded American Woman Suffrage Association with Lucy Stone and others (1869); following a move to Los Angeles (1875), founded the city's 1st Unitarian congregation with husband; established New England Woman's Club (1868) and Friday Morning Club in Los Angeles (1891); acknowledged as the 1st woman to register to vote under California's new woman suffrage law (1911). ❖ See also *Women in World History.*

SÉVERINE (1855–1929). French writer and lecturer. Name variations: Caroline Rémy or Remy; Caroline Rémy Guebhard; Mme. Adrien Guebhard or Guébhard; Severine. Pronunciation: say-VREEN. Born Caroline Rémy, April 27, 1855, in Paris, France; died at Pierrefonds (Oise), April 24, 1929; dau. of Marie-Joseph-Onésime Rémy (civil servant) and Mlle Villiaume-Geniès; m. Antoine-Henri Montrobert, 1871 (div. c. 1885); m. Dr. Adrien Guebhard, 1885 (died 1924); children: Louis-Georges-Auguste Montrobert (b. 1872); (with Guebhard) Roland Guebhard (1880–1926). ❖ In her time the most famous female journalist in the world, was the 1st French woman to run a newspaper and to earn a living as a regularly featured columnist in major newspapers; fled Paris with parents during the Commune and married to escape from home (1871); had a son with Adrien Guebhard and met Jules Vallès (1880); tried to commit suicide (1881); launched *Le Cri du Peuple* with Vallès and began to write (1883); directed *Le Cri du Peuple* (1885–88); descended into a mine to report on a disaster (1890); interviewed Pope Leo XIII (1892); raised money for unfortunates (1894–96); came under severe personal attack during the Lebaudy Affair (1896); covered the Dreyfus Affair for *La Fronde* (1898–99); became converted to political rights for women (1900); was especially active in peace and women's causes (1912–14); advocated a negotiated peace (1916–18); spoke in honor of the Russian Revolution (1917); spoke at a women's reception for President Wilson, and joined *l'Humanité* (1919); joined and then left the Communist Party (1921–23); gave last speech, at a rally protesting death sentences for Sacco and Vanzetti (1927); published her last article (1929); wrote more than 6,000 articles over a span of 46 years and attained a place no woman before her had reached in the thoroughly suffocating, masculine world of *la grande presse.* ❖ See also autobiographical novel, *Line (1855–1867)* (1921); and *Women in World History.*

SEVERN, Margaret (1901–1997). American ballet and interpretive dancer and choreographer. Born 1901 in Birmingham, Alabama; died in Vancouver, British Columbia, 1997; dau. of Dr. Elizabeth Severn (suffragist and psychologist). ❖ At 9, moved to London where she trained with Léon and Edouard Espinosa; made solo debut at Hotel Savoy (1914) before moving to New York, where she continued training with Mikhail Fokine and Luigi Albertieri, and took classes at Denishawn School; at 15, appeared at Metropolitan Opera in *Aida*; was a soloist in Ruth St. Denis recitals (1917); appeared on Broadway in *Linger Longer Letty* (1919), *As You Were* (1920), and *Greenwich Village Follies of 1920*; appeared in vaudeville on Keith and Orpheum circuit, using character masks in most performances; created works for Ballets Russes de Ida Rubinstein and Ballets Russes de Paris (1935–36), among them *Rhapsodie* and *Bolero*; played important role in unionization of dancers (late 1930s) and was founding president of The Dancers' Club; retired to Vancouver (1971). ❖ See also (documentary) *Dance Masks: The World of Margaret Severn* (1981).

SEVERSON, Kim (1973—). American equestrian. Name variations: Kimberly Vinoski-Severson. Born Kimberly Lyda Severson, Aug 22, 1973, in Tucson, AZ; dau. of Ed Severson (features writer for Arizona Daily Star) and Jackie Severson. ❖ Placed 1st for 3-day event (team) at World Equestrian Games (2002); on Winsome Adante, won a bronze medal for indiv. eventing and a silver medal for team eventing at Athens Olympics (2004).

SEVIER, Clara Driscoll (1881–1945). *See Driscoll, Clara.*

SÉVIGNÉ, Marie de (1626–1696). French letter writer. Name variations: Marie Rabutin-Chantal; Marie de Rabutin Chantal; Madame de Sévigné; Marquise de Sevigne. Born in Paris, France, Feb 5, 1626; died April 17, 1696, at Les Rochers, Provence; dau. of Celse-Bénigne de Rabutin-Chantal (1596–1627) and Marie de Coulanges (1603–1633); granddau. of Jeanne Françoise de Chantal (1572–1641); m. Henri, Marquis de

Sévigné (1623–1651), Aug 4, 1644; children: Françoise-Marguerite, future countess de Grignan (1646–1705); Charles (Mar 12, 1648–Mar 26, 1713). ❖ Aristocrat and landowner best known for the lively series of letters which she wrote to her daughter over the course of more than 20 years; born into the French aristocracy but orphaned at 7; raised by her extended family and given a good education; at 18, married a noble (1644); after husband was killed in a duel (1651), raised her children and administered her estates while maintaining independence; became deeply attached to daughter and wrote to her whenever the 2 were separated after daughter's marriage (1670). Her letters are her main claim to fame; witty, dramatic, poetic, and boldly descriptive, they provide a unique perspective on the high politics of the reign of the magnificent Sun King, while they are also rich in the details of everyday life, revealing the feelings of a mother far away from the daughter she loves. ❖ See also Harriet Ray Allentuch, *Madame de Sévigné: A Portrait in Letters* (Johns Hopkins Press, 1963); Frances Mossiker, *Madame de Sévigné: A Life and Letters* (Knopf, 1983); Jeanne A. Ojala and William T. Ojala, *Madame de Sévigné: A Seventeenth-Century Life* (St. Martin, 1990); and *Women in World History.*

SEVILLA, Carmen (1930—). Spanish actress, singer and dancer. Born María del Carmen García Galisteo, Oct 16, 1930, in Seville, Andalucia, Spain; m. Augusto Algueró, 1961. ❖ Star of stage, screen and nightclubs, made film debut in *Jalisco canta en Sevilla* (1948); other films include *La Guitarra de Gardel, Cuentos de la Alhambra, Andalousie, Le désir et l'amour, Violetas imperiales, Pluma al viento, La Belle de Cadix, Congreso en Sevilla, Requiebro, La fierecilla domada, El amor de Don Juan, Gli amanti del deserto, La venganza, Spanish Affair, Europa di notte, King of Kings* and *Antony and Cleopatra.*

SEVILLE, Carolina Ada (1874–1955). New Zealand nurse, hospital matron and founder. Name variations: Caroline Ada Insull, Kitty Seville. Born Feb 18, 1874, in Birmingham, England; died May 7, 1955, in Morrinsville, New Zealand; dau. of Walter Horace Insull and Sarah Caroline (King) Insull; m. George Edward Seville (physician), 1902 (died 1933); children: 1 daughter. ❖ Trained as nurse at General Hospital in Birmingham; established Morrinsville's first hospital, Loloma (1911), and served as manager, matron, and midwife; was active in volunteer relief organizations during WWI, and gave lectures to Red Cross and St John Ambulance Brigade during WWII. Member of British Empire (1953). ❖ See also *Dictionary of New Zealand Biography* (Vol. 3).

SEVILLE, Kitty (1874–1955). *See Seville, Carolina Ada.*

SEVOSTYANOVA, Nadezhda (1953—). Soviet rower. Born Sept 1953 in USSR. ❖ At Montreal Olympics, won a bronze medal in coxed fours (1976).

SEWALL, Lucy Ellen (1837–1890). American physician and feminist. Born April 1837 in Roxbury, Massachusetts; died Feb 13, 1890; dau. of Samuel Edmund Sewall (abolitionist and advocate of women's rights) and Louisa Maria (Winslow) Sewall (abolitionist, died 1850); graduate of New England Female Medical College, 1862; studied in London and Paris; never married; no children. ❖ One of the 1st women to become a medical doctor in US, became resident physician of New England Hospital for Women and Children (1863); spent much of her time with poor women and was well respected for her work in obstetrics; resigned residency (1869) to become one of two attending physicians at the hospital and devote more time to her private practice. ❖ See also *Women in World History.*

SEWALL, May Wright (1844–1920). American educator, suffragist, club founder, writer, and pacifist. Born May Eliza Wright, May 27, 1844, in Greenfield, Wisconsin; died July 23, 1920, in Indianapolis, Indiana; dau of Philander Montague Wright and Mary Weeks (Brackett) Wright; Northwestern Female College, Mistress of Science, 1866, Master of Arts, 1871; m. Edwin W. Thompson (mathematics teacher), 1872 (died 1875); m. Theodore Lovett Sewall (educator), 1880 (died 1895); no children. ❖ Co-founded Indianapolis Equal Suffrage Society (1878) and the Girls' Classical School of Indianapolis (1882); helped found Western Association of Collegiate Alumnae (1883); served as chair of executive committee of National Women Suffrage Association (1882–90); helped establish National Council of Women and International Council of Women (1888); founded General Federation of Women's Clubs (1889); headed World Congress of Representative Women (1893); appointed US representative to Paris Exposition by President William McKinley (1900); an active member of American Peace Society, accompanied Rosika Schwimmer on the "Peace Ship" (*Oscar II*), funded by Henry Ford, in an attempt to end the war in Europe (1915); writings include *Women, World War, and Permanent Peace* (1915) and *Neither Dead Nor Sleeping* (1920); for several years, edited a women's column in *Indianapolis Times*. ❖ See also *Women in World History.*

SEWARD, Anna (1742–1809). English poet. Name variations: "Swan of Lichfield"; Benvolio. Born in Eyam, Derbyshire, England, Dec 12, 1742; died at the Bishop's Palace, in Lichfield, Staffordshire, Mar 25, 1809; dau. of Thomas Seward (rector of Eyam and later canon of Lichfield and Salisbury) and Elizabeth Hunter Seward (whose father had been headmaster of Lichfield Grammar School and the teacher of Dr. Samuel Johnson); never married; no children. ❖ Began to write in her mid-30s and was a frequent contributor to *Gentlemen's Magazine*; was a well-known figure at literary salons; supplied Boswell with details about the early years of Dr. Samuel Johnson; her dislike for Johnson was well known when she parodied his letters in the *Gentlemen's Magazine* under the signature Benvolio; published poetical novel *Louisa* (1782); published poem "Llangollen Vale," (1796), which describes a visit she made to Lady Eleanor Butler and Sarah Ponsonby, the Ladies of Llangollen; bequeathed her poetical works to Sir Walter Scott, who had them published with a memoir in 3 vols. in 1810. ❖ See also E. V. Lucas, *A Swan and Her Friends* (1907); Margaret Ashmun, *The Singing Swan* (1931); H. Pearson, *The Swan of Lichfield* (1936); and *Women in World History.*

SEWELL, Anna (1820–1878). English writer. Born Mar 30, 1820, in Yarmouth, Norfolk, England; died in Old Catton, near Norwich, England, April 25, 1878; dau. of Isaac Sewell (bank manager) and Mary Wright Sewell (writer); never married. ❖ Writer whose sole published work, *Black Beauty,* became both a bestselling children's classic and a rallying cry for 19th-century organizations which campaigned for the humane treatment of animals; moved to Dalston, where she was given horse-riding lessons (1822); moved to Stoke Newington, where she eventually injured an ankle while running during a rainstorm (1832); moved to Brighton (1836); moved to Wick and began teaching a class in biology to workingmen (1848); only able to walk with a crutch, received hydrotherapy treatments in Germany (1846 and 1856); moved to Old Catton (1867); began writing *Black Beauty: The Autobiography of a Horse* (1871); completed manuscript for *Black Beauty* and was paid £20 for the story, which was issued during the Christmas season (1877); favorable reviews appeared, and 30,000 copies were sold at time of her death (1878); eventually sold more than 30 million copies, becoming one of the most enduring popular literary works from the 19th century. ❖ See also Margaret J. Baker, *Anna Sewell and Black Beauty* (1956); Susan Chitty, *The Woman Who Wrote* Black Beauty*: The Life of Anna Sewell* (Hodder & Stoughton, 1971); and *Women in World History.*

SEWELL, Edna (1881–1967). American advocate for farm women. Born Edna Belle Scott in Ambia, Indiana, Aug 1, 1881; died in Lafayette, Indiana, 1967; dau. of Clinton Scott (farmer) and Emma (Albaugh) Scott; m. Charles W. Sewell, 1897 (died 1933); children: Greta Geneive Sewell (b. 1900); Gerald Scott Sewell (1904–1945). ❖ Organized and helped direct 1st home improvement tours ever conducted in US; was instrumental in prompting the American Farm Bureau Federation (AFBF) to welcome women as members; served as board member of Indiana Farm Bureau; headed Associated Women of the AFBF (1934–50). ❖ See also *Women in World History.*

SEWELL, Elizabeth Missing (1815–1906). British novelist and children's writer. Born Feb 19, 1815, in Newport, Isle of Wight; died Aug 17, 1906, in Bonchurch, Isle of Wight; dau. of Thomas Sewell (solicitor) and Jane (Edwards) Sewell; sister of William Sewell (1804–1874), a leading figure in the Oxford Movement; another brother was the 1st premier of New Zealand; another the warden of New College; educated in Newport and Bath; never married; no children. ❖ Strongly influenced by brother William, published 1st book, *Stories, Illustrative of the Lord's Prayer* (1840); wrote 3-part *Laneton Parsonage* (1846–48) to teach children about the use of the Catechism; when John Henry Newman, one of the leaders of Oxford Movement, converted to Roman Catholicism, wrote the anti-Catholic novel *Margaret Percival* (1847); though her novels *Amy Herbert* (1844), written for young girls, and *Katharine Ashton* (1854) stress moral and religious duty, wrote about her own childhood in her most popular book, *The Experience of Life* (1852); also wrote travel books, devotional works, and school textbooks; established St. Boniface School for girls at Ventnor (1866), based on her liberal views on women's education, which she discussed in *Principles of Education* (1865). ❖ See also *Autobiography* (1907); Eleanor M. Sewell, ed. *The Autobiography of Elizabeth M. Sewell* (1907).

SEWELL, Mary Wright (1797–1884). English author. Born Mary Wright in England, 1797; died 1884; dau. of John Wright (Quaker); m. Isaac Sewell (bank manager), 1819; children: Anna Sewell (1820–1878, writer); Philip Sewell (b. 1822). ❖ Wrote verses and stories of a moral nature, including her poem collections *Stories in Verse* (1861) and *Poems and Ballads* (1886). ❖ See also *Women in World History.*

SEXBURGA (c. 627–673). Queen of Wessex. Name variations: Seaxburg; Seaxburh; Sexburh. Born c. 627; died in 673; m. Kenwealh, also seen as Coinwalch or Cenwalh, king of West Saxons or Wessex (r. 643–672). ❖ Following death of husband (672), reigned as queen of Wessex (672–73); deposed because her nobles refused to obey the orders of a woman. ❖ See also *Women in World History.*

SEXBURGA (d. around 699). Queen of Kent, 2nd abbess of Ely, and saint. Name variations: Saint Sexburga; Sexburga of East Anglia. Born in East Anglia; died c. 699; dau. of Saewara and Anna, king of East Anglia (r. 635–654); sister of Elthelthrith (630–679) and Withburga; half-sister of Ethelburga (d. 665); m. Earconbert also known as Ercombert, king of Kent (r. 640–664), around 640; children: Egbert, king of Kent (r. 664–673); Hlothere, king of Kent (r. 673–685); Earcongota; Ermenilda (who m. Wulfhere, king of Mercia). ❖ Founded a monastery for nuns in Isle of Sheppey and became its abbess; on death of sister Elthelthrith (c. 679), the 1st abbess of Ely, succeeded her; tenure ran for around 20 years. Feast day is July 6. ❖ See also *Women in World History.*

SEXTON, Alice (1868–1959). *See Sexton, Elsie Wilkins.*

SEXTON, Anne (1928–1974). American poet. Name variations: Anne Gray Harvey. Born Anne Gray Harvey, Nov 9, 1928, in Newton, Massachusetts; committed suicide, Oct 4, 1974; dau. of Ralph Churchill Harvey (businessman) and Mary Gray (Staples) Harvey; m. Alfred Muller Sexton II; children: Linda Gray Sexton (b. 1953); Joyce Ladd Sexton (b. 1955). ❖ One of the most important English-speaking poets of mid-20th century and a founding mother of the variously celebrated and maligned confessional school of poetry, spent the better portion of her 46 years tortured by life and flirting with death, branded, as she was from the onset of adulthood, by mental illness; began treatment with Martin Orne (1956), after the 1st of what would prove to be a series of suicide attempts and subsequent hospitalizations, and it was he who urged her to write poetry; published 1st volume, *To Bedlam and Part Way Back* (1960), which was nominated for a National Book Award; writing in a period of pre-feminism and eschewing such labels, nevertheless connected her poetry to her marginalized position as a woman and a housewife; followed success of 1st book with another success, *All My Pretty Ones* (1962), which won *Poetry*'s Levinson Prize and the National Book Award; taught poetry in workshops, 1st at Harvard University (1961), then Radcliffe; published *Selected Poems* (1964), followed by *Live or Die* (1966), which won Pulitzer Prize; began lecturing at Boston University (1967), a position that ultimately became a full professorship; wrote *Love Poems* and worked on American Place Theater production of her play *Mercy Street* (1969); issued another volume of poetry, *Transformations* (1971), one of her most popular books, which was an adaptation of the fairy tales of the Brothers Grimm; published *The Book of Folly* (1972) and *The Death Notebooks* (1974); took her own life after numerous failed attempts; posthumous publications include *The Awful Rowing Toward God* (1975), *45 Mercy Street* (1976) and *Words for Dr. Y.* (1978). Elected fellow of Royal Society of Literature (1965). ❖ See also Diane Wood Middlebrook, *Anne Sexton: A Biography* (Houghton, 1991); Linda Sexton, *Searching for Mercy Street* (Little, Brown, 1994); and *Women in World History.*

SEXTON, Elsie Wilkins (1868–1959). English zoologist and artist. Name variations: E. W. Sexton; Alice Sexton. Born Alice Wilkins Wing, April 27, 1868; died Feb 18, 1959; studied at Cornwall's Truro School of Art; m. Louis E. Sexton (dentist). ❖ Based in Plymouth at the Marine Biological Association, was invited to illustrate worms and other invertebrates for Dr. J. E. Allen's publications; published her 1st illustrations (1902); identified shrimps (amphipods) from Allen's collecting cruise in the Bay of Biscay (1906); published a popular study on the life history and genetics research of a shrimp species (*G. chevreuxi,* 1924); served as a director's research assistant and as a zoologist at Plymouth Marine Laboratory (1924–48); pursued genetic work until 1936; was a fellow of Linnean Society for 43 years.

SEY, Jennifer (1969—). American gymnast. Born Feb 23, 1969; trained with Parkettes in Allentown, PA. ❖ Placed 2nd at Canadian Classic (1982) and US Classic (1985); won US nationals (1986).

SEYFERT, Gabriele (1948—). East German skater. Name variations: Gaby Seyfert. Born 1948 in East Germany; daughter of Jutta Mueller (her mother and also her coach). ❖ Won a silver medal at the Grenoble Olympics (1968); won the World championships (1969 and 1970) and European championship (1967). ❖ See also autobiography (in German) *Da muss noch was sein: Mein Leben, mehr als Pflicht und Kür* (1998).

SEYLER, Athene (1889–1990). English actress. Born in London, England, May 31, 1889; died 1990; dau. of Clarence H. Seyler and Clara (Thies) Seyler; attended Bedford College; studied at Academy of Dramatic Art; married James Bury Sterndale-Bennett (died); married Nicholas Hannen. ❖ Comedic actress, made debut at Kingsway Theatre as Pamela Grey in *The Truants* (1909); had long, successful stage career in such roles as Rosalind in *As You Like It* (1920), Polly in *Kind Hearts and Coronets* (1920), Gabrielle in *The Coming of Gabrielle* (1923), Beatrice in *Much Ado About Nothing* (1924), Hermia in *A Midsummer Night's Dream* (1924), Miss Moffatt in *The Corn is Green* (1939), Madame Ranevska in *The Cherry Orchard* (1941), Fanny Farrelly in *Watch on the Rhine* (1942), Veta Louise Simmons in *Harvey* (1949) and Amy Beringer in *First Person Singular* (1952); films include *The Citadel* (1938), *Dear Octopus* (1943), *Nicholas Nickleby* (1947), *Pickwick Papers* (1953), *The Inn of the Sixth Happiness* as Mrs. Lawson (1958), *Make Mine Mink* (1959) and *Nurse on Wheels* (1963); also directed for the stage and authored (with Stephen Haggard) *The Craft of Comedy* (1944); elected president of Royal Academy of Dramatic Art (1950) and Theatrical Ladies Guild (1950). Received CBE (1959).

SEYMOUR, Anne (c. 1532–1587). British poet. Born c. 1532; died 1587; dau. of Edward, duke of Somerset, and Anne Stanhope (1497–1587); sister of Margaret Seymour and Jane Seymour; niece of Jane Seymour, queen of England; m. John Dudley (son of the earl of Warwick), 1550; m. Sir Edward Union, 1555. ❖ With sisters Margaret and Jane, wrote Latin elegy to Margaret of Angoulême published by Nicolas Denisot in collection called *Annae, Margaritae, Iannae, sororum virginum, heroidum Anglarum, in mortem Diuae Margaritae Valesiae, navarrorum Reginae, Hecadostichon* (1550), the 1st encomium in English by women for a woman. The poem, which was immediately successful and translated into Greek, Italian, and French, was republished in French volume *Le Tombeau de Marguerite de Valois, Royne de Navarre, Faict premierement en Distiques latins par les trois Soeurs Princesses en Angleterre. Depit traduictz en Grec, Italien, & François par plusiers Odes, Hymnes, Cantiques, Epitaphes, sur le mesme subject* (1551).

SEYMOUR, Anne (1909–1988). American stage, tv, and screen actress. Born Anne Eckert, Sept 11, 1909, in New York, NY; died Dec 8, 1988, in Los Angeles, CA; dau. of May Davenport Seymour (actress and museum curator, died 1967); sister of John Seymour and James Seymour (both actors). ❖ Made stage debut (1928); appeared on Broadway in *Mr. Moneypenny, School for Scandal, Troilus and Cressida, The Seagull* and *Sunrise at Campobello*; films include *All the King's Men, Desire Under the Elms, Home from the Hill, Pollyanna, Sunrise at Campobello, Good Neighbor Sam, Mirage, Fitzwilly* and *Field of Dreams*; appeared with her mother for 9 years on radio's "Against the Storm."

SEYMOUR, Arabella (1575–1615). See Stuart, Arabella.

SEYMOUR, Catherine (c. 1540–1568). See Grey, Catherine.

SEYMOUR, Clarine (1898–1920). American actress. Born Dec 9, 1898, in Brooklyn, NY; died April 25, 1920, in New Rochelle, NY, after an emergency operation for "strangulation of the intestines." ❖ Light comedian, made film debut (1917); appeared in 4 films of D. W. Griffith, *The Girl Who Stayed Home, True Heart Susie, Scarlet Days* and *The Idol Dancer*; at the time of her death, was working on the movie *Way Down East*, as Kate Brewster.

SEYMOUR, Elizabeth (d. 1776). See Percy, Elizabeth.

SEYMOUR, Ethel (1881–1963). English gymnast. Born 1881 in UK; died Nov 13, 1963. ❖ At Amsterdam Olympics, won a bronze medal in team all-around (1928).

SEYMOUR, Frances (d. 1674). See Devereux, Frances.

SEYMOUR, Frances (d. 1679). Countess of Holderness. Died 1679; interred on Jan 5, 1680, in Westminster Abbey, London; dau. of Frances Devereux (d. 1674) and William Seymour (1587–1660), 2nd duke of Somerset (r. 1660–1660); m. Richard Molyneux, 2nd viscount Molyneux; m. Thomas Wriothesly (1607–1667), 5th earl of Southampton (r. 1624–1667); m. Conyers Darcy, 2nd earl of Holderness, in 1676; stepchildren: Rachel Russell (1636–1723).

SEYMOUR, Frances Thynne (1699–1754). English poet, patron of letters, and countess of Hertford. Name variations: Frances Thynne; duchess of Somerset. Born May 10, 1699, in Longleat, Warminster, Wiltshire, England; died July 7, 1754, at Percy Lodge, Iver, Buckinghamshire, England; interred in Westminster Abbey; dau. of Honorable Henry Thynne (died 1708) and Grace Strode Thynne; m. Algernon Seymour (b. 1684), Baron Percy, earl of Hertford and later 7th duke of Somerset, on Mar 1, 1715 (died 1750); children: Elizabeth Percy (1716–1776), duchess of Northumberland; George Seymour (1725–1744), Lord Beauchamp. ❖ When husband was named to House of Peers (1723), was appointed Lady of the Bedchamber to princess of Wales, later Queen Caroline of Ansbach, a position she would hold until 1737; became an intimate of the queen and other noblewomen who shared her literary interests; wrote 1st known verses (c. 1723), and throughout her life would often exchange verses with correspondents; allowed some to be printed (1725), though anonymously, in *A New Miscellany*; despite praise, always considered writing a pastime and resisted publication; following deaths of son and husband, her letters and verses were devoted more to pious themes. ❖ See also Helen Sard Hughes, *The Gentle Hertford: Her Life and Letters* (Macmillan, 1940); and *Women in World History*.

SEYMOUR, Georgiana (d. 1884). Duchess of Somerset. Name variations: Lady Georgiana Seymour; Georgiana Sheridan; Jane Seymour; Lady Seymour. Born Jane Georgiana Sheridan around 1809; died on Dec 14, 1884; dau. of Thomas Sheridan (a public official) and Caroline Henrietta (Callander) Sheridan (1779–1851, novelist); granddau. of Richard Brinsley Sheridan and Elizabeth Linley (1754–1792); sister of Caroline Norton (1808–1877) and Helen Selina Blackwood, Lady Dufferin (1807–1867); m. Edward Adolphus Seymour (1804–1885, trustee of the British Museum and first lord of the Admiralty), 12th duke of Somerset and earl of St. Maur, on June 10, 1830; children: Edward Adolphus (b. 1835), earl of St. Maur; Edward Percy (b. 1841, diplomat); Jane Hermione Seymour (d. 1909, who m. Frederick Ulric, 3rd baronet of Netherby); Ulrica Seymour (d. 1916, who m. Henry Frederick Thynne, Rt. Hon. PC MP); Helen Guendolen Seymour (d. 1910, who m. Sir John William Ramsden, 5th baronet). ❖ See also *Women in World History*.

SEYMOUR, Jane (c. 1509–1537). Queen of England. Born c. 1509 (some sources cite 1506) in England; died from puerperal fever at Hampton Court on Oct 24, 1537; dau. of Sir John Seymour (a courtier) and Margaret Wentworth (d. 1550); m. Henry VIII (1491–1547), king of England (r. 1509–1547), in 1536; children: Edward VI (1537–1553), king of England (r. 1547–1553). ❖ Third wife of Henry VIII who gave birth to the king's only male heir, Edward VI, was lady-in-waiting for queens Catherine of Aragon and Anne Boleyn; began to receive the attentions of Henry VIII (1535); married him (1536); though she was not to become as heavily involved in state affairs as her predecessor, was responsible for reconciling the king with his eldest daughter, Mary (I); was beloved by both her husband and the English people; died 12 days after giving birth (1537). ❖ See also *Women in World History*.

SEYMOUR, Jane (1541–1560). British poet. Born 1541; died 1560; dau. of Edward, duke of Somerset, and Anne Stanhope (1497–1587); sister of Margaret Seymour and Anne Seymour; niece of Jane Seymour, queen of England. ❖ With sisters Margaret and Anne, wrote Latin elegy to Margaret of Angoulême published by Nicolas Denisot in collection called *Annae, Margaritae, Iannae, sororum virginum, heroidum Anglarum, in mortem Diuae Margaritae Valesiae, navarrorum Reginae, Hecadostichon* (1550), the 1st encomium in English by women for a woman.

SEYMOUR, Jane (d. 1679). English noblewoman. Name variations: Lady Jane Seymour; Lady Clifford. Died Nov 23, 1679; dau. of Frances Devereux (d. 1674) and William Seymour (1587–1660), 2nd duke of Somerset (r. 1660–1660); m. Charles Boyle, 2nd Lord Clifford, on May 7, 1661; children: Mary Boyle (1671–1709, who m. James Douglas, 2nd duke of Queensbury); Charles Boyle, 3rd earl of Cork.

SEYMOUR, Jane (d. 1884). See Seymour, Georgiana.

SEYMOUR, Jane (c. 1898–1956). Canadian-born stage, tv, and screen actress. Born c. 1898 in Hamilton, Ontario, Canada; died Jan 30, 1956, in New York, NY. ❖ Made stage debut in a road company of *Within the Law* (1913); on Broadway, appeared in *The Enemy, Paris Bound, The House Beautiful, Invitation to Murder, Remember the Day, The Women, The Moon is Down* and *The Show Off*.

SEYMOUR, Jane (1951—). English-born actress. Born Joyce Penelope Wilhelmina Frankenberg, Feb 15, 1951, in Hayes, Hayes and Harlington, Middlesex, England; dau. of John Frankenberg (British obstetrician) and Mieke van Trigt (Dutch); m. Michael Attenborough, 1971 (div. 1973); m. Geoffrey Planer, 1977 (div. 1978); m. David Flynn, 1981 (div. 1992); m. James Keach (actor), 1993; children: (3rd m.) Katherine and Sean; (4th m.) twins, John and Kristopher. ❖ Began career as a ballerina, making professional debut at 13 with London Festival Ballet; made film debut in the chorus of *Oh, What a Lovely War* (1969); in England, appeared on stage as well as tv, including in "Far from the Madding Crowd," "Young Winston" and "The Onedin Line"; on Broadway, originated the role of Constanza Weber in *Amadeus*; moved to US; on tv, starred on "War and Remembrance" (1988) and "Dr. Quinn, Medicine Woman" (1993–98) and in many tv movies; films include *Live and Let Die* (1973), *Somewhere in Time* (1980), and *The New Swiss Family Robinson* (1998); became international ambassador for Childhelp USA, an organization dedicated to the prevention and treatment of child abuse; also worked with American Red Cross Measles Initiative, which vaccinates children in Africa; became US citizen (2005). Named OBE (1999).

SEYMOUR, Lynn (1939—). Canadian ballet dancer. Born Lynn Berta Springbett, Mar 8, 1939, in Wainwright, Alberta, Canada; studied dance in Vancouver, British Columbia, and earned scholarship to Sadler's Wells Ballet School (now Royal Ballet School) in England; married Colin Jones (photographer); children: 3 sons. ❖ Danced with the Covent Garden Opera Ballet (1956), then joined Sadler's Wells Opera Ballet (1957); created 1st solo role, in Kenneth Macmillan's ballet *The Burrow* (1958); received acclaim not only for her dramatic roles, but also for such comedic and romantic roles as the lead in Frederick Ashton's *Two Pigeons* (1960) and Juliet in Macmillan's *Romeo and Juliet* (1965); danced with the Berlin State Opera Ballet (1967–70), but returned to the Royal Ballet to appear in *Anastasia* (1974), *Seven Deadly Sins* (1974), and *Rituals* (1975); was guest artist with American Ballet Theatre and Alvin Ailey Company; with Robert North of the London Contemporary Dance Theatre, choreographed *Gladly, Sadly, Madly, Badly* (1975); retired from the ballet (1980), but continued performing as an actress and rock musician; appeared as the wicked stepmother in *Cinderella*, a spoof by Matthew Bourne's ballet company (1997). Named Commander of the Order of the British Empire (1976).

SEYMOUR, Margaret (c. 1533—). British poet. Born c. 1533; dau. of Edward, duke of Somerset, and Anne Stanhope (1497–1587); sister of Anne Seymour and Jane Seymour; niece of Jane Seymour, queen of England. ❖ With sisters Anne and Jane, wrote Latin elegy to Margaret of Angoulême published by Nicolas Denisot in collection called *Annae, Margaritae, Iannae, sororum virginum, heroidum Anglarum, in mortem Diuae Margaritae Valesiae, navarrorum Reginae, Hecadostichon* (1550), the 1st encomium in English by women for a woman.

SEYMOUR, Margaret (d. 1550). See Wentworth, Margaret.

SEYMOUR, Marjory (d. 1550). See Wentworth, Margaret.

SEYMOUR, Mary (d. 1673). Countess of Winchelsea. Name variations: Countess of Winchilsea. Died before April 10, 1673; dau. of Frances Devereux (d. 1674) and William Seymour (1587–1660), 2nd duke of Somerset (r. 1660–1660); became 1st wife of Heneage Finch, 3rd earl of Winchelsea (r. 1639–1689), before 1653. Heneage Finch was also m. to Diana Willoughby, Catherine Norcliffe (d. 1679), and Elizabeth Ayres (d. 1745).

SEYMOUR, Mary F. (1846–1893). American entrepreneur and journalist. Born Mary Foot Seymour in Aurora, Illinois, 1846; died in New York, NY, Mar 21, 1893; dau. of Ephraim Sanford Seymour (lawyer and writer, died 1851) and Rosette (Bestor) Seymour. ❖ Established the Union School of Stenography in New York City (1879); soon expanded her business to 4 schools, a company that employed 25 stenographers, and an employment bureau, the Union Stenographic and Typewriting Association; launched the bimonthly *Business Women's Journal* (1889), which later became the *American Woman's Journal*; was an advocate of woman suffrage. ❖ See also *Women in World History*.

SEYMOUR, May Davenport (d. 1967). American actress and museum curator. Died Oct 5, 1967, age 83, in New York, NY; dau. of William Seymour (actor and stage manager) and May Davenport; m. William Eckert, 1908; children: John Seymour (actor), James Seymour (actor), Anne Seymour (1909–1988, actress). ❖ As an actress, appeared on stage in *The Lady of the Lyons, The Little Princess, A Doll's House, Alice Sit-by-*

the-Fire and *The Evangelist*, among others; retired (1908); later appeared with her daughter for 9 years on radio's "Against the Storm"; founded and was curator of the theater collection at the Museum of the City of New York.

SEYRIG, Delphine (1932–1990). Lebanese-born French stage and screen actress. Born April 10, 1932, in Beirut, Lebanon, to French Alsatian parents; died of lung disease, Oct 15, 1990, in Paris, France; sister of Francis Seyrig (composer); children: one son. ❖ Built her reputation on Paris stage before arriving in America (1956); in New York, studied at Actors Studio, performed on tv, and appeared in underground 16mm film *Pull My Daisy* (1958), written by Jack Kerouac; returning to France, made professional film debut in Resnais' *L'Année dernière à Marienbad* (*Last Year at Marienbad*, 1961), which advanced her career considerably; throughout 1960s and 1970s, played major and minor roles in international films of note, including Buñuel's *The Discreet Charm of the Bourgeoisie* (1972); a dedicated feminist, also appeared in films of a number of women directors, notably Marguerite Duras' *India Song* and Chantal Akerman's *Jeanne Dielman* (both 1975); directed her own major film, *Soi belle et tais-toi* (1977), as well as a number of experimental videotaped shorts; made last appearance in *Window Shopping*, which was released posthumously (1994). ❖ See also *Women in World History*.

S. F. E. (c. 1670–1723). See Egerton, Sarah Fyge.

SFINGI, Mrs. (1924—). See Hanson, Beverly.

SFORZA, Angela (fl. 1500s). Milanese noblewoman. Dau. of Carlo Sforza (b. 1461) and Bianca Simonetta Sforza; m. Ercole di Sigismondo d'Este; children: Sigismondo d'Este (d. 1579).

SFORZA, Anna (1473–1497). Duchess of Ferrara. Name variations: Anna d'Este. Born in 1473; died in 1497; dau. of Bona of Savoy (c. 1450–c. 1505) and Galeazzo Maria Sforza (1444–1476), 5th duke of Milan (r. 1466–1476); m. Alfonso I d'Este (1476–1534), 3rd duke of Ferrara and Modena, in 1491; no children. ❖ Alfonso I's 2nd wife was Lucrezia Borgia (1480–1519).

SFORZA, Battista (1446–1472). Duchess of Urbino. Born in 1446; died in 1472; dau. of Allesandro Sforza (1409–1473), lord of Pesaro and Cottignola, and Costanza Sforza; m. Federigo Montefeltro (1422–1482), 1st duke of Urbino; children: Giovanna Montefeltro (who m. Giovanni della Rovere); Guidobaldo (1472–1508, who m. Elisabetta Montefeltro [d. 1526]); Elisabetta Montefeltro (who m. Roberto Malatesta). ❖ Federigo's 1st wife was Gentile Brancaleone.

SFORZA, Beatrice (1427–1497). See Este, Beatrice d'.

SFORZA, Bianca Maria (1423–1470). See Visconti, Bianca Maria.

SFORZA, Bianca Maria (1472–1510). Holy Roman empress. Born April 5, 1472, in Milan; died Dec 31, 1510, in Innsbruck; dau. of Bona of Savoy (c. 1450–c. 1505), duchess of Milan, and Galeazzo Maria Sforza (1444–1476), 5th duke of Milan (r. 1466–1476); half-sister of Caterina Sforza (c. 1462–1509); became 2nd wife of Maximilian I (1459–1519), Holy Roman emperor (r. 1493–1519), in 1494; stepchildren: Margaret of Austria (1480–1530). Maximilian was 1st m. to Mary of Burgundy (1457–1482). ❖ During marriage, was all but confined to her quarters in the palace at Innsbruck. ❖ See also *Women in World History*.

SFORZA, Bianca Simonetta (fl. 15th c.). Milanese noblewoman. Married Charles also known as Carlo Sforza (b. 1461); children: Ippolita Sforza (who m. Alessandro Bentivoglio); Angela Sforza (who m. Ercole di Sigismondo d'Este).

SFORZA, Bona (1493–1557). Queen of Poland and duchess of Bari. Name variations: Bona of Poland. Born in Jan 1493 (some sources cite 1494) in Milan, Italy; died Nov 19, 1557 (some sources cite 1558), at Bari, Italy; dau. of Giangaleazzo or Gian Galeazzo Sforza, duke of Milan (died 1496), and Isabella of Naples (1470–1524); became 2nd wife of Zygmunt I Stary also known as Sigismund I the Elder (1467–1548), king of Poland (r. 1506–1548), in Dec 1517; children: Zygmunt August also known as Sigismund II Augustus (1520–1572), king of Poland (r. 1548–1572); Isabella of Poland (1519–1559, who m. John Zapolya, king of Hungary [r. 1526–1540]); Zofia also known as Sophia (who m. Henry, duke of Brunswick); Catherine Jagello (1525–1583, who m. John III, king of Sweden); Anna Jagello (1523–1596, who m. Stephen Bathory, king of Poland-Lithuania). Sigismund I the Elder's 1st wife was Barbara Zapolya (mother of Hedwig of Poland who m. Joachim II of Brandenburg). ❖ Was 3 years old when father died (1496) and mother was forced out of Milan; raised in an intellectual climate at the court of

Bari, absorbed the Renaissance values of scholarship and humanism, along with mother's strong political ambition; was married to the recently widowed Sigismund I, king of Poland (1518); became a major influence in his reign—politically, economically, and culturally; brought Italian writers, painters, architects, and musicians to her court; had architects design castles and palaces, and redesign existing ones in the new Renaissance style; also established art studios and workshops for the foreign artists to teach their crafts; became involved in the political struggles emerging between the crown, aristocracy, and landholding gentry; supported Sigismund's desire to strengthen royal power and centralize authority in the king; earned the animosity of the old noble and gentry classes, who traditionally opposed any increase in royal power or centralization of royal authority. ❖ See also *Women in World History.*

SFORZA, Cammilla (fl. 15th c.). Milanese noblewoman. Name variations: Camilla or Cammilla Marzano. Married Costanzo Sforza (1447–1483). Costanzo had an illegitimate son Giovanni Sforza (1466–1510), lord of Pessaro.

SFORZA, Caterina (c. 1462–1509). Countess of Forlì. Name variations: Caterine Sforza; Catherine Sforza, countess of Forli and Imola or Imolo; Caterina de Medici; Caterina Sforza Riario. Born Caterina Sforza in late 1462 or early 1463 in Milan, Italy; died in Florence, Italy, in 1509; illeg. dau. of Galeazzo Maria Sforza (1444–1476), duke of Milan, and Lucrezia Landriani (wife of Giampietro Landriani); m. Girolamo Riario, in 1477 (died 1488); began liaison with Giacomo Feo, in 1489 (died 1495); m. Giovanni de Medici, in 1497 (died 1498); children: (1st m.) Bianca Riario (b. 1478), Ottaviano Riario (b. 1479), Cesare Riario (b. between 1480 and 1482), Giovanni Livio Riario (b. 1484), Galeazzo Riario (b. 1485), Francesco Sforza Riario (b. 1487), and a daughter who died in infancy; (liaison with Feo) Bernardino, later called Carlo (b. 1490); (2nd m.) Ludovico, later called Giovanni delle Bande Nere (1498–1526). ❖ The "most famous virago of the Renaissance" who conducted military operations and defended besieged fortresses in 15th-century Italy; lived with birth mother until 1466, when she was transferred together with siblings to father's household; betrothed at age 10 to Girolamo Riario; married him at 14 and moved to Rome (1477); became countess of Forlì (1481), and thereafter lived primarily in Forlì and Imola; had 1st bout of quartan fever (1482); during chaotic papal succession (1484), rode into Rome and seized the Castel Sant'Angelo to try to retain the power and prestige of her family; acted as judge against those involved in an assassination conspiracy against husband, and imposed severe punishments (1487); husband Girolamo Riario assassinated (1488); successfully held the fortress of Ravaldino during revolt of Forlì after assassination, even when children were threatened (1488); served as regent for oldest son, ruling Imola and Forlì (1488–1500); exacted bloody retribution after assassination of lover Giacomo Feo in Forlì (1495); negotiated with Niccolò Machiavelli, envoy of Florence (1499); defended Ravaldino in Forlì against Cesare Borgia (1499–1500); captured and imprisoned in Rome (1500–01); retired to Florence (1501–09). ❖ See also Ernst Breisach, *Caterina Sforza: A Renaissance Virago* (U. of Chicago Press, 1967); and *Women in World History.*

SFORZA, Chiara (b. around 1464). Milanese noblewoman. Born c. 1464; illeg. dau. of Galeazzo Maria Sforza (1444–1476), duke of Milan, and Lucrezia Landriani (wife of Giampietro Landriani); sister of Caterina Sforza (c. 1462–1509).

SFORZA, Christierna (1521–1590). *See Christina of Denmark.*

SFORZA, Costanza (fl. 1445). Noblewoman of Pesaro. Name variations: Constanza or Costanza Varano. Flourished around 1445; m. Allesandro Sforza (1409–1473), lord of Pesaro and Cottignola; children: Battista Sforza (1446–1472); Costanza Sforza (1447–1483); Allesandro also had an illegitimate daughter, Ginevra Sforza (d. 1507).

SFORZA, Ginevra (1440–1507). Noblewoman of Pesaro. Name variations: Ginevra Bentivoglio. Born Jan 1440; died May 17, 1507; illeg. dau. of Allesandro Sforza (1409–1473), lord of Pesaro and Cottignola; m. Sante Bentivoglio; m. Giovanni Bentivoglio.

SFORZA, Ginevra Tiepolo (fl. 16th c.). Noblewoman of Pesaro. Born Ginevra Tiepolo; became 3rd wife of Giovanni Sforza (1466–1510), lord of Pesaro. ❖ Giovanni's 1st wife was Maddalena Sforza (1472–1490); his 2nd was Lucrezia Borgia.

SFORZA, Ippolita (1446–1484). *See Ippolita.*

SFORZA, Ippolita (fl. 15th c.). Milanese noblewoman. Name variations: Ippolita Bentivoglio. Dau. of Carlo Sforza (b. 1461) and Bianca Simonetta Sforza; m. Allesandro Bentivoglio.

SFORZA, Isabella (1470–1524). *See Isabella of Naples.*

SFORZA, Maddalena (1472–1490). Noblewoman of Pesaro. Name variations: Maddalena Gonzaga. Born 1472; died 1490; dau. of Margaret of Bavaria (1445–1479) and Frederigo also known as Federico Gonzaga (1441–1484), 3rd marquis of Mantua (r. 1478–1484); sister of Elisabetta Montefeltro (1471–1526); 1st wife of Giovanni Sforza (1466–1510), lord of Pesaro. ❖ Giovanni's 2nd wife was Lucrezia Borgia; his 3rd Ginevra Tiepolo Sforza.

SFORZA, Margherita (1375–?). *See Margaret of Attenduli.*

SFORZA, Polissena (fl. 15th c.). Ferrarese noblewoman. Name variations: Polissena Malatesta. Second wife of Sigismondo Pandolfo Malatesta (1417–1486). ❖ Sigismondo's 1st wife was Ginevra d'Este (1414–1440).

SFORZA, Seraphina (1434–1478). Italian Catholic saint. Born in Urbino, Italy, in 1434; died 1478; dau. of Guido Sforza, count of Montefeltro, and Catherine Colonna (niece of Pope Martin V, died around 1440); m. Allesandro Sforza (1409–1473), lord of Pesaro and Cottignola, in 1448. ❖ Orphaned at an early age, was raised in Rome at the Colonna Palace; after husband started an affair with a doctor's wife, was often beaten by him; when he attempted to poison her, was left half-paralyzed for rest of life; was kept captive in the convent of the Poor Clares in Pesaro; entered Franciscan order (c. 1457); eventually was made abbess and lived a praiseworthy life counseling her sisters in the religious community until her death. ❖ See also *Women in World History.*

SHAARAWI, Huda (1879–1947). Egyptian political activist and feminist. Name variations: Sh'arawi; Hoda Charaoui. Born Nur al-Huda Sultan on father's estate, near Minya (Minia), Egypt, 1879; died in Cairo, 1947; dau. of Sultan Pasha (wealthy landowner who eventually became president of Egypt's Chamber of Deputies) and Iqbal Hanim (a Turco-Circassian); tutored at home, becoming fluent in several languages; m. Ali Shaarawi (a cousin many years her senior who was active in the Wafd Party), in 1892 (died 1922); children: daughter Bathna (b. 1903); son Muhammad (b. 1905). ❖ Reformer who worked to end marriage for underage girls, the institution of the harem, and the wearing of the veil, and founded the Egyptian Feminist Union, the country's preeminent voice for women for many decades; married at age 13 (1892); after 15 months of marriage, returned to live with mother for next 7 years (c. 1894); traveled with husband to Paris, and witnessed the freedom of European women (c. 1901); founded the Intellectual Association of Egyptian Women (1914); led demonstrations against British colonial rule (1919); became prominent in the Wafd political party which sought independence; was elected president of the Wafdist Women's Central Committee (1920), passing resolutions that demanded the end of martial law and voting for an economic boycott against the British; as founder and president of the Egyptian Feminist Union, led a delegation to the International Alliance of Women in Rome and stopped wearing her veil (1923); founded Club of the Women's Union (1925); worked to limit the easy access that men had to divorce, restrict the practice of polygamy, and increase women's access to education; became the 1st president of the newly founded Arab Feminist Union (1944); is widely recognized for bringing permanent changes in the status of women in Egypt and to the entire Muslim world. Awarded the Nishan al-Kamal, Egypt's highest state decoration (1945). ❖ See also *Harem Years: The Memoirs of an Egyptian Feminist, 1879–1924* (1987); and *Women in World History.*

SHABANOVA, Anna (1848–1932). Russian physician and feminist. Name variations: Anna Nikitichna Shabanova. Born 1848 in Russia; died 1932; dau. of a wealthy landowner. ❖ Spent 6 months in prison for radical political activities (1865); studied medicine at Women's Medical Academy; became one of the 1st women in Russia to qualify as a doctor (1878); researched children's diseases; was one of the founders of the Russian Women's Mutual Philanthropic Society (1905), which advocated suffrage; organized several campaigns for education and social reform and, with Maria Pokrovskaya, led campaign against legalized prostitution; during WWI, organized voluntary agencies; met Emmeline Pankhurst (1914); after Russian Revolution, returned to pediatric research and publishing.

SHABANOVA, Rafiga (1943—). Soviet handball player. Born Oct 31, 1943, in USSR. ❖ At Montreal Olympics, won a gold medal in team competition (1976).

SHABAZZ, Betty (1936–1997). African-American civil-rights and education activist. Name variations: Betty Sanders; Sister Betty X. Born May 28, 1936, in Detroit, Michigan; died June 23, 1997, in New York, NY; attended Tuskegee Institute; Brooklyn State Hospital School of Nursing, RN; Jersey City State College, MA in public health administration; University of Massachusetts, PhD in education administration; m. Malcolm Little, known as Malcolm X, also known as Malik El-Shabazz (1925–1965, the Black Muslim leader), in 1958; children: 6 daughters, Attallah, Qubilah, Makaak, Malikah, Gamilah and Ilayasah Shabazz. ❖ Following husband's assassination (1965), raised her 6 children, continued with his civil-rights and political work, and went on to become a dedicated leader on educational issues; made speaking appearances throughout US; became associate professor of health education at Medgar Evers College in Brooklyn (1976), then director of department of communications and public relations and head of the school's office of institutional advancement; after 12-year-old grandson Malcolm, whom she had been caring for, set fire to her apartment in Yonkers, NY, suffered third-degree burns and died. ❖ See also Jamie Foster Brown, ed. *Betty Shabazz: A Sisterfriends' Tribute in Words and Pictures* (Simon & Schuster, 1998); and *Women in World History.*

SHABELSKA, Maria (1898–1980). Russian ballet dancer and teacher. Name variations: Maria Yakovleff. Born Sept 7, 1898, in St. Petersburg, Russia; died May 14, 1980, in Brattleboro, VT; m. Alex Yakovleff (ballet dancer, died 1930s). ❖ Performed with Diaghilev Ballet Russe, most notably as The Little American Girl in Massine's *Parade*; with husband, performed at Teatro Colon in Buenos Aires and taught classes at Ned Wayburn Studio in NY (1920s); joined Detroit Civic Opera where she served as resident choreographer and ballet master (1930s).

SHABELSKAIA, A. S. (b. 1845). See Montvid, A. S.

SHACKLETON, Mary (1758–1826). See Leadbetter, Mary.

SHADD, Mary Ann (1823–1893). See Cary, Mary Ann Shadd.

SHAFER, Helen Almira (1839–1894). American educator and college president. Born Sept 23, 1839, in Newark, New Jersey; died Jan 20, 1894, in Wellesley, Massachusetts; dau. of a Congregational minister; graduate of Oberlin College, 1863; never married. ❖ Taught in New Jersey; taught mathematics at St. Louis High School under William Torrey Harris; offered chair in mathematics at newly founded Wellesley College (1877); succeeding Alice Freeman Palmer, served as president of Wellesley (1888–94); worked to reorganize and broaden the college's curriculum; established a psychological laboratory, the 1st in a women's college and one of the earliest in any college (1891); presided over a liberalization of the college's social life, restoring some sororities and overseeing the introduction of the college periodicals. ❖ See also *Women in World History.*

SHAFFER, Alexandra (1976—). American Alpine skier. Born Jan 23, 1976, in Park City, UT. ❖ Won US championship for slalom and giant slalom (1999).

SHAFIK, Doria (1908–1975). Egyptian feminist. Name variations: Durriyah or Dori'a Shafiq; Doria Chafik. Born Doria Chafik in Tanta, Gabiyya, Dec 14, 1908; committed suicide by leaping from 6th floor of her apartment building in Cairo, Egypt, Sept 20, 1975; dau. of Ahmad Chafik Sulaiman Effendi (civil engineer) and Ratiba Nasif Qassabi Bey (member of a prominent family); attended Notre Dame des Apôtres; attended Sorbonne in Paris, 1930–32, returned to obtain a doctorate, 1936–39; m. Nour Ragai (Egyptian lawyer), 1937; children: daughters Aziza (b. 1942) and Jihan (b. 1944). ❖ Leading Egyptian feminist and founder of the Bint al-Nil Union, which fought for women's right to vote (granted in 1956 largely as a result of her hunger strike), who was condemned for protesting Nasser's dictatorial powers and isolated politically for almost 20 years; was 2nd in her country in baccalauréat examinations (1929); began work as the inspector for French languages in secondary schools throughout Egypt (1942); founded Bint al-Nil Union, 1st as a magazine, then as political organization (1948); organized the closing of the Egyptian Parliament by women (1951); organized the storming of Barclay's Bank that led to the final downfall of British colonial rule (1952); went on 1st hunger strike for women's right to vote (1954); placed under house arrest for protesting dictatorial powers of Nasser government (1957); name was banned forever in the media, and the Bint al-Nil Union was closed; lived final years in self-imposed seclusion until committing suicide (1975); was a nationalist who loved her country and a moderate who advocated a balance between Islamic teaching and feminist reform. ❖ See also *Women in World History.*

SHAFIQ, Dori'a or Durriyah (1908–1975). See Shafik, Doria.

SHAFTESBURY, countess of. See Lamb, Emily (d. 1869).

SHAGINIAN, Marietta (1888–1982). Russian poet, author, dramatist, and literary critic. Name variations: Marietta Shaginyan; Marietta Sergeyevna Shaginyan; Mariètta Sergeevna Shaginián; (pseudonym) Jim [Dzhim] Dollar; "Re." Born Marietta Sergeevna Shaginian in Moscow, Russia, Mar 21, 1888; died in Moscow, Mar 21, 1982; dau. of a physician (died 1902); educated in Germany; m. Y. S. Khachatryants (Ia. S. Khachatriants, philologist); children: 1 daughter. ❖ One of the most prolific, versatile and best-known women authors of the Soviet era, published 1st poem (1903); self-published 1st collection of poems, *Pervye vstrechi* (1st Encounters, 1909); for several years, was an informal member of the neo-Christian circle led by Gippius; with 2nd vol. of poems, *Orientalia* (1912), found the literary renown she had been seeking; sent songs to pianist Rachmaninoff which were later published as Fourteen Songs, Op. 34 (the last of these would be the famous *Vocalise*); during 1914, wrote *Puteshestvie v Veimar* (Journey to Weimar), which because of war and revolution would not be published until 1923; though she considered herself a Christian and did not apply for membership in the Communist Party until 1941, greeted the Bolshevik revolution of Nov 1917 with enthusiasm; under pseudonym "Jim Dollar," wrote the popular serialized novel *Mess-Mend, ili Ianki v Petrograde* (*Mess-Mend, Yankees in Petrograd*), which appeared in 10 installments (1924); published 2 "agitation-adventure novellas" as sequels to *Mess-Mend: Lori Lane, Metallworker* and *The International Car* (1925); was the lone voice of protest at a meeting of the Writers' Union when she disagreed with Stalinist guidelines for book reviewers (1935); novel about Lenin, *Bilet po istorii, Chast' I: Sem'ia Ul'yanovykh* (Ticket to History, Part I: The Ulyanov Family) was published in Moscow (1938), but banned by Politburo; by end of 1950s, was the doyenne of Soviet letters; wrote about 70 other books, including biographical studies of William Blake, Goethe, Sergei Rachmaninoff and Taras Shevchenko. Awarded Lenin Prize (1972); honored with a 10-kopeck postage stamp (April 2, 1988). ❖ See also memoirs (in Russian) *Chelovek i vremia* (*Man and Time*); and *Women in World History.*

SHAGINYAN, Marietta (1888–1982). See Shaginian, Marietta.

SHAGRAT AL-DURR (d. 1259). See Shajar al-Durr.

SHAHEEN, Jeanne (1947—). American politician. Born Jan 28, 1947, in St. Charles, Missouri; graduate of Shippensburg University, 1969; University of Mississippi, MA in political science, 1973; m. Bill Shaheen; children: 3. ❖ Taugh high school in Mississippi and New Hampshire; elected to NH state senate (1990), serving 3 terms; became the 1st female governor of New Hampshire (1996), serving for 3 terms until Jan 2003.

SHAHN, Bernada Bryson (1903–2004). See Bryson, Bernarda.

SHAIN, Eva (1917–1999). American heavyweight referee. Born Eva Inwood, Nov 24, 1917, in Jersey City, New Jersey; died Aug 19, 1999, in Englewood, NJ; attended New York University; m. 2nd husband Frank Shain (ring announcer); children: (1st m.) Harvey Schultz and Barbara Brocklehurst. ❖ Received license as boxing judge from NY State (1975); as 1st woman to judge world heavyweight bout refereed Muhammad Ali vs. Ernie Shavers at Madison Square Garden, NY (1977), voting 9 to 6 in favor of Ali (Ali won unanimous 15-round decision); judged thousands of fights before retirement in 1998.

SHAJAR AL-DURR (d. 1259). Sultana of Egypt. Name variations: Shajar al Durr; Shajarat; Shagrat al-Durr; Spray of Pearls. Born into a Turkish family; died in 1259 (some sources cite 1258) in Cairo; m. Najm ad Din, also known as al-Salih Ayyub or Salih II Ayyub, Ayyubid sultan of Egypt, in 1240 (died 1249); m. Aybak, Mamluk sultan of Egypt, in 1250; stepchildren: Turan or al-Muazzam Turanshah. ❖ One of the few women in Muslim history to have ruled as sultana, played an important role in the defeat of 7th Crusade; acted as regent of Egypt while husband was on military campaign in Damascus (1249); after French king Louis IX's Crusading army captured Damietta (June 1249), organized the Egyptian army against him; when husband died shortly after his return (Nov 1249), concealed his death; ruled alone in his name, until stepson Turan returned from Syria to take power; with stepson, organized defense of Cairo against Louis (1250), defeating the Crusaders and capturing the king; when stepson was assassinated by Mamluk (Turkish) military officers of the Egyptian army (May 1250), became the 1st Mamluk (Turkish) sultan of Egypt and the 1st female sultan to rule in her own name; forced to abdicate after only a few months, married her successor

Aybak and together they consolidated Mamluk rule in Egypt, making a new capital at Cairo; eventually had husband assassinated when he tried to take a 2nd wife (1259); was murdered at instigation of Aybak's son. ❖ See also *Women in World History.*

SHAKESPEARE, Anne (1556–1623). *See Hathaway, Anne.*

SHAKHOVSKAYA, Eugenie M. (1889–?). Russian aviator. Name variations: Princess Eugenie M. Shakhovskaia; Shakhowaskaya or Schakovskoy. Born 1889 in St. Petersburg, Russia; niece or cousin of Tsar Nicholas II; date of death unknown. ❖ The 1st woman to become a military pilot, flew with Vladimir Lebedev at Gatchina, then moved to Germany to train with Vsevolod Abramovitch, chief pilot of the Wright Company; received her license on a Farman at Johannistal, near Berlin (Aug 1912); became a Wright aircraft demonstrator in St. Petersburg; crashed a Wright at Johannistal (April 1913), killing Abramovitch; under a personal order from Tsar Nicholas II, was given the rank of ensign in the 1st aerial squadron of the Imperial Russian Air Service (Nov 1914); some say it was an honorific; others say she flew reconnaisance during WWI and executed "audacious raids" above German lines; wounded, was decorated with the Military Order of Saint George (1916); became a member of secret police during the Russian Revolution and was later named chief executioner of Kiev for the revolutionary general Tchecka.

SHAKHOVSKAYA, Zinaida (1906–2001). Russian novelist, poet and historian. Name variations: Princess Shakhovskaia; (pseudonym) Jacques Croise. Born Zinaida Alekseevna Shakhovskaya, 1906, in Moscow, Russia; died June 11, 2001, in Paris, France; sister of Natalie Shakhovskaya (who m. Vladimir Nabokov's cousin, composer Nikolas Nabokov). ❖ Following the Revolution, left Russia with family (1920), settling in Brussels, then Paris; was in the French resistance during WWII; after the war, lived in Moscow for some time, where her husband worked for the Belgian embassy; works include novel *Europe et Valerius,* as well as poetry, literary criticism, and memoirs; edited *emigré* journal *Russian Thought* (1968–78) and co-founded *Russian Almanac* (1981) in Paris.

SHAKIRA (1977—). Colombian pop singer. Name variations: Shakira Mebarak. Born Shakira Isabel Mebarak Ripoll, Feb 2, 1977, in Barranquilla, Colombia; dau. of William Mebarak (of Lebanese descent) and Nidia Ripoll de Mebarak (a native Colombian). ❖ Singing in Spanish and Portuguese, became the preeminent female superstar of Latin America; released 1st album, *Magia,* at 13 (1991), followed by *Peligro;* recorded the international smash hit "Pies Descalzos"; hit US charts with 1st English-language CD, *Laundry Service* (2001), which included the hit "Underneath Your Clothes"; won the Best Latin Pop Album Grammy for her *MTV Unplugged* (2001); became engaged to Antonio de la Rúa, a Buenos Aires lawyer and the son of the president of Argentina (2002).

SHAKUR, Assata (1948—). *See Chesimard, Joanne.*

SHALALA, Donna (1941—). American government official. Born Dona Edna Shalala, Feb 14, 1941, in Cleveland, Ohio, of Lebanese ancestry; twin sister of Diane Fritel (high school principal); Western College for Women, AB, 1962; Syracuse University, PhD, 1970. ❖ As a Peace Corps volunteer, served in Iran (1962–64); was professor of politics, Bernard Baruch College (1970–72); professor of politics and education at Columbia University Teachers College (1972–79); as treasurer of the Municipal Assistance Corporation (1970s), helped bail New York City out of a financial jam; was president of Hunter College (1980–87), then chancellor of University of Wisconsin–Madison (1987–93); appointed secretary of Health and Human Services by President Bill Clinton (1993), served in that capacity for 8 years, the longest serving HHS secretary in US history; became professor of political science and president of University of Miami (2001).

SHALAMAR. *See Watley, Jody.*

SHALAMOVA, Elena (1982—). Russian rhythmic gymnast. Name variations: Yelena Chalamova. Born 1982 in USSR. ❖ Won a team World championship (1998, 1999) and a team gold medal at Sydney Olympics (2000); won 2 team European championships.

SHALER, Eleanor (1900–1989). American actress, singer and dancer. Name variations: Eleanor Shaler Dickson. Born June 17, 1900, in Indianapolis, IN; died Dec 22, 1989, in Gladwyn, PA; graduate of Vassar College; m. Colonel Benjamin Abbott Dickson; children: Colin Campbell Dickson; William D. S. Dickson (died 2003). ❖ Dance satirist, was trained in ballet and other dance techniques; appeared in

Garrick Gaieties of 1926, The Manhatters (1927), *Pardon My English* (1932), and other revues; wrote novels *Wake and Find a Stranger* and *Gaunt's Daughter,* among others.

SHAMBAUGH, Jessie Field (1881–1971). *See Field, Jessie.*

SHAMIRAM (fl. 8th c. BCE). *See Sammuramat.*

SHAMRAY-RUDKO, Galina (1931—). Soviet gymnast. Name variations: Galina Rudko. Born Oct 1931 in USSR. ❖ At Helsinki Olympics, won a silver medal in teams all-around, portable apparatus, and a gold medal in team all-around (1952).

SHAN YING (1978—). Chinese swimmer. Born 1978 in Guangzhou, China. ❖ Won a silver medal for 4 x 100-meter relay and a bronze for 4 x 100-meter medley relay at Atlanta Olympics (1996); won 50-meter freestyle and 2 other gold medals at Asian Games (1998); won bronze medals in the 50- and 100-meter freestyle at World championships (1998); tested positive for a performance-enhancing drug before leaving for Sydney Olympics (Chinese authorities withdrew her from the national team); suspended by FINA after testing positive for a steriod in another drug test (2002).

SHANE, Mary Driscoll (c. 1949—). American sports radio broadcaster. Born Mary Driscoll c. 1949; graduate of University of Wisconsin–Madison. ❖ Taught high-school history; served as Milwaukee representative of Women's Political Caucus at Democratic National Convention (1972); began to specialize in sports for WMAQ radio (all-news NBC affiliate), Chicago, IL (1975); assigned to Chicago White Sox games as 1st woman to perform play-by-play broadcasts of baseball games (1976).

SHANE, Tamara (1902–1983). *See Shayne, Tamara.*

SHANGE, Ntozake (1948—). African-American writer. Born Paulette Williams, Oct 18, 1948, in Trenton, New Jersey; dau. of Paul Williams (sports physician) and Eloise Williams (educator and psychiatric social worker); Barnard College, BA, 1970; University of Southern California, MA, 1973; m. David Murray (musician), 1977; children: Savannah. ❖ Took name Ntozake Shange during graduate school (1971); began performing poetry, music and dance in and around San Francisco, often with African-American dance troupe Third World Collective; joined Halifu Osumare's dance company; moved to NY; wrote the hugely successful choreographed poem, *For Colored Girls Who Have Considered Suicide/ When the Rainbow is Enuf,* which was produced off-Broadway at New Federal Theater (1975), moved to Booth Theater on Broadway (1976), won an Obie and Outer Circle Award, and nominated for a Tony; served as artist-in-residence for New Jersey State Council of Arts, creative writing instructor at City College of New York, and professor of drama at University of Houston; poetry collections include *Nappy Edges* (1978), *A Daughter's Geography* (1983), *From Okra to Greens* (1984), *The Love Space Demands: A Continuing Saga* (1992); choreopoetry includes *Spell #7* (1979), *A Photograph: Lovers in Motion* (1979) and *Boogie Woogie Landscapes* (1979); novels include *Sassafras, Cypress, and Indigo* (1982), *Betsy Brown* (1985) and *Liliane: Resurrection of the Daughter* (1994); plays include *Black and White Two Dimensional Planes* (1979) and *Three views of Mt. Fuji* (1987); children's books include *I Live in Music* (1994), *Whitewash* (1997), *Float Like a Butterfly: Muhammad Ali* (2002) and *Daddy Says* (2003). ❖ See also Y. S. Saradha, *Black Women's Writing: Quest for Identity in the plays of Lorraine Hansberry and Ntozake Shange* (Prestige, 1998).

SHANGRI-LAS, The.
See Ganser, Marge.
See Ganser, Mary Ann.
See Weiss, Liz.
See Weiss, Mary.

SHANNON, Effie (1867–1954). American actress. Born May 13, 1867, in Cambridge, MA; died July 24, 1954, in Bay Shore, LI, NY. ❖ Made NY debut as Edith Ainsley in *Tangled Lives* (1886); starred opposite Herbert Kelcey in hit play *The Moth and the Flame* (1898); also appeared in *Manon Lescaut* (title role), *Widower's Houses, Children of Earth, At Sunrise, Heartbreak House, Trelawny of the Wells, L'Aiglon, Merry Andrew, The Admirable Crichton, The Truth about Blayds, Parnell* and *Arsenic and Old Lace* (as Martha Brewster); films include *The Man Who Played God, Bright Lights of Broadway* and *The Wiser Sex.*

SHANNON, Molly (1859–1943). *See Bock, Amy Maud.*

SHANNON, Peggy (1907–1941). American actress. Born Winona Sammon, Jan 10, 1907, in Pine Bluff, AR; died May 11, 1941, in

North Hollywood, CA; m. Allan Davis; m. Albert G. Roberts, 1940 (killed himself 19 days after her death). ❖ Made NY debut as a dancer in the *Ziegfeld Follies* (1923); also appeared in *Earl Carroll Vanities, What Ann Brought Home, High Gear, Back Here, The Cross Roads, Napi, Page Miss Glory* and *Alice Takat*; films include *The Man I Marry, Youth on Parole, Girls on Probation, Blackwell's Island, The Adventures of Jane Arden* and *Fixer Dugan*.

SHANTÉ, Roxanne (1970—). African-American rap singer. Name variations: Roxanne Shante. Born Lolita Shanté Gooden, Mar 8, 1970, in New York, NY; children: 1 daughter. ❖ At 14, recorded hit debut single, "Roxanne's Revenge," a response to U. T. F. O.'s sexist song, "Roxanne, Roxanne"; other hit singles include "Queen of Rox (Shanté Rox On)," "Go on Girl" and "Loosey's Rap"; released album, *Bad Sister* (1989); as Shanté, released unsuccessful album, *The Bitch Is Back* (1992); performed in revue, *Old School Throwdown III,* in NY (1995); released *Greatest Hits* (1995), which included new single, "Queen Pin"; released single, "Bite This" (1996).

SHAPIR, Olga (1850–1916). Russian novelist and short-story writer. Name variations: Olga Andreevna Shapír. Born 1850; died 1916; grew up on the Gulf of Finland near St. Petersburg; married a physician (exiled for political activism). ❖ Attended one of first public secondary schools for girls in Russia; worked for women's emancipation and pacifist ideals; novels include *Without Love* (1886) and *In the Stormy Years* (1907); also wrote shorter fiction and plays.

SHAPIRO, Betty Kronman (1907–1989). American-Jewish activist. Name variations: Rebecca Shapiro. Born Rebecca Kronman in Washington, DC, Sept 26, 1907; died in Washington, DC, Mar 18, 1989; dau. of Nathan Kronman (grocer) and Monya "Mollie" (Bogorod) Kronman (active in numerous Jewish community organizations); attended George Washington University and Cornell University; m. Michael Shapiro, July 5, 1936 (died Nov 23, 1976); no children. ❖ International president of B'nai B'rith Women, worked as school secretary (1924–29) and office manager, Washington, DC, branch, Hebrew Immigrant Aid Society (1929–43); served as president, National Council of Jewish Juniors, Washington, DC, Section (1936); founded and served as officer, Service Council of the Jewish Community Center, Washington, DC, during WWII; had over 40 years of activism with B'nai B'rith Women, including founder and member, Abram Simon Chapter, Washington, DC (1952–89), president, Argo Chapter, Washington, DC (1952–53), regional president, Eastern Seaboard District 5 (1955–56), and international president (1968–71). Inducted into District of Columbia Commission on Women's Hall of Fame (1988). ❖ See also *Women in World History*.

SHAPIRO, Erin (1939—). See *Pizzey, Erin*.

SHAPIRO, Margarita (1930—). See *Glantz, Margo*.

SHAPOSHNIKOVA, Natalia (1961—). Soviet gymnast. Name variations: Natalya Shaposhnikova. Born June 24, 1961, in Rostov-on-Don, USSR; m. Pavel Sut (gymnast). ❖ At USSR nationals, placed 3rd (1976, 1977) and 1st (1979); won USSR Cup (1977, 1979); at World championships, won a gold for team all-around and bronze for all-around (1978); at European championships, won a gold for balance beam, silver for floor exercise, and bronze for vault and all-around (1979); at Moscow Olympics, won gold medals for vault and team all-around, a bronze medal for balance beam, and tied with East Germany's Maxi Gnauck for a bronze medal in floor exercise (1980); was the 1st female to perform giant swings on uneven bars.

SHAPOVALOVA, Lyudmila (1947—). See *Aksyonova-Shapovalova, Lyudmila*.

SHARAFF, Irene (1910–1993). American costume designer. Pronunciation: SHAR-eff. Born in Boston, Massachusetts, in 1910; died in New York, NY, Aug 16, 1993; studied at New York School of Fine and Applied Arts, Art Students League, and Grande Chaumière in Paris; never married; no children. ❖ Over the course of her 50-year career, worked on some of America's most significant musicals, often producing costumes for the stage and film productions of the same work, such as *Flower Drum Song, Funny Girl, West Side Story* and *The King and I*; also designed for non-musicals, among them the films *The Sandpiper* (1955), *The Great White Hope* (1970) and *Mommie Dearest* (1981); known for her stylish creations and her use of color, also worked in tv, ballet, nightclubs and fashion illustration; other films include *Girl Crazy* (1943), *Meet Me in St. Louis* (1944), *Yolanda and the Thief* (1945), *The Best Years of Our Lives* (1946), *The Secret Life of Walter Mitty* (1947), *An*

American in Paris (1951), *Call Me Madam* (1953), *A Star Is Born* (1954), *Brigadoon* (1954), *Guys and Dolls* (1955), *Les Girls* (1957), *Porgy and Bess* (1959), *Can-Can* (1960), *Cleopatra* (1963), *Who's Afraid of Virginia Woolf?* (1966), *The Taming of the Shrew* (1967) and *Hello Dolly!* (1969). ❖ See also *Women in World History*.

SHARAPOVA, Darcie. See *Dohnal, Darcie*.

SHARAPOVA, Maria (1987—). Russian tennis player. Born April 19, 1987, in Nyagan, Russia (in Siberian region). ❖ At 17, won singles title at Wimbledon (2004), the 3rd youngest winner in Wimbledon history; had a 55–15 match record (2004), including the WTA title.

SHARELLI (fl. 1275 BCE). See *Akhat-milki*.

SHARIYYA (b. around 815). Arabian singer. Born in Basra (now Iraq) c. 815. ❖ Celebrated for centuries in Arabian history and folklore, sang in the romantic Persian style; at 7, already known as a singer, was sold as a slave to Ibrahim ibn al-Mahdi, one of the most significant musicians of that period; was then freed to marry him so that she could not be taken from him; on his death, was sold to a succession of caliphs—al-Mutasim (r. 833–842), al-Watiq (r. 842–847), al-Mutawakki (r. 847–862), al-Muntasir (r. 861–862), al-Mustain (r. 862–866), Al-Mutazz (r. 866–869), and al Mutamid (r. 870–892); set the latter's poems to music, for which she was richly rewarded; grew to be famous and powerful. ❖ See also *Women in World History*.

SHARMAN, Helen (1963—). English astronaut. Born Helen Patricia Sharman, May 30, 1963, in Sheffield, England; dau. of J. D. Sharman; Sheffield University, BS in chemistry, 1984; attended Birkbeck College. ❖ England's 1st astronaut, began career as research technologist for Mars Confectionery (1987); beat out over 13,000 applicants to become UK cosmonaut on Soviet space mission Project Juno; endured 18 months of grueling training at Yuri Gagarin Cosmonaut Training Center in Moscow's Star City; became 1st Briton in space (1991), spending 8 days at Mir Space Station, conducting scientific experiments. Received Order of British Empire (OBE, 1992). ❖ See also (with Christopher Priest) *Seize the Moment: Autobiography of Britain's First Astronaut* (Gollancz, 1994).

SHARMAN, Lucy (1965—). See *Tyler-Sharman, Lucy*.

SHARMAY, Lyubov (1956—). Soviet basketball player. Born April 15, 1956, in USSR. ❖ At Moscow Olympics, won a gold medal in team competition (1980).

SHARP, Jane (fl. 1671). British midwife. Fl. in 1671 in England. ❖ The 1st Englishwoman to write a book on midwifery and gynecology, published *The Midwives Book* (1671).

SHARP, Katharine Lucinda (1865–1914). American librarian. Name variations: K. L. S. Born May 21, 1865, in Elgin, Illinois; dau. of John William Sharp and Phebe (Thompson) Sharp; died in Saranac Lake, New York, June 1, 1914; Northwestern University, PhB, 1885, PhM, 1889; New York State Library School, BLS, 1892, MLS, 1907. ❖ Established libraries in Wheaton, Illinois, and Xenia, Ohio (1890s); served as head of the Armour Institute of Technology's department of library economy; transferred the Armour Institute's library school to the University of Illinois and created the Illinois State Library School (1897); published *Illinois Libraries* (1906–08); advanced the teaching of librarianship in late 19th and early 20th centuries. ❖ See also *Women in World History*.

SHARP, Margery (1905–1991). British author. Born Jan 25, 1905, to British parents living on the island of Malta; died Mar 14, 1991, in London, England; dau. of J. H. Sharp; Bedford College of London University, BA, 1929; m. Geoffrey L. Castle (major in British army), 1938 (died 1990). ❖ Published 1st novel, *Rhododendron Pie* (1930); tried her hand as a playwright, and several of her works were produced in London (1930s–40s); had a bestseller with novel *The Nutmeg Tree* (1937), which was filmed as *Julia Misbehaves* (1948); published *Cluny Brown* (1944), which was also filmed; her Victorian-era melodrama *Britannia Mews* (1946) was filmed as *Forbidden Street* (1949), and short story "The Tenant" was filmed as *The Notorious Landlady* (1962); wrote children's book *The Rescuers* (1959), which introduced the elegant and refined white mouse named Miss Bianca; wrote 7 more books featuring Miss Bianca and her faithful friend Bernard the pantry mouse. ❖ See also *Women in World History*.

SHARP, May (1876–1929). See *Churchill, May*.

SHARP, Sarah (1830–1923). See *Higgins, Sarah*.

SHARP, Susie M. (1907–1996). American chief justice. Name variations: Susie Marshall Sharp. Born July 7, 1907, in Rocky Mount, NC; died Mar 1, 1996, in Raleigh, NC. ❖ Was the only woman in her graduating class at University of North Carolina Law School (1926); practiced law in Reidsville, NC (1929–49); was the 1st woman to be appointed superior court judge in North Carolina (1949) and served until she was appointed to Supreme Court by Governor Terry Sanford (1962); was also the 1st woman elected to the post of chief justice of a state supreme court, serving NC Supreme Court (c. 1974–79).

SHARPE, May (1876–1929). See Churchill, May.

SHASHKOVA, Liubov (1977—). See Chachkova, Lioubov.

SHATTUCK, Lydia (1822–1889). American naturalist, botanist, and educator. Born Lydia White Shattuck, June 10, 1822, in East Landaff, New Hampshire; died Nov 2, 1889, in South Hadley, Massachusetts; dau. of Timothy Shattuck (farmer) and Betsy (Fletcher) Shattuck; never married; no children. ❖ Graduated from Mt. Holyoke with honors (1851) and remained on campus to become an instructor; quickly became one of the most highly regarded teachers there; was instrumental in the creation of the school's herbarium and botanical gardens; traveled extensively in her capacity as a botanist, visiting Canada, Europe, the western US, and Hawaii in search of new and rare plants, but her primary contribution to the field of botany was as a classifier of plant species; retired as professor emeritus (1888). ❖ See also *Women in World History.*

SHAVELSON, Clara Lemlich (1888–1982). See Lemlich, Clara.

SHAVER, Dorothy (1897–1959). American business executive. Born July 29, 1897, in Center Point, Arkansas; died June 28, 1959, in Hudson, New York; dau. of James D. Shaver (lawyer) and Sallie (Borden) Shaver; attended University of Arkansas and University of Chicago; never married; no children. ❖ President of Lord & Taylor for many years, began working there in 1924; served as general consultant to Office of the Quartermaster General (1942–45); became president of Lord & Taylor stores (1945) at salary of $110,000, the largest ever paid to an American woman at the time; was responsible for the store's rise in sales from $30 million to $100 million by 1959; voted outstanding woman in business by Associated Press (1946, 1947); received American Woman's Association award for feminist achievement (1950); recognized for "outstanding support of American design" by the Society of New York Dress Designers (1953). ❖ See also *Women in World History.*

SHAW, Anna Howard (1847–1919). American social reformer, feminist, physician, and cleric. Born Anna Howard Shaw, Feb 14, 1847, in Newcastle-upon-Tyne, England; died July 2, 1919, in Moylan, Pennsylvania; dau. of Thomas Shaw and Nicolas (Stott) Shaw; attended Albion College, 1873–76; graduate of School of Theology, Boston University, 1878; Boston University, MD, 1886. ❖ Methodist cleric, who won credibility for the women's suffrage movement at a crucial time through her extraordinary public-speaking skills, was 1st licensed to preach in Methodist Episcopal Church (1871); became minister of the Wesleyan Methodist Church in East Dennis, Massachusetts (1878); ordained a cleric in the Methodist Protestant Church (1880); resigned pastorate (1885) to become, 1st, a freelance lecturer for suffrage and then a national lecturer for the Women's Christian Temperance Union; became vice-president of National American Woman Suffrage Association (1892) and served as president (1904–15); began tenure as chair of Woman's Committee of the Council of National Defense (1917); embarked on final lecture tour for League to Enforce Peace (1919); able to combine new ideas with old values, affirmed Christianity, patriotism and motherhood, yet passionately supported the right of women to vote and to speak from the pulpit and lecture platform; gave over 10,000 speeches during her career and was praised by suffragist Carrie Chapman Catt as "the greatest orator among women the world has ever known." ❖ See also memoir *The Story of a Pioneer* (Harper & Brothers, 1915); Mary D. Pellauer, *Toward a Tradition of Feminist Theology: The Religious and Social Thought of Elizabeth Cady Stanton, Susan B. Anthony and Anna Howard Shaw* (Carlson, 1991); and *Women in World History.*

SHAW, Clara S. Weeks (1857–1940). See Weeks-Shaw, Clara S.

SHAW, Elizabeth (fl. 1500s). Scottish mistress. Mistress of James V (1512–1542), king of Scotland (r. 1513–1542); children: (with James V) James Stewart (b. around 1529), abbot of Kelso and Melrose.

SHAW, Elizabeth (1920–1992). Irish writer and illustrator. Name variations: Elizabeth Shaw-Graetz. Born in Belfast, Northern Ireland, 1920; died 1992; studied under Henry Moore and Graham Sutherland at Chelsea Art School in London; m. Rene Graetz (Swiss activist), in 1946. ❖ During WWII, distinguished herself as an illustrator and cartoonist, contributing to such publications as *Our Time* and *Lilliput*; after moving to Germany (1946), established her reputation with caricatures of East Berlin's intelligentsia; collaborated with Bertha Waterstradt for 2 decades on *Das Magazin,* which published the work of women writers and artists; wrote and illustrated children's books, earning international acclaim for illustrations for a collection of Bertolt Brecht's verse for children; wrote several travel books. Won Käthe Kollwitz Prize (1981). ❖ See also autobiography, *Irish Berlin* (1990).

SHAW, Fiona (1958—). Irish actress. Born Fiona Mary Wilson, July 10, 1958, in Co. Cork, Ireland; graduate of Royal Academy of Dramatic Art. ❖ Came to prominence as Julia in the National Theatre production of *The Rivals* (1983), followed by *The Taming of the Shrew* and *Hyde Park,* for the RSC; acclaimed for performances in *Electra* (1988), *The Good Person of Sichuan,* and *Hedda Gabler,* winning 3 Olivier Awards; starred as Richard in *Richard II* (1996), the 1st woman to play the deposed king; named Best Actress at Evening Standard Theatre Awards for *Machinal* (1993) and *Medea* (2002); on tv, appeared on "Gormenghast" (2000), among others; films include *My Left Foot* (1989), *Mountains of the Moon* (1990), *Three Men and a Little Lady* (1990), *Super Mario Brothers* (1993) and *Persuasion* (1995); also appeared as Aunt Petunia in *Harry Potter and the Sorcerer's Stone* (2001), *Harry Potter and the Chamber of Secrets* (2002) and *Harry Potter and the Prisoner of Azkaban* (2004). Awarded CBE (2001).

SHAW, Flora (1852–1929). British journalist. Name variations: Lady Lugard; Dame Flora Shaw. Born Flora Louise Shaw, Dec 1852, in Kimmage, Ireland; died in Abinger, England, Jan 25, 1929; dau. of George Shaw (general) and Marie (de Fontaine) Shaw; m. Sir Frederick Lugard, June 11, 1902. ❖ Staunch advocate of imperialism, whose articles played a vital role in educating both the public and politicians about the British Empire, 1st wrote children's books in effort to support herself and siblings (1874–85); published the semi-autobiographical *Castle Blair* (1877), which received universally favorable reviews; began writing short stories and articles for a variety of journals and newspapers; developed attitudes about imperialism while researching unfinished history of England, and was soon a potent and learned force in imperial politics; became colonial editor for *The Times* (1893); was implicated in scandal over Jameson Raid against the Boers when she printed a forged telegram to justify the Raid (1895); was joint founder of War Refugee Committee during WWI; had an enormous impact on British public opinion and imperial affairs; also wrote *Hector* (1883), *A Sea Change* (1885), *Colonial Chiswick's Campaign* (1886), *The Story of Australia* (1898) and *A Tropical Dependency* (1905), among others. Made Dame of the British Empire (1918). ❖ See also E. Moberly Bell, *Flora Shaw* (Constable, 1947); Margary Perham, *Lugard* (2 vols., Collins, 1956); and *Women in World History.*

SHAW, Flora Madeline (1864–1927). Canadian nurse. Born Flora Madeline Shaw, Jan 15, 1864, in Perth, Ontario, Canada; died of a pulmonary embolism while participating at an International Council of Nurses conference in Liverpool, England, Aug 27, 1927; graduate of Montreal General Hospital Training School for Nurses, 1896; dau. of Flora Madeline (Matheson) Shaw and Henry Dowsley Shaw (businessman). ❖ Served as assistant superintendent of Montreal General Hospital Training School for Nurses (1896–99, 1900–1903); was 1st secretary-treasurer of Canadian Nurses Association (1908); appointed 1st director of McGill School for Graduate Nurses in Montreal (1920); served as president of Canadian Association of Nursing Education (1922–24) and president of Association of Registered Nurses of the Province of Quebec (1922–26); elected president of Canadian Nurses Association (1926).

SHAW, Helen (1913–1985). New Zealand poet and short-story writer. Name variations: Hella Hofmann. Born Helen Lilian Shaw, Feb 20, 1913, in Timaru, New Zealand; dau. of Jessie Helen (Gow) Shaw and Walter Shaw (solicitor, killed in France 1916); died June 13, 1985, in Auckland; Canterbury College, BA, 1936; m. Frank Simon Hofmann (Jewish refugee from Prague, later photographer), Dec 24, 1941 (died 1989); children: 2 sons. ❖ Published *The Orange Tree and Other Stories* (1957), *Out of Dark: Poems* (1968), *The Girl of the Gods* (1973), *The Word and Flower* (1975), *The Gipsies and Other Stories* (1978), *Ambitions of Clouds* (1981), *Time Told from a Tower* (1985), and *Leda's Daughter*

(1985); wrote critical essays; also edited letters exchanged between Lady Ottoline Morrell and D'Arcy Cresswell (1983).

SHAW, Mary G. (1854–1929). American actress and suffragist. Born Jan 25, 1854, in Boston, Massachusetts; died in New York, NY, May 18, 1929; dau. of Levi W. Shaw (carpenter and builder) and Margaret (Keating) Shaw; m. 2nd husband Duc de Brissac (div.); children: (1st m.) Arthur Shaw (actor). ❖ Joined Boston Museum stock company (1879); appeared with Helena Modjeska for several seasons; recognized as one of the leading dramatic actresses of her time, appeared in many notable New York productions (1890–1910); was one of the 1st actresses to present Ibsen on US stage, when she portrayed Mrs. Alving in *Ghosts*; starred in Elizabeth Robins' play *Votes for Women* (1909) and advanced the cause of women's suffrage with lectures throughout the country.

SHAW, Nancy Langhorne (1879–1964). *See Astor, Nancy Witcher.*

SHAW, Patricia Hearst (b. 1954). *See Hearst, Patricia Campbell.*

SHAW, Pauline Agassiz (1841–1917). Swiss-American philanthropist and educator. Born Pauline Agassiz, Feb 6, 1841, in Neuchâtel, Switzerland; died Feb 10, 1917, in Jamaica Plain, Massachusetts; dau. of Louis Agassiz (naturalist) and Cécile (Braun) Agassiz; stepdau. of Elizabeth Cary Agassiz; educated at her stepmother's school for girls in Boston; m. Quincy Adams Shaw (businessman), Nov 13, 1860 (died 1908); children: Louis Agassiz; Pauline; Marian; Quincy Adams; Robert Gould. ❖ Advocate of early childhood education, opened 2 kindergartens in Boston (1877); within 6 years, was supporting and overseeing 31 kindergartens scattered throughout Boston area, a number of them housed within the public schools (in 1888, 14 of her schools were accepted into Boston's public school system, beginning the city's commitment to public kindergarten); began organizing day nurseries for working mothers, which became full-fledged community centers; also founded an industrial training school (1881) and Civic Service House, both in the North End of Boston (1901); became a proponent of women's suffrage, contributing substantial sums to the cause if not actually marching in parades; founded Boston Equal Suffrage Association for Good Government (1901), serving as its president for rest of life; helped keep afloat *Woman's Journal,* the weekly suffrage paper. Inducted into Women's Hall of Fame (2000). ❖ See also *Women in World History.*

SHAW, Reta (1912–1982). American character actress of stage, tv, and screen. Born Sept 13, 1912, in South Paris, ME; died Jan 8, 1982, in Encino, CA; m. William Forester (actor); children: daughter. ❖ Made Broadway debut in *It Takes Two* (1947); films include *Picnic, Pajama Game, All Mine to Give, Pollyanna, Batchelor in Paradise, Mary Poppins, The Ghost and Mrs. Muir* and *Escape to Witch Mountain.*

SHAW, Susan (1929–1978). English actress. Born Patsy Sloots, Aug 29, 1929, in Norwood, England; died Nov 27, 1978, in Middlesex, England; m. Albert Lieven (actor) 1949 (div. 1953); m. Bonar Colleano (actor), 1954 (died 1958); children: Mark Colleano (b. 1955, actor). ❖ Star of British films (1950s), including *Jassy, Holiday Camp, Dulcimer Street, My Brothers Keeper, It Always Rains on Sunday, Quartet, The Huggetts Abroad, Waterfront, Marry Me, The Intruder, Fire Maidens from Outer Space, Carry On Nurse* and *The Switch.*

SHAW, Victoria (1935–1988). Australian actress. Name variations: Jeanette Elphick. Born Jeanette Elphick, May 25, 1935, in Sydney, NSW, Australia; died Aug 17, 1988, near Sydney; m. Roger Smith (actor), 1956 (div. 1965); m. Elliott Alexander (actor), 1966; children: (1st m.) 3. ❖ Began career as a model in Sydney; made film debut in *The Phantom Stockman* (1953), followed by *Cattle Station, The Eddy Duchin Story, Edge of Eternity, The Crimson Kimono, I Aim at the Stars, To Trap a Spy, Alvarez Kelly* and *Westworld,* among others; on tv, appeared as Moire Gilmore on Australia's "Shimmering Light" (1978).

SHAW, Wini (1910–1982). American dancer and singer. Name variations: Winifred Shaw. Born Winifred Lei Momi Lokelani-Shaw, Feb 25, 1910, in San Francisco, CA; died May 2, 1982 in New York, NY; sister of Princess Lei Lokelani; m. Leo Cummins; m. William O'Malley, 1955; children: 3. ❖ As youngest member in The Shaw Family, made performance debut in their Hawaiian dance act; on Broadway, performed as dancer and vocalist in *Rain or Shine* (1928), *Simple Simon,* and *Ziegfeld Follies of 1931;* films include *Sweet Adeline* (1935), *The Singing Kid* (1936), *In Caliente* (1935), in which she sang "The Lady in Red," and Busby Berkeley's *Gold-Diggers of 1935,* in which she sang "Lullaby of

Broadway"; made USO tour to Europe with Jack Benny's "Five Jerks in a Jeep."

SHAWLEE, Joan (1926–1987). American actress. Name variations: Joan Fulton. Born Mar 5, 1926, in Forest Hills, NY; died Mar 22, 1987, in Hollywood, CA. ❖ Made film debut in *House of Horrors* (1946); other films include *Lover Come Back, The Marrying Kind, A Star is Born, A Farewell to Arms, The Apartment, Irma La Douce, Critic's Choice, Tony Rome* and *Willard;* probably best remembered as Sweet Sue in *Some Like It Hot;* on tv, was a regular on "The Abbott and Costello Show" and appeared as Peaches on "The Dick Van Dyke Show."

SHAYKH, Hanan al- (1945—). Lebanese novelist and playwright. Born 1945 in Beirut, Lebanon; brought up in Ras al-Naba; attended American College for Girls in Cairo, 1963–66. ❖ One of the foremost writers of the Arab world, began career as a journalist in Beirut, working for the magazines *al-Hasna* and *al-Nahar* (1968–75); published 1st book *Intihar rajul mayyit* (1970); left Lebanon because of civil war (1976), living in Saudi Arabia until 1982, then moved to London; came to international prominence with *Hikayat Zahrah* (*The Story of Zahra,* 1980), followed by *Misk al-ghazal* (*Women of Sand and Myrrh,* 1989); other writings, which focus on the limitations imposed on women in a patriarchal society, include *Barid Bayrut* (*Beirut Blues,* 1992), *Only in London* (2000) and a collection of short stories *I Sweep the Sun off Rooftops* (1998); works have often been banned in the Arab world.

SHAYLE GEORGE, Frances (c. 1827–1890). New Zealand teacher and writer. Name variations: Frances Southwell. Born Frances Southwell, c. 1827–1829, at Clifton, Gloucestershire, England; died Sept 8, 1890, in Auckland, New Zealand; dau. of John Southwell (solicitor) and Martha Southwell; m. Thomas Shayle George, 1848 (died 1868); children: 5. ❖ Immigrated with husband to New Zealand (1850); opened Wye-Cottage Seminary (1852); wrote poetry, short pieces and letters to newspapers; published "From a Settler's Wife" in Charles Dickens' *Household Words* (1852); opened school for girls in Shortland Crescent (1867). ❖ See also *Dictionary of New Zealand Biography* (Vol. 1).

SHAYNE, Tamara (1902–1983). Russian actress. Name variations: Tamara Shane. Born Nov 25, 1902, in Perm, Russia; died Oct 23, 1983, in Los Angeles, CA; sister of Konstantine Shayne (actor); m. Akim Tamiroff (actor, died 1972). ❖ Made film debut in *Ninotchka* (1939); also appeared in *Mission to Moscow, The Jolson Story, It Happened in Brooklyn, Northwest Outpost, The Snake Pit, Walk a Crooked Mile, The Red Danube, Anastasia* and *Romanoff and Juliet.*

SHAZAR, Rachel (1888–1975). *See Katznelson-Shazar, Rachel.*

SHCHEGOLEVA, Tatiana (1982—). Russian basketball player. Born Feb 9, 1982, in Moscow, Russia. ❖ Center, won a team bronze medal at Athens Olympics (2004); placed 2nd at World championships (2002) and 1st at European championships (2003).

SHCHELKANOVA, Tatyana (1937—). Soviet track-and-field athlete. Born April 18, 1937, in USSR. ❖ At Tokyo Olympics, won a bronze medal in the long jump (1964).

SHCHEPKINA-KUPERNIK, Tatiana (1874–1952). Russian playwright, translator and poet. Name variations: Tatiana L'vovna Shchépkina-Kupérnik, Tatiana Lvovna Shchepkina-Kupernik. Born Jan 24, 1874, in Moscow, Russia; died July 27, 1952, in Moscow; dau. of Lev Kupernik (barrister); mother was a pianist; great-granddau. of Mikhail Shchepkin (famed actor); studied at University of Lausanne, 1896. ❖ Began career as an actress with Korsh Drama Theater, Moscow; wrote a play and a number of short stories; traveled to Italy and France, met Edmond Rostand, and translated one of his plays into Russian (1894–95); published 1st collection of stories, *Pages from a Life* (1898), followed by *Unposted Letters* (1906); married and moved to St. Petersburg (1904); repelled by the extremism after the Bolshevik coup (1917), but decided to remain in Russia; translated 59 foreign classical plays into Russian; wrote 3 books of memoirs: *The Days of My Life* (1928), *About Maria Yermolova* (1940), and *The Theater in My Life* (1948); plays, which often focus on class issues, role of art in life, and friendships between women, include *Summer Picture* (1892) and *A Happy Woman* (1911); poetry includes *From Women's Letters* (1898), *My Poems* (1901), *Clouds* (1912), and *Echoes of War* (1915); short-story collections include *This Happened Yesterday* (1907). Received Griboedov Prize and order of Labor of the Red Banner (1944).

SHCHETININA, Lyudmila (1951—). Soviet volleyball player. Born Jan 1951 in USSR. ❖ At Montreal Olympics, won a silver medal in team competition (1976).

SHEA, Lynda Lee (c. 1939—). See Mead, Lynda Lee.

SHEAHAN, Marion (1892–1994). American nurse. Name variations: Marion Sheahan Bailey. Born Marion Winifred Sheahan, Sept 5, 1892, in New York, NY; died Mar 17, 1994, in Albany, NY; dau. of Catherine (Nolan) Sheahan and James C. Sheahan; m. Frank W. Bailey, Mar 17, 1935 (died 1947). ❖ Public health administrator, began career as a private duty-nurse in Albany, NY; worked at Lillian Wald's Henry Street Visiting Nurse Service (from 1917) and New York State Department of Health (1920–48); served as assistant director and director of the Division of Public Health Nursing (1932–48); was a visiting nursing professor at University of California, Berkeley; served as director of Division of Nursing Services for National League for Nursing (NLN), then as deputy general director until 1963; was the 1st nurse to be president of American Public Health Association (APHA, 1960). Received Sedgwick Award (1969), APHA's greatest honor.

SHEALEY, Courtney (c. 1978—). American swimmer. Born c. 1978 in Columbia, SC; attended University of Georgia. ❖ Won a gold medal for 4 x 100-meter freestyle relay at Sydney Olympics (2000); won gold medals in 100-meter freestyle and 400-meter freestyle relay and a silver in 100- meter backstroke at Pan American Games (2003).

SHEARER, Janet (1958—). New Zealand yacht racer. Born July 17, 1958. ❖ At Barcelona Olympics, won a silver medal in 470 class (1992).

SHEARER, Jill (1936—). Australian playwright. Name variations: Jill Patricia Shearer; (pseudonym) Flora McKay. Born April 14, 1936, in Melbourne, Victoria, Australia; lived mainly in Queensland. ❖ Wrote several full-length and one-act plays; works include *Catherine* (1977), *The Foreman* (1978), *The Boat* (1978), *The Family,* and *Shimada* (1989), which was produced on Broadway (1992); also wrote *Georgia,* about Georgia O'Keeffe (2005). ❖ See also autobiography, *Nowhere but Broadway.*

SHEARER, Moira (1926–2006). Scottish ballerina and actress. Name variations: Mrs. Ludovic Kennedy. Born Moira Shearer King, Jan 17, 1926, in Dunfermline, Fifeshire, Scotland; died Jan 31, 2006, in Oxford, England; dau. of Harold Charles King (civil engineer) and Margaret Crawford (Reid) Shearer; m. Ludovic Kennedy (writer and lecturer), 1950. ❖ Joined the International Ballet Company (1941), and danced as the Fairy of Song Birds in *Aurora's Wedding* and the Guardian Swallow in *Planetomania;* danced with the Vic-Wells Ballet in the Pas de deux in *Orpheus and Eurydice,* and became soloist (1942), dancing such roles as the Serving Maid in *The Gods Go a-Begging,* the Pas de deux in *Les Patineurs,* the Nightingale in *The Birds,* Pride in *The Quest,* Pas de trois and Rendezvous pas de deux in *Promenade* (all 1943), the Polka in *Façade,* The Butterfly in *Le Festin d'araignée,* the Young Girl in *Spectre de la rose,* Chiarina in *Le Carnaval,* and A Lover in *Miracle in the Gorbals* (all 1944), Odile in *Swan Lake,* Mlle Théodore in *The Prospect Before Us,* Lover in *The Wanderer,* Countess Kitty in *Les Sirèns,* and the Dancer in *The Rake's Progress* (all 1945); earned rank of ballerina (1946); made film debut in *The Red Shoes* (1948), which was an enormous international success; danced the title role in *Giselle* at Edinburgh Festival (1948) to great success; appeared on stage and in film (1948–62); retired from dancing (1954), except for a single tv appearance in Gillian Lynne's *A Simple Man;* choreographed for the Northern Ballet Theater (1987); on theatrical stage, performed for an entire season with the Bristol Old Vic (1955–56); appeared in title role in *Major Barbara* in London (1956); wrote *Balletmaster: A Dancer's View of George Balanchine* (1986); her success as a dancer and actress in films tends to overshadow her achievements in ballet. Films include *Tales of Hoffmann* (1951), *The Story of Three Loves* (1953), *The Man Who Loved Redheads* (1954), *Peeping Tom* (1960) and *Black Tights* (1962). ❖ See also *Women in World History.*

SHEARER, Norma (1900–1983). Canadian-born actress. Born Edith Norma Shearer, Aug 10, 1900, in Montreal, Canada; died June 12, 1983, in Woodland Hills, CA; dau. of Andrew Shearer and Edith Mary (Fisher) Shearer; sister of Athole Shearer; m. Irving G. Thalberg (film producer), 1928 (died 1936); m. Martin Arrouge (ski instructor), 1942 (died Aug 8, 1999); children: (1st m.) Irving Thalberg; Katharine Thalberg. ❖ One of the major stars of 1930s Hollywood, won the Oscar as Best Actress for performance in *The Divorcee* (1930); made silent film debut in *The Stealers* (1920); made MGM film debut in *Pleasure Mad* (1923); appeared as Consuelo in *He Who Gets Slapped* (1924), opposite

Lon Chaney; starred in some of MGM's finest movies, including *Idiot's Delight* and *The Women* (both 1939), and 5 for which she received Oscar nominations: *Their Own Desire* (1929), *A Free Soul* (1931), *The Barretts of Wimpole Street* (1934), *Romeo and Juliet* (1936), and *Marie Antoinette* (1938); turned down starring roles in *Gone With the Wind* and *Mrs. Miniver,* appearing instead in back-to-back flops, *We Were Dancing* and *Her Cardboard Lover* (both 1940); retired from the screen (1942). ❖ See also *Women in World History.*

SHEBA, Queen of (fl. 10th c. BCE). Ethiopian queen. Name variations: Balkama; Balkis, Bilkas, or Bilkis; Balqis or Bilqis; Makeda; Nicaula; Panther in the Blossom; Queen of the South (Eteye of Azeb); Saba, Sabbe, or Seba; Sibyl or Sibylla. ❖ Queen of Axum in Ethiopia and Sheba in southern Arabia who is known in the Jewish, Christian, and Islamic traditions as peer and lover of Solomon, king of Israel, and maternal ancestor of Ethiopia's royal dynasty. The earliest mention of the queen comes from the Old Testament where she undertakes a diplomatic trading mission to King Solomon in Israel from the territories she ruled in modern-day Ethiopia and Yemen. From the Biblical source, legends of the queen developed in Jewish, Christian, and Islamic literature. She was said to have been the lover of Solomon, and Ethiopians claim her as the ancestor of their royal line. In the West, she is associated with the legend of the True Cross upon which Jesus was crucified. ❖ See also Post Wheeler, *The Golden Legend of Ethiopia: The Love-Story of Makeda Virgin Queen of Axum and Sheba and Solomon the Great King* (1936); E.A. Wallis Budge, *The Queen of Sheba and Her Only Son Menyelek* (1892); Nicholas Clapp, *Sheba: Through the Desert in Search of the Legendary Queen* (Houghton, 2001); Miguel Serrano, *The Visits of the Queen of Sheba* (Routledge & Kegan Paul, 1972); and *Women in World History.*

SHEED, Maisie (1889–1975). See Ward, Maisie.

SHEEHAN, Margaret Flavin (d. 1969). Welsh-born actress. Born in Wales; died Mar 18, 1969, age 88, in Boston, MA. ❖ Known as Boston's Million Dollar Beauty, appeared in *Prince of Pilsen, Yankee Consul, Defender* and *The Big Stick;* retired (1927).

SHEEHAN, Patty (1956—). American golfer. Born Patty Sheehan, Oct 27, 1956, in Middlebury, VT; daughter of a ski coach; attended San Jose State. ❖ Was Nevada State Amateur (1975–78) and California State Amateur (1978–79); won several LPGA tournaments, including Mazda Japan Classic (1981), Orlando Lady, Safeco, and Inamori classics (1982), Corning, Henredon, and Inamori classics, and LPGA championship (1983), Elizabeth Arden, McDonald's, and Henredon classics, and LPGA championship (1984), Safeco Classic (1990); won US Open (1992). ❖ See also *Women in World History.*

SHEEHY, Kathy (1970—). American water-polo player. Born April 26, 1970, in San Diego, CA. ❖ Won a team silver medal at Sydney Olympics (2000).

SHEEHY-SKEFFINGTON, Hanna (1877–1946). Irish feminist and nationalist. Name variations: Johanna Mary Sheehy; Hanna Sheehy; Mrs. Sheehy-Skeffington. Born Johanna Sheehy, May 24, 1877, in Co. Cork, Ireland; died in Dublin, Ireland, April 20, 1946; dau. of David Sheehy (member of Irish Parliamentary Party) and Elizabeth (McCoy) Sheehy; Royal University of Ireland, BA, 1899, MA, 1902; m. Frank Sheehy-Skeffington, 1903 (died 1916); children: Owen (b. 1909). ❖ Irish reformer whose feminist and nationalist aspirations were often in conflict, though she pursued both with dedication and courage, co-founded Irish Women's Franchise League (1908); helped establish *The Irish Citizen* (1912); imprisoned as a militant suffragist (1912 and 1913); husband killed in Easter Rising (1916); made lecture tour of US to raise money for the nationalist organization Sinn Fein (1916–18), and met with President Wilson (1918); imprisoned in Liverpool, Dublin, and Holloway (1918); served as judge during War of Independence (1919–21); made lecture tour of US and Canada (1922–23); visited League of Nations (1923); attended Women's International League for Peace and Freedom Conference in Prague (1929); journeyed to Moscow (1930); imprisoned in Armagh (1933); made lecture tour to US and Canada (1933–34); established Women's Social and Political League (1937); toured US (1937–38); was a candidate in general election (1943); as a journalist, published hundreds of articles, and wrote *Impressions of Sinn Fein In America* (1919) and *Ireland—Present and Future* (1919); just as she was not inhibited by the British military after they murdered her husband, so too, in independent Ireland, was not inhibited by the repressive Catholic State and spoke out for the rights of women in a nation which largely eschewed them. ❖ See also Levenson and Naderstad, *Hanna Sheehy Skeffington* (Syracuse U. Press, 1986); Maria Luddy, *Hanna Sheehy-Skeffington* (1995); Cliona Murphy, *The Women's Suffrage Movement and Irish Society in the Early Twentieth Century* (Temple U. Press, 1989); and *Women in World History*.

SHEEN, Gillian (1928—). English fencer. Born Aug 21, 1928, in England. ❧ At Melbourne Olympics, won a gold medal in indiv. foil (1956).

SHEEPSHANKS, Mary (1872–1958). British feminist and pacifist. Born Mary Sheepshanks, 1872, in Liverpool, England; died 1958; dau. of a Church of England vicar who was bishop of Norwich. ❧ Studied at Newnham College, Cambridge, and became social worker; was vice-principal, then principal (1897), of Morley College for Working Men and Women; attended International Woman Suffrage Association congress in Holland (1908), became its secretary in London (1913), and began to edit and distribute its journal *Jus Suffragii*; lectured widely in Europe on women's emancipation and non-violence; during WWI, was secretary of Fight the Famine Council; became international secretary of Women's International League for Peace and Freedom (1927); organized 1st international scientific conference on Modern Methods of Warfare and the Protection of Civilians (1929). Unpublished memoirs *The Long Day's Task* are held in Fawcett Library.

SHEILA E. (1957—). *See Escovedo, Sheila.*

SHEINA, Svetlana (1918–2005). Soviet ballet dancer. Born Dec 26, 1918, in Odessa; died Jan 19, 2005. ❧ Became principal dancer at Leningrad Maly Theater (1938), where she danced in 19th-century classics as well as contemporary works; created roles for Boris Fenster's *Youth* (1949) and *Twelve Months* (1954); became repiteur there (1959); joined staff of St. Petersburg Mussorgsky State Opera and Ballet.

SHELBY, Juliet (1902–1984). *See Minter, Mary Miles.*

SHELDON, Joan Mary (1943—). Australian politician. Born April 29, 1943, in Bundaberg, Queensland, Australia. ❧ Was a physiotherapist (1979–90); as a member of the Liberal Party, elected to the Queensland Parliament for Landsborough (1990–92), then Caloundra (1992—); shadow minister for Employment, Training, Industrial Relations and the Arts (2000–01); served as Liberal Party Leader (1991–98), the 1st woman to lead a political party.

SHELDON, Jorja (1923–1985). *See Curtright, Jorja.*

SHELDON, Mary Downing (1850–1898). *See Barnes, Mary Downing.*

SHELDON, May French (1847–1936). American explorer and traveler. Born May French, May 10, 1847, in Bridgewater, PA; died 1936 in London, England; dau. of Colonel Joseph French (civil engineer) and Elizabeth J. Poorman French; educated in NY and Italy; m. Eli Lemon Sheldon (US banker and publisher in London), 1876 (died 1892). ❧ Managed own publishing company, Saxon and Co., and published novel *Herbert Severence* (1889); traveled alone to Africa (1891), the 1st white woman to visit parts of eastern and central Africa; made several descents to Lake Chala, a volcanic crater on the side of Mt. Kilimanjaro, and punted its unexplored waters; elected fellow of Royal Geographic Society (1892); made safari to Belgian Congo (1894); conducted research in Congo and raised money in US for Belgian Red Cross during WWI, for which she was made Chevalier de l'Ordre de la Couronne by King Albert of Belgium; also wrote *Sultan to Sultan: Adventures Among the Masai and Other Tribes of East Africa* (1892).

SHELDON AMOS, Bonté (1874–1960). *See Elgood, Cornelia.*

SHELDON AMOS, Cornelia (1874–1960). *See Elgood, Cornelia.*

SHELEST, Alla (1919–1998). Soviet ballerina. Born Feb 26, 1919, in Smolensk, Russia; died Dec 7, 1998, in St. Petersburg, Russia; studied at the Leningrad Ballet (1927–37); m. Yuri Grigorovich. ❧ Performed with Kirov Ballet for 26 years, dancing solo roles at the outset; 1st prominent role was that of the Girl-Swan in Agrippina Vaganova's *Swan Lake* (1938–39); appeared as Zarema in *The Fountain of Bakhchisary*, Nikia in *La Bayadère*, Juliet in *Romeo and Juliet*, Myrtha in *Giselle*, the Lilac Fairy and Aurora in *The Sleeping Beauty*, Yekaterina in *The Stone Flower*, Bird-Girl in *Shurale*, and the Tsar-Maiden in *The Humpbacked Horse*; during 1960s, appearances became less frequent; became ballet master of Kirov Ballet.

SHELLEY, Barbara (1933—). English actress. Name variations: Barbara Kowin. Born Barbara Kowin, 1933, in London, England. ❧ Began career as a model; under name Barbara Kowin, made film debut in *Mantrap* (1953); changed name to Barbara Shelley and appeared in 7 Italian films (1954–56); other films include *Cat Girl*, *The Camp on Blood Island*, *Blood of the Vampire*, *The Solitary Child*, *Village of the Damned* (*Anthea Zellaby*), *Shadow of the Cat*, *Death Trap*, *The Gorgon*, *The Secret of Blood Island*, *Dracula: Prince of Darkness*, *Rasputin: The Mad Monk* and *More Than a Messiah*.

SHELLEY, Harriet (1795–1816). *See Westbrook, Harriet.*

SHELLEY, Mary (1797–1851). English writer. Name variations: Mary Godwin Shelley; Mary Wollstonecraft Shelley. Born Mary Wollstonecraft Godwin, Aug 30, 1797, in London, England; died in Chester Square, London, Feb 1, 1851; dau. of William Godwin (political philosopher) and Mary Wollstonecraft (1759–1797, author of *A Vindication of the Rights of Woman*); m. Percy Bysshe Shelley (poet), 1816; children: William (died young); Clara (died young); Percy. ❧ Author of *Frankenstein* and other texts who is as notable for her influence on Percy Bysshe Shelley as she is for her own writings; learned that her half-sister Fanny had committed suicide by taking laudanum and that Shelley's wife Harriet had drowned herself; eloped with Shelley (1814); composed her famous story of Dr. Frankenstein and his monster when she was just 18 (1815–16), which was a a phenomenal success; with Lord Byron, John Keats, and Shelley, became a major figure in the "second generation" of Romantics; by 1822, had lost 2 of her children and her husband in quick succession; edited *Posthumous Poems of Percy Bysshe Shelley* (1824); an established woman of letters, nevertheless struggled for acceptance in a prudish and unforgiving British society; was attentive to social injustice and, in particular, the oppression of women; succumbed to a brain tumor and eventual death (1851); other writings include *History of a Six Weeks' Tour* (1817), *Matilda* (1820), *Proserpine* (1820), *Midas* (1820), *Valperga* (1823), *The Last Man* (1826), *The Fortunes of Perkin Warbeck* (1830), *Lives of the Most Eminent Literary and Scientific Men of Italy, Spain and Portugal* (1835), *Lodore* (1835) and *Rambles in Germany and Italy* (1844). ❧ See also *The Journals of Mary Shelley 1814–1844* (Ed. by Feldman and Scott-Kilvert, 2 vols., Clarendon, 1987); *The Letters of Mary Wollstonecraft Shelley* (Ed. by Betty T. Bennett, 3 vols., Johns Hopkins U. Press, 1980, 1983, 1988); William St. Clair, *The Godwins and the Shelleys: A Biography of a Family* (Norton, 1989); Emily Sunstein, *Mary Shelley: Romance and Reality* (Johns Hopkins U. Press, 1989); and *Women in World History*.

SHELTON, Karen (1957—). American field-hockey player. Born Nov 14, 1957, in Honolulu, Hawaii; dau. of James Shelton (lieutenant colonel in the army); attended West Chester State College; m. Willie Scroggs (athletic director); children: William. ❧ At Los Angeles Olympics, won a bronze medal in team competition (1984); became head coach of field hockey at University of North Carolina (1981). Was US Field Hockey's Athlete of the Year (1983); inducted into USFHA Hall of Fame (1989).

SHEMANSKAYA, Vera (1981—). *See Shimanskaya, Vera.*

SHEN RONG (1935—). Chinese novelist. Born 1935 in China. ❧ Studied Russian at Beijing Foreign Languages Institute; taught briefly in middle school; novellas, which explore social issues and lives of modern Chinese women, include *Everlasting Spring* (1979), *At Middle Age* (1980), *Yang Weiwei and Sartre* (1984), and *Divorce? Why Bother?* (1989).

SHEPARD, Helen Miller (1868–1938). American philanthropist. Name variations: Helen Miller Gould. Born Helen Miller Gould in New York, NY, June 20, 1868; died 1938; eldest dau. of Jay Gould (1836–1892, the financier) and Helen Day (Miller) Gould; briefly attended New York Law University; m. Finley Johnson Shepard (1867–1942, executive of the Missouri Pacific Railway), Jan 22, 1913; children: Olivia Margaret, Finley Fay, and Helen Anna Shepard. ❧ Inherited part of the family fortune (1892); became known for her charity; contributed $100,000 to victims of St. Louis cyclone (1896), and funded a library and the Hall of Fame building at New York University, as well as the naval branch of Brooklyn YMCA; also gave generously to Rutgers, Vassar, and Mt. Holyoke colleges; during Spanish-American War (1898), contributed $100,000 to US government for relief of soldiers at Camp Wycoff, Long Island.

SHEPARD, Mary (1909–2000). English illustrator. Name variations: Mary Eleanor Jessie Knox. Born Mary Eleanor Jessie Shepard, Dec 25, 1909, in Surrey, England; died in London, Sept 4, 2000; dau. of Ernest H. Shepard (illustrator) and Florence Eleanor (Chaplin) Shepard (artist); attended Slade School of Art; m. Edmund George Valpy Knox (editor for *Punch*), Oct 2, 1937 (died Jan 2, 1971); children: (stepdaughter)

Penelope Knox (died 1999) who wrote novels as Penelope Fitzgerald. ❖ Following in footsteps of her father who had illustrated A. A. Milne's "Winnie the Pooh" series, began illustrating P. L. Travers' "Mary Poppins" series (1932). ❖ See also *Women in World History.*

SHEPARDSON, Mary Thygeson (1906–1997). American cultural anthropologist. Born Mary Thygeson, May 26, 1906, in St. Paul, MN; died Mar 30, 1997, in Palo Alto, CA; dau. of Nels Marcus Thygeson and Sylvie Thompson Thygeson (1868–1975, reproductive rights activist); graduate of Stanford University, 1928; also studied at Sorbonne and London School of Economics; m. Dwight Shepardson (physician), 1942 (died 1967). ❖ At 54, received PhD from University of California, Berkeley, with dissertation *Navajo Ways in Government* (published 1963); collaborated with Blodwen Hammond on *The Navajo Mountain Community* (1970); performed studies on Navajo law; taught at San Francisco State University; performed fieldwork with Hammond on Bonin Islands, Japan (1971); with Lakota anthropologist Bea Medicine, organized symposium on American Indian women.

SHEPHARD, Gillian (1940—). British politician. Born Gillian Watts, Jan 22, 1940, in Norfolk, England; grew up in a rural area of eastern England; dau. of Reginald Watts (cattle farmer) and Bertha Watts; St. Hilda's College, Oxford, MA, 1961; m. Thomas Shephard, 1975. ❖ As a member of Conservative Party, was elected to Norfolk County Council (West Norfolk, 1977), and became chair of the council's social services committee; appointed deputy leader of the council (1981); became chair of Norwich Health Authority (1985); elected to Parliament (1987); during 1st years in Parliament, was a member of the Select Committee on Social Services, and appointed under-secretary of state in the Department of Social Security (1989); was named minister of state at the Treasury (1990) and deputy chair of the Conservative Party (1991); joined Cabinet as secretary of state for unemployment (1992); became minister of agriculture, food and fisheries (1993); appointed secretary of state for education (1994), then named secretary of state for education and employment (1995); despite sweeping defeat at polls for Conservative Party (1997), won reelection and was named shadow leader of the House of Commons; served as shadow secretary of state for environment, transport, and the regions (1998–99); while still a member of Parliament, published *Shephard's Watch: Illusions of Power in British Politics* (2000).

SHEPHERD, Cybill (1949—). American model and actress. Born Cybill Lynne Shepherd, Feb 18, 1949, in Memphis, TN; m. David Ford, 1978 (div. 1982); m. Bruce Oppenheim, 1987 (div. 1990); children: (1st m.) Clementine; (2nd m.) twins, Ariel and Zachariah. ❖ Had highly successful career as a model; came to prominence as actress in *The Last Picture Show* (1971); other films include *The Heartbreak Kid* (1972), *Daisy Miller* (1974), *At Long Last Love* (1975), *Taxi Driver* (1976) and *Texasville* (1990): with film career on the decline, made comeback on tv with enormous hit, "Moonlighting" (1985–89), then starred on "Cybill" (1995–98). ❖ See also memoir *Cybill Disobedience* (2000).

SHEPHERD, Dolly (d. 1983). British parachutist and balloonist. Born in England; died 1983. ❖ Known as Britain's "Parachute Queen," made 1st jump from a gas-filled balloon after only 30 minutes of training; soon joined a troupe of parachutists which toured Britain performing daredevil jumps; was injured several times. ❖ See also Peter Hearn and Molly Sedgwick, *When the 'Chute Went Up: Adventures of a Pioneer Lady Parachutist* (1997); and *Women in World History.*

SHEPHERD, Karen (1940—). American politician. Born July 5, 1940, in Silver City, Grant Co., New Mexico; University of Utah, BA, 1962; Brigham Young University, MA, 1963. ❖ Taught high school English (1963–75); founded and owned a magazine publishing company (1978–88); was a Utah state senator (1991–93); representing Utah, elected as a Democrat to US House of Representatives (1992); lost bid for reelection (1994).

SHEPHERD, Mary (c. 1780–1847). Scottish philosopher. Name variations: Lady Mary Shepherd; Lady Mary Primrose. Born Mary Primrose, c. 1780; died Jan 7, 1847; 2nd dau. of Neil Primrose, 3rd earl of Rosebery; m. Henry John Shepherd, April 11, 1808 (died Jan 7, 1847). ❖ Wrote *An Essay on the Relation of Cause and Effect, Controverting the Doctrine of Mr. Hume, Concerning the Nature of that Relation* (1824), *Essays on the Perception of an External Universe and Other Subjects Connected with the Doctrine of Causation* (1827), essays critical of the views of John Fearn in *Parriana* (1829), and a response to Fearn in *Fraser's Magazine* (1832). ❖ See also *Women in World History.*

SHEPHERD-BARRON, Dorothy (1897–1953). English tennis player. Name variations: Dorothy Barron. Born Nov 24, 1897, in UK; died Feb 20, 1953. ❖ At Paris Olympics, won a bronze medal in mixed doubles–outdoors and a bronze medal in singles (1924).

SHEPITKO, Larissa (1938–1979). Soviet filmmaker. Name variations: Larisa Shepitko or Shepit'ko. Born Jan 6, 1938, in Artyomovsk, eastern Ukraine; died June 2, 1979, in an automobile accident outside Moscow; educated at VGIK state film school; studied with Alexander Dovzhenko; m. Elem Klimov (film director); children: 1 son. ❖ Acclaimed director, made 1st successful feature, *Znoi* (Heat, 1963), at age 22; received guarded praise from Soviet press for *Krylya* (Wings, 1966), which focused on a celebrated fighter pilot during World War II as she adjusts to the more traditional role expected of a woman in postwar Soviet society; completed 1st color film, *Ty i ya* (You and I, 1971); though her films were unofficially suppressed in Soviet Union, received international attention; was frequently compared to Alain Resnais. Won a Golden Bear for *Voskhozdenie* (The Ascent) at Berlin Film Festival (1977). ❖ See also *Women in World History.*

SHEPLEY, Ruth (1892–1951). American actress. Born May 29, 1892, in Providence, RI; died Oct 16, 1951, in New York, NY; m. Gordon Sarre; m. Dr. Beverly Chew Smith. ❖ Made Broadway debut as Diana Dinwiddie in *All for a Girl* (1908); appeared in many other plays, including *A Gentleman of Leisure, The Brute, The Boomerang, Three in One,* and as Mrs. Campbell in *Ladies and Gentlemen* (with Helen Hayes); films include *When Knighthood was in Flower;* retired (1939).

SHEPPARD, Kate (1847–1934). British-born suffragist and temperance leader. Name variations: Mrs. K. W. Sheppard. Born Catherine Wilson Malcolm, probably on Mar 10, 1847, in Liverpool, England; died July 13, 1934, in Riccarton, Christchurch, New Zealand; dau. of Andrew Wilson Malcolm (lawyer) and Jemima Crawford (Souter) Malcolm; m. Walter Sheppard, 1870 (died 1915); m. William Lovell-Smith (printer and author), 1925; children: (1st m.) Douglas (1880–1910). ❖ A key figure in gaining enfranchisement for women in New Zealand, was 21 when she moved with widowed mother and siblings to Christchurch, New Zealand; soon became involved in Women's Christian Temperance Union (WCTU); as president of New Zealand WCTU, founded the Franchise Department (1886), devoted to the enfranchisement of women; wrote articles and pamphlets, organized countless meetings with women in small towns throughout New Zealand, and lobbied widely with politicians and other public figures; edited women's page of *Prohibitionist* (1891–94); became head of economics department of Canterbury Women's Institute and de facto head of the institute's push for suffrage (1892); after passage of a suffrage bill (1893), continued advocating for improvement of women's condition; became president of the National Council of Women on its founding (1896); edited *White Ribbon* (1898–1903). ❖ See also Judith Devaliant, *Kate Sheppard—A Biography* (Penguin, 1992); and *Women in World History.*

SHEPPARD, Kellye Cash (c. 1965—). See Cash, Kellye.

SHER, Lisa (1969—). American mountain biker. Born April 16, 1969, in Chicago, IL. ❖ Six-time US World's Team member, specializes in downhill; results include 7th in Downhill at Winter X Games (1997), 4th in World championships (Quebec, 1998), 7th and 8th respectively in NORBA National standing for Downhill and Dual Slalom (1998), and 6th in Downhill and 7th in Speed at Winter X Games (1998).

SHEREMETA, Liubov (1980—). Ukrainian gymnast. Born Jan 17, 1980, in Lvov, Ukraine. ❖ Won a bronze medal for floor exercises at the World championships (1996); won Gym Coupes and Salamunov Memorial (1997).

SHEREMETSKAIA, Natalia (1880–1952). Russian empress. Name variations: Sheremetskaya; Nathalie Brasova; Countess Brassovna; Natasha. Born June 27, 1880; died in automobile accident in Sept 1952; dau. of Serge Scheremetersky; m. Mamontov; m. Wulfert; m. Michael Aleksandrovich Romanov (1878–1918, son of Alexander III, tsar of Russia, and Marie Feodorovna), grand duke Thronfolger, in July 1912; children: George M. (1910–1931, died in automobile accident). ❖ A beautiful Russian divorcée and nonroyal, created a scandal when she married Michael (1912); was empress for one day, when brother-in-law Nicholas II abdicated (1917) and husband became tsar in the middle of the revolution but abdicated within hours. ❖ See also Rosemary and Donald Crawford's *Michael and Natasha: The Life and Love of Michael II, the Last of the Romanov Tsars* (Scribner, 1997).

SHERIDAN, Ann (1915–1967). American actress. Name variations: The Oomph Girl; Clara Lou Sheridan. Born Clara Lou Sheridan, Feb 21, 1915, in Denton, TX; died Jan 21, 1967, in San Fernando Valley, CA; m. Edward Norris (actor), 1936 (div. 1939); m. George Brent (actor), 1942 (div. 1943); m. James Owens, 1956 (div.); m. Scott McKay (actor), 1966. ❖ Leading lady of stage and screen, won a beauty contest in Texas (1933), which included a trip to Hollywood and bit part in the film *Search for Beauty*; appeared in many films (until 1935 under Clara Lou Sheridan), including *Dodge City, King's Row, George Washington Slept Here, The Man Who Came to Dinner, Angels with Dirty Faces* and *I Was a Male War Bride*; also appeared on NBC series "Another World."

SHERIDAN, Bonnie (1944—). *See Bramlett, Bonnie.*

SHERIDAN, Caroline (1808–1877). *See Norton, Caroline.*

SHERIDAN, Caroline Henrietta Callander (1779–1851). English author. Name variations: Caroline Campbell; Caroline Henrietta Callander. Born Caroline Henrietta Callander in 1779; died 1851; dau. of Colonel Callander, afterwards Sir James Campbell (1745–1832); m. Thomas Sheridan (1775–1817, poet, public official, and son of playwright Richard Brinsley Sheridan), in 1805; children: Helen Selina Blackwood, Lady Dufferin (1807–1867); Caroline Norton (1808–1877); and Lady Georgiana Seymour (later duchess of Somerset). ❖ A celebrated beauty, produced 3 novels, including *Carwell, or Crime and Sorrow* (1830). ❖ See also *Women in World History.*

SHERIDAN, Clare (1885–1970). English sculptor, journalist, and travel writer. Name variations: Clare Frewen Sheridan. Born Clare Consuelo Frewen, Sept 9, 1885, in London, England; died 1970 in Brede, England; dau. of Moreton Frewen and Clara (Jerome) Frewen (sister of Jennie Jerome Churchill [1854–1921]); m. Wilfred Sheridan, Oct 10, 1910 (killed in action during WWI, 1915); children: Margaret (b. 1911); Elizabeth (1912–1913); Richard (1915–1936). ❖ Set up a studio in London (1915), launching a career as a professional sculptor; initially, sold only decorative pottery, but soon connections to London elite led to commissions for portrait busts in marble and bronze; by 1920, was well established; traveled secretly to Moscow (1920), where she modeled busts of Lenin, Trotsky and other Russian political figures; on return home (1921), learned that London society had branded her a traitor; published a memoir, *Mayfair to Moscow*; moved to New York; went to Mexico to write articles for *New York World* on life there; sent to England as correspondent on European affairs for *New York World* (1922); over next 2 years, interviewed top political figures, including Kemal Ataturk and Benito Mussolini; returned to Europe as permanent correspondent to Germany for the *World* (1923), but continued to travel across Europe as events unfolded; lived in Bikstra in the Sahara (1927–31), where she produced several novels as well as travel books on her experiences in Europe and Russia, and continued to sculpt as well; moved back to England, then Galway, Ireland, where her sculptures, mostly large-scale religious works in wood or stone, often portraying madonnas, are still on display in Galway churches. ❖ See also memoir *To the Four Winds* (Deutsch, 1957); Anita Leslie, *Cousin Clare: The Tempestuous Career of Clare Sheridan* (Hutchinson, 1976); and *Women in World History.*

SHERIDAN, Dinah (1920—). English actress. Born Dinah Nadyejda Mec, Sept 17, 1920, in Hampstead, England; dau. of James Mec and Lisa Mec (both photographers); attended Sherrards Wood School; trained at Italia Conti school; married Jimmy Hanley (actor), May 8, 1942 (div. 1952); m. Sir John Davis (executive at Rank), 1954 (div. 1965); m. Jack Merivale (actor), 1986 (died 1990); m. Aubrey Ison, 1992; children: (1st m.) Jeremy Hanley (b. 1945, member of Parliament), Jenny Hanley (b. 1947, model and actress); and daughter who died at birth. ❖ Star of the comedy classic *Genevieve*, made London stage debut at 12; joined a tour of *Peter Pan*, playing Wendy to Elsa Lanchester's Peter; throughout teens, continued acting in theater; made 1st film, *Irish and Proud of It* (1936), at 16; appeared in films regularly, including *Get Cracking* (1943) with George Formby, but never quite made it to stardom; filmed 23rd movie, *Genevieve* (1953), which was a huge hit; retired from the screen on marriage (1954); following divorce (1965), returned to stage and film; played the mother in *The Railway Children* (1972); made last on-screen appearance (1980), in *The Mirror Crack'd*. ❖ See also *Women in World History.*

SHERIDAN, Elizabeth Ann (1754–1792). *See Linley, Elizabeth.*

SHERIDAN, Frances (1724–1766). Irish novelist and dramatist. Born Frances Chamberlaine in Dublin, Ireland, in 1724; died in Blois, France, Sept 26, 1766; dau. of Philip Chamberlaine (Irish cleric) and Anastasia Whyte; m. Thomas Sheridan (well-known actor-manager), in 1747; children: 3 sons, including Richard Brinsley Sheridan (1751–1816, Irish dramatist and parliamentary orator), and 3 daughters, including writers Alicia Lefanu (1753–1817) and Elizabeth Lefanu (1758–1837). ❖ At urging of friend Samuel Richardson, published the highly successful *Memoirs of Miss Sidney Biddulph* (1761); also wrote the play *The Discovery*, which starred her husband and David Garrick, and the less-successful *The Dupe*, starring Kitty Clive (1763–64); one year before her sudden death, completed novel, *A Trip to Bath* (1765), which when finally published (1902), was discovered to contain an antecedent to her son's famous character Mrs. Malaprop. ❖ See also *Women in World History.*

SHERIDAN, Helen Selina (1807–1867). *See Blackwood, Helen Selina.*

SHERIDAN, Jane Georgiana (d. 1884). *See Seymour, Georgiana.*

SHERIDAN, Margaret (1889–1958). Irish soprano. Name variations: Margaret Burke Sheridan; Margaret Burke-Sheridan. Born Margaret Burke Sheridan, Oct 15, 1889, in Castlebar, Co. Mayo, Ireland; died in Dublin, April 16, 1958; dau. of John Burke Sheridan (postmaster) and Mary Ellen (Cooley) Burke Sheridan; educated at Royal Academy of Music, London, 1909–11; studied in Rome with Alfredo Martino, 1916–18; never married. ❖ Made triumphant operatic debut at Rome's Constanzi Opera House in what was to be her most celebrated role, as Mimi in *La Bohème* (1918); appeared at Covent Garden in *La Bohème, Madama Butterfly*, and London premiere of Mascagni's *Iris* (1919); became one of the supreme exponents of Puccini's work, as the composer himself recognized; was coached by Puccini for part of Manon in a new performance of *Manon Lescaut*, 1st given in Rimini (1923); following a successful season at San Carlo theater in Naples, was invited to join the company of La Scala, under its director Toscanini (1922); made La Scala debut in revival of Catalani's *La Wally* (1922); returned to La Scala for world premiere of Respighi's *Belfagor* (1923); also appeared there in Primo Riccitelli's comic opera *I compagnacci* (1923), and as Maddalena in *Andrea Chenier* (1924), but worsening relations with Toscanini cut short her stay; appeared at Covent Garden in *Madama Butterfly* and *Andrea Chenier* (1925), followed by great success in *Bohème* and as Lauretta in *Gianni Schicci* (1926); made a number of records, of operatic arias and of Irish songs, for HMV (1927) and performed on the 1st complete recording of *Butterfly*, with Lionelo Cecil (1930); at Covent Garden, scored a notable triumph in title role of *Manon Lescaut* (1929); performed for the last time in Italy, singing *Gianni Schicchi* in Turin (1930); because of ill health, made last appearance on the operatic stage, at Covent Garden, as Desdemona (1930); effectively retired, moved to Dublin (1940). ❖ See also Anne Chambers, *Adorable Diva: Margaret Burke Sheridan, Irish Prima-Donna, 1889–1958* (Wolfhound, 1989); and *Women in World History.*

SHERIDAN, Mrs. Richard Brinsley (1754–1792). *See Linley, Elizabeth.*

SHERIF, Carolyn Wood (1922–1982). American social psychologist. Name variations: Carolyn Wood. Born Carolyn Wood, June 26, 1922, in Loogootee, Indiana; died 1982; Purdue University, BS with highest honors, 1943; State University of Iowa, MA, 1944; attended Columbia University; University of Texas, PhD, 1961; m. Muzafer Sherif (social psychologist), 1945; children: Sue (b. 1947); Joan (b. 1950); Ann (b. 1955). ❖ Pioneer in research methods, particularly in the study of the psychology of women, was a research associate at Institute of Group Relations at University of Oklahoma; published, in conjunction with husband, some of her most influential books: *Intergroup Conflict and Cooperation: The Robbers Cave Experiment* (1961, which for over 20 years remained one of the most cited studies in the field), *Reference Groups: Exploration into Conformity and Deviation of Adolescents* (1964), *Problems of Youth* (1965), and *Attitude and Attitude Change* (1965); became visiting faculty member in psychology department at Penn State University (1965) and earned a full professorship (1970); published famous study "Bias in Psychology," as a chapter in *The Prism of Sex* (1979); was a key figure in the creation of both a course on women and psychology and a women's studies program at Penn State. Elected fellow in American Psychological Association (1976); received the American Psychological Foundation's Award for Distinguished Contributions to Education in Psychology. ❖ See also *Women in World History.*

SHERIF, William (1848–1944). *See Bain, Wilhelmina Sherriff.*

SHERK, Cathy (1950—). Canadian golfer. Name variations: Cathy Graham Sherk. Born Cathy Graham, June 17, 1950, in Niagara Falls,

Ontario, Canada. ❖ Won Canadian Amateur (1977, 1978), North South Amateur (1978), and US Women's Amateur Open (1978); won Women's CPGA championship (1986, 1987, 1990), Ontario PGA championship (2000); was national coach of the CLGA (1995–99). Inducted into Canadian Golf Hall of Fame (1995) and Ontario Hall of Fame (2000).

SHERKAT, Shahla (c. 1956—). Iranian journalist, publisher and women's rights advocate. Born c. 1956 in Iran; married; children: 2 daughters. ❖ A major voice for reform, was dismissed from her position as editorial director at *Zan-e Rouz,* a government-owned weekly, because she wanted to change the way it depicted women; founded (1991) and serves as editor of the popular monthly magazine, *Zanan* (Women), in Tehran; was fined and sentenced to prison for 4 months for "anti-Islamic" activities (2001), though she did not have to serve time; outspoken in her demands for basic rights for women, was given the Courage in Journalism Award from the International Women's Media Foundation (2005).

SHERLOCK, Sheila (1918–2001). British physician and educator. Name variations: Dame Sheila Sherlock. Born Sheila Patricia Violet Sherlock, Mar 31, 1918, in Dublin, Ireland; died Dec 30, 2001, in London, England; graduate of Edinburgh University, 1941; m. Geraint James (physician), 1951; children: 2 daughters. ❖ One of the founders of modern hepatology, who pioneered the study of liver disease, began career as clinical assistant to Sir James Learmonth in Edinburgh; moved to London; worked as Beit Research fellow at Hammersmith Hospital (1942–47), before attending Yale University on Rockefeller fellowship; served as professor of medicine at London's Royal Free Hospital School of Medicine (1959–83), the 1st woman professor of medicine in UK; pioneered use of percutaneous liver biopsy and was one of the first to appreciate importance of immunological mechanisms in pathogenesis of cirrhosis and hepatitis; wrote *Diseases of the Liver and Biliary System* (1954), which ran to 11 editions and has been translated into several languages; was also the 1st woman to serve as vice-president of Royal College of Physicians. Named Dame of British Empire (DBE, 1978); elected fellow of Royal Society of Edinburgh (1989) and fellow of Royal Society (2000).

SHERMAN, Lydia (d. 1878). American serial killer. Born in Burlington City, NJ, 1824 (some sources cite 1830); died in Wethersfield Prison, May 16, 1878; m. Edward Struck (murdered); Dennis Hurlburt (or Hurlbut, murdered); Horatio Sherman (murdered); children: many. ❖ Dubbed "Queen Poisoner" and "Borgia of Connecticut" by the press, killed at least 3 of her husbands and 7 of her children; tried and convicted of 2nd-degree murder (1872), spent rest of life in prison.

SHERMAN, Mary Belle (1862–1935). American activist. Born Mary Belle King, Dec 11, 1862, in Albion, New York; died Jan 15, 1935; dau. of Rufus King and Sarah Electa (Whitney) King; educated at St. Xavier's Academy and Park Institute in Chicago; m. John Dickinson Sherman (newspaper editor), Feb 10, 1887 (died 1926); children: John King. ❖ Clubwoman who lobbied on behalf of the national-parks movement, served as recording secretary for Chicago Woman's Club and General Federation of Women's Clubs; became enough of an expert on parliamentary law to write the handbook *Parliamentary Law at a Glance* (1901) and serve as an instructor in the field at John Marshall Law School in Chicago; became chair of the conservation department of General Federation (1914) and began lobbying for formation of the National Park Service; known as the "National Park Lady," was responsible for the creation of a number of park areas in the Grand Canyon and in parts of the Rocky Mountains; served as president of the General Federation of Women's Clubs (1924–28). ❖ See also *Women in World History.*

SHERMAN, Yvonne (1930–2005). American figure skater. Name variations: Yvonne C. Sherman; Yvonne Sherman Tutt. Born May 3, 1930, possibly in New York; died Feb 2, 2005, in Colorado Springs, CO; m. William Thayer Tutt (1912–1989), skater and president of the International Ice Hockey Federation. ❖ Won the US National title (1949, 1950); at World championships, placed 6th (1948) and 2nd (1949); with Robert Swenning, won the US National pairs title (1947), placed 2nd at North American championships (1947) and 5th at World championships (1948). Inducted into US Figure Skating Hall of Fame (1991).

SHERMAN-KAUF, Patti (1963—). American skier. Name variations: Patti Sherman Kauf. Born April 6, 1963, in Spokane, WA; married; children: 2. ❖ Won bronze in Skier X at X Games (1999, 2000, and 2002); placed 1st at World Pro Mogul Tour (in Moguls, 1993 and 1995), Budweiser World championships (in Moguls, 1998 and 1999), and Grand Nationals, Big Sky, MT (in Skiercross, 2001), among others.

SHERWIN, Belle (1868–1955). American suffragist and civic leader. Born Mar 25, 1868, in Cleveland, Ohio; died July 9, 1955; dau. of Henry Alden Sherwin (founder of Sherwin-Williams Paint Co.) and Mary Frances (Smith) Sherwin; Wellesley College, BS, 1890; never married; no children. ❖ Became president of Cleveland Suffrage Association (1919); after ratification of 19th Amendment, moved to Washington, DC, to serve as 2nd national president of League of Women Voters (NLWV, 1924); during 10-year presidency, was responsible for the NLWV's reputation for evenhanded accuracy of its research and its evolvement into the non-partisan educational organization that it remains today; accepted an appointment to Consumers' Advisory Board of the National Recovery Administration (1934); also served on the Federal Advisory Committee of the US Employment Service. ❖ See also *Women in World History.*

SHERWOOD, Mrs. John (1826–1903). *See Sherwood, Mary Elizabeth.*

SHERWOOD, Josephine (1886–1957). *See Hull, Josephine.*

SHERWOOD, Katharine Margaret (1841–1914). American journalist, poet and civic leader. Name variations: Kate Brownlee; Kate Brownlee Sherwood. Born Katharine Margaret Brownlee, Sept 24, 1841, in Poland, Ohio; died Feb 15, 1914; dau. of James Brownlee (Scottish immigrant and judge) and Rebecca (Mullen) Brownlee; educated at Poland Union Seminary; m. Isaac Ruth Sherwood (journalist who later served in Congress), 1859; children: Lenore and James. ❖ During Civil War, while husband worked his way up to the rank of brigadier general in Union Army, took over his duties with the *Williams County Gazette* in Bryan, Ohio; helped him edit the *Toledo Journal* (1875–1885); was one of the founders of the Woman's Relief Corps (WRC), an auxiliary of the Grand Army of the Republic (1883), and later served as national president; published 2 vols. of poetry: *Camp-Fire, Memorial-Day, and Other Poems* (1885) and *Dream of Ages: A Poem of Columbia* (1893); worked as a Washington (DC) correspondent for a newspaper syndicate, serving as editor of women's department of *National Tribune,* a Washington newspaper; wrote satires on politics for *New York Sun;* was the 1st president of the Ohio Newspaper Women's Association (1902). ❖ See also *Women in World History.*

SHERWOOD, Madeline (1899–1989). *See Hurlock, Madeline.*

SHERWOOD, Martha (1775–1851). *See Sherwood, Mary Martha.*

SHERWOOD, Mary (1856–1935). American doctor and public health advocate. Born Mar 31, 1856, in Ballston Spa, New York; died May 24, 1935, in Baltimore, Maryland; dau. of Thomas Burr Sherwood (lawyer and farmer) and Mary Frances (Beattie) Sherwood; sister of Margaret Pollock Sherwood, English literature professor at Wellesley College, and Sidney Sherwood, associate professor of economics at Johns Hopkins University; educated at State Normal School in Albany, NY; Vassar College, AB, 1883; University of Zurich, MD, 1890. ❖ With Dr. Lilian Welsh, opened a private medical practice in Baltimore (1892); also ran the Evening Dispensary for Working Women and Girls of Baltimore, a charitable clinic (1893–1910); was medical director of Bryn Mawr School for girls in Baltimore (1894–1935); served as the 1st director of the Baltimore City Health Department's Bureau of Child Welfare (1919–24), the 1st woman in the city to head a municipal bureau. ❖ See also *Women in World History.*

SHERWOOD, Mary Elizabeth (1826–1903). American author and etiquette expert. Born Mary Elizabeth Wilson in Keene, New Hampshire, Oct 27, 1826; died New York, NY, Sept 12, 1903; dau. of James Wilson (lawyer, politician, and member of Congress) and Mary Lord (Richardson) Wilson; m. John Sherwood (lawyer), Nov 12, 1851 (died 1895); children: James Wilson (died in childhood); Samuel (b. 1853); Arthur Murray (b. 1856); John Philip (died 1883); grandmother of playwright Robert E. Sherwood. ❖ Became part of New York society, attending Anne C. L. Botta's literary salon, traveling in style to fashionable places, and working on such charitable causes as fund raising for the restoration of Mount Vernon; began publishing pieces on etiquette, as well as short stories, in such respected magazines as *Frank Leslie's Weekly* and *Appleton's Journal,* though 1st novel, *The Sarcasm of Destiny* (1878), received little attention; 2nd effort, *A Transplanted Rose* (1882), proved popular; turned from novels to publish her most popular work, *Manners and Social Usages* (1884), which went through a number of reprintings; published 3rd novel, *Sweet-Brier* (1889), as well as a book of poetry and another social guide, *The Art of Entertaining* (1892). ❖ See also memoirs, *An Epistle to Posterity—Being Rambling Recollections of Many Years of My Life* (1897) and *Here & There & Everywhere* (1898); and *Women in World History*.

SHERWOOD, Mary Martha (1775–1851). British children's author. Name variations: Martha Sherwood. Born Mary Martha Butt, May 6, 1775, in Stanford, Worcestershire, England; died Sept 20, 1851, in London; dau. of Dr. George Butt (chaplain to George III) and Martha Sherwood; sister of Lucy Lyttleton Cameron (1781–1858) who also wrote for children; educated at Reading Abbey; married her cousin, Henry Sherwood (army officer), in 1803; children: 5, including Sophia Kelly (writer); adopted 3 more. ❖ Lived in India with husband (1805–16), where she taught in an army school and cared for orphans; wrote about 400 stories and morality tales for children; had 1st popular success with *History of Susan Gray* (1802), a tale aimed at bolstering religion among the poor; career took off with publication of *The Story of Henry and His Bearer*, which proved to be wildly successful and went through nearly 100 editions; most famous book was *The History of the Fairchild Family* (1818). ❖ See also *Life of Mrs. Sherwood* (1854); and *Women in World History*.

SHERWOOD, Maud Winifred (1880–1956). New Zealand and Australian painter. Name variations: Maud Winifred Kimbell. Born Dec 22, 1880, at Dunedin, New Zealand; died Dec 1, 1956, at Katoomba, NSW, Australia; dau. of Alfred Charles Kimbell and Eliza (Palmer) Kimbell; New Zealand Academy of Fine Arts, teacher's certificate, 1899; m. Alfred Charles Sherwood, 1917 (div. 1920). ❖ Major contributor to Australian and New Zealand art world, began exhibiting at New Zealand Academy of Fine Arts (1898); taught design, still-life, and sketching classes at Wellington Technical School (early 1900s); studied in Europe and returned to Australia and New Zealand (c. 1913); had solo exhibition at New Zealand Academy of Fine Arts, Wellington (1925); returned briefly to Australia and then worked and exhibited in Italy, France, Spain, and Tunisia; elected to Society of Artists, Sydney (1933); exhibited at National Centennial Exhibition of New Zealand Art (1940). Received Coronation Medal (1937) and Australian 150th Anniversary Exhibition Medal (1938). ❖ See also *Dictionary of New Zealand Biography* (Vol. 3).

SHERWOOD, Rosetta (1865–1951). *See Hall, Rosetta Sherwood.*

SHERWOOD, Sheila (1945—). English track-and-field athlete. Name variations: Sheila Parkin. Born Sheila Parkin, Oct 22, 1945; m. John Sherwood (Olympic bronze medal winner); children: David Sherwood (tennis player). ❖ Won North of England championships in long jump (1961–67); at Mexico City Olympics, won a silver medal in the long jump (1968); placed 1st at Commonwealth games in long jump (1970).

SHERWOOD-HALL, Rosetta (1865–1951). *See Hall, Rosetta Sherwood.*

SHESHENINA, Marina (1985—). Russian volleyball player. Born June 26, 1985, in USSR. ❖ Won a team silver medal at Athens Olympics (2004).

SHESTOV, Xenia (1560–1631). *See Martha the Nun.*

SHETTER, Liz (1947—). *See Allan-Shetter, Liz.*

SHEVCHENKO, Elena (1971—). Soviet gymnast. Name variations: Yelena Shevchenko. Born Oct 7, 1971, in Russia; m. Vladislav Olenin (speedskater). ❖ Won USSR Spartakiade (1986); won gold medal for team all-around and silver medal for vault at the Goodwill Games (1986); placed 3rd at USSR nationals and won European Cup (1988); at Seoul Olympics, won a gold medal for team all-around (1988); at Australian Grand Prix won a gold medal for team all-around and a silver medal for all-around (1989).

SHEVCHENKO, Lyudmyla (1975—). Ukrainian handball player. Born Feb 4, 1970, in USSR. ❖ Won a team bronze medal at Athens Olympics (2004).

SHEVTSOVA, Lyudmila (1934—). Soviet runner. Born Nov 26, 1934, in USSR. ❖ At Rome Olympics, won a gold medal in the 800 meters (1960), with a time of 2:04.50.

SHEWCHUK, Tammy Lee (1977—). Canadian ice-hockey player. Born 1977 in Canada. ❖ Won a gold medal at World championships (2001) and a gold medal at Salt Lake City Olympics (2002).

SHE-WOLF OF FRANCE. *See Isabella of France (1296–1358).*

SHI GUIHONG. Chinese soccer player. Born in Guangdong, China. ❖ Won a team silver medal at Atlanta Olympics (1996).

SHIBAKI, Yoshiko (b. 1914). Japanese novelist. Born 1914 in Tokyo, Japan; married. ❖ Wrote *Fresh Produce Mart*, which won the Akutagawa Prize (1941); other writings include *Paradise, Suzaki* (1954), *River Sumida* (1961), *The Eighth Building in Marunouchi* (1962), *Twilight on the River Sumida* (1984), which won the Prize for Japanese Literature, and *Dancing Snow* (1987), which won the Mainichi Prize.

SHIBATA, Ai (1982—). Japanese swimmer. Born May 14, 1982, in Japan. ❖ Won a gold medal for 800-meter freestyle at Athens Olympics (2004).

SHIBUKI, Ayano (1941—). Japanese volleyball player. Born Mar 29, 1941, in Japan. ❖ At Tokyo Olympics, won a gold medal in team competition (1964).

SHIELDS, Carol (1935–2003). Canadian novelist and short-story writer. Born Carol Warner, June 2, 1935, in Oak Park, Illinois; died of breast cancer, July 16, 2003, in Victoria, British Columbia, Canada; Hanover College, BA; attended University of Exeter in England; University of Ottowa, MA; m. Donald Hughes Shields (professor of civil engineering), 1957; children: 5. ❖ Moved with Canadian husband to Canada (1957); taught literature at universities of Ottawa and British Columbia; served as editor for journal *Canadian Slavonic Papers*; lived with family in Winnipeg after 1980, working as professor of English and chancellor at University of Manitoba; won Pulitzer Prize for *The Stone Diaries* (1993); works include *Small Ceremonies* (1976), *The Box Garden* (1977), *Happenstance* (1980), *A Fairly Conventional Woman* (1982), *Various Miracles* (1985), *Swann* (1987), *The Orange Fish* (1989), *Larry's Party* (1997), *Dressing Up for the Carnival* (2001), and the bestselling *Unless* (2002); also wrote a book of literary criticism, *Susanna Moodie: Voice and Vision* (1977), and a biography, *Jane Austen*, which won the Charles Taylor prize for literary nonfiction (2002).

SHIELDS, Ella (1879–1952). American-born English music-hall star. Born Ella Buscher, Sept 26, 1879, in Baltimore, MD; died Aug 5, 1952, in Lancaster, England; m. William Hargreaves. ❖ Debuted on the British variety stage (1904); famed as a male impersonator in top hat, white tie and tails; best remembered for song "Burlington Bertie from Bow"; other songs include "Waltz Time," "The Girl in White," "When You've Got Money in Your Pocket" and "Just One Kill, Just Another One."

SHIELDS, Margaret (1941—). New Zealand politician. Born Margaret Porter, Dec 18, 1941; m. Pat Shields; children: 2. ❖ Elected Labour MP for Kapiti (1981); was one of two women in the Labour Cabinet (1984), and the 1st woman appointed a minister after only 3 years in the House; concerned with childcare and pay equity; lost seat (1990); became director of a UN agency working for the advancement of women, and chair of Wellington Regional Council.

SHIELDS, Susan (1952—). American swimmer. Name variations: Susan Shields White. Born Susan Marie Shields, Feb 1952; grew up in Louisville, KY. ❖ At Mexico City Olympics, won a bronze medal in the 100-meter butterfly (1968).

SHIGE, Yumiko (1965—). Japanese sailor. Born Aug 4, 1965, in Karatsu, Japan. ❖ Won a silver medal for double-handed dinghy (470) at Atlanta Olympics (1996).

SHIGEKO (1925–1961). Japanese princess. Born in 1925; died 1961; eldest dau. of Nagako (1903–2000) and Hirohito (1901–1989), emperor of Japan (r. 1924–1989); m. Prince Morihiro (son of Prince Higashikunim, the 1st postwar prime minister); children: 1 son.

SHIKIBU, Murasaki (c. 973–c. 1015). *See Murasaki Shikibu.*

SHIKOLENKO, Natalya (1964—). Soviet track-and-field athlete. Born Aug 1, 1964, in USSR. ❖ At Barcelona Olympics, won a silver medal in the javelin throw (1992).

SHILEY, Jean (1911–1998). American high jumper. Name variations: Jean Newhouse. Born Nov 20, 1911, in Harrisburg, PA; died Mar 11, 1998, in Los Angeles, CA; graduate of Temple University, 1933. ❖ Competed in Amsterdam Olympics, placing 4th in high jump (1928); won national titles (1929, 1930, 1931); won a gold medal for high jump at Los Angeles Olympics (1932), beating favorite Babe Didrikson Zaharias. ❖ See also *Women in World History*.

SHILLING, Beatrice (1909–1990). English aeroengineer. Name variations: Tilly Shilling. Born Mar 8, 1909, in Waterlooville, Hampshire, England; died Nov 18, 1990; dau. of a butcher; attended Manchester University; m. George Naylor. ❖ Aeroengineer who worked on aircraft engines and aircraft safety challenges, enjoyed a long career at the Royal Air Establishment at Farnborough (1933–69); researched and solved a serious defect in the Rolls-Royce Merlin engine design; investigated aircraft dangers, such as wet runways and their effect on breaking; worked on rocket propulsion and on supersonic aircrafts; pursued an interest in racing and won a Gold Star for lapping a track at over 100 mph on a self-altered motorbike at the Brooklands circuit (1930s). Made an Officer of the Order of the British Empire (1948).

SHILLING, Tilly (1909–1990). See Shilling, Beatrice.

SHILOVA, Irina (1960—). Soviet shooter. Born Feb 22, 1960, in USSR. ❖ At Seoul Olympics, won a gold medal in air rifle (1988).

SHIM EUN-JUNG (1971—). Korean badminton player. Born June 8, 1971, in South Korea. ❖ At Barcelona Olympics, won a bronze medal in doubles (1992).

SHIMAKAGE, Seiko (1949—). Japanese volleyball player. Born Feb 16, 1949, in Japan. ❖ At Munich Olympics, won a silver medal in team competition (1972).

SHIMANSKAYA, Vera (1981—). Russian rhythmic gymnast. Name variations: Shemanskaya or Shimanskaia. Born 1981 in Moscow, Russia. ❖ Won a team World championship (1998, 1999) and a team gold medal at Sydney Olympics (2000); won European championships twice. Named Honored Master of Sports.

SHINDLE, Kate (1979—). Miss America. Born Katherine Shindle, Jan 31, 1979, in Toledo, Ohio; Northwestern University, BA, 1999. ❖ Named Miss America (1998), representing Illinois; advocate for AIDS education; an actress, has appeared in numerous plays; made film debut in *The Stepford Wives* (2004).

SHINN, Millicent Washburn (1858–1940). American psychologist and author. Born in Niles, California, April 15, 1858; died in Niles, Aug 13, 1940; dau. of James and Lucy Ellen (Clark) Shinn; sister of Charles Howard Shinn, writer and key figure in the early Western conservation movement; cousin of Edmund Clark Sanford, prominent psychologist; University of California, AB, 1880, PhD, 1898; the 1st woman to receive a PhD there. ❖ Served as editor of *Overland Monthly* (1883–94), contributing poems and stories; when brother's wife gave birth to a daughter (1890), began keeping a journal of the infant's mental and physical development; published *Notes on the Development of a Child* (1893), one of the few systematic observations of infant development available in English at end of 19th century; also wrote *The Biography of a Baby* (1900). ❖ See also *Women in World History.*

SHINODA, Miho (1972—). Japanese gymnast and singer. Born May 18, 1972, in Tachikawa City, Tokyo, Japan. ❖ Won NHK Cup (1985, 1987, 1988) and Japanese nationals (1986, 1987); became a singer with a well-known pop music group in Japan.

SHINOZAKI, Yoko (1945—). Japanese volleyball player. Born Jan 29, 1945, in Japan. ❖ At Tokyo Olympics, won a gold medal in team competition (1964).

SHIOKAWA, Michiko (1951—). Japanese volleyball player. Born Jan 26, 1951, in Japan. ❖ At Munich Olympics, won a silver medal in team competition (1972).

SHIONO, Nanami (1937—). Japanese novelist. Born 1937 in Tokyo, Japan; graduate of Gakushuin University; lives in Florence, Italy. ❖ Specializing in medieval Italian history, wrote such novels as *The Story of a City Facing the Sea* and *My Friend, Machiavelli and a Collection of His Sayings.* Received Kan Kikuchi Prize (1983); won the Shinchosha Gakugei Prize (1993), for the 1st novel in her series titled *Romajin no Monogatari* (Tales of the Romans).

SHIPLEY, Debra (1957—). English politician and member of Parliament. Born June 22, 1957, in UK. ❖ Writer and lecturer; representing Labour, elected to House of Commons for Stourbridge (1999, 2001); successfully introduced a bill to register child abusers which must be checked by childcare organizations taking on new staff; left Parliament (2005).

SHIPLEY, Jenny (1952—). Prime minister of New Zealand. Born Jennifer Mary Robson, Feb 4, 1952, in Gore, NZ; m. Burton Shipley (farmer), 1973; children: two. ❖ Elected National MP for Ashburton, later renamed Rakaia (1987); served as minister of Social Welfare (1990–93), minister of Health (1993–96), and minister of Women's Affairs (1990–96); elected New Zealand's 1st woman prime minister (1997–99); retained the seat of Rakaia and was the Leader of the Opposition (1999–2001); retired (2001); liberal in social policy, conservative economically.

SHIPLEY, Ruth B. (1885–1966). American government official. Born Ruth Bielaski in Montgomery Co., Maryland, April 20, 1885; died in Washington, DC, Nov 3, 1966; dau. of Alexander Bielaski (Methodist minister) and Roselle Woodward (Israel) Bielaski; sister of A. Bruce Bielaski, head of the FBI; m. Frederick William van Dorn Shipley, 1909 (died 1919); children: Frederick William. ❖ Hired as a clerk, began 41-year career at Department of State (1914); appointed special assistant to Assistant Secretary A. Adee, then assistant to the chief of the Office of Coordination and Review, Margaret M. Hanna; became 1st permanent chief of the Passport Division (1928), the 1st woman to head a major division of the State Department; as a staunch anti-Communist, contributed to the drafting of the McCarran Internal Security Act (1950) and used her power to restrict the travel of many leftist figures, including Paul and Eslanda Robeson, Linus Pauling, Arthur Miller, Rockwell Kent, Elizabeth Gurley Flynn and W. E. B. Du Bois, whether they were admitted Communists or not; her role in the McCarthyism of the Cold War era drew harsh criticism from liberal America, and the power of her position was gradually dismantled (1950s–60s). ❖ See also *Women in World History.*

SHIPMAN, Nell (1892–1970). Canadian-born actress and filmmaker. Name variations: Helen Foster Barham. Born Helen Foster Barham in Oct 1892 in Victoria, British Columbia, Canada; died Jan 1970 in Cabazon, California; m. Ernest Shipman (writer), 1911 (div. 1920); m. Charles Ayers (artist), 1925 (div. 1934); children: (1st m.) Barry Shipman (b. 1912); (2nd m.) twins Daphne and Charles (b. 1926). ❖ Established herself as a writer for the early film industry's major studios, including Vitagraph, Selig and Universal; gained popularity as a film star with the release of *God's Country and the Woman* (1916), a wildlife adventure film which she also produced and directed; formed Nell Shipman Productions (1920); wrote, produced, and starred in numerous other films, including *Baree, Son of Kazan* (1918), *Back to God's Country* (1919), *Something New* (1920), *A Boy, a Bear and a Dog* (1921), *The Grub Stake* (1922), *Trail of the North Wind* (1923) and *The Golden Yukon* (1927); wrote screenplay for *Wings in the Dark* (1935); also wrote novels, including *Get the Woman* (1930). ❖ See also autobiography, *The Silent Screen and My Talking Heart* (1987); and *Women in World History.*

SHIPP, Ellis Reynolds (1847–1939). American physician. Born Ellis Reynolds, Jan 20, 1847, in Davis Co., IA; died Jan 31, 1939, in Salk Lake City, UT; dau. of Anna (Hawley) Reynolds and William Fletcher Reynolds; m. Milford Bard Shipp, May 5, 1866 (as a Mormon, took 3 additional wives); children: at least 6. ❖ At age 18, after her parents joined the Mormon church (1851), lived for a time with Brigham Young and his family in Salt Lake City, UT, and kept a diary; with Young's encouragement, graduated from the Woman's Medical College of Pennsylvania (1878); opened a Salt Lake City practice and established a midwifery school, training at least 500 women during her career; served as a Deseret Hospital staff member (1882–90); delivered 6,000 babies and practiced medicine for nearly 60 years.

SHIPPEN, Nancy (1763–1841). See Livingston, Anne Shippen.

SHIPPEN, Peggy (1760–1804). American socialite. Name variations: Margaret Shippen Arnold; Peggy Shippen Arnold; Mrs. Benedict Arnold; Margaret Shippen. Born Margaret Shippen, 1760, in Philadelphia, Pennsylvania; died Aug 24, 1804, in Epping, Essex, England; dau. of Edward Shippen (judge); became 2nd wife of Benedict Arnold (1741–1801, military governor of Pennsylvania who defected to the British in 1780), April 8, 1779; children: Edward Shippen Arnold; James Robertson Arnold; Sophia Arnold; George Arnold; William Fitch Arnold. Benedict Arnold was 1st married to Margaret Mansfield (died 1775). ❖ Wife of Benedict Arnold who was aware of husband's treasonous activities during the Revolutionary War and may, or may not, have aided him; lived most of her life amid the enmity caused by his treason. ❖ See also *Women in World History.*

SHIPTON, Mother (1488–1561). English witch and prophet. Name variations: Ursula Southill, Sonthiel or Southeil. Born Ursula Southiel in 1488, near Knaresborough, North Yorkshire, England; died 1561 in Clifton, Yorkshire, England; illeg. dau. of Agatha Southeil; m. Toy

Shipton (carpenter), 1512. ❖ Prophet whose visions and predictions gained notoriety in her day and beyond, is believed to have been born in a riverside cave, known as "The Petrifying Well," now a tourist attraction; was given to foster mother at age 2, while her own mother spent remainder of life in convent in Nottingham; rumored to have special powers from childhood, was said to have performed many acts of magic; provided herbal medicines and potions to community as well; said to have prophesied many events, such as the collapse of York's Trinity Church, deaths of prominent citizens, and the great fire of London (1666).

SHIRAI, Takako (1952—). Japanese volleyball player. Born July 18, 1952, in Japan. ❖ Won a silver medal at Munich Olympics (1972) and a gold medal at Montreal Olympics (1976), both in team competition.

SHIRASU TOSHIKO (1939—). See Aihara, Toshiko.

SHIRELLES, The.
See Coley, Doris.
See Harris, Addie.
See Lee, Beverly.
See Owens, Shirley.

SHIRLEY (1819–1906). See Clapp, Louise.

SHIRLEY, Anne (1917–1993). American actress. Name variations: Dawn O'Day. Born Dawn Evelyeen Paris, April 17, 1917, in New York, NY; died July 4, 1993, in Los Angeles, CA; m. John Payne (actor), 1937 (div. 1942); m. Adrian Scott (producer), 1945 (div. 1948); m. Charles Lederer (screenwriter), 1949 (died 1976); children: (1st m.) Julie Payne; (3rd m.) 1 son. ❖ As a child, worked as Dawn O'Day in Pola Negri's *The Spanish Dancer*; was also cast in *The Fast Set* (1924), *Riders of the Purple Sage* (1925), *Mother Knows Best* (1928) and *Liliom* (1930); played Anastasia in *Rasputin and the Empress* (1932); after getting breakthrough role of film adaptation of *Anne of Green Gables*, changed her name to that of the movie's heroine, Anne Shirley; within months, was the juvenile lead on the RKO lot; in addition to the sequel, *Anne of Windy Poplars*, was featured in *Chasing Yesterday* (1935), *Chatterbox* (1936), *Mother Carey's Chickens* (1938), *Career* (1939), *Saturday's Children* (1940), *The Powers Girl* (1942) and *Murder, My Sweet* (1944); had another memorable role as Barbara Stanwyck's daughter Laurel in *Stella Dallas*, which earned her an Oscar nomination for Best Supporting Actress (1937); quit acting at 27. ❖ See also *Women in World History*.

SHIRLEY, Dorothy (1939—). English track-and-field athlete. Born May 15, 1939, in UK. ❖ At Rome Olympics, won a silver medal in the high jump (1960).

SHIRLEY, Elizabeth (c. 1568–1641). British biographer and devotional writer. Born c. 1568, possibly in Leicestershire, England; died Sept 1, 1641, in Louvain, Flanders; dau. of John Shirley of Leicestershire. ❖ Converted to Roman Catholicism and became recusant; was one of the founders of St. Monica's Monastery in Louvain (1606), where she was subprioress for 28 years; wrote *Life of Margaret Clement* (1611).

SHIRLEY, Penn (1840–1929). See Clarke, Sarah Jones.

SHIRLEY, Selina (1707–1791). See Hastings, Selina.

SHIRREFF, Emily (1814–1897). English writer and educationalist. Born Emily Anne Eliza Shirreff, Nov 3, 1814, in England; died Mar 20, 1897, in London, England; sister of Maria Georgina Grey (writer). ❖ Pioneer of women's education, wrote novels *Passion and Principle* (1841) and *Love and Sacrifice* (1868) with sister, as well as *Thoughts on Self-Culture Addressed to Women* (1850), laying out arguments for women's education and criticizing ways in which women were trained to be dependent; wrote *Intellectual Education and Its Influence on the Character and Happiness of Women* (1858); with Maria, co-founded National Union for Promoting the Higher Education of Women (1871) and co-edited *Journal of the Women's Education Union*; served as mistress of Girton College (1870–97); co-founded Girl's Public Day School Company with sister (1872), enabling creation of girls' public schools by trusts or companies; set up 1st girls' public school with Maria (1877); became proponent of ideas of Friedrich Froebel, serving as president of Froebel Society (1875–97); published works on kindergarten and Froebel system, including *Principles of the Kindergarten System* (1876), *The Kindergarten at Home* (1884) and *Principles of Froebel's System* (1887), as well as biography, *A Short Sketch of the Life of Friedrich*

Fröebel; helped sister establish Maria Grey College (1878), a teachers' training college for middle-class women, which is still extant in the form of Twickenham campus of Brunel University.

SHIRREFF, Maria Georgina (1816–1906). See Grey, Maria Georgina.

SHISHIGINA, Olga (1968—). Kazakhstan hurdler. Born Dec 23, 1968, in Kazakhstan. ❖ Won a gold medal for 100-meter hurdles at Sydney Olympics (2000); at World championships, won a silver (1995) and bronze (2001), both for 100-meter hurdles.

SHISHIKURA, Kunie (1946—). Japanese volleyball player. Born July 13, 1946, in Japan. ❖ At Mexico City Olympics, won a silver medal in team competition (1968).

SHISHOVA, Albina (1966—). Russian gymnast. Born Oct 17, 1966, in Zaporozhie, USSR. ❖ Won Dynamo Spartakiade and Riga International (1981); at European championships, won a bronze medal in all-around (1983); at World championships, won a gold medal in team all-around (1983).

SHISHOVA, Lyudmila (1940—). Soviet fencer. Born June 1940 in USSR. ❖ Won a gold medal at Rome Olympics (1960) and a silver medal at Tokyo Olympics (1964), both in team foil.

SHIUBHLAIGH, Maire Nic (1884–1958). Irish actress. Born Mary Elizabeth Walker in Dublin, Ireland, in 1884 (some sources cite 1888); died in Drogheda, Co. Louth, Ireland, Sept 9, 1958; dau. of Matthew Walker (printer and newsagent) and Marian (Doherty) Walker; sister of Ann and Gypsy Walker, who acted under stage names Eileen O'Doherty and Betty King; m. Eamon Price (major-general), 1928. ❖ The 1st actor to use the Irish form of her name for stage purposes, joined Maud Gonne's Inghinidhe na hEireann (Daughters of Ireland), a valuable launching ground for theatrical careers; played the Mother in *Deirdre* and replaced Gonne as Delia Cahill in *Kathleen Ni Houlihan* (1902), for Irish Literary Theatre; a founder member of Irish National Theatre Society (1903), was on the management committee; at the Abbey, played lead roles in 1st performances of Yeats' *The Hour Glass* and Lady Gregory's *Twenty-Five* (1903); created roles in 2 more Yeats plays, *The King's Threshold* (1903) and *The Shadowy Waters* (1904), and in 2 plays of John Millington Synge, *In the Shadow of the Glen* (in which she introduced the role of Nora Burke) and *Riders to the Sea*; was lead actress for Theatre of Ireland (1904–12); became increasingly involved with various amateur dramatic groups; as political events moved to a crisis in Ireland with the passing of Home Rule Bill (1914), joined the nationalist Cumann na mBan (the Women's League) and did concert work for the organization. ❖ See also memoirs, *The Splendid Years* (1955); and *Women in World History*.

SHIVAKIER (1876–1947). See Chewikar.

SHIVE, Natalya (1963—). Russian speedskater. Name variations: Natalya Shive-Glebova; Natalia Glebova. Born April 30, 1963, in USSR. ❖ At European championships, won a bronze medal for small allround (1982); won a bronze medal for the 500 meters at Sarajevo Olympics (1984); won a World sprint bronze (1984); competed at Calgary Olympics, but did not medal (1988).

SHIZUKA GOZEN (fl. 12th c.). Japanese mistress. Pronunciation: She-zoo-kah Goe-zen. Flourished in the later 12th century; no other details are known. ❖ One of the great tragic, romantic heroines of Japanese history, was the mistress of Minamoto no Yoshitsune; her story is a romantic legend, written in numerous works of medieval fiction which chronicle the Minamoto-Taira War (1180–1185). ❖ See also *Women in World History*.

SHKAPSKAIA, Mariia (1891–1952). Russian poet, journalist and children's writer. Name variations: Mariia Mikhailovna Shkápskaia or Shkapskaya. Born Mariia Mikhailovna Andreyevsky, 1891, in St. Petersburg, Russia, of well-to-do parents; died 1952; sister of Ivan Mikhailovich Andreyevsky (writer who wrote as I. M. Andreyev). ❖ Was arrested before 1905 Revolution for political activism; published 6 books of poetry (1920s), including *Mater Dolorosa* (1921); after her female-centered works were criticized under the Soviet regime as decadent, turned to journalism (1925); was also a frequent reviewer of children's literature and wrote about the cruelties of fascism in WWII, *It Actually Happened* (1942).

SHKURNOVA, Olga (1962—). Soviet volleyball player. Born Mar 23, 1962, in USSR. ❖ At Seoul Olympics, won a gold medal in team competition (1988).

SHMONINA, Marina (1965—). Soviet runner. Born Feb 9, 1965, in USSR. ❖ At Barcelona Olympics, won a gold medal in 4 x 400-meter relay (1992).

SHNEURSON, Zelda (1914–1984). See Mishkowsky, Zelda Shneurson.

SHOCHAT, Manya (1878–1961). Jewish socialist and revolutionary. Name variations: Mania Shochat; Manya Wilbushevitz; Manya Shochat-Vilbushevich. Born 1878 in Lososna, Russia; died 1961; m. Yisrael Shochat, 1908; children: Geda and Anna. ❖ Helped settle Eretz Israel, the area of Palestine that would eventually become the state of Israel; was instrumental in arming Jews to protect them from Arab aggression; with husband, founded kibbutz (collective farm) movement; campaigned for the Zionist cause and worked to improve Arab-Jewish relations. ❖ See also Rachel Yanait Ben-Zvi, Before Golda: Manya Shochat (Biblio, 1989); and Women in World History.

SHOCKLEY, Ann Allen (1925—). African-American novelist and literary critic. Born Ann Allen, June 21, 1927, in Louisville, KY; dau. of Henry Allen and Bessie Lucas; m. William Shockley, 1949. ❖ Began work as Librarian of Special Collections and University Archivist at Fisk University (1969); published Loving Her (1974), now regarded as the 1st black American lesbian novel and the 1st about love between a white woman and a black woman; fiction includes The Black and White of It (1980) and Say Jesus and Come to Me (1982); edited Living Black Authors: A Biographical Directory (1973), A Handbook for Black Librarianship (1977), and Afro-American Women Writers (1746–1933): An Anthology and Critical Guide (1988).

SHOCKLEY, Marian (1911–1981). American stage and radio actress. Name variations: Marian Collyer. Born Oct 10, 1911, in Kansas City, MO; died Dec 14, 1981, in Los Angeles, CA; sister-in-law of June Collyer (actress); m. Bud Collyer (actor). ❖ Made Broadway debut in Dear Old Darling (1936); starred with her husband in 2 radio serials, "Road of Life" and "Guiding Light."

SHOEMAKER, Agnes (1913–1993). See Reinders, Agnes.

SHOEMAKER, Ann (1891–1978). American radio, stage, tv and screen actress and vaudevillian. Born Jan 10, 1891, in Brooklyn, NY; died Sept 18, 1978, in Los Angeles, CA; m. Henry Stephenson (British actor); children: daughter. ❖ Made Broadway debut in Nobody's Widow (1910), followed by The Great God Brown, Speakeasy, Whispering Friends, Tonight at 12, Silent Witness, Ah Wilderness!, Dream Girl, The Bad Seed and Separate Tables, among others; films include Alice Adams, Shall We Dance, Stella Dallas, The Life of the Party, Babes in Arms, The Farmer's Daughter, Seventeen, Strike Up the Band, Sunrise at Campobello and Magic Town.

SHOEMAKER, Betty Nuthall (1911–1983). See Nuthall, Betty.

SHOEMAKER, Carolyn (1929—). American astronomer. Born June 24, 1929, in Gallup, New Mexico; Chico State College in California, BA, MA; Northern Arizona University, PhD, 1990; m. Eugene Shoemaker (1928–1997, geologist and astronomer), Aug 18, 1951; children: 3. ❖ With husband and David Levy, discovered the Shoemaker-Levy 9 comet (1993); has discovered over 800 asteroids; holds the world record for number of comets—32—discovered by a living astronomer (as of 2001); became a research professor of astronomy at Northern Arizona University (1989); also serves on the staff of the Lowell Observatory in Flagstaff, Arizona; her self-taught skill at scanning telescopic photographs of the night sky is credited with her high number of comet discoveries. Named a fellow of American Academy of Arts and Sciences. ❖ See also Women in World History.

SHŌKEN KŌTAIGŌ (1850–1914). See Haruko.

SHON MI-NA (1964—). Korean handball player. Born Oct 8, 1964, in South Korea. ❖ Won a silver medal at Los Angeles Olympics (1984) and a gold medal at Seoul Olympics (1988), both in team competition.

SHONAGON, Sei (c. 965–?). See Sei Shonagon.

SHONINGER, Katherine (1894–1974). See Murray, Katherine.

SHOPP, BeBe (1930—). Miss America. Born Beatrice Bella Shopp, Aug 17, 1930. ❖ Named Miss America (1948), representing Minnesota, the 1st to be crowned in an evening gown; became a licensed lay minister. ❖ See also Frank Deford, There She Is (Viking, 1971).

SHORE, Dinah (1917–1994). American pop singer and tv personality. Born Frances Rose Shore, Mar 1, 1917, in Winchester, TN; died Feb 24, 1994, in Beverly Hills, CA; attended Vanderbilt University; m. George Montgomery (actor), 1943 (div. 1962); m. Maurice Smith (businessman), 1963 (div. 1964); children: (1st m.) Melissa Montgomery (b. 1948); John David (adopted, 1954). ❖ Offered a job on one of Nashville's WSM musical programs; moved to NY the next year and began auditioning as Dinah Shore; won recording contracts with NBC and RCA and had 1st hit single, "Yes, My Darling Daughter" (1939); had 1st national network job on Eddie Cantor's radio show (1940) and became one of the nation's most popular entertainers throughout radio's Golden Age; released recording of "Blues in the Night," which quickly sold a million copies (1942); made film debut in Thank Your Lucky Stars (1943), followed by Up in Arms (1944), Follow the Boys (1944), Belle of the Yukon (1944), Till the Clouds Roll By (1946) and Aaron Slick from Punkin Crick (1952), among others; hosted her own radio show (1943) and entertained troops during WWII; starred on "The Dinah Shore Chevy Show" on NBC (1951–61), singing the show's theme song, "See the USA in your Chevrolet," blowing her audience her trademark goodnight kiss, and winning 2 Emmy Awards along the way; had a series of popular "Dinah Shore TV Specials" (1964–65, 1969); as an accomplished golfer and promoter of the sport, hosted the Ladies Professional Golf Association (LPGA) Dinah Shore Classic, which soon became a major tv event on the tour; starred on "Dinah's Place" (1970–74), earning 3 more Emmys, followed by "Dinah!" (1976) and "A Conversation with Dinah" (1990–92). ❖ See also Women in World History.

SHORE, Elizabeth (fl. 1460s). See Lucy, Elizabeth.

SHORE, Henrietta (1880–1963). Canadian-born American painter. Born 1880 in Toronto, Canada; died 1963 in Carmel, California; studied at Art Students League (NY) under William Merrit Chase and Robert Henri; studied at Heatherley's Art School in London. ❖ First studied art under Laura Muntz in Toronto; influenced by Robert Henri, developed a modernist style of abstracted realism; moved to West Coast (1913), where she quickly made a name for herself as an innovator in West Coast art; won a silver medal at Panama-Pacific Exposition in San Diego (1915); established Los Angeles Society of Modern Artists; returned to New York City (1921); was honored as one of 25 representatives of American art in Paris (1924); was a founding member of New York Society of Women Artists (1925); produced such semi-abstract works as Source and The unfolding of life, though as the decade progressed, turned more and more to simplified landscapes of rock formations, shells and desert plants; began living in the art colony at Carmel, California (1930). ❖ See also Women in World History.

SHORE, Jane (c. 1445–c. 1527). English royal mistress. Born Jane Wainstead c. 1445; died c. 1527; dau. of Thomas Wainstead (a London mercer); m. William Shore (goldsmith); mistress of the marquis of Dorset, Lord Hastings, and Edward IV. ❖ Legendary mistress of Edward IV, king of England, used her influence with the king to petition the pope for an annulment of his marriage on the grounds of impotence; on the death of Edward (1483), was accused of witchcraft by his brother Richard III and hauled before the bishop of London's court for harlotry; had to to forfeit all material possessions, then walk the streets of London barefoot, wearing a white sheet and carrying a lighted candle. ❖ See also Women in World History.

SHORE, Lynne Jewell (1959—). See Jewell, Lynne.

SHORINA, Anna (1982—). Russian synchronized swimmer. Born Aug 26, 1982, in USSR. ❖ At World championships, won team gold medals (2003); won a team gold medal at Athens Olympics (2004).

SHORT, Clare (1946—). English politician and member of Parliament. Name variations: Rt. Hon. Clare Short. Born Clare Short, Feb 15, 1946, in Birmingham, England, of Irish ancestry; attended universities of Keele and Leeds; m. Andrew Moss, 1964 (div. 1971); m. Alex Lyon (MP, 1966–83), 1982 (died 1993). ❖ Representing Labour, elected to House of Commons for Birmingham Ladywood (1982, 1987, 1992, 1997, 2001, 2005); was secretary of state for International Development (1997–2003); wrote An Honourable Deception? New Labour, Iraq, and the Misuse of Power (2004).

SHORT, Elizabeth (1925–1947). American murder victim. Name variations: The Black Dahlia. Born in Medford, Massachusetts, in 1925; dau. of Phoebe Short; murdered in Los Angeles, California, on Jan 15, 1947. ❖ Hollywood hopeful, known as "The Black Dahlia," whose body was found hacked in two at the waste and the initials "B. D." carved deeply into one thigh. Theories abound as to the name of Short's killer in one of the most famous unsolved crimes in American history. ❖ See also James

Ellroy, *The Black Dahlia* (1985); John Gilmore, *Severed: The True Story of the Black Dahlia Murder* (Amok, 1998); Steve Hodel, *Black Dahlia Avenger* (2003); and *Women in World History*.

SHORT, Florence (1889–1946). American screen actress. Born May 19, 1889, in Springfield, MA; died July 10, 1946, in Los Angeles, CA; dau. of Lew Short (actor); sister of Antrim Short (actor) and Gertude Short (actress). ❖ Made film debut in *Damaged Goods* (1914), followed by *When You and I Were Young, The Outsider, Public Defender, The Hohenzollerns, Way Down East, The Light of New York* and *The Enchanted Cottage*, among others.

SHORT, Gertrude (1902–1968). American comedic actress. Born Carmen Gertrude Short, April 6, 1902, in Cincinnati, OH; died July 31, 1968, in Hollywood, CA; dau. of Lew Short (actor); sister of Antrim Short (actor) and Florence Short (actress); m. Scott Pembroke (director, writer). ❖ Age 5, made stage debut; made film debut with Edison Company; films include *Rent Free, Beggar on Horseback, Tillie the Toiler, Adam and Evil, Golddiggers of Broadway, The Telephone Girl* (series), *Son of Kong, The Key* and *Woman Wanted*; retired to work at Lockheed during WWII and remained there.

SHORTALL, Róisín (1954—). Irish politician. Name variations: Roisin Shortall. Born April 25, 1954, in Drumcondra, Ireland; m. Seamus O'Byrne; children: 3 daughters. ❖ Began career as primary school-teacher of the deaf; representing Labour, elected to the 27th Dáil (1992–97) for Dublin North West; returned to 28th Dáil (1997–2002) and 29th Dáil (2002–07); was Labour spokesperson on Health and Children (1997).

SHORTEN, Monica (1923–1993). Zoologist. Name variations: M. Shorten. Born Monica Ruth Shorten, 1923; died 1993; m. A. D. Vizoso. ❖ A gray squirrel expert, 1st worked with Charles Elton at the Bureau of Animal Population, studying the ecology of rats, among other topics; was asked by Elton to investigate gray squirrel distribution, a research project that spanned 10 years; began research for Ministry of Agriculture, Fisheries, and Food (MAFF) on toxic chemicals and squirrels (1954); employed to study the woodcock by the Game Conservancy. Wrote *Squirrels* (1954) and (with F. Barkalow) *The World of the Grey Squirrel* (1973).

SHORTER, Mrs. Clement (1866–1918). *See Sigerson, Dora.*

SHORTER, Dora (1866–1918). *See Sigerson, Dora.*

SHORTT, Elizabeth Smith (1859–1949). Canadian physician. Name variations: Elizabeth Smith. Born Elizabeth Smith, Jan 18, 1859, at Mountain Hall, Vinemount, Canada; died Jan 14, 1949, in Ottawa, Canada; dau. of Isabella (McGee) Smith and Sylvester Smith (a Winona, Ontario-based farmer); m. Adam Shortt (professor), Dec 3. 1886; children: 3, including Muriel Shortt Clarke (fruit farmer) and Lorraine Shortt (social worker). ❖ Began career as a teacher; graduated with the 1st class from Queen's University's Women's Medical College (1884); opened a private practice; served as president of the 1st YWCA in Canada; moved with family to Ottawa (1908), where she helped establish the Victorian Order of Nurses and the Women's Canadian Club; served as vice chair of Ottawa Provincial Board of Mother's Allowances, which helped fatherless families (1920–49). ❖ See also V. Strong-Boag, ed. *A Woman with a Purpose: The Diaries of Elizabeth Smith, 1872–1884* (U. of Toronto Press, 1980).

SHOSHI (fl. 990–1010). Japanese empress. Name variations: Shōshi. Dau. of Fujiwara no Michinaga (966–1028, head of the famous Fujiwara family during their period of greatest power and influence) and Rinshi; had sisters Kenshi, Ishi, and Kishi, and brother Yorimichi (who became emperor); m. Emperor Ichijo (died, autumn 1011); children: 2 sons born between 1008 and 1010.

SHŌTOKU, Empress (718–770). *See Kōken-Shōtoku.*

SHOUAA, Ghada (1972—). Syrian heptathlete. Name variations: Ghada Shou'aa. Born 1972 in Mehardi, Syria. ❖ Won a gold medal at World championships (1995); won a gold medal at Atlanta Olympics (1996), the 1st gold medal ever won by Syria.

SHOUSE, Kay (1896–1994). American philanthropist. Name variations: Mrs. Jouett Shouse; Catherine Filene Shouse. Born Catherine Filene Shouse, 1896, in Boston, Massachusetts; died in Naples, Florida, Dec 1994; dau. of A. Lincoln Filene (Boston philanthropist and department store owner) and Therese Filene; Wheaton College, BA, 1918; Harvard University, MEd, 1923; became 2nd wife of Jouett Shouse (Kansas

congressional representative, newspaper publisher, and assistant secretary of US Treasury who was 1st m. to Marion Edwards Shouse and had 2 children), on Dec 2, 1932. ❖ Received the 1st master's degree in education awarded to a woman by Harvard University (1923); appointed by President Coolidge as chair of 1st federal prison for women, focused on rehabilitation and created a job-training program for inmates; was also actively involved in the Democratic Party, co-founding the Women's National Democratic Club with Florence Jaffray Harriman (1922); bought about 56 acres of land in Fairfax County, Virginia, in an area near the stream commonly known as Wolf Trap Creek (1930), to which she would add a little over 100 acres more in the next 3 decades; donated 100 acres of the farm, as well as money for construction of an amphitheater, to the National Park Service (1965), resulting in Wolf Trap Farm Park, the only national park for the performing arts in America; remained actively involved in managing Wolf Trap almost until the end of her long life. Made Dame Commander of the British Empire (1976); received Presidential Medal of Freedom (1977); made an Officier dans l'Order des Arts et des Lettres in France (1985); given Medal of Honor from Austria (1992). ❖ See also *Women in World History*.

SHOWA EMPRESS. *See Nagako (1903–2000).*

SHOWALTER, Elaine (1941—). American literary critic and educator. Born Elaine Cottler, Jan 21, 1941, in Cambridge, MA; University of California, Davis, PhD. ❖ Taught at Rutgers University (1969–84), then Princeton; developed a school of feminist criticism, which incorporates female experience into literary criticism; writings include *A Literature of Their Own: British Women Novelists from Brontë to Lessing* (1977), *The Female Malady: Women, Madness, and English Culture, 1830–1980* (1985) and *Sexual Anarchy* (1991); edited several works, including *The New Feminist Criticism* (1986), *Speaking of Gender* (1989) and *These Modern Women: Autobiographical Essays from the Twenties* (1989).

SHREWSBURY, countess of.
See Stafford, Catherine (d. 1476).
See Hastings, Anne (d. after 1506).
See Talbot, Elizabeth (1518–1608).
See Talbot, Mary (d. 1632).
See Talbot, Nadine (1913–2003).

SHRIMPTON, Jean (1942—). British fashion model. Born Nov 7, 1942, in High Wycombe, Buckinghamshire, England; m. Michael Cox (photographer), 1979; children: son Thaddeus (b. 1979). ❖ One of the top models of the mid-'60s, appeared on the covers of numerous fashion magazines, most prominently *Vogue*, and was featured on the cover of *Newsweek* (May 1965). ❖ See also *Jean Shrimpton: An Autobiography* (1990); and *Women in World History*.

SHRIVER, Eunice Kennedy (1921—). American advocate and founder. Name variations: Eunice Kennedy. Born Eunice Mary Kennedy in Brookline, Massachusetts, July 10, 1921; dau. of Joseph Patrick Kennedy (financier, diplomat, and head of several government commissions) and Rose (Fitzgerald) Kennedy; sister of John F. Kenney (US president); granted a bachelor's degree in sociology from Stanford University, 1943; m. (Robert) Sargent Shriver, in 1953; children: Robert Sargent Shriver III (b. 1954, investor and film producer); Maria Shriver (b. 1955, NBC correspondent); Timothy Perry Shriver (b. 1959, CEO of the Special Olympics); Mark Kennedy Shriver (b. 1963, Maryland legislator and telephone executive); Anthony Paul Kennedy Shriver (b. 1965, mental-retardation activist and president of a drug-delivery company). ❖ Pioneer in advocacy for the mentally and physically challenged, president for many years of the Joseph Kennedy Foundation, and a founder and organizer of the Special Olympics; worked in the US State Department (1943–45); became foundation director of the Joseph P. Kennedy Jr. Foundation for the care and research of the disabled (1957); campaigned for brother John F. Kennedy for presidency of US (1960); during Kennedy's presidency, became advocate for the developmentally challenged (1962); instituted private day camp for the retarded (1963); joined others in establishing the Special Olympic Summer Games (1968); retired as president of the organization (1988). ❖ See also Laurence Leamer, *The Kennedy Women* (Villard, 1994); and *Women in World History*.

SHRIVER, Maria (1955—). American broadcaster. Name variations: Maria Shriver Schwarzenegger. Born Maria Owings Shriver, Nov 6, 1955, in Chicago, IL; dau. of Eunice Kennedy Shriver and (Robert) Sargent Shriver (US ambassador to France, 1968–70); cousin of Pam Shriver (tennis player); m. Arnold Schwarzenegger (actor and governor of California), April 26, 1986; children: Katherine, Christina, Patrick and Christopher. ❖ TV newscaster, became correspondent for "The American Parade" (1984); co-anchored "CBS This Morning" (1985–86) and NBC's "Sunday Today" (1987–90); anchor of "Main Street" (1987–88); contributing anchor for "Dateline NBC" (1992–2004); became first lady of California (2003); wrote *Ten Things I Wish I'd Known–Before I Went Out Into the Real World* (2000), among others.

SHRIVER, Pam (1962—). American tennis player. Born July 4, 1962, in Baltimore, MD; cousin of Maria Shriver; m. 2nd husband George Lazenby (actor), 2002; children: George Lazenby (b. 2004). ❖ At Seoul Olympics, won a gold medal in doubles (1988); on WTA Tour, won 21 singles titles and 106 doubles titles; won Grand Slam doubles titles (1982–89); was on the Wightman Cup Team (1978–81, 1983, 1985, 1987) and US Fed Cup Team (1986–87, 1989, 1992); does tennis commentary for ESPN.

SHROEDER, Cynthia Goyette (1946—). *See Goyette, Cynthia.*

SHTARKELOVA, Margarita (1951—). Bulgarian basketball player. Born July 5, 1951, in Bulgaria. ❖ At Montreal Olympics, won a bronze medal in team competition (1976).

SHTEREVA, Nikolina (1955—). Bulgarian runner. Born Jan 21, 1955, in Bulgaria. ❖ At Montreal Olympics, won a silver medal in 800 meters (1976).

SHTERN, Lina (1878–1968). Russian physiologist. Name variations: Lina Solomonovna Shtern; Lina Solomonovna Stern; Lina Salomonowna Schtern; Lina Sterna. Born Aug 26, 1878, in Liepaja (Libava), Latvia, Russia; died in Moscow, Mar 7, 1968; educated at University of Geneva. ❖ Was a professor at University of Geneva; returned to Russia (1925), and became a major figure in Soviet medical research; was the 1st woman admitted to the USSR Academy of Sciences; survived the anti-Semitic purges of the late Stalin era; lived to an advanced age as the most illustrious woman scientist of the USSR; was noted for her discovery of the hematoencephalic barrier and other major scientific breakthroughs. ❖ See also *Women in World History.*

SHUB, Esther (1894–1959). Soviet film editor and director. Name variations: Esfir Shub. Born Esfir Ilyianichna Shub, Mar 3, 1894, in Chernigovsky district, Ukraine; died Sept 21, 1959, in Moscow; attended Institute for Women's Higher Education in Moscow. ❖ One of the 1st film editors to use montage editing to create compilation films, worked in the experimental theaters of Mayakovsky and Meyerhold at beginning of career; edited more than 200 films, mostly foreign films that needed to be recut and retitled for Soviet audiences to comply with censorship guidelines; became so skilled in montage editing that she virtually created the compilation method of documentary filmmaking, a technique that influenced Eisenstein; made 1st and most famous compilation film, *The Fall of the Romanov Dynasty* (1927), followed by *The Great Road* (1927); when movies began to use sound, created an ultrarealistic style, predating *cinema verité* by 30 years; co-directed, with Vsevolod Pudovkin, *Twenty Years of Soviet Cinema* (1940); became chief editor of the *News of the Day* serial at the Central Studio for Documentary Film in Moscow (1942); other films include *The Russia of Nicholas II and Leo Tolstoy* (1928), *Today* (1930), *Komsomol* (1932), *Moscow Builds the Metro* (1934), *Land of the Soviets* (1937), *Spain* (1939), *Fascism Will Be Defeated* (1941), *Native Land* (1942), *The Trial in Smolensk* (1946) and *Across the Araks* (1947). ❖ See also *Women in World History.*

SHUBINA, Lyudmila (1948—). Soviet handball player. Born Oct 1948 in USSR. ❖ At Montreal Olympics, won a gold medal in team competition (1976).

SHUBINA, Mariya (1930—). Soviet kayaker. Born May 12, 1930, in USSR. ❖ At Rome Olympics, won a gold medal in K2 500 meters (1960).

SHUBINA, Yelena (1974—). Soviet swimmer. Born Sept 8, 1974, in USSR. ❖ At Barcelona Olympics, won a bronze medal in 4 x 100-meter medley relay (1992).

SHUHUA LING (1904–1990). *See Ling Shuhua.*

SHUI QINGXIA (1976—). Chinese soccer player. Born Dec 18, 1976, in Shanghai, China. ❖ Selected to Chinese national team (1985); won a team silver medal at Atlanta Olympics (1996).

SHULER, Nettie Rogers (1862–1939). American suffragist. Born Nov 8, 1862, in Buffalo, NY; died Dec 2, 1939, in New York, NY; dau. of Alexander Rogers (clerk) and Julia Antoinette (Houghtaling) Rogers; m. Frank J. Shuler (bookkeeper), Mar 31, 1887 (died 1916); children:

1 daughter. ❖ Helped organize referendum campaigns for suffrage amendment in western NY for New York Woman Suffrage Party (1913–15, 1916–17); served as corresponding secretary for National American Woman Suffrage Association (1917–21); was co-author, with Carrie Chapman Catt, of *Woman Suffrage and Politics* (1923).

SHULL, Elizabeth (1913—). *See Russell, Elizabeth S.*

SHULMAN, Alix Kates (1932—). American novelist and feminist. Born 1932 in Cleveland, OH; attended Case Western Reserve; New York University, MA in humanities; children: 2. ❖ An early member of Redstockings and NY Radical Feminists, published *Memoirs of an Ex-Prom Queen* (1972), on being female in the 1950s, which was nominated for a National Book Award and regarded as the 1st important novel of the women's movement of 1970s; other works include *To the Barricades: The Anarchist Life of Emma Goldman* (1971), *Burning Questions* (1978), *On The Stroll* (1981), *In Every Woman's Life* (1987) and *Drinking the Rain* (1995). ❖ See also memoir, *A Good Enough Daughter* (1999).

SHUNN, Iris (1915–1980). *See Meredith, Iris.*

SHURR, Gertrude (c. 1920—). American modern dancer and teacher. Born c. 1920 in Riga, Latvia. ❖ Trained at Denishawn school in New York City; was charter member of Humphrey/Weidman Group; danced in Martha Graham's early company, where she created roles in Graham's *Heretic* (1930), *Bacchanale* (1931), *American Provincials* (1934), *Horizons* (1936), and *American Lyric* (1937); retired from performance career, but taught at High School of Performing Arts in New York City and University of Utah.

SHUSHUNOVA, Elena (1969—). Soviet gymnast. Name variations: Yelena. Born May 23, 1969, in Leningrad (now St. Petersburg), Russia. ❖ Won USSR Cup (1983, 1985–88), Moscow News (1985, 1988), World Cup (1986), USSR nationals and University Games (1987), and French International (1988); at European championships, won gold medals for all-around, vault, uneven bars and floor exercise and a bronze for beam (1985) and a bronze in all-around and a gold in vault (1987); at World championships, won gold medals in all-around, team, and vault, a silver in floor, and a bronze in beam (1985) and gold medals in vault and floor (1987); at Seoul Olympics, won a bronze medal in uneven bars, silver medal in balance beam, and gold medals in indiv. all-around and team all-around (1988).

SHUTTA, Ethel (1896–1976). American actress and singer. Born Ethel Schutte, Dec 1, 1896, in New York, NY; died Feb 5, 1976, in New York, NY; m. George Olsen (orchestra leader), 1929 (div. 1936); m. George Kirksey. ❖ At 5, made stage debut with parents in vaudeville, dancing the cake walk at Madison Square Garden; made Broadway debut in *The Passing Show of 1922*, followed by *Louie the 14th, Whoopee, Marjorie, Jennie*, and several editions of the *Ziegfeld Follies*; sang with her 1st husband's band on radio, including "The Jack Benny Show"; also remembered as Eddie Cantor's nurse in the film *Whoopee*; made a Broadway comeback in Sondheim's *Follies* (1971).

SHUVAYEVA, Nadezhda (1952—). Soviet basketball player. Born Sept 1952 in USSR. ❖ Won a gold medal at Montreal Olympics (1976) and a gold medal at Moscow Olympics (1980), both in team competition.

SHVAYBOVICH, Yelena (1966—). Soviet basketball player. Born Feb 3, 1966, in USSR. ❖ At Barcelona Olympics, won a gold medal in team competition (1992).

SHVYGANOVA, Tatyana (1960—). Soviet field-hockey player. Born Nov 1960 in USSR. ❖ At Moscow Olympics, won a bronze medal in team competition (1980).

SHYNKARENKO, Tetyana (1978—). Ukrainian handball player. Born Oct 26, 1978, in Ukraine. ❖ Won a team bronze medal at Athens Olympics (2004).

SIBERIA, princess of (1805–1863). *See Volkonskaya, Maria.*

SIBIRSKII, N. (1876–1921). *See Samoilova, Konkordiya.*

SIBLEY, Antoinette (1939—). English ballerina. Born in Bromley, England, Feb 27, 1939; m. Michael Somes; studied at Arts Educational School until 1949, then the Royal Ballet School. ❖ Entered the company of the Royal Ballet (1956); became a soloist (1959), then principal (1960); roles include Odette/Odile, Giselle, and the betrayed girl in *The Rake's Progress*; also created the role of Titania for Frederick

Ashton's *The Dream* and was one of the Juliets in Kenneth Macmillan's *Romeo and Juliet*.

SIBYL or SIBYLLA (fl. 10th c. BCE). *See Sheba, Queen of.*

SIBYLLA. *Variant of Sybilla.*

SIBYLLA (1160–1190). Queen of Jerusalem. Name variations: Sibyl, Sybil, or Sybilla. Born in 1160 in Jerusalem; died in 1190 in Jerusalem; dau. of Almaric I, king of Jerusalem (r. 1162–1174), and Agnes of Courtenay (1136–1186); sister of Baldwin IV, king of Jerusalem (r. 1174–1183); m. William of Montferrat, count of Jaffa and regent of Jerusalem, in 1176 (died 1180); m. Guy of Lusignan, later king of Jerusalem (r. 1186–1192), in 1180; children: (1st m.) Baldwin V (b. 1179), king of Jerusalem (r. 1185–1186); (2nd m.) 2 daughters, names unknown, who both died in 1190. ❖ Was crowned queen by popular acclaim (1186), but her new subjects refused to accept her corrupt and imprudent husband Guy of Lusignan as their king; had him crowned anyway; when husband was taken prisoner by Saladin, surrendered Jerusalem after a siege (Oct 1187), effectively ending the Crusader kingdom which had lasted almost a century. ❖ See also *Women in World History.*

SIBYLLA OF ARMENIA (fl. 1200s). Countess of Tripoli. Married Bohemund VI, prince of Antioch (r. 1251–1268), count of Tripoli (r. 1251–1275); children: Lucia, countess of Tripoli (r. 1288–1289); Bohemund VII (d. 1287), prince of Antioch and count of Tripoli (r. 1275–1287).

SIBYLLE DU FAUBOURG SAINT-GERMAIN, La (1772–1843). *See Lenormand, Marie Anne Adélaïde.*

SIBYLLE ELIZABETH OF WURTTEMBERG (1584–1606). Electress of Saxony. Born April 10, 1584; died Jan 20, 1606; dau. of Sibylle of Anhalt (1564–1614) and Frederick, duke of Wurttemberg-Mompelga; sister of Louis Frederick (b. 1586), duke of Wurttemberg; m. John George I, elector of Saxony, on Sept 16, 1604.

SIBYLLE OF ANHALT (1564–1614). Duchess of Wurttemberg-Mompelga. Born Sept 20, 1564; died Nov 16, 1614; dau. of Joachim Ernst (b. 1536), prince of Anhalt, and Agnes of Barby (1540–1569); sister of Elizabeth of Anhalt (1563–1607); m. Frederick, duke of Wurttemberg-Mompelga, on May 22, 1581; children: Sibylle Elizabeth of Wurttemberg (1584–1606); Louis Frederick (b. 1586), duke of Wurttemberg.

SIBYLLE OF BRUNSWICK-LUNEBURG (1584–1652). Duchess of Brunswick-Dannenberg. Born June 3, 1584; died August 5, 1652; dau. of Dorothy of Denmark (1546–1617) and William the Younger, duke of Luneburg; m. Julius Ernst, duke of Brunswick-Dannenberg, on Dec 18, 1617.

SIBYLLE OF BURGUNDY (1065–1102). Duchess of Burgundy. Name variations: Sibylle de Bourgogne. Born in 1065; died Mar 23, 1102; dau. of William I, count of Burgundy, and Etienette de Longwy; sister of Gisela of Burgundy (fl. 1100s); m. Eudes I the Red (1058–1103), duke of Burgundy (r. 1079–1103), in 1080; children: Helie also known as Ela (b. 1080); Florine of Burgundy (b. 1083); Hugh II (b. 1085), duke of Burgundy (r. 1102–1143); Henry of Burgundy (b. 1087), a priest.

SIBYLLE OF BURGUNDY (1126–1150). Queen of Sicily. Name variations: Sibylle de Bourgogne. Born in 1126; died Sept 19, 1150; dau. of Hugh II (b. 1085), duke of Burgundy (r. 1102–1143), and Mathilde de Mayenne; became 3rd wife of Roger II, king of Sicily (r. 1103–1154), duke of Apulia (r. 1128–1154), in 1149. Roger II's 1st wife was Beatrice of Rethel; his 2nd was Elvira (d. 1135).

SICHELGAITA OF SALERNO (1040–1090). Duchess of Apulia. Born 1040 in Salerno; died 1090 in Normandy; dau. of the duke of Salerno; sister of Gisulf II, Lombard prince of Salerno; 2nd wife of Robert Guiscard (d. 1085), a Frankish noble, duke of Apulia and Calabria, count of Sicily (r. 1057–1085), whose 1st wife was Aubrey of Buonalbergo; children: Roger Gorsa or Borsa, duke of Apulia and Calabria (r. 1085–1111); Helena (betrothed to Constantine, son of the emperor Michael VII); Matilda (who m. Raymond Berengar II, count of Barcelona); Mabel (who m. William of Grandmesnil); Emma (who m. Odo, the marquis); and others. ❖ Was husband's most valuable ally in the constant wars in which he engaged; rode beside him, dressed in armor, urging on their troops; even ordered some retreating Normans to return to the fight, chasing after them with a spear until she managed to herd them back into the battle. ❖ See also *Women in World History.*

SICILY, queen of.
See Elvira (d. 1135).
See Sibylle of Burgundy (1126–1150).
See Beatrice of Rethel (fl. 1150s).
See Margaret of Navarre (fl. 1154–1172).
See Constance of Sicily (1154–1198).
See Joanna of Sicily (1165–1199).
See Constance of Aragon (d. 1222).
See Beatrice of Savoy (fl. 1240s).
See Helena of Epirus (fl. 1250s).
See Marguerite de Bourgogne (1250–1308).
See Beatrice of Provence (d. 1267).
See Blanche of Naples (d. 1310).
See Lenore of Sicily (1289–1341).
See Constance of Aragon (c. 1350–?).
See Maria of Sicily (d. 1402).
See Blanche of Navarre (1385–1441).
See Maria of Castile (1401–1458).
See Anne-Marie d'Bourbon-Orleans (1669–1728).
See Maria Carolina (1752–1814).
See Marie Isabella of Spain (1789–1848).

SICILY, regent of.
See Adelaide of Savona (d. 1118).
See Margaret of Navarre (fl. 1154–1172).
See Yolande of Aragon (1379–1442).

SIDDAL, Elizabeth (1829–1862). English painter, writer, and artist's model. Name variations: Elizabeth Rossetti; Mrs. Dante Gabriel Rossetti. Born Elizabeth Eleanor Siddal, July 25, 1829, in Holborn, England; died of overdose of laudanum, Feb 11, 1862, in London; dau. of Charles Siddal and Elizabeth (Evans) Siddal; m. Dante Gabriel Rossetti (the painter and poet), May 23, 1860; children: 1 daughter (stillborn). ❖ Model for the Pre-Raphaelite Brotherhood of mid-19th century painters, was also a painter in her own right; first modeled for painter Walter Deverall, an artist associated with the Pre-Raphaelite artists' fraternity (1849); can be identified in many paintings and drawings by Holman Hunt, John Everett Millais, for whom she posed for his famous *Ophelia,* and Dante Gabriel Rossetti, who painted her numerous times, most often as Dante's beloved Beatrice (Portinari); by 1852, was working regularly with Rossetti, who was the 1st to encourage her own artistic interests; was painted by Rossetti so often that her face came to signify the Pre-Raphaelite movement; had 1st public showing (1857), when some of her watercolors were included in an exhibition of Pre-Raphaelite work. ❖ See also Jan Marsh, *Elizabeth Siddal 1829–1862: Pre-Raphaelite Artist* (Ruskin Gallery, 1991); and *Women in World History.*

SIDDEN, Marguerite (1872–1968). *See Seddon, Margaret.*

SIDDONS, Mrs.
See Siddons, Sarah (1755–1831).
See Siddons, Harriet (1783–1844).

SIDDONS, Harriet (1783–1844). British actress. Name variations: Mrs. Siddons. Born Harriet Murray, 1783; died 1844; dau. of Charles Murray; m. Henry Siddons (b. 1774, actor and the son of Sarah Siddons). ❖ Shakespearean actress of note, was seen regularly at London's Covent Garden (1798–1805); performed at Drury Lane (1805–09), at which time she appeared with the popular actor Robert William Elliston, playing Juliet to his Romeo; assisted husband, who managed the Edinburgh Theater (1809–15).

SIDDONS, Sarah (1755–1831). English actress. Name variations: Sarah Kemble; Mrs. Siddons. Born Sarah Kemble, July 5, 1755, in Brecon, Powys, England; died June 8, 1831, in London; eldest child of Roger Kemble (actor-manager) and Sarah "Sally" (Ward) Kemble; sister of actors John Philip Kemble (1757–1823), Stephen Kemble (1758–1822), Charles Kemble (1775–1854), and Eliza Kemble (1761–1836, known as Mrs. Whitlock); aunt of Fanny Kemble (1809–1893); m. William Siddons, Nov 26, 1773 (died Mar 11, 1808); children: Henry Siddons (b. 1774); Sarah Martha Siddons, known as Sally (b. 1775); Maria Siddons (b. 1779); Frances Emilia Siddons (b. 1781 and died in infancy); Eliza Ann Siddons (1782–1788); George John Siddons (b. 1785); Cecilia Siddons (b. 1794). ❖ Tragic actress who, by the dramatic power of her performances and the moral rectitude of her private life, helped to raise the status of the theater in Britain; gave moving performance of *Venice Preserved* (1774); endured London debut failure as Portia in *The Merchant of Venice* (Dec 29, 1775); joined the

Theater Royal, Bath (1778); began lifelong friendship with artist Thomas Lawrence (c. 1780); made triumphant return to Drury Lane (Oct 10, 1783) and would remain the undeposed Queen of Tragedy until her retirement in 1812; moved to Covent Garden (1803); gave farewell performance as Lady Macbeth (June 22, 1812); some of her most popular roles were Isabella in *Isabella* by Southerne, Euphrasia in *The Grecian Daughter* by Murphy, Jane in *Jane Shore* by Rowe, Calista in *The Fair Penitent* by Rowe, Belvidera in *Venice Preserved* by Otway, Isabella in *Measure for Measure*, Constance in *King John*, Zara in *The Mourning Bride* by Congreve, Lady Macbeth in *Macbeth*, Volumnia in *Coriolanus*, Mrs. Haller in *The Stranger* by Kotzebue. ❖ See also Roger Manvell, *Sarah Siddons: Portrait of an Actress* (Heinemann, 1970); Yvonne French, *Mrs Siddons: Tragic Actress* (Verschayle, 1954); Oswald G. Knapp, *An Artist's Love Story: Told in the Letters of Sir Thomas Lawrence, Mrs. Siddons and her Daughters* (Allen, 1905); and *Women in World History*.

SIDERI, Cornelia (1938—). Romanian kayaker. Born Dec 29, 1938, in Romania. ❖ At Tokyo Olympics, won a bronze medal in K2 500 meters (1964).

SIDGWICK, Eleonora Mildred (1845–1936). Scottish suffragist and women's education campaigner. Name variations: Nora Sidgwick, Eleanor Mildred Balfour; Nora Balfour. Born Eleanor Mildred Balfour, Mar 11, 1845, in East Lothian, Scotland; died Feb 10, 1936 in England; sister of Arthur Balfour (British prime minister); m. Henry Sidgwick (professor, ethicist, proponent of women's education), 1870 (died 1900). ❖ Married Henry Sidgwick, her brother's tutor from Cambridge, and through husband was drawn into the development of Newnham College, Cambridge, which was designed specifically for women; served as math teacher and principal of Newnham College (1892–1910); a major financial supporter of Newnham, campaigned to have women admitted to Cambridge on the same basis as men (through university examinations) and to have equal access to degrees, but failed in both efforts; was also interested in scientific analysis of occult, helping husband to found Society for Physical Research (1882) and conducting investigations; deplored tactics of militant suffragists, preferring moderate campaign tactics, but was a well-known speaker on women's rights and a formidable, if quiet, adversary when riled. ❖ See also Ethel Sidgwick, *Mrs Henry Sidgwick* (Sigwick & Jackson, 1936).

SIDGWICK, Nora (1845–1936). See Sidgwick, Eleonora Mildred.

SIDHWA, Bapsi (1938—). Pakistani novelist. Born Aug 11, 1938, in Karachi, Pakistan; brought up in Lahore; graduate of Kinnaird College for Women, Lahore; lives in Houston, Texas; children: 3. ❖ Taught at University of Houston, Rice University, Columbia University, Brandeis, and Mt. Holyoke College; in English, wrote *The Crow Eaters* (1982), *The Bride* (1983), *Cracking India* (1991), and *An American Brat* (1993). Awarded Sitari-I-Imtiaz (1991), Harvard Fellowship, and Lila Wallace–Reader's Digest Award (1993).

SIDNEY, Dorothy (1617–1684). Countess of Sunderland. Name variations: Lady Dorothy Sidney; Lady Dorothy Spencer; Lady Sunderland; Sacharissa. Born in 1617 in Scion House in England; baptized on Oct 5, 1617, in Isleworth, Middlesex; died 1684 and buried on Feb 25 at Brington; eldest of eight daughters of Robert Sidney, 2nd earl of Leicester, and Dorothy Percy (dau. of the 9th earl of Northumberland); sister of Lady Lucy Sidney; m. Henry, 3rd Lord Spencer (later created earl of Sunderland), on July 11, 1639 (killed in battle, 1643); m. Robert Smythe (a Kentish gentleman), in July 1652; children: (1st m.) Dorothy Spencer (who m. George, Viscount Halifax); Robert Spencer; Henry Spencer; Penelope Spencer (died young). ❖ Celebrated as "Sacharissa" in poems of Edmund Waller. ❖ See also *Women in World History*.

SIDNEY, Margaret.
See Hoby, Margaret (1571–1633).
See Lothrop, Harriet (1844–1924).

SIDNEY, Mary (1561–1621). See Herbert, Mary.

SIDNEY, Sylvia (1910–1999). American actress. Born Sophia Kosow, Aug 8, 1910, in the Bronx, New York; died July 1, 1999; dau. of Russian Jewish immigrants; studied acting at Theater Guild School; m. Bennett Cerf (publisher), 1935 (div. 1936); m. Luther Adler (actor), 1938 (div. 1947); m. Carlton Alsop (publicist), 1947 (div. 1950); children: Jacob Adler (died). ❖ At 16, made professional stage debut in Washington in *The Challenge of Youth*, then replaced the lead in New York production of *The Squall*; made screen debut in *Thru Different Eyes* (1929); signed with Paramount (1931); often cast as the downtrodden girl of the working class, played an innocent whose boyfriend becomes involved in racketeering in *City Streets* (1931), an unmarried mother in *Confessions of a Co-Ed* and again in *An American Tragedy* (both 1931), a prisoner in *Ladies of the Big House* (1932), a fugitive in *Mary Burns—Fugitive* (1935), the girlfriend of a fugitive in *Fury* (1936), and the sister of a criminal in *Dead End* (1937); left Hollywood (1956); made film comeback in *Summer Wishes, Winter Dreams* (1973), for which she was nominated for Academy Award for Best Supporting Actress; other films include *I Never Promised You a Rose Garden* (1977), *Damien: Omen II* (1978) and *Beetlejuice* (1988). Received Golden Globe and nominated for Emmy for performance in tv movie "An Early Frost" (1986); received Life Achievement award from Film Society of Lincoln Center (1990). ❖ See also *Women in World History*.

SIDORENKO, Tatyana (1966—). Soviet volleyball player. Born July 4, 1966, in USSR. ❖ At Seoul Olympics, won a gold medal in team competition (1988).

SIDOROVA, Evgenyia (c. 1935—). Russian Alpine skier. Name variations: Eugenie, Evgenia, Evguenia, Jejgenija, Yevgenia, or Yevgeniya Sidorova. Born in USSR. ❖ Won a bronze medal for slalom at Cortina Olympics (1956).

SIDOROVA, Tatyana (1936—). Russian speedskater. Name variations: Tatiana or Tatjana. Born July 25, 1936, in USSR. ❖ Won a bronze medal for the 500 meters at Innsbruck Olympics (1964).

SIDOROVA-BUROCHKINA, Valentina (1954—). Soviet fencer. Born May 1954 in USSR. ❖ Won a gold medal at Montreal Olympics (1976) and a silver medal at Moscow Olympics (1980), both in team foil.

SIEBERT, Gloria (1964—). East German runner. Born Jan 13, 1964, in East Germany. ❖ At Seoul Olympics, won a silver medal in 100-meter hurdles (1988).

SIEBERT, Muriel (1932—). American business executive. Born 1932 in Cleveland, Ohio; dau. of Irwin J. Siebert (dentist) and Margaret Eunice (Roseman) Siebert; attended Western Reserve University (now Case Western Reserve University), 1949–52; never married; no children. ❖ Financial company executive and New York State banking commissioner, who was the 1st woman to own a seat on the New York Stock Exchange, began career as a securities analyst (1954); advanced rapidly on Wall Street, changing firms whenever her salary increases did not match those of her male colleagues; became the 1st woman of the New York Stock Exchange (Dec 28, 1967) and was highly successful with Muriel Siebert & Co., Inc.; named New York State banking commissioner by Governor Hugh Carey (1969), the 1st woman so appointed; became a founding member of the National Women's Forum; created the Siebert Philanthropic Program (1990). Received the Women's Hall of Fame's inaugural Emily Warren Roebling Award (1984). ❖ See also memoir, *Changing the Rules: Adventures of a Wall Street Maverick* (2002); and *Women in World History*.

SIEBOLD, Charlotte Heidenreich von (1788–1859). German physician. Name variations: Charlotte von Siebold Heidenreich; Charlotte Heidenreich-von Siebold; Henriette Charlotte T. Heidenreich von Siebold; Dr. Charlotte Heidenreich. Born Marianna Theodore Charlotte von Siebold, Sept 12, 1788, in Heiland, Germany; died July 8, 1859, in Darmstadt, Germany; dau. of Josepha von Siebold (1771–1849, obstetrician) and Damian von Siebold. ❖ Earned doctorate from University of Giessen (1917), with thesis on ectopic pregnancy; worked with mother in charitable practice and assisted at births of several eminent people, including that of Queen Victoria.

SIEBOLD, Josepha von (1771–1849). German obstetrician. Name variations: Regina Josepha von Siebold. Born Regina Josepha Henning, 1771, in Germany; died 1849; m. Damian von Siebold, 1795. ❖ Worked as midwife and assistant to husband; studied obstetrics in Wurzburg and gained permission from Archducal Medical College, Darmstadt, to practice obstetrics and pox vaccination; became 1st woman to earn doctorate in obstetrics from German university (University of Giessen, 1815) and ran charitable practice assisted by daughter, Charlotte Heidenreich von Siebold.

SIECH, Birte (1967—). German rower. Born Mar 19, 1967, in Germany. ❖ At Seoul Olympics, won a gold medal in coxed fours (1988); at Barcelona Olympics, won a bronze medal in coxless fours (1992).

SIEDEBERG, Emily Hancock (1873–1968). New Zealand physician, anaesthetist, and hospital superintendent. Name variations: Emily Hancock McKinnon. Born Feb 17, 1873, at Clyde, New Zealand; died

June 13, 1968, at Oamaru, New Zealand; dau. of Franz David Siedeberg and Anna (Thompson) Siedeberg; University of Otago Medical School, 1896; m. James Alexander McKinnon (banker), 1928 (died 1949). ❖ Served as medical officer at Caversham Industrial School (1907–30), anaesthetist at Dental School (1921–31), and medical officer and superintendent of St Helens Hospital, Dunedin (1905–38); opened New Zealand's 1st antenatal clinic (1918), and worked with Plunket Society; helped to establish Dunedin branch of National Council of Women of New Zealand (1918); founding president of New Zealand Medical Women's Association (1921). Received King George V Silver Jubilee Medal (1935); Named Commander of the British Empire (1949). ❖ See also *Dictionary of New Zealand Biography* (Vol. 3).

SIEFERT, Silvia (1953—). East German handball player. Born July 19, 1953, in East Germany. ❖ At Montreal Olympics, won a silver medal in team competition (1976).

SIEGELAAR, Sarah (1981—). Dutch rower. Born Oct 4, 1981, in the Netherlands. ❖ Won a bronze medal for coxed eights at Athens Olympics (2004).

SIEGL, Siegrun (1954—). East German pentathlete. Born Oct 29, 1954, in East Germany. ❖ At Montreal Olympics, won a gold medal in pentathlon (1976).

SIEMON, Kirsten (1961—). *See Emmelmann-Siemon, Kirsten.*

SIEMS, Margarethe (1879–1952). Polish-German soprano. Born Dec 30, 1879, in Breslau (now Wroclaw), Poland; died April 13, 1952, in Dresden, Germany; studied with Aglaja von Orgéni and Pauline Viardot. ❖ Made debut in Prague as Marguerite in *Les Huguenots* (1902); joined Prague Opera (1902) and Dresden Court Opera (1908); was the leading dramatic coloratura soprano in Dresden (1908–20); created roles of Chrysothemis in *Elektra* (1909) and of the Marshallin in *Der Rosenkavalier* (1911), both in Dresden; created role of Zerbinetta in *Ariadne auf Naxos* in Stuttgart (1912); made Covent Garden debut (1913); taught at Berlin Conservatory and then in Dresden and Breslau.

SIEPMANN, Mary (1912–2002). *See Wesley, Mary.*

SIERENS, Gayle (1954—). American sportscaster and newsanchor. Born 1954; Florida State University, BS; married; children: 3. ❖ For WFLA News Channel 8 (FL), became weekend sports anchor and reporter (1977), 11pm weekday sports anchor (1983), and co-anchor of 5, 6, and 11pm newscasts; as 1st woman to do play-by-play coverage of National Football League games, covered her 1st game for NBC between Kansas City Chiefs and Seattle Seahawks (1987); freelanced for ESPN as play-by-play announcer. Won a Florida Emmy Award for Sports Reporting (1984).

SIERING, Lauri (1957—). American swimmer. Born Feb 23, 1957; grew up in Modesto, CA. ❖ At Montreal Olympics, won a silver medal in 4 x 100-meter medley relay (1976).

SIERRA, Stella (1917–1997). Panamanian poet. Born July 5, 1917, in Aguadulce, Panama; died 1997; dau. of Alejandro Tapia Escobar and Antonia Sierra Jaén de Tapia. ❖ Works include *Sinfonia jubilosa en doce sonetos* (1942), *Canciones de mar y luna* (1943), *Himno para la glorificación de F. D. Roosevelt* (1946), *Libre y cautiva* (1947), *Cinco poemas* (1949), and *Tamarindos.*

SIEVEKING, Amalie (1794–1859). German humanitarian, charity worker and educator. Born Amalie Wilhelmine Sieveking in Hamburg, Germany, July 25, 1794; died in Hamburg, April 1, 1859; never married. ❖ Orphaned at an early age (1809), her mother dying when she was 4 and her father when she was 15; during cholera epidemic of 1831, volunteered as a nurse at the plague hospital; joined by 12 other women, founded the Weiblicher Verein für Armen- und Krankenpflege (Female Association for the Care of the Poor and Sick, 1832); played an important role in making philanthropic activities more available to German Lutheran women. Postage stamp of the Federal Republic of Germany was issued in her honor (Nov 15, 1955). ❖ See also Emma Poel, *Life of Amelia Wilhelmina Sieveking* (ed. by Catherine Winkworth, 1863); and *Women in World History.*

SIEVWRIGHT, Margaret Home (1844–1905). New Zealand feminist and political activist. Name variations: Margaret Richardson. Born Margaret Richardson, Mar 19, 1844, in East Lothian, Scotland; died Mar 9, 1905, at Whataupoko, Poverty Bay, New Zealand; dau. of John Richardson and Jane Law (Home) Richardson; m. William Sievwright (lawyer), 1878; children: 1 daughter. ❖ Immigrated to New Zealand

(1878); was appointed to Waiapu Licensing Board and organized local branch of New Zealand Women's Christian Temperance Union; presented petition with 32,000 signatures to leading suffrage supporter, who took it to House of Representatives, where Electoral Bill became law (1887–92); served as president of Gisborne Women's Political Association (1901–05); established Local Council of Waiapu Women, which promoted women's causes internationally (1901); also advocated for reform in marriage and divorce laws. ❖ See also *Dictionary of New Zealand Biography* (Vol. 2).

SIGBRIT or SIGBRITT, Mother (fl. 1507–1523). *See Willums, Sigbrit.*

SIGEA, Luisa (c. 1531–1560). Spanish poet. Born c. 1531 in Spain; died 1560. ❖ Knew Latin, Greek, and Hebrew at young age; became teacher in household of Infanta Maria de Portugal (1521–1577) until 1555; returned to Spain after marriage and died in childbirth; wrote long Latin poem *Sintra* (1546).

SIGERSON, Dora (1866–1918). Irish poet and novelist. Name variations: Dora Sigerson Shorter; Mrs. Clement Shorter. Born in Dublin, Ireland, Aug 16, 1866; died Jan 16, 1918, in Buckinghamshire, England; eldest dau. of George Sigerson (scholar, surgeon, and writer) and Hester (Varian) Sigerson (poet and novelist); sister of Hester Sigerson Piatt (writer); m. Clement King Shorter (editor of *Illustrated London News*), July 1895. ❖ On marriage (1895), moved to London where she remained homesick for the rest of her life; during Easter Rising in Ireland (1916), worked tirelessly for her imprisoned compatriots and strained her health in the process; published *Verses* (1894), *The Fairy Changeling and Other Poems* (1897), *My Lady's Slipper and Other Poems* (1899), *Ballads and Poems* (1899), *The Father Confessor* (1900) and *The Woman Who Went to Hell and Other Poems* (1901).

SIGERSON, Hester (d. 1898). Irish novelist and poet. Born Hester Varian in Cork, Ireland; died 1898; dau. of Amos Varian of Cork; m. Dr. George Sigerson (writer and historian), 1861; children: Dora Sigerson (1866–1918, writer); Hester Sigerson Piatt (poet). ❖ Was a frequent contributor to *The Boston Pilot, The Gael,* and *Irish Fireside*; published only novel *A Ruined Race* (1889).

SIGNORET, Simone (1921–1985). French actress and social activist. Born Simone Henriette Charlotte Kaminker, Mar 25, 1921, in Wiesbaden, Germany; died Sept 30, 1985, in Normandy, France; dau. of André and Georgette (Signoret) Kaminker; Vannes lycée, baccalauréate in philosophy (1940); m. Yves Allegret (director), 1948 (div. 1949); m. Yves Montand (singer-actor and activist), 1950; children: (with Allegret) Catherine Allegret (actress, b. 1947). ❖ Academy-award winning French actress and social activist who appeared in a number of film classics during 40-year career, moved to Paris with family while still a child; was forced to work as a typist to support family when Nazis invaded Paris and her Jewish father fled to London; was cast by Marcel Carné in her 1st significant, though non-speaking, role in *Les Visiteurs du Soir* (1942); appeared in Allegret's *Démons de l'Aube (Demons of Dawn,* 1947), followed by *Dédée d'Anvers* and *Impasse des Deux Anges*; with Yves Montand, became prominent in protests against the testing and development of atomic weapons and France's colonial war in Indochina; returned to films in Ophuls' *La Ronde* and Becker's *Casque d'Or (The Golden Helmet,* 1952); her performance in Carné's *Thérèse Racquin* (1953), in which she played Zola's doomed heroine, was received to great acclaim; followed that with the classic suspense thriller *Diabolique*; won British Film Association Award and Academy Award for Best Actress for *Room at the Top* (1958); published 2 vols. of memoirs and a novel, *Adieu Volodia.* Other films include *Les Sorcières de Salem (The Crucible,* 1957), *Le Mauvais Coups* (1961), *Term of Trial* (1962), *Ship of Fools* (1964), *Paris Brûle-t-il?* ("Is Paris Burning?," 1966), *Games* (1967), *The Sea Gull* (1968), *L'Americain* (1969), *Le Chat* (1970), *La Veuve Couderc* (1970), *Rude Journée pour la Reine* (1973), *La Vie devant soi (Madame Rosa,* 1977), *Une Femme dangereuse* (1978), *Judith Therpauve* (1978), *L'Adolescente* (1980), *L'Étoile du Nord* (1982) and *Guy de Maupassant* (1982). ❖ See also Catherine David, *Simone Signoret* (trans. by Sally Sampson, Bloomsbury, 1992); and *Women in World History.*

SIGOLENA OF ALBI (fl. 7th c.). French deaconess and saint. Flourished 7th century in Albi, France. ❖ One of the early female saints, founded a monastery, became its leader, and was consecrated as a deaconess; is known because an anonymous admirer, probably a monk or nun over whom she had held office, wrote of her life. ❖ See also *Women in World History.*

SIGOURNEY, Lydia H. (1791–1865). American author and poet. Born Lydia Howard Huntley, Sept 1, 1791, in Norwich, Connecticut; died June 10, 1865, in Hartford, Connecticut; dau. of Ezekiel Huntley (gardener) and Zerviah or Sophia (Wentworth) Huntley; m. Charles Sigourney (hardware merchant), June 16, 1819 (died 1854); children: Mary (b. 1827); Andrew (b. 1831); and 3 others (stillborn). ❖ Known as "the sweet singer of Hartford," was the one of the best-known poets publishing in the early-to-mid-19th century, but her vast popularity, which influenced other women writers of her day, did not survive into 20th century; produced her most famous book, *Letters to Young Ladies* (1833); other writings include *Moral Pieces, in Prose and Verse* (1815), *The Square Table* (1819), *Sketch of Connecticut, Forty Years Since* (1824), *The Farmer and the Soldier* (1833), *Pocahontas, and Other Poems* (1841), *The Voice of Flowers* (1846), *The Weeping Willow* (1847), *Olive Leaves* (1852), *Past Meridian* (1854), *The Daily Counsellor* (1859) and *The Man of Uz, and Other Poems* (1862). ❖ See also autobiography, *Letters of Life* (1866); and *Women in World History*.

SIGRID THE HAUGHTY (d. before 1013). Queen of Denmark. Born in Sweden; died before 1013; dau. of Tosti-Skogul; m. Eric VI the Victorious, king of Sweden; became 2nd wife of Sven or Sweyn I Forkbeard, king of Denmark (r. 985–1014), king of England (r. 1014), around 996 (div.); also had a liaison with Vissavald, prince of Kiev; children: (1st m.) Olof or Olaf Sköttkonung or Skötkonung, king of Sweden (r. 994–1022); Holmfrid Ericsdottir (who m. Svein, earl of Ladir); (2nd m.) Svantoslava; Estrith (fl. 1017–1032). ❖ Sweyn's 1st wife was Gunhilda of Poland (d. around 1015).

SIGURANA, Caterina (fl. 1543). Italian heroine. Name variations: Catherine. Flourished in Nice. ❖ When Francis I of France began a 2-month siege of Nice aided by Muslim Turks (1543), attacked a Turkish standard-bearer and stole his flag, spurring fellow defenders to renewed efforts; has been remembered ever since as a hero of the city.

SIGURDSEN, Gertrud (1923—). Swedish politician. Born Jan 11 (also seen as Jan 10), 1923, in Nävekvarn, Sweden; children: 2 sons. ❖ Began 40-year career in Swedish politics (1949), serving as secretary for the Confederation of Trade Unions, before becoming information secretary of the Information Division (1964); elected as a Social Democrat to Parliament (1969), where she served as minister for Internal Development Assistance (1973–76) and was a member of the Parliament Standing Committee on Foreign Affairs until 1982; focusing attention on public health issues, became minister for Public Health and Medical Services (1982) and served as minister for Health and Social Affairs (1985–89); retired (1989).

SIHANOUK, Norodom Monineath (1936—). *See Norodom Monineath Sihanouk.*

SIKAKANE, Joyce Nomafa (1943—). South African journalist and anti-apartheid activist. Name variations: Joyce Sikhakane. Born Joyce Nomafa Sikakane, 1943, in Soweto, South Africa; dau. of Amelia Nxumalo and Jonathan Sikakane; m. Kenneth Rankin (Scottish physician); children: Nkosinathi; Nomzamo; Samora; Vikela. ❖ Worked as a reporter for the *World*, Johannesburg (1960–68); was a freelance reporter for *Rand Daily Mail* and a staff reporter with the *Post* and the *Drum* (1968); became the 1st African female staff reporter at *Rand Daily Mail* (1968); detained under Terrorism Act (May 12, 1969), because she was involved in the welfare of political prisoners; was among 21 activists charged under Suppression of Communism Act (Dec 1, 1969); after 17 months in prison, released with banning orders (Sept 14, 1970); went into exile in Zambia (July 1973); was reunited with family and finally able to marry Kenneth Rankin (mixed-race marriage was illegal in South Africa); with family, lived in Scotland and then Zimbabwe, writing and campaigning, continuing to fight against the injustices of apartheid. ❖ See also autobiography *A Window on Soweto* (1977); and *Women in World History*.

SIKES, Mrs. (1839–1909). *See Logan, Olive.*

SIKOLOVA, Helena (1949—). Czech cross-country skier. Name variations: Helena Sikolová; Helena Sikolova-Balatkova. Born in 1949 in Czechoslovakia. ❖ Won a bronze medal for the 5 km at Sappora Olympics (1972).

SIKVELAND, Annette (1972—). Norwegian biathlete. Name variations: Anette Sikveland. Born April 25, 1972, in Stavanger, Norway. ❖ Placed 4th for 4 x 7.5 km relay at Lillehammer Olympics (1994); won a bronze medal for 4 x 7.5 km relay at Nagano Olympics (1998).

SILAI, Ileana (1941—). Romanian runner. Born Oct 14, 1941, in Romania. ❖ At Mexico City Olympics, won a silver medal in 800 meters (1968).

SILANG, Gabriela (1731–1763). Filipino revolutionary. Name variations: Josefa Gabriela Silang. Born Maria Josefa Gabriela Silang, Mar 19, 1731, Caniogan, Santa, Ilocos Sur, Philippines; executed by hanging, Sept 20, 1763, in Vigan, Ilocos Sur; father was an Ilocano peasant; mother was an Itneg; married a rich widower, c. 1751 (died); m. Diego Silang (leader of the Ilocano or Ilokano revolution), c. 1757 (assassinated May 28, 1763); no children. ❖ Leader of a revolt in the Ilocos region of the Philippines, was separated from her pagan mother in early childhood; reared as a Christian (her father's religion) by the town's parish priest; betrothed by father to a rich widower (c. 1751) who died shortly after their marriage; married Diego Silang (c. 1757); when British seized Manila from the Spanish (1762), viewed their arrival as an opportunity to gain independence; under British protection, husband assumed the position of captain-general and local governor in Vigan and proclaimed the independence of the Ilocos region, but he was assassinated (May 28, 1763); assumed leadership of the rebellion against Spanish colonial rule until her defeat and execution. Her story, celebrated in poetry and song, has inspired other women of the Philippines to leadership in revolutionary movements; a monument of Silang on horseback stands in a public square in Makati, metropolitan Manila. ❖ See also *Women in World History*.

SILANPÄÄ, Miina (1866–1952). *See Sillanpää, Miina.*

SILESIA, duchess of.
See Hedwig of Silesia (1174–1243).
See Anna of Bohemia (fl. 1230s).

SILHANOVA, Olga (1920–1986). Czech gymnast. Born Dec 31, 1920; died Aug 27, 1986. ❖ At London Olympics, won a gold medal in team all-around (1948).

SILINGA, Annie (1910–1983). South African anti-apartheid activist. Born 1910 in the Transkei, South Africa; died in Langa, South Africa, 1983; married; children. ❖ Member of the African National Congress (ANC), organizer of the 1st Federation of South African Women's conference, and lifelong opponent of pass laws, moved with husband to Cape Town, Somerset West (1937); joined the Langa branch of the ANC, arrested during Defiance Campaign (1952); was part of group that planned the 1st Federation of South African Women's conference in Cape Town (1953); led women of the Western Cape in anti pass-law protests (1954); arrested for refusing to carry a pass (1955); deported to Namaqualand, returned to Cape Town and was arrested again, one of 156 activists arrested and charged with treason (1956); released after charges were dropped (1957); elected president of the Cape Town ANC Women's League (1958); was one of those arrested after the police massacred Africans during demonstrations protesting the pass-laws in Sharpeville and Langa townships (1960); was released without being charged. ❖ See also *Women in World History*.

SILIVAS, Daniela (1970—). Romanian gymnast. Name variations: Dana Silivas. Born May 9, 1970, in Deva, Romania. ❖ Won Peace Cup (1982), Blume Memorial (1984, 1989), Champions All (1985), International Championships of Romania (1985, 1986, 1988), Romanian nationals (1986, 1987, 1989), Swiss Cup (1987), Chunichi Cup (1988), and French International (1989); placed 1st all-around at European championships (1987) and 2nd all-around (1989); scored 5 perfect 10's at World championships, placing 1st in team, uneven bars, and floor in 3rd in all-around (1987) and 1st in uneven bars, beam, and floor (1989); at Seoul Olympics, won a bronze medal in vault, silver medals in team all-around and indiv. all-around, and gold medals in floor exercises, balance beam, and uneven bars (1988); moved to Atlanta, GA. Inducted into International Gymnastics Hall of Fame (2002).

SILKE, Ellen (c. 1845–1930). *See Crowe, Ellen.*

SILKO, Leslie Marmon (1948—). Native American writer. Born Mar 5, 1948, in Albuquerque, New Mexico, of Pueblo, Laguna, Mexican, and caucasian descent; grew up on Laguna Pueblo reservation; University of New Mexico, BA, 1969. ❖ One of the most important contemporary Native American writers, published 1st work, *Tony's Story* (1969), and 1st book of poetry, *Laguna Women Poems* (1974), drawing on legends passed down from Laguna elders, which brought national attention; was hailed as 1st Native American woman novelist after publishing *Ceremony* (1977), still considered to be her most important novel; released *Storyteller* (1989), which combines poetry, fiction, memoir, legend and photographs to depict family history; received MacArthur Foundation fellowship; published *Almanac of the Dead* (1992), which deals with European conquest; also wrote *Yellow Woman* (1993) and *Yellow Woman and a Beauty of the Spirit* (1996); taught in New Mexico, Alaska, and Arizona and has held academic appointments at universities of New Mexico and Arizona; also wrote *Western Stories* (1980), *Delicacy and Strength of Lace* (letters, 1986), *Sacred Water Narratives and Pictures* (1993), *Love Poem and Slim Man Canyon* (1999) and *Gardens in the Dunes* (1999).

SILKWOOD, Karen (1946–1974). American whistleblower. Born Karen Gay Silkwood, Feb 19, 1946, in Longview, Texas; died in car accident on way to Oklahoma City, Oklahoma, Nov 13, 1974; dau. of William Silkwood (paint contractor); attended Lamar College in Beaumont; m. Bill Meadows, 1966 (div. 1972); children: 3. ❖ Lab technician who—possibly armed with information that proved tampering in quality control at Kerr-McGee plutonium plant in Oklahoma City—was killed while driving to meet a reporter from *The New York Times*; interested in science, had taken lab technician courses before applying to work in Kerr-McGee's Cimarron nuclear facility in Oklahoma City (1972); became suspicious of a poor plant safety record of 17 contamination incidents involving 77 employees, all the more so after she was contaminated (1974); determined to prove the need for better safeguards for workers, gathered information to deliver to David Burnham, a reporter; killed in an auto accident (1974); no trace of the information she was carrying was ever found. ❖ See also Howard Kohn, *Who Killed Karen Silkwood?* (Summit, 1981); Richard Rashke, *The Killing of Karen Silkwood: The Story Behind the Kerr-McGee Plutonium Case* (Houghton Mifflin, 1981); (film) *Silkwood* (1983); and *Women in World History*.

SILL, Anna Peck (1816–1889). American educator. Born Anna Peck Sill, Aug 9, 1816, in Burlington, New York; died June 18, 1889, in Rockford, Illinois; dau. of Abel Sill (farmer) and Hepsibah (Peck) Sill (dau. of a prominent New York judge, Jedediah Peck); attended Miss Phipps' Union Seminary, Albion, NY; never married; no children. ❖ Was head of the female department of the Cary Collegiate Institute in Oakfield, New York (1844–1849); opened a private girls' school, Rockford Female Seminary (later Rockford College), in Rockford, Illinois (1849), and served as principal; sought to establish the seminary as an exemplar of Christian values and of service to the community; exerted authoritarian control over the institution but adapted to shifting educational needs; managed to elevate Rockford Female Seminary to collegiate status (1882); retired (1884). ❖ See also *Women in World History*.

SILLANPÄÄ, Miina (1866–1952). Finnish politician, journalist, and activist. Name variations: Miina Sillanpaa; Miina Silanpaa. Born 1866; died 1952. ❖ One of the most important politicians in early 20th-century Finland, began 40-year career in Parliament while the country was still under Russian control (1907); following WWI, edited *Working Women*, a trade union periodical, while simultaneously performing her duties as a Helsinki city councillor; as Finland's 1st woman member of Parliament, served as minister of Social Affairs (1926–28) and chaired the Social Democratic Women's League (1931); also served as speaker of Parliament (1936–47); devoted much of her energy to improving social conditions, especially for working women with children; active in the co-operative movement, chaired the Ensi Kotien Liito, a group of homes for single mothers (1945–52).

SILLIMAN, Lynn (1959—). American rower. Born April 24, 1959. ❖ At Montreal Olympics, won a bronze medal in coxed eights (1976).

SILLITOE, Ruth (1931—). *See Fainlight, Ruth.*

SILLS, Beverly (1929—). American opera singer and director. Born Belle Miriam Silverman, May 25, 1929, in Brooklyn, NY; studied with Estelle Liebling for 34 years; m. Peter B. Greenough, 1956; children: Meredith Greenough (b. 1959); Peter Greenough (b. 1961). ❖ Coloratura soprano, who gained wide recognition for her superb handling of classic "bel canto" roles and her strong dramatic instincts; began singing on radio at age 3 (1932); at 7, sang the aria "Caro nome" from Verdi's *Rigoletto* on the Major Bowes Amateur Hour and became a regular on the show for next 3 years; trilled the country's 1st commercial jingle, for Rinso laundry soap ("Rinso white, Rinso white, happy little washday song"); began formal vocal studies with Liebling; made operatic debut in Philadelphia as Frasquita in *Carmen* (1947), followed by several years of touring with small repertory companies before appearing with New York City Opera (1955), singing Rosalinda in Strauss' *Die Fledermaus*; sang with New York City Opera (1955–70); to great acclaim, sang the title role

in Douglas Moore's *The Ballad Of Baby Doe* (1958) and Cleopatra in Handel's *Guilio Cesare* (1966); debuted in Vienna as Queen of the Night in *Die Zauberflöte* (1967); debuted at Teatro alla Scale as Pamira in Rossini's *Le Siège de Corinthe* (1969) and at Covent Garden and Berlin's Deutsche Opera (1970); made formal debut at Metropolitan Opera in a reprise of her Pamira (1975); took on the more difficult *bel canto* roles, including all 3 of "Donizetti's queens"—Elizabeth in *Roberto Devereaux*, Anne in *Anna Bolena*, and Mary in *Maria Stuarta*; became general director of New York City Opera (1979), rescuing it from financial insolvency and building its artistic reputation during 8-year term; retired from the stage (1980); named chair of New York's Lincoln Center (1994); began hosting "Live From Lincoln Center" tv series. Received President's Medal of Freedom from Jimmy Carter (1980). ❖ See also autobiography (with Lawrence Linderman) *Beverly* (Bantam, 1987); and *Women in World History*.

SILOS, The. *See Rowell, Mary (1958—).*

SILVA, Benedita da (1942—). *See Silva, Benedita da.*

SILVA, Branca (1966—). *See Silva, Maria Angelica.*

SILVA, Clara (1905–1976). Uruguayan poet and novelist. Born 1905 in Montevideo, Uruguay; died 1976; m. Zum Felde (critic). ❖ Well known as a poet of *La cabellera oscura* (1945) and *Memoria de nada* (1948), did not write her 1st novel, *La sobreviviente*, until 1951; also wrote *Los delirios* (1954), *Las bodas* (1960), *Aviso a la población* (1964), *Habitación testigo* (1967), *Juicio final* (1971), *La astúcia mística* (1974) and *Los juicios del sueño* (1975).

SILVA, Francisca Julia da (1871–1920). *See Júlia, Francisca.*

SILVA, Jackie (1962—). Brazilian beach volleyball player. Name variations: Jacqueline Cruz Silva. Born Feb 13, 1962, in Rio de Janeiro, Brazil. ❖ With Sandra Pires Tavares, won a gold medal at Atlanta Olympics (1996) and was FIVB Tour champion (1996, 1996). Named WPVA Best Setter (1992) and AVP MVP (1994).

SILVA, Luisa del Valle (1896–1962). *See Valle Silva, Luisa del.*

SILVA, Maria Angelica (1966—). Brazilian basketball player. Name variations: Maria Angélica Gonçalves da Silva or Maria Angelica Goncalves da Silva; also known as Branca Silva. Born Jan 10, 1966, in Osvaldo Cruz, São Paulo, Brazil; sister of Paula Silva (basketball player). ❖ Won a team silver medal at Atlanta Olympics (1996).

SILVA, Maria Helena Vieira da (b. 1908). *See Vieira da Silva, Maria Elena.*

SILVA, Maria Tereza Cayetana de (1762–1802). *See Cayetana, Maria del Pilar Teresa.*

SILVA, Paula (1962—). Brazilian basketball player. Name variations: Maria Paula Silva; Maria Paul Gonçalves de Silva; Magic Paula. Born Mar 11, 1962, in Osvaldo Cruz, São Paulo, Brazil; sister of Cássia Silva. ❖ A Brazilian superstar, won a team gold medal at Pan American Games (1992) and World championships (1994); won a team silver medal at Atlanta Olympics (1996).

SILVA, Raquel (1978—). Brazilian volleyball player. Born April 30, 1978, in Brazil. ❖ Outside hitter, won a team bronze medal at Sydney Olympics (2000).

SILVA E ORTA, Teresa M. da (c. 1711–1793). Brazilian-born novelist. Name variations: Teresa Margarida da Silva e Orta; (pseudonym) Dorothea or Dorotéia Engrássia Tavareda Dalmira. Born c. 1711 in São Paulo, Brazil; died 1793 in Portugal; dau. of José Ramos da Silva and Catarina Horta; sister of Matias Aires Ramos da Silva (writer); m. Pedro Jansen von Praet. ❖ Moved with family to Portugal (1716); married at 16 against wishes of family and was disinherited; one of the leading intellectual women in Portugal, wrote a study on the expulsion of Jesuits from Brazil and Portugal; under the name Dorotéia Engrássia Tavareda Dalmira, wrote the political and philosophical *roman à clef, Máximas de Virtude e Formosura de Tebas, Venceram os Mais Apertados Lances da Desgraça* (Maximas of Virtue and Beauty with which Diófanes, Climeneia and Hemirena, Princes of Thebes, Overcame the Most Rigorous Trials of Adversity, 1752), the only anti-absolutist work published in Portugal in this period. A 2nd edition was published as *Aventuras de Diófanes*; by the 3rd edition the title page attributed the work to the diplomat Alexandre de Gusmão; it was not until Ernesto Enes wrote a definitive biography of her in 1938 that her authorship was acknowledged.

SILVA VILA, María Inés (1926—). Uruguayan novelist and short-story writer. Name variations: Maria Ines Silva Vila. Born 1926 in Uruguayan. ❖ Works include *La mano de nieve* (1951), *Felicidad y otras tristezas* (1964), *Salto Cancan* (1969), and *Los rebeldes del 800* (1971).

SILVAIN, Louise (1883–1970). *See Sylvie.*

SILVER, Joan Micklin (1935—). American film producer, screenwriter, and director. Born Joan Micklin, May 24, 1935, in Omaha, Nebraska; dau. of Russian-Jewish immigrants, Maurice David Micklin (businessman) and Doris (Shoshone) Micklin; Sarah Lawrence College, BA, 1956; m. Raphael D. Silver (b. 1930, real-estate entrepreneur), June 28, 1956; children: Dina Silver (producer); Marisa Silver (director); Claudia Silver (director). ❖ Wrote and directed several educational shorts for the Learning Corporation of America, including *The Immigrant Experience*; formed Midwest Film Productions with husband and made directorial feature debut with *Hester Street* (1975), a multimillion-dollar sleeper; also directed *Between the Lines* (1977), *Head Over Heels* (1979), which was re-released as *Chilly Scenes of Winter* (1982), *Crossing Delancey* (1988) and *Loverboy* (1990); for tv, directed "Bernice Bobs Her Hair" (1976) and "Finnegan Begin Again" (1985); for stage, developed and directed musical revue *Maybe I'm Doing It Wrong* and feminist revue *A . . . My Name Is Alice*. ❖ See also *Women in World History*.

SILVIA SOMMERLATH (1943—). Queen of Sweden. Name variations: Queen Silvia. Born Silvia Renate Sommerlath on Dec 23, 1943, in Heidelberg, Baden-Wurttemberg, Germany; grew up in Brazil; dau. of Alice Soares de Toledo (Brazilian) and Walter Sommerlath (German industrialist); graduated from the Munich School of Interpreting, 1969; m. Carl XVI Gustavus, also known as Charles XVI Gustavus (1946–1973), king of Sweden (r. 1973—), on June 19, 1976, at Storkyrkan Cathedral, Stockholm; children: Victoria (b. 1977); Carl Philip (b. 1979); Madeleine (b. 1982). ❖ Moved to Germany with family (1957); became an interpreter for a Spanish firm at international conventions; as chief hostess of Munich Olympics (1972), met Prince Carl Gustav of Sweden (Carl XVI Gustavus); engaged (Mar 1976); became 25th queen of Sweden (June 19); introduced new economy measures to the castle and disposed of excess ceremony attached to her station, such as curtsying at court; a believer in gender equality, successfully urged husband to support legislation to change the laws of monarchical succession from 1st son to 1st child (1979); advocated on behalf of disabled and disadvantaged children; took part in 1st World Congress against Commercial Sexual Exploitation of Children, held in Stockholm (1996); established World Childhood Foundation. Received "Deutsche Kulturpreis" (1990) and Chancellor's Medal from University of Massachusetts. ❖ See also *Women in World History*.

SILVIE, Louise (1883–1970). *See Sylvie.*

SIM, Sheila (1922—). English actress. Name variations: Sheila Attenborough. Born Sheila Beryl Grant Sim, June 5, 1922, in Liverpool, England; sister of actor Gerald Sim; m. Richard Attenborough (actor), 1945; children: Charlotte Attenborough (actress), Michael Attenborough (director) and Jane Attenborough (killed in tsunami while vacationing in Phuket, Thailand, 2004). ❖ Made stage debut at Croyden in *1066 and All That* (1939); succeeded Nova Pilbeam as Fenella in *This Was a Woman* (1944); other plays include *Tomorrow's Child, St. Joan* (title role), *Oak Leaves and Lavender, School for Spinsters* and *Double Image*; co-starred opposite husband in original production of Agatha Christie's *The Mousetrap* (1952); films include *A Canterbury Tale, Great Day, The Guinea Pig, Dear Mr. Prohack, West of Zanzibar* and *The Night My Number Came Up.*

SIMAGINA, Irina (1982—). Russian jumper. Born May 25, 1982, in Ryazan, USSR. ❖ Won a silver medal for long jump at Athens Olympics (2004).

SIMAITE, Ona (1899–1970). Lithuanian hero. Name variations: Ona Simajte. Born 1899 in Lithuania; died 1970 in France. ❖ During World War II, was a librarian at Vilnius University; used her position to aid Jews in Vilna Ghetto (1941–44); entered the ghetto under the pretext of recovering library books; smuggled food and other provisions in, and literary and historical documents out; was arrested and tortured (1944); deported to Dachau, then a concentration camp in southern France; lived in France after the war. Named "Righteous Among the Nations" by Yad Vashem.

SIMBERG, Wyomia (1945—). *See Tyus, Wyomia.*

SIMCOX, Edith (1844–1901). British journalist, labor activist, and social reformer. Name variations: (pseudonym) H. Lawrenny. Born Aug 21, 1844; died Sept 15, 1901; dau. of Jemima Haslope and George Price Simcox (merchant). ❖ Perhaps best remembered as one of novelist George Eliot's (Mary Anne Evans) most ardent admirers, earned esteem for her own substantial contributions to economic theory and social reform in England; for more than 25 years, contributed reviews under pseudonym "H. Lawrenny" on literature and economics to the distinguished journal *The Academy*; developed her own socialist ideas, which formed the basis of her work on behalf of women and laborers; with Emma Paterson, formed Shirt and Collar Makers' Union (1875); also partnered with Mary Hamilton in creating a cooperative shirt-making workshop, Hamilton and Co., which provided women with useful employment under humane conditions (1875); elected to London School Board as the Radical candidate (1879); writings include *Natural Law: An Essay in Ethics* (1877), *Episodes in the Lives of Men, Women and Lovers* (1882) and *Primitive Civilizations; or, Outlines of the History of Ownership in Archaic Communities* (1894). ❖ See also *A Monument to the Memory of George Eliot: Edith Jemima Simcox's Autobiography of a Shirtmaker* (ed. by Fulmer and Barfield, Garland, 1998); and *Women in World History*.

SIMEONI, Sara (1953—). Italian high jumper. Born April 19, 1953, in Verona, Italy. ❖ Won a silver medal at Montreal Olympics (1976) and a gold medal at Moscow Olympics (1980); won a bronze medal at European championships (1982) and a silver medal at Los Angeles Olympics (1984). ❖ See also *Women in World History*.

SIMIONATO, Giulietta (1910—). Italian mezzo-soprano. Born Giulietta Simionato, May 12, 1910, in Forlì, Italy; studied in Rovigo with Locatello and in Milan with Palumbo; grew up on island of Sardinia. ❖ Won 1st place in a bel canto competition in Florence (1933); sang in premiere of Pizzetti's *Orsèolo* (1933); debuted at Teatro alla Scala in Milan, singing Beppe in *L'Amico Fritz* (1936); continued to sing secondary roles at La Scala for next 8 years, then struck out on her own; performed throughout Italy in such leading roles as Carmen (1944–57); debuted at Edinburgh Festival (1947); invited back to La Scala, sang title role in *Mignon* (1947) and remained a star in Milan for the rest of her career, particularly acclaimed for roles in such operas as *Anna Bolena, Il Barbiere di Siviglia, La Favorita* and *I Capuleti ed i Montecchi*; also performed internationally, singing to wide praise in Salzburg, London, Vienna, Mexico City, Paris, Madrid, Geneva and Rio de Janeiro, among other cities; sang for 1st time in US (1954), in Bellini's *Norma* with Maria Callas at Chicago Lyric Opera; made successful Metropolitan Opera debut as Azucena in *Il Trovatore* and continued to perform there until her retirement (1966). ❖ See also *Women in World History*.

SIMKHOVITCH, Mary (1867–1951). American social reformer. Born Mary Melinda Kingsbury, Sept 8, 1867, in Chestnut Hill, Massachusetts; died Nov 15, 1951, in New York, NY; dau. of Isaac Franklin Kingsbury and Laura (Holmes) Kingsbury; Boston University, BA, 1890; m. Vladimir Gregorievitch Simkhovitch (economics professor), Jan 1899; children: Stephen (b. 1902); Helena (b. 1904). ❖ Key figure in the settlement house movement during 1st half of 20th century, founded the Association of Neighborhood Workers (1901); established Greenwich House (1902), which under her 45 years of guidance became a primary influence in the settlement house movement; active in politics, served on the Mayor's Public Recreation Commission (1911), on the executive board of the National Consumers' League starting 1917, and was a member of the New York City Recreation Committee (1925); appointed vice chair of the New York City Housing Authority (1934); writings include *The City Worker's World* (1917), *Neighborhood: My Story of Greenwich House* (1938), *Group Life* (1940) and *Here is God's Plenty* (1949). ❖ See also *Women in World History*.

SIMKINS, Modjeska M. (1899–1992). African-American civil-rights activist and educator. Born Mary Modjeska Monteith, Dec 5, 1899, in South Carolina; died April 5, 1992; dau. of Henry Clarence Monteith and Rachel Evelyn (Hull) Monteith; Benedict College, AB, 1921; also attended Columbia University, Morehouse College, University of Michigan, and Eastern Michigan University (then Michigan State Normal School); m. Andrew Whitfield Simkins (businessman). ❖ Taught at Booker T. Washington School in Columbia, South Carolina; served as "Director of Negro Work" for South Carolina Tuberculosis Association (1931–42); when the state senate demanded that all state employees break from NAACP, refused and was fired; began her long campaign as an agitator for civil rights.

SIMMERN, Anne (1616–1684). *See Gonzaga, Anne de.*

SIMMERN, duchess of. *See Marie of Brandenburg-Kulmbach (1519–1567).*

SIMMERN, Elizabeth (1618–1680). *See Elizabeth of Bohemia.*

SIMMONS, Coralie (1977—). American water-polo player. Born Mar 1, 1977, in Hemet, CA. ❖ Won a team silver medal at Sydney Olympics (2000).

SIMMONS, Erin (1976—). Canadian snowboarder. Born July 9, 1976, in Vancouver, British Columbia, Canada. ❖ Won silver in Snowboarder X at X Games (Winter 2001 and 2002); received ISF World Ranking of 3rd in Boardercross for Season End 2001; finished 1st at USASA National championship, Mammoth Mountain, CA, in Boardercross (2002).

SIMMONS, Gertrude (1876–1938). *See Bonnin, Gertrude Simmons.*

SIMMONS, Jean (1929—). English actress. Born Jean Merilyn Simmons, Jan 31, 1929, in Crouch Hill, London, England; dau. of Charles Simmons (physical education teacher) and Winifred Ada (Loveland) Simmons; m. Stewart Granger (actor), Dec 20, 1950 (div. 1960); m. Richard Brooks (director), Nov 1, 1960 (div. 1977); children: (1st m.) Tracy Granger; (2nd m.) Kate Brooks. ❖ At 15, made film debut in *Give Us the Moon* (1944); at 16, played Estella in *Great Expectations* (1946); appeared as Ophelia in Laurence Olivier's film of *Hamlet* (1948), for which she won Best Actress at Venice Festival and was nominated for Academy Award; made US film debut in *Androcles and the Lion* (1953); made 3 other films in 1953—*The Actress, Young Bess* and *The Robe*—all considered to be among her best; appeared in historical dramas *The Egyptian* and *Desiree* (both 1954); became US citizen (1956); made *Elmer Gantry* (1960), one of her most memorable films, followed by *All the Way Home* (1963); received 2nd Oscar nomination for *The Happy Ending* (1969); toured in musical *A Little Night Music* (1970s); other films include *Black Narcissus* (1947), *Guys and Dolls* (1955), *Hilda Crane* (1956), *This Could Be the Night* (1957), *Until They Sail* (1957), *Spartacus* (1960) and *The Grass Is Greener* (1960). ❖ See also *Women in World History.*

SIMMONS, Ruth J. (1945—). African-American educator. Born Ruth Jean Stubblefield, July 3, 1945, in Grapeland, Texas, in a sharecropper's shack; dau. of Isaac and Fannie Stubblefield; Dillard University, BA, 1967; Harvard University, AM, 1970, PhD in romance languages, 1973; m. Norbert Simmons, 1968 (div. 1989); children: daughter Khari; (adopted) Maya. ❖ Was an instructor in French at George Washington University (1968–69), then admissions officer at Radcliffe College (1970–72); at University of New Orleans, was assistant professor of French (1973–75) and assistant dean of the college of liberal arts (1975–76); was assistant dean of graduate school of University of Southern California (1979–82), then associate dean (1982–83); was an administrator at Princeton for 7 years (1983–90); served as provost of Spelman College (1990–92), then vice provost at Princeton (1992–95); was president of Smith College (1995–2000); became president of Brown University (2000), the 1st black president of an Ivy League institution.

SIMMONS-CARRASCO, Heather (1970—). American synchronized swimmer. Name variations: Heather Simmons Carrasco. Born May 25, 1970, in Mountain View, CA. ❖ Won a team gold medal at Atlanta Olympics (1996).

SIMMS, Florence (1873–192?). American industrial/social reformer. Name variations: Daisy Florence Simms. Born Daisy Florence Simms, April 17, 1873, in Rushville, ID; died Jan 6, 1923, in Mattoon, IL; dau. of Michael M. Simms (farmer) and Jennie (Taylor) Simms. ❖ Joined YWCA American Committee as national secretary in college department (1895); established and served as director of YWCA's new industrial department (from 1909); formed "industrial clubs," which provided religious, labor, and recreational programs in factories, mills, and other workplaces across US; headed War Work Council's Industrial Commission and traveled across Europe to explore possibility of creating international labor standards for women; helped create 1st National Assembly of Industrial Girls. ❖ See also Richard Roberts, *Florence Simms: A Biography* (1926).

SIMMS, Ginny (1915–1994). American band singer and actress. Born May 25, 1915, in San Antonio, TX; raised in CA; died April 4, 1994, in Palm Springs, CA; attended Fresno State College; m. Hyatt von Dehn, 1945 (div. 1951); m. Bob Calhoun, 1951 (div. 1952); m. Don Eastvold, 1962; children: 7. ❖ Band singer and actress, was featured with Kay Kyser's orchestra; had her own radio show on NBC; became an MGM contract player in 1940s; films include *That's Right You're Wrong, You'll*

Find Out, Playmates, Hit the Ice, Shady Lady, Seven Days Leave, Broadway Rhythm and *Night and Day*; retired from films (1951); recorded such songs as "It Could Happen to You," "There Goes that Song Again," "Cuddle Up a Little Closer," "In the Still of the Night," "You'd Be So Nice to Come Home To," "The Man I Love," "Till the End of Time" and "My Heart Sings."

SIMMS, Hilda (1920–1994). African-American stage and screen actress. Born Hilda Moses, April 15, 1920, in Minneapolis, MN; died Feb 6, 1994, in Buffalo, NY; m. Richard Angarola (div.). ❖ Made stage debut in St. Paul in *Kiss the Boys Goodbye* (1937); made NY debut in *Three's a Family* (1944); probably best remembered for performance in the title role in *Anna Lucasta* (1944), which ran for 2 years; other plays include *The Cool World, The Gentle People, Tambourines to Glory* and *The Madwoman of Chaillot*; had her own radio program, "Ladies' Day with Hilda Simms" (1954–57); on tv, had recurring role on "The Nurses" (1962); films include *The Joe Louis Story.*

SIMMS, Ruth Hanna McCormick (1880–1944). *See McCormick, Ruth Hanna.*

SIMON, Carly (1945—). American musician. Born June 25, 1945, in New York, NY; sister of Lucy Simon (folksinger and composer) and Joanna Simon (opera singer); attended Sarah Lawrence College; m. James Taylor (musician), Nov 3, 1972 (div. 1983); m. James Hart, Dec 23, 1987; children: (1st m.) Sally and Ben. ❖ Performed in NY with sister, Lucy, as folk duo, the Simon Sisters, who had minor hit with "Winken, Blinken and Nod" (1964); pursued solo career; hit #10 with "That's the Way I've Always Heard It Should Be" from debut LP; released successful album, *Anticipation* (1971), with hit title track, winning Best New Artist Grammy; released gold albums, *No Secrets* (1972) and *Hotcakes* (1973); other hit songs include "You're So Vain" (1972), "You Belong to Me" (1978), and "Why" (1982); other albums include *Playing Possum* (1974), *Spoiled Girl* (1985), and *Film Noir* (1997); recorded theme song, "Nobody Does It Better," for James Bond film *The Spy Who Love Me* (1977), which hit #2; released 1st platinum album, *Boys in the Trees* (1978); composed music for films, hitting Top 20 with "Coming Around Again" from *Heartburn* (1987), and winning Best Original Song Grammy for "Let the River Run" from *Working Girl* (1988); was diagnosed with breast cancer (1997), undergoing mastectomy and chemotherapy, and dealt with experience on album, *The Bedroom Tapes* (2000); wrote several children's books, including *Amy the Dancing Bear* (1989) and *Midnight Farm* (1997).

SIMON, Else (1900–1942). *See Yva.*

SIMON, Jennifer Jones (b. 1919). *See Jones, Jennifer.*

SIMON, Kate (1912–1990). Polish-born American autobiographer and travel writer. Born Kaila Grobsmith, Dec 5, 1912, in Warsaw, Poland; died Feb 4, 1990, in New York, NY; dau. of Jacob Grobsmith (shoemaker) and Lina Babica (corsetiere); Hunter College, BA, 1935; lived with Stanley F. Goldman (physician, died 1942); m. Robert Simon (publisher), 1947 (div. 1960); children: daughter Alexandra (died 1954). ❖ Widely praised for her lively and entertaining prose, established literary reputation as a travel writer with publication of her successful *New York Places and Pleasures* (1959), and went on to write similar guides for such cities as Mexico, Paris, London and Italy; was considered a master of the genre; writings include *Italy: the Places in Between* (1970, 1984), *England's Green and Pleasant Land* (1974), *Fifth Avenue: A Very Social History* (1978) and *A Renaissance Tapestry: The Gonzaga of Mantua* (1988). Received awards from National Book Critics Circle and the English Speaking Union. ❖ See also memoirs *Bronx Primitive: Portraits in a Childhood* (1982), *A Wider World: Portraits in an Adolescence* (1986) and *Etchings in an Hour Glass* (1990); and *Women in World History.*

SIMON, Lidia (1973—). Romanian marathon runner. Name variations: Lidia Slavuteanu-Simon. Born Lidia Slavuteanu, Sept 4, 1973, in Targu Carbunesti, Romania. ❖ Won a silver medal at Sydney Olympics (2000) and a gold medal at World championships (2001).

SIMON, Simone (1910–2005). French actress. Born April 23, 1910, in Béthune, France; died Feb 22, 2005, in Paris, France; dau. of engineer father and Italian mother; never married; no children. ❖ Worked briefly as a fashion designer and model before being discovered by Russian director Victor Tourjansky, who offered her a part in *Le Chanteur inconnu* (1931); after roles in several additional French films, among them *Mam'zelle Nitouche* (1931), *Le Lac aux Dames* (1934) and *Les Beaux Jours* (1935), made US debut in *Girls' Dormitory* (1936), followed by

Seventh Heaven (1937), *Love and Hisses* (1937) and *Josette* (1938); despite growing popularity in US, returned to France; following her glowing performance in Claude Renoir's *La Bête humaine* (*The Human Beast*, 1938), returned to Hollywood for *Cat People* (1942) and its sequel *Curse of the Cat People* (1943), now considered classics; continued to make French, English and European movies (mid-1950s), then was not seen on screen again until 1973, when she appeared in *La Femme en Bleu*; also appeared in *La Ronde* (1950), *Olivia* (*Pit of Loneliness*, 1951) and *La Plaisir* (*House of Pleasure*, 1952), among others. ❖ See also *Women in World History.*

SIMONE (1877–1985). See Simone, Madame.

SIMONE, Kirsten (1934—). Danish ballet dancer. Born July 1, 1934, in Copenhagen, Denmark. ❖ Trained under Vera Volkova and Gerda Karstens at Royal Danish Ballet before joining company (1952); promoted to soloist (1956) and first solist (1966); danced principal roles in Bournonville repertory to great acclaim, including in *A Folk Tale*, *The King's Volunteers on Amager*, and *Napoli*; had leading roles in *Swan Lake*, *Sleeping Beauty*, *Giselle*, Petit's *Cyrano de Bergerac*, Ashton's *Romeo and Juliet*, and Balanchine's *Four Temperaments*, *Apollo* and *Bourée Fantasque*; created roles in Flindt's *The Three Musketeers* (1966), von Rosen's *Don Juan* (1967) and Lander's *Fête polonaise* (1970); guested with American Ballet Theatre and London Festival Ballet.

SIMONE, Madame (1877–1985). French actress. Name variations: Simone; Mme Simone; Mme Simone Le Bargy; Pauline Benda. Born Pauline Benda, April 3, 1877, in Paris, France; died in 1985; m. Claude Casimir-Perier, 1909. ❖ Made stage debut at the Théâtre Molière in Brussels; than appeared in Paris in Bernstein's *Le Détour* (1902); appeared in several plays by Bernstein and two by Rostand (*Chantecler* and *L'Aiglon*); made London debut in an English version of *L'Adversaire* (1905) and NY debut in *The Thief* (1911); other plays include *Frou-Frou*, *The Paper Chase*, *Le Secret*, *Pétard*, *La jeune fille aux Jones Roses*, *La Rafale*, *Le Passé* and *Les femmes savantes.*

SIMONE, Nina (1933–2003). African-American singer, songwriter, and pianist. Born Eunice Kathleen Waymon, Feb 21, 1933, in Tryon, NC; died April 21, 2003, in Carry-le-Rouet, France; dau. of John Divan Waymon (day laborer) and Mary Kate Irvin (minister); attended Juilliard School in NY; m. Donald Ross, 1958 (div. 1959); m. Andy Stroud, 1961 (div. 1970); children: Lisa Celeste Stroud (b. 1961, singer as Lisa Simone Kelly). ❖ Perhaps one of the most difficult singers to categorize, began playing piano at 3; intent on becoming the 1st black concert pianist, earned scholarship to Juilliard; when racism intervened, played and sang in a nightclub (1954), changing name to Nina Simone; cut album *Little Girl Blue* (1957), which included "I Loves You, Porgy," a Top-20 hit; had 1st concert at NY's Town Hall; released at least 9 albums, half of which were live (1960s), then 7 more in a 3-year period; wrote "Mississippi Goddam" which became an anthem for the civil-rights movement; for the rest of the decade, was regarded as the singer of the civil-rights movement, with songs like "Sunday in Savannah," "Backlash Blues," and the ballad "To Be Young, Gifted, and Black"; tired of racism in US, began a 15-year exile (1970), residing in Switzerland, Liberia, Barbados, France and England; recorded little with the exception of the critically acclaimed album *Baltimore* (1978); returned to US (1985), performing in several concerts and recording album *Nina's Back*; re-release of her 1958 rendition of "My Baby Just Cares for Me" became a hit in Europe (1987); settled in Bouc-Bel-Air in south of France (1991); signed with Elektra, recording *A Single Woman*, and was featured on soundtrack of film *Point of No Return* (1993). ❖ See also autobiography (with Stephen Cleary), *I Put a Spell on You* (1991); and *Women in World History.*

SIMONETTA, Bianca. See Sforza, Bianca Simonetta.

SIMONETTO DE PORTELA, Noemi (1926—). Argentinean long jumper. Born Feb 1, 1926, in Buenos Aires, Argentina. ❖ At London Olympics, won a silver medal in the long jump (1948); won 21 national titles and 11 South American championships.

SIMONIS, Anita (1926—). American gymnast. Name variations: Anita Zetts. Born Mar 1926. ❖ At London Olympics, won a bronze medal in team all-around (1948).

SIMONOVICH-EFIMOVA, Nina (1877–1948). Russian artist and puppet maker. Name variations: Nina Efimova Simonovich or Simonovicha. Born Nina Yakovlevna Simonovicha, 1877, in St. Petersburg, Russia; died 1948; dau. of Yakov Mironovich Simonovich (pediatrician) and Adelaida Semyonovna Bergman (kindergarten advocate); niece of

composer Valentina Serova; cousin of painter Valentin Serov; studied painting with O. Shmerling, and in the Paris studios of Delécluze, Eugene Carrière, and Henri Matisse; m. Ivan Efimov (sculptor), 1906; children: Adrian. ❖ Found true calling after she and husband opened their 1st puppet theater (1918); created innovative rod-puppets that were detailed and vivid enough to communicate high drama; with husband, gave 1,500 puppet theater performances (1918–36) and also staged several of Shakespeare's plays, with *Macbeth* considered the standout. ❖ See also *Women in World History.*

SIMONS, Ann (1980—). Belgian judoka. Born Sept 28, 1980, in Belgium. ❖ Won a bronze medal for -48 kg extra-lightweight at Sydney Olympics (2000).

SIMONS, Beverly (1938—). Canadian playwright. Name variations: Beverly Rosen Simons. Born 1938 in Flin Flon, Manitoba, Canada. ❖ Studied at McGill University and University of British Columbia; works include *Crabdance* (1969), *The Green Lawn Rest at Home* (1973), *Preparing/Crusader/Triangle* (1975) and *Leela Means to Play* (1976).

SIMONS, Frieda Hennock (1904–1960). See Hennock, Frieda B.

SIMONS, Judikje (1904–1943). See Themans-Simons, Judikje.

SIMONS, Nancy (1938—). American swimmer. Name variations: Nancy Joan Simons. Born May 20, 1938. ❖ At Melbourne Olympics, won a silver medal in 4 x 100-meter freestyle relay (1956).

SIMONS DE RIDDER, Alexandra (1963—). German equestrian. Name variations: Alexandra Simons-de Ridder. Born Alexandra Simons, Oct 29, 1963, in Köln, Germany; m. Ton de Ridder. ❖ Won a gold medal for team dressage at Sydney Olympics (2000), on Chacomo.

SIMPSON, Adele (1903–1995). American fashion designer. Born Adele Smithline, Dec 8, 1903, in New York, NY; died Aug 23, 1995, in Greenwich, Connecticut; dau. of Latvian immigrants; studied design at Pratt Institute; m. Wesley Simpson (textile executive), 1927 (died 1976); children: Jeffrey Simpson; Joan Simpson Raines (who succeeded her mother as head of Adele Simpson). ❖ Began working as a dress designer at Ben Gershel's 7th Avenue design house, which made ready-to-wear dresses (early 1920s); enjoyed meteoric rise, becoming NY's highest paid designer by age 21 and replacing older sister Anna as head designer at Gershel's; moved to Mary Lee Fashions (1928), where she began designing a line of clothing under her own label; purchased Mary Lee Fashions and renamed it Adele Simpson (1949); created Adele Simpson line, featuring classically cut suits and matching jacket and dress ensembles, dressing celebrities, as well as a generation of upper-middle-class American women, in her meticulously constructed ready-to-wear fashions; was so popular that first ladies Lady Bird Johnson and Pat Nixon considered her their favorite designer; retired (1985). Won Coty American Fashion Critics award (1947). ❖ See also *Women in World History.*

SIMPSON, Carole (1940—). African-American broadcast journalist. Name variations: Carole Simpson Marshall. Born Dec 7, 1940, in Chicago, Illinois; University of Michigan, BA in journalism, 1962; m. James Marshall; children: Adam and Mallika. ❖ Served as Washington correspondent on "NBC Nightly News" (1974–82); was substitute news anchor on "Good Morning America" (1988–95) and Sunday anchor on "ABC Evening News" (1988–2003).

SIMPSON, Edna Oakes (1891–1984). American politician. Born Oct 26, 1891, in Carrollton, Greene Co., Illinois; died May 15, 1984, in Alton, Illinois; m. Sidney E. Simpson (8-term US congressional representative, died 1958). ❖ Following husband's death during his 8th term as a Republican US congressional representative from Illinois 20th Congressional District (Nov 1958), won election in his place; served a single term (Jan 3, 1959–Jan 3, 1961), then declined to seek reelection. ❖ See also *Women in World History.*

SIMPSON, Elspeth (1738–1791). See Buchan, Elspeth.

SIMPSON, Fiona (1965—). Australian politician. Name variations: Fiona Stuart Simpson. Born April 18, 1965, in Sea Lake, Victoria, Australia. ❖ As a member of the National Party, elected to the Queensland Parliament for Maroochydore (1992); named shadow minister for Tourism (2001).

SIMPSON, Harriet Maria (1818–1907). See Ritchie, Harriet Maria.

SIMPSON, Helen (1897–1940). Australian-born British writer. Born Helen de Guerry Simpson, Dec 1, 1897, in Sydney, Australia; died during

German bombing of London, Oct 14, 1940; dau. of Edward Percy Simpson (solicitor) and Anne (de Lauret) Simpson; m. Denys (or Denis) John Browne, in 1927; children: daughter Clemence. ❖ Best known for her detective novels, worked as a decoder (1914–18), unscrambling secret messages for the British Admiralty during WWI; produced a wide range of work, including plays, novels, translations from the French, histories, biographies, and even recipe books; claim to fame, however, rests in her 5 mystery or detective novels, 3 of which were written in collaboration with Clemence Dane: *Enter Sir John* (1928), *Printer's Devil* (1930) and *Re-Enter Sir John* (1932); used an Australian setting for 2 of her most famous works of fiction: *Boomerang* (1932) and *Under Capricorn* (1937); also wrote *Saraband for Dead Lovers* (1935), a translation from the French of *Heartsease and Honesty, being the Pastimes of the Sieur de Grammont, Steward to the Duc de Richelieu in Touraine* (1935), and (with Dane) a biography of Mary Kingsley, *A Woman Among Wild Men* (1938). Won James Tait Black Memorial Prize for *Boomerang*. ❖ See also *Women in World History*.

SIMPSON, Helen Ann (1793/94–1871). *See Wilson, Helen Ann.*

SIMPSON, Janet (1944—). English runner. Born Sept 1944 in UK. ❖ At Tokyo Olympics, won a bronze medal in 4 x 100-meter relay (1964).

SIMPSON, Juliene (1953—). American basketball player. Born Jan 20, 1953; attended John F. Kennedy College in Nebraska; married Mike Simpson; children: Jennifer and Shannon. ❖ Was 4-time AAU All-American; at Montreal Olympics, won a silver medal in team competition (1976); coached at Arizona State University (1979–87), Whitworth College (1988–91), Bucknell University (1991–97), Marshall (1997–2000) and East Stroudsburg University. Inducted into Women's Basketball Hall of Fame (2000).

SIMPSON, Mary Elizabeth (1865–1948). New Zealand religious teacher, healer, and writer. Name variations: Mary Elizabeth Gething. Born Mary Elizabeth Gething, June 10, 1865, at Christchurch, New Zealand; died Sept 19, 1948, at Christchurch; dau. of Joseph Brunt (innkeeper) and Hannah Gething; m. William Simpson (wood turner), 1884 (died 1943); children: 2 daughters, 1 son. ❖ Considered the founder of Christian Science church in New Zealand, was active in social and political work; joined Canterbury Women's Institute (1895); began holding Christian Science meetings in her home (early 1900s); formed Christian Science Society (1907); trained in Sydney, Australia, as accredited practitioner (1910), and became 1st Christian Science practitioner from New Zealand listed in *Christian Science Journal* (1911); traveled to Boston to train as authorized teacher (1913); devoted time to religious healing and lecturing before leaving Christian Science church due to rift (1925); founded Divine Science Fellowship and became its leader, traveling to US to teach and lecture; published *New Zealand Bellbird* and wrote several books as forum for her beliefs, including *Daily Doses of Mental Tonic* (1940). ❖ See also *Dictionary of New Zealand Biography* (Vol. 3).

SIMPSON, Mary Michael (1925—). American priest and psychotherapist. Born Dec 1, 1925, in Evansville, Indiana; dau. of Link Wilson Simpson and Mary Garrett (Price) Simpson; Texas Women's University, BA, BS, 1946; graduate of New York Training School for Deaconesses, 1949, and Westchester Institute Training in Psychoanalysis and Psychotherapy, 1976. ❖ Began career with Episcopal Church as a missionary at Holy Cross Mission in Bolahun, Liberia (1950); returned to US (1952); served as academic head of Margaret Hall School, a girls' school run by the Episcopal Order of St. Anne in Versailles, KY (1958–61); a member of the Order of St. Helena (offshoot of Order of St. Anne), then served as sister in charge of the Convent of St. Helena mission in Liberia (1962–67) and as director of novices there (1968–74); returned to US (1974) to become a pastoral counselor on staff of Cathedral of St. John the Divine in New York City; opened her own private practice as a psychoanalyst (1974), adding on a directorship of the Cathedral Counseling Service (1975); was the 1st American nun to be ordained an Episcopal priest (1977); added to her duties at Cathedral of St. John the Divine by becoming a canon there, the 1st woman canon in American Episcopal Church (1977); was 1st ordained woman invited to preach at Britain's Westminster Abbey (1978); wrote *The Ordination of Women in the American Episcopal Church: The Present Situation* (1981). ❖ See also *Women in World History*.

SIMPSON, Mrs. (1895–1986). *See Windsor, Wallis Warfield, duchess of.*

SIMPSON, Nicole Brown (1959–1994). American murder victim. Born May 19, 1959, in Dana Point, CA; murdered June 12, 1994; sister of Denise Brown; m. O. J. Simpson, 1985 (div. 1992); children: Sydney (b. 1985) and Justin (b. 1988). ❖ Suffered from domestic violence during marriage; was found murdered with Ronald Goldman (1994); ex-husband O. J. Simpson was charged with the crime but acquitted after sensational trial (though he was found liable for the deaths in a civil trial).

SIMPSON, Ryllis Barnes (1906–1978). *See Hasoutra.*

SIMPSON, Sherone (1984—). Jamaica runner. Born Aug 12, 1984, in Jamaica. ❖ Won a gold medal for the 4 x 100-meter relay at Athens Olympics.

SIMPSON, Valerie (1946—). African-American songwriter, pop singer, and record producer. Born in the Bronx, NY, Aug 26, 1946; sister of Ray Simpson, lead vocalist for Village People; studied music at Chatham Square School; m. Nickolas Ashford (songwriter), 1974. ❖ Joined with future husband to become the writing team of Ashford and Simpson (1964); had 1st success with "Let's Go Get Stoned" (1966), sung by Ray Charles; signed with Motown and wrote a series of hits, including Marvin Gaye and Tammi Terrell's duets "Ain't No Mountain High Enough" and "You're All I Need to Get By" and Diana Ross' "Reach Out and Touch (Somebody's Hand)"; also made 2 solo albums, *Exposed!* (1971) and *Valerie Simpson* (1972); with Ashford, launched a performing career as Nick & Valerie (1973); had breakthrough with gold album *Send It* (1977), which included Top-10 hit "Don't Cost You Nothing"; followed that with another gold-seller, *Is It Still Good to Ya?* and a 3rd gold album, *Stay Free* (1979), which contained the single "Found a Cure"; had biggest hit album with *Solid* (1984); continued to create hits for such singers as Diana Ross, Gladys Knight, and Whitney Houston. ❖ See also *Women in World History*.

SIMPSON, Wallis Warfield (1895–1986). *See Windsor, Wallis Warfield, duchess of.*

SIMPSON-SERVEN, Ida (c. 1850s–c. 1896). American dance teacher. Name variations: Ida Serven. Born c. 1850s; died c. 1896, in Chicago, IL. ❖ Worked with Steele MacKaye (an acclaimed student of François Delsarte), teaching Delsarte theory and elocution to his New York City theater company; moved to Denver, CO, possibly due to family sickness; served on faculty of O. E. Howell's Conservatory of Music in Denver, taught at University of Denver, and later became principal of Denver Conservatory; taught Delsarte theories at Denver Chautauqua, where she worked with children, adults, professionals, and more; moved to Chicago, IL (1893), where she taught at Hart Conway School of Dramatic Arts; said to be of great importance for development of Delsarte theories in the West, but rarely receives credit.

SIMS, Joan (1930–2001). English comedic actress. Born Irene Joan Marian Sims, May 9, 1930, in Laindon, Essex, England; died June 27, 2001, from cardiac arrest in London. ❖ Starred in many revues, including *Intimacy at 8:30* and *High Spirits,* and more than 2 dozen "Carry On" films; appeared with Judi Dench in *The Last of the Blonde Bombshells* and the series "As Time Goes By"; other appearances include "Before the Fringe," "The Kenneth Williams Show" and as a regular on "The Floggits" and "London Lights." ❖ See also autobiography *High Spirits* (Partridge).

SIMS, Naomi (1948—). African-American entrepreneur and fashion model. Born Mar 30, 1948, in Oxford, Mississippi; graduate of Westinghouse High School in Pittsburgh; studied briefly at New York's Fashion Institute of Technology; m. Michael Findlay (art dealer); children: John Phillip. ❖ Fashion model, accepted a *New York Times* assignment that placed her on the cover of its *Fashion of the Times* supplement—the 1st for a black model; became the 1st black model published on the covers and in the pages of such Anglo-American bastions of fashion as *Vogue, Ladies' Home Journal, Life* and *Cosmopolitan* (late 1960s); dissatisfied with the quality of wigs available to African-American women, founded Naomi Sims Collection (1973); founded Naomi Sims Beauty Products (1985), with wares exclusively formulated for African-American women; also wrote several books, including *All About Health and Beauty for the Black Woman* (1975), *How to Be a Top Model* (1979) and *All about Success for the Black Woman* (1983). Named Model of the Year (1969 and 1970). ❖ See also *Women in World History*.

SIMSON, Lady (1872–1957). *See Ashwell, Lena.*

SINAIDA. *Variant of Zinaida.*

SINATRA, Nancy (1940—). American singer. Born June 8, 1940, in Jersey City, NJ; dau. of Frank Sinatra (singer and actor) and Nancy Sinatra; attended University of Southern California; m. Tommy Sands (singer and actor), Sept 11, 1960 (div. 1965); m. Hugh Lambert, Dec 12, 1970 (died Aug 18, 1985); children: (2nd m.) Angela Jennifer and Amanda. ❖ Appeared in several films, including *For Those Who Think Young* (1964), *The Wild Angels* (1966) and *Speedway* (1968); released several singles, including "Like I Do" and "Think of Me," which became hits abroad but not in US; began working with songwriter-producer Lee Hazelwood and had #1 hit with "These Boots Are Made for Walking" (1966); other hits include "Sugar Town" (1966), "Summer Wine" (1966), and the duet "Jackson" (1967); early albums include *Boots* (1966) and *Nancy and Lee* (1968); recorded popular title song for James Bond film, *You Only Live Twice* (1967); with father, had duet #1 hit with "Somethin' Stupid" (1967); retired (1968); revived career with albums *One More Time* (1995) and *California Girl* (2003); sang "Bang Bang—My Baby Shot Me Down" for film, *Kill Bill: Vol. 1* (2003).

SINCLAIR, Betty (1907–1983). English-born actress. Name variations: Bijou Sinclair. Born Feb 7, 1907, in Liverpool, England; died Sept 20, 1983, in Tenafly, NJ. ❖ Appeared on stage in England for many years; made Broadway debut in *The Winslow Boy* (1947), followed by *The Deep Blue Sea, The Doctor's Dilemma, The Apple Cart, Auntie Mame, Port-Royal, Lord Pengo, Ivanov, The Sea Gull* and *The Crucible*, among others.

SINCLAIR, Bijou (1907–1983). See Sinclair, Betty.

SINCLAIR, Catherine (fl. 1475). Duchess of Albany. Flourished around 1475; dau. of Elizabeth Douglas (d. before 1451) and William Sinclair, earl of Orkney and Caithness; m. Alexander Stewart (c. 1454–1485), 1st duke of Albany, around 1475 (div. due to propinquity of blood in 1477); children: Alexander (b. around 1477), bishop of Moray; Margaret Stewart (d. after July 5, 1542, who m. Patrick Hamilton of Kincavil); Andrew. ❖ Alexander's 2nd wife was Anne de la Tour (d. 1512).

SINCLAIR, Catherine (1780–1864). Scottish novelist and children's writer. Born April 17, 1780, in Edinburgh, Scotland; died Aug 6, 1864, in London, England; 4th dau. of Sir John Sinclair (politician and agriculturist) and Diana (Macdonald) Sinclair; aunt of Lucy Walford (1845–1915); never married; no children. ❖ Prolific and popular writer whose early children's book *Holiday House: A Series of Tales* (1839) marked a turning point in the history of children's literature, served as her father's secretary (1814–35); wrote several guidebooks, including *Shetland and the Shetlanders* and *Scotland and the Scotch* (both 1840), which are steeped in the history and folklore of the regions; following father's death, produced 2 lengthy but well-received novels, *Modern Accomplishments, or the March of the Intellect* (1836) and its conclusion, *Modern Society: or, The March of Intellect* (1837); a devout Protestant, strongly anti-Catholic, used her writing to expose "papists" in *Popish Legends or Bible Truths* (1852), *Modern Superstition* (1857), and the scathing *Beatrice* (1852); also wrote a number of religious tracts; her final and most popular projects were her *Letters* (1861–64) for children. ❖ See also *Women in World History.*

SINCLAIR, Catherine (1817–1891). English-American actress. Name variations: Catherine Norton Sinclair; Mrs. C. N. Sinclair; Catherine Forrest or Catherine Norton Sinclair Forrest. Born Catherine Norton Sinclair, Feb 20, 1817, in London, England; died June 9, 1891, in New York, NY; dau. of John Sinclair (ballad and operatic singer) and Catherine (Norton) Sinclair; m. Edwin Forrest (actor), June 23, 1837 (div. 1852, died 1872); children: 4 (all died at birth). ❖ Arrived in US following marriage (1837); traveled the theatrical circuit with well-known actor husband (1837–49); was charged by husband with infidelity (1849); received widespread newspaper coverage during divorce trial (Dec 1851–Jan 1852), winning the case; appearing as "Mrs. C. N. Sinclair, the late Mrs. Forrest" despite lack of experience as an actress, played Lady Teazle in *The School for Scandal* in NY (1852); was actress-manager at Metropolitan Theatre in San Francisco, CA (1853–55) and for Edwin Booth at Sacramento and Forrest Theatres, Sacramento, CA (1855–56); performed in Australia and England (1856–57); retired (1860).

SINCLAIR, Eleanor (d. 1518). Countess of Atholl. Died in 1518; dau. of William Sinclair, earl of Orkney and Caithness; m. John Stewart also known as John of Balveny (c. 1440–1512), 1st earl of Atholl; children: Anne Stewart (fl. 1515). John Stewart was 1st m. to Margaret Douglas (b. around 1427), the "Fair Maid of Galloway."

SINCLAIR, Elizabeth McHutcheson (1800–1892). Scottish-born farmer and plantation owner. Name variations: Often misspelled McHutchison; Eliza or Elizabeth McHutcheson. Born Elizabeth McHutcheson, April 26, 1800, in Glasgow, Scotland; died Oct 16, 1892, in Makaweli, Kauai, Hawaii; dau. of James McHutcheson (merchant) and Jean (Robertson) McHutcheson; probably aunt of Isabella McHutcheson Sinclair (nature artist and illustrator); m. Francis Sinclair (ship's captain), 1824 (died 1846); children: George, Jane, James, Helen, Francis and Anne. ❖ Immigrated with family to New Zealand (1840), settling on South Island; after death of husband at sea, established farm at Pigeon Bay (1849); left New Zealand for Vancouver Island, Canada, finally settling in Hawaii (1863); bought the Hawaiian Island of Niihau with her sons (1864), became its matriarch, and cultivated sugar cane. ❖ See also *Dictionary of New Zealand Biography* (Vol. 1) and *Notable Women of Hawaii.*

SINCLAIR, Jo (1913–1995). See Seid, Ruth.

SINCLAIR, Madge (1938–1995). Jamaican-born actress. Born April 28, 1938, in Kingston, Jamaica; died Dec 20, 1995, in Los Angeles, CA; m. Royston Sinclair (div. 1969); children: 2 sons. ❖ Appeared in *Iphigenia* at the NY Shakespeare Festival (1971); films include *Conrack, I Will I Will . . . For Now, Star Trek IV: The Voyage Home*, and *The Lion King* (as the voice of Lion Queen, Sarabi); had recurring role on "Trapper John, M. D." Won an Emmy for the series "Gabriel's Fire" (1990); nominated for Emmy for performance as Belle in "Roots" (1977).

SINCLAIR, Mary Amelia St. Clair (1863–1946). See Sinclair, May.

SINCLAIR, Mary Ann (1864–1948). See Sutherland, Mary Ann.

SINCLAIR, May (1863–1946). English novelist, critic, suffragist, and philosopher. Name variations: Mary Amelia St. Clair Sinclair; (pseudonym) Julian Sinclair. Born Mary Amelia St. Clair Sinclair in Rock Ferry, Cheshire, England, 1863; died in Aylesbury, Buckinghamshire, England, Nov 14, 1946; dau. of William Sinclair (shipowner) and Amelia (Hind) Sinclair; never married; no children. ❖ Influential writer of early 20th century, created a transitional literature between Victorianism and Modernism; published novel *The Divine Fire* (1904), which transformed her overnight from a struggling, almost anonymous figure into a novelist famous throughout the English-speaking world; prolific and energetic, wrote 24 novels, using several distinct styles: early works on philosophical idealism, a "middle period" series advocating social reform, and a later group bringing the insights of Freudian psychology to a wide popular audience; pioneered in "stream of consciousness" writing and specialized in depictions of the intense, suppressed emotionality of English family life; was also a poet, critic, and essayist, befriended many of the great literary modernists, including Ezra Pound and T. S. Eliot, and helped them in their early struggles for publication and recognition. Writings include (novels) *Mr. and Mrs. Nevill Tyson* (1898), *The Helpmate* (1907), *The Creators* (1910), *The Belfry* (1916), *The Tree of Heaven* (1917), *Mary Olivier: A Life* (1919), *Life and Death of Harriet Frean* (1922), *The Allinghams* (1927); (biography) *The Three Brontës* (1912), as well as a fictionalized version of their lives, entitled *The Three Sisters* (1914); also published a number of collections of short stories, including *Uncanny Stories* (1923) and *The Intercessor and Other Stories* (1931). ❖ See also autobiography, *A Journal of Impressions in Belgium* (1915); Theophilus E. M. Boll, *Miss May Sinclair: Novelist* (Fairleigh Dickinson U. Press, 1973); Hrisey D. Zegger, *May Sinclair* (Twayne, 1976); and *Women in World History.*

SINCLAIR, Ruth (1894–1984). See Cummings, Ruth.

SINCLAIR BURNS, Berta (1893–1972). See Burns, Violet Alberta Jessie.

SINDEN, Topsy (1878–1951). English dancer, actress and singer. Born Dec 15, 1878, in UK; died 1951; sister of Bert Sinden (1877–1911), actor and dancer. ❖ Made debut as a child (1884), performing at Empire Theatre in London in numerous productions staged by Lanner, among them *The Paris Exhibition, Dolly,* and *Cecilia*; engaged at Gaety Theatre as principal dancer in *Cinder-Ellen Up Too Late, In Town, A Gaiety Girl,* and others; danced solo in such musicals as *The Yakima* (1897) and *San-Toy* (1899); performed principal boy hero roles at London's Brittania and other theaters; replaced Adeline Genée in *The Belle of the Ball* (1908); retired around 1930.

SINGA. See Njinga.

SINGER, Eleanor (1903–1999). English doctor. Born Nov 12, 1903, in Hampstead, London, England; died Sept 10, 1999; University College London, MS, 1929; m. Sidney Fink (Communist Party organizer in

Great Britain, died 1943); m. Michael Barratt Brown (economist), 1948. ❖ Important family-planning doctor, 1st qualified as a doctor (1941); conducted research on vitamins; served as the head of Save the Children Fund, the medical unit for postwar relief in the Balkans until 1948; after marriage to Michael Barratt Brown (1948), settled and worked in Colchester and later Sheffield and Derbyshire (1948–83); played an important role in the creation of the Young People's Consultation Centres, which offered advice on the then-controversial topic of birth control; taught at University of California, Berkeley. Decorated by Marshal Tito for work with women and children in Sarajevo.

SINGER, Elizabeth (1674–1737). *See Rowe, Elizabeth Singer.*

SINGER, Heike (1964—). East German kayaker. Born July 14, 1964, in East Germany. ❖ At Seoul Olympics, won a gold medal in K4 500 meters (1988).

SINGER, Margaret (1921–2003). American psychologist. Name variations: Margaret Thaler Singer. Born Margaret Thaler, July 29, 1921, in Denver, CO; died Nov 23, 2003, in Berkeley, CA; dau. of chief operating engineer at US Mint; mother was a secretary to a federal judge; University of Denver, PhD in clinical psychology, 1943; m. Jerome R. Singer (professor of physics); children: Sam and Martha. ❖ One of the world's leading experts on cults and brainwashing, began career at Walter Reed Army Institute of Research, where, during Korean War, she specialized in studying returning American prisoners of war who had renounced the US during captivity; was a clinical psychologist and professor of psychology at University of California, Berkeley (1964–91); served as an expert witness in many high-profile trials, including that of Patricia Hearst; was also known for her work on schizophrenia.

SINGER, Winnaretta (1865–1943). American-born artist, musician, and patron of the arts. Name variations: Princess Edmond de Polignac; Princesse de Polignac; Princess Winnie; Princess de Scey-Montbéliard. Born Winnaretta Eugénie Singer, Jan 8, 1865, in Yonkers, New York; died Nov 26, 1943, in London, England; dau. of Isaac Merritt Singer (millionaire creator of the Singer sewing-machine, died 1875) and Isabelle Eugénie Boyer Singer of Paris, France; m. Prince Louis de Scey-Montbéliard, July 27, 1887 (annulled 1892); m. Prince Edmond de Polignac, Dec 15, 1893 (died Aug 8, 1901); no children. ❖ Patron of avant-garde culture, who presided over one of the most illustrious salons in Paris, moved there with family (1866); studied art in studio of Félix Barrias; exhibited paintings in Salon (1885–90); bought a large mansion on avenue Henri-Martin (1890), now home of the Fondation Singer-Polignac; bought palace in Venice (1894); translated Thoreau's *Walden,* published in *La Renaissance latine* (1903–04); established Polignac Prize in the Royal Society of Literature, London (1911); created Fondation Singer-Polignac to foster and endow artistic and scientific projects (1928); collected Impressionist paintings before they were publicly acclaimed, commissioned works by modern composers, such as Eric Satie and Igor Stravinsky, and developed friendships with Marcel Proust, Jean Cocteau, and Anna de Noailles; her generous financial subsidies ensured the success of Sergei Diaghilev's Ballets Russes in Europe. ❖ See also Michael de Cossart, *The Food of Love: Princesse Edmond de Polignac (1865–1943) and Her Salon* (Hamish Hamilton, 1978); and *Women in World History.*

SINGLETON, Anne (1887–1948). *See Benedict, Ruth.*

SINGLETON, Mary.
See Brooke, Frances (1724–1789).
See Currie, Mary Montgomerie (1843–1905).

SINGLETON, Mildred (1933—). *See McDaniel, Mildred.*

SINGLETON, Penny (1908–2003). American actress. Name variations: Dorothy McNulty. Born Mariana Dorothy McNulty, Sept 15, 1908, in Philadelphia, Pennsylvania; died Nov 12, 2003, in Sherman Oaks, CA; niece of former Postmaster General James Farley; attended Columbia University; m. Lawrence Singleton (dentist), in 1937 (div. 1939); m. Bob Sparks (film producer), 1941; children: 2 daughters. ❖ Best remembered for her portrayal of Blondie, the long-suffering wife of Dagwood Bumstead, launched her show-business career as a singer and dancer, appearing in several Broadway musicals before making her way to Hollywood; under name Dorothy McNulty, made movie debut in *Good News* (1930); made first appearance in *Blondie* (1938), which spawned 28 sequels, a long-running radio show, and 2 short-lived tv sitcoms (1957, 1968); became a union activist for American Guild of Variety Artists (AGVA); other films include *After the Thin Man* (1936), *The Mad Miss Manton* (1938), *Go West Young Lady* (1941) and *The Best*

Man (1964); was also the voice of Jane Jetson for Hanna-Barbera cartoons and feature film *Jetsons: The Movie* (1990). ❖ See also *Women in World History.*

SINGSTAD, Karin (1958—). Norwegian handball player. Born Dec 29, 1958, in Norway. ❖ At Seoul Olympics, won a silver medal in team competition (1988).

SINKO, Andrea (1967—). Hungarian rhythmic gymnast. Born Feb 11, 1967, in Budapest, Hungary; m. Laszlo Beres (pentathlete). ❖ Placed 6th in all-around at Seoul Olympics (1988); was Hungary's 6-time national champion.

SINN, Pearl (1967—). South Korean golfer. Name variations: Pearl Sinn-Bonanni. Born July 17, 1967, in Seoul, Korea; m. Greg Bonanni, 2002. ❖ Won US Women's Amateur championship (1988) and State Farm Rail Classic (1998); crossed the $1 million mark in career earnings (2002). Inducted into Arizona State University Hall of Fame (2002).

SINNIGE, Clarinda (1973—). Dutch field-hockey player. Born Jan 14, 1973, in Amsterdam, Netherlands. ❖ Goalkeeper, won a team bronze medal at Sydney Olympics (2000) and a team silver at Athens Olympics (2004); won Champions Trophy (2000) and European championship (2003).

SINOVA, Matylda (1933—). *See Matouskova-Sinova, Matylda.*

SINTENIS, Renée (1888–1965). German sculptor and engraver. Name variations: Renee Sintenis. Born Renate Alice Sintenis in Glatz, Silesia, Mar 20, 1888; died in Berlin, April 22, 1965; dau. of Bernhard Sintenis (attorney); studied art at Stuttgart Academy, 1902–05, and Berlin's School of Applied Arts, 1908–12, under Leo von König; studied sculpture with Wilhelm Haverkamp; m. Emil Rudolf Weiss (painter and printmaker, 1875–1942); no children. ❖ Artist whose sculptures of young animals and children in motion were extremely popular in pre-Nazi Germany but removed from museums as "degenerate art" during Third Reich, was awarded Olympia Prize for bronze of *The Runner Nurmi* (1932); had created other sports-inspired works, including *The Boxer* (1925), *The Football Player* (1927), and *The Polo Player* (1929); also created a number of portrait busts, including ones depicting André Gide, Joachim Ringelnatz, and Ernst Toller; created the 1st of several small bear figurines (1932), especially the "Berlin bear" which became immensely popular; an outspoken anti-Nazi, was regarded by the Third Reich as an "un-German" artist; during Allied bombing of Berlin (May 1, 1945), her studio was destroyed; after the war, taught at Academy for the Graphic Arts, becoming a full professor (1955). In US, a number of her works are held by major museums, including 2 lithographs, *Girl Seated* and *Profile of a Woman,* both in collection of National Gallery of Art; her *Bronze Donkey* is located at Farnsworth entrance of Detroit Institute of Arts. Was the 1st sculptor elected to Prussian Academy of the Arts; became a member of Order of the Pour le Mérite (1952); awarded Federal Cross for Achievement of Federal Republic of Germany (1953). ❖ See also *Women in World History.*

SINUÉS, Maria del Pilar (1835–1893). Spanish novelist. Name variations: Maria del Pilar Sinues y Navarro; Maria del Pilar Sinués de Marco. Born 1835 in Zaragoza; died 1893 in Madrid, Spain. ❖ Wrote over 100 popular novels, most of which focused on women's lives.

SIPILÄ, Helvi (1915—). Finnish lawyer and feminist. Name variations: Helvi Sipila. Born Helvi Linnea Sipilä, May 5, 1915, in Helsinki, Finland; dau. of Vilho Sipilä and Sanni Maukola; attended University of Helsinki; m. Sauli Sipilä, in 1939; children: 1 daughter, 3 sons. ❖ International advocate for women's rights, worked as an acting judge in Finland's rural districts (1941–42); served as secretary of Finland's Ministry of Supply (1943); opened her own law office (1943), only 2nd woman in Finland with a private practice; became president of International Federation of Women Lawyers (1954); served as chief commissioner of Finnish Girl Guides (1952–69); chaired the Finnish Refugee Council (1965–72); was a member of Finnish delegation to United Nations General Assembly (1966–72), member of the Council of the Human Rights Institute in Strasbourg (from 1969), and vice-president of the International Council of Women (from 1970); was Finnish representative to UN Commission on Status of Women (1960–68, 1971–72); became Assistant Secretary-General for Social Development and Humanitarian Affairs at UN (1973), the 1st woman to hold that post; served as Secretary General for UN World Conference in Mexico City (1975); retired from UN (1980), though she remained active in the Finnish commission of the UN Development Fund for Women (UNIFEM); became 1st woman to run for president of Finland (1981); spoke at opening ceremony of the

4th World Congress on Women in Beijing (1995). Received Commander of Finland's White Rose (1977), the Great Cross of Finland's Lion (1989), the inaugural Helvi Sipilä Award from US Committee for UNIFEM (1999), and International Bar Association's 1st lifetime achievement award for women, the Outstanding International Women's Award (2001).

SIPPRELL, Clara (1885–1975). Canadian-born photographer. Born Clara Estelle Sipprell in Tillsonburg, Canada, Nov 1, 1885; died in Bennington, Vermont, April 1975. ❖ Established her own studio in New York's Greenwich Village (1915); work appeared in numerous magazines, including *American Magazine of Art, American Girl, Mentor,* and *Revue du vrai et du beau;* exhibited at the 2nd and 3rd National Salon of Pictorial Photography at the Albright Art Gallery in Buffalo (1921 and 1922), the International Salon of the Pictorial Photographers of America in New York City, and at various locations in Europe, where she traveled extensively; did portraits of Gustav V of Sweden, Robert Frost, Pearl S. Buck, Sergei Rachmaninoff, and Alfred Stieglitz, among others. ❖ See also Mary Kennedy McCabe, *Clara Sipprell: Pictorial Photographer* (Amon Carter Museum); and *Women in World History.*

SIRANI, Elizabetta (1638–1665). Italian painter. Name variations: Elisabeth Sirani. Born in Bologna, Italy, 1638; died Aug 1665; dau. of Gian Andrea Sirani (1610–1670, Bolognese artist); never married; no children. ❖ Created some 170 works, including paintings, drawings, and etchings, before her suspicious death at 27; consciously modeling her style on that of Guido Reni, was known for her incredible speed; turned professional at 17 and by 1662 had about 90 works to her credit; finished another 80 or so before her death, working mostly for private patrons, though she also had some public commissions, including a large *Baptism* for the chapel of a Bolognese church; became a local celebrity and something of a tourist attraction; produced such paintings as *Judith Triumphant* (1658), *The Penitent Magdalene in the Wilderness* (1660), *Porcia Wounding her Thigh* (1664) and *Madonna and Child,* and such etchings as *St. Eustace Kneeling before a Crucifix* (1656) and *The Beheading of St. John* (1657). ❖ See also *Women in World History.*

SIRCH, Cornelia (1966—). East German swimmer. Born Oct 23, 1966, in East Germany. ❖ At Seoul Olympics, won a bronze medal in 200-meter backstroke, bronze medal in 100-meter backstroke, and gold medal in 4 x 100-meter medley relay (1988).

SIRIKIT (1932—). Queen and regent of Thailand. Name variations: Princess Mom Rajawongse Sirikit Kitiyakara or Mom Rajawong Sirikit Kitiyakara; Sirikit Kitiyakara. Born in Bangkok, Thailand, Aug 12, 1932; dau. of Prince Chandaburi Suranath (Nakkhatra Mongkol Kitiyakara), a diplomat, and Mom Luang Bua (Snidwongse) Kitiyakara; m. Bhumibol Adulyadej, also known as King Rama IX, April 28, 1950; children: Princess Ubol Ratana (b. 1951); Prince Ma Ha Vajiralongkorn (b. 1952); Crown Princess Sirindhorn (b. 1955); Princess Chulabhorn (b. 1957). ❖ Crowned queen of Thailand (1950); acted as regent (1956); was active in Thai Red Cross and public health issues; promoted Thai cottage industries by establishing the Foundation for the Promotion of Supplementary Occupations and Related Techniques (1976); as a member of the World Wildlife Fund, promoted the afforestation of one of Thailand's most arid regions and worked to protect wildlife habitats, particularly those of endangered species; was an untiring advocate for the well-being of the people of Thailand, whether it be their access to adequate health care or promotion of their livelihoods; retired from public life (1985). Received UN's Ceres Medal for her work among rural Thai women (1979) and Borobudur Gold Medal (1992) for her efforts to preserve Thailand's cultural heritage; became 1st foreigner to receive the International Humanitarian Award from Friends of the Capital Children's Museum of Washington, DC (1991). ❖ See also *Women in World History.*

SIRIMAVO (1916–2000). See Bandaranaike, Sirimavo.

SIRIN (1874–1925). See Gertsyk, Adelaida.

SIROKA, Marie (1912–1987). See Vetrovska, Marie.

SIROTA, Beate (1923—). Austrian-born feminist and opera impresario. Name variations: Beate Sirota Gordon. Born Oct 25, 1923, in Vienna, Austria; grew up in Japan; dau. of Leo Sirota (concert pianist) and Augustine (Horenstein) Sirota; m. Joseph Gordon (Japanese expert), Jan 15, 1948; children: Nicole (b. 1954); Geoffrey (b. 1958). ❖ Longtime leader in Japanese-American cultural relations, is also well known as the woman who wrote women's equality into the Japanese constitution; moved to US to attend Mills College (1939); fluent in Japanese, German,

Russian, French, Spanish, and English, found work as a translator of Japanese radio broadcasts for Office of War Information in San Francisco during World War II; following Japanese surrender (1945), returned to Japan and was employed in the American occupation government division; was assigned to write the articles on women's rights for the Civil Rights Commission during the secret drafting of the new constitution (1946); though most of her articles on women's and child social welfare were eliminated, her fundamental statements of gender equality in legal status, marriage, divorce, and property rights, and her article on academic freedom, were finally accepted; had a long association with the Asia Society (1960–93), becoming director of its performing arts program (1970). Received John D. Rockefeller III Award for her outstanding contribution to the modern Asian arts. ❖ See also memoir *The Only Woman in the Room: A Memoir* (Kodansha, 1997); and *Women in World History.*

SIRRIDGE, Marjorie S. (1921—). American physician. Born Oct 6, 1921, in Kingman, KS; m. William Sirridge (physician); graduate of Kansas State University premedical program, 1942 and University of Kansas' medical school, 1944; children: 4. ❖ Specialist in hematology, was assistant clinical professor at University of Kansas (1958–71); practiced privately with husband; was a founding faculty member of University of Missouri-Kansas City Medical School (UMKC, 1971); with husband, endowed and served as director of Sirridge Office of Medical Humanities (1992–2004); wrote *Laboratory Evaluation of Hemostasis and Thrombosis.*

SISI, empress. See Elizabeth of Bavaria (1837–1898).

SISK, Mildred Gillars (1900–1988). See Gillars, Mildred E.

SISOWATH KOSSAMAK NEARIREATH (1904–1975). See Kossamak.

SISSI (1967—). Brazilian soccer player. Name variations: Sisleide do Amor Lima. Born Sisleide do Amor Lima, June 2, 1967, in Esplanada, Brazil. ❖ Midfielder; member of the Brazilian national team; was co-scoring leader (with Sun Wen) at World Cup (1999); played for Vasco da Gama; signed with WUSA's San Jose SyberRays (2000). Named to All-WUSA First Team (2001, 2002); named WUSA Humanitarian of the Year (2002).

SISSI, empress. See Elizabeth of Bavaria (1837–1898).

SISSON, Hilda Strike (1910–1989). See Strike, Hilda.

SISTARE, Lucy Way (1801–1885). See Say, Lucy Sistare.

SISTER OLIVE (1875–1973). See Williams, Matilda Alice.

SISTER SLEDGE
See Sledge, Debra (1955—).
See Sledge, Joni (1957—).
See Sledge, Kathy (1959—).
See Sledge, Kim (1958—).

SISULU, Albertina (1918—). South African anti-apartheid activist. Name variations: Nontsikelelo Albertina Sisulu; Mama Sisulu. Born Oct 21, 1918, among the Xhosa people, in Tsomo, Transkei, South Africa; dau. of Benjamin Boniliawe and Nonani Thethiwe; certified as a nurse; m. Walter Sisulu (ANC official), July 17, 1944 (died 2003); children: daughters Nonkululeko, Lindiwe, and Beryl (adopted); sons Max, Mlungisi, Zwelakhe (prominent journalist), Jonqumzi (adopted), Gerald (adopted), and Samuel (adopted). ❖ African National Congress (ANC) official, called the "mother of the nation" for her role in the struggle against apartheid, began learning about the injustice of apartheid when she started working in the black hospital in Johannesburg and was required to be under the supervision of white nurses, even when she held seniority over them; worked as a nurse in Johannesburg (1944–81); joined the ANC's Women's League (1940s), serving as deputy president (1954–63); helped form the multiracial Federation of South African Women (FSAW, 1954), of which she would later become president (1980); with FSAW, led huge demonstrations against the extension to women of the hated pass laws and against the introduction of the infamous Bantu education system; shared 1st jail sentence (1958) with Winnie Madikizela-Mandela; after husband was incarcerated for life in prison on Robben Island with Nelson Mandela and 6 other ANC leaders (1964), endured 17 years of continuous bans, including 10 years during which she was subject to dusk-to-dawn house arrest; was arrested again (1983) and sentenced to 4 years' imprisonment for leading ANC songs, distributing its literature, and displaying its black, green, and gold flag; managed to get freedom pending appeal and suspension of half the sentence; helped found United Democratic Front (UDF, 1983), incorporating hundreds of anti-apartheid groups, and was elected one of its three co-presidents while in jail; with other anti-apartheid activists, traveled to US (1983), using the 1st passport granted to her by South African government; was the 1st South African black nationalist leader to meet with a US president; became president of World Peace Council in Johannesburg (1992); was elected a member of Parliament (1994). ❖ See also *Women in World History*.

SITEMAN, Isabella Flora (c. 1842–1919). New Zealand farmer and philanthropist. Name variations: Isabella Coupar. Born Isabella Coupar, c. 1842 or 1843, near Dundee, Angus, Scotland; died Mar 18, 1919, in Dannevirke, New Zealand; dau. of Robert Coupar and Margaret (Mitchell) Coupar; m. James Cruikshank (railway shunter), 1868 (died 1870); m. William Jacob Siteman (team driver), 1872 (died 1917); children: (1st m.) 2. ❖ Immigrated to New Zealand soon after death of 1st husband (1871); farmed an initial 233 acres with 2nd husband; gradually acquired large land holdings, which upon her death formed the foundation of a scholarship in her name to provide better assistance to those who wished to obtain a university education. ❖ See also *Dictionary of New Zealand Biography* (Vol. 2).

SITHA (1218–1275). See *Zita of Lucca*.

SITHOLE-NIANG, Idah (1957—). Zimbabwean biochemist and geneticist. Name variations: Idah Sithole-Niang; Idah Niang; Idah Sithole. Born Oct 2, 1957, in Zimbabwe; University of London, BS in biochemistry, 1982; Michigan State University, PhD, 1988; m. Cheikh I. Niang; children: 1. ❖ Conducted genetic studies of plants and viruses at Michigan State University (1988); became lecturer in biochemistry at University of Zimbabwe (1992), and focused research on affects of potyvirus on growth of vegetable called cowpeas, a chief food crop in Zimbabwe.

SITI, Beata (c. 1974—). Hungarian handball player. Name variations: Beáti. Born c. 1974 in Hungary; sister of Eszter Siti (handball player). ❖ Won a team bronze medal at Atlanta Olympics (1996) and a team silver medal at Sydney Olympics (2000). Named EURO 2000's Best Player.

SITI BINTI SAAD (c. 1880–1950). See *Saad, Siti binti*.

SITOE, Aline (c. 1920–1944). See *Aline Sitoe*.

SITTERLY, Charlotte Moore (1898–1990). American astronomer and spectroscopist. Name variations: Charlotte Emma Moore Sitterly, Charlotte Emma Moore. Born Charlotte Emma Moore, Sept 24, 1898, in Enciltoun, Pennsylvania; died Mar 3, 1990, in Washington, DC; Swarthmore College, BA, 1920; University of California, Berkeley, PhD, 1931; m. Bancroft W. Sitterly (physics professor, astronomer and mathematician). ❖ Became assistant to Henry Norris Russell at Princeton University and co-authored papers on binary stars (1920–25); with Charles E. St. John and Harold D. Babcock, worked at Mt. Wilson Observatory (late 1920s), studying solar spectrum and publishing revision of Henry Rowland's table of wavelengths of solar spectrum (1928); back at Princeton (1931–45), produced 1st comprehensive spectroscopic compilation, *A Multiplet Table of Astrophysical Interest* (1933); studied and documented spectra at National Bureau of Standards (NBS) as member of Atomic Spectroscopy Section (1945–68); published *Ultraviolet Multiplet Tables* (1946) and *Atomic Energy Levels* (1949–58); documented thousands of wavelengths, creating tables of data which have been invaluable in development of new laser technology.

SITWELL, Edith (1887–1964). British poet. Born Edith Louisa Sitwell, Sept 7, 1887, in Scarborough, England; died Dec 9, 1964, in Keat's Grove, Hampstead, England; 1st and only dau. of Sir George Reresby Sitwell (British aristocrat) and Lady Ida (Denison) Sitwell; sister of Osbert and Sacheverell Sitwell; never married; no children. ❖ Major 20th-century British poet, who was co-creator, with Sir William Walton, of groundbreaking music and poetry "entertainment" *Facade*; published 1st collection of poems, *The Mother and Other Poems* (1915); was introduced to Bloomsbury circle members (1916); served as editor of *Wheels* (1916–21); participated in failed 1st performance of *Fanfare* at home of brother Osbert (1922); published *Bucolic Comedies* (1923); scored success with public performance of *Fanfare* (1926); published *Street Song* (1942) and *The Shadow of Cain* (1947), generally considered her best work of poetry; participated in unsuccessful project to produce motion-picture script from her *Fanfare for Elizabeth* (1948); published *Collected Poems* (1954); converted to the Roman Catholic Church (1955); also wrote such prose as *Aspects of Modern Poetry*

(1934), *Victoria of England* (1936), *I Live Under a Black Sun* (1937) and *The Queen and the Hive* (1962); despite a childhood that she believed was an "unqualified hell," used her memories to fashion a successful, and ultimately eminent, career as a poet. Named Dame Commander of the Order of the British Empire (1948). ❖ See also *Taken Care Of: The Autobiography of Edith Sitwell* (Atheneum, 1965); Elizabeth Salter, *The Last Years of a Rebel: A Memoir of Edith Sitwell* (Hutchinson, 1967) and *Edith Sitwell* (Oresko, 1979); *The Sitwells and the Arts of the 1920s and 1930s* (U. of Texas Press, 1996); Victoria Glendinning, *Edith Sitwell: A Unicorn among Lions* (Knopf, 1981); John Lehmann, *A Nest of Tigers: The Sitwells in Their Times* (Little, Brown, 1968); and *Women in World History*.

SITZBERGER, Jeanne (1946—). See *Collier, Jeanne*.

SIUKALO, Ganna (1976—). Ukrainian handball player. Born Sept 12, 1976, in Ukraine. ❖ Won a team bronze medal at Athens Olympics (2004).

SIVALI (d. 93). Queen of Ceylon. Executed in 93; dau. of Āmandagāmani Abhaya, ruler of Ceylon (modern-day Sri Lanka); granddau. of Mahādāthikamahānāga, ruler of Ceylon; sister of Cūlābhaya. ❖ During a brief reign, was one of a line of pious rulers of the Vijaya dynasty whose capital was at Anuradhapura; was dethroned by cousin Ilanāga and executed. ❖ See also *Women in World History*.

SIVKOVA, Anna (1982—). Russian fencer. Born April 12, 1982, in USSR. ❖ Won a gold medal for épée team at Athens Olympics (2004); at World championships, placed 1st for team épée (2001, 2003).

SIVUSHENKO, Elena (1982—). See *Slesarenko, Yelena*.

SIXSMITH, Jane (1967—). English field-hockey player. Born Sept 1967 in Sutton Coldfield, England. ❖ At Barcelona Olympics, won a bronze medal in team competition (1992); over course of career, scored over 100 goals and won 165 caps for England and 158 for Great Britain; was the only British female hockey player to appear at 4 Olympics, including Sydney in 2000. Awarded an MBE.

SIZOVA, Alla (1939—). Soviet ballet dancer. Name variations: Alla Ivanovna Sizova. Born Sept 22, 1939, in Moscow, USSR; grew up in Leningrad where she studied at the Vaganova School under Natalia Kamkova. ❖ Famed for her Aurora, danced with the Kirov Ballet throughout career; made professional debut as Queen of the Dryads in *Don Quixote* (1958); partnered with Rudolf Nureyev, danced Princess Florine in *The Sleeping Beauty* and the pas de deux from *Le Corsaire*; after Nureyev's defection (1961), regularly performed with Mikhail Baryshnikov and Yuri Soloviev; danced Princess Aurora for the film *Spyashchaya krasavitsa* (Sleeping Beauty, 1964); also lauded for performances as The Girl in Belsky's *Leningrad Symphony*, Ophelia in Sergeyev's *Hamlet* (1970) and Juliet and Giselle; gave final performance at Kirov (1988); joined the faculty of the Vaganova School.

SJÖBERG, Johanna (1978—). Swedish swimmer. Name variations: Sjoberg. Born Mar 8, 1978, in Kiaby, Sweden. ❖ At SC European championships, won a gold medal for 100-meter butterfly (1999); won a bronze medal for 4 x 100-meter freestyle relay at Sydney Olympics (2000).

SJOEQVIST, Laura (1903–1964). Swedish diver. Born Sept 23, 1903, in Sweden; died Aug 1964. ❖ At Amsterdam Olympics, won a bronze medal in platform (1928).

SJURSEN, Helen Schifano (b. 1922). See *Schifano, Helen*.

SKACHKO-PAKHOVSKAYA, Tatyana (1954—). Soviet track-and-field athlete. Name variations: Tatyana Pakhovskaya. Born Aug 18, 1954, in USSR. ❖ At Moscow Olympics, won a bronze medal in the long jump (1980).

SKAKUN, Nataliya (1981—). Ukrainian weightlifter. Born Aug 3, 1981, in Ukraine. ❖ Placed 1st for 63 kg and 63 kg clean & jerk at World championships (2003); won a gold medal for 63 kg at Athens Olympics (2004).

SKALA, Carole Jo (1938—). See *Callison, Carole Jo*.

SKALA, Lilia (1896–1994). Viennese stage, tv, and screen actress. Born Nov 28, 1896, in Vienna, Austria; died Dec 18, 1994, in Bay Shore, LI, NY. ❖ Toured with Max Reinhardt; fled Austria for US at start of WWII (1939); made Broadway debut in *Letters to Lucerne* (1941), followed by *With a Silk Thread, Call Me Madam, Diary of Anne Frank, Threepenny Opera* (1965), *Zelda, 40 Carats* and *Shop on Main Street,* among others; films include *Roseland, Ship of Fools, Charly, The End of August, Caprice, Flashdance* and *House of Games.* Nominated for Academy Award as Best Supporting Actress for film *Lilies of the Field* (1963).

SKALDASPILLIR, Sigfridur (1944—). *See Broxon, Mildred Downey.*

SKALDINA, Oksana (1972—). Soviet rhythmic gymnast. Born May 24, 1972, in Kiev, Ukraine; m. Dmitry Svatkovsky (pentathlete). ❖ At the World championships, won a silver team medal, bronze all-around, and gold medals in hoop, rope, ribbon (1989) and the indiv. all-around (1991); won the Intervision Cup, Goodwill Games, USSR nationals, and World Cup (1990); at Barcelona Olympics, won a bronze medal in rhythmic gymnastics, all-around (1992).

SKANDHALAKI, Ivi (c. 1907–c. 1991). *See Melissanthi.*

SKARBEK, Krystina (1915–1952). *See Granville, Christine.*

SKARI, Bente (1972—). *See Martinsen, Bente.*

SKAVRONSKA, Marta (1684–1727). *See Catherine I.*

SKAVRONSKY, Catherine (1684–1727). *See Catherine I.*

SKEFFINGTON, Hanna Sheehy (1877–1946). *See Sheehy-Skeffington, Hanna.*

SKERLATOVA, Girgina (1954—). Bulgarian basketball player. Born Mar 25, 1954, in Bulgaria. ❖ At Montreal Olympics, won a bronze medal in team competition (1976).

SKILLMAN, Hope (c. 1908–1981). *See Schary, Hope Skillman.*

SKILLMAN, Melanie (1954—). American archer. Name variations: Melanie Skillman-Hull. Born Sept 23, 1954. ❖ At Seoul Olympics, won a bronze medal in team round (1988); won NAA Athlete of the Year Award (1985).

SKINNER, Constance Lindsay (1877–1939). Canadian-born American author and historian. Born Constance Annie Skinner, Dec 7, 1877, in Quesnel, British Columbia, Canada; died Mar 27, 1939, in New York, NY; dau. of Robert James Skinner (agent for Hudson's Bay Co.) and Annie (Lindsay) Skinner; never married. ❖ Upon moving to California, became a music and theater critic, while also covering fires and murders for such papers as the *San Francisco Examiner* and *Los Angeles Times*; spent 3 years in Chicago, writing for *Chicago American,* before moving to NY where she wrote poetry and essays for *Bookman, North American Review, Poetry,* and other magazines, garnering poetry prizes; was asked to contribute to the 50-volume Yale University "Chronicles of America" series, for which she wrote *Pioneers of the Old Southwest* (1919) and *Adventurers of Oregon* (1920); produced a popular series of historical adventure tales for children, all based on frontier life, drawn from the experiences of her own childhood, including *Silent Scot, Frontier Scout* (1925), *Becky Landers, Frontier Warrior* (1926), *Ranch of the Golden Flowers* (1928) and *Debby Barnes, Trader* (1932); published well-received collection of poetry, *Songs of the Coast Dwellers* (1930); began editing a series of historical books for Farrar & Rinehart, designed to highlight the importance of America's major rivers (1935). Annual Constance Lindsay Skinner Award was established by Women's National Book Association (1940). ❖ See also *Women in World History.*

SKINNER, Cornelia Otis (1901–1979). American stage actress and author. Born May 30, 1901, in Chicago, Illinois; died July 9, 1979, in New York, NY; dau. of Otis Skinner (actor) and Maud (Durbin) Skinner (actress); attended Bryn Mawr College; m. Alden Sanford Blodget, Oct 1928; children: Otis. ❖ Made 1st professional stage appearance in Buffalo, performing a small part in *Blood and Sand,* with father in starring role (1921); moved with show to Broadway; appeared in several plays (1920s), while fostering a writing talent that 1st blossomed with *Captain Fury* (1925), a play written for her father; found niche in writing monologue-driven character sketches in which she also performed; toured US and eventually England with one-woman shows, including *The Wives of Henry VIII* (1931), *The Empress Eugénie* (1932), *The Loves of Charles II* (1933) and *Edna, His Wife* (1937); had 14 different roles in musical revue *Paris '90* (1952), another solo show; starred in Shaw's *Candida* (1935), *The Searching Wind* (1944), and *The Pleasure of His Company* (1958), which she co-wrote with Samuel Taylor; also wrote books based on her experiences, starting with *Tiny Garments* (1932); with Emily Kimbrough, co-authored the bestselling *Our Hearts Were Young and Gay* (1942); also wrote *Elegant Wits and Grand Horizontals* (1962) and *The Life of Lindsay and Crouse* (1976); was a longtime contributor of

essays and light verse to magazines, including *The New Yorker* and *Harper's Bazaar.* ❖ See also *Women in World History.*

SKINNER, Julie (1968—). Canadian curler. Born April 23, 1968, in Calgary, Alberta, Canada. ❖ As skip, won a bronze medal at Albertville Olympics (1992); won a World championship (2000) and a team bronze medal at Salt Lake City Olympics (2002).

SKINNER, Mollie (1876–1955). Australian novelist. Name variations: (pseudonym) R. E. Leake. Born in Perth, Western Australia, 1876; died 1955; educated in England. ❖ Worked in India during WWI, which provided background for 1st novel, *Letters of a V. A. D.* (1918), published under pseudonym R. E. Leake; collaborated with D. H. Lawrence on her most famous book, *The Boy in the Bush* (1924); later works include *Black Swans* (1925), *Men Are We* (1927), *Tucker Sees India* (1937), *WX—Corporal Smith: A Romance of the A. I. F. in Libya* (1941) and *Where Skies Are Blue* (1946). ❖ See also autobiography, *The Fifth Sparrow* (1972); and *Women in World History.*

SKIPWORTH, Alison (1863–1952). English stage and screen actress. Born Alison Groom, July 25, 1863, in London, England; died July 5, 1952, in New York, NY; m. Frank Markham Skipworth (artist). ❖ Made London debut in *A Gaiety Girl* (1894); debuted on Broadway in *The Artist's Model* (1895); became a member of Daniel Frohman's company (1897); other plays include *The Swan, The Enchanted April, The Torch Bearers, The Grand Duchess and the Waiter* and *Marseilles*; made film debut (1930); appeared in over 100 films, including *Raffles, Outward Bound, Madame Racketeer, Song of Songs, Alice in Wonderland, Becky Sharp* and *Ladies in Distress*; was W. C. Fields' foil in *If I Had a Million, Tillie and Gus* and *Six of a Kind.*

SKIRVING, Angie (1981—). Australian field-hockey player. Born Feb 1, 1981, in Toowoomba, Queensland, Australia. ❖ Defender, won a team gold medal at Sydney Olympics (2000).

SKJELBREID, Ann-Elen (1971—). Norwegian biathlete. Name variations: Ann Elen Skjelbreid. Born Sept 13, 1971, in Bergen, Norway; sister of Liv Grete Poiree (biathlete). ❖ Won a silver medal for spring at World championships (1996); won a bronze medal at Nagano Olympics (1998) and a silver medal at Salt Lake City Olympics (2002), both for the 4 x 7.5 km relay.

SKJELBREID, Liv Grete (1974—). *See Poiree, Liv Grete.*

SKLENICKOVA, Miroslava (1951—). Czech gymnast. Born Mar 11, 1951. ❖ At Mexico City Olympics, won a silver medal in team all-around (1968).

SKLODOWSKA, Manya or Marie (1867–1934). *See Curie, Marie.*

SKOBLIKOVA, Lydia (1939—). Russian speedskater. Name variations: Lidija Skoblikova. Born Mar 8, 1939, in Zlatoust, Chelyabinsk, Soviet Union. ❖ Won six Olympic gold medals: took the 1,500 and 3,000 meters at Squaw Valley (1960) and the 1,000, 1,500, 3,000, and 500 meters at Innsbruck (1964), the 1st athlete to win 4 gold medals in a Winter Olympics; won gold medals at the World championship in the 500, 1,000, 1,500, and 3,000-meters (1963); won women's all-around World championship once more (1964).

SKOBTSOVA, Maria (1891–1945). Latvian Russian Orthodox nun, essayist, poet and hero. Name variations: Mother Mariia or Maria; Mother Maria Skobtsóva; Elizaveta Kuzmina-Karavaeva; Elizabeta or Elizaveta Iur'evna Kuz'mina-Karavaeva; Liza Kuzmin-Karaviev; Elizabeta Iurievna Kuzmina-Karavaeva Skobtsova; Elizaveta Skobtsóva. Born Elizaveta Pilenko, 1891, in Riga, Latvia; died in Ravensbrück concentration camp, Mar 30, 1945; dau. of Sophia Pilenko; attended Theological Academy of Alexander Nevsky Monastery, St. Petersburg; m. Dimitri Kuzmin-Karaviev (Bolshevik intellectual), 1910; m. Daniel Skobtsóva (schoolmaster); children: Gaiana Kuzmin-Karaviev, Yuri Skobtsóva, Anastasia Skobtsóva, George. ❖ Had early career as a painter and poet; participated in Union of Youth Exhibition (1912); joined Social Revolutionary Party and participated in modernist literary groups; moved to Paris (1920), where she painted murals for two churches; wrote *Scythian Crocks* (1912), *Ruth* (1916), 2-volume work on lives of saints (1927), book on Russian religious philosopher Vladimir Solov'ev (1929), and religious poetry; took the veil (1926); worked for Russian émigré community; during WWII, rescued Jews during Nazi occupation; arrested with son and others (1943); collection of work published posthumously (1947); canonized by Russian Orthodox Church (2003). ❖ See also Laurence Varant, *Mother Maria Skobtsova* (Perrin, 2000).

SKÖLD, Beri. (1939—). Swedish ballet dancer. Born 1939 in Stockholm, Sweden. ❖ Trained at school of Royal Swedish Ballet, then joined the company (1956), performing there throughout career; best known for role of The Mistress of the Copper Mountain in Grigorovitch's *The Stone Flower* (1962) and title role in Birgit Cullberg's *Lady from the Sea.*

SKOLIMOWSKA, Kamila (1982—). Polish hammer thrower. Born Nov 4, 1982, in Warsaw, Poland. ❖ Won a gold medal at Sydney Olympics (2000); at European championships, won a silver medal (2002).

SKORIK, Irene (1928—). French ballet dancer. Born Irène Beaudemont, Jan 27, 1928, in Paris, France. ❖ Trained with Olga Preobrazhenskaya, Lyubov Egorova, and Boris Kniaseff; danced with Les Ballets des Champs Elysée (1945–60), where she created a role in Serge Lifar's *Chota Rostaveli* (1946) and had great success in *La Sylphide*; danced in Petit's Ballets de Paris (1950); also created roles with the Munich Opera for Victor Gsovsky's *Hamlet* (1950) and *La Legende de Joseph* (1951) and with Berlin Stadtopera for Tatiana Gsovsky's *Fleurenville* (1956) and *Etudes* (1961).

SKORONEL, Vera (1909–1932). Swiss modern dancer. Born May 28, 1909, in Zurich, Switzerland; died Mar 24, 1932, in Berlin, Germany. ❖ Trained with German expressionist pioneers Mary Wigman and Rudolf von Laban; opened dance studio in Berlin with Bertha Trumpy (c. 1926) and founded her own dance troupe.

SKOTVOLL, Annette (1968—). Norwegian handball player. Born Sept 1, 1968, in Norway. ❖ Won a silver medal at Seoul Olympics (1988) and a silver medal at Barcelona Olympics (1992), both in team competition.

SKOV, Rikke (1980—). Danish handball player. Born Sept 7, 1980, in Denmark. ❖ Left back, won a team gold medal at Athens Olympics (2004).

SKOVORONSKI, Marta (1684–1727). *See Catherine I.*

SKRABATUN, Valentina (1958—). Belarusian rower. Born July 23, 1958, in Belarus. ❖ Won a bronze medal for coxed eights at Atlanta Olympics (1996).

SKRAM, Amalie (1846–1905). Norwegian writer. Name variations: Bertha Skram. Born Bertha Amalie Alver in Bergen, Norway, 1846; died in Copenhagen, Denmark, Mar 13, 1905; dau. of Mons Monsen Alver and Ingeborg Lovise (Sivertsen) Alver; m. Bernt Ulrik August Müller (ship's captain), 1864 (div. 1882); m. Erik Skram (Danish writer), April 3, 1884 (sep. 1890, div. 1900); children: (1st m.) Jakob and Ludvig; (2nd m.) Johanne Skram. ❖ One of the leading Nordic naturalistic writers of her time, published 1st story "Madam Höiers Leiefolk" ("Mrs. Höier's Renters," 1882); had breakthrough as novelist with *Constance Ring* (1885), based on experiences in her 1st marriage; married Erik Skram, who brought her to Copenhagen (1884); wrote her major work, the tetralogy *Hellemyrsfolket* (tr. *The People of Hellemyr*, 1887–98), the 1st great Norwegian novel; close to a nervous breakdown, was declared insane and detained against her will at Saint George Hospital in Copenhagen; released when another doctor found no evidence of insanity; wrote 2 vols. about her stay in the psychiatric ward (*Professor Hieronimus* and *At Saint George*), which were scathing in their criticism (1895); left husband but remained in Copenhagen the last 5 years of her life (1900–05). Other writings include *Bön og anfägtelse* (*Prayer and Temptation*, 1885), *Knut Tandberg* (1886), *Lucie* (1888), *Fjäldmennesker* (*Mountain People*, 1889), *Bornefortællinger* (children's stories, 1890), *Fru Ines* (*Mrs. Ines*, 1891), *Forraadt* (tr. *Betrayed*, 1892), *Agnete* (1893), *Sommer* (*Summer*, 1899), *Julehelg* (*Christmas Celebration*, 1900) and *Mennesker* (*People*, 1902–05). ❖ See also *Women in World History.*

SKRBKOVA, Milada (1897–1965). Czech tennis player. Born May 30, 1897; died Oct 1935. ❖ At Antwerp Olympics, won a bronze medal in mixed doubles–outdoors (1920).

SKRINE, Agnes (c. 1865–1955). Irish poet, novelist and reviewer. Name variations: Agnes Higginson Skrine; Nesta Skrine; (pseudonym) Moira O'Neill. Born Agnes (Nesta) Shakespeare Higginson at Springmount, Cushendun, Co. Antrim, Ireland, c. 1865; died at Ferns, Co. Wexford, Ireland, Jan 22, 1955; dau. of Charles Henry Higginson and Mary Higginson; m. Walter Clarmont Skrine, June 5, 1895 (died 1930); children: 3 sons, 2 daughters, including novelist Molly Keane (1904–1996). ❖ Published 1st novel, *An Easter Vacation* (1893), followed by *The Elf Errant* (1894); published a highly successful collection of poems, *Songs of the Glens of Antrim* (1901), a number of which were set to

music, including "Loughareema"; wrote *More Songs of the Glens of Antrim* (1921); under pseudonym Moira O'Neill, wrote regularly for *Blackwood's Magazine*, one of the most prestigious literary journals of the day; published *Collected Poems of Moira O'Neill* (1933), written in the dialect of the Glens. ❖ See also *Women in World History.*

SKRINE, Mary Nesta (1904–1996). *See Keane, Molly.*

SKUJYTE, Austra (1979—). Lithuanian heptathlete. Born Aug 12, 1979, in Birzai, Lithuania; attended Kansas State University. ❖ Won a silver medal for heptathlon at Athens Olympics (2004).

SKURATOVA, Maria (d. 1605). *See Maria Skuratova.*

SLAGLE, Eleanor Clarke (1871–1942). American reformer and therapist. Born Ella May Clarke, Oct 13, 1871, in Hobart, New York; died Sept 18, 1942, in Philipse Manor, New York; dau. of John Clarke (sheriff) and Emmaline J. (Davenport) Clarke; attended Claverack College; was among the 1st to take a course in "Invalid Occupation" at what would later become the school of social work at University of Chicago (1908); m. Robert E. Slagle (div.); no children. ❖ Pioneer in occupational therapy, organized occupational therapy program at Phipps Psychiatric Clinic, Johns Hopkins Hospital (1913); by 1915, was director of Chicago's Henry B. Favill School of Occupations, which specialized in the training of occupational therapy aides; became Illinois Department of Public Welfare's superintendent of occupational therapy (1918), where she organized a therapy program for Illinois mental hospitals; became director of occupational therapy for New York State Hospital Commission (1922), and spent rest of career with the commission; her accomplishments became the model for institutions throughout US, and her guidance was frequently sought in the development of similar programs across the nation; helped found and served as an officer for National Society for the Promotion of Occupational Therapy (1917–37), later renamed the American Occupational Therapy Association. ❖ See also *Women in World History.*

SLAMET, Winarni Binti (1975—). Indonesian weightlifter. Born 1975 in Indonesia. ❖ Won World championship (1997); won a bronze medal 48–53 kg at Sydney Olympics (2000).

SLANCIKOVA, Bozena (1867–1951). Slovak playwright and short-story writer. Name variations: Božena Slančiková; Božena Slančiková-Timrava; (pen name) Timrava. Born Oct 20, 1867, in Polichno, Slovakia; died Nov 27, 1951, in Lucenec, Slovakia; never married. ❖ Writer of critical realism; stories include *Tapákavci* (1914), *Hrdinovia* (1902), and *Skon Pala Ročku.*

SLANEY, Mary Decker (1958—). American middle-distance runner. Name variations: Mary Decker. Born Mary Teresa Decker, Aug 4, 1958, in Bunnvale, NJ; m. Ron Tabb (marathoner), 1981 (div. 1983); m. Richard Slaney (British discus thrower), 1985; attended University of Colorado. ❖ At 13, qualified for US Olympic track team but was too young to compete (1972); set world records in New Zealand and US for the mile and 1,500-meter races respectively, then went on to break the world record for the 880-yard event and the US record for the 800-meter event at San Diego Invitational track meet (1980); qualified for Olympics in Moscow but could not compete due to US boycott (1980); at a European meet, ran the 10,000 meters for 1st time and beat US record by 42 seconds (1981); set 5 world records in indoor and outdoor races, including a 4:18 mile (1982); held every American distance record from 800 to 10,000 meters (1984); during Los Angeles Olympics (1984), in one of the most famous collisions in sports history, became entangled with Zola Budd, lost balance, and pulled a hip muscle; set a world record in indoor 2,000 meters and another world record for the mile (1985). Named female athlete of the year by Associated Press (1982); named Jesse Owens International Amateur Athlete of the Year, the 1st woman to be so honored (1982); received Amateur Sportswoman of the Year award from Women's Sports Foundation and named Sportswoman of the Year by *Sports Illustrated* (1983). ❖ See also *Women in World History.*

SLATER, Daphne Arden (1941—). *See Arden, Daphne.*

SLATER, Frances Charlotte (1892–1947). South African novelist. Name variations: (pseudonym) F. Bancroft or Francis Bancroft. Born 1892 on the family farm in the Eastern Cape, South Africa; died 1947. ❖ Lived in England for some time but returned to Eastern Cape and worked as journalist and novelist; works, which focus on women's suffrage, Temperance movement, gender issues, problems faced by Dutch and English settlers, and Anglo-Boer War, include *Of Like Passions* (1907), *The Veldt Dwellers* (1912), *Thane Brandon* (1913), *The Settler's Eldest*

Daughter (1920), *The Brandons* (1928), *Love's Bondage* (1929), *The Sure Years* (1931), and *Green Youth* (1933).

SLATON, Danielle (1980—). American soccer player. Born June 10, 1980, in San Jose, CA; attended college at Santa Clara. ❖ Won a silver medal at Sydney Olympics (2000); signed with Carolina Courage (2002). Named WUSA Defensive Player of the Year (2001).

SLATTER, Kate (1971—). Australian rower. Name variations: Kate Elizabeth Slatter. Born Nov 19, 1971, in South Australia; graduate of Australian National University. ❖ With Megan Still, went undefeated in national and international competition (1995), culminating in the World championship, and won a gold medal for coxless pair at Atlanta Olympics (1996), the 1st Australian oarswomen to do so; with Rachael Taylor, won a silver medal for coxless pair at Sydney Olympics (2000). Presented with Order of Australia (1997).

SLAUGHTER, Lenora S. (1906–2000). American pageant executive. Name variations: Lenora Slaughter Frapart. Born Lenora S. Slaughter, Oct 23, 1906; died Dec 4, 2000, in Arizona; m. Bradford Frapart (died Sept 1972). ❖ Served as executive director of the Miss America Pageant (1941–67), generally acknowledged as the one who changed it from a "girly" competition into a respected pageant; credited with many innovations, including college scholarships; backed Yolande Betbeze (Miss America, 1951) when she refused to pose in a swimsuit. ❖ See also Frank Deford, *There She Is* (Viking, 1971).

SLAUGHTER, Louise M. (1929—). American politician. Born Louise McIntosh, Aug 14, 1929, in Harlan County, KY; University of Kentucky, BS, 1951, MA in public health, 1953; m. Robert Slaughter; children: 3 daughters. ❖ Won a seat in the New York Assembly (1983), serving until 1986; as a Democrat representing NY, elected to US House of Representatives 100th Congress (1986); appointed to the House Rules Committee (1989); served on Select Committee on Aging; in 104th Congress, served on the Budget Committee and the Committee on Government Reform and Oversight; during 108th Congress, served as co-chair for Congressional Caucus on Women's Issues; elected to 10th term (2004); became ranking member of House Committee on Rules, the 1st woman from either party to hold this position; also sits on Select Committee for Homeland Security and is chair of Bipartisan Congressional Pro-Choice Caucus.

SLAVCHEVA, Evladiya (1962—). Bulgarian basketball player. Born Feb 25, 1962, in Bulgaria. ❖ At Moscow Olympics, won a silver medal in team competition (1980).

SLAVENSKA, Mia (1914–2000). Yugoslavian-born ballerina, choreographer, and teacher. Name variations: Mia Corak. Born Mia Corak or Corakin in Slavonski-Brod (then Brod-na Savi), Croatia or Austria-Hungary (later Yugoslavia), Feb 20, 1914; died Oct 5, 2002, in Los Angeles, CA; studied 7 years at Royal Academy of Music, Zagreb; had dance training in Zagreb, Vienna, Paris (under Bronislava Nijinska), and New York (under Vincenzo Celli); also studied modern dance with Harald Kreutzberg and Mary Wigmore; m. Kurt Neumann, 1946; children: Maria Ramas. ❖ At 5, debuted at Zagreb National Opera House (1921), became a soloist (1931) and prima ballerina (1933); joined Bronislava Nijinska's short-lived Théâtre de la Danse in Paris (1933), receiving acclaim from Parisian audiences; appeared in film *La Mort du Cygne* (*Ballerina,* 1936), considered one of the few classic movies about dance; became a lead dancer with Ballets Russes (1938), performing that season in *Les Sylphides, Gaite Parisienne, Les Elfes, Carnevale* and *Giselle,* in which she danced the title role; during WWII, formed Slavenska Ballet Variante in Hollywood; toured US, South America, and Canada (1944–52); became US citizen; with dancer Frederic Franklin (1952), formed Slavenska-Franklin Ballet and danced role of Blanche in their best-known production, *A Streetcar Named Desire*; was prima ballerina with Metropolitan Opera Ballet (1955–56), while also working with regional companies and at Jacob's Pillow Dance Festival. ❖ See also *Women in World History.*

SLAVIKOVA, Ludmila (1890–1943). Czech geologist. Name variations: Ludmila Slávíková; Ludmila Slavikova-Kaplanova. Born Ludmila Kaplanova, Feb 23, 1890, in Prague, Czechoslovakia; died at Auschwitz, Feb 18, 1943; Charles University in Prague, PhD in math and physics, 1914; m. Frantisek Slávík (professor), 1917. ❖ Noted geologist, researched crystals (in Bohemian pyrargyrite); with husband, wrote a monograph about Ordovician iron ores in Bohemia; wrote papers on the history of the National Museum's mineral collections in Prague and headed its department of Mineralogy and Petrology (1921–39); with

husband, was arrested by the Nazis and taken to Auschwitz (1943), where she died 14 days later.

SLAVUTEANU, Lidia (1973—). *See Simon, Lidia.*

SLEDGE, Debra (1955—). American singer. Name variations: Sister Sledge. Born 1955 in Philadelphia, PA; sister of Joni, Kathy and Kim Sledge (all singers); graduate of Temple University. ❖ With sisters, worked as background singer while in college, signed with Atlantic (1973), and released album, *We Are Family* (1979), which went gold and contained dance hits, "He's the Greatest Dancer" and "We Are Family"; other albums include *Circle of Love* (1975), *Love Somebody Today* (1980) and *When the Boys Meet the Girls* (1985); had last US hit with cover of Mary Wells song, "My Guy" (1982) and UK hit with "Frankie" (1985); with sisters minus Kathy, released album *African Eyes* (1998).

SLEDGE, Joni (1957—). American singer. Name variations: Sister Sledge. Born 1957 in Philadelphia, PA; sister of Debra, Kathy and Kim Sledge (all singers); graduate of Temple University. ❖ With sisters, formed Sister Sledge (late 1950s) in Philadelphia; released album, *We Are Family* (1979), which went gold and contained dance hits, "He's the Greatest Dancer" and "We Are Family."

SLEDGE, Kathy (1959—). American singer. Name variations: Sister Sledge. Born 1959 in Philadelphia, PA; sister of Debra, Joni and Kim Sledge (all singers); graduate of Temple University. ❖ With sisters, began singing at Second Macedonia Church in Philadelphia (late 1950s) and recorded song, "Time Will Tell" (1971); released album, *We Are Family* (1979), which went gold and contained dance hits, "He's the Greatest Dancer" and "We Are Family"; left Sister Sledge to pursue solo career (late 1980s), and had some success in Europe (early 1990s).

SLEDGE, Kim (1958—). American singer. Name variations: Sister Sledge. Born 1958 in Philadelphia, PA; sister of Debra, Joni and Kathy Sledge (all singers); graduate of Temple University. ❖ With sisters, formed the pop and R&B group, Sister Sledge (late 1950s) and released the hit album, *We Are Family* (1979), which contained the hits "He's the Greatest Dancer" and "We Are Family."

SLEEPER, Martha (1907–1983). American stage and screen actress. Born June 24, 1907, in Lake Bluff, IL; died Mar 25, 1983, in Beaufort, NC; m. Hardie Albright (actor), 1934 (div. 1940); m. Harry Dresser (Deutchbein), 1940; children: Victoria Albright. ❖ Began film career as a child actress in Hal Roach comedies; later appeared in *Danger Street, Our Blushing Brides, War Nurse, Madam Satan, Ten Cents a Dance, Huddle, Rasputin and the Empress, Broken Dreams, Spitfire, West of the Pecos, The Scoundrel* and *The Bells of St. Mary's*; made Broadway debut in *Stepping Out* (1929), followed by *Dinner at 8, Russet Mantel, Save Me the Waltz* and *Christopher Blake,* among others.

SLENCZYNSKA, Ruth (1925—). American pianist. Name variations: Ruth Slenczynski. Born in Sacramento, California, Jan 15, 1925; dau. of Josef Slenczynski (violinist and once head of the Warsaw Conservatory); studied with Marguerite Long, Artur Schnabel, Alfred Cortot and Egon Petri. ❖ Hailed as one of the great musical prodigies of the age, first played in public at age 6, in Berlin; performed a concerto in Paris 5 years later; by mid-teens, career disintegrated because of the psychological toll; after more than a decade of therapy, resumed public performances, to mostly positive reviews; taught at the University of Southern Illinois. ❖ See also memoir *Forbidden Childhood* (Doubleday, 1957); and *Women in World History.*

SLESARENKO, Yelena (1982—). Russian high jumper. Name variations: Elena Sivushenko. Born Feb 28, 1982, in Volgograd, USSR. ❖ Won a gold medal for high jump at Athens Olympics (2004), with an Olympic record of 6:9.1; won World Indoor championship (2004).

SLESINGER, Tess (1905–1945). American novelist and short-story writer. Born 1905 in New York, NY; died Feb 21, 1945; dau. of middle-class Jewish immigrant parents; attended Ethical Culture School; studied at Swarthmore College, 1923–25; Columbia School of Journalism, BLitt, 1927; m. Herbert Solow (leftist activist and writer), 1928; m. Frank Davis (film producer and writer), 1936; children: 2. ❖ Worked as an assistant fashion editor on New York *Herald Tribune* (1926), then became assistant on New York *Evening Post Literary Review*; co-founded *The Menorah Journal* with 1st husband; published novel *The Unpossessed* (1934) and collection of short stories *Time: The Present* (1935); marched in protests and spoke out on the inequities of economics and race; co-wrote screen adaptation of *The Good Earth* and screenplay for *The*

Bride Wore Red (both 1937); with 2nd husband, wrote the screen adaptation of *A Tree Grows in Brooklyn* (1945), which was nominated for an Academy Award; helped establish the Screenwriters Guild.

SLESSOR, Mary (1848–1915). Scottish missionary. Name variations: Mary Mitchell Slessor. Born Mary Mitchell Slessor, Dec 1848, in Gilcomston, near Aberdeen, Scotland; died Jan 13, 1915, in Use, the Calabar, Nigeria; dau. of Robert Slessor (shoemaker) and Mary Slessor (weaver and textile factory worker); never married; children: a number officially and unofficially adopted. ❖ Moved from Gilcomston to Dundee, Scotland (1859); left school at 14 to join mother in the textile factories, beginning to work a full factory schedule (1862); inspired by reports of David Livingstone in *Missionary Record,* a church publication, began to educate herself (1866); offered her services to Foreign Missions Board of the Scottish Presbyterian Church (1875), setting sail for the Calabar, West Africa (Aug 1876); served in the Calabar Mission Field, an area of Nigeria that included Duke Town, Old Town, Creek Town, and Okoyong, and far into the interior of Nigeria to Enyong Creek (1876–1915). Named honorary associate of Hospital Order of St. John of Jerusalem in England. ❖ See also James Buchan, *The Expendable Mary Slessor* (Saint Andrew, 1980); Ronald Syme, *Nigerian Pioneer: The Story of Mary Slessor* (Morrow, 1964); and *Women in World History.*

SLICK, Grace (1939—). American singer. Name variations: Jefferson Airplane; Starship. Born Grace Barnett Wing, Oct 30, 1939, in Chicago, IL; grew up in Palo Alto, CA; dau. of investment banker father and singer mother; attended Finch College and University of Miami; m. Jerry Slick, Aug 26, 1961 (div. 1971); m. Skip Johnson, Nov 29, 1976 (div. 1994); children: (with bandmate Paul Kantner) China Kantner (actress). ❖ Called the high priestess of rock, formed The Great Society (1965) and played in San Francisco clubs; became the main vocalist for the musical group Jefferson Airplane (1966), had a smash album *Surrealistic Pillow,* and scored such hits as "Somebody to Love" and "White Rabbit" (which she wrote); played piano, keyboards, and flute as well; with the band renamed Jefferson Starship, had hit "Miracles" (1975); went solo (1978); returned to the band, now named Starship (mid-1980s), and had hits "We Built This City" (1985), "Sara" (1986) and "Nothing's Gonna Stop Us Now" (1987); left the band once more (1988); quit the music business and turned to painting; rendered bestselling portraits of rock stars, such as Jimi Hendrix, Janis Joplin and Jerry Garcia. Inducted into Rock and Roll Hall of Fame (1996). ❖ See also autobiography, *Somebody to Love?* (1998).

SLICK, Jonathan (1810–1886). See Stephens, Ann S.

SLIOUSSAREVA, Olga (1969—). See Slyusareva, Olga.

SLITS, The.
See Albertine, Viv (1955—).
See Palmolive (1955—).
See Up, Ari (1962—).

SLIWKOWA, Maria (1935—). Polish volleyball player. Born Dec 1935 in Poland. ❖ At Tokyo Olympics, won a bronze medal in team competition (1964).

SLIZOWSKA, Barbara (1938—). Polish gymnast. Born Barbara Wilk, June 29, 1938, in Poland. ❖ At Melbourne Olympics, won a bronze medal in teams all-around, portable apparatus (1956).

SLOAN, Susan (1958—). Canadian swimmer. Name variations: Susan Sloan Kelsey. Born April 1958 in Stettler, Alberta, Canada; Arizona State University, BSc in physical education, 1982; earned law degree from University of British Columbia, 1986; m. Chris Kelsey; children: John and Mark. ❖ At Montreal Olympics, won a bronze medal in the 4 x 100-meter medley relay (1976).

SLOCUM, Frances (1773–1847). American captive. Name variations: Maconaqua; Maconaquah. Born Mar 4, 1773, in Warwick, Rhode Island; died Mar 9, 1847, in Indiana; dau. of Jonathan Slocum and Ruth (Tripp) Slocum (Quaker farmers); m. a Delaware tribesman, in 1791 (div.); m. Shepancanah (a Miami chief), c. 1794 (died 1832); children: daughters Kekesequa (b. 1800) and Ozahshinqua (b. 1809); 2 sons who died in childhood. ❖ During Revolutionary War, was taken captive when a small group of Delaware tribesmen attacked the Slocum home (1778), near what is now Wilkes-Barre, Pennsylvania; taken to a village near Niagara Falls, was adopted by a Delaware couple whose daughter had recently died; gradually she forgot how to speak English, married and had children; after 2nd husband's death (1832), well respected within the Native American community, continued to manage their sizable farm in Indiana on her own, raising cattle and some 100 horses; revealed her identity to a fur trader (1835); was reunited with some siblings (1837), who had been searching for her for 59 years. ❖ See also *Women in World History.*

SLOMAN, Mary (1891–1980). See Lavater-Sloman, Mary.

SLOSS, Elizabeth Butler- (1933—). See Butler-Sloss, Elizabeth.

SLOSSON, Annie Trumbull (1838–1926). American entomologist. Born 1838 in Stonington, Connecticut; died 1926; dau. of Gurdon Trumbull and Sarah Trumbull; educated in Hartford, Connecticut; married Edward Slosson, 1867. ❖ Made her mark as an entomologist with a collection of unusual insects which she gathered at her homes in Florida and New Hampshire; presented many then-unknown specimens to specialists for analysis; also wrote descriptions of the physical characteristics and habits of insects she collected, and published several stories about natural history intended for lay readers.

SLOW, Mrs. Clive (1898–1984). See Taylor, Mary.

SLOWE, Lucy Diggs (1885–1937). American educator. Born July 4, 1885, in Berryville, Virginia; died Oct 21, 1937, in Washington, DC; dau. of Henry Slowe and Fannie (Porter) Slowe; graduate of Howard University, 1908; Columbia University, MA in English, 1915; lived with Mary Burrill, public school teacher and playwright, 1922–37. ❖ The 1st African-American woman dean of Howard University, was also one of the founders of Alpha Kappa Alpha Sorority, the 1st Greek-letter organization for black women; was appointed principal at District of Columbia's 1st junior high school for black children (1919); appointed dean of women at Howard University (1922), also served as a professor of English and education; became the 1st president of National Association of College Women (NACW, 1923), an organization of black women college graduates; organized National Association of Deans of Women and Advisors to Girls in Negro Schools (1929), which became independent of NACW (1935) as the number of women advisors and deans of black colleges grew; with Mary McLeod Bethune, helped found National Council of Negro Women and served as its 1st executive secretary. ❖ See also *Women in World History.*

SLUPIANEK, Ilona (1956—). East German track-and-field athlete. Born Sept 24, 1956, in East Germany. ❖ At Moscow Olympics, won a gold medal in the shot put (1980).

SLUTSKAYA, Irina (1979—). Russian figure skater. Pronunciation: SLOOT-skaya. Born Feb 9, 1979, in Moscow, Russia; m. Sergei Mikheyev. ❖ Won Russian Jr. championship (1993) and Jr. World championship (1995); at World championships, won gold medals (2002, 2005), silver medals (1998, 2000, 2001) and a bronze medal (1996); won European championships (1996, 1997, 2000, 2001, 2003, 2005); won Skate Canada (1997, 2001) and Cup of Russia (1997, 1998, 2000, 2001, 2002, 2005), Russian nationals (2000, 2001, 2002), NHK Trophy (2001), Grand Prix Final (2001, 2002), and Goodwill Games (2002); at Salt Lake City Olympics, won a silver medal (2002); won a bronze medal at Torino Olympics (2006).

SLUTSKAYA, Vera (1874–1917). Russian revolutionary. Name variations: Vera Slutskaia; Vera Kliment'evna Slutskaia. Born Berta Bronislavovna Slutskaya in Minsk, Sept 17, 1874; killed in action in Tsarskoe Selo (now Pushkin), Nov 12, 1917. ❖ A dentist by profession, joined Russian revolutionary movement (1898) and the Bolshevik faction of Russian Social Democratic Labor Party (RSDLP), later known as the Communist Party (1902); participated in the revolution in Minsk and St. Petersburg (1905–07), as a member of the military organization of the RSDLP; served as a delegate to 5th congress of RSDLP (1907); lived in exile in Germany and Switzerland (1909–12); resumed party work in St. Petersburg (1913), and was arrested several times by the tsarist police; was exiled to the Caucasus (1914); after the overthrow of the tsar (early 1917), became a member of the St. Petersburg (now named Petrograd) committee of the Bolsheviks; was a delegate to 6th congress of the RSDLP; took part in the armed uprising in Petrograd during October revolution (1917); killed in a skirmish with anti-Bolshevik forces. ❖ See also *Women in World History.*

SLY, Wendy (1959—). English runner. Name variations: Wendy Smith. Born Wendy Smith, Nov 5, 1959, in UK. ❖ At Los Angeles Olympics, won a silver medal in 3,000 meters (1984); placed 1st in 3,000 meters at UK championships (1988).

SLY AND THE FAMILY STONE.
See Robinson, Cynthia (1946—).
See Stone, Rosie (1945—).

SLYE, Maud (1869–1954). American pathologist. Born Maud Caroline Slye, Feb 8, 1869, in Minneapolis, Minnesota; died Sept 17, 1954, in Chicago, Illinois; dau. of Florence Alden (Wheeler) Slye and James Alvin Slye (lawyer and writer); attended the University of Chicago; Brown University, BA, 1899; never married; no children. ❖ Among the 1st scientists to demonstrate that cancer is inheritable, became graduate assistant in biology department at University of Chicago (1908); began performing breeding experiments with mice to research a possible heredity link to cancer; joined staff of Sprague Memorial Institute at University of Chicago (1911), where she was provided more money to conduct her research; presented 1st paper to American Society for Cancer Research (1913), refuting the idea that cancer was a contagious disease; appointed director of the Cancer Laboratory at University of Chicago (1919), then served as associate professor of pathology (1926–44); also published 2 vols. of poetry, *Songs and Solaces* (1934) and *I in the Wind* (1936). ❖ See also *Women in World History*.

SLYUSAREVA, Olga (1969—). Ukrainian cyclist. Name variations: Olga Slioussareva; Olga Rostovteva. Born April 28, 1969, in Kharkov, Ukraine; m. Mikhail Rostovtev (her coach). ❖ Set the world record for the flying 200-meter sprint at 10.831s (1993); representing Russia, won a bronze medal for points race at Sydney Olympics (2000); at World championships, won gold medals for points race (2001, 2002, 2003, 2004) and silver medals for pursuit (2001, 2002); representing Russia, won gold medal for points race and a silver medal for road race at Athens Olympics (2004).

SMABERS, Hanneke (1973—). Dutch field-hockey player. Born Oct 19, 1973, in the Netherlands. ❖ Won a team bronze medal at Sydney Olympics (2000).

SMABERS, Minke (1979—). Dutch field-hockey player. Born Mar 22, 1979, in Den Haag, Netherlands. ❖ Won a team bronze medal at Sydney Olympics (2000) and a team silver medal at Athens Olympics (2004); won Champions Trophy (2000) and European championship (2003).

SMALL, Kim (1965—). Australian field-hockey player. Born April 13, 1965, in Australia. ❖ At Seoul Olympics, won a gold medal in team competition (1988).

SMALL, Mary Elizabeth (1812/13–1908). New Zealand market produce gardener and farmer. Name variations: Mary Elizabeth Philport, Mary Elizabeth Phipps. Born c. 1812 or 1813, in Kent, England; died at Governors Bay, New Zealand, May 23, 1908; m. Stephen Small, 1841; children: 6. ❖ Immigrated with husband to NSW, Australia (1849); treated badly by husband, sailed for New Zealand with children and assumed name of Phipps (1859); survived by gardening and selling fruit and produce at market; bought land for family to farm (1870s). ❖ See also *Dictionary of New Zealand Biography* (Vol. 1).

SMALL, Sami Jo (1976—). Canadian ice-hockey player. Born 1976 in Winnipeg, Manitoba, Canada. ❖ Goaltender, won gold medals at World championships (1999, 2000) and a gold medal at Salt Lake City Olympics (2002).

SMALLEY, Mrs. Philips (1881–1939). See Weber, Lois.

SMALLWOOD, Norma (c. 1908–1966). Miss America. Name variations: Norma Bruce. Born Norma Descygne Smallwood c. 1908; died May 1966; attended Oklahoma State College; m. Thomas Gilcrease (art collector and oilman), Sept 3, 1928 (div. Oct 3, 1933); m. George H. Bruce (pres. of Aladdin Petroleum, Wichita); children: (1st m.) daughter. ❖ Was the first Native American (Cherokee) to be named Miss America (1926), representing Oklahoma. ❖ See also Frank Deford, *There She Is* (Viking, 1971).

SMALLWOOD-COOK, Kathryn (1960—). English runner. Name variations: Kathy Cook; Kathryn Smallwood. Born May 3, 1960, in UK. ❖ At Moscow Olympics, won a bronze medal in 4 x 100-meter relay (1980); at Los Angeles Olympics, won a bronze medal in 4 x 100-meter relay and a bronze medal in the 400 meters (1984).

SMART, Elizabeth (1913–1986). Canadian-born novelist and poet. Born Dec 27, 1913, in Ottawa, Ontario, Canada; died Mar 4, 1986, in London, England; dau. of Russel Smart (patent lawyer) and Emma Louise Parr; attended King's College in England; never married; children: (with poet George Barker) Georgina, Christopher, Sebastian and Rose. ❖ Wrote *By Grand Central Station I Sat Down and Wept* (1945), a lyrical novel in 1st person with loosely autobiographical plot; moved to England (1943) and over next 20 years supported herself and children with a variety of jobs in journalism, including writing for fashion magazines and doing advertising copywriting; had long struggle with writer's block; published collection of poems, *A Bonus* (1977), and 2nd novel, *The Assumption of the Rogues and Rascals* (1978), followed by *Ten Poems* (1981) and *Eleven Poems* (1982); issued *In the Meantime* (1984), a varied collection which includes the story, "Dig a Grave and Let Us Bury Our Mother," one of her most powerful works; died shortly after publication of her journals as *Necessary Secrets*. ❖ See also *Autobiographies* (1987); Rosemary Sullivan, *By Heart: The Life of Elizabeth Smart* (Flamingo, 1991); and *Women in World History*.

SMART, Pamela Wojas (1967—). American murderer (accused). Born Pamela Ann Wojas, Aug 16, 1967, in Miami, FL; m. Gregory Smart (murdered May 1, 1990). ❖ Accused of masterminding plot to murder husband, convicted in sensational trial in New Hampshire, after 4 teenagers arrested for the crime, one of them her lover, testified against her; sentenced to life in prison with no chance of parole (1991). ❖ See also tv movie "Murder in New Hampshire: The Pamela Wojas Smart Story" (1991).

SMEAL, Eleanor (1939—). American feminist. Name variations: Ellie. Born Eleanor Cutri, July 30, 1939, in Ashtabula, Ohio; raised in Erie, Pennsylvania; dau. of Peter Cutri (home builder, developer, and owner of a General Insurance agency) and Josephine Cutri; graduated Phi Beta Kappa from Duke University, 1961; University of Florida, MA in political science and public administration, 1963; m. Charles Smeal, 1963; children: Tod (b. 1964, PhD in molecular biology), Lori (b. 1968, lawyer). ❖ President of the Feminist Majority and former president of the National Organization for Women (NOW), who led the national ERA campaign, discovered the gender gap in voting, and spearheaded feminist drives for more than a quarter of a century; joined National Organization for Women (1970); founded South Hills Chapter of NOW (1971) and served as its president (1971–73); was a founder and member of the board of South Hills NOW Day Nursery School (1972–77); was Pennsylvania NOW state coordinator and president (1972–75); served as NOW national board member (1973–75); served as member of the Bylaws, Budget, Financial Development and Conference Implementation Committees (1973–75); served as chair of NOW national board (1975–77); served as president of NOW (1977–82, 1985–87); with Peg Yorkin, co-founded the Fund for the Feminist Majority and Feminist Majority Foundation (1987), and became president (1987); writings include *Why and How Women Will Elect the Next President* (1984). Awarded honorary doctor of law degree from Duke University (1991). ❖ See also *Women in World History*.

SMEDLEY, Agnes (1892–1950). American writer. Born Agnes Smedley, Feb 23, 1892, in Campground, Missouri; died in Oxford, England, May 6, 1950; dau. of Charles H. Smedley (itinerant laborer) and Sarah (Ralls) Smedley (washerwoman); m. Ernest George Brundin, Aug 14, 1912 (div. 1916); common-law marriage with Virendranath Chattopadhyaya, 1921–25; no children. ❖ Foreign correspondent and leading defender of the People's Republic of China, who used her talents to aid the Chinese Communist armies in their fight against Nationalist and Japanese forces, began as an activist for India liberation in New York (1917–20) and Berlin (1920–28); left Germany for China (1928), a land she saw as the focal point of the coming showdown between Asian nationalists and European imperialists; served as correspondent for *Frankfurter Zeitung* (1928–32) and *Manchester Guardian* (1938–41); published an English-language weekly *China Forum* (1932–34); lived in Soviet Union (1933–34), then China (1934–41), where she won fame by her crusade to publicize the suffering produced by the Japanese invasion and to make the cause of Chinese Communists (CCP) known to the outside world; sustained the longest tour in China of any foreign journalist, man or woman; returning to US, met with tremendous popularity (1943–44), until she became more overtly pro-CCP, in the process attacking Guomindang leaders; came under scrutiny of FBI; moved to Wimbledon, England (1949). Writings include the semi-autobiographical *Daughter of Earth* (1929), as well as *Chinese Destinies* (1933), *China's Red Army Marches* (1934), *China Fights Back: An American Woman with the Eighth Route Army* (1938), *Battle Hymn of China* (1943) and *The Great Road: The Life and Times of Chu Teh* (1956). ❖ See also MacKinnon and MacKinnon, *Agnes Smedley: The Life and Times of an American Radical* (U. of California Press, 1988); and *Women in World History*.

SMEDLEY, Menella Bute (c. 1820–1877). English poet and novelist. Name variations: (pseudonym) S. M. Born c. 1820 in Great Marlow, Buckinghamshire, England; died May 25, 1877, in London, England; dau. of Edward Smedley (encyclopedia editor, poet, and cleric) and Mary (Hume) Smedley; sister of writer Frank Smedley; never married; no children. ❖ Was a writer of poetry, novels, stories, and plays and a philanthropist devoted to the education and training of poor children; wrote several books for children, such as *Poems Written for a Child* (1868), *Child-World* (1869) and *Silver Wings and Golden Scales* (1877); other writings include *The Maiden Aunt* (1848), *The Story of a Family* (1851), *Nina: A Tale for the Twilight* (1853), *Lays and Ballads from English History* (1856), *The Story of Queen Isabel, and Other Verses* (1863), *Twice Lost* (1863), *Linnet's Trial* (1864) and *The Colville Family* (1867). ❖ See also *Women in World History*.

SMEKALOVA, Hana (1918–1978). See Marly, Florence.

SMELLIE, Elizabeth Lawrie (1884–1968). Canadian nurse. Born Elizabeth Lawrie Smellie, Mar 22, 1884, in Port Arthur, Ontario, Canada; died Mar 5, 1968, in Toronto; dau. of Janet Eleanor Lawrie Smellie and Dr. Thomas Stewart Traill Smellie; graduate of Johns Hopkins Training School for Nurses, 1909. ❖ During WWI, served as a nursing sister with Canadian Army Medical Corps and as matron of Moore Barracks Hospital in England (1915–18); served as assistant matron-in-chief with Canadian National Nursing Service (1918–20); was director's assistant at McGill School of Graduate Nursing (1921–24); served as chief superintendent of Victorian Order of Nurses (VON, 1924–47); was vice president of American Public Health Association (1939); during WWII, was matron-in-chief and lieutenant colonel, then appointed the 1st Canadian woman colonel in Royal Canadian Army (1944). Received Canadian Nurses Association's Mary Snively Memorial Medal (1938).

SMENDZIANKA, Regina (1924—). Polish pianist. Born 1924; studied with Zbigniew Drzewiecki in Warsaw. ❖ Besides carrying on an important concert career, recorded a superb performance of Sonata No. 2 by Polish composer Grazyna Bacewicz; also recorded Bacewicz's piano *Etudes*. ❖ See also *Women in WorldHistory*.

SMET, Miet (1943—). Belgian politician. Born April 5, 1943, in St. Niklaas, Belgium. ❖ Served as chair of the European Union of Christian Democratic Workers (1995–97), member of the House of Representatives (1978–95), member of the Senate (1995), minister of Employment, Labour and Equal Opportunities for Men and Women (1992–99); minister of state (2002); as a member of the European People's Party (Christian Democrats) and European Democrats, elected to 5th European Parliament (1999–2004). Awarded Knight of the Order of Leopold (1985) and Grosses Verdienstkreuz mit Stern (2002).

SMETANINA, Raisa (1929—). Russian cross-country skier. Name variations: Raissa Smetanina. Born Feb 29, 1952, in Russia. ❖ Won 10 winter Olympics medals: at Innsbruck, won gold medals for 10 km and 4 x 5 km relay and a silver medal for 5 km (1976); at Lake Placid, won a gold medal for 5 km and a silver medal for 4 x 5 km relay (1980); at Sarajevo, won silver medals for 10 km and 20 km (1984); at Calgary, won a silver medal for 10 km and a bronze medal for 20 km (1988); at Albertville, won a gold medal for 4 x 5 km relay (1992), the oldest woman to win a Winter gold.

SMIDOVA, Lenka (1975—). Czechoslovakian sailor. Born Mar 26, 1975, in Havlickuv Brod, Czechoslovakia; dau. of sailors; attended University of Economics in Prague. ❖ Won a silver medal for single-handed dinghy (Europe) at Athens Olympics (2004).

SMIETON, Mary (1902–2005). English civil servant. Name variations: Dame Mary Smieton. Born Mary Guillan SmietonDec 5, 1902, in Cambridge, England; died Jan 23, 2005, in England; dau. of librarian and bursar of Westminster College, Cambridge; graduate of Lady Margaret Hall, Oxford; never married. ❖ Only the 2nd woman to head a government department, was appointed permanent secretary in the Ministry of Education (1959), serving until 1963; was also UK representative on the board of UNESCO. Named DBE (1949).

SMILEY, Jane (1949—). American novelist and short-story writer. Born Sept 26, 1949, in Los Angeles, California; raised in suburbs of St. Louis, Missouri; Vassar College, BA, 1971; University of Iowa, MA, 1975, MFA, 1976, PhD, 1978; m. John Whiston, 1970 (div. 1975); m. William Slag, 1978 (div. 1986); m. Stephen Mortensen, 1987 (div. 1997); children: (2nd m.) Phoebe and Lucy Slag; (3rd m.) A. J. Mortenson. ❖ Taught at Iowa State University (1981–96); published 1st novel, *Barn Blind* (1980); won Pulitzer Prize for novel

A Thousand Acres (1991), a reworking of *King Lear* set in a farming community in Iowa; also wrote the novels *The Greenlanders* (1988), *Moo* (1995), *The All-True Travels and Adventures of Lidie Newton* (1998), *Horse Heaven* (2000) and *Good Faith* (2003); short story collections include *The Age of Grief* (1987) and *Ordinary Love and Good Will* (1989).

SMIRNOVA, Irina (1968—). Soviet volleyball player. Born Aug 3, 1968, in USSR. ❖ Won a gold medal at Seoul Olympics (1988) and a silver medal at Barcelona Olympics (1992), both in team competition.

SMIRNOVA, Ludmila (1949—). Russian pairs skater. Name variations: Lyudmila or Liudmila. Born July 21, 1949, in USSR; m. Alexei Ulanov (skater). ❖ With Andrei Suraikin, won 3 World championship silver medals (1970–72), 3 European championship silver medals (1970–72), and a silver medal at Sapporo Olympics (1972); with Alexei Ulanov, placed 2nd at World championships (1973, 1974).

SMIRNOVA, Sofia (1852–1921). Russian novelist and short-story writer. Name variations: Sofia Ivanovna Smirnóva. Born 1852 in Russia; died 1921; m. Nikolai Sazanov (actor), 1877. ❖ Wrote novels, popular in their day, including *A Small Light* (1871), *The School District Administrator* (1873), *Strength of Character* (1876) and *Through Fire and Water* (1893); also wrote plays, including *The Anthill* (1896), and several short stories.

SMIRNOW, Zoya (fl. 1914). Russian fighter. Born in Moscow, Russia. ❖ During WWI, left school in Moscow with 11 other girls and made way to Lemberg, where they dressed as soldiers and joined the Russian army; fought in Galacia and the Carpathians; wounded and sent to hospital, was the only survivor of her group.

SMIT, Gretha (1976—). Dutch speedskater. Born Jan 20, 1976, in Rouveen, Netherlands. ❖ Won a silver medal for the 5,000 meters at Salt Lake City Olympics (2002).

SMITA (1955–1986). See Patil, Smita.

SMITH, Abby (1797–1878). American political activist and social reformer. Name variations: Abba. Born Abby Hadassah Smith, June 1, 1797, in Glastonbury, Connecticut; died July 23, 1878; dau. of Zephaniah Hollister Smith (cleric turned lawyer, died 1836) and Hannah Hadassah Hickok Smith (died 1850); sister of Julia Smith (1792–1886); never married; no children. ❖ Lifelong social and political reformer who, with sister Julia Smith, refused to pay taxes unless she could vote and in consequence had livestock seized; moved back to Glastonbury with family (1795); lived at home with parents and 4 other sisters, learning and teaching; did charitable work among free blacks (1819); with family, joined Hartford Anti-Slavery Society, hosted abolitionists, distributed literature, initiated petitions (1830s–60s); helped Julia translate the Bible 5 times (1847–1855); unfairly taxed by town of Glastonbury (1869), traveled with Julia to Connecticut Woman's Suffrage Association in Hartford (1869); after Julia tried to register to vote and was denied (1873), joined her in refusing to pay taxes (1873); spoke before town meeting (1873); with Julia, spoke in public on suffrage (1873–78) and bought back 7 Alderney cows beloved as pets which were seized for auction by the tax collector, causing a sympathetic uproar across the region and then the nation (1874); addressed a crowd outside town meeting from a wagon, after having been refused a voice inside the building (1874), and spoke before the Woman Suffrage Committee of the Connecticut State Legislature (1874); with Julia, fought town's attempt to auction off Smith land (1874), then bought back cows seized for auction twice more (1876); with Julia, won court appeal and regained land (1876). ❖ See also Kathleen L. Housley, *The Letter Kills But the Spirit Gives Life: The Smiths—Abolitionists, Suffragists, Bible Translators* (Historical Society of Glastonbury, 1993); and *Women in World History*.

SMITH, Ada (1894–1984). African-American jazz singer. Name variations: Bricktop; Brickie; Ada Smith Ducongé or Duconge. Born Beatrice Queen Victoria Louise Virginia Smith in Alderson, WV, Aug 14, 1894; died in New York, NY, Jan 31, 1984; m. Peter Ducongé (saxophonist), 1929 (sep. 1933, never div.). ❖ Celebrated Parisian club owner, began dancing and singing in Chicago as a child; at 14, was in the chorus at Pekin Theater, the 1st theater of consequence in Chicago to devote its playbill to black drama; by 16, was touring with Theater Owners' Booking Association (TOBA) under name Bricktop, because of her flaming red hair and freckles; by 20, had traveled throughout US and moved on to Europe; opened club on Rue Pigalle in Paris (1920), which she called Chez Bricktop, where such celebrities as John Steinbeck, Ernest

Hemingway and Josephine Baker flocked; married and settled into an estate in Bougival, outside Paris (1929); opened a bigger Bricktop (1931), hiring constant companion Mabel Mercer as assistant, and regularly performing Cole Porter's "Miss Otis regrets"; with Nazis poised to invade, was one of the last US entertainers to leave France (1939); opened Brittwood on 140th Street in Harlem (1940), becoming a well-known host in café society; lived in Mexico City (1943–49); returned to Paris (1949) and opened a new Bricktop (1950), but it closed shortly thereafter; left for Rome (1951) and opened a club on Via Veneto; became involved in Italian charities, raising money for the housing of war orphans; returned to US (1964); released her only recording, "So Long, Baby" (1970); made documentary, *Honeybaby, Honeybaby!* (1973). ❖ See also autobiography (with James Haskins), *Bricktop* (Atheneum, 1983); and *Women in World History*.

SMITH, Ada. English gymnast. Born in UK. ❖ At Amsterdam Olympics, won a bronze medal in team all-around (1928).

SMITH, Alexis (1921–1993). Canadian-born actress. Born Gladys Smith, June 8, 1921, in Penticton, British Columbia, Canada; died June 9, 1993, in Los Angeles, California; attended Los Angeles City College; m. Craig Stevens (actor), in 1944; no children. ❖ Statuesque beauty who played leads or 2nd leads, appearing in such movies as *Dive Bomber* (1941), *The Constant Nymph* (1943), *Doughgirls* (1944), *San Antonio* (1945), *The Horn Blows at Midnight* (1945), *Rhapsody in Blue* (1945), *Night and Day* (1946), *Stallion Road* (1947), *The Two Mrs. Carrolls* (1947), *The Woman in White* (1948), *Any Number Can Play* (1949), *Beau James* (1957), *This Happy Feeling* (1958) and *The Young Philadelphians* (1959); retired from films (1959); made a stunning Broadway comeback in *Follies* (1971), for which she won a Tony Award as Best Actress; following triumph, appeared in *Jacqueline Susann's Once Is Not Enough* (1975) and on Broadway in *The Women, Summer Brave,* and the musical *Platinum*; also had a recurring role in tv series "Dallas" (1984) and in the short-lived "Hothouse" (1988). ❖ See also *Women in World History*.

SMITH, Alys Pearsall (1866–1951). See Russell, Alys Smith.

SMITH, Amanda Berry (1837–1915). American missionary. Born Amanda Berry, Jan 23, 1837, in Long Green, Maryland; died in Sebring, Florida, Feb 24, 1915; dau. of Samuel Berry and Miriam Matthews, slaves on adjoining farms; m. Calvin Devine, Sept 1854; m. James Smith, 1863; children: (1st m.) Mazie; (2nd m.): Nell, Thomas Henry, and Will. ❖ Slave-born Protestant evangelist and missionary, began career as itinerant evangelist in Holiness circles (1869); traveled to England to preach (1878) and left to become missionary to India (1879); worked as missionary in West Africa (1882–89), primarily in Liberia and Sierra Leone; traveled to Great Britain before returning to US and settling in Chicago area; began work on establishment of orphanage for African-American children (1895); opened Amanda Smith Orphan's Home for Colored Children (1899); moved to Florida (1912). ❖ See also *An Autobiography; The Story of the Lord's Dealings with Mrs. Amanda Smith the Colored Evangelist* (Oxford U. Press, 1988); Marshall William Taylor, *The Life, Travels, Labors and Helpers of Mrs. Amanda Smith; the Famous Negro Missionary Evangelist* (c. 1886); M. H. Cadbury, *The Life of Amanda Smith* (1916); and *Women in World History*.

SMITH, Amey (c. 1829–1920). See Daldy, Amey.

SMITH, Angela (1959—). English politician and member of Parliament. Born Angela Evans, Jan 7, 1959, in London, England; m. Nigel Smith, 1978; Leicester Polytechnic, BA. ❖ Representing Labour/Co-operative, elected to House of Commons for Basildon (1997); named assistant government whip and parliamentary under-secretary of state, Northern Ireland Office.

SMITH, Anna Deavere (1950—). African-American playwright and actress. Born Sept 18, 1950, in Baltimore, Maryland; attended Beaver College; American Conservatory Theatre, MFA, 1976; never married. ❖ Taught at Carnegie-Mellon, Yale, Stanford, Harvard and New York universities; came to national prominence for solo shows, *Fire in the Mirror* (1993) and *Twilight, Los Angeles: 1992,* for which she was nominated for Tony Awards for Best Actress and Best Play; had a recurring role as Nancy McNally on "West Wing" (2000–04); received MacArthur Foundation "genius" grant (1996); wrote *Talk to Me: Travels in Media and Politics* (2000).

SMITH, Anna Young (1756–1780). American poet. Name variations: Anna Young; (pseudonym) Sylvia. Born Anna Young, 1756, in Philadelphia, PA; died April 3, 1780; dau. of Jane Graeme Young (died 1756); raised by aunt, Elizabeth Graeme Ferguson (poet); m. Dr. William Smith, 1775. ❖ Wrote poems "An Ode to Gratitude, Inscribed to Miss Eliza Graeme by her Niece, Anna Young," "An Elegy to the Memory of American Volunteers" (1775), and "On Reading Swift's Works," all published posthumously.

SMITH, Annette. American singer. Name variations: The Chantels. ❖ Sang with the Veneers; replaced Arlene Smith (no relation) as lead vocalist for the doo-wop group The Chantels (late 1950s), one of 1st and most well-received girl groups; her hits with The Chantels included "Look in My Eyes" and "Well, I Told You" (both 1961).

SMITH, Annie Lorrain (1854–1937). Scottish botanist. Born 1854 in Dumfriesshire, Scotland; died 1937; educated in Germany and France. ❖ Studied botany with D. H. Scott at South Kensington; assisted W. C. Carruthers at the British Museum of Natural History and worked in the botany department (1902–34); served as president of British Mycological Society (1907 and 1917); published the textbook, *Lichens.* Made Officer of the Order of the British Empire (1934).

SMITH, Arlene (1941—). American singer. Name variations: The Chantels. Born Oct 5, 1941, in New York. ❖ Sang with Lois Harris, Sonia Goring, Jackie Landry and Rene Minus in their Bronx, NY, parochial school choir, then became lead singer for their group The Chantels (1956), one of 1st and most well-received girl groups; released album *We Are the Chantels* (1958); left Chantels for solo career; reformed the group with new members (early 1970s); appeared with original group in reunion performances (1990s). Chantels biggest hit was "Maybe" (1958).

SMITH, Barbara Leigh (1827–1891). See Bodichon, Barbara.

SMITH, Bathsheba (1822–1910). American religious leader. Born Bathsheba Wilson Bigler, May 3, 1822, in Shinnston, Harrison Co., Virginia (now West Virginia); died 1910; dau. of Mark Bigler and Susannah (Ogden) Bigler; m. George A. Smith (elder of Church of Jesus Christ of Latter-day Saints and leader of Utah Territorial legislature), July 26, 1841 (died 1875); children: George A. Smith Jr. (1842–1860); Bathsheba Smith, known as Kate (b. 1844, who m. Clarence Merrill); John Smith (1847–1847). ❖ General president of Relief Society of the Church of Jesus Christ of Latter-day Saints, became a charter member of Nauvoo Female Relief Society (1842); settled in what would become Salt Lake City, Utah (1849); at a meeting of Salt Lake City women (early 1870), proposed "that we demand of the Governor the right of franchise" which ultimately led to women in Utah being the 1st in the nation to exercise the right to vote; after Brigham Young organized the churchwide Retrenchment Society, was selected as one of its 3 women leaders; elected to the board of directors of Deseret Hospital (1882); served as general president of the Relief Society (1904–10); at time of death, was granted a funeral service in the Mormon Tabernacle, the 1st woman to be so honored. ❖ See also *Women in World History*.

SMITH, Becky (1959—). See Smith, Rebecca.

SMITH, Bessie (1894–1937). African-American blues and jazz singer. Born Bessie Smith, April 15, 1894, in Chattanooga, TN; died in Clarksdale, MS, Sept 26 (some sources cite the 27th), 1937, from injuries suffered in an automobile accident while touring; m. Earl Love (died c. 1920); m. Jack Gee (Philadelphia night watchman), 1923 (estranged at time of her death). ❖ One of America's greatest jazz singers, known as "Empress of the Blues," began singing for traveling shows in segregated venues throughout the South; turned Atlanta's famous "81" theater into home base for several years, then headed north to play Baltimore (1918), before moving to Philadelphia (1920); signed with Columbia (1923) and recorded "Gulf Coast Blues," "T'Ain't Nobody's Business If I Do" and "Down Hearted Blues," the latter selling nearly 800,000 copies on its release; quickly became the best-known blues performer, playing scores of theaters to huge crowds throughout Northeast, Midwest and South, singing such songs as "I'm Wild About That Thing" with gleeful abandon; at height of career (1925), traveled from city to city in her own railroad car with her 1st *Harlem Frolics* vaudeville show; with advent of swing and fall of the stock market, saw career begin a downward spiral (1929), the same year Columbia released her signature song, "Nobody Knows You When You're Down and Out"; starred in a short, 17-minute film, *St. Louis Blues*, then starred on Broadway in an all-black musical, *Pansy*, but it closed after 3 performances; contract with Columbia was not renewed (1931); modified repertoire to include swing numbers (1935) and resumed recording for Columbia; in demand again, appeared at The

Famous Door in Manhattan; while on tour in the South with *Broadway Rastus*, was killed when her Packard collided with the rear of a trailer truck (1937). ❖ See also Chris Albertson, *Bessie* (Stein & Day, 1972); Elaine Feinstein, *Bessie Smith* (Viking, 1985); Angela Y. Davis, *Blues Legacies and Black Feminism: Gertrude "Ma" Rainey, Bessie Smith, and Billie Holiday* (Pantheon, 1998); and *Women in World History*.

SMITH, Betty (1896–1972). American novelist and playwright. Born Elisabeth Keogh on Dec 15, 1896, in Brooklyn, New York; died Jan 17, 1972; dau. of John Keogh and Catherine (Wehner) Keogh; attended University of Michigan, 1927–30; attended Yale University Drama School, 1930–34; m. George H. E. Smith, June 1924 (div. 1938); m. Joseph Piper Jones (journalist), 1943 (div. 1951); m. Robert Finch, June 1957 (died 1959); children: (1st m.) Nancy, Mary. ❖ Wrote articles for the *Detroit Free Press* and the NEA syndicate; won University of Michigan's prestigious Avery Hopwood Award for one-act plays; wrote over 70 one-act plays (all either produced or published) and was involved in the theater in a variety of ways, including acting, playreading, and a brief stint as a radio performer (1930s–40s); published 1st novel, *A Tree Grows in Brooklyn* (1943), which sold some 6 million copies by early 1970s, was translated into 16 languages, and was required reading for millions of American schoolchildren; also wrote *Tomorrow Will Be Better* (1948), *Maggie-Now* (1958), and the autobiographical *Joy in the Morning* (1963). ❖ See also *Women in World History*.

SMITH, Bev (1960—). Canadian basketball player and coach. Born April 4, 1960, in Armstrong, British Columbia, Canada; graduate of University of Oregon, 1982. ❖ Considered one of the best basketball players in Canada, led her team to a 3rd-place finish at World championships (1979); competed as an athlete at Los Angeles and Atlanta Olympics (1984, 1996) and as a coach at Sydney Olympics (2000); played professionally in Italy for 12 years; became head coach of the University of Oregon women's basketball team. Inducted into Canadian Basketball Hall of Fame (2001) and Canadian Olympic Hall of Fame (2003).

SMITH, Bill (1886–1975). Australian jockey. Name variations: Wilhelmina Smith. Born 1886 in Australia; died near Cairns, Australia, 1975. ❖ Known in North Queensland, Australia, for skill with riding racehorses, won Australia's St. Leger Quest Derby (1902), Jockey Club Derby (1903), and Victorian Oaks Derby (1909–10); was discovered to have been a woman only after she died (1975), the year after women jockeys were allowed to race in Australia. ❖ See also *Women in World History*.

SMITH, Bronwyn. *See Mayer, Bronwyn.*

SMITH, Mrs. Bunty (1924–1978). *See Stephens, Frances.*

SMITH, Caroline (1906—). American diver. Name variations: Carol Smith. Born July 21, 1906; trained with Los Angeles AC. ❖ At Paris Olympics, won a gold medal in platform (1924), the 1st woman to win the event; also placed 1st at US nationals (1925). Honored by International Swimming Hall of Fame (1988).

SMITH, Charlotte (1749–1806). English novelist and poet. Name variations: Charlotte Turner Smith. Born Charlotte Turner in London, England, May 4, 1749; died in Tilford, near Farnham, Surrey, Oct 28, 1806; dau. of Nicholas Turner of Stoke House, Surrey, and Anna (Towers) Turner; sister of Catherine Ann Dorset (c. 1750–c. 1817, noted writer of children's books); m. Benjamin Smith (director of East India Co.), 1765 (died 1806); children: 12, one of whom, Lionel Smith (1778–1842), was governor of the Windward and Leeward Islands (1833–39). ❖ To support a feckless husband, published *Elegiac Sonnets and other Essays* (1784), dedicated to her friend, poet William Hayley, and printed at her own expense; translated Prévost's *Manon Lescaut* (1785) and *The Romance of Real Life* (1786); devoted herself to novel writing and financially assisting her children and husband until his death in Berwick jail; chief works are *Emmeline, or the Orphan of the Castle* (1788), *Ethelinde* (1789), *Celestina* (1791), *Desmond* (1792), *The Old Manor House* (1793), *The Young Philosopher* (1798) and *Conversations introducing Poetry* (1804). ❖ See also F. M. A. Hilbish, *Charlotte Smith: Poet and Novelist* (1941); and *Women in World History*.

SMITH, Chloethiel Woodard (1910–1992). American architect and city planner. Name variations: often incorrectly spelled Cloethiel. Born Feb 2, 1910, in Peoria, Illinois; died Dec 30, 1992, in Washington, DC; dau. of Oliver Ernest Woodard and Coy Blanche (Johnson) Woodard; University of Oregon, Bachelor of Architecture, with honors, 1932; Washington University, Master of Architecture

in city planning, 1933; m. Bromley Keables Smith, April 5, 1940; children: Bromley Keables Smith; Susanne Woodard Smith. ❖ One of the nation's most successful woman architects, was a partner in Keyes, Smith, Satterlee & Lethbridge (1951–56), then Satterlee & Smith (1956–63); founded Chloethiel Woodard Smith & Associated Architects (1963); projects ranged from US Chancery and ambassador's residence in Asunción, Paraguay, to Crown Towers in New Haven, Connecticut; became especially well known for urban renewal work and community planning projects on waterfront in Washington, DC, La Clede Town in St. Louis, Missouri, and a complex of townhouses in Reston, Virginia. Elected to the College of Fellows of American Institute of Architects (1960). ❖ See also *Women in World History*.

SMITH, Christine Anne (1946—). Australian politician. Born Oct 11, 1946, in Sydney, Australia. ❖ As a member of the Australian Labor Party, elected to the Queensland Parliament for Burleigh (2001).

SMITH, Clara (1894–1935). African-American blues singer. Born in Spartanburg, SC, 1894; died Feb 21, 1935, in Detroit, Michigan; m. Charles Wesley (baseball manager), 1926. ❖ Known as Queen of the Moaners, began singing in Southern vaudeville and eventually became a popular performer on Theater Owners' Booking Association (TOBA) circuit; opened her own club (1924), the Clara Smith Theatrical Club; recorded mostly for Columbia (1925–28), backed by such jazz artists as Louis Armstrong on cornet, Coleman Hawkins on sax, Don Redman on clarinet, and James P. Johnson on piano; also recorded 2 duets with Bessie Smith; recorded over 125 songs in her career, including "Every Woman's Blues" and "Awful Moaning Blues." ❖ See also *Women in World History*.

SMITH, Delia (1941—). English food writer and broadcaster. Born 1941 in Woking, Surrey, England; m. Michael Wynn Jones (newspaper editor). ❖ Began writing food column for *Daily Mirror* magazine (1969); published 1st cookbook, *How to Cheat at Cooking* (1971); wrote for *Evening Standard* (1972–84); began tv career with BBC1 series "Family Fare" (1973), with easy-to-follow recipes and unintimidating style; wrote *Frugal Food* (1976) and *Delia Smith's Book of Cakes* (1977); published 3-part *Delia Smith's Cookery Course* (1985, 1990, 1993), as well as the wildly popular *Delia Smith's Winter Collection* (1995), which was accompanied by 12-part BBC2 tv series; served as consultant food editor for award-winning *Sainsbury's The Magazine* which she launched with husband (1993). Received Order of British Empire (OBE, 1995). ❖ See also Alison Bowyer, *Delia: The Biography* (Carlton, 1999).

SMITH, Dodie (1896–1990). English playwright and novelist. Name variations: (pseudonyms) C. L. Anthony, Charles Henry Percy. Born Dorothy Gladys Smith, May 3, 1896, in Whitefield, Lancashire, England; died Nov 24, 1990; dau. of Ernest Walter Smith and Ella (Furber) Smith; studied at Royal Academy of Dramatic Art; m. Alec Macbeth Beesley (her business manager), 1939 (died 1987). ❖ Popular English playwright, noted for her humorous insights into ordinary lives, is probably best remembered for *The Hundred and One Dalmatians* and *Dear Octopus*; wrote 1st one-act, *British Talent* (1924); under pseudonym C. L. Anthony, wrote breakthrough play, the romantic comedy *Autumn Crocus* (1931); had similar success with 2 other plays written under C. L. Anthony, *Service* and *Touch Wood*; under real name, wrote *Call It a Day* (1935), which ran for almost 200 performances in NY and more than 500 performances in London; returned with *Dear Octopus* (1938), which became the best known of all her plays; during WWII, lived in US; wrote play *Lovers and Friends* (1943), as well as film scripts; published 1st novel, *I Capture the Castle* (1948), a bestseller; returned to England (1953) and, in addition to her other writing, began to write several stories for children, penning *The Hundred and One Dalmatians* (1956). ❖ See also autobiographies *Look Back with Love: A Manchester Childhood* (1974), *Look Back with Mixed Feelings* (1978), *Look Back with Astonishment* (1979) and *Look Back with Gratitude* (1985); Valerie Grove, *Dear Dodie: The Life of Dodie Smith* (Pimlico, 1997); and *Women in World History*.

SMITH, Donalda (d. 1998). Canadian syncronized swimming judge and official. Died Nov 1998; children: Margaret MacLennan (synchronized swimmer). ❖ Moved to Vancouver (1934); coached synchronized swimming, then became a judge and official; served on the technical committee of FINA (1972–80); played a fundamental role in getting sport included in Olympics; served on the inaugural judging panel at Los Angeles Olympics (1984). Named Officer of the Order of Canada (1983); inducted into the Canadian Aquatics Hall of Fame (1991).

SMITH, Dorothy Greenhough (1875–1965). *See Greenhough, Dorothy.*

SMITH, Edith Blackwell (1871–1920). *See Holden, Edith B.*

SMITH, Elaine (1963—). Scottish politician. Born May 7, 1963, in Coatbridge; m. Vann Smith; children: son. ❖ As a Labour candidate, elected to the Scottish Parliment for Coatbridge and Chryston (1999, 2003).

SMITH, Eliza Roxey Snow (1804–1887). American religious leader and poet. Name variations: Eliza Roxey Snow; middle name sometimes spelled "Roxcy" or "Roxcey." Born Eliza Roxey Snow, Jan 21, 1804, in Becket, Berkshire Co., Massachusetts; died Dec 5, 1887, in Salt Lake City, Utah; dau. of Oliver Snow III (farmer) and Rosetta Leonora (Pettibone) Snow; sister of Lorenzo Snow (president of the Mormon Church, 1898–1901); became a plural wife of Joseph Smith (1805–1844, founder of Church of Jesus Christ of Latter-day Saints), June 1842 (died June 1844); became a plural wife of Brigham Young (1801–1877, leader of Church of Jesus Christ of Latter-day Saints), June 1849; no children. ❖ Called "mother of Mormonism," played a crucial part in establishing the role of women in Mormon Church; was a founding member of Women's Relief Society (1842) and pioneered "temple work" that became part of the religion's permanent tradition; while the church became riven with factionalism in aftermath of 1st husband's death, went to live in family home of Brigham Young; was one of thousands who traveled west with him from Nauvoo to Salt Lake Valley (1846–47); became one of Young's many plural wives (1849); appointed president of the Endowment House (1855); having continued to work with Women's Relief Society in Utah, became the society's general president (1866); oversaw opening of the Deseret Hospital for women (1882); was put in charge of the newly formed Young Ladies' Retrenchment Association (1869), turning it into the Young Ladies' Mutual Improvement Association, one of the main women's organizations in the church; organized and directed a meeting in defense of polygamy (1878); named president of Mormon women's organizations throughout the world (1880); writings include *Poems, Religious, Historical and Political* (1856 and 1877) and *Biography and Family Record of Lorenzo Snow* (1884); also wrote a number of hymns, the best known being "O My Father, Thou That Dwellest." ❖ See also *Women in World History.*

SMITH, Elizabeth (1859–1949). *See Shortt, Elizabeth Smith.*

SMITH, Elizabeth (c. 1948—). *See Primrose-Smith, Elizabeth.*

SMITH, Elizabeth "Betsy" (1750–1815). Sister of Abigail Adams. Name variations: Betsy Shaw, Betsy Peabody, Betsy Smith. Born 1750; died 1815; dau. of the Reverend William Smith (pastor, 1706–1783) and Elizabeth (Quincy) Smith (1721–1775); sister of Abigail Adams (1744–1818); m. Reverend John Shaw (died 1794); m. Reverend Stephen Peabody. ❖ See also *Women in World History.*

SMITH, Elizabeth Oakes (1806–1893). American author. Born Elizabeth Prince, near Portland, Maine, 1806; died 1893; descended from distinguished Puritan ancestry; m. Seba Smith (American satirist who founded and edited the *Portland [Maine] Courier*). ❖ Published *The Sinless Child and Other Poems* (1843), which had originally appeared in *Southern Literary Messenger*; also wrote *The Western Captive* (1842), *Bald Eagle: Or, The Last of the Ramapaughs* (1867), *The Newsboy, Sagamore of Saco, The Two Wives, Kitty Howard's Journal, Destiny: A Tragedy, Jacob Leisler, The Salamander: A Legend for Christmas,* and a tragedy in 5 acts, *The Roman Tribute*; a prominent advocate of women's rights, published *Woman and Her Needs* (1851).

SMITH, Elizabeth Quincy (1721–1775). Mother of Abigail Adams. Name variations: Elizabeth Quincy. Born 1721; died 1775; dau. of Colonel John Quincy (speaker of the House of Representatives) and Elizabeth Norton; m. Reverend William Smith (1706–1783, a pastor); children: Mary Smith Cranch (1741–1811); Abigail Adams (1744–1818); William "Billy" (1746–1787); Elizabeth "Betsy" Smith (1750–1815). ❖ See also *Women in World History.*

SMITH, Emily James (1865–1944). *See Putnam, Emily James.*

SMITH, Emma Hale (1804–1879). American mormon. Name variations: Emma Hale Smith Bidamon. Born Emma Hale, July 10, 1804, in Harmony, Pennsylvania; died April 20, 1879, in Nauvoo, Illinois; dau. of Isaac Hale (farmer) and Elizabeth (Lewis) Hale; m. Joseph Smith (1805–1844, founder of the Church of Jesus Christ of Latter-day Saints), Jan 18, 1827; m. Major Lewis Crum Bidamon, April 1847; children: (1st m.) 3 (all died young); Joseph Smith III (b. 1832, later president of Reorganized Church of Jesus Christ of Latter-Day Saints); Frederick; Alexander; Don Carlos (died young); David; (adopted twins)

Joseph Murdock (died young) and Julia Murdock. ❖ Wife of Joseph Smith, founder of the Church of Jesus Christ of Latter-day Saints, who was one of her husband's earliest converts but later broke with the church over the doctrine of polygamy. ❖ See also Norma J. Fischer, *Portrait of a Prophet's Wife: Emma Hale Smith* (Silver Leaf, 1992); Linda King Newell, *Mormon Enigma: Emma Hale Smith, Prophet's Wife, "Elect Lady," Polygamy's Foe, 1804–1879* (Doubleday, 1984); and *Women in World History.*

SMITH, Erminnie A. Platt (1836–1886). American ethnologist. Born Ermina Adele Platt, April 26, 1836, in Marcellus, New York; died June 9, 1886; dau. of Joseph Platt (farmer and Presbyterian deacon) and Ermina (Dodge) Platt; graduate of Troy Female Seminary, 1853; studied at universities in Strassburg and Heidelberg and attended the School of Mines in Freiburg, Germany; m. Simeon H. Smith (lumber dealer), 1855; children: Simeon, Willard, Carlton and Eugene. ❖ The 1st woman to practice in the field of ethnology, focused her studies on the Iroquois Nation, and spent most of her time among the Tuscarora tribe; devoted summers to traveling to reservations in NY and Canada under the auspices of the Smithsonian Institution's Bureau of American Ethnology (1880–85); compiled an Iroquois dictionary of more than 15,000 words and recorded a collection of legends, published as *Myths of the Iroquois* (1883); was the 1st woman elected a fellow of New York Academy of Sciences (1885) and the 1st woman to hold an office (secretary of the anthropology section) in the American Association for the Advancement of Science; became a member of the London Scientific Society. ❖ See also *Women in World History.*

SMITH, Ethel (1907–1979). Canadian runner. Name variations: Ethel Smith Stewart. Born July 5, 1907, in Toronto, Ontario, Canada; died Dec 31, 1979, in Toronto. ❖ At Amsterdam Olympics, won a bronze medal in 100 meters and a gold medal in 4 x 100-meter relay (1928).

SMITH, Eunice (1757–1823). American writer. Born 1757 in MA; died 1823. ❖ Wrote religious works that reflect her strong Baptist beliefs, including *Some Arguments Against Worldly-Mindedness* (1791), *Some Exercises of a Believing Soul* (1793) and *Some Motives to Engage Those Who Have Professed the Name of the Lord Jesus* (1798).

SMITH, Evelyn E. (1922–2000). American science-fiction writer. Name variations: (pseudonym) Delphine Lyons or Delphine C. Lyons. Born July 25, 1922, possibly in NY; died July 4, 2000, in New York, NY. ❖ Wrote "Miss Melville" series, including *Miss Melville Regrets* (1986) and *Miss Melville Rides a Tiger* (1991); also wrote *The Perfect Planet* (1962), *Valley of Shadows* (1968), *Unpopular Planet* (1975) and *The Copy Shop* (1985); short stories appeared in *Beyond, Fantasy and Science Fiction, Fantastic Universe, Galaxy,* and other magazines and anthologies; was also a crossword puzzle compiler.

SMITH, Fanny Louise (1878–1948). *See Irvine-Smith, Fanny Louise.*

SMITH, Fiona (1973—). Canadian ice-hockey player. Born Oct 31, 1973, in Edam, Saskatchewan, Canada. ❖ Won a gold medal at World championships (1997); won a team silver medal at Nagano (1998), the 1st Olympics to feature women's ice hockey; also won a team bronze medal at the National Fastball championships (1991).

SMITH, Florence Margaret (1902–1971). *See Smith, Stevie.*

SMITH, Frances (1924–1978). *See Stephens, Bunty.*

SMITH, Frances Hagell (1877–1948). New Zealand missionary and welfare worker. Name variations: Frances Hagell Every, Fan Every. Born Feb 21, 1877, at Oamaru, New Zealand; died Nov 1, 1948, at Gore, New Zealand; dau. of Frederick Every (builder) and Henrietta (Jeffreys) Every; m. Ethelbert Cann Smith, 1911 (died 1947); children: 1 daughter, 2 sons. ❖ Entered foreign mission service of Presbyterian Church (1909); active in Dr. Barnado's Homes, English children's charity, and in Gore branch of Women's Christian Temperance Union of New Zealand; also belonged to Gore branch of Plunket Society. ❖ See also *Dictionary of New Zealand Biography* (Vol. 3).

SMITH, Francie Larrieu (b. 1952). *See Larrieu, Francie.*

SMITH, Geraldine (1961—). English politician and member of Parliament. Born Geraldine Smith, Aug 29, 1961. ❖ Postal officer (1980–97); representing Labour, elected to House of Commons for Morecambe and Lunesdale (1997, 2001, 2005).

SMITH, Gina (1957—). Canadian equestrian. Born Nov 11, 1957, in Saskatoon, Saskatchewan, Canada. ❖ At Seoul Olympics, won a bronze medal in team dressage (1988); on Fledermaus, won the Grand Prix Champion title (1997, 1999).

SMITH, Gladys Eastlake (1883–1941). *See Eastlake-Smith, Gladys.*

SMITH, Grace Cossington (1892–1984). Australian painter. Name variations: Grace Cossington-Smith. Born Grace Cossington Smith, April 20, 1892, in Neutral Bay, NSW, Australia; died Dec 10, 1984, in Turramurra, Australia; dau. of Ernest (rector) and Grace Smith; attended Dattilo Rubbo's Art School, 1909–12, 1914–26; studied with Albert Collins, Alfred Coffey and Nora Simpson; never married. ❖ Pioneer of modernist movement, credited with introducing post-Impressionism to Australia, co-founded Contemporary Group (1926) and was a leader among Sydney modernist painters; painted in bright colors with square brush strokes, a style which was not yet popular and can be seen in *The Sock Knitter* (1915), a key work in Australian modernist movement; focused on form and color in such landscapes as *The Bridge In-Curve* (1930), in such domestic scenes as *The Lacquer Room* (1935) and in such urban scenes as *Soldiers Marching* (1917); held 1st solo exhibition (1928) and received scathing reviews, though same works are now considered among Australia's finest; exhibited at London's Walker Gallery (1932) and at New English Art Club, Redfern Gallery and Royal Academy (1950); held 12 exhibitions at Macquarie Galleries in Sydney (1932–72); widely recognized for her talent by 1970, included in survey exhibitions of Australian women artists at Ewing and George Paton Galleries, University of Melbourne and touring public galleries (1975); featured at The Great Australian Art Exhibition and A Century of Women Artists 1840s–1940s at Deutscher Fine Art, Melbourne (1993); lived most of life with sisters in Sydney, spending final years at family home in Sydney suburb of Turramurra. Won Mosman prize (1952), Bathurst prize (1958 and 1960); awarded Order of British Empire (OBE, 1973).

SMITH, Hannah Whitall (1832–1911). American religious leader and writer. Born Hannah Whitall in Philadelphia, Pennsylvania, Feb 7, 1832; died May 1, 1911, in Iffley, near Oxford, England; dau. of Quakers, John M. Whitall (wealthy glass manufacturer) and Mary (Tatum) Whitall; sister of Mary Whitall Thomas (mother of M. Carey Thomas); m. Robert Pearsall Smith (brother of librarian Lloyd Pearsall Smith), in 1851 (died 1898); children: Nelly (died at age 5); Logan Pearsall Smith (1865–1946, English essayist); Franklin (died 1872, at 18, of typhoid); Rachel (died 1879, age 11); Mary Berenson (who m. Bernard Berenson); Alice or Alys Smith Russell (who m. Bertrand Russell); grandmother of Ray Strachey (1887–1940). ❖ Wrote the religious classic *The Christian's Secret of a Happy Life* (1875); preached with husband in Germantown, Pennsylvania, then Millville, New Jersey; moved to England with family (1874) and continued evangelical work; also wrote *The Record of a Happy Life: Being Memorials of Franklin Whitall Smith* (1873) and *The Unselfishness of God and How I Discovered It* (1903). ❖ See also *Women in World History.*

SMITH, Hazel Brannon (1914–1994). American journalist, newspaper publisher and civil-rights activist. Name variations: Hazel Brannon. Born Feb 4, 1914, in Gadsden, Alabama; died May 14, 1994, in Cleveland, Tennessee; dau. of Doc Boad Brannon (electrical contractor) and Georgia Parthenia Brannon; University of Alabama, BA in journalism, 1935; m. Walter Dyer Smith, 1950 (died 1982); no children. ❖ White Southern newspaper owner and editor, one of the few journalists in her region to oppose racism during early desegregation efforts, who was the 1st woman editor to win a Pulitzer Prize; became a reporter and then advertising representative for *Etowah Observor* (1930–32); was managing editor of University of Alabama student newspaper, *Crimson-White* (1932–33); purchased 1st newspaper in Mississippi, the *Durant News* (1936); bought *Lexington Advertiser* (1943), and later owned papers in towns of Flora and Jackson; campaigned editorially against corruption in her local Holmes County (1951–54), earning enemies among some of the more wealthy and powerful citizens; campaigned against racist economic, political and legal policies in the county and state, which made her a target of financial and personal harassment; took on the White Citizens Council, which had been formed to intimidate blacks, and endured loss of advertising, boycotts, lawsuits, vandalism, and bombings during an 11-year siege; became the printer for the *Mississippi Free Press,* a civil-rights newspaper, and sat on a local advisory committee of the Civil Rights Commission; awarded Pulitzer Prize for editorial writing (1964). ❖ See also (tv movie) "A Passion for Justice: The Hazel Brannon Smith Story," starring Jane Seymour (1994); and *Women in World History.*

SMITH, Helen Hay (1873–1918). New Zealand clothing manufacturer and retailer. Name variations: Helen Hay Broad. Born Aug 29, 1873, at McMaster's Flat, South Otago, New Zealand; died Nov 17, 1918, at Oamaru, New Zealand; dau. of James Smith (farmer) and Jessie (Haigie) Smith; m. Alfred Evans Broad, 1915. ❖ Established clothing manufacturing company, H.&J. Smith, with brother John Smith (1900); company grew to include mail-order service and imported clothing; opened new shop and factory that contained innovative improvements, such as well-lighted workrooms and gas heating (1910). ❖ See also *Dictionary of New Zealand Biography* (Vol. 3).

SMITH, Hilda. English gymnast. Born in UK. ❖ At Amsterdam Olympics, won a bronze medal in team all-around (1928).

SMITH, Jacqui (1962—). English politician. Born Nov 3, 1962; m. Richard Timney, 1987. ❖ Economics teacher; representing Labour, elected to House of Commons for Redditch (1997, 2001, 2005); named minister of state for Community, Department of Health.

SMITH, Janet Adam (1905–1999). *See Adam Smith, Janet.*

SMITH, Jean Kennedy (1928—). American diplomat. Born Jean Ann Kennedy in Boston, Massachusetts, 1928; dau. of Joseph P. Kennedy (1888–1969, financier and diplomat) and Rose Fitzgerald Kennedy (1890–1995); sister of Patricia Kennedy Lawford, Eunice Kennedy Shriver, John Fitgerald Kennedy (president of US), Robert F. Kennedy and Ted Kennedy (US senator); m. Stephen Smith (attorney), 1956 (died 1990); children: Stephen Edward Smith Jr. (b. 1957, conflict-resolution consultant); William Kennedy Smith (b. 1960, doctor); Amanda Mary Smith (b. 1967, writer); Kym Maria Smith (b. 1972). ❖ The youngest of the Kennedy sisters, was appointed ambassador to Ireland by President Bill Clinton (1993). ❖ See also *Women in World History.*

SMITH, Jennifer Lee (1948—). *See Lee Smith, Jenny.*

SMITH, Jessie Willcox (1863–1935). American painter and illustrator. Born Jessie Willcox Smith, Sept 8, 1863, in Philadelphia, Pennsylvania; died May 3, 1935, in Philadelphia; dau. of Charles Henry Smith (investment broker) and Katherine DeWitt (Willcox) Smith; attended School of Design for Women (later Moore College of Art), Philadelphia, 1885; attended Pennsylvania Academy of the Fine Arts, 1885–88; studied under Howard Pyle at Drexel Institute of Arts and Sciences, 1894; never married; no children. ❖ One of the most popular and financially successful women artists of the Victorian era, and certainly one of the most prolific, created illustrations for over 200 *Good Housekeeping* magazine covers as well as for numerous children's books, including *At the Back of the North Wind, The Princess and the Goblin, The Water Babies, Little Women* and *A Child's Garden of Verses;* after early training, did several drawings for *St. Nicholas* magazine, but it was during her study with Pyle that she received her 1st book commissions; particularly acclaimed for her images of children (each was individualized with a distinctive personality), brought a new standard of realism to the art of illustration; did advertisements and illustrations for periodicals, including *Ladies' Home Journal, Collier's, Scribner's,* and *Harper's;* spent entire life in Philadelphia area, living for many years in a communal home with two other well-known women artists, Elizabeth Shippen Green and Violet Oakley. ❖ See also Michael S. Schnessel, *Jessie Willcox Smith* (Crowell); Alice A. Carter, *The Red Rose Girls: An Uncommon Story of Art and Love* (Abrams, 2000); and *Women in World History.*

SMITH, Jewel (1943–2005). *See Smith, Sammi.*

SMITH, Joslyn (1954—). *See Hoyte-Smith, Joslyn Y.*

SMITH, Julia (1792–1886). American political activist and social reformer. Born Julia Evelina Smith, May 27, 1792, in Glastonbury, Connecticut; died in Hartford, Connecticut, Mar 6, 1886; dau. of Zephaniah Hollister Smith (cleric turned lawyer, died 1836) and Hannah Hadassah Hickok Smith (died 1850); sister of Abby Smith (1797–1878); m. Amos Parker, April 9, 1879; no children. ❖ Lifelong social and political reformer who, with sister Abby Smith, refused to pay taxes unless she could vote and in consequence had livestock seized; moved back to Glastonbury with family (1795); did charitable work among free blacks (1819); taught at Troy Female Seminary (1823) and returned home (1824); with family, joined Hartford Anti-Slavery Society, hosted abolitionists, distributed literature, initiated petitions (1830s–60s); with Abby's aid, translated the Bible 5 times (1847–55); unfairly taxed by town of Glastonbury (1869); with Abby, traveled to the Connecticut Woman's Suffrage Association in Hartford (1869); tried to register to vote and was refused (1873); with Abby, refused to pay taxes (1873), began to speak in public on suffrage (1873–78), and bought back 7 Alderney cows which were seized for auction by tax collector, causing a sympathetic uproar across the region and then the nation (1874); spoke at Worcester Convention for Woman's Suffrage (1874); with Abby, fought town's attempt to auction off Smith land (1874); spoke at the National Woman Suffrage Association (1876); with Abby, bought back cows seized for auction twice more (1876), won court appeal and regained land (1876); addressed the Congressional Committee on Privileges and Elections (1878); husband auctioned off the contents of the Smith house (1884); writings include *The Holy Bible: Containing the Old and New Testaments; Translated Literally From the Original Tongues* (1876) and *Abby Smith and Her Cows, With A Report of the Law Case Decided Contrary to Law* (1877). ❖ See also Kathleen L. Housley, *The Letter Kills But the Spirit Gives Life: The Smiths—Abolitionists, Suffragists, Bible Translators* (Historical Society of Glastonbury, 1993); Susan J. Shaw, *A Religious History of Julia Evelina Smith's Translation of the Holy Bible: Doing More Than Any Man Has Ever Done* (Mellen, 1993); and *Women in World History*.

SMITH, Julia Frances (1911–1989). American composer. Born Julia Frances Smith in Denton, Texas, Jan 25, 1911; died April 27, 1989, in New York, NY; dau. of Julia (Miller) Smith (piano teacher) and James Willis Smith (professor of mathematics); North Texas State College, BA; New York University, MA, 1933; m. Oscar Vielehr (engineer), April 23, 1938. ❖ Studied with Rubin Goldmark at Juilliard; began teaching at Hamlin School in New Jersey; as a member of the Orchestrette Classique, an all-women's orchestra, composed several works; composed *Cynthia Parker* which premiered (1939), the 1st of several operas; wrote a book on Aaron Copland (1955), and *Directory of American Women Composers* (1970); premiered the opera *Daisy* based on the life of Juliette Gordon Low (1973), which was performed more than 30 times in the next 6 years; also wrote works for piano, voice, organ, chamber groups, chorus and orchestra. ❖ See also *Women in World History*.

SMITH, Julie (1968—). American softball player. Born May 10, 1968, in Glendora, CA. ❖ Won a team gold medal at Atlanta Olympics (1996).

SMITH, Kate (1907–1986). American pop singer. Born Kathryn Elizabeth Smith in Greenville, VA, May 1, 1907; died in Raleigh, NC, June 17, 1986; never married. ❖ Made Broadway debut in *Honeymoon Lane* (1926), before recording several songs from the show for Columbia Records, which were the 1st of some 3,000 records she would make over the next 50 years; made a short for Warner Bros., *Kate Smith: Songbird of the South* (1929), singing "Carolina Moon"; met Ted Collins, recording executive with Columbia Records, who became her manager, the beginning of a professional friendship that would turn Kate Smith into a national institution; had her own show on CBS 3 times a week (1931), introducing what would become her theme song, "When the Moon Comes Over the Mountain," opening each show with "Hello, everybody! This is Kate Smith!" and ending with "Thanks for listenin'!"; was on the air nearly constantly for next 20 years; on a show dedicated to the WWI Armistice, introduced the song that became hers and hers alone—"God Bless America" (1938); during WWII, raised some $600 million for the war effort; began appearing on NBC-TV's "The Kate Smith Hour" (1950), in addition to radio commitments; forced to retire because of health problems (mid-1970s); made few public appearances thereafter. Received a special Emmy Award for her contributions to tv, and Medal of Freedom from President Ronald Reagan (1982). ❖ See also autobiography *Living Life in a Great Big Way* (Blue Ribbon, 1938); and *Women in World History*.

SMITH, Katie (1974—). American basketball player. Born June 4, 1974, in Logan, OH; graduate of Ohio State, 1996. ❖ Guard; finished collegiate career at Ohio State as Big Ten Conference's all-time career scoring leader—male or female—with 2,437 points; played for Columbus Quest of the ABL; after folding of ABL, allocated to the Minnesota Lynx of the WNBA (1999); set 7 single-season WNBA records (2001); won team World championships (1998, 2002); won a team gold medal at Sydney Olympics (2000) and a team gold medal at Athens Olympics (2004); became the 1st US woman to score 5,000 points in professional basketball career (2005).

SMITH, Keely (1932—). American pop and jazz singer. Born Dorothy Jacqueline Keely, Mar 9, 1932, in Norfolk, VA; m. Louis Prima (bandleader and singer), 1953 (div. 1961); m. Jimmy Bowen (record producer), 1965 (div.); m. Bobby Milano; children: Toni and Luanne Prima. ❖ At 18, became bandsinger for Louis Prima, as well as deadpan

foil for his jokes; came to prominence with "That Ol' Black Magic," sung with Prima; also had solo hit with "I Wish You Love"; films include *Thunder Road* (1958).

SMITH, Kendra (1960—). American musician and singer. Name variations: Dream Syndicate; Opal. Born Mar 14, 1960, in San Diego, CA. ❖ With Steve Wynn, Karl Precoda, and Dennis Duck, formed psychedelic band, the Dream Syndicate, in Los Angeles, CA (1981), playing bass; with group, gained local recognition with self-released debut album, *The Dream Syndicate* (1982), and national success with *The Days of Wine and Roses* (1982); quit Dream Syndicate after *Tell Me When It's Over* (1983), and joined band, Opal (later Mazzy Star), as a singer; with Opal, released *Northern Line* (1985), *Happy Nightmare Baby* (1987), and *Early Recordings* (1989); quit Opal and released solo venture, *Kendra Smith Presents the Guild of Temporal Adventures* (1992), and acclaimed solo album, *Five Ways of Disappearing* (1995).

SMITH, Lillian (1897–1966). American writer and civil-rights activist. Born Lillian Eugenia Smith, Dec 12, 1897, in Jasper, Florida; died in Atlanta, Georgia, Sept 28, 1966; dau. of Annie (Hester) Smith and Calvin Warren Smith (merchant and later children's camp administrator); attended Piedmont College, 1916, Peabody Conservatory, 1917–20, and Columbia University Teachers College, 1927–28; longtime companion of Paula Snelling, 1930–66. ❖ Southerner who dedicated her life to educating Americans about the evils of prejudice broadly defined and to pressing white Southerners to recognize that segregation harmed them also; moved with family to Rabun County, Georgia (1915); helped father run Laurel Falls Hotel on Old Steamer Mountain; served as director of music at a Methodist academy for wealthy Chinese girls in Zhejiang Province (1922–25); directed Laurel Falls Camp (1925–48); elected president, Macon Writers Club (1935); founded, with Paula Snelling, *Pseudopodia* (1936), later named *North Georgia Review* (1937), then *The South Today* (1942); traveled the South with Snelling as Rosenwald Fund fellows to investigate racial and class divisions in education and employment; was an active member of the board of Southern Conference of Human Welfare (1942–44); published *Strange Fruit*, which created an immediate sensation when it was banned in Boston and catapulted her into national prominence as a writer and passionate opponent of segregation and racial and sexual prejudice (1944); joined boards of NAACP, ACLU, and CORE (mid-1940s); joined *Chicago Defender* as weekly columnist (1948); saw library, manuscripts and correspondence destroyed when teenage arsonists set fire to her home; wrote *Now is the Time* to urge the South to comply with *Brown v. Board of Education* (1955); elected vice-chair, ACLU (1956); actively supported Montgomery Bus Boycott; became advisor to Student Nonviolent Coordinating Committee (1960); was traveling with Martin Luther King Jr. when he was arrested in Atlanta (1960); defended Julian Bond's right to be seated in Georgia Legislature (1965); other writings include *Killers of the Dream* (1949), *The Journey* (1954), *One Hour* (1959) and *Memory of a Large Christmas* (1961). ❖ See also Margaret Rose Gladney, ed. *How Am I To Be Heard?: Letters of Lillian Smith* (U. of North Carolina, 1993); Anne C. Loveland, *Lillian Smith: A Southerner Confronting the South* (1986); and *Women in World History*.

SMITH, Liz (1923—). American gossip columnist. Born Feb 2, 1923, in Fort Worth, TX; m. George Beeman, 1945 (div. 1947); m. Fred Lister, 1957 (div. 1962). ❖ Began career writing for *Modern Screen* (1949); was associate producer at CBS-Radio (1953–55) and "Wide, Wide World" on NBC-TV (1955–58); was associate for "Cholly Knickerbocker" gossip column (1959–64); served as editor and film critic for *Cosmopolitan* (1964–78); became syndicated gossip columnist (1976); was commentator for NBC-TV (1978–91), Fox-TV (1991–99), and E! (1993–99). ❖ See also memoir *Natural Blonde* (2000).

SMITH, Louise (1819–1906). See Clapp, Louise.

SMITH, Lucy Masey (1861–1936). New Zealand editor, feminist, and temperance worker. Name variations: Lucy Lovell-Smith; (pseudonym) Vesta. Born June 1, 1861, in Christchurch, New Zealand; died Mar 3, 1936, in St. Albans, New Zealand; dau. of James Thomas Smith (compositor) and Eleanor Phoebe (Macleod) Smith. ❖ Was active in New Zealand Women's Christian Temperance Union (WCTU) and Canterbury Women's Institute and supported their campaigns for women's rights; edited WCTU's page in *Prohibitionist*, writing under pseudonym Vesta (1894); helped establish WCTU's *White Ribbon*, which she edited (1903); also edited National Council of Women of New Zealand's magazine, *Bulletin* (1928–29); changed name to Lovell-Smith (1926). ❖ See also *Dictionary of New Zealand Biography* (Vol. 2).

SMITH, Mabel (1924–1972). African-American blues singer. Name variations: Big Maybelle; Big Maybelle Smith. Born Mabel Louise Smith, May 1, 1924, in Jackson, TN; died Jan 23, 1972, in Cleveland, OH. ❖ Developed her powerful vocal style singing in church, accompanying herself on piano; traveled with a number of bands before hooking up with Tiny Bradshaw (1947); recorded for King, Okeh, Savoy and Rojac, with several songs landing on the rhythm-and-blues charts; also appeared in *Jazz on a Summer Day,* a film about the Newport Jazz Festival (1959); performed regularly at the Harlem Savoy (1960s), but complications from diabetes kept her from public appearances after 1967. ❖ See also *Women in World History.*

SMITH, Madeleine Hamilton (1835–1928). Scottish woman tried for murder. Born 1835 in Glasgow, Scotland; died in US, April 12, 1928; daughter of socially prominent Glasgow architect; m. George Wardle (artist-publisher), 1861; married once more. ❖ Became lovers with packing clerk, Pierre Emile L'Angelier (June 1856), to whom she wrote passionate letters; when her ardor cooled, demanded letters back, but he refused and threatened to disclose them; after Emile took ill (Feb 1857) and died of arsenic poisoning (Mar 23), her letters to him were discovered; arrested (Mar 31), was tried in Edinburgh, but freed under a cloud of suspicion after a verdict of "not proven" (July 9); moved to London, where she was a popular social figure, then immigrated to US. Known as trial of the century, the case made headlines in London, Paris and New York, and debate over her innocence continues to this day. ❖ See also Douglas MacGowarn, *Murder in Victorian Scotland* (Westport, CT: Greenwood, 1999).

SMITH, Maggie (1934—). English stage and screen actress. Name variations: Dame Maggie Smith. Born Margaret Natalie Smith, Dec 28, 1934, in Ilford, Essex, England; m. Robert Stephens (actor), 1967 (div. 1974); m. Beverley Cross (screenwriter), 1975 (died 1998); children: Toby Stephens (b. 1969, actor) and Christopher Stephens (actor under name Chris Larkin). ❖ Made NY stage debut in the revue *New Faces '56* and London stage debut in the revue *Share My Lettuce* (1957); appeared with Old Vic Company (1959–60, 1963–66); other plays include *Rhinoceros, The Rehearsal, The Beaux Strategem, The Three Sisters, Hedda Gabler* and *Antony and Cleopatra*; films include *Oh What a Lovely War, The V. I. P.s, The Pumpkin Eater, Young Cassidy, Murder by Death, Death on the Nile, Clash of the Titans, Love and Pain, Sister Act, The Secret Garden, Quartet, Ladies in Lavender* and 3 Harry Potter films. Received *Evening Standard* award as Best Actress for *The Private Ear and the Public Eye* (1962) and Variety Club award as Best Actress for *Mary Mary* (1963) and *Private Lives* (1972); received an Oscar as Best Actress for *The Prime of Miss Jean Brodie* (1969) and as Best Supporting Actress for *California Suite* (1978); nominated for an Oscar as Best Actress for *Travels with My Aunt* (1972), and as Best Supporting Actress for *Othello* (1965) and *Room with a View* (1985); won British Film Award as Best Actress for *A Private Function* (1984) and *The Lonely Passion of Judith Hearne* (1987); won a Tony award for *Lettice and Lovage* (1993); nominated for an Emmy for Best Actress for "Suddenly Last Summer" (1993); named Commander of the British Empire (CBE, 1970) and Dame Commander of the Order of the British Empire (DBE, 1990). ❖ See also Michael Coveney, *Maggie Smith: A Bright Particular Star* (1994).

SMITH, Mamie (1883–1946). African-American blues recording artist and actress. Born Mamie Robinson Smith, May 26, 1883, in Cincinnati, OH; died Oct 30, 1946, in New York, NY; m. William "Smitty" Smith, 1912; m. Sam Gardner, 1920; m. Jack Goldberg, 1929. ❖ Called the "Queen of the Blues," also enjoyed a career as an actress in film and on the vaudeville stage; left Cincinnati (1893) to join a touring dance troupe, the Four Dancing Mitchells; appeared as part of Tutt's Smart Set dance company (1912); became a popular performer in nightclubs in Harlem; appeared at Lincoln Theater in musical *Maid in Harlem* (1918); made a test record of Perry Bradford's "That Thing Called Love" which was bootlegged and became popular in NY; for Okeh Records, recorded "You Can't Keep a Good Man Down," "It's Right Here for You," and "Crazy Blues," (1920) the 1st commercial blues record, which sold over 1 million copies in its 1st year, setting off a recording boom in "race records" and opening the way for such blues singers as Bessie Smith; continued making blues with her band, the Jazz Hounds (1920s); toured in musical *Yelping Hounds* (1932–34); performed in Europe (1936); films include *Paradise in Harlem* (1939), *Sunday Sinners* (1940) and *Murder on Lenox Avenue* (1941). ❖ See also *Women in World History.*

SMITH, Margaret (fl. 1660). American letter writer. A Quaker who lived in Massachusetts. ❖ With Mary Traske, wrote "Joint Letter from Mary Traske and Margaret Smith . . . to . . . John Endicott" (1660) about Puritan persecution of Quakers; was imprisoned 10 months in Boston with Traske for speaking out about Quaker beliefs.

SMITH, Margaret.
See Smith, Wiffi (1936—).
See Court, Margaret Smith (1942—).

SMITH, Margaret (1961—). Scottish politician. Born Feb 18, 1961 in Edinburgh, Scotland; Edinburgh University, MA in Arts, 1983; divorced; children: 1 son, 1 daughter. ❖ As a Liberal Democrat, elected to the Scottish Parliment for Edinburgh West (1999, 2003).

SMITH, Margaret Bayard (1778–1844). American journalist. Born Margaret Bayard in Philadelphia, Pennsylvania, Feb 20, 1778; died in Washington, DC, 1844; dau. of Colonel John Bayard of the Revolutionary Army; m. Samuel Harrison Smith, 1800. ❖ Reporter of Washington social and political scene, was the author of *A Winter in Washington; or, the Seymour Family* (2 vols. 1827) and *What is Gentility?* (1830); was also a frequent contributor to Sarah Josepha Hale's *Godey's Lady's Book* magazine.

SMITH, Margaret Charles (b. 1906). African-American midwife. Born Sept 12, 1906, in Green County, AL; dau. of Beulah Sanders; raised by grandmother, Margaret Charles; m. Randolph Smith. ❖ A "granny" midwife in Alabama, received a state permit (1940s); worked for 28 years in prenatal care at the Green County Health Department; with Linda Janet Holmes, wrote *Listen to Me Good: The Life Story of an Alabama Midwife* (1996).

SMITH, Margaret Chase (1897–1995). American politician. Born Margaret Madeline Chase, Dec 14, 1897, in Skowhegan, Maine; died in Skowhegan, May 29, 1995; dau. of George Emery Chase (barber) and Carrie Matilda (Murray) Chase; m. Clyde Harold Smith (US congressional representative), May 14, 1930 (died 1940); no children. ❖ Republican US congressional representative and 4-term senator, known as the "conscience of the Senate," who was the 1st senator to publicly oppose Joseph McCarthy and the 1st woman candidate for a major party nomination for the US presidency; served as husband's secretary during his 2 terms in US House of Representatives; elected to House of Representatives to succeed him (1940), and for 3 more terms; elected to US Senate (1948), and for 3 more terms, becoming the 1st woman to serve more than 2 Senate terms; specialized in issues related to the armed forces and defense, as well as labor; became known as the "Mother of the Waves," because she waged a long and early struggle for women's rights within the military, and introduced the legislation which 1st allowed WAVES (Woman Accepted for Volunteer Emergence Service) to serve in hospitals and offices overseas during WWII; was noted for an "independent" voting record, often supporting Democratic as well as Republican measures in Congress; elected to the Senate by the widest margins in Maine's history; issued a ringing "Declaration of Conscience" in which she expressed alarm at the activities of fellow Republican Senator Joseph McCarthy (1950); became the 1st woman candidate for a major party's presidential nomination (1964); served in the Senate until her retirement (1973). Was voted "Woman of the Year" several times and thrice rated by the Gallop Poll as one of the ten most admired women in the world. ❖ See also autobiography with William A. Lewis Jr., *Declaration of Conscience* (Doubleday, 1964); Frank Graham Jr. *Margaret Chase Smith: Woman of Courage* (Day, 1964); Patricia Ward Wallace, *The Politics of Conscience: A Biography of Margaret Chase Smith* (Praeger, 1995); and *Women in World History.*

SMITH, Marilyn (1929—). *See Smith, Marilynn.*

SMITH, Marilynn (1929—). American golfer. Name variations: (incorrectly) Marilyn Smith. Born Marilynn Louise Smith, April 13, 1929, in Topeka, KS. ❖ Won Intercollegiate tournament and joined pro tour (1949); helped found the LPGA; won 22 LPGA tournaments, including Fort Wayne Open (1954), Titleholders (1963–64), Pabst Classic (1972); member of the President's Physical Fitness Council; president of LPGA (1958–60) and founding member of the Teaching Division. Inducted into Kansas Golf Hall of Fame (1991) and Texas Golf Hall of Fame (1997).

SMITH, Mary Ellen (1861–1933). Canadian politician and social reformer. Name variations: Mary Ellen Spear. Born Oct 11, 1861, in Devonshire, England; died May 3, 1933, in Vancouver, British Columbia, Canada; married to a Liberal member of the British Columbia legislature (died 1917). ❖ Immigrated to Canada with husband (early 1890s); after husband died in office (1917), won his seat (1918), serving as the 1st woman elected to British Columbia

Legislative Assembly (1918–28); as a member of the Liberal Party, won subsequent elections by sizable majorities (1920 and 1924); was the 1st woman in the British Empire appointed minister (1921) and 1st woman to serve as Acting Speaker of the Legislature (1928). ❖ See also *Women in World History.*

SMITH, Mary Louise (1914–1997). American political organizer and women's-rights activist. Born Mary Louise Epperson, Oct 6, 1914, in Eddyville, Iowa; died Aug 22, 1997, in Des Moines, Iowa; graduate of University of Iowa, 1935; m. Elmer M. Smith. ❖ Began career working for Employment Relief Administration in Iowa City; became membership chair of Iowa Council of Republican Women (1961), then vice-chair of Wright County Republican Central Committee (1962); served as national committeewoman for Iowa (1964–84); after the Watergate scandal, was appointed chair of the Republican National Committee by President Gerald Ford, the 1st woman to hold that post (1974); was also the 1st woman to organize a presidential nominating convention (1976); appointed vice chair of the US Commission on Civil Rights (1981), by Ronald Reagan; a social liberal, was a staunch advocate of the Equal Rights Amendment.

SMITH, Mary Pearsall (1864–1944). *See Berenson, Mary.*

SMITH, Melanie Ainsworth (b. 1949). *See Taylor, Melanie Smith.*

SMITH, Michele (1967—). American softball player. Born June 21, 1967; graduate of Oklahoma State University, 1990. ❖ Won team gold medals at Atlanta Olympics (1996) and Sydney Olympics (2000); was MVP in a Japanese League (1999).

SMITH, Michelle (1969—). Irish swimmer. Name variations: Michelle Smith de Bruin (also seen as deBruin or De Bruin). Born Michelle Marie Smith, Dec 16, 1969, in Rathcoole, Co. Dublin, Ireland; graduate of University of Houston, 1992; m. Erik de Bruin (her coach), 1996. ❖ At European championships, won the 200-meter butterfly and indiv. medley, the 1st Irish woman to win European titles in those events (1995); won gold medals for 200-meter indiv. medley, 400-meter freestyle, and 400-meter indiv. medley and a bronze medal for 200-meter butterfly at Atlanta Olympics (1996), the 1st Irish competitor to win a swimming medal and the 1st Irish woman to win a medal of any color, and passed all tests when accused of using performance-enhancing drugs; won 2 gold medals at European championships (1997); suspended for 4 years by FINA for tampering with a urine sample (1998); ban upheld by the Court of Arbitration for Sport (1999); retired (1999).

SMITH, Mother (1904–1994). *See Smith, Willie Mae Ford.*

SMITH, Muriel Burrell (1923–1985). African-American actress and singer. Born Feb 23, 1923, in New York, NY; died Sept 13, 1985, in Richmond, VA. ❖ Made Broadway debut originating the title role in *Carmen Jones* to enormous success (1943), reprising the role (1956); other appearances include *Our Lan', The Cradle Will Rock, Sojourner Truth, Hippolytus, South Pacific* and *The King and I*; sang Bizet's Carmen at London's Covent Garden (1956–57); films include *Moulin Rouge.* Received the arts award from the National Council of Negro Women (1984).

SMITH, Naomi Gwladys Royde-. *See Royde-Smith, Naomi.*

SMITH, Nixola (1880–1919). *See Greeley-Smith, Nixola.*

SMITH, Nora Archibald (1859?–1934). American educator. Born c. 1859 in Philadelphia, Pennsylvania; died in 1934; dau. of Robert Noah Smith and Helen Elizabeth (Dyer) Smith; sister of Kate Douglas Wiggin (1856–1923); graduated from Santa Barbara College. ❖ With sister Kate Douglas Wiggin, helped run California Kindergarten Training School and Silver Street Kindergarten, then took over Silver Street (1881) and the training school (1884), following sister's marriage; with Wiggin, also co-authored *Kindergarten Principles and Practice* (1896) and co-edited a 5-vol. collection of fairy tales and fables; wrote *Kate Douglas Wiggin as Her Sister Knew Her* (1925).

SMITH, Oceana (b. 1835). *See LaBelle Oceana.*

SMITH, Patsy Adam- (1924–2001). *See Adam-Smith, Patsy.*

SMITH, Patti (1946—). American singer, songwriter and poet. Born Dec 30, 1946, in Chicago, IL; m. Fred "Sonic" Smith (guitarist), 1980 (died 1994); children: Jackson (b. 1982) and Jessie (b. 1987). ❖ Innovative performance artist, who redefined roles open to women in the male-dominated rock scene, began performing her poetry (1971), accompanied by guitar and piano; formed band and released album *Horses* (1975), which received critical raves, and *Radio Ethiopia* (1976); while recuperating from neck injuries after falling off stage during performance in Tampa, FL (1977), wrote 4th book of poetry, *Babel* (1978); released 1st Top-20 LP, *Easter* (1978), with her only hit single, "Because the Night"; married and withdrew from music industry and moved to Detroit, MI; resurfaced with album, *Dream of Life* (1988), but did not tour; published book of poetry, *Early Work: 1970–1979* (1994) and prose poem, *The Coral Sea* (1996); other albums include *Gone Again* (1996), *Peace and Noise* (1997), *Gung Ho* (2000) and *Trampin'* (2004); published *Patti Smith Complete: Lyrics, Reflections & Notes for the Future* (1998). ❖ See also Victor Bockris and Roberta Bayley, *Patti Smith: A Biography* (1999).

SMITH, Pauline (1882–1959). South African-born writer. Born in Oudtshoorn, South Africa, in 1882; died in 1959; dau. of British parents; educated in Britain. ❖ Left South Africa at age 12; lived mostly in Dorset, on England's south coast; wrote of South Africa in 1st collection of short stories, *The Little Karoo* (1925), and novel *The Beadle* (1926); also published a collection of children's stories, *Platkops Children* (1935).

SMITH, Phylis (1965—). English runner. Name variations: Phylis Watt. Born Sept 29, 1965, in UK. ❖ At Barcelona Olympics, won a bronze medal in the 4 x 400-meter relay (1992).

SMITH, Phyllis Ida (1903–1980). *See Barclay-Smith, Phyllis.*

SMITH, Queenie (1898–1978). American actress, singer, and ballet dancer. Born Sept 8, 1898, in New York, NY; died Aug 5, 1978, in Burbank, CA; m. Robert Garland (div.). ❖ Began career as a ballet dancer, dancing solo with the Metropolitan Opera Company in *Aida, Samson and Delilah,* and *La Traviata*; starred on Broadway in such musical comedies as *Just Because, Orange Blossoms, Cinders, Helen of Troy, Sitting Pretty, Judy, The Greeks Had a Word For It, Tip Toes, The Street Singer* and *Hit the Deck*; films include *Show Boat, On Your Toes, The Killers, My Sister Eileen, The Snake Pit, Sweet Smell of Success* and *Foul Play*; also appeared often on tv and coached acting.

SMITH, Rebecca (1959—). Canadian swimmer. Name variations: Becky Smith. Born June 1959 in Canada. ❖ At Montreal Olympics, won a bronze medal in the 4 x 100-meter freestyle relay and a bronze medal in the 400-meter indiv. medley (1976).

SMITH, Robyn (1942—). American jockey. Name variations: Melody Dawn Miller; Caroline Smith; Robyn Caroline Smith; Robyn Astaire. Born Melody Dawn Miller, Aug 14, 1942, in San Francisco, CA; m. Fred Astaire (actor and dancer), 1980 (died 1987). ❖ Received jockey's license (1969); rode in 1st race at Golden Gate Park and finished 2nd (April 5, 1969); went on to ride in 40 races on the California country fair circuit; raced at the prestigious Aqueduct track in Queens (Dec 5, 1969), managing a 5th-place finish in a close race on Exotic Bird; won 18–20% of her races against horses with better records (early 1970s); became a regular rider for Alfred Gwynne Vanderbilt's stable; was the 1st woman jockey to win a stakes race (Mar 1, 1973), riding North Sea to victory in the $27,450 Paumanok Handicap at the Aqueduct; retired (1975). ❖ See also Lynn Haney, *The Lady is a Jock* (Dodd, 1973); Fern G. Brown, *Racing Against the Odds: Robyn C. Smith* (juvenile, 1976); and *Women in World History.*

SMITH, Robyn (1948—). *See Archer, Robyn.*

SMITH, Ronetta (1980—). Jamaican runner. Born May 2, 1980, in Kingston, Jamaica. ❖ Won a bronze medal for 4 x 400-meter relay at Athens Olympics (2004).

SMITH, Rosamond (1938—). *See Oates, Joyce Carol.*

SMITH, Ruby Doris (1942–1967). *See Robinson, Ruby Doris Smith.*

SMITH, Samantha (1972–1985). American peace advocate. Born 1972; died in a plane crash in Auburn, Maine, Aug 25, 1985; dau. of Arthur and Jane Smith; attended Manchester Elementary School, Manchester, Maine. ❖ At 10, wrote a letter to then Soviet leader Yuri V. Andropov, expressing her fears and concerns about the threat of nuclear war (1982); received an answer from Andropov (1983), who invited her and her parents to visit the Soviet Union that summer, as guests of the country; when she did, became a national celebrity; wrote *Journey to the Soviet Union.* ❖ See also Anne Galicich, *Samantha Smith: A Journey for Peace* (Dillon, 1987); and *Women in World History.*

SMITH, Sammi (1943–2005). American country singer. Name variations: Jewel Smith. Born Jewel Fay Smith, Aug 5, 1943, in Orange, CA; died Feb 12, 2005, in Oklahoma City, OK; Jody Payne (div.);

children: 4, including Waylon Payne (actor-singer). ❖ Recorded "Help Me Make It Through the Night," which earned her a Grammy as Best Female Country Vocalist (1971); had her 1st hit with "So Long Charlie Brown" (1967) and also recorded "Today I Started Loving You Again" (1975).

SMITH, Sara Yarborough (1950—). *See Yarborough, Sara.*

SMITH, Sarah (1832–1911). *See Stretton, Hesba.*

SMITH, Scottie Fitzgerald (1921–1986). *See Fitzgerald, Frances Scott.*

SMITH, Shannon (1961—). Canadian swimmer. Born Sept 28, 1961, in Canada. ❖ At Montreal Olympics, won a bronze medal in the 400-meter freestyle (1976).

SMITH, Shawntel (1971—). Miss America. Name variations: Shawntel Smith Wuerch. Born Sep. 17, 1971; graduate of Northeastern State University; Oklahoma City University, MBA. ❖ Named Miss America (1996), representing Oklahoma; appointed ambassador to National School to Work by US Department of Education and Labor.

SMITH, Sheila Kaye- (1887–1956). *See Kaye-Smith, Sheila.*

SMITH, Sophia (1796–1870). American philanthropist. Born in Hatfield, Massachusetts, Aug 27, 1796; died in Hatfield, June 12, 1870; dau. of Joseph Smith (farmer and Revolutionary War soldier) and Lois (White) Smith; niece of Oliver Smith (founder of Smith charities in Northampton); never married; no children. ❖ Though she herself had been denied an education, became the 1st woman to found and endow a women's college, bequeathing her considerable fortune to found Smith College in Northampton, Massachusetts (1870). Inducted into Women's Hall of Fame at Seneca Falls (2000). ❖ See also *Women in World History.*

SMITH, Stevie (1902–1971). English writer. Name variations: Florence Margaret Smith; Peggy Smith. Born Florence Margaret Smith in Hull, Yorkshire, England, Sept 20, 1902; died in Ashburton, Devonshire, England, Mar 7, 1971; dau. of Charles Ward Smith and Ethel (Spear) Smith; never married; no children. ❖ Novelist, book reviewer, short-story writer, and "poet of frozen anguish," who was a literary celebrity, a kind of cult figure among youthful radicals, and one of the most anthologized British female poets; worked as secretary for London publishing firm (1923–53); began writing poetry (1924), though it would be 11 years before she had anything published; in the meantime, toiled at her "demeaning" job, lived with her maiden aunt in a London suburb, and dreamed of entering the ranks of the British literary set; had 6 poems published in *New Statesman* (1935); published *Novel on Yellow Paper* (1936), which was widely reviewed and well received; published 1st book of poetry, *A Good Time Was Had by All* (1938); attempted suicide (1953); other writings include *Over the Frontier* (1938), *Mother, What is Man?* (1942), *The Holiday* (1949), *Harold's Leap* (1950), *Not Waving but Drowning* (1957), *Some Are More Human Than Others* (1958), *Cats in Colour* (1959), *The Frog Prince and Other Poems* (1966), *The Best Beast* (1968), and the radio play, *A Turn Outside* (1959). Received Cholmondeley Award for Poetry (1966); awarded Gold Medal for Poetry by Queen Elizabeth II (1969). ❖ See also Sanford Sternlicht, ed. *In Search of Stevie Smith* (Syracuse U. Press, 1991); Barbera and McBrien, *Stevie* (Heinemann, 1985); Kay Dick, *Ivy and Stevie: Ivy Compton-Burnett and Stevie Smith* (Duckworth, 1971); Frances Spalding, *Stevie Smith* (Norton, 1989); *Stevie: A Play from the Life and Work of Stevie Smith* by Hugh Whitemore (1977) and *Stevie* (film), starring Glenda Jackson, based on the play (1978); and *Women in World History.*

SMITH, Susan (1847–1918). *See Steward, Susan McKinney.*

SMITH, Tricia (1957—). Canadian rower. Born April 14, 1957, in Canada; dau. of Marshall Smith (rugby player) and Pat McIntosh Smith (rower); University of British Columbia, BA, 1981, law degree, 1985. ❖ At Los Angeles Olympics, won a silver medal in coxless pairs (1984); won a gold medal at Commonwealth Games (1986) and 7 World championship medals; became a lawyer.

SMITH, Trixie (1895–1943). African-American blues singer. Born in Atlanta, GA, 1895; studied at Selma University; died in New York, NY, Sept 21, 1943. ❖ Moved to NY (1915) and appeared in numerous vaudeville shows, eventually becoming a featured vocalist; when blues became the rage (1920s), recorded on Black Swan label; entered a blues contest in NY and won 1st place with "Trixie's Blues" (1922) which was also recorded by Black Swan; particularly remembered for "Railroad

Blues" and "The World Is Jazz Crazy and So Am I" which featured Louis Armstrong on cornet. ❖ See also *Women in World History.*

SMITH, Virginia Dodd (1911–2006). American politician. Born Virginia Dodd in Randolph, Fremont County, Iowa, June 30, 1911; died Jan 23, 2006, in Sun City, Arizona; graduate of University of Nebraska, Lincoln, 1936; m. a Nebraska wheat farmer. ❖ Republican US congressional representative from Nebraska, chaired the women's bureau of American Farm Bureau Federation (1955–74) and was active in American Country Life Association; was a member of US Department of Agriculture's Home Economics Research Advisory Committee (1950–60); was active in Nebraska Republican Party, serving as a delegate to Republican National conventions (1956–72); was appointed a delegate to White House Conference on Children and Youth (1960); served on US Department of Health, Education, and Welfare's Clearinghouse on Rural Education and Small Schools Advisory Board (1972–74); served on US Department of Commerce's Census Advisory Committee on Agricultural Statistics (1973); won election as a representative from Nebraska to 94th Congress (1975), and was reelected to 7 succeeding terms; became the ranking Republican member of the Subcommittee on Rural Development, Agriculture and Related Agencies, and worked assiduously to promote the interests of farmers and ranchers; retired (1991).

SMITH, Virginia Thrall (1836–1903). American social worker. Born Tryphena Virginia Thrall in Bloomfield, Connecticut, Aug 16, 1836; died in Hartford, Connecticut, Jan 3, 1903; dau. of Hiram Thrall (businessman and surveyor) and Melissa (Griswold) Thrall; educated at the Suffield (Connecticut) Institute, the Hartford Female Seminary, and Mt. Holyoke Seminary; m. William Brown Smith (businessman), Dec 31, 1857 (died 1897); children: Oliver (b. 1859), Edward (b. 1861), Lucy (b. 1865), Kate (b. 1867), William (b. 1871) and Thomas (b. 1874). ❖ A pioneer in the field of child care in Connecticut, was named administrative head of Hartford City Mission (1876); was instrumental in establishing kindergartens in Connecticut public schools; appointed to State Board of Charities (1882); became director of Connecticut Children's Aid Society (1892); established Home for Incurables (1898), later named the Newington Hospital for Crippled Children. ❖ See also *Women in World History.*

SMITH, Wendy (1959—). *See Sly, Wendy.*

SMITH, Wiffi (1936—). American golfer. Name variations: Margaret Smith. Born Margaret Smith, Sept 28, 1936, in Redlands, CA. ❖ Won Women's Championship of Mexico (1952); won USGA Junior Girls' championship (1954), World Women's Amateur (1955), British and French Women's Amateur (1956), and Trans-Mississippi (1956); member of Curtis Cup team (1956); joined LPGA tour; won Dallas Open (1957); won Royal Crown Open (1960); won Peach Blossom Open (1961). Inducted into Michigan Golf Hall of Fame (1987). ❖ See also Mona Void, *Different Strokes: The Lives and Teachings of the Game's Wisest Women.*

SMITH, Willie Mae Ford (1904–1994). African-American gospel singer. Name variations: Mother Smith. Born in Rolling Fort, MS, June 23, 1904; died in St. Louis, MO, 1994; m. James Peter Smith (owner of a small business), 1924 (died 1950); children: Willie James Smith, Jacquelyn Smith Jackson, (adopted) Bertha Smith. ❖ Debuted with sisters in Ford Sisters quartet (1922); performed with Ford Sisters at National Baptist Convention (1924); established and became director of National Convention of Gospel Choirs and Choruses Soloists Bureau (1932); toured extensively throughout US (1930s–40s); sang with Mahalia Jackson at Easter Sunrise Service, Hollywood Bowl, CA (late 1940s); ordained as minister in Lively Stone Apostolic Church, St. Louis, MO (mid-1950s); served for 17 years as director of Education Department of National Baptist Convention; featured in documentary film *Say Amen, Somebody* (1982); received National Endowment for the Arts Heritage Award as outstanding American folk artist (1988). ❖ See also *Women in World History.*

SMITH, Winifred Lily (1865–1939). *See Boys-Smith, Winifred Lily.*

SMITH, Zilpha Drew (1851–1926). American social worker. Born Jan 25, 1851, in Pembroke, Massachusetts; died Oct 12, 1926, in Boston; dau. of Silvanus Smith (carpenter) and Judith Winsor (McLauthlin) Smith. ❖ Became registrar of Associated Charities of Boston (1879) and served as general secretary (1886–1903); was also active in the National Conference of Charities and Correction, and lectured at New York School of Philanthropy; served as associate director of Boston School for Social Workers (1904–18), which set a milestone in the development of the social-work field by requiring a full year's academic training; did much to professionalize charity work at end of 19th century. ❖ See also *Women in World History*.

SMITH COURT, Margaret (b. 1942). *See Court, Margaret Smith.*

SMITH-ROBINSON, Ruby Doris (1942–1967). *See Robinson, Ruby Doris Smith.*

SMITH-ROSENBERG, Carroll. American historian and educator. Columbia University, PhD, 1968. ❖ Leading historian, whose work played an important role in drawing attention to the marginalizing of women in historical texts (1970s), taught at University of Pennsylvania and University of Michigan; writings include *Religion and the Rise of the American City* (1971) and *Disorderly Conduct: Visions of Gender in Victorian America* (1985).

SMITHER, Elizabeth (1941—). New Zealand poet and novelist. Born 1941 in New Plymouth, New Zealand. ❖ Poetry collections include *Here Come the Clouds* (1975), *The Sarah Train* (1980), *Casanova's Ankle* (1981), *Professor Musgrove's Canary* (1986), *A Pattern of Marching* (1989), *A Cortège of Daughters* (1993), *The Tudor Style* (1993), and *The Lark Quartet* (1999); novels include *First Blood* (1983), *Mr. Fish* (1994), and *The Sea Between Us* (2003); journals published as *The Journal Box* (1996); short-story collections include *The Mathematics of Jane Austen* (1997) and *Listening to the Everly Brothers* (2002). Won New Zealand Book Award (1990) and Montana New Zealand Book Award (2000).

SMITHSON, Alison (1928–1993). British architect. Born June 22, 1928, in Sheffield, England; died Aug 16, 1993, in London, England; studied at Edinburgh and Durham universities; m. Peter Smithson, 1949; children: 3. ❖ Set up architecture practice with husband in London and co-founded Independent Group; with husband, designed Hunstanton Secondary School, Norfolk (1949–54), Economist Building, London (1964), and housing complex at Robin Hood Gardens, London (1972). With husband, wrote works on architecture, including *Urban Structuring* (1967), *Without Rhetoric* (1974), *The Shift* (1983), *Changing the Art of Inhabitation* (1994), and *The Charged Void–Architecture* (2001); also wrote novel, *Portrait of the Female Mind as a Young Girl* (1966).

SMITHSON, Harriet Constance (1800–1854). Irish actress. Name variations: Henrietta Constance Smithson; Madame Berlioz. Born in Ennis, Ireland, 1800; died Mar 3, 1854; dau. of a theatrical manager; m. Hector Berlioz (the composer), Oct 1833 (sep. 1840). ❖ Debuted at Crow Street Theatre in Dublin as Lady Teazle in *The School for Scandal* (1815); appeared at London's Drury Lane Theatre as Letitia Hardy (1818); appeared in Paris with William Macready (1828, 1832); played such roles as Jane Shore, Desdemona, Juliet and Ophelia.

SMITHSON, Henrietta Constance (1800–1854). *See Smithson, Harriet Constance.*

SMOLEYEVA, Nina (1948—). Soviet volleyball player. Born Mar 28, 1948, in USSR. ❖ Won a gold medal at Mexico City Olympics (1968), gold medal at Munich Olympics (1972), and silver medal at Montreal Olympics (1976), all in team competition.

SMOLLER, Dorothy (c. 1901–1926). American theatrical ballet dancer. Born c. 1901, in Memphis, TN; stricken with tuberculosis, committed suicide, Dec 10, 1926, in New York, NY. ❖ Worked with Tom Rector as his ballroom dance partner in Oriental tour (1915); danced as apprentice with company of Anna Pavlova, where she performed at the New York Hippodrome in *The Sleeping Beauty*; opened danced studio with sister in Washington, DC, where she taught for brief period; appeared on Broadway as featured ballet dancer in *Seesaw* (1919), *What's in a Name?* (1920), *Up in the Clouds* (1921), *The Hotel Mouse* (1922) and *The Fantastic Fricasee* (1922).

SMOSARSKA, Jadwiga (1898–1971). Polish actress. Born Jadwiga Asmosarska, Sept 23, 1898, in Warsaw, Poland; died Nov 1, 1971, in Warsaw; m. Zygmunt Protasiewicz (engineer). ❖ The most famous actress in Poland from 1918 to 1939, starred in the first film produced in independent Poland, *Cud nad Wisla* (*Miracle on the Vistula*, 1921); appeared in over 17 films, including as Lucyna in the Polish comedy, *Czy Lucyna to dziewczyna* (1934).

SMUCKER, Barbara (1915–2003). American-born children's writer. Born Sept 1, 1915, in Kansas; died July 29, 2003, in New York, NY; married a Mennonite minister and professor; children: 3. ❖ Moved with husband to Ontario, Canada (1969); worked as reporter, teacher, and librarian; works include *Underground to Canada* (1977), *Days of Terror* (1979), *Amish Adventure* (1983), *White Mist* (1985), *Jacob's Little Giant* (1987), *Incredible Jumbo* (1990) and *Selina and the Bear-Paw Quilt* (1995). Received Canada Council Children's Literature Prize (1979) and Vicky Metcalf Award (1988).

SMULDERS, Marlies (1982—). Dutch rower. Born Feb 22, 1982, in Amstelveen, Netherlands. ❖ Won a bronze medal for coxed eights at Athens Olympics (2004).

SMUROVA, Elena (1973—). Russian water-polo player. Born May 22, 1973, in USSR. ❖ Won a team bronze medal at Sydney Olympics (2000).

SMYLIE, Elizabeth (1963—). Australian tennis player. Born April 11, 1963, in Australia. ❖ At Wimbledon, won doubles championship with Kathy Jordan (1985) and mixed doubles with John Fitzgerald (1991); at Seoul Olympics, won a bronze medal in doubles (1988); with Todd Woodbridge, won mixed doubles at US Open (1990).

SMYTH, Donna (1943—). Canadian playwright and novelist. Born 1943 in Kimberley, British Columbia, Canada; attended universities of Victoria, Toronto and London. ❖ Co-founded journal *Atlantis: A Woman's Studies Journal* (1976); taught at Acadia University in Nova Scotia; plays include *Susanna Moodie* (1976), *Giant Anna* (1978–79) and *Subversive Elements* (1986); novels include *Quilt* (1982); with Margaret Conrad and Toni Laidlaw, edited *No Place Like Home: Diaries and Letters of Novia Scotia Women* (1988).

SMYTH, Ethel (1858–1944). British composer. Name variations: Dame Ethel Smyth. Born Ethel Mary Smyth in Marylebone, England, April 22, 1858; died in Woking, England, May 9, 1944; dau. of a major-general in the British army; studed at Conservatory in Leipzig; never married; no children. ❖ Major 20th-century composer, who produced highly charged music of astonishing breadth and power, began formal music training with Alexander Ewing (1875); studied orchestration with Heinrich von Herzogenberg, the Austrian composer (1878); wrote orchestral work "Serenade," which was given its 1st major performance at Crystal Palace (1890); composed Mass in D, which was presented by Royal Choral Society at Royal Albert Hall (Jan 18, 1893); wrote 1st opera, *Fantasio*, which premiered in Weimar, Germany (1898); wrote 2nd opera, *Der Wald*, produced in Berlin and Covent Garden (1902) and in NY (1903); wrote *The Wreckers* (1906); participated in the women's suffrage movement and served a jail term for her activities (1910–13); composed "March of the Women," with words by Cicely Hamilton, which became the "Marseillaise" of the suffrage movement; began to go deaf after 1913; wrote final work, *The Prison*, for orchestra and chorus (1931); also wrote the operas *The Boatswain's Mate* (1913–14), *Fete Galante* (1923) and *Entente Cordiale* (1925); wrote 10 books whose well-penned portraits of public figures of her day made them bestsellers; by end of long life, could not hear at all. Made Dame of the British Empire (1922). ❖ See also *The Memoirs of Ethel Smyth* (Viking, 1987); and *Women in World History*.

SMYTH, Patty (1957—). American singer. Born June 26, 1957, in New York, NY; m. Richard Hell (musician, div.); m. John McEnroe (tennis player), 1997; children: (1st m.) Ruby (b. 1985); (with McEnroe) Anna (b. 1995) and Ava (b. 1999). ❖ As a teenager, formed band, Patty and the Planets; became lead vocalist for pop band Scandal and released the album *Scandal* (1982), which included singles "Goodbye to You" and "Love's Got a Line on You," and went on to become bestselling EP in Columbia Records' history; co-wrote material for album, *The Warrior* (1984), but quit band; made solo debut with album, *Never Enough* (1987); released gold album, *Patty Smyth* (1992), which included the Top-10 hit "Sometimes Love Just Ain't Enough," a duet with Don Henley; nominated for Academy Award for song, "Look What Love has Done," from film *Junior* (1994); cut back on music career, but sometimes sings with Johnny Smyth's Band, where her husband plays guitar.

SMYTHE, Emily Anne (c. 1845–1887). English relief worker and author. Name variations: Viscountess Strangford. Born Emily Anne Beaufort, c. 1845; died at sea, 1887; dau. of Sir Francis Beaufort (1774–1857, rear admiral and hydrographer); m. Percy Ellen Frederick William Smythe, 8th viscount Strangford of Ireland, 1862. ❖ Active in relief work, organized a fund for relief of Bulgarian peasants (1875); during war in Turkey, established and supervised a hospital for Turkish soldiers (1877); writings include *Egyptian Sepulchres and Syrian Shrines* (1861) and a work about eastern shores of the Adriatic.

SMYTHE, Maria Anne (1756–1837). *See Fitzherbert, Maria Anne.*

SMYTHE, Pat (1928–1996). English equestrian and show jumper. Name variations: Patricia Smythe; Pat Koechlin-Smythe. Born near Richmond-upon-Thames, England, 1928; died 1996; m. Sam Koechlin (Swiss lawyer), 1963; children: 2 daughters. ❖ Became the 1st female rider on a Nations Cup Team, and won the Prince of Wales Cup for England (1952); victorious in a record 8 British Show Jumping championships; became the 1st female member of an Olympic show jumping team, and won a bronze medal for England at the Stockholm Games (1956); won European Ladies' championship (1957, 1961–63); won British Jumping Derby (1962); also published several children's books. Made an Officer of the British Empire (OBE). ❖ See also autobiography *Jumping Life's Fences* (1992).

SNAP! *See Harris, Jackie.*

SNELL, Belinda (1981—). Australian basketball player. Born Jan 10, 1981, in Mirboo North, Australia. ❖ Forward/guard, placed 1st at Oceania championships (2003); won a team silver medal at Athens Olympics (2004); played for Sydney Flames.

SNELL, Hannah (1723–1792). English soldier. Born April 23, 1723, in Worcester, England; died in Bethlehem Hospital, Feb 8, 1792; dau. of a hosier; m. James Summs (sailor); children: 1. ❖ Orphaned at 17; was abused by husband who abandoned her when she was pregnant; determined to find him, disguised herself as a man and joined the infantry regiment battling supporters of Bonnie Prince Charlie; in Portsmouth, using name James Gray, joined the crew of sloop *Swallow* which accompanied Boscawen's fleet to East Indies (1747); though wounded in battle, succeeded in removing the bullet herself, so that the surgeon would not learn her gender; served on *Tartar* and *Eltham*, distinguishing herself in action; upon discovering that husband was dead, retired from soldiering, receiving a government pension for her service; wrote a somewhat exaggerated account of her adventures, *The Female Soldier, or the Surprising Adventures of Hannah Snell* (1750); also gave exhibitions on the London stage, dressed in full military regalia; opened an inn. ❖ See also *Women in World History.*

SNELLING, Lilian (1879–1972). English botanical artist. Born June 8, 1879; died Oct 12, 1972; studied with Sir Isaac Bayley Balfour at the Royal Botanic Garden, Edinburgh. ❖ Main artist for *Curtis's Botanical Magazine* (1922–52), was also noted for her lily drawings for Grove and Cotton's *Supplement to Elwes' Monograph of the Genus Lilium* (1933–40); illustrated Stoker's *Book of Lilies* (1943) and Stern's *Study of the Genus Paeonia* (1946). Received Royal Horticultural Society's Victoria Medal (1955).

SNEP-BALAN, Doina Liliana (1963—). Romanian rower. Name variations: Doina Balan. Born Dec 10, 1963, in Romania. ❖ At Los Angeles Olympics, won a silver medal in coxed eights (1984); at Seoul Olympics, won a bronze medal in coxed fours and a silver medal in coxed eights (1988); at Barcelona Olympics, won a silver medal in coxed eights (1992).

SNITE, Betsy (1938–1984). American Alpine skier. Name variations: Betsy Snite Riley. Born Dec 20, 1938, in Norwich, VT; died June 1984, in Stowe, VT. ❖ Won a silver medal for slalom at Squaw Valley Olympics (1960).

SNITINA, Natalia (1971—). *See Snytina, Natalia.*

SNITKINA, Anna (1846–1918). *See Dostoevsky, Anna.*

SNIVELY, Mary Agnes (1847–1933). Canadian nurse. Born Nov 12, 1847, in St. Catharines, Ontario, Canada; died Sept 25, 1933; dau. of Susan M. (Copeland) Snively and Martin Snively; graduate of Bellevue Hospital Training School in NY, 1884. ❖ As superintendent of Toronto General Hospital (1885–1910), created a nurses' residence (1887), enlisted physicians to teach nursing classes, including nursing ethics, and expanded the course of study for nurses in training; advocated state registration; helped found (1893) and was president (1897) of the American Society of Superintendents of Training Schools for Nurses of the United States and Canada, later the National League for Nursing; helped found and served as a president of the Canadian Association of Trained Nurses (1924), later the Canadian Nurses Association.

SNOEKS, Jiske (1978—). Dutch field-hockey player. Born May 19, 1978, in the Netherlands. ❖ Won European championship (2003); forward, won a team silver medal at Athens Olympics (2004).

SNOW, Eliza Roxey (1804–1887). *See Smith, Eliza Roxey.*

SNOW, Helen Foster (1907–1997). American activist and writer. Name variations: (pseudonym) Nym Wales. Born in Cedar, Utah, Sept 21, 1907; died in Guilford, Connecticut, Jan 1997; dau. of John Moody (lawyer) and Hanna (Davis) Foster (teacher); attended University of Utah, 1925–27, and Yenching University and Tsinghua University, Peking, 1934–35; m. Edgar Snow (d. 1972, author, foreign correspondent, and photographer), Dec 25, 1932 (div. 1949). ❖ Began career as a string correspondent for Scripps-Canfield League of Newspapers in Seattle, Washington (1931); was a foreign correspondent and activist in China (1931–38); with husband, helped establish Chinese Industrial ("Gung Ho") Cooperatives in Shanghai (1938); during WWII, worked as a book reviewer for *Saturday Review of Literature*; served as vice-chair of board of directors of American Committee in Aid of Chinese Industrial Cooperatives (1941–52); under pseudonym Nym Wales, wrote a number of books about China, including *Inside Red China* (1939), *Red Dust: Autobiographies of Chinese Communists* (1952) and *Notes on the Chinese Student Movement, 1935–36* (1959). Nominated for Nobel Peace Prize (1981). ❖ See also memoir *My China Years* (1984); and *Women in World History.*

SNOW, Lady (1912–1981). *See Johnson, Pamela Hansford.*

SNOW, Marguerite (1889–1958). American silent-screen actress. Born Sept 9, 1889, in Salt Lake City, UT; died Feb 17, 1958, in Woodland Hills, CA; dau. of a comedian in vaudeville; m. James Cruze (actor-director), 1913 (div. 1922); m. Neely Edwards (comedian), 1925. ❖ One of Thanheuser's top stars (1911–15), films include *Carmen, The Woman in White, East Lynne, Lucile, Undine, She, Potiphar's Wife* and *Daughters of Kings*; co-starred opposite George M. Cohan in his 1st film, *Broadway Jones*; also appeared in the noted serial *The Million Dollar Mystery*; retired from the screen (1925).

SNOW, Phoebe (1952—). American singer. Name variations: Phoebe Laub. Born Phoebe Laub, July 17, 1952, in New York, NY; children: Valerie. ❖ Began performing blues, folk and pop music in NY's Greenwich Village (1970s); released gold debut LP, *Phoebe Snow* (1974), which included Top-5 single, "Poetry Man"; sang on hit gospel single, "Gone at Last," with Paul Simon; released 2nd LP, *Second Childhood* (1976), which included "Two-Fisted Love" and also went gold; had less success with subsequent albums, *Against the Grain* (1977), *Something Real* (1989), *I Can't Complain* (1998), and *Natural Wonder* (2003); performed with Donald Fagen's Rock and Soul Revue (early 1990s) and with gospel group at Woodstock (1994).

SNOW, Sarah Ellen Oliver (1864–1939). New Zealand political activist, feminist, and welfare worker. Name variations: Sarah Ellen Oliver Murphy. Born Feb 16, 1864, in Wellington, New Zealand; died Feb 13, 1939, in Wellington; dau. of Michael James Murphy (police officer) and Jessie (Flighty) Murphy; m. Clarence Herbert Snow (laborer), 1892; children: 4 sons, 3 daughters. ❖ Interests in women's domestic issues, political representation, and social-welfare issues grew out of her life as working-class wife and mother; served as president of Wellington Housewives' Union (early 1910s); active in charitable work with Wellington Hospital Board; worked to include feminist issues, including sex-equality legislation, onto labor movement's national agenda; was a Labor representative (1919–23 and 1933–39); advocated for welfare reform and worked to build New Zealand welfare state (1930s). ❖ See also *Dictionary of New Zealand Biography* (Vol. 4).

SNOW, Valaida (c. 1903–1956). African-American jazz singer, dancer, and trumpeter. Name variations: Valaida Edwards; sometimes performed simply as Valaida. Born in Chattanooga, TN, June 2, sometime between 1903 and 1909; died in New York, NY, May 30, 1956; m. Ananias Berry, 1934; m. Earle Edwards, 1943. ❖ Best known of the early female jazz horn players (1920s–50s), made Broadway debut in *Chocolate Dandies* (1924); toured Far East with drummer Jack Carter's band (1926–28); toured Europe, Russia and Middle East (1929); co-starred with Ethel Waters in *Rhapsody in Black* (1931); cut 1st record, with the Washboard Rhythm Kings (1932); led a group that included Earl Hines at Grand Terrace Ballroom in Chicago (1933); appeared in London in musical *Blackbirds* (1934); moved to Los Angeles, where she began to appear in movies, including *Take It from Me, Irresistible You,* and the French film *L'Alibi* (1935); taken prisoner by the Nazis while working in Copenhagen (1941); freed from a concentration camp in a prisoner exchange after 18 months and returned to NY (1943); made performance comeback, including an appearance at Apollo Theater (1943), Town Hall (1949) and Palace Theater (1956). ❖ See also *Women in World History.*

SNOWDEN, Leigh (1929–1982). American actress. Born Martha Lee Estes, June 23, 1929, in Memphis, TN; died May 11, 1982, in Los Angeles, CA; m. Dick Contino (accordionist), 1956; children: 5. ❖ Began career as a model; films include *Kiss Me Deadly, Francis in the Navy, All That Heaven Allows, I've Lived Before* and *The Creature Walks Among Us*; retired (1956).

SNOWE, Olympia J. (1947—). American politician. Born Olympia Jean Boucles, Feb 21, 1947, in Augusta, Kennebec Co., Maine; dau. of George Bouchles and Georgia (Goranites) Bouchles; University of Maine, BA, 1969; m. John R. McKernan Jr. (governor of Maine). ❖ Served in Maine House of Representatives (1973–76), then Maine State Senate (1976–78); elected as a Republican to 96th US Congress (1978); reelected for 7 succeeding congresses (Jan 3, 1979–Jan 3, 1995) and served as co-chair of the Congressional Caucus for Women's Issues; elected to the US Senate (1994), the 1st Greek-American woman elected to the Senate; reelected (2000); chair of the Committee on Small Business and Entrepreneurship; a leading moderate, focuses on building bipartisan consensus on key issues; known for her work on budget deficit reduction, fiscal issues, health care, domestic violence, women's issues and foreign affairs.

SNYDER, Alice D. (1887–1943). American educator. Born Alice Dorothea Snyder, Oct 29, 1887, in Middletown, Connecticut; died Feb 17, 1943, at her Vassar College campus apartment; dau. of Peter Miles Snyder (minister) and Grace Evelyn (Bliss) Snyder (pianist and mathematics teacher); sister of Franklyn Bliss Snyder (president of Northwestern University) and Edward Douglas Snyder (professor of English at Haverford College); Vassar College, AB, 1909, AM, 1911; University of Michigan, PhD in English and philosophy, 1915; never married; no children. ❖ Became an instructor in English at Vassar (1912); was an assistant in rhetoric at University of Michigan (1914), then returned to Vassar, where she helped to develop educational policy and served on the College Entrance Examination Board committee; over the years, authored several books on Samuel Taylor Coleridge. ❖ See also *Women in World History.*

SNYDER, Ruth (1893–1928). American murderer. Born Ruth Brown in New York, 1893; executed Jan 12, 1928, in NY; dau. of Josephine Brown; m. Albert Snyder (art editor for *Motor Boating* magazine), 1915 (murdered 1927); children: Lorraine Snyder (b. 1918). ❖ Subject of one of the most sensational murder cases of the 1920s, made more so by the intense media war between New York's tabloid newspapers; was electrocuted at Sing Sing prison for the murder of husband (Jan 12, 1928), while a reporter scored an exclusive with an unauthorized camera tied to his ankle, snapping the shutter as the lethal current surged through her body (the illicit photograph is still considered the most remarkable, albeit repulsive, exclusive in the history of criminal photojournalism). ❖ See also *Women in World History.*

SNYTINA, Natalia (1971—). Russian biathlete. Name variations: Natalia Snitina. Born Aug 16, 1971, in Russia. ❖ Won a gold medal for 4 x 7.5 km relay at Lillehammer Olympics (1994).

SOAD, Aisha Rateb (1928—). *See Rāteb, Aisha.*

SOAEMIAS, Julia (d. 222). *See Julia Soaemias.*

SOAMES, Lady (b. 1922). *See Churchill, Mary.*

SOARES, Manuel (1892–1958). *See Lisboa, Irene.*

SOBAKIN, Marta (d. 1571). Russian empress. Died Nov 13, 1571; dau. of Vassili Sobakin; became third wife of Ivan IV the Terrible (1530–1584), tsar of Russia (r. 1533–1584), on Oct 28, 1571. ❖ Was empress for less than one month.

SOBEK-NEFERU (fl. 1680–1674 bce). Egyptian pharoah. Name variations: Nefrusobek; Scemiophris; Sebek-neferu; Sebekneferu; Sebeknefru; Sobekneferu. Dau. of Amenemhet III (pharaoh); sister of Amenemhet IV. ❖ Female pharaoh who was the last ruler of ancient Egypt's 12th Dynasty and co-builder of the famous Labyrinth, one of the Seven Wonders of the ancient world; was the 1st female known to carry a complete set of kingly titles and is portrayed in sculpture wearing the kingly *nemes* headdress and a male kilt over her own dress. ❖ See also *Women in World History.*

SOBIESKI, Clementina (1702–1735). Polish princess. Name variations: Mary, Marie, or Maria Sobieska; Clementine or Clementina Sobiewski; Clementina Sobieska; Maria Clementina Stewart or Stuart. Born Marie Casimir Clementina on July 18, 1702, in Silesia; died of scurvy on Jan 18, 1735, at the Apostolic Palace, Rome; interred in St. Peter's Basilica, Vatican; dau. of Prince James Sobieski (son of John III, king of Poland, and Marie Casimir) and Hedwig Wittelsbach; m. Prince James Francis Edward Stuart (1688–1766), duke of Cornwall, known as the Old Pretender, on Sept 1, 1719; children: Charles Edward Stuart (1720–1788), known as Bonnie Prince Charlie, the Young Pretender; Henry Stuart (1725–1807), cardinal of York. ❖ Married English prince James Edward Stuart, exiled son of Mary of Modena and the deposed Catholic king James II, who was struggling to win back the throne; while husband was concerned only with the military efforts needed to try to secure his throne, turned more and more to her religious devotions; lived in a convent (1725–27), which caused a major scandal across Europe, and served to weaken the Stuart cause abroad. ❖ See also *Women in World History.*

SOBIESKI, Cunigunde (fl. 1690s). *See Cunigunde Sobieska.*

SOBIESKI, Marie (1702–1735). *See Sobieski, Clementina.*

SOBIESKI, Teresa. *See Cunigunde Sobieska.*

SOBOTKA, Ruth (1925–1967). Vienna-born ballet dancer and costume designer. Name variations: Ruth Sobotka Kubrick; Born Aug 4, 1925 in Vienna, Austria; died June 18, 1967, in New York, NY; trained at Carnegie Institute of Technology and School of American Ballet; m. Stanley Kubrick (film director), 1954 (div. 1957). ❖ Joined Ballet Society (1947); also danced with New York City Ballet, where she created a major role in Balanchine's *Tyl Eulenspiegel* (1951) and danced in revivals of Tudor's *Time Table,* Robbins' *Interplay,* and Christensen's *Jinx*; served as costume designer for Francisco Moncion's *Pastorale* (1957), *Les Biches* (1960), and *Night Song* (1966), among others; also designed for Erick Hawkins, John Taras, Kazuko Hirabayashi, and Richard Rodham, as well as for tv and films.

SOBOTTA, Barbara (1936—). *See Janiszewska, Barbara.*

SOBRAL, Leila (1974—). Brazilian basketball player. Name variations: Laiza de Souza Sobral. Born Nov 22, 1974, in São Paulo, Brazil; sister of Márcia and Marta Sobral. ❖ Won a team gold medal at World championships (1994) and a team silver medal at Atlanta Olympics (1996).

SOBRAL, Marta (1964—). Brazilian basketball player. Name variations: Marta de Souza Sobral. Born Mar 23, 1964, in São Paulo, Brazil; sister of Márcia and Leila Sobral. ❖ Center; won a team gold medal at World championships (1994), a team silver medal at Atlanta Olympics (1996) and a team bronze medal at Sydney Olympics (2000); joined ABL's Philadelphia Rage.

SOBRERO, Kate (1976—). American soccer player. Name variations: Kate Markgraf. Born Kathryn Michele Sobrero, Aug 23, 1976, in Pontiac, Michigan; attended Notre Dame University; married. ❖ Won a silver medal at Sydney Olympics (2000); won a team gold medal at World Cup (1999); was a founding member of the Women's United Soccer Association (WUSA); signed with Boston Breakers (2001); won a team gold medal at Athens Olympics (2004). Received WUSA Humanitarian award (2001).

SOBTI, Krishna (1925—). Indian novelist and short-story writer. Name variations: (pseudonym) Hashmat. Born Feb 18, 1925, in Gujarat, Pakistan. ❖ Served as honorary fellow at Punjab University (1980–82); works include *Mitro Marjani* (*Damn you, Mitro* 1967), *Surajmukhi Andhere Ke* (*Blossoms in Darkness,* 1979), *Zindaginama,* and *Dil-o-Danish* (*Heart and Mind,* 1993). Received Sahitya Shiromani Award, Sahitya Akademi Award, and Katha Chudamani Award for Lifetime Literary Achievement (1999).

SOD DOK MAI (1905–1963). *See Nimmanhemin, M. L. Bupha Kunjara.*

SÖDERBAUM, Kristina (1912—). Swedish actress. Name variations: Kristina Soderbaum or Soederbaum. Born in Djursholm-Stockholm, Sweden, Sept 5, 1912 (one source cites 1909); dau. of Henrik Söderbaum; m. Veit Harlan (director, died 1964); children: sons, Caspar and Kristian. ❖ Star of German films during Nazi era, moved to Berlin to study art history (1930); made film debut in *Onkel Bräsig* (1936); came to prominence in Veit Harlan's *Jugend* (Youth) and

Verwehte Spuren (Covered Tracks, both 1938); appeared in the popular *Das unsterbliche Herz* (The Immortal Heart, 1939); also appeared in *Die Reise nach Tilsit* (The Journey to Tilsit, 1939), which was strongly influenced by Nazi ideology; appearance in the anti-Semitic *Jud Süss* (1940) was to haunt her for the rest of her life; was featured in several more large-budget films, including *Die goldene Stadt* (The Golden City, 1942), only the 2nd film to be made in color by a German studio, *Immensee* (1943), *Opfergang* (Sacrifice, 1943), and the patriotic epic *Kolberg* (1945); following WWII, starred in 7 more films (1951–58), often receiving good reviews; made one final screen appearance, in Hans Jürgen Syberberg's *Karl May* (1974). ❖ See also *Women in World History*.

SÖDERGRAN, Edith (1892–1923). Finnish poet. Born in St. Petersburg, Russia, April 4, 1892; died at Raivola on June 24, 1923; dau. of Matts and Helena (Holmroos) Södergran; never married; no children. ❖ Though her work went relatively unrecognized in her lifetime, now acknowledged as a germinal poet and a major liberating force for Scandinavian poetry; spent her life in Raivola, Finland, with her mother as companion; attended the girls' division of the German *Hauptschule* in St. Petersburg, where she began to write poetry (1902–09); was a recurring patient at sanatoriums, treated for tuberculosis (1909–14); published 4 politically and stylistically controversial collections of poetry as well as a book of aphorisms (some of her poems translated into German by Nelly Sachs); writings include *Dikter* (Poems, 1916), *Septyran* (The September Lyre, 1918), *Rosenaltaret* (The Rose Altar, 1919), *Brokiga iakttagelser* (*Manifold Observations*, 1919) and *Framtidens skugga* (The Shadow of the Future, 1920); major works are in Swedish, which was the language spoken at her home. ❖ See also George C. Schoolfield, *Edith Södergran: Modernist Poet in Finland* (Greenwood, 1984); and *Women in World History*.

SODERMANLAND, duchess of. *See Marie Pavlovna (1890–1958).*

SÖDERSTRÖM, Elisabeth (1927—). Swedish soprano. Name variations: Elizabeth Soderstrom or Soederstroem. Born May 7, 1927, in Stockholm, Sweden; studied with Andrejeva von Skilodz at Royal Academy of Music and Opera School in Stockholm; m. Sverker Olow, 1950. ❖ Debuted at Stockholm (1947), Glyndebourne (1957), Metropolitan Opera (1959), and Covent Garden (1960); performed such modern roles as the Governess in *The Turn of the Screw,* Jenny in Richard Rodney Bennett's *The Mines of Sulphur,* Daisie Doody in Blomdahl's *Aniara,* Elisabeth Zimmer in Henze's *Elegy for Young Lovers,* and the aging prima donna in Argento's *The Aspern Papers*; became artistic director of the Drottningholm Court Theater (1990). ❖ See also autobiography *In My Own Key* (1979); and *Women in World History*.

SÖDERSTRÖM, Marit (1962—). Swedish yacht racer. Name variations: Marit Soederstroem or Soderstrom. Born Oct 25, 1962, in Sweden. ❖ At Seoul Olympics, won a silver medal in 470 class (1988).

SOEDERSTROEM, Marit (1962—). *See Söderström, Marit.*

SOERENSEN, Inge (1924—). *See Sorensen, Inge.*

SOERLIE, Else-Marthe (1978—). *See Sørlie, Else-Marthe.*

SOETERMEER, Bernardina Adriana (1900–1987). *See Schramm, Bernardina Adriana.*

SOFIA. *Variant of Sophia or Sophie.*

SOFIA MAGDALENA (1746–1813). *See Sophia of Denmark.*

SOFIA OF SPAIN (b. 1938). *See Sophia of Greece.*

SOFIE. *Variant of Sophia or Sophie.*

SOFOLA, Zulu (1935–1995). Nigerian playwright and educator. Born 1935 in Delta State, Nigeria; died 1995; dau. of Igbo/Edo parents; received a degree in English from Virginia Union Baptist Seminary in Nashville, TN; studied drama at Catholic University in Washington, DC. ❖ Nigeria's 1st woman playwright, served as head of department of performing arts at University of Ilorin, Nigeria; works include *The Deer Hunter, and the Hunter's Pearl* (1969), *Wedlock of the Gods* (1973), *The Wizard of the Law* (1975), *The Sweet Trap* (1977), *Memories in the Moonlight* (1986), and *Song of a Maiden* (1986).

SOFRONIE, Daniela (1988—). Romanian gymnast. Born Feb 12, 1988, in Constanta, Romania. ❖ Won a gold medal for team all-around and a silver medal for floor exercise at Athens Olympics (2004).

SOFRONOVA, Antonina (1892–1966). Russian artist. Name variations: Antonina Fedorovna; Antonina Fyodorovna Sofronova. Born in 1892 in Droskovo in Orel Province, Russia; dau. of a doctor; studied art at School of Feodor Rerberg in Moscow, 1910; studied under Ilya Mashkov, 1913. ❖ Best remembered for her cityscapes, had work exhibited in the "Knave of Diamonds" show (1914); paintings were also featured at "World of Art" exhibition (1917); focused on figurative paintings early on, but style became more Expressionistic; during 1920s, taught with Mikhail Sokolov at State Art Studios in Tver; went on to become an artist of the urban landscape, and cities show up as a recurrent theme in her works; completed watercolors and ink drawings titled *Moscow Street Types* (1924–25); participated in Group 13's exhibition (1931), but rarely showed her work in public after a restrictive decree issued by the government abolished all official art groups (1932). ❖ See also *Women in World History*.

SOHIER, Elizabeth Putnam (1847–1926). American advocate for libraries. Born 1847; died 1926. ❖ Persuaded the Massachusetts legislature to establish the Free Public Library Commission (1890), the 1st state agency of its kind in the nation, charged with establishing libraries across the state; was appointed to the board and served as its secretary until her death 36 years later. ❖ See also *Women in World History*.

SOHNEMANN, Kate (1913—). German gymnast. Born May 1913 in Germany. ❖ At Berlin Olympics, won a gold medal in team all-around (1936).

SOHONIE, Kamala (1911—). Indian biochemist. Born Kamala Bhagwat, July 18, 1911; University of Bombay, BS, 1933; University of Cambridge's Institute of Biochemistry, PhD, 1939; m. Madhav Sohonie, 1947. ❖ The 1st Indian woman to earn a PhD in science and the 1st Indian woman to head a scientific research institute, successfully challenged Nobel Prize-winning physicist C.V. Raman and his policy of not accepting women at his Indian Institute of Science, Bangalore, becoming its 1st female student and completing the course with distinction; at Cambridge, worked with Frederick Gowland Hopkins, a Nobel Prize winner; established, served as a director (1965–69) and taught (1949–69) at the Biochemistry Department at the Institute of Science in Mumbai; focused research interests on paddy flour's nutritive qualities, on palm juice biochemistry and on Indian legumes.

SOIA, Elena (1981—). Russian synchronized swimmer. Born Nov 9, 1981, in USSR. ❖ Won a team gold medal at Sydney Olympics (2000).

SOISSONS, countess of. *See Mancini, Olympia (c. 1639–1708).*

SOISSONS, queen of. *See Fredegund (c. 547–597).*

SOJOURNER TRUTH (c. 1797–1883). *See Truth, Sojourner.*

SOKHANSKAIA, Nadezhda (1823–1884). Russian short-story writer. Name variations: Nadezhda Stepanovna Sokhánskaia or Sokhanskaya; (pseudonym) Kokhanovskaia. Born 1823 in Kharkov, Ukraine; died 1884. ❖ Lived in Ukraine and wrote fiction that reflects the history and folklore of region; wrote her *Autobiography* (1847–48), but it was not published unitl 1896; other works include *The Rusty Linchpin* (1856, trans. 1887) and *After-Dinner Guests* (1858, trans. as *Luboff Archipovna,* 1887).

SOKOLOVA, Elena. Russian gymnast. Name variations: Yelena. Born in Russia. ❖ At Sydney Olympics, won a silver medal for all-around team and a bronze medal for balance beam (2000).

SOKOLOVA, Elena (1980—). Russian figure skater. Name variations: Yelena. Born Feb 15, 1980, in Moscow, Russia. ❖ Placed 3rd at Russian nationals (1997), 2nd at Skate America (1998) and 7th at Nagano Olympics (1998); won Nations Cup and Cup of Russia (1998).

SOKOLOVA, Eugenia (1850–1925). Russian ballet dancer. Born 1850 in St. Petersburg, Russia; died 1925 in St. Petersburg. ❖ Trained at school of Imperial Ballet; danced with Maryinsky Ballet (1869–86), where she appeared in Petipa's *Fille du Pharon, Don Quixote, Le Corsaire, Esmeralda,* and *Offrandes à l'Amour* (1886); trained numerous acclaimed Russian dancers during her near 20 years as ballet teacher.

SOKOLOVA, Lioubov (1977—). *See Chachkova, Lioubov.*

SOKOLOVA, Lydia (1896–1974). English ballet dancer. Name variations: Hilda Munnings, Hilda Munningsova; Mrs. Nicholas Kremnev. Born Hilda Munnings in Wanstead, Essex, England, Mar 4, 1896;

died at Sevenoaks, England, Feb 5, 1974; received early training at Steadman's Academy in London; studied under Anna Pavlova; m. Nicholas Kremnev (dancer), 1917; children: daughter, Natasha Kremnev (b. 1917). ❖ Dancer who performed with Sergei Diaghilev's Ballet Russe, the company with which her name is always associated, made debut in pantomime *Alice in Wonderland* (1910); toured US with Mordkin's Imperial Russian Ballet (1911–12); toured Germany and Austria-Hungary with Theodore Kosloff Co. (1912–13); as one of its best character dancers, danced with Ballet Russe (1913–29), appearing as the Polovetsian Maid in *Polovetsian Dances* from *Prince Igor*, in *Les Sylphides*, and as a nymph in *L'Après-midi d'un Faune* (1913–14), as Papillon in *Le Carnaval* and in *Le Soleil de Nuit* (1915), in *Las Meninas* (1916), as Ta-Hor in *Cléopatre*, as a bacchante in *Narcisse*, as Kikimora in *Contes Russes*, as Apple Woman in *Til Eulenspiegel* (1917), as Tarantella dancer in *La Boutique Fantasque*, in finale of *Le Tricorne* (1919), as Chosen Virgin in *Le Sacre du Printemps*, as Death in *Le Chant du Rossignol*, as Miller's Wife in *Le Tricorne*, in a character pas de deux in *Le Astuzie Femminili* (1920), as La Bouffonne in *Chout*, as Cherry Blossom fairy and Red Riding Hood in *The Sleeping Princess* (1921); was a principal dancer in London revue *You'd be Surprised* (1923); appeared as Chloe in *Daphnis and Chloe*, as Chanson dansée in *Les Biches*, as sorceress in *Night on Bald Mountain*, as Perlouse in *Le Train Bleu*, and as a principle dancer in *Les Sylphides* (1924); appeared as a muse in *Zéphire et Flore*, as The Friend in *Les Matelots*, as a soloist in *Polovetsian Dances* (1926), as Nurse in *Romeo and Juliet*, as a goddess in *Triumph of Neptune* (1926), as a dancer in *Le Bal* (1929); retired (1929); reemerged to perform with Woizikowsky Co. (1935), and in Ivor Novello musical *Crest of the Wave* (1937); choreographed *Russki-Plasski* for Ballet de la Jeunesse Anglaise (1939); retired again; returned as Marquise Silvestra in *The Good-Humoured Ladies* (1962). ❖ See also memoir *Dancing for Diaghilev* (ed. by Richard Buckle, 1960); and *Women in World History*.

SOKOLOVA, Lyubov (1921–2001). Soviet actress. Name variations: Lyubov Sergeyevna Sokolova. Born July 31, 1921, in Ivanovo, USSR; died on June 6, 2001, in Moscow, Russia; m. Georgi Arapovsky, 1940 (died 1941 in WWII); m. Georgi Daneliya (director), 1958 (div. 1984); children: son (died 1985). ❖ Appeared in over 300 films after WWII, generally as a wife or mother; made film debut in *The Genuine Human Being* (1948); best-known films in the West are *Worker's Quarters* (1965) and *Asya's Happiness* (1967), which were shown at film festivals.

SOKOLOVA-KULICHKOVA, Natalya (1949—). Soviet runner. Name variations: Natalya Kulichkova. Born Oct 1949 in USSR. ❖ At Montreal Olympics, won a bronze medal in the 4 × 400-meter relay (1976).

SOKOLOW, Anna (1910–2000). American dancer, choreographer and teacher. Born Feb 9, 1910, in Hartford, Connecticut; died Mar 29, 2000, at her home in Manhattan; dau. of Samuel Sokolow and Sara (Cohen) Sokolow; never married; no children. ❖ Choreographer and teacher who was an innovator in the field of modern dance and introduced modern dance to Mexico and Israel; studied dance with Martha Graham and choreography with Louis Horst at Neighborhood Playhouse; was a dancer with Graham's 1st company (1929–37); assisted Horst in dance composition classes; formed her own company, the Dance Unit (1933); studied ballet with Margaret Curtis at Metropolitan Opera House (1938); on Broadway, choreographed for the musical *Street Scene* (1947), Marc Blitzstein's *Regina*, Tennessee Williams' *Camino Real*, and Leonard Bernstein's *Candide*; off-Broadway, choreographed the rock musical *Hair* (1967); best known for *Rooms* (1955), with a jazz score by Kenyon Hopkins; taught at Herbert Berghof acting studio, the American National Theater and Academy, and Juilliard School, in addition to numerous universities, including Ohio State University, University of Utah, City College, and New York University; enjoyed a lengthy and prodigious international career that changed the course of modern dance. Received Aztec Eagle—the highest Mexican civilian honor given to a foreigner (1988), and Samuel E. Scripps Lifetime Achievement Award (1991); inducted into C. V. Whitney Hall of Fame at National Museum of Dance (1998). ❖ See also Larry Warren, *Anna Sokolow: The Rebellious Spirit* (Harwood, 1991); and *Women in World History*.

SOKOLOWSKA, Beata (1974—). Polish kayaker. Name variations: Beata Sokolowska-Kulesza or Beata Sokolowska Kulesza. Born Jan 10, 1974, in Gorzow Wielkopolski, Poland. ❖ Placed 1st at World championships for K2 500 (1999); won a bronze medal for K2 500 meters at Sydney Olympics (2000); won a silver medal for K2 500 at Athens Olympics (2004).

SOLANO, Solita (1888–1975). American novelist, journalist, editor, and translator. Born Sarah Wilkinson in Troy, New York, 1888; died in Orgeval, France, Nov 22, 1975; dau. of Almadus Wilkinson (lawyer); m. Oliver Filley, 1904 (annulled, 1913); no children. ❖ Writer who rebelled against her puritanical, patriarchical middle-class family, loved women and travel, and lived much of her adult life in Paris; lived in the Philippines (1904–08); tried stage career in New York (1908); had career as journalist for Boston *Traveler*, Boston *Journal* and New York *Tribune* (1914–20); met and fell in love with Janet Flanner (1918–19); was on assignment for *National Geographic* magazine in Europe (1921–22); settled in Paris with Flanner (1922); met Nancy Cunard (1924); published 3 novels (1924–27), none of which sold well; was secretary to George I. Gurdjieff, Russian mystic (1932); still in Paris, was a reporter for *Detroit Athletic Club News* (1932); during WWII, lived in US; returned to France (1952, 1954–75); spent last decade collecting and organizing the private and professional documents that comprise the Flanner-Solano Papers in the Library of Congress; writings include *The Uncertain Feast* (1924), *The Happy Failure* (1925), *This Way Up* (1927) and *Statue in a Field* (1934). ❖ See also *Women in World History*.

SOLBERG, Trine (1966—). See Hattestad, Trine.

SOLEDAD (1854–1928). See Zamudio, Adela.

SOLEIL, Germaine (1913–1996). French astrologer. Name variations: Madame Soleil. Born July 18, 1913, in the Loire Valley region, France; died Oct 1996 in Paris, France. ❖ Astrologer whose radio program was immensely popular for over 2 decades, appealing to both the cultural and political elite and a mass public.

SOLER, Yolanda. Spanish judoka. Born in Spain. ❖ Won European championship (1994–96); won a bronze medal for -48 kg extra-light-weight at Atlanta Olympics (1996).

SOLEY, Elizabeth Jane (1805–1897). See Hamilton, Elizabeth Jane.

SOLINAS DONGHI, Beatrice (1923—). Italian novelist and short-story writer. Born 1923 in Genoa, Italy; studied at Genoa University. ❖ Works include *L'estate della menzogna* (1956), *Natale non mio* (1961), *L'uomo fedele* (1965), *Le fiabe incantate* (1967), *Fiabe a Genova* (1972), *La grande fiaba intrecciata* (1972) and *Città d'esilio* (2003).

SOLJAK, Miriam Bridelia (1879–1971). New Zealand teacher, political activist, feminist, and journalist. Name variations: Miriam Bridelia Cummings. Born June 15, 1879, at Thames, New Zealand; died Mar 28, 1971, at Auckland, New Zealand; dau. of Matthew Cummings (carpenter) and Annie (Cunningham) Cummings; m. Peter Soljak (restaurant keeper), 1908 (div., 1939); children: 7. ❖ Taught at Taumarere Native School in Northland, and Pakuru School (c. 1900), and maintained interest in Maori culture and language; unknowingly forfeited British nationality by marriage to foreigner and advocated for independent nationality on agenda of New Zealand Labor Party (1920s); was executive member of Auckland women's branch of Labor Party (late 1920s); worked to sustain unemployment benefit for women workers; became freelance journalist and public speaker, working with urban Maori (1930s); was founding member of New Zealand Family Planning Association (1940). ❖ See also *Dictionary of New Zealand Biography* (Vol. 4).

SOLLMANN, Melitta. East German luge athlete. Name variations: Melitta Sollmann-Schack. Born in East Germany. ❖ Won a silver medal for singles at Lake Placid (1980); won World championships (1979, 1981).

SOLMS, princess de (1830–1902). See Rute, Mme de.

SOLMS, Thérèse de (1840–1907). See Blanc, Marie-Thérèse.

SOLNTSEVA, Yulia (1901–1989). Russian actress and director. Name variations: Iuliia Ippolitovna Solntseva; Yuliya Solntseva. Born August 7, 1901, in Moscow, Russia; died Oct 1989; studied philosophy at Moscow University; graduate of State Institute of Music and Drama in Moscow; m. Aleksandr Dovzhenko (film director), 1927 (died 1956). ❖ One of the most beautiful actresses of the Soviet's post-Revolution years, gained fame in title role of Protazanov's science-fiction melodrama *Aelita* (1924), and as the cigarette girl in Zhelyabuzhsky's *Cigarette-Girl from Mosselprom*; made final appearance on screen in husband's *Earth/Soil* (1930); began co-directing with him; most notable early works are documentaries that focus on the Ukraine and the beginnings of World War II; was sole director of documentary *Bucovina-Ukrainian Land*

(1940), then collaborated with Yakov Avdeyenko on *The Battle for Our Soviet Ukraine* (1943), and with husband on *Victory in the Ukraine and the Expulsion of the Germans from the Boundaries of the Ukrainian Soviet Earth* (1945); following husband's death (1956), completed his *Poem of an Inland Sea*, the 1st part of a trilogy, which eventually received the Lenin Prize; further dedicated herself to finishing and filming all his unrealized work; also created *The Golden Gate* (1969), about her relationship with husband, and *Such High Mountains* (1974), which focused on education. Named Honored Artist of the Republic (1935). ❖ See also *Women in World History*.

SOLOGNE, Madeleine (1912–1995). French actress. Born Madeleine Vouillon, Oct 27, 1912, in La Ferté–Imbault, France; died Mar 31, 1995, in Virezon, France. ❖ Star of French films; made debut in *La vie est à nous* (1936), followed by *Adrienne Lecouvreur, Conflit, Le monde tremblera, Départ à zéro, Fièvres, Croisières sidérales, Les hommes sans peur, Le loup des Malveneur, L'Éternel retour, Vautrin, Mademoiselle X, Marie la Misère, Un ami viendra ce soir, La foire aux chimères, Le dessous des cartes, Figure de proue, Une grande fille toute simple, Les Naufrageurs, Il suffit d'aimer* and *Le temps des loups*, among others.

SOLOMON, Hannah Greenebaum (1858–1942). American welfare worker and community activist. Born Jan 14, 1858, in Chicago, Illinois; died Dec 7, 1942, in Chicago; dau. of Michael Greenebaum and Sarah (Spiegel) Greenebaum; studied piano with Carl Wolfsohn; m. Henry Solomon, May 14, 1879 (died 1913); children: Herbert, Helen and Frank. ❖ One of the 1st Jewish members of the Chicago Woman's Club (1877), participated in the founding of the National Council of Jewish Women and served as its 1st president (1890–1905); established more than 50 local chapters within 6 years; co-founded the Illinois Federation of Women's Clubs (1896); was a founding member of Women's City Club (1910); published *A Sheaf of Leaves* (1911), a collection of her speeches. ❖ See also autobiography, *Fabric of My Life* (1946); and *Women in World History*.

SOLOMONIA (fl. 16th c.). Grand princess of Moscow. Name variations: Salome Saburova. Dau. of Yuri Saborov; became 1st wife of Vasili also known as Basil III Ivanovich (1479–1534), grand prince of Moscow (r. 1505–1534), on Sept 4, 1505 (div. in 1526); no children. ❖ Following divorce, was sent to a convent.

SOLOV'EVA, Poliksena (1867–1924). Russian writer. Name variations: Poliksena Soloveva or Solovieva; (pseudonym) Allegro. Born Poliksena Sergeevna Solov'eva in 1867; died 1924; dau. of the president of Moscow University; sister of philosopher and theologian Vladimir Solov'ev or Soloviev (1853–1900); studied art and voice; lived with N. I. Manaseina. ❖ Published her 1st poems (1885); under pseudonym Allegro, published *Hoarfrost*, which won Pushkin prize (1908); with her companion N. I. Manaseina, a children's writer, published a highly respected children's magazine (1906–13). ❖ See also *Women in World History*.

SOLOVOVA, Olga (1953—). Soviet volleyball player. Born July 22, 1953, in USSR. ❖ At Moscow Olympics, won a gold medal in team competition (1980).

SOLTESOVA, Elena Marothy- (1855–1939). *See Marothy-Soltesova, Elena.*

SOMER, Hilde (1922–1979). Austrian pianist. Born in Vienna, Austria, Feb 11, 1922; died in Freeport, the Bahamas, Dec 24, 1979. ❖ Fled Nazis with family (1938) and settled in US; studied with Rudolf Serkin at Curtis Institute in Philadelphia and privately with Claudio Arrau; known for performances of modern works and innovative concert techniques, succeeded with the largely neglected Latin American repertoire, bringing such compositions as Juan José Castro's *Sonatina española* to the attention of musical public; commissioned a number of piano concertos from contemporary composers, including John Corigliano Jr. and Antonio Tauriello (1968), and made several acclaimed recordings of music by Argentinean composer Alberto Ginastera (1973); performed a "Spatial Concerto" by Henry Brant (1978). ❖ See also *Women in World History*.

SOMERS, Ann (1932–1983). *See Gorham, Kathleen.*

SOMERS, Armonía (1914–1994). Uruguayan writer and educator. Name variations: Armonía Liropeya Etchepare Locino, Armonía Etchepare de Henestrosa; Armonia Somers. Born Armonía Liopeya Etchepare Locino, Oct 7, 1914, in Pando, Uruguay; died Mar 1, 1994, in Uruguay; dau. of Pedro Etchepare and María Judith Locino; m. Rodolfo Henestrosa, 1955. ❖ Writer of complex and imaginative fiction under pseudonym Armonía Somers and academic texts under

real name Armonía Etchepare de Henestrosa, began teaching in Montevideo (1933); published a book on Helen Keller's teacher, *Ana Sullivan Macy: La forja en noche plena* (Ana Sullivan Macy: The Forge in the Darkest Night, 1944); served as assistant director of Library and Pedagogical Museum of Uruguay (1957–61) and was named director of Pedagogical Museum (1961); served as director of Uruguayan National Center for Pedagogical Documentation and Information (1962–71); completed studies of pedagogical documentation (1964–65) for UNESCO in Paris, Dijon, Geneva and Madrid; as Armonía Somers, wrote such novels as *La mujer desnuda* (The Naked Woman, 1950), which critics initially attributed to others; once it was established that the author was indeed a Uruguayan woman, became a national legend for her daring. Additional works include *El derrumbamiento* (1953) and many short stories. ❖ See also Rómulo Cosse, ed., *Armonía Somers, papeles críticos: Cuarenta años de literatura* (Librería Linardi y Risso, 1990).

SOMERS, Jane (b. 1919). *See Lessing, Doris.*

SOMERSET, Anne (1631–1662). English noblewoman. Name variations: Anne Howard. Born in Oct 1631 at Raglan Castle; died in 1662; dau. of Edward Somerset, 2nd marquess of Worcester, and Elizabeth Dormer (d. 1635); sister of Elizabeth Somerset; m. Henry Howard (1628–1683), 6th duke of Norfolk (r. 1667–1683), in 1652; children: Henry Howard (1655–1701), 7th duke of Norfolk (r. 1683–1701); Thomas Howard; Elizabeth Howard (d. 1732, who m. George Gordon, 1st duke of Gordon). Henry Howard, 6th duke of Norfolk, was also married to Jane Bickerton.

SOMERSET, Blanche (1583–1649). *See Arundel, Blanche.*

SOMERSET, countess of.
See Holland, Margaret (1385–1429).
See Beauchamp, Margaret (d. 1482).
See Howard, Frances (1593–1632).

SOMERSET, duchess of.
See Beauchamp, Eleanor (1408–1468).
See Stanhope, Anne (1497–1587).
See Devereux, Frances (d. 1674).
See Percy, Elizabeth (1667–1722).
See Seymour, Frances Thynne (1669–1754).
See Seymour, Georgiana (d. 1884).

SOMERSET, Elizabeth (fl. 1650). Baroness Powys. Name variations: Elizabeth Herbert; Lady Elizabeth Somerset. Dau. of Elizabeth Dormer (d. 1635) and Edward Somerset, 2nd marquess of Worcester; sister of Anne Somerset (1631–1662); m. William Herbert (1617–1696), 1st marquis of Powis, 3rd baron Powis or Powys; children: Mary Herbert (who m. Sir George Maxwell); Frances Herbert (who m. Lord Seaforth); Anne Herbert (who m. Viscount Carrington); William Herbert, 1st marquis of Powis or Powys; Lucy Herbert (1669–1744); Winifred Maxwell (1672–1749).

SOMERSET, Henrietta (1669–1715). Countess of Suffolk. Name variations: Lady Henrietta Somerset; Henrietta Howard. Born in 1669; died Aug 2, 1715; dau. of Henry Somerset, 1st duke of Beaufort, and Mary Capell (1630–1714); m. Henry Horatio O'Brien (1670–1690), Lord O'Brien, on June 24, 1686 (died of smallpox); m. Henry Howard (1670–1718), 6th earl of Suffolk (r. 1709–1718), in April 1705; children: (1st m.) Henry O'Brien (b. 1688), 8th earl of Thomond; Elizabeth O'Brien (1689–1689); Mary O'Brien (d. 1716); Margaret O'Brien. Henry Howard was also married to Auberie Anne Penelope O'Brien (1668–1703), Lady Walden.

SOMERSET, Henrietta (d. 1726). Duchess of Grafton. Name variations: Lady Henrietta Somerset. Died in 1726; dau. of Rebecca Child (d. 1712) and Charles Somerset, marquess of Worcester; m. Charles Fitzroy (1683–1757), 2nd duke of Grafton (r. 1690–1757); children: Charles Henry Fitzroy (b. 1714), earl of Euston; George Fitzroy, earl of Euston (b. 1715); Augustus Fitzroy (b. 1716); Charles Fitzroy (b. 1718); Caroline Fitzroy (d. 1784, who m. William Stanhope, 2nd earl of Harrington); Isabel Fitzroy (1726–1782); Harriet Fitzroy (d. 1735).

SOMERSET, Lady Henry (1851–1921). *See Somerset, Isabella.*

SOMERSET, Isabella (1851–1921). British philanthropist and temperance leader. Name variations: Lady Henry Somerset; Isabel Somerset; Isabella Caroline Cocks. Born Isabella Caroline Cocks in London, England, Aug 3, 1851; died Mar 12, 1921; eldest dau. of Charles Somers Cocks (1819–1883), viscount Eastnor and 3rd earl of Somers, and Virginia Pattle (d. 1910); sister of Adeline Cocks (later the duchess of Bedford); m. Lord Henry Richard Charles Somerset (comptroller of Queen Victoria's household [1874–79] and member of Parliament for Monmouthshire [1871–80]), on Feb 6, 1872 (div. 1878); children: Henry Charles Somers Augustus Somerset (1874–1945). ❖ Served as president of British Women's Temperance Association (1890–1903); founded Duxhurst, a home for inebriate women near Reigate, which was the 1st institution of its kind in England to treat the women as patients rather than criminals (1895); served as president of World's Women's Christian Temperance Union (1898–1906). ❖ See also *Women in World History*.

SOMERVILLE, E. (1858–1949). Irish writer. Name variations: Edith Somerville. Born Edith Œnone Somerville, May 2, 1858, in Corfu, Greece; died in Castletownshend, Co. Cork, Ireland, Oct 8, 1949; dau. of Thomas Henry Somerville and Adelaide (Coghill) Somerville; never married; no children. ❖ Collaborator with cousin Violet Martin on novels and other writings which chronicled the declining fortunes of their class, the Anglo-Irish gentry, in the decades before Irish independence; spent most of life at family home in Castletownshend, Co. Cork; studied art (1870s–80s); met cousin Violet Martin (1886) and began their literary collaboration; published 1st collaborative novel, *An Irish Cousin* (1889) and between then and Martin's death (1915) published 10 books and numerous articles in British and Irish periodicals; published *The Real Charlotte* (1893), considered the best work; published *Some Experiences of an Irish R. M.* (1899), an enormous success; continued the collaboration after Martin's death with the help of spiritualism and seances and wrote 14 other books; had exhibitions of her paintings and also had a horse-coping business (1920s–30s); writings include *Through Connemara in a Governess Cart* (1893), *In The Vine Country* (1893), *Further Experiences of an Irish R. M.* (1908), *In Mr Knox's Country* (1915), *Irish Memories* (1917), *Mount Music* (1919), *Wheeltracks* (1923), *The Big House of Inver* (1999) and *The States through Irish Eyes* (1930). Elected to Irish Academy of Letters (1933); received Gregory Gold Medal, Irish Academy of Letters (1941). ❖ See also Geraldine Dorothy Cummins, *Dr E.Œ Somerville* (Andrew Dakers, 1952); Maurice Collis, *Somerville and Ross: A Biography* (Faber & Faber, 1968); John Cronin, *Somerville and Ross* (Bucknell U. Press, 1972); *The Selected Letters of Somerville and Ross* (ed. by Gifford Lewis, Faber & Faber, 1989); and *Women in World History*.

SOMERVILLE, Mary Fairfax (1780–1872). Scottish mathematical physicist. Born Mary Fairfax, Dec 26, 1780, in Jedburgh, Scotland; died Nov 29, 1872, in Naples, Italy; dau. of Margaret (Chartres) Fairfax (sister-in-law of Dr. Thomas Somerville who wrote *My Own Life and Times*) and William George Fairfax (vice-admiral); m. Samuel Greig (Russian consular agent), 1804 (died 1807); married maternal cousin William Somerville (doctor and inspector of army medical board), 1812 (died 1860); children: (1st m.) Woronzow Greig (1805–1865), William Greig (1806–1814); (2nd m.) Margaret Farquhar Somerville (1813–1822), Thomas Somerville (1814–1815), Martha Chartres Somerville (b. 1815), Mary Charlotte Somerville (b. 1817). ❖ Scientific writer whose ability to popularize science earned her unparalleled popularity, as well as a reputation for thoroughness of intellect and depth of understanding; enrolled at Miss Primrose's Academy for Girls, Musselburgh, Scotland (1789); moved to Edinburgh (1793); on marriage, moved to London (1805); on death of husband (1807), returned to Scotland and resumed her education, reading Isaac Newton's *Principia Mathematica*, and studying physical astronomy and mathematics; awarded silver medal by editors of *Mathematical Repository* magazine for her solution to a problem on Diaphantine equations (1811); moved to London where she soon began to frequent scientific circles (1815); undertook experiments in magnetism (1825), the subject of her 1st scientific paper, which was submitted to Royal Society (1826); received request to write a popular version of Pierre de Laplace's *Celestial Mechanics* for the Society for the Diffusion of Useful Knowledge (1827), which resulted in *Mechanism of the Heavens* (1831), an instant success; published *On the Connection of the Physical Sciences* (1834), which proved to be an even greater success; with Caroline Herschel, elected the 1st female members to Royal Astronomical Society (1835); awarded royal pension (1835); because of husband's faltering health, moved to Italy (1838), where she spent the remaining 34 years of her life; produced *Physical Geography* (1848), her most successful work, used in universities for next 50 years; elected member of American Geographical and Statistical Society (1857); published *On Molecular and Microscopic Science* (1869); elected member of American Philosophical Society (1869); elected to Italian Geographical Society

(1869). Awarded Victoria Gold Medal by Royal Geographical Society (1869). ❖ See also Elizabeth C. Patterson, *Mary Somerville and the Cultivation of Science, 1815–1840* (Nijhoff, 1983) and *Mary Somerville, 1780–1872* (Oxford U. Press, 1979); Martha Somerville, *Personal Recollections of Mary Somerville* (1874); and *Women in World History*.

SOMERVILLE, Nellie Nugent (1863–1952). American suffragist and politician. Born Eleanor White Nugent, Sept 25, 1863, near Greenville, Mississippi; died July 28, 1952, in Ruleville, Mississippi; dau. of William Lewis Nugent and Eleanor Fulkerson (Smith) Nugent; attended Whitworth College in Brookhaven, Mississippi; Martha Washington College in Abingdon, Virginia, AB, 1880; m. Robert Somerville (civil engineer) 1885 (died 1925); children: Robert Nugent Somerville (b. 1886); Abram Douglas Somerville (b. 1889); Eleanor Somerville (b. 1891); Lucy Somerville Howorth (1895–1997). ❖ Named corresponding secretary of the Mississippi Women's Christian Temperance Union (1894); became chair of the Mississippi Woman Suffrage Association (1897); elected vice-president of the National American Woman Suffrage Association (1915); a powerful figure in Mississippi's Democratic Party, became the 1st woman elected to the Mississippi state legislature (1923), serving until 1927; served as a delegate from Mississippi to the national convention of the Democratic Party (1925). ❖ See also *Women in World History*.

SOMERVILLE AND ROSS.
See Somerville, E. (1858–1949).
See Martin, Violet (1862–1915).

SOMMER, Renate (1958—). German agriculturist and politician. Born Sept 10, 1958, in Bochum, Germany. ❖ As a member of the European People's Party (Christian Democrats) and European Democrats, elected to 5th European Parliament (1999–2004).

SOMOGI, Judith (1937–1988). American chorale and orchestra conductor. Born Judith Somogi, May 13, 1937, in Brooklyn, NY; died Mar 23, 1988, in Rockville Center, LI, NY; Juilliard School of Music in New York, MM degree, 1961; never married. ❖ Joined New York City Opera as a rehearsal pianist (1966); between opera seasons, worked as assistant conductor at Spoleto in Italy and at American Symphony Orchestra in NY; was assistant conductor to Thomas Schippers and Leopold Stokowski before debut as 1st female conductor of New York City Opera (1974), conducting *The Mikado* and *La Traviata*; appeared in San Francisco, San Diego, Los Angeles, Pittsburgh and San Antonio, conducting orchestra and operatic productions (1970s); made European debut in Saarbrücken (1979); conducted both Tulsa Philharmonic and Oklahoma City Orchestra; after conducting *Madama Butterfly* in West Germany (1981), was offered the position of 1st Kappelmeister (principal conductor) at Frankfurt Opera (1982); was the 1st woman to conduct in a major Italian opera house, when she directed Gluck's *Orfeo ed Euridice* at Teatro La Fenice in Venice (1984); remained at Frankfurt Opera until administrative changes and declining health caused her to retire (1987); died at 47. ❖ See also documentary, "On Stage with Judith Somogi," which aired on PBS; and *Women in World History*.

SONDERGAARD, Gale (1899–1985). American actress. Name variations: Gale Biberman. Born Edith Holm Sondergaard in Litchfield, Minnesota, Feb 15, 1899; died in Woodland Hills, California, Aug 1985; dau. of a professor; graduate of University of Minnesota School of Drama, 1921; m. Neill O'Malley, 1922 (div. 1930); m. Herbert Biberman (stage director and writer), 1930 (died 1971); children: (2nd m.) daughter (died 1965). ❖ Began career with Jessie Bonstelle's stock company; made Broadway debut as replacement for Judith Anderson in *Strange Interlude*; signed 3-year contract with Theater Guild; was the 1st woman to receive Academy Award for Best Supporting Actress (1936), for portrayal of Faith in *Anthony Adverse*, her 1st film; went on to supporting parts, often cast as the villain in such films as *Spider Woman* (1944) and *The Spider Woman Strikes Back* (1946); received 2nd Academy Award nomination for supporting role of Lady Thiang in *Anna and the King of Siam* (1946), starring Irene Dunne; film career came to a halt when she was blacklisted following House Un-American Activities Committee hearings (HUAC), and her husband, one of the "Hollywood Ten," was sent to prison for refusing to testify; reemerged in off-Broadway one-woman show *Woman* (1965); had a 6-month run on tv soap "The Best of Everything"; returned to the screen in *Slaves* (1969), *Pleasantville* and *The Return of a Man Called Horse* (both 1976), and *Echoes* (1983). Other films include *Maid of Salem* (1937), *Seventh Heaven* (1937), *The Life of Emile Zola* (1937), *Juarez* (1939), *The Cat and the*

Canary (1939), *Sons of Liberty* (1939), *The Blue Bird* (1940), *The Mark of Zorro* (1940), *The Letter* (1940), *The Black Cat* (1941), *Paris Calling* (1941), *My Favorite Blonde* (1942), *A Night to Remember* (1943), *Appointment in Berlin* (1943), *Follow the Boys* (1944), *The Invisible Man's Revenge* (1944), *The Climax* (1944), *Enter Arsene Lupin* (1944) and *East Side, West Side* (1949). ❖ See also *Women in World History.*

SONG AILING (1890–1973). Chinese financier and philanthropist. Name variations: Soong Eling, Eye-ling, or Ai-ling; Sung Eling; Madame H. H. Kong or Madame H. H. Kung. Pronunciation: Soong EYE-ling. Born Dec 12, 1890, in Shanghai, China; died Oct 20, 1973, in New York City; eldest child of Han Chiao-shun, universally known as Charlie Jones Song (publisher of Bibles) and Ni Guizhen (Ni Kwei-tseng, known later as Song Guizhen); elder sister of Song Qingling and Song Meiling; educated at Wesleyan College, Georgia, 1904–09; m. financier Kong Xiangxi also spelled K'ung Hsiang-hsi (1880–1967), April 1914 (in the West, he was known as H. H. Kung, and she was therefore known as Madame Kung; he died 1967); children: Ling-i (known is Rosamund, b. 1916); Ling-ki'an (David, b. 1917); Ling-wei (Jeannette, b. 1918); Ling-chieh (Louie, b. 1919). ❖ Receiving her degree in US (1909), returned to Shanghai, where she took part in charity activities; became secretary to Dr. Sun Yat-sen; as the respectable Madame Kung, was more interested in business than politics; with husband, lived in Shanghai and rapidly expanded their business in large Chinese cities, including Hong Kong; a shrewd entrepreneur who usually stayed away from publicity, was often said to be the mastermind of the Song family; brokered Meiling's marriage to Chiang Kai-shek and played a crucial role in directing American foreign policy in the 20th century; fled China with husband (1947), taking most of her wealth with her; remained in US, never returning to China or even Taiwan. ❖ See also Roby Eunson, *The Soong Sisters* (Watts, 1975); Emily Hahn, *The Soong Sisters* (Doubleday, 1941); Sterling Seagrave, *The Soong Dynasty* (Harper & Row, 1985); and *Women in World History.*

SONG, Mrs. Charles Jones (c. 1869–1931). *See Ni Guizhen.*

SONG CHING LING (1893–1981). *See Song Qingling.*

SONG ELING (1890–1973). *See Song Ailing.*

SONG GUIZHEN (c. 1869–1931). *See Ni Guizhen.*

SONG JI-HYUN (1969—). Korean handball player. Born Jan 23, 1969, in South Korea. ❖ At Seoul Olympics, won a gold medal in team competition (1988).

SONG MEILING (1897–2003). Chinese first lady. Name variations: Soong or Sung May-ling, Mayling, or Mei-ling; Madame Chiang, Madame Chiang Kai-shek or Madame Chiang Kaishek; Mme. Jiang Jieshi; Chiang Mei-ling. Pronunciation: Soong MAY-ling. Born Mar 5, 1897, in Shanghai, China; died Oct 23, 2003, in New York, NY; youngest dau. of Charlie Jones Song (business leader and philanthropist born Hon Chao-Shun or Jia-shu Song) and Ni Guizhen (Ni Kweitseng, dau. of a wealthy scholar family in Shanghai who believed in Christianity, also known as Song Guizhen); sister of Song Ailing (1890–1973), Song Qingling (1893–1981) and T. V. Song; educated at Miss Potwin's preparatory school in Summit, New Jersey; attended Wesleyan College in Georgia; graduate of Wellesley College, 1917; m. Chiang Kai-shek (1887–1975, nationalist leader and ruler of China, 1927–49), on Dec 1, 1927 (died 1975). ❖ Wife of Generalissimo Chiang Kai-shek and leading member of the most influential Chinese family of 1st half of 20th century, was undoubtedly the most powerful woman of her time; spent school years in US and spoke English with a lilting Georgia accent; returning to Shanghai (1917), became one of the city's leading socialites; community-minded, was the 1st woman and the 1st Chinese national to serve on Municipal Council's child labor committee, which issued a damning report on sweatshop conditions (1924); met Chiang Kai-shek (1921), whose armies controlled much of China; married and moved to Nanjing (Nanking), where Chiang was selected to head Guomindang government (1927); as First lady of China, organized hospitals, nursing corps, and schools for orphans; served continually on government committees, made inspection tours, and frequently accompanied Chiang to front lines, where he was 1st fighting warlords and then Communists; was the spearhead of Chiang's "New Life Movement"; since he spoke no English, served as his interpreter and voice to the Western world, thereby possessing untold influence in crucial diplomatic negotiations; now known as Madame Chiang Kai-shek, was an enormous asset in molding Western opinion; during war with Japan, organized the evacuation of thousands of Hankou (Hankow) factory workers and their

families (1938), led the National Refugee Children's Association, and with sister Ailing, started the Women's Advisory Committee, an effective war-relief group; often broadcast to US, pleading with Americans to boycott Japanese goods and to stop supplying oil to Japan; her books saturated the American market, including *Messages in War and Peace* (1938), *This Is Our China* (1940), *China Shall Rise Again* (1941) and *We Chinese Women* (1943); with China as a US ally, addressed both houses of Congress separately (Feb 1943), appealing to US to alter its wartime priorities by defeating Japan before tackling Germany; toured US, asking for aid; was also in US to secure American military aid for Chiang's war against the Communist forces of Mao Zedong (1948–50); returned to Asia, this time not to China, which was under Mao's rule, but to the island fortress of Taiwan, where husband had set up a rump government (Jan 1950); continued involvement in social work, particularly orphanages, schools, and groups advancing the welfare of women; following death of husband (1975), settled in Lattingtown, Long Island, at estate of nephew David Kung. ❖ See also Roby Eunson, *The Soong Sisters* (Watts, 1975); Emily Hahn, *The Soong Sisters* (Doubleday, 1941); Sterling Seagrave, *The Soong Dynasty* (Harper & Row, 1985); and *Women in World History.*

SONG NINA (1980—). Chinese volleyball player. Born April 7, 1980, in Anshan, China. ❖ Setter, won a team gold medal at Athens Olympics (2004).

SONG QINGLING (1893–1981). Chinese political leader. Name variations: Madame Sun Yat-sen or Sun Yatsen; Soong Ching Ling; Soong Qingling; Song Chingling or Ching-ling; Sung Chingling. Born Jan 27, 1893, in Shanghai; died May 29, 1981, in Beijing; 2nd dau. of Han Chiao-shun, universally known as Charlie Jones Song (publisher of Bibles) and Ni Guizhen (Ni Kwei-tseng, known later as Song Guizhen); sister of Song Ailing and Song Meiling; educated at Potwin's private school in Summit, New Jersey, and at Wesleyan College, 1907–13; m. Sun Yat-sen (father of the Chinese Revolution), in 1915 (died 1925). ❖ Pro-Communist wife of Sun Yat-sen and vice chair of the People's Republic of China, who was a direct and powerful participant in the 20th-century struggle between Nationalists and Communists that changed both China and the world; joined husband in campaigns against warlords and encouraged women to participate in Chinese revolution by organizing women's training schools and associations; elected executive member of Guomindang Central Committee (1926); went on 4-year self exile (1927–31); with sisters, gave radio broadcasts to American audience on the Anti-Japanese War in China (1940); was isolated from the rest of family when the Communists, led by Mao Zedong and Zhou Enlai, won her allegiance as Sun Yat-sen's widow as they destroyed the regime of Chiang Kai-shek and confiscated the Chinese property of the Kung and Song families; remained in China, leading the China Welfare League to establish new hospitals and provide relief for wartime orphans and famine refugees; when Chinese Communists established a united government in Beijing (1949), was invited as a non-Communist to join the new government and elected vice chair of the People's Republic of China; awarded the Stalin International Peace Prize (1951); while active in the international peace movement and Chinese state affairs (1950s), never neglected her work with China Welfare and her lifelong devotion to assisting women and children; was one of the most respected women in China, who inspired many of her contemporaries as well as younger generations; made honorary president of the People's Republic of China (1981). ❖ See also Liu Jia-quan, *Biography of Song Qingling* (1988); Roby Eunson, *The Soong Sisters* (Watts, 1975); Emily Hahn, *The Soong Sisters* (Doubleday, 1941); Sterling Seagrave, *The Soong Dynasty* (Harper & Row, 1985); and *Women in World History.*

SONG XIAOBO (1958—). Chinese basketball player. Born May 8, 1958, in China. ❖ At Los Angeles Olympics, won a bronze medal in team competition (1984).

SONIC YOUTH.
See DeMarinis, Ann.
See Gordon, Kim.

SONJA (1907–2000). *See Kuczinski, Ruth.*

SONJA (1937—). Queen of Norway. Name variations: Sonja Haraldsen. Born Sonja Haraldsen on July 4, 1937, in Oslo, Norway; dau. of Dagny (Ulrichsen) Haraldsen and Carl August Haraldsen (a clothing shop proprietor, died 1959); studied dressmaking and tailoring at the Oslo Vocational School, 1954–55; attended Swiss Ecole Professionelle des Jeunes Filles, a women's college in Lausanne, Switzerland; University of Oslo, BA, 1971; studied English at Cambridge University, England;

m. Prince Harald of Norway, later Harald V, king of Norway (r. 1991—), on Aug 29, 1968; children: Martha Oldenburg (b. 1971); crown prince Haakon Oldenburg (b. 1973). ❖ A commoner, 1st met Prince Harald (later Harald V) at an officers' ball and a romance developed; kept apart by parents, met him in secret for 10 years; allowed to wed only after Harald threatened to renounce his right to the throne; devoted a great deal of time to charitable causes, especially work with disabled children; served as president of Norwegian Red Cross' children's aid division, a role which expanded to include the vice-presidency of the larger organization (1987); became queen of Norway (1991); exhibiting the qualities necessary for the position of First lady of the kingdom, became well regarded for her intelligence, charm, elegance, and many works of goodwill. Awarded Nansen Medal by UN High Commissioner for Refugees (1982). ❖ See also *Women in World History.*

SONNEMANN, Emmy (1893–1973). *See Goering, Emmy.*

SONNING, Noelle (1895–1986). *See Streatfeild, Noel.*

SONO, Ayako (1931—). Japanese novelist. Born 1931 in Tokyo, Japan; baptized a Christian at age 17; m. Miura Shumon (novelist), 1953. ❖ Awarded Holy Cross Prize by Vatican for work on religious themes; served as participant on government committees; works include *The Guests from a Distant Country* (1954), *Rio Grande* and *A Miracle*; also wrote essay *For Whose Sake is Love* (1970).

SONTAG, Henriette (c. 1803–1854). German soprano. Name variations: Henrietta Sontag; Jetterl Sontag; Countess Lauenstein; Countess de Rossi or di Rossi. Born in Coblenz (Koblenz) in the German Rhineland, Jan 3, probably 1803; died of cholera, June 17, 1854, in Mexico City; dau. of Franz Sontag (stage actor and comedian) and Franziska von Markloff Sontag (singer and actress); attended Royal Conservatorium of Prague, 1815–1820; m. Count Carlo di Rossi, 1828. ❖ One of the era's stellar performers on the European and American opera and concert stages, made debut as child actress (1807) and child singer (1809); settled in Prague (1815); debuted as an opera star in Prague (1820); appeared in Vienna, Berlin, Paris and London (1823–30); elevated to Prussian nobility as Countess Lauenstein (1828); became one of the most famous women in Europe; formally presented as Countess di Rossi, journeyed via Poland to Russia (1830); saw husband named Sardinian minister to German Confederation (1834); joined him on diplomatic assignment to Russia (1838–43); cared for sister Nina (1843–46); lost family fortune during European revolutions (1848); renewed career as a singer (1849); toured US (1852–54); made trip to Mexico (1854); major roles and appearances include Agathe in *Der Freischütz* (1823), Pamina in *The Magic Flute* (1823), Rosina in *The Barber of Seville* (1823), title role in *Euryanthe* (1823), Isabella in *L'Italiana in Algeri* (1825), title role in *Semiramide* (1828), Desdemonda in *Othello* (1828), Donna Anna in *Don Giovanni* (1829), title role in *Linda di Chamounix* (1849), Susanna in *The Marriage of Figaro* (1849), Miranda in *The Tempest* (1850), Zerlina in *Don Giovanni* (1853) and Princess Isabella in *Roberto il Diavolo* (1853). ❖ See also *Women in World History.*

SONTAG, Susan (1933–2004). American novelist, essayist, critic, film-maker and short-story writer. Born Susan Rosenblatt, Jan 16, 1933, in New York, NY; died Dec 28, 2004, in New York, NY; dau. of Jack Rosenblatt (fur trader, died in China of TB in 1938) and Mildred (Jacobson) Sontag (whose 2nd husband was Nathan Sontag); m. Philip Rieff (instructor in social theory), 1950 (div. 1959); children: Davie Rieff (b. 1952, writer). ❖ Studied at University of California at Berkeley, Harvard University, and University of Paris; taught philosophy at City College of New York, Sarah Lawrence, and Columbia University; provocative liberal commentator on American art and culture, came to prominence with her contentious essay, "Notes on Camp," in the *Partisan Review* (1964); works include *Freud: The Mind of the Moralist* (with Philip Rieff, 1959), *The Benefactor* (1963), *Against Interpretation* (1966), *Death Kit* (1967), *The Style of Radical Will* (1969), *On Photography* (1976), *Illness as Metaphor* (1977), *I, Etcetera* (1978), *AIDS and its Metaphors* (1988), *The Volcano Lover* (1992), *In America* (1999), *Where the Stress Falls* (2001) and *Regarding the Pain of Others* (2003); wrote and directed the film *Duet for Cannibals* (1969). Received National Book Critics Circle Award (1977), Academy of Sciences and Literature Award (Germany, 1979), and fellowship from MacArthur Foundation (1990).

SONTHIEL, Ursula (1488–1561). *See Shipton, Mother.*

SOO-NYUONG KIM (1971—). *See Kim Soo Nyung.*

SOONG. *See Song.*

SOONG CHINGLING (1893–1981). *See Song Qingling.*

SOONG ELING (1890–1973). *See Song Ailing.*

SOONG MAY-LING (b. 1897). *See Song Meiling.*

SOPER, Eileen Louise (1900–1989). New Zealand journalist, writer, and Girl Guide commissioner. Name variations: Eileen Louise Service, Phillida. Born Dec 14, 1900, in Sydney, NSW, Australia; died Oct 24, 1989, at Otago, New Zealand; dau. of Edwin Curwen Service (chemist's assistant) and Olga Louise (Varcoe) Service; University of Otago, BA, early 1920s; m. Frederick George Soper (professor), 1938 (died 1982). ❖ Worked as women's editor of *Otago Daily Times* and *Witness* (1924–32); under pseudonym Phillida, penned column "Notes for Women"; was Otago's provincial commissioner of Girl Guides Association (1941–54); published: *The Otago of Our Mothers* (1948), children's novel, *Young Jane* (c. 1948), and memoirs *The Green Years* (1968) and *The Leaves Turn* (1973). ❖ See also *Dictionary of New Zealand Biography* (Vol. 4).

SOPHIA. *Variant of Sofia and Sophie.*

SOPHIA (fl. early 2nd c.). Saint. Name variations: Sofia; St. Wisdom. Flourished early 2nd century in Rome; married and widowed; children: daughters Pistis, Elpis and Agape. ❖ Nothing is known of Sophia; her name, or pseudonym, was found on a tomb in a cemetery reserved for martyrs on the Aurelian Way; thus, it was assumed that she had died for her faith. Feast day is August 1 (Sept 30 in the Roman Martyrology).

SOPHIA (c. 525–after 600). Empress of Byzantium and Rome. Born c. 525; died after 600; dau. of Sittas and Comitona (sister of Empress Theodora); niece of Empress Theodora (c. 500–548); m. Flavius Justinus or Justin II (son of Emperor Justinian I's sister, Vigilantia), emperor of Byzantium and Rome (r. 565–578); children: son Justus; daughter Arabia. ❖ When husband exhibited signs of mental illness (574), began to assert herself in running of the empire; grew as husband diminished, principally in the contentious arena of court politics; concerned herself with the problem of husband's successor; became the 1st late Roman Augusta to be portrayed on imperial coins—a symbolic recognition of her imperial significance; was especially engaged in the economic affairs of the empire; though charity was an imperial virtue expected of emperors and empresses, was zealous in shouldering this responsibility; with Tiberius at her side, dominated the imperial court and its day-to-day business (574–78); before death, urged husband to appoint Tiberius as a full Augustus; was shocked when Tiberius cast her aside on his accession; after attempting to replace Tiberius, was removed from the central court and placed under house arrest in a residence of her own; was, however, always shown respect by Tiberius, and he continued to permit her use of title Augusta; when his health rapidly declined (582), was called in for advice regarding his successor; successfully recommended Maurice Tiberius; following Tiberius death, was returned to her freedom. ❖ See also *Women in World History.*

SOPHIA (fl. 1211). Landgravine of Thuringia. Name variations: Sophie; Sophia of Thuringia or Thüringia. Married Hermann I, landgrave of Thuringia (died 1216); children: Louis IV also known as Ludwig IV, landgrave of Thuringia; Agnes of Thuringia (mother of Jutta of Saxony).

SOPHIA (1464–1512). *See Sophie of Poland.*

SOPHIA (fl. 1500s). Duchess of Brunswick. Name variations: Zofia. Dau. of Bona Sforza (1493–1557) and Zygmunt I Stary also known as Sigismund I the Elder (1467–1548), king of Poland (r. 1506–1548); m. Heinrich also known as Henry, duke of Brunswick.

SOPHIA (1630–1714). Electress of Hanover. Name variations: Sophia or Sophie Simmern; Sophie von Hannover; Sophia Wittelsbach. Born in Wassenaer Court, The Hague, Netherlands, on Oct 13 or 14, 1630; died at Schloss Herrenhausen, Hanover, Germany, on June 8, 1714; interred at the Chapel of Schloss Herrenhausen; 12th child of Frederick V, king of Bohemia, and Elizabeth of Bohemia (1596–1662, the winter queen and dau. of James I, king of England); m. Ernst August also known as Ernest Augustus (d. 1698), elector of Hanover and duke of Brunswick-Lüneburg, on Sept 30, 1658; children: George Louis, later George I (1660–1727), king of England (r. 1714–1727); Frederick (1661–1690); Maximilian (1666–1726); Sophie Charlotte of Hanover (1668–1705); Charles (1669–1691); Christian (1671–1703); Ernest (1674–1728), duke of York and Albany. ❖ Had an unhappy marriage: husband was unfaithful, 3 of her children were stillborn, and 3 of her 6 sons died in battle; also had a long-lived animosity with daughter-in-law Sophia Dorothea of Brunswick-Celle, wife of eldest son George Louis (future

George I, king of England); as a Stuart and a granddaughter of James I, officially became heir to English throne in Act of Settlement of 1701, in the likelihood that there were no children of William III or Queen Anne. ❖ See also *Women in World History.*

SOPHIA (1868–1927). Countess of Torby. Name variations: Countess de Torby. Born June 1, 1868; died Sept 14, 1927; dau. of Natalie Alexandrovna Pushkin (dau. of the poet Alexander Pushkin) and Nicholas of Nassau (1832–1905); m. Michael Michaelovitch (grandson of Tsar Nicholas I), on Feb 26, 1891; children: Nadejda Michaelovna (1896–1963), countess of Torby (who m. George Mountbatten, 2nd marquess of Milford Haven).

SOPHIA (1957—). Romanian princess. Name variations: Sophia Hohenzollern. Born Oct 29, 1957, in Tatoi, near Athens, Greece; dau. of Michael (b. 1921), king of Romania (r. 1927–1930, 1940–1947), and Anne of Bourbon-Parma (b. 1923).

SOPHIA, countess of Chotek (1868–1914). *See Chotek, Sophie.*

SOPHIA, queen of Spain (1938—). *See Sophia of Greece.*

SOPHIA ALEKSEYEVNA (1657–1704). Russian princess and regent. Name variations: Tsarevna Sophia; Regent Sophia; Susanna; Sofya Alekseevna, Aleksyeevna, Alexeevna, or Alexinova. Born Sophia Alekseyevna, Sept 17, 1657, in Moscow, Russia; died at the Convent of Novodevichy in Moscow, July 3, 1704; dau. of Tsar Alexis I (Aleksei of Alexius) Mikhailovich Romanov (1629–1676) and Maria Miloslavskaia (1626–1669); sister of Fyodor (Theodore) III and Ivan V, both tsars; educated informally at her father's court and tutored by Simeon Polotsky and Sylvester Medvedev; never married; no children. ❖ Able and ambitious daughter of Tsar Alexis who served as regent of Russia for her brother Ivan V and half-brother Peter I (1682–89); when brother Fyodor III died (1682) and 10-year-old half-brother Peter was proclaimed tsar, made accusations that Fyodor had been poisoned and her younger brother, the feeble-minded Ivan (V), was being passed over in the succession; incited the *streltsy* (palace troops) to revolt and murder several members of Peter's side of the family; calmed the *streltsy* and the populace by arranging for 16-year-old Ivan to become co-ruler with Peter, with Ivan as senior tsar; with approval of the *zemsky sobor* (national assembly), assumed the role of regent for both; served as the 1st female ruler during the imperial period of Russian history; ruled with competence and success during the transitory period prior to the reign of Peter the Great. ❖ See also Lindsey A. J. Hughes, *Sophia: Regent of Russia 1657–1704* (Yale U. Press, 1990); C. Bickford O'Brien, *Russia Under Two Tsars, 1682–1689: The Regency of Sophia* (U. of California Press, 1952); Z. Schakovskoy, *Precursors of Peter the Great: The Reign of Tsar Alexis, Peter the Great's Father, and the Young Peter's Struggle Against the Regent Sophia for the Mastery of Russia* (Cape, 1964); and *Women in World History.*

SOPHIA CARLOTTE (1673–1725). Countess of Platen. Name variations: Sophia Charlotte of Kielmansegge. Born in 1673; died in 1725; had liaison with King George I (1660–1727), king of England (r. 1714–1727).

SOPHIA DOROTHEA OF BRANDENBURG (1736–1798). Duchess of Wurttemberg. Name variations: Dorothea Frederica of Brandenburg-Schwedt; Princess Dorothea. Born Dec 18, 1736; died Mar 9, 1798; m. Frederick II Eugene, duke of Wurttemberg; children: Frederick II (1754–1816), duke of Wurttemberg (r. 1797–1802), elector of Wurttemberg (r. 1802–1806), also known as Frederick I, king of Wurttemberg (r. 1797–1816); Ludwig also known as Louis Frederick Alexander (1756–1817), duke of Wurttemberg; Eugene (b. 1758), duke of Wurttemberg; Sophia Dorothea of Wurttemberg (1759–1828), also known as Marie Feodorovna, empress of Russia; William (b. 1761); Freiderike (1765–1785, who m. Peter Frederick Louis I, duke of Oldenburg); Elizabeth of Wurttemberg (1767–1790); Alexander (1771–1833), duke of Wurttemberg.

SOPHIA DOROTHEA OF BRUNSWICK-CELLE (1666–1726). Duchess of Ahlden and the "uncrowned queen" of England. Name variations: Sophie of Brunswick-Zell; Sophia Dorothea of Brunswick-Lüneberg or Luneberg; princess of Ahlden; electress of Hanover. Born Sept 5, 1666, at Celle Castle, Germany; died Nov 13, 1726, at Castle of Ahlden, Hanover, Germany; interred at Celle Church, Germany; dau. of George William, duke of Celle and Brunswick-Lüneberg, and his morganatic wife Eleanor Desmier (1639–1722); m. George Louis of Hanover, later George I (1660–1727), king of England (r. 1714–1727), on Nov 21, 1682 (div. 1694); associated with Philip Christopher, count

von Königsmarck; children: George II (1683–1760), king of England (r. 1727–1760); Sophia Dorothea of Brunswick-Lüneburg-Hanover (1687–1757). George I also had children with Ehrengard Melusina, baroness Schulenburg. ❖ Intelligent and high-spirited, married 1st cousin George Louis of Hanover (later George I, king of England), son of her uncle Ernst August, duke of Hanover (1682); following birth of son (later George II, king of England), began to spend more time apart from husband (1683); was despised by mother-in-law, the electress Sophia (1630–1714), a feeling soon shared by George; began correspondence with a Swedish count, Philip von Konigsmarck (1690), who was serving in Hanoverian army; took him as a lover (1692), an open secret at Hanover court; pressed George for a divorce; when Konigsmarck left Hanoverian army for a position in army of Saxony (1694), enemy to house of Hanover, and was assassinated, became a virtual prisoner at remote castle of Ahlden in the duchy of Celle; was divorced and confined at Ahlden for rest of her life; never saw children again. ❖ See also W. H. Wilkins, *The Love of an Uncrowned Queen: Sophie Dorothea, Consort of George I* (Duffield, 1906); and *Women in World History.*

SOPHIA DOROTHEA OF BRUNSWICK-LÜNEBURG-HANOVER (1687–1757). Queen of Prussia. Name variations: Sophia Guelph; Sophia Dorothea Hanover; Sophia Dorothea of England. Born Mar 16 (or 26), 1687 (some sources cite 1685), in Hanover, Germany; died June 29, 1757, in Monbijou Palace, near Berlin, Germany; buried in Potsdam, Brandenburg, Germany; dau. of George I (1660–1727), king of England (r. 1714–1727), and Sophia Dorothea of Brunswick-Celle (1666–1726); m. Frederick William I (1688–1740), king of Prussia (r. 1713–1740); children: Frederick Louis (1707–1708); Wilhelmina (1709–1758, who m. Frederick of Bayreuth); Frederick William (1710–1711); Frederick II the Great (1712–1786), king of Prussia (r. 1740–1786); Charlotte Albertine (1713–1714); Frederica Louise (1715–1784, who m. Charles William, margrave of Ansbach); Philippine Charlotte (1716–1801); Louis Charles William (1717–1719); Sophia Dorothea Maria (1719–1765); Louisa Ulrica of Prussia (1720–1782, who m. Adolphus Frederick, king of Sweden); Anna Amalia of Prussia (1723–1787); Augustus William Hohenzollern (1722–1758); Henry (1726–1802, who m. Wilhelmina of Hesse-Cassel [1726–1808]); Ferdinand (1730–1813, who m. Anne Elizabeth Louise, princess of Schwedt [1738–1820]). ❖ With the help of tutors and against husband's wishes, secretly taught music, the arts, literature, and philosophy to son Frederick (Frederick II the Great), who thus became acquainted with Enlightenment literature and philosophy (he even became an accomplished flutist).

SOPHIA DOROTHEA OF WURTTEMBERG (1759–1828). Russian empress. Name variations: Marie Feodorovna; Maria Feodorovna or Fyodorovna; Mariia Fedorovna; Sophia Dorothea of Württemberg. Born Sophia Dorothea Augusta Louisa on Oct 14 (o.s.) or Oct 25, 1759, in Stettin, Pomerania; died Nov 5 (o.s.) or Nov 12, 1828, probably in St. Petersburg, Russia; dau. of Frederick II Eugene (b. 1732), duke of Wurttemberg (r. 1795–1797), and Sophia Dorothea of Brandenburg (1736–1798); educated at home; m. Paul I (1754–1801), tsar of Russia (r. 1796–1801, who was the son of Catherine II the Great), on Sept 26 (o.s.) or Oct 7, 1776; children: Alexander I (1777–1825), tsar of Russia; Constantine (1779–1831, who m. Anna Juliana of Saxe-Coburg); Alexandra Pavlovna (1783–1801); Helena Pavlovna (1784–1803, who m. Frederick Louis of Mecklenburg-Schwerin); Marie Pavlovna (1786–1859, who m. Charles Frederick, duke of Saxe-Weimar); Olga (1792–1795); Catherine of Russia (1788–1819, who m. William I of Württemberg); Anna Pavlovna (1795–1865, who m. William II, king of the Netherlands); Nicholas I (1796–1855), tsar of Russia (r. 1825–1855); Michael (1798–1849), grand duke. ❖ Married Paul Petrovich (later Paul I), only son of Catherine II the Great (1776); in conformity with Russian custom, converted from Lutheranism to Orthodoxy and took name Marie Feodorovna; for 1st 20 years of marriage, lived the comfortable but isolated existence of a grand duchess as husband waited for his mother to die; after this finally happened (1796), spent a brief but often unhappy 5 years as the wife of the reigning tsar and as empress of Russia; following Paul's assassination (1801), became a formidable dowager empress and a force for conservatism in Russia until her own death in 1828. ❖ See also *Women in World History.*

SOPHIA MATILDA (1773–1844). English royal. Name variations: Sophia Guelph. Born Sophia Matilda on May 29, 1773 (some sources cite 1772), at Gloucester House, Grosvenor Street, London, England; died Nov 29, 1844, at Ranger's House, Blackheath, Kent, England; buried at St. George's Chapel, Windsor; dau. of William Henry, 1st duke of Gloucester and Edinburgh (brother of George III, king of England), and Maria Walpole (1736–1807).

SOPHIA MATILDA (1777–1848). Princess royal of England. Name variations: Princess Sophia, Sophia Guelph. Born Sophia Matilda on Nov 3, 1777, at Buckingham House, London, England; died May 27, 1848, at Kensington, London, England; dau. of George III (1738–1820), king of England (r. 1760–1820), and Charlotte of Mecklenburg-Strelitz (1744–1818); sister of George IV (1762–1821), king of England (r. 1820–1830); children: (with General Thomas Garth) Thomas Garth (b. 1800). ❖ In a family plagued by scandals, had a child fathered by an unknown man—gossipmongers hatefully spread the name of her brother Ernest Augustus, the duke of Cumberland. ❖ See also *Women in World History.*

SOPHIA OF BAVARIA (fl. 1390s–1400s). Queen of Bohemia. Dau. of John II of Munich, duke of Bavaria (r. 1375–1397) and Catherine of Gorizia; 2nd wife of Wenceslas IV the Drunkard (1361–1419), duke of Luxemburg (r. 1383–1419), king of Bohemia (r. 1378–1419), and (as just Wenceslas) Holy Roman emperor (r. 1378–1400).

SOPHIA OF BAYREUTH (1700–1770). Queen of Denmark and Norway. Name variations: Sophie Magdalene of Brandenburg-Kulmbach; Sofie-Magdalene of Kulmbach-Bayreuth. Born Nov 28, 1700; died May 27, 1770, in Christianborg, near Copenhagen, Denmark; dau. of Christian Henry, margrave of Brandenburg-Kulm; m. Christian VI, king of Denmark and Norway (r. 1730–1746); children: Frederick V (1723–1766), king of Denmark and Norway (r. 1746–1766); Louise (1724–1724); Louise of Saxe-Hilburghausen (1726–1756).

SOPHIA OF BYZANTIUM (1448–1503). Russian empress. Name variations: Sofia or Sophie Paleologa, Paleologue, or Paleologos; Sophia Palaeologus; Zoë or Zoe Palaeologus. Born Zoë Paleologus in Byzantium in 1448; died in Moscow on April 7, 1503; dau. of Thomas Paleologus, despot of Morea, and Catherine of Achaea (d. 1465); niece of Constantine XI (r. 1448–1453), Byzantine emperor; educated in Rome; became 2nd wife of Ivan III the Great (1440–1505), grand prince of Moscow (r. 1462–1505), on Nov 12, 1472; children: Helene of Moscow (1474–1513, who m. Alexander, king of Poland); Theodosia of Moscow (1475–1501); Vasili also known as Basil III (1479–1534), tsar of Russia (r. 1505–1534); Yuri (b. 1480); Dimitri of Uglitsch (b. 1481); Eudoxia of Moscow (1483–1513, who m. Peter Ibragimovich, prince of Khazan); Simeon of Kaluga (b. 1487); Andrei also known as Andrew of Staritza (b. 1490). ❖ Was the niece of the last two Byzantine emperors, the ward of two popes in Rome, the wife of Grand Prince Ivan III the Great of Moscow, and the mother of his successor Basil III; brought with her to Russia both her Byzantine and Roman heritage, and left her mark on Ivan's court and on the architecture of his capital. ❖ See also *Women in World History.*

SOPHIA OF DENMARK (1217–1248). Margravine of Denmark. Name variations: Sophia Valdemarsdottir or Waldemarsdottir. Born in 1217; died Nov 3, 1248; dau. of Berengaria (1194–1221) and Valdemar also known as Waldemar II the Victorious, king of Denmark and Norway (r. 1202–1241); m. John I, margrave of Brandenburg, in 1231. ❖ John I's 2nd wife was Jutta of Saxony.

SOPHIA OF DENMARK (1746–1813). Queen of Sweden. Name variations: Sofia Magdalena or Sophia Magdalena Oldenburg. Born July 3, 1746; died Aug 21, 1813; dau. of Louise of England (1724–1751) and Frederick V (1723–1766), king of Denmark (r. 1746–1766); sister of Christian VII, king of Denmark (r. 1766–1808); m. Gustavus III (1746–1792), king of Sweden (r. 1771–1792); children: Gustavus IV Adolphus (b. 1778), king of Sweden (r. 1792–1809); Charles Gustaf (b. 1782).

SOPHIA OF GANDERSHEIM (c. 975–1039). Abbess of Gandersheim. Born in 975 or 978 in Germany; died in 1039 at abbey of Gandersheim, Germany; dau. of Otto II (955–983), Holy Roman emperor (r. 983–983), king of Germany (r. 973–983), and Theophano of Byzantium (c. 955–991); sister of Otto III (980–1002), Holy Roman emperor (r. 983–1002) and Adelaide of Quedlinburg; never married; no children. ❖ Showing a great piety early on, left the royal palaces of her parents and entered a convent; after some years, became abbess of the large, powerful religious establishment at Gandersheim. ❖ See also *Women in World History.*

SOPHIA OF GREECE (b. 1914). Princess of Greece and Denmark. Name variations: Sophia Oldenburg; Sophia of Spain; Sophia von Schleswig-Holstein-Sonderburg-Glücksburg. Born June 26, 1914, in Corfu, Greece; dau. of Prince Andrew of Greece and Alice of Battenberg (1885–1969); m. Christopher Ernest, prince of Hesse-Cassel, in 1930; m. George Guelph, prince of Hanover, in 1946; children: (1st m.) Christine of Hesse-Cassel (b. 1933), Dorothea Charlotte (b. 1934); Karl (b. 1937); Rainer (b. 1939); Clarissa (b. 1944); (2nd m.) Welf (b. 1947), George (b. 1949) and Frederike (b. 1954).

SOPHIA OF GREECE (1938—). Queen of Spain. Name variations: Sophia Oldenburg; Sophia of Spain; Sophie of Spain; Sofia; Sofia of Spain. Born Nov 2, 1938, in Psychiko, near Athens, Greece; dau. of Frederika (1917–1981) and Paul I (1901–1964), king of the Hellenes (r. 1947–1964); sister of Constantine II, king of Greece (r. 1964–1973); m. Juan Carlos I (1938—), king of Spain (r. 1975—), on May 14, 1962; children: Elena (b. 1963); Cristina (b. 1965); Felipe or Philip, prince of the Asturias (b. 1968). ❖ Went into exile with parents when Nazi Germany invaded Greece during World War II and only returned following referendum that reinstated the monarchy in 1946; became engaged to Juan Carlos de Borbón y Borbón (later Juan Carlos I), son of Juan de Borbón, the pretender to the Spanish throne, despite concern that he was Catholic and she Greek Orthodox (1961); with husband, became monarch of Spain (1975); has done much to patronize and promote Spanish arts and culture, especially music. Received Wiesenthal Prize (1994), for efforts with husband to improve relations with Jewish and Islamic peoples, who had flourished in Spain during Middle Ages but had been driven out by militant Catholicism; honored with Grameen Foundation USA's humanitarian award for efforts in fighting poverty (2000). ❖ See also *Women in World History.*

SOPHIA OF KIEV (fl. 1420s). Queen of Poland. Fourth wife of Jagiello (1377–1434), grand duke of Lithuania, who became Vladislav also known as Ladislas II (or V) Jagello, king of Poland (r. 1386–1434); children: Ladislas III or VI (1424–1444, also known as Vladislav), king of Poland (r. 1434–1444) and Hungary (r. 1440–1444); Casimir IV (1427–1492), king of Poland (r. 1447–1492). ❖ Jagiello's 1st wife was Jadwiga (1374–1399); his 2nd wife was Anna of Cilli; his 3rd was Elzbieta.

SOPHIA OF MALINES (d. 1329). Duchess of Guelders. Died 1329; m. Renaud, also known as Rainald or Reginald II the Black Haired (d. 1343), duke of Guelders (also known as count of Gelderland), count of Zutphen; children: Margaret of Guelders (d. 1344); Isabella of Graventhal, abbess of Graventhal; Matilda of Guelders (d. 1380); Mary of Guelders (d. 1405, who m. William VI, duke of Julicrs). ❖ Renaud's 2nd wife was Eleanor of Woodstock (1318–1355).

SOPHIA OF MECKLENBURG (1508–1541). Duchess of Lüneburg. Born in 1508; died June 17, 1541; dau. of Ursula of Brandenburg (1488–1510) and Henry III, duke of Mecklenburg; m. Ernest the Pious of Zelle, duke of Lüneburg, on June 2, 1528; children: Francis Otto (b. 1530), duke of Brunswick; Henry (b. 1533), duke of Danneburg; William the Younger (b. 1535), duke of Lüneburg.

SOPHIA OF MECKLENBURG (1557–1631). Queen of Denmark and Norway. Name variations: Sophia of Mecklenburg-Gustrow. Born Sept 4, 1557; died Oct 4, 1631, in Nykobing; dau. of Ulrich III (b. 1528), duke of Mecklenburg, and Elizabeth of Denmark (1524–1586); m. Frederick II (1534–1588), king of Denmark and Norway (r. 1559–1588), on July 20, 1572; children: Elizabeth of Denmark (1573–1626); Anne of Denmark (1574–1619); Christian IV (1577–1648), king of Denmark and Norway (r. 1588–1648); Ulrich (b. 1578); Amelia of Denmark (1580–1639); Hedwig of Denmark (1581–1641); Johann (b. 1583).

SOPHIA OF MECKLENBURG (1758–1794). Princess of Denmark. Name variations: Sophia Fredericka; Sophia Frederica; Sofie Frederikke of Mecklenburg-Schwerin. Born Sophia Fredericka on August 24, 1758; died Nov 29, 1794; dau. of Louis of Mecklenburg-Schwerin and Charlotte Sophie of Saxe-Coburg-Saalfeld (1731–1810); m. Frederick Oldenburg (1753–1805), prince of Denmark (son of Frederick V, king of Norway and Denmark, and Maria Juliana of Brunswick), in 1774; children: Julian Marie (1784–1784); Christian VIII (1786–1848), king of Denmark (r. 1839–1848); Juliane (1788–1850, who m. William, landgrave of Hesse); Charlotte Oldenburg (1789–1864, who m. William of Hesse-Cassel).

SOPHIA OF NASSAU (1824–1897). Grand Duchess of Saxe-Weimar. Name variations: Sophie von Nassau. Born April 8, 1824; died Mar 23, 1897; dau. of Anna Pavlovna (1795–1865) and William II (1792–1849), king of the Netherlands (r. 1840–1849); m. Charles Alexander, grand duke of Saxe-Weimar, on Oct 8, 1842; children: Charles Augustus (b. 1844), grand duke of Saxe-Weimar; Marie Alexandrine of Saxe-Weimar (1849–1922), who m. Henry VII, prince Reuss of Kostritz; Elizabeth Sybilla of Saxe-Weimar (1854–1908, who m. John, duke of Mecklenburg-Schwerin).

SOPHIA OF NASSAU (1836–1913). Queen of Sweden. Born Sophia Wilhelmina Marianne on July 9, 1836, in Biebrich; died Dec 30, 1913, in Stockholm, Sweden; dau. of William George (b. 1792), duke of Nassau, and Pauline of Wurttemberg (1810–1856), granddau. of Frederick I; m. Oscar II (1829–1907), king of Sweden (r. 1872–1907), on June 6, 1857; children: Gustavus V (1858–1950), king of Sweden (r. 1907–1950); Oscar Charles Augustus, count of Wisborg (1859–1953); Charles of Sweden (1861–1951, who m. Ingeborg of Denmark); Eugene Bernadotte (1865–1947), duke of Närke.

SOPHIA OF POMERANIA (1498–1568). Queen of Denmark and Norway. Name variations: Sofie; Sophie of Pommerania. Born in 1498; died May 13, 1568, in Keil; dau. of Bogislav also known as Boleslav X, duke of Pomerania; became 2nd wife of Frederik or Frederick I (1471–1533), king of Denmark and Norway (r. 1523–1533), on Oct 9, 1518; children: Johann (1521–1580); Elizabeth of Denmark (1524–1586); Anna Oldenburg (d. 1535); Adolf (1526–1586, of the Holstein-Gottorp line); Dorothea of Denmark (1528–1575); Frederick (1532–1556), baron von Hildesheim.

SOPHIA OF SCHLESWIG-HOLSTEIN-SONDERBURG-GLÜCKSBURG (b. 1914). See Sophia of Greece.

SOPHIA OF SPAIN.
See Sophia of Greece (b. 1914).
See Sophia of Greece (1938—).

SOPHIA OF SWEDEN (1801–1865). Grand duchess of Baden. Born May 21, 1801; died July 6, 1865; dau. of Gustavus IV Adolphus (1778–1837), king of Sweden (r. 1792–1809), and Frederica Dorothea of Baden (1781–1826); m. Leopold (1790–1852), grand duke of Baden (r. 1830–1852), on July 25, 1819; children: 8, including Alexandrina of Baden (1820–1904, who m. Ernest II, duke of Saxe-Coburg-Saalfeld); Louis II of Baden, grand duke of Baden (b. 1824); Frederick I (1826–1907), grand duke of Baden; William of Baden (1829–1897); Mary of Baden (1834–1899); Cecilia of Baden (1839–1891, also known as Olga Feodorovna); Charles of Baden (b. 1832).

SOPHIA OF THURINGIA (fl. 1211). See Sophia.

SOPHIA OF THURINGIA (1224–1284). German duchess and founder of landgraviate of Hesse. Name variations: Sophie von Thuringen or Thüringen. Born Mar 20, 1224; died May 29, 1284 (some sources cite 1275); dau. of St. Elizabeth of Hungary (1207–1231) and Ludwig IV of Thuringia; niece of Henry Raspe IV of Thuringia; became 2nd wife of Henry II (1207–1248), duke of Brabant (r. 1235–1248), around 1240; children: Elizabeth of Brabant (1243–1261); Henry I (b. 1244), landgrave of Hesse (Henry I was 1st male ruler of Hesse). ❖ After their cousin Henry of Meissen fought against her and husband over Thuringia and was triumphant, was given Hesse as a consolation. Henry II's 1st wife was Marie of Swabia (c. 1201–1235).

SOPHIA OF WURTTEMBERG (1818–1877). Queen of the Netherlands. Born Sophie Frederica Mathilde on June 17, 1818, in Stuttgart, Germany; died June 3, 1877, at Het Loo, Apeldoorn; dau. of Catherine of Russia (1788–1819) and William I (b. 1781), king of Wurttemberg (r. 1816–1864); became 1st wife of William III (1817–1890), king of the Netherlands (r. 1849–1890), on June 18, 1839; children: William Nicholas (1840–1879); Maurice (1843–1850); Alexander (1851–1884). ❖ Following her death (1877), William III married Emma of Waldeck, mother of Queen Wilhelmina (1879).

SOPHIA OF ZAHRINGEN (fl. 12th c.). Saxon noblewoman. Flourished in 12th century in Saxony; dau. of Henry the Black (d. 1126), duke of Saxony and Bavaria, and possibly Wolfida of Saxony (c. 1075–1126); sister of Judith of Bavaria, Welf also known as Guelph VI (d. 1191), and Henry the Proud (d. 1139), duke of Bavaria, one of the most significant men in west European politics in 12th century; m. Bertold of Zahringen. ❖ A Saxon noblewoman, came from a powerful German ruling family which held the duchies of Saxony and Bavaria; always a loyal supporter of brother Henry's royal claims, aided him in military and financial ways after husband died; was even put in command of at least one of his sieges.

SOPHIE (fl. 1200s). Scandinavian royal. Dau. of Richeza Eriksdottir and Niels of Werle, also known as Nicholas II von Werle; granddau. of Erik V Klipping or Clipping, king of Denmark (r. 1259–1286); m. Gerhard.

SOPHIE (1734–1782). French princess. Name variations: Madame Sophie. Born Sophie Elizabeth Justine; youngest dau. of Louis XV (1710–1774), king of France (r. 1715–1774), and Marie Leczinska (1703–1768); sister of Adelaide (1732–1800), Louise Elizabeth (1727–1759), and Victoire (1733–1799).

SOPHIE (1965—). See Rhys-Jones, Sophie.

SOPHIE AMALIE OF BRUNSWICK-LÜNEBERG (1628–1685). Queen of Denmark. Name variations: Sophia of Lüneburg; Sophia Amelia of Brunswick; Sophia Amelia of Brunswick-Luneburg. Born Mar 24, 1628, in Herzberg; died Feb 20, 1685, in Copenhagen, Denmark; dau. of George Guelph (b. 1582), duke of Brunswick-Lüneburg (d. 1641) and Anne-Eleanor of Hesse-Darmstadt (1601–1659); m. Frederick III (1609–1670), king of Denmark and Norway (r. 1648–1670), on Oct 1, 1643; children: Ulrik Frederik Gyldenlove; Christian V (1646–1699), king of Denmark and Norway (r. 1670–1699); Anna Sophia of Denmark (1647–1717, who m. John George III of Saxony); Jørgen or George of Denmark (who m. Queen Anne of England); Frederica Amalie (1649–1704); Wilhelmine (1650–1706); Frederick (1651–1652); Ulrica Eleanora of Denmark (1656–1693, who m. Charles XI, king of Sweden); Dorothea (1657–1658).

SOPHIE CAROLINE (1737–1817). Margravine of Brandenburg. Born Sophie Caroline Marie on Oct 8, 1737; died Dec 23, 1817; dau. of Philippine Charlotte (1716–1801) and Charles, duke of Brunswick-Wolfenbüttel; m. Frederick, margrave of Brandenburg, on Sept 20, 1759.

SOPHIE CHARLOTTE OF HANOVER (1668–1705). Queen of Prussia. Name variations: Sophia Charlotte; Sophie Charlotte of Brunswick-Luneberg or Brunswick-Lüneberg; also baby-named "Figuelotte." Born Sophie Charlotte or Sophia Charlotte on Oct 20, 1668 (some sources cite Oct 12, 1662), in Schloss Iburg, near Osnabruck; died Feb 1, 1705 (some sources cite Jan 21, 1706), in Hanover, Lower Saxony, Germany; interred at the Royal Chapel, Berlin; dau. of Ernst August, duke of Brunswick, who was elevated to elector of Hanover, and the duchess Sophia (1630–1714), electress of Hanover (granddau. of King James I of England); sister of George I (1660–1727), king of England (r. 1714–1727); became 2nd wife of Frederick III (1657–1713), elector of Brandenburg (r. 1688–1701), later Frederick I, king of Prussia (r. 1701–1713), on Oct 8, 1684; children: Frederick William I (1688–1740), king of Prussia (r. 1713–1740). Frederick's 1st wife was Elizabeth Henrietta of Hesse-Cassel (1661–1683). ❖ Queen who brought her Hanoverian cultural heritage to the backward Prussian court; became patron, pupil, and good friend of the great mathematician and philosopher Gottfried Wilhelm Leibniz, spurring him toward the publication of his *Theodicy*, the only formal work he ventured to publish in his lifetime; was the 1st non-French host of the female-dominated salon culture of the European Enlightenment; her cultural aspirations were vindicated by the intellectual and artistic accomplishments of a grandson, who came to the throne as Frederick II and became known to history as Frederick II the Great. ❖ See also *Women in World History*.

SOPHIE CHARLOTTE OF OLDENBURG (1879–1964). Duchess of Oldenburg. Born Feb 2, 1879, in Oldenburg; died Mar 29, 1964, in Westerstede, Oldenburg; dau. of Frederick Augustus, grand duke of Oldenburg, and Elizabeth Anna Hohenzollern (1857–1895); m. Eitel-Frederick, prince of Prussia, on Feb 27, 1906 (div. 1926); m. Harald von Hedemann, on Nov 24, 1927.

SOPHIE ELISABETH, Duchess of Brunswick-Lüneburg. See *Braunschweig-Lüneburg, Sophie Elisabeth (1613–1676)*.

SOPHIE HEDWIG (1677–1735). Danish princess. Name variations: Sophie Hedwig Oldenburg. Born August 28, 1677; died Mar 13, 1735; dau. of Charlotte Amalia of Hesse (1650–1714) and Christian V (1646–1699), king of Norway and Denmark (r. 1670–1699).

SOPHIE LOUISE OF MECKLENBURG (1685–1735). Queen of Prussia. Born May 16, 1685; died July 29, 1735, in Grabow; became third wife of Frederick III (1657–1713), elector of Brandenburg (r. 1688–1701), later Frederick I, king of Prussia (r. 1701–1713), on Nov 28, 1708. ❖ Frederick's 1st wife was Elizabeth Henrietta of Hesse-Cassel; his 2nd was Sophie Charlotte of Hanover.

SOPHIE OF AUSTRIA (1805–1872). See Sophie of Bavaria.

SOPHIE OF BAVARIA (1805–1872). Archduchess of Austria. Name variations: Sophia; Sophie of Austria. Born Jan 27, 1805, in Munich, Germany; died May 28, 1872, in Vienna, Austria; dau. of Maximilian I Joseph of Bavaria, elector of Bavaria (r. 1799–1805), king of Bavaria (r. 1805–1825), and Caroline of Baden (1776–1841); twin sister of Maria of Bavaria (1805–1877); m. Franz Karl also known as Francis Charles (son of Francis II, emperor of Austria); children: Franz Josef also known as Francis Joseph (1830–1916), emperor of Austria; Maximilian (1832–1867), emperor of Mexico; Karl Ludwig also known as Charles Louis (1833–1896, who m. Maria Annunziata of Naples); Ludwig Viktor also known as Louis Victor (1842–1919).

SOPHIE OF BAVARIA (1847–1897). *See Sophie of Bayern.*

SOPHIE OF BAYERN (1847–1897). Duchess of Alençon. Name variations: Sophie of Bavaria; duchess of Alencon. Born Feb 22, 1847; perished in the fire of the Paris charity bazaar on May 4, 1897; dau. of Ludovica (1808–1892) and Maximilian Joseph (1808–1888), duke of Bavaria; sister of Elizabeth of Bavaria (1837–1898); m. Ferdinand, duke of Alençon, on Sept 28, 1868; children: Louise of Orleans (b. 1869, who m. Alfons of Bavaria); Emanuel (b. 1872), duke of Vendôme. ❖ Was once betrothed to Ludwig II, king of Bavaria.

SOPHIE OF BRANDENBURG (1568–1622). Electress of Saxony. Born June 6, 1568; died Dec 7, 1622; dau. of Sabine of Brandenburg-Ansbach (1529–1575) and John George (1525–1598), elector of Brandenburg (r. 1571–1598); m. Christian I, elector of Saxony, April 25, 1582; children: Christian II (b. 1583), elector of Saxony; John George (b. 1585), elector of Saxony.

SOPHIE OF DENMARK (d. 1286). Queen of Sweden. Name variations: Sophie Eriksdottir. Died in 1286; dau. of Jutta of Saxony (d. around 1267) and Erik or Eric IV Ploughpenny (1216–1250), king of Dennmark (r. 1241–1250); m. Waldemar I, king of Sweden (r. 1250–1275), in 1260; children: Ingeborg (d. around 1290, who m. Gerhard II, count of Plön); Eric (b. 1272); Ryksa (fl. 1288); Katherina; Marina (who m. Rudolf, count von Diephold in 1285); Margaret, a nun.

SOPHIE OF HOHENBERG (1868–1914). *See Chotek, Sophie.*

SOPHIE OF HOLSTEIN-GOTTORP (1569–1634). Duchess of Mecklenburg. Born June 1, 1569; died Nov 14, 1634; dau. of Adolf (1526–1586), duke of Holstein-Gottorp (r. 1544–1586), and Christine of Hesse (1543–1604); m. John V, duke of Mecklenburg, on Feb 17, 1588; children: Adolf Frederick I (b. 1588), duke of Mecklenburg-Schwerin.

SOPHIE OF HUNGARY (d. 1095). Duchess of Saxony. Died July 18, 1095; dau. of Richesa of Poland (fl. 1030–1040) and Bela I, king of Hungary (r. 1060–1063); sister of St. Ladislas I (1040–1095), king of Hungary (r. 1077–1095) and Geza I, king of Hungary (r. 1074–1077); m. Magnus (c. 1045–1106), duke of Saxony (r. 1072–1106), around 1071; children: Wolfida of Saxony (c. 1075–1126); Eilica of Saxony (c. 1080–1142, who m. Otto von Ballenstadt).

SOPHIE OF LIEGNITZ (1525–1546). First wife of the elector of Brandenburg. Born in 1525; died Feb 6, 1546; dau. of Frederick III, duke of Liegnitz; became 1st wife of John George (1525–1598), elector of Brandenburg (r. 1571–1598), on Feb 15, 1545; children: Joachim Frederick (1546–1608), elector of Brandenburg (r. 1598–1608). ❖ John George's 2nd wife was Sabine of Brandenburg-Ansbach (1529–1575); his 3rd was Elizabeth of Anhalt (1563–1607).

SOPHIE OF LITHUANIA (1370–1453). Princess of Moscow. Born in 1370; died June 15, 1453; dau. of Vitold, prince of Lithuania; m. Basil I, prince of Moscow, on Jan 9, 1392; children: Basil II the Blind (b. 1415), prince of Moscow; Anna of Moscow (1393–1417); Yuri (b. 1395); Ivan (b. 1396); Anastasia of Moscow (b. around 1398, who m. Odellko, prince of Kiev, in 1417); Daniel (b. 1401); Vasilissa of Moscow (b. around 1403, who m. Alexander of Susdal); Simeon (b. 1405); Marie of Moscow (who m. Yuri, prince of Lithuania).

SOPHIE OF MONTFERRAT (fl. 15th c.). Byzantine empress. Name variations: Sophia Monteferrata; Monferrato; Empress of Nicaea. Born of Italian ancestry; became 2nd wife of her cousin John VIII Paleologus (1391–1448), emperor of Nicaea (r. 1425–1448), then divorced. ❖ John VIII's 1st wife was Anna of Moscow (1393–1417); his 3rd was Maria of Trebizond.

SOPHIE OF NASSAU (1902–1941). Princess of Saxony. Name variations: Sophie von Nassau. Born Feb 14, 1902; died May 31, 1941; dau. of Marie-Anne of Braganza (1861–1942) and William IV (1852–1912), grand duke of Luxemburg; m. Ernest Henry (b. 1896), prince of Saxony, on April 12, 1921; children: Dedo (b. 1922); Timo (b. 1923); Gero (b. 1925).

SOPHIE OF POLAND (1464–1512). Margravine of Ansbach. Name variations: Sophia or Zofia. Born May 6, 1464; died Oct 5, 1512; dau. of Elizabeth of Hungary (c. 1430–1505) and Casimir IV Jagiellon, grand duke of Lithuania (r. 1440–1492), king of Poland (r. 1446–1492); m. Frederick V of Ansbach, margrave of Ansbach, on Feb 14, 1479; children: Albert of Prussia (b. 1490), duke of Prussia (r. 1526–1568); George of Ansbach (b. 1484), margrave of Ansbach; Casimir (b. 1481), margrave of Brandenburg.

SOPHIE OF PRUSSIA (1870–1932). Queen of the Hellenes. Name variations: Sophia; Sophia Hohenzollern; queen of Greece. Born Sophie Dorothea Ulrika Alice on June 14, 1870, in Potsdam, Brandenburg, Germany; died Jan 13, 1932, in Frankfurt-am-Main, Germany; buried in Nov 1936 in Tatoi, near Athens, Greece; third dau. of Frederick III (1831–1888), emperor of Germany (r. 1888), and Victoria Adelaide (1840–1901, dau. of Queen Victoria); sister of Kaiser Wilhelm II of Germany (r. 1888–1918); m. Constantine I (1868–1923), king of the Hellenes (r. 1913–1917, 1920–1922), on Oct 27, 1889; children: George II (1890–1947), king of Greece (r. 1922–1923, 1935–1947); Alexander I (1893–1920), king of Greece (r. 1917–1920); Helen of Greece (1896–1982, who m. Carol II, king of Romania); Paul I (1901–1964), king of Greece (r. 1947–1964); Irene (b. around 1904, who m. the duke of Aosta); Catherine.

SOPHIE OF RUSSIA (c. 1140–1198). Queen of Denmark. Name variations: Sophie of Polotzk. Born c. 1140; died May 5, 1198; dau. of Vladimir, prince of Novgorod, and Richizza of Poland (1116–1185); m. Valdemar also known as Waldemar I the Great (1131–1182), king of Denmark (r. 1157–1182), in 1157; children: Canute VI (1163–1202), king of Denmark (r. 1182–1202); Waldemar II the Victorious (b. 1170), king of Denmark (r. 1202–1241); Sophie (d. 1208, who m. Siegfried III, count of Orlamunde, in 1181); Richizza of Denmark (d. 1220); Margaret (a nun at Roskilde); Marie (a nun at Roskilde); Helen of Denmark (d. 1233); Ingeborg (c. 1176–1237/38, who m. Philip II Augustus, king of France); and another daughter who m. Philip of Swabia, king of the Romans.

SOPHIE OF SOLMS-LAUBACH (1594–1651). Margravine of Ansbach. Born May 15, 1594; died May 16, 1651; dau. of John George I of Solms-Laubach; m. Joachim Ernst (1583–1625), margrave of Ansbach (r. 1603–1625), on Oct 14, 1612; children: Albert (b. 1620), margrave of Ansbach.

SOPHIE VALDEMARSDOTTIR (d. 1241). Princess of Mecklenburg-Rostok. Died in 1241; dau. of Leonor of Portugal (1211–1231) and Valdemar or Waldemar the Younger (1209–1231), king of Denmark (r. 1215–1231); m. Henry Burwin III, prince of Mecklenburg-Rostok.

SOPHONISBA (c. 225–203 BCE). Carthaginian noblewoman. Name variations: Sophoniba; Sophonisbe. Born c. 225 BCE; committed suicide in 203 BCE; dau. of the Carthaginian Hasdrubal (son of Gisgo and one of the generals who sought to keep Rome from seizing Spain from Carthage [214–206 BCE]); m. Syphax, a Numidian chieftain, c. 206 BCE (died in captivity, 201 BCE); m. Masinissa (another Numidian chieftain and a rival of Syphax), in 203 BCE. ❖ During the 2nd Punic War fought between Rome and Carthage (218–201 BCE), abandoned husband Syphax for his victorious rival Masinissa; when Scipio Africanus ordered Masinissa to send her to him as a legitimately won war captive, chose suicide over Roman slavery; she foreshadowed the fate of her native city. Too proud to submit to absolute Roman dominion, Carthage would also one day opt for honorable destruction over Roman bondage. ❖ See also *Women in World History.*

SORABJI, Cornelia (1866–1954). Indian lawyer. Born Nov 15, 1866, in Nasik, in the Bombay presidency, India; died July 6, 1954, in London, England; dau. of Rev. Sorabji Karsedji Langrana (ex-Zoroastrian and a Parsi who converted to Christianity) and Francina (also seen as Franscina); elder sister of Susie Sorabji, educational reformer (died 1931); graduate of Decca College in Poona, 1886; studied at Somerville College in Oxford, England; received Bachelor of Civil Law (BCL) in 1922. ❖ The 1st Indian woman to become a lawyer, was also the 1st female student at Decca College in Poona; determined to improve the condition of India's widows, orphans and wives, became an advocate for women in the court system; writings include *Love and Life Behind the*

Purdah (1901), *Sun-Babies* (1904), *Between the Twilights* (1908), *Social Relations: England and India* (1908), *Indian Tales of the Great Ones Among Men, Women and Bird-People* (1916), *Therefore* (1924), *Susie Sorabji, A Memoir* (1932), *India Calling* (1934) and *India Recalled* (1936). Her legal work for hundreds of women, as well as her efforts on behalf of infant welfare and nursing, earned her the Kaisar-i-Hind gold medal (1909). ❖ See also *Women in World History.*

SORAY, Turkan (1945—). Turkish actress. Name variations: Türkan Soray. Born June 28, 1945, in Istanbul, Turkey; sister of Nazan Soray (actress); m. Cihan Ünal, Dec 2, 1983 (div. Dec 15, 1987); children: Yagmur Unal (b. 1984). ❖ Legendary movie star who had a profound influence on popular culture throughout the Middle East, began acting at age 15; often called the "sultan of Turkish cinema," made over 200 films; received the Gramel Prix from Rome Film Festival (1999).

SORAYA (b. 1932). *See Pahlavi, Soraya.*

SOREL, Agnes (1422–1450). French royal mistress. Name variations: Agnès Sorel. Born 1422 in France; died in 1450 in France; dau. of Jean Soreau, lord of Coudun, and Catherine de Maignelais; never married; children: (with Charles VII, king of France) Charlotte de Brézé (c. 1444/49–?, whose son Louis de Breze m. Diane de Poitiers); Jeanne de France (who associated with Antoine de Bueil, count of Sancerre); Marie de Valois, also seen as Marguerite de France (who associated with Olivier Coëtivy). ❖ Powerful mistress to King Charles VII of France, was lady-in-waiting to Isabelle of Lorraine, queen of Naples, when she met Charles, soon becoming his mistress and moving to Paris (1444); exerted great power at the court and over Charles' actions; held much more influence than did the queen, Marie of Anjou, whose position she more or less usurped; died suddenly and suspiciously at 28. ❖ See also Jehanne D'Orliac, *The Lady of Beauty: Agnes Sorel* (Lippincott, 1931); and *Women in World History.*

SOREL, Cécile (1873–1966). French actress. Name variations: Cecile Sorel. Born Sept 17, 1873, in Paris, France; died Sept 3, 1966, in Deauville, France; m. Viscomte de Segur. ❖ Made stage debut in Paris; appeared at the Vaudeville in *Lysistrata* (1892), then in the title role of *Flipote*, Queen of Naples in *Madame Sans-Gêne*, and Claudine in *Viveurs*; appeared in numerous productions at the Odéon (1898–1901), then embarked on a long career with the Comédie Française (1901–35), appearing in such roles as the Marquise in *Les Affrontes*, Célimène in *Le Misanthrope*, Elmire in *Tartuffe*, the Comtesse in *Le Mariage de Figaro*, and the leads in *Sapho*, *L'Abbe Constantin*, *Le Paon*, *Notre Jeunesse*, *Chacun sa vie*, *Les Deux Hommes*, *Vouloir* and *Le Roi Christine*, among others; became a sociétaire (1904); left the stage (1950) and was admitted as a novice of the 3rd order of the Franciscans, Bayonne.

SOREL, Claudette (1930—). French pianist and teacher. Born in Paris on Oct 10, 1930; studied with Olga Samaroff. ❖ Noted for her performances of little-known Romantic works, had a light, delicate touch, playing with imagination and sensitivity; also showed an affinity for Russian composers and recorded several solo works by Sergei Rachmaninoff; as a musical scholar, edited the works of such lesser-known Russians as Anton Arensky; taught.

SOREL, Felicia (1904–1972). American concert dancer and choreographer. Born 1904 in New York, NY; died 1972 in Las Vegas, Nevada; m. Senia Gluck-Sandor (dancer). ❖ Trained in ballet, modern dance, and Spanish dance, performed in concert recitals with husband (1920s–30s), mainly under title of Dance Center; performed leading roles with Dance Center—which was also a larger company at times—in such works as *Petrouchka* (1931), *Tempo* (1932), *Afternoon of a Faun* (1932), and *El Amor Brujo*; performed at Radio City Music Hall with Demetrios Vilan; for theater, choreographed Marc Connelly's *Everywhere I Roam* and *Our Honor and Our Strength* (1939) for Theater Guild, as well as *La Belle Hélène* (1941) and *Lysistrata* (1946).

SOREL, Ruth (1907–1974). *See Abrahamowitsch, Ruth.*

SORENSEN, Inge (1924—). Danish swimmer. Name variations: Inge Soerensen, Inge Sörensen. Born in July 18, 1924 in Denmark. ❖ At Berlin Olympics, won a bronze medal in the 200-meter breaststroke (1936).

SORENSEN, Jette Hejli (1961—). Danish rower. Born Mar 25, 1961, in Denmark. ❖ At Los Angeles Olympics, won a bronze medal in quadruple sculls with coxswain (1984).

SORENSEN, Patsy (1952—). Belgian politician. Name variations: Patsy Sörensen or Soerensen. Born Oct 1, 1952, in Antwerp, Belgium.

❖ Served as deputy mayor of Antwerp (1995–99); representing Group of the Greens/European Free Alliance, elected to 5th European Parliament (1999–2004).

SORENSON, Carol (1942—). American golfer. Name variations: Mrs. William Flenniken; Carol Sorenson Flenniken. Born Carol Sorenson, Nov 15, 1942, in Janesville, WI; m. William Flenniken. ❖ Won Women's Western Junior and USGA Junior Girls' championships (1960); won Women's National Collegiate (1960), while attending Arizona State; won Western Amateur (1962); won British Women's Amateur and Trans-Mississippi (1964); member of Curtis Cup team (1964, 1966) and World Cup team (1964). Inducted into Colorado Hall of Fame.

SORENSTAM, Annika (1970—). Swedish golfer. Born Oct 9, 1970, in Stockholm, Sweden; dau. of Tom and Gunilla Sorenstam; sister of Charlotta Sorenstam (golfer); attended University of Arizona; m. David Esch, 1997. ❖ Began playing golf at 12; was a member of the Swedish national team (1987–92); was World Amateur champion (1992); won 7 collegiate titles; joined LPGA tour (1993); won US Open (1995, 1996); won Heartland Classic, Samsung World championship (1995, 1996, 2004), Betsy King Classic (1996, 1997), Chrysler-Plymouth Tournament of Champions (1997), Hawaiian Ladies Open (1997), ITT LPGA Tour championship (1997), Michelob Light Classic (1997, 1998, 1999), LPGA Classic (1998, 2000), SAFECO Classic (1998), Sara Lee Classic (1999), Circle K championship (2000, 2001), Kroger Classic (2000), Big Apple Classic (2000), Safeway LPGA championship (2000, 2003), Kraft Nabisco championship (2001, 2002, 2005), Mizuno Classic (2000, 2001, 2003), McDonald's LPGA championship (2003, 2004, 2005), Canadian Open (2001), British Open (2003), Corning Classic (2004), among others; was the 1st player in LPGA history to finish a season with a sub-to scoring average (69.99) in 1998; had 8 wins, 6 second-place finishes, and 20 top-10 finishes (2001); won 11 tournaments (2002), joining Mickey Wright as the only players to win 11 tournaments in one season; competed on the Solheim Cup Team; won the ANZ Ladies Masters in Australia (2002) and Compaq Open in Sweden (2002); set or tied 22 LPGA records (2003); became the 1st woman since 1945 to compete on the men's PGA Tour (2003). Was Rookie of the Year (1994); won Athlete of the Year award in Sweden (1995); named Rolex Player of the Year (1995, 1997, 1998, 2001, 2002, 2003, 2005); won Vare Trophy (1995, 1996, 1998, 2001, 2002, 2005); received ESPY Aard (1996, 1998–99, 2002–03); won LPGA's Patty Berg award (2003); inducted into World Golf Hall of Fame (2003).

SORENSTAM, Charlotta (1973—). Swedish golfer. Born April 16, 1973, in Stockholm, Sweden; dau. of Tom and Gunilla Sorenstam; sister of Annika Sorenstam (golfer); attended University of Texas. ❖ Was a member of the Swedish national team for 7 years; won European team championship (1993); won NCAA title (1993); turned pro (1994); competed on European Tour (1995–96); won Standard Register PING (2000); won Hyundai Securities Ladies Open on Korean LPGA tour (2001); tied LPGA record for most holes-in-one in a single season with 3 (2002).

SORGDRAGER, Winnie (1948—). Dutch politician. Born in The Hague, the Netherlands, April 6, 1948; studied law at Groningen University; received doctorate in 1971. ❖ Became a public prosecutor at Almelo, rising to the position of advocate-general (1986) and procurator-general (1993); served as minister of justice as a Democrat in the Kok government (1994–98). ❖ See also *Women in World History.*

SORGERS, Jana (1967—). East German rower. Born Aug 4, 1967, in East Germany. ❖ Won a gold medal at Seoul Olympics (1988) and a gold medal at Atlanta Olympics (1996), both for quadruple sculls without coxswain.

SORIANO, Elena (1917–1996). Spanish novelist. Name variations: Elena Soriano Jara. Born Feb 4, 1917, in Fuentidueña del Tajo, Madrid, Spain, of Andalusian parents; died 1996 in Madrid; m. Juan José Arnedo Sánchez. ❖ Published the 1st novel of her trilogy "Mujer y hombre" (Woman and Man), *La playa de los locos* (1955), but it was censored by the Franco regime and not published until 1984 (the other 2 novels, *Espejismos* [Mirages] and *Medea*, were published in 1986); founded and directed the magazine *El Urogallo* (1969–76); also wrote *Caza menor* (1951), *La vida pequeña: Cuentos de antes y de hora* (1989), and *Tres sueños y otros cuentos* (1996).

SORKIN, Naomi (1948—). American ballet dancer. Born Oct 23, 1948, in Chicago, IL. ❖ Trained with Sybil Shearer, Eric Braun, Walter

Camryn, Carmelita Maracchi and Maggie Black; danced with Ruth Page's Chicago Opera Ballet as adolescent; joined American Ballet Theater in New York City where she appeared in classical as well as contemporary works, including *Swan Lake, Giselle, Les Sylphides* and José Limón's *The Moor's Pavanne*; danced for choreographers Eliot Feld, Dennis Nahat, and Michael Smuin while in residence at Ballet Theater, and later in their respective companies.

SØRLIE, Else-Marthe (1978—). Norwegian handball player. Name variations: Sorlie or Soerlie. Born Sept 11, 1978, in Gjøvik, Norway. ❧ Won a team bronze medal at Sydney Olympics (2000).

SORMA, Agnes (1862–1927). German actress. Name variations: Agnes, Gräfin von Mio da Minotto. Born Agnes Martha Karoline Zaremba, 1862, in Germany; died 1927. ❧ Began acting as child; originated the part of Rita in Germany in Ibsen's *Little Eyolf* (1895); made New York debut (1897) and toured Europe and Scandinavia; worked with Max Reinhardt in Berlin (1904–07); during WWI, entertained troops at the front.

SORNOSA MARTÍNEZ, María (1949—). Spanish politician. Name variations: Maria Sornosa Martinez. Born June 15, 1949, in Manises, Valencia. ❧ Was a member of the municipal council of Manises, with responsibility for Health (1979); as a European Socialist, elected to 4th and 5th European Parliament (1994–99, 1999–2004). Wrote *Viajes, memoria parlamentaria.*

SOROKINA, Anna (1976—). Ukrainian diver. Name variations: Ganna Sorokina. Born Mar 31, 1976, in Zaporozhye, Ukraine. ❧ Won European championship for synchronize springboard (1999); won a bronze medal for synchronized 3-meter springboard at Sydney Olympics (2000).

SOROKINA, Nina (1942—). Soviet ballet dancer. Born May 13, 1942, in Moscow, Russia. ❧ Trained with Bolshoi Ballet and danced there throughout her career; best known for her performances in the Soviet repertory, in such works as Natalia Kasatkina and Vladimir Vasiliov's *Sacre du Printemps, Poème Heroique,* and *War and Peace*; also noted for her Masha in *The Nutcracker* and Kitri in *Don Quixote.*

SORRENTINA, La (d. 1973). *See Frasca, Mary.*

S. O. S. BAND.
See Davis, Mary.
See Ford, Penny.

SOSA, Mercedes (1935—). Argentine folksinger. Born July 9, 1935, in Tucuman Province in central Argentina; m. Oscar Matus (musician), 1957. ❧ Sang on a local radio station at age 15; appeared at festivals and theaters in smaller towns, particularly in nearby Uruguay and Chile, before becoming well known in Buenos Aires; recorded over 16 albums (mid-1970s) and was known throughout South America; sang accompanied only by guitar and drum, wearing a poncho; because she often sang protest songs, was in constant danger, especially in 1970s, when thousands of Argentineans disappeared, often killed by right-wing death squads; was called "The Voice of the Americas." ❧ See also *Women in World History.*

SOSIPATRA (fl. 4th c.). Ephesian philosopher. Born in Ephesus in Asia Minor; educated by two male guardians who were seers; m. Eustathius (orator and diplomat); children: (with Eustathius) 3 sons, including Antoninus. ❧ A towering pagan intellectual, during an age when Christians were doing all they could to expunge paganism, whose wisdom made that of her husband seem insignificant by comparison; after his death, became the consort of the philosopher Aedesius, a noted neo-Platonic philosopher, and they founded a school of philosophy together. ❧ See also *Women in World History.*

SOSTORICS, Colleen (1979—). Canadian ice-hockey player. Born Dec 17, 1979 in Kennedy, Saskatchewan, Canada; attended University of Calgary. ❧ Won a gold medal at World championships (2001), gold medal at Salt Lake City Olympics (2002), and a gold medal at Torino Olympics (2006).

SOSULJA, Vera. *See Zozula, Vera.*

SOTERIOU, Dido (1909–2004). *See Sotiriou, Dido.*

SOTHERN, Ann (1909–2001). American actress and singer. Name variations: acted under real name Harriette Lake until 1934. Born Harriette Arlene Lake on Jan 22, 1909, in Valley City, North Dakota; died Mar 15, 2001, in Ketchum, Idaho; dau. of Walter Lake (actor) and Annette Yde-Lake (concert singer and vocal coach at Warner Bros.); granddau. of Hans Nilson, Danish concert violinist, and Simon Lake, who invented the modern submarine; attended University of Washington; m. Roger Pryor (actor-bandleader), Sept 27, 1936 (div. 1943); m. Robert Sterling (actor), May 23, 1943 (div. 1949); children: (2nd m.) daughter, Patricia Ann Sterling (actress). ❧ The wisecracking Maisie Ravier in popular "Maisie" movie series (1940s), and the similarly spunky Susie McNamara on tv series "Private Secretary" (1953–57), made film debut in a bit part in *The Show of Shows* (1929); made Broadway debut in *America's Sweetheart* (1931), in which she introduced the song "I've Got Five Dollars" with Jack Whiting; went on to appear on Broadway in *Everybody's Welcome* (1931); for RKO, appeared in a quartet of bland romantic comedies with Gene Raymond; had breakthrough role in *Trade Winds* (1938), followed by title role in *Maisie* (1939), which spawned 9 sequels and a radio version; also appeared in *Lady Be Good* (1940), in which she introduced the song "The Last Time I Saw Paris," which won an Oscar for Best Song of 1941; snagged best dramatic role in *A Letter to Three Wives* (1949), followed by *Shadow on the Wall* (1950); other films include *Brother Orchid* (1940), *Dulcy* (1940), *Panama Hattie* (1942), *Thousands Cheer* (1943), *Cry Havoc* (1943), *Words and Music* (1948), *The Blue Gardenia* (1953), *The Best Man* (1964), *Lady in a Cage* (1964), *Sylvia* (1965) and *Crazy Mama* (1975); made dramatic tv debut on "Schlitz Playhouse of Stars" (1952); also starred in sitcom, "The Ann Sothern Show." Nominated for Academy Award for Best Supporting Actress for *The Whales of August* (1988). ❧ See also *Women in World History.*

SOTHERN, Mrs. E. H. (1866–1950). *See Marlowe, Julia.*

SOTHERN, Georgia (1912–1981). American dancer and ecdysiast. Name variations: Georgia Diamond. Born Hazel Eunice Finklestein (some sources cite Hazel Anderson), Oct 24, 1912, in Dunganon, GA; died Oct 14, 1981, in New York, NY; m. John J. Diamond (attorney), 1955. ❧ Made theater debut as a child at age 4 in Atlanta, GA; performed with a vaudeville act until age 12, where she specialized in acrobatic and barefoot toe dancing; 1st appeared in burlesque at Bijou Theater in Philadelphia, PA (1931); performed at nightclubs and in burlesque shows throughout Northeast (1940s), including at The Republic in New York for 15 years, as well as the Old Howard Theater in Boston and Billy Rose's Casino de Paris. ❧ See also autobiography, *My Life in Burlesque* (1973).

SOTHERTON, Kelly (1976—). British heptathlete. Born Nov 13, 1976, in Newport, England. ❧ Won a bronze medal for heptathlon at Athens Olympics (2004).

SOTIRIOU, Dido (1909–2004). Greek novelist, feminist and journalist. Name variations: Dido Soteriou. Born Dido Pappas, Feb 18, 1909, a Greek in Audin, Turkey; died Sept 23, 2004; dau. of an industrialist; sister of Elli Pappas (who was imprisoned for 16 years [1950–66] because of her relationship with KKE leader Nikos Beloyianis, shot as a traitor by the conservative government); m. Plato Sotiriou (uncle of the author Alki Zei); studied literature at the Sorbonne; children: raised her sister's son, Nikos. ❧ Was the 1st woman to write about the the Greco-Turkish War (1919–22), the destruction of Smyrna (now Izmir, Turkey) and the expulsion of about 1 million Greeks by the forces of Atatürk; published *Matomena Chomata* (Bloodied Earth, 1962), reprinted in English as *Farewell Anatolia* (1991), which chronicled her family's flight from Turkey and the later exchange of populations between Greece and Turkey (the book has been republished 65 times); since her parents died soon after the enforced exodus, was raised in Athens, Greece, by an aunt; began writing career as the French correspondent for several Greek newspapers and magazines, one of the 1st Greek women to break into journalism; joined Greek Communist Party (mid-1930s), became editor of its newspaper *Rizospastis* (1945), but later expelled for voicing dissent; during WWII, was active in the resistance; also wrote *The Dead Are Waiting* (1959), Electra (1961), and *The Command* (1976). Awarded Greece's highest honor for a writer, the prize of the Athens Academy.

SOTNIKOVA, Yuliya (1970—). Russian runner. Name variations: Yulia Sotnikova. Born Nov 18, 1970, in Russia. ❧ Won a bronze medal for 4 x 400-meter relay at Sydney Olympics (2000).

SOTO, Miriam Blasco (1963—). *See Blasco Soto, Miriam.*

SOTOMAYOR, Maria de Zayas y (1590–c. 1650). *See Zayas y Sotomayor, María de.*

SOUBIRAN, Marie-Thérèse de (1834–1889). *See Marie-Thérèse de Soubiran.*

SOUBIROUS, Bernadette (1844–1879). *See Bernadette of Lourdes.*

SOUEZ, Ina (1903–1992). American soprano. Born Ina Rains, June 3, 1903, in Windsor, CO; died Dec 7, 1992, in Santa Monica, CA; studied with Florence Hinman. ❖ Of Cherokee descent, debuted as Mimì in *Ivrea* (1928); performed at Covent Garden, London (1929, 1935); was prima donna at Glyndebourne Festival (1934–39); performed at City Opera in New York (1945); most acclaimed performances were her Mozartean roles as Donna Anna in *Don Giovanni* and Fiordiligi in *Così fan tutte*; after WWII, appeared with Spike Jones' music and comedy troupe for 10 years, then taught voice in San Francisco and Los Angeles. ❖ See also *Women in World History.*

SOULE, Aileen (1906–2002). *See Riggin, Aileen.*

SOULE, Caroline White (1824–1903). American author and Universalist minister. Born Caroline White on Sept 3, 1824, in Albany, New York; died Dec 6, 1903, in Glasgow, Scotland; dau. of Nathaniel White and Elizabeth (Mèrselis) White; graduate of Albany Female Academy, 1841; m. Henry Birdsall Soule (Unitarian Universalist minister), Aug 28, 1843 (died of smallpox, 1852); children: 5. ❖ After publishing a biography of late husband (1852), became a popular contributor to a variety of Universalist publications, including *Rose of Sharon* and *Ladies' Repository*; became assistant editor of *Ladies' Repository* (1865); moved to NY to edit her own Sunday school paper, *The Guiding Star* (1867), for Unitarian congregations; named 1st president of Women's Centenary Association (WCA, 1871–80), the 1st national organization of church women in US; went to Scotland as a missionary in employ of WCA (1878), and was named minister of St. Paul's Universalist Church in Glasgow (1879); officially ordained as a Unitarian Universalist minister (1880); wrote *Home Life* (1855), *The Pet of the Settlement* (1860) and *Wine or Water* (1862). ❖ See also *Women in World History.*

SOUMET, Gabrielle (1814–1886). *See Beauvain d'Althenheim, Gabrielle.*

SOUNDARYA (1972–2004). Indian actress. Name variations: Saundarya. Born Sowmya, July 18, 1972, in Bangalore, Karnataka, India; killed in plane crash near Bangalore, April 17, 2004; dau. of Satyanarayana (producer-director); m. Raghu Sridhar (software engineer), April 2003. ❖ Made film debut in *Gandharva* (1992); made more than 90 movies in her 12-year career, acting in the south Indian languages of Kannada, Telugu, Tamil and Malayalam (majority of her hits were in Telugu); produced the Kannada film *Dweepa* (2002), for which she won the national award for Best Actor.

SOURDIS, Isabelle de (fl. 16th c.). French noblewoman. Name variations: Isabelle Babou de Sourdis. Born Isabelle Babou; one of seven daughters of Jean Babou (prominent soldier, politician, and diplomat in the reign of Henry II); sister of Françoise Babou de la Bourdaisière d'Estrées; aunt of Gabrielle d'Estrées; m. M. de Sourdis (governor of Chartre). ❖ Married to the governor of Chartre and mistress of Armand de Chiverny, promoted her niece's relationship with Henry IV of France, primarily to achieve her own ambitions to join the royal court. ❖ See also *Women in World History.*

SOUSA, Auta de (1876–1901). *See Souza, Auta de.*

SOUSA, Noemia de (1926—). *See de Sousa, Noémia.*

SOUSA Y MELO, Beatriz de (c. 1650–1700). *See Souza e Mello, Beatriz de.*

SOUTHAMPTON, countess of. *See Villiers, Barbara.*

SOUTHCOTT, Joanna (1750–1814). English prophet. Born in Tarford, Devonshire, England, 1750; died in London, Dec 27, 1814; dau. of William Southcott and Hannah Southcott; received no formal education; never married; no children. ❖ Prophet and sectarian who believed that the Holy Spirit spoke through her and promised the imminent end of the world and Christ's Second Coming; was a domestic servant until age 42, then a prophet, a writer inspired by the Holy Spirit, a preacher, and an interpreter; printed a collection of her prophecies, *The Strange Effects of Faith* (1801), which caused a sensation and enabled her fame to spread widely; moved to London (1802) where her gatherings often brought together a thousand or more followers, named "Johannas" or "Southcottians," who were buoyed by her preaching of universal salvation; asked for a "trial" in London to quiet allegations that she was a fraud (1804); toured English provinces, preaching; in her *Third Book of Wonders* (1813), announced that she was going to give birth to "Shiloh," the "Second Christ" (1814); gave every sign of imminent maternity but died and was found to have had no more than a phantom pregnancy. ❖ See also G. R. Balleine, *Past Finding Out: The Tragic Story of Joanna Southcott and Her Successors* (S. P. C. K., 1956); James K. Hopkins, *A Woman to Deliver Her People: Joanna Southcott and English Millenarianism in an Era of Revolution* (U. of Texas Press, 1982); and *Women in World History.*

SOUTHERN, Eileen Jackson (1920–2002). African-American pianist and musicologist. Born Feb 19, 1920 in Minneapolis, Minnesota; died Oct 13, 2002, in Port Charlotte, FL; University of Chicago, undergraduate degree, 1940, MA, 1941; New York University, doctorate in musicology, 1961; m. Joseph Southern; children: Edward and April Myra. ❖ An authority on Renaissance and African-American music, was Harvard University's 1st black female tenured professor; studied piano as a child, playing her 1st concert in Chicao at age 7; taught at Prairie View University, Southern University, Brooklyn College and City University of New York; became a lecturer at Harvard (1974), full professor (1976), and chaired the department of Afro-American studies (1975–79); retired (1987); wrote *The Music of Black Americans, a History* (1970), among others.

SOUTHERN, Jeri (1926–1991). American jazz singer and pianist. Born Genevieve Lillian Hering, Aug 5, 1926, in Hering's Mill, Royal, Nebraska; died Aug 4, 1991, in Los Angeles, CA; children: Kathy King. ❖ Silky-voiced singer, called the Greta Garbo of jazz, had such hit singles as "You Better Go Now" (1951), "Joey" (1954), and "When I Fall in Love"; albums include *The Very Thought of You, Southern Breeze* and *Jeri Southern Meets Cole Porter*; sang title song for film *Fire Down Below* (1957); quit performing to teach (1965).

SOUTHESK, countess of. *See Carnegie, Maud (1893–1945).*

SOUTHEY, Caroline Anne (1786–1854). British poet and prose writer. Name variations: Caroline Bowles. Born Caroline Anne Bowles, Oct 7, 1786, in Lymington, Hampshire, England; died July 20, 1854, in Lymington; only child of Captain Charles Bowles (of East India Company) and Anne (Burrard) Bowles; m. Robert Southey (poet), 1839 (died 1843). ❖ Parents died when she was a child; having lost most of inheritance through improper dealings of a guardian, wrote to supplement her income; submitted metric tale *Ellen Fitzarthur*, which would be published anonymously, to poet Robert Southey (1820); enjoyed further literary success with her poetry collections *The Widow's Tale* (1822) and *Solitary Hours* (1826); also contributed a collection of stories in serial form to *Blackwood's Magazine* (1829), which was published as a book, *Chapters on Churchyards*; exhibited an interest in social issues, publishing *Tales of the Factories* (1833); married Robert Southey (1839), soon after the death of his 1st wife Edith Fricker Southey; regarded husband's death with a sense of relief (1843). ❖ See also *The Correspondence of Robert Southey with Caroline Bowles* (1881); Virginia Blain, *Caroline Bowles Southey, 1786–1854: The Making of a Woman Writer* (Ashgate, 1997); and *Women in World History.*

SOUTHIEL or SOUTHILL, Ursula (1488–1561). *See Shipton, Mother.*

SOUTHILL, Ursula (1488–1561). *See Shipton, Mother.*

SOUTHWELL, Frances (c. 1827–1890). *See George, Frances Shayle.*

SOUTHWORTH, E. D. E. N. (1819–1899). American novelist. Born Emma Dorothy Eliza Nevitte, Dec 26, 1819, in Washington, DC; died in Georgetown, Washington, DC, June 30, 1899; dau. of Charles Le Compte Nevitte and his 2nd wife, Susannah (Wailes) Nevitte; sister of Frances Henshaw Baden; graduate of stepfather Joshua L. Henshaw's school, 1835; m. Frederick Hamilton Southworth (inventor), 1840 (sep. 1844); children: Richmond, Charlotte Emma. ❖ Abandoned by husband, wrote to support family; serialized 1st story, *The Irish Refugee*, in *Baltimore Sunday Visitor* (1846); published 1st novel, *Retribution*, in both serial and book form (1849), which subsequently increased her success as a writer; wrote for *Saturday Evening Post* for 8 years, then began writing for *New York Ledger* (1857); as the *New York Ledger* became one of the bestselling periodicals in the US, became one of the most popular novelists of her era; published most popular novel, *The Hidden Hand* (1859); writing 73 books, deftly used the machinations of the Gothic romance style to create stories brimming with melodramatic conventions, which appealed to readers, while also developing protagonists with greater depth of character than their counterparts in typical stories of the day; often featured heroines who were on the margins of society, who were abused or neglected by their spouses, or were constrained by the patriarchal culture of the 19th century; was also a feminist and abolitionist. ❖ See also *Women in World History.*

SOUTHWORTH, Helen (1956—). English politician and member of Parliament. Born Nov 13, 1956; m. Edmund Southworth. ❖ Representing Labour, elected to House of Commons for Warrington South (1997, 2001, 2005); was PPS to Paul Boateng, chief secretary to the Treasury (2001–05).

SOUZA, Adele de (1761–1836). *See Souza-Botelho, Adélaïde Filleul, marquise of.*

SOUZA, Auta de (1876–1901). Brazilian poet. Name variations: Auta de Sousa; (pseudonyms) Ida Salúcio; Hilário das Neves. Born Sept 12, 1876, in Macaiba, Rio Grande do Norte, Brazil; died of tuberculosis, Feb 7, 1901, in Rio Grande do Norte. ❖ Was member of *O Biscoito* literary group in Rio Grande do Norte state and wrote for newspapers; deeply religious, published her only volume of poetry, *Horto* (1900).

SOUZA, Helia (1970—). Brazilian volleyball player. Name variations: Helia Rogerio Souza; (nickname) Fofao. Born Mar 10, 1970, in Brazil. ❖ Setter; won team World Grand Prix (1994, 1996, 1998); won South American championship (1991, 1995, 1997, 1999, 2001); won team bronze medals at Atlanta Olympics (1996) and Sydney Olympics (2000). Named Best Setter at Sydney (2000).

SOUZA-BOTELHO, Adélaïde Filleul, marquise of (1761–1836). French writer. Name variations: Adelaide Marie Emilie Filleul, marquise of Souza Botelho; Adele de Souza; Sousa. Born Adélaïde-Marie-Émilie Filleul in Paris, France, May 14, 1761; died April 10, 1836; dau. of Marie Irène Catherine de Buisson de Longpré (dau. of the seigneur of Longpré, near Falaise) and a middle-class man of Falaise named Filleul (who was one of the king's secretaries); had older sister Julie, who m. the marquis of Marigny, brother of Madame de Pompadour; married Alexandre Sebastien de Flahaut de la Billarderie, count of Flahaut (soldier of some reputation, who was many years her senior), on Nov 30, 1779 (died at the guillotine during Reign of Terror, 1793); m. José Maria de Souza Botelho Morão e Vasconcellos (Portuguese minister plenipotentiary in Paris), in 1802; children: (with Charles Maurice de Talleyrand) Charles Auguste (b. April 21, 1785), count of Flahaut de la Billardérie. ❖ French aristocrat who had a son with Talleyrand, survived the Revolution to become a popular author, and was the mother of general and diplomat Charles Auguste, count of Flahaut; with onset of French Revolution, fled France for Great Britain (1792); sold off her jewels and began writing novels; published 1st novel, *Adèle de Sénange* (1794); moved to Germany (1795); returned to France under protection of Talleyrand (1797); flourished during Napoleon's reign; published *Emilie et Alphonse* (1800); later novels depicted aristocratic society, especially during Napoleonic and Bourbon Restoration periods, the most famous of which was *Eugène de Rothelin* (1808); other works, which contain finely crafted descriptions of French aristocratic life, include *Eugénie et Mathilde ou Mémoires de la famille du comte de Revel* (1811), *Mademoiselle de Tournon* (1820), *La Comtesse de Fargy* (1822), and *La Duchesse de Guise* (1831). ❖ See also *Women in World History.*

SOUZA E MELLO, Beatriz de (c. 1650–1700). Portuguese playwright. Name variations: Doña Beatriz de Sousa y Melo. Born c. 1650, near Lisbon, Portugal; died c. 1700 in Torres Novas, Portugal; dau. of D. Lorenzo de Souza e Mello (commander of the Order of Cristo) and Ana Cordeiro. ❖ As a lay person, entered the convent of Espíritu Santo de Torres Novas, where she lived until her death; wrote the comedies *La vida de Santa Elena, y invención de la Cruz* and *Yerros enmendados, y alma arrepentida.*

SOVETNIKOVA, Galina (1955—). Soviet rower. Born Nov 14, 1955, in USSR. ❖ At Moscow Olympics, won a bronze medal in coxed fours (1980).

SOWERBY, Githa (1876–1970). English playwright and author. Name variations: Katherine Githa Sowerby. Born Katherine Githa Sowerby, 1876, in England; died 1970; dau. of Amy Margaret (Hewison) Sowerby and John G. Sowerby (illus); sister of Millicent Sowerby (illustrator); m. John Kaye Kendall. ❖ Wrote such plays as *Rutherford & Son, Sheila, The Stepmother,* and *The Policeman's Whistle;* collaborated with younger sister on a number of books for children.

SOWERBY, Millicent (1878–1967). British illustrator. Born in 1878, possibly in Gateshead, Colchester, England; died 1967; dau. of John G. Sowerby (illustrator who flourished between 1876 and 1914); younger sister of author Githa Sowerby. ❖ One of the best loved postcard artists of the Edwardian age, illustrated "Postcards for the Little Ones" series and children's books including *Alice in Wonderland* (1907), *A Child's Garden of Verses* (1908), and many others; illustrated many children's books written by sister Githa. ❖ See also *Women in World History.*

SOW FALL, Aminata (1941—). Senegalese novelist. Name variations: Aminata Sow-Fall. Born 1941 in Saint-Louis, Senegal; earned a licence in modern languages in France; married, 1963. ❖ Served as director of la Propriété littéraire in Dakar (1979–88); founded and served as director of the Centre Africain d'Animation et d'Échanges Culturels and the Khoudia publishing house in Fann, Dakar; works include *Le Revenant* (The Ghost, 1976), *La Grève des Bottu* (The Beggar's Strike, 1979), *L'Appel des arènes* (The Call of the Wrestling Arenas, 1982), *Le Jujubier du Patriarche* (The Patriarch's Jujubier, 1993), *Douceurs du bercail* (Home Sweet Home, 1998) and *Un grain de vie et d'espérance* (Food for thought and Tomorrow's Life, 2002). Awarded honorary doctorate from Mount Holyoke College, MA (1997).

SOYER, Ida (1909–1970). American modern dancer. Born 1909 in US; died July 4, 1970, in Hamptons, NY; dau. of Russian immigrants; m. Moses Soyer (1899–1974, artist), c. 1927; sister-in-law of Raphael Soyer (1899–1987, artist); children: David Soyer (b. 1928). ❖ As an original member of Helen Tamiris' concert group (1931–44), danced in Tamiris' *Olimpus Americanus* (1932), *Mourning Ceremonial* (1932), and *Towards the Night* (1934); performed for other choreographers, notably in Dorothy Barret's *Last Spring* (1938).

SOYSAL, Sevgi (1936–1976). Turkish novelist, memoirist and short-story writer. Born 1936; died 1976. ❖ Studied philosophy at Ankara University and drama and archeology in Germany; published the novel *Yurumek* (1970), about a sexually unfulfilled wife, which won a state prize but was then removed from stores for obscenity; also wrote the novels *Yenisehir'de Bir Ogle Vakti* (1974) and *Safak* (1975), the short-story collections *Tutkulu Percem* (1962) and *Tante Rosa* (1968) and the memoir *Yildirim Bolge Kadinlar Kogusu* (1976).

SPACEK, Sissy (1949—). American actress. Born Mary Elizabeth Spacek, Dec 25, 1949, in Quitman, TX; cousin of actor Rip Torn; m. Jack Fisk (art director), 1974; children: Schuyler and Madison Fisk. ❖ Nominated for 5 Academy Awards during her career, made film debut in *Prime Cut* (1972); came to early prominence in *Badlands* (1973), followed by *Carrie* (1976), *3 Women* (1977) and *Welcome to L. A.* (1977); won an Academy Award for Best Actress for *Coal Miner's Daughter* (1980); other films include *Raggedy Man* (1981), *Missing* (1982), *The River* (1984), *'Night Mother* (1986), *Crimes of the Heart* (1986), *JFK* (1991), *In the Bedroom* (2001), *Tuck Everlasting* (2002) and *The Ring Two* (2005); for tv, starred in "Verna: USO Girl" (1978), among others.

SPAFFORD, Belle Smith (1895–1982). American social worker. Born Marion Isabelle Sims Smith in Salt Lake City, Utah, Oct 8, 1895; died Feb 2, 1982, in Salt Lake City; dau. of Hester (Sims) Smith and John Gibson Smith; graduate of University of Utah Normal School, 1914; m. Willis Earl Spafford, Mar 23, 1921 (died 1963); children: Mary (b. 1923); Earl (b. 1926). ❖ Social work advocate, served as editor of *Relief Society Magazine* (1937–45); served as general president of Relief Society (1945–71); was vice-president of the National Council of Women (1948–56); served as a delegate to triennial meetings of International Council of Women at Philadelphia (1947), Montreal (1957), and Washington, DC (1963); was chair of US delegation to the ICW triennial meetings at Helsinki (1954), Teheran (1966), and Bangkok (1969); served as president of National Council of Women (1968–70); was a member of National Advisory Committee to the White House Conference on Aging; served as vice-president of the American Mothers Committee; was the 1st female member of the board of governors of LDS Hospital and of the board of trustees of Brigham Young University; became an officer of the board of directors of National Association for Practical Nurses; was a special lecturer at the School of Social Work at the University of Utah. ❖ See also *Women in World History.*

SPAGNUOLO, Filomena (1903–1987). American actress. Name variations: Mary Spinell. Born Nov 2, 1903, in New York, NY; died July 30, 1987, in New York, NY; children: Joe Spinell (actor). ❖ Character actress, appeared in over 50 films, including *The Godfather, The Godfather II, Next Stop Greenwich Village, Gloria, Moscow on the Hudson* and *The Last Horror Film.*

SPAHN, Helen May (1867–1957). *See Butler, Helen May.*

SPAIN, Elsie (1879–1970). English actress and singer. Born 1879 in England; died May 28, 1970. ❖ As a child, made stage debut in

Anerley as Theresa in *The Mountebanks* (1897); made professional debut as understudy for Isabel Jay as Sally Hook in *Miss Hook of Holland* (1907); was a member of the D'Oyly Carte Opera Co. (1908–10), appearing as Josephine in *H. M. S. Pinafore*, Phyllis in *Iolanthe*, Yum-Yum in *The Mikado*, Gianetta in *The Gondoliers* and Else Maynard in *The Yeomen of the Guard*; other plays include *The Islander*, *The Chocolate Soldier*, *The Quaker Girl*, *The Dancing Mistress*, *The Best Man* and *Fun and Fancy*.

SPAIN, Fay (1932–1983). American actress. Born Oct 6, 1932, in Phoenix, AZ; died May 8, 1983, in Los Angeles Co., CA; m. John Altoon (div. 1962); m. Philip Fulmer Westbrook, 1968; children: 1 son. ❖ Film and tv actress, made screen debut in *The Crooked Circle* (1957); also appeared in *The Abductors, God's Little Acre, Al Capone, Flight to Fury* and *The Grove*.

SPAIN, Jayne (1927—). American manufacturer and reformer. Name variations: Mrs. John A. Spain. Born Jayne Baker, Mar 28, 1927, in San Francisco, California; dau. of Lawrence I. Baker (businessman) and Marguerite (Buchanan) Baker (died 1984); attended University of California, 1944–47, and University of Cincinnati, 1947–50; Edgecliff College in Cincinnati, LLD, 1969; m. John Spain (b. 1923, lawyer), July 14, 1951; children: Jeffry Alan (b. 1953, physician); Jon Kimberly (b. 1955, business manager). ❖ Inherited a controlling interest in Alvey-Ferguson, manufacturer of conveyor systems (1950); turned Alvey-Ferguson into a model of employee involvement and opportunity for handicapped workers, especially the blind; traveled worldwide promoting employment of handicapped, women's rights, and American business practices; appointed vice-chair of the President's Civil Service Commission by President Richard Nixon (1971); was executive professor in residence at George Washington University (1980s); often named one of the Fifty Most Influential Women in America. ❖ See also *Women in World History*.

SPAIN, queen of.
See Isabella of Portugal (1503–1539).
See Elizabeth of Valois (1545–1568).
See Anne of Austria (c. 1550–1580).
See Margaret of Austria (c. 1577–1611).
See Elizabeth Valois (1602–1644).
See Maria Anna of Austria (c. 1634–1696).
See Marie Louise d'Orleans (1662–1689).
See Maria Anna of Neuberg (1667–1740).
See Marie Louise of Savoy (1688–1714).
See Farnese, Elizabeth (1692–1766).
See Louise Elizabeth (1709–1750).
See Maria Barbara of Braganza (1711–1758).
See Maria Amalia of Saxony (1724–1760).
See Maria Luisa Teresa of Parma (1751–1819).
See Bonaparte, Julie Clary (1771–1845).
See Maria Josepha of Saxony (1803–1829).
See María Christina I of Naples (1806–1878).
See Isabella II (1830–1904).
See Maria Christina of Austria (1858–1929).
See Maria de las Mercedes (1860–1878).
See Ena (1887–1969).
See Sophia of Greece (b. 1938).

SPALDING, Catherine (1793–1858). American nun and activist. Name variations: Mother Catherine. Born in Charles Co., Maryland, Dec 23, 1793; died in Louisville, Kentucky, Mar 20, 1858; parents may have been Edward and Juliet (Boarman) Spalding. ❖ Known most of her life as Mother Catherine, was a pioneer who helped to establish schools, orphanages, and a hospital on the Kentucky frontier; entered the sisterhood (1812); elected 1st mother superior of the Sisters of Charity of Nazareth (1813); took vows (1816); established what became St. Catherine's Academy in Lexington, Kentucky (1823); opened Presentation Academy in Louisville (1831); established St. Joseph's Hospital (1832) and St. Vincent's Orphan Asylum (1833); directed construction of convent church at Nazareth, Kentucky (1850–56). ❖ See also *Women in World History*.

SPALDING, Eliza (1807–1851). American missionary. Born Eliza Hart, Aug 11, 1807, near Berlin, Connecticut; died of TB, Jan 7, 1851, near Brownsville, Oregon; dau. of Levi Hart (farmer) and Martha (Hart) Hart; m. Henry Harmon Spalding, Oct 13, 1833 (died 1874); children: Eliza Spalding (b. 1837, the 1st white child born in what is now Idaho); Henry Hart Spalding (b. 1839); Martha Jane Spalding (b. 1845); Amelia Lorene

Spalding (b. 1846). ❖ One of the 1st white women to cross the Rocky Mountains by wagon train, traveled West with Marcus and Narcissa Whitman to establish Presbyterian missions (1836); with husband, established a Protestant mission among the Nez Percé Indians in eastern Oregon Territory, now Washington State. ❖ See also *Women in World History*.

SPANKY AND OUR GANG. *See McFarlane, Elaine.*

SPARA, Hieronyma (d. 1659). Italian poisoner. Name variations: La Spara. Born in Rome, Italy; hanged 1659. ❖ Called La Spara, sold poison to young wives looking to do away with their husbands; after several women disclosed their killings in the confessional, and the papacy learned of the secret society which met nightly at her home (1659), was arrested with companions, including La Gratiosa; apparently refused to confess under torture; found guilty, was hanged along with Gratiosa and 3 other women. More than 30 other members of La Spara's sisterhood were publicly whipped through the streets of Rome; an additional 9 women were hanged for poisoning a few months later; and a 2nd group was whipped through the streets.

SPARK, Muriel (1918–2006). English novelist. Born Muriel Sarah Camberg, Feb 1, 1918, in Edinburgh, Scotland; died Apr 13, 2006, in Florence, Italy; dau. of Bernard (Barney) Camberg (Jewish mechanical engineer) and Sarah (Cissy) Uezzell Camberg; attended Heriot-Watt College, 1936; m. Sydney Oswald Spark (S. O. S.), in 1937 (div. 1942); lives with Penelope Jardine (sculptor); children: 1 son, Robin Spark. ❖ Prominent English novelist and a convert to Roman Catholicism, whose works focus on moral conflicts and religious belief, moved to Rhodesia (1937); returned to England (1944); became secretary of Poetry Society and editor of *Poetry Review* (1947); founded her own magazine, *Forum* (1949); received prize for short story "The Seraph and the Zambesi" (1951); published *The Fanfarlo and Other Verse* (1952); baptized into Anglican Church (1953); received into Roman Catholic Church (1954); published 1st novel *The Comforters* (1957), followed by *Memento Mori* (1959), *The Bachelors* (1960), *The Prime of Miss Jean Brodie* (1961); lived in Israel (1961) and New York (1962–66); published *The Girls of Slender Means* (1963) and *The Mandelbaum Gate* (1965); moved to Rome (1966); moved to rural Tuscany (1985); other novels include, *The Abbess of Crewe* (1974), *Territorial Rights* (1979), *Loitering with Intent* (1981), *The Only Problem* (1984), *A Far Cry from Kensington* (1988), *Symposium* (1990), *Reality and Dreams* (1997) and *Aiding and Abetting* (2001); also wrote children's books, short stories, and biographies. Awarded Order of the British Empire (1967). ❖ See also *Curriculum Vitae: Autobiography* (1992); Alan Bold, *Muriel Spark* (Methuen, 1986); Norman Page, *Muriel Spark* (Macmillan, 1990); Ruth Whittaker, *The Faith and Fiction of Muriel Spark* (St. Martin, 1982); Peter Kemp, *Muriel Spark* (Harper & Row, 1975); Derek Stanford, *Muriel Spark: A Biographical and Critical Study* (Centaur, 1963); and *Women in World History*.

SPARKS, Donita (1963—). American singer. Born April 8, 1963, in Chicago, Illinois. ❖ With Suzi Gardner, Jennifer Finch and Demetra (Dee) Plakas, formed band L7 (1988) and released album *Smell the Magic* (1990), with hit single "Shove/Packin' A Rod"; had major success with *Bricks Are Heavy* (1992), featuring international pop hit "Pretend We're Dead"; appeared in mockumentary *The Beauty Process*.

SPAZIANI, Maria Luisa (1924—). Italian poet and journalist. Born 1924 in Turin, Italy. ❖ Taught German language and literature at University of Messina and worked as journalist for newspapers and radio; published scholarly works on Ronsard and Prudhomme; works include *Primavera a Parigi* (1954), *Luna lombarda* (1959), *Utilità della memoria* (1966), *L'occhio del ciclone* (1970), *Poesia* (1979), *Geometria del disordine* (1981), *La stella del libero arbitrio* (1986), *I fasti dell'ortica* (1996) and *La traversata dell'oasi* (2002). Won Città di Firenze Prize for *Il gong* (1962).

SPEARE, Elizabeth George (1908–1994). American author. Born Nov 21, 1908, in Melrose, Massachusetts; died in Tucson, Arizona, Nov 15, 1994, of an aortic aneurysm; dau. of Harry Allan and Demetria (Simmons) George; attended Smith College, 1926–27; Boston University, AB, 1930, MA, 1932; m. Alden Speare (industrial engineer), Sept 26, 1936; children: Alden Jr., Mary Elizabeth. ❖ Taught English in high schools in Rockland, MA (1932–35), and Auburn, MA (1935–36); published her 1st historical novel, *Calico Captive* (1957); followed that with *Witch of Blackbird Pond* (1958), which won the Newbery Medal; awarded another Newbery for *The Bronze Bow* (1961).

SPEARS, Britney (1981—). American singer. Born Britney Jean Spears, Dec 2, 1981, in Kentwood, LA; dau. of Jamie (building contractor) and Lynne Spears (schoolteacher); m. Jason Allen Alexander, Jan 3, 2004 (div. Jan 5, 2004); m. Kevin Federline, Sept 18, 2004. ❖ As child, appeared in commercials and attended Professional Performing Arts School in NY; performed in off-Broadway show, *Ruthless* (1991), and on Disney Channel's "The New Mickey Mouse Club" (1993–94); signed with Jive Records at age 15; released 1st single, ". . . Baby One More Time" (1998), which debuted at #1, followed by album of the same name (1999), which also debuted at #1 and included other singles, "(You Drive Me) Crazy" and "Sometimes"; released hit album, *Oops! . . . I Did It Again* (2000), which included singles "Lucky," "Stronger," and title track; appeared in films *Longshot* (2000) and *Crossroads* (2002); released hit albums, *Britney* (2001) and *In the Zone* (2003).

SPEARS, Charlotte (1880–1969). *See Bass, Charlotta Spears.*

SPECTOR, Ronnie (1943—). American musician. Name variations: Veronica Bennett, Veronica Spector; The Ronettes. Born Veronica Bennett, Aug 10, 1943, in New York, NY; sister of Estelle Bennett (singer); m. Phil Spector (music producer), 1966 (div. 1974); m. Jonathan Greenfield; children: (2nd m.) Austin Drew and Jason Charles. ❖ With sister Estelle Bennett and cousin Nedra Talley, sang as the Darling Sisters, then signed with Phil Spector as the Ronettes for his Phillies label (1963); with group, released #2 hit, "Be My Baby" (1963), followed by "Baby I Love You" (1963), "Walking in the Rain" (1964) and "Is This What I Get For Lovin' You?" (1965); revived career (1973), releasing solo albums, *Siren* (1980), *Unfinished Business* (1987) and *She Talks to Rainbows* (1999); had hit with "Take Me Home Tonight," duet with Eddie Money (1986); returned to recording and touring (late 1990s). ❖ See also autobiography (with Vince Waldron), *Be My Baby* (1986).

SPEED, Janet (1864–1947). *See Gillies, Janet.*

SPEIRS, Annie (1889–1926). English swimmer. Born July 14, 1889, in UK; died Oct 1926. ❖ At Stockholm Olympics, won a gold medal in 4 x 100-meter freestyle relay (1912).

SPEGHT, Rachel (1597–c. 1630). English writer. Born in London, England, 1597; died c. 1630; dau. of Reverend James Speght; m. William Procter (a gentleman), 1621; children: 2. ❖ Polemicist and poet; wrote in support of women's spiritual equality to men with her *A Mouzell for Melastomus: The Cynicall Bayter of, and Foule Mouthed Barker against Evahs Sex* (1617), in response to a notorious attack on women written by Joseph Swetnam; published a 2nd work, *Mortalities Memorandum, with a Dreame Prefix'd, Imaginarie in Manner, Reall in Matter* (1621). ❖ See also *Women in World History.*

SPELLMAN, Gladys Noon (1918–1988). American politician. Born Gladys Blossom Noon in New York, NY, Mar 1, 1918; died in Rockville, Maryland, June 19, 1988; dau. of Henry Noon and Bessie G. Noon; attended George Washington University and graduate school of US Department of Agriculture; m. Reuben Spellman; children: Stephen, Richard, Dana, and Eric. ❖ Elected to Prince Georges County Board of Commissioners (1962 and 1966); after a 3-year term as councilwoman-at-large (1971–74), was catapulted into a bid for Maryland's Fifth District seat in US House of Representatives as a Democrat; won election to the 1st of 3 terms in Congress (Jan 3, 1975–Feb 24, 1981); focused much of her attention on the civil service during career in Congress. ❖ See also *Women in World History.*

SPELMAN, Caroline (1958—). English politician and member of Parliament. Born Caroline Cormack, May 4, 1958; m. Mark Spelman, 1987. ❖ As a Conservative, elected to House of Commons for Meriden (1997, 2001, 2005); named shadow secretary of state for International Development and shadow minister for Women.

SPENCE, Catherine (1825–1910). Australian writer, journalist, reformer, and public speaker. Born Catherine Helen Spence near Melrose, Scotland, Oct 31, 1825; died in Australia, 1910; dau. of David Spence (lawyer and banker) and Helen (Brodie) Spence; never married. ❖ Became 1st successful woman novelist in Australia with publication of *Clara Morison: A Tale of South Australia during the Gold Fever* (1854); was active in work with destitute children, the women's suffrage movement, and electoral reform; wrote 1st social studies textbook used in Australia, *The Laws We Live Under* (1880); was the 1st woman in Australia to run for public office (1897); her work was a major catalyst in creating a more progressive environment in Australia in late 19th century. ❖ See also *Women in World History.*

SPENCE, Judith (1957—). Australian politician. Name variations: Hon. Judith Caroline Spence. Born May 19, 1957, in Brisbane, Australia. ❖ As a member of the Australian Labor Party, elected to the Queensland Parliament for Mt Gravatt (1989); named minister for Aboriginal and Torres Strait Island Policy (1998), minister for Disability Services (2001), and minister for Seniors (2002).

SPENCER, Anna (1851–1931). American minister, reformer, lecturer, and writer. Born in Attleboro, Massachusetts, April 17, 1851; died in New York, NY, Feb 12, 1931; dau. of Francis Warren Garlin and Nancy Mason (Carpenter) Garlin; m. William Henry Spencer, Aug 15, 1878 (died 1923); children: Fletcher Carpenter Spencer (b. 1879, died in infancy); Lucy Spencer (b. 1884). ❖ The 1st woman minister in Rhode Island, served as associate director and lecturer at New York School of Philanthropy (1903); was associate director of New York Society for Ethical Culture (1904); worked for child labor and factory inspection laws; was special lecturer at University of Wisconsin and director of the Institute of Municipal and Social Service in Milwaukee (1908–11); as a pacifist, was president of Woman's International League for Peace and Freedom after World War I; wrote over 70 magazine articles on various aspects of social services, including best known book, *Woman's Share in Social Culture* (1913). ❖ See also *Women in World History.*

SPENCER, Anne (1882–1975). African-American poet and salonnière. Name variations: Annie Bethel Scales. Born Anne Bethel Bannister in Henry County, Virginia, Feb 6, 1882; died July 27, 1975; dau. of freed slaves Joel Cephus Bannister and Sarah Louise (Scales) Bannister; graduate of Virginia Seminary, 1899; m. Edward Spencer, May 15, 1901; children: 2 boys, 1 girl. ❖ A founding member of the Harlem Renaissance, published 1st poem, "Before the Feast at Shushan" (1920s); home became a salon for African-American artists, including Langston Hughes, W. E. B. Du Bois, James Weldon Johnson and Claude McKay; a civil-rights activist and feminist, helped found Lynchburg's 1st NAACP chapter, started a suffrage club, refused to ride segregated public transportation, and was the librarian at Dunbar High School for over 20 years, so that black children would be exposed to books otherwise unavailable. ❖ See also J. Lee Greene, *Time's Unfading Garden: Anne Spencer's Life and Poetry* (Louisiana State U. Press, 1977); and *Women in World History.*

SPENCER, Barbara (d. 1721). English coiner. Born in St. Giles, England; died at Tyburn, July 5, 1721. ❖ Received death sentence for coining, then a crime of treason against Crown; was pelted with stones and dirt by mob of spectators before being strangled and then burned at stake at Tyburn.

SPENCER, Cornelia Phillips (1825–1908). American writer and education reformer. Born Cornelia Ann Phillips, Mar 20, 1825, in Harlem, NY; died Mar 11, 1908, in Cambridge, MA; dau. of James (mathematics professor and minister) and Judith Vermeule Phillips; sister of Samuel Phillips (solicitor general of US); m. James Monroe Spencer (lawyer), June 20, 1855 (died 1861); children: Junc Spencer Love; grandmother of Cornelia Spencer Love (librarian at Univ. of North Carolina, 1917–1948). ❖ Contributed series "The Last Ninety Days of the War in North Carolina" to *Watchman* magazine (1866); wrote articles and letters to influential people in a campaign to reopen University of North Carolina.

SPENCER, Diana (1961–1997). *See Diana.*

SPENCER, Dorothy (1617–1684). *See Sidney, Dorothy.*

SPENCER, Dorothy (b. 1909). American film editor. Born in Covington, Kentucky, Feb 2, 1909. ❖ Enjoyed a career that spanned 5 decades, and included such films as *Foreign Correspondent* (1940), *To Be or Not to Be* (1942), *Heaven Can Wait* (1943), *Lifeboat* (1944), *A Tree Grows in Brooklyn* (1945), *Dragonwyck* (1946), *Cluny Brown* (1946), *My Darling Clementine* (1946), *The Ghost and Mrs. Muir* (1947), *The Snake Pit* (1948), *Down to the Sea in Ships* (1949), *Three Came Home* (1950), *The Left Hand of God* (1955), *The Man in the Gray Flannel Suit* (1956), *A Hatful of Rain* (1957), *The Young Lions* (1958) and *Von Ryan's Express* (1965); collaborated with some of Hollywood's best directors, including John Ford, Alfred Hitchcock, Ernst Lubitsch, and Elia Kazan. Received 4 Academy Award nominations: for *Stagecoach* (1939), *Decision Before Dawn* (1951), *Cleopatra* (1963), and *Earthquake* (1974). ❖ See also *Women in World History.*

SPENCER, Elizabeth (1921—). American novelist and short-story writer. Born in Carrollton, Mississippi, July 19, 1921; dau. of James L.

Spencer (farmer) and Mary J. (McCain) Spencer; Belhaven College, BA, 1942; Vanderbilt University, MA, 1943; m. John Rusher (educator), Sept 29, 1956. ❖ Best known for her short stories and for her novel *The Light in the Piazza*, taught English and creative writing at several schools: Northwest Mississippi Junior College in Senatobia (1943–44), Ward-Belmont in Nashville (1944–45), and for several years at University of Mississippi; also served a stint as a reporter for *Nashville Tennessean* (1945–46); published *Fire in the Morning* (1948), followed by *This Crooked Way* (1952) and *The Voice at the Back Door* (1956), a cycle of novels that, taken together, portray the social and political circumstances of the rural South during 1st half of 20th century; lived in Italy (1953–56) and wrote 4 novels about North Americans in Europe, including *The Light in the Piazza* (1960), *Knights and Dragons* (1965) and *No Place for an Angel* (1967); published *The Snare* (1972); moved to Montreal, Canada (1958), where she taught at Concordia University (1976–86); returned to the South (1986) and was a professor in creative writing at University of North Carolina in Chapel Hill (1986–92). ❖ See also autobiography, *Landscapes of the Heart* (1998); and *Women in World History*.

SPENCER, Georgiana (1757–1806). *See Cavendish, Georgiana.*

SPENCER, Henrietta Frances (1761–1821). Countess of Bessborough. Name variations: Lady Bessborough; Viscountess Duncannon; Henrietta Frances Ponsonby. Born Henrietta Frances Spencer, June 16, 1761; died Nov 1, 1821; dau. of John Spencer, 1st earl Spencer, and Georgiana (Poyntz) Spencer (eldest dau. of Stephen Poyntz); sister of Georgiana Cavendish (1757–1806); m. Frederick Ponsonby, 3rd earl of Bessborough, on Nov 27, 1780; children: John Ponsonby, 4th earl of Bessborough; Major-General Sir Frederick Ponsonby; Caroline Lamb (1785–1828); William Ponsonby, 1st Lord De Mauley. ❖ See also *Women in World History*.

SPENCER, Jane (1957—). British royal. Name variations: Jane Fellowes; Lady Jane Spencer. Born Cynthia Jane Spencer in 1957; dau. of Edward John VIII Spencer (b. 1924), viscount Althorp, and Frances Burke Ruth Roche (Fermoy) Spencer, viscountess Althorp, later known as Frances Shand Kydd; sister of Diana, princess of Wales (1961–1997); m. Sir Robert Fellowes (the Queen's private secretary), in Mar 1978; children: Laura Jane Fellowes (b. 1980).

SPENCER, Lilly Martin (1822–1902). British-born American painter. Born Angélique Marie Martin in Exeter, England, Nov 26, 1822; died in New York City on May 22, 1902; dau. of Giles Marie Martin (French teacher) and Angélique (le Petit) Martin; attended Academy of Design in NY; studied painting informally with Charles Sullivan and Sala Bosworth in Marietta, Ohio, and John Insco Williams in Cincinnati, Ohio; m. Benjamin Rush Spencer, Aug 1844 (died 1890); children: Benjamin Martin, Angelo Paul, Charles, William Henry, Flora, Pierre, and Lilly Caroline. ❖ Immigrated to US as a child (1830); had 1st show, in Marietta, Ohio (1841); studied in Cincinnati (beginning 1841) and became established as leading local genre artist; launched as nationally known genre artist by the American Art-Union; commissioned to illustrate Elizabeth F. Ellet's *Women of the American Revolution*; completed *Truth Unveiling Falsehood*, which was acclaimed as her masterwork (1869); better-known paintings include *Domestic Happiness* (1849), *The Jolly Washerwoman* (1851), *Peeling Onions* (1852), *Shake Hands* (1854), *"This Little Pig Went to Market"* (1857) and *The Gossips* (1857). ❖ See also *Women in World History*.

SPENCER, Sarah (1955—). British royal. Name variations: Sarah McCorquodale; Lady Sarah Spencer. Born Elizabeth Sarah, Lady Spencer, in 1955; dau. of Edward John VIII Spencer (b. 1924), viscount Althorp, and Frances Burke Ruth Roche (Fermoy) Spencer, viscountess Althorp, later known as Frances Shand Kydd; sister of Diana, princess of Wales (1961–1997); m. Neil Edward McCorquodale, in May 1980.

SPENCER BOWER, Olivia (1905–1982). New Zealand artist. Name variations: Olivia Spencer Bower. Born Catherine Olivia Orme Spencer Bower, April 13, 1905, in St. Neots, Huntingdonshire, England; died July 8, 1982, at Christchurch, New Zealand; dau. of Anthony Spencer Bower and Agnes Rosa Marion (Dixon) Bower. ❖ Immigrated to New Zealand with family (1920); studied art at Canterbury College School of Art and Slade School of Fine Art, University College, London (1920s); exhibited primarily at Canterbury Society of Arts, where she served as executive member (1940–46, 1959–62, 1967–68, 1978 and 1980) and became president (1980); known primarily as watercolorist.

SPENCER-CHURCHILL. *See Churchill.*

SPENCER-CHURCHILL, Baroness (1885–1977). *See Churchill, Clementine.*

SPENCER-CHURCHILL, Clarissa (b. 1920). *See Eden, Clarissa.*

SPENCER-CHURCHILL, Clementine (1885–1977). *See Churchill, Clementine.*

SPENCER-CHURCHILL, Consuelo (1877–1964). *See Vanderbilt, Consuelo.*

SPENCER SMITH, Joan (1891–1965). New Zealand Anglican deaconess. Born Joan Elizabeth Spencer Smith, June 27, 1891, in London, England; died April 10, 1965, in London; dau. of Charles Spencer Smith (clerk) and Charlotte Owen (Gaze) Spencer Smith. ❖ Ordained and licensed as head deaconess (1933); was acting head deaconess of St Hilda's House in Melbourne (1937), and head deaconess of St Faith's (1938–43); during WWII, pioneered ecumenical work among women through National Council of Churches in New Zealand and chaired numerous committees. ❖ See also *Dictionary of New Zealand Biography* (Vol. 4).

SPENDER, Dale (1943—). Australian historian, literary critic, educator and feminist. Born 1943 in Newcastle, NSW, Australia; educated at University of Sydney and London University. ❖ Taught at American and Canadian universities and was visiting professor at University of London; founded Women's Studies International Forum and Pandora Press, London; co-founded the international data base on women, *Women's International Knowledge: Encyclopedia and Data*; writings, which seek to re-evaluate women's history and writing, include *Women of Ideas and What Men Have Done to Them* (1982), *Man Made Language* (1980, 1985), *There's Always Been a Women's Movement* (1985), *Writing a New World: Two Centuries of Australian Women Writers* (1988) and *Nattering on the Net: Women, Power and Cyberspace* (1996).

SPENSER, Violet (d. 1910). *See Cook, Edith Maud.*

SPERANI, Bruno (1843–1923). *See Speraz, Beatrice.*

SPERANZA (c. 1821–1896). *See Wilde, Jane.*

SPERAZ, Beatrice (1843–1923). Italian novelist. Name variations: (pseudonym) Bruno Sperani. Born 1843 in Italy; died 1923. ❖ Works, which address position of women in Milanese society, include *Nell'ingranaggio* (1885), *Numeri e sogni* (1887) and *La fabbrica* (1908).

SPERBER, Sylvia (1965—). West German shooter. Born Feb 9, 1965, in West Germany. ❖ At Seoul Olympics, won a silver medal in air rifle and a gold medal in smallbore rifle 3 positions (1988).

SPERLING, Hilde (1908–1981). German tennis player. Name variations: Hilde Krahwinkel. Born Hilde Krahwinkel, Mar 26, 1908, in Essen, Germany; died Feb 14, 1981; m. Sven Sperling (Danish tennis star). ❖ Greatly respected player on the international tennis circuit in 1930s, won the French Open (3 times) and Swiss championships; was runner-up at Wimbledon (1931). ❖ See also *Women in World History*.

SPERREY, Eleanor Catherine (1862–1893). New Zealand artist. Name variations: Eleanor Catherine Mair, E. K. Mair. Born Eleanor Catherine Sperrey, Jan 7, 1862, in Victoria, Australia; died April 23, 1893, in Belheim, New Zealand; dau. of John Sperrey (timber merchant) and Eleanor (Maunder) Sperrey; m. Gilbert Mair, 1888; children: 1 son, 1 daughter. ❖ Arrived in New Zealand with family (1863); studied portraiture in Rome, Paris and London (1881–82); returned to New Zealand (1884) and established studio (1886); painted numerous prominent political figures and Maori subjects; after marriage, signed paintings, E. K. Mair. ❖ See also *Dictionary of New Zealand Biography* (Vol. 2).

SPESSIVTZEVA, Olga (1895–1980). Russian ballerina. Name variations: Olga Spessivtseva. Born in Rostov, Russia, 1895; died 1980; dau. of an opera singer; graduate of Imperial Maryinsky Theater ballet school in 1913, where she had studied under Michel Fokine and Agrippina Vaganova. ❖ Reputedly the greatest Russian Romantic ballerina of her generation, joined Maryinsky Ballet (1913); promoted to ballerina (1918), dancing principal roles for next 5 years in *Esmeralda, Giselle, Chopiniana (Les Sylphides), The Nutcracker, Paquita, Le Corsaire, Bayaderka, The Sleeping Beauty, The Daughter of Pharoah, Don Quixote,* and *Swan Lake*; also toured US with Ballet Russe (1916), dancing with Vaslav Nijinsky in *Blue Bird* and *Le Spectre de la Rose*; rejoined Ballet Russe (1921), dancing Aurora in *Sleeping Beauty*; left Russia for good (1923); worked with Teatro Colón in Buenos Aires for one year, before joining Paris Opéra where she remained until 1932, rising to *première danseuse étoile* (1931); during Australian tour with Victor Dandré-Alexander Levitov company, began to reveal 1st signs of chronic depression; suffered a nervous breakdown and was confined to a mental hospital for 20 years (1943–63).

SPEWACK, Bella (1899–1990). Romanian-born American playwright and screenwriter. Name variations: Bella Cohen. Born Bella Cohen in Transylvania on Mar 25, 1899; died in New York, NY, April 27, 1990; dau. of Adolph Cohen and Fanny (Lang) Cohen; m. Samuel Spewack (writer), c. 1922 (died 1971); no children. ❖ As a playwright, made her mark with the musical *Kiss Me Kate* (1949), which she co-wrote with husband; worked 1st as a journalist, starting at the socialist newspaper *The New York Call*, then writing for *The New York Times*, *The New York Herald Tribune*, and the *Evening Mail*; with husband, served as a foreign correspondent in Moscow for *The World*; collaborated with husband on such plays as *Clear All Wires* (1932), *Boy Meets Girl* (1935) and *My Three Angels* (1953), and such films as *Vogues of 1938* (1938), *My Favorite Wife* (1940), *Weekend at the Waldorf* (1945), *Kiss Me Kate* (1953) and *Move Over Darling* (1963). ❖ See also autobiography *Streets: A Memoir of the Lower East Side*; and *Women in World History*.

SPEYER, Ellin Prince (1849–1921). American philanthropist and socialite. Name variations: Mrs. John A. Lowery; Mrs. James Speyer. Born Ellin L. Prince in Lowell, Massachusetts, Oct 14, 1849; died in New York, NY, Feb 23, 1921; dau. of John Dynely Prince (chemist) and Mary (Travers) Prince; m. John A. Lowery, Oct 1871 (died 1892); m. James Speyer (1861–1941, banker and philanthropist), Nov 11, 1897; no children. ❖ Was one of the founders of the United Hospital Fund (1881); helped establish the New York Skin and Cancer Hospital (1886); founded club for working girls (1883); with husband, gave $100,000 to Columbia University Teachers College to found an experimental school which was named after them (1902); organized girls' branch of Public School Athletic League (1906); founded the New York Women's League for Animals (1910), heading the organization for the remainder of her life; was chair of subcommittee on unemployment among women (1915); raised funds for the Lafayette Street Hospital for animals, later named the Ellin Prince Speyer Free Hospital for Animals. ❖ See also *Women in World History*.

SPEYER, Leonora (1872–1956). American poet and violinist. Born Leonora Von Stosch in Washington, DC, Nov 7, 1872; died in New York, NY, Feb 10, 1956; dau. of Count Ferdinand Von Stosch and Julia (Thompson) Von Stosch; married in 1893 (div.); m. Edgar Speyer (banker), 1902; children: (1st m.) Enid (who m. Robert Hewitt), Pamela (who m. Count Hugo Moy), Leonora Speyer (d. 1987, who lived with Maria Donska), and Vivien. ❖ Began career as a concert violinist playing with the Boston Symphony Orchestra (1890), and appeared later with the New York Philharmonic; when a severe bout of neuritis stopped her from playing, started writing poetry; won Pulitzer Prize for poetry for *Fiddler's Farewell* (1927), which was especially noted for its wit and understanding of the feminine character; taught poetry at Columbia University; other works include *A Canopic Jar* (1921), *Naked Heel* (1931) and *Slow Wall: New and Selected Poems* (1939). ❖ See also *Women in World History*.

SPHEERIS, Penelope (1945—). American film director. Name variations: P. Spheeris. Born Dec 2, 1945, in New Orleans, Louisiana; University of California at Los Angeles, BA; children: (with Robert Schoeller) Anna. ❖ Had great success with 1st major project as director, writer and producer, *The Decline of Western Civilization* (1981), a punk-rock documentary, followed by sequels *Decline of Western Civilization Part II, The Metal Years* (1988) and *Part III* (1998); changed career course with blockbuster screwball comedy, *Wayne's World* (1992); other films include *The Boys Next Door* (1986), *Dudes* (1987), *Thunder and Mud* (1990), *The Beverly Hillbillies* (1993), *The Little Rascals* (1994), *Black Sheep* (1996), *Senseless* (1998), *The Thing in Bob's Garage* (1998), *Hollywierd* (1999), *We Sold Our Souls for Rock 'n Roll* (2001) and *Posers* (2001).

SPHINX, The (1862–1933). See Leverson, Ada.

SPICE GIRLS
See Beckham, Victoria.
See Brown, Melanie.
See Bunton, Emma.
See Chisholm, Melanie.
See Halliwell, Geri.

SPIDER WOMAN, The (1894–1970). See Glaum, Louise.

SPIEL, Hilde (1911–1990). Austrian writer. Born Hilde Maria Spiel in Vienna, Austria, Oct 19, 1911; died in Vienna, Nov 29, 1990; dau. of Hugo Spiel and Marie (Gutfeld) Spiel; graduate of University of Vienna, 1936; attended Eugenie Schwarzwald's school; graduate of University of Vienna, 1936; m. Peter de Mendelssohn (writer), 1936; m. Hans Flesch Edler von Brunningen; children: Christine and Anthony. ❖ At 22, published 1st novel, *Kati auf der Brücke* (Cathy on the Bridge), which won the Julius Reich Prize; with the rise of Nazism, immigrated with husband to England (1936); in English, published novel *Flute and Drums* (1939); wrote biography of Fanny von Arnstein; regarded by many as Vienna's *femme de lettres*, reported on Austrian affairs, both literary and political, in *New Statesman* as well as in *Die Welt*. Received the Goethe Medal (1990). ❖ See also autobiographies (in German): *Die hellen und die finsteren Zeiten: Erinnerungen 1911–1946* (The Bright and the Dark Times: Memoirs 1911–1946) and *Welche Welt ist meine Welt? Erinnerungen 1946–1989* (Which World is My World? Memoirs 1946–1989); and *Women in World History*.

SPIER, Erna Gunther (1896–1982). See Gunther, Erna.

SPIES, Daisy (1905–2000). German ballet dancer and choreographer. Born Dec 29, 1905, in Moscow, Russia; died Sept 9, 2000, in Berlin, Germany. ❖ Joined the Berlin State Opera (1924), where she performed in works by Jens Keith, among others; also choreographed works for Keith's troupe, including *Traumwalzer* and *Freitagszauber*; began dancing with East Berlin State Opera (1951), where she created the production of *Aschenbroedel*; choreographed for Hamburg Operetta Theater and served as teacher at Wigman school in Berlin.

SPIESS, Riki (1924—). See Mahringer, Erika.

SPILLANE, Joan (1943—). American swimmer. Name variations: Joan Postma. Born Jan 31, 1943; attended University of Michigan; m. Peter Postma; children: Perri and Robert. ❖ At Rome Olympics, won a gold medal in 4 x 100-meter freestyle relay (1960); taught middle schoolers for 29 years in Houston, Texas.

SPINELL, Mary (Spagnuolo, Filomena). See 1903–1987.

SPINELLI, Evelita Juanita (1889–1941). American murderer. Name variations: Mrs Evelita Juanita Spinelli. Born 1889; died in gas chamber at San Quentin, CA, Nov 21, 1941. ❖ Gang leader known as the Duchess, organized robberies in San Francisco; after members of her gang murdered an owner of a barbecue stand during a hold-up, killed 19-year-old Robert Sherrard to keep him from talking; sent to gas chamber, the 1st woman officially executed in California.

SPINK (1876–1964). See Austen, Winifred.

SPIRA, Camilla (1906–1997). German actress. Born in Hamburg, Germany, Mar 1, 1906; died in Berlin, Aug 25, 1997; dau. of Fritz (formerly Jacob) Spira (1881–1943, Viennese-born singer and comic actor) and Wilhelmine Emilie Charlotte (Lotte) Andresen Spira (actress known as Lotte Spira-Andresen, 1883–1943); sister of Steffie Spira (1908–1995); married; children: 2 sons. ❖ Was a singing and acting star in various operettas, including *Im Weissen Rössl* (White Horse Inn, 1930); starred in film *Morgenrot* (Break of Dawn, 1933); because of her mixed parentage, could only perform for the Nazi-approved Jüdischer Kulturbund (Jewish Culture League); fled Nazi Germany with family (1938); while in Amsterdam, was interned in Westerbork concentration camp (1943); spent remainder of war in hiding in Amsterdam; returned to West Berlin (1947), where she was a highly successful actress on Berlin and West German stage, as well as in films; in later years, had motherly roles on tv; when the Berlin Wall ceased to divide Germans (1989), was able to reconcile with sister. ❖ See also *Women in World History*.

SPIRA, Steffie (1908–1995). Austrian-born German actress and author. Name variations: Steffi Spira; Steffie Spira-Ruschin. Born Steffanie Spira in Vienna, Austria, June 2, 1908; died in Berlin, May 10, 1995; dau. of Fritz (formerly Jacob) Spira (1881–1943, Viennese-born singer and comic actor of Jewish ancestry) and Wilhelmine Emilie Charlotte (Lotte) Andresen Spira (actress known as Lotte Spira-Andresen, 1883–1943); sister of Camilla Spira (1906–1997); m. Günter Ruschin (1904–1963, actor of Jewish ancestry), 1931 (died 1963); children: Thomas; Rutta (died 1941). ❖ Appeared in small role in premiere of Brecht's *Mann ist Mann* (Man is Man, 1928); joined Communist Party of Germany (KPD, 1931); with husband, joined Gustav von Wangenheim's Truppe 31, an actors' collective that presented agitprop productions; after husband was arrested, fled to Zurich with son (1933);

on husband's release due to clerical error, moved to Paris; had a major role in world premiere of Brecht's *Die Gewehre der Frau Carrar* (Mrs. Carrar's Rifles, 1937); starred in *99%: Bilder aus dem Dritten Reich* (99%: Pictures from the Third Reich, 1938); after months in internment camps, lived with family in Mexico (1941–46); resumed career in East Berlin (1949), particularly at Deutsches Theater and Volksbühne (People's Playhouse), where she became a favorite for such roles as Mutter Wolffen in *Der Biberpelz* (The Beaver Fur) and Frau Hassenreuther in *Der gute Mensch von Sezuan* (*The Good Woman of Szechuan*); also starred in a number of GDR films, including *Schneewittchen: Ein Märchenfilm nach den Gebrüdern Grimm* (Snow White: A Fairy Tale Film Taken from the Grimm Brothers, 1961), *Die Grosse Reise der Agathe Schweigert* (Agathe Schweigert's Long Trip, 1972) and *Die Beunruhigung* (Apprehension, 1982); spoke at the mass Alexanderplatz demonstration against Honecker regime (Nov 4, 1989); when the Berlin Wall ceased to divide Germans (1989), was able to reconcile with sister. ❖ See also (in German) *Trab der Schaukelpferde: Autobiographie* (1991); and *Women in World History*.

SPIRCU, Doina (1970—). Romanian rower. Name variations: Doina Tudora Spircu. Born July 24, 1970, in Bucharest, Romania. ❖ Won a gold medal for coxed eights at Atlanta Olympics (1996).

SPIRIDONOVA, Maria (1884–1941). Russian political assassin. Name variations: Mariya Spiridovna or Spiridinova. Born Maria Alexandrovna Spiridonova, Oct 16, 1884, in Tambov, Russia; shot to death by Soviet secret police, Sept 1941 in Ural town of Orel; dau. of Alexander Alexandrovich (provincial civil servant) and Alexandra Yakovlevna; never married; no children. ❖ Revolutionary hero of the Russian peasantry, who faced the wrath of both tsarist and Soviet governments, and spent the vast majority of her adult life in captivity; shot a government official at the behest of the Russian Socialist Revolutionary Party (SRs, 1906); jailed until the country's political prisoners were amnestied (1917); became a leading figure of the LSRs (the leftist faction of the SRs), who 1st supported, then opposed the Bolshevik-led Soviet government; accused the Bolsheviks of betraying the cause of the peasantry, and of being more interested in abstract theories than in the needs of the poor; organized the assassination of the German ambassador to Russia, which almost resulted in the overthrow of the Bolsheviks (1918); most of the rest of her life spent in exile or in jail. ❖ See also Isaac Steinberg, *Spiridonova: Revolutionary Terrorist* (Methuen, 1935); and *Women in World History*.

SPITZ, Sabine (1971—). German cyclist. Born Dec 27, 1971, in Bad S., Germany; m. Ralf Schaeuble. ❖ At World championships, placed 1st for cross country (2003); placed 2nd overall for World Cup ranking in cross country (2002, 2003); won a bronze medal for cross country at Athens Olympics (2004).

SPIVAK, Gayatri Chakravorty (1942—). American literary critic and translator. Born Gayatri Chakravorty, Feb 24, 1942, in Calcutta, West Bengal, India; graduate of University of Calcutta with 1st class honors; Cornell University, MA in English; University of Iowa, PhD; m. Talbot Spivak (an American, div.). ❖ Foremost post-colonial theorist and pioneer in subaltern studies, came to prominence with her translation of, and introduction to, Jacques Derrida's *Of Grammatology* (1974); taught at University of Iowa; became an Avalon Foundation professor at Columbia; other works include *Myself Must I Remake: The Life and Poetry of W. B. Yeats* (1974), *In Other Worlds: Essays in Cultural Politics* (1987), *The Post-Colonial Critic: Interviews, Strategies, Dialogues* (1990), *Outside in the Teaching Machine* (1993) and *The Spivak Reader* (1996); with Ranajit Guha, edited *Selected Subaltern Studies* (1988).

SPIVEY, Victoria (1906–1976). African-American blues singer and songwriter. Name variations: Victoria Regina Spivey; Vicky Spivey; Queen Victoria; occasionally recorded as Jane Lucas. Born Oct 15, 1906, in Houston, TX; died Oct 3, 1976, in New York, NY; dau. of Grant Spivey (musician) and Addie (Smith) Spivey (nurse); m. Reuben Floyd, 1928 (div. early 1930s); m. William Adams (dancer), mid-1930s (div. c. 1951); m. twice more. ❖ Made 1st recording for Okeh label (1926) and had 1st hit, "Black Snake Blues," now considered a classic; within 2 years, recorded about 38 songs for Okeh, including such hits as "Spider Web Blues," "Dirty Woman Blues" and "TB Blues"; performed in revues, including *Hits and Bits from Africana* (1927) and, on occasion, with sisters Addie "Sweet Pea" Spivey, Elton "Za-Zu" Spivey, and Leona Spivey; moved to Chicago (1930), performing with such musicians as Sonny Boy Williamson, Memphis Minnie (Lizzie Douglas), and Big Bill Broonzy; with 2nd husband, dancer Bill Adams, appeared in revue *Hellzapoppin*; also appeared at Apollo, and recorded with Decca and

Vocalion labels (sometimes using the name Jane Lucas); toured with Louis Armstrong (mid-1930s); retired from stage (1952); set up recording company, Spivey, reissuing a number of her own albums and reintroducing such singers as Alberta Hunter, Lucille Hegamin and Hannah Sylvester, and introducing Luther Johnson, Lucille Spann, Olive Brown, Memphis Slim, Big Joe Williams, and a young Bob Dylan (who also played on a few of her albums); appeared in "Philadelphia Folk Festival" broadcast on PBS (1974) and performed on BBC's "The Devil's Music—A History of the Blues" (1976). ❖ See also *Women in World History*.

SPIVY, Mme. (1906–1971). See LaVoe, Spivy.

SPOFFORD, Grace Harriet (1887–1974). American music educator. Born Grace Harriet Spofford, Sept 21, 1887, in Haverhill, MA; died June 5, 1974, in New York, NY; dau. of Harry Hall Spofford (salesman) and Sarah G. (Hastings) Spofford; attended Mount Holyoke College, 1905, and Smith College, 1909; studied piano at Peabody Conservatory of Music, 1913, and organ, 1916. ❖ Taught piano at Heidelberg College in Tiffin, Ohio, and gave recitals (1910–12); worked at Peabody Conservatory of Music in Baltimore, MD, teaching piano (1916–18) and serving as executive secretary (1917–24); wrote music criticism for newspaper, *Baltimore Sun* (1923–24); was 1st dean of Curtis Institute of Music (1924–31); worked as executive secretary for Olga Samaroff's Layman's Music Courses, as manager for Curtis String Quartet, and in radio music education, in NYC (early 1930s); was associate director of New York College of Music (1934–38) and lecturer on music at Katherine Gibbs School (1936–59); was director of Music School of Henry Street Settlement (1935–54), creating model for similar schools; served 3 terms as elected chair of music of International Council of Women (1954–63).

SPOFFORD, Harriet Prescott (1835–1921). American author. Name variations: Harriet Elizabeth Spofford. Born Harriet Elizabeth Prescott, April 3, 1835, in Calais, Maine; died Aug 14, 1921, on Deer Island, in Amesbury, Massachusetts; dau. of Joseph Newmarch Prescott (attorney and lumber merchant) and Sarah Jane (Bridges) Prescott; attended Pinkerton Academy, Derry, New Hampshire; m. Richard S. Spofford, 1865 (died 1888); children: Richard (died in infancy). ❖ First caught the attention of critics when her short story "In a Cellar" appeared in *Atlantic Monthly* (1859); by late 1800s, was one of the most popular women writers in US; her short stories, published in such collections as *The Amber Gods* (1863) and *New England Legends* (1871), came to define the "Gothic" tale with their reliance upon legend, mystery, and elements of mysticism and the supernatural; in addition to *A Scarlet Poppy, and Other Stories* (1894) and *Old Madame, and Other Tragedies* (1900), published poetry collection *In Titian's Gardens* (1897), the children's book *The Fairy Changeling* (1910), and essay collection *A Little Book of Friends* (1916). ❖ See also *Women in World History*.

SPOLIN, Viola (1906–1994). American acting teacher and author. Born Nov 7, 1906; died Nov 22, 1994, in Los Angeles, CA; children: Paul Sills (b. 1927, actor). ❖ Considered the doyenne of improvisational comedy, taught dramatics to children and adults (1930s), then published *Improvisations for the Theatre*, which has been used to train generations of actors; son Paul Sills used the techniques while molding Compass Players, Second City, and his revue *Story Theatre*.

SPONER, Hertha (1895–1968). German physicist. Born 1895 in Germany; died 1968; University of Göttingen, PhD, 1920; m. James Franck (physicist), 1946. ❖ Investigated quantum mechanics as well as its application to atomic and molecular physics; worked as an assistant at the Physics Institute in Göttingen (1921–25); at University of Göttingen, taught and researched (1925–32) and worked as a physics professor (1932–34); was a visiting professor at University of Oslo (1934–36), and professor at Duke University (1936–66); worked with M. Bruch-Willstater on the lattice energy of carbon dioxide; elected a fellow of New York Academy of Sciences, Optical Society of America and American Physical Society.

SPONG, Hilda (1875–1955). English-born actress. Born May 14, 1875, in London, England; died May 16, 1955, in Norwalk, CT; dau. of W. B. Spong (painter). ❖ Made stage debut in Sydney, Australia, in *Joseph's Sweetheart* (1890), London debut as Sibyl Grey in *The Duchess of Coolgardie* (1896), and NY debut as Imogen Parrott in *Trelawny of the Wells* (1898); for the most part, remained in US, appearing in such plays as *Notre Dame, Iris, Imprudence, Lord and Lady Algy, Sherlock Holmes, John Hudson's Wife* and *Dear Brutus*; had title roles in *Candida* and *Lady Jim*, among others.

SPOONER, Cecil (1875–1953). American actress. Born Jan 29, 1875, in New York, NY; died May 13, 1953, in Sherman Oaks, CA; dau. of Mary Gibbs Spooner (ran a theater in Brooklyn); sister of Edna May Spooner (actress) and F. E. Spooner (actor); m. Charles E. Blaney, 1909. ❖ Made stage debut as a child; made NY debut in *My Lady Peggy Goes to Town* (1903); played stock engagements at the Metropoollis Theater and the Cecil Spooner Theater in NY; also appeared in *A Child of the Regiment*, *The House of Bondage*, and *Arms and the Woman*; toured in *The Brat* (1918–19); wrote, directed and starred in the film *Nell of the Circus* (1914).

SPOONER, Edna May (1873–1953). American actress. Born May 10, 1873, in Centerville, IA; died July 14, 1953, in Sherman Oaks, CA; dau. of Mary Gibbs Spooner; sister of Cecil Spooner (actress) and F. E. Spooner (actor); m. Arthur Behrens (Whaley). ❖ Made stage debut as a child in her parents' company; was principally connected to her mother's theater in Brooklyn, appearing in such roles as Zaza, Camille, Magda, Juliet, Dorothy Vernon, Nell Gwynne, Leah, and Du Barry; headed the Proctor Stock Company at the Fifth Avenue Theater (1907); wrote the play *1776*.

SPOONER, Mary Florence (1914–1997). *See Spooner, Molly.*

SPOONER, Molly (1914–1997). English marine biologist. Name variations: Mary Florence Mare; Mary Florence Spooner. Born Mary Florence Mare, July 10, 1914, in Birmingham, England; died Aug 27, 1997; Newnham College, Cambridge, MA, PhD, 1941; m. Malcolm Spooner (zoologist), May 14, 1943; children: 2. ❖ Internationally recognized expert on oil spills, served as a researcher at the Scottish Marine Biological Association Laboratory, Milport (1942–45), as a part-time Plymouth school teacher (1955–58) and as a Marine Biological Association Laboratory researcher at Plymouth (1967–76); researched food chains of a marine benthic community for PhD and the antifouling of ships; assisted husband on a study of dwarf oak trees in Wistman's Wood; after the *Torrey Canyon* accident west of the Scilly Isles, worked with a team to study the effects of the oil spill; was one of the 1st to recognize that the use of dispersants could cause more harm than the effects of the oil alone; appointed advisor on oil pollution precautions and procedures for Department of the Environment (1973). Made Member of the Order of the British Empire (1977).

SPORN, Rachael (1968—). Australian basketball player. Born May 26, 1968, in Murrayville, South Australia; attended University of South Australia. ❖ Forward; won a team bronze medal at Atlanta Olympics (1996), a team silver at Sydney Olympics (2000) and a team silver at Athens Olympics (2004); played for Adelaide Lightning in WNBL; played for Detroit Shock in WNBA (1998–99, 2001). Named WNBL MVP (1996, 1997).

SPORTY SPICE (1974—). *See Chisholm, Melanie.*

SPOTSWOOD, Claire Myers (1896–1983). *See Owens, Claire Myers.*

SPOTTISWOODE, Alicia Ann (1810–1900). Scottish poet and composer. Name variations: Lady John Scott; Alicia Ann Spottiswood. Born Alicia Ann Spottiswoode (or Spottiswood) at Lauder in Berwickshire, 1810; died Mar 13, 1900; m. Lord John Scott (son of duke of Buccleugh), 1836 (died 1860). ❖ Under the name Lady John Scott, wrote the words and music for many popular Scotch songs of 19th century, including "Douglas Tender and True," "Durisdeer," "The Comin' o' the Spring," "Ettrick," and the popular "Annie Laurie."

SPRAGUE, Kate Chase (1840–1899). American socialite. Name variations: Catherine Jane Chase; Kate Chase. Born Catherine Jane Chase, Aug 13, 1840, in Cincinnati, Ohio; died July 31, 1899, near Washington, DC; dau. of Salmon Portland Chase (US senator and secretary of the treasury, died 1873) and Eliza Ann (Smith) Chase; m. William Sprague (US senator), in 1863 (div. 1882); children: William (b. 1865), Ethel (b. 1869), Portia (b. 1872) and Kitty Sprague (b. 1873). ❖ When father was appointed secretary of the treasury under Abraham Lincoln (1860), moved with family to Washington, DC, where she acted as his host, becoming one of the city's most prominent; 10 years into marriage, took a lover, New York senator Roscoe Conkling, who was driven from her home at gunpoint by husband, creating a national scandal; went into seclusion; became impoverished. ❖ See also *Women in World History*.

SPRAGUE, Kristin Babb (1968—). *See Babb-Sprague, Kristen.*

SPRAY OF PEARLS (d. 1259). *See Shajar al-Durr.*

SPRIGG, June (1903–1984). *See Marlowe, June.*

SPRINGFIELD, Dusty (1939–1999). British-born pop singer. Born Mary Isobel Catherine Bernadette O'Brien in Hampstead, England, April 16, 1939; died of breast cancer, Mar 2, 1999, in Henley-on-Thames, England; sister of Tom O'Brien (musician); never married. ❖ Began performing in an all-girl trio called The Lana Sisters (1958); joined brother and a friend to form a group called The Springfields (1960), their release of "Silver Threads and Golden Needles" becoming an international bestseller; released 1st record as a solo performer, "I Only Want to Be with You" (1963), and followed it with a string of successful, folk-rock singles that included "I Just Don't Know What to Do with Myself," "Stay Awhile," "Little by Little," "Wishin' and Hopin'," and "You Don't Have to Say You Love Me"; had her own BBC tv show; signed with Atlantic Records, resulting in album some consider her best, *Dusty in Memphis* (1968); saw career slip (1970s–80s), but returned to charts (late 1980s) through recording of "Do I Deserve This?" with the Pet Shop Boys; seemed destined for rediscovery. Named Best Female Vocalist in Britain's *New Musical Express* (1964–67, 1969); inducted into Rock and Roll Hall of Fame (1998); just weeks before death, was awarded the Order of the British Empire. ❖ See also Lucy O'Brien, *Dusty* (Rev. ed. Sidgewick & Jackson, 1999); and *Women in World History*.

SPRY, Constance (1886–1960). British floral designer. Born Constance Fletcher, Dec 5, 1886, in Derby, England; died Jan 3, 1960; educated at Alexandra School and College, Dublin. ❖ Began career as a professional flower arranger (1920s); founded a school of floristry (1930s), followed by a cooking school and finishing school after WWII; served as an advisor on the decorations for numerous London weddings and galas, including the coronation of Queen Elizabeth II at Westminster Abbey (1953); lectured and published several books on flower arranging and cooking; through the Royal Gardeners' Orphan Fund, used her considerable influence to raise large sums of money to aid needy children throughout Great Britain. ❖ See also E. Coxhead, *Constance Spry* (1975); and *Women in World History*.

SPURGEON, Caroline F. E. (1869–1942). English educator and writer. Born Caroline Frances Eleanor Spurgeon in Punjab, India, in 1869; died Oct 24, 1942; educated at Cheltenham College, England; Oxford University, BA, 1899. ❖ An authority on Chaucer and Shakespeare, was a lecturer at England's Bedford College for Women (1901–06), head of its English literature department (1913–29); was a lecturer at the University of London (1906–13), before becoming the 1st woman to hold a professorship there (1913–29); while a visiting professor at Barnard College in NY (1920–21), helped organize the International Federation of University Women and became its 1st president (1920–24); major writings include *Mysticism in English Literature* (1913), *Five Hundred Years of Chaucer Criticism and Allusion* (1920–25), *Keats's Shakespeare* (1928) and *Shakespeare's Imagery, and What It Tells Us* (1935).

SPURGIN, Patricia (1965—). American shooter. Name variations: Pat Spurgin; Pat Spurgin Pitney. Born Aug 10, 1965; attended Murray State University in Kentucky. ❖ At Los Angeles Olympics, won a gold medal in air rifle (1984); was an 8-time All-American.

SPUZICH, Sandra (1937—). American golfer. Born Sandra Ann Spuzich, April 3, 1937, in Indianapolis, IN; graduate of University of Indiana, 1959. ❖ Joined pro tour (1962); won Haig & Haig and USGA Women's Open (1966), Buckeye (1968), Lady Tara (1974); Lady Keystone (1977); Barth Classic (1980); Corning Classic and Mary Kay Classic (1982). Inducted into the Indiana Golf Hall of Fame.

SPYRI, Emily Kempin (1853–1901). Swiss lawyer. Born 1853 in Switzerland; died 1901; niece of Johanna Spyri (writer); University of Zurich, doctorate of law, 1887; married with children. ❖ The 1st woman in Europe to earn a doctorate of law degree, was prohibited because of her gender to practice law in Switzerland; immigrated with family to NY (1888), where she established and taught the 1st law classes for women; persuaded by husband and children to return to Zurich (1891), was still not allowed to pursue a law career; collapsed and spent the remainder of her life in an asylum. ❖ See also Eveline Hasler, *Flying with Wings of Wax: The Story of Emily Kempin Spyri* (1993).

SPYRI, Johanna (1827–1901). Swiss writer. Name variations: Joanna. Pronunciation: Spee-REE. Born Johanna Heusser, July 12, 1827, in Hirzel, Switzerland; died July 7, 1901, in Zurich; dau. of Dr. Johann Jakob Heusser and Meta (Schweizer) Heusser; aunt of Emily Kempin Spyri (1853–1901); m. Bernhard Spyri (town clerk), 1852 (died 1884);

children: Bernhard Diethelm Spyri (b. 1852). ❖ Author who changed the course of children's literature with her book *Heidi*, penned 1st stories (1870), at age 43; published 1st story for adults, "A Leaf on Vrony's Grave" (1871); published *Heidi: Her Years of Wandering and Learning* (anonymously, 1880) and *Heidi Makes Use of What She Has Learned* (1st work under own name, 1881), which were combined into one book (early 1880s); also wrote *Red-Letter Stories* (1884), *Rico and Wiseli* (1885), *Uncle Titus* (1886), *Grittli's Children* (1887), *Dorris and Her Mountain Home* (1902), *Moni the Goat Boy* (1906), *Heimatlos* (1912), *Chel* (1913), *The Rose Child* (1916), *Little Miss Grasshopper* (1918), *Little Curly Head: The Pet Lamb* (1919), *Cornelli* (1920), *Toni: The Little Wood-Carver* (1920), *Erick and Sally* (1921), *Maezli* (1921), *Trini: The Little Strawberry Girl* (1922), *Jo: The Little Machinist* (1923), *Vinzi* (1924), *Joerli: The Story of a Swiss Boy* (1924), *Veronica and Other Friends* (1924), *Francesca at Hinterwald* (1925), *Eveli: The Little Singer* (1926), *Eveli and Beni* (1926), *Peppino* (1926) and *Renz and Margritli* (1931), among others. ❖ See also Anna Ulrich, *Recollections of Johanna Spyri's Childhood* (trans. by Helen B. Dole, Crowell, 1925); and *Women in World History*.

SQUIER, Miriam (1836–1914). *See Leslie, Miriam Folline Squier.*

SQUIRE, Rachel (1954–2006). British politician and member of Parliament. Born Rachel Anne Squire, July 13, 1954, in Carshalton, Surrey, England; died Jan 5, 2006; University of Durham, BA in anthropology; m. Allan Lee Mason, 1984. ❖ Representing Labour, elected to House of Commons for Dunfermline West (1992, 1997, 2001, 2005); defended industry and Scottish regiments.

SQUIRES, Catharine (1843–1912). New Zealand church leader. Name variations: Catharine Dewe, Kate Squires. Born Catharine Dewe, July 13, 1843, in Warwickshire, England; died July 15, 1912, in Bluff, Southland, New Zealand; dau. of John Dewe (bookseller) and Eliza Matilda (Woodhead) Dewe; m. John Squires, 1860 (died 1901); children: 1. ❖ Immigrated with family to New Zealand (1848); adopted Brethren faith, holding home prayer meetings and preaching on Sundays; eventually led schism (1894). ❖ See also *Dictionary of New Zealand Biography* (Vol. 1).

SQUIRES, Helena E. (1879–1959). Canadian politician. Name variations: Lady Helena E. Strong Squires. Born Helena E. Strong in 1879 in Little Bay Islands, Newfoundland; died 1959 in Toronto, Canada; dau. of James Strong (supplier to the fishing industry); attended Mount Allison University; m. Richard Squires (later prime minister of Newfoundland), in 1905; children: 7. ❖ Though she was an opponent of women's suffrage, became the 1st woman to campaign for and win a seat in the Newfoundland House of Assembly (1930); was ousted (1932); when Newfoundland officially became a part of Canada (1949), was elected the 1st president of the Liberal Association of Newfoundland.

SQUIRES, Kate (1843–1912). *See Squires, Catharine.*

SRAMKOVA, Iveta (1963—). Czech field-hockey player. Born Oct 1963. ❖ At Moscow Olympics, won a silver medal in team competition (1980).

SRI, Indriyani (1978—). Indonesian weightlifter. Born 1978 in Indonesia. ❖ Won World championships (1996, 1997); won a bronze medal for -48 kg at Sydney Olympics (2000).

SRI DELIMA (1936—). *See Amin, Adibah.*

SRNCOVA, Bozena (1925—). Czech gymnast. Born June 11, 1925. ❖ Won a gold medal at London Olympics (1948) and a bronze medal at Helsinki Olympics (1952), both in team all-around.

SRPKINJA, Milica Stojadinović- (1830–1878). *See Stojadinovic-Srpkinja, Milica.*

ST. *See Saint.*

STAAL, Flossie (1946—). *See Wong-Staal, Flossie.*

STAAL, Mme de (1684–1750). *See Staal de Launay, Madame de.*

STAAL-DELAUNAY, Mme de (1684–1750). *See Staal de Launay, Madame de.*

STAAL DE LAUNAY, Madame de (1684–1750). French writer. Name variations: Madame de Staal; Madame de Staal-Delaunay; Baronne de Staal-Delaunay; Rose Delaunay; Rose Delaunay, Baronne de Staal; Rose Staal de Launay; Marguerite Cordier de Launay. Pronunciation: der-low-NAY der STALL. Born Marguerite-Jeanne Cordier in Paris, France, Aug 30, 1684; died June 15, 1750, in Gennevilliers (Seine) or Sceaux (Seine); 2nd dau. of Cordier (artist) and Rose de Launay Cordier, known as Rose de Launay; m. Baron de Staal, in 1734 or 1735; no children. ❖ Writer whose memoirs and letters furnish a candid view of French high society in the 18th century and the frustrations experienced by a talented woman confronting obstacles of gender and class; began to live at the Convent of Saint-Louis (1691); fell in love with the Marquis de Silly (c. 1700); took employment with the Duchess of Maine (1711); earned welcome notoriety for letter to Fontenelle on the Tétar affair (1713); organized the "Grand Nights of Sceaux" (1714–15); imprisoned in the Bastille as a participant in the Cellamare Conspiracy (1718–20); was in love with the Chevalier de Ménil (1719–c. 1721); after death of Dacier ruined a probable marriage (1722), entered a loveless marriage to Baron de Staal (1734–35); a splendid stylist with a true gift for acute observation, wrote her memoirs (c. 1736–41), which were published 5 years after her death and recognized at once as a classic of French literature. ❖ See also *Mémoires de Madame de Staal-Delaunay* (4 vols.) and *Memoirs of Madame de Staal de Launay* (trans. by Selina Bathurst, 1877); and *Women in World History*.

STABENOW, Debbie (1950—). American politician. Name variations: Deborah Ann Stabenow. Born April 29, 1950, in Gladwin, Michigan; Michigan State University, BS, 1972, MSW, 1975; m. Tom Athans (div.); children: Todd and Michelle. ❖ Was the youngest and 1st woman chair of the Ingham County Commission (1977–78); served as state representative for 12 years (1979–90) and state senator for 4 years (1991–94); lost primary in run for governor (1994); as a Democrat, elected to US House of Representatives (1996); elected to US Senate (2000), the 1st woman from Michigan to fill that post; authored the 1st ban on drilling for oil and gas in the Great Lakes.

STACE, Helen McRae (1850–1926). New Zealand school matron. Name variations: Helen McRae Mowat. Born Helen McRae Mowat, Oct 26, 1850, in Marlborough, New Zealand; died Jan 19, 1926, in Blenheim, New Zealand; dau. of Alexander Mowat (sheepfarmer) and Marjory (McRae) Mowat; m. Henry Joseph Stace (station manager), 1874 (died 1924); children: 2 daughters, 6 sons. ❖ With husband, established Robin Hood Bay Public School, a boarding school for boys, and managed day-to-day activities (1886–1917). ❖ See also *Dictionary of New Zealand Biography* (Vol. 2).

STACEY, Kim (1980—). American skier and snowboarder. Born May 3, 1980, in Concord, NH. ❖ Received 4 AST Halfpipe titles (2002); won bronze medal in Ski Superpipe at X Games Global championships (2003); other placements include 4th in Superpipe at X Games (Winter 2000), 2nd in Halfpipe at Ripzone Invitational (2002), and 3rd in Superpipe (ski) at US Open (2003).

STACHOW, Danuta (1934—). Polish gymnast. Born Danuta Nowak, Aug 22, 1934, in Poland. ❖ At Melbourne Olympics, won a bronze medal in teams all-around, portable apparatus (1956).

STACHOWSKI, Amber (1983—). American water-polo player. Born Mar 14, 1983, in Mission Viejo, CA; attended University of California, Los Angeles. ❖ Won World championship (2003); driver, won a team bronze medal at Athens Olympics (2004).

STACK, Chelle (1973—). American gymnast. Born July 23, 1973, in Philadelphia, PA; trained with Bela Karolyi. ❖ Won a silver medal in all-around and a gold medal in floor exercises at Pan American Games (1991).

STACKER, Brenann (1987—). American rhythmic gymnast. Born Jan 3, 1987, in Chicago, IL. ❖ Won Jr. nationals (2000) and a gold medal in clubs at US nationals (2001).

STACY, Hollis (1954—). American golfer. Born Mar 16, 1954, in Savannah, Georgia; attended Rollins College. ❖ Won USGA Junior Girls' championship (1969–71); won North and South (1970); member of Curtis Cup team (1972); joined LPGA tour (1974); won Lady Tara and Rail Charity Classic (1977); won US Women's Open (1977, 1978, 1984); won Birmingham Classic (1978), Mayflower Classic (1979), and CPC International (1980, 1984); won West Virginia LPGA Classic (1981, 1982), Whirlpool championship (1982), S&H Classic (1982, 1983), Peter Jackson Classic (1983), Mazda Classic of Deer Creek (1985), Crestar-Farm Fresh Classic (1991), WSGT Shopko Great Lakes Classic (2001); designed Blackhawk Golf Course in Austin, Texas.

STAD-DE JONG, Xenia (1922—). Dutch runner. Name variations: Xenia de Jong. Born Xenia Stad, Mar 4, 1922, in Semarang (former Dutch East Indies). ❖ At London Olympics, won a gold medal in 4 x 100-meter relay (1948).

STADE, Frederica von (1945—). *See Von Stade, Frederica.*

STADE, Richardis von (d. 1152). Abbess of Bassum. Died Oct 29, 1152, at Bassum Abbey, Germany; dau. of the noble family of Stade; sister of Hartwig, archbishop of Bremen; never married; no children. ❖ Born into a noble German family and sent to a convent as a child; is best known for her many years at the convents of Disibodenberg and Rupertsberg, where she served as secretary and advisor under abbess, Hildegard of Bingen; translated and edited Hildegard's visionary writings and prepared them for production as manuscripts; became abbess at the convent of Bassum. ❖ See also *Women in World History.*

STAËL, Germaine de (1766–1817). French writer. Name variations: Anne Louise Germaine Necker; Madame de Stael or Staël; Baronne or Baroness de Staël von Holstein; (nickname) Minette. Born in Paris, France, April 22, 1766; died in Paris, July 14, 1817; dau. of Jacques Necker (financier and director general of finance for Louis XVI) and Suzanne (Curchod) Necker (governess); cousin of Albertine Necker de Saussure (1766–1841); m. Eric Magnus, baron de Staël von Holstein (Swedish ambassador to France), Jan 14, 1786; secretly married John Rocca, Oct 10, 1816; children: (1st m.) Gustavine (b. 1787, died young); (with Louis, comte de Narbonne-Lara) Auguste (b. 1790) and Albert (b. 1792); (with Benjamin Constant) Albertine, Duchesse de Broglie (b. 1797); (in secret with John Rocca) Louis Alphonse Rocca (b. 1812). ❖ A precursor of Romanticism and modern literary criticism whose liberalism reflected 18th-century thought and made her an active adversary of Napoleon Bonaparte; while husband was Swedish ambassador to France, established her own salon, attended by a new generation of thinkers whose major interest was politics, a circle that included Thomas Jefferson, the Marquis de Lafayette, and Charles Maurice de Talleyrand-Perigord; after her *Letters on the Writings and Character of Jean-Jacques Rousseau* was published (1788), was recognized as a writer of distinction; present at opening of Estates-General, Versailles (May 5, 1789); father resigned as French finance minister (Sept 3, 1790); published *Sophia, or the Secret Feelings* (Oct 1790); with overthrow of the monarchy (Aug 1792), was arrested but released after an appeal to a political acquaintance; published *Reflections on Peace* (1794), which excoriated Robespierre and the Terror; reopened salon in Paris and strove to influence the course of events (1795); published *On the Influence of the Passions* (1796); met Napoleon Bonaparte (Dec 6, 1797), who became her *bête noire*, while she became an irritating thorn under his imperial crown; published *On Literature* (1800); published *Delphine* (1802) which explored issues such as religion and marriage and divorce as they affect society, especially women; exiled from France (1802–14); published *Corinne or Italy* (1807), a great success; attempted to publish *On Germany* in France, but Napoleon forbade it, and the manuscript and proof pages were seized; instead, published *On Germany* in London (1813); published *Ten Years of Exile* (1813); suffered a stroke in Paris (Feb 21, 1817). ❖ See also J. Christopher Herold, *Mistress to an Age: A Life of Madame de Staël* (Bobbs-Merrill, 1958); Renée Winegarten, *Mme de Staël* (Berg, 1985); M. Gutwerth, *Mme de Staël, Novelist: The Emergence of the Artist as Woman* (U. of Illinois Press, 1978); David Glass Larg, *Madame de Staël: Her Life as Revealed in Her Work, 1766–1800* (trans. by Veronica Lucas, Knopf, 1926); and *Women in World History.*

STAFFORD, Anne (c. 1400–1432). Duchess of Huntington and Exeter. Name variations: Anne Holland; Anne Mortimer; countess of Mar. Born c. 1400; died Sept 20, 1432; dau. of Edmund Stafford, 5th earl of Stafford, and Anne Plantagenet (1383–1438); m. Edmund Mortimer, 5th earl of March, about 1415; m. John Holland (1395–1447), duke of Huntington (r. 1416–1447), duke of Exeter (r. 1443–1447), before Mar 5, 1427; children: Henry Holland, 2nd duke of Exeter; Anne Holland (fl. 1440–1462). ❖ Following her death, John Holland married Beatrice of Portugal (d. 1439), then Anne Montacute (d. 1457).

STAFFORD, Anne (d. 1472). English noblewoman. Died c. April 14, 1472; interred at Lingfield; dau. of Humphrey Stafford, 1st duke of Buckingham, and Anne Neville (d. 1480); m. Aubrey de Vere (son of the 12th earl of Oxford), in April 1460; children: Thomas, Lord Cobham.

STAFFORD, Anne (d. 1480). *See Neville, Anne.*

STAFFORD, Catherine (d. 1419). Countess of Suffolk. Name variations: Catherine de la Pole. Died April 8, 1419; interred at Wingfield Church, Suffolk; dau. of Hugh Stafford (c. 1344–1386), 2nd earl of Stafford (r. 1351–1386), and Philippa Stafford; m. Michael de la Pole (1368–1415), 2nd earl of Suffolk (r. 1385–1415, who died at the siege of Harfleur); children: Michael de la Pole (c. 1395–1415, killed in battle at Agincourt), 3rd earl of Suffolk; William de la Pole (1396–1450, murdered), duke of Suffolk; John de la Pole; Alexander de la Pole; Thomas de la Pole.

STAFFORD, Catherine (d. 1476). Countess of Shrewsbury. Died Dec 26, 1476; dau. of Anne Neville (d. 1480) and Humphrey Stafford, 1st duke of Buckingham, 1st earl of Stafford; m. John Talbot, 3rd earl of Shrewsbury, around 1467; children: George Talbot (b. 1468), 4th earl of Shrewsbury.

STAFFORD, Catherine (fl. 1530). Countess of Westmoreland. Dau. of Eleanor Percy (d. 1530) and Edward Stafford (1478–1521), 3rd duke of Buckingham (executed on May 17, 1521); m. Ralph Neville (1497–1555), 4th earl of Westmoreland (r. 1499–1555); children: Henry Neville, 5th earl of Westmoreland; Dorothy Neville (d. around 1546, who m. John de Vere, 16th earl of Oxford); Margaret Neville (d. 1559, who m. Henry Manners, 2nd earl of Rutland).

STAFFORD, Constance (d. 1474). Countess of Wiltshire. Name variations: Constance Greene. Died Mar 2, 1474; dau. of Margaret Roos and Henry Green; m. John Stafford, 9th earl of Wiltshire (r. 1469–1473), in 1458; children: Edward Stafford (b. 1470), 10th earl of Wiltshire.

STAFFORD, countess of.
 See Audley, Margaret (fl. 1340s).
 See Stafford, Philippa (d. before 1386).
 See Anne Plantagenet (1383–1438).

STAFFORD, Eleanor (d. 1530). *See Percy, Eleanor.*

STAFFORD, Elizabeth (d. 1532). Royal mistress. Name variations: Countess of Essex. Died before May 11, 1532; interred at Boreham, Essex; dau. of Henry Stafford (1455–1483), 2nd duke of Buckingham (r. 1460–1483), and Katherine Woodville (c. 1442–1512); m. Robert Fitzwalter (c. 1483–1542), earl of Essex, on July 23, 1505; children: Henry Radcliffe, 2nd earl of Sussex; George Radcliffe; Humphrey Radcliffe. Following her death, Robert Fitzwalter married Margaret Stanley. ❖ Was mistress of Henry VIII, king of England.

STAFFORD, Elizabeth (1494–1558). Duchess of Norfolk. Born in 1494; died in 1558; dau. of Edward Stafford (1478–1521), 3rd duke of Buckingham (executed on May 17, 1521), and Eleanor Percy (d. 1530); m. Thomas Howard (1473–1554), 3rd duke of Norfolk (r. 1524–1554), on Jan 8, 1512 or 1513; children: Henry Howard (1517–1547), earl of Surrey; Mary Fitzroy (c. 1519–1557); Thomas Howard, Viscount Bindon. Thomas Howard's 1st wife was Anne Howard (1475–1511).

STAFFORD, Jean (1915–1979). American writer. Born in Covina, California, July 1, 1915; died in White Plains, New York, Mar 26, 1979; dau. of John Richard Stafford (writer) and Mary Ethel McKillop; University of Colorado, BA and MA; studied at University of Heidelberg, 1936–37; m. Robert (Cal) Lowell (poet), April 2, 1940 (div. 1948); m. Oliver Jensen (editor at *Life* magazine), Jan 28, 1950 (div. 1953); m. A. J. Liebling (writer), April 3, 1959 (died 1963); no children. ❖ Pulitzer Prize-winning novelist, short-story writer, essayist, and journalist; taught at Stephens College (1937–38); had 1st story published (1939); published 1st novel *Boston Adventure*, which was an immediate success (1944); with her marriage failing, signed herself into Payne Whitney Psychiatric Clinic in New York Hospital (1946); began a decade-long association with *The New Yorker* (1947); wrote *The Catherine Wheel*; published 1st collection of short stories, *Children Are Bored on Sunday*, to great success (1953); received O. Henry award for "In the Zoo" (1955); named a fellow at the Center for Advanced Studies, Wesleyan University (1964–65); released collection *Bad Stories*; published her only nonfiction work, *A Mother in History*; taught at Columbia University (1967–68); received Pulitzer Prize for *Collected Stories* (1970); suffered a stroke (1976). Elected to National Academy of Arts and Letters (1970). ❖ See also Ann Hulbert, *The Interior Castle: The Art and Life of Jean Stafford* (Knopf, 1992); Charlotte Margolis Goodman, *Jean Stafford: The Savage Heart* (U. of Texas Press, 1990); David Roberts, *Jean Stafford* (Little, Brown, 1988); and *Women in World History.*

STAFFORD, Jo (1920—). American pop singer. Name variations: Cinderella G. Stump and Darlene Edwards. Born Jo Elizabeth Stafford, Nov 12, 1920, in Coalinga, CA; dau. of Grover Cleveland Stafford (oilman) and Anna (York) Stafford (highly acclaimed 5-string banjoist); sister of Christina and Pauline Stafford (singers); m. John Huddleston (div.); m. Paul Weston (arranger-conductor), 1952. ❖ Began career on radio, singing with her sisters; joined 7 male singers in a short-lived group called the Pied Pipers, which were hired by Tommy Dorsey (1938); joined 3 other singers (also called the Pied Pipers) and continued working with Dorsey for the next 3 years; on her own, recorded "I'll Never Smile Again" with Frank Sinatra; with the Pipers, left Dorsey (1942) and worked successfully on various radio shows, including "Your Hit Parade"; went solo (1944) and was signed by Johnny Mercer for his radio show and to record with his Capitol Records; quickly became one of the most popular female singers in the country; launched her own radio series, "Chesterfield Supper Club" (1946); launched her own tv series, "The Jo Stafford Show" (1954); was the 1st recording artist to sell 25 million records, with such hits as "You Belong to Me," "Whispering Hope" (with Gordon MacRae), "Shrimp Boats," "Make Love to Me" and "Jambalaya"; also moonlighted as Cinderella G. Stump with "Timtayshun," which sold 1 million copies, a hillbilly version of the 1933 hit "Temptation"; with husband Paul Weston as Jonathan Edwards, also recorded 4 albums as Darlene Edwards, parodying all the mediocre pianists and lounge singers they had encountered in their travels and winning a Grammy with *Jonathan and Darlene in Paris.* Was one of the few performers to have 3 plaques on Hollywood's Boulevard of the Stars: for radio, tv, and recordings. ❖ See also *Women in World History.*

STAFFORD, Margaret (d. 1396). Countess of Westmoreland. Name variations: Margaret Neville; Margaret de Stafford. Born before 1364; died June 9, 1396; dau. of Philippa Stafford (d. before 1386) and Hugh Stafford, 2nd earl of Stafford; m. Ralph Neville (b. 1363), 1st earl of Westmoreland; children: John Neville (b. 1387); Ralph Neville (d. 1457); Anne Neville (who m. Gilbert de Umfreville, 3rd baron of Umfreville); Margaret Neville (d. 1464, who m. Richard Scrope, 3rd Lord Scrope). ❖ See also *Women in World History.*

STAFFORD, Mary (d. 1543). See *Boleyn, Mary.*

STAFFORD, Mary (1872–1932). See *Mayor, Flora M.*

STAFFORD, Philippa (d. before 1386). Countess of Stafford. Name variations: Philippa Beauchamp; Philippe Beauchamp. Died before April 6, 1386; dau. of Thomas Beauchamp (b. 1313), 3rd earl of Warwick (some sources cite 11th earl of Warwick), and Catherine Mortimer (c. 1313–1369); m. Hugh Stafford, 2nd earl of Stafford, on Mar 1, 1350; children: Ralph Stafford, Lord Stafford; Margaret Stafford (d. 1396, who m. Ralph Neville, 1st earl of Westmoreland); Joan Stafford (d. 1442, who m. Thomas Holland, 3rd earl of Kent); Thomas Stafford (c. 1368–1392), 3rd earl of Stafford; William Stafford (b. 1375); Catherine Stafford (d. 1419, who m. Michael de la Pole, 2nd earl of Suffolk); Edmund Stafford (1378–1403), 5th earl of Stafford.

STAGECOACH MARY (c. 1832–1914). See *Fields, Mary.*

STAGEL, Elsbeth (c. 1300–c. 1366). Swiss nun and writer. Born c. 1300 in Switzerland; died c. 1366. ❖ Wrote history of Dominican convent of Töss, *Das Leben der Schwestern zu Töss.*

STAHL, Lesley (1941—). American television journalist. Born Dec 16, 1941, in Lynn, MA; dau. of Louis (paint salesman) and Dolly Stahl; graduate of Wheaton College, 1963; m. Aaron Latham (writer), 1977; children: daughter Taylor. ❖ Began career at NBC News in NY as a writer and researcher (1967); took a job as reporter with CBS in Washington (1972), and came to prominence while covering Watergate; named CBS White House correspondent (1978); was co-anchor of "The CBS Morning News" (1977–79); hosted "Face the Nation" (1983–91); anchored "America Tonight" (1990); became correspondent on "60 Minutes" (1991); was also host of "48 Hours" (2002–04). ❖ See also memoir, *Reporting Live* (1999).

STAHL, Michelle (1966—). See *Akers, Michelle.*

STAHL, Rose (1870–1955). Canadian-born stage star. Born Oct 29, 1870, in Montreal, Canada; died July 16, 1955, in Queens, LI, NY; m. William Bonelli (actor). ❖ Made 1st stage appearance in Philadelphia; played leads for many stock companies; gained prominence in the role of Patricia O'Brien in a sketch later lengthened into the 4-act play *The Chorus Lady,* which she performed 1,676 times (1904–11); starred in other plays, including *Maggie Pepper, A Perfect Lady, Moonlight Mary,*

Our Mrs. McChesney and *Pack Up Your Troubles;* toured with the all-star cast of *Out There* during WWI; retired (1919).

STAHL-IENCIC, Ecaterina (1946—). Romanian fencer. Name variations: Ecaterina Iencic. Born July 31, 1946, in Romania. ❖ Won a bronze medal at Mexico City Olympics (1968) and a bronze medal at Munich Olympics (1972), both in team foil.

STAHR-LEWALD, Fanny (1811–1889). See *Lewald, Fanny.*

STAICULESCU, Doina (1967—). Romanian rhythmic gymnast. Born Dec 7, 1967, in Romania. ❖ At Los Angeles Olympics, won a silver medal in rhythmic gymnastics, all-around (1984).

STALEY, Dawn (1970—). African-American basketball player. Born May 4, 1970, in Philadelphia, PA; graduate of University of Virginia, 1992. ❖ Guard; won a team gold medal at Atlanta Olympics (1996), Sydney Olympics (2000) and Athens Olympics (2004); played with the American Basketball League's Philadelphia Rage (1996–97); selected to play for the Charlotte Sting in WNBA 1st-round draft (1999); became 1st woman in US pro-basketball history to record 1,000 assists (2001). Named most outstanding player of (NCAA) Final Four playoffs (1991); named Kodak All-American (thrice) and Naismith Player of the Year (twice). ❖ See also *Women in World History.*

STALIN, Nadezhda (1901–1932). See *Alliluyeva-Stalin, Nadezhda.*

STALIN, Svetlana (b. 1926). See *Alliluyeva, Svetlana.*

STALLER, Ilona (1951—). See *Cicciolina.*

STALLMAIER, Veronika (1966—). Austrian Alpine skier. Name variations: Veronika Wallinger or Stallmaier Wallinger. Born July 30, 1966, in St. Kolomann, Austria. ❖ Placed 10th in downhill at Sarajevo Olympics (1984); won a bronze medal for downhill at Albertville Olympics (1992).

STALMAN, Ria (1951—). Dutch track-and-field athlete. Born Dec 11, 1951. ❖ At Los Angeles Olympics, won a gold medal in discus throw (1984).

STAM-BEESE, Charlotte (1903–1988). See *Beese, Lotte.*

STAMMERS, Kay (1914–2005). English tennis player. Name variations: Katherine Menzies; Kay Stammers Menzies; Kay Bullitt. Born Kay Stammers, April 3, 1914, in St. Albans, Hertsfordshire, England; died Dec 23, 2005, m. Michael Menzies, 1939 (div. 1975); m. Thomas W. Bullitt (of Louisville, KY, died 1991). ❖ Was the 1st 17-year-old to compete at Wimbledon (1931); with Freda James, won Wimbledon doubles championships (1935, 1936); represented Great Britain against US in Wightman Cup for 5 years (1934–39), beating such players as Helen Hull Jacobs and Alice Marble; won the Surrey hard-court singles championship (1932–34, 1936); was the 1st British player to beat Helen Newington Wills in 11 years (1935).

STAMP, Jane Tregunno (1962—). See *Tregunno, Jane.*

STAMP TAYLOR, Edith (1904–1946). English stage and screen actress and singer. Name variations: Enid Stamp-Taylor. Born June 12, 1904, in Monkseaton, England; died Jan 13, 1946, in London from a fall; dau. of Agnes (Pagan) and George Stamp Taylor; m. Sydney Colton (div.). ❖ Made stage debut in London in the chorus of *A to Z* (1922), followed by *Madame Pompadour, Midnight Follies, R. S. V. P., The Cocoanuts, Wonder Bar, Paulette* and *The Voice;* films include *Blind Man's Bluff, House Broken, Take a Change, Underneath the Arches, Feather Your Nest, Blondes for Danger, Stepping Toes, Old Iron, Action for Slander, Climbing High, Hatter's Castle* and *The Lambeth Walk.*

STAMPA, Gaspara (1523–1554). Italian poet. Born 1523 in Padua, Italy; died April 23, 1554, in Venice, possibly a suicide; dau. of Bartolomeo Stampa (gold merchant, died 1530) and Cecilia Stampa; sister of Baldassare Stampa and Cassandra Stampa (singer); studied classics, history, philosophy, music, Latin, and Greek; never married; no children. ❖ Widely regarded as the greatest Italian woman poet, was born at the height of the Italian Renaissance; when young, sang, played music, and recited poetry for the distinguished scholars and artists who gathered at the family home and was considered the most talented of her talented siblings; underwent a spiritual crisis on the death of her beloved brother (1544) and withdrew from social activities; in 1548, at height of fame, fell in love with Collatino di Collalto, count of Treviso; had an affair, immortalized in the majority of her surviving poems, which lasted off and on for 3 years; became a poet of considerable originality and eloquence, praising her lover but also expressing her physical passion and the emotional turmoil his inconstancy caused her; eventually fell in love again, with the wealthy Venetian patrician Bartolomeo Zen, a far more devoted lover than the half-hearted Collalto, and they remained together for 2 years; suffering from ill health, moved to Florence to regain strength (1553); returned to Venice (April 1554), dying from an undiagnosed illness 2 weeks later; sister Cassandra edited the 1st edition of Stampa's sonnets, published as *Rime d'amore* (Love Sonnets). ❖ See also Fiora Bassanese, *Gaspara Stampa* (Twayne, 1982); Frank Warnke, *Three Women Poets: Renaissance and Baroque* (Associated U. Presses, 1987); and *Women in World History.*

STANCIU, Anisoara (1962—). Romanian track-and-field athlete. Name variations: Anisoara Stanciu-Cusmir. Born June 29, 1962, in Romania. ❖ At Los Angeles Olympics, won a gold medal in the long jump (1984).

STANFIELD, Agnes (1836–1874). *See Clare, Ada.*

STANFORD, Jane (1828–1905). American philanthropist. Name variations: Mrs. Leland Stanford. Born Jane Lathrop, Aug 25, 1828, in Albany, New York; died of a heart attack on Feb 28, 1905, in Honolulu, Hawaii, while on a cruise (though some suspect strychnine poisoning); dau. of Dyer Lathrop (businessman) and Jane Ann (Shields) Lathrop; educated at Albany, New York, Female Academy, 1840–41; m. Leland Stanford (attorney and governor of California), 1850 (died 1893); children: Leland Stanford Jr. (1868–1884). ❖ Co-founder of Stanford University, moved from New York to Sacramento, where husband was elected governor of California (1861); after son's death (1884), devoted the family fortune to the establishment of Stanford University in Palo Alto; after husband's death (1893), was given a great deal of power in determining matters regarding the planning and growth of the campus as well as in the choice of curriculum and faculty at the college; relinquished her powers under a trusteeship (1903). ❖ See also Robert Cutler, *The Mysterious Death of Jane Stanford* (Stanford U. Press, 2003); and *Women in World History.*

STANFORD, Mrs. Leland (1828–1905). *See Stanford, Jane.*

STANG, Dorothy (1931–2005). American nun and activist. Name variations: Sister Dorothy Stang. Born June 7, 1931, in Dayton, Ohio; murdered Feb 14, 2005, near Anapu, Brazil. ❖ Joined Sisters of Notre Dame de Namur (1948); took her vows (1956); sent to Brazil as a missionary (1966); began working for the CPT in the Amazon, the Roman Catholic church's Pastoral Land commission (1982); became a naturalized Brazilian; testified in Brazilia about deforestation, naming logging companies who were invading state areas (2004); was shot by 2 gunmen on an Amazon road, as she walked to a meeting of poor farmers. Thousands attended her funeral.

STANGELAND, Karin Michaëlis (1872–1950). *See Michaëlis, Karin.*

STANHOPE, Anne (1497–1587). English duchess. Name variations: Duchess of Somerset. Born in 1497; died in 1587; m. Edward Seymour, duke of Somerset (the Lord Protector and brother of Jane Seymour); children: Edward Seymour (1st earl of Hertford), Anne Seymour (c. 1532–1587), Margaret Seymour, Jane Seymour (niece of queen Jane Seymour (1541–1560), Mary Seymour, Katherine Seymour, & Elizabeth Seymour.

STANHOPE, Hester (1776–1839). English traveler and humanitarian. Name variations: Lady Hester Stanhope. Born Hester Lucy Stanhope, Mar 12, 1776, at Chevening, Kent, England; died at Djoun, Lebanon, June 23, 1839; dau. of Charles, Viscount Mahon, later 3rd earl Stanhope (radical politician) and Hester Pitt, Lady Mahon (dau. of William Pitt the Elder); niece of William Pitt the Younger (prime minister, died 1806); never married; no children. ❖ Aristocratic traveler, who pioneered Western access to remote areas of the Middle East and later settled in the region, performing humanitarian services and acquiring a reputation for wisdom and sanctity; lived with uncle while he was prime minister and served as his host (1804–06); was the confidante of leading politicians, soldiers, and diplomats who admired her for her wit, intelligence and candor; suffered the deaths of her uncle (1806), as well as her favorite half-brother and a soldier she had befriended, both killed at the battle of Corunna (1809); embarked on a foreign tour, initially with no clear destination in mind, though she would never return to England (1810); lived in Constantinople and was shipwrecked off the island of Rhodes (1811); embarked for Egypt and adopted the loose-fitting costume of the Turkish male as her mode of attire; journeyed to Syria, where she made a dramatic entry into Damascus, still something of a forbidden city for Europeans; ignoring the danger, became 1st European woman to enter Syrian city of Palmyra (1813); settled in Lebanon (1820s), becoming

object of a romantic cult; her career foreshadowed that of T. E. Lawrence (Lawrence of Arabia), whose daring exploits alongside his Arab allies in WWI brought him the kind of fleeting fame that Stanhope had enjoyed over 100 years before. ❖ See also Ian Bruce, *The Nun of Lebanon: The Love Affair of Lady Hester Stanhope and Michael Bruce* (Collins, 1951); Duchess of Cleveland, *The Life and Letters of Lady Hester Stanhope* (Murray, 1914); Charles Lewis Meryon, *Memoirs of the Lady Hester Stanhope as related by Herself in Conversation with Her Physician* (Colburn, 1846); Virginia Childs, *Lady Hester Stanhope: Queen of the Desert* (Weidenfeld & Nicolson, 1990); Joan Haslip, *Lady Hester Stanhope: A Biography* (Cobden Sanderson, 1934); and *Women in World History.*

STANHOPE, Lady (d. 1667). *See Kirkhoven, Catherine.*

STANISLAVSKI, Maria Lilina (b. around 1870). Russian actress. Name variations: Maria Petrovna Perevozchikova; Maria Lilina Perevozchikova or Perevoshchikova; Mme Stanislavsky; Maria Stanislavski or Stanislavskaya; acted under the name Maria Lilina. Born Maria Lilina Petrovna Perevostchikova, c. 1870; dau. of Petrov Perevostchikov (well-known lawyer); m. Constantin Stanislavski (1863–1938, actor, director, and teacher of acting), July 5, 1889; children: Xenia (died in infancy); Kira Stanislavski; Igor Stanislavski. ❖ Met Constantin Stanislavski when she made her acting debut with him in a charity performance of *Spoiled Darling* (1888); at his invitation, joined his Society of Art and Literature; appeared with him in the society's production of Schiller's *Kabale and Liebe*; married (1889); when not pregnant, took to the stage whenever possible and may have been involved with the design elements of his productions; also knew English and frequently interpreted for him; remained a member of the company of the Moscow Art Theater, though Olga Knipper-Chekova emerged as the company's leading actress; in later years, as husband became famous, protected him from an eager public and helped manage his busy schedule. ❖ See also *Women in World History.*

STANITSKII, N. (c. 1819–1893). *See Panaeva, Avdotia.*

STANKOWITCH, Countess of. *See La Grange, Anna de (1825–1905).*

STANLEY, Charlotte (1599–1664). French heroine. Name variations: Charlotte de la Trémoille; countess of Derby. Born Charlotte de la Trémoille in 1599; died 1664; dau. of Duc de Thouars; granddau. of William the Silent (1533–1584), prince of Orange; m. James Stanley, 7th earl of Derby (known as Lord Strange until 1642). ❖ French Huguenot and Royalist heroine during the English Civil Wars, was said to have been a better soldier than husband; left in charge of Lathom House (1643), refused to surrender the stronghold to local Parliamentary forces, which began a bombardment; held out for 3 months until relieved by Royalist forces; was notorious in 17th-century England. ❖ See also *Women in World History.*

STANLEY, Kim (1925–2001). American actress. Born Patricia Kimberley Reid, Feb 11, 1925, in Tularosa, New Mexico; died Aug 20, 2001, in Santa Fe, NM; dau. of J. T. Reid (professor of philosophy) and Ann (Miller) Reid (painter and interior decorator); University of Texas, BA in psychology, 1945; studied acting at Pasadena Playhouse, 1945–46, and Actors Studio; m. Bruce Franklin Hall (actor), 1948 (div.); m. Curt Conway (actor-director, div. 1956); m. Alfred Ryder (actor-director), Aug 1958; children: (2nd m.) 1 daughter, 1 son; (3rd m.) 1 daughter. ❖ A product of the Actors Studio and the Method, made New York debut in *The Dog Beneath the Skin* (1948), by Auden and Isherwood; subsequently appeared in *him* by e.e. cummings and *Yes Is For a Very Young Man* by Gertrude Stein; made Broadway debut replacing Julie Harris in *Montserrat* (1949); also appeared in *The House of Bernarda Alba* and *The Chase,* then won the Drama Critics' Award for Best Supporting Actress for *Picnic* (1953); following another acclaimed performance in *The Traveling Lady,* appeared as Cherie in *Bus Stop* (1955), for which she received the Donaldson Award and New York Drama Critics Award as Best Actress; made triumphant London debut as Maggie in *Cat on a Hot Tin Roof* (1958); appeared in 5 films during career, winning Academy Award nominations for 3 of them: *The Goddess* (1958), *Seance on a Wet Afternoon* (1964) and *Frances* (1982); preferred tv, however, and by 1955 had appeared in some 75 different roles; received an Emmy for performance in "A Cardinal Act of Mercy," an episode on "Ben Casey" (1963); left the stage to teach drama at College of Santa Fe, New Mexico (1966), after which she made only occasional appearances on screen and tv. ❖ See also *Women in World History.*

STANLEY, Louise (1883–1954). American home economist and federal administrator. Born June 8, 1883, in Nashville, Tennessee; died July 15, 1954, in Washington, DC; dau. of Gustavus Stanley and Eliza (Winston) Stanley; Peabody College at University of Nashville, AB, 1903; University of Chicago, BEd, 1906; Columbia University, AM, 1907; Yale University, PhD, 1911; never married; children: (adopted) 1 daughter. ❖ Joined staff of home economics department at University of Missouri (1907), and served as department chair (1917–23); became known both academically and professionally for her efforts to improve the quality of life in American homes, particularly with regard to nutrition of the poor; was selected the 1st female bureau chief of US Department of Agriculture (1923); developed diet plans, compiled data to be used in the base-year consumer price index, and encouraged the standardization of clothing sizes; directed nutritional education programs throughout Latin America; retired from government service (1953). ❖ See also *Women in World History.*

STANLEY, Margaret (fl. 16th c.). Countess of Essex. Name variations: Margaret Radcliffe. Dau. of Anne Hastings (c. 1487–?) and Thomas Stanley, 2nd earl of Derby; interred at St. Lawrences Pountney, London; m. Robert Fitzwalter Radcliffe, earl of Essex, in 1532; children: Sir John Radcliffe.

STANLEY, Martha M. (1867–1950). American playwright. Born Nov 20, 1867, in Cape Cod, MA; died Jan 15, 1950, in Los Angeles, CA. ❖ With Adelaide Matthews, co-wrote such plays as *Nightie Night* (1919), *Puppy Love* (1927), *The Wasp's Nest* (1927), *Scrambled Wives, The Teaser,* and *Let and Sub-Let*; also wrote *My Son* (filmed in 1925).

STANLEY, Mary (1919–1980). New Zealand poet. Born 1919 in New Zealand; died 1980 in New Zealand; m. 2nd husband Kendrick Smithyman (poet). ❖ Published the collection *Starveling Year and Other Poems* (1950). Won the Jessie Mackay Memorial Award (1945).

STANLEY, Rosalind Frances (1845–1921). *See Howard, Rosalind Frances.*

STANLEY, Una Isabel (1890–1954). *See Carter, Una Isabel.*

STANLEY, Winifred Claire (1909–1996). American attorney and politician. Born Winifred Claire Stanley, Aug 14, 1909, in the Mount Hope section of the Bronx, New York; died Feb 29, 1996, in Kenmore, New York; dau. of John Francis Stanley and Mary (Gill) Stanley; University of Buffalo, BA, magna cum laude, 1930, LLB, 1933, JD, 1933; never married. ❖ One of four women to graduate from University of Buffalo's law school (1933), was honored with the Edward Thompson award for the highest scholastic average over a 3-year period; admitted to Bar of State of New York (1934), practiced law in Buffalo for 4 years before becoming 1st woman to be appointed as Erie County's assistant district attorney (1938); successfully ran for US House of Representatives on Republican ticket (1942); serving in Congress (1943–45) in an at-large seat that was eliminated (1945), voted along the lines of fellow Republicans against several of the New Deal policies; served as counsel to New York State Employee's Retirement System (1945–55); was assistant attorney general for state of New York (1955–79). ❖ See also *Women in World History.*

STANNARD, Mrs. Arthur (1856–1911). *See Winter, John Strange.*

STANNARD, Henrietta (1856–1911). *See Winter, John Strange.*

STANNUS, Edris (1898–2001). *See de Valois, Ninette.*

STANSFIELD, Grace (1914–). *See Walsh, Kay.*

STANSFIELD, Lisa (1966–). English rhythm-and-blues singer. Born April 11, 1966, in Rochdale, England; m. Ian Devaney (musician). ❖ Began singing in early teens; hosted British children's tv program, *Razzamatazz* (early 1980s); formed and was lead singer for the group Blue Zone (1983), releasing album, *Big Thing* (1988), as well as several singles, including "Jackie" (1988), which reached US charts; began solo career (1989), generating international hit with debut album, *Affection* (1989), which included singles "This Is the Right Time," "All Around the World" and "You Can't Deny It"; won Best British Female Artist at BRIT Awards (1991); released album, *Real Love* (1991), which included moderately successful singles, "Change," "All Woman," and "A Little More Love"; other albums include *Lisa Stansfield* (1997), *Face Up* (2001) and *Biography* (2003); appeared in film *Swing* (1999), and sang several songs for soundtrack, including "Mack the Knife."

STANTON, Elizabeth Cady (1815–1902). American writer and suffragist. Name variations: "Cady." Born Nov 12, 1815, at Johnstown, New York; died Oct 26, 1902, in New York, NY; dau. of Daniel Cady (associate justice of New York Supreme Court) and Margaret (Livingston) Cady; attended Emma Willard's Troy Female Seminary, 1831–33; m. Henry Stanton (abolitionist and lawyer), May 1, 1840; children: (2 daughters, 5 sons), including Daniel Cady Stanton (b. 1842) and Harriot Stanton Blatch (1856–1940). ❖ Women's rights activist, journalist, reformer, polemicist, and historian, co-convener of the 1848 Seneca Falls Convention, whose lifelong efforts on behalf of women's rights won her worldwide admiration; attended World Anti-Slavery convention in England (1840), where she met Lucretia Mott; collaborated with Mott in calling 1st women's rights convention at Seneca Falls, NY (1848); teamed up with Susan B. Anthony in what would prove a lifelong friendship and women's rights partnership (1851); co-founded and edited *The Revolution,* a women's rights newspaper, with Anthony (1868–70); co-founded and led National Woman Suffrage Association (1869–90); served as president of National American Woman Suffrage Association (1890–92); co-wrote and edited 3-vols. of *History of Woman Suffrage* (1881–86); wrote the highly controversial *The Woman's Bible* (1895), which stirred up a hornet's nest and marked the end of her association with the organized suffrage movement. ❖ See also autobiography, *Eighty Years and More: Reminiscences, 1815–1897* (1898); *The Selected Papers of Elizabeth Cady Stanton and Susan B. Anthony* (Rutgers U. Press, 1997); Ann D. Gordon, ed. *The Selected Papers of Elizabeth Cady Stanton and Susan B. Anthony: Vol. 1: In the School of Anti-Slavery, 1840–1866* (Rutgers U. Press, 1996); Ellen Carol DuBois, ed. *The Elizabeth Cady Stanton-Susan B. Anthony Reader: Correspondence, Writings, Speeches* (rev. ed., Northeastern U. Press, 1992); Elisabeth Griffith, *In Her Own Right: The Life of Elizabeth Cady Stanton* (Oxford U. Press, 1984); Alma Lutz, *Created Equal: A Biography of Elizabeth Cady Stanton, 1815–1902* (Day, 1940); Theodore Stanton and Harriot Stanton Blatch, eds. *Elizabeth Cady Stanton as Revealed in Her Letters, Diary and Reminiscences* (Harper, 1922); and *Women in World History.*

STANTON, Nora (1883–1971). *See Barney, Nora.*

STANULET, Mihaela (1966–). Romanian gymnast. Born July 16, 1966, in Sibiu, Romania. ❖ Won Balkan championships (1982); won a silver medal in team all-around at World championships and a bronze medal in balance beam at European championships (1983); at Romanian International, placed 3rd in indiv. all-around (1983, 1984); at Los Angeles Olympics, won a gold medal in team all-around (1984).

STANWOOD, Cordelia (1865–1958). American ornithologist. Born Cordelia Stanwood, 1865, in Ellsworth, Maine; died 1958 in Maine; educated at a New England teachers' college; never married; no children. ❖ Fascinated by birds, began taking notes and photographs (1906); published many articles in *Bird Lore,* attracting the attention of other ornithologists; her meticulous notes and over 900 photographs served as a major contribution to ongoing studies of North American bird life; family estate in Maine later became the Stanwood Wildlife Sanctuary. ❖ See also *Women in World History.*

STANWYCK, Barbara (1907–1990). American actress. Born Ruby Katharine Stevens in Brooklyn, NY, July 16, 1907; died Jan 20, 1990, in Santa Monica, California; dau. of Byron Stevens (construction worker) and Catherine (McGee) Stevens; m. Frank Fay (song-and-dance man), Aug 26, 1928 (div. Feb 1936); m. Robert Taylor (actor), May 14, 1939 (div. Feb 1952); children: (adopted) son Dion Fay. ❖ Actress who spent 55 years in front of the camera playing saucy dames, was performing in the chorus of Ziegfeld Follies by age 15 (1922); became an experienced hoofer, dancing the Black Bottom in *George White's Scandals of 1926*; changed name to Barbara Stanwyck and landed part in 1st straight play, *The Noose* (1926); made film debut with *Broadway Nights,* a silent with sound effects (1927); had Broadway breakthrough in *Burlesque* (1927); made sound film breakthrough with Frank Capra's *Ladies of Leisure* (1930); made movie after movie (1930s), including *So Big, The Bitter Tea of General Yen, Ladies They Talk About, Gambling Lady, The Secret Bride, The Woman in Red* and *A Lost Lady*; nominated for Academy Award as Best Actress for *Stella Dallas* (1937); appeared in 3 successful light comedies, *The Lady Eve, Meet John Doe* (both 1941) and *Ball of Fire* (1942), for which she was nominated for Academy Award; continued making comedies, notably *Lady of Burlesque*; had another career shift with *Double Indemnity* (1944), for which she received Oscar nomination for Best Actress; appeared in *Sorry, Wrong Number* (1948), which brought her 4th Oscar nomination; turned to tv for "The Barbara Stanwyck Show" (1960) and played the matriarch in "The Big Valley" (1965–69), appearing in 105 of the 112 episodes; also appeared in "Dynasty II: The Colbys" (1985) and miniseries "The Thorn Birds" (1982); other films include *Annie Oakley* (1935), *A Message to Garcia* (1936), *The Plough and the Stars* (1937), *The Mad Miss Minton* (1938), *Golden Boy* (1939), *Remember the Night* (1940), *Hollywood Canteen* (1944), *Christmas in Connecticut* (1945), *The Strange Love of Martha Ivers* (1946), *The Two Mrs. Carrolls* (1947), *B. F.'s Daughter* (1948), *The File on Thelma Jordan* (1950), *Clash by Night* (1952), *Jeopardy* (1953), *Titanic* (1953), *Cattle Queen of Montana* (1955) and *Walk on the Wild Side* (1962). Awarded honorary Oscar (1982) and American Film Institute's Lifetime Achievement Award (1986). ❖ See also Axel Madsen, *Stanwyck* (HarperCollins, 1994); and *Women in World History*.

STAPLE SINGERS, The.
See Staples, Cleo.
See Staples, Mavis.
See Staples, Pervis.
See Staples, Yvonne.

STAPLES, Cleo (1934—). African-American singer. Name variations: The Staple Singers, The Staples. Born 1934 in Mississippi; dau. of Roebuck "Pops" Staples (singer) and Oceola Staples (singer); sister of Mavis, Yvonne, and Pervis Staples (all singers). ❖ With family, began singing at early age and recorded gospel, then pop music, and appeared in documentaries, *Soul to Soul* (1971), *Wattstax* (1973) and *The Last Waltz* (1978); found success with album, *Bealtitude: Respect Yourself* (1972); hits included "Respect Yourself" and "I'll Take You There," both of which went gold, and "If You're Ready (Come Go With Me)," which became #1 R&B hit (1973); had number 1 R&B and pop hit with title track from film, *Let's Do It Again*, which also contained their hit, "New Orleans" (1974); with group, adopted name The Staples and released Top-20 singles, "Love Me, Love Me, Love Me" (1976) and "Unlock Your Mind" (1978); other albums include *Turning Point* (1984), *Freedom Highway* (1991), and *Uncloudy Day* (2004). Inducted into Rock and Roll Hall of Fame (1999).

STAPLES, Mavis (1940—). African-American singer. Name variations: The Staple Singers, The Staples. Born 1940 in Chicago, IL; dau. of Roebuck "Pops" Staples (singer) and Oceola Staples (singer); sister of Cleo, Yvonne and Pervis Staples (all singers). ❖ Sang with family on album *Bealtitude: Respect Yourself* (1972); had such hits as "Respect Yourself," "I'll Take You There" and "If You're Ready (Come Go With Me)" (1973); also had hit with title track from film, *Let's Do It Again*, and "New Orleans" (1974); with group, adopted name The Staples and released Top-20 singles, "Love Me, Love Me, Love Me" (1976) and "Unlock Your Mind" (1978); released several solo albums, including *Only for the Lonely* (1976), *Time Waits for No One* (1984), and *Spirituals and Gospel: Dedicated to Mahalia Jackson* (with Lucky Peterson, 1996); performed with Prince, Aretha Franklin, and Ray Charles, among others. Inducted into Rock and Roll Hall of Fame (1999).

STAPLES, Yvonne (1939—). African-American singer. Name variations: The Staple Singers, The Staples. Born 1939 in Chicago, IL; dau. of Roebuck "Pops" Staples (singer) and Oceola Staples (singer); sister of Cleo, Mavis and Pervis Staples (all singers). ❖ With family, sang gospel and pop in early years; appeared in documentaries, *Soul to Soul* (1971), *Wattstax* (1973), and *The Last Waltz* (1978); had success with album *Bealtitude: Respect Yourself* (1972); had hit singles with "Respect Yourself," "I'll Take You There," "If You're Ready (Come Go With Me)," "Let's Do It Again" and "New Orleans"; with group, adopted name The Staples and released Top-20 singles, "Love Me, Love Me, Love Me" (1976) and "Unlock Your Mind" (1978). Inducted into Rock and Roll Hall of Fame (1999).

STAPLES-BROWNE, Makereti (1873–1930). *See Papakura, Makereti.*

STAPLETON, Maureen (1925–2006). American actress. Born Lois Maureen Stapleton in Troy, New York, June 21, 1925; died Mar 13, 2006, in Lenox, Massachusetts; m. Max Allentuck (producer), 1949 (div. 1959); m. David Rayfiel (playwright), May 1965 (div.); children: (1st m.) Cathy Allentuck; Danny Allentuck. ❖ Emmy, Oscar, and Tony winner, who slipped easily between drama and comedy in a career that spanned almost 5 decades, made NY debut as Sarah Tansey in *The Playboy of the Western World* (1946); became charter member of Actors Studio; had breakthrough role as Serafina in Tennessee Williams' *The Rose Tattoo* (1951), for which she won Tony Award as Best Actress; following appearances in *The Emperor's Clothes*, *The Crucible*, and *The Sea Gull* (1953–54), created roles in 2 additional plays by Williams: Flora in *Twenty-Seven Wagons Full of Cotton* and Lady Torrance in *Orpheus Descending*; appeared as Carrie in *Toys in the Attic* (1960) and Georgie Elgin in *The Country Girl* (1972); launched film career with an Oscar

nomination for *Lonelyhearts* (1959), as well as for her work in *Airport* (1970) and *Interiors* (1978); won Oscar for portrayal of Emma Goldman in *Reds* (1981); on tv, won Sullivan Award for performance as Sadie Burke in *All the King's Men* (1958) and Emmy for *Save Me a Place at Forest Lawn* (1967); had 3 roles in Neil Simon's comedy *Plaza Suite* (1970) and appeared as Evy Meara in his *The Gingerbread Lady*; appeared in *The Glass Menagerie* (1975); other films include *The Fugitive Kind* (1960), *Bye Bye Birdie* (1963), *Plaza Suite* (1971), *The Runner Stumbles* (1979), *The Fan* (1981), *Cocoon* (1985), *The Money Pit* (1986), *Heartburn* (1986), *Nuts* (1987), *Cocoon: The Return* (1988) and *Passed Away* (1992). ❖ See also autobiography (with Jane Scovell) *A Hell of a Life?* (1995); and *Women in World History*.

STAPLETON, Ruth Carter (1929–1983). American evangelist and faith healer. Name variations: Ruth Carter. Born Ruth Carter, Aug 7, 1929, in Archery, Georgia; died Sept 26, 1983, in Hope Mills, North Carolina; dau. of Earl Carter and Lillian (Gordy) Carter; sister of Jimmy Carter (president of US); University of North Carolina, MA in English; m. Robert Stapleton (veterinarian), Nov 14, 1948; children: Lynn, Scott, Patti, and Michael. ❖ Popular Christian evangelist, suffered from depression for years; after undergoing psychoanalysis, found the inner peace she sought in Christian theology; taught Bible classes at Fort Bragg, establishing a large following in Fayetteville area with a dynamic preaching style that combined theology with elements of psychoanalysis; became a born-again Christian and developed a therapy of "inner healing" based on her own experience; with husband's aid, began preaching across the South and earned a reputation for faith healing; was careful to maintain that she did no healing herself, that all healing came from God; instrumental in the conversion of older brother Jimmy, became involved as a campaigner in his political races; founded a retreat, Holovita Ranch, near Dallas, Texas (1978); wrote *The Gift of Inner Healing* (1976), *Experiencing Inner Healing* and *In His Footsteps*. ❖ See also *Women in World History*.

STARBIRD, Kate (1975—). American basketball player. Born July 30, 1975, in West Point, NY; grew up in Tacoma, WA; granddau. of Charles Leonard and Alfred Starbird (both pentathletes at Berlin Olympics, 1936); graduate of Stanford University, 1997. ❖ Guard, set a PAC-10 record with 753 points (1996–97); played for the Seattle Reign in the ABL; signed with Sacramento Monarchs (1999); traded to Miami Sol, then Utah Starzz (1999); traded to Seattle Storm (2002). Named College Player of the Year (1997).

STARBUCK, Mary Coffyn (1644/45–1717). American minister. Born Feb 20, 1644 or 1645, in Haverhill, Massachusetts; died Nov 13, 1717, in Nantucket, Massachusetts; dau. of Tristram Coffyn (magistrate) and Dionis (Stevens) Coffyn; m. Nathaniel Starbuck (farmer), c. 1663; children: Mary, Elizabeth, Nathaniel, Jethro, Barnabas, Eunice, Priscilla, Hepzibah, Ann, and Paul. ❖ Moved with family to island of Nantucket (166), after father implemented plans to purchase and colonize the tiny island; married and had 10 children; welcomed the arrival of several Society of Friends (Quaker) missionaries to the island (1698–1704) and accepted their request that she host weekly religious services for family and friends; was instrumental in helping the island boast a substantial Quaker presence by 1710; a capable public speaker, became Nantucket's 1st minister, as well as an active voice in community affairs and local politics. ❖ See also *Women in World History*.

STARK, Freya (1893–1993). British explorer and author. Name variations: Dame Freya Stark. Born Freya Madeline Stark, Jan 31, 1893, in Paris, France; died May 9, 1993, in Asolo, Italy; dau. of Robert Stark (sculptor) and Flora Stark (artist); attended Bedford College, University of London and London School of Oriental and African Studies; m. Stewart Perowne, 1947. ❖ Adventurer who made several journeys to remote areas of the Middle East and whose knowledge of the people and the area proved invaluable to the Allied cause during WWII; fluent in English, Italian, German, and French, 1st set foot in Asia (1927) when she settled for the winter in Brummana in Lebanon, as well as in Damascus; returned to Lebanon to undertake 3 solo journeys—2 in Luristan and 1 in Mazanderan, south of the Caspian Sea (1929–31); out of these travels, published *The Valley of the Assassins* which established her as a writer; traveled into Arabic interior (1934–35), only the 5th European woman to undertake such a journey; fluent in Arabic also understood local customs; preferred to travel alone, though she often had one male guide; began a 2nd journey from Mukalla on the Arabian coast (1937–38), then recorded adventures in *The Southern Gates of Arabia* (1936), for which she received the Royal Scottish Geographical Society's Mungo Park Medal; during WWII, offered services to British

Foreign Office; posted to Aden as an Arabist attached to Ministry of Information (1939), devised an effective strategy to counter German influence in the area; efforts in the war only increased her fame; began visiting classical sites in Persia and coast of Western Turkey (1947), resulting in *Ionia: A Quest, The Lycian Shore* and *Alexander's Path*; explored Roman frontiers in Asia and recorded adventures in *Riding to the Tigris*; at 77, embarked on 1st of 3 mounted treks into Himalayan foothills; also ventured to the Cambodian temples of Angkor Wat before going on to China; was in Afghanistan, traveling by Land Rover (1968); in her 90s, confined herself mostly to Europe; embarked on final journey at age 100 (May 9, 1993). Received Cross of the British Empire (1953); made Dame of the British Empire (1972). ❖ See also Jane Fletcher Geniesse, *Passionate Nomad: The Life of Freya Stark* (Random House, 1999); Caroline Moorehead, *Freya Stark* (Penguin, 1985); Malise Ruthven, *Traveller Through Time: A Photographic Journey with Freya Stark* (Viking, 1986); and *Women in World History*.

STARK, Pauline (1900–1977). *See Starke, Pauline.*

STARKE, Pauline (1900–1977). American actress. Name variations: Pauline Stark. Born Jan 10, 1900, in Joplin, MO; died Feb 3, 1977, in Santa Monica, CA; m. George Sherwood (producer), 1928. ❖ Made film debut as a dancing extra in D. W. Griffith's *Intolerance* (1916), then appeared in *Birth of a Nation*; starred in *Salvation Nell, A Connecticut Yankee in King Arthur's Court, Dante's Inferno, Little Church around the Corner, Devil's Cargo, Man without a Country* and *The Viking*; retired (1928) with advent of sound.

STARKE, Ute (1939—). East German gymnast. Born Jan 14, 1939, in Germany. ❖ At Mexico City Olympics, won a bronze medal in team all-around (1968).

STARKEY, Phyllis (1947—). English politician and member of Parliament. Born Phyllis Williams, Jan 4, 1947; m. Hugh Walton Starkey, 1969. ❖ Served as science policy administrator, Biotechnology and Biological Sciences Research Council (1993–97); representing Labour, elected to House of Commons for Milton Keynes South West (1997, 2001, 2005); named PPS to Denis MacShane as minister of State, Foreign and Commonwealth Affairs.

STARKIE, Enid (1897–1970). Irish literary critic. Born Enid Mary Starkie, Aug 18, 1897, in Killiney, Co. Dublin, Ireland; died April 21, 1970, in Oxford, England; dau. of W(illiam) J(oseph) M(yles) Starkie (classicist) and Mary Walsh Starkie; sister of Walter Starkie (writer); received undergraduate degree at Alexander College, Dublin; Sorbonne, doctorate in French literature, 1928; Somerville College, University of Oxford, Doctorate of Letters, 1939. ❖ Taught modern languages at Oxford from 1929; played an important role in establishing the reputation of Rimbaud; works include *Baudelaire* (1933, 1957), *Arthur Rimbaud in Abyssinia* (1937), *A Critical Edition of Baudelaire's "Les Fleurs du Mal"* (1947), *Petrus Borel* (1954), *From Gautier to Eliot: The Influence of France on English Literature, 1854–1954* (1954), and *Flaubert: The Master* (1971); elected to Irish Academy of Letters. Received Chevalier of French Legion of Honor (1948); made CBE (1967). ❖ See also memoir, *A Lady's Child* (1941).

STARLETS, The. *See Jansen, Linda.*

STAROVOITOVA, Galina (1946–1998). Russian politician. Pronunciation: Sta-ro-VOI-to-va. Born Galina Vasil'evna in Cheliabinsk, RSFSR, May 17, 1946; assassinated in St. Petersburg, Russia, Nov 20, 1998; dau. of Vasilii Stepanovich (professor and Party organizer who held an important position in the defense industry) and Rimma Iakovlevna; Leningrad College of Military Engineering, BA, 1966; Leningrad State University, MA in social psychology, 1971; Institute of Ethnography of the USSR Academy of Sciences, PhD in psychology, 1980; m. Grigorii Borshevskii; m. Andrei Volkov (physicist), 1998; children: (1st m.) son, Platon Grigor'evich Borshevskii. ❖ Advisor to Boris Yeltsin, was a member of the USSR Congress of People's Deputies (1989–91), a member of the Russian Congress of People's Deputies (1990–93) and an advisor to Boris Yeltsin on inter-ethnic affairs (1991–92); was also a member of Russian State Duma (1995–98); ran for president of the Russian Federation (1996); a popular public figure among the citizenry (on the day of her funeral, more than 10,000 mourners came to pay their respects as she lay in state), wrote numerous articles and gave interviews in the press on the political situation in the former Soviet Union (1988–98); writings include *Ethnic Groups in the Modern Soviet City* (1987). ❖ See also *Women in World History*.

STARR, Belle (1848–1889). American bandit. Born Myra Maybelle (or Maebelle) Shirley, Feb 5, 1848, in Jasper County, Missouri; gunned down on Feb 3, 1889, en route to Younger's Bend; dau. of John Shirley (horse breeder and tavern owner) and Elizabeth "Eliza" (Pennington) Shirley; m. Jim Reed (outlaw), Nov 1, 1866 (killed 1874); (possibly) m. Bruce Younger, May 15, 1880 (marriage ended after 3 weeks); m. Sam Starr, June 5, 1880 (shot to death, 1886); m. Jim July (some sources cite Bill July), in 1886 (killed 1889); children: (1st m.) Rosie Lee Reed (b. 1868, known as Pearl Starr, speculated to be the illeg. dau. of Cole Younger); Edward "Eddie" Reed (b. 1871, horse thief). ❖ Confederate sympathizer, rancher and convicted horse thief, who associated with outlaws and made an enduring name for herself as the "Bandit Queen" of the Old West; charged with horse stealing (July 31, 1882); tried by "Hanging Judge" Isaac Parker and sentenced to two 6-month prison terms; released for good behavior after 9 months; her lifestyle was so unusual for a woman of her time that she captured the imagination of writers who were hoping to entertain their 19th-century readership; her death, still an unsolved mystery, deepened the intrigue she had inspired in life. ❖ See also S. W. Harman, *Belle Starr: The Female Desperado* (Frontier, 1954); Burton Rascoe, *Belle Starr: "The Bandit Queen"* (Random House, 1941); Phillip Steele, *Starr Tracks: Belle and Pearl Starr* (Pelican, Gretna, 1989); Glenn Shirley, *Belle Starr and her Times: The Literature, the Facts, and the Legends* (U. of Oklahoma Press, 1982); Robert G. Winn, *Two Starrs: Belle the Bandit Queen, Pearl, Riverfront Madame* (1979); and *Women in World History*.

STARR, Billie (1916–2002). *See Dawn, Dolly.*

STARR, Eliza Allen (1824–1901). American writer. Name variations: Eliza Ann Starr. Born Eliza Ann Starr, Aug 29, 1824, in Deerfield, Massachusetts; died Sept 7, 1901, in Durand, Illinois; dau. of Oliver Starr (dyer and farmer) and Lovina Allen Starr; aunt of Ellen Gates Starr (1859–1940), socialist reformer and co-founder of Hull House; studied painting under Caroline Negus Hildreth; never married; no children. ❖ Poet, lecturer on art and religion, and teacher of art, wrote verse and articles on Christian art for periodicals; works on Christian art include *Patron Saints* (1st series, 1871, 2nd series, 1881), *Pilgrims and Shrines* (2 vols., 1885) and *The Three Archangels and the Guardian Angel in Art* (1899); published collected poems as *Songs of a Lifetime* (1887). Received Notre Dame University's Laetare Medal (1885) and medallion from Pope Leo XIII (1899). ❖ See also *Women in World History*.

STARR, Ellen Gates (1859–1940). American labor activist and social reformer. Born in Laona, Illinois, Mar 19, 1859; died in Suffern, New York, Feb 10, 1940; dau. of Caleb Allen Starr and Susan (Gates) Starr; niece of Eliza Allen Starr (1824–1901); attended Rockford (IL) Seminary, 1877; never married; no children. ❖ Settlement house worker and labor supporter who co-founded Hull House and remained there for 20 years; became increasingly involved in labor organizing; participated in 1st strike (1896), assisting Chicago women textile workers; joined the Women's Trade Union League (1903) and took part in several more strikes, including a 1914 strike of Chicago waitresses during which she was arrested. ❖ See also *Women in World History*.

STARR, Frances Grant (1886–1973). American stage and screen actress. Born June 6, 1886, in Oneonta, NY; died June 11, 1973, in New York, NY; m. Haskell Coffin (div.); m. Robert G. Donaldson (died); m. Emil Churchill Wetten. ❖ Made stage debut in stock; had 1st success as Juanita in Belasco's *The Rose of the Rancho* (1908), and was considered one of Belasco's brightest stars; other plays include *Music Master, The Easiest Way, The Case of Becky, Marie—Odile, Tiger! Tiger!, The Lake, Claudia, The Second Flame, Midnight Bell, Little Lady in Blue* and *Ladies of the Corridor*; made film debut in *Five Star Final* (1931).

STARR, Kay (1922—). American pop and band singer. Born Katherine LaVerne Starks, July 21, 1922, in Dougherty, OK; dau. of Harry Starks (laborer and full-blooded Iroquois) and Annie Starks (of Irish descent). ❖ Had her own radio show, "Starr Time," on WREC in Memphis and was a featured singer on the station's "Saturday Night Jamboree"; began singing with Joe Venuti's band (1937); also sang with orchestras of Bob Crosby, Glenn Miller, and Charlie Barnet; while with Barnet, made 1st recordings, most notably "Share Croppin' Blues"; contracted pneumonia and lost voice (1945); upon recovery, was left with a deeper, huskier sound, a sound that would become her trademark; signed with Capitol (1947); had 1st hit with her cover of Russ Morgan's "So Tired" (1949), followed by such hits as "Hoop-Dee-Doo," "Bonaparte's Retreat," "I'm the Lonesomest Gal in Town," "Side by Side," "Angry," "I'll Never Be Free" (with Tennessee Ernie Ford), "Changing Partners," and "Wheel of

Fortune," which earned her her 1st gold record and was the #2 top-selling single of 1952; featured in the revue *4 Girls 4* (1980s). ❖ See also *Women in World History.*

STARR, Mae Faggs (1932–2000). *See Faggs, Mae.*

STARR, Muriel (1888–1950). Canadian-born actress. Born Feb 20, 1888, in Canada; died April 19, 1950, backstage at the Golden Theater in NY during matinee performance of *The Velvet Glove*; m. William Hartwell Johnson. ❖ Made NY debut as Jeanne Chapin in *Going Some* (1909); sailed for Australia (1913) where she became a star, touring for many years in New Zealand and Australia in such plays as *Within the Law, The Chorus Lady, Madame X, The Yellow Ticket, The Bird of Paradise, The Easiest Way, The 13th Chair* and *The Garden of Allah*; returned to Broadway and appeared in *The Star Wagon, On the Rocks* and *Johnny Belinda.*

STARRE, Katie (1971—). Australian field-hockey player. Name variations: Kate Starre. Born Sept 18, 1971, in Armadale, Western Australia. ❖ Midfielder; won team gold medals at Atlanta Olympics (1996) and Sydney Olympics (2000).

STARSHIP. *See Slick, Grace.*

STASIUK, Natalia. *See Stasyuk, Natalia.*

STASOVA, Elena (1873–1966). Russian revolutionary. Born Elena Dmitrievna Stasova into an aristocratic family in St. Petersburg, Russia, Oct 15, 1873; died in Moscow, Dec 31, 1966; dau. of Dmitri Vasilievich Stasov (lawyer) and Poliksena Stepanovna Stasova (well-known feminist); niece of feminist Nadezhda Stasova (1822–1895). ❖ Bolshevik revolutionary and Communist leader, taught among the poor and joined revolutionary movement (1890s); avoided capture by police for 5 years; joined V. I. Lenin's group; exiled to Siberia (1913–16); elected secretary of Bolshevik Party Central Committee (1919) but resigned post in protest over intrigues she regarded as directed against her (1920); worked in Germany for Comintern (1921–25); worked for MOPR (1927–37), which assisted imprisoned and exiled revolutionaries; served as editor of *International Literature* (1938–46); retired (1946) and was briefly imprisoned, but continued to speak out on basic political issues; after Stalin's death (1953), was long honored as one of the last of the Old Bolsheviks. ❖ See also *Women in World History.*

STASOVA, Nadezhda (1822–1895). Russian philanthropist and feminist. Born Nadezhda Vasil'evna Stasova, June 12, 1822, in Tsarskoe Selo, Russia; died Sept 27, 1895, in St. Petersburg; dau. of Vasilii P. Stasov (court architect and academician); sister of Vladimir Vasilievich Stasov (art critic) and Dmitri Vasilievich Stasov (lawyer); aunt of Elena Stasova (1873–1966); never married; no children. ❖ Leading 19th-century Russian activist, ran Sunday School for working women (1860–62); helped establish Society to Provide Cheap Lodgings for women in St. Petersburg (1861); co-founded women's Publishing Workshop (1863); promoted the establishment of the Vladimir Courses (1870); was 1st director of the Bestuzhev Courses (1878); served as chair of the Society for Assistance to Graduate Science Courses; was president of the Russian Women's Mutual Philanthropic Society (1894); helped establish Children's Aid Society in St. Petersburg (1894); for over 35 years, was one of the leaders of the nascent women's movement in Russia. ❖ See also *Women in World History.*

STASSIOUK, Natalia. *See Stasyuk, Natalia.*

STASYUK, Natalia (1969—). Belarusian rower. Name variations: Natalya Stasiuk or Stassiouk. Born Jan 21, 1969, in Belarus. ❖ Won a bronze medal for coxed eights at Atlanta Olympics (1996).

STATHAM, Edith May (1853–1951). New Zealand preservationist. Born April 13, 1853, at Bootle, Lancashire, England; died Feb 13, 1951, in St Heliers, New Zealand; dau. of William Stratham (lawyer) and Ellen Allen (Hadfield) Stratham. ❖ Active in Victoria League, and worked to restore graves of soldiers who had died during New Zealand wars of 1840s and 1860s; also worked with Medical Service Corps of National Reserve. ❖ See also *Dictionary of New Zealand Biography* (Vol. 3).

STATHEM, Vivian (1915–2000). *See Bullwinkel, Vivian.*

STATILIA MESSALINA (fl. 66–68 CE). *See Messalina, Statilia.*

STATIRA I (c. 425–? BCE). Persian queen. Name variations: Stateira. Born c. 425 BCE; death date unknown; dau. of Hydarnes (Persian noble); half-sister of Teritouchones; m. Arsaces, later known as Artaxerxes II Mnemon, king of Persia (d. 359); children: probably sons Darius,

Ariaspes, and Ochus (who was later known as Artaxerxes III); possibly daughters Atossa and Amestris. ❖ Was apparently Artaxerxes' only legitimate wife, a fact which pit her against mother-in-law Parysatis, as both sought to be the dominant political influence in Artaxerxes' life; perhaps becoming *too* influential, was poisoned at the command of Parysatis. ❖ See also *Women in World History.*

STATIRA II (c. 360–331 BCE). Persian queen and warrior. Name variations: Stateira. Born c. 360 BCE; died in 331 BCE; probably dau. of Persian noble Arsanes but not dau. of his wife Sisygambis; sister of a Persian noble named Pharnaces; m. Darius III Codomannus (possibly her half-brother), king of Persia; children: 2 daughters, Statira III and Drypetis; son Ochus. ❖ In her prime, was said to have been the most beautiful woman in Asia; is also the only attested wife of Darius III, who fought his way to the Persian throne (336); in Persian fashion, accompanied Darius in his initial attempt to ward off Alexander the Great's invasion of the Persian Empire; captured by Alexander after the Battle of Issus (333), remained in his custody until she died. ❖ See also *Women in World History.*

STATIRA III (fl. 324 BCE). Macedonian queen. Name variations: Stateira. Dau. of Darius III Codomannus, king of Persia, and Statira II (c. 360–331 BCE); sister of Drypetis; m. Alexander III the Great (356–323 BCE), in 324 BCE. ❖ Accompanied father when he advanced against Alexander III the Great during the campaign which ended in the Persian defeat at the Battle of Issus (333 BCE); along with the rest of her family, except her father, fell captive to the Macedonian conqueror; was married to Alexander at a ceremony at Susa (324) and introduced into a polygamous household; following Alexander's death, was put to death by orders of Roxane. ❖ See also *Women in World History.*

STAUFFENBERG, Litta von (c. 1905–1945). German aviator. Name variations: Litta Schiller; Melitta Gräfin Schenk von Stauffenberg. Born Melitta Schiller in Krotoschin, Germany (later Poland), c. 1905; shot down by American fighter plane near Strasskirchen, Germany, April 8, 1945; earned a degree in civil engineering from Munich Institute of Technology, 1927; m. Alexander Graf Schenk von Stauffenberg; sister-in-law of Claus von Stauffenberg (member of a plot to assassinate Adolf Hitler). ❖ Test pilot who, though she was of Jewish origin, was exempted from the anti-Semitic Nuremberg Laws because of her abilities as an aviator; acquired several pilot's certificates; became involved in aerodynamics research (1927), making test flights to check instruments that control dives; worked at several facilities, including the German Aviation Testing Institute at Berlin-Adlershof, Askania Works at Berlin-Friedenau, and starting in Oct 1937, at Air War Academy at Berlin-Gatow; before and during WWII, flew well over 2,000 diving missions in Ju (Junkers) 87 and Ju 88 dive bombers, an accomplishment surpassed by only one German male test pilot; awarded Air Captain's commission (1937), also received Iron Cross class II (1943) and Pilot's Badge in Gold with Diamonds; nominated for Iron Cross class I (1944); was sympathetic to brother-in-law Claus attempt to assassinate Hitler (1944) but avoided discovery; performed test dives with the Junkers 88 and night flights with the Arado 96, the Focke-Wulf 190 and the revolutionary new turbo-jet fighter, the Messerschmidt 262 (1944); also worked on night-landing instruments, inventing a number of useful new devices; flying a slow and unarmed Bücker 181 trainer, was shot down from behind by an American fighter near Strasskirchen.

STAUFFER, Brenda (1961—). American field-hockey player. Born April 6, 1961, in New Holland, PA; attended Penn State University. ❖ At Los Angeles Olympics, won a bronze medal in team competition (1984).

STAUNER, Gabriele (1948—). German lawyer and politician. Born April 22, 1948, in Wolfratshausen, Germany. ❖ Qualified as an interpreter in English, French, and Russian (1972); served as official of the foreign service of the Federal Republic of Germany (1987–90); as a member of the European People's Party (Christian Democrats) and European Democrats, elected to 5th European Parliament (1999–2004).

STAUPERS, Mabel (1890–1989). African-American nurse and activist. Name variations: Mabel Keaton Staupers; Mabel Doyle Keaton Staupers. Born Mabel Doyle, Feb 27, 1890, in Barbados, West Indies; died Nov 29, 1989; dau. of Thomas and Pauline Doyle; graduate of Freedmen's Hospital School of Nursing (now Howard University College of Nursing), 1917; m. James Max Keaton, 1917 (div.); m. Fritz C. Staupers, 1931 (died 1949); no children. ❖ One of most significant figures in the history of African-Americans in American nursing profession, was responsible for gaining black nurses admittance into the American military; migrated to US (1903); began career as a private-duty nurse (1917); helped organize Booker T. Washington Sanitarium (1920), the 1st in-patient center in Harlem for black tuberculosis sufferers; instrumental in establishing the Harlem Committee of New York Tuberculosis and Health Association, served as the committee's executive secretary for 12 years; elected executive secretary of National Association of Colored Graduate Nurses (NACGN, 1934) and formed a productive partnership with president Estelle Masse Riddle that was to continue for 15 years; led the struggle of black nurses to win full integration into the American nursing profession; played a crucial role in the desegregation of the military's nursing corps during WWII; published *No Time for Prejudice: A Story of the Integration of Negroes in the United States* (1961). Received Spingarn medal (1951). ❖ See also *Women in World History*.

STAVELEY, Dulcie (1898–1995). English radiologist. Born 1898 in UK; died 1995; Royal Free School of Medicine, MD, 1922; University Medical College, medical radiology and electrotherapy diploma, 1923. ❖ The Royal Free Hospital's 1st woman radiologist, served as a University College radiologist (1924–26); established a private radiology practice while working as a senior radiologist at the Royal Free Hospital (1926–58); as a Royal Army Medical Corps (RAMC) major, employed in army hospitals in Belgium and Germany (1939–44); retired to Alford, Lincolnshire.

STAVER, Julie (1952—). American field-hockey player. Born April 4, 1952, in Hershey, PA; attended University of Pennsylvania. ❖ At Los Angeles Olympics, won a bronze medal in team competition (1984).

STAW, Sala (d. 1972). Polish-born actress. Born in Poland; died Nov 3, 1972, in Torrance, CA; m. Otto Albertson. ❖ Came to US (1927); appeared with Eva Le Gallienne's Civic Rep and the Federal Theatre Project; starred in one-woman show *The Five Queens*; founder and director of the Foundation for Classic Theatre and Academy.

STEAD, Christina (1902–1983). Australian novelist. Born Christina Ellen Stead, July 17, 1902, in Sydney, Australia; died Mar 31, 1983, in Glebe, Australia; dau. of David Stead (Australian scientist and politician) and Ellen (Butters) Stead; attended Sydney Teachers' College; m. William Blake (Blech), in 1952, after living with him since 1929; no children. ❖ Novelist whose book *The Man Who Loved Children* is regarded by many critics as a forgotten 20th-century masterpiece, was a student, then teacher (1921–25), then office worker in Australia (1925–28); left hometown of Sydney (1928) and stayed away from Australia for 41 years, moving restlessly between Britain, Europe and America; was an office worker in London and Paris (1928–33); published *Seven Poor Men of Sydney* and the short stories, *The Salzburg Tales* (1934), both to critical acclaim; published *The Beauties and the Furies* (1936); like many left-wing intellectuals during the Great Depression of 1930s, became deeply involved in radical causes; published *The Man Who Loved Children* (1940), one of the most harrowing yet persuasive 20th-century descriptions of life in a dysfunctional family, which biographers have shown is quite closely based on her childhood; also wrote *For Love Alone* (1944), and *Letty Fox: Her Luck* (1946), which was banned in Australia; was belatedly honored in Australia; also wrote *Cotter's England* (1967, published in US as *Dark Places of the Heart*), *The People With the Dogs* (1952) and *I'm Dying Laughing* (1986). Received Patrick White Prize for literature (1974). ❖ See also Diana Brydon, *Christina Stead* (Macmillan, 1987); Joan Lidoff, *Christina Stead* (Ungar, 1982); Hazel Rowley, *Christina Stead: A Biography* (Holt, 1993); Susan Sheridan, *Christina Stead* (Indiana U. Press, 1988; Chris Williams, *Christina Stead: A Life of Letters* (Virago, 1989); and *Women in World History*.

STEARNS, Lutie (1866–1943). American librarian and reformer. Born Lutie Eugenia Stearns, Sept 13, 1866, in Stoughton, MA; died Dec 25, 1943, in Milwaukee, WI; dau. of Isaac Holden Stearns (physician) and Catherine (Guild) Stearns. ❖ Appointed superintendent of circulation department of Milwaukee Public Library (1890) and campaigned for creation of state library commission; was 1st paid staff member of Free Library Commission (1897); helped organize 100 public libraries and more than 1,400 traveling libraries in Wisconsin; lectured and campaigned for woman suffrage, state prohibition, and child labor laws throughout US.

STEARNS, Sally (c. 1915—). American coxswain. Born c. 1915. ❖ Served as coxswain for all-male Rollins College (Winter Park, FL) varsity scull team during their defeat of Manhattan College (Bronx, NY), becoming 1st woman coxswain of a men's college varsity crew (1936).

STEBBING, L. Susan (1885–1943). British philosopher. Name variations: Lizzie Susan Stebbing. Born Dec 2, 1885, in Wimbledon, Surrey, England; died Sept 11, 1943, in London, England; dau. of Alfred Charles Stebbing (barrister) and Elizabeth (Elstob) Stebbing; attended Girton College, Cambridge; University of London, MA, 1912, DLit, 1931; never married. ❖ Began lecturing in philosophy at King's College, London (1913); taught at Bedford College, University of London, Columbia University in NY, and Kingsley Lodge School for Girls in Hampstead, where she served as principal (1915–43); wrote the 1st text to make the advancements in logic generally accessible, *A Modern Introduction to Logic* (1930); firmly believing that the application of reason could eradicate evil, expounded on this idea in *Ideals and Illusions* (1941).

STEBBINS, Alice. See Wells, Alice Stebbins.

STEBBINS, Emma (1815–1882). American sculptor and painter. Born Sept 1, 1815, in New York, NY; died Oct 24, 1882, in New York, NY; dau. of John Stebbins (New York banker) and Mary (Largin) Stebbins; sister of Henry George Stebbins, president of New York Stock Exchange; studied painting in NY with Henry Inman and sculpture in Rome under Benjamin Paul Akers; lifetime companion of Charlotte Cushman; never married. ❖ Created the celebrated fountain *The Angel of the Waters* (also known as the Bethesda Fountain) installed in New York City's Central Park (1873); other works include *Columbus* (1867), originally erected in Central Park at 102nd Street, now in the Brooklyn Civic Center, and the innovative *Industry* (1859) and *Commerce* (1860), which depict a miner and a sailor, respectively, in modern dress; wrote *Charlotte Cushman: Her Letters and Memories of Her Life* (1878). ❖ See also *Women in World History*.

STEBER, Eleanor (1914–1990). American soprano. Born Eleanor Steber, July 17, 1914, in Wheeling, WV; died Oct 3, 1990, in Langhorne, PA; dau. of William Charles Steber (bank cashier) and Ida A. (Nolte) Steber (singer); studied at New England Conservatory with Paul Althouse and William Whitney; m. Edwin L. Bilby, 1938. ❖ Debuted in Boston (1936); won Metropolitan Radio Auditions (1936); debuted at the Met (1936) and remained there (1936–62), becoming known for performances of Mozart and Strauss; debuted at Bayreuth and Vienna (1953); sang in the 1st performance of Samuel Barber's *Knoxville: Summer of 1915* (1948) and premiered the title role of Barber's *Vanessa* (1958); sang Miss Wingrave in American premiere of Britten's *Owen Wingrave* (1973); taught at Cleveland Institute of Music, Temple University, New England Conservatory, and Juilliard. ❖ See also *Women in World History*.

STEBLOVNIK, Jolanda (1976—). See Ceplak, Jolanda.

STECHER, Renate (1950—). East German track-and-field champion. Name variations: Renate Meissner or Stecher-Meissner. Born Renate Meissner, May 12, 1950, in Süptitz, East Germany; m. Gerd Stecher (a hurdler). ❖ Top international sprinter, went undefeated in the 100 and 200 meters (1970–74); won 100 and 200 meters at European championships (1971); won gold medals for the 100 and 200 meters and 4 x 100-meter relay at Munich Olympics (1972); won silver medals for the 100 meters and 4 x 100-meter relay and a bronze for the 200 meters at Montreal Olympics (1976); ran the first sub-11-second 100 meters ever (1973).

STEDING, Katy (1967—). American basketball player. Born Dec 11, 1967, in Tualatin, OR; graduate of Stanford University, 1990; m. John Jeub, 1997. ❖ Forward; won an NCAA title (1990) and 2 Pac-10 titles while at Stanford; played professionally in Japan (1990–93) and Spain (1993–94); won a team gold medal at Atlanta Olympics (1996); joined the Portland Power of the ABL; played for Sacramento Monarchs of the WNBA (2000), then Seattle Storm (2001); opened a basketball academy.

STEDMAN, Myrtle (1885–1938). American actress. Born Mar 3, 1885, in Chicago, IL; died Jan 8, 1938, in Hollywood, CA; m. Marshall Stedman (actor, div. 1920); children: Lincoln Stedman (b. 1907, actor). ❖ Began career with Selig (1912), under direction of her husband; was a feature player (1920s) and character actress (1930s); films include *The Valley of the Moon*, *Jane*, *The Call of the Cumberlands*, *Sex*, *Reckless Youth*, and *Alias the Deacon*.

STEED, Gitel P. (1914–1977). American cultural anthropologist. Name variations: Gitel Poznanski Steed. Born Gertrude Poznanski, May 3, 1914, in Cleveland, OH; grew up in the Bronx, NY; died 1977; dau. of Sara Auerbach Poznanski and Jakob Poznanski (businessman); New York University, BA, 1938; Columbia University, PhD, 1969; m. Robert

Steed (artist), 1947; children: Andrew Hart Steed. ❖ Served as editor and researcher for explorer Vilhjalmur Stefansson; was a member of the Jewish Black Book Committee which submitted the report, *The Black Book: The Nazi Crime Against the Jewish People* (1946) to the UN War Crimes Commission; worked under direction of Ruth Bunzel among Chinese immigrants in NY (beginning 1947), as part of Columbia Research in Contemporary Cultures Project; taught at Hunter College and Fisk University; as director of Columbia University Research in Contemporary India Project, took team to India for fieldwork (1949–51); published "Notes on an Approach to A Study of Personality Formation in a Hindu Village in Gujarat" (1955); joined staff of Hofstra College (now University) in 1962; made second trip to India (1970). Portrait of her by Rafael Soyer, "Girl in White Blouse" (1932), is located at Metropolitan Museum of Art.

STEELE, Danielle (1947—). American novelist. Born Danielle Fernande Schuelein-Steel, Aug 14, 1947, in New York, NY; studied at Parsons School of Design; m. Claude-Eric Lazard, 1965 (div. 1974); m. Danny Zugelder, 1975 (div. 1978); m. William George Toth, 1978 (div. 1981); m. John Traina, 1981 (div. 1996); m. Thomas J. Perkins, 1998 (sep.); children: (1st m.) 1; (3rd m.) 1; (4th m.) 5. ❖ Bestselling novelist, began career as a copywriter for the Grey Advertising Agency in San Francisco; wrote over 60 romance novels, including *Going Home* (1973), *Now and Forever* (1978), *The Promise* (1979), *Summer's End* (1980), *Once in a Lifetime* (1982), *Full Circle* (1984), *Wanderlust* (1986), *Daddy* (1989), *Jewels* (1992), and *Ransom* (2004); had over 20 of her novels adapted for tv; also wrote *His Bright Light: The Story of Nick Traina* (1998), an account of her son who committed suicide after years of battling mental illness; recognized for work with mentally ill children. Made Chevalier of Distinguished Order of Arts and Letter by French government (2002). ❖ See also Vickie Bane and Lorenzo Benet, *The Lives of Danielle Steel* (1994).

STEEL, Dawn (1946–1997). American film executive. Born Aug 19, 1946, in New York; died Dec 20, 1997, in Los Angeles, California; dau. of Nat Steel and Lillian Steel (electronics executive); m. Ronald Rothstein (financial investor), Dec 31, 1975 (div. 1977); m. Chuck Roven (producer), May 30, 1985; children: Rebecca Roven. ❖ The 1st woman to head a major studio, moved to Los Angeles (1978), where she landed a job in the merchandising department at Paramount; named vice-president of feature productions, was one of the few who believed in her 1st project, *Flashdance,* which made her name in the industry; as senior vice-president of Paramount (1983–85) and president of production (1985–87), oversaw such hits as *Footloose, Top Gun, Beverly Hills Cop II, The Untouchables,* and *Fatal Attraction;* served as president of Columbia Pictures (1987–91); left Columbia (1991), opting for a less demanding job as an independent producer; produced the film *Cool Runnings,* the surprise hit of 1993. ❖ See also autobiography *They Can Kill You . . . But They Can't Eat You* (1993); and *Women in World History.*

STEEL, Dorothy (1884–1965). British croquet player. Born 1884 in UK; died 1965. ❖ Won women's croquet championship 15 times (1919–39) and won Open Croquet championship 4 times; won several other contests, including Beddows Cup, Open and Mixed Doubles, and the MacRobertson Trophy (1925, 1928, and 1937).

STEEL, Flora Annie (1847–1929). English novelist. Born Flora Annie Webster at Sudbury Priory, Harrow-on-the-Hill, England, April 2, 1847; died April 12, 1929; dau. of George Webster (sheriff clerk of Forfarshire) and Isabella (Macallum) Webster (heiress of a Jamaican sugar planter); m. Henry William Steel (with the Indian civil service), in 1867; children: daughter (b. 1870). ❖ Lived in India (1868–89), where she advocated education for Indian women, was 1st inspector of girls' schools, and served on the Provincial Educational Board (1884); became interested in Indian culture and history and, writing about those subjects for British reading public, published 1st book, *Wide Awake Stories,* a collection of Indian folk tales; after return to England (1889), wrote bestselling novel about the Indian Mutiny of 1857, *On the Face of the Waters;* with Grace Gardiner, co-authored *The Complete Indian Housekeeper and Cook,* which was one of the most influential 19th-century texts in shaping the role of the colonial woman; lived in North Wales (1900–13); best work is contained in 2 collections of short stories: *From the Five Rivers* (1893) and *Tales from the Punjab* (1894); later works are *In the Permanent Way* (1897), *Voices of the Night* (1900), *The Hosts of the Lord* (1900), *In the Guardianship of God* (1903) and *A Sovereign Remedy* (1906). ❖ See also autobiography, *The Garden of Fidelity* (1929).

STEEL, Mary Nicol Neill (1902–2000). *See Armour, Mary Nicol Neill.*

STEELE, Alison (c. 1937–1995). American radio personality. Name variations: The Nightbird. Born c. 1937 in Brooklyn, New York; died in New York, NY, Sept 1995; sister of Joyce Loman (who operated a feline boutique with her sister); m. Ted Steele (bandleader, div.). ❖ One of the 1st female rock 'n' roll disc jockeys in America, began broadcasting career at 14; worked her way up to associate producer at a New York radio station; chosen from 800 applicants for an all-woman lineup of disc jockeys (1966), a publicity stunt organized by New York station WNEW-FM, was the only woman asked to stay on; known to her loyal listeners as "the Nightbird" because of her specialty graveyard shifts, was the 1st female winner of *Billboard* magazine's FM Personality of the Year (1976); worked for several different New York stations and her distinctively sultry voice, inviting listeners to "Come fly with me," was much in demand for radio and tv voice-overs. Inducted into Rock 'n' Roll Hall of Fame.

STEELE, Anne (1717–1778). English hymn writer. Name variations: Theodosia. Born at Broughton, Hampshire, England, in 1717; died 1778. ❖ Published *Poems on Subjects chiefly devotional* under name "Theodosia" (1760); though she was a Baptist, some of her hymns, like "Father of mercies, in Thy word," found their way into the collections of other churches; her complete works (144 hymns, 34 metrical psalms, and 50 moral poems) appeared in one volume in London (1863).

STEELE, Barbara (1937—). English actress and producer. Born Dec 29, 1937, in Trenton Wirrall, England; m. James Poe (screenwriter). ❖ Made film debut in *Bachelor of Hearts* (1958), followed by *Sapphire, The Pit and the Pendulum, 8½, Caged Heat, They Came From Within, I Never Promised You a Rose Garden, Piranha* and *The Silent Scream,* among others; starred in several Italian horror films, including the cult classics *La Maschera del Demonio* (*Black Sunday,* 1960) and *L'Orrible Segreto del Dr. Hitchcock* (*The Horrible Dr. Hitchcock,* 1962); on tv, appeared on "Dark Shadows" (1991) and briefly in "War and Remembrance" (1988) and won an Emmy as one of its producers.

STEELE, Joyce. Australian politician. Born in Australia; children: Christopher Steele. ❖ A Liberal, was the 1st elected to the South Australian Parliament (1959), the 1st woman Opposition Whip (1966) and the 1st woman Cabinet minister (1968); held the seat of Burnside (1959–70) and Davenport (1970–72).

STEELE, Micki (1954—). American bassist and singer. Name variations: Michael Steele; The Runaways; The Bangles. Born Michael Susanne Steele, June 2, 1955, in Pasadena, CA. ❖ Bassist, played with all-girl, hard-rock band, the Runaways (1975–83), before joining pop group, the Bangles; with Bangles, released critically acclaimed album, *All Over the Place* (1984), which included classic, "Hero Takes a Fall"; followed that with hit album, *Different Light* (1985), which included "Walk Like an Egyptian" and "Walking Down Your Street"; also had hit singles "Manic Monday" (1986) and "Hazy Shade of Winter" which could be heard on soundtrack of film *Less Than Zero* (1987); with Bangles, released *Everything* (1988), which included hits "In Your Room" and "Eternal Flame"; though Bangles disbanded (1989), reunited with band to record "Get the Girl," for the film *Austin Powers: The Spy Who Shagged Me* (1999).

STEELEYE SPAN (1947—). *See Prior, Maddy.*

STEEN, Karl (1844–1940). *See Daudet, Julia.*

STEENBERGHE, Florentine (1967—). Dutch field-hockey player. Born Nov 11, 1967, in Netherlands. ❖ Won a team bronze medal at Atlanta Olympics (1996).

STEER, Irene (1889–1947). English swimmer. Born Aug 10, 1889, in UK; died April 18, 1947. ❖ At Stockholm Olympics, won a gold medal in 4 x 100-meter freestyle relay (1912).

STEEVENS, Grissell (1653–1746). Irish founder. Name variations: Grizell Steevens; Grizel Steevens; Grisilda Steevens; Madam Steevens. Born Grissell Steevens in 1653, probably in England; died in Dublin, Mar 18, 1746; dau. of Rev. John Steevens and Constance Steevens; twin sister of Richard Steevens (Dublin physician); never married; no children. ❖ Co-founder, with her brother, of Dr. Steevens's Hospital, one of the 1st public hospitals in Ireland; moved as a child with family to Ireland, where her father became rector of Athlone (1660); inherited brother's fortune on his death (1710); surrendered most of her share of the inheritance in order to permit the fulfillment of his desire for the erection of a hospital in Dublin for the care of the sick poor; helped fund and supervise the building of Dr. Steevens's Hospital, which opened 1733; was involved in the management of the institution until she died, at age 93; remained a legendary figure in Dublin long after. ❖ See also Cheyne Brady, *The History of Steevens's Hospital* (1865); T. P. C. Kirkpatrick, *History of Dr. Steevens's Hospital, Dublin 1720–1920* (U. Press, 1924); and *Women in World History.*

STEFAN, Maria (1954—). Romanian kayaker. Born Feb 16, 1954, in Romania. ❖ At Los Angeles Olympics, won a gold medal in K4 500 meters (1984).

STEFAN, Verena (1947—). Swiss novelist, poet, and feminist. Born Mar 10, 1947, in Berne, Switzerland; dau. of a Sudeten German father and German-Swiss mother; attended University of Berlin. ❖ Moved to Berlin (1967), where she was closely involved with the student movement and became a physiotherapist; published the bestselling *Häutungen* (*Shedding,* 1975), a narration of the radical transformation of a young woman during the women's, civil rights, and health-care movements, which became a feminist manifesto; also wrote short stories *Literally Dreaming* and *Es ist reich gewesen: Bericht vom Sterben meiner Mutter* (*Times Have Been Good,* 1993), in honor of her mother; moved to Montreal (1999), where she writes in English and German. Received Prix de la Ville de Berne (1988, 1994).

STEFANEK, Gertrud (1959—). Hungarian fencer. Born July 1959 in Hungary. ❖ Won a bronze medal at Moscow Olympics (1980) and a bronze medal at Seoul Olympics (1988), both in team foil.

STEFANSKA, Halina Czerny (1922—). *See Czerny-Stefanska, Halina.*

STEFFIN, Christel (1940—). East German swimmer. Born April 4, 1940, in Germany. ❖ At Rome Olympics, won a bronze medal in 4 x 100-meter freestyle relay (1960).

STEGEMANN, Kerstin (1977—). German soccer player. Born Sept 29, 1977, in Rheine-Mesum, Germany. ❖ Midfielder; won a team bronze medal at Sydney Olympics (2000); played for FFC Heike Rheine; won team European championships (1997, 2001).

STEGGALL, Zali (1974—). Australian Alpine skier. Pronunciation: STEEG-ul. Born April 14, 1974, in Manly, Australia. ❖ Won a bronze medal for slalom at Nagano Olympics (1998); won a gold medal for slalom at World championships (1999).

STEICHEN, Mary (1904–1998). *See Calderone, Mary Steichen.*

STEIFF, Margarete (1847–1909). German entrepreneur. Name variations: Gretel Steiff. Born Margarete Steiff in Giengen on the Brenz, Baden-Württemberg, Germany, in 1847; died in 1909; sister of Fritz Steiff. ❖ Contacted polio when she was 18 months old which left her paralyzed, except for left hand and arm; enrolled in a local sewing school and excelled at needlework; opened a dressmaking business (1872); with its success, opened a factory (1877); created 1st Steiff toy animal (1879); with brother, founded their family toy business, Margarete Steiff GmbH, in Giengen (1904); created most popular toy, the teddy bear, which started a craze that has not ceased. ❖ See also *Women in World History.*

STEIN, Charlotte von (1742–1827). German playwright. Name variations: Charlotte von Schardt; Baroness von Stein. Born Charlotte Albertine Ernestine von Schardt, Dec 25, 1742, in Saxe-Weimar, Germany; died Jan 6, 1827, near Weimar; dau. of Johann Wilhelm von Schardt (master of ceremonies) and Concordia (Irving) von Schardt; m. Baron Josias von Stein (the duke of Saxe-Weimar's chief equerry), May 8, 1764 (died 1793); children: Karl (b. 1765); Ernst (b. 1767); Fritz (b. 1772); and 4 daughters who did not survive infancy. ❖ Dramatist and intellectual figure at the Weimar court, is remembered for her long friendship with Johann Wolfgang von Goethe, whose letters to her have made her almost mythical; served as lady-in-waiting to Duchess Anna Amalia of Saxe-Weimar; on marriage, spent most of next 10 years at von Stein family castle at Kochberg, outside Weimar, in relative isolation; gave birth to 7 children (1765–75) and suffered from constant loneliness and depression; met Goethe (1775); began an intimate relationship which was to influence much of his later writing; was the inspiration for idealized visions of her in his plays *Iphigenia* and *Tasso*; on death of husband (1793), continued to be an active figure in the intellectual life at Weimar ducal court, and took up writing as well; wrote 1st drama, *Dido,* followed by *Rino: A Play in Five Acts* and *Die Zwey Emilien.* ❖ See also Johann Goethe, *Selections from Goethe's Letters to Frau von Stein 1776–89* (ed. and trans. by Robert M. Browning, Camden House, 1990); and *Women in World History.*

STEIN, Edith (1891–1942). German philosopher, nun, and saint. Name variations: Sister Teresa Benedicta of the Cross; Sister Teresia Benedicata; Saint Teresa Benedicta. Born Oct 12, 1891, in Breslau, Germany (now Wroclaw, Poland); died Aug 9, 1942, in a gas chamber in Auschwitz; dau. of Siegfried Stein (owned lumber business) and Auguste Courant Stein; sister of Rosa Stein; attended Victoria School in Breslau, University of Breslau, and Göttingen University; awarded doctorate from University of Freiburg, 1916. ❖ Philosopher, interpreter of the phenomenologist Edward Husserl and Jewish convert to Catholicism, served with the wartime Red Cross (1916); worked as personal assistant to Edward Husserl (1916–18); baptized a Roman Catholic (1922); translated the letters of the Catholic convert and English cardinal John Henry Newman into German (1928); wrote a comparison of the philosophy of the 13th-century theologian St. Thomas Aquinas and phenomenology (1929); taught at St. Magdalena in Speyer (1923–31); career as a lecturer before Catholic groups took her to France, Switzerland, and Austria; appointed a lecturer at German Institute for Scientific Pedagogy in Münster (1932), a position terminated (April 19, 1933), when the Nazi Party banned Jews from teaching; entered a Discalced Carmelite convent in Cologne, Germany (Oct 14, 1933); tried, unsuccessfully, to persuade Pope Pius XI to speak out against Nazi genocide against the Jews (1933); for her safety and that of her fellow nuns, was transferred to Echt in the Netherlands (1938); with her sister, was summoned for questioning by SS police (spring 1942); arrested with sister (Aug 2); deported from the Westerbork detention camp to Auschwitz (Aug 7); declared venerable, 1st step in the process of being canonized a Roman Catholic saint (Jan 26, 1987); 2nd step, beatified (May 1, 1987); elevated to sainthood by Pope John Paul II (Oct 11, 1998); writings include *Life in a Jewish Family, 1891–1916* (1986) and *Finite and Eternal Being* (1950). ❖ See also Susanne M. Batzdorff, ed. and trans. *Edith Stein Selected Writings* (Templegate, 1990); Waltraud Herbstrith, *Edith Stein* (trans. by Bernard Bonowitz, Harper & Row, 1986); and *Women in World History.*

STEIN, Gertrude (1874–1946). American writer. Born in Allegheny, Pennsylvania, Feb 3, 1874; died in Neuilly, France, July 27, 1946; dau. of Daniel Stein and Amelia (Keyser) Stein; Harvard, BA, 1898; attended Johns Hopkins Medical School, 1897–1901; lived with Alice B. Toklas for 39 years (died Mar 7, 1967); never married. ❖ Novelist, poet, short-story writer, librettist, memoirist, and art collector, whose house on the Left Bank of Paris became a salon for the "Lost Generation," 1st settled in Paris at 27 rue de Fleurus with brother Leo (1903); became solidly entrenched in the artistic and literary life of her adopted country; met Pablo Picasso (1905) and Alice B. Toklas (Sept 8, 1907); filled the walls with modern art by obscure young artists such as Picasso, Matisse, Cézanne, Renoir and Gauguin; published *Three Lives* (1909), which drew praise; between the wars, became close with such writers as Ernest Hemingway, Sherwood Anderson, and F. Scott Fitzgerald; published her 1,000-page epic, *The Making of Americans* (1925), bringing increased recognition of her unique contribution to literature, though without financial rewards; went on lecture tour, Cambridge and Oxford universities (1926); though accepted as a leading figure among "modernist" writers, never won the popular acclaim of Joyce or Pound; established "Plain Edition" publishing company (1930); published the highly successful *The Autobiography of Alice B. Toklas* (1933), in which she chronicled her own life in Paris over a quarter of a century; wrote libretto for opera, *Four Saints in Three Acts,* 1st performed in New York (1934); by now a celebrity, went on lecture tour of US (1934–35); published *Everybody's Autobiography* (1937) and *Paris France* (1940); spent war years in Bilignin, France (1939–44); described wartime experiences in *Wars I Have Seen* (1945). ❖ See also Alice B. Toklas, *What Is Remembered* (1963); Janet Hobhouse, *Everybody Who Was Anybody: A Biography of Gertrude Stein* (Putnam, 1975); Diana Souhami, *Gertrude and Alice* (Pandora, 1991); John Malcolm Brinnin, *The Third Rose: Gertrude Stein and Her World* (Addison-Wesley, 1987); James R. Mellow, *Charmed Circle: Gertrude Stein & Company* (Praeger, 1974); Brenda Wineapple, *Sister Brother: Gertrude and Leo Stein* (Putnam, 1996); and *Women in World History.*

STEIN, Marion (1926—). Countess of Harewood. Name variations: Marion Thorpe. Born Mary Donata Nanetta Pauline Gustava Erwina Wilhelmina in Vienna, Austria, on Oct 18, 1926; m. George Lascelles, 7th earl of Harewood, on Sept 29, 1949 (div. 1967); m. Jeremy Thorpe (an English Liberal politician), on Mar 14, 1973; children: (1st m.) David Lascelles, viscount Lascelles (b. 1950); James Lascelles (b. 1953); Robert Lascelles (b. 1955); Mark Lascelles (b. 1964).

STEINBACH, Angela (1955—). West German swimmer. Born Mar 31, 1955. ❖ At Munich Olympics, won a bronze medal in 4 x 100-meter freestyle relay (1972).

STEINBACH, Sabina von (fl. 13th c.). Austrian sculptor. Flourished in 13th century in Strasbourg. ❖ Popular, talented sculptor, was trained in the arts by father, who was himself a sculptor, and eventually gained her own patrons; continued to assist father on his largest commissions; worked on the intricate stone carvings of the great cathedral of Strasbourg, her only known commissioned project.

STEINBACH, Sabine (1952—). East German swimmer. Born July 18, 1952. ❖ At Mexico City Olympics, won a bronze medal in 400-meter indiv. medley (1968).

STEINBECK, Janet (1951—). Australian swimmer. Born Feb 27, 1951, in Brisbane, Australia. ❖ At Mexico City Olympics, won a silver medal in 4 x 100-meter medley relay (1968).

STEINDORF, Ute (1957—). East German rower. Born Aug 26, 1957, in East Germany. ❖ At Moscow Olympics, won a gold medal in coxless pairs (1980).

STEINEM, Gloria (1934—). American writer and feminist. Pronunciation: STY-nem. Born Gloria Marie Steinem, Mar 25, 1934, at Clark Lake, Michigan; dau. of Leo Steinem (antique dealer) and Ruth (Nuneviller) Steinem; Smith College, BA, 1956; m. David Bale (entrepreneur and political activist and father of actor Christian Bale), Sept 3, 2000 (died Dec 30, 2004); no children. ❖ Best-known leader and speaker for the feminist movement during 1970s, who was a founder and editor of *Ms.* magazine, as well as a co-founder of the Ms. Foundation, Women's Action Alliance, and Women's Political Caucus, obtained 1st job in publishing (1960); earned 1st byline, *Esquire* magazine (1962); briefly became an undercover Playboy bunny to write article for *Show* (1963); served as staff writer for *New York* magazine (1968–72) and had regular column, "The City Politic"; wrote "After Black Power, Women's Liberation," award-winning article on the women's movement, for *New York* magazine (1969); covered the Harlem riots and the tumultuous Democratic National Convention in Chicago (1968); participated in the Women's Strike for Equality March (1969); served as editor of *Ms.,* the 1st feminist women's magazine (1972–88); became one of the most well-known speakers for the feminist movement; was a major force behind language changes, coining the expression "reproductive rights" and pointing out that "battered woman" and "sexual harassment" were new terms for old ideas ("Ten years ago," she told audiences, "it was just called life"); was a visible presence in many cities where battles for the ERA were being waged; helped form the Coalition of Labor Union Women (1974); operated on for breast cancer (1986); left *Ms.* to write several books (1988); writings include *A Thousand Indias* (1957), *The Beach Book* (1963), *Outrageous Acts and Everyday Rebellions* (1983), *Marilyn* (1986), *Revolution from Within* (1992) and *Moving Beyond Words* (1994). ❖ See also Sondra Henry and Emily Taitz, *One Woman's Power: A Biography of Gloria Steinem* (Dillon, 1987); Carolyn G. Heilbrun, *The Education of a Woman: The Life of Gloria Steinem* (Dial, 1995); and *Women in World History.*

STEINES, Leanza (c. 1971—). See Cornett, Leanza.

STEINROTTER, Diann (1967—). See Roffe, Diann.

STEINSEIFER, Carrie (1968—). American swimmer. Name variations: Carrie Steinseifer Bates. Born Feb 12, 1968, in San Francisco, CA; dau. of Bob an Lois Steinseifer; m. Mike Bates; children: 2 daughters. ❖ Won 3 gold medals at Pan American Games (1983); at Los Angeles Olympics, won gold medals in 4 x 100-meter medley relay and 4 x 100-meter freestyle relay, and tied with Nancy Hogshead for a gold medal in 100-meter freestyle (1984); won 2 US national championships in 100-meter freestyle (1983, 1985); won 2 NCAA titles while attending University of Texas.

STEINWACHS, Ginka (1942—). German novelist and literary critic. Born Oct 31, 1942, in Göttingen, Germany. ❖ Taught at University of Vincennes and was writer-in-residence at University College Dublin (1999); works include *George Sand: Eine Frau in Bewegung, Die Frau von Stand* (1980), *Der schwimmende Österreicher* (1985), *Rolling Stein* (1997) and *Barnarella oder das Herzkunstwerk in Flammen* (1998).

STEINWEHR, Christiane Mariane von (1695–1760). See Ziegler, Christiane Mariane von.

STELLA.
See Rich, Penelope (c. 1562–1607).
See Johnson, Esther (1681–1728).
See Lewis, Estelle Anna (1824–1880).

STELLA, Claudine Bousonnet (1636–1697). French engraver. Name variations: Claudine Stella-Bouzzonet or Bouzinnet. Born 1636 at Lyons, France; died Oct 1, 1697, in Paris; niece of Jacques Stella (1596–1657, artist); sister of Françoise Bousonnet Stella and Antoinette Stella (both engravers) and Antoine Bousonnet Stella (painter). ❖ Distinguished herself with her engravings of the works of her uncle Jacques Stella and those of Nicolas Poussin; was especially successful in rendering the spirit of the pictures of Poussin, and her plates were much esteemed.

STELLMACH, Manuela (1970—). East German swimmer. Born Feb 22, 1970, in East Germany. ❖ At Seoul Olympics, won a bronze medal in 200-meter freestyle and gold medals in 4 x 100-meter medley relay and 4 x 100-meter freestyle relay (1988); at Barcelona Olympics, won a bronze medal in 4 x 100-meter freestyle relay (1992).

STELMA, Jacoba (1907—). Dutch gymnast. Born July 1907 in Netherlands. ❖ At Amsterdam Olympics, won a gold medal in team all-around (1928).

STELOFF, Frances (1887–1989). American bookseller. Name variations: Fanny Steloff. Born Ida Frances Steloff, Dec 31, 1887, in Saratoga Springs, New York; died April 15, 1989, in New York, NY; married David Moss (div. around 1930); no children. ❖ The day after 33rd birthday, opened her own store, the Gotham Book Mart, in the basement of a brownstone on 45th Street in New York City, stocked with her own collection of out-of-print theater books (1920); her bookstore became a haven for the literati between the wars; an early supporter of authors like John Steinbeck and William Faulkner, helped launch the work of Gertrude Stein, e.e. cummings, Anais Nin and Ezra Pound; was one of the founders of the James Joyce Society, which made the Gotham Book Mart its meeting place; championed new and controversial works, illegally importing and selling such banned books as D. H. Lawrence's *Lady Chatterley's Lover* and Henry Miller's *Tropic of Cancer.* ❖ See also *Women in World History.*

STEN, Anna (1908–1993). Russian-born actress. Born Annel (Anjuschka) Stenskaja Sudakevich, Dec 3, 1908, in Kiev, Ukraine; died in New Yorkm NY, Nov 12, 1993; dau. of a Russian ballet master and a Swedish mother; m. Fedor Ozep (director), c. 1930 (div.); m. Dr. Eugene Frenke (director-producer, div.). ❖ Began acting career with the famed Moscow Art Theater; acted in a number of Russian films, including the comedies *The Girl With the Hat Box* (1927) and *The Yellow Ticket* (1928); made her way to Germany where her performance as Grushenka in the film *The Brothers Karamazov* (1931) caught the attention of Samuel Goldwyn; made US debut in *Nana* (1934), but never quite caught on at the box office; turned to painting; films include *We Live Again* (*Resurrection,* 1934), *Exile Express* (1939), *The Man I Married* (1940), *So Ends Our Night* (1941), *Chetniks* (1943), *Three Russian Girls* (1944), *Let's Live a Little* (1948), *Soldier of Fortune* (1955), *Runaway Daughters* (1956) and *The Nun and the Sergeant* (1962). ❖ See also *Women in World History.*

STENINA, Valentina (1936—). Russian speedskater. Born Valentina Sergeyevna Miloslavova, Dec 29, 1936, in Bobruysk (now Belarus); m. Boris Stenin (champion skater, died 2001). ❖ At World championships, won a silver medal (1959) and gold medals (1960, 1961, 1966), all for allround; won a silver medal at Squaw Valley Olympics (1960) and a silver at Innsbruck Olympics (1964), both for the 3,000 meters; won 4 Soviet titles; retired (1968).

STENZEL, Ursula (1945—). Austrian journalist and politician. Born Sept 22, 1945, in Vienna, Austria. ❖ Journalist and presenter with ORF-TV (1972–99); as a member of the European People's Party (Christian Democrats) and European Democrats, elected to 4th and 5th European Parliament (1994–99, 1999–2004); chaired the Delegation to the EU–Czech Republic Joint Parliamentary Committee. Awarded the Schuman Prize.

STEPAN, Mary Louise (1935—). American swimmer. Born Feb 2, 1935. ❖ At Helsinki Olympics, won a bronze medal in 4 x 100-meter freestyle relay (1952).

STEPANOVA, Maria (1979—). Russian basketball player. Born Feb 23, 1979, in Stavropol, USSR. ❖ Center, won a team bronze medal at Athens Olympics (2004); placed 2nd at World championships (1998) and 1st at European championships (2003); in WNBA, played for Phoenix Mercury (1998–2001).

STEPANOVA, Varvara (1894–1958). Russian artist. Name variations: Warwara Stepanowa; (pseudonym) Varst. Born Varvara Feodorovna Stepanova, Oct 1894, in Kovno, Lithuania (Russia); died in Moscow, May 20, 1958; studied painting at Kazan Art School, 1911; studied at studios of Konstantin Yuon and Ivan Dudin, Moscow, 1912, and Stroganov School of Applied Art, Moscow, 1913; m. Alexander Rodchenko (artist); children: 1 daughter. ❖ Constructivist artist, teacher and theorist, worked primarily in the areas of textiles, apparel, graphics, and theater set designs, frequently in concert with husband, artist and designer Alexander Rodchenko; worked with director Vsevolod Meyerhold on a set design for his reinterpretation of the classic play *The Death of Tarelkin* (1922), then designed the costumes to integrate with the geometric forms of the set as well; work in costume design soon expanded into designing for the clothing industry; began working in a Moscow textile print factory in an attempt to convert these designs into clothing (1923); is especially noted for her innovative graphic designs of contemporary magazines such as *Cine-Photo, Soviet Cinema,* and *Red Student Life,* as well as various books. ❖ See also *Women in World History.*

STEPANOWA, Warwara (1894–1958). *See Stepanova, Varvara.*

STEPANSKAYA, Galina (1949—). Russian speedskater. Born Jan 27, 1949, in USSR. ❖ Won a gold medal for 1,500 meters at Innsbruck Olympics (1976); placed 2nd for small allround at World championships (1977, 1978).

STEPHANIE (1837–1859). Queen of Portugal. Name variations: Stephanie Hohenzollern. Born July 15, 1837; died July 17, 1859; dau. of Josephine of Baden (1813–1900) and Charles Anthony I of Hohenzollern-Sigmaringen (1811–1885), prince of Romania; m. Pedro V or Peter V (1837–1861), king of Portugal (r. 1853–1861), on May 18, 1858.

STEPHANIE DE BEAUHARNAIS (1789–1860). Vicomtesse de Beauharnais and grand duchess of Baden. Born Aug 28, 1789; died Jan 29, 1860; dau. of Claude (1756–1819), count de Beauharnais; adopted as a daughter by Napoleon I Bonaparte (1769–1821), emperor of France; m. Charles Ludwig, grand duke of Baden, on April 8, 1806; children: Louise of Baden (1811–1854), princess of Baden; son (1812–1812); Josephine of Baden (1813–1900); Marie of Baden (1817–1888), princess of Zahringen; Alexander (1816–1817).

STEPHANIE OF BELGIUM (1864–1945). Belgian princess. Name variations: Stephanie Saxe-Coburg. Born May 21, 1864; died in 1945; dau. of Leopold II, king of the Belgians (r. 1865–1909), and Maria Henrietta of Austria (1836–1902); m. Rudolf (1858–1889), crown prince of Austria and Hungary, on May 10, 1881; m. Elemer, prince Lonyai de Nagy, on Mar 22, 1900; children: (1st m.) Elizabeth von Habsburg (1883–1963). ❖ First husband died at Mayerling, along with his mistress Marie Vetsera, as the result of a suicide pact (1889). ❖ See also memoir, *I Was to Be an Empress* (1937).

STEPHANIE OF MONACO (1965—). Princess of Monaco. Name variations: Stephanie Grimaldi. Born Stephanie Marie Elizabeth Grimaldi, Feb 1, 1965, in Monaco; dau. of Princess Grace (Grace Kelly) and Rainier III, Prince of Monaco; sister of Caroline of Monaco and Prince Albert II of Monaco; m. Daniel Ducruet, July 1, 1995 (div. Sept 1996); m. Adans López Peres (circus acrobat), 2003 (sep.); children: (1st m.) Louis (b. 1992) and Pauline (b. 1994); (with Jean Raymond Gottlieb) Camille Marie Kelly (b. 1998). ❖ Pursued brief careers as a model, fashion designer and pop singer; her song "Irresistible" reached #2 on Germany's charts.

STEPHANSEN, Elizabeth (1872–1961). Norwegian mathematician. Name variations: Mary Ann Elizabeth Stephansen; Trasa Stephansen. Born Mar 10, 1872, in Bergen, Norway; died Feb 23, 1961; graduate of Eidgenössische Polytechnikum Zurich in Switzerland, 1896; University of Zurich, PhD, 1902. ❖ The only Norwegian to pass the Eidgenössische Polytechnikum Zurich entrance exam and the 1st Norwegian woman to obtain a doctorate, served as a teacher in Bergen (1896–98); published a doctoral thesis in *Archiv for Mathematik og Naturvidenskab* (1902); awarded a Norwegian travel grant to study at the University of Göttingen in Germany (1902–03); worked as a teacher in Oslo (1904–06); as an employee of the Norwegian College of Agriculture (Landbrukshoiskole) at As, worked as an assistant and taught math and physics (1906–21) and later served as a math docent

(1921–37); retired (1937). Fluent in German, was awarded the King's Medal of Service for assisting Norwegians in the German prisoner-of-war camp Espeland during WWII.

STEPHANSEN, Mary (1872–1961). *See Stephansen, Elizabeth.*

STEPHEN, Julia Prinsep (1846–1895). British children's writer and essayist. Name variations: Julia Duckworth; Julia Jackson Duckworth Stephen; Mrs. Leslie Stephen. Born Julia Prinsep Jackson, Feb 7, 1846, in Calcutta, India; died May 5, 1895, in London, England; dau. of John Jackson and Maria Pattle Jackson; niece of Julia Margaret Cameron; m. Herbert Duckworth, 1867 (died); m. Leslie Stephen, 1878; children: (1st m.) George, Gerald and Stella Duckworth; (2nd m.) Vanessa Bell (b. 1879), Thoby Stephen (b. 1880), Adeline Virginia Stephen (b. 1882), also known as Virginia Woolf (the writer), and Adrian Stephen (b. 1883); stepdaughter Harriet Thackeray. ❖ Published various essays, as well as an entry on Julia Margaret Cameron for *The Dictionary of National Biography* (1882) and a nursing tract, *Notes From Sick Rooms* (1883); her letters are included in *Leslie Stephen's Life in Letters* (1993); wrote several children's stories not published in lifetime. ❖ See also D. F. Gillespie and E. Steele (eds.), *Julia Duckworth Stephen* (Syracuse U., 1987).

STEPHEN, Mrs. Leslie (1846–1895). *See Stephen, Julia Prinsep.*

STEPHEN, Vanessa (1879–1961). *See Bell, Vanessa.*

STEPHEN, Virginia (1882–1941). *See Woolf, Virginia.*

STEPHENS, Alice Barber (1858–1932). American illustrator. Born July 1, 1858, near Salem, New Jersey; died July 13, 1932, in Rose Valley, Pennsylvania; dau. of Samuel Clayton Barber and Mary (Owen) Barber; studied engraving at Philadelphia School of Design for Women; studied life drawing and portraiture under Thomas Eakins at Pennsylvania Academy of Fine Arts; studied at Académie Julian and Filippo Colarossi's school in Paris; m. Charles Hallowell Stephens (art instructor), June 1890; children: Daniel Owen Stephens (b. 1893). ❖ One of the best-known illustrators of her day, worked for such publications as *Century, Cosmopolitan* and *Frank Leslie's Weekly;* became accomplished in a wide variety of media, including oils, charcoal and watercolors; was a regular illustrator for *Ladies' Home Journal* and a number of publishers, including Houghton Mifflin and Thomas Y. Crowell; illustrated books by Louisa May Alcott, Margaret Deland and Sir Arthur Conan Doyle, as well as special editions of Longfellow's *The Courtship of Miles Standish,* Nathaniel Hawthorne's *The Marble Faun* and George Eliot's *Middlemarch.* ❖ See also *Women in World History.*

STEPHENS, Ann S. (1810–1886). American writer. Name variations: Ann Winterbotham Stephens; Jonathan Slick. Born Ann Sophia Winterbotham, Mar 30, 1810, in Humphreysville (later Seymour), Connecticut; died in Newport, Rhode Island, Aug 20, 1886; dau. of John Winterbotham and Ann (Wrigley) Winterbotham (both British immigrants); m. Edward Stephens (merchant), 1831; children: Ann (b. 1841); Edward (b. 1845). ❖ Founded and edited the *Portland Magazine* (1835–37) and the *Portland Sketch Book* (1836), a collection of miscellanies by Maine writers; known for her humor, wrote many novels, including *Fashion and Famine* (1854), and edited the *Pictorial History of the War for the Union* (1865–66) in 2 vols.; also wrote a goodly amount of frontier adventure tales, including *Malaeska: The Indian Wife of the White Hunter* (1860), the 1st dime novel, which sold 500,000 copies and upped her visibility.

STEPHENS, Bunty (1924–1978). *See Stephens, Frances.*

STEPHENS, Catherine (1794–1882). English soprano and actress. Name variations: Catherine Capell-Coningsby, countess of Essex. Born in London, England, Sept 18, 1794; died in London, Feb 22, 1882; m. earl of Essex, 1838 (died 1839). ❖ Began studying singing with Gesualdo Lanza (1807); sang small parts with an Italian company at the Pantheon in London (1812); made debut as Mandane in Arne's *Artaxerxes* at Covent Garden (1813); sang in ballad operas, operas, and other entertainments at Covent Garden (1813–22), Drury Lane (1822–28), then Covent Garden; fashioning herself as a singer with an "English style based on Italian rudiments," became one of the most popular artists of the period; sang Susanna in the 1st London performance of Mozart's *Le nozze di Figaro* (1819); retired (1835). ❖ See also *Women in World History.*

STEPHENS, Frances (1924–1978). English golfer. Name variations: Frances Smith; Bunty Stephens; Mrs. Bunty Smith. Born Frances Stephens, 1924, in Bootle, Lancashire, England; died 1978; m. Roy

Smith, 1955 (test pilot who was killed in a flying accident, 1957); children: 1 daughter. ❖ Won the Lancashire Ladies championship 10 times (1948–55, 1959–60); won Engish Women's championship (1948, 1954–55) and British Open (1949 and 1954); during 5 Curtis Cup matches with US, was undefeated in singles between 1950 and 1958, and won 3 of her foursomes with Elizabeth Price; was president of English Ladies Golf Association. Received OBE (1977).

STEPHENS, Helen (1918–1994). American runner. Name variations: Helen Herring Stephens. Born Feb 3, 1918, in Fulton, MO; died Jan 17, 1994. ❖ Known as the "Missouri Express," won gold medals for the 100 meters and 4 x 100-meter relay at Berlin Olympics (1936); ran races against Jesse Owens, the famed African-American track star. ❖ See also *Women in World History.*

STEPHENS, Kate (1853–1938). American feminist writer, editor and university professor. Born Feb 27, 1853, in Moravia, New York; died May 10, 1938, in Concordia, Kansas; dau. of Nelson Timothy Stephens (lawyer) and Elizabeth (Rathbone) Stephens; University of Kansas, MA in Greek, 1878; engaged to Byron Caldwell Smith (professor), 1874 (died 1877); never married; no children. ❖ Wrote polemical works, including *A Curious History in Book Editing* (1927) and *Lies and Libels of Frank Harris* (1929); wrote several books on Kansas, including *American Thumb-Prints: Mettle of Our Men and Women* (1905); wrote epistolary fiction in *A Woman's Heart* (1906), republished as *Pillar of Smoke,* and feminist essays in *Workfellows in Social Progression* (1916); her love letters from Byron Caldwell Smith were published as *The Professor's Love-Life: Letters of Ronsby Maldclewith* (1919), and republished (1930) as *The Love-Life of Byron Caldwell Smith*; published *Truths Back of the Jimmy Myth in a State University in the Middle West* (1924) which argued her father's claim to founding the University of Kansas law school over that of her brother-in-law, Dr. James Green. ❖ See also *Women in World History.*

STEPHENSON, Elsie (1916–1967). English nurse. Born 1916 in Co. Durham, England; died 1967 in Ireland; trained as nurse at West Suffolk General Hospital; attended Toronto University, 1946; m. William Henry Gardner, 1964. ❖ Qualified in midwifery at Queen Charlotte's Hospital in London (1938), then trained as fever nurse and health visitor (1938–42); during WWII, served with Red Cross in Egypt, Italy, Yugoslavia and Germany (1944–46); studied advanced public health administration at Toronto University (1946); became deputy chief matron of British Red Cross Society (1947–48) and undertook missions to Germany, Singapore, North Borneo, Brunei and Sarawak; served as county nursing officer in East Suffolk (1948), then Newcastle-upon-Tyne (1950–56), creating links between hospital and community; with others, produced influential Jameson Report, *An Inquiry into Health Visiting* (1956); became 1st director of nursing studies unit at Edinburgh University (1956), pioneering academic nursing studies in Europe. ❖ See also Sheila Allan, *Fear Not to Sow–A Life of Elsie Stephenson* (Jamieson, 1990).

STEPHENSON, Jan (1951—). Australian golfer. Born Dec 22, 1951, in Sydney, NSW, Australia; attended Hales Secretarial School in Sydney; lives in Islamorada, FL; m. Eddie Vossler. ❖ Was 5-time winner of the New South Wales (NSW) Schoolgirl championships (1964–69); won the NSW Jr. championships (1969–72); won NSW Amateur twice and named NSW "Woman Athlete of the Year" (1971); turned pro (1972) and played the Australian LPGA tour before joining US tour full time; won Australian LPGA title (1973, 1977); in US, won the Sarah Coventy-Naples Classic and the Birmingham Classic (1976), Women's International (1978), Sun City Classic (1980), Peter Jackson Classic and Mary Kay Classic (1981), LPGA championship and Lady Keystone (1982), Lady Keystone and US Open (1983), Safeco Classic (1987), and J. C. Penney LPGA Skins Game (1990); became 1st woman pro to design golf courses. Named Rookie of the Year (1974). ❖ See also *Women in World History.*

STEPHENSON, Karen Moras (1954—). *See Moras, Karen.*

STEPHENSON, Marjory (1885–1948). English biochemist. Born Jan 24, 1885, in Burwell, Cambridge, England; died Dec 12, 1948; attended Newnham College, 1903–06; studied under F. G. Hopkins; awarded a Beit Memorial fellowship for medical research. ❖ The foremost authority on bacterial metabolism (1930s–40s), was appointed to the permanent staff of the Medical Research Council (1929); was a reader in chemical microbiology at the University of Cambridge; was one of the 1st two women (with Kathleen Lonsdale) to be elected fellow of the Royal Society (1945); served as president of the Society of General Microbiology; wrote *Bacterial Metabolism* (1930), considered a standard work.

STEPNEY, Catherine (1785–1845). British novelist. Name variations: Lady Catherine or Catharine Stepney; Mrs. Manners. Born Catharine or Catherine Pollok, 1785, in Grittleton, Wiltshire, England; died April 14, 1845, in London, England; dau. of Reverend Thomas Pollok and Susannah (Palmer) Pollok; m. C. Russell Manners; m. Sir Thomas Stepney, 1813 (died 1825); children: 1. ❖ Wrote Gothic novels and novels about nobility, including *Castle Nuovier, Or Henry and Adelina* (1806), *The Lords of Erith* (1809), *The New Road to Ruin* (1833), *The Heir-Presumptive* (1835), *The Courtier's Daughter* (1838) and *The Three Peers* (1841).

STEPNIK, Ayelen (1975—). Argentinean field-hockey player. Name variations: Ayelén Stepnik. Born Ayelén Stepnik, Nov 22, 1975, in Rosario, Argentina; sister of German and Gustavo Stepnik (both hockey players); attended University of Rosario. ❖ Midfielder, won a team silver medal at Sydney Olympics (2000) and a team bronze medal at Athens Olympics (2004); won Champions Trophy (2001), World Cup (2002), and Pan American Games (2003).

STEPTOE, Lydia (1892–1982). *See Barnes, Djuna.*

STERBINSZKY, Amalia (1950—). Hungarian handball player. Born Sept 29, 1950, in Hungary. ❖ At Montreal Olympics, won a bronze medal in team competition (1976).

STERKEL, Jill (1961—). American swimmer. Born May 27, 1961, in Hacienda Heights, CA; attended University of Texas. ❖ At Montreal Olympics, won a gold medal in 4 x 100-meter freestyle relay (1976); at Los Angeles Olympics, won a gold medal in 4 x 100-meter freestyle relay (1984); at Seoul Olympics, won a bronze medal in 50-meter freestyle and a bronze medal in 4 x 100-meter freestyle relay (1988); won 20 US national championships and 21 NCAA championships; became swimming coach at University of Texas. Inducted into International Swimming Hall of Fame (2002).

STERLING, Jan (1921–2004). American stage, tv and screen actress. Name variations: Jane Adrian; Jane Sterling. Born Jane Sterling Adriance, April 3, 1921, in New York, NY; died Mar 26, 2004, in Woodland Hills, CA; m. John Merivale (actor), 1941 (div. 1948); m. Paul Douglas (actor), 1950 (died 1959); children: Adams Douglas (1955–2003). ❖ Under name Jane Sterling, made Broadway debut in *Bachelor Born* (1938) and appeared in *When We Were Married, Grey Farm, Panama Hattie* and *Over 21*; as Jan Sterling, appeared in *The Rugged Path* (1945), followed by *Dunnigan's Daughter, This Too Shall Pass, Present Laughter, Two Blind Mice, Born Yesterday, The Perfect Setup* and *The Front Page,* among others; made film debut in *Johnny Belinda* (1948), followed by *Caged, Union Station, Appointment with Danger, Split Second, The Human Jungle, Women's Prison, Female on the Beach, The Harder They Fall, Slaughter on 10th Avenue, Love in a Goldfish Bowl, The Angry Breed* and *First Monday in October,* among others. Nominated for an Oscar as Best Supporting Actress for *The High and the Mighty* (1954).

STERLING, Jane (1921–2004). *See Sterling, Jan.*

STERN, Catherine Brieger (1894–1973). German-born American educational innovator. Name variations: Käthe Brieger. Born Käthe Brieger, Jan 6, 1894, in Breslau, Germany; died Jan 8, 1973, in New York, NY; dau. of Oscar Brieger (physician) and Hedwig (Lyon) Brieger; University of Breslau, PhD in mathematics and physics, 1918; studied Montessori teaching method; m. Rudolf Stern, 1919 (died 1962); children: daughter Toni Stern Gould (b. 1920); son Fritz Stern (b. 1926). ❖ Wrote on the theoretical framework of her teaching experiences in *Methodik der täglichen Kinderhauspraxis* (1932) and on the practicalities of running a kindergarten in *Wille, Phantasie und Werkgestaltung* (1933); wrote on her theories and Gestalt principles in *Children Discover Arithmetic* (1949) and her materials published for classroom use as *Structural Arithmetic* (1951, 1965, 1966); with daughter Toni Stern Gould, wrote *The Early Years of Childhood: Education Through Insight* (1955) and *Children Discover Reading* (1965). ❖ See also *Women in World History.*

STERN, Daniel (1805–1876). *See Agoult, Marie d'.*

STERN, Edith Rosenwald (1895–1980). American philanthropist. Name variations: Mrs. Edgar Rosenwald Stern; Effie Stern. Born Edith Rosenwald in Chicago, Illinois, May 31, 1895; died in Sept 1980 in New Orleans, LA; dau. of Julius (J.R.) Rosenwald and Augusta (Nusbaum) Rosenwald; sister of Marion Rosenwald Ascoli and Adele

Rosenwald; m. Germon Sulzberger, 1913 (div.); m. Edgar Bloom Stern (died 1959); children: Philip, Edgar Jr., Audrey. ❖ Known especially for her charities and reforms in New Orleans, built the Newcomb Nursery School, then the Metairie Country Day School; helped prop up black voter registration; was made a trustee of Dillard University, a black college, and founded the New Orleans repertory theater, the Symphony Society, and the Isaac Delgado Museum of Art; with husband, founded the Stern Fund, which supported philanthropic activities for 20 years. ❖ See also *Women in World History*.

STERN, Elizabeth (1915–1980). Canadian-American pathologist. Born Sept 19, 1915, in Cobalt, Ontario, Canada; died Aug 9, 1980, in Los Angeles, CA; m. Solomon Shankman, 1940. ❖ Received medical degree from University of Toronto, Ontario (1939), and immigrated to US the following year; was among 1st specialists in cytopathology (study of diseased cells); published case report that linked the virus herpes simplex to cervical cancer (1963), the 1st person to link a specific virus to a specific cancer; discovered that prolonged use of birth-control pills was linked to cervical dysplasia (often a precursor of cervical cancer) and published findings in *Science* (1973); provided information about specific progression of cells from normal to advanced stage of cervical cancer, which made possible improved screening techniques for cervical cancer.

STERN, Frances (1873–1947). American social worker and dietitian. Born July 3, 1873, in Boston, Massachusetts; died Dec 23, 1947, in Newton, Massachusetts; dau. of Louis Stern (dealer in boots and shoes) and Caroline (Oppenheimer) Stern; graduate of Garland Kindergarten Training School, 1897; studied food chemistry and sanitation at Massachusetts Institute of Technology, 1909–12; studied at London School of Economics, 1922; never married. ❖ Founded Boston Dispensary Food Clinic (1918), now known as the Frances Stern Nutrition Center; wrote a number of books and articles on diet and health, including *Food for the Worker* (with Gertrude T. Spitz, 1917), *Food and Your Body: Talks with Children* (with Mary Pfaffman, 1932, revised as *How to Teach Nutrition to Children*, 1942), and *Applied Dietetics* (1936). ❖ See also *Women in World History*.

STERN, G. B. (1890–1973). English novelist, short-story writer and playwright. Name variations: Gladys Bronwyn Stern; Gladys Bertha Stern. Born Gladys Bertha Stern, June 17, 1890, in London, England; died Sept 19, 1973; dau. of Albert Stern (gem dealer) and Elizabeth (Schwabacher) Stern; educated in Germany and Switzerland; spent 2 years at Academy of Dramatic Art; m. Geoffrey Lisle Holdsworth (journalist from New Zealand), 1919 (div.). ❖ Published 1st novel, *Pantomime*, at 20; came to prominence with 2nd novel *Twos and Threes* (1916); wrote over 40 novels which appeared every 2 or 3 years in regular succession, with several reprinted in US; best known for a multi-volume saga of the Jewish family Rakonitz, based on her own family, collected as *The Rakonitz Chronicles* (1932) and *The Matriarch Chronicles* (1936); chronicled her conversion to Catholicism in *All in Good Time* (1947). ❖ See also autobiographical memoirs *Monogram* (1936), *Another Part of the Forest* (1941), *Trumpet Voluntary* (1944), *Benefits Forgot* (1949) and *A Name to Conjure With* (1953); and *Women in World History*.

STERN, Irma (1894–1966). South African painter. Born in Schweizer-Reneke, Transvaal, South Africa, in 1894, to German-Jewish parents; died in Cape Town, South Africa, 1966; studied at Weimar Academy in Germany under Carl Fritjof Smith, 1913; studied at Levin-Funcke Studio in Berlin with Gari Melchers and Martin Brandenburg, 1914; studied at Bauhaus in Weimar; m. Johannes Prinze, 1926 (div. 1935). ❖ Regarded as one of the most eminent 20th-century artists in South Africa, moved to Germany with family (1901); was a founding member of Novgruppe (1916), exhibiting work in Berlin, at the Freie Sezession (1918) and at Fritz Gurlitt Gallery (1919); at age 26, returned to South Africa, where she would reside permanently; rendered still-lifes, landscapes, and portraits, often of the black inhabitants of her country; introduced Expressionism to South Africa; by 1940s, had secured her place in the history of South African art. Following her death, her Cape Town home was converted into the Irma Stern Museum. ❖ See also *Women in World History*.

STERNE, Stuart (1845–1905). See Bloede, Gertrude.

STERNHAGEN, Frances (1930—). American stage, tv, and screen actress. Born Jan 13, 1930, in Washington DC; m. Thomas A. Carlin, 1956 (died 1991); children: 6. ❖ Began career as a teacher at the Milton Academy (MA); made professional stage debut at Bryn Mawr as Laura in *The Glass Menagerie* (1948); appeared with Arena Stage in Washington

DC (1953–54); made NY debut as Eva in *Thieves Carnival* (1955), followed by *The Skin of Our Teeth, The Country Wife, Ulysses in Night Town, Great Day in the Morning, The Right Honorable Gentleman, The Cocktail Party, A Slight Ache, The Playboy of the Western World, Enemies, Equus, On Golden Pond, Driving Miss Daisy* and *Mornings at Seven*; made film debut in *Up the Down Staircase* (1967); other films include *The Tiger Makes Out, The Hospital, Two People, Fedora, Starting Over, Outland, Independence Day, Misery, Doc Hollywood* and *The Grass Harp*; frequent appearances on tv include "Spencer," "The Road Home" and "ER." Nominated for 5 Tonys, won for *The Good Doctor* (1973); received Clarence Derwent and Obie awards for *The Admirable Bashville* and an Obie for *The New Pinter Plays*.

STERRY, Mrs. A. (1871–1966). See Cooper, Charlotte.

STETSENKO, Tatyana (1957—). Soviet rower. Born Feb 1957 in USSR. ❖ At Moscow Olympics, won a silver medal in coxed eights (1980).

STETSON, Augusta (1842–1928). American religious leader. Born Augusta Emma Simmons, Oct 12, 1842, in Waldoboro, Maine; dau. of Peabody Simmons (carpenter and architect) and Salome (Sprague) Simmons; died Oct 12, 1928, in Rochester, New York; educated at Lincoln Academy, New Castle, Maine; m. Captain Frederick J. Stetson (shipbuilder), 1864 (died 1901); no children. ❖ After a pivotal experience (1884), became a practitioner in the Christian Science religion; at Mary Baker Eddy's request, traveled to New York City (1886), reluctantly leaving her family, to organize the church there; was formally ordained as a pastor (1890), a title that later was changed to 1st Reader of the First Church of Christ, Scientist, New York City; founded the New York City Christian Science Institute to train practitioners who treated patients and formed the core of support within the congregation (1891); oversaw the building of a new church at 96th Street and Central Park West, an imposing granite structure costing more than $1 million which was dedicated in 1903; when rumors circulated that her ultimate desire was to depose Eddy as leader of the church, her license as a teacher and practitioner was revoked (1909); continued to teach her own version of Christian Science tenets, which she called the Church Triumphant; published her major work, *Sermons Which Spiritually Interpret the Scriptures and Other Writings on Christian Science* (1924); began broadcasting 5 times weekly on radio, interspersing her own religious messages with Christian Science music and readings from the Bible and Eddy's works (1925); used the forum to promulgate her own propaganda: the preservation of Nordic supremacy in America, traditional American virtues, and the belief that the founding documents of the US were "divinely inspired" to protect the country from Catholicism; claiming immortality, also predicted her own resurrection as well as that of Mary Baker Eddy; other writings include *Reminiscences, Sermons, and Correspondence* (1913) and *Vital Issues in Christian Science* (1914), in which she chronicled the controversy of her experiences in the Church. ❖ See also *Women in World History*.

STETSON, Charlotte Perkins (1860–1935). See Gilman, Charlotte Perkins.

STETSON, Helen (1887–1982). American golfer. Name variations: Mrs. Helen Stetson. Born Sept 23, 1887, in Media, PA; died Jan 1982 in Pennsylvania; married the son of the founder of Stetson hats. ❖ Won Whitemarsh Cup (1925, 1927, 1933, 1934, 1936, 1937) and Philadelphia Women championship (1924, 1928); won USGA Women's Amateur and Women's Eastern (1926); represented Huntingdon Valley C. C. in interclub matches for over 30 years.

STETTHEIMER, Florine (1871–1944). American artist. Born in Rochester, New York, Aug 19, 1871; died in New York, NY, May 11, 1944; dau. of Joseph Stettheimer (banker) and Rosetta (Walter) Stettheimer; sister of Stella, Ettie and Carrie Stettheimer; studied painting at Art Students League, and in Munich, Berlin and Stuttgart; never married. ❖ Artist whose lavish, satirical paintings were rediscovered to great acclaim 50 years after her death, when the Whitney Museum mounted "Manhattan Fantastica," an exhibit of her paintings (1995); sometimes described as "rococo subversive" because of the subtle social satire hidden within them, her paintings provide a whimsical view of the Americana that comprised her rarefied world, from Wall Street to high fashion to the art establishment which she ultimately rejected; also designed the sets and costumes for the avant-garde opera *Four Saints in Three Acts*, for an all-black cast (1934); works include *Portrait of Carl Van Vechten* (1922), *Spring Sale at Bendel's* (1922), *Portrait of Myself* (1923), *Beauty Contest* (1924), *Natatorium Undine* (1927), *Bouquet for Ettie* (1927), *Portrait of Stieglitz* (1928), *Cathedrals of Broadway* (1929),

Family Portrait No. 2 (1933) and *Cathedrals of Wall Street* (1939). ❖ See also *Women in World History.*

STEUER, Anni (b. 1913). German runner. Born Feb 12, 1913. ❖ At Berlin Olympics, won a silver medal in 80-meter hurdles (1936).

STEURER, Florence (1949—). French Alpine skier. Born Nov 1, 1949, in Lyon, France. ❖ Placed 4th for giant slalom at Grenoble (1968); won a bronze medal for slalom at Sapporo Olympics (1972); at World championships, won a bronze medal for giant slalom (1966) and silver medals for combined (1970, 1972); at World Cup, placed 3rd overall (1968, 1970) and 2nd overall (1969).

STEVENS, Alzina (1849–1900). American labor leader, journalist, and settlement worker. Born Alzina Ann Parsons, May 27, 1849, in Parsonsfield, Maine; died in Chicago, Illinois, June 3, 1900; dau. of Enoch Parsons (farmer and manufacturer) and Louise (Page) Parsons; married a man named Stevens (div.). ❖ Organized and was 1st president of Working Woman's Union No. 1 in Chicago (1877); moved to Toledo, Ohio (1882), where she advanced quickly to positions of correspondent and editor of the *Toledo Bee*; became a leader in the Knights of Labor in Toledo; was such an important figure in the Ohio labor movement that she was chosen to represent northwestern Ohio's labor organizations at Populist Party's national convention (1892); returned to Chicago (1892) to co-ownership and co-editorship of the short-lived *Vanguard*, a weekly publication devoted to economic and industrial reform; also became associated with Hull House and led in lobbying for child-labor laws; became 1st probation officer at Cook County Juvenile Court in Chicago (1899); helped organize new unions for the American Federation of Labor. ❖ See also *Women in World History.*

STEVENS, Connie (1938—). American actress and singer. Born Concetta Rosalie Ann Ingolia, Aug 8, 1938, in Brooklyn, NY; sister of John Megna; m. James Stacy (actor), 1963 (div. 1966); m. Eddie Fisher (singer), 1967 (div. 1969); children: Joely Fisher (b. 1967, actress) and Tricia Leigh Fisher (b. 1968, actress). ❖ Began career with singing group, The Three Debs; made film debut in *Young and Dangerous* (1957), followed by *Parrish, Susan Slade, Palm Springs Weekend, Never Too Late, Sgt. Pepper's Lonely Hearts Club Band, Grease 2, Back to the Beach* and *Tapeheads,* among others; starred as Cricket Blake on "Hawaiian Eye" (1959–63) and appeared on Broadway in *Star Spangled Girl*; made several recordings, including the Top-10 hit, "Sixteen Reasons" (1961).

STEVENS, Constance (1916—). See Gray, Sally.

STEVENS, E. S. (1879–1972). See Drower, E. S.

STEVENS, Emily (1882–1928). American actress. Born Feb 27, 1882, in New York, NY; died Jan 2, 1928, in New York, NY; dau. of Robert E. Stevens (stage director) and Emma (Maddern) Stevens; niece of Minnie Maddern Fiske (actress); sister of Robert Stevens (actor). ❖ Made stage debut in Bridgeport, CT, with her aunt's troupe in *Becky Sharp* (1900), remaining with the company for 8 more years; made NY debut in *Miranda of the Balcony* (1901); other plays include *The Devil, The Boss, Modern Marriage, Within the Law, The Unchastened Woman, The Gentle Wife, Sophie* (title role), *A Lesson in Love* and *Fata Morgana*; starred in film debut in *Cora*, then played a dual role in *The House of Tears.*

STEVENS, Georgia Lydia (1870–1946). American music teacher and nun. Born May 8, 1870, in Boston, MA; died Mar 28, 1946, in New York, NY; dau. of Henry James Stevens (lawyer) and Helen (Granger) Stevens; began training as violinist at Hoch Conservatorium in Germany, 1888. ❖ Converted to Roman Catholicism (1894); entered Society of the Sacred Heart at Kenwood in Albany, NY (1906); took teaching post at Sacred Heart's Manhattanville school in New York (1914); founded and was active teacher at Chair of Liturgical Music, later known as Pius X Institute and Pius X School of Liturgical Music of Manhattanville College of the Sacred Heart (1916); started publishing "Tone and Rhythm" series (1932). Her school was instrumental in spurring interest in Gregorian chant.

STEVENS, Inger (1934–1970). Swedish-born stage, tv, and screen actress. Born Inger Stensland, Oct 18, 1934, in Stockholm, Sweden; died of barbiturate poisoning, April 30, 1970, in Los Angeles, CA; m. Anthony Soglio, 1955 (div. 1957); m. (secretly) Isaac (Ike) Jones (African-American musician), 1961. ❖ At 13, came to US; began career as a chorine at the Latin Quarter; made Broadway bow in *Debut* (1957); films include *Man on Fire, Cry Terror, The Buccaneer, The World of the Flesh and the Devil, Guide for the Married Man, Madigan* and *A Dream of Kings*; starred in tv series "The Farmer's Daughter" (1963–66); other tv appearances include the episode "Going My Way?" on "The Twilight Zone," where she played a woman who kept passing the same hitchhiker.

STEVENS, Julie (1916–1984). American stage and radio actress. Name variations: Julia Stevens; Helen Trent. Born Nov 23, 1916, in St. Louis, MO; died Aug 26, 1984, in Wellfleet, MA. ❖ On Broadway, appeared in *Snookie, Brooklyn USA, Proof through the Night, The World's Full of Girls, The Male Animal* and *Sleep My Pretty One,* among others; on radio, played the title role in "The Romance of Helen Trent" (1944–60).

STEVENS, K. T. (1919–1994). American actress. Name variations: Katharine Stevens, Baby Gloria Wood. Born Gloria Wood, July 20, 1919, in Hollywood, CA; died June 13, 1994, in Brentwood, CA; dau. of Clara L. (Roush) Wood and Sam Wood (director); sister of Jeane Wood (actress, 1909–1997); m. Hugh Marlowe (actor), 1946 (div. 1968); children: 2 sons, including Chris Marlowe (sportscaster). ❖ Began career as Baby Gloria Wood in the film *Peck's Bad Boy* (1921); under the name Katharine Stevens, made Broadway debut in *Land is Bright* (1941); as K. T. Stevens, appeared in such films as *Address Unknown, Port of New York, Harriet Craig, Bob and Carol and Ted and Alice,* and *Corrina, Corrina;* on tv, appeared as Vanessa Prentiss on the long-running soap "The Young and the Restless."

STEVENS, Katharine (1919–1994). See Stevens, K. T.

STEVENS, Lillian (1844–1914). American temperance reformer. Born Lillian Marion Norton Ames, Mar 1, 1844, in Dover, Maine; died April 6, 1914, in Portland, Maine; dau. of Nathaniel Ames (teacher) and Nancy Fowler (Parsons) Ames; educated at Foxcroft Academy and Westbrook Seminary in Portland; m. Michael T. Stevens (grain and salt dealer), 1865; children: Gertrude Mary Stevens. ❖ Helped found the Maine Woman's Christian Temperance Union (1875), and advanced from her position as its 1st treasurer to the presidency (1878); an especially influential figure in the National Woman's Christian Temperance Union (WCTU), rose to the presidency upon Frances Willard's death (1898); elected vice-president of the World's Women's Christian Temperance Union (1903). ❖ See also *Women in World History.*

STEVENS, Marilyn Buferd (1925–1990). See Buferd, Marilyn.

STEVENS, May (1924—). American painter and feminist. Born 1924 in Boston, MA; studied at Massachusetts College of Art, Art Students League, New York, and Académie Julien, Paris; m. Rudolf Baranik (artist); children: 1 son (committed suicide). ❖ Pop-style painter, had 1st individual exhibition in Paris (1951); taught at New York High School of Music and Art (1953–57), then at Parson's School of Design; became involved in feminist movement; worked on her "Big Daddy" paintings (1967–76), about sexism, racism and militarism, and her "Sea of Words" series (1990–91), among others; works held in the Whitney and Brooklyn Museum of Art.

STEVENS, Nettie Maria (1861–1912). American scientist. Born July 7, 1861, in Cavendish, Vermont; died May 4, 1912, in Baltimore, Maryland; dau. of Ephraim Stevens (carpenter) and Julia (Adams) Stevens; Stanford University, BA, 1899, MA, 1900; Bryn Mawr College, PhD, 1903. ❖ First scientist to demonstrate that gender is determined by a particular chromosome, was a Carnegie research fellow in biology at Bryn Mawr (1903–05), and associate in experimental morphology (1905–12), during which time she worked with prominent German biologist Theodor Boveri (1908–09); published widely in the fields of cytology and experimental physiology. ❖ See also *Women in World History.*

STEVENS, Risë (1913—). American mezzo-soprano. Name variations: Rise Stevens. Born Risë Steenbjorg, June 11, 1913, in the Bronx, NY; dau. of Christian Steenbjorg, also seen as Steenberg (Norwegian), and an American mother; studied with Anna Schoen-René at Juilliard School of Music and in Salzburg with Marie Gutheil-Schoder and Herbert Graf; m. Walter G. Surovy, 1939 (died 2001); children: Nicolas Vincent Surovy. ❖ Debuted in Prague (1936), Metropolitan Opera as Octavian in *Der Rosenkavalier* (1938), Glyndebourne Festival (1939) and Teatro alla Scala (1954); virtually owned the roles of Delilah and Carmen; appeared in the films *The Chocolate Soldier* (1941), opposite Nelson Eddy, and *Going My Way,* starring Bing Crosby (1944); retired from singing (1964); served as co-director of Metropolitan Opera National Company (1965–67); was president of Mannes College of Music (1975–78); became managing director of Metropolitan Opera (1988).

Voted best female vocalist in radio (1947, 1948); honored at the Kennedy Center (1990). ❖ See also *Women in World History*.

STEVENS, Rochelle (1966—). American runner. Born Sept 8, 1966, in Memphis, TN; dau. of Beatrice Holloway Davis (her coach); graduate of Morgan State, 1988. ❖ Won US Indoor championship in the 200 meters (1991); at Barcelona Olympics, won a silver medal in 4×400-meter relay (1992); won a gold medal for the 4×100-meter relay at Atlanta Olympics (1996).

STEVENS, Stella (1936—). American tv and screen actress and director. Born Estelle Caro Eggleston, Oct 1, 1936, in Yazoo City, MS; m. Noble Herman Stephens, 1954 (div.); children: Andrew Stevens (b. 1955, actor). ❖ Made film debut in *Say One For Me*, but came to prominence with *Li'l Abner* (both 1959); other films include *Too Lates Blues, Girls! Girls! Girls!, The Courtship of Eddie's Father, The Nutty Professor, The Silencers, Advance to the Rear, Synanon, The Ballad of Cable Hogue, The Poseidon Adventure, Arnold* and *Nickelodeon*; on tv, had recurring roles on "Surfside Six," "Ben Casey," "Flamingo Road" and "General Hospital"; produced and directed the 90-minute documentary *The American Heroine* (1979) and directed the Canadian feature *The Ranch* (1989).

STEVENS, Yvette Marie (1953—). *See Khan, Chaka.*

STEVENSON, Anne (1933—). British poet. Born Jan 3, 1933, in Cambridge, England; dau. of C(harles) L(eslie) Stevenson (American philosopher) and Louise (Destler) Stevenson; attended University of Michigan; m. R. L. Hitchcock, 1955; m. Mark Elvin, 1962; m. Michael Farley, 1984; m. Peter Lucas, 1987; children: 3. ❖ Educated in Ann Arbor, Michigan, but lived adult life in England, Scotland and Wales; was a fellow at Radcliffe Institute for Independent Women (1970–71), and a fellow of Lady Margaret Hall, Oxford (1975–77); works include *Living in America* (1965), *Correspondence: A Family History in Letters* (1974), *Enough of Green* (1977), *Minute by Glass Minute* (1982), *The Fiction-Makers* (1985), *The Other House* (1990), *Four and a Half Dancing Men* (1993), and *Granny Scarecrow* (2000); also wrote 2 radio plays, "Correspondences" (1975) and "Child of Adam" (1976), and biographies *Elizabeth Bishop* (1966) and *Bitter Fame: A Life of Sylvia Plath* (1989). Received Northern Arts Writer Award (2002).

STEVENSON, Dawn (1971—). *See Stevenson, Nicole.*

STEVENSON, Fanny (1840–1914). American literary celebrity. Name variations: Frances Vandegrift or Frances Van de Grift; Frances or Fanny Osbourne. Born Frances Vandegrift in 1840 in Indianapolis, Indiana; died Feb 1914 in Santa Barbara, California; dau. of Jacob Vandegrift or Van de Grift (farmer and lumber merchant); attended Grez School of Art in France; m. Samuel Osbourne, 1857 (div.); m. Robert Louis Stevenson (the writer), 1880 (died 1894); children: (1st m.) Belle, Samuel Lloyd, Hervey (died 1876). ❖ Wife and caretaker of Robert Louis Stevenson, who defied convention to marry him and is credited with a strong influence on his work; followed silver-mining 1st husband to California; moved to San Francisco where she joined a circle of intellectuals and adventurers; accompanied by her 3 children, went to Paris to study art (1875); while staying at Hotel Chevillon of Grez-sur-Loing in French countryside (1876), met 24-year-old writer Robert Louis Stevenson who had not yet achieved literary fame; began to live openly with him (1877); started her nearly 20-year quest to save him from his frequent bouts of consumption; settled in an artists' colony in Monterey, California (1879) and married him (1880); lived in England (1884–87), then traveled the South Seas from the Marquesas Islands to Tahiti and Hawaii (1888–89); eventually settled on Samoa. ❖ See also Alexandra Lapierre, *Fanny Stevenson: A Romance of Destiny* (Carroll & Graf, 1995); and *Women in World History*.

STEVENSON, Frances (1888–1972). *See Lloyd George, Frances Stevenson.*

STEVENSON, Greta Barbara (1911–1990). New Zealand botanist, mycologist, mountaineer, and teacher. Name variations: Greta Barbara Cone. Born June 10, 1911, in Auckland, New Zealand; died Dec 18, 1990, in London, England; dau. of William Stevenson (clerk) and Grace Mary (Scott) Stevenson; University of Otago, BSc, 1932, MSc, 1933; Imperial College of Science and Technology, London, PhD, 1934; m. Edgar Cone (chemical engineer) 1936 (div. 1966); children: 2. ❖ Worked as analyst for Wellington City Council (late 1930s); taught science at various secondary schools; active in numerous New Zealand botanical societies; helped initiate Wellington Botanical Society's *Bulletin*, 1941; wrote articles and scholarly papers on mycology and published 3 popular self-illustrated books on ferns and fungi; was

research fellow at Cawthron Institute in Nelson (1954–57); became research assistant at Imperial College of Science and Technology in London (1958); returned to New Zealand and served as research officer in botany at Victoria University (1970); also worked at University of Canterbury's botany department (early 1980s); member of New Zealand Alpine Club (1934–49), and made numerous ascents, including that of first significant climb in New Zealand by all-woman party, east peak of Mt. Earnslaw at Lake Wakatipu (1933); active member of New Zealand Women Writers' Society. ❖ See also *Dictionary of New Zealand Biography* (Vol. 4).

STEVENSON, Juliet (1956—). English actress. Born Juliet Anne Stevenson, Oct 30, 1956, in Essex, England; attended Royal Academy of Dramatic Arts. ❖ Made tv debut as Barbara Mallen in "The Mallens" (1978); also starred on "A Doll's House" (1992) and "The Politician's Wife" (1995), among many others; on stage, appeared as Isabella in *Measure for Measure* (1983–84) and earned the Laurence Olivier Theatre Award for Best Actress for performance in *Death and the Maiden* (1992), among others; films include *Drowning by Numbers* (1988), *Truly Madly Deeply* (1991), *Emma* (1996), *Bend It Like Beckham* (2002), *Food of Love* (2002), *Nicholas Nickleby* (2002), *Mona Lisa Smile* (2003) and *Being Julia* (2004). Named Commander of the Order of the British Empire.

STEVENSON, Margaret Beveridge (1865–1941). New Zealand religious reformer. Born Nov 30, 1865, in Onehunga, Auckland, New Zealand; died Feb 11, 1941, at Auckland; dau. of William Stevenson (storekeeper) and Margaret (Trumbull) Stevenson. ❖ Raised Presbyterian but became first New Zealander to convert to teachings of Bahi'i faith (1913), a religion that stresses the unity of all people and the abolition of prejudice; served as president of small Baha'i group formed in 1924 which became first Spiritual Assembly of the Baha'is of Auckland; was acknowledged as "Mother of the Cause" in New Zealand. ❖ See also *Dictionary of New Zealand Biography* (Vol. 4).

STEVENSON, Matilda (1849–1915). American anthropologist. Name variations: Matilda Coxe Stevenson; Tilly Stevenson. Born Matilda Coxe Evans, May 12, 1849, in San Augustine, Texas; died in Oxon Hill, Maryland, June 24, 1915; dau. of Maria Matilda (Coxe) Evans and Alexander H. Evans; m. Colonel James Stevenson (explorer and ethnologist), 1872 (died 1888). ❖ Accompanied husband, an officer of the US Geological Survey (1879), on an expedition to Mexico to study the Zuñi for the newly founded Bureau of American Ethnology; for several years, continued to work alongside him with little recognition, until famed British anthropologist Edwin B. Taylor brought her contributions to light (1884); continued her research on the Zuñi, with particular attention to the roles, duties and rituals of Zuñi women; became founder and 1st president of Women's Anthropological Society of America (1885); appointed to the staff of the Bureau of American Ethnology (1888); undertook a study of the small tribe at the Sia pueblo in New Mexico (1889); her major work, *The Zuñi Indians: Their Mythology, Esoteric Fraternities, and Ceremonies,* a 600-page study with hundreds of illustrations, appeared in the *Twenty-third Annual Report* of the Bureau of American Ethnology (1901–02). ❖ See also *Women in World History*.

STEVENSON, Nicole (1971—). Australian swimmer. Name variations: Dawn Stevenson. Born Nicole Dawn Stevenson, June 24, 1971. ❖ At Barcelona Olympics, won a bronze medal in 200-meter backstroke (1992); won a silver medal for 4×100-meter medley relay and a bronze medal for 800-meter freestyle relay at Atlanta Olympics (1996).

STEVENSON, Mrs. R. H. S. (1906–1944). *See Menchik, Vera.*

STEVENSON, Rona (1911–1988). New Zealand politician. Born Rona Cade, Feb 13, 1911, in Wellington, NZ; died Sept 4, 1988; m. Andrew Stevenson (engineer), 1937. ❖ Spent years involved with Women's Division of Federated Farmers; representing Taupo, served as National Party MP (1963–72); retired (1972). Awarded an MBE (1976).

STEVENSON, Sara Yorke (1847–1921). American archaeologist and Egyptologist. Born Sara Yorke in Paris, France, 1847; died 1921; granted ScD, University of Pennsylvania, the 1st ever conferred on a woman by that institution; m. Cornelius Stevenson, 1870. ❖ Came to US (1862); sent to Egypt for the American Exploration Society to investigate archaeological work in Nile Valley (1898); was curator of the Mediterranean Section of the University of Pennsylvania Museum; writings include *Maximilian in Mexico* and *The Book of the Dead*.

STEVENSON, Sarah Hackett (1841–1909). American physician. Born Sarah Ann Hackett Stevenson, Feb 2, 1841, in Buffalo Grove (now Polo),

Ogle Co., Illinois; died Aug 14, 1909, in Chicago, Illinois; dau. of John Davis Stevenson (merchant and farmer) and Sarah T. (Hackett) Stevenson; educated at Mount Carroll Seminary; graduate of State Normal University (now Illinois State University), 1863; Woman's Hospital Medical College of Chicago, MD, 1874; studied with Thomas Huxley at South Kensington Science School in London; never married; no children. ❖ Opened her medical practice in Chicago (1875); was one of the delegates of Illinois State Medical Society to the national convention of American Medical Association (AMA) in Philadelphia (1876), the 1st female member of the AMA; also became the 1st woman appointed to the staff of Chicago's Cook County Hospital (1881), and the 1st woman appointed to the Illinois State Board of Health (1893); was professor of physiology and histology (1875–80), and of obstetrics (1880–94), at Woman's Hospital Medical College, which became Northwestern University Woman's Medical School in 1891; co-founded Illinois Training School for Nurses (1880); published a popular work, *The Physiology of Woman* (1880). ❖ See also *Women in World History*.

STEVENSON, Vera (1906–1944). *See Menchik, Vera.*

STEWARD, Natalie (1943—). English swimmer. Born April 30, 1943, in UK. ❖ At Rome Olympics, won a bronze medal in the 100-meter freestyle and a silver medal in the 100-meter backstroke (1960).

STEWARD, Susan McKinney (1847–1918). African-American physician. Name variations: Susan Maria Smith McKinney Steward; Dr. Susan McKinney; Dr. Susan Smith. Born Susan Maria Smith, 1847, in Brooklyn, NY; died Mar 7, 1918, at Wilberforce in Ohio; dau. of Anne (Springsteel) Smith and Sylvanus Smith (prosperous pig farmer); m. Rev. William G. McKinney, 1871; m. Theophilus Gould Steward (army chaplain), 1896. ❖ The 3rd African-American woman physician in US and the 1st to practice in New York state, graduated from Clemence Lozier's New York Medical College and Hospital for Women (1870); practiced in Manhattan, then Brooklyn until 1895; helped found and served on staff of the Brooklyn Woman's Homeopathic Hospital and Dispensary (1881–95); was board member and physician at Brooklyn Home for Aged Colored People (1892–95); conducted postgraduate work at Long Island Medical College Hospital (1887–88), the only woman in her class; spent latter part of career as resident physician and member of the faculty of Wilberforce University; was also active in the temperance and suffrage movements.

STEWART. *See also Stuart (in Scotland, the spelling of the surname Stewart was changed to Stuart by brothers Matthew and John Stewart, who adopted the French spelling in 1537).*

STEWART, Adela Blanche (1846–1910). New Zealand diarist. Name variations: Adela Blanche Anderson. Born Adela Blanche Anderson, Jan 1, 1846, at Clifton, Bristol, England; died Feb 12, 1910, at Katikati, New Zealand; dau. of James Anderson and Eliza Catherine (Dick) Anderson; m. Hugh Stewart (military officer), 1870 (died 1909); children: 1 son. ❖ Lived in England, Scotland, Ireland, and Channel Islands, the Mediterranean, West Indies, and Bermuda before immigrating with husband and son to New Zealand (1878); settled and farmed 300 acres near Katikati, and supplemented income by selling plants and dairy products at market; returned to England (1906); published diary detailing their settlement experience, *My Simple Life in New Zealand* (1906). ❖ See also *Dictionary of New Zealand Biography* (Vol. 2).

STEWART, Alexandra (1939—). Canadian-born actress. Born June 10, 1939, in Montreal, Quebec, France; children: (with Louis Malle) 1. ❖ Star and featured player in many French and international films, including *Les Motards, Exodus, The Fire Within* (Solange), *Only When I Larf, Obsessions, Ils, The Man Who Had Power Over Women, The Black Moon, Climats, Mickey One, The Bride Wore Black, Day for Night, In Praise of Older Women, Chanel Solitaire, Intimate Moments, Under the Cherry Moon* and *Frantic*.

STEWART, Alice (1906–2002). British epidemiologist. Born Alice Mary Naish, Oct 4, 1906, in Sheffield, England; died June 23, 2002, in Oxford, England; dau. of Albert Ernest Naish (an internist) and Lucy Wellburn Naish (physician); attended Cambridge and London universities; m. Ludovick Stewart (div. 1950); children: 2, including Anne Marshall (physician). ❖ Scientist condemned by government and the medical community for much of her career, who proved the link between prenatal X-rays and childhood cancers, contradicting the professed safety of low-dose radiation and challenging an establishment which wished time and again that she would just go away; qualified as a doctor (1931);

began work at Oxford University's Department of Social Medicine (1945); was the 1st woman elected to both the Association of Physicians and Royal College of Physicians (1947); published Oxford Survey of Childhood Cancers (1958); officially retired from Oxford University and became research fellow at University of Birmingham (1974); with Mancuso and Kneale, published results of their mortality study of US nuclear workers at Hanford Nuclear Reservation in Washington State in *Health Physics* (1977), concluding that "Hanford workers were dying of cancer from cumulative radiation exposures far below the standards established as safe"; ostracized by the medical and scientific community (1970s); studied with Kneale the effects of radiation on Japanese atom-bomb survivors (1988); testified before US Senate and House committee hearings, warning of flaws in Department of Energy's standards for assessing radiation hazards (1988, 1989); resumed study of Hanford data (1990); though it was thanks to her research and perseverance that the dangerous practice of administering pelvic X-rays to pregnant women stopped in late 1970s, received little professional reward for preventing leukemia and other cancers resulting from exposure to low levels of radiation. Received Right Livelihood Prize (1986); received the Ramazzini Prize for epidemiology (1991). ❖ See also Gayle Greene, *The Woman Who Knew Too Much: Alice Stewart and the Secrets of Radiation* (U. of Michigan Press, 1999); and *Women in World History*.

STEWART, Anastasia (1883–1923). Princess of Greece. Born Jan 20, 1883, in Cleveland, Ohio; died August 29, 1923; dau. of W. E. Stewart; m. William Bateman Leeds; became 1st wife of Prince Christopher Oldenburg of Greece (1888–1940), on Feb 1, 1920. ❖ Christopher's 2nd wife was Françoise of Guise (1902–1953).

STEWART, Anita (1895–1961). American actress. Name variations: Anna Stewart. Born Anna Stewart in Brooklyn, New York, Feb 7, 1895; died May 4, 1961, in Beverly Hills, CA; sister-in-law of director-actor Ralph Ince; sister of silent film actor George Stewart and actress Lucille Lee Stewart. ❖ Joined Vitagraph (1911); eventually became one of the company's major silent screen stars, appearing in dozens of films; sometimes billed by given name Anna Stewart, was usually paired on screen with actor Earle Williams; became focus of a landmark lawsuit in actor-studio relations, when Vitagraph sued her for breach of contract; with advent of talkies, retired from acting to assume control of her own production company, with Louis B. Mayer as her production executive; wrote novel *The Devil's Toy*; films include *The Swan Girl* (1913), *The Goddess* (serial, 1915), *Mary Regan* (1919), *In Old Kentucky* (1919), *A Question of Honor* (1922), *The Great White Way* (1924), *The Prince of Pilsen* (1926), *Wild Geese* (1927), *Romance of a Rogue* (1928) and *Sisters of Eve* (1928). ❖ See also *Women in World History*.

STEWART, Anna (1895–1961). *See Stewart, Anita.*

STEWART, Annabella (d. after 1471). Countess of Huntly. Name variations: Annabella Stuart. Died after 1471; dau. of James I (1394–1437), king of Scotland (r. 1406–1437), and Joan Beaufort (c. 1410–1445); m. Louis, count of Geneva, on Dec 14, 1447 (div. 1458); m. George Gordon, 2nd earl of Huntly, before Mar 10, 1459 (div. 1471); children: (2nd m.) Isabella Gordon (who m. William Hay, 3rd earl of Erroll); Janet Gordon; Elizabeth Gordon; Margaret Gordon; Agnes Gordon; Alexander, earl of Huntly. ❖ See also *Women in World History*.

STEWART, Anne (fl. 1515). Countess of Lennox. Name variations: Anne Stuart; some sources show her as Lady Elizabeth Stuart. Dau. of John Stewart (c. 1440–1512), 1st earl of Atholl (John of Balveny), and Eleanor Sinclair (d. 1518, dau. of the earl of Orkney and Caithness); m. John Stewart (d. 1526), 3rd earl of Lennox (r. 1473–1526, murdered by Sir James Hamilton of Finnart), on Jan 19, 1511; m. Ninian, 3rd Lord Ross, on Dec 9, 1529; children: (1st m.) Matthew Stuart (1516–1571), 4th earl of Lennox (father of Lord Darnley); Robert Stewart (c. 1516–1586), 6th earl of Lennox; John Stuart (d. 1567), 5th Lord of Abigney; Helen Stewart (who m. William Hay, 6th earl of Erroll); Elizabeth Stewart (mistress of James V [1512–1542], king of Scotland).

STEWART, Arabella (1575–1615). *See Stuart, Arabella.*

STEWART, Beatrice (d. around 1424). Countess of Douglas. Name variations: Beatrix Stuart; Beatrix Sinclair. Died c. 1424; dau. of Robert Stewart of Fife (c. 1339–1420), 1st duke of Albany (and brother of Robert III, king of Scotland), and Margaret Graham (d. 1380), countess of Menteith; m. James Douglas, 7th earl of Douglas.

STEWART, Catherine Campbell (1881–1957). New Zealand welfare worker, political activist, and politician. Name variations: Catherine Campbell Sword. Born Catherine Campbell Sword, Aug 15, 1881, in

Glasgow, Scotland; died April 2, 1957, in Glasgow; dau. of William Baird Sword (journeyman ironfitter) and Margaret Christina (Neilson) Sword; m. Charles Stewart (foreman ironfitter), Mar 23, 1900 (died 1948); children: 3 sons. ❖ Worked for Labor candidates in Glasgow and founded Women's Co-operative Guild; also involved with British suffrage movement; was a member of Women's Social and Political Union; with family, immigrated to New Zealand at age 40 (1921); was executive member of Wellington After-care Association for intellectually impaired children (1920s); active in women's branch of New Zealand Labor Party; helped establish Women's Central Co-operative Committee and Wellington District Co-operative Society (1930s); served as Labour MP from Wellington West (1938–43), the 2nd woman to be elected to the New Zealand Parliament and, until 1960, the only woman to win a seat without the help of a by-election; returned to Glasgow (1950). ❖ See also *Dictionary of New Zealand Biography* (Vol. 4).

STEWART, Cora Wilson (1875–1958). American educator. Name variations: The Moonlight-School Lady. Born in Farmers, Kentucky, 1875; died 1958; attended Morehead Normal School (later Morehead State University) and University of Kentucky. ❖ Leader in the movement against adult illiteracy, taught for a time in Rowan Co., Kentucky; began serving as school superintendent of the county (1901); reelected (1909); opened 50 schoolhouses in Rowan Co. to be used to teach adults at night, a highly successful campaign later known as the movement for Moonlight Schools (1911); became the director of the National Illiteracy Crusade (1913); was the 1st woman president of the Kentucky Education Association and served as chair of the Commission on Illiteracy during the Hoover administration in the early years of the Great Depression. ❖ See also Willie Nelms, *Cora Wilson Stewart: Crusader against Illiteracy* (McFarland, 1997); and *Women in World History*.

STEWART, Egidia (d. after 1388). Lady Nithsdale. Died after 1388; dau. of Robert II (1316–1390), king of Scotland (r. 1371–1390), and Euphemia Ross (d. 1387, his 2nd wife); m. William Douglas of Nithsdale, in 1387; children: William, lord of Nithsdale; Egidia Douglas (who m. Henry, earl of Orkney).

STEWART, Egidia (fl. 14th c.). Scottish princess. Name variations: Edgitha Stewart; Egidia Stuart. Dau. of Robert III (1337–1406), king of Scotland (r. 1390–1406), and Annabella Drummond (1350–1401).

STEWART, Elaine (1929—). American actress. Born Elsa Steinberg, May 31, 1929, in Montclair, NJ. ❖ Made film debut in *Sailor Beware* (1951), followed by *The Bad and the Beautiful, Young Bess* (as Anne Boleyn), *Brigadoon, Night Passage, The Rise and Fall of Legs Diamond* and *Most Dangerous Man Alive,* among others.

STEWART, Eleanor (1427–1496). Archduchess of Austria. Name variations: Eleanor Stuart; Eleonore von Osterreich. Born Oct 26, 1427; died in 1496 (some sources cite Nov 20, 1480); dau. of James I (1394–1437), king of Scotland (r. 1406–1437), and Joan Beaufort (c. 1410–1445); m. Sigismund von Tirol, archduke of Austria, on Feb 12, 1449.

STEWART, Eleanor (1868–1920). See Porter, Eleanor H.

STEWART, Eliza Daniel (1816–1908). American temperance leader. Name variations: Mother Stewart. Born Eliza Daniel, April 25, 1816, in Piketon, Ohio; died Aug 6, 1908, in Hicksville, Ohio; dau. of James Daniel (farmer) and Rebecca (Guthery) Daniel; attended Granville and Marietta, Ohio, seminaries; m. Joseph Coover (died); m. Hiram Stewart, 1848; children: (2nd m.) 5 who died in infancy. ❖ Established the 1st Woman's Temperance League, the predecessor of the Woman's Christian Temperance Union (WCTU), in Osborn, Ohio (1873); took her message to Great Britain in support of the British Women's Temperance Association and the Scottish Christian Union (1876); delivered opening speech to World's WCTU convention in London (1895); wrote *Memories of the Crusade: A Thrilling Account of the Great Uprising of the Women of Ohio in 1873, against the Liquor Crime* (1888) and *The Crusader in Great Britain; or, The History of the Origin and Organization of the British Women's Temperance Association* (1893). ❖ See also *Women in World History*.

STEWART, Elizabeth (fl. 1300s). English noblewoman. Name variations: Elizabeth Stuart; Elizabeth de la Haye. Flourished in the 1300s; dau. of Elizabeth Muir (d. before 1355) and Robert II (1316–1390), earl of Atholl, earl of Strathearn (r. 1357–1390), king of Scots (r. 1371–1390); m. Thomas Hay also known as Thomas de la Haye, great constable of Scot, before Nov 7, 1372; children: William; Gilbert of Dronlaw;

Elizabeth de la Haye (who m. George Leslie of Rothes); Alice de la Haye (who m. Willam Hay of Locharret).

STEWART, Elizabeth (c. 1390–?). Scottish noblewoman. Born c. 1390; dau. of Robert Stewart, 1st duke of Albany, and Muriel Keith (d. 1449); m. Malcolm Fleming.

STEWART, Elizabeth (d. before 1411). Lady of Dalkeith. Name variations: Elizabeth Douglas; Elizabeth Stuart; Lady Dalkeith. Died before 1411; dau. of Sir John Stewart of Kyle, later known as Robert III (1337–1406), king of Scotland (r. 1390–1406), and Annabella Drummond (1350–1401); m. James Douglas, lord of Dalkeith, around 1387; children: William Douglas (b. 1390); James, 2nd lord of Dalkeith; Henry Douglas.

STEWART, Elizabeth (fl. 16th c.). Royal mistress. Dau. of John Stewart, 3rd earl of Lennox, and Lady Anne Stewart (fl. 1515); mistress of James V (1512–1542), king of Scotland (r. 1513–1542); children: Adam Stewart, prior of Charterhouse. ❖ See also *Women in World History*.

STEWART, Elizabeth (fl. 1578). Countess of Lennox and countess of Arran. Name variations: Lady Elizabeth Stewart; Elizabeth Stuart. Flourished around 1578; dau. of John Stewart, 4th earl of Atholl, and Elizabeth Gordon (dau. of George Gordon, 4th earl of Huntly, and Elizabeth Kieth); m. Hugh Fraser, 6th Lord Lovat; m. Robert Stewart (c. 1516–1586), 6th earl of Lennox (r. 1578–1586), on Dec 6, 1578 (div.); m. James Stewart, earl of Arran, on July 6, 1581.

STEWART, Ellen (c. 1920—). African-American producer. Name variations: Mama Stewart. Born c. 1920 in Alexandria, Louisiana; educated at Arkansas State University. ❖ Theater producer, manager, and director who founded the pioneer La Mama Experimental Theater Company, spawning the "off-off-Broadway" renaissance and originating one of the most important experimental theaters in the world; worked as a freelance fashion designer until 1961; rented a basement on 9th Street, started her own theater which she named La Mama, and premiered 1st production, Tennessee Williams' *One Arm* (July 27, 1962); began producing original plays; started workshops to teach acting and added more directors and actors to the company; began an intensive exchange program, in which La Mama would travel abroad and foreign theater groups would perform at La Mama in New York (by 1981, there were 4 La Mama theaters in the NY area and branches in Boston, Amsterdam, Bogota, Israel, London, Melbourne, Morocco, Munich, Paris, Tokyo, Toronto and Vienna). Received MacArthur Foundation's "genius" grant (1985); inducted into the Theater Hall of Fame (1993). ❖ See also *Women in World History*.

STEWART, Ethel Smith (1907–1979). See Smith, Ethel.

STEWART, Euphemia (c. 1375–1415). Countess of Strathearn and countess of Caithness. Born c. 1375; died in Oct 1415; dau. of David Stewart, earl of Strathearn; m. Patrick Graham of Kilpont, before 1406; children: Malise Graham (d. before 1490), 1st earl of Strathearn; Euphemia Graham (d. 1469); Elizabeth Graham (who m. John Lyon of Glamis).

STEWART, Frances Ann (1840–1916). New Zealand social activist. Name variations: Frances Ann Carkeek. Born Frances Ann Carkeek, June 18, 1840, at Sydney, Australia; died Nov 12, 1916, at Wanganui, New Zealand; dau. of Stephen Carkeek and Martha (Piotti) Carkeek; m. John Tiffin Stewart (provincial engineer), 1865 (died 1913); children: 5 daughters, 5 sons. ❖ Active in community affairs, supported temperance and women's suffrage movements, and advocated better training of nurses; affiliated with Wanganui Orphanage (1889); donated land to establish Wanganui Girls' College; donated her home, which became known as Stewart Karitane Home, to the care of children; was 1st woman member of hospital board (1897). ❖ See also *Dictionary of New Zealand Biography* (Vol. 2).

STEWART, Frances Teresa (1647–1702). See Stuart, Frances.

STEWART, Isabel (fl. 1390–1410). Countess of Ross. Dau. of Robert Stewart of Fife (c. 1339–1420), 1st duke of Albany (and brother of Robert III, king of Scotland), and Margaret Graham (d. 1380), countess of Menteith; m. Alexander Leslie, 7th earl of Ross (some sources cite 9th earl of Ross), before 1398 (died 1402); m. Walter of Dirleton, Lord Haliburton, around 1405; children: (1st m.) Euphemia Leslie (d. after 1424), countess of Ross; (2nd m.) Walter Haliburton; Christina Haliburton.

STEWART, Isabel (d. around 1410). Scottish princess and countess of Douglas. Name variations: Isabel Stewart; Isabella Stuart; Isabel Douglas; Isabel Edmondstone. Died c. 1410; dau. of Robert II (1316–1390), king of Scots (r. 1371–1390), and Elizabeth Muir (d. before 1355); m. James Douglas, 2nd earl of Douglas, after Sept 24, 1371; m. John Edmondstone, around 1389; children: (2nd m.) 1.

STEWART, Isabel (d. 1494). Duchess of Brittany. Name variations: Isabella, duchess de Bretagne; Isabel Stuart. Died in 1494; dau. of James I (1394–1437), king of Scotland (r. 1406–1437), and Joan Beaufort (c. 1410–1445); m. Francis duc de Bretagne also known as Francis I (b. 1414), duke of Brittany, on Oct 30, 1442; children: Marguerite de Foix (fl. 1456–1477); Marie of Dreux (who m. John, viscount de Rohan).

STEWART, Isabel Maitland (1878–1963). Canadian nurse and educator. Born Jan 14, 1878, in Raleigh, Ontario, Canada; died Oct 5, 1963, in Chatham, New Jersey; dau. of Francis Beattie Stewart (Presbyterian missionary) and Elizabeth (Farquharson) Stewart; attended Winnipeg General Hospital School of Nursing, 1900–03; graduate of Columbia University Teachers College, BS, 1911, AM, 1913. ❖ Was supervisor of nursing at Winnipeg General Hospital; trained under Mary Adelaide Nutting at Columbia Teachers College (1908), then remained at the college as an instructor; became director of nursing department as the Helen Hartley Jenkins Foundation Professor of Nursing Education, succeeding Nutting (1925); turned the program into the best of its kind in the nation; helped to establish Association of Collegiate Schools of Nursing (1932); wrote *Opportunities in the Field of Nursing* (1912), as well as *The Education of Nurses: Historical Foundations and Modern Trends* and the 5-vol. set *A Short History of Nursing*; retired (1947). ❖ See also *Women in World History*.

STEWART, Jean (d. after 1404). Scottish princess. Name variations: Lady Jean Stuart. Died after 1404; interred at Scone Abbey, Perthshire; dau. of Robert II (1316–1390), king of Scots (r. 1371–1390), and Elizabeth Muir; m. Sir John Keith, on Jan 17, 1373; m. Sir John Lyon of Glamis, chamberlain of Scotland, in 1379; m. Sir James Sandilands of Calder, in Nov 1384; children: (1st m.) Sir Robert Keith; Robert, lord of Strathkyn; (2nd m.) Sir John Lyon; (3rd m.) Sir James of Calder.

STEWART, Jean (d. 1486). Scottish noblewoman. Name variations: Jean Stuart; Joan Stewart or Stuart; Joan "the Dumb Lady." Born a deaf mute; died after Oct 16, 1486; dau. of James I (1394–1437), king of Scotland (r. 1406–1437), and Joan Beaufort (c. 1410–1445); m. James Douglas, 3rd earl of Angus, on Oct 18, 1440; m. James Douglas, 1st earl of Morton, before May 15, 1459; children: (2nd m.) John Douglas, earl of Morton; Janet Douglas; James Douglas; Elizabeth Douglas.

STEWART, Jean (1930—). New Zealand swimmer. Born Dec 23, 1930, in New Zealand. ❖ At Helsinki Olympics, won a bronze medal in 100-meter backstroke (1952).

STEWART, Joan (fl. 15th c.). Scottish royal. Dau. of Robert Stewart of Fife (c. 1339–1420), 1st duke of Albany (and brother of Robert III, king of Scotland), and Margaret Graham (d. 1380), countess of Menteith; m. Robert Stewart of Lorn, 1st Lord Lorn, after Sept 27, 1397; children: John Stewart, 2nd Lord Lorn; Walter, 3rd Lord Lorn; Alan; David; Robert; Isabel Stewart.

STEWART, Katherine (d. after 1394). Scottish princess. Died after 1394; dau. of Elizabeth Muir (d. before 1355) and Robert II (1316–1390), earl of Atholl, earl of Strathearn (r. 1357–1390), king of Scots (r. 1371–1390); m. Sir Robert of Restalrig.

STEWART, Katherine (fl. 14th c.). Scottish princess. Name variations: sometimes referred to as Jean or Elizabeth; Katherine Lindsay; Catherine Stuart. Dau. of Robert II (1316–1390), king of Scots (r. 1371–1390), and Euphemia Ross (d. 1387); m. David Lindsay, 1st earl of Crawford, in 1380; children: Alexander, earl of Crawford; David, lord of Newdosk; Gerard; Ingelram, bishop of Aberdeen; Marjory Lindsay; Elizabeth Lindsay; Isabella Lindsay.

STEWART, Katherine (c. 1861–1949). English stage actress. Born c. 1861 in Kent, England; died Jan 24, 1949, in New York, NY. ❖ Accompanied Lillie Langtry's company to NY; later appeared with John Drew and Olga Nethersole; plays include *The Age of Innocence, Ode to Liberty, Tonight or Never* and *I Married an Angel*.

STEWART, Louisa (1752–1824). *See Louise of Stolberg-Gedern.*

STEWART, Margaret (fl. 1350). Scottish princess. Dau. of Robert II (1316–1390), king of Scotland (r. 1371–1390), and Elizabeth Muir (d. before 1355); m. John MacDonald, lord of the Isles, after June 14, 1350; children: Donald, lord of the Isles; John Ian Mor Tanistier; Alexander; Angus; Hugh, thane of Glentilt; Marcus; Mary MacDonald; Elizabeth (sometimes referred to as Margaret) MacDonald.

STEWART, Margaret (fl. 14th c.). Scottish royal. Name variations: Margaret of Albany. Dau. of Robert Stewart of Fife (c. 1339–1420), 1st duke of Albany (and brother of Robert III, king of Scotland), and Margaret Graham (d. 1380), countess of Menteith; m. Sir John Swinton, around 1392. ❖ Is often shown married to Robert Stewart, Lord of Lorn, but she is probably being confused with her sister Joan Stewart.

STEWART, Margaret (d. before 1456). Scottish princess. Died before 1456; dau. of Sir John Stewart of Kyle, later known as Robert III (1337–1406), king of Scotland (r. 1390–1406) and Annabella Drummond (1350–1401); m. Archibald Douglas, 4th earl of Douglas; children: Archibald Douglas, 5th earl of Douglas; Elizabeth Douglas (d. before 1451).

STEWART, Margaret (fl. 1460–1520). Scottish princess. Name variations: Margaret Stuart. Flourished between 1460 and 1520; dau. of Mary of Guelders (1433–1463) and James II (1430–1460), king of Scotland (r. 1437–1460); abducted by William Crichton; m. William Crichton, 3rd lord Crichton (div. 1520); children: Margaret Crichton (d. before 1546, who m. William Todrik, George Halkerstoun, and George Lesley, earl of Rothes).

STEWART, Maria Clementina (1702–1735). *See Sobieski, Clementina.*

STEWART, Maria W. (1803–1879). African-American women's-rights and civil-rights activist. Born Frances Maria Miller, 1803, in Hartford, Connecticut; died Dec 17, 1879, in Washington, DC; dau. of a free black couple named Miller; educated through Sabbath schools; m. James W. Stewart (shipping agent), Aug 10, 1826 (died Dec 17, 1829); no children. ❖ Orphaned at 5, was indentured as a servant to a cleric until age 15; began to speak publicly, urging blacks to become educated and actively pursue their rights; published *Religion and the Pure Principles of Morality, the Sure Foundation on Which We Must Build,* a 12-page pamphlet (1831); continued to express her views through public-speaking engagements and is remembered for 4 notable addresses (1832–33), which were published together with other essays and poems, as *Productions of Mrs. Maria W. Stewart* (1835); financed the publishing of a 2nd edition of her speeches, *Meditations from the Pen of Mrs. Maria W. Stewart* (1879); was the 1st American-born woman to speak on political themes to audiences of both men and women and probably the 1st African-American woman to speak in defense of women's rights. ❖ See also Marilyn Richardson, ed. *Maria W. Stewart, America's First Black Woman Political Writer: Essays & Speeches* (Indiana U. Press, 1987); and *Women in World History*.

STEWART, Marjorie (d. after 1417). Countess of Moray. Name variations: Marjory Stuart. Died after May 6, 1417; dau. of Robert II (1316–1390), king of Scots (r. 1371–1390), and Elizabeth Muir (d. before 1355); m. John Dunbar, 1st earl of Moray, after July 11, 1370 or 1371; m. Sir Alexander Keith of Grantown or Grandown, before April 24, 1403; children: (1st m.) Thomas, earl of Moray; Alexander; James; Euphemia Dunbar (who m. Alexander Cumming); (2nd m.) Christina Keith (who m. Sir Patrick Ogilvy).

STEWART, Marjory (d. before 1432). Scottish royal. Name variations: Marjorie; sometimes referred to as Marcellina. Died before August 1432; dau. of Robert Stewart, 1st duke of Albany, and Muriel Keith (d. 1449); m. Duncan Campbell, 1st lord Campbell of Lochawe.

STEWART, Marlene (1934—). *See Streit, Marlene Stewart.*

STEWART, Martha (1941—). American designer, tv host and entrepreneur. Born Martha Helen Kostyra, Aug 3, 1941, in Jersey City, NJ; dau. of Edward and Martha Kostyra (1st generation Polish-Americans); graduate of Barnard College; m. Andrew Stewart (publisher), 1961 (div. 1990); children: Alexis (b. 1965). ❖ Was one of the 1st female stockbrokers on Wall St. (1968–75); for years, built up a catering business from her Westport (CT) basement; had syndicated tv show "Martha Stewart Living" (1991–2004); launched magazine *Martha Stewart Living*; had regular segments on NBC's "Today" (1990–87) and CBS's "Early Show" (1999–2002); had a syndicated "Ask Martha" column; sent out mail-order catalogs; signed with Kmart to produce her own name-brand goods; became the wealthiest self-made woman in media when Martha Stewart Living Omnimedia went public (1999); convicted of 4 felony charges (Mar 5, 2004), served a 5-month sentence with more panache than anyone had given her credit for.

STEWART, Mary (d. 1458). Scottish princess. Name variations: Mary Stuart. Died in 1458; interred at Strathblane Church, Scotland; dau. of Sir John Stewart of Kyle, later known as Robert III (1337–1406), king of Scotland (r. 1390–1406), and Annabella Drummond (1350–1401); m. George Douglas, 13th (1st) earl of Angus, in 1387; m. Sir James Kennedy of Dunure, in 1405; m. Sir William Cunningham, in July 1409; m. William of Kincardine, later known as 1st Lord Graham, on Nov 13, 1413; m. William Edmonstone or Edmondstone of Duntreath, in 1425; children: (1st m.) William (b. around 1398), 2nd earl of Angus; Elizabeth Douglas (who m. Sir David Hay of Yester); (2nd m.) James Kennedy (b. 1405), bishop of Dunkeld; Gilbert (b. around 1406), Lord Kennedy; Sir John Kennedy; (4th m.) Patrick Graham, archbishop of St. Andrews; Robert Graham.

STEWART, Mary (d. 1465). Countess of Buchan. Name variations: Mary Stuart. Died Mar 20, 1465; interred at Sandenburg-ter-Veere, Zeeland; dau. of James I (1394–1437), king of Scotland (r. 1406–1437), and Joan Beaufort (c. 1410–1445); m. Wolfaert van Borselen, count of Grandpre, in 1444; children: two sons. ❖ See also *Women in World History.*

STEWART, Mary (c. 1451–1488). Scottish princess. Name variations: Mary Stuart. Born c. 1451; died in May 1488; dau. of Mary of Guelders (1433–1463) and James II (1430–1460), king of Scotland (r. 1437–1460); sister of James III, king of Scotland (r. 1460–1488); m. Thomas Boyd, 1st earl of Arran, on April 26, 1467 (div. 1473); m. James Hamilton, 1st Lord Hamilton, in April 1474; children: (1st m.) James, 2nd Lord Boyd; Margaret (Gizelda) Boyd (c. 1470–after 1516, who m. Alexander, 4th Lord Forbes, and David Kennedy, 1st earl of Cassilis); (2nd m.) James Hamilton; Elizabeth Hamilton (who m. Matthew Stewart, 2nd earl of Lennox); Patrick Hamilton of Kincavil; Robert Hamilton, seigneur d'Aubigny. ❖ See also *Women in World History.*

STEWART, Mary (1542–1587). See *Mary Stuart.*

STEWART, Mary (1916—). British novelist. Born Mary Florence Elinor Rainbow, Sept 17, 1916, in Sunderland, Co. Durham, England; dau. of Frederick Albert Rainbow and Edith Matthews Rainbow; Durham University, BA and MA; m. Sir Frederick Henry Stewart (chair of the geology deparment, Edinburgh University), 1945. ❖ Won British Crime Writer's Association Award for *My Brother Michael* (1959) and Mystery Writers of America Award for *This Rough Magic* (1964); her bestselling novels, generally praised by critics, include *Madam, Will You Talk?* (1955), *Nine Coaches Waiting* (1958), *The Moon-Spinners* (1968), *Thornyhold* (1988) and *Rose Cottage* (1997); wrote children's books *The Little Broomstick* (1971) and *Ludo and the Star Horse* (1974); also known for her trilogy on Merlin, including *The Last Enchantment*; elected fellow of Royal Society of the Arts (1968).

STEWART, Mary Downie (1876–1957). New Zealand political host and welfare worker. Born Nov 13, 1876, in Dunedin, New Zealand; died Mar 27, 1957, in Dunedin; dau. of William Downie Stewart (lawyer and politician) and Rachel (Hepburn) Stewart; sister of William Downie Stewart, mayor of Dunedin, and later minister of customs and minister of finance. ❖ Served as political host for brother (1913–33); was active in New Zealand Society for the Protection of Women and Children and Ladies' Benevolent Advisory Committee of Otago Hospital Board. ❖ See also *Dictionary of New Zealand Biography* (Vol. 3).

STEWART, Mother (1816–1908). See *Stewart, Eliza Daniel.*

STEWART, Muriel (d. 1449). See *Keith, Muriel.*

STEWART, Nellie (1858–1931). Australian singer and actress. Name variations: Eleanor Stewart Towzey. Born Eleanor Stewart Towzey, Nov 22, 1858, in Wolloomooloo, Sydney, Australia; died June 20, 1931, in Sydney; dau. of Richard Towzey (actor who changed his last name to Stewart) and Theodosia Stewart (actress); m. Richard Goldsborough Row, 1884 (div.); lived with George Musgrove until his death in 1916. ❖ At 5, made acting debut with father in *The Stranger* in Melbourne; played principal boy in *Sinbad the Sailor* (1881); after a successful run as drummer boy in *La Fille du Tambour Major*, was cast in leads for Royal Comic Opera, formed by J. C. Williamson, A. Garner, and George Musgrove; traveled to England with Musgrove (1887); returned to Australia to star in popular Gilbert and Sullivan productions directed by Musgrove; also appeared as Marguerite in *Faust* (1888); had

an 80-show run in *Blue-Eyed Susan* at Prince of Wales in London (1891) and bigger successes at Drury Lane pantomimes (1898, 1899); returned to Australia, where her performance as Nell Gwynn in *Sweet Nell of Old Drury* became the role for which she is most famous; also appeared in film *Sweet Nell* and released recordings; opened Nellie Stewart School of Acting. ❖ See also autobiography *My Life's Story* (1923); and *Women in World History.*

STEWART, Olga Margaret (1920–1998). Scottish botanist and botanical artist. Born Olga Margaret Mounsey, July 1, 1920, in Edinburgh, Scotland; died Aug 6, 1998; m. Frank Stewart (lawyer), Nov 28, 1946. ❖ Prolific field botanist, studied architecture at the Art College in Edinburgh, Scotland (1938–39) and engineering at Dalhousie University in Halifax, Canada (1939–40); served as a Naval Dockyard draftswoman for the National Research Council of Canada in Halifax (1940–43); worked for the Royal Navy in Edinburgh, Scotland (1943–45); joined (1947) and served as a branch secretary of the Wild Flower Society; recorded plants in a diary (more than 3,400 total); joined (1965) and served as a Kirkcudbrightshire (Scotland) vice-county recorder for the Botanical Society of the British Isles; created most of the drawings for Mary McCallum Webster's *Flora of Moray, Nairn and East Inverness* (1978).

STEWART, Rachelina Hepburn (1873–1955). See *Armitage, Rachelina Hepburn.*

STEWART, Rosie (1970–2003). See *Gallagher, Rosie.*

STEWART, Sarah (1906–1976). American viral oncologist. Born Aug 16, 1906, in Tecalitlan, Mexico; grew up in New Mexico; died of cancer, Nov 27, 1976; dau. of George (mining engineer) and Maria Andrade Stewart; New Mexico State University, AB, 1927; University of Chicago, PhD, 1939; Georgetown University, MD. ❖ Joined the Microbiology Laboratory of the National Institute of Health (NIH) where she researched bacteria (1936–44); transferred to the NIH's National Cancer Institute (1947) but lost her position when she returned to school to earn her MD; with Bernice Eddy, discovered the SE polyoma virus (named after Stewart and Eddy), which caused cancer in mammals (the discovery, which initially met with widespread skepticism, was eventually regarded as a major scientific breakthrough); received Federal Women's Award by President Lyndon Johnson (1965).

STEWART, Sarah (1911—). Scottish swimmer. Born July 19, 1911, in Scotland. ❖ At Amsterdam Olympics, won a silver medal in 4 x 100-meter freestyle relay (1928).

STEWART, Sophie (1908–1977). Scottish stage, radio, and screen actress. Born Mar 5, 1908, in Crieff, Perthshire, Scotland; died June 6, 1977, in London, England; m. Ellis Irving. ❖ Originally pursued a career in ballet until an accident intervened; had long and successful career on stage in England and Australia, especially in the title role of *Marigold*; made over 40 films, including *Things to Come, Murder in the Old Red Barn, As You Like It, Nurse Edith Cavell, Things to Come, My Son, My Son!* and *The Inheritance.* Nominated for TV Actress of the Year in Melbourne, Australia, for her performance in "Fly By Night" (1962).

STEWART, Mrs. Thomas (b. 1926). See *Lear, Evelyn.*

STEWART-MACKENZIE, Maria (1783–1862). Scottish matriarch. Name variations: Lady Hood. Born Maria Elizabeth Frederica Mackenzie in 1783; died in 1862; m. Sir Samuel Hood (1724–1816), an admiral, created Baron Hood of Catherington (an Irish peerage) in 1782, created 1st viscount Hood and governor of Greenwich in 1796 (died 1815); m. James Alexander Stewart of Glasserton, in 1817. ❖ Succeeded to the headship of clan Mackenzie (1815); was also a friend of Sir Walter Scott.

STEWART-MURRAY, Katharine (1874–1960). Duchess of Atholl and public servant. Name variations: Katharine Ramsay. Born in Edinburgh, Scotland, in 1874; died 1960; dau. of James Ramsay, 10th baronet of Bamff (East Perthshire), and Charlotte (Stewart) Fanning Ramsay; half-sister of Agnata Frances Ramsay; educated at Wimbledon High School and Royal College of Music; married John George Stewart-Murray, marquess of Tullibardine, later duke of Atholl, in 1899 (died 1942); no children. ❖ Became involved in local government and Scottish social service, for which she was made Dame Commander of the Order of the British Empire (1918); as a Conservative, became the 1st Scottish woman elected to House of Commons (1923), and quickly advanced to a ministerial position as parliamentary secretary for Board of Education (1924); as a crusader against cruelty and oppression, ignored party loyalties and prejudices, thereby alienating her peers; with Eleanor Rathbone, battled against the practice of genital mutilation of women in Africa (1929), the same year she concluded her duties with Board of Education; published *Women in Politics* and *The Conscription of a People* (1931); temporarily surrendered the party whip when she spoke against the government's plan for a new constitution for India, and lost it permanently after she criticized the Conservative government's tolerance of fascism in Spain, causing her to be termed the "Red Duchess"; resigned seat in Parliament (1938) to protest Chamberlain's appeasement of Hitler; became known as the "fascist beast" because of her alignment with right-wing forces against Stalinism and Communist oppression of refugees, as well as her apprehension over plight of several Eastern European countries (1950s); served as chair of British League for European Freedom (1944–60). ❖ See also autobiography, *Working Partnership* (1958); and *Women in World History*.

STEWART-RICHARDSON, Lady Constance (1883–1932). Scottish interpretive dancer. Born Lady Constance Mackenzie in 1883; died Nov 24, 1932, in London, England; dau. of Francis Leveson Gower, 2nd earl of Cromarty, and Lilian Janet Macdonald; m. Edward Stewart-Richardson, 15th baronet, April 19, 1904; m. Dennis Luckie Matthew, Aug 4, 1921; children: (1st m.) Ian Rorie Hay Stewart Richardson (b. 1904) and Torquil (1909–1961). ❖ Under the spell of Isadora Duncan, began performing as an interpretive dancer (1909), and dedicated herself to trying to establish own Duncanesque school without success; appeared in annual London recitals where she danced in her own works (starting 1910), but the scandal of a woman of the nobility dancing in diaphanous gowns overwhelmed her choreographic reputation; performed at The Empire in London, where she presented *Judith* (1915) and *The Wilderness* (1915), among others; performed in US at Hammerstein theaters and on Keith circuit (1919); toured US with Gertrude Hoffmann, Mlle Polaire, and Evan Burrows-Fontaine, but had little success due to fading popularity of interpretive dance; retired and taught dance to factory workers in England; also fought for educational reforms.

STEWART STREIT, Marlene (b. 1934). *See Streit, Marlene Stewart.*

STICH-RANDALL, Teresa (1927—). American soprano. Born Teresa Stich, Dec 24, 1927, in West Hartford, CT; studied at the Hartford School of Music, Columbia University, and University of Perugia (Italy). ❖ While a student at Columbia, created the role of Gertrude Stein in Virgil Thomson's opera *The Mother of Us All*, a performance that attracted considerable attention (1944); sang in *Aïda* and *Falstaff* with NBC Symphony Orchestra under Arturo Toscanini; debuted with Vienna State Opera (1952), then Metropolitan Opera (1961); one of the great Mozart singers of the mid-20th century, had a range as a lyric soprano that was also suited to Strauss; recording of Sophie in *Der Rosenkavalier* for EMI, conducted by Herbert von Karajan, remains a classic. Was the 1st American singer to be named an Austrian *Kammersängerin* (1962). ❖ See also *Women in World History*.

STICKER, Josephine (1894—). Austrian-Jewish swimmer. Born July 7, 1894, in Austria; death date unknown. ❖ At Stockholm Olympics, won a bronze medal in 4 x 100-meter freestyle relay (1912).

STICKLE, Hannah (1839–1940). *See Retter, Hannah.*

STICKLES, Terri Lee (1946—). American swimmer. Born May 11, 1946. ❖ At Tokyo Olympics, won a bronze medal in 400-meter freestyle (1964).

STICKNEY, Dorothy (1896–1998). American actress. Born Dorothy Hayes Stickney, June 21, 1896, in Dickinson, North Dakota; died in New York, NY, June 2, 1998; dau. of Dr. Victor Hugo Stickney and Margaret (Hayes) Stickney; niece of William Stickney (Vermont governor); studied drama at North Western Dramatic School, Minneapolis; m. Howard Lindsay (actor and playwright), 1927. ❖ Starred with husband in *Life with Father* (1939–44), the longest running non-musical show in Broadway history; made NY stage debut in *Toto*; made Broadway debut as Liz in *Chicago* (1926); also appeared as Cherry in *The Beaux' Strategem* (1928), Mollie Molloy in *The Front Page* (1928), Mincing in *The Way of The World* (1931), and Granny in *On Borrowed Time* (1938); films include *The Little Minister* (1934), *The Remarkable Mr. Pennypacker* (1959) and *I Never Sang for My Father* (1970); was also seen on tv, as well as in her solo show, *A Lonely Light*, in which she presented the writings of Edna St. Vincent Millay.

STICKNEY, Sarah (d. 1872). *See Ellis, Sarah Stickney.*

STIEFL, Regina (1966—). German mountain biker. Name variations: Regina Stifl. Born Oct 11, 1966, in Grainau, Germany. ❖ Began career as a skier; won nearly all titles in downhill (1990s), including Grundig World Cup (1993, 1995). Inducted into Mountain Bike Hall of Fame (1999).

STIFL, Regina (1966—). *See Stiefl, Regina.*

STIFLE, June (1940—). *See Campbell, Maria.*

STIGNANI, Ebe (1903–1975). Italian mezzo-soprano. Name variations: Ebi Stignani. Born July 11, 1903, in Naples, Italy; died Oct 5, 1975, in Imola, near Bologna; studied with Agostino Roche, San Pietro di Maiella Conservatory, Naples; m. Alfredo Sciti (engineer), 1940. ❖ Debuted in Naples (1925); one of Italy's greatest singers, was the leading mezzo at Teatro alla Scala (1926–53); sang all the great Verdi roles, some Rossini, and the popular Bellini and Donizetti works; also made recordings; retired (1958). ❖ See also *Women in World History*.

STIHLER, Catherine (1973—). Scottish politician. Born July 30, 1973, in Bellshill, Scotland. ❖ Served as researcher and facilitator to Anne Begg, MP (1997–99) and as Young Labour representative on the Labour Party Scottish Executive Committee (1993–95) and the National Executive Committee (1995–97); as a European Socialist, elected to 5th European Parliament (1999–2004) from UK.

STILL, Caroline (1848–1919). *See Anderson, Caroline Still.*

STILL, Megan (1972—). Australian rower. Name variations: Megan Leanne Still. Born Oct 19, 1972, in NSW, Australia. ❖ Won NSW state titles (1989); with Kate Slatter, went undefeated in national and international competition (1995), culminating in the World championship, and won a gold medal for coxless pair at Atlanta Olympics (1996), the 1st Australian oarswomen to do so; retired (1997). Named ACT Sportstar of the Year (1995, 1996); inducted into ACTSPORT Hall of Fame (2000).

STILLINGS, Betsy Beard (1961—). *See Beard, Betsy.*

STIMSON, Julia (1881–1948). American nurse and military leader. Born Julia Catherine Stimson, May 26, 1881, in Worcester, Massachusetts; died Sept 29 or 30, 1948, in Poughkeepsie, NY; dau. of Henry A. Stimson (minister) and Alice Wheaton (Bartlett) Stimson; cousin of Henry Lewis Stimson, secretary of war and later secretary of state; sister of Dr. Phillip Moen Stimson, specialist in communicable diseases, and Dr. Barbara E. Stimson, specialist in orthopedic surgery; Vassar College, BA, 1901; attended Columbia University, 1901–03; graduate of New York Hospital Training School, 1908; Washington University, AM, 1917. ❖ The 1st woman in US Army to receive rank of major, served as superintendent of nurses and head of department at Harlem Hospital (1908–11); served as acting social service administrator for Barnes and Children's Hospitals, associated with Washington University, where she became superintendent of nurses (1913); became involved with Red Cross as a nurse (1909) and became a member of National Committee on Red Cross Nursing (1914); during WWI, joined Army Nurse Corps; was chief of Red Cross Nursing Service in France and coordinator of Red Cross and Army Nursing; named director of nursing for the American Expeditionary Forces; named acting superintendent (1919), and later permanent superintendent, of Army Nurse Corps and dean of Army School of Nursing; received relative rank of major (1920); retired from position (1937); called back into active service during WWII to recruit nurses into the Army; promoted to full commissioned rank of colonel on retired list (1948). Received Distinguished Service Medal, awarded by General John J. Pershing, and a citation from the Allied Expeditionary Forces by Field Marshal Douglas Haig. ❖ See also *Women in World History*.

STINDT, Hermine (1888–1974). German swimmer. Born Jan 3, 1888, in Germany; died Feb 19, 1974. ❖ At Stockholm Olympics, won a silver medal in 4 x 100-meter freestyle relay (1912).

STINE INGSTAD, Anne (c. 1918–1997). *See Ingstad, Anne-Stine.*

STINSON, Katherine (1891–1977). American aviator. Name variations: Katherine Stinson Otero; Kate Stinson. Born Feb 14, 1891, in Ft. Payne, Alabama; died July 8, 1977, in Santa Fe, New Mexico; dau. of Edward Anderson and Emma (Beaver) Stinson (with daughter, formed Stinson Aviation); sister of aviators Marjorie Stinson (1894–1975), Edward Stinson Jr. and Jack Stinson; m. Miguel A. Otero Jr. (judge and WWI pilot), in 1928 (died Oct 2, 1977); no children. ❖ Was the 1st woman pilot in the world to perform a loop and the 1st to sky-write (1915); was the 1st woman pilot to fly at night (1915), the 1st woman to fly a plane propelled by a jet engine, and the 1st woman pilot to tour China and Japan (1917). ❖ See also *Women in World History.*

STINSON, Marjorie (1894–1975). American aviator. Name variations: The Flying Schoolmarm; Madge Stinson. Born July 5, 1894, at Fort Payne, AL; died April 15, 1975, in Washington, DC; dau. of Emma Beavers Stinson (who served as business manager for family flight school); sister of Katherine Stinson (aviator), Eddie Stinson (airplane designer), and Jack Stinson (pilot). ❖ At 18, enrolled in Wright School at Dayton; received pilot's license (1914 [some sources cite 1913]); served as chief flying instructor at family's flight school in San Antonio, TX; inducted (as only woman) into US Aviation Reserve Corps (1915); when refused position as pilot in US Army, and family school shut down due to ban on civilian flying, served as draftsman with Aeronautical Division of US Navy, Washington, DC.

STIRLING, Alexa (1897–1977). *See Fraser, Alexa Stirling.*

STIRLING, Mary Anne (1815–1895). English actress. Name variations: Fanny Clifton; Mary Anne Kehl; Fanny Stirling; Lady Gregory. Born Mary Anne Kehl, 1815, in Mayfair, London; died Dec 30, 1895, in London; dau. of Captain Kehl; m. Edward Stirling (also known as Edward Lambert, actor, theater manager, and playwright), c. 1835 (died 1894); m. Sir Charles Hutton Gregory (civil engineer in railroads), in 1894. ❖ Made London debut at Coburg Theater under name Fanny Clifton (1832); performed regularly with husband at Adelphi Royal Theater, which he managed in London (1830s–40s); also played at Theater Royal Drury Lane (1840s–50s); was critically acclaimed for her Cordelia in *King Lear* (1845); had greatest role as Peg Woffington in *Masks and Faces,* a role she created at Haymarket (1852); appeared in company of St. James's Theater playing mostly in comedy (1860s); celebrated for her Nurse in *Romeo and Juliet* at Lyceum (1882) and for final role, as Martha in *Faust* (1885); at height of fame, performed and taught elocution at Royal Academy of Music in London.

STIRLING, Mihi Kotukutuku (1870–1956). New Zealand tribal leader. Name variations: Mihi Kotukutuku. Born Mihi Kotukutuku, Oct 30, 1870, at Pohaturoa, in Bay of Plenty, New Zealand; died Nov 14, 1956, at Raukokore, New Zealand; dau. of Maaka Te Ehutu and Ruiha Rahuta; m. Duncan Stirling, 1896; children: 10. ❖ As local chief, participated in seasonal rituals, and promoted traditional practices; used considerable land holdings as collateral to establish Te Kaha Dairy Factory and promoted dairy farming among her people; performed health and welfare work among people in her district; presented to Queen Elizabeth at Rotorua (1953). Received George V coronation medal (1911). ❖ See also *Dictionary of New Zealand Biography* (Vol. 3).

STIRLING-MAXWELL, Caroline (1808–1877). *See Norton, Caroline.*

STIRNEMANN, Gunda (1966—). *See Niemann, Gunda.*

STIVES, Karen (1950—). American equestrian. Born Nov 3, 1950, in Wellesley, MA. ❖ On Ben Arthur, won Olympic individual silver and team gold in three-day event in Los Angeles (1984). ❖ See also *Women in World History.*

STJERNSTEDT, Rosemary (1912–1998). English architect. Born June 11, 1912, in Birmingham, England; died Oct 31, 1998; married a Swedish lawyer named Stjernstedt, 1930s. ❖ Important architectural designer of British public housing and the 1st woman architect to earn the senior grade 1 status in a British county council division (1950), 1st served for 6 years as an architect and town-and-country planning officer in Stockholm, Sweden (1930s); as a London County Council architect and senior grade 1 architect, worked on the Alton East estate at Roehampton, an important council development; for the Lambeth Council, led the team of the large Central Hill housing development; worked for the Ministry of Housing and Local Government (1964); retired to Wales.

STÖBE, Ilse (1911–1942). German resistance leader and spy. Name variations: Ilse Stobe; Ilse Stoebe. Born Ilse Müller in Berlin, Germany, May 17, 1911; executed Dec 22, 1942, in Berlin. ❖ Worked in Warsaw as a correspondent for German and Swiss newspapers; as an anti-Nazi, passed important information through the Soviet intelligence network (1931–39), even before the Nazis came to power; while working at German Foreign Ministry (1939), supplied Moscow with valuable intelligence on Nazi political and military plans, including the date for the Nazi invasion of USSR. ❖ See also *Women in World History.*

STOBS, Shirley (1942—). American swimmer. Name variations: Shirley Stobs Davis. Born May 20, 1942, in Florida. ❖ At Rome Olympics, won a gold medal in the 4 x 100-meter freestyle relay (1960).

STOCKBAUER, Hannah (1982—). German swimmer. Born Jan 7, 1982, in Nuremberg, Germany. ❖ At World championships, won gold medals for 800-meter freestyle and 1,500-meter freestyle (2001) and for 400-meter freestyle, 800-meter freestyle, and 1,500-meter freestyle (2003); won a bronze medal for 4 x 200-meter freestyle relay at Athens Olympics (2004).

STOCKENSTRÖM, Wilma (1933—). South African poet, novelist and actress. Name variations: Wilma Stockenstrom or Stockenstroem. Born 1933 in Napier, South Africa; received degree in drama from University of Stellenbosch. ❖ Worked in film and on stage; writings explore African landscape and issues of race; poetry includes *Vir die Bysiende Leser* (1970), *Spieël van Water* (1973), *Van Vergetelheid en van Glans* (1975), *Monsterverse* (1984), and *Die Heengaanrefrein* (1988); other works include *Dawid die Dik Dom Kat* (1971), *Trippens se Patatta* (1971), *Die Laaste Middagmaal* (1978), *Die Kremetartsekspedisie* (1981, trans. as *Expedition to the Baobab Tree,* 1983), *Kaapse Rekwisiete* (1987), and *Abjater wat so Lag* (1991). Received Hertzog Prize, CNA Prize, and Grinzane Cavour Prize.

STÖCKER, Helene (1869–1943). *See Stoecker, Helene (1869–1943).*

STOCKERT-MEYNERT, Dora von (1870–1947). Austrian playwright and biographer. Born May 5, 1870, in Vienna, Austria; died Jan 3, 1947 (some sources cite 1949), in Vienna; dau. of Johanna Meynert (social worker, died 1879) and Theodor Meynert (psychiatrist and poet); m. Leopold Stockert; children: 3 daughters, 1 son. ❖ Works include play, *Die Blinde* (The Blind One, 1907), novels, and an important work about her father, *Theodor Meynert und seine Zeit* (1930).

STOCKFLETH, Maria Katharina (c. 1633–1692). German poet and novelist. Name variations: Maria Catharina Stockfleth. Born c. 1633 in Nuremberg, Germany; died 1692; m. 2nd husband Heinrich Arnold Stockfleth (1643–1708, theologian and poet), 1669. ❖ Wrote poetry as well as a sequel to her husband's novel, *Die Kunst–und Tugendgezierte Macarie* (1673), which was recently discovered.

STOCKLEY, Cynthia (1872–1936). Rhodesian writer. Born 1872 in Bloemfontein, South Africa; died 1936. ❖ Lived with husband in Rhodesia and then traveled to London, North America, and Paris; novels, which were popular because of racy content and lively narrative, include *Poppy: The Story of a South African Girl* (1910), *The Claw* (1911), *Ponjola* (1923), *The Leopard in the Bush* (1927), *Kraal Baby* (1933), and *Perilous Stuff* (1936); published short-story collections, *Wild Honey: Stories of South Africa* (1914) and *Blue Aloes: Stories of South Africa* (1918).

STÖCKLIN, Franziska (1894–1931). Swiss poet and painter. Name variations: Franziska Stocklin or Stoecklin. Born 1894 in German-speaking Switzerland; died 1931. ❖ Works include *Gedichte* (1920), *Traumwirklichkeit* (1923), *Liebende: Zwei Novellen* (1923), and *Die singende Muschel* (1925).

STOCKS, Mary Danvers (1891–1975). English baroness and activist. Name variations: Baroness of Kensington and Chelsea. Born July 25, 1891, in Kensington, London, England; died in London, July 6, 1975; dau. of Roland Danvers Brinton (physician) and Helen Constance Rendel; London School of Economics, BSc in economics, 1913; m. John Leofric Stocks (professor in philosophy at Manchester University, then vice-chancellor of Liverpool University), 1913 (died 1937); children: 1 son, 2 daughters. ❖ Feminist, college administrator, social reformer, and writer, became heavily involved with Manchester University Settlement and the birth-control clinic she had opened in 1925, the 1st in the area; active in National Union of Women's Suffrage Societies (NUWSS), which had become the National Union of Societies for Equal Citizenship (NUSEC), jointly edited its journal, *Woman's Leader* (early 1920s); though personally opposed to abortion, persuaded the organization to expand its policy to include issue of birth control; worked briefly as general secretary of London Council of Social Service, then accepted position of principal of Westfield College (1939); came to public prominence as a broadcaster on such radio programs as "The Brains Trust," "Petticoat Line" and "Any Questions"; retired (1951); bestowed a peerage (1966), earned respect of her peers in House of Lords, assuming Labor Party whip; writings include *Eleanor Rathbone* (1949), *The Workers' Educational Association, the First Fifty Years* (1953), *A Hundred Years of District Nursing* (1960) and *Ernest*

Simon of Manchester (1963). ❖ See also autobiography, *My Commonplace Book* (1970); and *Women in World History*.

STOCKTON, Annis Boudinot (1736–1801). American poet. Born Annis Boudinot, 1736, in Darby, PA; died 1801; dau. of Elias Boudinot and Catherine Williams; m. Richard Stockton, 1757 (died 1781); children: 6. ❖ Owing to husband's position as member of landed elite and signer of Declaration of Independence, enjoyed privileged position in Princeton, NJ; one of the most frequently published women poets of the 18th century, was a member of a prominent writing circle. Poems published in *The Poetry of Annis Boudinot Stockton* (ed. by Carla J. Mulford, 1994).

STOCKTON, Betsey (c. 1798–1865). African-American educator. Born c. 1798 into slavery; died Oct 24, 1865, in Princeton, New Jersey; informally educated; never married; no children. ❖ Grew up in the home of Reverend Ashbel Green, president of Princeton College; was baptized a Presbyterian around age 20 and freed by the Greens at approximately the same time; traveled with a Presbyterian missionary and his family to Hawaii (1823), where she founded a missionary school in Lahaina, Maui, serving as both superintendent and teacher to about 30 students; is believed to have been the 1st black woman to arrive in Hawaii (Sandwich Islands); taught at an infant school in Philadelphia, organized a school for Indians in Canada, and founded Witherspoon Street Colored School in Princeton. ❖ See also *Women in World History*.

STOCKUM, Hilda van (b. 1908). *See van Stockum, Hilda.*

STODDARD, Cora Frances (1872–1936). American temperance leader. Born Sept 17, 1872, in Irvington, Nebraska; died May 13, 1936, in Oxford, Connecticut; dau. of Emerson Hathaway Stoddard (farmer) and Julia Frances (Miller) Stoddard (president of Women's Christian Temperance Union, WCTU, in Brookline, Massachusetts); Wellesley College, AB, 1896. ❖ Moved to Boston, where she worked as secretary to Mary Hanchett Hunt, director of Department of Scientific Temperance Instruction of national WCTU; following Hunt's death, co-founded the Scientific Temperance Federation (STF) to continue Hunt's work (1906); served as STF's executive secretary for 30 years, compiling statistics, writing pamphlets and articles on the effects of alcohol, and editing the quarterly *Scientific Temperance Journal*; became active in Anti-Saloon League; returned to WCTU as director of its Bureau of Scientific Temperance Investigation (1918) and later its Department of Scientific Temperance Instruction. ❖ See also *Women in World History*.

STODDARD, Elizabeth Drew (1823–1902). American novelist and poet. Name variations: Elizabeth Stoddard; Elizabeth Drew Barstow Stoddard. Born Elizabeth Drew Barstow, 1823, in Mattapoisset, MA; m. Richard Stoddard (poet); children: 3. ❖ Wrote column for San Francisco *Alta* (1854–58) as "Lady Correspondent" and published short stories in *Harper's*; wrote novels *The Morgesons* (1862), *Two Men* (1865), and *Temple House* (1867) and book of children's stories, *Dolly Dinks' Doings* (1874). ❖ See also Lawrence Buell and Sandra Zagarell, eds., *"The Morgesons" and Other Writings, Published and Unpublished, by Elizabeth Stoddard* (1984).

STODDART, Margaret Olrog (1865–1934). New Zealand painter. Born Oct 3, 1865, at Diamond Harbour, Canterbury, New Zealand; died Dec 10, 1934, at Hanmer, New Zealand; dau. of Mark Pringle Stoddart and Anna Barbara (Schjött) Stoddart; Canterbury College School of Art, second-grade full certificate, 1889. ❖ Regarded as one of New Zealand's best flower painters (Canterbury Museum acquired 12 of her botanical paintings in 1890), traveled throughout Europe, sketching in France, Switzerland, Norway and Italy (1897); exhibited at Salon of the Société des artistes fran̂cais, Société nationale des beaux-arts, and Baillie Gallery, London; belonged to several art societies, including School of Art Sketch Club, National Art Association of New Zealand, and Canterbury Society of Arts and Society for Imperial Culture. ❖ See also *Dictionary of New Zealand Biography* (Vol. 3).

STOECKEL, Ellen Battell (1851–1939). American philanthropist. Name variations: Ellen Battell Terry. Born Ellen Mar 10, 1851, in Norfolk, CT; died May 5, 1939, in Norfolk; dau. of Robbins Battell (CT state comptroller) and Ellen Ryerson (Mills) Battell; m. Frederick Peet Terry, Feb 5, 1873 (died 1874); Carl Stoeckel (organist and Yale music teacher), May 6, 1895); children: (1st m.) 1 son. ❖ With husband, founded Litchfield County Choral Union (1899); built private, 1,500-seat auditorium in Norfolk to accommodate popular choral union and Norfolk musical festivals (1906); willed entire family estate to Yale University to establish

summer schools of music and art. Norfolk Festivals became model for other summer music festivals in New England.

STOECKER, Helene (1869–1943). German feminist and pacifist. Name variations: Helene Stöcker. Pronunciation: STIR-kir. Born Nov 13(?), 1869, in Elberfeld, Germany; died Feb 24, 1943, in New York City; dau. of Ludwig Stoecker (textile merchant) and Hulda (Bergmann) Stoecker; took four years of college preparatory work in feminist-sponsored courses in Berlin, and college work at Universities of Berlin and Bern; University of Bern, PhD, 1901; never married; no children. ❖ President and guiding spirit of the League for the Protection of Motherhood and Sexual Reform, and editor of the journal *Neue Generation* (*The New Generation*), rejected her parents' Calvinism because of its obsession with "sin and damnation" (1883), at age 14; at 21, arrived in Berlin planning to prepare for a teaching career (1892) and became involved in women's causes; studied at University of Berlin with philosopher Wilhelm Dilthey (1896); left because one professor refused to accept female students (1899); earned PhD at Bern (1901); returned to Berlin and became an officer in social reform organizations (1902); assumed leadership of the League for the Protection of Motherhood and Sexual Reform (1905); founded the journal *The New Generation* (1908); attended conference of the Women's League for Peace and Freedom at the Hague (1915); founded War Resisters League (1921); founded War Resisters International and co-founded the Group of Revolutionary Pacifists (1926); refused to live in Germany after the Nazi accession to power, living in Switzerland and other countries before settling in New York City (1941); writings include *Die Liebe und die Frauen* (1909) and *Die Frau und die Heiligkeit des Lebens* (1921); was one of the most politically involved women in Germany during the 1st 40 years of the 20th century. ❖ See also *Women in World History*.

STOECKLIN, Franziska (1894–1931). *See Stöcklin, Franziska.*

STOECKLIN, Stephane (1969—). French handball player. Born Jan 12, 1969, in France. ❖ At Barcelona Olympics, won a bronze medal in team competition (1992).

STOERE, Heidi (1973—). Norwegian soccer player. Name variations: Støre or Store. Born July 4, 1963, in Rade, Norway. ❖ Midfielder; joined Norway's national team (1980); won team championships at UEFA European (1987, 1993), FIFA Invitational (1988) and FIFA World Cup (1995); as captain, won a team bronze medal at Atlanta Olympics (1996); retired after 17-year-career (1997), the most capped player in the history of the world, having made 151 international appearances.

STOEVA, Vasilka (1940—). Bulgarian track-and-field athlete. Born Jan 14, 1940, in Bulgaria. ❖ At Munich Olympics, won a bronze medal in the discus throw (1972).

STOJADINOVIĆ-SRPKINJA, Milica (1830–1878). Serbian poet. Name variations: Milica Stojadinovic-Srpkinja. Born 1830; died 1878. ❖ The 1st Serbian woman poet, wrote on nationalist themes and tried to conceal her female identity.

STOKE NEWINGTON, baroness of (1942—). *See Blackstone, Tessa.*

STOKES, Caroline Phelps (1854–1909). American philanthropist. Born Caroline Phelps Stokes, Dec 4, 1854, in New York, NY; died April 26, 1909, in Redlands, California; dau. of James Boulter Stokes and Caroline (Phelps) Stokes (helped found the Colored Orphan Asylum of New York); sister of Olivia Phelps Stokes; educated at Miss Porter's School; never married; no children. ❖ With sister, funded Yale University, New York Zoological Society, New York Botanical Garden, Berea College, St. Paul's Chapel at Columbia University, Peabody Home for Aged and Infirm Women in Ansonia, Connecticut, and many missionary causes; bequeathed money to build chapels at such notable African-American educational institutions as Tuskegee Institute and Calhoun Colored School in Alabama; also endowed a fund at Hampton Institute in Virginia to educate blacks and Native Americans. ❖ See also *Women in World History*.

STOKES, Olivia Phelps (1847–1927). American philanthropist. Name variations: Olivia Egleston Phelps. Born Olivia Egleston Phelps Stokes, Jan 11, 1847, in New York, NY; died Dec 14, 1927, in Washington, DC; dau. of James Boulter Stokes and Caroline (Phelps) Stokes (helped found the Colored Orphan Asylum of New York); sister of Caroline Phelps Stokes; never married; no children. ❖ With sister, contributed substantial sums to various causes, particularly in the improvement of opportunities for African-Americans, through the establishment of the

Phelps-Stokes fund; wrote several books, including *Pine and Cedar: Bible Verses* (1885), *Forward in the Better Life* (1915), *Saturday Nights in Lent* (1922) and *Letters and Memories of Susan and Anna Bartlett Warner* (1925). ❖ See also *Women in World History*.

STOKES, Rose Pastor (1879–1933). Polish-American politician. Name variations: Rose Pastor (took the name Pastor from stepfather). Born Rose Harriet Wieslander, July 18, 1879, in Augustów, Russian Poland; died June 20, 1933, in Frankfurt-am-Main, Germany; dau. of Jacob and Anna (Lewin) Wieslander; m. James Graham Phelps Stokes (wealthy Socialist and nephew of Olivia and Caroline Phelps Stokes), July 18, 1905 (div. 1925); m. Isaac Romaine (also known as V. J. Jerome, language teacher and Communist), 1927; no children. ❖ Socialist and Communist leader, moved with family to US at 11, settling in Cleveland, Ohio, where she worked in a cigar factory; became a contributor to *Jewish Daily News* in New York (1900), joining paper's staff when family moved to the Bronx (1903); on marriage, became active in Intercollegiate Socialist Society and Socialist Party; a lecturer and labor organizer, was active in New York hotel and restaurant workers' strike (1912); contributed articles, reviews and poems to *Independent, Everybody's, Arena* and *Century*; trans. Morris Rosenfeld's Yiddish *Songs of Labor and Other Poems* (1914); as a pacifist, was indicted under Espionage Act for writing to *Kansas City Star*: "I am for the people, while the Government is for the profiteers" (Mar 1918), resulting in a 10-year sentence for interfering with military recruitment, which was overturned on appeal (her case became a symbol of anti-radical harassment); aligned herself with the more radical leftist elements and joined Communist Party (1919), where she labored on behalf of African-American workers; often contributed to *Pravda* and the *Worker* (later the *Daily Worker*). ❖ See also *I Belong to the Working Class: The Unfinished Autobiography of Rose Pastor Stokes* (Shapiro and Sterling, eds., U. of Georgia Press, 1992); Zipser and Zipser, *Fire and Grace: The Life of Rose Pastor Stokes* (U. of Georgia Press, 1989); and *Women in World History*.

STOKES, Shelly (1967—). American softball player. Born Oct 26, 1967, in Sacramento, CA. ❖ Won a team gold medal at Atlanta Olympics (1996).

STOKOWSKI, Olga (1882–1948). *See Samaroff, Olga.*

STOLER, Shirley (1929–1999). American stage and screen actress. Born Mar 30, 1929, in Brooklyn, NY; died Feb 17, 1999, in New York, NY. ❖ Made Broadway debut in *Lolita* (1981), followed by regional tour of *The Music Man*; off-broadway, appeared with such experimental companies as Caffe Cino, LaMama, and Living Theater; portrayed the serial murderer in *The Honeymoon Killers*; other films include *Seven Beauties, The Deer Hunter, Sticky Fingers* and *Miami Blues*.

STOLITSA, Liubov (1884–1934). Russian poet and playwright. Name variations: Liubov Nikitishna (or Nikitichna) Stolitsa. Born 1884; died 1934. ❖ Immigrated with family to Sofia, Bulgaria (1920), where poetry appeared in *émigré* journals; poetry collections, which draw on folklore, the Russian landscape, and Russian Orthodoxy, include *Rainia* (1908) and *Lada* (1912); also wrote 5 full-length plays in verse, including *The Blue Carpet*.

STOLK, Gloria (1918–1979). Venezuelan poet, novelist and short-story writer. Born 1918 in Venezuela; died 1979; studied at Sorbonne and Smith College. ❖ Works include *Rescate y otros poemas* (Ransom and Other Poems, 1950), *El arpa* (The Harp, 1951), *Bellas Vegas* (Beautiful Plains, 1953), *Amargo el fondo* (1957), *Diamela* (1960), *Angel de piedra* (Stone Angel, 1962), *La casa del viento* (The House of the Wind, 1965), and *Manual de buenos modales* (Manual of Good Manners, 1967).

STOLZ, Teresa (1834–1902). Bohemian soprano. Born Teresina (Terezie) Stolzová in Elbekoteletz (now Kostelec nad Labem), Bohemia, 1834; died Aug 23, 1902, in Milan; sister of twins Francesca (Fanny) Stolz and Ludmilla (Lidia) Stolz, both sopranos (b. 1827); aunt of Adelaide Ricci (1850–1871); studied at Prague Conservatory, with Luigi Ricci in Trieste, and with Lamperti in Milan. ❖ Debuted in Tbilisi (1857), Spoleto (1864), Teatro alla Scala (1865) and Milan (1874); appeared throughout Italy singing numerous Giuseppe Verdi roles (1864–72), including Elisabetta at La Scala in 1st Italian version of *Don Carlo* (1868) and the title role in Italy's 1st Aïda; closely associated with the work of Verdi, influenced him both professionally and personally, and played a major role in creating a voice type now known as a "Verdi soprano"; retired (1879). ❖ See also *Women in World History*.

STOMPOROWSKI, Katrin (1975—). *See Rutschow, Katrin.*

STONE, Barbara Gwendoline (1962—). Australian politician. Born Jan 28, 1962, in Brisbane, Australia. ❖ As a member of the Australian Labor Party, elected to the Queensland Parliament for Springwood (2001).

STONE, Beth (1940—). American golfer. Name variations: Elizabeth Stone. Born May 15, 1940, in Harlingen, TX. ❖ Was the 1st girl to win varsity letter at University of Oklahoma, by being on men's golf team; joined LPGA tour (1961); with JoAnn Prentice, runs the Gulf Stop in Tucson, Arizona.

STONE, Carol (1915—). American actress. Born Feb 1, 1915, in New York, NY; dau. of Aileen (Crater) Stone and Fred Stone (actor); sister of Dorothy Stone (actress) and Paula Stone (actress and producing manager); m. Robert W. McCahon (div.). ❖ Made NY stage debut as Augustina Bastida in *Spring in Autumn* (1933); other plays include *Mackerel Skies, Jayhawker, As You Like It, Lady Behave, Dark of the Moon, They Knew What They Wanted* and *Desire Under the Elms*; also appeared on tv.

STONE, Constance (1856–1902). Australian physician and feminist. Name variations: Emma Constance Stone. Born Emma Constance Stone, Dec 4, 1856, in Hobart, Tasmania, Australia; died of TB, Dec 29, 1902; dau. of William Stone and Betsey (Haydon) Stone; sister of Grace Clara Stone and cousin of Emily Mary Page Stone, both doctors; attended Woman's Medical College of Pennsylvania; University of Trinity College in Toronto, MD; studied at Licentiate of Society of Apothecaries in London; m. David Egryn Jones (minister); children: Bronwen. ❖ Since the University of Melbourne barred women from medical studies, had to leave her native Australia to study abroad; became the 1st woman to be registered with the Medical Board of Victoria (1890); paved the way for women doctors in Melbourne and co-founded the Queen Victoria Memorial Hospital for women (1895). ❖ See also *Women in World History*.

STONE, Dannette Young- (1964—). *See Young, Dannette.*

STONE, Dorothy (1905–1974). American musical-comedy singer and dancer. Born June 3, 1905, in Brooklyn, NY; died Sept 24, 1974, in Montecito, CA; dau. of Allene Crater (d. 1957) and Fred Stone (both theatrical performers); sister of Carol Stone (actress) and Paula Stone (1912–1997, actress and producing manager); m. Charles Collins (dancer), 1930. ❖ At 16, made stage debut with parents in *Stepping Stones* (1923); subsequently appeared in *Criss-Cross, Three Cheers* and *Show Girl*; danced with husband as a ballroom team in cabarets and in such shows as *Smiling Faces, The Gay Divorcee, As Thousands Cheer, You Can't Take It With You* and *The Red Mill*.

STONE, Elizabeth (1940—). *See Stone, Beth.*

STONE, Grace Zaring (1896–1991). American novelist. Name variations: (pseudonym) Ethel Vance. Born Jan 9, 1896, in New York, NY; died Sept 29, 1991, in Mystic, Connecticut; dau. of Charles Wesley Zaring (lawyer) and Grace (Owen) Zaring (died 1896); great-granddau. of Socialist reformer Robert Owen; attended Isadora Duncan School of Dancing in Paris; m. Ellis S. Stone (naval officer), 1917; children: Eleanor Stone Perényi, later Baroness Perényi. ❖ Began writing in course of her travels, as husband was posted throughout the world, including Europe, Asia, and South Seas; wrote 1st book, *Letters to a Djinn* (1922), though later rarely acknowledged it and credited *The Heaven and Earth of Doña Elena* (1929) as 1st novel; following a trip to China, wrote bestselling 3rd novel, *The Bitter Tea of General Yen* (1930); wrote bestselling *Escape* (1939), an anti-Nazi novel written under pseudonym "Ethel Vance" to protect husband, who was a military attaché in France during WWII, and daughter Eleanor, who was living in occupied Czechoslovakia as Baroness Perényi; other writings include *The Almond Tree* (1931), *The Cold Journey* (1934), *Reprisal* (1942), *Winter Meeting* (1946), *The Secret Thread* (1949), *The Grotto* (1951), *Althea* (1962) and *Dear Deadly Cara* (1968); hosted literary salons in Rome and NY that boasted such notables as Robert Lowell, Gore Vidal and Mary McCarthy. Named a fellow of Royal Society of Literature in Great Britain; elected to Council of the Authors League (1956). ❖ See also *Women in World History*.

STONE, Hannah (1893–1941). American physician. Name variations: Hannah Mayer Stone. Born Hannah Mayer, Oct 15, 1893, in New York, NY; died July 10, 1941, in New York, NY; dau. of Golda (Rinaldo) Mayer and Max Mayer (pharmacist); graduate of New York Medical College, 1920; m. Dr. Abraham Stone. ❖ Served as director of America's 1st legal birth control clinic, Margaret Sanger's Birth Control Clinical Research Bureau (1925–41); with 4 other staff members, was arrested and charged with illegally spreading contraceptive information (April 1929); successfully won the *United States* v. *One Package* trial, which concerned birth-control devices sent from Japan to Stone via Sanger; was director of New Jersey Birth Control League; practiced gynecology privately; with husband, created a marriage consultation center in NYC's Labor Temple (1930).

STONE, Janet Moreau (1927—). *See Moreau, Janet.*

STONE, Lucinda Hinsdale (1814–1900). American educator. Born Sept 30, 1814, in Hinesburg, Vermont; died Mar 14, 1900, in Kalamazoo, Michigan; dau. of Aaron Hinsdale (woolen mill owner) and Lucinda (Mitchell) Hinsdale; educated at Hinesburg Academy and female seminaries in Vermont; m. James Andrus Blinn Stone (Baptist minister and educator), June 10, 1840 (died 1888); children: Clement Walker, Horatio Hackett, and James Helm. ❖ As principal of Kalamazoo College's "Female Department," secured speakers on such topics as abolitionism and women's rights, as well as such celebrities as Ralph Waldo Emerson; expanded these gatherings to include other women in the community as the Kalamazoo Ladies' Library Association (1852); also organized women's travel clubs throughout Michigan, as well as the Michigan Women's Press Association; became known as the "mother of clubs," and her weekly column, "Club Talks," was featured in many Michigan newspapers; was instrumental in convincing the University of Michigan to admit women (1870) and to hire women faculty members (1896). ❖ See also *Women in World History.*

STONE, Lucy (1818–1893). American suffragist and abolitionist. Name variations: Lucy Stone Blackwell. Born Lucy Stone, Aug 13, 1818, in West Brookfield, Massachusetts; died Oct 18, 1893, in Dorcester, Massachusetts; dau. of Francis Stone (tanner and farmer) and Hannah (Matthews) Stone; attended Mt. Holyoke Seminary; Oberlin College, AB, 1847; sister-in-law of Elizabeth Blackwell (1821–1910), Emily Blackwell (1826–1910), and Antoinette Brown Blackwell (1825–1921); m. Henry Browne Blackwell, May 1855; children: Alice Stone Blackwell (1857–1950). ❖ Activist whose pioneering lectures on suffrage and work to change the legal status of women regarding property, custody, and voting rights earned her the movement's title of "morning star"; was refused church voting rights as a teenager because of gender; became 1st woman from Massachusetts to obtain a college degree (1847); hired as a public lecturer by Massachusetts Anti-Slavery Society (1847); expelled from her home church for her anti-slavery position (1851); wedding ceremony included a protest against the legal dominance of husbands (1855); called attention to suffrage issue by protesting against taxation without representation in New Jersey (1858); was a founding member of American Equal Rights Association (1866); was a founder of American Woman's Suffrage Association (1869); cofounded the weekly *Woman's Journal* newspaper (1870); was a member of New England Women's Press Association and Association of Collegiate Alumnae; at a time when the public was bitterly divided about the issue of slavery, and largely unwilling even to consider the question of what was known then as woman's rights, was one of the abolitionists who recognized similarities between the positions of "free" women and of slaves. ❖ See also Andrea Moore Kerr, *Lucy Stone: Speaking Out for Equality* (Rutgers U. Press, 1992); Alice Stone Blackwell, *Lucy Stone: Pioneer Woman Suffragist* (Little, Brown, 1930); Elinor Rice Hays, *Morning Star: A Biography of Lucy Stone, 1818–1893* (Harcourt, 1961); Leslie Wheeler, ed. *Loving Warriors: Selected Letters of Lucy Stone and Henry B. Blackwell, 1853 to 1893* (Dial, 1981); Carol Lasser and Marlene Merrill, eds. *Soul Mates: The Oberlin Correspondence of Lucy Stone and Antoinette Brown, 1846–1850* (Oberlin College, 1983); and *Women in World History.*

STONE, Marius (1859–1927). *See Janitschek, Maria.*

STONE, Miriam (1920–1995). *See Harwood, Gwen.*

STONE, Nikki (1971—). American freestyle skier. Born Feb 4, 1971, in Westborough, MA. ❖ Won the gold medal for aerials at Nagano (1998), the 1st American medalist in that event; was two-time World Cup aerials champion (1995, 1998) and World Cup freestyle champion (1998).

STONE, Paula (1912–1997). American actress and producer. Born Jan 20, 1912, in NYC; died Dec 23, 1997, in Sherman Oaks, CA; dau. of Aileen (Crater) Stone and Fred Stone (actor); sister of Carol Stone and Dorothy Stone (both actresses); m. Duke Daley (dec.); m. Michael Sloan. ❖ Made NY stage debut in *Ripples* (1931); appeared in vaudeville and films; produced *The Red Mill, Sweethearts,* and *Top Banana*; wrote,

directed and appeared in her own radio series (1943) and on her own tv series (1955), "The Paula Stone Show"; served as moderator on radio's "Leave It to the Girls" (1945).

STONE, Rosie (1945—). African-American musician. Name variations: Sly and the Family Stone. Born Mar 21, 1945, in Vallejo, CA; sister of Sly Stone (musician) and Freddie Stone (musician). ❖ Pianist and back-up singer who, as a member of Sly and the Family Stone, released debut single, "I Ain't Got Nobody," backed with "I Can't Turn You Loose"; had hit with title track of 2nd album, *Dance to the Music* (1968), and with single, "Everyday People," which went to #1 on both pop and R&B charts; with group, also released hit album, *Stand* (1969), which included songs "Don't Call Me Nigger Whitey," "Somebody's Watching You" and "I Want to Take You Higher," and the more political *There's a Riot Goin' On* (1971), which went to #1 and included "Family Affair"; other hit singles include "Hot Fun in the Summertime" and "Thank You (Falenttinme Be Mice Elf Agin)"; other albums include *Fresh* (1973), *Small Talk* (1974), *Back on the Right Track* (1979) and *Ain't But the One Way* (1983). With Sly and the Family Stone, inducted into Rock and Roll Hall of Fame (1993).

STONE, Ruth (1915—). American poet. Born Ruth Perkins, June 8, 1915, in Roanoke, VA; dau. of Roger McDowell Perkins and Ruth Ferguson Perkins; m. Walter Stone (poet and novelist); children: 3 daughters. ❖ Moved to England; husband committed suicide (1958), an event which influenced Stone's later poetry; taught at universities in US, including Indiana University, New York University, Old Dominion, Brandeis, and State University of New York at Binghamton; works include *In an Iridescent Time* (1959), *Topography and Other Poems* (1971), *Cheap* (1975), *Second-Hand Coat* (1987), *Who is the Widow's Muse* (1991), and *Nursery Rhymes from Mother Stone* (1992); won the National Book Critics Circle Award for *Ordinary Words* (1999) and the National Book Award for *In the Next Galaxy* (2003). Received Shelley Memorial Award (1964), Delmore Schwartz Award (1983), Whiting Writer's Award (1986), Paterson Poetry Prize (1988) and Wallace Stevens Prize (2003).

STONE, Sharon (1958—). American actress and activist. Born Sharon Vonne Stone, Mar 10, 1958, in Meadville, PA; dau. of a factory worker; graduate of Edinboro State University of Pennsylvania; m. George Englund Jr. (div.); m. Michael Greenburg (tv producer), 1984 (div. 1987); m. Phil Bronstein (exec editor of *San Francisco Examiner*), 1998 (div. 2004); children: (adopted) Roan and Laird. ❖ Began career as a Ford model; had non-speaking part in Woody Allen's *Stardust Memories* (1980); worked for a decade in tv and B movies; came to prominence in *Total Recall* (1990) and *Basic Instinct* (1992); earned an Oscar nomination for *Casino* (1995); other films include *Sliver* (1993), *The Quick and the Dead* (1995), *Diabolique* (1996), *Last Dance* (1996), *The Mighty* (1998), *The Muse* (1999), *Gloria* (1999), *Basic Instinct II* (2006); an AIDS, human rights and gay rights activist, appeared on "If These Walls Could Talk 2" (2000) for tv; with younger sister Kelly, co-founded Planet Hope, an organization that helps the homeless.

STONE, Toni (1921–1996). African-American baseball player. Name variations: Marcenia Lyle Alberga. Born Marcenia Lyle in 1921; died Nov 2, 1996, in Alameda, CA; m. Aurelious Alberga (Army officer), 1950 (died 1988). ❖ Played second base in the Negro American League, the 1st woman to play as a regular on a big-league professional team. Inducted into Women's Sports Foundation's International Women's Sports Hall of Fame (1985). ❖ See also *Women in World History.*

STONEHOUSE, Ruth (1892–1941). American silent-film actress and director. Born Sept 28, 1892, in Denver, CO; died May 12, 1941, in Hollywood, CA. ❖ At 8, began career as a dancer in vaudeville; as an actress, formed a partnership with Bronco Billy Anderson at Essanay Studios of Chicago; by 1911, was one of the company's leading players, appearing opposite such silent-screen stars as Francis X. Bushman, Harry Houdini and Norma Shearer; feeling typecast in submissive "little girl" roles, began working behind the camera; joined Universal Studios to write, direct, and star in her own films (1916); returned to acting in supporting roles for Universal and other studios (early 1920s); retired (1928); as an actress, films include *Neptune's Daughter* (1912), *Sunshine* (1912), *An Angel Unaware* (1914), *The Hand That Rocks the Cradle* (1914), *Night Hawks* (1914), *The Adventures of Peg o' the Ring* (serial, 1916), *The Phantom Husband* (1917), *The Masked Rider* (serial, 1919), *The Master Mystery* (serial, 1919), *A Girl of the Limberlost* (1924) and *The Fugitive* (1925). ❖ See also *Women in World History.*

STONEMAN, Abigail (c. 1740–?). American innkeeper. Name variations: Abigail Treville. Born sometime after 1740, in Newport, RI; probably married Samuel Stoneman (died c. 1760); m. John Treville (English aristocrat), Aug 1774. ❖ Was proprietress of the Merchant's Coffee House in Newport, RI (1767); applied for license and opened the coffee-house Royal Exchange in Boston, MA (1770); was the only woman in Newport to receive license to keep tavern and sell spirits (1772–73); opened King's Arms tavern and inn in Newport (1774); established business in New York (1777); was 1st Newport woman to marry a titled Englishman.

STONEMAN, Bertha (1866–1943). American educator and botanist. Born Bertha Stoneman, 1866, in Lakewood, NY; died April 1943 in Wellington, South Africa; Cornell University, AB, 1894, PhD in botany, 1896. ❖ Became science teacher at Huguenot University College in Wellington, South Africa (1897), and built herbarium there; wrote popular textbook on South African plants (1915); helped to found South African Association of University Women; was the last American to head Huguenot University College, retiring from presidency in 1932.

STONES, Elsie Margaret (1920—). See Stones, Margaret.

STONES, Margaret (1920—). Australian botanical artist. Name variations: Elsie Margaret Stones. Born Elsie Margaret Stones, Aug 28, 1920, in Colac, Victoria, Australia; 3rd dau. of Frederick and Agnes Stones; studied at Swinburne and National Gallery Art Schools in Melbourne, and at the University of Melbourne. ❖ Internationally recognized botanical artist, moved to Britain (1951) and began freelancing as a botanical artist at the Herbarium, Royal Botanical Gardens, Kew (1951); illustrated volumes of *The Endemic Flora of Tasmania* (1967–78); was artist-in-residence at Louisiana State University; was commissioned to create 200 watercolor drawings of state flora, which were shown at Louisiana State Museum's "Naturally Louisiana" exhibit (1985); served as principal illustrator of *Curtis Biological Magazine*. Made a Member of the Order of Australia (1988).

STONE THE CROWS (1945—). See Bell, Maggie.

STOPA, Wanda (1899–1925). American murderer. Born 1899; committed suicide, 1925. ❖ Respected Chicago attorney, was rebuffed by her artistic mentor Y. K. Smith; fired shots at Smith's wife, and a stray bullet killed the Smiths' caretaker, 68-year-old Henry Manning; fled the scene; was later traced to Detroit where she swallowed poison as detectives were attempting entry into her hotel room.

STOPES, Marie (1880–1958). English reproductive-rights activist. Born Marie Carmichael Stopes, Oct 15, 1880, in Edinburgh, Scotland; died Oct 2, 1958, in Surrey, England; dau. of Charlotte Carmichael Stopes (Shakespearean scholar and suffragist) and Henry Stopes (architect); University College of London University, BSc, 1902; University of Munich, PhD, 1903; London University, DSc, 1905; m. Reginald Gates, Mar 18, 1911 (div. 1916); m. Humphrey Verdon Roe, May 16, 1918; children: (2nd m.) Harry Verdon Stopes-Roe. ❖ Founder of the 1st birth-control clinic in the British Empire who helped popularize the idea that women could and should enjoy sexually satisfying relationships, of which one component must be women's ability to control their own reproductive functions; after earning undergraduate and graduate degrees in botany, became a lecturer at Manchester University; appointed lecturer in paleobotany at University College, London (1911); became one of the most eminent paleobotanists in Britain and a noted expert on coal formation; after failure of 1st marriage, wrote *Married Love*, describing the importance of women's sexuality, the 1st of several bestselling publications discussing questions of human sexuality and contraception; opened the Mothers' Clinic for Constructive Birth Control, the 1st birth control clinic in the British Empire, and founded the Society for Constructive Birth Control to spread her ideas about birth control and eugenics (1921); brought a well-publicized defamation suit against the author of an anti-birth control book (1923); devoted the conclusion of her life to writing poetry and plays and assisting poets such as Alfred Douglas and Walter de la Mare; also wrote *Wise Parenthood* (1918), *The Truth About VD* (1920) and *Radiant Motherhood* (1920). ❖ See also Muriel Box, ed. *The Trial of Marie Stopes* (Femina, 1967); Eaton and Warnick, *Marie Stopes: A Checklist of Her Writings* (Croom Helm, 1977); Ruth Hall, *Passionate Crusader* (Harcourt, 1977); Aylmer Maude, *The Authorized Life of Marie C. Stopes* (1924); June Rose, *Marie Stopes and the Sexual Revolution* (Faber & Faber, 1992); and *Women in World History*.

STOPFORD GREEN, Alice (1847–1929). Irish historian and nationalist. Name variations: Mrs. Stopford Green. Born Alice Sophia Amelia Stopford, May 30, 1847, in Kells, Co. Meath, Ireland; died May 28, 1929, in Dublin; dau. of Edward Stopford (rector of Kells and archdeacon of Meath) and Ann (Duke) Stopford; m. John Richard Green (historian), 1877 (died 1883). ❖ Served as husband's research assistant and collaborator; following his death, produced a revised edition of his *Short History of the English People*, followed by a life of Henry II (1888) and the 2-volume study *Town Life in the Fifteenth Century* (1894) and *Women's Place in the World of Letters* (1913); traveled to St. Helena to visit camps for Boer prisoners of war (1900) and helped found the African Society (1901); became a supporter of Irish nationalist cause; produced a new account of Irish history, *The Making of Ireland and Its Undoing* (1908), which celebrated the Gaelic inheritance and justified nationalist aspirations, followed by *Irish Nationality* (1911); joined Roger Casement in an unsuccessful effort to rally Protestant support for home rule, but disapproved of the republican uprising (1916); supported the Anglo-Irish Treaty which ended the War of Independence and was a member of the pro-Treaty women's organization Cumann na Saoirse (League of Freedom) and a founding member of the political party, Cumann na nGael; nominated to the 1st Irish Senate as one of four women members, served on a committee for the publication of Irish-language manuscripts and supported the retention of the right to divorce. ❖ See also R. B. McDowell, *Alice Stopford Green: A Passionate Historian* (Figgis, 1967).

STORACE, Anna (1765–1817). See Storace, Nancy.

STORACE, Nancy (1765–1817). English soprano. Name variations: Anna or Ann Storace. Born Ann Selina Storace, Oct 27, 1765, in London; died Aug 24, 1817, in London; sister of composer Stephen Storace (1762–1796); m. John Abraham Fisher (composer), 1783; lived with John Braham (tenor). ❖ Studied with Sacchini and Rauzzini in London; was a prima donna at Vienna's Burgtheater (1783–87); premiered role of Susanna in her friend Mozart's *Le nozze di Figaro*; performed many operas by her brother (1787–1808); retired (1808). ❖ See also *Women in World History*.

STORBECK, Hestrie (1978—). See Cloete, Hestrie.

STORCHIO, Rosina (1876–1945). Italian soprano. Born May 19, 1876, in Venice; died July 24, 1945, in Milan; studied under A. Giovannini and G. Fatuo at Milan Conservatory. ❖ Debuted at Teatro del Verme Milan and Teatro alla Scala (1895); created role of Musetta in Leoncavallo's *Bohème* in Venice (1897); a great favorite of Italian audiences, performed in many premieres, including *Zazà* (1900) and Giordano's *Siberia* (1903), both at La Scala, Mascagni's *Lodoletta* in Rome (1917), and the disastrous debut of Puccini's *Madame Butterfly* at La Scala (Feb 17, 1904), a role she understood better than her 1st audience; toured South America, North America, and Europe. ❖ See also *Women in World History*.

STORCZER, Beata (1969—). Hungarian gymnast. Born July 10, 1969, in Budapest, Hungary. ❖ Placed 1st in floor exercises at Kosice International (1987) and 5th in floor exercises at Seoul Olympics (1988).

STORE, Heidi (1973—). See Stoere, Heidi.

STORER, Maria (1849–1932). American arts patron and ceramist. Name variations: Maria Nichols; Maria Longworth Nichols. Born Maria Longworth, Mar 20, 1849, in Cincinnati, Ohio; died April 30, 1932, in Paris, France; dau. of Joseph Longworth (arts patron) and Ann Maria (Rives) Longworth; aunt of Nicholas Longworth who married Alice Roosevelt Longworth; m. George Ward Nichols (journalist), 1868 (died 1885); m. Bellamy Storer (US congressional representative, and minister to Belgium), 1889 (died 1922); children: (1st m.) Joseph Ward Nichols; Margaret Rives Nichols (who married the marquis de Chambrun). ❖ Took up ceramic painting (1873) and experimented with different techniques; wrote a manual of pottery-making (1876); opened Ohio's 1st art pottery, calling it Rookwood after the family's estate (1880); assembled a staff of designers and artists, a Staffordshire potter, and a chemist, who developed a number of notable glazes, colors, and designs that earned the pottery national acclaim and a gold medal at Paris Exposition (1889); earned another gold medal at Paris Exhibition for her decorative bronze work (1890); writings include *Probation* (1910), *Sir Christopher Leighton* (1915), *The Borodino Mystery* (1916) and *In Memoriam Bellamy Storer* (1923). ❖ See also *Women in World History*.

STOREY, Edith (1892–1955). American actress. Born Mar 18, 1892, in New York, NY; died Oct 9, 1967, in Northport, LI, NY. ❖ Popular star for Vitagraph (1909–17); films include *A Florida Enchantment, A Tale of*

Two Cities, The Troublesome Stepdaughters, The Island of Regeneration, The Silent Woman and *The Greater Profit*; retired from the screen (1921).

STOREY, Elizabeth Allen (1894–1976). *See Pudney, Elizabeth Allen.*

STORM, Gale (1922—). American tv and screen actress. Born Josephine Owaissa Cottle, April 5, 1922, in Bloomington, TX; m. Lee Bonnell (actor), 1941 (died 1986); m. Paul Masterson (died 1996); children: (1st m.) Phillip, Peter, Paul, Susie. ❖ Made film debut in *Tom Brown's School Days* (1940), followed by *Red River Valley, Jesse James at Bay, Nearly 18, Smart Alecks, Rhythm Parade, Revenge of the Zombies, Where Are Your Children?, Forever Yours, G. I. Honeymoon, Sunbonnet Sue* and *Swing Parade of 1946*, among others; came to prominence on tv, starring in "My Little Margie" (1952–56) and "The Gale Storm Show," retitled "Oh Susanna!" (1956–60). ❖ See also autobiography *I Ain't Down Yet* (1981).

STORM, Lesley (1898–1975). Scottish playwright and novelist. Born 1898 in The Manse, Maud, Aberdeenshire, Scotland; died Oct 19, 1975, in London, England; dau. of Rev. William Cowie and Christian (Ewen) Cowie; m. James Doran Clark (died). ❖ Wrote such plays as *Tony Draws a Horse* (1939), *A Night in Venice, Great Day, Black Chiffon, Favonia, Time and Yellow Roses, The Paper Hat* and *Roar Like a Dove*; wrote screenplays for *East of Piccadilly* (adaptation), *Tonight and Every Night* (adapted from her play *Heart of a City*), *The Heart of the Matter* (adapted from Graham Greene novel), *The Golden Salamander* (adaptation), *Personal Affair* (adapted from her play *A Day's Mischief*), and *The Spanish Gardener* (adaptation), among others; novels include *Lady What of Life?* (1927) and *Just As I Am* (1933).

STORMS, Jane (1807–1878). *See Cazneau, Jane McManus.*

STORNI, Alfonsina (1892–1938). Argentine writer and social activist. Name variations: (pseudonyms) Tao-Lao and Alfonsina. Born Alfonsina Storni, May 29, 1892, in Sala Capriasca, Canton Ticino, Switzerland; died a suicide in Mar del Plata, Argentina, Oct 25, 1938; dau. of Alfonso Storni (small-time businessman, died 1906) and Paulina Martignoni de Storni (teacher); Escuela Normal Mixta de Maestros Rurales (Mixed Normal School for Rural Teachers) in Coronda, Santa Fe, teaching certificate, 1910; never married; children: Alejandro (b. April 21, 1912). ❖ One of her nation's most celebrated poets, began teaching career in Rosario, Province of Santa Fe, and published 1st poems in local literary press, *Mundo Rosarino* (The Rosario World) and *Monos y monadas* (Clowns and Monkeyshines); moved to Buenos Aires (1911), after becoming pregnant; contributed items to magazine *Caras y Caretas* (Faces and Masks); established reputation as a poet with publication of *La inquietud del rosal* (The Restlessness of the Rose Bush, 1916) and, within a year, found a new occupation as director of teachers in Colegio Marcos Paz; won a National Council of Women prize for *Canto a los niños* (Song for Children, 1917); became one of the leaders of the Asociación pro Derechos de la Mujer (Association for the Rights of the Woman) and a regular correspondent for the prestigious Buenos Aires daily newspaper *La Nación*, writing under pen-names Tao-Lao and Alfonsina; became Argentine citizen (1920); was named professor at Escuela Normal de Lenguas Vivas (Normal School of Living Languages, 1923); composed some of her best work (1930s), but under the shadow of breast cancer; major works include *El dulce daño* (Sweet Mischief, 1918), *Irremediablemente* (Irremediably, 1919), *Languidez* (Languor, 1920), for which she won several prizes, *Ocre* (Ochre, 1925), *El mundo de siete pozos* (The World of Seven Wells, 1934) and *Mascarilla y trébol* (Mask and Trefoil, 1938). ❖ See also Rachel Phillips, *Alfonsina Storni: From Poetess to Poet* (Tamesis, 1975); and *Women in World History*.

STORY, Gertrude (1929—). Canadian short-story writer. Born 1929 in Saskatchewan, Canada. ❖ Grew up in Lutheran farming community, which is reflected in work; also wrote children's fiction, radio plays, and nonfiction, and worked for CBC Radio; writings include *The Book of Thirteen* (1981), *The Way to Always Dance* (1983), *It Never Pays to Laugh Too Much* (1984), *Black Swan* (1986), *After Sixty: Going Home* (1991), and *The Last House on Main Street*.

STOTHARD, Anna Eliza (1790–1883). *See Bray, Anna Eliza.*

STOTHARD, Sarah Sophia (1825/26–1901). New Zealand teacher. Name variations: Sophia Stothard. Born Sarah Sophia Stothard, c. 1825–1826, in London, England; died Aug 29, 1901, in Auckland, New Zealand; dau. of Thomas Stothard (sculptor). ❖ Earned English teacher's certificate and taught for several years in England and Wales before immigrating to New Zealand (1860); advocated for establishment of a secondary school for girls in Auckland, becoming 1st principal of

Auckland Girls' Training and High School (1876); replaced by board with a man (1878); returned to private teaching. ❖ See also *Dictionary of New Zealand Biography* (Vol. 1).

STOTHARD, Sophia (1825/26–1901). *See Stothard, Sarah Sophia.*

STOUDER, Sharon (1948—). American swimmer. Name variations: Sharon Stouder Clark. Born Sharon Marie Stouder, Nov 9, 1948, in Altadena, CA; m. Kenyon Clark, Sept 8, 1979. ❖ Among the 1st of the California "water babies" who would win many international events, began swimming at age 3; won gold medals for 100-meter butterfly, 4 x 100-meter freestyle relay, and 4 x 100-meter medley relay and a silver medal for 100-meter freestyle at Tokyo Olympics (1964). ❖ See also *Women in World History*.

STOUT, Anna Paterson (1858–1931). New Zealand feminist and social activist. Name variations: Anna Paterson Logan. Born Anna Paterson Logan, Sept 29, 1858, in Dunedin, New Zealand; died May 10, 1931, at Hanmer Springs, New Zealand; dau. of John and Jessie Alexander (Pollock) Logan; m. Robert Stout (politician), 1876 (died 1930); children: 6. ❖ Joined New Zealand Women's Christian Temperance Union (1885); elected president of Women's Franchise League (1892); became vice president of National Council of Women of New Zealand (1896); helped to found Wellington branch of New Zealand Society for Protection of Women and Children (1897); lived in England while children attended school and aligned herself with Women's Social and Political Union (WSPU, early 1900s); contributed articles to *Votes for Women* and *Englishwoman*, republished as pamphlets later used by several suffrage groups. ❖ See also *Dictionary of New Zealand Biography* (Vol. 2).

STOUT, Mrs. C. T. (1884–1960). *See Hecker, Genevieve.*

STOUT, Juanita Kidd (1919–1998). African-American judge. Name variations: J. K. Stout. Born 1919 in Wewoka, OK; died Aug 21, 1998, in Philadelphia, PA; received bachelor's degree from University of Iowa and studied law at Indiana University; m. Charles Otis Stout (died 1988). ❖ The 1st black woman to serve as judge in Pennsylvania, began career as a music teacher in Oklahoma; established a law practice in Philadelphia (1954); appointed to District Attorney's office (1956); appointed to the Philadelphia Municipal Court (1959), and 2 months later became the 1st black woman in the nation to win election to a court of record; appointed to Philadelphia Court of Common Pleas; received an interim appointment to Pennsylvania Supreme Court (1988), the 1st black woman in the nation to be a judge on a state's highest court; held that position until mandatory retirement age of 70, then returned to the bench in Philadelpha.

STOUTE, Jennifer (1965—). English runner. Born April 16, 1965, in Bradford, England; m. John Regis; children: Alicia. ❖ At Barcelona Olympics, won a bronze medal in 4 x 400-meter relay (1992); appeared as Rebel on the tv program "Gladiators" (1996).

STOVBCHATAYA, Ludmila (1974—). Ukrainian gymnast. Born Mar 1, 1974, in Odessa, Ukraine, USSR; m. Vladimir Shamenko (gymnast). ❖ Won Jr. USSR nationals (1988); at European championships, won a bronze medal for balance beam (1992); won a gold medal for team all-around, silver medals for all-around and beam, and bronze medals for bars and floor at University Games (1993).

STOVE, Betty (1945—). Dutch tennis player. Born June 24, 1945, in Rotterdam, the Netherlands. ❖ With Wendy Turnbull, won doubles at Roland Garros (1979), US Open (1977 and 1979) and Italian Open (1979); with Billie Jean King, won doubles at Wimbledon and Roland Garros (1972); with Françoise Durr, won doubles at US Open (1972); with Frew McMillan, won mixed doubles at Wimbledon (1978 and 1981) and US Open (1977, 1978); was on the Dutch Fed Cup Team (1966, 1969–72, 1976–80, 1982–83); on WTA Tour, won 2 singles titles and 11 doubles titles; served 3 terms as president of WTA Tour Players Association.

STOVER, Mary Johnson (1832–1883). American first daughter. Name variations: Mary Johnson Brown. Born Mary Johnson in 1832; died 1883; dau. of Eliza McCardle Johnson (1810–1876) and Andrew Johnson (1808–1875, 17th president of US, 1865–69); sister of Martha Johnson Patterson (1828–1901); m. Daniel Stover (1826–1864, colonel killed in Civil War); m. William Ramsey Brown (div.); children: (1st m.) 3. ❖ During father's presidency, provided care for mother while her sister handled most of the social duties.

STOVER-IRWIN, Juno (1928—). American diver. Name variations: Juno Irwin. Born Juno Stover, Nov 22, 1928, in Los Angeles, CA; attended Glendale Community College, 1947–49; m. Russ Irwin; children: 5. ❖ Won a bronze medal at Helsinki Olympics (1952), while 3½ months pregnant, and a silver medal at Melbourne Olympics (1956), both in platform; competed on US swim team in 4 Olympics and was ranked as one of the top four divers in US (1947–60). Inducted into International Swimming Hall of Fame (1980).

STOWE, Augusta (1857–1943). *See Gullen, Augusta Stowe.*

STOWE, Emily Howard (1831–1903). Canadian physician and feminist. Name variations: Emily Jennings Stowe. Born Emily Howard Jennings in South Norwich, Upper Canada (now Ontario), May 1, 1831; died April 30, 1903, in Muskoka, north of Toronto, Canada; dau. of Solomon and Hannah (Howard) Jennings; New York College of Medicine for Women, MD, 1867; m. John Stowe, 1856; children: Augusta Stowe Gullen (1857–1943, physician). ❖ Became a teacher (1847); applied to Victoria College in Coburg, Ontario, but was refused because of gender; appointed principal of the public school in Brantford, Ontario, the 1st woman principal in Canada; after graduating from New York's College of Medicine, returned to Canada, established an unlicensed medical practice in Toronto, and launched her 13-year fight to be admitted to the College of Physicians and Surgeons in Ontario; finally allowed to take classes at the Toronto Faculty of Medicine, became the 1st licensed female physician in Canada (1880); a leading suffragist, was also the founder and 1st president of the Dominion Woman Suffrage Association.

STOWE, Harriet Beecher (1811–1896). American writer. Born Harriet Beecher, June 14, 1811, in Litchfield, Connecticut; died July 1, 1896, in Hartford, Connecticut; dau. of Lyman Beecher (died 1863, cleric) and Roxana (Foote) Beecher (died 1816); sister of Catharine Beecher; attended Litchfield Female Academy, 1819–24, and Hartford Female Seminary where she became a full-time instructor in 1829; m. Calvin Ellis Stowe, Jan 6, 1836 (died 1886); children: Eliza and Harriet (twins, b. 1836); Henry Ellis (1838–1857); Frederick William (b. 1840); Georgiana May (b. 1843); Samuel Charles (1848–1849); Charles Edward (b. 1850, author and his mother's biographer). ❖ Author whose best-known work, *Uncle Tom's Cabin,* helped to change the course of American history, published 1st writings in *Western Monthly Magazine* (1833); moved with husband and children to Brunswick, Maine (1850); published *Uncle Tom's Cabin* (1852); moved with family to Andover, Massachusetts (1852), then traveled to Europe for 1st time (1853); published 2nd novel *Dred* (1856); oldest son Henry drowned (1857); wrote 1st New England novel, *The Minister's Wooing* (1859); published *The Pearl of Orr's Island* (1862); met with President Abraham Lincoln at White House who, on introduction, said, "So this is the little woman who wrote the book that made this big war" (1862); moved with family to Hartford, Connecticut (1864); wrote *Lady Byron Vindicated* (1870); published last novel, *Poganuc People* (1878). ❖ See also Anne Fields, *Life and Letters of Harriet Beecher Stowe* (Houghton, 1898); Catherine Gilbertson, *Harriet Beecher Stowe* (Appleton-Century, 1937); Charles Edward Stowe, *Life of Harriet Beecher Stowe* (Houghton, 1890); Forrest Wilson, *Crusader in Crinoline: The Life of Harriet Beecher Stowe* (Lippincott, 1941); Joan D. Hedrick, *Harriet Beecher Stowe: A Life* (Oxford U. Press, 1994); Johanna Johnston, *Runaway to Heaven: The Story of Harriet Beecher Stowe* (Doubleday, 1963); and *Women in World History.*

STOWELL, Belinda (1971—). Zimbabwean-born Australian sailor. Born May 28, 1971, in Harare, Zimbabwe; moved to Perth, Western Australia. ❖ Won World championship in 420 class (1995); crewed the all-female Elle Racing entry for the Whitbread 60 around-the-world race (1996); won a gold medal for double-handed dinghy (470) at Sydney Olympics (2000); won World championships in double-handed dinghy class (2002). Named Western Australian Sailor of the Year.

STOYANOVA, Boriana (1968—). Bulgarian gymnast. Born July 3, 1968, in Sofia, Bulgaria. ❖ At European championships, won bronze medals for vault and floor exercises (1983); won a gold medal for vault and a bronze for floor at World championships (1983); won Champions All (1984), Golden Sands International and Medico Cup (1987); placed 2nd all-around at European Cup (1988).

STOYANOVA, Mariya (1947—). Bulgarian basketball player. Born July 19, 1947, in Bulgaria. ❖ At Montreal Olympics, won a bronze medal in team competition (1976).

STOYANOVA, Penka (1950—). Bulgarian basketball player. Born Jan 21, 1950, in Bulgaria. ❖ Won a bronze medal at Montreal Olympics (1976) and a silver medal at Moscow Olympics (1980), both in team competition.

STOYANOVA, Radka (1964—). Bulgarian rower. Born July 1964, in Bulgaria. ❖ At Seoul Olympics, won a silver medal in coxless pairs (1988).

STRACHEY, Pippa (1872–1968). British suffragist. Name variations: Philippa Strachey. Born Philippa Strachey in 1872; died 1968; dau. of Sir Richard Strachey (1817–1908) and Lady Jane Maria (Grant) Strachey (1840–1928); sister of Elinor Strachey (1860–1944), Dorothy Strachey (1865–1960, writer who m. Simon Bussy), Oliver Strachey (1874–1960), Marjorie Strachey (1882–1964), Joan Pernel Strachey (1876–1951), and Lytton Strachey (1880–1932); aunt of Julia Strachey (1901–1978, writer, dau. of Oliver Strachey and Ruby Meyer Strachey); sister-in-law of Ray Strachey; never married. ❖ Joined mother in National Union of Women's Suffrage Societies (NUWSS) and served as secretary, working mainly in the background to organize demonstrations; often collaborated with sister-in-law Ray Strachey on feminist causes, particularly as they related to labor issues, but was usually the long-term strategist behind the scenes; acted as secretary to the Women's Service Bureau when it became the London Society for Women's Service following end of WWI; also saw the founding of a club for the society, the Women's Service House, which was later renamed the Fawcett Society. Named Commander of the British Empire (CBE, 1951). ❖ See also Brian Harrison, *Prudent Revolutionaries: Portraits of British Feminists between the Wars* (Clarendon, 1987); and *Women in World History.*

STRACHEY, Ray (1887–1940). British suffragist. Name variations: Rachel Mary Costelloe; Rachel Strachey. Born Rachel Mary Costelloe, June 4, 1887; died July 1940; dau. of Frank (died 1899) and Mary Pearsall (Smith) Costelloe, also known as Mary Berenson (1864–1944, who later married Bernard Berenson); granddau. of Hannah Whitall Smith; sister of Karin Costelloe Stephen (1889–1953, one of the 1st British psychoanalysts, who m. Adrien Stephen, brother of Virginia Woolf); niece of Alys Russell (1866–1951); sister-in-law of Pippa Strachey; educated at Newnham College and Bryn Mawr College; became 2nd wife of Oliver Strachey (1874–1960), May 31, 1911; children: Barbara Strachey (b. 1912); Christopher Strachey (1916–1975); stepchildren: Julia Strachey (1901–1978, writer). ❖ Often working with sister-in-law Pippa Strachey, took a high-profile position both in National Union of Women's Suffrage Societies (NUWSS) and the Women's Service Bureau; negotiated for passage of 1918 suffrage bill that granted the vote to women over 30; stood unsuccessfully for a seat in Parliament (1918, 1922 and 1923); served as parliamentary secretary for Nancy Astor; assumed control of the Women's Employment Federation (1935), a natural progression from her early days with the Women's Service Bureau; edited suffrage paper *The Common Cause* (later renamed the *Women's Leader*); published most famous book, *The Cause* (1928), a germinal work on the history of British women's movement. ❖ See also Barbara Strachey, *Remarkable Relations: The Story of the Pearsall Smith Women* (Universe, 1982); Brian Harrison, *Prudent Revolutionaries: Portraits of British Feminists between the Wars* (Clarendon, 1987); and *Women in World History.*

STRADNER, Rose (1913–1958). Viennese-born actress. Name variations: Rose Mankiewicz. Born July 31, 1913, in Vienna, Austria; died Sept 27, 1958, a suicide, in Mt. Kisco, NY; m. Joseph Mankiewicz (producer). ❖ Made film debut as Rosi in *Hochzeit am Wolfgangsee* (1933); other films include *Keys of the Kingdom* (as Mother Maria-Veronica), *Blind Alley* and *The Last Gangster.*

STRAIGHT, Beatrice (1914–2001). American stage and screen actress. Born Beatrice Whitney Straight, Aug 2, 1914, in Old Westbury, NY; died April 7, 2001, in Los Angeles, CA; dau. of Willard Dickerman Straight (banker and diplomat) and Dorothy Payne Whitney (1887–1968, philanthropist); sister of Michael Straight (writer and editor of *The New Republic*); cousin of Gloria Vanderbilt; m. Louis Dolivet (div. 1949); m. Peter Cookson (actor), 1949 (died 1990); children: Gary Cookson (actor) and Tony Cookson (writer-director). ❖ Made NY debut in *Bitter Oleander* (1935); other plays include *Twelfth Night* (Viola), *Land of Fame, Eastward in Eden, Macbeth* (Lady Macduff), *The Heiress* (succeeding Wendy Hiller as Catherine Sloper), *The Grand Tour, Phèdre* (title role), *Everything in the Garden* and *Ghosts*; made film debut in *Phone Call from a Stranger* (1952), followed by *Patterns, The Nun's Story, The Promise, Endless Love, Poltergeist, Power, Two of a Kind* and *Under Seige,* among others; on tv, had recurring role of Lynda Carter's mother on "Wonder Woman." Won a Tony Award as Best Supporting Actress for role of Elizabeth Proctor in *The Crucible,* a part she originated (1953); nominated for Emmy for "The Dain Curse" (1978); won Oscar as Best Supporting Actress for *Network* (1976).

STRAIGHT, Dorothy (1887–1968). *See Whitney, Dorothy Payne.*

STRAKER, Karen (1964—). English equestrian. Name variations: Karen Dixon. Born Sept 17, 1964, in UK; dau. of Elaine Straker (her trainer); sister of Matthew and Nick Straker (equestrians); m. Andrew Dixon; children: 2. ❖ On Running Bear, was Jr. European champion (1982); at Seoul Olympics, won a silver medal in team 3-day event (1988), on Get Smart; on Get Smart, won team silver at Stockholm World Games (1990) and team gold and individual bronze at Europeans (1991); came in 6th at Barcelona Olympics; on Too Smart, won British Open championship (1994). Received MBE.

STRANDBERG, Britt. Swedish cross-country skier. Born in Sweden. ❖ Won a gold medal for 3 x 5 km relay at Squaw Valley Olympics (1960); won silver medals for 3 x 5 km relay at Innsbruck Olympics (1964) and Grenoble Olympics (1968).

STRANG, Elise (c. 1879–1959). *See L'Esperance, Elise Strang.*

STRANG, Ruth (1895–1971). American educator and writer. Born Ruth May Strang, April 3, 1895, in Chatham, New Jersey; died Jan 3, 1971, in Amityville, New York; dau. of Charles Garret Strang (farmer) and Anna (Bergen) Strang; Columbia University Teachers College, BS, 1922, MA, 1924, PhD, 1926; never married. ❖ At Columbia, was supervisor of health education at Horace Mann School (1924) and research assistant in psychology (1925), then began her 3-decade career at Teachers College as an assistant professor of education (1929), becoming an associate professor (1936) and a full professor (1940); served as a professor of education and head of the reading development center at University of Arizona (1960–68); published *An Introduction to Child Study* (1930), the 1st of some 400 articles, monographs, books and pamphlets; edited the influential *Journal of the National Association for Women Deans, Administrators, and Counselors* (1938–60); also wrote *Educational Guidance: Its Principles and Practices* (1947), *The Role of the Teacher in Personnel Work* (1953), *Explorations in Reading Patterns* (1942), and *The Adolescent Views Himself: A Psychology of Adolescence* (1957); served for several years as a director of the American Association for Gifted Children. ❖ See also *Women in World History.*

STRANGE, Michael (1890–1950). American writer. Name variations: Blanche Marie Louise Oelrichs; Blanche Oelrichs Thomas Barrymore Tweed. Born Blanche Marie Louise Oelrichs, Oct 1, 1890, in New York, NY; died Nov 5, 1950, in Boston, Massachusetts; dau. of Blanche (de Loosey) Oelrichs and Charles May Oelrichs; m. Leonard Moorhead Thomas (first secretary of American legation to Madrid), Jan 1910 (div. 1919); m. John Barrymore (actor), Aug 1920 (div. 1928); m. Harrison Tweed (lawyer and yachtsman), May 1929 (div. 1942); children: (1st m.) sons Leonard Moorhead Thomas Jr. (b. 1911) and Robin May Thomas (1915–1944); (2nd m.) Diana Barrymore (1921–1960), actress). ❖ Actress and playwright who wrote poetry, dressed in men's shirts and ties, and was married to the hugely popular John Barrymore; published *Miscellaneous Poems* (1916), under name Michael Strange; continued to use this pseudonym for the rest of her life, in both her literary and stage careers; wrote the play *Redemption* (1918), an adaptation of Tolstoy's *The Living Corpse,* which had a successful run on Broadway and starred John Barrymore; published 2nd collection of poetry (1919); as an actress, appeared in Strindberg's *Easter,* Wilde's *The Importance of Being Earnest,* Sophocles' *Electra,* and on Broadway in Rostand's *L'Aiglon;* toured on lecture circuit, reading poetry set to music; also appeared on radio. ❖ See also autobiography *Who Tells Me True* (1940); and *Women in World History.*

STRANGFORD, Viscountess (c. 1845–1887). *See Smythe, Emily Anne.*

STRASBERG, Paula (1911–1966). American actress, director, and drama coach. Name variations: Paula Miller. Born Paula Miller, 1911, in New York, NY; died April 29, 1966, in New York, NY; m. Lee Strasberg (actor and acting teacher), 1934; children: John Strasberg (actor) and Susan Strasberg (actress, 1938–1999). ❖ As Paula Miller, 1st appeared with Le Gallienne's Civic Rep (1928), then with the Group Theatre; plays include *Till the Day I Die, Waiting for Lefty, Case of Clyde Griffiths, Johnny Johnson* and *Me and Molly;* taught, directed, and was one of the founders of the Actors Studio.

STRASBERG, Susan (1938–1999). American actress. Born May 22, 1938, in New York, NY; died in New York, NY, Jan 21, 1999; dau. of Lee Strasberg (acting teacher) and Paula Strasberg (actress); attended Actors Studio; m. actor Christopher Jones (div.); children: Jennifer. ❖ Considered an accomplished actress at an early age, grew up around the Actors Studio; at 17, created role of Anne Frank in Broadway hit *The Diary of Anne Frank* (1955); also appeared in *Time Remembered* (1957); in a career that spanned 4 decades, acted in over 30 films, including *Stage Struck, The Cobweb, Picnic* and *Morning Glory,* made nearly 2 dozen tv appearances, and performed in many plays. ❖ See also memoir, *Bittersweet* (1980), and the autobiographical *Marilyn and Me: Sisters, Rivals, Friends* (1992); and *Women in World History.*

STRATAS, Teresa (1938—). Canadian soprano. Born Anastasia Strataki of Greek descent, May 26, 1938, in Toronto, Ontario, Canada; studied with Irene Jessner at Toronto, 1956–59; graduate of University of Toronto, Faculty of Music, 1959. ❖ Began singing in Greek cafes in Toronto; at 12, admitted to Royal Academy of Music; debuted with Canadian Opera in Toronto (1958); won Metropolitan Opera Auditions of the Air (1959) and began a swift ascent in the opera world; debuted at Metropolitan Opera (1959), Covent Garden (1961), and Teatro alla Scala (1962); performed title role in 1st 3-act production of Berg's *Lulu* in Paris (1979); also starred with Placido Domingo in Zeffirelli's film version of *La Traviata* (1983); made Broadway debut in musical *Rags* (1986), for which she won a Tony Award for Best Actress. Made an Officer of the Order of Canada (1972); won 3 Grammy awards and 1 Emmy. ❖ See also Harry Rasky, *Stratas: An Affectionate Tribute* (Oxford U. Press, 1989); and *Women in World History.*

STRATEMEYER, Harriet (c. 1893–1982). *See Adams, Harriet Stratemeyer.*

STRATHEARN, countess of. *See Stewart, Euphemia (c. 1375–1415).*

STRATHEARN, duchess of. *See Horton, Ann (1743–1808).*

STRATHMORE, Lady. *See Cavendish-Bentinck, Nina.*

STRATONICE I (c. 319–254 BCE). Seleucid queen. Name variations: Stratoniki or Stratonike. Born c. 319; died in 254 BCE; dau. of Demetrius Poliorcetes (Macedonian general-king) and his 1st wife Phila I (dau. of Antipater); m. Seleucus I Nicator (c. 360–280 BCE, Macedonian general and founder of the Seleucid Empire, covering most of Asia Minor, Syria, Persia, and Bactria), c. 298 BCE; m. Antiochus I Soter (324–261 BCE), in 294; children: (1st m.) daughter, Phila II (b. around 300 BCE); (2nd m.) Seleucus; Apama (born c. 290 BCE, mother of Berenice II of Cyrene); Antiochus II Theos (286–247 BCE); Stratonice II (c. 285–228 BCE). ❖ While married to Seleucus I Nicator, became the beloved of her stepson Antiochus I Soter, who was 5 years older and pining away to the point of illness; husband Seleucus divorced her so that she could marry Antiochus, then proclaimed that she and Antiochus would henceforth assume the status of "queen" and "king" and rule jointly over Seleucus' territories to the east of the Euphrates River; as queen, maintained a very high profile, being especially zealous in her dedications at such religious sites as Delos; her subjects even came to worship her, usually in association with the goddess Aphrodite; upon Seleucus' death (280), assumed rule with Antiochus over the entire Seleucid realm. ❖ See also *Women in World History.*

STRATONICE II (c. 285–228 BCE). Seleucid princess. Name variations: Stratoniki or Stratonike. Born c. 285; died in 228 BCE; dau. of the Seleucid king and queen, Antiochus I Soter and Stratonice I (c. 319–254 BCE); sister of Antiochus II Theos; m. her cousin-nephew Demetrius II, king of Macedonia, in 255 BCE (marriage ended, 239); children: Apama. ❖ After husband succeeded to Macedonian throne and married 2nd wife Phthia of Epirus, took offense at his 2nd marriage and returned to the kingdom of her birth; back in Asia, made a beeline for Antioch, the capital of the Seleucid Empire, where she: 1) offered herself in marriage to the reigning king, her nephew Seleucus II; and 2) encouraged him to avenge her flight from Macedon by warring on Demetrius II; after Seleucus declined to act upon either of her suggestions, set out to topple Seleucus from his throne; her revolt quickly faded and she was put to death. ❖ See also *Women in World History.*

STRATONICE III (fl. 250 BCE). Seleucid princess. Name variations: Stratoniki or Stratonike. Born c. 250 BCE; dau. of Antiochus II Theos and Laodice I (c. 285–236 BCE); sister of Antiochus Hierax and Seleucus II; niece of Stratonice I; m. Ariarathes III, Persian ruler of Cappadocia. ❖ See also *Women in World History.*

STRATONIKE. *Variant of Stratonice.*

STRATONIKE. *See Olympias (c. 371–316 BCE).*

STRATONIKI. *Variant of Stratonice.*

STRATTON, Dorothy (b. 1899). American educator and military leader. Name variations: Dorothy Constance Stratton. Born Mar 24, 1899, in Brookfield, Missouri; dau. of Richard Lee Stratton (Baptist minister) and Anna (Troxler) Stratton; Ottawa University, Kansas, BA, 1920; University of Chicago, MA, 1924; Columbia University, PhD, 1932. ❖ Appointed dean of women and associate professor of psychology at Purdue University (1932), then promoted to a full professor (1940); during WWII, left Purdue to serve on the selection board of the Women's Army Auxiliary Corps (1942), and entered the Women Appointed for Volunteer Emergency Service (WAVES); became the 1st director and 1st woman officer, with rank of lieutenant commander, of the Coast Guard Women's Reserve upon its creation (1942); served as director of personnel at the International Monetary Fund (1947–50); served as national executive director of the Girl Scouts of America (1950–60); at age 105, was living in West Lafayette, Indiana. ❖ See also *Women in World History.*

STRATTON, Helen (fl. 1891–1925). British children's book illustrator. Flourished between 1891 and 1925. ❖ A popular turn-of-the-century illustrator, lent her art-nouveau style to numerous works of fairy tale and folklore; provided 167 illustrations for Walter Campbell's folklore collection, *Beyond the Border* (1898); was at the height of her career when she illustrated *The Fairy Tales of Hans Christian Andersen* (1899); also illustrated *Grimm's Fairy Tales, Heroic Legends, A Book of Myths, The Princess and the Goblin* and *The Princess and Curdie.*

STRATTON, Mercy Lavinia (1841–1919). *See Warren, Lavinia.*

STRATTON-PORTER, Gene (1863–1924). American writer. Name variations: Gene Stratton Porter. Born Geneva Grace Stratton, Aug 17, 1863, in Wabash County, Indiana; died Dec 6, 1924, in Los Angeles, California; dau. of Mark Stratton (farmer and minister) and Mary (Schallenberger) Stratton; m. Charles Darwin Porter (chemist), April 21, 1886; children: Jeanette Porter-Meehan (b. 1888). ❖ Naturalist who publicized her concern for the threatened wildlife habitats of North America through enormously successful magazine columns, novels, photograph collections, and films; began publishing photographs and nature essays in magazines (1900); published 1st book, *The Song of the Cardinal* (1903); was a bestselling fiction author and sought-after columnist (1905); began financing and producing films based on her work (1922); during 1st two decades of the 20th century, was one of the most famous women in US; writings include *The Song of the Cardinal: A Love Story* (1903), *Freckles* (1904), *At the Foot of the Rainbow* (1907), *A Girl of the Limberlost* (1909), *Music of the Wild* (1910), *The Harvester* (1911), *Moths of the Limberlost* (1912), *After the Flood* (1912), *Laddie: A True Blue Story* (1913), *Michael O'Halloran* (1915), (self-illustrated) *Morning Face* (1916), *A Daughter of the Land* (1918), *Homing with the Birds: The History of a Lifetime of Personal Experiences with the Birds* (1919), *Her Father's Daughter* (1921), *The Fire Bird* (1922), *The White Flag* (1923), *The Keeper of the Bees* (1925) and *The Magic Garden* (1927). ❖ See also Judith Reick Long, *Gene Stratton Porter: Novelist and Naturalist* (1990); Jeanette Porter-Meehan, *The Lady of the Limberlost: The Life and Letters of Gene Stratton-Porter* (Doubleday, 1928); Sydney Landon Plum, *Coming Through the Swamp: The Nature Writings of Gene Stratton Porter* (U. of Utah Press, 1996); and *Women in World History.*

STRAUCH, Annegret (1968—). German rower. Name variations: Annegret Strauch-Lamers. Born Dec 1, 1968, in Germany. ❖ Won a gold medal at Seoul Olympics (1988) and a bronze medal at Barcelona Olympics (1992), both in coxed eights.

STRAUS, Ida (1849–1912). American philanthropist. Born Rosalie Ida Blun, Feb 6, 1849, in Worms, Hessen, Germany; died April 15, 1912; m. Isidor Straus; children: 6, including Jesse Isidor Straus (b. 1872, an ambassador), Percy Selden Straus (b. 1876), and Nathan Straus. ❖ With husband, owned Macy's department store and was well-known for philanthropy; was on the *Titanic* (April 15, 1912); as the ship foundered, urged her maid Ellen Bird to take her place in the lifeboat. ❖ See also *Women in World History.*

STRAUSS, Astrid (1968—). East German swimmer. Born Dec 24, 1968, in East Germany. ❖ At Seoul Olympics, won a silver medal in 800-meter freestyle (1988).

STRAUSS, Jennifer (1933—). Australian poet, literary critic, and educator. Born Jan 30, 1933, in Heywood, Victoria, Australia; educated at universities of Melbourne and Glasgow; Monash University, PhD; children: 3. ❖ Taught at universities of Melbourne and Monash; works include *Children and Other Strangers* (1975), *Winter Driving* (1981), and *Labour Ward* (1988).

STRAUSS, Sara Milford (1896–1979). American dancer, teacher and choreographer. Born 1896 in New York, NY; died July 7, 1979, in Wilmington, DE. ❖ Published *The Dance and Life* (c. 1916); performed in a series of concert dance recitals, including *Formlessness, Consciousness* (1928), and *Space Limitation* (1933); served as chair of Concert Dancers' League in NY and helped overturn the city's blue law that banned dance performances on Sunday; staged acts for *Ziegfeld Follies*; best known for her breathing and movement classes for stage actors.

STRAUSS UND TORNEY, Lulu von (1873–1956). German writer. Born Sept 20, 1873, in Bückeburg, Germany; died June 19, 1956, in Jena, East Germany; dau. of a general major who served as adjunct to the duke of Schaumburg-Lippe; m. Eugen Diederichs (publisher), 1916 (died 1930). ❖ Prolific and popular writer of poetry, prose, criticism and correspondence, whose work is deeply linked to the northern region of Germany where she was born, published such poetry collections as *Reif steht die Saat* (The Crop is Ripe, 1919), and *Erde der Väter* (Our Forefathers' Soil, 1936); novels include *Luzifer* (1907), *Judas* (1911), and *Der jüngste Tag* (Judgment Day, 1922), which is regarded as her masterpiece; short stories include *Bauernstolz* (Peasant's Pride, 1901), *Das Meerminneke* (The Sea Maid, 1906), and *Auge um Auge* (Eye for Eye, 1933); nonfiction includes *Das Leben der Heilingen Elisabeth* (The Life of Saint Elisabeth, 1926), *Eugen Diederichs, Leben und Werk* (Eugen Diederichs, Life and Work, 1936), and *Annette von Droste-Hülshoff* (1936); though her heroic ballads are considered among the best of the early 20th century, her poetry and fiction, permeated by mythology, heroic human struggles, and romanticized "sons of the soil," found much favor with members of the Nazi Party, perhaps the largest reason why even her best writing is now little read. ❖ See also memoirs, *Das verborgene Angesicht, Erinnerungen* (The Veiled Face, Memories, 1943); and *Women in World History.*

STRAZHEVA, Olga (1972—). Soviet gymnast. Born Nov 12, 1972, in Zaporozhie, USSR. ❖ Won Konica Cup (1988), USSR nationals (1988), and USSR Cup (1989); at Seoul Olympics, won a gold medal in team all-around (1988); at European championship, won a silver medal in uneven bars and a bronze medal in all-around (1989); at Worlds, won a gold medal in team all-around and bronze medals in all-around and uneven bars (1989).

STREATFEILD, Noel (1895–1986). British novelist and children's writer. Name variations: (pseudonyms) Noelle Sonning, Susan Scarlett. Born Dec 24, 1895, in Amberley, near Arundel, Sussex, England; died Sept 11, 1986, in London; dau. of William Champion Streatfeild (vicar and later a bishop) and Janet Nancy (Venn) Streatfeild; attended St. Leonard's College and Laleham School in Eastbourne, Hastings; graduate of Royal Academy of Dramatic Art in London; never married; no children. ❖ Began career as an actress, including tours in South Africa and Australia (1929), gaining knowledge of the theater world that would later lend authenticity to such books as *The Whicharts* (1931) and *Curtain Up* (1944); published 1st children's book, *Ballet Shoes: A Story of Three Children on the Stage* (1936), which proved hugely popular; wrote *The Circus Is Coming* (1938), which was awarded the Carnegie Medal; often wrote about vocations, including *The Painted Garden* (1949) and *White Boots* (1951); wrote a series of novels for adults under pseudonym Susan Scarlett, many of them dealing with such issues as illegitimacy and homosexuality, including *The Man in the Dark* (1941) and *Murder While You Work* (1944); using her own name, published the adult novel *I Ordered a Table for Six* (1942), concerning the aftereffects of unexpected death; worked in radio with a popular serial about the Bells, the family of a small-town vicar (1950s), which was later made into a tv series and spawned 2 of her children's books, *The Bell Family* (1954) and *New Town* (1960); wrote biographies of E. Nesbit and Queen Victoria; published *The Growing Summer* (also released as *The Magic Summer*, 1966), which is considered one of her best; other writings include *The House in Cornwall* (1940), *The Children of Primrose Lane* (1941), *Grass in Piccadilly* (1947), *Gemma* (1968) and *Meet the Maitlands* (1978). ❖ See also autobiographical trilogy: *The Vicarage Family* (1963), *Away from the Vicarage* (1965) and *Beyond the Vicarage* (1971); and *Women in World History.*

STREB, Elizabeth (1950—). American dancer and choreographer. Born Feb 23, 1950, in Rochester, NY; State University of New York, Brockport, BS in modern dance, cum laude, 1972; studied with

Susannah Payton, Daniel Nagrin, Irma Plyshenko, and Mary Edwards. ❖ Danced with Margaret Jenkins in San Francisco (1972–74); founded Streb/Ringside dance company in Ringside, NY (1985); premiered her signature piece *Little Ease* (1985); began to intertwine the disciplines of dance, athletics, extreme sports, and Hollywood stunt work for a choreography she called POPACTION; received 3 New York Dance and Performance (Bessie) awards (1988–90); awarded a MacArthur Foundation "genius" grant (1997).

STREB, Marla (1965—). American mountain biker. Born June 24, 1965, in Baltimore, MD. ❖ Turned pro at age 28 (1990); won gold in Downhill (Winter 1998) and silver in Speed (Winter 1997) at X Games; became Singlespeed Women's World champion (1999); won bronze at World championships in Downhill (2000); made 2nd-place finish at Red Bull Race to the Center of the Earth, Austria (2001), 1st-place finish at Sea Otter Classic Downhill (2001), and 1st-place finish at 1st race of National Series (2001) in Big Bear, CA.

STRECEN-MASEIKAITE, Sigita (1958—). Soviet handball player. Born Sept 24, 1958, in USSR. ❖ At Moscow Olympics, won a gold medal in team competition (1980).

STREEP, Meryl (1949—). American actress. Born Mary Louise Streep, June 22, 1949, in Summit, New Jersey; Vassar College, BA, 1971; Yale Drama School, MFA, 1975; m. Don Gummer (sculptor), 1978; children: Henry, Mary Willa, Grace and Louisa. ❖ Just out of Yale Drama School, moved to New York and landed lead in Joseph Papp's production of *Trelawney of the Wells* (1975); earned Tony nomination for *27 Wagons Full of Cotton* and Obie Award for *Alice at the Palace*; made film debut in *Julia* (1977); nominated for Academy Awards for *The Deer Hunter* (1978), *The French Lieutenant's Woman* (1981), *Silkwood* (1983), *Out of Africa* (1985), *A Cry in the Dark* (1988), *Postcards from the Edge* (1990), *The Bridges of Madison County* (1995), *One True Thing* (1998), *Music of the Heart* (1999) and *Adaptation* (2002), becoming the most nominated actor in history; won Academy Award for Best Actress for *Kramer vs. Kramer* (1979) and *Sophie's Choice* (1982); nominated for Golden Globes for *The Hours* (2002) and *The Manchurian Candidate* (2004); on tv, appeared in "Angels in America" (2003), for which she won Emmy; received American Film Institute's Life Achievement Award (2004); other films include *The Still of the Night* (1980), *Heartburn* (1986), *Ironweed* (1987), *She-Devil* (1989), *Death Becomes Her* (1992), *The House of the Spirits* (1993), *Marvin's Room* (1996), *Dancing at Lughnasa* (1998) and *Lemony Snicket's A Series of Unfortunate Events* (2004). ❖ See also Pfaff and Emerson, *Meryl Streep: A Critical Biography* (McFarland, 1987).

STREET, Jessie (1889–1970). Australian feminist and diplomat. Name variations: Jessie Lillingston; Jessie Mary Grey Street; Lady Street. Born Jessie Lillingston, April 18, 1889, in Chota Nagpur, India; died July 2, 1970; dau. of Charles Lillingston (British civil servant) and Mabel (Ogilvie) Lillingston; Women's College of Sydney University, BA, 1910; m. Kenneth Whistler Street (justice of Supreme Court of NSW who was made a Knight Commander of the Order of St. Michael and St. George), in 1916; children: 4. ❖ At 7, moved with family to a station (ranch) near the Clarence River in NSW; helped to establish the country's 1st Social Hygiene Association (1916); joined League of Nations Union (1918) while maintaining her activities in various women's groups, including National Council of Women, of which she served as secretary (1920), then president; founded United Associations of Women (UAW, 1929) and spent most of the next 20 years as its president; stood unsuccessfully as Labor candidate for a seat in Australian Parliament (1943 and 1946); was the only woman in Australia's delegation to San Francisco conference on the foundation of United Nations (1945), where she advocated the formation of the Commission on the Status of Women, then served as vice-chair of the commission until 1949; became a constituent member of the Federal Council for Aboriginal Advancement; founded and was a frequent contributor to *The Australian Women's Digest* (1944–48). ❖ See also memoirs *Truth or Repose* (1966); and *Women in World History*.

STREET, Picabo (1971—). American Alpine skier. Born April 3, 1971, in Triumph, ID. ❖ Won a silver medal at the World championships and a gold medal at the US championships (1993); won a silver medal in the downhill at Lillehammer Olympics (1994); won a World Cup downhill title, the 1st American woman to accomplish that feat (1995), then another (1996); won the downhill title at the World championships (1996); won a gold medal for super-G at Nagano Olympics

(1998); competed at Salt Lake City Olympics but did not medal (2002). ❖ See also Christina Lessa, *Women Who Win* (Universe, 1998).

STREETER, Alison (1964—). English long-distance swimmer. Born 1964 in Nutfield, Surrey, England; dau. of Freda Streeter (schoolteacher). ❖ Known as "Queen of the Channel," took up swimming to help with asthma; just shy of 18th birthday, crossed English Channel for 1st time; was the 1st woman to swim from Ireland to Scotland, the 1st person to swim from Scotland to Ireland, and the 1st British woman to swim Channel both ways; other long-distance routes include Ireland to Scotland, Capri to Naples, tidal length of Thames River from Richmond to Gravesend (and back) and around Manhattan Island; became overall record-holder (man or woman) for most cross-channel swims (40) in 1995; awarded MBE (1991).

STREETER, Roberta (1944—). See Gentry, Bobbie.

STREETER, Ruth Cheney (1895–1990). American military leader. Born Oct 2, 1895, in Brookline, Massachusetts; died Sept 1990 in Morristown, New Jersey; dau. of Charles Paine Cheney and Mary Ward (Lyon) Cheney Schofield; attended Bryn Mawr College, 1914–16; m. Thomas Winthrop Streeter (lawyer, banker, and utility executive), 1917; children: Frank Sherwin; Henry Schofield; Thomas Winthrop Jr.; Lilian Carpenter. ❖ As World War II raged in Europe, began taking flying lessons (1940), then served with the Civil Air Patrol; after Congress approved creation of a Women's Reserve (WR) of the Marine Corps in order to free up Marines for combat duty (1943), was commissioned a major and named director of the WR, overseeing some 1,000 officers and 18,000 enlisted women by 1944; reached rank of colonel (1945); also served as national president of the Society of Colonial Dames (1948–52). ❖ See also *Women in World History*.

STREETIN, Mary Ann (c. 1759–1888). See Buxton, Mary Ann.

STREICH, Rita (1920–1987). German coloratura soprano. Born Dec 18, 1920, in Barnaul, Russia; died Mar 20, 1987, in Vienna, Austria; studied with Willi Domgraf-Fassbänder, Maria Ivogün, and Erna Berger. ❖ Sang with Berlin Staatsoper (1946–51) and Berlin Städtische Oper (1951–53); debuted in London (1957); made American debut in San Francisco (1957); was especially remembered for her Sophie in Strauss' *Der Rosenkavalier* and Zerbinetta in *Ariadne auf Naxos*; joined the Folkwang-Hochschule faculty in Essen (1974). ❖ See also *Women in World History*.

STREIDT, Ellen (1952—). East German runner. Born July 27, 1952, in East Germany. ❖ At Montreal Olympics, won a bronze medal in 400 meters and a gold medal in 4 x 400-meter relay (1976).

STREISAND, Barbra (1942—). American singer, actress and film producer and director. Born Barbara Joan Streisand, April 24, 1942, in Brooklyn, NY; dau. of Emanuel and Diana (Rosen) Streisand (later Kind); half-sister of Roslyn Kind (singer); m. Elliot Gould (actor), 1963 (div. 1971); m. James Brolin (actor), 1998; children: (1st m.) Jason Gould (actor). ❖ Made Broadway debut in *I Can Get It For You Wholesale*, for which she was nominated for a Tony Award; won 2 Grammy Awards for debut album, *The Barbra Streisand Album* (1963); starred on Broadway (1964), then on film (1968) in *Funny Girl*, for which she won an Academy Award for Best Actress; won an Emmy for 1st tv special, "My Name is Barbra" (1965), an achievement repeated with "Barbra Streisand: The Concert" (1995) and "Barbra Streisand: Timeless, Live in Concert" (2001); became the 1st female composer to win an Academy Award with "Evergreen," written for her film *A Star is Born* (1976); became the 1st woman to produce, direct, write and star in a major motion picture with *Yentl* (1983); directed and starred in *The Prince of Tides* (1991), the 1st film directed by its female star to receive a Best Director nomination from Directors Guild, as well as 7 Academy Award nominations; released numerous hit albums, including *Guilty* with Barry Gibb (1980), and had #1 albums in each of the last 4 decades; received American Film Institute's Life Achievement Award (2001); other film appearances include *Hello, Dolly!* (1969), *On a Clear Day You Can See Forever* (1970), *The Owl and the Pussycat* (1970), *What's Up, Doc?* (1972), *Up the Sandbox* (1972), *The Way We Were* (1973), *Funny Lady* (1975), *The Main Event* (1979), *Nuts* (1987), *The Mirror Has Two Faces* (1996), for which she co-wrote the song "I Finally Found Someone," and *Meet the Fockers* (2004).

STREIT, Marlene (1934—). Canadian golfer. Name variations: Marlene Stewart. Born Marlene Stewart, Mar 9, 1934, in Cereal, Alberta, Canada; Rollins College, BA, 1956; m. J. Douglas Streit, 1957; children: Darlene Louise Streit; Lynn Elizabeth Streit. ❖ Won the Canadian

Women's Open (1951, 1954–56, 1958–59, and 1963); won the USGA Women's Amateur (1956); won the British Women's Amateur (1953), Australian Women's Amateur (1963), and the World Women's Amateur (1966); was the 1st woman ever to win the amateur championships of Canada, US, Britain, and Australia; captained Canada's Commonwealth championship team in Perth, Australia (1979). Named Canadian Woman Athlete of the Year (1951, 1953, 1956, 1960, 1963) and Canadian Outstanding Athlete of the Year (1951, 1956); elected to the Canadian Sports Hall of Fame (1962); named an Officer of the Order of Canada (1967). ❖ See also *Women in World History.*

STRENGELL, Marianne (1909–1998). Finnish-born American textile designer. Name variations: Marianne Hammarstrom. Born in Helsinki, Finland, in 1909; died May 8, 1998, in Wellfleet, Massachusetts; trained in design at Institute of Industrial Arts in Helsinki; m. Olav Hammarstrom; children: son Chris Dusenbury. ❖ An innovator in the development of American commercial-production textiles, was among the 1st to utilize synthetics in combination with natural fibers; worked in Copenhagen as a rug, fabric, and furniture designer before immigrating to US (1936); became an instructor in the weaving and textile design department and then department head at Michigan's Cranbrook Academy; remained at Cranbrook until her retirement (1961); work appeared in more than 70 solo exhibitions and in Metropolitan Museum of Art, Art Institute of Chicago, and National Museum of American Art. ❖ See also *Women in World History.*

STREONAESHALCH, abbess of. See Hilda of Whitby (614–680).

STREPPONI, Giuseppina (1815–1897). Italian soprano. Name variations: Giuseppina Verdi. Born Giuseppina Clelia Maria Josepha Strepponi, Sept 8, 1815, in Lodi; died at Sant'Agata, Nov 14, 1897; trained at Milan Conservatory; became 2nd wife of Giuseppe Verdi (Italian composer), 1859. ❖ Made operatic debut (1834); was Verdi's mistress (1847–59), then wife (1859), and appeared in his 1st opera *Oberto*; had greatest successes with roles of Amina in *La Sonnambula* and Lucia in *Lucia di Lammermoor*; retired (1846) and turned to teaching. ❖ See also *Women in World History.*

STRESHNEV, Eudoxia (1608–1645). See Eudoxia Streshnev.

STRETTON, Hesba (1832–1911). English novelist and children's writer. Name variations: Sarah Smith. Born Sarah Smith, July 27, 1832, in Wellington, Shropshire; died Oct 8, 1911, in Ham, Surrey; dau. of Benjamin Smith (bookseller and publisher) and Anne (Bakewell) Smith; never married; no children. ❖ Under pseudonym Hesba Stretton, was an ardent advocate for the welfare of impoverished children through both her writing and volunteer work; published 1st story in Charles Dickens' *Household Words* (1859); moved to Manchester (1863), where numerous factories had spawned a desperate underclass, many of them women and children; published *The Children of Cloverley* (1865), which featured what would become her frequent theme of Christian children who, through their virtues and innocent example, show their lost elders the true path; moved to London (1866) where she came to international prominence with novel *Jessica's First Prayer*, which would be translated into numerous languages and sell nearly 2 million copies over next 40-odd years; follow-up children's books included *Pilgrim Street, a Story of Manchester Life* (1867) and *Alone in London* (1869); published 1st work for adults, *Paul's Courtship* (1867), followed by *David Lloyd's Last Will* (1869); over following 36 years, continued to publish both children's and adult novels, often with an underlying political as well as Christian theme; though books are strongly moralistic and didactically Christian, skillfully drew readers' attention to a common problem which many well-bred people might have preferred to ignore; books were quite popular, several of them immensely so. ❖ See also *Women in World History.*

STRICKLAND, Agnes (1796–1874). English historian and writer. Born Agnes Strickland, Aug 19, 1796, in London, England; died July 13, 1874, in Southwold, Suffolk; dau. of Thomas Strickland of Reydon Hall, Suffolk (shipper, died 1818), and Elizabeth (Homer) Strickland; sister of Elizabeth Strickland (1794–1875), Jane Margaret Strickland (1800–1888), Catherine Parr Traill (1802–1899), Susanna Moodie (1803–1885), and Samuel Strickland (1809–1867), all writers; never married. ❖ Authored historical romances in verse, including *Worcester Field* and *Demetrius and Other Poems* (1833), before writing prose histories, among them *Historical Tales of Illustrious British Children* (1833) and *Tales and Stories from History* (1836), for children; served as coeditor of *Fisher's Juvenile Scrapbook*; with sister Elizabeth as a silent partner, wrote the 12-vol. *Lives of the Queens of England* (1840–48); edited *Letters*

of Mary, Queen of Scots (1843); also wrote *Lives of the Queens of Scotland, Lives of the Bachelor Kings of England, Lives of the Seven Bishops Committed to the Tower in 1688,* and *Lives of the Tudor Princesses.* ❖ See also *Women in World History.*

STRICKLAND, Catherine (1802–1899). See Traill, Catherine Parr.

STRICKLAND, Mabel (1899–1988). Maltese newspaper publisher and politician. Born Mabel Edeline Strickland on Malta, Jan 8, 1899; died in Lija, Malta, Nov 29, 1988; dau. of Baron Gerald Strickland of Sizergh Castle, Kendal (6th count della Catena of Malta), and Lady Edeline Sackville Strickland; never married. ❖ Newspaper publisher and politician who was regarded as the most powerful woman in the Mediterranean region for a period after WWII; during father's tenure as Malta's prime minister (1927–32), played an important role as his advisor, helping withstand the growing pressure from Fascist Italy to lay claim to the island; starting 1935, took on the Italians on a daily basis in the family-owned newspapers she edited, *The Times of Malta* and the Italian-language *Il-Berqa*; after Italian air attacks in WWII destroyed the offices of both newspapers, printed them in a cavern beneath the capital city of Valletta; when father died (1940), became de facto leader of his Constitutional Party, and also managed the family's business interests, particularly its 2 newspapers; in final months of WWII, served as a war correspondent for her newspapers, attached to 21st Army Group of British Army of the Rhine; resigned editorial positions to make a successful run for a seat in the Legislative Assembly as candidate of a revived Constitutional Party (1950); reelected (1951); founded Progressive Constitutional Party (PCP, 1953); for PCP, served in Legislative Assemby (1962–66); defeated in a bitterly contested election (1971); her *Times of Malta* was firebombed (1979). Awarded Order of the British Empire (1944). ❖ See also Joan Alexander, *Mabel Strickland* (Progress, 1996); and *Women in World History.*

STRICKLAND, Shirley (1925–2004). Australian track-and-field athlete. Name variations: Shirley de la Hunty; Shirley de la Hunty-Strickland. Born Shirley Strickland, July 18, 1925, in Guildford, Western Australia; died Feb 17, 2004, at her home in Perth, Australia; dau. of David Strickland (professional sprinter); m. Laurence de la Hunty (Perth geologist), 1950 (died 1980); children: 4, including Philip (b. 1953). ❖ Won 7 Olympic medals in track and field: a silver medal for 4 x 100-meter relay and bronze medals for 100 meters and 80-meter hurdles at London Olympics (1948), a bronze medal for 100 meters and gold medal for 80-meter hurdles at Helsinki Olympics (1952), and gold medals for 4 x 100-meter relay and 80-meter hurdles at Melbourne Olympics (1956), the 1st woman to successfully defend an Olympic title; later discovered to have won the bronze medal in the 200 meters at the London Olympics (1948), when a photograph of the finish emerged (1975), but was never recognized for it officially; her record was equaled only by Poland's Irena Szewinska; also won 3 golds and 2 silvers at the Empire Games in Auckland (1950); was a torchbearer at the opening of the Sydney Olympics (2000); taught academic mathematics at Claremont Teachers College (now Edith Cowan) for 30 years. Awarded MBE (1951); received the Olympic Order from the International Olympic Committee for fundraising efforts (1952); inducted into Athletics Australia Hall of Fame (2000).

STRIKE, Hilda (1910–1989). Canadian runner. Name variations: Hilda Strike Sisson. Born Sept 1, 1910, in Montreal, Quebec, Canada; died Mar 9, 1989; m. Fred Sisson, 1935. ❖ At Los Angeles Olympics, won a silver medal in 4 x 100-meter relay and a silver medal in 100 meters (1932); won silver medal in 100 yards and silver medal in 4 x 110-yard relay at British Empire Games (1934). ❖ See also *Women in World History.*

STRINDBERG, Mrs. August.
See Strindberg, Siri (1850–1912).
See Uhl, Frida (1872–1943).
See Bosse, Harriet (1878–1961).

STRINDBERG, Frida (1872–1943). See Uhl, Frida.

STRINDBERG, Siri (1850–1912). See von Essen, Siri.

STRINGER, C. Vivian (1948—). African-American coach. Name variations: Vivian Stringer. Born in Edenborn, Pennsylvania, Mar 16, 1948; attended Slippery Rock State College, Pennsylvania; m. gymnast Bill Stringer (died 1992); children: David, Janine, and Justin. ❖ The 1st women's basketball coach in US to take 2 different college teams to NCAA Final Four and the 3rd all-time winningest Division I coach in women's basketball, spent 11 seasons at Cheyney State University (1971–

82), where she took the team to the finals of 1st Final Four when the National Collegiate Athletics Association (NCAA) started a women's championship tournament (1981); served as head coach of the Hawkeyes, the University of Iowa's women's basketball team (1983–95), where she had 10 straight 20-victory seasons and won 6 conference championships; became 1 of only 5 active coaches with 500 career victories (1994); accepted a base salary of $150,000 a year (higher than any male coach at Rutgers) to become women's basketball coach at Rutgers University (1995); by 1997–98, racked up a 20-win season and an NCAA Tournament bid; took her Rutger's Team to the Final Four (2000); won 700th game (2004). Named Naismith National Coach of the Year (1993); received the Carol Eckman Award; named national coach of the year 3 times. ❖ See also *Women in World History*.

STRINGFIELD, Bessie B. (1912–1993). African-American motorcyclist. Name variations: BB; Motorcycle Queen of Miami. Born Mar 5, 1912, in Kingston, Jamaica; died Feb 1993 in Opalocka, FL; married and divorced 6 times. ❖ Motorcycling pioneer, rode 1st bike (1928 Indian Scout) at 16; took 8 long-distance solo rides across America (1930s–40s); during WWII, served as civilian motorcycle dispatch rider; worked as stunt rider; settled in Miami, FL, and became a licensed practical nurse and founder of the Iron Horse Motorcycle Club; featured at inaugural exhibit of American Motorcycling Association (AMA) on Women in Motorcycling (1990); owned 27 Harleys in her lifetime. The Bessie Stringfield Award of the AMA honors women leaders in motorcycling; inducted into Motorcycle Hall of Fame (2002).

STRITCH, Elaine (1925—). American stage, tv and screen actress. Born Feb 2, 1925, in Detroit, Michigan; m. John Bay (English actor), 1972 (died 1982). ❖ Made NY debut in *Loco* (1946), followed by *Made in Heaven, The Little Foxes, Yes M'Lord, Pal Joey, On Your Toes, Bus Stop, Sail Away!, Who's Afraid of Virginia Woolf, Wonderful Town, Small Craft Warnings* and *The Gingerbread Lady,* among others; created the role of Joanne in Stephen Sondheim's *Company,* introducing the song "Ladies Who Lunch"; films include *The Scarlet Hour, Three Violent People, Farewell to Arms, Who Killed Teddy Bear?, The Sidelong Glances of a Pigeon Kicker, Providence, Cocoon: The Return* and *Out to Sea*; on tv, co-starred as Ruth on "My Sister Eileen" (1960–61). Won a Tony award for one-woman show *Elaine Stritch at Liberty* (2002).

STRITT, Marie (1856–1928). German feminist. Born Feb 18, 1856, in Schaessburg, Germany; died Sept 16, 1928, in Dresden, Germany. ❖ Key activist for women's rights in Germany at turn of century, joined Hedwig Kessler's women's group Reform (1891), to promote educational, marital and occupational equality, and became its leader (1895); created 1st legal protection association for women in Dresden (1894); a radical campaigner for women's rights, joined Federation of German Women's Associations, serving as its president (1899–1910); was president of Germain Imperial Suffrage Union (1911–22) and World League for Women's Right to Vote (1913–20), as well as delegate to international congress in Geneva (1899–1921); engaged in dispute with conservative elements of suffragist movement headed by Gertrud Bäumer; was a leader in Helene Stoecker's Association for Sexual Reform and Protection of Mothers; became town councilor for German Democratic Party and pressed for equality in local policies of Dresden (1919–22); became chair of City Federation of Dresden Women's Association (1925).

STROESCU, Silvia (1985—). Romanian gymnast. Born May 8, 1985, in Bucharest, Romania. ❖ Won the Swiss Cup (2001); at World championships, won a gold medal for team all-around (2001); won a team all-around gold medal at Athens Olympics (2004).

STROGANOVA, Nina (1919—). Danish ballet dancer. Name variations: Nina Rigmor Dokoudovsky or Dokoudovski. Born Nina Rigmor Strøm, Oct 21, 1919, in Copenhagen, Denmark; m. Vladimir Dokoudovsky (1919–1998, ballet dancer, div.). ❖ Trained with Jenny Moller in Denmark, Olga Preobrazhenska in Paris, and Bronislava Nijinska, Mikhail Mordkin, and Anatole Vilzak in New York; performed with Ballet de l'Opéra Comique de Paris in France; moved to US (c. 1937); was soloist with Mordkin Ballet in New York City (1937–40), creating roles in his *The Goldfish* (1939) and *Voices of Spring* (1940); as a charter member of Ballet Theater (1940), created roles for Adolf Bolm's *Peter and the Wolf* (1940) and Anton Dolin's *Quintet* and *Capriccioso* (1940); danced with Original Ballet Russe (1942–50) where she was in *Swan Lake, Les Sylphide,* and Fokine's *Petrouchka*; taught at Ballet Arts in Carnegie Hall, New York Conservatory of Dance, and City Center Theater Studios.

STROIEVA, Vera (b. 1903). See Stroyeva, Vera.

STRONG, Ann Monroe Gilchrist (1875–1957). New Zealand professor of home science. Name variations: Ann Monroe Gilchrist. Born July 29, 1875, in Carthage, Illinois, USA; died June 23, 1957, in Dunedin, New Zealand; dau. of Charles Allen Gilchrist (civil engineer) and Lucy Ellen (Walker)Gilchrist; Columbia University, BS, 1904; m. Benjamin Rush Strong, 1907 (div.). ❖ Helped found American Home Economics Association (1899); immigrated to New Zealand (1907); taught home economics in Cincinnati, Ohio; taught graduate course at Baroda College in India (1917–20); returned to New Zealand (1921); taught household arts at School of Home Science, University of Otago (1921), becoming dean of faculty of home science (1924); helped found Otago Home Economics Association (1923), and helped organize branches of Women's Division of New Zealand Farmers' Union. Received bronze medal of Carnegie Corporation (1936), OBE (1936) and Coronation Medal (1937). ❖ See also *Dictionary of New Zealand Biography* (Vol. 4).

STRONG, Anna Louise (1885–1970). American journalist. Born Anna Louise Strong, Nov 24, 1885, in Friend, Kansas; died Mar 29, 1970, in Beijing, China; dau. of Sydney Dix Strong (Congregationalist minister) and Ruth Maria (Tracy) Strong (lay missionary leader); Oberlin College, AB, 1905; University of Chicago, PhD, 1908; common-law marriage to Joel Shubin, late 1931 (died 1942); no children. ❖ Ardent defender of the Soviet Union (1920s–40s) and People's Republic of China (1950s–60s), served as feature editor, *Seattle Record* (1918–21); became correspondent, American Friends Relief Mission in Russia (1921–22); served as correspondent, *Hearst's International Magazine* for Central and Eastern Europe (1922–25); worked as correspondent, North American Newspaper Alliance in Russia (1925), and for Federated Press (1925); founded *Moscow Daily News* (1930), the 1st English-language daily in the Soviet Union; worked as editor, *Today* (1951–56); wrote newsletter *Letter from China* (1962–70); for almost half a century, promoted Communist regimes with evangelical zeal; also wrote a learned treatise on prayer, acted as a spearhead of the Seattle General Strike of 1919, was a friend of Leon Trotsky, and dined in the White House with Franklin and Eleanor Roosevelt; writings include *Children of the Revolution* (1925), *China's Millions* (1928), *Red Star in Samarkand* (1929), *The Road to the Grey Pamirs* (1931), *The Soviets Conquer Wheat* (1931), *Spain in Arms* (1937), *The Soviets Expected It* (1941), *Wild River* (1943), *I Saw the New Poland* (1946), *The Stalin Era* (1956) and *Cash and Violence in Laos and Vietnam* (1962). ❖ See also autobiography, *I Change Worlds* (1935); Tracy B. Strong and Helene Keyssar, *Right in Her Soul: The Life of Anna Louise Strong* (Random House, 1983); and *Women in World History*.

STRONG, Eithne (1923–1999). Irish novelist, poet and short-story writer. Born 1923 in Limerick, Ireland; died Aug 1999 in Dublin, Ireland; m. Rupert Strong, 1943; children: 9. ❖ Taught creative writing and helped found Runa Press; wrote in both English and Irish; poetry includes *Songs of Living* (1961), *Sarah, in Passing* (1974), *Cirt Oibre* (1980), *The Greatest Sin* (1982), *Fuil agus Fallaí* (1983), *My Darling Neighbour* (1985), *An Sagart Pinc* (1990) and *Let Live* (1990).

STRONG, Harriet (1844–1929). American agriculturist and civic leader. Name variations: Hattie Russell. Born Harriet Russell, July 23, 1844, in Buffalo, New York; died Sept 16, 1929, in auto accident near Whittier, California; dau. of Henry Pierpont Russell and Mary Guest (Musier) Russell; m. Charles Lyman Strong (mine superintendent), Feb 26, 1863 (committed suicide, 1883); children: Harriet Russell, Mary Lyman, Georgina Pierpont, and Nelle de Luce. ❖ Following husband's death (1883), turned to farming their 220 acres in southern California; undertook a study of irrigation, water storage, and flood control to successfully grow walnuts, citrus fruits, pomegranates, and pampas grass on her Rancho del Fuerte, which would become more popularly known as the Strong Ranch; later used her understanding of water control for the benefit of Los Angeles County, as an advocate of flood control and specific water-supply measures; filed patents on sequential water storage dams (1887, 1894), followed by patents for a number of household inventions; won national attention at World's Columbian Exposition of 1893; a staunch feminist, was the 1st woman elected to Los Angeles Chamber of Commerce. ❖ See also *Women in World History*.

STRONG, Judy (1960—). American field-hockey player. Born Mar 26, 1960; graduate of University of Massachusetts. ❖ At UMass, played on the lacrosse team that won the Division I New England championship (1979–80); at Los Angeles Olympics, won a bronze medal in field-hockey team competition (1984); became field hockey coach at Smith College.

STRONG, Lady (1930–2003). See Oman, Julia Trevelyan.

STRONG, Lori (1972—). Canadian gymnast. Born Sept 12, 1972; m. Steve Ballard (brother of gymnast Julie Ballard Clark). ❖ Won Canadian Jr. nationals (1985), Canadian nationals (1988, 1989) and Commonwealth Games (1990); does sports commentary for CBS and Fox Sport Net. Received the Elaine Tanner Award (1987).

STRONG, Shirley (1958—). English hurdler. Born Nov 18, 1958, in Northwich, Cheshire, England. ❖ At Los Angeles Olympics, won a silver medal in 100-meter hurdles (1984); at Commonwealth games, won a silver medal for 100-meter hurdles (1978) and gold medal for 100-meter hurdles (1982).

STROSSEN, Nadine (1950—). American lawyer and writer. Born in Jersey City, New Jersey, Aug 18, 1950; dau. of Woodrow John Strossen and Sylvia (Simicich) Strossen; graduated Phi Beta Kappa from Harvard-Radcliffe College, 1972; graduated magna cum laude from Harvard Law School, 1975; m. Eli Michael Noam (professor), 1980. ❖ At Harvard Law School, assumed the editorship of the *Law Review*; become a law clerk for Supreme Court of Minnesota (1975); joined staff at New York University School of Law (1984), where she eventually became associate professor of clinical law and supervising attorney of the Civil Rights Clinic, then full professor of law (1988); became involved with American Civil Liberties Union (ACLU), as a member of the board of directors (1983) and as national general counsel (1986); rose to the presidency (1991), becoming the 1st woman and the youngest individual so elected; wrote *Defending Pornography* (1995) and *Speaking of Race, Speaking of Sex: Hate Speech, Civil Rights, and Civil Liberties* (1996). Named to *National Law Journal's* list of "100 most influential lawyers in America" (1991 and 1994); earned Media Institute's Freedom of Speech Award (1994) and the "Women of Distinction" award from Women's League for Conservative Judaism. ❖ See also *Women in World History*.

STROUD, Gloria Brewster (1918–1996). *See Brewster, Gloria.*

STROYEVA, Vera (b. 1903). Ukrainian film director and screenwriter. Name variations: Vera Stroieva. Born 1903 in Kiev, Ukraine (then part of Russian empire); m. Grigori Roshal (director). ❖ Began career as a screenwriter (1926); collaborated with husband on numerous films before becoming a director in her own right, specializing in musicals and opera adaptations; directed *Pravo ottsov, Peterburgskaya noch, Pokolenije pobeditelej, V poiskakh radosti, Boyevoj kinosbornik 12, Marite, Bolshoj kontsert, Boris Godunov, Veselye zhvezd', Polyushko pole, Khovanschina, My russkij narod* and *Serdtse Rossii*.

STROZZI, Alessandra (1406–1469). Florentine writer. Name variations: Alessandra Macinghi; Alessandra Macinghi Strozzi. Born Alessandra Macinghi in 1406 in Florence; died 1469 in Florence; m. Matteo di Simone Strozzi, 1422 (died 1436); children: 4 surviving sons. ❖ After husband was banished from Florence by Cosimo de Medici (1434), followed him into exile with their children; returned to Florence following husband's death (1436); dedicated herself to the onerous task of re-establishing the honor and good name of the Strozzis; since all of her sons were subject to banishment when they came of age (13), continued to work for their eventual return, and spent much of her time writing letters to each son, giving advice and counsel; managed the family's holdings carefully and made investments which were usually profitable; eventually regained the family fortune lost when husband was banished. ❖ See also *Women in World History*.

STROZZI, Barbara (1619–1664). Italian composer. Born in Venice, Italy, 1619; died in Venice, 1664; dau. of Isabella Briega (some sources cite Garzoni) and stepdau. of Giulio Strozzi (famous poet, librettist, and dramatist); studied with Francesco Cavalli. ❖ At 9, adopted by stepfather Giulio Strozzi, since her biological father had not married her mother; showcased most of her compositions, mainly vocal chamber music, in homes rather than at court or on stage; one of the era's most prolific composers, published 1st volume of madrigals on texts by stepfather (1644); published over 100 works in 8 vols., mostly arias and secular cantatas (1644–64). ❖ See also *Women in World History*.

STROZZI, Clarice (1493–1528). *See Medici, Clarice de.*

STROZZI, Kay (1899–1996). American actress. Born Nov 25, 1899, in Swan's Point Plantation, VA; died Jan 18, 1996, in New Rochelle, NY. ❖ Made NY debut in *The Living Mask* (1924), followed by *Ink, The Crown Prince, Heavy Traffic, The Silent Witness* and *St. Helena,* among others.

STROZZI, Marietta Palla (fl. 1468). Florentine noblewoman. Flourished around 1468; dau. of Lorenzo Palla Strozzi. ❖ As a young heiress, brought disfavor because she "lived where she liked and did what she would." Her features were immortalized by Desiderio.

STRUCHKOVA, Raissa (1925–2005). Soviet ballet dancer. Name variations: Raisa Struchkova. Born Raissa Stepanovna Struchkova, Oct 5, 1925, in Moscow, Russia; died May 2, 2005, in Moscow; m. Aleksandr Lapauri (ballet dancer, died 1975). ❖ Trained at Bolshoi Ballet school, principally with Yelisaveta Gerdt, and created title role in *The Little Stork* (1937), while a student; graduated into Bolshoi company (1944) and danced as Lise, Giselle, Juliet, Cinderella, Odette/Odile and Aurora, and heroines of such Soviet classics as *The Red Poppy*; partnered husband Aleksandr Lapauri in pas de deux on tour, including in his *Moszkowski Waltz* and *Spring Waters*; was editor of *Soviet Ballet* magazine (1981–85); served as artistic director of the faculty of choreography of Russian Academy of Theatre Arts.

STRUG, Kerri (1977—). American gymnast. Born Nov 19, 1977, in Tucson, AZ. ❖ Won American Classic (1989, 1990, 1993); at World championships, won a silver medal (1991) and bronze medal (1995), both for team all-around; at Barcelona Olympics, won a bronze medal in team all-around (1992); at Atlanta Olympics, won a gold medal in team all-around (1996), performing the last vault on an injured ankle; won US Olympic Festival (1995) and American Cup (1996). Won Olympic Spirit Award (1996).

STRUNNIKOVA, Natalya (1964—). Soviet swimmer. Born Mar 14, 1964, in USSR. ❖ At Moscow Olympics, won a bronze medal in 4 x 100-meter medley relay (1980).

STRUPPERT, Barbel (1950—). East German runner. Born Sept 26, 1950, in East Germany. ❖ At Munich Olympics, won a silver medal in 4 x 100-meter relay (1972).

STRUTHER, Jan (1901–1953). *See Maxtone Graham, Joyce.*

STRUTHERS, Karen Lee (1963—). Australian politician. Born Feb 19, 1963, in Adelaide, Australia. ❖ As a member of the Australian Labor Party, elected to the Queensland Parliament for Archerfield (1998–2001), then Algester (2001); named chair of the Legal, Constitutional and Administrative Review Committee (2001).

STUART. *See also Stewart (in Scotland, the spelling of the surname Stewart was changed to Stuart by brothers Matthew and John Stewart, who adopted the French spelling in 1537).*

STUART, Aimée (c. 1885–1981). Scottish playwright and screenwriter. Name variations: Aimee Stuart. Born c. 1885 in Glasgow, Scotland; died April 17, 1981, in Brighton, England; dau. of William and Mercie (Baker) McHardy; m. Philip Stuart (writer). ❖ Wrote such plays as *Melodrama, Summer Snow, Jeannie, London W.1., This Virtue, Lace on Her Petticoat, Fair Passenger, Gaily We Sinned* and *Oh Benjamina*; plays written with husband include *The Cat's Cradle, No Gentleman, Clara Gibbings, Her Shop, Nine Till Six, Supply and Demand, Sixteen* and *Full Circle*; collaborated on over 10 screenplays, including *Fanny by Gaslight, Jeannie* and *Nine Till Six.*

STUART, Arabella (1575–1615). English princess. Name variations: Lady Arabella Stuart; Arbella Stuart; Arabella or Arbella Seymour. Born Oct 1575 in London, England; died Sept 25, 1615, in Tower of London; dau. of Charles Stuart (1555–1576), 5th earl of Lennox, and Elizabeth Cavendish (d. 1582); cousin of King James I; m. William Seymour (1587–1660), 2nd duke of Somerset (r. 1660–1660), on June 22, 1610; no children. ❖ Royal princess whose unhappy life was dominated by the political exigencies of 2 wary monarchs, despite her disinterest in claiming the throne; at birth, held a strong claim to the crown through her father, who was 3rd in the line of succession, as strong a claim as Elizabeth I's eventual successor, James I; as well, her father was brother-in-law of Elizabeth's enemy and rival monarch, the Catholic Mary Stuart, queen of Scots, who held the strongest claim to succeed Elizabeth; by age 2, was stripped of title and estates by royal revocation; was championed by maternal grandmother Elizabeth Talbot, countess of Shrewsbury; after becoming the center of an unsuccessful plot, in which Catholic nobles planned to kidnap her, marry her to a Catholic and put her on the throne, was confined to grandmother's home in Derbyshire (1592–1601); chafing under grandmother's care, made a number of poor decisions and attempted to escape; when James I came to the throne (1603), was allowed at court in Queen Anne of Denmark's retinue for 6 years; against the king's wishes, married William Seymour in a secret ceremony (June 22, 1610) and was arrested (July 9); in an attempt to escape with William (June 3, 1611), set out on an ill-fated voyage across the English Channel for France, from which she returned to London as a prisoner; remained a prisoner in the Tower, but was never charged with any crime; died of starvation in the Tower at age 39. ❖ See also *The Letters of Lady Arbella Stuart* (ed. by Sara Jayne Steen, Oxford U. Press, 1994); David N. Durant, *Arbella Stuart: A Rival to the Queen* (Weidenfeld & Nicholson, 1978); P.M. Handover, *Arbella Stuart* (Eyre & Spottiswoode, 1957); Ian McInnes, *Arabella: the Life and Times of Lady Arabella Seymour* (W. H. Allen, 1968); and *Women in World History*.

STUART, Bathia Howie (1893–1987). New Zealand actress, singer, journalist, and film producer. Name variations: Bathia Tighe-Umbers. Born on May 10, 1893, in Hastings, New Zealand; died on June 22, 1987, at South Laguna, California, USA; dau. of Alexander Stuart (draper) and Ellen Elizabeth (Downie) Stuart; m. Crofton Gordon Tighe-Umbers (accountant, d. 1918), 1913; children: 1 son. ❖ Joined Tom Pollard's juvenile opera company (early 1900s), became writer for *New Zealand Illustrated Sporting and Dramatic Review* (1920s); worked for Henry Hayward, owner of chain of movie theaters in New Zealand, and produced several theatrical shows, including *Bathie Stuart and Her Musical Maids* and *Bathie Stuart and her Maori Maids*; played female lead in silent film, *The Adventures of Algy* (1925); visited California and was invited by Universal Studios to record prologue for *Under the Southern Cross*, shot in New Zealand (1927); served as travel agent and tourist representative for New Zealand Railways; wrote narration and edited *Away to the South Seas* (1950s); began shooting own footage in South Pacific locations for her films. Received Queen's Service Medal (1986). ❖ See also *Dictionary of New Zealand Biography* (Vol. 4).

STUART, Cora Wilson (1875–1958). *See Stewart, Cora Wilson.*

STUART, Elizabeth (1596–1662). *See Elizabeth of Bohemia.*

STUART, Elizabeth (d. 1673). Countess of Arundel. Died Jan 23, 1673; dau. of Esme or Esmé Stuart (b. 1579), 3rd duke of Lennox, and Baroness Katherine Clifton; m. Henry Frederick Howard, earl of Arundel, in 1626; children: Thomas Howard (b. 1627), 5th duke of Norfolk; Henry Howard (b. 1628), 6th duke of Norfolk; Cardinal Philip Howard (b. 1629); Charles Howard of Greystoke (b. 1630), Lord of the Manor; Bernard Howard (b. 1641); Catherine Howard; Talbot Howard; Edward Howard (b. 1637); Francis Howard (b. 1639); Esmé Howard (b. 1645); Elizabeth Howard (1651–1705, who m. Alex Macdonnel and Bartholomew Russell).

STUART, Elizabeth (1635–1650). *See Elizabeth Stuart.*

STUART, Frances (1647–1702). Duchess of Richmond and Lennox. Name variations: Frances Blantyre; Frances Stewart; known as La Belle Stuart. Born Frances Teresa Stuart in 1647 (some sources cite 1648) in Scotland; died Oct 15, 1702, in London; dau. of Walter Stuart (or Stewart) and Sophia Stuart; m. Charles Stuart, duke of Richmond and Lennox, in 1667 (died 1672); no children. ❖ One of the most popular of the court women, was appointed a lady-in-waiting to the queen, Catherine of Braganza (1662); became a good friend of both the queen and the queen's rival, Charles II's mistress Barbara Villiers, but soon found herself the object of the king's attentions; encouraging his attachment, soon usurped Villiers' place, becoming the most important woman at court after the queen; despite her youth and inexperience, refused the king's attempts to make her his mistress, apparently recognizing the danger and instability of such a position; against the king's wishes, eloped with Charles Stuart, young duke of Richmond and Lennox (1667); reconciled with the king (1668) and was appointed a Lady of the Bed-Chamber; following husband's death (1672), her titles and properties reverted to King Charles, except for Cobham Hall in Kent which she inherited; was left deeply in debt, but through careful planning and management of her small estates, expanded her properties considerably and created a personal fortune. ❖ See also Cyril H. Hartmann, *La Belle Stuart: Memoirs of court and society in the times of Frances Teresa Stuart, duchess of Richmond and Lennox* (Dutton, 1924); and *Women in World History*.

STUART, Gisela (1955—). English politician and member of Parliament. Born Gisela Gschaider, Nov 26, 1955, in Velden/Vilsbiburg, Germany; attended Staat Realschule Vilsbiburg, Manchester Polytechnic and London University; m. Robert Scott Stuart, 1980 (div. 2000). ❖ Lawyer, translator and lecturer; representing Labour, elected to House of Commons for Birmingham Edgbaston (1997, 2001, 2005); was parliamentary undersecretary of State in Department of Health (1999–2001).

STUART, Gloria (1909—). American screen star. Born Gloria Stewart Finch, July 14, 1909, in Santa Monica, CA; m. Blair Gordon Newell, 1930 (div. 1934); m. Arthur Sheekman (drama critic and screenwriter), 1934 (died 1978); children: Sylvia Sheekman. ❖ Began acting career with Pasadena Players; made film debut in *Street of Women* (1932); played leads or was featured in such movies as *The Old Dark House*, *Back Street*, *Girl in 419*, *The Invisible Man*, *The Kiss Before the Mirror*, *Roman Scandals*, *Gift of Gab*, *Gold Diggers of 1935*, *The Prisoner of Shark Island*, *The Poor Little Rich Girl*, *The Crime of Dr. Forbes*, *Girl Overboard*, *Rebecca of Sunnybrook Farm*, *The Three Musketeers*, *The Whistler*, *My Favorite Year* and *Mass Appeal*. Nominated for an Oscar for performance in *Titanic* (1998). ❖ See also autobiography, *Gloria Stuart: I Just Kept Hoping* (1999).

STUART, Helen Campbell (1839–1918). *See Campbell, Helen Stuart.*

STUART, Jane (1812–1888). American artist. Born 1812; died 1888 in Newport, Rhode Island; youngest of 4 daughters of Gilbert Stuart (1755–1828, portraitist of George Washington) and Charlotte (Coates) Stuart (b. around 1768); sister of Anne Stuart; self-trained by assisting her father in his painting studio; never married. ❖ Best known for her copies of her father's famous paintings, one of which is hung in the Kennedy School of Government at Harvard University in Boston; had her own distinctive style for such original paintings as *Scene from a Novel* (1834) and *Caroline Marsh* (1840). ❖ See also *Women in World History*.

STUART, Jay Allison (1905–1972). *See Tait, Dorothy.*

STUART, Jeanne (1908–2003). *See Rothschild, Jeanne de.*

STUART, Jessie Bonstelle (1871–1932). *See Bonstelle, Jessie.*

STUART, Louisa (1752–1824). *See Louise of Stolberg-Gedern.*

STUART, Louisa (1757–1851). British letter writer and memoirist. Born 1757 in London, England; died 1851 in London; dau. of John, 3rd earl of Bute, and Mary (1718–1794), countess of Bute; granddau. of Mary Wortley Montagu. ❖ Though kept from intellectual pursuits by family, read widely and corresponded with such figures as Sir Walter Scott; works include "Introductory Anecdotes" to *The Letters and Works of Lady Mary Wortley Montague* (J.A.S. Wharncliffe, ed., 1837), *Gleanings from an Old Portfolio* (Mrs. Godfrey Clark, ed., 1895–98), *Selections from the Manuscripts of Lady Louisa Stuart* (J. A. Home, ed., 1899), *Letters of Lady Louisa Stuart to Miss Louisa Clinton* (J. A. Home, ed., 1901–03), *The Letters of Lady Louisa Stuart* (R. B. Johnson, ed., 1926), and *Memoir of Frances, Lady Douglas* (J. Rubenstein, ed., 1985).

STUART, Maria Clementina (1702–1735). *See Sobieski, Clementina.*

STUART, Mary (1542–1587). *See Mary Stuart.*

STUART, Mary (1926–2002). American actress. Born Mary Stuart Houchins, July 4, 1926, in Miami, FL; died Feb 28, 2002, in New York, NY; grew up in Tulsa, OK; m. 2nd husband, Richard Krolik, 1951 (div. 1966); m. Wolfgang Neumann (architect), 1986; children: (2nd m.) 2. ❖ Starred on tv soap operas for over 50 years; had a 35-year run as Jo on "Search for Tomorrow" (1951–86) and was the 1st and only actor nominated for a prime-time Emmy for a daytime serial (1962); also appeared on "Guiding Light." ❖ See also autobiography, *Both of Me* (1980).

STUART, Marten (1888–1979). *See Scott, Mary Edith.*

STUART, Miranda (c. 1795–1865). British physician and soldier. Name variations: James Barry; Miranda Stuart Barry. Born Miranda Stuart or Miranda Stuart Barry around 1795; died c. the age of 70 in London, July 25, 1865; Edinburgh College, MD, 1812. ❖ Born in an era when women were traditionally denied any profession outside the home, posed as a man named James Barry, becoming the 1st female doctor in UK, and had a distinguished medical career in the British military; served in the military in South Africa, the West Indies, Canada, and the Crimea. ❖ See also *Women in World History*.

STUART, Ruth McEnery (c. 1849–1917). American writer. Born Mary Routh McEnery in Marksville, Louisiana, on May 21, 1849 (some sources cite 1856); died in White Plains, New York, on May 6, 1917; dau. of James McEnery (cotton merchant, planter, and slaveholder) and Mary Routh (Stirling) McEnery; m. Alfred O. Stuart (merchant and planter), Aug 5, 1879 (died 1883); children: Stirling McEnery (1882–1905). ❖ At 7, moved with family to New Orleans, where she was exposed to Italians, Creoles, and African-Americans in the old French Market area, which is vividly reflected in her later stories; following husband's death, turned to fiction writing as a means of earning a living, and drew on her impressive mastery of New Orleans dialects to create colorful characters in short stories; published "Uncle Mingo's 'Speculations,'" in *New Princeton Review* (1888); wrote and published more stories in the same local-color style for various periodicals, including "Lamentations of Jeremiah Johnson" in *Harper's New Monthly Magazine*; published 1st book, *A Golden Wedding and Other Tales* (1893) and her best-known work *In Simpkinsville: Character Tales* (1897). ❖ See also *Women in World History*.

STUART, Wilhelmina Magdalene (1895–1985). New Zealand telegraphist. Born Aug 9, 1895, in Dunedin, New Zealand; died July 3, 1985, in Dunedin; dau. of Abraham Francis Stuart (compositor) and Wilhelmina Catherine (Bohning) Stuart (tailor). ❖ Joined Post and Telegraph Department (1915), and worked on manual telegraph equipment, transmitting and receiving messages in Morse code; became 1st woman in Dunedin to operate new multiplex machine-printing telegraph system (1925); after fighting lack of advancement because of her gender, saw her appeal upheld (1944), and was promoted, receiving increase in salary from £15 to £320 per year. ❖ See also *Dictionary of New Zealand Biography* (Vol. 4).

STUART-WORTLEY, Emmeline (1806–1855). English poet and travel writer. Born Emmeline Charlotte Elizabeth Manners, May 2, 1806; died in Beirut, Nov 1855; dau. of John Henry Manners, 5th duke of Rutland, and Lady Elizabeth Howard (d. 1825, dau. of Frederick Howard, 5th earl of Carlisle, and Margaret Leveson); sister of Lord John Manners (1818–1906); m. the Honourable Charles Stuart-Wortley, 1831; children: 3. ❖ Published 1st collection of poems (1833); drew on her travels in Europe for several of her volumes of poetry, including *Travelling Sketches in Rhyme* (1835), *Impressions of Italy* (1837) and *Sonnets* (1839); extended travels to include US and Middle East, which also served as material for her poetic imagination when she published a 3-vol. account, *Travels in the United States*. ❖ See also *Women in World History*.

STUBNICK, Christa (1933—). East German runner. Born Dec 12, 1933, in Germany. ❖ At Melbourne Olympics, won a silver medal in 200 meters and a silver medal in 100 meters (1956).

STÜCKELBERGER, Christine (1947—). Swiss equestrian in dressage. Name variations: Christine Stueckelberger or Stuckelberger. Born in Wallisellen, a village north of Zurich, Switzerland, May 22, 1947; father was a doctor; mother was the daughter of the president of Switzerland. ❖ On Merry Boy, won European championships (1969, 1971, and 1973) and World championship (1972); on Granat, won European championships (1975, 1977), Olympic gold medal in Montreal (1976), Olympic team silver in Montreal (1976), and World championship (1978); on Gauguin de Lully, won Olympic team silver in Los Angeles (1984), silver medal in World championship (1986), and Olympic individual bronze in Seoul (1988); while she was training a young stallion (1989), was thrown against a wall when the horse bucked, breaking her back in two places, effectively ending her career. ❖ See also *Women in World History*.

STUDDIFORD, Grace (b. 1873). See Van Studdiford, Grace.

STUDER, Claire (1891–1977). See Goll, Claire.

STUDIFORD, Grace (b. 1873). See Van Studdiford, Grace.

STUDNEVA, Marina (1959—). Soviet rower. Born Feb 1959 in USSR. ❖ At Moscow Olympics, won a bronze medal in coxed fours (1980).

STUECKELBERGER, Christine (1947—). See Stückelberger, Christine.

STUKALAVA, Tatsiana (1975—). Belarusian weightlifter. Born Oct 3, 1975, in USSR. ❖ Won a bronze medal for 63 kg at Athens Olympics (2004).

STUNYO, Jeanne (1936—). American diver. Born April 11, 1936; trained at the Detroit Athletic Club. ❖ At Melbourne Olympics, won a silver medal in springboard (1956).

STURE-VASA, Mary Alsop (1885–1980). See O'Hara, Mary.

STURGEON, Nicola (1970—). Scottish politician. Born July 19, 1970, in Irvine, Ayrshire, Scotland; Glasgow University, LLB, 1992, diploma in Legal Practice, 1993. ❖ As an SNP candidate, elected to the Scottish Parliament for Glasgow (1999).

STURGES, Ethel (1866–1954). See Dummer, Ethel Sturges.

STURGIS, Caroline (1819–1888). See Tappan, Caroline Sturgis.

STURGIS, Ellen (1812–1848). See Hooper, Ellen Sturgis.

STURGIS, Katharine Boucot (1903–1987). American physician. Name variations: Katharine Rosenbaum; Katharine Rosenbaum Boucot; Katharine Rosenbaum Boucot Sturgis. Born Katharine Rosenbaum, Sept 3, 1903, in Philadelphia, PA; died Mar 28, 1987; dau. of Morris Rosenbaum; graduate of Woman's Medical College of Pennsylvania; m. Arthur Guest, 1922 (div.); Joseph Boucot, 1945 (died 1962); Dr. Samuel Booth Sturgis, 1964 (died 1983); children: (1st m.) 2. ❖ The 1st female chief editor of the American Medical Association's *Archives of Environmental Health* (1960–71) and the 1st woman president of American College of Preventative Medicine (1969), completed a tuberculosis residency at Herman Kiefer Hospital in Detroit (1944–45); with Dr. David Cooper, investigated the diabetes-tuberculosis relationship (1945–47) and established the Philadelphia Pulmonary Neoplasm Research Project to study lung cancer; began to teach at Woman's Medical College (1943) and became chair of Department of Preventative Medicine (1952); taught radiology and internal medicine at the University of Pennsylvania (1947–63).

STURM, J. C. (1927—). New Zealand poet and short-story writer. Name variations: Jacqueline Cecilia Sturm. Born 1927 in Opunake, New Zealand; m. James K. Baxter, 1948. ❖ Maori writer, published stories and poetry in magazines and anthologies; best known for story collection, *The House of the Talking Cat* (1985), also wrote *Dedications* (1996) and *Postscripts* (2000); poems collected in *How Things Are* (1996).

STURRUP, Chandra (1971—). Bahamian runner. Born Chandra Vanessa Sturrup, Sept 12, 1971, in Nassau, Bahamas; graduate of Norfolk State University. ❖ Known as one of the "Golden Girls," won a silver medal Atlanta Olympics (1996) and a gold medal at Sydney Olympics (2000), both for 4 x 100-meter relay; won a gold medal for 4 x 100-meter relay at World championships (1999); won gold medals for the 100 meters at Commonwealth Games (1998) and Pan American Games (1999); won a gold medal for the 60 meters at World Indoor championships (2001), the 1st Bahamian to win an indiv. gold medal for track. Given the Silver Jubilee Award (1998) and the Bahamas Order of Merit (2000).

STYLE, Sarah Maria (c. 1823–1895). See Barraud, Sarah Maria.

STYOPINA, Viktoriya (1976—). Ukrainian high jumper. Born Feb 21, 1976, in Zaporozhye, Ukraine. ❖ Won a bronze medal for high jump at Athens Olympics (2004).

STYRENE, Poly (c. 1962—). English singer. Name variations: Marion Elliot, X-Ray Spex. Born Marion Elliot, c. 1962, in London, England. ❖ Raw-voiced lead vocalist for punk bank, X-Ray Spex, had singles "Oh Bondage, Up Yours," "The Day the World Turned Dayglo" and "Identity"; with band, released only album, *Germ Free Adolescents* (1978), then disbanded group (1978); as Marion Elliot, released album, *Translucence* (1980); later issued *God's and Goddesses* (1986).

STYRIA, duchess of. See Mary of Bavaria (d. 1608).

SU HSUEH-LIN (1897–1999). Chinese essayist and literary critic. Name variations: Su Xuelin. Born 1897 in China; died April 21, 1999, in southern Taiwan. ❖ Renowned scholar, critic and journal writer, was involved in the May Fourth student movement (1919); wrote *The Bitter Heart* (1929); her *The Diary of Su Hsueh-lin*, covering 1948 and 1996, and comprising 15 volumes, was published in Chinese in 1999.

SU HUI (fl. 4th c.). Chinese poet. Name variations: Ruolan. Born in China during the Eastern Ching dynasty. ❖ Married to a general at 16; after being abandoned by husband, wrote palindromic verses on cloth which could be read forwards, backwards, slantwise, upwards, downwards, and by alternate words.

SU HUIJUAN (1964—). Chinese volleyball player. Born April 3, 1964, in China. ❖ Won a gold medal at Los Angeles Olympics (1984) and a bronze medal at Seoul Olympics (1988), both in team competition.

SU XUELIN (1897–1999). See Su Hsueh-lin.

SUAREZ, Paola (1976—). Argentinean tennis player. Born June 23, 1976, in Pergamino, Argentina. ❖ Won doubles titles at Roland Garros (2001, 2002, 2004), Australian Open (2004) and US Open (2002, 2003); with Patricia Tarabini, won the bronze medal for doubles at Athens Olympics (2004); was a semifinalist for singles championship at Roland Garros (2004).

SUAVEGOTTA (fl. 504). Queen of Reims and Metz (Austrasia). Dau. of Sigismond, king of the Burgundians; m. Thierry also known as Theuderic or Theodoric I (c. 490–534), king of Reims and Metz (r. 511–534); children: Thibert also known as Theodebert or Theudebert I (504–548), king of Metz (Austrasia, r. 534–548).

SUBBULAKSHMI, M. S. (1916–2004). Indian singer. Name variations: Madurai Shanmugavadivu Subbulakshmi. Born Subbulakshmi, Sept 16, 1916, in Madurai, in southern Tamil Nadu; died Dec 11, 2004; dau. of Shanmugavadivu (mother who played the lute-like veena); m. Thiyagaraja Sadasivam (freedom fighter), 1940 (died 1997). ❖ One of India's greatest musicians, was a vocalist in the classical Carnatic style of southern India; had a career that spanned 6 decades; also acted in a few Tamil films, including *Seva Sadanam* (1938) and *Meera* (1945); was the 1st female vocalist to be honored with the title Sangita Kalanidhi (music maestro) by the Music Academy of Chennai (1968); received the Magsaysay award for public service (1974), Indira Gandhi award (1990) and the Bharat Ratna (1996), India's highest civilian honor.

SUBE, Karola (1964—). East German gymnast. Born April 28, 1964, in East Germany. ❖ At Moscow Olympics, won a bronze medal in team all-around (1980).

SUBLIGNY, Marie-Thérèse Perdou de (1666–1736). French ballerina. Name variations: Marie-Therese Perdou de Subligny. Born 1666; died 1736; dau. of an actor-playwright who is reputed by some to have edited *Letters of a Portuguese Nun* (Mariana Alcoforado), published in Paris in 1669. ❖ For 17 years, was the lead ballerina at the Opéra de France, until replaced by Françoise Prévost (1705); was the 1st French *danseuse* to have a career on both sides of the English Channel. ❖ See also *Women in World History*.

SUCHER, Rosa (1847–1927). German operatic soprano. Born Rosa Hasselbeck (or Haslbeck) in Germany, 1847 (some sources cite 1849); died 1927; m. Josef Sucher (conductor-composer known for his interpretation of Wagnerian music), 1876. ❖ Famed for her performances in Wagner's operas; appeared for 2 successful seasons in London (1882, 1892) and sang in Hamburg (1879–88) and at Bayreuth (1886, 1888); in later years, appeared principally on opera stages of Berlin; retired (1903); is especially remembered for her portrayal of Isolde. ❖ See also *Women in World History*.

SUCHOCKA, Hanna (1946—). Polish politician. Pronunciation: HAHN-nah sue-HUT-ska. Born April 3, 1946, in Pleszew, Poland; received a law and doctoral degree from Poznan University; also studied at Institute of Public Law in Heidelberg, Germany; never married; no children. ❖ The 1st woman to lead Poland since Queen Jadwiga in the 14th century, served as the 5th post-Communist prime minister of Poland (July 10, 1992–Oct 26, 1993); elected to the Sejm (lower house of Parliament) on the Democratic Party ticket (1980); joined the Solidarity labor movement and soon became its legal adviser; after voting against the government's decision to outlaw Solidarity (1984), left the party; following the collapse of Communist rule in Poland (1989), returned to the Sejm, this time as a member of the Civic Committee; was reelected (1991) as a member of the Democratic Union, a center-left party founded by Suchocka and a group of Solidarity leaders; nominated by Lech Walesa, became prime minister (1992); succeeded in holding the diversified political parties together for 15 months, longer than any of her predecessors had been able to do; continued to serve as a member of Parliament. ❖ See also *Women in World History*.

SUCKLING, Sophia Lois (1893–1990). New Zealand optician and family planning reformer. Name variations: Sophia Lois Anthony. Born Aug 12, 1893, in Bondi, Sydney, Australia; died June 20, 1990, in Auckland, New Zealand; dau. of Stephen Anthony (formerly Nowinsky) and Clara Emma (Ackland) Anthony; m. Walter Edgar Suckling (optician), 1914 (died 1944); children: 5. ❖ Became 1st woman in New Zealand to qualify as registered optometrist (1924); helped found Sex Hygiene and Birth Regulation Society (now New Zealand Family Planning Association, 1936); active in Wellington branch of National Council of Women of New Zealand; founding member of Soroptomist International; active in Friends of the Soviet Union and Fabian Society; after husband's death, practiced in England for 18 years. ❖ See also *Dictionary of New Zealand Biography* (Vol. 4).

SUCKOW, Ruth (1892–1960). American writer. Pronunciation: SOO-koh. Born Aug 6, 1892, in Hawarden, Iowa; died in Claremont, California, Jan 1960; dau. of William John Suckow (Congregational minister) and Anna Mary (Kluckhohn) Suckow; University of

Denver, AB, 1917, AM, 1918; m. Ferner Nuhn (writer and critic), Mar 1929. ❖ Regional writer, whose short story "Uprooted" brought her to the attention of journalist H. L. Mencken (1921); serialized novella *Country People* in *The Century Magazine* (1924), which was then published in book form; 1st stories appeared as *Iowa Interiors* (1926); also wrote *The Bonney Family* (1928), *Cora* (1929), *The Kramer Girls* (1930) and *The Folks* (1934), which covered 30 years in the life of the Ferguson family, and was equally as sweeping in its portrayal of the emotional relationships of its characters. ❖ See also *Women in World History*.

SUDDUTH, Jill (1971—). American synchronized swimmer. Born Sept 9, 1971, in Baltimore, MD. ❖ Won a team gold medal at Atlanta Olympics (1996).

SÜDERMANNLAND, duchess of. See Ingeborg (c. 1300–c. 1360).

SUDLOW, Joan (1892–1970). American stage, tv, and screen actress. Born Mar 15, 1892, in Minnesota; died Feb 1, 1970, in Laurel Canyon, CA. ❖ Films include *The Pride of St. Louis* and *A Fine Madness*.

SUDRE, Margie (1943—). French politician. Born Oct 17, 1943, in Vinh, Vietnam. ❖ Anaesthetist; served as chair of the Réunion Island Regional Council (1993–98) and state secretary for the French-Speaking World (1995–97); as a member of the European People's Party (Christian Democrats) and European Democrats, elected to 5th European Parliament (1999–2004). Named Knight of the Legion of Honour (1999).

SUESS, Birgit (1962—). East German gymnast. Name variations: Birgit Süss. Born May 29, 1962, in East Germany. ❖ At Moscow Olympics, won a bronze medal in team all-around (1980).

SUESSE, Dana (1909–1987). American composer and pianist. Name variations: Dana DeLinks; (nickname) "Sally of Tin Pan Alley." Born Nadine Dana Suesse, Dec 3, 1909, in Kansas City, MO; died Oct 16, 1987, in New York, NY; m. H. Courtney Burr, 1940 (div. 1954); m. Edward DeLinks, 1971 (died 1981). ❖ Musical prodigy, composed 1st song and gave 1st piano concert at 8; at 10, won a prize for composition from National Federation of Music; moved to NY and began composing popular tunes; had 1st hit, "Syncopated Love Song," (1930), followed by "Ho Hum" (1931), recorded by Bing Crosby, and *Jazz Nocturne*, popularized with lyrics by Edward Heyman as "My Silent Love" (1932); an excellent pianist as well as composer, made debut at Carnegie Hall performing her Concerto in Three Rhythms (1932); subsequently wrote orchestral works *Symphonic Waltzes* and *Blue Moonlight*; composed numerous popular songs, including "The Night is Young and You're So Beautiful," "This Changing World," and "Yours for a Song" (1930s); collaborating with Heyman, wrote the music for "You Oughta Be in Pictures," (1934) an unofficial Hollywood theme song; also scored several films, including *Sweet Surrender* (1935), *Young Man with a Horn* (1950) and *The Seven Year Itch* (1955); turned to classical work exclusively, studying in Paris with Nadia Boulanger (1947–50); returning to US, wrote Jazz Concerto in D Major (1956); was honored with a concert of her works at Carnegie Hall (1974). ❖ See also *Women in World History*.

SUFFOLK, countess of.
See Montacute, Joan (fl. 1300s).
See Stafford, Catherine (d. 1419).
See Somerset, Henrietta (1669–1715).
See Howard, Henrietta (1688–1767).
See Ufford, Margaret de.
See Crawford, Mimi (d. 1966).

SUFFOLK, duchess of.
See Chaucer, Alice (fl. 1400s).
See Pole, Elizabeth de la (1444–1503).
See Neville, Margaret (b. 1466).
See Mary Tudor (1496–1533).
See Brandon, Frances (1517–1559).
See Bertie, Catharine (1519–1580).

SUGAWARA, Noriko (1972—). Japanese judoka. Born Sept 27, 1972, in Kanagawa, Japan. ❖ Won a bronze medal at Atlanta Olympics (1996) and a silver medal at Sydney Olympics (2000), both for 48–52 kg half-lightweight.

SUGAWARA, Risa (1977—). Japanese gymnast. Born Aug 15, 1977, in Bijogi, Toda, Japan; dau. of Hiroshi Sugawara (gymnast) and mother Takako Hasegawa (who competed as a gymnast at 1972 Olympics). ❖ Won Japanese nationals (1994, 1996, 1997, 1998, 1999); won Aloha Gymfest (1995), NHK Cup (1997, 1998) and Pitari Cup (1997).

SUGGIA, Guilhermina (1888–1950). Portuguese cellist. Born Guilhermina Suggia, June 27, 1888, in Oporto, Portugal; died July 31, 1950, in Oporto; m. Dr. José Mena (X-ray specialist); studied with Julius Klengel at Leipzig Conservatory (1902); sister of Virginia Suggia (pianist). ❖ At 7, made debut at the Palácio de Cristal; at 10, played before Pablo Casals; at 12, was the leader of the Porto City Symphony Orchestra's cello section; debuted with the Gewandhaus concerts (1902); moved to Paris (1906); studied with Casals and later lived with him for 7 years before establishing herself as one of the world's finest cellists; immortalized in Augustus John's portrait of her. ❖ See also *Women in World History*.

SUGGS, Louise (1923—). American golfer. Born Mae Louise Suggs, Sept 7, 1923, in Atlanta, GA. ❖ Won the USGA Women's Amateur (1947); won the British Women's Amateur, 3 North and South Amateurs and 3 Western Amateurs, as well as being a member of the US Curtis Cup team (1948); won 50 LPGA events, including the Titleholders championship (1946, 1954, 1956, 1959), USGA Women's Open (1949, 1952), and LPGA championship (1957). Was the 1st member of the LPGA Hall of Fame (1951) and 1st woman elected to Georgia Hall of Fame (1966); inducted into World Golf Hall of Fame; won Vare trophy (1957); won Patty Berg Award (2000). ❖ See also *Women in World History*.

SUGIMOTO, Sonoko (1925—). Japanese novelist. Born 1925 in Tokyo, Japan. ❖ Historical novels include *An Embarkation Filled with Distress* (1962), *Takazawa Bakin*, and *Magnificent Hell*. Won Naoki Prize (1962) and Yoshikawa Eiji Prize for Literature.

SUGIYAMA, Kayoko (1961—). Japanese volleyball player. Born Oct 31, 1961, in Japan. ❖ At Los Angeles Olympics, won a bronze medal in team competition (1984).

SUH HYO-SUN (1966—). Korean field-hockey player. Born Sept 20, 1966, in South Korea. ❖ At Seoul Olympics, won a silver medal in team competition (1988).

SUH KWANG-MI (1965—). Korean field-hockey player. Born Feb 1, 1965, in South Korea. ❖ At Seoul Olympics, won a silver medal in team competition (1988).

SUHARTO, Siti (1923–1996). Indonesian first lady. Name variations: Ibu Tien. Born Siti Hartinah in Solo, Central Java, Aug 23, 1923; died in Jakarta, April 28, 1996; marriage arranged by family to General Thojib N. J. Suharto (later president of Indonesia), in 1947; children: 3 daughters, including Siti Hardiyanti Rukmana, known as Tutut (b. 1948) and Siti Hadiati Harijadi, known as Titik (b. 1958); 3 sons, Sigit (b. 1951), Hutomo Mandala Putra, known as Tommy (b. 1961), and Bambang Trihatmodjo (b. 1952). ❖ Worked side-by-side with husband during Indonesia's fight for independence from Dutch rule (1945); throughout tenure as first lady of Indonesia (1968–1996), stayed out of politics, except on one issue: led a women's organization that pushed through a law making it illegal for a Muslim man in Indonesia to add a 2nd wife without permission from his 1st wife. ❖ See also *Women in World History*.

SÜHBAATARYN YANJMAA (1893–1962). *See Yanjmaa, Sühbaataryn.*

SUI XINMEI. Chinese shot putter. Born in China. ❖ Won a silver medal at Atlanta Olympics (1996).

SUIHKONEN, Liisa (1943—). Finnish cross-country skier. Born July 7, 1943, in Suonenjoki, Finland. ❖ Won a silver medal for 4 x 5 km relay at Innsbruck Olympics (1976).

SUIKO (554–628). Japanese empress. Name variations: Suiko-tenno. Pronunciation: Sue-e-koe. Reigned from 592 to 628; born in Asuka Village, Japan, in 554; died in Nara, Japan, in 628; dau. of Emperor Kimmei and a woman from the politically powerful Soga family; sister of Emperor Yomei; empress-consort to her half-brother Emperor Bidatsu. ❖ The 1st woman sovereign of Japan, ascended to the throne following a period of political and religious conflicts in which her predecessor had been killed; established Buddhism as the religion of Japanese rulers and initiated steps to centralize the state under imperial rule. ❖ See also *Women in World History*.

SUI SIN FAR (1865–1914). *See Eaton, Edith.*

SUISTED, Laura Jane (1840–1903). New Zealand journalist and writer. Name variations: Laura Eyre. Born Laura Eyre, Jan 1, 1840, in Yorkshire, England; died Sept 7, 1903, in Westport, New Zealand; dau. of Abel Eyre (plumber) and Mary (Lee) Eyre; m. James Samuel Suisted (station manager), 1864. ❖ Immigrated to New Zealand (1862); contributed stories, poems, and sketches to *Otago Witness* (1878); became parliamentary note-taker in Wellington (1884); admitted to New Zealand Institute of Journalists (1891); acted as correspondent to several newspapers and was corresponding member of Royal Geographical Society of Australasia; became member of British Institute of Journalists; journey to Scandinavia resulted in book, *From New Zealand to Norway* (1894). ❖ See also *Dictionary of New Zealand Biography* (Vol. 2).

SUK EUN-MI (1976—). South Korean table tennis player. Born Dec 25, 1976, in Seoul, South Korea. ❖ Won a silver medal for table tennis doubles at Athens Olympics (2004); ranked 2nd in doubles on ITTF Pro Tour (2004).

SUK MIN-HEE (1968—). Korean handball player. Born Sept 7, 1968, in South Korea. ❖ At Seoul Olympics, won a gold medal in team competition (1988).

SUKARNOPUTRI, Megawati (1947—). Indonesian leader. Born Jan 23, 1947, in Jakarta; dau. of Sukarno (1901–1970, founder and 1st president of Independent Indonesia) and Fatmawati; m. Surendro (air force pilot who disappeared in action over Irian Jaya); briefly m. Hassan Gamal Ahmad Hassan (Egyptian businessman); m. Taufik Kiemas; children: 3. ❖ Joined the opposition to President Suharto (1987), a general who had sent her father to internal exile in 1965; when Suharto tried to remove her as leader of the Indonesia Democratic Party (PDIP, 1996), emerged as a national hero because of demonstrations in the capital; after Suharto's resignation (May 1998), relaunched the PDIP; in the country's 1st free parliamentary election (1999), her party won the most votes but the national assembly denied her the top job in favor of Abdurrahman Wahid; became his vice-president; became president of Indonesia (July 2001), when Wahid was dismissed for incompetence; failed to win reelection (2004).

SUKHARNOVA, Olga (1955—). Soviet basketball player. Born Feb 14, 1955, in USSR. ❖ Won a gold medal at Montreal Olympics (1976) and a gold medal at Moscow Olympics (1980), both in team competition.

SUKOVA, Helena (1965—). Czech tennis player. Born Feb 23, 1965, in Praha, Czechoslovakia; dau. of Cyril Suk (pres. of the Czech Tennis Federation) and Vera Sukova (tennis player); sister of Cyril Suk Jr. (often her doubles partner). ❖ Won doubles championships at Wimbledon (1987, 1989, 1990, 1996); won doubles championships at Australian Open (1990, 1992), US Open (1985, 1993), and French Open (1990); won mixed doubles championships at Wimbledon (1994, 1996, 1997), US Open (1993) and French Open (1991); won a silver medal for doubles at Seoul Olympics (1988) and a silver for doubles at Atlanta Olympics (1996).

SUKOVA, Vera (1931–1982). Czech tennis player and women's coach. Born June 13, 1931, in Uherske Hradiste, Czechoslovakia; died of a brain tumor, May 13, 1982, in Prague; m. Cyril Suk (pres. of the Czech Tennis Federation); children: Cyril Suk Jr. and Helena Sukova (both tennis players). ❖ Won doubles championship at Wimbledon (1962); was an early coach of Martina Navratilova.

SULKA, Elaine (1933–1994). American actress, director, and theater founder. Born in New York, NY, c. 1933; died Dec 24, 1994, age 61, in NYC; m. Philip Meister (died 1982). ❖ Made off-Broadway debut in *Hop Signor!* (1962), followed by *Brotherhood, Brothers, Last Prostitute* and *The Courting*; on Broadway, appeared in *Passion of Josef D* and *Medea*; with husband, co-founded the National Shakespeare Company (1963) and NYC's Cubiculo Theatre.

SULLAM, Sara Coppia (1590–1641). Italian Renaissance figure. Name variations: Sara Copio Sullam. Born Sara Coppia or Copio in Venice, Italy, 1590; died 1641; could read Latin, Greek, Spanish, Hebrew, and Italian by age 15; m. Joseph Sullam. ❖ Able to perform on the lute and harpsichord, was also known as a gifted poet, though very little of her work has survived; following marriage, turned her home into one of the most popular literary salons in Venice, frequented by distinguished people of the era; often entertained by reading her own poetry and performing music; as a Jew, defended her religious beliefs, writing the pamphlet *Manifesto of Sara Coppia Sullam, Jewess*, in which she refutes the opinion denying immortality of the soul, falsely attributed to her by Sr. Bonifaccio (1621). ❖ See also *Women in World History*.

SULLAVAN, Margaret (1911–1960). American actress. Born Margaret Brooke Sullavan, May 16, 1911, in Norfolk, VA; died Jan 1, 1960, of an overdose of barbiturates; dau. of Cornelius H. Sullivan (broker) and Garland (Council) Sullavan; attended Sullins College; m. Henry Fonda (actor), 1930 (div. within a year); m. William Wyler (director), 1934 (div. 1936); m. Leland Hayward (producer-agent), 1936 (div. 1947); m. Kenneth Wagg (businessman), 1950; children: daughters, Brooke Hayward (author) and Bridget Hayward. ❖ Versatile actress who was successful on both stage and screen, is remembered primarily for her wrenching performance in the film *Three Comrades* (1938), her portrayal of the struggling young actress in the play *The Voice of the Turtle* (1943), for which she won New York Drama Critics' award, and her light touch in the classic film, *The Shop Around the Corner* (1940); made stage debut as Isabella Parry in *Strictly Dishonorable* (1930) and Broadway debut in the lead in *A Modern Virgin* (1931); made film debut in *Only Yesterday* (1933), followed by *Little Man What Now?* (1934), *Back Street* (1941), *So Ends Our Night* (1941), *Cry Havoc* (1943), and *No Sad Songs for Me* (1950), among others; turned her back on Hollywood at height of success, but continued to work on stage, including *The Deep Blue Sea* (1952), though advancing deafness made it necessary for her to read lips in order to continue to perform. ❖ See also *Women in World History*.

SULLEROT, Evelyne (1924—). French sociologist and journalist. Born Evelyne Annie Henriette Pasteur, Oct 10, 1924, in Montrouge, France; dau. of André Pasteur and Georgette (Roustain) Pasteur; educated at Compiègne, Royan and Uzès, and then at universities of Paris and Aix-en-Provence; married François Sullerot, in 1946; children: 3 sons, 1 daughter. ❖ Was a teacher at the French Press Institute, as well as a professor at the Free University of Brussels and head of the Faculty of Letters at University of Paris; co-founded the French Family Planning Association (1955), serving as secretary-general of the organization (1955–58), then as honorary president; served as an advisor to UN, the International Labour Organization, and the European Economic Community; authored several books on women's issues, including *La vie des femmes* (1964), *Demain les femmes* (1965), *Histoire et sociologie du travail féminin* (1968), *La femme dans le monde moderne* (1970), *Les françaises aux travail* (1973), *Histoire et mythologie de l'amour* (1976) and *L'âge de travailler* (1986).

SULLIVAN, Annie (1866–1936). See Macy, Anne Sullivan.

SULLIVAN, Carryn (1955—). Australian politician. Born Sept 6, 1955, in Millmerran, Australia. ❖ Primary school teacher; as a member of the Australian Labor Party, elected to the Queensland Parliament for Pumicestone (2001).

SULLIVAN, Mrs. Cornelius (1877–1939). See Sullivan, Mary Quinn.

SULLIVAN, Cynthia Jan (1937—). American golfer. Name variations: Silky Sullivan. Born Cynthia Jan Sullivan, Sept 15, 1937, in Harrisburg, PA; attended Coker College. ❖ Turned pro (1959); served as LPGA president (1969–70, 1972–73).

SULLIVAN, Denny G. (1908–2001). See Griswold, Denny.

SULLIVAN, Jean (1923–2003). American actress, musician, ballet and flamenco dancer. Born May 26, 1923, in Logan, UT; died Feb 27, 2003, in Woodland Hills, CA; m. Tom Poston (comedic actor), 1955 (div. 1968); children: Francesca Poston. ❖ Starred in screen debut opposite Errol Flynn in *Uncertain Glory* (1944), followed by *Roughly Speaking* and *Escape in the Desert*; moved to NY to study acting and ballet; became a principal dancer for the American Ballet Theatre; played Spanish guitar and performed flamenco at Latin nightclubs and on tv; also played cello and piano.

SULLIVAN, Kathryn (1951—). American astronaut. Born Kathryn Dwyer Sullivan, Oct 3, 1951, at Paterson, New Jersey; dau. of Donald P. Sullivan (aerospace design engineer) and Barbara K. Sullivan; University of California at Santa Cruz, BS, 1973, Dalhousie University, PhD, 1978. ❖ Selected for 1st group of women astronauts (1978) and flew on 3 missions (1984); was the 1st American woman to walk in space (1990, 1992), and the 1st female payload commander; wrote foreword in *Your Future in Space: The US Space Camp Training Program* (1986); served as chief scientist of the National Oceanographic and Atmospheric Administration (1992–96); was appointed to head the nonprofit Center of Science and Industry in Columbus, OH (1996). ❖ See also *Women in World History*.

SULLIVAN, Leonor Kretzer (1902–1988). American politician. Born Leonor Kretzer, Aug 21, 1902, in St. Louis, MO; died in St. Louis, Sept 1, 1988; dau. of Frederick William and Nora (Jostrand) Kretzer; attended Washington University; m. John Berchmans Sullivan (legislator and politician), Dec 27, 1941 (died Jan 1951). ❖ Following marriage to John Sullivan (1941), US representative of 11th District in Missouri, served as his campaign manager and administrative aide until his death in 1951; ran for Democratic congressional nomination in her own right (1952), defeating incumbent Claude I. Bakewell, who had been appointed to serve out her husband's term; won a seat in 82nd Congress, the only woman representative from Missouri; earned a reputation as a defender of consumers, and worked throughout her nearly 25-year career in Congress to protect the American public from hazardous substances, harmful cosmetics, food-color additives, and tainted meat; was also instrumental in passage of Consumer Credit Protection Act (1968), which mandated "truth in lending"; was a member of the Committee on Banking and Currency, Committee on Merchant Marine and Fisheries, and Joint Committee on Defense Production; won reelection 12 times. ❖ See also *Women in World History*.

SULLIVAN, Mary Quinn (1877–1939). Art collector and founder. Name variations: Mrs. Cornelius Sullivan. Born Mary Josephine Quinn in Indianapolis, IN, Nov 24, 1877; died Dec 5, 1939; dau. of Thomas Quinn and Anne (Gleason) Quinn; studied at Pratt Institute in New York City and at Slade School for Fine Art of University College, London; m. Cornelius Joseph Sullivan (attorney and art collector), Nov 21, 1917 (died 1932); no children. ❖ One of the founders of the Museum of Modern Art (MOMA), began career as a teacher and was selected by NY City Board of Education to travel to Europe to observe art schools (1902); while in France and Italy, came to appreciate Impressionist and Post-Impressionist paintings; became instructor of design and household arts and sciences at Pratt Institute (1910); with husband, began to collect rare paintings, purchasing such works as Cézanne's *Madame Cézanne*, Toulouse-Lautrec's *Woman in the Garden of Mr. Forest*, Rouault's *Crucifixion*, Modigliani's *Sculptured Head of a Woman*, and a Picasso; with art-patron friends, created Museum of Modern Art and was among the 7 trustees to sign the charter for the museum, then housed in a NY brownstone (1929); during last 10 years of her life, was involved in gallery work, presenting solo shows for such artists as Peter Hurd in her own gallery on East 56th Street. ❖ See also *Women in World History*.

SULLIVAN, Maxine (1911–1987). African-American pop singer. Name variations: Marietta Williams. Born Marietta Williams in Homestead, PA, May 13, 1911; died April 7, 1987, in New York, NY; trained as a nurse in 1950s; m. John Kirby (bandleader), 1938 (div. 1941); m. Cliff Jackson (pianist), 1950 (died 1970). ❖ Famed for rendition of Scottish folk song "Loch Lomond," made professional debut at a small Pittsburgh speakeasy; moved to NY and sang at the famed Onyx Club (1936); with her light voice, was well suited to singing classic folk songs, which she adapted to a swinging beat; recorded "I'm Coming, Virginia," "Annie Laurie," "Blue Skies," and the hit "Loch Lomond" (1937); appeared in Hollywood film musicals *Going Places* (opposite Louis Armstrong) and *St. Louis Blues* (both 1938); appeared on Broadway in *Swingin' the Dream* (1939), a jazz version of *A Midsummer Night's Dream*, with Louis Armstrong and Benny Goodman; included in her repertoire such pop tunes as "I've Got the World on a String," "Wrap Your Troubles in Dreams," and "I Got a Right to Sing the Blues"; with husband John Kirby, worked on her CBS radio show, "Flow Gently, Sweet Rhythm," that aired for 2 years; toured with Benny Carter orchestra, then launched solo act, performing in late 1940s with Johnny Long and Glenn Miller before returning to NY for 6 years at Le Ruban Bleu and 4 years at Village Vanguard; occasionally performed at clubs in the Bronx with such musicians as Bobby Hackett, Charlie Shavers, Earl Hines, and Bob Wilber; earned Tony Award nomination for musical *My Old Friends* (1979); recorded 11 albums, all of which were well received and earned her Grammy nominations (1982, 1985, and 1986). ❖ See also *Women in World History*.

SULLIVAN, Silky (1937—). See Sullivan, Cynthia Jan.

SULLIVAN, Whetu Tirikatene (1932—). Tirikatene-Sullivan, Whetu.

SULNER, Hanna (1917–1999). Hungarian document analyst and handwriting expert. Born Hanna Fischof in Budapest, Hungary, Feb 17, 1917; died in New York, NY, Jan 5, 1999; dau. of Professor Julius Fischof (handwriting analyst); studied criminology, earned special degree to teach document examination; m. Laszlo Sulner (handwriting analyst), Nov 1947 (died 1950); children: Andrew (document expert).

❖ One of the world's leading authorities in the field of handwriting analysis, spent her life analyzing and authenticating documents, many of them at issue in important legal cases; studied handwriting analysis with father from age 16; took over father's handwriting analysis work (1944); without at 1st being aware of it, was drawn into Communist government plot to frame Cardinal Jozsèf Mindszenty (c. 1947); denounced trial after escaping to Vienna (1949); published *Disputed Documents* (1966). ❖ See also *Women in World History.*

SULPICIA I (fl. 1st c. BCE). Roman poet. Fl. in the 1st century BCE; possibly niece of M. Valerius Messalla Corvinus. ❖ Moved in the cultural circle surrounding the Roman M. Valerius Messalla Corvinus, patron of poets Ovid and Tibullus; authored 6 elegiac poems that survived with the works of Tibullus. ❖ See also *Women in World History.*

SULPICIA II (fl. 1st c. CE). Roman poet. Married Calenus. ❖ Wrote graphic lyric poems celebrating her love for husband Calenus, and was compared favorably to the famous Sappho by Roman poet Martial. ❖ See also *Women in World History.*

SULZBERGER, I. O. (1892–1990). American civic leader and newspaper publisher. Born Iphigene Ochs; Iphigene Ochs Sulzberger; Mrs. Arthur H. Sulzberger. Born Iphigene Bertha Ochs, Sept 19, 1892, in TN; died Feb 26, 1990, in Stamford, CT; dau. of Adolph Ochs (newspaper publisher) and Iphigenia (Wise) Ochs (dau. of Isaac Mayer Wise, founder of American Reform Judaism); attended Barnard College; m. Arthur Sulzberger (president and publisher of *The New York Times*), Nov 17, 1917 (died 1968); children: Marian Sulzberger Heiskell (b. 1918); Ruth Sulzberger Holmberg (b. 1921); Judith P. Sulzberger (b. 1923); Arthur Sulzberger (b. 1926). ❖ Known as the "matriarch of *The New York Times*," remained a constant in the leadership of the paper as management shifted; served as the quiet "conscience" of the *Times* for over 70 years; father purchased the *New York Times* (1896); married Arthur Hays Sulzberger (1917), who joined her father at *The Times*; after father died (1935), inherited prominent leadership position at *The Times* with husband; following father's wishes, remained on the sidelines when it came to running the paper, except for a stint as director of special events during WWII, when she coordinated programs to assist the war effort; was also a tireless worker in civic affairs, concentrating on the conservation of public parks and education. ❖ See also *Women in World History.*

SUMAC, Yma (1927—). Peruvian-born singer. Born Emperatriz Chavarri, Sept 10, 1927, in Ichocan, Peru; m. Moises Vivanco (musician and composer), 1942 (div. 1958); became US citizen (1955). ❖ Known for her 4-octave vocal range and exotic repertoire, was discovered by Moises Vivanco, a musician, composer, and director of Peruvian National Board of Broadcasting, who took over management of her singing career; became part of his performing troupe, Moises' Compañia, and with them made her radio debut (1942); toured with troupe in Rio de Janeiro, Buenos Aires, and Mexico City; with Vivanco, and her cousin Cholita Rivero, arrived in NY, where they began performing as the Inca Taky Trio (1946); signed with Capital Records (1950) and released album *Voice of Xtabay*, which featured melodies in the Quechua Indian language and was an instant bestseller (as were subsequent albums *Mambo* and *Legend of the Sun Virgins*); played an Arabian princess in Broadway musical *Flahooley* (1951) and appeared in 2 Hollywood films: *Secret of the Incas* (1954) and *Omar Khayyam* (1957); performed ancient Andean folk themes as well as arias from *The Magic Flute, Lakmé,* and *La Traviata* in concert at Hollywood Bowl, Constitution Hall in Washington, and Carnegie Hall in NY, among other venues; performed at Montreal International Jazz Festival (1997). ❖ See also *Women in World History.*

SUMAKO, Matsui (1886–1919). Japanese actress. Born in 1886 in Japan; died 1919. ❖ Was at the center of the shingeki (modern theater) movement in early 20th century Japan; introduced Ibsen's Nora to Tokyo (1911); hailed as a pioneer in the women's movement. ❖ See also Phyllis Birnbaum, *Modern Girls, Shining Stars, The Skies of Tokyo* (Columbia U. Press, 1999); (film) *Joyu Sumako no koi* (Love of Sumako the Actress, 1947), starring Kinuyo Tanaka.

SUMII, Sue (1902–1997). Japanese novelist. Born Jan 7, 1902; died June 16, 1997, Ushiku City, Japan. ❖ Fought for rights of workers in Japan and opposed imperial system; works include *A Conflict* (1921), *Dawn and Morning Gloom* (1954), *A River Without Bridges* (6 vols, 1961–73), and *My Life: Living, Loving, and Fighting* (1961).

SUMMER, Donna (1948—). African-American singer. Born Adrian Donna Gaines, Dec 31, 1948, in Boston, MA; dau. of Mary Ellen

and Andrew Gaines (electrician); sister of Mary Ellen Bernard (singer); m. Helmut Sommer (actor), 1971 (div. 1976); m. Bruce Sudano (singer), July 16, 1980; children: (1st m.) Mimi Summer (b. 1974); (2nd m.) Brook Lyn Sudano (actress) (b. 1981) and Amanda Sudano (b. 1982). ❖ Disco star of 1970s, had 21 #1 hits on Billboard Disco-Dance charts, and was 1st female performer to have 3 consecutive US #1 albums; as child, sang in churches in Boston, MA; performed in German production of musical, *Hair*, in Munich (1967); had huge hit with title track from debut album, *Love to Love You Baby* (1975), and followed up with several successful albums, including *A Love Trilogy* (1976), *I Remember Yesterday* (1977), and double platinum *Bad Girls* (1979); appeared in film *Thank God It's Friday* (1978), winning Grammy for soundtrack song, "Last Dance"; had hit with album, *She Works Hard for the Money* (1983), and title track went to #1 on R&B charts; after several bleak years, began performing again (1996); moved to Nashville, TN, and began writing songs for other performers, including Dolly Parton and Reba McEntire.

SUMMERS, Essie (1912–1998). New Zealand novelist. Born July 24, 1912, in Christchurch, New Zealand; died Aug 27, 1998, in Taradale, Hawkes Bay, New Zealand; dau. of Edwin Summers and Ethel Summers; m. Bill Flett; children: 2. ❖ Works of romantic fiction include *Bachelors Galore* (1958), *The Lark in the Meadow* (1959), *Moon Over the Alps* (1960), *The House of the Shining Tide* (1962), *Through All the Years* (1976). ❖ See also autobiography, *The Essie Summers Story* (1974).

SUMMERS, Leonora (1897–1976). American comedic actress and dancer. Born Dec 12, 1897, in New York, NY; died June 29, 1976, in Woodland Hills, Ca; m. Mushy Callahan (junior welter-weight champion). ❖ Began career on Broadway; arrived in Hollywood (1925) and was featured in numerous Mack Sennett comedies; other films include *Sea Beast, Ben-Hur* and *Hoboken to Hollywood.*

SUMMERS, Merna (1933—). Canadian short-story writer. Born 1933 in Alberta, Canada. ❖ Worked as journalist and reporter; served as writer-in-residence at several institutions and on faculty at Banff Center Writing Program; writings include *The Skating Party* (1974), *Calling Home* (1982), and *North of the Battle* (1988). Received Marian Engel Award and Writers' Guild of Alberta award for best book of short fiction.

SUMMERSBY, Kay (1908–1975). Irish paramour. Name variations: Kay Summersby Morgan. Born 1908 in Co. Cork, Ireland; died 1975. ❖ Was the chauffeur, and claimed to be the wartime mistress, of Dwight Eisenhower in her book, *Past Forgetting: My Love Affair with Dwight D. Eisenhower* (1976), though she admitted that the affair did not go beyond kissing; also wrote *Ike Was My Boss* (1948).

SUMMERSKILL, Edith (1901–1980). English politician, doctor, and author. Born Baroness Summerskill. Born Edith Clara Summerskill on April 19, 1901, in London; died 1980; dau. of William Summerskill (physician and radical politician) and Edith Summerskill; educated at King's College, London; studied at Charing Cross Hospital; m. (Edward) Jeffrey Samuel (physician), in 1924 or 1925; children: Michael and Shirley Summerskill (Labour MP). ❖ As a member of Parliament (1938–55), successfully campaigned for a wide array of women's rights; followed father into medicine, becoming a member of the Royal College of Surgeons and a licentiate of Royal College of Physicians; became involved with Socialist Medical Association, a group of doctors dedicated to the establishment of a free national health service, and served as its vice-president for many years; won 1st of many political campaigns as a Labour candidate, a seat on the Middlesex county council (1934); ran in national campaigns for Parliament in Putney and Lancashire, though she was unsuccessful until she defeated the Conservative candidate in a by-election in West Fulham (1938); as a member of Parliament, supported women's rights in the areas of equal pay, birth control, and property rights; though controversial, gained an international reputation during WWII, successfully campaigned for women's admission into Britain's Home Guard (1943); appointed under-secretary at Ministry of Food (1945) and campaigned for the 1949 Clean Milk Act, which she hailed as her finest achievement; named minister of National Insurance (1950), becoming the 1st married woman to reach a Cabinet ranking; having served as a member of the Labour Party's National Executive Committee since 1944, became its chair (1954); as representative from Warrington (1955), made social security a special cause as a member of the shadow cabinet until 1957; was honored with a life peerage (1961), becoming Baroness Summerskill of Kenwood, which gained her entrance into the House of Lords; made a Companion of Honour (1966); continued to battle on behalf of women's rights in the House of Lords, particularly as president of the Married Women's Association; won significant victories for women in the area of property rights with the passage of the Married Women's Property Act (1964) and the Matrimonial Homes Act (1967). ❖ See also *Women in World History*.

SUMMERTON, Laura (1983—). Australian basketball player. Born Dec 13, 1983, in Adelaide, Australia. ❖ Forward/center, played for Adelaide Lightning; placed 1st at Oceania championships (2003); won a team silver medal at Athens Olympics (2004). Voted WNBL Rookie of the Year (2001).

SUMMITT, Pat (1952—). American basketball player and coach. Name variations: Pat Head; Patricia Summitt. Born Patricia Sue Head, June 14, 1952, in Henrietta, TN; dau. of Richard and Hazel (Albright) Head; University of Tennessee at Martin, BS, 1974; University of Tennessee at Knoxville, MA; m. Ralph B. Summitt (bank president), 1980; children: Tyler. ❖ While a student at University of Tennessee-Martin, led Lady Pacers to a 64–29 record over 4 years and had most career points (1,405), most career free throws (361), and most points in a season (530 in 1971–72); at Montreal Olympics, won a silver medal in team competition (1976); coached Olympic gold-medal team (1984); as head coach of University of Tennessee Lady Vols, won 990 games as of Jan 2006, becoming college basketball's winningest coach; won 6 NCAA titles (1987, 1989, 1991, 1996, 1997, 1998) and had appeared in all 25 NCAA tournaments as of 2006. Was the 1st female coach to receive the John Bunn Award given by the Basketball Hall of Fame (1990); inducted into the International Women's Sports Hall of Fame (1990); finished the 1997–1998 season with a perfect 39–0 record and was named coach of the year by Associated Press (1998); inducted into Basketball Hall of Fame (2000); named Naismith College Basketball Women's Coach of the Century (2001). ❖ See also Nancy Lay, *The Summitt Season* (Leisure Press, 1989); and *Women in World History*.

SUMNER, Helen Laura (1876–1933). See Woodbury, Helen Sumner.

SUMNER, Jessie (1898–1994). American politician. Born in Milford, IL, July 17, 1898; died in Watseka, IL, Aug 10, 1994; dau. of A. T. Sumner and Elizabeth (Gillan) Sumner; Smith College, degree in economics, 1920; studied law at University of Chicago, Columbia University, Oxford University, and University of Wisconsin; studied at School of Commerce at New York University. ❖ US Republican congressional representative whose 8 years in Congress were marked by her fiscal conservatism, her opposition to US involvement in WWII, and her conviction that the Soviet Union would politically influence the countries it liberated; admitted to the bar (1923), entered practice in Chicago; became the 1st female judge in the state of Illinois when she was elected to finish the rest of uncle's term as judge of Iroquois County (1937); on an anti-New Deal platform, won a seat in US House of Representatives (1938); an unyielding isolationist before and after the war, argued against endorsing US involvement in the formation and funding of international relief organizations such as the UN Relief and Rehabilitation Administration; declared the US entry into the World Bank and the International Monetary Fund to be the worst fraud in American history; was reelected to her 4th term (Nov 1944), but decided against seeking renomination (1946). ❖ See also *Women in World History*.

SUMNERS, Rosalynn (1964—). American figure skater. Born April 20, 1964, in Palo Alto, CA. ❖ Won US nationals (1982, 1983, 1984); won World championship (1983); won a silver medal at Sarajevo Olympics (1984); as a professional, won US Open championship (1991). Inducted into Skating Hall of Fame.

SUMNIKOVA, Irina (1964—). Soviet basketball player. Born Oct 15, 1964, in USSR. ❖ Won a bronze medal at Seoul Olympics (1988) and a gold medal at Barcelona Olympics (1992), both in team competition.

SUN DANDAN. Chinese short-track speedskater. Born in Jilin Province, China. ❖ Won a silver medal at Nagano Olympics (1998) and a silver medal at Salt Lake City Olympics (2002), both for the 3,000-meter relay; began coaching in Jilin Province (2004).

SUN FUMING (1974—). Chinese judoka. Born April 14, 1974, in Tieling, Liaoning Province, China. ❖ Won a gold medal for +72 kg heavyweight at Atlanta Olympics (1996); placed 1st at World championships for +78 kg (2003); won a bronze medal for +78 kg at Athens Olympics (2004).

SUN JIN (1980—). Chinese table tennis player. Born Mar 10, 1980, in China. ❖ Won a silver medal for doubles at Sydney Olympics (2000).

SUN QINGMEI. Chinese soccer player. Born in Hebei, China. ❖ Won a team silver medal at Atlanta Olympics (1996).

SUN TIAN TIAN (1981—). Chinese tennis player. Born Oct 12, 1981, in Henan, China. ❖ Won a gold medal for doubles at Athens Olympics (2004).

SUN WEN (1973—). Chinese soccer player. Born April 6, 1973, in Shanghai, China. ❖ Joined national team (1990); won a team silver medal at Atlanta Olympics (1996); won Asian Cup (1991, 1993, 1995, 1997) and Asian Games championships (1994, 1998); won World Cups (1991, 1995); as captain of the Chinese national team, won a team silver and was co-scoring leader (with Sissi) at World Cup (1999). Named International Football Federation's Women's Player of the Year (1999) and Asian Football Player of the Year (2000), the 1st woman to receive the honor.

SUN XIULAN (1961—). Chinese handball player. Born Mar 27, 1961, in China. ❖ At Los Angeles Olympics, won a bronze medal in team competition (1984).

SUN YAT-SEN, Mme. (1893–1981). See Song Qingling.

SUN YUE (1973—). Chinese volleyball player. Born Mar 15, 1973, in China. ❖ Outside hitter, won team Asian championship (1995, 1997); won a team silver medal at Atlanta Olympics (1996).

SUNDAL, Heidi (1962—). Norwegian handball player. Born Oct 30, 1962, in Norway. ❖ Won a silver medal at Seoul Olympics (1988) and a silver medal at Barcelona Olympics (1992), both in team competition.

SUNDBY, Siren (1982—). Norwegian sailor. Born Dec 2, 1982, in Lørenskog, Norway. ❖ Won a gold medal for single-handed dinghy (Europe) at Athens Olympics (2004) and at World championships (2003 and 2004). Has twice won the Norwegian Female Sailor of the Year award.

SUNDERLAND, countess of.
See Sidney, Dorothy (1617–1684).
See Churchill, Anne (1684–1716).

SUNDERLAND, Nan (1898–1973). American actress. Name variations: Ninetta Sunderland; Mrs. Walter Huston. Born April 13, 1898; died Nov 32, 1973, in New York, NY; m. Walter Huston (actor), 1931 (died 1950); children: (stepson) John Huston (actor-director). ❖ Made Broadway debut in *The Baby Cyclone* (1927); other plays include *Othello, Elmer the Great*, and *Dodsworth*.

SUNDHAGE, Pia (1960—). Swedish soccer player. Born Feb 13, 1960, in Ulrichshamn, Sweden. ❖ Considered one of the world's all-time great footballers, led her team to a World title (1977); over 21 years, made 146 international appearances; named head coach of WUSA's Boston Breakers (2002). Finished 6th in voting for the FIFAF Woman Player of the Century.

SUNDSTROM, Becky (1976—). American speedskater. Born Rebecca Sundstrom, May 10, 1976, in Glen Ellyn, IL; sister of Tama Sundstrom (b. 1968, skater) and Shana Sundstrom (skater). ❖ Won World Jr. championships for allround (1995); placed 6th for the women's 1000 meters at Nagano Olympics (1998).

SUNDSTROM, Shana (1973—). American short-track speedskater. Born Feb 11, 1973, in USA; sister of Tama Sundstrom (b. 1968, skater) and Becky Sundstrom (skater). ❖ Won a bronze medal for the 3,000-meter relay at Lillehammer Olympics (1994).

SUNESEN, Gitte (1971—). Danish handball player. Name variations: Gitte Sunesen Vilhelmsen. Born Dec 11, 1971, in Denmark. ❖ Won a team gold medal at Atlanta Olympics (1996); won team European championships (1994, 1996) and World championships (1997).

SUNG. See also Song.

SUNG JUNG-A (1965—). Korean basketball player. Born Dec 25, 1965, in South Korea. ❖ At Los Angeles Olympics, won a silver medal in team competition (1984).

SUNG KYUNG-HWA (1965—). Korean handball player. Born July 20, 1965, in South Korea. ❖ Won a silver medal at Los Angeles Olympics (1984) and a gold medal at Seoul Olympics (1988), both in team competition.

SUNN, Rell (1951–1998). American surfer. Name variations: Ruella Sunn-Parmenter. Born Ruella Kapoliokaʻehukai (means "heart of the sea") Sunn, 1951, in Makaha, Oahu, HI; died Jan 2, 1998 of breast cancer in Makaha. ❖ Known as a pioneer of women's professional surfing, was Hawaii's #1 female surfer for 5 years; co-founded Women's International Surfing Association (WISA, 1975); co-formed Women's Pro Surfing (WPS, 1979); ranked #1 in world on longboard (1982); was also Hawaii's 1st female lifeguard. Inducted into International Surfing Museum's Walk of Fame. ❖ See also "Heart of the Sea" (documentary, PBS) and Andrea Gabbard, *Girl in the Curl* (Seal Press).

SUNNICHILD (d. 741). Bavarian princess. Name variations: Suanehilde; possibly Kunehilda. Died in 741; possibly dau. of Theodebert, duke of Bavaria, and Folcheid; sister of Guntrud of Bavaria; became 2nd wife of Charles Martel, mayor of Austrasia and Neustria (r. 714–741), in 725; children: Grifo; daughter Chiltrud; and possibly Adeloga Martel.

SUNOHARA, Vicky (1970—). Canadian ice-hockey player. Born May 18, 1970, in Scarborough, Ontario, Canada. ❖ Played for Brampton Thunder; won a team silver medal at Nagano (1998), the 1st Olympics to feature women's ice hockey; won team gold medals at World championships (1997, 2001); won a team gold medal at Salt Lake City Olympics (2002) and a team gold medal at Torino Olympics (2006). Was an All-American at Northeastern University (1988–90) and Rookie of the Year at University of Toronto (1990).

SUNSHINE, Marion (1894–1963). American actress, vaudevillian, and songwriter. Born Mary Tunstall Ijames, May 15, 1894, in Louisville, KY; died Jan 25, 1963, in New York, NY; sister of Claire Lillian Ijames (who performed as Florence Tempest). ❖ At age 5, made stage debut in *Two Little Waifs* with sister; headlined vaudeville with sister for years as "Tempest and Sunshine"; appeared in such plays as *Ziegfeld Follies of 1907, Broadway to Paris, The Beauty Shop, Going Up, The Girl from Home, Daffy Dill* and *Captain Jinks*; made film debut (1908), and often appeared in support of Mary Pickford; helped popularize Latin American music in US; also wrote songs, including "Hot Tamales," "I've Got a Guy," "Have You Seen My Love," and the lyrics for "The Peanut Vendor."

SUNTAQUE, Andreia (1977—). Brazilian soccer player. Name variations: Andreia. Born Sept 14, 1977, in Brazil; attended University of Campo Mourao. ❖ Goalkeeper, won a team silver medal at Athens Olympics (2004).

SUPERVIA, Conchita (1895–1936). Spanish mezzo-soprano. Name variations: Lady Rubenstein. Born Dec 9, 1895, in Barcelona, Spain; died in childbirth, Mar 30, 1936, in London, England; studied at Colegio de las Damas Negras in Barcelona; m. Sir Ben Rubenstein, 1931. ❖ At 15, debuted in Buenos Aires in Bretón's *Los amantes de Teruel* (1910); was the youngest singer to professionally sing Octavian, in Rome premiere of *Der Rosenkavalier*; assisted conductor Vittorio Gui in reviving Rossini's bel canto operas; known especially for her Carmen, was the 1st contralto to be regarded as a prima donna; sang with Chicago Opera (1915–16); debuted at Teatro alla Scala (1924); made London debut at Covent Garden in Rossini's *La Cenerentola* (1934); appeared in screen version of *La Bohème* and in British film *Evensong*, starring Evelyn Laye (1934). ❖ See also *Women in World History*.

SUPLICY, Marta (c. 1946—). Brazilian psychoanalyst and politician. Born Marta Teresa Smith, c. 1946, in São Paulo, Brazil; studied psychology in Brazil and at Michigan State University; m. Eduardo Matarazzo Siplicy (economist and senator), 1964; m. Luis Favre; children: (1st m.) 3 sons, including rock star Supla. ❖ Operated a psychoanalytic practice, specializing in therapy for couples and children; came to public attention as a moderator on daily sexual advice program on Brazilian tv; tangled with military and church censors, but gained a public following; elected to Congress (1994), where she sponsored bills to set candidate quotas for women and to legalize civil unions for homosexuals; representing the leftist Workers' Party, elected mayor of São Paulo (2000), with 58 percent of the vote; lost bid for reelection (2004).

SUPREMES, The.
See Ballard, Florence.
See Birdsong, Cindy.
See Ross, Diana.
See Wilson, Mary.

SURAIYA (1929–2004). Indian actress and singer. Name variations: Suraiya Mubin. Born Suraiya Jamal Sheikh, 1929, in Lahore, Punjab, British India (now Pakistan); died Jan 31, 2004, in Bombay, India; never married. ❖ Know as the Queen of Melody, made screen debut at 12 in

Taj Mahal (1941), playing the young Mumtaz Mahal; first sang in the film *Sharda* (1942) and came to prominence in *Omar Khayyam* (1946); became India's most sought after singing film star; career peaked in 1948–49 with box-office hits *Pyar Ki Jeet* (The Triumph of Love), *Badi Behan* (Big Sister) and *Dillagi* (Mischief); acclaimed for film *Mirza Ghalib* (1954); starred opposite Dev Anand in *Jeet* (Victory, 1949) and *Do Sitare* (Two Stars, 1951); retired at age 34.

SURANGKHANANG, K. (b. 1911). See Kiengsiri, Kanha.

SURANOVA-KUCMANOVA, Eva (1946—). Czech track-and-field athlete. Name variations: Eva Kucmanova. Born April 24, 1946, in Czechoslovakia. ❖ At Munich Olympics, won a bronze medal in the long jump (1972).

SURAPHAN, Nakhon (b. 1911). See Kiengsiri, Kanha.

SURRATT, Mary E. (c. 1820–1865). American accused conspirator. Born Mrs. Surratt; also seen as Mary Seurat. Born Mary Eugenia Jenkins near Waterloo, Prince George's Co., Maryland, c. 1820 (some sources cite 1817, others 1823); hanged in Washington, DC, July 7, 1865; dau. of Samuel Isaac Jenkins; m. John Harrison Surratt (farmer), 1835 (died 1862); children: Isaac Douglas Surratt (b. 1841); Anna Eugenia Surratt (b. 1843); John Harrison Surratt (b. 1844, who became a secret dispatch rider for the Confederacy). ❖ Maryland woman hanged, despite little evidence of guilt, for involvement in Lincoln's assassination; owned a boarding house, which became the meeting place of John Wilkes Booth, her son John H. Surratt, and other conspirators as they plotted to kill Lincoln. ❖ See also *Women in World History*.

SURREY, countess of.
See Gundred (d. 1085).
See Isabel of Vermandois (d. before 1147).
See Isabel de Warrenne (c. 1137–1203).
See Marshall, Maud (d. 1248).
See Alice le Brun (d. 1255).
See Joan de Vere (fl. 1280s).
See Tylney, Elizabeth (d. 1497).
See Tylney, Agnes (1476–1545).

SURRIAGE, Agnes (1726–1783). See Frankland, Agnes.

SURUAGY, Sandra (1963—). Brazilian volleyball player. Name variations: Sandra Maria Lima Suruagy. Born April 7, 1963, in Brazil. ❖ Won team World Grand Prix (1996, 1998); won a team bronze medal at Atlanta Olympics (1996).

SURVILLE, Laure (1800–1871). French author. Born Laure de Balzac in 1800; died 1871; sister of famous French novelist Honoré de Balzac; married to a civil engineer. ❖ Wrote *Balzac, sa vie et ses Oeuvres d'après sa correspondance* (1858).

SUSAN OF POWYS (fl. 1100s). Queen of Powys. Dau. of Gruffydd ap Cynan, king of Gwynedd, and Angharad (d. 1162); m. Madog ap Maredudd, king of Powys; children: four, including Marared (mother of Llywelyn II the Great, Ruler of All Wales).

SUSANN, Jacqueline (1921–1974). American author. Born in Philadelphia, PA, Aug 20, 1921; died in New York, NY, Sept 21, 1974; dau. of Robert Susann (portrait painter) and Rose (Jans) Susann (teacher); m. Irving Mansfield (press agent and radio-tv producer), 1939; children: Guy (b. 1946). ❖ Using her show-business background, drew on personal relationships and experiences to produce wildly popular novels that were generally reviled by book critics as one dimensional; writings include *Every Night, Josephine!* (1963), *Valley of the Dolls* (1966), *The Love Machine* (1969), *Once Is Not Enough* (1973), *Dolores* (1976) and *Yargo* (1979). At the time of her death, *Valley of the Dolls* was ranked as the bestselling book of all time by the *Guinness Book of Records*. ❖ See also *Lovely Me: The Life of Jacqueline Susann*; and *Women in World History*.

SUSANNA (fl. 6th c. BCE). Biblical woman. Name variations: Susannah. Dau. of Hikiah; m. Joakim. ❖ According to versions of the Book of Daniel, spurned the advances of 2 elders; was accused by them of adultery; condemned to death, was saved by the young prophet Daniel who protested the undo haste of the trial and elicited discrepancies in the elders testimony. ❖ See also *Women in World History*.

SUSANNE DE BOURBONNE (1491–1521). See Suzanne of Bourbon.

SUSANTI, Susi (1971—). Indonesian badminton player. Name variations: Susi Susanti Haditono. Born Feb 11, 1971, in Malaysia. ❖ Ranked best in the world, won a gold medal at Barcelona Olympics (1992) and a bronze medal at Atlanta Olympics (1996), both for singles; won record-breaking 4th consecutive World/Grand Prix title (1994), along with the Indonesian, Malaysian, Thailand, Japanese and Chinese Taipei Opens, the World Cup, and All-England championship; retired (1998).

SUSANU, Viorica (1975—). Romanian rower. Born Oct 29, 1975, in Galati, Romania. ❖ Won a gold medal for coxed eights at Sydney Olympics (2000) and at Athens Olympics (2004); at World championships, won gold medals for coxed eights (1997, 1998, 1999) and coxless pair (2001, 2002); won a gold medal for coxless pair at Athens Olympics (2004).

SUSLOVA, Nadezhda (1845–1916). Russian doctor. Born in Russia, 1845; died 1916; dau. of a serf; attended Medical Faculty, University of Zurich, qualifying in 1867. ❖ Russian medical pioneer, studied medicine at the University of Zurich and became the 1st Russian woman physician. ❖ See also *Women in World History.*

SÜSS, Birgit (1962—). *See Suess, Birgit.*

SUSSEX, countess of.
See Howard, Elizabeth (d. 1534).
See Palmer, Anne (1661–1722).

SUSSIEK, Christine (1960—). West German runner. Born Mar 4, 1960, in West Germany. ❖ At Los Angeles Olympics, won a bronze medal in 4 x 400-meter relay (1984).

SUSSLAR, Julia. *See Darvas, Julia.*

SÜSSMUTH, Rita (1937—). German academic and politician. Name variations: Rita Sussmuth; Rita Suessmuth. Born Feb 17, 1937, in Wuppertal, Germany; educated at universities of Münster, Tübingen, and Paris; m. Hans Süssmuth (a professor); children: 1 daughter. ❖ Taught at several German universities, including those at Stuttgart and Osnabrück (1963–66), Pädagogische Hochschule Ruhr (1966–69, 1971), and University of Dortmund (1980); aligned with Christian Democratic Union Party, rose through the ranks and worked on several governmental committees devoted to women, children, marriage, and family affairs (1970s–80s); served as director of the research institute Frau und Gesellschaft (Women and Society) in Hanover before assuming the role of chair of Christian Democratic Union Women's Association (1986), and minister of Youth, Family Affairs, Women and Health (1987); joined the Bundestag (1987) and became its president (1988), heading the governing body until 1999; was a persuasive advocate for social justice.

SUTA, Khassaraporn (1971—). Thai weightlifter. Born 1971 in Thailand. ❖ Won a bronze medal for 53–58 kg at Sydney Olympics (2000).

SUTCLIFF, Rosemary (1920–1992). English novelist and children's writer. Born Dec 14, 1920, in West Clandon, Surrey, England; died July 23, 1992; dau. of a naval officer; attended Bideford School of Art, 1935–39. ❖ At 2, contracted Still's disease, an arthritic condition that ultimately restricted her to a wheelchair; considered one of the most important writers of historical fiction for young people, produced breakthrough work, *The Eagle of the Ninth* (1954), which describes the journey of Marcus Aquila to recover the eagle standard of his father's 9th Hispana Legion after the legion vanished mysteriously in the country north of Hadrian's Wall; followed this with other novels that focused on later generations of the Aquila family, including *The Silver Branch* (1957), *The Lantern Bearers* (1959) and *Frontier Wolf* (1980); convinced of the historical existence of King Arthur, wrote the trilogy: *The Light Beyond the Forest: The Quest for the Holy Grail* (1979), *The Sword and the Circle: King Arthur and the Knights of the Round Table* and *The Road to Camlann: The Death of King Arthur* (1981); other books include *Outcast* (1955), *The Shield Ring* (1955), *Dawn Wind* (1962) and *Song for a Dark Queen* (1978), about Boadicea (Boudica). Named an officer (1975) and commander of the Order of the British Empire (1992). ❖ See also autobiography, *Blue Remembered Hills* (1983); and *Women in World History.*

SUTCLIFFE, Alice (c. 1600–?). British devotional writer. Born c. 1600 in England; dau. of Luke Woodhouse of Kimberly, Suffolk (related to Sir Thomas Woodhouse, attendant in the court of James I); m. John Sutcliffe (court groom). ❖ Wrote *Meditations of Man's Mortalitie: Or, A Way to True Blessednesse* (1634) not only as spiritual work but also, apparently, to promote family's position at court.

SUTHERLAND, duchess of.
See Leveson-Gower, Elizabeth (1765–1839).
See Leveson-Gower, Harriet Elizabeth Georgiana (1806–1868).

SUTHERLAND, Efua (1924–1996). Ghanaian poet, author, theater director and filmmaker. Name variations: Efua Nyankoma; Efua Theodora Morgue; Efua Theodora Sutherland. Born June 27, 1924, in Cape Coast, in the British colony of the Gold Coast; died Jan 2, 1996; attended St. Monica's School and Training College, the Gold Coast; Homerton College, Cambridge University, BA, and School of Oriental and African Studies, University of London; m. William Sutherland, in 1954; children: Esi Reiter Sutherland; Muriel Amowi Sutherland; Ralph Gyan Sutherland. ❖ Prominent writer and theater professional who also held academic and government positions sponsoring the development of the arts in her newly independent country; studied abroad and returned to the Gold Coast (1951); was a teacher at St. Monica's School (1951–54); after the Gold Coast became the independent state of Ghana, organized Ghana Society of Writers (1957); began publication of literary magazine *Okyeame* (Spokesman, 1959); founded Ghana Experimental Players (1958) and Ghana Drama Studio (1961); appointed research fellow in Literature and Drama, University of Ghana (1963); quest for folk tales led her to the small, impoverished Fante village of Atwia, with a population of 700, in the Central Region of Ghana (1964); helped build the community theater Kodzidan (The Story House) in Atwia (1966) and Atwia began an economic as well as a cultural revival; founded Kusum Players (1968), a group of professional actors with its home at the Ghana Drama Studio which toured the country presenting plays to groups of various ages; writings include *The Roadmakers* (1961), *Playtime in Africa* (1962), and *New Life at Kyerefaso* (1964), and the plays *Edufa* (1962), *Foriwa* (1962) and *The Marriage of Anansewa* (1975); was the dominant presence in theater in Ghana for more than 30 years. ❖ See also *Women in World History.*

SUTHERLAND, Joan (1926—). Australian-born opera singer. Name variations: Dame Joan Sutherland. Born Nov 7, 1926, in Sydney, Australia; attended Rathbone School of Dramatic Art, Sydney; Covent Garden Opera school, London; m. Richard Bonynge (conductor), 1954. ❖ Particularly renowned for work in bel canto operas, became one of the most celebrated opera stars of 20th century; made public debut as singer in chorus of Bach's *Christmas Oratorio* (1946); made solo debut the same year in concert performances of Henry Purcell's *Dido and Aeneas* and Handel's *Acis and Galatea*; moved to London (1951), enrolling in Royal College of Music; hired by Covent Garden Opera, London (1952); began to establish her famed versatility, appearing in 3 different roles in Offenbach's *The Tales of Hoffmann*; also appeared in von Weber's *Der Freitschutz* to critical praise (1954) and in Zeffirelli's production of Handel's *Alcina* in Venice (1960); as Lucia, debuted at Paris Opera (1960), and La Scala Opera in Milan and NY's Metropolitan Opera (1961); now in demand, began a 30-year, globe-trotting career; triumphed in 1st return tour of her native Australia (1965); retired from performing (1990), making final appearances in Sydney Opera House in *Les Huguenots,* followed by a gala appearance at Covent Garden in which she sang duets with Pavarotti and Marilyn Horne; throughout long career, most notable roles include title role in *Lucia di Lammermoor,* Donna Anna in *Don Giovanni,* title role in *Alcina,* Amina in *La Sonnambula* (her favorite), Elvira in *I Puritani,* title role *Norma,* and Marie in *La Fille du Regiment.* Named Commander of the Order of the British Empire (1961) and Dame Commander (DBE, 1979), the 2nd Australian singer to be honored (the 1st being Nellie Melba, 1918); named Companion of the Order of Australia (1975) and "Australian of the Year" (1989). ❖ See also autobiography *A Prima Donna's Progress* (Regnery, 1997); Brian Adams, *La Stupenda: A Biography of Joan Sutherland* (Hutchinson, 1980); Russell Braddon, *Joan Sutherland* (St. Martin, 1962); Norma Major, *Joan Sutherland* (Queen Anne Press, 1987); Richard Bonynge, *Joan Sutherland and Richard Bonynge: With the Australian Opera* (Gordon & Breach, 1990); and *Women in World History.*

SUTHERLAND, Lucy Stuart (1903–1980). Australian-born English historian and administrator. Name variations: Dame Lucy Sutherland. Born Lucy Stuart Sutherland in Geelong, Australia, June 21, 1903; died in Oxford, England, Aug 20, 1980; dau. of Alexander Charles Sutherland (mining engineer) and Margaret Mabel (Goddard) Sutherland; educated at Roedean School and the University of Witwatersrand in South Africa; graduate of Somerville College, Oxford; never married. ❖ Spent most of her young life in South Africa; became the 1st woman to address the Oxford Union (1926), in a speech supporting women's colleges; at Oxford (1945), accepted the post of principal of Lady Margaret Hall; served as pro-vice-chancellor of the university (1961–69), the 1st woman to assume such a position; writings include *The East India Company in Eighteenth Century Politics* (1952); also edited part of *The Correspondence of Edmund Burke* (1960), and cooperated in the preparation of *History of Parliament.* Named Commander of the British Empire (CBE, 1947) and Dame of the British Empire (DBE, 1969); received a fellowship at British Academy (1954).

SUTHERLAND, Margaret (1897–1984). Australian composer. Born Margaret Ada Sutherland in Adelaide, South Australia, Nov 20, 1897; died in Melbourne, Aug 12, 1984; dau. of Alice (Bowen) Sutherland and George Sutherland (leader writer on *The Age*); attended Marshall Hall Conservatorium; also studied with Edward Goll and Fritz Hart; m. Dr. Norman Albiston, 1926 (div. 1948). ❖ At 19, invited to Sydney by Belgian conductor and violinist Henri Verbrugghen to perform Beethoven's G major Piano Concerto; went to London to study with Arnold Bax (1923); while there, composed her Sonata for Violin and Piano; after 2 years' study in London, Paris and Vienna, returned to Australia (1925), where she would struggle to gain recognition for next 4 decades; taught at Melbourne Conservatory as well as privately; finally saw her Sonata for Violin and Piano published (1935); completed *Suite on a Theme of Purcell*, a work that received many performances under direction of George Szell (1935); composed *Dithyramb* (1937), followed by String Quartet, *House Quartet, Pavan for Orchestra, The Soldier,* and *Prelude for Jig*; following divorce (1948), composed 9 orchestral works, 12 chamber works, a chamber opera, and many smaller pieces; successfully submitted Concerto for String Orchestra under name "M. Sutherland." for publication (when publisher discovered the "M." stood for Margaret, however, the offer was withdrawn); premiered *The Haunted Hills* (1951), which was recorded by Melbourne Symphony Orchestra, as was orchestral suite, *Three Temperaments* (1958); organized the Camerata Society; collaborated with Lady Maie Casey on *The Young Kabbarli*, a chamber opera based on life of Daisy May Bates (1965), the 1st Australian opera to be recorded in Australia; toward end of life, finally began to gain the recognition long denied; received 1st commission and an honorary doctorate from University of Melbourne, at age 70; was made an Officer of the British Empire Order, at 73. ❖ See also *Women in World History.*

SUTHERLAND, Margaret (1941—). New Zealand novelist and short-story writer. Born 1941 in New Zealand; twice married. ❖ Trained as a nurse and received registration (1979); migrated to Australia (1980s), where she worked as an education officer with the Newcastle Migrant Health Unit; works include *The Fledgling* (1974), *The Love Contract* (1976), *Getting Through and Other Stories* (1977), *The Fringe of Heaven* (1984) and *The City Far from Home* (1991).

SUTHERLAND, Mary (1893–1955). New Zealand forester and botanist. Born May 4, 1893, in London, England; died Mar 11, 1955, in Wellington, New Zealand; dau. of David and Nellie (Miller) Sutherland; University College of North Wales, BSc, 1916. ❖ First woman in UK to complete degree in forestry; served in Women's Land Army and worked as forester on estates in Scotland; immigrated to New Zealand (early 1920s); became forestry assistant at New Zealand State Forest Service (1923–32); made a member of Empire Forestry Association (1924) and charter member of New Zealand Institute of Foresters (1928); served on Council of New Zealand Institute of Foresters (1935), and Council of New Zealand Forestry League (1936); secured position with Dominion Museum in Wellington, becoming botanist (1933); transferred to Department of Agriculture as sole farm forestry officer (1946); wrote significant series of articles for *New Zealand Journal of Agriculture* on benefits of tree farming (1950s). ❖ See also *Dictionary of New Zealand Biography* (Vol. 4).

SUTHERLAND, Mary Ann (1864–1948). New Zealand farmer and landowner. Name variations: Mary Ann Sinclair. Born Jan 29, 1864, at Pirinoa, southern Wairarapa, New Zealand; died Oct 21, 1948, in Featherston, New Zealand; dau. of Donald and Katherine (McCallum) Sinclair; m. Donald Sinclair Sutherland (shepherd), 1895 (died 1927); children: 3. ❖ Purchased brother's share in Sinclair and Te Whaiti holdings, which included Whatarangi coastal station (late 1890s); inherited additional land from father (1914); accumulated and controlled additional vast holdings of land throughout area. ❖ See also *Dictionary of New Zealand Biography* (Vol. 3).

SUTHERLAND, Nellie (1864–1943). *See Glyn, Elinor.*

SUTHERLAND, Selina Murray McDonald (1839–1909). New Zealand nurse and social worker. Born Dec 26, 1839, at Sutherlandshire, Scotland; died Oct 8, 1909, in Melbourne, Australia; dau. of Baigrie (farm servant) and Jane (McDonald) Sutherland. ❖ Immigrated to New Zealand (1865); provided medical services to Maori and Pakeha communities in central Wairarapa area; established hospital in Masterton by soliciting donations (1879); appointed matron of Wellington Hospital (1879); relocated to Australia and began caring for destitute children, initiating Neglected Children's Aid Society (1881); helped form Victorian Neglected Children's Aid Society (1894); presented to Queen Victoria (1897) and received diamond brooch, which she sold to raise money for charitable activities; formed Sutherland Homes for Orphans, Neglected and Destitute Children (1908). ❖ See also *Dictionary of New Zealand Biography* (Vol. 2).

SUTLIFFE, Irene H. (1850–1936). American nurse. Born Nov 12, 1850, in Albany, NY; died Dec 10, 1936; dau. of Charlotte (Ramsey) Sutliffe and George Washington Sutliffe; graduate of New York Hospital School of Nursing, 1880. ❖ Noted nursing education administrator who taught some of the most famous nurses of the early 1900s, Lillian Wald, Annie Goodrich and Mary Beard, 1st established an Erie (PA) school of nursing at the Hamot Hospital, and the Long Island Hospital School of Nursing in Brooklyn, NY (c. 1886); served as director of New York Hospital School of Nursing (1886–1902) and became dean emerita (1932); organized and directed an emergency hospital in response to a polio outbreak in NY (1916); presented a paper at the Conference of Charities, Correction, and Philanthropy at the World's Fair, Chicago (1893), which led to the creation of the National League for Nursing.

SUTOWSKI, Sonia (1927–2001). *See Arova, Sonia.*

SUTTER, Linda (1941–1995). American cartoonist. Born in Greenwich, Connecticut, in 1941; died in Cambridge, Massachusetts, Dec 18, 1995; dau. of Clifford S. Sutter and Suzanne T. Sutter; graduate of Vassar College, 1971; married; children: son Joshua C. Empson. ❖ Former tv reporter for Channel 5 in New York City (1970s), drew the "Brenda Starr" comic strip (1982–85). ❖ See also *Women in World History.*

SUTTNER, Bertha von (1843–1914). Austrian writer, pacifist, and baroness. Name variations: Countess Kinsky; Baroness von Suttner. Pronunciation: SOOT-ner. Born Bertha Felicie Sophie Kinsky in Prague, June 9, 1843; died June 21, 1914; dau. of Count Franz Joseph Kinsky von Wehinitz and Tettau (field marshal in Austrian army) and Countess Sophie Wilhelmina Kinsky (dau. of a cavalry captain); m. Baron Arthur von Suttner (1850–1902, novelist), June 12, 1876; no children. ❖ Baroness whose antiwar novel *Die Waffen Nieder!* became a bestseller in late 19th-century Europe, laying the basis for peace societies in central Europe and winning the Nobel Peace Prize for its author, the 1st woman so honored; served as private secretary to Alfred Nobel (1876); lived with husband in the Caucasus section of Russia (1876–85); published 1st major book, *Das Maschinenzeitalter* (*The Machine Age*, 1889); published *Die Waffen Nieder!* (*Lay Down Your Arms!* 1889), which had an impact in Europe equivalent to the influence of Harriet Beecher Stowe's *Uncle Tom's Cabin* in US; with the pacifist Alfred Fried, co-founded the journal *Die Waffen Nieder!* (1892), later titled *Friedens-Warte* (1899); founded Austrian Peace Society (1891); attended the Hague Peace Congresses (1899 and 1908); visited US, partly to secure funding for peace activities (1904 and 1911); won Nobel Peace Prize (1905); was one of the most famous women of the late 19th century. ❖ See also *Memoiren* (Deutsche Verlags-Anstalt, 1901); Beatrix Kempf, *Suffragette for Peace: The Life of Bertha von Suttner* (trans. by R. W. Last, Wolff, 1972); Emil Lengyel, *And All Her Paths were Peace: The Life of Bertha von Suttner* (Nelson, 1975); Caroline E. Playne, *Bertha von Suttner and the Struggle to Avert the World War* (Allen & Unwin, 1936); and *Women in World History.*

SUTTON, Carol (1933–1985). American journalist and editor. Born June 29, 1933, in St. Louis, Missouri; died Feb 19, 1985, in Louisville, Kentucky; graduate of University of Missouri School of Journalism (Columbia) in 1955; m. Charles Whaley (communications director); children: Carrie and Kate. ❖ The 1st woman to head the news staff of a major American daily newspaper, was hired as secretary at *Courier-Journal* in Kentucky (1955), and within a year promoted to reporter; named editor of women's section (1963); became managing editor (1974); promoted to assistant to the publisher of *Courier-Journal* and *Louisville Times* (1976), then served as senior editor (1979–85). ❖ See also *Women in World History.*

SUTTON, Eve (1906—). New Zealand children's writer. Name variations: Evelyn Mary Sutton. Born 1906 in England; married; children: 3 sons. ❖ Immigrated to New Zealand (1949); with Lynley Stuart Dodd, wrote *My Cat Likes to Hide in Boxes* (1973), which won the Esther Glen medal; also wrote *Green Gold, Tuppenny Brown, Moa Hunter* and *Valley of Heavenly Gold*, among others. Awarded New Zealand Children's Literature Association prize (1991).

SUTTON, May (1887–1975). American tennis player. Name variations: May Sutton Bundy. Born May Godfray Sutton in Plymouth, England, Sept 25, 1887 (some sources wrongly cite 1886); died Oct 4, 1975, in Santa Monica, CA; sister of tennis players Ethel, Adele, Florence and Violet Sutton; m. Thomas Bundy (tennis star), 1912; children: 3 sons and daughter Dorothy Bundy Cheney (tennis player). ❖ Moved to US at age 6; won US singles title (1904, 1907), the youngest national champion in history before Maureen Connolly; became Wimbledon's 1st foreign champion (1905), then won again (1907). ❖ See also *Women in World History.*

SUYIN HAN (b. 1917). *See Han, Suyin.*

SUZANNE OF BAVARIA (1502–1543). Margravine of Brandenburg. Born April 2, 1502; died April 23, 1543; dau. of Albert IV the Wise (1447–1508), duke of Bavaria (r. 1465–1508); m. Casimir, margrave of Brandenburg, Aug 24, 1518; children: Marie of Brandenburg-Kulmbach (b. 1519).

SUZANNE OF BOURBON (1491–1521). Duchess of Bourbon. Name variations: Susanne of Bourbon, Susanne de Bourbonne. Reigned as duchess of Bourbon or Bourbonnais from 1503 to 1521; born May 10, 1491; died April 28, 1521; dau. of Anne of Beaujeu (c. 1460–1522) and Pierre II de Bourbon, lord of Beaujeu; m. Charles II, count of Montpensier and later duke of Bourbon (constable of France), on May 10, 1505; children: 3 sons who died young. ❖ A painting of Suzanne of Bourbon is in the Robert Lehman Collection, Metropolitan Museum of Art. ❖ See also *Women in World History.*

SUZE, Henriette de Coligny, comtesse de la (1618–1683). *See Coligny, Henriette de.*

SUZMAN, Helen (1917—). South African anti-apartheid activist. Name variations: Dame Helen Suzman. Pronunciation: Sooz-man. Born Helen Gavronsky, Nov 7, 1917, in Germiston, South Africa; dau. of Samuel Gavronsky (businessman) and Frieda (David) Gavronsky; University of the Witwatersrand, B.Commerce, 1941; m. Moses Meyer (Mosie) Suzman (physician), Aug 13, 1937; children: Frances Suzman; Patricia Suzman. ❖ Parliamentary opponent of apartheid, who championed human rights and the rule of law, 1st came to public attention as a leading figure in Women's Action (1952), an organization to mobilize women against the Nationalist government; as a United Party (UP) candidate, stood for nomination for the parliamentary seat of Houghton (1952); won the nomination, and in the 1953 general election was returned as a member of the House of Assembly; was member of Parliament (MP) for Houghton (1953–89); as an opposition member, believed her main role was to hold the government to account; used her parliamentary platform to speak out against the horrors of apartheid and to try to help its victims; also campaigned on behalf of women's rights: her 1st speech in Parliament, where for 6 years she was the only woman among 166 MPs, was in the debate on the Matrimonial Affairs Bill, an early milestone on the road to legal equality for women; continued to fight for such equality, making major contributions in Parliament (1975, 1984, and 1988), and pleading for the participation of more women at the 1st meeting of the Convention for a Democratic South Africa (CODESA, 1991); often at war with the conservative elements in her party, showed 1st act of defiance when her party initially supported the Separate Amenities Bill (1953), which provided for racial segregation in public places; resigned from the UP in disgust when it voted against the grant of more land to Africans (1959) and helped form the Progressive Party (PP), which opposed racial segregation root and branch; was in effect the entire parliamentary opposition, for the UP offered little or no resistance as many key apartheid laws were enacted; a woman of great political courage, was left to battle alone. Of South Africans of the 20th century, only General Jan Smuts, Archbishop Tutu, and Nelson Mandela were more honored internationally; invested as a Dame of the British Empire (1989). ❖ See also memoirs *In No Uncertain Terms* (Ball, 1993); P. Lewsen, ed. *Helen Suzman: The Solo Years* (Ball, 1991); J. Strangewayes-Booth, *A Cricket in the Thorn Tree: Helen Suzman and the Progressive Party* (Hutchinson, 1976); and *Women in World History.*

SUZMAN, Janet (1939—). English actress and director. Born Feb 9, 1939, in Johannesburg, South Africa; niece of anti-apartheid activist Helen Suzman; attended Kingsmead College and University of Witwaterstrand; trained at London Academy of Music and Dramatic Art; m. Trevor Nunn (actor, film director), 1969 (div. 1986); children: Joshua. ❖ Made 1st London stage appearance in *Billy Liar* and joined Royal Shakespeare Company (1962); became one of the RSC's most distinguished players, winning acclaim for her Rosalind, Portia, Ophelia, Beatrice and Kate, and for work in plays by Ibsen, Chekhov, Fugard and Pinter; starred in film *A Day in the Death of Joe Egg* (1970) and nominated for Academy Award for portrayal of Empress Alexandra Feodorovna in *Nicholas and Alexandra* (1971); won London Evening Standard Award for performance in stage productions of *Antony and Cleopatra* (1973) and *The Three Sisters* (1976); made directorial debut with *Othello* (1987).

SUZUKI, Emiko (1981—). Japanese synchronized swimmer. Born Nov 12, 1981, in Japan. ❖ At World championships, placed 1st in free routine combination (2003); won a team silver medal at Athens Olympics (2004).

SVARTZ, Helga (1890–1964). *See Martinson, Moa.*

SVEDBERG, Ruth (1903–2004). Swedish track-and-field athlete. Born April 14, 1903; died Jan 2003. ❖ At Amsterdam Olympics, won a bronze medal in the discus throw (1928).

SVEDOVA-SCHOENOVA, Lydmila (1936—). Czech gymnast. Name variations: Lydmila Schoenova or Schönova. Born Nov 13, 1936. ❖ At Rome Olympics, won a silver medal in team all-around (1960).

SVENDSEN, Cathrine (1967—). Norwegian handball player. Born Sept 23, 1967, in Norway. ❖ Won a silver medal at Seoul Olympics (1988) and a silver medal at Barcelona Olympics (1992), both in team competition.

SVENSSON, Tina (1970—). Norwegian soccer player. Born Jan 25, 1970, in Norway. ❖ Won a team bronze medal at Atlanta Olympics (1996).

SVET, Mateja (1968—). Slovenian Alpine skier. Born Aug 16, 1968, in Ljubljana, Slovenia. ❖ Won the World Cup giant slalom title (1988); won a silver medal for slalom at Calgary Olympics (1988); at World championships, won a gold medal for slalom (1989), silver medal for giant slalom (1987), and bronze medals for slalom and super-G (1987) and giant slalom (1989).

SVETLA, Caroline (1830–1899). Czech author and feminist. Name variations: Karolina Svetla or Karolína Světlá; Johanna Mužáková or Johanna Muzakova; Johanna Rotová. Born Johanna Rotová on Feb 24, 1830, in Prague; died Sept 7, 1899; m. Petr Mužák (teacher). ❖ One of her nation's most influential writers in the 19th century, was a prominent member of the Máj circle of Czech writers, who sought to create a revolutionary literature based on their own liberal views and political nationalism; published 1st writings in Máj journals; devoted much of her career to composing tales of the Prague middle class or stories about the rural lifestyle of those living in the mountains of northern Bohemia; in later years, wrote political stories about the revolutions of 1848; also founded the 1st serious Czech women's association, the Women's Work Club (1871); suffered from nearly total blindness (1875); for remainder of life, had to dictate her work to a niece; credited with introducing poetic realism to Czech literature; writings include *The Cross by the Stream* (1868) and *A Village Novel* (1869).

SVETLOVA, Marina (1922—). French ballet dancer. Born Yvette von Hartmann, May 3, 1922, in Paris, France. ❖ Trained at studios of Olga Preobrazhenska, Lyubov Egorova, and Vera Trefilova in Paris; joined Original Ballet Russe (1939), where she was featured in Massine's *Symphonie Fantastique* and Lichine's *Protée*, among others; in NY, danced one season with Ballet Theater, and for an extended period at Metropolitan Opera in such works as *La Traviata, Carmen*, and *Aïda*; was guest artist with Irish National Ballet and London Festival troupe; served as chair of ballet department at University of Indiana, Bloomington, upon retiring from performance career.

SVILOVA, Elizaveta (1900–1975). Soviet film editor and filmmaker. Name variations: Yelizaveta Svilova. Born Sept 5, 1900, in Russia; died Nov 11, 1975; m. Dziga Vertov, considered the "father" of Soviet documentary (died 1954). ❖ Was a member of the influential Kino-eye group, dedicated to a formalist technique of film editing known as Soviet montage; collaborated on husband's films *Man with a Movie Camera* (1929), a landmark in experimental cinema, *Enthusiasm*

(1930), and *Three Songs of Lenin* (1934); won Stalin Prize for *Fascist Atrocities* (1946). ❖ See also *Women in World History.*

SVOBODOVA, Gabriela (1953—). Czech cross-country skier. Name variations: Svobodová; Gabriela Svobodova-Sekajova. Born Feb 27, 1953, in Kremnica, Czechoslovakia. ❖ Won a silver medal for 4 x 5 km relay at Sarajevo Olympics (1984).

SVOBODOVA, Martina (1983—). Slovakian skater. Born Oct 25, 1983. ❖ Won gold (2001 and 2002) and silver (2000) at X Games in Street/ Park; won gold at Gravity Games in Street (2000); other 1st-place finishes in Street include: YOZ, Munich (2000), UBI Open Skate championships, London (2000), ASA World championships, Las Vegas, NV (2000), ASA, Woodward, PA (2000), and Euro X Qualifier, Barcelona (2001).

SVOLOU, Maria (d. 1976). Greek feminist, Communist, and anti-Nazi activist. Died 1976; m. Alexander Svolou (law professor). ❖ At a young age, became an active member of the women's movement in Greece; served as editor of magazine *Woman's Struggle*; during General Ioannis Metaxa's dictatorship, sent into exile for political views (1936–40, 1948); during WWII, joined the resistance and spent a year as a member of the National Council, the independent government convened in the mountains of free Greece; was twice elected member of Parliament representing Greek Leftist Party, and served as a member of its Central Committee. ❖ See also *Women in World History.*

SVUBOVA, Dagmar. Czech cross-country skier. Name variations: Schvubova, Svubová, or Svybova; Dagmar Svubova-Paleckova. Born in Czechoslovakia. ❖ Won a silver medal for 4 x 5 km relay at Sarajevo Olympics (1984).

SVYBOVA, Dagmar. See Svubova, Dagmar.

SWAAB, Ninna (1940—). Swedish equestrian. Born June 26, 1940, in Sweden. ❖ At Munich Olympics, won a bronze medal in team dressage (1972).

SWAGERTY, Jane (1951—). American swimmer. Name variations: Jane Swagerty-Hill. Born July 30, 1951. ❖ At Mexico City Olympics, won a bronze medal in 100-meter backstroke (1968).

SWAIL, Julie (1972—). American water-polo player. Born Dec 27, 1972, in Placentia, CA. ❖ Won a team silver medal at Sydney Olympics (2000).

SWAIN, Clara A. (1834–1910). American medical missionary. Born Clara Swain, July 18, 1834, in Elmira, NY; died Dec 25, 1910, in Castile, NY; dau. of John Swain and Clarissa (Seavey) Swain; attended Female Seminary in Canandaigua, NY, and Castile Sanitarium; graduate of Woman's Medical College of Pennsylvania, 1869; never married. ❖ Missionary, sailed for Bareilly, northwest India (1869); helped found the Clara Swain Hospital, the 1st women's hospital in India (1874), designed so that women in seclusion could come without breaking caste rules; became the court appointed physician for the rani (1885); retired from active missionary service (1896); as the 1st female missionary physician to minister especially to woman and children, not only established better health care for women in India but also provided them with educational and employment opportunities. ❖ See also Dorothy Clarke Wilson, *Palace of Healing: The Story of Dr. Clara Swain* (McGraw-Hill, 1968); and *Women in World History.*

SWAINSON, Edith Stanway (1844–1903). See Halcombe, Edith Stanway.

SWAINSON, Mary Anne (c. 1833–1897). New Zealand teacher and headmistress. Name variations: Mary Anne Arrowsmith. Born Mary Anne Arrowsmith, c. 1833 (baptized on July 19, 1833, in Westmoreland, England); died Aug 3, 1897, at Thorndon, Wellington, New Zealand; dau. of Henry Abel Arrowsmith (schoolmaster) and Isabella (Parkin) Arrowsmith; m. George Frederick Swainson (surveyor), 1859 (died 1870); children: 2 sons, 3 daughters. ❖ Immigrated to New Zealand (1856); opened girls' school, The Terrace, in Thorndon (1869); established successful boarding school, Fitzherbert Terrace School (1878); less involved in teaching toward end of her life, remained headmistress until her death. ❖ See also *Dictionary of New Zealand Biography* (Vol. 2).

SWALLOW, Ellen Henrietta (1842–1911). See Richards, Ellen Henrietta.

SWANBOROUGH, Baroness (1894–1971). See Isaacs, Stella.

SWANK, Hilary (1974—). American actress. Born Hilary Ann Swank, July 30, 1974, in Lincoln, Nebraska; grew up in Bellingham, Washington; dau. of Judy Swank; m. Chad Lowe (actor), Sept 28, 1997. ❖ On tv, had recurring roles on "Growing Pains" and "Beverly Hills, 90201"; made film debut in *Buffy the Vampire Slayer* (1992), followed by a starring role in *The Next Karate Kid* (1994); came to prominence with *Boys Don't Cry* (2000), for which she won an Academy Award for Best Actress; won 2nd Oscar for *Million Dollar Baby* (2004); other films include *The Gift* (2000), *The Affair of the Necklace* (2001), *Insomnia* (2002), *Red Dust* (2004) and *The Black Dahlia* (2006).

SWANN, Caroline Burke (d. 1964). American producer, writer and actress. Name variations: Caroline Burke. Died Dec 5, 1964, age 51, in New York, NY; m. Erwin D. Swann. ❖ As actress, appeared on Broadway in *Brooklyn USA* and *Heart of a City*; produced (on Broadway) *The Tenth Man* and *The Hostage*, (off-Broadway) *The Dumbwaiter, The Collection, The Room, A Slight Ache,* and *One Way Pendulum*; worked as a producer, writer, and director for NBC (1946–56).

SWAN OF LICHFIELD (1742–1809). See Seward, Anna.

SWANSON, Gloria (1897–1983). American actress. Born Gloria May Josephine Swenson, Mar 27, 1897, in Chicago, IL; died April 4, 1983; dau. of Adelaide (Klanowski) Swenson and Joseph Theodore Swenson; m. Wallace Beery (actor), 1916 (div. 1919); m. Herbert K. Somborn, 1920 (div. 1925); m. Henri, Marquis de la Falaise de la Coudraye, 1925 (div. 1930); m. Michael Farmer (Irish sportsman), Aug 16, 1931 (div. 1934); m. William N. Davey (investment broker), 1945 (div. 1945); m. William Dufty, 1976; children: (2nd m.) Gloria Somborn Anderson (b. 1920); (4th m.) Michele Farmer (b. 1932); (adopted) Joseph Swanson. ❖ Film star, whose lasting legacy was her outsized performance as the ex-movie queen in 1950 classic *Sunset Boulevard*, made 1st silent film (1914); made 1st film in which she was billed by name, *The Fable of Elvira and Farina and the Meal Ticket* (1915); gave other notable performances in *The Danger Girl* (1916), in which she drove a racing car and did her own stunts, *Teddy at the Throttle* (1917), in which she was tied to a railroad track and slipped into a hole between the rails at the last moment while a steam train rolled over her, *Shifting Sands* (1918), an anti-German propaganda film during WWI, *Don't Change Your Husband* (1919), the 1st of her films directed by Cecil B. De Mille, *Beyond the Rocks,* which co-starred Rudolph Valentino, *Madame Sans-Gêne* (1925), the 1st American feature film shot abroad on location (in France), *The Love of Sunya* (1927), the 1st film she produced, *Sadie Thompson* (1928), source of one of her many run-ins with the censorious Hays Office but also of her 1st Oscar nomination, *The Trespasser* (1929), her 1st talkie, in which she also sang songs, and source of her 2nd Oscar nomination, *Father Takes a Wife* (1941), her only film between 1934 and 1950—a commercial failure, and *Sunset Boulevard* (1950), her masterpiece, which unwittingly traced her own fall from silent star; made at least 70 films. ❖ See also autobiography *Swanson on Swanson* (1980); and *Women in World History.*

SWANSON, Pipsan Saarinen (1905–1979). Finnish-American interior, glassware and textile designer. Name variations: Pipsan Saarinen; Pipsan Saarinen-Swanson; Eva Lisa Saarinen Swanson. Born Eva Lisa Saarinen, Mar 3, 1905, in Finland; died Oct 1979 in Michigan; dau. of architect Eliel Saarinen (1873–1950) and sculptor Loja (Gesellius) Saarinen (1879–1968); sister of architect Eero Saarinen (1910–1961); sister-in-law of Aline B. Saarinen (1914–1972); m. Robert Swanson (architect). ❖ Studied weaving and other crafts in Helsinki; with family, moved to US (1923), settling at Cranbrook Academy of Art in Bloomfield Hills, MI (1925); taught there until 1935; a designer in the tradition of Scandinavian modernism, left Cranbrook to head the interior design department at husband's office; specialized in furniture, textile and glassware design, and also served as a color consultant to various companies, including Barwick Mills, Goodall Fabrics, and Pittsburgh Plate Glass. ❖ See also *Women in World History.*

SWANWICK, Anna (1813–1899). British translator, feminist, and philanthropist. Born in Liverpool, England, June 22, 1813; died at Tunbridge Wells, Kent, Nov 2, 1899; dau. of John Swanwick; University of Aberdeen, LLD. ❖ Journeyed to Berlin to study German, Greek, and Hebrew (1839); on return to London (1843), took up mathematics; published 1st vol. of translations, *Selections from the Dramas of Goethe and Schiller* (1843), then a translation of Schiller's *Jungfrau von Orleans* (1847); also published a complete translation of both parts of *Faust* in blank verse (1878) which ran through several editions; turned attention to translating from the Greek, issuing a blank verse translation of Aeschylus' *Trilogy* (1865), followed by a complete edition of Aeschylus (1873); though chiefly remembered for her translations, published original prose: *Books, our Best Friends and Deadliest Foes* (1886), *An Utopian Dream and How it May Be Realized* (1888), *Poets, the Interpreters of their Age* (1892) and *Evolution and the Religion of the Future* (1894); was also involved in social and philanthropic movements. ❖ See also M.L. Bruce, *Anna Swanwick: A Memoir* (1904); and *Women in World History.*

SWANWICK, Helena (1864–1939). British suffragist and pacifist. Born Helena Maria Lucy Sickert, 1864, in Munich, Germany; died 1939; dau. of Oswald Sickert; m. Frederick Swanwick, 1888. ❖ Staunch advocate of pacifism and disarmament, studied Moral Sciences at Girton College and became psychology lecturer and journalist; joined North England Suffrage Society (1900) but opposed militancy; edited suffragist newspaper, *The Common Cause,* and later contributed to *The Manchester Guardian, The Observer, The Nation,* and *The Daily News;* became chair of Women's International League for Peace (1915); after WWI, was delegate to League of Nations (1924, 1929) and became vice-president of League of Nations Union; writings include *The Future of the Women's Movement* (1913), *Builders of Peace* (1924), *Collective Insecurity* (1937) and *Roots of Peace* (1938). ❖ See also autobiography, *I Have Been Young* (1935).

SWARTHOUT, Gladys (1904–1969). American mezzo-soprano. Born Dec 25, 1904, in Deepwater, MO; died July 7, 1969, in Florence, Italy; dau. of Frank Leslie Swarthout and Ruth (Wonser) Swarthout; Bush Conservatory of Music in Chicago, doctorate in music, 1923; m. Harry Richmond Kern, 1925 (died 1931); m. Frank M. Chapman Jr., 1932 (died 1966). ❖ By 1923, was an accomplished concert singer, having given recitals throughout US, often performing with older sister Roma Swarthout; made operatic debut with Chicago Civic Opera, singing 22 roles in 50 performances in 1924–25 season; after successful stint with Ravinia Park Opera in Chicago (late 1920s), debuted at NY's Metropolitan Opera (1929), as La Cieca in *La Gioconda,* one of her best-known roles; quickly became one of the Met's leading mezzo-sopranos, featured in US premiere of *Sadko* and taking over many roles from retiring Marion Telva; with a repertoire of over 25 operas, excelled in *Mignon* and *Carmen* but was also celebrated for performances in *Norma, Peter Ibbetson* and *La Forza del Destino;* spent much of late 1930s in Hollywood, appearing in such films as *Rose of the Rancho* (1936), *Give Us This Night* (1936), *To Have and to Hold* (1937) and *Romance in the Dark* (1938); found greatest fame on radio, singing on "Chase and Sanborn Hour," "Caravan," and "Ford Sunday Evening," and had her own program on WEAF in NYC; was named "#1 Female Singer of Classics" on radio for 5 successive years. ❖ See also memoirs, *Come Soon, Tomorrow* (1945); and *Women in World History.*

SWARTZ, Maud O'Farrell (1879–1937). Irish-born labor activist. Born May 3, 1879, in Co. Kildare, Ireland; died Feb 22, 1937, in New York, NY; dau. of William J. O'Farrell and Sarah Matilda (Grace) O'Farrell; m. Lee Swartz (printer), 1905 (sep.). ❖ Became secretary of National Women's Trade Union League (1916), then president (1922); became secretary of International Congress for Working Women (later International Federation of Working Women), 1919, then American vice-president; appointed secretary of New York State Department of Labor (1931), where she expanded its activities among female workers and served as referee in compensation cases.

SWAYNE-GORDON, Julia (1878–1933). See Gordon, Julia Swayne.

SWEDEN, queen of.
See Lathgertha (b. around 665).
See Astrid of the Obotrites (c. 979–?).
See Helen (fl. 1100s).
See Ulfhild (fl. 1112).
See Christina Stigsdottir (fl. 1160s).
See Richizza of Denmark (d. 1220).
See Sophie of Denmark (d. 1286).
See Martha of Denmark (c. 1272–1341).
See Hedwig of Holstein (d. 1325).
See Blanche of Namur (d. 1363).
See Philippa (1394–1430).
See Katarina of Saxe-Lüneburg (1513–1535).
See Margareta Leijonhufvud (1514–1551).
See Catherine Jagello (1525–1583).
See Katarina Stenbock (1536–1621).
See Anna of Styria (1573–1598).
See Christina of Holstein-Gottorp (1573–1625).

See Maria Eleonora of Brandenburg (1599–1655).
See Christina of Sweden (1626–1689).
See Hedwig of Holstein-Gottorp (1636–1715).
See Ulrica Eleanora of Denmark (1656–1693).
See Ulrica Eleanora (1688–1741).
See Louisa Ulrica of Prussia (1720–1782).
See Sophia of Denmark (1746–1813).
See Charlotte of Oldenburg (1759–1818).
See Désirée (1777–1860).
See Frederica Dorothea of Baden (1781–1826).
See Josephine Beauharnais (1807–1876).
See Louise of the Netherlands (1828–1871).
See Sophia of Nassau (1836–1913).
See Victoria of Baden (1862–1930).
See Louise Mountbatten (1889–1965).
See Silvia Sommerlath (b. 1943).

SWEDEN, regent of. See Margaret I of Denmark (1353–1412).

SWEENEY, Mrs. See Margaret (d. 1993), duchess of Argyll.

SWEENY, Violet Pooley (1886–1965). See Pooley, Violet.

SWEET, Blanche (1895–1986). American silent-film actress. Born June 18, 1895, in Chicago, IL; died Sept 6, 1986, in New York, NY; dau. of theatrical parents; m. Marshall "Mickey" Neilan (director), 1922 (div. 1929); m. Raymond Hackett (actor), 1936 (died 1958). ❖ One of the earliest and greatest silent actresses, began stage career as a small child and was a seasoned veteran by the time she began her film career (1909); worked for Biograph in Manhattan and, along with Mary Pickford, became D. W. Griffith's 1st major dramatic star; played feisty, determined heroines, most memorably in 2 of Griffith's landmark films, *The Lonedale Operator* (1911) and *Judith of Bethulia* (1913); joined Famous Players-Lasky (c. 1915), to star for Cecil B. De Mille and work for 1st husband; made over 70 films, but her best performances were in the title role of the 1st screen adaptation of *Anna Christie* (1923) and in *Tess of the D'Urbervilles* (1924); made only 3 "talkies" (1930) before retiring to a successful vaudeville career; had brief comeback in some small movie roles (late 1950s). ❖ See also *Women in World History.*

SWEET, Rachel (1963—). American singer. Born 1963 in Akron. OH; m. Tom Palmer, 1997; children: 2. ❖ At 5, won talent contest in Akron, and went on to appear in tv commercials and at club shows with Mickey Rooney and Bill Cosby; released debut album, *Fool Around* (1979); while in high school, had minor hit with "Who Does Lisa Like?"; other albums include *Protect the Innocent* (1980), *. . . And Then He Kissed Me* (1981), and *Blame It on Love* (1982); appeared in films *Sing* (1989), *Gypsy* (1993) and *The Investigator* (1994); hosted own tv show, "The Sweet Life" (1989–90); became voice of animated Barbie.

SWEET, Winifred (1863–1936). See Black, Winifred Sweet.

SWENSON, May (1913–1989). American poet. Born May 28, 1913; died at Bethany Beach, Delaware, Dec 4, 1989; dau. of Dan Arthur Swenson and Margaret (Hellberg) Swenson, members of a Mormon family of Swedish immigrants, in Logan, Utah; attended Utah State Agricultural College (later Utah State University), 1930–34; never married; lived with Rozanne R. Knudson (1967–89); no children. ❖ Major poet who presented much of her imaginative and sensual poetry using vivid visual patterns; moved to NY (1936); had initial stay at Yaddo writers' colony (1950); published highly successful 1st volume of poetry, *Another Animal* (1954); served as editor at New Directions Press (1956–66); published *A Cage of Spines,* her 2nd collection of verse (1958); received Amy Lowell fellowship for travel in Europe (1960); was poet-in-residence at Purdue University (1966–67); wrote and delivered Phi Beta Kappa poem at Harvard University commencement ceremony (1982); gave Theodore Roethke reading at University of Washington (1989); over course of career, wrote prose, translations, and published 450 poems in 11 volumes, including *To Mix with Time* (1963), *Poems to Solve* (1966), *Half Sun Half Sleep* (1967), *Iconographs* (1970), *In Other Words* (1987), *The Love Poems of May Swenson* (1991) and *Nature* (1994). Elected to National Institute of Arts and Letters (1970); received Bollingen Prize in Poetry from Yale University (1981) and MacArthur Foundation fellowship (1987). ❖ See also R. R. Knudson and Suzanne Bigelow, *May Swenson: A Poet's Life in Photos* (Utah State U. Press, 1996); and *Women in World History.*

SWETCHINE, Anne Sophie (1782–1857). Russian mystic, writer, and salonnière. Name variations: Madame Swetchine. Pronunciation: SVYEE-chen. Born Anne Sophie Soymanof, Soymonoff, or Soymanov in Moscow, Russia, 1782; died 1857; m. General Swetchine, 1799. ❖ Came under influence of Joseph de Maistre and converted to Roman Catholicism (1815); settling in Paris (1816), fostered her religious leanings by maintaining a private chapel (a rare Church indulgence) and a salon famed not only for its courtesy and brilliance but for its spiritual atmosphere; her *Life and Works*, marked by mysticism, was published posthumously by M. de Falloux in 2 vols. (1860), followed by 2 vols. of her *Letters* (1861).

SWETT, Jane (b. 1805). American murderer. Born 1805; m. Charles Swett (Baptist minister). ❖ In Maine, killed husband of 30 years (Sept 23, 1866), by mixing morphine into his whiskey; received 6-year prison sentence.

SWIATOWIAK, Izabela (1968—). *See Dylewska, Izabella.*

SWIEBEL, Joke (1941—). Dutch politician. Born Nov 28, 1941, in Den Haag, Netherlands. ❖ Served as head of political sciences library, University of Amsterdam (1972–77), executive official, Ministry of Culture, Recreation and Social Work (1977–82), executive official, Ministry of Social Affairs and Employment (1982–99), and vice-chair of the UN Commission on the Status of Women (1992–93); as a European Socialist, elected to 5th European Parliament (1999–2004).

SWIFT, Anne (1829/35–?). New Zealand prostitute. Name variations: Anne Carte. Born c. 1829–1835, probably in Lancashire, England; children: 2. ❖ Arrived in Canterbury, New Zealand, as a free immigrant (1867); refused situation as servant upon arrival and was officially considered a prostitute (1867); sent to Auckland (1868), where she had a child with a man named Massey; had another child, calling herself Carte (1870); appeared in Auckland police records as late as 1895. ❖ See also *Dictionary of New Zealand Biography* (Vol. 1).

SWIFT, Delia (fl. 1850s). American murderer. Name variations: Bridget Fury. Possibly born in Cincinnati, Ohio. ❖ Reportedly became prostitute at age 12 in Cincinnati; known as Bridget Fury, worked in Mary Jane (Bricktop) Jackson's brothel in New Orleans' French Quarter, and was noted for her violence; sentenced to life imprisonment for the 1858 axe-murder of customer who wouldn't meet her price.

SWIFT, Jane M. (1965—). American politician. Born Feb 24, 1965, in Massachusetts; m. Charles Hunt; children: 3. ❖ A Republican, was lieutenant governor of Massachusetts; became acting governor (April 2001), with the resignation of Governor Paul Cellucci; as the 1st woman to be governor of MA, was also the 1st governor to give birth while in office (May 15, 2001), with the arrival of twins; in the face of poor poll ratings and a tough primary challenge from Republican Mitt Romney, dropped out of the race for governor (2002).

SWINBURNE, Nora (1902–2000). English stage and screen actress. Name variations: Elinor Johnson; Elnora B. Johnson. Born Elinore Johnson, July 24, 1902, in Bath, England; died May 1, 2000, in London; m. Francis Lister (div.); m. Edward Ashley-Cooper (div.); m. Esmond Knight (actor), 1946 (died 1987). ❖ Made London debut in *Paddly Pools* (1916), followed by *Suzette, Yes Uncle, Scandal, Tilly of Bloomsbury* (title role), *The Bat, In the Next Room, The Best People, Outward Bound, Fame, Murder on the Second Floor, The 9th Man, Dodsworth, Lot's Wife, Dear Brutus, A Month in the Country, Watch on the Rhine, The Years Between, A Woman of No Importance* and *Music at Midnight*, among others; made NY debut in *The Mountebank* (1923); films include *Conspiracy of Hearts, Decision at Midnight, A Man Could Get Killed, Interlude, Anne of the 1,000 Days, Quo Vadis?* (as Pomponia), *Betrayed* and *Helen of Troy* (as Hecuba).

SWINDLER, Mary Hamilton (1884–1967). American archaeologist. Born Mary Hamilton Swindler, Jan 3, 1884, in Bloomington, IN; died Jan 16, 1967, in Haverford, PA; dau. of Harrison T. Swindler and Ida Hamilton Swindler; University of Indiana at Bloomington, AB, 1905, AM in Greek, 1906; Bryn Mawr College, PhD, 1912; never married. ❖ One of the most influential classical archaeologists in the US, began teaching at Bryn Mawr College (1906), where she remained nearly all her life, helping to make it a distinguished archaeological center (1906); became a professor of classical archaeology (1931); wrote *Ancient Painting* (1929); was the 1st woman editor-in-chief of *American Journal of Archaeology* (1932–46); was a fellow of both the Royal Society of the Arts, London, and the German Archaeological Institute. ❖ See also *Women in World History*.

SWINFEN, Lady (1912–2002). *See Wesley, Mary.*

SWINFORD, Catherine (c. 1350–1403). *See Swynford, Catherine.*

SWING OUT SISTER. *See Drewery, Corinne.*

SWIRSKAYA, Tamara. *See De Swirska, Tamara.*

SWISSHELM, Jane Grey (1815–1884). American newspaper publisher, abolitionist and suffragist. Name variations: Jane Grey Cannon. Born Dec 6, 1815, in Wilkensburg, near Pittsburgh, PA; died in Pennsylvania, 1884; dau. of Thomas Cannon and Marcy (Scott) Cannon; m. James Swisshelm, 1836 (div. 1857); children: Mary Henrietta Swisshelm (b. 1851). ❖ Feisty and outspoken, began career in journalism by contributing stories, poems and articles to Philadelphia and Pittsburgh newspapers; launched her own paper, the *Saturday Visiter* [sic], in Pittsburgh (1848); came to national attention with her editorials supporting the abolitionist cause; also published practical advice and advocated equal education and property rights for women, though she resisted affiliation with any of the suffrage movement's organizations; hired by Horace Greeley, editor of the *New York Daily Tribune*, became the 1st woman correspondent in Washington, representing both his paper and her own; on discovering that women were barred from the Senate Press Gallery (1850), successfully campaigned for equal rights for women reporters; left husband and moved to Minnesota (1857), where she began publishing another anti-slavery paper, *St. Cloud Visitor*, later relaunched as *St. Cloud Democrat*; in Washington, started a 3rd newspaper (1865), *Reconstructionist*. ❖ See also memoir, *Reminiscences of Half a Century* (1880); and *Women in World History*.

SWITZER, Kathy (1947—). American marathon runner. Name variations: Kathy Miller. Born Kathrine Virginia Switzer, Jan 5, 1947; attended Lynchburg College; Syracuse University, BA, 1968, MS, 1972; m. Tom Miller (hammer thrower). ❖ Because of the 100-year "no women allowed" rule in the Boston Marathon, registered for the race as K. V. Switzer and kept running to the finish (1967), though an official tried to stop her, thus helping to pave the way for women to enter the premiere event (1972); won the New York City Marathon with a time of 3:07:29 (1974). Inducted into National Distance Runner Hall of Fame.

SWITZER, Mary E. (1900–1971). American government official. Born Mary Elizabeth Switzer, Feb 16, 1900, in Newton Upper Falls, MA; died Oct 16, 1971, in Washington, DC; dau. of Julius F. Switzer and Margaret (Moore) Switzer; Radcliffe College, AB in international law, 1921; never married; no children; lifelong companion of Isabella Stevenson Diamond. ❖ Served as executive secretary of the Women's International League for Peace and Freedom, then entered the federal civil service; became a junior economist in Treasury Department (1922); assigned to oversee the US Public Health Service (1934); helped consolidate health and welfare programs into the Federal Security Agency (FSA), which later became the Department of Health, Education and Welfare and is now the Department of Health and Human Services; helped set up World Health Organization; appointed director of Office of Vocational Rehabilitation (OVR, 1950), one of the highest positions then given to a woman in the federal government; transformed the program by including in its ranks those with severe disabilities who would have been rejected for rehabilitation prior to her tenure, including those with mental illnesses or retardation; successfully campaigned for the landmark Vocational Rehabilitation Act (1954). Received the President's Certificate of Merit and Albert Lasker Award (1960). ❖ See also *Women in World History*.

SWOOPES, Sheryl (1971—). African-American basketball player. Born Mar 25, 1971, in Brownsfield, TX; attended South Plains Junior College; graduate of Texas Tech in Lubbock; m. Eric Jackson. ❖ Forward; led Texas Tech Lady Rangers to NCAA championship (1993), setting an NCAA record for most points scored by any basketball player (47) in Final Four history; won a team gold medal at Atlanta Olympics (1996), Sydney Olympics (2000) and Athens Olympics (2004); was a founding player in the Women's National Basketball Association (WNBA); led the Houston Comets to 3 straight WNBA championships beginning with the inaugural season (1997). Was the 1st woman to have her own athletic shoe named for her (Nike "Air Swoopes"); named WNBA Most Valuable Player (2000, 2002, 2005) and WNBA Defensive Player (2000, 2002, 2003). ❖ See also Christina Lessa, *Women Who Win* (Universe, 1998); and *Women in World History*.

SWORD, Catherine Campbell (1881–1957). *See Stewart, Catherine Campbell.*

SWYNFORD, Catherine (c. 1350–1403). Duchess of Lancaster. Name variations: Katherine Rouet; Catherine de Ruet or Catherine de Roet; Katherine Swynford. Born c. 1350; died May 10, 1403; interred at

Lincoln Cathedral; dau. of Sir Payne Roelt (a knight from Hainault, France, who arrived in England with the train of Edward III's queen Philippa of Hainault); sister of Philippa RoUet who m. Geoffrey Chaucer (the poet); m. Sir Hugh Swynford of Lincolnshire (d. 1372), c. 1367; was mistress, as of 1388, before becoming 3rd wife of John of Gaunt, duke of Lancaster, Jan 13, 1396; children: (1st m.) Thomas (c. 1368–1433, friend and companion of Henry IV and supposed murderer of Richard II); Blanche Swynford (b. around 1370); (2nd m.) 4, all of whom were born before the marriage but were declared legitimate in 1396 and 1397: John Beaufort (c. 1373–1410), earl of Somerset; Henry (1375–1447); Cardinal Beaufort (b. around 1375); Thomas (c. 1377–1426), earl of Dorset and chancellor of England; Joan Beaufort (c. 1379–1440). ❖ Catherine Swynford's children took the name Beaufort from one of her husband's castles in Anjou.

SYAMOUR (1857–1945). *See Gagneur, Marguerite.*

SYBIL (fl. 1030). *See Elflaed.*

SYBIL OF CONVERSANO (d. 1103). Duchess of Normandy. Name variations: Sybilla. Died in Feb 1103 at Rouen, France; buried at Caen Cathedral, Normandy, France; dau. of Geoffrey, count of Conversano; m. Robert II (some cite III) Curthose (c. 1054–1134), duke of Normandy (r. 1087–1106), in 1100, in Apulia, Italy; children: William III the Clito (1101–1128), count of Flanders (r. 1127–1128); Henry of Normandy (b. 1102).

SYBILLA (d. 1122). Queen of Scots. Born c. 1092, in Domfront, Normandy; died July 12, 1122, at Loch Tay, Scotland; buried at Dunfermline Abbey, Fife, Scotland; illegitimate dau. of Henry I, king of England (r. 1100–1135), and Sybilla Corbert; m. Alexander I (1078–1124), king of Scots (r. 1107–1124), around 1107; children: Malcolm, earl of Ross (b. around 1110).

SYBILLA OF ANJOU (1112–1165). Countess of Boulogne. Name variations: Sybilla de Gatinais; Sybil of Anjou; countess of Flanders (very briefly). Born in 1112 (some sources cite 1114 or 1116); died in 1165 at the Abbey of St. Lazarus, in Bethlehem, Israel; interred at the abbey; dau. of Fulk V the Younger, count of Anjou and king of Jerusalem, and Ermentrude (d. 1126), countess of Maine; m. William III the Clito (1101–1128), count of Flanders (r. 1127–1128), in 1123 (annulled 1124); m. Theodore of Alsace, count of Flanders, in 1134; children: (2nd m.) Philip of Alsace, count of Flanders (r. 1157–1191); Matthew I, count of Boulogne (d. 1173); Margaret of Alsace (c. 1135–1194). Eventually, Sybilla took the veil in the Abbey of St. Lazarus in Bethlehem. William III the Clito's 2nd wife was Joan of Montferrat (d. 1127).

SYBILLA OF BRANDENBURG (fl. 1500). Duchess of Juliers. Fl. around 1500; m. William III (or IV), duke of Juliers (Jülich) and Berg; children: Maria of Julich-Berg (mother of Anne of Cleves).

SYBILLA OF CLEVES (1514–1554). Sister of Anne of Cleves. Born in 1514; died in 1554; dau. of John III, duke of Cleves (r. 1521–1539), and Maria of Julich-Berg; sister of Anne of Cleves (who m. Henry VIII, king of England); m. John Frederick I, elector of Saxony.

SYBILLA OF SAXE-COBURG-GOTHA (1908–1972). Duchess of Westerbotten. Name variations: Sibylla; Sibylla Saxe-Coburg; princess Wettin. Born Sybilla Calma Mary Alice Bathildis Feodore, Jan 18, 1908, in Gotha, Thuringia, Germany; died Nov 28, 1972, in Stockholm, Sweden; dau. of Charles Edward Saxe-Coburg, 2nd duke of Albany, and Victoria Adelaide of Schleswig-Holstein (1885–1970); m. Gustav Adolphus, duke of Westerbotten, on Oct 19, 1932; children: Margaret Bernadotte (b. 1934, who m. John Ambler); Birgitta of Sweden (b. 1937, who m. Johann Georg of Hohenzollern); Desiree Bernadotte (b. 1938, who m. Niclas Silferschiöld); Christina Bernadotte (b. 1943); Charles also known as Carl XVI Gustavus (b. 1946), king of Sweden (r. 1973—).

SYDOR, Alison (1966—). Canadian mountain biker. Born Alison Jane Sydor, Sept 9, 1966, in Edmonton, Alberta, Canada. ❖ Won World Cup cross-country (1990); won Canadian National road race championships (1993, 1994) and MTB championships (1994–98); won World MTB championships (1994, 1995, 1996); won Pan American Games (1995); won a silver medal for cross-country at Atlanta Olympics (1996). Named Canadian Female Athlete of the Year and Velonews International Cyclist of the Year (1996).

SYDNEY, Margaret (1917–2004). *See Jefferis, Barbara.*

SYDOW, Madame (1758–1800). *See Monbart, Marie-Joséphine de Lescun.*

SYERS, Madge Cave (1881–1917). English figure skater. Name variations: Madge Syers-Cave. Born Florence Madeline Cave, 1881, in England; died Sept 1917, age 35; m. Edgar W. Syers (her coach, 1863–1946). ❖ With husband-coach Edgar Syers, won the 1st English National pairs competition (1899); entered the all-male World championship (1902), placing 2nd to Ulrich Salchow, causing officials to ban women from the competition until 1906, when a separate competition was held; won the 1st singles championship in Britain (1903) and defended her title against her husband (1904); won the World championship for women (1906, 1907); won a figure-skating gold medal for singles and a bronze for pairs with Edgar Syers at London Olympics (1908).

SYKES, Bobbi (1943—). Australian poet and Aboriginal-rights activist. Name variations: Roberta Sykes. Born 1943 in Townsville, Queensland, Australia. ❖ Was 1st Aborigine to receive PhD from Harvard and 1st Aboriginal columnist of *Nation Review*; participated in Aborigine movement, co-founded Redfern Aboriginal Medical Service, and became first secretary of Aboriginal Tent Embassy representing Aboriginal land claims; also co-founded Black Women's Action Group; writings include *Love Poems and Other Revolutionary Actions* (1979), *Snake Cradle* (1997), *Snake Dancing* (1998), and *Snake Circle* (2001); nonfiction includes *Black Power in Australia* (1975), *Incentive, Achievement and Community* (1986), *Black Majority* (1989), *Eclipse* (1996). Awarded Australian Human Rights Medal (1994).

SYKES, Mrs. (1839–1909). *See Logan, Olive.*

SYKOROVA, Marie (1952—). Czech field-hockey player. Born Nov 18, 1952. ❖ At Moscow Olympics, won a silver medal in team competition (1980).

SYLPHE, La. *See La Sylphe.*

SYLVA, Carmen (1843–1916). *See Elizabeth of Wied.*

SYLVAIN, Louise (1883–1970). *See Sylvie.*

SYLVIA (1756–1780). *See Smith, Anna Young.*

SYLVIE (1883–1970). French stage and screen character actress. Name variations: Louise Sylvie; Madame Sylvie; Louise Silvain. Born Louise Mainquéne, Jan 3, 1883, in Paris, France; died Jan 5, 1970, in Compiègne, Oise, Picardie, France; dau. of Louise (Morel) and M. Mainquéne; studied at the Conservatoire under M. Silvain. ❖ Made stage debut at the Odéon as Agnes in *École des femmes* (1902), followed by *Resurrection, Les Appeleurs, Madame Scarron, Son Père, La flamme, Jacques Aban, Diane de Poitiers, Les Corbeaux, Troilus et Cressida, La foi, Faust, Un Grand Bourgeois, Monsieur Brotonneau,* and *La Possession*; films include *Crime et châtiment* (as Catherine Ivanova), *Un Carnet de Bal, Le Corbeau, Nous sommes tous des assassins, Thérèse Raquin* and *La vieille dame indigne* (*The Shameless Old Lady*, 1965).

SYLVIE, Louise (1883–1970). *See Sylvie.*

SYLWAN, Kari (1959—). Swedish ballet dancer and actress. Born Oct 15, 1940 in Stockholm, Sweden. ❖ Joined Royal Swedish Ballet (1959), where she was best known for performances of powerful women in works by Birgit Cullberg, including Eve in *Eden*, Elida in *The Lady from the Sea*, and title role in *Miss Julie*; became a charter member of Cullberg's company (c. 1965); on film, appeared as Anna in Ingmar Bergman's *Cries and Whispers* (1972).

SYMBORSKA, Wislawa (b. 1923). *See Szymborska, Wislawa.*

SYMS, Nancy Roth (1939—). American golfer. Born Mar 30, 1939, in Elkhart, IN. ❖ Five-time winner of Florida state championship (1961–68); won Doherty Challenge (1963, 1964, 1966), North and South (1963, 1966), Southern Amateur (1964), Eastern Women's Amateur (1963–65), and Broadmoor (1972, 1975); won British Women's Amateur (1975); member of Curtis Cup team (1964, 1966, 1976), and non-playing captain (1980). Inducted into Colorado Golf Hall of Fame.

SYMS, Sylvia (1916–1992). American stage actress and singer. Born Sylvia Blagman, Dec 13, 1916, in Brooklyn, NY; died May 10, 1992, in New York, NY. ❖ Noted nightclub performer, made Broadway debut in *Diamond Lil* (1949), followed by *Dream Girl, South Pacific, Whoop Up,* and *Camino Real*; often confused with British actress Sylvia Syms (1934—).

SYMS, Sylvia (1934—). English actress. Born Jan 6, 1934, in London, England; m. Alan Edney, 1956 (div. 1989); children: 2, including Beatie

Edney (b. 1962, actress). ❖ Films include *My Teenage Daughter, The Moonraker, Expresso Bongo, Conspiracy of Hearts, The World of Suzie Wong, East of Sudan, Operation Crossbow, Hostile Witness, The Desperados, Run Wild Run Free, Born to Win, Asylum, Shirley Valentine, Shining Through* and *What a Girl Wants*; on tv, appeared on "Nancy Astor," "Natural Lies," "Peak Practice" and "At Home with the Braithwaites"; often confused with American singer Sylvia Syms (1916–1992). Nominated for British Academy Awards for *Woman in a Dressing Gown* (1957), *No Trees in the Street* (1958) and *The Tamarind Seed* (1974).

SYNADENE OF BYZANTIUM (c. 1050–?). Queen of Hungary. Born Sophia or Zsofia. Born c. 1050; death date unknown; m. Geza I, king of Hungary (r. 1074–1077); children: Coloman or Koloman (1070–1114), king of Hungary (r. 1095–1114); Almos, duke of Croatia (who m. Ingeborg of Sweden).

SYNNOEVE, Hilde. *See Lid, Hilde Synnove.*

SYNTYCHE. Biblical woman. Pronunciation: SIN-tih-keh. ❖ A member of the church of Philippi, possibly a deaconess, got into an argument with Euodia, at which time the apostle Paul beseeched them to "be of the same mind in the Lord."

SYREETA (1946–2004). *See Wright, Syreeta.*

SYRIA, queen of.
See Laodice I (c. 285–c. 236 BCE).
See Mavia (c. 350–c. 430 CE).

SYRO-PHOENICIAN. Biblical woman. Pronunciation: sigh-row feh-KNEE-shun. ❖ Gentile from Phoenicia, brought her afflicted daughter to Jesus to be healed; was tested by his silence, refusal, and reproach, but stood firm in her faith, and her petition was granted.

SZABO, Ecaterina (1966—). Romanian gymnast. Name variations: Kati Szabo; Ekaterina Szabo. Born Jan 22, 1966, in Zagon, Romania; m. Christian Tamas (rower), 1991. ❖ Won Jr. European championships (1980, 1982), Chunichi Cup (1980), Ennia Cup (1982), Romanian International (1983, 1985), Balkan championships (1984), and Europeans (1987); at Los Angeles Olympics, won a silver medal in indiv. all-around and gold medals in balance beam, team all-around, floor exercises, and vault (1984); at World championships, won a team gold (1987); retired (1987) and turned to coaching. Inducted into International Gymnastics Hall of Fame (2000).

SZABO, Gabriela (1975—). Romanian runner. Born Nov 14, 1975, in Bistrita, Romania. ❖ Won a silver medal for 1,500 meters at Atlanta Olympics (1996); won a gold medal for 5,000 meters and a bronze for 1,500 meters at Sydney Olympics (2002); at World championships, won gold medals for the 5,000 meters (1997, 1999, 2001); at Europeans, won silver medals for the 5,000 (1998) and 1,500 (2002).

SZABÓ, Herma (1902–1986). *See Planck-Szabó, Herma.*

SZABÓ, Magda (1917—). Hungarian novelist and poet. Name variations: Magda Szabo. Born 1917 in Debrecen, Hungary; received teacher's diploma from Lajos Kossuth University; m. Tibor Szobotka. ❖ Regarded as one of most important Hungarian writers after WWII, 1st worked as a teacher and for the ministry of education; won Prix Femina Roman du Roman Étranger (2003); writings include *Freszkó* (1950, Fresco), *Az öz* (1959, The Fawn), *Disznótor* (1960, Night of the Pig-Killing), and *Az ajto* (1975, The Door); has been translated in over 30 languages. Won Attila Jozsef Prize (1959) and Lajos Kossuth Prize (1978).

SZABO, Reka (1967—). Romanian fencer. Name variations: Reka Zsofia Szabo-Lazar. Born Mar 11, 1967, in Pais, Romania. ❖ Won a bronze medal at Barcelona Olympics (1992) and a silver medal at Atlanta Olympics (1996), both for team foil.

SZABO, Szilvia (1978—). Hungarian kayaker. Name variations: Szilvia Szabó. Born Oct 24, 1978, in Hungary. ❖ Won a silver medal for K2 500 meters and K4 500 meters at Sydney Olympics (2000); at World championships, placed 1st for K4 200 and 500 (1999), K4 500 and 1000 and K2 500 (2001), K4 500 and 200, K2 500 and 1000 (2002), K4 200 and 500 and K2 500 (2003); won a silver medal for K4 500 at Athens Olympics (2004).

SZABO, Tünde (1974—). Hungarian swimmer. Name variations: Tuende or Tunde Szabo. Born May 31, 1974, in Hungary. ❖ At Barcelona Olympics, won a silver medal in 100-meter backstroke (1992).

SZABO, Violette (1921–1945). British secret agent. Name variations: (code name) Louise. Born Violette Reine Elizabeth Bushell (some sources cite Bushnell), June 26, 1921 (some sources cite 1918), in Paris, France; executed at Ravensbrück concentration camp sometime between Jan 25 and Feb 5, 1945 (some sources cite Jan 26); dau. of Charles Bushell (Englishman who operated a fleet of tourist taxis) and a French mother (name unknown); m. Etienne Michel René Szabo (French soldier), Aug 1940 (killed in action, Oct 24, 1942); children: daughter Tania (b. June 8, 1942). ❖ British secret agent in France during WWII, who single-handedly held off a Nazi SS infantry regiment so her partner, a local leader of the Maquis, could escape with information important to the Allies; was captured and sent to Paris for interrogation; though tortured in Nazi prisons, never revealed the identity of any of her contacts; was sent with 2 other women agents to Ravensbrück concentration camp in Germany, where all 3 were executed. Awarded the George Cross for courage, for her work in Normandy and around Limoges (1946); awarded the Croix de Guerre (1947). ❖ See also R. J. Minney, *Carve Her Name with Pride* (London, 1956) and film *Carve Her Name with Pride*, starring Virginia McKenna as Szabo (1958); and *Women in World History*.

SZABO-ORBAN, Olga (1938—). Romanian fencer. Name variations: Olga Orban. Born Oct 9, 1938, in Romania. ❖ At Melbourne Olympics, won a silver medal in indiv. foil (1956); at Mexico City Olympics, won a bronze medal in team foil (1968); at Munich Olympics, won a bronze medal in team foil (1972).

SZALAY HORVATHNE, Gyongyi. Hungarian fencer. Name variations: Gyöngyi or Gyoengyi Szalay-Horvathne; Gyongyi Szalay. Born in Hungary. ❖ Won a bronze medal for indiv. épée at Atlanta Olympics (1996).

SZANTO, Anna. Hungarian handball player. Born in Hungary. ❖ Won a team bronze medal at Atlanta Olympics (1996).

SZANTON, Beatrice. *See Tobey, Beatrice.*

SZARVADY, Wilhelmine Clauss (1834–1907). *See Clauss-Szárvady, Wilhelmina.*

SZASZ, Barbara Maria (1841–1916). *See Baker, Florence von Sass.*

SZATKOWSKA, Zofia or Zofdja de (1890–1968). *See Kossak, Zofia.*

SZCZEPANSKA, Aneta (1972—). Polish judoka. Name variations: Szczepanska-Rosiak or Rosiak-Szczepanska. Born in 1972 in Poland. ❖ Won a silver medal for 61–66 kg middleweight at Atlanta Olympics (1996).

SZCZERBINSKA, Halina (1900–1989). *See Konopacka, Halina.*

SZCZERBINSKA-KROLOWA, Lidia (1935—). Polish gymnast. Name variations: Lidia Król; Lidia Szczerbinska-Krol; Lidia Krolowa. Born 1935 (some sources cite 1934) in Poland. ❖ At Melbourne Olympics, won a bronze medal in teams all-around, portable apparatus (1956).

SZCZESNIEWSKA, Zofia (1943–1988). Polish volleyball player. Born Aug 31, 1943; died Dec 1988. ❖ Won a bronze medal at Tokyo Olympics (1964) and a bronze medal at Mexico City Olympics (1968), both in team competition.

SZCZEPINSKA, Czeslawa (1959—). *See Koscianska, Czeslawa.*

SZCZUCKA, Zofia (1890–1968). *See Kossak, Zofia.*

SZÉCHENYI, Countess (1886–1965). *See Vanderbilt, Gladys Moore.*

SZEKELY, Eva (1927—). Hungarian swimmer. Born April 3, 1927, in Hungary. ❖ Won a gold medal at Helsinki Olympics (1952) and a silver medal at Melbourne Olympics (1956), both in 200-meter breaststroke.

SZEKELY, Violeta (1965—). *See Beclea-Szekely, Violeta.*

SZEKELYNE-MARVALICS, Gyorgyi (1924—). Hungarian fencer. Name variations: Gyorgyi Marvalics. Born Dec 1924 in Hungary. ❖ At Rome Olympics, won a silver medal in team foil (1960).

SZENES, Chana (1921–1944). *See Senesh, Hannah.*

SZENES, Katalin (b. 1899). Mother of Hannah Senesh. Name variations: Catherine, Kató, Catalin Szenes; Katalin Senesh. Born Katalin Salzberger in 1899; m. Béla (r.n. Schlesinger) Szenes (writer); children: Hannah Senesh (1921–1944); Gyuri (George, b. 1920). ❖ After fleeing a Nazi death march and a successful search for the grave of her daughter (1945), narrowly made it through the closing borders of the new occupier of

Hungary: the Russians; made it to Palestine by way of Romania. ❖ See also *Women in World History*.

SZEWCZYK, Barbara (1970—). Polish fencer. Name variations: Barbara Szewczyk-Wolnicka or Wolnicka-Szewczyk. Born Barbara Szewczyk, 1970, in Poland. ❖ Won a silver medal for team foil at Sydney Olympics (2000).

SZEWINSKA, Irena (1946—). Polish-Jewish track-and-field athlete. Name variations: Irene Kirszenstein; Irena Kirszenstein-Szewinska; Irena Szewinska-Kirszenstein. Born Irena Kirszenstein, May 24, 1946, in Leningrad (now St. Petersburg), Russia; m. Junusz Szewinski (runner who became her coach), 1967. ❖ Won medals at 4 Olympics, a feat no man or woman had ever accomplished: won silver in long jump, silver in 200 meters, gold in 4 x 100-meter relay at Tokyo Olympics (1964), won bronze in 100 meters, gold in 200 meters at Mexico City Olympics (1968), won bronze in 200 meters at Munich Olympics (1972), won gold in 400 meters at Montreal (1976); became the 1st woman to break 50 seconds in the 400 meters, breaking tape at 49.9 seconds (1974); at European championships, won gold medals in the 200 meters, long jump, and 400-meter relay as well as a silver medal in the 100 meters (1966), a bronze medal in the 200 meters (1971) and gold medals in the 100- and 200-meters (1974); won the 400 meters at the World championships in 49.0 seconds, a new world record (1977).

SZILAGYI, Katalin. Hungarian handball player. Born in Hungary. ❖ Won a team bronze medal at Atlanta Olympics (1996).

SZOCS, Zsuzsanna (1962—). Hungarian fencer. Born April 10, 1962, in Hungary. ❖ Won a bronze medal at Moscow Olympics (1980) and a bronze medal at Seoul Olympics (1988), both in team foil.

SZOKE, Katalin (1935—). Hungarian swimmer. Born Aug 17, 1935, in Hungary. ❖ At Helsinki Olympics, won a gold medal in 4 x 100-meter freestyle relay and a gold medal in 100-meter freestyle (1952).

SZOLD, Henrietta (1860–1945). American-Jewish Zionist and founder. Pronunciation: Zold. Born Henrietta Szold, Dec 21, 1860, in Baltimore, MD; died Feb 13, 1945, in Palestine; dau. of Benjamin Szold (rabbi of Oheb Shalom Congregation, Baltimore, MD) and Sophie Schaar Szold; attended Jewish Theological Seminary, NY, 1902–05; never married. ❖ Fiercely practical founder of Hadassah, the Women's Zionist Organization of America, who established a comprehensive network of public health services in pre-Israel Palestine; became a Baltimore correspondent for *New York Jewish Messenger* (1877); taught at Misses Adams' French and English School for Girls, Baltimore (1878–92); worked as editor and translator, Jewish Publication Society of America (1888–1916); founded Russian night school, Baltimore (1889–93); was a founding member of Zionist Association of Baltimore (1893); made 1st visit to Palestine (1909); was honorary secretary for Jewish Agricultural Station, Palestine, and Federation of American Zionists (1910); founded Hadassah, Women's Zionist Organization of America, NY (1912), and was president (1912–26); helped organize American Zionist Medical Unit (1916); was executive in charge of Health and Education, World Zionist Organization (1927–30); elected member of Vaad Leumi (General Jewish Council), Palestine (1931–33); served as director, Department of Social Welfare, Vaad Leumi, Palestine (1932–37); served as director, Youth Aliyah (1933–45); established Children's Foundation in Palestine (1941). ❖ See also Joan Dash, *Summoned to Jerusalem: The Life of Henrietta Szold* (Harper & Row, 1979); Alexandra Levin, *The Szolds of Lombard Street: A Baltimore Family, 1859–1909* (1960); Irving Fineman, *Woman of Valor: The Story of Henrietta Szold* (Simon & Schuster, 1961); Nachum T. Gidal, *Henrietta Szold: The Saga of an American Woman* (Gefen, 1996); and *Women in World History*.

SZOLNOKI, Maria (1947—). Hungarian fencer. Born June 16, 1947, in Hungary. ❖ At Munich Olympics, won a silver medal in team foil (1972).

SZÖNYI, Erzsebet (1924—). Hungarian composer, choral conductor, pianist, and lecturer. Name variations: Szonyi or Szoenyi. Born in Budapest, Hungary, April 25, 1924. ❖ Known worldwide for work in music education, studied at Liszt Academy with Janos Viski and Ernö Szegedi (1942–47); won a scholarship to Paris Conservatoire to study with Nadia Boulanger, Tony Aubin, and Olivier Messiaen, then won the conservatoire's prix de composition (1948); returned to Budapest and taught at Ferenc Liszt Academy, becoming director of its school of music (1960); also won the Liszt (1947) and Erkel (1959) prizes; began composing opera, beginning with *Dalma* (1952); a prolific composer with over 100 works for orchestra, voice, piano and theater, also composed works for children, such as the ballets *Garden Tale* (1949) and *The Cricket and the Ants* (1953); collaborated with Hungarian composer Zoltan Kodaly, in order to implement his ideas for music education in Hungary's schools; was soon known as an international expert on musical education for children; became supervisor of Hungarian music conservatories (1951) and served on board of directors of International Society for Music Education; also wrote several volumes translated into English, German, and Japanese about teaching music to young children. ❖ See also *Women in World History*.

SZUMIGALSKI, Anne (1922–1999). Canadian poet. Born 1922 in London, England; died 1999 in Canada. ❖ During WWII, served as interpreter, welfare officer and medical auxiliary; immigrated to Canada (1951) and helped found Saskatchewan Writer's Guild and the literary journal *Grain*; works include *Woman Reading in Bath* (1974), *A Game of Angels* (1980), *Risks* (1984), *Dogstones: Selected and New Poems* (1986), *Rapture of the Deep* (1991), and *On Glassy Wings: Poems, New and Selected* (1997); also wrote the play *Z: A Meditation on Oppression, Desire, and Freedom*. Received Governor General's Award for Poetry for *Voice* (1995).

SZUMOWSKA, Antoinette (1868–1938). Polish pianist. Born in Lublin, Poland, Feb 22, 1868; died in Rumson, NJ, Aug 18, 1938; began formal piano studies at the Warsaw Conservatory with Aleksander Michailowski; continued education with Ignace Jan Paderewski in Paris (1890–95); m. Joseph Adamowski (cellist), 1896. ❖ Made Paris debut (1891); settled in US (1895), where the bulk of her career was spent as pianist with the Adamowski Trio (whose cellist she married), a group that garnered a reputation for excellence in chamber music; also taught privately and at New England Conservatory. ❖ See also *Women in World History*.

SZWAJGER, Adina Blady (1917–1993). Polish-Jewish pediatrician and anti-Nazi activist. Born 1917 in Poland; died 1993 in Lodz, Poland. ❖ Revealed in her memoirs that during WWII, confined to the Warsaw Ghetto, she tried to ease the plight of sick children destined for concentration camps by feeding them fatal doses of morphine. ❖ See also memoir, *I Remember Nothing More: The Warsaw Children's Hospital and the Jewish Resistance* (1990).

SZYDLOWSKA, Irena (1928–1983). Polish archer. Born Jan 28, 1928, in Poland; died Aug 14, 1983. ❖ At Munich Olympics, won a silver medal in double FITA round (1972).

SZYMANOWSKA, Maria Agata (1789–1831). Polish composer, pianist, and teacher. Name variations: Szymanowski; Shimanovskaya. Born Maria Agata Wolowska in Warsaw, Poland, Dec 14, 1789; died of cholera in St. Petersburg, Russia, July 24, 1831; m. Theophilus Jozef Szymanowski (Polish landowner), 1810 (div. 1820); children: 3, including daughter Celina Szymanowska, who m. Adam Mickiewicz, the poet. ❖ Known especially for her nocturnes, was the 1st Polish pianist and composer to gain a European reputation; when husband did not support her concert career, left him, taking their 3 children (1820), and sustained her family through concerts and compositions; was one of Johann Wolfgang von Goethe's last passions (he wrote his *Aussöhnung* for her); appointed pianist to Russian imperial court (1822), won the admiration of Russian intellectuals, including poet Alexander Pushkin and composer Mikhail Glinka; as one of the 1st composers to use Polish dance forms such as the mazurka and polonaise as the basis for her compositions, had an enormous influence on the young Chopin. ❖ See also *Women in World History*.

SZYMBORSKA, Wislawa (1923—). Polish poet, essayist and translator. Name variations: Wisawa Szymborska; Wislava Symborska; (pseudonym) Stanczykowna. Pronunciation: Vee-SWAH-vah Shim-BOR-skah. Born July 2, 1923, in Prowent-Bnin, Poland; dau. of Wincenty Szymborski and Anna (Rottermund) Szymborska; attended schools in Cracow (Kraków); attended a Polish underground school during German occupation in WWII; granted an undergraduate degree from Jagiellonian University, Cracow; m. Adam Wlodek or Wodek (div.); m. Kornel Flipowicz (also seen as Filipowicz), a poet and prose writer (died 1990). ❖ One of the leading poets, and the leading woman poet, in post-WWII Poland, won the Nobel Prize for Literature (1996); published 1st poem in a supplement to *Dziennik Polski* (*Polish Daily*, 1945); published some 30 poems in the *Daily* (1945–48); worked on the staff of the literary newspaper *Życie Literackie* (*Literary Life*, 1952–81); was criticized for writing elitist poetry, in violation of Socialist Realism, when she attempted to publish her 1st book of poems (1948); accepted Stalinist-era Socialist Realism and criticized Western countries in *Dlatego żyjemy* (*That's Why We Live* (1952) and *Pytania zadawane sobie* (*Questioning*

Oneself, 1954); repudiated Socialist Realism in *Wolanie do Yeti* (*Calling Out to Yeti,* 1957); completely omitted pre-1956 poems from her collected works of poetry, *Poezje* (*Poetry,* 1970); emerged as a mature poet with *Sto pociech* (*A Hundred Laughs,* 1967); considered not only Poland's most eminent woman poet of the 20th century but also one of its three greatest poets of the century. Received Goethe Award (1991) and Polish PEN Poetry award (1996). ❖ See also *Women in World History.*

T

⟡

TAAFE, Alice (1899–1987). *See Terry, Alice.*

TABA, Hilda (1902–1967). Estonian-American educator. Born on Dec 7, 1902, in Estonia; died July 6, 1967, in Burlingame, California; dau. of Robert Taba (teacher and farmer) and Liisa (Leht) Taba; University of Tartu, Estonia, BA, 1926; Bryn Mawr College, MA, 1927; Columbia University, PhD, 1933. ❖ Appointed assistant professor at Ohio State University (1936) and at University of Chicago (1938); took a leave from University of Chicago (1945–48) to study intergroup relations from perspective of race, religion, and ethnic background; continued this work as director of the Center for Intergroup Education at University of Chicago (1948–51); appointed professor of education at San Francisco State College (1951), where she wrote her most important book, *Curriculum Development: Theory and Practice* (1962); published the Taba Program in Social Science, a series of textbooks for grades 1 through 8 (1970s); wrote or co-wrote nearly 2 dozen books; her pioneering work influenced those who followed her in the field of curriculum development. ❖ See also *Women in World History.*

TABAKOVA, Maja (1978—). Bulgarian rhythmic gymnast. Name variations: Maia Tabakova. Born May 11, 1978, in Bulgaria. ❖ Won a silver medal for team all-around at Atlanta Olympics (1996).

TABAKOVA, Yuliya (1980—). Russian runner. Born May 1, 1980, in Kaluga, USSR. ❖ Won a silver medal for 4 x 100-meter relay at Athens Olympics (2004).

TABANKIN, Margery Ann (c. 1948—). American activist. Born c. 1948 in Newark, NJ; graduate of University of Wisconsin–Madison, 1971. ❖ At 19, began activist career with anti-Vietnam War and civil-rights activities; became 1st woman president of National Student Association (NSA, 1971 or 1972); served as executive director of Youth Project of Volunteers in Service to America (VISTA, 1977–81), executive director of Arca Foundation, Washington, DC (1981–88), and executive director of Hollywood Women's Political Committee (HWPC, 1988–94); served as executive director of Steven Spielberg's Righteous Persons Foundation and of The Streisand Foundation. Produced documentary films *Village by Village; A Student's Journey to Vietnam* (1972) and *Heartstrings: Peter Paul & Mary in Central America* (1984).

TABBS (c. 610–c. 683). *See Ebba.*

TABEI, Junko (1939—). Japanese mountaineer. Born Junko Ishibashi in Miharu Machi, in the Fukushima prefecture, Japan, in 1939; graduate of Showa Women's College, Tokyo, 1962; m. Masanobu Tabei (mountaineer), 1959; children: daughter Noriko (b. 1972); son Shinya (b. 1978). ❖ With Rumie Saso, made 1st all-female ascent of Central Buttress on Tanigawa-Dake (1965); was the 1st woman to climb Mt. Everest (May 16, 1975). ❖ See also memoir *Everest Mother* (Shinco-Sha, 1982); and *Women in World History.*

TABER, Gladys (1899–1980). American writer. Born Gladys Leonae Bagg on April 12 (some sources cite April 24), 1899, in Colorado Springs, Colorado; died Mar 11, 1980, in Hyannis, Massachusetts; dau. of Rufus Mather Bagg and Grace Sibyl (Raybold) Bagg; Wellesley College, BA, 1920; Lawrence College, MA, 1921; graduate study at Columbia University, 1931–33; m. Frank Albion Taber Jr. (teacher), 1922; children: Constance Anne Taber. ❖ Taught English at Randolph Macon Women's College (1925–26) and creative writing at Columbia University (1936–43); published a collection of poetry, *Lyonnesse* (1926); with husband, children, sister and sister's 2 children, moved to Stillmeadow, a 17th-century farmhouse in the Connecticut countryside, which would become her inspiration for numerous books and articles about country living; publised 1st novel *Late Climbs the Sun* (1934), which was favorably reviewed; published *Harvest at Stillmeadow* (1940), her initial collection of essays on day-to-day country living, followed by *The Book of Stillmeadow* (1948) and *Stillmeadow Seasons* (1950); also

published books on such topics as raising cocker spaniels and flower arranging, as well as cookbooks, historical and romance novels, children's books, and a biography of her impetuous father, *Especially Father* (1949); in addition to contributing more than 200 short stories to periodicals in US and abroad, wrote "Diary of Domesticity" column for *Ladies' Home Journal* (1938–58), where she also served as an assistant editor (1946–58), and authored "Butternut Wisdom" column for *Family Circle.* ❖ See also autobiographies *Harvest of Yesterdays* (1976) and *Still Cove Journal* (1981); and *Women in World History.*

TABER, Mrs. Robert (1866–1950). *See Marlowe, Julia.*

TABITHA (fl. 37 CE). *See Dorcas.*

TABOUIS, Geneviève (1892–1985). French writer. Name variations: Genevieve Tabouis; Cassandra. Pronunciation: JAWN-vee-ev Tah-BOO-ee. Born Geneviève Rapatel Le Quesne, Feb 23, 1892, in Paris, France; died Sept 22, 1985, in Paris; dau. of Fernand Le Quesne (well-known artist) and a mother of the French upper class named Cambon; niece of Paul Cambon (diplomat) and Jules Cambon (French ambassador to Germany); spent 3 years at Sorbonne and School of Archaeology at the Louvre; m. Robert Tabouis (administrator of French radio), 1916; children: 1 daughter, 1 son. ❖ French columnist, one of the 1st women to achieve international distinction as a journalist, was read throughout Europe and America between WWI and WWII and despised by Hitler; gained favorable reputation for journalistic work (after 1924); became foreign news editor for French daily, *L'Oeuvre* (1932), and her columns were syndicated throughout Europe, UK and US; an idealist and realist, was a fighter for peace and an ardent supporter of League of Nations; in her writings, was one of the 1st voices raised against the threat of the growing movement in Germany known as National Socialism; throughout 1930s, as Adolf Hitler proceeded with systematic takeover of Germany, anticipated his actions in ways that sometimes disrupted his carefully laid plans; with Germany's invasion of France, escaped to US (1939); was tried for treason in absentia; wrote *Pour la Victoire,* the weekly French-language magazine she had founded in New York (1940–45); returned to Paris (1945); remained active in journalism until a late age; also wrote *Nebuchadnezzar, Private Life of Tutankhamen, Solomon, Blackmail or War, Perfidious Albion—Entente Cordiale,* and *A Life of Jules Cambon.* Made an Officier de la Légion d'honneur and awarded Commandeur de l'orde national du Mérite. ❖ See also memoirs, *They Called Me Cassandra* (1942) and *Vingt ans de 'suspense' diplomatique;* and *Women in World History.*

TACHE, Christin (1961—). *See Cooper, Christin.*

TACHIBANA, Miya (1974—). Japanese synchronized swimmer. Born Dec 12, 1974 in Kyoto, Japan; attended Doshisha University in Kyoto. ❖ Won a team bronze medal at Atlanta Olympics (1996) and silver medals for duet and team at Sydney Olympics (2000); at World championships, won a gold medal for duet (2001) and silver medals for team (1998, 2003) and duet (1994, 1998, 2003); placed 2nd for World Cup solo and duet in Zurich (2002); with Miho Takeda, won a silver medal for duet at Athens Olympics (2004), as well as a team silver medal.

TAE, Satoya (1976—). Japanese skier. Born June 12, 1976, in Japan. ❖ Won a gold medal in freestyle skiing at Nagano Olympics (1998), the 1st Japanese woman to win an Olympic gold medal in the Winter Games; won a bronze medal in freestyle skiing at Salt Lake City Olympics (2002).

TAEUBER, Irene Barnes (1906–1974). American demographer. Born Irene Barnes, Dec 25, 1906, in Meadville, Missouri; died Feb 24, 1974, in Hyattsville, Maryland; dau. of Ninevah D. Barnes (farmer and barber) and Lily (Keller) Barnes; University of Missouri, BA, 1927; Northwestern University, MA, 1928; University of Minnesota, PhD, 1931; m. Conrad Taeuber (demographer), 1929; children: Richard Conrad (b. 1933); Karl Ernst (b. 1936). ❖ The 1st woman president of the Population Association of America (PAA, 1953), coedited the Population Association of America's *Population Index*; joined Princeton University's Office of Population Research (1936) and was appointed senior research demographer (1961); coauthored 16 books and monographs on demography and population; published *The Population of Japan* (1958), a landmark demographic analysis; was 1st woman elected vice-president of International Union for the Scientific Study of Population (1961). ❖ See also *Women in World History*.

TAEUBER-ARP, Sophie (1889–1943). *See Tauber-Arp, Sophie.*

TAFOYA, Margaret (1904–2001). Tewa folkartist. Name variations: Corn Blossom. Born Maria Margarita Tafoya, Aug 13, 1904, in Santa Clara Pueblo, near Santa Fe, New Mexico; died Feb 25, 2001, in Santa Clara Pueblo; dau. of Sara Fina Gutierrez Tafoya, known as Autumn Leaf (Tewa potter), and Geronimo, known as White Flower; had 7 siblings, 4 of whom were also potters; m. Alcario Tafoya (professional cook), 1924; children: 6 daughters, 3 sons. ❖ Earned a global reputation for her black-on-black and red-on-red pottery; was the matriarch of the Santa Clara Pueblo potters; named folk artist of the year by National Endowment for the Arts (1984). ❖ See also Mary Ellen and Laurence Blair, *Margaret Tafoya: A Tewa Potter's Heritage and Legacy* (Schiffer, 1986).

TAFT, Helen Herron (1861–1943). American first lady. Name variations: Mrs. William Howard Taft; Nellie Taft. Born June 2, 1861, in Cincinnati, Ohio; died May 22, 1943, in Washington, DC; dau. of John Williamson Herron (lawyer) and Harriet (Collins) Herron; attended University of Cincinnati; m. William Howard Taft (1857–1930, 27th president of US), June 19, 1886; children: Robert Alphonso Taft (1889–1953, senator from Ohio); Helen Herron Taft Manning (1891–1987, president of Bryn Mawr College); Charles Phelps Taft (1897–1983, lawyer, civic leader, and mayor of Cincinnati). ❖ The primary force behind husband's political career, spent 4 years in Philippines while he headed a commission and was governor-general (1899–1904); though husband longed for a position on the Supreme Court, had eyes only for the White House; when a vacancy on the court appeared (1906), arranged a meeting with Theodore Roosevelt to discuss husband's future, and William was hand picked by Roosevelt to run for the presidency on the Republican ticket (1908); as first lady (1909–13), continued to influence his decisions, especially at the beginning of his term, and accompanied him on political trips; 2 months into her tenure, her influence in the White House was cut short by a debilitating stroke from which she never fully recovered. By far the most well received and permanent of Helen Taft's contributions to her nation was her plan to enhance Potomac Park with the planting of 3,500 cherry trees, which were donated by the mayor of Tokyo. ❖ See also *Women in World History*.

TAFT, Jessie (1882–1960). American psychologist and social services educator. Born Julia Jessie Taft, June 24, 1882, in Dubuque, Iowa; died June 7, 1960, in Philadelphia, Pennsylvania; dau. of Charles Chester Taft (wholesale fruit seller) and Amanda May (Farwell) Taft; Drake University, BA, 1904; University of Chicago, PhB, 1905, PhD, 1913; companion of Virginia Robinson (psychologist and writer), 1912–1960; children: (adopted) 2. ❖ Became director of Social Services Department of the New York State Charities Aid Association's Mental Hygiene Committee (1915), where she developed mental health programs for the state of NY and carried a caseload at New York Hospital Mental Hygiene Clinic; also established the Farm School in New Jersey for children who were having problems in school; in Philadelphia, was appointed director of Seybert Institution's Department of Child Study, a shelter for children awaiting placement (1918); met Otto Rank (1924) and underwent analysis with him (1926); appointed professor of social casework at Pennsylvania School of Social Work (later part of University of Pennsylvania, 1934), where she established the curriculum and influenced its practical philosophy, known as functionalism; wrote extensively about functionalism and its application to social work education, and published *The Dynamics of Therapy in a Controlled Relationship* (1933); also published a biography of Rank and a 2-vol. translation of his work. ❖ See also *Women in World History*.

TAFT, Mrs. Josiah (c. 1711–1778). *See Taft, Lydia.*

TAFT, Lydia (c. 1711–1778). American voter. Name variations: Mrs. Josiah Taft. Born c. 1711 in Mendon, MA; died Nov 9, 1778 in Uxbridge, MA; m. Captain Josiah Taft (died Sept 30, 1756); children: Josiah (b. 1733), Ebenezer (b. 1739), Caleb (b. 1738), Asahael (b. 1740), Joel (b. 1742), Bezaleel (b. 1750), Chloa (b. 1753). ❖ While taking the place of her minor son, voted for levying a town tax in Uxbridge, MA, casting the 1st recorded vote by a woman (1756).

TAGASKOUITA (1656–1680). *See Tekakwitha, Kateri.*

TAGGARD, Genevieve (1894–1948). American poet. Born in Washington state on Nov 28, 1894; died on Nov 8, 1948, in New York City; dau. of Alta Gale (Arnold) Taggard and James Nelson Taggard (both schoolteachers); graduated fromm the University of California at Berkeley in 1920; m. Robert L. Wolf (a writer), on Mar 21, 1921 (div. 1934); m. Kenneth Durant (who worked for Tass, the Soviet news agency), on Mar 10, 1935; children: (1st m.) Marcia Sarah Wolf (b. 1922). ❖ Though her poetry was well known in her time to both literary and popular audiences, now is best known as the author of *The Life and Mind of Emily Dickinson* (1930); in addition to poetry and scholarly work, wrote short stories, reviews, essays, and articles on poetic theory, and edited literary journals and anthologies; in prose work, was a tireless crusader for more involvement—in liberal causes, in art, in life; her 1st commitment was to the writing of poetry, however, and at her best, produced some fine poems containing imagery still vivid today; her best poetry, on art, woman's experience, and social injustice, has much in common with the work of later poets such as Sylvia Plath and especially Adrienne Rich. Writings include *For Eager Lovers* (1922), *Hawaiian Hilltop* (1923), *Words for the Chisel* (1926), *Travelling Standing Still: Poems, 1918–1928* (1928), *Monologue for Mothers (Aside)* (1929), *The Life and Mind of Emily Dickinson* (1930), *Remembering Vaughan in New England* (1933), *Not Mine to Finish: Poems 1928–1934* (1934), *Calling Western Union* (1936), *Collected Poems, 1918–1938* (1938), *Long View* (1942), *A Part of Vermont* (1945), *Slow Music* (1946), (edited) *May Days: An Anthology of Masses-Liberator Verse, 1912–1924* (1925), (edited) *Circumference: Varieties of Metaphysical Verse, 1456–1928* (1929). ❖ See also *Women in World History*.

TAGGART, Edith Ashover (1909–1997). Northern Ireland politician. Born Edith Ashover Hind, Nov 11, 1909, in Nottingham, England; died 1997; niece of John Andrews, 1st PM of Northern Ireland; m. Redmond Thibeaudeau Taggart. ❖ As a Unionist, elected to the Northern Ireland Senate in a by-election (1970–72), the 1st woman to serve in the Northern Ireland Parliament; was a founder of Age Concern (1976). Appointed OBE (1964).

TAGGART, Michele (1970—). American snowboarder and skier. Born May 6, 1970, in Salem, OR. ❖ Won gold (Winter 1999) and silver (Winter 1999) in Halfpipe at X Games; won 6 ISF World championship titles in Alpine and Freestyle; other 1st-place finishes include Vans World championships, Kirkwood, CA, in Halfpipe (1998), US Grand Prix, Mt. Bachelor, OR, in Quarterpipe (1998), FIS World Cup, Tandadalan, Sweden, in Halfpipe (1998), and USSA Grand Prix, Sunday River, ME, in Halfpipe (1999).

TAGLIABUE, Elena (1977—). Italian Alpine skier. Born Dec 12, 1977, in Edolo, Italy. ❖ Placed 5th at World Cup in super-G (2000).

TAGLIAFERRO, Magda (1893–1986). Brazilian-French pianist. Name variations: Magda Tagliafero. Born in Petropolis, Brazil, Jan 19, 1893; died in Rio de Janeiro, Sept 9, 1986; her father was a French pianist of note. ❖ Made Paris recital debut (1908); accompanied composer Gabriel Fauré on tour (1910), playing his *Ballade* with him at a 2nd piano; especially known for her performances of Fauré, made 1st recording of his *Ballade* for Piano and Orchestra (1929) and last recording, in digital sound, of same *Ballade* in its 2-piano version (with Daniel Varsano, 1981); also championed the works of Heitor Villa-Lobos and Reynaldo Hahn; had one of the longest musical careers in history—over 75 years—and was still able to delight audiences in her 90s. ❖ See also *Women in World History*.

TAGLIONI, Louisa (1823–1893). Italian ballet dancer. Born 1823 in Milan or Naples, Italy; died 1893 in Naples, Italy; dau. of Salvatore Taglioni; cousin of Maria Taglioni. ❖ Trained by father Salvatore Taglioni and later by Jean-Baptiste Coulon; at Paris Opéra danced principal roles in Jean Perrot's *Catarina, ou la fille du Bandit, Lalla Rookh*, and *Le Jugement de Paris*; returned to Naples upon retiring from performance career, and served as director of ballet studio there.

TAGLIONI, Maria (1804–1884). Italian ballerina. Name variations: Marie Taglioni; countess de Voisins; countess of Voisins. Born in Stockholm, Sweden, April 23, 1804; died in Marseilles, France, April 23, 1884; dau. of Filippo Taglioni (1778–1871, dancer and choreographer) and Sophia (Karsten) Taglioni (Swedish dau. of opera singer Christoffer Karsten); sister of Paul Taglioni (dancer and choreographer);

niece of Salvatore Taglioni (1780–1868, principal dancer and ballet master at Naples); aunt of Marie Taglioni (1833–1891, ballet dancer); m. Count Gilbert de Voisins, 1832 (sep. 1835); children: Marie ("Nini," b. 1836); Georges (b. 1843, father unknown). ❖ One of the most acclaimed dancers of the Romantic period, began studying ballet with her father's teacher at 12; made debut in Vienna in *La Réception d'une nymphe au temple de Terpsichore*, a ballet staged especially for the occasion (1822); spent 3 years performing in Stuttgart, perfecting her point technique and her famed *ballonné* style; made 1st trial appearance at Paris Opéra (July 12, 1827), dancing the *pas* in *Le Sicilien*; popularity increased, culminating with her triumphant performance in title role of *La Sylphide* (1832), the ballet that would be associated with her; signed 6-year contract with the Opéra, at which time her father also became ballet master; danced in Russia (1837–42); agreed to appear with 3 of her rival performers—Carlotta Grisi, Fanny Cerrito, and Lucile Grahn—in *Pas de Quatre* in London; retired from stage (1847); confirmed as Inspectrice de la danse at the Paris Opéra (1859), a position she retained until 1870, and as such taught advanced classes. ❖ See also *Women in World History.*

TAGLIONI, Marie (1833–1891). German ballet dancer. Name variations: Marie Paul Taglioni. Born Oct 27, 1833, in Berlin, Germany; died Aug 227, 1891, in Neu-Aigen, Austro-Hungary; dau. of Paul Taglioni (Austrian ballet dancer and choreographer) and Amalia Galster; niece of Maria Taglioni (1804–1884). ❖ Trained by father in Berlin and London; performed a season at Her Majesty's Theatre in London in his *Théa, ou la Fée aux fleurs* (1848) and Jules Perrot's *Les Quatre Saisons* (1848), among others; danced at Berlin State Opera in other ballets of her father, including *Flik und Flok* and *La Fantasma.*

TAGWERKER, Andrea. Austrian luge athlete. Born in Austria. ❖ Won a bronze medal for singles at Lillehammer Olympics (1994); won World championship (1997).

TAIA (c. 1400–1340 BCE). See *Tiy.*

TAIAROA, Tini Kerei (c. 1846–1934). New Zealand tribal leader. Name variations: Tini Pana, Jane Burns. Born Tini Pana, c. 1845 or 1847, at Moeraki, North Atago, New Zealand; died Sept 4, 1934, at Taumutu, New Zealand; dau. of Richard Burns (Riki Pana) and Pukio Iwa; m. Hori Kerei Taiaroa (tribal leader and politician), late 1850s or early 1860s (died c. 1904); children: 6 sons. ❖ Important behind-the-scenes participant in Maori affairs in Canterbury and Otago, managed farm and business affairs when husband became member of House of Representatives for Southern Maori (1871); after husband's death, was active in tribal and community activities. ❖ See also *Dictionary of New Zealand Biography* (Vol. 2).

TAILLEFERRE, Germaine (1892–1983). French composer. Name variations: Germaine Taillefere; Germaine Taileferre; Germaine Taillefesse. Born Germaine Marcelle Taillefesse, April 19, 1892, in Parc Saint-Maur, outside Paris; died Nov 7, 1983, in Paris; admitted to Paris Conservatoire, 1904; m. Ralph Barton, 1925 (div. 1931); m. Jean Lageat, 1931; children: (2nd m.) Françoise Lageat. ❖ As a member of Les Six, emancipated herself from the musical constraints of academic training to create lively, crisp, straightforward music that echoed jazz; was 1st admitted to Paris Conservatoire (1904), then forced by father to attend convent school (1906); reinstated at conservatory (1914), studying under Maurice Ravel, Claude Debussy, and Charles-Marie Widor; proclaimed a musical protegee of Erik Satie (1917); was a member, with Darius Milhaud, Arthur Honegger, Louis Durey, Francis Poulenc and Georges Auric, of the famous group of modern musicians known as Les Six (1920–24); invited by Leopold Stokowski to perform her Sonata for Violin and Piano in NY's Aeolian Hall (1925); wrote several well-known compositions, including String Quartet, *Images, Jeu de plein air, Ballade, Deux Valses* for two pianos, *Pavane, Nocturne, Finale* for orchestra, the ballet *Le Marchand d'oiseaux,* and an exuberant Overture, which many judge to be her finest piece; also wrote *Six Chansons Françaises* (1929); wrote and performed her Concerto for Two Pianos, Chorus, and Orchestra (1934); premiered ballet *Parisiana* in Copenhagen (1953); appeared in musical exhibit sponsored by International Council of Music featuring Les Six (1952); honored with other members of Les Six at a celebration of their 35th anniversary in Paris (1954). Awarded Grand Prix Musical from Académie des Beaux Arts (1973) and a 2nd Grand Prix Musical by City of Paris (1978). ❖ See also *Women in World History.*

TAILLON, Jacinthe (1977—). Canadian synchronized swimmer. Born Jan 1, 1977, in St.-Eustache, Quebec, Canada. ❖ Placed 1st for duet and team at Commonwealth Games; won a team bronze medal at Sydney Olympics (2000).

TAIMUR, Aichat Asmat (1840–1902). See *Taymuriyya, 'A'isha 'Ismat al-.*

TAISHO EMPRESS (1885–1951). See *Sadako.*

TAIT, Agnes (c. 1897–1981). American artist. Name variations: Mrs. William McNulty. Born c. 1897 (some sources cite 1894) in Greenwich Village in New York, NY; died 1981 in Santa Fe, New Mexico; educated at National Academy of Design; m. William McNulty (journalist), 1933. ❖ Noted for decorative panels; active in a number of Depression-era federal art programs, for which she executed mural paintings and created *Skating in Central Park*; selected to exhibit at New York World's Fair (1939); later turned to printmaking and illustrating children's books, such as *Peter and Penny of the Island* (1941), Johanna Spyri's *Heidi* (c. 1950) and *Paco's Miracle* (1961), among others. ❖ See also *Women in World History.*

TAIT, Dorothy (1905–1972). American novelist and biographer. Name variations: (pseudonyms) Ann Fairbairn; Jay Allison Stuart. Born Mar 1, 1905; died Feb 1972 in Pacific Grove, Monterey, California. ❖ Former newspaper columnist, met jazz musician George Lewis (1952), fell in love and took over managership of his band; under name Jay Allison Stuart, wrote his biography as *Call Him George* (1961), though she used the Fairbairn pseudonym in 2nd edition (1969); as Ann Fairbairn, wrote *Five Smooth Stones* (1966) and *That Man Cartwright* (1969).

TAITU (c. 1850–1918). See *Taytu.*

TAJIMA, Yasuko (1981—). Japanese swimmer. Born May 8, 1981, in Kanagawa, Japan. ❖ Won a silver medal for 400-meter indiv. medley at Sydney Olympics (2000).

TAJOLMOLOUK (1896–1981). Queen of Iran. Name variations: HM Queen Tajolmolouk; Taj al Molouk; HM The Empress Mother. Born Nimtaj Ayramlu on Mar 17, 1896; died in California in 1981; dau. of Brigadier General Tadfel Molouk; became 2nd wife of Reza Shah Pahlavi, shah of Iran (r. 1925–1941, abdicated), in Feb 1915 (div. April 1924); children: Shams Pahlavi (1917–1996); (twins) Muhammad Reza Pahlavi also known as Riza I Pahlavi, shah of Iran (r. 1941–1979, deposed), and Asraf Pahlavi (1919—); Ali Reza Pahlavi (1921–1954). ❖ Reza Shah Pahlavi's 1st wife was his cousin Maryam Khanum (m. 1903); his 3rd and 4th wives were Touran Amir Soleimani Saltaneh (1904–1995) and Queen Esmat.

TAKÁCS, Eva (1779–1845). Hungarian education reformer. Name variations: Eva Takacs. Born 1779; died 1845; children: Teréz Karács (1808–1892, educator). ❖ With daughter Teréz Karács, advocated education reform in Hungary.

TAKAGI, Tokuko Nagai (1891–1919). Japanese actress and dancer. Born 1891 in Tokyo, Japan; died 1919 in Japan; dau. of a junior technician working for the Ministry of Finance; m. Chimpei Takagi, 1906. ❖ The 1st Japanese film actress, made 4 short features for Thanhouser in NY, which were released in US and England (1911–12); returned to Japan where she introduced toe dancing and promoted modified versions of European operettas.

TAKAHASHI, Kaori (1974—). Japanese synchronized swimmer. Born 1974 in Japan. ❖ Won a team bronze medal at Atlanta Olympics (1996).

TAKAHASHI, Naoko (1972—). Japanese marathon runner. Born May 6, 1972, in Gifu, Japan. ❖ Won Japanese nationals and Asian Games (1998); won a gold medal for the marathon at Sydney Olympics (2000); at Berlin marathon, placed 1st with a time of 2:19.46, breaking the previous best time by 57 seconds and becoming the 1st woman to break the elusive 2:20 barrier (Sept 30, 2001); subject of a comic strip in Japan called "Kazekko" (daughter of the wind).

TAKAHASHI, Takako (1932—). Japanese novelist. Born Mar 2, 1932, in Kyoto, Japan; m. Takahashi Kazumi, 1954 (died 1971). ❖ Writings, which are often semi-autobiographical, include *The End of the Sky* (1973), which won the Tamura Toshiko Prize, *Tempter* (1976), which won the Izumi Kyoka Prize, *Doll Love* (1976), *Child of Wrath*, which won the Yomiuri Prize, and *Lonely Woman*; moved to Paris (1980) and entered Carmelite convent (1986).

TAKAKO DOI (b. 1928). See *Doi, Takako.*

TAKALO, Helena (1947—). Finnish cross-country skier. Name variations: Anni Helena Takalo. Born 1947 in Finland. ❖ Won a silver medal for 3 x 5 km relay at Sapporo Olympics (1972); won a gold medal for 5 km and silver medals for 10 km and 4 x 5 km relay at Innsbruck Olympics (1976); won a bronze medal for 10 km at Lake Placid Olympics (1980).

TAKAMINE, Hideko (1924—). Japanese actress. Name variations: Takama Yoshio. Pronunciation: Ta-ka-me-nay He-day-koe. Born Takama Yoshio, Mar 27, 1924 in Hakodate, Hokkaido, Japan; dau. of Hirayama Kinji (restaurant owner); adopted by Hirayama Shige (her paternal aunt) and Ogino Ichiji (both of whom were *benshi*, a professional narrator for silent films before the introduction of sound); m. Matsuyama Zenzo (film director and screenwriter), Mar 1955; no children. ❖ Popular child actress, known as "the Japanese Shirley Temple," who in adulthood worked with Japan's most accomplished film directors, portraying a wide variety of roles; at 5, made film debut in *Mother*; managing to avoid the pitfalls of a popular child performer trying to sustain a career, became a popular "pin-up girl" as a teenager; following the war, maintained her popularity with appearances in critically acclaimed films, which include *Tsuzurikata kyoshitsu* (Composition Class, 1938), *Nijushi no hitomi* (Twenty-four Eyes, 1954), and *Na mo naku mazushiku utsukushiku* (Nameless, Poor, Beautiful, 1961). ❖ See also autobiography, *Watashi no tosei nikki* (1976); and *Women in World History*.

TAKANO-TENNO (718–770). *See Kōken-Shōtoku.*

TAKARU, Princess (594–661). *See Kōgyoku-Saimei.*

TAKAYAMA, Aki (1970—). Japanese synchronized swimmer. Born Mar 12, 1970, in Japan. ❖ At Barcelona Olympics, won a bronze medal in duet (1992).

TAKAYAMA, Juri (1976—). Japanese softball player. Born Oct 21, 1976, in Yokosuka, Japan. ❖ Pitcher, won a team silver medal at Sydney Olympics (2000) and a team bronze at Athens Olympics (2004).

TAKAYAMA, Suzue (1946—). Japanese volleyball player. Born Dec 12, 1946, in Japan. ❖ At Mexico City Olympics, won a silver medal in team competition (1968).

TAKAYANAGI, Shoko (1954—). Japanese volleyball player. Born Sept 13, 1954, in Japan. ❖ At Montreal Olympics, won a gold medal in team competition (1976).

TAKEDA, Miho (1976—). Japanese synchronized swimmer. Born Sept 13, 1976, in Kyoto, Japan; attended Ritsumeikan University in Kyoto. ❖ Won a team bronze medal at Atlanta Olympics (1996) and silver medals for duet and team at Sydney Olympics (2000); at World championships, won a gold medal for duet (2001) and silver medals for team (1998, 2001, 2003) and duet (1998, 2003); with Miya Tachibana, won a silver medal for duet at Athens Olympics (2004), as well as a team silver medal.

TAKEI, Kei (1946—). Japanese choreographer and dancer. Born Keiko Takei, Dec 30, 1946, in Tokyo, Japan; studied dance on a Fulbright at Juilliard in NY, 1967–69; studied with Alfred Corvino, Trisha Brown, Anna Halprin and at the Merce Cunningham Studio and the Alwin Nikolais School. ❖ Won 1st choreography prize at age 12 for *March of Good Friends*; founded her own company, Moving Earth, in NY (1969), later named Moving Earth Orient Sphere and rebased in Tokyo; choreographed 1st of ongoing series of dances entitled *Light* (1969), a series that contains over 30 individual parts with subtitles including *Wind Field, Rice Field, Dream Catcher's Diary,* and *Pilgrimage*; also choreographed for Nederlands Dans Theater, Inbal Dance Theater, Shaliko Theater Company (NY), Shinjinkai Theater Co. (Japan), among others. Further works include *Playing this everyday Life* (1971), *The Dreamcatchers* (1982), *Whirlwind Field* (1982), *Wild Grass River Festival* (1989), and *Time Diary* (1994).

TAKENISHI, Hiroko (1929—). Japanese novelist and sociologist. Born 1929 in Hiroshima, Japan. ❖ Studied Japanese classical literature and published social criticism; works, which often focus on the suffering of atom bomb victims, include *The Rite* (1963), *Two Ways Between the Ancient and the Contemporary Times* (1964) and *Barracks* (1980); also wrote *A Theory on the Tales of Genji*; her selected works, *Takenishi Hiroko chosakushu*, were published in 6 volumes (1995). Received Tamura Toshiki Prize (1964) and Kawabata Yasunari Prize (1980).

TAKIHORA (c. 1842–1893). *See Lord, Lucy Takiora.*

TAKOUK, Diana (1977—). *See Romagnoli, Diana.*

TALALAYEVA, Lyubov (1953—). Soviet rower. Born Jan 24, 1953, in USSR. ❖ At Montreal Olympics, won a silver medal in coxed eights (1976).

TALANOVA, Nadejda (1967—). Russian biathlete. Born April 17, 1967, in Udmurtja, Russia. ❖ Won a gold medal for 4 x 7.5 km relay at Lillehammer Olympics (1994); at World championships, won a silver medal for sprint (1993) and a silver medal for relay (1999).

TALAVERA, Tracee (1966—). American gymnast. Born Sept 1, 1966, in San Francisco, CA. ❖ Won Emerald Empire Cup (1978, 1982), Rose Cup (1978), Fiesta Bowl and National Sports Festival (1979), American Cup and KIPS Invitational (1980), US nationals (1981, 1982), Caesar's Palace Invitational (1982); won a bronze medal for balance beam at World championships (1981); at Los Angeles Olympics, won a silver medal in team all-around (1984).

TALBERT, Mary Morris (1866–1923). African-American educator and civil-rights activist. Name variations: Mary Burnett Talbert. Born Mary Morris Burnett in Oberlin, Ohio, Sept 17, 1866; died in Buffalo, New York, Oct 15, 1923; dau. of Cornelius J. Burnett and Caroline (Nichols) Burnett; Oberlin College, SP degree, 1886, BA, 1894; m. William Talbert (city clerk and realtor), 1891; children: Sarah May Talbert (who became an accomplished pianist and composer). ❖ Became assistant principal of Bethel University (1887), the 1st woman in the state to hold that position; was principal of Union High School in Little Rock (1888); moved to Buffalo and became active in African-American community there; was also a charter member in Phillis Wheatley Club; with husband, was prominent in the black protest movement, founding the Michigan Avenue Baptist Church (1892), and frequently sharing home with reformers, including Booker T. Washington, W. E. B. Du Bois, and Nannie Helen Burroughs; also worked regularly alongside Anna J. Cooper and Mary Church Terrell in National Association of Colored Women (NACW), serving as its president (1916–20); as vice-president of National Association for the Advancement of Colored People (NAACP), took on a national crusade to support the Dyer Anti-Lynching Bill (1921); was the 1st woman to receive the Spingarn Medal from NAACP.

TALBOT, Anne (d. 1440). Duchess of Devon. Name variations: Anne Courtenay. Died Jan 16, 1440; dau. of Richard Talbot, 4th lord Talbot, and Ankaret Lestrange Talbot (1361–1413); m. or associated with Hugh Courtenay, 4th earl of Devon; associated with John Botreaux; children: (with Hugh Courtenay) Thomas Courtenay (1414–1458), 5th earl of Devon.

TALBOT, Catherine (1721–1770). English Bluestocking, essayist, and letter writer. Born May 1721 in Berkshire, England; died Jan 9, 1770, in London; dau. of Edward Talbot (archdeacon of Berkshire) and Mary (Martyn) Talbot; grew up in the family of Edward Secker, bishop of Oxford and later archbishop of Canterbury; never married; no children. ❖ Deeply devout, wrote treatises on scripture and other religious topics but refused to allow the publication of all except one, which appeared in Samuel Johnson's *Rambler* (1750); well known in London literary circles, belonged to the group of women writers and scholars called the Bluestocking Circle; was also a prolific correspondent, and many of her letters to her Bluestocking friends have been preserved, including almost 30 years of letters to her closest friend, poet Elizabeth Carter; collected essays, *Reflections on the Seven Days of the Week* and *Essays on Various Subjects*, were published posthumously. ❖ See also Montagu Pennington, ed. *A Series of Letters between Mrs. Elizabeth Carter and Catherine Talbot, from the year 1741 to 1770* (Rivington, 1809); and *Women in World History*.

TALBOT, Elizabeth (d. 1487). Baroness Lisle. Died 1487; dau. of John Talbot, 1st Viscount Lisle or L'Isle, and Joan Chedder; m. Edward Grey, viscount L'Isle (r. 1483–1492); children: Elizabeth Grey (fl. 1482–1530), 6th baroness Lisle; John Grey (b. 1480), 4th viscount Lisle; Anne Grey (who m. Sir John Willoughby); Margaret Grey (who m. Edward Stafford, 10th earl of Wiltshire).

TALBOT, Elizabeth (d. around 1506). Duchess of Norfolk. Name variations: Elizabeth Mowbray. Died c. 1506; dau. of John Talbot (1384–1453), 1st earl of Shrewsbury (r. 1442–1453), and Margaret Beauchamp (1404–1467); m. John Mowbray, 4th duke of Norfolk, before Nov 27, 1448; children: Anne Mowbray (1472–1481).

TALBOT, Elizabeth (1518–1608). Countess of Shrewsbury. Name variations: Bess of Hardwick; Bess of Hardwick Hall; Elizabeth of Hardwick; Elizabeth Hardwick; Elizabeth Shrewsbury. Born in 1518 in Derbyshire,

England; died on Feb 13, 1608 (some sources cite 1607); interred at Allhallows, Derby; 4th daughter and co-heiress of John Hardwick of Hardwick, Derbyshire, and Elizabeth Leake; m. Robert Barlow, in 1532 (died 1533); m. Sir William Cavendish, later 1st earl of Devonshire, in 1549 (died); m. Sir William St. Loe (died); m. George Talbot (1522–1591), 6th earl of Shrewsbury, on Feb 9, 1567 (separated 1583); children: (2nd m.) Henry Cavendish (MP for Derby); William Cavendish (b. 1552), earl of Devonshire; Charles Cavendish; Frances Cavendish; Elizabeth Cavendish (d. 1582); Mary Talbot (d. 1632); grandchildren: Arabella Stuart. ❖ Renowned for her financial acuity, passion for building, and 4 shrewd marriages, was one of the wonders of the Elizabethan age; widely called Bess of Hardwick, was among the richest women in England (2nd only to the queen), and knew how both to increase and to spend her money; built grand mansions on a spectacular scale, and her masterpiece, Hardwick Hall in Derbyshire, is considered perhaps the finest extant house of the era; was also an intimate of Queen Elizabeth I England, a longtime "custodian" of Mary Stuart, queen of Scots, an occasional partner in court intrigue, a mother who assiduously promoted her children's interests, and an energetic business-woman who did not suffer fools lightly. ❖ See also David N. Durant, *Bess of Hardwick: Portrait of an Elizabethan Dynast* (Weidenfeld & Nicolson, 1977); and *Women in World History*.

TALBOT, Elizabeth (1581–1651). *See Grey, Elizabeth.*

TALBOT, Gloria (1931–2000). *See Talbott, Gloria.*

TALBOT, Marion (1858–1948). American educator and founder. Born on July 31, 1858, in Thun, Switzerland; died Oct 20, 1948, in Chicago, Illinois; dau. of Israel Tisdale Talbot (1st dean of Boston University Medical School) and Emily (Fairbanks) Talbot (helped establish Girls' Latin School in Boston); Boston University, BA, 1880; Massachusetts Institute of Technology, BS, 1888. ❖ With others, organized the Association of Collegiate Alumnae, which eventually became the American Association of University Women, serving as 1st secretary and later president (1895–97); became involved in domestic science, co-editing, with Ellen Swallow Richards, *Home Sanitation: A Manual for Housekeepers* (1887); appointed instructor in domestic science at Wellesley College (1890); became dean of undergraduate women and assistant professor of sanitary science in department of social science and anthropology at University of Chicago (1892), then associate professor (1895), then dean of women (1899); made a full professor in the department of household administration (1905), which she created and which included Alice Peloubet Norton and Sophonisba P. Breckinridge; also served as acting president of Constantinople Woman's College in Turkey (1927–28, 1931–32); other writings include (with Richards) *Food as a Factor in Student Life* (1894), *The Education of Women* (1910) and (with Breckinridge) *The Modern Household* (1912). ❖ See also *Women in World History*.

TALBOT, Mary (d. 1632). Countess of Shrewsbury. Name variations: Mary Cavendish. Interred on April 14, 1632, at St. Peter's, Sheffield, England; dau. of Elizabeth Talbot (1518–1608), countess of Shrewsbury, and Sir William Cavendish, 1st earl of Devonshire; m. Gilbert Talbot (1552–1616), 7th earl of Shrewsbury, on Feb 9, 1567; children: Mary Talbot (d. 1649); Elizabeth Talbot (d. 1651); Lady Alathea Talbot (d. 1654, who m. Thomas Howard, earl of Arundel).

TALBOT, Mary Anne (1778–1808). British soldier and sailor. Born 1778 in UK; died 1808. ❖ At 14, became enamored of a British Army captain, by some accounts her husband, and followed him into the army; joined the 82nd regiment of infantry, where she served in Flanders disguised as a drummer boy and a foot boy; with the army, served in Caribbean city of Santo Domingo and in Valenciennes, France; deserted the army and joined the navy as a "powder monkey"; also served as cabin boy on the *Le Sage* and on the *Brunswick* and was with Lord Howe during war with France; was wounded in battle (June 1, 1794); captured, was imprisoned for 18 months; identity was discovered and her fighting career ended (1796); became a servant for Robert S. Kirby, who wrote of her history in *Wonderful Museum* (1804).

TALBOT, Nadine (1913–2003). English countess and opera singer. Name variations: Nadine, Countess of Shrewsbury and Waterford; Nadine Credi. Born 1913; died Feb 19, 2003, in Leightonn Buzzard, London, England; m. John George Charles Henry Altonn Alexander Chetwynd, 21st earl of Shrewsbury and Waterford (div. 1963); children: six. ❖ Under name Nadine Talbot, made debut as a soprano in a recital at Wigmore Hall, London (1954); helped start Opera at Ingestre, a festival that featured Sir John Pritchard conducting; in a celebrated divorce case, was sued for adultery by husband but judge refused the petition because the earl had committed adultery himself with Nina Mortlock (1959); resumed career under name Nadine Credi (short for Crediton).

TALBOT, Nancy (1825–1901). *See Clark, Nancy Talbot.*

TALBOTT, Gloria (1931–2000). American actress. Name variations: Gloria Talbot. Born Feb 7, 1931, in Glendale, CA; died Sept 19, 2000, in Glendale; sister of Lori Talbott (actress). ❖ Starred in cult sci-fi film *I Married a Monster from Outer Space* (1958); other films include *We're No Angels, Lucy Gallant, All That Heaven Allows, The Oregon Trail* and *An Eye for an Eye*; on tv, appeared as Abbie Crandall in the premiere season of "The Life and Legend of Wyatt Earp" (1955–56).

TALCOTT, Eliza (1836–1911). American missionary teacher. Born May 22, 1836, in Vernon, CT; died Nov 1, 1911, in Kobe, Japan; dau. of Ralph Talcott (woolen manufacturer) and Susan (Bell) Talcott. ❖ Dubbed the "Florence Nightingale of Japan," volunteered for missionary work and traveled to Japan (1873); founded and served as principal of girls' boarding school Kobe Home (later Kobe College, 1875–80); became housemother and head of nurses' training school at Doshisha University in Kyoto (1885); tended to wounded soldiers on both sides of Sino-Japanese War at Hiroshima (from 1894); was missionary teacher to Japanese workers in Hawaiian islands (1900–02).

TALEVA, Ivelina (1979—). Bulgarian rhythmic gymnast. Born Mar 22, 1979, in Bulgaria. ❖ Won a silver medal for team all-around at Atlanta Olympics (1996).

TALIAFERRO, Edith (1893–1958). American stage and radio actress. Born Dec 21, 1893, in Richmond, VA; died Mar 2, 1958, in Newton, CT; dau. of Robert and Anna (Barriscale) Taliaferro; sister of Mabel Taliaferro (actress, 1887–1979); cousin of actress Bessie Barriscale; m. Earle Brown (div.); m. House B. Jameson (actor). ❖ Made NY debut as a child in *Shore Acres* (1896); succeeded her sister as Lovey Mary in *Mrs. Wiggs of the Cabbage Patch* (1906); best remembered for title role in *Rebecca of Sunnybrook Farm* (1910); other plays include *Mother Carey's Chickens* and *Private Lives*; devoted later years exclusively to radio.

TALIAFERRO, Mabel (1887–1979). American stage and silent-screen actress. Born Maybelle Evelyn Taliaferro, May 21, 1887, in New York, NY; died Jan 24, 1979, in Honolulu, HI; dau. of Robert and Anna (Barriscale) Taliaferro; sister of Edith Taliaferro (1893–1958, stage and screen actress); cousin of actress Bessie Barriscale; m. Frederick W. Thompson (stage manager, div. 1912); m. Thomas J. Carrigan (div.); m. Joseph O'Brien (div.); m. Robert Ober. ❖ Began career at age 2 in *Blue Jeans*, then appeared in juvenile and adult leads on Broadway; made film debut in title role in *Cinderella* (1911); other films include *When Rome Ruled, The Three of Us, The Slacker, A Magdalene of the Hills, The Snowbird, God's Half Acre, Sentimental Tommy* and *My Love Came Back*; retired (1921).

TALKING HEADS. *See Weymouth, Tina.*

TALLCHIEF, Maria (1925—). Native American ballerina. Name variations: Betty Marie Tall Chief. Born Elizabeth Marie Tall Chief, Jan 24, 1925, in Fairfax, Oklahoma; dau. of Alexander Tall Chief (real estate investor) and Ruth (Porter) Tall Chief; sister of Marjorie Tallchief (b. 1927, dancer); m. George Balanchine (choreographer), 1946 (annulled 1950); m. Elmourza Natirboff (charter plane pilot), 1952 (div. 1954); m. Henry D. Paschen Jr. (construction company executive), 1956; children: (3rd m.) Elise Maria Paschen (b. 1959). ❖ World-renowned Osage dancer, noted for many roles with the Ballet Russe de Monte Carlo and New York City Ballet, who was the 1st Native American to achieve the stature of prima ballerina in the US; made 1st appearance as a soloist in *Chopin Concerto*, in Los Angeles (1940); toured with corps de ballet of Ballet Russe de Monte Carlo, then joined the company (1942); premiered 2 roles with Ballet Russe (1946); joined husband George Balanchine at Paris Opera, where she danced Terpsichore in premiere of *Apollo* to stunning success (1947), the 1st American to dance with Paris Opera Ballet since 1839; joined Ballet Society, soon renamed New York City Ballet (1947); clothed in the flame-colored costume of the Firebird, stunned both audiences and critics with her technique and fire in premiere of Balanchine's *Firebird* (1948); danced with André Eglevsky (1951), creating a dazzling new partnership for Balanchine's *pas de deux* roles; appeared in film *The Million Dollar Mermaid* (1952); became prima ballerina (1954); retired from New York City Ballet (1965); after period as artistic director for Chicago Lyric Opera Ballet, co-founded Chicago City Ballet with sister (1980); other notable roles include ice-fairy queen in *Le Baiser de la Fée* and Coquette in *Night Shadow*, for Ballet Russe de Monte Carlo, and Eurydice in *Orpheus*, Swan Queen in *Swan Lake*, and Sugar Plum Fairy in *The Nutcracker* for Ballet Society–New York City Ballet. Commemorated for lifetime achievement by President Bill Clinton at Kennedy Center Honors (1996). ❖ See also autobiography (with Larry Kaplan) *Maria Tallchief: America's Prima Ballerina* (Holt, 1997); Olga Maynard, *Bird of Fire: The Story of Maria Tallchief* (Dodd, 1961); Tobi Tobias, *Maria Tallchief* (Crowell, 1970); and *Women in World History*.

TALLCHIEF, Marjorie (1927—). Native American ballerina. Name variations: Marjorie Tall Chief; Marjorie Skibine. Born in Denver, CO, Oct 19, 1927; raised in Fairfax, OK; dau. of Alexander Tall Chief (real-estate investor) and Ruth (Porter) Tall Chief; sister of Maria Tallchief (b. 1925, dancer); m. George Skibine (dancer), 1947; children: Alex and George. ❖ Osage ballerina, noted for her romantic dance style, danced with the Los Angeles Civic Opera Ballet, Ballet Theater, Original Ballet Russe, Grand Ballet du Marquis de Cuevas, Paris Opera, and the Ruth Page Chicago Opera Ballet; joined sister to co-found the Chicago City Ballet (1980). ❖ See also *Women in World History*.

TALLEY, Marion (1906–1983). American opera singer. Born Marion Nevada Talley, Dec 20, 1906, in Nevada, MO; died Jan 3, 1983, in Beverly Hills, CA; studied voice with Ottley Cranston in Kansas City and Frank LaForge in NY; also studied piano and violin; m. Michael Baucheisen (German pianist), 1932 (annulled 1933); m. Adolph Eckstrom, 1935. ❖ Made highly publicized Metropolitan Opera House debut (1926), as Gilda in *Rigoletto*, but did not live up to expectations; sang "Caro Nome" from *Rigoletto* with NY Philharmonic Symphony Orchestra, the 1st woman to sing in a film (1926); remained with the Met for 3 seasons and performed in several operas, including *Lucia*, *The Magic Flute*, and *Le Chant du Rossignol*; appeared as a featured singer in film *Follow Your Heart* (1936); also recorded arias by Rossini and Verdi as well as concert songs on Victor label. ❖ See also *Women in World History*.

TALLEY, Nedra (1946—). American musician. Name variations: The Ronettes. Born Jan 27, 1946, in New York, NY. ❖ With cousins Ronnie Spector and Estelle Bennett, sang as the Darling Sisters, then danced and sang at Peppermint Lounge in NY (1961), and recorded for Colpix as Ronnie and the Relatives, then as the Ronettes (1962); with group, signed with Phil Spector's Phillies label (1963) and sang background vocals for other performers, including Darlene Love, before releasing own hits: "Be My Baby" (1963), "Baby I Love You" (1963), "Walking in the Rain" (1964), and "Is This What I Get For Lovin' You?" (1965); after Ronettes disbanded (1966), married NYC radio station-programming director.

TALLIEN, Thérésa (1773–1835). French political adventurer. Name variations: Theresa Tallien; Thérèsia Tallien; Thérèse or Teresa Cabarrus; Theresia de Tallien; Madame Jean-Lambert Tallien; formerly Marquise de Fontenay; later Comtesse de Riquet-Caraman and Princesse de Chimay. Pronunciation: tall-YEH. Born Juana-Maria-Ignacia-Teresa Cabarrus, later Jeanne-Marie-Ignace-Thérésa Cabarrus, July 31, 1773, at the château of San Pedro de Carabanchel de Arriba, near Madrid; died 1835 at Chimay, Belgium; daughter of François (Francisco) Cabarrus (1752–1810, banker) and Maria-Antonia (Galabert) Cabarrus (1756–1827); m. Marquis Jean-Jacques Devin de Fontenay, 1788 (div. 1793); m. Jean-Lambert Tallien (1767–1820), Dec 26, 1794 (secretary of the Paris Commune, who lead in the overthrow of Robespierre, in 1802); m. Comte (François-) Joseph de Riquet-Caraman (b. 1771), later Prince de Chimay, in 1805; children: (with Fontenay) Théodore (1789–1815); (with Tallien) Joséphine (1795–1862); (with Gabriel-Julien Ouvrard, but surnamed Cabarrus) Clémence-Isaure (1800–1884), Édouard (1801–1862), Clarisse (1802–1877), and Stéphanie (1803–1887); (with Prince Joseph de Chimay) Prince Joseph (1808–1866), Alphonse (1810–1866), Marie-Louise (1813–1814), and Marie-Louise-Thérésa-Valentine (1815–1876). ❖ One of the most controversial women in French history, famed for her beauty, marriages, and liaisons, who intervened on behalf of supplicants during Reign of Terror and was queen of high society during the Thermidorean Reaction and the Directory; hosted a salon frequented by leading political figures (1788–93); in Bordeaux with future 2nd husband, aided many people in avoiding trial or execution, mitigating the Terror through her influence over him (1793–94); her countless intercessions to obtain passports or commute or remit sentences played a signal role in sparing Bordeaux the worst; imprisoned in Paris, refused to testify against future husband (June 1794); played a role in the fall of Robespierre (1794); was the

leading social figure during the Thermidorean Reaction (1794–95); answered a litany of pleas, especially from returned émigrés and ex-nobles but also from distressed souls of the humblest sort; also worked to smooth relations between political opponents; rejected Napoleon as a suitor; while mistress of Paul Barras, then the most powerful man in France, continued as leader of high society during the Directory (1795–99); was in Egypt and England (1798–1801); was mistress of "the richest man in France," Gabriel-Julien Ouvrard, but ostracized from court by Napoleon (1800–04); while married to the Prince de Chimay, continued to entertain notable figures, especially from the world of music, and engaged in numerous charitable activities (1805–35); resided principally in Belgium (1815–35); in a society whose moral compass was swinging wildly, remained in heart uncorrupted, a woman sincerely mourned by the legions she had helped in the course of a turbulent existence. ❖ See also *Women in World History*.

TALMA, Madame (1771–1860). French actress. Name variations: Mlle Vanhove; Madame Petit-Vanhove; Madame Talma; Caroline or Charlotte Vanhove. Born Cécile Caroline Charlotte Vanhove, Sept 10, 1771, at The Hague, Netherlands; died April 11, 1860, in Paris, France; m. François Joseph Talma (1763–1826, famed actor), 1802. ❖ One of the most famous actresses of her day, appeared at the Comédie-Française as Mlle Vanhove (1777–79, 1785–94), Madame Petit-Vanhove (1794–1802) and as Madame Talma (1802–11).

TALMA, Louise (1906–1996). French-born American composer. Born in Arcachon, France, Oct 31, 1906; died Aug 13, 1996; attended Columbia University; studied at Institute of Musical Art in NY under Howard Brockway, George Wedge, Helen Whily and Percy Goetschius; studied piano with Isidor Philipp; studied under Nadia Boulanger at Fontainebleau School of Music. ❖ Known as the dean of American women composers, was the 1st woman to receive a Guggenheim grant for composition; taught at Hunter College; received a 20-minute ovation at premiere at Frankfurt-am-Main for her opera *The Alcestiad*, adapted from Thornton Wilder's play *Life in the Sun* (1962), the 1st American woman to have an opera staged at a major European opera house; composed many works which have been performed in recitals and concert halls throughout Europe and America; was the 1st woman to be elected to music department of National Institute of Arts and Letters and the only American to teach at Fontainebleau in 1930s. Was 1st woman to win Sibelius Award in composition. ❖ See also *Women in World History*.

TALMADGE, Constance (1897–1973). American silent-film actress. Born April 19, 1897, in Brooklyn, NY; died Nov 23, 1973, in Los Angeles, California; youngest dau. of Fred Talmadge and Peg Talmadge; sister of actresses Norma Talmadge and Natalie Talmadge; m. John Pialoglou (tobacco exporter), 1920 (div. 1922); m. Alistair MacIntosh (captain in Her Majesty's Horse Guards), 1926 (div. 1927); m. Townsend Metcher (department store tycoon), 1929 (div. 1931); m. Walter Giblon (stockbroker), 1939 (died 1964). ❖ Star of sophisticated comedies, reached height of career in 1920s, but faded into obscurity with advent of sound; entered films (1914), and for 2 years played in comedy shorts opposite Billy Quirk; break came when cast as the Mountain Girl in Griffith's *Intolerance* (1916); starred in a series of comedies, many of which were written by Anita Loos and John Emerson, including *A Virtuous Vamp* (1919) and *Learning to Love* (1925); established Constance Talmadge Film Co., which turned out 12 films over 6-year period; retired from films (1929); also appeared in *Two Weeks* (1920), *Polly of the Follies* (1922), *Dulcy* (1923), *Her Night of Romance* (1924), *Sybil* (1926), *Venus of Venice* (1927) and *Breakfast at Sunrise* (1927). ❖ See also Anita Loos, *The Talmadge Girls: A Memoir* (Viking, 1978); and *Women in World History*.

TALMADGE, Natalie (1897–1969). American silent-film actress. Born April 29, 1899, in Brooklyn, NY; died June 19, 1969, in Santa Monica, CA; middle dau. of Fred Talmadge and Peg Talmadge; sister of actresses Constance Talmadge and Norma Talmadge; m. Buster Keaton (actor), 1921 (div. 1933); children: 2 sons. ❖ Unlike superstar sisters, was a reluctant actress, at 1st eschewing the profession to become private secretary of Roscoe "Fatty" Arbuckle; eventually appeared in small roles, usually in her sisters' films; also appeared with husband Buster Keaton in *Our Hospitality* (1923). ❖ See also Anita Loos, *The Talmadge Girls: A Memoir* (Viking, 1978); and *Women in World History*.

TALMADGE, Norma (1893–1957). American silent-film actress. Born May 26, 1893, in Jersey City, New Jersey; died in Las Vegas, Nevada, Dec 24, 1957; eldest dau. of Fred Talmadge and Peg Talmadge; sister of Constance Talmadge and Natalie Talmadge (actresses); m. Joseph M. Schenck (film producer), Nov 1916 (sep. 1928, div. 1934); m. George

Jessel (actor, comic and producer), 1934 (div. 1937 or 1939); m. Carvel James (physician), 1946. ❖ Made film debut at Vitagraph Studio in Flatbush (1910); break came with performance in original screen version of *A Tale of Two Cities* (1911); while working at Vitagraph, played a variety of roles, then signed with Triangle; released 1st film with husband Joseph Shenck, *Panthea* (1917), which met with enormous success, propelling her to stardom; was one of the most popular actresses on the screen, whose nearest rival was sister Constance; appeared in over 164 films, including *Poppy* (1917), *Smilin' Through* (1922), *Within the Law* (1923), *Camille* (1927) and *The Dove* (1928); her limited range as an actress, as well as her strong Brooklyn accent, became apparent with advent of sound and after starring in *New York Nights* (1929) and *Du Barry—Woman of Passion* (1930), retired from films with large personal fortune. ❖ See also Anita Loos, *The Talmadge Girls: A Memoir* (Viking, 1978); and *Women in World History*.

TALON, Zoe (1785–1852). *See Cayla, Comtesse du.*

TALVACE, Adela (d. 1174). Duchess of Salisbury. Name variations: Ala Talvas. Died on Oct 4, 1174; dau. of William Talvace, count of Ponthieu, and Helie Borel (b. 1080); m. William de Warrenne (1119–1148), 3rd earl of Warrenne and Surrey (r. 1138–1148), a crusader who died in the Holy Land; m. Patrick, 1st earl of Salisbury, in 1152; children: (1st m.) Isabel de Warrenne (c. 1137–1203); Beatrice de Warrenne (1st wife of Hubert de Burgh).

TALVJ (1797–1870). *See Robinson, Therese Albertine Louise von Jakob.*

TALVO, Tyyne (b. 1919). Finnish ballet dancer and choreographer. Name variations: Tyyne Talvo-Cramér. Born 1919 in Helsinki, Finland; m. Ivo Cramer (dancer and choreographer). ❖ Danced in companies of husband, such as Dance Company of 1945, Swedish Dance Theater, and Ny Norsk Ballet and Dance Company (1970s); created own works for Ny Norsk, including *The Hill of the Winds* (c. 1979) and *Bright Night* (1972); also choreographed *Sauna* (1968), *Carvings* (1970), *As Time Passes . . .* (1975) and *Among Pucks and Trolls* (1976).

TALYSHEVA-TREGUB, Tatyana (1937—). Soviet track-and-field athlete. Name variations: Tatyana Andreyevna Talysheva. Born Oct 15, 1937, in USSR. ❖ At Mexico City Olympics, won a bronze medal in the long jump (1968).

TAMAIRANGI (fl. 1820–1828). New Zealand tribal leader and poet. Dau. of Te Ronaki and Kahukura-a-Tane; m. Whanake (Te Huka-tai-o-Ruatapu); children: 2. ❖ Highly regarded leader from Porirua to Cape Palliser, and the northern parts of South Island; captured by party of Ngati Mutunga during period of tribal unrest (c. 1824); sang a moving waiata she had composed to bid farewell to her lands, and was released by captors. ❖ See also *Dictionary of New Zealand Biography* (Vol. 1).

TAMAR (fl. 1000 BCE). Biblical woman. Dau. of King David and Maacah; sister of Absalom. ❖ Was raped by half-brother Amnon (her brother Absalom then lured Amnon to a party and murdered him).

TAMAR (fl. 1000 BCE). Biblical woman. Dau. of Absalom. ❖ Was the only surviving dau. of Absalom and the grandmother of Abijah (2 Sam. 14:27).

TAMAR (fl. 1100 BCE). Biblical woman. Married Er (son of Judah, died); married his brother Onan (son of Judah, died); children: (with Judah) twin sons, Perez and Zerah.

TAMAR (1929–1990). *See Rubinstein, Renate.*

TAMARA (1160–1212). Queen of Georgia. Name variations: Thamar; Tamara the Great. Born Tamara in 1160 in Georgia; died in Georgia in 1212 (some sources cite 1207); dau. of a princess of Osseti and Giorgi III, also known as Giorgi III (descendant of Georgia's ruling Bagrationi line), king of Georgia; m. George Bogolyubskoi, also seen as George Bogolyubski (Kievan prince and son of Prince Andrew of Suzdal), in 1185 or 1187 (div. 1188 or 1189); m. David Soslan also seen as David Sosland, an Ossetian prince, in 1189 or 1190; children: (2nd m.) son Giorgi (b. 1194), later George IV, king of Georgia; daughter Rusudani (b. 1195), later queen of Georgia. ❖ Queen of the ancient kingdom of Georgia, renowned for the military exploits which increased her mountainous holdings from the Black to the Caspian seas, whose reign encompassed a flourishing of literature and the arts that marked the country's golden age; began rule as co-regent with father (1178); assumed full power on his death (1184), the only remaining descendant in Bagrationi line; often turned for advice to her aunt Rusudani, a

particularly powerful influence during her reign; was a good administrator, a steady soldier, and a careful diplomat, wise as well as pious, gentle, and humane; was often described as forceful but maternal, and was obeyed by her subjects out of love and respect—though to do otherwise would have been foolish; divorced and exiled 1st husband George Bogolyubskoi (1188); defeated and banished 1st husband once more for his attempt to usurp her power (1191); quelled another insurgency (1193); defeated Bogolyubskoi for the last time (1200); including her years as co-ruler, reigned for 34 years, greatly expanding her kingdom and increasing its prosperity; died at height of power and popularity and was deeply mourned. ❖ See also *Women in World History*.

TAMARA (1907–1943). Russian-born actress. Born Tamara Drasin, 1907, in Poltava, Odessa, Russia; died Feb 22, 1943, in plane crash in Portugal; educated in Ukraine and at Hunter College; m. Erwin D. Swann. ❖ Moved to US (1912); became popular on radio; made stage debut in *Crazy Quilt* (1931) and came to prominence in *Roberta* (1933); other plays include *Free For All, Americana, They All Come to Moscow, Tide Rising* and *Leave It to Me*; films include *Sweet Surrender* and *No No Nanette*; was one of 24 casualties in a plane crash near Lisbon during WWII (Jane Froman survived).

TAMAS, Angela (1972—). *See Alupei, Angela.*

TAMATI, Arihia Kane (1879–1929). *See Ngata, Arihia Kane.*

TAMIRIS (fl. 550–530 BCE). Scythian queen. Name variations: Tamyris, Tomyris. Warrior queen and ruler of the nomadic Massagetae tribe in Persia (now Iran), who lived beyond the lower Oxus River by the Aral Sea. ❖ According to Herodotus, spurned a marriage offer from Cyrus II the Great, founder of the Persian Empire, who was after her kingdom along with her hand; with her son at the helm, sent her armies to abort Cyrus' invasion (530 BCE); after son was slain, led the army in his stead; defeated Cyrus who was killed in battle (July 530 BCE). ❖ See also *Women in World History*.

TAMIRIS, Helen (1902–1966). American dancer and choreographer. Name variations: Helen Becker. Pronunciation: Ta-MEER-iss. Born Helen Becker, April 24, 1902, in New York, NY; died Aug 4, 1966, in New York, NY; dau. of Isor Becker (tailor) and Rose (Simoneff) Becker (both Russian-Jewish immigrants); m. Daniel Nagrin, Sept 3, 1943 (sep. 1964); no children. ❖ As notable for her political dynamism as for her appearances onstage, energized the burgeoning modern-dance movement in America with her concern for social issues, including racism; made NY solo concert debut (1927); created and led Dance Repertory Theater (1930–32); was a primary choreographer for Dance Project within the Federal Theater Project of the Works Progress Administration (WPA); elected the 1st president of American Dance Association (1935); formed Tamiris-Nagrin Dance Company with husband (1960); remained involved in raising the status of African-Americans in dance; concert dances include "Subconscious" (1927), *Manifesto* (1927), *Negro Spirituals* (1929), *Walt Whitman Suite* (1934), *Harvest 1935* (1935), *How Long Brethren?* (1937), *Trojan Incident* (1938), *Adelante* (1939), *Dance for Walt Whitman* (1958); choreographed for Broadway musicals *Annie Get Your Gun* (1946), *Inside USA* (1948), *Fanny* (1954) and *Plain and Fancy* (1955); her career encompassed various dance styles, from vaudeville to modern dance and the Broadway stage, and her captivating stage presence enlivened her performances, but it was ultimately her role as an organizer that had the greater impact on the dance field. Won Tony Award for *Touch and Go* (1949). ❖ See also *Women in World History*.

TAMMES, Tine (1871–1947). Dutch geneticist. Name variations: Jantine Tammes. Born 1871 in Netherlands; died 1947. ❖ Scientist, who made an early contribution to Mendelian genetics, entered University of Groningen (1890), earning teacher's certificates (1892 and 1897); assisted professor J. W. Moll in the Botany department there (1897–99), was a botany practical classes supervisor (1912–17) and served as a variability and hereditary professor (1919–37), only the 2nd Dutch woman to serve as a university professor; visited noted geneticist Hugo de Vries in Amsterdam; studied the characteristics of cultivated flax (*Linum usitatissimum*); studied inheritance of characteristics (e.g., flower color) using flax.

TAMOTO, Hiroko (c. 1974—). Japanese softball player. Born c. 1974 in Japan. ❖ Won a team silver medal at Sydney Olympics (2000).

TAMURA, Ryoko (1975—). Japanese judoka. Name variations: Ryoko Tani-Tamura; Ryoko Tani. Born Sept 6, 1975, in Fukuoka, Japan; m. Yoshitomo Tani (professional baseball player). ❖ Won silver medals at Barcelona Olympics (1992) and Atlanta Olympics (1996) and a gold medal at Sydney Olympics (2000), all for extra-lightweight 48 kg; was World champion in 48 kg class (1993–99); won a gold medal for 48 kg at Athens Olympics (2004).

TAMYRIS (fl. 550–530 BCE). *See Tamiris.*

TAN, Amy (1952—). Asian-American writer. Born Feb 19, 1952, in Oakland, California; dau. of John (electrical engineer) and Daisy Tan (Chinese immigrants); San Jose State University, BA, MA; attended University of California, Santa Cruz, and University of California, Berkeley; m. Louis DeMattei (lawyer), 1974. ❖ Won admission to Squaw Valley writer's workshop with 1st short story "Endgame," which was printed in *FM* magazine; traveled to China with mother (1987), who, having escaped from the Chinese civil war, had been forced to leave behind 3 daughters; using mother's story, wrote 1st novel, *The Joy Luck Club* (1989), which was a bestseller and finalist for National Book Award; published 2nd novel, *The Kitchen God's Wife* (1991), which also enjoyed brisk sales; also wrote children's books, *The Moon Lady* and *The Chinese Siamese Cat*, novels *The Hundred Secret Senses* (1998) and *The Bonesetter's Daughter* (2001), as well as *The Opposite of Fate: A Book of Musings* (2003); nominated for BAFTA Award and Writer's Guild Award for screenplay for *The Joy Luck Club* (1993).

TAN XUE (1984—). Chinese fencer. Born Jan 30, 1984, in Tianjin, China. ❖ At World championship, won a gold medal for indiv. sabre (2002) and placed 2nd for indiv. sabre and team sabre (2003); won a silver medal for indiv. sabre at Athens Olympics (2004).

TANABE, Seiko (1928—). Japanese novelist. Born 1928 in Osaka, Japan. ❖ Works include *Watching Flowers* (1959), *Sentimental Journey* (1964), *Woman's Sundial, The Diary of a Faithful Wife*, and *Scenes From My Osaka*; also wrote scenarios for radio and tv.

TANABE, Yoko (1966—). Japanese judoka. Born Jan 28, 1966, in Ibaragi, Japan. ❖ Won silver medals at Barcelona Olympics (1992) and Atlanta Olympics (1996), both for half-heavyweight 72 kg.

TANAKA, Junko (1973—). Japanese synchronized swimmer. Born 1973 in Japan. ❖ Won a team bronze medal at Atlanta Olympics (1996).

TANAKA, Keiko (1933—). *See Ikeda, Keiko.*

TANAKA, Kinuyo (1907–1977). Japanese actress and director. Born Nov 28 (also seen as Nov 29), 1907 (also seen as 1909 and 1910), in Shinomoseki, Japan; died Mar 21, 1977, in Japan; m. Hiroshi Shimizu (director), 1929 (div.); no children. ❖ The only woman film director in Japan during 1950s, began career as an actress in the silent era and acted in more than 240 films, including Japan's 1st talkie and 1st color film; won the Japan Kinema Jumpo Award for Best Actress for her work in *Ballad of Narayama* (1958) and Best Actress Award at Berlin Festival for *Sandakan 8* (1975); met with vehement opposition, particularly from the directors' union, when she set out to direct; brought a female sensitivity to previously established cinematic forms in *The Moon Has Risen* (1955) and *Love Under the Crucifix* (1962); had feminist writer Sukie Tanaka script 2 of her films, *The Eternal Breasts* (1955) and *Girls of the Night* (1961); faced with continued professional hostility and audience indifference, abandoned directoral pursuits (1962) but continued to act in films until 1975. ❖ See also *Women in World History.*

TANAKA, Masami (1979—). Japanese swimmer. Born Jan 5, 1979, in Tokyo, Japan. ❖ Won a gold medal for 200-meter breaststroke at Asian Games (1998); at SC World championships, won gold medals for 50- and 100- and 200-meter breaststroke (1999); won a bronze medal for 4 x 100-meter medley relay at Sydney Olympics (2000).

TANAKA, Miyako (1967—). Japanese synchronized swimmer. Born Feb 20, 1967, in Japan. ❖ At Seoul Olympics, won a bronze medal in duet (1988).

TANAKA, Satoko (1942—). Japanese swimmer. Born Feb 3, 1942, on the island of Kyushu, Japan. ❖ Battled childhood bronchitis and beriberi to become the world's greatest 200-meter backstroke swimmer of her time, holding the Japanese record (1958–70) and the World record (1959–64); at Rome Olympics, won a bronze medal in 100-meter backstroke (1960), though the 200-meter backstroke was not yet an Olympic event.

TANAQUIL (fl. late 7th–early 6th BCE). Etruscan noblewoman. Name variations: Caia Caecilia. Died after 579 BCE; probably from the Etruscan city of Tarquinii, and of noble birth; m. Lucumo, later known as Lucius Tarquinius Priscus (or Tarquin, king of Rome); children: sons Lucius and Arruns; daughters (names unknown); son-in-law Servius Tullius (578–535 BCE, king of Rome). ❖ Shadowy figure from Rome's regal period,

probably a figure of history and not merely of myth, who was the reason husband and son-in-law became the 1st two Etruscan kings of Rome; highly ambitious, convinced husband to immigrate to Rome and adopt a new name; saw husband appointed guardian of the king's sons (traditionally 617 BCE), then take the throne on death of king; just as she had been germinal to his own accession, allegedly played the dominant role in the selection of husband's successor, raising Servius Tullius (578–535 BCE) as if he were a member of their own family, then marrying him to their daughter; the instant husband was assassinated after a 38-year reign, decisively acted to procure Rome's political stability by ordering Servius Tullius to do as she commanded: to take vengeance upon his enemies, to protect her interests in a world which had been suddenly redefined, and to follow the "guidance" of the gods, then told the crowd waiting below that husband was still alive but needed time for recovery and that he had appointed Servius Tullius as his royal proxy. Though her liberality as a queen was revered for centuries after her death, the name "Tanaquil" had become a readily accepted synonym for an "imperious woman" by the 1st century of the common era. ❖ See also *Women in World History.*

TANAQUILLE (d. 696). Queen of the Franks. Died in 696; m. Clovis III (680–695), king of all Franks (r. 691–695).

TANASE, Anca (1968—). Romanian rower. Born 1968 in Romania. ❖ Won a gold medal for coxed eights at Atlanta Olympics (1996).

TANCHEVA, Galina (1987—). Bulgarian rhythmic gymnast. Born May 18, 1987, in Varna, Bulgaria; twin sister of Vladislava Tancheva (rhythmic gymnast). ❖ Won team all-around bronze medal at Athens Olympics (2004).

TANCHEVA, Vladislava (1987—). Bulgarian rhythmic gymnast. Born May 18, 1987, in Varna, Bulgaria; twin sister of Galina Tancheva (rhythmic gymnast). ❖ Won team all-around bronze medal at Athens Olympics (2004).

TANDERUP, Anne Dorthe (1972—). Danish handball player. Name variations: Dörthe Tanderup. Born April 24, 1972, in Denmark. ❖ Won a team gold medal at Atlanta Olympics (1996); won team European championships (1994, 1996) and World championships (1997).

TANDERUP, Dörthe (1972—). *See Tanderup, Anne Dorthe.*

TANDY, Jessica (1909–1994). British-born actress of stage and screen. Born in London, England, June 7, 1909; died in Easton, Connecticut, Sept 11, 1994; dau. of Harry Tandy (rope manufacturer) and Jessie Helen (Horspool) Tandy; trained at Ben Greet Academy of Acting in London, 1924–27; m. Jack Hawkins (actor), 1932 (div. 1940); m. Hume Cronyn (actor), 1942; children: (1st m.) Susan Hawkins (who m. John Tettemer); (2nd m.) Christopher Cronyn (b. 1943), Tandy Cronyn (b. 1945, actress). ❖ In an acting career that spanned 6 decades, won 2 Academy Awards, 3 Tonys, and was nominated for a tv Emmy on night of her death, but her most impressive accolades came for her work on the stage; made professional debut in *The Manderson Girls* (1927), at a small theater in Soho; came to attention of English audiences in *Children in Uniform* (1932); appeared as Ophelia opposite John Gielgud in *Hamlet*, in London (1934); to escape war in England, immigrated to US with daughter (1940), where she lent her voice to radio as Princess Nada on "Mandrake the Magician"; was the original Blanche DuBois in *A Streetcar Named Desire* on Broadway (1947), earning her 1st Tony as Best Actress (1948); worked in London and US and Canadian regional theaters; starred opposite husband Hume Cronyn in *The Fourposter, The Physicists, A Delicate Balance, Noel Coward in Two Keys, The Gin Game, Foxfire*, and *The Petition*; later films include *The Seventh Cross* (1944), *Forever Amber* (1947), *Light in the Forest* (1958), *The Birds* (1963), *Butley* (1974), *The World According to Garp* (1982), *The Bostonians* (1984), *Cocoon* (1985), and *Used People* (1992). Earned Tonys for Best Actress in *The Gin Game* (1978) and *Foxfire* (1983); won Academy Award for Best Actress for *Driving Miss Daisy* (1990) and a 2nd Oscar, for Best Supporting Actress, in *Fried Green Tomatoes* (1992); nominated for Emmy for "To Dance with the White Dog" (1994); accepted 1st-ever Tony given for Lifetime Achievement (1994). ❖ See also *Women in World History.*

TANG GONGHONG (1979—). Chinese weightlifter. Born Mar 5, 1979, in China. ❖ At World championships, placed 1st for + 75 kg and + 75 kg clean & jerk (1998); won a gold medal for + 75 kg at Athens Olympics (2004).

TANG JIUHONG (1969—). Chinese badminton player. Born Feb 14, 1969, in China. ❖ At Barcelona Olympics, won a bronze medal in singles (1992).

TANG LIN (1975—). Chinese judoka. Born 1975 in Sichuan, China. ❖ Won a gold medal for 70–78 kg half-heavyweight at Sydney Olympics (2000).

TANG YONGSHU. Chinese badminton player. Born in China. ❖ Won a bronze medal for doubles at Atlanta Olympics (1996).

TANGER, Helen (1978—). Dutch rower. Born Aug 22, 1978, in the Netherlands. ❖ Won a bronze medal for coxed eights at Athens Olympics (2004).

TANGERAAS, Trine (1971—). Norwegian soccer player. Born Feb 26, 1971, in Norway. ❖ Won a team bronze medal at Atlanta Olympics (1996).

TANGNEY, Dorothy (1911–1985). Australian politician. Name variations: Dorothy Margaret Tangney. Born Mar 13, 1911, in Perth, Western Australia; died June 1, 1985. ❖ Began career as a schoolteacher; joined the Labor Party of for Western Australia; was the 1st woman elected to the federal Senate (Aug 21, 1943), serving in Parliament until June 30, 1968; was on the Joint Committee on Social Security (1943–46); was also the 1st Western Australian woman to be appointed Dame Commander of the British Empire (1968).

TANGUAY, Eva (1878–1947). French-Canadian singer and silent-film actress. Born Aug 1, 1878, in Marbleton, Quebec, Canada; died Jan 11, 1947, in Hollywood, CA; dau. of Octave and Adele (Pajean) Tanguay; m. John Ford (member of her acting troupe), 1913 (div. 1917); m. Chandos Ksiazkewacz (pianist, also known as Allan Parado), 1927 (annuled). ❖ At 6, moved with family to Holyoke, MA; at 8, joined Francesca Redding Co. in juvenile lead of *Little Lord Fauntleroy* and toured with the company for 5 years before receiving a small part in *The Merry World*; made NY debut in *My Lady* (1901); headlined in *The Office Boy* and *The Chaperones* (1903), *A Good Fellow* (1906), *The Follies of 1909* (1909), *The Sun-Dodgers* (1912), *Miss Tobasco* (1914), and *The Girl Who Smiles* (1916), introducing such songs as "I've Got to Be Crazy," "I Want Someone to Go Wild with Me," "It's All Been Done Before but Not the Way I Do It," and the song that brought her national fame, "I Don't Care," which anticipated the flapper era. ❖ See also *The I Don't Care Girl* (film), starring Mitzi Gaynor (1953); and *Women in World History*.

TANGUY, Katherine Sage (1898–1963). See Sage, Kay.

TANGWYSTL (fl. 1180–1210). Welsh royal mistress. Name variations: Tangwystyl Goch. Flourished around 1180 to 1210; m. Ednyfed Fychan ap Kendrig, Lord of Brynffenigl; mistress and possibly later wife of Llywelyn II the Great (1173–1240), Ruler of All Wales; children: (with Ednyfed Fychan) many; (with Llywelyn) 6, including Gruffydd, Lord of Lleyn (born before 1205–1244); Gladys the Black (d. 1251); Angharad; possibly Ellen of Wales, countess of Huntingdon and Chester (d. 1253). ❖ Paramour of King Llywelyn II the Great. Llywelyn II was married to Joan of England (d. 1237), and there is some confusion between Joan of England and Tangwystl as to who had which children.

TANI, Ryoko (1975—). See Tamura, Ryoko.

TANIA.
See Bunke, Tamara (1937–1967).
See Hearst, Patricia Campbell (1954—).
See Pereira Ribeiro, Tania (1974—).

TANIDA, Kuniko (1939—). Japanese volleyball player. Born Sept 18, 1939, in Japan. ❖ At Tokyo Olympics, won a gold medal in team competition (1964).

TANIMOTO, Ayumi (1981—). Japanese judoka. Born Aug 4, 1981, in Japan. ❖ Placed 3rd at World championships for 63 kg (2001); won a gold medal for 63 kg at Athens Olympics (2004).

TANNENBAUM, Jane Belo (1904–1968). American anthropological photographer. Name variations: Jane Belo. Born Jane Belo, Nov 3, 1904, in TX; died 1968. ❖ Traveler, artist, photographer and fieldworker, was noted as pioneer in anthropological photography.

TANNER, Beatrice or Stella (1865–1940). See Campbell, Mrs. Patrick.

TANNER, Clara Lee (1905–1997). American cultural anthropologist. Born Clara Lee Fraps, May 28, 1905, in Biscoe, NC; died Dec 22, 1997, in Tucson, AZ; dau. of Joseph Conrad Fraps and Clara Dargon Lee Fraps; University of Arizona, BA, 1927, MA, 1928; m. John F. Tanner, 1936; children: Sandra Lee. ❖ Known primarily for work on Southwestern Indian arts and crafts, taught at University of Arizona for 50 years (1928–78); writings include *Southwest Indian Craft Arts* (1969), *Southwest Indian Painting, A Changing Art* (1974), and *Prehistoric Southwestern Craft Arts* (1976) and *Indian Baskets of the Southwest* (1984).

TANNER, Elaine (1951—). Canadian swimmer. Name variations: Elaine Tanner Nahrgang. Born Feb 22, 1951, in Vancouver, British Columbia, Canada; m. Ian Nahrgang, 1971. ❖ Won 4 gold medals, 3 silver, and broke 2 world records at Commonwealth Games (1966); won 2 gold medals, 3 silver, and broke 2 world records at Pan American Games (1967); at Mexico City, won a bronze medal in 4 x 100-meter freestyle relay, silver medal in 200-meter backstroke, and silver medal in 100-meter backstroke (1968), the 1st Canadian woman to win 3 Olympic medals; retired from competition (1968); did commentary for the CBC. Given Lou Marsh Award (1966); inducted into Canada's Sports Hall of Fame (1971).

TANNER, Ilona (1895–1955). Hungarian novelist. Name variations: (pseudonym) Sophié Török or Sophie Torok. Born Dec 10, 1895, in Budapest, Hungary; died Jan 28, 1955, in Budapest; m. Babits Mihály (1883–1941, poet), 1921. ❖ Wrote *Hintz tanárségéd úr* (Mr. Hintz the Professor's Assistant), about marriage, motherhood, and passing of youth.

TANNER, Marion (1891–1985). American actress. Name variations: Auntie Mame, Mame Dennis. Born Mar 6, 1891, in Buffalo, NY; died Oct 30, 1985, in New York, NY; aunt of Edward Everett Tanner, 3rd (writer under pseudonym Patrick Dennis). ❖ Was the basis for the character Auntie Mame, who 1st appeared in a novel written by her nephew; on Broadway, appeared in *Fires of Spring, The Cat and the Canary, Knickerbocker Holiday* and *Tobacco Road*.

TANNER, Vera (b. 1906). English swimmer. Born 1906 in UK; George Dupre Crozier Murrell (1894–1979), 1930; children: Julia de Burley Murrell (b. 1934). ❖ Won a silver medal at Paris Olympics (1924) and a silver medal at Amsterdam Olympics (1928), both in 4 x 100-meter freestyle relay.

TANNING, Dorothea (b. 1910). American artist. Name variations: Dorothea Tanning Ernst. Born 1910 in Galesburg, Illinois; attended Knox College and Art Institute of Chicago; m. Max Ernst (artist), 1946 (died 1976). ❖ Surrealist painter, graphic artist and sculptor, moved to New York (1936); became part of surrealist circle of artists; also appeared in surrealist film *Dreams That Money Can Buy* (1944–46); exhibited her work at Julian Levy Gallery and created scenery and costume designs for Ballet Russe de Monte Carlo and New York City Ballet; included in exhibition "31 Women" at Art of This Century (1943); on marriage, moved to Sedona, Arizona (1946), then established permanent residency in France (1952); became highly acclaimed throughout Europe where she was given a retrospective exhibition at Centre National d'Art Contemporain in France (1974); on death of husband, returned to NY (1976); at 90, enjoyed 1st one-woman exhibition in US when the Philadelphia Museum of Art presented "Dorothea Tanning: Birthday and Beyond" (2000–01); works include *Children's Games* (1942), *Hotel du Pavot* (1942), *Max in a Blue Boat* (1946), *Eine Kleine Nachtmusik* (1946), *The Great Room* (1950–52), *Interior with Sudden Joy* (1951) and *Family Portrait* (1954). ❖ See also *Women in World History*.

TANZINI, Luisa (b. 1914). Italian gymnast. Born July 14, 1914, in Italy. ❖ At Amsterdam Olympics, won a silver medal in team all-around (1928).

TAO HUA. Chinese softball player. Born in China. ❖ Won a silver medal at Atlanta Olympics (1996).

TAO LUNA (1974—). Chinese shooter. Born Feb 1974, in Shanghai, China. ❖ Won a gold medal for 10 m air pistol and a silver medal for 25 m pistol at Sydney Olympics (2000); won 10 m air pistol at Asian Games (2000).

TAO-LAO (1892–1938). See Storni, Alfonsina.

TAORMINA, Sheila (1969—). American swimmer and triathlete. Born Mar 18, 1969, in Livonia, Michigan; University of Georgia, business degree, 1992, MBA, 1994. ❖ Won a gold medal for 800-meter freestyle relay at Atlanta Olympics (1996); began competing as an Olympic triathlete (1998); placed 1st at ITU World Cup (2002).

TAPLEY, Rose (1881–1956). American actress. Born Rose Elizabeth Tapley, June 30, 1881, in Petersburg, VA; died Feb 23, 1956, in Woodland Hills, CA. ❖ Came to prominence on stage as Queen Victoria in *The Victoria Cross* (1912); made film debut (1905); films include *Vanity Fair, The Illumination, Java Head, The Pony Express, Resurrection,* and *It.*

TAPPAN, Caroline Sturgis (1819–1888). American transcendentalist poet. Name variations: Carrie Tappan; Caroline Sturgis. Born Caroline Sturgis, Aug 1819, in Boston, Massachusetts; died Oct 20, 1888, in Lenox, Massachusetts; dau. of William Sturgis (sea captain and merchant) and Elizabeth Marston (Davis) Sturgis (dau. of Judge John Davis); sister of Ellen Sturgis Hooper (1812–1848) and Susan Sturgis; aunt of Clover Adams (1843–1885); m. William Aspinwall Tappan (walking companion of Henry David Thoreau), Dec 12, 1847; children: Ellen Sturgis Tappan (b. 1849); Mary Aspinwall Tappan (b. 1851). ❖ Contributed verse to the *Dial* under pseudonym "Z"; though her contributions to the Transcendentalist movement were minor, is remembered for her close associations with its leaders; spent summers with the Emersons in Concord (Ralph was then married to Lidian Jackson Emerson) or with Margaret Fuller traveling the Great Lakes to Niagara and Fishkill-on-the-Hudson; throughout travels, wrote and published several children's books. The "Little Red House," where Nathaniel Hawthorne wrote *The House of Seven Gables,* was situated on the Tappans' estate in Lenox, eventually renamed Tanglewood. ❖ See also *Women in World History.*

TAPPAN, Eva March (1854–1930). American educator and writer. Born Dec 26, 1854, in Blackstone, Massachusetts; died Jan 29, 1930 (one source indicates Jan 30), in Worcester, Massachusetts; dau. of Edmund March Tappan (minister) and Lucretia Logée Tappan (teacher); Vassar College, BA, 1875; University of Pennsylvania, MA, 1895, PhD, 1896. ❖ Teacher, children's author, and anthologist; taught Latin and German at Wheaton College in Massachusetts (1876–80); was also associate principal at Raymond Academy in Camden, NJ (1884–94) and began teaching at English High School in Worcester, Massachusetts (1897); retired from teaching (1904) to devote more time to writing, focusing on works for grade-school and high-school students (many of her books were used in schools); brought to life kings and queens, Greek and Roman societies, folk heroes, and historical and literary figures, translated folk tales from other countries, and edited *The Children's Hour,* a 15-vol. collection of myths, adventure and nature stories. ❖ See also *Women in World History.*

TAPPIN, Ashley T. (1974—). American swimmer. Born Dec 18, 1974, in Louisiana. ❖ At Barcelona Olympics, won a gold medal in 4 x 100-meter freestyle relay (1992); became a swimming coach.

TAPPING, Sydney (1872–1941). *See Fairbrother, Sydney.*

TAPSELL, Hine-i-turama (c. 1818–1864). *See Hine-i-turama.*

TAPSELL, Ngatai Tohi Te Ururangi (1844–1928). New Zealand tribal leader. Name variations: Ngatai Tohi Te Ururangi. Born Ngatai Tohi Te Ururangi, 1844, in Ohinemutu, New Zealand; died Jan 1928 at Maketu, New Zealand; dau. of Tohi Te Ururangi and Taniko Te Haukau; m. Retireti Tapsell (tribal leader), early 1860s; children: 7 sons, 1 daughter. ❖ Among the few Maori women to testify in Te Arawa Native Land Court hearing, was a major shareholder of Te Arawa tribal lands. ❖ See also *Dictionary of New Zealand Biography* (Vol. 2).

TARABINI, Patricia (1968—). Argentinean tennis player. Born Aug 6, 1968, in La Plata, Argentina. ❖ With Paola Suarez, won the bronze medal for doubles at Athens Olympics (2004); turned professional (1986).

TARABOTTI, Arcangela (1604–1652). Italian writer and nun. Name variations: Elena Cassandra Tarabotti; Suor or Sor Arcangela; (pseudonyms) Galerana Barcitotti and Galerana Baratotti. Born Elena Cassandra Tarabotti in Venice, Feb 24, 1604; died in Venice, Feb 28, 1652; dau. of Stefano Bernardino Tarabotti (minor aristocrat) and Maria (Cadena) Tarabotti; never married. ❖ Venetian Benedictine nun and writer known for her controversial pamphlets concerning the conditions of women; became an *educanda* (boarder) in Sant'Anna monastery (1617); took the veil without vocation (Sept 8, 1620); made her religious profession (1623); had 5 works published (1643–52), including *Il paradiso monacale* (The Monastic Paradise, 1643), *Lettere familiari e di complimento* (Informal and Greeting Letters, 1650), and *Che le donne siano della spezie degli uomini, difesa delle donne* (Are Women of the same Species as Men? A Defence of Women, 1651); her works are informed both by the particularity of her experience as an enclosed nun and by the

similarity of women's limited experiences within society, a condition she bitterly denounced. Posthumous work *La semplicità ingannata* (Simplicity Tricked, 1654), was formally placed on the Index of Forbidden Books (1660). ❖ See also (in Italian) Francesca Medioli, *"L'Inferno monacale" di Arcangela Tarabotti* (Rosenberg e Sellier, 1990); and *Women in World History.*

TARAKANOVA, Nelli (1954—). Soviet rower. Born Sept 1954 in USSR. ❖ At Montreal Olympics, won a silver medal in coxed eights (1976).

TARAN, Ruslana (1970—). Ukrainian sailor. Born Oct 27, 1970, in Evpatoria, Ukraine; m. Dmytro Tsalik. ❖ Won European championship for 470 (1993, 1995); won bronze medals for double-handed dinghy (470) at Atlanta Olympics (1996) and Sydney Olympics (2000); won a silver medal for Yngling class at Athens Olympics (2004), a debut event.

TARAN-IORDACHE, Maricica Titie (1962—). Romanian rower. Name variations: Maricica Titie Iordache. Born Jan 1962 in Romania. ❖ At Los Angeles Olympics, won a gold medal in quadruple sculls with coxswain (1984).

TARANINA, Viktoria. Russian short-track speedskater. Name variations: Viktoria Troitskaya or Troitskaia. Born in USSR. ❖ Won a bronze medal for 3,000-meter relay at Albertville Olympics (1992).

TARASOVA, Alla (1898–1973). Ukrainian-born actress. Name variations: Alla Konstantinovna Tarasova; Alla K. Tarasova. Born Jan 25, 1898, in Kiev, Ukraine; died April 4, 1973, in Moscow, Russia. ❖ Became a member of the Moscow Art Theatre (1916), later touring America and Europe in such parts as Irina in *The Three Sisters,* Sonya in *Uncle Vanya,* Nastya in *Lower Depths,* and Grushenka in *The Brothers Karamozov* (1922–24); created the roles of Ustinya in *Pugachevshchina,* Parasha in *Ardent Heart,* Negina in *Talents and Admirers,* Masha in *Armoured Train 14–69,* and Makarova in *Fear;* also appeared in title role in *Anna Karenina,* as Tatyana in *Enemies,* Maria in *Maria Stuart,* Madame Ranevskaya in *The Cherry Orchard,* and Zabelina in *Kremlin Chimes;* films include *Storm, Guilty But Innocent, The Conquest of Peter the Great* (as Catherine I) and *Anna Karenina* (title role, 1953). Created People's Artist of the USSR (1937); was deputy to USSR Supreme Soviet in the 3rd, 4th, and 5th sessions.

TARBELL, Ida (1857–1944). American journalist. Name variations: (pseudonym) Iderem. Pronunciation: tar-BELL. Born Ida Minerva Tarbell, Nov 5, 1857, in Hatch Hollow, Erie Co., Pennsylvania; died in Bridgeport, Connecticut, Jan 6, 1944; dau. of Franklin Sumner Tarbell (carpenter) and Esther Ann (McCullough) Tarbell (schoolteacher); Allegheny College, AB, 1880, MA, 1883; never married; no children. ❖ Journalist and editor whose exposé of the Standard Oil Co. made her name synonymous with the appellation muckraker; worked as associate editor, *The Chautauquan* (1883–91); attended the Sorbonne (1891–94); was an editor on staff and associate editor, *McClure's Magazine* (1894–1906); launched the most sensational 18-part serial to appear in an American magazine, an exposé on John D. Rockefeller's Standard Oil Co., full of ciphers, spies, arson, and kickbacks (Nov 1902); in the process, became one of the most successful magazine writers in America; was associate editor, *The American Magazine* (1906–15); was a member of women's committee, Council on National Defense (1917), President Woodrow Wilson's Industrial Conference (1919), President Warren G. Harding's Unemployment Conference (1921) and National Women's Committee for Mobilization of Human Needs (1933–36); authored well-received biographies of Napoleon and Lincoln; other writings include *Madame Roland* (1896), *History of the Standard Oil Company* (2 vols., 1904), *The Tariff in Our Times* (1911), *The Rising of the Tide: The Story of Sabinsport* (1919), *Peacemakers—Blessed or Otherwise* (1922), *Life of Judge Gary: The Story of Steel* (1925), *A Reporter for Lincoln: The Story of Henry E. Wing, Soldier and Newspaperman* (1927), *Owen D. Young—A New Type of Industrial Leader* (1932), *The Nationalizing of Business, 1878–1898* (1936), and *Women at Work: A Tour Among Careers* (1939). Inducted into Women's Hall of Fame at Seneca Falls, New York (autumn 2000). ❖ See also *All in a Day's Work: An Autobiography* (1939); Kathleen Brady, *Ida Tarbell: Portrait of a Muckraker* (Putnam, 1984); and *Women in World History.*

TARIACURI, La (1923–2001). *See Mendoza, Amalia.*

TARKIAINEN, Maria (1880–1943). *See Jotuni, Maria.*

TARN, Pauline M. (1877–1909). *See Vivien, Renée.*

TARNOW, Fanny (1779–1862). German short-story writer. Name variations: Franziska Tarnow. Born Franciska Christiane Johanne Frederike

Tarnow, Dec 17, 1779, in Güstrow, Mecklenburg-Schwerin; died July 4, 1862; aunt of Amely Bolte. ❖ Worked as governess and teacher and maintained friendships with several literary figures; wrote stories for women's magazines and edited the journal *Iduna* with Helmina von Chézy (1820).

TARNOWSKA, Maria (1878–1923). Russian countess convicted of murder. Name variations: Countess Maria Tarnowska. Born in St. Petersburg, Russia, 1878; died 1923; m. Count Vassili Tarnowska (div.); children: 2. ❖ As sole beneficiary of his life insurance policy, planned murder of her lover Count Paul Kamarovsky; arranged for another lover Nicholas Naumov to commit the crime, of which her attorney Donat Prilukov, another beau, was aware (early Sept 1907); along with Naumov and Prilukov, stood trial for the murder in Venice, Italy (Mar 1910); sentenced to 8 years; served short time at Trani Prison and was released (Aug 1912). The public was transfixed by the trial of Tarnowska, who earned names like "Sphinx in Crepe" and "Russian Vampire."

TARO, Gerda (1910–1937). German-Jewish photojournalist. Name variations: Gerda Pohorylle; Gerta Taro. Born in Stuttgart, Germany, Aug 1, 1910; severely injured near the front lines near Brunete, Spain, July 25, 1937, and died on July 26; dau. of Heinrich (Hersch) Pohorylle and Gisela (Ghittel) Boral Pohorylle (both Polish Jews); companion of Robert Capa (b. 1913, photographer). ❖ First woman war photographer to die in combat, whose photographs of the Spanish Civil War brought powerful images to the attention of a public unable to fully grasp the growing menace of fascist aggression; with Hitler's rise to power (1933), became active in anti-Nazi movement in Leipzig; arrested and taken into "protective custody" (*Schutzhaft*, Mar 19, 1933), was released because of her Polish citizenship (April 4); fled to Paris (1933); met and moved in with Hungarian photographer Robert Capa (1934); found a job with the photographic agency Alliance Photo (1935); when Republican Spain was threatened by a military coup led by Francisco Franco, arrived in Barcelona with Capa to photograph soldiers and the hastily erected barricades in and around Barcelona (Aug 5, 1936); often appeared with her Rolliflex in the midst of Republican soldiers, ignoring the bullets that flew from all directions; did a series of photos of Madrid's destroyed buildings, documentation of the 1st city to be bombed; also captured on film one of the Spanish Republic's most heartening victories, the battle of Guadalajara (Mar 1937). Alberto Giacometti designed her tomb in the Père-Lachaise cemetery, though her name was deleted during the Nazi occupation. ❖ See also Robert Capa, *Death in the Making* (1938); and *Women in World History*.

TARPLEY, Lindsay (1983—). American soccer player. Born Sept 22, 1983, in Madison, WI; attended University of North Carolina. ❖ Forward, won a team gold medal at Athens Olympics (2004).

TARRANT, Margaret (1888–1959). British illustrator and painter. Born Margaret Winifred Tarrant, 1888, in Battersea, south London, England; died July 28, 1959; dau. of Percy Tarrant (well-known landscape painter and illustrator) and Sarah (Wyatt) Tarrant; studied at Heatherley's School of Art; attended Guildford School of Art, 1935; lifelong friend of Molly Brett (artist). ❖ At 20, illustrated Charles Kingsley's *The Water-Babies* (1908); with Marion St. John Webb, popularized "Flower Fairies" (1920), issuing a series of books on this theme; her religious paintings became very popular, while her best-known painting, *The Piper of Dreams*, was also reproduced, selling thousands; other illustrated books include *Fairy Stories from Hans Christian Andersen* (1910), Robert Browning's *The Pied Piper of Hamelin* (1912), Lewis Carroll's *Alice's Adventures in Wonderland* (1916), Eleanor Farjeon's *An Alphabet of Magic* (1928), *The Margaret Tarrant Birthday Book* (1932) and *The Margaret Tarrant Story Book* (1951). ❖ See also *Women in World History*.

TARRY, Ellen (b. 1906). African-American writer. Born 1906 in Birmingham, Alabama; attended Alabama State College for Negroes and Bank Street College Writers' Laboratory; children: Elizabeth. ❖ Journalist, teacher, social worker, and writer, 1st served as deputy assistant to the Regional Administrator for Equal Opportunity, Department of Housing and Urban Development; co-founded Friendship House (Chicago); worked for Archdiocese of New York; wrote weekly column, "Negroes of Note," for the *Birmingham Truth*; contributed to many Catholic periodicals; writings, which were heavily influenced by her involvement in the civil-rights movement, include *Janie Belle* (1940), *Hezekiah Horton* (1942), (with Marie Hall Ets) *My Dog Rinty* (1946), *The Runaway Elephant* (1950), *Katharine Drexel: Friend of the Neglected*

(1958), *Martin de Porres: Saint of the New World* (1963), *Young Jim: The Early Years of James Weldon Johnson* (1967), *The Other Toussaint: A Modern Biography of Pierre Toussaint, a Post-Revolutionary Black* (1981), and *Pierre Toussaint: Apostle of Old New York* (1998); was one of the 1st authors to use African-Americans as main characters in books for children. ❖ See also *The Third Door: The Autobiography of an American Negro Woman* (McKay, 1955); and *Women in World History*.

TARSOULI, Athena (1884–1974). Greek travel writer. Born 1884 in Athens, Greece; died 1974. ❖ Folklore historian, published *Castles and Cities of Morea* (1934), *Dodecanese* (1947), *White Islands* (1948), and *Greek Women Poets* (1953).

TASCHAU, Hannelies (1937—). German poet and novelist. Born April 26, 1937, in Hamburg, Germany. ❖ Works include *Verworrene Route* (1959), *Die Taube auf dem Dach* (1967), *Landfriede* (1978), *Luft zum Atmen* (1978), *Erfinder des Glücks* (1981), *Nahe Ziele* (1985), *Dritte Verführung* (1992), *Mein letzter Mann* (1992), and *Das Sommerhaus* (1995).

TASCHER DE LA PAGERIE, Marie-Josèphe (1763–1814). *See Josephine.*

TASHMAN, Lilyan (1899–1934). American screen star. Born Lillian Tashman, Oct 23, 1899, in Brooklyn, NY; died Mar 21, 1934, in New York, NY; sister of Kitty Tashman (actress, died 1931); m. Edmund Lowe (died 1971). ❖ Began career as an artist's model and came to prominence when she sat for Raphael Kirchner; appeared in Ziegfeld Follies (1916 and 1917); made film debut in *Experience* (1921); played the lead or was featured in *The Garden of Weeds*, *Pretty Ladies*, *This is Paris*, *Camille*, *French Dressing*, *Manhattan Cocktail*, *Craig's Wife*, *The Trial of Mary Dugan*, *Bulldog Drummond*, *No No Nanette*, *Puttin' on the Ritz*, *The Cat Creeps*, *Murder by the Clock* and *Frankie and Johnny*, among others.

TASKER, Marianne Allen (1852–1911). New Zealand domestic servant, feminist, and trade unionist. Name variations: Marianne Allen Manchester. Born Marianne Allen Manchester, Nov 13, 1852, in Sussex, England; died Feb 4, 1911, in Wellington, New Zealand; dau. of James (shoemaker) and Matilda (Gillet) Manchester; m. John Tasker (clerk), 1874 (died 1910); children: 5 daughters, 2 sons. ❖ Immigrated to New Zealand (1871); broke from Women's Social and Political League (WSPL) and formed Women's Democratic Union (WDU), which worked to better women's position in society through legislative reform and education (1895); founded Wellington branch of New Zealand Workers' Union and proposed separate division for women workers (1895); tried unsuccessfully to establish domestic workers' union (1906); served as president of WSPL (1911). ❖ See also *Dictionary of New Zealand Biography* (Vol. 2).

TASMA (1848–1897). *See Couvreur, Jessie.*

TASTU, Amable (1798–1885). French poet. Born Sabine Casimire Amable Voïart in 1798 in Metz, France; died 1885; married; children: 1 son. ❖ Especially adept at writing elegiac poetry, also wrote children's stories, educational texts, literary criticism, and translated *Robinson Crusoe* into French (1835); published "Le Narcisse" (The Narcissus) in *Mercure de France* (French Mercury, 1816), which led to her friendship with Adelaïde de Dufrénoy; writings include *Poésies* (Poems, 1826), *Le Livre des enfants* (The Children's Book, 1836–37), *Tableau de la littérature italienne* (List of Italian Literature, 1843) and *Voyage en France* (French Travel, 1845).

TATAPANUM OR TATATANUM (c. 1650–1676). *See Wetamoo.*

TATE, Ellalice (1906–1993). *See Hibbert, Eleanor.*

TATE, Mavis (1893–1947). British politician. Born Maybird Hogg, Aug 17, 1983; died June 5, 1947; m. Captain G. H. Gott, 1915 (div. 1925); m. Henry Tate, 1925 (div. 1944). ❖ As a member of the Conservative Party, elected to House of Commons for West Willesden (1931); moved to Frome constituency (1935); championed women's causes; was a member of the pro-German Right Club, an organization that sought to purge the Conservative Party of "Jewish influence"; suffered a nervous breakdown (1940); on recovery, abandoned pro-German beliefs and broke away from members of the Right Club; visited factories to investigate women's working conditions during World War II; was the only woman member of a group of MPs to visit German concentration camps, and was deeply affected by what she saw; lost her seat in House of Commons (1945).

TATE, Phyllis (1911–1987). British composer. Born in Gerrard's Cross, England, April 6, 1911; died May 20, 1987; studied at Royal Conservatory of Music, 1928–32; m. Alan Frank, 1935. ❖ Joined Composers' Guild (1959); served on board of Performing Rights Society's Members' Fund, the 1st woman to do so (1976–81); received many commissions from such sponsors as BBC and Royal Academy of Music; wrote Concerto for Saxophone and Strings (1944), the opera *The Lodger*, based on story of Jack the Ripper (1960), and *Serenade to Christmas* for soprano, chorus and orchestra (1972); other works include a cello concerto entitled *St. James Park—A Lakeside Reverie* (1933), *Apparitions—Ballade for Tenor, Harmonica, String Quartet and Piano* (1968), and *St. Martha and the Dragon* (1976), a work for narrator, soloists, chorus and orchestra. ❖ See also *Women in World History*.

TATE, Sharon (1943–1969). American actress. Born Sharon Marie Tate, Jan 24, 1943, in Dallas, Texas; murdered Aug 9, 1969, in Beverly Hills, California; dau. of Paul Tate (soldier) and Doris Tate; m. Roman Polanski (film director), Jan 20, 1968. ❖ Called "generous-hearted" by those who knew her, had small parts in films *Adventures of a Young Man* (1961), *Barrabas* (1961), *The Wheeler Dealers* (1963), *The Americanization of Emily* (1964), *The Sandpiper* (1965), *Eye of the Devil* (1966), before being cast in Roman Polanski's comic horror film *The Fearless Vampire Killers* (1966); co-starred in an adaptation of Jacqueline Susann's smash bestseller *Valley of the Dolls* (1967); 2 weeks before her baby was due, was murdered in her Beverly Hills home by members of Charles Manson's "Family." ❖ See also *Women in World History*.

TATENO, Chiyori (1970—). Japanese judoka. Born June 25, 1970, in Japan. ❖ At Barcelona Olympics, won a bronze medal in lightweight 56 kg (1992).

TATHAM, Reidun (1978—). Canadian synchronized swimmer. Born Mar 20, 1978, in Calgary, Alberta, Canada. ❖ Won a team bronze medal at Sydney Olympics (2000).

TATIANA (1897–1918). Russian grand duchess. Name variations: Tatiana Nicholaevna. Born Tatiana Nicholaevna Romanov (Romanoff or Romanovna) on June 10, 1897, in St. Petersburg, Russia; executed by the Bolsheviks on July 16–17, 1918, at Ekaterinburg, in Central Russia; dau. of Alexandra Feodorovna (1872–1918) and Nicholas II (tsar of Russia). ❖ See also *Women in World History*.

TATSUMI, Juri (1979—). Japanese synchronized swimmer. Born Sept 5, 1979, in Osaka, Japan. ❖ Won a team silver medal at Sydney Olympics (2000); at World championships, placed 1st in free routine combination (2003); won a team silver medal at Athens Olympics (2004).

TATTERSALL, Philippa (c. 1975—). British soldier. Born c. 1975 in London, England; grew up in Tarland, Aberdeenshire, Scotland; attended Roedean School and Chester College; attended the Royal Military Academy at Sandhurst. ❖ British army captain; became the 1st woman soldier to win the coveted Royal Marines' green beret, on her 3rd and final attempt, during the 8-week commando course, regarded as the world's toughest (May 31, 2002).

TAUBER, Ulrike (1958—). East German swimmer. Born June 16, 1958, in East Germany. ❖ At Montreal Olympics, won a silver medal in 200-meter butterfly and a gold medal in 400-meter indiv. medley (1976); at World championships, won gold medal for 400-meter indiv. medley (1975), then silver (1978).

TAUBER-ARP, Sophie (1889–1943). Swiss artist. Name variations: Sophie Taeuber or Sophie Taeuber-Arp; Sophie Täuber or Sophie Täuber-Arp. Born 1889 in Davos, Switzerland; died because of a faulty heater in her bedroom in 1943 in Zurich, Switzerland; m. Jean Arp (sculptor), 1921. ❖ Member of the Dadaist movement, who used purely geometric forms repeated many times against a plain background, taught weaving and embroidery at School of Arts and Crafts in Zurich (1916–29); also joined the Dadaists at the Café Voltaire in Zurich, mainly as a dancer but also collaborating with husband on the café's abstract interior decorations; created theatrical sets, marionettes, stained glass, embroideries, collages and furniture designs; coauthored and published *Dessin et arts textiles* (1927), a book about decorative arts, and founded a short-lived magazine on the subject (1937); also became interested in abstract painting (1915) and wood relief sculpture (1931); with husband, created abstract designs in embroidery and weaving and experimented in torn-paper work (1914–18); 1st abstract paintings were watercolors and drawings of rectangles and curved forms; gradually reduced this to rectangles and triangles, culminating in the powerful large-scale *Triptych: Vertical-Horizontal Composition with Reciprocal Triangles*

(1918), then employed a softer and more fluid approach in *Little Triptych, Free Vertical-Horizontal Rhythms, Cut and Pasted on a White Ground* (1919); associated with Cercle et Carre group and Abstraction-Creation group (1930s), both advocates of non-figural art. ❖ See also *Women in World History*.

TAURASI, Diana (1982—). American basketball player. Born Diana Lurena Taurasi, June 11, 1982, in Glendale, CA; dau. of Liliana and Mario Taurasi. ❖ As guard at University of Connecticut, led her team to 4 NCAA Final Fours (2000–2003), where they won 3 titles (2000, 2002, 2003); as the 1st draft pick in the WNBA, drafted by the Phoenix Mercury (2004); won a team gold medal at Athens Olympics (2004). Named Naismith National Player of the Year (2003, 2004) and AP Player of the Year (2003); won Wade Trophy (2003); named Kodak All-American (2002–04); named NCAA Final Four Most Outstanding Player (2003).

TAUSERET (c. 1220–1188 BCE). Egyptian pharaoh. Name variations: Tausert; Twosret. Born c. 1220 BCE; died 1188 BCE; sister-wife of Seti II, king of Egypt; children: (stepson) Siptah. ❖ Wife of Egyptian pharaoh Seti II, was briefly the ruler of the country in her own right (1196–1188 BCE); as the last legitimate member of the royal family of the brilliant 19th Dynasty of Egypt, may have 1st enjoyed a joint rule with brother-husband Seti II but then apparently attempted to assume the rulership of Egypt upon husband's death; constructed a large funerary temple for herself at ancient Thebes and a tomb in the Valley of the Kings, where no other woman of her dynasty was buried; for a time, was regent on behalf of her stepson, the young Siptah, who then ruled briefly by himself; afterwards, again ruled alone as a female pharaoh, but only for a short time.

TAUSKEY, Mary Anne (1955—). American equestrian. Born Dec 3, 1955. ❖ On Marcus Aurelius, won gold medal in team 3-day event at Pan American Games (1975) and Montreal Olympics (1976); named USEA Rider of the Year (1977).

TAUSSIG, Helen Brooke (1898–1986). American physician. Pronunciation: TOE-sig. Born Helen Brooke Taussig, May 24, 1898, in Cambridge, Massachusetts; died in auto accident in Kennett Square, Pennsylvania, May 21, 1986; dau. of Frank William Taussig (professor of economics at Harvard University) and Edith (Guild) Taussig; attended Radcliffe College, 1917–19; graduate of University of California, Berkeley, 1921; studied at Boston University, 1922–24; graduate of Johns Hopkins University School of Medicine, 1927; never married; no children. ❖ Renowned pediatric cardiologist and authority on congenital cardiac malformations who helped develop a surgical procedure that saved the lives of thousands of children; published 1st scientific article while in medical school (1925); was a fellow in cardiology and intern in pediatrics, Johns Hopkins Hospital (1927–29); was physician-in-charge, Harriet Lane Home Cardiac Clinic, Johns Hopkins Hospital (1930–63), began to discover that certain malformations created specific clinical signs and symptoms in children; 1st operated on a blue baby (1944), at Johns Hopkins Hospital (at least 12,000 children were eventually saved before advances in cardiac surgery reduced the need for the Blalock-Taussig procedure); was instructor in pediatrics, Johns Hopkins University School of Medicine (1930–46), associate professor of pediatrics (1946–59), professor of pediatrics (1959–63), professor emeritus (1963–86); published landmark textbook *Congenital Malformations of the Heart* (1947); was founding member of the Board of Pediatric Cardiology (1960); began investigation of birth deformities caused by thalidomide and other drugs (1962) and publicized conclusions in scientific articles, in medical meetings, and before Kefauver Committee in Congress; was 1st woman and 1st pediatric cardiologist to serve as president of American Heart Association (1965–66); more than any other person, was responsible for the development of pediatric cardiology as a medical specialty. Received Chevalier Légion d'Honneur (France, 1947), Feltrinelli Prize (Italy, 1954), Albert Lasker Award (1954), Eleanor Roosevelt Achievement Award (1957), Gairdner Foundation Award of Merit (Canada, 1959) and Medal of Freedom of US, presented by President Lyndon B. Johnson (1964). ❖ See also Joyce Baldwin, *To Heal the Heart of a Child: Helen Taussig, M.D.* (Walker, 1992); and *Women in World History*.

TAUTARI, Mary (d. 1906). New Zealand teacher, postmistress, and interpreter. Name variations: Mary Perry. Born Mary Perry at Mahia, New Zealand; died Jan 2, 1906, at Rawene, New Zealand; dau. of Robert Perry (trader) and Harieta Haumu; m. Hemi Tautari (trader), 1861 (died 1883). ❖ Established boarding school at Taumarere (1875–83); was granted subsidy to open day school for children (1883); acted as interpreter and postmistress at Taumarere, where she and husband owned property. ❖ See also *Dictionary of New Zealand Biography* (Vol. 2).

TAUTI (c. 1850–1918). *See Taytu.*

TAUTPHOEUS, Baroness von (1807–1893). Irish novelist. Name variations: Jemima Montgomery; Jemima Tautphoeus. Born Jemima Montgomery, Oct 23, 1807, at Seaview, in Co. Donegal, Ireland; died Nov 12, 1893; dau. of a landowner; m. Baron von Tautphoeus of Marquartstein (chamberlain to king of Bavaria), 1838 (died 1885); children: 1 son who also died in 1885. ❖ Wrote several novels that dealt with the manners and history of Bavarian scene; principal works include *The Initials* (1850), which is considered her best, *Cyrilla* (1854), *Quits* (1857) and *At Odds* (1863).

TAVAREDA DALMIRA, Dorotéia Engrássia (c. 1711–1793). *See Silve e Orta, Teresa M. da.*

TAVARES, Salette (1922–1994). Portuguese poet. Born 1922 in Lourenço Marques, Mozambique; died 1994. ❖ Studied in France and Italy; participated in experimental poetry movements *Poesia Experimental* and *Hidra*; works include *Espelho Cego* (1958), *Comcerto em Mi Maior para Clarinete e Bateria* (1961), *Tempo* (1965), *Quadrada* (1967) and *Lex Icon* (1971).

TAVERNER, Sonia (1936—). English ballet dancer. Born 1936 in Byfleet, England. ❖ Danced with Sadler's Wells Ballet for 1 season; immigrated to Canada with family (1956), and joined Gwynneth Lloyd's newly established Royal Winnipeg Ballet; danced in almost all of company's repertory works for more than a decade, in such 19th century classics as *Giselle* and such contemporary works as Fernand Nault's *Carmina Burana* and Benjamin Harkavy's *Fête Brillante* (1957), among others; made guest appearances in 19th-century works across US and Canada, notably in *Swan Lake*.

TAVERNIER, Nicole (fl. 1594). French saint. Born in France. ❖ Arrived in Paris from Reims (1594) and began preaching and healing on streets; became famous for performing miracles and was championed by aristocracy; organized religious procession through city.

TAYLAN, Nurcan (1983—). Turkish weightlifter. Born Oct 29, 1983, in Ankara, Turkey. ❖ At World championships, placed 2nd at 48 kg, 48 kg snatch, and 48 kg clean and jerk (2002); won a gold medal for 48 kg at Athens Olympics (2004).

TAYLOR, Alma (1895–1974). English actress. Born Jan 3, 1895, in London, England; died Jan 23, 1974, in London. ❖ Popular child star then leading lady, made film debut in *His Daughter's Voice* (1906), followed by *The Little Flower Girl, Tilly the Tomboy Goes Boating, Oliver Twist, David Copperfield, The Old Curiosity Shop, Trelawny of the Wells, Sweet Lavender, Iris, Annie Laurie, The Cobweb, The American Heiress, Sheba, South Sea Bubble, Deadlock, Everybody Dance* and *Blue Murder at St. Trinian's,* among others.

TAYLOR, Angella (1958—). Canadian runner. Name variations: Angella Issajenko. Born Sept 28, 1958, in St. Andrew, Jamaica; m. Tony Issajenko (sprinter). ❖ Won a gold medal for the 100 meters at the Commonwealth Games (1982) and a gold medal for the 200 and a bronze for the 100 (1986); won a silver medal in the 4 x 100-meter relay at Los Angeles Olympics (1984).

TAYLOR, Ann (1782–1866). English writer. Name variations: Ann Gilbert; Mrs. Gilbert. Born Jan 30, 1782, in London; died Dec 20, 1866, in Nottingham; dau. of Reverend Isaac Taylor (Congregational minister) and Ann Martin Taylor (1757–1830, writer); sister of writer Jane Taylor (1783–1824); m. Reverend Joseph Gilbert (Nonconformist), in 1813; children: 8, including Josiah (b. 1814) and Joseph (b. 1817). ❖ With sister, became one of the most popular English writers for children of early 19th century, shaping the way children's literature has been written ever since; co-published a volume of children's verses as *Original Poems for Infant Minds* (1805), which became immensely popular in England, remaining in print continuously into 1880s, and was translated and published abroad as well; wrote additional books of poetry and reading primers, both individually and jointly, which often included their engravings as illustrations; though marriage and motherhood left little time for writing, still contributed essays and reviews periodically to Christian journals, and published hymns; composed a short biography on husband after his death in 1853, and became a social activist, involved in the abolition movement and in the rehabilitation of former prostitutes. ❖ See also Christina D. Stewart, *The*

Taylors of Ongar: An Analytical Bio-bibliography (Garland, 1975); and *Women in World History.*

TAYLOR, Ann (1947—). Scottish politician and member of Parliament. Born Winifred Ann Walker, July 2, 1947, in Motherwell, Scotland; attended Bradford and Sheffield universities; m. David Taylor, 1966. ❖ Trained as a teacher, was a tutor at Open University; representing Labour, entered Parliament for Bolton West (1974–83); elected to House of Commons for Dewsbury (1987, 1992, 1997, 2001); served as chair, Modernisation of the House of Commons committee (1997–98) and Intelligence and Security committee (2001–05); was government whip (1977–79), shadow Housing minister (1981–83), shadow minister for Environmental Protection (1990–92), shadow secretary of State for Education (1992–94), shadow leader of House of Commons (1994–97), leader of House of Commons (1997–98) and government chief whip (1998–2001); did not stand for reelection (2005).

TAYLOR, Ann Martin (1757–1830). English writer. Name variations: Ann Martin. Born June 20, 1757, in Kensington, England; died June 4, 1830, in Ongar, England; m. Reverend Isaac Taylor (engraver, book illustrator and Congregational minister), in 1781 (died 1829); children: Ann Taylor (1782–1866, writer); Jane Taylor (1783–1824, writer); Isaac Taylor (b. 1787); Jefferys Taylor (b. 1792); Jemima Taylor (b. 1798); 6 who died young. ❖ Best known as the author of conduct books, published *Maternal Solicitude,* with a preface by daughter Ann, to critical acclaim (1814); collaborated with daughter Jane on *Correspondence between a Mother and Her Daughter at School;* also wrote *Practical Hints to Young Females* (1815) and *The Present of a Mistress to a Young Servant;* published 2 bestselling fictional works, *The Family Mansion* (1819) and *Retrospection* (1821); wrote last book, *Itinerary of a Traveller in the Wilderness,* a series of essays meditating on preparation for death and the afterlife (1825). ❖ See also Christina D. Stewart, *The Taylors of Ongar: An Analytical Bio-bibliography* (Garland, 1975); and *Women in World History.*

TAYLOR, Anna Edson (c. 1858–c. 1921). American adventurer. Name variations: Annie Taylor. Born c. 1858; died c. 1921; lived in Bay City, Michigan. ❖ First person to survive going over Niagara Falls in a barrel, went over the 167' high Horseshoe Falls (on Canadian side of Niagara Falls) in a 4½'x3' barrel (Oct 24, 1901). ❖ See also *Women in World History.*

TAYLOR, Annie Royle (1855–c. 1920). British missionary. Born 1855 in Egremont, Cheshire, England; died c. 1920. ❖ Worked for China Inland Mission for 3 years around Yangtze River, Lanchow, and near Tibetan border (1884–1887); after illness in Australia, went to Darjeeling and worked among Tibetans (1887–91); disguised as a pilgrim, traveled with young convert Pontso on treacherous 7-month journey to Tibet (1892), but was turned away by army chief at Lhasa; returned with group of men to Darjeeling and later opened shop in Yatung; was the 1st European woman to enter Tibet.

TAYLOR, Betty (1916–1977). Canadian track-and-field athlete. Born Elizabeth Taylor, Feb 22, 1916; died Feb 2, 1977; raised in Hamilton, Ontario, Canada; attended McMaster University in Hamilton. ❖ Won a bronze medal for the 80-meter hurdles at Berlin Olympics (1936). Won Canadian Press Award and Velma Springstead Memorial Trophy, and named Best Canadian female athlete (1936). ❖ See also *Women in World History.*

TAYLOR, Brenda (1934—). English ballet dancer. Born 1934 in London, England. ❖ Trained at school of Sadler's Wells Ballet, then joined the company (1951), which became the Royal Ballet; danced with company for over 10 years and was celebrated for her Lilac Fairy in *The Sleeping Beauty* and Myrthe in *Giselle.*

TAYLOR, Brenda (1962—). Canadian rower. Born Oct 28, 1962, in Canada. ❖ At Barcelona Olympics, won a gold medal in coxed eights and a gold medal in coxless fours (1992).

TAYLOR, Dari (1944—). English politician and member of Parliament. Born Dec 13, 1944; dau. of Phyllis Jones and Daniel Jones (MP for Burnley, 1959–83); m. David E. Taylor, 1970. ❖ Representing Labour, elected to House of Commons for Stockton South (1997, 2001, 2005); named PPS to parliamentary under secretaries Lewis Moonie and Lord Bach, Ministry of Defence; served as PPS to Hazel Blears, Home Office minister (2003–05).

TAYLOR, Edith Stamp (1904–1946). *See Stamp Taylor, Edith.*

TAYLOR, Elizabeth (d. 1708). British poet. Name variations: Mrs. Taylor; Lady Wythens; (pseudonym) Olinda. Fl. in 1685; died 1708; dau. of Sir Thomas Taylor; m. Sir Frances Wythens, 1685; m. Sir Thomas Colepeper, 1704. ❖ Poems include "Ode: Ah poor Olinda never boast," "Song, Made by Mrs. Taylor: Ye Virgin Pow'rs defend my heart," "Song, by Mrs. Taylor: Strephon has Fashion, Wit and Youth," and "To Mertill who desired her to speak to Clorinda of his Love."

TAYLOR, Elizabeth (1912–1975). English novelist and short-story writer. Born in Reading, Berkshire, England, July 3, 1912; died Nov 19, 1975; dau. of Oliver Coles and Elsie Coles; m. John William Kendal Taylor (manufacturer), 1936; children: son Renny (b. 1937); daughter Joanna (b. 1941). ❖ While husband was in Royal Air Force, lived in Scarborough, Yorkshire (1940–45); published 1st 2 autobiographical novels, *At Mrs. Lippincote's* (1945) and *Palladian* (1946); last novel, *Blaming,* published posthumously (1976); often wrote about outwardly respectable, well-to-do, well-bred people who inhabit the Thames Valley, emphasizing their lives rather than plot or setting; other writings include *A View of the Harbour* (1947), *A Wreath of Roses* (1949), *A Game of Hide-and-Seek* (1951), *The Sleeping Beauty* (1953), *Hester Lilly and Twelve Short Stories* (1954), *Angel* (1957), *The Blush and Other Stories* (1958), *In a Summer Season* (1961), *The Soul of Kindness* (1964), *A Dedicated Man and Other Stories* (1965), *Mossy Trotter* (1967), *The Wedding Group* (1968), *Mrs. Palfrey at the Claremont* (1971), *The Devastating Boys* (1972) and *Blaming* (1976). ❖ See also Robert Liddell, *Elizabeth and Ivy* (Peter Owen, 1986); and *Women in World History.*

TAYLOR, Elizabeth (1916–1977). *See Taylor, Betty.*

TAYLOR, Elizabeth (1932—). English-born American actress. Born Feb 27, 1932, in London to American parents; dau. of Francis Taylor (art dealer) and Sara (Warmbrodt) Taylor (who officially changed name to Sara Sothern when she began acting in stock companies); m. Conrad "Nicky" Hilton Jr. (hotelier), 1950 (div. 1951); m. Michael Wilding (actor), 1952 (div. 1957); m. Michael Todd (producer), 1957 (died 1958); m. Eddie Fisher (singer), 1959 (div. 1964); m. Richard Burton (actor), 1964 and 1975 (div. 1973 and 1976); m. John Warner (US senator), 1976 (div. 1982); m. Larry Fortensky (construction worker), 1991 (div. 1996); children: (2nd m.) Michael Wilding Jr. (b. 1953); Christopher Wilding (b. 1955); (3rd m.) Elizabeth Frances Todd (b. 1957); (5th m.) adopted, Maria Burton. ❖ Academy Award-winning actress who remains a respected and much-loved celebrity around the world, particularly after raising millions of dollars for AIDS research, though later career was less spectacular and marked by numerous health problems; moved with parents to Los Angeles at outbreak of WWII (1939); made screen debut in *There's One Born Every Minute* (1942); was 1st noticed in *Lassie Come Home* (1943), followed by *Jane Eyre* (1944) and *The White Cliffs of Dover* (1944); had 1st starring role in *National Velvet* (1944); while under contract to MGM (1942–62), starred in numerous movies, including *Courage of Lassie* (1946), *Cynthia* (1947), *Life with Father* (1947), *A Date with Judy* (1948), *Julia Misbehaves* (1948), *Little Women* (1949), *Father of the Bride* (1950), *Father's Little Dividend* (1951), *A Place in the Sun* (1951), *Ivanhoe* (1952), *Elephant Walk* (1954), *The Last Time I Saw Paris* (1954), *Giant* (1956), *Raintree County* (1957), *Cat on a Hot Tin Roof* (1958) and *Suddenly, Last Summer* (1959); as one of the world's most glamorous actresses, became as famous for her off-screen life, especially during filming of *Cleopatra* (1963); won Academy Awards for *Butterfield 8* (1960) and *Who's Afraid of Virginia Woolf?* (1966); also appeared on stage in *Private Lives* with Richard Burton; other films include *The VIPs* (1963), *The Sandpiper* (1965), *The Taming of the Shrew* (1967), *Reflections in a Golden Eye* (1967), *The Comedians* (1967), *Boom!* (1968), *Under Milkwood* (1971), *A Little Night Music* (1977), *The Mirror Crack'd* (1980) and *The Visit* (1999). Named Dame of the Order of the British Empire by Queen Elizabeth II (2000). ❖ See also Alexander Walker, *Elizabeth* (Grove, 1990); C. David Heymann, *Liz: An Intimate Biography of Elizabeth Taylor* (Birch Lane, 1995); Donald Spoto, *A Passion for Life: The Biography of Elizabeth Taylor* (HarperCollins, 1995); and *Women in World History.*

TAYLOR, Elizabeth Best (1868–1941). New Zealand temperance worker and social reformer. Name variations: Elizabeth Best Ellison. Born Sept 21, 1868, at Lyttelton, New Zealand; died April 27, 1941, in Dunedin; dau. of Robert Best Ellison and Rachel (Robinson) Ellison; m. Thomas Edward Taylor (politician), 1892 (died 1911); children: 6. ❖ Active in New Zealand Women's Christian Temperance Union (WCTU), and in other organizations that focused on issues involving children, women, and world peace; became justice of peace and associate magistrate to Children's Court; one of New Zealand delegates to 1st Pan-Pacific Women's Conference (1928). Received King George V Silver Jubilee Medal (1935). ❖ See also *Dictionary of New Zealand Biography* (Vol. 3).

TAYLOR, Enid Stamp (1904–1946). *See Stamp Taylor, Enid.*

TAYLOR, Estelle (1894–1958). American silent-film actress. Born Estelle Boylan, May 20, 1894, in Wilmington, DE; died April 15, 1958, in Hollywood, CA; m. Kenneth M. Peacock (banker), 1913 (div.); m. Jack Dempsey (boxer), 1925 (div. 1931); m. Paul Small (film producer, div.). ❖ Only stage appearance was with husband Jack Dempsey in *The Big Fight* (1928); began in movies as a double for Dorothy Dalton; films include De Mille's *The Ten Commandments* (as Miriam, sister of Moses), *While New York Sleeps, Blind Wives, Monte Cristo, The Alaskan, Dorothy Vernon of Haddon Hall, Lady Raffles, Don Juan* (as Lucretia Borgia), *Cimarron, Mahattan Madness, Street Scene* (as Sylvia Sidney's mother), *Mary, Queen of Scots* and *Where East is East;* retired from film (1945).

TAYLOR, Eva (1879–1966). British science historian and geographer. Born Eva Germaine Rimington Taylor, June 22, 1879, in Highgate, England; died July 5, 1966, in Wokingham, England; dau. of Charles Richard Taylor (solicitor) and Emily Jane (Nelson) Taylor; Royal Holloway College, BS, 1903, DSc, 1929; earned diploma with distinction at Oxford University, 1908; married; children: 3 sons. ❖ Following graduation from Oxford, remained there as a research assistant to A. J. Herbertson, head of the geography school (1908–10); was a lecturer at Clapham Training College for Teachers and at Froebel Institute; moved on to a lecturing post at East London College (1920), then a similar post at Birkbeck College (1921), where she was appointed the school's chair of geography (1930) and enjoyed a brilliant reputation as a lecturer during 15-year career there; published *Tudor Geography, 1485–1583* (1930) and *Late Tudor and Early Stuart Geography, 1583–1650* (1934); served Britain during and immediately after WWII by contributing her expertise in geography to Association for Planning and Regional Reconstruction, for which the Royal Geographical Society awarded her the Victoria Medal (1947); retired from Birkbeck (1944), then was elected one of the 1st fellows of Birkbeck (1960); also received a fellowship from the Royal Geographical Society (1965). ❖ See also *Women in World History.*

TAYLOR, Eva (1895–1977). African-American singer, dancer, and radio show host. Name variations: Irene Gibbons; Catherine Henderson. Born Irene Gibbons, Jan 22, 1895, in St. Louis, MO; died Oct 31, 1977, in Mineola, NY; dau. of Frank Gibbons and Julia (Evans) Gibbons; m. Clarence Williams (musician), 1921 (died 1965). ❖ At 3, began singing and dancing in vaudeville, performing with Josephine Gassman and Her Pickaninnies at St. Louis' Orpheum Theater, then toured with troupe in US and abroad; in NY, appeared in chorus of *Vera Violetta* (1911); rejoined Gassman troupe (1914), touring as ballad singer and dancer; following marriage (1921), performed in clubs and theaters in NY, singing ballads and blues with husband's group, the Clarence Williams Trio; appeared on stage in such shows as *Queen of Hearts, Step On It* and *Shuffle Along* (1922); sang at the Apollo, Carnegie Hall, Madison Square Garden, Savoy Ballroom and Harlem Casino (1923–30); other stage appearances include the musical revue *Melodies of 1933, Bottomland* and *Keep Shufflin';* became the 1st black American female soloist to broadcast nationally and internationally on radio (1929); hosted the "Eva Taylor, Crooner Show" (1932–33); as staff soloist at WEAF-WJZ, often sang with Knickerbockers Orchestra, but also appeared on "Harlem" (with Cab Calloway Orchestra), "The Eveready Hour" (with Nat Shilkret), "Slow River Show" (with Lil Hardin Armstrong), and "Kraft Music Hall" (with Paul Whiteman Orchestra); recorded under names Eva Taylor, Irene Gibbons, and Catherine Henderson. ❖ See also *Women in World History.*

TAYLOR, Florence M. (1879–1969). British-born Australian architect, engineer, and publisher. Born Florence Mary Parsons, 1879, in Bristol, England; died Feb 13, 1969; dau. of John Parsons (government employee) and Eliza (Brooks) Parsons; educated at Sydney Technical College and University of Sydney Engineering School; m. George Augustine Taylor (architect), 1907 (died 1928). ❖ Moved with family to Australia (1888); was chief draftsperson for John Burcham Clamp, the Diocesan architect; became Australia's 1st qualified female architect (1920); with husband, helped to found the Town Planning Association of Australia and established a publishing company that produced 11 trade journals (1913); following his death (1928), reduced the number of publications to 3: *Building* (renamed *Building, Lighting, and Engineering), Construction,* and *The Australasian Engineer;* continued to conceive and execute ideas, including a subway in Sydney, an airport in Newport, and an expressway to link the downtown area of Sydney with the suburbs. Named Officer of the Order of the British Empire (OBE, 1939) and Commander of the Order of the British Empire (CBE, 1961). ❖ See also *Women in World History.*

TAYLOR, Harriet (1807–1858). English philosopher and feminist. Name variations: Harriet Taylor Mill. Born Harriet Hardy in London, England, Oct 8, 1807; died Nov 3, 1858; dau. of Harriet (Hurst) Hardy and Thomas Hardy (surgeon); educated at home by father; m. John Taylor (died 1849); m. John Stuart Mill (the philosopher), April 1851; children: (1st m.) 2 sons and daughter, Helen Taylor (1831–1907). ❖ Recognized not only for her philosophical treatments of marriage and of women's political equality, but also for her contributions to John Stuart Mill's political writings; was acknowledged by Mill as the co-author of *The Principles of Political Economy* and *On Liberty* (though this assertion is disputed to some extent); published her "Enfranchisement of Women" in the utilitarian journal, *The Westminster Review* (July 1851), in which she argued that women have a right to both education and the self-development that comes with it, and maintained that a woman's role as a wife or mother should not limit her pursuit of other careers; likely inspired the writing of Mill's *On the Subjection of Women*, the only feminist treatise written by a man for many centuries. ❖ See also Alice S. Rossi, ed. *Essays on Sex Equality: John Stuart Mill and Harriet Taylor* (U. of Chicago Press, 1970); F. A. Hayek, *John Stuart Mill and Harriet Taylor: Their Friendship and Subsequent Marriage* (Routledge & Kegan Paul, 1951); and *Women in World History.*

TAYLOR, Harriette Deborah (1807–1874). *See Lacy, Harriette Deborah.*

TAYLOR, Helen (1831–1907). British suffragist and social reformer. Born 1831; died 1907 in Torquay, England; dau. of Harriet Taylor (1807–1858, feminist) and John Taylor; stepdau. of John Stuart Mill (the philosopher and economist). ❖ Was already an adult when mother married John Taylor (1851); joined Mill in Avignon after mother died there (1858); helped Mill produce *The Subjection of Women* (1869); also edited the works of historian Henry Thomas Buckle (1872) and Mill's autobiography (1873); after Mill died (1873), moved to London and became involved in politics and social issues; was considered a proficient public speaker; was a member of the London School Board (1876–84) and helped to institute radical changes in London's industrial schools; was also president of Prisoners' Sustentation Fund; vigorously opposed the Liberal government's policy of Irish coercion (1880–85); was a promoter of land nationalization, taxation of land values, and women's suffrage movement; helped establish Democratic Federation (1881). ❖ See also *Women in World History.*

TAYLOR, Jane (1783–1824). English writer. Born Sept 23, 1783, in London; died April 12, 1824, in Ongar; dau. of Reverend Isaac Taylor (Congregational minister) and Ann Martin Taylor (1757–1830, writer); sister of writer Ann Taylor (1782–1866); never married. ❖ With sister, published the bestselling *Rhymes for the Nursery* (1806), which included her verse "Twinkle, twinkle, little star," still one of the best-known verses in English; also co-published *Hymns for Infant Minds* (1811), among others; her 1st novel, *Display*, established her reputation as an independent writer (1815); remained a prolific author throughout life and contributed essays on various moral themes to *Youth's Magazine* until 1822. ❖ See also Christina D. Stewart, *The Taylors of Ongar: An Analytical Bio-bibliography* (Garland, 1975); *Memoirs and Poetical Remains of the late Jane Taylor* (1825); and *Women in World History.*

TAYLOR, Janet (1804–1870). English nautical teacher and writer. Born Jane Ann Ionn, May 13, 1804, in Wolsingham, England; died of bronchitis, Jan 26, 1870, in London; 5th of 8 children of Peter Ionn (cleric) and Joyce Ionn; m. George Taylor Jane (brewer who agreed to drop his surname so she would not be Jane Jane), 1825 (died 1853); children: 5, including Herbert (b. 1831). ❖ Mathematician, astronomer, meteorologist, writer and instrument maker, set up home in East Street, Lion Square, London, at time of marriage, where she began Mrs. Janet Taylor's Nautical Academy and Navigation Warehouse (c. 1830); taught merchant navy officers navigation techniques; learned principles of navigation at her father's free grammar school; taught algebra, astronomy and geometry; adjusted compasses in iron merchant ships; published *Lunar Tables for Calculating Distances* (3rd ed., c. 1840) and a pilot book for the Brazilian coast. Received gold medals from kings of Prussia and Holland.

TAYLOR, June (1917–2004). American dancer and choreographer. Born Dec 14, 1917, in Chicago, IL; died May 16, 2004, in Miami, FL; sister of Marilyn Taylor (who married Jackie Gleason); m. Sol Lerner (died 1986). ❖ Made performance debut at 13 in *George White Scandals* in Chicago; danced with The Chez Pare Adorables until age 17; performed in cabarets in England with Ted Lewis Band until c. 1938; choreographed works for precision dance troupe performing at Chicago nightclubs and later on tour around US; appeared on tv with June Taylor Dancers on Ed Sullivan's "The Toast of the Town," followed by "Cavalcade of Stars" (1950–52), "Jackie Gleason Show" (1953–59, 1962–70) and "American Scene Magazine." Won an Emmy for choreography on "Jackie Gleason Shjow" (1954).

TAYLOR, Kamala (1924–2004). British novelist. Name variations: Kamala Purnaiya Taylor; (pseudonym) Kamala Markandaya. Born Kamala Purnaiya in 1924 (one source cites 1923), in Chimakurti, Mysore, India; died at home, May 16, 2004, in London, England; her family was Brahmin, the highest Hindu caste; graduate of University of Madras; m. Bertrand Taylor (died 1986); children: Kim. ❖ One of the 1st women writers from the Indian subcontinent to achieve renown, studied history at Madras University and became a journalist; moved to Britain (1948); came to prominence with 1st novel, *Nectar in a Sieve* (1954), which was a bestseller, particularly in US, followed by *Some Inner Fury* (1955) and *A Silence of Desire* (1960), considered one of her best works; wrote 7 other novels, including *A Handful of Rice* (1966), *The Nowhere Man* (1972), *Two Virgins* (1973), *The Golden Honeycomb* (1977), and *Pleasure City* (1982, published as *Shalimar* in US, 1983). ❖ See also *Women in World History.*

TAYLOR, Knox (1814–1835). American first daughter. Name variations: Sallie Knox Taylor; Sarah Knox Taylor; Knox Davis. Born Sarah Knox Taylor in 1814; died of malaria, Sept 15, 1835; dau. of Zachary Taylor (army major, Mexican war hero, and president of US) and Margaret Mackall Smith Taylor; m. Jefferson Davis (president of the Confederacy), June 17, 1835. ❖ See also *Women in World History.*

TAYLOR, Koko (1935—). African-American singer. Name variations: Ko Ko Taylor. Born Cora Walton, Sept 28, 1935, in Memphis, TN; m. Robert "Pops" Taylor, 1953 (died 1988); m. Hays Harris, 1996. ❖ At 18, moved to Chicago and started singing with Buddy Guy/Junior Wells Blues Band; discovered by Willie Dixon (1962), had smash hit with song, "Wang Dang Doodle" (1965); formed own band, the Blues Machine (1975); appeared in films *The Blues Is Alive and Well in Chicago* (1970), *Wild at Heart* (1990) and *Blues Brothers 2000* (1998); albums include *I Got What It Takes* (1975), *Queen of the Blues* (1985), and *Royal Blue* (2000); opened nightclub, Koko Taylor's Celebrity, in Chicago (1999); won 19 W. C. Handy awards, more than any other female blues singer.

TAYLOR, Laurette (1884–1946). American actress. Born Loretta Cooney, April 1, 1884, in New York, NY; died Dec 7, 1946, in New York, NY; dau. of James Cooney and Elizabeth Cooney; married Charles A. Taylor (producer), 1901 (div. 1910); m. J. Hartley Manners (English playwright), 1911 (died 1928); children: (1st m.) Dwight (b. 1902); Marguerite (b. 1904). ❖ Stage actress, considered one of the finest of the early 20th century, whose often troubled career ended in triumph with her creation of Amanda Wingfield in *The Glass Menagerie*; made professional stage debut (c. 1900); made NY debut as lead in *The Great John Ganton* (1909); became toast of Broadway starring in *Peg o' My Heart* (1912), the longest-running dramatic play up to that time; starred in other plays by husband, including *The Harp of Life* (1917), *Out There* (1918), *One Night in Rome* (1919) and *The National Anthem* (1922); adapted and starred in Fannie Hurst's *Humoresque*; her career, built on a series of simple-hearted characters created by husband, languished during more cynical 1920s, forcing her retirement from stage; turned increasingly to alcohol; after closing in Zoe Akins' *The Furies* (1928), entered a sanitarium for treatment of her disease; returned briefly to the stage (late 1930s–early 1940s), most notably in revivals of *Alice Sit by the Fire* (1932) and *Outward Bound* (1939), and with her portrayal of Amanda Wingfield in the original production of *The Glass Menagerie* (1945), for which she was awarded Critics Circle Award for Best Actress (1946); films include *Peg o' My Heart* (1922), *Happiness* (1924) and *One Night in Rome* (1924). ❖ See also Marguerite Courtney, *Laurette* (Atheneum, 1968); and *Women in World History.*

TAYLOR, Lily Ross (1886–1969). American educator. Born Aug 12, 1886, in Auburn, Alabama; killed by hit-and-run driver, Nov 18, 1969, in Bryn Mawr, Pennsylvania; dau. of William Dana Taylor (railway engineer and professor) and Mary (Ross) Taylor; University of Wisconsin, AB, 1906; attended American Academy in Rome, 1917–20; Bryn Mawr College, PhD, 1912. ❖ Classicist who helped develop the influential 20th-century view of Roman political history and religion, including the areas of the Roman Republic's political structure and religious cults; became a Latin instructor at Vassar College (1912), where she remained until 1927, eventually earning title of professor; became 1st woman to receive a fellowship at American Academy in Rome (1917); appointed professor and chair of Latin department at Bryn Mawr (1927), then named dean of graduate school (1942); became 1st woman appointed Sather Professor of Classics at University of California (1947); served as director of Classical School of American Academy in Rome (1952–55), then returned to Bryn Mawr; was Jerome Lecturer at American Academy in Rome and University of Michigan (1964–65); writings include *Local Cults in Etruria* (1932), *The Divinity of the Roman Emperor* (1931), *Party Politics in the Age of Caesar* (1949) and *Roman Voting Assemblies* (1966); was associate editor for *Classical Philology* (1940s). Received *Life* Magazine Teachers Award (1952). ❖ See also *Women in World History.*

TAYLOR, Louisa Jane (1846–1883). English murderer. Born 1846; hanged at Maidstone Prison, Jan 2, 1883. ❖ After husband's death (Mar 1882), boarded with the elderly William and Mary Ann Tregillis, in exchange for nursing 82-year-old Mary Ann; used sugar of lead (lead acetate) to slowly poison Mrs. Tregillis.

TAYLOR, Lucy Hobbs (1833–1910). American dentist. Born Lucy Beaman Hobbs, probably in Franklin Co., rather than Clinton Co., NY, Mar 14, 1833; died in Lawrence, Kansas, Oct 3, 1910; dau. of Lucy (Beaman) and Benjamin Hobbs; Ohio College of Dental Surgery, DDS, 1866; m. James Myrtle Taylor (dentist who apprenticed under her), April 24, 1867 (died 1886); no children. ❖ The 1st woman in the world to earn a dental degree, graduated from Franklin Academy, Malone, NY (1849); moved to Cincinnati, Ohio, where she was refused admission to Eclectic College of Medicine due to her gender (1859); was tutored privately by Charles A. Cleaveland, professor of materia medica and therapeutics at Eclectic, who suggested she pursue a career in dentistry, a field more accessible to women; was also refused admission to Ohio College of Dental Surgery (1859 and 1861); was tutored privately by Jonathan Taft, dean of the college, then was accepted as an apprentice to a dentist in private practice, Dr. Samuel Wardle; opened her own practice in Cincinnati (1861), then Bellevue, Iowa (1861), then McGregor, Iowa (1863), where her reputation spread; graduated from Ohio College of Dental Surgery (1866); became the 1st woman in the world to become a Doctor of Dental Surgery (1866); was the 1st woman to address a state dental association (July 1866); moved to Chicago, opened a practice, and was elected to Illinois State Dental Society (1866); moved to Lawrence, Kansas, where dentists were much in demand, and opened a practice (1867), which grew into one of the largest in the state; joined Rebekah Lodge of the Independent Order of Odd Fellows (1871), becoming the 1st female Noble Grand of Degree of the order; joined Adah Chapter of Order of the Eastern Star (1875); went into semiretirement (1886); retired (1907); much like Elizabeth Blackwell in the field of medicine, held open the door for women to enter the field of dentistry. ❖ See also *Women in World History.*

TAYLOR, Margaret (1917—). *See Burroughs, Margaret Taylor.*

TAYLOR, Margaret Smith (1788–1852). American first lady. Name variations: Peggy Taylor. Born Margaret Mackall Smith, Sept 21, 1788, in Calvert Co., Maryland; died Aug 18, 1852, in Pascagoula, Mississippi; dau. of Walter Smith (planter and veteran of Revolutionary War) and Ann (Mackall) Smith; m. Zachary Taylor (1784–1850, 12th president of US), June 21, 1810; children: 8, including Ann Mackall Taylor (b. 1811); (Sarah) Knox Taylor (b. 1814, who m. Jefferson Davis); Octavia Pannill Taylor (b. 1816); Margaret Smith Taylor (b. 1819); Mary Elizabeth Taylor Bliss (1824–1909); Richard Taylor (b. 1826). ❖ As first lady (1849–1850), was an "invisible" presence in the White House; welcomed friends and relatives in her private upstairs sitting room, ate with the family, and worshipped regularly at St. John's Episcopal Church, but all official social functions were presided over by youngest daughter Mary Elizabeth Taylor Bliss, 2nd wife of her former son-in-law Jefferson Davis; her fears that the presidency would take her husband's life were not unfounded (he died in office [July 9, 1850]); left Washington shortly after the funeral and never spoke of the White House again. ❖ See also *Women in World History.*

TAYLOR, Maria Jane (1844–1933). *See Mackay, Maria Jane.*

TAYLOR, Mary (1817–1893). English traveler. Born in Yorkshire, England, Feb 26, 1817; died in Gomersal, England, Mar 1, 1893; dau. of Joshua and Ann Tickell Taylor; attended boarding school in Roe Head, Mirfield; immigrated to New Zealand (1845); returned to England (1859). ❖ A friend of Charlotte Brontë, journeyed to New Zealand to seek her fortune and temporarily found it as a shopkeeper; traveled, lectured, and wrote on behalf of women; protested a society that kept middle-class women from earning a living, and her anger informs her only novel *Miss Miles: A Tale of Yorkshire Life Sixty Years Ago.* ❖ See also *Women in World History.*

TAYLOR, Mary (1898–1984). English radio researcher and mathematician. Name variations: Mrs. Clive Slow. Born July 15, 1898, in Sheffield, England; died May 26, 1984; Girton College, Cambridge, BS, 1920, MA, 1924; University of Göttingen, PhD, 1926; m. (Ernest) Clive Slow, 1934; children: 2 daughters. ❖ The 1st woman to research radio as a profession, studied with Edward Appleton at Cambridge; wrote a doctoral thesis on electromagnetic waves in German; awarded a Yarrow fellowship to conduct research at University of Göttingen with professor Richard Courant; abstracted and translated papers for *Wireless Engineer* (1930–40); served as a scientific officer at Radio Research Station in Slough (1929–34); joined London Mathematics Society and Cambridge Philosophical Society.

TAYLOR, Mary Isabella (1871–1939). *See Lee, Mary Isabella.*

TAYLOR, Mary Scott (1751–1793). *See Scott, Mary.*

TAYLOR, Maud Ruby (1879–1963). *See Basham, Maud Ruby.*

TAYLOR, Megan (1920–1993). British figure skater. Born Oct 25, 1920 in UK; died July 23, 1993, in Glen Head, NY. ❖ One of Great Britain's greatest female athletes in 1930s, competed in 1932 Olympics at Lake Placid, at age 11, and finished 7th; known for her spinning, won World championships (1938 and 1939) and 2 British championships; moved to US to teach.

TAYLOR, Melanie Smith (1949—). American equestrian in show jumping. Name variations: won her titles until 1985 as Melanie Ainsworth Smith. Born Melanie Ainsworth Smith in Litchfield, Connecticut, Sept 23, 1949; m. Lee Taylor (polo player), 1985. ❖ Was the 1st American Grandprix Association Rider of the Year (1978); riding Calypso, won the Grand Prix of Paris (1980), the American Gold Cup, American Invitational, and World Cup (1982), and was on the US team that won the Nations Cup and World Cup (1983); again riding Calypso, was on the 1st American equestrian team to win an Olympic gold medal in team jumping, at Los Angeles (1984); after retiring from competition, became a tv commentator for equestrian events. ❖ See also *Women in World History.*

TAYLOR, Penny (1981—). Australian basketball player. Born Penelope Jane Taylor, May 24, 1981, in Melbourne, Australia. ❖ Forward, played for the WNBL Dandenong Rangers (1998–2002); placed 1st at Oceania championships (2003); won a team silver medal at Athens Olympics (2004); selected by the Cleveland Rockers in the 1st round of WNBA draft (2001), then signed with Phoenix Mercury (2004).

TAYLOR, Rachael (1976—). Australian rower. Born May 6, 1976, in Australia. ❖ With Kate Slatter, won a silver medal for coxless pair at Sydney Olympics (2000).

TAYLOR, Renée (1933—). American comedic actress and writer. Name variations: Renee Taylor. Born Renee Wexler, Mar 19, 1933, in New York, NY; m. Joseph Bologna (actor, comedian), 1965. ❖ With husband, co-wrote and starred in the Broadway hit *Lovers and Other Strangers* (1968); films include *Made for Each Other* (also co-wrote screenplay), *Cops and Robbers, Mixed Company, The Big Bus, Chapter Two, My Favorite Year, Blame It on Rio, The Woman in Red, Transylvania 6-5000, It Had to Be You* (also co-directed and co-wrote screenplay), *Coupe De Ville* and *Love Is All There Is* (also co-wrote screenplay); co-created and co-wrote tv series "Calucci's Dept." Nominated for Oscar for Best Adaptation for *Lovers and Other Strangers* (1970).

TAYLOR, Ruth (1908–1984). American actress. Name variations: Ruth Zuckerman. Born Jan 13, 1908, in Grand Rapids, Michigan; died April 12, 1984, in Palm Springs, CA; children: Buck Henry (b. 1930, actor-writer). ❖ Films include *Gentlemen Prefer Blondes, Just Married, The College Coquette* and *This Thing Called Love.*

TAYLOR, Sallie (1814–1835). *See Taylor, Knox.*

TAYLOR, Sarah Knox (1814–1835). *See Taylor, Knox.*

TAYLOR, Sophia Louisa (1847–1903). New Zealand suffragist and landowner. Name variations: Sophia Louisa Davis. Born July 2, 1847, in Kaitaia, New Zealand; died Jan 24, 1930, at Alberton, New Zealand; dau. of John Davis and Mary Ann (Cryer) Davis; m. Allan Kerr Taylor,

1865 (died 1890); children: 6 daughters, 4 sons. ❖ Member of first committee of Auckland branch of Women's Franchise League (1892); also active in Women's Christian Temperance Union (WCTU), despite opposing prohibition. ❖ See also *Dictionary of New Zealand Biography* (Vol. 3).

TAYLOR, Stella (1929–2003). English-American long-distance swimmer. Born 1929 in England; died Feb 11, 2003 in Fort Lauderdale, FL. ❖ Moved to Canada, then Buffalo, where she spent 4 years at Sister of Mercy Convent preparing to be a nun; moved to Fort Lauderdale; set several records, including records for swimming the English Channel, Loch Ness, and the straits between the Bahamas and Florida; at age 52 (April 1982), swam laps in the 55-yard pool at the International Swimming Hall of Fame in Ft. Lauderdale for 65 hours, having traversed the length of the pool and back 3,120 times, an estimated 175 miles, which shattered her old record. ❖ See also *Women in World History.*

TAYLOR, Susie King (1848–1912). African-American memoirist. Born Susie Baker, Aug 6, 1848, on Isle of Wight off Savannah, Georgia; died Oct 6, 1912, in Boston, Massachusetts; dau. of Raymond Baker and Hagar Ann (Reed) Baker (slaves on the Grest farm); m. Sergeant Edward King, early 1860s (died Sept 1866); m. Russell L. Taylor, 1879 (died c. 1902); children: (1st m.) 1 son (died 1898). ❖ Author of *Reminiscences of My Life in Camp,* the only Civil War memoir by an African-American woman veteran, was born a slave; escaped to freedom during Civil War (April 1862); joined the 1st South Carolina Volunteers, later the 33rd US Colored Troops, as a laundress, nurse and teacher; was a teacher and house servant in Savannah, Georgia (1866–74); moved to Boston (1874); organized the Women's Relief Corps (1886); was president of local WRC (1893); wrote *Reminiscences of My Life in Camp* (1902). ❖ See also *Women in World History.*

TAYLOR, Valerie (1902–1988). English actress. Born Nov 10, 1902, in Fulham, England; died Oct 24, 1988, in London; m. Hugh Sinclair (div.); m. Desborough William Saunders (died). ❖ Made London debut in *Storm* (1924); other London plays include *The Show, Berkeley Square, The House of the Arrow, The Seagull, Call It a Day, The Children's Hour, Dear Octopus, Skylark, Venus Observed, The Happy Man, Mary Stuart* and *Time Present;* made NY debut in *Berkeley Square* (1929), followed by *Peter Ibbetson, Love of Women* and *The Gioconda Smile,* among others; co-authored the film *Take My Life.*

TAYLOR, Valerie (1935—). Australian scuba diver and filmmaker. Name variations: Valerie Hughes. Born Valerie May Hughes, 1935, in Sydney, Australia; m. Ron Taylor (an underwater filmmaker and photographer). ❖ First began swimming as therapy after a bout of poliomyelitis; also started snorkeling and spearfishing at an early age; won Australian women's scuba title (1963), as well as Australian Women's Spearfishing Open championship 3 times; with husband, began to concentrate on underwater photography (c. 1968); was hired by Peter Gimbel to film his search for the great white shark, *Blue Water—White Death;* also filmed the live shark segments for *Jaws* (1974); with husband, had tv series in Australia, "Taylor's Innerspace." ❖ See also *Women in World History.*

TAYLOR-GREENFIELD, Elizabeth (c. 1819–1876). See *Greenfield, Elizabeth Taylor.*

TAYLOR-QUINN, Madeleine (1951—). Irish politician. Born Madeleine Taylor, May 1951, in Kilkee, Co. Clare, Ireland; dau. of Frank Taylor (TD for Clare, 1969–81); m. George Quinn. ❖ Began career as a secondary schoolteacher; elected as a Fine Gael candidate to the 22nd Dáil (1981–82), the 1st woman to represent Clare; returned to 23rd–26th Dáil (1982–92); elected to Seanad from Cultural and Educational Panel (1982, 1993, 1997, 2002).

TAYLOR-SMITH, Shelley (1961—). Australian long-distance swimmer. Born 1961 in Perth, Australia; won a scholarship to the University of Arkansas, graduating with a degree in physical education. ❖ Began setting local and state swimming records at the Surat Swim Club while still in teens; began setting marathon swimming records, breaking the women's 4-mile time (1983); was the 1st woman to finish the 25-kilometer swim at Seal Beach (1985); won the Manhattan Island swim 4 times, setting a record in that event; won Australian marathon titles (1988–90) and women's world marathon championship in Perth (1991).

TAYMOR, Julie (1952—). American director, costume designer and puppet creator. Born Dec 15, 1952, in Newton, MA; dau. of Melvin (gynecologist) and Betty Taymor (political activist); graduate of Oberlin College; m. Elliot Goldenthal (composer). ❖ Lived in Indonesia, where she was exposed to Javanese shadow puppets and founded an acting company; won Obie for stage version of Thomas Mann's *The Transposed Heads* (1986); directed *Oedipus Rex* for Saito Kinen Festival in Japan (1992); awarded MacArthur Foundation "genius grant" (1991); received Tony nominations as Best Director and Best Scenic Designer for *Juan Darien: A Carnival Mass* (1997); won Tony Award for Best Director in a Musical, the 1st woman to receive that award, and Best Costume Designer, for *Lion King* (1998); directed film *Frida* (2002).

TAYMURIYYA, 'A'isha 'Ismat al- (1840–1902). Egyptian writer. Name variations: 'A'isha Taymur; Aichat Asmat Taimur; Aisha Esmat al-Taymuriyya. Pronunciation: AY-sha IS-mat at-tay-moo-REE-a. Born 1840 in Cairo, Egypt; died in Cairo, 1902; dau. of Isma'il Pasha Taymour (Turkish notable of Kurdish origin who served as a government official in Egypt, died 1882) and his Circassian concubine; began education in Turkish, Arabic, and Persian at home when quite young; m. Mahmud Bey al-Islambuli (Turkish notable), 1854 (died 1885); children: daughter, Tawhida (died 1873, age 18). ❖ Poet and essayist, who advocated the education of women and was celebrated by later authors as one of the founders of feminist expression in Arabic, stopped writing upon marriage and did not resume until after the death of husband and father; published essays in Egyptian press and corresponded with other female intellectuals, such as the Syrian poet Warda al-Yaziji (1838–1924); resumed her own education; writings in Arabic include: *Nata'ij al-Ahwal fi al-Aqwal wa-al-Af al* (*The Results of Circumstances in Words and Deeds,* 1887), *Mir'at al-Ta'amul fi al-Umur* (*The Mirror of Contemplation on Things,* published during the last 10 years of her life), and a collection of poetry, *Hilyat al-Tiraz* (*Embroidered Ornaments,* 1885); also published a collection of Turkish poetry, *Shakufa* (*Blossom*); has been called the "mother of Egyptian feminism" because her work inspired later generations of feminist writers, but with the exception of her publications she never ventured into the public sphere. ❖ See also (in Arabic) Mayy Ziyadah, *'A'isha Taymur: Sha'irat al-Tali'ah* ('A'isha Taymur: A Vanguard Poet, Cairo: Matba'at al-Muqtataf, 1926); and *Women in World History.*

TAYTU (c. 1850–1918). Empress of Ethiopia. Name variations: Taitu; Tauti; Queen of Shoa. Pronunciation: TIE-too. Born Taytu Betul Hayle Maryam, probably in 1850 or 1851, probably in Mahdere Maryam in Begemder, Ethiopia; died Feb 11, 1918, in Addis Ababa; dau. of Betul (warrior) and a mother whose 2nd marriage was to a lay administrator of the monastery at Debre Mewi; was married at age 10, to an officer in the army of Emperor Tewodros II; married Kenyazmach Zikargatchew, c. 1881–82; married 3 more times, the last in April 1883, to Sahlé Maryam, who became Emperor Menelik II (or Menilek), in one of history's most remarkable alliances; no children. ❖ Important contributor to the modernization of her country, who led troops in battle and devised strategies crucial in defeating the Italian army in 1896; upon marriage to Sahlé Maryam, became queen of Shoa (1883); with husband's ascent to imperial throne, became empress of Ethiopia (1889); during the struggle against Italian armies, devised the strategy which defeated the fort at Adigrat (Feb 1896); led troops at the Battle of Adwa, Italy's final humiliating defeat (March 1, 1896); increased her power as regent after Menelik suffered a stroke (1906); lost the battle to guarantee the throne for a member of her own family after the death of Menelik (1913). ❖ See also Chris Prouty, *Empress Taytu and Menelik II: Ethiopia 1883–1910* (1986); and *Women in World History.*

T. CH. (1830–1880). See *Márchenko, Anastasiia.*

TCHACHINA, Irina (1982—). Russian rhythmic gymnast. Name variations: Irina Chaschina. Born April 24, 1982, in Omsk, USSR. ❖ At World championships, placed 1st in team all-around (1999, 2003); won a silver medal for indiv. all-around at Athens Olympics (2004).

TCHEMERZIN, Monika (1924—). See *Tcherina, Ludmilla.*

TCHEPALOVA, Julija (1976—). Russian cross-country skier. Name variations: Julia Tschepalova. Born Dec 23, 1976, in Komsomolski/Amur, Russia, m. Dmitri Linschanko; children: Olesja. ❖ Won a gold medal for 30 km at Nagano Olympics (1998); won a gold medal for 1.5 km sprint and a bronze medal for 10 km at Salt Lake City Olympics (2002); won a gold medal for 4 x 5 km relay and a silver medal for 30 km at Torino Olympics (2006).

TCHEPELEVA, Anna (1984—). See *Chepeleva, Anna.*

TCHERIAZOVA, Lina (1968—). See *Cheryazova, Lina.*

TCHERINA, Ludmilla (1924–2004). French ballerina and actress. Name variations: Ludmila or Ludmilla Tchérina; Monique Audran, Monika Tchemerzin. Born Monique Tchemerzine (or Tchemerzina), Oct 10, 1924, in Paris, France; died Mar 21, 2004, in Paris; dau. of a French mother and Georgian general; trained at the school of the Paris Opéra; m. Edmond Audran (actor, died 1951); m. Raymond Roi. ❖ At Paris Opéra, created role of Juliet in Serge Lifar's *Romeo and Juliet* (1942); danced with Opéra de Marseilles and was a prima ballerina with Monte Carlo Ballet, where she created roles in Lifar's *Mephisto Valse* (1946); starred in French and foreign films, including *Un revenant, The Red Shoes, La Belle que voilà, The Tales of Hoffman, The Legend of Parsifal, Spartacus, The Daughter of Mata Hari, Sign of the Pagan, Oh Rosalinda!, Lune de Miel, Les amants de Teruel* and *Une ravissante idiote*.

TCHERKASSKY, Marianna (1955—). American ballet dancer. Born 1955 in Glen Cove, Long Island, NY. ❖ Trained at School of American Ballet; danced a season with Eglevsky Ballet; joined American Ballet (1970) and performed successfully in classical as well as contemporary works; danced Swanilda and Giselle, and had principal roles in *Les Sylphides, Spectre de la Rose,* and others; featured in van Dantzig's *Monument for a Dead Boy* and Darrell's *The Nutcracker*; retired (1996); taught for Bartholin Institute in Copenhagen and University of Cincinnati; became ballet mistress at Pittsburgh Ballet Theatre.

TCHERNICHEVA, Lubov (1890–1976). Russian-born British ballerina. Name variations: Liubov Pavlovna Chernysheva; Luba Tchernicheva. Born Lubov Pavlovna Tchernicheva in St. Petersburg, Russia, Sept 17, 1890; died in Richmond, Surrey, England, Mar 1, 1976; studied at St. Petersburg's Imperial Ballet Academy, graduating 1908; m. Sergei Grigoriev (stage and rehearsal director), 1909 (died 1968). ❖ Major figure in 20th-century classical ballet, joined Maryinsky Theater (1908); moved to Paris with husband (1911) and joined Diaghilev's Ballets Russes; within a few years, was the company's leading dancer, particularly distinguished in the repertory of Michel Fokine; became ballet mistress to Diaghilev's Ballets Russes (1926), then joined de Basil's Ballet Russe of Monte Carlo (1932); danced for more than 3 decades, well past the retirement age of most ballerinas; as late as 1937, was creating the role of Francesca in David Lichine's *Francesca da Rimini*; enjoyed great success in such roles as Zobeide in *Scheherazade* and the Miller's wife in *The Three Cornered Hat*; remained active in de Basil company until it was disbanded (1952); with husband, staged productions of great ballet classics from Diaghilev repertory, including *The Firebird* (Sadler's Wells Ballet, 1954) and *Petrushka* (Royal Ballet, 1957); made last appearance on stage (1959), creating the role of Lady Capulet in John Cranko's *Romeo and Juliet* at La Scala, Milan; continued to teach at Sadler's Wells Ballet and London Festival Ballet. ❖ See also Cyril Beaumont, *The Art of Lubov Tchernicheva* (C. W. Beaumont, 1921); and *Women in World History*.

TE AITANGA-A-MAHAKI (1932—). *See Hineira, Arapera.*

TEALE, Nellie (1900–1993). American naturalist. Born Nellie Imogene Donovan, Sept 13, 1900, in Colorado Springs, Colorado; died in Windham, Connecticut, July 18, 1993; educated at Earlham College; m. Edwin Way Teale (1899–1980, naturalist author), 1923; children: David Allen Teale (killed in action in Germany, 1945). ❖ Collaborated with husband Edwin Way Teale on a series of nature books that have been acclaimed as modern classics; with husband, developed an insect garden near their home in Baldwin, on Long Island, which became the basis for his 1st book, *Grassroot Jungles* (1937); helped husband with research and editing of his 4-vol. series "The American Seasons" (1947–65), by which time the couple had traveled 76,000 miles across the US; purchased a farm outside the village of Hampton, Connecticut, and named their property Trail Wood (1959); eventually donated the land for a wildlife sanctuary, the Trail Wood Audubon Sanctuary; continued to live in the old farmhouse at Trail Wood until her death. ❖ See also *Women in World History*.

TE AMA, Maikara (1863–1937). *See Te Whaiti, Kaihau Te Rangikakapi Maikara.*

TE AO AHITANA, Kiti Karaka (1870–1927). *See Riwai, Kiti Karaka.*

TEASDALE, Sara (1884–1933). American writer. Born in St. Louis, Missouri, Aug 8, 1884; committed suicide in New York, NY, Jan 29, 1933; dau. of John Warren Teasdale (wealthy businessman) and Mary Elizabeth (Willard) Teasdale; m. Ernest Filsinger (St. Louis businessman), Dec 19, 1914 (div. Sept 5, 1929, died May 1937); no children. ❖ One of the foremost lyric poets in the early decades of the 20th century, was also shy, sensitive, physically frail, ambitious and talented; with a few other women, had an arts group, the Potters (1904–07); with mother, traveled to Europe and Near East (1905); contributed a prose sketch, "The Crystal Cup," to William Morris Reedy's weekly, *The Mirror* (1906); published *Sonnets to Duse and Other Poems* (1907); selected for membership in Poetry Society of America in New York (1910); published *Helen of Troy and Other Poems* (1910); wrote short story, "The Sentimentalist," her only prose piece, which was published in *Smart Set* (1916); published *Rivers to the Sea*, which received glowing reviews (1916); now an acclaimed poet, moved to NY (1916); her collection of poems for children, *Rainbow Gold* was also an immediate success (1922); other writings include *Flame and Shadow* (1920), *Dark of the Moon* (1926), *Strange Victory* (1933), *The Collected Poems of Sara Teasdale* (1937), and (ed. by William Drake) *Mirror of the Heart, Poems of Sara Teasdale* (1984). Won Poetry Society of America award (June 1917); awarded Columbia Poetry Prize (1918) and Brookes More Prize for poetry (1921). ❖ See also William Drake, *Sara Teasdale: Woman & Poet* (Harper & Row, 1979); Margaret Haley Carpenter, *Sara Teasdale: A Biography* (Schulte, 1960); and *Women in World History*.

TEASDALE, Verree (1904–1987). American stage and screen actress. Name variations: Verree Menjou; Verrée Teasdale. Born Mar 15, 1904, in Spokane, WA; died Feb 17, 1987, in Culver City, CA; cousin of Edith Wharton (the writer); m. William O'Neal (div.); m. Adolph Menjou (actor), 1934 (died 1963). ❖ Made Broadway debut as Augusta Winslow-Martin in *The Youngest* (1924), followed by *The Morning After, The Master of the Inn, The Constant Wife, Elizabeth and Essex, The Greeks Had a Word for It* and *Experience Unnecessary*, among others; films include *Syncopation, The Sap from Syracuse, Payment Deferred, Roman Scandals, Fashions of 1934, Madame Du Barry, A Midsummer Night's Dream, Topper Takes a Trip* and *Come Live with Me*.

TE ATI AWA (1937—). *See Grace, Patricia.*

TEBA, countess of. *See Eugénie (1826–1920).*

TEBALDI, Renata (1922–2004). Italian soprano. Born in Pesaro, Italy, Feb 1, 1922; died Dec 19, 2004, in the Republic of San Marino; dau. of Giuseppina (Barbieri) Tebaldi and Teobaldo Tebaldi (cellist); studied with Brancucci and Campogalliani at Parma Conservatory, and with Carmen Melis and Giuseppe Pais at Pesaro Conservatory; never married. ❖ Possessed with one of the most beautiful voices of the mid-20th century, debuted in the small but significant role of Elena in Boïto's *Mefistofele* at Rovigo (1944); next appeared at Trieste Opera as Desdemona in Verdi's *Otello* (1946); chosen by Toscanini to perform in a gala concert of Verdi's *Te Deum* at the reopening of Teatro alla Scala (1946); made La Scala stage debut in starring role of Eva in Wagner's *Die Meistersinger von Nürnberg*, sung in Italian as *I maestri cantori* (1947); debuted at Covent Garden as Desdemona and San Francisco as *Aïda* (1950); made Metropolitan Opera debut (1955) and sang there regularly until 1972, giving more than 250 performances; going beyond standard Verdi and Puccini roles, displayed her mastery of title roles in such operas as *Andrea Chénier*, Catalani's *La Wally*, Spontini's *Olympia*, Handel's *Giulio Cesare*, and Verdi's rarely performed *Giovanna d'Arco*; retired (1976). ❖ See also Carlamaria Casanova, *Renata Tebaldi: The Voice of an Angel*, trans. and ed. by Connie Mandracchia DeCaro (Baskerville, 1995); Walter Panofsky, *Renata Tebaldi* (Berlin: Rembrandt, 1961); Victor Seroff, *Renata Tebaldi: The Woman and the Diva* (1970); and *Women in World History*.

TEBENIKHINA, Irina (1978—). Russian volleyball player. Born Dec 5, 1978, in Fergana, USSR. ❖ Placed 3rd at World championships (1998); won a team silver medal at Athens Olympics (2004).

TECK, duchess of. *See Mary Adelaide (1833–1897).*

TECSON, Trinidad (1848–1928). Philippine revolutionary. Born Nov 18, 1848, in San Miguel de Mayumo Bulacan, Philippines; died in Manila, Jan 28, 1928; buried in Manila's Tomb of the Veterans; dau. of Rafael Tecson and Monica S. Perez; m. 2nd husband Julian Alcantara (Philippine nationalist, died); m. Doroteo Santiago (died); m. Francisco Empained; children: (1st m.) 2 died young. ❖ Hero of the Philippine Revolution, joined the Katipunan, a revolutionary nationalist army (1895); participated in battles against Spanish army under generals Llanera, del Pilar, and Soliman, and was wounded several times; while husband and others defended the fort of Biak-na-Bato in Bulacan from attack, established a field hospital at Biak-na-Bota for injured soldiers; went on to create nursing stations on the battle sites of the southern Philippine provinces, organizing and training nationalist women to serve in her hospitals. Honored by American Red Cross. ❖ See also *Women in World History.*

TECUICHPO (d. 1551). Aztec princess. Name variations: Tecuichpoch; Miahuaxochitl; (baptismal name) Isabel; Doña Isabel. Dau. of Moctezuma II (c. 1480–1520), Aztec emperor (r. 1502–1520); m. Alonso de Grado; m. Pedro Gallego; m. Juan Cano de Suavedra, in 1531; some sources claim also married Cuauhtemoc, last emperor of the Aztecs; children: (with Hernán Cortés) daughter Leonor Cortés Motecuhzoma, also known as Marina. ❖ See also *Women in World History.*

TEER, Barbara Ann (1937—). African-American actress, dancer and theater founder. Born June 18, 1937, in East St. Louis, IL. ❖ Trained with Mary Wigman, Alwin Nikolais, Syvilla Fort, and others; danced early in Alvin Ailey company, including with touring company in *Pearl Bailey Dance Revue*; performed in concert groups of Agnes de Mille and Louis Johnson; served as director of workshops at Harlem School of the Arts; important figure in development of theater in NY, co-founded Group Theater Workshop which later grew into Negro Ensemble Company, and National Black Theatre (NBT).

TEERLINC, Levina (c. 1520–1576). Flemish artist. Born Levina Benninck c. 1520 (some sources cite 1515) in Bruges, Flanders (now a part of Belgium); died 1576 in Stepney, England; dau. of Simon Benninck (painter of miniatures and book illuminator); married; children: Marcus. ❖ Achieved some fame in Flanders before migrating to England (c. 1546) to accept an annuity from the court of Henry VIII; stayed at court for a number of years, working for Edward VI, Mary I, and Elizabeth I, whose portrait she 1st painted in 1551; became an English subject (1566) and made her home in Stepney with husband; was the only Flemish miniature painter known to be at the English court (1546–76); was also the most important miniaturist between the death of Hans Holbein the Younger (1543) and the ascent of her successor, Nicolas Hilliard. Miniatures thought to be from her hand are *Portrait of a Young Woman* (1549), *Katherine, Countess of Hertford*, and a portrait of Elizabeth I in her coronation robes that dates to approximately 1559. ❖ See also *Women in World History.*

TEETERS, Nancy Hays (1930—). American economist. Born July 29, 1930, in Marion, Indiana; Oberlin College, AB in economics, 1952; University of Michigan, MA in economics, 1954. ❖ The 1st woman on the board of governors of the Federal Reserve Bank, served as a staff economist in the government finance section of board of governors of Federal Reserve System in Washington, DC (1957–66); served as an economist for Bureau of the Budget (1966–70), and was a senior fellow of Brookings Institute (1970–73); served as president of National Economists Club (1974–75); was also chief economist for US House of Representatives Committee on the Budget (1974–78); was a member of Federal Reserve's board of governors (1978–84); became vice-president and chief economist at IBM.

TEEUWEN, Josepha (1974—). Dutch field-hockey player. Name variations: Margje Teeuwen. Born May 21, 1974 in Netherlands. ❖ Won team bronze medals at Atlanta Olympics (1996) and Sydney Olympics (2000).

TEFFI, N. A. (1872–1952). Russian writer. Name variations: Nadezhda Aleksandrovna Teffi; Nadezhda Aleksandrovna Lokhvitskaia or Lokhvitskaya; Nadezhda Aleksandrovna Buchinskaia, Buchinskaya, or Buczynska; (pseudonym) Teffi. Born Nadezhda Aleksandrovna Lokhvitskaia in St. Petersburg, Russia, May 9, 1872; died in Paris, France, Oct 6, 1952; dau. of Aleksandr Lokhvitskii (prominent St. Petersburg lawyer); sister of poet Mirra Lokhvitskaia (1869–1905) and writers Varvara Lokhvitskaia and Elena Lokhvitskaia; m. Vladislav Buchinskii, c. 1890; children: daughters Valeriia (b. 1892) and Elena; son Jan. ❖ One of the most popular women writers in Russia at the turn of the century, best known for her comic short stories and feuilletons, continued to enjoy a large readership even after emigrating from Russia in 1919; left husband Buchinskii (c. 1900) and began a writing career in St. Petersburg; published 1st poem (1901); served on editorial staff of journal *The New Life* (1905); published 1st book, *Seven Fires*, which consisted of 39 poems in the Symbolist vein and 1 play on an oriental theme (1910); met with immense success with 1st volume of prose, *Humorous Stories* (1910), which took the difficulties of daily life as its subject; published 6 more major collections of comic stories which were well received by critics and readers alike (1911–18); also continued to publish in *The Satyricon* and became a regular contributor to the Moscow paper, *The Russian Word*, a period that marked the height of

"Teffimania" in Russia; published a volume of "serious" stories entitled *The Lifeless Beast* (1916), which were later reprinted in exile as *The Quiet Backwater*; emigrated from Russia (1919) and settled in Paris (1920), where she flourished as an émigré writer; prepared 19 volumes of short stories (some of which were reprints) as well as 2 collections of poetry, a novel, memoirs, and a collection of plays (1920–40); saw 2 of her full-length plays, *A Moment of Fate* and *Nothing of the Sort*, produced in Paris (1937 and 1939); wrote regularly for the Parisian émigré paper *The Latest News*, as well as for its conservative competitor *La Renaissance*; was one of the 1st members of the Russian émigré community to establish an active literary salon in Paris; also played a key role in organizing various foundations for Russian writers and artists. ❖ See also *Women in World History.*

TEGAKWITHA (1656–1680). See Tekakwitha, Kateri.

TEGART, Judy. See Dalton, Judy Tegart.

TE HIKAPUHI (1860/71?–1934). See Hikapuhi.

TE HUINGA (1852/56?–1930). See Carroll, Heni Materoa.

TEITEL, Carol (1923–1986). American stage, radio, tv actress. Born Carolyn Sally Kahn, Aug 1, 1923, in Brooklyn, NY; died July 27, 1986, in Camden, NJ, from complications following an auto accident; m. Nathan R. Teitel (playwright). ❖ Made Broadway debut in *The Country Wife* (1957); other NY plays include *The Entertainer, Hamlet, Marat/de Sade, A Flea in Her Ear, Crown Matrimonial, The Little Foxes, The Marriage of Figaro, The Misanthrope, Long Day's Journey into Night, Every Good Boy Deserves Favor* and the title role in *Juana La Loca*; on tv, appeared in "Edge of Night," "The Guiding Light," and "Lamp unto My Feet," among others; was a founding member of American Conservatory Theater in San Francisco. Won Obie awards for *A Country Scandal* and *Under Milk Wood.*

TEIXEIRA DA SILVA, Katia Cilene (1977—). See Katia.

TEKAHIONWAKE (1861–1913). See Johnson, E. Pauline.

TE KAHUHIAPO, Rahera (1820s?–1910). New Zealand tribal leader. Born probably in 1820s, near Lake Rotoiti, New Zealand; died Oct 12, 1910, at Ngapeke, New Zealand; dau. of Te Nia and Rangiawhao; m. Hone Te Atirau, mid-1860s (died early 1880s); m. Eru Netana, 1885; children: 1 daughter. ❖ Held in high esteem due to connection with several tribes; inherited control of large land holdings upon death of husband, and wielded great influence among her people. ❖ See also *Dictionary of New Zealand Biography* (Vol. 2).

TE KAKAPI, Ripeka Wharawhara-i-te-rangi (?–1880). New Zealand tribal leader. Name variations: Wharawhara-i-te-rangi. Died Jan 4, 1880; m. Ihaka Ngahiwi. ❖ Instrumental in bringing peace to warring Waimarama and Hereaungu peoples (c. 1852). ❖ See also *Dictionary of New Zealand Biography* (Vol. 1).

TEKAKWITHA, Kateri (1656–1680). Mohawk nun and saint. Name variations: Tagaskouita; Tegakwitha; also known as Lily of the Mohawks, The Genevieve of New France, La Bonne Catherine, Katherine or Catherine Tekakwitha. Pronunciation: KAT-e-ree Tek-a-QUEE-ta. Born 1656 at Ossernenon, a Mohawk settlement situated near the site of present-day Auriesville, New York; died April 17, 1680, at Caughnawaga, New France (near Montreal, Quebec, Canada); 1st child of Kenhoronkwa (a Mohawk chief) and Kahenta (an Algonquin); given no formal education; never married; no children. ❖ Mohawk who was the 1st native woman to be beatified by the Roman Catholic Church; at about 4, father, mother, and infant brother all died of smallpox, and she was left with both a severely disfigured face and very poor eyesight; baptized into the Catholic faith (1676) and given the name by which she is now popularly known, Kateri (Katherine); with family and neighbors exerting a strong pressure to recant her beliefs, traveled to the St. François Xavier mission (1677); found refuge with Anastasia Tegonhatsihongo, an Algonquin native and a previous friend of her mother; though she was not permitted to become a nun, took a vow of perpetual chastity (Mar 1679); became a figure of veneration among her fellow natives, Jesuit priests, and local French settlers; as she lay dying, exhorted visitors to follow the principles of Christian virtue; was beatified by the Vatican on the basis of numerous favors reputedly granted to those who had sought her intercession through prayer (June 22, 1980). Following her death, one of her closest advisors reported that her face, so severely marked by the smallpox virus, had miraculously become "beautiful." ❖ See also Marie Cecelia Buehrle, *Kateri of the Mohawks* (All Saints Press, 1962); Rachel Jodoin, *Kateri Tekakwitha* (Lidec, 1983);

Ellen Walworth, *The Lily of the Mohawks, 1656–1680* (Peter Paul and Brother, 1893); Karen Anderson, *Chain Her by One Foot* (Routledge, 1991); and *Women in World History.*

TEKAKWITHA, Katherine (1656–1680). *See Tekakwitha, Kateri.*

TE KANAWA, Kiri (1944—). New Zealand soprano. Name variations: Dame Kiri Janette Te Kanawa. Born Mar 6, 1944, in Gisborne, North Island, New Zealand, of Maori and British parentage; m. Desmond Park, 1967. ❖ Began career as a pop singer in night clubs in New Zealand and was accepted at London Opera Centre without audition; joined Royal Opera Company (1970) and appeared to critical acclaim as the Countess in Mozart's *Marriage of Figaro* (1971); debuted at Metropolitan Opera as Desdemona in Verdi's *Otello* (1974); appeared with most major companies in US, Europe and Australia; acclaimed roles include Mimì in Puccini's *La Bohème,* Tatyana in Tchaikovsky's *Eugene Onegin,* Micaela in Bizet's *Carmen,* and Donna Elvira in Mozart's *Don Giovanni;* released several recordings of classical and popular music, including *Blue Skies* (1986), *Italian Opera Arias* (1991), and *Our Christmas Songs for You* (1996); wrote *Land of the Long White Cloud: Maori Myths and Legends* (1989). Made DBE (1982).

TE KIRI, Rahui (?–1913). *See Tenetahi, Rahui Te Kiri.*

TE KIRI KARAMU, Heni (1840–1933). New Zealand tribal leader, teacher, warrior, and interpreter. Name variations: Heni Pore, Jane Foley, Jane Russell. Born Nov 14, 1840, at Mokoia Island, New Zealand; died June 24, 1933, in New Zealand; dau. of either Richard Russell or Thomas William Kelly and Maraea; m. Te Kiri Karamu; m. Denis Stephen Foley, 1869; children: 11. ❖ Taught at boarding school for Maori children in Auckland; during tribal wars, translated captured military documents for Wiremu Tamihana (1863–64); recognized as tribal warrior and supported government against Pai Marire movement (1865–66); worked as licensed interpreter and became secretary of Maori mission (1880s). ❖ See also *Dictionary of New Zealand Biography* (Vol. 1).

TELALKOWSKA, Wanda (1905–1986). Polish designer and printmaker. Born 1905 in Poland; died 1986 in Poland; Academy of Fine Arts, diploma, 1931. ❖ Active in modernist movement, began career as member of Polish design group LAD; organized and ran production department for Poland's ministry of culture after WWII; while serving as director of Warsaw's Institute of Industrial Design (1950–56), protected and sponsored many modernist designers during Stalinist era; organized collaborative projects, bringing together professional designers, folk artists and children and producing many creative textiles and ceramics.

TELEKI, Blanka (1806–1862). Hungarian countess and education reformer. Born July 3, 1806, at Kövarhosszufalu, Hungary; died Oct 23, 1862, in Paris; dau. of Count Imre Teleki (1782–1848) and Karolina Brunswick (1782–1843); studied arts in Munich and Paris. ❖ Known as the Revolutionary Countess, was a pioneer in women's education; founded the 1st secondary girls' school in Hungary (1846), in Pest; after Hungarian revolution against the Habsburgs (1848–49), was imprisoned for 5 years for hiding refugees (1853–57). Painting *Blanka Teleki in Prison* rendered by Viktor Madarasz (1867).

TELES, Leonor (c. 1350–1386). *See Leonora Telles.*

TELES, Lígia Fagundes (b. 1923). *See Telles, Lygia Fagundes.*

TELESILLA (fl. 6th or 5th c. BCE). Poet from Argos. Name variations: Telessilla. ❖ Led the women of Argos in a successful defense of their city against the army of Cleomenes, a Spartan king. A statue was erected in her honor before a temple of Aphrodite in Argos. ❖ See also *Women in World History.*

TELKES, Maria (1900–1995). Hungarian-born American scientist. Name variations: Maria de Telkes. Born Maria de Telkes, Dec 12, 1900, in Budapest, Hungary; died Dec 2, 1995, in Budapest; dau. of Aladar de Telkes and Maria (Laban) de Telkes; naturalized US citizen, 1937; Budapest University, BA, 1920, PhD, 1924; never married; no children. ❖ Physical chemist who investigated the practical uses of solar energy, taught physics in a Budapest school (1923–24); came to US (1925); as a biophysicist, was on the staff of Cleveland Clinic Foundation (1925–37), working for a time with Dr. George Crile on a series of experiments which led to the invention of a photoelectric mechanism for recording the energy of the human brain; also collaborated with Crile on his book *Phenomena of Life;* became a US citizen (1937); was employed for 2 years as a research engineer at the laboratories

of Westinghouse Electrical Co. in East Pittsburgh, Pennsylvania; became a research associate in solar energy conversion program at Massachusetts Institute of Technology (MIT, 1939); during WWII, served as civilian adviser to US Office of Scientific Research and Development and developed a system for distilling fresh water from sea water, to be used on life rafts; wrote many scholarly articles on solar heating, thermoelectric generators and distillers, and electrical conductivity of solids and electrolytes; died in Budapest on her 1st return visit since 1925. ❖ See also *Women in World History.*

TELL, Alma (1892–1937). American stage and screen actress. Born Mar 27, 1892, in New York, NY; died Dec 29, 1937, in Hollywood, CA; sister of Olive Tell (actress, 1894–1951); m. (William) Stanley Blystone (actor). ❖ Made NY debut as Ethel in *Peg o' My Heart* (1914); also appeared as Harriett in *Our Children* (1915), Susan Lenox in *The Rise and Fall of Susan Lenox* (1920), Annie Laurie in *When We Were Young* (1920), and Carol Kennicott in *Main Street* (1921); films include *On with the Dance, Paying the Piper, Broadway Rose, Saturday's Children* and *The Right to Love.*

TELL, Olive (1894–1951). American stage and screen actress. Born Sept 27, 1894, in New York, NY; died June 8, 1951, in New York, NY; sister of Alma Tell (1892–1937, actress). ❖ Appeared on stage (1914–23) in such plays as *Cousin Lucy, A King from Nowhere, The Intruder, The Fountain of Youth, Nemesis, Whispering Wires* and *The Mollusc* (with George Arliss); also appeared in films, including *Who is Sylvia?, Her Sister, Secret Strings, Worlds Apart, Zaza, The Trial of Mary Dugan, Lawful Larceny* and *Ten Cents a Dance.*

TELLERIA GONI, Maider (1973—). Spanish field-hockey player. Born July 14, 1973, in Spain. ❖ At Barcelona Olympics, won a gold medal in team competition (1992).

TELLES, Leonora (c. 1350–1386). *See Leonora Telles.*

TELLES, Lygia Fagundes (1923—). Brazilian lawyer, novelist and short-story writer. Name variations: Ligia or Lígia Fagundes Teles. Born 1923 in São Paulo, Brazil; educated in São Paulo and Rio de Janeiro. ❖ Was a lawyer in São Paulo; works include *Porões e sobrados* (Above and Below Stairs, 1938), *O cacto vermelho* (The Red Cactus, 1949), *Histórias do desencontro* (Stories of Missed Encounters, 1958), *Histórias escolhidas* (1961), *As Meninas* (The Girl in the Photograph, 1973), *Seminário dos ratos* (Seminar of the Rats, 1977), *A disciplina do amor* (1980), and *Tigrela e outras histórias* (1986); contributed to many important newspapers, including *Letras e Artes;* elected to the Brazilian Academy of Letters.

TELLES, Maria (d. 1379). Duchess of Valencia. Name variations: Maria de Menezes; Maria de Telles. Murdered by her husband in 1379; dau. of Martin Afonso Telles de Meneses and Aldonza de Vasconcelhos also spelled Aldonsa de Vasconcelos; older sister of Leonora Telles (c. 1350–1386); m. John (c. 1349–1397), duke of Valencia, in 1376. ❖ See also *Women in World History.*

TELLEZ, Dora Maria (1957—). Nicaraguan revolutionary. Born in 1957 in Nicaragua; dau. of a government administrator and Maria Dora Tellez; studied medicine at the University of Leon. ❖ Became involved in the activities of the Sandinista National Liberation Front (FSLN), known as the Sandinistas, a revolutionary group opposed to the repressive government of Anastasio Somoza Debayle (late 1960s); went underground (1976), as more and more political prisoners were taken; following assassination of Somoza opponent Pedro Joaquin Chamorro (husband of Violeta Chamorro, 1978), was "Commander Two" in the FSLN's occupation of the National Palace; was also one of the leaders who took the city of Leon for the FSLN and became a hero to many who had opposed the Somoza government.

TELLEZ, Eleanor or Leonor (c. 1350–1386). *See Leonora Telles.*

TELLEZ DE MENESES, Eleanor (c. 1350–1386). *See Leonora Telles.*

TELLEZ PALACIO, Dulce M. (1983—). Cuban volleyball player. Born Sept 12, 1983, in Cuba. ❖ Won a team bronze medal at Athens Olympics (2004).

TELLIER, Nicole (1972—). *See Koolen, Nicole.*

TELTSCHER, Gudrun (1907–1982). *See Baudisch-Wittke, Gudrun.*

TELVA, Marion (1897–1962). American contralto. Born in St. Louis, MO; died Oct 23, 1962, in Norwalk, CT. ❖ Made debut at the

Metropolitan Opera in *Manon Lescaut* (1920); became a popular Wagnerian singer; retired (1931).

TEMES, Judit (1930—). Hungarian swimmer. Born Oct 10, 1930, in Hungary. ❖ At Helsinki Olympics, won a gold medal in 4 x 100-meter freestyle relay and a bronze medal in 100-meter freestyle (1952).

TEMPEST, Florence (c. 1891–?). American dancer. Name variations: Florenze Tempest. Born Claire Lillian Ijames, c. 1891, in Richmond, VA; sister of Mary Ijames, known professionally as Marion Sunshine. ❖ Made performance debut with sister Marion Sunshine in *The Two Little Waifs* (1901); headlined vaudeville with sister for years as "Tempest and Sunshine"; on Broadway, received acclaim for portrayal of The Candy Kid in *Little Nemo* (1908); also appeared in *Ziegfeld Follies of 1907* and *H. M. S. Pinafore* (1911); danced in numerous vaudeville shows without sister, including *College Town* (1913), *Our American Boy* (1914) and *One of the Boys* (1915).

TEMPEST, Marie (1864–1942). English actress. Born Mary Susan Etherington on July 15, 1864, in London, England; died Oct 14, 1942; studied singing at Royal Academy of Music; m. Alfred E. Izard (div.); m. Cosmo Gordon-Lennox (actor and playwright), 1898 (died 1921); m. William Graham Browne (actor-director), 1921 (died 1937); no children. ❖ Celebrated stage actress who 1st graced the stage as a singer in operas and musical comedies before taking up serious acting, at which she was also immensely successful; made London debut (1885), in the role of Fiametta in the comic opera *Boccaccio*; after leading roles in *The Fay o' Fire*, *Erminie*, and *La Béarnaise*, took over title role in *Dorothy* (1887), remaining in the part for 2 years, then won great acclaim as Kitty Carroll in *The Red Hussar*; made American debut in same role, opening at New York's Palmer Theater (1889), to the delight of critics; toured US and Canada with J. C. Duff Opera Co., taking roles in several well-known operas, including Arline in *The Bohemian Girl*, title role in *Mignon*, and Mabel in *The Pirates of Penzance*; returned to NY (1891), where she was in constant demand for next 3 years; now considered the queen of musical comedy, began 5-year engagement at Daly's Theater, London (1895), then under management of George Edwardes; because of a falling out with Edwardes (1899), walked away from Daly's and musical comedy as well; opened as Nell Gwynn in *English Nell* (1900), a play directed by Dion Boucicault, who also helped her make the transition to straight plays, then appeared in title role in *Peg Woffington*, and as Becky Sharp in an adaptation of *Vanity Fair* (both 1901); had huge success as Kitty Silverton in *The Marriage of Kitty*, which her 2nd husband had adapted from the French (1902); became manager of Playhouse Theater in London (1913), where she opened in title role in *Mary Goes First*; set off on 8-year world tour (Oct 1914); had next unqualified hit as Judith Bliss in Coward's *Hay Fever* (1925), which ran for 337 performances and was followed by *The Cat's Cradle* (1926), another solid hit; last appearance on London stage was as Dora Randolph in *Dear Octopus* (1938), a successful venture that ran for 373 performances; her phenomenal popularity lay not so much in her creative genius, but in her unique ability to bring much of her own personality and temperament to the characters she portrayed. Made a Dame Commander of the British Empire (DBE, 1937). ❖ See also *Women in World History*.

TEMPLE, Dorothy (1627–1695). See Osborne, Dorothy.

TEMPLE, Shirley (b. 1928). See Black, Shirley Temple.

TEMPLETON, Fay (1865–1939). American stage actress. Born Dec 25, 1865, in Little Rock, Arkansas; died Oct 3, 1939, in San Francisco, California; dau. of John and Alice (Vane) Templeton (both actors); m. William H. "Billy" West (minstrel-show performer), in 1883 (div. 1883); possibly m. Howell Osborn (wealthy New Yorker), in 1885; m. William Joshua Patterson (well-to-do contractor from Pittsburgh), Aug 1, 1906 (died 1932). ❖ Born in Little Rock while her theatrical parents were on tour; made 1st stage appearance as an infant and by 5 had 1st speaking role; appeared as Puck in Augustin Daly's production of *A Midsummer Night's Dream* and as Juliet in *Romeo and Juliet* before age 10; in early years, also performed in *East Lynne* and several comic operas; came to prominence as Gabriel in revival of *Evangeline* (1885); 1st appeared in London (1886), then toured with the play *The Corsair* (1888), earning praise; appeared with Weber and Fields in their comedies *Hurly Burly* (1898), *Fiddle-dee-dee* (1900), in which she introduced the songs "Ma Blushin' Rosie" ("Rosie, You Are Ma Posie"), *Hoity Toity* and *Twirly Whirly*; starred in musical, *The Runaways* (1903), and reached peak of career playing the lead in George M. Cohan's *Forty-five Minutes from Broadway*, in which she sang "Mary is a Grand Old Name" (1906); though semi-retired during last marriage, frequently appeared as Buttercup in Gilbert and Sullivan's *H. M. S. Pinafore*, made the Hollywood film, *Broadway to Hollywood* (1933), and appeared as Aunt Minnie in Jerome Kern's *Roberta* (1933). ❖ See also *Women in World History*.

TEMPLETON, Olive (1883–1979). American stage, tv, and screen actress. Born Oct 19, 1883; died May 29, 1979, in New York, NY; m. John L. Flannery, 1919. ❖ Made stage debut in *Peer Gynt* (1899), followed by *The Philadelphia Story*, *The Swan*, *Happy Hunting* and *Uncle Vanya*, among others; was a regular on the tv series "Mr. Peepers."

TEMPLETON, Rini (1935–1986). American-born artist and social activist. Born Lucille Corinne Templeton in Buffalo, New York, July 1, 1935; died in Mexico City, Mexico, June 15, 1986; dau. of Corinne (Flaacke) Templeton and Richard Templeton III; attended Laboratory School of the University of Chicago; briefly married Alistair Graham (Scottish musician), 1956; m. a Cuban artist in early 1960s (presumably div. shortly thereafter); m. John DePuy (painter), July 16, 1966 (sep. by 1973). ❖ Artist who used her talents to create art for the masses while living in Mexico, spent early years as a "Quiz Kid" on NBC's popular radio —and later tv—show (1947–49); published *Chicagoverse* (1949); lived in Taos, New Mexico (1958–60), working as art editor for progressive newspaper *El Crepúsculo* (The Dawn); studied sculpture with Harold Tovish, and printmaking at *La Esmeralda*, a workshop in Mexico City; taught etching by Isidoro Ocampo, and also studied in Mexican state of Guerrero; was in Cuba (1959–64), where she helped found the Taller de Grabado de Catedral de La Habana (Havana Cathedral Printmaking Workshop), and published articles and letters defending the revolution in *The National Guardian* (1961–62); moving to Taos, New Mexico, area, became involved with Native American life and culture; with husband, held numerous exhibitions of sculptures and silkscreens (1968–74); working closely with Chicano movement, was staff artist for newspapers *El Grito del Norte* and *New Mexico Review*; turning away from sculpture, moved to Mexico City to study printmaking (late 1974); joined the Taller de la Gráfica Popular (TGP, Popular Graphic Workshop); designed the books *450 Years of Chicano History* and *Beyond the Border: Mexico and the US Today*; at time of death, left behind sculptures, dozens of silkscreen prints, over 100 sketchbooks, over 9,000 drawings, and the oft-repeated saying, "Where there is life and struggle, there is Rini Templeton." ❖ See also *El Arte de Rini Templeton: The Art of Rini Templeton* (The Real Comet Press, n.d.); and *Women in World History*.

TENAGNEWORQ (1913–2003). Ethiopian princess. Name variations: Tenagne Worq. Born Jan 29, 1912 at Harar, Abyssinia; died April 6, 2003, in Addis Ababa; eldest dau. of Empress Menen (1899–1962) and Ras Tafari, later known as Haile Selassie I (1892–1975), emperor of Ethiopia (r. 1930–1974); m. Ras Desta Bamtaw, 1924 (killed in Italo-Ethiopian War, 1936); m. Ras Andargathcew Massai, 1944; children: (1st m.) sons Amha (died in adolescence) and Alexander (as commander of the Imperial Ethiopian Navy, was shot by revolutionaries, Nov 1974); daughters Aida, Ruth, Seble and Sofya. ❖ Said to be strong in adversity, was an influence on her father; after the revolution (1974), was incarcerated with daughters in Akaki Prison without trial (1974–89), living in cramped, fetid cells for years.

TEN BOOM, Corrie (1892–1983). Dutch Holocaust rescuer. Born April 15, 1892, in Haarlem, Holland; died April 15, 1983, in Orange County, California; dau. of Casper ten Boom (watchmaker) and Cornelia ten Boom; sister of Willem, Nollie, and Betsie ten Boom (died Dec 1944); never married; no children. ❖ Devout Christian, trained as a watchmaker (1920–22), became the 1st woman watchmaker licensed in Holland; during WWII, was an organizer for Haarlem underground; with family, saved over 700 Jews, and protected scores of Dutch underground workers (1943–44); was arrested, along with 5 other members of her family, and taken to prison (Feb 28, 1944); was sent to Scheveningen Prison, where her father died, then transferred 1st to Vught, then to Ravensbrück in Germany, where her sister Betsie died; survived and was released from the camp through a clerical error; in response to many invitations to share her experiences, began a traveling ministry, taking her message to Christian groups and prisons in 60 countries over next 32 years; wrote the bestselling *The Hiding Place* (1971). ❖ See also Carole C. Carlson, *Corrie ten Boom: Her Life, Her Faith* (Ravell, 1983); Pamela Rosewell, *Five Silent Years of Corrie ten Boom* (Zondervan, 1986); Ellen de Kroon Stamps, *My Years with Corrie* (Revell, 1978); Sam Wellman, *Corrie ten Boom* (Barbour, 1995); (film) *The Hiding Place* (1975); and *Women in World History*.

TENCIN, Claudine Alexandrine Guérin de (1685–1749). French writer and salonnière. Name variations: Madame de Tencin; Marquise de Tencin. Born 1685; died 1749; sister of Madame de Ferriol; mistress of Philippe II also known as Philip or Philippe Bourbon-Orleans (1674–1723), 2nd duke of Orléans and regent for Louis XV (1710–1774), king of France (r. 1715–1774); children: illeg. son, Jean Le Rond d'Alembert (1717–1783), was the famous editor of the *Encyclopédie*. ❖ Audacious and ambitious, liberal and déclassé society leader who was famed for organizing the notorious fêtes at Saint-Cloud; fond of intrigue, highly intelligent, and imaginative, held the 1st salon where writers and artists were elevated to the same status as aristocrats (Fontenelle, Marivaux, Montesquieu, Chesterfield, and Grimm were among those who frequented). ❖ See also *Women in World History.*

TENELLA (1827–1886). *See Clarke, Mary Bayard.*

TEN ELSEN, Eva-Maria (1937—). East German swimmer. Born Sept 14, 1937. ❖ At Melbourne Olympics, won a bronze medal in 200-meter breaststroke (1956).

TENETAHI, Rahui Te Kiri (d. 1913). New Zealand tribal leader. Name variations: Rahui Te Kiri. Born Rahui Te Kiri, prior to 1840s, in Pakiri, on east coast of Northland; died 1913; dau. of Te Kiri (tribal chief) and Pepei; m. Te Rua (Roa), died late 1850s; m. Te Heru Tenetahi; children: 10. ❖ Settled on Little Barrier Island with 2nd husband, where they served as joint chiefs (late 1860s); using boat built for them, began trading with mainland; successfully petitioned courts for rights to island (1886); eventually lost island to the Crown; removed from island, remained uncompensated for their possessions. ❖ See also *Dictionary of New Zealand Biography* (Vol. 2).

TENG (r. 105–121). *See Deng.*

TENG, Teresa (1953–1995). Taiwanese pop singer. Name variations: Little Teng. Born 1953 in Taiwan; died May 8, 1995, in Chiang Mai, Thailand. ❖ Became a Chinese superstar after China became more open (late 1970s), one of the 1st foreign artists to gain such a following; was a capitalist symbol in eyes of authorities and saw her Mandarin love songs banned in Beijing during crackdowns (1980s); with an easing of China's cultural climate, enjoyed renewed sales and fame. ❖ See also *Women in World History.*

TENG YINGCHAO OR YING-CH'AO (1903–1992). *See Deng Yingchao.*

TENG YÜ-CHIH (b. 1900). *See Deng Yuzhi.*

TENNANT, Eleanor (1895–1974). American tennis coach. Name variations: Teach Tennant. Born Feb 12, 1895, in San Francisco, CA, to English parents; died May 1974 in La Jolla, CA. ❖ Often called "Hollywood's best-known coach," ranked 3rd among American women tennis players in 1920, before becoming a highly regarded professional tennis coach; pupils included champions Maureen Connolly, Alice Marble, Pauline Betz, and Bobby Riggs, as well as such non-champions as Clark Gable and Carole Lombard. ❖ See also *Women in World History.*

TENNANT, Emma (1937—). British writer. Name variations: Catherine Aydy. Born Oct 20, 1937, in London, England; dau. of Baron Glenconnor and Elizabeth Lady Glenconnor; great-niece of Margot Tennant Asquith; children: 3. ❖ Was founding editor of periodical *Bananas* (1975) and general editor of *In Verse* (1982); fiction explores apocalyptic themes and often reinterprets canonical texts from feminist and revisionist perspective; works include *The Colour of Rain* (1964), *The Time of the Crack* (1973), *Hotel de Dream* (1976), *The Bad Sister* (1978), *Wild Nights* (1980), *Alice Fell* (1980), *The Ghost Child* (1984), *Two Women in London* (1989), *The Magic Drum: An Excursion* (1989), *An Unequal Marriage* (1991), *Faustine* (1992), *Tess* (1993), and *Emma in Love* (1996). ❖ See also memoirs, *Strangers: A Family Romance* (1998), *Girlitude: A Memoir of the 50s and 60s* (1999), and *Burnt Diaries* (1999).

TENNANT, Kylie (1912–1988). Australian writer. Name variations: Kylie Tennant Rodd. Born Kathleen Tennant, Mar 12, 1912, in Manly, NSW, Australia; died Feb 28, 1988, in Sydney, Australia; dau. of Thomas Walter Tennant and Kathleen (Tolhurst) Tennant; attended Brighton College and University of Sydney; m. Lewis Charles Rodd (headmaster), Nov 21, 1932 (died 1979); children: (daughter) Benison Rodd; John Laurence Rodd (died 1978). ❖ Noted author of social-realist fiction, wrote novels offering spirited and authentic portrayals of Australian life; worked at various jobs (1928–32); was a full-time writer (1935–59, 1969–88); worked as journalist, editor, and publishing adviser (1959–69); was a lecturer for Commonwealth Literary Fund (1957–58) and

member of advisory board (1961–73); was a member of board, Australian Aborigines Cooperatives; made appearances on Australian tv and radio; novels include *Foveaux* (1939), *Ride on, Stranger* (1943), *Time Enough Later* (1943), *Lost Haven* (1946), *The Joyful Condemned* (1953, complete version published as *Tell Morning This*, 1968), *The Honey Flow* (1956) and *Tantavallon* (1983); also wrote short stories, nonfiction, plays, children's books and criticism. Received S. H. Prior Memorial Prize for *Tiburon* (1935) and *The Battlers* (1941); gold medal, Australian Literary Society for *The Battlers* (1941); Commonwealth Jubilee Stage Play Award for *Tether a Dragon* (1952); Children's Book of the Year Award (1960), for *All the Proud Tribesmen*; named Officer of the Order of Australia (1980). ❖ See also *The Missing Heir: The Autobiography of Kylie Tennant* (Macmillan, 1986); Margaret Dick, *The Novels of Kylie Tennant* (Rigby, 1966); and *Women in World History.*

TENNANT, Margaret Mary (1869–1946). English social worker. Name variations: May Tennant. Born Margaret Mary Edith Abraham in 1869; died 1946; m. Harold John Tennant (Liberal member of Parliament), in 1896 (died 1946). ❖ Pioneer in the field of public reform, was the 1st woman in England to serve as a factory inspector (1893–96); served as a member of the Central Committee on Women's Employment (1914–39). Named a Companion of Honor (1917).

TENNANT, May (1869–1946). *See Tennant, Margaret Mary.*

TENNANT, Veronica (1946—). English-born ballet dancer, actress and tv host. Born Jan 15, 1946, in London, England. ❖ Prima ballerina, trained at Cone-Ripman School in London, England, before immigrating to Toronto, Canada; joined National Ballet of Canada (1963), and performed principal roles in such classics as *La Sylphide, Les Sylphides, Cinderella, Giselle,* Ashton's *The Sleeping Beauty,* Cranko's *Romeo and Juliet,* and others; also danced in contemporary works, such as Petit's *Kraanerg,* Neumeier's *Don Juan* and Feld's *Intermezzo;* gave farewell performance as Juliet (1989); became host for "Sunday Arts Entertainment" on CBC-TV; films include *Satie and Suzanne,* for which she was nominated for a Gemini Award; also produces and writes.

TENNENT, Madge Cook (1889–1972). British-born artist and musician. Born Madeline Grace Cook, June 22, 1889, in Dulwich, England; died Feb 5, 1972, in HI; dau. of Arthur Cook (architect) and Agnes Cook (writer and publisher); educated at Academie Julian in Paris; studied with William Bouguereau; m. Hugh Cowper Tennent (accountant), 1915 (died 1967). ❖ Served as headmistress of art at assorted schools in Capetown, South Africa; began exhibiting her works (early 1900s); established her own art school and gave piano recitals; appointed head instructor of Government School of Art, New Zealand; began devoting herself to artistic documentation of the Hawaiian culture (1923). ❖ See also *Women in World History.*

TENNET, Elizabeth. New Zealand politician. Name variations: Liz Tenne, Elizabeth Patricia Tennet. Victoria University, BA Honors. ❖ Worked as a official at the Department of Labour and as a trade-union organizer; representing Labour Party, 1st entered Parliament as MP for Wellington electorate of Island Bay (1987), retaining this seat until 1996; was the 3rd woman to give birth while an MP, and lobbied successfully for a parliamentary creche to meet the needs of parliamentary staff (1992).

TENNEY, Tabitha Gilman (1762–1837). American author. Born Tabitha Gilman, April 7, 1762, in Exeter, New Hampshire; died May 2, 1837, in Exeter; dau. of Samuel Gilman and Lydia Robinson (Giddinge) Gilman; m. Samuel Tenney (surgeon and US congressional representative), 1788 (died 1816). ❖ Published *The New Pleasing Instructor,* a manual of poetry and classical selections for use in the education of young women (1799); is best known for 2-vol. fictional work, *Female Quixotism: Exhibited in the Romantic Opinions and Extravagant Adventures of Dorcasina Sheldon* (1801), widely viewed as one of the best parodies of Cervantes' *Don Quixote.* ❖ See also *Women in World History.*

TENNILLE, Toni (1943—). American singer. Name variations: Captain and Tenille. Born Catheryn Antoinette Tennille, May 8, 1943, in Montgomery, AL; attended Auburn University; m. Daryl Dragon (musician, aka the "Captain"), Nov 11, 1975. ❖ Had enormous success with husband as pop duo Captain and Tennille with such hits as "Love Will Keep Us Together" (#1, 1975), "The Way I Want to Touch You" (#4, 1975), "Lonely Night" (#3, 1976), "Muskrat Love" (#4, 1976), and "Do That to Me One More Time" (#1, 1979); with husband, hosted ABC prime-time series (1976–77); hosted daytime talk show; recorded solo albums of standards; starred in the national tour of *Victor/Victoria* (1998).

TENNYSON, Emily (1813–1896). English amanuensis. Name variations: Lady Tennyson; Baroness Tennyson; Emily Sellwood. Born Emily Sarah Sellwood in 1813 in England; died Aug 10, 1896; eldest dau. of Henry Sellwood (solicitor); m. Alfred, Lord Tennyson (1809–1892, the writer), June 13, 1850; children: 2 sons, Hallam and Lionel. ❖ Intelligent and well-read, served as husband's secretary or amanuensis; 1st met husband (1830), thus beginning an on-again-off-again courtship that lasted for 20 years; during 42-year marriage, managed several households, handled husband's correspondence, copied his poems and helped to prepare them for publication, entertained visitors, and generally protected the poet from distractions of daily life; also kept a running journal of her life with Alfred (1850–74); an accomplished pianist, sometimes set husband's poems to music, of which several were printed, including "The Song of the Alma River," "The City Child" and "Minnie and Winnie"; gave permission to pianist Natalia Janotha to perform several of her songs in concert at St. James's Hall (1891); following Alfred's death (1892), assisted son Hallam in the preparation of the Tennyson *Memoir*; also prepared her own final Journal. ❖ See also James O. Hoge, ed. *Lady Tennyson's Journal* (U. Press of Virginia, 1981); and *Women in World History*.

TEOTOCHI-ALBRIZZI, Isabella (1760–1836). See *Albrizzi, Isabella Teotochi, Contessa d'.*

TE PAEA.
See *Hinerangi, Sophia (c. 1830–1911).*
See *Cherrington, Te Paea (1877/78?–1937).*

TE PAEA TIAHO (1820s?–1875). New Zealand tribal leader. Name variations: Sophia Tiaho, Princess Sophia. Born Te Paea Tiaho, c. early 1820s, in Waikato, New Zealand; died Jan 22, 1875, at Te Kuiti, New Zealand; dau. of Potatau Te Wherowhero (first Maori king) and Whakawi (senior wife) or Raharaha (junior wife). ❖ As a child, sent by father as a hostage for peace to the leader of a warring tribe and was allowed to return to her people to signal acceptance of peace; continued to favor moderation and peace in her leadership; considered an influential leader of the King movement at Kawhia and Te Kuiti; referred to as "Princess Sophia" by Europeans. ❖ See also *Dictionary of New Zealand Biography* (Vol. 2).

TE PIKINGA (c. 1800–after 1868). Maori tribal leader. Born c. 1800, south of Wanganui, New Zealand; died after 1868; m. Te Rangihaeata. ❖ Captured during a tribal battle, was wed to the chief of the opposing tribe, thereby securing freedom for her people and the preservation of their lands through her marriage alliance. ❖ See also *Dictionary of New Zealand Biography* (Vol. 1).

TEPLOVA, Nadezhda Sergeevna (1814–1848). Russian poet. Name variations: Nadezhda Sergevna Teplóva. Born in 1814 into a wealthy Russian family of merchants; died in 1848; sister of Serafima Teplova (poet). ❖ With sister, was among the few recognized female poets associated with the Golden Age of Russia; best-known works include "A Confession," "Advice," and "Spring."

TE PUEA, Princess (1883–1952). See *Herangi, Te Kirihaehae Te Puea.*

TERABUST, Elisabetta (1946—). Italian ballet dancer. Born Elisabetta Terabust Maglie, Aug 5, 1946, in Varese, Italy; trained with Atila Radice at school of Rome Opera Ballet. ❖ Joined Rome Opera Ballet (1963) where she rose to prima ballerina and danced in *Giselle, La Sylphide, Les Biches,* Balanchine's *Symphony in C,* and others; was guest dancer with Roland Petit's Ballet on numerous occasions before joining his company (1977) and appearing in *Casse-Noisette, Carmen, Arlesienne,* and *Notre Dâme de Paris;* partnered Rudolf Nureyev; was director of Ballet of La Scala (1993–96).

TERÁN, Ana Enriqueta (1919—). Venzuelan poet and short-story writer. Name variations: Ana Enriqueta Teran. Born 1919 in Venezuela. ❖ One of Venezuela's best known poets, worked as diplomat and lived in Uruguay and Argentina; published more than a dozen books of poetry; works include *Al norte de la sangre* (1946), *Cuaderona Cabriales, I* (1949), *Presencia terrena* (1949), *Testimonio* (1954), and *De bosque a bosque* (1970). Awarded Premio Nacional de Literatura (1989).

TE RANGI PAI (1868–1916). See *Howie, Fanny Rose.*

TE RANGI-I-PAIA II (fl. 1818–1829). Maori tribal leader. Born probably at Tokomaru Bay, New Zealand; dau. of Te Pori-o-te-rangi and Hinerori; m. Nga-rangi-tokomauri (tribal chief, died 1818); m. Pomare I (died 1826); m. Te Kariri; children: (1st m.) 1 daughter; (2nd m.) several; (3rd m.) 1 son. ❖ After attack by rival tribe (1818), was captured

and taken in marriage by Pomare I, who accepted Christianity, introducing it to East Coast; after husband was killed during a raid, married again and had son, Mohi Turei, who became a famous Anglican minister on East Coast. ❖ See also *Dictionary of New Zealand Biography* (Vol. 1).

TE RANGIMARIE, Puna Himene (fl. 1908–1911). New Zealand tribal leader, nurse, and healer. Married Hopu Nga Oka. ❖ Served as spiritual leader to her people; also began to practice traditional healing (c. 1908); became 1st Maori woman to be prosecuted under Tohunga Suppression Act (1910); though allowed to continue to practice as nurse, was forced to stop practicing tohungaism. ❖ See also *Dictionary of New Zealand Biography* (Vol. 3).

TE RAU-O-TE-RANGI, Kahe (?–c. 1871). Maori tribal leader, trader, and innkeeper. Name variations: Kahe Nicoll, Kahe Nicholl, Peti Nicoll, Peti Nicholl. Died c. 1871; dau. of Te Maroha and Te Hautonga; m. John (Scotch Jock) Nicoll (Nicholl), 1841 (died 1886); children: 5. ❖ Worked with husband as trader; became famous for swimming 7 miles from Kapiti to the mainland with child strapped to her back to warn people of impending attack; was one of 5 women who signed Treaty of Waitangi (1840); kept inn with husband at Paekakariki (1845). ❖ See also *Dictionary of New Zealand Biography* (Vol. 1).

TER BEEK, Carin (1970—). Dutch rower. Born Dec 29, 1970, in Almelo, Netherlands. ❖ Won a silver medal for coxed eight at Sydney Olympics (2000).

TEREKHOV, Yvonne (b. 1929). See *Chouteau, Yvonne.*

TERENTIA (fl. 69–45 BCE). Roman noblewoman. Married Marcus Tullius Cicero (106–40 BCE), Roman orator and consul, in 76 BCE (div. 45 BCE); children: Tullia (c. 79–45 BCE); Marcus.

TERESA. *Variant of Theresa or Thérèse.*

TERESA, Mother (c. 1766–1846). Irish-born American religious leader and educator. Born Alice Lalor, c. 1766, in Ballyragget, Co. Kilkenny, Ireland (some sources cite Co. Queens, now Co. Laois); died Sept 9, 1846, in Georgetown, District of Columbia. ❖ Immigrated to US with elder sister and settled in Philadelphia, Pennsylvania (1795); under auspices of a religious order called the Pious Ladies, established the oldest surviving school for girls in the original 13 colonies (1796); in Georgetown, District of Columbia, embraced the lifestyle of the Visitation nuns of the Catholic Church and formally established the 1st American community of that order under the sanction of the pope (1808); assumed position of the 1st mother superior of the cloister, after which she became known as Mother Teresa.

TERESA, Mother (1794–1861). See *Ball, Frances.*

TERESA, Mother (1910–1997). Albanian nun. Name variations: Agnes Bojaxhiu (1910–31); Sister Teresa (1931–50); Mother Teresa (1950–97); Mother Teresa of Calcutta. Born Gonxha Agnes Bojaxhiu, Aug 27, 1910, in Skopje, Macedonia (then part of Ottoman Empire); died in Calcutta, Sept 5, 1997; dau. of Drana and Nikola Kole Bojaxhiu (both Albanians); never married; no children. ❖ The most famous nun in the world whose uncompromising dedication to the poor, destitute, and dying made her a Catholic celebrity throughout Europe and the Americas, though most of her work was done in India, a country with only a tiny Christian population, where she cared for the homeless population of Calcutta; at 18, joined Sisters of Loreto in Dublin (1928); sailed to India for novitiate (1929); adopted name Teresa with vows as a nun, and began teaching in St. Mary's School, Calcutta (1931); proved herself an able teacher and administrator, rising to position of school principal; took final vows (1937); during violent years of Indian independence movement (1947), responded to the emergency by venturing onto the streets in search of food, an experience which catalyzed her growing sense of restlessness at her work; accorded exclaustration to begin work with the poor (1948); studied with Medical Missionary Sisters, founded by another pioneering nun, Mother Anna Dengel, learning basic medical and nutritional techniques; for next 2 years, now wearing a white *sari* with a blue edge rather than her convent black, tramped the slums of Calcutta's Motijhil district, setting up an ad hoc school for homeless children, giving 1st aid to the sick and wounded; began to recruit helpers; founded Missionaries of Charity (1950) and was made its mother superior; did not make Christian evangelization a priority and ensured that Muslim and Hindu patients in the hospitals would each have access to their own religious rites; opened Nirmal Hriday, home for the dying in Calcutta (1954); established Nirmala Shishu Bhavan, an orphanage (1955); was an extremely capable administrator and fund raiser, hard-nosed in negotiations with civic authorities when necessary, systematic in planning and organization, and able after a few years to command and direct a complicated system; founded the International Association of the Co-Workers of Mother Teresa, a group of lay volunteers, donors, and publicists, who helped fund the missions (1969); stepped down as head of Missionaries of Charity (Mar 1997); published *A Gift for God* and *My Life for the Poor*. Awarded Nobel Peace Prize (1979); awarded US Presidential Medal of Freedom (1985) and Congressional Gold Medal (1997). ❖ See also Joan G. Clucas, *Mother Teresa* (Chelsea, 1988); Eileen Egan, *Such a Vision of the Street* (Doubleday, 1985); Edward Le Joly, *Mother Teresa of Calcutta* (Harper & Row, 1977); B. Srinivasa Murthy, *Mother Teresa and India* (Long Beach, 1979); David Porter, *Mother Teresa, the Early Years* (Eerdman, 1986); Anne Sebba, *Mother Teresa: Beyond the Image* (Doubleday, 1997); (tv movie) "Mother Teresa: In the Name of God's Poor" (1997); and *Women in World History*.

TERESA BENEDICTA OF THE CROSS (1891–1942). *See Stein, Edith.*

TERESA CRISTINA OF BOURBON (1822–1889). Empress of Brazil. Name variations: Theresa; Thereza Christina of Naples; Teresa Christina Maria; Theresa of Sicily. Born Teresa Cristina Maria on Mar 14, 1822; died Dec 28, 1889, soon after arriving in Portugal, having been exiled from Brazil; dau. of Francis I, king of Naples and Sicily (r. 1825–1830), and Marie Isabella of Spain (1789–1848); sister of Maria Cristina I of Naples (1806–1878), queen of Spain; m. Pedro II of Braganza (1825–1891), emperor of Brazil (r. 1831–1889), Sept 4, 1843; children: Afonso (1845–1847); Isabel of Brazil (1846–1921); Leopoldine (1847–1871, who m. August, prince of Saxe-Coburg-Gotha); Pedro also known as Peter Alfons (1848–1850). ❖ See also *Women in World History*.

TERESA DE CARTAGENA (fl. 1400). Spanish nun and writer. Flourished in 1400 in Cartagena, Spain; never married; no children. ❖ Born deaf, had an intense devotion to God, and experienced mystical trances and visions, which she wrote about for the enlightenment of others; authored 2 books, in which she chronicles her own spiritual growth and gives guidance to others seeking the same path; also wrote about physical deformities and handicaps, and created a cosmology in which the physically disabled could, by virtue of their suffering and unique experiences, play an important role in leading others to God.

TERESA D'ENTENZA (fl. 1319). Aragon noblewoman. Name variations: Theresa de Entenza. Flourished c. 1319; 1st wife of Alphonso IV, king of Aragon (r. 1327–1336); children: Jaime, count of Urgel; Pedro IV also known as Peter IV the Ceremonious (b. 1319), king of Aragon (r. 1336–1387). ❖ Alphonso's 2nd wife was Eleanor of Castile (1307–1359).

TERESAH (1877–1964). *See Gray, Teresa.*

TERESA OF ARAGON (1037–?). Princess of Aragon. Born in 1037; death date unknown; dau. of Gilberga (d. 1054) and Ramiro I, king of Aragon (r. 1035–1069); m. William VI, count of Provence.

TERESA OF AVILA (1515–1582). Spanish mystic and religious reformer. Name variations: Teresa de Jesús; Santa Teresa; Teresa of Jesus; Teresa of Ávila; Theresa de Jesus des Carmes-Dechausses; Santa Teresa de Avila. Born Teresa de Cepeda y Ahumada, Mar 28, 1515, at Avila, Spain; died Oct 4, 1582, at Alba de Tormes, Spain; dau. of Alonso Sánchez de Cepeda (*converso*, or New Christians, meaning a former Jew who had converted to Christianity) and Beatriz de Ahumada (died 1528); never married; no children. ❖ Mystic and monastic reformer, influential writer on spirituality, founder of the Discalced Carmelite order of Roman Catholic nuns, and canonized saint, who was the 1st woman to be proclaimed a Doctor of the Church; professed as a Carmelite sister at Avila's convent of La Encarnación (1537); during a prolonged absence from the convent due to illness (1538), read Francis of Osuna's *Abecedario espiritual* (Spiritual Alphabet, 1527), which provided her introduction to the so-called Devotio Moderna, a movement for spiritual renewal within the Church which had its roots in Christian humanism; in the years that followed, read heavily in the classics of Christian spiritual literature; resided at Carmelite convent off and on for about 20 years, but became increasingly dissatisfied with her surroundings; began to experience visions (1540s); experienced the famous Transverberation, a powerful vision in which she believed that an angel had pierced her through the heart with a fiery arrow (1559); withdrew from La Encarnación with 4 young followers to found reformed convent of St. Joseph at Avila (1562); sought to return to a purer and more primitive regime, which she modeled on Peter of Alcántara's so-called discalced (or barefoot) reform movement in the Franciscan order, where lives were to be devoted to silent prayer and spiritual discipline and growth, and applicants would be judged on their aptitude for the rigorous spiritual life, rather than on the

economic status; founded 16 additional reformed convents in other Spanish cities (1567–82); traveled extensively throughout Spain directing the work of her religious reform movement; beatified (1614); canonized (1622); proclaimed Doctor of the Church (1970); a talented writer, found time to produce a number of works which have become classics of Western spiritual literature, including *El camino de la perfección* (The Way of Perfection), *El libro de su vida* (autobiography), *Las moradas, o el castillo interior* (The Dwelling Places, or the Interior Castle), *El libro de las fundaciones* (The Foundations) and *Cuentas de conciencia* (Spiritual Testimonies); was one of the outstanding personalities of her time, and a major presence in the history both of Spain and of Roman Catholicism. ❖ See also *The Life of Teresa of Jesus: The Autobiography of St. Teresa of Avila* (trans. by E. Allison Peers, Doubleday, 1960); Jodi Bilinkoff, *The Avila of St. Teresa: Religious Reform in a Sixteenth-Century City* (Cornell U. Press, 1989); Victoria Lincoln, *Teresa* (ed. by Rivers and de Nicolás, State U. of New York Press, 1984); E. Allison Peers, *Mother of Carmel: A Portrait of St. Teresa of Jesus* (Morehouse-Barlow, 1944); Stephen Clissold, *St. Teresa of Avila* (Sheldon, 1979); Cathleen Medwick, *Teresa of Avila: The Progress of a Soul* (Knopf, 1999); Alison Weber, *Teresa of Avila and the Rhetoric of Femininity* (Princeton U. Press, 1990); Rowan Williams, *Teresa of Avila* (Morehouse, 1991); and *Women in World History*.

TERESA OF CALCUTTA (1910–1997). *See Teresa, Mother.*

TERESA OF CASTILE (c. 1080–1130). Countess of Portugal and queen regnant. Name variations: Theresa; Teresa of Portugal. Born c. 1080 in Castile; died on Nov 1, 1130, in Portugal; illeg. dau. of Alphonso VI (Alfonso), king of Castile, and Jimena Munoz (c. 1065–1128); half-sister of Urraca of Leon-Castile (c. 1079–1126); m. Henry, count of Burgundy, in 1095 (died 1112); m. Fernando or Ferdinand, count of Trastamara, in 1124; children: (1st m.) Urraca (c. 1096–1130); Sancha (b. around 1098, who m. Fernando de Braganza); Teresa (b. around 1102, who m. Sancho de Barbosa); Alphonso I Enriques or Henriques (c. 1110–1185), 1st king of Portugal (r. 1139–1185). ❖ Played a vital role in the establishment of the kingdom of Portugal; was given the title countess of Portugal and married to Henry of Burgundy (1095), to cement an alliance between Castile and Burgundy; after husband died (1112), acted as her son's regent, turning her attention to her holdings in Portugal, and spending the rest of her life working towards Portugal's independence from Spain; enjoyed widespread popularity until her long-term affair with the noble Fernando Peres became public. ❖ See also *Women in World History*.

TERESA OF JESUS (1515–1582). *See Teresa of Avila.*

TERESA OF LISIEUX (1873–1897). *See Thérèse of Lisieux.*

TERESA OF PORTUGAL (1157–1218). Portuguese princess. Born in 1157; drowned off Flanders on May 6, 1218; dau. of Matilda of Maurienne (c. 1125–1157) and Alphonso I Henriques, also known as Alphonso I, king of Portugal (r. 1139–1185); sister of Urraca of Portugal (c. 1151–1188), Sancho I, king of Portugal (r. 1185–1211), and Matilda of Portugal (c. 1149–1173); m. Philip the Great, count of Flanders and Artois, in 1183; m. Eudes III, duke of Burgundy, in 1194 (div. 1195).

TERESA OF PORTUGAL (1793–1874). Princess of Beira and duchess of Molina. Born April 29, 1793, in Queluz; died on Jan 17, 1874, in Trieste; dau. of Carlota Joaquina (1775–1830) and John VI, king of Portugal; interred in Trieste Cathedral; m. Pedro Carlos de Alcantra, on May 13, 1810; became 2nd wife of Don Carlos also known as Charles (1788–1855), duke of Molina, Oct 20, 1838. ❖ Teresa's sister Francisca of Portugal was the 1st wife of Charles of Molina.

TERESA OF THE LITTLE FLOWER (1873–1897). *See Thérèse of Lisieux.*

TERESA OF TUSCANY (1801–1855). *See Maria Theresa of Tuscany.*

TERESA SOBIESKA (fl. 1690s). *See Cunigunde Sobieska.*

TERESHCHUK-ANTIPOVA, Tetiana (1969—). Russian runner. Born Oct 11, 1969, in Lugansk, Ukraine. ❖ Placed 1st at 400-meter hurdles at Grand Prix in London (2001) and at Golden League in Saint-Denis, France and Oslo, Norway (2001); won a bronze medal for 400-meter hurdles at Athens Olympics (2004).

TERESHKOVA, Valentina (1937—). Soviet cosmonaut. Name variations: Valya Nikolayeva-Tereshkova. Pronunciation: Ter-yesh-KOH-vah. Born Valentina Vladimirovna Tereshkova, Mar 6, 1937, in Maslennikovo, near Yaroslavl, USSR; dau. of Vladimir Aksyonovich Tereshkov (farmer) and Yelena (Fyodorovna) Tereshkova; graduated from Zhukovsky Aviation

Academy as military engineer, 1969; m. Andrian Grigoryevich Nikolayev (cosmonaut), 1963 (div. 1977, died July 2004); children: Yelena (b. 1964). ❖ The world's 10th astronaut and 1st woman in space, who served as chair of the Committee of Soviet Women and a member of the Central Committee of the Communist Party, started work at 16 in a tire factory; worked at Yaroslavl textile factory, Krasny Perekop (1955–60); joined local airclub (1958) and made 1st parachute jump (1959); completed 160 parachute jumps; became one of the 5 women accepted for cosmonaut training because her qualification as a parachute jumper was nearly as important as experience as a pilot or engineer (1962); joined Communist Party of the Soviet Union (1962); made spaceflight piloting the Vostok 6, which circled the Earth 114–144 miles above the surface, completing an orbit every 89 minutes (June 16, 1963), spending nearly 71 hours in orbit (her flight had been longer than all 4 flights by American astronauts combined); having become a Soviet international star, was sent all over the world to make speeches and meet heads of state and world leaders; spoke at World Congress of Women in Moscow (1963); served as head of the Committee of Soviet Women (1968–87); elected member of the Central Committee (1971); became a member of Soviet Presidium (1974); gained permission to hold a National Congress of Women, dedicated to public discussion of women's issues in the Soviet Union (1986); elected chair of Union of Soviet Friendship Societies (1987). Awarded Hero of the Soviet Union and Order of Lenin. ❖ See also *Women in World History.*

TERESIA BENEDICTA OF THE CROSS (1891–1942). *See Stein, Edith.*

TERGIT, Gabrielle (1894–1982). German writer and journalist. Name variations: Gabriele Tergit; (pseudonym) Christian Thomasius. Born Elise Hirschmann, Mar 4, 1894, in Berlin, Germany; died July 25, 1982, in London, England. ❖ Came to prominence (1920s) as a reporter for the *Berliner Tageblatt* (Berlin Daily News), where she earned a reputation for compelling reportage of courtroom cases; published one novel *Käsebier erobert den Kurfürstendamm* (*Cheese and Beer Conquer the Kurfürstendamm,* 1931); of Jewish heritage, was forced underground during Nazi rule and later wrote memoirs, *Etwas Seltenes überhaupt, Erinnerungen* (*Something Quite Special, Recollections* 1983), a well-regarded chronicle of her life during the Holocaust.

TERHUNE, Mary Virginia (1830–1922). American novelist. Name variations: Mrs. E. P. Terhune; (pseudonym) Marion Harland. Born Mary Virginia Hawes, Dec 21, 1830, in Dennisville, Virginia; died June 3, 1922, in New York, NY; dau. of Samuel Pierce Hawes (merchant and magistrate) and Judith Anna (Smith) Hawes; m. Edward Payson Terhune (Presbyterian minister), Sept 2, 1856 (died 1907); children: Edward Terhune (b. 1857); Christine Terhune Herrick (1859–1944, an author); Alice Terhune (b. 1863); Virginia Belle Terhune Van de Water (b. 1865, author); Myrtle Terhune (b. 1869); Albert Payson Terhune (b. 1872, popular author who married pianist Anice Morris Terhune). ❖ Had a career as a home economics writer and novelist that spanned 8 decades; under name Marion Harland, published 1st full-length story, *Alone,* to critical and popular acclaim, followed by 2nd successful novel, *The Hidden Path* (both 1856); published regularly (1856–73), and occasionally after that, making Marion Harland a household name among readers in the US; began to concentrate on nonfiction (1878), especially advice based on the new field of "domestic science," publishing books of domestic advice and household management for wives; served as a copy editor for *Home-Maker* (1888–90) and *Housekeeper's Weekly;* in 1900, began to write a syndicated column of domestic advice which appeared in 27 daily newspapers across US, including *Chicago Tribune* (1911–17); composed a book of personal philosophy, *Looking Westward* (1914); wrote 25 novels. ❖ See also *Women in World History.*

TERK-DELAUNAY, Sonia (1885–1979). *See Delaunay, Sonia.*

TERMEULEN, Johanna (1929–2001). Dutch swimmer. Name variations: Johanna Maria Termeulen-Boomstra; Hannie Termeulen. Born Feb 18, 1929, in Wiesbaden; died Mar 1, 2001, in Amsterdam. ❖ At London Olympics, won a bronze medal in 4 x 100-meter freestyle relay (1948); at Helsinki Olympics, won a silver medal in 4 x 100-meter freestyle relay and a silver medal in 100-meter freestyle (1952).

TERNAN, Frances Eleanor (c. 1803–1873). English actress and writer. Name variations: Frances Eleanor Trollope; Frances Eleanor Jarman; Mrs. Ternan. Born Frances Eleanor Jarman, c. 1803; died 1873; 2nd wife of Thomas Adolphus Trollope (1810–1892, a novelist); daughter-in-law of Frances Milton Trollope (1779–1863). ❖ Made stage debut at Bath, England (1815); appeared as Juliet to Charles Kemble's Romeo at Covent Garden (1827–28); accompanied 1st husband on US and Canadian tour (1834–36); appeared as Pauline in *The Winter's Tale* (1855) and as blind Alice in *The Bride of Lammermoor* (1866); following 2nd marriage to Thomas Trollope, left the stage, settled in Florence, and wrote *Aunt Margaret's Trouble* (1866), *Black Spirits and White* (1877) and *That Unfortunate Marriage* (1888); with husband, also published *Homes and Haunts of the Italian Poets* (1881).

TERNINA, Milka (1863–1941). Croatian soprano. Born Dec 19, 1863, in Vezišce, Croatia; died May 18, 1941, in Zagreb, Croatia; studied voice 1st in Zagreb under Ida Winterberg, then with Joseph Gänsbacher at Vienna Conservatory. ❖ At 19, debuted to strong acclaim in role of Amelia in *Ballo in Maschera* in Zagreb (1882); enjoyed long contracts with opera companies in German cities of Leipzig (1883–84), Graz (1884–86), Bremen (1886–90), and Munich (1890–1906); performed throughout Europe (1882–1906); made American debut in Boston with Damrosch Opera Co. (1896); made debut at Covent Garden (1898), singing role of Tosca in 1st London performance of Puccini's opera; performed in US at Metropolitan (1899–1904), premiering *Tosca* (1901) and performing 15 roles in 74 other productions; mastered a range of major roles, including Aïda, Tosca, Donna Anna, Kundry, Leonore, Isolde, Brünnhilde and Elsa; struck with partial facial paralysis, retired from performing and began teaching (1906). ❖ See also *Women in World History.*

TE ROHU (fl. 1820–1850). Maori tribal leader. Dau. of Mananui Te Heuheu Tukino II and Nohopapa; m. Te Pareihe or Kurupo Te Moananui. ❖ Remained with father and participated in numerous campaigns and peacetime activities; negotiated several tribal peace agreements and land disputes. ❖ See also *Dictionary of New Zealand Biography* (Vol. 1).

TERPSTRA, Erica (1943—). Dutch swimmer and politician. Name variations: Erica Georgine Terpstra. Born May 26, 1943, in The Hague, Netherlands. ❖ At Tokyo Olympics, won a bronze medal in 4 x 100-meter freestyle relay and a silver medal in 4 x 100-meter medley relay (1964); liberal politician, entered Parliament for the Volkspartij voor Vrijheid en Democratie (VVD, 1977); served as secretary of Health, Well-Being and Sports (1994–98) and vice-chair of the Tweede Kamer (1998–2002).

TERRELL, Mary Church (1863–1954). African-American activist. Born Mary ("Mollie") Eliza Church, Sept 23, 1863, in Memphis, Tennessee; died in Highland Beach, Maryland, July 24, 1954; dau. of Robert Reed Church (saloon owner who later became a millionaire) and Louisa (Ayers) Church (hair store proprietor); Oberlin College, BA, 1884; m. Robert Heberton Terrell, Oct 28, 1891; children: Phyllis and Mary (adopted), and 3 who died in infancy. ❖ First president of the National Association of Colored Women, who championed such causes as racial justice, woman's suffrage, and internationalism, 1st taught at Wilberforce University (1885–87), then M Street Colored High School in Washington, DC (1887–88, 1890–91); was a member of the District of Columbia Board of Education (1895–1901, 1906–11); served as president of National Association of Colored Women (1896–1901); was a founding member of NAACP (1910); was a lecturer at Brooklyn Institute of Arts and Science (1911–13); was a delegate to the founding conference of WILPF, Zurich (1919); appointed director of the Work among Colored Women in the East for the Republican National Committee (1920); was the 1st African-American member of American Association of University Women (1949); chaired the Coordinating Committee for Enforcement of District of Columbia's Anti-Discrimination Laws (1949–53); was one of the most prominent African-American activists in the country, whose ultimate goal was gender and racial equality; as her disappointments mounted in both areas, grew increasingly confrontational, battling segregation on picket lines and organizing sit-ins during last years of her long life. ❖ See also autobiography, *A Colored Woman in a White World* (1940); Beverly Washington Jones, *Quest For Equality: The Life and Writings of Mary Eliza Church Terrell, 1863–1954* (Carlson, 1990); Gladys Byram Sheppard, *Mary Church Terrell—Respectable Person* (Human Relations, 1959); and *Women in World History.*

TERRELL, Tammi (1946–1970). African-American singer. Name variations: Thomasina Montgomery. Born Thomasina Montgomery, Jan 24, 1946, in Philadelphia, PA; died Mar 16, 1970, in Philadelphia; studied psychology at University of Pennsylvania (early 1960s). ❖ At 15, recorded 1st single, "If You See Bill" (1961), followed by "The Voice of Experience" (1962); joined James Brown revue; reached R&B Top 30 with "I Can't Believe You Love Me" (1965); with Marvin Gaye, had numerous hits, including "Your Precious Love" (1967), "You're All I Need to Get By" (1968), and "What You Gave Me" (1969); diagnosed with brain tumor (1967); released solo album, *Irresistible Tammi Terrell* (1969); albums with Gaye include *United* (1967), *You're All I Need* (1968), and *Easy* (1969); stopped touring because of illness, but continued to record with Gaye, though he revealed years later that most songs on *Easy,* including "Good Lovin' Ain't Easy to Come By" and "What You Gave Me," had been sung by Valerie Simpson.

TERRIS, Norma (1904–1989). American stage actress. Born Norma Allison, Nov 13, 1904, in Columbus, KS; died Nov 15, 1989, in Lyme, CT; m. Max Hoffman Jr. (div.); m. Dr. Jerome Wagner (died); m. once more. ❖ Made NY debut in the chorus of *The Ziegfeld Midnight Frolic* (1920); toured in vaudeville with 1st husband as Junior and Terris; had 1st major role on tour in *Little Nellie Kelly* (1923–24); created the part of Magnolia in *Show Boat* (1927); served on board of directors for Goodspeed Opera House for 30 years.

TERRISS, Ellaline (1871–1971). English actress and singer. Name variations: Ellaline Lewin; Lady Hicks. Born Ellaline Lewin, April 13, 1871, at Ship Hotel, Stanley, Falkland Islands; died June 16, 1971, in London, England; dau. of William Terriss (actor) and Amy (Fellowes) Terriss; sister of Tom Terriss (1874–1964, actor); m. Sir Seymour Hicks (actor, writer, and impresario), 1893 (knighted 1935, died 1949); children: Betty Seymour Hicks (b. 1904, actress). ❖ Popular actress and singer who appeared on the English stage for over 40 years, often with husband; made professional debut as Mary Herbert in *Cupid's Messenger* (1888); signed with Charles Wyndham (1888); came to prominence in the role of Cinderella (1893); other noted roles include the lead in *The Shopgirl, The Circus Girl,* as well as in *The Runaway Girl,* which ran for almost 600 performances; maintained an extensive repertoire, including *The Man in Dress Clothes, Sleeping Partners* and *Bluebell in Fairyland;* with husband, opened their 1st theater, The Aldwych (Dec 1905), followed by Hicks Theater (1906), where they starred in *The Beauty of Bath,* which ran for 341 performances; films include *Masks and Faces* (1917), *Blighty* (1927), *Land of Hope and Glory* (1927), *Atlantic* (1929), *A Man of Mayfair* (1931), *Glamour* (1931), *The Iron Duke* (1934), *The Royal Cavalcade* (1935) and *The Four Just Men* (1939); also made numerous gramophone recordings. ❖ See also autobiographies *Ellaline Terriss, by Herself and With Others* (1928) and *Just a Little Bit of String* (Hutchinson, 1955); also Seymour Hicks' memoirs, *Me and the Missus.*

TERRÓN I CUSÍ, Anna (1962—). Spanish politician. Born Oct 6, 1962, in Barcelona, Spain. ❖ Served as European and International Policy secretary for the Executive Committee of the Party of Catalan Socialists (PSC-PSOE, 1990–2000); as a European Socialist, elected to 4th and 5th European Parliament (1994–99, 1999–2004).

TERRY, Alice (1899–1987). American actress. Name variations: Alice Taafe. Born Alice Frances Taafe, July 24, 1899, in Vincennes, IN; died Dec 22, 1987, in Burbank, CA; m. Rex Ingram (director), 1921 (died 1950). ❖ Starred opposite Valentino in *Four Horsemen of the Apocalypse*; starred in features directed by husband; films include *Not My Sister, The Arab, Old Wives for New, Turn to the Night, The Prisoner of Zenda, Where the Pavement Ends, Scaramouche, The Garden of Allah, The Great Divide* and *The Magician*; was co-director on *Love in Morocco* (1933); retired after husband's death (1950).

TERRY, Beatrice (b. 1890). English stage actress. Born 1890 in London, England; dau. of Charles and Margaret Terry; sister of Minnie Terry (actress); niece of Kate, Marion, Florence, and Ellen Terry (all actresses); m. Leonard Mudie (div.). ❖ Made stage debut with Henry Irving and Ellen Terry as the Baby in *Olivia* (1893); other plays include *The Man from Blankley's, Peter Pan* (title role), *Toddles, The Scarlet Pimpernel* and *Henry of Navarre* (as Marie); appeared with Annie Horniman's Company (1913–14); moved to America (1916), appearing in such NY plays as *Hamlet* (as Ophelia), *Somebody's Language,* and *Children of the Moon;* toured with Laurette Taylor in *Happiness;* was a member of Eva Le Gallienne's Civic Rep (1926–27, 1932–33).

TERRY, Ellen (1847–1928). English actress. Name variations: Mrs. George Frederic Watts (1864–78); Mrs. Charles Claverine Kelly (1878–85); Mrs. James Carew (1907–09); Dame Ellen Terry. Born Ellen Alice Terry, Feb 27, 1847; died July 21, 1928; dau. of Benjamin Terry (1818–1896, actor) and Sarah Ballard Terry (1819–1892, actress who performed as Miss Yerret); sister of Kate Terry (1844–1924), Marion Terry (1852–1930) and Florence Terry (1854–1896), all actresses; aunt of Phyllis Neilson-Terry (1892–1977) and Beatrice Terry (both actresses); great-aunt of John Gielgud; sister-in-law of Julia

Neilson (1868–1957); m. George Frederic Watts (painter), 1864 (div. c. 1878); m. Charles Wardell (actor who performed under name Charles Kelly), 1878 (div. c. 1885); m. James Usselman (1876–1938, American actor who performed under name John Carew), 1907 (div. c. 1909); children: (with Edward Godwin) Edith Craig (1869–1947, actress, costume designer, stage director); (Edward) Gordon Craig (b. 1872, stage designer). ❖ Foremost actress who is best remembered for her Shakespearean roles, in particular her interpretation of Portia in *The Merchant of Venice*; as a child performer, made debut as Mamillius in *The Winter's Tale* (1856); had 1st success as Prince Arthur in *King John* (1858); appeared at Haymarket opposite E. H. Sothern in *The Little Treasure* (1862); remained with Haymarket until 1864; retired (1867–74); returned to the stage (1874), as Katherine opposite Henry Irving's Petruchio in *The Taming of the Shrew*; in a partnership that would last for 24 years and become legendary in the annals of the London stage, played Ophelia to Irving's Hamlet, Portia to his Shylock, and Henrietta Maria to his Charles the First, and toured with him extensively, including appearances in US, until his death (1905); was a great friend of the Anglo-Irish playwright George Bernard Shaw; undertook management of Imperial Theater (1903), where she staged and appeared in *Much Ado About Nothing,* made a rare appearance in an Ibsen play, *The Vikings,* played Alice Grey in *Alice Sit-by-the-Fire* (1905) and Lady Cicely in *Captain Brassbound's Conversion* (1906), a part especially written for her by Shaw. Was the 2nd actress (after Genevieve Ward) to be created Dame Commander of the British Empire (1925). ❖ See also autobiography, *The Story of My Life* (1908); Nina Auerbach, *Ellen Terry Player in Her Time* (1987); Roger Manvell, *Ellen Terry* (1968); Christopher St. John, *Ellen Terry and Bernard Shaw: A Correspondence* (1931); E. G. Craig, *Ellen Terry and Her Secret Self* (1931); T. Edgar Pemberton, *Ellen Terry and her Sisters* (1902); and *Women in World History.*

TERRY, Ellen Battell (1851–1939). See Stoeckel, Ellen Battell.

TERRY, Hazel (1918–1974). English actress. Name variations: Hazel Neilson-Terry. Born Hazel Neilson-Terry, Jan 23, 1918, in London, England; died Oct 12, 1974, in London; dau. of Dennis Neilson-Terry (actor) and Mary Glynne (actress); granddau. of Fred Terry (actor-manager) and Julia Neilson; niece of Phyllis Neilson-Terry (actress); m. Geoffrey Keen (div.); m. David Evans. ❖ Made stage debut in London as the Page in *King Henry IV: Part I* (1935), followed by *The Last Trump, Behold the Bride, The Brothers Karamazov, Peace in Our Time, Adventure Story* (as Statira), and *The Seagull* (as Masha); made NY debut in *Time and the Conways* (1938); appeared as Ophelia to John Gielgud's Hamlet (1944); films include *The Marriage of Corbal, Our Fighting Navy, Kill or Cure* and *The Servant.*

TERRY, June (1920–1984). See Preisser, June.

TERRY, Kate (1844–1924). English stage actress. Born April 21, 1844; died Jan 6, 1924; dau. of Benjamin Terry (1818–1896, actor) and Sarah Ballard Terry (1819–1892, actress who performed as Miss Yerret); sister of actors George, Charles and Fred Terry and actresses Ellen Terry (1847–1928), Marion Terry (1852–1930) and Florence Terry (1854–1896); m. Arthur James Lewis; children: Mabel Terry-Lewis (1872–1957, actress). ❖ Made London debut as Robin in *The Merry Wives of Windsor* (1851), then appeared as Prince Arthur in *King John* at a Command Performance for Queen Victoria (1852); toured with sister Ellen; came to prominence as Mrs. Union in *Friends or Foes* (1862); other plays include *The Duke's Motto, Bel Demonio, Hamlet* (as Ophelia), *The Hidden Hand, Settling Day, Everybody's Friend, The Serf, Money, The Lady of Lyons, A Sheep in Wolf's Clothing, A Sister's Penance* and *Dora* (title role); greatly acclaimed, retired from the stage (1867).

TERRY, Lucy (c. 1730–1821). See Prince, Lucy Terry.

TERRY, Marion (1852–1930). English stage actress. Born Oct 16, 1852, in London, England; died Aug 21, 1930; dau. of Benjamin Terry (1818–1896, actor) and Sarah Ballard Terry (1819–1892, actress who performed as Miss Yerret); sister of actors George, Charles and Fred Terry and actresses Ellen Terry (1847–1928), Kate Terry (1844–1924) and Florence Terry (1854–1896). ❖ Made London debut as Isabelle in *A Game of Romps* (1873), followed by *Fame, The Vagabond, The Two Orphans, Gretchen* (title role), *Duty, Money, Peg Woffington* (title role), *Mimi* (title role), *Broken Hearts, The Millionaire, The Red Lamp, Faust* (as Margaret), *Little Lord Fauntleroy, Lady Windermere's Fan, The Piper* and *Our Betters.*

TERRY, Megan (1932—). American playwright. Born 1932 in Seattle, WA. ❖ Was founding member of La Mama Theatre and Open Theatre in New York and founder of Magic Theatre in Omaha, Nebraska; wrote over 60 plays, including the 1st rock musical, *Viet Rock* (1966), as well as *Hothouse* (1974), *Babes in the Bighouse* (1974), *100,001 Horror Stories of the Plains* (1975), *The Tommy Allen Show* (1978), *Brazil Fado* (1978), *American King's English for Queens* (1978), *Kegger* (1985), and *Amtrak* (1988). Awarded Obie for Best Play for *Approaching Simone* (biography of Simone Weil, 1970).

TERRY, Minnie (b. 1882). English stage actress. Born 1882; dau. of Charles and Margaret Terry; sister of Beatrice Terry (actress); niece of Kate, Marion, Florence, and Ellen Terry (all actresses); m. Edmund Gwenn (actor), 1901 (div. within hours). ❖ Made stage debut in *Frou-Frou* (1885), followed by 7 more years of children's roles; took time off for school and stagework in Australia (1892–1904); reappeared on the London stage in *The Courage of Silence* (1905), followed by *What the Butler Saw, Sweet Kitty Bellairs, Lady Frederick, Dame Nature, The 12 Pound Look,* and *The Will,* among others; served as leading lady at the English Theater, Paris (1921–22).

TERRY, Olive (1884—). English stage actress. Born April 22, 1884, in London, England; dau. of William Morris and Florence Terry (actress); niece of Kate, Marion, and Ellen Terry (all actresses); cousin of Beatrice and Minnie Terry (both actresses). ❖ Made stage debut as Lady Gerania in *Dr. Wake's Patient* (1906); other appearances include *Macbeth, In the Workhouse* and *Godefroi and Yolande.*

TERRY, Rose (1827–1892). *See Cooke, Rose Terry.*

TERRY-LEWIS, Mabel (1872–1957). English stage and screen actress. Name variations: Mabel Gwynedd Terry-Lewis; Mabel Terry Lewis. Born Mabel Gwynedd Lewis, Oct 28, 1872, in London, England; died Nov 28, 1957; dau. of Arthur James Lewis and Kate Terry (actress); niece of actors George, Charles and Fred Terry and actresses Ellen Terry (1847–1928), Marion Terry (1852–1930) and Florence Terry (1854–1896); m. Captain Ralph C. Batley. ❖ Made London stage debut as Lucy Lorimer in *A Pair of Spectacles* (1895), followed by *The Master, School, Ours, Caste, You Never Can Tell, English Nell, After All,* and *My Lady of Rosedale,* among others; retired from the stage (1904–20); made comeback, appearing in *Getting Married, Dear Brutus, If Winter Comes, The Grain of Mustard Seed, Easy Virtue, The Skin Game, The Importance of Being Earnest* (as Lady Bracknell), *Death Takes a Holiday, Dinner at 8,* and *Kind Lady;* films include *The Scarlet Pimpernel, Jamaica Inn,* and *They Came to a City.*

TERVAPÄÄ, Juhani (1886–1954). *See Wuolijoki, Hella.*

TERWILLEGAR, Erica (1963—). American luge champion. Born in Nelsonville, New Jersey, in April 8, 1963. ❖ First US woman to win a medal in international luge competition, was one of the few American lugers who grew up in the sport; won a silver medal in international junior competition (1982); at World championships, finished 5th (1983); won national championship (1983).

TERYOSHINA, Yelena (1959—). Soviet rower. Born Feb 1959 in USSR. ❖ At Moscow Olympics, won a silver medal in coxed eights (1980).

TERZIAN, Alicia (1938—). Argentine composer, conductor, musicologist, pianist and lecturer. Born July 1, 1938, in Córdoba, Argentina, of Armenian descent; graduated from National Conservatory in Buenos Aires, 1958, with a 1st prize and a gold medal, having studied under A. Ginastera, R. Gonzalez, R. Garcia Morillo, F. Ugarte, and G. Gilardi. ❖ Completed studies in 4th- to 12th-century medieval religious Armenian music in Venice under Padre Dr. Leoncio Dayan; won several prizes, including Outstanding Young Woman of Argentina Prize (1970); wrote numerous orchestral and vocal works as well as 2 ballets; also directed many festivals of contemporary music. ❖ See also *Women in World History.*

TESKE, Charlotte (1949—). West German marathon runner. Born Nov 23, 1949, in Munich, Germany. ❖ Won Boston Marathon (1982).

TESKE, Rachel (1972—). Australian golfer. Name variations: Rachel Hetherington. Born Rachel Hetherington, April 23, 1972, in Sunnybank Hills, Queensland, NSW, Australia; m. Dean Teske, 1998. ❖ Won NSW Amateur; turned pro (1994); wins include Ford Ladies Challenge in Denmark (1994), Spanish Open and German Open (1995), Betsy King Classic (1998), Myrtle Beach Classic (1999), Evian Masters (2001), Kroger Classic (2002), Wegmans Rochester (2003).

TESKY, Adeline Margaret (c. 1850–1924). Canadian novelist and short-story writer. Born c. 1850 in Appleton, Ontario, Canada; died

1924. ❖ Wrote *A Little Child Shall Lead Them* (1911), *The Yellow Pearl: a Story of the East and the West* (1911) and *Candlelight Days* (1913).

TESLENKO, Olga (1981—). Ukrainian gymnast. Born May 23, 1981, in Kirovgrad, Ukraine; sister of Inna Teslenko (gymnast). ❖ At European championships, won a silver medal in balance beam (1998); placed 5th for team all-around at Atlanta Olympics (1996).

TESS, Giulia (1889–1976). Italian soprano. Born Feb 19, 1889, in Milan, Italy; died Mar 17, 1976, in Milan; studied singing under Bottagisio; m. Giacomo Armani (conductor). ❖ Debuted as a mezzo-soprano at Prato (1904); performed in Venice and in Prague (1909); also made appearances in Vienna and St. Petersburg; retrained and expanded her vocal range to that of a soprano (1922), appearing in such roles as Mignon, Salome, and Elektra; retired from stage (1940) and taught such students as Tagliavini and Fedora Barbieri. ❖ See also *Women in World History.*

TE TAIAWATEA RANGITUKEHU, Maata (1848/49?–1929). New Zealand tribal leader. Born in 1848 or 1849, probably near Lake Tarawera, New Zealand; died June 27, 1929, at Te Teko, New Zealand; dau. of Rangitukehu Hatua and Rangitowhare; m. Te Haroto Whakataka Riini Manuera, late 1860s; children: at least 7. ❖ Assumed tribal responsibilities of father (1880s); fought to return confiscated lands to her people and for tribal ownership of land; renovated Ruataupare meeting house and built dining hall as gift to her people. ❖ See also *Dictionary of New Zealand Biography* (Vol. 3).

TE TAI, Meri (1868–1920). *See Mangakahia, Meri Te Tai.*

TETBERGA (fl. 9th c.). Queen of Lorraine. Name variations: Theutberga of Valois. Flourished in the 9th century in Lorraine, also known as Lotharingia; sister of Hubert, abbot of Saint-Maurice; m. Lothar also known as Lothair II (c. 826–869), king of Lorraine (r. 855–869), in 855; no children. ❖ Was involved in a divorce case which altered the patterns of marriage in the Frankish empire; came from a politically important noble family and married King Lothair II; had not given birth after 2 years, which led Lothair to decide to divorce her and marry his mistress Waldrada who had given birth; was adamantly opposed to the divorce, as were most Church officials, the dissolution of which lasted several years and became known across Western Europe; was 1st accused of incest with her brother Hubert, abbot of Saint-Maurice, one of the few acceptable reasons for an annulment; defiantly maintained her innocence, and even suffered through an ordeal by fire to prove it; imprisoned, was forced to "confess" in public to incest, aborting a fetus, and various other sins; because husband was under immense political pressure from the pope, was brought out from her prison cell and made queen again. ❖ See also *Women in World History.*

TETER, Hannah (1987—). American snowboarder. Born Jan 27, 1987, in Belmont, VT. ❖ Placed 1st at USASA National championship, Mammoth Mountain, CA, in Boardercross (2001), Grand Prix #1, Park City, UT, in Halfpipe (2002), FIS Junior World championships, Rovaniemi, Finland, in Halfpipe (2002), Grand Prix #2, Breckenridge, CO, in Halfpipe (2003), and Yahoo! Big Air & Style, Breckenridge, CO, in HIP—TIE (2003); won a bronze medal in Superpipe at X Games (Winter 2003); won a gold medal for Halfpipe at Torino Olympics (2006).

TETRAZINI, Baby (1909–1987). *See Clyde, June.*

TETRAZZINI, Eva (1862–1938). Italian operatic soprano. Born in Mar 1862 in Milan, Italy; died Oct 17, 1938, in Parma, Italy; sister of Luisa Tetrazzini (1871–1940) and Elvira Tetrazzini; studied under Ceccherini; m. Cleofonte Campanini (conductor). ❖ Lesser-known older sibling of soprano Luisa Tetrazzini, made debut as Marguerite in Florence (1882), after training with Ceccherini; appeared in NY (1888, 1908) and London (1890); performed many roles, including Aïda, Valentine, Fedora and Desdemona; not to be confused with other sister, soprano Elvira Tetrazzini, who recorded under name E. Tetrazzini. ❖ See also *Women in World History.*

TETRAZZINI, Luisa (1871–1940). Italian coloratura soprano. Born June 29, 1871, in Florence, Italy; died April 28, 1940, in Milan; sister of Eva Tetrazzini (1862–1938) and Elvira Tetrazzini; studied with Ceccherini at Liceo Musicale; m. Giuseppe Scalaberni (opera manager); m. Pietro Vernati; m. once more. ❖ An international opera star, acclaimed for dramatic and comedic skills as well as for pure soprano, began studying voice at the Liceo Musicale in Florence (1890) and appeared there as Inéz (1890); made professional debut as lead in *L'Africaine* at the Pagliano, which led to a command performance for

Margaret of Savoy, queen of Italy, in Rome; went on an extended Italian tour; debuted in US in San Francisco (1904); made London debut at Covent Garden (1907), playing to sold-out houses; with Enrico Caruso, published *The Art of Singing* (1909); starred at Manhattan Opera House (1908–10); published *How To Sing* (1923); sang farewell concert (1933); retired, age 64, and settled in Milan (1934). ❖ See also autobiography *My Life of Song* (1921); Charles Neilson Gattey, *Luisa Tetrazzini: The Florentine Nightingale* (Amadeus, 1995); and *Women in World History*.

TETZEL, Joan (1921–1977). American stage, radio, and screen actress. Born Joan Margaret Tetzel, June 21, 1921, in New York, NY; died Oct 31, 1977, in Sussex, England; m. John E. Mosman (radio producer, div.); m. Oscar Homolka (actor, died 1978). ❖ At 16, made Broadway debut in *Dramatic School*, followed by *Liliom, Happy Days, The Damask Cheek, Peepshow, I Remember Mama, The Masterbuilder, One Flew Over the Cuckoo's Nest* (as Nurse Ratchett), and *How the Other Half Loves,* among others; films include *Duel in the Sun, The Paradine Case, File on Thelma Jordan* and *Joy in the Morning*.

TETZNER, Gerti (1936—). East German novelist. Born Nov 29, 1936, in Germany; m. Reiner Tetzner. ❖ Works include *Karen W.* one of the 1st East German novels to explore the status of women in socialist society.

TEUFFEL, Countess von (1847–1898). *See Howard, Blanche Willis.*

TEUSCHER, Cristina (1978—). American swimmer. Born Mar 12, 1978, in New Rochelle, NY; graduate of Columbia College, 2000. ❖ Won a gold medal for 200-meter freestyle at Pan American Games (1995); won a gold medal for 800-meter freestyle relay at Atlanta Olympics (1996); won a bronze medal for 200-meter indiv. medley at Sydney Olympics (2000); won a gold medal for 800-meter freestyle relay at World championships (2001). Awarded Honda-Broderick Cup (2000).

TEUTA (c. 260–after 228 BCE). Queen of Illyria. Born possibly around 260 BCE; died after 228 BCE; m. Agron, king of the Illyrian tribe of the Ardiaioi. ❖ Powerful queen whose successful piracy and sieges in Greece were checked only by Roman military intervention; had succeeded husband on his death (231 BCE). ❖ See also *Women in World History*.

TEWDR, Nesta. *See Nesta Tewdr.*

TE WHAITI, Kaihau Te Rangikakapi Maikara (1863–1937). New Zealand tribal leader. Name variations: Maikara Iraia, Maikara Te Ama. Born 1863, probably in lower Wairarapa Valley, New Zealand; died Jan 19, 1937, in Greytown, New Zealand; dau. of Hohepa Aporo and Maikara Paranihia; m. Iraia Te Ama-o-te-rangi Te Whaiti, 1881 (died 1918); children: 13. ❖ Leader who accumulated vast land holdings and represented herself and siblings in Native Land Court; trained in traditional Maori customs and genealogy. ❖ See also *Dictionary of New Zealand Biography* (Vol. 3).

TE WHEROWHERO, Piupiu (1886/87?–1937). New Zealand tribal leader. Born in 1886 or 1887, at Whatiwhatihoe, Waikato, New Zealand; died Oct 29, 1937, at Arapuni, New Zealand; dau. of Te Wherowhero Tawhiao and Tamirangi Manahi; m. Kainuku Vaikai; m. Hiroka Hetet; children: at least 10. ❖ Established new community, Kenana, on her own land; worked to alleviate problems of her people; promoted allegiance to Ratana faith. ❖ See also *Dictionary of New Zealand Biography* (Vol. 3).

TEWKESBURY, Joan (1936—). American screenwriter and director. Name variations: Joan Maguire. Born April 8, 1936, in Redlands, CA. ❖ Appeared as a dancer in the film *The Unfinished Dance* (1947); understudied for Mary Martin in *Peter Pan* (1954–55); directed and choreographed in small theaters around Los Angeles; taught dance, drama, and film; was a script supervisor for Robert Altman on *McCabe and Mrs. Miller* (1971); wrote screenplays for *Thieves Like Us, Nashville,* and *A Night in Heaven*; wrote and directed teleplays "The Acorn People," "Cold Sassy Tree," "Elysian Fields," and "Scattering Dad" and the off-Broadway play *Cowboy Jack* (1978); directed *Old Boyfriends,* and *Strangers,* as well as numerous tv episodes for such shows as "Alfred Hitchcock Presents," "Felicity," and "The Guardian."

TEXAS TESSIE (1897–1973). *See Douglas, Lizzie.*

TEXIDOR, Greville (1902–1964). English-born short-story writer. Name variations: Greville Foster; Mrs. Droescher. Born Margaret Foster, 1902, in Hampstead, England; committed suicide, 1964, in Australia; married 1st husband, a Spaniard; m. Werner Droescher (anarchist); children: 2. ❖ Lived Bohemian life in England, traveled extensively and married a Spaniard in South America; lived in Spain during

Civil War; became anarchist before leaving for New Zealand with 2nd husband Werner Droescher (1940); moved to Australia with family (1948); lived in Europe (1953–63); wrote about politics, relationships, and migration; published *These Dark Glasses* (1949) and *In Fifteen Minutes You Can Say a Lot* (ed. Kendrick Smithyman, 1987).

TEY, Josephine (1896–1952). English writer. Name variations: Elizabeth Mackintosh; (pseudonym) Gordon Daviot. Born Elizabeth Mackintosh at Inverness, 1896; died in London, Feb 13, 1952; dau. of Colin Mackintosh (greengrocer) and Josephine Horne Mackintosh (schoolteacher); educated at Anstey Physical Training College in Birmingham, 1915–18; never married; no children. ❖ Writer best known for the 8 mystery novels she wrote between 1929 and 1951, the 1st as Gordon Daviot and the rest as Josephine Tey, but who 1st achieved fame writing plays, all of them under pseudonym Gordon Daviot; began as a physical-training instructor at schools near Liverpool and at Tunbridge Wells in England; after mother's death (1926), abandoned teaching to care for invalid father in Inverness; published 1st mystery novel *The Man in the Queue* (under pseudonym Gordon Daviot) in London and NY (1929), followed that same year by publication of the 1st of her 4 non-mystery novels, *Kif: An Unvarnished History,* also as Gordon Daviot; turned attention to playwriting and achieved instant fame with *Richard of Bordeaux,* which, with John Gielgud as actor and producer, ran for hundreds of performances in London (1932–33); had less success with play *Queen of Scots* (1934); returned to mystery writing, and published 1st crime novel as Josephine Tey, *A Shilling for Candles* (1936); wrote little during WWII, but then completed a number of plays, 6 mystery novels and 1 historical novel (1946–52); was a master of suspense, whose books include (as Daviot) *The Expensive Halo* (1931), *Richard of Bordeaux* (1933), *The Laughing Woman* (1934), *Claverhouse* (1937), *The Stars Bow Down* (1939), *Leith Sands and Other Short Plays* (1946) and *The Privateer* (1952); (as Tey) *Miss Pym Disposes* (1946), *The Franchise Affair* (1948), *Brat Farrar* (1949), *To Love and Be Wise* (1950), *The Daughter of Time* (1951) and *The Singing Sands* (1952). After her death, a number of her plays were presented at drama festivals and on radio and tv. ❖ See also *Women in World History*.

TEYE (c. 1400–1340 BCE). *See Tiy.*

TEYTE, Maggie (1888–1976). British operatic soprano. Name variations: Dame Maggie Teyte. Born Margaret Tate, April 17, 1888, in Wolverhampton, England; died May 26, 1976, in England; dau. of Jacob James Tate (hotel owner) and Maria (Doughty) Tate (singer); attended Royal College of Music; studied with Jean de Reszke, Paris, 1904–06; m. Eugène de Plùmon, 1909 (div. 1915); m. Walter Sherwin Cottingham, 1921 (div. 1931). ❖ Known in her day as the preeminent living interpreter of modern French songs, debuted in Paris (1906); debuted in opera at Monte Carlo (1907); performed at Opéra-Comique, Paris (1908–10), becoming especially known for portrayal of Mélisande in *Pelléas et Mélisande,* for which she trained with Debussy; collaborated with Beecham in world premiere of English adaptation of Eugen d'Albert's *Tiefland* (1910); performed with Beecham Opera and British National Opera, London (1911–14, 1936–38); made US debut as Cherubino in *Le Nozze di Figaro* at Philadelphia Metropolitan Opera and created role of Cinderella for US premiere of *Cendrillon* in Chicago (1911); performed same role at NY Metropolitan Opera House (1912); performed in US repeatedly (1911–19, 1940s), as Lygia in *Quo Vadis,* Antonia in *Les Contes d'Hofmann,* and *Mignon*; appeared as Lady Mary Carlisle in *Monsieur Beaucaire* at London's Princess Theater (1915) and followed this with a series of light operas; also appeared in lead in *The Little Dutch Girl* at the Lyric; retired after farewell concert at Royal Festival Hall (1955); other great opera roles included Zerlina, Blonde, Marguerite, Mimi and Butterfly. Received Croix de Lorraine (1943); made a Chevalier of the Légion d'honneur (1957); made a Dame of the British Empire (1958). ❖ See also autobiography *Star on the Door* (1958); Garry O'Connor, *The Pursuit of Perfection: A Life of Maggie Teyte* (Atheneum, 1979); and *Women in World History*.

THACHER, Edith (1910–1997). *See Hurd, Edith Thacher.*

THACKERAY, Anne (1837–1919). *See Ritchie, Anne Isabella.*

THACKREY, Dorothy Schiff (1903–1989). *See Schiff, Dorothy.*

THADEN, Louise (1905–1979). American aviator. Name variations: Louise McPhetridge. Born Iris Louise McPhetridge, Nov 12, 1905, in Bentonville, Arkansas; died Nov 9, 1979, in High Point, North Carolina; dau. of Roy and Edna (Hobs) McPhetridge; m. Herbert von Thaden (army pilot and engineer), July 21, 1928 (died 1969); children: Bill

(b. 1930); Pat (b. 1933). ❖ Celebrated pilot of the golden age of American aviation, as well known in her time as Amelia Earhart, began flying lessons (1927); was issued solo pilot's license, signed by Orville Wright (1928), making her one of the 1st women to achieve pilot status; set a new world record for women's high altitude flying (1928), followed by a short-lived endurance record for a 22-hour flight (Mar 1929); also set a women's aviation speed record of 156 mph; won the 1st Powder Puff Derby (1929); with Earhart, co-founded the Ninety-Nines (1930); served as director of women's division of Pennsylvania School of Aeronautics; with co-pilot Blanche Noyes, became 1st women to enter and win Bendix Cup Race, flying from NY to Los Angeles in a record-setting 14 hours, 54 minutes (1936), for which she received the Harmon Trophy (1936); set world speed record of 197 mph (1937); worked as a representative for Beech Aircraft; during WWII, served as a pilot in Civilian Air Patrol, reaching rank of lieutenant-colonel; was vice-president and director of husband's Thaden Molding Corp. (1955–56), and became partner in Thaden Engineering (1961); after husband's death (1969), ran company as sole owner. Inducted into National Aviation Hall of Fame (1999) and Women in Aviation International's Pioneer Hall of Fame (2000). ❖ See also memoirs *High, Wide, and Frightened* (1938); and *Women in World History.*

THAIS (fl. 331 BCE). **Greek courtesan.** Name variations: Thaïs. Married Lagus (father of Ptolemy I Soter). ❖ Accompanied Alexander III the Great on his campaign out of Egypt in his war with the Persians (331 BCE); when his armies met with resistance at Persepolis, is credited with persuading Alexander to set fire to the Persian palace and city. Though the authenticity of this account is doubtful, it is the subject of John Dryden's *Ode to Saint Cecilia's Day;* numerous anecdotes and witticisms were attributed to Thais in *The Deipnosophists,* the 15 books of the Greek scholar Athenaeus.

THALESTRIS (fl. 334 BCE). **Queen of the Amazons.** Name variations: Minythyia. Possibly flourished around 334 BCE. ❖ Legendary Amazon queen who is reported to have traveled 25 days with 300 attendants through populous lands, so as to meet the famous Macedonian king Alexander the Great in Hyrcania (northern Iran), in order conceive a child with him. The story as related by Justin is based on the discredited account of Onesicratus, a philosopher-pilot-writer who accompanied Alexander on his eastern expedition. ❖ See also *Women in World History.*

THAMAR. *Variant of Tamar.*

THAMAR (1160–1212). *See Tamara.*

THAMARIS. *See Timarete.*

THANE, Elswyth (1900–1984). **American novelist and playwright.** Name variations: Elswyth Beebe; Mrs. William Beebe; Elswyth Thane Ricker. Born Helen Ricker, May 16, 1900, in Burlington, IA; m. Dr. William Beebe (naturalist and explorer), 1927. ❖ Began career as a freelance writer (1925); wrote such plays as *The Tudor Wench* (1933) and *Young Mr. Disraeli* (1934); novels include *Riders of the Wind, Echo Answers, His Elizabeth, Cloth of Gold, Bound to Happen* and *Tryst;* also wrote biographies of George and Martha Washington.

THANET, Octave (1850–1934). *See French, Alice.*

THANHOUSER, Gertrude (1880–1951). *See Homan, Gertrude.*

THANHOUSER TWINS.
See Fairbanks, Madeline.
See Fairbanks, Marion.

THÁNOU, Ekateríni (1975—). **Greek runner.** Name variations: Ekaterini Thanou. Born Feb 1, 1975, in Athens, Greece. ❖ Won a silver medal for 100 meters at Sydney Olympics (2000); at European championships, won a gold medal for 100 meters (2002).

THANT, Mme (1900–1989). **Burmese wife of U Thant.** Name variations: Daw Thein Tin; Ma Thein Tin. Born Ma Thein Tin in Mandalay, Burma (now Myanmar), 1900; died in 1989; dau. of U Khinn (lawyer) and Daw Kye; m. Maung Thant (U Thant, secretary-general of United Nations during Cold War era), Nov 1934 (died Nov 1974); children: Maung Boh (b. 1936, died in infancy); Saw Lwin (adopted); Aye Aye; Maung Tin Maung (d. 1962); grandchildren: Thant Myint U (b. Jan 31, 1966). ❖ When husband became Burma's representative to UN, moved to New York City (1957); was unhappy there, but husband's growing importance in international politics prevented her from returning to Burma; while husband served as secretary-general of UN (1962–71),

her health broke down because of homesickness and death of son Maung Tin Maung (1962); unable to return to Burma, even for the funeral of her son, grew increasingly withdrawn; rarely attended official events with husband, preferring to remain quietly at home, and received few visitors. ❖ See also *Women in World History.*

THARP, Twyla (1941—). **American choreographer and director.** Born July 1, 1941, in Portland, Indiana; m. Bob Huot (painter, div.); children: 1 son. ❖ Pioneering ballet and modern-dance choreographer, studied at Barnard College and then with Igor Schwezoff, Richard Thomas, Barbara Fallis, Martha Graham, Merce Cunningham and Eugene Lewis; debuted with Paul Taylor company (1963); headed Twyla Tharp Dance Group (1964–88); became known for innovative use of space, technical brilliance, and the combining of classical ballet with modern dance forms; disbanded company and became artistic associate at American Ballet Theatre (1988); choreographed the film *Hair* (1979), as well as *Ragtime* (1981), *Amadeus* (1984), *White Nights* (1985), and *The Catherine Wheel* (1992); received 2 Emmys for "Baryshnikov by Tharp" (1985); received Tony Award for Best Choreographer and Tony nomination for Best Director for *Movin' Out* (2003); other choreographic works include *The Fugue* (1970), *Deuce Coupe* (1973), *As Time Goes By* (1973), *When We Were Very Young* (1980), *Sinatra Suite* (1984), *Cutting Up* (1991), *The Beethoven Sonata* (2000), *Brief Fling* and *In the Upper Room.* Received Barnard College Medal of Distinction (1982) and MacArthur Fellowship (1992). ❖ See also autobiography, *Push Comes to Shove* (1992).

THARPE, Rosetta (1915–1973). **African-American singer and guitarist.** Name variations: Sister Rosetta Tharpe. Born Rosetta Nubin, Mar 20, 1915, in Cotton Plant, AR; died in Philadelphia, PA, Oct 9, 1973; dau. of Kate Bell Nubin; married a pastor named Thorpe, 1934; m. Forrest Allen, 1940s; m. Russell Morrison, 1951. ❖ The 1st gospel singer to sign with a major recording company, came to national attention with Decca hit "Rock Me" (1938), recorded with Lucky Millender; performed with Cab Calloway Revue and appeared at Café Society, then unleashed her talent in Carnegie Hall during historic "Spirituals to Swing" concert (1938); popularized gospel music to a wider audience, one among a handful of gospel prima donnas who spread the sound to the country; was the 1st gospel singer to engage in extensive European travel (1950s); appeared at Antibes Festival (1960) and performed at Paris Jazz Festival (1968) and Newport Jazz Festival; received Grammy nominations. ❖ See also *Women in World History.*

THATCHER, Annie (c. 1837–?). *See Vitelli, Annie.*

THATCHER, Margaret (1925—). **British prime minister.** Name variations: Margaret Roberts; Mrs. Thatcher; Lady Thatcher. Born Margaret Roberts in Grantham, England, Oct 13, 1925; dau. of Alfred Roberts (shopkeeper and mayor of Grantham) and Beatrice Roberts; attended Somerville College, Oxford, 1943–47; m. Denis Thatcher (London businessman), Dec 1951; children: (twins) Carol and Mark (b. 1953). ❖ First female Conservative Party leader and prime minister (1979–90), who made as strong a mark on British politics as any 20th-century prime minister; while attending Somerville College, became president of the University's Conservative Association—the 1st woman to hold that office; worked as a research chemist (1947–51); ran unsuccessfully for a seat in Parliament (1950), in the pro-Labour constituency of Dartford, Kent; passed the bar (1954); practiced law, concentrating on tax cases (1954–59); after several more unsuccessful bids for a parliamentary seat, won position of MP for Finchley (part of north London, 1959), when Conservatives were in power; appointed junior minister in the Ministry of Pensions and National Insurance (1961), where she was soon a dominant presence; when the Conservatives lost the General Election of 1964, served as parliamentary opposition speaker 1st on Pensions, then on Housing, Finance, Transport, and finally Education (1964–70); served as secretary of state for Education and Science (1970–74); elected Conservative Party leader (1975); gained international prominence as an outspoken leader of the opposition (1975–79); elected prime minister, the 1st woman to hold Britain's highest political office (1979); in following decade, known as "The Iron Lady," carried out a conservative revolution even more dramatic than that of her friend and counterpart Ronald Reagan, denationalizing primary industries, curbing union power, and selling public-housing units to their occupants; won the war in the Falkland Islands (1982); reelected prime minister (1983 and 1987), thereby winning 3 consecutive general elections, which no British premier had done since early 19th century, and dominating her party more completely than any other politician of the century; introduced a ruinously unpopular "poll tax," changing the local taxation structure and imposing the burden less progressively than hitherto; also remained suspicious of Britain's role in European Economic Community; losing support of her party, resigned as prime minister (1990); elevated to a life peerage as Lady Thatcher (1992), became one of the elder chiefs of state of the Western world. ❖ See also memoirs *The Downing Street Years* (HarperCollins, 1993) and *The Path to Power* (HarperCollins, 1995); E. Bruce Geelhoed, *Margaret Thatcher: In Victory and Downfall* (Prager, 1992); Penny Junor, *Margaret Thatcher: Wife, Mother, Politician* (Sidgwick & Jackson, 1983); Dennis Kavanagh, *Thatcherism and British Politics* (Oxford U. Press, 1990); Alan Watkins, *A Conservative Coup: The Fall of Margaret Thatcher* (Duckworth, 1991); Leo Abse, *Margaret, Daughter of Beatrice* (Cape, 1989); and *Women in World History*.

THATCHER, Molly Day (d. 1963). American playwright. Name variations: Molly Kazan. Died Dec 14, 1963, age 56, in New York, NY; m. Elia Kazan (director). ❖ Plays include *The Egghead, Rosemary* and *The Alligator*.

THATE, Carole (1971—). Dutch field-hockey player. Born Dec 6, 1971, in Utrecht, Netherlands. ❖ Won team bronze medals at Atlanta Olympics (1996) and Sydney Olympics (2000).

THAW, Evelyn Nesbit (1884–1967). *See Nesbit, Evelyn.*

THAXTER, Celia Laighton (1835–1894). American poet. Born in Portsmouth, New Hampshire, June 29, 1835; died Appledore, one of the Isles of Shoals, off Portsmouth, Aug 26, 1894; dau. of Thomas B. Laighton (newspaperman) and Eliza (Rymes) Laighton; m. Levi Lincoln Thaxter (lawyer), Sept 30, 1851 (died 1884); children: Karl, John and Roland Thaxter (1858–1932, well-known botanist at Harvard). ❖ Grew up about 10 miles off the coast of Portsmouth, NH, on White Island, on the isolated Isles of Shoals—which would serve to color the best of her verse; after father built a summer hotel on Appledore Island (1845), the 1st of its kind along New England coast, met many of the leading writers and artists of the period who flocked to its doors; in later years, separated from husband, joined her brothers who had inherited the summer hotel on Appledore, where she became the center of a salon for the best minds of New England, including John Greenleaf Whittier, William Morris Hunt, and Edwin Arlington Robinson; had 1st printed poem, "Land-Locked," published by James Russell Lowell in *Atlantic Monthly*; also wrote prose sketches, including *Among the Isles of Shoals* (1873), *Driftweed*, a book about floriculture, *An Island Garden* (1894), and stories and poems for children while contributing articles to *St. Nicholas* magazine. ❖ See also *Women in World History*.

THAXTER, Phyllis (1921—). American stage, tv and screen actress. Born Phyllis St. Felix Thaxter, Nov 20, 1921, in Portland, ME; dau. of Sidney S. F. Thaxter (Maine Supreme Court justice) and Marie Phyllis Schuyler Thaxter (Shakespearean actress); m. James T. Aubrey (producer), 1944 (div. 1963); m. Gilbert Lea; children: Skye Aubrey (actress). ❖ Made NY debut in *What a Life* (1938), followed by *There Shall Be No Night, Heartsong* and *Take Her She's Mine*, among others; films include *30 Seconds over Tokyo, Weekend at the Waldorf, Sea of Grass, Bewitched, The World of Henry Orient, No Man of Her Own, The Breaking Point, Jim Thorpe—All American, Springfield Rifle, She's Working Her Way Through College, Women's Prison* and *Superman*.

THAYER, Ann (1932—). *See Bannon, Ann.*

THAYER, Caroline Matilda Warren (1785–1844). *See Warren, Caroline Matilda.*

THEA (c. 165–121 BCE). *See Cleopatra Thea.*

THEANO (fl. 6th c. BCE). Greek composer, poet, and philosopher. Name variations: Theano of Crotona. Married Pythagoras (c. 582–c. 500 BCE, Greek philosopher and mathematician who was devoted to the reformation of politics, morality, and society); children: daughters Arignote, Myia, and Damo; sons Telauges and Mnesarchus. ❖ Taught husband that the spheres and stars of heaven moved in eternal song and dance; organized rites for her followers, so that they could achieve inner harmony through movement to the music. ❖ See also *Women in World History*.

THEANO II (fl. 5th c. BCE). Poet. Flourished in the 5th century BCE. ❖ Writer of lyric verse who was mentioned in the 10th-century *Suda* and Eustathius.

THEATO, Diemut R. (1937—). German politician. Born April 13, 1937, in Kleinröhrsdorf/Dresden, Germany. ❖ Worked as interpreter and translator (English and Portuguese, 1960–87); as a member of the European People's Party (Christian Democrats) and European Democrats, elected to 4th and 5th European Parliament (1994–99, 1999–2004); named chair of the Committee on Budgetary Control. Awarded Order of Merit of Federal Republic of Germany (1995).

THEBOM, Blanche (b. 1918). American mezzo-soprano. Born Sept 19, 1918, in Monessen, PA, to Swedish-American parents; studied under Margaret Matzenauer and Edyth Walker. ❖ Made professional debut at a recital in Sheboygan, WI (1941); sang with the Philadelphia Orchestra as well as in countless small towns, followed by contracts with Minneapolis Symphony (1943) and NY's Town Hall (1944); appeared in musical sequence in film *When Irish Eyes Are Smiling* (1944); debuted at Metropolitan Opera (1944), then performed regularly at the Met, usually in dramatic roles, to rave reviews; made numerous recordings and was frequently featured on classical radio programs; was the 1st American to sing with Bolshoi Opera in Moscow; joined music faculty of University of Arkansas (1960s); retired from stage (1970); named director of Hot Springs National Park Foundation for Performing Arts (1973); founded Opera Arts Training Program in San Francisco (1988) and served as its director. ❖ See also *Women in World History*.

THECLA (fl. 1st c. CE). Anatolian saint. Name variations: Thecla of Seleucia. Born at Iconium, a small town in Cilicia (southern Anatolia); dau. of Theocleia. ❖ Early Christian, follower of St. Paul and one of the best-known saints of the Greek Church, whose miraculous escapes from certain death became a famous legend; as reported in the *Acts of Paul and Thecla*, was ordered to be put to death by immolation, but a downpour doused the flames; was lashed to a lion, but it licked her feet; had a lioness and a bear set loose on her, but the lioness protectively positioned itself between Thecla and the bear. A sanctuary at Seleucia in her honor became a popular site of pilgrimage during the Middle Ages and thereafter, and her purported accomplishments became institutionalized among Greek Orthodox Christians. Feast day is Sept 24. ❖ See also *Women in World History*.

THECLA (c. 775–c. 823). Byzantine empress. Name variations: Thekla. Born c. 775; died c. 823; dau. of a general; 1st wife of Michael II of Amorion, Byzantine emperor (r. 820–829); children: Theophilus I (r. 829–842). ❖ Growing up in a military household, was almost certainly an iconoclast, as was her husband, though when he ruled he would be somewhat moderate in his approach to iconodules; stood at husband's side when he was crowned emperor (Dec 25, 820); with him, established a dynasty (the Amorion, or Phrygian), an accomplishment unmatched by Michael II's 3 imperial predecessors; at her death, was mourned by husband deeply (Michael's 2nd wife was Euphrosyne [c. 790–c. 840]). ❖ See also *Women in World History*.

THECLA (c. 810–c. 860). *See Theodora the Blessed.*

THECLA (c. 823–c. 870). Possible co-regent of the Byzantine Empire. Name variations: Saint Thecla. Born c. 823; died c. 870; dau. of Theophilus I, Byzantine emperor (r. 829–842), and Empress Theodora the Blessed (c. 810–c. 860); sister of Michael III the Drunkard (c. 836–867), Byzantine emperor (r. 842–867), and Mary (or Maria), Anna, Anastasia, and Pulcheria; mistress of Basil I, Byzantine emperor (r. 867–886). ❖ At brother Michael's urging, served as Basil's mistress, beginning when she was about 43 years of age; after the murderous accession of Basil, became the mistress of one John Neatocometes, for which she suffered beatings and the confiscation of her considerable property. ❖ See also *Women in World History*.

THEILADE, Nini (b. 1915). Danish ballet dancer and choreographer. Name variations: Nina Theilade. Born June 15, 1915, in Poerwoherto, Java, Dutch East Indies; dau. of Johanna (Dom) and Hans Theilade; studied ballet in Denmark and in Paris with Lyubov Egorova; was trained in modern dance by Harald Kreutzberg. ❖ Made stage debut as a solo dancer in Amsterdam (1929), then toured with her own dance recitals in principal European cities; was 1st solo dancer and ballet-mistress with Max Reinhardt (1931–33); made London debut in Reinhardt's production of *A Midsummer Night's Dream* (1933); toured in America (1933–34), then joined the Ballet Russe de Monte Carlo, creating roles in Massine's *Seventh Symphony* (1938), *Nobilissima Visione* (1938), and *Bacchanale* (1939), as well as her own *Les Nuages* (1940); danced in such plays as *Comus, Psyche, Chloridia* (title role), and *The Laughing Cavalier*; choreographed and appeared in such films as *A Midsummer Night's Dream* (1935) and *Lotusblomsten*; taught in Brazil for many years, before opening a school in Svendborg, Denmark (1970). Decorated by the king of Denmark with royal Gold Medal of the First Class, with Crown (1936).

THEKLA. *Variant of Thecla.*

THEKLA (1815–1876). *See Düringsfeld, Ida von.*

THEMANS-SIMONS, Judikje (1904–1943). Dutch-Jewish gymnast. Name variations: Judikje Simons. Born Aug 20, 1904, in Netherlands; killed at Sobibor concentration camp, Mar 3, 1943, with husband, 3-year-old son Leon and 5-year-old daughter Sonja. ❖ At Amsterdam Olympics, won a gold medal for team all-around (1928), the 1st time women's gymnastics made the Olympic program (no indiv. medals were awarded).

THEOCTISTA (c. 740–c. 802). Byzantine nun. Born c. 740; died c. 802; dau. of a Byzantine bureaucrat; sister of Plato, a monk; m. Photinus; children: 3 sons, Theodore, Joseph and Euthymius; 1 daughter (name unknown). ❖ Nun whose religious scruples helped to bring about the downfall of Emperor Constantine VI; was greatly affected by the Iconoclastic Controversy which raged throughout her lifetime; when Irene of Athens, a devotee of icons, became regent for Constantine VI, was reunited with brother Plato, a monk of some standing, who returned to the capital and its court; energized by brother, threw open her house to icon-venerating monks; under Plato's influence, sold most of her property and retired with the rest of her family to an estate at Saccudium in Bithynia, where she lived under Plato's rule; when Constantine VI sought to divorce his 1st wife (Maria of Amnia) to marry Theodota, a close relative of Theoctista, opposed the marriage and was imprisoned, though her punishment only served to make a martyr of her in the eyes of the capital's masses; freed by Irene who had staged a coup (797), returned to Saccudium where she lived an ascetic life. ❖ See also *Women in World History.*

THEODELINDA (568–628). Queen of Lombardy. Name variations: Theodolinda; Theolinde. Born in 568 in Bavaria; died in 628 in Lombardy; dau. of Garibald I; m. Authari also known as Autarie, king of Lombardy (died); m. Flavius Agiluphus of Pavia, also known as Ago (died); children: at least 1 son. ❖ As queen-regent of Lombardy for son, was both an excellent queen and a devout woman; encouraged agriculture and instituted policies to increase Lombardy's economic stability; was also responsible for the construction of many churches, monasteries and nunneries; successfully encouraged her subjects to turn back to orthodoxy from the spreading heresy of Arianism (whose members denied that Christ was divine); gained such a reputation for intelligence and faith that Pope Gregory I the Great dedicated one of his works, the *Dialogues*, to her.

THEODELINDE (1814–1857). Countess of Wurttemberg. Name variations: Théodelinde; Theodolinde; Theolinde de Beauharnais. Born April 13, 1814; died April 1, 1857; dau. of Amalie Auguste (1788–1851) and Eugene de Beauharnais (1781–1824), duke of Leuchtenburg; sister of Josephine Beauharnais (1807–1876), queen of Sweden; m. Count William of Württemberg, on Feb 8, 1841.

THEODERADE. *See Theodorade.*

THEODORA (fl. 3rd c.). Roman noblewoman. Flourished in late 200s CE; dau. of Eutropia (fl. 270–300 CE) and Afranius Hannibalianus; stepdau. of Maximian, the senior Roman emperor of the West; half-sister of Fausta (d. 324); 2nd wife of Constantius I Chlorus, Roman emperor of the West, c. 292 (died 306); children: Constantia (c. 293–?); Flavius Dalmatius; Flavius Julius Constantius; Hannibalianus; Eutropia (fl. 330s); and Anastasia (who m. Bassianus).

THEODORA (d. 304). Egyptian saint. Name variations: Saint Theodora. Died in 304. ❖ At the height of the Great Persecution of Christians sanctioned by Diocletian (303–311), was arrested for her religion; refusing to acknowledge the pagan gods, was sentenced to a life of prostitution in a common brothel; was discovered there by a pagan named Didymus, who was so moved by the cruelty of this sentence that he determined both to convert to Christianity and to rescue her from her debasement; discovered in an attempt to escape, was martyred with Didymus. Feast day is April 28.

THEODORA (c. 500–548). Byzantine empress. Born Theodora on Cyprus, or more likely in Syria, c. 500; died 548; dau. of Acacius (keeper of the Green faction's bears in Constantinople's Hippodrome) and a mother of low status; sister of Comitona and Anastasia; m. Justinian I, Byzantine emperor (r. 527–565); children: (before marriage) 2 illeg. (son John and a daughter whose name is unknown). ❖ Empress, known for her courage and sharp political skills, wielded enormous power as the wife of Justinian I and strongly influenced his policies and actions during their joint rule of the world's greatest existing empire; with sisters, was introduced to the stage at a time when the word *actress* was a synonym for *prostitute*; her fortunes, however, rapidly improved, for her beauty, wit and intelligence attracted the attention of the best heeled of Constantinople's pleasure-loving population; became mistress of Hecebolus, governor of Pentapolis; sent packing, made her way to Alexandria, the 2nd city of the Byzantine Empire, where she became involved with religiosity and religious issues; returned to Constantinople, where she met and probably seduced Justinian (I), about 15 years her senior (c. 522); as his mistress, was officially enrolled as one of the empire's aristocracy; married to Justinian with full ecclesiastical approval (c. 523); with husband, expanded dominance over the imperial court as virtual colleagues; for 3 years, helped Justinian ward off the attacks of rivals, in the process learning the ins and outs of "Byzantine" politics; efforts paid off when Justinian was designated heir-apparent (525); with husband, was co-regent of Byzantium (r. 527–548); meticulously constructed a network of allies, mostly women, through whom she hoped to extend her influence; played 2 great roles at Justinian's side: counciled husband not to flee during the Nika riot (532), and was an important stimuli to Justinian's great recodification of Roman law; was especially interested in the rights of women, paying special attention to access to property through inheritance, to the usufruct of dowries, and to the division of estates after divorce; having overcome her lowly birth, was probably the most powerful Byzantine woman ever. ❖ See also A. Bridge, *Theodora* (Academy Chicago, 1978); R. Browning, *Justinian and Theodora* (Thames & Hudson, 1987); C. Diehl, *Theodora: Empress of Byzantium* (Ungar, 1972); and *Women in World History.*

THEODORA (fl. early 900s). Byzantine empress. Married Romanos I Lekapenus or Romanus I Lecapanus, emperor of Byzantium (r. 919–944); children: Christopher; Stephen; Constantine; Theophylact; Helena Lekapena (c. 920–961).

THEODORA (fl. late 900s). Byzantine empress. Dau. of Helena Lekapena (c. 920–961) and Constantine VII Porphyrogenetos (c. 906–959), Byzantine emperor (r. 913–959); sister of Romanus II, Byzantine emperor (r. 959–963); m. John I Tzimisces, Byzantine emperor (r. 969–976).

THEODORA, Efua (1924–1996). *See Sutherland, Efua Theodora.*

THEODORA, Saint (1096–1160). *See Christina of Markyate.*

THEODORA I OF ROME (c. 875–c. 925). *See Theodora of Rome.*

THEODORA II OF ROME (c. 900–c. 950). *See Theodora the Younger.*

THEODORA III OF ROME (c. 875–c. 925). *See Theodora of Rome.*

THEODORA BATATZAINA (fl. 1200s). *See Theodora Ducas.*

THEODORA CANTACUZENE (fl. 14th c.). Byzantine princess. Dau. of Irene Asen and John VI Cantacuzene, emperor of Nicaea (r. 1347–1354); m. Orchan.

THEODORA COMNENA (fl. 1080s). Byzantine princess. Dau. of Alexius I Comnenus, Byzantine emperor (r. 1081–1118) and Irene Ducas (c. 1066–1133); sister of Anna Comnena (1083–1153/55); m. Constantine Angelus; children: John and Andronicus.

THEODORA COMNENA (fl. 1140). Byzantine royal. Dau. of Andronicus Comnenus (1104–1142); niece of Manuel I Comenus (c. 1120–1180), Byzantine emperor (r. 1143–1180); children: (with Manuel I) illeg. son, Alexius Comnenus.

THEODORA COMNENA (1145–after 1183). Queen of Jerusalem. Born in 1145; died after 1183; dau. of Isaac Comnenus; granddau. of the Byzantine emperor John II Comnenus (r. 1118–1143); niece of Manuel I Comnenus (c. 1120–1180), emperor of Byzantium (r. 1143–1180); m. Baldwin III, king of Jerusalem (r. 1143–1162), in 1158; children: (with Andronicus I Comnenus) Alexius; Irene Comnena. ❖ Byzantine noblewoman, briefly queen of Jerusalem, who later was associated with Andronicus I Comnenus, future emperor of Byzantium; at 13, was married to Baldwin, king of Jerusalem, with a dowry of 100,000 gold coins (1158); in the marriage negotiations, was endowed with the city of Acre and its revenues, to be her private possession if she outlived Baldwin and if he died childless; husband died childless after a short illness (1162); as a beautiful widow, just 16 years old, settled into her possession at Acre, remaining there for 5 years; at 21, met 46-year-old 2nd cousin, Andronicus I Comnenus, and fell in love, but was far too closely related for legitimate ecclesiastical authorities even to consider the sanction of marriage; abandoned Acre for Beirut, where she took up residence as

Andronicus' mistress; with Andronicus, slipped into Syria and spent next few years (excommunicated by Christian authorities) wandering around the Islamic middle east; kidnaped with children by Nicephorus Palaeologus, the governor of Trebizond, and held hostage against Andronicus' return to Byzantium; when Andronicus agreed to do so, to spare their lives, her period of intimacy with him was over (Andronicus ascended the Byzantine throne in 1183). ❖ See also *Women in World History.*

THEODORA CRESCENTII THE ELDER (c. 875–c. 925). *See Theodora of Rome.*

THEODORA CRESCENTII THE YOUNGER (c. 900–c. 950). *See Theodora the Younger.*

THEODORA DUCAS (fl. 11th c.). Byzantine princess. Dau. of Eudocia Macrembolitissa (1021–1096) and Constantine X Ducas (d. 1067), Byzantine emperor (r. 1059–1067).

THEODORA DUCAS (fl. 1200s). Byzantine empress. Name variations: Theodora Doukaina; Theodora Batatzaina. Flourished in the 1200s; dau. of John Ducas; m. Michael VIII Paleologus (1224–1282), emperor of Nicaea (r. 1261–1282); children: Irene Paleologina (fl. 1279–1280, who m. Ivan Asen III of Bulgaria); Andronicus II (1259–1332), emperor of Nicaea (r. 1282–1328); Constantine; Eudocia (c. 1260–?, who m. John of Trebizond). ❖ Michael VIII also had an illegitimate daughter, Euphrosyne, who married Nogaj. ❖ See also *Women in World History.*

THEODORA OF BYZANTIUM (c. 989–1056). *See Theodora Porphyrogenita.*

THEODORA OF ROME (c. 875–c. 925). Roman noblewoman. Name variations: Theodora the Elder; Theodora I the Elder of Rome; Theodora III; Theodora Crescentii; Theodora Crescentii the Elder; Theodora the Senatrix. Probably born in or near Rome around 875, likely of noble birth; died probably in or near Rome around 925; m. Theophylactus from Tusculum (died c. 925), also known as Theophylact Crescentii and Theophylacte, governor of the Roman senate; children: Marozia Crescentii (885–938); Theodora the Younger (c. 900–950). ❖ Roman woman, influential in Italy and in Papal affairs, was the wife and political ally of Theophylacte, one of the most prominent Roman officials of his generation; shared the public spotlight with husband; with Theophylacte, was a close political ally of Pope Sergius III (r. 904–911) and, after death of Sergius, was instrumental in elevating John X (r. 914–928) to the papacy. Even her supporters admit, however, that she was excessively ambitious and perhaps a bit too avaricious for beatification. ❖ See also *Women in World History.*

THEODORA OF THE KHAZARS (fl. 700s). Byzantine empress. Name variations: Theodoar. Sister of the khagan of the Khazars; 2nd wife of Justinian II Rhinotmetos, Byzantine emperor (r. 685–695 and 705–711). ❖ As the wife of Justinian II, was the 1st Byzantine empress to hail from a barbarian tribe outside the frontiers of the empire. ❖ See also *Women in World History.*

THEODORA OLDENBURG (1906–1969). Margravine of Baden. Name variations: Théodora; Princess Mountbatten. Born May 30, 1906, in Athens, Greece; died Oct 16, 1969, in Budingen; dau. of Alice of Battenberg (1885–1969) and Andrew, prince of Greece and Denmark; m. Berthold Frederick William, margrave of Baden; children: Margaret of Baden (b. 1932); Maximilian Andrew Frederick (b. 1933), margrave of Baden; Louis William George Ernest, prince (b. 1937).

THEODORA PALEOLOGINA (fl. 1200s). Byzantine noblewoman. Name variations: Palaeologina. Flourished around the 1200s; dau. of Irene and Alexius Paleologus; m. Andronicus Paleologus; children: Michael VIII Paleologus, emperor of Nicaea (r. 1261–1282); John; Constantine; Maria Paleologina (who m. Nicephorus Tarchaneiotes); Eulogia Paleologina. ❖ Was the matriarch of the Paleologi family.

THEODORA PALEOLOGINA (fl. 14th c.). Byzantine princess. Dau. of Michael IX Paleologus (d. 1320), Byzantine emperor, co-emperor of Nicaea (r. 1295–1320) and Maria of Armenia; m. Theodore Svetoslav; m. Michael Shishman or Sisman.

THEODORA PORPHYROGENITA (c. 989–1056). Co-empress of Byzantium. Name variations: Augusta Theodora; Theodora of Byzantium. Co-empress of Byzantium (r. 1042–1056). Born c. 989 in Byzantium (some sources cite 981); died in 1056 or 1057 in Byzantium; youngest dau. of Constantine VIII, Byzantine emperor (r. 1025–1028), and Helena of Alypia; sister of Empress Zoë Porphyrogenita (980–1050)

and Eudocia (c. 978–?); never married; no children. ❖ Despite living in a convent, aided empress sister Zoë Porphyrogenita through her indirect influence, bringing a high sense of morality to the administration and a belief that the ruler of the empire had an obligation to better the life of its citizens; following death of sister (1050) and brother-in-law Constantine IX (1055), was brought out of the convent by popular opinion and onto the throne; reigned alone (1055–57); by her firm administration, frustrated an attempt to supersede her on behalf of the general Nicephorus Bryennius; controlled the unruly nobles and checked numerous abuses but marred her reputation by being excessively severe towards her enemies and by employing menials for advisers; even so, was a well-respected and well-loved empress, who left a high standard for moral rule when she died.

THEODORA THE BLESSED (c. 810–c. 860). Empress of Byzantium. Name variations: Thecla or Thekla; St. Theodora; Theodora of Paphlagonia; Theodora the Blessed. Born c. 810, a princess of Paphlagonia, a region of the Byzantine empire situated on the Black Sea; died c. 860 in Byzantium; sister of Bardas (Bardus); m. Theophilus I, emperor of Byzantium, in 829 (died 842); children: Mary (or Maria); Thecla; Anna; Anastasia (fl. 800s); Pulcheria; Constantine; Michael III (b. around 836), later known as Michael the Drunkard, emperor of Byzantium (r. 842–867). ❖ Served as empress and regent of the Byzantine Empire and was made a saint by the Eastern Orthodox Church; was chosen to be the wife of the emperor Theophilus I (c. 830); noted for her courage and thoughtfulness, became quite popular; widowed (842), was made regent for son Michael III; during 14 years as regent, restored religious orthodoxy, though she showed considerable patience and moderation in doing so, refusing to sanction violence against the heretics as a means of stamping them out; carried on the government with a firm and judicious hand, replenishing the treasury, and repelling the Bulgarians during an attempted invasion; when it came to her son, made some important mistakes which would ultimately end her reign: to ensure her power, neglected his education, encouraged him to pursue a life of pleasure, and refused to allow him to co-rule with her. ❖ See also *Women in World History.*

THEODORA THE ELDER (c. 875–c. 925). *See Theodora of Rome.*

THEODORA THE YOUNGER (c. 900–c. 950). Roman noblewoman. Name variations: Theodora II of Rome; Theodora Crescentii the Younger. Born c. 900; died c. 950; dau. of Theophylactus from Tusculum (died c. 925), also known as Theophylact Crescentii and Theophylacte, governor of the Roman senate, and Theodora of Rome (c. 875–c. 925); sister of Marozia Crescentii; m. John (a bishop); children: John (who was Pope John XIII from 965 to 972); Crescentius. ❖ Member of the influential Crescentii family and mother of Pope John XIII, was an active partisan in the politics of Rome, like her mother and sister, but unlike both, was not the target of sensationalist slander. ❖ See also *Women in World History.*

THEODORADE (fl. 9th c.). Queen of France. Name variations: Theoderade; Théodor-ade. Married Odo, also known as Eudes (860–898), count of Paris and king of France (r. 888–898).

THÉODORE, Mlle (1760–1796). *See Crespé, Marie-Madeleine.*

THEODORE, Mother (1798–1856). *See Guérin, Mother Theodore.*

THEODORE, Sister (1798–1856). *See Guérin, Mother Theodore.*

THEODORESCU, Monica (1963—). West German equestrian. Born Mar 2, 1963, in Halle, Germany; m. George Theodorescu (trainer). ❖ Won gold medals at Seoul Olympics (1988), Barcelona Olympics (1992) and Atlanta Olympics (1996), all in team dressage; won team gold medals at World championships (1990) and European championships (1993).

THEODOROPOULOU, Avra (1880–1963). Greek pianist, women's-rights activist, and critic. Born 1880; died in 1963; m. Agis Theros (poet). ❖ Founded School for Working Women (1911); founded Soldier's Sister (1918); founded and was president of Greek League for Women's Rights (1920–57). ❖ See also *Women in World History.*

THEODOSIA. *Variant of Feodosia.*

THEODOSIA (fl. 1220). Russian princess. Dau. of Mystislav the Gallant, Prince of Novgorod, one of the greatest warriors of his day; m. Yaroslav II, grand prince of Moscow and grand duke of Vladimir (r. 1238–1246); children: Andrew or Andrei II (c. 1220–1263), grand duke of Moscow (r. 1246–1252); Alexander Nevski, grand prince of Moscow (r. 1252–

1263); Michael; Yaroslav III, prince of Tver and grand prince of Moscow (r. 1263–1272); Basil or Vasili Kostroma, grand prince of Moscow (r. 1272–1277); Michael Khorobrit.

THEODOSIA OF MOSCOW (1475–1501). Russian princess. Name variations: Feodosia. Born May 29, 1475 (some sources cite 1488); died Feb 19, 1501; dau. of Sophia of Byzantium (1448–1503) and Ivan III the Great (1440–1505), grand prince of Moscow and tsar of Russia (r. 1462–1505); m. Vassili, prince Cholinksi, on Feb 13, 1500.

THEODOTA (c. 775–early 800s). Byzantine empress. Name variations: Theodote. Born c. 775; died in early 800s; was a close relative of monks Plato and Theodore and the nun Theoctista; became 2nd wife of Constantine VI Porphyrogenitus, Byzantine emperor (r. 780–797), in Aug 795 (Constantine VI's 1st wife was Maria of Amnia). ❖ Empress whose marriage prompted the coup that ended her husband's reign; a beauty who served in Irene of Athens's courtly entourage, was encouraged by Irene to marry her son, though he was already married to Maria of Amnia; lived out the rest of her days in obscurity after Irene engineered a successful coup. ❖ See also *Women in World History.*

THEODRADA (b. between 783 and 794). Abbess of Argenteuil. Name variations: Theodrada of Argenteuil. Born between 783 and 794; dau. of Fastrada (d. 794) and Charles I also known as Charlemagne (742–814), king of the Franks (r. 768–814), and Holy Roman emperor (r. 800–814).

THEOPHANE, Sister (1913–1993). *See Reinders, Agnes.*

THEOPHANO (c. 866–c. 897). Byzantine empress and saint. Name variations: Saint Theophano. Born in Constantinople around 866 (some sources cite 865); died c. 897 (some sources cite 893, 895 or 896); dau. of the patrician Constantine Martinacius; mother's name unknown; 1st of four wives of Leo VI the Wise, Byzantine emperor (co-ruled 870–886, r. 886–912); children: 1 daughter. ❖ Chosen as the 1st wife of Byzantine Emperor Leo VI by Eudocia Ingerina (Leo's mother) at the imperial Bride Show, a kind of beauty contest (881–882); though she supported Leo, spent her time in prayer and religious contemplation, neglected the political side of her position, and seemed to prefer a chaste life to one which embraced the responsibility of providing for an imperial heir, though she did give birth to a daughter; died young, presenting as much of a problem for Leo as she had in life, for her piety made her a popular symbol among the devout masses; was recognized as a saint soon after her demise, a fact which forced Leo to construct a sanctuary for her relics and to honor her holy memory. These relics were the objects of devotion for centuries. Leo VI was also married to Zoë Zautzina, Eudocia Baiane, and Zoë Carbopsina. ❖ See also *Women in World History.*

THEOPHANO (c. 940–?). Byzantine empress. Name variations: Theophano of Byzantium. Born c. 940 (some sources cite 941) in Constantinople; died after 976; dau. of Anastaso (a publican); became 2nd wife of Romanos or Romanus II, Byzantine emperor (r. 959–963), around 956; m. Nicephorus II Phocas or Nikephoros II Phokas, Byzantine emperor (r. 963–969); children: (1st m.) Theophano of Byzantium (c. 955–991); Basil II (957–1025), Byzantine emperor (r. 976–1025); Constantine VIII (c. 960–1028), Byzantine emperor (r. 1025–1028); Anna of Byzantium (963–1011, who m. Vladimir I, grand-duke of Kiev, around 989). ❖ Married Romanus II, son of Byzantine emperor Constantine VII (c. 956); became the power behind Romanus, inciting him to place his 5 sisters (including Agatha and Theodora [fl. late 900s]) in convents and to break with his mother Helena Lekapena, so that she would face no opposition from the women of his family; having established herself at court, is said to have lived a dissolute life; soon after death of Romanus, married Nicephorus (II) Phocas and was germinal in his elevation to the imperial office; was officially established as regent for her young sons, Basil and Constantine; possibly plotted the assassination of Nicephorus with John Tzimiskes (Nicephorus' cousin) (969); charged with murder and adultery among other crimes, was committed to a convent until recalled to Constantinople (976) in the midst of the contested accession of her son, Basil. ❖ See also *Women in World History.*

THEOPHANO OF ATHENS (fl. 800s). Byzantine empress. Born c. 790; died probably much after 812; m. Stavrakios or Stauracius, Byzantine emperor (r. 811); cousin of Irene of Athens (c. 752–803). ❖ Was engaged and actually living with her betrothed, when Emperor Nicephorus I (r. 802–811) forced her to participate in a Bride Show (a contest through which a suitable wife was procured for a Byzantine emperor or his heir, 807); was chosen for his son Stauracius because of

her kinship to Irene, with whose political and religious policies Nicephorus wished to be associated; as an Augusta, was politically active, if not always in her husband's interests. ❖ See also *Women in World History.*

THEOPHANO OF BYZANTIUM (c. 955–991). Holy Roman empress and regent of Germany. Name variations: Theophanu. Born c. 955 or 956 in Constantinople; died June 15, 991; dau. of Romanus II, Byzantine emperor (r. 959–963), and Theophano (c. 940–?); sister of Constantine VIII (r. 1025–1028) and Basil II (r. 976–1025), both Byzantine emperors, and Anna of Byzantium (963–1011); niece of John Tzimiskes; m. Otto II (955–983), Holy Roman emperor (r. 973–983), king of Germany (r. 973–983), on April 14, 972; children: Sophia of Gandersheim (c. 975–1039), abbess of Gandersheim; Otto III (980–1002), Holy Roman emperor (r. 983–1002); Adelaide of Quedlinburg (977–1045); Matilda of Saxony (978–1025); one who died young. ❖ Married Otto II (972), with southern Italy constituting a large part of her dowry, and influenced the cultural blossoming in Germany; with husband, traveled to Italy where they received imperial coronations (980); after husband died (983), became regent for 3-year-old Otto III, making him more Byzantine than German, a fact which was of significance to his reign; was an effective regent and did everything necessary to demonstrate who was in control during her 8-year reign. ❖ See also *Women in World History.*

THEOPHANU. *Variant of Theophano.*

THÉORET, France (1942—). Canadian feminist and literary critic. Name variations: France Theoret. Born 1942 in Montreal, Canada. ❖ Studied in Canada and France and taught for 19 years before becoming full-time writer; works include *Nous parlerons comme on écrit* (1982) and *Homme qui peignait Staline* (1991); with Nicole Brossard and Marie Claire Blais, wrote *La Nef des Sorcières* (1976).

THEORIN, Maj Britt (1932—). Swedish politician. Born Dec 22, 1932, in Göteborg, Sweden. ❖ Member of the Riksdag (1971–95) and special ambassador on disarmament issues and chair of the Swedish disarmament delegation to the UN (1982–91); served as president of the International Peace Bureau, Geneva (1982—), chair of the UN Commission of Experts on Nuclear Weapons (1989–90), the UN Expert Committee on the Reallocation of Military Spending to the Environment (1990–91), and the UN Commission of Experts on Equality and the Agenda for Peace (1994); as a European Socialist (PSE), elected to 4th and 5th European Parliament (1994–99, 1999–2004).

THÉOT, Catherine (d. 1794). French visionary. Name variations: Catherine Theot. Born at Barenton (Manche); died in prison on Sept 1, 1794. ❖ Following a long period of religious asceticism in the convent of the Miramiones in Paris, suffered from dementia and was placed under restraint; after she was freed (1782), early delusions accelerated; convinced that she was chosen to be the mother of the new Messiah, described to her followers the coming of Paradise on earth; was soon hailed as the "Mother of God"; during the revolution, was accused of being involved in a conspiracy with Robespierre by those who resented his theocratic aims. ❖ See also *Women in World History.*

THEOXENA (fl. 315 BCE). Macedonian noblewoman. Dau. of Berenice I (c. 345 BCE–c. 275 BCE) and a Macedonian noble named Philip; m. Agathocles (the tyrant of Syracuse).

THERBUSCH, Anna (1721–1782). *See Lisiewska, Anna.*

THERESA (1767–1827). Queen of Saxony. Name variations: Theresa Habsburg-Lotharingen; Maria Theresia. Born Jan 14, 1767, in Florence; died Nov 7, 1827, in Leipzig; dau. of Maria Louisa of Spain (1745–1792) and Leopold II (1747–1792), count of Tuscany, ruler of Florence (r. 1765–1790), Holy Roman emperor (r. 1790–1792); m. Anthony I Clement (1755–1836), king of Saxony (r. 1827–1836), on Oct 18, 1787. ❖ Anthony I Clement was also married to Maria Charlotte of Sardinia (c. 1761–c. 1786).

THERESA, Saint (1515–1582). *See Teresa of Avila.*

THERESA HENRIQUES (c. 1176–1250). Queen of Leon. Name variations: Teresa of Portugal; Theresa Enriques or Enriquez. Born c. 1176; died June 18, 1250, in Lorvano; dau. of Sancho I (1154–1211 or 1212), king of Portugal (r. 1185–1211 or 1212), and Douce of Aragon (1160–1198); m. Alfonso or Alphonso IX (1171–1230), king of Leon (r. 1188–1230), on Feb 15, 1191 (annulled 1198); children: Fernando (b. after 1192–1214); Sancha of Castile (b. after 1193–died before 1243); Dulce or Douce of Castile (b. 1194–died after 1243). ❖ Alphonso IX's 1st wife was Berengaria of Castile (1180–1246).

THERESA OF AUSTRIA (1816–1867). Queen of the Two Sicilies. Name variations: Marie Therese of Austria. Born July 31, 1816; died August 8, 1867; became 2nd wife of Ferdinand II, king of the Two Sicilies (r. 1830–1859), on Jan 9, 1837; children: Louis, count of Trani (1838–1886); Albert (b. 1839); Alfonso (1841–1934), count of Caserta; Maria Annunziata (1843–1871); Maria Immaculata of Sicily (1844–1899); Gaetano (1846–1871), count of Girgenti; Joseph of Sicily (b. 1848); Pia of Sicily (1849–1882); Vinzenz (b. 1851); Pascal (b. 1852), count of Bari; Louise of Sicily (1855–1874, who m. Henry of Parma, count of Bardi); Gennaro of Sicily (b. 1857).

THERESA OF AVILA (1515–1582). *See Teresa of Avila.*

THERESA OF LIECHTENSTEIN (1850–1938). Princess of Liechtenstein. Born July 28, 1850; died Mar 13, 1938; dau. of Aloysius II, prince of Liechtenstein; m. Arnulf Wittelsbach (1852–1907), on April 12, 1882; children: Henry Wittelsbach (b. 1884).

THERESA OF MODENA (1801–1855). *See Maria Theresa of Tuscany.*

THERESA OF SAVOY (1803–1879). Duchess of Parma and Piacenza, queen of Etruria. Born Sept 19, 1803; died July 16, 1879; dau. of Maria Teresa of Austria (1773–1832) and Victor Emmanuel I, king of Sardinia (r. 1802–1821); m. Charles Louis also known as Charles II of Parma (1799–1883), duke of Parma and Piacenza, king of Etruria, on Sept 5, 1823; children: Louise (1821–1823); Charles III (b. 1823), duke of Parma.

THERESA OF SAXE-ALTENBURG (1836–1914). Princess of Saxe-Altenburg. Born Dec 21, 1836; died Nov 9, 1914; dau. of Edward (b. 1804), prince of Saxe-Altenburg; m. August Bernadotte (son of Oscar I, king of Sweden, and Josephine Beauharnais), on April 16, 1864.

THERESA OF SAXONY (1792–1854). Queen of Bavaria. Name variations: Princess Theresa of Saxe-Hildburghausen. Born July 8, 1792, in Hildburghausen; died Oct 26, 1854, in Munich; interred at St. Boniface Church in Munich; m. Louis I Augustus also known as Ludwig I (1786–1868), king of Bavaria (r. 1825–1848, abdicated), on Oct 12, 1810; children: Maximilian II (1811–1864), king of Bavaria (r. 1848–1864); Princess Matilda (1813–1862, who m. Louis III of Hesse-Darmstadt); Otto I (1815–1867), king of Greece (r. 1833–1862, deposed); Luitpold (1821–1912, regent [1886–1912]); Theodolinde (1816–1817); Adelgunde of Bavaria (1823–1914); Hildegarde of Bavaria (1825–1864); Adalbert (1828–1875).

THERESA OF SPAIN (1651–1673). *See Margaret Theresa of Spain.*

THERESE. *Variant of Teresa.*

THERESE OF AUSTRIA (1801–1855). *See Maria Theresa of Tuscany.*

THERESE OF BOURBON (1817–1886). Countess of Chambord. Name variations: Thérèse or Therese of Modena; Maria Theresia. Born July 14, 1817, in Modena; died Mar 25, 1886, in Gaz; eldest dau. of Maria Beatrice of Sardinia (1792–1840) and Francis IV (1779–1846), duke of Modena (r. 1814–1846); m. Henry V (1820–1883), count of Chambord, on Nov 16, 1846.

THÉRÈSE OF LISIEUX (1873–1897). French saint. Name variations: Saint Therese of Lisieux; Thérèse de Lisieux; Teresa of the Little Flower; The Little Flower of Jesus; St. Thérèse of the Child Jesus and of the Holy Face (Soeur Thérèse de l'Enfant Jésus et de la Sainte Face). Pronunciation: LEEZ-yair. Born Marie Françoise-Thérèse Martin in Alençon, Normandy, France, Jan 2, 1873; died of TB, Sept 30, 1897; dau. of Louis Martin (watchmaker, died 1893) and Zélie (Guérin) Martin (lacemaker). ❖ Carmelite nun who, in her brief 24 years, left behind "the little path" for the devout to follow; was born into a pious household; at around 4, mother died (1877); from ages 5 to 13, was an unhappy, sickly child; a week before 14th birthday, had what she called a "conversion" (Christmas eve, 1886), convinced she would be a saint; at 15, was welcomed into the cloistered walls of Carmelite convent at Lisieux (April 9, 1888), where she and 20 other nuns shared little food, slept on beds made of planks, and had no heat, save one stove in a communal room, during the harsh French winters; was determined to walk the ordinary path, to be an example to the world that piety was available to everyone, that the joys she knew in her spiritual life were joys that everyone could experience; began to cough, suffering a hemorrhage that soaked a handkerchief with her blood (1896); wrote chapters for her autobiographical *Story of a Soul*; was beatified (April 29, 1923) and canonized (May 17, 1925). Her sayings, published as *Novissima Verba*,

included "I will spend my heaven doing good upon earth" and "After my death I will let fall a shower of roses." ❖ See also autobiography, *The Story of a Soul* (1898); Dorothy Day, *Thérèse: A Life of Thérèse of Lisieux* (Templegate, 1960); Henri Gheon, *The Secret of the Little Flower* (Sheed & Ward, 1944); and *Women in World History*.

THERESE OF NASSAU (1815–1871). Duchess of Oldenburg. Name variations: Therese von Nassau. Born April 17, 1815; died Dec 8, 1871; dau. of William George, duke of Nassau, and Louise of Saxe-Altenburg (1794–1835); m. Peter, duke of Oldenburg, on April 23, 1837; children: Alexandra of Oldenburg (1838–1900); Nikolaus (b. 1840); Cecilie (1842–1843); Alexander (b. 1844); Katharine (1846–1866); Georg (b. 1848); Konstantin (b. 1850); Therese of Oldenburg (1852–1883, who m. Georg, duke of Leuchtenberg). ❖ See also *Women in World History*.

THERESIA. *Variant of Theresa.*

THERMUTHIS (fl. 1500 BCE). Biblical woman. Born and lived around 1500 BCE; dau. of either the pharaoh Seti I or Ramses II; foster mother of Moses. ❖ In the Old Testament, is recognized as the foster mother of Moses, a childless woman who rescued him as an infant and raised him as her own son in the pharaoh's palace.

THÉROIGNE DE MÉRICOURT, Anne-Josèphe (1762–1817). French feminist and activist. Name variations: Theroigne de Mericourt; Mme Campinado. Pronunciation: tay-ROYN der MERRY-coor. Born Anne-Josèphe Terwagne, Aug 13, 1762, in Marcourt (Luxembourg), Belgium (*Terwagne* was the Walloon spelling of a common name whose Frenchified version was *Théroigne*; the addition *de Méricourt,* which she never used, was invented by the royalist press during the Revolution and was a corruption of Marcourt, her native village); died in Paris, June 8, 1817; dau. of Pierre Terwagne (1731–1786, peasant proprietor) and Anne-Elisabeth Lahaye (1732–1767); never married; children: (with unknown man) Françoise-Louise Septenville (d. 1788). ❖ Activist during French Revolution, notably advocating equality for women, including the right to bear arms, who became the subject of numerous legends, and, tragically, a prominent figure in the history of insanity; became a companion to Mme Colbert (1778); an ambitious, courageous woman, escaped from peasant drudgery only to fall into a life as a courtesan; had liaisons with an English officer, who had promised marriage (1782–87?), and the Marquis de Persan (c. 1784–c. 1793); went to Italy with the castrato Tenducci (1788–89); embracing the Revolution's promise of liberty, took to dressing like a man; was in Paris during fall of the Bastille and at Versailles during October march of the women, though she did not participate as her royalist enemies claimed (1789); began to conduct a salon; helped found Les Amis de la loi and spoke at the Cordeliers Club to enthusiastic applause, discovering her gift for oratory; became the butt of vicious attacks by royalist papers, starting on Nov 10, 1789, in *Les Actes des apôtres*; went to Belgium to avoid possible arrest (1790); abducted by French émigrés, imprisoned and questioned by Austrian authorities, but released in Vienna (1791); returned to France and became an activist, advocating further revolution and the arming of women, and participated in the assault on the Tuileries (Aug 10) which overthrew the monarchy (1792); tried to preach political reconciliation but was whipped as a Girondin by a mob of Jacobin women (1793), a psychological wound from which she never fully recovered; arrested during the Great Terror but was certified as insane (1794); was confined in asylums, including the Hôtel-Dieu and La Salpêtrière (1795–1817). ❖ See also Frank [Fanny] Hamel, *A Woman of the Revolution: Théroigne de Méricourt* (Brentano, 1911); Elisabeth Roudinesco, *Théroigne de Méricourt: A Melancholic Woman during the French Revolution* (trans. by Martin Thom, Verso, 1991); and *Women in World History*.

THESMAR, Ghislaine (1943—). French ballet dancer. Born Mar 18, 1943, in Beijing, China; m. Pierre Lacotte (choreographer and dancer). ❖ Trained at studios of Solange Schwarz, Peggy Van Praagh, and Marie Rambert; danced with International Ballet du Marquis de Cuevas; began appearing with Les Ballets de Pierre Lacotte (1961), dancing in numerous works by husband, including *Hôtel des Etrangers* (1962), *Intermèdes* (1965), and *La Proie* (1967); appeared on tv in Lacotte revivals of classical works, most notably *La Sylphide* (1972); danced in many premieres, including Nicholas Zverev's *Sérénade* with Marquis de Cuevas (1962), and at Paris Opéra in Petit's *Formes* (1967), MacDonald's *Variations Diabelli* (1974), and Balanchine's *Chaconne* and *Orpheus* (1975).

THESSALONIKE (c. 345–297 BCE). Macedonian queen. Born c. 345 BCE; murdered in 297 BCE; dau. of Philip II, king of Macedonia, and Nicesipolis (niece of Jason of Pherae); m. Cassander, king of Macedonia;

children: Philip, Antipater (I), and Alexander (V). ❖ Shortly after she was born, her mother died; was reared by Olympias, Philip's chief wife and the mother of 2 of his children, Alexander III the Great and Cleopatra (b. 354 BCE), both of whom were older than Thessalonike; following Alexander the Great's death, was forced to marry Cassander after he had taken Pydna, had Olympias judicially executed, and put Alexander IV under "protective" custody; since she was the last to have any direct tie with the defunct Argead house, was the primary reason why Cassander was able to rule Macedonia proper; was immortalized by Cassander when he founded a city in her name (the modern Thessaloniki); after Cassander died of consumption (297) and sons Antipater and Alexander became rivals for the vacant throne, attempted to divide the kingdom between the two which led to her murder by Antipater. ❖ See also *Women in World History.*

THEUDESINDA (fl. 700). Wife of Grimoald. Married Grimoald II, mayor of Neustria and Austrasia (d. 714); children: Theudoald, mayor of Austrasia.

THEUERKAUFF-VORBRICH, Gudrun (1937—). West German fencer. Born April 8, 1937, in Germany. ❖ At Tokyo Olympics, won a bronze medal in team foil (1964).

THEURER, Elisabeth (1956—). Austrian equestrian. Name variations: Sissy Theurer; Elisabeth Max-Theurer. Born Sept 20, 1956, in Linz, Austria; m. Hans Max (her coach), 1983; children: Victoria (equestrian) and Johannes. ❖ Won European championship (1970: at Moscow Olympics, on Mon Cherie, won a gold medal in indiv. dressage (1980), the only gold medal for Austria; became president of Austrian Federation for Reiten und Fahren (2002); named to Austrian Olympic executive committee (2005).

THEUTBERGA (fl. 9th c.). *See Tetberga.*

THIAM, Awa (1936—). Senegalese feminist. Born 1936 in Senegal. ❖ Works include *La parole aux négresses* (1978, trans. as *Speak Out, Black Sisters,* 1986), about female genital mutilation and child marriage, and *Continents noirs* (1987), about race.

THIELEMANN, Ursula (1958—). West German field-hockey player. Born Jan 5, 1958, in Germany. ❖ At Los Angeles Olympics, won a silver medal in team competition (1984).

THIEME, Jana (1970—). German rower. Born July 6, 1970, in Hallesaale, Germany. ❖ At World championships, won gold medal for quadruple sculls (1995, 1997, 1998, 1999); won a gold medal for double sculls at Sydney Olympics (2000).

THIEN, Margot (1971—). American synchronized swimmer. Born Dec 29, 1971, in San Diego, CA. ❖ Won a team gold medal at Atlanta Olympics (1996).

THIESS, Ursula (1924—). German actress. Born May 15, 1924, in Hamburg, Germany; m. Robert Taylor (actor), 1954 (died 1969). ❖ Made film debut in *Nachtwache* (1949), followed by *Monsoon, Bengal Brigade, The Iron Glove, The Americano, Bandido* and *Left Hand of Gemini;* appeared on tv series "The Detectives starring Robert Taylor."

THIGPEN, Lynne (1948–2003). African-American actress. Name variations: Lynne Richmond. Born Lynne Richmond, Dec 22, 1948, in Joliet, IL; died Mar 12, 2003, in Los Angeles, CA. ❖ Made NY stage debut in *Godspell* (1973); on tv, appeared as Grace Keeper on "All My Children" (1993–2000), and starred as the Chief in the PBS children's show "Where in the World is Carmen Sandiego?" (1991) and as Ella Mae Farmer on "The District" (2000–03); films include *The Insider, Shaft, Random Hearts, Lean on Me, Bob Roberts, Tootsie* and *Anger Management.* Won Tony award for *An American Daughter* (1997), Obie awards for *Boesman and Lena* (1992) and *Jar the Floor* (2000), and Los Angeles Drama Critics Award for *Fences;* nominated for a Tony for *Tintypes* (1981).

THIJN, Mercedes (1962—). *See Coghen Alberdingk, Mercedes.*

THIMELBY, Gertrude Aston (c. 1617–1668). British letter writer and poet. Name variations: Mrs. Henry Thimelby, Esq. Born c. 1617 in Tixall, Staffordshire, England; died 1668 in Louvain, Flanders, dau. of Walter, 1st baron of Forfar, and Gertrude Sadler Aston; m. Henry Thimelby, Esq.; children: 1. ❖ English recusant who, upon death of husband and child, became canoness at St. Monica's convent in Louvain; writing, which shows influence of St. Augustine and of medieval Flemish

mystics, includes *Tixall Poetry* (1813) and *Tixall Letters* (1815), both edited by Arthur Clifford.

THIMIG, Helene (1889–1974). Austrian actress. Name variations: Helene Thimig-Reinhardt; "Helene Werner." Born Ottilie Helene Thimig in Vienna, Austria, June 5, 1889; died in Vienna, Nov 6, 1974; dau. of Hugo Thimig (actor and director of Vienna's Burgtheater) and Fanny (Hummel) Thimig; sister of Hans and Hermann Thimig (both actors); studied with Hedwig Bleibtreu; m. Paul Kalbeck; became 2nd wife of Max Reinhardt (1873–1943, actor, manager, and stage director), in 1935 (Max Reinhardt's 1st wife was Else Heims); m. Anton Edthofer. ❖ Member of a great theatrical family and one of the leading actresses of Central Europe for half a century, whose career was closely linked for several decades to the achievements of her 2nd husband Max Reinhardt; made stage debut in Baden bei Wien (1907) and for next several years was apprenticed with Germany's Meiningen Players; by 1911, had moved to Berlin, where she became one of the stars of Reinhardt's Deutsches Theater; starred in such roles as Gretchen in *Faust,* Solveig in *Peer Gynt,* and Elisabeth in *Maria Stuart;* at Salzburg Festival, appeared yearly in the morality play *Jedermann* (Everyman, 1920–30s), then helped revive it after WWII; created many roles in world premieres, including Hugo von Hofmannsthal's Der Schwierige and Max Mell's *Das Apostelspiel;* with rise of Nazi Germany, immigrated with husband to California (1937); made English-language movies while in exile in US: *The Hitler Gang* (1944), *None But the Lonely Heart* (1944), *Cloak and Dagger* (1946) and *The Locket* (1947); returned to Austria (1946), where she resumed her career both in Vienna's Burgtheater and at Salzburg Festival; also taught acting. ❖ See also *Women in World History.*

THIMM-FINGER, Ute (1958—). West German runner. Name variations: Ute Finger. Born July 10, 1958, in Germany. ❖ At Los Angeles Olympics, won a bronze medal in 4 x 400-meter relay (1984).

THIRKELL, Angela (1890–1961). English novelist and short-story writer. Name variations: (pseudonym) Leslie Parker. Born Margaret Angela Mackail, Jan 30, 1890, in London, England; died Jan 30, 1961, in Bramley, England; dau. of John W. Mackail (professor of poetry) and Margaret Burne-Jones Mackail; granddau. of Pre-Raphaelite artist Edward Burne-Jones and Georgiana Macdonald, painter; m. James Campbell McInnes (famed singer), 1911 (div. 1917); m. George Thirkell (Australian soldier), 1918 (div. 1929); children: (1st m.) Graham, Colin, and 1 daughter (died); (2nd m.) Lance. ❖ Prolific writer whose career spanned 3 decades; on 2nd marriage, traveled to Australia in a troopship (1920), then settled in Melbourne, where she befriended such Australian notables as Nellie Melba, John Monash, and Thea Parker; left husband and returned to England (1929); published memoirs, *Three Houses* (1931); published *Ankle Deep, High Rising* and *Wild Strawberries* (1933), then continued to publish one or more novels each year, with few exceptions, until her death; better-known novels include *Pomfret Towers, The Brandons* and *Marling Hall;* though she borrowed 18th-century novelist Anthony Trollope's fictional Bartsetshire for settings, wrote predominantly about characters in modern times; books were popular with audiences in both Great Britain and US. ❖ See also Margot Strickland, *Angela Thirkell, Portrait of a Lady Novelist* (Duckworth, 1977); and *Women in World History.*

THIROUX D'ARCONVILLE, Marie-Geneviève-Charlotte d'Arlus (1720–1805). *See d'Arconville, Geneviève.*

THISTLETHWAITE, Bel (1857–1940). *See Wetherald, Ethelwyn.*

THOBURN, Isabella (1840–1901). American missionary. Born Mar 29, 1840, near St. Clairsville, Ohio; died Sept 1, 1901, in Lucknow, India; dau. of Matthew Thoburn (d. 1850, farmer) and Jane Lyle (Crawford) Thoburn; educated at Wheeling Female Seminary in Wheeling, Virginia (now West Virginia); spent 1 year at Cincinnati Academy of Design. ❖ Methodist evangelist, missionary, and educator, taught in several public and private schools; went to India as missionary (1869); began work in Lucknow (1870); opened the Lal Bagh Boarding School (1871); served as principal of girls' school in Cawnpore (1874); returned to US on furlough to travel and lecture on missionary work (1880–82); suggested Lal Bagh become the Girls' High School and add a collegiate department (1887); during 2nd furlough, worked in Chicago with Lucy Meyer and taught at Chicago Training School for City, Home, and Foreign Missions (1887–88); in Cincinnati, helped organize the Elizabeth Gamble Deaconess Home and Training School and helped direct Christ Hospital; returned to Lucknow and Lal Bagh (late 1890); helped establish the Wellesley School for girls in Naini Tal (1891); granted charter for Lucknow Woman's College (1895). Lucknow Woman's College was renamed Isabella Thoburn College (1903), and later became women's college of Lucknow University. ❖ See also *Women in World History*.

THOC-ME-TONY (1844–1891). See Winnemucca, Sarah.

THOM, Linda (1943—). Canadian shooter. Born Dec 30, 1943, in Ottawa, Canada; children: 2. ❖ At Los Angeles Olympics, won a gold medal in sport pistol (1984), with a score of 297 out of 300.

THOM, Margaret Pattison (1873–1930). See Papakura, Makereti.

THOMAS, Agnes (fl. 1878–1926). English stage actress. Fl. between 1878 and 1926; m. Harry Lees-Craston; m. E. J. Malyon; children: (1st m.) Eily Malyon (1879–1961, actress). ❖ On stage for over 50 years, made London debut in *A Treaty of Peace* (1878) and NY debut as Ariadne in *Beauty* (1885); other appearances include *Elizabeth* (with Adelaide Ristori), *Bondage, The Wrong Door, The Guardsman, The World, The Wild Duck* (as Gina Ekdal), *The Passing of the Third Floor Back, Em'ly, Man and Superman, Rutherford and Son, The Wynmartens, David Copperfield* (as Betsy Trotwood), and *Pygmalion*.

THOMAS, Mrs. Albert (1900–1993). See Thomas, Lera Millard.

THOMAS, Alice (fl. 1670s). Colonial tavernkeeper. Lived in Boston, MA. ❖ Considered the 1st woman tavernkeeper in America, ran tavern in Boston (early 1670s); was arrested and convicted for several crimes, including selling liquor without license, receiving stolen goods, profaning the Sabbath, and "frequent secret and unreasonable entertainment in her house to Lewd Lascivious and Notorious persons of both sexes, giving them opportunity to commit Carnale Wickedness"; fined, whipped, and sent to prison; made significant financial contribution to city of Boston which apparently appeased authorities.

THOMAS, Alma (1891–1978). African-American teacher and painter. Born Sept 22, 1891, in Columbus, Georgia; died Feb 25, 1978; dau. of John Harris Thomas (businessman) and Amelia (Cantey) Thomas (teacher); Howard University, BS, 1924; graduate of Columbia University Graduate School, 1934. ❖ Taught art classes at Shaw Junior High School, Washington, DC (1924–60); became associated with Barnett-Aden Gallery, an artistic center which played an important role in the development of African-American visual culture; retired from teaching (1960) and began to paint full time; painted series of works, including *Earth Paintings* and *Space Paintings*; held a solo exhibition, Du Pont Theater Art Gallery, Washington, DC (1960); exhibited at Whitney Museum in NY (1972). ❖ See also *Women in World History*.

THOMAS, Audrey (1935—). Canadian novelist. Name variations: Audrey Grace Thomas. Born Audrey Grace Callahan, Nov 17, 1935, in Binghamton, NY; Smith College, BA, 1957, University of British Columbia, MA, 1963; m. Ian Thomas (Scottish sculptor and art teacher); children: 3 daughters. ❖ With husband, immigrated to Canada (1959), settling in British Columbia; lived with husband in Ghana (1964–66), where he taught; taught creative writing and traveled extensively; works include *Ten Green Bottles* (1967), *Mrs. Blood* (1970), *Blown Figures* (1974), *Latakia* (1979), *Real Mothers* (1981), *Intertidal Life* (1984), *The Wild Blue Yonder* (1990), *Coming Down from Wa* (1995), *Isobel Gunn* (1999) and *The Path of Totality* (2001). Received Marian Engle Award (1987) and Canada-Australia Prize (1990).

THOMAS, Caitlin (1913–1994). British writer. Born Caitlin Macnamara, Dec 8, 1913, in London, England; died July 31, 1994, in Catania, Sicily, Italy; dau. of Francis Macnamara (Irish artist) and Yvonne (Majolier) Macnamara; m. Dylan Thomas (poet), July 11, 1937 (died 1953); lived with or m. Guiseppe Fazio (film director); children: (with Dylan Thomas) Llewelyn (b. 1939), Aeronwyn (b. 1943), Colm (b. 1949); (with Giuseppe Fazio) Francesco Thomas (b. 1963). ❖ The wife of Dylan Thomas, was also a poet and writer in her own right; in her teens, was an art model for her neighbor, painter Augustus John; also had a brief career as a dancer; settled in Wales with husband (1937); had a stormy marriage, struggling with poverty and high debts; in early 1950s, her marriage collapsed entirely, though she did not divorce; moved to Catania, Sicily (1957), where she published the 1st of her memoirs, *Left Over Life to Kill* (1957), recalling her marriage; published *Not Quite Posthumous Letter to My Daughter* (1963); battling alcoholism, lived out the rest of her years in relative obscurity with Sicilian film director Giuseppe Fazio in Sicily; wrote a 3rd book of memoirs, *Life With Dylan Thomas* (1986). ❖ See also Paul Ferris, *Caitlin: The Life of Caitlin Thomas* (Pimlico, 1995); and *Women in World History*.

THOMAS, Carey (1857–1935). See Thomas, M. Carey.

THOMAS, Carla (1942—). African-American singer. Born Dec 21, 1942, in Memphis, TN; dau. of Rufus Thomas (musician). ❖ "Queen of Memphis Soul," made professional debut singing duet with father, "Cause I Love You" (1960); released hit album, *Gee Whiz* (1961), with title track which went to #5 on R&B charts and helped establish label, Stax Records; had numerous hits, including "I'll Bring It Home to You" (1962), "B-A-B-Y" (1966), "I'll Always Have Faith in You" (1967), and "I Like What You're Doing to Me" (1969); recorded several hit duets with Otis Redding, including "Tramp" and "Knock on Wood" (1967); other albums include *Queen Alone* (1967), *Love Means* (1971), and *Sugar* (1994). Received Pioneer Award from Rhythm and Blues Foundation (1993).

THOMAS, Caroline (1825–1913). See Dorr, Julia Caroline.

THOMAS, Clara (1919—). Canadian literary critic and educator. Name variations: Clara McCandless Thomas. Born 1919 in Strathroy, Ontario, Canada; University of Western Ontario, BA, 1941, MA, 1944; University of Toronto, PhD, 1962; m. Morley Thomas, 1942; children: Stephen and John. ❖ Taught English at York University (1961–84) and served on editorial boards of many literary journals; works include *Love and Work Enough: The Life of Anna Jameson* (1967), *Ryerson of Upper Canada* (1969), *The Manawaka World of Margaret Laurence* (1972), *William Arthur Deacon: A Canadian Literary Life* (with John Lennox, 1982), *All My Sisters: Essays on the Work of Canadian Women Writers* (1994), and *Chapters in a Lucky Life* (1999); became fellow of Royal Society of Canada (1983).

THOMAS, Debi (1967—). African-American figure skater. Born Mar 25, 1967, in Poughkeepsie, NY; Stanford University, BA, 1991; attended Northwestern University Medical School; m. Brian Vanden Hogen, Mar 15, 1988 (div.); m. Christopher Bequette (attorney), 1997. ❖ Won US nationals (1986, 1988) and World championships (1986); won a bronze medal at Calgary Olympics (1988), the 1st African-American in history to medal at the Winter Games; won bronze medal at World Figure Skating championships, Budapest (1988); skated with Stars on Ice; became an orthopedic surgeon. ❖ See also *Women in World History*.

THOMAS, Edith Matilda (1854–1925). American poet and translator. Born Aug 12, 1854, in Chatham, Ohio; died Sept 13, 1925, in New York, NY; dau. of Frederick Thomas (died 1861) and Jane (Sturges) Thomas (died 1887); graduate of Geneva Normal Institute, 1872; never married; no children. ❖ One of the best-known American poets at turn of 20th century, briefly attended Oberlin College but dropped out to teach school; began to publish poetry in NY magazines; published 1st collection, *A New Year's Masque* (1885); published subsequent collections regularly over next 30 years, including *The Inverted Torch* (1890) and *The Guest at the Gate* (1909); was much in demand by NY publishers for her verses, which were classic both in form and subject. ❖ See also *Women in World History*.

THOMAS, Edna (1885–1974). African-American actress. Born Edna Lewis, Nov 1, 1885, in Lawrenceville, Virginia; died July 22, 1974, in New York, NY; m. Lloyd Thomas. ❖ Stage and screen actress, made her name as part of the Harlem Renaissance; made stage debut in *Turn to the Right* with the Lafayette Players, a touring dramatic troupe (1920); in NY, appeared in *Comedy of Errors* (1923), *Porgy* (1927), *Lulu Belle, Shuffle Along, Run, Little Chillun* (1933) and *Stevedore* (1934); appeared as Lady Macbeth in the all-black cast of the Federal Theater Project production of *Macbeth* (1936–37), directed by Orson Welles; went on to perform again with Federal Theater Project in *Androcles and the Lion* with Dooley Wilson (1938); appeared on Broadway in *Harriet* with Helen Hayes (1944–45), in *Strange Fruit* (1945), and *A Streetcar Named Desire* (1946); also appeared in the film. ❖ See also *Women in World History*.

THOMAS, Elean (1947–2004). Jamaican poet and activist. Born Sept 18, 1947, in St. Catherine, Jamaica; died May 27, 2004; dau. of David Thomas (Pentecostal bishop); mother was a health worker; attended University of the West Indies and Goldsmiths College, London; m. Lord Gifford (radical lawyer, div. 1998); children: (adopted) daughter. ❖ Worked as a reporter for *Jamaica Gleaner*; served on the executive of Press Association of Jamaica; was a founder-member of Workers Party of Jamaica; sat on editorial board of Prague-based *World Marxist Review*; protested the US invasion of Grenada (1983); published 1st poetry collection, *Word Rhythms from the Life of a Woman* (1986), followed by *Before They Can Speak of Flowers* (1988); wrote novel *The Last Room* (1991), which won the Ruth Hadden Prize.

THOMAS, Elizabeth (1675–1731). British poet. Name variations: (pseudonym) Corinna. Born in 1675 (one source cites 1677) in England; died Feb 5, 1731, in London, England; dau. of Emmanuel Thomas (lawyer, died 1677) and Elizabeth (Osborne) Thomas. ❖ At 24, impressed the celebrated poet John Dryden with her verses, and they began a long correspondence; used the pen name "Corinna," suggested by Dryden, the rest of her life; 1st published poems appeared in *Luctus Britannici* (1700), a collection of elegies on Dryden's death; other literary acquaintances included Mary Lee Chudleigh, Mary Astell, Henry Cromwell and Alexander Pope; published *Miscellany Poems on Several Subjects* (1722); had a falling out with Pope when she sold some of his original letters to the libelous publisher Edmund Curll, who immediately published them (1726); lost some patrons over the episode, even spending time in debtors' prison at Fleet (1727); in response to Pope's attack on her in his satirical *The Dunciad*, wrote *Codrus, or the Dunciad Dissected* (1729). ❖ See also *Women in World History.*

THOMAS, Elizabeth (1910–1963). *See Brousse, Amy.*

THOMAS, Helen (1920—). American journalist. Born Aug 4, 1920, in Winchester, Kentucky; dau. of George Thomas and Mary Thomas; grew up in Detroit; Wayne State University, BA, 1942; m. Douglas B. Cornell (journalist), Oct 11, 1971 (died 1982); no children. ❖ Journalist who covered the White House through 8 presidential administrations and 4 decades, becoming one of the most respected members of the American press; joined the national staff of United Press International (UPI) and began covering the Justice Department (1956); named chief White House correspondent, one of American journalism's most coveted assignments (1970); was the only print journalist to accompany Richard Nixon to China (1972); promoted to White House bureau chief by UPI (1974), the 1st woman to head the White House Bureau for a national wire service; elected 1st woman president of White House Correspondents Association (1975); elected 1st woman head of Gridiron Club (1975); remained chief correspondent until her retirement from UPI (June 2000), the day after it was purchased by News World Communications, a company founded by Reverend Sun Myung Moon; was hired by Hearst News Service (July 2000). ❖ See also memoirs *Dateline: White House* (1975) and *Front Row at the White House* (1999); and *Women in World History.*

THOMAS, Joyce Carol (1938—). African-American poet and novelist. Born May 25, 1938, in Ponca City, OK; grew up in Tracy, CA. ❖ Traveled throughout North and South America and Australia and taught at several universities in US; writings include *Bittersweet* (1973), *Marked by Fire* (1982), *Bright Shadow* (1983), *The Golden Pasture* (1986), *Water Girl* (1986), and *Journey* (1988). Received National Book Award, Coretta Scott King Honors, Governor's Awards, International Reading Association Award, and Oklahoma Lifetime Achievement Award.

THOMAS, Lera Millard (1900–1993). American politician. Name variations: Mrs. Albert Thomas. Born Aug 3, 1900, in Nacogdoches, Texas; died July 23, 1993, in Nacogdoches; attended Brenau College and University of Alabama; m. Albert Thomas (US congressional representative, 1936–66), in 1922 (died 1966); children: Ann; Lera; and James. ❖ Following husband's death (1966), won his house seat in a special election; served in US House of Representatives, 89th Congress (1966–67), continuing efforts of husband, particularly in support of NASA programs, as well as Houston area economic initiatives; retired (1967).

THOMAS, Lillian Beynon (1874–1961). Canadian suffragist, novelist and playwright. Name variations: Lillian Beynon; (pseudonym) Lillian Laurie. Born Lillian Beynon in 1874 in southern Ontario; died Sept 4, 1961, in Winnipeg, Manitoba, Canada; elder sister of Francis Marion Beynon; married A. Vernon Thomas (journalist), 1911. ❖ One of the most influential women on the Canadian prairies, taught for 9 years in rural communities; in Winnipeg, joined the staff of *Manitoba Weekly Free Press* (1905), where she developed the women's page and wrote the column "Home Loving Hearts" under pseudonym Lillian Laurie; used her columns to lobby for changes in divorce and child-custody laws, property rights of farm women, and rights of unwed mothers; was also for temperance; with sister and Nellie McClung and others, helped form the Political Equality League (1912) and served as its 1st president; moved to NY (1917), then returned to Winnipeg (1920s); was later active in establishing a theater in Manitoba and became a successful novelist and playwright. ❖ See also *Women in World History.*

THOMAS, Margaret Haig (1883–1958). *See Rhondda, Margaret.*

THOMAS, Marlo (1937—). American actress, producer, and feminist. Born Margaret Julia Thomas, Nov 21, 1937, in Detroit, Michigan; dau. of Rose Marie (Cassaniti) and Danny Thomas (comedian); m. Phil Donahue, 1980. ❖ On tv, starred as Ann Marie and produced "That Girl" (1966–71), the 1st series to center around a single, independent woman; co-produced and narrated "Free to Be...You and Me"; appeared in such tv-movies as "It Happened One Christmas" (1977) and "The Lost Honor of Kathryn Beck" (1984); films include *Jenny, Thieves,* and *Playing Mona Lisa*; made Broadway debut in *Thieves* (1974), followed by *Social Security*; active in the women's rights movement, also promoted St. Jude's Children's Hospital. Won Emmys for "Free to Be... You and Me" (1974), "The Body Human: Facts for Girls" (1981) and "Nobody's Child" (1986).

THOMAS, M. Carey (1857–1935). American educator. Name variations: Min or Minnie; Carey Thomas. Born Martha Carey Thomas, Jan 2, 1857, in Baltimore, Maryland; died in Philadelphia, Pennsylvania, Dec 2, 1935; dau. of James Carey Thomas (doctor) and Mary Whitall Thomas; niece of Hannah Whitall Smith; Cornell University, BA; University of Zurich, PhD, 1882 (1st woman and 1st foreigner to be awarded the degree at Zurich); lived with Mamie Gwinn (co-founder of Bryn Mawr) and Mary Garrett; never married; no children. ❖ Important player in the transformation of higher education for women, was co-founder of the Bryn Mawr School for girls, the 1st woman president of Bryn Mawr College and its primary architect for many years, and instrumental in opening the Johns Hopkins Medical School to women; co-founded and was board member of the Bryn Mawr School (1878); served as dean of Bryn Mawr (1884–94); served as president of Bryn Mawr (1894–1922), emerging as a major public voice for the higher education of women, advocating greater access and equal academic standards; served as 1st woman trustee at Cornell University (1897–1901); participated in Women's Medical School Fund, with Mary Garrett, which underwrote the Johns Hopkins University School of Medicine, open to both men and women; was active in the National American Woman Suffrage Association, National College Equal Suffrage League, and National Women's Party (1906–20); founded, with Mary Anderson and Rose Schneiderman, the Bryn Mawr Summer School for Women Workers (1921). ❖ See also Marjorie Housepian Dobkin, ed. *The Making of a Feminist: Early Journals and Letters of M. Carey Thomas* (Kent State U. Press, 1979); Edith Finch, *Carey Thomas of Bryn Mawr* (Harper and Row, 1947); Helen Lefkowitz Horowitz, *The Power and Passion of M. Carey Thomas* (Knopf, 1994); and *Women in World History.*

THOMAS, Mary (1932–1997). Welsh mezzo-soprano. Born 1932 in Swansea, Wales; died 1997; studied at Royal Academy of Music, London. ❖ Played a key role in introducing audiences to many of the major compositions of Sir Peter Maxwell Davies; her performances of the aging, ravaged bride in Maxwell Davies' *Miss Donnithorne's Maggot* was an international triumph for both the singer and the composer; joined the faculty of Royal Academy of Music.

THOMAS, Mary (1946—). American singer. Name variations: The Crystals. Born 1946 in Brooklyn, NY. ❖ As an original member of the Crystals, had hit singles "There's No Other (Like My Baby)" (1961), "Uptown" (1962), "Da Doo Ron Ron" (1963) and "Then He Kissed Me" (1964). However, the Crystals #1 hit "He's a Rebel" was recorded by session singers the Blossoms. Crystals albums include *He's a Rebel* (1963) and *The Best of the Crystals* (1992).

THOMAS, Mary Myers (1816–1888). American physician and activist. Born Mary Frame Myers, Oct 28, 1816, in Bucks Co., Pennsylvania; died Aug 19, 1888; dau. of Samuel Myers (teacher and abolitionist) and Mary (Frame) Myers; Penn Medical University, MD, 1856; half-sister of Hannah E. Longshore; m. Owen Thomas (physician), 1839 (died 1886); children: Laura; Pauline Heald; Julia Josephine (Thomas) Irvine. ❖ One of the 1st woman physicians in America, who contributed to many social reform movements, practiced medicine in Richmond, Indiana (1856); during Civil War, served as a nurse, assistant surgeon to husband in Nashville, Tennessee, and on the governor's Sanitary Commission; served on the city board of public health of Richmond, Indiana, for 8 years; resurrected Indiana Woman Suffrage Association (1869) and edited 2 feminist newspapers, *The Mayflower* and Amelia Bloomer's *The Lily*; admitted to the Indiana State Medical Society, becoming 1st woman regular (1876); elected president of American Woman Suffrage Association (1880); elected president of Wayne County Medical Society (1887); was also a leader in the temperance movement. ❖ See also *Women in World History.*

THOMAS, Olive (1884–1920). American actress, dancer and model. Born Oliveretta Elaine Duffy, Oct 29, 1884, in Charleroi, PA; died Sept 10, 1920, of a drug overdose, in Neuilly-sur-Seine, France; m. Bernard Krug Thomas, 1911 (div. 1913); m. Jack Pickford (brother of Mary Pickford), 1916. ❖ Began career modeling for *Vogue* and *Vanity Fair*; starred in *Ziegfeld Follies* (1915, 1916) and posed nude for Peruvian artist Alberto Vargas; starred in a series of Triangle films, including *Betty Takes a Hand* and *Madcap Madge*; became a contract player for Myron Selznick's production company and starred in such films as *Beatrix Fairfax, Broadway Arizona, Youthful Folly, The Follies Girl, Footlights and Shadows, Everybody's Sweetheart* and *The Flapper*.

THOMAS, Petria (1975—). Australian swimmer. Born Aug 25, 1975, in Mullumbimby, NSW, Australia; attended University of Canberra; married. ❖ Won a silver medal for 200-meter butterfly at Atlanta Olympics (1996); won a gold medal for 100-meter butterfly and 4 x 100-meter medley relay at Commonwealth Games (1998); won a bronze medal for 200-meter butterfly and silver medals for 4 x 100-meter medley and 800-meter freestyle relay at Sydney Olympics (2000); at LC World championships, won gold medals for 100- and 200-meter butterfly (2001); at SC World championships, won a gold medal for 200-meter buttefly (2002); won gold medals for 200-meter butterfly, 4 x 100-meter freestyle relay and 4 x 100-meter medley relay and a silver medal for 200-meter butterfly at Athens Olympics (2004).

THOMAS, Rozonda (1971—). African-American singer. Name variations: Rozonda "Chilli" Thomas, TLC. Born Rozonda Ocelean Thomas, Feb 27, 1971, in Atlanta, GA; dau. of Abdul Ali and Ava Thomas; children: (with Dallas Austin, music producer) Tron. ❖ With Lisa Lopes and Tionne Watkins, as TLC, released album *Oooooooohhh . . . On the TLC Tip* (1992), which went to #3 on R&B charts and included Top-10 hits, "Ain't 2 Proud 2 Beg," "Baby-Baby-Baby," and "What About Your Friends"; appeared in film, *House Party 3* (1994); with group, released album, *CrazySexyCool* (1994), which went platinum, won 2 Grammy Awards, and included hits, "Creep," "Waterfalls," "Red Light Special" and "Diggin' On You"; with TLC, released enormously popular album, *Fanmail* (1999), which entered charts at #1 and included #1 pop hits "No Scrubs" and "Unpretty"; after death of Lopes, released tribute album, *3D* (2002), with Watkins.

THOMAS-MAURO, Nicole (1951—). French politician. Born June 6, 1951, in Reims, France. ❖ Representing Union for Europe of the Nations Group (UEN), elected to 5th European Parliament (1999–2004).

THOMASCHINSKI, Simone (1970—). German field-hockey player. Born April 1970 in Germany. ❖ At Barcelona Olympics, won a silver medal in team competition (1992).

THOMASIUS, Christian (1894–1982). *See Tergit, Gabrielle.*

THOMASSE (fl. 1292). Book illustrator and innkeeper. Flourished in 1292 in Paris. ❖ Professional manuscript illuminator, was an exceptionally talented artist, well respected for her work; also owned and managed a Parisian inn and tavern.

THOMPSON, Annie E. (1845–1913). Canadian first lady. Name variations: Lady Thompson. Born Annie E. Affleck, June 26, 1845, in Halifax, Nova Scotia, Canada; died April 10, 1913; m. John Sparrow David Thompson (prime minister of Canada, 1892–94), July 5, 1870 (died in office, Dec 12, 1894); children: John Thomas (1872–1952), Joseph (1874–1935), Mary Aloysia (Babe, 1876–1917), Mary Helena (1878–1944), Annie Mary (1879–1880), Frances Alice (Frankie, 1881–1947), David Anthony (1883–1885).

THOMPSON, Blanche Edith (1874–1963). New Zealand piano teacher, cyclist, and social reformer. Name variations: Blanche Edith Lough. Born Mar 18, 1874, at Brown's Ridge, North Canterbury, New Zealand; died Jan 19, 1963, in Wellington; dau. of Henry Lough and Harriet (Watters) Lough; m. Horace Thompson (piano manufacturer and retailer), 1893 (c. 1934); children: 3 daughters, 2 sons. ❖ Helped organize Atalanta Cycling Club for women (1892); advocated for appropriate dress for women in sports; learned to drive automobile and participated in competitive events of Canterbury Automobile Association; supported kindergarten movements and was active in Richmond Free Kindergarten in Christchurch. ❖ See also *Dictionary of New Zealand Biography* (Vol. 3).

THOMPSON, Carol Semple (1948—). American golfer. Name variations: Carol Keister Semple. Born Carol Keister Semple, Oct 27, 1948, in Sewickley, PA; dau. of Harton Semple (USGA president). ❖ Won USGA Women's Amateur (1973), was runner-up (1974); won British Women's Amateur (1974); member of World Amateur and Curtis Cup teams (1974); won Western Pennsylvania Women's championship (1965, 1967, 1971, 1973); won US Women's Mid-Amateur (1990, 1997); won USGA Senior Women's Amateur (1999, 2000, 2001, 2002); playing in her 12th Curtis Cup team, scored the winning point (2002).

THOMPSON, Clara (1893–1958). American psychiatrist. Born Clara Mabel Thompson, Oct 3, 1893, in Providence, Rhode Island; died Dec 20, 1958, in New York, NY; dau. of T. Franklin Thompson (tailor and salesman) and Clara (Medbery) Thompson; attended Pembroke College; graduate of Brown University, 1916; Johns Hopkins Medical School, MD, 1920. ❖ Leading psychoanalyst for over 25 years, opened her own psychoanalytic practice in Baltimore and became an associate of analyst Harry Stack Sullivan (c. 1925); moved to Budapest to study under Sandor Ferenczi (1931), who was both teacher and analyst to her; opened practice in NY (1933) and became part of a small group of psychoanalysts known as the Zodiac Group, which included Sullivan, Karen Horney, and Erich Fromm; devoted most of her research over next 20 years to questions about female sexuality and development; with Fromm, in conjunction with the Washington School of Psychiatry, established a psychiatric school in New York (1943), which in 1945 was renamed the William Alanson White Institute of Psychiatry. ❖ See also *Women in World History.*

THOMPSON, Donielle (1981—). American gymnast. Born Feb 17, 1981, in Wheatridge, CO. ❖ Won Mexican Olympic Festival (1992) and US Olympic Festival (1994); won a bronze medal at World championships and a gold medal at Pan American Games (1995), both for team all- around.

THOMPSON, Dorothy (1893–1961). American journalist. Born Dorothy Celène Thompson, July 9, 1893, in Lancaster, New York; died in Lisbon, Portugal, Jan 30, 1961; dau. of Peter Thompson (Methodist minister) and Margaret (Grierson) Thompson; Syracuse University, BA cum laude, 1914; m. Josef Bard, April 26, 1923 (div. 1927); m. Sinclair Lewis (novelist), May 14, 1928 (sep. 1937, div. 1942); m. Maxim Kopf (artist), June 16, 1943; children: (2nd m.) Michael Lewis. ❖ Foreign correspondent, columnist, and radio commentator who was the foremost woman journalist of her time; moved to London (1920), then Paris, then Vienna (1921), to make her mark as a foreign correspondent; served as foreign correspondent for Curtis-Martin newspapers, *Philadelphia Public-Ledger* and *New York Evening Post* (1920–28), scoring interviews with such European leaders as Thomas Masaryk, Ramsay MacDonald, Aristide Briand, Kemal Ataturk, Leon Trotsky, and Marie of Rumania; transferred to Berlin (1925); contributed highly successful column, "On the Record," for *New York Herald Tribune* (1936–41); added monthly column in *Ladies' Home Journal* (1937); had radio program over NBC, where she reached 5.5 million listeners; sought to alert Americans to the dangers of fascism and Germany; gave much attention to plight of Europe's refugees, particularly Jews; after *New York Herald Tribune* dropped her for supporting Roosevelt, wrote column for Bell newspaper syndicate (1941–58), which distributed it to over 200 papers, including *New York Post*; a woman of great courage and absolute integrity, was a crack correspondent in a great age of frontline reporting and 2nd to few in her knowledge of Central Europe, though she lacked the kind of philosophical base that would have given cohesion to her often disparate opinions; writings include *The New Russia* (1928), *"I Saw Hitler!"* (1932), *Refugees: Anarchy or Organization?* (1938), *Let the Record Speak* (1939), *Listen, Hans* (1942) and *The Courage to Be Happy* (1957). ❖ See also Peter Kurth, *American Cassandra: The Life of Dorothy Thompson* (Little, Brown, 1990); Marion K. Sanders, *Dorothy Thompson: A Legend in Her Time* (Houghton, 1973); Vincent Sheean, *Dorothy and Red* (Houghton, 1963); and *Women in World History.*

THOMPSON, Edith (c. 1894–1923). English accused murderer. Born c. 1894; hanged at Holloway Prison, Jan 9, 1923; m. Percy Thompson. ❖ Began extramarital affair with Freddie Bywaters (1921), to whom she wrote numerous letters; was traveling with husband Percy from London to Ilford, when Bywaters stabbed him repeatedly before fleeing (early Oct); her letters to Bywaters—in which she had written about her own apparent attempts to kill Percy—were found; during a sensational trial, was tried for husband's murder along with Bywaters (Dec 1922), found guilty and condemned to death; her execution at Holloway Prison (Jan 9, 1923) did not go smoothly. Because Bywaters never wavered in his assertion that she had no hand in the actual murder, nor in inciting him to kill Percy, debate over her guilt or innocence continues to this day. ❖ See also René Weis, *Criminal Justice: the True Story of Edith Thompson* (Penguin, 2001); (film) *Another Life* (2001).

THOMPSON, Eliza (1816–1905). American reformer. Born Eliza Jane Trimble, Aug 24, 1816, in Hillsboro, Ohio; died Nov 3, 1905, in Hillsboro; dau. of Allen Trimble (governor of Ohio) and Rachel (Woodrow) Trimble; m. James Henry Thompson (lawyer), Sept 21, 1837; children: Allen, Anna, John, Joseph, Maria, Mary, Henry and John Thompson. ❖ Methodist reformer who assisted in the founding of the National Woman's Christian Temperance Union, became involved in the temperance movement (1873); was a celebrity figure at the founding of the National Woman's Christian Temperance Union (WCTU) in Cleveland, Ohio, where the efforts of her Hillsboro temperance activists were hailed as the beginning of a new morality in American society (1874). ❖ See also *Women in World History.*

THOMPSON, Elizabeth Rowell (1821–1899). American philanthropist. Born Elizabeth Rowell, Feb 21, 1821, in Lyndon, Vermont; died July 20, 1899, in Littleton, New Hampshire; dau. of Samuel Rowell and Mary (Atwood) Rowell; m. Thomas Thompson, Jan 1844 (died 1869); no children. ❖ Patron of the arts, scientific research, and women's political causes, underwrote the Chicago–Colorado Colony of Longmont, Colorado, designed to provide a cooperative, self-supporting community for residents of overpopulated urban areas (1871); was also the principal patron of the communal farm in Salina, Kansas, known as the Thompson Colony; enrolled as the 1st patron of the American Association for the Advancement of Science (1873); subsidized the establishment of the Yellow Fever Commission (1878); founded the Elizabeth Thompson Science Fund (1885). ❖ See also *Women in World History.*

THOMPSON, Elizabeth Southerden (1846–1933). See Butler, Elizabeth Thompson.

THOMPSON, Eloise Bibb (1878–1928). African-American writer and journalist. Born Eloise Bibb, June 29, 1878, in New Orleans, Louisiana; died Jan 8, 1928; dau. of Charles H. Bibb (customs inspector) and Catherine Adele Bibb; graduate of Teachers College of Howard University, 1908; m. Noah Thompson (historian and journalist), Aug 4, 1911. ❖ Teacher, writer, and religious activist, published *Poems* (1895); taught public school in Louisiana (1901–02); headed the Social Settlement at Howard University, Washington, DC (1908–11); wrote for *Los Angeles Tribune* and *Morning Sun,* and also wrote poetry and fiction for Catholic journals such as *The Tidings* and *Out West;* sold 1st work of drama, *A Reply to Clansmen* (1915); wrote 4 plays, 3 of which were produced in Los Angeles with black casts for black audiences— *Caught* (1920), *Africannus* (1922), and *Cooped Up* (1924); also wrote numerous short stories on racial themes, including the critically acclaimed "Mademoiselle 'Tasie—A Story," (1925). ❖ See also *Women in World History.*

THOMPSON, Emma (1959—). English actress and screenwriter. Born April 15, 1959, in Paddington, London, England; dau. of Eric Thompson (stage director and creator of children's program *The Magic Roundabout*) and Phyllida Law (actress); sister of Sophie Thompson (actress); Newnham College, Cambridge, BA, 1982; m. Kenneth Branagh (actor, director), 1989 (div. 1995); m. Greg Wise (actor), 2003; children: Gaia Romilly Wise. ❖ The only person to win Academy Awards for both acting and writing, spent student years at Cambridge acting in Footlights student theater and co-writing, co-producing and co-directing university's 1st all-female revue (1982); spent several years as stand-up comic; joined former Footlights colleagues Hugh Laurie and Stephen Fry in tv comedy "Alfresco" (1983), leading to tv special "Up For Grabs"; starred in "Tutti Frutti" (1987) and in 1st dramatic role for miniseries "Fortunes of War" (1988), with Kenneth Branagh; on stage, performed in long-running West End musical *Me and My Girl* (1985–86); with Branagh, starred on stage in *Look Back in Anger* (1989) and on film in *Henry V* (1989), *Dead Again* (1991), *Peter's Friends* (1992) and *Much Ado About Nothing* (1993); won Oscar and BAFTA Award for Best Actress for *Howards End* (1992), followed by Academy Award nominations for Best Supporting Actress for *In the Name of the Father* and Best Actress for *The Remains of the Day* (both 1993); won Academy Award for Best Screenplay for *Sense and Sensibility,* as well as Oscar nod for Best Actress (1995); appeared with mother in *The Winter Guest* (1997); other films include *Carrington* (1995), *Primary Colors* (1998), *Maybe Baby* (2000), *Love Actually* (2003) and *Harry Potter and the Prisoner of Azkaban* (2004); on tv, appeared in "Wit" (2001) and

nominated for Screen Actors Guild Award for miniseries "Angels in America" (2003). ❖ See also Chris Nickson, *Emma: Many Faces of Emma Thompson* (Taylor, 1997).

THOMPSON, Era Bell (1906–1986). African-American journalist. Born Aug 10, 1906, in Des Moines, Iowa; died Dec 29, 1986, in Chicago, Illinois; dau. of Steward C. Thompson (farmer and laborer) and Mary (Logan) Thompson; attended North Dakota State University; graduate of Morningside College, 1933; attended Medill School of Journalism, Northwestern University. ❖ Long-time editor for *Ebony* magazine, contributed articles to *Chicago Defender;* won Newbery fellowship (1945) and Bread Loaf Writer's fellowship (1949); served as managing editor of *Negro Digest* (1947–51); served as managing editor, then promoted to international editor, *Ebony* (1951–86); writings include *Africa, Land of My Fathers* (1954). Inducted into Iowa Hall of Fame (1978). ❖ See also autobiography, *American Daughter* (U. of Chicago Press, 1946); and *Women in World History.*

THOMPSON, Estelle (1911–1979). See Oberon, Merle.

THOMPSON, Flora (1876–1947). English writer. Born Flora Jane Timms, Dec 5, 1876, at Juniper Hill, Brackley, Oxfordshire, England; died at Brixham, England, May 21, 1947; dau. of Albert Timms (stonemason) and Emma (Lapper) Timms; attended a village school at Cottisford, Oxfordshire; married John Thompson (post-office clerk); children: Basil, Winifred, and Peter. ❖ Writer, unrecognized for much of her career, whose autobiographical trilogy about rural peasant life in late 19th century is now treasured as a literary classic; was born at Juniper Hill, a hamlet on the boundary between Oxfordshire and Northamptonshire; educated at the school in the neighboring village of Cottisford; at 14, left home to work as assistant to the post-office clerk in nearby Fringford; later worked in the post office at Grayshott in Hampshire; lived in Bournemouth (1903–16); began writing for magazines when her children grew beyond infancy; moved to Liphook (1916); published *Bog Myrtle and Peat,* a volume of verse (1921); moved to Dartmouth (1928); began to write sketches of her childhood (1937): *Lark Rise* (1939), *Over to Candleford* (1941), and *Candleford Green* (1943), later published as the trilogy of rural life in 1880s and 1890s, *Lark Rise to Candleford* (1945); did not gain a reputation as a serious and established writer until she was in her 60s; also wrote *Still Glides the Stream* (1948). ❖ See also Gillian Lindsay, *Flora Thompson: The Story of the Lark Rise Writer* (Robert Hale, 1990); and *Women in World History.*

THOMPSON, Frank (1841–1898). See Edmonds, Emma.

THOMPSON, Freda (1906–1980). Australian aviator. Born 1906 in Melbourne, Australia; died of cancer 1980 in Australia; dau. of a banker. ❖ The 1st Australian woman to fly solo from England to Australia (Sept 28–Nov 6, 1934), obtained pilot's license (1930), commercial license (1932), and became the 1st female flying instructor in Australia and the British Empire (1933); won 47 trophies; appointed commandant of the Victoria branch of the Women's Air Training Corps (1940). Made OBE. ❖ See also Joan Palmer, *Goggles and God Help You: Pioneer Airwoman Freda Thompson OBE and Some of Her Contemporaries* (1986).

THOMPSON, Georgia Ann (1893–1978). See Broadwick, Tiny.

THOMPSON, Gertrude Caton (1888–1985). See Caton-Thompson, Gertrude.

THOMPSON, Gertrude Hickman (1877–1950). American executive and philanthropist. Name variations: Mrs. William Boyce Thompson. Born Gertrude Hickman in 1877 in Virginia City, Montana; died Aug 27, 1950, in Yonkers, New York; m. William Boyce Thompson, wealthy railroad owner and president of Magma Copper Co. (died June 27, 1930). ❖ Contributed money to help civilians in France, Belgium, and Italy during WWI; following husband's death, named chair of the board of the Bryce Thompson Institute for Plant Research in Yonkers, NY, chair of the Magma Arizona Railroad and a director of husband's Newmont Mining Corp. (1930); established the Mrs. William Boyce Thompson Foundation; during WWII, established an organization to make and distribute clothing to Allied military personnel.

THOMPSON, Grace Gallatin Seton (1872–1959). See Seton, Grace Gallatin.

THOMPSON, Helen (1908–1974). American musician and orchestra manager. Born Helen Mulford, June 1, 1908, in Greenville, IL; died June 25, 1974, in Carmel, CA; attended DePauw University, Indiana, 1926–27; University of Illinois, Phi Beta Kappa, 1932; m. Carl Denison Thompson (research chemist), 1933; children: Charles Denison

(b. 1940). ❖ Was a violinist with Charleston Symphony (1940); became affiliated with Chicago-based American Symphony Orchestra League (ASOL, 1943), serving as executive secretary (1950–63) and vice-president (1963–70); was consultant to Ford Foundation (1966); served as manager for NY Philharmonic (1970–73); authored various studies, including *The Community Symphony Orchestra: How to Organize and Develop It* (1952). ❖ See also *Women in World History.*

THOMPSON, Jennie (1981—). American gymnast. Born July 29, 1981, in Wichita Falls, TX. ❖ Won US Classic (1996, 1998), Visa Cup (1999); won a bronze medal for team all-around and a silver for all-around at Pan American Games (1999). ❖ See also Christina Lessa, *Women Who Win* (Universe, 1998).

THOMPSON, Jennifer (1973—). See Thompson, Jenny.

THOMPSON, Jenny (1973—). American swimmer. Name variations: Jennifer Thompson. Born Jennifer Thompson, Feb 26, 1973, in Georgetown, MA; graduate of Stanford University, 1995; attended Columbia University School of Medicine. ❖ Won a gold medal at Pan American Games (1987); helped win 19 NCAA titles and 4 team titles during college career at Stanford; set a world record in 100-meter freestyle at US Olympic Trials (1992); at Barcelona Olympics, won a silver medal in 100-meter freestyle and gold medals in 4 x 100-meter medley relay and 4 x 100-meter freestyle relay (1992); won 6 gold medals at Pan Pacific Games (1993); won 5 US national titles (1993); won 2 gold medals at US national championships (1994); won 3 individual and 2 relay events at NCAA championships (1995); at Atlanta Olympics, won gold medals for the 4 x 100-meter medley relay, 4 x 100-meter freestyle relay and 800-meter freestyle relay (1996); won gold medals for the 100-meter freestyle and 100-meter butterfly and 2 relay gold medals at World championships, Perth (1998); won 3 gold medals and 1 silver medal and set a world record at World Short Course championships (1999); won 2 gold medals and 1 silver medal and set a world record at World Short Course championships (2000); at Sydney Olympics, won gold medals in 4 x 100-meter freestyle relay, 4 x 100-meter medley relay, and 800-meter freestyle relay and a bronze medal in the 100-meter freestyle (2000); won silver medals for 4 x 100-meter freestyle and 4 x 100-meter medley relay at Athens Olympics (2004). Named US Swimmer of the Year (1993).

THOMPSON, Jessica (1894–1995). See Blackburn, Jessy.

THOMPSON, Joanne (1965—). English field-hockey player. Born May 13, 1965, in UK. ❖ At Barcelona Olympics, won a bronze medal in team competition (1992).

THOMPSON, Mrs. John G. (1846–1891). See Armour, Rebecca.

THOMPSON, Katharina Kuipers (1916–2004). See Dalton, Katharina.

THOMPSON, Kay (1908–1998). American entertainer and writer. Born Katherine L. Fink, Nov 9, 1908, in St. Louis, Missouri; died in New York, NY, July 2, 1998; m. William Spier (div.); m. Jack Jenny (div.); no children. ❖ Though best remembered as the creator of books featuring Eloise, the mischievous denizen of the Plaza Hotel, was also an acclaimed entertainer; landed a radio gig as a vocalist with Mills Brothers (1929), then sang and arranged for Fred Waring band; produced the short-lived radio show, "Kay Thompson and Company," with Jim Backus; was an arranger and composer at MGM; created her own night-club act, backed by the Williams Brothers, an act that opened at Ciro's in Hollywood (1947) and toured for 6 years; opened one-woman show at New York's Plaza Hotel (1954); published *Eloise: A Book for Precocious Grown Ups* (1955), followed by *Eloise in Paris* (1957); produced 3 additional sequels: *Eloise at Christmastime* (1958), *Eloise in Moscow* (1959) and *Eloise Takes a Bawth* (1964); on film, appeared in *Funny Face* (1956) and *Tell Me That You Love Me, Junie Moon* (1970); also wrote *Miss Pooky Peckinpaugh and Her Secret Private Boyfriends Complete with Telephone Numbers* (1970). ❖ See also *Women in World History.*

THOMPSON, Lady (1845–1913). See Thompson, Annie E.

THOMPSON, Lesley (1959—). Canadian rower. Born Lesley Allison Thompson, Sept 20, 1959, in Toronto, Ontario, Canada. ❖ At Los Angeles Olympics, won a silver medal in coxed fours (1984); won a gold medal at Barcelona Olympics (1992), silver medal at Atlanta Olympics (1996), and bronze medal at Sydney Olympics (2000), all for coxed eights.

THOMPSON, Linda (1948—). Scottish folk-rock singer. Name variations: Linda Peters, Linda Peters Thompson. Born Linda Pettifer, Aug 23, 1948, in Hackney, England, of Scottish parentage; grew up in Glasgow, Scotland; m. Richard Thompson (musician), 1972 (div. 1983); m. Steve Kenis (American agent), mid-1980s; children: (1st m.) 3. ❖ Changed name to Linda Peters and released single "You Ain't Going Nowhere" (c. 1969); with 1st husband, released numerous albums, including *I Want to See the Bright Lights Tonight* (1974), *Pour Down Like Silver* (1975), and *Shoot Out the Lights* (1982); named female singer of the year by *Rolling Stone* magazine (1983); released 1st solo album, *One Clear Moment* (1985), which included song, "Telling Me Lies"; stopped performing for 11 years; released solo albums, *Dreams Fly Away* (1996), *Give Me a Sad Song* (2001) and *Fashionably Late* (2002).

THOMPSON, Linda Brown (1943—). See Brown, Linda.

THOMPSON, Linda Chavez- (1944—). See Chavez-Thompson, Linda.

THOMPSON, Louise (1901–1999). African-American educator, labor organizer, and social reformer. Name variations: Louise Patterson. Born Louise Alone Thompson on Sept 9, 1901, in Chicago, Illinois; died Aug 27, 1999, in New York, NY; graduate of University of California at Berkeley, 1923; m. Wallace Thurman (novelist and playwright), Aug 1928 (sep. 1929, died 1934); m. William Patterson (lawyer), 1940 (died 1980); children: (2nd m.) Mary Louise Patterson (b. 1943). ❖ Leading figure in the civil-rights and social-reform movements of 1930s and 1940s, was also associated with New York's Harlem Renaissance, mainly through her marriage to Wallace Thurman, her 1st husband, and her long-time association as secretary of poet Langston Hughes, who dedicated his 1942 collection of poems, *Shakespeare in Harlem*, to her. ❖ See also *Women in World History.*

THOMPSON, Lydia (1836–1908). British actress and dancer. Born in London, England, Feb 9, 1836; died Nov 1908 in London. ❖ In a career that lasted almost 50 years and spanned 4 continents, made debut in title role of *Little Flaxen-hair* at Her Majesty's Theater in London (1852); performed at provincial theaters (1864–65) and appeared in London at Drury Lane (1865) and at Prince of Wales Theater (1866); with her troupe of pantomime performers, toured Australia, Russia and India; toured US on 3 separate occasions (1867–68, 1872–73, and 1887–88) with her "British Blondes" (Pauline Markham, Rose Coghall, and Eliza Weathersby); in London, performed in a satire of *Bluebeard* (1874); also appeared in *The Sultan of Mocha* at London's Strand Theater (1886); was a major influence on American costuming and staging.

THOMPSON, Marie (1758–1836). See Lavoisier, Marie.

THOMPSON, Marilou Bonham (1936—). See Awiakta.

THOMPSON, Marion Beatrice (1877–1964). New Zealand school teacher, principal, and memoirist. Name variations: Marion Beatrice Thomson. Born Nov 22, 1877, in Dunedin, New Zealand; died June 12, 1964, in Feilding, New Zealand; dau. of Andrew Thomson and Margaret (Hamilton) Thomson; Dunedin Training College, MA, 1899; m. Laurence Thompson (cleric), 1909 (died 1929); children: 1 daughter, 2 sons. ❖ Taught at Waitaki Girls' High School, Oamaru, at Prince Albert College, Auckland, and at Southland Girls' High School; helped establish Solway College, where she served as principal (1916–42); published *We Built a School* (1956). ❖ See also *Dictionary of New Zealand Biography* (Vol. 3).

THOMPSON, Mary Harris (1829–1895). American surgeon and professor. Born April 15, 1829, in Washington Co., New York; died May 21, 1895; dau. of John Harris (mine owner) and Calista (Corbin) Thompson; attended Ford Edward Collegiate Institute; graduate of New England Female Medical College, 1863; Chicago Medical College, MD, 1870. ❖ One of the 1st American women to become a professional surgeon, helped to establish the Chicago Hospital for Women and Children (1865); cofounded and taught hygiene, obstetrics, and gynecology, Woman's Hospital Medical College (beginning 1870); founded a nurse training school (1874); elected vice-president, Chicago Medical Society (1881); elected to membership, American Medical Association (1886). ❖ See also *Women in World History.*

THOMPSON, May (d. 1978). English-born musical-comedy star. Died Nov 18, 1978, in Devon, PA; m. twice. ❖ At 16, came to US to dance in *The Half Moon*; subsequent appearances include *You're in Love, Fancy Free, Oui Madame, Angel Face, Katinka* and *Century Revue.*

THOMPSON, Pauline Elaine (1966—). See Davis-Thompson, Pauline.

THOMPSON, Rebecca (1846–1891). See Armour, Rebecca.

THOMPSON, Ruth (1887–1970). American judge and politician. Born Sept 15, 1887, in Whitehall, Michigan; died April 5, 1970, in Allegan

County, Michigan; graduate of Muskegon Business College, 1905; studied law in night school. ❖ Admitted to the bar of Michigan (1924); elected judge of Muskegon County Probate Court (1925–37); served as a representative, Michigan House of Representatives (1939–41); started private law practice in Michigan (1946); as a Republican from Michigan's 9th District (1950), was the 1st woman elected to Congress from Michigan; served in 82nd through 84th Congresses (1951–57); served on the House Judiciary Committee, the 1st woman to do so, as well as on the Joint Committee on Immigration and Nationality Policy; on national issues, consistently voted with conservative Republicans against the Truman administration, opposing domestic social programs and executive powers while supporting aid to non-Communist nations. ❖ See also *Women in World History.*

THOMPSON, Sada (1929—). American actress. Born Sept 27, 1929, in Des Moines, Iowa; dau. of Hugh Woodruff and Corlyss Elizabeth (Gibson) Thompson; attended Carnegie Institute of Technology; m. Donald E. Stewart. ❖ Made professional stage debut at University Playhouse, Mashpee, Massachusetts, as Harmony Blue-blossom in *The Beautiful People* (1947); made 1st tv appearance on "Goodyear TV Playhouse" (1951); made New York debut (1953); appeared in 1st film, *You Are Not Alone* (1961); appeared in best-known stage role, as Beatrice in Paul Zindel's *The Effect of Gamma Rays on Man-in-the-Moon Marigolds* (1970); had 4-character part in *Twigs* (1971), which brought her a Tony Award for Best Actress (1971); appeared as Mary Todd Lincoln in tv miniseries "Sandburg's Lincoln," for which she was nominated for an Emmy (1976); received 2nd Emmy nomination for performance in "The Entertainer" (1976); appeared as matriarch Kate Lawrence in "Family" (1976), winning Emmy Award for Outstanding Lead Actress in a Drama Series (1978); guest-starred on comedy series "Cheers" (1991), for which she was again nominated for an Emmy; starred in 15 made-for-tv movies and miniseries, most notably in "Our Town" (1977), "Alex Haley's Queen" (1993), "Any Mother's Son" (1997) and "Indictment: The McMartin Trial" (1995), which brought her her 6th Emmy Award nomination; also appeared in the San Diego Globe production of Thornton Wilder's *The Skin of Our Teeth,* broadcast live on PBS (Dec 1982). ❖ See also *Women in World History.*

THOMPSON, Sarah (1774–1852). American countess. Name variations: Sara Thompson; Sarah Thomson; countess of Rumford. Born Oct 18, 1774, in Concord, NH; died Dec 2, 1852, in Concord; dau. of Benjamin Thompson (1753–1814, physicist), count of Rumford, and Sarah Walker Rolfe (died Jan 19, 1972); granddau. of Timothy Walker (founder of Concord); stepdau. of Marie Lavoisier (1758–1836). ❖ As the countess of Rumford, became the 1st American countess when her father was dubbed count of Rumford by Charles Theodore, elector of Bavaria (1791); joined her father in London (1796); was received by the Bavarian elector as a countess (1797); divided her time between London, Paris and Concord; with father, established the Rolfe and Rumford asylums for the poor and needy, particularly motherless girls, in Concord.

THOMPSON, Sylvia (1902–1968). English writer. Born Sept 4, 1902, in Scotland; died April 27, 1968; dau. of Norman Thompson; attended Somerville College, Oxford; m. Theodore Luling (American artist), in 1926; children: 3 daughters. ❖ At 16, published 1st novel, *Rough Crossing* (1918), the story of a flapper; published *A Lady in Green Gloves* (1924), followed by *The Hounds of Spring* (1926); released popular novels every year or two until the war, including *Breakfast in Bed* (1934) and *A Silver Rattle* (1935); with Victor Cunard, wrote play *Golden Arrow* (1935), which was performed at London's Whitehall Theater, starring Greer Garson and Laurence Olivier. ❖ See also *Women in World History.*

THOMPSON, Tina (1975—). African-American basketball player. Born Tina Marie Thompson, Feb 10, 1975, in Los Angeles, CA; attended Morningside High School and University of Southern California. ❖ Forward, was the top pick in the WNBA draft (1997); playing for Houston Comets, was the 2nd player in WNBA history to surpass the 3,000-point plateau (2003); named MVP of All-Star game (2000); won a team gold medal at Athens Olympics (2004).

THOMPSON, Mrs. William Boyce (1877–1950). See Thompson, Gertrude Hickman.

THOMS, Adah B. (c. 1863–1943). African-American nurse and activist. Name variations: Adah Belle Thoms; Adah Smith. Born Adah Belle Samuels in Richmond, Virginia, Jan 12, c. 1863 (some sources cite 1870); died in Harlem, Feb 21, 1943; dau. of Harry and Melvina Samuels; graduate of Woman's Infirmary and School of Therapeutic

Massage in NY, 1900; graduate of Lincoln Hospital and Home school of nursing in NY, 1905; m. 2nd husband Henry Smith, 1920s (died 1 year later). ❖ Appointed assistant superintendent of nurses at Lincoln Hospital (1905), remaining in that position for 18 years; with Martha Franklin, helped organize the National Association of Colored Graduate Nurses (NACGN), 1908), serving as president (1916–23); during WWI, campaigned for acceptance of black nurses in the American Red Cross as well as US Army Nurse Corps; appointed to Women's Advisory Council on Venereal Disease of US Public Health Service (1921). Was 1st nurse to receive Mary Mahoney Award from National Association of Colored Graduate Nurses (1936). ❖ See also *Women in World History.*

THOMSEN, Camilla Ingemann (1974—). Danish handball player. Born Nov 19, 1974, in Denmark. ❖ Pivot, won a team gold medal at Athens Olympics (2004).

THOMSEN, Ellen Osiier (1890–1962). See Osiier, Ellen.

THOMSON, Elaine (1957—). Scottish politician. Born 1957 in Inverness, Scotland; grew up in Aberdeen; Aberdeen University, BSc in Science. ❖ As a Labour candidate, elected to the Scottish Parliment for Aberdeen North (1999); defeated for reelection (2003).

THOMSON, Jane (1858–1944). New Zealand mountaineer. Name variations: Jane Coutts. Born May 18, 1858, at Kaiapoi, New Zealand; died July 17, 1944, in Christchurch, New Zealand; dau. of Donald Coutts (farmer) and Anne (Mackay) Coutts; m. John Thomson (civil engineer), 1879 (died 1923); children: 1 son. ❖ Began mountaineering in her mid-40s and was one of first women to cross Copland Pass through Southern Alps; made numerous ascents and was second woman to successfully climb Mt. Cook (1916); member of New Zealand Alpine Club. ❖ See also *Dictionary of New Zealand Biography* (Vol. 3).

THOMSON, Kirsten (1983—). Australian swimmer. Born 1983 in Sydney, Australia; attended Sydney University. ❖ Won a silver medal for 800-meter freestyle relay at Sydney Olympics (2000); won the 100- and 200- and 400-meter freestyle at Australian University Games (2002). Named Australian University Sport Female Athlete of the Year (2003).

THOMSON, Marion Beatrice (1877–1964). See Thompson, Marion Beatrice.

THOMSON, Muriel (1954—). Scottish golfer. Born Dec 12, 1954, in Aberdeen, Scotland; sister of Anne Bowman (golfer). ❖ One of triplets, recorded 10 top-10 finishes in 1st season on pro tour; won Canadian Foursome (1978); member of Curtis Cup team (1978); won Elizabeth Ann Classic and Hambro Life Order of Merit (1981); spent 11 years on the Ladies' European tour; was the 1st woman to be appointed a Club Professional in Scotland.

THOMSON, Sarah (1774–1852). See Thompson, Sarah.

THONGSUK, Pawina (1979—). Thai weightlifter. Born April 18, 1979, in Si Khoraphum, Thailand. ❖ At World championships, placed 1st for 69 kg and 69 kg clean & jerk and 2nd for 69 kg snatch (2002); won a gold medal for 75 kg at Athens Olympics (2004), setting an Olympic and World record with 272.5.

THORA (fl. 900s). Danish wife of Harald Bluetooth. One of 3 wives of Harald Bluetooth (c. 910–986), king of Denmark (r. 940–986). ❖ Harald was also married to Gyrid and a Gunhilde.

THORA (fl. 1100s). Queen of Norway. Name variations: Thora Guthormsdottir. Married Harald IV Gille, also known as Harald IV Gilchrist, king of Norway (r. 1130–1136); children: Sigurd II Mund also known as Sigurd II Mouth (1133–1155), king of Norway (r. 1136–1155).

THORA (fl. 1100s). Norwegian mistress. Associated with Harald IV Gille, also known as Harald IV Gilchrist, king of Norway (r. 1130–1136); children: Haakon II the Broadshouldered (b. 1147), king of Norway (r. 1157–1162). ❖ A workwoman, had a liaison with Harald IV. ❖ See also *Women in World History.*

THORA JOHNSDOTTIR (fl. 1000s). Associated with two kings. Concubine or wife of Harald III Haardrade (1015–1066), king of Norway (r. 1047–1066); became 2nd wife of Svend II Estridsen (d. 1076), also known as Sweyn Estridsen, king of Denmark (r. 1047–1074); children: (with Harald III) Magnus II Bareleg, king of Norway (r. 1066–1069); Olaf III Kyrri (the Peaceful), king of Norway (r. 1066–1093); (with Svend II) Ingirid (fl. 1067, illeg.), queen of Norway. ❖ There are 16 children attributed to Svend II, who had 4 wives or paramours (Gunhild of

Norway, Gyde, Elizabeth of Kiev, and Thora Johnsdottir); any one of the 4 could be the mother of Svend's royal offspring: Harald Hén, king of Denmark (r. 1074–1080); St. Knud or Canute the Holy, king of Denmark (r. 1080–1086); and Oluf or Olaf Hunger, king of Denmark (r. 1086–1095).

THORBORG, Kerstin (1896–1970). Swedish contralto. Born May 19, 1896, in Hedemora, in northern Sweden; died April 12, 1970, in Falun, Dalarna; dau. of a newspaper editor father and an amateur pianist mother; studied at Royal Conservatory in Stockholm; m. Gustav Bergman (general manager of Gothenburg Opera). ❖ Considered one of the great Orfeos in opera history, made debut at Royal Theater, Stockholm (1924); sang in Prague, Berlin, Salzburg and Vienna; debuted at Covent Garden (1936); made a famous appearance in Vienna with Bruno Walter to perform Mahler's song-cycle *Das Lied von der Erde* (1936), from which the 1st recording was made; debuted at NY's Metropolitan Opera as Fricka in *Die Walküre* (1936), singing there until 1950; took part in radio broadcast Gluck's *Orfeo ed Eurydice*; taught voice in Stockholm after retirement (1950). ❖ See also *Women in World History*.

THORBURN, June (1930–1967). English actress. Born June 30, 1931, in Kashmir, India; died in a plane crash, Nov 4, 1967, in England; m. Aldon Bryce-Harvey; m. Morton Smith-Petersen, 1957; children: 2 daughters. ❖ Appeared in over 30 films, including *Gulliver's Travels, Tom Thumb, Pickwick Papers, Don't Bother to Knock, Transatlantic* and *The Scarlet Blade.*

THORESEN, Cecilie (1858–1911). Norwegian activist. Name variations: Cecilie Krog; Ida Cecilie Thoresen. Born Ida Cecilie Thoresen in Eidsvoll, Norway, 1858; died 1911; m. Fredrik Arentz Krog (1844–1923, lawyer); children: son Helge Krog (1889–1962, dramatist). ❖ Pioneer in the campaign for women's rights, was the 1st woman to study at Oslo University (1882); also studied science at University of Copenhagen; was voted to membership of the Norwegian Students' Union (1883), the 1st woman to be admitted; founded a discussion group for "the advancement of the women's cause," and became a board member of other women's associations (1883). ❖ See also *Women in World History*.

THORN, Robyn (1945—). Australian swimmer. Name variations: Robyn Risson; Robyn Thorn-Risson. Born Robyn Thorn, Jan 6, 1945, in Queensland, Australia. ❖ At Tokyo Olympics, won a silver medal in 4 x 100-meter freestyle relay (1964).

THORN, Tracey (1962—). English vocalist. Name variations: Everything But the Girl; Marine Girls. Born Sept 26, 1962, in Hertfordshire, England. ❖ Made 2 albums with Marine Girls; with Ben Watt, formed duo Everything But the Girl (1981), which 1st made UK charts with "Each and Everyone" (1984), had hit with "I Don't Want to Talk About It" (1988) and success with album *The Language of Life* (1990). Other albums with Everything But the Girl include *Worldwide* (1991), *Acoustic* (1992), *Amplified Heart* (1994), *Walking Wounded* (1996) and *Temperamental* (1999).

THORNDIKE, Eileen (1891–1954). English actress. Born Jan 31, 1891, in Rochester, Kent, England; died April 17, 1954; dau. of Canon Arthur John Webster Thorndike and Agnes Macdonald (Bowers) Thorndike; sister of Russell Thorndike (1885–1972, actor and playwright) and Sybil Thorndike (actress); m. Maurice Ewbank, 1920 (died). ❖ Made stage debut as a walk-on in *As You Like It* (1909), then joined Annie Horniman's company in Manchester; appeared at Liverpool Rep (1912–17), then Ben Greet's company (1917–19); retired from stage (1920–30), reappearing in *Madame Plays Nap*; other plays include *Saint Joan, Fire, The Brontës of Haworth* (as Charlotte), *The Cathedral, The Family Reunion, Mandragola* and *Hindle Wakes*; served as principal of Embassy School of Acting (1933–39) and producer at Central School of Speech at the Albert Hall.

THORNDIKE, Sybil (1882–1976). English actress. Name variations: Lady Lewis Casson; Dame Sybil Thorndike. Born Agnes Sybil Thorndike, Oct 24, 1882, Gainsborough, Lincolnshire, England; died June 6, 1976; dau. of Canon Arthur John Webster Thorndike and Agnes Macdonald (Bowers) Thorndike; sister of Eileen Thorndike (actress) and Russell Thorndike (1885–1972, actor and playwright); m. Lewis Casson (actor and director), 1908 (died 1969); children: John, Christopher, Mary Casson (actress) and Ann Casson (actress). ❖ Made debut in Oxford in *My Lord from Town* (1904); spent 4 years touring US with Ben Greet (1904–08); made London debut in *The Marquise* (1908); with husband, joined Annie Horniman's company in Manchester, performing

in classic and modern plays, including Shaw's *The Devil's Disciple*; with husband, appeared in NY with John Drew in *Smith* (1910); appeared as Beatrice Farrar in *Hindle Wakes* (1912), under husband's direction, followed by title role in *Jane Clegg* to great success; had 2nd success in *The Shadow*; spent 4 years at Old Vic, appearing as Adrianna in *The Comedy of Errors,* Imogen in *Cymbeline,* Viola in *Twelfth Night,* Constance in *King John,* Beatrice, Rosalind, Portia and Lady Macbeth, among others; appeared in *The Trojan Women* (as Queen Hecuba), Medea, Beatrice of Cenci in *The Cenci*; starred in *Saint Joan* (1924), written for her by George Bernard Shaw; also appeared in *Major Barbara* (1929), as Emilia in the now-famed production of *Othello,* starring Paul Robeson, as Evie Millward in *The Distaff Side,* as Volumnia in *Coriolanus,* as Mary Herries in *Kind Lady,* as Miss Moffat in *The Corn is Green,* and as Queen Jocasta to Olivier's Oedipus; films include: *Major Barbara, Stage Fright, Britannia Mews, The Prince and the Showgirl, Separate Tables, The Chalk Garden,* and *A Passage to India*; helped inaugurate the Sybil Thorndike Theater, Leatherhead, Surrey (1969); was active in advancement of religious drama, the peace movement, trade unionism, women's rights, and election of Socialist and Labour Party candidates for Parliament. Created Dame Commander of the British Empire (1931); made a Companion of Honour to Queen Elizabeth II (1970). ❖ See also J. C. Trewin, *Sybil Thorndike* (1955); John Casson, *Lewis and Sybil* (1962); Russell Thorndike, *Sybil Thorndike* (1970); Elizabeth Sprigges, *Sybil Thorndike Casson* (1971); Sheridan Morley, *Sybil Thorndike: A Life in the Theater* (1977).

THORNE, Florence (1877–1973). American labor researcher and editor. Born Florence Calvert Thorne, July 28, 1877, in Hannibal, Missouri; died Mar 16, 1973, in Falls Church, Virginia; dau. of Stephen Thorne (teacher) and Amanthis Belle (Mathews) Thorne; University of Chicago, PhB, 1909; never married; lived with longtime companion and AFL research associate Margaret Scattergood. ❖ Taught liberal arts (1899–1912); employed as a researcher, writer, and executive assistant to American Federation of Labor (AFL) president Samuel Gompers (1912–17); served on Subcommittee on Women in Industry of the Advisory Committee of Council of National Defense (1917); served as assistant director of Working Conditions Service, War Labor Administration, US Department of Labor (1918); was director of research, AFL (1933–53); during WWII, served as a delegate to Federal Advisory Commission for Employment Security; served as adviser to International Labor Organization; wrote *Samuel Gompers, American Statesman* (1957). ❖ See also *Women in World History*.

THORNE, Harriet V. S. (1843–1926). American photographer. Name variations: Harriet van Schoonhoven Horne. Born Harriet Smith van Schoonhoven in 1843 in Troy, New York; died 1926 in Bridgehampton, NY; great-grandmother of Rollie McKenna (b. 1918); m. Jonathan Thorne (businessman), 1867 (died 1920); children: Josephine (b. 1869, died in infancy); Victor Corse (b. 1871); Samuel "Brink" Brinckerhof (b. 1873). ❖ Photographed a variety of subjects, including Native Americans, architecture, wildlife, and flora; joined the New York Camera Club (1888–89); works exhibited posthumously at Yale University (1979). ❖ See also *Women in World History*.

THORNE, Olive (1831–1918). *See Miller, Olive Thorne.*

THORNING-SCHMIDT, Helle (1966—). Danish politician. Born Dec 14, 1966, in Copenhagen, Denmark. ❖ Served as consultant on EU affairs with the Danish Federation of Trade Unions (1997–99); as a European Socialist, elected to 5th European Parliament (1999–2004).

THORNTON, Alice (1626–c. 1707). British memoirist. Name variations: Alice Wandesford Thornton. Born Alice Wandesford, Feb 13, 1626 (some sources cite 1627), in Kirklington, Yorkshire, England; died 1706 or 1707 in East Newton, Yorkshire, England; dau. of Christopher Wandesford and Alice (Osborne) Wandesford; m. William Thornton, 1651. ❖ Wrote *The Autobiography of Mrs. Alice Thornton, of East Newton, Co. York* (ed., C. Jackson, 1875), a lively account of the life of a 17th-century woman and of the politics of the period.

THORNTON, Karen (1952—). *See Moe, Karen.*

THORNTON, Kathryn (1952—). American astronaut. Born Kathryn Ryan Cordell, Aug 17, 1952, at Montgomery, Alabama; dau. of William Carten Thornton and Elsie Elizabeth Ryan Cordell (restaurant owners); Auburn University, BS, 1974, University of Virginia, MS, 1977, PhD, 1979; m. Stephen Thomas Thornton; children: Carol Elizabeth (b. 1982), Laura Lee (b. 1985), Susan Annette (b. 1990); (stepsons) Kenneth (b. 1963) and Michael (b. 1965). ❖ Selected by

NASA (1984); flew on 3 missions (1989); became the 1st female astronaut to fly on a classified Department of Defense mission (1992), achieving the female spacewalking record; helped repair the Hubble telescope (1993); went on 4th mission as payload commander of the 2nd US Microgravity Laboratory (1995). ❖ See also *Women in World History.*

THORNTON, Willie Mae (1926–1984). African-American blues singer. Name variations: Big Mama Thornton. Born Dec 11, 1926, in Montgomery, AL; died in Los Angeles, CA, July 25, 1984. ❖ Began singing in amateur shows throughout Alabama; toured Gulf Coast with Sammy Green's Hot Harlem Revue (1941); settled in Houston, TX, performing at Eldorado Club (1948); made 1st recording with E&W Records (1951); joined Johnny Otis' Rhythm and Blues Caravan and often performed with Johnny Ace; released recording "Hound Dog" which became No. 1 rhythm-and-blues song (1953), reaping $500 for Thornton (3 years later Elvis Presley recorded the same song, selling over 1 million copies and launching his career); in frustration, moved to San Francisco, appearing at local clubs (1957); sang at Monterey Jazz Festival (1964); toured with American Folk Blues Festival (1965) and re-recorded "Hound Dog"; released album *Big Mama Thornton with the Chicago Blues Band* (1967); also appeared on "The Dick Cavett Show," "The Della Reese Show," "The Midnight Special" and "Rock 1." ❖ See also *Women in World History.*

THOROGOOD, Alfreda (1942—). English ballet dancer. Born Aug 17, 1942, in Lambeth, London, England. ❖ Trained at Royal Ballet School in London, before joining its touring company (1960); danced with Royal Ballet on tour in *Swan Lake, Sleeping Beauty,* and Ashton's *The Two Pigeons;* created roles for Geoffrey Cauley's *Symphonie Pastorale* and *Beginning* (1969), and Tudor's *Knight Errant* (1968); joined Royal Ballet proper (1970), where she performed numerous principal female roles, including Swanilda and Aurora, to great acclaim.

THORPE, Elizabeth (1910–1963). *See Brousse, Amy.*

THORPE, Kamba (1839–1900). *See Bellamy, Elizabeth Whitfield.*

THORPE, Rose Hartwick (1850–1939). American poet. Born July 18, 1850, in Mishawaka, Indiana; died July 19, 1939, in San Diego, California; dau. of William Morris (tailor) and Mary Louisa (Wight) Hartwick; m. Edmund Carson Thorpe (carriage maker), Sept 11, 1871; children: Lulo May Thorpe (illustrator); Lillie Maud. ❖ Penned the popular poem "Curfew Must Not Ring Tonight" (1870); wrote for *St. Nicholas, Wide Awake, Youth's Companion,* and *Detroit Free Press;* was employed as periodical editor for *Temperance Tales, Well-Spring,* and *Words of Life;* wrote 5 children's novels; published an anthology, *The Poetical Works of Rose Hartwick Thorpe* (1912); also wrote the well-known poem, "Remember the Alamo." ❖ See also *Women in World History.*

THORS, Astrid (1957—). Finnish lawyer and politician. Born Nov 6, 1957, in Helsingfors, Finland. ❖ Served as policy advisor, Ministry of Justice (1986–87) and Ministry of Defence (1987–89), and vice-chair of the Swedish People's Party (1992–2000); as a member of the European Liberal, Democrat and Reform Party, elected to 4th and 5th European Parliament (1994–99, 1999–2004) and named vice-chair of the Committee on Petitions.

THORSNESS, Kristen (1960—). American rower. Born Mar 10, 1960, in Anchorage, Alaska. ❖ At Los Angeles Olympics, won a gold medal in coxed eights (1984).

THORUP, Kirsten (1942—). Danish poet, novelist and short-story writer. Born Feb 9, 1942, in Gelsted, on the island of Fyn, Denmark. ❖ Published a collection of modernist poems, *Indeni–udenfor* (1967, Inside–Outside); in the style of psychological realism, published her 1st novel in the "Jonna" series, *Lille Jonna* (Little Jonna, 1977), followed by *Den lange sommer* (The Long Summer, 1979), *Himmel og helvede* (Heaven and Hell, 1982), and *Den yderste grænse* (The Uttermost, 1989); also wrote (short stories) *I dagens anledning* (In Honor of the Occasion, 1968), (poetry) *Love from Trieste* (1969), (poetry) *Idag er det Daisy* (It's Daisy Today, 1971), (novel) *Baby* (1973), which won the Pegasus Prize, (novel) *Elskede Ukendte* (1994), and plays for tv and film.

THOST, Nicola (1977—). German half-pipe snowboarder. Born May 3, 1977, in Munich, Germany. ❖ Placed 1st at half-pipe at US Open (1998, 1999); was 1st in World ranking (1998); at Nagano, won the 1st gold medal ever awarded for women's half-pipe snowboarding at Winter Olympics (1998); placed 1st at European X-Games (2000) and Nippon

Open and World championships (2001); placed 11th at Salt Lake City Olympics (2001).

THRALE, Hester Lynch (1741–1821). *See Piozzi, Hester Lynch.*

THREE MARIAS, The.
 See Barreno, Maria Isabel (1939—).
 See Horta, Maria Teresa (1937—).
 See Velho de Costa, Maria (1938—).

THREE RIBBONS AND A BOW, The.
 See Hutchinson, Jeanette.
 See Hutchinson, Sheila.
 See Hutchinson, Wanda.

THROWER, Norma (1936—). Australian hurdler. Born Feb 5, 1936, in South Australia. ❖ At Melbourne Olympics, won a bronze medal in 80-meter hurdles (1956); won a gold medal in 80-meter hurdles at Commonwealth Games (1958); won Australian nationals (1955, 1957, 1959).

THUEMER, Petra (1961—). East German swimmer. Name variations: Petra Thümer. Born Jan 29, 1961, in East Germany. ❖ At Montreal Olympics, won a gold medal in 800-meter freestyle and a gold medal in 400-meter freestyle (1976).

THUEMMLER-PAWLAK, Doerte (1971—). East German gymnast. Name variations: Dörte Thümmler-Pawlak. Born Oct 29, 1971, in Berlin, East Germany. ❖ At Seoul Olympics, won a bronze medal in team all-around (1988); at World championships, won a gold medal for uneven bars (1987).

THUERIG, Karin (1972—). Swiss cyclist. Name variations: Karin Thurig or Thürig. Born July 4, 1972, in Rothenburg, Switzerland. ❖ Won a bronze medal for indiv. time trial at Athens Olympics (2004).

THULIN, Ingrid (1926–2004). Swedish actress. Born Jan 27, 1926, in Solleftea, Sweden; died Jan 7, 2004, in Stockholm; studied acting at Royal Dramatic Theater, Stockholm; studied pantomime with Etienne Decroux in Paris; m. Harry Schein (founder of the Swedish Film Institute). ❖ One of Sweden's finest stage and screen actresses, began film career in *Where the Winds Blow* (1948), but it was her work with director Ingmar Bergman—both at the Malmö Municipal Theater and in films—that brought her international recognition with *Wild Strawberries* (1957), *The Magician* (1958), *Winter Light* (1963), *The Silence* (1963), *Hour of the Wolf* (1968), *The Ritual* (1969) and *Cries and Whispers* (1972); also worked with France's Alain Resnais (*La Guerre est finie,* 1966) and Italy's Luchino Visconti (*The Damned,* 1969); directed several films, including the short *Devotion* (1975), in which she also acted, and 2 features: *One and One* (1978) and *Brusten Himmel* (Broken Sky, 1982); other films include *Foreign Intrigue* (1956), *The Judge* (1960), *The Four Horsemen of the Apocalypse* (1962), *Night Games* (1966), *La Cage* (1975), *The Cassandra Crossing* (1977), *At the Rehearsal* (1984) and *La Casa del Sorriso* (House of Smiles, 1991). Won Best Actress award at Cannes Film Festival (1958), for Bergman's *Brink of Life.*

THUMB, Mrs. Tom (1841–1919). *See Warren, Lavinia.*

THÜMER, Petra (1961—). *See Thuemer, Petra.*

THÜMMLER-PAWLAK, Dörte (1971—). *See Thuemmler-Pawlak, Doerte.*

THUN, Kjersti (1974—). Norwegian soccer player. Born June 18, 1974, in Norway. ❖ Won a team bronze medal at Atlanta Olympics (1996).

THURBER, Jeannette (1850–1946). American music patron. Born Jan 29, 1850, in New York, NY; died Jan 2, 1946, in Bronxville, NY; dau. of Henry Meyer(s) and Anne Maria Coffin (Price) Meyer(s); m. Francis Beattie Thurber (merchant and attorney), Sept 15, 1869; children: Jeannette M., Marianna Blakeman, Francis Beattie. ❖ Obtained a charter from the state of New York to found the 1st National Conservatory of Music, which opened in New York City as the American School of Opera (1885); oversaw the establishment of the National Conservatory of Music (1891), which was headed by Antonin Dvorak (1892–95). ❖ See also *Women in World History.*

THURIG, Karen (1972—). *See Thuerig, Karin.*

THURINGIA, landgravine of.
 See Sophia (fl. 1211).
 See Elizabeth of Hungary (1207–1231).
 See Margaret of Germany (1237–1270).

THURMAN, Karen L. (1951—). American politician. Born Jan 12, 1951, in Rapid City, South Dakota; University of Florida, BA, 1973; m. John Thurman. ❖ Was a mayor of Dunnellon, Florida (1979–81); served as a state senator (1983–93); elected as a Democrat to US House of Representatives (1993), serving 5 terms; lost her bid for reelection when her district was gerrymandered by Florida's Republican Legislature (2002); elected chair of Florida Democratic Party (2005).

THURMAN, Sue (1903–1996). African-American civic leader and religious worker. Name variations: Sue Bailey Thurman. Born Sue Bailey, Aug 26, 1903, in Pine Bluff, Arkansas; died in San Francisco, California, Dec 25, 1996; dau. of Isaac George Bailey (minister and educator) and Susie (Ford) Bailey (educator); Oberlin College, BS, 1926, the 1st black student to receive a degree in music there; m. Howard Thurman (minister and theology professor), June 12, 1932 (died 1981); children: (stepdau.) Olive Thurman (b. 1932); Anne Thurman Chiarenza (b. 1933). ❖ Taught music at Hampton Institute in Virginia (1927–28); became traveling secretary of national YWCA based in NY (1930); studied at University of Santineeketan in Bengal, India, with poet Rabindranath Tagore, and met privately with Mohandas Gandhi (1936); returning to US, began an ambitious lecture tour about Indian culture at American and Canadian colleges; founded and edited *Aframerican Women's Journal* (1940); with husband, founded Church for the Fellowship of All Peoples, San Francisco (1944), the nation's 1st racially integrated and internationally oriented church; edited *International Cuisine* (1957). ❖ See also *Women in World History.*

THURMAN, Tracey. American woman who inspired the Thurman Law. Married Charles Thurman (div.); children: at least 1 son. ❖ In Torrington, CT, was stabbed 13 times by ex-husband, while an on-the-scene police officer did nothing (1983); sued Torrington Police Department for violating her civil rights and became 1st battered wife to win a civil suit (1985); was awarded $2.3 million, while her 3-year-old son, a witness to the crime, was awarded $300,000; ex-husband was sentenced to 15 years for assault. The Thurman Law requires police to treat domestic abuse in the same manner as any other assault. ❖ See also (tv movie) *A Cry for Help: The Tracey Thurman Story* (1989).

THURMAN, Uma (1970—). American Actress. Born Uma Karuna Thurman, April 29, 1970, in Boston, MA; dau. of Robert (Buddhist scholar) and Nena Thurman (Swedish model and psychotherapist who was once married to Timothy Leary); m. Gary Oldman, 1990 (div. 1992); m. Ethan Hawke (actor), 1998 (div. 2004); children: (2nd m.) Roan and Maya. ❖ Had breakthrough film roles as Cecile de Volanges in *Dangerous Liaisons* (1988) and June in *Henry and June* (1990); nominated for Academy Award for Best Supporting Actress for *Pulp Fiction* (1994), directed by Quentin Tarantino; collaborated with Tarantino on *Kill Bill: Vol. 1* (2003) and *Kill Bill: Vol. 2* (2004); other films include *Get Shorty* (1995), *The Avengers* (1998), *Sweet and Lowdown* (1999), *Tape* (2001), *Paycheck* (2003), *Be Cool* (2005) and *The Producers: The Movie Musical* (2005); won Golden Globe for tv movie "Hysterical Blindness" (2002).

THURN AND TAXIS, princess of.
See Helene of Bavaria (1834–1890).
See Margaret Clementine (1870–1955).

THURNER, Helene. Austrian luge athlete. Born in Austria. ❖ Won a bronze medal for singles at Innsbruck Olympics (1964).

THURSBY, Emma (1845–1931). American concert singer. Born Emma Cecilia Thursby, Feb 21, 1845, in Williamsburg, NY; died July 4, 1931, in New York, NY; studied singing with Julius Meyer, Achille Errani, Francesco Lamperti, Antonio Sangiovanni, and Erminia Mansfield-Rudersdorff. ❖ Sang as a church soloist (1865–77), including 3 years for Rev. Henry Ward Beecher's Plymouth Church in Brooklyn; performed with Brooklyn Musical Association in Haydn's *Creation* (1868); turned gradually from choir music to performing in classical music concerts in various East Coast cities, becoming especially well known for interpretations of Mozart; rose to national celebrity while touring with Patrick S. Gilmore's 22nd Regiment Band (1874–75); appeared in concert with Hans von Bülow (1875); toured North America (1877–78); made London debut (1878), then Paris debut (1879) and enjoyed enormous popularity across western Europe; went on German tour (1880); retired to teach (1895–1924); was a professor at NY Institute of Musical Art (1905–11). Received medal of Société des Concerts, Paris Conservatoire (1881). ❖ See also *Women in World History.*

THURSTON, Katherine (1875–1911). Anglo-Irish novelist. Name variations: Katherine Cecil Madden. Born Katherine Cecil Madden, April 18, 1875, in Co. Cork, Ireland; died Sept 5, 1911, in Co. Cork; dau. of Paul Madden (Anglo-Irish banker and mayor of Cork) and Catherine (Barry) Madden; married Ernest Charles Temple Thurston (novelist), 1901 (div. 1910). ❖ Popular literary figure in England and Ireland, published 1st novel, *The Circle* (1903), with little success; serialized 2nd work, *The Masquerader* (titled *John Chilcote, M. P.* in England) in American magazine *Harper's Bazaar*, which became a bestseller when it was published in US in book form (1904); her 3rd novel, *The Gambler,* also appeared in serial form in *Harper's Bazaar* before being published as a book (1906). ❖ See also *Women in World History.*

THURSTON, Lucy (1795–1876). American missionary. Born Lucy Goodale, Oct 29, 1795, in Marlborough, Massachusetts; died Oct 13, 1876, in Honolulu, HI; dau. of Abner Goodale (farmer and deacon in Congregational Church) and possibly Mary Howe (died 1818); graduate of Bradford Academy in Massachusetts where she taught until her marriage; m. Asa Thurston (Congregationalist minister), Oct 21, 1820 (died Mar 11, 1868); children: 6, including Thomas G. Thurston (missionary) and Persis G. Taylor; grandson Lorrin Andrews Thurston was envoy to US from Hawaii. ❖ Congregationalist missionary, sailed with husband and 15 other missionaries to the Sandwich Islands (now Hawaii), landing in Kailua (1821); spent majority of life doing missionary work in Kailua, moving to Honolulu only after retiring (1862). ❖ See also *Life and Times of Mrs. Lucy G. Thurston, Wife of Rev. Asa Thurston, Pioneer Missionary to the Sandwich Islands, Gathered from Letters and Journals Extending Over a Period of More than Fifty Years* (S. C. Andrews, 1934); and *Women in World History.*

THURSTON, Mabel (1869–1960). New Zealand nurse, hospital matron, and army nursing administrator. Born July 22, 1869, in Manea, Cambridgeshire, England; died July 23, 1960, in London England; dau. of Frederick Thurston (pharmaceutical chemist) and Mary Ann (Green) Thurston. ❖ Became registered nurse (1904); served as matron at Grey River Hospital (1906–08), Christchurch Hospital (1908–16), New Zealand Military Hospital at Walton-on-Thames, England, and British-based New Zealand Army Nursing Service (1916–20), King George V Military Hospital at Rotorua (1920–23), Queen Mary Hospital in Hanmer Springs (1923–24) and Pukeora Sanatorium, Waipukurau (1924–27); during WWI, was official visitor for New Zealand War Services Association. Received Royal Red Cross, first class (1917). ❖ See also *Dictionary of New Zealand Biography* (Vol. 3).

THURSTON, Matilda (1875–1958). American educator and missionary. Born Matilda Smyrell Calder, May 16, 1875, in Hartford, Connecticut; died April 18, 1958, in Auburndale, Massachusetts; dau. of George (carpenter) and Margery (Patterson) Calder; Mt. Holyoke College, BS, 1896; m. John Lawrence Thurston (missionary), 1902 (died 1904). ❖ Taught in Connecticut secondary schools (1896–1900); volunteered for foreign mission work (1900); taught at Central Turkey College for Girls, Marash, Turkey (1900–02); traveled to China with husband (1902); taught at Yale mission in Zhangsha, China (1903); returned to China with support from Presbyterian Board of Foreign Missions (1913); founded Ginling College for Women (1913) and served as school's 1st president (1913–28); lived in US (1936–39), returning to China to work with war and relief efforts (1940–43); when the Japanese took over Nanjing (Nanking), was interned, then repatriated to Auburndale, Massachusetts (1943). ❖ See also *Women in World History.*

THUSNELDA (fl. 1st c. CE). Germanic warrior and military advisor. Probably born at end of 1st century BCE; died early in the 1st century CE. ❖ Known for her bravery, served as the key military advisor to Hermann of Germany (Arminius) during the 1st two decades of the 1st century; during their fight against the Romans, was captured, put in chains, and taken to Rome.

THWAITE, Lady Alice (1896–1953). See Rawlings, Marjorie Kinnan.

THWAITES, Minnie (1868–1894). See Knorr, Frances.

THYGESON, Sylvie Thompson (1868–1975). American birth-control activist. Born Sylvie Thompson, 1868, in Forreston, IL; died 1975; m. Nels Marcus Thygeson; children: 4, including Mary Thygeson Shepardson (anthropologist). ❖ Became activist in Woman's Welfare League; held informal "parlor" gatherings at her home to discuss and provide information about women's issues; inspired by Margaret Sanger, organized birth-control clinic in St. Louis, despite law prohibiting distribution of birth control; supported women's rights, including legalization of contraception and suffrage.

THYNNE, Frances (1699–1754). *See Seymour, Frances Thynne.*

THYRA (d. 940). Queen of Denmark. Name variations: Thyri Klacksdottir; Tyra Dannebod. Died 940; dau. of Klack-Harald, king of Jutland; possibly the wife of Gorm the Old of Jutland, king of Denmark (r. c. 883–940) or possibly the wife of Harald Bluetooth; children: possibly Harald Bluetooth (c. 910–986), king of Denmark (r. 940–986); Knut "Danaást." ❖ Raised a great wall, parts of which are still extant, called the Danneverke, which served as a bastion of defense in the southern region of Denmark for centuries to come. ❖ See also *Women in World History.*

THYRA (d. 1018). Countess of Wessex. Name variations: Thyra Sveynsdottir. Born c. 993; died in 1018; dau. of Gunhilda of Poland (d. around 1015) and Sven or Sweyn I Forkbeard, king of Denmark (r. 985–1014) and king of England (r. 1014); 1st wife of Godwin of Wessex (d. 1053), earl of Wessex and Kent (r. 1018–1053). ❖ Godwin's 2nd wife was Gytha (fl. 1022–1042).

THYRA OF DENMARK (d. 1000). Queen of Norway. Name variations: Thyre. Flourished around 999; died Sept 18, 1000; dau. of Harald Bluetooth (c. 910–985), king of Denmark (r. 940–985), and Gyrid; grandmother of Gytha; sister of Sveyn or Sweyn I Forkbeard, king of Denmark (r. 986–1014), king of England (r. 1014); m. Styrbjörn (son of Olaf, king of Sweden); betrothed to and possibly m. King Burislaf of Wendland; m. Olav I Tryggvason (968–1000), king of Norway, in 998 or 999; children: (1st m.) Thorgils Sprakalegg. ❖ Fled from Wendland to Norway, appalled at the prospect of married life with an old pagan king such as Burislaf; married Olaf Tryggvason and begged him to go to Burislaf to retrieve her dowry, which he did (1000). ❖ See also *Women in World History.*

THYRA OF DENMARK (1880–1945). Danish princess. Born Thyra Louise Caroline Amelia in 1880; died Nov 1, 1945; dau. of Louise of Sweden (1851–1926) and Frederick VIII (1843–1912), duke of Schleswig-Holstein-Sonderburg-Augustenburg (r. 1869–1880), king of Denmark (r. 1906–1912); sister of Christian X, king of Denmark (r. 1912–1947).

THYRA OLDENBURG (1853–1933). Princess of Denmark and duchess of Cumberland. Name variations: Thyra, duchess of Cumberland and Teviotdale. Born Thyra Amelia Caroline Charlotte Anne on Sept 29, 1853, in Copenhagen, Denmark; died Feb 26, 1933, in Gmunden, Austria; dau. of Louise of Hesse-Cassel (1817–1898) and Christian IX (1818–1906), king of Denmark (r. 1863–1906); sister of Marie Feodorovna and Alexandra of Denmark; m. Ernest Augustus, 3rd duke of Cumberland and Teviotdale, on Dec 21, 1878; children: Marie Louise (1879–1948, who m. Maximilian Alexander, prince of Baden); George William, earl of Armagh (1880–1912); Alexandra Guelph (1882–1963); Olga (1884–1958); Christian (1885–1901); Ernest Augustus, duke of Brunswick-Luneburg (1887–1953).

THYRE. *Variant of Thyra.*

THYSSEN, Marianne L. P. (1956—). Belgian lawyer and politician. Born July 24, 1956, in Sint-Gillis-Waas, Belgium. ❖ Granted law degree (1979); as a member of the European People's Party (Christian Democrats) and European Democrats, elected to 4th and 5th European Parliament (1994–99, 1999–2004).

TIAHO, Sophia (1820s?–1875). *See Te Paea Tiaho.*

TIBBETTS, Margaret Joy (1919—). American diplomat and ambassador to Norway. Born Aug 26, 1919, in Bethel, Maine; dau. of Raymond R. Tibbetts (physician) and Pearl (Ashby) Tibbetts (nurse); Wheaton College, BA, 1941; Bryn Mawr College, MA, 1942, PhD in history, 1944. ❖ Career foreign service officer, was a research analyst for Office of Strategic Services (1944–45) and US Department of State, Washington (1945–49); served as attaché to the American Embassy in London (1949–51, 1951–54); served as officer in charge, US consulate general of Belgian Congo, Leopoldville (now Kinshasa, Congo, 1954–56); served as special assistant to the director, ICA (1959–61); served as 1st secretary at American Embassy in Brussels, Belgium (1961–65); served as US ambassador to Norway (1964–69); was deputy assistant secretary, Foreign Service, Bureau of European and Canadian Affairs (c. 1969–71); became a college professor (1970s). ❖ See also *Women in World History.*

TIBBLES, Susette (1854–1902). *See La Flesche, Susette.*

TIBORS (b. around 1130). European troubadour. Born c. 1130 and grew up in the castle of Sarenom, known as Serignan, near Grasse in the Alpes Maritimes; dau. of a noble family; sister of troubadour Raimbuat d'Orange, or Rambaud of Orange; m. Bertrand de Baux (assassinated 1181). ❖ Only one of her songs survives. ❖ See also *Women in World History.*

TIBURZI, Bonnie (1948—). American pilot. Name variations: Bonnie Tiburzi Caputo. Born 1948; lived in Pompano Beach, FL. ❖ Grew up in family of pilots and taught to fly by father; became 1st woman hired as jet pilot by major US airline, when employed as pilot (third officer) on Boeing 727 jet operated by American Airlines (1973). ❖ See also autobiography *Takeoff: The Story of America's First Woman Pilot for a Major Airline* (1986).

TICHENET, Madame (1667–c. 1750). *See Montour, Isabelle.*

TICHO, Anna (1894–1980). Israeli artist. Born 1894 in Brno, Czechoslovakia; died Feb 29, 1980, in Israel; educated in Austria; married cousin Dr. Avraham Albert Ticho (ophthalmologist), 1912 (died 1960). ❖ Moved to Vienna with family (1904); with husband, moved to Jerusalem (1912); lived in Damascus (1917–19), while husband served in Austrian army; one of the great masters of drawing, found fame depicting the landscape and desert flowers of Palestine/Israel; sketched the hills of Jerusalem for 65 years; her Arab-style home became part of the Israel Museum.

TICHTCHENKO, Elizaveta (1975—). Russian volleyball player. Born Feb 7, 1975, in Kiev, Ukraine. ❖ Made national team debut (1991); won European team championship (1993, 1997, 1999, 2001) and World Grand Prix (1997, 1999, 2002); placed 3rd at World championships (1994, 1998, 2002); won a team silver medal at Sydney Olympics (2000) and a team silver at Athens Olympics (2004). Named Spiker of the Year (2002).

TICKELL, Mary (1758–1787). *See Linley, Mary.*

TICKEY, Bertha (1925—). American softball player. Born Mar 13, 1925, in Dinuba, CA. ❖ Was a member of 11 national championship teams—the Orange, California Lionettes (1950–52 and 1955) and the Raybestos Brakettes (1958–60, 1963, 1966–68); over length of career, pitched 757 winning games and lost 88. Won Most Valuable Player award 8 times; named to National Softball Hall of Fame (1972) and Connecticut Hall of Fame (1973). ❖ See also *Women in World History.*

TICKNOR, Anna Eliot (1823–1896). American educator and reformer. Born Anna Eliot Ticknor in Boston, Massachusetts, in 1823; died 1896; dau. of George Ticknor (1791–1871, 1st professor of modern languages at Harvard and founder of the Boston Public Library) and Anna Eliot Ticknor (1800–1885, hosted a famous literary salon); cousin of historian Samuel Eliot; never married; no children. ❖ Founded Boston's Society to Encourage Studies at Home (1873), a school that offered instruction in 24 subjects and remained open until 1887; also authored the children's book *An American Family in Paris,* published anonymously (1869); was instrumental in editing and publishing her father's letters and journals. ❖ See also *Women in World History.*

TIDD, Rachel (1984—). American gymnast. Born May 20, 1984, in Escondido, CA. ❖ Won a bronze medal for team all-around at World championships (2001).

TIDWELL-LUCAS, Gypsy (c. 1975—). American inline skater. Name variations: Gypsy Lucas; Gypsy Tidwell. Born c. 1975. ❖ Won gold in Women's Downhill at X Games (1996 and 1997).

TIECK, Sophie (1775–1833). *See Bernhardi, Sophie.*

TIEDEMANN, Charlotte (1919–1979). Duchess of Segovia. Born Charlotte Auguste Luise Tiedemann, Jan 2, 1919, in Konigsberg, Prussia; died July 3, 1979, in Berlin, Germany; dau. of Otto Eugen Tiedemann and Luise Amalia Klein; married a man named Buchler; married a man named Hippler, 1939 (div. 1940); m. Jaime (1908–1975), duke of Segovia (renounced claim to the throne of Spain in 1939), on Aug 3, 1949; children: Helga Hippler.

TIEMPO, Edith L. (1919—). Filipino poet, novelist and short-story writer. Born April 22, 1919, in Bayombong, Nueva Vizcaya, Philippines; m. Edilberto K. Tiempo (died). ❖ Was a literary critic and teacher; with husband, founded Silliman National Writers Workshop in Dumaguete City (1962), which has produced many fine writers; works include *Abide, Joshua, and Other Stories* (1964), *The Tracks of Babylon and Other Poems* (1966), *A Blade of Fern* (1978), *His Native Coast* (1979), *The Alien Corn* (1992), and *The Charmer's Box and Other Poems* (1993); was the 1st woman awarded the title of National Artist for Literature.

TIERNAN, Frances Fisher (1846–1920). American author. Name variations: Frances Christine Fisher; (pseudonym) Christian Reid. Born Frances Christine Fisher, July 5, 1846, in Salisbury, North Carolina; died Mar 24, 1920, in Salisbury; dau. of Charles Frederic Fisher (newspaper editor and Civil War colonel killed at Battle of Bull Run) and Elizabeth Ruth (Caldwell) Fisher; m. James Marquis Tiernan (mineralogist), Dec 29, 1887 (died 1898); no children. ❖ Author of 45 books with a deeply Catholic perspective, published 1st novel *Valerie Aylmer* (1870), under pseudonym Christian Reid; traveled to Europe (1879–80); lived in Mexico (1887–97); as Reid, also wrote *Morton House* (1871), *Hearts of Steel* (1883), *Armine* (1884), *Carmela* (1891), *The Land of the Sun* (1894), *The Man of the Family* (1897), *Under the Southern Cross* (1900), *A Daughter of the Sierra* (1903), *Princess Nadine* (1908), *The Wargrave Trust* (1912), *Daughter of a Star* (1913), *A Far-Away Princess* (1914) and *The Secret Bequest* (1915). Received University of Notre Dame's Laetare Medal (1909). ❖ See also *Women in World History*.

TIERNEY, Gene (1920–1991). American actress. Name variations: Gene Lee. Born Gene Eliza Tierney, Nov 19, 1920, in Brooklyn, NY; died in Houston, Texas, Nov 6, 1991; dau. of Howard Tierney (insurance broker) and Belle (Taylor) Tierney; m. Oleg Cassini (fashion designer), June 1, 1941 (div. Feb 1952); m. W. Howard Lee (oil executive), July 1960; children: (1st m.) 2 daughters, Daria (born blind and deaf) and Christina Cassini. ❖ Tall brunette with chiseled cheekbones, slanted blue-green eyes, and famed overbite, was one of 20th Century-Fox's lineup of stars (1940s); on stage, had breakthrough role of the kid sister in *The Male Animal* (1940); made film debut as female lead in *The Return of Jesse James* (1940); best known for performances in title roles of *Laura* (1944) and *The Ghost and Mrs. Muir* (1947); hospitalized for a nervous breakdown (1955–58); other films include *Tobacco Road* (1941), *Belle Starr* (1941), *Heaven Can Wait* (1943), *A Bell for Adano* (1945), *Dragonwyck* (1946), *The Razor's Edge* (1946), *Whirlpool* (1950), *Night and the City* (1950), *Where the Sidewalk Ends* (1950), *Close to My Heart* (1951), *Plymouth Adventure* (1952), *Black Widow* (1954), *The Egyptian* (1954), *The Left Hand of God* (1955), *Advise and Consent* (1962), *Toys in the Attic* (1963) and *The Pleasure Seekers* (1964). Received Oscar nomination for performance in *Leave Her to Heaven* (1945). ❖ See also autobiography (with Mickey Herskowitz) *Self-Portrait* (Wyden, 1979); and *Women in World History*.

TIETJENS, Eunice (1884–1944). American poet, journalist, and writer. Born Eunice Strong Hammond, July 29, 1884, in Chicago, Illinois; died Sept 6, 1944, in Chicago; dau. of William Andrew Hammond (banker) and Idea Louise (Strong) Hammond; m. Paul Tietjens (composer), May 1904 (div. 1914); m. Cloyd Head (playwright and director), Feb 1920; children: (1st m.) Idea (died in childhood), Janet Tietjens (b. 1907); (2nd m.) Marshall (b. 1920), 1 daughter (died shortly after birth). ❖ Poet, war correspondent, and author of children's books, wrote with an international spirit derived from her travels to Asia, Europe, northern Africa, and the South Seas; went to Europe after death of father (c. 1897); began work with Harriet Monroe on *Poetry* magazine (1913), where her legacy in the literary world would be based more on her influence on other writers than on her own works; traveled to China for 6 months (1916); served as war correspondent in France for the *Chicago Daily News* (1917); lived in Tunisia (early 1920s); taught poetry at University of Miami (1933–35); writings include *Profiles from China* (1917), *Body and Raiment* (1919), *Jake* (1921), (play, with husband Cloyd Head) *Arabesque* (1925), *Boy of the Desert* (1928), *The Romance of Antar* (1929), *Leaves in Windy Weather* (1929), (with daughter Janet Tietjens) *The Jaw-Breaker's Alphabet of Prehistoric Animals* (1930), and *Boy of the South Seas* (1931). ❖ See also autobiography, *The World at My Shoulder* (1938); and *Women in World History*.

TIETJENS, Therese (1831–1877). German operatic soprano. Name variations: surname sometimes spelled Titiens. Born Thérèse Johanne Alexandra Tietjens, July 17, 1831, in Hamburg, Germany; died Oct 3, 1877, in London, England; studied music in Vienna with Dellessie, Babing, and Proch. ❖ Debuted in Hamburg as Erma in Auber's *Maçon* (1848) and went on to success in title role of Donizetti's *Lucrezia Borgia* (1849); made London debut as Valentine in *Les Huguenots* (1858) and achieved great fame on the English stage; further distinguished herself by performing in the provinces, an unusual effort for

an internationally acclaimed prima donna; performed throughout Europe (1858–69), appearing in opera houses in Vienna, London, Paris and Naples; most famous roles include Fidelio, Medea in Cherubini's opera, Donna Anna in Mozart's *Don Giovanni*, Elvira, Norma, Lucia, Ortud, and Leonore. ❖ See also *Women in World History*.

TIETZ, Marion (1952—). East German handball player. Born Nov 17, 1952, in East Germany. ❖ Won a silver medal at Montreal Olympics (1976) and a bronze medal at Moscow Olympics (1980), both in team competition.

TIFFANY (1971—). American singer. Name variations: Tiffany Renee Darwish, Tiffany Renee. Born Tiffany Renee Darwish, Oct 2, 1971, in Norwalk, CA; m. Bulmaro "Junior" Garcia (makeup artist), April 4, 1992 (div. 2003); m. Ben George, Aug 4, 2004; children: Elijah (b. 1992). ❖ At 9, began performing with country bands; released debut album, *Tiffany* (1987), which, after a slow start, hit #1 on pop charts and included hit singles "Could've Been," "I Think We're Alone Now," and "I Saw Her Standing There"; released *Hold an Old Friend's Hand* (1988) and *The Color of Silence* (2000); was the voice of Judy Jetson in *The Jetsons: The Movie* (1990).

TIGER WOMAN, The (1894–1970). *See Glaum, Louise.*

TIGHE, Mary (1772–1810). Irish poet. Born Mary Blachford in Dublin, Ireland, Oct 9, 1772; died Mar 24, 1810, at Woodstock; dau. of Reverend William Blachford and Theodosia (Tighe) Blachford; m. Henry Tighe of Woodstock (member of the Irish Parliament), in 1793. ❖ Left fatherless shortly after birth, received education from mother who had participated in the Methodist movement in Ireland and was unusually well educated for a woman of her time; was the author of *Psyche, or the Legend of Love*, a poem of unusual merit which was privately printed (1805) and published posthumously (1811), along with some other poems. ❖ See also *Women in World History*.

TIGHE, Virginia (1923–1995). American reincarnate. Name variations: Bridey Murphy; Virginia Tighe Morrow. Born Virginia Tighe in Chicago, Illinois, in 1923; died July 12, 1995; married. ❖ Colorado housewife whose apparent recollection of a past life fascinated the nation; after being hypnotized by Morey Bernstein to relieve her allergies (1952), spoke in a thick Irish brogue, claiming to have lived before as Bridey Murphy, a red-headed, 19th-century Irishwoman born in Cork 158 years previous; was able to detail people, places, and customs with an accent and in words that seemed totally foreign to her; endured enormous notoriety when Bernstein published the bestselling *The Search for Bridey Murphy* (1956). ❖ See also *Women in World History*.

TIGHE-UMBERS, Bathia (1893–1987). *See Stuart, Bathia Howie.*

TII (c. 1400–1340 BCE). *See Tiy.*

TIIT, Cecilia (1962—). Peruvian volleyball player. Born Mar 15, 1962, in Peru. ❖ At Seoul Olympics, won a silver medal in team competition (1988).

TIKHONINA, Tamara (1934—). Soviet volleyball player. Born Feb 22, 1934, in USSR. ❖ At Tokyo Olympics, won a silver medal in team competition (1964).

TIKHONOVA, Tamara (1964—). Russian cross-country skier. Born June 13, 1964, in Kovalyovo, Russia. ❖ Won cross-country gold medals for 20 km and 4 x 5 km relay and a silver medal for 5 km at Calgary Olympics (1988); at World championships, won gold medals (1985, 1991), a silver medal (1989), and bronze medals (1989, 1991).

TIKKANEN, Märta (1935—). Finnish-Swedish poet and novelist. Name variations: Marta Tikkanen. Born April 3, 1935, in Helsinki, Finland; dau. of a professor; m. Henrik Tikkanen (1924–1989, writer); children: 5. ❖ One of the best-known woman writers in Finland, worked as teacher, editor, and was head of Helsinki's Swedish Institute for Workers (1972–81); writes in Swedish; published a novel in 2 volumes, *Nu imorron* (Now Tomorrow, 1970) and *Ingenmansland* (No Man's Land, 1972); published (poems) *Århundradets kärlekssaga* (Love Story of the Century, 1978) and novels *Rödluvan* (Little Red Riding Hood, 1986) and *Storfangeren* (The Great Hunter, 1990); also wrote *Man kan inte valdtas* (Manrape, 1979).

TILBERIS, Liz (1947–1999). British fashion-magazine editor. Born Elizabeth Kelly, Sept 7, 1947, in Alderly Edge, England; died April 21, 1999, in New York, NY; dau. of Thomas Stuart-Black Kelly (eye surgeon) and Janet (Caldwell) Kelly; attended Jacob Kramer College of Art in Leeds; graduate of Leicester Polytechnic Art School with a degree in fashion design; m. Andrew Tilberis (artist), 1971; children: (adopted) Robbie (born c. 1981) and Chris (born c. 1985). ❖ Editor of two of the most influential magazines in the fashion industry, was known for her sharp eye for style and fashion photography; began career as an intern at British *Vogue* (1969), becoming an assistant editor (1971), fashion editor and executive fashion editor, then editor-in-chief (1989); on becoming editor-in-chief of *Harper's Bazaar* (1992), moved to Manhattan; received Editor of the Year citation from *Advertising Age* (1993); diagnosed with ovarian cancer (1993); for next 6 years, continued to edit *Harper's Bazaar,* often from her hospital bed; became president of the nonprofit Ovarian Cancer Research Fund. ❖ See also memoir, *No Time to Die* (1998); and *Women in World History.*

TILBURY, Zeffie (1863–1950). English-born actress. Born Nov 20, 1863, in London, England; died July 24, 1950, in Los Angeles, CA; m. Arthur Lewis; m. L. E. Woodthorpe. ❖ Made stage debut in Brighton in *Nine Points of the Law* (1881) and London debut in *Pluto* (1882); other plays include *Ruth's Romance* (title role), *Family Ties,* and *The Overland Route*; joined Mary Anderson's company in US, making NY debut as Celia in *As You Like It* (1885), remaining there for many years; appeared in 70 films, including *Camille, Charlie Chan Carries On, Bulldog Drummond Comes Back, The Story of Alexander Graham Bell, Comin' Round the Mountain* and *Tobacco Road* (as Grandma Lester).

TILGHMAN, Shirley M. (1946—). Canadian biochemist and educator. Born Sept 17, 1946, in Toronto, Ontario, Canada; Queen's University, BSc, 1968; Temple University, PhD in biochemistry, 1975. ❖ Was secondary schoolteacher in Sierra Leone (1968–70); was a fellow at National Institutes of Health (1975–77); was assistant professor at Temple University School of Medicine (1978–79); was a member of Institute for Cancer Research (1979–86); served as adjunct associate professor of human genetics and biochemistry at University of Pennsylvania (1980–86); served as Howard Prior Professor of Life Sciences at Princeton University (1986–2001), then became Princeton's 19th president (2001); was a leader in the field of molecular biology and one of the founding members of the National Advisory Council of the Human Genome Project Initiative for the National Institutes of Health.

TILL, Mamie (1921–2003). *See Mobley, Mamie Till.*

TILLER, Nadja (1929–). Viennese actress. Born Maria Nadja Tiller, Mar 16, 1929, in Vienna, Austria; m. Walter Giller (film actor), 1956. ❖ Named Miss Austria and made film debut in *Eroica* (1949); other films include *Illusion in Moll, Die Kaiserin von China, Ich suche dich, Sie, Hotel Adlon, Mozart, Griff nach den Sternen, Die Barrings, Ball im Savoy, Das Bad auf der Tenne, Friederike von Barring* (title role), *El Hakim, Le désordre et la nuit, Das Mädchen Rosemarie* (title role), *Labyrinth, Buddenbrooks, The Rough and the Smooth, L'Affaire Nina B.* (title role), *Anima nera, Lulu* (title role), *Du rififi à Paname, Poppies Are Also Flowers, Tendre voyou, L'Estate,* and *Lady Hamilton.*

TILLEY, Vesta (1864–1952). English performer and male impersonator. Name variations: Lady de Freece; Great Little Tilley; Pocket Sims Reeves; London Idol. Born Matilda Alice Powles in 1864 in Worcester, England; died Sept 16, 1952, in Monte Carlo (some sources cite London); dau. of a variety-hall manager who went by the name of Harry Ball; m. Sir Walter de Freece (music-hall owner and member of Parliament), in 1890 (died 1935). ❖ Probably the best-known music-hall performer in England of her day, made debut in Gloucester, at age 3 or 4, as "The Great Little Tilley"; at 10, made 1st London appearance; performed on London stage (1874–1920); in her signature top hat and tails, anticipated 1920s cabarets, entertaining audiences with faultless performances in roles she researched herself; appeared in *Sinbad* (1882) and *Beauty and the Beast* (1890); toured America (after 1898), earning critical acclaim in NY and Chicago; featured in the 1st royal command performance of music-hall entertainers (1912); became known for such songs as "Burlington Bertie," "Jolly Good Luck to the Girl Who Loves a Soldier," "Following in Father's Footsteps," "After the Ball," "The Army of Today's All Right," and "Algy—The Piccadilly Johnny with the Little Glass Eye." ❖ See also *Women in World History.*

TILLION, Germaine (b. 1907). French ethnologist. Pronunciation: TEE-YEE-OH. Born at Allègre (Haute-Loire), May 30, 1907; dau. of Lucien Tillion (d. 1925, magistrate) and Émilie (Cussac) Tillion (1875–1945, art historian); educated at Lycée Jeanne-d'Arc in Clermont-Ferrand and Institut d'Ethnologie (Sorbonne). ❖ Pioneering French ethnologist, a student of Algerian desert tribes, who was an early leader in the French Resistance during WWII, survived internment at the Ravensbrück concentration camp, wrote a germinal study of the camp system, and worked for peace during the Algerian War for Independence; lived with a Berber tribe in southeastern Algeria (1934–40); joined the Resistance (1940); arrested and imprisoned (1942–43); interned at the Ravensbrück concentration camp (1943–45); published 1st edition of *Ravensbrück* (1946); sent on a mission to Algeria and founded the Centres sociaux (1954–56); published *L'Algérie en 1957* and had secret meetings with Algerian leaders (1957); organized education for prisoners while at the Ministry of Education (1959–60); published *Le Harem et les cousins,* a study of the treatment of women in Mediterranean cultures (1967); published revised edition of *Ravensbrück,* responding to revisionist theses on the camp system (1973); ended teaching career at the École des Hautes Études en Sciences Sociales (1977); named president of the French Section of the Minority Rights Group (1978); published 3rd edition (rev.) of *Ravensbrück* (1988). ❖ See also *Women in World History.*

TILLOTSON, Queena (1896–1951). *See Mario, Queena.*

TILLY, Dorothy (1883–1970). American civil-rights activist. Born Dorothy Eugenia Rogers, June 30, 1883, in Hampton, Georgia; died of respiratory arrest, Mar 16, 1970, in Atlanta, Georgia; dau. of Richard Wade Rogers (Methodist minister) and Frances (Eubank) Rogers; graduate of Reinhardt College, 1899; Wesleyan College, AB, 1901; m. Milton Eben Tilly (chemical distributor), Nov 24, 1903 (died 1961); children: Eben Fletcher (b. 1904). ❖ Crusader to eliminate poverty and racism, served as secretary of children's work, Women's Missionary Society (1910s–20s); became member of executive committee, Association of Southern Women for the Prevention of Lynching (c. 1931); elected president of Georgia chapter of Committee on the Cause and Cure of War (1936); appointed member of Presidential Committee on Civil Rights by Harry Truman (1945); served as director of women's work for Southern Regional Council (late 1940s); also campaigned against Ku Klux Klan, resulting in the legislatures of Georgia and South Carolina passing antimask laws; founded Fellowship of the Concerned (1949); was a delegate to Israel, American Christian Palestine Committee (1949). ❖ See also *Women in World History.*

TILNEY, Agnes (1476–1545). *See Tylney, Agnes.*

TILNEY, Elizabeth (d. 1497). *See Tylney, Elizabeth.*

TILTON, Elizabeth (1834–c. 1896). Notorious American. Name variations: Mrs. Theodore Tilton; Lib Tilton. Born in 1834; died around 1896 or 1897; m. Theodore Tilton (a lecturer and journalist), in 1851; probably lived in Brooklyn, New York. ❖ Was at the center of a sensational 6-month adultery trial that began in 1875, because of her liaison with abolitionist preacher Henry Ward Beecher. ❖ See also Richard Wightman Fox, *Trials of Intimacy: Love and Loss in the Beecher-Tilton Scandal* (U. of Chicago Press, 1999); and *Women in World History.*

TILTON, Martha (1915—). American band singer and actress. Born Nov 14, 1915, in Corpus Christi, TX; m. an aerospace executive, 1953. ❖ Sang in Al Lippan's band; appeared on Benny Goodman's radio show (1940s); appeared in films *Sunny* (1941), *Swing Hostess* (1944), *Crime, Inc.* (1945), and *The Benny Goodman Story* (1956); began hosting "Liltin' Martha Tilton Time" on NBC Radio (1948); with Curt Massey, sang on CBS Radio (1951–59), then continued performing with him for another 5 years on NBC-TV; had such hit recordings as "And the Angels Sing," "Time After Time," "I'll Walk Alone" and "How Are Things in Glocca Mora." ❖ See also *Women in World History.*

TIMANOFF, Vera (1855–1942). Russian pianist. Born Feb 18, 1855, in Russia; died in 1942; studied with Anton Rubinstein, Carl Tausig, and Franz Liszt. ❖ A superb pianist, was *"la crème de la crème"* of all Liszt's students; never developed a significant concert career, however, perhaps because of stage fright; became a teacher in St. Petersburg. ❖ See also *Women in World History.*

TIMARETE (fl. 3rd c. BCE). Ancient Greek painter. Name variations: Timareta; Thamaris; Thamar. Pronunciation: teem-aret-AY. Probably born after the 90th Olympiad (420–417 BCE), perhaps in Syracuse in the 3rd century BCE; probably dau. of the artist Micon. ❖ The 1st woman painter in Pliny the Elder's list, which is given in reverse alphabetical order, painted a portrait of the goddess Artemis at Ephesus. ❖ See also *Women in World History.*

TIMBERLAKE, Margaret (c. 1799–1879). *See Eaton, Peggy.*

TIMMER, Marianne (1974—). Dutch speedskater. Born Maria Aaltje Timmer, Oct 3, 1974, in Sappemeer, Netherlands. ❖ Won a gold medal for the 1,500 meters, with a time of 1:57.58, and a gold medal for the 1,000 meters, with a time of 1:16.51, at Nagano Olympics (1998); won a gold medal for 1,000 meters at Torino Olympics (2006).

TIMMS, Michelle (1965—). Australian basketball player. Name variations: (nickname) Timmsy. Born June 28, 1965, in Australia; attended Burwood College. ❖ Point guard; began career in Australia's WNBL with the Bulleen Boomers (1984); was part of 4-straight WNBL championships while playing for Nunawading Spectres (1985–89); won 5th WNBL title with the Perth Breakers (1991); played in Italy and Germany; won a team bronze medal at Atlanta Olympics (1996) and a silver medal at Sydney Olympics (2000); played for Phoenix Mercury of WNBA (1997–2001), the 1st Australian to play professional basketball abroad; retired (2002). Named WNBL Player of the Year (1995, 1996).

TIMMS, Sally (1959—). English singer. Name variations: The Mekons. Born Nov 29, 1959, in Leeds, England. ❖ Joined Mekons (1985), and sang on celebrated album, *Fear and Whiskey* (1985), released in US as *Original Sin* (1989); with Mekons, released moderately successful albums, *The Edge of the World* (1986), *Honky Tonkin'* (1987) and *So Good It Hurts* (1988), the critically acclaimed *The Mekons Rock 'n' Roll* (1989) and *Journey to the End of the Night* (2000); also released solo albums, *Someone's Rocking My Dreamboat* (1988), *To the Land of Milk and Honey* (1995) and *Cowboy Sally's Twilight Laments...For Lost Buckaroos* (1999).

TIMOCHENKO, Alexandra (1972—). Ukrainian rhythmic gymnast. Name variations: Aleksandra Timoshenko. Born Feb 18, 1972, in Boguslav, Ukraine. ❖ Won European championships (1988, 1990); won a bronze medal at Seoul Olympics (1988) and a gold medal at Barcelona Olympics (1992), both in rhythmic gymnastics, all-around; at World championships, won 5 out of 6 golds (1989).

TIMOCLEA (c. 370–? BCE). Hero of Thebes. Born c. 370 BCE; sister of Theagenes of Thebes, who commanded his city's army against Philip II of Macedon at the battle of Chaeronea (338 BCE) and died there. ❖ Woman of Thebes whose act of revenge against a marauding soldier won the respect of Alexander the Great. ❖ See also *Women in World History.*

TIMOSHENKO, Aleksandra (1972—). *See Timochenko, Alexandra.*

TIMOSHKINA-SHERSTYUK, Natalya (1952—). Soviet handball player. Born May 25, 1952, in USSR. ❖ Won a gold medal at Montreal Olympics (1976) and a gold medal at Moscow Olympics (1980), both in team competition.

TIMOTHY, Ann (c. 1727–1792). Colonial American newspaper publisher and printer. Born Ann Donovan, c. 1727, probably in Charleston, South Carolina; died Sept 11, 1792, in Charleston; thought to be a descendant of Daniel Donovan (South Carolina settler); m. Peter Timothy (publisher), Dec 8, 1745 (died 1783); children: possibly 15, including Peter (d. 1770), Sarah, Robert, Elizabeth Anne (who m. Peter Valton), Frances Claudia (who m. Benjamin Lewis Merchant), and Benjamin Franklin Timothy; and 7 who died in infancy. ❖ The 2nd woman in South Carolina to become a newspaper publisher (the 1st was her mother-in-law Elizabeth Timothy), published the *Gazette of the State of South Carolina* (1783–92), which had started life as the *South-Carolina Gazette;* served as "Printer to the State" of South Carolina (1785–92). ❖ See also *Women in World History.*

TIMOTHY, Elizabeth (d. 1757). Colonial American newspaper publisher and printer. Born in the Netherlands; died c. May 1757 in Charleston, South Carolina; educated in the Netherlands; m. Lewis Timothy (publisher, died 1738); children: Peter (c. 1725–1782); Louisa (Mrs. James Richards); Charles (d. Sept 1739); Mary Elizabeth (Mrs. Abraham Bourquin); Joseph (d. Oct 1739); Catherine (Mrs. Theodore Trezevant). ❖ The 1st woman in America to publish a newspaper, immigrated to Philadelphia (1731); moved to Charleston, South Carolina (1733); following death of husband Lewis, was publisher of *South-Carolina Gazette* (1737–46), a paper that ranked among the most prominent in the colonies; was proprietor of book and stationery shop (1747); also published at least 20 books and pamphlets by other writers (1739–45). ❖ See also *Women in World History.*

TIMOXENA (fl. 2nd c.). Greek philosopher. Lived in Boetian town of Chaeronea; m. Plutarch (born c. 46, writer, lecturer, philosopher, priest of the Delphic Oracle who wrote *Parallel Lives*); children: 4 sons and daughter Timoxena who died in infancy. ❖ Plutarch claims she wrote *On the Love of Adornment,* written in the form of letter to a woman called Aristylla.

TIMRAVA (1867–1951). *See Slančikova, Božena.*

TINAYRE, Marcelle (c. 1870–1948). French writer and journalist. Pronunciation: tee-NAIR. Born Marguerite-Suzanne-Marcelle Chasteau at Tulle (Corrèze) in 1870 (or possibly 1871 or 1872); died at Grosrouvre, near Montfort-l'Amaury (Seine-et-Oise), Aug 23, 1948; dau. of Chasteau Fourichon (businessman [*négociant*]) and Louise Fourichon (c. 1850–1926, teacher); dau.-in-law of Marguerite Tinayre (1831–?); m. Julien Tinayre (1859–1923, engraver), 1889 (died 1923); children: Louise (b. 1890); Suzanne (1891–1896); Noël (b. 1896); Lucile (b. 1899). ❖ One of France's most praised and popular novelists during early 20th century whose numerous novels dealt especially with the effects of love on women's freedom and development; published *Avant l'amour* (Before Love), her 1st novel under her own name (1897); joined staff of Marguerite Durand's *La Fronde* (1898); received a prize for *Hellé* and was hailed by critics as one of the "new princesses" of literature (1900); published most praised work, *La Maison du péché* (The House of Sin, 1902); bought a country home (1905); denied the Legion of Honor after making some controversial remarks about it (1909); became editor of *La Nouvelle Revue féminine* (1933); received Prix Barthou from Académie Française (1938); was a daring feminist by the standards of the time, which in France were modest; writings include *La Rançon* (1898), *L'Oiseau d'orage* (1900), *La Vie amoureuse de François Barbazanges* (1904), *La Rebelle* (1905), *Le Paysage de Port-Royal* (1910), *Napoléon et la reine Hortense* (1910), *Madeleine au miroir: Journal d'une femme* (1912), *Perséphone* (1920), *Les Lampes voilées: Laurence-Valentin* (1921), *Le Bouclier d'Alexandre* (1922), *Un Drame de famille* (1925), *L'Ennemi intime* (1931), *Gérard et Delphine I: La Porte rouge* (1936) and *Gérard et Delphine II: Le Rendez-vous du soir* (1938). ❖ See also *Women in World History.*

TINAYRE, Marguerite (1831–?). French educator and political radical. Name variations: (pseudonym) Jules Paty. Pronunciation: tee-NAIR. Born Marguerite-Victoire Guerrier at Issoire (Puy-de-Dôme) on Mar 6, 1831; date of death unknown; married a notary's clerk named Tinayre (died 1871); children: 1 daughter and 4 sons, including engraver Julien (1859–1923, who m. novelist Marcelle Tinayre), and painter (Jean-Paul-)Louis (b. 1861). ❖ Licensed as an elementary teacher (1856); under pen name Jules Paty, published 2 turgid novels, *La Marguerite* (1864) and *Un Rêve de femme;* founded the Société des Équitables de Paris, a consumer cooperative (1867); during Franco-Prussian War and the siege of Paris (July 1870–Jan 1871), continued advocating left-wing causes; joined the revolt (Mar–May 1871) of the Paris Commune against the government and was named inspector of girls' schools in the 12th arrondissement; after husband was shot and killed, was in exile in Switzerland, Saxony, and Hungary as a governess and teacher (1871–79); condemned *in absentia* to deportation (1874); sentence remitted (1879); returned to Paris (1880). ❖ See also *Women in World History.*

TINDALL, Gillian (1938—). British novelist and biographer. Born May 4, 1938, in London, England; m. R. G. Lansdown. ❖ Novels include *No Name in the Street* (1959), *The Edge of the Paper* (1963), *The Youngest* (1967), *Fly Away Home* (1971), *The Intruder* (1979), *To the City* (1987); nonfiction includes *The Born Exile: George Gissing* (1974), *The Fields Beneath: The History of One English Village* (1977) and *City of Gold: The Biography of Bombay* (1982); also published essays and reviews for magazines and journals. Won Mary Elgin Prize and Somerset Maugham Prize for *Fly Away Home.*

TING LING (1904–1985). *See Ding Ling.*

TINGLEY, Katherine (1847–1929). American theosophist leader. Name variations: Katherine Westcott; Katherine Westcott Tingley. Born Katherine Augusta Westcott, July 6, 1847, in Newbury, Massachusetts; died from injuries sustained in auto accident, July 11, 1929, in Visingsö, Sweden; dau. of James P. L. Westcott (merchant and hotelkeeper) and Susan Ordway (Chase) Westcott; m. Richard Henry Cook (printer), 1867 (div. 1867); m. George W. Parent (railroad investigator), c. 1880 (div. c. 1887); m. Philo Buchanan Tingley (mechanical engineer), April 25, 1888. ❖ Founded Society for Mercy (1887) and "Do-Good Mission" in Manhattan (1890s); was named Outer Head of Esoteric Section, Theosophical Society in America (1896); toured with Theosophical Society world crusade (1896); founded Point Loma Theosophical community in California (1897); founded International Brotherhood League (1897); formed War Relief Corps (1898). ❖ See also *Women in World History.*

TINKER, Alice (1886–1968). *See McLean, Alice.*

TINNÉ, Alexandrine (1839–1869). Dutch explorer in Africa. Name variations: Alexandrine Tinne. Born Alexandrine Petronella Francina Tinné at The Hague, the Netherlands, Oct 17, 1839; killed Aug 1, 1869; dau. of Philip F. Tinné (Dutch merchant) and Baroness Van Steengracht-Capellan (dau. of Admiral van Capellan). ❖ With death of father when she was 5, became one of the richest heiresses in the country; devoted fortune and energies to the cause of geographical discovery, to report on the slave trade, and to help the oppressed people of the "dark continent"; in Egypt, ascended the Nile, a trek that saw the deaths of her mother and aunt (1860s); also made trips to Algeria, Tunisia, and additional locations of the Mediterranean; began her last and fatal expedition (Jan 1869), departing with a caravan from Tripoli intending to reach the upper Nile; en route from Murzuk to Ghat (Aug 1), was murdered along with her 3 European attendants. ❖ See also *Women in World History*.

TINSLEY, Annie Turner (1808–1885). British poet and novelist. Name variations: Mrs. Charles Tinsley. Born Anne Turner in 1808 in Preston, Lancaster, England; died 1885; dau. of Thomas Milner Turner; mother's maiden name was Carruthers; m. Charles Tinsley, 1833; children: 6. ❖ Wrote *The Children of the Mint* (1840), *The Priest of the Nile* (1840), *Lays for the Thoughtful and Solitary* (1848), *Margaret* (1853) and *Women as They Are, by One of Them* (1854).

TINSLEY, Mrs. Charles (1808–1885). See Tinsley, Annie Turner.

TINSLEY, Pauline (1928—). English operatic soprano. Born Mar 23, 1928, in Wigan, England; studied with Dillon in Manchester and Joan Cross at London Opera Center, as well as with Keeler, Henderson, and Turner. ❖ Made debut in London in Rossini's *Desdemona* (1951); joined Welsh National Opera and sang Elsa in Wagner's *Lohengrin*, Susanna in Mozart's *Le nozze di Figaro*, title roles in *Aïda* and *Turandot*, and Lady Macbeth in Verdi's *Macbeth*; joined Sadler's Wells Opera (1963), where she sang the Countess in *Figaro*, Fiordiligi in *Così fan tutte*, Donna Elvira in *Don Giovanni*, Queen Elizabeth in Donizetti's *Maria Stuarda*, and Leonore in Beethoven's *Fidelio*; toured widely, performing in Berlin, Hamburg, Amsterdam, Zurich, Verona and NY; was considered particularly memorable as Lady Billows in Britten's *Albert Herring* at Covent Garden (1989); other repertory roles include Queen of the Night, Anna Bolena, Leonora (in *Trovatore* and *Forza*), Brunnhilde, Zerlina, Donna Anna, Kundry, Kostelnicka and Elektra. ❖ See also *Women in World History*.

TIOMKIN, Albertina (1896–1967). See Rasch, Albertina.

TIOURINA, Elena (1971—). Russian volleyball player. Name variations: Elena or Yelena Batoukhtina or Batukhtina. Born April 12, 1971, in Sverdlovsk, USSR. ❖ At Barcelona Olympics, won a silver medal in team competition (1992); won a team silver medal at Sydney Olympics (2000) and a team silver medal at Athens Olympics (2004); placed 3rd at World championships (2002).

TIPO, Maria (1931—). Italian pianist. Born in Naples, 1931; dau. of Ersilia Cavallo, pianist who gave the Naples premiere of Tchaikovsky 1st Piano Concerto. ❖ Known for her Romantic performances, studied with mother; won 1st prize in Geneva Piano Competition (1948); toured US (1955) to great success; in Europe, built up a reputation with stylish performances of Mozart, Bach and Scarlatti. ❖ See also *Women in World History*.

TIPPER, Constance (1894–1995). English metallurgist. Born Constance Figg Elam in 1894; died Dec 14, 1995, in Penrith, in northwest England; obtained doctorate from Cambridge University; m. George Tipper (geologist), 1928 (died 1947). ❖ During WWII, created the "Tipper test," a way to determine the brittleness of metal, to keep the British merchant marine's Liberty vessels afloat. ❖ See also *Women in World History*.

TIPPER, Elizabeth (fl. late 17th c.). British poet. Born Elizabeth Tipper; fl. in 1690s in England; dau. of William Tipper and Elizabeth Tipper. ❖ Wrote *The Pilgrim's Viaticum: or, The Destitute, but not Forlorn* (1698).

TIPTON, Billy (1914–1989). Cross-dressing American jazz pianist and saxophonist. Born Dorothy Lucille Tipton in Oklahoma City, OK, Dec 29, 1914; died in Spokane, Washington, Jan 21, 1989; dau. of George Tipton (aviator) and Reggie Tipton; studied organ, piano, and saxophone in school; married at least 5 times, including Betty Cox and Kitty Kelly. ❖ Learned to play the piano, organ, and sax, but quickly concluded that a woman could never be successful in the jazz world; assuming the persona of a man, lent tenor voice to a group known as the Banner Cavaliers; performed with the Jack Teagarden, Russ Carlyle, and Scott Cameron bands; formed the Billy Tipton Trio (1951) and released 2 albums—*Sweet Georgia Brown* and *Billy Tipton Plays Hi-Fi on Piano*. ❖ See also Diane Middlebrook, *Suits Me: The Double Life of Billy Tipton* (1998); and *Women in World History*.

TIRCONNELL, queen of. See MacDonald, Finula (fl. 1569–1592).

TIRIKATENE-SULLIVAN, Whetu (1932—). New Zealand politician. Name variations: Whetu Tirikatene, Whetu Tirikatene Sullivan, Whetu Sullivan. Born Whetu Tirikatene, Jan 9, 1932, in Ratana Pa, NZ; dau. of Eruera Tirikatene (MP); m. Denis Sullivan (lecturer in physics). ❖ One of the longest serving members in the New Zealand House of Representatives, male or female, represented Labour for Southern Maori (1967–96); was the 1st woman to give birth while an MP (1970); appointed Minister for Tourism (1972), becoming the 1st Maori woman Cabinet minister.

TIRLEA-MANOLACHE, Ionela (1976—). Romanian runner. Name variations: Ionela Manolache. Born Feb 9, 1976, in Romania. ❖ Won gold medal for 200 meters at World Indoor championships (1999); won a silver medal for 400-meter hurdles at Athens Olympics (2004); at Super Grand Prix, placed 1st in 400 meters (2003) and 400-meter hurdles (2004).

TIROL, countess of. See Margaret Maultasch (1318–1369).

TIRZAH. Biblical woman. Youngest of the 5 daughters of Zelophehad, of the Manasseh tribe; sister of Milcah, Mahlah, Noah and Hoglah. ❖ After father died without any male heirs, joined with her 4 older sisters to request permission from Moses to inherit their father's property (Moses granted their request, stipulating only that the sisters marry within their father's tribe; his judgment concerning the inheritance eventually became general law).

TISSOT, Alice (1895–1971). French stage and screen actress. Born Jan 1, 1895, in Paris, France; died May 5, 1971, in Paris. ❖ Appeared with Fernandel in several movies; made over 125 films, including *Women in Green Hats, Ignace, The Glory of Faith, Last Desire* and *Mirages of Paris*.

TITBOALD, Anne (c. 1825–1896). See Ward, Anne.

TITCUME, Natalie (1975—). Australian softball player. Born Dec 6, 1975, in Sydney, Australia; attended Australian College of Physical Education. ❖ Won a team bronze medal at Sydney Olympics (2000) and a team silver medal at Athens Olympics (2004).

TITHERADGE, Madge (1887–1961). Australian-English actress. Born July 2, 1887, in Melbourne, Australia; died Nov 14, 1961, in Fetcham, Surrey, England; m. Charles Quartermaine (div.); m. Edgar Park (died). ❖ Made stage debut in London in *The Water Babies* (1902); starred on the London stage for over 30 years, in such plays as *Trilby, Toddles, French as He is Spoke, Faust, King Henry V, Bevis, Bardelys the Magnificent, The Garden of Allah* and *Bluebeard's Eighth Wife*; Broadway appearances include *The Butterfly on the Wheel* and *The Patriot*; made films (1919–20).

TITLIC, Ana (1952—). Yugoslavian handball player. Born June 13, 1952, in Yugoslavia. ❖ At Moscow Olympics, won a silver medal in team competition (1980).

TITO, Jovanka Broz (1924—). Croatian revolutionary fighter and first lady of Yugoslavia. Name variations: Jovanka Broz; Jovanka Budisavljevic Broz; Jovanka Budisavljevic. Born Jovanka Budisavljevic, Dec 7, 1924, in rural Croatia near Bosnian border; dau. of Miko Budisavljevic (laborer); attended University of Belgrade; became 3rd wife of Josip Broz Tito (1892–1980, president of Yugoslavia), on April 25, 1952 (sep. 1977). ❖ At 16, joined Communist underground (1940); became a private in the partisan army (1942) and fought in guerilla campaigns in the mountains; contracted typhus and was brought to the field hospital at headquarters of commander in chief, Josip Broz Tito; assuming a more subordinate role after her marriage, was first lady of Yugoslavia (1953–80); hailed as attractive, elegant and vivacious, traveled often with Tito and attended numerous public functions; furthered her own interrupted education and was particularly involved in the issue of women's rights; after husband died, was prevented from inheriting his wealth; when Slobodan Milosevic was in power, was kept under virtual house arrest, watched by secret police and denied visitors; attended a wreath-laying ceremony at the memorial to husband in Belgrade (2000). Josip Broz Tito was 1st married to Pelagia Belousova (or Belousnova), then Herta Hass. ❖ See also *Women in World History*.

TITOVA, Ludmila (1962—). Russian speedskater. Name variations: Lyudmila Titova. Born Sept 26, 1962, in USSR. ❖ Won a gold medal for 500 meters and a silver medal for 1,000 meters at Grenoble Olympics (1968); won a bronze medal for 500 meters at Sapporo Olympics (1972); won ISU sprint championships (1970); at European championships, won a silver medal for small allround (1971).

TITUS, Shirley Carew (1892–1967). American nurse. Born Shirley Carew Titus, April 28, 1892, in Alameda, CA; died Mar 21, 1967, in San Francisco, CA; dau. of Sarah (Simmons) Titus and Henry Titus; graduate of St. Luke's Hospital School of Nursing in San Francisco, 1915; Columbia University Teachers College, BS, 1920; University of Michigan, MA, 1930; lived with Mary Dodd Giles (colleague from Vanderbilt). ❖ Became director of the nursing school and nursing service at University of Michigan (1925); as a professor and a dean of Vanderbilt University's new nursing school, encouraged the incorporation of liberal arts in nursing studies; as executive director of the California Nurses' Association (CNA, 1942–56), led the 1st collective bargaining for nurses and successfully pushed for nurses rights, including the implementation of a 40-hour work week.

TIY (c. 1400–1340 BCE). Queen of Egypt. Name variations: Taia, Teye, Tii, Tiye, and Tiyi. Pronunciation: Tee. Born c. 1400 BCE to a leading family from Akhmim, a provincial town in Middle Egypt; died 1340 BCE, possibly from plague; was 1st buried at the new capital city of Akhetaten (Tell el-Amarna) which her son had built and dedicated to his sole god, the sun disk or Aten; later reburied in Valley of the Kings at Thebes, probably during reign of Tutankhamun; dau. of mother Tjuya (chief of female celebrants in temple of Amun at Karnak) and father Yuya (master of royal stud farm and lieutenant general of royal charioteers); common-born wife of the pharaoh Amenhotep III (Amenophis); mother-in-law of Nefertiti; children: princesses Satamun, Isis, Henuttaneb, and Nebetah, and princes Thutmose (died young) and Amenhotep IV (known as Akhenaten). ❖ Ancient queen who was the highly influential wife of the pharaoh Amenhotep III, the world's most powerful monarch in the 1st half of the 14th century BCE, and mother of the enigmatic monotheistic pharaoh Akhenaten; universally deemed by scholars as energetic, bright, and imperious as well as beautiful, was the 1st queen to create a position more powerful than that of King's Mother; was worshipped as a goddess with her own temples during her life; her power and presence at court did not end with the death of her husband, but continued well into the reign of her remarkable son. Up to her time, no queen was so frequently depicted in art at the side of her husband. ❖ See also Barbara S. Lesko, *The Remarkable Women of Ancient Egypt* (3rd ed., B. C. Scribe, 1996); and *Women in World History.*

TIYE or TIYI (c. 1400–1340 BCE). See Tiy.

TIZARD, Catherine (1931—). New Zealand educator and politician. Name variations: Dame Cath Tizard. Born Catherine Anne Maclean on April 4, 1931; only child of Neil Maclean and Helen Maclean (both Scottish immigrants); educated at Waharoa Primary School, Matamata College, University of Auckland (BA); m. Robert James Tizard, in 1951 (div. 1983); children: Anne Francis, Linda Catherine, Nigel Robert and Judith Tizard (politician). ❖ Lecturer in zoology at Auckland University who was the 1st woman to be elected mayor of Auckland and the 1st woman to be appointed governor-general of New Zealand; grew up in a working-class community in New Zealand; met and became engaged to Robert (Bob) Tizard during the 2nd year of her Arts Degree at Auckland University; married (1951) and had 4 children within 6 years; left in charge of home and family, while husband's political career flourished and he spent much of his time in Wellington (capital of New Zealand); returned to university and took courses in zoology (1961); eased herself into university teaching; took an interest in civic affairs; elected to the Auckland City Council (1971); made several tv appearances and widely broadened her public-speaking experience; elected mayor of Auckland, New Zealand's largest city—the 1st Labour mayor and the 1st woman to hold the post (1983); re-elected twice and, during 3rd term of office, was offered the position of governor-general of New Zealand (1990), an appointment she held until Mar 1996. Named Dame commander of the British Empire (DBE, 1985); received Freedom of the City of London (1990); named Dame Grand Cross of the Order of St. Michael and St. George (GCMG, 1990) and Dame Grand Cross of the Royal Victorian Order (GCVO, 1995); received Companion of the Queen's Service Order (QSO, 1996). ❖ See also *Women in World History.*

TIZARD, Judith (1956—). New Zealand politician. Born Judith Ngaire Tizard, Jan 3, 1956, in Avondale, NZ; dau. of Robert James Tizard (politician) and Cath Tizard, 1st woman governor-general of New Zealand. ❖ Elected Labour MP for Panmure for 43 and 44th Parliament (1990–96), then Auckland Central (1996), for 45th–47th Parliament; served as associate minister for Arts, Culture, and Heritage and associate minister of Commerce.

TJIPTAWAN, Mia (1979—). *See Audina, Mia.*

TJOERHOM, Linda (1979—). Norwegian biathlete. Name variations: Linda Tjørhom or Tjörhom. Born Sept 13, 1979, in Stavanger, Norway. ❖ Won a silver medal for 4 x 7.5 km relay at Salt Lake City Olympics (2002).

TJÖRHOM, Linda (1979—). *See Tjoerhom, Linda.*

TJUGUM, Heidi (1973—). Norwegian handball player. Born Heidi Maire Tjugum, Sept 5, 1973, in Drammen, Norway. ❖ Won a team silver medal at Barcelona Olympics (1992) and a team bronze at Sydney Olympics (2000).

TKACHENKO, Marina (1965—). Soviet basketball player. Born Aug 29, 1965, in USSR. ❖ At Barcelona Olympics, won a gold medal in team competition (1992).

TKACHENKO, Nadezhda (1948—). Soviet pentathlete. Born Sept 19, 1948, in USSR. ❖ At Moscow Olympics, won a gold medal in pentathlon (1980).

TKACIKOVA-TACOVA, Adolfina (1939—). Czech gymnast. Born April 19, 1939, in Czechoslovakia. ❖ Won a silver medal at Rome Olympics (1960) and a silver medal at Tokyo Olympics (1964), both in team allaround.

TLALI, Miriam (1933—). South African novelist and short-story writer. Born 1933 in Doornfontein, Transvaal, South Africa. ❖ First black woman to publish novel in English in South Africa; championed woman writers and served on board of Skotaville Press; worked as editor of women's literary magazine *Straight Ahead International;* later works focus on experiences of black women in a racist, sexist society; works include *Muriel at Metropolitan* (1975), *Amandla* (1981), *Mihloti* (1984), and *Footprints in the Quag: Stories and Dialogues from Soweto* (1989); co-founded *Staffrider* magazine for which she wrote a regular column.

TLC.
See Lopes, Lisa (1971–2002).
See Thomas, Rozonda (1971—).
See Watkins, Tionne (1970—).

TOA, Ngati (1937—). *See Grace, Patricia.*

TOBEY, Beatrice (d. 1993). American artist. Name variations: B. Szanton. Born Beatrice Szanton in New York, NY; died June 19, 1993, in New York, NY; dau. of Viennese immigrants; attended Art Students League, studying with Yasuo Kuniyoshi; m. Barney Tobey (cartoonist), 1928 (died 1989); children: David and Natasha. ❖ Developed an Expressionistic style and exhibited in NY galleries; contributed 11 covers to *The New Yorker* (1959–69), signing them B. Szanton.

TOBIN, Genevieve (1899–1995). American stage and screen actress. Born Nov 29, 1899, in New York, NY; died July 31, 1995, in Pasadena, CA; sister of George Tobin (actor) and Vivian Tobin (actress); m. William Keighley (director), 1938 (died 1984). ❖ Made stage debut as a child (1912); played leads in such plays as *Little Old New York, Dear Sir,* and *50 Million Frenchmen* (1920–30); made film debut in *A Lady Surrenders* (1930), followed by *One Hour With You, Cohens and Kellys in Hollywood, The Petrified Forest, The Great Gambini, Zaza* and *No Time for Comedy,* among others.

TOBIN, Vivian (1902–2002). American actress. Born Aug 12, 1902, in New York, NY; died Aug 6, 2002, in Rancho Palos, CA; sister of George Tobin (actor) and Genevieve Tobin (actress); m. Karl O. Von Hagen. ❖ Appeared on Broadway; made film debut in *The Avalanche* (1915), followed by *The Sign of the Cross, Kennedy's Castle, Stage Fright* and *Home Work,* among others.

TOCCO, Magdalena-Theodora (fl. mid-1400s). First wife of Constantine XI. Dau. of Leonardo Tocco; 1st wife of Constantine XI Paleologus, emperor of Nicaea (r. 1448–1453).

TOCHENOVA, Klavdiya (1921—). Soviet track-and-field athlete. Born Nov 16, 1921, in USSR. ❖ At Helsinki Olympics, won a bronze medal in the shot put (1952).

TOC-ME-TO-NE (1844–1891). *See Winnemucca, Sarah.*

TOD, Isabella (1836–1896). Irish feminist campaigner and journalist. Born Isabella Maria Susan Tod in Edinburgh, Scotland, May 18, 1836; died in Belfast, Ireland, Dec 8, 1896; dau. of James Banks Tod and Maria Isabella (Waddell) Tod; never married; no children. ❖ First came to public prominence with her paper, "On advanced education for girls of the upper and middle classes" (1867); also championed the campaign to amend the Married Women's Property Act; was active in the movement to repeal the Contagious Diseases Act; was vice-president of the British Women's Temperance Association (1877–92); spoke at meetings up and down the country and produced a stream of articles for Irish newspapers and journals; was "the outstanding advocate of women's rights" in the critical last 4 decades of the 19th century. ❖ See also *Women in World History.*

TODD, Ann (1909–1993). English stage, tv, and screen actress. Born Jan 24, 1909, in Hartford, Cheshire, England; died May 6, 1993, in London; m. Victor Neill Malcolm (grandson of Lillie Langtry, div.); m. Nigel Tangye (div. 1949); m. David Lean (director), 1949 (div. 1957). ❖ Made stage debut (1928), later appearing as Lady Macbeth with the Old Vic; achieved international prominence in film *The Seventh Veil* (1945); other films include *South Riding, The Paradine Case, Bulldog Drummond, Madeleine, Breaking the Sound Barrier, Time Without Pity* and *The Human Factor.* ❖ See also autobiography *The Eighth Veil* (1980).

TODD, Ann (1931—). American actress. Name variations: Ann E. Todd. Born Anne Todd Mayfield, Aug 26, 1931, in Denver, CO. ❖ Child star, made film debut as Toto in *Zaza* (1939), followed by *The Zero Hour, Intermezzo, Destry Rides Again, The Blue Bird, All This and Heaven Too, Brigham Young, Blood and Sand, How Green Was My Valley, Kings Row, Margie,* and *Three Daring Daughters,* among many others; retired from film (1951).

TODD, E. L. (fl. early 1900s). American airplane inventor. Name variations: E. Lillian Todd. ❖ Was the 1st woman to invent an airplane, but never learned to fly; 1st worked as stenographer in US Patent Office, Washington, DC; designed an airplane built by Wittemann Brothers that was exhibited at aero show at Madison Square Garden (1906); organized 1st Junior Aero Club in US (1908); had working model of a collapsible airplane exhibited at air show at Brighton Beach racetrack, Brooklyn, NY (1908); had test flight across Garden City aviation field of a biplane she had built, which was piloted by Didier Masson (NY, 1910).

TODD, Irene (1901–1981). *See Baird, Irene.*

TODD, Mabel Loomis (1858–1932). American poet, editor, and writer of travel books. Born Mabel Loomis, Nov 10, 1858, in Cambridge, Massachusetts; died Oct 14, 1932; dau. of Eben J. Loomis (poet-astronomer) and Mary Alden (Wilder) Loomis (direct descendant of John Alden); graduate of Georgetown Seminary; studied music and painting in Boston; married David Todd (professor of astronomy and director of observatory at Amherst), 1879; children: Millicent Todd Bingham (1880–1968, m. Walter Van Dyke Bingham). ❖ Accompanied professor-husband to Japan to serve as his assistant, while observing the total eclipse of the sun (1887), then wrote of the expedition for several American newspapers and magazines; with husband, traveled to West Africa to view another eclipse (1889), then followed the sun for almost 20 years—to Tripoli, Dutch East Indies, Chile, and Russia—while continuing to write of experiences; while living in Amherst, cultivated a relationship with Emily Dickinson and became romantically involved with Emily's brother Austin; following Dickinson's death, edited and published 2 volumes of Dickinson's poetry (which included biographical prefaces). ❖ See also Polly Longsworth, *Austin and Mabel: The Amherst Affair and Love Letters of Austin Dickinson and Mabel Loomis Todd* (Holt, 1984); and *Women in World History.*

TODD, Margaret G. (1859–1918). Scottish physician and novelist. Name variations: (pseudonym) Graham Travers. Born Margaret Georgina Todd, 1859, in Glasgow, Scotland; died Sept 3, 1918, in London, England; dau. of James Cameron Todd; lived with Sophia Jex-Blake (physician). ❖ Studied in Edinburgh, Glasgow, and Berlin before entering Edinburgh School of Medicine for Women; graduated 1894 and became assistant to Sophia Jex-Blake with whom she lived from 1895; practiced medicine intermittently after 1895; wrote *Mona Maclean, Medical Student* (1892), *Fellow Travellers* (1896), *Windyhaugh* (1898), *The Way of Escape* (1902), *Growth* (1906), and *The Life of Sophia Jex-Blake* (1918).

TODD, Marion Marsh (1841–post 1913). American lawyer, political activist, and writer. Born Mar 1841 in Plymouth, Chenango Co., New York; lived until at least 1914, with no record available of her death; dau. of Abner Kneeland Marsh (Universalist preacher) and Dolly Adelia (Wales) Marsh; educated at Ypsilanti State Normal School (now Eastern Michigan University) and Hastings Law College, San Francisco; m. Benjamin Todd (reformist lawyer), 1868 (died 1880); children: Lula Todd. ❖ Pioneer in women's rights and reformist politics, gave up teaching to devote her time to public lectures on temperance, women's suffrage, and economic reform; moved with family to California (late 1870s), where she enrolled in Hastings Law College in San Francisco; admitted to California bar (1881), opened a law practice in San Francisco; elected a member of the Greenback Labor Party's platform committee (1882); received the party's nomination for state attorney general, making her one of the 1st women to run for statewide office; wrote political works, including *Protective Tariff Delusions* (1886) and *Railways of Europe and America* (1893); also wrote 3 novels that protested capitalist exploitation, human profligacy, and religious hypocrisy: *Rachel's Pitiful History* (1895), *Phillip: A Romance* (1900) and *Claudia* (1902). ❖ See also *Women in World History.*

TODD, Mary (1818–1882). *See Lincoln, Mary Todd.*

TODD, Olga Taussky (1906–1995). Austrian-American mathematician. Name variations: Olga Taussky-Todd. Born Aug 30, 1906; died in Pasadena, California, Oct 7, 1995. ❖ Trained in number theory, worked with David Hilbert at the University of Göttingen; during the Nazis' early years in power, immigrated to America around the same time as other members of the Hilbert school, including Emmy Noether.

TODD, Thelma (1905–1935). American actress. Born July 29, 1905, in Lawrence, MA; died, possibly of carbon monoxide poisoning, Dec 16, 1935, in Santa Monica, CA. ❖ Sometimes called the "Vamping Venus" or "The Hot Toddy," starred with Marx Brothers in *Monkey Business* (1931) and *Horse Feathers* (1932); also appeared in comedy shorts and dramatic feature films, including *Vamping Venus* (1928), *The Haunted House* (1928), *Naughty Baby* (1929), *Follow Thru* (1930), *Swanee River* (1931), *Aloha* (1931), *The Maltese Falcon* (1931), *This is the Night* (1932), *Klondike* (1932), *Sitting Pretty* (1933), *Counsellor-at-Law* (1933), *Hips Hips Hooray* (1934), *Palooka* (1934), *Bottoms Up* (1934) and *The Bohemian Girl* (1936); at 30, was at the height of her career when her body was found in her garage slumped over the steering wheel of her parked car. Though it appears clear that Todd's death was a murder and not a suicide, the exact circumstances of her last moments have never been determined. ❖ See also *Women in World History.*

TODI, Luiza Rosa (1753–1833). Portuguese mezzo-soprano. Born Luiza Rosa Aguiar in Setubal, Portugal, Jan 9, 1753; died in Lisbon, Oct 1, 1833. ❖ Was an actress at 15 before becoming a pupil of Lisbon conductor Davide Perez; sang in London (1772) and to great success in Madrid (1777); was a court singer in Berlin (1780); provoked a famous rivalry with Gertrud Mara (1783). ❖ See also *Women in World History.*

TODORA. *Variant of Theodora.*

TODOROVA, Rita (1958—). Bulgarian rower. Born Aug 18, 1958, in Bulgaria. ❖ At Moscow Olympics, won a silver medal in coxed fours (1980).

TODTEN, Jaqueline (1954—). East German track-and-field athlete. Born May 29, 1954, in East Germany. ❖ At Munich Olympics, won a silver medal in the javelin throw (1972).

TOETSCHNIG, Brigitte (1954—). *See Totschnig, Brigitte.*

TOFANA (1653–1723). Italian poisoner. Name variations: La Toffania. Born in 1653; died in 1723. ❖ Supplied poison to high-born ladies who wished to get rid of unwanted husbands, facilitating as many as 600 deaths before she was discovered and tried by the authorities. ❖ See also *Women in World History.*

TOFFANA *See Tofana.*

TOFTE, Brit. *See Pettersen, Brit.*

TOFTS, Catherine (c. 1685–1756). English operatic soprano. Name variations: Katherine Tofts. Born c. 1685; died in 1756 in Venice; m. John Smith (British consul to Venice). ❖ One of the earliest English prima donnas, sang in concert (1703–04); sang at Drury Lane (1705–09), in *Arsinoe* (1705), *Rosamond, Love's Triumph,* and other operas, and also in such pasticcios as *Camilla, Thomyris* and *Phyrrus and Demetrius;* retired to Venice (1709); a rival of Margherita de l'Épine, was the 1st English-born singer to perform Italian opera in England, and her pleasant voice and graceful stage presence was admired by such critics as Cibber and Burney. ❖ See also *Women in World History*.

TOGURI, Iva (1916—). American-born broadcaster. Name variations: Tokyo Rose; Ann; Orphan Annie; Iva Ikuko Toguri d'Aquino. Born Iva Ikuko Toguri in Los Angeles, California, July 4, 1916; dau. of June Toguri (shopkeeper and importer) and Fumi (Iimuro) Toguri; graduate of University of California, Los Angeles, 1940; m. Felipe d'Aquino, in Tokyo, 1945; children: 1 (stillborn). ❖ American-born woman of Japanese descent, known as Tokyo Rose, who broadcast over Tokyo Radio during World War II and later was wrongly convicted of treason to America; responded to a Japanese aunt's invitation to visit the old country (1941); after bombing of Pearl Harbor, had to register as a foreign citizen; pressured by the Japanese authorities to declare herself a Japanese citizen, refused to do so; worked as a translator and typist at Japanese news agency (1942–43); was recruited by Allied prisoners of war to work on a propaganda radio show with Tokyo Radio (in their attempts to vitiate the propaganda); cooperated with the prisoners of war in their efforts to damage, rather than boost, Japanese propaganda; introduced light entertainment shows, with words written by one of the prisoners of war, for Tokyo Radio (1943–45); as a scapegoat, was singled out as Tokyo Rose, though she was only one among the 20 or more female English-speaking broadcasters; convicted of treason, though some of the government's witnesses were involved in perjury and a cover-up, was a prisoner of the US government (1949–56); became a shopkeeper in Chicago (1956); was granted a full pardon from President Gerald Ford (1977). ❖ See also Masayo Duus, *Tokyo Rose: Orphan of the Pacific* (trans. by Peter Duus, Harper & Row, 1979); Russell Warren Howe, *The Hunt for Tokyo Rose* (Madison, 1990); and *Women in World History*.

TOHI TE URURANGI, Ngatai (1844–1928). See *Tapsell, Ngatai Tohi Te Ururangi*.

TOKAREVA, Viktoria (1937—). Russian cinematographer, scriptwriter and short-story writer. Name variations: Viktoriia Samoilovna Tókareva. Born Nov 20, 1937, in Leningrad, USSR; attended Moscow Institute of Cinematography. ❖ A cinematographer by trade, came to prominence with 1st story "A Day Without Lives" (1964); other popular stories include "Centre of Gravity," "Nothing Special," and "Dry Run"; also wrote screenplays, tv scripts and the novella *A Long Day*.

TOKLAS, Alice B. (1877–1967). American companion of Gertrude Stein. Born Alice Babette Toklas in San Francisco, California, on April 30, 1877; died Mar 7, 1967; 1st child and only dau. of Ferdinand Toklas (wholesaler in dry goods) and Emma (Levinsky) Toklas (died 1897); attended Miss Lake's School for Girls; studied music at Washington University; lived with Gertrude Stein for 39 years. ❖ Met Gertrude Stein (1907); had a strong nature and a great deal of sway over Stein, despite her unassuming presence. ❖ See also *Women in World History*.

TOKOUN, Elena (1974—). Russian water-polo player. Born Mar 15, 1974, in USSR. ❖ Won a team bronze medal at Sydney Olympics (2000).

TOKYO ROSE (b. 1916). See *Toguri, Iva*.

TOLKACHEVA, Irina (1982—). Russian synchronized swimmer. Born Nov 29, 1982, in Russia. ❖ At World championships, won team gold medals (2001, 2003); won a team gold medal at Athens Olympics (2004).

TOLKOUNOVA, Irina (1971—). Russian water-polo player. Born June 2, 1971, in USSR. ❖ Won a team bronze medal at Sydney Olympics (2000).

TOLSTAIA, Natalia (1888–1963). See *Krandievskaya, Natalia*.

TOLSTAIA, Tatiana (1951—). See *Tolstaya, Tatyana*.

TOLSTAYA, Natalia (1888–1963). See *Krandievskaya, Natalia*.

TOLSTAYA, Tatyana (1951—). Russian short-story writer. Name variations: Tania or Tatiana Mikhailovna Tolstaia. Born Tatyana Mikhailovna Tolstaya, 1951, in St. Petersburg, Russia; dau. of Nikita Tolstoy (physicist) and Ina Lozinskaya (dau. of Mikhail Lozinsky, noted translator); granddau. of Natalia Krandievskaya (writer) and A. N. Tolstoy (writer); great-granddau. of Anastasiia Krandievskaya (writer); sister of Mikhail Tolstoy (legislator) and Natalya Tolstaya (philologist and expert on German literature); graduate of Department of Philology, Leningrad University; married. ❖ Worked at the Nauka Publishing House in the Oriental Literature Department for 8 years; gained fame

in Russia with her 1st story (1983); with husband, moved to US to teach creative writing and Russian literature (1988); stories appeared in a collected translation, *On the Golden Porch* (1989); published 1st novel *Kys* (2000), followed by the story collection *Izyum*; with Dunya Smirnova, became a tv co-host in Russia (2002); also wrote *The Slynx* and *Pushkin's Children*. ❖ See also *Women in World History*.

TOLSTOI. *Variant of Tolstoy.*

TOLSTOY, Alexandra (1884–1979). Russian lecturer, writer, and activist. Name variations: Sasha Tolstoi or Tolstaya; Alexandra Tolstoj. Born Alexandra Lvovna Tolstoy, July 1, 1884, at family estate, Yasnaya Polyana, in Russia; died at her Tolstoy Foundation estate, Reed Farm (an American Yasnaya Polyana), near Valley Cottage, New York, Sept 26, 1979; dau. of Count Leo Nikolaevich Tolstoy (author) and Sophia (Sonya) Andreyevna (Behrs) Tolstoy (1844–1919); aunt of Vera Tolstoy (1903–1999, who worked with Voice of America); never married; no children. ❖ Daughter and secretary of Leo Tolstoy who tried to perpetuate his ideas through lectures, writing, and as president of the anti-Communist Tolstoy Foundation which aided Russian refugees coming to US; served as secretary to Leo Tolstoy (1901–10); edited Tolstoy's posthumous works (1911–14); during WWI, served as nurse in All-Union Zemstvo Medical Service, a detachment of Russian Red Cross; sent to fight an outbreak of typhus, typhoid, and malaria among the troops fighting the Turks on the Caucasian front (1914–17) and was awarded the Medal of St. George, 4th class; founded Society for the Dissemination and Study of Tolstoy's Works (1918–28); became curator of the Tolstoy estate, Yasnaya Polyana Museum (1921–29); founded 6 schools (1921–29); a staunch anti-Communist and a devout member of the Russian Orthodox Church, was arrested 5 times by Soviet government and spent 1 year in prison (1920–29); was a writer and lecturer in Japan (1929–31); entered US (1931); served as president of the Tolstoy Foundation (1939–79); became US citizen (1941); writings include *Tragedy of Tolstoy* (1933); *I Worked for the Soviet* (1934) and *Tolstoy: A Life of My Father* (1953). ❖ See also *Women in World History*.

TOLSTOY, Sonya (1844–1919). Russian countess. Name variations: Countess Tolstoy or Tolstoi; Sonia, Sophie, Sofya, Sofia, Sofiya, Sofie Anreevna; Sophie Behrs. Born Sophia Andreyevna Behrs in 1844; died 1919; dau. of Lyubov Alexandrovna Behrs (who was the illeg. dau. of Princess Kozlovsky) and a Dr. Behrs; m. Count Leo Nikolaevich Tolstoy (the novelist and social and moral philosopher), Sept 23, 1862; children: 13 (6 died young), Sergei or Sergey Lvovich (1863–1947); Tatyana Tolstoy Sukhotina (1864–1950); Ilya (1866–1933, whose daughter Vera Tolstoy [1903–1999] worked for Voice of America); Lev (1869–1945); Marya (1871–1906); Pyotr (1872–1873); Nikolai (1874–1875); Varvara (1875–1875); Andrei (1877–1916); Mikhail (1879–1944); Alexei (1881–1886); Alexandra Tolstoy (1884–1979); Ivan (1888–1895). ❖ Diarist and wife of Tolstoy, who, within 2 months of her marriage, became obsessed with husband and would remain obsessed; spent 1st years of their lives together paying homage to his genius, copying his manuscripts, serving as his business manager, and bearing their children, and the last years begging to be recognized as her own person, with her own wants and needs. ❖ See also Anne Edwards, *Sonya: The Life of Countess Tolstoy* (Simon & Schuster, 1986); William L. Shirer, *Love and Hatred: The Troubled Marriage of Leo and Sonya Tolstoy* (Simon & Schuster, 1994); and *Women in World History*.

TOM, Constance (1948—). See *Noguchi, Constance*.

TOMA, Celestina (b. 1970). See *Popa, Celestina*.

TOMA, Sanda (1956—). Romanian rower. Born Feb 24, 1956, in Romania. ❖ Won World championship (1979, 1981); at Moscow Olympics, won a gold medal in single sculls (1980); retired (1981).

TOMA, Sanda (1970—). Romanian kayaker. Born 1970 in Romania. ❖ Won a bronze medal for K4 500 meters at Sydney Olympics (2000).

TOMANN, Rozalia (1950—). See *Lelkesne-Tomann, Rozalia*.

TOMASHOVA, Tatyana (1975—). Russian runner. Born July 1, 1975, in Perm, USSR. ❖ Won World Athletics Final for 3,000 meters (2001) and World championship for 1,500 meters (2003); won a silver medal for 1,500 meters at Athens Olympics (2004).

TOMASZEWICZ-DOBRSKA, Anna (1854–1918). Polish doctor. Name variations: Anna Tomaszewiczowna. Born 1854 in Poland; died 1918. ❖ The 1st woman to practice medicine in Poland, studied medicine in Zurich, and qualified as a doctor in Switzerland (1878); did graduate work briefly in Vienna, Berlin, and St. Petersburg, where she qualified to practice medicine (1879); returning to Warsaw, married a physician and began working as a doctor; despite objections from the medical establishment, was made chief of Lying-In Hospital No. 2 in Warsaw, a facility for obstetric patients, and remained there until it closed in 1911; also maintained a private practice; was recognized by the Warsaw Medical Society (1896); an advocate of women's rights, was also a founding member of the Society of Polish Culture.

TOMBLESON, Esmé (1917—). New Zealand politician. Name variations: Esme Tombleson. Born Esmé Lawson, Oct 1, 1917, in Sydney, Australia; m. Thomas Tombleson (farmer), 1950. ❖ Served as National Party MP for Gisborne (1960–72); founded the Multiple Sclerosis Society (1961), serving as national president (1975–82).

TOMIOKA, Taeko (1937—). Japanese poet and novelist. Born 1937 in Osaka, Japan; graduate of Osaka Women's University; m. Ikeda Masuo (woodblock artist, div. 1971). ❖ Published 1st collection of poems, *Return Present*; shifted focus from poetry to fiction; other works include *An Opening Day for a Story* (1961), which won the Muro Saisei Prize, *The Festival for Plants* (1973), *Family in Hell*, and *A Lover's Suicide–Ten no Tsunashima*; also writes for tv, film and the stage. Received Tamura Toshiko Prize.

TOMLIN, Lily (1939—). American actress. Born Mary Jean Tomlin, Sept 1, 1939, in Detroit, Michigan; dau. of Guy Tomlin (toolmaker) and Lillian May Ford; attended Wayne State University; studied mime with Paul Curtis; partner of writer-director Jane Wagner since 1971. ❖ Made tv debut on "The Garry Moore Show"; came to prominence as a regular on "Rowan and Martin's Laugh-In" (1970–73), with such characterizations as the toddler Edith Ann and the telephone operator Ernestine; made numerous comedy recordings, including *This Is a Recording* (1971), which won a Grammy; made film debut in *Nashville* (1975), for which she was nominated for an Oscar and won New York Film Critics award; other films include *The Late Show* (1977), *Nine to Five* (1980), *All of Me* (1984), *Tea With Mussolini* (1999), *Orange County* (2002) and *I ♥ Huckabees* (2004); on stage, performed in Tony Award-winning solo shows, *Appearing Nitely* (1977) and *The Search for Signs of Intelligent Life in the Universe* (1985–86); was regular on "Murphy Brown" (1996) and "The West Wing" (2002). ❖ See also Jeff Sorenson, *Lily Tomlin: Woman of a Thousand Faces* (St. Martin, 1989).

TOMOE GOZEN (fl. c. 12th c.). Japanese warrior. Pronunciation: Toe-mow-eh Go-zen. Was the concubine of Kiso Yoshinaka, commander of the Minamoto forces. ❖ Legendary woman warrior, said to have been both beautiful and valiant, who displayed military prowess equal to that of any man during the Taira-Minamoto war (1180–85); accompanied Yoshinaka into battle and was said to have personally commanded a force of 1,000 warriors. ❖ See also *Women in World History*.

TOMPKINS, Sally Louisa (1833–1916). American military nurse. Born Nov 9, 1833, in Poplar Grove, Mathews Co., Virginia; died July 25, 1916, in Richmond, Virginia; dau. of Christopher and Maria Boothe (Patterson) Tompkins. ❖ The 1st woman commissioned as an officer in the Confederate Army, opened and operated the 25-bed Robertson Hospital in Richmond during Civil War; when the surgeon general of the Confederacy recommended that private hospitals in Richmond be closed, was commissioned a captain of cavalry by Jefferson Davis, which enabled her to keep her hospital open as a military facility; recorded only 73 deaths out of 1,333 admissions (1861–65), a record unmatched by any other hospital in either the North or the South. ❖ See also *Women in World History*.

TOMSON, Graham R. (1860–1911). See Watson, Rosamund.

TOMYRIS (fl. 550–530 BCE). See Tamiris.

TONE, Lel (c. 1971—). Swiss-born skier. Name variations: Lesley Tone. Born c. 1971 in Switzerland; married. ❖ Was on skis by age 2; moved with family to Maine at 10; served as a member of ski patrol in CA; became powder guide for Pointes North Heli-Adventures in Cordova, Alaska, then joined Chugach Powder Guides of Girdwood; competed in pro circuit as cross-country mountain bike racer; climbed Denali (2001).

TONE, Matilda (c. 1769–1849). Wife of Irish nationalist Wolfe Tone. Born Martha Witherington, exact date and place unknown, c. 1769; died Mar 18, 1849, in Washington, DC; dau. of William Witherington and Catherine (Fanning) Witherington (dau. of a wealthy Church of Ireland cleric, Edward Fanning); sister of Edward Witherington, Kitty Witherington and Harriet Witherington Reynolds (who married

Thomas Reynolds); m. Theobald Wolfe Tone (Irish nationalist), July 21, 1785 (died 1798); m. Thomas Wilson (Scottish doctor), Aug 8, 1816 (died 1824); children: (1st m.) Maria Tone (1786–1803); William Tone (b. 1791); Frank Tone (b. 1793). ❖ Having eloped with Wolfe Tone, was eventually cut out of her grandfather's will; when husband's revolutionary activities led to his exile from Ireland (1795), accompanied him to America, along with children and his sister Mary Tone; settled in Princeton, NJ; left America with children (end of 1796) and arrived in Hamburg (Jan 1797); lived happily outside Paris until Sept 1798, when husband embarked on another expedition to Ireland; after he was caught in Ireland and slit his throat rather than be executed (Nov 11, 1798), led a hardscrabble life in France, except for a brief 2nd marriage; joined son William in America (1817); with him, published 2-vol. biography, *Life of Theobald Wolfe Tone*, based on his memoirs, journals and writings (1826), a work of great historical significance; after son died (1828), stayed on in Washington, becoming something of a celebrity. ❖ See also *Women in World History*.

TONELLI, Annalena (1943–2003). Italian humanitarian. Born April 2, 1943, in Forli, Italy; murdered Oct 5, 2003, in Borama, Somalia. ❖ Was a lawyer; earned diplomas in tropical medicine, community medicine and TB control; devoted 33 years to helping poor Somalis; ran a 200-bed hospital in Borama, in the northwestern region known as Somaliland; worked against female circumcision and for AIDS/HIV prevention; won the Nansen Medal, the highest honor given by the UN for humanitarian efforts on behalf of refugees (April 2003); 6 months later, was shot twice in the head by an unidentified gunman when leaving her hospital for tuberculosis patients in Borama.

TONGA, queen of. See Salote Topou III (1900–1965).

TONGE, Jenny (1941—). English politician and member of Parliament. Name variations: Dr. Jenny Tonge. Born Jennifer Smith, Feb 19, 1941, in West Midlands; m. Keith Tonge, 1964. ❖ Served as manager, Community Health Services (Ealing, 1992–96); as a Liberal Democrat, elected to House of Commons for Richmond Park (1997, 2001); named Liberal Democrat spokeswoman for International Development (1999–2003); caused an uproar for comments made about Palestinian suicide bombers: "If I had to live in that situation*and I say that advisedly* I might just consider becoming one myself" (Jan 2004); did not stand for reelection (2005).

TONKOVIC, Marija (1959—). Yugoslavian basketball player. Born Nov 23, 1959, in Yugoslavia. ❖ At Moscow Olympics, won a bronze medal in team competition (1980).

TONNA, Charlotte Elizabeth (1790–1846). British novelist and editor. Name variations: Charlotte Elizabeth Browne or (incorrectly) Brown; Mrs. Tonna; Mrs. Phelan; (pseudonyms) Charlotte Elizabeth, C. E. Born Charlotte Elizabeth Browne, Oct 1, 1790, in Norwich, Norfolk, England; died July 12, 1846, in Ramsgate, Kent, England; dau. of Michael Browne (rector); m. George Phelan, 1813 (died 1837); m. Lewis Henry Joseph Tonna, 1841. ❖ Writer of religious-historical novels, children's stories, poems, songs, travel narratives, and social-protest fiction whose works focus on working women, industrialization, and social decay; writings include *The Shepherd Boy and the Deluge* (1823), *Anne Bell: or, the Faults* (1826), *Little Frank, The Irish Boy* (1827), *The Burying Ground* (1830), *A Letter to a Friend, Containing a Few Heads for Consideration, on Subjects that Trouble the Church* (1831), *The Simple Flower* (1840), *Helen Fleetwood* (1841), *Judah's Lion* (1843), *The Wrongs of Women* (1843–44), *War with the Saints* (1848), *Stories for Children* (1854) and *The Two Servants*.

TONNERRE, countess of.
See Mahaut II de Dampierre (1234–1266).
See Yolande of Burgundy (1248–1280).
See Marguerite de Bourgogne (1250–1308).
See Jeanne of Chalon (1300–1333).

TONOLLI, Livia (1909–1985). Italian freshwater biologist. Name variations: Livia Pirocchi; Livia Pirocchi-Tonolli. Born Livia Pirocchi, Sept 15, 1909; died Dec 15, 1985; graduate of University of Milan, 1932; m. Vittorio Tonolli (director of Pallanza Institute, died 1967). ❖ International hydrology expert, served as a lecturer at the University of Milan's Institute of Zoology (1968–72); became assistant professor at Institute of Hydrobiology in Pallanza, Italy (1939), then deputy director, and served as director (1967–78, after husband's death; was a founding member, then president of Italian Association for Oceanography and Limnology (1976–78); edited Pallanza Institute journal *Memorie*; established the International Vittorio Tonolli Memorial Fund and the Vittorio Tonolli Foundation for Cardiological Culture. Received Silver Medal for Merit in Culture, Science, and Art (1974) from president of Italy, the Italian Ecological Society's Gold Medal and the Societas Internationalis Limnologiae's E. Naumann–A. Thieneman Medal (1983).

TOOK, Belladonna (1898–1996). *See Chapman, Vera.*

TOOMER, Barbara (1944—). *See Parritt, Barbara.*

TOOMEY, Mary (b. 1940). *See Rand, Mary.*

TOOR, Frances (1890–1956). American writer. Name variations: Paca Toor; Panchita Toor. Born in Plattsburgh, New York, 1890; died in New York, NY, June 16, 1956; University of California, Berkeley, BA and MA in anthropology; m. J. L. Weinberger (dentist, div. early 1920s). ❖ Publisher, anthropologist and ethnographer whose books and journal *Mexican Folkways* introduced Americans to the folk traditions and art of revolutionary Mexico; writings include (with Carlos Mérida) *Frescoes in Ministry of Education* (1937), *Modern Mexican Artists* (1937), *A Treasury of Mexican Folkways* (1947), *The Three Worlds of Peru* (1949), *Festivals and Folkways of Italy* (1953), *The Golden Carnation, and Others Stories Told in Italy* (1960) and *Frances Toor's Guide to Mexico, including Lower California* (1967). ❖ See also *Women in World History.*

TOOTH, Liane (1962—). Australian field-hockey player. Born Liane Marianne Tooth, Mar 13, 1962, in New South Wales, Australia. ❖ Defender, won team gold medals at Seoul Olympics (1988) and Atlanta Olympics (1996).

TOPEORA, Rangi Kuini Wikitoria (?–1865/73). Maori tribal leader, poet, and composer. Died c. 1865–1873, at Otaki, New Zealand; dau. of Te Ra-ka-herea and Waitohi; m. Te Ra-Tu-tonu, 1818 (died c. 1822); m. Rangikapiki; m. Te Wehi-o-te-rangi; m. Hauturu; children: (2nd m.) 1 son; (3rd m.) 1 daughter. ❖ Noted poet and composer of waiata; participated in numerous tribal negotiations and was one of 5 women who signed Treaty of Waitangi (1840). ❖ See also *Dictionary of New Zealand Biography* (Vol. 1).

TOPHAM, Mirabel (d. 1980). British racecourse owner. Name variations: (pseudonym) Hope Hillier. Died 1980; m. Arthur Topham (1922). ❖ Elected to board of Aintree racecourse (1935) and took over company (1936); purchased racecourse (1949) and became embroiled in legal battles with family, bookmakers, and BBC until racecourse was sold to Walton Group (1973).

TOPPAN, Jane (1854–1938). American nurse and mass murderer. Born Nora Kelley in 1854 in Boston, Massachusetts; died Aug 17, 1938, in Taunton, Massachusetts; dau. of Peter Kelley (tailor); attended nursing school in Cambridge, Massachusetts; adopted by Mr. and Mrs. Abner Toppan, 1859, who changed her name to Jane, and raised her in comfortable surroundings in Lowell, Massachusetts. ❖ As a private nurse (1880–1901), worked for scores of families throughout New England, poisoning patients in her care with morphine and atropine; charged with murder, named 31 persons she claimed to have killed; following trial (1902), was sent to the Taunton State Asylum for the Criminally Insane, where she lived until her death. ❖ See also *Women in World History.*

TOPPERWEIN, Elizabeth "Plinky" (c. 1886–1945). American sharpshooter. Name variations: Mrs. Ad; Auntie Plinky Topperwein. Born Elizabeth Servanty, c. 1886, possibly in CT; died Jan 15, 1945, in San Antonio, TX; m. Adolph "Ad" Topperwein (sharpshooter), c. 1904 (died 1962); children: 1 son. ❖ Was the 1st woman to break 100 straight traps (1904), and repeated that feat 200 times; broke 200 straight 14 times; in contest of endurance, broke 1,952 of 2,000 targets (an average of 98%) in 5 hrs. 20 min. (1916) with no rest (though the heat of the gun blistered her hand she still broke 98 of the last 100); appeared on the vaudeville circuit with her husband (1930s). Inducted into the National Trapshooting Hall of Fame (1969). Annie Oakley thought her the greatest female sharpshooter of all time.

TOPPING, Jenny (1980—). American softball player. Born May 30, 1980, in Whittier, CA; attended California State University, Fullerton. ❖ Catcher/outfielder, won team gold medal at Athens Olympics (2004).

TORBY, countess of (1896–1963). *See Nadejda Michaelovna.*

TORDASI SCHWARCZENBERGER, Ildiko (1951—). Hungarian track-and-field athlete. Name variations: Ildiko Tordasi; Ildiko Tordasi-Schwarczenberger; Ildiko Schwarczenberger. Born Ildiko

Tordasi, Sept 9, 1951, in Hungary; dau. of a Hungarian Olympic masseur. ❖ Was 6-time Hungarian national champion; won team gold at World championships (1973); at Munich Olympics, won a silver medal in team foil (1972); at Montreal Olympics, won a bronze medal in team foil and a gold medal in indiv. foil (1976); at Moscow Olympics, won a bronze medal in team foil (1980); was seriously wounded in an accident and forced to withdraw from competition; became a trainer.

TORELLI, Maria (1846–1920). *See Torriani, Maria Antonietta.*

TOREN, Marta (1926–1957). Swedish actress. Name variations: Märta Torén. Born May 21, 1926, in Stockholm, Sweden; died Feb 19, 1957, in Stockholm. ❖ Contracted by Universal, brought to Hollywood to appear in such films as *Sword of the Desert, Casbah, Rogues Regiment, Illegal Entry, One Way Street* and *Deported*; returned to Sweden for stage debut (1957), but died one month later of leukemia at age 31.

TORGERSSON, Therese (1976—). Swedish yacht racer. Born Mar 28, 1976, in Gothenburg, Sweden. ❖ Won World championship for 470 class (2004); won a bronze medal for double-handed dinghy (470) at Athens Olympics (2004).

TORLESSE, Elizabeth Henrietta (1835/36–1922). New Zealand founder of refuge. Name variations: Elizabeth Henrietta Revell. Born Elizabeth Henrietta Revell, c. 1835 or 1836, in Co. Wicklow, Ireland; died Sept 22, 1922, in Christchurch, New Zealand; dau. of Thomas and Margaret Elizabeth (Bradell) Revell; m. Henry Torlesse, 1857 (died 1870); children: 8 daughters, 2 sons. ❖ Immigrated with family to New Zealand (1853); lived at sheep run near Rangiora with husband; relocated to Christchurch when husband's health failed; cofounded and helped operate refuge for prostitutes (1864). ❖ See also *Dictionary of New Zealand Biography* (Vol. 1).

TORLONIA, Beatriz (1909–2002). *See Beatriz of Spain.*

TORLUEMKE, Judy (b. 1945). *See Rankin, Judy.*

TORNABUONI, Lucrezia (1425–1482). *See Medici, Lucrezia de.*

TORNEY, Lulu von Strauss und (1873–1956). *See Strauss und Torney, Lulu von.*

TORNIKIDU, Yelena (1965—). Soviet basketball player. Born May 27, 1965, in USSR. ❖ At Barcelona Olympics, won a gold medal in team competition (1992).

TORNIMPARTE, Alessandra (1916–1991). *See Ginzburg, Natalia.*

TORO, Maria Teresa (d. 1803). Wife of Simon Bolivar. Name variations: Maria Teresa Rodríguez del Toro. Born into a prominent family; died of yellow fever in 1803, 6 months after her marriage; m. Simon Bolivar (1783–1830, liberator of Venezuela), in 1802.

TÖRÖK, Sophie (1895–1955). *See Tanner, Ilona.*

TORREALVA, Gina (1961—). Peruvian volleyball player. Born Nov 16, 1961, in Peru. ❖ At Seoul Olympics, won a silver medal in team competition (1988).

TORRENCE, Gwen (1965—). African-American track-and-field athlete. Born June 12, 1965, in Atlanta, GA; graduated from University of Georgia, 1987; m. Manley Waller (sprinter and coach). ❖ Won a gold medal and set meet record (6.57 seconds) in 55-meter dash, Millrose Games (1986); won NCAA championships in 55 meters, 100 meters, and 200 meters (1987); won gold medals in 100 and 200 meters, World University Games (1987); won a gold medal in 200 meters at US outdoor championships (1991); won gold medals for 200-meter sprint and 4 x 100-meter relay and a silver medal for 4 x 400-meter relay at Barcelona Olympics (1992); won gold medals for 100 and 200 meters at US outdoor championships (1995); won a gold medal for 100 meters at World championships (1995); won a gold medal for 4 x 100-meter relay and a bronze medal for 100-meter sprint at Atlanta Olympics (1996). ❖ See also *Women in World History.*

TORRES, Dara (1967—). American swimmer. Born April 15, 1967, in Los Angeles, CA; attended University of Florida. ❖ At Los Angeles Olympics, won a gold medal in 4 x 100-meter freestyle relay (1984); at Seoul Olympics, won a silver medal in 4 x 100-meter medley relay and a bronze medal in 4 x 100-meter freestyle relay (1988); at Barcelona Olympics, won a gold medal for 4 x 100-meter freestyle relay (1992); won gold medals for 4 x 100-meter freestyle and 4 x 100-meter medley relay and bronze medals for 100-meter butterfly, 50-meter freestyle, and

100-meter freestyle at Sydney Olympics (2000), the 1st American to swim in 4 Olympics and the oldest woman swimmer to win a medal.

TORRES, Lolita (1930–2002). Argentinean actress and singer. Born Beatriz Mariana Torres, Mar 26, 1930, in Avellana, Argentina; died Sept 14, 2002, in Buenos Aires, Argentina; m. Santiago Rodolfo Burastero (died 1959); m. Julio Caccia; children: Santiago, Angélica, Marcelo, Mariana and Diego (pop star). ❧ Leading actress and singer, began career at age 11, singing folk songs from Spain at the Avenida Theater in Buenos Aires; had small role in the film *The Dance of Fortune* (1944) and soon gained renown in musical comedies; had international hit with *La Edad del amor* (The Age of Love, 1954); appeared in 17 films before retiring as an actress (1972); pursued singing career with such hits as "Gitano Jesus" (Gypsy Jesus).

TORRES, Raquel (1908–1987). Mexican-born actress. Born Paula Marie Osterman, Nov 11, 1908, in Hermosillo, Mexico; died Aug 10, 1987, in Malibu, CA; m. Stephen Ames (film producer), 1935 (died 1955); m. Jon Hall (actor), 1959. ❧ Made film debut in the classic *White Shadows of the South Seas* (1928); other films include *The Bridge of San Luis Rey, The Desert Rider, Under a Texas Moon* and *Duck Soup*.

TORRES, Regla (1975—). Cuban volleyball player. Name variations: Regla R. Torres Herrera. Born Feb 12, 1975, in Cuba. ❧ Middle blocker/hitter, won a gold medal at Barcelona Olympics (1992), the youngest player in history (19) to win an Olympic gold in volleyball; won a team World championship (1994); won team gold medals at Atlanta Olympics (1996) and Sydney Olympics (2000). Named MVP at Senior World championships (1994).

TORRES, Vanessa (1986—). American skateboarder. Born July 17, 1986, in Anaheim, California. ❧ Won gold medal for Skateboard Park at X Games (Summer 2003); starred in film *AKA: Girl Skater* (Globe/Gallaz, 2002); other 1st-place finishes include The Mountain Dew National championships of Skateboarding (Vert, 2002), All Girl Skate Jam (2003, 2004), Slam City Jam (Street).

TORRES, Xohana (1931—). Spanish novelist. Born 1931 in Santiago de Compostela, Spain. ❧ Participated in Galician cultural movement and created first Galician radio program; works include *Do sulco* (1957), *Polo mar van as sardiñas* (1968), *Adiós, Maria* (1971), *Pericles e a balea* (1984), and *Tempo de Ria* (1992).

TORRES MARQUES, Helena (1941—). Portuguese politician. Name variations: D. Helena Torres Marques. Born May 8, 1941, in Lisbon, Portugal. ❧ Served as a member of the Assembly of the Republic (1983–94) and vice-chair of the parliamentary party of the PS (1991–94); as a European Socialist (PSE), elected to 4th and 5th European Parliament (1994–99, 1999–2004). Awarded Grand Cross of the Infante D. Henrique (1998).

TORREZÃO, Guiomar (1844–1898). Portuguese novelist, editor, playwright and feminist. Name variations: Guiomar Delfina de Noronha Torrezão. Born 1844 in Portugal; grew up in Cape Verde; died 1898; dau. of a customs official. ❧ One of first Portuguese women to earn living as writer, was an ardent supporter of women's rights and wrote about women's issues, especially education; works include *Uma Alma de Mulher* (1869) and *A Família Albergaria* (1874); founded magazine *Alamanaque das Senhoras* (1871) and edited *Ribaltas e Gambiarras*; also wrote plays.

TORRIANI, Maria Antonietta (1840–1920). Italian novelist. Name variations: Anna Maria Torriani; Maria Torelli-Torriani; Maria Antonietta Torriani Torelli-Viollier; (pseudonyms) La Marchesa Colombi; Marchioness Colombi. Born Maria Antonietta Torriani, Jan 1, 1840, in Novara, Italy; died 1920 in Milan, Italy; m. Eugenio Torrelli Viollier, founder and editor of *Corriere della Sera* (sep.). ❧ Concerned about exploitation of women laborers and campaigned on behalf of women's education; works include *In risaia* (1878), *Un matrimonio in provincia* (1885), and *Il tramonto d'un ideale*.

TORRIE, Malcolm (1901–1983). See Mitchell, Gladys.

TORS, Mrs. Ivan (1920–1969). See Dowling, Constance.

TORVILL, Jayne (1957—). English pairs skater. Born Oct 7, 1957, in Nottingham, England. ❧ With Michael Hutchinson, won British Pairs championship (1971); with Christopher Dean, won British Ice Dance championships (1978–84), gold medals at European championships (1981, 1982, 1984, 1993) and World championships (1981, 1982, 1984); finished 5th at Lake Placid Olympics (1980); skating to

Maurice Ravel's "Bolero," won a gold medal at Sarajevo Olympics (1984), the 1st to use one piece of music through an entire free-dance program, the 1st to sustain a mood, the 1st to capture 12 6.0s for artistic impression, highest scores ever recorded in an international ice dancing competition; won a bronze medal at Lillehammer Olympics (1994). Named Member of the British Empire (MBE, 1981) and Officer of the Order of the British Empire (OBE, 2000).

TORY, Louise (1933–1994). See Troy, Louise.

TOSATTI, Barbara Maria (1891–1934). Italian poet. Born 1891 in Modena, Italy; died 1934. ❧ Published some poetry in *Nuova Antologia* and a collection in 1932; brother edited writings for posthumous collection *Canti e preghiere. Liriche, pensieri, lettere* (1939).

TOSELLI, Louisa (1870–1947). Princess of Saxony. Name variations: Louise Antoinette; Louise of Habsburg-Lotharingen; Louise of Tuscany; Marie Louise; princess of Tuscany; countess Montignoso. Born Louisa or Louise Antoinette on Sept 2, 1870, in Salzburg, Austria; died Mar 23, 1947, in Brussels, Belgium; 2nd dau. of Alicia of Parma (1849–1935) and Ferdinand IV (1835–1908), titular grand duke of Tuscany (r. 1859–1908); m. Frederick Augustus III (1865–1932), king of Saxony (r. 1904–1918, abdicated in 1918), on Nov 21, 1891 (div. 1903); m. Enrico Toselli (a composer); children: (1st m.) George (b. 1893); Frederick Christian (b. 1893, who m. Elizabeth of Thurn and Taxis); Ernest Henry (b. 1896), prince of Saxony; Margaret; Maria; Anna.

TOSHIKO, Princess (1740–1814). See Go-Sakuramachi.

TOSHIKO SHIRASU (1939—). See Aihara, Toshiko.

TOSTEVIN, Lola Lemire (1937—). Canadian poet. Born June 15, 1937, in Timmins, Ontario, Canada, of French-speaking parents. ❧ Studied in Paris and Canada; works, which reflect francophone upbringing and often explore questions of women and language, include *Color of Her Speech* (1982), *Gyno Text* (1983), *Double Standards* (1985), *Sophie* (1988), *Frog Moon* (1994), and *Cartouches* (1995); published *Subject to Criticism* (1995).

TOSUN, Hamide (1978—). See Bikcin, Hamide.

TOTENOHL, Josefa Berens (1891–1969). See Berens-Totenohl, Josefa.

TOTH, Beatrix. Hungarian handball player. Name variations: Beatrix György-Toth. Born in Hungary. ❧ Won a team bronze medal at Atlanta Olympics (1996).

TOTH, Judit (b. 1906). Hungarian gymnast. Born Dec 27, 1906, in Hungary. ❧ At Berlin Olympics, won a bronze medal in team all-around (1936).

TOTH, Noemi (1976—). Hungarian-Italian water-polo player. Born June 7, 1976, in Szentes, Hungary. ❧ At World championships, won team gold medal for Hungary (1994) and team silver medal for Italy (2003); representing Italy as center back, won a team gold medal at Athens Olympics (2004).

TOTH HARSANYI, Borbala (1946—). Hungarian handball player. Born Aug 1946 in Hungary. ❧ At Montreal Olympics, won a bronze medal in team competition (1976).

TOTHNE-KOVACS, Annamaria (1945—). Hungarian pentathlete. Name variations: Annamaria Kovacs. Born Sept 14, 1945, in Hungary. ❧ At Mexico City Olympics, won a bronze medal in the pentathlon (1968).

TOTSCHNIG, Brigitte (1954—). Austrian Alpine skier. Name variations: Tötschnig or Totschnigg; Brigitte Toetschnig-Habersatter. Born Aug 30, 1954, in Filmoos, Austria. ❧ Won a silver medal for downhill at Innsbruck Olympics (1976); won World Cup titles in the downhill (1976, 1977).

TOUKAN, Fadwa (1917–2003). See Tuqan, Fadwa.

TOULOUSE, countess of.
See Elvira (fl. 1080s).
See Constance Capet (c. 1128–1176).
See Joan of Toulouse (d. 1271).

TOUMANOVA, Tamara (1919–1996). Russian ballerina, actress, and choreographer. Name variations: Tumanova, Tata. Born Tamara Vladimirovna Toumanova in Siberia, between Ekaterinburg and Tyumen, Mar 2, 1919; died May 29, 1996, in Santa Monica,

California; dau. of Vladimir Toumanov (colonel in Russian Imperial Army, died 1963) and Evgeniia Khacidovitch (died 1988); studied with Olga Preobrazhenska; m. Casey Robinson (movie producer), 1943 (div. 1953); no children. ❖ Internationally known dancer, choreographer, and film actress who, as 1 of the 3 "baby ballerinas" of 1920s, became the personification of a Russian prima ballerina; debuted in Paris in *L'Evantail de Jeanne*, a children's ballet (1927); signed with Ballet Russe de Monte Carlo (1932–38); appeared with Original Ballet Russe and with Ballet Theater (1940–45); danced with Grand Ballet du Marquis de Cuevas (1949), with Festival Ballet (1951–52, 1956), and with Paris Opera (1947–52, 1956); became US citizen and settled in Southern California (1944); at La Scala, created the ballet *La legenda di Guiseppe* for Margarethe Wallmann, as well as *The Legend of St. Joseph, La Vita Del'uomo*, and *Setter Piccati* (1953); also choreographed von Karajan's presentation of Richard Strauss' *Salome* (1956); danced in such ballets as *L'Evantail de Jeanne* (1927), *Cotillon* (1932), *Concurrence* (1932), *Le Bourgeois Gentillhomme* (1932), *Jeux d'Enfants* (1932), *Mozartiana* (1933), *Songes* (1933), *Petrouchka* (1934), *Symphonie fantastique* (1936), *Firebird* (1940), *Spectre of the Rose* (1940), *Aurora's Wedding* (1940), *Les Sylphides* (1940), *Balustrade* (1940–41), *Swan Lake* (1941), *Magic Swan* (1942), *Giselle* (1944–45), *The Nutcracker* (1944–45), *Le Palais de Cristal* (1947), *Le Baiser de la Fee* (1947), *La legenda di Guiseppe* (1951) and *Phedre* (1952); films include *Days of Glory* (1944), *Tonight We Sing* (1953), *Deep in My Heart* (1954), *Invitation to the Dance* (1956), *Torn Curtain* (1966) and *The Private Life of Sherlock Holmes* (1970). ❖ See also *Women in World History*.

TOUMINE, Nesta (c. 1912–1995). English ballet dancer and teacher. Name variations: Nesta Williams; Nesta Maslova. Born Nesta Williams, c. 1912, in England; died in 1995; raised in Ottawa, Canada; m. Sviatoslav Toumine (mime and designer). ❖ Trained and worked with Gwendolyn Osbourne in Canada, and Margaret Craske, Nicholai Legat, Olga Preobrazhenska and Lyubov Egorova in Europe; made performance debut in London musical *The Golden Troy* (1932), directed by Ninette De Valois; danced with Ballets Russes de Paris as Nesta Williams; performed in US with Ballet Russe de Monte Carlo; opened Classical Ballet Studio in Ottawa (1949), and later founded own company (1958), the predecessor of Ballet Imperial de Canada (1965); created own works for this company, including *Gymnopédies* (c. 1960), *Mozartiana* (1961), and *The Seasons* (1962), but is better known for staging Fokine repertory.

TOUPIN, Marie (c. 1790–1850). See Dorion, Marie.

TOURAY, Josephine (1979—). Danish handball player. Born Oct 6, 1979, in Denmark. ❖ Left wing, won a team gold medal at Athens Olympics (2004).

TOUR DU PIN, Henriette de la (1770–1853). See La Tour du Pin, Henriette de.

TOUREL, Jennie (1899–1973). American operatic mezzo-soprano. Born June 22, 1899, in Vitebsk, Russia; died Nov 23, 1973, in New York, NY; dau. of Solomon Davidson (banker) and Pauline (Schulkin) Davidson; studied music privately and with Anna El-Tour; m. Bernhard Michlin (div.); m. Leo Michaelson (artist, later div.); m. Harry Gross (cardiac specialist), 1955 (div. 1957); became naturalized US citizen (1946). ❖ Considered one of the best recitalists of her era, debuted at Opera-Russe, Paris (1931); made US debut with Chicago Opera (1930–31), singing in Ernest Moret's *Lorenzaccio* and performing role of Lola in Mascagni's *Cavelleria Rusticana*; also appeared with Mary Garden in world premiere of Hamilton Forrest's *Camille*; performed title role of *Carmen* at Paris Opéra-Comique (1933), followed by Charlotte in Massenet's *Werther*, and title roles in Thomas' *Mignon*, Rossini's *La Cenerentola* and Bizet's *Kjamileh*; sang under baton of Arturo Toscanini in Berlioz's *Roméo et Juliette* with New York Philharmonic (1942), an event that launched her American career; went on to perform with Boston Symphony under Serge Koussevitzky, with Leopold Stokowski and NBC Symphony in US premiere of Prokofiev's *Alexander Nevsky Cantata* (1943), and with Stokowski again in Bach's *St. Matthew Passion* at Met (1943); created role of Baba the Turk in Venice premiere of Stravinsky's *The Rake's Progress* (1951) and sang in premiere of Bernstein's *Jeremiah* in Pittsburgh (1944); began offering master classes at Carnegie Recital Hall (1963) and joined faculty of Juilliard School (1964). ❖ See also *Women in World History*.

TOURISCHEVA, Ludmila (1952—). Soviet gymnast. Name variations: Liudmila or Ludmilla or Lyudmila Turishcheva, Turischeva, or Turitscheva. Born Ludmila Ivanovna Tourischeva, Oct 7, 1952, in Grozny, USSR; m. Valery Borzov (track-and-field champion). ❖ Won USSR Cup (1967); at Mexico City Olympics, won a gold medal in team all-around (1968); at World championships, won gold medals in all-around (1970, 1974), balance beam (1974), and floor exercises (1970, 1974); won European championships (1971, 1973); at Munich Olympics, won a bronze medal in vault, a silver medal in floor exercises, and gold medals in team and indiv. all-around (1972); won USSR championships (1972, 1974); won World Cup (1975); at Montreal Olympics, won a bronze medal indiv. all-around, silver medal in vault and floor exercises and gold medal in team all-around (1976); battled Nadia Comaneci and Olga Korbut for the spotlight toward the end of career; became head of the Ukrainian Gymnastics Federation. Awarded Order of Lenin. ❖ See also V. Golubev, *Liudmila Turishcheva* (Moscow, 1977); and *Women in World History*.

TOURKY, Loudy (1979—). Australian-Israeli diver. Born July 7, 1979, in Haifa, Palestine; grew up in Brisbane; Sydney University, BA. ❖ Won a bronze medal for synchronized platform diving at Sydney Olympics (2000); became the 1st diver to win gold in the same event at 3 FINA diving championships (Canada, Mexico and US, 2003); placed 2nd for sychronized platform at World championships (2003); for 10-meter platform, placed 1st in Grand Prix ranking (2003) and 2nd (2004); placed 2nd at Grand Prix Super Final for 10-meter platform (2004); won a bronze medal for 10-meter platform at Athens Olympics (2004).

TOURNEMIRE, Elizaveta Salhias de (1815–1892). *See Salhias de Tournemire, Elizaveta.*

TOUROVER, Denise (1903–1980). *See Ezekiel, Denise Tourover.*

TOURTEL, Mary (1874–1948). English writer and illustrator. Born Mary Caldwell, Mar 15, 1874, in Canterbury, England; died Jan 28, 1948, in England; dau. of stained glass artist and stone mason; attended Canterbury Art School; m. Herbert Tourtel (newspaper editor). ❖ Creator of the popular cartoon character Rupert the Bear, began career as professional illustrator of children's books (1890s); with husband, embarked on many adventures, including a flight in a Handley-Page airplane which broke flight-time record from Hounslow to Brussels (1919); challenged by husband to create cartoon character to rival competing newspaper's Teddy Tail, came up with Rupert the Bear cartoon strip, published both in *The Daily Express* (1920–35) and in some 50 books, beginning with *The Adventures of Rupert the Little Lost Bear* (1921); retired due to failing eyesight (1935).

TOUSEK, Yvonne (1980—). Canadian gymnast. Born Feb 23, 1980, in Ontario, Canada. ❖ Won Elite Canada (1998) and Buckeye Classic (1999).

TOUSSAINT, Anna Louisa (1812–1886). *See Bosboom-Toussaint, Anna.*

TOUSSAINT, Cheryl (1952—). African-American runner. Born Dec 16, 1952, in Brooklyn, NY; graduate of New York University, 1974. ❖ Won the AAU 990-yard title (1970, 1971) and AAU indoor 800 yards (1973, 1973); won a silver medal for the 4 x 400-meter relay at Munich Olympics (1972). ❖ See also *Women in World History*.

TOUW, Daphne (1970—). Dutch field-hockey player. Born Jan 13, 1970, in Sint Oedenrode, Netherlands. ❖ Won a team bronze medal at Sydney Olympics (2000).

TOVSTOGAN, Yevgeniya (1965—). Soviet handball player. Born April 3, 1965, in USSR. ❖ At Seoul Olympics, won a bronze medal in team competition (1988).

TOWER, Joan (1938—). American composer. Name variations: Joan Peabody Tower. Born Sept 6, 1938, in La Rochelle, New York; father was amateur violinist and mining engineer; raised in South America; Bennington College, BA, 1967; Columbia University, PhD, 1967. ❖ Among the most successful woman composers of all time, co-founded and performed as pianist in Da Capo Chamber Players (1969–84), which commissioned and introduced many of her most popular works, including *Breakfast Rhythms I and II* (1974–75) and *Petroushskates* (1980); taught at Bard College and served as composer-in-residence with Orchestra of St. Luke's and at Deer Park Valley Institute in Utah; created 1st orchestral work, *Sequoia* (1981), which led to appointment by Leonard Slatkin as composer-in-residence of St. Louis Symphony Orchestra (1985–88); wrote award-winning *Silver Ladders* for St. Louis Symphony (1986), which was later choreographed by Helgi Tomasson and performed by San Francisco Ballet (1998); created *Fanfare for the Uncommon Woman* (1987), commissioned by Houston Symphony Orchestra; commissioned to write fanfares No. 2 for Absolut Vodka

(1989), No. 3 for Carnegie Hall's 100th anniversary (1991), No. 4 for 50th anniversary of Kansas City Symphony (1992) and No. 5 for Aspen Music Festival (1993); wrote many other celebrated works, such as *Concerto for Violin* (1991), solo piano piece for John Browning *Vast Antique Cubes/Throbbing Still* (2000), and string quartets *Night Fields* (1994) and *In Memory*, premiered by Tokyo String Quartet (2002); served as co-artistic director of Yale/Norfolk Chamber Music Festival and composer-in-residence at Tanglewood; featured in retrospective at Carnegie Hall, *Making Music* (2005). Inducted into American Academy of Arts and Letters (1998) and Academy of Arts and Sciences at Harvard University (2004).

TOWERS, Julie (1976—). Australian field-hockey player. Born Oct 12, 1976, in Taree, NSW, Australia. ❖ Forward; won a team gold medal at Sydney Olympics (2000).

TOWLE, Charlotte (1896–1966). American social worker and educator. Born Charlotte Helen Towle, Nov 17, 1896, in Butte, Montana; died Oct 1, 1966, in North Conway, New Hampshire; dau. of Herman Augustus Towle (jeweler) and Emily (Kelsey) Towle (schoolteacher); graduate of Goucher College, 1919; graduate study at New York School for Social Work (later Columbia University School of Social Work), 1926–27. ❖ Became assistant professor at University of Chicago's School of Social Service Administration (SSA, 1932), then associate professor (1935), and full professor (1944); developed new courses and wrote several important journal articles, as well as her 1st book, *Social Case Records from Psychiatric Clinics* (1941); insisted that all social workers needed thorough training in psychiatric theory, and instituted a curriculum that replaced separate courses with one generic course covering family, child welfare, medical, and psychiatric issues, an innovation soon implemented by other schools; held significant advisory positions with Veterans Administration (1946–48), American Red Cross (1945–48), and US Public Health Service's Mental Health Division (1947–49 and 1953); also wrote *Common Human Needs* (1945) and *The Learner in Education for the Professions* (1954). ❖ See also *Women in World History*.

TOWLE, Katherine (1898–1986). American educator and US Marine Corps officer. Born Katherine Amelia Towle, April 30, 1898, in Towle, California; died 1986; dau. of George Gould Towle and Katherine (Meister) Towle; University of California, Berkeley, BA (*cum laude*), 1920, MA, 1935; graduate study at Columbia University, 1922–23. ❖ Became resident dean at a private girls' school in Piedmont, California (1927), then headmistress (1929); was assistant to the manager and then senior editor of University of California Press (1935–42); accepted a commission in Women's Reserve of US Marine Corps (1943), becoming one of the 1st women officers in that branch of the military service; commissioned as a captain, was called to active duty (Feb 1943); promoted to major (1944) and named assistant director of the Women's Reserve; elevated to lieutenant colonel (Mar 1945), then colonel (Dec 1945) and assigned to succeed Ruth Cheney Streeter as director of the Women's Reserve; served as director (1945–46, 1948–53); at University of California, Berkeley, served as dean of women and associate dean of students (1953–62), then named dean of students (1962), a position she held until her retirement. Awarded US Navy's Letter of Commendation, with Ribbon (1946); received American Campaign Medal and World War II Victory Medal. ❖ See also *Women in World History*.

TOWNE, Laura Matilda (1825–1901). American educator and abolitionist. Born May 3, 1825, in Pittsburgh, Pennsylvania; died of influenza on Feb 22, 1901, on St. Helena Island, South Carolina; dau. of John Towne (businessman, died 1851) and Sarah (Robinson) Towne (died 1833); educated in Boston and Philadelphia; studied homeopathic medicine privately and enrolled in the Penn Medical University. ❖ Taught at charity schools and practiced medicine (1850s–61); during Civil War, became a teacher on the Sea Islands of South Carolina (1862), working with freed slaves; on St. Helena Island, co-founded and taught at the Penn School (1862–1901), one of the 1st schools for former slaves, which provided the only secondary education available to the African-Americans who lived on the Sea Islands. ❖ See also *Women in World History*.

TOWNLEY, Mary K. (1905–1990). See Campbell, Mary Katherine.

TOWNSEND, Cathy (1937—). Canadian bowler. Born June 8, 1937, in Campbellton, New Brunswick, Canada. ❖ Placed 1st in the World Cup (1975), 1st Canadian woman to do so; placed 1st in all events, 1st in mixed foursome, and 3rd in singles at the Tournament of the Americas (1976). Inducted into Canada's Sports Hall of Fame (1976).

TOWNSEND, Jacquelyn Mayer (c. 1942—). *See Mayer, Jacquelyn.*

TOWNSEND, Sue (1946—). British novelist, playwright and children's writer. Born Susan Lilian Johnstone, April 2, 1946, in Leicester, England; dau. of John and Grace Johnstone (Leicester bus conductors); m. Keith Townsend, 1964; m. Colin Broadway, 1986. ❖ Began the bestselling "Adrian Mole" series with *The Secret Diary of Adrian Mole, Aged 13¾* (1982), followed by *The Growing Pains of Adrian Mole* (1984) and *Adrian Mole, From Minor to Major* (1991); also wrote *Womberang* (1979), *Ear, Nose, and Throat* (1989), *Ten Tiny Fingers, Nine Tiny Toes* (1990), (play) *The Queen and I* (1992), and *Ghost Children* (1997); struck with diabetes-induced blindness; launched web site providing counseling and services for people with sight problems (2002).

TOWNSEND WARNER, Sylvia (1893–1978). *See Warner, Sylvia Townsend.*

TOWZEY, Eleanor Stewart (1858–1931). *See Stewart, Nellie.*

TOXOPEUS, Jacqueline (1968—). Dutch field-hockey player. Born Jan 1, 1969, in Netherlands. ❖ One of the finest goalkeepers in Dutch women's field hockey history, won a team bronze medal at Atlanta Olympics (1996).

TOYE, Wendy (1917—). English director, choreographer and dancer. Born May 1, 1917, in London, England; studied with Marie Rambert; m. Edward Selwyn Sharp (div.). ❖ At 10, produced a ballet at the London Palladium; made stage debut at the Old Vic as Mustard Seed in *A Midsummer Night's Dream* (1929); danced with Ninette de Valois' Vic-Wells Ballet Company (1930 on) and toured with Anton Dolin and Alicia Markova; received 1st major choreography credit on *These Foolish Things* (1938); other stage appearances include *Toad of Toad Hall*, *The Miracle*, *Tulip Time*, *Best Bib and Tucker*, *Panama Hattie*, and *Follow the Girls*; arranged dances for all George Black productions (1938–45); directed plays, musicals, operas and ballets, such as *Big Ben*, *Bless the Bride*, *Tough at the Top*, *Peter Pan*, *And So to Bed*, *Second Threshold*, *Wild Thyme*, *Lady at the Wheel*, *Fledermaus*, *As You Like It*, *A Majority of One*, *Orpheus in the Underworld*, and *Show Boat*; directed such films as *The Stranger Left No Card*, *The Teckman Mystery*, *The King's Breakfast*, *The 12th Day*, *Raising a Riot*, *All for Mary*, *True as a Turtle* and *We Joined the Navy*; also directed for tv.

TOYEN (1902–1980). Czech painter and printmaker. Name variations: Marie Cermínová; Marie Cerminova. Born Marie Cermínová in Prague, Czechoslovakia, Sept 21, 1902; died in Paris, Nov 9, 1980; studied at Prague's School of Fine Arts with Emanuel Dite, 1919–22; lived with Jindrich Styrsky (Czech modernist artist, died 1942), 1922–42. ❖ Leading Surrealist, generally regarded as the most important 20th-century woman artist from the Czech lands, joined avant-garde Devetsil group (1923); lived in Paris with Jindrich Styrsky (1925–29), where she found her work becoming ever more Surrealistic in content and spirit; illustrated a Czech translation of Marquis de Sade's *Justine* (1932), signaling the beginning of an interest in the erotic that would inform her work; started a formal organization of Czech Surrealists (1934), and helped put together its 1st exhibition (1935); now a well-regarded Surrealist artist, was able to participate in all of the major Surrealist exhibitions, including ones held in London (1936) and Paris (1938), presenting such works as *Prometheus* (1934) and *The Abandoned Corset* (1937); during Nazi occupation of Czech lands (1939–45), worked underground, producing a series of book illustrations for works of major authors, including Georg Büchner's *Lenz*, Queen Margaret of Angoulême's *L'Heptaméron*, Apollinaire's *Alcools* and selections of poems, Joseph Conrad's *Chance*, as well as Czech versions of books by Pearl S. Buck and Simonetta Buonaccini; also did a set of lithographs, *Tir* (The Shooting Gallery, 1939–40); by end of WWII, her erotic works of Surrealism had become more veiled and mysterious than those of Czech male Surrealists; with the Communist takeover of Czechoslovakia, renounced Czech citizenship and lived in France as a refugee (1948–80); posthumous exhibitions were held at Paris' Centre Georges Pompidou (1982) and at Prague (2000), which was accompanied by publication of a catalogue of her artistic oeuvre totaling 360 pages. ❖ See also *Women in World History*.

TOYS, The.
See Harris, Barbara (1945—).
See Monteiro, June (1946—).
See Parritt, Barbara (1944—).

TRAA, Kari (1974—). Norwegian freestyle skier. Born Jan 28, 1974, in Voss, Norway. ❖ Won a bronze medal for moguls at Nagano Olympics (1998); won FIS World Cup Grand Prix for moguls (1998); placed 14th at Albertville Olympics in the 1st official Olympic mogul competition (1992); won 5 of 7 events to take the freestyle World championship (2001); won moguls and dual moguls at World championships (2003); won a gold medal for moguls at Salt Lake City Olympics (2002) and a silver medal for moguls at Torino Olympics (2006).

TRABA, Marta (1930–1983). Argentinean novelist and critic. Born Jan 5, 1930, in Buenos Aires, Argentina; died Nov 27, 1983, in an airplane crash en route from Paris, France, to Bogotá, Colombia; dau. of Spanish immigrants to Argentina; graduated with a degree in philosophy and the history of art from University of Buenos Aires; studied in Chile; m. Alberto Zalamea (div. 1967); m. Angel Rama (literary critic, died Nov 27, 1983). ❖ Published 1st book of poems, *Historia natural de la alegría* (Natural History of Happiness, 1951); moved to Colombia (1954); founded *Prisma* magazine; founded Museum of Modern Art, Bogotá (1965); published 1st novel, *Las ceremonias del verano* (Summer Ceremonies), which met critical acclaim and was awarded the Casa de las Américas Prize (1966); taught art and literature at universities in Latin America and North America; wrote about Latin America in poetry, essays, novels, and critical works; opposed tyranny and corruption while advocating human rights, democracy, and women's rights; expelled from Colombia following anti-military protests (1967); was the 1st Latin American woman to voice opinions in novel form about the political kidnappings and torture of political prisoners in Latin America when she published *Homérica Latina* (Homeric Latin, 1979); also addressed these issues in the 1st two novels of a trilogy, *Conversación al sur* (Conversation to the South, 1981) and *En cualquier lugar* (In Any Place, 1984). ❖ See also *Women in World History*.

TRACY, Hannah Conant (1815–1896). See Cutler, Hannah Conant.

TRACY, Honor (1913–1989). British novelist and travel writer. Name variations: Honor Lilbush Wingfield Tracy. Born Honor Lilbush Wingfield, Oct 19 (some sources cite Dec 19), 1913, in Bury St. Edmunds, East Anglia, England; died June 13, 1989, in Oxford, England; dau. of Humphrey Wingfield (surgeon) and Christabel May Clare (Miller) Tracy. ❖ Sent to Ireland by *Evening Standard* as special correspondent (1950); spent 10 years there and gleaned material for novels from experiences with Irish justice system; works include *Kakemono: A Sketch Book of Post-War Japan* (1950), *Mind You, I've Said Nothing: Forays in the Irish Republic* (1953), *The Prospects are Pleasing* (1958), *A Season of Mists* (1961), *Men at Work* (1966), *The Quiet End of Evening* (1972), *Winter in Castile* (1973) and *The Heart of England* (1983).

TRACY, Martha (1876–1942). American physician. Born April 10, 1876, in Plainfield, NJ; died Mar 22, 1942, in Philadelphia, PA; dau. of Jeremiah Evarts Tracy (lawyer) and Martha Sherman (Greene) Tracy; Woman's Medical College of Pennsylvania, medical degree, 1904; University of Pennsylvania, PhD in public hygiene, 1917. ❖ Studied under William B. Coley and assisted in development of "Coley's Fluid" at Cornell Medical College; named dean of Woman's Medical College of Pennsylvania (1917); appointed assistant director of public health for city of Philadelphia (1940).

TRACY, Mona Innis (1892–1959). New Zealand journalist, poet, short-story writer, and novelist. Name variations: Mona Innis Mackay; (pseudonym) Sally Forth. Born Jan 24, 1892, at Kensington, Adelaide, South Australia; died Feb 22, 1959, at Christchurch, New Zealand; dau. of John William Mackay and Catherine Julia (Bilston) Mackay (novelist); m. William Francis Tracy (barrister), 1921; children: 1 daughter, 1 son. ❖ Worked at *Auckland Weekly News* and Christchurch *Times* (1910s); contributed to *Weekly Press*, Auckland *Sun*; contributed "The Voice of the Enzed Woman" column to Australian magazine *Aussie* under pen-name Sally Forth (1920s); published collection of short stories, *Piriki's Princess* (1925), children's novel *Rifle and Tomahawk* (1927), historical fiction *Lawless Days* (1928), and novel *Martin Thorn—Adventurer* (1930); produced several school history texts and generated series of radio broadcasts, which were gathered in *West Coast Yesterday* and published in 1960. ❖ See also *Dictionary of New Zealand Biography* (Vol. 4).

TRACY, Paula (1939—). American ballet dancer. Born 1939 in San Francisco, CA; m. Michael Smuin. ❖ Performed with San Francisco Ballet (1956–62), where she created a role in Lew Christensen's *Emperor Norton* (1957); with husband, toured as an adagio team; appeared on Broadway in *Little Me* (1962) and *No Strings* (1962); joined American Ballet Theater (1966), where she created roles for Eliot Feld's *A Soldier's Tale* and Smuin's *Pulcinella Variations*, among others; returned to San Francisco Ballet when husband became co-artistic director there (1973), and created roles in his *Songs of Mahler* (1976), *Mozart's C Minor Mass* (1978), and *Shinju* (1978) and for Lew Christensen's *Filling Station* and William Christensen's *Nothing Doing Bar*.

TRADER, Ella King (1838–1919). See Newsom, Ella King.

TRAFFORD, F. G. (1832–1906). See Riddell, Charlotte.

TRA HIEU NGAN See Tran Hieu Ngan.

TRAILINE, Helen (1928—). French ballet dancer. Born Oct 6, 1928, in Bombas, Lorraine, France. ❖ Prima ballerina, trained with Julie Sedova, Olga Preobrazhenska, and Lyubov Egorova; performed in numerous ballet companies throughout France, such as Nouveau Ballet de Monte Carlo (1946), Les Ballets des Champs-Elysées (1949–50), Les Ballet Janine Charrat, and French Ballet Russe de Monte Carlo; danced in repertory works of Maurice Béjart, Aurel Milloss, Charrat, and in numerous classical works including *Giselle, Lac des Cygnes,* and *The Nutcracker*; created roles for Charrat's *Electre* (1960) and Béjart's *Haut Voltage* (1956).

TRAILL, Catherine Parr (1802–1899). English-born Canadian author, botanist, and pioneer. Name variations: Catherine Strickland. Born Catherine Parr Strickland, Jan 9, 1802, in London, England; died Aug 29, 1899, in Lakefield, Ontario, Canada; dau. of Thomas Strickland of Suffolk, England (landowner and shipper) and Elizabeth (Homer) Strickland; sister of Susanna Moodie (1803–1885), Agnes Strickland (1796–1874), Elizabeth Strickland (1794–1875), Jane Margaret Strickland (1800–1888), and Samuel Stickland, all writers; m. Thomas Traill (military officer), 1832 (died 1859). ❖ At 16, while still in England, wrote 1st book, *The Tell Tale: An Original Collection of Moral and Amusing Stories*; before age 30, also wrote over a dozen children's books and works on natural history, including *The Young Emigrants: or, Pictures of Life in Canada* (1826); immigrated to Upper Canada shortly after marriage (1832), living primarily in Ontario, which was then a wilderness; published her best-known book, *The Backwoods of Canada: Being Letters from the Wife of an Emigrant Officer; Illustrative of the Domestic Economy of British America* (1836); also wrote a number of children's stories and published sketches that were widely circulated; wrote *The Female Emigrant's Guide, and Hints on Canadian Housekeeping* (1854), which was later retitled *The Canadian Settler's Guide* and printed in several editions; also published many nature studies and works about botany later in life, including her best-known *Canadian Wild Flowers* (1868), *Studies of Plant Life in Canada* (1885) and *Pearls and Pebbles; or, Notes of an Old Naturalist* (1895). ❖ See also *Women in World History*.

TRALOW, Charlotte (1905–1982). See Keun, Irmgard.

TRAMBLEY, Estela (1936–1999). See Portillo-Trambley, Estela.

TRANDENKOVA-KRIVOSHEVA, Marina (1967—). Soviet runner. Born Jan 7, 1967, in USSR. ❖ At Barcelona Olympics, won a silver medal in 4 x 100-meter relay (1992).

TRAN HIEU NGAN (1974—). Vietnamese taekwondo player. Name variations: Tra Hieu Ngan. Born 1974 in Tuy Hoa, Vietnam. ❖ Won a silver medal for 49–57 kg at Sydney Olympics (2000), the 1st medal won by a Vietnamese in Olympic competition.

TRANI, countess of. See Mathilde of Bavaria (1843–1925).

TRAN LE XUAN (b. 1924). See Nhu, Madame.

TRANQUILLI, Allison (1972—). See Cook, Allison.

TRAPANI, Antonia von (b. 1851). Countess of Caserta. Born Mar 16, 1851; dau. of Franz, count of Trapani; m. Alphonse of Sicily (1841–1934), count of Caserta, on June 8, 1868; children: Ferdinand Pio, duke of Calabria (1869–1934); Charles or Carlos (1870–1949), prince of Bourbon-Sicily; Franz (1873–1876); Maria Immaculata (b. 1874, who m. John George of Saxony); Maria Cristina of Sicily (1877–1947); Maria Pia (b. 1878, who m. Louis d'Eu); Maria Josephine (b. 1880); Gennaro (b. 1882); Reiner (1883–1973), duke of Castro; Philipp (b. 1885); Franz (1888–1914); Gabriel (b. 1897).

TRAPANI, countess of. See Maria Isabella (1834–1901).

TRAPNEL, Anna (fl. 1642–1661). English prophet and writer. Birth date and place unknown; date of death unknown but evidence suggests she was still alive in 1661; dau. of William Trapnel (shipwright); married, possibly in 1661. ❖ Achieved some fame as a prophet while Oliver Cromwell served as Lord Protector of England (1653–58); her 1st book, *The Cry of a Stone; or a Relation of Something Spoken in Whitehall by Anna Trapnel . . . Uttered in Prayers and Spiritual Songs, by an Inspiration Extraordinary, and Full of Wonder* (1654), consists of verse prophecies that she spoke during a trance, which were written down by an attendant; for calling Cromwell the "little horn" on the head of the Beast, was arrested and imprisoned in Plymouth; while there, wrote *A Legacy for Saints: Being Several Experiences of the Dealings of God with Anna Trapnel* and *Anna Trapnel's Report and Plea: or a Narrative of her Journey from London into Cornwall* (both 1654); also wrote *Strange and Wonderful Newes from White-hall* (1654) and *A Voice for the King of Saints* (1657). ❖ See also *Women in World History.*

TRAPP, Maria von (1905–1987). *See Von Trapp, Maria.*

TRASCA, Marioara (1962—). Romanian rower. Born Oct 29, 1962, in Romania. ❖ At Los Angeles Olympics, won a silver medal in coxed eights (1984); at Seoul Olympics, won a silver medal in coxed eights and a bronze medal in coxed fours (1988).

TRASK, Kate Nichols (1853–1922). American writer and philanthropist. Name variations: Katrina Trask. Born May 30, 1853, in Brooklyn, New York; died Jan 8, 1922, at Yaddo, near Saratoga Springs, New York; dau. of George Little Nichols (importer) and Christina Mary (Cole) Nichols; m. Spencer Trask (banker-financier and chair of *The New York Times*), Nov 12, 1874 (died 1909); m. George Foster Peabody (financier and philanthropist), Feb 6, 1921. ❖ During 1st marriage, had 4 children, but all died in infancy or early childhood; turned to writing for solace (1888); anonymously published *Under King Constantine* (1892), a trio of long love poems which achieved success (used name Katrina Trask on a later edition); wrote poems, sonnets, novels, blank verse, and plays (1892–1915), including the novel *Free, Not Bound* (1903), the blank-verse narrative *Night & Morning* (1907), and *King Alfred's Jewel* (1908), a historical drama written in blank verse; a pacifist, also wrote the antiwar play *In the Vanguard* (1914), her best-known work; with husband, entertained writers and artists at Yaddo, their 300-acre country estate near Saratoga Springs, NY; made public her plans for developing the property as an artists' residence on her death (1913). ❖ See also *Women in World History.*

TRASK, Katrina (1853–1922). *See Trask, Kate Nichols.*

TRASKE, Mary (fl. 1660). American letter writer. A Quaker who lived in Massachusetts. ❖ With Margaret Smith, wrote "Joint Letter from Mary Traske and Margaret Smith . . . to . . . John Endicott" (1660) about Puritan persecution of Quakers in Massachusetts, and was imprisoned 10 months in Boston.

TRASTAMARA, Eleanor (d. 1415). *See Eleanor Trastamara.*

TRAUBEL, Helen (1899–1972). American soprano. Born in St. Louis, MO, June 20, 1899; died in Santa Monica, CA, July 28, 1972; dau. of Clara Stuhr Traubel (singer) and Otto Ferdinand Traubel (druggist); m. Louis Franklin Carpenter (car salesman), 1922 (div.); m. William L. Bass (her manager). ❖ One of America's greatest singers, began by performing in church choirs, then took voice lessons with Louise Vetta-Karst (1916); debuted with St. Louis Symphony Orchestra (1924); made Metropolitan Opera debut (1937), appearing with Kirsten Flagstad; sang on NBC radio, becoming more widely known throughout US; temporarily retired to study with Giuseppe Boghetti, then debuted at NY's Town Hall (1939); after Kirsten Flagstad returned to Norway (1941), reigned supreme as the Met's "Queen of the German Wing," particularly known for her Wagnerian repertoire for which her large voice and big frame seemed ideally suited; was the 1st entirely American-trained singer to do Isolde and all 3 Brünnhildes in a season; during WWII, performed light music for troops in USO concerts; with advent of tv, appeared with Jimmy Durante, Red Skelton and Ed Sullivan; also performed in 3 films, made numerous recordings for RCA and Columbia, and was the 1st singer to record with Arturo Toscanini and his NBC Symphony Orchestra; wrote detective stories, including *The Metropolitan Opera Murders* (1951). ❖ See also autobiography *St. Louis Woman* (Duell, 1959); and *Women in World History.*

TRAURIG, Christine (1957—). German-born equestrian. Born Mar 13, 1957, in Germany; lives in Carlsbad, CA; m. Bernie Traurig (show

jumper, div.). ❖ Won a team bronze medal for dressage at Sydney Olympics (2000), on Etienne.

TRAVA, Teresa Fernandez de (fl. 1170). Queen of Leon. Became 2nd wife of Fernando or Ferdinand II (1137–1188), king of Leon (r. 1157–1188), before Oct 7, 1178; children: Fernando of Leon (born after 1179).

TRAVELL, Janet G. (1901–1997). American physician. Name variations: Janet Powell. Born Janet Graeme Travell, Dec 17, 1901, in New York, NY; died Aug 1, 1997, in Northampton, Massachusetts; dau. of Willard (physician) and Janet (Davidson) Travell; sister of Virginia Travell, pediatrician; Wellesley College, BA, 1922; Cornell University Medical College, MD, 1926; m. John W. G. Powell (investment counselor), June 1929; children: Janet Powell McAlee; Virginia Powell Street. ❖ Noted for her work in the field of neuromuscular pain, was the 1st woman to serve as personal physician to a US president; served as an ambulance surgeon while an intern and resident at New York Hospital, an affiliate of Cornell University Medical College (1927–29); served as house physician at New York Hospital (1929–61); became expert in the use of digitalis to treat pneumonia, arterial disease, and pain; was an instructor, then associate professor in pharmacology, Cornell Medical College (1930–61); as personal physician to John F. Kennedy, was appointed to serve as personal physician to the president of US (1961); one of her other patients was Barry Goldwater; remained White House physician after Kennedy's assassination, serving until 1965; published, with David G. Simons, *Travell and Simons' Myofascial Pain and Dysfunction: The Trigger Point Manual* (2 vols., 1983). ❖ See also *Women in World History.*

TRAVERS, Graham (1859–1918). *See Todd, Margaret G.*

TRAVERS, Linden (1913–2001). English actress. Born Florence Linden-Travers, May 27, 1913, in Houghton-le-Spring, Durham, England; died Oct 23, 2001, in Cornwall, England; sister of Bill Travers (actor); m. Guy Leon (div.); m. James Holman, 1948 (died 1974); children: Jennifer Leon (b. 1939); Sally Linden Holman (b. 1949). ❖ Made stage debut at Newcastle-on-Tyne in *Cynara* (1933) and London debut in *Murder in Mayfair* (1934); other plays include *No Orchids for Miss Blandish* (title role on stage and in film), *Quality Street* and *My Friend Lester*; made 25 films, including *Brief Ecstasy, The Lady Vanishes, Jassy, Quartet* and *Don't Ever Leave Me*; became a credentialed and practicing hypnotist and psychologist.

TRAVERS, Mary (1894–1941). *See Bolduc, Marie.*

TRAVERS, Mary (1936—). American singer. Name variations: Peter, Paul and Mary. Born Nov 7, 1936, in Louisville, KY; dau. of Virginia Coigney (social activist and journalist who also wrote for tv soap "Edge of Night"); father wrote novels; m. 3rd husband Ethan Robbins (restaurateur), 1991; children: Erika and Alicia. ❖ Sang on Broadway in *The Next President* (1957); while working in Greenwich Village, met Peter Yarrow and Noel Paul Stookey and formed Peter, Paul and Mary (1961); with trio, signed with Warner Bros. and released debut LP, *Peter, Paul and Mary* (1962), which went #1 and included hits "Lemon Tree" and "If I Had a Hammer"; other single hits include "Puff the Magic Dragon" (1963), "Blowin' in the Wind" (1963), "I Dig Rock and Roll Music" (1967), "Day Is Done" (1969), "Leaving on a Jet Plane" (1969); albums include *A Song Will Rise* (1965), *Late Again* (1968), *Flowers and Stones* (1990), and *Around the Campfire* (1998); hosted radio talk show and BBC tv series after group disbanded (1970); with trio, began 40th anniversary tour of US (2000); known for commitment to political and social issues.

TRAVERS, P. L. (1906–1996). Australian-English writer. Name variations: Pamela Lyndon Travers. Born Helen Goff Travers, Aug 9, 1906, in Queensland, Australia; died April 23, 1996, in London; dau. of Robert and Margaret (Goff) Travers (Irish-Scottish ranchers); never married; no children. ❖ Theater and literary critic, writer on mythology and spirituality, whose success with her "Mary Poppins" books overshadowed her other literary accomplishments; was a writer, actress and dancer in Australia; was a freelance writer in England (1924–40); wrote regularly for *New English Weekly*; with illustrations by Mary Shepard, published *Mary Poppins* (1934), which was an instant success; lived in America (1940–45) and England (1945–65); was writer-in-residence at Radcliffe College (1965–66), Smith College (1966–67), and Scripps College (1970); returned to England (1976); wrote 12 books for children, including *Mary Poppins* (1934), *Mary Poppins Comes Back* (1935), *Happy Ever After* (1940), *I Go by Sea, I Go by Land* (1941), *Mary Poppins Opens the Door* (1943), *Mary Poppins in the Park* (1952), *Two Pairs of Shoes* (1980) and *Mary Poppins in Cherry Tree Lane* (1982), and 7 books for adults, including *Moscow Excursion* (1935), *Aunt Sass* (1941), *In Search of the Hero: The Continuing Relevance of Myth and Fairy Tale* (1970), (translator with Ruth Lewinnek) Karlfried Montmartin's *The Way of Transformation* (1971) and *George Ivanovitch Gurdjieff* (1973). ❖ See also Patricia Demers, *P. L. Travers* (Twayne, 1991); and *Women in World History*.

TRAVERS, Susan (1909–2003). French legionnaire. Born 1909 in London, England; died 2003 in France; dau. of a naval officer; m. Nicholas Schlegelmilch (legion NCO), 1947 (died 1995); children: 2 sons. ❖ The only woman to serve in French Foreign Legion, joined the Free French Forces who were fighting in North Africa during WWII; after withstanding Rommel's siege of the desert fortress of Bir Hakeim for 15 days (1942), played a key role in the breakout of the troops, including 650 legionnaires; awarded the Croix de Guerre; applied to join the legion officially (1945), omitting gender from the form, and was accepted; resigned (1947). ❖ See also memoir (with Wendy Holden), *Tomorrow to be Brave* (2001).

TRAVERSA, Lucia (1965—). Italian fencer. Born May 31, 1965, in Italy. ❖ At Seoul Olympics, won a silver medal in team foil (1988).

TRAVERSE, Madlaine (1875–1964). American silent-film star. Born Madlaine Businsky, Aug 1, 1875, in Cleveland, OH; died Jan 7, 1964, in Cleveland. ❖ Films include *Leah Kleschna, Fruits of Desire, Ben-Hur, Snares of Paris, The Hell Ship, Poor Little Rich Girl, Beyond the Horizon, Seven Keys to Baldpate* and *Gambling Souls*; retired after Klieg lights seriously damaged her eyesight.

TREBLE, Lillian M. (1854–1909). Canadian philanthropist. Born Lillian Massey in 1854; died in 1909; dau. of H. A. Massey; m. John Mill Treble. ❖ Organized classes in domestic science which led to the adoption of a complete curriculum in household science in various women's colleges throughout Canada; gave a handsome, spacious structure called the "Lillian Massey Household Science and Art Building," to Toronto University, which opened in 1913.

TREE, Mrs. Beerbohm (1858–1937). *See Tree, Maud Holt.*

TREE, Clare (d. 1954). *See Major, Clare Tree.*

TREE, Dolly (1899–1962). American costume designer. Name variations: Dorothy Tree. Born Dorothy Marian Isbell, Mar 17, 1899, in Bristol, England; died May 17, 1962, in Long Island, NY. ❖ Began career on Broadway (1920s), where she designed Mae West's costumes for *Diamond Lil* (1927); also designed for Capitol Stage and Paramount Circuit Shows (1927); moved to Los Angeles (1929); at MGM, designed costumes for over 200 movies (1932–42), including *Manhattan Melodrama* (1934), *The Thin Man* (1934), *Evelyn Prentice* (1934), *David Copperfield* (1934), *Age of Indiscretion* (1935), *A Night at the Opera* (1935), *Ah, Wilderness!* (1935), *A Tale of Two Cities* (1935), *After the Thin Man* (1936), *The Good Earth* (1936), *Night Must Fall* (1937), *A Day at the Races* (1937), *Rosalie* (1937), *Ice Follies of 1939* (1938), *Test Pilot* (1938), *Young Tom Edison* (1939), *Maisie* (1939), *On Borrowed Time* (1939), *Babes in Arms* (1939), *Andy Hardy Meets Debutante* (1940), *Wyoming* (1940), *Dr. Kildare Goes Home* (1940), *Strike up the Band* (1940), *Hullabaloo* (1940), *Little Nellie Kelly* (1940), *The Trial of Mary Dugan* (1940), *Billy the Kid* (1941) and *Tales of Manhattan* (1942). ❖ See also *Women in World History*.

TREE, Dorothy (1906–1992). American stage and screen actress. Born Dorothy Estelle Triebitz, May 21, 1906, in Brooklyn, NY; died Feb 13, 1992, in Englewood, NJ. ❖ Featured player on Broadway and in films; made film debut in *Husband's Holiday* (1931), followed by *The Man with Two Faces, The Case of the Howling Dog, Madame DuBarry, The Woman in Red, A Night at the Ritz, The Great Garrick, Trade Winds, Zaza, Abe Lincoln in Illinois, Knute Rockne All American,* and *The Asphalt Jungle,* among others; was a founding member of the Screen Actor's Guild; became a voice teacher and wrote a guide for public speaking, *A Woman's Voice.*

TREE, Ellen (1805–1880). *See Kean, Ellen.*

TREE, Mrs. Herbert Beerbohm (1858–1937). *See Tree, Maud Holt.*

TREE, Lady (1858–1937). *See Tree, Maud Holt.*

TREE, Marietta (1917–1991). American diplomat and social activist. Born Mary Endicott Peabody on April 12, 1917, in Lawrence, Massachusetts; died Aug 15, 1991, in New York, NY; dau. of Malcolm E. Peabody (Episcopal bishop) and Mary (Parkman) Peabody; attended University of Pennsylvania, 1936–39; m. Desmond FitzGerald (lawyer), Sept 2, 1939 (div. 1947); m. Arthur Ronald Lambert Tree (investment

broker who had been a Conservative member of British Parliament for 13 years and married to Nancy Lancaster), July 28, 1947; children: (1st m.) Frances FitzGerald (journalist who won Pulitzer Prize for *Fire in the Lake*); (2nd m.) Penelope Tree (well-known model). ❖ The 1st woman to serve as a chief US delegate and a permanent ambassador to the UN, was a civil-rights activist (beginning 1940s); helped found Sydenham Hospital in New York City (1944), the 1st voluntary inter-racial hospital in US; on 2nd marriage, lived in England (1947–49); as a Democrat, worked on congressional and presidential election campaigns; appointed to serve as chief US delegate to the United Nations (1961); became ambassador to the UN on the Human Rights Commission (1964); worked at UN Secretariat as a member of the staff of Secretary General U Thant (1966–67). ❖ See also Caroline Seebohm, *No Regrets: The Life of Marietta Tree* (Simon & Schuster, 1998); and *Women in World History*.

TREE, Maud Holt (1858–1937). English stage actress. Name variations: Maud Holt; Lady Tree; Mrs. Beerbohm Tree; Mrs. Herbert Beerbohm Tree. Born Helen Maud Holt, Oct 5, 1858, in London, England; died Aug 7, 1937, in London; m. Herbert Beerbohm Tree (actor-director and founder of RADA), 1883 (died 1917); children: Viola Tree (actress). ❖ Made stage debut in London as Jenny in *Sweethearts* and came to prominence as Hester Gould in *The Millionaire* (both 1883); other plays include *The Magistrate, Clancarty, The Red Lamp, The Pompadour* (title role), *Hamlet* (as Ophelia), *A Woman of No Importance, A Woman's Reason, Trilby* (title role), *The Musketeers, Julius Caesar, Nero, Captain Swift, What Every Woman Knows, The Admirable Crichton, Mayfair and Montmartre, Diplomacy,* and *The Rivals* (as Mrs. Malaprop); starred in NY debut opposite husband in *The Red Lamp* (1895) and later appeared there with Mrs. Patrick Campbell in *Electra* (1908); films include *Little Dorrit, Such is the Law, Wedding Rehearsal, Early to Bed, Her Imaginary Lover* and *The Private Life of Henry VIII.* Named Officer of the British Empire (OBE).

TREE, Nancy (1897–1994). *See Lancaster, Nancy.*

TREE, Viola (1884–1938). English actress, singer and playwright. Born July 17, 1884, in London, England; died Nov 15, 1938, of pleurisy in London; dau. of Herbert Beerbohm Tree (actor- director and founder of RADA) and Maud Holt Tree (actress); m. Alan Parsons. ❖ Made London debut as Viola in her father's production of *Twelfth Night* (1904); appeared as Eurydice in Gluck's opera *Orpheus* to great success (1912); assumed the management of the Aldwych (1919–20, 1921), appearing there in *Sacred and Profane Love, Pygmalion, The Tempest,* and *Olivia;* other plays include *Agatha, A Woman of No Importance, Hamlet* (as Ophelia), *Loyalty, The Truth Game, Strange Orchestra, Fresh Fields, Jill Darling* and *Symphony in Two Flats;* appeared in such films as *Unmarried, For the Love of Mike* and *Heart's Desire;* co-wrote with Gerald Du Maurier the play *The Dancers* and wrote *The Swallow* (Everyman, 1925). ❖ See also reminiscences *Castles in the Air* (1926).

TREEN, Mary (1907–1989). American tv and screen actress. Name variations: Mary Louise Treen; Mary Lou Treen. Born Mary Louise Summers, Mar 27, 1907, in St. Louis, MO; died July 20, 1989, in Newport Beach, CA. ❖ Began career in musicals and vaudeville; made over 150 films, mostly in small parts, including *Babbitt, A Night at the Ritz, Kitty Foyle, So Proudly We Hail* and *Who's Minding the Store;* also appeared as Cousin Tilly in *It's a Wonderful Life.*

TREFILOVA, Vera (1875–1943). Russian ballerina and actress. Born 1875 in St. Petersburg, Russia; died July 11, 1943 in Paris, France; parentage and family history unknown; graduated from St. Petersburg Imperial School of Ballet, 1894; m. A. I. Butler (died); m. N. V. Soloviev (died); m. Valerian Svetlov (ballet critic and author, died 1934). ❖ At Maryinsky Theater of St. Petersburg, became a ballerina (1904), debuting as Princess Aurora in Tchaikovsky's *The Sleeping Beauty;* was prima ballerina of the Maryinsky (1906–10); resigned from the company after a final appearance as Odette-Odile in Tchaikovsky's *Swan Lake* (1910); returned to the stage as a dramatic actress at the Imperial Mikhailovsky Theater in St. Petersburg (1915); with the Russian Revolution (1917), left Russia and opened a ballet studio in Paris; returned to ballet with Diaghilev's Ballet Russe in Paris (1921), dancing as Princess Aurora, her last appearance as a prima ballerina; lived rest of life in Paris and died during the German occupation. ❖ See also *Women in World History*.

TREFUSIS, Violet (1894–1972). English novelist, memoirist, and salonnière. Born Violet Keppel in London, England, June 6, 1894; died in Florence, Italy, Mar 1, 1972; dau. of Colonel George Keppel (army officer and brother of the earl of Albemarle) and Alice

(Edmonstone) Keppel (1869–1947, acknowledged mistress of King Edward VII); sister of Sonia Keppel (1900–1986); m. Denys Robert Trefusis (cavalry officer with Royal Horse Guards), June 16, 1919 (died summer 1929); no children. ❖ Had affair with Vita Sackville-West (1918–21), the defining episode in Violet's life; with husband, settled in Paris where they became part of Parisian high society (1921); presided over a salon that attracted well-known writers, such as Jean Cocteau and Max Jacob, diplomats and politicians, including Paul Reynaud (future prime minister of France), the couturiers Christian Dior and Pierre Balmain, and European royalty; published 1st novel, *Sortie de Secours* (Emergency Exit, 1929), which was a success, followed by *Echo* (1931), which became a bestseller and received good reviews; also wrote *Tandem* and *Hunt the Slipper* (1930s); published last work in French, *Les Causes Perdues* (*Lost Causes*), which appeared in German-occupied Paris (1940); was one of the few English writers to have written equally well in French. Awarded Legion of Honor in France (1950); received Order of Commendatore from Italian government (early 1960s). ❖ See also memoir *Don't Look Round* (1952); Sonia Keppel, *Edwardian Daughter* (Hamilton, 1958); Henrietta Sharpe, *A Solitary Woman: A Life of Violet Trefusis* (Constable, 1981); Diana Souhami, *Mrs. Keppel and Her Daughter* (St. Martin, 1997); Philippe Jullian and John Phillips. *The Other Woman: A Life of Violet Trefusis* (Houghton, 1976); Philippe Jullian, *Violet Trefusis: Life and Letters* (Hamilton, 1976); *The Last Edwardians: An Illustrated History of Violet Trefusis and Alice Keppel* (Athenaeum, 1985); and *Women in World History*.

TREGUNNO, Jane (1962—). Canadian rower. Name variations: Jane Tregunno Stamp. Born Sept 9, 1962; McMaster University, BSc, 1986. ❖ At Los Angeles Olympics, won a silver medal in coxed fours (1984).

TREIBER, Birgit (1960—). East German swimmer. Born Feb 26, 1960, in East Germany. ❖ At Montreal Olympics, won a silver medal in 200-meter backstroke and a silver medal in 100-meter backstroke (1976); at Moscow Olympics, won a bronze medal in 200-meter backstroke (1980).

TRELLING, Ursula (1900–1993). See Anderson, Regina M.

TREMAIN, Rose (1943—). British novelist, historian and playwright. Born 1943 in London, England; attended East Anglia University and the Sorbonne; married twice; children: daughter. ❖ Taught creative writing at University of East Anglia (1988–95); works include *Sadler's Birthday* (1976), *The Cupboard* (1981), *Journey to the Volcano* (1985), *Restoration* (1989), *Evangelista's Fan and Other Stories* (1994), *The Way I Found Her* (1997) and *The Colour* (2003); won James Tait Black Memorial Prize for *Sacred Country* (1992) and Whitbread Novel Award (1999) for *Music and Silence*; also wrote *The Fight for Freedom for Women* (1973), as well as radio and tv plays.

TRENCH, Melesina (1768–1827). Irish writer. Born Melesina Chenevix, Mar 22, 1768, in Dublin, Ireland, to parents of Huguenot descent; died May 27, 1827, in Dublin; raised by paternal grandfather, the bishop of Waterford, then maternal grandfather, Archdeacon Gervais; m. Richard St. George (colonel), 1786 (died 1788); m. Richard Trench (barrister), in 1803; children: (1st m.) 1 son; (2nd m.) 3 sons, including Francis Chenevix Trench (1806–1886, essayist) and Richard Chenevix Trench (1807–1886, poet, theologian, and archbishop of Dublin). ❖ Celebrated beauty, spent 10 years living in Germany and France (1797–1807), where she met leaders and prominent citizens from all over Europe, including Lord Horatio Nelson and Lady Emma Hamilton; during this time, wrote a series of journals and letters, edited and released under the title *Remains* by son Richard (1862), which are now hailed as both important historical documents and literary achievements; while in Europe, married Richard Trench, who was later captured and imprisoned in France by Napoleon; escaped with husband to Dublin (1807), where she wrote novels, poetry, and essays until her death. ❖ See also *Women in World History*.

TRENT, Helen (1916–1984). See Stevens, Julie.

TRENTINI, Emma (1878–1959). Italian opera star. Born in 1878; died Mar 23, 1959, in Milan, Italy. ❖ Sang at La Scala and Metropolitan Opera; starred on Broadway in the operetta *Naughty Marietta*, written expressly for her by Victor Herbert, and in Rudolf Friml's *The Firefly*; toured America in vaudeville for several years.

TRETTEL, Lidia (1973—). Italian snowboarder. Born April 5, 1973, in Italy. ❖ Won a bronze medal for giant parallel slalom at Salt Lake City (2002).

TRETTIN, Christine (1956—). See Errath, Christine.

TREVERTON, Ruth (1917—). See van Heyningen, Ruth.

TREVILLE, Abigail (c. 1740–?). See Stoneman, Abigail.

TREVOR, Claire (1909–2000). American actress. Born Claire Wemlinger on Mar 8, 1909, in New York City; died April 8, 2000, in Newport Beach, California; attended Columbia University and American Academy of Dramatic Arts; m. Clark Andrews (producer), 1938 (div. 1942); m. Cylos William Dunsmoore (div. 1947); m. Milton Bren (producer), 1948 (died 1979); children: (2nd m.) Charles Dunsmoore (died 1978). ❖ Blonde, sultry-voiced veteran of over 100 films, who proved to be a highly accomplished actress when given the opportunity, is probably best remembered for her portrayal of the boozy mistress of gangster Edward G. Robinson in *Key Largo* (1948), for which she received an Academy Award as Best Supporting Actress; also received Oscar nominations for roles in *Dead End* (1937) and *The High and the Mighty* (1954) and critical acclaim for performance in the classic *Stagecoach* (1939); won Emmy Award for tv performance in "Dodsworth" (1956); other films include *Baby Take a Bow* (1934), *Dante's Inferno* (1935), *The Amazing Dr. Clitterhouse* (1938), *Dark Command* (1940), *Honky Tonk* (1941), *The Adventures of Martin Eden* (1942), *Murder My Sweet* (1944), *Johnny Angel* (1945), *Crack-Up* (1946), *Born to Kill* (1947), *The Babe Ruth Story* (1948), *The Velvet Touch* (1948), *Hard Fast and Beautiful* (1951), *Lucy Gallant* (1955), *The Mountain* (1956), *Marjorie Morningstar* (1958), *Two Weeks in Another Town* (1962) and *Kiss Me Goodbye* (1982). ❖ See also *Women in World History*.

TREVOR-JONES, Mabel (fl. 1904–1921). Australian golfer. Name variations: Lady Halse Rogers. Born in New South Wales, Australia. ❖ Won Australian Women's Amateur (1904); led in the formation of the Australian Ladies Golf Union (1921).

TREWAVAS, Ethelwynn (1900–1992). Freshwater biologist and ichthyologist. Born Nov 5, 1900, Penzance, Cornwall, England; died Aug 16, 1992; University College, Reading, BS, 1921; King's College for Women, DSc, 1934; attended Queen Elizabeth College, University of London. ❖ International freshwater fish expert and the 1st woman deputy keeper of zoology at the British Museum of Natural History, 1st worked at King's College of Household and Social Science (1925–28); at British Museum, was research assistant for Tate Regan (1928–35), then assistant freshwater fish keeper (1935–37), permanent keeper (1937–46), principal scientific officer (1946–58) and deputy keeper in zoology (1958–61); compiled fish section of the zoological record; traveled to Africa several times for fish-searching expeditions; studied deep-sea fishes and cichlid fishes from Lakes Malawi and Tanganyika; elected fellow of Linnean Society (1991).

TRICKEY, Minnijean Brown (b. 1942). See Brown, Minnijean.

TRIER MØRCH, Dea (1941—). Danish essayist, novelist and illustrator. Name variations: Dea Trier Morch or Trier Moerch. Born Dec 9, 1941, in Copenhagen, Denmark; dau. of an unmarried mother who was an architect; attended art colleges in Eastern Europe; children: 3. ❖ Participated in socialist artists' collective *Røde Mor*; came to prominence with self-illustrated novel *Vinterbørn* (1976, Winter's Child, 1986); also wrote *Sørgmunter realisme* (1968, Realism of Joy and Sorrow), *Kastaniealleen* (1978, Chestnut Avenue), *Den indre* (1980, The Inner City), and *Aftenstjernen* (1982, Evening Star).

TRIEU, Lady (225–248 CE). See Ba Trieu.

TRIEU AU (225–248 CE). See Ba Trieu.

TRIEU THI CHINH (225–248 CE). See Ba Trieu.

TRIEU THI TRINH (225–248 CE). See Ba Trieu.

TRIEU TRING NUONG (225–248 CE). See Ba Trieu.

TRIGÈRE, Pauline (1912–2002). French-born American couturiere. Name variations: Pauline Trigere. Pronunciation: Tree-JAIR. Born Nov 4, 1912, in Paris, France; died Feb 13, 2002, in New York, NY; dau. of Alexandre Trigère (tailor) and Cécile (Coriene) Trigère (seamstress); Collège Victor Hugo, BA; m. Lazar Radley (Russian-born tailor), 1929 (sep. 1941, eventually div.); children: Jean-Pierre and Philippe. ❖ Worked in the Place Vendôme salon of Martial et Armand; moved to US (1937); worked for local fashion houses, including those of Hattie Carnegie and Ben Gershel (1937–42); with brother, launched clothing-design business in a New York City loft, Trigère Inc. (1942); though noted especially for the reserved elegance of her clothes, is credited with the development of such fashion innovations as the sleeveless coat, reversible coat, mobile collar, and spiral jacket; became US citizen (1944); was at the forefront of American fashion, releasing some 80 outfits a year in 4 seasonal collections (1950s–60s); remained a significant presence on American fashion scene (1970s–80s); kept her design firm in business for over 50 years. Received 3 Coty Awards (1949, 1951, 1959) and inducted into Coty Fashion Hall of Fame (1959); received Silver Medal of the City of Paris (1972) and Lifetime Achievement Award from Council of Fashion Designers of America (1993); named chevalier of Legion of Honor (2001). ❖ See also *Women in World History.*

TRILLING, Diana (1905–1996). American writer. Born Diana Rubin in New York, NY, July 21, 1905; died in New York, NY, Oct 23, 1996; dau. of Joseph Rubin (businessman) and Sadie Helene (Forbert) Rubin; Radcliffe College, AB, 1925; m. Lionel Trilling (critic and professor of English), June 12, 1929 (died Nov 5, 1975); children: James Lionel Trilling. ❖ Trenchant observer of NY literary and cultural scene (1930s–70s) who emerged from the shadow of her husband to become a notable and iconoclastic critic in her own right; met Lionel Trilling (1927); began work for National Committee for the Defense of Political Prisoners (1932), but became convinced that many of the funds raised by the committee were being used for political purposes by Communist Party; caused a stir in NY political and literary circles when she and husband resigned from Committee (1933) and praised Stalin's rival Leon Trotsky; involved in controversy among NY litterateurs for years to come; now an avowed anti-Communist, worked as a fiction reviewer for *The Nation* (1942–49), mixing political commentary in the reviews; began writing criticism for *Partisan Review,* where she became known for her independent viewpoints (1950); chaired Committee for Cultural Freedom (1955–57); was a columnist for *New Leader* (1957–59); wrote reviews and articles for a wide variety of journals and magazines, including *Commentary, American Scholar, Harper's, Vogue,* and *Harper's Bazaar,* as well as such newspapers as *The New York Times* and *New York Herald Tribune;* nominated for Pulitzer Prize for *Mrs. Harris: The Death of the Scarsdale Diet Doctor* (1981); articles eventually appeared in her collections *Claremont Essays* (1964), *We Must March My Darlings: A Critical Decade* (1977) and *Reviewing the Forties* (1978); also edited many of husband's essays. ❖ See also memoir *The Beginning of the Journey: The Marriage of Diana and Lionel Trilling* (Harcourt, 1993); and *Women in World History.*

TRILLINI, Giovanna (1970—). Italian fencer. Born May 17, 1970, in Jesi, Italy. ❖ At Barcelona Olympics, won gold medals in team foil and indiv. foil (1992), the 1st female fencer to win two gold medals at the same Olympics; won indiv. foil at World Cups (1991, 1993, 1998); at World championships, won for team foil (1997, 2001, 2004) and indiv. and team foil (1990, 1996); won a gold medal for team foil and a bronze for team foil at Atlanta Olympics (1996); won a bronze medal for indiv. foil and a gold medal for team foil at Sydney Olympics (2000); won a silver medal for indiv. foil at Athens Olympics (2004).

TRIMMER, Sarah (1741–1810). English writer. Name variations: Sarah Kirby. Born Sarah Kirby, Jan 6, 1741, in Ipswich, England; died Dec 15, 1810, in London; dau. of John Joshua Kirby (artist) and Sarah (Bull) Kirby; m. James Trimmer (government bureaucrat of Kew), in 1762; children: 6 daughters, 6 sons. ❖ Believing many of the educational texts then available to be frivolous or amoral, began writing her own lessons, combining them with stories of religious instruction; published stories as *Easy Introduction to the Knowledge of Nature* (1780), which went into numerous editions and was well received; continued to publish stories, including her most popular book, *The History of the Robins;* pioneered in the use of illustrations as an aid in learning; also wrote treatises on educational issues, and gradually emerged as an active proponent of religiously oriented popular education; helped establish local schools to teach vocational subjects to the poor; assisted by husband and older children, published the popular *Family Magazine* (1778–89), followed by *Guardian of Education,* a periodical review of new children's literature; also issued the illustrated *New and Comprehensive Lessons,* which was continuously in print until 1830. ❖ See also D. M. Yarde, *The Life and Works of Sarah Trimmer, a Lady of Brentford* (1971).

TRINQUET, Pascale (1958—). *See Hachin-Trinquet, Pascale.*

TRINQUET, Veronique (1956—). French fencer. Born June 15, 1956, in France. ❖ At Montreal Olympics, won a silver medal in team foil (1976).

TRINTIGNANT, Nadine (1934—). French film director and screenwriter. Name variations: N. Marquand or Nadine Marquand. Born Nadine Marquand on Nov 11, 1934, in Nice, France; sister of

Serge Marquand (actor) and Christian Marquand (actor-director); became 2nd wife of Jean-Louis Trintignant (actor), in 1960; children: Marie Trintignant (1962–2003, character actress) and Vincent Trintignant (b. 1973, assistant director). ❖ Pursuing an early interest in the cinema, dropped out of school at age 15 to become an assistant in a film lab; subsequently worked as an assistant editor and script clerk before becoming editor for such directors as Serge Bourguignon, Jacques Doniol-Valcroze, and Jean-Luc Godard; launched her own directing career with a few shorts and a number of tv productions, then undertook 1st feature film, *Mon Amour, Mon Amour* (1967); wrote her own scripts, which frequently starred husband Jean-Louis; other films include *Le Voleur de Crimes* (1969), *Ça n'arrive qu'aux autres* (*It Only Happens to Others,* 1971), *Defense de savoir* (1973), *Le Voyage de Noces* (*Jalousie,* 1976), *Premier Voyage* (1979), *L'Ete Prochain* (*Next Summer,* 1984), *Le Maison de Jade* (1988) and *Lumière et compagnie* (1995); also directed the tv miniseries "Colette, une femme libre" (2004). ❖ See also *Women in World History.*

TRIOLET, Elsa (1896–1970). French writer and resistance fighter. Name variations: Mme Aragon. Born Elsa Yureyevna Kagan in Moscow, Russia, Sept 24, 1896; died in Saint-Arnoult, France, June 18, 1970; dau. of Yuri Alexandrovich Kagan (Lithuanian Jew and lawyer) and Yelena (Borman) Kagan (Latvian Jew); sister of Lili Kagan Brik; m. Pierre-Marie-André Triolet (French diplomat), 1918 (div. 1939); m. Louis Aragon (poet and writer), Feb 26, 1939 (died Dec 24, 1982); no children. ❖ Novelist and short-story writer, met and befriended poet Vladimir Mayakovsky (1911); studied painting at Institute of Architecture, Moscow (1913–17); met André Triolet at French Embassy in Moscow (1917); though she supported the revolution, left Russia to marry (July 1918); with husband, journeyed to Tahiti (1919); separated from husband and returned to Paris (1921), where she would live among the Surrealists and Dadaists in Montparnasse; inhabited two worlds, her beloved Russia and her adopted country, France; published 1st books, *In Tahiti* and *Wild Strawberry,* the latter based on childhood memories, in Moscow (1925); also wrote *Camouflage* (1927); met Louis Aragon (Nov 1928) and would remain with him until her death; published 1st book in French, *Goodnight, Thérèse* (1938), which received favorable reviews; during German occupation of France, was a member of the French Resistance (1941–44) and helped establish the National Committee of Writers (1941); with husband, became part of a clandestine organization of intellectuals in Lyons called "Les Étoiles" (The Stars); worked on *The White Horse,* her most autobiographical work to date, and illegally published "The Lovers of Avignon" (1943); with the advent of peace and the Cold War, detailed her disillusionment in novels *Nobody Loves Me, Armed Ghosts* and *The Inspector of Ruins;* now a famous writer, became an icon, through Aragon's poems, especially *Elsa's Eyes* (1942); other novels include *The Red Horse* (1953), *The Monument* (1957) and *The Grand Never* (1965). Awarded Prix Goncourt for collection of short stories, *The First Tear Costs Two Hundred Francs* (1945). ❖ See also Lachlan Mackinnon, *The Lives of Elsa Triolet* (Chatto & Windus, 1992); and *Women in World History.*

TRIPE, M. E. R. (1870–1939). *See Tripe, Mary Elizabeth.*

TRIPE, Mary Elizabeth (1870–1939). New Zealand painter and art teacher. Name variations: Mary Elizabeth Richardson, signed paintings M. E. R. Tripe and M. E. R. T. Born Sept 14, 1870, at Opawa, Christchurch, New Zealand; died Sept 21, 1939, in Wellington; dau. of Edward (civil engineer and politician) and Frances Mary Elizabeth (Corke) Richardson; Wellington Technical School, art master's certificate, 1894; m. Joseph Albert Tripe (lawyer), 1900 (died 1926); children: 2 sons. ❖ Nationally important portrait painter, studied in London; exhibited throughout New Zealand and at Paris Salon of the Société des artistes français, Royal Academy of Arts, and Royal Society of Portrait Painters, London; was the 1st woman appointed to council of New Zealand Academy of Fine Arts (1893). Received Coronation Medal (1937). ❖ See also *Dictionary of New Zealand Biography* (Vol. 3).

TRIPOLI, countess of.
See Hodierna of Jerusalem (c. 1115–after 1162).
See Lucia (r. 1288–1289).

TRIPP, Grace (1691–1710). English murderer. Born in Barton, Lincolnshire, 1691; executed at Tyburn, Mar 27, 1710. ❖ Employed as maid in London at mansion of Lord Torrington, was persuaded by a man named Peters to assist him in robbing the house; when the 2 were discovered by a housekeeper during the robbery, held a candle to provide Peters with enough light to cut the housekeeper's throat; with Peters, made off with household silverware and about 30 guineas; condemned to death for her part in the crime, was executed at age 19. Likely due to the status of Torrington, a respected Lord, the case was a London sensation.

TRISLER, Joyce (1934–1979). American modern dancer. Born 1934 in Los Angeles, CA; died Oct 13, 1979, in New York, NY. ❖ Trained with Lester Horton before joining his Dance Theater during adolescence; created roles for his *Seven Scenes with Ballabilli, Prado de Pena,* and *Dedication in Our Times* (1952); trained with Antony Tudor at Juilliard; danced on freelance basis with companies of Alvin Ailey, John Wilson, Valerie Bettis, and at 92nd Street YMHA, among others; considered among the foremost experts of Horton technique and repertory, was widely known for recreations of his works, as well as works of Ruth St. Denis and Ted Shawn; formed own group Danscompany, staging Denishawn repertory works for extended periods; choreographed and staged productions for San Francisco Opera, New York Opera, Boston Opera, and at annual New York Shakespeare Festival in Central Park (1967–71).

TRISTAN, Flora (1803–1844). French activist. Name variations: Madame Chazal. Born Flore-Célestine-Thérèse-Henriette Tristan Moscoso, April 7, 1803, in Paris, France; died in Bordeaux, France, Nov 14, 1844; dau. of Mariano de Tristan y Moscoso (Peruvian noble, died 1807) and Anne-Pierre Laisnay (French); m. André-François Chazal (lithographer), Feb 3, 1821 (sep. 1824); children: a son (b. ca. 1822); Ernest-Camille (b. 1824); Aline-Marie Chazal (b. 1825, mother of artist Paul Gauguin). ❖ Campaigner for women's rights and the rights of working people, who attempted to found a "Universal Union of Working Men and Women," married her employer at 17 (1821); at 21, agreed to separate (1824); traveled in Europe as a ladies' maid (1825–28); applied successfully to the courts for a separation of property, to prevent husband and his creditors from seizing control of her savings or income (1828); husband began to seek custody of their 2 surviving children (1831); traveled to Peru to unsuccessfully seek inheritance (1833–34); her daughter, who had never met her father, was abducted by him on the way to school (1835); began to campaign for women's rights and became linked with French socialist movement (1835); attended feminist salons (1836); published *Pérégrinations d'une Paria 1833–1834* (*Peregrinations of a Pariah,* 1837), which made her a minor celebrity; after daughter alleged that her father was sexually abusing her (1837), petitioned for the legalization of a divorce (1837); was seriously injured in a murder attempt by estranged husband (1838); completed 2nd major work, the novel *Méphis* (1838); petitioned for the abolition of capital punishment (1838); traveled to England to study social conditions (1839), then published *Promenades dans Londres* (*The London Journal of Flora Tristan,* 1840); devised a plan for a "workers' union" (1843), contained in *L'Union ouvrière, chez tous les libraires* (*The Workers' Union*); toured France to promote the workers' union (1844); also wrote *Nécessité de faire un bon accueil aux femmes étrangères* (The need to extend a warm welcome to foreign women, 1835). ❖ See also Máire Cross and Tim Gray, *The Feminism of Flora Tristan* (Berg, 1992); and *Women in World History.*

TRIVULZIO, Cristina (1808–1871). See Belgioso, Cristina.

TRIX, Bino (1908–1987). See Ward, Polly.

TROCMÉ, Magda (1901–1996). Italian-French Holocaust rescuer. Name variations: Magda Trocme; The "Good Samaritan of Le Chambon." Born Magda Grilli in Florence, Italy, 1901; died in Paris, Oct 10, 1996; dau. of an Italian engineer and Russian mother; m. André Trocmé (Protestant minister), 1926; children: daughter Nelly; son Jacques. ❖ Along with husband and the entire village of Le Chambon-sur-Lignon, in southcentral France, relied on nonviolent resistance to save 5,000 men, women and children from Nazi annihilation; married André Trocmé, a pacifist, who had been a conscientious objector during World War I (1926); moved to Le Chambon-sur-Lignon (1934), where husband was appointed pastor to the Reformed church; with husband, founded the Collège Cévenol (1938), a private non-denominational secondary school whose mission would be to serve as an international center for peace and reconciliation; taught Italian at the Collège Cévenol. Honored as one of the Righteous Gentiles by Yad Vashem. ❖ See also Philip P. Hallie, *Lest Innocent Blood be Shed: The Story of the Village of Le Chambon and How Goodness Happened There* (Harper, 1994); (documentary) *Weapons of the Spirit* (1994); and *Women in World History.*

TROCTULA. See Trotula.

TROES, Olga (1914—). Hungarian gymnast. Born Aug 1914 in Hungary. ❖ At Berlin Olympics, won a bronze medal in team all-around (1936).

TROFIMOVA-GOPOVA, Nina (1953—). Soviet kayaker. Born May 1953 in USSR. ❖ Won a gold medal at Montreal Olympics (1976) and a silver medal at Moscow Olympics (1980), both in K2 500 meters.

TROITSKAIA, Viktoria. See Taranina, Viktoria.

TROLL-BOROSTYANI, Irma von (1847–1912). Austrian writer and women's rights activist. Name variations: Irma von Troll-Borostyáni; (pseudonym) Veritas Leo Bergen. Born Marie von Troll, Mar 31, 1847, in Salzburg, Austria; died Feb 10, 1912, in Salzburg; sister of Wilhelmina von Troll; married a man named Borostyani. ❖ Moved to Vienna (1870), where she began to write and became involved with women's rights; captured widespread attention with an essay published under pseudonym Veritas Leo Bergen, *Die Mission unseres Jahrhunderts: Eine Studie über die Frauenfrage* (The Mission of Our Century: A Study on the Woman Question, 1878); returned to Salzburg and, with sister, became the center of a large coterie of intellectuals; published the pseudonymous collections *Die Gleichstellung der Geschlechter und die Reform der Jugenderziehung* (The Equality of the Sexes and Reform in Education, 1887) and *Katechismus der Frauenbewegung* (The Catechism of the Women's Movement, 1903).

TROLLOPE, Eleanor (c. 1803–1873). See Ternan, Frances Eleanor.

TROLLOPE, Frances Eleanor (c. 1803–1873). See Ternan, Frances Eleanor.

TROLLOPE, Frances Milton (c. 1779–1863). English writer. Born Mar 10, c. 1779 (some sources cite 1778 or 1780), in Heckfield, near Bristol, England; died Oct 6, 1863, in Florence, Italy; dau. of William Milton (minister) and Frances (Gelsey) Milton; m. Thomas Anthony Trollope (lawyer), May 23, 1809 (died 1835); children: Thomas Adolphus (1810–1892, novelist who m. Theodosia Garrow Trollope and Frances Eleanor Ternan); Henry (1811–1834); Arthur (b. 1812); Emily (b. 1813, died in infancy); Anthony Trollope (1815–1882, novelist); Cecilia Trollope Tilley (1816–1849, who wrote one novel); Emily Trollope (1818–1836). ❖ Novelist and travel writer who began writing in middle age out of dire financial necessity and went on to enjoy wide popularity in a career that lasted over 20 years; grew up much better educated than most young Englishwomen of her time; with sister Mary, moved to London (1802); husband disinherited (1820); befriended Frances "Fanny" Wright, a radical utopian socialist (1823); with husband suffering from poor health, financial situation worsened; 1st traveled to US (1827), invited by Fanny Wright to join the work at Nashoba, Mississippi, a community of white social activists seeking to educate former slaves; to raise funds in US, opened Trollope Bazaar, a combination retail-residential-cultural building in Cincinnati (1828); returned to England (1831); published 1st book, *Domestic Manners of the Americans* (1832), which became a bestseller; published 1st novel, *The Refugee in America* (1832), followed by *The Abbess* (1833), then *Belgium and Western Germany* (1834); published antislavery novel set in America, *Jonathan Jefferson Whitlaw* (1836), one of her best works; retired in Florence (1844); published last book, *Fashionable Life* (1856); an extremely prolific writer, published 34 novels and 6 travel books. ❖ See also Eileen Bigland, *The Indomitable Mrs. Trollope* (Lippincott, 1954); Helen Heineman, *Mrs. Trollope: The Triumphant Feminine in the 19th Century* (Ohio U. Press, 1979); Pamela Neville-Sington, *Fanny Trollope: The Life and Adventures of a Clever Woman* (Viking, 1998); and *Women in World History.*

TROLLOPE, Theodosia (1825–1865). English writer. Born Theodosia Garrow in 1825; died in 1865; m. Thomas Adolphus Trollope (1810–1892, the novelist), in 1848; daughter-in-law of Frances Milton Trollope (1779–1863). ❖ Wrote on "Social Aspects of the Italian Revolution" for the *Athenaeum;* also contributed to other periodicals and was the center of a salon in Florence.

TRONCONI, Carolina (b. 1913). Italian gymnast. Born May 22, 1913, in Italy. ❖ At Amsterdam Olympics, won a silver medal in team all-around (1928).

TROT, Dame. See Trotula.

TROTMAN, Julia (1968—). American yacht racer. Name variations: Julia Trotman Brady. Born Mar 25, 1968; graduate of Harvard University, 1989. ❖ At Barcelona Olympics, won a bronze medal in European class (1992); won US women's single-handed championship (1992). Named Rolex/US Yachtswoman of the Year (1993).

TROTSKY, Natalia Ivanovna (1882–1962). Russian revolutionary. Name variations: Natalia Ivanovna Sedova-Trotsky; Natalia Sedova; Natasha Trotsky. Born Natalia Ivanovna Sedova in Russia in 1882; died 1962; became 2nd wife of Lev Bronstein, also known as Leon Trotsky (1879–1940, Russian socialist and revolutionary), 1903 (killed in Mexico City, Aug 21, 1940); children: Leon and Sergei. ❖ After meeting Leon Trotsky in Paris, became his lifelong companion (he was 1st married to Marxist Alexandra Sokolovskaya); was in Mexico City with husband when a Soviet agent buried an ice axe in his skull (1940); portrayed by Valentina Cortese in Joseph Losey's *The Assassination of Trotsky* (1972). ❖ See also *Women in World History*.

TROTTA (c. 1040s–1097). *See Trotula.*

TROTTA, Margarethe Von (1942—). *See Von Trotta, Margarethe.*

TROTTER, Catharine (1679–1749). *See Cockburn, Catharine Trotter.*

TROTTER, Deedee (1982—). American runner. Name variations: De'Hashia Trotter. Born Dec 8, 1982, in US; graduate of University of Tennessee, 2005. ❖ Won gold medals for 4 x 400-meter relay at World championships (2003) and at Athens Olympics (2004); was NCAA outdoor champion (2004); won US indoor championship in 400 meters (2005).

TROTTER, Mildred (1899–1991). American physical anthropologist. Born Feb 3, 1899, in Monaca, PA; died 1991. ❖ Among the most eminent physical anthropologists of the 20th century, was responsible for contributing much of the current knowledge about human skeletal structure and density, especially characteristics of long limb bones; taught more than 4,000 students during career at Washington University School of Medicine and became 1st woman to be named full professor at that institution (1946). Her formulas for estimating stature are still in use by the FBI.

TROTTER, Virginia Yapp (1921–1998). American educator. Born Nov 29, 1921, in Boise, ID; died Oct 11, 1998, in Athens, GA; Kansas State University, BA, 1943, MA, 1947; Ohio State University, PhD, 1960. ❖ Served as teacher and administrator in home economics at universities of Nebraska, Utah, and Vermont; became 1st woman to fill highest education position in US government, as assistant secretary for education (1974–77); at University of Nebraska, served as head of School of Economics (from 1963) and vice chancellor of academic affairs (from 1972); served as 1st woman vice president of academic affairs at University of Georgia (1977–86).

TROTULA (c. 1040s–1097). Italian physician and educator. Name variations: Troctula; Trotta; Dame Trot; Trotula Platearius. Pronunciation: TROH-too-lah. Born probably shortly before 1050, in Salerno; died 1097; said to have been married to Giovanni Plateario (fellow physician); children: said to have had 2 sons who became noted doctors. ❖ Professor of medicine at University of Salerno, who wrote several works on medicine, including a text on obstetrics and gynecology that was used in Europe for at least 6 centuries; her most important text, *De mulierum passionibus or De passionibus mulierum* (*On the diseases of women*), enjoyed great success in Europe and was translated into Irish, French, German, Old and Middle English, Flemish, and Catalan; her name became a byword for a wise woman, especially a healer, and the "Dame Trot" encountered in several English nursery rhymes probably derives from Trotula; also wrote *De ornatu mulierum* (On beautifying women) and *De passionibus mulierum ante, in et post partum* (On the diseases of women before, during, and after birth). ❖ See also *Women in World History*.

TROTZIG, Birgitta (1929—). Swedish novelist and literary critic. Born Birgitta Kjellén in 1929 in Göteborg, Sweden; m. Ulf Trotzig (an artist); children. ❖ Studied literature and art history, then worked as an art critic; at 22, published novel *Ur de älskandes liv* (From the Lives of the Lovers, 1951), followed by *Bilder* (Images, 1954); became firmly established with *De utsatta* (The Exposed, 1957); also wrote *En berättelse från kusten* (A Tale from the coast, 1961); lived with husband and children in Paris (1954–69), where she converted from her childhood Protestantism to Catholicism, a turning point in light of her growing preoccupation with the spiritual well-being of characters in later writing; published *Levande och döda* (The Living and the Dead, 1964), *Sveket* (The Betrayal, 1966) and *Sjukdomen* (The Sickness, 1972), as well as collected essays in *Ordgränser* (Word Limits, 1968) and *Jaget och världen* (The Ego and the World, 1977). ❖ See also *Women in World History*.

TROUBETZKOY, Amélie (1863–1945). *See Rives, Amélie.*

TROUHANOVA, Natalia (1885–1956). Russian dancer. Born 1885 in Kiev; died Aug 25, 1956, in Moscow, Russia. ❖ Performed as interpretive dancer in private recitals in Russia early on; moved to Paris, where she presented recitals to works she commissioned from leading composers, poets, and artists; worked with Ivan Clustine in evening concert, where she presented Vincent D'Indy's *Istar of the Seven Gates*, Paul Dukas' *La Péri*, and Florenz Schmitt's *La Tragédie de Salomé*, among others, to great acclaim; danced with Theodore Cherer-Bekefi and Leo De Carva; retired from performance career (1914) but remained in France for many years.

TROUILLOT, Ertha Pascal- (1943—). *See Pascal-Trouillot, Ertha.*

TROUP, Augusta Lewis (c. 1848–1920). American labor union executive. Name variations: Augusta Lewis. Born c. 1848 in New York, NY; died Sept 14, 1920, in New Haven, Connecticut; dau. of Charles and Elizabeth (Rowe) Lewis; orphaned as an infant, raised by Isaac Baldwin Gager; graduated with honors from the convent school of the Sacred Heart in Manhattanville; m. Alexander Troup (labor activist and newspaper publisher), June 12, 1874 (died 1908); children: daughters Marie Grace, Augusta Lewis (died in infancy), Jessie (died in infancy), George Bernardine, and Elsie; sons Alexander and Philip. ❖ Worked as a reporter for New York City newspapers, including New York *Sun*; became an apprentice typesetter at the *Era*; joined typesetting staff at New York *World*; quickly became expert in her newfound trade, though she continued to work as a reporter as well; cofounded the New York Working Women's Association (1868); became founder and president, Women's Typographical Union No. 1, New York (1868); elected corresponding secretary of the International Typographical Union (1870), making her the 1st woman to be elected to an executive position in a national labor union. ❖ See also *Women in World History*.

TROUP, Margaret (1913–1999). *See Casson, Margaret MacDonald.*

TROUSER BUTTON (1891–1994). *See Harsant, Florence Marie.*

TROUT, Jenny Kidd (1841–1921). Scottish-Canadian physician. Born Jenny Kidd Gowanlock, April 21, 1841, in Kelso, Scotland; died 1921 in Los Angeles, CA; dau. of Elizabeth and Andrew Gowanlock; graduate of Woman's Medical College of Pennsylvania in Philadelphia, 1875; m. Edward Trout (worked in publishing field), 1865; children: adopted 2 (grandniece and a grandnephew). ❖ The 1st licensed woman medical practitioner in Canada, immigrated with family to Canada (1847); earned a teaching certificate (1861); taught around Stratford, Ontario, until 1865; settled in Toronto after marriage (1865); earned medical license (1876); created the Therapeutic and Electrical Institute (1877); retired (1882); moved with husband to Los Angeles (1908) to do mission work; helped establish and fund a women's medical college at Queen's University in Kingston and successfully pushed for a women's medical college at University of Toronto.

TROY, Doris (1937–2004). African-American rhythm-and-blues singer. Name variations: Doris Payne. Born Doris Higgensen, Jan 6, 1937, in The Bronx, NY; died Feb 16, 2004; dau. of Barbadian Pentecostal minister. ❖ Came to prominence in US with hit "Just One Look" (1963), followed by "What'cha Gonna Do About It"; nicknamed Mama Soul, moved to London and had successful career in Britain, singing "I'll Do Anything (He Wants Me To Do)"; had a solo spot on Pink Floyd's *Dark Side of the Moon* (1973); returned to US (1974); her younger sister Vy Higgensen wrote and produced the hit stage musical, *Mama, I Want to Sing* (1983), about Troy's life (Troy sang the role of their mother, Geraldine).

TROY, Louise (1933–1994). American stage, tv and screen actress and singer. Name variations: Louise Tory. Born Nov 9, 1933, in New York, NY; died May 5, 1994, in NY; m. Werner Klemperer (actor); m. Douglas Seale (actor). ❖ Made notable stage debut in NY in *The Infernal Machine* (1954), followed by *Merchant of Venice, Conversation Piece, Salad Days, A Doll's House, Heartbreak House, Pipe Dream, A Shot in the Dark, Tovarich, High Spirits, Walking Happy, Equus, Woman of the Year, Design for Living*, and *42nd Street*, among others; appeared as Sue Rollins in the tv serial "Love of Life."

TROYANOS, Tatiana (1938–1993). Greek-American mezzo-soprano. Born Tatiana Troyanos, Sept 12, 1938, in New York, NY; died of cancer, Aug 21, 1993, in NY; studied with Hans Heinz and at Juilliard School of Music. ❖ Debuted at New York City Opera as Hippolyta in Benjamin Britten's *Midsummer Night's Dream* (1963), also appearing as Jocasta in Stravinsky's *Oedipus Rex*; was a member of the Hamburg State Opera (1965–75), where she sang a number of popular mezzo-soprano roles;

made 1st major European debut (1966), at Aix-en-Provence, as the Composer in *Ariadne auf Naxos*; debuted at Covent Garden (1969), singing Octavian in *Rosenkavalier*, which became a standard of her repertoire as did other "trouser roles," such as Cherubino in *Le Nozze di Figaro* and Romeo in Bellini's *I Capuletti e I Montecchi*; debuted at Metropolitan Opera (1976), once again as Octavian, and subsequently became a regular on their roster, appearing in such roles as Countess Geschwitz in *Lulu*, Sesto in *Clemmenza di Tito*, Charlotte in *Werther*, Adalgisa in *Norma*, and Dorabella in *Cosi fan tutte*; also became a noted Handel stylist and one of very few singers to take on the roles of both Cleopatra and Caesar in *Giulio Cesare*; premiered role of Queen Isabella in Philip Glass's *Voyage* (1992). ❖ See also *Women in World History*.

TRUAX, Sarah (1877–1958). American actress. Born Feb 12, 1877, in Cincinnati, OH; died April 25, 1958, in Seattle, WA; m. C. S. Albert. ❖ Made stage debut in Chicago with Otis Skinner's company in *His Grace de Grammont* (1894) and NY debut in *The Double Life* (1906); other plays include *The Garden of Allah* and *My Son*.

TRUBNIKOVA, Mariia (1835–1897). Russian philanthropist and feminist. Name variations: Maria Trubnikov; Marya Trubnikova. Pronunciation: Troob-nih-KO-vah. Born Mariia Vasil'evna Ivasheva, Jan 6, 1835, in Chita, eastern Siberia; died April 28, 1897, in Tambov, Russia; dau. of V. V. Ivashev (exiled Decembrist who died 1840) and Camille LeDantieux (who followed husband into exile and died during childbirth in 1839); with younger sister Vera Ivasheva, moved to Samara where they were brought up by a wealthy aunt, Princess Ekaterina Khovanskaia; m. K. V. Trubnikov (newspaper editor), 1854 (sep. 1869); children: 7, including daughter O. K. Bulanova-Trubnikova, and 3 who died in infancy. ❖ Leading 19th-century progressive, was active in Sunday School movement (1859–62); for a while, helped husband edit his liberal newspaper, *Birzhevye vedomosti* (The Stock Exchange News), and their St. Petersburg apartment became a meeting place for those seeking change in Russian society; developed contacts with feminist groups in Western Europe and US and started to write articles for various European journals; with Nadezhda Stasova and Anna Filosofova, sought ways of helping less fortunate women in the Russian capital; served as 1st chair of St. Petersburg's Society to Provide Cheap Lodgings for women (1861); co-founded women's Publishing Workshop (1863), a co-operative that employed several dozen women as writers, translators, typesetters and binders; with others, called for the establishment of a women's university or at least the opening of courses at Russian universities to women; active in the establishment of the Vladimir Courses (1870) and Bestuzhev Courses (1878) for women; had nervous breakdown brought on by domestic troubles; died in a mental institution at age 62. ❖ See also (in Russian) O. K. Bulanova-Trubnikova, *Tri pokoleniia* (Three Generations, Moscow, 1928); and *Women in World History*.

TRUDEAU, Margaret (1948—). Canadian first lady. Name variations: Margaret Kemper. Born Margaret Sinclair, Sept 10, 1948; dau. of James Sinclair (Liberal fisheries minister); m. Pierre Elliott Trudeau (prime minister of Canada, 1968–79), Mar 4, 1971 (sep. 1977, div. 1984, died 2000); m. Fred Kemper (real-estate developer), 1984 (sep. 1999); children: (1st m.) Justin (b. 1971), Alexandre (Sasha, b. 1973), and Michel (b. 1975, drowned 1998); (2nd m.) 2. ❖ Married Pierre Trudeau at age 22, becoming the youngest first lady in the world, and one of the most troubled; chafed under the scrutiny and violated protocol; walked out on the marriage while husband was still in office, though they would remain close; became a photographer, actress, writer and tv host, while social life became a popular topic for tabloids; subject of a CBC documentary "Passion Before Reason: Life & Times of Margaret Trudeau" (1998). ❖ See also autobiography *Beyond Reason* (Paddington, 1979) and *Consequences*.

TRUEMAN, Paula (1900–1994). American stage and screen actress and dancer. Born April 25, 1900, in New York, NY; died Mar 23, 1994, in NY. ❖ Made Broadway stage debut in *Thunderbird* (1922) and dramatic debut as Madanika in *The Little Clay Cart* (1925); appeared in numerous musicals and comedies in NY, including *Grand Street Follies*, *Sweet and Low*, *Grand Hotel*, *You Can't Take It With You*, *George Washington Slept Here*, *Kiss and Tell*, *Gentlemen Prefer Blondes*, *Solid Gold Cadillac*, *Mrs. McThing* and *Wonderful Town*; films include *Crime without Passion*, *Paint Your Wagon*, *The Outlaw Josey Wales*, *Dirty Dancing*, *The Anderson Tapes* and *The Stepford Wives*.

TRUEX, Sylvia Field (1901–1998). *See Field, Sylvia.*

TRUGANINI (1812–1876). Tasmanian Aborigine. Name variations: Truccanini or Traucanini; also known as Trugernanner; "Lalla Rookh" or "Lallah Rookh." Born 1812 (some sources cite 1803) at Recherche Bay, Tasmania; died May 8, 1876, in Hobart, Tasmania; dau. of Mangerner (a Lyluequonny man and an elder of southeast Aboriginal tribe); mother's name unknown (slain by whalers); sister of Moorinna who had been kidnapped and shot by sealers; m. Wooraddy (member of the Nuenonne tribe), July 1829 (died c. 1842). ❖ After martial law was declared and whites were permitted to kill on sight all Aborigines they saw near "settled" land, assisted secular missionary George Augustus Robinson in relocating Tasmania's remaining Aborigines to nearby Flinders Island (1830–35); following a visit to the settlement where many were dying, began to urge her fellow Aborigines to remain in Tasmania (1836); after Robinson was named protector of the Aborigines in Australia's Port Phillip district (1839), was forced with husband and others to accompany him to his new posting near Melbourne; escaped from the Port Phillip mission in the company of 2 Aboriginal men and 2 Aboriginal women and went on a rampage (c. 1842); as punishment, was shipped back to Flinders Island (c. 1842), then relocated with others to an abandoned settlement at Oyster Bay, some 20 miles south of Hobart in Tasmania (1847); became last of that group to survive and one of the last full-blooded Tasmanian Aborigines. By 1904, her bones had been strung together in a full skeleton and placed on display at a Hobart museum, where they were the most visited exhibit for years. ❖ See also *Women in World History*.

TRUITT, Anne (1921–2004). American artist and writer. Born Anne Dean, Mar 16, 1921, in Baltimore, Maryland; died Dec 23, 2004, in Washington, DC; dau. of Duncan Witt Dean and Louisa Folsom (Williams) Dean; Bryn Mawr College, BA in psychology, 1943; studied art with Alexander Giampetro and Kenneth Noland at Institute of Contemporary Art, 1948–50, and with Octavo Medillin in Dallas; m. James McConnell Truitt (journalist), Sept 19, 1947; children: Alexandra; Mary; Samuel. ❖ Sculptor and painter of the minimalist school, was a potent force in American art through several decades, helping to shape the modern era of abstract art; her sculpture, and paintings masquerading as sculpture, were in the advance guard of the literalist-minimalist art movement that took a firm hold (1960s); though her work is clearly linked with the minimalist school, is more precisely a proponent of the Washington, DC, art movement known as "Color Field"; with her trademark boxes, had 1st one-woman show at Andre Emmerich Gallery in NY (1963); had solo shows at Whitney Museum in NY (1973) and Corcoran in Washington (1974); works include *Autumn Dryad* and *Spring Snow*. ❖ See also (journals) *Daybook* (1982) and *Turn* (1986); and *Women in World History*.

TRUMAN, Bess (1885–1982). American first lady. Name variations: Bess Wallace. Born Elizabeth Virginia Wallace, Feb 13, 1885, in Independence, Missouri; died Oct 18, 1982, in Independence; dau. of David Willock Wallace (merchant) and Margaret Elizabeth (Gates) Wallace; m. Harry S. Truman (president of US), June 28, 1919 (died Dec 26, 1972); children: (Mary) Margaret Truman (b. 1924, writer). ❖ One of the least-known first ladies in modern times (April 12, 1945–Jan 20, 1953), was often guarded from public attention by husband, though he credited her as "a full partner in all my transactions—political and otherwise"; at 18, her father committed suicide, after years of financial woes and bouts with alcoholism; was bitterly opposed to husband's run for vice-president (1944); when he succeeded to the presidency after Roosevelt's death (April 12, 1945), entered the White House determined to hang on to privacy; in one of her 1st official acts, canceled the weekly press conference in favor of informal teas, held with the understanding that anything she said was off the record; privately carried out all the customary duties; often tempered husband's "shoot from the hip" responses and his notorious public swearing; agreed to another campaign (1948), because she knew husband wanted to finish what he had started—and probably because she believed, along with many others, that he could not possibly win reelection; in one of the major upsets in American political history, found herself back in the White House for 4 more years; back in Independence (1953), edited and organized husband's memoirs and set up the Truman Library. ❖ See also *Women in World History*.

TRUMAN, Margaret (1924—). American writer, singer, and first daughter. Name variations: Margaret Truman Daniel. Born Mary Margaret Truman in Independence, Missouri, Feb 17, 1924; dau. of Harry S. Truman (president of US) and Bess Truman (1885–1982); George Washington University, BA, 1946; m. (E.) Clifton Daniel (award-winning foreign correspondent and managing editor of *The*

New York Times), 1956 (died Feb 2000); children: Clifton Truman Daniel (b. around 1957); William Wallace Daniel (died Sept 4, 2000, age 41); Harrison Gates Daniel; Thomas Washington Daniel. ❖ Viewed her brief residency in the White House as a mixed blessing: enjoyed meeting interesting people, but deplored the lack of privacy; following college, embarked on a concert career, making professional singing debut with Detroit Symphony Orchestra (Mar 16, 1947), on its weekly network radio program; made stage debut with Eugene Ormandy and Hollywood Bowl Symphony (1947), then toured some 30 cities; made tv appearance on Ed Sullivan's "Toast of the Town" (1950); conducted her own radio show, "Authors in the News," for 7 years and co-hosted the radio show "Weekday," with Mike Wallace; wrote biographies *Harry S. Truman* (1973) and *Bess W. Truman* (1986), collective biography, *Women of Courage* (1976), as well as a series of mystery novels, all set in Washington, DC. ❖ See also autobiography, *Margaret Truman's Own Story*; and *Women in World History*.

TRUMBULL, Alice (1904–1971). *See Mason, Alice Trumbull.*

TRUNG SISTERS (d. 43 CE). Vietnamese resistance leaders. Name variations: Hai Ba Trung (Two Ladies Trung); Trung Nu Vuong or Trung Vuong (She-king Trung); Truong sisters. Pronunciation: TCHUNG sisters. Born in village of Me Linh in Son Tay region in Vietnam (dates of birth unknown); died in 43 CE; daughters of a local chief and Ba Man Thien, reputed descendant of the Hung kings; Trung Trac married Thi Sach (a local chieftain assassinated by the Chinese); marital status of Trung Nhi unknown. ❖ Two sisters, considered models and inspiration for centuries of Vietnamese resistance against foreign domination, who led the 1st Vietnamese insurrection against foreign occupation by the Chinese feudalists and ruled Vietnam for two years before being overthrown by the Chinese; led insurrection against Chinese rule (39 CE); commanded an army of 80,000 soldiers; defeated Chinese; liberated 65 fortresses and proclaimed themselves joint queens (40 CE); upon defeat by a Chinese general, threw themselves into the river (43 CE). The Trungs' memory is honored throughout Vietnam, with streets, schools, and hospitals bearing their name; on the southern outskirts of Hanoi sits the Den Hai Ba Trung (Trung Sisters Temple), built in 1142 and restored in 19th and 20th centuries; every year, on the 16th day of the 2nd moon, people in Vietnam celebrate the anniversary of their death. ❖ See also *Women in World History*.

TRUNNELLE, Mabel (1879–1981). American actress. Born Nov 8, 1879, in Dwight, IL; died April 29, 1981, in Glendale, CA; m. Herbert Prior (actor). ❖ Star of the Edison Company (1910–17), often co-starred with husband; films include *A Modern Cinderella, The Man He Might Have Been, Eugene Aram, The Heart of the Hills* and *The Ghost of Morro.*

TRUONG SISTERS (d. 43 CE). *See Trung Sisters.*

TRUSCA, Gabriela (1957—). Romanian gymnast. Born July 28, 1957, in Romania. ❖ Won a silver medal in team all-around at Montreal Olympics (1976). ❖ See also *Women in World History*.

TRUSSEL, Elizabeth (1496–1527). Countess of Oxford. Name variations: Elizabeth de Vere. Born in 1496; died before July 1527; dau. of Edward Trussell and Margaret Dun; m. John de Vere, 15th earl of Oxford, around 1508; children: Frances de Vere (d. 1577); John de Vere (b. around 1516), 16th earl of Oxford; Aubrey de Vere; Robert de Vere; Geoffrey de Vere; Elizabeth de Vere (who associated with Thomas Darcy, 1st Lord Darcy); Anne de Vere (who associated with Edmund Sheffield, 1st Lord Sheffield, and John Brock).

TRUSTA, H. (1815–1852). *See Phelps, Elizabeth Wooster Stuart.*

TRUTH, Sojourner (c. 1797–1883). African-American abolitionist and feminist. Name variations: Isabella Bomefree or Isabella Baumfree; Isabella Van Wagener or Isabella Van Wagenen. Born Isabella Bomefree, c. 1797, in Ulster Co., NY; died Nov 26, 1883, in Battle Creek, Michigan; dau. of Elizabeth and James Bomefree (both slaves of Colonel Johannes Hardenbergh); m. Robert, a slave owned by a man named Catlin, sometime between 1810 and 1817 (relationship terminated by Catlin soon thereafter); m. another fellow slave named Thomas about 1817; children: (1st m.) Diana (b. 1815); (2nd m.) Peter, James, Elizabeth and Sophia. ❖ Former slave from NY who gained her freedom in 1827 and subsequently became a renowned religious reformer, public speaker, and activist on behalf of abolition and women's rights; upon death of 2nd master, Charles Hardenbergh (1808), was sold away from parents to John Neely, also of Ulster Co.; a few months later, was purchased by Martin Schryver, a local tavernkeeper; was sold again (1810), to John J. Dumont of New Paltz, NY; ran away from

Dumont's plantation with her infant child (1826) and sought asylum with Maria and Isaac Van Wagener, who purchased her freedom from Dumont; went to court to reclaim her son Peter, who had been illegally sold to a Southern plantation (1828); joined a utopian religious commune called the Kingdom, led by Robert Matthias (1832); after the Kingdom disintegrated, moved to New York City where she worked to support herself and her son; changed name to Sojourner Truth and became a traveling preacher (1843); entered a Massachusetts utopian community called the Northampton Association for Education and Industry (1843), where she was introduced to the principles of feminism and abolitionism; gave 1st speech on abolition (1844); spoke to American Anti-Slavery Society in NY (1845); dictated life story to fellow Association member Olive Gilbert (1846) and had it printed by William Lloyd Garrison (1850); commenced formal association with the growing circuit of antislavery agitators in Northeast and Midwest (1851); gave a speech on female equality at Akron meeting of Ohio Women's Rights Convention (May 1851); moved to Harmonia, a Progressive Friends (spiritualist) settlement near Battle Creek, Michigan (1857); upon outbreak of Civil War, made numerous speeches in support of Union cause (1861); met Abraham Lincoln (1864); engaged in refugee relief work at the many camps established by the National Freedmen's Relief Association and the Freedmen's Bureau (1864–68); attended and spoke at Equal Rights Association meeting in NY (1867); undertook a petition campaign agitating for the federal government to provide western land grants to emancipated slaves (beginning 1868); nearly 6 feet tall, with a deep voice and dramatic persona, convincingly presented her opinions about religion, slavery, and equality to captivated audiences throughout the North during the height of the anti-slavery movement of the 1850s. ❖ See also *Narrative of Sojourner Truth* (1878); Carleton Mabee, *Sojourner Truth: Slave, Prophet, Legend* (New York U. Press, 1993); Nell Irvin Painter, *Sojourner Truth: A Life, A Symbol* (Norton, 1996); Stetson and David, *Glorying in Tribulation: The Lifework of Sojourner Truth* (Michigan State U. Press, 1994); Bell Hooks, *Ain't I a Woman: Black Women and Feminism* (South End, 1981); and *Women in World History*.

TRUTHGEBA (700–779). *See Lioba.*

TRYON, Amy (1970—). American equestrian. Born Feb 24, 1970, in Redmond, WA. ❖ Placed 1st for 3-day event (team) at World Equestrian games (2002); on Poggio II, won a bronze medal for team eventing at Athens Olympics (2004).

TRYTKO, Maria (1913—). *See Kwadzniewska, Maria.*

TSAGARAYEVA, Larisa (1958—). Soviet fencer. Born Oct 1958 in USSR. ❖ At Moscow Olympics, won a silver medal in team foil (1980).

TSAHAI HAILE SELASSIE (1919–1942). Ethiopian princess and nurse. Name variations: Princess Tsahai Worq; Tsahaiwork; Tsehai. Born Oct 13, 1919, in Addis Ababa, Ethiopia; died Aug 17, 1942, in Lekemti, Ethiopia; dau. of Tafari Makonnen, later Haile Selassie I (1892–1975), emperor of Ethiopia (r. 1930–1974), and Waizero Menen (1889–1962); trained as a nurse at London's Great Ormond Street Hospital for Sick Children; graduated as a registered state children's nurse, 1939; m. Colonel Abiye Ababa (military officer), April 26, 1942; no children. ❖ Upon father's coronation as emperor (1930), became involved in royal activities of palace life, accompanying him on official tours and frequently filling in for mother at official dinners; with Italy threatening (1935), took an active role in the country's defense, sponsoring the Ethiopian Women's Welfare Work Association (EWWWA); also worked with the Ethiopian Red Cross; worked as a volunteer with the 1st field ambulance of the emperor's army following Italian invasion; while living in exile for 5 years, served as an interpreter for parents and also became a spokesperson for Ethiopia, speaking about the plight of her people; at 17, became the 1st Ethiopian woman to train as a nurse (1936), graduating as a State Registered Children's Nurse (1939); returned to Ethiopia (1941) and went to work with the British Red Cross unit, setting up headquarters in Dessie, which had suffered a massive air raid; reactivated the Ethiopian Women's Welfare Work Association; died of a hemorrhage suffered during a miscarriage. ❖ See also *Women in World History*.

TS'AI CH'ANG (1900–1990). *See Cai Chang.*

TS'AI YEN (c. 162–239). *See Cai Yan.*

TSANG, Tasha (1970—). Canadian rower. Born Oct 17, 1970, in Saskatoon, Saskatchewan, Canada. ❖ Won a silver medal for coxed eights at Atlanta Olympics (1996).

TSATITSA (1898–1990). *See Bunzel, Ruth.*

TSCHECHOWA, Olga (1897–1980). Russian-born German film actress. Name variations: Olga Chekhova. Born April 26, 1897, in Aleksandropol, Russia; died Mar 9, 1980, in Munich, Germany; dau. of an engineer and a painter; studied sculpture and engraving in schools in Moscow and St. Petersburg; took acting lessons at Constantin Stanislavski's Moscow Art Theater school; niece of playwright Anton Chekhov and actress Olga Knipper-Chekova; m. her cousin Michael Chekhov (an actor), c. 1913 (marriage ended c. 1916); children: daughter Ada Chekhova. ❖ Because of the turmoil that followed Russia's Bolshevik Revolution, moved to Berlin (1921); was discovered by F. W. Murnau who cast her in a leading role in his *Schloss Vogelöd* (Haunted Castle), a film that launched a career spanning 3 decades and earned her the title, "Grand Dame of German film"; teamed with German boxing champion Max Schmeling to star in *Liebe im Ring* (Love in the Ring, 1930); co-starred in Max Ophuls' very successful *Liebelei* (Flirtation, 1933), then appeared with Paula Wessely in Willi Forst's masterpiece *Maskerade* (Masquerade in Vienna, 1934); costarred with Werner Krauss in *Burgtheater* (Town Theater, 1936); despite the Nazi edict calling for the production of German historical epics, preferred working in such American-style comedies as *Die gelbe Flagge* (The Yellow Flag, 1937) and *Verliebtes Abenteuer* (Amorous Adventure, 1938); was similarly disposed towards musicals and fantasy films, such as *Die Welt ohne Maske* (The World Unmasked, 1934) and *Die unheimlichen Wünsche* (Sinister Desires, 1939); also appeared in *Zwei Frauen* (Two Women, 1938), *Befreite Hände* (Unfettered Hands, 1939) and *Gefährlicher Frühling* (Dangerous Spring, 1943); starred in an episode of the German tv series "Duell zu dritt" (Duel for Three, 1971); founded cosmetics company (early 1950s), which would boast branches in Helsinki, Milan, Vienna, and US by 1990. ❖ See also autobiography (in German) *Meine Uhren gehen anders* (My Clocks Tell Different Times); and *Women in World History*.

TSCHEPALOVA, Julia (1976—). *See Tchepalova, Julija.*

TSCHITSCHKO, Helene (1908–1992). Austrian politician. Born Jan 10, 1908 in Timenitz (Kärnten), Austria; died Aug 1, 1992, in Klagenfurt, Austria. ❖ Was presiding officer of the Austrian Parliament (Jan 1, 1965–Dec 30, 1965, July 1, 1969–Dec 31, 1969 and Jan 1, 1974–June 30, 1974).

TSEBRIKOVA, M. K. (1835–1917). Russian literary critic, translator and memoirist. Name variations: Mariia Konstantinovna Tsébrikova; used 11 pseudonyms. Born 1835 in Russia; died 1917. ❖ Translated works from German, French, English, and American literature and history; edited children's magazine and wrote about education, women's rights, and class; printed abroad "Open Letter to Alexander III" (1889), about conditions under his reign; worked tirelessly for women's rights and was exiled for criticism of Alexander and descriptions of repressive conditions in Russia.

TSE-HI (1835–1908). *See Cixi.*

TSERBE-NESSINA, Valentyna (1969—). Ukrainian biathlete. Name variations: Valentina Tserbe Nessina. Born Jan 8, 1969, in Ukraine. ❖ Won a bronze medal for 7.5 km at Lillehammer Olympics (1994).

TSHIRKOVA, Svetlana (1945—). *See Tsirkova, Svetlana.*

TSHOMBE, Dawn (1968—). *See Robinson, Dawn.*

TSIRKOVA, Svetlana (1945—). Soviet fencer. v: Svetlana Chirkova or Tshirkova; Svetlana Tsirkov-Lozovaja. Born Nov 5, 1945, in Tsuvassias. ❖ Won a gold medal at Mexico City Olympics (1968) and a gold medal at Munich Olympics (1972), both in team foil.

TSJERJASOVA, Lina (1968—). *See Cheryazova, Lina.*

TSOTADZE, Liana (1961—). Soviet diver. Born June 1961 in USSR. ❖ At Moscow Olympics, won a bronze medal in platform (1980).

TSOULFA, Emilia (1973—). Greek yacht racer. Name variations: Aimilia Tsoulfa. Born May 15, 1973, in Athens, Greece; attended Sports Sciences University. ❖ Won World championships for 470 class (2001, 2002, 2003); won a gold medal for double-handed dinghy (470) at Athens Olympics (2004). With Sofia Bekatorou, named ISAF Female World Sailor of the Year (2002).

TSOUMELEKA, Athanasia (1982—). Greek track-and-field athlete. Born Jan 2, 1982, in Preveza, Greece. ❖ For 20 km road walk, placed 1st at European championships (2001, 2003) and Greek championships (2002, 2003, 2004); won a gold medal for 20 km road walk at Athens Olympics (2004).

TSU-HSI (1835–1908). *See Cixi.*

TSUKADA, Maki (1982—). Japanese judoka. Born Jan 5, 1982, in Japan; attended Tokai University. ❖ Placed 2nd at World championships for + 78 kg (2003); won a gold medal for + 78 kg at Athens Olympics (2004).

TSUKAHARA, Cheko. *See Oda, Cheko.*

TSUKASA, Yoko (1934—). Japanese actress. Name variations: Yôko Tsukasa. Born Aug 20, 1934, in Tottori, Japan. ❖ Leading lady of Japanese films, began career as a cover girl; made film debut in *Forever Be Mine* (1954), followed by *Tenka taihei, Oen-san, Brother and Sister, Iwashigumo* (Summer Clouds), *Nippon tanjo, Girl in the Mist, Akibiyori, Yojimbo, Honkon no yoru, Early Autumn, Onna no za, Horoki, Chushingura (47 Samurai), Kojiro, Samurai Rebellion, Midaregumo, Admiral Yamamoto, Goyokin, Shinsengumi* (Band of Assassins), and *Island of Horrors*, among others.

TSU-MANA (c. 1860–1942). *See Nampeyo.*

TSUMURA, Setsuko (1928—). Japanese novelist. Born 1928 in Kukui, Nagano Prefecture, Japan; m. Akira Yoshimura. ❖ Works include *Saihate* (1964), *Gangu* (1965), *Chieko Tobu* (1998). Received Akutagawa Award (1965) and Selected Artists Award of Minister of Education.

TSUNODA, Fusako (1914—). Japanese memoirist. Born 1914 in Tokyo, Japan. ❖ Studied at Sorbonne; works include *Hilda in East Germany* (1961), which won Bungei Shunju Prize (1961), *The Windy Border*, which won Fujin Koron Prize, and *Captain Amakasu*.

TSUPER, Alla (c. 1980—). Belarusian freestyle skier. Born c. 1980 in Belarus. ❖ Placed 5th for aerials at Nagano Olympics for Ukraine (1998) and 11th at Salt Lake City Olympics for Belarus (2002); won Europa Cup for aerials (1997) and FIS World Cup for aerials (2002).

TSURU AOKI (1892–1961). *See Aoki, Tsuru.*

TSUSHIMA, Yuko (1947—). Japanese writer. Born 1947 in Tokyo, Japan; dau. of Osamu Dazai (postwar novelist who committed suicide in 1948). ❖ One of the 1st Japanese writers to achieve popular success while addressing women's issues, published *Choji* (1978, *Child of Fortune*, 1983); won Kawabata Award for *Silent Traders*; works, translated into English by Geraldine Harcourt, include *Woman Running in the Mountains* (1992) and *The Shooting Gallery & Other Stories* (1997).

TSVETAEVA, Marina (1892–1941). Russian poet. Name variations: Marina Cvetaeva; Marina Tsvetayeva or Tsvétaieff; Marina Tswetajewa-Efron. Pronunciation: Tsve-TAH-ye-va. Born Marina Ivanovna Tsvetaeva in Moscow, Russia, Sept 26, 1892 (according to Julian calendar); committed suicide, Aug 31, 1941, in Yelabuga, USSR; dau. of Maria A. Meyn (pianist, died 1906) and Ivan V. Tsvetaev (authority on classical languages, died 1913); sister of Anastasia Tsvetaeva, known as Asya; m. Sergei Efron (writer), Jan 1912 (shot 1941); children: Ariadna Efron (b. 1912); Irina Efron (1917–1920); Georgii Efron (b. 1925). ❖ Innovative Russian poet, long undervalued for political reasons, who is now generally recognized as a national treasure; published 1st book of poems, *Evening Album* (1910), at 18, followed by *The Magic Lantern* (Moscow, 1912); as poetry grew more mature, won a Moscow literary prize and occasionally published in journals; published a selection from 1st two books, *From Two Books* (1913), but the next book would not appear until several years after 1917 Revolution; poetry leaped in significance during her intense love affair with an older poet, Sophia Parnok, whom she traveled, read, wrote and quarreled with (1914–16); husband became an officer in White Army (1917); published *Mileposts* (1921 and 1922); after the Whites were decisively defeated, joined husband near Prague, and their émigré life began (1922); receiving a subsidy as a poet, published *Mileposts I* (1922), *The End of Casanova: A Dramatic Study* (1922), *Parting* (1922), *Poems to Blok* (1922), *The Tsar-Maiden* (1922), *Psyche Romanticism* (1923), and *The Swain* (1924); now a recognized poet, moved to Paris (Nov 1, 1925), where she continued to write short lyric poems and long narrative poems about what she loved, regardless of political expediency; published *After Russia* (1928); with the depression, wrote more critical and autobiographical prose, which sold and paid better than poetry; her last cycle of poems was a passionate protest against Hitler's occupation of Czechoslovakia; returned to USSR (1939); on arrival, learned that sister was in a labor camp; daughter Alya, nearly 27, was arrested and disappeared into the Stalinist system of prisons and camps

(Aug 1939), followed by husband (Oct 1939); got work as a literary translator; committed suicide (1941); until the "thaw" after Stalin's death (1953), remained a "non-person" in the Soviet Union; by end 1970s, was recognized as one of Russia's greatest 20th-century poets. ❖ See also Simon Karlinsky, *Marina Tsvetaeva: The Woman, Her World and Her Poetry* (Cambridge U. Press, 1986); Viktoria Schweitzer, *Tsvetaeva* (HarperCollins, 1992); Pasternak, Pasternak, and Azadovsky, eds. *Letters Summer 1926: Correspondence Between Pasternak, Tsvetaeva and Rilke* (Oxford U. Press, 1985); Jane Taubman, *A Life Through Poetry: Marina Tsvetaeva's Lyric Diary* (Slavica, 1988); and *Women in World History*.

TSYGITSA, Olena (1975—). Ukrainian handball player. Born April 8, 1975, in Ukraine. ❖ Won a team bronze medal at Athens Olympics (2004).

TSYHULEVA, Oksana. Ukrainian trampolinist. Born in Ukraine. ❖ Won a silver medal at Sydney Olympics (2000).

TSYLINSKAYA, Natallia (1975—). Belarusian cyclist. Born Aug 30, 1975, in Minsk, USSR. ❖ At World championships, placed 1st for 500-meter time trial (2000, 2002, 2003) and for sprint (2000, 2003); won a bronze medal for 500-meter time trial at Athens Olympics (2004); placed 1st overall in World Cup ranking for 500-meter time trial (2001, 2003) and for sprint (2001, 2004).

TSZE HSI AN (1835–1908). *See Cixi.*

TUA-O-RANGI (1845–1903). *Bullock, Margaret.*

TUBBS, Alice (1851–1930). American gambler. Name variations: Poker Alice; Alice Ivers; Alice Huckert; Alice Duffield; Corduroy Alice. Born Alice Ivers, Feb 17, 1851, in Sudbury, England; died Feb 27, 1930, in Sturgis, South Dakota; only dau. of a schoolmaster and a housewife; moved with family to Virginia in late 1860s, then to Colorado; m. Frank Duffield (mining engineer), c. 1870; m. W. G. (George) Tubbs, 1907; m. George Huckert, after 1910; no children. ❖ First and most successful professional woman gambler in the American West, who played at casinos from Oklahoma Territory to the Rocky Mountains in a career that spanned decades; began professional gambling in Lake City, Colorado (1876), as means of support after husband was killed in mine accident; traveled the West as gambler and ran roadhouses in Deadwood and Sturgis, South Dakota; retired (early 1920s). ❖ See also Nolie Mumey, *Poker Alice: Alice Ivers, Duffield, Tubbs, Huckert, 1851–1930: History of a Woman Gambler in the West* (Artcraft, 1951); and *Women in World History*.

TUBMAN, Harriet (1821–1913). African-American abolitionist. Name variations: Araminta "Minty" Ross; Harriet Ross. Born Araminta Ross in 1821 on the Edward Brodas plantation near Bucktown, Dorchester Co., Maryland; died Mar 10, 1913, in Auburn, NY; dau. of Harriet Greene and Benjamin Ross (slaves of Edward Brodas); m. John Tubman (slave), 1844 (estranged 1848); m. Nelson Davis (Civil War veteran), 1869; no children. ❖ Legendary runaway slave from Maryland who, once free, returned to the South 19 times to guide as many as 300 enslaved African-Americans to freedom through the secret network known as the Underground Railroad; escaped from slavery (1849), traveling only at night, following the north star for days until she realized that she had crossed the border between the slaveholding and non-slaveholding states; convinced that slavery was an evil willed by man, not by God, had an unwavering belief that she was destined to lead her people out of the "jaws of hell" and into the land of freedom, or die in the effort; planned and executed liberation excursions into slaveholding territory (1850s); eventually rescued both her parents and settled them in a house she purchased in Auburn, New York (1858); raised funds for John Brown's raid on Harper's Ferry, Virginia; moved to Beaufort, South Carolina (1862), where she worked for 3 years as a nurse, scout, and spy on behalf of the Union Army; moved to Virginia where she cared for wounded black soldiers as the matron for the Colored Hospital at Fortress Monroe (1865); collaborated with Sarah Bradford to write her autobiography, which was published as *Scenes in the Life of Harriet Tubman* (1868); was a delegate to the National Association of Colored Women's 1st annual convention (1896); converted her family home in Auburn into the Harriet Tubman Home for Aged and Indigent Colored People; garnered almost mythological status even during her lifetime. ❖ See also Sarah Bradford, *Harriet Tubman: The Moses of Her People* (1886); and *Women in World History*.

TUCHMAN, Barbara (1912–1989). American historian. Pronunciation: TUCK-man. Born Barbara Wertheim, Jan 30, 1912, in New York, NY; died Feb 6, 1989, in Greenwich, Connecticut; dau. of Maurice Wertheim and Alma (Morgenthau) Wertheim; Radcliffe College, BA, 1933; m. Dr. Lester R. Tuchman, 1940; children: Lucy, Jessica, Alma. ❖ Two-time winner of the Pulitzer Prize whose writings have become popular bestsellers and are celebrated for their vivid style; served as research assistant, Institute of Public Relations, NY and Tokyo (1934–35); worked as editorial assistant, *The Nation*, in NY (1936); stationed in Madrid to cover Spanish Civil War (1937); was staff writer, *War in Spain*, London (1937–38); served as American correspondent, *New Statesman and Nation*, London (1939); worked on Far East news desk, Office of War Information, NY (1944–45); made trustee of Radcliffe College (1960); awarded Pulitzer Prize for *The Guns of August* (1962) and *Stillwell and the American Experience in China* (1971); served on Smithsonian Council (1971–89); decorated, Order of Leopold 1st Class (Belgium); fellow, American Academy of Arts and Letters (president, 1978–80); awarded AAAL Gold Medal for History (1978); served as president of Society of American Historians (1971–73); contributed to *Foreign Affairs, Atlantic Monthly, American Heritage, Harper's, The New York Times,* and other magazines and journals. Other writings include: *Bible and Sword: England and Palestine from the Bronze Age to Balfour* (1956), *The Zimmerman Telegram* (1958), *The Proud Tower* (1962), *The March of Folly: From Troy to Vietnam* (1984), *A Distant Mirror: The Calamitous 14th Century* (1984) and *The First Salute* (1988). ❖ See also *Women in World History*.

TUCKER, C. DeLores (1927–2005). African-American politician and civil-rights activist. Born Oct 4, 1927, in Philadelphia, Pennsylvania; died Oct 12, 2005; in Philadelphia, Pennsylvania; dau. of Whitfield Nottage (minister) and Captilda (Gardiner) Nottage (entrepreneur); attended Temple University, Pennsylvania State University, and University of Pennsylvania; m. William J. Tucker (real-estate executive), July 1951; no children. ❖ Took part in the march from Selma to Montgomery, Alabama, and the White House Conference on Civil Rights (1965); served as secretary of the Commonwealth of Pennsylvania, becoming the highest-ranking black woman in any state government at the time (1971–77); was cofounder and chair of National Political Caucus of Black Women; was founding member of National Women's Caucus; served as vice-president of Pennsylvania chapter of NAACP and board member of NAACP's Special Contribution Fund; committed to feminism as well as to civil rights. ❖ See also *Women in World History*.

TUCKER, Charlotte Maria (1821–1893). English children's writer and missionary. Name variations: (pseudonyms) A. L. O. E., A Lady of England. Born May 8, 1821, in Barnet, England; died Dec 2, 1893, in Amritsar, India; dau. of Henry St. George Tucker (civil servant and financier) and Jane (Boswell) Tucker (Scottish-born dau. of an Edinburgh attorney who was related to James Boswell); never married; no children. ❖ Under pseudonym A. L. O. E., published 1st book, *Claremont Tales; or Illustrations of the Beatitudes* (1852), a well-received collection of morality tales aimed at children; published some 140 books for the young under that pseudonym, and donated proceeds to charity; served as a Church of England missionary in India (1875–93); writings include *The Rambles of a Rat* (1854), *Wings and Stings* (1855), *Old Friends with New Faces* (1858), *The Story of a Needle* and *The Giant Killer* (1868) and *Cyril Ashley* (1870). ❖ See also *Women in World History*.

TUCKER, Corin (1972—). American musician. Name variations: Sleater-Kinney. Born Nov 9, 1972, in State College, PA; graduate of Evergreen State College, Olympia, WA; m. Lance Bangs (cinematographer), June 19, 2000; children: 1 son, Marshall Tucker Bangs. ❖ Singer-guitarist, formed Sleater-Kinney, in Olympia, WA, with Carrie Brownstein and drummer Lora McFarlane (1994); with group, released debut album, *Sleater-Kinney* (1995), which addressed sexism and sexual abuse, followed by *Call the Doctor* (1996), which included song, "I Wanna be Your Joey Ramone," and was voted best album of the year by critics; other acclaimed albums include *Dig Me Out* (1997), *The Hot Rock* (1999) and *All Hands on the Bad One* (2000), which included songs, "#1 Must Have" and "The Ballad of a Ladyman"; with Sarah Dougher, released *Introducing Cadallaca* (1998) and *Out West* (2000).

TUCKER, Eugenia (c. 1834–1928). *See Fitzgerald, Eugenia Tucker.*

TUCKER, Sophie (1884–1966). American entertainer. Born Sophia Kalish (later known as Sophia Abuza), Jan 13, 1884, in Russia; died Feb 9, 1966, in New York, NY; dau. of Charles Abuza (restaurateur originally named Kalish) and Jennie (Yacha) Abuza; m. Louis Tuck (beer-wagon driver), 1903 (div. 1913); m. Frank Westphal (her pianist), 1914 (div. 1919); m. Albert Lackey (personal manager), 1928 (div. 1933);

children: (1st m.) 1 son, Bert. ❖ Self-proclaimed "Last of the Red Hot Mamas," began career in vaudeville (1906), then sang and kibitzed her way through next 6 decades, performing at NY's Latin Quarter 4 months before her death; appeared in *Ziegfeld Follies of 1909*; began touring William Morris circuit with great success, particularly in Chicago, where she was billed as "The Mary Garden of Ragtime"; had flamboyant, frequently racy act that capitalized on her music-hall voice and rotund frame; began to introduce songs filled with the double-entendre which came to be associated with her (tunes like "Nobody Loves a Fat Girl, But Oh How a Fat Girl Can Love" and "You've Got To See Mama Ev'ry Night"); made one of her earliest recordings, "Some of These Days," which became her theme song; also noted for "My Yiddishe Mama"; played the Palace in NY (1914); owned a nightclub in NY, Sophie Tucker's Playground, and headlined *Earl Carroll's Vanities of 1924*; on radio, starred on "Sophie Tucker and Her Show" (1938–39); appeared on Broadway in *Leave It to Me* (1931) and *The High Kickers* (1941); films include *Honky Tonk* (1928), *Follow the Boys* (1944) and *The Joker is Wild* (1957). ❖ See also autobiography *Some of These Days* (1945); and *Women in World History*.

TUCKER, Tanya (1958—). American country singer. Born Tanya Denise Tucker, Oct 10, 1958, in Seminole, TX; children: Presley Tanita (b. 1989) and Beau Grayson (b. 1991). ❖ At 13, appeared in film, *Jeremiah Johnson* (1972); had hits with title tracks of *Delta Dawn* (1972) and *What's Your Mama's Name* (1973), and with "Blood Red and Goin' Down"; released *Would You Lay With Me (in a Field of Stone)* (1974), with title track becoming #1 C&W single; released rock album, *TNT* (1978), which went gold, but soon returned to country music; appeared in films *The Georgia Peaches* (1980) and *Hard Country* (1981); other hit songs include "Just Another Love" (1986), "Highway Robbery" (1988), "Some Kind of Trouble" (1992) and "Soon" (1993); other albums include *Girls Like Me* (1986), *Tennessee Woman* (1990) and *Complicated* (1997); released platinum records, *What Do I Do With Me* (1991) and *Can't Run From Yourself* (1992). ❖ See also autobiography, *Nickel Dreams* (1997).

TUCKWELL, Gertrude (1861–1951). English trade unionist. Born Gertrude Mary Tuckwell in Oxford, England, in 1861; died in 1951; dau. of a parson who was master of New College School. ❖ Following a 7-year stint teaching in elementary schools in London (1885–93), became secretary to her aunt, Lady Emily Dilke (1893); served as president of Women's Trade Union League (1904–1921); led crusades against white lead poisoning and organized the Sweated Goods Exhibition (1906), spurring the Trade Boards Act of 1909; was the 1st woman justice of the peace for County of London (1920); founded the maternal Mortality Committee (1927); was president of the Women Sanitary Inspectors and the National Association of Probation Officers; and sat on the Central Committee on Women's Training and Employment; also published *The State and its Children* (1894), *Women in Industry* (1908), and (with Stephen Gwynn) a biography of Sir Charles Wentworth Dilke (1917).

TUCKWELL, Patricia (b. 1926). See Lascelles, Patricia.

TUDOR, Elizabeth (1533–1603). See Elizabeth I.

TUDOR, Margaret.
See Beaufort, Margaret (1443–1509).
See Margaret Tudor (1489–1541).

TUDOR, Mary.
See Mary Tudor (1496–1533).
See Mary I (1516–1558).

TUDOR-HART, Edith (1908–1978). Austrian photographer. Born Edith Suschitzky, 1908, in Vienna, Austria; died 1978; sister of Wolfgang Suschitzky; m. Alex Tudor-Hart. ❖ Social documentarian, trained at Dessau Bauhaus and as Montessori teacher; became known in Europe as Modernist photographer before fleeing Austria for London (1933), where she opened a photo studio (1936); worked for such magazines as *The Listener*, *The Social Scene*, and *Design Today*; focused on social issues, Spanish Civil War, working women, and industrial decline; later did stories on care of disabled children for *Picture Post*.

TUDORAN, Ioana (1948—). Romanian rower. Born Aug 3, 1948, in Romania. ❖ At Montreal Olympics, won a bronze medal in quadruple sculls with coxswain (1976).

TUENI, Nadia (1935–1983). Lebanese poet. Born 1935 in Beirut, Lebanon; died 1983. ❖ Educated in French schools in Beirut and Athens; became literary editor of French supplement of Beirut paper, *al-Nahar*; works include *Juin et les Mécreants* (1968), *Poèmes pour une Histoire* (1972), *Le Revêur de Terre* (1975), *Archives Sentimentales d'une Guerre au Liban* (1982), *La Terre Arretée* (1984), and *La Prose Oeuvres Complètes* (1985).

TUETING, Sarah (1976—). American ice-hockey player. Born April 26, 1976, in Winnetka, IL; attended Dartmouth College. ❖ Goaltender, named Ivy League Rookie of the Year and Dartmouth's Rookie of the Year (1994–95); won a team gold medal at Nagano (1998), the 1st Olympics to feature women's ice hockey; won team silver medals at World championships (1997, 2000, 2001); won a team silver medal at Salt Lake City Olympics (2002). ❖ See also Mary Turco, *Crashing the Net: The U. S. Women's Olympic Ice Hockey Team and the Road to Gold* (HarperCollins, 1999); and *Women in World History*.

TUFAN-GUZGANU, Elisabeta (1964—). Romanian fencer. Born Aug 8, 1964, in Romania. ❖ Won a silver medal at Los Angeles Olympics (1984) and a bronze medal at Barcelona Olympics (1992), both in team foil.

TUFNELL, Meriel (1948–2002). British jockey. Born Dec 12, 1948, in England; died of cancer, Oct 14, 2002; m. Glenn Humphrey (div.). ❖ England's 1st champion female jockey, became the 1st woman to ride a winner in England under the Rules of Racing, when she won the Goya Stakes on Scorched Earth (May 6, 1972); rode 2 more winners (1972), at Folkestone (on Scorched Earth) and Newbury (on Hard Slipper); became an owner. Named MBE.

TUFTY, Esther Van Wagoner (1896–1986). American journalist and war correspondent. Born Esther Van Wagoner, July 2, 1896, in Kingston, Michigan; died May 4, 1986, in Alexandria, Virginia; dau. of James Van Wagoner and Florence (Loomis) Van Wagoner; attended Michigan State College, 1914–15; University of Wisconsin (Madison), BA, 1921; m. Harold Guilford Tufty Sr. (electrical engineer), Sept 17, 1921 (div. 1947); children: Harold Guilford Tufty Jr. (b. 1922); James Van Wagoner Tufty (b. 1929). ❖ Established the Tufty News Service in Washington, DC (1935), for which she served as writer, editor, and president; originally set up to serve 26 Michigan newspapers, over time her news agency came to feed reports to more than 300 US newspapers; covered the Washington political scene, as well as Nazi air assaults on Britain, the Berlin airlift, and both the Korean and Vietnam wars (1935–85); began work as tv and radio commentator for NBC (1952); served as president of Women's National Press Club, American Newspaper Women's Club, and American Women in Radio and Television; became 1st woman member of National Press Club (1971). ❖ See also *Women in World History*.

TUGURLAN, Mirela (1980—). Romanian gymnast. Born Sept 4, 1980, in Focsani, Romania. ❖ At Atlanta Olympics, won a bronze medal in team all-around (1996).

TUIÚ, Cintia (1975—). See dos Santos, Cintia.

TULA, María Teresa (1951—). Salvadoran political activist. Name variations: Maria Teresa Tula. Born April 23, 1951, in Izalco, El Salvador; m. José Rafael Canales Guevara (blacksmith and labor organizer, murdered 1980); children: 6 (4 survived). ❖ After husband was imprisoned for labor organizing, joined COMADRES (The Mothers and Relatives of Political Prisoners, Disappeared, and Assassinated) and participated in demonstrations, as well as the takeover of Red Cross and UN buildings and many Catholic Churches, to draw attention to cause; became full-time activist after husband was executed by right-wing death squad (1980); was further steeled by 1980 assassination of Archbishop Romero who had played a key role in founding and supporting COMADRES; fled with children to Mexico City, where she continued activism; traveled to Canada (1983) and Europe (1985), speaking out against brutalization of El Salvador's civilian population, interacting with feminists and developing ideas about Salvadoran grassroots feminism; returned to El Salvador (1986); because of continued COMADRES work, was imprisoned, tortured and raped by government forces; released due to international pressure, escaped to US with family (1987); lived in Washington, DC, working with COMADRES office; engaged in 7-year fight for political asylum (1987–94), hindered by official US support for El Salvador's government; moved to Minneapolis (1995); continued political work through COCODA (Companion Communities in Development), which links US municipalities to sister communities in El Salvador. ❖ See also (with Lynn Stephen) *Hear My Testimony: María Teresa Tula, Human Rights Activist of El Salvador* (South End, 1994);.

TULES, La (c. 1820–1852). *See Barcelo, Gertrudis.*

TULI, Felix (1886–1954). *See Wuolijoki, Hella.*

TULLIA (fl. 535 BCE). **Roman queen.** Dau. of Servius Tullius (578–535 BCE), 6th king of Rome; sister of another Tullia, said to be gentle and subservient, who married Lucius (brother of Arruns); m. Arruns; m. Lucius, later known as Tarquinius Superbus, the Etruscan king; children: Sextus Tarquinius (Tarquin); and others. ❖ Infamous queen of Rome, who became a byword for female villainy throughout Roman history; married Arruns, a son of Tarquin and Tanaquil, who had been denied inheritance to the throne in favor of her father; since Arruns was apparently content with his unkingly lot, approached her brother-in-law Lucius with a proposal: they should both kill their spouses and then themselves marry, the better to work together to achieve power; after the deeds were done and Arruns and her sister were killed, married Lucius; with husband, conspired to dispossess her father and seize the crown; when father was killed in the struggle, reputedly drove over his body as it lay unburied in the street; as queen, gained an evil reputation among the citizens of Rome, both for the murder of her father and for the wanton lifestyle ascribed to her.

TULLIA (c. 79–45 BCE). **Roman noblewoman.** Born c. 79 BCE; died in childbirth in 45 BCE; dau. of Terentia and Marcus Tullius Cicero (106–40 BCE), Roman orator and consul; m. Calpurnius Piso; m. 2nd husband; m. 3rd husband Publius Cornelius Dolabella (consul, 44 BCE), in 50 BCE. ❖ Died in childbirth, which devastated her father Cicero, as we know from the poignant letters (still extant) written shortly after her death. ❖ See also *Women in World History.*

TULLIS, Julie (1939–1986). **British mountaineer.** Born Julie Palau in 1939 in Surrey, England; died 1986; m. Terry Tullis, 1959; children: 2. ❖ Began climbing as teenager in England and later took up martial arts, becoming black belt in karate and aikido; embarked on 1st climbing expedition to Peruvian Andes (1974), and went on to climb in Yosemite and Himalayas; worked as filming partner to Kurt Diemberger and with him climbed K2; climbed Broad Peak to become 1st British woman to climb 8,000-meter Himalayan mountain; was 1st British woman on Everest expedition (1985); died of cerebral edema during descent of K2. Wrote *Clouds from Both Sides* (1986).

TULLY, Alice (1902–1993). **American opera singer and philanthropist.** Born Sept 11, 1902; died Dec 10, 1993, in NY, NY; dau. of William J. Tully (state senator) and Clara (Houghton) Tully (Corning heiress); maternal granddau. of Amory Houghton, who founded the Corning Glass Works; studied in Paris with Jean Perier and Miguel Fontecha. ❖ Fairly successful as a mezzo-soprano and later as a dramatic soprano in opera and recitals (1920s–40s), was also a specialist in French repertory; contributed to museums, libraries, and the arts, and was a patron, friend, and supporter of other singers, pianists and composers; founded the Maya Corporation, which made anonymous gifts to the arts; was the main donor for the $4.5 million Alice Tully Hall, a visually and acoustically impressive chamber-music concert hall that opened at Lincoln Center for the Performing Arts (1969); also subsidized the formation of the hall's resident ensemble, the Chamber Music Society of Lincoln Center. ❖ See also *Women in World History.*

TULLY, Mary Jean Crenshaw (1925–2003). **American feminist and lawyer.** Born Mary Jean Crenshaw, Dec 15, 1925, in Fort Sill, OK; died Dec 27, 2003, in White Plains, NY; attended Stanford University, University of Texas at Austin, and University of Chicago; Wayne State University, MA; m. C. Robert Tully, 1947 (div. 1991); children: Bruce C., Scott P., Andrew G., Laura L. and N. Linsey Tully. ❖ Lectured in sociology at Long Island University (1960s); co-founded the Westchester chapter of National Organization for Women (NOW); served as president of NOW's Legal Defense and Education Fund (1971–77); was president of the Fund for Women's Rights (1971–81); founded Midlife Institute at Marymount Manhattan College and directed it (1981–86); funded the Tully Crenshaw Feminist Oral History Project.

TULU, Derartu (1969—). **Ethiopian runner.** Born Mar 21, 1972, a member of the Oromo ethnic group, in Bokoji, in the Arsi region of central Ethiopia. ❖ Won the 10,000 meters at Barcelona (1992), becoming the 1st black African woman to win a gold medal at the Olympics; at the African Games, won the 3,000 meters and 10,000 meters (1992); at World Cup, became the 1st female distance runner to win 2 races: the 3,000 meters and 10,000 meters (1992); placed 4th at Atlanta Olympics (1996); at World Cross Country championships, placed 1st (1997, 2000); won a gold medal for 10,000 meters at

Sydney (2000), the 1st woman to win 2 gold medals in Olympic distance races; at World championships, won a gold medal for the 10,000 (2001); won a bronze medal for 10,000 meters at Athens Olympics (2004). Received Runner of the Year award (1992).

TUMIATI, Lucia (1926—). **Italian novelist and children's writer.** Born 1926 in Venice, Italy. ❖ Participated in Resistance in Venice; studied in Florence and contributed to Italian newspapers and magazines; works include *Terra d'oggi* (1959), *Saltafrontiera* (1962), *Una cartella di sogni* (1968), *Una scuola da bruciare* (1972), *Fiabe di libertà* (1980), and *Fiabe più belle* (1988).

TUOMAITE, Vitalija (1964—). **Soviet basketball player.** Born Nov 22, 1964, in USSR. ❖ At Seoul Olympics, won a bronze medal in team competition (1988).

TUPPER, Frances (1826–1912). **Canadian first lady.** Name variations: Lady Tupper. Born Frances Amelia Morse, 1826, in Amherst, Nova Scotia, Canada; died May 11, 1912; dau. of Silas Hibbert Morse, Esq; m. Charles Tupper (premier of Nova Scotia, then prime minister of Canada, 1896–96, created a baronet), Oct 8, 1846; children: Emma (b. 1847), Elizabeth Stewart (1849–1849), James Stewart (1851–1915), Sir Charles Hibbert (1855–1927, MP 1882–1904), Sophy Almon (1858–1863), William Johnston (1862–1947, lt-gov of Manitoba, 1934–40). ❖ Celebrated 50th wedding anniversary in Ottawa (1896).

TUQAN, Fadwa (1917–2003). **Palestinian poet and feminist.** Name variations: Fadwa Toukan. Born Mar 1, 1917, in Nablus on the West Bank; died Dec 12, 2003, in Nablus; dau. of a soap manufacturer; studied with brother, poet Ibrahim Tuqan (died 1941); attended Oxford University, 1962–64; never married; no children. ❖ One of the Arab world's most distinguished poets, lived childhood in seclusion; moved to Jerusalem to live with poet brother and his wife, where she met and corresponded with many other writers; had to return home when brother died (1941), resulting in *My Brother Ibrahim* (1946); when political turmoil erupted in Palestine (1948), joined factional and literary movements, and began to infuse her poetry with politics; writings include *Wahdi m'a al-Ayyam* (Alone with the Days, 1955), *Amam al-Bab al-Mughlaq* (Before the Closed Door, 1967), *al-Layl Wa-al Fursan* (Night and the Horsemen, 1969), *Ala Qimmat al-Dunya Wahidan* (Alone, at the Top of the World, 1973) and *Kabus al-Layl Wa al-Nahar* (Nightmare in Daylight, 1974). ❖ See also autobiography *A Mountainous Journey* (trans. by Olive Kenny, 1990); and *Women in World History.*

TUR, Evgeniia (1815–1892). *See Salhias de Tournemire, Elizaveta.*

TURCHINA, Zinaida (1946—). **Soviet handball player.** Born May 17, 1946, in USSR. ❖ Won a gold medal at Montreal Olympics (1976), gold medal at Moscow Olympics (1980), and bronze medal at Seoul Olympics (1988), all in team competition.

TURECK, Rosalyn (1914–2003). **American pianist and musicologist.** Born Rosalyn Tureck, Dec 14, 1914, in Chicago, IL; died July 17, 2003, in Riverdale, the Bronx, NY; studied with Sophia Brilliant-Liven, 1925–29, Jan Chiapasso, 1929–31, Leon Theremin, 1931–32; graduated cum laude from Juilliard School of Music, 1935. ❖ An authority on music of Johann Sebastian Bach, received a 4-year fellowship to Juilliard, at age 16, where she studied with Olga Samaroff, among others; debuted at NY's Carnegie Hall with Philadelphia Orchestra, playing Brahm's Concerto in B-Flat (1935); performed her 1st series of all-Bach recitals at NY's Town hall (1937), executing the 48 Preludes and Fugues of the *Well-Tempered Clavier*, the "Goldberg Variations," and miscellaneous works; devoted much of her concert career to Bach, performing his works on the piano rather than the harpsichord or clavichord; wrote a 3-vol. study, *An Introduction to the Performance of Bach*, and recorded much of his music; also played the works of Liszt, Chopin, Weber, Tchaikovsky, Debussy, Albeniz, Ravel and Rachmaninoff, as well as contemporary composers, such as Paul Nordoff; was the 1st woman to conduct the NY Philharmonic (1958); taught at Philadelphia Conservatory of Music (1935–42), Juilliard (1943–55) and at University of California, San Diego (1966–72); founded International Bach Institute, NY (1966) and Tureck Bach Research Foundation, Oxford (1993). ❖ See also *Women in World History.*

TURELL, Jane (1708–1735). **American poet.** Born Jane Colman, Feb 25, 1708, in Boston, Massachusetts; died Mar 26, 1735, in Medford, Massachusetts; dau. of Benjamin Colman (pastor) and Jane (Clark) Colman; m. Ebenezer Turell (pastor), Aug 11, 1726; children: 3 who died in infancy, and Samuel (who died in childhood). ❖ Had intense religious upbringing; composed her 1st hymn at 11, then went on to compose her own rhymed paraphrases of the psalms, as well as reverent meditations and prayers. After her death, husband published a biography of her, *Reliquiae Turellae et Lachrymae Paternal*, which includes several of her poems, letters, diary entries, and essays. ❖ See also *Women in World History*.

TURHAN (1627–1683). *See Hadice Turhan*

TURIKATUKU (d. 1827). New Zealand tribal leader. Died in 1827; dau. of Matunga II; m. Hongi Hika (died 1828); children: 2. ❖ Senior wife of Hongi Hiki, was considered his chief adviser; participated in numerous campaigns against warring tribes. ❖ See also *Dictionary of New Zealand Biography* (Vol. 1).

TURISCHEVA or TURISHCHEVA, Ludmila (1952—). *See Tourischeva, Ludmila.*

TURISINI, Valentina (1969—). Italian shooter. Born Aug 16, 1969, in Italy. ❖ Won a silver medal for 50 m rifle 3 positions at Athens Olympics (2004).

TURITSCHEVA, Ludmila (1952—). *See Tourischeva, Ludmila.*

TURKAN (1627–1683). *See Hadice Turhan*

TURKOVIC, Ingrid. *See Wendl, Ingrid.*

TURLINGTON, Christy (1969—). American model. Born Jan 2, 1969, in Walnut Creek, California; dau. of American father and Salvadoran mother; Gallatin School at New York University, BA, 1999. ❖ Supermodel, signed with Eileen Ford and landed spots in US *Vogue* at 16; came to prominence after appearing on cover of Italian *Vogue* (1987); considered a fresh new face for designers at Chanel, Christian Lacroix, Gianni Versace, and Azzedine Alaïa; signed with Calvin Klein for perfume *Eternity* (1989) and Maybelline.

TURNBO-MALONE, Annie (1869–1957). *See Malone, Annie Turnbo.*

TURNBULL, Julia Anne (1822–1887). American ballet dancer and actress. Born June 18, 1822, in Montreal, Canada; died of TB, Sept 11, 1887, in Brooklyn, New York; dau. of John D. Turnbull (actor and playwright); studied ballet with French dancer Mme LeComte and LeComte's brother, Jules Martin, and with James Sylvain. ❖ At 3, made stage debut as an actress in Albany with sisters Emily and Caroline; at 6, appeared in *The Wandering Boys* in Albany, sharing the stage with Louisa Lane Drew; became a regular player in stock company at Park Theater in NY, simultaneously studying ballet; debuted in 1st leading dance role in *The Sisters* at Bowery Theater (1839); was a soloist in Fanny Elssler's touring company (1840); launched her own solo tour; returned to Bowery Theater (1847), where she joined the stock company and had a great hit as star of *The Naiad Queen*; also danced *Giselle,* for which she received rave reviews (1847), one of the earliest American women to dance the classic title roles of *Giselle* and *Esmeralda*; after her rivalry with Italian dancer Giovanna Ciocca resulted in an audience riot at Bowery Theater (Aug 1848), left the company and continued to dance with great success, assuming more acting roles and earning accolades for these as well; retired from the stage (1857). ❖ See also *Women in World History*.

TURNBULL, Karen (1967—). *See Gillon, Karen.*

TURNBULL, Wendy (1952—). Australian tennis player. Born Nov 26, 1952, in Brisbane, Australia. ❖ At Seoul Olympics, won a bronze medal in doubles (1988); won back-to-back mixed doubles titles at Wimbledon with John Lloyd (1983–84); ranked in Top 20 for 10 consecutive years (1977–86) and in Top 10 (1977–84); won 9 Grand Slam doubles and mixed doubles championships and 14 Senior Grand Slam doubles titles.

TURNER, Anne (1576–1615). English murderer. Born 1576; executed by hanging in 1615 in Tyburn, England; was a friend of the astrologer Simon Forman and may actually have been his daughter; m. George Turner. ❖ Helped Frances Howard, countess of Somerset, to poison Sir Thomas Overbury (1613). ❖ See also *Women in World History*.

TURNER, Cathy (1962—). American short-track speedskater. Born April 10, 1962, in Rochester, NY. ❖ Won a gold medal for 500 meters and silver medal in 3,000-meter relay at Albertville Olympics (1992); won a gold medal for 500 meters and a bronze medal for the 3,000-meter relay at Lillehammer Olympics (1994).

TURNER, Debbye (1966—). Miss America and TV host. Born 1966 in Mexico, Missouri; Arkansas State University, BS; University of Missouri-Columbia, doctor of veterinary medicine, 1991. ❖ Named Miss America (1990), representing Missouri; was a contributor to "The Early Show," CBS; hosted series on pets and veterinary medicine for PBS, "The Gentle Doctor."

TURNER, Dumitrita (1964—). Romanian gymnast. Born Feb 12, 1964, in Romania. ❖ At World championships, placed 1st in team all-around and vault (1979); at Moscow Olympics, won a silver medal in team all-around (1980).

TURNER, Eliza Sproat (1826–1903). American author and suffragist. Name variations: Eliza L. Sproat Randolph Turner. Born Eliza L. Sproat, 1826, in Philadelphia, PA; died June 20, 1903, in Chadds Ford, PA; dau. of a farmer and Maria (Lutwyche) Sproat; m. Nathaniel Randolph (lumber merchant), 1855 (died Sept 1858); Joseph C. Turner (attorney and dairy farmer), 1864; children: (1st m.) 1 son. ❖ Wrote reform-minded fiction and poetry in magazines such as *Christian Keepsake*, *Sartain's*, *Graham's*, and *National Era* (1847–55); published collection of poetry, *Out-of-Door Rhymes* (1872); helped organize Pennsylvania Woman Suffrage Association (1869); wrote suffrage tract, *Four Quite New Reasons Why You Should Wish Your Wife to Vote* (1875); organized Children's Country Week Association of Philadelphia (1875); served as corresponding secretary and president (1879–81) of New Century Club in Philadelphia; established evening classes and community center for working women and girls (1881), which eventually became New Century Guild of Working Women.

TURNER, Elizabeth (1774–1846). English children's writer. Name variations: Mrs. Turner. Born 1774 in England; died 1846 in Whitchurch, Salop, England. ❖ One of the most popular children's book authors in the early and middle 19th century, wrote many moral tales in verse, which she called "cautionary stories"; writings include *The Daisy* (1807), *The Cowslip* (1811), *The Blue Bell* (1838) and *The Crocus* (1844).

TURNER, Ethel (1872–1958). Australian children's author and novelist. Born Ethel Burwell, Jan 24, 1872, in Doncaster, Yorkshire, England; died April 8, 1958, in Sydney; dau. of G. W. Burwell (died 1874); sister of Lilian Turner (1870–1956); attended Sydney Girls' High School; m. Herbert Curlewis (a judge), in 1896; children: Jean Curlewis (1899–1930). ❖ After father died, mother married Henry Turner; served as editor of the children's column of *Illustrated Sydney News* and began writing her own books, which were similar to those of Louisa May Alcott and Charlotte Mary Yonge, but with characteristically Australian, middle-class settings and values; best-known books are *Seven Little Australians* and *The Family at Misrule*; also wrote *The Little Duchess* (1896), *The Little Larrikin* (1896), *The Camp at Wandinong* (1898), *Gum Leaves* (1900), *Betty & Co.* (1903), *A White Roof-Tree* (1905), *The Stolen Voyage* (1907), *Fair Ines* (1910), *Fifteen and Fair* (1911), *The Secret of the Sea* (1913), *The Cub* (1915), *Captain Cub* (1917), *Laughing Water* (1920), *King Anne* (1921), *Jennifer J.* (1922), *Nicola Silver* (1924) and *The Ungardeners* (1925), among others. ❖ See also *Women in World History*.

TURNER, Eva (1892–1990). English soprano. Name variations: Dame Eva Turner. Born Mar 10, 1892, in Oldham, England; died June 16, 1990, in London; studied with Dan Rootham, Giglia Levy, Edgardo Levy, Mary Wilson, and Albert Richards-Broad. ❖ Sang in the chorus of Carl Rosa Opera (1915), later establishing herself as prima donna of this provincial English touring company; debuted in London (1916); sang at La Scala (1924), the only English opera singer to achieve international status during interwar years; especially remembered for her role of Turandot; made debut at Covent Garden (1928); saw career curtailed by WWII; taught at University of Oklahoma (1949–59); joined faculty at the Royal Academy of Music (1959). Named Dame Commander of the Order of the British Empire (1962). ❖ See also *Women in World History*.

TURNER, Florence E. (c. 1888–1946). American actress, producer, and director. Born Jan 6, c. 1888, in New York, NY; died of cancer, Aug 28, 1946, in Los Angeles, California; dau. of William Clifton Turner (artist) and Frances Louise (Bowles) Turner (actress). ❖ Applied at Vitagraph studios in NY and secured the lead in a short comedy, *How to Cure a Cold* (1907); was the 1st American film actor to receive a contract; as "The Vitagraph Girl," was often paired with Maurice Costello and Wallace Reid; formed her own company, Turner Films, Ltd., in England (1913), where she produced a small but well-received collection of films and became a popular actress (1915); during WWI, returned to US and worked regularly as an actor, writer, and director for Universal and MGM; back in England (1920), appeared as the lead in several comedies produced by W. W. Jacobs; also produced a two-reel comedy, *Film Favorites* (1924); in US, played character parts and comedy roles

(1925–46), and was a member of the MGM stock company (1936–46). ❖ See also *Women in World History*.

TURNER, Mrs. G. D. (1882–1973). *See Wilson, Margaret W.*

TURNER, Helen Newton (1908–1995). *See Newton Turner, Helen.*

TURNER, Mrs. Henry E. (1903–1961). *See Robertson, E. Arnot.*

TURNER, Jane (before 1640–after 1660). British devotional writer. Born before 1640 in England; died after 1660; m. John Turner. ❖ Wrote spiritual autobiography about experiences as Baptist, *Choice Experiences of the Kind Dealings of God before, in and after Conversion; laid down in six general heads. Together with some brief observations upon the same. Whereunto is added a description of the experience* (1653).

TURNER, Kathleen (1954—). American actress. Born Mary Kathleen Turner, June 19, 1954, in Springfield, MO; attended Southwest Missouri State University; University of Maryland, BFA, 1977; m. David Guc, 1977 (div. 1982); m. Jay Weiss, 1983; children: (2nd m.) Rachel Ann (b. 1987). ❖ Had recurring role on "The Doctors" (1978–79); appeared in film *Body Heat* (1981); came to prominence with *Romancing the Stone* (1984); other films include *Crimes of Passion* (1984), *Prizzi's Honor* (1985), *The Jewel of the Nile* (1985), *Peggy Sue Got Married* (1986), *Who Framed Roger Rabbit* (1988), *The War of the Roses* (1989), *V. I. Warshawski* (1999), *Serial Mom* (1994), *The Virgin Suicides* (1999) and *Without Love* (2004); appeared on Broadway in *Cat on a Hot Tin Roof* (1990). Nominated for Tony Award for Best Actress for *Who's Afraid of Virginia Woolf?* (2005).

TURNER, Kim (1961—). African-American runner. Born Mar 21, 1961, in Detroit, Michigan; attended University of Texas. ❖ At Los Angeles Olympics, tied with Michele Chardonnet for a bronze medal in the 100-meter hurdles (1984).

TURNER, Lana (1921–1995). American actress. Born Julia Jean Mildred Frances Turner, Feb 8, 1921, in Wallace, Idaho; died June 29, 1995, in Los Angeles, California; dau. of John Virgil Turner (mine overseer) and Mildred (Cowan) Turner; m. Artie Shaw (bandleader), 1940 (div. 1941); m. Stephen Crane (actor turned restaurateur), 1942 (annulled, then div. 1943); m. Bob Topping (millionaire), 1948 (div. 1952); m. Lex Barker (actor), 1953 (div. 1957); m. Fred May; m. Robert Eaton; m. Ronald Dante, also known as Ronald Peller (hypnotist), 1968; children: (2nd m.) daughter, Cheryl Crane (b. 1943). ❖ Hollywood "Sweater Girl" who blossomed into one of the most glamorous, popular stars of 1940s and 1950s, made film debut as walk-on in *A Star is Born* (1937); had 1st small role in *They Won't Forget* (1937); appeared in such films as *Love Finds Andy Hardy* (1938), *Ziegfeld Girl* (1941), *Dr. Jekyll and Mr. Hyde* (1941) and *Honky-Tonk* (1941); popularity soared during WWII, when she ranked among the nation's top "pin-up girls"; in postwar years, made such notable films as *Green Dolphin Street* (1947), *Cass Timberlane* (1947), *The Three Musketeers* (1948) and *The Bad and the Beautiful* (1956), but turned in most credible performance in *The Postman Always Rings Twice* (1946); kept career afloat through a tumultuous private life that included 7 marriages and a scandal which involved her teenage daughter protecting her with an 8-inch kitchen knife by stabbing Johnny Stompanato to death because he was beating her (1958); with career seemingly over, came back to star in remake of *Imitation of Life* (1959), which was an enormous hit, followed by *Portrait in Black* (1960) and *Madame X* (1966); retained star power well into 1980s, when she played a recurring role in "Falcon Crest"; other films include *Slightly Dangerous* (1943), *Week-End at the Waldorf* (1945), *The Merry Widow* (1952), *The Rains of Ranchipur* (1955) and *By Love Possessed* (1962). Nominated for an Academy Award for her performance in *Peyton Place* (1957). ❖ See also memoir *Lana: The Lady, the Legend, the Truth* 1982; Cheryl Crane (with Cliff Jahr) *Detour: A Hollywood Story* (Arbor, 1988); and *Women in World History*.

TURNER, Lesley (1942—). Australian tennis player. Born 1942 in Sydney, Australia; m. Bill Bowrey (tennis player). ❖ Was a member of Australia's inaugural Federation Cup team (1963) and runner-up for the Australian Open title (1964, 1967); won 13 Grand Slam events, including 2 French singles titles (1963, 1965), Wimbledon doubles (1964) and French Open doubles (1964, 1965), both with Margaret Court, as well as mixed doubles at Wimbledon with Fred Stolle (1961, 1964) and women's doubles at US Open with Darlene Hard (1961).

TURNER, Mary (d. 1918). African-American lynching victim. Died May 19, 1918, near Valdosta, Georgia; m. Hayes Turner (died May 18, 1918). ❖ Eight months' pregnant, was lynched at Folsom's Bridge over the Little River, in Brooks Co., north of Valdosta, Georgia, in order "to teach her a lesson," her offense being that she had made "unwise remarks" by suggesting that those who had lynched her husband Hayes Turner—a man innocent of any crime—should be brought to justice; her death turned the nation's attention to a savage tradition, serving to galvanize efforts to pass federal anti-lynching legislation, and her martyrdom has been commemorated and memorialized in African-American novels, poetry and works of art. ❖ See also *Women in World History*.

TURNER, Reather "Dimples" Dixon (1945—). *See Dixon, Reather.*

TURNER, Sherri (1956—). American golfer. Born Oct 4, 1956, in Greenville, SC; attended Furman University. ❖ Was Carolinas Junior champion (1974–75); joined LPGA tourn (1983); won LPGA championship and Corning Classic (1988); won Orix Hawaiian Open (1989). Inducted in Furman Athletic Hall of Fame (1989) and NutraSweet Hall of Fame (1990).

TURNER, Tina (1938—). African-American rock-and-roll singer. Born Anna Mae Bullock, Nov 26, 1938, in Nut Bush, TN; m. musician Ike Turner (sep. 1976, div. 1978); companion of Erwin Bach, EMI record company executive, for many years; children: (Raymond) Craig Turner; (with Ike Turner) Ronald Renelle Turner. ❖ After meeting Ike Turner, began performing professionally while attending high school in St. Louis, MO; became featured singer of Ike and Tina Turner Revue, recording "A Fool in Love" (1960) and "River Deep, Mountain High" (1965); with band, opened for Rolling Stones during US tour (1969), which resulted in several pop chart hits: "I've Been Loving You Too Long," "Got to Take You Higher," "Bold Soul Sister," "Honky Tonk Woman" and "Proud Mary" (1970); appeared in film version of The Who's rock opera *Tommy* (1974); abandoned both Turner and his band because of Ike's abusive treatment (1976), refusing all compensation as part of their divorce; rebuilt career performing 6 nights a week in small clubs; after meeting an Australian manager who promoted her, released album *Private Dancer* (1984), which included "What's Love Got to Do With It"; soon far eclipsed whatever fame she had achieved previously with Turner's band; appeared in film *Mad Max—Beyond Thunderdome* (for which she sang the title song, "We Don't Need Another Hero"); went on tour which earned nearly $25 million (1997). At Grammys, awarded Best Female Pop Vocal for "What's Love," while her work on the album *Better Be Good to Me* earned Best Female Rock Vocal and "What's Love" was named Best Record of the Year (1984); inducted into the Rock and Roll Hall of Fame (1991). ❖ See also autobiography (with Kurt Loder) *I, Tina* (Morrow, 1986); (film) *What's Love Got to Do With It?*, starring Angela Bassett, based on autobiography (1993); and *Women in World History*.

TURNER-WARWICK, Margaret (1924—). Immunologist and thoracic doctor. Born Margaret Moore, Nov 19, 1924, in London, England; Oxford University, BA, 1946; University College Hospital Medical School in London, MD, 1956, PhD, 1961; m. Richard Trevor Turner-Warwick (surgeon), 1950. ❖ The 1st woman president of Royal College of Physicians (1989–92), completed junior doctor posts at University College and Brompton Hospitals (1950–57); worked as a general medicine consultant at Elizabeth Garrett Anderson Hospital (1960–67); employed as senior lecturer at Institute of Diseases of the Chest at Brompton Hospital (1963–72); served as a medical professor at the Cardiothoracic Institute, then director of department of thoracic medicine (1972–87) and dean (1984–87); was chair of Royal Devon and Exeter Health Trust (1992–95); with Deborah Doniach and Jack Pepys, wrote *Immunology of the Lung* (1978). Made Dame Commander of the Order of the British Empire (1991).

TURNLEY, Christopher (1894–1958). *See Ellis-Fermor, Una Mary.*

TURPIE, Marion (d. 1967). American golfer. Name variations: Marion Turpie Lake; Marion McNaughton. Born Marion Turpie; died Feb 27, 1967, in New Orleans, LA. ❖ Won the Women's Southern Amateur (1926, 1928, 1931) and Eastern Amateur (1941).

TURPIN, Luci Baines (b. 1947). *See Johnson, Luci Baines.*

TURUNKU BAKWA (fl. 1530s). Queen of Zaria. Flourished 1530s as the queen of Zazzau (later Zaria) in central Nigeria; children: Amina (c. 1533–c. 1598) and Zaria (both would rule Zaria). ❖ Member of a warlike matriarchal clan, was queen (*sarauniya*) of Zazzau, the large empire of the Hasau people, though she was not originally Hasau but a Fulani; founded the city of Zaria in northcentral Nigeria (1536).

TUSAP, Srbuhi (1841–1901). Armenian poet, novelist, and feminist. Born 1841 in Constantinople; died 1901; m. Paul Tusap (her music teacher), 1871; children: Dorine (d. 1890). ❖ During 1880s, gained recognition as a writer, social activist, and public speaker; the leader of a literary salon, and a member of the group of writers known as the "Renascence Generation," wrote 3 novels, dozens of poems and articles, and encouraged writers to use the Armenian language; her 1st book, *Mayda* (1883), was the 1st novel in Armenian written by a woman, as well as the 1st to espouse women's rights; also wrote novels *Siranoush* (1885) and *Arak'sya kam Varjouhin* (A. or the Teacher, 1887).

TUSCANY, countess of. See Matilda of Tuscany (1046–1115).

TUSCANY, grand duchess of.
See Joanna of Austria (1546–1578).
See Cappello, Bianca (1548–1587).
See Martelli, Camilla (fl. 1570s).
See Christine of Lorraine (c. 1571–1637).
See Maria Magdalena of Austria (1589–1631).
See Medici, Vittoria de (d. 1694).
See Marguerite Louise of Orleans (c. 1645–1721).
See Medici, Anna Maria de (d. 1741).
See Bonaparte, Elisa (1777–1820).

TUSCANY, Matilda of (1046–1115). See Matilda of Tuscany.

TUSCANY, princess of. See Toselli, Louisa (1870–1947).

TUSCHAK, Katalin (1959—). Hungarian fencer. Born June 13, 1959, in Hungary. ❖ At Seoul Olympics, won a bronze medal in team foil (1988).

TUSQUETS, Esther (1936—). Spanish novelist. Born Aug 30, 1936, in Barcelona, Spain. ❖ Studied philosophy and history at universities of Barcelona and Madrid; directed publishing house Editorial Lumen, then started own publishing house; works, which focus on themes of love and sexual identity, include *El mismo mar de todos los veranos* (1978), *El amor es un juego solitario* (1979), *Varada tras el último naufragio* (1980), *Recuerdo de Safa* (1982), *Olivia* (1986), *Después de Moisés* (1989), *La reina de los gatos* (1993), *La niña lunática y otros cuentos* (1996), *Con la miel en los labios* (1997), and *Ser Madre* (2000). Received City of Barcelona Prize.

TUSSAUD, Marie (1761–1850). English artist and entrepreneur. Name variations: known as Marie Grosholtz (1767–95), Marie Tussaud (1795–1850). Born Anna-Maria Grosholtz (also seen as Gresholtz) in Strasbourg, Germany, Dec 7, 1761; died in London, England, April 15, 1850; dau. of Anna Maria (Walder) Grosholtz, of Strasbourg, and Johannes Grosholtz (German officer from Frankfurt); m. François Tussaud (civil engineer), Oct 20, 1795; children: daughter (who died in infancy); 2 sons, Joseph Tussaud and François, known as Francis Tussaud (1800–1873). ❖ Talented artist in the unusual medium of dyed wax and far-sighted entrepreneur who created one of London's most popular attractions, Madame Tussaud's; father, wounded in battle, died before she was born; adopted by Dr. Philippe Curtius of Berne, where her mother was cook and housekeeper; moved to Paris and tutored by Curtius, a doctor who made anatomical models in wax (1767); taught wax modeling to Madame Élisabeth of France, sister of King Louis XVI; lived and worked with the princess, who was unmarried, at Versailles and Montreuil (1781–88); through Curtius, met Robespierre, Danton, Marat and Sieyes; modeled heads of guillotine victims, including Marie Antoinette, Robespierre and Charlotte Corday (1792–93); inherited Curtius' fortune (1794); after maneuvering through the hazards of the French Revolution, being close to all its central figures but avoiding their fate on the guillotine, started a new life in Britain at age 40 and made an even greater triumph there than she had in her native land (1802); narrowly lost part of her collection when her boat was shipwrecked en route to Ireland (1822); founded permanent exhibition in London (1835). ❖ See also Pauline Chapman, *Madame Tussaud's Chamber of Horrors* (Constable, 1984) and (with Anita Leslie) *Madame Tussaud: Waxworker Extraordinary* (Hutchinson, 1978); Francis Herve, *Madame Tussaud's Memoirs and Reminiscences of France* (London, 1838); John Theodore Tussaud, *The Romance of Madame Tussaud's* (Odhams, 1919); and *Women in World History.*

TUTHILL, Louisa Huggins (1799–1879). American writer. Born Louisa Caroline Huggins, July 6, 1799, in New Haven, Connecticut; died June 1, 1879, in Princeton, New Jersey; dau. of Ebenezer Huggins (merchant) and Mary (Dickerman) Huggins; educated at seminaries for girls in New Haven and Litchfield, Connecticut; m. Cornelius Tuthill (editor), Aug 6, 1817 (died 1825); children: Charles Henry (b. 1818); Cornelia Louisa (b. 1820); Mary Esther (b. 1822); Sarah Schoonmaker (b. 1824). ❖ Took up writing following death of husband (1825); wrote more than 30 books, publishing her 1st works, including *James Somers: The Pilgrim's Son* (1827), anonymously; wrote several books providing guidance in moral living, manners, aesthetic and spiritual improvement, housekeeping, and child rearing; also wrote *History of Architecture from the Earliest Times* (1848), the 1st history of architecture to be published in US; edited 2 collections of John Ruskin's work: *The True and the Beautiful in Nature, Art, Morals, and Religion* (1859) and *Precious Thoughts: Moral and Religious* (1866).

TUTIN, Dorothy (1930–2001). British actress. Name variations: Dame Dorothy Tutin. Born April 8, 1930, in London, England; died Aug 6, 2001, in London; attended RADA; m. Derek Waring (actor); children: Nicholas and Amanda Waring (both actors). ❖ Had breakthrough role as Rose Pemberton in Graham Greene's *The Living Room* (1953); appeared as Sally Bowles in *I Am a Camera* (1954), Joan of Arc in *The Lark* (1955), Hedvig in *The Wild Duck* (1955), Queen Victoria in *Portrait of a Queen* (1965); appeared in 3 of Pinter's plays, *Old Times, A Kind of Alaska* and *Party Time,* and in many Shakespearean roles, including Ophelia, Juliet, Portia, Viola, Rosalind, and Lady Macbeth; on film, appeared as Cecily in *The Importance of Being Earnest* (1952), as Polly Peachum in *The Beggar's Opera,* and in *The Shooting Party.* Named Commander of the British Empire (CBE, 1967) and Dame Commander of the Order of the British Empire (DBE, 2001).

TUTIN, Winifred (1915—). See Pennington, Winifred.

TUTT, Yvonne Sherman. See Sherman, Yvonne.

TUTTLE, Lurene (1906–1986). American stage, radio, tv and screen actress. Name variations: Lurene Ruick. Born Aug 29, 1906, in Pleasant Lake, IN; died May 28, 1986, in Encino, CA; m. Mel Ruick; children: Barbara Ruick (1930–1974, actress). ❖ Once called the "first lady of radio," was the voice of Effie Perrine on "Adventures of Sam Spade" (1946–51); films include *Heaven Only Knows, Macbeth, Mr. Blandings Builds His Dream House, Don't Bother to Knock, Niagara, The Affairs of Dobie Gillis, Sweet Smell of Success* and *Psycho.*

TUTWILER, Julia Strudwick (1841–1916). American educator and prison reformer. Born Aug 15, 1841, in Tuscaloosa, Alabama; died Mar 24, 1916, in Birmingham, Alabama; dau. of Henry Tutwiler (educator and school administrator) and Julia (Ashe) Tutwiler; maternal granddau. of Pascal Paoli Ashe, steward of the University of Alabama; attended Madame Maroteau's boarding school (Philadelphia), Vassar College, and Deaconesses' Institute (Kaiserswerth, Germany). ❖ Joined the faculty of Tuscaloosa Female College (1876) and taught modern languages and English literature for 5 years; became well known as an educator and was appointed co-principal of the Livingston (Alabama) Female Academy (1881); through her urging (1883), helped establish the Alabama Normal College for Girls at Livingston Academy (later named Livingston Normal College) and became its principal (1890), a position she held for next 2 decades; elected president of department of elementary education of National Education Association (NEA, 1891); persuaded Alabama legislature to establish an industrial school for girls (later known as Alabama College at Montevallo); convinced trustees at University of Alabama to admit women at the sophomore level (1893) and as freshmen (1897); also organized the Tuscaloosa Benevolent Association, which worked toward prison reform (1880); her poem "Alabama" was later adopted as the state song. ❖ See also *Women in World History.*

TUVE, Rosemond (1903–1964). American scholar and educator. Born Rosemond Tuve, Nov 27, 1903, in Canton, SD; died Dec 20, 1964, in Bryn Mawr, PA; dau. of Anthony Gulbrandssen Tuve (president of Augustana College, Canton, SD, and mathematician) and Ida Marie (Larsen) Tuve (music teacher); University of Minnesota, AB, 1924; Bryn Mawr College, AM, 1925, PhD, 1931; attended Somerville College, Oxford, 1928. ❖ Awarded Bryn Mawr European fellowship (1925); taught at Goucher College (1926–28); received American Association of University Women fellowship and attended Somerville College, Oxford, in England (1928); taught at Vassar College (1929–31), and at Bryn Mawr Summer School for Women Workers in Industry; published *Seasons and Months: Studies in a Tradition of Middle English Poetry* (1933), *Elizabethan and Metaphysical Imagery* (1947), *A Reading of George Herbert* (1952), and *Allegorical Imagery* (1966); taught at Connecticut College, and established reputation as leading American literary scholar of Renaissance (1934–62); was visiting lecturer at

University of Minnesota (1952), Harvard University (1956), University of Aarhus, Denmark (1960), and Princeton University (1961); joined faculty of University of Pennsylvania (1963).

TUYAA, Nyam-Osoryn (1958—). Mongolian politician. Name variations: Nyam-Osoriyn or Nyam-Osorin Tuyaa. Born 1958 in Mongolia. ❖ Member of the MÜAN/MNDP, was minister of Foreign Affairs (1998–2000); served as acting prime minister of Mongolia (July 22–July 1999); was an unsuccessful candidate in the Aïmag Xäntiie 50 constituency (2000).

TUYLL, Isabella van (1740–1805). *See Charriere, Isabelle de.*

TWAIN, Shania (1965—). Canadian singer. Name variations: Eileen Regina Edwards. Born Eileen Regina Edwards, Aug 28, 1965, in Windsor, Canada; dau. of Clarence and Sharon Edwards; m. Robert John "Mutt" Lange (music producer), 1993; children: Eja (b. Aug 12, 2001). ❖ At 6, adopted by stepfather Jerry Twain, an Ojibway Indian, later taking name, Shania, Ojibway for "I'm on my way," to honor him; by 8, was singing at social events; at 21, lost mother and stepfather in auto accident, and began singing at resort in Deerhurst, Ontario, to support younger brothers; moved to Nashville (1991) and released moderately successful eponymous album (1993); released 2nd album, *The Woman in Me* (1995), which sold 12 million copies and contained 7 hit singles, including "Any Man of Mine" and "(If You're Not In It for Love) I'm Outta Here"; outdid earlier success with *Come on Over* (1997), which generated 9 hit singles, including "You're Still the One" and "That Don't Impress Me Much," won Grammy Awards for Best Country Song and Best Female Country Performance, and went 20 times platinum in US, becoming the bestselling C&W album in history; released album *Up!* (2002); sold more records than any other female C&W singer ever.

TWEED, Blanche Oelrichs (1890–1950). *See Strange, Michael.*

TWEEDIE, Jill (1936–1993). British feminist, journalist and satirist. Name variations: Jill Sheila Tweedie. Born May 22, 1936, in Egypt; died of MND (motor neurone disease), Nov 12, 1993, in London, England; at 18, m. a Hungarian count; m. 3rd husband Alan Brien; children: (1st m.) 2; (2nd m.) son. ❖ Became a regular columnist on liberal, humanist and feminist issues for the *Guardian* (1969–1988); wrote several volumes on feminist themes, including the bestselling *Letters from a Fainthearted Feminist* (1982) and *More from Martha: Further Letters from a Fainthearted Feminist* (translated into a BBC2 sitcom, "The Fainthearted Feminist," starring Lynn Redgrave). ❖ See also autobiography, *Eating Children: Young Dreams and Early Nightmares* (1993).

TWEEDY, Hilda (b. 1911). Irish feminist and consumer affairs campaigner. Born Hilda Anderson in Clones, Co. Monaghan, Ireland, Aug 26, 1911; dau. of James Ferguson Anderson (Church of Ireland cleric) and Muriel Frances Victoria (Swayne) Anderson; educated at Alexandra School and College, Dublin, and at University of London; m. Robert Massy Tweedy, July 18, 1936; children: 1 son, 1 daughters. ❖ Cofounded the Irish Housewives' Committee (IHC, 1942), which was reorganized as the Irish Housewives' Association (IHA, 1946), to (1) unite housewives in order to ensure their right to play an active part in community planning; (2) establish real equality of liberties, status and opportunity for everyone; and (3) defend consumers' rights in the supply, distribution and price of essential commodities; represented Ireland at International Alliance of Women (IAW) congresses (1949–86); became a founder member and the 1st chair of the Council for the Status of Women (1972); wrote *A Link in the Chain: The Irish Housewives' Association 1942–1992* (1992). Received honorary doctorate, Trinity College, Dublin (1990). ❖ See also *Women in World History.*

TWEEDY, May (1882–1978). *See Mellanby, May.*

TWELVETREES, Helen (1908–1958). American actress. Born Helen Marie Jurgens, Dec 25, 1908 (some sources cite 1907), in Brooklyn, New York; died of a drug overdose on Feb 13, 1958, near Harrisburg, Pennsylvania; dau. of William Jurgens (in advertising) and Helen (Kelly) Jurgens; trained at American Academy of Dramatic Arts; m. Clark Twelvetrees (actor), 1927 (div. 1931); m. Frank Woody (realtor), 1931 (div. 1936); m. Conrad Payne (Air Force officer), c. 1946; children: (2nd m.) Jack Bryan (b. 1932). ❖ Made NY debut as Sondra in an adaptation of Theodore Dreiser's *An American Tragedy*; made 3 undistinguished films for Fox before signing with Pathé, where her film career began to flourish with *Her Man* (1930), a box-office hit, and *Millie* (1931); starred opposite Spencer Tracy in *Now I'll Tell* (1934); went to Australia (1936), where her role in *Thoroughbred* made her the 1st American star of the "talkies" to film there; filmed last 2 pictures with Paramount (1939), then

returned to the stage, where over the years she appeared in several plays, including *Arsenic and Old Lace, A Streetcar Named Desire* and *The Man Who Came to Dinner.* ❖ See also *Women in World History.*

TWIGG, Rebecca (1963—). American cyclist. Born Mar 26, 1963, in Honolulu, HI; University of Washington, BS in biology, 1985; Colman College, San Diego, AA in computer science, 1989; attended graduate school at University of Colorado at Colorado Springs, 2000. ❖ Was 4-time jr. national champion; won National championship in indiv. pursuit (1981–82, 1984, 1986, 1992, 1995); won World championship in indiv. pursuit (1982, 1984–85, 1987, 1992, 1995); won National championship in indiv. time trial (1982, 1993–94); won National championship in kilometer time trial (1984, 1986, 1995); won silver medal for road race at Los Angeles Olympics (1984); won bronze medal for indiv. pursuit at Barcelona Olympics (1992); was 16-time Senior National champion. Named USCF Senior Female Athlete of the Year (1985, 1987, 1993, 1995); nominated for James E. Sullivan Award (1987, 1992, 1995). ❖ See also *Women in World History.*

TWIGGY (1946—). British fashion model and actress. Name variations: Twiggy Lawson. Born Lesley Hornby, Sept 19, 1946, in Neasden, England; m. Michael Witney, 1977 (died 1983); m. Leigh Lawson (director), 1988; children: (1st m.) daughter Carly. ❖ Pop icon of late 1960s, began modeling under the name Twiggy for a fashion known as "Mod" (1967); razor thin, with large mascara-enhanced eyes, was often seen on magazine covers; starred in Ken Russell's film of the Broadway musical hit *The Boyfriend* (1971); retiring from modeling (mid-1970s), reappeared on Broadway as the star of the musical *My One and Only* (1983); subsequently co-starred with Shirley MacLaine in film *Madame Sousatzka* (1988); appeared off-Broadway in the musical *If Love Were All* (1999); other films and TV movies include *There Goes the Bride* (1980), *The Doctor and the Devils* (1985), *Club Paradise* (1986) "The Little Match Girl" (1987), "The Diamond Trap" (1988), *Young Charlie Chaplin* (1988) and *Istanbul* (1989).

TWINING, Louisa (1820–1912). British reformer. Born 1820 in London, England; died 1912 in Tunbridge Wells, England; dau. of Robert Twining. ❖ Trained as artist and published *Symbols and Emblems of Early and Medieval Art* (1952); began working among poor and organized workhouse visiting scheme which was implemented after publication of her "Practical Lectures to Ladies" (1855); was active in Workhouse Visiting Society and workhouse reform, delivering paper to Social Science Association (1857) and giving evidence on Poor Schools to Poor Law Boards; set up hostel for workhouse girls (1861) and Workhouse Infirmary Nursing Association (1870); became member of board of guardians of Society for Promoting Employment of Women (1884) and was one of founders of Bedford College; wrote *Workhouses and Women's Work* (1858), *Recollections of Life and Work* (1895), and *Workhouses and Pauperism* (1898)l; also supported suffrage movement.

TWINING, Marion (1924–1996). *See Barone, Marian E.*

TWOMEY, Mary (b. 1940). *See Rand, Mary.*

TWO SICILIES, queen of.
See Maria Carolina (1752–1814).
See Maria Clementina of Austria (1777–1801).
See Migliaccio, Lucia (1770–1826).
See Christina of Sardinia (1812–1836).
See Theresa of Austria (1816–1867).
See Maria Sophia Amalia (1841–1925).

TWOSRET (c. 1220–1188 BCE). *See Tauseret.*

TY-CASPER, Linda (1931—). Filipino-American lawyer, novelist and short-story writer. Name variations: Linda Ty Casper. Born Linda Ty, Sept 17, 1931, in Manila, Philippines; dau. of Francisco Figueroa Ty (civil engineer) and Catallina (Velasquez) Ty (educator and writer) University of the Philippines, AA, 1951, LLB, 1955; Harvard University, LLM, 1957; m. Leonard Casper (writer and professor), 1956; children: 2. ❖ A lawyer, who resides mainly in US, published *The Peninsulars* (1964), considered one of her best; also wrote *The Three-Cornered Sun* (1979), *Dread Empire* (1980), *The Hazards of Distance* (1981), *Awaiting Trespass* (1985), *Fortress in the Plaza* (1985), *Wings of Stone* (1986), *Ten Thousand Seeds* (1987) and *A Small Party in the Garden* (1988); published short stories in *Asia Magazine, New Mexico Quarterly, Solidarity* and in several anthologies, including *The Transparent Sun and Other Stories* (1963) and *The Secret Runner and Other Stories* (1974).

TYABJI, Kamila (1918–2004). Indian lawyer, social reformer and women's-rights activist. Born Feb 14, 1918, in Bombay (now Mumbai), India; died May 17, 2004; dau. of Faiz Badruddin Tyabji (chief justice); attended St. Hugh's College, Oxford, possibly the 1st Muslim woman to go to Oxford. ❖ Practiced law in London for 25 years, and was the 1st woman lawyer to argue a case before the privy council; returned to India to set up the Women's Indian Trust (WIT), a charity providing women with training and employment (1968); represented India on the UN commission into the status of women and helped draft its declaration of rights for women.

TYLER, Adeline Blanchard (1805–1875). American nurse and hospital administrator. Born Dec 8, 1805, in Billerica, MA; died Jan 9, 1875, in Needham, MA; dau. of Jeremiah Blanchard (farmer) and Mary (Gowen) Blanchard; m. John Tyler (auctioneer), 1826 (died 1853). ❖ Became Episcopalian deaconess (c. 1853); studied nursing at Deaconesses' Institute in Kaiserswerth, Germany; established (1856) and supervised infirmary in Baltimore, MD, for St. Andrew's Church; tended to wounded Union soldiers after they were attacked by pro-Southern mob in Baltimore (1861); hired as superintendent of Camden Street federal military hospital in Baltimore (1861); served as head nurse at National Hospital in Chester, PA (1862–63) and Naval School Hospital in Annapolis, MD (later US General Hospital, Division No. 1) (1863–64); was "lady superintendent" of Children's Hospital in Boston, MA (1869–72).

TYLER, Alice S. (1859–1944). American librarian and educator. Born Alice Sarah Tyler, April 27, 1859, in Decatur, Illinois; died April 18, 1944, in Cleveland, Ohio; dau. of John William Tyler (minister) and Sarah (Roney) Tyler (died 1893); graduate of Armour Institute Library School, 1895. ❖ At 36, received professional certificate; moved to Cleveland, Ohio, where she worked as head cataloguer in the public library; became secretary of Iowa State Library Commission (1900); during 13-year tenure, saw the number of public libraries in Iowa nearly triple; also served as director of a summer school for training librarians at State University of Iowa (1901–12); worked as secretary of 1st executive committee of League of Library Commissions and served as its president (1906–07); became director of Library School at Western Reserve University in Cleveland (1913); instituted a combined 4-year library science course that resulted in a bachelor's degree (1915); became dean of the school (1925), receiving the title of professor of library science; served as president of Ohio Library Association (1916–17), Association of Library Schools (1918–19), and American Library Association (1920). ❖ See also *Women in World History.*

TYLER, Anne (1941—). American novelist and short-story writer. Born Oct 25, 1941, in Minneapolis, MN; dau. of Lloyd Parry Tyler (industrial chemist) and Phyllis Mahon Tyler (social worker); raised in Raleigh, North Carolina; graduate of Duke University; married, 1963; children: 2. ❖ Grew up in Quaker community, was a bibliographer at Duke University, and worked in the law library at McGill University; on marriage, settled in Baltimore; published 1st novel *If Morning Ever Comes* (1964), followed by *Earthly Possessions* (1977) and *Dinner at the Homesick Restaurant* (1982); won National Book Critics Circle Award (1986) for *The Accidental Tourist* (1985), which was filmed; also wrote *Breathing Lessons* (1988), *Saint Maybe* (1991), *Ladder of the Year* (1996), *A Patchwork Planet* (1998), *Back When We Were Grownups* (2001) and *The Amateur Marriage* (2003).

TYLER, Audrey (1926–1996). See Patterson, Audrey.

TYLER, Danielle (1974—). American softball player. Name variations: Dani Tyler. Born Oct 23, 1974, in River Forest, IL; graduate of Drake University, 1997. ❖ Won a team gold medal at Atlanta Olympics (1996).

TYLER, Dorothy J. (1920—). English high jumper. Name variations: competed as Dorothy Odam in 1936; as Dorothy Tyler in 1948; Dorothy Odam-Tyler. Born Dorothy Odam, Mar 14, 1920, in Great Britain. ❖ Won a silver medal at Berlin Olympics (1936) and a silver medal at London Olympics (1948), both in high jump. Awarded MBE (2001). ❖ See also *Women in World History.*

TYLER, Judy (1933–1957). American actress. Born Judith Mae Hess, Oct 9, 1933, in Milwaukee, WI; died in auto accident along with husband, July 3, 1957, near Billy the Kid, Wyoming; dau. of a trumpeter father and a Ziegfeld Follies mother; m. Colin Romoff (musical director), 1950 (div. 1956); m. Greg Lafayett, 1957. ❖ On tv, appeared as Princess Summerfall Winterspring on "Howdy Doody"; made stage debut in

lead role on Broadway in *Pipe Dream* (1956); also appeared in Elvis Presley film *Jailhouse Rock.*

TYLER, Julia Gardiner (1820–1889). American first lady. Born May 4, 1820, in Gardiner Island, New York; died July 10, 1889, in Richmond, Virginia; dau. of David Gardiner (lawyer and state senator in New York) and Juliana (McLachlen) Gardiner (dau. of a wealthy Scottish brewer of New York City); attended Chagaray Institute in New York City; became 2nd wife of John Tyler (president of US), June 26, 1844 (died 1862); children: David Gardiner Tyler (b. 1846); John Alexander Tyler (b. 1848); Julia Gardiner Tyler (b. 1849); Lachlan Tyler (b. 1851); Lyon Gardiner Tyler (b. 1853, who became president of College of William and Mary in Virginia); Robert Fitzwalter Tyler (b. 1856); Pearl Tyler (b. 1860). ❖ First lady (1844–45) who brought an air of royalty to the White House, provided outspoken support for husband's Confederate views, and lobbied for pensions for presidential widows; a trend setter, even as a debutante, had created a fashion craze by wearing a diamond on her forehead held in place by a gold chain; was invited by Tyler to sail on a test run of the 1st propeller-driven warship, the USS *Princeton,* where an accidental misfiring of the ship's main gun resulted in the deaths of 6 men, including her father; at 24 (1844), married the 54-year-old widower John Tyler (whose 1st wife was Letitia Tyler); filled her 8 months as first lady with a flurry of social activities; also hired a NY press agent, to insure favorable publicity, and entertained lavishly in the European court tradition; was her husband's staunchest ally, lobbying openly for the annexation of Texas, which was enacted before the end of his term in 1845; during Civil War, continued to support the Confederate causes of states' rights and the institution of slavery; took up residence in Washington (late 1870s), where she lobbied for federal pensions for president's widows. ❖ See also Robert Seager II, *And Tyler Too: A Biography of John and Julia Gardiner Tyler* (1963); and *Women in World History.*

TYLER, Letitia (1790–1842). American first lady. Born Letitia Christian, Nov 12, 1790, in New Kent Co., Virginia; died Sept 10, 1842, in Washington, DC (the 1st wife of a president to die while husband was in office); dau. of Robert Christian (planter) and Mary (Brown) Christian; became 1st wife of John Tyler (president of US), Mar 29, 1813, in New Kent Co., Virginia; children—9, 7 of whom survived infancy: Mary Tyler (b. 1815); Robert Tyler (b. 1816, who would later earn distinction as an Alabama newspaper editor and political figure); John Tyler (b. 1819); Letitia Tyler Semple (b. 1821); Elizabeth Tyler (b. 1823); Alice Tyler (b. 1827); Tazewell Tyler (b. 1830). All 3 sons served the Confederacy during Civil War. ❖ First lady who had a brief tenure in the White House (1841–42), secluded in an upstairs room; as husband's political career had advanced, 1st in the Senate, then as governor of Virginia, then as vice president, remained in background, appearing socially only when necessary; after a crippling stroke (1838), was confined at 48 to a wheelchair; with sudden death of William Harrison (1841), lived the last few years of her life in seclusion in the White House, appearing publicly only once, at the wedding of her daughter Elizabeth Tyler in Jan 1842 (social duties were assumed by her daughter-in-law, Priscilla Cooper Tyler, and her daughter, Letitia Tyler Semple); succumbed to complications of her stroke (Sept 1842). John Tyler also married Julia Gardiner Tyler. ❖ See also *Women in World History.*

TYLER, Margaret (d. 1595). British translator. Born in 1530s or 1540s; died 1595 in Castle Camps, near Cambridge, England; m. possibly John Tyler; children: possibly 2. ❖ Translated part of Diego Ortunez de Calahorra's *Espejo de principes y cavalleros* as *The First Part of the Mirrour of Princely Deeded and Knighthood* (1578, 1580, 1599); also wrote preface and letter to reader defending women's reading and writing.

TYLER, Odette (1869–1936). American actress and playwright. Born Sept 26, 1869, in Savannah, GA; died Dec 8, 1936; dau. of Susan (Hardee) and General William W. Kirkland; m. R. D. McLean (actor, r.n. Shepherd), 1897. ❖ Made stage debut in NY in the title role of the spectacle *Sieba* (1884), followed by *Caprice, Featherbrain, Shenandoah, The Councilor's Wife, The Girl I Left Behind Me, The Man Upstairs, Secret Service,* and *The Red Carnation*; often appeared in vaudeville and toured with husband; wrote *The Red Carnation* and *Boss: A Story of Virginia Life.*

TYLER, Priscilla Cooper (1816–1889). White House hostess. Born Elizabeth Priscilla Cooper, June 14, 1816, in New York, NY; died Dec 29, 1889; dau. of Thomas Abthorpe Cooper (British actor) and Mary (Fairlee) Cooper (popular socialite); m. Robert Tyler (son of Letitia Tyler and John Tyler, US president, and editor of *Montgomery Mail and*

Advertiser), Sept 12, 1839; children: Mary Fairlie Tyler (d. 1845); John Tyler (d. 1845); Letitia Christian Tyler (born in the White House); Grace Tyler; Thomas Cooper Tyler (died in infancy); Priscilla Tyler; Elizabeth Tyler; Julia Campbell Tyler; Robert Tyler. ❖ Because of the illness and subsequent death of first lady Letitia Tyler, filled in at the White House; quite beautiful, made a charming and gracious host, but was happy to turn her duties over to Julia Gardiner Tyler when her father-in-law remarried (1844).

TYLER-SHARMAN, Lucy (1965—). Australian-American cyclist. Name variations: Lucy Tyler Sharman; Lucy Tyler. Born Lucy Tyler, June 6, 1965, in USA; m. Graeme Sharman. ❖ Won a bronze medal for points race at Atlanta Olympics (1996); placed 1st at World championships for 3,000-meter indiv. pursuit and 1st at World Cup in Canada (1998); became an Australian citizen, thus holding dual citizenship; unhappy with deeply divided team, wanted to represent the US at Sydney Olympics but request was denied by Cycling Australia; returned to US.

TYLICKA, Justyna Budzynska (1876–1936). *See Budzynska-Tylicka, Justyna.*

TYLNEY, Agnes (1476–1545). Duchess of Norfolk and countess of Surrey. Name variations: Agnes Tilney; Agnes Howard. Born in 1476; died in May 1545; dau. of Hugh Tylney; m. Thomas Howard (1443–1524), earl of Surrey and 2nd duke of Norfolk (r. 1514–1524), Aug 17, 1497; children: William Howard, first Baron of Effingham (b. around 1510); Thomas Howard, Lord Howard; Dorothy Howard, countess of Derby; Anne Howard (d. 1559); Catherine Howard (related to Queen Catherine Howard); Elizabeth Howard (d. 1534); step-grandmother of Catherine Howard (who m. Henry VIII).

TYLNEY, Elizabeth (d. 1497). Countess of Surrey. Name variations: Elizabeth Tilney; Elizabeth Howard. Died April 4, 1497; dau. of Frederick Tylney and Elizabeth Cheney; m. Henry, also seen as Humphrey, Bourchier, 2nd baron Berners; m. Thomas Howard (1443–1524), earl of Surrey and 2nd duke of Norfolk (r. 1514–1524), on April 30, 1472; children: (2nd m.) Thomas Howard, 3rd duke of Norfolk (1473–1554); Edward Howard (c. 1477–1513), Lord High Admiral; Edmund Howard (c. 1478–1539); Muriel Howard (who m. John Grey, 2nd viscount L'Isle); Elizabeth Howard (?–1538; mother of Anne Boleyn); John Howard.

TYMOSHENKO, Yulia (1960—). Ukrainian politician. Name variations: Yulia Volodymyrivna Tymoshenko. Born Nov 27, 1960, in Dnipropetrovs'k, Ukraine; earned a degree in economics. ❖ Called the "Goddess of the Revolution," was one of the key leaders of Ukraine's Orange Revolution (2004), and a close ally of Viktor Yushchenko who became president; 1st worked as an engineer-economist in a machine-building plant in Dnipropetrovs'k; served as president of the United Energy System of Ukraine Corporation (1995–97); elected people's deputy of Ukraine (1997); elected people's deputy to the Verkhovna Rada of Ukraine (1998) and headed the budget committee; elected head of All-Ukrainian Batkivschyna Party (1999); was vice prime minister of Ukraine (Dec 1999–Jan 2001); became prime minister (2005).

TYNAN, Katharine (1861–1931). Irish writer. Name variations: Katharine Hinkson; Katharine Tynan-Hinkson. Born Katharine Tynan, Jan 23, 1861, in Dublin, Ireland; died in London, England, April 2, 1931; dau. of Andrew Cullen Tynan (farmer) and Elizabeth (O'Reilly) Tynan; attended Dominican Convent, Drogheda, 1871–74; m. Henry Albert Hinkson (barrister and author), 1893; children: Theobald Henry Hinkson; Giles Aylmer Hinkson; Pamela Mary Hinkson. ❖ Poet, novelist and author of 5 volumes of autobiography, which offer a valuable insight into late 19th- and early 20th-century Irish political and literary life, began to write poetry (1878); published *Louise de la Valliere and Other Poems* (1885), the 1st of over 160 books which included novels, poetry and short stories; as a supporter of Parnell and a constitutional nationalist, was a member of the Ladies' Land League (1881–82); was also associated with the Irish literary renaissance (1880s–90s); moved to London on her marriage (1893) and continued writing career; returned to Ireland with family (1912) and lived for a number of years in Co. Mayo, where Henry Hinkson was a resident magistrate; after husband's death (1919), traveled widely, living mainly in London, where she died. ❖ See also autobiographies *Twenty-five Years: Reminiscences* (1913), *The Middle Years* (1916), *The Years of the Shadow*

(1919), *The Wandering Years* (1922), and *Memories* (1924); Marilyn Gaddis Rose, *Katharine Tynan* (Associated U. Presses, 1974); W. B. Yeats, *Letters to Katharine Tynan* (1953); and *Women in World History*.

TYNAN, Kathleen (1937–1995). British journalist, screenwriter and biographer. Born Kathleen Jeanette Halton, Jan 25, 1937, in England; died Jan 10, 1995, in London, England; m. Kenneth Tynan (drama critic), 1967 (died 1980); children: Matthew and Roxana. ❖ Began career as a journalist for the *Observer*; wrote several novels and screenplay for film *Agatha* (1979), based on her fictionalization of the disappearance and search for Agatha Christie; probably best known for *The Life of Kenneth Tynan* (1987).

TYNG, Lila (1899–1999). *See Luce, Lila.*

TYPHOID MARY (1867–1938). *See Mallon, Mary.*

TYRA DANNEBOD (d. 940). *See Thyra.*

TYROL, countess of. *See Margaret Maultasch (1318–1369).*

TYSHKEVICH, Tamara (1931—). Soviet track-and-field athlete. Born Mar 31, 1931, in USSR. ❖ At Melbourne Olympics, won a gold medal in the shot put (1956).

TYSON, Cicely (1933—). African-American stage, tv, and screen actress. Born Dec 19, 1933, in New York, NY; m. Miles Davis (jazz trumpeter), 1981 (div. 1988). ❖ Began career as a model; made NY stage debut in *The Cool World* (1960), followed by *The Blacks, Moon on a Rainbow Shawl, Tiger Tiger Burning Bright, Trumpets of the Lord, A Hand is on the Gates, Carry Me Back to Morningside Heights,* and *To Be Young Gifted and Black,* among others; made film debut in *A Man Called Adam* (1966); other films include *The Heart is a Lonely Hunter* (as Portia), *The Comedians, The River Niger, The Blue Bird, A Hero Ain't Nothin' But a Sandwich, Bustin' Loose, Fried Green Tomatoes, The Grass Harp,* and *Hoodlum;* on tv, appeared on "East Side West Side" (1963–64), "Roots" (1977), "King" (as Coretta Scott King, 1978), "The Marva Collins Story" (1981), and "Oldest Living Confederate Widow Tells All" (1994); co-founded the Dance Theatre of Harlem with Arthur Mitchell. Nominated for Oscar as Best Actress for *Sounder* (1972); won Emmy for "The Autobiography of Miss Jane Pittman" (1974).

TYSON, Miriam (1904–1951). *See Horn, Miriam Burns.*

TYSSE, Kjersti (1972—). *See Plaetzer, Kjersti.*

TYSZKIEWICZOWA, Maria Anna (1904–1950). *See Ordonówna, Hanka.*

TYURINA, Lyubov (1943—). Soviet volleyball player. Born May 25, 1943, in USSR. ❖ At Munich Olympics, won a gold medal in team competition (1972).

TYUS, Wyomia (1945—). African-American runner. Name variations: Wyomia Tyus Simberg. Born Aug 29, 1945, in Griffin, GA; graduate of Tennessee State University. ❖ Trained at Tennessee State University; won a gold medal in the 100 meters and a silver medal in the 4 x 100-meter relay at Tokyo Olympics (1964); at Mexico City Olympics, won a gold medal in the 4 x 100-meter relay and a gold medal in the 100 meters, becoming the 1st athlete ever to win two consecutive gold medals in the same event (1968); won 8 National AAU championships. Elected to the National Track and Field Hall of Fame (1980) and the Women's Sports Hall of Fame (1981); inducted into the Olympic Hall of Fame (1985); was a founding member of the Women's Sports Association. ❖ See also *Women in World History*.

TZAVELLA, Moscho (1760–1803). Greek heroine. Born in 1760; died in 1803; came from a family of Greek guerrilla fighters who had led insurgents against the Turkish conquerors. ❖ Known for her extreme bravery, commanded an uprising against Ali Pascha, the Albanian ruler of western Greece, who attacked her mountain village of Souli; was given the title of *capetanios* (captain), participated in the village councils of war and advised the guerrillas on military tactics.

TZE HSI (1835–1908). *See Cixi.*

TZELILI, Miréla (1976—). *See Manjani-Tzelili, Miréla.*

TZ'U-AN (1837–1881). *See Ci'an.*

TZU HSI, T'zu Hsi, or Tz'u-hsi (1835–1908). *See Cixi.*

U

UBAIDA (fl. c. 830). **Arabian singer and tunbur player.** Name variations: Ubayda; Obeidet. Flourished around 830. ❖ Considered the best instrumentalist of her time, the golden age of classical Arabian culture; learned to play the tunbur (a skin-bellied stringed instrument) from Al-Zubaidi al-Tunburi. ❖ See also *Women in World History.*

UCA, Feleknas (1976—). **German politician.** Born Sept 17, 1976, in Celle, Germany. ❖ Representing the Confederal Group of the European United Left/Nordic Green Left (GUE/NGL), elected to 5th European Parliament (1999–2004).

UCHIDA, Christine (1952—). **American ballet dancer.** Born April 20, 1952, in Chicago, IL. ❖ Trained at School of American Ballet and American Ballet Center in New York, NY; performed with City Center Joffrey Ballet for many years, creating featured roles in Gerald Arpino's *Chabriesque* (1972) and *Sacred Grove on Mount Tamalpais* (1972), Eliot Feld's *Jive* (1973), and Twyla Tharp's *Deuce Coupe I* and *As Time Goes By* (1973); joined Twyla Tharp's company, where she created roles in *From Hither and Yon* (1976), *Mud* (1977), *Baker Dozen* (1979), and others.

UCHIDA, Mitsuko (1948—). **Japanese pianist.** Born in Tokyo, Japan, Dec 20, 1948. ❖ Known as a Mozart specialist, received initial musical training in Tokyo, then traveled to Vienna (1961), to study with Richard Hauser at the Vienna Academy of Music; also studied with Stefan Askenase and Wilhelm Kempff; won the Beethoven Competition (1968) and came in 2nd in Chopin Competition in Warsaw (1970); by 1980s, had developed into a superb Mozart performer, winning raves for her survey of Mozart's piano concertos, which she performed with the English Chamber Orchestra (she also conducted from the keyboard), during the 1985–86 concert season in London; gave New York recital debut (Feb 1987); her performances of Chopin, Debussy, Bartok and Schoenberg were also of rare distinction.

UCHIDA, Yoshiko (1921–1992). **American writer.** Name variations: Yohziko Uchida. Pronunciation: Oo-CHEE-dah. Born Nov 24, 1921, in Alameda, California; died June 21, 1992, in Berkeley, California; dau. of Dwight Takashi Uchida (businessman) and Iku (Umegaki) Uchida; University of California, Berkeley, AB (cum laude), 1942; Smith College, MEd, 1944. ❖ Writer of many books on Japanese culture for readers of all ages, was a senior at University of California, Berkeley, when her family was sent to Tanforan Racetracks, a Japanese relocation center where thousands of Japanese-Americans lived in stables and barracks after the bombing of Pearl Harbor; was then moved to Topaz, a guarded camp in the Utah desert, where she taught elementary school (1942–43); taught in Frankford Friends' School, Philadelphia, Pennsylvania (1944–45); wrote *Desert Exile: The Uprooting of a Japanese-American Family* (1982); writings for children include *The Dancing Kettle and Other Japanese Folk Tales* (1949), (self-illustrated) *The Magic Listening Cap—More Folk Tales from Japan* (1955), (self-illustrated) *The Full Circle* (1957), *Takao and Grandfather's Sword* (1958), *The Promised Year* (1959), *Mik and the Prowler* (1960), *Rokubei and the Thousand Rice Bowls* (1962), *Sumi's Prize* (1964), *The Sea of Gold, and Other Tales from Japan* (1965), *Sumi's Special Happening* (1966), *In-Between Miya* (1967), *Hisako's Mysteries* (1969), *Sumi and the Goat and the Tokyo Express* (1969), *Makoto, the Smallest Boy* (1970); *Journey to Topaz* (1971), *Journey Home* (sequel to *Journey to Topaz*, 1978), *A Jar of Dreams* (1981), *The Best Bad Thing* (sequel to *A Jar of Dreams,* 1983); *Tabi* (1984); *The Happiest Ending* (sequel to *The Best Bad Thing,* 1985); *The Two Foolish Cats* (1987); *The Terrible Leak* (1990); *The Magic Purse* (1993); *The Bracelet* (1993) and *The Wise Old Woman* (1994). ❖ See also *Women in World History.*

UCOK, Bahriye (d. 1990). **Turkish educator and politician.** Name variations: Bahriye Üçok. Born in Turkey; killed by a bomb, Oct 6, 1990. ❖ Secularist dean of the Theological Faculty, Ankara University, was one of the rare female professors there; wrote a book on woman governors in Islamic history; as a member of the Social Democratic Populist Party, was also a prominent figure in the Turkish Parliament; had frequently spoken and written against the wearing of headscarves in educational establishments and government offices, for which she received death threats; was assassinated by fundamentalists who sent a package to her home that contained a bomb.

UDALTSOVA, Nadezhda (1885–1961). **Russian artist.** Name variations: Nadezhda Andreevna Udaltsova. Born in 1885 in Orel, Russia; died 1961; studied at Moscow School of Painting, at a school run by Konstantin Yuon, and with various artists in Paris and in Russia; m. 2nd husband Aleksandr Drevin (painter), in 1920s (died in concentration camp, 1938). ❖ Studied the principles of Cubism with Karol Kish (1909); with Liubov Popova, went to Paris (1912), where they studied with Cubist painters for a year; upon return to Russia (1913), was involved with 3 major exhibitions and established herself as a prominent Cubist painter; though this avant-garde art received a mixed critical reception, published a persuasive essay defending the techniques and style of the movement; despite executing a series of reliefs entitled *Painterly Constructions* for the State Tretyakov Gallery (1915), did not follow other artists into Constructivism but remained interested in the use of color and texture on canvas; was, therefore, more aligned with Suprematism; after Russian Revolution (1917), became an assistant at the Free State Studios; by 1920, had become a professor and senior lecturer at Vkhutemas, the former Higher Artistic and Technical Studios, where she would teach until 1934; also became a member of the Institute of Artistic Culture (Inkhuk, 1920); during 1920s, her art became more representational and included more landscapes; with husband, traveled across Russia, painting the Ural and Altai Mountains, Armenia, and Central Asia (mid-1930s). ❖ See also *Women in World History.*

UDHAM BAI (fl. 1748–1754). **Queen and co-ruler of Mughal India.** Dau. of Farrukh-Siyar; m. Muhammad Shah, leader of the Mughal Empire; children: Ahmad Shah Badahur (b. 1725). ❖ Married Muhammad Shah, the 4th in a line of weak rulers of the Mughal Empire, which was in serious decline; when husband died (1748), manipulated 23-year-old son's weakness and lack of responsibility and assumed de facto control of the rulership, which eventually led to her downfall; her son fled the invading Marathas rather than face them, thus abandoning her and the other women of the family and allowing them to be captured.

UELAND, Clara Hampson (1860–1927). **American suffragist and reformer.** Born Oct 10, 1860, in Akron, OH; died Mar 1, 1927, in Minneapolis, MN; dau. of Henry Oscar Hampson and Eliza (Osborn) Hampson; m. Andreas Ueland (lawyer and probate judge), June 19, 1885; children: 4 sons, 4 daughters. ❖ As a prominent socialite, was an invaluable advocate and fund raiser in the cause of woman suffrage in Minnesota; was part of group of mothers that campaigned for 1st public school kindergarten in Minneapolis (1897); helped create and served as trustee of Minneapolis Institute of Arts (formerly Minneapolis Society of Fine Arts); elected president of Minnesota Woman Suffrage Association (1914); was 1st president of Minnesota League of Women Voters (1919).

UENO, Chizuko (1948—). **Japanese feminist and educator.** Born in 1948 in Toyama Prefecture, Japan. ❖ Influenced by Michael Foucault and Claude Levi-Strauss, became a post-modernist; published *Sekushi Gyaru no Daikenkyu* (*A Study of Sexy Girls,* 1982), followed by her translation of *The Challenge of Marxist Feminism* (1983); was a lecturer, then associate professor, at Heian Women's College (1979–89); was an associate professor, then professor, Department of Humanities, Kyoto Seika University (1989–94); became professor of sociology, Graduate School of Humanities and Sociology, University of Tokyo (1995); writings include *Patriarchy and Capitalism* (1990), the Suntory prizewinning *Kindai Kazoku no Seiritsu to Shuen* (*The Rise and Fall of the Japanese Modern Family,* 1994), (ed.) *Risky Business: A Dangerous Relationship* *between Women and Capitalism* (1994), and *Nationalism and Gender* (1998). ❖ See also *Women in World History.*

UENO, Masae (1979—). Japanese judoka. Born Jan 17, 1979, in Japan. ❖ Placed 1st at World championships for 70 kg (2001, 2003); won a gold medal for 70 kg at Athens Olympics (2004).

UENO, Yukiko (1982—). Japanese softball player. Born July 22, 1982, in Fukuoka, Japan. ❖ Pitcher, won a team bronze at Athens Olympics (2004).

UFFORD, Joan de (fl. 1300s). *See Montacute, Joan.*

UFFORD, Margaret de (fl. 14th c.). Countess of Suffolk. Name variations: Baroness Ferrers of Groby. Married Robert de Ufford (1298–1369), 1st earl of Suffolk; m. William Ferrers, 3rd baron Ferrers of Groby; children: Margaret Ferrers; Henry Ferrers (d. 1388), 4th baron Ferrers of Groby.

UFFORD, Maud de (fl. 1360s). *See Vere, Maud de.*

UGA, Elisa (1968—). Italian fencer. Born Feb 27, 1968, in Vercelli, Italy. ❖ Won a silver medal for épée team at Atlanta Olympics (1996); at European championships, won a gold medal for indiv. (1998).

UGGAMS, Leslie (1943—). African-American singer and actress. Born May 25, 1943, in New York, NY; m. Grahame Pratt, 1965; children: 2. ❖ At 6, made national tv debut in series "Beulah" (1950); won a Tony Award for Best Actress in a Musical for *Hallelujah, Baby!* (1968); nominated for Tony as Best Actress in a Play for *King Hedley II* (2001); appeared as Kizzy on "Roots" (1977) and starred on "The Leslie Uggams Show" (1969).

UHDE, Sonia (1885–1979). *See Delaunay, Sonia.*

UHL, Frida (1872–1943). Austrian-born journalist. Name variations: Frida Strindberg. Born in Austria in 1872; died 1943; dau. of Friedrich Uhl (publisher of Austria's government newspaper *Wiener Zeitung* and theater critic); m. August Strindberg (1849–1912, playwright), 1893 (div. 1895); children: (with Strindberg) 1 daughter; (with playwright Frank Wedekind) 1 child. ❖ At 20, while still a fledgling journalist, met and married August Strindberg, who was 20 years her senior and had recently separated from his wife Siri von Essen (he would later marry Harriet Bosse); for 2 years, subjugated herself for his career, arranging for translations and productions of his work in England and managing the household and his business affairs, while Strindberg in return was cruel and abusive; following her divorce (1895), held a series of jobs, but behavior grew increasingly erratic; published a memoir of her years with Strindberg (1937), translated as *Marriage With Genius.* ❖ See also Monica Strauss, *Cruel Banquet: The Life and Loves of Frida Strindberg* (2000); and *Women in World History.*

UHLIG, Elsa (1888–1948). *See Brandstrom, Elsa.*

UHLIG, Petra (1954—). East German handball player. Born July 22, 1954, in East Germany. ❖ Won a silver medal at Montreal Olympics (1976) and a bronze medal at Moscow Olympics (1980), both in team competition.

UJLAKINE, Ildiko (1937—). *See Sagine-Ujlakine-Rejto, Ildiko.*

UKRAINKA, Lesya (1871–1913). Ukrainian poet and playright. Pronunciation: LESS-ya oo-CRYEN-ka. Name variations: Laryssa Kosach; Laryssa Kosach-Kvitka; Lesia or Lessya Ukrainka; Lesëiia Ukrainka; Lesja Ukrajinka; Lesia Ukraïnka; Lesya Ukrayinka. Born Laryssa Kosach on Feb 26 (sometimes given as Feb 25), 1871, in Zvyahel' in Volynia, Ukraine; died Aug 15, 1913, in Surami, near Tbilisi; dau. of Petro Antonovych Kosach (lawyer and landowner) and Olha Petrivna Drahomaniv (writer and political activist who wrote under name Olena Pchilka); m. Klyment Kvitka (ethnographer and musicologist), 1907. ❖ Prominent Ukrainian poet whose body of work presents both universal themes and a reflection of her homeland's struggle for greater freedom; moved with family to Kovel (1878); after her aunt was arrested by the tsarist police for political agitation, wrote 1st poem to protest the event (1879); afflicted with tuberculosis (1881); under pseudonym Lesya Ukrainka, published 1st collection of poems, *Na krylakh pisen'* (*On Wings of Song*, 1892), followed by *Nevilnychi pisni* (*Songs of Slaves*, 1893); went to Berlin for surgery on her legs, but the tuberculosis had spread to her lungs, then kidneys (1897); made 1st trip to Italy for her health (1901–02); had further medical treatment in Berlin (1908); made 1st trip to Egypt (1909); often exuded an irrepressible nationalism in her work, including her play, *Boiarina* (*The Boiar's Wife* 1910), which was

explicitly anti-Russian and banned; returned to Egypt and published her best work *Lisova pisnia* (*Song of the Forest,* 1911); considered by many critics to be the greatest female poet in the Ukrainian language, used a variety of poetic tools; as well, her stage plays have occupied a prominent role in the repertoire of such émigré companies as the Ukrainian Theater of America. Other poetry collections include *Dumy i mriyi* (*Thoughts and Dreams,* 1899) and *Vidhuky* (*Echoes,* 1902). ❖ See also Constantine Bida, *Lesya Ukrainka: Life and Work* (U. of Toronto Press, 1968); and *Women in World History.*

ULANOVA, Galina (1910–1998). Russian ballerina. Name variations: Galya. Pronunciation: Ga-LEEN-ah oo-LAHN-ova. Born Galina Sergeievna Ulanova on Jan 10 (some sources cite Jan 8), 1910, in St. Petersburg; died in Moscow, April 25, 1998; dau. of Sergei Nikolaevich Ulanov and Maria Fedorovna (Romanova) Ulanova (both professional dancers); attended Leningrad School of Choreography, 1919–28; m. Vadim Rindin (chief set designer of the Bolshoi Theater); no children. ❖ Prominent ballerina from late 1920s to early 1960s who flourished in both the classic and the newly composed propagandistic ballets that formed the repertoire of the Soviet dance world; joined Leningrad State Theater (later Kirov Theater) of Opera and Ballet and debuted in *The Sleeping Beauty* (1928); debuted as star dancer in *Swan Lake* (1929); starred as Princess Maria in newly created *The Fountain of Bakhchisary* (1934); gave 1st guest performance with the Bolshoi Ballet (1935); joined Bolshoi (1944); performed in Italy (1950), then China (1952); made London debut (1956); toured US (1959); gave final performance with Bolshoi (1960); retired and began career as teacher (1961); awarded title of Heroine of Soviet Labor (1974); enjoyed gala performance by Bolshoi in honor of her 80th birthday (1990); other roles include title roles in *The Dying Swan, Giselle* and *Romeo and Juliet,* as well as Masha in *The Nutcracker,* Princess Aurora in *The Sleeping Beauty,* and Tao Hoa in *The Red Poppy;* was the most prominent and widely hailed Soviet ballerina of her time. ❖ See also Albert E. Kahn, *Days with Ulanova* (Simon & Schuster, 1979); Léon Nemenschousky, *A Day with Galina Ulanova* (trans. by Margaret McGregor, Cassell, 1960); M. I. Sizòva, *Ulanova: Her Childhood and Schooldays* (trans. by Marie Rambert, A&C Black, 1962); and *Women in World History.*

ULANOVA, Maria (1886–1954). *See Romanova, Maria.*

ULASI, Adaora Lily (1932—). Nigerian novelist and journalist. Born 1932 in Nigeria; descended from the Royal House of Nnewi; University of Southern California, BA. ❖ Educated in Nigeria and US; was one of the 1st women journalists in Nigeria and the 1st woman there to write detective fiction; immigrated to UK (1967); worked for Voice of America and BBC; works include *Many Thing You No Understand* (1970), *Many Thing Begin for Change* (1971), *The Night Harry Died* (1974), *The Man from Sagamu* (1978), and *Who is Jonah?* (1978).

ULAYYA (fl. 800s). Arabian singer. Dau. of Maknuna (slave singer) and Caliph al-Mahdi (r. 775–785); half-sister of Harun al-Rashid, Ibrahim ibn al-Mahdi, and Abassa; stepdau. of Khaizaran. ❖ Talented musician, became a leader of the Persian romantic music movement which sought to replace the classical conservative school; preferring others to perform her work, wrote many songs which were sung by Oraib; covered a forehead blemish with a fillet set with jewels which became known as the fillet *à la Ulayya,* and was soon adopted by Muslims as the fashion of the day. ❖ See also *Women in World History.*

ULFELDT, Leonora Christina (1621–1698). Danish writer and princess. Name variations: Eleonora Ulfeldt; Leonora Ulfeld. Pronunciation: OOL-felt. Born Eleonora Christina on July 8, 1621, at the Castle of Frederiksborg in Hillerod, Denmark; died at Maribo Abbey, Denmark, on Mar 16, 1698; dau. of Christian IV, king of Denmark and Norway (r. 1588–1648), and his 2nd wife Kirsten Munk (1598–1658); m. Corfitz Ulfeldt (high steward), in 1636; children: presumably 10, of whom 7 reached adulthood. ❖ Writer of *A Monument to Suffering,* which records her 22-year imprisonment in the Blue Tower of Copenhagen on the charge of conspiracy to treason; father died and stepbrother Frederick III ascended the throne (1648); when husband was accused of graft, left Copenhagen to seek the support and protection of Queen Christina of Sweden (July 1651); made several unsuccessful attempts at reconciliation with King Frederick; was living in exile (1651–60), when husband joined Christina's successor, Charles X, in his war against Denmark (1657); with husband, was arrested for treason by Frederick and imprisoned at the island of Bornholm (1660), then released a year and a half later (1662); spent time in Denmark and abroad; husband again plotted against the Danish king and died while fleeing; was arrested and brought to the Blue Tower of Copenhagen (1663); released by Frederick's son, Christian V (1685); spent last 13 years as head of her household at Maribo Abbey (1685–98); during prison term, wrote *French Biography* and drafted a large part of *A Monument to Suffering*, as well as a series of biographical sketches of women in history and mythology; has held her place among the illustrious names in Danish history for the past 300 years. ❖ See also *Women in World History*.

ULFHILD (fl. 1112). Queen of Sweden and Denmark. Name variations: Ulvhild. Married Inge (d. 1112), king of Sweden and co-regent (r. 1080–1112); became 2nd wife of Niels, king of Denmark (r. 1104–1134); possibly mother of Magnus (Niels' 1st wife was Margarethe of Vastergotland). ❖ An important Christian founder in her capacity as queen of Sweden, succeeded in using her authority and influence to found several Cistercian houses in Sweden, both convents and monasteries.

ULFHILD OF DENMARK (d. before 1070). Duchess of Saxony. Died before 1070; dau. of Ingigerd Haraldsdottir and Olaf I Hunger, king of Denmark (r. 1086–1095); m. Ordulf, duke of Saxony, in 1042; children: Magnus, duke of Saxony (b. about 1045).

ULFSDATTER, Merete (fl. 1320–1370). *See Merete Ulfsdatter.*

ULION, Gretchen (1972—). American ice-hockey player. Born May 4, 1972, in Marlborough, CT; graduate of Dartmouth College. ❖ Set 11 Dartmouth and 4 Ivy League records during college career; named Ivy League Player of the Year (1992–93, 1993–94); won a team gold medal at Nagano (1998), the 1st Olympics to feature women's ice hockey; won a team silver medal at World championships (1997). ❖ See also Mary Turco, *Crashing the Net: The U. S. Women's Olympic Ice Hockey Team and the Road to Gold* (HarperCollins, 1999); and *Women in World History*.

ULLMAN, Tracey (1959—). English singer, comedian and actress. Born Dec 30, 1959 in Slough, Berkshire, England; attended Italia Conti Academy of Theatre Arts; m. Allan McKeown, 1983; children: Mabel and John. ❖ Began career as professional dancer with a ballet company in Berlin; turned to musical theater, performing in *Grease!* and *Elvis*; earned London Theater Critics' Most Promising Actress Award for *Four in a Million* (1981); starred in her own tv series "Three of a Kind" (1981); cut album *You Broke My Heart in 17 Places* (1984); made film debut in *Give My Regards to Broad Street* (1984), but got the reviews for her turn in *Plenty* (1985); other films include *Jumpin' Jack Flash* (1986), *I Love You to Death* (1990), *Death Becomes Her* (1992), *Household Saints* (1993), *I'll Do Anything* (1994), *Small Time Crooks* (2000) and *A Dirty Shame* (2004); launched US tv career with "The Tracey Ullman Show" (1987–90), earning 3 Emmys; co-starred with Woody Allen in Oscar-Winning hit *Bullets Over Broadway* (1994); won Emmy for "Tracey Takes On..." (1996–99) and guest roles on "Ally McBeal" (1998–99) and "Love & War" (1997).

ULLMANN, Liv (1939—). Norwegian actress and director. Born Liv Johanne Ullmann in Tokyo, Japan, Dec 16, 1939; dau. of Viggo Ullmann (aircraft engineer, died 1943) and Janna (Lund) Ullmann; attended Oslo's Theatre School; m. Jappe Stang (physician), 1960 (div. 1965); m. Donald Saunders (real-estate developer), in 1985 (div. 1995, then reconciled, though not remarried); children: (with Ingmar Bergman) daughter Linn Ullmann (b. 1966, writer). ❖ Internationally acclaimed actress and director who is particularly known for her work with Ingmar Bergman, made theater debut as Anne Frank in rep company at Stavanger (1956); made 1st film with Bergman, *Persona*, which was released to great international acclaim (1964); lived with Bergman (1964–69) and filmed *The Hour of the Wolf* (1968), *Shame* (1968), *The Passion of Anna* (1969), *Cries and Whispers* (1971) and *Autumn Sonata* (1978); won Tony Award as Best Actress for Broadway debut in *A Doll's House* (1975); returned to Broadway in *Anna Christie* (1977), the musical version of *I Remember Mama* (1979), *Ghosts* (1982) and *Old Times* (1985); became the 1st goodwill ambassador for UNICEF (1980); co-wrote and directed film *Sofie* (1992), followed by screen adaptation of *Kristen Lavransdatter*, a huge hit in Norway (1995); directed *Private Confessions* (*Private Conversations*, 1996) and *Faithless*, both from screenplays by Bergman (2001); other films include *The Emigrants* (1972), *Pope Joan* (1972), *Lost Horizon* (1973), *40 Carats* (1973), *Scenes from a Marriage* (1974), *The Abdication* (1974), *The Serpent's Egg* (1978), *Richard's Things* (1980), *The Wild Duck* (1983), *Dangerous Moves* (1985), *Time of Indifference* (1987), *The Ox* (1991) and *The Long Shadow* (1992). ❖ See also memoirs *Forandringen* (*Changes*, 1976) and *Choices* (1984); and *Women in World History*.

ULLMANN, Regina (1884–1961). Swiss novelist. Born Dec 14, 1884, of German-speaking Jewish parents, in St. Gallen, Switzerland; died Jan 6, 1961; children: (with Viennese economist Hanns Dorn) 1; (with psychoanalyst Otto Gross) Camilla Ullmann (1908–2000). ❖ With mother, frequented literary circles in Munich and Vienna; was protégée of Rainer Maria Rilke.

ULLRICH, Kay (1943—). Scottish politician. Born 1943 in Prestwick. ❖ As an SNP candidate, elected to the Scottish Parliment for West of Scotland (1999); served as SNP Parliamentary Group chief whip; retired (2003).

ULLRICH, Luise (1911–1985). Austrian actress. Born Aloisa Ullrich, Oct 31, 1911, in Vienna, Austria; died Jan 22, 1985, in Munich, Germany; dau. of a count who was a major in Austro-Hungarian army; studied acting at Vienna Theater-Akademie; m. Wulf Diether, count of Castell-Rudenhausen (airport director). ❖ As a teenager, was offered a 2-year contract with Vienna Volkstheater; also appeared in *Rauhnacht* (Brawly Night) at Lessing-Theater in Berlin; made film debut as the lead in *Der Rebell* (The Rebel, 1932); appeared in *Liebelei* (Flirtation, 1933), *Versprich mir nichts!* (Promise Me Nothing!, 1937), *Ich liebe Dich* (I Love You, 1938), and *Annelie: Die Geschichte eines Lebens* (Annelie: The Story of a Life, 1941), considered her best film; also made *Nora* (1944), a distorted version of *A Doll's House*; after WWII, continued to appear in tv series and films; also published a novel *Ricarda* (1954), and several short stories. ❖ See also memoirs, *Komm auf die Schaukel, Luise; Balance eines Lebens* (Come onto the Swing, Luise: Appraisal of a Life, 1943); and *Women in World History*.

ULMANN, Doris (1882–1934). American photographer. Born 1882 in New York, NY; died 1934 in New York, NY; dau. of Bernard Ulmann and Gertrude (Maas) Ulmann; studied with Lewis Hine at Ethical Culture School, 1900–03; studied psychology and law at Columbia University; studied photography with Clarence White; m. Charles H. Jaeger (doctor), before 1917 (div. 1925). ❖ Published photographs in *Portraits, College of Physicians and Surgeons* (1920), *Portraits, Medical Faculty, Johns Hopkins University* (1922) and *A Portrait Gallery of American Editors* (1925); began to shoot scenes of rural life (1925), especially of people who lived in Dunkard, Mennonite, and Shaker communities in NY, Pennsylvania, Virginia, and New England; photographed the people of Appalachia (1927); turned attention to Gullah people on islands of South Carolina (1929–30), publishing 70 of their portraits in *Roll, Jordan, Roll* (1933), with text by Julia Peterkin; with Allen Henderson Eaton, photographed people engaged in traditional crafts in Southern Highlands of US (1933); also contributed photographs to *Theatre Art Monthly, Bookman, Spur,* and *Vanity Fair*. ❖ See also *Women in World History*.

ULMER, Sarah (1976—). New Zealand cyclist. Born Mar 14, 1976, in Auckland, NZ; dau. of Gary Ulmer; Auckland University, Bachelor of Sports Science. ❖ Won a gold medal and set a world record in the 3,000-meter indiv. pursuit at World championships (2004); won World Cup overall for indiv. pursuit (2003, 2004); won gold medal at Athens Olympics for 3,000-meter individual pursuit (2004), beating her own world record at 3:24.537. Won the Lonsdale Cup (2002); named New Zealand's Sportswoman of the Year (1994).

ULPIA MARCIANA (fl. 98–117 CE). Roman noblewoman. Name variations: Marciana. Born Ulpia Marciana; dau. of M. Ulpius Traianus; sister of the Roman emperor Trajan; m. C. Salonius Matidius Patruinus; children: Matidia I.

ULRIC, Lenore (1892–1970). American stage and screen actress. Born Lenore Ulrich, July 21, 1892, in New Ulm, MN; died Dec 30, 1970, in Orangeburg, NY; m. Sidney Blackmer (actor), 1928 (div. 1939). ❖ Joined the Essanay film company (1911); made NY stage debut in *The Mark of the Beast* (1915) and appeared in productions by David Belasco, especially *Tiger Rose* (1917); films include *Tiger Rose, Frozen Justice, Kilmeny, The Heart of Paula, South Sea Rose, Camille, Notorious, Two Smart People* and *Northwest Outpost*.

ULRICA ELEANORA (1688–1741). Queen of Sweden. Name variations: Ulrika Eleanor; Ulrika Eleanora; Ulrica Eleanora von Simmern; Ulrike Eleonore. Born Jan 23, 1688, at Stockholm palace; died Nov 24, 1741, in Stockholm; dau. of Carl XI or Charles XI (1655–1697), king of Sweden (r. 1660–1697), and Queen Ulrica Eleanora of Denmark (1656–1593); sister of Charles XII (1682–1718), king of Sweden (r. 1697–1718); m. Frederick (1676–1751), landgrave of Hesse-Cassel, later Frederick I, king of Sweden (r. 1720–1751), on Mar 24, 1715; no children.

Frederick's 1st wife was Louise Dorothea of Brandenburg (1680–1705). ❖ One of 3 reigning queens in Swedish history, was also the last monarch of the Pfalz dynasty; when brother Charles XII was killed in battle (Nov 1718), proclaimed herself queen, but the Swedish senate would not recognize her claim because she was married; after negotiations between the senate and her supporters, was elected queen (Jan 23, 1719), her 31st birthday; in return, had to agree to relinquish much of the absolutist royal authority previously held by Swedish monarchs, and accept a new constitution establishing parliamentary government with authority over royal policy decisions; crowned (Mar 17, 1719), was forced to abdicate after only 1 year, the shortest reign in Swedish history, and husband eagerly accepted the crown as King Frederick I; was active as a patron of the arts, sciences, and literature during her 20 years as queen-consort. ❖ See also *Women in World History*.

ULRICA ELEANORA OF DENMARK (1656–1693). Queen of Sweden. Name variations: Ulrica Eleanor the Elder; Ulrika Eleanor or Ulrika Eleanora. Born Sept 11, 1656; died Aug 6, 1693; dau. of Frederick III (1609–1670), king of Denmark and Norway (r. 1648–1670), and Sophie Amalie of Brunswick-Lüneburg (1628–1685); m. Carl XI or Charles XI (1655–1697), king of Sweden (r. 1660–1697); children: Hedwig Sophia (1681–1708, who m. Frederick IV of Holstein-Gottorp); Charles XII (1682–1718), king of Sweden (r. 1697–1718); Ulrica Eleanora (1688–1741), queen of Sweden (r. 1719–1720); Gustav (b. 1683); Ulrich (b. 1684); Frederick (b. 1685); Charles Gustav (b. 1686).

ULRIKA or ULRIKE. *Variant of Ulrica.*

ULSTER, countess of.
See Margaret de Burgh (d. 1303).
See Maud Plantagenet (c. 1310–c. 1377).
See Elizabeth de Burgh (1332–1363).
See Mortimer, Philippa (1355–1382).

ULTROGOTTE (fl. 558). See Vultrogotha.

ULVAEUS, Agnetha (1950—). See Fältskog, Agnetha.

ULVHILD (fl. 1112). See Ulfhild.

ULYANOVA, Marie (1878–1937). Russian revolutionary and journalist. Name variations: Maria, Mariia or Mariya Ul'lanova, Ulianova or Uljanova. Born Maria Ilyichina Ulyanova in 1878; died 1937; dau. of Ilya Nikolayevich Ulyanov (school administrator, 1832–1886) and Maria Alexandrovna (Blank) Ulyanova (1835–1916); sister of Olga Ulyanova (1871–1891), Ana Yelizarova, journalist (1864–1935), Vladimir Ulyanov, known to the world as V.I. Lenin (1870–1924), Dimitri Ulyanov, physician (1874–1943), and Alexander Ulyanov who was arrested for plotting the assassination of Tsar Alexander III and was executed in 1887. ❖ Communist journalist, served as chief of the Central Educational Department in the Bolshevik government.

UMANETS, Nina (1956—). Soviet rower. Born May 1956 in USSR. ❖ At Moscow Olympics, won a silver medal in coxed eights (1980).

UMA NO NAISHI (fl. 10th c.). Japanese poet. Probably born c. the mid-10th century. ❖ A contemporary of Sei Shonagon, also served women at court; near the close of her life, took Buddhist vows and withdrew to a temple.

UMEH, Stella (1975—). Canadian gymnast. Born May 27, 1975, in Mississauga, Canada; dau. of a Nigerian father and Guyanan mother; sister of Stacey Umeh-Lees (coach). ❖ Won Jr. Pacific Alliance (1989), Elite Canada (1991), Canadian nationals (1992, 1993); at Commonwealth Games, won gold medals in all-around and vault, silver in team and uneven bars; joined Cirque du Soleil (1999).

UMEKI, Miyoshi (1929—). Japanese-born actress. Born April 3, 1929, in Otaru, Hokkaido, Japan; married Randall Hood, director (div.). ❖ Began working as a radio and nightclub singer when she was still a teenager in Japan; came to US (1950s), where she 1st appeared on tv; had break-through role in *Sayonara* (1957), for which she won an Academy Award for Best Supporting Actress, the 1st Asian actor so honored; appeared on Broadway in *Flower Drum Song*; returned to tv in "The Courtship of Eddie's Father," and made a number of other films, including *Cry for Happy* (1961), *Flower Drum Song* (1961), *The Horizontal Lieutenant* (1962) and *A Girl Named Tamiko* (1963); retired and moved to Hawaii. ❖ See also *Women in World History*.

UMILITA or UMILTA (1226–1310). See Humilitas of Faenza.

UM KALTHUM (c. 1898–1975). Egyptian singer. Name variations: Um Kalthoum; Oum Kalsoum; Umm Kulthum; Umm Thulum; Star of the East. Born Fatma el-Zahraa Ibrahim in the Egyptian delta village of Tamay al-Zahirah (or Tammay al-Zahayrah) probably 1898 but possibly 1900; died Feb 3, 1975; m. Dr. Hassan el-Hifnawi (skin specialist), 1954. ❖ After WWI, went to Cairo and eventually gave public performances; took stage name Um Kalthum; a star while still in her early 20s, added an orchestra, unbound her hair, donned Western dress, and clutched a silk scarf in her hand that became a trademark; toured Libya, Lebanon, Syria and Paris (1932); gave 1st broadcast for Radio Egypt (1934); awarded highest decoration an Egyptian woman could receive, the Al-Kamal medal, from King Farouk (1944); a dominant force in the Arab world for several decades, gained influence in Gamal Abdel Nasser's government (1950s); when a goiter threatened her voice, had successful surgery in US and made a number of broadcasts on the Voice of America's Arab-language service in gratitude (1954); made recordings that are still widely listened to, and continued to give concerts until her death, which was mourned by millions. ❖ See also Virginia Louise Danielson, *"The Voice of Egypt": Umm Kulthum, Arabic Song, and Egyptian Society in the Twentieth Century* (U. of Chicago Press, 1997); *Umm Thulum: A Voice Like Egypt*, documentary by Michal Goldman, 1996 (English and Arabic with English subtitles); and *Women in World History*.

UMM AL-HAKIM (c. 590–c. 640). See Zaynab bint Jahsh.

UMM AL-MU'MININ (c. 613–678). See A'ishah bint Abi Bakr.

UMM KULTHUM (c. 1898–1975). See Um Kalthum.

UMM NIZAR (1908–1953). See Malaika, Salma al-.

UMM RUMAN (fl. 7th c.). Mother of A'ishah bint Abi Bakr. Married Abu Bakr who had at least 3 other wives; children: A'ishah bint Abi Bakr (c. 613–678). ❖ See also *Women in World History*.

UMM SALAMAH (fl. 7th c.). Wife of Muhammad. Name variations: Hind bint Abi 'mayyah. Sixth cousin of Muhammad; m. Abu Salamah (who died of wounds suffered earlier at the battle of Uhud); m. Muhammad in 626; children: (1st m.) several. ❖ See also *Women in World History*.

UMM THULUM (c. 1898–1975). See Um Kalthum.

UNDER, Marie (1883–1980). Estonian poet. Born 1883 in Tallinn, Estonia; died Sept 25, 1980, in Stockholm, Sweden; dau. of Fredrich Under (teacher) and Leena (Kerner) Under; attended school in Germany; m. Carl Hacker (accountant), 1902 (div. 1917); m. Artur Adson (1889–1977, poet), 1924; children: (1st m.) 2 daughters. ❖ Considered perhaps the finest poet in the Estonian language, published 1st collection of verse, *Sonetid* (Sonnets, 1917); published *Eeloitseng* (Budding, 1918), *Sinine puri* (Blue Sail, 1918), *Verivalla* (A Flowing of Blood, 1920), and *Onnevarjutus* (The Eclipse of Happiness, 1929); turned to lyric verse, with *Lageda taeva all* (Under the Open Sky, 1930) and *Kivi südamelt* (A Stone from My Heart, 1935); wrote of her mother's death, the destruction brought about by World War II and the occupation of her country in *Mureliku suuga* (With Careworn Lips, 1942); with 2nd husband, moved to Sweden (1944), where she wrote about the Soviet occupation of her homeland once more in *Sädemed tuhas* (Sparks in the Ashes, 1954). ❖ See also *Women in World History*.

UNDERHILL, Evelyn (1875–1941). English poet, novelist, and writer on mysticism. Name variations: (pseudonym) John Cordelier. Born Dec 6, 1875, in Wolverhampton, England; died June 15, 1941, in Hampstead, London; dau. of Sir Arthur Underhill (barrister) and Alice Lucy (Ironmonger) Underhill; educated at King's College for Women, London; m. Hubert Stuart Moore (barrister), 1907. ❖ One of the leading writers on mysticism, wrote numerous books on the subject, including 2 that are considered classics, *Mysticism* (1911) and *Worship* (1936); experienced a religious conversion (1907) and began studying the lives of the mystics; published novels and light verse, but came to prominence with *Mysticism: A Study in the Nature and Development of Man's Spiritual Consciousness*, which brought her to the attention of many prominent theologians and writers, including Baron von Hügel, who would be her mentor; lectured at Manchester College, Oxford (1921); became the 1st woman to be appointed an outside lecturer at Oxford University (1927), when she was made a fellow of King's College; was a prolific writer, producing a book each year for 14 years; including *Grey World: A Novel* (1904), *The Column of Dust* (1909), (under pseudonym John Cordelier) *The Path of Eternal Wisdom* (1911), *Ruysbroeck* (1915),

Theophanies: A Book of Verses (1916), *Jacopone da Todi* (1919), *The Essentials of Mysticism* (1920), *The Mystics of the Church* (1925), *Man and the Supernatural* (1927), *The House of the Soul* (1929), *Abba* (1940), and *Fruits of the Spirit* (1942).

UNDERHILL, Miriam O'Brien (1898–1976). *See O'Brien, Miriam.*

UNDERHILL, Ruth Murray (1883–1984). American ethnographer and author. Born Ruth Murray Underhill, Aug 22, 1883, in Ossining, NY; died Aug 1984 in Denver, CO; dau. of Abram Sutton Underhill (lawyer) and Anna Murray Underhill (both Quakers and pacifists); Vassar College, AB, 1905; attended London School of Economics and University of Munich; Columbia University, PhD, 1939; m. Charles Crawford (div.). ❖ At Columbia University, provided with funding by Franz Boas for research among the Papago; assisted in recording the 1st published life history of a Southwestern Indian woman, Maria Chona, which was issued as *Autobiography of a Papago Woman* (1936); worked in various capacities with Bureau of Indian Affairs (BIA); taught in anthropology department at University of Denver (1948–52); taught at New York State Teachers College in New Paltz (now State University of New York College at New Paltz) and Colorado Women's College. Other works include *White Moth* (novel, 1920); *Singing for Power* (1938); *The Northern Paiute Indians of California and Nevada* (1941); *Red Man's America* (1953); and *Red Man's Religion* (1965).

UNDERWOOD, Agness Wilson (1902–1984). American journalist. Name variations: Aggie Underwood. Born Agness Wilson, Dec 17, 1902, in San Francisco, California; died July 3, 1984, in Greeley, Colorado; dau. of Cliff Wilson and Mamie (Sullivan) Wilson; married and div.; children: Mary Evelyn Underwood (who m. William A. Weed); H. George M. Underwood. ❖ The 1st woman city editor of a major daily newspaper, worked as a reporter for *Los Angeles Review* (1931–35); served as police-beat reporter for *Los Angeles Herald-Express* (1935–47, which later became the *Los Angeles Herald-Examiner*); became the paper's city editor (1947), the 1st woman to hold that job at any major daily in the country; appointed assistant managing editor of *Herald-Examiner* (1964), a post she held until retirement (1968). ❖ See also autobiography, *Newspaper Woman* (1949).

UNDERWOOD, Lillias (1851–1921). American physician and missionary. Name variations: Lillias Stirling Horton; Stirling Horton. Born Lillias Stirling Horton, June 21, 1851, in Albany, NY; died Oct 29, 1921, in Seoul, Korea; dau. of James Mandeville Horton (hardware merchant) and Matilda (McPherson) Horton; Woman's Medical College of Chicago, MD, 1887; m. Horace Grant Underwood (missionary), Mar 13, 1889 (died Oct 1916); children: 1 son. ❖ Volunteered for Presbyterian Board of Foreign Missions; traveled to Korea to supervise women's department and dispensary for government hospital and to serve as personal physician to Queen Min (1888); due to close association with Min and royal court, was occasionally involved in Korea's political turmoil; with husband, created Frederick Underwood Shelter to treat people with infectious diseases (1893); published *Fifteen Years Among the Top-knots* (1904), *With Tommy Tompkins in Korea* (1905), and biography of husband, *Underwood of Korea* (1918).

UNDERWOOD, Sophie Kerr (1880–1965). *See Kerr, Sophie.*

UNDSET, Sigrid (1882–1949). Norwegian writer. Born in Kalundborg, Denmark, May 20, 1882; died in Lillehammer, June 10, 1949; dau. of Ingwald Undset (archaeologist) and (Anna) Charlotte (Gyth) Undset; m. Anders Castus Svarstad (painter), 1913 (marriage annulled); children: Anders (b. 1913); Maren Charlotte (b. 1915); Hans (b. 1919). ❖ Writer of novels, short stories and essays who was awarded the Nobel Prize for literature (1928) and honored by her country with the Norwegian Grand Cross of the Order of Saint Olav (1945), presented as much for her patriotic activities as for her writing; though probably most well known for her *Kristin Lavransdatter* (1920–22), spent decades writing and exploring questions of morality, loyalty, sexuality and spirituality with particular focus on the relationship between wife and husband; her childhood exposure to history, and later meticulous research, made possible the powerful Middle Ages settings in which her most lauded works often found expression; an ardent patriot and anti-Nazi, housed refugees during WWII, and lost one of her sons to the war after the Nazis landed in Norway in 1940; writings include *Martha Oulie* (1907), *Gunnar's Daughter* (1909), *Jenny* (1911), *Tales of King Arthur* (1914), *The Wise Virgins* (1918), *Olav Audunsson in Hestviken* (1925), *Olav Audunsson and His Children* (1927), *The Wild Orchid* (1929), *The Burning Bush* (1931), *Ida Elisabeth* (1932), *The Longest Years* (1934), *The Faithful Wife* (1936), *Madame Dorthea* (1939), *Articles and Tales from Wartime* (1952) and

Catherine of Siena (1954). ❖ See also Mitzi Brunsdale, *Sigrid Undset: Chronicler of Norway* (St. Martin, 1988); A. H. Winsness, *Sigrid Undset: A Study in Christian Realism* (Sheed & Ward, 1953); and *Women in World History.*

UNGER, Caroline (1803–1877). Austrian operatic mezzo-soprano. Name variations: Karoline Unger; Caroline Unger-Sabatier; Caroline Sabatier. Born Oct 28, 1803, in Stuhlweissenburg, Austria; died Mar 23, 1877, in Florence, Italy; studied with Mozatti, Lange, Vogl, and Ronconi; m. François Sabatier (writer). ❖ One of the most outstanding and intelligent singers of her time, had an immense vocal range, from A to high D; in Vienna, made 1st appearance (1819), official debut (1821), and sang there until 1824; performed in Naples (1825–26), Milan (1827–30), Paris (1833), and again in Vienna (1839–40), appearing in such roles as Zerlina, Rosina, and Isabella in *L'italiana*; also created roles of Isoletta in *La straniera*, Donizetti's Parisina, Maria di Rudenz, and Antonina in *Belisario*, and sang the alto solo in premiere performance of Beethoven's Ninth Symphony, which was conducted by the composer; made last appearance on opera stage in Dresden (1843), then retired, though she sang in concerts under married name Caroline Unger-Sabatier. ❖ See also *Women in World History.*

UNGER, Gladys B. (c. 1885–1940). American playwright and screenwriter. Born c. 1885, in San Francisco, CA; died May 25, 1940, in New York, NY; m. Kai Kushrou Ardaschir (div.). ❖ Wrote such plays as *Edmund Kean* (1903), *Mr. Sheridan, The Knave of Hearts, Henry of Lancaster, In an Arab Garden, Inconstant George* (from the French), *Betty* (with Frederick Lonsdale), *Toto, The Highwaymen, The Werewolf* (from the German), *The Virgin of Bethulia* (from the French), and *Nona*; contributed to, or wrote screenplays for, *Music is Magic, Strange Wives, The Mystery of Edwin Drood, Rendezvous at Midnight, Miss Mary Dow, Sylvia Scarlett* and *Daughter of Shanghai,* among others.

UNGER, Mary Ann (1945–1998). American sculptor. Born May 10, 1945, in New York, NY; died Dec 28, 1998, in New York, NY; dau. of William and Dorothy Unger; Mt. Holyoke College, BA in art, 1967; attended University of California, Berkeley; Columbia University, MFA, 1975; m. Geoffrey Biddle (photographer); children: Eve Biddle. ❖ Began sculpting as a child; studied with George Sugarman and Ronald Bladen at Columbia; received public commissions and exhibited at solo shows; work is held in permanent collections of Hirschorn Museum and Sculpture Garden in Washington, DC, the Brooklyn Museum of Art, and the Philadelphia Museum of Art. ❖ See also *Women in World History.*

UNGUREANU, Corina (1980—). Romanian gymnast. Born Aug 29, 1980, in Polesti, Romania. ❖ At European championships, won a gold medal for floor exercises (1998).

UNGUREANU, Teodora (1960—). Romanian gymnast. Born Nov 13, 1960, in Resita, Romania; m. Sorin Cepoi (gymnast). ❖ Won Romanian Jr. nationals (1973), Japan Cup (1975), Champions All (1976, 1977), Milan Grand Prix and Milk Meet (1976), Coca-Cola International (1978) and University Games (1979); at Montreal Olympics, won a bronze medal for balance beam, a silver for uneven bars, and a silver for team all-around (1976); at World championships, won a team silver (1978). Inducted into International Gymnastics Hall of Fame (2001).

UNO, Chiyo (1897–1996). Japanese novelist. Born 1897 in Yamaguchi prefecture, Japan; died June 10, 1996, in Tokyo, Japan; married 3 times; children: 1 (died at birth). ❖ Well-known Japanese writer who had several tumultuous love affairs with other writers and artists, including painter Seiji Togo, who had attempted suicide (by slashing his throat) with his previous lover; further shocked the conservative nation by cutting her hair short (1927); won the Prize of Jijishinpo for *A Powdered Face* (1921); published novel *Confessions of Love* (1935), which was based on Togo's love affairs; with another lover, Kitahara Takeo, founded Japan's 1st fashion magazine, *Style* (1936); earned the Noma Prize for Literature for *Ohan*, a story about the relationship between two women who share the same lover (1957); other novels include *A Dollmaker, Tenguya Hisakichi, A Cherry of Pale Pink,* and *To Stab*; became a member of the Japanese Academy of Arts (1972); awarded the Kikuchi Kan Prize (1982); memoir, *I Will Go On Living* (1983), became a Japanese bestseller and a tv movie; despite her scandalous past, was recognized as a "person of cultural merit" by Japanese government (1990) and received a title from the emperor. ❖ See also *Women in World History.*

UNSOELD, Jolene (1931—). American politician. Born Jolene Bishoprick, Dec 3, 1931, in Corvallis, Oregon; educated at primary schools in Shanghai, China, 1938–40, and public schools in Portland, Oregon; attended Oregon State University, Corvallis, 1949–51; married an educator. ❖ US congressional representative (Jan 3, 1989–Jan 3, 1995); with husband, who was a mountain climber and educator, lived in Kathmandu, Nepal (1962–67); was director of the English Language Institute in Kathmandu for 2 years; as a lobbyist in Olympia, Washington, worked for campaign finance reform and environmental issues; was a member of the Democratic National Committee (1983–88); served in Washington state House of Representatives (1984–89); during tenure, ran a successful campaign to set more stringent guidelines for cleanup of toxic waste sites in the state; elected to US Congress from 3rd Congressional District (1988), a seat she held from the 101st Congress through the 103rd; served on the Committee on Merchant Marine and Fisheries, Committee on Education and Labor, and Select Committee on Aging; ran unsuccessfully for reelection (1994).

UNZER, Johanne Charlotte (1725–1782). German poet. Born 1725 in Halle, Germany; died 1782; married a doctor, 1751. ❖ Published *Scherzgedichte* (1751), *Sittliche und zärtliche Gedichte* (1754), and *Fortgesetzte Versuche in sittlichen un zärtlichen Gedichten* (1766); also wrote book of advice for young women, *Grundrißeiner Weltweisheti für das Frauenzimmer* (1751) and a book on the role of women, *Historie und eigentlichen Naturlehre für das Frauenzimmer* (1767).

UP, Ari (1962—). German-English singer. Name variations: The Slits. Born Ariana Forster, 1962, in Munich, Germany. ❖ German-English vocalist who was lead singer for English punk rock band, the Slits (formed 1976 in London); with group, released debut album, *Cut* (1978), which included song, "Typical Girls"; other Slits releases include *Return of the Giant Slits* (1981), *The Peel Sessions* (1989), and *In the Beginning* (1997); after Slits disbanded (1981), joined experimental funk and reggae group, New Age Steppers.

UPDEGRAFF, Edith (1884–1956). See Kelley, Edith Summers.

UPHOFF, Nicole (1967—). German equestrian. Born Jan 25, 1967, in Germany. ❖ At Seoul Olympics, won a gold medal in team dressage and a gold medal in indiv. dressage (1988); at Barcelona Olympics, won a gold medal in team dressage and a gold medal in indiv. dressage (1992).

UPPINGTON, Mrs. (1889–1973). See Randolph, Isabel.

UPTON, Harriet Taylor (1853–1945). American suffragist, political leader, and author. Name variations: Mrs. George Upton. Born Dec 17, 1853, in Ravenna, Ohio; died Nov 2, 1945, in Pasadena, California; dau. of Ezra Booth Taylor (judge and US congressional representative) and Harriet M. (Frazer) Taylor; m. George Whitman Upton (lawyer), July 9, 1884 (died 1923). ❖ Joined the National American Woman Suffrage Association (NAWSA, 1890); was treasurer of NAWSA (1894–1910); ran the association from its headquarters in Warren, Ohio (1903–09); also testified before Congressional hearings and edited the group's monthly paper, *Progress* (1902–10); presided over Ohio Woman Suffrage Association (1899–1908, 1911–20) and managed the campaign that led to the Ohio legislature's ratification of the 19th Amendment granting women the vote; wrote numerous political articles for newspapers and magazines, including *Woman's Home Companion, Harper's Bazaar,* and *Outlook*; also wrote local histories *A Twentieth Century History of Trumbull County, Ohio* (1909) and the 3-vol. *History of the Western Reserve* (1910); was vice-chair of the Republican National Executive Committee when Warren G. Harding ran for president, one of the 1st women to hold such a high party post. ❖ See also *Women in World History*.

UPTON, Mary (1810–1881). See Ferrin, Mary Upton.

UPTON, Mary (1946—). Irish politician. Born May 30, 1946, in Kilrush, Co. Clare, Ireland; sister of Pat Upton (senator, 1989–92, TD, 1992–99). ❖ Representing Labour, elected to the 28th Dáil in a by-election (1999–2002) for Dublin South Central, following the death of her brother; returned to 29th Dáil (2002).

URAIB (797–890). See Oraib.

URBANIAK, Dorota (1972—). Canadian rower. Born May 6, 1972, in Lask-Kolunna, Poland; lives in Toronto, Ontario, Canada. ❖ Won a bronze medal for coxed eights at Sydney Olympics (2000).

URBANOVA, Marta (1960—). Czech field-hockey player. Born Oct 14, 1960. ❖ At Moscow Olympics, won a silver medal in team competition (1980).

URBANOVICH, Galina (1917—). Soviet gymnast. Born Sept 1917 in Russia. ❖ At Helsinki Olympics, won a silver medal in teams all-around, portable apparatus, and a gold medal in team all-around (1952).

URBINO, duchess of.
See Sforza, Battista (1446–1472).
See Montefeltro, Elisabetta (1471–1526).
See Gonzaga, Eleonora (1493–1543).
See Madeleine de la Tour d'Auvergne (1501–1519).
See Este, Lucrezia d' (1535–1598).
See Medici, Vittoria (d. 1694).

URBINO, princess of. See Medici, Claudia de (1604–1648).

URE, Mary (1933–1975). Scottish-born stage and screen actress. Born Feb 18, 1933, in Glasgow, Scotland; died April 3, 1975, of accidental mixture of alcohol and barbiturates in London, England, hours after successfully opening in a new play; m. John Osborne (playwright, div. 1963); m. Robert Shaw (actor), 1963; children: 4. ❖ Leading lady of the English stage, made London debut as Amanda in *Time Remembered* (1954); had enormous success as Alison Porter in *Look Back in Anger* in London and NY; also appeared as Ophelia in *Hamlet* and in *The Crucible, Duel of Angels* and *Old Times*; films include *Storm Over the Nile, Look Back in Anger, The Luck of Ginger Coffey* and *Where Eagles Dare.* Nominated for Oscar for performance as Clara Dawes in *Sons and Lovers* (1960).

URECAL, Minerva (1894–1966). American actress. Name variations: Minerva Holtzer. Born Sept 22, 1894, in Eureka, CA; died Feb 26, 1966, in Glendale, CA; m. Max Holtzer. ❖ Began career in radio; appeared in such films as *Her Husband's Secretary, Love in a Bungalow, Lost Moment, Wake Up and Dream, The Trap* and *Seven Faces of Dr. Lao*; appeared on tv as Tugboat Annie.

URIBE, Cenaida (1964—). Peruvian volleyball player. Born Dec 2, 1964, in Peru. ❖ At Seoul Olympics, won a silver medal in team competition (1988).

URQUHART, Cora (1857–1936). See Potter, Cora.

URQUHART, Eliza (1877–1938). See Gordon, Eliza.

URQUHART, Leilah (1877–1938). See Gordon, Eliza.

URRACA (1033–1101). Princess of Castile. Born in 1033; died in 1101; dau. of Sancha of Leon (1013–1067) and Ferdinand I (c. 1017–1065), king of Castile (r. 1038–1065).

URRACA (c. 1079–1126). Queen of Castile and Aragon. Born c. 1079 (some sources cite 1081); died Mar 8, 1126, in Saldaña; was the 1st surviving child of Queen Constance of Burgundy (c. 1046–c. 1093) and Alphonso VI (c. 1030–1109), king of Leon (r. 1065–1109), king of Castile (r. 1072–1109); m. Raymond of Burgundy, in 1087 (died 1107); m. Alphonso I the Battler (1073–1134), king of Aragon (r. 1104–1134), in 1109 (annulled in 1114); children: (1st m.) Princess Sancha (born by 1095–1159); Alphonso VII Raimúndez (1105–1157), king of Castile and Leon (r. 1126–1157); illeg. children with Count Pedro González de Lara. ❖ Queen who governed the Iberian kingdoms of Galicia, Leon and Castile, and through her marriage to Alphonso I of Aragon briefly united almost all of medieval Christian Spain; married (1087); by 1090, named countess of Galicia and Portugal; husband died (1107); after father died (June 30, 1109), was recognized as queen of Leon-Castile; married Alphonso the Battler, king of Aragon (Oct 1109); at odds with husband, skillfully maneuvered to protect her crown and realms during a civil war (1112–14); with marriage annulled (1114), ruled personally over her kingdoms (1114–26); reigned longer than any other queen of a major Western European kingdom during the High Middle Ages, then bequeathed to her son Alphonso VII a stable and peaceful realm. ❖ See also Bernard F. Reilly, *The Kingdom of León-Castilla under Queen Urraca, 1109–1126* (Princeton U. Press, 1982); and *Women in World History*.

URRACA (c. 1096–c. 1130). Countess of Trastamara. Born c. 1096; died after 1130; dau. of Teresa of Castile (c. 1080–1130) and Henry, count of Burgundy (r. 1093–1112); sister of Alphonso I Henriques, king of Portugal (r. 1139–1185); m. Bermudo, count of Trastamara, before 1120.

URRACA OF ARAGON (fl. 11th c.). Princess of Aragon. Dau. of Gilberga (d. 1054) and Ramiro I, king of Aragon (r. 1035–1069). ❖ Became a nun.

URRACA OF CASTILE (d. 1179). Queen of Navarre. Born after 1126; died Oct 12, 1179 (some sources cite 1189), in Palencia; illeg. dau. of Alfonso also known as Alphonso VII (1105–1157), king of Castile (r. 1126–1157), and Gontrada Perez; m. Garcia Ramirez IV, king of Navarre (r. 1134–1150), on June 24, 1144; children: Sancha (who m. Gaston V, vicomte of Bearn, and Peter, vicomte of Narbonne); Rodrigo, count of Montescaglioso. Garcia's 1st wife was Marguerite de l'Aigle (d. 1141).

URRACA OF CASTILE (c. 1186–1220). Queen of Portugal. Born in 1186 or 1187 in Castile; died in 1220; dau. of Alfonso or Alphonso VIII, also known as Alphonso III (1155–1214), king of Castile (r. 1158–1214), and Eleanor of Castile (1162–1214, dau. of Henry II of England and Eleanor of Aquitaine); sister of Berengeria of Castile (1171–1246) and Blanche of Castile (1187–1252); m. Alfonso or Alphonso II the Fat (1185–1223), king of Portugal (r. 1211–1223), in 1206; children: Sancho II (1207–1248), king of Portugal (r. 1223–1248); Alphonso III (1215–1279), king of Portugal (r. 1248–1279); Leonor of Portugal (1211–1231); Fernando or Ferdinand (1217–1246, who m. Sancha de Lara); Vicente (b. 1219, died young). ❖ An excellent queen, was popular, pious, and a believer in the responsibilities inherent in kingship (or queenship); involved herself in the daily functions of the administration, and presided over a large and intellectual court; also used her own wealth to found hospitals and convents. ❖ See also *Women in World History*.

URRACA OF PORTUGAL (c. 1151–1188). Queen of Leon. Born c. 1151; died Oct 16, 1188; dau. of Matilda of Maurienne (c. 1125–1157) and Alphonso I Henriques, king of Portugal (r. 1139–1185); sister of Sancho I, king of Portugal (r. 1185–1211), Matilda of Portugal (c. 1149–1173), and Teresa of Portugal (1157–1218); became 1st wife of Fernando or Ferdinand II (1137–1188), king of Leon (r. 1157–1188), in 1165 (div. 1175); children: Alfonso or Alphonso IX (1171–1230), king of Leon (r. 1188–1230).

URRUTIA, Maria Isabel (1965—). Colombian weightlifter. Born Mar 25, 1965, in Candelaria, Colombia. ❖ Won World championship (1990, 1994); won a gold medal for 69–75 kg at Sydney Olympics (2000); won South American championship (2000).

URSELMANN, Wiltrud (1942—). West German swimmer. Born May 12, 1942, in Germany. ❖ At Rome Olympics, won a silver medal in 200-meter breaststroke (1960).

URSINS, Marie Anne (c. 1642–1722). *See Marie-Anne de la Trémouille.*

URSINS, Princess of the (c. 1642–1722). *See Marie-Anne de la Trémouille.*

URSINUS, Sophie (1760–1836). German murderer. Born Sophie Charlotte Elizabeth Weingarten in 1760; died April 4, 1836; dau. of an Austrian diplomat; m. Ursinus of Berlin (privy counselor), in 1779 (died Sept 11, 1800). ❖ Had an affair with a Dutch officer named Rogay, which ended with his death (1800); husband died (Sept 11, 1800), then her aunt Christina Regina Witte died mysteriously (Jan 21, 1801); having killed all 3, unsuccessfully tried to kill her servant, Benjamin Klein; sent to prison, lived out her life in grand style, with the fortune inherited from husband and the money gained from death of her murdered aunt. ❖ See also *Women in World History*.

URSO, Camilla (1842–1902). French violinist. Born in Nantes, France, June 13, 1842; died 1902; eldest child of Salvator Urso (organist and flutist from Palermo, Italy) and Emilie Girouard (from Portugal). ❖ One of the great virtuosi of her day, gave 1st concert and was the 1st female allowed to enter the Paris Conservatoire, both at age 7; studied there for 3 years, principally under Massart; went on 3-month tour of Germany and appeared in public concerts in Paris; at 10, gave 1st concert in NY (1852), the 1st woman violinist to appear in concert in US; joined Henriette Sontag's US tour (1853–54); following a series of losses, including the death of Sontag, retired from stage (1856–63); at 21, made comeback at NY Philharmonic, one of the 1st female child prodigies to continue performing as an adult; often played Mendelssohn and Beethoven during a period when they were considered to be "modern" composers; also enjoyed ensemble playing, devoting concerts to string quartets and chamber orchestras; appeared with Paris Conservatoire orchestra (1866), the 1st woman to do so; elected an "honorary member" of all-male Philadelphia Philharmonic Society; was honorary president of Women's String Orchestra, one of the 1st female symphony orchestras. ❖ See also Charles Barnard, *Camilla: A Tale of a Violin* (Loring, 1874); and *Women in World History*.

URSULA (fl. 3rd or 5th c.). British saint and martyr. Birth date unknown; died in either 238, 283, or 451; dau. of a British prince. ❖ The patron saint of maidens, who is especially honored in Cologne, the place of her Christian martyrdom; according to legend, while leading a group of virgins on a pilgrimage to Rome, was massacred along with her charges by the Huns at Cologne; in another version, was fleeing Great Britain and the atrocities of the invading Saxons. The numbered dead is also in wide dispute; some sources assign the total of young girls martyred at 11,000, while others claim as few as 5. Omer Englebert, in his *Lives of the Saints*, suggest that 11 is more probable, and he offers the names Ursula, Pinnosa, Martha, Saula, Brittica, Gregoria, Saturnina, Sabatia, Palladia, Sentia, and Saturia. Feast day is Oct 21.

URSULA (1908–1998). *See Noach, Ilse.*

URSULA OF BRANDENBURG (1488–1510). Duchess of Mecklenburg. Born Oct 17, 1488; died Sept 18, 1510; dau. of Margaret of Saxony (1449–1501) and Joachim I, elector of Brandenburg (r. 1486–1499); m. Henry III, duke of Mecklenburg, on Feb 16, 1507; children: Sophia of Mecklenburg (1508–1541); Magnus of Mecklenburg-Schwerin (b. 1509).

URSULEAC, Viorica (1894–1985). Romanian soprano. Born in Czernowitz, Romania, Mar 26, 1894; died in Ehrwald, Tyrol, Oct 23, 1985; m. Clemens Krauss (conductor). ❖ Trained and lived in Vienna; created the leading soprano roles in several of Richard Strauss' operas, in *Arabella* in Dresden (1933), in *Friedenstag* in Munich (1938), and in *Capriccio* in Munich (1942); all told, gave 506 performances in 12 Strauss roles; mainly a Central European performer, appeared only once at Covent Garden (1934), where she sang in English premieres of *Arabella* and *Svanda the Bagpiper*; had 83 roles in her repertory over a long career; was a notable Tosca and Turandot as well as Senta and Sieglinde. ❖ See also *Women in World History*.

USHAKOVA, Irina (1954—). Soviet fencer. Born Sept 24, 1954, in USSR. ❖ At Moscow Olympics, won a silver medal in team foil (1980).

USOVA, Maia (1964—). Russian ice dancer. Name variations: Maya Usova. Born May 22, 1964, in Gorki, Russia; m. Alexandr Zhulin (skating partner, sep. 1994 but continued to skate together). ❖ With Alexandr Zhulin, won World championship and European championship (1993), a bronze medal at Albertville Olympics (1992) and a silver medal at Lillehammer Olympics (1994); became partners with Evgeny Platov (1998), winning the Professional Ice Dance championship (1998).

USTINOV, Nadia (1896–1975). *See Benois, Nadia.*

USTINOVA, Natalya (1944—). Soviet swimmer. Born Dec 22, 1944, in USSR. ❖ At Tokyo Olympics, won a bronze medal in 4 x 100-meter medley relay (1964).

USTROWSKI, Betina (1976—). German swimmer. Born July 27, 1976. ❖ At Barcelona Olympics, won a silver medal in 4 x 100-meter medley relay (1992).

USTVOLSKAYA, Galina (1919—). Russian composer. Name variations: Galina Ivanovna Ustvolskaya. Born June 17, 1919, in St. Petersburg, Russia; attended Leningrad Arts School, 1937–39), and Leningrad Conservatory, 1939–47; m. Konstantin Makukhin (1966). ❖ Reclusive composer, taught composition classes at Leningrad Conservatory and Rimsky-Korsakov Music School (1948–77); pressured by Soviet state, composed music in Socialist Realist genre, including cantatas, *Stepan Razin's Dream* (1948), *Hail, Youth!* (1950), *Dawn Over the Homeland* (1952) and *Man from the High Mountains* (1952), and symphonic poems, *Young Pioneers* (1950), *Children's Suite* (1955), *The Hero's Exploit* (1957), *Sports* (1958) and *Fire on the Steppes* (1958); purged Socialist Realist works from opus list, preferring to recognize only "pure" spiritual music, which numbers 21 works, including *Song of Praise* for boys' choir, trumpets, percussion, and piano (1964), Duet for violin and piano (1968), *Dona nobis pacem* for piccolo, tuba, and piano (1975), *Benedictus, Qui venit* for 4 flutes, 4 bassoons, and piano (1977); probably best known for symphonic cycle begun in 1955 and continued with Symphonies Two: *True and Eternal Bliss* for orchestra and solo voice (1979), Three: *Jesus Messiah, Save Us!* for orchestra and soloist (1983), Four: *Prayer* (1985–87) and Five: *Amen* (1989–90); had "true" music performed for 1st time outside of Russia at Wiener Festwochen (1986), and later at festival in Heidelberg, Germany (1988) and achieved breakthrough in west with concerts at Holland Festival in Amsterdam (1989) and Festival of Huddersfield (1992).

USTYUZHANINA, Tatyana (1965—). *Soviet rower.* Born May 6, 1965, in USSR. ❖ At Barcelona Olympics, won a bronze medal in quadruple sculls with coxswain (1992).

UTA OF PASSAU (fl. 11th c.). *Duchess of Carinthia.* Dau. of Udalrich, count of Passau; m. Ingelbert II, duke of Carinthia; children: Maud Carinthia (c. 1105–1160).

UTLEY, Freda (1898–1977). *English-American journalist and author.* Born Freda Utley, Jan 23, 1898, in London, England; died in Washington, DC, Jan 21, 1977; dau. of Willie Herbert Utley (journalist) and Emily (Williamson) Utley; King's College, London University, BA, 1923; Westfield College, London University, MA, 1925; doctorate, Russian Academy of Sciences, 1933; common-law marriage with Arcadi Berdichevsky, 1930 (died Mar 30, 1938); children: John (Jon) Basil. ❖ Ardent critic of USSR and People's Republic of China, was a research fellow, London School of Economics (1926–28); worked as special correspondent, *Manchester Guardian Commercial,* in Japan (1928–29); employed in the Soviet Union by the Comintern, the Commissariat of Foreign Trade, the Commissariat of Light Industry, and the Institute of World Economy and Politics (1930–36); common-law husband was carted off in the night (April 10, 1936), sentenced without trial to 5 years hard labor, and never returned (did not learn facts of his death until 1963); ever afterwards, fervently condemned Stalinist and Maoist rule and attacked any Westerners whom she perceived as favoring an accommodation to world communism; was special correspondent, *London News-Chronicle,* China war zone (1938); was an accredited correspondent, *Reader's Digest,* China (1945–46), Germany (1948); writings include *An Illustrated History of the Russian Revolution* (1928), *Japan's Gamble in China* (1938), *The Dream We Lost: Soviet Russia Then and Now* (1940), *Lost Illusion* (1948), *The China Story: How We Lost Four Hundred Million Allies* (1951) and *Will the Middle East Go West?* (1957). ❖ See also *Odyssey of a Liberal: Memoirs* (Washington National Press, 1970); Justus D. Doenecke, *Not to the Swift: The Old Isolationists in the Cold War Era* (Bucknell U. Press, 1979); and *Women in World History.*

UTONDU, Beatrice (1969—). *Nigerian runner.* Born Nov 23, 1969, in Nigeria. ❖ At Barcelona Olympics, won a bronze medal in 4 x 100-meter relay (1992).

UTSUGI, Reika (1963—). *Japanese softball player.* Born June 1, 1963, in China; grew up in China; attended Gumma Women's College. ❖ Infielder, won a team silver medal at Sydney Olympics (2000) and a team bronze at Athens Olympics (2004).

UTTER, Suzanne (1865–1938). *See Valadon, Suzanne.*

UTTLEY, Alison (1884–1976). *English writer.* Name variations: Alice Jane Taylor Uttley. Born Alice Jane Taylor, Dec 17, 1884, in Cromford, Derbyshire, England; died May 7, 1976, in High Wycombe, Buckinghamshire, England; dau. of Henry Taylor (farmer) and Hannah (Dickens) Taylor; Manchester University, BSc, 1906; attended Ladies' Training College (later Hughes Hall), Cambridge, 1907; m. James Arthur Uttley (civil engineer), 1911 (committed suicide, 1930); children: John (1915–1978). ❖ Prolific writer who is primarily known for her "Little Grey Rabbit" series, worked as a physics teacher at Fulham Secondary School in London (1908), where she became interested in socialism and was active in the women's suffrage movement; published 1st work, *The Squirrel, the Hare and the Little Grey Rabbit* (1929), which was written for her son John who had just left for boarding school; after husband committed suicide (1930), took up pen to support herself and son, publishing *The Country Child* and producing over 100 books in the course of the next 4 decades; her "Little Grey Rabbit" series, which grew to include over 30 titles, are tales of anthropomorphic animals, a mode that she used throughout her career (other popular animal characters, Sam Pig, Tim Rabbit, Brock the Badger, and Fuzzypeg the Hedgehog, also inhabited a rural Victorian village similar to the one in which Uttley was raised); also wrote adult books, including *A Traveller in Time* (1939). ❖ See also Denis Judd, *The Life of a Country Child (1884–1976): The Authorized Biography* (M. Joseph, 1986); Elizabeth Saintsbury, *The World of Alison Uttley* (Baker, 1980); and *Women in World History.*

UVAROV, Olga (1910–2001). *Russian-born veterinary surgeon.* Name variations: Olga Nikolaevna Uvarov; Dame Olga Uvarov. Born July 9, 1910, in Russia; died Aug 29, 2001; trained at Royal College of Veterinary Surgeons. ❖ After most of her family perished in the Revolution, was brought to England by an uncle (1917); served as an assistant in general mixed practice (1934–43); owned a small animals practice (1944–53); as a clinical researcher at Glaxo Industries' laboratories (1953–67), created a line of (betamethasone) skin and eye ointments, tablets, injections and eye and ear droplets for animals; was head of the Veterinary Advisory Group in Glaxo (1967–70); served as a president of Veterinary Teachers and Research Workers (1967–68); elected fellow of Royal College of Veterinary Surgeons (1973) and Institute of Biology (1983); was the 1st woman president of the Royal College of Veterinary Surgeons (1976–77). Named Commander of the Order of the British Empire (1978), Dame Commander of the Order of the British Empire (1983); received Central Veterinary Society's Victory Gold Medal (1965).

UWILINGIYIMANA, Agathe (1953–1994). *Rwandan interim prime minister.* Born in 1953 in Nyaruhengeri, Rwanda; assassinated by opposition soldiers on April 7, 1994; earned master's degree in chemistry; married a university employee; children: 5. ❖ Taught science for 10 years at the high-school level; named to a government post as director for small- and medium-sized industries in the Ministry of Commerce of Industry; was a member of the moderate, multiethnic Rwandan Democratic Movement; was also a member of the minority Tutsi tribe that had traditionally ruled the country before the majority Hutus took power in the 1960s; as minister of higher education, was a strong advocate of equal educational opportunity for everyone, regardless of ethnic group, a view that earned her many enemies; was beaten and raped by assailants who broke into her home (April 1993); served as interim prime minister (July 18, 1993–April 1994); when Rwanda exploded into violence, prepared to address the nation, asking for calm after the president's death, but was killed (husband was also murdered in front of their 5 children). ❖ See also *Women in World History.*

UZÈS, Anne, Duchesse d' (1847–1933). *French aristocrat.* Name variations: Anne, duchess of Uzes; (pseudonym) Manuela. Pronunciation: dew-ZEH. Born (Marie-Adrienne) Anne-Victurnienne-Clémentine de Rochechouart-Mortemart, Feb 10, 1847, in Paris; died Feb 3, 1933, at the Château de Dampierre (Seine-et-Oise); dau. of (Anne-Victurnien) Louis-Samuel de Rochechouart, Comte de Mortemart (1809–1873) and Marie-Clémentine Le Riche de Chevigné (1818–1877); m. (Amable-Antoine-Jacques-) Emmanuel de Crussol, 12th Duc d'Uzès (1840–1878), May 11, 1867; children: Jacques, 13th Duc d'Uzès (b. 1868); Simone, Duchesse de Luynes (b. 1870); Louis-Emmanuel, 14th Duc d'Uzès (b. 1871); and Mathilde-Renée, Duchesse de Brissac (b. 1875). ❖ Immensely wealthy French aristocrat who, after failing to restore the monarchy by financing General Boulanger's political schemes, emerged as one of the most original women of her time—a sculptor, renowned hunter, generous supporter of charitable works, and an advocate and exemplar of the liberation of women; married to the Duc d'Uzès (1867–78); maintained the leading hunt in France, the Rallye Bonnelles (1880s–1933); received honorable mention for sculpture at the Paris Salon (1887); involved in financing the political campaigns of General Georges Boulanger in hopes of restoring the monarchy (1888–89); was at the peak of her literary and sculpting activities (1890–1914); joined "L'Avant-Courrière" and began feminist activities (1894); became the 1st Frenchwoman to obtain an automobile driver's license (1898); helped launch *La Française* and the Union Française pour le Suffrage des Femmes (1907–09); ran a hospital and nursed during WWI (1914–18); was the 1st woman made Wolf Lieutenant (1923); founded the Automobile-Club Féminin de France (1926); made vice-president of Groupe Féminin de l'Aéro-Club (1932); writings include *Le Coeur et le sang* (3-act play, 1890), *Pauvre Petite* (novel, 1890), *Julien Masly* (novel, 1891), *L'Arrondissement de Rambouillet* (history, 1893), *Voyage de mon fils au Congo* (history, 1894), *Paillettes grises* (poems, 1909), *La Chasse à courre* (history, 1912) and *Souvenirs de la duchesse d'Uzès née Mortemart* (1934). ❖ See also *Women in World History.*

V

V.

See Vardill, Anna Jane (1781–1852).
See Clive, Caroline (1801–1873).
See Currie, Mary Montgomerie (1843–1905).

VAA, Aslaug (1889–1965). Norwegian poet and dramatist. Born 1889 at Rauland in Telemark, Norway; died Nov 28, 1965, in Oslo; dau. of a farmer; studied in Paris and Berlin, 1909; m. Ola Raknes (philologist and psychoanalyst), 1911 (div. 1938); children: 5. ❖ Published 1st a collection of poems, *Nord i leite* (In the North Horizon), and a play, *Steinguden* (God of Stone, 1934), which brought her to prominence; following divorce (1938), supported 5 children by working as a housekeeper and a translator; wrote 7 poetry collections, 4 plays, and more than 150 articles and essays; writings include *Skuggen og strendan* (1935), *Villarkonn* (1936), *På vegakanten* (1938), *Tjugendagen* (1947), *Fotefar* (Footprints, 1947), *Munkeklokka* (The Monastery Bell, 1950), *Skjenkarsveinens visur* (The Innkeeper's Songs, 1954), *Bustader* (Living Quarters, 1963), *Dikt i utval* (1964), *Honningfuglen og leoparden* (1965) and *Munkeklokka* (1966).

VAANDRAGER, Wiljon (1957–). Dutch rower. Born Aug 27, 1957, in Netherlands. ❖ At Los Angeles Olympics, won a bronze medal in coxed eights (1984).

VACCARO, Brenda (1939–). American stage, tv and screen actress. Born Nov 18, 1939, in Brooklyn, NY; m. Guy Hector; m. William Bishop, 1977. ❖ Made professional stage debut at Margo Jones Theatre in Dallas in *The Willow Tree* (1961); made NY debut in *Everybody Loves Opal* (1961); other plays include *The Affair, The Natural Look* and *Father's Day*; made film debut in *Where It's At* (1969), followed by *Midnight Cowboy, I Love My Wife, Going Home, Summertree, Capricorn One, Airport '77, The House by the Lake* and *Ten Little Indians,* among others; on tv, starred on "Sara" (1976) and guest starred on numerous episodic shows. Nominated for Tony awards for *Cactus Flower* (1966), *How Now Dow Jones* (1968) and *The Goodbye People* (1969); nominated for Oscar as Best Supporting Actress for *Jacqueline Susann's Once Is Not Enough* (1975); won Emmy for "The Shape of Things" (1976).

VACCARONI, Dorina (1963–). Italian fencer. Born Sept 24, 1963, in Italy. ❖ At Los Angeles Olympics, won a bronze medal in indiv. foil (1984); at Seoul Olympics, won a silver medal in team foil (1988); at Barcelona Olympics, won a gold medal in team foil (1992).

VACHELL, Eleanor (1879–1948). Welsh botanist. Born Eleanor Vachell, 1879, in Wales; died Dec 6, 1948; dau. of Dr. C. T. Vachell (botanist, died 1914). ❖ Collected specimens with father; observed all but 13 out of 1,800 species of native British plants; during WWI, cared for National Museum of Wales' herbarium; for a time, was the only female member of National Museum of Wales' court of governors and council; discovered a microspecies (early 1930s), which was named in her honor (*Taraxacum vachellii*); discovered a new hybrid, mudwort (*Limosella*); observed Italian lords-and-ladies (*Arum italicum neglectum*), a rare species, in the Dinas Powis area; left a wildflower collection and funding to National Museum of Wales; wrote a weekly column on wildflowers for *Western Mail* (1921–40s); was 1st female member of Cardiff Naturalists' Society (1903) and served as its 1st woman president (1932–33); elected fellow of Linnean Society (1917) and Wild Flower Society.

VACHETTA, Roseline (1951–). French politician. Born Dec 12, 1951, in Le Mans, France. ❖ Teacher of children with special needs (1973–91); representing the Confederal Group of the European United Left/Nordic Green Left (GUE/NGL), elected to 5th European Parliament (1999–2004).

VADASZNE-VANYA, Maria (1950–). Hungarian handball player. Born Jan 1950 in Hungary. ❖ At Montreal Olympics, won a bronze medal in team competition (1976).

VADKERTI-GAVORNíKOVÁ, Lydia (1932–1999). Slovak poet. Name variations: Lydia Vadkerti-Gavornikova. Born Mar 30, 1932, in Modra; died May 22, 1999, in Bratislava, Czech Republic. ❖ Worked as teacher and magazine editor; works include *Pohromnice* (1966), *Kolovrátok* (1972), *Kameň a džbán* (1973), and *Trvanie* (1979).

VAELBE, Elena (1968–). *See Välbe, Elena.*

VAESSEN, Marie-Louise (1928–1993). *See Linssen-Vaessen, Marie-Louise.*

VAGANOVA, Agrippina (1879–1951). Russian ballet dancer and teacher. Born Agrippina Yakovlevna Vaganova, June 26, 1879 (June 12 according to Julian calendar), in St. Petersburg, Russia; died in Leningrad, Nov 5, 1951; attended Ballet School (1889–97). ❖ Dancer and teacher who was the virtual founder of Soviet ballet, one of the greatest dance traditions of all time; studied under Lev Ivanov, Nicholas Legat, and Ekaterina Vazem, learning much from watching the classes of Enrico Cecchetti and later those of Olga Preobrazhenska; entered Maryinsky Company (1897), performing such roles as Hebe in *The Awakening of Flora* (1900), Chinese Doll in *The Fairy Doll* (1903), Thaw in *The Seasons* (1907), Mazurka in *Chopiniana*, principal dancer in *The Whisper of Flowers* (1910), Naila in *La Source*, title role in *The Pearl* (1911), Odette-Odile in *Swan Lake* (1913), Tsar-Maiden in *The Little Humpbacked Horse* (1915) and title role in *Giselle* (1916); taught at Miklos School, Petrograd (1917), at Volynsky School of Russian Ballet (1920), and at Theater School of Petrograd (1920–22); taught and coached at State Academic Theater of Opera and Ballet (GATOB, later the Kirov Theater and Ballet, 1917–51); served as artistic director of Kirov Ballet (1931–37); taught in the pedagogical departments of Leningrad Ballet school (1934–41) and at Leningrad Conservatory (1946–51); attained near-mythic status as a teacher. Granted title Peoples' Artist of the Russian Soviet Federation (1934) and State Prize of the USSR (1946); Leningrad Choreographic School was renamed the Vaganova School in her honor (1957). ❖ See also *Women in World History.*

VAGUE, Vera (1906–1974). American comedic actress in radio, tv and film. Name variations: Barbara Jo Allen; Barbara "Vera Vague" Allen. Born Barbara Jo Allen, Sept 2, 1906, in New York, NY; died Sept 14, 1974, in Santa Barbara, CA; m. Norman Morell; children: daughter. ❖ Began career in serious drama on Broadway; appeared on Bob Hope radio shows, adopting name Vera Vague; films include *Lake Placid Serenade, Earl Carroll Sketchbook, Kiss the Boys Goodbye, The Mad Doctor, Design for Scandal* and *Melody Ranch.*

VAIL, Myrtle (1888–1978). American actress. Born Jan 7, 1888, in Joliet, Illinois; died Sept 18, 1978, in Kansas City, Missouri; m. George Damerel (actor), 1907 (died 1936); children: Donna Damerel (1908–1941, actress); George. ❖ Screen, vaudeville, and radio actress, had an act with husband as "Damerel & Vail & Co.," which became "The Three of Us" when daughter joined them on stage; co-starred with daughter on the long-running radio show "Myrt and Marge" (1931–42), the most popular dramatic program on radio; had bit parts in films *Bucket of Blood* (1959) and *Little Shop of Horrors* (1960). ❖ See also *Women in World History.*

VAILLANDE-DOUVILLIER, Suzanne (1778–1826). *See Douvillier, Suzanne.*

VAKALO, Eleni (1921–). Greek poet and art critic. Born in 1921 in Athens, Greece; attended university in Athens and the Sorbonne, Paris; m. George Vakalo (stage designer), 1944 (died 1991). ❖ With husband, founded the School of Fine Arts in Athens (1958), and taught there for several years; in addition to being a poet, was one of the most well-known art critics in Greece and wrote extensively on the topic; works include numerous reviews and articles, as well as the verse collections *Themes and Variations* (1945) and *Recollections from a Nightmarish City* (1948); also wrote *The Forest* (1954), *Description of the Body* (1959), *How to Endanger Ourselves* (1966), *The Palavers of Ma'am Rodalina* (1984), and *Epilegomena* (1997); translated work of Marianne Moore into Greek.

VALA, Katri (1901–1944). *See Heikel, Karin Alice.*

VALADON, Suzanne (1865–1938). French artist and model. Name variations: Maria; Suzanne Utter. Pronunciation: Va-la-DAWN. Born Marie-Clémentine Valadon, Sept 23, 1865, at Bessines-sur-Gartempe, France; died April 7, 1938, in Paris; dau. of Madeleine Valadon (unmarried seamstress) and unknown father; m. Paul Mousis (Parisian businessman), 1896 (div. c. 1909); m. André Utter (painter), 1914; children: (possibly with Miguel Utrillo y Molins, a Spanish artist) illeg. son, Maurice Utrillo (b. 1883, the artist). ❖ Artist's model who rose from an impoverished background to become a notable figure on the French art scene of early 20th century; with mother, settled in Montmartre (1866); began work as an artist's model (c. 1881), posing for some of the most brilliant painters of the era, including Henri Toulouse-Lautrec and Auguste Renoir; completed 1st known works (1884); gave birth to son Maurice (Dec 1883); showed samples of her work to Degas (c. 1887); son Maurice was formally adopted by Miguel Utrillo (1891); completed 1st paintings (1892); distinguished by her lack of formal training, drew on her native talent, as well as her experiences as a model; produced still lifes, landscapes, and realistic views of women; had love affair with Erik Satie (1893); had initial exhibition of her work at Salon de la Nationale (1894); married (1896); son committed for the 1st time to an insane asylum (1901); started affair with André Utter and began to confine her work to painting (1909); had one-woman exhibition at Weill gallery in Paris (1915); had 1st joint exhibition with Utter and Utrillo (1917); signed lucrative contract with art dealer Bernheim (1924); though she lived in an era in which European painting was dominated by such movements as Cubism, went her own way and never became closely linked with them, though she may have been somewhat influenced by later trends, such as Post-Impressionism and Fauvism; work was characterized by its energy, realism verging on brutality, and rich color; major works include *Adam and Eve* (1909), *Joy of Living* (1911), *The Fortuneteller* (1912), *Casting of the Net* (1914), *The Blue Room* (1923), and *The Church of St. Bernard* (1929). ❖ See also John Storm, *The Valadon Drama: The Life of Suzanne Valadon* (Dutton, 1959); Jeanine Warnod, *Suzanne Valadon* (Crown, 1981); Sarah Baylis, *Utrillo's Mother* (Rutgers U. Press, 1986); June Rose, *Suzanne Valadon: The Mistress of Montmartre* (St. Martin, 1999); and *Women in World History*.

VALAIDA (c. 1903–1956). *See Snow, Valaida.*

VALASCA (fl. 738). Military leader of Bohemia. Name variations: Dlasta. Flourished around 738 in Bohemia. ❖ A bold military leader, began career as a soldier in the army of Queen Libussa; made a general, became one of Libussa's most trusted aides; led a coup d'etat against her queen, taking the throne for herself (c. 738); was an aggressive queen and ruled a highly centralized government until her death. ❖ See also *Women in World History*.

VÄLBE, Elena (1968—). Russian cross-country skier. Name variations: Yelena Valbe or Vaelbe; Yelena Walbe. Born Elena Trubitsina, April 24, 1968, in Magadan, Siberia; m. Urmas Välbe (Estonian skier), 1987 (div.); children: Franz (b. 1987). ❖ Won 7 World championships; won 5 World Cups for overall cross-country; won a gold medal for the 4 x 5 km relay and bronze medals for 5 km, 10 km pursuit, 30 km, and 15 km at Albertville Olympics (1991); won gold medals at Lillehammer Olympics (1994) and Nagano Olympics (1998), for 4 x 5 km relay.

VALDES, Carmen (1954—). Cuban runner. Born Nov 23, 1954, in Cuba. ❖ At Munich Olympics, won a bronze medal in 4 x 100-meter relay (1972).

VALDEZ, Kristen (c. 1965—). *See Lignell, Kristen.*

VALDINE, Blanche (c. 1862–1948). *See D'Alessandri-Valdine, Blanche.*

VALEGRA, Dorothy (1904–1993). *See Revier, Dorothy.*

VALENCIA, duchess of. *See Telles, Maria (d. 1379).*

VALENCIANO MARTÍNEZ-OROZCO, María Elena (1960—). Spanish politician. Born Sept 18, 1960, in Madrid, Spain. ❖ Served as vice-president of the Foundation "Mujeres" and vice-chair of the Women's Association of Southern Europe; as a European Socialist, elected to 5th European Parliament (1999–2004).

VALENTÍ, Helena (1940—). Spanish novelist. Name variations: Helena Valenti. Born 1940 in Barcelona, Spain; received doctorate from Cambridge University. ❖ Works include *L'amor adult* (1977), *La solitud d'Anna* (1981), and *La dona errant* (1986).

VALENTINA (1899–1989). Russian-born fashion designer. Name variations: Valentina Schlee. Born Valentina Nicholaevna Sanina, April 18, 1899, in Russia; died Sept 14, 1989, in New York, NY; m. George Schlee (died 1964). ❖ Was one of America's most glamorous dressmakers for the theater as well as private clients, including Katharine Hepburn, Gloria Swanson, Irene Selznick, Gertrude Lawrence, Greta Garbo and Lynn Fontaine; was a great friend of Garbo, until Garbo commandeered her husband; closed her couture house (1957).

VALENTINE, Grace (1884–1964). American actress. Born Feb 14, 1884, in Springfield, OH; died Nov 14, 1964, in New York, NY. ❖ Made Broadway debut in *Yosemite* (1914); appeared in numerous plays, including *Johnny Get Your Gun, Lombardi Ltd., The Fabulous Invalid, George Washington Slept Here* and *Anna Christie*; appeared in films (1915–16, 1929–34); worked in tv and radio.

VALENTINE, Lila (1865–1921). American educational reformer and suffragist. Born Lila Hardaway Meade, Feb 4, 1865, in Richmond, Virginia; died July 14, 1921, in Richmond; dau. of Richard Hardaway Meade (founder of wholesale drug firm) and Kate (Fontaine) Meade; m. Benjamin Batchelder Valentine (banker), Oct 28, 1886 (died 1919); children: 1 (stillborn). ❖ With others, founded the Richmond Education Association (1900), dedicated to the improvement of public schools, and served as president until 1904; as president of the Richmond Training School for Kindergartners, helped introduce kindergartens and vocational training into Richmond's schools and obtained a city grant for a new high school; also supported education for African-Americans; appointed to executive committee of Co-operative Educational Association of Virginia, a citizens' organization devoted to raising the standards of schools in the state; also founded Instructive Visiting Nurse Association of Richmond and organized Anti-Tuberculosis Auxiliary, which led the 1st major campaign against tuberculosis in Virginia; served as president of Equal Suffrage League of Virginia for 11 years. ❖ See also *Women in World History*.

VALENTINE, Winifred Annie (1886–1968). New Zealand teacher and education reformer. Born on May 5, 1886, at Hawksbury, Otago, New Zealand; died Aug 6, 1968, in Wellington, New Zealand; dau. of Archibald Valentine (road inspector) and Mary (Maxwell) Valentine. ❖ Trained in New York and London to administer intelligence quotient tests (early 1920s); worked with New Zealand Department of Education to investigate children in special education classes (1923); changed focus of special education to one that segregated, educated, and then placed children who could be helped in suitable environment; produced 1st instructional manual for special-class teachers (1926); was supervisor of special classes (1929–42), and continued to fight for rights to education for children with special needs. ❖ See also *Dictionary of New Zealand Biography* (Vol. 4).

VALENTINE OF MILAN (1366–1408). *See Visconti, Valentina.*

VALENTINO, Jean Acker (1893–1978). *See Acker, Jean.*

VALENTINO, Natacha (1897–1966). *See Rambova, Natacha.*

VALENTINO, Mrs. Rudolph (1897–1966). *See Rambova, Natacha.*

VALENTINOIS, duchess of. *See Diane de Poitiers (1499–1566).*

VALENZUELA, Luisa (1938—). Argentinean novelist and short-story writer. Born Nov 26, 1938, in Buenos Aires, Argentina; dau. of Pablo Francisco Valenzuela and Luisa Mercedes Levinson; m. Theodore Marjak, 1958 (div. 1963). ❖ Worked as journalist in Buenos Aires from age of 17; won Fulbright scholarship and Guggenheim fellowship and studied in US; left Argentina after death of Peron and worked as writer-in-residence at Columbia and New York universities and as director of New York Institute for the Humanities; returned to Argentina (1989); works, which have been widely published and translated, often focus on political and feminist themes, include *Hay que sonreir* (1966), *El gato eficaz* (1972), *Aqui pasan cosas raras* (1975; trans. as *Here Strange Things Happen: Twenty Six Short Stories and a Novel,* 1979), *Como en la guerra* (1977), *Donde viven las águilas* (1983), *Cola de lagartija* (1983), *Black Novel (With Argentines)* (1992), and *La travesia* (2001).

VALERIA, Empress (c. 23–48 CE). *See Messalina, Valeria.*

VALERIA MESSALINA (c. 23–48 CE). *See Messalina, Valeria.*

VALERIE, Joan (1911–1983). American actress. Name variations: Helen Valkis. Born July 15, 1911, in Rhinelander, WI; died Jan 30, 1983, in Long Beach, CA; children: daughter. ❖ Made more than 40 films, including *A Trip to Paris, Submarine Patrol, Daytime Wife, Lillian Russell, The Great Profile* and *Rio Rita.*

VALÉRY, Violetta (1824–1847). *See Plessis, Alphonsine.*

VALESKA, Countess (1786–1817). *See Walewska, Marie.*

VALETTE, Aline (1850–1899). French activist. Pronunciation: va-LET. Born Alphonsine Goudeman in Lille (Nord), Oct 4, 1850; died of TB at Arcachon (Gironde), Mar 21, 1899; dau. of a railway worker and grand-dau. of a college dean; educated to be a teacher; married to a lawyer, separated, and widowed; children: 2 sons. ❖ Organizer, writer, and speaker who was a leading figure in the formative years of French socialist movement; elected secretary of newly founded teacher's union (1878); joined French Workers' Party (1879); published a widely circulated home economics text, *La Journée de la petite ménagère* (The Little Housewife's Day, 1883); became a substitute inspector of child labor (1887); named secretary of National Federation of Feminist Societies, and founded and directed *L'Harmonie sociale* (1892); was the 1st woman to sit on National Council of the French Workers' Party (POF) and published *Socialism and Sexualism* (1893); elected permanent secretary of French Workers' Party (1896); contributed articles on women's labor to *La Fronde* (1897–98); with Louise Michel, Paule Mink and Eugénie Potonié-Pierre, was one of the most prominent women socialists in France in late 19th century. ❖ See also *Women in World History.*

VALETTE RACHILDE, Mme Alfred (1860–1953). *See Vallette, Marguerite.*

VALEYEVA, Natalya (1969—). Soviet archer. Born Nov 16, 1969, in USSR. ❖ At Barcelona Olympics, won bronze medals in team round and double FITA round (1992).

VALKIS, Helen (1911–1983). *See Valerie, Joan.*

VALLA, Trebisonda (1916—). Italian hurdler. Name variations: Ondina Valla. Born May 20, 1916, in Bologna, Italy. ❖ At Berlin Olympics, won a gold medal in the 80-meter hurdles (1936), the 1st Italian woman to win an Olympic gold medal.

VALLANCE, Agnes (1859–1943). *See Bock, Amy Maud.*

VALLAYER-COSTER, Anne (1744–1818). French artist. Name variations: Anna Vallayer-Coster. Born Anne Vallayer in France in 1744; died 1818; dau. of a goldsmith; m. Jean Pierre Coster (lawyer), 1781. ❖ Still-life painter, the 1st woman to become a member of France's Royal Academy, executed 1st known painting (1762); submitted *Allegory of the Visual Arts* and *Allegory of Music* (now in Louvre, Paris) to Académie Royale and was unanimously elected a member (1770); greatly admired in her day, was both versatile and resourceful and had many influential patrons; was responsible for some 450 works which are attributed to her, including portraits of flower arrangements, table settings, musical instruments, tureens of soup, bread, wine, lobsters, and plums in a basket—all in simple or elaborate configurations. ❖ See also *Women in World History.*

VALLE, Inger-Louise (1921—). Norwegian politician. Name variations: Inger Valle. Born 1921 in Oslo, Norway. ❖ Studied law and became head of legal and economic section of Consumer Council (1958–71); was member of Labor Party and elected to Baerum Municipal Council (1967–71); became Minister of Family and Consumer Affairs (1971) and later appointed to Ministry of Justice (1973, 1976, 1979) and Ministry of Local Government and Labor (1979).

VALLE SILVA, Luisa del (1896–1962). Venezuelan poet. Born 1902 in Spain; died 1962; lived in Venezuela. ❖ Combined classicism with modern forms; works include *Ventanas de ensueño* (1930), *Amo* (1941), *Humo* (1941), *En silencio* (1961), *Poesía* (1962), *Sin tiempo y sin espacio* (1963) and *Amanecer* (1968).

VALLETTE, Marguerite (1860–1953). French novelist and literary critic. Name variations: Mme Alfred Vallette or Valette; Mme Alfred Valette Rachilde; Marguerite Eymery; (pseudonym) Rachilde (pronounced RAH-sheeld). Born Marguerite Eymery, Feb 11, 1860, near Périgueux in southwest France; died 1953; only child of a career army officer and a mother whose father was a newspaper editor; m. Alfred Vallette (co-founder and editor of *Mercure de France*). ❖ Wrote erotic novels under pseudonym Rachilde; with husband, founded *Le Mercure de France*, one of the best-known literary review journals of the Symbolists;

writings include *Monsieur Vénus* (1884, which was banned in Belgium), *Nono* (1885), *Mme Adonis* (1888), *Les Hors Nature* (Nature's Outcasts, 1897), *L'Heure sexuelle* (The Sexual Hour, 1898), *La Tour d'Amour* (The Tower of Love, 1899), *La Jongleuse* (The Juggler, 1900), *La Souris japonaise* (The Japanese Mouse, 1912), *La Tour d'Amour* (1914), *La Maison Vierge* (1920), *Refaire l'Amour* (1928), and *L'Homme au Bras de Feu* (1931). ❖ See also autobiography, *Pourquoi je ne suis pas féministe* (Why I Am Not a Feminist, 1928), and memoirs, *Quand j'étais jeune* (When I Was Young, 1948); and *Women in World History.*

VALLI, Alida (1921–2006). Italian actress. Name variations: sometimes acted under name Valli. Born Alida Maria Laura von Altenburger, May 31, 1921, in Pola, Istria, Italy (now Pula, Croatia), to an Austrian journalist father and an Italian mother (killed 1945); died May 31, 2006, in Rome, Italy; briefly studied at Rome's Centro Sperimentale di Cinematografia; m. Oscar de Mejo (pianist-composer), in 1944 (sep.). ❖ Made film debut in *T'ameròsempre* (1933); her haunting beauty and natural charm soon made her a star, one of Italy's highest paid young actresses; during WWII, refused to continue working for the Fascist film industry and was forced into hiding; after war, appeared in popular American films, *The Miracle of the Bells* (1948), *The Paradine Case* (1948), and *The Third Man* (1949), for which she won international acclaim; career suffered a brief setback (1953), when she served as an alibi for a politician implicated in the unsolved murder of Wilma Montesi; other films include *Eugenia Grandet* (1946), *The White Tower* (1950), *Walk Softly Stranger* (1950), *Ultimo Incontro* (1951), *Siamo Donne* (1953), *Les Bijoutiers du Clair de Lune* (The Night Heaven Fell, 1958), *Les Yeux sans Visage* (The Horror Chamber of Dr. Faustus, 1960), *Les Dialogue des Carmélites* (1960), *El Vale de Las Spades* (The Castilian, 1963), *Edipo Re* (Oedipus Rex, 1967), *1900* (1976), *The Cassandra Crossing* (1977), *Suspiria* (1977), *La Luna* (1979), *Inferno* (1979), *Aspern* (1982), *Segreti Segreti* (1984), *Hitchcock* (1985), *A Month By the Lake* (1994), *Il dolce rumore della vita* (1999) and *La Grande strada azzura* (2001). ❖ See also *Women in World History.*

VALLI, Valli (1882–1927). German actress. Born née Knust, Feb 11, 1882, in Berlin, Germany; died Nov 4, 1927, in Hampstead, England; sister of Lulu and Ida Valli; educated in London; m. Louis Dreyfuss. ❖ Made stage debut in London in *Gentle Ivy* (1894), then appeared in Berlin in *Morocco Bound* to great success (1895); other plays include *Olivia, The Physician, Alice in Wonderland, School, The Power and the Glory, Quo Vadis?, Véronique, A Waltz Dream, The Merry Widow, Kitty Grey, Hullo London!* and *The Purple Road*; often appeared in America; also appeared in music halls and vaudeville; films include *The High Road* and *Her Debt of Honor.*

VALLI, Virginia (1895–1968). American silent-film actress. Born Virginia McSweeney, 1895, in Chicago, IL; died Sept 24, 1968, in Palm Springs, CA; m. Charles Farrell (actor), 1932. ❖ Universal contract star, came to prominence in *The Storm* (1922); other films include *Escape, A Lady of Quality, His Father's Wife, The Black Circle, Sentimental Tommy, The Shock,* and a starring role in Alfred Hitchcock's 1st feature, *The Pleasure Garden* (1925); retired (1930s).

VALLIER, Hélène (1932–1988). French actress. Name variations: Helene Vallier. Born Militza de Poliakoff-Baidaroff (also seen as Baidarov), Feb 2, 1932, in Paris, France; died Aug 1, 1988, in Marseille, France; sister of Odile Versois, Marina Vlady, and Olga Poliakoff (all actresses). ❖ Made film debut in *Penne nere* (1952), followed by *Saadia, Sophie et le crime, Le dialogue des Carmélites, La maison des Bories, Le Sauveur, Beau masque, Toute une vie, Love and Death, Le Portrait de Dorian Gray* and *L'Adolescente,* among others; on tv, appeared as Raissa Klarsfeld in "Nazi Hunter: The Beate Klarsfeld Story" (1986).

VALLIN, Ninon (1886–1961). French soprano. Name variations: Nina Vallin. Born Sept 8, 1886, in Montalieu-Vercieu, France; died Nov 22, 1961, in Lyons; studied at Lyons Conservatory. ❖ Known especially for recordings of 20th-century composers, debuted in premiere of Debussy's *Le martyre de Saint Sébastien* (1911); sang with Opéra-Comique (1912–16); debuted at Teatro Colón in Buenos Aires (1916), Paris Opéra (1920); sang with Teatro Colón (1916–36); specialized in the work of Massenet, Charpentier, Hahn, Nin, de Falla, Respighi and Fauré. ❖ See also *Women in World History.*

VALLOT, Ingrid (1961-). *See Berghmans, Ingrid.*

VALMAI, Gwenyth (b. 1907). *See Meredith, Gwen.*

VALMORE, Marceline (1785–1859). *See Desbordes-Valmore, Marceline.*

VALOIS, countess of.
See Margaret of Anjou (c. 1272–1299).
See Jeanne of Burgundy (1293–1348).
See Catherine de Courtenay (d. 1307).
See Mahaut de Chatillon (d. 1358).

VALOIS, duchess of. See Margaret of Valois (1553–1615).

VALOIS, Ninette de (1898–2001). See de Valois, Ninette.

VALOVA, Elena (1963—). Russian pairs skater. Name variations: Yelena Valova. Born Jan 4, 1963, in St. Petersburg, Russia; m. German Galusha, 1994. ❖ Skated with partner Oleg Vassiliev for 20 years, winning 3 World titles (1983, 1985, 1988), a gold medal at Sarajevo Olympics (1984), and a silver medal at Calgary Olympics (1988); retired to coach (1994).

VALPY, Catherine Henrietta Elliot (1829–1919). See Fulton, Catherine Henrietta Elliot.

VALPY, Ellen (1827–1904). See Jeffreys, Ellen Penelope.

VAN ALMSICK, Franziska (1978—). German swimmer. Name variations: Franzi van Almsick. Born April 5, 1978, in Berlin, Germany. ❖ At Barcelona Olympics, won bronze medals in 100-meter freestyle and 4 x 100-meter freestyle relay and silver medals in 200-meter freestyle and 4 x 100-meter medley relay (1992); at European championships, placed 1st in 50-meter freestyle (1993), 100-meter freestyle (1993, 1995, 2002), 200-meter freestyle (1993, 2002) and 400-meter freestyle (1995); at LC World championships, won a gold medal for 200-meter freestyle (1994); at Atlanta Olympics, won a silver medal for 200-meter freestyle and 800-meter freestyle relay and a bronze medal for 4 x 100-meter freestyle relay (1996); won a bronze medal for 800-meter freestyle relay at Sydney Olympics (2000); won bronze medals for 4 x 100-meter medley relay and 4 x 200-meter freestyle relay at Athens Olympics (2004).

VAN ALSTYNE, Frances (1820–1915). See Crosby, Fanny.

VAN BAALEN, Coby (1957—). Dutch equestrian. Born April 6, 1957, in the Netherlands. ❖ Won a team silver medal at Sydney Olympics (2000), on Ferro.

VAN BLARCOM, Carolyn (1879–1960). American nurse and midwife. Born Carolyn Conant Van Blarcom, June 12, 1879, in Alton, Illinois; died Mar 20, 1960, in Arcadia, California; dau. of William Dixon Van Blarcom (financier) and Fanny (Conant) Van Blarcom (linguist and pianist); graduate of Johns Hopkins Hospital Training School for Nurses, 1901. ❖ Was an instructor of obstetrics and assistant superintendent of nurses, Johns Hopkins Hospital Training School (1901–05); served as director of sanitariums in Maryland and Massachusetts; served as secretary, New York Committee for the Prevention of Blindness (beginning 1909); became America's 1st licensed midwife (1913); helped establish a school for midwives (1914); published textbooks and popular health books. ❖ See also Women in World History.

VAN BREMPT, Kathleen (1969—). Belgian sociologist and politician. Born Nov 18, 1969, in Wilrijk, Belgium. ❖ Sociologist; served as political secretary, Socialist Party (1997–99) and deputy head of the office of Renaat Landuyt, Flemish minister for Employment and Tourism (1999); as a European Socialist, elected to 5th European Parliament (1999–2004).

VANBRUGH, Irene (1872–1949). English actress. Name variations: Irene Boucicault; Dame Irene Vanbrugh. Born Irene Barnes, Dec 2, 1872, in Exeter, England; died Nov 30, 1949; dau. of Reginald H. Barnes (vicar of Heavitree and prebendary of Exeter Cathedral) and Frances M. E. (Nation) Barnes; sister of Violet Vanbrugh (1867–1942) and Kenneth and Angela Barnes; studied acting with Sarah Thorne and John Toole; m. Dion Boucicault the Younger (1859–1929, actor), 1901 (died 1929). ❖ Made professional debut as Phoebe in As You Like It at Sarah Thorne's Theatre Royal in Margate (1888), where sister Violet was a star performer; made London debut at the Olympic, playing the White Queen in Alice in Wonderland (1888); traveled to Australasia with John Toole's company (1890), and returned to Toole's Theatre in London, where she played small parts for next 2 years; opened at Haymarket as Lettice in The Tempter (1893); appeared with George Alexander's company at St. James's Theatre (1894), where she created role of Gwendolyn Fairfax in The Importance of Being Earnest; made NY debut as Dulcie in The Chili Widow (1896); returned to London (1897), and for next several years moved from company to company and created role of Sophie Fullgarney in Pinero's The Gay Lord Quex; with husband, was associated

with Charles Frohman at Duke of York's Theatre for 13 years, earning critical acclaim and leading roles and originating the part of Lady Mary Lasenby in The Admirable Crichton; after husband became manager of the New Theatre (1916), played major roles in several productions and spent some time working on an all-star film of Masks and Faces; film credits include Escape Me Never, Knight Without Armour, Wings of the Morning and I Lived in Grosvenor Square. Created a Dame Commander of the British Empire (1941). ❖ See also Women in World History.

VANBRUGH, Prudence (1902—). English actress. Born Prudence Bourchier, Mar 1, 1902, in London, England; dau. of Arthur Bourchier (actor and theater manager) and Violet Vanbrugh (actress); m. James Blomfield Dixon. ❖ Made stage debut in London as Curley in Peter Pan (1912) and grown-up debut as Mrs. Darling in Peter Pan (1922); appeared at Stratford as Lady Anne in Richard III, Hippolita in A Midsummer Night's Dream, and Hecate in Macbeth (1922–23); other plays include The Prisoner of Zenda, The Flame, The Letter of the Law, Captain Banner, The Three Sisters, Wooden Shoes and Little Lord Fauntleroy; often toured with mother.

VANBRUGH, Violet (1867–1942). English actress. Name variations: Dame Violet Vanbrugh. Born Violet Augusta Mary Barnes, June 11, 1867, in Exeter, England; died Nov 10, 1942; dau. of Reginald H. Barnes (vicar of Heavitree and prebendary of Exeter Cathedral) and Frances M. E. (Nation) Barnes; sister of Irene Vanbrugh (1872–1949) and Kenneth and Angela Barnes; studied acting with Sarah Thorne; m. Arthur Bourchier (actor and theater manager), 1894 (div. 1917); children: Prudence Vanbrugh (b. 1902, actress). ❖ Known as "Britain's greatest Shakespearean actress" during her lifetime, played almost every important female part in the Bard's works; appeared with Sarah Thorne's repertory company (1886–88), during which time she became a star player; then toured US with W. H. Kendal and Dame Madge Kendal (1889–91), and played Anne Boleyn in Henry Irving's production of Henry VIII (1892); with husband, took over management of Royalty Theatre in London (1895); most notable roles include Queen Katherine in Henry VIII (1910) and Mistress Ford in The Merry Wives of Windsor (1911); also appeared in a few films, including Pygmalion. Created a Dame Commander of the British Empire (1942). ❖ See also Women in World History.

VAN BRUGGEN, Carry (1881–1932). See Bruggen, Carry van.

VAN BUREN, Abigail (b. 1918). See Friedman, Pauline Esther.

VAN BUREN, Mrs. Abraham (1816–1878). See Van Buren, Angelica.

VAN BUREN, Adeline (1894–1949). American motorcyclist. Born 1894 in Brooklyn, NY; died 1949; sister of Augusta Van Buren (motorcyclist). ❖ With sister Augusta, became 1st woman to cross continental US on solo motorcycles (1916) and 1st to climb Pike's Peak (CO); departed from Sheepshead Bay racetrack (Brooklyn, NY) and arrived 60 days later in San Francisco (their trip was meant to show US government that women could serve as dispatch riders if US entered WWI); inducted into AAA Motorcycle Hall of Fame (2002). With sister, was once arrested for wearing trousers in public.

VAN BUREN, Angelica (1816–1878). American first daughter-in-law. Name variations: Mrs. Abraham Van Buren; Angelica Singleton. Born Angelica Singleton in 1816; died 1878; cousin of Dolley Madison (1768–1849); m. Abraham Van Buren (son of Martin Van Buren, 8th president of US, and Hannah Hoes Van Buren), in 1838. ❖ While husband served as his father's secretary, was a gracious White House host during Van Buren administration (1837–41); portrait, painted by Henry Inman (1842), still hangs there. ❖ See also Women in World History.

VAN BUREN, Augusta. American motorcyclist. Born in Brooklyn, NY; sister of Adeline Van Buren (motorcyclist). ❖ With sister Adeline, became 1st woman to cross continental US on solo motorcycles (1916) and 1st to climb Pike's Peak (CO); departed from Sheepshead Bay racetrack and arrived 60 days later in San Francisco; inducted into AAA Motorcycle Hall of Fame (2002).

VAN BUREN, Hannah Hoes (1783–1819). American wife of Martin Van Buren. Born Mar 8, 1783, in Kinderhook, New York; died Feb 5, 1819, in Albany, New York; dau. of John Dircksen Hoes and Maria (Quackenboss) Hoes; m. Martin Van Buren (8th president of US), Feb 21, 1807; children: 5; four boys lived to adulthood, including the eldest Abraham. ❖ Devoted countless hours to church work, aiding the poor and needy; fell ill with tuberculosis soon after the birth of her 5th child

(1817); died just before 36th birthday. ❖ See also *Women in World History*.

VAN BUREN, Mabel (1878–1947). American screen actress. Born July 17, 1878, in Chicago, IL; died Nov 4, 1947, in Hollywood, CA; m. James Gordon; m. Ernest Joy. ❖ Following a stage career, made film debut (1914); starred in *The Girl in the Golden West*; retired (1941).

VAN BUREN, Mrs. Martin (1783–1819). See Van Buren, Hannah Hoes.

VANCASPEL, Venita (1922—). American financial planner. Name variations: Venita Walker VanCaspel; Venita W. VanCaspel Harris. Born Venita Walker, Oct 3, 1922, in Sweetwater, OK; dau. of Leonard Rankin Walker and Ella Belle Walker; attended Duke University, 1944–46; University of Colorado, BA, 1948; attended New York Institute of Finance, 1962; m. 2nd or 3rd husband, Lyttleton T. Harris IV, 1987. ❖ Became president and founder of stock brokerage firm VanCaspel & Co, Inc., and 1st woman member of Pacific Stock Exchange (1968); established affiliate companies VanCaspel Wealth Management, Inc., and VanCaspel Planning Service; became senior vice president of investments at Raymond James & Associates; served as moderator on national PBS tv shows, including "The Money Makers" and "Profiles of Success." Author of best-selling books on financial planning, including *Money Dynamics for the 1990s*.

VANCE, Clara (1826–1911). See Denison, Mary Andrews.

VANCE, Danitra (1954–1994). African-American comedic actress and performance artist. Born July 13, 1954, in Chicago, IL; died Aug 21, 1994, in Markham, IL. ❖ Appeared off-Broadway in *Danitra Vance and the Mel-O-White Boys*, *Colored Museum* and *Marisol*, and in the performance piece *The Radical Girl's Guide to Radical Mastectomy*; films include *Sticky Fingers*, *The War of the Roses*, *Hangin' with the Homeboys*, *Little Man Tate* and *Jumpin' at the Boneyard*; was the 1st female African-American cast member on tv's "Saturday Night Live" but became so frustrated for being typecast as a maid or hooker that she quit after 1 season (1985–86). Won Obie Award for *Spunk* (1991).

VANCE, Ethel (1896–1991). See Stone, Grace Zaring.

VANCE, Nina (1914–1980). American theatrical producer and director. Born Nina Eloise Whittington, Oct 22, 1914, in Yoakum, Texas; died in Houston, Texas, Feb 18, 1980; only dau. of Calvin Perry Whittington (cotton broker) and Minerva (DeWitt) Whittington; Texas Christian University in Fort Worth, BA in public speaking, 1935; postgraduate work at University of Southern California in Los Angeles, 1935, American Academy of Dramatic Art, and Columbia University, 1936; m. Milton Vance (lawyer), Aug 30, 1941 (div. 1960); no children. ❖ Director and producer who founded the Alley Theater in Houston, helping to spawn the nationwide movement that revolutionized theater and cultural life in America; was founder and artistic director of Houston Jewish Community Center's Players Guild (1945–47); was founder and artistic director of Alley Theater (1947–80); was active in Theater Communications Group (TCG), 1st as a member of its advisory board and later on its executive committee (1961–71); invited by President John F. Kennedy to serve on advisory committee for proposed National Center for the Performing Arts (1961); appointed to US Advisory Commission on International Education and Cultural Affairs (1963); produced US premiere of Mikhail Roschin's *Echelon*, directed by Galina Volchek of Moscow's Sovremenik Theater, the 1st collaboration between a US and Soviet theater (1978); directed over 125 plays during course of career, including the highly acclaimed Eugene O'Neill's *Desire under the Elms* (1949) and *The Iceman Cometh* (1959), and Edward Albee's *Tiny Alice* (1976); world premieres include Ronald Alexander's *Season with Ginger* (1950), James Lee's *Career* (1956), Paul Zindel's *The Effect of Gamma Rays on Man-in-the-Moon Marigolds* (1965), and Shirley Lauro's *The Contest* (1975). Recognized by American Theater Association as a pioneer in the field of resident professional theater (1975). ❖ See also N.J. Stanley, "Nina Vance: Founder and Artistic Director of Houston's Alley Theatre, 1947–1980" (PhD diss., Indiana University, 1990); and *Women in World History*.

VANCE, Norma (1927–1956). American ballet dancer. Name variations: Norma Kaplan. Born May 1927 in New York, NY; died in plane crash, April 15, 1956. ❖ Trained with Mikhail Mordkin and Maria Yurievna-Swoboda during adolescence; danced with Ballet Theater (1946–52), where she created a role in William Dollar's *Jeux* (1950), among others; danced in Antony Tudor repertory to great acclaim, among them *Gala Performance* and *Pillar of Fire*.

VANCE, Vivian (1909–1979). American actress. Born Vivian Roberta Jones in Cherryvale, Kansas, July 26, 1909; died Aug 17, 1979, in Belvedere, California; dau. of Robert A. and Mae (Ragan) Jones; grew up outside of Albuquerque, New Mexico; m. Philip Ober (actor), 1941 (div. 1959); m. John Dodds (literary agent and publishing executive), 1961. ❖ Played Ethel Mertz on tv series "I Love Lucy" (1951–59); featured on Broadway in *Hooray for What* (1937) and *Let's Face It* (1941); films include *The Secret Fury* (1950), *The Blue Veil* (1951) and *The Great Race* (1965); was chair of the Connecticut Mental Health Association. Won Emmy (1953) and Genii Award (1964). ❖ See also Frank Castelluccio and Alvin Walker. *The Other Side of Ethel Mertz: The Life Story of Vivian Vance* (1998); and *Women in World History*.

VAN CHU-LIN (1893/94?–1946). New Zealand shopkeeper. Name variations: Mary Chun. Born probably in 1893 or 1894, in Zengcheng province, China; died Nov 12, 1946, in Wellington, New Zealand; dau. of Van Poy Wah (oil vendor) and Ah Day; m. Chun Yee Hop (shopkeeper), 1915; children: 11 daughters, 7 sons. ❖ Promised to husband as his secondary wife, arrived in New Zealand (1915); lost court case over Immigration Restriction Act of 1908 based on improper naturalization papers procured by husband; marginalized socially, her life was severely circumscribed by numerous pregnancies, family duties, and heavy jobs in husband's shop; used name Mary Chun after arriving in New Zealand. ❖ See also *Dictionary of New Zealand Biography* (Vol. 3).

VAN CITTERT, Truus (1903–1988). See Eymers, Truus.

VAN CLEVE, Edith (1894–1985). American actress and theatrical agent. Born Oct 11, 1894; died Oct 10, 1985, in Boston, MA. ❖ Made Broadway debut in Jane Cowl's *Romeo and Juliet* (1923); other plays include *Antony and Cleopatra*, *The Depths*, *Broadway*, *American Dream*, *June Moon*, *Three Men on a Horse*, *Front Page*, *Boy Meets Girl* and *Goodbye in the Night*; for many years, was assistant to George Abbott; became a major theatrical agent, representing, among others, Marlon Brando, Montgomery Clift, and Grace Kelly.

VAN CORTLANDT, Annetje Lockermans (c. 1620–after 1665). Dutch Colonial inventor. Born c. 1620 in the Netherlands; immigrated to New Amsterdam colony in 1642; died sometime after 1665; m. Oloff Van Cortlandt (military officer); children: 3. ❖ Unable to get officials of the then-village of Manhattan to improve the dirt road (Brower Street) in front of her house, instructed servants to pave the road with cobblestones (1648), which became the 1st paved street in America. ❖ See also *Women in World History*.

VAN COTT, Margaret (1830–1914). American evangelical. Name variations: Maggie Van Cott. Born Margaret Ann Newton, Mar 25, 1830, in New York, NY; died Aug 29, 1914, in Catskill, New York; dau. of William K. Newton (real-estate broker) and Rachel A. (Primrose) Newton; m. Peter P. Van Cott (store owner and businessman), Jan 23, 1848 (died 1866); children: Rachel (died in infancy); Sarah Ellen Conselyea. ❖ The 1st female Methodist Episcopal evangelist in America, had a conversion experience that drew her to prayer meetings at the Duane Street Methodist Episcopal Church in Manhattan (1858); following husband's death (1866), joined the church and began to lead prayer meetings and Bible study classes at the nondenominational mission founded by Phoebe Worrall Palmer in New York's Five Points slum area; successful in winning converts, accepted an invitation from a Methodist minister to hold revival meetings at his church in Durham, NY (1868); received an Exhorter's License (1868) and a Local Preacher's License (1869), making her 1st woman licensed to preach in the Methodist Episcopal Church in US; preached at revivals for many denominations throughout US; for more than 30 years, traveled up to 7,000 miles a year, converting over 2,000 people. ❖ See also *Women in World History*.

VANCUROVA, Vera (1932—). Czech gymnast. Name variations: Vera Vancurova-Markova. Born Sept 17, 1932. ❖ At Helsinki Olympics, won a bronze medal in team all-around (1952).

VANDAMM, Florence (1883–1966). British portrait photographer. Born Florence Van Damm in 1883 in London, England; died 1966 in New York City; m. George R. Thomas (American photographer), 1918 (died 1944); children: Robert. ❖ Opened a photographic studio in London (1883), and also worked as a miniaturist and portrait painter; elected a fellow of the Royal Photographic Society of Great Britain (1919); went into partnership with husband, who would use the name Tommy Vandamm professionally (1919); specialized in studio portraits of actors; with high unemployment in England, moved to New York City

(1923); with husband, worked for *Vogue* and *Vanity Fair* and became important photographers for Theater Guild, covering over 2,000 Broadway productions (1925–50); donated her archives to the New York Public Library (1961). ❖ See also *Women in World History*.

VANDECAVEYE, Gella (1973—). Belgian judoka. Born June 5, 1973, in Kortrijk, Belgium. ❖ Won a silver medal for 56–61 kg half-middleweight at Atlanta Olympics (1996); won European championships (1994, 1996, 1997, 1998, 1999, 2000, 2001); won World championships (1993, 2001); won a bronze medal for 57–63 kg at Sydney Olympics (2000).

VANDEGRIFT, Frances (1840–1914). *See Stevenson, Fanny.*

VAN DE KIEFT, Fleur (1973—). Dutch field-hockey player. Born Oct 22, 1973, in Amsterdam, Netherlands. ❖ Won team bronze medals at Atlanta Olympics (1996) and Sydney Olympics (2000); retired (2002).

VAN DEMAN, Esther (1862–1937). American archaeologist. Born Esther Boise Van Deman, Oct 1, 1862, in South Salem, Ohio; died May 3, 1937, in Rome, Italy; dau. of Joseph Van Deman (farmer) and Martha (Millspaugh) Van Deman; University of Michigan, AB, 1891, AM, 1892; graduate work at Bryn Mawr College, 1892–93; University of Chicago, PhD, 1898. ❖ The 1st woman field archaeologist, began study of Roman buildings (1907); discovering that different bricks were used at different points in Roman history, applied her dating method to many buildings and works and wrote about her findings in *The Atrium Vestae* (1909), then studied Roman aqueducts, a neglected subject; during 30 years spent in Rome, became the leading authority on ancient Roman building methods, setting forth her methodology in "Methods of Determining the Date of Roman Concrete Monuments" (1912), which remains the standard. ❖ See also *Women in World History*.

VAN DEMAN, Irene (1889–1961). Canadian-American airplane passenger. Name variations: Mrs. Ralph Henry Van Deman. Born Irene Kingcombe, Oct 27, 1889, in Vancouver, British Columbia, Canada; died Mar 30, 1961, in San Diego County, CA; m. Ralph Henry Van Deman (1865–1952, major general in US Army, regarded as the father of military intelligence), Mar 3, 1917. ❖ Became 1st woman airplane passenger in US (Oct 27, 1909), on a 4-minute flight at College Park, MD, with Wilbur Wright as pilot.

VAN DEN BERG, Jacomina (b. 1909). *See Berg, Jacomina van den.*

VAN DEN BOOGAARD, Dillianne (1974—). Dutch field-hockey player. Born Aug 9, 1974, in Veghel, Netherlands. ❖ Won team bronze medals at Atlanta Olympics (1996) and Sydney Olympics (2000).

VAN DEN BOS, Alida (1902—). *See Bos, Alida van den.*

VAN DEN BURG, Ieke (1952—). Dutch politician. Born Mar 6, 1952, in Apeldoorn, Netherlands. ❖ Served as policy adviser (1986–90) and administrator (1990–97) for FNV (Netherlands Trade Union Confederation); as a European Socialist, elected to 5th European Parliament (1999–2004).

VANDENHENDE, Severine (1974—). French judoka. Born Jan 12, 1974, in Dechy, France. ❖ Won World championship (1997); won a gold medal for 57–63 kg half-middleweight at Sydney Olympics (2000).

VANDENHOECK, Anna (1709–1787). German book publisher. Name variations: Anna Van den hoek; Anna van Hoeck. Pronunciation: fahnden'hœk (German); fahn-den-hook (Dutch). Born Anna Parry, May 24, 1709, in London, England; died Mar 5, 1787, in Göttingen, Germany; m. Abraham Vandenhoeck, in 1720s (died 1750); no children. ❖ Head of the most active academic publishing house in Germany, which prospered during the Enlightenment under her guidance; moved with husband, Dutch bookseller and printer, to Hamburg (1732); with husband (1734), opened firm in Hanover which quickly became recognized for producing books of distinguished quality (2 of its earliest works were an edition of the Bible using Martin Luther's translation "with useful summaries" and a 3-vol. edition of the works of Terence); succeeded husband as head of the publishing house at time of his death (1750), taking the helm of a failing business enterprise and turning it into one of Germany's most outstanding and longlived publishing houses; ran the company for 37 years (1750–87); printed the work of Johan David Michaelis and Gottfried Less; brought out the 2-vol. work by botanist Carl von Linné, or Linnaeus, that established the system of botanical classification still followed today (1772). ❖ See also *Women in World History*.

VANDERBECK, Mrs. Clarence H. (1884–1935). *See Vanderbeck, Florence.*

VANDERBECK, Florence (1884–1935). American golfer. Name variations: Mrs. Clarence H. Vanderbeck. Born May 1884; died Oct 1935. ❖ From Philadelphia, won USGA Women's Amateur (1915); won the Eastern (1915, 1921).

VAN DER BEN, Helena (1964—). Dutch field-hockey player. Born July 25, 1964. ❖ At Seoul Olympics, won a bronze medal in team competition (1988).

VANDERBILT, Alice Gwynne (1845–1934). American socialite. Name variations: Mrs. Cornelius Vanderbilt II. Born Alice Claypoole Gwynne in 1845; died in 1934; m. Cornelius Vanderbilt II (1843–1899, a banker, investor, and philanthropist); children: Alice Gwynne Vanderbilt (1869–1874); William Henry Vanderbilt II (1872–1892); Cornelius Vanderbilt III (1873–1942); Gertrude Vanderbilt Whitney (1875–1942); Alfred Gwynne Vanderbilt (1877–1915, killed while on board the *Lusitania* when it was torpedoed and sunk); Reginald Claypoole Vanderbilt (1880–1925, father of Gloria Vanderbilt); and Gladys Moore Vanderbilt (1886–1965, who m. Count Laszlo Szechenyi). ❖ Commissioned architect Richard Morris Hunt who, with her considerable input, designed The Breakers, a more-stately mansion overlooking Cliff Walk in Newport, Rhode Island, now on the tourist circuit (1892); because of Newport's gusty ocean winds, determined that rather than a center courtyard, she would have an interior courtyard, a center hall 45 feet high with a trompe l'oeil sky filled with billowing clouds on its ceiling. ❖ See also *Women in World History*.

VANDERBILT, Alva Smith (1853–1933). *See Belmont, Alva Smith.*

VANDERBILT, Amy (1908–1974). American etiquette expert. Born July 22, 1908, in Staten Island, New York; died in Dec 1974 in New York City; dau. of Joseph Mortimer Vanderbilt and Mary Estelle (Brooks) Vanderbilt; attended Institute Heubi, Lausanne, Switzerland, Packer Collegiate Institute in Brooklyn, and special student in school of journalism, New York University, 1926–28; m. Robert S. Brinkerhoff, in 1929; m. Morton G. Clark, in 1935; m. Hans Knopf, in 1945; children: (second marriage) Lincoln Clark; (3rd m.) Paul Vanderbilt Knopf; Stephen John Knopf. ❖ Columnist who wrote on good manners for two decades, challenging Emily Post's dominant position in this field in the years after World War II; worked as society and feature writer for Staten Island *Advance* (1927–29); was assistant advertising publicity director, H.R. Mallison Co. (1929–30); was an advertising account executive, New York City (1930–33); was a columnist, International News Service, and business and literary manager of *American Spectator* (1933); worked as home service director, Tower magazines (1934); served as 1st vice president, Publicity Assos., New York City (1937–40); president (1940–45); was entertaining etiquette advisor, Royal Crest Sterling (1940–64); had a syndicated daily column, "Amy Vanderbilt's Etiquette," United Feature Syndicate (1954–74); was a tv host on "It's Good Taste" (1954–56); was a consultant, Bristol Inc., New York City (1960–65); wrote many books on etiquette.

VANDERBILT, Consuelo (1877–1964). American heiress and duchess of Marlborough. Name variations: Consuelo Churchill. Born Mar 2, 1877, in New York; died in 1964; dau. of William Kissam Vanderbilt I (1849–1920) and Alva (Smith) Vanderbilt, later Alva Smith Belmont (1853–1933); m. Charles Richard Spencer Churchill (1871–1934), 9th duke of Marlborough and cousin of Winston Churchill, Nov 6, 1895 (sep. 1905, div. 1920); m. (Louis) Jacques Balsan (1868–1956, French lieutenant-colonel in the cavalry), July 4, 1921; children: (1st m.) John Albert William (b. 1897); Ivor Charles (1898–1956). ❖ Following divorce from duke of Marlborough (1920), became immersed in charity work, corralling donors for the Young Women's Christian Association; also supported women's suffrage and the movement to improve the minimum wage for women factory workers; during WWI, assisted the Red Cross and organized an employment service to help secure jobs for the 400,000 servants displaced when mansions were shut down; with 2nd marriage, lived in Paris and oversaw a salon for a glittering set of writers, artists, diplomats and dignitaries; built a sanitarium on her property large enough to house 80 sick children; at outbreak of WWII, returned to US. ❖ See also James Brough, *Consuelo: Portrait of an American Heiress* (Coward, McCann, 1979); and *Women in World History*.

VANDERBILT, Mrs. Cornelius.
See Vanderbilt, Sophia Johnson (1797–1868).
See Vanderbilt, Alice Gwynne (1845–1934).

VANDERBILT, Gertrude (1875–1942). *See Whitney, Gertrude Vanderbilt.*

VANDERBILT, Gertrude (1880–1960). American musical-comedy actress. Born 1880; died Feb 19, 1960, in New York, NY. ❖ Appeared in *Ziegfeld Follies of 1917*; replaced Ina Claire in *The Gold Diggers* (1920); other appearances include *Our Miss Gibbs*, *The Jolly Batchelors*, *The Red Widow*, *The Lady in Red*, and *Fifty-Fifty Ltd.*

VANDERBILT, Gladys Moore (1886–1965). American socialite. Name variations: Countess Széchenyi. Born in 1886; died in 1965; dau. of Cornelius Vanderbilt II and Alice Gwynne Vanderbilt (1845–1934); m. Count Laszlo Szechenyani, also seen as Lásló Széchenyi (Hungarian minister to US and Britain); children: 5 daughters, including Alice Széchenyi (who also married a count).

VANDERBILT, Gloria (1924—). American actress, artist, and designer. Name variations: Gloria Vanderbilt-Cooper; Mrs. Wyatt E. Cooper. Born Gloria Laura Vanderbilt in New York, NY, Feb 20, 1924; dau. of Reginald Claypoole Vanderbilt (1880–1925) and Gloria Mercedes (Morgan) Vanderbilt (1904–1965); m. Pasquale (Pat) De Cicco (1909–1979, actor's agent), 1941 (div. April 24, 1945); m. Leopold Stokowski (1882–1977, the conductor), April 25, 1945 (div. Oct 1955); m. Sidney Lumet (b. 1924, film director), Aug 27, 1956 (div. Aug 1963); m. Wyatt E. Cooper, Dec 24, 1963 (died Jan 5, 1978); children: (2nd m.) Stanley and Christopher Stokowski; (4th m.) Carter Vanderbilt Cooper (died 1988) and Anderson H. Cooper (newsanchor for CNN). ❖ Heiress to the fortune amassed by her great-grandfather Cornelius Vanderbilt, was just 1 year old when her father died (1925), leaving her a multimillion-dollar trust fund from which she received a monthly allotment; became a contested child in an infamous custody battle (1934); made 1st appearance on Broadway in a small role in *Time of Your Life* (1955); continued to perform in summer stock and regional theater and on tv; wrote *Love Poems* (1955); had solo shows as an artist at Barbara Shaeffer Gallery in New York (1954), Juster Gallery (1956), Hammer Gallery (1966); as creative director of Gloria Vanderbilt Designs, began transferring the colorful motifs of her paintings to a line of products, including table linens, bathroom accessories, china, and wallpaper (1972); added to business empire with a line of jeans carrying her signature logo: her name and a swan motif (1978). Received Neiman-Marcus fashion award (1969), Fashion Hall of Fame award (1970), and gold medal from Society of Arts and Letters (1976). ❖ See also autobiographies, *Once Upon a Time* (1985), *Black Knight, White Knight* (1987) and *A Mother's Story* (1996); Barbara Goldsmith, *Little Gloria... Happy at Last* (Knopf, 1980); and *Women in World History.*

VANDERBILT, Maria (1821–1896). American socialite. Name variations: Mrs. William Henry Vanderbilt I. Born Maria Louisa Kissam in 1821; died 1896; m. William Henry Vanderbilt I (1821–1885); children: 9, including Cornelius Vanderbilt II (1843–1899) and William Kissam Vanderbilt I (1849–1920).

VANDERBILT, Sophia Johnson (1797–1868). American socialite. Name variations: Mrs. Cornelius Vanderbilt I. Born in 1797; died in 1868; m. Cornelius Vanderbilt I, called the Commodore (1794–1877); children: 13, including William Henry Vanderbilt I (1821–1885). ❖ Cornelius' 2nd wife was Frances Armstrong (Frank) Crawford (1839–1885), known as Frances Vanderbilt.

VANDERBILT, Mrs. William K. (1853–1933). See Belmont, Alva Smith.

VANDERBILT I, Mrs. Cornelius (1797–1868). See Vanderbilt, Sophia Johnson.

VANDERBILT II, Mrs. Cornelius (1845–1934). See Vanderbilt, Alice Gwynne.

VANDERBILT-COOPER, Gloria (b. 1924). See Vanderbilt, Gloria.

VAN DERBUR, Marilyn (c. 1937—). Miss America. Name variations: Marilyn Van Derbur Atler. Born Marilyn Elaine Van Derbur, c. 1937, in Denver, CO; University of Colorado, Phi Beta Kappa; m. Larry Atler (attorney); children: 1 daughter. ❖ Named Miss America (1958), representing Colorado; went public about surviving her father's sexual abuse from age 5 to 18; was a guest lecturer and frequent keynote speaker; established an adult survivor program; produced "Once Can Hurt a Lifetime," a video for teenagers on the trauma of sexual abuse shown often on PBS stations. Named to Colorado Women's Hall of Fame. ❖ See also Frank Deford, *There She Is* (Viking, 1971).

VANDERBURG, Helen (1959—). Canadian synchronized swimmer. Born Jan 12, 1959, in Calgary, Alberta, Canada. ❖ Won a gold medal in solo and gold medal in duet at World Aquatic championship (1978); won a gold medal in solo and gold medal in duet at Pan American Games

(1979) and World Cup (1979); won a gold medal at Pan Pacific Games (1979).

VANDERBUSH, Carin (1940—). See Cone, Carin.

VAN DER GOES, Frederica. South African swimmer. Name variations: Frederica Johanna Van Der Goes. Born in South Africa. ❖ At Amsterdam Olympics, won a bronze medal in the 4 x 100-meter freestyle relay and finished 5th in the 400 m freestyle (1928).

VAN DER KADE-KOUDIJS, Gerda (1923—). Dutch runner. Name variations: Gerda Koudijs. Born Gerda Koudijs, Oct 29, 1923, in Rotterdam, Netherlands. ❖ At London Olympics, won a gold medal in the 4 x 100-meter relay (1948).

VAN DER KAMP, Anna (1972—). Canadian rower. Born June 19, 1972, in Abbotsford, British Columbia, Canada. ❖ Won a silver medal for coxed eights at Atlanta Olympics (1996).

VAN DER KOLK, Kirsten (1975—). Dutch rower. Born Dec 18, 1975, in the Netherlands. ❖ Won a bronze medal for lightweight double sculls at Athens Olympics (2004).

VAN DER MARK, Christine (1917–1969). Canadian novelist. Born Sept 17, 1917, in Calgary, Alberta, Canada; died 1969; dau. of Mary Van der Mark (writer); children: Dorothy Wise. ❖ Works include *In Due Season* (1947), *Hassan* (1960), and *Honey in the Rock* (1966).

VAN DER OOSTEN, Gertrude (d. 1358). See Gertrude of Ostend.

VAN DER PLAATS, Adriana (1971—). Dutch swimmer. Born Aug 12, 1971. ❖ At Seoul Olympics, won a silver medal in the 4 x 100-meter freestyle relay (1988).

VANDERPOOL, Sylvia (1936—). African-American singer and guitarist. Name variations: Sylvia Robinson; Mickey and Sylvia. Born Sylvia Vanderpool on Mar 6, 1936, in New York, NY; m. Joe Robinson, 1956. ❖ Learned guitar from blues guitarist, Mickey Baker, and partnered with him as Mickey and Sylvia, releasing such hits as "Love Is Strange" (1956), "There Oughta Be a Law" (1957) and "Baby You're So Fine" (1961); split up when Baker went to Europe (1961), but briefly reunited (1965); with husband, founded All Platinum Records (late 1960s), and produced such hits as Moments' gold single "Love on a Two-Way Street" (1970) and Shirley and Company's "Shame, Shame, Shame" (1976); returned to singing, and had hits with "Pillow Talk" (1973), "Sweet Stuff" (1978) and "Automatic Lover" (1978); renamed troubled All Platinum label Sugar Hill, and gathered group of rap vocalists called Sugar Hill Gang, who went on to have smash hit with "Rappers Delight" (1979); served as producer for many successful rap bands, including Grandmaster Flash and the Furious Five, and Funky Four Plus One.

VAN DER SCHRIECK, Louise (1813–1886). See Schrieck, Louise van der.

VAN DER VAART, Macha (1972—). Dutch field-hockey player. Born April 17, 1972 in Alkmaar, Netherlands. ❖ Won a team bronze medal at Sydney Olympics (2000) and a team silver at Athens Olympics (2004); won Champions Trophy (2000) and European championship (2003).

VAN DER VEGT, Anna (1903–1983). Dutch gymnast. Born Dec 1903; died April 13, 1983. ❖ At Amsterdam Olympics, won a gold medal in team all-around (1928).

VAN DER WIELEN, Suzan (1971—). Dutch field-hockey player. Born Oct 30, 1971, in Emmen, Netherlands. ❖ Won team bronze medals at Atlanta Olympics (1996) and Sydney Olympics (2000).

VAN DER WILDT, Paulina (1944—). Dutch swimmer. Born Jan 29, 1944. ❖ At Tokyo Olympics, won a bronze medal in 4 x 100-meter freestyle relay (1964).

VANDERWOUDE, Wendy (1964—). See Wyland, Wendy.

VANDEUIL, Dame de (1573–1599). See Estrées, Gabrielle d'.

VAN DEURS, Brigitte (1946—). Duchess of Gloucester. Name variations: Bridget van Deurs. Born June 20, 1946, in Odensee, Denmark; dau. of Asger Henriksen and Vivian van Deurs; m. Richard Windsor (b. 1944), 2nd duke of Gloucester, on July 8, 1972; children: Alexander Windsor (b. 1974), earl of Ulster; Davina Windsor (b. 1977); Rose Windsor (b. 1980).

VAN DE VATE, Nancy (1930—). American composer. Born in Plainfield, NJ, Dec 30, 1930; received Rochester Prize scholarship and George Eastman scholarship to attend Eastman School of Music; graduated with a degree in music theory from Wellesley College, master's degree in composition from University of Mississippi, and doctorate in music from Florida State University. ❖ Premiered *Six Etudes for Solo Vila* at Lincoln Center; challenged granting procedures of Rockefeller Foundation, National Endowment for the Arts, and John F. Kennedy Center for the Performing Arts, which she felt were biased against women; served as chair of International League of Women Composers; was a professor of music at University of Mississippi, Memphis State University, University of Tennessee, and University of Hawaii. Awarded 6 American Society of Composers, Authors, and Publishers awards. ❖ See also *Women in World History.*

VAN DISHOECK, Pieta (1972—). Dutch rower. Born May 13, 1972, in Amsterdam, Netherlands. ❖ Won silver medals for double sculls and coxed eights at Sydney Olympics (2000).

VAN DOORN, Marieke (1960—). Dutch field-hockey player. Born June 15, 1960. ❖ At Los Angeles Olympics, won a gold medal in team competition (1984); at Seoul Olympics, won a bronze medal in team competition (1988).

VAN DOREN, Irita (1891–1966). American editor. Born Irita Bradford in Birmingham, Alabama, Mar 16, 1891; died Dec 18, 1966; dau. of John Taylor Bradford (merchant and owner of a sawmill) and Ida Henley (Brooks) Bradford (accomplished musician); graduate of Florida State College for Women at Tallahassee, 1908; Columbia University, PhD; m. Carl Van Doren (literary critic and Pulitzer Prize-winning biographer), Aug 1912 (div. 1935); children: Anne Van Doren (b. 1915); Margaret Van Doren (b. 1917); Barbara Van Doren (b. 1920). ❖ Was on the editorial staff of *The Nation* (1919–22), becoming advertising manager (1922–23) and literary editor (1923–24); moved to New York *Herald Tribune* as assistant to Stuart P. Sherman (1924); on his death (1926), succeeded him as editor of the weekly book review section, a powerful position.

VAN DOREN, Mamie (1931—). American actress and singer. Name variations: Joan Olander. Born Joan Lucille Olander, Feb 6, 1931, in Rowena, SD; m. Jack Newman, 1950 (div. 1950); m. Ray Anthony (bandleader), 1955 (div. 1961); m. Lee Meyers, 1966 (div. 1967); m. Ross McClintock, 1972 (div. 1973); m. Thomas Dixon, 1979. ❖ Named Miss Palm Springs (1948); began career as a dance-band singer; made film debut in *The All American* (1953), followed by *Untamed Youth, Francis Joins the WACS, High School Confidential, Born Reckless, Teacher's Pet, The Navy vs. The Night Monsters* and *Boarding School,* among others. ❖ See also autobiography *Playing the Field* (1987).

VAN DOVER, Cindy (1954—). American marine biologist. Born Cindy Lee Van Dover, May 16, 1954, in Red Bank, NJ; dau. of James K. and Virginia Van Dover; Rutgers University, BS in environmental science, 1977; University of California, Los Angeles, MA in ecology, 1985. ❖ Contributor of research about life and ecosystem on ocean's floor, was 1st scientist and 1st woman to receive license as a navy certified submersible pilot-commander; piloted 48 dives in the submersible *Alvin* (1990–92); led scientific team beneath Indian Ocean (2001); had lifelong affiliation with Woods Hole; worked as visiting scholar at Duke University in NC (1994–95), as associate professor at University of Alaska at Fairbanks (1995–98), as West Coast National Undersea Center science director, and as assistant professor at College of William and Mary in Virginia (since 1998); writings include *Deep-Ocean Journeys: Discovering Life at the Bottom of the Sea* (1997) and *The Ecology of Deep-Sea Hydrothermal Vents* (2000).

VAN DROGENBROEK, Marieke (1964—). Dutch rower. Born Dec 16, 1964. ❖ At Los Angeles Olympics, won a bronze medal in coxed eights (1984).

VAN DUYN, Mona (1921–2004). American poet. Born May 9, 1921, in Waterloo, Iowa; died Dec 2, 2004, in University City, Missouri; dau. of Earl George Van Duyn (businessman) and Lora (Kramer) Van Duyn; University of Northern Iowa, BA, 1942; University of Iowa, MA, 1943; m. Jarvis A. Thurston (professor of English), Aug 31, 1943. ❖ Poet laureate and Pulitzer Prize winner, taught English at University of Iowa and University of Louisville in Kentucky; with husband, founded *Perspective: A Quarterly in Literature* (1947), which she edited (1947–67); taught English at Washington University in St. Louis, Missouri (1950–67); taught and lectured at various other universities in US and in Salzburg, Austria (1970s); won National Book Award for Poetry for *To See, To Take* (1971); became a member of Academy of American Poets (1981) and 1 of 12 chancellors for life (1985); at 70, won Pulitzer Prize for poetry collection, *Near Changes* (1991); became 1st woman poet laureate (consultant in poetry) for US Library of Congress (1992);

works include *Valentines to the Wide World* (1959), *A Time of Bees* (1964), *Bedtime Stories* (1972), *Merciful Disguises* (1973), *Letters from a Father, and Other Poems* (1982), *If It Be Not I: Collected Poems 1959–1982* (1994) and *Firefall* (1994). Received Eunice Tietjens Memorial Prize (1956) and Harriet Monroe Memorial Prize (1968), both from *Poetry* magazine; received Hart Crane Memorial Award from American Weave Press (1968); won Yale University Library's Bollingen Prize (1970); won the National Institute of Arts and Letters' Loines Prize (1976). ❖ See also *Women in World History.*

VAN DYKE, Vonda Kay (c. 1944—). Miss America. Name variations: Vonda Scoates. Born c. 1944; attended Arizona State University; m. David Tyler Scoates (minister); children: 1 daughter. ❖ Named Miss America (1965), representing Arizona, the 1st ventriloquist to compete; as a singer and entertainer, recorded albums; published numerous children's books, including *That Girl in Your Mirror.* ❖ See also Frank Deford, *There She Is* (Viking, 1971).

VAN DYKEN, Amy (1973—). American swimmer. Born Feb 15, 1973, in Englewood, CO; attended University of Arizona, 1992–94; graduate of Colorado State University, 1997; m. Alan McDaniel, Oct 14, 1995. ❖ Won a gold medal for 50-yard freestyle at NCAA championships (1994); won a gold medal for 50-meter freestyle at US National championships (1995); won gold medals in 50-meter freestyle, 100-meter butterfly, 4 x 100 freestyle relay, and 4 x 100 medley relay at Atlanta Olympics (1996); won gold medals in 50-meter freestyle, 4 x 100 freestyle relay, and 4 x 100 medley relay at World championships (1998); won a gold medal for 4 x 100-freestyle relay at Sydney Olympics (2000). Named Sportswoman of the Year (1996). ❖ See also *Women in World History.*

VANE, Daphne (1918–1966). American ballet dancer. Born 1918; died Dec 15, 1966, in New York, NY; m. Richard Day (film art director). ❖ Danced at Radio City Music Hall; joined American Ballet (1935) and was a lead dancer at Metropolitan Opera House in premieres of Balanchine works, including *Mozartiana* and *Orpheus and Eurydice*; danced "Romeo and Juliet ballet" in film *Goldwyn Follies* (1938); appeared on Broadway in *Keep Off the Grass* (1940).

VANE, Lady Frances Emily (1822–1899). See Churchill, Fanny.

VANE-TEMPEST, Frances Anne Emily (d. 1865). Marchioness of Londonderry and countess of Antrim. Name variations: Lady Frances Anne Londonderry. Born Frances Anne Emily Vane-Tempest; died Jan 20, 1865; dau. of Sir Henry Vane-Tempest and Anne Katherine MacDonnell, countess of Antrim; m. Charles William Vane, 3rd marquess of Londonderry, April 3, 1819; children: George (1821–1884), 5th marquess of Londonderry; Frances Anne Emily Vane, later known as Fanny Churchill (1822–1899), duchess of Marlborough, and Adolphus (1825–1864).

VANE-TEMPEST-STEWART, Edith (1878–1949). Marchioness of Londonderry. Name variations: Lady Edith Helen Vane-Tempest-Stewart Londonderry. Born Edith Helen Chaplin, Dec 3, 1878 (some sources cite 1879); died April 23, 1949 (some sources cite 1959); dau. of Henry Chaplin, 1st viscount Chaplin, and Florence Leveson-Gower (dau. of 3rd duke of Sutherland); m. Charles Stewart Henry Vane-Tempest-Stewart, 7th marquess of Londonderry, Nov 28, 1899 (died 1949); children: Maureen (1900–1942), Edward (1902–19550, 8th marquess of Londonderry, and Mairi (b. 1921).

VANE-TEMPEST-STEWART, Theresa (1856–1919). Irish political host. Name variations: Lady Theresa Vane-Tempest-Stewart Londonderry. Born Theresa Susey Helen Talbot, 1856, in Ireland; died Mar 16, 1919; dau. of Charles Chetwynd-Talbot, 19th earl of Shrewsbury, and Anna Theresa Cockerell; m. Charles Stewart Vane-Tempest-Stewart, 6th marquess of Londonderry, Oct 2, 1875; children: Helen Mary Theresa Vane-Tempest-Stewart (b. 1876), Charles Vane-Tempest-Stewart (1878–1949), 7th marquess of Londonderry. ❖ Called one of the most striking and dominating women of her time, was the foremost Tory political hostess of 19th-century Ireland, entertaining royalty at her 2 residences: Wynyard Park, Co. Durham, and Mount Stewart, Co. Down. ❖ See also Hyde, H. Montgomery. *The Londonderrys: A Family Portrait* (1979).

VAN ETTEKOVEN, Harriet (1961—). Dutch rower. Born Jan 6, 1961. ❖ At Los Angeles Olympics, won a bronze medal in coxed eights (1984).

VAN EUPEN, Marit (1969—). Dutch rower. Born Sept 26, 1969, in Arnhem, Netherlands. ❖ Won a bronze medal for lightweight double sculls at Athens Olympics (2004).

VAN FLEET, Jo (1919–1996). American actress. Born Dec 30, 1919, in Oakland, California; died June 8, 1996, in New York, NY; dau. of Roy H. Van Fleet and Elizabeth (Gardner) Van Fleet; College of the Pacific, in Stockton, California, BA; studied at Neighborhood Playhouse with Sanford Meisner and at Actors Studio with Elia Kazan; m. William Bales (dancer and choreographer, died 1990); children: 1 son, Michael. ❖ Veteran of stage, screen and tv, acclaimed for her portrayals of tough, complex women, made professional debut in a touring production of *Uncle Harry* (1945), and NY debut as Dorcas in *The Winter's Tale* (1946); won Tony Award for performance as Jessie Mae Watts in *The Trip to Bountiful* (1953); won Academy Award as Best Supporting Actress for role as James Dean's mother in *East of Eden* (1955), her 1st film; on stage, also appeared as Miss Foster in *Flight Into Egypt* (1952), Marguerite Gautier in *Camino Real* (1953), Eliza Grant in *Look Homeward Angel* (1957), Amanda Wingfield in *The Glass Menagerie* (1959), and Madame Rosepettle in *Oh Dad, Poor Dad, Mama's Hung You in the Closet and I'm Feelin' So Sad* (1962); was also the wicked stepmother in tv revival of Rodgers and Hammerstein's *Cinderella* (1965); other films include *I'll Cry Tomorrow* (1955), *The Rose Tattoo* (1955), *The King and Four Queens* (1956), *Gunfight at the O. K. Corral* (1957), *Wild River* (1950), *Cool Hand Luke* (1967), *I Love You Alice B. Toklas!* (1968), and *The Gang That Couldn't Shoot Straight* (1971). ❖ See also *Women in World History*.

VAN GEENHUIZEN, Miek (1981—). Dutch field-hockey player. Born Dec 17, 1981, in Eindhoven, Netherlands. ❖ Won Champions Trophy (2000) and European championship (2003); won a team silver medal at Athens Olympics (2004).

VAN GELDER, Betty (1866–1962). See Holtrop-van Gelder, Betty.

VANGELOVSKA, Stojna (1965—). Yugoslavian basketball player. Born Feb 5, 1965. ❖ At Seoul Olympics, won a silver medal in team competition (1988).

VAN GENNIP, Yvonne (1964—). Dutch speedskater. Name variations: Yvonne van Gennip. Born May 1, 1964, in Haarlem, Netherlands. ❖ Won gold medals for 1,500, 3,000, and 5,000 meters at Calgary Olympics (1988); at European championships, won silver medals (1985, 1986, 1987) and bronze medals (1988, 1991), all for all-around; at World championships, won bronze medals for all-around (1987, 1989) and a silver (1988).

VAN GORDON, Cyrena (1896–1964). American contralto. Born Sept 4, 1896, in Camden, Ohio (nee Pocock); died April 4, 1964, in New York, NY. ❖ Made debut with Chicago Opera as Amneris in *Aïda* (1913); debuted at the Metropolitan (1934); most famous roles were Ortud, Erda, Fricka, Brunnhilde, Azucena, Venus, and Delilah.

VAN GRIPPENBERG, Alexandra (1859–1913). Finnish feminist and legislator. Name variations: Baroness Alexandra Grippenberg. Born in 1859; died in 1913. ❖ A member of the temperance movement, was also a founding member of Finsk Kvinneførening (Finnish Women's Association, 1884); served as vice-president on International Council of Women; was elected a member of the Finnish Diet (1909), where she argued against legislation protecting women, on the grounds that total equality between the sexes would not be achieved if either of them received special protection; founded the Finnish National Council of Women (1912) and was elected its 1st president.

VAN GRUNSVEN, Anky (1968—). Dutch equestrian. Born Jan 2, 1968, in Erp, Netherlands. ❖ Won Dutch national championships (1990–2000, 2003); at Barcelona Olympics, won a silver medal for team dressage (1992); won a gold medal at World championships (1994); won a silver medal for indiv. dressage and a silver medal for team dressage at Atlanta Olympics (1996), on Bonfire; carried the Dutch flag in opening ceremonies and won a gold medal for indiv. dressage and a silver medal for team dressage at Sydney Olympics (2000), on Bonfire; on Salinero, won a gold medal for indiv. dressage at Athens Olympics (2004); also has a World record number of World Cup championships; won European championship (1999); held superstar status in the Netherlands. Named Rider of the Century (2000) and Rider of the Year (2001).

VANGSAAE, Mona (1920–1983). Danish ballet dancer. Born Mona Elly Hou Vangsaae, April 29, 1920, in Copenhagen, Denmark; died May 17, 1983; dau. of Albert Carl Hou Vangsaae and Boline Andersen Vangsaae; m. Børge Angelo Jahncke, 1942; m. Frank Schaufuss (ballet dancer), 1946 (div. 1977); children: Liselotte (b. 1943) and Peter (b. 1949). ❖ Trained at Royal Danish Ballet school in Copenhagen; joined Royal Danish Ballet and performed there throughout most of career; danced in numerous Bournonville works, including *Konservatoriet*, *La Ventana*, and *Napoli*,

and in European classics such as Fokine's *Chopiniana* and *Giselle*; created title role for Frederick Ashton's *Romeo and Juliet* (1955) and role of Aili in Birgit Cullberg's *Moon Reindeer* (1957).

VAN HAMEL, Martine (1945—). Dutch ballet dancer. Born Nov 16, 1945, in Brussels, Belgium; dau. of a Dutch diplomat. ❖ Trained in Denmark, the Netherlands and Venezuela, and in Canada with Betty Oliphant; performed with National Ballet of Canada; moved to NY and danced with City Center Joffrey Ballet; joined American Ballet Theater (1971), where she remained through most of career; danced in company revivals of *Giselle*, *Swan Lake*, *The Sleeping Beauty*, and the Rudolf Nureyev production of *Raymonda*; also danced in premieres of Nahat's *Some Times* (1972) and Tharp's *Push Comes to Shove* (1975).

VAN HEMESSEN, Caterina (c. 1528–c. 1587). See Hemessen, Caterina van.

VAN HEYNINGEN, Ruth (1917—). Welsh ophthalmologist. Name variations: Ruth Eleanor Treverton; Ruth Eleanor van Heyningen. Born Ruth Eleanor Treverton, Oct 16, 1917, in Newport, Monmouthshire, Wales; attended Newnham College, Cambridge, 1937–40, University of Cambridge, PhD in biochemistry, 1951, DSc, 1972; m. Dr. William Edward van Heyningen (Oxford University reader), June 24, 1940. ❖ An expert on the biochemical process of cataract formation, worked as a research assistant at the Lister Institute in London (1943–48) and researcher for University of Oxford's Department of Anatomy (1948–52); at Nuffield Laboratory of Ophthalmology, served as a research assistant (1952–69) and as a senior research officer (1969–77); with Antoinette Pirie, wrote *Biochemistry of the Eye* (1956).

VAN HOFWEGEN, Wilma (1971—). See van Rijn, Wilma.

VANHOOK, Mary Ann (1823–1899). See Lee, Mary Ann.

VAN HOOSEN, Bertha (1863–1952). American physician. Born Mar 26, 1863, in Stony Creek, Michigan; died June 7, 1952, in Romeo, Michigan; dau. of Joshua Van Hoosen (homesteader) and Sarah Ann (Taylor) Van Hoosen (teacher); University of Michigan, AB, 1884, medical degree, 1888; additional medical training in Detroit and Kalamazoo, Michigan, and in Boston. ❖ Surgeon who was the 1st woman to head a medical division of a coeducational university; was an instructor of medicine, Women's Medical School of Northwestern University (1888–1902); established private practice in Chicago (1892); was a professor at University of Illinois College of Medicine (1902–12); became chief of gynecological staff of Cook County Hospital, Chicago (1913), then chief of obstetrical staff (1920); cofounded and was 1st president of American Medical Women's Association (1915); was a professor and head of obstetrics, Loyola University (1918–37). ❖ See also autobiography, *Petticoat Surgeon* (1947); and *Women in World History*.

VAN HOUTEN, Leslie (1949—). American murderer (accused). Born Aug 23, 1949, in Los Angeles, CA. ❖ Joined cult of Charles Manson (1968) and was involved in murders of Leno and Rosemary LaBianca (1969); sentenced to life in prison and was denied parole several times despite record as model prisoner.

VANHOVE, Caroline or Charlotte (1771–1860). See Talma, Madame.

VAN KESSEL, Lieve (1977—). Dutch field-hockey player. Born Sept 17, 1977, in the Netherlands. ❖ Won European championship (2003); won a team silver medal at Athens Olympics (2004).

VAN KLEECK, Mary Abby (1883–1972). American reformer. Born in 1883; died in Woodstock, New York, in 1972; grew up in New York City; graduate of Smith College, 1904. ❖ Began studies on status of working women, sponsored by Russell Sage Foundation (1908), which exerted a powerful influence on labor reform; published 1st book, *Artificial Flower Makers* (1913), concerning immigrant women, which was followed by *Women in the Bookbinding Trade* (1913), *Wages in the Military Trade* (1914), *Working Girls in Evening Schools* (1914), and *A Seasonal Industry* (1917); hired to advise the army Ordnance Department and to serve as a member of the War Labor Policies Board (1917), helped form the Women's Bureau of the Department of Labor, which she headed briefly; returned to her work with the Russell Sage Foundation (1919); served on 2 presidential commissions on unemployment; chaired the National Interracial Conference (1928); co-authored *The Negro in American Civilization* (1930); and presided over the International Conference of Social Work in Germany (1932); as she grew older, swung more to the political left, putting forth her views in *Creative America* (1936) and *Technology and Livelihood* (1944).

VAN LANCKER, Anne E. M. (1954—). Belgian sociologist and politician. Born Mar 4, 1954, in Temse, Belgium. ❖ Served as deputy head, then head of office of the Flemish Minister of Employment (1989–92) and head of private office to the Minister of Employment and Social Affairs (1992–94); as a European Socialist, elected to 4th and 5th European Parliament (1994–99, 1999–2004).

VAN LANGEN, Ellen (1966—). Dutch runner. Born Feb 9, 1966, in Oldenzaal, Netherlands. ❖ At Barcelona Olympics, won a gold medal in 800 meters (1992).

VAN LAWICK-GOODALL, Jane (b. 1934). *See Goodall, Jane.*

VAN LEW, Elizabeth (1818–1900). American abolitionist and spy. Name variations: Crazy Bet. Born Oct 17, 1818, in Richmond, Virginia; died Sept 25, 1900, in Richmond; dau. of John Van Lew (hardware merchant) and Elizabeth (Baker) Van Lew; educated in Philadelphia and at home. ❖ Longtime opponent of slavery, even before the Civil War began, maintained loyalty to the Union despite her home state of Virginia's being a Confederate stronghold; during Civil War, assisted inmates at Libby Prison, a confederate prison camp for federal officers, and smuggled their letters back to their families; with mother, helped more than 100 of them to escape, hiding them in a secret room in the Van Lew house; was the Union's most valuable spy; obtained Confederate military information at Libby, then passed it on to Union forces; because she came from such a prominent Richmond family, was trusted and allowed access to many places, including Jefferson Davis' Confederate White House, where, to gain even more information, she placed as a servant the former slave whose education she had sponsored, Mary Elizabeth Bowser. ❖ See also *Women in World History.*

VAN MANEN, Aletta (1958—). Dutch field-hockey player. Born Oct 20, 1958. ❖ Won a gold medal at Los Angeles Olympics (1984) and a bronze medal at Seoul Olympics (1988), both in team competition.

VAN MERKEN, Lucretia Wilhelmina (1721–1789). *See Merken, Lucretia Wilhelmina van.*

VAN MOORSEL, Leontien (1970—). Dutch cyclist. Name variations: Leontien Zijlaard-Van Moorsel. Born Mar 22, 1970, in Boekel, Netherlands; m. Michael Zijlaard (her trainer since 1994), Oct 1995. ❖ At World championships, placed 1st at pursuit (1990, 2001, 2002, 2003), road race (1991, 1993) and indiv. time trial (1998, 1999); won gold medals for indiv. road race, indiv. time trial, and indiv. pursuit (3,000 meters) and a silver medal for points race at Sydney Olympics (2000); won a bronze medal at 3,000-meter indiv. pursuit and a gold medal for indiv. time trial at Athens Olympics (2004), retiring from the games as the most successful cyclist in Olympic history. Named Dutch Sportswoman of the Year 4 times.

VAN NES, Eeke (1969—). Dutch rower. Born April 17, 1969. ❖ Won a bronze medal for double sculls at Atlanta Olympics (1996) and silver medal for double scull and coxed eight at Sydney Olympics (2000).

VANO, Donna (c. 1955—). American inline skater and snowboarder. Name variations: Donna Dennis Vano. Born Donna Dennis, c. 1955, in Watts, Los Angeles, CA; m. Alan Vano (pro-skater). ❖ Began inline competition around age 36 (1991) and helped pioneer sport for women; won many skating and snowboarding competitions; made Guinness Book of World Records as world's oldest female inline skater.

VAN OOSTERWYCK, Maria (1630–1693). *See Oosterwyck, Maria van.*

VANOZZA, Rosa (1442–1518). *See Cattanei, Vannozza.*

VANN, Jesse Matthews (c. 1890–1967). African-American publisher. Born Jesse Ellen Matthews around 1890; died in 1967; m. Robert Lee Vann (publisher), 1910 (died 1940). ❖ When husband died (1940), inherited the *Pittsburgh Courier,* a major source of information for African-Americans, and for next 2 decades served as its publisher. ❖ See also *Women in World History.*

VAN PRAAGH, Peggy (1910–1990). British-born ballet dancer. Name variations: Dame Margaret van Praagh; Dame Peggy van Praagh. Born Margaret van Praagh, Sept 1, 1910, in London, England; died in Melbourne, Australia, Jan 15, 1990. dau. of a physician; trained under a series of dancers and dance teachers; received diploma from Cecchetti Society, 1932. ❖ Largely responsible for the development of the Australian Ballet, made her debut at London Coliseum (1929), opposite

Anton Dolin in *Revolution*; danced for Camargo Society (1930–33), in ballets *Revolution* (1929) and *Adam and Eve* (1932); danced with Ballet Rambert (1933–38), in *Mephisto Waltz* (1934), *Valentine's Eve* (1935), *Circus Wives* (1935), *The Planets* (1937), *Dark Elegies* (1937), *Jardin aux Lilas* (1938) and *Gala Performance, Soirée Musicale*; was co-director of London Ballet with Maude Lloyd (1939–40); was a teacher and dancer with the Sadler's Wells Ballet (1941–46), for ballets *Coppélia, Les Patineurs*; was producer and ballet mistress with the same company (1946–52); served as associate director of the company (1952–55); was a freelance producer and tv dance director (1955–62); served as director, Borovansky Ballet, Melbourne (1960); was artistic director of the Australian Ballet (1963–74, 1978–79), with Robert Helpmann from 1965; retired (1979); devoted the last half of her professional life to sowing the seeds that would lead to the successful development of 2 national ballets of international stature, one in Canada and the other in Australia. Named Commander of the Order of the British Empire (1966), Officer of the Order of the British Empire (1966) and Dame Commander of the Order of the British Empire (1970). ❖ See also *How I Became a Dancer* (1954); Christopher Sexton, *Peggy van Praagh: A Life of Dance* (1985); and *Women in World History.*

VAN RANDWIJK, Petronella (1905–1978). Dutch gymnast. Born Sept 14, 1905; died Sept 21, 1978. ❖ At Amsterdam Olympics, won a gold medal in team all-around (1928).

VAN RENSSELAER, Catherine (1734–1803). *See Schuyler, Catherine Van Rensselaer.*

VAN RENSSELAER, Maria Van Cortlandt (1645–c. 1688). Colonial American administrator. Born Maria Van Cortlandt, July 20, 1645, in New Amsterdam (later New York City); died Jan 24, 1688 or 1699, in Albany, New York; dau. of Oloffe Stevense Van Cortlandt (merchant and city official) and Anna (Loockermans) Van Cortlandt; m. Jeremias Van Rensselaer (1st patroon, or proprietor, of Rensselaerswyck), July 12, 1662 (died 1674); children: Kiliaen, Anna, Hendrick, Maria, Johannes, Jeremias. ❖ When husband died (1674), took over as administrator of the Dutch patroonship of Rensselaerswyck, their 24-square-mile estate, near Albany, New York, and fought the claims of others; by the time she died, had successfully secured title to the estate—the richest land patent in the colony—for her children. ❖ See also *Women in World History.*

VAN RENSSELAER, Mariana (1851–1934). American writer. Name variations: M. G. Van Rensselaer; Mrs. Schuyler Van Rensselaer. Born Mariana Alley Griswold, Feb 21, 1851, in New York, NY; died Jan 20, 1934, in New York, NY; dau. of George and Lydia (Alley) Griswold; m. Schuyler Van Rensselaer (engineer), April 14, 1873 (died 1884); children: George Griswold (1875–1894). ❖ Began writing career with publication of a poem in *Harper's Magazine* (1876) and an article on art in *American Architect and Building News*; published other articles and reviews of art exhibitions in New York City; a devotee of pictorial realism, published *Book of American Figure Painters* and *American Etchers* (1886); following husband's death (1884), moved to NY and started her 1st important work in the field of architectural criticism, a series entitled "Recent American Architecture" for *Century Magazine,* which led to the publication of *Henry Hobson Richardson and His Works* (1888), a classic study of the architect's work; published studies of Renaissance and modern artists in *Six Portraits* (1899), and was elected an honorary member of American Institute of Architects (1900); published *English Cathedrals* (1892), based on a series she had done for *Century Magazine,* followed by an introduction to landscape gardening, *Art Out of Doors* (1893); published well-received 2-vol. *History of the City of New York in the Seventeenth Century* (1909); also served as president of the Public Education Association of New York City (1899–1906). Received gold medal from American Academy of Arts and Letters (1923). ❖ See also *Women in World History.*

VAN RENSSELAER, Martha (1864–1932). American home economist and educator. Born June 21, 1864, in Randolph, New York; died May 26, 1932, in New York, NY; dau. of Henry Killian Van Rensselaer (storekeeper and insurance agent) and Arvilla A. (Owen) Van Rensselaer (schoolteacher and boardinghouse manager); educated at Chamberlain Institute; Cornell University, AB, 1909. ❖ Elected one of two school commissioners of Cattaraugus County (1893 and 1896); as commissioner, assisted the efforts of the agricultural extension program at Cornell University, including Anna Botsford Comstock's work using nature study to promote farming; organized an extension program for farmers' wives, a project that evolved into the New York State College of

Home Economics at Cornell University; published the 1st bulletin of the "Farmers' Wives' Reading Course" (1901); appointed co-chair of department of home economics which was formed within the College of Agriculture at Cornell (1906); became professor (1911); served as president of American Home Economics Association (1914–16); also worked as homemaking editor for the journal *Delineator* (1920–26). ❖ See also *Women in World History.*

VAN RENSSELAER, Mrs. Schuyler (1851–1934). *See Van Rensselaer, Mariana.*

VAN RIJN, Wilma (1971—). Dutch swimmer. Name variations: Wilma van Rijn-van Hofwegen. Born July 17, 1971, in the Netherlands. ❖ Won a silver medal for 4 x 100-meter freestyle relay at Sydney Olympics (2000).

VAN ROOIJEN, Manon (1982—). Dutch swimmer. Born July 7, 1982, in Westdorpe, Holland, Netherlands; attended University of Miami. ❖ Won a silver medal for 4 x 100-meter freestyle relay at Sydney Olympics (2000).

VAN ROOST, Dominique (1973—). Belgian tennis player. Name variations: Dominique Monami. Born Dominique Monami, May 31, 1973, in Verviers, Belgium; m. Bart van Roost, 1995. ❖ Reached quarterfinals of Australian Open (1997); won a bronze medal for doubles at Sydney Olympics (2000);.

VAN RUMPT, Annemarieke (1980—). Dutch rower. Born April 29, 1980, in the Netherlands. ❖ Won a bronze medal for coxed eights at Athens Olympics (2004).

VAN RUMT, Hendrika (b. 1897). Dutch gymnast. Born Aug 28, 1897, in Netherlands. ❖ At Amsterdam Olympics, won a gold medal in team all-around (1928).

VAN RUNKLE, Theadora (1940—). American costume designer. Name variations: Thea Van Runkle. Born 1940 in Los Angeles, CA. ❖ Began career as an illustrator for store ads and catalogs; came to prominence and spawned a fashion trend for designs for *Bonnie and Clyde* (1967); other films include *The Thomas Crown Affair, Bullitt, Myra Breckinridge, Mame, Godfather Part II, Nickelodeon, New York New York, Same Time Next Year, Heaven Can Wait, S. O. B., Peggy Sue Got Married, Stella,* and *Leap of Faith.* Nominated for 3 Academy Awards.

VAN SCHURMANN, Anna Maria (1607–1678). Dutch scholar and artist. Name variations: Anna Maria van Schuurman or Schuurmann; van Schurman. Born Nov 5, 1607, in Cologne, Germany; died May 14, 1678, in Wieuwerd, Friesland; dau. of Frederik van Schurmann (died 1623) and Eva (von Harff) van Shurmann (died 1637); never married; no children. ❖ Writer, philosopher, theologian, and artist, was perhaps the most learned woman of 17th-century Europe; born in religious exile in Cologne, returned with family to the Netherlands, settling in Utrecht (1610); studied largely on her own, mastering variety of subjects, including geography, astronomy, music, mathematics and theology; composed poetry on religious issues in Dutch and excelled in painting, engraving, and embroidery; best known for her knowledge of languages: Dutch, French, German, Latin, Greek and Hebrew; also studied Eastern languages, including Turkish, Syrian, Arabic and Ethiopian; gained early fame in Netherlands and among intellectual circles of Europe, where her accomplishments as a scholar stimulated debate over the natural intelligence and capabilities of women; became part of wide network of learned men and women who contested philosophical and theological ideas through extensive correspondence; conducted one such debate with theologian André Rivet on the question of whether women should be educated, published as a *Dissertation* (1641); allowed to attend lectures at University of Utrecht, the only woman given the privilege; continued to correspond with philosophers and theologians across Europe, including René Descartes, with whom she debated the nature of knowledge and reason; published a collection of these letters (1648); was one of the earliest supporters of Pietism; published *Euklerion* (1673), an autobiographical and spiritual work in which she explained her decision to join the Labadists as part of her spiritual path to God and in which she renounced much of her life's work. ❖ See also Mirjam De Baar, *et al.,* eds. *Choosing the Better Part: Anna Maria van Schurman (1607–1678)* (Kluwer Academic, 1996); and *Women in World History.*

VANSITTART, Henrietta (1840–1883). English engineer. Born Henrietta Lowe, 1840, in London, England; died Feb 8, 1883, of acute mania and anthrax, a few months after she was discovered wandering the streets and sent to a county lunatic asylum (near Newcastle); dau. of a machinist; m. William Vansittart, 1855. ❖ The 1st woman engineer in Britain, was involved in a secret affair, then long friendship, with Edward Bulwer Lytton, later 1st earl of Lytton (1858–71); after father's death (1866), pursued some patents to earn recognition for his inventions; registered patent 2,877 for the Lowe-Vansittart propeller (1868), which was used on HMS *Druid* in Admiralty trials and awarded a 1st class diploma at 1871 Kensington Exhibition; presented her 1st speech (1876), at London Association of Foreman Engineers and Draughtsmen's anniversary dinner; presented paper, "The Screw Propeller of 1838 and Its Subsequent Improvements" (1876); developed the propeller but failed to pay its renewal patent fee (£600).

VANSOVA, Terezia (1857–1942). Slovak novelist and playwright. Name variations: Terézia Vansová. Born Terezia Medvecka, 1857, in Zvolenska Slatina, Slovakia; died 1942 in Banská Bystrica; married. ❖ Edited 1st Slovak women's paper, *Dennica* (Morning Star, 1898–1907), wrote 1st novel by a Slovak woman, *Sirota Podhradských* (1889, *The Podhradskys' Orphan*), and organized the women's movement; also wrote *Kliatba* (Curse, 1927), and *Sestry* (Sisters, 1930), as well as verse and a travel book on Prague; translated Božena Němcová's novel *Babička* (1855).

VAN STAVEREN, Petra (1966—). Dutch swimmer. Born June 2, 1966, in Kampen, Netherlands. ❖ At Los Angeles Olympics, won a gold medal in 100-meter breaststroke (1984).

VAN STOCKUM, Hilda (b. 1908). Dutch-born writer and illustrator. Name variations: Hilda Van Stockum. Born Feb 9, 1908 in Rotterdam, Netherlands; dau. of Abraham John van Stockum and Olga (Boissevain) van Stockum; attended Dublin School of Art and Amsterdam Academy of Art; studied briefly at Corcoran School of Art, 1937; m. Ervin Ross Marlin (American aviator), June 27, 1932; children: Olga, Brigid, Randal, Sheila, John and Elisabeth. ❖ On marriage (1932), moved to New York City, where she taught at a Montessori school; wrote and illustrated 1st children's novel, *A Day on Skates: The Story of a Dutch Picnic* (1934), which received the Newbery Honor Award (1935); moved to Washington, DC, and taught art and writing at Institute of Lifetime Learning, while continuing to write herself; became a US citizen (1936); with husband, moved to Canada, where she concentrated on writing and illustrating children's books, over 20 in all; her books, set in Ireland, US, and Holland, draw heavily on her childhood experiences as well as on her own children; continued to illustrate for other authors, and translated numerous children's books into English; was also well known for her paintings, mainly still-life and portraiture, which were exhibited in one-woman shows from Dublin to Netherlands to US (1950s–70s); returned to Washington (1960s), where she became president of the Children's Book Guild; retired to Hertfordshire, England (1980s). ❖ See also *Women in World History.*

VAN STUDDIFORD, Grace (1873–1927). American actress and singer. Name variations: Grace Studdiford; Grace Studiford. Born Grace Quivey, Jan 8, 1873, in North Manchester, IN; died Jan 29, 1927. ❖ Made stage debut in Chicago as Minna in *The Black Hussar;* made opera debut at the Metropolitan in title role of *Martha* (1900), followed by Michaela in *Carmen,* Marguerite in *Faust,* Fleur-de-Lys in *Esmeralda,* Josephine in *H. M. S. Pinafore,* Leonora in *Il Trovatore;* appeared in title roles in *Maid Marion* (1903) and *Lady Teazle,* and had a huge success in *The Red Feather;* also appeared at leading music halls; on Broadway, starred in *The Golden Butterfly, The Bohemian Girl, A Bridal Trip* (renamed *The Paradise of Mahomet*), *La Belle Paree,* and *Oh Oh Delphine;* as Grace Studdiford, appeared in such films as *The Land of Promise* and *Pardon My French.*

VAN TUYLL, Isabelle (1740–1805). *See Charriere, Isabelle de.*

VAN UPP, Virginia (1902–1970). American screenwriter and producer. Born Jan 13, 1902, in Chicago, IL; died Mar 25, 1970, in Los Angeles, CA. ❖ Began career as a child actress in early silent films, then became script girl, cutter, reader and casting director for Paramount; named executive producer at Columbia, a protégée of Harry Cohn (1945); screenplays include *The Pursuit of Happiness, So Red the Rose, Poppy, Easy to Take, Swing High Swing Low, St. Louis Blues, You and Me, Cafe Society, Honeymoon in Bali, Virginia, One Night in Lisbon, Bahama Passage, The Crystal Ball, Cover Girl, The Impatient Years, Together Again* (also producer), *She Wouldn't Say Yes* (also producer), *Here Comes the Groom,* and *Affair in Trinidad;* also produced *Gilda* and helped shape the career of Rita Hayworth.

VAN VALKENBURGH, Elizabeth (1799–1846). American poisoner. Born in Bennington, VT, July 1799; hanged Jan 24, 1846; m. 2nd husband John Van Valkenburgh, Mar 1834 (died Mar 16, 1845);

children: (1st m.) 4; (2nd m.) at least 2. ❖ Condemned to death in Fulton, NY, made full confession to murdering 2nd husband with arsenic because he was "addicted to liquor" and "misused the children when under its influence"; denied murdering 1st husband, but in a subsequent statement did confess to poisoning him with arsenic about a year before his death.

VAN VECHTEN, Fania (1890–1971). *See Marinoff, Fania.*

VAN VELSEN, Wilma (1964—). Dutch swimmer. Born Mar 22, 1964. ❖ Won a bronze medal at Moscow Olympics (1980) and a silver medal at Los Angeles Olympics (1984), both in 4 x 100-meter freestyle relay.

VAN VLIET, Petronella (1926—). Dutch swimmer. Born Jan 17, 1926. ❖ At London Olympics, won a gold medal in 200-meter breaststroke (1948).

VAN VOORN, Koosje (1935—). Dutch swimmer. Born Jan 15, 1935. ❖ At Helsinki Olympics, won a silver medal in 4 x 100-meter freestyle relay (1952).

VAN VORST, Marie Louise (1867–1936). American author and reformer. Born Nov 23, 1867, in New York, NY; died Dec 16, 1936, in Florence, Italy; dau. of Hooper Cumming Van Vorst (judge) and Josephine (Treat) Van Vorst; m. Count Gaetano Cagiati (an Italian), Oct 16, 1916; children: (adopted) Frederick John. ❖ With sister-in-law Bessie McGinnis Van Vorst, wrote a light novel, *Bagsby's Daughter* (1901); published a more serious novel, *Philip Longstreth* (1902); investigating the plight of factory workers, secured jobs with Bessie, then wrote *The Woman Who Toils; Being the Experiences of Two Ladies as Factory Girls* (1903), an exposé of the poor living and working conditions faced by women and children; with such books as *Amanda of the Mill* (1905), a well-received novel set in a factory in the Blue Ridge Mountains, became more widely known than Bessie; wrote articles on "Rivers of the World," for *Harper's Monthly* (1906–09), requiring her to travel to Europe and Africa; also wrote poetry and fiction, including 15 more novels, which were not as well received; during WWI, wrote *War Letters of an American Woman* (1916) and became head of a commission that coordinated war relief for Italy (1918). ❖ See also *Women in World History.*

VAN WAGENER, Isabella (c. 1797–1883). *See Truth, Sojourner.*

VAN WATERS, Miriam (1887–1974). American prison reformer. Born Oct 4, 1887, in Greensburg, Pennsylvania; died Jan 17, 1974, in Framingham, Massachusetts; dau. of George Browne Van Waters (Episcopal minister) and Maude (Vosburg) Van Waters; University of Oregon, AB, 1908, AM, 1910; Clark University, PhD, 1913; children: Sarah Ann (adopted 1932). ❖ A leader in women's corrections (1920s–40s), became an agent of Boston Children's Aid Society and was placed in charge of young girls who were appearing before the court (1913); worked to improve court health-care services and to find foster homes for the girls; was appointed superintendent of the county juvenile home in Los Angeles (1917), and successfully improved conditions there, leading to her appointment to head El Retiro, another county home for delinquent girls (1919); published *Where Girls Go Right* (1922), *Youth in Conflict* (1925) and *Parents on Probation* (1927); passed California Bar Exam and appointed referee of Los Angeles Juvenile Court (1920); became a consultant to National Commission on Law Enforcement (1929); in *The Child Offender in the Federal System of Justice* (1932), wrote about the failure of district courts to use juvenile court procedures or to supervise juvenile reformatories; became superintendent of Massachusetts Women's Reformatory in Framingham (1932), where she continued the liberal policies instituted by the previous superintendent, Jessie Hodder; served as superintendent until 1957, earning praise and honors. ❖ See also Estelle B. Freedman, *Maternal Justice: Miriam Van Waters and the Female Reform Tradition, 1887–1974* (University of Chicago Press, 1996); and *Women in World History.*

VAN WEERDENBURG, Wilhelmina (1946—). Dutch swimmer. Born Oct 1946. ❖ At Tokyo Olympics, won a bronze medal in 4 x 100-meter freestyle relay (1964).

VAN WIE, Virginia (1909–1997). American golfer. Born Feb 9, 1909, in Chicago, IL; died Feb 18, 1997; lived with Janet E. Towne (Chicago obstetrician and gynecologist, died 1999). ❖ Won Chicago District GA championship (1926–28); won USGA Women's Amateur three times in a row (1932–34); member of Curtis Cup team (1932, 1934); then retired from golf. Named Associated Press Female Athlete of the Year (1934).

VAN WINTER, Lucretia Wilhelmina (1721–1789). *See Merken, Lucretia Wilhelmina van.*

VAN ZANDT, Marie (1858–1919). American opera singer. Born Oct 8, 1858, in New York, NY; died Dec 31, 1919, in Cannes, France; dau. of James Rose Van Zandt (clerk) and Jennie Van Zandt (concert singer); studied singing with her mother, Adelina Patti, and Francesco Lamperti; m. Mikhail Petrovitch de Tscherinoff (Russian state councilor and professor), 1898. ❖ Debuted in Turin as Zerlina in *Don Giovanni* and in London as Amina in *La Sonnambula* (1879); sang in Paris (1880) and her performance in *Mignon* led to a 5-year contract with the Opéra-Comique; with that company, rapidly achieved fame, most notably in title role in Léo Delibes' *Lakmé*, an opera said to be written specifically for her; experienced a disaster losing voice during a performance of *Il Barbiere di Siviglia* (*The Barber of Seville*, 1884); though friends attributed cause to overwork, others maintained incorrectly that she was drunk, and her reputation suffered; went to St. Petersburg, where she was welcomed; also sang at London's Covent Garden and in various venues in America, including Metropolitan Opera, before spending remainder of career in Europe; enjoyed successful season at Opéra-Comique (1896–97); on marriage, retired from stage (1898). ❖ See also *Women in World History.*

VANZETTA, Bice (1961—). Italian cross-country skier. Born Mar 7, 1961, in Italy. ❖ Won a bronze medal at Albertville (1992) and a bronze medal at Lillehammer Olympics (1994), both for 4 x 5 km relay.

VARADY, Julia (1941—). Romanian operatic soprano. Born Sept 1, 1941, in Oradea, Romania; studied in Bucharest with Florescu; married Dietrich Fischer-Dieskau (an opera singer), in 1977. ❖ Made debut with opera company of Cluj (1962), remaining there until 1972; appeared in Cologne and Munich, Germany; 1st sang at the Metropolitan Opera in NY (1977) as Donna Elvira in Mozart's *Don Giovanni* and also appeared at La Scala in Milan (1984); as a performer and singer, was noted for her warmth and intensity, which is well-suited to the Mozart, Verdi, and Puccini roles she plays; also noted as Judith in Béla Bartók's *Duke Bluebeard's Castle.*

VARANO, Costanza (fl. 1445). *See Sforza, Costanza.*

VARCOE, Helen (b. 1907). English swimmer. Name variations: Helen Nicholls. Born Feb 18, 1907, in Croyden, Surrey, England; m. Gordon Nicholls. ❖ At Los Angeles Olympics, won a bronze medal in 4 x 100-meter freestyle relay (1932).

VARDA, Agnes (1928—). French filmmaker. Name variations: Agnès Varda. Born in Ixelles, Belgium, May 30, 1928; raised in France; dau. of Eugène Jean Varda (engineer) and Christiane (Pasquet) Varda; m. Jacques Demy (filmmaker), Jan 8, 1962 (died 1990); children: Rosalie and Mathieu Demy. ❖ Award-winning director-producer whose films, a creative mixture of both fictional and documentary styles, anticipated the French New Wave; made 1st film, *La Pointe-Courte* (1954), a major influence on the French cinema movement of 1960s; after a series of shorts, released 2nd feature-length film, *Cléo de cinq à sept* (*Cleo from 5 to 7*), which brought international attention and was her 1st commercial success (1961); followed that with *Le Bonheur* (*Happiness*, 1964), one of her best-known films, which won the Silver Bear at Berlin film festival; other films include *Les Créatures* (*The Creatures*, 1966), *Loin du Vietnam* (1967), *The Black Panthers* (short, 1968), *Daguerreotypes* (1975), *Plaisir d'amour en Iran* (1976), *L'une chante, l'autre pas* (*One Sings, the Other Doesn't*, 1976), *Mur Murs* (1980), *Documenteur* (1980), *Une minute pour une image* (*One Minute for One Image*, 1982), *Ulysse* (1982), *Le Dites-Caryatides* (*The So-called Cariatids*, 1984), *7P., cuis., S. de B...* (*7 rooms, kitchen, bath*, 1984), *T'as de beaux escaliers, tu sais* (1986), *Le Petit Amour* (1987), *Kung Fu Master* (1987), *Jane B. par Agnès V* (1988), *Jacquot de Nantes* (1990), *Les demoiselles on eu 25 ans* (1992), *L'Univers de Jacques Demy* (*The Universe of Jacques Demy*, 1993), *Les 101 nuits* (*The One Hundred and One Nights*, 1994), *Les glaneurs et la glaneuse* (*The Gleaners and I*, 1999). *Sans toit ni loi* (*Without Roof or Law*, also called *Vagabond*, 1985) won the Golden Lion at Venice Film Festival (1985). ❖ See also Alison Smith, *Agnes Varda* (St. Martin, 1998); and *Women in World History.*

VARDEN, Evelyn (1893–1958). American stage and screen actress. Born June 12, 1893, in Adair, Craig County, OK; died July 11, 1958, in New York, NY. ❖ Made NY debut as Alice Adams in *The Nest Egg* (1910); other stage credits include *Our Town, Family Portrait, Candle in the Wind, Dream Girl, Present Laughter, Hilda Crane,* and *The Bad Seed;*

had great success in London in *Roar Like a Dove*; films include *Cheaper by the Dozen, Pinky, Stella, Hilda Crane* and *The Bad Seed*.

VARDEN, Norma (1898–1989). English stage, tv, and screen actress. Born Jan 20, 1898, in London, England; died Jan 19, 1989, in Santa Barbara, CA. ❖ Played the murder victim in Billy Wilder's *Witness for the Prosecution*; other films include *Random Harvest, Casablanca, The White Cliffs of Dover, National Velvet, Strangers on a Train, The Sound of Music* and *Doctor Dolittle*.

VARDILL, Anna Jane (1781–1852). British poet and translator. Name variations: (pseudonyms) A. J. V.; V. Born Nov 10, 1781, in London, England; died June 4, 1852, in Skipton, Yorkshire, England; dau. of Rev. John Vardill (writer); m. James Niven, 1822 (died 1830); children: 1. ❖ Published *Poems and Translations from the Minor Greek Poets and Others* (1809) and *The Pleasures of Human Life* (1812); also published poems, stories, and essays in *European Magazine* (1813–22); became well known for sequel to Coleridge's poem "Christabel" which appeared in *European Magazine* and *London Review* (1815).

VARE, Glenna Collett (1903–1989). American golfer. Name variations: Glenna Collett. Born June 20, 1903, in New Haven, CT; grew up in Narrangansett, RI; died Feb 3, 1989, in Gulfstream, FL; m. Edward Vare, 1931. ❖ Won the Berthellyn Cup (1921); won US Women's Amateur championship (1922, 1925, 1928–30, 1935); won Canadian Women's Amateur (1923–24); won 59 out of the 60 events (1924); instrumental in organizing Curtis Cup matches and selected for 5 Curtis Cups squads, twice as captain (1932–50); won the Rhode Island State championship at age 56; participated in her 62nd straight Rhode Island Invitational Tournament at age 83; though she never turned pro, won more amateur golf championships than any other athlete and brought a new power and accuracy to the game. Inducted into World Golf Hall of Fame (1975); honored by LPGA with founding of the Vare trophy (1953), for golfer with lowest stroke average at season's end; given the Bob Jones Award by WSGA (1965). ❖ See also autobiography *Ladies in the Rough* (Knopf, 1928); and *Women in World History*.

VARGANOVA, Svetlana (1964—). Soviet swimmer. Born Nov 19, 1964, in USSR. ❖ At Moscow Olympics, won a silver medal in 200-meter breaststroke (1980).

VARGAS, Chavela (1919—). Mexican singer. Born Isabel Vargas Lizano, April 19, 1919, in Santa Bárbara de Heredia, Costa Rica; dau. of Francisco Vargas and Herminia Lizano. ❖ Grand Dame of Mexican Music, ran away at 14 after family moved to Mexico; took up with Mexican intellectuals such as Diego Rivera, Juan Rulfo, and Agustín Lara; had love affair with Frida Kahlo, living with Kahlo and Diego Rivera for several years; started performance career relatively late in life (mid-30s), singing with José Alfredo Jiménez (1950s); recorded 1st album (1961); became internationally famous for interpretations of sentimental Mexican ranchera music, touring worldwide; battled alcoholism (1970s), periodically attempting to make comebacks, including stellar performances in Olympia Theater of Paris, Palacio de Bellas Artes in Mexico, and Palau de la Música in Barcelona (1981); retired again (1980s), unable to conquer addiction; was tracked down by Spanish filmmaker Pedro Almodóvar (1990s) who helped her rebuild career; produced music for soundtrack for Almodóvar's *Tacones Lejanos* and appeared in cameos in his other films, as well as in Julie Taymor's *Frida* (2000); gave triumphant concert before 20,000 in Mexico City's main plaza, Zócalo (1999); awarded Spain's Great Cross of Isabel la Católica (2000); made Carnegie Hall debut at 83 (2003). Signature songs include "La Llorona" (The Crybaby), "Somos" (We Are), "Luz de luna" (The Light of the Moon), "Canción de las simples cosas" (Song of the Simple Things), "Macorina," "Piensa en mí" (Think of Me), "Se me hizo fácil" (It Was Easy for Me), "Volver volver" (Return, Return), "Angelitos negros" (Little Black Angels), "Amanecí en tus brazos" (I Woke Up in Your Arms), "Vámonos" (Let's Go), "Un mundo raro" (A Strange World), and "El último trago" (The Last Drink); albums include *Chavela Vargas Le Canta a México* (1995), *Colección de Oro* (2002) and *En Carnegie Hall* (2004). ❖ See also Chavela Vargas, *Y si quieres saber de mi pasado* (And If You Want to Know of My Past, 2002).

VARGAS, Virginia (1945—). Peruvian feminist activist. Born July 23, 1945, in Lima, Peru; m. Juan Veas Rossi, 1968 (died 1979); m. Valente; children: 1 daughter. ❖ Moved to Chile to be with 1st husband (1968) and worked as sociology professor while organizing for Salvador Allende's Socialist Popular Unity Party; forced to leave Chile after 1973 coup in which Allende was deposed by military dictator Pinochet; worked in Peru at National Cultural Institute and continued solidarity work with Chile;

pursued graduate studies in economics; helped found Flora Tristán Center for Peruvian Women (1979); served as the center's coordinator and then as director until 1990, offering programs on domestic violence, reproductive rights, abortion, sexual freedom, local government empowerment and citizenship; published magazine *Viva* (Live) for 10 years through the center's research institute; participated in women's economic development projects of non-governmental organizations, helping found Latin American section of Development Alternatives for a New Era (DAWN); as international feminist leader, helped to organize *Encuentros* (meetings) of Latin American and Caribbean Women in Peru to strengthen development of local feminism (1981 and 1983); served as visiting professor at many universities and for Women's Program at Social Studies Institute at The Hague; was Latin American representative to 4th Women's World Conference in Beijing (1995); continued to work for advancement of women and sustainable development, collaborating with Women's Council of the Interamerican Bank of Development, Council on Gender of the World Bank and Women's World Forum. Received Monseñor Proaño Award from the Latin American Association for Human Rights (1995), UNIFEM award (1995), and Spain's Progressive Woman Award (1995).

VARLAMOVA, Inna (1922–1990). *See Landau, Klavdia Gustavovna.*

VARLEY, Isabella (1821–1887). *See Banks, Isabella.*

VARLEY, Mrs. (1918—). *See Brown, Margaret Elizabeth.*

VÁRNAY, Astrid (1918—). Swedish-born American operatic soprano. Name variations: Astrid Varnay. Born Ibolyka Astrid Várnay, April 25, 1918, in Stockholm, Sweden; came to US (1923) and became a naturalized citizen (1943); dau. of Alexander Várnay (tenor and stage director) and Maria (Yavor) Várnay (coloratura soprano); studied voice with mother, and later with Weigert; m. Hermann O. Weigert (conductor), 1944. ❖ Made debut at Metropolitan Opera in *Die Walküre* and sang the part of Sieglinde when Lotte Lehmann became ill (1941); continued to sing with the Met for rest of career; known for interpretations of Wagner and Richard Strauss, especially the roles of Herodias and Klytemnestra in *Salome* and *Elektra*, also added Italian roles from *Aïda, La Gioconda*, and *Otello* to repertoire; made acclaimed recordings of the *Ring* cycle; began singing mezzo-soprano roles (1962); retired (1979). ❖ See also *Women in World History*.

VARNHAGEN, Rahel (1771–1833). Jewish-German salonnière and letter writer. Name variations: Rahel Levin changed to Rahel Robert in 1810, baptized Antonie Friederike in 1814, married name Rahel Varnhagen or Rahel Varnhagen von Ense. Born Rahel Levin, May 19, 1771, in Berlin, Germany; died in Berlin, 1833; dau. of Chaie Levin and Markus Levin (Jewish Berlin banker); converted from Judaism to Christianity in 1814; m. Karl August Varnhagen von Ense, 1814; no children. ❖ Salonnière whose Berlin salons (1789–1806 and 1819–33) attracted many well-known personages—men and women—of various social classes, religions, and occupations; drew to her 1st salon such luminaries as August Wilhelm Schlegel, Friedrich Schlegel, Alexander and Wilhelm von Humboldt, Ludwig Tieck, Friedrich Schleiermacher, Johann G. Fichte, Friedrich de la Motte Fouqué, Heinrich von Kleist, Prince de Ligne, Pauline Wiesel and Rebecca Friedländer; held 2nd salon for Leopold Ranke, Georg Hegel, Alexander von Humboldt, and Fürst Pückler, and then later Heinrich Heine and Bettina von Arnim; published some of her letters anonymously in Cotta's "Morgenblatt für die gebildete Stände" (1812) and in various journals until her death. Posthumous collections of her letters with various people, include David Veit (1861), Karl Varnhagen von Ense (1874–75), Karoline von Humboldt (1896), Alexander von der Marwitz (1925), Pauline Wiesel (1982), and Rebecca Friedländer (1988). ❖ See also Hannah Arendt, *Rahel Varnhagen: The Life of a Jewish Woman* (rev. ed., Harcourt, 1974); Ellen Key, *Rahel Varnhagen: A Portrait* (Putnam, 1913); Heidi Thomann Tewarson, *Rachel Levin Varnhagen: The Life and Work of a German Jewish Intellectual* (U. of Nebraska Press, 1999); and *Women in World History*.

VARO, Remedios (1906–1963). Spanish artist. Name variations: Maria de los Remedios Varo y Uranga. Born Maria de los Remedios Varo y Uranga, Dec 16, 1906, in Anglés, Spain; died of a heart attack, Oct 8, 1963; dau. of Rodrigo Varo y Zejalbo and Ignacia Uranga y Bergareche; studied art at the Academy of San Fernando; m. Gerardo Lizárraga (artist), in 1930; m. Benjamin Péret (French Surrealist poet), in 1942; m. Walter Gruen, around 1952. ❖ Twentieth-century Surrealist painter in Spain and Mexico, displayed a talent for drawing and painting at an early age and a fascination with a magical world that would later infuse her Surrealism; with 1st husband, settled in Barcelona; during Spanish

Civil War, lived in Paris (1937–39); during WWII, managed to escape France, ending up in Mexico where she remained; painted prolifically, her works evolving from the Surrealism of the 1930s. In Mexico City, the Palace of Fine Arts and the Museum of Modern Art held major retrospective exhibitions of her paintings, to great popular acclaim (1964, 1971, and 1983). ❖ See also Janet A. Kaplan, *Unexpected Journeys: The Art and Life of Remedios Varo* (Abbeville, 1988); and *Women in World History*.

VARSI, Diane (1937–1992). American actress. Born Diane Marie Varsi, Feb 23, 1937, in San Mateo, CA; died Nov 19, 1992, in Los Angeles, CA; m. James Dickson, 1955 (div. 1958); m. Michael Hausman (producer), 1961 (div. 1965); children: 2. ❖ Films include *From Hell to Texas, 10 North Frederick, Compulsion, Wild in the Streets, Bloody Mama, Johnny Got His Gun* and *I Never Promised You a Rose Garden*; broke contract with Fox and moved to Vermont (1959), seriously impairing career in films. Nominated for Academy Award for Best Supporting Actress for portrayal of Allison MacKenzie in *Peyton Place* (1957).

VARST (1894–1958). *See Stepanova, Varvara.*

VARTIO, Marja-Liisa (1924–1966). Finnish novelist and poet. Born 1922 at Säminge, Finland; died 1966; m. Paavo Haavikko. ❖ Poetry includes *Häät* (1952) and *Seppele* (1953); novels, which enjoyed a wide readership in Finland, include *Mies kuin mies, tyttö kuin tyttö* (1958), *Kaikki naiset näkevät unia* (1962), and *Hänen olivat linnut* (1967).

VASALIS, M. (1909–1998). *See Fortuyn-Leenmans, Margaretha Droogleever.*

VASARHELYI WECKINGER, Edit (1923—). Hungarian gymnast. Born May 25, 1923, in Hungary. ❖ At London Olympics, won a silver medal in team all-around (1948); at Helsinki Olympics, won a silver medal in team all-around and a bronze medal in teams all-around, portable apparatus (1952).

VASCO, María (1975—). Spanish track-and-field athlete. Name variations: Maria. Born Dec 26, 1975, in Barcelona, Spain. ❖ Won a bronze medal for the 20 km road walk at Sydney Olympics (2000).

VASCONCELLOS, Karoline Michaëlis de (1851–1925). Portuguese educator and scholar. Name variations: Carolina Michaëlis de Vasconcelos. Born Karoline Wilhelmina Michaëlis in 1851 in Germany; died in 1925; m. Joaquim de Vasconcellos (Portuguese historian), 1876. ❖ On marriage, became a Portuguese citizen (1876); was known for her broad scholarship in the philology of Romance languages; became the 1st woman appointed to a university chair in Portugal (1911); best known for her 2-vol. work *Cancioneiro da Ajuda* (1904), which discusses the role of women in the creation of early Portuguese poetry; also known for *A Infanta Dona Maria de Portugal e as Suas Damas* (The Infanta Dona Maria of Portugal and Her Ladies, 1902); believed in the necessity for education for women and for educational reform, and wrote extensively on the subject, particularly in *O Movimiento Feminista em Portugal* (The Feminist Movement in Portugal, 1901).

VASEVA, Lilyana (1955—). Bulgarian rower. Born Aug 12, 1955, in Bulgaria. ❖ At Montreal Olympics, won a silver medal in coxed fours (1976).

VASEY, Jessie (1897–1966). Australian social reformer. Born Jessie Mary Halbert, Oct 19, 1897, in Roma, Queensland, Australia; died Sept 22, 1966; dau. of Joseph Halbert (pastoralist) and Jessie (Dobbin) Halbert; University of Melbourne, BA, 1921; m. George Alan Vasey (army officer), early 1920s (died 1945); children: George Alan (b. 1925), Robert (b. 1932). ❖ Was a founding member of the Australian Imperial Forces Women's Association; established the War Widows' Craft Guild to improve plight of Australia's war widows (1946). Named an Officer of the British Empire (1950) and Commander of the British Empire (1963). ❖ See also *Women in World History*.

VASHTI (fl. 5th c. BCE). Biblical woman and queen of Persia. Name variations: Astin; Vastis; Vasthi; Wasti. Pronunciation: (Hebrew) wasti; (English) Vashti. Was the wife of King Xerxes I (Ahasuerus in the Biblical text), and may have been associated with Persian nobility (though the wives of Persian kings were required to come from specific Persian noble families, this was not always the case); what is known about Vashti is contained in the scroll of *Esther*, one of the writings in the Hebrew Scriptures. ❖ Queen of Persia in the Biblical story of *Esther* who, by defying her husband, was deposed and replaced by the compliant Esther; her brief, but significant, story comprises the 1st 27 verses of this "early Jewish novella." The fact that Amestris, rather than Vashti, is recorded as Xerxes' queen during the period under study has raised questions about

Vashti's historicity. However, given the numerous concubines and mistresses the king enjoyed, it is not implausible for him to have had more than one queen. ❖ See also *Women in World History*.

VASILCHENKO, Olga (1956—). Soviet rower. Born Nov 1956 in USSR. ❖ At Moscow Olympics, won a silver medal in quadruple sculls with coxswain (1980).

VASILEVSKAIA, Elena (1978—). Russian volleyball player. Name variations: Yelena Vassilevskaia. Born Feb 27, 1978, in Ekaterinburg, Russia. ❖ Made national team debut (1997); won European team championship (1997, 1999, 2001) and World Grand Prix (1997, 1999); won a team silver medal at Sydney Olympics (2000).

VASILI, Paul (1836–1936). *See Adam, Juliette.*

VASILIEVA, Yulia (1978—). Russian synchronized swimmer. Name variations: Julia Vasilieva. Born Sept 6, 1978, in USSR. ❖ Won a team gold medal at Sydney Olympics (2000).

VASILKOVA, Elvira (1962—). Soviet swimmer. Born May 15, 1962, in USSR. ❖ At Moscow Olympics, won a silver medal in 100-meter breaststroke and a bronze medal in 4 x 100-meter medley relay (1980).

VASIUKOVA, Olga (1980—). *See Vassioukova, Olga.*

VASSAR, Queenie (1870–1960). Scottish-born musical-comedy star. Born Oct 28, 1870, in Glasgow, Scotland; died Sept 11, 1960, in West Los Angeles, CA; m. Joseph Cawthorn (comedian, died 1949). ❖ Came to US (1884); worked for Tony Pastor; Broadway appearances include *A Trip to Chinatown, The Country Fair, Belle of New York, The Toreador* and *Sister Mary*.

VASSILEVSKAIA, Elena or Yelena (1978—). *See Vasilevskaia, Elena.*

VASSILIEVA, Ekaterina (1976—). Russian water-polo player. Born May 30, 1976, in USSR. ❖ Won a team bronze medal at Sydney Olympics (2000).

VASSILTSCHIKOV, Anna (16th c.). Russian empress. Fifth wife of Ivan IV, tsar of Russia. Ivan IV also m. Anastasia Romanova (d. 1560) in Feb 1547; Maria of Circassia (d. 1569) in August 1561; Marta Sobakin (d. 1571) in Oct 1571; Anna Koltoskaia (d. 1626) in April 1572 (div. 1574); Maria Nagaia (d. 1612); and Vassilissa Malentieva c. 1576 (div. 1577).

VASSIOUKOVA, Olga (1980—). Russian synchronized swimmer. Name variations: Olga Vasiukova. Born May 8, 1980, in USSR. ❖ Won a team gold medal at Sydney Olympics (2000).

VASTIS (fl. 5th c. BCE). *See Vashti.*

VATACHKA, Vjara (1980—). Bulgarian rhythmic gymnast. Name variations: Viara Vatashka. Born Feb 20, 1980, in Bulgaria. ❖ Won a silver medal for team all-around at Atlanta Olympics (1996).

VATASHKA, Vjara (1980—). *See Vatachka, Vjara.*

VATASOIU, Emilia (1933—). *See Lita-Vatasoiu, Emilia.*

VAUCHER, Yvette (1929—). Swiss mountaineer. Born Yvette Pilliard in Vallorbe, northeast of Geneva, Switzerland, in 1929; m. Michel Vaucher (a mountaineer), in 1962. ❖ Began rock climbing at the Salève (1951); moved to Neuchâtel (1955), took up free-fall parachuting, and made over 100 descents; formed a climbing team with Michel Vaucher; made many important climbs: Piz Badile, Triolet, Drus, Eiger, and Grandes Jorasses; also climbed Ninagougo in Zaire and the West Ridge of Mt. McKinley in Alaska; made 1st direct ascent of North Face of Dent Blanche (1966); made 1st female ascent of North Face of the Matterhorn; was a member of the disastrous International Everest Expedition (1971) during which one man died of exposure.

VAUGHAN, Gladys (d. 1987). American stage director. Name variations: Gladys Regier. Born Gladys Eileen Regier in IA; died Dec 30, 1987, age 64, in NYC; m. Stuart Vaughan (director, actor, playwright, div.). ❖ With producton of *Richard II* (1961), became the 1st woman to direct at the New York Shakespeare Festival; others include *Macbeth, King Lear, The Winter's Tale, Othello, Coriolanus, Measure for Measure, Richard III*, and a co-directing credit with Joseph Papp on *The Merchant of Venice*.

VAUGHAN, Helen Gwynne- (1879–1967). *See Gwynne-Vaughan, Helen.*

VAUGHAN, Hilda (1892–1985). Welsh playwright and novelist. Born in 1892 in Builth, Breconshire, Wales; died in 1985; dau. of Hugh Vaughan Vaughan and Eva (Campbell) Vaughan; m. Charles Langbridge Morgan (novelist and drama critic), 1923 (died 1958); children: two. ❖ Wrote such plays as *She Too Was Young* and *Forsaking All Others* (both with Laurier Lister) and the novel *The Soldier and the Gentlewoman* (dramatized by Lister and Dorothy Massingham); also wrote romantic novels, including *The Battle to the Weak, Here Are Lovers, The Invader, Her Father's House, A Thing of Nought, The Curtain Rises, Harvest Home, Pardon and Peace, The Candle and the Light* and *Iron and Gold* (1948), now considered a classic work of Welsh feminism. ❖ See also Christopher Newman, *Hilda Vaughan* (Univ. of Wales Press, 1981).

VAUGHAN, Janet (1899–1993). English pathologist, administrator and radiobiologist. Name variations: Dame Janet Vaughan. Born Janet Maria Vaughan, Oct 18, 1899, in Clifton, Bristol, England; died Jan 9, 1993; dau. of William Wyamar Vaughan (headmaster at Rugby) and Margaret Madge Symonds Vaughan (author and friend of Virginia Woolf); Somerville College, Oxford, BSc, 1922; m. David Gourlay (Wayfarers' Travel Association founder), 1930; children: 2. ❖ Received medical training at University College Hospital (1922–24); studied hematology and the application of statistical techniques with Cecil Price-Jones at University College Hospital; worked with George Minoti on pernicious anemia treatments at Boston Memorial Hospital; collaborated with H. M. Turnball and Donald Hunter on blood and bone diseases; studied celiac disease (a chronic nutritional disorder); during WWII, played an important role in establishing blood transfusion depots in London; with Rosalind Pitt-Rivers and Charles Dent, sent to Europe after the war to assess value of concentrated protein solutions in treating starvation; served as principal of Somerville College (1945–67); worked for Medical Research Council Unit for Bone-seeking Isotopes, Churchill Hospital, Oxford (1947–67); elected fellow of Royal Society (1979); wrote *The Anaemias* (1934), *The Physiology of Bone* (1971) and *The Effects of Irradiation on the Skeleton* (1973). Made Officer of the Order of the British Empire (1944) and Dame Commander of the Order of the British Empire (1957).

VAUGHAN, Kate (c. 1852–1903). English actress and dancer. Born Catherine Candellon c. 1850 or 1852; died in Johannesburg, South Africa, Feb 21, 1903. ❖ Debuted as a dancer (1870); had 1st success in *Magic Toys* at the Adelphi (1874), then appeared at Princess Theater and Drury Lane; was a headliner in burlesques at the Gaiety Theater in London (1876–83); for 2 years, worked with her own company, the Vaughan-Conway Comedy troupe, and inaugurated the modern school of skirt dancing, before performing on stage in the roles of Lady Teazle and Lydia Languish; sailed to Johannesburg, South Africa, in hopes of improving her declining health (1902).

VAUGHAN, Lucile (1935—). See Wheeler, Lucile.

VAUGHAN, Sarah (1924–1990). African-American jazz and pop singer. Born Sarah Vaughan, Mar 27, 1924, in Newark, NJ; died April 4, 1990, in CA; m. George Treadwell, 1946 (div. 1958); m. Clyde B. Atkins, 1958 (div. 1962); m. Waymon Reed, 1978 (div. 1981); children: (adopted) Debra, known professionally as Paris Vaughan. ❖ By early teens, played and sang at local nightclubs and ballrooms; appeared at Harlem's Apollo Theater, where she sang "Body and Soul" on amateur night and won 1st prize (1942); was hired to sing with Earl "Fatha" Hines' band (1943), then Billy Eckstine's band (1944), before striking out as a solo artist; made 1st recording, "I'll Wait and Pray" (1944); made some of her best recordings for Musicraft, including her 1st jazz recording to cross over to pop charts, "Tenderly" (1947), and "It's Magic," which stayed at #11 for nearly 3 months; known for her unique combination of jazz, pop, and classical styles, gained international reputation under guidance of 1st husband and manager, and began a nearly 50-year career; discovered by a new generation, singing a series of all-Gershwin concerts under baton of Michael Tilson Thomas, which brought her her 1st Grammy (1982); other hits include "Don't Blame Me," "Make Believe," "I Cried for You" and "Broken-Hearted Melody." Inducted into Jazz Hall of Fame (1988); awarded special Grammy for lifetime achievement (1989); won Emmy for one of the Gershwin concerts that had been presented on PBS. ❖ See also Leslie Gourse, *Sassy: The Life of Sarah Vaughan* (Scribner, 1993); and *Women in World History*.

VAUGHN, Hilda (1898–1957). American character actress. Born Dec 27, 1898, in Baltimore, MD; died Dec 28, 1957, in Baltimore. ❖ Broadway appearances include *Only the Heart, Jacobowsky and the Colonel, On Whitman Avenue, The Devil's Disciple* and *Medea*; films include *Three Live Ghosts, Susan Lenox, Dinner at 8* and *Anne of Green Gables*.

VAUGHT, Wilma L. (1930—). American general. Born 1930 in Scottsville, Illinois; graduate of University of Illinois, 1957. ❖ Air Force brigadier general, was the Air Force's 1st female general and one of the most decorated women to serve in the military; served as chair of NATO women in the Allied Forces Committee (1983–85); was the senior woman military representative to the Defense; retired (1985); was instrumental in building a memorial to the nearly 2 million women who have served in the US military: the Women in Military Service Memorial at the entrance to Arlington National Cemetery (1997). Inducted into the Women's Hall of Fame at Seneca Falls, NY (2000).

VAUSSARD, Christiane (1923—). French ballet dancer. Born 1923 in Neuilly-sur-Seine, France. ❖ Trained with Carlotta Zambelli, among others, at ballet school of Paris Opéra; joined Paris Opéra (1940) and danced in Zambelli's roles in revivals of *Giselle* and *Deux Pigeons*, and others; also danced in contemporary works such as *Le Chevalier Errant* (1950), *Firebird* (1954), and *Pas de Quatre* (1960), all by Serge Lifar; upon retiring from performance career, served as ballet teacher at Paris Opéra school.

VAUTIER, Catherine (1902–1989). New Zealand netball player, teacher, and sports administrator. Born Catherine Wilhelmina Vautier, Aug 27, 1902, in Palmerston North, New Zealand; died June 12, 1989, in Palmerston North; dau. of Reginald de Jersey Vautier (farmer) and Ada (Wallis) Vautier. ❖ Taught at Palmerston North Technical School (1927–67); helped found Manawatu Basketball Association (1928); active in all aspects of game, including coaching, managing, officiating, announcing, publicizing, and fund raising; made life member of New Zealand Basketball (later Netball) Association (1967). Named OBE (1977). ❖ See also *Dictionary of New Zealand Biography* (Vol. 4).

VAUTRIN, Minnie (1886–1941). American missionary. Born Sept 27, 1886, in Secor, IL; died May 14, 1941, in Indianapolis, IN; dau. of Edmond Louis Vautrin and Pauline (Lohr) Vautrin. ❖ Served as principal of girls' school in Luchow, China (from 1914); became head of department of education and acting president at Ginling College in Nanking (1919); oversaw care of thousands of women and children refugees on grounds of Ginling College during attack of Nanking (Nanjing) by Japanese army (1937–38), saving hundreds of lives.

VAUX, Anne (fl. 1605–1635). British radical. Flourished between 1605 and 1635; 3rd dau. of William Vaux, 3rd Baron Vaux. ❖ A recusant, often taunted the ecumenical and secular laws of the Church of England; under name Mrs. Perkins, sheltered the Jesuit Henry Garnett and was imprisoned at Hindlip (1606) when Garnett was arrested at her home; also held company with gunpowder plotters, who gathered at her home in Wandsworth (1604) and in Enfield (1605); after establishing a school for Roman Catholic youth near Derby, was forced by the Privy Council to close it (1635).

VAUX, Clotilde de (1815–1846). French writer. Born in Paris, April 3, 1815; died in Paris, April 5, 1846; 1st child of Captain Joseph Marie and Countess Henriette-Josephine de Ficquelmont; m. Amenee de Vaux (tax collector); beloved by philosopher Auguste Comte. ❖ When husband left Paris for Belgium after embezzling 15,000 francs, refused to join him there; despite her poverty, enjoyed her independence and concentrated on writing, publishing several essays, and a novel *Lucie* in the journal *The National*; became ill with tuberculosis; met philosopher Auguste Comte (Aug 1844); her affection for him was genuine, if not romantic, and their friendship intensified as her illness progressed; received poor medical treatment, which probably hastened her death. Comte adopted her as a model of saintly womanhood and credited her with having inspired his new religious philosophy, the "Religion of Humanity." ❖ See also *Women in World History*.

VAYTSEKHOVSKAYA, Yelena (1958—). Soviet diver. Born Mar 1958 in USSR. ❖ At Montreal Olympics, won a gold medal in platform (1976).

VAZ DE CARVALHO, Maria Amália (1847–1921). Portuguese poet and novelist. Name variations: Maria Amalia Vaz de Carvalho. Born Feb 1, 1847, in Lisbon, Portugal; died 1921. ❖ Wrote didactic works on such issues as women's education, marriage, and religion; works include *Una Primavera de Mulher* (1867), *Cartas a Uma Noiva* (1871), and *Cartas a Luíza*; also wrote biography of Duke of Palmela, *Vida de Duque de Palmela*. Carvalho and Carolina Michaëlis de Vasconcelos were first women inducted into Lisbon Academy of Sciences (1912).

VAZ DIAS, Selma (1911–1977). Dutch actress and writer. Born Nov 23, 1911, in Amsterdam, Netherlands; died Aug 30, 1977; studied at RADA; m. Hans W. Egli. ❖ Made stage debut in London as Nina Verganskaia in *Red Rust* (1929), followed by *The Matriarch, Phèdre, The Anatomist,*

Young Mr. Disraeli (as Sarah Disraeli), *'Tis Pity She's a Whore, Thunder Rock, A Bell for Adano, Dark Summer, The Balcony, Little Eyolf,* and *Jacques,* among others; translated *The Wise Cat* and adapted the novel *Good Morning Midnight* for BBC.

VAZEM, Ekaterina (1848–1937). Russian ballet dancer. Name variations: Ykaterina Vazem. Born Jan 13, 1848, in Moscow, Russia; died 1937 in Leningrad, Russia. ❖ Graduated from Imperial Ballet in St. Petersburg (1876); performed in numerous Petipa works and helped create roles for his *Le Corsaire (Le Slave)* (1868), *Le Papillon* (1874), *Les Bandits* (1875), *La Bayadère* (1877), and *La Fille du Neige* (1879), among others; upon retiring from performance career (1884), served as teacher at Imperial Ballet school, where she trained numerous dancers in Petipa repertory, including Anna Pavlova and Tamara Karsavina.

VAZ FERREIRA, María Eugenia (1875–1924). Uruguayan poet and short-story writer. Born 1875 in Montevideo, Uruguay; died 1924; sister of Carlos Vaz Ferreira (1872–1958, philosopher). ❖ Wrote romantic verse and was part of *modernismo* group of Uruguayan writers; in later life, shunned publicity and eventually suffered nervous breakdown. Most of her works were published posthumously by her brother, including *La isla de los cánticos* (1925).

VEAZIE, Carol (1895–1984). Canadian-born stage, screen and tv actress. Name variations: Carol Eberts Veazie. Born July 27, 1895, in Canada; died July 19, 1984, in Carmel, CA. ❖ Films include *The Catered Affair, A Cry in the Night, Designing Women, Auntie Mame, Baby, the Rain Must Fall* and *Cat Ballou.*

VECHESLOVA, Tatiana (1910–1991). Soviet ballet dancer. Born 1910 in St. Petersburg, Russia; died in 1991; dau. of Yevgenia Snietkova (teacher at the Kirov); studied at Vaganova School with Agrippina Vaganova and Marie Romanova. ❖ Danced with Kirov Ballet throughout career, where she performed leading female roles in range of repertory works, including *Esmeralda,* Zarema in *The Fountain of Bakhchisarai,* Manizhe in *Heart of the Hills* (1938), and Paskuala in *Laurencia* (1939); was the 1st Soviet ballerina to tour abroad (1934); retired from stage (1953); served as teacher at Kirov and its ballet school for many years.

VECHTOVA, Eva (1931–1991). *See Bosakova-Vechtova, Eva.*

VECSEI, Eva (1930—). Canadian architect. Born 1930 in Vienna, Austria; m. Andrei Vecsei. ❖ Educated at University of Technical Sciences, Budapest; immigrated to Canada (1957) and worked for architectural firm in Montreal; designed huge commercial complex, Place Bonaventure (opened 1967), and 7-acre development, La Cité (opened 1977); became Member of Order of Architects of Quebec, fellow of Royal Architectural Institute of Canada, and honorary fellow of American Institute of Architects; received *Canadian Architect* award of excellence (1983).

VÉDRÈS, Nicole (1911–1965). French director, novelist, and essayist. Name variations: Nicole Vedres. Born Sept 4, 1911, in Paris, France; died Dec 1965. ❖ Made the probing feature-length documentary *Paris 1900* (1947), followed by 2 shorts: *La vie commence demain (Life Begins Tomorrow)* and *Aux frontières de l'homme* (with Jean Rostand).

VEENSTRA, Myrna (1975—). Dutch field-hockey player. Born Mar 4, 1975, in Netherlands. ❖ Won a team bronze medal at Sydney Olympics (2000).

VEGA, Ana Lydia (1946—). Puerto Rican writer. Born Dec 6, 1946, in Santurce, Puerto Rico; dau. of Virgilio Vega and María Santana (grade-school teacher); m. Robert Villanúa (French poet); children: 1. ❖ Writer of fiction and nonfiction, who sought to distinguish a Caribbean identity and create a distinctively Puerto Rican literature, studied literature in France (1968–78); returned to Puerto Rico and published feminist critique *Vírgenes y mártires* (Virgins and Martyrs, 1982); wrote film scripts, including *La Gran Fiesta* (The Big Party, 1987); combined autobiographical essays and social commentary in *Esperando a Loló y otros delirios generacionales* (Waiting for Loló and Other Generational Deliriums, 1994). Received Emilio S. Belaval Award for short story "Pollito Chicken" (Little Chicken Chicken, 1978), Circle of Iberoamerican Writers and Poets award (1979) for short story "Puerto Principe Abajo" (Down Puerto Principe), Casa de las Américas award for *Encancaranublado y otros cuentos de naufragio* (Encancaranublado and Other Stories of Shipwreck, 1982), and Juan Rulfo International Award (1984). ❖ See also David J. Labiosa, *Ana Lydia Vega: Linguistic Women and Another Counterassault, or Can the Master(s) Hear?* (1996).

VEGA, Elvira de la (fl. late 1300s). Mistress of the king of Castile. Born Elvira Iniguez de la Vega; mistress of Henry II of Trastamara, king of Castile (r. 1369–1379); children: Constanza (who m. John, duke of Valencia); Juana (who m. Denis, count of Villar-Dompardo).

VEGA, Suzanne (1959—). American singer. Name variations: Vega. Born Suzanne Nadine Vega, Aug 12, 1959, in New York, NY; studied literature at Barnard College; m. Mitchell Froom (music producer and musician), Mar 17, 1995 (div. 2000); children: Ruby (b. 1994). ❖ At 16, began performing her songs in Greenwich Village coffeehouses; released eponymous debut album (1985), which hit #11 on British pop charts; recorded "Left of Center" for film *Pretty in Pink* (1986); released *Solitude Standing* (1987), which went to #11 in US and #2 in UK, and included song, "Luka," which was nominated for 3 Grammys; other albums include *99.9°* (1992), *Nine Objects of Desire* (1996) and *Songs in Red and Gray* (2001); published *The Passionate Eye: The Collected Writings of Suzanne Vega* (1999).

VEIGEL, Eva-Maria (1724–1822). Austrian-born English dancer, actress, and Bluestocking. Name variations: Eva Maria Veigel; Eva-Maria Garrick; Eva Maria Violetti or Violette; (stage name) La Violette. Born in 1724 in Vienna, Austria; died 1822 in London, England; m. David Garrick (the actor), June 22, 1749 (died 1779); no children. ❖ Moved to London (1746), where she worked as a dancer at the Haymarket Opera House; met David Garrick, London's most celebrated actor-manager of the popular Drury Lane theater (1747); declined his offer to dance at the theater, but agreed to marry him and retire (1749); with husband, became well known among high society and regulars in the literary clubs flourishing in London, often reciting scenes to amuse their audience; after husband's death (1779), shared a home with Hannah More, the poet; when she came out of mourning (1781), again joined in the salons of London's Bluestockings.

VEIL, Simone (1927—). French politician. Pronunciation: VAY, the L is sounded but truncated. Born Simone-Annie-Liline Jacob in Nice, France, July 13, 1927; dau. of André Jacob (1890–c. 1944, architect) and Yvonne Steinmetz Jacob (1900–1945); sister of Denise Jacob; m. Antoine Veil (b. 1926), 1946; children: Jean (b. 1947); Claude-Nicolas (b. 1949); François-Pierre (b. 1954). ❖ Most important female politician in France in 20th century, the 1st woman minister of the Fifth Republic, who saw to passage of the laws on adoption and abortion (the *loi Veil*) and was the 1st president of the European Parliament after the office became elected by popular vote; at 16, during a roundup of Jews in Nice, was deported to Auschwitz (1944), then Bergen-Belsen (1945); received diploma from Institut d'Études Politiques and law license from the Faculty of Law (Sorbonne, 1948); qualified as a magistrate (1956); was attaché at Ministry of Justice with the Administration of Prisons (1957–64) and at the Ministry of Justice's Office of Civil Affairs (1964–68); saw passage of the Adoption Law (1966); served as secretary-general of Conseil Supérieur de la Magistrature (1970–79); was minister of Health in Jacques Chirac's cabinet (1974–76); saw passage of the Abortion Law (1974–75); was minister of Health and Social Security in Raymond Barre's cabinet (1976–79); was a member of European Parliament (1979–93), and its president (1979–82); chaired Legal Affairs Committee of European Parliament (1982–84) and Liberal and Democratic and Reforming Group of European Parliament (1984–89); was minister of Health, Social Affairs, and Urban Affairs in Édouard Balladur's cabinet (1993–95); signed the Manifesto of Ten (1996); became a member of the Conseil Constitutionnel (1998); forged an extraordinary political career by being "an independent personality," as she put it; participated to some degree in party affairs through the Union for French Democracy (UDF) but was never comfortable there; won a unique place in French politics and public opinion as someone free of ordinary political ties. ❖ See also (in French) Michel Sarazin, *Une femme Simone Veil* (Laffont, 1987) and Maurice Szafran, *Simone Veil: Destin* (Flammarion, 1994); and *Women in World History.*

VEJJABUL, Pierra (b. 1909). Thai physician. Name variations: Dr. Pierra Vejabul. Born Kunying Pierra Hoontrakul, Nov 27, 1909, in Lampang, Siam (now Thailand); dau. of Thongkich Hoontrakul (teak merchant) and Phon He Hoontrakul; Sorbonne, Paris, MB, 1934, MD with Silver Medal, diploma of hygiene, 1936. ❖ Following completion of medical studies, returned to Bangkok (1937) and began working as a medical officer in the division of venereal diseases at the Hospital of the Ministry of Public Health; founded Pierra Maternity and Child Welfare Foundation (1938), which provided free medical care and lodging to needy mothers; through the Ministry and later through her own foundation, joined in international effort to solve global medical and social welfare problems; helped found Association of Women Physicians in Thailand (1950); worked for the Ministry of the Interior in fighting venereal diseases (late 1930s); founded Institute for Social Welfare for Women, an organization dedicated to rehabilitating prostitutes, and played a pivotal role in securing the enactment of legislation that abolished legal prostitution; published *Mother and Child Magazine* and gave weekly radio talks on child care, child guidance, the protection of children, and venereal diseases; through Pierra Foundation, also legally adopted children whose parents were unable to provide for them; by 1963, had fostered 660 children, 77 of whom were still living with her; when her family objected to having all of these children bear their name, was bestowed with the name "Vejjabul," which means "complete doctor," by Thai Premier Luang Pibul Songram; joined governing body of International Family Planning Association (1956) and helped found Thai Family Planning Association, for which she served as vice-president; also served on executive committee of International Union Against Venereal Diseases and Treponematosis (1957). ❖ See also *Women in World History.*

VELARDE, Pablita (1918—). Native American artist. Name variations: Tse Tsan (Golden Dawn). Born Sept 1918 at Santa Clara Pueblo, New Mexico; dau. of Herman and Marianita Velarde (died 1921); often stayed with paternal grandmother Qualupita, a medicine woman; attended St. Catherine's Indian School; graduate of Bureau of Indian Affairs' Santa Fe Indian School, 1936; studied under Dorothy Dunn; m. Herbert Hardin (non-Indian night watchman at the Bureau), in 1942 (div. 1959); children: Helen Bagsaw Hardin (1943–1984, artist); Herbert Hardin Jr. (b. 1944). ❖ One of the most prominent Tewa painters from the Santa Clara Pueblo in New Mexico, began to paint from her tribal experience and to master the tribal symbols (1932); turned artistic attention to Native ceremonials, capturing them with photographic detail; at 15, was selected to work with artist Olive Rush on murals for Chicago World's Fair (1933); painted archaeological and ethnological murals for Bandelier National Monument Visitors' Center (1939); wrote and illustrated *Old Father, Story Teller* (1960), a book of Tewa tribal legends; completed 4 panels for Museum of New Mexico and a large acrylic mural, *The Herd Dance,* for Indian Pueblo Cultural Center in Albuquerque (1970s); in a career that spanned more than 50 years, exhibited widely and received many awards, including the Philbrook Art Center's Grand Prize (1948) and a special trophy for Outstanding Contributions to Indian Art (1968), the 1st woman to be so honored. A retrospective of her work, "Woman's Work: The Art of Pablita Velarde," was held at the Wheelwright Museum in Santa Fe (1993). ❖ See also *Women in World History.*

VELÁSQUEZ, Loreta (1842–1897). Cuban-born American Confederate soldier. Name variations: Loreta Janeta Velasquez; Loretta Velasquez; Loreta Velazquez. Born 1842 in Cuba; died 1897; educated in Louisiana; married an American Confederate Army officer (died in battle). ❖ Determined to accompany husband into battle, disguised herself as a man and enlisted with a group of independent volunteer scouts; fought valiantly at Battle of Bull Run (1861) and several times penetrated Northern lines as a spy and blockade runner; remained in active combat and earned praise from General Stonewall Jackson, who never discovered her identity; arrested by her own forces as a federal spy, talked her way out of imprisonment; joined the 21st Louisiana Regiment, engaging in guerrilla warfare before she was wounded; was fined $10 and sentenced to 10 days in jail by Confederate officers, for her misrepresentations; published *The Woman in Battle: A Narrative of the Exploits, Adventures, and Travels of Madame Loreta Velásquez* (1876). ❖ See also *Women in World History.*

VELÁSQUEZ, Lucila (1928—). Venezuelan poet and essayist. Born 1928 in San Fernando de Apure, Venezuela. ❖ Works include *Color de tu recuerdo* (1949), *Amada tierra* (1955), *Tarde o temprano* (1964), *Indagación de dia* (1969), and *Claros enigmas* (1973).

VELAZQUEZ, Consuelo (1916–2005). Mexican composer and songwriter. Born Aug 21, 1916, in Ciudad Guzman, Jalisco, Mexico; died Jan 22, 2005, in Mexico City; dau. of army officer; m. Mariano Rivera Conde (recording executive), 1944 (died 1977); children: Sergio and Mariano Rivera. ❖ Began career as a concert pianist at 20; started writing popular songs and ran a classical music program for radio station XEQ; had a huge hit with her composition, "Bésame Mucho" (1941), which was subsequently recorded by Frank Sinatra, Joao Gilberto, Cesaria Evora, the Beatles, Placido Domingo, Elvis Presley and Diana Krall; also wrote other Mexican hit *boleros,* including "Amar y Vivir" (To Love and To Live) and "Verdad Amarga" (Bitter Truth).

VELÁZQUEZ, Loreta (1842–1897). *See Velásquez, Loreta.*

VELDHUIS, Marleen (1979—). Dutch swimmer. Born June 29, 1979, in Netherlands. ❖ Won a bronze medal for 4 x 100-meter freestyle relay at Athens Olympics (2004).

VELEY, Margaret (1843–1887). British novelist and poet. Born May 12, 1843, in Braintree, Essex, England; died Dec 7, 1887. ❖ Victorian novelist and poet whose output was slender but well regarded; began to contribute prose and poetry to some of the leading literary magazines of the day (1870); published 1st novel, *For Percival* (1878), which remained the best known from her works; moved to London (1880), where she published *Mitchelhurst Place* (1884) and *A Garden of Memories* (1887). After her death, her poetry was collected and published as *A Marriage of Shadows.* ❖ See also *Women in World History.*

VELEZ, Lisa (1967—). American singer. Name variations: Lisa Lisa. Born Jan 15, 1967, in New York, NY; sister of Raymond Velez. ❖ As Lisa Lisa and the Cult Jam, released 1st single, "I Wonder If I Take You Home," an international disco hit; followed with more hit singles, "Can you Feel the Beat" and "All Cried Out" and released platinum debut album *Lisa Lisa and Cult Jam with Full Force* (1985), followed by the even more popular platinum album *Spanish Fly* (1987), which incorporated dance, funk, salsa and doo-wop; released *Straight Out of Hell's Kitchen* (1991), yielding #1 hit "Let the Beat Hit 'Em"; dissolved band and made solo debut with mildly popular single "Skip to My Lu" (1993) and largely ignored album *LL77* (1994); on tv, starred as Gloria in Nickelodeon show "Taina" (2004).

VELEZ, Lupe (1908–1944). Mexican-American actress. Born Maria Guadalupe Velez de Villalobos, July 18, 1908, in San Luis Potosí, Mexico; committed suicide, Dec 13, 1944, in Beverly Hills, CA; m. Johnny Weissmuller (actor and swimmer), 1933 (div. 1938); no children. ❖ Known as "The Mexican Spitfire," performed as a dancer in both Mexico and Hollywood during teen years; hired for a group of comedy shorts directed by Hal Roach (1926); appeared with Laurel and Hardy in *Sailors Beware* (1927); came to prominence starring opposite Douglas Fairbanks Sr. in *The Gaucho* (1927); played a series of passionate women onscreen and lived an equally passionate existence in real life, having affairs with actors John Gilbert and Gary Cooper; had stormy marriage with *Tarzan* star Johnny Weissmuller; riding high through much of the 1930s, career suffered a decline in 1940s; films include *Tiger Rose* (1929), *The Storm* (1930), *Resurrection* (1931), *The Cuban Love Song* (1931), *The Squaw Man* (1931), *Palooka* (1934), *Strictly Dynamite* (1934), *Laughing Boy* (1934), *The Girl from Mexico* (1939), *Mexican Spitfire* (1940), *Six Lessons from Madame La Zonga* (1941), *Playmates* (1941), *Honolulu Lu* (1941), *Ladies' Day* (1943), *Redhead from Manhattan* (1943) and *Nana* (1944). ❖ See also Floyd Conner, *Lupe Velez and Her Lovers* (Barricade, 1993); and *Women in World History.*

VELHO DA COSTA, Maria (1938—). Portuguese writer and feminist. Name variations: The Three Marias. Born in Lisbon, Portugal, June 26, 1938; granted degree in German philology from University of London; married with children. ❖ Taught in high school; employed in the National Institute of Industrial Research; with Maria Teresa Horta and Maria Isabel Barreno, wrote and published *Novas Cartas Portuguesas* (*The New Portuguese Letters,* 1972), which led the modern feminist literary movement in Portugal and achieved notoriety because of the government's attempt to suppress the work; arrested on charges of pornography and offenses against public morality, went on trial as one of the "The Three Marias," as they became known internationally (1971–74); following the ousting of the Portuguese dictatorship, was declared innocent with all charges dismissed (1974); won the City of Lisbon Prize for novel *Casas Pardas* (1977); shared the D. Dinis Prize for her *Lucialima* (1983). ❖ See also *The Three Marias: New Portuguese Letters* (trans. by Helen R. Lane, Doubleday, 1975); and *Women in World History.*

VELICHKOVSKAIA, Tamara Antonovna (1908–1990). Russian poet and literary critic. Name variations: Tamara Antonovna Velichkóvskaia; Tamara Velichkovskaia-Zhaba; Tamara Antonovna Jaba or Zhaba. Born 1908 in Russia; died 1990. ❖ Grew up in Yugoslavia and moved to France (1942); encouraged by many, including Ivan Bunin, to publish, contributed poetry to *emigré* journals and anthologies; published *The White Staff* (1952).

VELINOVA, Iskra (1953–). Bulgarian rower. Born Aug 8, 1953, in Bulgaria. ❖ At Moscow Olympics, won a silver medal in coxed fours (1980).

VELLAMO, Katri (1914–2002). *See Parviainen, Katri.*

VELTMAN, Vera (1905–1973). *See Panova, Vera.*

VENABLE, Evelyn (1913–1993). American stage and screen actress. Born Oct 18, 1913, in Cincinnati, OH; died Nov 16, 1993, in Post Falls, ID; m. Hal Mohr (cinematographer, died 1974). ❖ Joined Walter Hampton's stock company; Broadway credits include *Dear Brutus, Cyrano de Bergerac, Hamlet* and *Romeo and Juliet*; made film debut in *Cradle Song* (1933), followed by *Death Takes a Holiday, Mrs. Wiggs of the Cabbage Patch, Alice Adams, The Little Colonel, The Frontiersman* and *He Hired the Boss*, among others; taught ancient Greek and Latin at UCLA and organized the production of Greek plays. Served as the model for Columbia's torchbearer logo.

VENCIENÉ, Vida. Soviet-Lithuanian cross-country skier. Name variations: Vida Venciene or Ventsene. Born in Lithuania. ❖ Won a gold medal for 10 km and a bronze medal for 5 km at Calgary Olympics (1988).

VENDÔME, countess of.
See Euphrosine (d. 1102).
See Jeanne de Castile (r. 1366–1374).
See Catherine of Vendôme (r. 1374–1412).
See Marie of Luxemburg (d. 1546).

VENDÔME, duchess of. *See Henrietta of Belgium (1870–1948).*

VENEMA, Anneke (1971—). Dutch rower. Born Jan 19, 1971, in the Netherlands. ❖ Won a silver medal for coxed eight at Sydney Olympics (2000).

VENGEROVA, Isabelle (1877–1956). Russian pianist and teacher. Name variations: Izabelle Vengérova. Born Isabella Afanasievna in Minsk, Russia, Mar 1, 1877; died in 1956; sister of Zinaida Vengerova (1867–1941). ❖ Studied at Vienna Conservatory with Joseph Dachs, and privately with Theodor Leschetizky; returning to Russia, completed musical education with Annette Essipova, then began teaching at the St. Petersburg Conservatory (1906); left Russia (1920), 1st touring Europe and then settling in US (1923); joined faculty of Curtis Institute in Philadelphia (1924), mentoring such students as Leonard Bernstein, Samuel Barber, Lilian Kallir, Gary Graffman, Leonard Pennario and Lukas Foss. ❖ See also *Women in World History.*

VENGEROVA, Zinaida (1867–1941). Russian literary critic. Name variations: Zinaida Vengérova; Zinaida Afanas'evna Vengérova. Born 1867 in Russia; died in New York, NY, 1941; sister of Isabelle Vengerova (1877–1956, pianist); educated at universities in Russia and England and at Sorbonne in Paris; m. N. M. Minskii (poet and critic), 1925 (died 1937). ❖ Literary critic and translator who built bridges between the Russian and Western European modernist literary and artistic worlds; translated the latest writings from Western Europe into Russian; also wrote essays on such influential figures as Henrik Ibsen, Paul Verlaine, Arthur Rimbaud, Gerhard Hauptmann, H. G. Wells and Ezra Pound; for 15 years, wrote a column on European literature for Russian periodical *The Herald of Europe*; her essays filled a 3-vol. collection, *Literary Characteristics* (1897–1910); also published *English Writers of the 19th Century* (1913); spent WWI in England, where she frequently lectured and gave interviews; returned to Russia following the Communist Bolshevik takeover (1917); left Russia for good (1921). ❖ See also *Women in World History.*

VENICE, princess of (1969—). *See Courau, Clotilde.*

VENIER-BAFFO, Cecelia (1525–1583). *See Nurbanu.*

VENTCEL, Elena Sergeevna (1907–2002). *See Venttsel, Elena Sergeevna.*

VENTÓS I CULLELL, Palmira (1862–1917). Spanish novelist. Name variations: Palmira Ventos i Cullell; (pseudonym) Felip Palma. Born 1862 in Barcelona, Spain; died 1917. ❖ Writings, which often depict harshness of village life in rural Catalonia, include *La caiguda* (1907) and the posthumous collection *Asprors de la vida* (1924).

VENTRE, Fran (1941—). American nurse-midwife. Name variations: Fran Katz. Born Aug 14, 1941, in Brooklyn, NY; dau. of Sonia and Fred Katz; University of Wisconsin, BS, 1962; Montgomery College, nursing degree, 1977; graduate of Georgetown University nurse-midwifery program, 1978; Boston University, MA in public health, 1991; m. Robert Ventre, c. 1963; children: 2. ❖ Helped found the Home Oriented Maternity Experience (HOME) for women interested in home births (1970s); contributed immensely to the successful block of a bill that threatened midwifery licensing (1978); volunteered in Senegal (West Africa) and worked with Doctors of the World in Kosovo, Serbia; opened the 1st freestanding birth centers in the state of MA (1980) and Brooklyn, NY (1999).

VENTSEL, Elena Sergeevna (1907–2002). *See Venttsel, Elena Sergeevna.*

VENTSENE, Vida. *See Venciené, Vida.*

VENTTSEL, Elena Sergeevna (1907–2002). Russian mathematician and short-story writer. Name variations: Elena Sergeevna Ventsel; Elena Sergeevna Ventcel; (pseudonym) I. Grékova or Grekova; Irina Nikolaevna Grekova. Born 1907 in Russia; died 2002. ❖ Lectured in mathematics; used pseudonym I. Grekova for writing and real name Elena Sergeevna Venttsel as a mathematician; published 1st short story "Behind the Checkpoint" (1962); other stories, which offer insight into aspects of Soviet life and often depict independent and successful women, published in *Russian Women* (1963), *Image of Women in Contemporary Soviet Fiction* (1965), and *Soviet Women Writing* (1988); also wrote *The Hotel Manager* (1976) and *The Ship of Widows* (1981).

VENTURELLA, Michelle (1973—). American softball player. Born May 11, 1973, in South Holland, Illinois; graduate of Indiana University, 1996. ❖ Catcher, won a team gold medal at Sydney Olympics (2000); was on US national team (1995–2000); became a coach at Indiana University.

VENTURINI, Fernanda (1970—). Brazilian volleyball player. Name variations: Fernanda Porto Venturini. Born Oct 24, 1970, in Araraquara, Brazil. ❖ Setter, won team World Grand Prix (1993, 1994, 1996, 1998); won South American championship (1991, 1995, 1997); won a team bronze medal at Atlanta Olympics (1996). Twice awarded Best Setter at World Grand Prix.

VENTURINI, Tisha (1973—). American soccer player. Name variations: Tisha Venturini-Hoch. Born Tisha Lea Venturini, Mar 3, 1973, in Modesto, CA; graduate of University of North Carolina, 1995; m. Casey Hoch. ❖ Midfielder; won a gold medal at Atlanta Olympics (1996); won a team gold medal at World Cup (1999); was a founding member of the Women's United Soccer Association (WUSA); signed with the San Jose CyberRays (2001).

VENUTA, Benay (1911–1995). American stage and screen actress, singer, and dancer. Born Benvenuta Rose Crooke, Jan 27, 1911, in San Francisco, CA; died Sept 1, 1995, in New York, NY; m. Kenneth Kelly (div.); m. Armand S. Deutsch (div.); m. Fred Clark, 1952 (div.). ❖ Made Broadway debut replacing Ethel Merman in *Anything Goes* (1935), followed by *Kiss the Boys Goodbye, By Jupiter, Nellie Bly, Hazel Flagg, Dear Me the Sky is Falling, Carousel* and *Annie Get Your Gun*, among others; films include *Annie Get Your Gun, Call Me Mister* and *Bullets over Broadway*.

VERA.
See West, Vera (1900–1947).
See Neumann, Vera (1907–1993).

VERA CONSTANTINOVNA (1854–1912). Duchess of Wurttemberg. Name variations: Vera Romanov. Born Feb 4, 1854; died April 11, 1912; dau. of Alexandra of Saxe-Altenburg (1830–1911) and Constantine Nicholaevitch (son of Nicholas I of Russia and Charlotte of Prussia); m. Eugene, duke of Wurttemberg, on May 8, 1874.

VERA-ELLEN (1920–1981). American dancer and actress. Born Vera-Ellen Westmeyer Rohe, Feb 16, 1920, in Cincinnati, Ohio; died Aug 30, 1981, in Los Angeles, California; dau. of Martin F. Rohe (piano tuner) and Alma (Westmeyer) Rohe; m. Robert Hightower (dancer; div.); m. Victor Rothschild (oilman), Nov 19, 1954 (div. 1966). ❖ Appeared as a Rockette at Radio City Music Hall (1930s); made stage debut in *Very Warm for May* (1939); signed to MGM and made film debut opposite Danny Kaye in *The Wonder Man* (1945); performed in "Slaughter on Tenth Avenue" ballet segment of *Words and Music* (1948); receiving consistently high marks for her abilities, danced opposite Gene Kelly, Fred Astaire, and others in a series of musicals, including *The Kid from Brooklyn* (1946), *Three Little Girls in Blue* (1946), *Carnival in Costa Rica* (1947), *On the Town* (1949), *Love Happy* (1950), *Three Little Words* (1950), *Happy Go Lucky* (1951), *The Belle of New York* (1952), *Call Me Madam* (1953), *The Big Leaguer* (1953), *White Christmas* (1954) and *Let's Be Happy* (1957); retired from film (1957). ❖ See also *Women in World History.*

VERANES, Sibelis (1974—). Cuban judoka. Born Feb 5, 1974, in Santiago de Cuba. ❖ Won a gold medal for 63–70 kg middleweight at Sydney Olympics (2000); won World championship (1999).

VERBEEK, Tonya (1977—). **Canadian wrestler.** Born Aug 14, 1977, in Grimsby, Canada. ❖ Won Pan American championships (2003) for 55 kg freestyle; won a silver medal for 55 kg freestyle at Athens Olympics (2004).

VERBITSKAIA, Anastasiia (1861–1928). **Russian novelist, playwright and short-story writer.** Name variations: Anastasia or Anastasiia Alekseevna Verbítskaia or Verbitskaya. Born 1861 in Russia; died 1928, living in obscurity in Moscow. ❖ Wrote the hugely popular saga *The Keys to Happiness* (6 vols., 1909–13), which was filmed twice and outsold *War and Peace*; also wrote *Discord* (1887), *Spirit of the Times* (1907), plays, children's fiction, and autobiographies, *To My Reader* and *My Reminiscences*; after the 1917 Revolution, her books were removed from stores for allegedly being counter-revolutionary.

VERBITSKY, Eva (1934–1980). *See Hunt, Eva Vervitsky.*

VERBRUGGEN, Susanna (c. 1667–1703). **English actress.** Born c. 1667; died in 1703; dau. of an actor named Percival; m. William Mountfort (English actor and playwright), in 1686 (stabbed to death by a jealous suitor of actress Anne Bracegirdle, 1692); m. John Verbruggen (fl. 1688 c. 1707, actor). ❖ Made 1st recorded stage appearance in D'Urfey's *Sir Barnaby Whig* (1681), then played at Dorset Garden and Theatre Royal; by 1690, was one of the leading actresses in Thomas Betterton's company. ❖ See also *Women in World History.*

VERCESI, Ines (1916–1997). **Italian gymnast.** Born Jan 5, 1916, in Pavia, Italy; died in 1997. ❖ At Amsterdam Olympics, won a silver medal in team all-around (1928).

VERCHERES, Madeleine de (1678–1747). **Canadian hero.** Name variations: Madeleine Jarrett Tarieu. Born Madeleine Jarrett Tarieu in 1678 in Canada; died 1747. ❖ Sometimes referred to as the Canadian Joan of Arc, grew up on family lands in Vercheres, not far from present-day Montreal; became an accomplished markswoman; left alone at 14 when Iroquois braves attacked the French-held fort of Vercheres (early 1690s), rose to the occasion, loading guns that were scattered around the fortification and firing them in random patterns so that the attackers could not tell from where the next shot might come; in the end, repulsed the entire Iroquois force in this way.

VERCHININA, Nina (1910–1995). **Russian ballet dancer, choreographer, and teacher.** Born Jan 20, 1910, in Moscow, Russia; died Dec 16, 1955; trained in Paris by Olga Preobrazhenska, Lyubov Egorova, Mathilde Kshesinskaia, and Bronislave Nijinska. ❖ Made stage debut at Covent Garden in the corps de ballet in *Le Martyre de Saint-Sébastien* with Ida Rubinstein; came to prominence while dancing with Colonel de Basil's Monte Carlo Ballets Russes (1932–37), creating roles in Massine's *Les Présages* and *Choreartium* (both 1933), and *Symphonie Fantastique* (1936); was also featured in *Jeux d'Enfants, Le Beau Danube, Les Cents Baisers* and Balanchine's *La Concurrence* and *Les Sylphides*; taught and coached in Rio de Janeiro, Buenos Aires, and Copacabana, Argentina.

VERDE. *Variant of Virida.*

VERDECIA, Legna (1972—). **Cuban judoka.** Name variations: Legna Verdecia Rodriguez. Born Oct 29, 1972, in Havana, Cuba. ❖ Won World championship (1993); won a bronze medal at Atlanta Olympics (1996) and a gold medal at Sydney Olympics (2000), both for 48–52 kg half lightweight.

VERDI, Giuseppina (1815–1897). *See Strepponi, Giuseppina.*

VERDON, Gwen (1925–2000). **American dancer, singer, and actress.** Born Gwyneth Evelyn Verdon, Jan 13, 1925, in Los Angeles, CA; died Oct 18, 2000, in Woodstock, VT; dau. of Joseph (stage electrician at MGM) and Gertrude (Strandring) Verdon (Denishawn dancer); m. James Henaghan (Hollywood journalist), 1942 (div. 1947); m. Bob Fosse (dancer-choreographer), 1960 (sep. 1971, died 1987); children: (1st m.) James Henaghan Jr.; (2nd m.) Nicole Fosse. ❖ Irrepressible redhead with a crackling voice, made Broadway debut in *Alive and Kicking* (1950); stood out with an Apache dance in *Can-Can* (1953) and won 1st Tony Award; appeared as Lola in *Damn Yankees* (1955), winning 2nd Tony and bringing house down with "Whatever Lola Wants"; won 2 subsequent Tonys for roles in *New Girl in Town* (1957) and *Redhead* (1959), both of which were directed and choreographed by Bob Fosse; after a hiatus, returned to stage in *Sweet Charity* (1966), which ran for 600 performances; starred in original production of *Chicago* (1975); served as supervisor on Fosse's musical *Dancin'* (1978) and worked on his autobiographical film *All That Jazz* (1979); appeared in

several films, notably *Cocoon* (1985), *Cocoon: The Return* (1988) and *Marvin's Room* (1996). ❖ See also *Women in World History.*

VERDUGO, Elena (1926—). **American actress.** Born Elena Angela Verdugo, April 20, 1926, in Hollywood, CA; m. Charles R. Marion, 1946 (div. 1955); m. Charles R. Rockwell, 1972; children: Richard Marion (actor-director). ❖ Began career as a band singer, singing briefly with Xavier Cugat's band and recording the song "Tico-Tico"; starred in tv series "Meet Millie" (1952–56) and "Marcus Welby, M. D." (1969–76); films include *Down Argentine Way, Belle Starr, The Moon and Sixpence, House of Frankenstein, Song of Scheherazade, Tuna Clipper, The Lost Volcano, Cyrano de Bergerac, Knights of the Round Table, Panama Sal, How Sweet It Is!* and *Angel in My Pocket.*

VERDUN, Maud de (fl. 1200s). *See Fitzalan, Maud.*

VERDY, Violette (1931—). **French ballet dancer.** Born Nelly Guillerm, Dec 1, 1931, in Pont-l'Abbé-Lambour, France. ❖ Trained with Carlotta Zambelli and Victor Gsovsky in Paris; danced under name Guillerm with Ballets des Champs-Elysées, creating roles for Roland Petit's *Les Forains* (1945), *Rendez-Vous* (1945), and *Triste Dances* (1947), and David Lichine's *Orpheus* (1948); joined American Ballet Theater in NY—as Violette Verdy—and danced principal roles in *Swan Lake, The Nutcracker, Les Sylphides,* Cullberg's *Miss Julie* and Tudor's *Gala Performance,* among others; danced with New York City Ballet (late 1950s) and was acclaimed for performances in Balanchine's *Symphony in C, Orpheus, Allegro Brillante, Stars and Stripes,* and others; created numerous roles for Balanchine throughout career, including in *Episodes* (1959), *The Figure in the Carpet* (1960), *Jewels* (1967) and *Glinkiana* (1967); returned to France and served as director of Paris Opéra Ballet (1977–80); worked as co-artistic director of Boston Ballet in Massachusetts.

VERE, Anne de (1556–1589). *See Cecil, Anne.*

VERE, Diana de (d. 1742). **English aristocrat.** Name variations: Lady Diana de Vere; Lady Diana Beauclerk. Died in 1742; only child of Aubrey de Vere, 20th earl of Oxford, and Diana Kirke (d. 1719); m. Charles Beauclerk (1670–1726), 1st duke of St. Albans (son of Nell Gwynn), on April 13, 1694; children: Charles Beauclerk, 2nd duke of St. Albans (b. 1696); William, Lord Beauclerk (b. 1698); Baron Vere Beauclerk of Hanworth (b. 1699); Col. Henry Beauclerk (b. 1701); James Beauclerk, Lord Bishop of Hereford (b. 1702); Sidney Beauclerk (b. 1703, vice-chamberlain and MP); Lt. Gen George Beauclerk (b. 1704); Cmdr. Aubrey Beauclerk (b. 1711).

VERE, Elizabeth de.
See Howard, Elizabeth (c. 1410–1475).
See Trussel, Elizabeth (1496–1527).

VERE, Frances de (d. 1577). **Countess of Surrey.** Name variations: Frances Howard. Died June 30, 1577; dau. of John de Vere, 15th earl of Oxford, and Elizabeth Trussel (1496–1527); m. Henry Howard (1517–1547), earl of Surrey; m. Thomas Staynings; children: (1st m.) Thomas Howard (b. 1537), 4th duke of Norfolk; Catherine Howard (d. 1596); Henry Howard, earl of Northampton; Jane Howard (d. 1593); Margaret Howard (d. 1592, who m. Henry, Lord Scrope of Bolton).

VERE, Margaret de (fl. 14th c.). **Baroness Beaumont.** Name variations: Margaret Beaumont. Dau. of John de Vere, 7th earl of Oxford, and Maud Badlesmere (d. 1366); m. Henry Beaumont (1340–1369), 3rd baron Beaumont; children: John Beaumont (b. 1361), 4th baron Beaumont; Eleanor Beaumont (who m. Richard de Molines).

VERE, Maud de (d. 1366). *See Badlesmere, Maud.*

VERE, Maud de (fl. 1360s). **Countess of Oxford.** Name variations: Maud de Ufford. Born Maud de Ufford; dau. of Maud Plantagenet (c. 1310–c. 1377) and Ralph de Ufford; m. Thomas de Vere (1337–1371), 8th earl of Oxford; children: Robert de Vere, 9th earl of Oxford and duke of Ireland (1362–1392).

VERED, Ilana (1939—). **Israeli pianist.** Born in Tel Aviv, Dec 6, 1939. ❖ Studied at Paris Conservatoire with Vlado Perlemuter and Jeanne-Marie Darré, then with Rosina Lhévinne and Nadia Reisenberg at Juilliard School in NY; established a solid career, concertizing widely in America and Europe (1970s). ❖ See also *Women in World History.*

VERENA, Sophie (1826–1892). *See Alberti, Sophie.*

VERES-IOJA, Viorica (1962—). Romanian rower. Born Feb 26, 1962, in Romania. ❖ At Los Angeles Olympics, won a silver medal in coxed eights and a gold medal in coxed fours (1984).

VEREY, Rosemary (1918–2001). British garden designer and horticulturist. Born Rosemary Isabel Baird Sandilands in 1918; died May 31, 2001, in London, England; dau. of a colonel; attended University College, London; m. David Verey (architectural historian), 1939 (died 1984); children: 2 sons, 2 daughters. ❖ Created her own garden in a 17th-century former rectory called Barnsley House in the Cotswolds; designed for Prince Charles at Highgrove, lectured widely in US, and wrote 17 books, many of which are now classics, including *The Classic Garden* and *The Garden in Winter.*

VERGELYUK, Maryna (1978—). Ukrainian handball player. Born June 24, 1978, in Ukraine. ❖ Won a team bronze medal at Athens Olympics (2004).

VERGILIA (late 6th c.–mid-5th c. BCE). *See Volumnia.*

VERGNIAUD PIERRE-NOËL, Loïs M. (1905–1998). *See Jones, Loïs Mailou.*

VERGOVA, Mariya (1950—). *See Petkova-Vergova, Mariya.*

VERIKO (1900–1987). *See Andjaparidze, Veriko.*

VERINA (fl. 437–483). Byzantine empress. Name variations: Verina Augusta. Birth date unknown; died before 484; sister of the general Basiliscus; m. Leo I, emperor of Byzantium (r. 457–474); children: Ariadne (fl. 457–515); Leontia (b. after 457). ❖ Like husband (the future Leo I), was of humble birth (one legend has it that they once worked together in a butcher shop in Constantinople).

VERMIROVSKA, Zdena (1913—). Czech gymnast. Born June 27, 1913, in Koprivinice, Czechoslovakia. ❖ Won a silver medal at the Berlin Olympics (1936) and a gold medal at the London Olympics (1948), both in team all-around.

VERNE, Kaaren (1918–1967). German actress. Name variations: Karen Verne. Born April 6, 1918, in Berlin, Germany; died Dec 23, 1967, in Hollywood, CA; m. James Powers; children: (adopted) daughter. ❖ Member of German State Theater; moved to London and appeared in British films, including *Ten Days in Paris;* came to US (1940), appearing in such films as *King's Row, All Through the Night, Seventh Cross, Madame X, Ship of Fools* and *Torn Curtain.*

VERNE, Mathilde (1865–1936). English pianist. Born Mathilde Wurm, May 25, 1865, in Southampton, England; died in London, June 4, 1936; dau. of Bavarian music teachers; sister of Alice Verne Bredt (1868–1958) and Adela Verne (1877–1952); cousin of artist Sir Hubert von Herkomer; studied with Franklin Taylor and Clara Schumann. ❖ Had a successful career in England, giving chamber music concerts (1907–36); established her own school (1909), which produced many excellent pianists. ❖ See also autobiography *Chords of Remembrance* (Hutchinson, 1936); and *Women in World History.*

VERNEUIL, Marquise de (1579–1633). *See Entragues, Henriette d'.*

VERNEY, Margaret Maria (1844–1930). British historical writer. Name variations: Lady Verney. Born Margaret Maria Williams in 1844; died 1930; m. E. H. Verney (naval officer and baronet), in 1868. ❖ Chronicled the long history of husband's family and investigated the small-town life and the educational system that surrounded her in the regions of Anglesey, Wales, and Buckinghamshire, England; gained the designation of Lady Verney when husband received title of 3rd baronet (1868); planned and executed a series of *Memoirs of the Verney Family* that eventually ran to 6 vols. (1892–1930).

VERNIZZI, Laura (1985—). Italian rhythmic gymnast. Born Sept 12, 1985, in Como, Italy. ❖ Won team all-around silver medal at Athens Olympics (2004).

VERNON, Anne (1924—). French actress. Born Edith Antoinette Alexandrine Vignaud, Jan 24, 1924, in Saint-Denis, France. ❖ Leading player and supporting actress, made film debut in *Le mannequin assassiné* (1947), followed by *Warning to Wantons, Shakedown, Édouard et Caroline, Rue des Saussaies, A Tale of 5 Cities, Massacre en dentelles, Song of Paris, Time Bomb, The Love Lottery, L'Affaire des poisons, Bel Ami, Le long des trottoirs, Les suspects, Il Conte Max, Arsène Lupin contre Arsène Lupin, Umbrellas of Cherbourg, Patate* and *Therese und Isabell.*

VERNON, Barbara (1910–2003). *See Bailey, Barbara Vernon.*

VERNON, Barbara (1916–1978). Australian writer. Born Barbara Mary Vernon, July 25, 1916, in Invernell, NSW, Australia; died April 1978 in Sydney, Australia; dau. of Murray Menzies Vernon (doctor) and Constance Emma (Barling) Vernon; attended University of Queensland; never married; no children. ❖ Screenwriter, dramatist, broadcaster, and novelist, worked in radio and tv, both as a scriptwriter and as an on-air personality; began broadcast career at radio station 2NZ in hometown, where she organized a children's hour and staged several plays, including her own works, *The Multi-Coloured Umbrella* and *The Passionate Pianist,* which would later be performed on tv; moved to Sydney (1959), finding success when the national Australian Broadcasting Corporation produced a serial radio play she had written about the life of George Sand; was best known for creating a long-running tv series "Bellbird" (1960s–70s) and 2 novels, *Bellbird: The Story of a Country Town* (1970) and *A Big Day at Bellbird* (1972), the latter of which was made into the film *Country Town;* wrote many other stage plays, some of them for children.

VERNON, Billie (1901–1994). *See Cagney, Frances.*

VERNON, Frances (1901–1994). *See Cagney, Frances.*

VERNON, Lillian (1927—). *See Katz, Lillian.*

VERNON, Mabel (1883–1975). American suffragist and peace advocate. Born Sept 10, 1883, in Wilmington, Delaware; died Sept 2, 1975, in Washington, DC; dau. of George Washington Vernon (newspaper publisher) and Mary (Hooten) Vernon; Swarthmore College, BA, 1906; Columbia University, MA in political science, 1924. ❖ Key figure in both the women's rights and pacifist movements, was one of the 1st suffrage activists to spend time in jail for the cause; became an organizer at the national level for the Congressional Union for Woman Suffrage (1913); interrupted speech by President Woodrow Wilson in Washington, DC, an act that signaled a new boldness in the efforts of suffragists (1916); joined Women's International League for Peace and Freedom (1930); was present as inter-American committee delegate at founding of the United Nations (1945). ❖ See also *Women in World History.*

VÉRONE, Maria (1874–1938). French lawyer, journalist, and activist. Pronunciation: mah-REE-ah vay-ROHN. Born in Paris, France, June 20, 1874; died in Paris, May 24, 1938; dau. of an accountant and a shop clerk; educated at Faculty of Law (Sorbonne); married and div.; m. Georges Lhermitte (attorney), 1908; children: (1st m.) 2. ❖ Leading trial lawyer in France in a time when female attorneys were exceedingly rare and almost never appeared in open court, was best known to the public as an advocate of women's rights, especially the right to vote; worked as a substitute teacher in Paris (1894–97); wrote for *La Fronde* (1897–1902); named secretary-general of the French League for Women's Rights (LFDF, 1904); helped reestablish *Le Droit des femmes* and served as its editor (1906–38); admitted to Paris bar (1907) and would be the 1st woman lawyer in France to plead in the criminal courts; sponsored Jeanne Laloë's candidacy for Paris Municipal Council (1908); authored a report to the National Council of French Women (CNFF), which formed the basis for the women's suffrage bill (1909); left Socialist Party (1912); served as president of Suffrage Section of CNFF (1913–20); involved with Jeanne Halbwachs trial and Condorcet demonstration (1914); served as president of LFDF (1918–38); was a columnist for *L'Oeuvre* (1918–35); named president of Legal Section of the CNFF (1921); when Senate defeated the women's suffrage bill, became "Madame Quand-même" (1922); was convener of the Suffrage Section of the International Council of Women (1927–36); arrested in a suffragist demonstration (1928); wrote an Open Letter to Premier André Tardieu, and was a founder of Open Door International (1929); represented CNFF at The Hague Conference on Codification of Law (1930); was a founder of the Sexological Educational and Studies Association (1931); assisted La Femme Nouvelle (1934–36); opposed Blum's project of a National Feminist Council (1936); saw final passage of the Renoult Law on women's civil rights (Feb 18, 1938). Received France's Legion of Honor. ❖ See also *Women in World History.*

VERONICA (fl. 1st c. CE?). Saint. Name variations: Berenice or Bernice; Berenike or Beronike. Possibly flourished around 1st century CE. ❖ Acknowledged as a saint, allegedly met Jesus on the day of his crucifixion as he agonized his way to Calvary; feeling compassion for his pain and predicament, is said to have wiped his face with a cloth, upon which thereafter was left a permanent likeness. Feast Day is July 12. ❖ See also *Women in World History.*

VERONICA OF CORREGGIO (1485–1550). *See Gambara, Veronica.*

VERRETT, Shirley (1931—). American mezzo-soprano. Name variations: known professionally as Shirley Verrett-Carter until 1963. Born Shirley Verrett, May 31, 1931, in New Orleans, LA; received AA degree from Ventura (California) College, 1951; studied with Anna Fitziu and Hall Johnson; studied with Marian Szekely-Freschl at Juilliard, graduating 1961; m. 2nd husband Louis Frank LoMonaco (painter and illustrator), 1963. ❖ One of the foremost singers of her time, made NY debut at New York City Opera as Irina in Weill's *Lost in the Stars* (1958); performed in 1st recital at NY's Town Hall, singing arias by Handel, Bach and Mozart, as well as works by Chausson, Brahms, Purcell and Persichetti (1958); sang role of Carmen with New York City Opera (1964) to great acclaim; appeared as Athaliah, Queen of Judea, in world premiere at Lincoln Center (1964); sang Carmen at Teatro alla Scala debut (1966); performed Ulrica in Verdi's *Un Ballo in Maschera* for triumphant Covent Garden debut; debuted at Metropolitan (1968), again as Carmen, and continued to sing at Met regularly for more than 2 decades, making musical history when she appeared as both Cassandra and Dido in Berlioz's *Les Troyens*; also appeared at Met as both Norma and Azucena in Bellini's *Norma*, and as Tosca, Eboli, Lady Macbeth, Amneris and Azucena; made Broadway debut as Nettie Fowler in *Carousel* (1994); joined faculty at University of Michigan as James Earl Jones Distinguished University Professor of Music (1996). ❖ See also *Women in World History.*

VERRILL, Conchita (1922—). *See Cintrón, Conchita.*

VERSCHOOR, Annie Romein- (1895–1978). *See Romein-Verschoor, Annie.*

VERSOIS, Marina (1938—). *See Vlady, Marina.*

VERSOIS, Odile (1930–1980). French actress. Born Katiana de Poliakoff-Baidaroff, also seen as Baidarov, June 14, 1930, in Paris, France; died 1980; dau. of a painter; sister of actresses Hélène Vallier (Militza de Poliakoff-Baidaroff), Marina Vlady and Olga Poliakoff. ❖ Actress whose popularity crossed national boundaries, was a European film star of mid-20th century; took to the stage as a child, winning a place in the ballet troupe of Paris Opera; at 16, made film debut; often played leads, usually in gentle, optimistic roles; appeared in films not only in her native France (*Dernières Vacances*, 1948, *Fantômas contre Fantômas*, 1949, *Mademoiselle Josette ma Femme*, 1951, *Belle Amour*, 1951, *Le Rendez-vous*, 1961, and *Le Dernier Tiercé*, 1964, among others), but in Britain (*A Day to Remember*, 1953, *The Young Lovers*, 1954, *To Paris with Love*, 1955, *Passport to Shame*, 1959, and more), Germany (*Herrscher ohne Krone*, 1957), and Italy (*Paolo e Francesca*, 1950).

VERSTAPPEN, Annemarie (1965—). Dutch swimmer. Born Oct 3, 1965, in Rosmalen, Netherlands. ❖ At Los Angeles Olympics, won bronze medals in 20-meter freestyle and 100-meter freestyle and a silver medal in 4 x 100-meter freestyle relay (1984).

VERTEN, Jennie (1855–1875). *See Whiteside, Jane.*

VERTUA GENTILE, Anna (1850–1927). Italian novelist and short-story writer. Born 1850 in Como, Italy; died 1927. ❖ Wrote popular works, mostly addressed to children and young girls, including *Come dettava il cuore* (1871), *Silvana* (1886), *La potenza della bonità* (1912), *Voce d'esperienza* (1913), *Castellacio* (1924) and *Le due cugine* (1930).

VESAAS, Halldis Moren (1907–1995). Norwegian poet, prose writer and translator. Born Halldis Moren, 1907, in Trysil, Norway; died Aug 9, 1995, in Oslo, Norway; dau. of Sven Moren (1871–1938, writer); graduate of a teachers' college; m. Tarjei Vesaas (Norwegian novelist, poet and Nordic prizewinner), in 1934; children: son Olav Vesaas; daughter Guri Vesaas. ❖ One of the 1st strong female voices in the modern poetry of Norway, worked as a teacher in Oslo, Norway, and Geneva, Switzerland; also worked for Norwegian consulate in Vevey, Switzerland; was a translator of such widely different plays for the Norwegian stage as those by Shakespeare, Racine, and Claudel, and published such works as *The Threepenny Opera* and A.A. Milne's *Winnie the Pooh*; best remembered for her many volumes of lyric poetry that spanned more than 60 years; published 1st collection, *Harpe og dolk* (Harp and Dagger, 1929); other collections include *Morgonen* (Morning, 1930), *Tung tids tale* (The Voice of Tragic Times, 1945), *Treet* (The Tree, 1947), and *I ein annan skog* (In a Different Forest, 1955); received many literary prizes; named Commander of the Order of St. Olav for her services to literature. ❖ See also *Women in World History.*

VESELITSKAIA, Lidiia Ivanovna (1857–1936). Russian translator and short-story writer. Name variations: Lidiia Ivanovna Veselitskaia or Veselítskaya; (pseudonym) V. Mikulich. Born 1857 in Russia; died 1936. ❖ Works, which turned from social realism to focus on characters' individual psychology, include series of novellas about young women, trilogy *Mimochka*, and various stories such as "Bird Cherry" (1898) and "In Venice" (1901).

VESELKOVA-KIL'SHTET, M. G. (1861–1931). Russian poet, novelist and playwright. Name variations: Mariia Grigorevna Veselkóva-Kilshtét; M. G. Veselkovoj-Kil'shtet. Born 1861 in Russia; died 1931. ❖ Works include the historial novel *The Kolychevs' Patrimony* (1911) and its sequel, *On Native Soil* (1914); poetry collections include *Songs of a Forgotten Estate* and *The Yellowed Pages* (1916); career ceased with the Revolition in 1917.

VESENIEV, Iv. (1828–1865). *See Khvoshchinskaia, Sofia.*

VESEY, Elizabeth (c. 1715–1791). Irish writer and Bluestocking. Name variations: Elizabeth Vessey. Born Elizabeth Vesey, c. 1715, in Ireland; died 1791 in London, England; dau. of Bishop Sir Thomas Vesey and Mary (Muschamp) Vesey; m. William Handcock (member of Parliament), c. 1730 (div.); m. cousin Agmondesham Vesey (member of Parliament and accountant-general of Ireland), in 1746 (died 1785); no children. ❖ Prominent social host and member of the Bluestockings' literary circle of London, whose parties brought together London's female intellectuals with members of "The Club," a circle of prominent male writers, scholars, and philosophers, including Horace Walpole, Samuel Johnson, and her husband; was also a prolific correspondent. ❖ See also *Women in World History.*

VESPASIA POLLA (fl. 50 CE). Roman mother of Vespasian. Married T. Flavius Sabinus; children: Flavius Sabinus (who m. Arretina); Vespasian, Roman emperor (r. 69–79 CE).

VESPUCCI, Simonetta (d. 1476). Italian artist's model. Name variations: Simonetta de' Vespucci; Simonetta de Vespucci; Simonetta Cattaneo. Born Simonetta Cattaneo in Genoa, Italy, in 1453; died of TB, April 26, 1476, in Florence; dau. of Gasparo Cattaneo; m. Marco Vespucci (a Florentine), in 1469; no children. ❖ Famous in her own time as "la Bella Simonetta," was long thought to have been the model for Botticelli's famous painting *The Birth of Venus* (though this theory is now discredited, it is still thought that she served as his inspiration); was considered by many the most beautiful woman in Florence, and numerous court poets and writers, including Poliziano, wrote works in praise of her beauty and charm; was the mistress of the powerful Giuliano di Piero de Medici. ❖ See also *Women in World History.*

VESSEL, Anne Marie (1949—). Danish ballet dancer. Name variations: Anne Marie Vessel Schlüter. Born May 1, 1949, in Copenhagen, Denmark; dau. of Poul Vessel (ballet dancer). ❖ Trained by father and Vera Volkova, among others, at Royal Danish Ballet; joined the company (1967) and danced there to great acclaim in numerous French and Russian classical repertory works such as *Coppélia* and *The Nutcracker*; also noted for her work in Bournonville repertory, including *Flower Festival in Genzano*, *La Ventana*, *The Kermesse in Bruges*, and *The King's Volunteers on Amager*; became a teacher (1979); served as director of the Royal Danish Theatre Ballet School (1988–2001).

VESTA
See Smith, Lucy Masey (1861–1936).
See Henderson, Stella May (1871–1962).

VESTERGAARD, Mette (1975—). Danish handball player. Name variations: Mette Vestergaard Larsen. Born Nov 27, 1975, in Denmark. ❖ Back, won a team European championship (1996); won team gold medals at Sydney Olympics (2000) and Athens Olympics (2004); was top scorer in the Danish League (2000–01) and captained the Danish national team.

VESTLY, Anne-Cath (1920—). Norwegian children's writer. Name variations: Anne-Catharina Vestly. Born Feb 15, 1920, in Rena, Norway; m. Johan Vestly (artist). ❖ Made radio broadcasts for children (1950s), which were published as stories; wrote over 40 books of realist fiction which have had great influence on children's literature in Norway; all books illustrated by husband.

VESTOFF, Floria (1920–1963). American theatrical dancer. Born 1920; died Mar 18, 1963, in Hollywood, CA; dau. of Genrik and Jennie Vestoff (dancer and teacher); great-grand-niece of Veronine Vestoff (ballet dancer). ❖ Performed early on as tap dancer in nightclubs; made dance stage debut in New York City at Latin Quarter, then appeared at Astor Hotel Roof, Café Mirador, El Morocco, and Paramount Theater; on tv, appeared as the dancing Old Gold cigarette box in a popular commercial; retired from dance career, but continued in tv as writer for song and comedy.

VESTRIS, Lucia (1797–1856). English actress, singer and theatrical manager. Name variations: Mrs. Armand Vestris; Eliza or Elizabeth Vestris; Madame Vestris; Mrs. Charles Mathews or Matthews; Lucia Elizabeth Mathews. Born Lucia Elizabetta Bartolozzi, Mar 3, 1797, in London, England; died in London, Aug 8, 1856; granddau. of famous engraver Francesco Bartolozzi; dau. of Gaetano Stefano Bartolozzi (music teacher) and Theresa Janssen Bartolozzi (German musician and music teacher); married Armand Vestris (1787–1825, dancer and ballet master), 1813; m. Charles James Mathews Jr. (1803–1878, actor and son of the actor Charles Mathews, sometimes seen as Charles James Matthews), 1838; no children. ❖ Had a great influence on development of stage-craft, insisting on realism in scenery and furnishings and historical accuracy in costume; made stage debut in title role in von Winter's opera *Il Ratto di Proserpina* (1815); performed at Comédie Française (1816–19), appearing in both comedy and tragedy with the celebrated François Joseph Talma; had 1st London success in *Giovanni in London,* a satire on Mozart's *Don Giovanni* (1820); became highly popular as a singer of ballads and a comedian in light opera specializing in male roles, especially that of Macheath in *The Beggar's Opera*; appeared next in *Tom and Jerry, or Life in London* (1821) and *Paul Pry* (singing "Cherry Ripe," 1825); made mark in English theatrical history as a manager of Covent Garden (1831), assembling a company that included such well-known performers as Julia Glover, J. Vining, F. Mathews, John Liston, and Maria Foote (1831); after 1st success, managed Olympic Theater (1831–39), introducing realism in scenery, abandoning the grotesque costumes and acting styles long associated with burlettas, and making use of the latest technical advances; is also credited with adding the 1st ceiling used in a stage setting; with husband, ran Covent Garden (1840–45), opening in the hit *London Assurance,* then took control of Lyceum Theater (1847–55); retired (1855); not to be confused with another Madame Vestris, the French actress Françoise-Rose Gourgaud (1743–1804). ❖ See also A. A. Appleton, *Madame Vestris and the London Stage* (1974); Charles Pearce, *Madame Vestris and her Times* (London, 1923); and *Women in World History.*

VESTRIS, Madame (1797–1856). *See Vestris, Lucia.*

VESTRIS, Thérèse (1726–1808). French-Italian ballerina. Name variations: Therese Vestris. Born 1726; died 1808; sister of Gäetan Vestris (a ballet dancer) and Angelo Vestris (a dancer). ❖ At 21, arrived in Paris with another and 5 of her 8 siblings (1747); with his enormous talent, brother Gäetan's star ascended; sharing his arrogance but not his talent, had an affair with the Opera's ballet master Lany and focused her competitive energy on Mlle Puvigny, who was premiere danseuse; was forced out after the directors grew tired of her scheming; from then on, used her skills as a courtesan; her only loyalty was to her family.

VETO, Madame (1755–1793). *See Marie Antoinette.*

VETROVSKA, Marie (1912–1987). Czech gymnast. Name variations: Marie Siroka. Born June 26, 1912, in Czechoslovakia; died May 21, 1987. ❖ At Berlin Olympics, won a silver medal in team all-around (1936).

VETSERA, Marie (1871–1889). Austrian baroness. Name variations: Marie Alexandrine; Baroness Mary Vetsera. Born Mar 19, 1871, in Vienna, Austria; died Jan 29, 1889, at Mayerling, near Vienna; dau. of Baron Albin Vetsera (career diplomat) and Helene Baltazzi Vetsera; never married; no children. ❖ Met Austrian crown prince Rudolf, son of Elizabeth of Bavaria and Emperor Franz Joseph (c. 1885); became infatuated with the unstable prince, who was 13 years her senior and married to Stephanie of Belgium; at 17, became one of his numerous mistresses, visiting him frequently but covertly at the emperor's palace in Vienna; when Rudolf's mental state deteriorated because of syphilis, agreed to die with him; at isolated hunting lodge of Mayerling, outside Vienna, was shot by Rudolf, who then shot himself (1889), an event which shocked Austria and Europe. The tragedy has been the subject of numerous plays, books, and films. ❖ See also Franz Judtmann, *Mayerling: The Facts Behind the Legend* (trans. by Ewald Osers, Harrap, 1971); Georg Markus, *Crime at Mayerling: the Life and Death of Mary Vetsera* (trans. by Carvel de Bussy, Ariadne Press, 1995); and *Women in World History.*

VETURIA (late 6th c.–mid-5th c. BCE). Mother of Coriolanus. Name variations: Volumnia. Mother of Gnaeus Marcius, later named Coriolanus (Roman soldier). ❖ Patrician mother of Coriolanus who, along with Volumnia, convinced him not to fight with Rome. (In William Shakespeare's *Coriolanus,* 1st presented around 1609, the character of Volumnia is the mother of Coriolanus; the character of Virgilia is his wife.) ❖ See also *Women in World History.*

VEYRINAS, Françoise de (1943—). *See de Veyrinas, Françoise.*

VEYSBERG, Yuliya (1878–1942). Russian composer. Name variations: Yuliya Weissberg; Yuliya Rimskaya-Korsakova. Born Yuliya Lazarevna Veysberg in Orenburg, Dec 23, 1878; died in the siege of Leningrad (now St. Petersburg), Mar 1, 1942; m. Andrei Rimsky-Korsakov (son of the composer). ❖ Attended St. Petersburg Conservatory, studying under Nikolai Rimsky-Korsakov and Alexander Glazunov; politically liberal, was expelled from conservatory for taking part in a demonstration against its director during revolutionary upheavals (1905); lived in Germany (1907–12), completing her musical education there before returning to St. Petersburg; considered the composer most like Glazunov, wrote one of her most successful pieces, to Alexander Blok's poem "The Twelve" (1923); drawn to subjects like the Arabian Nights, wrote numerous works for children, including operas, a cantata, partsongs, and songs; translated the musical writings of Romain Rolland, which appeared in print in Moscow (1938). ❖ See also *Women in World History.*

VEZIN, Jane Elizabeth (1827–1902). British actress. Name variations: Mrs. Charles Young. Born Jane Elizabeth Thompson in 1827; died 1902; m. Charles Frederick Young (comedian), 1846 (div. 1862); m. Hermann Vezin (actor), 1863. ❖ Important Shakespearean actress of 19th century, appeared on stage as a singer and dancer when young; toured Australia with a theatrical company (1855); made London stage debut (1857); over next several years, took several leading roles in Shakespeare's plays; played Desdemona in *Othello* (1864), and continued to earn marquee roles for most of the next 2 decades; appeared opposite Edwin Booth (1880–81).

VEZZALI, Valentina (1974—). Italian fencer. Born Feb 14, 1974, in Jesi, Italy. ❖ Won a gold medal for team foil and a silver medal for indiv. foil at Atlanta Olympics (1996); at World championships, won a gold medal for team foil (1995, 1997, 1998, 2001, 2004) and indiv. foil (1998, 2001, 2003); won World Cups (1995, 1998, 1999, 2000, 2001); won European championship, for indiv. foil (1999, 2000); won gold medals for indiv. and team foil at Sydney Olympics (2000); won a gold medal for indiv. foil at Athens Olympics (2004).

VIA DUFRESNE, Begona (1971—). Spanish sailor. Born Feb 13, 1971, in Barcelona, Spain; sister of Natalia Via Dufresne (sailor). ❖ Won World championships for 470 (1993, 1994, 1995, 1996); won European championship (1994); won a gold medal for double-handed dinghy (470) at Atlanta Olympics (1996).

VIA DUFRESNE, Natalia (1973—). Spanish yacht racer. Name variations: Natalia Via Dufresne Perena. Born June 10, 1973, in Barcelona, Spain; sister of Begona Via Dufresne (sailor); attended University of Raon Llull. ❖ At Barcelona Olympics, won a silver medal in European class (1992); won European SPA Regatta (1995); won a silver medal for double-handed dinghy (470) at Athens Olympics (2004).

VIARDOT, Louise (1841–1918). French contralto. Name variations: Louise Héritte-Viardot or Louise Heritte-Viardot. Born Louise-Pauline-Marie on Dec 14, 1841; died 1918; dau. of Pauline Viardot (1821–1910) and Louis Viardot; married a diplomat. ❖ Was a professor at the St. Petersburg School of Music and later at Frankfurt, Berlin, and Heidelburg. ❖ See also autobiography *Une Famille de grands musiciens: Memoirs de Louise Héritte-Viardot* (Paris: Stock, 1923); and *Women in World History.*

VIARDOT, Pauline (1821–1910). French-born opera singer, composer, and teacher. Name variations: Pauline Garcia; Pauline Viardot-Garcia or Viardot-García. Born Louise-Ferdinande-Michelle-Pauline Garcia in Paris, France, July 18, 1821; died in Paris, May 18, 1910; dau. of Manuel del Popolo Vincente Rodriguez Garcia (1775–1832, opera singer and teacher) and (Maria) Joaquina Stiches di Mendi (1780–1862, singer); sister of Maria Malibran (1808–1836, singer); m. Louis Viardot (1800–1883, critic, director, and author), 1840; children: Louise Viardot (1841–1918, contralto), Claudie Viardot Chamerot (1852–1914), Marianne Viardot Duvernoy (1854–?), Paul-Louis-Joachim Viardot (1857–1941). ❖ One of history's greatest opera stars, was also a composer, teacher, and for 40 years the intimate friend of Russian writer

Turgenev; debuted in concert in Brussels (1837); made opera debut in London in Rossini's *Otello* (1839); went to Central Europe (1843); made 1st Russian tour and met Turgenev (1843–44); had highly acclaimed seasons in Berlin and London (1846–49); debuted at Paris Opéra in Meyerbeer's *Le Prophète* (1849); debuted in Gounod's *Sapho* (1851), Gluck's *Orphée*, her artistic summit (1859), and Gluck's *Alceste* (1861); retired from Paris opera stage (1863); lived in Baden-Baden (1863–70); ended public career (c. 1875); went into retirement in Paris but continued to teach (1883–1910); operatic repertoire included Leonore in *Fidelio*,, title role in *Norma*, Amina in *La Sonnambula*, Fidalma in *Il Matrimonio Segreto*, Alina in *Alina, Regina de Golconda*, Norma in *Don Pasquale*, Adina in *L'Elisir d'amore*, Leonore in *La Favorita*, Lucia in *Lucia di Lammermoor*, Mafio Orsini in *Lucrezia Borgia*, Maria in *Maria de Rohan*, Iphigénie in *Iphigénie en Tauride*, Valentine in *Les Huguenots*, Zerlina, Donna Anna, and Donna Elvira in *Don Giovanni*, Rosina in *Il Barbieri di Siviglia*, Cenerentola in *La Cenerentola*, Ninette in *La Gazza ladra*, Desdemona in *Otello*, Arsace in *Semiramide*, Tancredi in *Tancredi*, Lady Macbeth in *Macbeth*, and Azucena in *Il Trovatore*. ❖ See also April FitzLyon *The Price of Genius: A Life of Pauline Viardot* (Calder, 1964); and *Women in World History*.

VIBIA AURELIA SABINA (b. 166). Roman noblewoman. Born in 166 CE; dau. of Faustina II (130–175 CE) and Marcus Aurelius, Roman emperor (r. 161–180).

VIBIA PERPETUA (181–203). *See Perpetua.*

VIBIA SABINA (88–136 CE). *See Sabina.*

VIBORADA (d. 925). Frankish recluse and saint. Born in France; killed by Hungarian troops in 925 in France; never married; no children. ❖ After a pilgrimage to Rome, had a cell built for her at a nearby church; as an ascetic, kept only the barest supplies she needed to maintain life, and gave the rest to the poor; moved to another cell at a more remote church (c. 891), no longer receiving visitors and speaking to almost no one; made an exception for a young woman named Rachilda, who was suffering from an undiagnosed disease; requested that Rachilda be brought to her, and insisted that she would be healed if she remained as a recluse with her; for over 30 years, lived with Rachilda, who was indeed cured, which served to increase Viborada's already widespread renown; canonized (1047). ❖ See also *Women in World History*.

VICARIO, Arantxa Sanchez (1971—). *See Sanchez Vicario, Arantxa.*

VICARIO, Leona (1789–1842). Mexican revolutionary. Born María de la Soledad Leona Camila Vicario Fernández de San Salvador (but from childhood known simply as Leona Vicario), April 10, 1789, in Mexico City; died in Mexico City, Aug 21, 1842; dau. of Gaspar Martín Vicario (wealthy merchant born in Spain) and Camila Fernández de San Salvador y Montiel (of a distinguished family of Toluca, Mexico); m. Andrés Quintana Roo (the future statesman), 1813; children, Genoveva (b. 1817); María Dolores (b. 1820). ❖ Heroic insurrectionist, born in an age of upheaval in Europe and the Americas, who became the most notable woman of wealth and privilege to join the struggle for Mexican independence from 1810 to 1821; was orphaned and an heiress at 18 (1807); learned of French occupation of Spain (mid-1808); sympathized with educated Mexicans' efforts (late 1808) to establish a national congress; deplored Spaniards' violent removal of viceroy from office (Sept 15, 1808), for supporting Mexicans' desire for a voice in their government; after independence movement began (Sept 16, 1810), contacted and aided the revolutionaries (1811–13); was detected (Feb 28, 1813); fled Mexico but was recaptured and imprisoned in a convent in Mexico (Mar 11, 1813); freed by patriots (late April 1813); joined insurgents and married Andrés Quintana Roo, one of the intellectual lights of Mexican independence (late 1813); with husband, suffered incredible hardships eluding enemy for 4 years; gave birth to 1st child in a hovel (1817); accepted pardon (1818); returned to Mexico City (early 1820) where 2nd child was born; after independence was achieved (1821), her husband served in cabinet, legislature, and supreme court while she retired to private life; her letters in defense of her role in the Mexican independence movement appeared in the newspaper *El Federalista Mexicano* (Feb–Mar 1831); admired by patriots and scorned by traditionalists, challenged most of the stereotypes concerning "the weaker sex" and "woman's sphere." Since her death and for over 150 years, she has been an icon of Mexican history. ❖ See also *Women in World History*.

VICENT, Tania (1976—). Canadian short-track speedskater. Born Jan 13, 1976, in Montreal, Quebec, Canada. ❖ Won bronze medals at Nagano Olympics (1998) and Salt Lake City Olympics (2002), both for the 3,000-meter relay; won a silver medal for 3,000-meter relay at Torino Olympics (2006).

VICENTE, Paula (1519–1576). Portuguese playwright and actress. Born 1519 in Portugal; died 1576; dau. of Gil Vicente (1465–1536?, dramatist and poet) and Melícia Roiz. ❖ Appeared as actress and musician in father's plays; wrote plays as well as a guide, *Arte de lengua inglesa y holandesa*.

VICKERS, Janeene (1968—). American hurdler. Born Oct 3, 1968; grew up in Pomona, CA; attended University of California, Los Angeles. ❖ At Barcelona Olympics, won a bronze medal in 400-meter hurdles (1992).

VICKERS, Martha (1925–1971). American actress. Name variations: Martha MacVicar. Born Martha MacVicar, May 28, 1925, in Ann Arbor, Michigan; died Nov 2, 1971, in Hollywood, CA; m. Mickey Rooney (actor), 1949 (div. 1952); m. Manuel Rojas, 1954 (div. 1965); children: Teddy Rooney (b. 1950, actor). ❖ Made screen debut in *Frankenstein Meets the Wolf Man*, billed as Martha MacVicar (1942); billed as Martha Vickers in films after 1945, including *The Big Sleep*, *Daughter of the West*, *Alimony*, *That Way with Women*, *Love and Learn* and *Bad Boy*.

VICKERY, Betsy (1860–1950). *See Cowie, Bessie Lee.*

VICKERY, Joyce (1908–1979). Australian botanist. Name variations: Joyce Winifred Vickery. Born Dec 15, 1908, in Australia; died May 1979; dau. of Elizabeth (Rossbach) Vickery and George Begg Vickery; University of Sydney, BS, 1931, MS, 1933, DSc, 1959; never married. ❖ Appointed assistant botanist at the National Herbarium in Sydney (1936), the 1st woman in Australia to be appointed a scientific officer in the public service; served as assistant botanist (1936–64), senior botanist (1964–71) and honorary research fellow (1973–79); endowed the Joyce Vickery Fund (later administered by the Linnean Society of New South Wales). Made a Member of the Order of the British Empire; received Clarke Medal from Royal Society of New South Wales.

VICOL, Maria (1935—). Romanian fencer. Born Oct 17, 1935, in Romania. ❖ At Rome Olympics, won a bronze medal in indiv. foil (1960); at Mexico City Olympics, won a bronze medal team foil (1968).

VICTOIRE, Duchesse de Nemours (1822–1857). *See Victoria of Saxe-Coburg.*

VICTOIRE, Madame (1733–1799). French princess. Born Victoire Louise Marie Thérèse at Versailles, France, in 1733; died June 8, 1799; dau. of Louis XV (1710–1774), king of France (r. 1715–1774), and Marie Leczinska (1703–1768); sister of Adelaide (1732–1800) and Louise Marie (1737–1787), as well as Louis le dauphin (father of Louis XVI). ❖ Youngest and jolliest of King Louis XVI's aunts, blindly obeyed her elder sister Adelaide; when her father came down with smallpox, however, was the one with the courage to nurse him, staying with him until he died.

VICTOR, Frances (1826–1902). American novelist and historian. Name variations: Frances Fuller; Frances Auretta Fuller Victor; (pseudonym) Florence Fane. Born Frances Fuller, May 23, 1826, in Rome, New York; died Nov 14, 1902, in Portland, Oregon; dau. of Adonijah Fuller and Lucy A. (Williams) Fuller; sister of Metta Victor (1831–1885, author); educated at a female seminary in Wooster, Ohio; m. Jackson Barritt, 1853 (div. Mar 1862); m. Henry Clay Victor (naval engineer), May 1862 (died in a shipwreck, 1875); no children. ❖ Published the adventure romance *Anizetta, the Guajira: or the Creole of Cuba* (1848); moved to New York with younger sister Metta (1848); wrote poetry and fiction (late 1840s); moved west to a homestead in Nebraska with 1st husband (1853); left husband and moved back to NY; wrote for "Dime Novels" series (1862); moved west to Oregon with 2nd husband (1864); wrote historical works on Western subjects which are still considered fundamental to further study of these regions (1870s–90s), including *The River of the West* (1870), *All Over Oregon and Washington* (1872, rev. ed. published as *Atlantis Arisen*, 1890), *The History of Oregon* (2 vols., 1886–88), *The History of Washington, Idaho, and Montana* (1890), *The History of Nevada, Colorado, and Wyoming* (1890), and *The Early Indian Wars of Oregon* (1894). ❖ See also *Women in World History*.

VICTOR, Lucia (1912–1986). American director, producer, and playwright. Born Jan 8, 1912, in Iowa; died Mar 22, 1986, in Chappaqua, NY. ❖ Was associated with David Merrick for many years, stage managing *Take Me Along, Becket, The Rehearsal*, and *Carnival*; assisted Gower Champion on *Hello Dolly!* and *42nd St.* and directed their touring companies; on Broadway, directed *Billy Noname, Exodus,* and *Heathen*; produced *The Milky Way* and *Boy Meets Girl*; wrote and produced *Detour after Dark* and *Eye for an I.*

VICTOR, Metta (1831–1885). American writer. Name variations: Metta Victoria Fuller Victor. Born Metta Victoria Fuller, Mar 2, 1831, in Erie, Pennsylvania; died June 26, 1885, in Ho-Ho-Kus, New Jersey; dau. of Adonijah Fuller and Lucy A. (Williams) Fuller; sister of Frances Victor (1826–1902, author); graduated from an all-female school in Wooster, Ohio; m. Orville J. Victor (editor who published the Beadle and Adams "Dime Novels"), July 1856; children: Lillian (b. 1857); Alice (b. 1859); Bertha (b. 1860); Winthrop (b. 1861); Lucy (b. 1863); Guy (b. 1865); Metta (b. 1866); twins Vivia and Florence (b. 1872). ❖ Prolific creator of over 100 dime novels, whose readership included not only ordinary Americans but also one as renowned as Abraham Lincoln; published 1st novel, *The Last Days of Tul,* at 15; moved with sister Frances to New York City (1848); published a pro-temperance novel, *The Senator's Son, or, The Maine Law: A Last Refuge* (1851), which launched her literary career in earnest; with husband, edited *Cosmopolitan Art Journal* (late 1850s); also edited *Home* (from 1859); anonymously or under a pseudonym, wrote dime novels and other works of fiction (1860–85), including *Maum Guinea, and Her Plantation "Children"* which was widely popular and played a role in the antislavery movement at the height of the Civil War; sometimes worked outside the dime novel genre, as with *Miss Slimmens' Window* (1859), a collection of short satires, and *The Blunders of a Bashful Man* (1875), and continued to contribute to the numerous periodicals of the day. ❖ See also *Women in World History.*

VICTOR, Wilma (1919–1987). Native American educator. Name variations: Wilma L. Victor. Born a full-blooded Choctaw in Idabel, Oklahoma, on Nov 5, 1919; died in Idabel on Nov 15, 1987; attended University of Kansas; Milwaukee State Teachers College (now University of Wisconsin-Milwaukee), BA; University of Oklahoma, MA in education. ❖ Took a Federal Bureau of Indian Affairs (BIA) teaching post at the Intermountain School in Utah, on Navajo land (1940s); spent 13 years there, then moved to Santa Fe, where she assisted in the establishment of the Institute of American Indian Arts; played a key role in developing the curriculum there, which focused on Native artistic traditions, and came to believe strongly in the capacity of Native Americans to create their own solutions to the social problems that faced them; returned to Intermountain School, as its supervisor (1960s); received Federal Women's Award (1967) and was a keynote speaker at 1st National Indian Workshop for Indian Affairs; named special assistant to Rogers C. B. Morton, secretary of the interior under President Richard Nixon (1971), a post that made her the highest-ranking Native American woman in government at the time. Received the Indian Achievement Award (1970). ❖ See also *Women in World History.*

VICTORIA (d. around 253 CE). Italian martyr and saint. Executed in or about 253 CE; dau. of noble Tivoli parents; sister of Anatolia; never married; no children. ❖ A Christian, was betrothed to the pagan Eugenius, while sister was betrothed to the pagan Titus Aurelius; with sister, refused to marry in favor of chastity (both sisters were eventually killed). Feast day is Dec 23. ❖ See also *Women in World History.*

VICTORIA (1819–1901). Queen of England. Born Alexandrina Victoria, May 24, 1819, in Kensington Palace, London, England; died Jan 22, 1901, at Osborne House, Isle of Wight, England; dau. of Edward Guelph, duke of Kent (4th son of King George III) and Victoria of Coburg; niece of George IV and William IV, kings of England; m. Prince Albert of Saxe-Coburg, on Feb 10, 1840 (died 1861); children: Victoria Adelaide (1840–1901); Albert Edward (1841–1910, future Edward VII, king of England, r. 1901–1910, who m. Alexandra of Denmark); Alice Maud Mary (1843–1878, mother of Alexandra Feodorovna of Russia); Alfred (1844–1900, who m. Marie Alexandrovna [1853–1920]); Helena (1846–1923); Louise (1848–1939); Arthur (1850–1942); Leopold Albert (1853–1884, duke of Albany, and father of Princess Alice of Athlone [1883–1981]); Beatrice (1857–1944). ❖ Queen who presided over the most confident years of British imperial and industrial dominance; following death of William IV, succeeded to throne at 18 (1837); was coronated (June 28, 1838); ruled Britain and its expanding empire for the next 64 years, restored the sagging prestige of the monarchy, worked tirelessly, and came to impart a moral and aesthetic style to an entire age and way of life; confirmed Prime Minister Lord Melbourne in his office and enjoyed his tutelage through the early years of her reign; with Sir Robert Peel, developed a mutual respect after he became prime minister (1841); managed to work effectively with her prime ministers (Lord John Russell, Lord Palmerston,

William Gladstone, Lord Salisbury, and especially Benjamin Disraeli), even with those she did not particularly like; ruled through the Irish Potato Famine (1845–49), Crimean War (1853–56), Indian Mutiny (1857), and South African War (1899–1902); husband's death came to her as a shattering blow (1861); though she lived on for another 40 years, never subsequently cast off her mourning clothes; also withdrew from public life; for many years, declined even to preside at the official opening of Parliament; named empress of India (1877); in the last years of her reign, emerged from self-imposed seclusion; celebrated her Diamond Jubilee (1897); died at age 81 (1901), having reigned 63 years (1837–1901), and the fact that her name was attached to the age, and to an entire way of life, "Victorian," suggests the breadth and durability of her influence. Descendants include H. M. Queen Elizabeth II and the House of Mountbatten-Windsor; Wilhelm II of Hohenzollern, last German emperor; kings Carl XVI Gustaf of Sweden and Juan Carlos I of Spain, and Queen Margrethe II of Denmark; the former kings of Greece, Romania, and Yugoslavia; the head of the former Russian imperial house of Romanov. ❖ See also Theo Aronson, *Heart of a Queen: Queen Victoria's Romantic Attachments* (Murray, 1991); Dulcie Ashdown, *Victoria and the Coburgs* (Hale, 1981); Elizabeth Longford, *Victoria R. I.* (Pan, 1976); Mullen and Munson, *Victoria: Portrait of a Queen* (BBC Books, 1987); Giles St. Aubyn, *Queen Victoria: A Portrait* (Sinclair-Stevenson, 1991); (film) *Mrs. Brown,* starring Judi Dench (1997); (play) *Victoria Regina* by Laurence Housman (1935); and *Women in World History.*

VICTORIA (1866–1929). Prussian princess. Name variations: Victoria Hohenzollern. Born Frederica Amelia Wilhelmina Victoria on April 12, 1866, in Potsdam, Brandenburg, Germany; died Nov 13, 1929, in Bonn, Germany; dau. of Victoria Adelaide (1840–1901) and Frederick III (1831–1888), emperor of Germany (r. 1888); sister of Wilhelm II, emperor of Germany (r. 1888–1918); m. Adolph of Schaumburg-Lippe, on Nov 19, 1890; m. Alexander Anatolievitch Zoubkoff, on Nov 19, 1927.

VICTORIA (1868–1935). Princess Royal. Name variations: Victoria Saxe-Coburg. Born Victoria Alexandra Olga Mary on July 6, 1868, in London, England; died Dec 3, 1935, in Iver, Buckinghamshire, England; dau. of Edward VII, king of England (r. 1901–1910), and Alexandra of Denmark (1844–1925). ❖ See also *Women in World History.*

VICTORIA (1977—). Swedish crown princess and duchess of Västergötland. Name variations: Victoria Bernadotte. Born Victoria Ingrid Alice Désirée on July 14, 1977, in Stockholm, Sweden; dau. of Carl XVI Gustavus, king of Sweden, and Silvia Sommerlath (1943—); studied French at a French university in 1996; studied political science at Uppsala University. ❖ See also *Women in World History.*

VICTORIA ADELAIDE (1840–1901). Princess royal of Great Britain and German empress. Name variations: Vicky; Victoria; Victoria Adelaide Mary Louise; Empress Frederick. Born Victoria Adelaide Mary Louise on Nov 21, 1840, in Buckingham Palace, London, England; died of cancer on August 5, 1901, in Friedrichshof, Germany; eldest child of Queen Victoria (1819–1901) and Prince Albert Saxe-Coburg; sister of King Edward VII of England; educated by a French governess and her father; m. Friedrich Wilhelm also known as Frederick III (1831–1888), emperor of Germany (r. 1888), on Jan 25, 1858; children: Wilhelm (William) II (1859–1941), emperor of Germany; Charlotte of Saxe-Meiningen (1860–1919); Henry of Prussia (1862–1929); Sigismund (1864–1866); Victoria (1866–1929); Waldemar (1868–1879); Sophie of Prussia (1870–1932, who m. Constantine I, king of the Hellenes); Margaret Beatrice (1872–1954). ❖ Following marriage, her outspoken views on the benefits of constitutional government were unwelcome in Germany, and she chafed under the surveillance of mother-in-law Augusta of Saxe-Weimar; enjoyed a strong influence over husband, which made her increasingly unpopular in court circles; found herself constantly in opposition to Bismarck over issues; became the focus of anti-English opinion during Franco-Prussian war of 1870–71, despite efforts recruiting nurses and organizing hospitals for wounded Germans; a keen artist, was elected a member of the Berlin Academy (1860) and founded Berlin Industrial Art Museum; also founded the Victoria House and Nursing School (1881) and the Victoria Lyceum, the 1st institution in Germany dedicated to women's higher education; founded over 40 educational or philanthropic institutions; just 3 months after his accession (1888), husband died, leaving her isolated and estranged from both Bismarck and eldest son, now Emperor Wilhelm II. ❖ See also Daphne Bennett, *Vicky: Princess Royal of England and German Empress* (St. Martin, 1971); Jerrold M. Packard, *Victoria's*

Daughters (St. Martin, 1998); Hannah Pakula, *An Uncommon Woman: Empress Frederick, Daughter of Queen Victoria, Wife of the Crown Prince of Prussia, Mother of Kaiser Wilhelm* (Simon & Schuster, 1995); and *Women in World History.*

VICTORIA ADELAIDE OF SCHLESWIG-HOLSTEIN (1885–1970). Duchess of Albany. Name variations: Victoria Adelheid, princess von Schleswig-Holstein. Born Victoria Adelaide of Schleswig-Holstein-Saxe-Coburg-Glucksburg on Dec 31, 1885, in Grunholz, Holstein, Germany; died Oct 3, 1970, in Coburg, Bavaria, Germany; dau. of Frederick Ferdinand (1855–1934), duke of Schleswig-Holstein-Glucksburg (r. 1855–1934) and Caroline Matilda of Schleswig-Holstein (1860–1932); m. Charles Edward Saxe-Coburg, 2nd duke of Albany, on Oct 11, 1905; children: John Leopold (b. 1906), prince of Saxe-Coburg; Sybilla of Saxe-Coburg-Gotha (1908–1972); Hubertus Frederick (b. 1909, a pilot in the Luftwaffe); Caroline Matilda Schnirring (1912–1983, who m. Max Otto Schnirring, a captain in the Luftwaffe), duchess of Saxony; Frederick (b. 1918).

VICTORIA ALEXANDRA ALICE MARY (1897–1965). *See Mary.*

VICTORIA EUGENIA (1887–1969). *See Ena.*

VICTORIA EUGENIE OF BATTENBERG (1887–1969). *See Ena.*

VICTORIA FREDERICA OF SCHLESWIG-HOLSTEIN (1860–1932). *See Caroline Matilda of Schleswig-Holstein.*

VICTORIA LOUISE (1892–1980). Duchess of Brunswick-Lüneburg. Born Victoria Louise Adelaide Matilda Charlotte on Sept 13, 1892, at Marble Palace, Potsdam, Brandenburg, Germany; died Dec 11, 1980, in Hanover, Lower Saxony, Germany; dau. of Augusta of Schleswig-Holstein (1858–1921) and Wilhelm II (1859–1941), emperor of Germany (r. 1888–1918); m. Ernest Augustus of Cumberland (1887–1953), duke of Brunswick-Luneburg (r. 1923–1953), on May 24, 1913; children: Ernest Augustus (1914–1987); George (b. 1915); Fredericka (1917–1981, queen of Greece); Christian (1919–1981); Welf-Henry (b. 1923); Monika of Solms-Laubach (b. 1929).

VICTORIA LOUISE SOPHIA AUGUSTA AMELIA HELENA (1870–1948). *See Helena Victoria.*

VICTORIA MARY LOUISA (1786–1861). *See Victoria of Coburg.*

VICTORIA MARY OF TECK (1867–1953). *See Mary of Teck.*

VICTORIA MELITA OF SAXE-COBURG (1876–1936). Grand duchess of Hesse-Darmstadt. Name variations: Victoria of Saxe-Coburg; Grand Duchess Kiril or Cyril; (nickname) Ducky; known as Marie Feodorovna following her 2nd marriage. Born in Malta on Nov 25, 1876; died of a stroke in Amorbach, Germany, on Mar 2, 1936; dau. of Alfred Saxe-Coburg, duke of Edinburgh, and Marie Alexandrovna (1853–1920); sister of Alexandra Saxe-Coburg (1878–1942), Beatrice of Saxe-Coburg (1884–1966), duchess of Galliera, and Marie of Rumania (1875–1938); m. Ernest Louis, grand duke of Hesse-Darmstadt, on April 19, 1894 (div. 1901); m. Cyril Vladimirovitch (grand duke and grandson of Alexander II of Russia), on Oct 8, 1905; children: (1st m.) Elizabeth of Hesse-Darmstadt (1895–1903) and one son (1900–1900); (2nd m.) Marie of Russia (1907–1951); Kira of Russia (1909–1967); Vladimir Cyrillovitch (1917–1992). ❖ See also Michael John Sullivan, *A Fatal Passion: The Story of Victoria Melita, the Uncrowned Last Empress of Russia* (Random House, 1997).

VICTORIA OF BADEN (1862–1930). Queen of Sweden. Born Sophia Mary Victoria on Aug 7, 1862, in Karlsruhe, Baden-Wurttemberg, Germany; died April 4, 1930, in Rome, Italy; buried in Stockholm, Sweden; dau. of Frederick I, grand duke of Baden, and Louise of Baden (dau. of William or Wilhelm I, emperor of Germany, and Augusta of Saxe-Weimar); m. Gustav or Gustavus V (1858–1950), king of Sweden (r. 1907–1950), on Sept 20, 1881; children: Gustavus VI Adolphus (1882–1973), king of Sweden (r. 1950–1973); William Bernadotte, prince of Sweden (b. 1884, who m. Marie Pavlovna of Russia); Eric Gustaf Louis, duke of Vestmanland (1889–1918).

VICTORIA OF BATTENBERG (1887–1969). *See Ena.*

VICTORIA OF COBURG (1786–1861). Duchess of Kent. Name variations: Victoria of Leiningen; Victoria of Saxe-Coburg; Victoria Mary Louisa von Saxe-Coburg. Born Victoria Mary Louisa of Saxe-Coburg-Saalfeld on Aug 17, 1786, in Coburg, Bavaria, Germany; died Mar 16, 1861, in Windsor, Berkshire, England; interred at Frogmore, Windsor; dau. of Francis, duke of Saxe-Coburg-Saalfeld, and Augusta of Reuss-

Ebersdorf (1757–1831); sister of Leopold I, king of the Belgians; m. Emich, 2nd prince of Leiningen, on Dec 21, 1803; m. Edward Guelph also known as Edward Augustus, duke of Kent, on July 11, 1818, at Kew Palace, Surrey; children: (1st m.) Charles, 3rd prince of Leiningen, and Feodore of Leiningen (1807–1872); (2nd m.) Queen Victoria (1819–1901). ❖ See also Jerrold M. Packard, *Victoria's Daughters* (St. Martin, 1998).

VICTORIA OF HESSE-DARMSTADT (1863–1950). Princess of Hesse-Darmstadt. Name variations: Princess Victoria, marchioness of Milford Haven. Born Victoria Alberta Elizabeth Matilda Mary on April 5, 1863, in Windsor Castle, Berkshire, England; died Sept 24, 1950, in Kensington Palace, London, England; dau. of Grand Duke Louis IV of Hesse-Darmstadt and Princess Alice Maud Mary (dau. of Queen Victoria); m. Louis of Battenberg, 1st marquess of Milford Haven, on April 30, 1884; children: Alice of Battenberg (1885–1967); Louise Mountbatten (1889–1965, who m. Gustavus VI Adolphus); George, 2nd marquess of Milford Haven (1892–1938); Lord Louis Mountbatten (1900–1979, who m. Edwina Ashley Mountbatten).

VICTORIA OF MECKLENBURG-STRELITZ (1878–1948). Prussian aristocrat. Born Victoria Marie Augusta Louise Antoinette Caroline Leopoldine on May 8, 1878; died Oct 14, 1948, in Obercassel; dau. of Adolphus Frederick V, grand duke of Mecklenburg-Strelitz, and Elizabeth of Anhalt-Dessau; m. George Jametel, on June 22, 1899 (div. 1908); m. Julius of Lippe, in August 1914; children: (1st m.) 2; (2nd m.) 2.

VICTORIA OF SAXE-COBURG (1822–1857). Duchess of Nemours. Name variations: Victoria of Saxe-Coburg-Gotha. Born Feb 14, 1822; died Nov 10, 1857; dau. of Ferdinand Saxe-Coburg (b. 1785) and Antoinette Kohary (1797–1862); sister of Ferdinand Saxe-Coburg (1816–1885, who m. Maria II da Gloria, queen of Portugal); cousin of Queen Victoria (1819–1901); m. Louis (1814–1896, son of Louis Philippe I, king of France), duke of Nemours, on April 27, 1840; children: Gaston (b. 1842), count of Eu; Ferdinand (b. 1844), duke of Alençon; Margaret d'Orleans (1846–1893, who m. Ladislaus Czartoryski); Blanka d'Orleans (1857–1932).

VICTORIA OF SAXE-COBURG (1876–1936). *See Victoria Melita of Saxe-Coburg.*

VIDAL, Doriane (1976—). French snowboarder. Born April 16, 1976, in Limoges, France. ❖ Placed 12th at Nagano Olympics (1998); won a silver medal for halfpipe at World championships (2000); won a silver medal for halfpipe at Salt Lake City (2002); won the halfpipe World championship (2003).

VIDAL, Ginette (b. 1931). French murderer. Born 1931. ❖ Moved in with married-lover Gerard Osselin in Clichy-sous-Bois (1972); made a written pact with him that, if either had relations with another, then the betrayed party had the right to take the other's life; in accordance with pact, murdered Osselin in his sleep with .22 rifle after he had begun seeing his wife again; dismayed by court's rejection of signed murder pact, received 10-year sentence.

VIDAL, Mary Theresa (1815–1869 or 1873). British-born Australian writer. Born in 1815 in Devon, England; died in 1869 or 1873; relative of portraitist Joshua Reynolds; married a minister; children. ❖ One of the 1st women to write fiction in Australia, moved with husband to Australia (1840); though not set in Australia, published *Tales for the Bush* (1845), a collection of moralistic short stories that warned servants and other working folk against drink and dereliction; returned to England (1845); created 2 works set in Australia, a story called "The Cabramatta Store" (1850) and the novel *Bengala: Or, Some Time Ago* (1860), and 8 other works of fiction. ❖ See also *Women in World History.*

VIDALI, Lynn (1952—). American swimmer. Name variations: Lynn Vidali Gautschi. Born May 26, 1952; trained with Santa Clara Swim Club. ❖ At Mexico City Olympics, won a silver medal in 400-meter indiv. medley (1968); at Munich Olympics, won a bronze medal in 200-meter indiv. medley (1972).

VIDAR, Jorunn (1918—). Icelandic composer, pianist and teacher. Born in Reykjavik, Iceland, Dec 7, 1918; studied music 1st with mother, then Pall Isolfsson; later enrolled at Reykjavik College of Music, studying with Arni Kristjansson and graduating, 1936; studied at Berlin Hochschule für Musik, 1936–38; continued musical education at Juilliard School in NY, 1943–45; studied piano in Vienna with Viola Tern, 1959–60.

❖ Pioneer in Icelandic music, whose compositions combined traditional Icelandic melodies with the subtleties of the prevailing international style, was often featured on Icelandic radio and tv; best-known works include the ballet *Fire* (1951), *Five Meditations on Icelandic Themes* for piano (1965), and a Suite for Violin and Piano to commemorate the 1,100-year-old settlement of Iceland (1973). ❖ See also *Women in World History.*

VIDOR, Florence (1895–1977). American actress. Name variations: Mrs. Jascha Heifetz; Florence Cobb. Born Florence Cobb (changed to Florence Arto when mother remarried), July 23, 1895, in Houston, TX; died Nov 3, 1977, in Pacific Palisades, CA; m. King Vidor (director), 1915 (div. 1925); m. Jascha Heifetz (violinist), 1928 (div. 1946); children: 2 daughters, 1 son. ❖ Starred in numerous silent films, including *A Tale of Two Cities, The Patriot, The Virginian, Barbara Frietchie* (title role), *Old Wives for New, Hail the Woman, Alice Adams* (title role), *The World at Her Feet,* and *Main Street*; career ended with her 1st talkie *Chinatown Nights* (1929), when voice proved inadequate for sound.

VIEBIG, Clara (1860–1952). German novelist and short-story writer. Name variations: Clara Viebig Cohn. Born 1860 in Trier, Germany; died 1952 in Berlin, Germany; educated in Düsseldorf and at Berlin High School of Music; m. Fritz Theodor Cohn (publisher). ❖ Used the Eifel region, the area of her birth, for the settings of her early novels, an area that had been featured very rarely in earlier German literature; published *Die Wacht am Rhein* (The Watch on the Rhine, 1902), which received the greatest international acceptance and acclaim of all her books (not to be confused with Lillian Hellman's later play); was one of Germany's most read novelists, and many of her works were translated into English; writings include *Kinder der Eifel* (Children of the Eifel, 1897), *Das Weiberdorf* (Village of Women, 1900), *Das tägliche Brot* (1900, published in English as *Our Daily Bread,* 1909), *Das schlafende Heer* (1904, published in English as *The Sleeping Army,* 1929), *Einer Mutter Sohn* (1907, published in English as *The Son of His Mother,* 1913), *Das Kreuz im Venn* (The Cross in Venn, 1908), *Die vor den Toren* (Those Outside the Gates, 1910), *Töchter der Hekuba* (1917, published in English as *Daughters of Hecuba,* 1922), *Insel der Hoffnung* (1933), and *Der Vielgeliebte und die Vielgehasste* (1936). ❖ See also *Women in World History.*

VIEHOFF, Valerie (1976—). German rower. Born Feb 16, 1976, in Germany. ❖ Won a silver medal for lightweight double sculls at Sydney Olympics (2000).

VIEIRA, Maruja (1922—). Colombian poet. Name variations: Maruja Vieira de Vivas. Born 1922 in Manizales, Colombia. ❖ Works include *Palabras de la ausencia* (1953), *Ciudad Remanso* (1956), *Clave mínima* (1958), *Los poemas de enero* (1961), *Campanario de lluvia* (1974), and *Sombra del amor.*

VIEIRA DA SILVA, Maria Elena (1908–1992). Portuguese-born French painter. Name variations: Maria Helena. Born June 13, 1908, in Lisbon, Portugal; died Mar 6, 1992, in Paris, France; only child of Marcos Vieira da Silva (economist) and Maria (Graca) Vieira da Silva; studied in Paris, learning sculpture with Bourdelle and Despiau, engraving with Hayter, and painting with Friesz and Léger; m. Arpad Szénes (Hungarian painter), Feb 22, 1930. ❖ In Paris, held the 1st of her several one-woman shows (1933); had a semi-abstract style notable for its soft colors, gentle light, and often poetic moods; spent WWII in Rio de Janeiro, Brazil (1939–47), creating murals for the University of Agriculture, but lived the vast majority of her adult life in France, ultimately becoming a French citizen; exhibited at the Venice and Sao Paolo Biennales, as well as in London, Paris and NY (1940s–50s); paintings hang in major museums and galleries around the world; works include *Forest of Errors* (1941), *The City* (1948), *Morning Mist* (1952), *Iron Bridges* (1953), *Theatre* (1953), *Nocturnal Space* (1954) and *Overhead Railway* (1955).

VIERDAG, Maria (b. 1905). Dutch swimmer. Name variations: Marie or Rie Vierdag; Marie Smit-Vierdag. Born Sept 22, 1905, in Amersfoort, Netherlands. ❖ At Los Angeles Olympics, won a silver medal in 4 x 100-meter freestyle relay (1932); turned 99 (2004).

VIEREGG, Elizabeth Helene (fl. 17th c.). Queen of Denmark and Norway. Second wife of Frederick IV (1671–1730), king of Denmark and Norway (r. 1699–1730); no children. Frederick IV had two other wives: Louise of Mecklenburg-Gustrow and Anne Sophie Reventlow.

VIERTEL, Salka (1889–1978). Galician screenwriter and salonnière. Born Salomea Sara Steuerman or Steuermann in 1889 in Sambor, Galicia (part of the Austro-Hungarian Empire); died Oct 20, 1978, in Klosters, Switzerland; dau. of a prominent Jewish attorney and town mayor; m. Berthold Viertel (stage and film director), April 30, 1918 (later sep., died 1953); children: John Viertel; Peter Viertel (b. 1920, writer who m. Deborah Kerr); Thomas Viertel. ❖ Central European actress and writer, now known chiefly for her screenplays for Greta Garbo, who hosted a brilliant salon in Hollywood and provided aid to European refugees in the years before and during World War II; after sudden death of fiancé, went to Vienna at 16 to study theater (1905); landed a position with Deutsches Theater led by Max Reinhardt; with husband, founded acting ensemble Die Truppe in Berlin; driven by rising anti-Semitism, left Germany with family for Hollywood (1928); became a screenwriter, chiefly for Garbo, writing the scripts for *Queen Christina* (1933), *Anna Karenina* (1935) and *Conquest* (1937), among others; established a salon at her house in Santa Monica where actors and intellectuals from Europe and US gathered, including Albert Einstein, the brothers Heinrich and Thomas Mann, André Malraux, Sergei Eisenstein, Upton Sinclair, Aldous Huxley, and Charlie Chaplin; over 2 decades, worked on many films; with less work available after House Un-American Activities Committee implied she was a Communist, moved to Switzerland (1953). ❖ See also autobiography *The Kindness of Strangers* (1969); and *Women in World History.*

VIEUVILLE, Marquise de La (b. 1731). *See Saint-Chamond, Claire-Marie Mazarelli, Marquise de La Vieuville de.*

VIEUX, Marie (1916–1973). *See Chauvet, Marie.*

VIGANÒ, Renata (1900–1976). Italian poet, journalist and novelist. Name variations: Renata Vigano. Born 1900 in Bologna, Italy; died 1976 in Bologna; married with children. ❖ Worked as nurse during WWII and participated in Italian Resistance, resulting in her best known novel *L'Agnese va a morire* (1949, Agnes Goes Off to Die), which won the Viareggio Prize; other writings include *Ginestra in fiore* (1913), *Piccola fiamma* (1916), *Il lume spento* (1933), *Mondine* (1952), *Arriva la cicogna* (1954), *Donne della Resistanza* (1955), *Ho conosciuto Ciro* (1959), *Una storia di ragazze* (1962) and *Matrimonio in brigata* (trans. into English as *Partisan Wedding*).

VIGÉE-LE BRUN, Elisabeth (1755–1842). French painter. Name variations: Elisabeth Vigee; Elisabeth Vigee LeBrun; Mme Le Brun, le Brun, or Lebrun. Born Marie Anne Élisabeth Louise Vigée on April 16, 1755, in Paris, France; died 1842 in Paris; dau. of Louis Vigée (pastel and oil painter) and Jeanne (Maissin) Vigée; m. Jean Baptiste Pierre Le Brun (painter and picture dealer), 1776 (died 1813); children: Jeanne Lucie Louise Le Brun Nigris (1780–1819). ❖ Celebrated painter during late 18th and early 19th centuries who is best known for her portraits of Marie Antoinette and other members of the French court prior to the French Revolution; left convent school (1767); father died (1768); elected to Royal Academy of Painting (1783); fled France during French Revolution and traveled throughout Europe (1789–1801), beginning in Italy, and settling for a time in Naples, Rome, Berlin, Vienna, and St. Petersburg; as she traveled, made her living by painting; elected to the Academy and Institute of Bologna (1789); elected to St. Petersburg Academy (1795); returned to Paris (1801), then lived in London (1802–05); returned to Paris (1805); used her incredible talents and personal charm to make acquaintances among the most famous figures in Europe; rendered over 660 portraits and other paintings, some of the most famous of which are *Madame Vigée-Le Brun and Her Daughter, Mother Love, The Girl With the Muff, Venus Tying the Wings of Love,* several self-portraits, portraits of Marie Antoinette and the Royal Family, and portraits of members of the French and European aristocracy. ❖ See also *Memoirs of Mme. Elisabeth Louise Vigée-Le Brun* (c. 1834); Mary D. Sheriff, *The Exceptional Woman: Elizabeth Vigée-Lebrun and the Cultural Politics of Art* (U. of Chicago Press, 1996); and *Women in World History.*

VIGILANTIA (c. 485–?). Byzantine royal. Born c. 485; dau. of swineherds; sister of Emperor Justinian I (482–565); children: Justin II, emperor of Byzantium and Rome (r. 518–527, who m. Sophia [c. 525–after 600]). ❖ See also *Women in World History.*

VIGRI, Caterina dei (1413–1463). *See Catherine of Bologna.*

VIJAYA LAKSHMI PANDIT (1900–1990). *See Pandit, Vijaya Lakshmi.*

VIK, Bjørg (1935—). Norwegian playwright and short-story writer. Born Sept 11, 1935, in Oslo, Norway. ❖ Works, which focus on sexuality as way of understanding human relationships, include *Søndag ettermiddag* (1963), *Nødrop fra en myk sofa* (1966), *Ferie* (1966), *Kvinneakvariet* (1972), *En håndfull lengsel* (1979), and *Snart er det høst* (1982); also published stage and radio plays.

VIKE-FREIBERGA, Vaira (1937—). President of Latvia. Name variations: Vaira Vīķe-Freiberga; Vaira Vīke-Freibergs. Born in Riga, Latvia, on Dec 1, 1937; dau. of Karlis and Annemarie (Rankis) Vike; University of Toronto, BA, 1958, MA, 1960; McGill University, PhD, 1965; m. Imants F. Freibergs, on July 16, 1960; children: Karl Robert; Indra Karoline. ❖ During WWII, immigrated with family to Canada; was a clinical psychologist at Toronto Psychiatric Hospital (1960–61); was an assistant professor, department of psychology, at University of Montreal (1965–72), then associate professor (1972–77) and became professor (1977); became an expert in Latvian folklore and culture, and lobbied Western governments not to recognize the annexation of the Baltics by the Soviet Union; was director of Latvian Youth Ethnic Heritage Seminars Divreiizdivi (1979) and president of the Social Science Federation of Canada (1980); served as chair of NATO special program panel on human factors (1980); returned to Latvia; was sworn in as president of Latvia (July 8, 1999), the 1st democratically elected woman president in Eastern Europe; reelected (2003). ❖ See also *Women in World History.*

VIKTORIA. *Variant of Victoria.*

VILAGOS, Penny (1963—). Canadian synchronized swimmer. Born April 17, 1963, in Brampton, Ontario, Canada; twin sister of Vicky Vilagos (synchronized swimmer). ❖ At Barcelona Olympics, won a silver medal in duet (1992).

VILAGOS, Vicky (1963—). Canadian synchronized swimmer. Born April 17, 1963, in Brampton, Ontario, Canada; twin sister of Penny Vilagos (synchronized swimmer). ❖ At Barcelona Olympics, won a silver medal in duet (1992).

VILANDER, Sirkka (b. 1927). *See Polkunen, Sirkka.*

VILARIÑO, Idea (1920—). Uruguayan poet, essayist and educator. Name variations: Idea Vilarino. Born Aug 18, 1920, in Montevideo, Uruguay. ❖ Works include *La suplicante* (1945), *Paraíso perdido* (1949), *Por aire sucio* (1951), *Nocturnos* (1955), *Poemas de amor* (1957), *Las letras de tango* (1965), *Pobre mundo* (1966), and *No* (1980); translated works from English and French into Spanish. Received several awards including City of Montevideo Prize.

VILBUSHEVICH, Manya (1878–1961). *See Shochat, Manya.*

VILHELMINA or VILHELMINE. *Variant of Wilhelmina or Wilhelmine.*

VILHELMSEN, Gitte (1971—). *See Sunesen, Gitte.*

VILINSKA, Mariya (1834–1907). Ukrainian short-story writer, translator and editor. Name variations: Mariia Aleksandrovna Markovich; Mariya Oleksandrivna Vilinska; Mariia or Maria Vilinska or Vilinskaia; Mariaa Vilinska Markovych Zhuchenko; (pseudonym) Marko Vovchók or Vovchok. Born 1834 (some sources cite 1833) in Ukraine; died 1907; m. A. V. Markovych. ❖ Wrote short stories in Ukrainian and Russian; works include *Ukrainskie narodnye razskazy* (*Ukrainian Folk Tales*, 1857), which was praised by Ukrainian nationalists and Russian radicals and translated by Turgenev into Russian, as well as *Tales from Russian Folk Life* (1859), and *Notes of a Junior Deacon* (1869–70); lived abroad and worked as editor and translator; continued to write stories about all classes but the most popular were about peasant life.

VILJOEN, Lettie (b. 1948). *See Winterbach, Ingrid.*

VILLA, Brenda (1980—). American water-polo player. Born April 18, 1980, in Commerce, CA; attended Stanford University. ❖ Attacker/driver, won a team silver medal at Sydney Olympics (2000) and a team bronze at Athens Olympics (2004); won World championship (2003).

VILLAMEUR, Lise (1905–2004). French secret agent and heroine. Name variations: Lise de Baissac; (code name) Odile and Marguerite. Born Lise de Baissac, May 11, 1905, in Mauritius; died Mar 28, 2004; moved to Paris when young; m. Henri Villameur (artist), 1950 (died 1978); no children. ❖ As a member of the British Special Operations Executive (SOE), landed by parachute in the Loire and Cher region of France, the 1st woman to be parachuted into occupied France (1942); under code-name Odile, established a small resistance network in Poitiers (1942–43); under codename Marguerite, joined her brother Claude de Baissac in Normandy, where she set up more resistance groups (1944). Awarded MBE and Chevalier de la Légion d'Honneur Croix de Guerre avec Palme.

VILLARD, Fanny Garrison (1844–1928). American philanthropist, suffragist, and activist. Name variations: Helen Frances Garrison. Born Helen Frances Garrison, Dec 16, 1844, in Boston, Massachusetts; died July 5, 1928, in Dobbs Ferry, New York; dau. of William Lloyd Garrison (the abolitionist) and Helen Eliza (Benson) Garrison; m. Henry Villard (publisher of New York *Evening Post* and *Nation*), Jan 3, 1866 (died 1900); children: Helen Villard; Oswald Garrison Villard (liberal editor of New York *Evening Post*); Harold Garrison Villard; Henry Hilgard Villard. ❖ Joined the suffragist movement (1906); cofounded the National Association for the Advancement of Colored People (1909); founded Women's Peace Party with Jane Addams (1915); founded Women's Peace Society (1919); concerned with the educational opportunities for blacks and women, took an active role in the founding of both Barnard and Radcliffe colleges, the American College for Women in Constantinople, and numerous schools for black students in NY and the South, including Hampton Institute in Virginia; published *William Lloyd Garrison and Non-Resistance* (1924). ❖ See also *Women in World History.*

VILLARINO, María de (1905–1994). Argentinean poet and short-story writer. Name variations: Maria de Villarino. Born Maria de Chivilcoy Villarino, 1905, in Chivilcoy, Argentina; died June 6, 1994, in Buenos Aires ❖ Taught at University of La Plata and wrote for Argentinean and foreign newspapers; works include *Calle apartada* (1930), *Junco sin sueño* (1935), *Tiempo de angustia* (1937), *Una antigua historia de la niña-niña* (1941), *Puebla de la niebla* (1943), *La iluminada* (1946), *La rosa no debe morrir* (1950), *Los espacios y los símbolos* (1960), *La dimensión oculta* (1972), and *Los nombres de la vida* (1981).

VILLEDIEU, Catherine des Jardins, Mme de (c. 1640–1683). French novelist and playwright. Name variations: Madame de Villedieu; Marie Catherine Desjardins or Marie-Catherine Desjardins; Marie-Catherine Boesset; Marie-Catherine de Chaste. Born Marie-Catherine Hortense Desjardins or des Jardins around 1640, probably in Alençon, France; died 1683 in Paris; dau. of Guillaume Desjardins and Catherine (Ferrand) Desjardins; associated with Antoine de Boesset de Villedieu, sire of Villedieu (lieutenant in the regiment of Picardy, died in battle 1667); m. Claude-Nicolas de Chaste, sire of Chalon, in 1677 (died c. 1679); children: Louis de Chaste (b. 1678). ❖ Grew up and was educated in household of Madame de Montbazon, where her mother was a maid; at 18, published a sonnet, "Jouissance," in a Parisian journal, followed by the publication of several essays and more poetry; published to critical success *Alcidamie* (1661), an unfinished romance; increasing popularity led to publication of a collection of poetry (1662), 2 plays (both tragedies), and a 2nd novel (1663); solemnized her relationship with Antoine de Boesset with a formal engagement (1664) and referred to herself as Madame de Villedieu; though de Boesset disavowed his promise of marriage and married another (1667), insisted that she continue to be referred to as Madame de Villedieu; her 3rd play, *Le Favori* (The Favorite, 1664), brought her the friendship of Molière, who staged the drama to great success at the Palais Royal (1665), the 1st by a female playwright to be honored by a command performance by the king; also enjoyed the patronage of Marie d'Orleans, duchess of Nemours, who would remain her good friend and patron for many years; published 1st major novel, *Cléonice* (1669), earning her a place among France's most popular writers; is credited with creating a new kind of French novel, the "nouvelle galante" (gallant novel), which broke away from the predominant genre of heroic adventure novels set in exotic lands; published *Les desordres de l'amour* (*The Disorders of Love*, 1675). ❖ See also Nancy D. Klein, ed. *Selected writings of Madame de Villedieu* (Lang, 1995); and *Women in World History.*

VILLEGAS, Micaela (1748–1819). Peruvian actress, singer, and mistress. Name variations: La Périchole, La Perricholi, or La Pirricholi; (nickname) Miquita. Born in Lima, Peru, Sept 28, 1748; died May 16, 1819, in Lima; dau. of José Villegas and Teresa Hurtado de Mendoza; m. Vicente Fermín Echarri y Gorózabal, 1795. ❖ The most celebrated Peruvian woman of her age, known as "La Perricholi," became comic actress (c. 1763); starred at the Coliseo, where she met Viceroy Manuel de Amat (1766) and became his mistress; had a son and daughter; banned from the stage by Amat because of her hot temper (1773); reconciled with Amat and returned to stage (1775); withdrew from public life when Amat was replaced as viceroy and returned to Spain (1776); with Vicente Echarri y Gorózabal, became theatrical entrepreneur (1780s); idolized in popular legend, became the subject of Jacques Offenbach's opera *La Périchole*, and the romantic drama by M. Théaulon, *La Périchole*; also figured prominently in Thornton Wilder's *The Bridge of San Luis Rey*. ❖ See also *Women in World History.*

VILLEMS, Sigbrit (fl. 1507–1523). *See Willums, Sigbrit.*

VILLENA, Isabel de (1430–1490). Spanish abbess and author. Born 1430; died 1490 in Valencia, Spain; illeg. dau. of Enric de Villena (a noble and writer); educated at the court of Alphonso V (1396–1458), king of Aragon (r. 1416–1458); never married; no children. ❖ Served as abbess of Trinity Convent in Valencia (1463–90); became an increasingly important voice in Valencian society, particularly after the accession of the "Catholic kings," Isabella I of Castile and Ferdinand II of Aragon; best known for her work *Vita Christi*, which was published posthumously (1497).

VILLENEUVE, Gabrielle-Suzanne de (c. 1695–1755). French novelist. Name variations: Mme de Villeneuve; Gabrielle-Suzanne Barbot Gallon de Villeneuve. Born c. 1695; died 1755; widowed c. 1730. ❖ Widowed and left with a small income, supported herself by writing, producing over 12 vols. during the latter half of her life; is credited with writing the fairy tale *Beauty and the Beast* (*La Belle et la bête*, in vol. XXVI of *Cabinet des fées*); portraying lower-class women as admirable heroines, also wrote *Le Phénix conjugal* (The Phoenix of Marriage, 1733) and *La Jardinière de Vincennes* (The Gardener of Vincennes, 1753), considered her best work. ❖ See also *Women in World History*.

VILLERS, Mme (fl. late 18th c.). French artist. Active in the late 18th and early 19th centuries; maiden name was either Lemoine or Nisa; studied with an artist named either Giraudet (an unknown figure), Girardet (one of a large family of Swiss artists), or possibly Anne Louis Girodet-Trioson (1767–1824). ❖ Enigmatic figure in the history of French art, exhibited a handful of paintings at the Paris Salon (1799, 1801, and 1802), including *A Baby in its Cradle* (1802) and *Portrait of Mme Soustras*, which was possibly also exhibited in 1802 under the title *A Study of a Woman from Nature*.

VILLIERS, Anne (d. 1688). Countess of Portland. Died Nov 30, 1688; dau. of Sir Edward Villiers and Lady Frances Villiers (c. 1636–1677); sister of Elizabeth Villiers (c. 1657–1733); m. Hans William Bentinck, earl of Portland, on Feb 1, 1678; children: Mary Bentinck (1679–1726, who m. Algernon Capell, 2nd/22nd earl of Essex, and Hon. Sir Conyers D'Arcy); William Bentinck (b. 1681); Henry Bentinck (b. 1682), 1st duke of Portland; Anne Margaretta Bentinck (1683–1763, who m. Arend de Wassenaer-Duvenvoirde, Baron de Wassenaer); Frances Wilhemina Bentinck (1684–1712, who m. William Byron, 4th Baron Byron); Eleanor Bentinck (b. 1687), a nun; Isabella Bentinck (1688–1728, who m. Evelyn Pierrepont, duke of Kingston-on-Hull).

VILLIERS, Barbara (d. 1708). Viscountess FitzHardinge. Died Sept 19, 1708; interred on Sept 23, 1708, at Westminster Abbey, London; dau. of Sir Edward Villiers and Lady Frances Villiers (c. 1636–1677); m. John Berkeley, 4th Viscount FitzHardinge.

VILLIERS, Barbara (c. 1641–1709). Countess of Castlemaine, duchess of Cleveland, and paramour. Name variations: Barbara Palmer; Lady Castlemaine; Countess of Southampton; Baroness Nonsuch. Born autumn 1641 (some sources cite 1640 or 1642) at Westminster, England; died at Chiswick on Oct 9, 1709; only dau. of William Villiers, 2nd Viscount Grandison, and Mary (Bayning) Villiers; m. Roger Palmer (a Royalist), in 1659 (died 1705); became mistress of King Charles II, in 1660; m. Robert (Beau) Feilding or Fielding (d. 1712), on Nov 25, 1705; children: (with Charles II) Anne Palmer (b. 1661); Charles, duke of Southampton (1662–1730); Henry, 1st duke of Grafton (1663–1690); Charlotte Fitzroy (1664–1717); George, duke of Northumberland (1665–1716); (with John Churchill) Barbara Palmer (b. 1672). ❖ The powerful and influential mistress of Charles II of England for over 10 years, moved to London in early teens; married Roger Palmer (1659); became mistress of Charles II (1660); was created countess of Castlemaine (1662) and appointed lady-in-waiting to Queen Catherine of Braganza; converted to Catholicism (1663); husband acknowledged her children with Charles II as his own, then retreated from court to concentrate on his career as a member of Parliament; realizing that she would have to share her royal lover with other women, continued to hold a powerful sway over the king; given large pension and created Baroness Nonsuch, countess of Southampton, and duchess of Cleveland (1669); was removed from queen's household due to Test Act which prohibited anyone who was not a member of the Church of England from holding public office (1672); with influence over the king dwindling, particularly as a succession of women had supplanted her as royal mistress, had affair with John Churchill, duke of Marlborough (1672); moved to Paris (1677) and lived there for several years; remained at court during reigns of James II and William and Mary; married Robert Feilding (Nov 1705), a union which was declared void after a bigamy trial (May 24, 1707), as Feilding had a wife, Mary Wadsworth; fell ill (July 1709) and died from dropsy (Oct 1709). ❖ See also Allen Andrews, *The Royal Whore: Barbara Villiers, Countess of Castlemaine* (Chilton, 1970); Margaret Gilmour, *The Great Lady: A Biography of Barbara Villiers, Mistress of Charles II* (Knopf, 1941); Elizabeth Hamilton, *The Illustrious Lady: A Biography of Barbara Villiers, Countess of Castlemaine and Duchess of Cleveland* (Hamish Hamilton, 1980); and *Women in World History*.

VILLIERS, Elizabeth (c. 1657–1733). Countess of Orkney. Name variations: Elizabeth Hamilton, Countess of Orkney; Mrs. Villiers. Born c. 1657; died in London on April 19, 1733; dau. of Colonel Sir Edward Villiers of Richmond and Frances (Howard) Villiers (c. 1633–1677); sister of Anne Villiers (d. 1688) and Edward Villiers (1656–1711), 1st earl of Jersey, and master of the horse; m. cousin, Lord George Hamilton (5th son of the 3rd duke of Hamilton), 1st earl of Orkney (r. 1696–1737), on Nov 25, 1695; children: Anne Hamilton (b. 1694), countess of Orkney; Henrietta Hamilton. ❖ With sister Anne, was among the maids of honor who accompanied Mary (II) to The Hague on her marriage to William III, prince of Orange (future William III of England); became William's acknowledged mistress (1680); though no great beauty, had intelligence and wit; had a large share of the confiscated Irish estates of King James II conferred on her by King William, but grant was revoked by Parliament (1699); following marriage, husband was granted the titles of earl of Orkney, viscount of Kirkwall, and Baron Dechmont. ❖ See also *Women in World History*.

VILLIERS, Frances (c. 1633–1677). Duchess of Richmond. Name variations: Lady Frances Howard. Born c. 1633 (one source cites c. 1636); died Nov 27, 1677; interred at Westminster Abbey, London; dau. of Theophilus Howard (1584–1640), 2nd earl of Suffolk (r. 1626–1640), and Elizabeth Hume (c. 1599–1633); m. Colonel Sir Edward Villiers of Richmond; children: Edward Villiers (1656–1711), 1st earl of Jersey; Henry Villiers; Elizabeth Villiers (c. 1657–1733); Katherine Villiers (who m. Colonel William Villiers and Louis James Le Vasseur, marquess de Purissar); Barbara Villiers (d. 1708); Anne Villiers (d. 1688, who m. Hans William Bentinck, earl of Portland); Henrietta Villiers (d. 1719, who m. John Campbell, 2nd earl of Breadalbane); Mary Villiers (d. 1753, who m. William O'Brien, 3rd earl Inchiquin). ❖ See also *Women in World History*.

VILLIERS, Margaret Elizabeth Child- (1849–1945). English philanthropist and countess. Name variations: Margaret Elizabeth Leigh, countess of Jersey. Born Margaret Elizabeth Leigh on Oct 29, 1849, in Stoneleigh Abbey, England; died May 22, 1945; dau. of William Henry Leigh (b. 1824), 2nd Baron Leigh, and Caroline Amelia (Grosvenor) Leigh; m. Victor Albert George Child-Villiers (1845–1915), 7th earl of Jersey (r. 1859–1915), on Sept 19, 1872; children: George Henry Robert Child-Villiers (b. 1873), 8th earl of Jersey; Margaret (1874–1874); Margaret Child-Villiers (b. 1875, who m. Walter FitzUryan Rhys, 7th baron Dynevor); Beatrice Child-Villiers (b. 1880); Arthur George Child-Villiers (b. 1883). ❖ Known for much of her life as a society hostess, entertaining widely at both Middleton Park, Bicester, and Osterley Park, Isleworth, took an active interest in children's welfare; was the founder and served as president of Victoria League (1901–27). Named Dame Commander of the British Empire (DBE, 1927). ❖ See also *Women in World History*.

VILLIERS, Susan (fl. 17th c.). Countess of Denbigh. Dau. of Sir George Villiers and Mary Beaumont, countess of Buckingham; m. William Fielding, 1st earl of Denbigh (r. 1622–1643), around 1607; children: Basil Fielding, 2nd earl of Denbigh; George Fielding, 1st earl of Desmond; Mary Hamilton (1613–1638); Anne Fielding (d. 1636, who m. Baptist Noel, 3rd viscount Campden); Elizabeth Fielding, countess of Guildford (who m. Lewis Boyle, viscount Kynalmeaky). ❖ See also *Women in World History*.

VILLIERS, Theresa (1968—). English barrister and politician. Born Mar 5, 1968, in London, England. ❖ Served as barrister in chambers, Lincoln's Inn (1994–95), and lecturer in law, King's College, London (1995–99); as a member of the European People's Party (Christian Democrats) and European Democrats, elected to 5th European Parliament (1999–2004), from UK.

VILLINGER, Hermine (1849–1917). German novelist and short-story writer. Name variations: (pseudonym) H. Willfried. Born Feb 6, 1849, in Freiburg, Germany; died Mar 3, 1917, in Karlsruhe. ❖ Known for her stories of village life, writings include *Der lange Hilarius* (1885),

Sommerfrischen (1887), *Mutter und Tochter* (1905), and *Die Dachprinzeß* (1908).

VILLOING, Mme (1819–1884). *See Lachman, Thérèse.*

VILLOMS, Sigbrit (fl. 1507–1523). *See Willums, Sigbrit.*

VILMORIN, Louise de (1902–1969). French novelist and poet. Born 1902 in Verrières-le-Buisson, France; died in 1969; m. 2nd husband, Count Paul Palffy, late 1930s. ❖ Published her 1st, largely autobiographical novel, *Sainte-Unefois* (Saint Onetime, 1934); published 1st poetry collection, *Fiançailles pour rire* (Betrothal in Jest, 1939); though she was to publish more poetry, received most acclaim for her novels, a number of which were filmed, including *Le Lit à colonnes* (The Tapestry Bed, 1941), *Julietta* (1951), and *Madame de . . .* (1951); other popular successes include *La Fin des Villavides* (The Last of the Villavides, 1938), *La Lettre dans un taxi* (Letter in a Taxi, 1958), and *Le Retour d'Erica* (Erica's Return, 1948). Awarded Grand Prix Littéraire de Monaco (1955).

VINCE, Marion Lloyd (1906–1969). American fencer. Name variations: Mrs. Joseph Vince. Born Marion Lloyd, April 16, 1906, Brooklyn, NY; died Nov 2, 1969; m. Joseph Vince (fencer). ❖ Won national championship (1928, 1931); was the 1st American woman to reach the finals at the Olympics (1932); was a member of the Salle Vince team, directed by her husband, which won 10 consecutive national team championships. Inducted into Helms Hall of Fame. ❖ See also *Women in World History.*

VINCENS, Mme Charles (1840–1908). *See Barine, Arvède.*

VINCENT, Mrs. James R. (1818–1887). *See Vincent, Mary Ann.*

VINCENT, Madge (b. 1884). English actress and singer. Born 1884 in Norfolk, England; dau. of Henry Vincent Bunn; younger sister of Ruth Vincent (actress and singer); m. Henry Frankiss (tenor). ❖ Appeared with sister at the D'Oyly Carte Opera Company (1898–1900); on London stage, appeared in *San Toy, The Toreador, The Wicked Uncle, Three Little Maids, The Medal and the Maid,* and *Véronique* (as Sophie); toured in musical comedy (1908–21).

VINCENT, Marjorie (c. 1965—). Miss America. Born Marjorie Judith Vincent c. 1965; dau. of Haitian immigrants; attended Duke University; married; children: Cameron. ❖ African-American, named Miss America (1991), representing Illinois; worked as newsanchor in Peoria, IL, and Columbus, OH.

VINCENT, Mary Ann (1818–1887). British-born American actress. Name variations: Mrs. Vincent; Mrs. J. R. Vincent; Mrs. James R. Vincent. Born Mary Ann Farlow on Sept 18, 1818, in Portsmouth, England; died Sept 4, 1887, in Boston, Massachusetts; dau. of John Farlow (naval worker); m. James R. Vincent (actor), in 1835 (committed suicide, June 11, 1850); m. John Wilson (expressman), Dec 16, 1854 (deserted 1866, later div.); no children. ❖ Made stage debut in Cowes, Isle of Wight, as the chambermaid Lucy in *The Review, or the Wags of Windsor* (1835); at 16, married and began working with husband as traveling players in England, Ireland and Scotland; known as Mrs. Vincent, sailed for US, where she appeared with William Pelby's National Theater in Boston (1846–52); when the National burned down (1852), moved to Boston Museum theater, beginning a long association with that institution which would last until her death; enjoyed a popular and long-lived career that was founded on a wide repertoire, from Shakespeare to classical comedy to melodrama; was most noted for her roles in comedies, particularly *She Stoops to Conquer* and *The Rivals.* ❖ See also *Women in World History.*

VINCENT, Mother (1819–1892). Irish-born Australian nun and educator. Name variations: Sister Mary Vincent; Ellen Whitty. Born Ellen Whitty on Mar 3, 1819, near Oilgate, Co. Wexford, Ireland; died Mar 9, 1892, in Brisbane, Australia; dau. of William Whitty (farmer) and Johanna (Murphy) Whitty; trained as a teacher. ❖ At 19, joined a religious order of the Sisters of Mercy and was known after 1840 as Sister Mary Vincent; became novice mistress and bursar before her election (1849) as Reverend Mother; invited to become one of the 1st women religious in the newly formed diocese of Queensland, Australia, arrived in Brisbane with 5 sisters (May 1861); appointed assistant to the Queensland head of the Order (1870), an office she held for rest of life; created 26 Mercy schools in Queensland, with 222 sisters and 7,000 pupils, as well as a Mercy Training College for teachers; also started All Hallow's, the state's 1st Catholic secondary school. ❖ See also *Women in World History.*

VINCENT, Ruth (1877–1955). English actress and soprano. Born Mar 22, 1877, in Grand Yarmouth, Norfolk, England; died July 4, 1955, in London, England; dau. of Henry Vincent Bunn; elder sister of Madge Vincent (actress and singer); m. John Fraser (of the Royal Horse Guards). ❖ Made stage debut with the D'Oyly Carte Opera in the chorus of *The Chieftain* (1894); remaining with D'Oyly Carte (1894–99), created the small part of Gretchen in *The Grand Duke* and role of Dorothea in *His Majesty* (1897) and appeared as Kate in the 1st revival of *The Yeomen of the Guard* (1897), Casilda in *The Gondoliers,* Laine in *The Beauty Stone,* and Laoula in *The Lucky Star,* among others; on the London stage, starred in *Véronique, A Girl on the Stage, Trial by Jury, Amäsis, Tom Jones, The Belle of Brittany,* and *A Persian Princess*; appeared in grand opera at Covent Garden and made concert tours.

VINCENT, Sarah (1833–1898). *See Curzon, Sarah Anne.*

VINE, Barbara (1930—). *See Rendell, Ruth.*

VINGE, Joan D. (1948—). American science-fiction and short-story writer. Name variations: Joan Carol Dennison Vinge. Born April 2, 1948, in Baltimore, MD; earned degree in anthropology from San Diego State University; m. Vernor Vinge, 1972 (div. 1979); m. James R. Frenkel, 1980. ❖ Works include *The Outcasts of Heaven's Belt* (1978), *Eyes of Amber* (1979), *Psion* (1982), *The Snow Queen* (1982), *World's End* (1984), *Ladyhawke* (1987), *The Summer Queen* (1991), and *Tangled Up in Blue* (2000); wrote novelizations of such films as *Star Wars* and *Mad Max.* Received Hugo Award (1978, 1981).

VINING, Elizabeth Gray (1902–1999). American writer and royal tutor. Name variations: Elizabeth Janet Gray. Born Oct 6, 1902, in Philadelphia, Pennsylvania; died Nov 27, 1999, in Kennett Square, Pennsylvania; dau. of John Gordon Gray (businessman) and Anne Moore (Iszard) Gray (both Quakers); educated at Germantown Friends School; Bryn Mawr College, AB, 1923; Drexel Institute School of Library Science, BS, 1926; m. Morgan Vining (educator), Jan 31, 1929 (died). ❖ Tutor to the crown prince of Japan who wrote many books for children and adults; at 17, contributed story to *Young Churchman* (1919); wrote several books under name Elizabeth Janet Gray; won Newbery Medal for *Adam of the Road* (1943); was recipient of *Herald Tribune* Spring Festival award for book *Sandy* (1945); tutored Crown Prince Akihito and other members of the royal family of Japan (1946–50), then wrote bestselling book, *Windows for the Crown Prince* (1952), and *Return to Japan* (1960), about her experiences; wrote more than 60 books for children and adults, including biographies, contemporary fiction, and historical novels; served as vice-president of trustees of Bryn Mawr (1951–71). Given the Third Order of the Sacred Crown, an award with eight possible degrees of merit, by the Japanese goverment. ❖ See also autobiographies (under Elizabeth Gray Vining) *Quiet Pilgrimage* (1970) and *Being Seventy: The Measure of a Year* (1978); and *Women in World History.*

VINOSKI-SEVERSON, Kimberly (1973—). *See Severson, Kim.*

VINSON, Helen (1907–1999). American stage and screen actress. Born Helen Rulfs, Sept 17, 1907, in Beaumont, TX; died Oct 7, 1999, in Chapel Hill, NC; m. Henry Neilson Vickerman (div.); m. Fred Perry (English tennis pro, div.); m. once more. ❖ Made NY debut in *Los Angeles* (1927); other plays include *Death Takes a Holiday, Berlin,* and *The Fatal Alibi*; made film debut in *Jewel Robbery* (1932), followed by *I Am a Fugitive from a Chain Gang, Second Hand Wife, Grand Slam, The Power and the Glory, The Kennel Murder Case, Gift of Gab, Broadway Bill, Reunion, Vogues of 1938, In Name Only, The Lady and the Monster* and *The Thin Man Goes Home,* among others.

VINSON-OWEN, Maribel (1911–1961). *See Owen, Marible Vinson.*

VINTIMILLE, Pauline Félicité, Marquise de (1712–1741). French mistress of Louis XV. Born 1712; died in childbirth in 1741; dau. of Louis, marquis de Nesle (whose family name was Mailly) and Madame de Nesle (lady-in-waiting to Queen Marie Leczinska); sister of Louise, comtesse de Mailly (1710–1751), Marie Anne de Mailly-Nesle, Duchesse de Châteauroux (1717–1744), and the Duchesse de Lauraguais; children: (with Louis XV) son (the comte de Luc, b. 1741). ❖ During 3-year liaison with Louis XV, became pregnant and died while giving birth to their son, the Comte de Luc. Her sister, Louise, comtesse de Mailly, adopted the baby, while Louis turned for affection to another of her sisters, Marie Anne, duchesse de Châteauroux.

VIOLA, Emilia Ferretti (1844–1929). Italian novelist and essayist. Name variations: (pseudonym) Emma. Born 1844 in Italy; died 1929.

❖ Under the pseudonym Emma, wrote *Un fra tante* (One Among Many, 1878) about prostitution, and *Mediocrità* (1884); was a frequent contributor to periodical *La Nuova Antologica*.

VIOLANTE. *Variant of Violet, Yolanda or Yolande.*

VIOLANTE DO CÉU (1601–1693). Portuguese poet. Name variations: Violante do Ceo; Soror Violante do Ceu; Violante Montesino. Born Violante Montesino in 1601; died 1693. ❖ Major poet of Baroque period, considered a proponent of *conceptismo* because of intellectual density of work; took Dominican vows (1630) and often wrote anonymously because of frank treatment of love in poems; works include *Rimas Várias* (1646) and *Parnaso Lusitano de Divinos e Humanos Versos* (1733); poems also appear in *Fénix Renascida* (1716–28).

VIOLANTE OF BAVARIA (d. 1731). *See Medici, Violante Beatrice.*

VIOLANTE OF HUNGARY (1215–1251). *See Iolande of Hungary.*

VIOLANTE OF MONTFERRAT (fl. 1300). *See Irene of Montferrat.*

VIOLANTE VISCONTI (c. 1353–1386). *See Visconti, Violet.*

VIOLETTE, La (1724–1822). *See Veigel, Eva-Maria.*

VIOLETTI, Eva Maria (1724–1822). *See Veigel, Eva-Maria.*

VIOLET VISCONTI OF MILAN (c. 1353–1386). *See Visconti, Violet.*

VIOLLIER, Maria Torelli (1846–1920). *See Torriani, Maria Antonietta.*

VIONNET, Madeleine (1876–1975). French fashion designer. Born in 1876 in Chileurs aux Boix, near Paris, France; died 1975; dau. of a plumber and a café owner. ❖ Worked in ateliers of Kate Reilly, Callot Soeurs, and Jacques Doucet; began own fashion house (1912); a dominant influence in women's fashion, designed the 1st of her tubular dresses which slipped over the head, developing the revolutionary bias-cut dresses that were to become her trademark (1919); also pioneered the use of flowing fabrics like crepe and silk and popularized "handkerchief point" skirts; had to shut down business permanently after German invasion of Paris (1940). Awarded Chevalier of the Legion of Honor (1929). ❖ See also *Women in World History.*

VIPSANIA AGRIPPINA (?–20 CE). Roman matron. Died in 20 CE; dau. of Marcus Vipsanius Agrippa and his 1st wife Pomponia; half-sister of Agrippina the Elder; m. (future emperor) Tiberius (div. 11 BCE); m. Asinius Gallus; children: (1st m.) Drusus the Younger. ❖ At the order of Caesar Augustus in 14 CE, her doting husband Tiberius was forced to divorce her and marry the emperor's own daughter Julia (39 BCE–14 CE). ❖ See also *Women in World History.*

VIRDIMURA OF SICILY (fl. 1376). Jewish physician of Sicily. Flourished in 1376 in Sicily; m. Pasquale of Catania (doctor). ❖ Was tutored by husband in the art of surgery and herbal medicine; eager to build a lawful practice and win recognition for her healing abilities, petitioned the court for the right to treat patients as a professional; was granted a license to practice medicine throughout the state by the Sicilian royal court (1376); chose not to work among the wealthy nobles who could afford to pay her well, but instead healed the poor of Sicily, often for free or for a very reduced fee.

VIRGILIA. *See Volumnia.*

VIRGINIA (c. 1899–1971). *See O'Hanlon, Virginia.*

VIRGIN MARY (20 BCE–40 CE). *See Mary the Virgin.*

VIRGIN QUEEN, The (1533–1603). *See Elizabeth I.*

VIRGO (1891–1994). *See Harsant, Florence Marie.*

VISCONTI, Agnes (c. 1365–1391). Italian noblewoman. Name variations: Agnese; Agnesina; Agnes Gonzaga. Born c. 1365 in Milan; beheaded in Feb 7, 1391, in Mantua (some sources cite 1395); dau. of Bernabo Visconti, lord of Milan (r. 1354–1385), and Beatrice della Scala (1340–1384); sister of Catherine Visconti (c. 1360–1404) and Virida Visconti (c. 1354–1414); m. Francesco Gonzaga (1366–1407), 4th captain general of Mantua (r. 1382–1407) and lord of Mantua (r. 1388–1407), in 1381; children: daughter Alda Visconti (b. 1391). ❖ Was married to Francesco Gonzaga, heir to Ludovico, ruler of the city-state of Mantua and a powerful player in Italian politics; was caught up in the Visconti family's political struggles with the Gonzagas (1380s); her refusal to put the Gonzagas' interests before her own family, coupled with her failure to bear sons to secure the succession, led her into a precarious position at the Mantuan court; along with several of her

retinue, was arrested and confined to her apartments (Jan 1391); found guilty of adultery, a questionable charge, was beheaded, while her supposed lover was strangled in prison. ❖ See also *Women in World History.*

VISCONTI, Beatrice (d. 1334). *See Este, Beatrice d'.*

VISCONTI, Bianca Maria (1423–1470). Duchess of Milan. Name variations: Bianca Maria Sforza; Blanca Maria. Born in 1423 in Milan, Italy; died in 1470 (some sources cite 1468) in Milan; dau. of Duke Filippo Maria Visconti (r. 1402–1447), duke of Milan, and his mistress Agnes del Maino; m. Francesco Sforza (1401–1466), 4th duke of Milan (r. 1450–1466), in 1441; grandmother of Caterina Sforza (c. 1462–1509); children: Galeazzo Maria Sforza (1444–1476), 5th duke of Milan (r. 1466–1476); Ascanio (1445–1505, a cardinal); Ippolita (1446–1484, who m. Alphonso II, king of Naples); Sforza Maria (1449–1479), duke of Bari; Lodovico il Moro Sforza (1451–1508, who m. Beatrice d'Este [1427–1497]); Ottaviano. Francesco had two illegitimate children: Sforza "Secondo" (1433–1501), count of Borgonovo, and Tristano (d. 1477, who m. Beatrice d'Este da Correggio [1427–1497]). ❖ Married her father's ally, the Italian noble Francesco Sforza (1441); after father named Alphonso II of Aragon as his heir (1447), went to war with Alphonso for the right of succession; with husband, emerged victorious (1450), and co-ruled Milan until Francesco's death (1466); continued to rule with eldest son, Galeazzo Maria, before retiring; was also responsible for the upbringing of Caterina Sforza, who would become a powerful force in Italian politics; known for her generous patronage of artists and charitable contributions to religious establishments, was also adored by the people as a champion of the oppressed. ❖ See also *Women in World History.*

VISCONTI, Caterina (c. 1360–1404). *See Visconti, Catherine.*

VISCONTI, Catherine (c. 1360–1404). Duchess and regent of Milan. Name variations: Caterina Visconti; Caterina di Bernabo Visconti. Born c. 1360 in Milan; died Oct 1404 in Monza, Italy; 3rd dau. of Barnabas, Barnabo or Bernabo Visconti, lord of Milan (r. 1354–1385), and Beatrice della Scala (1340–1384); sister of Virida Visconti (c. 1354–1414) and Agnes Visconti (c. 1365–1391); m. her cousin Giangaleazzo or Gian Galeazzo Visconti, later 1st duke of Milan (r. 1396–1402), in Nov 1380 (Gian Galeazzo was 1st married to Isabelle of France [1349–1372], dau. of John II, king of France, and Bona of Bohemia; he also had many illeg. children, including son Gabriele Maria Visconti with Agnese Mantegazza and possibly two other sons with a woman named Lusotta); children: Gian Maria Visconti (1388 or 1389–1412), duke of Milan (r. 1402–1412); Filippo Maria Visconti (1392–1447), duke of Milan (r. 1402–1447). ❖ Because father wanted to add her future husband's lands to his own, was married to Gian Galeazzo Visconti, count of Pavia, her 1st cousin and her father's political rival (1380); became much more of an asset to her husband than to her father; advised husband on policy issues and was given some authority in his administration, responsible for appointing state officials; also fulfilled the responsibilities more common to aristocratic women, presiding over the court of Pavia and patronizing artists and writers; after mother died (1384), put forth a legitimate claim to rule the city of Verona, and husband overthrew her father (1385); husband named the 1st duke of Milan (1395); with husband, reigned in a time of prosperity, pride, and peace for Lombardy; following his death (1402), was named regent for 10-year-old son Giovanni Maria, the 2nd duke of Milan; with sons, spent most of the next two years besieged in fortress in Milan, attempting to fight off one invading army after another; son turned against her (1404); fled Milan but son had her captured and imprisoned at Monza to prevent her from exercising influence. ❖ See also *Women in World History.*

VISCONTI, Elizabeth (d. 1432). Duchess of Bavaria. Name variations: Elisabetta Visconti. Died in 1432; dau. of Bernabo Visconti, lord of Milan (r. 1354–1385), and Beatrice della Scala (1340–1384); m. Ernst or Ernest (1373–1438), duke of Bavaria (r. 1397–1438); children: Albert III the Pious (b. 1401, sometimes referred to as Albert II), duke of Bavaria (r. 1438–1460).

VISCONTI, Regina (1340–1384). *See della Scala, Beatrice.*

VISCONTI, Sylvia (1913–1995). *See Ballesteros, Mercedes.*

VISCONTI, Thaddaea (d. 1381). Duchess of Bavaria. Name variations: Taddea; Thaddia. Died Sept 28, 1381; dau. of Bernabo Visconti, lord of Milan (r. 1354–1385), and Beatrice della Scala (1340–1384); m. Stephen III the Magnificent, duke of Bavaria (r. 1375–1413), on Oct 13, 1364; children: Isabeau of Bavaria (1371–1435); Louis VII the Bearded (1365–1447), duke of Bavaria (r. 1413–1443, deposed). Stephen III m. Elizabeth of Cleves (dau. of Adolf III, count of Cleves) on Jan 16, 1401.

VISCONTI, Valentina (1366–1408). Duchess of Orléans. Name variations: Valentina of Milan; Valentine Visconti; Valentine of Milan. Born in 1366 in Milan; died in 1408 in France; dau. of John Galeas Visconti also known as Gian Galeazzo Visconti, lord of Milan (r. 1378–1402), duke of Milan (r. 1396–1402), and Isabelle of France (1349–1372); m. Louis (1372–1407), duke of Orléans, in 1388 (died 1407); children: Charles (1391–1465), duke of Orléans; Jean or John (b. 1404), count of Angoulême; Philippe, count of Vertus; Marguerite of Orleans (d. 1466). ❖ Highly literate, read and spoke Latin, French, and German fluently, collected books and manuscripts throughout her life, and was an accomplished harpist; married Louis, duke of Orléans (brother of French king Charles VI), in 1388; once in France, developed a great rivalry with the French queen Isabeau of Bavaria (1371–1435); as the wife of the popular and powerful Louis, was in an influential position almost similar to Isabeau's; moreover, was a popular duchess, respected as a kind and beautiful woman, while Isabeau made enemies all her life and was perhaps France's most despised queen; when Louis was assassinated (1407), tried to re-establish herself in Paris with some success, based on her previous good reputation and popularity. ❖ See also *Women in World History*.

VISCONTI, Violante (c. 1353–1386). *See Visconti, Violet.*

VISCONTI, Violet (c. 1353–1386). Duchess of Clarence. Name variations: Violante. Born c. 1353; died in Nov 1386 (some sources cite 1404); dau. of Galeazzo II, lord of Milan (r. 1354–1378), and Blanche of Savoy (c. 1337–?); became 2nd wife of Lionel of Antwerp (1338–1368), duke of Clarence, on May 28, 1368 (died); m. Marquis of Montferrat (died); m. Louis also known as Ludovico Visconti (son of Bernabo Visconti), in 1380. Lionel of Antwerp's 1st wife was Elizabeth de Burgh (c. 1332–1363).

VISCONTI, Virida (c. 1354–1414). Archduchess of Austria. Name variations: Verde Visconti; Virda Visconti; Viridis Visconti. Born c. 1354 (some sources cite 1350 and 1351) in Milan, Italy; died in 1414 in Sittich, Karnten; dau. of Bernabo Visconti, lord of Milan (r. 1354–1385), and Beatrice della Scala (1340–1384); sister of Catherine Visconti (c. 1360–1404), and Agnes Visconti; m. Leopold of Habsburg also known as Leopold III (1351–1386), archduke of Austria, Styria, and Carniola, co-emperor of Austria (r. 1365–1379), on Feb 23, 1365; children: Friedrich IV (b. 1368); William (b. 1369, who m. Joanna II of Naples); Margarethe (1370–c. 1400), margravine of Moravia; Leopold IV (1371–1411); Archduke Ernst or Ernest the Iron (1377–1424, who m. Cimburca of Masovia); Elisabeth (b. 1378); Katharine (b. 1380); Friedrich or Frederick IV (1382–1439), duke of Austria-Tyrol. ❖ See also *Women in World History*.

VISCOPOLEANU, Viorica (1939—). Romanian long jumper. Name variations: Viorica Viscopoleanu-Belmega. Born Aug 8, 1939, in Romania. ❖ Won a gold medal at Mexico City Olympics (1968), with a world record jump of 6.82 m, and a silver at European championships (1969), both for long jump; placed 7th at Munich Olympics (1972); retired (1973).

VISE, Hollie (1987—). American gymnast. Born Dec 6, 1987, in Dallas, TX. ❖ Won team World championship (2003).

VISEU, duchess of. *See Beatrice of Beja (1430–1506).*

VISHNEVSKAYA, Galina (1926—). Russian soprano. Name variations: Vishnevskaiia; Galina Rostropovich. Born Galina Pavlovna Vishnevskaya in Leningrad (now St. Petersburg), USSR, Oct 25, 1926; m. Mstislav Rostropovich (cellist and conductor), 1955. ❖ Trained in Leningrad (St. Petersburg) by Vera Garina; joined Bolshoi Theater's operatic staff in Moscow (1952); frequently appeared in concert with cellist Mstislav Rostropovich, then married him; appeared with Metropolitan Opera in NY (1961); with husband, had repeated political clashes with Communist government, especially when they welcomed dissident Aleksander Solzhenitsyn into their home; immigrated to West (1974), settling in Washington, DC; stripped of Soviet citizenship (1978) but saw citizenship restored (1990); performed and recorded Benjamin Britten's *War Requiem* with Peter Pears and Dietrich Fischer-Dieskau, conducted by the composer (considered by many to be one of the great recordings of the 20th century). ❖ See also autobiography *Galina: A Russian Story* (1984); and *Women in World History*.

VISKI, Erzsebet (1980—). Hungarian kayaker. Born Feb 22, 1980, in Verocemaros, Hungary. ❖ Won a silver medal for K4 500 meters at Sydney Olympics (2000); at World championships, placed 1st for K4 200 (1998), K4 200 and 500 (1999), K4 200, 500 and 1000 (2001), K4 500 (2002), and K4 200 and 500 (2003); won a silver medal for K4 500 at Athens Olympics (2004).

VISNJIC, Biserka (1953—). Yugoslavian handball player. Born Oct 10, 1953. ❖ Won a silver medal at Moscow Olympics (1980) and a gold medal at Los Angeles Olympics (1984), both in team competition.

VISSER, Adriana (1961—). Dutch speedskater. Name variations: Ria Visser. Born Adriana Johanna Visser, July 20, 1961, in the Netherlands. ❖ Won a silver medal for the 1,500 meters at Lake Placid Olympics (1980).

VITELLI, Annie (c. 1837–?). New Zealand singer and entertainer. Name variations: Ann Day, Annie Thatcher. Born Ann Day, c. 1837 (baptized May 7, 1837, in London, England); dau. of Francis John Day (merchant) and Margaret (Tilley) Day; m. Giovanni Whittle Vitelli, 1855 (died 1859); m. Charles Robert Thatcher (singer, died 1878); children: (1st m.) 1 daughter; (2nd m.) 2 daughters. ❖ Toured throughout Australia and New Zealand as Madame Vitelli, performing romantic opera and singing lyrical ballads; thought to have returned to England. ❖ See also *Dictionary of New Zealand Biography* (Vol. 1).

VITORINO, Virginia (1897–1967). Portuguese poet and playwright. Name variations: Virginia Vila Nova de Sousa Vitorino. Born 1897 (some sources cite 1898) in Portugal; died 1967. ❖ Wrote mostly romantic poems and love sonnets, as well as comedies about middle class; works include *Namorados* (1921, Lovers), *Apaixonadamente* (1923, Passionately), *Renúncia* (1926, Renunciation), *A Volta* (1930), and *Manuela* (1934).

VITRICHENKO, Elena (1976—). Ukrainian rhythmic gymnast. Name variations: Olena Vitrichenko or Yelena Vitrichenko; Yelena Vytrychenko. Born Nov 25, 1976, in Odessa, Ukraine; dau. of Nina Vitrichenko (Elena's trainer). ❖ Won a bronze medal for all-around at Atlanta Olympics (1996); at World championships, won gold medals for ball (1994), clubs (1995) and all-around (1997); at European championships, won gold medals for team all-around, rope, hoop, and ribbon (1994), team all-around (1996), all-round (1997), club (1998); at Atlanta Olympics, won a bronze medal in indiv. all-around (1996); placed 4th all-around at Sydney Olympics (2000).

VITTADINI, Rita (1914–2000). Italian gymnast. Born Mar 19, 1914, in Italy; died in 2000. ❖ At Amsterdam Olympics, won a silver medal in team all-around (1928).

VITTI, Monica (1931—). Italian actress and director. Born Maria Luisa Ceciarelli on Nov 3, 1931, in Rome, Italy; graduate of National Academy of Dramatic Art, 1953. ❖ Extremely famous in Italy, made stage debut in Machiavelli's *La mandragora* (1953); joined director Michelangelo Antonioni's theater group (mid-1950s) and appeared as Sally Bowles in his version of *I am a Camera* (1957); made film debut in Anton's *Ridere, Ridere, Ridere* (Laugh, Laugh, Laugh, 1955); is particularly known for her leading roles in Antonioni films *L'avventura* (1960), *La Notte* (The Night, 1961), *L'eclisse* (The Eclipse, 1962), and *Il deserto rosso* (Red Desert, 1964); also appeared in Vadim's *Chateau en Suede* (Nutty, Naughty Chateau, 1963), Losey's *Modesty Blaise* (1966), and Jansco's *La pacifista* (1971); continued appearing in films throughout 1970s and 1980s, writing the scripts for *Flirt* (1983) and *Francesca e mia* (1986); also directed and co-wrote film, *Scandalo Segreto* (Secret Scandal, 1989). ❖ See also *Women in World History*.

VITTORIA DELLA ROVERE (d. 1694). *See Medici, Vittoria de.*

VIVANTI, Annie (1868–1942). Italian poet and novelist. Born 1868 in London, England; died 1942 in Turin, Italy; dau. of an Italian father and Anna Lindau (German writer); trained as a teacher of singing and languages; m. John Chartres (Irish lawyer), 1908; children: 1 daughter (died in aerial bombardment during WWII). ❖ In Italy, became intimate with Giosuè Carducci, dean of Italian poets, who sponsored both her 1st book of poetry, *Lirica* (Lyric, 1890) and her novel *Marion, artista da caffè concerto* (Marion, Café Entertainer, 1891); published a novel in English, *The Devourers* (1910, issued in Italian as *I divoratori*, 1911), then followed it with over 20 books, including novels, short stories, plays, and travelogues.

VIVAS, Rosie (c. 1954—). *See Ruiz, Rosie.*

VIVIAN. *See Bibiana (d. 363).*

VIVIAN, Ruth (c. 1883–1949). English-born actress. Born c. 1883 in London, England; died Oct 24, 1949, in New York, NY. ❖ Came to America with the Ben Greet Co.; appeared on Broadway in *The Strings,*

And Now Good-Bye, Sweet Aloes, The Man Who Came to Dinner, The Damask Cheek, I Remember Mama and *Goodbye, My Fancy.*

VIVIEN, Renée (1877–1909). French poet. Name variations: Renee; (real name) Pauline Tarn. Born Pauline Mary Tarn in Paddington, England, in 1877; died at age 32 of self-induced starvation in 1909; dau. of a Michigan heiress and John Tarn, an English gentleman from Kent. ❧ After wandering in the East, settled permanently in Paris where she translated the ancient poetry of Sappho and other women of Lesbos, published as *Les Kitharèdes* (1904); published her own French verse as *Cendres et poussières* (*Cinders and Dust,* 1902), *Evocations* (1903), and *Les Flambeaux éteints* (*Extinguished Torches,* 1907); novelized her turbulent relationship with Natalie Clifford Barney in *Une Femme m'apparut* (*A Woman Appeared to Me,* 1904); published 12 vols. of her poetry, *Poésies complètes* (1901–10). ❧ See also Karla Jay, *The Amazon and the Page: Natalie Clifford Barney and Renée Vivien* (Indiana U. Press, 1988); and *Women in World History.*

VIVONNE DE SAVELLI, Catherine de (1588–1665). *See Rambouillet, Catherine de Vivonne, Marquise de.*

VIXEN.
See Gardner, Janet.
See Kuehnemund, Jan.
See Pedersen, Share.
See Petrucci, Roxy.

VJERA. *Variant of Vera.*

VLACHOS, Helen (1911–1995). Greek publisher and legislator. Name variations: Eleni Vlachou. Born Dec 18, 1911, in Athens, Greece; died Oct 14, 1995, in Athens; dau. of George Vlachou (newspaper publisher); m. Costas Loundras. ❧ Legend in Greek journalism, began career as reporter (1935); wrote a witty political column in *Kathimerini,* in which she regularly criticized the government (late 1940s); assumed control of influential daily, *Kathimerini,* as well as *Messimvrini,* another daily newspaper, and the weekly picture magazine *Eikones* (1951); published *Kathimerini* (1951–87); in a dramatic move that garnered international attention, closed her 3 newspapers after military takeover, rather than submit to censorship (1967); escaped to London while under house arrest (1967); returned to Greece after the junta fell, and elected to Parliament as a member of the conservative New Democracy Party (1974). ❧ See also autobiography *The House Arrest* (1970); and *Women in World History.*

VLADIMIR, grand duchess (1854–1920). *See Maria of Mecklenburg-Schwerin.*

VLADY, Marina (1938—). French actress. Name variations: Marina Versois; Marina. Born Marina de Poliakoff-Baidaroff (also seen as Baidarov), Mar 10, 1938, in Clichy, France; sister of Hélène Vallier, Olga Poliakoff, and Odile Versois (all actresses); m. Robert Hossein (director-actor), 1955 (div.); m. Vladimir Vysotsky, 1969 (died 1980). ❧ Star of French and international films; made film debut in *Orage d'été* (1949), followed by *Pardon My French, Penne nere, Le Infedeli, Cavalcade of Song, Sie, Musoduro, Le Avventure di Giacomo Casanova, Sophie et le crime, Le Crâneur, La Sorcière, Crime et châtiment, La sentence, Les canailles, La Princesse de Clèves* (title role), *La ragazza in vetrina, The Seven Deadly Sins, Climats, La Cage, Le temps de vivre, La nuit Bulgare, Sappho,* and *Le complot;* frequently seen on tv. Won Best Actress award at Cannes for *Una storia moderna* (*The Conjugal Bed,* 1963).

VLASEK, June (b. 1915). *See Lang, June.*

VLASOVA, Yulia. Russian short-track speedskater. Name variations: Julia or Ioulia Vlasova or Vlassova. Born in USSR. ❧ Won a bronze medal for 3,000-meter relay at Albertville Olympics (1992).

VLASSOVA, Julia. *See Vlasova, Yulia.*

VLASTO, Didi (1903–1985). French tennis player. Name variations: Julie Vlasto. Born Pénélope Julie Vlasto, Aug 8, 1903, in Marseille, France; died 1985; m. Jean Baptiste Serpieri. ❧ At Paris Olympics, won a silver medal in singles (1924); with Suzanne Lenglen, won the French Open doubles championship (1926).

VLASTO, Dominique (1946—). French politician. Born Dominique Fleury, Aug 14, 1946, in Marseille, France; m. Michel "Micky" Vlasto. ❧ Member of Marseilles Municipal Council (1983–89), district councillor (1989–95), and deputy mayor with responsibility for building permits and land rights (1995–98) and responsibility for tourism, conferences and festivals (1999—); as a member of the European People's Party (Christian Democrats) and European Democrats, elected to 5th European Parliament (1999–2004). Named Knight of the Order of Merit (1995).

VLASTO, Julie (1903–1985). *See Vlasto, Didi.*

VLIEGHUIS, Kirsten (1976—). Dutch swimmer. Born May 17, 1976, in Hengelo, Netherlands. ❧ Won bronze medals for 400- and 800-meter freestyle at Atlanta Olympics (1996).

VODOPYANOVA, Natalia (1981—). Russian basketball player. Born June 4, 1981, in Leningrad, USSR. ❧ Forward, won a team bronze medal at Athens Olympics (2004).

VOEGTLIN, Marie (1845–1916). *See Vögtlin, Marie.*

VOELKER, Sabine (1973—). German speedskater. Born May 11, 1973, in Erfurt, Germany. ❧ Placed 2nd at the World championships at Berlin (1998); won a silver medal for the 1,000 meters at World Single Distance championships (2001); won silver medals in the 1,000 and 1,500 meters and a bronze medal in the 500 meters at Salt Lake City Olympics (2002); won a gold medal for Team Pursuit at Torino Olympics (2006).

VOELKER, Sandra (1974—). *See Völker, Sandra.*

VOELKNER, Iris (1960—). West German rower. Name variations: Iris Völkner. Born Oct 16, 1960, in Germany. ❧ At Los Angeles Olympics, won a bronze medal in coxless pairs (1984).

VOETEN-MENCO, Sara (1920—). *See Menco, Sara.*

VOGEL, Dorothy (1935—). American art collector. Born Dorothy Hoffman, May 14, 1935, in Elmira, New York; dau. of a stationery store owner; studied at University of Buffalo, 1953–55; Syracuse University, BA, 1957; University of Denver, MA in library studies, 1958; m. Herbert Vogel (postal worker), in 1962. ❧ With husband, made 1st important art purchase, one of the earliest works that Sol LeWitt—a founding member of the minimal school—ever sold (1965), then concentrated on minimalism and conceptualism, eventually amassing a collection of more than 2,000 paintings, drawings, and sculptures, all housed in their one-bedroom apartment in New York; bequeathed their collection to the National Gallery of Art in Washington, DC (1992). ❧ See also *Women in World History.*

VOGEL, Renate (1955—). East German swimmer. Born June 30, 1955, in East Germany. ❧ At Munich Olympics, won a silver medal in 4 x 100-meter medley relay (1972).

VOGELSTEIN, Julie (1883–1971). *See Braun-Vogelstein, Julie.*

VÖGTLIN, Marie (1845–1916). Swiss physician. Name variations: Marie Heim-Vögtlin; Marie Vogtlin or Marie Voegtlin. Born in Bözen, Canton Aargau, Switzerland, on Oct 7, 1845; died of tuberculosis in Zurich, Nov 7, 1916; dau. of a minister; attended University of Zurich, 1868–72, University of Leipzig (where she was the only woman among 3,200 students), and University of Dresden, then passed her doctoral examination in Zurich (July 11, 1874); m. Albert Heim (1849–1937, geologist), in 1876; children: Helene and Arnold; (foster daughter) Hanneli. ❧ Medical pioneer, the 1st woman in Switzerland to earn a medical degree, served as director of the pediatric division of Zurich's Swiss Nurses' School; opened her medical practice in gynecology (1874) and quickly became well known throughout Zurich; with Anna Heer and Ida Schneider, opened the Swiss Nurses' School (Schweizerischen Pflegerinnenschule, 1901). ❧ See also *Women in World History.*

VOGUE.
See Ellis, Terry.
See Herron, Cindy.
See Jones, Maxine.
See Robinson, Dawn.

VOIGT, Angela (1951—). East German track-and-field athlete. Born May 18, 1951, in East Germany. ❧ At Montreal Olympics, won a gold medal in the long jump (1976).

VOIGT, Franka (1963—). German gymnast. Born Aug 2, 1963, in Germany. ❧ Was Germany's balance-beam champion (1982); won Moncada Cup (1983).

VOIGT-DIEDERICHS, Helene (1875–1961). German novelist and short-story writer. Born in 1875 in Marienhoff, a family estate in Schleswig-Holstein, Germany; died 1961; m. Eugen Diederichs (Leipzig publisher), 1898 (sep. 1911). ❧ Published her only volume of poetry, *Unterstrom* (Undercurrents), and the novel *Regine Vosgerau* (1901), beginning a writing life that was to span 50 years; based many of her books on her own experiences, like *Regine Vosgerau* and *Dreiviertel Stund vor Tag* (Three-Quarters of an Hour Before Daybreak, 1905); described mother's life in *Auf Marienhoff: das Leben einer deutschen Mutter* (Marienhoff, the Life of a German Mother, 1925); explored marital conflicts in the stories in *Mann und Frau* (Husband and Wife, 1921) and in novel *Ring um Roderich* (A Ring about Roderich, 1929); is also known for her stories about children, such as *Kinderland* (The Land of Children, 1907) and *Der grüne Papagei* (The Green Parrot, 1934), and for her travel books *Wandertage in England* (Wandering in England, 1912) and *Gast in Siebenbürgen* (Visitor in Siebenbürgen, 1936).

VOILQUIN, Suzanne (1801–1877). French feminist, midwife, and writer. Born 1801 in France; died 1877 in France; married and divorced. ❖ Trained as midwife; practiced in France, Egypt, and Russia; was editor of *Tribune des femmes* (Women's Tribune, 1832–34); was a member of the Saint-Simonian movement; published Claire Démar's *Ma loi d'avenir* (My Law for the Future, 1834); wrote autobiography *Souvenirs d'une fille du peuple* (Memories of a Daughter of the People, 1866). ❖ See also *Women in World History.*

VOINEA, Camelia (1970—). Romanian gymnast. Name variations: Cami. Born Mar 1, 1970, in Constanta, Romania. ❖ Placed 1st for team all-around and 2nd for all-around at Balkan championships (1985) and 1st for all-around at Champions All (1987); at World championships, placed 1st for team all-around (1987); at European championships, won a silver medal for floor exercises (1987); at Seoul Olympics, won a silver medal in team all-around (1988); was the 1st gymnast to tumble a double layout to punch front somersault; retired (1989).

VOISIN, La. See *Deshayes, Catherine (d. 1680).*

VOISINS, countess of. See *Taglioni, Maria (1804–1844).*

VOIT, Eszter (1916—). Hungarian gymnast. Born Jan 11, 1916, in Hungary. ❖ At Berlin Olympics, won a bronze medal in team all-around (1936).

VOJINOVIC, Zorica (1958—). Yugoslavian handball player. Born June 27, 1958. ❖ At Moscow Olympics, won a silver medal in team competition (1980).

VOKES, May (d. 1957). American comedic actress. Died Sept 13, 1957, in Stamford, CT. ❖ Made Broadway debut in *My Friend from India* (1896); appeared in numerous plays, including *A Fool and His Money, Checkers, A Knight for a Day, When Dreams Come True, Cold Feet,* and *Dr. X*; best remembered as Lizzie, the frightened maid, in *The Bat.*

VOLCHEK, Natalya. Belarusian rower. Born in Belarus. ❖ Won a bronze medal for coxed eights at Atlanta Olympics (1996).

VOLCHETSKAYA, Yelena (1943—). Soviet gymnast. Born Dec 1943 in USSR. ❖ Won an all-around team gold medal at Tokyo Olympics (1964). ❖ See also *Women in World History.*

VOLHARD, Christiane (b. 1942). See *Nüsslein-Volhard, Christiane.*

VOLK, Helen (1954—). Zimbabwean field-hockey player. Born Mar 29, 1954. ❖ At Moscow Olympics, won a gold medal in team competition (1980).

VÖLKER, Sandra (1974—). German swimmer. Name variations: Sandra Voelker. Born April 1, 1974, in Lubeck, Germany. ❖ Won a silver medal for 100-meter freestyle and bronze medals for 50-meter freestyle and 4 x 100-meter freestyle relay at Atlanta Olympics (1996); at European championships, won a gold medal for 100-meter freestyle (1997), 50-meter backstroke (1998, 1999) and 100-meter backstroke (1998, 1999).

VÖLKNER, Iris (1960—). See *Voelkner, Iris.*

VOLKONSKAYA, Maria (1805–1863). Russian aristocrat and Decembrist. Name variations: Maria Raveskaya, Princess of Siberia; Maria Volkonsky. Pronunciation: Vole-kun-SKY-ya. Born Maria Raveskaya, Dec 25, 1805, on family estate in Ukraine; died Aug 10, 1863, in St. Petersburg; dau. of Nikolai Nikolaevich Ravesky (military officer in campaign against Napoleon) and Sophia Konstantinova Raveskaya (descendant of poet and scientist M. V. Lomonosov); m. Prince Sergei Volkonsky, Jan 12, 1825; children: Nicholas (b. Jan 2, 1826, died young); son Misha and daughter Elena. ❖ Aristocrat who joined husband in Siberian exile and became known as the Princess of Siberia, the savior of the Decembrists, for her leadership and charitable work among the exiled families; became friends during adolescence with celebrated poet Alexander Pushkin; married Prince Sergei Volkonsky

(1825) who was implicated in a revolt against the tsar (Dec 14, 1825); followed Volkonsky into exile, leaving son behind (1827); after husband's 10-year imprisonment, was allowed to live in a Siberian town, staffing a large house with servants in Irkurtsk; returned from exile to St. Petersburg, where Decembrists were fêted for their courage and ideals (1856). ❖ See also Christine Sutherland, *The Princess of Siberia: The Story of Maria Volkonsky and the Decembrist Exiles* (Farrar, 1984); Anatole G. Mazour, *Women in Exile: Wives of the Decembrists* (Diplomatic Press, 1975); and *Women in World History.*

VOLKONSKY, Maria (1805–1863). See *Volkonskaya, Maria.*

VOLKOVA, Vera (1904–1975). Russian ballet dancer and master teacher. Name variations: Mrs. Hugh Finch Williams. Born Vera Volkova, June 7, 1904, in St. Petersburg, Russia; died in Copenhagen, Denmark, May 5, 1975; dau. of a Russian military officer in an elite hussar regiment (died in combat 1917); attended Smolny Institute; m. Hugh Finch Williams (British architect), 1936. ❖ Trained the finest dancers of her day in the Vaganova technique of which she was the leading exponent in the West; entered the Russian Choreographic School (1920); was a member of the State Theater for Opera and Ballet (1925–29); toured the Soviet Far East (1928); made 2nd tour, including China and Japan (1929); defected while on a tour of the Far East (1929); settled in Shanghai (1929); moved to Hong Kong (1932), then London (1937); danced with International Ballet (1941); founded a school in London (1943); taught at Sadler's Wells Ballet (1943–50); was advisor to Teatro La Scala, Milan (1950); was a guest teacher at Royal Danish Ballet, Copenhagen (1951), then artistic director (1952) and permanent instructor in dance (1952–75), where she had a profound influence on such dancers as Erik Bruhn, Lis Jeppsen, Henning Kronstram, Adam Lüder, Peter Martins, Peter Schaufuss, and Kirsten Simone; toured US with the Royal Danish Ballet; was guest instructor with Joffrey Ballet (1958) and Harkness Ballet (1964, 1965). Granted title Knight of Dannebrog by the Danish government (1956); received Carlsberg Memorial Legacy (1974). ❖ See also *Women in World History.*

VOLKOVA, Yelena (1960—). Soviet volleyball player. Born April 13, 1960, in USSR. ❖ At Seoul Olympics, won a gold medal in team competition (1988).

VOLLERTSEN, Julie (1959—). American volleyball player. Born Mar 1, 1959, in Syracuse, Otoe Co., Nebraska. ❖ At Los Angeles Olympics, won a silver medal in team competition (1984); was on US national team (1979–84); played professionally for 4 years.

VOLLMAR, Jocelyn (1925—). American ballet dancer. Born Nov 25, 1925, in San Francisco, CA. ❖ Trained at school of San Francisco Ballet with Harold and William Christensen, among others; performed there in Bolm's *Mefisto,* and Christensen's *Farranda, Coppélia,* and *Sonata Pathétique* (1948–49); joined Ballet Theater in NY where she danced in *Swan Lake,* Balanchine's *Theme and Variations* and Ashton's *Les Patineurs,* among others; danced with Grand Ballet du Marquis de Cuevas and Borvcansky Ballet in Australia; returned to San Francisco Ballet, where she created roles for Lew Christensen's *Lady of Shallott* (1958) and *Fantasma* (1963) and danced as Sugar Plum Fairy in *The Nutcracker*; retired from performance career (1972), but remained at San Francisco Ballet as a teacher.

VOLLMER, Dana (1987—). American swimmer. Born Nov 13, 1987, in Granbury, TX. ❖ Won a gold medal for 4 x 200-meter freestyle relay at Athens Olympics (2004).

VOLLMER, Lula (d. 1955). American playwright and radio writer. Born in Keyser, NC; died May 2, 1955, in New York, NY; dau. of Virginia (Smith) and William Sherman Vollmer; never married. ❖ Moved to NY (1918); wrote plays centering on North Carolina mountain life, including *Sunup, The Shame Woman, The Dunce Boy, Trigger, Sentinels* and *The Hill Between*; wrote radio serials for NBC: "Moonshine and Honeysuckle" (1930–33), "Grits and Gravy" (1934), and "The Widow's Sons" (1935–37).

VOLNER, Jill (1943—). See *Wine-Banks, Jill.*

VOLOSHENKO, P. S. (1853–1935). See *Ivanovskaia, Praskovia.*

VOLPI, Giulia (1970—). Italian gymnast. Born Jan 30, 1970, in Brescia, Italy; dau. of Carol and Franca Volpi (literary agent). ❖ Won Italian nationals (1987, 1988, 1991, 1992).

VOLUMNIA (late 6th c.–mid-5th c. BCE). Wife of Coriolanus. Name variations: Vergilia or Virgilia. Married Gnaeus Marcius Coriolanus

(Roman soldier). ❖ Patrician wife of Coriolanus who, along with Veturia, convinced him not to fight with Rome. (In William Shakespeare's *Coriolanus*, 1st presented around 1609, the character of Volumnia is the mother of Coriolanus; the character of Virgilia is the wife.) ❖ See also *Women in World History.*

VON ARNIM, Bettina (1785–1859). *See Arnim, Bettine von.*

VON ARNIM, Elizabeth (1866–1941). *See Arnim, Elizabeth von.*

VON ARNSTEIN, Baroness (1758–1818). *See Arnstein, Fanny von.*

VON AROLDINGEN, Karin (1941—). German ballet dancer. Born July 9, 1941, in Greiz, Germany. ❖ Joined Frankfurt Opera Ballet (1959), appearing in Tatiana Gsovsky's productions of *The Sleeping Beauty* (1960) and *The Seven Deadly Sins* (1962); upon the recommendation of Lotte Lenya, came to US and joined Balanchine's repertory (1962), dancing featured roles in *Serenade, Concerto Barocco, Western Symphony, Jewels, Agon* and most notably as The Siren in *Prodigal Son*; created roles for Balanchine in *Who Cares?* (1970), *Stravinsky violin Concert* (1972), *Kammermusik No. 2* (1978), and *Vienna Waltzes* (1978).

VON BACHERACHT, Therese (1804–1852). *See Bacheracht, Therese von.*

VON BERLEPSCH, Emilie (1755–1830). *See Berlepsch, Emilie von.*

VON BINGEN, Hildegard (1098–1179). *See Hildegard of Bingen.*

VON BREDEN, Christiane (1839–1901). *See Breden, Christiane von.*

VON BREMEN, Wilhelmina (1909–1976). American runner. Born Aug 13, 1909; died July 16 (some sources cite July 23), 1976. ❖ At Los Angeles Olympics, won a bronze medal in 100 meters and a gold medal in the 4 x 100-meter relay (1932).

VON BRIEST, Karoline (1774–1831). *See Fouqué, Karoline Freifrau de la Motte.*

VON BRONSART, Ingeborg (1840–1913). *See Bronsart, Ingeborg von.*

VON BÜLOW, Cosima (1837–1930). *See Wagner, Cosima.*

VON BUSING, Fritzi (c. 1884–1948). American actress and singer. Born c. 1884; died Mar 6, 1948, in New York, NY. ❖ Appeared on stage in *The Great White Way, The Chocolate Soldier, The Merry Countess,* and *Alone at Last*; was a member of the St. Louis Municipal Opera and the Aborn Opera.

VON DER LIPPE, Susan (1965—). *See Rapp, Susan.*

VON DER RECKE, Elisa (1754–1833). *See Recke, Elisa von der.*

VON DONNERSMARCK, Countess (1819–1884). *See Lachman, Thérèse.*

VON EHRENWEISEN, Baroness Hilla Rebay (1890–1967). *See Rebay, Hilla.*

VON ENGELTHAL, Christina (1277–1355). *See Ebner, Christine.*

VON ERTMANN, Dorothea (1781–1849). German-Austrian pianist. Born in Offenbach am Main, Germany, May 3, 1781; died in Vienna, Austria, Mar 16, 1849. ❖ Moved to Vienna and quickly established herself as a performer and member of that city's cultivated social elite; studied with Beethoven briefly (1803) and often performed his new compositions in concerts and recitals (his great Sonata No. 28 in A major, Op. 101, is dedicated to her). ❖ See also *Women in World History.*

VON ESSEN, Siri (1850–1912). Swedish actress and acting teacher. Name variations: Baroness Siri von Essen Wrangel; Siri von Essen-Strindberg. Born Sigrid Sofia Mathilda Elisabet von Essen, Aug 17, 1850, in Finland; died April 21, 1912; m. Baron Carl Gustaf Wrangel (military officer), 1872 (div. 1876); became the 1st wife of August Strindberg (playwright; he later married Frida Uhl and Harriet Bosse), Dec 30, 1877 (div. 1891); children: (with Strindberg) Hans (b. 1884), Karin (b. 1880), Greta (b. 1881) and another daughter who died in infancy. ❖ Made acting debut at the Royal Dramatic Theater (1877); created title role in *Miss Julie* (1889); later taught acting (one of her pupils was Martha Hedman). Strindberg wrote *A Madman's Defence* about his 1st marriage.

VON FURSTENBERG, Diane (1946—). Belgian-American fashion designer. Born Diana Simone Michelle Halfin, Dec 31, 1946, in Brussels, Belgium; dau. of Leon and Liliane Nahmias Halfin (an Auschwitz survivor); studied economics at University of Geneva; m. Prince Egon von Furstenberg, July 16, 1969 (div. 1983, died 2004);

children: Alexandre (who m. Alexandra Miller von Furstenberg) and Tatiana von Furstenberg (b. 1971). ❖ Famed designer, began career designing easy knit dresses (1972); created the fragrance Tatiana (1975); sold 5 million wrap dresses (1976); introduced Style for Living collection of home furnishings (1977); licensed dress business (1979); moved to Paris and founded Salvy, a French-language publishing house (1985); returned to US (1990); became a contributing editor to *Vanity Fair* (1993); returned to retail with signature dresses (1997); became naturalized US citizen (2002). ❖ See also autobiography, *Diane: A Signature Life* (1998).

VON GREIFFENBERG, Catharina Regina von (1633–1694). *See Greiffenberg, Catharina Regina von.*

VON HAHN-HAHN, Ida (1805–1880). *See Hahn-Hahn, Ida, countess von.*

VON HARBOU, Thea (1888–1954). German screenwriter, novelist, director and actress. Born Dec 27, 1888, in Tauperlitz bei Hof, Bavaria; died in West Berlin, July 1, 1954; dau. of Theodor von Harbou (chief forester) and Clotilde (d'Alinge) von Harbou; m. Rudolf Klein-Rogge (actor), 1914; m. Fritz Lang (director), c. 1918 (div. 1934). ❖ Best known for her novel and screenplay *Metropolis,* published the novel *Die nach uns kommen* (The Next Generation, 1910), earning good reviews and healthy sales; published 2 dozen novels, with conservative and nationalistic emphasis, many of which became bestsellers (1910–52), including *Der Krieg und die Frauen* (War and Women, 1913), *Deutsche Frauen* (German Women, 1914), *Der unsterbliche Acker* (Immortal Soil, 1915), *Der junge Wacht am Rhein* (The Young Watch on the Rhine, 1915) and *Die deutsche Frau im Weltkrieg* (The German Woman in the World War, 1916); became a well-known personality of the extreme right; began writing screenplays for Fritz Lang, beginning with his 1920 film *Das wandernde Bild* (Wandering Image); wrote 10 screenplays (1920–33), of which the best known are *Dr. Mabuse, der Spieler* (*Dr. Mabuse, the Gambler,* 1922), *Die Nibelungen* (1922–24), *Metropolis* (1927), *M* (1931) and *Das Testament des Dr. Mabuse* (The Testament of Dr. Mabuse); by mid-1920s, was the leading writer of the German cinema; her successful novel *Frau im Mond* (The Girl in the Moon, 1928) was transformed by Lang into a popular film (1929); had a successful career in the Third Reich; by end of WWII, become notorious as a last-ditch Nazi, particularly because of her screenplay for *Kolberg,* a historical epic that appealed to the German people to fight to the bitter end (1945); declared a Nazi by German courts, was banned from working in films for several years, but by late 1940s was once more active in the industry, writing dubbing scripts for Deutsche London Film. ❖ See also *Women in World History.*

VON HAYNAU, Edith (1884–1978). Italian novelist, illustrator and essayist. Name variations: Edith von Haynau-Arnaldi; (pseudonym) Rosa Rosà. Born Edith von Haynau, 1884, in Vienna, Austria; died 1978 in Rome, Italy; married Ulrico Arnaldi (Italian futuristic poet) and moved to Italy. ❖ Wrote series of articles for futurist magazine *L'Italia futurista,* but unlike most futurists was a feminist; published 2 novels, *Una donna con tre anime* (1918) and *Non c'è che te!* (1919), whose female characters rebel against male domination; also illustrated books.

VON HEYGENDORF, Frau (1777–1848). *See Jagemann, Karoline.*

VON HILLERN, Wilhelmine (1836–1916). *See Hillern, Wilhelmine von.*

VON KÄRNTEN, Margarete (1318–1369). *See Margaret Maultasch.*

VON KRÜDENER, Baroness (1764–1824). *See Krüdener, Julie de.*

VON KRUSENSTJERNA, Agnes (1894–1940). *See Krusenstjerna, Agnes von.*

VON LA ROCHE, Sophie (1730–1807). *See La Roche, Sophie von.*

VON LE FORT, Gertrud (1876–1971). *See Le Fort, Gertrud von.*

VON LENGEFELD, Karoline (1763–1847). *See Wolzogen, Karoline von.*

VON MECK, Nadezhda (1831–1894). Russian patron of music. Name variations: Naddezhda, Nadeja, or Nadejda von Meck; Madame von Meck. Born Nadezhda Philaretovna Frolovskaya (also seen as Frolowskaya) in Znamenskoye, near Smolensk, Russia, Feb 10, 1831; died Jan 13, 1894, in Wiesbaden, Germany; m. Karl Fyodorovich von Meck (engineer), 1847; children: 18, of whom 11 survived. ❖ Wealthy Russian patron of music who supported one of her country's greatest composers during a critical period in his career, maintaining years of correspondence that provide valuable insights into the daily life and creative mind of Tchaikovsky; married at 16, encouraged husband to strike out as a railroad entrepreneur; after husband had garnered an enormous fortune, widowed by his sudden death; turned to music, commissioning pieces from the young composer Peter Ilyich Tchaikovsky, who entreated his patron for a subsidy that would allow him to devote himself entirely to composing; began an intense 14-year correspondence with Tchaikovsky (1876); ended the relationship suddenly for reasons unknown (1890); died two months after the death of Tchaikovsky (1894). ❖ See also Catherine Drinker Bowen and Barbara von Meck, *"Beloved Friend": The Story of Tchaikowsky and Nadejda von Meck* (Random House, 1937); Edward Garden and Nigel Gotteri, eds. *"To my best friend": Correspondence between Tchaikovsky and Nadezhda von Meck 1876–1878* (trans. by Galina von Meck, Clarendon, 1993); and *Women in World History*.

VON MISES, Hilda (1893–1973). *See Geiringer, Hilda.*

VON MOLTKE, Freya (b. 1911). German anti-Nazi and memoirist. Name variations: Freya Deichmann. Born Freya Deichmann, 1911, in Germany; m. Count Helmuth James von Moltke (great-great nephew of Helmuth von Moltke, the German field marshal). ❖ During WWII, husband was an anti-Nazi, even though he served in the German High Command, and did what he could to rescue Jews; served as hostess when husband had meetings at their farm in Kreisau with a cadre of resisters known as the "Kreisau Circle"; husband executed after his role in attempt to assassinate Hitler (Jan 1945); moved to Vermont; wrote *Memories of Kreisau and the German Resistance* (1998, published in English in US 2004). ❖ See also *Letters to Freya.*

VON NAGEL, Ida (1917–1971). West German equestrian. Born May 15, 1917; died Aug 29, 1971. ❖ At Helsinki Olympics, won a bronze medal in team dressage (1952).

VON NAGY, Käthe (1909–1973). Hungarian-born film actress. Name variations: Kathe von Nagy; Kate de Nagy; Kató Nagy. Born April 4, 1909, in Szabadka (near Budapest), Austria-Hungary; died Dec 20, 1973, in Los Angeles, CA; dau. of a bank director; attended school in St. Christiania (Frohsdorf); m. Constantin J. David (German film director, div. 1935); m. Jacques Fattini, c. 1935. ❖ Worked briefly at Hungarian newspaper *Pester Hirlop*; made acting debut on Hungarian stage; made film debut in Germany in *Männer von der Ehe* (Men Before Marriage, 1927); appeared in German, French, and Italian films of both silent and early sound eras; was associated with Nazi-era German cinema, particularly comedies; films include *Republik der Backfische* (Teenager's Republic, 1928), *Rotaie* (Rails, 1929), *Der Andere* (The Other One, 1930), *Ronny* (1931), *Der Sieger* (The Victor, 1932), *Ich bei Tag, Du bei Nacht* (I by Day, You by Night, 1932), *Flüchtlinge* (Refugees, 1933), *Prinzessin Turandot* (1934), *Liebe, Tod und Teufel* (Love, Death and the Devil, 1934), *La Route impériale* (The Imperial Road, 1935), and *Unser kleine Frau* (Our Little Wife, 1938); with end of 1st marriage, moved to Paris, married a Frenchman, and began to also appear in French films, including *La belle aventure, Un jour viendra, Ave Maria* and *Nuits de princes.* ❖ See also *Women in World History.*

VON NISSEN, Constanze (1762–1842). *See Mozart, Constanze.*

VONNOH, Bessie Potter (1872–1955). American sculptor. Name variations: Bessie Potter. Born Bessie Onahotema Potter, Aug 17, 1872, in St. Louis, Missouri; died Mar 8, 1955, in New York, NY; studied at Art Institute of Chicago under Lorado Taft; m. Robert W. Vonnoh (well-known painter), in 1899. ❖ Traveled to Paris (1895); best known for small genre subjects like *The Young Mother* (1896), *Girl Dancing* (1897), *Enthroned* (1902), *A Modern Madonna* (1905), and *Beatrice* (1906); moved to New York City (1899); held one-woman show at Brooklyn Museum (1913); work of the 1920s and 1930s includes the *Burnette Fountain* in Central Park and a fountain for the Roosevelt Bird Sanctuary in Oyster Bay, Long Island; portrait commissions include *Major General S. Crawford* for the Smith Memorial, Philadelphia, and *James S. Sherman* for the US Capitol; elected an associate of the National Academy of Design (1906) and a member (1921). Awarded a bronze medal at Paris (1900) and a gold medal at St. Louis (1904). ❖ See also *Women in World History.*

VON REIBNITZ, Marie-Christine (b. 1945). *See Michael of Kent.*

VON RICHTHOFEN, Else (1874–1973). German intellectual and social activist. Name variations: Else Jaffe. Born Elisabeth Helene Amalie Sophie Freiin von Richthofen, in the French city of Metz, in Lorraine, Oct 8, 1874; died Dec 22, 1973; eldest of 3 daughters of Friedrich von Richthofen (civil engineer) and Anna (Marquier) von Richthofen; sister of Frieda Lawrence (1879–1956) and Johanna "Nusch" von Richthofen;

Heidelberg University, PhD, 1901; m. Edgar Jaffe (teacher of political economy), 1902 (died 1921); children: (with Edgar Jaffe) 3; (with psychologist Otto Gross) 1 son (b. 1907). ❖ Eldest and brainiest of the 3 von Richthofen sisters, was the 1st woman appointed by the state to monitor the rights of women factory workers; won respect and admiration of country's feminists and, as a scholar, was a respected member of the intellectual community; went to live with sociologist Alfred Weber (1921), becoming his reader, translator, and traveling companion until his death (1958); occasionally turns up in a D. H. Lawrence story: as Mary Lindley, for example, in "Daughters of the Vicar," which also explores her marriage to Jaffe. ❖ See also Martin Green, *The von Richthofen Sisters: The Triumphant and the Tragic Modes of Love* (Basic, 1974); and *Women in World History.*

VON RICHTHOFEN, Frieda (1879–1956). *See Lawrence, Frieda.*

VON ROSEN, Elsa Marianne (1924—). Swedish ballet dancer and choreographer. Born April 21, 1924, in Stockholm, Sweden; dau. of Reinhold von Rosen and Elisabeth Osteryd; m. Allan Sigurd Monies Fridericia (ballet historian), 1950; children: Elisabeth (b. 1963). ❖ Danced with the Oscars Teatrum in Stockholm; performed with Swedish Ballet (1950); joined Royal Swedish Ballet where she danced principal roles in Massine's *Gaité Parisienne* and *Le Tricorne,* Cullberg's *Medea,* and Lander's *The Woman in Rhapsody,* which she also helped create; choreographed or staged numerous works for Royal Swedish Ballet and other companies throughout Scandinavia, Russia, and England; choreographed *Prometheus* (1958), *Helios* (1960), *The Virgin Spring* (1964), *Jenny Von Westfalen* (1965), *Don Juan* (1967), *Romeo and Juliet* (1972) and *A Girl's Story* (1975).

VON ROSEN, Maud (1925—). Swedish equestrian. Born Dec 24, 1925, in Sweden. ❖ At Munich Olympics, won a bronze medal in team dressage (1972).

VON SALTZA, Chris (1944—). American swimmer. Name variations: Chris Von Saltza Olmstead. Born S. Christine von Saltza, Jan 3, 1944, in San Francisco, CA; granddau. of Count Philip of Sweden (making her Baroness von Saltza); graduate of Stanford University, 1966; m. Robert Olmstead. ❖ Won gold medals for the 400-meter freestyle, 4 x 100 medley and 4 x 100 freestyle and a silver for the 100-meter freestyle at Rome Olympics (1960).

VON SCHLEGEL, Dorothea (1764–1839). *See Mendelssohn, Dorothea.*

VON SECK-NOTHNAGEL, Anke (1966—). German kayaker. Born Sept 10, 1966, in Germany. ❖ At Barcelona Olympics, won a silver medal in K4 500 meters and a gold medal in K2 500 meters (1992).

VON SIEBOLD, Charlotte (1788–1859). *See Siebold, Charlotte Heidenreich von.*

VON SIEBOLD, Josepha (1771–1849). *See Siebold, Josepha von.*

VON STADE, Frederica (1945—). American mezzo-soprano. Born June 1, 1945, in Somerville, NJ; studied with Engelberg. ❖ Made debut in NY at the Metropolitan Opera as Second Boy in *Zauberflöte* (1970); debuted at Paris Opera (1973), Covent Garden (1975), and Milan (1976); created the role of Tina in Dallas Opera's world premiere of Argento's *The Aspern Papers,* as well as the role of Mme de Merteuil in Susa's *Dangerous Liaisons* and Mrs. Patrick De Rocher in Heggie's *Dead Man Walking,* both for San Francisco Opera; best known for Cherubino, Sesto, Dorabella, Mignon, Périchole, Rosina, Cenerentola, Composer, Octavian, Charlotte and Melisande; has made over 70 recordings.

VON STADE, Richardis (d. 1152). *See Stade, Richardis von.*

VON STEINBACH, Sabina (fl. 13th c.). *See Steinbach, Sabina von.*

VON STRAUSS UND TORNEY, Lulu (1873–1956). *See Strauss und Torney, Lulu von.*

VON SUTTNER, Bertha (1843–1914). *See Suttner, Bertha von.*

VON TEUFFEL, Countess (1847–1898). *See Howard, Blanche Willis.*

VON TRAPP, Maria (1905–1987). Austrian-born singer. Name variations: Baroness Maria Von Trapp. Born Maria Augusta Kutschera, Jan 26, 1905, on a train en route to Vienna, Austria; died Mar 28, 1987, in Morrisville, VT; dau. of Karl Kutschera and Augusta (Rainer) Kutschera; graduate of State Teachers College for Progressive Education, Vienna; m. Baron Georg Ritter Von Trapp (1880–1947), 1927; children: Rosmarie (b. 1929); Eleonore (b. 1931); Johannes (b. 1939); stepchildren: Rupert (1911–1992); Agathe (b. 1913); Maria (b. 1914); Werner (b. 1915);

Hedwig (1917–1972); Johanna (1919–1994); Martina (1921–1951). ❖ Mother of the world-famous Trapp Family Singers, whose flight from Nazi-occupied Austria (1938) inspired the musical play and motion picture *The Sound of Music*; went on worldwide concert tours with the Trapp Family Singers (1935–56); emigrated with family from Salzburg, Austria, to US (1938); organized and directed Trapp Family Music Camp, Stowe, VT (1944–56); organized Trapp Family Austrian Relief, Inc. (1947); recorded with family for RCA Victor, Concert Hall Society and Decca recording companies (1938–59); lectured and appeared on radio and tv (1938–84); managed Trapp Family Lodge, Stowe (1948–69). Given Austrian Honorary Cross for Science and Art (1967). ❖ See also autobiographies *The Story of the Trapp Family Singers* (1949), *Yesterday, Today and Forever* (1952), *Around the Year with the Trapp Family* (1955), *A Family on Wheels* (1959), and *Maria: My Own Story* (1972); and *Women in World History*.

VON TROTTA, Margarethe (1942—). German actress and film director. Born Feb 21, 1942, in Berlin, Germany; m. Felice Laudadio, 1964 (div. 1970); m. Volker Schlöndorff (film director), 1971 (div. 1991); children: (1st m.) 1. ❖ Moved to Paris (1960s), where she worked for film collectives and pursued an acting career, starring in films of Fassbinder and Volker Schlöndorff; co-wrote many scripts for 2nd husband's films; with him, co-directed *Verlorene Ehre der Katharina Blum oder* (*The Lost Honor of Katharina Blum*, 1975); directed *Das Zweite Erwachen der Christa Klages* (1978, The Second Awakening of Christa Klages); came to prominence directing *Die Bleierne Zeit* (*Marianne and Juliane*, 1981); also directed *Heller Wahn* (1983), *Rosa Luxemburg* (1986), *Paura e amore* (1988), *L'Africana* (1990), *Il Lungo silenzio* (1993), *Das Versprechen* (1995) and *Rosenstrasse* (2003), as well as for tv.

VON WATTEVILLE, Benigna (1725–1789). *See Watteville, Benigna von.*

VON WEDEMEYER, Maria (c. 1924–1977). *See Wedemeyer, Maria von.*

VON WEILER, Sophie (1958—). Dutch field-hockey player. Born Dec 24, 1958, in Netherlands. ❖ Won a gold medal at Los Angeles Olympics (1984) and a bronze medal at Seoul Olympics (1988), both in team competition.

VON WESTPHALEN, Jenny (1814–1881). *See Marx, Jenny von Westphalen.*

VON WIEGAND, Charmion (1896–1993). American abstract painter and collage artist. Born Charmion von Wiegand, 1896, in Chicago, Illinois; died 1993; dau. of an editor for Hearst newspapers; studied at Barnard College, 1915; attended Columbia University; m. 2nd husband Joseph Freeman (editor of *New Masses*), in 1932. ❖ Grew up in San Francisco; inspired by theosophy and Tibetan Buddhism, began painting (1926); wrote for art magazines; met friend and mentor Piet Mondrian (1941); learned to paint Chinese characters and developed abstract collage style (1940s); organized Kurt Schwitter's exhibition of collages (1948). ❖ See also *Women in World History*.

VOORBIJ, Aartje (1940—). Dutch swimmer. Name variations: Atie Voorbij. Born Sept 20, 1940, in Hilversum, Netherlands. ❖ Became world record holder in the 100-meter butterfly with a time of 1:10.5 (1956); won Netherlands nationals in the 100-meter butterfly (1955–58, and 1960); won a silver medal in 100-meter butterfly at European championship (1958).

VORLOVA, Slavka (1894–1973). Czech composer, conductor, pianist, singer and teacher. Name variations: Miroslava; (pseudonym) Mira Kord. Born in Nachod, Czechoslovakia, Mar 15, 1894; died in Prague, Aug 24, 1973. ❖ Lost voice while studying singing under Rosa Papier at Vienna's Music Academy, so she studied composition under Vitezslav Novak and piano under Vaclav Stephan in Prague; studied composition at Prague Conservatory, becoming 1st woman to receive a degree in composition in Czechoslovakia (1948); was a prolific composer who wrote over 100 works which cover a wide range of styles, including *Rozmarynka*, a folk opera set in a 19th-century Czech village; using name Mira Kord, also composed many jazz works and songs. ❖ See also *Women in World History*.

VORONINA, Zinaida (1947—). Soviet gymnast. Name variations: Zinaida Druzhinina. Born Zinaida Druzhinina, Dec 10, 1947, in USSR; m. Mikhail Voronin (gymnasts, div.). ❖ At World championships, won a silver medal in team all-around and bronze for floor exercises (1966) and a gold medal for team all-around and bronze medals for all-around, uneven bars, and floor exercises (1970); at European championships, won a silver medal for all-around and bronze medals for beam and

floor (1967); at Mexico City Olympics, won bronze medals in uneven bars and vault, a silver medal in indiv. all-around and a gold medal in team all-around (1968).

VORONOVA, Natalya (1965—). *See Pomoshchnikova, Natalya.*

VORONTSOVA, Ekaterina (1744–1810). *See Dashkova, Ekaterina.*

VOROS, Zsuzsanna (1977—). Hungarian pentathlete. Born May 4, 1977, in Szekesfehervar, Hungary. ❖ At World championships, placed 1st in indiv. (2003, 2004), 1st in relay (2000, 2003), and 1st in team (2002); was 3rd in indiv. overall World Cup ranking (2001) and 1st (2004); won gold medal at Athens Olympics (2004).

VORSE, Mary Heaton (1874–1966). American labor journalist. Born in New York, NY, Oct 9, 1874; died in Provincetown, Massachusetts, June 14, 1966; only child of Hiram Heaton and Ellen (Blackman) Heaton; m. Albert White Vorse (sailor, explorer and writer), 1898 (died 1910); m. Joe O'Brien (radical journalist), in 1912 (died 1915); children: (1st m.) Heaton Vorse (b. 1901) and Ellen Vorse (b. 1907); (2nd m.) Joel O'Brien (1914). ❖ Her coverage of the 1912 Lawrence, Massachusetts, "Bread and Roses" textile strike established her as a sympathetic, even at times participatory reporter; worked as an editor for the radical journal the *Masses*; for 40 years, traveled from one strike to the next, reporting the horrible conditions of labor which drove workers to strike, and the police brutality they frequently faced on the picket line; wrote hundreds of articles and short stories, two plays, and 16 books, including *Men and Steel* (1920), *Strike!* (1930) and *Time and Town* (1942). ❖ See also Dee Garrison, *Mary Heaton Vorse: The Life of an American Insurgent* (Temple U. Press, 1989); and *Women in World History*.

VOSE, Harriet L. (1856–1886). *See Bates, Harriet Leonora.*

VOSKES, Elles (1964—). Dutch swimmer. Name variations: Elles van der Werf-Voskes. Born Aug 3, 1964. ❖ At Los Angeles Olympics, won a silver medal in 4 x 100-meter freestyle relay (1984).

VOSKUIJL, Bep (d. 1983). Dutch Holocaust rescuer. Name variations: Elli Vossen. Born Elisabeth Voskuijl; died in 1983. ❖ Young typist who helped the family of Anne Frank; appears in the original diary under the name Elli Vossen. ❖ See also *Women in World History*.

VOSS, Christina (1952—). East German handball player. Born July 1952 in East Germany. ❖ At Montreal Olympics, won a silver medal in team competition (1976).

VÖTEN-MENCO, Sara (1920—). *See Menco, Sara.*

VOUTILAINEN, Katrina (1975—). American snowboarder. Name variations: Katrina Warnick. Born Katrina Warnick, May 23, 1975, in Salt Lake City, UT; m. Ami Voutilainen (Finnish pro snowboarder). ❖ Won bronze medal in Boarder X at X Games (Winter 1998); has had 5 top-ten finishes in all disciplines at Winter X Games, including 4th in Big Air (1998) and 4th in Slopestyle (2001).

VOVCHOK, Marko (1834–1907). *See Vilinska, Mariya.*

VOYNICH, Ethel (1864–1960). Irish-born British writer and translator. Born Ethel Lilian Boole in 1864 in Cork, Ireland; died in 1960 in New York, NY; dau. of George Boole (mathematician) and Mary Everest Boole (feminist philosopher); m. Wilfrid Michael Voynich (1865–1930, Polish nationalist), in 1891. ❖ Worked for periodical *Free Russia* in London; drew on husband's political experiences for the 1st and best known of her novels, *The Gadfly* (1897), made into a film in Soviet Union (1955); moved to US (1916); published other novels featuring revolutionary heroes, such as *Jack Raymond* (1901), the story of a rebel and a Polish patriot's widow, *Olive Latham* (1904), about an English nurse and a Russian revolutionary, and *An Interrupted Friendship* (1910), which continues the story of *The Gadfly*; also published 2 translations of Russian stories, *Stories from Garshin* (1893) and *The Humour of Russia* (1895), and a translation of Chopin's letters (1931). ❖ See also *Women in World History*.

VOZNESENSKAYA, Julia (1940—). Russian poet and short-story writer. Name variations: Iulia Nikolaevna Voznesénskaia or Voznesenskaya. Born 1940 in USSR. ❖ Active in the Leningrad Second Culture movement; her dissident views kept her writings out of the official press; was sent several times to prison and labor camps; after involvement with feminist magazine *Women and Russia*, received threats against her sons; immigrated with them to West Germany (1980); works, which focus on ills of Soviet regime, include *The Women's Decameron* (1986) and *The Star Chernobyl* (1987).

VRBA, Elisabeth (1942—). South African-American paleontologist. Born May 27, 1942, in Hamburg, Germany; dau. of a law professor who died when she was 2; with mother, moved to Namibia soon after; m. George Vrba. ❖ Raised in Namibia; studied zoology and statistics at University of Cape Town, South Africa (graduated with honors); taught high school after move to Pretoria (1967); began work as unpaid assistant at Transvaal Museum (1968) and became deputy director in charge of fossil hominids (human ancestors) collection; developed turnover pulse hypothesis, a theory based on studies of fossils hominids and fossil antelopes that claims climate changes led to evolution of humans and other species and fails to support Charles Darwins' survival of the fittest theory; relocated to US with family (1986); became tenured professor in Department of Geology and Geophysics at Yale University.

VREDENBURGH, Dorothy V. (1916–1991). *See Bush, Dorothy V.*

VREELAND, Diana (1903–1989). French magazine editor. Born Diana Dalziel in Paris, France, July 29, 1903; died in New York, NY, Aug 22, 1989; dau. of Frederick Y. Dalziel (Scottish stockbroker) and Emily Key (Hoffman) Dalziel (American socialite); m. T. Reed Vreeland (banker), 1924 (died 1966); children: Thomas R. Vreeland Jr. (architect); Frederick Vreeland (diplomat); grandchildren: Alexander Vreeland (US director of marketing for Giorgio Armani). ❖ Parisian-born fashion icon, style setter, and innovative editor of *Vogue* and *Harper's Bazaar*, who created the annual fashion exhibitions at Metropolitan Museum of Art as consultant to its Costume Institute; moved with family to New York during turmoil that led to WWI (1914); made debutante debut (1922); following marriage, lived in Albany where husband was a banker trainee (1924–28); moved to Europe; briefly ran an exclusive lingerie shop in London; returned to US (1936); began writing a column for *Harper's Bazaar*, "Why Don't You" (1937); served as fashion editor of *Harper's* (1937–62); incorporated the uncommon images of photographers like Man Ray and Richard Avedon, and developed a long working relationship with Louise Dahl-Wolfe, who photographed American fashion outdoors; moved to *Vogue* as fashion editor (1962), where she highlighted the work of photographers such as Avedon, Beaton, Irving Penn, and Deborah Turbeville; became editor-in-chief (1963); dismissed from *Vogue* (1971); took 4-month hiatus and traveled to Europe; became consultant to the Costume Institute of the Metropolitan Museum of Art (1972), producing a range of costume exhibitions for 14 years. ❖ See also memoirs *D. V.* (Knopf, 1984); Martin and Koda, *Diana Vreeland: Immoderate Style* (Metropolitan Museum of Art, 1993); and *Women in World History*.

VRONSKY, Vitya (1909–1992). Russian pianist. Name variations: Viktoria; Vitya Vronsky Babin. Born in Evpatoria, Russian Crimea, Aug 22, 1909; died June 28, 1992, in Cleveland, Ohio; studied at Kiev Conservatory and with Artur Schnabel and Egon Petri in Berlin and Alfred Cortot in Paris; m. Victor Babin (1908–1972, pianist), 1933. ❖ Began concert career (1930); with husband, established a highly successful duo-piano team (1933); immigrated to US (1937), where their joint career blossomed; made many recordings. ❖ See also *Women in World History*.

VRUGT, Johanna Petronella (1905–1960). Dutch writer. Name variations: (pseudonym) Anna Blaman. Born Johanna Petronella Vrugt in Rotterdam, Netherlands, Jan 31, 1905; died in Rotterdam, July 13, 1960. ❖ As Anna Blaman, became known for her controversial fiction which challenged traditional views; works include *Vrouw en vriend* (1941) (Woman and Friend), *Eenzaam avontuur* (Lonely Adventure, 1948), *Op leven en dood* (A Matter of Life and Death, 1954), *Overdag en andere verhalen* (A Day and Other Stories, 1957) and *De verliezers* (1960). Received P.C. Hooft Prize (1957) and Literature Prize of Amsterdam.

VUCANOVICH, Barbara F. (1921—). American politician. Born Barbara Farrell on June 22, 1921, in Camp Dix, New Jersey; graduate of Albany Academy for Girls, 1938; attended Manhattan College of the Sacred Heart, NY, 1938–39. ❖ Was a delegate to the Nevada State Republican conventions (1952–80); served as district staff assistant for US Senator Paul Laxalt (1974–82); was a delegate to the Republican National conventions (1976 and 1980); elected as Republican to the 98th through 104th Congresses (1983–97); focused on a number of issues of concern to her constituency, including federal wilderness and national park policy, public land use, and nuclear waste disposal; served on the Committee on Interior and Insular Affairs (where she was ranking Republican on the Subcommittee on General Oversight and Investigation) and the Committee on House Administration (where she was ranking Republican on the Subcommittee on Accounts); also served on the Committee on Appropriations, chairing the Subcommittee on Military Construction during her final term. ❖ See also *Women in World History*.

VUKOJICIC, Paola (1974—). Argentinean field-hockey player. Born Aug 28, 1974, in Buenos Aires, Argentina. ❖ Goalkeeper, won a team silver medal at Sydney Olympics (2000) and a team bronze medal at Athens Olympics (2004); won Champions Trophy (2001) and World Cup (2002); also played on the HC Rotterdam club in the Netherlands.

VUKOTICH, Milena (1847–1923). *See Milena.*

VULDETRADE (fl. 550). Queen of Metz (Austrasia). Name variations: Vuldetrada. Flourished around 550; dau. of Wacho, king of the Lombards; m. Thibaud also known as Theodovald or Theudebald (d. 555), king of Metz (Austrasia, r. 548–555); seventh wife of Chlothar, Clothaire, Clotar or Lothair I (497–561), king of Soissons and the Franks.

VULTROGOTHA (fl. 558). Queen of Paris. Name variations: Ultrogotte. Flourished around 558; m. Childebert (d. 558), king of Paris (r. 511–558), c. 558.

VUYK, Beb (1905–1991). Dutch novelist, journalist and short-story writer. Name variations: Elisabeth Vuyk. Born Feb 11, 1905; died 1991; m. Fernand de Willigen (died 1986). ❖ Moved from Holland to Dutch East Indies (1929) and, with family, spent war in Japanese internment camp; family settled in Java but was forced to return to Netherlands for political reasons; often wrote stories about adventure and life in Dutch East Indies; works include *Duizend eilanden* (1937), *Het laatste huis van de wereld* (1939), *het hout van Bara* (1947), *Verzameld Werk* (1972), and *Kamdaghoeken* (1989); also wrote cookery books and children's books. Received several literary awards.

VYDARINA, A. A. (1848–1927). *See Kirpishchikova, Anna.*

VYMAZALOVA, Lenka (1959—). Czech field-hockey player. Born June 15, 1959. ❖ At Moscow Olympics, won a silver medal in team competition (1980).

VYROUBOVA, Nina (1921—). Russian-born French ballerina. Born June 4, 1921, in Gourzouv or Gourzoff, Crimea, USSR; daughter of Irène Vyroubova (ballet teacher); educated at the Lycée Jules Perry, Paris; studied ballet with Vera Trefilova, Olga Preobrazhenska, Victor Gsovsky, Boris Kniaseff, Lyubov Egorova, Serge Lifar, Nicholas Zverev, and Yves Brieux. ❖ Made debut with a Chauve-Souris company (1939); appeared in Irene Lidova's *Soirées de la Danse* (1944); had 1st major success in *La Sylphide*, Les Ballets des Champs Élysées (1946); was première danseuse étoile of Paris Opéra (1949–56); ballerina with Grand Ballet du Marquis de Cuevas (1957–61); won Prix Pavlova of the Institut Chorégraphique de Paris (1957); was guest ballerina with Ballet Russe de Monte Carlo (1961–62), and ballet of the Colón Theater, Buenos Aires (1964). ❖ See also *Women in World History*.

VYTRYCHENKO, Yelena (1976—). *See Vitrichenko, Elena.*

VYUZHANINA, Galina (1952—). Soviet field-hockey player. Born Aug 1952 in USSR. ❖ At Moscow Olympics, won a bronze medal in team competition (1980).

W

WA SHI (1498–1560). Chinese military and political leader. Pronunciation: Wah Shrrr. Born Wa Shi in 1498; dau. of Cen Zhang (a great feudal lord of the Zhuang minority people of the Sino-Vietnamese frontier region of southern China); m. the Zhuang lord Cen Meng; children: son, Cen Bangzuo. ❖ Zhuang warrior, noted general, and shrewd political figure in southern China in the latter years of the Ming Dynasty, who became the most famous woman in the history of the Zhuang ethnic minority; trained in the art of combat and known for her strength, was briefly married to the most powerful and wealthy of the Zhuang lords; returned with her son to her father's court; after the death of her former husband at her father's hands, created shrewd alignments that allowed the Zhuang people to live in peace with the Chinese, gaining great influence for her family and protection for her people; chosen as the general to lead an army against Japanese pirates plaguing the Chinese coast, achieved military success (1557). ❖ See also *Women in World History.*

WAARA, Jennie (1975—). Swedish snowboarder. Born Jan 10, 1975, in Gallivare, Sweden. ❖ Won gold in Boarder X (Winter 1997) and Slopestyle (Winter 1998), silver in Halfpipe (Winter 1997), and bronze in Slopestyle (Winter 1997) at X Games.

WAARD, Elly de (1940—). Dutch poet. Born 1940 in Bergen, Netherlands. ❖ Helped organize festivals of women poets, *Amazone,* and direct *De Nieuwe Wilden* group of female poets; was co-founder of Anna Bijns Foundation to promote female writers in Holland; some works attracted controversy because of erotic treatment of lesbian love; writings include *Afstand* (1978), *Luwte* (1979), *Furie* (1981), *Strofen* (1983), *Een wildernis van verbindingen* (1986), *Onvoltooing* (1988), and *Anderling* (1998); wrote biography *Anna Bijns* (1985).

WACHTEL, Christine (1965—). East German runner. Born Jan 6, 1965. ❖ At Seoul Olympics, won a silver medal in 800 meters (1988).

WACHTER, Anita (1967—). Austrian Alpine skier. Born Feb 12, 1967, in Schruns, Austria. ❖ Won a gold medal for combined at Calgary Olympics (1988); won a silver medal for combined and a silver (tied with Diann Roffe) for giant slalom at Albertville Olympics (1992); placed 4th for giant slalom at Lillehammer Olympics (1994); at World championships, won silver medals for giant slalom (1993) and combined (1996); won World Cup giant slalom titles (1990, 1994) and overall (1993).

WACIUMA, Charity (1936—). Kenyan memoirist and children's writer. Born 1936 in Naaro village, Fort Hall, Kenya. ❖ Works focus on tension between traditional and western values; children's works incorporate Kikuyu folklore and storytelling tradition; writings include *Mwenu, the Ostrich Girl* (1966), *The Golden Feather* (1966), *Daughter of Mumbi* (1969), *Merry-Making* (1972), *Who's Calling* (1973) and *Mweru the Ostrich Girl.*

WADDELL, Helen (1889–1965). Irish scholar of medieval literature and poet. Born Helen Jane Waddell in Tokyo, Japan, May 31, 1889; died in London, England, Mar 5, 1965; dau. of Hugh and Jane Martin Waddell; graduated Queen's University with a 1st class BA in English language and literature, 1911, MA, 1912; also attended Somerville College, Oxford, 1920–22; never married; no children. ❖ Went to Paris on a Susette Taylor Traveling Scholarship to do research for 1st book; returned to London (1925) and released *The Wandering Scholars* (1927) to considerable acclaim; followed this with *Medieval Latin Lyrics* (1929); published *A Book of Medieval Latin* for schools (1931), which went into 10 editions over next 30 years; became a member of Royal Irish Academy (1932); published *Abelard* (1933), which went through 3 editions in 6 months and was translated into 9 languages; also wrote *The Desert Fathers* (1936); served as assistant to F. A. Voigt, editor of the journal *Nineteenth Century;* her Ker lecture at University of Glasgow (1947) on "Latin Poetry in the Dark Ages" was a great success.

Received A. C. Benson Foundation Medal from Royal Society of Literature (1928). ❖ See also Monica Blackett, *The Mark of the Maker: A Portrait of Helen Waddell* (Constable, 1973); and *Women in World History.*

WADDINGHAM, Dorothea (1899–1936). English murderer. Name variations: Dorothea Leech; Nurse Waddingham. Born Dorothea Nancy Waddingham in 1899 in England; hanged on April 16, 1936, in Nottingham, England; m. Thomas Willoughby Leech (died before 1935); lover of Ronald Joseph Sullivan. ❖ Opened her own private nursing home on Devon Drive in Nottingham (1935), though it's not certain she had any nursing training; was found guilty of killing her 1st two patients, a mother and daughter, for their estate. ❖ See also *Women in World History.*

WADDINGTON, Marianna Bacinetti-Florenzi (1802–1870). See *Bacinetti-Florenzi, Marianna.*

WADDINGTON, Miriam (1917–2004). Canadian poet. Born Miriam Dworkin, Dec 23, 1917, in Winnipeg, Canada; died Mar 3, 2004, in Vancouver, Canada; dau. of Isidore Dworkin and Mussia Dworkin; m. Patrick Waddington (journalist, sep., 1960). ❖ Studied at universities of Toronto and Pennsylvania; worked as social worker and then taught social work at McGill University and literature at York University; works include *Green World* (1945), *The Second Silence* (1955), *The Season's Lovers* (1958), *The Glass Trumpet* (1966), *Driving Home: Poems New and Selected* (1972), *The Price of Gold* (1976), *Mister Never* (1978), *The Visitants* (1981), *Collected Poems* (1986), *Apartment Seven: Essays New and Collected* (1989) and *The Last Landscape* (1992); edited *Canadian Jewish Short Stories* (1990). Won J.J. Segal Prize (1972, 1986) and Borestone Mountain Award (1963, 1966, 1974).

WADDINGTON, Sheila (1936—). See *Willcox, Sheila.*

WADDLES, Charleszetta (1912–2001). African-American religious leader and humanitarian. Name variations: Reverend Mother Charleszetta Waddles; Mother Waddles; Charleszetta Lena Campbell. Born Charleszetta Lena Campbell, Oct 7, 1912, in St. Louis, Missouri; died July 12, 2001, in Detroit, Michigan; dau. of Henry Campbell and Ella (Brown) Campbell; married 3 times; 1st to Clifford Walker (died c. 1922); last husband was Payton Waddles (died 1980); children: 10. ❖ Moved to Detroit (1940s); opened a "thirty-five cent restaurant" there (1950); opened her own church, the Perpetual Help Mission (1950s), founded on the principles of charity and humanitarianism; ordained a Pentecostal minister; established 10 non-profit urban missions, including 2 in Africa, assisting thousands of people with job training, health care, food distribution, budgeting and emergency aid; wrote several books, including 2 cookbooks; received more than 300 awards and honors; was the subject of PBS documentary *Ya Done Good* (1989). ❖ See also *Women in World History.*

WADDY, Charis (1909–2004). Islamic scholar and author. Born Sept 24, 1909, in Parramatta, Australia; died Aug 29, 2004; dau. of Stacy Waddy (headmaster); studied Arabic and Hebrew at Lady Margaret Hall, gaining a 1st-class degree; London University, PhD; never married. ❖ The 1st woman to graduate in oriental languages from Oxford University, wrote the groundbreaking book, *The Muslim Mind* (1976, 3rd ed., 1991); also wrote *Women in Muslim History* (1980); was held in high esteem by Muslims worldwide.

WADDY, Harriet (1904–1999). African-American military leader. Name variations: Harriet West; Harriet West Waddy. Born Harriet West on June 4, 1904; died Feb 21, 1999, in Las Vegas, Nevada. ❖ One of the highest-ranking black officers in the Women's Army Corps (WAC) during World War II, was also its wartime adviser on racial issues; after being promoted to major and named an aide to WAC director, Colonel Oveta Culp Hobby, lobbied to change the military's policy of segregation which forced many of the 6,500 enlisted black women into service as uniformed domestic servants, assigned to cleaning officers' clubs. ❖ See also *Women in World History*.

WADE, Jane (c. 1866–1935). *See Woodrow, Nancy.*

WADE, Margaret (1912–1995). American basketball player and coach. Born Dec 30, 1912, in McCool, Mississippi; died Feb 16, 1995; graduate of Delta State University, 1933. ❖ Legendary basketball coach of Delta State University, gave her name to the Wade Trophy, which is awarded annually to the top women's collegiate player; played in college and 2 years with Tupelo Red Wings, but a knee injury ended career; coached high school basketball in Mississippi (1933–54); coached Delta State (1973–79), winning 3 AIAW national championships (1975–77). Inducted into Basketball Hall of Fame (1985).

WADE, Virginia (1945—). English tennis player. Born Sarah Virginia Wade, July 10, 1945, in Bournemouth, England; daughter of an Anglican cleric. ❖ Known for aggressive play and ability to recover from mistakes, brought a sense of drama to the court and was tremendously popular with fans; learned to play tennis in South Africa, where her family moved when she was a child; 1st qualified for Wimbledon (1962); won US Open (1968), the 1st British woman to do so since 1930; finally won Wimbledon singles championship (1977); by the time she retired from professional play (1987), was 3rd in world rankings for number of titles won, including singles titles at Wimbledon and the US and Australian opens. Inducted into International Tennis Hall of Fame (1989). ❖ See also autobiography (with Mary Lou Mellace) *Courting Triumph* (Hodder & Stoughton, 1978); and *Women in World History*.

WADEMANT, Annette (1928—). Belgian screenwriter. Born Dec 19, 1928, in Brussels, Belgium. ❖ Worked with Jacques Becker and Max Ophuls, among others; screenplays include *Édouard et Caroline, Rue de l'estrapade, Lola Montès, Club de femmes, Typhon sur Nagasaki, Une parisienne, Une manche et la belle, Faibles femmes, Voulez-vous danser avec moi?, La Française et l'amour, Un soir sur la plage, Les Parisiennes, Comment réussir en amour, Comment trouvez-vous ma soeur?, La leçon particulière* and *L'Enfant secret*.

WADHAM, Doris (1919–1994). *See Gare, Nene.*

WAERA or WAERE, Keita (d. 1913). *See Wyllie, Kate.*

WAETFORD, Katerina (1903–1948). *See Nehua, Katerina.*

WAGAR, Dorothy (1938—). *See Lidstone, Dorothy.*

WAGNER, Allison (1977—). American swimmer. Born July 20, 1977; attended University of Florida at Gainesville. ❖ Won a silver medal for 400-meter indiv. medley at Atlanta Olympics (1996).

WAGNER, Aly (1980—). American soccer player. Born Aug 10, 1980, in San Jose, CA; attended Santa Clara University. ❖ Midfielder, played for Boston Breakers; won a team gold medal at Athens Olympics (2004).

WAGNER, Barbara (1938—). Canadian figure skater. Born 1938 in Toronto, Ontario; m. James Grogan (American skater, div.). ❖ With partner Robert Paul, won gold medals at the World championships (1957–60); awarded 7 firsts by judges at Squaw Valley Olympics (1960), the 1st non-European pair to win a gold medal at the Olympics; also won 5 Canadian senior championships; spent 3 years with Ice Capades. Inducted into Canadian Sports Hall of Fame (1957).

WAGNER, Catherina (1919—). Dutch swimmer. Born Dec 17, 1919. ❖ At Berlin Olympics, won a gold medal in 4x100-meter freestyle relay (1936).

WAGNER, Cosima (1837–1930). German founder. Name variations: Cosima Liszt; Cosima von Bulow or von Bülow. Born Cosima Liszt in Bellagio, on Lake Como, Dec 24, 1837; died in Bayreuth, Germany, April 1, 1930; illeg. dau. of Franz Liszt (pianist and composer) and Countess Marie d'Agoult (who wrote under the pseudonym Daniel Stern); m. Hans von Bülow (conductor), Aug 18, 1857 (div. 1870); m. Richard Wagner (composer), Aug 25, 1870 (died 1883); children: (1st m.) daughters Blandine von Bülow and Daniela von Bülow (Wagner); (conceived with Richard Wagner during 1st marriage) Isolde Wagner and Eva Wagner; (with Wagner before 2nd marriage) Siegfried Wagner. ❖ Daughter of one great musician and wife of another, who was instrumental in helping found Bayreuth, the festival featuring her husband's operas, and ensuring its survival as an annual event; though she was not a musician, her influence on the music world has been incalculable, and it was under her leadership particularly that the Bayreuth

Festival grew from a German event into one of international stature. ❖ See also *Cosima Wagner's Diaries* (2 vols., Gregor-Dellin and Mack, eds., 1978, 1980); Geoffrey Skelton, *Richard and Cosima Wagner: Biography of a Marriage* (Houghton, 1982); Alice Sojoloff, *Cosima Wagner, Extraordinary Daughter of Franz Liszt* (Dodd, 1969); and *Women in World History*.

WÄGNER, Elin (1882–1949). Swedish writer. Name variations: Elin Wagner. Born Elin Matilda Elisabeth Wägner in 1882 in Lund, Sweden; died 1949; dau. of a headmaster; m. John Landquist (critic), in 1910 (div. 1922). ❖ Began writing career as a journalist; a radical thinker who supported the causes of pacifism, women's emancipation and environmental preservation, wrote most of her novels as part of a public debate; published 1st book *Från det jordiska muséet* (From our Earthly Museum, 1907), followed by *Pennskaftet* (The Penholder, 1910), a work that was groundbreaking in its erotic insights and views on women's suffrage; during WWI, published pacifist novel *Släkten Jernploogs framgång* (The Success of the Family Ironplough, 1916) and also *Åsa-Hanna* (1918), considered her best work; continued to write novels and endorse causes throughout life, including the feminist *Väckarkloka* (Alarm Clock, 1941); for her biography of Selma Lagerlöf, was awarded a seat in the Swedish Academy (1944).

WAGNER, Friedelind (1918–1991). German author and lecturer. Born in Bayreuth, Germany, Mar 29, 1918; died in Herdecke, Germany, May 8, 1991; dau. of Siegfried Wagner (conductor and composer of operas and director of Bayreuth, died 1930) and Winifred (Williams) Wagner (1897–1980); granddau. of Richard Wagner (composer, died 1883) and Cosima Wagner (1837–1930); sister of Wieland, Wolfgang and Verena Wagner; never married. ❖ Granddaughter of Cosima and Richard Wagner, who broke with her family's tradition of nationalism and racism, while maintaining her influential link with Wagnerian scholarship; grew up with her mother's uncritical support of the Nazi ideology, though her father repudiated anti-Semitism; after father and grandmother died (1930), her mother enjoyed a close relationship with Hitler who assumed the role of a surrogate father for the Wagner children; spoke out against the use of the Wagner Festivals for Nazi propaganda; on eve of WWII, fled to Lucerne (1939), eventually arriving in US (1941); wrote articles in the musical press and spoke out in the media against Nazi Germany; published *Heritage of Fire: The Story of Richard Wagner's Granddaughter* (1945); invited by brother Wieland, was a lecturer and organizer of master classes at Bayreuth (1959–66). ❖ See also *Women in World History*.

WAGNER, Johanna (1826–1894). German soprano. Name variations: Johanna Jachmann-Wagner. Born Oct 13, 1826, in Lohnde, Germany; died Oct 16, 1894, in Würzburg, Germany; adopted dau. of tenor and producer Albert Wagner (1799–1874), composer Richard Wagner's brother; niece of Cosima Wagner (1837–1930); m. Alfred Jachmann. ❖ Began opera career (1844); performed in major opera houses in cities throughout Europe, including Hamburg, Berlin and London, in such roles as Tancredi, Lucrezia Borgia, Fidès and Ortrud; created the role of Elisabeth in *Tannhäuser*. ❖ See also *Women in World History*.

WAGNER, Katrin (1977—). German kayaker. Born Oct 13, 1977, in Brandenburg, Germany. ❖ At World championships, placed 1st for K4 200 and 500 (1997); placed 2nd overall in World Cup ranking in kayak (2002); won gold medals for K2 500 meters and K4 500 meters at Sydney Olympics (2000); won a gold medal for K4 500 at Athens Olympics (2004).

WAGNER, Lisa Rathgeber (1961—). *See Rathgeber, Lisa.*

WAGNER, Minna (c. 1800–1866). German actress. Born Minna Planer around 1800; died in Dresden, Germany, in Feb 1866; m. Richard Wagner (the composer), Nov 22, 1836; children: an illeg. daughter; (with Wagner) no children. ❖ Met Richard Wagner while he was assistant conductor with the Bethmann Company in Magdeburg and she was a young and sought-after actress in the company (1834); was almost 4 years older than Wagner and at 16 had had an illegitimate daughter whom she passed off as her sister; had a tumultuous relationship with husband as they fled borders and creditors; while he was in debtors' prison in France (1840), wrote desperate letters to friends who eventually bailed him out; but 15 years later, as she lay dying in Dresden, her now-affluent husband did not visit while he was in the city. ❖ See also *Women in World History*.

WAGNER, Sandra (1969—). German archer. Name variations: Sandra Sachse. Born Sandra Wagner, Sept 9, 1969, in Esloh, Germany. ❖ Won a silver medal for teams at Atlanta Olympics (1996) and a bronze medal for teams at Sydney Olympics (2000).

WAGNER, Winifred (1897–1980). British-born opera administrator. Born Winifred Williams in England in 1897; died 1980; at 10, was adopted by a German musician, Karl Klindworth, whose wife was a cousin of composer Richard Wagner; m. Siegfried Wagner (son of Cosima Wagner and composer Richard Wagner, died 1930); children: Wolfgang and Wieland Wagner (directors of Bayreuth Festival); Verena Wagner; Friedelind Wagner (1918–1991). ❖ Ran the Bayreuth Festival (1930s–40s) and played a key role in forging its alliance with Hitler, an association that has haunted both the Wagner family and the festival ever since. ❖ See also *Women in World History*.

WAGNER-STANGE, Ute (1966—). German rower. Born April 2, 1966. ❖ At Barcelona Olympics, won a bronze medal in coxed eights (1992).

WAGSTAFF, Elizabeth (1974—). American swimmer. Name variations: Janie Wagstaff. Born July 22, 1974; attended University of Florida. ❖ At Barcelona Olympics, won a gold medal in 4 x 100-meter medley relay (1992).

WAGSTAFF, Janie (1974—). See Wagstaff, Elizabeth.

WAHRHAFTIG, Alma (1897–1989). See Lavenson, Alma.

WAIF WANDER (fl. 1866–1910). See Fortune, Mary.

WAINE, Mary Elizabeth (1836–1920). See Gibbs, Mary Elizabeth.

WAINWRIGHT, Helen (1906—). American swimmer and diver. Born Mar 15, 1906. ❖ At Antwerp Olympics, won a silver medal in springboard diving (1920); at Paris Olympics, won a silver medal in 400-meter freestyle swimming (1924).

WAITAORO (c. 1848–1929). New Zealand tribal leader. Born c. 1848 or 1849, on Chatham Islands, New Zealand; died on Mar 26, 1929; dau. of Raniera and Rongorongo; m. Tahana Takiroa Coffee (Kawhe); children: 1 adopted daughter. ❖ Born during her peoples' thwarted attempt to return to ancestral lands, settled at Pukerauhe, where she became leader of her people and fostered several children. ❖ See also *Dictionary of New Zealand Biography* (Vol. 2).

WAITE, Catherine (1829–1913). American writer, suffragist, and lawyer. Born Catherine Van Valkenburg, Jan 30, 1829, in Dumfries, Ontario, Canada; died in Park Ridge, Illinois, Nov 9, 1913; dau. of Joseph and Margaret (Page) Van Valkenburg; attended Knox College; graduate of Oberlin College, 1853; attended Union College of Law (later Northwestern University Law School), 1885; admitted to the bar, June 1886; m. Charles B. Waite (Chicago lawyer), 1854; children: Lucy, Jessie, Margaret, Joseph, and Charles. ❖ For four years, lived with husband in Utah Territory, following his appointment to the Utah Territory Supreme Court by Abraham Lincoln; upon return to Chicago, wrote of her experiences in *The Mormon Prophet and His Harem* (1867), protesting the practice of polygamy; for 3 years, published the *Chicago Law Times*; also served as president of the International Woman's Bar Association.

WAITE, Elizabeth (fl. 1460s). See Lucy, Elizabeth.

WAITOHI (?–1839). New Zealand tribal leader. Died Aug or Sept 1839; dau. of Werawera and Parekowhatu; m. Te Ra-ka-herea; children: Te Rangihaeata (war leader and carver) and Rangi Topeora (tribal leader). ❖ Served as important representative of her people's issues during tribal migration and resettlement. ❖ See also *Dictionary of New Zealand Biography* (Vol. 1).

WAITZ, Grete (1953—). Norwegian marathon runner. Born Grete Andersen, Oct 1, 1953, in Oslo, Norway; m. Jack Waitz, 1975. ❖ At 16, won Norwegian Junior title in 400 and 800 meters; set a European Junior record in the 1,500 meters with a time of 4:17 (1971); competed in Olympics (1972) but failed to medal; set a record in the 3,000 meters (1975); won inaugural World Cup in 3,000 meters, placed 5th in the 1,500 meters in European championships, and won 5 World cross-country titles in Norway (1977); finished 1st in the NY marathon (1978), taking 2 minutes off world record; won 9 out of 11 NY marathons (1978–88); took 5 minutes off her 1978 record, becoming 1st woman to run a marathon in under 2:30 (1979); won London Marathon and 1st World Track and Field championship marathon in Helsinki (1983); was an Olympic silver medalist in Los Angeles (1984); formed Grete Waitz Foundation to help teenage girl runners. Selected Sportswoman of the Year by *Women's Sports* magazine; voted best female

distance runner of the past 25 years by *Runner's World* (1991). ❖ See also *Women in World History*.

WAIZERO (1876–1930). See Zauditu.

WAJS, Jadwiga (1912–1990). Polish track-and-field athlete. Name variations: Jadwiga Wajsowna or Wajs-Gretkiewicz or Wajsowna-Gretkiewicz; Jadwiga Marcinkiewicz. Born in 1912; died in 1990. ❖ Won a bronze medal at Los Angeles Olympics (1932) and a silver medal at the Berlin Olympics (1936), both in discus throw.

WAJSOWNA, Jadwiga (1912–1990). See Wajs, Jadwiga.

WAKA YAMADA (1879–1956). See Yamada, Waka.

WAKE, Margaret of Liddell (c. 1299–1349). See Margaret Wake of Liddell.

WAKEFIELD, Baroness of (1935–2001). See Denton, Jean.

WAKEFIELD, Deserie (1960—). See Baynes, Deserie.

WAKEFIELD, Priscilla (1751–1832). English writer of children's books. Born Priscilla Bell on Jan 31, 1751, in Tottenham, England; died Sept 12, 1832, in Ipswich, England; dau. of Daniel Bell of Stamford, Middlesex, and Catherine Barclay (both Quakers); aunt of prison reformer Elizabeth Fry; grandmother of politician Edward Gibbon Wakefield and colonist William Hayward Wakefield; m. Edward Wakefield (London merchant), in 1771 (died 1826); children: 1 daughter; 2 sons (who became well-known economists). ❖ Engaged in philanthropic activities (1770s–80s), creating a charity for lying-in women in Tottenham and promoting "frugality banks," savings banks for women and children, the 1st of their kind in Great Britain; specializing in natural history and travelogues, wrote chiefly instructive works for children, several of which became extremely popular and continued to be reprinted even after her death, including *An Introduction to Botany in a Series of Familiar Letters* (1796), *Juvenile Anecdotes founded on Facts* (2 vols., 1795–98), and *The Juvenile Travelers* (1801); other works included *Leisure Hours; or Entertaining Dialogues* (1794–96) and *A Family Tour through the British Empire* (1804); her one work for adults, *Reflections on the Present Condition of the Female Sex, with Suggestions for its Improvement* (1798), advocated greater educational and vocational opportunities for women. ❖ See also *Women in World History*.

WAKELING, Gwen (1901–1982). American movie costume designer. Born Mar 3, 1901, in Detroit, Michigan; died June 16, 1982, in Los Angeles, California. ❖ Worked for Cecil B. De Mille at Pathé and Paramount; served as head costume designer at Fox (1933–42); worked on over 120 films for a number of studios (1927–65); also designed for tv, stage plays and light opera companies; was costume designer for numerous Shirley Temple (Black) films, including *The Littlest Rebel, Poor Little Rich Girl, Dimples, Heidi, Rebecca of Sunnybrook Farm, Little Miss Broadway, Just Around the Corner, The Little Princess,* and *Young People;* also designed costumes for *King of Kings* (1927) and *The Grapes of Wrath* (1939). Nominated for Academy Award for *Samson and Delilah* (1950).

WAKOSKI, Diane (1937—). American poet. Born Aug 3, 1937, in Whittier, CA; dau. of John Joseph Wakoski and Marie Megel Wakoski; University of California at Berkeley, BA, 1960; m. S. Shepard Sherbell, 1965; m. Michael Watterlond, 1973 (div. 1975); m. Robert J. Turney, 1982. ❖ Began giving poetry readings in New York in 1960s and worked as writer-in-residence at US colleges and universities; joined faculty of Michigan State University (1976); works include *Coins and Coffins* (1962), *Discrepancies and Apparitions* (1966), *George Washington Poems* (1967), *Greed, parts one and two* (1968), *Emerald Ice, Selected Poems 1962–1987* (1988), *The Archeology of Movies and Books* (1991–98), and *Jason the Sailor* (1993).

WALASIEWICZ, Stanisława (1911–1980). See Walsh, Stella.

WALBE, Elena (1968—). See Välbe, Elena.

WALBERGA (c. 710–777). See Walpurgis.

WALBURG, Walburga, or Walburge (c. 710–777). See Walpurgis.

WALCAMP, Marie (1894–1936). American actress. Born July 27, 1894, in Dennison, OH; died by her own hand, Nov 17, 1936; m. Harland Tucker, 1920. ❖ Featured at Universal; films include *The Evil Power, Liberty, A Daughter of the U.S.A., Patria, The Blot* and *In a Moment of Temptation.*

WALCOTT, Mary Morris (1860–1940). American artist and naturalist. Born Mary Morris Vaux on July 31, 1860, in Philadelphia, Pennsylvania;

died Aug 22, 1940, in St. Andrews, New Brunswick, Canada; dau. of George Vaux and Sarah Humphreys (Morris) Vaux (both Quakers); sister of George Vaux Jr.; graduate of Friends Select School of Philadelphia, 1879; m. Charles Doolittle Walcott (secretary of Smithsonian Institution), June 30, 1914 (died 1927). ❖ Became 1st woman to climb Mount Stephen (1900); moved to Washington, DC, upon marriage (1914); published her wildflower paintings in *North American Wild Flowers* (1925); joined the Society of Woman Geographers (1926) and was elected national president of the Society (1933); appointed by President Calvin Coolidge to her deceased brother's seat on the Board of Indian Commissioners (1927), serving until 1932; contributed paintings to *Illustrations of North American Pitcher Plants* (1935). ❖ See also *Women in World History*.

WALD, Florence (1917—). American university administrator. Name variations: Florence S. Wald. Born Florence Schorske in New York, NY, April 19, 1917; dau. of Theodore Alexander Schorske and Gertrude (Goldschimdt) Schorske; graduate of Mt. Holyoke College, 1938; Yale University, MA in nursing, 1941; m. Henry J. Wald (health-facility planner); children: Joel David Wald; Shari Johanna Wald. ❖ Dean of Yale School of Nursing who played a key role in launching the hospice movement in the US; appointed to the faculty of the Yale University School of Nursing as director of the mental health and psychiatric nursing program (1957); served as dean of the nursing school (1958–67); established the 1st hospice in the US, the Connecticut Hospice, in Branford (1974). Inducted into National Women's Hall of Fame (1998). ❖ See also *Women in World History*.

WALD, Lillian D. (1867–1940). American reformer. Born Lillian D. Wald, Mar 10, 1867, in Cincinnati, Ohio; died Sept 1, 1940, in Westport, Connecticut; dau. of Max D. Wald (optical goods dealer) and Minnie (Schwartz) Wald; granted nursing diploma, New York Hospital Training School for Nurses, 1891; attended Woman's Medical College of New York, 1892–93; never married; no children. ❖ Public health nurse, social reformer, settlement house leader, and feminist who worked to improve the health and welfare of women and children; founded the Henry Street Settlement and organized the Henry Street Visiting Nurse Service (1893), to provide inhabitants of a poor neighborhood with nursing care and teach them the rudiments of healthy living; by 1913, had a thriving Visiting Nurses' Service consisting of 92 nurses who made more than 200,000 visits per year from the Henry Street headquarters and branch settlements in upper Manhattan and the Bronx; became involved in a nationwide movement to reform American nursing; founded the National Child Labor Committee (1904); helped establish a department of nursing and health at Columbia University Teachers College (1910); elected 1st president of National Organization for Public Health Nursing (1912); helped establish the Children's Bureau (1912); headed Committee on Home Nursing, Council of National Defense (1917–19); founded League of Free Nations Association (1919); retired as head of Henry Street Settlement (1933); was co-chair, Good Neighbor League (1936). ❖ See also autobiographies *The House on Henry Street* (1915) and *Windows on Henry Street* (1934); Clare Coss, ed. *Lillian D. Wald: Progressive Activist* (Feminist Press, 1989); Doris Groshen Daniels, *Always a Sister: The Feminism of Lillian D. Wald* (Feminist Press, 1989); Robert L. Duffus, *Lillian Wald: Neighbor and Crusader* (Macmillan, 1938); Sally M. Rogow, *Lillian Wald: The Nurse in Blue* (Jewish Publication Society, 1966); and *Women in World History*.

WALD, Patricia McGowan (1928—). American judge. Born Sept 16, 1928, in Torrington, Connecticut; dau. of Joseph F. McGowan and Margaret (O'Keefe) McGowan; Connecticut College for Women, BA, 1948; Yale Law School, LLB, 1951; m. Robert L. Wald, June 22, 1952; children: Sarah, Douglas, Johanna, Frederica and Thomas. ❖ Was admitted to Washington, DC, bar (1952); served as clerk for US Circuit Court of Appeals judge (1951–52), then associate at firm of Arnold, Fortas & Porter, Washington (1952–53); was a member of the DC Crime Commission (1964–65); worked at Department of Justice (1967); worked at Neighborhood Legal Service in Washington (1968–70); was co-director, Ford Foundation Project Drug Abuse (1970), Center for Law and Social Policy (1971–72), and Mental Health Law Project (1972); was assistant attorney general for legislative affairs, Department of Justice (1977–79); became judge, US Court of Appeals for DC (1979), then chief judge (1986).

WALD, Ruth (1924—). See Hubbard, Ruth.

WALDECK AND PYRMONT, duchess of. See Helen of Nassau (1831–1888).

WALDEGRAVE, Frances (1821–1879). English countess and society leader. Name variations: Countess Waldegrave. Born Frances Elizabeth Anne Braham in 1821; died 1879; dau. of well-known Jewish singer John Braham; m. John Waldegrave, in 1839; m. Lord George Waldegrave, 7th earl Waldegrave, in 1840 (died 1846); m. George Granville Harcourt, in 1847 (died 1861); m. Chichester (later Lord) Fortescue, in 1863. ❖ Following 3rd marriage, established herself as a London society leader; in addition to throwing frequent "galas" in her Carlton Gardens home, was skilled at politics and often hosted more serious gatherings of the influential Whigs and Liberals of her day; is also known for her restoration of Strawberry Hill.

WALDEGRAVE, Maria, dowager countess of. See Walpole, Maria (1736–1807).

WALDETRUDE (c. 628–688). See Wandru.

WALDMANN, Maria (1842–1920). Austrian opera singer. Born in 1842 in Vienna, Austria; died Nov 6, 1920; studied with Passy-Cornet in Vienna, and with Lamperti in Milan. ❖ Considered by Giuseppe Verdi to be the ideal mezzo-soprano, debuted in St. Petersburg (1865); sang in Milan, Paris, Moscow, Vienna, Trieste, and Cairo (1870s); sang Amneris in the 1st Italian *Aïda* and created the alto part in Verdi's *Requiem*; married and retired (1878). ❖ See also *Women in World History*.

WALDO, Carolyn (1964—). Canadian synchronized swimmer. Born Dec 11, 1964, in Montreal, Canada. ❖ Won a silver medal in solo at Los Angeles Olympics (1984); partnered with Michelle Cameron, won a gold medal in duet, then a solo gold medal at Seoul Olympics (1988); with Cameron, won Rome and Spanish Opens (1985), FINA World Cup (1985, 1987), Spanish Open (1986), Commonwealth Games (1986), World championships (1986) and Pan Pacific championships (1987). Inducted into International Swimming Hall of Fame; received Order of Canada (1989).

WALDO, Ruth Fanshaw (1885–1975). American advertising executive. Born Dec 8, 1885, in Scotland, Connecticut; died Aug 30, 1975, in Bridgeport, Connecticut; dau. of Gerald Waldo and Mary (Thomas) Waldo; graduate of Adelphi College, 1909; Columbia University, AM, 1910; never married. ❖ One of the industry's most prominent women in her day, worked for the J. Walter Thompson Company advertising agency (1915–60); appointed 1st female vice president of the Thompson Company (1944). ❖ See also *Women in World History*.

WALDORF, Wilella (c. 1900–1946). American drama critic. Born c. 1900; died Mar 12, 1946, in New York, NY. ❖ Became drama critic for the *New York Post* (1941), then the only woman first-string critic on a NY newspaper; also wrote popular column "Two on the Aisle."

WALDRADA (fl. 9th c.). Queen of Lorraine. Briefly 2nd wife of Lothair also known as Lothar II (b. 826–869), king of Lorraine, also known as Lotharingia (r. 855–869), after 855; children: Hugh (b. around 855).

WALELA.
See Coolidge, Priscilla.
See Coolidge, Rita.
See Satterfield, Laura.

WALENSKA, Maria (1786–1817). See Walewska, Marie.

WALENTYNOWICZ, Anna (1929—). Polish labor leader. Name variations: (nickname) "Mala" (the little one). Born Anna Lubczyk in 1929 in Wolyn (Volhynia) province, Poland (now Ukraine); orphaned at 10 and ended formal education in 4th grade; m. Kazimierz Walentynowicz (locksmith at the shipyard), in 1964 (died 1973); children: son, Janusz. ❖ Worker and labor leader at Lenin Shipyard in Gdansk, whose firing (Aug 1980) triggered a massive strike movement leading directly to the birth of Solidarity and set in motion a process that brought about the end of Communist rule in Poland; found employment as a welder at Lenin Shipyard (1950); having complained that women workers were not receiving the same work incentives as the men (1953), was arrested and interrogated for 8 hours; compelled by health problems to give up her job as a welder (1965), became a crane operator; respected for honesty and outspokenness, gained a reputation throughout shipyard for activism on behalf of fellow workers; as a member of her division's workers' council, as well as of the division commission (which she chaired for a time), uncovered corruption by management; played significant role (Dec 1970), as one of the leaders of a strike that succeeded in shutting down the shipyard; was a member of the strikers' presidium that gained concessions for shipyard workers (Jan 1971); helped distribute illegal biweekly newspaper, *Robotnik* (The Worker, 1977–79), which published the Charter of Workers' Rights (Dec 1, 1979), signed by 107 intellectuals and workers, including Walentynowicz and Walesa, that is regarded as a major step toward the Solidarity movement; was fired from her job (Aug 9, 1980); was arrested and interned. Despite the crucial role played in the Solidarity movement by Walentynowicz and countless other women, they quickly found themselves marginalized once its male leadership achieved recognition as a legitimate political force. ❖ See also *Women in World History*.

WALES, Ethel (1878–1952). American actress. Born April 4, 1878, in Passaic, NJ; died Feb 15, 1952, Hollywood, CA; children: Wellington Charles Wales. ❖ Specialized in older women for Paramount, most memorably in *Miss Lulu Bett*; films include *Bobbed Hair, The Covered Wagon, Merton of the Movies, Beggar on Horseback* and *The Girl in the Pullman.*

WALES, Nym (1907–1997). *See Snow, Helen Foster.*

WALES, princess of.
See Eleanor of Montfort (1252–1282).
See Joan of Kent (1328–1385).
See Anne of Warwick (1456–1485).
See Caroline of Ansbach (1683–1737).
See Augusta of Saxe-Gotha (1719–1772).
See Caroline of Brunswick (1768–1821).
See Charlotte Augusta (1796–1817).
See Alexandra of Denmark (1844–1925).
See Mary of Teck (1867–1953).
See Diana (1961–1997).

WALES, queen of.
See Edith (fl. 1063).
See Angharad (d. 1162).

WALESKA, Peggy (1980—). German rower. Born April 11, 1980, in Pirna, Germany. ❖ At World championships, won gold medals for quadruple sculls (2001, 2002); won a silver medal for double sculls at Athens Olympics (2004).

WALEWSKA, Marie (1786–1817). Polish countess. Name variations: Maria Walenska; Maria Walevska; Countess Valeska. Pronunciation: Va-LEV-skah. Born Marie Laczynska in Brodno, Poland, Dec 7, 1786; died in Paris, France, Dec 11, 1817; dau. of Matthew Laczynski and Eva (Zaborowska) Laczynska (members of Polish nobility); m. Anastase Colonna Walewski (Polish noble, landowner, and former chamberlain to King Stanislaus Poniatowski), probably on June 17, 1804 (div. 1812); m. General Philippe Antoine Ornano (cousin to Napoleon), Sept 7, 1815; children: (1st m.) Anthony Basil Rudolph; (2nd m.) Rodolphe Auguste; (with Napoleon) Alexander Florian Joseph Colonna Walewski. ❖ Polish noblewoman who became the mistress of Napoleon Bonaparte in order to promote the restoration of independence to her country; father died in battle of Maciejowice, defending Warsaw against the Russian army (1794); with the 3rd partition of Poland (1795), saw Poland vanish as a sovereign state; left family estate for schooling in Warsaw (1800), where she became a patriot and, like other patriots, looked to Napoleon as Poland's savior; while French army occupied Warsaw, worked in French military hospitals (1806); urged on by Polish nationalists, became the mistress of Napoleon and one of the greatest loves of his life (1807); saw the creation of Grand Duchy of Warsaw (1807) and tried to make him personally receptive to the hopes of the Polish people; visited Paris (1808); fled from Warsaw to Thorn during Austrian invasion of Poland and joined Napoleon in Vienna and Paris (1809); after Napoleon married Archduchess Marie-Louise of Austria, moved permanently to Paris (1810); presented at French imperial court (1811); when Napoleon invaded Russia, returned to Warsaw (1812), then Paris (1813); visited Napoleon on Elba (1814); had 2 final meetings with Napoleon (1815). ❖ See also Christine Sutherland, *Marie Walewska: Napoleon's Great Love* (Vendome, 1979); *Conquest* (film), starring Charles Boyer and Greta Garbo (1937); and *Women in World History*.

WALFORD, Lucy (1845–1915). Scottish novelist. Born Lucy Colquhoun, April 17, 1845, in Portobello, near Edinburgh, Scotland; died May 11, 1915; dau. of John Colquhoun (author) and Frances Sara (Fuller-Maitland) Colquhoun; niece of novelist Catherine Sinclair; m. Alfred Saunders Walford, 1869 (died 1907); children: 2 sons, 5 daughters. ❖ Following marriage, wrote secretly, contributing stories to *Blackwood's Magazine*; though her family voiced disapproval, published *Mr. Smith: A Part of his Life* (1874), which was a great success; went on to write 45 books; was particularly adept at light-hearted domestic comedy, as seen in her books *Pauline* (1877), *Cousins* (1885), *The History of a Week* (1886), *A Mere Child* (1888), *A Stiff-Necked Generation* (1889), *The Mischief of Monica* (1892) and *Sir Patrick the Puddock* (1899); also contributed to several London magazines, and worked as London correspondent for the New York *Critic* (1889–93).

WALKENSHAW, Clementina (c. 1726–1802). *See Walkinshaw, Clementina.*

WALKER, Ada Overton (1870–1914). African-American actress, dancer and singer. Name variations: Aida Overton Walker. Born 1870 in Richmond, VA; died Oct 11, 1914, in New York, NY; m. George Walker (singer and dancer), June 22, 1899 (died 1911). ❖ Performed on tours with Black Patti company but is thought to have received little formal training in dance; worked with great co-stars, including Bert Williams, George Walker and Sissieretta Jones; appeared on Broadway in *Sons of Ham* (1900), *In Dahomey* (1902), *In Abyssinia* (1906) and *Bandanna Land* (1908).

WALKER, A'Lelia (1885–1931). African-American hostess and literary patron. Name variations: Lelia Walker (changed her name to A'Lelia as an adult). Born Lelia McWilliams in Vicksburg, Mississippi, June 6, 1885; died in Long Branch, New Jersey, Aug 1931; dau. of Sarah (Breedlove) McWilliams (the future Madame C. J Walker) and Moses (Jeff) McWilliams (laborer); graduate of Knoxville College in Tennessee; m. a man named Robinson, c. 1905 (div. 1914); m. Wiley Wilson (physician), 1919 (div. 1923); m. James Arthur Kennedy (physician, div.); children: (adopted during 1st marriage) Mae Walker Robinson. ❖ Heiress, hostess and literary patron whose social gatherings brought together some of the most colorful figures of the Harlem Renaissance; dau. of Madame C. J. Walker, was raised in Indianapolis, Indiana; arrived in New York City to manage the Walker Corporation's Harlem headquarters (1914); mother died (1919); opened the Dark Tower, a literary and artistic salon in her New York townhouse (1928). ❖ See also *Women in World History*.

WALKER, Alice (1944—). American novelist, poet and short-story writer. Born Alice Malsenior Walker, Feb 8, 1944, in Eatonton, GA; dau. of Willie Lee Walker and Minnie Tallulah (Grant) Walker (sharecroppers); attended Spelman College; Sarah Lawrence College, BA, 1965; m. Melvyn Rosenman Leventhal (Jewish civil rights attorney), 1967 (div. 1977); children: Rebecca Grant (b. 1969). ❖ Works trace black history from slavery through Civil Rights Movement, rejecting role of victim for black characters, especially women; helped to develop black feminist literary criticism and bring neglected black women writers to attention of critics; founded publishing company Wild Trees Press; won Pulitzer Prize for *The Color Purple* (1982); other works include *The Third Life of Grange Copeland* (1970), *Revolutionary Petunias* (1973), *In Love and Trouble: Stories of Black Women* (1973), *Meridian* (1976), *You Can't Keep a Good Woman Down* (1981), *In Search of Our Mothers' Gardens: Womanist Prose* (1983), *Horses Make a Landscape Look More Beautiful* (1985), *The Temple of My Familiar* (1989), *Finding the Green Stone* (1991), *Possessing the Secret of Joy* (1992), *By the Light of My Father's Smile* (1998), *Absolute Trust in the Goodness of the Earth: New Poems* (2003), and *Now is the Time to Open Your Heart* (2004). ❖ See also Erma Davis Banks and Keith Byerman, *Alice Walker: An Annotated Bibliography, 1968–1986* (Garland, 1989); Henry Louis Gates and Anthony K. Appiah, eds, *Alice Walker: Critical Perspectives Past and Present* (Amistad, 1993).

WALKER, Barbara Jo (1926–2000). Miss America and TV host. Name variations: Barbara W. Hummel. Born Mar 12, 1926, in Memphis, TN; died June 7, 2000, in Memphis; graduate of University of Memphis, 1948; m. John V. Hummel (physician); children: 3. ❖ Named Miss Memphis (1947); named Miss America (1947), the last to be crowned in a swimsuit; was one of the 1st female daytime tv talk show hosts in the nation. ❖ See also Frank Deford, *There She Is* (Viking, 1971).

WALKER, Betty (1928–1982). American actress and comedian. Born Aug 7, 1928; died July 26, 1982, in New York, NY. ❖ Broadway appearances include *Springtime Folly, Middle of the Night, The Passion of Josef D,* and *Ready When You Are C. B.*; best known for comedy monologues that led off with "Hello, Ceil?"

WALKER, Madame C. J. (1867–1919). African-American entrepreneur. Name variations: Sarah Walker; Sarah Breedlove McWilliams Walker; Sarah Breedlove McWilliams. Born Sarah Breedlove on Dec 23, 1867, on a cotton plantation in Delta, Louisiana; died at the mansion she built in

Irvington, New York, May 25, 1919; dau. of Owen Breedlove and Minerva Breedlove (field hands and former slaves); m. Moses (Jeff) McWilliams (laborer), 1881 (died 1887); m. John Davis, c. 1890 (div. c. 1903); m. Charles J. Walker (journalist), Jan 4, 1906 (div. 1912); children: (1st m.) Lelia McWilliams, later A'Lelia Walker (b. 1885). ❖ Laundress and daughter of former slaves, who invented hair-care products for black women which she turned into a multimillion-dollar business; was orphaned at 7 during a yellow fever epidemic; moved to Vicksburg with her sister when she was 10 (1877); at 14, married Moses McWilliams (1881), who died in an accident (1887); with infant daughter, moved to St. Louis where she supported herself as a laundress and attended night school; managed to send her daughter to college after years of labor over a washtub; developed a formula to straighten hair, targeted to black female customers (1905); embarked on 18-month sales trip to 9 states, including New York, speaking in churches, Masonic and public halls to promote her product; established the headquarters of the Madame C. J. Walker Manufacturing Co. in Pittsburgh, to operate the mail-order business more efficiently (1908); with daughter, opened a training center for Walker agents in Pittsburgh and called it Lelia College; established a manufacturing plant in Indianapolis (1910); expanded operations to New York City (1913); became a speaker not only for her products, but for her race and gender; also worked to end lynching; as one of the greatest capitalists in America, amassed a personal fortune, contributing to various black causes, from education to social protest. ❖ See also A'Lelia Perry Bundles, *Madame C. J. Walker* (Chelsea House, 1991) and *On Her Own Ground: The Life and Times of Madam C. J. Walker* (Scribner, 2001); and *Women in World History.*

WALKER, Cath (1920–1993). *See Walker, Kath.*

WALKER, Charlotte (1876–1958). American stage and screen star. Born Dec 29, 1876, in Galveston, TX; died Mar 23, 1958, in Kerrville, TX; m. Dr. John Haden, 1896 (div. 1902); m. Eugene Walter, c. 1910 (div. 1930); children: Sara Haden (actress). ❖ Made stage debut with Richard Mansfield's company (1895); starred, or was featured, in *Sag Harbor, The Crisis, Betsy, Trilby, The Prince Chap, On Parole, The Warrens of Virginia, The Wolf, Just a Wife, The Skylark* and *A Sleeping Clergyman*; retired from the stage (1934); appeared in 30 films, including as June Tolliver in *The Trail of the Lonesome Pine* (1915).

WALKER, Colleen (1956—). American golfer. Born Aug 16, 1956, in Jacksonville, Fl; attended Florida State University; m. Ron Bakich. ❖ Won Mayflower Classic (1987), Boston Five Classic (1988), Circle K Tucson Open (1990), Lady Keystone Open (1991), Oldsmobile LPGA Classic, Corning Classic, and SAFECO Classic (1992), du Maurier Classic and Star Bank LPGA Classic (1997); won Hy-Vee Classic on Senior Tour (2001). Awarded Vare Trophy (1988).

WALKER, Dimples (1887–1975). *See Walker, Lillian.*

WALKER, Edith Campbell (d. 1945). *See Campbell, Edith.*

WALKER, Edyth (1867–1950). American opera singer and teacher. Born Minnie Edith Walker, Mar 27, 1867, in Hopewell, NY; died Feb 19, 1950, in New York, NY; dau. of Marquis de Lafayette Walker and Mary (Purdy) Walker; graduate of Rome Free Academy (NY), 1884; studied with Anna Aglaia Orgeni at Dresden Conservatory, Germany; never married. ❖ Taught school in Rome (NY) for several years; made opera debut in Berlin as Fidès in *Le Prophète* (1894); debuted at Vienna Opera (1896), where her starring performance in *Der Evangelimann* so dazzled Austrian emperor Franz Joseph that he made her a Kammersängerin, the highest honor given in Austria and Germany to an opera singer; was lead mezzo-soprano at Vienna's Imperial Opera (1898–1903); debuted at Metropolitan Opera in NY as Amneris in *Aïda* (1903) and stayed for 3 years; debuted at Covent Garden, London (1908), taking the lead in the English premiere of *Elektra*; appeared with Munich Opera (1912–17); retired from the stage (1918); taught at American Conservatory in Fontainebleau (1933–36) and in NY. ❖ See also *Women in World History.*

WALKER, Ethel (1861–1951). Scottish painter and sculptor. Name variations: Dame Ethel Walker. Born June 9, 1861, in Edinburgh, Scotland; dau. of Arthur Walker and Isabella Robertson; attended Ridley School of Art, Putney Art School and Westminster School of Art; attended Slade School of Fine Art, 1892–94, studying with Frederick Brown and Walter Sickert. ❖ Began exhibiting portraits at Royal Academy (1898); developed individual style which drew on Impressionists; lived in Chelsea, but also painted seascapes from cottage in Robin Hood's Bay and associated with group of artists there;

represented Britain at Venice Biennale (1930, 1932) and at World Trade Fair in Chicago (1939); noted for portraits of young girls, flower paintings, mythical subjects and seascapes, as well as for visionary works such as *Nausicaa* (1920) and *The Zone of Love* (1931–33). Created Dame of British Empire (1943).

WALKER, Helen (1710–1791). Scottish heroine. Name variations: Jeannie Deans. Born in 1710 in Kirkudbrightshire, Scotland; died 1791. ❖ Immortalized as Jeannie Deans by Sir Walter Scott in *The Heart of Midlothian*, testified at her younger sister Isabella's trial when she was accused of infanticide (her honest testimony did nothing to help Isabella); after Isabella was handed the death sentence, walked to London (14 days) and successfully pled her case.

WALKER, Helen (1920–1968). American actress. Born July 17, 1920, in Worcester, MA; died Mar 10, 1968, in North Hollywood, CA; married twice, div. twice. ❖ Appeared on Broadway; co-starred in film debut with Alan Ladd in *Lucky Jordan*; other films include *Brewster's Millions, Cluny Brown, Call Northside 777, Impact, Duffy's Tavern, Murder He Says* and *Nightmare Alley*; suffered from ill health after a serious auto accident (1946), which curtailed her career and eventually forced her retirement (1955).

WALKER, Jeannetta Margaret (1864–1955). *See Blackie, Jeannetta Margaret.*

WALKER, June (1900–1966). American stage and screen actress. Born June 14, 1900, in Chicago, IL; died Feb 3, 1966, in Los Angeles, CA; m. Geoffrey Kerr (actor), 1926 (div. 1943); children: John Kerr (b. 1931, actor). ❖ Made stage debut (1918) and remained on stage for 40 years; originated the part of Lorelei Lee in *Gentlemen Prefer Blondes* (1926); starred or was featured in such NY plays as *Waterloo Bridge, The Farmer Takes a Wife, Green Grow the Lilacs, They Knew What They Wanted, Ladies of the Corridor* and *The Glass Slipper*; last appeared in *Blue Denim* (1958); appeared in many films, including *War Nurse, Through Different Eyes, The Unforgiven* and *A Child Is Waiting.*

WALKER, Kath (1920–1993). Australian Aborigine poet. Name variations: Cath Walker; (Aboriginal name) Oodgeroo Noonuccal. Born Nov 3, 1920, on Minjerriba (North Stradbroke Island), Queensland, Australia; died 1993; educated to primary school level; children: 2 sons. ❖ Became the 1st Aborigine to publish a book of poems with the appearance of *We Are Going* (1964), in which she made a plea for human and Christian rights to be extended to Aborigines, and pointed to a long list of discriminatory practices; established an Aboriginal educational and cultural center on Stradbroke Island; lectured and tutored at several institutions, including University of the South Pacific; officially changed name to the Aboriginal Oodgeroo Noonuccal (1988); also wrote *The Dawn Is at Hand* (1966), *My People* (1970), (compilation of Aboriginal legends) *Stradbroke Dreamtime* (1972), *Father Sky and Mother Earth* (1981), *Little Fella: Poems by Kath Walker* (1987), *Kath Walker in China* (1988), *The Rainbow Serpent: O. N. and Kabul Oodgeroo Noonuccal* (1990), *My People: Oodgeroo* (1990) and *Shoemaker* (1994). Received Jesse Litchfield Award (1967) and Mary Gilmore Medal (1977); named Member of the Order of the British Empire (MBE, 1970), though she rejected the honor (1988) in protest of England's bicentennial celebrations of European settlement, one she described as "200 years of humiliation and brutality to the Aboriginal people." ❖ See also *Women in World History.*

WALKER, Laura (1970—). American swimmer. Born July 1970; attended University of Houston. ❖ At Seoul Olympics, won a bronze medal in 4 x 100-meter freestyle relay (1988).

WALKER, Lelia (1885–1931). *See Walker, A'Lelia.*

WALKER, Lillian (1887–1975). American silent-screen actress. Name variations: Dimples Walker. Born April 21, 1887, in Brooklyn, NY; died Oct 10, 1975, in Trinidad; m. Eugene W. Senior. ❖ Appeared in early Vitagraph comedies as Dimples Walker, often opposite John Bunny (1911–17); with her own company, Crest Productions (1918–22), appeared in more serious roles in such films as *The Inherited Taint, The Blue Envelope Mystery, Troublesome Stepdaughters, Kitty MacKay, The Grain of Dust* and *The Embarrassment of Riches.*

WALKER, Lucy (1836–1916). English mountaineer. Born in 1836; died in 1916; dau. of Francis Walker (mountaineer); sister of Horace Walker (a mountaineer); lived in Liverpool. ❖ Climbed Finsteraarhorn and the Monte Rosa (Dufourspitze), the 2nd highest peak in Europe (1862); climbed the Eiger, Rimpfischorn, and Balmhorn (1864), then ascended the Jungfrau, the Weisshorn, Dom des Mischabels, and the Mönch; ascended the Aiguille Verte (1870); climbed the Matterhorn by the Hörnli route (1871), the 19th ascent of the mountain and the 1st by a woman; missed only two climbing seasons (1858–79)—the 1st, when her father died in 1872; served as president of the Ladies' Alpine Club (1913–15). ❖ See also *Women in World History*.

WALKER, Lucy (1903–1987). *See Sanders, Dorothy Lucie.*

WALKER, Maggie Lena (1867–1934). African-American financier and activist. Born Maggie Lena, July 15, 1867, in Richmond, Virginia; died Dec 15, 1934; dau. of ex-slave Elizabeth Draper, later Elizabeth Draper Mitchell, and (likely) Irish-American abolitionist Eccles Cuthbert; m. Armstead Walker, Sept 14, 1886; children: Russell Eccles Talmage Walker (b. 1890); Armstead Mitchell Walker (1893–1893); Melvin DeWitt Walker (b. 1897). ❖ The 1st female bank president in US, was also a champion of racial and women's equality; mother married William Mitchell (May 27, 1868), who would become head waiter at the exclusive St. Charles Hotel in central Richmond; stepfather was robbed and murdered (Feb 1876); began helping mother take in laundry; at 14, joined mutual aid society, Independent Order of Saint Luke (1881); taught school (1883–86); served as executive secretary treasurer of Independent Order of St. Luke's (1899–1934), turning it into one of the most successful mutual benefit societies in the country; founded *St. Luke Herald* (1902); became president of Saint Luke Penny Savings Bank of Richmond (1903); founded department store, Saint Luke Emporium (1905); suffered debilitating fall that injured legs (1907); son Russell killed husband by accident (1915); ran unsuccessfully for Virginia state superintendent of public instruction on Lily-Black Republican Party ticket (1921); became chair of the board, Consolidated Bank and Trust Co. (1930). In Richmond, a street, theater, and high school bear the name of Maggie Walker; her home, at 110½ East Leigh Street, has been designated the Maggie L. Walker National Historic Site. ❖ See also Wendell P. Dabney, *Maggie L. Walker: Her Life and Deeds* (Dabney, 1927); and *Women in World History*.

WALKER, Margaret (1915–1998). African-American writer. Born Margaret Abigail Walker, July 7, 1915, in Birmingham, Alabama; died Nov 30, 1998, in Chicago, Illinois; dau. of Sigismund Walker (minister in United Methodist Church) and Marion Dozier Walker (music teacher); Northwestern University, BA, 1932; University of Iowa, MA, 1940, PhD, 1965; m. Firnist James Alexander (disabled veteran), June 13, 1943 (died c. 1979); children: Marion (b. 1944), Firnist Jr. (b. 1946), Sigismund (b. 1949) and Margaret (b. 1954). ❖ Writer whose poetry and prose, especially her novel *Jubilee*, have become a recognized part of the African-American literary canon; helped by W. E. B. Du Bois, had 1st poem, "Daydreaming," published in *The Crisis*; employed with WPA Writers' Project in Chicago, where she met Arna Bontemps, Gwendolyn Brooks and Richard Wright; worked closely with Wright, helping him research and edit his novel *Native Son*; left Chicago (1939); published *For My People* (1942), the 1st book of poetry by a black woman to be issued since Georgia Douglas Johnson's *The Heart of a Woman and Other Poems* (1918); began teaching career at Livingstone College in Salisbury, North Carolina (1941); was 1st black poet chosen for Yale University's Series of Younger Poets (1941); lectured and read poetry (1943–48); taught at Jackson State College in Mississippi (1949–79); published *Jubilee* (1966), based on her great-grandmother's life, which won the Houghton Mifflin Literary Fellowship Award, sold millions of copies, was translated into 6 languages, and produced as an opera; also published 3 more vols. of poetry: *Ballad of the Free* (1966), *Prophets for a New Day* (1970) and *October Journey* (1973); published the critical biography, *Richard Wright: Daemonic Genius* (1988), followed by *This Is My Century: New and Collected Poems* (1989). ❖ See also *How I Wrote Jubilee and Other Essays on Life and Literature* (Ed. by Maryemma Graham, Feminist Press, 1990); Nikki Giovanni and Margaret Walker, *A Poetic Equation: Conversations Between Nikki Giovanni and Margaret Walker* (Howard U. Press, 1974); and *Women in World History*.

WALKER, Mary Broadfoot (c. 1888–1974). Scottish pharmacologist. Name variations: Dr. Mary Broadfoot Walker. Born c. 1888 in Croft-an-Righ, Wigtown, Scotland; died Dec 7, 1974, in Wigtown; sister of Gracie Walker (physician); Glasgow & Edinburgh Medical College for Women, MBChB, 1913. ❖ Joined Royal Army Medical Corps and served as ward physician at 63rd General Hospital in Malta (1914–18); was assistant medical officer in Poor Law Service at St. Alfege's Hospital in Greenwich (1920–36); moved to St. Leonard's Hospital in Shoreditch (1936); became member of Royal College of Physicians (1932); focused on mysterious familial disease, myasthenia gravis (MG) which causes

chronic fatigue and muscle weakness and periodic paralysis; was 1st to recognize association between familial periodic paralysis and hypokalaemia; began treating patients with injections of physostigmine or neostigmine and demonstrated that treatment offered temporary relief. Created Dame of British Empire (1943); awarded Jean Hunter Prize from Royal College of Physicians.

WALKER, Mary Edwards (1832–1919). American surgeon. Born Nov 26, 1832, in Oswego, New York; died in Oswego, Feb 21, 1919; dau. of Alvah Walker (carpenter-farmer) and Vesta (Whitcomb) Walker; obtained medical degree from Syracuse Medical College, 1855, and 2nd medical degree from Hygeia Therapeutic College (NY), 1862; m. Dr. Albert Miller, in 1855 (div. 1869); no children. ❖ Surgeon awarded the Congressional Medal of Honor for her service during the Civil War, who asserted the rights of women in the medical profession, became an active supporter of suffrage and broader divorce rights for women, and challenged the impractical and unhealthy nature of women's dress; taught in Minetto, New York (1852); began medical practice in Columbus, Ohio (1855); moved practice to Rome, New York (1855); wrote letters to Dr. Lydia Sayer Hasbrouck's publication *Sybil* that helped to launch a crusade for dress reform (1857); spurned corsets and hoopskirts as uncomfortable, impractical, and such a hindrance to free movement as to limit women's labor potential; became volunteer assistant to Union Army surgeon at Patent Office Hospital in Washington, DC (1861); assigned to tent hospital near Fredericksburg (1862); assigned as surgeon to 52nd Ohio Infantry regiment in Tennessee (1863); captured by Confederates (April 10, 1864), was released after 4 months in prisoner exchange for a Confederate surgeon with the rank of major (Aug 1864); commissioned as acting assistant surgeon, the only female surgeon commissioned in the army (Oct 1864); awarded Congressional Medal of Honor by President Andrew Johnson (1866); elected president of National Dress Reform Association (1866); made lecture tour of England (1866); helped organize Women's Suffrage Association for Ohio (1869); published *Hit*, about divorce (1871), and *Unmasked, or the Science of Immorality*, about infidelity in men (1878); was a candidate for Congress (1890), then a candidate for US Senate (1891); was a delegate to Democratic National Convention (1892); published "Crowning Constitutional Argument," on women's franchise (1907). Inducted into Women's Hall of Fame at Seneca Falls (2000). ❖ See also *Women in World History*.

WALKER, Matilda R. (1917–2003). *See Peters, Roumania.*

WALKER, Michelle (1952—). English golfer. Born Dec 17, 1952, in Leeds, Yorkshire, England. ❖ Won British Open (1971, 1972); won Trans-Mississippi (1972), the 1st British woman in 36 years to an American tournament; won Spanish Open (1973); won Lambert and Butler Match Play (1980); member of Curtis Cup team (1972).

WALKER, Nancy (1922–1992). American actress, comedian, and director. Born Anna Myrtle Swoyer, May 10, 1922, in Philadelphia, Pennsylvania; died Mar 25, 1992, in Studio City, California; dau. of comedian Dewey Swoyer (stage name Dewey Barto) and Myrtle (Lawler) Swoyer (also a vaudevillian); m. Gar Moore (div.); m. David Craig (dancer and vocal coach); children: Miranda Craig. ❖ With her brassy, confident stage presence and talent for comedy, made stage debut on Broadway (1941), as Blind Date in *Best Foot Forward*; continued on Broadway (1941–60); appeared in several films (1943–76); made tv guest appearances (late 1950s); made directorial debut with *UTBU* on Broadway (1956); appeared in various tv series (1970–92), including "Family Affair" (1970), "McMillan and Wife" (1971–76), "The Nancy Walker Show" (1976), "Blansky's Beauties" (1976), "True Colors" (1991–92) and as Ida Morgenstern in "The Mary Tyler Moore Show" (1970s) and "Rhoda" (1973–78); directed tv series episodes (mid-1970s); known as the Bounty paper towel spokeswoman. Received Emmy nominations for work on "McMillan and Wife" (1973, 1974, 1975), and "Rhoda" (1975). ❖ See also *Women in World History*.

WALKER, Nella (1880–1971). American actress. Born Mar 6, 1880 (some sources cite 1886), in Chicago, IL; died Mar 22, 1971, in Los Angeles, CA; m. Wilbur Mack (actor, div.). ❖ With husband, began career in vaudeville as the Mack and Walker team; made film debut in *Tanned Legs* (1929); appeared in character roles in over 100 films, including *The Vagabond Lover*, *Seven Keys to Baldpate*, *Indiscreet*, *Reunion in Vienna*, *All of Me*, *Madame Du Barry*, *Captain January*, *Stella Dallas*, *Young Dr. Kildare*, *When Tomorrow Comes*, *Kitty Foyle*, *Back Street*, *Hellzapoppin* and *Sabrina*.

WALKER, Nellie (1891–1964). *See Larsen, Nella.*

WALKER, Olene S. (1930—). American politician. Born Nov 15, 1930, in Ogden, Utah; Brigham Young University, BA, MA, and PhD; m. Myron Walker; children: 7. ❖ A Republican, served as 1st female lieutenant governor of Utah for more than a decade; became the 1st female governor of Utah (Nov 5, 2003), replacing Michael Leavitt who resigned; served until Jan 2005.

WALKER, Polly (b. 1908). American actress. Born Heather Eulalie Walker, 1908, in Chicago, IL; dau. of Alice Ethel (Pflieger) and John Alexander Walker; m. Frederick H. Moran. ❖ At 3, made stage debut with parents in Chicago as Patience in *Starlight* (1911) and NY debut in vaudeville; starred opposite George M. Cohan in *The Merry Malones* and *Billie*; on film, starred in *Hit the Deck*.

WALKER, Roumania (c. 1918–2003). *See Peters, Roumania.*

WALKER, Sarah Breedlove (1867–1919). *See Walker, Madame C. J.*

WALKINSHAW, Clementina (c. 1726–1802). Countess of Alberstroff. Name variations: Clementina Walkenshaw. Born c. 1726; died in 1802; mistress of Prince Charles Edward Stuart (d. 1788), known as Bonnie Prince Charlie, the Young Pretender; children: Charlotte (b. 1753), countess of Albany. ❖ Was the mistress of Prince Charles Edward Stuart (d. 1788), also known as Bonnie Prince Charlie, the Young Pretender, and was alleged to have been a Hanoverian spy.

WALKOWIAK, Daniela (1935—). Polish kayaker. Name variations: Daniela Pilecka-Lewicka; Daniela Walkowiakowna. Born Daniela Walkowiak, May 24, 1935, in Poland. ❖ At Rome Olympics, won a bronze medal in K1 500 meters (1960).

WALKOWIAKOWNA, Daniela (1935—). *See Walkowiak, Daniela.*

WALL, Geraldine (1912–1970). American stage, tv, and screen actress. Born June 24, 1912, in Chicago, IL; died June 22, 1970, in Woodland Hills, CA. ❖ Appeared on Broadway in *Heat Lightning, Three Men on a Horse, Three Blind Mice* and *The Love Nest*; films include *Valley of Decision, Winged Victory* and *High Barbaree*; on tv, appeared on "Perry Mason" series.

WALL, Lyndsay (1985—). American ice-hockey player. Born May 12, 1985, in Churchville, NY; attended University of Minnesota. ❖ Won a team silver medal at Salt Lake City Olympics (2002) and a team bronze medal at Torino Olympics (2006).

WALLACE, Bronwen (1945–1989). Canadian poet and short-story writer. Born 1945 in Kingston, Ontario, Canada; died 1989. ❖ Founded women's bookstore in Windsor, Ontario, and was active in women's groups; was writer-in-residence at University of Western Ontario; works include *Bread and Chocolate/Marrying into the Family* (with Mary di Michele, 1980), *Signs of the Former Tenant* (1983), *Common Magic* (1985), *The Stubborn Particulars of Grace* (1987), *Keep That Candle Burning Bright and Other Poems* (1991), *People You'd Trust Your Life To* (1992), and *Arguments With the World* (1992); also made 2 films with Chris Whynot.

WALLACE, Jean (1923–1990). American actress. Born Jean Wallasek, Oct 12, 1923, in Chicago, IL; died Feb 14, 1990, in Beverly Hills, CA; m. Franchot Tone (actor), 1941 (div. 1948); m. Cornel Wilde (actor), 1951 (died 1989). ❖ Was featured in such films as *Louisiana Purchase, When My Baby Smiles at Me, Jigsaw, The Good Humor Man, Native Son,* and *Star of India*; also starred opposite husband Cornel Wilde in a number of his independent films, including *Maracaibo, Lancelot and Guinevere, Beach Red,* and *No Blade of Grass*.

WALLACE, Lila Acheson (1889–1984). Canadian-born philanthropist and publisher. Born Lila Bell Acheson, Dec 25, 1889, in Virden, Manitoba, Canada; died May 1984 in Mount Kisco, NY; dau. of T. Davis Acheson (Presbyterian minister) and Mary E. (Huston) Acheson; graduate of University of Oregon in Eugene, 1917; m. DeWitt Wallace (publisher), Oct 15, 1921. ❖ The co-founder and publisher of *Reader's Digest* magazine, taught high school for 2 years (1917–19) and managed a Young Women's Christian Association (YWCA) summer home on an island in Puget Sound; with husband, founded *Reader's Digest* (1921) and built a global publishing empire from an idea that was ridiculed by others in the industry. The Lila and DeWitt Wallace Foundation donated generously to many arts organizations and to media such as National Public Radio and educational television. Received Medal of Freedom from President Richard Nixon (1972). ❖ See also Peter Canning, *American Dreamers: The Wallaces and Reader's Digest: An Insider's Story* (Simon and Schuster, 1996); and *Women in World History*.

WALLACE, Lucille (1898–1977). American pianist. Born in Chicago, IL, Feb 22, 1898; died in London, England, Mar 21, 1977; educated at Bush Conservatory and Vassar College; m. Clifford Curzon (British pianist), 1931; raised the 2 orphaned sons of singer Maria Cebotari. ❖ Studied music history with Guido Adler and social history with Alfons Dopsch at University of Vienna (1923); studied with Nadia Boulanger in Paris (1924); studied harpsichord with Wanda Landowska in Paris and piano with Artur Schnabel in Berlin; a musical scholar as well as a performing artist, grappled with problems centering around the proper historical and musical interpretation of piano music. ❖ See also *Women in World History*.

WALLACE, Maicel (1969—). *See Malone, Maicel.*

WALLACE, Mary (1959—). Irish politician. Born June 1959 in Dublin, Ireland; dau. of Tom Wallace (councillor); m. Declan Gannon. ❖ Elected to Seanad from Administrative Panel (1987–89); representing Fianna Fáil, elected to the 26th Dáil (1989–92) for Meath; returned to 27th–28th Dáil (1992–2000) and 29th Dáil (2002).

WALLACE, Nellie (1870–1948). Scottish music-hall comedian. Born Mar 18, 1870 (some sources cite 1882), in Glasgow, Scotland; died Nov 24, 1948, in London, England; m. W. J. Liddy (died). ❖ Regarded as one of few great woman pantomime actors of 1920s and 1930s, made stage debut as a clog dancer in a Birmingham music hall (1888); as La Petite Nellie, toured as a dancer, then appeared as one of the Three Sisters Wallace in music halls throughout the UK; popularized such songs as "I Was Born on a Friday," "Where are You Going to My Pretty Maid?" and "I Lost Georgie in Trafalgar Square"; appeared in London in *Aladdin, Dick Whittington, The Whirl of the World, Sky High, The Golden Toy,* and *The Sleeping Beauty*; films include *The Wishbone* (1933) and *Radio Parade of 1935*; collapsed and died after appearance in Royal Variety Show.

WALLACE, Regina (1886–1978). American stage and screen actress. Born Sept 1, 1886, in Trenton, NJ; died Feb 13, 1978, in Englewood, NJ. ❖ Made stage debut in *Good Little Devil* (1913), followed by *Pagans, The Breaking Point, The Show-Off, Antony and Cleopatra, The Male Animal* and *My Fair Lady,* among others; made film debut in *Du Barry Did All Right* (1937); other films include *Adventures of Martin Eden, The Male Animal, Because of Him, I Surrender Dear, The Dark Corner* and *Rachel and the Stranger*.

WALLACE, Sippie (1898–1986). African-American blues singer and pianist. Name variations: Beulah Belle Wallace. Born Beulah Belle Thomas, Nov 1, 1898, in Houston, TX; died Nov 1986 in Alameda, CA; coached in music by older brother George Thomas Jr.; m. Frank Seals (div.); m. Matthew Wallace. ❖ Sang with small bands in TX; moved to Chicago and formed the Thomas trio, with younger brother Hersal Thomas, a piano prodigy, and niece Hociel Thomas; with trio, released 1st record "Shorty George" and "Up the Country Blues," which sold 100,000 copies; often wrote her own blues songs, including "Jack O' Diamond" (1926), which featured Louis Armstrong; moved to Detroit, where trio folded; solo, signed a contract with Victor Records (1920) and put out a few strong recordings, including "Mighty Tight Woman," but faded into anonymity for many years; made 2 recordings (1945, 1959); toured Europe on folk-blues festival circuit (1966) and sang at NY's Lincoln Center (1977). ❖ See also *Women in World History*.

WALLACE, Zerelda G. (1817–1901). American temperance and suffrage leader. Born Zerelda Gray Sanders, Aug 6, 1817, in Millersburg, Kentucky; died Mar 19, 1901, in Cataract, Indiana; dau. of John H. Sanders and Polly C. (Gray) Sanders; m. David Wallace (lieutenant governor of Indiana), Dec 26, 1836 (died 1859); children: Mary Wallace; Agnes Wallace Steiner (who m. John H. Steiner); David Wallace Jr.; 3 who died in childhood; and 3 stepchildren, including the writer General Lew Wallace. ❖ Organized the Indiana state Women's Christian Temperance Union (WCTU, 1874); served as Indiana WCTU president (1877, 1879–83); helped organize the Indianapolis Equal Suffrage Society and became 1st president (1878); headed Franchise (suffrage) Department of the national WCTU (1883–88); was the inspiration for the character of Ben-Hur's mother in the 1880 novel *Ben-Hur*, which was written by her stepson. ❖ See also *Women in World History*.

WALLACH, Yonah (1944–1985). Israeli poet. Born 1944 in Tel Aviv, Israel; died of breast cancer, 1985, in Israel. ❖ A central figure in Israel's bohemian art circles in 1960s, was considered one of the nation's most fascinating and controversial poets; works include *Devarim* (Things, 1966), *Shney Ganim* (Two Gardens, 1969), *Shira* (Poetry, 1976).

WALLADA (fl. 11th c.). Spanish poet. Name variations: Walladah bint al-Mustakfi. Came from a ruling Arabic family, the daughter of the caliph of

Cordova. ❖ Led a rather leisured life and spent most of her years in intellectual pursuits; gathered around her poets, artists, and scholars from across Arabic Spain, patronizing their works and composing her own verse; never married, instead taking lovers, including Ibn Zaidun, one of early medieval Spain's greatest poets; able to live fairly independent of male control, reportedly even refused to wear the traditional veil of her culture. Of the numerous poems of hers that have survived, all are part of poetic "conversations" she held with Ibn Zaidun.

WALLADAH BINT AL-MUSTAKFI (fl. 11th c.). *See Wallada.*

WALLENDA, Helen (1910–1996). German-born trapeze artist. Born Helen Kreis, Dec 11, 1910, in Germany; died May 9, 1996, in Sarasota, FL; m. Karl Wallenda (circus performer), 1935 (fell to his death, 1978). ❖ At 16, joined her husband-to-be's Flying Wallendas (also known as the Great Wallendas), a daredevil circus act famed for performing highwire stunts without a net; with group, came to US (1928); was the peak of the family's famed 3-tier, 7-man pyramid; retired (1956). Over the years, 8 of the Wallendas died while performing.

WALLER, Anne (c. 1603–1662). British diarist. Name variations: Lady Anne Waller; Lady Anne Harcourt. Born Anne Paget in England, c. 1603; died in 1662; dau. of Lettice Knollys (c. 1583–1655) and William Paget of Beaudasert; m. Simon Harcourt (1603–1642, Royalist officer in the king's army), c. 1632; m. William Waller (Puritan); children: Mary, Frederick, and Phillip Harcourt. ❖ During a Dublin rebellion, first husband landed there with an army and was slain at the siege of Carrickmines (Mar 1642); kept a religious diary from 1649 to April 1661; was imprisoned with 2nd husband who was a Puritan (1659).

WALLER, Florence (1862–1912). English actress and manager. Name variations: Florence West; Mrs. Lewis Waller. Born Florence Brandon, Dec 15, 1862, in England; died Nov 14, 1912; dau. of Horace Brandon (solicitor); sister of Margaret Clement-Scott (actress) and Lady Arthur; m. Lewis Waller (1860–1915, actor-manager). ❖ Made stage debut as Mary Belton in *Uncle Dick's Darling* (1883), followed by *Favette, Adrienne Lecouvreur* (with Modjeska), *In Danger, The Still Alarm, Gladys* (title role), *Gloriana* (title role), *An Ideal Husband, A Woman's Reason, The Three Musketeers,* and *Tess* (title role), among others; had great success in title role in *Zaza*; often toured with her own company.

WALLER, Judith Cary (1889–1973). American broadcasting executive. Born Feb 19, 1889, in Oak Park, Illinois; died Oct 28, 1973, in Evanston, Illinois; dau. of John Duke Waller and Katherine (Short) Waller. ❖ Became manager of radio station WGU, later WMAQ (1922); created a classical music format for WMAQ; produced 1st play-by-play radio broadcast of a college football game (1924); brought the "Amos 'n' Andy" show to WMAQ (1928); became vice-president and general manager of WMAQ (1929); was most well known for the program "University of Chicago Round Table" which was launched in 1931 on WMAQ and later picked up by NBC; became educational director of the National Broadcasting Company's (NBC) Central Division (1931); wrote *Radio, The Fifth Estate* (1946); developed educational programming, creating the 1st successful tv show for pre-schoolers, "Ding Dong School"; retired from NBC (1957). ❖ See also *Women in World History.*

WALLER, Mrs. Lewis (1862–1912). *See Waller, Florence.*

WALLEY, Joan (1949—). English politician and member of Parliament. Born Joan Lorraine Walley, Jan 23, 1949, in Congleton, Cheshire; m. Jan Ostrowski, 1981. ❖ Representing Labour, elected to House of Commons for Stoke-on-Trent North (1992, 1997, 2001, 2005); focused on the environment.

WALLIN, Magdalena (1967—). *See Forsberg, Magdalena.*

WALLINGER, Veronika (1966—). *See Stallmaier, Veronika.*

WALLIS, Diana (1954—). English politician. Born June 28, 1954, in Hitchin, Hertfordshire, England. ❖ Qualified as a solicitor (1983); member of the National Executive of Women's Liberal Democrats (1993–95); as a member of the European Liberal, Democrat and Reform Party, elected to 5th European Parliament (1999–2004) and 6th (2004).

WALLIS, Ellen Lancaster (b. 1856). *See Lancaster-Wallis, Ellen.*

WALLIS, Martha Hyer (1924—). *See Hyer, Martha.*

WALLIS, Mary Ann Lake (1821–1910). New Zealand orphanage matron, grocer, and school administrator. Name variations: Marianne Dockray, Mary Ann Lake Dockery, Mary Coster. Born Marianne Dockray, probably on Oct 17, 1821 (baptized, Nov 14, 1821), in Dartford, Kent, England; died May 24, 1910; dau. of Robert Thornton Dockray (gardener) and Marianne (Lake) Dockray; m. John Philip Coster, 1842 (died 1843); m. Richard Wallis, 1844 (died 1882); children: (1st m.) 1; (2nd m.) 10. ❖ Immigrated to New Zealand with 1st husband (1842); opened small grocery shop in Nelson (1843); with 2nd husband, opened small school for girls (1850s); moved to Motueka and opened their home as orphanage. ❖ See also *Dictionary of New Zealand Biography* (Vol. 2).

WALLIS, Ruth Sawtell (1895–1978). American physical anthropologist and novelist. Born Ruth Sawtell, Mar 15, 1895, in Springfield, MA; died Jan 21, 1978; dau. of Grace Quimby Sawtell and Joseph Otis Sawtell (haberdasher); attended Vassar College, 1913; Radcliffe College, BA, 1919, MA in anthropology, 1923; Columbia University, PhD; m. Wilson D. Wallis (cultural anthropologist), 1931. ❖ Known for analysis of Azilian skeletal remains from France, children's growth studies, and ethnography of Micmac Indians (eastern Canada), published scholarly work *Azilian Skeletal Remains from Montardit (Ariege) France* (1931) and popular account *Primitive Hearths in the Pyrenees* (with Ida Treat, 1927); with Mildred Totter, was one of only two women who became charter members of American Association of Physical Anthropologists (1930); taught at Hamline University, St. Paul (early 1930s); worked with Works Progress Administration (WPA, 1935–37); launched 2nd career as novelist with *Too Many Bones* (1943); with husband, published ethnography of the Micmac, *The Micmac Indians of Eastern Canada* (1955), and work on Malecite Indians, *The Malecite Indians of New Brunswick* (1957); at Annhurst College in CT, began lecturing in sociology (1957), then became full professor (1967), then retired as its 1st professor emerita (1974).

WALLIS, Shani (1933—). English actress and singer. Born April 5, 1933, in Tottenham, England; dau. of James John Wallis and Ethel Caroline Wallis; sister of Leon Roy (jazz drummer); m. Bernie Rich, 1965; children: Rebecca Rich. ❖ Made London musical debut as Princess Marie in *Call Me Madam* (1952), followed by *Happy as a King, London Laughs, Wish You Were Here, Wonderful Town* and *Irma La Douce* (title role); starred in the Melbourne production of *Bells Are Ringing* (1958); made Broadway debut in *A Time for Singing* (1966) and later appeared in *42nd St.* (1985–87); reappeared in London in *Always* (1997); films include *A King in New York, Oliver!* (as Nancy), *Arnold, Terror in the Wax Museum* and *Round Numbers.*

WALLISER, Maria (1963—). Swiss Alpine skier. Born May 27, 1963, in Mosnang, Switzerland. ❖ Won a silver medal for downhill at Sarajevo Olympics (1984); won bronze medals for combined and giant slalom at Calgary Olympics (1988); at World championships, won gold medals for downhill and super-G (1987), then downhill (1989); won World Cup downhill titles (1984, 1986), super-G and giant slalom (1987), and overall (1986, 1987).

WALLMANN, Margarethe (1901–19922). German-born dancer, choreographer, and teacher. Name variations: Margarita Wallmann; Margaret Wallmann; Margarete Wallmann; Margherita Wallmann. Born, probably in Berlin, July 22, 1901; died in Monte Carlo, Monaco, May 2, 1992; studied ballet in Berlin under Eugenia Eduardowa and Olga Preobrazhenska, and later in Munich with Heinrich Kröll and Anna Ornelli. ❖ Leading exponent of expressionist dance in pre-Hitler Germany and the 1st woman to achieve international acclaim as an opera director, moved to Dresden to study modern dance with Mary Wigman (1923); founded dance school based on Wigman's style (1927); by 1929, had founded her own dance company, the Tänzer-Kollektiv (Dancers' Collective); staged premiere of *Das jüngste Gericht* (The Last Judgment, 1931) to music by Händel; closed dance school (1932), after an accident ended her career as an expressionist dancer; debuted in Salzburg as an opera producer with Gluck's *Orpheus and Eurydice* and choreographed Max Reinhardt's *Faust* (1933); was a regular guest at Salzburg Festival until 1937, serving as its chief choreographer; fled Germany when Nazis came to power (1933); turned away from Wigman's ideas on modern dance, preferring more traditional ballet-oriented dance styles; appointed ballet mistress of Vienna's Staatsoper (State Opera, 1934); at La Scala, choreographed operas by Boïto, Gluck, and Verdi, and ballets by Respighi (*The Birds* and *Ancient Airs and Dances*); also choreographed Greta Garbo film *Anna Karenina* (1935); had last Vienna triumph with *Carmen* (1937); fled Austria for Buenos Aires (1938) and worked for next decade with Teatro

Colón; returned to Europe (1948); for next 4 decades, worked as an opera director; in Italy, directed an astonishing number of operas—14 by Verdi alone—many of these at La Scala; while directing operas across the range of the lyric repertory, including Maria Callas in *Norma* and *La Gioconda,* enjoyed specializing in modern works, including operas by contemporary composers such as Strauss, Stravinsky, Falla, Milhaud, Castelnuovo-Tedesco and Penderecki; directed world premiere of Poulenc's *Dialogues des Carmélites* (1957); also directed operas at Covent Garden, Metropolitan Opera and Chicago's Lyric Opera. ❖ See also *Women in World History.*

WALLMODEN, Amalie Sophie Marianne (1704–1765). German noblewoman and mistress of George II. Name variations: Sophia von Walmoden, Countess of Yarmouth; Amalie Sophie Marianne Wallmoden von Wendt. Born Amalie Sophie Marianne Wallmoden von Wendt in 1704 in Germany; died Oct 20, 1765 in Hanover, Germany; dau. of Johann Franz Dietrich von Wendt and Friederike Charlotte von dem Bussche-Ippenburg; children: Johann Ludwig Graf von Wallmoden-Gimborn (illeg. son of King George II). ❖ Mistress of George II, was born to German noble family; made acquaintance of monarch in Hanover and became the 3rd of his mistresses; brought to England upon death of his wife, Queen Caroline of Ansbach (1737); created countess of Yarmouth; her illegitimate son had success in the military and became a noted collector of art.

WALLWORK, Elizabeth (1883–1969). New Zealand artist and art teacher. Name variations: Elizabeth Donaldson. Born July 20, 1883, at Broughton, Lancashire, England; died June 4, 1969, at Christchurch, New Zealand; dau. of John Donaldson (fishmonger) and Elizabeth Ann (Hibbert) Donaldson; m. Richard Wallwork (artist), 1910; children: 1 daughter. ❖ Studied at Municipal School of Art, Manchester (1899–1906), and Slade School of Fine Art (1906–08); exhibited with husband at Royal Academy of Arts and Salon in Paris (1910); immigrated to New Zealand (1911); with husband, became working member of Canterbury Society of Arts; established career as portrait painter, later painting and exhibiting landscapes; taught at Canterbury College School of Art (1925 and 1946). ❖ See also *Dictionary of New Zealand Biography* (Vol. 4).

WALMODEN, Amalie Sophie Marianne (1704–1765). *See Wallmoden, Amalie Sophie Marianne.*

WALN, Nora (1895–1964). American journalist and author. Born June 4, 1895, in Grampian, Pennsylvania; died Sept 27, 1964; dau. of Thomas Lincoln Waln and Lilla (Quest) Waln (both Quakers); educated at Swarthmore College in Swarthmore, Pennsylvania; m. George Edward Osland-Hill (in British government service), in 1922; children: one daughter. ❖ Published *House of Exile* (1933), based on her experience of living with a Chinese family for two years (1920–22); on eve of World War II, published a perceptive book on Nazi Germany, *The Approaching Storm: One Woman's Story of Germany, 1934–1938* (released in US as *Reaching for the Stars,* 1939). ❖ See also *Women in World History.*

WALOWA, Natalia (1938—). *See Kotowna-Walowa, Natalia.*

WALPOLE, Dorothy Fanny (1826–1913). *See Nevill, Dorothy Fanny.*

WALPOLE, Maria (1736–1807). Countess of Waldegrave and duchess of Gloucester. Name variations: Maria, Lady Waldegrave; Maria, Dowager Countess of Waldegrave; Maria of Waldegrave; Maria Gloucester. Born Maria Walpole on July 10, 1736 (some sources cite 1735), at St. James's Palace, Westminster, London, England; died Aug 22, 1807, at Oxford Lodge, Brompton, Middlesex; illeg. dau. of Sir Edward Walpole (elder brother of Horace Walpole and son of British minister Robert Walpole) and his mistress Dorothy Clement (milliner's apprentice, died 1739); m. James, 2nd earl of Waldegrave (member of Parliament, Lord of the Treasury and tutor to the prince of Wales), May 15, 1759 (died 1763); m. William Henry Hanover (1743–1805), 1st duke of Gloucester and Edinburgh (brother of George III, king of England), on Sept 6, 1766; children: (1st m.) Anne Horatio Waldegrave (1759–1801, who m. Lord Hugh Seymour); Elizabeth Laura, countess of Waldegrave (1760–1816, who m. George, 4th earl of Waldegrave); Charlotte Maria Waldegrave (1761–1808, who m. George Henry, duke of Grafton); (2nd m.) Sophia Matilda (1773–1844); Caroline Augusta Mary (1774–1775); William Frederick (1776–1834), duke of Edinburgh and Gloucester. William Henry Hanover also had a daughter with Lady Almeria Carpenter: Louisa Maria (1762–1835, who m. Godfrey Bosville, 3rd baron of Slate). ❖ With 1st husband, worked on his memoirs (much of the original manuscript is in her handwriting); after he died (1763), was left in control of his copious correspondence, memoirs, and other papers, many of which were

eventually published and provide insight into daily politics of 18th-century England; was seen constantly in public with William Henry, duke of Gloucester (King George III's younger brother), for several years (the king, fearful that William Henry would marry the illegitimate Lady Waldegrave, issued the Royal Marriage Act of 1772, stipulating that no member of the royal family could marry without the consent of the crown); confessed to her father (1772) that she had already married the duke, in a private ceremony in 1766, and was pregnant; her marriage was validated by Parliament before the birth of her daughter; banned from court. ❖ See also Violet Biddulph, *The Three Ladies Waldegrave and Their Mother* (Peter Davies, 1938); and *Women in World History.*

WALPURA or WALPURGA (c. 710–777). *See Walpurgis.*

WALPURGIS (c. 710–777). English saint and missionary. Name variations: Walberga; Walburg; Walburga; Walburge; Walpura; Walpurga. Born c. 710; died in 777 (some sources cite 779) at the monastery of Heidenheim (also seen as Heidenham), Germany; dau. of a petty noble of Wessex; sister of St. Willibald and St. Winibald; never married; no children. ❖ Following father's death, entered the convent of Wimborne; along with Lioba and a number of other nuns, was chosen to accompany St. Boniface to Germany to help convert the Germanic tribes; spent 2 years traveling among the German people, then was made abbess over the nuns at the foundation of Heidenheim, a double monastery established several years earlier by Walpurgis' brothers, Saint Willibald and Saint Winibald; on Winibald's death, was given responsibility for the monks as well, putting her in a position of considerable power. Feast days are Feb 25 and May 1. ❖ See also *Women in World History.*

WALPURGIS, Maria Antonia (1724–1780). *See Maria Antonia of Austria.*

WALSH, Adela Pankhurst (1885–1961). *See Pankhurst, Adela.*

WALSH, Jill Paton (1937—). *See Paton Walsh, Jill.*

WALSH, Kay (1914–2005). English actress and dancer. Name variations: Grace Stansfield. Born Kathleen Walsh, Aug 27, 1914, in London, England; died April 16, 2005; m. David Lean (film director), Nov 23, 1940 (div. 1949). ❖ Began career as a dancer; starred in many British films before taking on character roles; films include *Meet Mr. Penny, Sons of the Sea, The Mind of Mr. Reeder, The Middle Watch, All at Sea, In Which We Serve, This Happy Breed, Oliver Twist* (as Nancy), *Stage Fright, Encore, Young Bess, Now and Forever, The Horse's Mouth, Greyfriars Bobby, Tunes of Glory, The Ruling Class, The L-Shaped Room* and *Scrooge.*

WALSH, Kerri (1978—). American volleyball player. Born Aug 15, 1978, in San Jose, CA; Stanford University, BA in American Studies. ❖ Competed in the Sydney Olympics with the US national volleyball team as outside hitter (2000); with Misty May, won World championship (2003, 2005) and had a 59-match winning streak going into the Athens Olympics, where they won a gold medal for beach volleyball (2004).

WALSH, Loretta (1898–c. 1988). American Navy officer. Born 1898 in Philadelphia, PA; died possibly Oct 11, 1988, in Philadelphia. ❖ At 18, became 1st woman to enlist in US Navy (Mar 21, 1917), at a time when Navy needed to hire women to ensure adequate staffing during WWI; became chief yeoman in charge of recruiting for Naval Coast Defense Reserve.

WALSH, María Elena (1930—). Argentinean poet and children's writer. Name variations: Maria Walsh. Born Feb 1, 1930, in Buenos Aires, Argentina. ❖ Praised by critics for rich lyricism; works include *Otoño imperdonable* (1947), *Apenas viaje* (1948), *Casi milagro* (1958), *Hecho a mano* (1965), *Cancionero contra el mal de ojo* (1976), *Los poemas* (1984), *Novios de antaño* (1990), and *Desaventuras en el País-Jardin-de-Infantes* (1993); also wrote children's books, including *Tutú Marambá* (1960), *Aire libre* (1967), *Angelito* (1974) and *Chaucha y palito* (1977).

WALSH, Mary (1929–1976). Irish politician. Born Oct 1929 in Tinahely, Co. Wicklow, Ireland; died Aug 1976. ❖ Representing Fine Gael, elected to Seanad from Cultural and Educational Panel (1973); died while in office.

WALSH, Stella (1911–1980). Polish-American runner. Name variations: Stanislava Walaciewicz; Stanislawa Walasiewicz; Stanislawa Walasiewicz-Olson. Born Stanislawa Walasiewicz, April 3, 1911, in Rypin, Poland; murdered Dec 4, 1980, in Cleveland, OH; m. briefly to Harry Olson. ❖ Track-and-field star, the 1st woman to run the 100-yard dash in under 11 seconds, who set numerous world records in 30 years of competition, was posthumously accused of being a man, and later cleared of this accusation by an Olympic Committee; collected 1,100 trophies in track and field over a 30-year career; astounded the track-and-field world by running the 50-yard dash in 6.1 seconds in Madison Square Garden (1930); ran 100 yards in 10.8 seconds (1930), the 1st time a woman clocked under 11 seconds; competed for Poland at Los Angeles Olympics, winning a gold medal in the 100 meters with a world-record time of 11.9 seconds (1932); won a silver medal for Poland at Berlin Olympics in the 100 meters with a time of 11.7 seconds (1936); broke AAU women's national record for 70 yards with a time of 8.2 seconds (1935); became an American citizen (1947); organized track, field and other women's sports and recreation programs for Cleveland recreation program (1970s); edited the sports section of a Polish newspaper in Cleveland. ❖ See also *Women in World History*.

WALSH, Waris (1967—). *See Dirie, Waris.*

WALSINGHAM, Frances (d. 1631). Countess of Essex. Name variations: Frances Devereux. Interred on Feb 17, 1631, at Tonbridge Church; dau. of Francis Walsingham and Ursula St. Barbe; m. Sir Philip Sidney; m. Robert Devereux, 2nd earl of Essex, in 1590; m. Richard de Burgh, 4th earl of Clanricarde, before April 8, 1603; children: (1st m.) Elizabeth Sidney; (2nd m.) Frances Devereux (d. 1674); Robert Devereux (b. 1591), 3rd/20th earl of essex; Dorothy Devereux (d. 1636, who m. Henry Shirley, Bt. 2nd); (3rd m.) Honora de Burgh.

WALTER, Anne (1865–1939). *See Fearn, Anne Walter.*

WALTER, Annika (1975—). German diver. Born Feb 5, 1975, in Rostock, Germany. ❖ Won a silver medal at Atlanta Olympics (1996); won FINA Grand Prix at Ronneby (2000).

WALTER, Cornelia Wells (1813–1898). American journalist. Born June 7, 1813, in Boston, Massachusetts; died Jan 31, 1898, in Boston; dau. of Lynde Walter and Ann (Minshull) Walter; m. William Bordman Richards (iron and steel dealer), Sept 22, 1847 (died 1877); children: Annie (died at age 3); Elise Bordman (b. 1848); twins (b. 1853) Walter (died at 6 months) and William Reuben; and possibly 1 other child. ❖ After older brother Lynde Minshull Walter's death (1842), took over his position as editor at *Boston Transcript*; wrote columns about Boston social and literary life, and spoke in opposition to female suffrage, unorthodox religious theories, the Mexican War, and the annexation of Texas, and in support of higher education for women; also traded barbs with author Edgar Allan Poe; upon marriage (1847), retired as editor and devoted herself to domestic duties, thereafter contributing occasionally to the *Transcript*; published a history of Cambridge's famous cemetery, *Mount Auburn Illustrated* (1847).

WALTER, Judith (1845–1917). *See Gautier, Judith.*

WALTER, Louisa (1978—). German field-hockey player. Born Dec 2, 1978, in Germany. ❖ Won a team gold medal at Athens Olympics (2004).

WALTER, Lucy (c. 1630–1658). Welsh mistress of Charles II. Name variations: Mrs. Barlow or Lucy Barlow; incorrectly Lucy Walters and Lucy Waters. Born c. 1630 in Paris, France; died in 1658 in Paris; dau. of Richard Walter of Haverfordwest; mistress of Colonel Robert Sidney, in 1644; mistress of Charles II (1630–1685), king of England (r. 1661–1685), from 1648 to 1650; mistress of Henry Bennet, in 1650; children: (with Charles II) James Crofts Scott, duke of Monmouth (April 9, 1649–1685); possibly Mary Crofts (b. May 6, 1651, who m. William Sarsfield). ❖ Went to The Hague (1644), where she was a colonel's mistress; became the famed mistress of England's King Charles II (1648–50); after 1650, was mistress to a succession of other men; was in Cologne when Charles' friends bribed her to return to England (1656), where she was arrested as a spy and sent back to Holland; died in Paris 2 years later. ❖ See also Elizabeth Goudge (historical novel), *The Child from the Sea* (1970); and *Women in World History*.

WALTER, Martina (1963—). East German rower. Born Oct 5, 1963, in East Germany. ❖ At Seoul Olympics, won a gold medal in coxed fours (1988).

WALTER, Silja (1919—). Swiss nun, poet and playwright. Name variations: Sister Maria Hedwig. Born Cécile Walter, April 23, 1919, in Rickenbach, Switzerland. ❖ Attended the seminary at Menzingen (1933–38); took Benedictine vows in the monastery of Fahr near Zurich (1949); became Sister Maria Hedwig and remained there for more than 50 years; works, characterized by religious themes, include *Die ersten Gediche* (1945), *Der Tanz des Geshorsams oder die Strohmatte:*

Gedichte (1970), *Die Feuertaube. Neue Gedichte fur meinen Bruder* (1985), *Feuerturm* (1987), and *Der Wolkenbaum* (1992).

WALTER, Steffi (1962—). *See Walter-Martin, Steffi.*

WALTER-MARTIN, Steffi (1962—). East German luge athlete. Name variations: Steffi Martin; Steffi Walter; Steffi Martin-Walter. Born Steffi Martin, Sept 17, 1962, in East Germany. ❖ Won a gold medal at Sarajevo Olympics (1984) and a gold medal at Calgary Olympics (1988), both for luge singles; won World championship (1983, 1985) and World Cup (1984).

WALTERS, Barbara (1929—). American tv journalist. Born Sept 25, 1929, in Boston, Massachusetts; dau. of Lou Walters (show-business entrepreneur) and Dena (Seletsky) Walters; Sarah Lawrence College, BA in English, 1951; m. Bob Katz (businessman), 1955 (div. 1958); m. Lee Gruber (producer), 1963 (div. 1976); m. Merv Adelman (movie studio executive), 1986 (div. 1992); children: (adopted) Jacqueline Gruber. ❖ Award-winning tv journalist, particularly known for her celebrity interviews and news specials, who was the 1st woman to co-host a major network news program; had 1st job in broadcasting writing press releases for WNBC in New York City; hired as a writer for "Today" (1961) and eventually given on-screen reporting segments on topics the network deemed of interest to women; improved journalistic fortunes when she became part of the press corps traveling to Egypt with Jacqueline Kennedy (1962); named co-host for "Today" (1974); became the industry's 1st news anchor to earn a salary of $1 million when she moved to ABC to co-anchor its evening newscast (1976); in the years since, has interviewed everyone from Fidel Castro to Ronald Reagan, co-hosted ABC's long-running news magazine show "20/20," as well as a string of Barbara Walters Specials and "The View," and was presented with 7 Emmy awards; by the end of the century, was the highest-paid and longest-employed woman in broadcasting. Received Peabody Award for interview with actor Christopher Reeve (1995); was the 1st woman inducted into American Academy of Television Arts and Sciences' Hall of Fame. ❖ See also Jerry Oppenheimer, *Barbara Walters: An Unauthorized Biography* (St. Martin, 1990); Henna Remstein, *Barbara Walters* (Chelsea House, 1999); and *Women in World History*.

WALTERS, Bernice R. (1912–1975). American physician in US Navy. Name variations: Bernice Nordstrom. Born Bernice Rosenthal, Sept 1, 1912, in New York, NY; died Feb 10, 1975, in Kailua, HI; dau. of Murray and Henrietta Rosenthal; Long Island University, BS, 1932; Woman's Medical College of Pennsylvania, MD, 1936; m. 3rd husband, Dr. H. C. Nordstrom, 1954. ❖ Joined Jacqueline Cochran's WASP; became one of 1st Navy WAVE Medical Officers and served for 14 years, eventually becoming commander; was 1 of 5 active-duty women doctors in Bureau of Medicine and Surgery of Navy; served on hospital ship *Consolation* during Korean War; arrived in Hawaii (1961) and served in several hospitals, including as chief of Anesthesiology Service at Queen's hospital (1967 and 1974).

WALTERS, Catherine (1839–1920). British courtesan. Name variations: Skittles Walters. Born 1839 in Liverpool, England; died 1920; dau. of a junior customs officer at the Liverpool docks. ❖ Moved to London sometime before 1859 and caused a stir because of affairs with powerful men, including the Liberal politician Lord Hartington, as well as Napoleon III and the Prince of Wales (later Edward VII); was the subject of the sonnet sequence *Esther* by poet Wilfred Scawen Blunt, with whom she had an affair and a lifelong friendship. ❖ See also Henry Blyth, *Skittles: The Last Victorian Courtesan, The Life and Times of Catherine Walters* (Newton Abbot, 1972).

WALTERS, Julie (1950—). English actress. Born Julia Mary Walters, Feb 22, 1950, in Birmingham, England; attended Manchester Polytechnic School of Theatre; m. Grant Roffey, 1997; children: Maisie. ❖ Began career at Liverpool Everyman Theatre; came to prominence in play (1980) and film (1983) of *Educating Rita*, for which she received an Academy Award nomination; other stage work includes *Macbeth* (1985), *Frankie and Johnny in the Clair de Lune* (1989), and *The Rose Tattoo* (1991), and won Laurence Olivier Best Actress award for *All My Sons* (2001); was a regular on tv series "The Secret Diary of Adrian Mole Aged 13¾" (1985) and "G. B. H." (1991); films include *Personal Services* (1987), *Prick Up Your Ears* (1987), *Buster* (1988), *Stepping Out* (1991), *Billy Elliot* (2000), *Harry Potter and the Sorcerer's Stone* (2001) and *Calendar Girls* (2003); wrote *Babytalk* (1990). Named OBE (1999).

WALTERS, Lisa (1960—). Canadian golfer. Name variations: Lisa Young. Born Jan 9, 1960, in Prince Rupert, BC, Canada; m. Mike Walters, 1988. ❖ Won British Columbia Junior (1977), British Columbia Amateur (1979, 1980, 1981), and All-American at Florida State University (1981); won Itoki Hawaiian Open (1992, 1993), and Oldsmobile Classic (1998).

WALTERS, Lucy (c. 1630–1658). See Walter, Lucy.

WALTERS, Skittles (1839–1920). See Walters, Catherine.

WALTON, Angie (1966—). American inline skater. Born Sept 18, 1966. ❖ Helped pioneer pro Vert skating for women; held unofficial ranking as top female Vert skater in world at a time when there were no competitions for women in US (1991–94); produced "Launch" festival (1992); founded 1st aggressive skate magazine, *Daily Bread* (1993); brought 1st multisport Vert exhibition to Lollapalooza (1994); helped found ASA (1995); won silver in Women's Vert at X Games (1995); served as athletic coordinator for Warped Tour (1995 and 1996).

WALTON, Dorothy (1908—). Canadian badminton champion. Born Dorothy McKenzie, Aug 7, 1908, in Swift Current, Saskatchewan, Canada; m. William Walton, 1931. ❖ As an undergraduate at University of Saskatchewan, won titles in diving, discus, javelin, high jump, long jump, and 220-yard track; won Western Canadian tennis titles; was Canadian singles badminton champion (1936, 1938, 1940); placed 1st in All-England championship in badminton (1939), the 1st Canadian to do so and the 1st Canadian to hold Canadian, American, and All-England titles simultaneously; won 64 singles and doubles titles in badminton (1936–40); won 6 tennis championships; named one of the 6 best Canadian women athletes in the half-century (1949). Awarded Coronation medal for work with Consumers Association of Canada (1953); inducted into Canadian Sports Hall of Fame.

WALTON, Florence (1891–1981). American exhibition ballroom dancer. Born 1891 in Wilmington, DE; died Jan 7, 1981; m. Maurice Mouvet (dancer), 1911 (div. 1920); m. Leon Leitrim. ❖ Made performance debut in *The Girl Behind the Counter,* a Lew Fields show (1907); made Broadway debut as featured soloist in *Miss Innocence* (1908); with 1st husband, billed as Maurice and Florence Walton, enjoyed worldwide fame as ballroom dancers, specializing in the tango and the Apache dance; moved to Paris after divorce and danced with Leon Leitrim (1920–26); with Leitrim, managed Marigny Théâtre; retired from performance career (1934).

WALTON, Nancy (1915—). See Bird, Nancy.

WALTON, Octavia (1811–1877). See Le Vert, Octavia.

WALWORTH, Ellen Hardin (1832–1915). American clubwoman. Born Oct 20, 1832, in Jacksonville, IL; died June 23, 1915, in Washington, DC; dau. of John J. Hardin (US congressman) and Sarah Ellen (Smith) Hardin; granddau. of Martin D. Hardin (US senator); m. Mansfield Tracy Walworth (lawyer and novelist), July 29, 1852 (died 1873); children: 3 sons, 5 daughters. ❖ Began study of law after son Frank shot her husband to death, then helped him get released from prison on insanity defense (1877); served as president of Shakespeare Club; was among 1st women to be elected and hold position on board of education in NY state; during 18-year stint, was sole female trustee of Saratoga Monument Association (1876–94); was 1 of 3 official founders of Daughters of American Revolution; became 1st editor of DAR's journal, *American Monthly Magazine* (1892).

WAMBACH, Abby (1980—). American soccer player. Born June 2, 1980, in Rochester, NY. ❖ Forward, played for Washington Freedom; won a team gold medal at Athens Olympics (2004). Named WUSA's Rookie of the Year (2002); voted MVP in Founders Cup (2003).

WAMBAUGH, Sarah (1882–1955). American author and lecturer. Born Mar 6, 1882, in Cincinnati, Ohio; died Nov 12, 1955; dau. of Eugene Wambaugh (specialist in constitutional and international law at Harvard Law School) and Anna S. (Hemphill) Wambaugh; Radcliffe College, BA, 1902, MA in international law and political science, 1917; began graduate study at London University School of Economics, 1920; studied in Europe, 1922–c. 1924. ❖ Consultant on international affairs, published *Monograph on Plebiscites* (1920), which became the standard text and was widely used in foreign offices as well as at US State Department; was a member of League of Nations secretariat (1920–21); served as expert advisor to Peruvian government on the Tacna-Arica plebiscite (1925–26); became professor of the French-language Academy of International Law in the Netherlands (1927); helped draft

the regulations for the Saar Plebiscite (1935), a vote held to decide the question of whether that industrial area would belong to Germany or France; lectured at Institute for Advanced International Studies in Geneva (1935); was technical adviser to 600 Americans designated to observe Greek elections (1946); writings include *La pratique des plébiscites internationaux* (1928), *Plebiscites Since the World War* (1933) and *The Saar Plebiscite* (1940). ❖ See also *Women in World History.*

WAMI, Gete (1974—). Ethiopian runner. Born Dec 11, 1974, in Debre Birhan, Chacha, Ethiopia; m. Getaneh Tessema (cross-country manager), 2000. ❖ Won World Cross-Country championships (1996, 1999); won a bronze medal for 10,000 meters at Atlanta Olympics (1996); won a silver medal for 10,000 meters and a bronze medal for 5,000 meters at Sydney Olympics (2000); won African championship and World championship (1999).

WANDA OF POLAND (fl. 730). Queen of Poland. Flourished in 730 in Poland; dau. of Krak, king of Poland. ❖ Inherited the kingdom of Poland as the only surviving child of the powerful King Krak, who founded Krakow (Cracow); spent her long and successful reign strengthening Poland's military forces, even leading battles herself; was a strong, intelligent, and politically acute monarch, and successfully repelled most of her enemies.

WANDER, Maxie (1933–1977). Austrian diarist and letter writer. Born 1933 In Vienna, Austria; died 1977 in Berlin, Germany; m. Dred Wander, 1958; children: 1. ❖ Published series of interviews with East German women, *Guten Morgen, du Schöne. Protokolle nach Tonband* (1977); diaries and letters about coming to terms with cancer published posthumously by husband as *Leben wär' eine prima Alternative* (1980).

WANDOR, Michelene (1940—). British poet, playwright and short-story writer. Born 1940 in London, England. ❖ Educated at Newnham College, Cambridge, and active in feminist movement from 1960s; worked with feminist theater groups, including Gay Sweatshop, Women's Theatre Group, and Monstrous Regiment; work concerned with interaction between feminism, socialism, and gay liberation; writings include *The Day After Yesterday* (1972), *Spilt Milk* (1972), *The Body Politic* (1972), *Penthesilea* (1977), *Sexual Politics in Theatre* (1980), *Upbeat: Poems and Stories* (1982), *Me and My Mother* (1985), *The Wandering Jew* (with Sara Maitland, 1987), *Once a Feminist: Stories of a Generation* (1991), and *Gardens of Eden Revisited* (1999).

WANDRU (c. 628–688). Belgian saint. Name variations: Waldetrude; Waldetrudis; Waldetrud; Waudru. Born c. 628 in Cousolre, Belgium; died April 9, 688, in Mons, Belgium; dau. of (Saint) Walbert, count of Hainault, and (Saint) Bertilia; sister of Saint Aldegund (c. 680–684); m. Madelgaire (the future St. Vincent Madelgar); children: (all saints) Landry or Landric; Dentlin or Dentilinus; Madelberte; Aldetrude. ❖ Late in life, encouraged husband to found a monastery at Haumont and supported his retirement into the abbey; two years later, retired to a small religious establishment which became known as Châteaulieu, or Castrilocus, in Monte, where she spent her time in prayer, becoming famous for her miracles of healing; her piety attracted settlers to Châteaulieu, which led to the founding of a Benedictine monastery where she served as abbess until her death (the town of Mons grew up around the abbey). ❖ See also *Women in World History.*

WANG CHAO-CHUN (52 BCE–18 CE). See Wang Zhaojun.

WANG CHENGYI (1983—). Chinese shooter. Born July 17, 1983, in China. ❖ Won a bronze medal for 50 m rifle 3 positions at Athens Olympics (2004).

WANG CHUNLU (1978—). Chinese short-track speedskater. Born Sept 27, 1978, in China. ❖ Won a silver medal for the 3,000-meter relay at Nagano Olympics (1998); won a silver medal for the 3,000-meter relay and a bronze medal for the 500 meters at Salt Lake City Olympics (2002).

WANG FANG (1967—). Chinese basketball player. Born Jan 14, 1967, in China. ❖ At Barcelona Olympics, won a silver medal in team competition (1992).

WANG GUANGMEI (1922—). Chinese politician. Born 1922 in US; m. Liu Shaoqi (leader of Chinese Communist Party), 1948 (died 1969); children: Liu Ting. ❖ Born in US but went to China as child; studied physics at Furen University; worked as interpreter for Communists in mediation talks with Guomindang (1949) and was appointed to Central Committee Foreign Affairs Department; traveled with husband to Indonesia, Burma, Cambodia, Vietnam, Pakistan, and Afghanistan, and helped start anti-corruption investigations known as Taoynan Experience; elected deputy for Hebei Province (1964) and directed Cultural Revolution activities at Qinhua University (1966); was criticized, tried, and imprisoned by Red Guards for suppressing students' revolutionary fervor; later elected member of Fifth Central Committee (1979) and became director of Foreign Affairs Bureau at Academy of Social Sciences.

WANG HEE-KYUNG (1970—). Korean archer. Born July 16, 1970, in South Korea. ❖ At Seoul Olympics, won a silver medal in double FITA round and a gold medal in team round (1988).

WANG HONG (1965—). Chinese archer. Born May 22, 1965, in China. ❖ At Barcelona Olympics, won a silver medal in team round (1992).

WANG HUIFENG (1968—). Chinese fencer. Born Jan 24, 1968, in China. ❖ At Barcelona Olympics, won a silver medal in indiv. foil (1992).

WANG JUN (1963—). Chinese basketball player. Born Aug 20, 1963, in China. ❖ At Los Angeles Olympics, won a bronze medal in team competition (1984).

WANG JUNXIA (1973—). Chinese runner. Born Jan 9, 1973, in Jilin, China; m. Zhan Yu (footballer), 2001. ❖ At World championships, won the 10,000 meters (1993); set a world record time for the 10,000 of 29:31.78 at National Games (1993), the 1st woman to cover the distance in less than 30 minutes; won a gold medal for the 5,000 meters and a silver medal for the 10,000 meters at Atlanta Olympics (1996); retired (1997). Won the Jesse Owens International Trophy (1994).

WANG LIHONG (1970—). Chinese softball player. Born 1970 in China. ❖ Won a silver medal at Atlanta Olympics (1996).

WANG LINA (1978—). Chinese volleyball player. Born Feb 5, 1978, in Yingkou, China. ❖ Spiker, joined the national team (1996); won a team silver medal at Atlanta Olympics (1996); placed 2nd at World championships (1998); as an outside hitter, won a team gold medal at Athens Olympics (2004). Named best server in the national league (1999).

WANG LINWEI (1956—). Chinese handball player. Born Aug 29, 1956, in China. ❖ At Los Angeles Olympics, won a bronze medal in team competition (1984).

WANG LIPING (1973—). Chinese soccer player. Born Nov 12, 1973, in Hebei, China. ❖ Defender and midfielder; selected to the Chinese national team (1992); won a team silver medal at Atlanta Olympics (1996); signed with WUSA's Atlanta Beat (2001).

WANG LIPING (1976—). Chinese track-and-field athlete. Born July 1976, in Hebei, China. ❖ Won a gold medal for 20 km road walk at Sydney Olympics (2000).

WANG MINGXING (1961—). Chinese handball player. Born Sept 5, 1961, in China. ❖ At Los Angeles Olympics, won a bronze medal in team competition (1984).

WANG NAN (1978—). Chinese table tennis player. Born Oct 23, 1978, in Liaoning Province, China. ❖ Won gold medals for singles and doubles at Sydney Olympics (2000); won World championship doubles and singles (1999, 2001, 2003) and team (1997, 2000, 2001, 2004); won a gold medal for doubles at Athens Olympics (2004). Named the Best Female Athlete and Most Popular Female Athlete in China (2002).

WANG QIANG (52 BCE–18 CE). See Wang Zhaojun.

WANG, Vera (1949—). Asian-American fashion designer. Born June 27, 1949, in New York, NY; dau. of Cheng Ching Wang and Florence Wu Wang (wealthy Chinese immigrants who built a pharmaceuticals company); graduate of Sarah Lawrence College; attended Sorbonne; m. Arthur Becker (investment banker); children: (adopted) Josephine and Cecilia. ❖ At 23, became the youngest fashion editor of *Vogue* magazine, then worked there for 17 years; served as design director for Ralph Lauren for 2 years; having spent her early years as a competitive ice skater, began costuming top-rated figure skaters; opened her 1st store on Madison Avenue (1990); launched her signature line of wedding gowns (1993); added evening wear (1998).

WANG XIANBO. Chinese judoka. Born in China. ❖ Won a bronze medal for 61–66kg middleweight at Atlanta Olympics (1996); won a gold medal at Asian Games (1998); won World A Class Competitions twice in Italy and once in Holland (2000).

WANG XIAOHONG (1968—). Chinese swimmer. Born Nov 20, 1968, in China. ❖ At Barcelona Olympics, won a silver medal in 200-meter butterfly (1992).

WANG XIAOZHU (1973—). Chinese archer. Born May 12, 1973, in China. ❖ At Barcelona Olympics, won a silver medal in team round (1992).

WANG XU (1985—). Chinese wrestler. Born Sept 27, 1985, in Beijing, China. ❖ Won Asian championships for 68 kg freestyle (2001) and a gold medal for 72 kg freestyle at Athens Olympics (2004).

WANG YAJUN (1962—). Chinese volleyball player. Born Aug 27, 1962, in China. ❖ At Seoul Olympics, won a bronze medal in team competition (1988).

WANG YAN (1971—). Chinese track-and-field athlete. Born 1971 in Liaoning Province, China. ❖ Won World Jr. 5 km walk (1987), the youngest champion of that event; won World Cup 10 km (1993); won a bronze medal for the 10 km walk at Atlanta Olympics (1996); won Chinese nationals for 10 km (1998).

WANG YI (1973—). Chinese volleyball player. Born May 21, 1973, in China. ❖ Won a team silver medal at Atlanta Olympics (1996).

WANG YING. Chinese softball player. Born in China. ❖ Won a silver medal at Atlanta Olympics (1996).

WANG ZHAOJUN (52 BCE–18 CE). Chinese poet, concubine and empress. Name variations: Wang Chao-chun; Wang Qiang; Empress Ninghu (empress who brought peace to a border tribe). Born in 52 BCE in Baoping, Xingsha County, Hubei, China; died in 18 CE in Inner Mongolia; dau. of a poor scholar; m. Huhanye, king of the southern Xiong Nu (died); married his eldest son, according to custom; children: (1st. m) son; (2nd m.) 2 daughters. ❖ A royal concubine (one of thousands) to Emperor Yuan (Xuan) of the Western Han dynasty, was portrayed harshly by the court painter (Mao Yen-Shou), when she refused to pay a bribe (he added a black mole); was married off to a barbarian Xiong Nu (Hun) chieftain as a bid for peace by Emperor Yuan; brought culture and refinement to her new country (Mongolia); after the death of the chieftain, married his son by another wife; wrote poetry to express longing for homeland; remembered in legend as bringer of peace between China and its border enemies. Called one of the four beauties in Chinese history, is the subject of countless songs, paintings, poems and plays, in the many differing versions of this story.

WANG ZILING (1972—). Chinese volleyball player. Born Jan 14, 1972, in China. ❖ Won a team silver medal at Atlanta Olympics (1996).

WANGER, Beatrice (c. 1900–1945). See Nadja.

WANGER, Justine (1895–1982). See Johnstone, Justine.

WARBURG, Agnes (1872–1953). English photographer. Born 1872 in London, England; died 1953 in Surrey, England; dau. of Frederick and Emma Warburg. ❖ One of the foremost pictorialists of the early 20th century, exhibited at the Photographic Salon of the Linked Ring (1900); continued showing with Linked Ring for 9 more years; helped found the Halyon Women's Club and exhibited there (1914); exhibited at the London Salon of the British Photographic Society and the Royal Photographic Society (1916); was a founding member of the Royal Photographic Society's Pictorial Group (1920); helped found the Royal Photographic Society's Colour Group (1927); left London during World War II. ❖ See also *Women in World History*.

WARD, Anne (c. 1825–1896). New Zealand temperance leader and welfare worker. Name variations: Anne Titboald, Mrs. Dudley Ward. Born Anne Titboald, c. 1825 or 1826, at Exeter, Devonshire, England; dau. of Thomas Titboald; m. Charles Dudley Robert Ward (lawyer), 1850. ❖ Immigrated to New Zealand with husband (1854); served as first national president of New Zealand Women's Christian Temperance Union (WCTU), and established branches in Wellington, Nelson, New Plymouth, Patea, Hawera, Wanganui and Ashburton; helped WCTU establish kindergarten in Auckland (1887); worked to address needs of disadvantaged. ❖ See also *Dictionary of New Zealand Biography* (Vol. 2).

WARD, Barbara (1914–1981). British economist. Name variations: Barbara Ward (1914–50, and thereafter in publications); Barbara Jackson (1950–73); Dame Barbara Ward (1974–76); Baroness Jackson of Lodsworth (1976–81). Born Barbara Ward, May 23, 1914, in York, England; died in Sussex, England, May 31, 1981; dau. of Walter Ward and Teresa Mary (Burge) Ward; attended Lycee Molière, Sorbonne, and

Somerville College, Oxford University; m. Sir Robert Gillman Jackson, 1950 (sep. 1973); children: Robert (b. 1956). ❖ Economist, intellectual journalist, and advocate of Third World development who was an influential figure in academia and politics throughout mid-20th century; while foreign editor of *The Economist* (1939–50), assimilated vast quantities of difficult information quickly and was able to summarize and explain it lucidly and persuasively; served as governor of British Broadcasting Corporation (BBC, 1946–50); was Harvard Professor of International Development (1958–67); was economic advisor to President Lyndon Johnson (1964–67), and Schweitzer Professor of International Economic Development, Columbia University (1968–73); served as president of International Institute for Environment and Development (1973–81); rarely ahead of her time, embodied the wisdom of the moment raised to its highest power: was fiercely anti-fascist in the 1930s, anti-Communist in late 1940s, anti-colonialist in the 1950s, a "global villager" in 1960s, and an environmentalist in 1970s; was also a consistent advocate of the rights of the individual, the needs of poor nations, and the sovereignty of the Roman Catholic Church; writings include *The International Share-Out* (1938), *Hitler's Route to Baghdad* (1939), *Turkey* (1941), *The West at Bay* (1948), *Policy for the West* (1951), *Faith and Freedom* (1954), *The Interplay of East and West* (1957), *Five Ideas that Change the World* (1959), *India and the West* (1961), *The Rich Nations and the Poor Nations* (1962), *Spaceship Earth* (1966), *Nationalism and Ideology* (1966), *The Lopsided World* (1968), *The Widening Gap* (1971), *Only One Earth* (with Rene Dubos, 1972), and *The Home of Man* (1976). ❖ See also *Women in World History*.

WARD, Catharine Barnes (1851–1913). American photographer, writer and lecturer. Name variations: Catharine Barnes. Born Catharine Weed Barnes in Albany, New York, Jan 10, 1851; died 1913 in Hadlow, England; granddau. of Thurlow Weed (journalist and New York politician); attended Vassar College, 1869–71; m. Henry Snowden Ward (British founder and editor of *Practical Photographer*), in 1893 (died 1911). ❖ Took up photography (1886); received a photographic diploma in Boston (1888); became associate editor of *American Amateur Photographer* (1890) and quickly built a reputation as an advocate for female photographers; with husband, founded several photography magazines; published and illustrated *Shakespeare's Town and Times* (1896); followed this with a series of other illustrated works, including books on Dickens, the Canterbury pilgrimages, and Exmoor, the land of Lorna Doone. ❖ See also *Women in World History*.

WARD, Claire (1972—). English politician and member of Parliament. Born May 9, 1972; attended University of Hertfordshire. ❖ Became a solicitor (1998); representing Labour, elected to House of Commons for Watford (1997, 2001, 2005); named PPS to John Hutton as minister of state, Department of Health; became assistant government whip (2005).

WARD, Clara Mae (1924–1973). African-American gospel singer. Born April 21, 1924, in Philadelphia, PA; died Jan 16, 1973, in Los Angeles, CA; dau. of George Ward and Gertrude May (Murphy) Ward (gospel singer); sister of Willa Ward (singer). ❖ Joined with mother and sister Willa to form the Ward Trio (1934); after performing with trio at National Baptist Convention in Philadelphia (1943), began to tour on gospel circuit extensively (1943–57); added Marion Ward and Henrietta Waddy to group to form the Ward Singers (1949), later the Clara Ward Singers; assumed control of the group, giving them a more sophisticated image, and soon saw them ranked among the most successful female gospel groups of the 1950s; produced a long list of bestselling gospel records, including "Surely, God Is Able," "How I Got Over," "Come in the Room" and "The Day Is Past and Gone"; established Ward's House of Music, a successful publishing company of music, booklets and song collections, including many of the over 500 songs she wrote; performed at Apollo Theater in Harlem (1955), Newport Jazz Festival (1957), and Village Vanguard in NY (1961), which resulted in engagements at Birdland and the Blue Angel; spent 40-weeks at New Frontier Hotel in Las Vegas (1961); often made tv guest appearances, popularizing gospel music in the mainstream music industry; performed at Philadelphia Academy of Music (1967)—the 1st gospel group do so. ❖ See also *Women in World History*.

WARD, Dorothy (1890–1987). British actress and singer. Born April 26, 1890, in Birmingham, England; died 1987; dau. of Edwin Ward and Eliza (Millichamp) Ward; educated at Cheltenham; m. Shaun Glenville (actor), 1910 (died 1968); children: Peter Glenville (b. 1913, actor and director). ❖ Music-hall star, 1st appeared on stage in Birmingham at 15 and in the West End at 16; became highly successful in music hall and comedy; enjoyed fame in such shows as *Jack and the Beanstalk* at the London Hippodrome (1922); toured UK and Europe with troupe of children and often appeared with husband in pantomimes; known for her stirring rendition of "We're Going to Hang Out Our Washing on the Siegfried Line" during WWII, toured with ENSA and became known as "Mademoiselle from the Maginot Line"; appeared in last performance at 69 at Old Pavilion, Liverpool.

WARD, Mrs. Dudley (c. 1825–1896). See Ward, Anne.

WARD, Elizabeth (1960—). See Gracen, Elizabeth.

WARD, Elizabeth Stuart Phelps (1844–1911). American author and social reformer. Name variations: Mary Gray Phelps; Lily. Born Mary Gray Phelps on August 31, 1844, in Boston, Massachusetts; died Jan 28, 1911, in Newton, Massachusetts; dau. of Austin Phelps (Congregational minister and later president of Andover Theological Seminary) and Elizabeth Wooster Stuart Phelps (1815–1852, writer); attended Abbott Academy and Mrs. Edwards' School; m. Herbert D. Ward (writer), Oct 1888; no children. ❖ Following mother's death when Elizabeth was 8, chose to be known thereafter by mother's name; after losing a friend in the Battle of Antietam during Civil War, turned the event into the story "A Sacrifice Consumed," which was published in *Harper's New Monthly* (1864); helping to usher in the genre of literary realism, wrote a fictional account of Andover's Pemberton Mill fire in which 88 young women died (1860), which was published in *The Atlantic Monthly* (1868); had most significant success with *The Gates Ajar* (1868), which rejected the harsh Calvinistic doctrine of predestination in favor of a more merciful God and became a cultural phenomenon, its popularity enduring for almost 30 years; for next 20 years, championed the rights of women in her narratives; produced more than 150 short stories and 20 adult novels, in addition to poetry, plays, essays, and children's books; also wrote a biography of her father, *Austin Phelps: A Memoir* (1891). ❖ See also autobiography, *Chapters from a Life* (1896); and *Women in World History*.

WARD, Fannie (1865–1952). American stage and silent-film star. Born Feb 22, 1865, in St. Louis, MO; died Jan 27, 1952, in New York, NY; m. Joseph Lewis (div.); m. John W. Dean. ❖ Made NY debut in *Pippino* (1890), followed by *Adonis, The Charity Ball, The New Lady Bantock, The Spendthrift* and *Madam President*, among others; starred in films for Lasky, including *The Cheat, The Marriage of Kitty, Tennessee's Pardner, Common Clay, The Yellow Ticket* and *Innocent*.

WARD, Geneviève (1838–1922). American actress and opera singer. Name variations: Genevieve Ward; Lucy Geneviève Teresa Ward; Ginevra Guerrabella; Dame Geneviève Ward. Born Lucy Geneviève Teresa Ward, Mar 27, 1838 (one source cites 1837), in New York, NY; died Aug 18, 1922; granddau. of Gideon Lee, former mayor of NY; studied with San Giovanni, Lamperti, and Fanny Persiani; m. Count Constantin de Guerbel, 1856. ❖ Made opera debut in title role of Donizetti's *Lucrezia Borgia* at La Scala (1857); under name Ginevra Guerrabella, toured Europe for 6 years in such roles as Elvira in *Don Giovanni*, Maid Marian in *Robin Hood*, and Elvira in *I Puritani*; returned to NY (1862) to play Violetta in *La Traviata* at Academy of Music; contracted diphtheria while touring Cuba (1862), which destroyed her singing voice; pursued a career as a stage actress under her real name, making her dramatic stage debut as Lady Macbeth at Manchester's Theatre Royal to rave reviews (1873); appeared in 2 plays written expressly for her: Lewis Wingfield's *Despite the World* and William G. Willis' *Sappho* (1875); had great early success in dual role of Blanche de Valois and Unarita in *The Prayer in the Storm*, a performance she repeated 162 times; was also lauded for such roles as Julia in *The Hunchback*, Countess Almaviva in *The School for Intrigue*, Rebecca in *Ivanhoe*, Margaret Elmore in *Love's Sacrifice*, Emilia in *Othello* and, most especially, Stephanie de Mohrivart in *Forget-Me-Not* (1879); spent majority of her acting career on English stage, returning to America only for brief engagements. Was the 1st actress to be named a Dame Commander of the British Empire (1921). ❖ See also *Women in World History*.

WARD, Mrs. H. O. (1824–1899). See Moore, Clara.

WARD, Hannah (1829–1898). See Barron, Hannah Ward.

WARD, Harriet (1808–c. 1860). South African novelist. Born 1808 in Norfolk, England; died c. 1860. ❖ Wrote account of time spent with husband in garrison town of Grahamstown, Eastern Cape, South Africa, during frontier wars, *Five Years in Kaffirland* (1848, 1851), which was republished as 3 novels *Jasper Lyle: A Tale of Kaffirland* (1951), *Lizzy Dorian: The Soldier's Wife* (1954), and *Hardy the Hunter* (1858); also wrote *Helen Charteris* (1848), *Memoirs of Colonel Tidy* (1849) and *Hester*

Fleming (1854); edited *Past and Future Emigration, or The Book of the Cape* (1849).

WARD, Henrietta (1832–1924). English painter. Name variations: Mrs. E. M. Ward. Born Henrietta Mary Ada Ward, June 1, 1832, in London, England; died July 12, 1924, in England; dau. of artists; granddau. of painter James Ward; attended Bloomsbury Art School and Sak's Academy; m. Edward M. Ward (painter, no relation), 1848 (died 1879); children: 8, including son Leslie Ward (portrait painter). ❖ Portrait painter who received numerous commissions from Queen Victoria and Prince Albert and taught royal children, opened London art school for girls; successfully fought for Royal Academy School to admit female students (1861); continued to exhibit late into life; work shown at Chicago Exposition (1893) and Royal Academy (1924). ❖ See also autobiography, *Memories of Ninety Years* (Holt, 1924).

WARD, Hortense (1872–1944). American lawyer and reformer. Born Hortense Sparks, July 20, 1872, near Simpsonville, Texas; died Dec 5, 1944; dau. of Frederick Sparks (cattleman, surname originally Funks) and Louisa Marie (La Bauve) Sparks; graduate of Nazareth Academy in Victoria, 1890; m. Albert Malsch (tinner), 1891 (sep. 1903, div. 1906); m. William Henry Ward (lawyer), 1909; children: (1st m.) Mary Louise, Marguerite, and Hortense. ❖ Was the 1st woman in Texas to pass the bar examination (1910); with 2nd husband, established firm of Ward & Ward, active in civil cases; fought for a married woman's property rights law, known as the Hortense Ward law upon passage (1913); was the 1st Texas woman admitted to practice before US Supreme Court (Feb 1915); also gained women the right to vote in political primaries in Texas (1918). ❖ See also *Women in World History*.

WARD, Mrs. Humphry (1851–1920). English writer. Name variations: Mary Augusta Arnold (1851–1871); Mary Augusta Ward (1871–1920); Mrs. Humphry Ward (in all publications). Born Mary Augusta Arnold in Hobart Town, Tasmania, June 11, 1851; died in London, England, Mar 24, 1920; dau. of Thomas Arnold (son of Dr. Thomas Arnold, headmaster at Rugby) and Julia (Sorrell or Sorell) Arnold (1826–1888); sister of Julia Arnold Huxley (1862–1908); m. T(homas) Humphry Ward (fellow of Brasenose College, Oxford), in 1872; children: Dorothy Ward (b. 1874), Arnold Ward (b. 1876, briefly a member of Parliament), and Janet Ward (b. 1879). ❖ Prolific novelist, critic, journalist, and memoirist who was the author of *Robert Elsmere* (1888), one of the most famous religious novels of 19th century; in her heyday (1890–1910), was one of the most influential novelists in the English-speaking world; published 25 novels and 15 other books of social and literary criticism, played a prominent role in the settlement house movement, was an active society hostess, and a leader in the campaign against women's suffrage; was declared by Tolstoy the greatest English novelist of her day and ranked by William Dean Howells as almost the equal of George Eliot (Mary Anne Evans); by end 20th century, was almost forgotten; writings include (trans.) *Journal Intime of Henri Frederic Amiel* (1885), *Helbeck of Bannisdale* (1898), *The Testing of Diana Mallory* (1908), *Daphne* (1909), *Delia Blanchflower* (1914), *England's Effort* (1916) and *A Writer's Recollections* (1918, 2 vols.). A revival of scholarly interest (1970s–80s) has restored to historians and literary critics an awareness of Mrs. Humphry Ward and an appreciation for her novels, but it has not restored her to the pre-eminence she enjoyed in her lifetime. ❖ See also Anne M. Bindslev, *Mrs. Humphry Ward: A Study in Late Victorian Feminine Consciousness* (Almqvist & Wiksell, 1985); Enid Huws Jones, *Mrs. Humphry Ward* (Heinemann, 1973); Esther M. G. Smith, *Mrs. Humphry Ward* (Twayne, 1980); John Sutherland, *Mrs. Humphry Ward: Eminent Victorian and Preeminent Edwardian* (Clarendon, 1990); and *Women in World History*.

WARD, Ida Caroline (1880–1949). British phonetician and West African language scholar. Born Oct 4, 1880, in Bradford, Yorkshire, England; died Oct 10, 1949, in Guildford, England; dau. of Samson Ward (wool merchant) and Hannah (Tempest) Ward; Durham University, BLitt, 1902; London University, PhD, 1933; never married. ❖ Specializing in African languages, earned a doctorate from London University's School of Oriental and African Studies on the strength of her scholarly research, published as *Phonetic and Tonal Structure of Efik*; focused scientifically on tonal importance of African language, a subject she pursued further with the groundbreaking *Introduction to the Ibo Language* (1936); appointed head of the university's new department of African languages and cultures (1937), turned it into an internationally recognized center for research on Africa; was instrumental in the development of International African Institute's *Handbook of African Languages*, and her other scholarly works, *Practical Phonetics for Students of African Languages* (1933) and *Introduction to the Yoruba Language* (posthumously published, 1952), were no less important to the field. Named a Commander of the British Empire (1948).

WARD, Irene (1895–1980). English politician. Name variations: Irene Mary Berwick Ward; Baroness Ward. Born in England, Feb 23, 1895; died April 26, 1980; dau. of architect A. J. Berwick Ward and Elvina M. Ellis Ward; educated at Newcastle Church High School. ❖ As a Conservative, was a member of Parliament (1931–45, 1950–74), which made her the longest serving woman member at the time; won election in the Wallsend campaign (1931) and retained her seat until 1945, when a Labour landslide ejected numerous Conservative incumbents; during WWII, was chair of the Woman Power Committee, a group that influenced the most effective utilization of women during the labor shortage; won re-election to Parliament (1950), representing Tynemouth, and held this seat for 24 years; was no respecter of parties when it came to calling the government to account on broken promises made to women; upon retirement (1974), was created a baroness, then served in the House of Lords (1974–80); was a lifelong advocate for disadvantaged women and, throughout political career, stretched the boundaries for women's rights. Named a Dame of the British Empire (1951), and a Companion of Honor (1973). ❖ See also *Women in World History*.

WARD, Maisie (1889–1975). British biographer and publisher. Name variations: Mary Josephine Ward; Maisie Sheed. Born Mary Josephine Ward, Jan 4, 1889, on Isle of Wight, England; died Jan 28, 1975, in New York, NY; dau. of Wilfrid Ward (biographer of John Henry Newman and editor of the *Dublin Review*) and Josephine Ward; m. Francis Joseph Sheed (Australian publisher), 1926; children: Rosemary Sheed; Wilfrid Sheed (novelist). ❖ With husband, started publishing house of Sheed & Ward (1926), specializing in Catholic writings, then opened a branch in New York (1933); works include *Father Martin* (1920), *The Oxford Group* (1937), *Gilbert Keith Chesterton* (1943), *The Young Mr. Newman* (1948), *Be Not Solicitous* (1953), *The Rosary* (1957), *Unfinished Business* (1964), *Robert Browning and His World* (1967), and *The Tragi-Comedy of Pen Browning* (1972).

WARD, Mary (1586–1645). English nun and founder. Born Feb 2, 1586 (some sources cite Jan 23, 1585), in Yorkshire, England; died Jan 20 (some sources cite Jan 30), 1645, in Hewarth, Yorkshire, England; dau. of Marmaduke Ward and Ursula (Wright) Ward. ❖ English nun and founder of the Institute of the Blessed Virgin Mary, a model for modern Catholic women's institutes, entered a Poor Clares convent in the Netherlands (1606) at age 20; left the convent to establish a new order, Institute of the Blessed Virgin Mary (IBVM), based upon that of the Jesuits, which augmented a contemplative life with good works; with followers, established a community for Englishwomen near Gravelines in northern France (1607); experienced tremendous persecution after Pope Urban VIII effectively suppressed the society, closing the IBVM in Rome (1624); even so, extended IBVM activities throughout France, Germany, Holland, Italy, Austria and England; was imprisoned for heresy (1631); returned to England (1637), and was granted permission by the pope to form a modified order there (1639). Officially recognized by the Catholic Church (1909) as the founder of the IBVM, was also acknowledged by Pope Pius XII for her religious work in England during the 17th century (1951). ❖ See also *Women in World History*.

WARD, Mary (1827–1869). Irish author, artist, naturalist, astronomer and microscopist. Name variations: Mary King. Born April 27, 1827, in Ferbane, Ireland; died in a steam carriage accident, Aug 31, 1869; m. Henry Ward, later 5th Viscount Bangor, in 1854. ❖ Noted astronomer and scientist, whose skill with microscopes and telescopes produced 2 significant works: *Sketches with the Microscope* and *Telescope Teachings* (1859); her numerous publications benefited from her gift as an illustrator, a talent she employed in works by other writers such as Sir David Brewster's *Life of Newton*. ❖ See also *Women in World History*.

WARD, Mary Augusta (1851–1920). *See Ward, Mrs. Humphry.*

WARD, Mary Josephine (1889–1975). *See Ward, Maisie.*

WARD, Nancy (1738–1822). *See Nanye'hi.*

WARD, Natalie (1975—). Australian softball player. Born Dec 24, 1975, in Newcastle, Australia; attended Newcastle College. ❖ Infielder, won team bronze medals at Atlanta Olympics (1996) and Sydney Olympics (2000) and a team silver medal at Athens Olympics (2004).

WARD, Penelope Dudley (1914–1982). *See Dudley-Ward, Penelope.*

WARD, Polly (1908–1987). English actress, singer, and dancer. Name variations: Bino (or Byno) Poluski; Bino; Bino Trix. Born Winifred Charlotte Govett, June 30, 1908, in Mitcham, Surrey, England; died Feb 23 (or 24), 1987, in Surrey; dau. of William Govett (Will Poluski of the Poluski Brothers) and Winifred Ward (music-hall artist); m. Robert S. Freeman. ❖ Made stage debut under name Bino Poluski in *The Punch Bowl* (1924); as Bino, appeared with Helen Trix in variety as "The Trix Sisters"; other plays include *The Song of the Sear, Wake Up and Dream, Savoy Follies, Here We Are Again, The 40 Thieves, Puss in Boots, Orchids and Onions, Babes in the Wood,* and *Hoopla!*; films include *Harmony Heaven, The Old Curiosity Shop, Feather Your Nest, It's in the Air* and *Bulldog Sees it Through.*

WARD, Winifred Louise (1884–1975). American children's theater specialist. Born Oct 29, 1884, in Eldora, Iowa; died following a stroke on August 16, 1975, in Evanston, Illinois; dau. of George Ward (lawyer and city official) and Frances Allena (Dimmick) Ward; graduated from Cumnock School of Oratory in Evanston, Illinois, 1905; University of Chicago, PhB in English, 1918; never married; lived with Hazel Easton, her colleague at Northwestern, for more than 50 years. ❖ Joined the faculty of the Cumnock School (1918), which became the Northwestern University School of Speech (1920); with the sponsorship of Northwestern University, co-founded and ran the Children's Theater of Evanston (1925–50), providing a venue for students to develop their technical skills and their proficiency in acting, directing, and producing; founded the influential Children's Theater Conference at Northwestern University (1944); wrote *Creative Dramatics* (1930), *Theatre for Children* (1939) and *Stories to Dramatize* (1952). ❖ See also *Women in World History.*

WARDER, Ann Head (1758–1829). American diarist. Born Ann Head, 1758, in England; died 1829; dau. of John Head; m. John Warder (1751–1828), 1779; children: Mary Ann Warder Bacon (1782–1865), Elizabeth Warder Janney (1793–1851), Caroline Warder Cadbury (1801–1868). ❖ Traveled with husband to North America and kept journal account for sister of life in Pennsylvania Quaker community; journals published as *Extracts from the Diary of Mrs. Ann Warder* (1893–94).

WARDHANI, Kusuma (1964—). Indonesian archer. Born Feb 20, 1964, in Indonesia. ❖ At Seoul Olympics, won a silver medal in team round (1988).

WARDLAW, Elizabeth (1677–1727). Scottish poet. Name variations: Elizabeth Halket. Born April 1677 in Fife; died 1727; dau. of Janet (Murray) Halket and Sir Charles Halket of Pitfarraine; m. Sir Henry Wardlaw of Pitcruivie, June 13, 1696. ❖ Best remembered as the supposed author of the ballad "Hardyknute," which she claimed to have discovered as a fragment in a vault in Dunfermline. It was published as an example of an ancient Scottish epic (1719) and Allan Ramsay published it in *The Ever Green* (1724). The authenticity of the ballad was called into question (1765), when it appeared in *Reliques of Ancient English Poetry* by Bishop Thomas Percy; the controversy gave rise to false speculation that Lady Wardlaw might also have reworked the ballad "Sir Patrick Spens."

WARDROPE, Anne W. (1869–1950). See Brigman, Anne W.

WARENNE. *Variant of Warrenne.*

WARFIELD, Irene (c. 1896–1961). American silent-film actress. Born c. 1896; died April 10, 1961, in New York, NY. ❖ Lead player for Essanay, co-starred with such actors as Francis X. Bushman and Bryant Washburn.

WARFIELD, Wallis (1895–1986). See Windsor, Wallis Warfield, duchess of.

WARING, Anna Letitia (1823–1910). Welsh hymnwriter. Name variations: Anna Laetitia Waring. Born April 19, 1823, in Plas-y-Velin, Neath, Glamorganshire, Wales; died May 10, 1910; dau. of Elijah and Deborah Waring (both active members of the Society of Friends); never married. ❖ Began writing hymns at an early age and followed in the footsteps of uncle, Samuel Miller Waring, a hymnwriter who left the Society of Friends to join the Church of England; also leaving the Society to join the Church of England, learned to read Hebrew and studied the Psalms on a daily basis, as well as the Hebrew poetry of the Old Testament; at 23, wrote "Father, I know that all my life," one of her most popular works (1846); her hymns were widely embraced and her volume *Hymns and Meditations* (1850), containing 18 hymns, was reprinted through many editions in both 19th and 20th centuries; was a prolific religious writer, whose works included *Additional Hymns* (1858) and *Days of Remembrance* (1886).

WARING, Laura Wheeler (1887–1948). African-American artist and educator. Born 1887 in Hartford, Connecticut; died Feb 3, 1948; dau. of Robert Foster Wheeler (minister of Talcott Street Congregational Church in Hartford) and Mary (Freeman) Wheeler; attended Pennsylvania Academy of Fine Arts; attended Académie de la Grande Chaumière in Paris, 1924; m. Walter E. Waring. ❖ Became director of the art and music departments at Cheyney State Teachers College (c. 1920), remaining there for 3 decades; during this tenure, produced many of her best-known portraits, including those of Leslie Pickney Hill, president emeritus of Cheyney; also produced excellent landscapes of Chester and Delaware County, Pennsylvania; was head of the Negro Art section at Sesquicentennial Exposition in Philadelphia (1926) and at Texas Centennial Exposition (1927); was also invited to exhibit in Pennsylvania Academy of Fine Arts, Philadelphia Museum of Art, Carlen Galleries, National Collection of Arts, Corcoran Gallery, Art Institute of Chicago, Brooklyn Museum and Howard University; held a one-woman show at Galerie du Luxembourg in Paris; known primarily as a portrait painter, preserved the images of many distinguished African-Americans, in particular W. E. B. Du Bois, John Haynes Holmes, Marian Anderson and Jessie Redmon Fauset. Won gold medal in annual Harmon Foundation Salon (1927). ❖ See also *Women in World History.*

WARING, Margaret (1887–1968). Northern Ireland politician. Born Margaret Alicia Parr, Nov 19, 1887, in Warrington, Herefordshire; died May 9, 1968; dau. of Joseph Charlton Parr; m. Major Holt Waring, 1914 (killed in action, 1918). ❖ Was justice of the peace for Co. Down; representing the Unionist Party for Iveagh, Co. Down, elected to the Northern Ireland House of Commons (1929–33); championed mentally handicapped children, clearing slums and improving housing. Named Commander of the British Empire (CBE, 1933).

WARING, Marilyn (1952—). New Zealand politician. Born Marilyn Waring, Oct 7, 1952, in Taipiri, NZ; Victoria University, BA in Political Science, 11973, PhD, 1989. ❖ Vocal in support of women's issues, especially abortion rights; internationally renowned for global feminist economics; served as National Party MP for Raglan (1975–78) and Waipa (1979–84); was the 1st woman to chair the Public Expenditure Committee; anti-nuclear activist, established the Disarmament and Arms Control Committee; retired from the House, age 31 (1984); became a lecturer in politics and women's studies at Waikato University; wrote *Women, Politics, and Power* and *Counting for Nothing.*

WARINGTON, Katherine (1897–1993). English botanist. Born Sept 5, 1897, in Harpenden, Hertfordshire, England; died July 3, 1993; Royal Holloway College, University of London, BS; attended University of Lund, Sweden. ❖ The 1st to demonstrate that boron (boric acid) is essential for healthy broad bean development, worked with Dr. Winifred Brenchley at the Rothamsted Experimental Station in Harpenden (1921–57); studied trace elements (e.g., manganese and molybdenum); with Brenchley, investigated germination time of weed species.

WARMOND, Ellen (1930—). Dutch poet. Born Sept 23, 1930, in Rotterdam, Netherlands. ❖ Works include *Proeftuin* (1953), *Warmte, een woonplaats* (1961), *Vragen stellen aan de stilte* (1984), *Vlucht stroken van de taal* (1988) and *Persoonbweijs voor inwoner* (1991); translations of poems published in *Change of Scene: Contemporary Dutch and Flemish poems in English Translation* (1969) and *The Shape of Houses: Women's Voices from Holland and Flanders* (1974). Won Anna Bijns Prize (1987).

WARMUS, Carolyn (1964—). American murderer (accused). Born Jan 1964 in Birmingham, Michigan; dau. of Elizabeth and Thomas Warmus (insurance executive); Columbia University, MA. ❖ Elementary schoolteacher, living in Manhattan, had affair with fellow schoolteacher Paul Solomon, who was married and had a daughter; became obsessed with Solomon; drove to Westchester and gunned down his wife, Betty Jeanne Solomon (Jan 15, 1989); saw 1st trial end in hung jury; in 2nd trial, was found guilty and sentenced to 25 years to life.

WARNER, Ann O'Connor (1842–1915). See Alabaster, Ann O'Connor.

WARNER, Anna Bartlett (1827–1915). American writer. Name variations: (pseudonym) Amy Lothrop. Born Anna Bartlett Warner, Aug 31, 1827, in New York, NY; died Jan 15, 1915, in Highland Falls, New York; dau. of Henry Whiting Warner (lawyer) and Anna (Bartlett) Warner; sister of Susan Bogert Warner (1819–1885). ❖ Published 1st book, *Dollars and Cents* (1852); also developed a popular educational card game called "Robinson Crusoe's Farm," which was sold for many years through the George P. Putnam store; went on to publish some 25 books, including children's fiction and religious subjects; also published the extremely popular *Gardening by Myself* (1872), which was reprinted 50 years after its 1st publication; religious works included verse and the words to several hymns, her best-known efforts being "Jesus Loves Me, This I Know" and "Jesus Bids Us Shine"; other writings include *Carl Krinken: His Christmas Stocking* (1853), *Say and Seal* (1860), *Wych Hazel* (1876), *The Gold of Chickaree* (1876), and a biography of her sister, *Susan Warner* (1909). ❖ See also *Women in World History.*

WARNER, Anne (1954—). American rower. Born Aug 29, 1954; attended Yale University. ❖ At Montreal Olympics, won a bronze medal in coxed eights (1976). ❖ See also (documentary) *A Hero for Daisy.*

WARNER, Anne Marie (1945—). Australian politician. Name variations: Hon. Anne Marie Warner. Born Dec 5, 1945, in Lucknow, India. ❖ Representing the Australian Labor Party, served in the Queensland Parliament for Kurilpa (1983–86), then South Brisbane (1986–95); was minister for Family Services and Aboriginal and Islander Affairs (1989–95); retired.

WARNER, Bonny (1962—). American luge athlete and bobsledder. Born April 7, 1962, in Mt. Baldy, CA. ❖ Was a member of American luge team at Winter Olympics in Sarajevo (1984); came in 6th in the Calgary Olympics, best US finish ever (1988); was 5-time US champion; retired from luge (1992) and took up bobsled; placed 3rd at US bobsled nationals (1998) and 1st (2001); captained a Boeing 737 for United Airlines.

WARNER, Deborah (1959—). English stage and opera director. Born May 12, 1959, in Oxford, England; raised as Quaker in Cotswold town of Burford; attended St. Clare's College, Oxford, and Central School of Speech and Drama. ❖ Best-known for daring takes on works of Shakespeare, Sophocles, Bach, Berg, Beckett, Brecht and Ibsen, as well as for long-time working relationship with Irish actress Fiona Shaw, started own theater troupe, Kick, at age 21; served as company's artistic director (1980–86) and achieved success at Edinburgh Festival Fringe; was director at Royal Shakespeare Company (1987–89), winning Olivier and London Evening Standard awards for *Titus and Andronicus* (1987); regarded as wunderkind, became associate director of Royal National Theater (1989); won Olivier and London Evening Standard awards (1989) for Royal National Theater production of *Electra* and Olivier Award for Ibsen's *Hedda Gabbler* at Abbey Theater in Dublin (1991); returned to Royal Shakespeare Company as director-in-residence and staged controversial *Richard II* (1995), starring Fiona Shaw as monarch; made New York stage directing debut with staging of poem *The Waste Land* (1996) with Shaw again in lead, for which both actress and director received Drama Desk Awards; began directing opera (1992), working at Salzburg Festival (1993) and Glyndebourne Festival (1994), as well as Royal Opera and English National Opera; made film debut with adaptation of Elizabeth Bowen's *The Last September* (1999) starring Shaw and Maggie Smith; returned to stage with *Medea* (Obie Award, 2003), *The Powerbook* (2003) and *Julius Caesar,* starring Ralph Fiennes as Mark Antony (2005); also directed BBC-TV productions of *Hedda Gabler* (1993), *The Wasteland* (1995) and *Richard* (1997).

WARNER, Estella Ford (1891–1974). American physician. Born Estella Ford, Dec 21, 1891, in Ironwood, Michigan; died Sept 10, 1974, in Albuquerque, NM; dau. of Estella (Green) Ford and Cortes Ford (banker and judge); graduate of University of Oregon School of Medicine, 1918; studied pediatrics in London; m. Douglas Holmes Warner, Mar 1918 (died Oct 1918 during the influenza epidemic). ❖ Served as director of Division of Child Hygiene at US Public Health Service (USPHS) in Washington, DC (1931–35); became senior surgeon of Commissioned Corps (1942), district medical officer of Office of Indian Affairs in Albuquerque (1937–42) and San Francisco (1942), and regional officer medical director in Kansas City, MO; established a public health department at American University in Beirut (1951); led American medical assistance program in India (1952); retired to Albuquerque, NM (1956).

WARNER, Gloria (c. 1914–1934). American theatrical dancer. Name variations: Gloria Kelly. Born c. 1914 in New York, NY; died June 8, 1934, in Los Angeles, CA. ❖ At age 5, as Gloria Kelly, made stage debut tap dancing and singing while training at Ned Wayburn's studio; performed in numerous short subjects at Warner Bros. Brooklyn studio, including dance specialty act in *School for Romance* (1927); as Gloria Warner, appeared on Broadway in *Hotcha* and *Take a Chance* (1932);

moved to Hollywood, where she continued to perform for Warner Bros., until leukemia took her life at age 19.

WARNER, Marina (1946—). English literary critic and feminist writer. Born Nov 9, 1946, in London, England; attended Lady Margaret Hall, Oxford; dau. of Italian mother and English father; m. William Shawcross (writer), 1971 (div.); children: 1 son. ❖ Influential feminist, who focused on "the feminine" in myth and history and set out to deconstruct and explain underlying meanings of female archetypes, wrote *The Dragon Empress: Life and Times of Tz'u-his 1835–1908* (1972), *Alone of All Her Sex: The Myth and the Cult of the Virgin Mary* (1976), *Joan of Arc: The Image of Female Heroism* (1981) and *Monuments and Maidens: The Allegory of the Female Form* (1985), which won the Fawcett Book Prize; also published well-received fiction such as *In a Dark Wood* (1977), *The Skating Party* (1982) and *The Lost Father* (1988), which was shortlisted for Booker Prize; was only the 2nd woman to deliver BBC's Reith Lectures (1994), resulting in *Managing Monsters: Six Myths of Our Time* (1994); also wrote children's books *The Impossible Day* (1981) and *The Wobbly Tooth* (1984) and libretti for children's opera, *The Legs of the Queen of Sheba,* produced by English National Opera (1991); was visiting professor of women's studies at University of Ulster (1994–95), Mellon Professor at Pittsburgh University (1997), visiting fellow commoner at Trinity College (1998), Tanner Lecturer at Yale University (1999), visiting fellow of All Souls' College, Oxford (2001) and professor of literature at University of Essex (2004); also wrote (novel) *The Leto Bundle* (2001), (short stories) *Murderers I Have Known* (2002) and (nonfiction) *Fantastic Metamorphoses, Other Worlds* (2002) and *Signs & Wonders: Essays on Literature & Culture* (2003); became fellow of Royal Society of Literature (1985).

WARNER, Susan Bogert (1819–1885). American writer. Name variations: (pseudonym) Elizabeth Wetherell. Born Susan Bogert Warner, July 11, 1819, in New York, NY; died Mar 17, 1885, in Highland Falls, New York; dau. of Henry Whiting Warner (lawyer) and Anna (Bartlett) Warner; sister of Anna Bartlett Warner (1827–1915). ❖ Writing under pseudonym Elizabeth Wetherell, published 1st book, *The Wide, Wide World* (1852), which featured a character not unlike a female Huck Finn and was phenomenally popular, making her the 1st American to sell over a million copies of a book; shedding pen name, followed this with 2 more moderately successful novels, *Queechy* (1852) and *The Law and the Testimony* (1853); published *The Hills of the Shatemuc* (1956), which sold 10,000 copies on the day of its release; a prolific writer, published at least one book each year from 1856 until her death. ❖ See also *Women in World History.*

WARNER, Sylvia Ashton (1908–1984). See Ashton-Warner, Sylvia.

WARNER, Sylvia Townsend (1893–1978). British writer. Born Sylvia Townsend Warner at Harrow, Middlesex, England, Dec 6, 1893; died in Maiden Newton, Dorset, May 1, 1978; dau. of George Townsend Warner (assistant master at Harrow School for Boys) and Eleanor Mary (Nora) Hudleston; lived with Valentine Ackland. ❖ Author who, over a period of 50 years, won critical acclaim and a large readership in England and US for her novels, poetry, short stories, and biography of writer T. H. White; during WWI, interrupted budding career as a composer to work as a shell machinist in munitions factory; served as 1 of 4 editors of 10-vol. *Tudor Church Music* (1917–29); published 1st vol. of poetry, *The Espalier* (1925); found fame and a comfortable income with 1st novel, *Lolly Willowes* (1926); published 2 other novels, *Mr. Fortune's Maggot* and *The True Heart,* which added to her reputation (1927–29); formed a relationship with poet Valentine Ackland that lasted until the latter's death in 1969 (1930); frustrated by continuing economic depression and appeasement of Hitler, joined Communist Party (1935); published 2 novels, *Summer Will Show* (1936) and *After the Death of Don Juan* (1939), which reflect her political commitment to Marxism and admiration for Spanish people's fight against Fascism; involved in war work in Dorset until Germany's surrender in May 1945; her novel about 14th-century nuns, *The Corner That Held Them,* revived interest in her work (1947), as did last novel, *The Flint Anchor* (1954); for remainder of life, wrote some poetry and many short stories published in both England and US; edited 2 vols. of Ackland's poems (early 1970s); published last collection of short stories, *Kingdoms of Elfin,* to wide acclaim (1977); as a writer, was known for her wit, humor, irony, compassion, clarity and marvelous imagery. ❖ See also Claire Harman, *Sylvia Townsend Warner: A Biography* (Chatto & Windus, 1989); Claire Harman, ed. *The Diaries of Sylvia Townsend Warner* (Chatto & Windus, 1994); William Maxwell, ed. *Sylvia Townsend Warner: Letters* (Viking, 1982); Wendy Mulford, *This Narrow Place: Sylvia Townsend Warner and Valentine Ackland: Life, Letters and Politics, 1930–1951* (Pandora, 1988); Michael Steinman, ed.

The Element of Lavishness: Letters of Sylvia Townsend Warner and William Maxwell, 1938–1978 (Counterpoint, 2001); and *Women in World History*.

WARNES, Jennifer (1947—). American musician. Name variations: Jennifer Jean Warnes. Born Jennifer Jean Warnes, Mar 3, 1947, in Seattle, WA. ❖ Performed on Los Angeles folk-music circuit (late 1960s); performed on tv program, "The Smothers Brothers Comedy Hour" (1968); appeared in musical *Hair* in Los Angeles (1969); released several successful albums, including *Jennifer Warnes* (1977), which included hit single, "The Right Time of the Night," *Famous Blue Raincoat* (1986), which had covers of Leonard Cohen songs, and *The Well* (2001); won Academy Award for song "It Goes Like It Goes" from film *Norma Rae* (1979); had #1 hits and won Oscars and Grammys for soundtrack duets, "Up Where We Belong" from *An Officer and a Gentleman* (1982) and "(I've Had) The Time of My Life" from *Dirty Dancing* (1987).

WARNICK, Katrina (1975—). *See Voutilainen, Katrina.*

WARNICKE, Heike (1966—). East German speedskater. Name variations: Heike Warnicke-Schalling. Born June 1, 1966, in Weimar, East Germany; m. Jürgen Warnick (skater), 1990. ❖ Won silver medals for 3,000 and 5,000 meters at Albertville Olympics (1992); at European championships, won bronze for all-around (1990, 1992) and silver (1991, 1993); at World championships, won a silver for all-around (1991) and bronze (1993); took World Cup titles for 3,000 and 5,000 meters (1989, 1991); retired, having participated in 11 European and 10 World championships (1998).

WARNOCK, Mary (1924—). British philosopher. Name variations: Baroness Helen Mary Warnock. Born Helen Mary Wilson, April 14, 1924, in Winchester, England; Oxford University, BA and DPhil; m. Sir Geoffrey James Warnock (philosopher), 1949; children: 5. ❖ Major contributor to 20th-century debates on ethics and education, was educated at Oxford where she became tutor in philosophy at St. Hugh's College; worked as headmistress of Oxford High School and returned to teach at Oxford (1972), before becoming mistress of Girton College, Cambridge; led government commissions into special education, animal experiments, environmental pollution, human fertilization and teaching; works include *Modern Ethics* (1960), *Sartre* (1963), *Existentialism* (1966), *Imagination* (1976), *Schools of Thought* (1977), *Education: A Way Forward* (1979), *A Question of Life* (1985), *Memory* (1987), *The Uses of Philosophy* (1992), and *Imagination and Time* (1994). Named Dame Commander of the British Empire (DEB, 1984); created baroness (1985).

WARREN, Althea (1886–1958). American librarian. Born Althea Hester Warren, Dec 18, 1886, in Waukegan, Illinois; died Dec 20, 1958; dau. of Lansing Warren and Emma Newhall (Blodgett) Warren; University of Chicago, PhB, 1908; University of Wisconsin Library School, BSLS, 1911. ❖ Served as president of California Library Association (1921–22); as city librarian, successfully maneuvered the Los Angeles Public Library through difficult eras of budget cuts; assumed directorship of Victory Book Campaign, collecting 5 million books for military personnel during WWII; served as president of the American Library Association (1943–44). ❖ See also *Women in World History*.

WARREN, Ann Brunton (1769–1808). *See Merry, Ann Brunton.*

WARREN, Caroline Matilda (1785–1844). American novelist and children's writer. Name variations: Caroline Matilda Warren Thayer. Born Caroline Matilda Warren, 1785, in Worcester, Massachusetts; died 1844; dau. of William Warren (1751–1831) and Robey Hathatway Warren. ❖ Works include didactic and religious works for children and the 2-vol. *The Gamesters, or Ruins of Innocence* (1805).

WARREN, Eleanor Clark (1913–1996). *See Clark, Eleanor.*

WARREN, Elinor Remick (1900–1991). American composer and pianist. Born Elinor Remick Warren in Los Angeles, CA, Feb 3, 1900; died April 27, 1991; dau. of Maude Remick Warren (amateur pianist) and James Garfield Warren (businessman); studied piano with Kathryn Cocke and Olga Steeb; studied theory and harmony with composer Gertrude Ross; after attending Mills College, studied in NY with Frank LaForge, Ernesto Beruman, and Clarence Dickenson; studied with Nadia Boulanger in Paris, 1959; m. Raymond Huntsberger (physician), 1925 (div. 1929); m. Z. Wayne Griffin (producer in radio, film, and tv), 1936 (died 1981). ❖ While still a schoolgirl, wrote "A Song of June," which was accepted by NY publisher Schirmer; toured as accompanist for opera

star Florence Easton; often performed with Lawrence Tibbett and Richard Crooks; occasionally appeared as a soloist with symphony orchestras and made piano recordings for Okeh label; premiered 1st orchestral work, *The Harp Weaver*, set to a poem by Edna St. Vincent Millay, at Carnegie Hall, conducted by Antonia Brico (1936); premiered *The Legend of King Arthur* (1940), conducted by Britain's Albert Coates with the Los Angeles Philharmonic, which was also broadcast over Mutual radio network; composed some of her most important works (1940s–50s), among them *The Sleeping Beauty, The Crystal Lake, Along the Western Shore, Singing Earth, Transcontinental, Suite for Orchestra* and *Abram in Egypt*; had triumphant premiere of *Requiem* (1966) at the Dorothy Chandler Pavilion in Los Angeles (1966); produced several additional major works (1970s), including *Symphony in One Movement* and *Good Morning, America!*, for chorus, narrator and orchestra. ❖ See also *Women in World History*.

WARREN, Josephine (1912–1999). *See Barnes, Josephine.*

WARREN, Lavinia (1841–1919). American performer. Name variations: Mrs. Tom Thumb; Mrs. Charles Sherwood Stratton; Mercy Lavinia Stratton. Born Mercy Lavinia Warren Bump or Bumpus, Oct 31, 1841, on a farm in Middleboro, Massachusetts; died Nov 25, 1919, in Middleboro; dau. of James S. Bump and Huldah (Warren) Bump; m. Charles Sherwood Stratton (also known as General Tom Thumb), Jan 10, 1863 (died 1883); m. Count Primo Magri (young Italian dwarf, piccolo player and pugilist who stood 3'9), 1885; children: none, though one was reported. ❖ Performer who turned her genetically endowed dwarfism to her advantage through the showmanship of P. T. Barnum; joined Barnum's American museum (1862); her romance with 3-foot-tall General Tom Thumb was a press agent's dream; following marriage at Manhattan's Grace Church (Feb 10, 1863), with 2,000 attendees, including Mrs. Cornelius Vanderbilt (Sophia Johnson Vanderbilt), honeymooned in Washington, DC, where she met Abraham Lincoln; with husband, set off on a world tour (1869) that lasted 3 years and covered 56,000 miles. ❖ See also *Women in World History*.

WARREN, Mehetabel (c. 1822–1908). *See Newman, Mehetabel.*

WARREN, Mercy Otis (1728–1814). Colonial American writer. Born Mercy Otis, Sept 25, 1728, in Barnstable, Massachusetts; died Oct 19, 1814, in Plymouth, Massachusetts; dau. of Mary Allyne Otis (1702–1767) and Colonel James Otis Sr. (1702–1778); sister of James Otis Jr. (radical leader); m. James Warren Sr. (1726–1808), Nov 14, 1754; children: James Jr. (1757–1821); Winslow (1760–1791); Charles (1762–1785); Henry (1764–1828); George (1766–1800). ❖ Articulate and eloquent poet, playwright, political thinker, and traditional Puritan homemaker who demonstrated convincingly that gender was no barrier to intellectual equality; married and took up residence in husband's family home on the Eel River near Plymouth (1754); purchased the Winslow House in Plymouth (1757); became involved (1760s), at 1st vicariously but later more directly, in the anti-English furor which eventually led to American independence; taking pen in hand to oppose Britain's continuing attacks on American liberty, published *The Adulateur, a Tragedy* in 2 installments in *Massachusetts Spy* (1772), an ill-disguised satire on the political situation in Massachusetts; continued the attack with *The Defeat, a Play* (1773); became Abigail Adams' female mentor and had long-time correspondence with English historian Catharine Macaulay; purchased the Thomas Hutchinson country estate in Milton (1781); sold Milton estate and returned to Plymouth town home and farm (1788); like most anti-federalists, felt that the Constitution of 1787 represented a betrayal of the American Revolution, and wrote of her grievances in *Observations on the New Constitution, and on the Federal Conventions* (1788); published *Poems, Dramatic and Miscellaneous* (1790), a vol. that reflected her growing maturity as a writer and her emergence as a leading advocate of women's rights; published *History of the Rise, Progress and Termination of the American Revolution* (1805), a tour de force consisting of 1,298 pages (31 chapters) in 3 vols. which was the 1st major published historical work written by an American woman; corresponded with John Adams regarding her unfavorable depiction of him in her *History* (1807); the 1st published woman historian in the US, demonstrated a talent, vitality, and determination which commanded attention in the male-dominated society of the American revolutionary era and early national period. ❖ See also Katharine Anthony, *First Lady of the Revolution: The Life of Mercy Otis Warren* (Kennikat, 1958); Alice Brown, *Mercy Warren* (Scribner, 1896); Rosemarie Zagarri, *A Woman's Dilemma: Mercy Otis Warren and the American Revolution* (Harland Davidson, 1995); and *Women in World History*.

WARREN AND SURREY, countess of.
See Isabel of Vermandois (d. before 1147).
See Marshall, Maud (d. 1248).
See Alice le Brun (d. 1255).
See Joan de Vere (fl. 1280s).

WARRENNE, Adelicia de (d. 1178). *See Adelicia de Warrenne.*

WARRENNE, countess of. *See Alice le Brun (d. 1255).*

WARRENNE, Eleanor de (c. 1250–?). *See Eleanor de Warrenne.*

WARRENNE, Gundred de (d. 1085). *See Gundred.*

WARRENNE, Isabel de.
See Isabel de Warrenne (c. 1137–1203).
See Isabel de Warrenne (b. 1253).
See Isabel de Warrenne (d. 1282).

WARRENNE AND SURREY, countess of.
See Isabel of Vermandois (d. before 1147).
See Marshall, Maud (d. 1248).
See Alice le Brun (d. 1255).
See Joan de Vere (fl. 1280s).

WARRICK, Ruth (1915–2005). American actress. Born June 29, 1915, in St. Joseph, MO; died Jan 15, 2005, in New York, NY; cousin of actress Mimi Kennedy; m. Erik Rolf (actor), 1938 (div. 1946); m. Carl Neubert (actor), 1949 (div.); m. Robert McNamara, 1953 (div.); m. L. Jarvis Cushing Jr.; children: (1st m.) Karen Rolf Langenwalter and Jon Rolf; (3d m.) Robert McNamara. ❖ Began career as a radio singer; made film debut as Emily Norton Kane in *Citizen Kane* (1941); other films include *Journey into Fear, The Corsican Brothers, Obliging Young Lady, Petticoat Larceny, The Iron Major, Mr. Winkle Goes to War, China Sky, Song of the South, Driftwood* and *Guest in the House*; made NY stage debut in *The Thorntons* (1956), followed by *Miss Lonelyhearts, Take Me Along, Misalliance* and *Irene*; on tv, appeared on "The Guiding Light" (1953–54), "As the World Turns" (1956–60), "Father of the Bride" (1961–62), as Hannah Cord on "Peyton Place" (1965–67), and as Phoebe Tyler on "All My Children" (1970–2003). ❖ See also autobiography *The Confessions of Phoebe Tyler* (1980).

WARTENBERG, Christiane (1956—). East German runner. Born Oct 27, 1956, in East Germany. ❖ At Moscow Olympics, won a silver medal in 1,500 meters (1980).

WARTHA, Vilma (1847–1922). *See Hugonnay, Vilma.*

WARWICK, countess of.
See Mortimer, Catherine (c. 1313–1369).
See Despenser, Isabel (1400–1439).
See Neville, Cecily (1415–1495).
See Beauchamp, Anne (1426–1492).
See Rich, Mary (1625–1678).
See Greville, Frances Evelyn (1861–1938).

WARWICK, Daisy (1861–1938). *See Greville, Frances Evelyn.*

WARWICK, Dionne (1940—). African-American pop singer. Name variations: Dionne Warwicke. Born Marie Dionne Warrick, Dec 12, 1940, in East Orange, NJ; dau. of Mancel (some sources cite Marcel) Warrick (chef and gospel music promoter) and Lee Warrick (manager of a gospel group); earned a master's degree in music from Hartt College of Music at University of Hartford, 1976; m. Bill Elliot (drummer and actor), 1967 (div. 1975). ❖ Five-time Grammy winner, formed a group called The Gospelaires with 2 cousins and sister Dee Dee (mid-1950s), performing as back-up for other singers, including The Drifters, which brought her to the attention of Burt Bacharach and Hal David; signed contract with Scepter Records and released Bacharach-David's "Don't Make Me Over" (1962), which immediately soared to #21 on *Billboard* charts; collaborated with Bacharach and David to produce nearly 20 bestselling albums and 30 hit singles, including "Anyone Who Had a Heart" and "Walk on By" (both 1964), "Message to Michael" (1966), "I Say a Little Prayer for You" (1968) and "This Girl's in Love with You" (1969); other hits included "Trains and Boats and Planes," "Alfie," "You'll Never Get to Heaven" and "Make It Easy on Yourself"; collaborated with the Spinners on single "Then Came You" (1974), which topped the *Billboard* chart; signed with Arista (1979) and released album *Dionne*, which included "I'll Never Love This Way Again" and "Deja Vu" (both songs earned Grammy Awards, making her the 1st female artist to win in both Pop Female Vocal and Rhythm and Blues Female Vocal categories); on tv, hosted "Solid Gold" (1980), co-hosted

and helped originate "The Soul Train Music Awards," and hosted "Dionne and Friends" and the Psychic Friends Network (1990s); brought together other artists to record "That's What Friends Are For," which raised an estimated $2 million for AIDS research (1986); was also involved in boosting awareness for Sudden Infant Death Syndrome (SIDS) and sickle-cell anemia. Won Grammy Award for "Do You Know the Way to San Jose?" (1968) and "I'll Never Fall in Love Again" (1970); appeared at a command performance for Queen Elizabeth II (1968), the 1st black female performer to be so honored. ❖ See also *Women in World History.*

WARWICK, Lyn (1946—). Australian politician. Name variations: Lynette Robyn Warwick. Born Oct 21, 1946, in Cairns, Australia. ❖ As a Liberal, served in the Queensland Parliament for Barron River (1995–98).

WASER, Anna (1678–1714). Swiss painter. Name variations: Anna Wasser. Born Oct 1678 (some sources cite 1675 or 1676) in Zurich, Switzerland; died after a fall, Sept 20, 1714 (some sources cite 1713); studied in Berne. ❖ Known for her portraits, flowers and miniatures, rendered a self-portrait at age 12; at 21, was appointed court painter to Count Solms; received commissions from Holland, Germany and England.

WASER, Maria (1878–1939). Swiss novelist and essayist. Born Oct 15, 1878, in Bern, Switzerland; died Jan 19, 1939; dau. of Walter Krebs; m. Otto Waser, 1904. ❖ Works include fiction and criticism on art history and the historical novel *Die Geschichte der Anna Waser* (1913), about 17th-century Zurich painter Anna Waser. Was first woman to win Literature Prize of City of Zurich (1938).

WASH, Martha. African-American singer. Name variations: Two Tons O' Fun, The Weather Girls. Born in San Francisco, CA. ❖ Joined gospel group, N. O. W. (News of the World); was backup vocalist for disco singer, Sylvester (1970s); with Izora Armstead, formed duo Two Tons O' Fun and released albums, *Two Tons O' Fun* (1979) and *Backatcha'* (1980); with Armstead, changed name to Weather Girls (1982) and released album *Success* (1983), with hit single, "It's Raining Men"; pursued solo career (early 1990s); sang on several dance hits, including Black Box's "Everybody, Everybody" and C+C Music Factory's "Gonna Make You Sweat," but because of her weight, was replaced by lip-synching models on videos, and not credited on albums; sued for fraud and won; solo albums include *Martha Wash* (1993), and *The Collection* (1998). Other Weather Girls albums include *Big Girls Don't Cry* (1985) and *Weather Girls* (1988).

WASHAM, Jo Ann (1950—). American golfer. Born May 24, 1950, in Auburn, WA; graduate of Washington State University, 1972. ❖ Joined LPGA tour (1973); won Patty Berg Classic and Portland Classic (1975), Rail Charity Classic (1979); on the circuit for 17 years; instructor in Florida.

WASHBOURNE, Mona (1903–1988). English stage and screen actress. Born Nov 27, 1903, in Birmingham, England; died Nov 15, 1988, in London, England; trained as a pianist at Birmingham School of Music. ❖ Made stage debut (1924) and appeared in numerous plays, including *Home*; many films include *Billy Liar, Night Must Fall, My Fair Lady, The Collector, The Winslow Boy, The Good Companions, Cast a Dark Shadow, Doctor in the House, Child's Play, Romeo and Juliet* and *The Blue Bird*; also appeared in PBS series "Brideshead Revisited."

WASHBURN, Margaret Floy (1871–1939). American psychologist. Born Margaret Floy Washburn, July 25, 1871, in Harlem, New York; died Oct 29, 1939, in Poughkeepsie, New York; dau. of Francis Washburn (businessman and Episcopal cleric) and Elizabeth (Floy) Davis Washburn; Vassar College, AB, 1891; Cornell University, PhD, 1894; studied with James McKeen Cattell, Wilhelm Wundt and Edward Bradford Titchener; Wittenberg College, honorary DSc, 1927; never married; no children. ❖ Experimental psychologist, one of the premier women in the field in the early 20th century, devoted her lifelong work to the understanding of human and animal emotions; was professor of psychology, philosophy and ethics at Wells College (1894–1900); co-translated Wilhelm Wundt's 3-vol. *Ethical Systems* from the German; was a warden at Sage College and instructor of social psychology and animal psychology at Cornell University (1900–02); headed the psychology department at University of Cincinnati (1902–03); was associate professor (1904–08) and then professor of psychology (1908–37) at Vassar College, where she established (1912) and served as 1st head of the psychology department; published *The Animal Mind: A Text-Book of Comparative Psychology* (1908), still considered among the greatest psychological treatises; published *Movement and Mental Imagery: Outlines of a Motor Theory of the Complexer Mental Processes* (1916); became the 2nd woman elected to National Academy of Sciences (1931); wrote over 200 articles and book reviews; actively edited numerous journals, serving as one of four coeditors of the *American Journal of Psychology* and initiating *Psychological Abstracts*. ❖ See also *Women in World History*.

WASHBURN, Mary (1907–1994). American runner. Name variations: Mary Washburn Conklin. Born Aug 4, 1907; died Feb 2, 1994, in Weymouth, MA; graduate of DePauw University, 1928. ❖ At Amsterdam Olympics, won a silver medal in 4 x 100-meter relay (1928); was one of the founders of the Long Island Field Hockey Team and played on the US women's lacrosse team for 7 years; coached at Beaver College for 11 years.

WASHINGTON, Bennetta (1918–1991). American educator and Job Corps pioneer. Born 1918 in Winston-Salem, NC; died May 28, 1991, in Washington, DC; m. Walter Washington (mayor of Washington, DC). ❖ As principal of Cardozo High School in Washington, DC, pioneered work-study program which was a model for National Teachers Corps (1961–64); under presidents John F. Kennedy and Lyndon B. Johnson, directed Cardozo Project in Urban Education, the President's Commission on Juvenile Delinquency (1961–64); at request of President Johnson, launched Job Corps program for women (1964); served as associate director of Job Corps, US Labor Department (1970–73); became assistant secretary for employment training at Job Corps (1974); received Human Rights and Fundamental Freedoms Award (1978).

WASHINGTON, Dinah (1924–1963). African-American blues and pop singer. Name variations: Ruth Jones. Born Ruth Lee Jones in Tuscaloosa, AL, Aug 8(?), 1924; died in Detroit, Michigan, Dec 14, 1963; m. John Young, 1941 (div. 1942); m. George Jenkins (drummer), 1946 (div. 1947); m. Robert Grayson, 1947 (div. 1948); m. a saxophonist (div.); m. a cabdriver, 1959 (div. 1960); m. an actor (div.); m. Dick Lane (quarterback for Detroit Lions), 1963. ❖ Moved with mother to Chicago at start of Great Depression; began playing piano and singing in church choirs as a young girl; after winning a singing contest, sang in a local club, the owner of which gave her the stage name by which she would be known (1939); began touring with Lionel Hampton Band as a blues singer (1942) and recorded "Evil Gal Blues" and "Blowtop Blues"; became such a popular rhythm-and-blues artist (mid-1940s) that she went solo; signed with Apollo Records and churned out 12 blues singles, recordings that featured such instrumentalists as Max Roach and Charles Mingus; signed with mainstream Mercury Records and released "Baby Get Lost" (1949), which hit No. 1 on R&B lists; released 2 pop albums, *Look to the Rainbow* (1956) and *Land of Hi-Fi* (1956); known for the intense emotionalism of her interpretations, crossed over to pop charts (1959) with recording of "What a Diff'rence a Day Makes," reaching a mainstream audience and winning a Grammy award that year as best R&B artist. ❖ See also Jim Haskins, *Queen of the Blues: The Story of Dinah Washington* (Morrow, 1987); and *Women in World History*.

WASHINGTON, Fredi (1903–1994). African-American actress and founder. Name variations: Edith Warren. Born Fredricka Carolyn Washington on Dec 23, 1903, in Savannah, Georgia, to a black mother and a white father; died June 28, 1994, in Stamford, Connecticut; attended Egri School of Dramatic Writing and Christophe School of Languages; m. trombonist Lawrence Brown (div.); m. dentist Anthony H. Bell (died). ❖ Typecast in mainstream films as the "tragic mulatto" during her early career, worked to improve dramatic roles for black actors through the Negro Actors Guild of America, which she founded, then served as its 1st executive secretary (1937–38); began stage career at 16 in the chorus of *Shuffle Along*; under stage name Edith Warren, earned critical notice for appearance in Broadway play *Black Boy* (1926); starred in several films, including *Hot Chocolates* and *Great Day* (both 1929); established herself as a dancer with film *Black and Tan Fantasy* (1929); with sister Isabell, starred on stage in *Singin' the Blues*, a melodramatic depiction of Harlem night life (1931); won a starring role in Hall Johnson's folk drama *Run, Little Chillun* (1933); one of the most prominent black dramatic actresses of her day (1930s), created strong roles in such movies as *The Emperor Jones*, *The Old Man of the Mountain* and *Mills Blue Rhythm Band* (all 1933), but it was the movie *Imitation of Life* (1934), based on the novel by Fannie Hurst, that would provide her greatest success; returned to Broadway in *Mamba's Daughters* (1939), *Lysistrata* (1946), *A Long Way From Home* (1948) and *How Long Til*

Summer (1949); also appeared on tv's "The Goldbergs," starring Gertrude Berg. ❖ See also *Women in World History*.

WASHINGTON, Josephine (1861–1949). African-American writer. Born Josephine Turpin on July 31, 1861, in Goochland County, Virginia; died 1949; dau. of Augustus A. Turpin and Maria V. Turpin; attended Richmond Institute (later Richmond Theological Seminary); graduate of Howard University, 1886; m. Samuel H. H. Washington (physician), 1888. ❖ A deeply religious woman, expressed her convictions through prose and poetry; also played a significant role in the development of Selma University in Alabama, founded in 1878 to train ministers and teachers. ❖ See also *Women in World History*.

WASHINGTON, Margaret Murray (c. 1861–1925). African-American educator and lecturer. Born Margaret James Murray on Mar 9, c. 1861 (though her tombstone is inscribed 1865); died June 4, 1925; dau. of Lucy Murray (washerwoman) and an unknown white father born in Ireland; became 3rd wife of Booker T. Washington (1856–1915, founder of Tuskegee Normal and Industrial Institute), Oct 12, 1892. ❖ Educator who, while married to Booker T. Washington, played a significant role in the administration of Tuskegee Institute; 1st met Booker T. Washington (1889), about a month after the death of his 2nd wife Olivia Davidson Washington (his 1st wife Fanny Norton Smith Washington died May 4, 1884); began teaching at Tuskegee (1889), then assumed the position of lady principal (1890); continued working at Tuskegee following marriage, serving in several capacities; became director of the department of domestic science (1900); was also involved in the development of Dorothy Hall, which housed the girls' industries; eventually became dean of women, continuing her service to the institution after her husband's death in 1915; was president of National Federation of Afro-American Women (1896); when the group merged with the Colored Women's League to become the National Association of Colored Women, served as secretary of the executive board, becoming president in 1914; also presided over the Alabama Association of Women's Clubs (1919–25). ❖ See also *Women in World History*.

WASHINGTON, Martha (1731–1802). American first lady. Born Martha Dandridge, June 2, 1731, at Chestnut Grove plantation, in New Kent Co., Virginia; died at Mount Vernon Plantation, Fairfax County, Virginia, May 22, 1802; dau. of John Dandridge (planter) and Frances (Jones) Dandridge; m. Daniel Parke Custis (died 1757), May 15, 1750 (some sources cite 1749); m. George Washington, Jan 6, 1759 (died 1799); children (1st m.) Daniel Parke Custis II (b. 1751, died in infancy); Frances Parke Custis (b. 1753, died in infancy); Martha "Patsy" Parke Custis (1754–1773); John "Jacky" or "Jackie" Parke Custis (1755–1781). ❖ First first lady of the US who, despite the loss of all 4 of her children, maintained a simple dignity as one of Washington's warmest hostesses; inherited one-third of large estate (dower right) upon 1st husband's death (1757); was courted by George Washington (spring 1758); married Washington (Jan 1759); became mistress of Mount Vernon plantation; spent winters at Washington's headquarters during the Revolutionary War; lived at the nation's capitals during Washington's presidency: New York (1789–90), and Philadelphia (1789–97); was responsible for management of Mount Vernon and the other plantations of George Washington after his death (1799–1802); her devotion to family and acceptance of public duty exemplified the virtues extolled by Americans during the era of the founding of a new nation; maintained throughout her life a plain style in appearance and in her relations with people. ❖ See also Elswyth Thane, *Washington's Lady* (Dodd, 1960); Anne H. Wharton, *Martha Washington* (Scribner, 1897); Alice C. Desmond, *Martha Washington: Our First Lady* (Dodd, 1942); Dorothy C. Wilson, *Lady Washington* (Doubleday, 1984); and *Women in World History*.

WASHINGTON, Olivia Davidson (1854–1889). African-American educator and founder. Name variations: Olivia America Davidson. Born Olivia America Davidson, June 11, 1854, in Mercer County, Virginia; died May 9, 1889, in Boston, Massachusetts; dau. of Elias Davidson (a free laborer and former slave) and Eliza (Webb) Davidson; attended Hampton Institute, 1878–79; graduated with honors from State Normal School in Framingham, MA, June 29, 1881; m. Booker T. Washington (1856–1915, one of the great African-American leaders), Aug 11, 1886; children: Booker T. Washington Jr. (b. 1887); Ernest Washington (b. 1889); stepdaughter Portia Washington. ❖ Co-founder of Tuskegee Institute, received a scholarship from Lucy Webb Hayes, wife of President Rutherford B. Hayes, to enroll in the senior class program at Hampton Institute (1878); with colleague Booker T. Washington, founded Tuskegee Institute in Alabama, an institute of higher learning for blacks; was instrumental in organizing fund-raising efforts; in the position of lady principal, oversaw the female students in all aspects of their on-campus lives—dormitory living, industrial work, and class work; as the equal partner of Booker T. Washington in the administration of the school, her influence was felt everywhere; following the death of his 1st wife, Fanny Norton Smith Washington, married him (1886). ❖ See also *Women in World History.*

WASHINGTON, Ora (1899–1971). African-American tennis and basketball player. Born Jan 16, 1899, in Philadelphia, PA; died in May 1971 in Philadelphia. ❖ Played in segregated tennis and basketball leagues (1920s and 1930s); was undefeated singles champion of the all-black American Tennis Association (ATA, 1929–35); played with the Philadelphia Tribune and the Germantown Hornets basketball teams. ❖ See also *Women in World History.*

WASHINGTON, Sarah Spencer (1889–?). African-American entrepreneur. Name variations: Sara Washington. Born in Berkley, Virginia, June 6, 1889; death date unknown; dau. of Joshua and Ellen (Douglass) Phillips; educated at the Lincoln Preparatory School in Philadelphia, and the Norfolk Mission College; studied beauty culture in York, Pennsylvania, and advanced chemistry at Columbia University. ❖ Starting out as a dressmaker, turned to the field of beauty culture (1913), founding a small hairdressing shop in Atlantic City, New Jersey; like Madame C. J. Walker and Annie Turnbo Malone before her, began a house-to-house campaign to sell her wares; by 1919, was the sole owner of Apex Hair and News Co., conducting classes and setting up supply stations throughout New York and New Jersey; by 1939, her regular staff had grown to 215, with 35,000 agents throughout US; was also generous with her money, giving often to the black community.

WASILEWSKA, Wanda (1905–1964). Polish-born Russian politician and writer. Name variations: Vanda L'vovna Vasilievskaia; Wanda Wassilewska. Born Jan 21, 1905, in Cracow (Kraków), Poland; died July 29, 1964, in Kiev, Ukraine; dau. of Leon Wasilewski (politician involved with Polish nationalist movement); graduated from University at Kraków, 1927; married a university student and revolutionary (died); m. Marion Bogatko (a mason); m. Ukrainian-born Alexander Korneichuk (Ukrainian-born playwright and novelist who became foreign minister of the new Ukrainian Republic in 1944); children: Eva. ❖ Published major novels with proletarian themes: *The Image of the Day* (1934), *Motherland* (1935), *Earth in Bondage* (1938), and the trilogy *Flames in the Marshes* (1939); after losing her job as editor of the Warsaw children's magazine *Płomyk* (1937), because of her Communist associations, began work with *Nowe Widnokręgi* (New Horizons), a radical Polish publication; when Nazi Germany annexed Poland, left for Soviet Russia (1939); though she became a Soviet citizen, maintained strong ties to her Polish origins, developing the Russian-sponsored Union of Polish Patriots, an organization composed of Polish leftists living in Russia (c. 1943); became editor of the Polish-language newspaper *Volna Polska* (Free Poland) and correspondent to the Red Army (1943); was head of the Soviet-backed Union of Polish Patriots and deputy chair of the Polish Committee of National Liberation, which later became the provisional government of Poland after its liberation from the Nazis; also wrote *The Rainbow* (1942), her only book to reach an American audience through an English translation. ❖ See also *Women in World History.*

WASSER, Anna (1678–1714). *See Waser, Anna.*

WASSERSTEIN, Wendy (1950–2006). American playwright. Born Oct 18, 1950, in Brooklyn, New York; died Jan 30, 2006, in New York, NY; dau. of Morris Wasserstein (textile manufacturer) and Lola Scheifer; Mount Holyoke College, BA, 1971; Yale Drama School, MFA, 1976; children: (adopted) Lucy Jane Wasserstein. ❖ Pulitzer Prize-winning playwright, had 1st play, *Any Woman Can't*, produced by Playwrights Horizons (1973); collaborated with David Hollister on musical *Montpelier Pa-Zazz* (produced at Playwrights Horizons, 1975) and with Christopher Durang on musical revue *When Dinah Shore Ruled the Earth* (1977); had 1st major success with *Uncommon Women and Others*, which opened off-Broadway at Marymount Manhattan Theater (1977), followed by *Isn't It Romantic?* (1983); wrote *The Heidi Chronicles* (1986), which had an extended run on Broadway and won a Tony Award and Pulitzer Prize (1988–89); also wrote *Bachelor Girls* (1990), *The Object of My Affection: A Screenplay* (1990), *The Sisters Rosensweig* (1994), *Pamela's First Musical* (children's book, 1996) and *An American Daughter* (1998).

WATANABE, Yoko (1953–2004). Japanese soprano. Born 1953 in Fukuoka, Kyushu, Japan; died of cancer, July 15, 2004, in Milan, Italy; graduate of Tokyo National University of Fine Arts and Music, 1976, then studied in Milan; m. Renato Grimaldi (Italian tenor). ❖ Renowned for her Cio-Cio-San, began career as a dancer and pianist; moved to Milan (1976); made professional debut as Nedda in Leoncavallo's *Pagliacci* in Treviso, Italy (1978); made La Scala debut as Liu in Puccini's *Turandot* (1985); during 20 year career, sang other Puccini heroines, as well as roles in works of Mozart, Verdi, Gounod and Bizet; as Cio-Cio-San in *Madama Butterfly*, made debuts at Royal Opera (1983), Lyric Opera of Chicago (1986) and Metropolitan Opera (1987); also sang at the Vienna Staatsoper; was the 1st Japanese to sing lead roles in the world's four major opera houses.

WATANNA, Onoto (1875–1954). *See Babcock, Winnifred.*

WATERBURY, Lucy McGill (1861–1949). *See Peabody, Lucy.*

WATERFORD, countess of (1913–2003). *See Talbot, Nadine.*

WATERS, Alice (1944—). American chef and culinary-arts writer. Born April 28, 1944, in Chatham, New Jersey; graduate of University of California, at Berkeley, 1967; trained at Montessori School, London; children: Fanny (b. 1983). ❖ Opened Chez Panisse (1971), offering a single fixed-price menu that changes daily, serving the highest quality food only when in season; created the Chez Panisse Foundation (1996); wrote 8 books, including *Chez Panisse Vegetables* and *Chez Panisse Café Cookbook*, and the children's book, *Fanny at Chez Panisse*; named Best Chef in America by James Beard Foundation (1992) and one of the 10 best chefs in the world by Cuisine et Vins de France (1986); won James Beard Humanitarian Award (1997). Chez Panisse was named Best Restaurant in America by *Gourmet* magazine (2001). ❖ See also Joan Reardon, *M. F. K. Fisher, Julia Child, and Alice Waters: Celebrating the Pleasures of the Table* (Harmony, 1994).

WATERS, Ethel (1896–1977). African-American singer and actress. Born Ethel Perry, Oct 31, 1896, in Chester, PA; died Sept 1, 1977, in Chatsworth, CA; illeg. dau. of Louise Anderson who had been raped at knifepoint at age 12 by John Waters; m. Merritt "Buddy" Punsley, in 1913 (div. 1915); m. Clyde Matthews, c. 1930 (div. c. 1933); m. Edward Mallory. ❖ At 17, began appearing as "Sweet Mama Stringbean" in vaudeville shows and nightclubs, often singing "St. Louis Blues," a song that would become her trademark; worked at Harlem's Lincoln Theater, signed with Black Swan Records, and toured with Fletcher Henderson; came to national attention with performance in *Plantation Revue* in Chicago (1924); made Broadway debut in musical *Africana* (1927); recorded with Tommy Dorsey and Benny Goodman; appeared in 1st film, *On with the Show* (1929), singing "Am I Blue?" and "Birmingham Bertha"; appeared at Harlem's Cotton Club, singing "Stormy Weather," and on Broadway in Irving Berlin's *As Thousands Cheer*, singing "Supper Time," "Heat Wave" and "Harlem on My Mind"; was then the highest paid female performer on Broadway; opened in *Mamba's Daughters* to nearly unanimous praise (1939) and is generally credited with being the 1st African-American woman to receive star billing in legitimate theater and, later, on screen; scored another triumph as Petunia in *Cabin in the Sky* (1940); appeared in the film version of *Cabin in the Sky*, as well as *Cairo* (1942) and *Stage Door Canteen* (1943); though nominated for Academy Award for Best Supporting Actress for portrayal of Aunt Dicey in film *Pinky* (1949), is best remembered for performance in both the stage and screen versions of *The Member of the Wedding*; starred in tv series "Beulah" and toured with one-woman show, *An Evening with Ethel Waters* (1957); in later years, frequently appeared with the Billy Graham Crusade. ❖ See also autobiographies (with Charles Samuels) *His Eye Is on the Sparrow* (Doubleday, 1951) and (with Eugenia Price and Joyce Blackburn) *To Me It's Wonderful* (Harper and Row, 1972); and *Women in World History.*

WATERS, Lucy (c. 1630–1658). *See Walter, Lucy.*

WATERS, Maxine (1938—). American politician. Born Aug 15, 1938, in St. Louis, Missouri; California State University, Los Angeles, BA, 1970; m. Sidney Williams (diplomat); children: 2. ❖ Was a teacher and volunteer in the Head Start program; elected to California State Assembly (1976) and re-elected every 2 years (1977–91); representing California's 35th District, elected to Congress (1990); drew attention to allegations of CIA involvement in drug trafficking in South Central Los Angeles and rose to prominence after Los Angeles riots (1992); served as chair of Congressional Black Caucus (1997–98); appointed chief deputy whip of Democratic Party and served on many committees; co-founded Black Women's Forum and founded several civil-rights and community development organizations; elected (2002) to her 7th term and named co-chair of House Democratic Steering Committee; noted for support of black business endeavors, encouragement of youth and women, championing of environmental concerns, and work among black communities in Los Angeles.

WATKINS, Frances Ellen (1825–1911). *See Harper, Frances E. W.*

WATKINS, Gladys Elinor (1884–1939). New Zealand pianist, carillonist, and composer. Name variations: Gladys Elinor Muir. Born Oct 20, 1884, in Akaroa, New Zealand; died Oct 30, 1939, in Wellington, New Zealand; dau. of Stephen Watkins (gardener) and Elizabeth Ellen (Pavitt) Watkins; m. Ernest Edward Muir (reporter), 1937. ❖ Performed as piano accompanist in Wellington (early 1910s); studied at Belgian national carillon school in Mechelen and performed in recital throughout Belgium, France, Holland, and in London; was 1st official carillonist of New Zealand's only carillon; made 2 recordings of 4 carillon arrangements for His Master's Voice (1930); also noted for original compositions, many of which were published by Dutch Carillon Society. ❖ See also *Dictionary of New Zealand Biography* (Vol. 4).

WATKINS, Linda (1908–1976). American stage and screen actress. Born May 23, 1908, in Boston, MA; died Oct 31, 1976, in Santa Monica, CA; m. Gabriel L. Hess (lawyer). ❖ Made Broadway debut at 16 in *The Devil in the Cheese* (1926) and subsequently appeared in over 20 productions, including *The Wild Duck, Hedda Gabler, Lady from the Sea, June Moon, Midnight* and *Janie*; arrived in Hollywood (1931); films include *Gay Caballero, Going Steady, 10 North Frederick, Cash McCall, Parent Trap* and *Good Neighbor Sam.*

WATKINS, Margaret (1884–1969). Canadian-born Scottish photographer. Name variations: Meta Gladys Watkins. Born 1884 in Hamilton, Canada, to Scottish parents; died 1969 in Glasgow, Scotland. ❖ Studied photography with Clarence White in New York City (1914–16); produced still lifes, portraits, landscapes and nudes and exhibited throughout US and abroad (1916–30); joined Pictorial Photographers of America and edited the organization's journal (1920); worked for J. Walter Thompson, where she did advertising photography for Macy's department store (1920s); traveled throughout Europe and Soviet Union (1928), producing documentary photos in both Moscow and Leningrad (1930); moved to Scotland (1931) and remained there for rest of life; her executor discovered over 200 photographs after her death.

WATKINS, Mrs. (1907—). *See Lackie, Ethel.*

WATKINS, Tionne (1970—). African-American singer. Name variations: Tionne "T-Boz" Watkins, T. T., T-bone, TLC. Born Tionne Tenese Watkins, April 26, 1970, in Des Moines, IA; m. Mack 10 (musician), Aug 19, 2000; children: 1 daughter, Chase Rolison (b. Oct 20, 2000). ❖ As a member of hugely successful R&B trio, TLC, released debut album, *Ooooooohhh . . . On the TLC Tip* (1992), which went to No. 3 on R&B charts and included Top-10 hits, "Ain't 2 Proud 2 Beg," "Baby-Baby-Baby" and "What About Your Friends"; with group, appeared in film *House Party 3* and released album *CrazySexyCool* (1994), which won 2 Grammy Awards and included hits, "Creep," "Waterfalls," "Red Light Special" and "Diggin' On You"; with TLC, released enormously popular album, *Fanmail* (1999), which entered charts at No. 1, and included hits, "No Scrubs" and "Unpretty"; after death of TLC's Lisa Lopes, released tribute album with Rozonda Thomas, *3D* (2002).

WATKINS, Yoko Kawashima (1933—). Japanese-American children's writer. Born Yoko Kawashima, 1933, in Harbin, Manchuria; dau. of a Japanese goverment official; m. Donald Watkins (US pilot), 1953; children: 4; (adopted) 2. ❖ Grew up in Nanam, North Korea; forced to flee to Japan by Korean Communist forces; moved with husband to US (1958) and lectured extensively on wartime experiences to children in US, Asia, and England; works include *So Far From the Bamboo Grove* (1986), about experiences of escape from North Korea to Japan.

WATKINSON, Angela (1941—). English politician. Born Angela Ellicott, Nov 18, 1941, in England; m. Roy Michael Watkinson, 1961. ❖ As a Conservative, elected to House of Commons at Westminster (2001, 2005) for Upminster.

WATLEY, Jody (1959—). African-American pop singer and dancer. Name variations: Shalamar. Born Jan 30, 1959, in Chicago, IL; m. Andre Cymone (musician, div. 1995); children: 2. ❖ As a teen, was a dancer on tv show "Soul Train" (1970s); helped form dance band Shalamar (1977); with group, had such hits as "The Second Time Around," "Right in the Socket," "Make That Move" and "Dancing in the Streets"; performed on Shalamar albums *Disco Gardens* (1978), *Go for It* (1981), and *The Look* (1983); quit band (1984); released eponymous

debut solo album (1987), which included hits "Looking for a New Love," "Don't You Want Me" and "Some Kind of Lover," and won Grammy for Best New Artist; released gold album, *Larger Than Life* (1989), which included hits "Real Love," "Everything" and "Friends"; set up own label, Avitone, and released album *Affection* (1995); appeared in Broadway production of *Grease* (1996); released singles "Off the Hook" (1998) and "I Love to Love" (2000).

WATLEY, Natasha (1981—). American softball player. Born Nov 27, 1981, in Canoga Park, CA; attended University of California, Los Angeles. ❖ Shortstop, won World championship (2002) and voted MVP; won team gold medal at Athens Olympics (2004).

WATSON, Ada (1859–1921). Australian prime-ministerial wife. Born Ada Jane Low, 1859, in England; died July 19, 1921, in Sydney, Australia; m. Chris Watson (prime minister of Australia, 1904), Nov 27, 1889. ❖ Probably instrumental in her husband's resigning from the Federal Parliamentary Labor Party (1907).

WATSON, Debbie (1965—). Australian water-polo player. Born Sept 28, 1965, in NSW, Australia. ❖ Made the Australian national team (1984), captained it (1991–94) and won a World Cup (1986); won a team gold medal at Sydney Olympics (2000).

WATSON, Debra (1950—). *See Watson, Pokey.*

WATSON, Edith (1861–1943). American photographer. Born 1861 in New England; died 1943, probably in Canada; companion of writer Victoria Hayward (1911–43). ❖ Created portraits, landscapes and social documentation in late 19th and early 20th centuries; traveled extensively through Canada, photographing Canadians at work (1890s–1930); especially well known for her work on the Quebecoises (1910) and the Doukhobors (1919) and her photographs of Mennonites in the prairies and clam diggers and fishermen in Cape Breton; work was widely published in magazines. ❖ See also *Women in World History.*

WATSON, Ella (1861–1889). *See Watson, Ellen.*

WATSON, Ellen (1861–1889). American frontierswoman. Name variations: Ella Watson; Ellen Liddy Pickell; "Cattle Kate"; also mistakenly known as Kate Champion and Kate Maxwell. Born Ellen Liddy Watson, July 2, 1861, in Arran Township, Ontario, Canada; died July 20, 1889, in Sweetwater Valley of Wyoming Territory, by hanging; dau. of Thomas Lewis (farmer) and Frances (Close) Watson; m. William A. Pickell, Nov 24, 1879 (div. 1886); m. James Averell or Averill, May 17, 1886; no children. ❖ Homesteader accused of cattle rustling who became the 1st woman lynched in Wyoming Territory, and only the 3rd in the frontier history of America's West (the other 2 had committed murder), in a hanging carried out by a group of ranchers for their self-interests; moved with family to farm near Lebanon, Kansas (1877); after leaving 1st marriage, worked as cook and domestic employee in Nebraska and Wyoming until filing a homestead claim in Sweetwater Valley, Wyoming; a victim of the range wars, was accused with Jim Averell of cattle rustling by cattle ranchers who seized and lynched them (1889); newspapers owned by cattle interests blacked her reputation to explain the lynching, charging her with being a prostitute and accepting stolen cattle as payment. ❖ See also George W. Hufsmith, *The Wyoming Lynching of Cattle Kate, 1889* (High Plains, 1993); and *Women in World History.*

WATSON, Janet Vida (1923–1985). English geologist. Born Sept 1, 1923, in Hampstead, London, England; died Mar 29, 1985, in Ashtead, England; dau. of David Meredith Seares Watson (paleontologist and professor of zoology and comparative anatomy at University of London) and Katherine Margarite Watson (scientist); graduated with 1st-class honors in biology and geology from Reading University, 1943; Imperial College in London, PhD, 1949; m. John Sutton (geologist and chair of geology department at Imperial College), in 1949; children: 2 daughters (both died at birth). ❖ Studied some of the world's most ancient rocks; wrote 2 foundation texts in the study of geology, *Introduction to Geology* (1962) and *Beginning Geology* (1966); was a professor of geology at Imperial College; served as 1st woman president of the Geological Society of London (1982–84); assisted H. H. Read and had a professional partnership with husband. Co-recipient with husband of the Bigsby medal and the Lyell medal from the Geological Society of London.

WATSON, Jean (1933—). New Zealand novelist and short-story writer. Born 1933 on a farm near Whangarei, New Zealand; graduate of Victoria University; m. Barry Crump (writer). ❖ Probably best known for *Stand* *in the Rain* (1965), which was reissued in 1985 and 1995; also wrote *The Balloon Watchers* (1975), *The World is an Orange and the Sun* (1978), *Address to a King* (1986) and *Three Sea Stories* (1994). ❖ See also memoir, *Karunai Illam: The Story of an Orphanage* (1992), about her involvement with the founding of an orphanage in southern India.

WATSON, Jill (1963—). American pairs skater. Born 1963 in Bloomington, IN. ❖ With partner Peter Oppegard (1984–89), won a bronze medal at Calgary Olympics (1988) and US National championships (1985, 1987, 1988).

WATSON, Keala O'Sullivan (1950—). See O'Sullivan, Keala.

WATSON, Lillian (1950—). See Watson, Pokey.

WATSON, Linda (1955—). Zimbabwean field-hockey player. Born Sept 15, 1965. ❖ At Moscow Olympics, won a gold medal in team competition (1980).

WATSON, Lucile (1879–1962). Canadian-born character actress. Born May 27, 1879, in Quebec, Canada; died June 24, 1962, in New York, NY; m. Louis Shipman (playwright, died 1934). ❖ Made Broadway debut in *Wisdom of the Wise* (1902); other NY shows include *Captain Jinks, The City, Under Cover, Heartbreak House, Yes My Darling Daughter, Dear Octopus, Ring Round the Moon*, and the revival of *The Bat* (1953); films include *What Every Woman Knows, Waterloo Bridge, Pride and Prejudice, Julia Misbehaves* and *Little Women* (1949). Nominated for Academy Award for her performance as Bette Davis' mother in *Watch on the Rhine* (1943).

WATSON, Lynette (1952—). Australian swimmer. Born Nov 22, 1952, in Australia. ❖ At Mexico City Olympics, won a silver medal in the 4 x 100-meter medley relay (1968).

WATSON, Mary (1948—). See Gordon-Watson, Mary.

WATSON, Maud (b. 1864). English tennis player. Born Maud Edith Eleanor Watson, 1864, in Harrow, Middlesex, England; daughter of a rector in Berkswell, England; sister of Lillian Watson (tennis player). ❖ Was the 1st woman champion at Wimbledon (1884), when she beat her older sister Lillian in a tough final; repeated her win, beating Blanche Bingley Hillward (1885); handily beat her sister once more (1886), a Wimbledon face-off between sisters that would not be repeated until 2000, when Venus Williams beat Serena in the semifinals on center court. ❖ See also *Women in World History*.

WATSON, Pokey (1950—). American swimmer. Name variations: Lillian Watson; Debra Watson. Born Lillian Debra Watson, July 11, 1950, in Mineola, LI, NY; m. Allen Richardson (all-American swimmer), 1971; children: 3. ❖ At Tokyo Olympics, age 14, won a gold medal in 4 x 100-meter freestyle relay (1964); won consecutive US national titles, 1st in the outdoor freestyle 100-meter event, then in the 200-meter event; at Mexico City Olympics, won a gold medal in the inaugural 200-meter backstroke (1968), with a time of 2:24.8 seconds.

WATSON, Rosamund (1860–1911). British poet and essayist. Name variations: Rosamund Marriott Watson; Mrs. G. Armytage; R. Armytage; (pseudonym) Graham R. Tomson. Born Rosamund Ball, Oct 6, 1860, in Hackney, London, England; died Dec 29, 1911, in Shere, Surrey, England; dau. of Benjamin William Ball and Sylvia (Good) Ball; m. George Francis Armytage, 1879 (div.); Arthur Graham Tomson, 1887 (div. 1896); children: 4. ❖ Apart from poetry, wrote essays on art, fashion, gardening, and interior design; writings include *Tares* (1884), *The Bird-Bride, and Other Poems* (1889), *A Summer Night and Other Poems* (1891), *The Patch-Work Quilt* (1891), *Vespertilia, and Other Poems* (1895), *The Art of the House* (1897), *An Island Rose* (1900), *After Sunset* (1904), *The Heart of a Garden* (1906), and *The Poems of Rosamund Marriott Watson* (1912).

WATSON, Sheila (1909–1998). Canadian novelist and short-story writer. Born Sheila Doherty, Oct 24, 1909, in New Westminster, British Columbia, Canada; died Feb 1, 1998, at Nanaimo, British Columbia; dau. of Charles Edward Doherty (physician); attended University of British Columbia; m. Wilfred Watson (poet and playwright), 1941 (died less than 2 months after his wife, 1998). ❖ Taught English in high schools before studying for PhD at University of Toronto under Marshall McLuhan; taught in department of English at University of Alberta, Edmonton; with husband, established periodical *The White Pelican* (1971); probably best known for her modernist novel *The Double Hook* (1959), also wrote *Four Stories* (1979), *And the Four Animals* (1980),

Five Stories (1984), and *Deep Hollow Creek* (1992). ❖ See also F.T. Flahiff, *Always Someone to Kill the Doves: A Life of Sheila Watson* (2005).

WATSON, Violet Alberta Jessie (1893–1972). See Burns, Violet Alberta Jessie.

WATT, Grace (1908–1986). See Hickling, Grace.

WATT, Kathryn (1964—). Australian cyclist. Born Sept 11, 1964, in Victoria, Australia. ❖ At Barcelona Olympics, won a silver medal in 3,000-meter indiv. pursuit and a gold medal in indiv. road race (1992).

WATT, Phylis (1965—). See Smith, Phylis.

WATTEVILLE, Benigna von (1725–1789). German-born countess and educator. Name variations: Benigna de Watteville; Benigna, Baroness von Watteville; Henrietta Benigna Justine Zinzendorf von Watteville; Countess Benigna von Zinzendorf; Benigna Zinzendorf; Countess of Zinzendorf and Pottendorf. Born Henrietta Benigna Justine Zinzendorf, Dec 28, 1725, in Berthelsdorf, Saxony; died May 11, 1789, in Berthelsdorf; dau. of Count Nicolaus Ludwig von Zinzendorf and Countess Erdmuthe Dorothea von Reuss; m. Baron Johann von Watteville (de Watteville) (Moravian cleric), 1746; children: 2 sons, 2 daughters; grandmother of noted American botanist Lewis David von Schweinitz (1780–1834). ❖ Organized what was probably 1st girls' boarding school in American colonies in Moravian community of Germantown, PA (1742); helped reorganize school to expand curriculum (1748) and open it to students outside Moravian church (1784).

WATTLES, Santha Rama Rau (b. 1923). See Rama Rau, Santha.

WATTLETON, Faye (1943—). African-American reproductive-rights activist. Name variations: Alyce Faye Wattleton. Born Alyce Faye Wattleton on July 8, 1943, in St. Louis, Missouri; dau. of George Edward Wattleton (factory worker) and Ozie (Garrett) Wattleton (seamstress and preacher); graduate of Ohio State University Nursing School, 1964; Columbia University, MS, 1967; m. Franklin Gordon (social worker), 1973 (div. 1981); children: Felicia Gordon (b. 1975). ❖ Was the 1st African-American, the 1st woman since founder Margaret Sanger, and the youngest individual to serve as president of the Planned Parenthood Federation of America (PPFA); worked as a consultant and assistant director of Public Health Nursing Services for Dayton, Ohio (1967); became executive director of the local Planned Parenthood board (1969); became chair of the national executive director's council of PPFA (1975) and was appointed to the presidency (1978); soon began to change the direction of Planned Parenthood, which until then had been recognized primarily for its 850 clinics in 46 states, serving some 3 million each year with everything from infertility counseling and birth control to prenatal care; was a strong advocate for women's rights and reproductive freedom, making numerous guest appearances on radio and tv talk shows to rally support; was president of PPFA (1978–92); established a women's policy think tank, the Center for Gender Equality, to promote a national dialogue on the economic, political, and educational aspects of women's lives in addition to health and reproductive rights (1995). Received American Humanist Award (1986) and the Jefferson Award for the Greatest Public Service Performed by a Private Citizen (1992); inducted into the National Women's Hall of Fame (1993). ❖ See also *Women in World History*.

WATTS, Heather (1953—). American ballet dancer. Born Sept 27, 1953, in Los Angeles, CA. ❖ Trained at School of American Ballet; danced with New York City Ballet throughout career; featured in numerous Balanchine works, including *Symphony in C, Concerto Barocco*, and *Symphony in Three Movements*, and Robbins' *Goldberg Variations* and *In the Night*; also created roles for Peter Martins' *Calcium Light Night* (1977), *Pas de Deux* and *A Sketch Book* (1978).

WATTS, Helen (1927—). Welsh contralto. Born Dec 7, 1927, in Milford Haven, southwest Wales; studied under Caroline Hatchard and Frederick Jackson at Royal Academy of Music in London. ❖ Known chiefly for oratorio and opera roles, was also an interpreter of lieder and 20th-century songs; debuted in choruses at Glyndebourne Festival and BBC; gave 1st solo performance (1953); performed Bach arias under baton of Sir Malcolm Sargent at London Promenade Concerts (1955), the springboard for a successful concert career on European and North American circuits; embarked on an opera career as Didymus in *Theodora* with Handel Opera Society (1958) and regularly performed with the society for next 6 years; debuted at Salzburg Festival as 1st Maid in *Elektra*; made American debut in *A Mass of Life* (1966); also appeared most notably as Lucretia during a tour of Russia with English Opera Group, as the 1st Norn in *Götterdammerung* in debut at Covent Garden (1965), and as

Mistress Quickly at Welsh National Opera (1969), where she enjoyed a long run as a leading member until her retirement in 1983. Named Commander of the Order of the British Empire (1978). ❖ See also *Women in World History*.

WATTS RUSSELL, Elizabeth Rose Rebecca (1833/34–1905). New Zealand society leader. Name variations: Elizabeth Rose Rebecca Bradshaw, Elizabeth Rose Rebecca Creyke. Born Elizabeth Rose Rebecca Bradshaw, c. 1833 or 1834, probably in Ireland; died Oct 7, 1905, at Horsham, Sussex, England; m. John Charles Watts Russell, c. 1850 (died 1875); m. Alfred Richard Creyke, 1875 (died 1893). ❖ Immigrated with 1st husband to New Zealand (1850); established 30-acre estate, which became social center for Canterbury elite (1851); traveled and became active in charitable activities; returned to England (1875). ❖ See also *Dictionary of New Zealand Biography* (Vol. 1).

WAUNEKA, Annie Dodge (1910–1997). Native American activist. Name variations: Anne Wauneka. Name variations: known to the Navajo nation as "Our Legendary Mother." Born April 10, 1910, near Sawmill, Arizona; died of Alzheimer's disease, Nov 10, 1997, in Flagstaff, Arizona; dau. of Henry Chee Dodge (Navajo rancher and politician) and K'eehabah (also seen as Kee'hanabah); University of Arizona, BS in public health; m. George Wauneka, Oct 1929; children: Georgia, Henry, Irma, Franklin, Lorencita and Sallie Wauneka; and 2 who died young. ❖ Navajo public health activist and tribal leader who was the 1st Native American to win US Presidential Medal of Freedom (1963); became the 1st woman elected to Navajo Tribal Council (1951), then reelected (1955 and 1959); as chair of the health committee, focused 1st on tuberculosis, the reservation's most pernicious problem; studied in the hospitals and laboratories of US Public Health Service; also wrote a Navajo dictionary to help her people understand the illnesses they faced, and the cures and treatments that were available; brought understanding to other health areas, including improved gynecological, obstetric, and pediatric care; advocated regular eye and ear exams, and fought alcohol abuse; served on New Mexico Committee on Aging and became a member of advisory boards of US Surgeon General and US Public Health Service; began hosting her own daily radio show on KGAK in Gallup, New Mexico (1960); served as an advisor to the Navajo Tribal Council into her 80s. Honored as the legendary mother of the Navajo people by Navajo council (1984); inducted into the Women's Hall of Fame at Seneca Falls, NY (2000). ❖ See also Carolyn Niethammer, *I'll Go and Do More: Annie Dodge Wauneka, Navajo Leader and Activist* (U. of Nebraska Press, 2001); and *Women in World History*.

WAY, Amanda M. (1828–1914). American preacher and social reformer. Born July 10, 1828, in Winchester, Indiana; died Feb 24, 1914; dau. of Matthew and Hannah (Martin) Way (both Quakers); attended Randolph Seminary in Winchester; never married. ❖ Worked on behalf of women's rights and for temperance in Indiana and Kansas; was vice-president and later president of the Indiana Woman's Rights Society; co-edited the *Woman's Tribune,* an Indianapolis newspaper; was the 1st woman to be elected Grand Worthy Chief Templar of the temperance-oriented Independent Order of Good Templars; became a licensed preacher of Methodist Episcopal Church (1871), to which she had converted from Quakerism several years before; served as 1st president of Women's Christian Temperance Union in Kansas; was a Quaker minister (1880–1914). ❖ See also *Women in World History*.

WAYBURN, Peggy (1917–2002). American conservationist. Name variations: Cornelia E. Wayburn. Born Cornelia Elliot, Sept 2, 1917, in New York, NY; died Mar 21, 2002, in San Francisco, CA; graduate of Barnard College, 1941; m. Dr. Edgar Wayburn (president of the Sierra Club); children: Diana, Laurie, Cynthia and William. ❖ With husband, helped preserve millions of acres, including the Redwood National Park, The Golden Gate National Recreation Area, the greenbelt from the Point Reyes National Seashore to Sweeney Ridge along the Pacific Coast, and the expansion of Mount Tamalpais State Park; also was influential in passage of the Alaska Lands Act (1980), the largest public lands bill in the history of Congress; wrote 5 books, including *The Edge of Life* and *Alaska: The Great Land*; was director of the Point Reyes Foundation and helped found People for Open Space.

WAYNE, Carol (1942–1985). American actress. Born Sept 6, 1942, in Chicago, IL; died Jan 13, 1985, by drowning in Santiago Bay, Manzanillo, Mexico; dau. of Merrill Roberts (actor); sister of Nina Wayne (actress); m. Barry Feinstein (div.); m. Burt Sugarman (div.); children: son. ❖ Began career skating with sister in Ice Capades; was a show girl in Las Vegas; best known as "The Matinee Girl" on "The

Johnny Carson Show"; films include *Viva Las Vegas, The Party* and *The Heartbreaker*.

WAYNE, Patricia (1926–1974). See Cutts, Patricia.

WAYTE, Elizabeth (fl. 1460s). See Lucy, Elizabeth.

WAYTE, Mary (1965—). American swimmer. Born Mar 25, 1965, in Mercer Island, Washington; attended University of Florida. ❖ At Los Angeles Olympics, won a gold medal in 200-meter freestyle (1984); at Seoul Olympics, won a bronze medal in 4 x 100-meter freestyle relay and a silver medal in 4 x 100-meter medley relay (1988); won 4 US national championships and 2 NCAA championships; became a color commentator for Sports Channel, NBC, and ESPN. Inducted into International Swimming Hall of Fame (2000).

WEAMES, Anne (fl. 1650s). See Weamys, Anna.

WEAMYS, Anna (fl. 1650s). British poet. Name variations: Anne Weames; (pseudonym) Mrs. A. W. ❖ Traditionally thought of as author of *A Continuation of Sir Philip Sydney's [sic] "Arcadia": Wherein is handled the Loves of Amphialus and Helena Queen of Corinth, Prince Plangus and Erona. With the Historie of the Loves of Old Claius and Young Strephon to Urania* (1651).

WEATHER GIRLS, The.
See Armstead, Izora.
See Wash, Martha.

WEATHERSPOON, Teresa (1965—). African-American basketball player. Name variations: Spoon; T-Spoon. Born Dec 8, 1965, in Pineland, TX; dau. of Rowena Weatherspoon and James Weatherspoon (minor-league baseball player for Minnesota Twins); Louisiana Tech University, degree in physical education, 1988. ❖ Was a member of 3 gold-medal basketball teams in international competition, the FIBA World championships (1986), Goodwill Games (1986), and World University Games (1987); led college basketball team, Lady Techsters, to NCAA championship (1988); won a team gold medal for US at Seoul Olympics (1988) and a team bronze medal at Barcelona Olympics (1992); played professionally in Italy for 8 years and in Russia for 2; joined the New York Liberty team in the inaugural season of the Women's National Basketball Association (1997); named the WNBA Defensive Player of the Year (1997, 1998); 4-time WNBA All-Star (1999–2002); signed with Los Angeles Sparks (2003). Co-wrote *Basketball for Girls*. ❖ See also *Women in World History*.

WEAVER, Ernestine (1938—). See Russell, Ernestine.

WEAVER, Harriet Shaw (1876–1961). English publisher. Born Harriet Shaw Weaver in 1876 in Frodsham, Cheshire, England; died 1961 in Saffron Walden, near Cambridge; dau. of Frederick Poynton Weaver. ❖ Volunteered to work for *The Freewoman*, which Dora Marsden had founded; when financial troubles caused the magazine to fold, revived it as *The New Freewoman*, and again as *The Egoist*, assuming editorship of the last incarnation in 1914; began serializing James Joyce's *A Portrait of the Artist as a Young Man* until 1915, then ensured that it was published in hardcover; with Sylvia Beach, began championing the publication of James Joyce's *Ulysses* (1922); also gave Joyce £20,500 over a period of years and a house in the country; as Joyce's literary executor, took on the burden of the care of his troubled daughter Lucia (1951). ❖ See also *Women in World History*.

WEAVER, Marjorie (1913–1994). American actress, dancer and singer. Born Mar 2, 1913, in Crossville, TN; died Oct 1, 1994, in Austin, TX; trained at Ned Wayburn studio in New York City on scholarship. ❖ Lead player, made film debut in *China Clipper* (1936) but came to prominence in *Sally, Irene, and Mary* (1938); other films include *I'll Give a Million, Hold that Co-ed, Young Mr. Lincoln* (as Mary Todd), *The Cisco Kid and the Lady, Charlie Chan's Murder Cruise, Maryland, Michael Shayne: Private Detective, Murder Among Friends, Just Off Broadway,* and *Leave it to Blondie*.

WEAVER, Sigourney (1949—). American actress. Born Susan Alexandra Weaver, Oct 8, 1949, in New York, NY; dau. of Sylvester L. (Pat) Weaver (tv producer, NBC president) and Elizabeth Inglis (actress); niece of actor Doodles Weaver; Stanford University, BA, 1972; Yale University School of Drama, MFA; m. Jim Simpson (theater director), 1984; children: Charlotte Simpson. ❖ Made stage debut in *Watergate Classics* (1973), followed by *The Nature and Purpose of the Universe* (1974), *Gemini* (1976), *Beyond Therapy* (1981), *The Marriage of Bette and Boo* (1985),

The Merchant of Venice (1986) and *Sex and Longing* (1996), among others; made film debut with bit part in Woody Allen's *Annie Hall* (1977); came to prominence as Ripley in *Alien* (1979); co-wrote (with Chris Durang) and starred in *Das Lusitania Songspiel* (1979–81); other films include *Eyewitness* (1981), *The Year of Living Dangerously* (1982), *Ghostbusters* (1984), *Aliens* (1986), *Ghostbusters II* (1989), *Alien III* (1992), *Dave* (1993), *Death and the Maiden* (1994), *Alien: Resurrection* (1997) and *The Ice Storm* (1997); received Tony nomination for performance in *Hurly Burly*; nominated for Academy Award for portrayal of Dian Fossey in *Gorillas in the Mist* (1988) and for performance in *Working Girl* (1988).

WEAVERS, The. *See Gilbert, Ronnie (b. 1926).*

WEBB, Beatrice (1858–1943). English social reformer. Name variations: Bee or Bo Potter; Beatrice Potter; Lady Passfield. Born Beatrice Potter, Jan 22, 1858, in Standish House, in Gloucestershire, England; died April 30, 1943, in Passfield Corner, England; dau. of Richard Potter (wealthy businessman) and Lawrencina or Laurencina (Heyworth) Potter; m. Sidney James Webb (socialist, Labour member of Parliament, and Cabinet member), July 23, 1892; no children. ❖ Social researcher and reformer who became a member of the Fabian Society and, with husband, helped instigate many of the welfare and educational reforms adopted in Great Britain in the early part of 20th century; studied the conditions of the dock workers, the "sweated trades," the co-operative movement, and the development of trade unions; by 1888, had gained some renown for her research-related articles, which appeared in a few newspapers and journals; studied the co-operative movement in Great Britain, which led to the publication of *The History of Co-operation in Great Britain* (1891); became a socialist; with husband, published their widely acclaimed *History of Trade Unionism* (1894); devoted her life to social investigation, writing, and reform programs; established, with husband, the London School of Economics and Political Science (1895); served on Royal Commission on the Poor Law (1905–09) and later on various other governmental commissions; with husband, founded weekly journal, *The New Statesman* (1913); made a fellow in the prestigious British Academy, the lone woman member (1931); kept a diary throughout most of life; writings include (Fabian tracts) *Women and the Factory Acts* (1896) and *The Abolition of the Poor Law* (1918), as well as *Men's and Women's Wages: Should They be Equal?* (1919), and many other works jointly authored with husband. ❖ See also autobiographies *My Apprenticeship* (1926) and (edited and published posthumously) *Our Partnership* (1948); Margaret I. Cole, *Beatrice Webb* (Longmans, 1945); Kitty Muggeridge and Ruth Adam, *Beatrice Webb: A Life, 1858–1943* (Secker & Warburg, 1967); Lisanne Radice, *Beatrice and Sidney Webb: Fabian Socialists* (St. Martin, 1984); Carole Seymour-Jones, *Beatrice Webb: A Life* (Dee, 1992); Barbara Caine, *Destined to be Wives: The Sisters of Beatrice Webb.* London: Oxford U. Press, 1987; and *Women in World History.*

WEBB, Catherine (1859–1947). English cooperative leader. Born 1859; died 1947; dau. of a coppersmith who was also director of the Cooperative Wholesale Society. ❖ Became a force in the women's cooperative movement in England towards the end of 19th century, through her establishment of the Battersea branch of the Women's Cooperative Guild in London (1886); published *Woman with a Basket* (1927), which detailed the history of the guild, and also contributed to its visibility through lectures; became a member of the Cooperative Union's Central Board and contributed to a better understanding of the cooperative movement in general with her editing of what became its standard text, *Industrial Co-operation* (1904); served as governor of Morley College in south London.

WEBB, Electra Havemeyer (1888–1960). American art collector and museum founder. Born Aug 16, 1888, in Babylon, Long Island, New York; died Nov 19, 1960; dau. of Henry O. Havemeyer (president and founder of American Sugar Refining Co.) and Louisine (Waldron) Elder Havemeyer (1855–1929, art collector); m. J(ames) Watson Webb (great-grandson of Sophia Johnson Vanderbilt and Cornelius Vanderbilt I), in 1910; children: 5. ❖ Collector of American folk art whose founding of the Shelburne Museum contributed to the popularization of "Americana" as fine art; began collecting American folk art at 18, when she purchased a cigar-store Indian; inherited mother's collection of Chinese bronzes and Tanagra figurines and such grand masters as Degas, Corot, and Manet; though she had developed a keen appreciation for this art, was happiest collecting the works of anonymous artisans, anticipating a trend; with husband, owned a magnificent estate in Shelburne, Vermont; eventually acquired more than 125,000 objects,

among them quilts, rugs, furniture, pewter, toys, carriages, sleighs, tools, folk art, clothes, and decoys; began to establish an outdoor museum at Shelburne Farms (1947). The Shelburne Museum, which occupies more than 40 acres of land and comprises nearly as many buildings, was opened to the public in 1952, and preserves an extraordinary record of America's heritage. ❖ See also *Women in World History.*

WEBB, Elida (1895–1975). African-American theatrical dancer. Name variations: Elida Webb-Dawson; Elida Dawson. Born Aug 9, 1895; died May 1, 1975, in New York, NY; m. Garfield "Strutter" Dawson (dancer). ❖ Performed in Eubie Blake and Noble Sissle musical *Shuffle Along*; created and staged musical dance numbers for *Running Wild* on Broadway (1921); staged and presented numerous club acts for black Prolog theaters and cabarets; had longest career of any black female choreographer of her day.

WEBB, Jane (1807–1858). *See Loudon, Jane Webb.*

WEBB, Karrie (1974—). Australian golfer. Name variations: Karrie rhymes with "starry." Born Dec 12, 1974, in Ayr, Queensland, Australia; dau. of Robert (home builder) and Evelyn Webb (cafe owner). ❖ Made the Australian junior team at 16; turned pro at 19; named LPGA Rookie of the Year (1996); became the 1st player in LPGA history to win $1 million in a single season (1996), and the 1st rookie of either gender to top the million mark; as of 2004, had over 30 LPGA victories, including British Open (1995, 1996, 2002); HEALTHSOUTH Inaugural (1996), Sprint Titleholders championship (1996), SAFECO Classic (1996, 1997), ITT LPGA tour championship (1996), Susan G. Komen International (1997), Australian Ladies Masters (1998, 1999, 2000), City of Hope Myrtle Beach Classic (1998), The Office Depot (1999, 2000), du Maurier Classic (1999), Nabisco championship (2000 and 2006), US Open (2000, 2001), Oldsmobile Classic (2000), McDonald's LPGA championship (2001) and Kellogg-Keebler Classic (2004). Won ESPY Award as Outstanding Women's Golf Performer of the Year (1997 and 2001); carried Olympic torch for Sydney Olympics (2000); won Vare Trophy (1997, 1999, 2000).

WEBB, Laura (1941–2001). American singer. Name variations: Laura Webb Childress; The Bobbettes. Born Nov 8, 1941; died Jan 8, 2001, in New York, NY. ❖ Was tenor with The Bobbettes, the 1st female vocal group with #1 R&B hit and Top-10 hit on pop charts: "Mr. Lee" (1957); with Bobbettes, toured with such artists as Clyde McPhatter and Ruth Brown. Other singles by Bobbettes include "Have Mercy, Baby" (1960), "Dance With Me, Georgie" (1960), and "I Don't Like It Like That, Part 1" (1961).

WEBB, Mary (1881–1927). English writer. Born Gladys Mary Meredith, Mar 25, 1881, in Leighton, Shropshire, England; died in St. Leonards, Sussex, Oct 8, 1927; dau. of George Edward Meredith (schoolmaster, died 1909) and Sarah Alice (Scott) Meredith; m. Henry Bertram Law Webb (schoolmaster), 1912; no children. ❖ Novelist and poet who absorbed the characteristics of the people of Shropshire and immortalized them in her novels, essays and poems; at age 1, moved with parents to The Grange, a small country house near Much Wenlock, Shropshire; between 12 and 21, lived at Stanton-on-Hine Heath, 6 miles from Shrewsbury, followed by 10 years in Meole Brace, 1 mile from Shrewsbury; after marriage, lived for 2 years in Weston-super-Mare, Somerset, before returning to Shropshire, to live in Pontesbury, where she was a market gardener, and Lyth Hill; published *The Golden Arrow* (1916), which enjoyed some success, followed by *The Spring of Joy* (1917), *Gone to Earth* (1917), *The House in Dormer Forest* (1920), and *Seven for a Secret* (1922); began to have a circle of discriminating readers, along with the approval of those critics who warmed to her vivid prose and a treatment of natural beauty that contrasted with the imperfections of humankind; produced what is usually regarded her finest piece of work, *Precious Bane* (1924), which was awarded the Femina Vie Heureuse; her work became widely celebrated only after her early death. Collected works were published by Cape in London and Dutton in New York (1928), and included the unfinished *Armour Wherein He Trusted.* ❖ See also Michèle Aina Barale, *Daughters and Lovers: The Life and Writings of Mary Webb* (Wesleyan U. Press, 1986); Gladys Mary Coles, *The Flower of Light: A Biography of Mary Webb* (Duckworth, 1978); Thomas Moult, *Mary Webb: Her Life and Work* (Cape, 1932); Dorothy P. H. Wrenn, *Goodbye to Morning: A Biographical Study of Mary Webb* (Wilding & Son, 1964); and *Women in World History.*

WEBB, Matilda (1813–1899). *See Furley, Matilda.*

WEBB, Phyllis (1927—). Canadian poet. Born Phyllis Bane, April 8, 1927, in Victoria, British Columbia, Canada; attended University of

British Columbia and McGill University. ❖ Leading Canadian poet, worked as executive producer of CBC radio program "Ideas" (1967–69) and as teacher and writer-in-residence at Canadian universities; writings, noted for elegance and restraint, include *Even Your Right Eye* (1956), *The Sea is Also a Garden* (1962), *Naked Poems* (1965), *Selected Poems* (1971), *Wilson's Bowl* (1980), *Talking* (1980), *The Vision Tree* (1982), for which she received the Governor General's Prize, *Water and Light: Ghazals and Anti Ghazals* (1984), and *Hanging Fire* (1990).

WEBB, Ron (1936—). *See Webb, Sharon.*

WEBB, Sarah (1977—). English sailor. Born Jan 13, 1977, in Weybridge, England. ❖ Won a gold medal for Yngling class at Athens Olympics (2004), a debut event.

WEBB, Sharon (1936—). American science-fiction writer. Name variations: (pseudonym) Ron Webb. Born Feb 29, 1936, in Tampa, FL; m. Bryan Webb, 1956; children: 3. ❖ Wrote *Earthchild* (1982), *Earth Song* (1983), *Ram Song* (1984), *The Adventures of Terra Tarkington* (1985), *Pestis 18* (1987) and *The Halflife* (1989).

WEBB, Stella (1902–1989). *See Gibbons, Stella.*

WEBB, Violet (1915—). English runner. Born Feb 1915 in UK. ❖ At Los Angeles Olympics, won a bronze medal in 4 x 100-meter relay (1932).

WEBBER, Eliza Jane (1835–1902). *See Cowie, Eliza Jane.*

WEBER, Aloysia (c. 1761–1839). *See Lange, Aloysia.*

WEBER, Christiane (1962—). West German fencer. Born Mar 17, 1962, in Germany. ❖ Won a gold medal at Los Angeles Olympics (1984) and a gold medal at Seoul Olympics (1988), both in team foil.

WEBER, Constanze (1762–1842). *See Mozart, Constanze.*

WEBER, Helene (1881–1962). German politician and social worker. Pronunciation: VEHB-err. Born Mar 17, 1881, in Elberfeld, Germany; died in Bonn, Germany, July 25, 1962; dau. of Wilhelm Weber (schoolteacher) and Agnes Christiane (van Gent) Weber. ❖ Pioneering social worker who was also a leading political figure in Germany's Catholic Center Party during 1920s and in its successor, the Christian Democratic Party, after World War II; taught at schools in Aachen and Elberfeld (1900–05); studied at the universities of Bonn and Grenoble (1905–10); taught at women's secondary schools in Bochum (1909); became principal of the Kaiserina Augusta School in Cologne (1911); assumed leadership of the new social welfare school of German Catholic Women's Federation (1916); became editor of Federation journal (1917); elected to the constitution-writing convention for Weimar Republic (1919); appointed to ministerial rank in Prussian Ministry for Social Welfare (1919); was a member of the Prussian Landtag (1922–24); served as a deputy in the Reichstag (1924–33); released from her ministerial position by the new Nazi government on the grounds of "political unreliability" (June 1933); moved to sister's home in Marburg after her home in Berlin was destroyed by bombing (1945); served as a member of the Landtag of the German state of North Rhine-Westphalia (1946); assumed a prominent role as party secretary when the Christian Democratic Party was founded after WWII, and was a member of the group which wrote the constitution for Federal Republic of Germany; served as a member of German Bundestag in West Germany (1949–62), as part of the Christian Democratic government of Chancellor Konrad Adenauer; served as president of women's branch of Christian Democratic Party (1949–58); became president of women's committee of the Bundestag (1957); received the West German government's highest civilian award, the Grosse Bundeverdienstyrenz (1957); though active in a political party which opposed the right to vote for women, played a role in convincing party leaders to accept suffrage for women. ❖ *See also Women in World History.*

WEBER, Helene Marie (b. 1824). European feminist. Name variations: Hélène Marie Weber. Born in 1824. ❖ Was known to plow her land during the day and write through the night on behalf of women's rights, specifically the right to retain property, to study in universities, to become ministers and priests, and to vote and engage in politics; was also known for her attire: a black coat and pantaloons. ❖ *See also Women in World History.*

WEBER, Jeanne (1875–1910). French murderer. Name variations: Ogre de la Goutte d'Or; Madame Moulinet; Marie Lemoine. Born 1875 in northern France; died 1910 in Mareville, France; married, 1893; children: 3. ❖ Infamous murderer responsible for the strangling deaths of 8 children in France, including her own 3 children (1905–08), may have

killed as many as 20; despite convincing evidence that the children in her charge had been strangled, managed to elude conviction (1906); was found innocent in a court of law not once, but twice, because of misguided sympathizers who supported her, and local doctors who misdiagnosed the cause of the deaths; was finally pronounced insane (1908), after she killed again. ❖ *See also Women in World History.*

WEBER, Jutta (1954—). West German swimmer. Born June 28, 1954. ❖ At Munich Olympics, won a bronze medal in 4 x 100-meter freestyle relay (1972).

WEBER, Lois (1881–1939). American film director. Name variations: Mrs. Phillips Smalley. Born Florence Lois Weber, June 13, 1881, in Allegheny City, Pennsylvania; died Nov 13, 1939, in Los Angeles, California; dau. of George Weber (decorator) and Mary Matilda (Snaman) Weber; m. Phillips Smalley, May 1905 (div. 1922); m. Captain Harry Gantz; no children. ❖ One of the most important and prolific film directors in the era of silent films, brought to the screen her concerns for humanity and social justice in over 400 films; toured as a concert pianist at age 17; joined a theatrical touring company, where she met Phillips Smalley; began work as writer, actor, and director for Gaumont film (c. 1907); working with Smalley as a team, moved from Gaumont to Reliance Studio, then to Rex Co. (1909); with Smalley, was put in charge of Rex, by then under control of Universal Studios, where she became important as a director (1912); elected mayor of Universal City; moved to Bosworth Co. (1914) where she completed several 4- and 5-reel films, including *False Colors* (1914), *It's No Laughing Matter* (1914) and *Sunshine Molly* (1915), melodramas dealing with family life, as well as *The Hypocrites* (1914); returned to Universal (1915) where she directed Anna Pavlova in *The Dumb Girl of Portici*, along with *Where Are My Children* and *The People vs. John Doe* (both 1916), among others; established own studio, Lois Weber Productions, with financial help from Universal (1917); signed contract with Paramount to direct 5 films (1920), but Paramount deal withdrawn (1921); divorced Smalley (1922); suffered nervous collapse, but returned briefly to directing (1926); worked as script doctor and directed screen tests at Universal (early 1930s); directed last film, *White Heat*, her only sound film (1934); a person of outstanding gifts, had a personal fragility that remained in evidence throughout career. ❖ *See also Women in World History.*

WEBER, Louise (1869–1929). *See Goulue, La.*

WEBER, Regina (1963—). West German rhythmic gymnast. Born April 12, 1963. ❖ At Los Angeles Olympics, won a bronze medal in rhythmic gymnastics, all-around (1984).

WEBER-KOSZTO, Monika (1966—). German fencer. Born Feb 7, 1966. ❖ Won a silver medal at Los Angeles Olympics (1984), silver medal at Barcelona Olympics (1992) and bronze medal at Sydney Olympics (2000), all for team foil.

WEBSTER, Alice (1876–1916). *See Webster, Jean.*

WEBSTER, Annabella Mary (1864–1955). *See Geddes, Annabella Mary.*

WEBSTER, Augusta (1837–1894). English poet, dramatist, and essayist. Name variations: Julia Augusta Davies; (pseudonym) Cecil Home. Born Julia Augusta Davies, Jan 30, 1837, in Poole, Dorset, England; died Sept 5, 1894, in Kew, London, England; dau. of George Davies (vice-admiral in British navy) and Julia Augusta (Hume) Davies; maternal granddau. of Joseph Hume; studied at Cambridge School of Art; m. Thomas Webster (lawyer), 1863; children: 1 daughter. ❖ Under pseudonym Cecil Home, published *Blanche Lisle and Other Poems* (1860); under name Augusta Webster, published the poem *Lilian Gray* and her only novel, *Lesley's Guardians* (both 1864), followed by *Dramatic Studies* (1866), a collection of dramatic monologues; issued well-received translations from the Greek of *Prometheus Bound* (1866) and *Medea* (1868); released *A Woman Sold and Other Poems* (1867); returned to the monologue form in the highly successful *Portraits* (1870), which highlighted her feminism; began to focus on plays and essays, and campaign for better education for women; served on London School Board (1879–82); plays include *The Auspicious Day* (1872), *Disguises* (1879), *In a Day* (1882) and *The Sentence* (1887); wrote a series of essays on women's suffrage which were published in the *Examiner*; also wrote *A Housewife's Opinions* (1878) and *Mother and Child*. ❖ *See also Women in World History.*

WEBSTER, Clara Vestris (1821–1844). English ballet dancer. Born 1821 in Bath, England; died Dec 17, 1844, in London, England; dau. of Benjamin Webster (ballet master of Theatre Royal in Bath). ❖ Named Vestris after father's former teacher, Gaetano Vestris; performed in Bath and Dublin (c. 1840); appeared on tours in Northern England with Fanny Cerrito and Antonio Guerra; danced in James Sylvain's version of *La Bayadère* (1843); performed with ballet company at Drury Lane, where she danced featured roles in *Le Corsaire* and *Lady Henrietta*, among others (1844); died soon after her costume caught fire while performing in Sylvain's *Revolt of the Harem* (Dec 1844).

WEBSTER, Jean (1876–1916). American writer. Born Alice Jane Chandler Webster, July 24, 1876, in Fredonia, New York; died soon after giving birth to her only child, June 11, 1916, in New York; dau. of Charles Webster (publisher of *Huckleberry Finn*) and Annie (Moffett) Webster (niece of Mark Twain); Vassar College, BA, 1901; m. Glenn Ford McKinney (lawyer), in 1915; children: Jean Webster McKinney (b. 1916). ❖ Published *When Patty Went to College*, a collection of Patty stories believed to be based on her friend Adelaide Crapsey (1903); her European travels became the basis for next 2 books: *The Wheat Princess* (1905), which told of her winter stay in an Italian convent, and *Jerry, Junior* (1907); while living in Greenwich Village, wrote what would become her most-loved book, *Daddy-Long-Legs* (1912), the story of a young woman raised in an orphanage who gets the opportunity to go to college with the sponsorship of an unknown, wealthy bachelor; last book, *Dear Enemy* (1914), a sequel to *Daddy-Long-Legs*, also became a bestseller. ❖ See also *Women in World History*.

WEBSTER, Kate (1849–1879). Irish murderer. Born 1849 in Killane, Co. Wexford, Ireland; hanged on July 29, 1879, in London, England; never married; children: 1 son. ❖ Began stealing when young; served a 4-year sentence for pickpocketing in Liverpool; became a maid, but also supported herself through prostitution; turned to lodging-house robbery; throughout mid-1870s, spent many days in jail, including an 18-month sentence in Wandsworth prison; in Richmond area of London, began work as a maid for the wealthy, reclusive Julia Martha Thomas (1879); fired within a month, killed Thomas with an axe, then boiled the body; was easily caught when she began to sell the house furnishings, among other things. The circumstances of her crime—particularly her grisly methods of disposing of the body—horrified all England, and her trial, begun on July 2, 1879, was widely covered in the papers. ❖ See also *Women in World History*.

WEBSTER, Lucile (1886–1947). See Gleason, Lucile.

WEBSTER, Margaret (1905–1972). American-born actress and director. Name variations: Peggy Webster. Born Mar 15, 1905, in New York, NY; died Nov 13, 1972, in London, England; dau. of Benjamin Webster III (actor) and Mary Louisa (Whitty) Webster, actress known as May Whitty (1865–1948); attended Etlinger Dramatic School, London; never married; no children. ❖ Once called "America's foremost Shakespearean director," made theatrical debut at 8; made professional debut in London in chorus of *The Trojan Women* (1924); joined Old Vic (1929), playing 2nd leads during 1st season, but returning 3 years later as Lady Macbeth; acted in 14 plays, among them *Queen of Scots, Parnell* and *Girl Unknown* (1934–36); directed 9 productions, most of them tryout plays, with exception of revival of Ibsen's *Lady from the Sea* (1935–36); directed Maurice Evans in Broadway production of *Richard II* to unanimous acclaim (1937); continued to work with Evans on productions of *Hamlet* (1938), *Henry IV, Part I* (1939), *Twelfth Night* (1940), and *Macbeth* (1941); also made American acting debut (1938), playing Masha in Theatre Guild's *The Seagull*; created a stir when she cast black actor Paul Robeson as the Moor in *Othello* (1942) and ballet dancer Vera Zorina as Ariel and black boxer Canada Lee as Caliban in *The Tempest* (1945), both box-office smashes; also directed *The Trojan Women* (1941), Tennessee Williams' *Battle of Angels* (1941), *The Cherry Orchard* (1942), and *Thérèse* (1945); joined with Eva Le Gallienne and Cheryl Crawford to found American Repertory Theater (1945); formed Margaret Webster Shakespeare Co. (1946), a troupe that toured US and Canada; directed successful production of Verdi's *Don Carlos* at Metropolitan Opera (1950), the 1st woman to direct for the Met; career suffered a severe blow (1951), when José Ferrer named her before the House Committee on Un-American Activities as a Communist; though eventually cleared of all charges, was blacklisted and had difficulty finding work in US. ❖ See also family memoir *The Same Only Different* (1969) and autobiography *Don't Put Your Daughter on the Stage* (1972); and *Women in World History*.

WEBSTER, Mary (1864–1955). See Geddes, Annabella Mary.

WEBSTER, Mary Louise "May" (1865–1948). See Whitty, May.

WEBSTER, Mary McCallum (1906–1985). British botanist. Born Dec 31, 1906, in Sussex, England; died Nov 7, 1985; granddau. of Louisa Wedgwood (botanist); educated by private governesses, then sent to finishing school in Brussels, Belgium. ❖ Noted botanist and talented tennis player (qualified for Wimbledon), joined the Wild Flower Society (1915); joined Botanical Society of the British Isles (1936), serving on the council (1960–66) and on the meetings committee (1960–76); joined the Botanical Society of Edinburgh (1954); visited her brother in Natal, then embarked on a 7-month safari and collected 5,000 species; elected a fellow of Linnean Society (1960); wrote the lauded *Flora of Moray, Nairn and East Inverness* (1978), based on 50 years of work.

WEBSTER, Mary Morison (1894–1980). South African novelist and poet. Born 1894 in Scotland; died 1980 in Johannesburg, South Africa. ❖ Immigrated to South Africa (1920) and lived in Johannesburg; published poetry collections *To-morrow* (1922), *The Silver Flute* (1931), *Alien Guest* (1933), *Garland in the Wind* (1938), *Flowers from Four Gardens* (1951), and *A Litter of Leaves* (1977); wrote novels *Evergreen* (1929), *The Schoolhouse* (1933), *The Slaves of the Lamp; or, The Moon was their Undoing* (1950), and *A Village Scandal* (1965); with sister Elizabeth Charlotte Webster, wrote satire *High Altitude: A Frolic* (1949).

WEBSTER, Peggy (1905–1972). See Webster, Margaret.

WEDDERBURN, Jemima (1823–1909). See Blackburn, Jemima.

WEDDINGTON, Sarah R. (1945—). American lawyer and politician. Born Sarah Ragle, Feb 5, 1945, in Abilene, Texas; dau. of Herbert Doyle Ragle (Methodist minister) and Lena Catherine (Morrison) Ragle; McMurry College, BS, 1965; University of Texas Law School, JD, 1967; m. Ron Weddington (div. 1974). ❖ Argued the case of *Roe v. Wade* before the Supreme Court (1971, 1972); elected to Texas House of Representatives (1972); during 1st term, co-sponsored a health care act that established life-saving procedures for kidney patients and also championed and passed House Bill 920, which made it illegal to deny credit or loans on the basis of gender; after being reelected, co-sponsored, with Kay Bailey Hutchison, House Bill 284, which made a woman's past sexual experiences inadmissible as evidence in rape cases; relected for a 3rd term; advised President Jimmy Carter on issues affecting women (1978–80); returned to private practice and became a popular college lecturer; wrote *A Question of Choice* (1992), both a history of *Roe v. Wade* and a reflection on the years since her victory in the case. ❖ See also *Women in World History*.

WEDEMEYER, Maria von (c. 1924–1977). German-born mathematician. Name variations: Maria von Wedemeyer-Weller. Born c. 1924 in Germany; died, age 53, Nov 16, 1977, in Boston, Massachusetts; father and brother died fighting on Russian front; studied math at University of Göttingen; Bryn Mawr, MA, 1950; m. Paul Schniewind, 1949 (div. c. 1955); m. Barton Weller, 1959 (div. 1965); children: (1st m.) Christopher; Paul; (stepdaughter) Sue M. Ryan. ❖ By 1943, was engaged to German pastor Dietrich Bonhoeffer; after he was arrested for his role in a plot to assassinate Hitler (April 1943), was able to visit him under the supervision of guards during his almost 2 years in Berlin's Tegel Prison; corresponded with him regularly in letters that document both their love and his philosophies, before he was hanged (April 9, 1945); immigrated to US (1948), where she kept her correspondence with Bonhoeffer in a bank vault, finally donating it to Harvard University (1967), under the stipulation that it would not be published for another 25 years; had successful career at Honeywell in Boston, where she worked as an engineer in the field of minicomputers; her correspondence with Bonhoeffer was published as *Love Letters from Cell 92* (1994). ❖ See also *Women in World History*.

WEDGWOOD, C.V. (1910–1997). British historian. Born Cicely Veronica Wedgwood, July 20, 1910, in Stocksfield, Northumberland, England; died Mar 9, 1997, in London; dau. of Sir Ralph Wedgwood (chief general manager of a British railroad) and Iris Veronica (Pawson) Wedgwood (author of books on history and topography); descendant of Staffordshire potter Josiah Wedgwood; studied at Bonn University in Germany and at Sorbonne, 1927–28; Lady Margaret Hall, Oxford, BA, 1931. ❖ One of England's premier historians, who specialized in 17th-century Europe, published 1st book, *Strafford, 1593–1641* (1935), a biography of Thomas Wentworth, advisor to Charles I; wrote *The Thirty Years War* (1938), which became the definitive work on the subject; also wrote *Oliver Cromwell* (1939) and *Oliver Cromwell and the Elizabethan Inheritance* (1970); received James Tait Black Prize for *William the Silent* (1944); recaptured events preceding the Civil War in

The Great Rebellion: The King's Peace, 1637–1641 (1955), those of the war itself in *The King's War, 1641–1647* (1958), and its conclusion *A Coffin for King Charles: The Trial and Execution of Charles I* (1964); published several studies of poetry and literature in their historical context, including *Seventeenth Century English Literature* (1950), *Poetry and Politics Under the Stuarts* (1960), *Milton and His World* (1969) and *The Political Career of Peter Paul Rubens* (1975), and translated several volumes from the German; was literary editor of journal *Time and Tide* (1944–50); also frequently lectured and spoke on the BBC; at 75, published *The Spoils of Time: A World History from the Dawn of Civilization through the Early Renaissance* (1985). Named Commander of the British Empire (1956), then Dame Commander (1968). ❖ See also *Women in World History.*

WEDGWOOD, Camilla H. (1901–1955). British social anthropologist. Name variations: Camilla Hildegarde Wedgwood. Born Mar 25, 1901, in Barlaston, England; died May 17, 1955, in Sydney, Australia; dau. of Josiah Wedgwood IV (Labour leader and MP) and Ethel Bowen Wedgwood (public figure and intellectual); attended Orme Girls' School in Staffordshire and Bedford College; graduate of Newnham College at Cambridge. ❖ Taught at numerous institutions including Bedford College, University of Capetown, London School of Economics, and University of Sydney, serving as principal at the Women's College (1935–44); performed fieldwork on Manam Island, New Guinea (1932); during WWII, as member of Women's Services of Australian Army, impacted Australian policy toward native education and contact issues in New Guinea; joined staff of School of Pacific Administration.

WEED, Ella (1853–1894). American educator. Born Jan 27, 1853, in Newburgh, New York; died Jan 10, 1894, in New York, NY; dau. of Jonathan Noyes Weed (banker) and Elizabeth Merritt (Goodsell) Weed; graduate of Vassar College, 1873; never married; no children. ❖ Taught in Springfield, Ohio (1875–82); taught at Miss Mackay's School (1882); became head of the day school at Anne Brown School in New York City (1884); was recruited by Annie Nathan Meyer to assist with founding of Barnard College (1888) and named chair of the academic committee (1889); set the standard for the college, both in curriculum and in entrance standards, while overseeing its early development (1889–94); wrote a satirical novel, *A Foolish Virgin* (1883). ❖ See also *Women in World History.*

WEED, Ethel (1906–1975). American military officer. Name variations: Ethel Berenice Weed. Born May 11, 1906, in Syracuse, New York; died June 6, 1975, in Newton, Connecticut; dau. of Grover Cleveland Weed (engineer) and Berenice (Benjamin) Weed; attended Western Reserve University, AB in English, 1929. ❖ Had an 8-year stint as a reporter for *Cleveland Plain Dealer,*; started public relations business (1941), which she conducted largely on behalf of women's groups and other civic organizations; during World War II, was commissioned as a 2nd lieutenant (Aug 1944); became one of only 20 women officers chosen for an assignment in Japan at end of the war; as Women's Information Officer in the Civil Information and Education Section (1945), with responsibility for drafting policies, focused on promoting women's suffrage in preparation for the 1st postwar election; launched a campaign that utilized press conferences, radio shows, motion pictures, and other techniques to motivate women to vote (67% of Japanese women voters turned out, electing an astonishing 39 women to seats in Parliament); resigned from WAC as a 1st lieutenant (1947) but continued crusading in Japan, playing an important role in the forming of a Women's and Minors' Bureau of the new Japanese Ministry of Labor; stayed with this task until the end of the Occupation (1952) to guarantee that funds were not compromised by the government. ❖ See also *Women in World History.*

WEEKES, Liz (1971—). Australian water-polo player. Born Elizabeth Weekes, Sept 22, 1971, in Sydney, NSW, Australia; attended University of Sydney. ❖ Goalkeeper, won team gold at World Cup (1995); won a team gold medal at Sydney Olympics (2000).

WEEKLEY, Frieda (1879–1956). *See Lawrence, Frieda.*

WEEKS, Ada May (1898–1978). American dancer and musical-comedy star. Name variations: Ada May, Ada-May, Ada Mae Weeks. Born Ada May Weeks, Mar 8, 1898, in Brooklyn, NY; died April 25, 1978, in New York, NY; sister of Marion Weeks (actress); trained by Malvina Cavallazzi at Children's Ballet of the Metropolitan Opera; m. Col. Wilson Potter (div.); m. Mario Castegnaro. ❖ As Ada May, made NY debut at Metropolitan Opera as a dancer in *Parsifal*; on Broadway, appeared in *Miss Springtime, Jim Jam Jems, The O'Brien Girl, Listen Lester, Rio Rita*

and numerous editions of *Ziegfeld Follies*; as Ada May Weeks, appeared in such films as *Dance Girl Dance* and Charlie Chaplin's *Monsieur Verdoux*; headlined at the Palace and in London.

WEEKS, Dorothy (1893–1990). American physicist and mathematician. Born 1893 in Philadelphia, PA; died June 4, 1990, in Wellesley, MA. ❖ Served at US Patent Office and National Bureau of Statistics; became 1st woman to receive PhD in mathematics from MIT (1930); served as professor and head of physics department at Wilson College in Chambersburg, PA, for 26 years; following retirement from Chambersburg (1956), coordinated program to develop radiological shielding materials against nuclear weapons, neutrons and gamma rays for US Army arsenal at Watertown, MA; served at Harvard College Observatory as spectroscopist (1964–76).

WEEKS, Helen C. (1839–1918). *See Campbell, Helen Stuart.*

WEEKS, Marion (1886–1968). American actress and singer. Born Nov 12, 1886; died April 20, 1968, in New York, NY; sister of Ada May Weeks (actress); m. Henri Barron (singer). ❖ Began career in vaudeville and appeared in several Thomas Edison films (1912–13); on Broadway, was seen in *The Student Prince, Blossom Time, The Women, Strange Bedfellows, Gentlemen Prefer Blondes* and *Two Blind Mice.*

WEEKS-SHAW, Clara S. (1857–1940). American nurse. Name variations: Clara S. Weeks Shaw; Clara S. Weeks. Born Clara Shaw Weeks, Feb 28, 1857, in Sanbornton, NH; died Jan 14, 1940, in Mountainville, NY; dau. of Anna Coe Weeks and Dr. Alpheus Weeks; graduate of New York Hospital, 1880; m. Cyrus W. Shaw, 1888. ❖ The 1st American nurse to write a nursing textbook, published *A Text-Book of Nursing for the Use of Training Schools, Families, and Private Students,* (1885), a book so popular that it sold more than 100,000 copies by 1946 and underwent 3 editions and 58 printings; organized and served as a superintendent of the Paterson General Hospital nursing school in Paterson, NJ (1883–88).

WEERSMA, Elizabeth Geertruida Agatha (1897–1951). *See Dyson, Elizabeth Geertruida Agatha.*

WEERSMA, Hedda (1897–1951). *See Dyson, Elizabeth Geertruida Agatha.*

WEGGEN, Hanja (1943—). *See Maij-Weggen, Hanja.*

WEGMAN, Froukje (1979—). Dutch rower. Born April 22, 1979, in the Netherlands. ❖ Won a bronze medal for coxed eights at Athens Olympics (2004).

WEGNER, Gudrun (1955—). East German swimmer. Born Feb 28, 1955, in East Germany. ❖ At Munich Olympics, won a bronze medal in 400-meter freestyle (1972).

WEHNER-LOEBINGER, Lotte (b. 1905). *See Loebinger, Lotte.*

WEHR-HÁSLER, Sabine (1967—). German snowboarder. Name variations: Sabine Wehr-Hasler; Sabine Hasler. Born Aug 7, 1967, in Germany. ❖ Began snowboarding (1989); was ISF Women's European Halfpipe champion (1993), ISF Women's Vice European Halfpipe champion (1996), World Cup Overall Winner Halfpipe (2001 and 2002) and Vice World Cup Overall Winner Halfpipe (1998 and 2002); other 1st-place finishes include ISF Women's Halfpipe World Cup Masters, Naeba, Japan (1995) and Women's Halfpipe World Cup Series, Oberstdorf (1995).

WEHSELAU, Mariechen (1906–1992). American swimmer. Name variations: Mariechen Wehselau Jackson. Born April 15, 1906, in Honolulu, HI; died in 1992. ❖ Won a gold medal for 4 x 100-meter freestyle and a silver medal for 100-meter freestyle at Paris Olympics (1924). Inducted into Hawaii Sports Hall of Fame (2002).

WEI HAIYING. Chinese soccer player. Born in China. ❖ Won a team silver medal at Atlanta Olympics (1996).

WEI KUO FU-JEN (1262–1319). *See Guan Daosheng.*

WEI JUNYI (1917–2002). Chinese editor and short-story writer. Born 1917 in China; died 2002. ❖ Co-founded magazine *China Youth* and headed People's Literature Publishing House; works include *Women* (1980) and *Frailty* (1983).

WEI, Madame (272–349). *See Wei Shuo.*

WEI NING (1982—). Chinese skeet shooter. Born Aug 5, 1982, in China. ❖ Won a World championship (2003) and a silver medal at Athens Olympics (2004), both for skeet shooting.

WEI QIANG. Chinese softball player. Born in China. ❖ Won a silver medal at Atlanta Olympics (1996).

WEI SHUO (272–349). Chinese calligrapher. Name variations: Lady Wei; Madame Wei; Maoyi. Born 272 in Hedong, Shanxi Province, during the Eastern Jin dynasty; died 349; dau. of Wei Zhan, or dau., niece or younger sister of Wei Heng (calligrapher); m. Li Ju (inspector of Ding Prefecture); children: Li Chong (also a calligrapher). ❖ Was a student of Zhong You; established consequential rules about the regular script; taught famed calligrapher, Wang Xizhi (Wang Hsi-Chih).

WEIDENBACH, Lisa Larsen (c. 1962—). American marathon runner. Name variations: Lisa Larsen; Lisa Weidenbach; Lisa Rainsberger. Born Lisa Larsen, c. 1962, in Hutchinson, KS; attended University of Michigan. ❖ Won Boston Marathon and Cherry Blossom 10-miler (1985); won Chicago marathons (1988, 1990).

WEIDLER, Virginia (1926–1968). American child actress. Born Mar 21, 1926, in Eagle Rock, CA; died July 1, 1968, in Los Angeles, CA; dau. of an architect and a German opera singer (known professionally as Margaret Theresa Louise); sister of George Weidler (actor); m. Lionel Krisel, 1947. ❖ At 4, made uncredited film debut in *After Tonight* (1933); immediately following, appeared as Europena Wiggs in *Mrs. Wiggs of the Cabbage Patch* (1934); other films include *Freckles, Peter Ibbetson, Big Broadcast of 1936* (and 1937), *Girl of the Ozarks, The Outcasts of Poker Flat, Mother Carey's Chickens, The Great Man Votes* (with John Barrymore), *The Women, Young Tom Edison, All This and Heaven Too, The Philadelphia Story,* and *Babes on Broadway;* retired from acting (1945).

WEIERMANN-LIETZ, Andrea (1958—). West German field-hockey player. Born Dec 15, 1958. ❖ At Los Angeles Olympics, won a silver medal in team competition (1984).

WEIGANG, Birte (1968—). East German swimmer. Born Jan 31, 1968. ❖ At Seoul Olympics, won silver medals in the 200-meter butterfly and 100-meter butterfly and a gold medal in the 4 x 100-meter medley relay (1988).

WEIGEL, Helene (1900–1971). Austrian-born actress and director. Name variations: Helen Weigel-Brecht. Pronunciation: WHY-gl. Born in Vienna, May 12, 1900; died in East Berlin, 1971; came from a well-off Jewish family; m. Bertolt Brecht (dramatist), 1929; children: Stefan Sebastian Brecht (b. 1924); Mari Barbara Brecht (b. 1930). ❖ Legendary stage actress and theater director who was the quintessential Brechtian actress; auditioned with Arthur Rundt and made small stage appearances in Vienna (1918–19); acted in Frankfurt (1919–23), where she received her 1st major role, as Marie in *Woyzeck* (1921); appeared in Berlin (1922–28), where she met Brecht (1923); acted at Staatstheater Berlin (1928–29); emigrated from Germany (1933), 1st to Prague, then Vienna, Switzerland, and Denmark; traveled to Moscow (1933); immigrated to Sweden (1939), Finland (1940), and US via the Soviet Union (1941); settled with Brecht and their children in California; returned to Switzerland (1947) and settled in the Communist-controlled East sector of Berlin (1948); co-founded the Berlin Ensemble with Brecht (1949); was a director of Berlin Ensemble and lead actress in numerous plays (1949–71); major roles include Klara in *Maria Magdalena* (1925), Grete in *Der deutsche Hinkemann* (1927), the Widow Bebick in *Man equals Man* (1927), title role in *The Mother* (1932 and 1951), Therese Carrar in *Die Gewehre der Frau Carrar* (*The Guns of Mrs. Carrar,* 1937), title role in *Antigone* (1948), title role in *Mother Courage* (1949), Natella in *The Caucasian Chalk Circle* (1954), and Mrs. Luckerniddle in *St. Joan of the Stockyards* (1968); with Berlin Ensemble in London, appeared as Mother Courage (1956) and as Natella (1965), at Old Vic. ❖ See also *Women in World History.*

WEIGELT, Liane (1956—). See Buhr-Weigelt, Liane.

WEIGL, Vally (1889–1982). Austrian-born American composer, music therapist, and lecturer. Name variations: Valery Weigl. Born Valery Pick, Sept 11, 1889, in Vienna, Austria; died in New York, NY, Dec 25, 1982; dau. of Josef Pick (prominent attorney); sister of Käthe Leichter (1895–1942, Austrian Social Democratic leader who was murdered at Ravensbrück); studied in Vienna under Richard Robert, Guido Adler and Karl Weigl; Columbia University, MA in musical therapy, 1955; m. Karl Weigl (1881–1949, composer). ❖ With husband, came to US as refugees from Nazi occupation (1938); taught at Institute for Avocational Music and American Theater Wing (1947–58); became chief music therapist at NY Medical College and taught at Roosevelt Cerebral Palsy School; also wrote music therapy programs for UNESCO; a peace activist, served as co-founder of the Friends' Arts for World Unity Committee and composed *Peace Is a Shelter* for Chorus, Soloist and Piano (1970) during Vietnam War; composed well over 100 vocal pieces, a number of which have been recorded. ❖ See also *Women in World History.*

WEIL, Simone (1909–1943). French-Jewish activist. Name variations: (pseudonym) Émile Novis. Pronunciation: VALE. Born Simone Adolphine Weil, Feb 3, 1909, in Paris, France; died in Ashford, Kent, England, Aug 24, 1943; dau. of Bernard Weil (physician) and Salomea (Selma) Reinherz Weil; received baccalauréat degree, Lycée Duruy, Paris, 1925; studied philosophy, Lycée Henry IV, Paris, 1925–28; École Normale Supérieure, 1928–31 (passed agrégation, 1931); never married; no children. ❖ Intellectual writer, political activist, and Christian mystic, "the saint of outsiders," whose interest in politics led to involvement with French workers, and trade union movements, and whose attraction to Catholicism produced some of her most lyrical and profound writings; from early age, minimized her gender and rejected her Jewishness; at Sorbonne, ranked at top of class (Simone de Beauvoir ranked 2nd); was the only woman admitted to the École Normale Supérieure (1928); taught at girls' lycée in Le Puy (1931–32), but devoted energies to encourage unity among workers' unions, Socialist and Communist; taught in Auxerre (1932–33), then Roanne (1933–34); worked in factories (1934–35), relating her experiences in "Reflections"; taught in Bourges (1935–36); active in Spanish Civil War (1936); held teaching post in Saint-Quentin, suburb of Paris (1937–38); after debilitating headaches compelled her to take a sick leave (1938), never taught again; contracted pleurisy (spring 1939); eschewed physical comforts, often denying her body nourishment and her soul a tranquil existence; with German occupation, fled Paris with family (June 1940), staying in Vichy (June–Sept 1940), then Marseille; published articles in journal *Cahiers du Sud,* using name Émile Novis; was arrested for handing out anti-Vichy literature and arraigned in court; sailed to New York (June 7, 1942); in a letter to Dominican priest Father Perrin, reiterated her reasons for not joining the Catholic Church despite her personal commitment to Christianity (a collection of her letters to Perrin, *Attente de Dieu,* was published in 1950, then translated as *Waiting for God,* 1951); left for England (1942), to work for Free French forces in London; published *L'Enracinement* (*The Need for Roots,* 1943); hospitalized with TB (mid-April 1943); an idealist in an age of the horrors of two world wars, economic depression, genocide, and forced exile, sympathized with the working classes and sought solace in Catholicism while deprecating the organized Church. ❖ See also Robert Coles, *Simone Weil: A Modern Pilgrimage* (1987); David McLellan, *Simone Weil: Utopian Pessimist* (1989); Thomas R. Nevin, *Simone Weil: Portrait of a Self-exiled Jew* (1991); Gabriella Fiori, *Simone Weil: An Intellectual Biography* (1989); Pat Little, *Simone Weil: Waiting on Truth* (1988); Dorothy Tuck McFarland, *Simone Weil* (1983); Simone Pétrement, *Simone Weil: A Life* (1988); Peter Winch, *Simone Weil: "The Just Balance"* (1989); and *Women in World History.*

WEILER, Barbara (1946—). German politician. Born Sept 17, 1946, in Düsseldorf, Germany. ❖ SPD (Social Democratic Party) member of the Bundestag (1987–94); as a European Socialist, elected to 4th and 5th European Parliament (1994–99, 1999–2004).

WEINBERG, Wendy (1958—). American swimmer. Born Wendy Weinbert, June 27, 1958. ❖ At Montreal Olympics, won a bronze medal in 800-meter freestyle (1976).

WEINBRECHT, Donna (1965—). American freestyle skier. Born April 23, 1965, in West Milford, NJ. ❖ Placed 2nd at World championships (1989, 1997), 1st (1991) and 5th (1995); won a gold medal in moguls at Albertville (1992), the 1st Olympic gold medalist in the sport; came in 7th in the moguls at Lillehammer Olympics (1994) and 4th at Nagano Olympics (1998); won US championships (1994, 1996), and placed 2nd (1997); won 45 World Cup races, more World Cups than any skier in history at the time.

WEINGARTEN, Violet (1915–1976). American novelist and short-story writer. Born Feb 23, 1915, in San Francisco, CA; died July 1976 in Mount Kisco, NY; dau. of William and Elvira (Fleischman) Brown; attended Cornell University, 1931–35; m. Victor Weingarten; children: 2. ❖ Wrote novels *Mrs. Beneker* (1968), *A Loving Wife* (1969), *A Woman of Feeling* (1972), and *Half a Marriage* (1976); also wrote advice books for parents, *You Can Take Them with You: A Guide to Traveling with Children in Europe* (1961), *The Mother Who Works Outside the Home* (1961), and *Life at the Bottom* (1965); children's books include *The Nile, Lifeline of Egypt* (1964), *The Jordan, River of the Promised Land* (1967), and *The Ganges, Sacred River of India* (1969). ❖ See also journal account of her struggle with cancer, *Intimations of Immortality* (1978).

WEINSTEIN, Hannah (1911–1984). American film producer and political activist. Born Hannah Dorner, June 23, 1911, in New York, NY; died Mar 9, 1984, in New York; dau. of Israel Dorner and Celia (Kaufman) Dorner; New York University, BA, 1927; m. Peter Weinstein (journalist), 1938 (div. 1955); children: Dina Weinstein; Lisa Weinstein (producer); Paula Weinstein (producer and 1st woman vice president at Warner Bros.). ❖ Early in career, worked for the *New York Herald Tribune* (1927–37); was a political speechwriter for Fiorello La Guardia; feeling the effects of blacklisting during McCarthy era, moved with daughters to London (1950); became interested in filmmaking, producing 1st feature, *Fait-Divers à Paris* (1952); in partnership with a British tv station, ran a production company which made 435 tv films and series, including the highly popular "Robin Hood" series (1952–62); returned to US (1962); co-founded Third World Cinema (1971), to make films about minorities with minority actors and technicians, and produced the films *Claudine* (1974), *Greased Lightning* (1977) and *Stir Crazy* (1980). Received Women in Film Life Achievement Award (1982) and the Liberty Hill Upton Sinclair Award (1984). ❖ See also *Women in World History*.

WEINZWEIG, Helen (1915—). Canadian novelist and short-story writer. Born 1915 in Radom, Poland. ❖ Came to Toronto at age 9; began writing at age 45; works include the novels *Passing Ceremony* (1973) and *Basic Black with Pearls* (1980), and (short stories) *A View From the Roof* (1989), which was a finalist for Governor General's Award.

WEIR, Amanda (1986—). American swimmer. Born Mar 11, 1986, in Snellville, GA; attended University of Georgia. ❖ Won a silver medal for 4 x 100-meter freestyle relay at Athens Olympics (2004).

WEIR, Irene (1862–1944). American artist and art educator. Born Jan 15, 1862, in St. Louis, Missouri; died Mar 22, 1944, in Yorktown Heights, New York; dau. of Walter Weir (teacher) and Annie Field (Andrews) Weir; Yale School of Fine Arts, BFA, 1906; received diploma from École des Beaux Arts Américaine, Fontainebleau, 1923; never married; no children. ❖ Taught drawing in grammar and high schools in New Haven, Connecticut (1887–90); served as director of Slater Museum School of Art in Norwich, CT; was teacher and then director of art instruction for Brookline, MA, public schools; published *The Greek Painters' Art* (1905); taught in the fine arts department of Ethical Culture School; founded the School of Design and Liberal Arts (1917), then served as its director (1917–29); best-known works were posters from 1890s, flower and landscape paintings, portraits (one of Marie Curie hangs at Memorial Hospital in NY), and powerful murals painted during 1920s, including *Child of Bethlehem* for the Washington Cathedral. ❖ See also *Women in World History*.

WEIR, Judith (1954—). British composer. Born 1954 in Aberdeenshire, Scotland. ❖ Studied composition with John Tavener in London, with Barry Vercoe at Massachusetts Institute of Technology (1973), with Robin Holloway at Cambridge University (1973–76), and at Tanglewood with Gunther Schuller (1975); taught composition at Glasgow University and held fellowships at Oxford and Princeton universities; was composer in association for City of Birmingham Symphony Orchestra (1995–98) and artistic director of Spitalfields Festival, London (1995–2000); works include *Where the Shining Trumpets Blow* (1973), *Out of the Air* (1975), *Several Concertos* (1980), *Music for 247 Strings* (1981), *Thread!* (1981), *The Black Spider* (1984), *The Consolations of Scholarship* (1985), *A Night at the Chinese Opera* (1987) and *The Welcome Arrival of Rain* (2001); collaborated with playwrights Caryl Churchill and Peter Shaffer, storyteller Vayu Naidu, and several theatrical companies, including Royal National Theatre and Peter Hall Company. Named CBE (1995).

WEIR, Molly (1910–2004). Scottish actress. Born Mar 17, 1910 in Springburn, Glasgow, Scotland; died Nov 28, 2004, in Pinner, Middlesex, England; sister of Tom Weir (broadcaster and naturalist); m. Sandy Hamilton; no children. ❖ Best known for her portrayal of Aggie McDonald in "Life with the Lyons" (1950–61), began career in Scottish radio (1939), then landed role of Ivy in "The McFlannels"; in London, joined the cast of Tommy Handley's "It's That Man Again," as Tattie; published 5 volumes of memoirs, including *Shoes Were for Sunday, Best Foot Forward* and *A Toe on the Ladder*; on tv, was Hazel the McWitch on children's tv sitcom "Rentaghost"; films include *Life with the Lyons, The Lyons in Paris, The Prime of Miss Jean Brodie* and *Scrooge*.

WEIS, Jessica McCullough (1901–1963). American politician. Name variations: Judy Weis; Mrs. Charles W. Weis, Jr. Born July 8, 1901, in Chicago, Illinois; died May 1, 1963, in Rochester, New York; dau. of Charles H. McCullough, Jr. (president of Lackawanna Steel Co.) and Jessie (Martin) McCullough; m. Charles William Weis, Jr. (stockbroker and businessman), Sept 24, 1921 (died 1958); children: Charles McCullough Weis; Jessica Weis Warren; Joan Weis Jameson. ❖ US congressional representative (Jan 3, 1959–Jan 3, 1963), served as vice-chair of the Citizens' Republican Finance Committee (1935); appointed to the New York State Republican Committee's executive committee (1938); elected president of the National Federation of Republican Women's Clubs, and served as delegate-at-large to Republican National Convention (1940); seconded the nomination of Thomas E. Dewey for president and was associate campaign manager, the 1st woman to achieve that level within a presidential campaign (1948); received appointment to the national advisory board of the Federal Civil Defense Administration (1954); elected to House of Representatives for New York's 38th District (1958, 1960); served on the Committee on Science and Astronautics and supported the Equal Rights Amendment to the Constitution; coordinated the Republican congressional campaign in New York State (1960); declined to run for 3rd term because of poor health. ❖ See also *Women in World History*.

WEISBERGER, Barbara (c. 1926—). American ballet dancer and company administrator. Born Barbara Linshen, c. 1926, in Brooklyn, NY. ❖ As a child, trained in Brooklyn with Marian Lehman; was 1st child admitted into Balanchine's School of American Ballet (c. 1934); trained with Catherine Littlefield in Philadelphia; ran own small company and school in Wilkes-Barre, PA (late 1940s); founded School of Pennsylvania Ballet in Philadelphia (1962) and served as its artistic director; considered unsurpassed in her efforts and achievements to further development of ballet in US.

WEISBLY, Keena (1957—). *See Rothhammer, Keena.*

WEISHOFF, Paula (1962—). American volleyball player. Name variations: Paula Hanold. Born May 1, 1962, in Torrance, CA; attended University of Southern California, 1978–79; m. Karl Hanold. ❖ Won a gold medal at NORCECA championships (1981, 1983); won a bronze medal at World championships (1982); won a silver medal at Pan American Games (1983); won a team silver medal at Los Angeles Olympics (1984); played professionally in Italy, Brazil, and Japan (1984–97); won a bronze medal at Goodwill Games (1986); won a silver medal at NORCECA championships (1991); won a team bronze medal at Barcelona Olympics and at the FIVB Super Four (1992); played professional beach volleyball (1993); won a gold medal at World Grand Prix (1995); was a member of Olympic volleyball team at Atlanta (1996). Inducted into US Volleyball Hall of Fame (1998). ❖ See also *Women in World History*.

WEISL, Martina (1882–1957). *See Wied, Martina.*

WEISS, Alta (1889–1964). American baseball player and physician. Born Feb 9, 1889, in Ragersville, OH; died Feb 12, 1964, in Ragersville; attended Wooster Academy, 1908–10; Starling College of Medicine (now Ohio State University Medical College), MD, 1914; m. John E. Hisrich (gas-station owner), 1927 (sep. c. 1938). ❖ Pitched for two male semipro teams—the Vermilion Independents (1907) and Weiss All-Stars (1908). ❖ See also *Women in World History*.

WEISS, Bianca (1968—). German field-hockey player. Born Jan 24, 1968. ❖ At Barcelona Olympics, won a silver medal in team competition (1992).

WEISS, Gisela (1943—). East German swimmer. Born Oct 16, 1943. ❖ At Rome Olympics, won a bronze medal in 4 x 100-meter freestyle relay (1960).

WEISS, Janet (1965—). American musician. Name variations: Sleater-Kinney. Born Sept 24, 1965, in Hollywood, CA; graduate of San Francisco State University; m. Sam Coomes (musician). ❖ Drummer and singer for critically acclaimed rock and punk group, Sleater-Kinney, also performs with ex-husband in pop duo, Quasi; with Sleater-Kinney, 1st played on acclaimed album *Dig Me Out* (1997), followed by *The Hot Rock* (1999) and *All Hands on the Bad One* (2000), which included songs, "#1 Must Have" and "The Ballad of a Ladyman."

WEISS, Jeanne Daniloff (1868–1891). Murderer in Algeria. Born 1868; died in prison, May 30, 1891; children: 3. ❖ With lover, engineer Felix Roques, planned murder of her husband; began administering arsenic to him (Oct 1890), while writing letters to Roques to update him on progress; her letter of Oct 9, in which she asked Roques to send an additional quantity of poison, was intercepted; with Roques, arrested for attempted murder; found guilty, received 20-year sentence, and poisoned herself a day later (Roques committed suicide in jail as well).

WEISS, Josephine (1805–1852). Austrian ballet dancer and choreographer. Born 1805 in Austria; died Dec 18, 1852, in Vienna, Austria. ❖ Served as ballet master at Karntnertor and Josephstadter court theaters in Vienna; managed numerous children's ballets, most notably Les Danseuses Vienoises (c. 1843–48), with which she toured to Paris, London, New York, and more; died at relatively young age.

WEISS, Liz. American singer. Name variations: Betty Weiss; The Shangri-Las. Sister of Mary Weiss (singer). ❖ Began singing with sister Mary, and twins Marge and Mary Ann Ganser, while in high school in Queens, NY, and together they formed the Shangri-Las (1964); released 1st hit, "Remember (Walkin' in the Sand)," followed by album *Leader of the Pack* (1964), which included #1 hit title track; other Shangri-Las albums include *Shangri-Las '65* (1965) and *I Can Never Go Home Anymore* (1966); other hit songs include "Maybe" (1964), "Out in the Streets" (1965) and "Past, Present and Future" (1966).

WEISS, Louise (1893–1983). French journalist, film producer, pacifist and feminist. Name variations: Pronunciation: VICE. Born in Arras (Pas-de-Calais) on Jan 25, 1893; died in Paris, France, May 26, 1983; dau. of Paul-Louis Weiss; mother's maiden name was Javal; educated at Lycée Molière, Lady Margaret Hall (Oxford), and Collège Sévigné, and earned an *agrégé* in literature; m. José Imbert, c. 1934 (div. around 1937); no children. ❖ One of the most eminent journalists of her time, was an advocate of realpolitik, peace, and European unity; served as editor at (1918–19), then editor-in-chief of *Europe Nouvelle* (1920–34); developed an incomparable network of sources and worked non-stop, writing, interviewing, soliciting funds, attending virtually every international conference and League of Nations annual session in a decade crammed with them; went to Russia to observe the Revolution (1921); founded École de Paix (School of Peace), a private foundation under a component of the Académie de Paris, which sought to develop a "science of peace" (1930); founded and ran La Femme Nouvelle, which was devoted to winning the vote (1934–38); was secretary-general of Refugee Committee (1938–40); was editor of Resistance gazette *La Nouvelle République* (1942–44); undertook a series of travels to Asia, the Mideast, North America, and Africa, resulting in books and documentary films (1946–65), which investigated human aggression, religion, politics, and the evils ravaging the world; won Literature Prize of Académie Française for her novel *La Marseillaise* (1947); was secretary-general of Institut de Polémologie (1964–70); published 6 vols. of memoirs (1968–80) which took 11 years to write; chosen by Jacques Chirac to lecture throughout Western Europe on European unity (1979); elected to European Parliament (1979), delivered an inspiring address as temporary president, then served (1979–83). ❖ See also Michael Bess, *Realism, Utopia, and the Mushroom Cloud: Four Activist Intellectuals and Their Strategies for Peace, 1945–1989: Louise Weiss (France), Leo Szilard (USA), E. P. Thompson (England), Danilo Dolci (Italy)* (U. of Chicago Press, 1993); and *Women in World History.*

WEISS, Mary. American singer. Name variations: The Shangri-Las. Sister of Liz Weiss (singer). ❖ With sister Liz, and twins Marge and Mary Ann Ganser, formed Shangri-Las (1964) and released hit, "Remember (Walkin' in the Sand)," which launched the Red Bird label (1964); with group, released *Leader of the Pack* (1964), which included #1 hit title track; other albums include *Shangri-Las '65* (1965) and *I Can Never Go Home Anymore* (1966); other hit songs include "Give Him a Great Big Kiss" (1964), "Give Us Your Blessings" (1965) and "Long Live Our Love" (1966).

WEISS, Rosemarie (1935—). See Scherberger-Weiss, Rosemarie.

WEISSENSTEINER, Gerda (1969—). Italian luge and bobsledder champion. Born Jan 3, 1969, in Italian Alps. ❖ Placed 4th at Albertville Olympics 91992); won a gold medal at Lillehammer Olympics (1994); carried the Italian flag at the opening ceremony at Nagano Olympics (1998); won World championship (1993); also won many titles at World Cup, and European championships; with Jennifer Isaaco, won bronze medal for bobsleigh at Torino Olympics (2006).

WEISSMAN, Dora (1881–1974). American stage, tv and screen actress. Born Dec 25, 1881; died May 21, 1974, in New York, NY; sister of Bessie Weissmann (actress-writer); m. Anshel Shorr (playwright, died). ❖ Appeared often on the Yiddish stage; made Broadway debut in Hitch

Your Wagon (1937); other English-speaking plays include *Two on an Island, The Man with Blond Hair, A New Life, Down to Miami* and *Biography*; was a regular on tv's "The Goldbergs."

WEIZMANN, Vera (1881–1966). First lady of Israel. Name variations: Vera Chatzmann. Born Nov 27, 1881, in Rostov-on-Don, Russia; died Sept 24, 1966, in Israel; educated at Marinskaya Imperial Gymnasium and Rostov Conservatoire of Music; studied medicine at University of Geneva; m. Chaim Weizmann (1874–1952, 1st president of the state of Israel), 1906; children: Benjamin (b. 1907) and Michael (1916–1942). ❖ Served as medical officer in Manchester, England (1913–16); founded WIZO (Women's International Zionist Organization, 1920); was joint chair, with Rebecca D. Sieff, of WIZO's world executive committee (1920–40); served as president of Youth Aliyah (1940s); was a Red Cross worker in London during World War II; became first lady of Israel when husband was elevated from the presidency of the Provisional State Council to the title of president of the State of Israel (1949); husband died (1952); involved in Israeli Red Cross and Youth Aliyah (1950s). ❖ See also memoir *The Impossible Takes Longer* (1967); and *Women in World History.*

WELCH, Ann (1917–2002). English pilot, writer and aviation historian. Name variations: Ann Courtenay Welch; Ann Edmonds or Ann Courtenay Edmonds. Born Ann Courtenay Edmonds, May 20, 1917, in London, England; died Dec 5, 2002; dau. of Lt.-Col. Edmonds, a railway engineer; m. Graham Douglas, 1938; Lorne Welch, 1953 (died 1998); children: (1st m.) 2; (2nd m.) 1. ❖ Expert glider pilot, earned a pilot's license at age 17 (1934); began to glide (1937); established (1938) and served as the head instructor of the Surrey Gliding Club (1938–39), later part of the Lasham Gliding Centre, the world's largest gliding club; during WWII, worked at Air Transport Auxiliary; taught air gliding (1944–84); managed the British gliding team in world championships in England (1948–68); held the British women's goal distance record of 528 km. (1961–98); served as the British delegate to Fédération Aeronautique Internationale (FAI); founded the Microlight and the Hang Gliding Commission; served as chair of Royal Aeronautical Society Light Aviation Group; wrote *New Soaring Pilot* (1968) and *The Story of Gliding* (1980) and 2 children's books. Made a Member of the Order of the British Empire (1953) and Officer of the Order of the British Empire (1966).

WELCH, Barbara (c. 1904–1986). English botanist and geologist. Name variations: Barbara Gullick. Born Barbara Gullick, c. 1904, in Cheltenham, Gloucestershire, England; died April 1986; m. Dr. F. B. A. Welch (geologist), Feb 1939. ❖ Served as an assistant curator in archaeology at the Salisbury and South Wiltshire Museum; became assistant secretary at Botanical Society of the British Isles (1953); volunteered for the British Museum's Botany department; joined the Wild Flower Society (1921) and the Botanical Society of the British Isles (1928); presented a series of drawings to the Salisbury and South Wiltshire Museum (1936); after marriage (1939), moved to Richmond in Surrey; retired to Cheltenham (1963); frequent contributor to magazines and books, won several prizes for diary recordings of plants.

WELCH, Elisabeth (1904–2003). African-American actress and singer. Born Feb 27, 1904, in New York, NY, to Scottish mother and African-American and Native American father; died July 17, 2003, in London, England; married briefly and divorced. ❖ One of the most loved figures on the British stage, began career in the chorus of Broadway shows, then appeared in *Runnin' Wild* (1923) and introduced the song, "Singing Charleston"; had breakthrough in *Blackbirds of 1928*, starring Bill "Bojangles" Robinson; traveled with *Blackbirds* to Paris, playing at Moulin Rouge nightclub to favorable reviews (1929); sang "Love for Sale" in Cole Porter's revue *The New Yorkers* (1930); appeared in Porter's *Nymph Errant* in London, singing "Solomon" (1933), which became her signature tune; remained in London, where she starred on stage in *Glamorous Night* (1935), singing "Shantytown," and *Arc de Triomphe* (1943), and in such films as *Song of Freedom* (1936) and *Big Fella* (1937), with Paul Robeson; a frequent broadcaster on BBC, had own radio program, "Soft Lights and Sweet Music"; garnered raves for musical *Pippin* (1970s); starred in Derek Jarman's film *The Tempest* (1980); won Obie Award for one-woman show *A Time to Start Living* (1986) and nominated for Tony Award for Broadway version of London hit *Jerome Kern Goes to Hollywood* (1986); recordings include *Elizabeth Welch Sings Irving Berlin* (1988), *Nymph Errant Original Soundtrack* (1990), *Elisabeth Welch Live in New York* (1995), *Harlem in My Heart* (2001) and *Carmen Jones–1962 Studio Cast* (2003).

WELCH, Georgiana (1792–1879). English radical. Name variations: Georgiana Ford; Georgiana Fletcher Welch. Born Georgiana Ford, 1792, in Staffordshire, England; grew up in London; died 1879; dau. of Francis Ford (Barbados sugar plantation owner and MP for Newcastle-under-Lyme, died 1801) and Mary Anson (granddau. of 1st Lord Vernon); sister of Sophia Chichester (1795–1847); m. Stephen John Fletcher Welch (heir to Ebworth Park estate in Sheepscombe, near Gloucester), 1816 (sep. 1820s). ❖ Following separation from husband, lived with sister at Ebworth Park; became critical of state and church that upheld unjust marriage laws; corresponded with Richard Carlile and was mentored by the mystic, James Pierrepont Greaves; attempted to enlighten the villagers near Ebworth Park by issuing tracts; financially supported radicals, including Robert Owen and James E. Smith.

WELCH, Joan Kemp (b. 1906). *See Kemp-Welch, Joan.*

WELCH, Priscilla (1944—). English marathon runner. Born Priscilla Mayes, Nov 22, 1944, in Dean, England. ❖ Won London Marathon (1987), breaking Great Britain's record; won New York City Marathon (1987). ❖ See also (with Bill Rodgers) *Masters Running and Racing* (1991).

WELCH, Raquel (1940—). American actress. Born Jo Raquel Tejada, Sept 5, 1940, in Chicago, Illinois, to Bolivian aerospace engineer father and American mother; attended San Diego State University; m. James Welch, 1959 (div. 1964); m. Patrick Curtis (publicist), 1967 (div. 1972); m. André Weinfeld (writer), 1980 (div. 1990), m. Richard Palmer (restaurateur), 1999; children: Tahnee Welch (b. 1961, actress), Damon Welch (actor). ❖ Studied ballet as child and began entering beauty contests as teenager; employed as billboard girl on tv show "Hollywood Palace"; made film debut in *A House Is Not a Home* (1964); shot to stardom in *One Million Years B.C.* (1966), followed by *Fathom* (1967), *Tony Rome* (1968), *Lady in Cement* (1968), and *100 Rifles* (1969); rarely challenged as an actress in film, gave evidence of abilities in *The Three Musketeers* (1974), winning Golden Globe for Best Actress; headlined musical revues in Las Vegas and NY (1970s–80s); performed on Broadway in *Woman of the Year* (1982) and *Victor/Victoria* (1990s); starred in tv-movie *Right to Die* (1987), winning Golden Globe nomination; other films include *Bedazzled* (1967), *The Biggest Bundle of Them All* (1968), *Flareup* (1969), *Bluebeard* (1972), *Kansas City Bomber* (1972), *The Wild Party* (1975), *Mother, Jugs & Speed* (1976), *Crossed Swords* (1978), *The Muppets Go Hollywood* (1979), *Legally Blonde* (2001) and *Forget About It* (2005).

WELCH, Tawney (c. 1957—). *See Little, Tawny.*

WELD, Angelina Grimké (1805–1879). *See Grimké, Angelina E.*

WELD, Theresa (1893–1978). *See Blanchard, Theresa Weld.*

WELD, Tuesday (1943—). American actress. Born Susan Ker Weld, Aug 27, 1943, in New York, NY; dau. of Lathrop Motley Weld (investment broker, died 1946) and Aileen (Ker) Weld; attended Hollywood Professional School; m. Claude Harz (writer), 1965 (div. 1971); m. Dudley Moore (actor), 1975 (div. 1980); m. Pinchas Zuckerman (violinist), 1985; children: (1st m.) Natasha Harz; (2nd m.) Patrick Moore. ❖ At a young age, began career modeling; quickly accumulated a number of tv roles on such shows as "Playhouse 90," "Kraft Theater," "Alcoa Theater" and "Climax"; at 13, made film debut in *Rock, Rock, Rock* (1956), followed by *The Wrong Man* (1956), *Rally 'Round the Flag, Boys!* (1958) and *The Five Pennies* (1959); featured as Thalia Menninger in popular tv series "The Many Loves of Dobie Gillis"; during early 1960s, starred as a troubled teenager in a string of films: *Because They're Young* (1960), *High Time* (1960), *The Private Lives of Adam and Eve* (1961), *Return to Peyton Place* (1961) and *Wild in the Country* (1961), starring Elvis Presley; began to earn a reputation as an actress of surprising range in such movies as *Soldier in the Rain* (1963), *The Cincinnati Kid* (1965) and *Lord Love a Duck* (1966); was 1st runner-up as Best Actress for New York Film Critics Circle Award for *Pretty Poison* (1968); won Best Actress honors at Venice Film Festival for *Play It As It Lays* (1972); other films include *Looking for Mr. Goodbar* (1977), *Who'll Stop the Rain* (1978), *Serial* (1980), *Thief* (1981), *Author! Author!* (1982), *Once Upon a Time in America* (1984), *Heartbreak Hotel* (1988), *Falling Down* (1993) and *Feeling Minnesota* (1996). ❖ See also *Women in World History.*

WELDON, Barbara (1829/30–1882). New Zealand prostitute. Born c. 1829 or 1830, in Co. Limerick, Ireland; died Oct 31, 1882, near Kumara, New Zealand. ❖ Immigrated to New Zealand via Australia (1869); was notorious for her raucous behavior and frequent incarcerations for vagrancy and solicitation, reports of which were often published by the *West Coast Times.* ❖ See also *Dictionary of New Zealand Biography* (Vol. 1).

WELDON, Fay (1931—). British novelist. Born Franklin Birkinshaw, Sept 22, 1931, in Alvechurch, Worcestershire, England; grew up in New Zealand; dau. of Frank T. Birkinshaw (physician) and Margaret (Jepson) Birkinshaw (1907–2003, novelist who wrote *Via Panama* and *Velvet and Steel,* among others); sister of Jane Birkinshaw (who married the printer Guido Morris and died in 1969); studied economics and psychology at University of St. Andrews; m. 2nd husband Ron Weldon, 1962 (div. 1994); m. Nick Fox (poet); children: 4 sons. ❖ With mother and sister, sailed for England following the war (1946); worked on the problem page for *Daily Mirror,* then as a copywriter for Foreign Office; became an advertising copywriter; wrote over 50 plays for radio, stage, and tv, the most well-known being episodes of "Upstairs, Downstairs"; published 1st novel, *The Fat Woman's Joke* (1967, released in US as . . . *and the wife ran away*); wrote many bestselling novels and plays, which often focus on complex female characters struggling with day-to-day difficulties, isolation, and failure, including *Down Among the Women* (1971), *In Memoriam* (1974), *Female Friends* (1975), *Polaris* (1978), *Praxis* (1978), *Life and Loves of a She-Devil* (1983), *Scaling Down* (1987), *Life Force* (1992), *Affliction* (1993), *Splitting* (1994), *Worst Fears* (1996), *The Bulgari Connection* (2001) and *Mantrapped* (2004). Named 1st writer-in-residence at Savoy Hotel, London (2002).

WELDY, Ann (1932—). *See Bannon, Ann.*

WELITSCH, Ljuba (1913–1996). Bulgarian soprano. Born Ljuba Velickova or Welitschkova, July 10, 1913, in Borissovo, Bulgaria; died in Vienna, Sept 1996; studied with Gyogy Zlatov in Sofia and with Lierhammer in Vienna. ❖ Sang at Hamburg (1941–43), the Vienna Volksoper (1940–44), and at Munich (1943–46); gave a special performance of Richard Strauss' *Salome* with Strauss conducting (1944); joined Vienna Staatsoper (1946); debuted at Covent Garden (1947), Glyndebourne (1948), and NY's Metropolitan Opera (1949). ❖ See also *Women in World History.*

WELLES, Gwen (1951–1993). American actress. Born Mar 4, 1951, in Chattanooga, TN; died Oct 13, 1993, in Santa Monica, CA. ❖ Appeared as hopeful country singer Sueleen Gay in Robert Altman's *Nashville;* other films include *A Safe Place, Desert Hearts, California Split* and *Eating.*

WELLESLEY, Dorothy (1889–1956). English poet. Name variations: Duchess of Wellington. Born Dorothy Violet Ashton in White Waltham, Berkshire, England, July 20, 1889; died in Withyham, Sussex, England, July 11, 1956; dau. of Robert Ashton and Lucy Cecilia Dunn Gardner Ashton; m. Lord Gerald Wellesley, 7th duke of Wellington; children: 1 daughter, 1 son. ❖ Considered somewhat of a rebel from her upperclass upbringing, wrote poetry at an early age; books include *Early Poems* (1913), *Pride* (1923), *Lost Lane* (1925), *Genesis: An Impression* (1926), *Matrix* (1928), *Deserted House* (1930), *Jupiter and the Nun* (1932), *Sir George Goldie, Founder of Nigeria* (1934), *Poems of Ten Years, 1924–1934* (1934), *Selections from the Poems of Dorothy Wellesley,* with an introduction by William Butler Yeats (1936), *Lost Planet* (1942), *The Poets* (1943), *Desert Wells* (1946), *Rhymes for Middle Years* (1954) and *Early Light: The Collected Poems* (1955). ❖ See also autobiography, *Far Have I Travelled* (1952).

WELLINGTON, duchess of. *See Wellesley, Dorothy (1889–1956).*

WELLMAN, Emily Ann (d. 1946). American actress. Died Mar 20, 1946, in New York, NY. ❖ Appeared in *The Prince Chap, Elevating a Husband, Rockbound, The Wasp* and *Miss Quis.*

WELLS, Ada (1863–1933). New Zealand teacher, feminist, and politician. Name variations: Ada Pike. Born April 29, 1863, near Henley-on-Thames, Oxfordshire, England; died Mar 22, 1933, at Christchurch; dau. of William Henry Pike (wheelwright) and Maria (Beckett) Pike; m. Harry Wells (organist), 1884 (died 1918); children: 3 daughters, 1 son. ❖ Immigrated with family to New Zealand (1873); accepted teaching positions to supplement family income; became active in women's rights issues (late 1880s) and local and national politics (1890s); helped found Canterbury Women's Institute (1892), and served as president for many years; became 1st national secretary of National Council of Women of New Zealand (1896); elected to Ashburton and North Canterbury United Charitable Aid Board (1899); member of National Peace Council of New Zealand and provided aid to conscientious objectors during World War I; was 1st woman elected to Christchurch City Council (1917). ❖ See also *Dictionary of New Zealand Biography* (Vol. 2).

WELLS, Alice (1927–1987). American photographer. Name variations: Alisa Wells. Born 1927 in Erie, Pennsylvania; died 1987 in Galisteo, New Mexico; attended Pennsylvania State University; m. Kenneth Carl Meyers (div. 1959); m. Richard Witteman, 1974 (sep. 1980); m. Roman Attenberger; children: (1st m.) 3. ❖ Known for her experimental work, began working for Kodak in a secretarial position (1952); took up photography (1959); studied with Nathan Lyons, then became his secretary at George Eastman House (1962); began creating photographs of abstract forms in nature using large-format cameras; had solo exhibition at Eastman House (1964); switched to hand-held 35-mm cameras (1965) and used urban areas as her subject; experimented with multiple exposures; also worked with solarization, toning, and hand coloring. ❖ See also *Women in World History.*

WELLS, Alice Stebbins (1873–1957). American police officer. Born 1873 in Kansas; died 1957; attended public schools in Kansas; attended Hartford Theological Seminary in Connecticut. ❖ The 1st woman police officer in US, launched her own ministry, traveling across the country and giving lectures on Christian topics; earned her own pastorates in Maine and Oklahoma—the 1st woman to do so in those states—before settling in California; combined her Christian principles with an interest in prison reform; was sworn in as the 1st woman police officer with full powers of arrest in Los Angeles, California (Sept 12, 1910); lectured throughout US on the benefits of women police officers (1910s); established the International Association of Policewomen (1916); retired (1940). ❖ See also *Women in World History.*

WELLS, Carolyn (1862–1942). American author and editor. Born June 18, 1862, in Rahway, New Jersey; died Mar 26, 1942, in New York, NY; dau. of William Edmund Wells (insurance salesman) and Anna Potter (Woodruff) Wells; m. Hadwin Houghton (of the Boston publishing family), 1918 (died 1919); no children. ❖ Published *At the Sign of the Sphinx* (1899), a book of charades, which marked the beginning of a prolific writing career; all told, produced about 180 works of humor, mystery, and children's books; became so well known for her parodies and facility with limericks that publishers sought to incorporate her name into titles of humor books, such as *The Carolyn Wells Year Book of Old Favorites and New Fancies for 1909*; in the mystery genre, which earned her the informal title "Dean of American Mystery Writers," created the character Fleming Stone (1909) who thereafter became the subject of 60 mysteries; also created other detectives, including Kenneth Carlisle, Alan Ford, Lorimer Lane, and Pennington Wise; made mark in the genre of children's literature by producing several popular series for girls such as her "Patty," "Marjorie," and "Two Little Women" narratives. ❖ See also *Women in World History.*

WELLS, Catherine (d. 1927). English author. Name variations: Amy Catherine Robbins. Born Amy Catherine Robbins; died 1927; married H. G. Wells (English novelist, sociological writer, and historian), in 1895; children: George Philip Wells (b. 1901); Frank Wells (b. 1903). ❖ Was 20 years old when she enrolled in a biology laboratory being taught by H. G. Wells at University Tutorial College in London (1892); lived with him until Wells divorced his 1st wife, Isabel Mary Wells (1893–95); apparently accepted with equanimity that husband was notoriously promiscuous with both long- and short-term partners; died of cancer (1927), after having suffered for some time (a year later, H. G. published her stories and poems in *The Book of Catherine Wells*). ❖ See also *Women in World History.*

WELLS, Charlotte Fowler (1814–1901). American phrenologist and publisher. Born Charlotte Fowler, Aug 14, 1814, in Cohocton, New York; died in West Orange, New Jersey, June 4, 1901; dau. of Horace (farmer) and Martha (Howe) Fowler; sister of Orson Squire Fowler and Lorenzo Niles Fowler, phrenologists; attended Franklin Academy in Prattsburg, New York; m. Samuel Robert Wells, 1844 (died 1875). ❖ Began a career in teaching before she was 20; became interested in the Austrian "science" of phrenology (early 1830s); joined brothers' phrenological center in New York City (1837); as an integral part of the center, taught the 1st regular class in phrenology in America, gave readings and helped manage all aspects of the family's publishing activities; believed in Spiritualism, which promoted faith based on science and the promise of social reform, and was a vocal supporter for the equal rights of women; also hosted meetings for New York Medical College for Women and was a member of its board of trustees from its founding in 1863 until her death; with husband, took over ownership of brothers' business (1855) and was instrumental in founding the American Institute of Phrenology; after husband's death (1875), was the sole proprietor and

president of the Fowlers and Wells Co. ❖ See also *Women in World History.*

WELLS, Doreen (1937—). English ballet dancer. Born June 25, 1937, in Walthamstow, England. ❖ Trained at Bush-Davies School and Sadler's Wells School; joined company of Theatre Ballet (1955) and soon thereafter Sadler's Wells Ballet (1956), where she remained throughout career; appeared on tours with Royal Ballet throughout England; partnered Rudolf Nureyev on numerous occasions, most notably at Spoleto Festival in his *Raymonda* (1964); performed classical roles of Aurora and Swanilda, among others, as well as contemporary roles in works by Ashton, Macmillan, and Layton; retired (1974).

WELLS, Emmeline B. (1828–1921). American suffragist and religious leader. Name variations: E. W.; Blanche Beechwood; Aunt Em. Born Emmeline Blanche Woodward, Feb 29, 1828, in Petersham, Massachusetts; died April 25, 1921, in Salt Lake City, Utah; dau. of David Woodward and Deiadama (Hare) Woodward; m. James Harvey Harris (son of the presiding elder of local Mormon church), 1843 (deserted, 1844); m. Newel K. Whitney (Mormon bishop), 1845 (died 1850); m. Daniel Hanmer Wells, 1852 (died 1891); children: (1st m.) Eugene Henri Harris (died in infancy, 1844); (2nd m.) Isabel Modelena (b. 1848), Melvina Caroline (b. 1850); (3rd m.) Emmeline (b. 1853), Elizabeth Ann (b. 1859), and Louisa Martha (b. 1862). ❖ Leader of Mormon women, was baptized into Mormon Church (1842); traveled with 1st husband to Mormon city of Nauvoo, Illinois (1844); became plural wife of presiding bishop of the Mormon Church, Newel K. Whitney (1845); joined exodus of Mormons from Nauvoo to Salt Lake City (1846); 2 years after death of Bishop Whitney, became 7th wife of Daniel Hanmer Wells, a high officer in the Mormon Church (1852); began to devote her time to the work of the church, journalism, and women's suffrage, after the birth of last child (1862); as a member of the Relief Society, the largest Mormon women's organization, began contributing to its publication, the *Woman's Exponent* (1873), serving as full editor (1877–1914); in her articles, written under names Aunt Em, E. W. or Blanche Beechwood, sought to present a balanced representation of Mormonism and to promote the rights of women; was vice-president of the Utah chapter of National Women Suffrage Association and a friend of Susan B. Anthony and Elizabeth Cady Stanton; co-founded Woman Suffrage Association of Utah (1889) to demand the return of their right to vote; became general secretary of Relief Society (1892) and its president (1910); edited *Charities and Philanthropies: Woman's Work in Utah* (1893); also published book of poetry, *Musings and Memories* (1896), and wrote the words for the Mormon song "Our Mountain Home So Dear." ❖ See also *Women in World History.*

WELLS, Fay Gillis (1908–2002). American aviator and journalist. Born Fay Gillis, Oct 15, 1908, in Minneapolis, MN; died Dec 2, 2002, in Fairfax, VA; m. Ellery Walter (writer); m. Linton Wells (foreign correspondent); children: Linton II (b. 1946). ❖ Became member of Caterpillar Club after making a parachute jump to safety (1929); was 1st American woman to fly a Soviet airplane and 1st foreigner to own a Soviet glider; was a charter member of Ninety Nines (group of women fliers); served as correspondent for *The Herald Tribune*; sent with 2nd husband to Africa by President Franklin D. Roosevelt on secret mission to look for possible location for postwar Jewish homeland (1941); served as White House reporter for Storer Broadcasting Co.; was among 3 women reporters who traveled with President Richard M. Nixon to China (1972); landed a plane on her 92nd birthday. ❖ See also Lillian F. Brinnon and Howard J. Fried, *Fay Gillis Wells: In the Air and On the Air* (Woodfield Press, 2002).

WELLS, Ida B. (1862–1931). See Wells-Barnett, Ida.

WELLS, Jacqueline (1914–2001). See Bishop, Julie.

WELLS, John J.
See Bradley, Marion Zimmer.
See Coulson, Juanita.

WELLS, Kate Gannett (1838–1911). American social reformer and anti-suffragist. Name variations: Catherine Boott Gannett. Born April 6, 1838, in London, England; died Dec 13, 1911; dau. of American parents Ezra Stiles Gannett (minister) and Anna (Tilden) Gannett; m. Samuel Wells (Boston lawyer), June 11, 1863; children: Stiles Gannett, Samuel, and Louisa Appleton. ❖ Was a member of the Massachusetts Moral Education Association, which sought to combat prostitution through better education; elected to Boston School Committee for 1 term (1875), and appointed to three 8-year terms on Massachusetts State

Board of Education beginning 1888; led Massachusetts Emergency and Hygiene Association in promotion of better health practices in working-class families; adamantly opposed women's suffrage, arguing that the addition of uneducated women to the voting rolls would foster confusion and unnecessary legislation, though she acknowledged that the future presence of educated women in the political process would be beneficial. ❖ See also *Women in World History.*

WELLS, Kitty (b. 1919). American country singer. Born Ellen Muriel Deason, Aug 30, 1919, in Nashville, TN; m. Johnny Wright (musician), 1937. ❖ Known as the "Queen of Country Music," sang for 1st time over the radio (1936); adopted Kitty Wells as stage name; moved to Knoxville with family and sang on station WNOX; moved to Raleigh, NC, and performed on station WPTF; appeared on initial performance of "The Louisiana Hayride" over station KWKH, Shreveport, LA (1948); made 1st RCA recordings (1949); moved to Nashville; recorded "It Wasn't God Who Made Honky Tonk Angels" (1952), becoming the 1st female vocalist to have a #1 country music song on national record charts; sang 1st duet with Red Foley (1953), Roy Acuff (1955), Webb Pierce (1956), and Roy Drusky (1960); premiered "The Kitty Wells–Johnny Wright Family Show" (1969); made 1st appearance in Britain at Wembley Festival (1974); went on last concert tour (April 2000). Elected to Country Music Hall of Fame (1976); received Academy of Country Music's Pioneer Award (1986) and National Academy of Recording Arts and Sciences' Lifetime Achievement Grammy Award (1991); elected to Grammy Awards Hall of Fame (1997). ❖ See also *Women in World History.*

WELLS, Marguerite Milton (1872–1959). American women's-rights activist. Born Feb 10, 1872, in Milwaukee, Wisconsin; died in Minneapolis, Minnesota, Aug 12, 1959; dau. of Edward Payson Wells (banker, railroad entrepreneur, and politician) and Nellie (Johnson) Wells; graduate of Smith College, 1895; never married. ❖ Third president of National League of Women Voters who sought to educate women on the issues and their political rights; became involved with the suffrage movement in its final stages as a member of the Minnesota Woman Suffrage Association (1917); joined the newly formed National League of Women Voters after ratification of the 19th Amendment (1920); became president of the League (1934). ❖ See also *Women in World History.*

WELLS, Mary (b. 1928). See Lawrence, Mary Wells.

WELLS, Mary (1943–1992). African-American rhythm-and-blues singer. Born Mary Esther Wells, May 13, 1943, in Detroit, Michigan; died in Los Angeles, CA, July 26, 1992; m. Herman Griffin (div. 1962); m. Cecil Womack, 1966 (div. 1977); children: (2nd m.) 4, including Stacey Womack. ❖ Known as the Queen of Motown, was the 1st woman to become a major R&B star on the Motown label; had a series of successful releases, including "'Bye 'Bye Baby" (1961), "You Beat Me to the Punch" (1962), "Two Lovers" (1963) and "My Guy" (1964); toured with the Beatles (1964); career declined, however, when she left Motown and signed with another label (1964); other songs include "Set My Soul on Fire" (1968), "Dear Lover" (1968), "Dig the Way I Feel" (1970), "Give a Man the World" (1970) and "Gigolo" (1982). ❖ See also *Women in World History.*

WELLS, Mary Ann (c. 1895–1971). American ballet teacher. Born c. 1895 in Appleton, WI; died Jan 11, 1971, in Seattle, WA. ❖ Started out teaching ballet at Cornish School in Seattle (1916) and was soon considered most influential ballet teacher of Pacific Northwest; served as ballet teacher for close to 50 years in Seattle area and trained some of most acclaimed ballet and theater performers of 20th century, including Margaret Petit, choreographer William Weslow, and ballet directors Gerald Arpino and Robert Joffrey.

WELLS, Melissa Foelsch (1932–). American ambassador. Born Meliza Foelsch in Tallinn, Estonia, Nov 18, 1932; dau. of Kuno Georg Foelsch (physicist) and Miliza (Korjus) Foelsch (singer); became naturalized US citizen, 1941; Georgetown University's School of Foreign Service, BS, 1956; m. Alfred Washburn Wells (officer in Foreign Service), 1960; children: Christopher, Gregory. ❖ Served as ambassador to Guinea-Bissau and Cape Verde (1976–77), Mozambique (1987–90), and Zaire, now the Republic of Congo (1991–93); became ambassador to Estonia (1998); took several positions with the United Nations, including under-secretary general of administration and management; was the 1st woman foreign service officer to have a child while at her post. ❖ See also *Women in World History.*

WELLS, Sharlene (c. 1964—). See Hawkes, Sharlene.

WELLS-BARNETT, Ida (1862–1931). African-American writer, editor, and organizer. Name variations: Ida B. Barnett; Ida B. Wells; Ida Wells Barnett. Born Ida Bell Wells, July 16, 1862, in Holly Springs, Mississippi; died in Chicago, Illinois, Mar 25, 1931; dau. of Elizabeth Warrenton Wells (slave, then domestic servant) and James Wells (slave, then carpenter); m. Ferdinand Lee Barnett (attorney, Republican politician, and editor), June 27, 1895; children: Charles Aked (b. 1896); Herman K. (b. 1897); Ida B. Wells (b. 1901); Alfreda M. Duster (b. 1904). ❖ Major crusader against lynching, began career as a weekly columnist for *American Baptist* (1886); was soon contributing to a host of African-American journals, including *A. M. E. Church Review, Indianapolis World, Kansas City Dispatch,* and *Conservator* of Chicago; invested savings to buy a 3rd interest in *Memphis Free Speech and Headlight* and was part owner and editor (1889–92); contributed to various African-American newspapers; served as secretary, National Colored Press Association (1891–93); became weekly contributor to Fortune's *New York Age,* the leading black paper in the nation, which published her lengthy attack on lynching, reprinted in pamphlet form as *Southern Horrors: Lynch Law in All Its Phases* (1892); in her writings on lynching, challenged the notion that lynching was perpetuated by poor whites, declaring that leading businessmen led the mobs; was a founder of Southern Afro-American Press Association (1893); organized Ida B. Wells Club, Chicago (1893); toured British Isles for several weeks in an attempt to mobilize sentiment abroad (1893); helped launch the London Anti-Lynching Committee, the 1st anti-lynching organization in the world (1894); was owner and editor, *Conservator* (Chicago, 1895–97); was a founder of National Association of Colored Women (1896); served as editor for *Women's Era* (1896); was a founder of National Afro-American League, a body established to fight lynch law and integrate public accommodations (1898), serving as secretary (1898–99); headed Anti-Lynching Bureau (1899–1903); was a founder of Frederick Douglass Center, Chicago (1904); was a participant at National Negro Conference (1909) and member of Committee of Forty; was a founder of Negro Fellowship League, Chicago (1910); was an early participant of National Association for the Advancement of Colored People (1909–14); served as president, Chicago bureau, National Equal Rights League (1914); was a national organizer, Illinois Colored Women of Colored Voters Division, Republican National Committee (1928); writings include *Southern Horrors: Lynch Law in All Its Phases* (1892), *A Red Record: Tabulated Statistics and Alleged Causes of Lynching in the US, 1892–1893–1894* (1895), (with Frederick Douglass, Garland Penn, and F. L. Barnett) *The Reason Why the Colored American is not in the World Columbian Exposition* (1893), *Lynch Law in Georgia* (1899), *Mob Rule in New Orleans* (1900), *The Arkansas Race Riot* (1920) and *The East St. Louis Massacre: The Greatest Outrage of the Century* (1917). ❖ See also Alfreda M. Duster, ed. *Crusade for Justice. The Autobiography of Ida B. Wells* (U. of Chicago Press, 1970); Linda O. McMurry, *To Keep the Waters Troubled: The Life of Ida B. Wells* (Oxford U. Press, 1998); Mildred I. Thompson, *Ida B. Wells-Barnett: An Exploratory Study of an American Black Woman, 1893–1930* (Carlson, 1990); Miriam DeCosta-Willis, ed. *The Memphis Diary of Ida B. Wells* (Beacon, 1995); Trudier Harris, comp. *Selected Works of Ida B. Wells-Barnett* (Oxford U. Press, 1991); and *Women in World History.*

WELSH, Jane (1905–2001). English actress. Born Jan 14, 1905, in Bristol, England; died Nov 27, 2001, in London; m. Henry Mollison, 1932 (div. 1934); m. Leonard Ritte, 1960. ❖ Made London debut in *Alf's Button* (1924), followed by *Ordeal, The Hottentot, Mr. Pepys, Alibi, The Flying Fool, Little Tommy Tucker, Night of the Garter* and *Lot's Wife,* among others; regularly appeared as Mrs. Darling in *Peter Pan;* made film debut in *Two Crowded Hours* (1931) and appeared as Mrs. Brown in 2 "Just William" movies.

WELSH, Jane Baillie (1801–1866). See Carlyle, Jane Welsh.

WELSH, Lilian (1858–1938). American physician and educator. Born in Columbia, Pennsylvania, Mar 6, 1858; died in Columbia, Feb 23, 1938; dau. of Thomas Welsh (merchant and later general in the army) and Annie Eunice (Young) Welsh; graduate of State Normal School of Millersville, Pennsylvania, 1875; graduate of Woman's Medical College of Pennsylvania, 1889; attended University of Zurich, 1889–90; never married; long-time companion of Mary Sherwood (died c. 1935). ❖ Became a physician at the State Hospital for the Insane in Norristown, Pennsylvania (1890); teamed up with Dr. Mary Sherwood to set up a private practice in Baltimore (1892), focusing on preventive medicine and the health of expectant mothers and babies; appointed professor of physiology and hygiene and physician to the students at Woman's College of Baltimore (later known as Goucher College, 1894); taught personal and public health matters and promoted physical exercise for women; with Sherwood, took control of the Evening Dispensary for Working Women and Girls, recently founded by Kate Campbell Hurd-Mead and Alice Hall; became secretary of newly formed Baltimore Association for the Promotion of the University Education of Women (1897), seeking to secure admission of women into graduate departments within Johns Hopkins University; also supported women's suffrage. ❖ See also *Women in World History.*

WELTER, Ariadna (1930–1998). Mexican-born actress. Name variations: Ariadne Welter. Born in 1930 in Mexico; died Dec 13, 1998, in Mexico City of cirhossis of the liver; sister of Linda Christian (actress); m. Gustavo Alatriste (div. 1960). ❖ Made film debut in *Prince of Foxes* (1949); other films include *Sombra verde, Ensayo de un crimen, El Ultimo rebelde, El Vampiro, The Devil's Hand, Estas ruinas que ves,* and *Escápate conmigo;* often appeared on series tv, including "Sor Juana Ines de la Cruz," "Las Momias de Guanajuato," "El Caminante," "Cita con la muerte," "Cristina Guzman" and "Gente bien."

WELTFISH, Gene (1902–1980). American anthropologist. Born Regina Weltfish, Aug 7, 1902, in New York, NY; died Aug 2, 1980; dau. of Abraham and Eve Furman Weltfish; attended Hunter College; graduate of Barnard College, 1925; attended Columbia University; m. Alexander Lesser (div. 1940); children: Ann. ❖ Studied with Franz Boas and became a dedicated Boasian anthropologist; performed linguistic field-work among Pawnee Indians (1928–30, 1935); organized exhibitions of Indian crafts in museums, including American Museum of Natural History, NY; began teaching in graduate anthropology department at Columbia University (1935); dedicated to racial equality, collaborated with Ruth Benedict on pamphlet "The Races of Man," which was used for US Army orientation but later labeled subversive; called to testify before McCarthy's Senate Internal Security Committee (1952–53) and questioned about participation in Women's International Democratic Federation and Congress of American Women (both deemed subversive); blacklisted, was notified her position at Columbia was terminated (early 1950s); published what became the standard ethnography on Pawnee culture, *The Lost Universe* (1965); taught at Fairleigh Dickinson University (becoming full professor in 1968), New School for Social Research, Manhattan School of Music, and Rutgers University; helped develop Gerontological Society of New Jersey and the Grey Panthers, NY.

WELTS, Anne Quast (1937—). *See Sander, Anne Quast.*

WELTS, Mrs. David (1937—). *See Sander, Anne Quast.*

WELTY, Eudora (1909–2001). American writer. Born Eudora Alice Welty on April 13, 1909, in Jackson, Mississippi; died in Jackson, July 23, 2001; dau. of Christian Webb Welty and Mary Chestina (Andrews) Welty; attended two years at Mississippi State College for Women, 1925–27; University of Wisconsin, BA in English literature, 1929; studied advertising at Columbia University School of Business, 1930–31; never married; no children. ❖ One of the greatest literary figures of the 20th century, whose short stories, novels, and essays evoke the vibrant culture of her native Mississippi; lived in New York City (1930–31); returned to Mississippi upon death of father (1931); served as publicity agent for Works Project Administration (1933–36); published 1st short stories (1936); published many short stories and novels (1940s–50s), while traveling throughout US and Europe; won Pulitzer Prize for short novel, *The Optimist's Daughter* (1973); gave William E. Massey lectures at Harvard University (1983), which resulted in the bestseller, *One Writer's Beginnings* (1984); resided throughout life in Jackson; her keen observations of the peculiarities of Southern life allowed her to capture the rural Southern attitudes, family structures, relations between races, and speech patterns which are now disappearing; works enjoyed wide appeal that continued after her death, not only with Southern audiences, but with Northern, Western, and European audiences as well; writings include (short stories) *A Curtain of Green* (Doubleday, 1941), (novel) *The Robber Bridegroom* (1942), (short stories) *The Wide Net and Other Stories* (1943), (short stories) *Delta Wedding* (1946), (short stories) *The Golden Apples* (1949), *Selected Stories* and *The Ponder Heart* (1954), *Three Papers on Fiction* (1962), (juvenile) *The Shoe Bird* (1964), (novel) *Losing Battles* (1970), (short novel) *The Optimist's Daughter* (1972), (nonfiction) *The Eye of the Story* (1978), and *The Collected Stories of Eudora Welty* (1980). Was 4-time winner of O. Henry Award; elected to National Institute of Arts and Letters (1952); received William Dean Howells Medal for *The Ponder Heart* (1954); served as honorary consultant to Library of

Congress (1958–61); elected to American Academy of Arts and Letters (1971); received Gold Medal for Fiction of National Institute of Arts and Letters (1972); received National Medal of Literature and Medal of Freedom (1981) and National Medal of Arts (1986); inducted into the Women's Hall of Fame at Seneca Falls, New York (2000). ❖ See also Elizabeth Evans, *Eudora Welty* (Ungar, 1981); Neil Isaacs, *Eudora Welty* (Steck-Vaughn, 1969); Louise Westling, *Eudora Welty* (Barnes & Noble, 1989); (unauthorized biography) Ann Waldron, *Eudora* (Doubleday, 1999); and *Women in World History.*

WEN JIERUO (1927—). Chinese editor and translator. Born 1927 in China; m. Xiao Qian (journalist), 1954. ❖ Studied Japanese in Japan and worked as translator and editor of Japanese literature; wrote *Autobiography of a Hag* (1990), about life with husband during Cultural Revolution, which was published in Taiwan; translations include Czech writer Julius Fuchik's *Under the Gallows* (1945).

WEN LIRONG (1969—). Chinese soccer player. Born Oct 2, 1969, in China. ❖ Defender; made 1st appearance on Chinese national team (1986) and has over 100 caps; won 7 Asian team championships; won a team silver medal at Atlanta Olympics (1996); signed by WUSA's Carolina Courage (2001) then traded to San Diego Spirit; retired from international competition (2002).

WEN XIAOYU (1938—). Chinese short-story writer. Born 1938 in Zhejiang Province, China; graduate of Bejing University, 1955; m. Wang Zhecheng (writer). ❖ Taught Chinese literature at University of Inner Mongolia; with husband, wrote *Farewell, Thistles* (1983).

WENCHENG (c. 620–680). Chinese princess and founder. Name variations: Wen Cheng. Pronunciation: WHEN-chin. Born Wencheng into family of Emperor Tang Taizong; adopted and raised by his Empress Zhangsun; given title of princess and provided with a classical Confucian education; enjoyed the educational advantages of Chang-An, then one of the most cosmopolitan capitals of the world; m. Songzan Ganbu (or, according to the Tibetan alphabet, Srongbtdan Sgam-po), king of Tibet. ❖ Chinese princess of the Tang Dynasty who married the 1st king of Tibet and founded the Jokhang Temple in Lhasa, making her instrumental in establishing Buddhism as the national religion of Tibet; in a marriage alliance, became the bride of Songzan Ganbu, king of Tibet; brought with her from China a gilded bronze statue of the Sakyamuni Buddha, and under her supervision the Jokhang Temple was built to house this sacred object (the Jokhang is now considered one of Tibet's holiest places); her faith and the construction of her temple helped to spread the Buddhist faith, and laid the foundations for the emergence of the Dalai Lamas and the rule of Tibet as a theocracy; from China, brought artisans to introduce the arts of papermaking, textile weaving and new techniques in metallurgy and architectural design; also introduced the principles of grinding wheat, making pottery, and constructing field tools; commemorated in legends, plays and songs in Tibet and China. ❖ See also *Women in World History.*

WENDELL, Krissy (1981—). American ice-hockey player. Born Sept 12, 1981 in Brooklyn Park, MN. ❖ Won team silver medals at World championships (1999, 2000, 2001); won a team silver medal at Salt Lake City Olympics (2002) and a team bronze medal at Torino Olympics (2006).

WENDL, Ingrid (1940—). Austrian figure skater. Name variations: Ingrid Turkovic-Wendl. Born Ingrid Wendl, May 17, 1940, in Vienna, Austria; m. Milan Turkovic (musician). ❖ Won a bronze medal at Cortina Olympics (1956); won European championship (1956, 1958); starred with the Vienna Ice Revue and Ice Capades for 12 years; became a spokesperson for ORF (1972) and a tv host, journalist, and sport commentator (1988). ❖ See also autobiography *Mein grosser Bogen* (My Large Elbow, 2002).

WENDT, Julia Bracken (1871–1942). American artist. Born Julia Bracken in Apple River, Illinois, June 10, 1871; died in Los Angeles, California, 1942; dau. of Andrew and Mary Bracken; attended Art Institute of Chicago, 1887, and studied with Lorado Taft, 1887–92; m. William Wendt (b. 1865, well-known California artist), June 26, 1906. ❖ One of the leading women sculptors of the American West, began career in Chicago, working as one of Lorado Taft's female assistants (1888–94); commissioned for a sculpture at Illinois Pavilion at Chicago World's Fair (1893), produced *Illinois Welcoming the Nations*, which was placed in the state capitol in Springfield; following marriage, shared a studio with husband in an art colony in Laguna Beach; her sculptures in bronze, wood and marble made her one of the more famous figures in California art community, particularly her series of relief portraits of famous men of the century such as Tolstoy, Emerson, and Lincoln; created one of her best-known pieces, an allegory sculpture for the rotunda of Los Angeles County Museum, *The Three Graces: History, Science and Art* (1914); taught at Otis Art Institute (1918–25). ❖ See also *Women in World History.*

WENGER, Lisa (1858–1941). Swiss novelist and painter. Born 1858 in Berne, Switzerland; died 1941 in Carona; educated in Paris, Florence and Dusseldorf. ❖ Founded school for porcelain painters in Basle and began writing late in life; known for lively fables and works about demonic powers of women; writings include *Das blaue Märchenbuch* (1905), *Die Wunderdoktorin* (1909), *Das Zeichen* (1914) and *Der Vogel im Käfig* (1922).

WENHAM, Jane (d. 1730). English accused of witchcraft. Name variations: Witch of Walkern. Died in 1730. ❖ Last woman convicted of witchcraft in England, was tried and found guilty by jury (1713), but the jury's decision to condemn Wenham to death was contrary to the judge's leading; was pardoned and her case was debated in legal pamphlets of the day. ❖ See also *Women in World History.*

WENTSCHER, Dora (1883–1964). German novelist and short-story writer. Born 1883 in Germany; died 1964. ❖ Worked in theater and as painter and sculptor; works include novel *Barbara Velten* (1920), travelogues, short stories, and play about Heinrich von Kleist; went into exile (1933).

WENTWORTH, Baroness (1837–1917). *See Blunt, Anne.*

WENTWORTH, Cecile de (c. 1853–1933). American portrait painter. Name variations: Mme C.-E. Wentworth; Mme C. E. Wentworth; Cecile Smith de Wentworth. Born Cecilia Smith in New York, NY, c. 1853; died in Nice, France, Aug 28, 1933; studied painting in Paris with Alexandre Cabanel and Edouard Detaille; m. Josiah Winslow Wentworth, c. 1887 (died 1931). ❖ Appeared in exhibition catalogue of Paris Salon (1889); for next 30 years, showed her works at the salon and maintained a studio on Champs Élysées, achieving her greatest fame in France; won bronze medal for portrait of Pope Leo XIII at Exposition Universelle in Paris (1900); roster of clients included Theodore Roosevelt, William Howard Taft, Queen Alexandra of Denmark and General John J. Pershing; received title of Grand Commander of Order of the Holy Sepulcher and papal title of Marchesa; awarded title of Chevalier of Legion of Honor (1901); was one of the few women artists to have works purchased by Luxembourg Museum. ❖ See also *Women in World History.*

WENTWORTH, Henrietta Maria (c. 1657–1686). British baroness. Name variations: Baroness Wentworth. Born c. 1657; died April 23, 1686; only child of Sir Thomas Wentworth (1613–1665), Baron Wentworth, and Lady Philadelphia Wentworth (d. 1696, dau. of Ferdinando Carey); mistress of James Crofts Scott (1649–1685), duke of Monmouth (son of Charles II and Lucy Walter, executed 1685). ❖ Mistress and supporter of James Scott, duke of Monmouth, who inherited the estate of her grandfather the earl of Cleveland and succeeded to the barony of Wentworth (1667); spent several years discharging his debts and establishing her rights; met James Scott, duke of Monmouth, while performing in a masque at court (1674); lived with him on her estate (1680); followed him to exile in Holland (1684); dissuaded him from entering imperialist service against the Turks and supplied funds for him to lead a failed rebellion against King James II (1685); returned to England (1685). ❖ See also *Women in World History.*

WENTWORTH, Margaret (d. 1550). English aristocrat. Name variations: Margaret Seymour; Marjory Wentworth. Died in 1550; dau. of Henry Wentworth; descendant of Edward III; m. Sir John Seymour (a courtier), before 1500; children: John Seymour (d. 1510); Edward Seymour (who m. Anne Stanhope); John Seymour (d. 1520); Thomas Seymour (c. 1506–1549, who m. Catherine Parr); Jane Seymour (c. 1509–1537, who m. Henry VIII); Henry Seymour; Anthony Seymour (d. 1520); Elizabeth Seymour (d. 1563); Marjory Seymour (d. 1520); Dorothy Seymour.

WENZEL, Hanni (1951—). Liechtenstein Alpine skier. Name variations: Hanny Wenzel. Born Dec 4, 1954, in Straubirn, Germany; sister of Andreas Wenzel and Petra Wenzel (both Alpine skiers). ❖ Won 32 World Cup titles, including giant slalom (1974, 1980), overall (1978, 1980), slalom (1978), combined (tied with Annemarie Proell-Moser in 1979, 1980, 1983); won 4 Olympic medals: bronze in slalom at Innsbruck (1976), silver in downhill, gold in slalom, gold in giant slalom

at Lake Placid (1980); at World championships, placed 1st in slalom (1974) and combined (1980). ❖ See also *Women in World History.*

WENZEL, Kirsten (1961—). East German rower. Born Feb 27, 1961, in East Germany. ❖ At Moscow Olympics, won a gold medal in coxed fours (1980).

WENZEL-PERILLO, Brigitta (1949—). German politician. Born Feb 24, 1949, in Bösdorf, Germany. ❖ Worked as a veterinary surgeon (1975–80); lived in Rome (1980–91); as a member of the European People's Party (Christian Democrats) and European Democrats, elected to 5th European Parliament (1999–2004).

WERBEZIRK, Gisela (1875–1956). Austrian actress and cabaret performer. Name variations: Giselle Werbesik. Born Gisela Werbezirk into a Jewish family in Pressburg (Poszonyi), Hungary (now Bratislava, Slovakia), April 8, 1875; died in Hollywood, California, April 16, 1956; m. Hans Piffl; children: son, Heinrich. ❖ Viennese superstar of stage and screen for several decades before 1938; with the looming threat from Hitler's Germany, immigrated to US (1938), changing stage name to Giselle Werbesik; acted in a number of Hollywood films, including Anna Seghers' *The Seventh Cross.* ❖ See also *Women in World History.*

WERBROUCK, Ulla (1972—). Belgian judoka. Born Jan 24, 1972, in Izegem, Belgium. ❖ Won World Jr. championship (1990); won European championships for half-heavyweight (1994–97); won a gold medal for 66–72 kg half-heavyweight at Atlanta Olympics (1996).

WERBURGA (d. 700?). Saint and abbess of Sheppey and Ely. Name variations: Werburga of Ely; Werburh. Died c. 700; dau. of Wulfhere, king of Mercia (r. 657–675), and Ermenilda (d. about 700, who was also abbess of Sheppey and Ely).

WERE, Miriam (1940—). Kenyan novelist. Born 1940 in Kakamega District, Kenya. ❖ Received degrees in humanities and medicine in US and Uganda; trained as physician at University of Nairobi and became professor of public health; represented Kenya at UN decade of Women Conference (1985); works include *The Boy in Between* (1969), *The High School Gent* (1969), *The Eighth Wife* (1972), and *Your Heart is My Altar* (1980); also wrote biography of Margaret Owanyoni, *Nurse With a Song* (1978).

WERFEL, Alma (1879–1964). *See Mahler, Alma.*

WERLEIN, Elizebeth Thomas (1883–1946). American preservationist. Born Elizebeth Thomas in Bay City, Michigan, Jan 28, 1883; died in New Orleans, Louisiana, April 24, 1946; dau. of Henry Thomas (dynamite manufacturer) and his 1st wife, Marie Louise Felton Smith; attended Detroit Conservatory of Music, and Miss White's School in Paris, France; m. Philip Werlein III (music publisher and instrument dealer), Aug 4, 1908 (died Feb 1917); children: Betty, Lorraine, Evelyn, and Philip. ❖ Socialite who was largely responsible for the preservation of the French Quarter in New Orleans, supported cultural organizations in New Orleans' French Quarter; sparked interest in restoration of French Quarter mansions (1920s); organized and became 1st president of Vieux Carré Property Owners Association (1930); was instrumental in preservation of Vieux Carré; made honorary member of American Institute of Architects (1942). ❖ See also *Women in World History.*

WERNER, Ilse (1918—). German actress. Born July 11, 1918, in Batavia (later Jakarta), Java, Indonesia; dau. of O. E. G. Still (Dutch exporter) and Lilly Werner (German national); studied with Max Reinhardt at Vienna's Theater-Akademie, 1936 and 1937; m. John de Forest (American journalist), 1948 (div. 1953); m. Josef Niessen (orchestra conductor), 1954 (div.). ❖ Actress who personified the ideal "Aryan girl" in Third Reich propaganda films during World War II, made stage debut in Max Dauthendey's *Glück* in Vienna (1937); invited to Berlin; achieved popularity with film *Wunschkonzert* (1940); starred in *Die schwedische Nachtigall* (The Swedish Nightingale), loosely based on life of Jenny Lind (1941), *Wir machen Musik* (We Make Music, 1942), *Münchhausen* (The Adventures of Baron Münchhausen, 1943), which proved highly popular; moved to California with husband (1948); returned to Germany (1953); had hit song with "Baciare" throughout Europe (1960); starred in tv series "Eine Frau mit Pfiff" (1967); appeared as Anna in German version of *The King and I* (1970); toured Germany and Switzerland in play directed by Marie Becker (1973); worked on tv as moderator and host (1970s). ❖ See also memoirs (in German) *Ich über mich* (I on Myself, 1941) and *So wird's nie wieder sein* (It Will Never Again be the Same, 1981); and *Women in World History.*

WERNER, Marianne (1924—). West German track-and-field athlete. Born Jan 4, 1924, in Germany. ❖ Won a silver medal at Helsinki Olympics (1952) and a bronze medal at Melbourne Olympics (1956), both in the shot put; won the European championship (1958).

WERNER, Ruth (1907–2000). *See Kuczinski, Ruth.*

WERREMEIER, Stefani (1968—). German rower. Born Oct 17, 1968. ❖ At Barcelona Olympics, won a silver medal in coxless pairs (1992).

WERTH, Isabell (1969—). German equestrian. Name variations: Isabell Regina Werth. Born July 21, 1969, in Sevelen, Germany. ❖ Won a silver medal in indiv. dressage and a gold medal in team dressage at Barcelona Olympics (1992), gold medals for indiv. dressage and team dressage at Atlanta Olympics (1996), and a silver medal for indiv. dressage and gold medal for team dressage at Sydney Olympics (2000), all on Gigolo; won every title to be won: German, European, World, World Cup, and Olympic.

WERTMÜLLER, Lina (1928—). Italian filmmaker. Name variations: Lina Wertmuller; (pseudonyms) Nathan Wich, George H. Brown. Pronunciation: VERT-mew-ler. Born Arcangela Felice Assunta Wertmüller von Elgg Español von Brauchich, Aug 14, 1928, in Rome, Italy; dau. of Frederico Wertmüller (lawyer) and Maria (Santamaria) Wertmüller; m. Enrico Job (art director), in 1968; no children. ❖ Award-winning filmmaker and writer whose stylish and often controversial films made her one of the 1st women directors to achieve international acclaim; worked as assistant director for Federico Fellini for film *8½* (1962); directed her own script of *The Lizards,* for which she received the Silver Sail at Locarno Film Festival (1963); 2nd film, *Let's Talk About Men,* garnered a Silver Ribbon for its male lead, Nino Manfredi (1965); wrote and directed *The Seduction of Mimi* (1971), starring Giancarlo Giannini, which received Best Director Award at Cannes (1972), followed by the much-lauded *Love and Anarchy,* also starring Giannini (1972); also wrote script for Zeffirelli's *Brother Sun, Sister Moon* (1972); had another smash hit with *Swept Away . . . by an Unusual Destiny in the Blue Sea of August* (1975); wrote and directed *Seven Beauties* which received 4 American Academy Award nominations: Best Foreign Film, Best Actor, Best Director and Best Screenplay (1976); also wrote, directed and produced for theater, tv and radio; other films include *Belle Starr* (1968), *All Screwed Up* (1974), *The End of the World in Our Usual Bed in a Night Full of Rain* (1977), *Blood Feud (Revenge,* 1978), *A Jealous Man* (1984), *Complicated Intrigue of Back Alleys and Crimes* (1985), *A Summer Night* (1986), *To Save Nine* (1989), *Saturday, Sunday and Monday* (1990), *Ciao Professore* (1992), *Ferdinando e Carolina* (1999) and *Peperoni ripieni e pesci in faccia* (2004). ❖ See also autobiography (in Italian) *Avrei Voluto Uno Zio Esibizionista*; and *Women in World History.*

WESLEY, Cynthia (d. 1963). One of the Birmingham Four. Murdered Sept 15, 1963, age 14. ❖ With Denise McNair (11), Addie Mae Collins (14), and Carol Robertson (14), was in the Sixteenth Street Baptist church basement in Birmingham, Alabama, preparing to attend Sunday school and the monthly Youth Day service, when a bomb went off, killing her and the others (Sept 15, 1963). ❖ See also Spike Lee documentary *4 Little Girls* (1998).

WESLEY, Emilia (1692–1771). Sister of John and Charles Wesley. Name variations: Emily. Born in South Ormsby, England, in 1692; died in London in 1771; 3rd child of Samuel Wesley (a curate) and Susanna Wesley (1669–1742); m. Robert Harper (a chemist); children: infant who in died 1740. ❖ As the eldest girl, was a 2nd mother to the younger Wesleys, including John and Charles, later the founders of Methodism; opened her own school in the Lincolnshire township of Gainsborough; deserted by husband, moved to London to live with John Wesley in Moorfields. ❖ See also *Women in World History.*

WESLEY, Martha (1706–1791). Sister of John and Charles Wesley. Name variations: Patty. Born in Epworth, England, in 1706; died in City Road, London, in 1791; 17th child of Samuel Wesley (a curate) and Susanna Wesley (1669–1742); m. Reverend Westley Hall, in 1735; children: out of 10 confinements only 1 child survived, a boy who died of smallpox at age 14. ❖ Solemn and level-headed, was exceptionally close to brother John; after a disastrous marriage, turned her attention to the Methodism of her brothers, while enjoying the friendship of Dr. Samuel Johnson and other literary personages in 18th-century London. ❖ See also *Women in World History.*

WESLEY, Mary (1912–2002). British novelist. Name variations: Mary Siepmann; Lady Swinfen. Born Mary Aline Mynors Farmar, June 24, 1912, in Englefield Green, near Windsor, Berkshire, England; died Dec 30, 2002, in Devon, England; dau. of Colonel Harold Mynors Farmar and Violet (Dalby) Farmar; cousin of the duke of Wellington; raised by maternal grandmother, Lady Dalby; attended Queen's College, London, 1928–30, and London School of Economics, 1930–31; m. Charles Swinfen Eady (1883–1977), 2nd baron Swinfen (London barrister who would later marry Averil Humphreys of Co. Cork who would write under the name Lady Swinfen), Jan 1937 (div. 1944); m. Eric Siepmann (journalist), 1952 (died 1970); children: (1st m.) 2 sons (2nd m.) 1 son, William Siepmann. ❖ During World War II, worked in Bletchley Park before moving to Kent; wrote 2 children's books, *Speaking Terms* (1969) and *The Sixth Seal* (1969); at age 70, published 1st adult novel, *Jumping the Queue* (1983), which was an instant success; also wrote *Haphazard House* (1983), *The Chamomile Lawn* (1984), *Harnessing Peacocks* (1985), *The Vacillations of Poppy Carew* (1986), *Not That Sort of Girl* (1987), *Second Fiddle* (1988), *A Sensible Life* (1990), *A Dubious Legacy* (1992), *An Imaginative Experience* (1994), and *Part of the Furniture* (1997). Made CBE (1995).

WESLEY, Mehetabel (1697–1750). Sister of John and Charles Wesley. Name variations: Hetty. Born in Epworth, England, in 1697; died in London in 1750; 8th child of Samuel and Susanna Wesley; m. William Wright (plumber), in 1725. ❖ Intellectually gifted, fell in love with a lawyer named William Atkins but her father refused permission to marry him; eloped with Atkins who promised to marry her following one night of bliss then backed out, leaving her a "ruined" woman; was married off to the next suitor; for rest of life, was forbidden contact with her entire family. ❖ See also *Women in World History.*

WESLEY, Susanna (1669–1742). Mother of Methodism. Born Susanna Annesley in London, England, 1669; died at Bunhill, London, 1742; dau. of Dr. Annesley (prominent dissenting minister); m. Samuel Wesley (London curate), 1689 (died 1735); children: of 19 confinements only 10 survived, including daughters Emilia Wesley (1692–1771); Susanna Wesley (1695–1764); Maria Wesley (1696–1734); Mehetabel Wesley (1697–1750); Anne Wesley (b. 1702); Martha Wesley (1706–1791); Kezziah Wesley (1709–1741); sons Samuel Wesley Jr. (b. 1690); John Wesley (b. 1703, founder of Methodism); Charles Wesley (b. 1708, co-founder of Methodism and writer of 6,500 hymns, including "Hark! The Herald-Angels Sing"). ❖ English mother of John and Charles Wesley whose "kitchen prayers" were thought to be the seed of the Methodist movement; educated all 10 of her children; when son John was saved at the last minute from the fire that destroyed the Epworth rectory (1706), was convinced that God had spared him for a special purpose; for John, her will was his law, her letters through college were his oracles, her life was his example; began to hold service every Sunday evening in the rectory kitchen for the benefit of her children and servants (1710); was soon preaching to around 200 people; after husband died (1735), continued her ways until her own death. ❖ See also Abel Stevens, *The Women of Methodism; Its Three Foundresses, Susanna Wesley, the Countess of Huntingdon, and Barbara Heck; With Sketches of Their Female Associates and Successors in the Early History of the Denomination* (Carlton & Porter, 1866); and *Women in World History.*

WESSEL, Helene (1898–1969). German politician. Name variations: Helen Wessel. Born July 6, 1898, in Dortmund, Germany; died Oct 1969 in Bonn, Germany. ❖ Political leader, was co-founder of the All-German People's Party (Gesamtdeutschen Volkspartei, GVP), which from 1950 through 1957 criticized the Cold War assumptions of Chancellor Konrad Adenauer and advocated an early version of detente and relaxation of East-West tensions; began career as a social worker; before and during WWII, worked for Catholic Social Work Associations; after the war, published the newspaper *Neuer Westfälischer Kurier*; became a member of the Bundestag (1949) and 1st chair of Zentrumspartei, the 1st woman in Germany's history to head a party; co-founded GVP (1952); when the party split up (1957), joined the SPD and was a member of the Bundestag until 1969.

WESSEL-KIRCHELS, Ute (1953—). West German fencer. Born Mar 18, 1953. ❖ At Los Angeles Olympics, won a gold medal in team foil (1984).

WESSELY, Paula (1907–2000). Austrian actress. Born in Fünfhaus, Vienna, Austria, Jan 20, 1907; died May 11, 2000, in Vienna; dau. of a butcher and a former ballerina of the Hofoper (Court Opera); niece of Josephine Wessely, an actress of reputation with Vienna Burgtheater; studied with Hungarian actress Valerie Gray; attended Vienna's Theater-Akademie; studied with Max Reinhardt; m. Attila Hörbiger (actor), 1935; children: Elisabeth, Christiane, and Maresa. ❖ One of the most celebrated actresses in Central Europe for over a half-century and one of the superstars of Vienna's Burgtheater, made 1st professional performance at Deutsches Volkstheater in Vienna (1924); was continually engaged in theaters in Vienna, Prague, and Berlin until 1945, most memorably as Gretchen in *Faust* in Salzburg (1935) and title role in *St. Joan* in Berlin (1936); made film debut in *Maskerade* (1934), which was a tremendous success and established her as a leading film actress; during WWII, made Nazi propaganda films, the most blatant of which was *Heimkehr* (Homecoming, 1941); formed own movie production company (1949); reestablished successful stage career (late 1940s); became member of the ensemble of Burgtheater in Vienna (1953); was held in great affection for her down-to-earth persona and exceptional talent. Received the Max-Reinhardt-Ring (1949), Josef-Kainz-Medaille (1960), and Goldmedaille der Stadt Wien (1967). ❖ See also *Women in World History*.

WESSEX, countess of.
See Thyra (d. 1018).
See Gytha (fl. 1022–1042).
See Rhys-Jones, Sophie (1965—).

WESSEX, queen of.
See Sexburga (c. 627–673).
See Engyth (fl. 7th c.).
See Eadburgh (c. 773–after 802).
See Redburga (fl. 825).
See Osburga (?–c. 855).
See Martel, Judith (c. 844–?).

WEST, Ann (1825–1922). See Robertson, Ann.

WEST, Claire (1893–1980). American costume designer. Name variations: Clare West. Born in 1893; died in 1980; graduated from college sometime in the 1910s; studied fashion in Paris. ❖ One of the 1st costume designers in the American film industry, worked for D.W. Griffith and Cecil B. De Mille on such films as *Intolerance* (1916), *The Affairs of Anatol* (1921), *Adam's Rib* (1923), *The Ten Commandments* (1924), and *The Merry Widow* (1925); worked closely with De Mille in dressing, on average, three pictures a year; became personal costumer for Talmadge sisters, Norma and Constance (1923). ❖ See also *Women in World History*.

WEST, Dorothy (1907–1998). African-American writer. Name variations: (pseudonyms) Mary Christopher; Jane Isaac. Born Dorothy West, June 2, 1907, in Boston, Massachusetts; died Aug 16, 1998, in Boston, Massachusetts; dau. of Isaac Christopher West (entrepreneur) and Rachel Pease (Benson) West; graduated from Girls' Latin School, 1923; attended Columbia University; never married; no children. ❖ Youngest writer of the Harlem Renaissance of the 1920s who went on to develop a literary career spanning 8 decades; wrote her 1st short story at age 7; began publishing stories in the *Boston Post* while still in teens; shared 2nd place award with Zora Neale Hurston in *Opportunity* writing contest (1926); moved to New York with cousin Helene Johnson during the height of the Harlem Renaissance; spent a year in Russia; founded *Challenge* magazine (1934) and *New Challenge* (1937); worked as a welfare investigator and as a writer for the Federal Writers' Project during the Depression; published more than 2 dozen short stories in New York *Daily News* (1940s–1950s); moved to the island of Martha's Vineyard (mid-1940s), where she wrote a column for the local newspaper; published 1st novel, the semi-autobiographical *The Living Is Easy* (1948); published a collection of stories and reminiscences, *The Richer, the Poorer*, and her highly praised 2nd novel, *The Wedding* (1995); was rediscovered by literary historians, critics, and general admirers and became greatly sought after for interviews and lectures; after more than 6 decades, as the oldest living survivor of the Harlem Renaissance, experienced a renaissance of her own. ❖ See also "As I Remember It: A Portrait of Dorothy West," directed by Saleem Merkuria for WGBH (1991); and *Women in World History*.

WEST, Dottie (1932–1991). American country-western singer and songwriter. Born Dorothy Marie Marsh in McMinnville, TN, Oct 11, 1932; died in Nashville, Sept 4, 1991; dau. of Hollis Marsh; Tennessee Technological University, BA in music; m. Bill West (guitarist, div. 1969); m. Byron Metcalf (drummer, div. 1980); m. Al Winters (sound technician), 1983 (div. 1991); children: 4, including country star Shelly West. ❖ Performed with 1st husband Bill West, including a regular slot on Cleveland tv show, "Landmark Jamboree"; signed with Starday Records (1959) and moved to Nashville; began writing songs and had 1st hit "Is This Me?," recorded by Jim Reeves (1961); had successful duet career with Reeves which included top-10 "Love is No Excuse"; signed with RCA (1962), and wrote 1st of her smash hits, "Here Comes My

Baby," earning a Grammy (1964), the 1st female country star to win the award; produced several other chart-topping songs, including "Would You Hold It Against Me?," "Paper Mansions," "Rings of Gold," "I was Born a Country Girl," "Gettin' Married Has Made Us Strangers," "What's Come Over My Baby?" and "Mommy, Can I Still Call Him Daddy?"; became a regular on "Grand Ole Opry" tv show and did guest spots on "The Jimmy Dean Show," "Country Music Hall" and "The Faron Young Show"; switched to United Artists (1976) and had hit single "When It's Just You and Me"; also recorded duets with Kenny Rogers, including the hit "Every Time Two Fools Collide," which led to a full album of West-Rogers songs which went gold; with Rogers, did follow-up album, *Classics* (1979), an even bigger success, and had several hit singles, such as "Anyone Who Isn't Me Tonight," "Til I Can Make It On My Own" and "All I Ever Need Is You"; also released solo albums *Special Delivery* (1980) and *Wild West* (1981), both of which yielded significant hits, such as "Are You Happy Baby?" and "A Lesson in Leavin'." ❖ See also "Big Dreams & Broken Hearts: The Dottie West Story" (tv movie), starring Michele Lee (1995); and *Women in World History*.

WEST, Elizabeth (fl. early 18th c.). Scottish diarist. Born in Scotland. ❖ Wrote *Memoirs or Spiritual Exercises of Elizabeth West* (1766).

WEST, Elizabeth (1927–1962). English ballet dancer. Born 1927, in Alassio, Italy; died Sept 28, 1962, on Valtournanche, while climbing in the Italian Alps. ❖ Trained with Edouard Espinosa and at Bristol Old Vic; choreographed numerous Shakespearean dance segments for Bristol Old Vic and Stratford-on-Avon Company; appeared in West End in *Salad Days*; co-founded Western Theatre Ballet with Peter Darrell (1957), for which she also created several works (the company transferred to Glasgow in 1969 and became the Scottish Ballet).

WEST, Florence (1862–1912). See Waller, Florence.

WEST, Harriet (1904–1999). See Waddy, Harriet.

WEST, Jane (1758–1852). British novelist and poet. Born Jane Iliffe in London, England, April 30, 1758; died in Little Bowden, Northamptonshire, Mar 25, 1852; dau. of John Iliffe and Jane Iliffe; m. Thomas West (farmer), c. 1780 (died 1823); children: 3 sons. ❖ Writer who achieved a measure of celebrity for her educational tracts and didactic novels in a career that spanned over 50 years; initially published books of poetry, *Miscellaneous Poetry* (1786) and *Miscellaneous Poems and a Tragedy* (1791); her 1st novels, *The Advantages of Education; or The History of Maria Williams* (1793) and *The Gossip's Story* (1796), pre-date the anti-sentimentality of Jane Austen's *Sense and Sensibility*; published *An Elegy on the Death of Edmund Burke* (1797) and *A Tale of the Times* (1799), the latter of which was declared by critics to be anti-Jacobin; also assailed atheism in *The Infidel Father* (1802); up until 1810, used the character Prudentia Homespun as a narrator for her novels; also wrote historical novels, including *The Loyalists* (1812), *Alicia de Lacey* (1814) and *Ringrove* (1827). ❖ See also *Women in World History*.

WEST, Jennie (1866–1949). See Macandrew, Jennie.

WEST, Jessamyn (1902–1984). American writer. Born Mary Jessamyn West near North Vernon, Indiana, July 2, 1902; died in Napa, California, Feb 23, 1984; dau. of Eldo Roy West and Grace Anna (Milhous) West; 2nd cousin of President Richard Milhous Nixon; Whittier College, BA in English, 1923; m. Harry Maxwell (Max) McPherson (founder and 1st president of Napa Valley College), Aug 16, 1923; became guardian for Ann McCarthy (Cash) from Limerick, Ireland (1955). ❖ Writer who gained particular renown for novels and short stories set in Quaker communities in the American West; with family, moved to California (1909), when father bought a lemon grove in Yorba Linda; brought up on Quaker principles which are embodied in her work; had a 4-year teaching career in Hemet; contracted TB and lingered in a sanitorium (1931–33); published 1st story, "99.6," about life in the sanitorium (1939); published 1st collection of stories, the international bestseller *The Friendly Persuasion* (1945), based on her Quaker ancestors in Indiana; served as technical director for film *Friendly Persuasion* (1956); in *Cress Delahanty* (1953), describes the problems of growing up, a "thinly disguised story of her girlhood" in Yorba Linda, according to one critic; after assisting sister Carmen West, who was in the terminal stages of intestinal cancer, in ending her life (Oct 26, 1963), published *A Matter of Time* (1966), which deals with euthanasia; wrote the bestseller *Except for Me and Thee*, sequel to *The Friendly Persuasion* (1969); other writings include *South of the Angels, The Pismire Plan* (1948), *The Woman Said Yes* (1976) and (poetry collection) *The Secret Look* (1974); also wrote screenplays for *Stolen Hours* and *The Big

Country. ❖ See also memoir *To See the Dream* (1957), *Hide and Seek* (1973) and *Double Discovery* (1980); Ann Dahlstrom Farmer, *Jessamyn West* (1982); Alfred S. Shivers, *Jessamyn West* (Twayne, 1992); and *Women in World History.*

WEST, Lillie (1855–1939). *See Leslie, Amy.*

WEST, Mae (1893–1980). **American actress, singer and comedian.** Name variations: May West; (pseudonym) Jane Mast. Born Mary Jane West, Aug 17, 1893, in Brooklyn, NY; died in Hollywood, CA, Nov 22, 1980; sister of Mildred West (sometime actress who appeared on stage as Beverly Osborn); m. Frank Wallace (né Szatkus), 1911 (div. 1942). ❖ One of the great figures of popular culture who was a legend in her lifetime, 1st appeared on stage at amateur night in Brooklyn singing "Movin' Day" (c. 1900); played children's roles with Hal Clarendon's Stock Co. (1901–04); appeared in NY as Maggie O'Hara in *A La Broadway and Hello Paris* (1911) and as Mame Dean in *Sometime* (1918); appeared as Margie LaMont in *Sex* (1926–27), until it was raided and she spent 10 days in jail; became the darling of the tabloid press; appeared in title role of *Diamond Lil* (1928), which ran for 9 months; published 1st novel *Babe Gordon* (reissued as *The Constant Sinner*, 1930); made film debut in *Night After Night* (1932), followed by *She Done Him Wrong* (1932), *I'm No Angel* (1933), *Belle of the Nineties* (1934), *Klondike Annie* (1936), *Go West Young Man* (1937), *My Little Chickadee* (1940) and *Sextette* (1976), among others, portraying women who knew what they wanted, saw nothing wrong in going after it, and suffered no pangs of remorse at story's end; debuted on radio on "Chase and Sanborn Hour" (1938); opened in play *Catherine Was Great* (1944); appeared as Leticia Van Allen in film *Myra Breckinridge* (1970); an unparalleled mistress of the "one-liner," had a genius for delivery and timing (her quip "Come up and see me sometime" becoming the most famed of invitations). ❖ See also memoirs *Goodness Had Nothing to Do With It* (Prentice-Hall, 1959); Eels and Musgrove *Mae West* (Morrow, 1982); Marybeth Hamilton, *"When I'm Bad, I'm Better"* (U. of California Press, 1996); and *Women in World History.*

WEST, Rebecca (1892–1983). **English feminist, novelist, and critic.** Name variations: Cicely Isabel Fairfield; "Cissie"; Mrs. Henry Maxwell Andrews; Corinne Andrews; Rachel East. Born Cicely Isabel Fairfield, Dec 21, 1892, in London, England; died at Kingston House, London, Mar 15, 1983; dau. of Charles Fairfield (journalist) and Isabella (Mackensie) Fairfield; attended Academy of Dramatic Art; m. Henry Maxwell Andrews, Nov 1, 1930; children: (with H.G. Wells) Anthony Panther West (b. 1914). ❖ Considered by many to be the leading woman journalist of her generation, was a teenage participant in suffragist demonstrations; made an unsuccessful attempt at an acting career; served on staff of feminist paper *The Freewoman*, later *The New Freewoman*, as an ardent feminist, suffragist, socialist, and anti-imperialist; to preserve family unity and to save her mother pain, adopted pseudonym Rebecca West (1912); joined staff of socialist paper *The Clarion*; for *The New Republic, The New Yorker,* and numerous other publications, wrote nearly a thousand reviews over the course of her professional life; had affair with H. G. Wells (1913–23); published 1st book of nonfiction, *Henry James* (1916); published 1st novel, *The Return of the Soldier* (1918), followed by 10 other novels, of which the autobiographical *The Fountain Overflows* (1956) has been the most popular; published major work of nonfiction *Black Lamb and Grey Falcon* (1941), when the approach of World War II already shadowed Europe and the Balkans; published *The Meaning of Treason* (1941) and *The New Meaning of Treason*; went on British Council lecture tours in Finland and Yugoslavia (1935–36); was a member of the 1st executive committee of PEN, the worldwide writers' organization; reported on Nuremberg trials (1946); was an eyewitness reporter at the siege of Iranian Embassy in London (1980), at age 87. Named Companion of the British Empire (1949) and Dame of the British Empire (1959). ❖ See also memoirs, *The Young Rebecca* (1982) and *Family Memories* (1988); Victoria Glendinning, *Rebecca West* (Weidenfeld & Nicolson, 1987); Carl Rollyson, *Rebecca West* (Scribner, 1996); Bonnie Kime Scott, ed. *Selected Letters of Rebecca West* (Yale U. Press, 2000); and *Women in World History.*

WEST, Rosemary (1953—). **English serial killer.** Name variations: Rosemary Letts, Rose West. Born Rosemary Letts, 1953, in England; m. Frederick West, 1972 (committed suicide in jail before trial, Jan 1, 1995); children: 7. ❖ Came to attention of police when authorities investigated disappearance of her daughter Heather (1992) and found her remains underneath the floor of the family home at 25 Cromwell Street, Gloucester; was implicated with husband in several other murders, after excavation of backyard and other sites revealed numerous body parts;

jailed and charged with 12 counts of murder (1994); husband confessed to 9 murders, denied her involvement (1994), then killed himself; was convicted and given life sentence for murder of 10 girls over 20-year period, including 16 year-old daughter, 8-year-old stepdaughter and husband's pregnant lover (Nov 1995); continues to deny any knowledge of killings. ❖ See also Brian Masters, *She Must Have Known: Trial of Rosemary West* (Corgi, 1997).

WEST, Sandy (1960—). **American drummer, guitarist and vocalist.** Born 1960. ❖ Drummer with all-girl rock band, the Runaways, which was formed in Los Angeles (1975), with Cherie Currie, Joan Jett, Vickie Blue, Lita Ford; with band, signed with Mercury and released debut album, *The Runaways* (1976), followed by *Queens of Noise* (1977) and *Live in Japan*, which earned 3 gold records in Japan; other Runaways albums included *Waitin' for the Night* (1977) and *Little Lost Girls* (1981); after band folded (1979), formed the Sandy West Band (1980s).

WEST, Vera (1900–1947). **American costume designer.** Name variations: Vera. Born in 1900; died June 29, 1947; educated at Philadelphia School of Design. ❖ Served as head costume designer for Universal Studios (1928–47); films include *Back Street* (1932), *Diamond Jim* (1935), *Magnificent Obsession* (1935), *That Certain Age* (1938), *The Sun Never Sets* (1939), *My Little Chickadee* (1939), *The Bank Dick* (1940), *Never Give a Sucker an Even Break* (1941), *Pardon My Sarong* (1942), *Frankenstein Meets the Wolfman* (1942), *Follow the Boys* (1943), *She Gets Her Man* (1944), *Terror By Night* (1945), *The Killers* (1946) and *Pirates of Monterey* (1947).

WEST, Victoria Mary Sackville- (1892–1962). *See Sackville-West, Vita.*

WEST, Winifred (1881–1971). **British-born Australian educator.** Born in Frensham, Surrey, England, Dec 21, 1881; died Sept 26, 1971; dau. of Charles William West (schoolmaster) and Fanny (Sturt) West; studied medieval and modern languages at Newnham College, Cambridge, 1900–03; studied art at Julian Ashton Art School. ❖ Progressive school founder, who opened a succession of schools in Australia which focused on encouraging independent thinking, freeing the creative spirit, and nurturing girls to become whole and physically healthy modern women; traveled to Sydney, Australia (1907); was an illustrator for the Australian Museum; convened 1st meeting of New South Wales Women's Hockey Association (1908); founded experimental and progressive Frensham boarding school (1913); opened Sturt school and arts center (1941); opened Gibgate primary school (1952); opened Holt physical education college for women (1953) and Hartfield boarding school (1968). Named Officer of the British Empire (OBE, 1953). ❖ See also *Women in World History.*

WESTBROOK, Harriet (1795–1816). **Wife of Percy Shelley.** Name variations: Harriet Shelley. Born Harriet Westbrook in 1795; drowned herself in Serpentine River, Nov 1816; dau. of a retired tavern keeper; m. Percy Bysshe Shelley (the poet), Aug 1811; children: daughter Ianthe Shelley (b. 1813); Charles Shelley (b. 1814). ❖ Resisted husband's preference for threesomes; abandoned by Shelley, committed suicide when she discovered she was carrying the child of another man. ❖ See also *Women in World History.*

WESTCOTT, Helen (1928–1998). **American stage and screen actress.** Born Myrthas Helen Hickman, Jan 1, 1928, in Hollywood, CA; died Mar 17, 1998, in Edmonds, WA; dau. of Gordon Westcott (actor). ❖ Made film debut as a child in *A Midsummer Night's Dream* (1935); other films include *Adventures of Don Juan, Three Came Home, Phone Call from a Stranger, With a Song in My Heart, God's Little Acre, Studs Lonigan* and *I Love My Wife.*

WESTENDORF, Anke (1954—). **East German volleyball player.** Born Feb 26, 1954. ❖ At Moscow Olympics, won a silver medal in team competition (1980).

WESTERBOTTEN, duchess of. *See Sybilla of Saxe-Coburg-Gotha (1908–1972).*

WESTERHOF, Marieke (1974—). **Dutch rower.** Born Aug 14, 1974. ❖ Won a silver medal for coxed eight at Sydney Olympics (2000).

WESTERMANN, Liesel (1944—). **West German track-and-field athlete.** Born Nov 2, 1944, in Germany. ❖ At Mexico City Olympics, won a silver medal in the discus throw (1968).

WESTLEY, Helen (1875–1942). **American actress.** Name variations: Helen Ransom. Born Henrietta Remsen Meserole Manney in Brooklyn, New York, Mar 28, 1875; died in Franklin Township, New

Jersey, Dec 12, 1942; dau. of Charles Palmer Manney and Henrietta (Meserole) Manney; educated at Emerson College of Oratory, 1894–95, and American Academy of Dramatic Art; m. Jack Westley (actor), Oct 31, 1900 (sep. 1912); children: Ethel Westley. ❖ One of the founders of the Theatre Guild, made NY stage debut with the stock company headed by Rose Stahl in *The Captain of the Nonesuch* (Sept 13, 1897); acted in vaudeville and stock companies; joined Greenwich Village's famous Liberal Club; with Lawrence Langner and others, formed the Washington Square Players (1915); as one of the founders of the Theatre Guild (1918), served actively on its board for next 15 years; had successful career in Hollywood beginning in 1934, acting in nearly 30 films, including *Moulin Rouge* (1934), *The House of Rothschild* (1934), *Death Takes a Holiday* (1934), *Roberta* (1935), *Showboat* (1936), *Heidi* (1937), *Rebecca of Sunnybrook Farm* (1938), *Alexander's Ragtime Band* (1938) and *My Favorite Spy* (1942). ❖ See also *Women in World History*.

WESTMACOTT, Mary (1890–1976). *See Christie, Agatha.*

WESTMAN, Nydia (1902–1970). American stage and screen actress. Born Feb 19, 1902, in New York, NY; died May 23, 1970, in Burbank, CA; dau. of Lily Wren Westman (actress and playwright) and Theodore Westman (actor and composer); m. Robert Sparks (div.). ❖ Began career as a child in vaudeville with The Westman Family: her parents, 2 sisters, and brother; made Broadway debut at 16 in *Pigs*; also appeared in *Lysistrata, Merchant of Yonkers, Life with Father, Madwoman of Chaillot, Endgame* and *Midgie Purvis*, among others; films include *Little Women, Craig's Wife, The Goldwyn Follies, The Late George Apley, The Velvet Touch, The Horse in the Gray Flannel Suit* and *Rabbit Run.*

WESTMORELAND, countess of.
See Stafford, Margaret (d. 1396).
See Beaufort, Joan (1379–1440).
See Percy, Elizabeth (d. 1437).
See Stafford, Catherine (fl. 1530).
See Howard, Jane (d. 1593).

WESTON, Agnes (1840–1918). English philanthropist. Name variations: Dame Agnes Elizabeth Weston; Aggie Weston; Mother Weston. Born Mar 26, 1840, in London, England; died Oct 23, 1918, in Devonport, England; dau. of Charles Henry Weston (barrister) and Sarah Agnes Weston. ❖ Philanthropist who founded Sailors' Rests in England, became active in temperance movement; started coffee bar in Bath for men of 2nd Somerset Militia; with Sophia Gertrude Wintz, opened 1st Sailors' Rest restaurant and hostel on Fore Street, Devonport (1876), which was an enormous success; opened another establishment at Portsmouth; though the Rests were intended to be temperance houses, welcomed all sailors, housing over 1,600 men each night; was publicly recognized for work when Queen Victoria endowed a room at Devonport and gave permission for prefix "Royal" to be added to name (1895); printed monthly letter to be distributed to those at sea, with circulation rising to 60,000 by 1918; published journal *Ashore and Afloat*; buried with full naval honors. Made Dame of the British Empire (1918). ❖ See also Doris Gulliver, *Dame Agnes Weston* (Phillimore, 1971).

WESTON, Allen (1912—). *See Norton, Andre.*

WESTON, Cecil (1889–1976). South African-born actress. Name variations: Cecile Weston. Born Sept 3, 1889, in South Africa; died Aug 7, 1976, in Hollywood, CA; m. Fred Balshofer (producer-cinematographer). ❖ Appeared in over 80 films, including *Dude Ranch, Huckleberry Finn, Behold My Wife, Banjo on My Knee* and *Mr. Belvedere Rings a Bell.*

WESTON, Elizabeth Jane (1582–1612). British scholar and writer. Born in London, England, Nov 2, 1582; died in Prague, Czechoslovakia, Nov 23, 1612; m. Johann Leon (lawyer), c. 1602; children: 3 daughters, 4 sons. ❖ A prodigy in languages, spent most of her life on the Continent, eventually settling in Prague; though her primary spoken language was German, did all her writing, both poetry and prose, in Latin; also spoke and wrote Greek, Italian and Czech; was ranked with Sir Thomas More among the best Latin poets of her day, and her reputation on the Continent was even higher; poems were collected and published in several volumes as *Parthenicon Elisabethae Joannae Westoniae, virginis nobilissimae, poetriae florentissimae, linguarum plurimarum peritissimae.* ❖ See also *Women in World History.*

WESTON, Jessie Edith (1867–1944). New Zealand novelist. Born 1867; died 1944. ❖ Wrote one of first novels to deal with Maori or part-Maori character, *Ko Meri* (1890); novel does not depart from western stereotypes of Maoris and expresses the belief that Maoris were a dying race.

WESTON, Jessie Laidlay (1850–1928). English folklorist. Born 1850 in UK; died Sept 29, 1928. ❖ Specializing in medieval Arthurian texts, wrote *The Legends of the Wagner Drama* (1896), *The Legend of Sir Gawain* (1897), *King Arthur and His Knights* (1899), *Morien* (1901), *Sir Gawain and the Green Knight* (1905), *The Legend of Sir Perceval* (1906), *The Quest for the Holy Grail* (1913), and *From Ritual to Romance* (1920), among others.

WESTON, Ruth (1906–1955). American stage and screen actress. Born Aug 31, 1906, in Boston, MA; died Nov 6, 1955, in Orange, NJ; m. Alfred Reginald Meade. ❖ Made Broadway debut replacing Ina Claire in *Biography*; other credits include *No More Ladies, The Dominant Sex, Forbidden Melody, The Country Wife, Pastoral, Three's a Family* and *George Washington Slept Here*; had a 39-month run as Aunt Eller in *Oklahoma*; also appeared in several films.

WESTOVER, Winifred (1899–1978). American silent-film actress. Name variations: Winnifred Westover. Born Nov 9, 1899, in San Francisco, CA; died Mar 19, 1978, in Los Angeles, CA; m. William S. Hart (Western star), 1921 (sep 1922, div.); children: William S. Hart Jr. ❖ Made film debut in *Intolerance* (1916), followed by *Don Quixote, The Fall of Babylon, Anne of Little Smoky* (title role), *The Microscope Mystery, Love's Masquerade,* and *Silkesstrumpan*; often starred opposite Willam S. Hart. Nominated for Academy Award for *Lummox* (1930).

WESTPHAL, Heidi (1959—). East German rower. Born July 5, 1959. ❖ At Moscow Olympics, won a silver medal in double sculls (1980).

WESTPHALEN, Jenny von (1814–1881). *See Marx, Jenny von Westphalen.*

WESTPHALIA, princess of. *See Mathilde (1820–1904).*

WESTPHALIA, queen of. *See Catherine of Wurttemberg (1783–1835).*

WEST SAXONS, queen of.
See Sexburga (c. 627–673).
See Eadburgh (c. 773–after 802).
See Redburga (fl. 825).
See Osburga (?–c. 855).
See Martel, Judith (c. 844–?).

WESTWOOD, Vivienne (1941—). English fashion designer. Born Vivienne Isabel Swire, April 8, 1941, in Glossopdale, Derbyshire, England; dau. of Gordon Swire and Dora Ball; sister of Gordon and Olga Swire; m. Derek John Westwood (airline steward), 1962 (div. 1966); children: (1st m.) Benjamin (b. 1963); (with Malcolm McLaren) Joseph (b. 1967). ❖ One of the most influential British fashion designers of 20th century, created the '70s punk look; opened memorabilia shop, Let It Rock, on fashionable King's Road with Malcolm McLaren (1971); began creating fashions to sell in shop, catering to budding punk-rock movement, dressing the Sex Pistols; gave shop a makeover, renamed it Seditionaries, and it became the birthplace of punk; had her 1st catwalk show with her romantic Pirates Collection (1981), and experienced great success; began showing designs in Paris (1983); shifted focus to haute couture (1990s); enjoyed considerable mainstream success, with stores in Paris, Moscow, Hong Kong and Seoul; retrospective held at Victoria and Albert Museum (2004). Named British Designer of the Year (1990, 1991); awarded Order of British Empire (OBE).

WETAMOO (c. 1650–1676). Native American leader. Name variations: Namumpam; Tatatanum; Tatapanum; Weetammo; Wetamou; Wetamoe; Weetamore; Queen Wetamoo; Squaw Sachem of the Pocasset. Born c. 1650 on tribal lands of the Pocassets (now parts of Tiverton, Rhode Island, and Fall River, Massachusetts); drowned Aug 1676; dau. of a Wampanoag Federation sachem, Chief Corbitant of the Pocasset tribe; m. Winnepurket, sachem of Saugus (died); m. Wamsutta, also known as Alexander (died 1662), grand sachem of Wampanoag Federation and brother to Metacom (King Philip); m. Quequequamanchet (Ben); m. Quinnapin (d. 1676); children: (with Wamsutta) 1 son (after he was taken hostage with Wamsutta, no record exists of his life). ❖ Sunksquaw of the Pocassets, inherited her position from father Corbitant, one of the most powerful *sachems* (chiefs) in the Wampanoag Federation; following death of husband Wamsutta, married Quequequamanchet, but left him when he sided with the colonists; then married Quinnapin, a Narraganset, who was captured by the English and put to death; a valiant, proud warrior, sided with Metacom in King Philip's War (1675–76); drowned while escaping when her camp was attacked by the British. ❖ See also *Women in World History*.

WETHERALD, Ethelwyn (1857–1940). Canadian poet and journalist. Name variations: (pseudonym) Bel Thistlethwaite. Born Agnes Ethelwyn Wetherald, April 26, 1857 in Rockwood, Ontario, Canada; died 1940; dau. of Rev. William Wetherald (English Quaker and founder of the Rockwood Academy); attended Friends' Boarding School (Union Springs, NY) and Pickering College. ❖ As Bel Thistlewaite, wrote for Toronto *Globe,* Toronto *Week,* and *Wives and Daughters;* published 1st book of verse, *The House of the Trees and Other Poems* (1895); other collections include *Tangled in Stars* (1902), *The Radiant Road* (1904), *The Last Robin: Lyrics and Sonnets* (1907), considered her best, as well as *Tree-top Mornings* (1921), and *Lyrics and Sonnets* (1931).

WETHERED, Joyce (1901–1997). English golfer. Name variations: Lady Heathcote-Amory. Born Nov 17, 1901, in Maldon, Surrey, England; died Nov 18, 1997, in London; sister of Roger Wethered (golf champion); m. Lord Heathcote-Amory. ❖ Won English Ladies' championship 5 times (1920–24); was a 4-time winner of British Women's Amateur championships (1922, 1924–25, 1929); with various partners, including her brother Roger, won the Worplesdon mixed foursomes (1922–23, 1927–28, 1931–33, 1936); thought by some to be the greatest woman golfer of all time. ❖ See also *Women in World History.*

WETHERELL, Elizabeth (1819–1885). *See Warner, Susan Bogert.*

WETHERELL, Emma Abbott (1850–1891). *See Abbott, Emma.*

WETHERILL, Louisa Wade (1877–1945). American explorer and trader. Name variations: Asthon Sosi (Slim Woman). Born Louisa Wade, 1877, in Nevada; grew up in Mancos, CO; died 1945; sister of Nellie Wade Coston; sister-in-law of Richard Wetherill (explorer); m. John Wetherill (explorer and trader); children: 1 son; adopted 2 Navajo girls, including Betty Rodgers. ❖ With husband, established trading post at Ojo Alamo in Chaco Canyon (Utah), where she befriended Navajo and learned to speak their language; with husband and their partner Clyde Colville, ran a trading post near Oljato, UT (1906–10); earned trust of Navajo and became an expert on Navajo culture; started Hacienda De La Osa (She Bear) Guest Ranch near Tucson, Arizona (1921); worked with anthropologist Frances Gillmor on *Traders to the Navajos* (1934) which is considered a classic; became known as Asthon Sosi (Slim Woman) among Navajo. Inducted into Arizona Women Hall of Fame. ❖ See also Mary Apolline Comfort, *Rainbow to Yesterday: The John and Louisa Wetherill Story* (Vantage, 1979).

WETMORE, Elizabeth Bisland (1863–1929). *See Bisland, Elizabeth.*

WETMORE, Joan (1911–1989). Australian-born stage and tv actress. Born Aug 29, 1911, in Sydney, Australia; died Feb 13, 1989, in New York, NY; m. Palmer Dixon. ❖ Made Broadway debut as Bella Manchester in *Two Bouquets* (1938); other plays include *Two on an Island, Kind Lady, Counsellor-at-Law, For Keeps, The Two Mrs. Carrolls, The Small Hours, A Very Rich Woman* and *The Great Indoors;* also appeared on tv.

WETZKO, Gabriele (1954—). East German swimmer. Born Aug 28, 1954. ❖ Won a silver medal at Mexico City Olympics (1968) and a silver medal at Munich Olympics (1972), both in 4 x 100-meter freestyle relay.

WEXLER, Nancy (1945—). American psychologist and medical researcher. Born Nancy Sabin Wexler, July 19, 1945, in Washington, DC; dau. of Milton (psychoanalyst) and Leonore Wexler; sister of Alice Wexler (writer); University of Michigan, PhD, 1974. ❖ Developed interest in inherited brain disorders after mother was diagnosed with Huntington's disease (formerly Huntington's chorea); cofounded Hereditary Disease Foundation with father (1974), to find a cure for Huntington's disease, and later served as president (1983); elected head of Human Genome Project research committee (1989) to research legal, ethical, and social implications of testing for inherited diseases; convinced 6 US and British laboratories to work with Huntington Disease Foundation, which led to successful location of Huntington disease gene (1993); became professor (1985), then full professor (1992) of Columbia University's College of Physicians and Surgeons; elected fellow of American Association for the Advancement of Science (2002).

WEYENS, Claire Haesaert- (1924—). *See Haesaert, Clara.*

WEYGAND, Hannelore (1924—). West German equestrian. Born Oct 30, 1924, in Germany. ❖ At Melbourne Olympics, won a silver medal in team dressage (1956).

WEYMOUTH, Tina (1950—). American musician. Name variations: Martina Weymouth, Talking Heads, The Heads, The Tom Tom Club. Born Martina Michéle Weymouth, Nov 22, 1950, in Coronado, CA; m. Chris Frantz (drummer), June 18, 1977. ❖ With David Byrne and Chris Frantz, formed the band Talking Heads (1975), and began performing at Country BlueGrass Blues club (CBGB) in New York; playing bass and synthesizer with band, released debut album *77* (1977), which reached Top 100, and included song, "Psycho Killer"; had 1st hit with "Take Me to the River," from *More Songs about Buildings and Food* (1978); with band, released *Speaking in Tongues* (1983), which reached #15 in charts, and included their biggest hit single, "Burning Down the House"; released soundtrack from tour documentary, *Stop Making Sense* (1984), which was on pop charts for almost 2 years; released *Little Creatures* (1985), which went platinum; after departure of Byrne, released album, *No Talking Just Head* (1996), as The Heads; helped form Tom Tom Club, and released eponymous platinum album (1981), which had disco hit with "Genius of Love," followed by *Boom Boom Chi Boom Boom* (1989) and *The Good the Bad and the Funky* (2000); co-founded own music label, Tip Top Music (1999). Talking Heads were inducted into the Rock and Roll Hall of Fame. (2002).

WEYMOUTH, Viscountess (1735–1825). *See Cavendish-Bentinck, Elizabeth.*

WHALEN, Eleanor Holm (1913–2004). *See Holm, Eleanor.*

WHALEN, Sara (1976—). American soccer player. Born April 28, 1976, in Natick, MA; attended University of Connecticut, then Fordham. ❖ Defender and midfielder; won a team gold medal at World Cup (1999); won a silver medal at Sydney Olympics (2000); was a founding member of the Women's United Soccer Association (WUSA); signed with New York Power (2001).

WHARAWHARA-I-TE-RANGI (?–1880). *See Te Kakapi, Ripeka Wharawhara-i-te-rangi.*

WHAREITI, Hariata (1868/69?–1947). *See Rongonui, Kahupake.*

WHARETUTU (fl. 1827–1870). *See Newton, Wharetutu Anne.*

WHARTON, Anne (1659–1685). English poet. Born in Ditchley, Oxfordshire, England, in 1659; died at age 26 (of a venereal disease caught from husband) in Adderbury, Oxfordshire, England, Oct 29, 1685; 2nd dau. of Sir Henry Lee (wealthy landowner) and Anne (Danvers) Lee; m. Thomas Wharton, marquis of Wharton and Whig leader, in 1673; no children. ❖ Though none of her work was published during her lifetime, was one of the best-known poets of the Restoration, because her poems had such wide private circulation; a wealthy orphan from birth, grew up under care of grandmother, Anne Wilmot, mother of John Wilmot, earl of Rochester; at 14, was married to Thomas Wharton, prominent figure in the Whig faction of Parliament, and one of the greatest rakes in all of England; began to send copies of her poetry to Gilbert Burnet, who distributed them to friends, resulting in praise from other eminent poets of the day such as John Dryden and Aphra Behn. ❖ See also *Women in World History.*

WHARTON, Anne Hollingsworth (1845–1928). American writer. Born in Pennsylvania, 1845; died 1928. ❖ A founder and 1st historian of the National Society of Colonial Dames of America, wrote a number of books on Colonial and Revolutionary times; was appointed a judge at the Chicago World's Fair (1893); was an honorary member of the Pennsylvania Historical Society; works include *St. Bartholomew's Eve, The Wharton Family* (1880), *Colonial Days and Dames* (1895), *An English Honeymoon* (1908), *A Rose of Old Quebec* (1913) and *English Ancestral Homes of Noted Americans* (1915).

WHARTON, Edith (1862–1937). American writer. Born Edith Newbold Jones, Jan 24, 1862, in New York, NY; died Aug 11, 1937, in Saint-Brice-sous-Foret, France; dau. of George Frederic Jones (real-estate investor, died 1881) and Lucretia (Rhinelander) Jones; sister of Frederic (b. 1848, father of Beatrix Jones Farrand) and Henry Edward (b. 1850); m. Edward Robbins Wharton, in 1885 (div. 1913); no children. ❖ Acclaimed writer whose novels, novellas and short stories meticulously document high society of New York and Europe during late 19th and early 20th centuries and the way in which lives are shaped and dominated by social strictures and community pressure; until age 10, spent childhood in Paris and Rome; published collection of short stories, *The Greater Inclination* (1898); completed a novella, *The Touchstone,* another book of short stories, *Crucial Instances,* and a massive 2-vol. novel, *The Valley of Decision*

(1900–02); sold more than 140,000 copies of *The House of Mirth* (1905), a satiric portrait of fashionable New York; published novella *Ethan Frome* (1911) and the novel *The Reef* (1912); remained in Paris and did not return to the US to live; serialized in *Scribner's Magazine* her most powerful novel to exploit her knowledge of prewar American and European society, *The Custom of the Country* (1913), and its reception confirmed her major importance as an American writer; published *The Age of Innocence* (1920), for which she was awarded the Pulitzer Prize, the 1st woman to be so honored; explored intergenerational relationships in novels like *The Mother's Recompense* (1925) and *The Children* (1928); made her mark in every literary genre, publishing poems, travel sketches, literary and dramatic criticism, and translations, as well as 3 plays of her own; other writings include *Sanctuary* (1903), *Madame de Treymes* (1907), *The Glimpses of the Moon* (1922), *Hudson River Bracketed* (1929), *The Gods Arrive* (1932), *The Buccaneers* (1938) and *Old New York: False Dawn* (The 'Forties), *The Old Maid* (The 'Fifties), *The Spark* (The 'Sixties), *New Year's Day* (The 'Seventies), in 4 vols. (1924). ❖ See also autobiography, *A Backward Glance* (1934); R. W. B. Lewis, *Edith Wharton* (Harper & Row, 1975); Percy Lubbock, *Portrait of Edith Wharton* (1947); Cynthia Griffin Wolff, *A Feast Of Words: The Triumph of Edith Wharton* (Oxford U. Press, 1977); and *Women in World History*.

WHEATCROFT, Georgina (1965—). Canadian curler. Born Nov 30, 1965, in Nanaimo, British Columbia, Canada. ❖ Won World championships (1987, 2000) and a team bronze medal at Salt Lake City Olympics (2002).

WHEATLEY, Phillis (c. 1752–1784). African-American writer. Name variations: Phillis Peters. Born c. 1752 in Gambia, West Africa; died of complications associated with childbirth in Boston, Massachusetts, Dec 5, 1784; dau. of unknown parents; renamed Phillis by master John Wheatley after enslavement in 1761; m. John Peters, in April 1778; children: 3 (all died in infancy). ❖ Leading poet of the Revolutionary era and the 1st African-American of either gender to publish a book, was captured by slavers in West Africa (1761), at age 7 or 8, and transported to Boston; purchased by merchant tailor John Wheatley as a domestic servant; compared to most slaves, experienced a privileged childhood in the Wheatley home; was tutored and treated like a daughter by Susanna Wheatley, who was influenced by the ideas of the Great Awakening and active in humanitarian concerns; at around 14, published 1st poem in the *Newport Mercury,* "On Messrs. Hussey and Coffin" (Dec 21, 1767), concerning an incident that occurred in the life of people she knew; published 1st notable poem, "On the Death of the Rev. Mr. George Whitefield" (1770), which received wide publication throughout the American colonies and in England; wrote a poem about the Boston massacre, "On the Affray in King-Street, on the Evening of the 5th of March," and other verse sympathetic to the patriot cause; drew inspiration for her poetry from a number of sources, including Scripture, the neoclassical verse of Alexander Pope and other English artists, and the work of American poets, primarily Samuel Cooper; with the help of England's Selina Hastings, published her only collection, *Poems on Various Subjects, Religious and Moral,* in London (1773); traveled to England as a literary celebrity (1773); desolate when Susannah Wheatley died (Mar 3, 1774), was granted her freedom by John Wheatley (1774); in a letter, attacked the hypocrisy of so-called "patriots" who pleaded for liberty but would deny the same to slaves; wrote notable poem commemorating George Washington's appointment as commander of Continental Army (1775); after John Wheatley died (1778), was left without a home; married John Peters, a charismatic free black shopkeeper of some means (1778); continually sought to have a 2nd volume of poems published, which she dedicated to Benjamin Franklin, but could not get backing in the middle of the Revolution. ❖ See also Julian D. Mason, ed. *The Poems of Phillis Wheatley* (U. of North Carolina Press, 1966); William H. Robinson, *Phillis Wheatley and Her Writings* (Garland, 1984); John C. Shields, ed. *The Collected Works of Phillis Wheatley* (Oxford U. Press, 1988); and *Women in World History*.

WHEATON, Anne (1892–1977). American press secretary. Born in Utica, New York, Sept 11, 1892; died in Mar 1977; dau. of John Williams (politician and labor commissioner) and Elizabeth Ann (Owen) Williams; attended Simmons College in Boston, 1911–12; m. Warren Wheaton (journalist), Feb 19, 1926 (div. Nov 1946). ❖ The 1st woman to serve as a spokesperson for the president of the US, worked for *Knickerbocker Press* (1912–21); was one of the 1st female political correspondents at New York state capitol; moved to Washington, DC (1924); served as public relations consultant to National League of Women

Voters (1924–39); was director of women's publicity for Republican National Committee (1939–57); was a public relations representative for wives of Republican presidential candidates; as associate press secretary for the White House during Dwight D. Eisenhower administration, served as the 1st female presidential spokesperson (1957–61); was public relations representative for Nelson Rockefeller's presidential campaign (1964). ❖ See also *Women in World History*.

WHEELDON, Alice (fl. 1917). British pacifist and socialist. Lived in Derby, England. ❖ Socialist, suffragist and pacifist who joined the No-Conscription Fellowship during World War I; was tried and found guilty in 1917 for having joined with Alfred and Winnie Mason in a plot to assassinate British Prime Minister David Lloyd George, whom they held responsible for the carnage of war; was later found to be innocent. ❖ See also Sheila Rowbotham, *Friends of Alice Wheeldon* (Monthly Review Press, 1986); and *Women in World History*.

WHEELER, Anna Doyle (1785–c. 1850). Irish feminist writer. Born Anna Doyle in Clonbeg, Co. Tipperary, Ireland, in 1785; died c. 1850; dau. of Nicholas Doyle (dean in diocese of Fenner and Leighlen) and Anna (Dunbar) Doyle; m. Francis Massey Wheeler, 1800 (sep. 1812, died 1820); children: Henrietta Wheeler (d. 1825); Lady Rosina Bulwer-Lytton (1802–1882). ❖ Abused and neglected by husband, moved to Caen, France (1816), where she became part of a group of social reformers and thinkers; returned to Ireland when husband died (1820), and for next few years moved between Dublin and London; in London, became acquainted with members of the cooperative movement who were strongly influenced by the ideas of Robert Owen; also got to know Utilitarian leader Jeremy Bentham; met Irishman William Thompson who was associated both with Owen and Bentham; with Thompson, wrote *Appeal of One Half of the Human Race, Women, Against the Pretensions of the Other Half, Men, to Retain Them in Political, and Thence in Civil and Domestic Slavery* (1825), a sustained analysis of the social and economic causes of sexual inequality which is now recognized as a key text in feminist history; also popularized the beliefs of utopian socialist François Fourier. ❖ See also *Women in World History*.

WHEELER, Anna Pell (1883–1966). American mathematician. Born Anna Johnson in Hawarden, Iowa, May 5, 1883; died Mar 26, 1966; dau. of Amelia (Frieberg) Johnson and Andrew Gustav Johnson (Swedish immigrants); University of South Dakota, AB, 1903; University of Iowa, AM, 1904; Radcliffe College, AM, 1905; University of Chicago, PhD, 1910; m. Alexander Pell (mathematics instructor), July 19, 1907 (died 1921); m. Arthur Leslie Wheeler (classicist professor), July 6, 1925 (died 1932). ❖ Analytical mathematician, educator, and administrator, longtime chair of the mathematics department at Bryn Mawr College, whose achievements helped to break down barriers for women; awarded Alice Freeman Palmer fellowship at Wellesley College (1906), used the money to study at Göttingen University under mathematicians David Hilbert and Felix Klein (1906 and 1908) and was particularly intrigued by integral equations; taught at University of South Dakota (1907); enrolled at University of Chicago (Jan 4, 1909); after husband Alexander Pell suffered a stroke (1911), took over his classes at Armour Institute of Technology; accepted a position at Mount Holyoke College (1911), and was then promoted to associate professor and published a paper on linear equations of infinite unknowns (1914); accepted a position at Bryn Mawr College (1918); was starred in *American Men of Science* (1921); succeeded Charlotte A. Scott as chair of the mathematics department, Bryn Mawr (1924); appointed to the Board of Trustees of American Mathematical Society (1923); promoted to full professor (1925); was the 1st woman to deliver the Colloquium Lectures at American Mathematical Society (1927); was editor of *Annals of Mathematics* (1927); was instrumental in securing a position at Bryn Mawr for prominent German mathematician Emmy Noether (1933); successfully petitioned for an American analog to the German journal *Zentralblatt für Mathematik und ihre Grenzgebiete* (1939); retired from Bryn Mawr (1948). ❖ See also *Women in World History*.

WHEELER, Candace (1827–1923). American designer. Born in Delhi, New York, Mar 24, 1827; died in New York, NY, Aug 5, 1923; dau. of Abner Gilman Thurber (dairy farmer and fur dealer) and Lucy (Dunham) Thurber; attended Delaware Academy in Delhi, NY; m. Thomas M. Wheeler (bookkeeper), June 28, 1844 (died 1895); children: Candace (1845–1876); James Cooper (b. 1853); Dora Wheeler Keith (1856–1940); Dunham (b. 1861). ❖ The 1st woman to work professionally in the decorative arts in America, was encouraged by Eastman Johnson to take up painting (1854); studied painting in Dresden, Germany; founded the Society of Decorative Art of New York

City (1877); founded the Women's Exchange with Mrs. William Choate (1878); invited to join Louis Comfort Tiffany, Samuel Coleman, and Lockwood de Forest in Associated Artists to create textiles and embroideries; left Tiffany and founded own Associated Artists (1883); worked on advisory council of Woman's Art School of Cooper Union; directed exhibit of women's work for Chicago World's Columbian Exposition and was color director of Women's Building (1893); retired from Associated Artists (1900); published an important and influential book, *Principles of Home Decoration* (1903); her legacy of opening the professions of textile design and interior decoration for women and giving higher status to American designers has lasted. ❖ See also autobiography, *Yesterdays in a Busy Life* (1918); and *Women in World History*.

WHEELER, Ella (1850–1919). See *Wilcox, Ella Wheeler*.

WHEELER, Lucile (1935—). Canadian alpine skier. Name variations: Lucille Wheeler, Lucile Wheeler Vaughan. Born Jan 14, 1935, in St. Jovite, Quebec, Canada; dau. of Harry Wheeler (Olympic medalist, 1932); m. Kaye Vaughan (Ottawa Roughrider football player), 1960. ❖ Won a bronze medal for downhill at Cortina Olympics (1956), the 1st Canadian to win a skiing medal; won gold medals in the downhill and the giant slalom and a silver medal in the combined at the World championship in Bad Gastein, Austria (1958), the 1st Canadian to win a skiing World championship. Awarded the Lou Marsh Trophy (1958) and Order of Canada (1976); inducted into Canadian Sports Hall of Fame. ❖ See also *Women in World History*.

WHEELER, Rosina (1802–1882). See *Bulwer-Lytton, Rosina, Lady*.

WHEELER, Ruth (1877–1948). American nutritionist. Born Aug 5, 1877, in Plains, PA; died Sept 29, 1948, in Poughkeepsie, NY; dau. of Jared Ward Wheeler (wholesale provision-house manager) and Martha Jane (Evans) Wheeler; Yale University, PhD in physiological chemistry, 1913. ❖ Taught nutrition at University of Illinois (1912–18); served as chair of national committee on nutrition of Red Cross (1917–32); helped organize (1917) and was president of American Dietetic Association (1924–26); headed new department of nutrition at College of Medicine of State University of Iowa (1921–26); worked as professor of physiology and nutrition at Vassar College (1926–44); published *American Red Cross Textbook on Food and Nutrition* (1927).

WHEELOCK, Lucy (1857–1946). American educator and founder. Born in Cambridge, Vermont, Feb 1, 1857; died in Boston, Massachusetts, Oct 2, 1946; dau. of Edwin Wheelock (Congregational minister) and Laura (Pierce) Wheelock; graduated from the Kindergarten Training School, 1879. ❖ Directed inaugural one-year training course for kindergarten teachers at Chauncy Hall School in Boston; served as 2nd president of International Kindergarten Union (1895–99); established Wheelock Training School in Boston (1896); expanded curriculum to include teacher training for primary grades (1899); appointed to committee on education of the National Congress of Mothers (1899), and became chair (1908); served as chair of the Committee of Nineteen (1905–09); organized and led group of American kindergarten teachers to the home of Friedrich Froebel in Germany (1911); erected 1st permanent building for Wheelock School (1914); visited 8 Southern states to promote the kindergarten movement (1916); included preparation for nursery school teachers in Wheelock Training School program (1926); served on the Educational Committee of the League of Nations (1929); incorporated Wheelock School as nonprofit institution (1939), which became Wheelock College (1941). ❖ See also *Women in World History*.

WHELAN, Arleen (1916–1993). American actress. Born Sept 1, 1916, in Salt Lake City, UT; died April 7, 1993, in Orange County, CA; m. Alex D'Arcy (actor, div.); m. twice more. ❖ Made film debut as Jean MacDonald in *Kidnapped* (1938), followed by *Young Mr. Lincoln, Charley's Aunt* (as Kitty), *Stage Door Canteen, Suddenly It's Spring, Passage West, Never Wave at a WAC, The Sun Shines Bright, The Women of Pitcairn Island* and *Raiders of Old California*, among others.

WHELAN, Cyprienne Gabel (d. 1985). American actress, dancer, and school director. Died Oct 10, 1985, age 61, in Boston, MA; sister of Susan Whelan (actress). ❖ Broadway appearances include *Annie Get Your Gun, Finian's Rainbow,* and *On the Town*; served as director of the American Academy of Dramatic Arts.

WHIFFIN, Blanche (1845–1936). English-born actress. Name variations: Blanche Galton; Mrs. Thomas Whiffin. Born Blanche Galton, Mar 12, 1845, in London, England; died Nov 25, 1936, in Montvale, VA; dau. of Joseph West Galton (secretary in London general post office) and Mary Ann (Pyne) Galton (singer and piano teacher and sister of Louisa Pyne

and Susan Pyne of the three well-known musical Pyne sisters); sister of Susan Galton; m. Thomas Whiffin (musician and actor), July 11, 1868 (died 1897); children: Thomas Whiffin (actor turned farmer); Peggy Whiffin (actress). ❖ Came to US (1868) and was the original Buttercup in the American production of Gilbert and Sullivan's *H. M. S. Pinafore*; joined the NY Lyceum Theater Co. (1887), later played at the Empire, and became a great favorite with the public.

WHIGHAM, Margaret. See *Margaret (1912–1993)*.

WHIPPLE, Mary (1980—). American rower. Born May 10, 1980, in Sacramento, CA; attended University of Washington. ❖ Won a gold medal for coxed eights at World championships (2002); won a silver medal for coxed eights at Athens Olympics (2004); won 2 World Cups for coxed eights (2003 and 2004).

WHITAKER, Mabel (1884–1976). New Zealand teacher and local historian. Name variations: Mabel Wilson. Born May 11, 1884, at Belfast, near Christchurch, New Zealand; died July 10, 1976, in New Plymouth, New Zealand; dau. of Edward Robert Ward Wilson (farmer) and Margaret (Boyce) Wilson; m. Walter Morris Whitaker (grocer), 1917 (died 1952); children: 2 sons. ❖ Taught at Kapuni School (1908), at Marco School near Kohuratahi (1909–13), and Norfolk Women's Institute (1931–35), and worked as substitute teacher at schools in and around New Plymouth until retirement (1957); founding member of Norfolk Women's Institute (1931); worked with St John Ambulance Brigade during WWII; produced booklet, "A Survey of the District, 1841–1939"; wrote and illustrated collection of stories and lyrics, "Pioneer Tales from Taranaki's Rough North-east Back Blocks." ❖ See also *Dictionary of New Zealand Biography* (Vol. 3).

WHITBREAD, Fatima (1961—). English track-and-field athlete. Born Fatima Vedad, Mar 3, 1961, in Hackney, London, of Cypriot extraction; abandoned by parents, brought up in a children's home, then adopted at 12 by Margaret Whitbread, a javelin thrower. ❖ Immensely popular in Britain, won a bronze medal at Los Angeles Olympics (1984) and a silver medal at Seoul Olympics (1988), both in javelin throw; won the World championship (1987); was the 1st woman to throw a javelin over 76 meters (1985), then 77 meters (1986). Awarded MBE (1987).

WHITBY, abbess of.
See *Hilda of Whitby (614–680)*.
See *Elflaed (d. 714)*.

WHITCHER, Frances Miriam Berry (1811–1852). American satirist and cartoonist. Name variations: Miriam Berry; Miriam Whitcher; Widow Bedott; (pseudonym) Frank. Born in Whitesboro, New York, Nov 1, 1811; died in Whitesboro, Jan 4, 1852; dau. of Lewis Berry (tavern owner) and Elizabeth (Wells) Berry; m. Benjamin W. Whitcher (Episcopal cleric), Jan 6, 1847; children: Alice Miriam (b. 1849). ❖ Creator of the characters of the Widow Bedott and Aunt Magwire, showed early talent for drawing caricatures and writing satirical verse and parodies; published "Widow Spriggins" in weekly paper in Rome, NY; began publishing "The Widow Bedott" monologues in *Neal's Saturday Gazette* (1846), the 1st American woman to publish a series of satirical sketches; submitted "Aunt Magwire's Experience" to *Godey's Lady's Book* (1847–49); her work appeared regularly in popular periodicals and was itself extremely popular, appearing in a posthumous collection *The Widow Bedott Papers* (1856), which sold over 100,000 copies; her characters were dramatized by "Petroleum V. Nasby" (David Ross Locke) as *The Widow Bedott, or a Hunt for a Husband,* an acting vehicle for Neil Burgess (1879). ❖ See also *Women in World History*.

WHITE, A. Lois (1903–1984). See *White, Anna Lois*.

WHITE, Alice (1904–1983). American actress and dancer. Born Alva White, Aug 28, 1904, in Paterson, NJ; raised in Los Angeles; died Feb 19, 1983, in Los Angeles, CA; trained with Ernest Belcher; m. William Hinshaw; m. Sy Bartlett (div.); m. Jack Roberts, 1941 (div. 1949). ❖ A leading lady of silent and early sound films; known as "The Pout," was featured in nearly 40 movies, including *The Sea Tiger, Man Crazy, The Girl from Woolworths, Broadway Babies, A Show Girl in Hollywood, American Beauty, Hot Stuff, Sweethearts on Parade, Murder at Midnight, Gift of Gab* and *Flamingo Road*; was the 1st to portray the Anita Loos character Lorelei Lee in *Gentlemen Prefer Blondes* (1928).

WHITE, Alma Bridwell (1862–1946). American religious leader and founder. Born Mollie Alma Bridwell on June 16, 1862, near Vanceburg, Lewis Co., Kentucky; died June 26, 1946, in Zarephath, New Jersey; dau. of William Moncure Bridwell (tanner and farmer) and

Mary Ann (Harrison) Bridwell; attended Vanceburg Seminary and Millersburg Female College, both in Kentucky; m. Kent White (Methodist minister), Dec 21, 1887 (sep. 1909, died 1940); children: Arthur Kent White (b. 1889, bishop in the Pillar of Fire), Ray Bridwell White (b. 1892). ❖ Founder of the Pillar of Fire Church and the 1st woman ordained a bishop in US, began preaching, leading meetings, and organizing prayer sessions; established an independent mission of the holiness movement within the Methodist Church (July 7, 1896); believing that Methodism had departed from true Christianity and was confined by its refusal to ordain women or affirm their right to preach, felt the need to sever ties with the Methodist Church; founded Pentecostal Union Church (Dec 29, 1901), a religious, educational, and benevolent organization soon known as the Pillar of Fire, and was ordained into it (Mar 16); moved church headquarters to Zarephath, New Jersey (1908); established the Zarephath Bible Training School (later known as Zarephath Bible Institute) and Zarephath Academy, later named the Alma Preparatory School; purchased Westminster College from the Presbyterian Church (1920) to found Alma White College (1921); while serving as an ordained minister and spiritual and administrative leader of Pillar of Fire, was consecrated a bishop (Sept 1, 1918). ❖ See also Alma White, The Story of My Life and the Pillar of Fire (5 vols., Pillar of Fire Church, 1935–43) and Looking back from Beulah (Garland, 1987); Susie Cunningham Stanley, Feminist Pillar of Fire: The Life of Alma White (Pilgrim, 1993); and Women in World History.

WHITE, Amy (1968—). American swimmer. Born Oct 20, 1968. ❖ At Los Angeles Olympics, won a silver medal in 200-meter backstroke (1984).

WHITE, Anna (1831–1910). American Shaker eldress and reformer. Born in Brooklyn, New York, Jan 21, 1831; died in New Lebanon, New York, Dec 16, 1910; dau. of Robert White (hardware merchant) and Hannah (Gibbs) White; in early teens, sent to Mansion Square Seminary in Poughkeepsie, New York. ❖ Raised as a Quaker, joined the Shaker community in New Lebanon, NY, as a member of the North Family (1849); appointed associate eldress (1865); became 1st eldress of the North Family (1887); worked for peace and women's rights outside the community; in over 60 years of Shaker life, created valuable documents on Shaker songs and history, compiled 2 books of Shaker music, including some of her own compositions, and collaborated with Eldress Leila S. Taylor on the book Shakerism: Its Meaning and Message (1904). ❖ See also Women in World History.

WHITE, Anna Lois (1903–1984). New Zealand painter and art teacher. Name variations: A. Lois White. Born Nov 2, 1903, in Auckland, New Zealand; died Sept 13, 1984, in Auckland; dau. of Arthur Herbert White (architect) and Annie (Phillipps) White. ❖ Taught at Elam School of Art (1928–63); was considered significant in mainstream Auckland art world (1930s–40s); exhibited with New Group, which she helped form in 1948; work housed by Auckland Art Gallery and Museum of New Zealand Te Papa Tongarewa ❖ See also Dictionary of New Zealand Biography (Vol. 4).

WHITE, Antonia (1899–1980). British novelist and translator. Name variations: Eirene Adeline Botting. Born Eirene Adeline Botting in London, England, Mar 31, 1899; died in London, April 10, 1980; dau. of Cecil George Botting (senior classics master at St. Paul's School in London) and Christine Julia (White) Botting; married, 1921 (annulled 1924); married, 1924 (annulled 1929); m. Tom (H. T.) Hopkinson (writer), 1930 (div. 1938); children: Susan Chitty and Lyndall. ❖ At 14, expelled from convent school; left St. Paul's Girls' School against father's wishes; attended Royal Academy of Dramatic Art for 1 year (1919–20), then acted in provincial repertory; had mental breakdown followed by 9 months in mental hospital (1921); saw 1st marriage annulled on grounds of non-consummation (1924); became fashion editor and drama critic; published her only commercial success, the highly autobiographical, Frost in May (1933), recounting her experiences at the convent school and including the details of her expulsion; tried Freudian analysis after another mental breakdown (1934), and credited it with ultimately curing her after 4 years of therapy; during WWII, wrote for BBC and worked in Foreign Office; became prolific translator (1949 on); published 1st vol. of the "Clara Batchelor" trilogy, The Lost Traveller (1950), followed by The Sugar House (1952) and Beyond the Glass (1954); received Clairouin Prize for translation (1950); became fellow of Royal Society of Literature (1957); published an account of her return to the Catholic Church as The Hound and the Falcon (1965). ❖ See also Women in World History.

WHITE, Barbara Fay (1940—). See Boddie, Barbara White.

WHITE, Carlette (1969—). See Guidry, Carlette.

WHITE, Carol (1942–1991). English tv and screen actress. Born April 1, 1942, in London, England; died Sept 16, 1991, in Miami, FL. ❖ Leading lady of British films, made debut in Circus Friends (1956); other films include Carry on Teacher, Linda (title role), A Matter of Who, Gaolbreak, Ladies Who Do, The Playground, Prehistoric Women, I'll Never Forget What's'isname, The Fixer, Poor Cow, Daddy's Gone A-Hunting, The Man Who Had Power Over Women, Up the Sandbox, The Squeeze, Nutcracker, Talking Walls and Eating.

WHITE, Chrissie (1894–1989). English silent-screen actress. Born May 23, 1894, in London, England; died Aug 18, 1989, in Hollywood, CA; m. Henry Edwards (actor, director). ❖ Began career as a child star in silents, then grew into leading lady roles; made film debut in The Cabman's Good Fairy (1909), then appeared as Sally in the "Tilly" series (1910–15); made over 90 films, including The Vicar of Wakefield, Drake's Love Story, Sweet Lavender, Molly Bawn, The Failure, Broken Threads, Anna, Barnaby Rudge (as Dolly Varden), Lily of the Alley and Call of the Sea.

WHITE, Donna (1954—). American golfer. Born April 7, 1954, in Kinston, NC. ❖ Won US Amateur (1976); joined LPGA tour (1977); won Florida Lady Citrus and Coca-Cola Classic (1980); won Sarasota (1983); golf manager for Special Olympics. Inducted into University of Florida and National Golf Coaches halls of fame.

WHITE, Eartha M. (1876–1974). African-American entrepreneur. Name variations: Eartha White; Eartha Mary Magdalene White; Eartha M. M. White. Born in Jacksonville, Florida, Nov 8, 1876; died in Jacksonville, Jan 18, 1974; dau. of Molly (or Mollie) Chapman (former slave) and a white father; adopted as an infant by Lafayette White and Clara (English) White; never married; no children. ❖ Major philanthropist in her hometown of Jacksonville, Florida, opened a department store aimed at African-American consumers (1904), the 1st of numerous entrepreneurial successes; over next 25 years, bought a variety of small businesses in succession, including an employment agency, a dry-goods store, a steam laundry, a general store, a janitorial service, and a real-estate business; funded a rest home for tuberculosis patients, the Harriet Beecher Stowe Community Center, a child placement center, a home for unmarried pregnant women, and the Clara White Mission, which is now a historic landmark (the only non-profit soup kitchen in Jacksonville), as well as a museum of African-American history; also established the Eartha M. White Nursing Home. ❖ See also Women in World History.

WHITE, Edna Noble (1879–1954). American educator and home economist. Born Edna Noble White, June 3, 1879, in Fairmount, IL; died May 4, 1954, in Highland Park, Michigan; dau. of Alexander L. White (town government official and business manager) and Angeline (Noble) White; University of Illinois, AB, 1906. ❖ Educator and home economist who believed in interdisciplinary approach to child development study; was on faculty of home economics department at Ohio State University, becoming full professor, head of department, and supervisor of home economics extension service (1908–late 1920s); with Ruth A. Wardall, wrote A Study of Foods (1914); served as president of American Home Economics Association (1918–20); founed and was director of child development research center, Merrill-Palmer Institute, in Detroit, MI (1920–47), which earned worldwide fame, bringing together pediatricians, nutritionists, psychologists, educators, home economists, and social workers for work on child development; served as chair of National Council on Parent Education (1925–37).

WHITE, Eliza Orne (1856–1947). American novelist and children's author. Name variations: (pseudonym) Alex. Born Aug 2, 1856, in Keene, New Hampshire; died Jan 23, 1947, in Brookline, Massachusetts; dau. of William Orne White (Unitarian minister) and Margaret Eliot (Harding) White; granddau. of portrait artist Chester Harding; never married; no children. ❖ By 18, had begun writing short stories for publications including The Christian Register and The Atlantic Monthly, using the pseudonym "Alex"; published a novel for adults, Miss Brooks (1890); wrote over 40 books, the most popular of which were aimed at young girls; writings include As She Would Have It (1873), When Molly was Six (1894), John Forsyth's Aunts (1901), Leslie Chilton (1903), The Enchanted Mountain (1911), Peggy in Her Blue Frock (1921), Diana's Rosebush (1927), The Green Door (1930), Where Is Adelaide (1933), Anne Frances (1935), Helen's Gift House (1938), I: The

Autobiography of a Cat (1941), *Training of Sylvia* (1942) and *When Esther Was a Little Girl* (1944). ❖ See also *Women in World History.*

WHITE, Ellen Gould (1827–1915). American religious founder. Name variations: Ellen Gould Harmon. Born Ellen Gould Harmon, Nov 26, 1827, in Gorham, Maine; died July 16, 1915, in northern California; dau. of Robert Harmon (hat maker) and Eunice Harmon; m. James White (Adventist), Aug 30, 1846 (died 1881); children: Henry (1847–1863); James Edson (1849–1928); William (1854–1937); Herbert (Sept 1860–Dec 1860). ❖ Religious leader who co-founded the Seventh-Day Adventist Church which she led for over 50 years, directing its expansion throughout North America, Europe, and Australia; grew up in the Methodist faith; as a teenager, became involved in Adventist movement (also known as the Millerites), which claimed that the Second Coming of Jesus Christ, was now at hand; at 17, started to have religious visions that she had been selected as the prophet through whom God would prepare the world for Christ's Second Coming; began public career as religious leader, traveling throughout Maine and New Hampshire, sharing her visions with others; religious visions increased in frequency and expanded in scope (1850s); joined with husband to found the Seventh-Day Adventist Church (1863) and began to have visions regarding health reform; traveled more extensively, establishing Adventist communities in Midwest and Western states while membership in the church increased 5-fold (1863–80), largely due to her effectiveness as an evangelist and her skill at mediating conflicts between church leaders; made vegetarianism and hydropathy defining characteristics of Seventh-Day Adventism; established the Western Health Reform Institute in Battle Creek, Michigan, which operated under the direction of John Harvey Kellogg (1866); established churches in Europe (1885–87); established churches and a Bible school in Australia (1891–1900); established the College of Medical Evangelists, later Loma Linda University and Medical Center, in southern California, the crown jewel in a rich network of schools and hospitals founded by White (1909); wrote 26 books and over 5,000 periodical articles, including *Spiritual Gifts* (1858), *Spirit of Prophecy* (1870), *Patriarchs and Prophets* (1890) and *Ministry of Healing* (1905). By 1990, her church could claim the largest Protestant, nonprofit health-care system in the country. ❖ See also autobiography, *Life Sketches of Ellen G. White* (1915); Ronald L. Numbers, *Prophetess of Health: Ellen G. White and the Origins of Seventh-day Adventist Health Reform* (U. of Tennessee Press, 1992); and *Women in World History.*

WHITE, Emily Louisa Merielina (1839–1936). New Zealand gardener and writer. Name variations: Emily Louisa Merielina Rogers, Mrs. Marshall-White. Born May 1, 1839, at Beyton, Suffolk, England; died Sept 18, 1936, at Wanganui, New Zealand; dau. of Michael Edward Rogers (cleric) and Emily Eliza (Blake) Rogers; m. John Hannath Marshall, 1863 (died 1879); m. Blanco White, 1882 (died 1888); children: (1st m.) 1 daughter, 4 sons. ❖ Immigrated to New Zealand (1876); continuing family interest in botany and horticulture (ancestors included Thomas and William Gage), established 5 unique gardens in England and New Zealand, which became showplaces at turn of 20th century; introduced several species into New Zealand; published *My New Zealand Garden, by A Suffolk Lady* (1902); was active in New Zealand Women's Christian Temperance Union (WCTU), promoting women's rights and social-welfare work; helped found Wanganui's 1st orphanage on land she donated. ❖ See also *Dictionary of New Zealand Biography* (Vol. 3).

WHITE, Frances (1896–1969). American singer and dancer. Born Jan 1, 1896, in Seattle, WA; died Feb 24, 1969, in Baldwin Hills, Los Angeles, CA; m. Frank Fay (actor); m. Clinton Donnelly. ❖ Vaudeville headliner, began career as a singer (1910); partnered dancer William Rock in vaudeville and on Broadway; debuted at the Palace (1916); starred in *Ziegfeld Follies* (1914–27); danced in *Hitchy-Koo of 1917* and *1918* and in English revues; had a cameo in film *The Great Ziegfeld* (1936).

WHITE, Hannah (1830–1903). *See Martin, Hannah.*

WHITE, Helen C. (1896–1967). American educator and writer. Born Helen Constance White, Nov 26, 1896, in New Haven, Connecticut; died June 7, 1967, in Norwood, Massachusetts; dau. of John White and Mary (King) White; Radcliffe College, AB, AM, 1916; University of Wisconsin, PhD, 1924; never married; no children. ❖ Hired as an English instructor at University of Wisconsin (1919), remained there for rest of working life, becoming a full professor in 1936—the 1st woman to achieve such status at the university—and ultimately chair of the English department; earned PhD with dissertation "The Mysticism of William Blake" (1924) which she published as a book (1927); in later

scholarly studies, focused on medieval and Renaissance literature in such works as *The Metaphysical Poets: A Study in Religious Experience* (1936), *Social Criticism in Popular Religious Literature of the Sixteenth Century* (1944) and *Prayer and Poetry* (1960); also published a number of novels, including *A Watch in the Night* (1933), *Not Built with Hands* (1935), *To the End of the World* (1939) and *Bird of Fire: A Tale of St. Francis of Assisi* (1958); served as president of American Association of University Women (1941–47). Received Laetare Medal from the University of Notre Dame (1942). ❖ See also *Women in World History.*

WHITE, Helen Magill (1853–1944). American educator. Name variations: Helen Magill. Born Nov 28, 1853, in Providence, Rhode Island; died Oct 28, 1944, in Kittery Point, Maine; dau. of Edward Hicks Magill (classicist and president of Swarthmore) and Sarah (Beans) Magill (both Quakers); graduated in the 1st class at Swarthmore College, 1873; Boston University, PhD in Greek, 1877; graduate studies at Newnham College, Cambridge, 1877–81; m. Andrew D. White (diplomat and former president of Cornell University), Sept 10, 1890 (died 1918); children: Karin Andreevna. ❖ The 1st American woman to receive a doctorate (1877), was principal of a private school in Johnstown, Pennsylvania; organized the Howard Collegiate Institute (1883–87), a newly established women's school in West Bridgewater, Massachusetts, then briefly held teaching positions at Evelyn College, a women's annex to Princeton University; lived with husband in Russia (1892–94) and Germany (1897–1903), where he served as ambassador; after witnessing the actions of militant suffragists in England (1913), became a public and vocal opponent of women's suffrage, which she believed would be detrimental to women's well being. ❖ See also *Women in World History.*

WHITE, Isabella (1894–1972). English diver. Born Sept 1894 in UK; died July 1972. ❖ At Stockholm Olympics, won a bronze medal in platform (1912).

WHITE, Karyn (1965—). African-American singer. Born Karyn Lay Vonne White, Oct 14, 1965, in Los Angeles, CA; dau. of Clarence and Vivian White; m. Terry Lewis (music producer); children: Ashley. ❖ Sang in Los Angeles group, Legacy, and was backup vocalist for R&B singer, O'Bryan; did session work for numerous performers, including Julio Iglesias, Patti LaBelle, and Gladys Knight; was lead singer on Jeff Lorber's "Facts of Love" (1986); released multi-platinum debut album, *Karyn White* (1988), which included hits, "The Way You Love Me," "Superwoman," and "Secret Rendezvous"; co-wrote 10 of 12 songs on *Ritual of Love* (1991), which included hits, "The Way I Feel About You" and "Romantic"; released *Make Him Do Right* (1994), which went to #22 on R&B charts.

WHITE, Katharine S. (1892–1977). American magazine editor. Name variations: Katharine S. Angell; Kay White. Born Katharine Sergeant in Winchester, Massachusetts, Sept 17, 1892; died in North Brooklin, Maine, July 20, 1977; dau. of Charles Spencer Sergeant (vice president of West End Railway Co., Boston) and Elizabeth Blake (Shepley) Sergeant; graduate of Bryn Mawr, 1914; m. Ernest Angell (lawyer), May 22, 1915 (div. 1929, died 1973); m. E(lwyn) B(rooks) White (the writer), Nov 13, 1929; children: (1st m.) Nancy Angell and Roger Angell; (2nd m.) Joel McCoun White. ❖ Longtime editor at *The New Yorker*, whose skill, eye for talent, and uncompromising taste helped to elevate the magazine to the near-mythic status it enjoyed in mid-20th century; joined the staff of *New Yorker* as a part-time manuscript reader (Aug 1925); 2 weeks later, was working full-time, and in the fall became an editor; as editor for over 36 years, sought out and encouraged promising young writers such as John Updike, J. D. Salinger, Jean Stafford, John O'Hara, and Vladimir Nabokov; retired (1961); wrote *Onward and Upward in the Garden* (1979). ❖ See also Linda H. Davis, *Onward and Upward: A Biography of Katharine S. White* (Harper & Row, 1987); and *Women in World History.*

WHITE, Margaret (c. 1888–1977). English meteorologist. Name variations: Margaret White Fishenden. Born Margaret White, c. 1888, in UK; died 1977; University of Manchester, MS, 1910 and DSc, 1919. ❖ Was a lecturer at Howard Estate Observatory (1910–11) and University of Manchester (1911–16); headed research team of Manchester Corporation's Air Pollution Advisory Board (1916–22); presented papers on meteorology at British Association for the Advancement of Science's annual meetings (1907, 1911).

WHITE, Margaret Bourke (1904–1971). *See Bourke-White, Margaret.*

WHITE, Marilyn Elaine (1944—). African-American runner. Name variations: Marilyn Milligan. Born Marilyn Elaine White, Oct 17,

1944, in Los Angeles, CA; Pepperdine University, BS, 1967, and University of California, MA, 1974; m. Leon Leroy Milligan, Jan 5, 1974. ❖ Won a gold medal for the 400-meter relay and a bronze medal for the 100 meters at Pan American Games; won a silver medal for the 4 x 100-meter relay at Tokyo Olympics (1964). ❖ See also *Women in World History.*

WHITE, Maude Valerie (1855–1937). English composer, translator, and songwriter. Name variations: Maude Valérie White. Born in Dieppe, France, June 23, 1855; died in London, England, Nov 2, 1937; studied with G. A. Macfarren at Royal Academy of Music in London, 1876–79; also studied with W. S. Rockstro and Oliver May. ❖ Best known for composing some 200 songs, most of them in the style of the Victorian drawing-room ballad; was the 1st woman to win the prestigious Mendelssohn Scholarship (1879); forced to give up scholarship because of ill health (1881), began traveling through Europe and South America in search of a curative climate; became an able translator, rendering several books into English, as well as poems by Hugo, Heine and others which she used as texts for her songs; set Byron's "So we'll go no more a roving," to music, which some critics consider her best work; also produced several French songs and wrote instrumental works and music for the ballet *The Enchanted Heart* (1913). ❖ See also autobiographies *Friends and Memories* (1914) and *My Indian Summer* (1932); and *Women in World History.*

WHITE, Morgan (1983—). American gymnast. Born June 27, 1983, in West Bend, WI. ❖ Won Jr. nationals (1998); at Pan American Games, won a gold medal for all-around (1999).

WHITE, Oona (1922–2005). Canadian dancer and choreographer. Born Mar 24, 1922, in Inverness, Nova Scotia, Canada; died April 8, 2005, in West Hollywood, CA; m. Larry Douglas (Broadway musical star); children: Stuart and Jennie Douglas. ❖ Trained and danced with San Francisco Ballet for 7 years; served as assistant for Michael Kidd, and danced in *Finian's Rainbow* (1947), *Guys and Dolls* (1950) and *Silk Stockings*; choreographed for such Broadway shows as *The Music Man* (1957), *Whoop-Up* (1958), *Take Me Along* (1959), *Irma La Douce* (1961), *Half a Sixpence* (1965), *Mame* (1966), *Illya Darling* (1967) and *I Love My Wife* (1977); choreographed film version of *The Music Man* (1962) and *Mame,* as well as stage and film versions of *Bye Bye Birdie* and *1776.* Nominated for 8 Tony Awards; won a special Oscar for choreography for film version of *Oliver!* (1969).

WHITE, Pearl (1889–1938). American actress. Born Pearl Fay White, Mar 4, 1889, in Green Ridge, Missouri; died Aug 4, 1938, in Paris, France; dau. of Lizzie G. (House) White and Edward Gilman White; m. Victor C. Sutherland (actor), 1907 (div. 1914); m. Wallace McCutcheon (actor), c. 1919 (div. 1921); no children. ❖ Best known for her starring role in the famous silent-film serial *The Perils of Pauline,* was launched in a hot air balloon, hoisted to 20th story of New York skyscraper, left to sink off a dock, and tied to railroad tracks in path of oncoming train; was one of the best-loved actresses of the 1910s, as her fans cheered her miraculous escapes; performed many of her own stunts; films include *The Girl from Arizona* (1910), *The Chorus Girl* (1912), *Pearl as a Detective* (1913), *Heroic Harold* (1913), *The Exploits of Elaine* (serial, 1915), *The Iron Claw* (serial, 1916), *The Fatal Ring* (serial, 1917), *The Lightning Raider* (serial, 1918), *The House of Hate* (serial, 1918), *Black Secret* (serial, 1919–20), *Broadway Peacock* (1922), *Plunder* (serial, 1923), and *Terreur* (Fr. serial, released in US as *The Perils of Paris,* 1924). ❖ See also *The Perils of Pauline* (film), starring Betty Hutton (1947) and *The Perils of Pauline* (film), starring Pamela Austin (1967); and *Women in World History.*

WHITE, Ruth (1914–1969). American stage, tv, and screen actress. Name variations: Ruth Godfrey. Born April 24, 1914, in Perth Amboy, NJ; died Dec 3, 1969, in Perth Amboy. ❖ Made Broadway debut in *The Ivy Green* (1949); other NY appearances include *The Ponder Heart, The Happiest Millionaire, Rashomon, Malcolm, Happy Days, Lord Pengo, Absence of a Cello* and *Little Murders*; films include *Up the Down Staircase, The Nun's Story, To Kill a Mockingbird, No Way to Treat a Lady* and *Midnight Cowboy.* Nominated for Tony award for performance in *The Birthday Party* (1968); won Emmy for the Hallmark production of "Little Moon of Alban."

WHITE, Sandra (1951—). Scottish politician. Born Aug 17, 1951, in Govan, Glasgow, Scotland. ❖ As an SNP candidate, elected to the Scottish Parliament for Glasgow (1999, 2003); served as SNP Parliamentary group whip.

WHITE, Sue Shelton (1887–1943). American lawyer, suffragist, and government official. Born May 25, 1887, in Henderson, Tennessee; died May 6, 1943, in Alexandria, Virginia; dau. of James Shelton White (lawyer and Methodist minister) and Mary Calista (Swain) White; educated at Georgia Robertson Christian College and West Tennessee Business College; Washington College of Law, LLB, 1923. ❖ One of the architects of Democratic policies in the Roosevelt era, served as a court reporter (1907–18) and private secretary to several members of the Tennessee supreme court; joined the radical National Woman's Party (NWP, 1917), the most militant branch of the suffrage movement; also became chair of Tennessee Woman's Party; was responsible for drafting Tennessee's 1st married women's property act, a mother's pension act, and an old-age pension provision, all of which eventually became law; began working in the nation's capital (1920), 1st as a clerk and later as secretary to Tennessee Senator Kenneth D. McKellar; received law degree and helped to draft the Equal Rights Amendment (1923); had a private practice in Jackson (1926–30); became executive assistant to the vice-chair of the Democratic National Committee in charge of women's issues (1930); became assistant chair of the Consumers' Advisory Board of National Recovery Administration (NRA, 1934), and also served on the National Emergency Council, as assistant director of that group's Consumers' Division; became attorney for the Social Security Board (later the Federal Security Agency, 1936), helping to lay the foundations of Social Security as it exists today. ❖ See also *Women in World History.*

WHITE, Susan Shields (1952—). *See Shields, Susan.*

WHITE, Willye B. (1939—). African-American track-and-field athlete. Born Willie White, Jan 1, 1939, in Money, MS. ❖ Tennessee Tigerbelle and AAU indoor champion (1962); participated in 5 Olympics (1956, 1960, 1964, 1968, and 1972); won an Olympic silver medal at Melbourne (1956), the 1st American woman to win an Olympic medal in the long jump; won an Olympic silver medal in 4 x 100-meter relay at Tokyo (1964); traveled to 150 countries as a member of 35 international teams; served on the President's Commission on Olympic Sports; was the 1st American woman to jump over 21' in the broad jump; established the Willye White Foundation to honor women high-school athletes. Named to the Black Sports Hall of Fame, was the 1st to receive the Pierre de Coubertin International Fair Play Trophy from France, and was inducted into the Women's Sports Foundation International Hall of Fame. ❖ See also *Women in World History.*

WHITEFIELD, Karen (1970—). Scottish politician. Born 1970 in Bellshill, Scotland; attended Glasgow Caledonian University. ❖ Was personal assistant to Rachel Squire (MP, 1992–99); as a Labour candidate, elected to the Scottish Parliament for Airdrie and Shotts (1999, 2003).

WHITEHEAD, Charlotte (1843–1916). *See Ross, Charlotte Whitehead.*

WHITEHEAD, Nancy Dickerson (1927–1997). *See Dickerson, Nancy.*

WHITEHOUSE, Davina (1912–2002). English-born New Zealand actress. Born Dec 16, 1912, in London, England; died Dec 25, 2002, in Auckland, NZ. ❖ Starred on London's West End (1930s); moved to New Zealand (1952); films include *Night Nurse, Sleeping Dogs* and *Braindead*; appeared frequently on New Zealand tv.

WHITE LADY OF CHENONCEAU. *See Louise of Lorraine (1554–1601).*

WHITELAW, Billie (1932—). English actress. Born June 6, 1932, in Coventry, England; dau. of Percival (electrician) and Frances Whitelaw; m. Peter Vaughan (actor), 1952 (div. 1964); m. Robert Muller (writer), c. 1983 (died 1998); children: (with Muller) Matthew (b. 1967). ❖ The leading exponent of playwright Samuel Beckett, came to prominence at a young age as Bunkle on the 5-year BBC series, "St. Jonathan's in the Country"; made London stage debut in *Hotel Paradise* (1959); as a result of performance in musical revue *England, Our England* (1961), received invitation to join National Theater, where she 1st encountered Beckett, appearing in his one-act *Play* (1964); with the National Theater, appeared as Maggie in *Hobson's Choice* and Desdemona to Olivier's Othello; also appeared with Royal Shakespeare Company; won British Film Academy Award for performance in *Charlie Bubbles* (1968); starred in Beckett's *Not I* at Royal Court (1972); as Beckett's favorite actress, went on to perform in *Footfalls* (1976), *Happy Days* (1979), and *Rockaby* (1982 and 1984), as well as in several tv productions written by the playwright; appeared as the young American revolutionary in Mercer's *After Haggerty* (1970) and turned in a highly acclaimed performance as the librarian in Frayn's comedy *Alphabetical Order* (1975); also appeared in *Tales of Hollywood* (1984) and played Martha in Albee's *Who's Afraid of*

Virginia Woolf? (1987); films include *Make Mine Mink* (1960), *The Adding Machine* (1969), *Start the Revolution Without Me* (1970), *Frenzy* (1972), *Night Watch* (1973), *The Omen* (1976), *The Water Babies* (1979), *The Secret Garden* (1987), *Maurice* (1987), *The Dressmaker* (1988), *The Krays* (1990) and *Quills* (2000). ❖ See also autobiography *Billie Whitelaw . . . Who He?* (St. Martin, 1995); and *Women in World History.*

WHITEMAN, Mrs. Paul. *See Hoff, Vanda.*

WHITESIDE, Jane (1855–1875). New Zealand tightrope dancer, gymnast, and magician. Name variations: Madame Blanche, Blanche Fane, Blanche Anderson, Jennie Anderson, Jennie Verten. Born Jane Whiteside, Feb 5, 1855, in Co. Down, Ireland; died Jan 17, 1875, in Oamaru, New Zealand; dau. of John (weaver) and Jane (Totten) Whiteside; m. Frank Verten (singer and dancer), c. 1874. ❖ Immigrated with family to New Zealand (1856); made debut stage appearance (1872); performed as gymnast, tightrope dancer, and magician throughout New Zealand as Madame Blanche, Blanche Fane, Blanche Anderson, and Jennie Anderson. ❖ See also *Dictionary of New Zealand Biography* (Vol. 2).

WHITESTONE, Heather (c. 1973—). Miss America. Name variations: Heather Whitestone McCallum. Born c. 1973; attended Jacksonville State University; m. John McCallum; children: 2. ❖ Deaf since infancy, named Miss America (1995), representing Alabama; motivational speaker and activist for Republican causes. ❖ See also autobiographies, *Listening with My Heart* and *Believing the Promise.*

WHITFIELD, Beverly (1954–1996). Australian swimmer. Name variations: Beverly Joy Whitfield. Born June 15, 1954, in Shellharbour, NSW, Australia; died 1996. ❖ Won two individual gold medals for the 100- or 200-meter breaststroke in the British Commonwealth Games (1970) and a team gold for the 800-meter medley relay; won a gold medal in the 200-meter breaststroke and a bronze in the 100-meter breaststroke at the Olympic Games in Munich (1972); over the years, won 8 individual Australian championships, all in the 100- or 200-meter breaststroke, in addition to 2 Australian relay championships.

WHITFORD, Annabelle (1878–1961). *See Annabelle.*

WHITING, Lilian (1847–1942). American journalist and writer. Born Emily Lillian Whiting, Oct 3, 1847, in Olcott, New York; died April 30, 1942, in Boston, Massachusetts; dau. of Lorenzo Dow Whiting (Republican member of Illinois state legislature) and Lucretia Calistia (Clement) Whiting; longtime companion of Kate Field (author and actress, 1838–1896). ❖ Spent a year at *Cincinnati Commercial* (1879); moved to Boston and worked as an art critic, then literary editor for a local newspaper, the *Traveler;* on assignment for the *Traveler,* met Kate Field, with whom she formed an attachment that lasted the rest of Field's life (c. 1880); served as literary editor of the *Traveler* (1885–90), then editor of the weekly *Boston Budget* (1890–93); began working as a freelance writer, contributing to many leading magazines and newspapers, including *Harper's* and *New York Graphic;* also wrote and published essays and poetry, including her most popular books, the 3-vol. *The World Beautiful* (1894–96), a detailing of her optimistic spiritual philosophy which ran to 14 editions, and the poetry collection, *From Dreamland Sent* (1895); in tribute to Field, published *After Her Death* (1897) and *Kate Field* (1899); also wrote *A Study of Elizabeth Barrett Browning* (1899), *The Spiritual Significance* (1900), *Boston Days* (1902) and the semi-autobiographical *The Golden Road* (1918). ❖ See also *Women in World History.*

WHITING, Margaret (1924—). American pop singer. Born July 22, 1924, in Detroit, Michigan; dau. of Richard Whiting (songwriter); sister of Barbara Whiting (singer and actress, d. 2004); m. Hubbell Robinson (executive at CBS, div. a year later); m. Lou Busch (pianist and conductor), 1950 (div. 1953); m. John Richard Moore (cinematographer, div.); children: (2nd m.) Debbie Whiting. ❖ Sang on Johnny Mercer's radio show as part of an anniversary tribute to her father (1941); by 16, was singing under contract with NBC on many musical shows; signed with Capitol (1943) and had 1st hit with "That Old Black Magic," followed by hit #2 "My Ideal"; during WWII, was a nationwide star, with recording of "Moonlight in Vermont" selling 2 million copies (1944); had 13 gold records and 40 hit songs, including "It Might As Well Be Spring," "Now is the Hour," "Faraway Places," "(I'm in Love with) A Wonderful Guy," "A Tree in the Meadow," "Baby, It's Cold Outside," and "Come Rain or Come Shine" (1946–54); teamed with country star Jimmy Wakely for a number of duets, including the #1 hit "Slippin' Around" (1949); was resident vocalist on "The Bob Hope Show" and costarred

with sister Barbara Whiting on their series, "Those Whiting Girls" (1955–56); was a longtime member of the touring revue *4 Girls 4,* which also featured Rosemary Clooney, Helen O'Connell, and Rose Marie. ❖ See also autobiography *It Might as Well Be Spring* (Morrow, 1987); and *Women in World History.*

WHITING, Sarah F. (1847–1927). American physicist and astronomer. Born Sarah Frances Whiting in Wyoming, New Jersey, Aug 23, 1847; died 1927; dau. of a physics teacher; attended Ingham University. ❖ While a professor of physics at Wellesley College (1876), attended classes in physics at Massachusetts Institute of Technology as a guest, the 1st woman to study physics at MIT; developed, with the help of Harvard's E. C. Pickering, one of the 1st undergraduate teaching laboratories in physics in the country; introduced an astronomy course, then called "applied physics," at Wellesley (1880); better known for her teaching than her research; was the 1st director of the Whitin Observatory; retired (1916). ❖ See also *Women in World History.*

WHITLAM, Margaret (1919—). Australian prime-ministerial wife. Born Margaret Elaine Dovey, Nov 19, 1919, in Sydney, Australia; graduate in social studies from University of Sydney; m. Gough Whitlam (prime minister of Australia, 1972–75), April 22, 1942; children: Anthony (b. 1944), Nicholas (b. 1945), Stephen (b. 1950), Catherine (b. 1954). ❖ A swimming champion, represented Australia at the 3rd Empire Games (1938); well-liked though outspoken, addressed the role of prime-ministerial wife as ambiguous, with undefined duties and loss of a separate identity; became a frequent guest speaker and appeared on radio and tv; contributed a regular column to *Woman's Day* (1973–75), championing women's rights and conservation; accompanied her husband on many tours; was an active member of the Labor Party Women's Conference; appointed to the International Women's Year Advisory Committee (1974–76). Awarded Order of Australia (1983); honored by Australia's National Trust as a "National Living Treasure" (1990s). ❖ See also autobiography *My Day* (Collins, 1973) and Diana Langmore's *Prime Ministers' Wives* (McPhee Gribble, 1992).

WHITLOCK, Mrs. Charles Edward (c. 1761–1836). *See Kemble, Eliza.*

WHITLOCK, Mrs. Elizabeth (c. 1761–1836). *See Kemble, Eliza.*

WHITMAN, Christine Todd (1946—). American politician. Name variations: Christie Whitman. Born Christine Todd, Sept 26, 1946, in New York; dau. of Webster B. Todd (chair of Republican Party) and Eleanor (Schley) Todd (Republican activist); bachelor's degree in government, Wheaton College, 1968; m. John Whitman (financial consultant and grandson of Charles S. Whitman Sr., governor of New York), 1974; children: Kate Whitman (b. 1977); Taylor Whitman (b. 1979). ❖ Scion of one of New Jersey's wealthiest and best-connected political families, worked in New York as a teacher and in Washington, DC, with the Republican National Committee, also serving in US Office of Economic Opportunity, an anti-poverty program of the Nixon administration (1970s); made 1st bid for elective office (1981), serving 2 terms on Somerset County Board of Chosen Freeholders, a board of supervisors; was president of New Jersey Board of Public Utilities (1988–90); made failed bid for US Senate against incumbent Bill Bradley (1990); as a moderate Republican running on a platform of economic revival and tax cuts, became the 1st woman governor in the history of New Jersey (1994); during career as governor, downsized government programs and provided a more conducive environment for private businesses (1994–2001); served as administrator of the Environmental Protection Agency (EPA) under George Bush (2001); resigned (2003). ❖ See also Art Weissman, *Christine Todd Whitman: The Making of a National Political Player* (Birch Lane, 1996); and *Women in World History.*

WHITMAN, Narcissa (1808–1847). American missionary. Born Narcissa Prentiss, Mar 14, 1808, in Prattsburg, New York; killed Nov 29, 1847, in Oregon Territory; dau. of Stephen Prentiss (landowner) and Clarissa (Ward) Prentiss; m. Dr. Marcus Whitman, Feb 1836; children: Alice Clarissa (b. 1837). ❖ The 1st white woman to cross the Rocky Mountains by wagon train on the Oregon Trail, had religious conversion at age 11; committed to missionary work with Presbyterian Church at 15; married a Protestant missionary at age 27 and immediately began 7-month journey to Pacific Northwest (1836); established Whitman mission, Waiilatpu, among Cayuse Indians in eastern Oregon Territory (1836); lost the emotional focal point of her life when daughter drowned in Walla Walla River (1839); took on care of 7 orphaned Sager children, an honorable means of retreat from the missionary work she found so unsatisfying (1844); saw rising unrest among Cayuse Indians, due to increasing waves of white settlers and a measles epidemic that killed 30

Cayuse (1847); killed along with husband and 12 settlers in what came to be known as the Whitman Massacre (Nov 29, 1847). ❖ See also Clifford Drury, *Marcus and Narcissa Whitman and the Opening of Old Oregon* (1986); Julie Roy Jeffrey, *Converting the West: A Biography of Narcissa Whitman* (1991); Thomas E. Jessett, *The Indian Side of the Whitman Massacre* (1973); Matilda J. Delaney Sager, *A Survivor's Recollections of the Whitman Massacre* (1966); *The Whitman Massacre of 1847: Recollections of Catherine, Elizabeth and Matilda Sager* (1981); and *Women in World History*.

WHITMAN, Sarah Helen (1803–1878). American transcendentalist, essayist, and journalist. Name variations: Sarah Power; Mrs. Whitman. Born Sarah Helen Power, Jan 19, 1803, in Providence, Rhode Island; died June 27, 1878, in Providence; dau. of Nicholas Power (merchant) and Anna (Marsh) Power; m. John Winslow Whitman (poet and magazine editor), July 10, 1828 (died 1833); no children. ❖ Journalist and poet who, for many years, was an important figure in American literary circles; at 21, became engaged to John Winslow Whitman who published some of her verses in the *Boston Spectator* under the name "Helen"; became part of the city's literary elite; following husband's death (1833), returned to family home in Providence, where she continued to publish, always under a pseudonym; having adopted the Transcendentalist philosophy, became an outspoken advocate and practitioner of metaphysical science and spirituality; held séances and consulted with leaders of the spiritualist movement; also became actively involved in a range of progressive causes, including utopianism, women's rights, and new ideas in education; published an anonymous valentine poem in *Home Journal* for Edgar Allan Poe (1848), who responded with a poem entitled "To Helen"; met Poe and agreed to marry him, but he died the following year; published 1st book, *Hours of Life, and Other Poems* (1853); also wrote widely in defense of the life and work of Poe, becoming one of the most important sources of information on the poet for his critics and biographers. ❖ See also *Women in World History*.

WHITMIRE, Kathy (1946—). American mayor. Name variations: Kathryn J. Whitmire. Born Kathryn J. Neiderhoffer, Oct 29, 1946, in Houston, TX; dau. of Ida Reeves and Carl Neiderhoffer (attorney); m. 2nd husband Alan J. Whelms. ❖ Was the 1st female city controller of Houston, Texas; served as mayor of Houston (1982–92), the only woman to hold that office; moved to Hawaii.

WHITMORE, Annalee (1916–2002). *See Fadiman, Annalee.*

WHITNEY, Adeline Dutton (1824–1906). American writer. Born Adeline Dutton Train, Sept 15, 1824, in Boston, Massachusetts; died Mar 21, 1906, in Milton, Massachusetts; dau. of Adeline (Dutton) Train and Enoch Train (Boston merchant and trader); m. Seth Dunbar Whitney (wool and leather trader), 1843 (died 1890); children: Mary Adeline (b. 1844); Theodore Train (b. 1846); Marie Caroline (b. 1848, died in infancy); Caroline Leslie (b. 1853). ❖ Wrote prose, poems and essays overflowing with sentimentalized depictions of a good and happy life spent entirely within the sphere of the home; published 1st book, a vol. of poetry, *Mother Goose for Grown Folks* (1859), followed by 2 novels for children, *Boys at Chequasset* (1862) and *Faith Gartney's Girlhood* (1863), the latter of which went through 20 editions; won even more widespread acclaim for a series of books she wrote over the ensuing years: *A Summer in Leslie Goldthwaite's Life* (1866), *We Girls* (1870), *Real Folks* (1871) and *The Other Girls* (1873), which were reissued as the "Real Folks" series; wrote a political tract, *The Law of Woman-Life,* excoriating the women's suffrage movement; published several more collections of poems, including *Pansies* (1872) and *White Memories* (1893), as well as a collection of advice and commentary on domestic issues, *Friendly Letters to Girl Friends* (1896). ❖ See also *Women in World History*.

WHITNEY, Anne (1821–1915). American sculptor, abolitionist and feminist. Born Sept 2, 1821, in Watertown, Massachusetts; died Jan 23, 1915, in Boston, Massachusetts; dau. of Nathaniel R. Whitney II and Sarah (Stone) Whitney; received private instruction from sculptor William Rimmer, 1862–64; studied sculpture in France and bronze casting in Munich; never married; no children. ❖ Taught school in Salem, Massachusetts (1847–49); exhibited marble bust of Laura Brown at the National Academy of Design (1860); commissioned by Commonwealth of Massachusetts to create a statue of Samuel Adams for the US Capitol, Statuary Hall (1873); won (then lost) competition for monument of Senator Charles Sumner (1875); produced 3 sculptures for Philadelphia Centennial Exhibition (1876); exhibited busts of Frances Willard, Mary Livermore, Harriet Beecher Stowe, and Lucy Stone at the

Woman's Building at the Columbian Exposition (1893); erected full-size bronze figure of Sumner in Harvard Square in Cambridge (1902); major works include *Lady Godiva* (1861), *Le Modèle* (1875), *Senator Charles Sumner* (1875), *William Lloyd Garrison* (1880), *Leif Ericson* (1889), *Roma* (1890) and *Frances E. Willard* (1892). ❖ See also *Women in World History*.

WHITNEY, Betsey Cushing Roosevelt (1908–1998). American socialite and philanthropist. Name variations: Betsey Cushing; Mrs. James Roosevelt; Mrs. John Hay Whitney. Born Betsey Maria Cushing, May 18, 1908; died in Manhasset, New York, Mar 25, 1998; dau. of Henry Cushing (neurosurgeon) and Katherine "Kate" (Crowell) Cushing; sister of Babe Paley (1915–1978) and Minnie Astor Fosburgh (1906–1978); m. James Roosevelt (eldest son of Franklin Delano and Eleanor Roosevelt), June 1930 (div. 1940); m. John Hay (Jock) Whitney (US ambassador to England); children: Sara Roosevelt; Kate Roosevelt. ❖ While married to James Roosevelt, often acted as a White House host during Eleanor Roosevelt's frequent absences; with 2nd husband, became the toast of London, hosting royalty and dignitaries with elegance and simplicity; supported the Museum of Modern Art, Yale University, and the North Shore Hospital. ❖ See also David Grafton, *The Sisters: The Lives and Times of the Fabulous Cushing Sisters* (Villard, 1992); and *Women in World History*.

WHITNEY, Charlotte Anita (1867–1955). American suffragist and political organizer. Born July 7, 1867, in San Francisco, California; died Feb 4, 1955; dau. of a lawyer; niece of Stephen J. Field, justice on the Supreme Court (1863–97), and financier Cyrus W. Field; graduate of Wellesley College, 1889. ❖ Became a social worker in the Oakland slums, and served as secretary of Council of Associated Charities of Alameda County (1901–06); elected president of the California College Equal Suffrage League as well as 2nd vice-president of National American Woman Suffrage Association (NAWSA, 1911); joined Socialist Party, and was also active in International Workers of the World (IWW), the radical labor union known as the Wobblies; as part of the most radical wing of the Socialist Party (1919), helped orchestrate its defection and the founding of a separate Communist Labor Party (CLP) which, after tweakings, would become the American Communist Party; arrested after giving a speech at a CLP convention in Oakland (1919), was a defendant in the 1st major prosecution of California's "criminal syndicalism" law; pardoned by California's governor (June 1927); became national chair of the Communist Party (1936). ❖ See also *Women in World History*.

WHITNEY, Dorothy Payne (1887–1968). American philanthropist. Name variations: Dorothy Straight; Dorothy Straight Elmhirst; Mrs. Willard Straight. Born April 1887 in Washington, DC; died 1968 in Devon, England; dau. of William Collins Whitney and Flora (Payne) Whitney (1843-1893); sister of Payne, Pauline, and Henry (Harry) Payne Whitney; m. Willard Dickerman Straight (financial advisor), Sept 7, 1911 (died 1919); m. Leonard Knight Elmhirst (president of Cosmopolitan Club at Cornell University), 1925; children: (1st m.) Whitney Straight; Beatrice Straight (1918–2001, actress); Michael Straight; (2nd m.) 2. ❖ On death of father (1904), became a wealthy young heiress and was placed in the guardianship of her brother Harry and his wife Gertrude Vanderbilt Whitney; began philanthropies, working with the Junior League, the drive for women's suffrage, the State Charities Aid, and the YWCA; also subsidized *The New Republic,* a weekly newspaper devoted to "the improvement of the democracy" which husband started with Herbert Croly in 1914; was also instrumental in starting the New School for Social Research (1918), of which she also served as a director; with 2nd husband, moved to England (1925), where they purchased Dartington Hall, a decaying mansion on 2,000 acres in Devon, and started a combined school and industrial-cultural center, which became famous as an advanced school, particularly in the arts; continued to support *The New Republic* until it was sold in 1953. ❖ See also W. A. Swanberg, *Whitney Father, Whitney Heiress* (Scribner, 1980); and *Women in World History*.

WHITNEY, Eleanore (1917—). American film tap dancer. Name variations: Eleanor Whitney. Born April 21, 1917 in Cleveland, OH. ❖ Danced solos in 3 Paramount films, *Rose Bowl* (1936), *Blonde Trouble* (1937), *June Moon* (1937); also appeared in *Turn Off the Moon* (1937) and *The Big Broadcast of 1937*; danced on Fanchon's Paramount circuit.

WHITNEY, Flora Payne (1897–1986). American sculptor and art patron. Name variations: Flora Whitney Miller. Born July 29, 1897; died in Nassau, New York, July 17, 1986; dau. of Harry Payne Whitney

(1872–1930) and Gertrude Vanderbilt Whitney (1875–1942, founder of Whitney Museum); m. Roderick Tower (1892–1961, oilman), 1920 (div. 1924); m. George Macculloch Miller (1887–1972, artist and businessman), Feb 24, 1927; children: (1st m.) Pamela Tower; Whitney Tower; (2nd m.) Flora Miller Biddle; Leverett Miller. ❖ Began sculpting in Paris and later in New York, exhibiting her work at the Society of Independent Artist and in the Whitney Studio Club's 10th Anniversary Exhibition; after death of mother (1942), took over the stewardship of the Whitney Museum of American Art (1948), serving as president for 25 years; oversaw museum moves (1954, 1966), the last to its present location on Madison Avenue; helped to expand the museum's collection and assisted fund-raising projects, often donating money from her own funds; also took a great interest in nurturing new artists. ❖ See also Flora Miller Biddle, *The Whitney Women and the Museum They Made: A Family Memoir* (Arcade, 1999); and *Women in World History.*

WHITNEY, Gertrude Vanderbilt (1875–1942). American sculptor, patron of the arts, and philanthropist. Name variations: Mrs. Henry Payne Whitney; Mrs. Harry Payne Whitney; Mrs. H. P. Whitney. Born Gertrude Vanderbilt, Jan 9, 1875, in New York, NY; died April 18, 1942, in NY, NY; dau. of Alice Gwynne Vanderbilt (1845–1934) and Cornelius Vanderbilt II (1843–1899, banker and philanthropist); studied sculpture under Hendrik Andersen and James E. Fraser, and under Andrew O'Connor in Paris; m. Henry (Harry) Payne Whitney, Aug 25, 1896; children: Flora Payne Whitney (b. July 29, 1897); Cornelius Vanderbilt Whitney (b. Feb 20, 1899); Barbara Whitney (b. Mar 21, 1903). ❖ Noted sculptor, patron of poverty-stricken artists, champion of American art at a time when few believed it had any worth, who founded the Whitney Museum with her own art collection and left her fortune to the museum upon her death; opened her 1st studio (1901); joined board of directors of Greenwich House Social Settlement (1903); enrolled at Art Students League and finished *American Athlete* to exhibit at St. Louis Exhibition (1904); organized Colony Club exhibition (1907); had *Paganisme Immortel* accepted by National Academy of Design and opened Paris studio (1910); exhibited *Head of Spanish Peasant* at the Paris Salon and *Study of a Head* at Independent Artists Show in NY (1911); received commission for *Titanic Memorial* (1912); exhibited 5 works at all-women artists show at Gorham Art Gallery, NY; bought Whitney Studio at 8 West 8th Street (1913); started Whitney Studio prize competition and received Medal of Award at Panama-Pacific Exhibition for *Fountain of El Dorado* (1915); made an associate member of National Sculpture Society (1916); created set design for Giovanitti's play *As It Was in the Beginning* (1917); formed Whitney Studio Club (1918); had own shows at Luxembourg Museum and McLean's Gallery in London (1921); exhibited at National Association of Women Painters and Sculptors Show (1922); won bronze medallion at Paris Salon for *Buffalo Bill* (1924); awarded French Legion of Honor medal (1926); opened Whitney Museum of American Art (1932); published *Walking the Dusk* (1932); involved with court battle over custody of Gloria Vanderbilt (1934–38); had solo exhibition at Knoedler's Gallery (1936); elected associate of National Academy of Design and won Medal of Honor of the National Sculpture Society (1940); made an enormous and far-reaching contribution to the cultural life of the US by her unflinching support for modern American art and artists. ❖ See also Flora Miller Biddle, *The Whitney Women and the Museum They Made: A Family Chronicle* (Arcade, 2000); Avis Berman, *Rebels on Eighth Street: Juliana Force and the Whitney Museum of American Art* (Atheneum, 1990); B.H. Friedman, *Gertrude Vanderbilt Whitney* (Doubleday, 1978); and *Women in World History.*

WHITNEY, Mrs. Harry Payne (1875–1942). See Whitney, Gertrude Vanderbilt.

WHITNEY, Helen Hay (1876–1944). American sportswoman and philanthropist. Name variations: Mrs. Payne Whitney. Born Helen Hay, Mar 11, 1876, in New York; died Sept 1944 in New York; dau. of John Hay (1838–1905, private secretary to Abraham Lincoln and US secretary of state) and Clara Louise (Stone) Hay; sister of Alice Hay Wadsworth Boyd; m. Payne Whitney (financier), Feb 6, 1902 (died 1927); children: Joan Whitney Payson (1903–1975); Jock Whitney. ❖ Known as the "first Lady of the American Turf" because of her lifelong interest in horse racing, founded the Greentree Stable which produced numerous thoroughbreds, including the 1931 Kentucky Derby winner Twenty Grand. ❖ See also W. A. Swanberg, *Whitney Father, Whitney Heiress* (Scribner, 1980); and *Women in World History.*

WHITNEY, Mrs. Henry Payne (1875–1942). See Whitney, Gertrude Vanderbilt.

WHITNEY, Isabella (fl. 1567–1575). English poet. Belonged to a family of the minor gentry with a country home in Coole Pilate, near Nantwich, Cheshire, England; believed to have been the sister of another early English author, Geoffrey Whitney, who published a well-known book *A Choice of Emblemes* in 1586. ❖ One of the 1st women to publish secular literature, published 1st book, *A Copy of a Letter lately written in Meeter by a Yonge Gentilwoman to Her Unconstant Lover* (1567), followed by a collection of poems, *A Sweet Nosegay, or Pleasant Posye: containing a hundred and ten Philosophicall Flowers* (1573); was essentially the 1st English woman to identify herself as a professional writer. ❖ See also *Women in World History.*

WHITNEY, Joan (1903–1975). See Payson, Joan Whitney.

WHITNEY, Mrs. John Hay (1908–1998). See Whitney, Betsey Cushing.

WHITNEY, Marilyn Corson (1954—). See Corson, Marilyn.

WHITNEY, Mary Watson (1847–1921). American astronomer and educator. Born Mary Watson Whitney, Sept 11, 1847, in Waltham, Massachusetts; died Jan 20, 1921, in Waltham; dau. of Samuel Buttrick Whitney and Mary Watson (Crehore) Whitney; Vassar College, BA, 1868, AM, 1872; attended lectures at Harvard and University of Zurich; never married; no children. ❖ Astronomy teacher, taught in Auburndale, Massachusetts (1868); was on staff at Dearborn Observatory, Chicago (1870); taught at Waltham High School (1876); was assistant to Maria Mitchell at Vassar College Observatory (1881–88), then succeeded Mitchell, serving as professor of astronomy and director of the observatory (1888–1910); writings include *Observations of Variable Stars Made During the Years 1901–12* (1913). ❖ See also *Women in World History.*

WHITNEY, Myra (1805–1885). See Gaines, Myra Clark.

WHITNEY, Mrs. Payne (1876–1944). See Whitney, Helen Hay.

WHITNEY, Phyllis A. (b. 1903). American writer. Born Phyllis Ayame Whitney, Sept 9, 1903, in Yokohama, Japan; dau. of Charles Whitney (American businessman) and Mary (Mandeville) Whitney; m. George A. Garner, 1925 (div. 1945); m. Lovell F. Jahnke, 1950 (died 1973); children: Georgia Whitney. ❖ Author of popular novels, spent portions of childhood living with family in the Philippines and China until father's death when she was 15; sold 1st short story to *Chicago Daily News* (1928); during WWII, began reign as one of the best-known American writers of romantic suspense in the latter half of the 20th century; her long career of writing for young people and adults produced more than 75 novels, a number of articles on the writing of fiction, and several textbooks for would-be writers of fiction; wrote her 1st adult book, *Red is for Murder* (1943), but did not begin writing regularly for adults until publication of *The Quicksilver Pool* (1955); edited children's book review pages for *Chicago Sun* and *Philadelphia Inquirer,* and taught writing courses at Northwestern University (1945) and New York University (1947–58); writings include *The Silver Inkwell* (1945), *Mystery of the Black Diamonds* (1954), *The Moonflower* (1958), *Sea Jade* (1965), *Columbella* (1966), *The Winter People* (1969), *The Stone Bull* (1977), *Rainbow in the Mist* (1989) and *Amethyst Dreams* (1997). Won Edgar Awards from Mystery Writers of America for *Mystery of the Haunted Pool* (1960) and *Mystery of the Hidden Hand* (1963). ❖ See also *Women in World History.*

WHITNEY, Ruth (1928–1999). American journalist and magazine editor. Born July 23, 1928, in Oshkosh, WI; died of Lou Gehrig's disease in Irvington, NY, June 4, 1999; dau. of Leonard and Helen Reinke; graduate of Northwestern University; m. Daniel Whitney, 1949; children: Philip Whitney. ❖ Served as editor in chief of *Glamour* for 31 years, regularly publishing thought-provoking articles; changed the annual college competition from the best dressed to the most accomplished.

WHITTELSEY, Abigail Goodrich (1788–1858). American magazine editor. Born Abigail Goodrich, Nov 29, 1788, in Ridgefield, Connecticut; died July 16, 1858, in Colchester, Connecticut; dau. of Reverend Samuel Goodrich and Elizabeth (Ely) Goodrich; sister of children's book author Samuel Griswold Goodrich (1793–1860), who wrote under pseudonym Peter Parley; m. Reverend Samuel Whittelsey, Nov 10, 1808 (died 1842); children: Samuel (b. 1809); Charles Chauncey (b. 1812); Elizabeth (b. 1815); Henry (b. 1821); Charles Augustus (b. 1823); Emily (b. 1825). ❖ Served as matron of a female seminary in upstate New York (1824–28); together with husband, founded a seminary for girls in Utica, NY (1828), and served as its matron; appointed editor of periodical *Mother's Magazine* (1833), which moved to New York City, where circulation reached 10,000 by 1837; resigned (1848); was founder, editor, and publisher, *Mrs. Whittelsey's Magazine for Mothers* (1850–52). ❖ See also *Women in World History*.

WHITTIER, Polly (1877–1946). American golfer. Name variations: Pauline Whittier. Born 1877; died Mar 30, 1946. ❖ At the Paris Olympics, won a silver medal in singles (1900).

WHITTLE, Jenny (1973—). Australian basketball player. Born Jennifer Whittle, Sept 5, 1973, in Australia. ❖ Center; won a team bronze medal at Atlanta Olympics (1996) and a silver medal at Sydney Olympics (2000); played for Perth Breakers in Australia; played for Washington Mystics in WNBA (2001).

WHITTON, Charlotte (1896–1975). Canadian politician. Born Mar 8, 1896, in Renfrew, Ontario, Canada; died Jan 25, 1975, in Ottawa, Ontario, Canada; dau. of John Edward Whitton (forestry official for the province of Ontario) and Elizabeth (Langin) Whitton; Queen's University, MA, 1917 (was the 1st female editor of the university newspaper); lived with Margaret Grier, from 1918 to 1947. ❖ The 1st female mayor of a major Canadian city, served in the social service sector, including as private secretary to Canada's minister in Trade and Commerce (1922–25) and as executive director of the Canadian Welfare Council (1926–41); was founder and editor of journal *Canadian Welfare*; authored several studies of Canadian social conditions, among them the extensive survey *The Dawn of Ampler Life* (1943), as well as more than 50 pamphlets, among them *Canadian Women in the War Effort* (1942), *Security for Canadians* (1942) and *Welfare Must Be Planned and Paid For* (1945); appointed, elected, then served as mayor of Ottawa (1951–56 and 1960–64); was columnist and essayist, with work published in Canadian newspapers; her book *A Hundred Years A-Fellin'* (1943) is a history on lumbering in Ontario's Ottawa Valley. Named Commander of the Order of the British Empire (1934); received Jubilee Medal (1935) and Coronation Medal (1937). ❖ See also *Women in World History*.

WHITTY, Ellen (1819–1892). *See Vincent, Mother.*

WHITTY, May (1865–1948). English actress. Name variations: Dame May Whitty. Born Mary Louise Whitty in Liverpool, England, June 19, 1865; died in Hollywood, California, May 29, 1948; dau. of Alfred Whitty (newspaper editor) and Mary (Ashton) Whitty; m. Benjamin Webster (lawyer turned actor), Aug 1892 (died 1947); children: Margaret Webster (1905–1972, actress and director). ❖ Celebrated for skill on stage and screen during a career that spanned over half a century, made stage debut in chorus of *The Mountain Sylph* (Liverpool, 1881), and London debut as Fillippa in *Boccaccio* (1882); joined Lyceum Co. (1895), then under management of Sir Henry Irving and Ellen Terry, and toured US with the company (1895–96); won some good notices for portrayal of Susan Throssell in *Quality Street* (1902); played Amelia in *The Madras House* (1910), the 1st of the character roles that would dominate the 2nd half of her career; the 1st actress to be created a dame, received DBE in 1918, for work in theater and charity work during WWI; managed the Florence Etlinger Dramatic School (1921–26); appeared as Mrs. Corsellis in *The Enchanted Cottage* (1922), Mrs. Henry Gilliam in *The Fool* (1924), and Mrs. Ebley in *The Last of Mrs. Cheyney* (1925), among others; scored major triumph as Mrs. Bramson in *Night Must Fall* (1935), which she brought to NY (1936), then reprised on film; was memorable in title role in film *The Lady Vanishes* (1938); other films include *The 13th Chair* (1937), *Conquest* (1937), *Raffles* (1940), *A Bill of Divorcement* (1940), *One Night in Lisbon* (1941), *Suspicion* (1941), *The Constant Nymph* (1943), *Lassie Come Home* (1943), *Madame Curie* (1943), *The White Cliffs of Dover* (1944), *Gaslight* (1944), *Devotion* (1946), *Green Dolphin Street* (1947) and *If Winter Comes* (1948); on stage, also appeared as Madame Raquin in *Thérèse* (1945). Nominated for Academy Awards for *Night Must Fall* and for portrayal of Lady Belden in *Mrs. Miniver* (1942). ❖ See also Margaret Webster, *The Same Only Different* (Knopf, 1969); and *Women in World History*.

WHITWORTH, Donna (c. 1942—). *See Axum, Donna.*

WHITWORTH, Kathy (1939—). American golfer. Name variations: Kathryne Whitworth. Born Kathryne Whitworth, Sept 27, 1939, in Monahans, TX. ❖ Dominated the pro circuit (1960s); won the New Mexico State Amateur championship (1957, 1958); won the Baltimore Kelly Girl Open (1962); won 8 tournaments (1963, 1965, 1967), 9 (1966), and 10 (1968); was the leading money winner (1965–68,

1970–73); at the Rochester International golf tournament, claimed her 85th career championship (1984), including 3 LPGA titles, surpassing Sam Snead's record for most professional golf tournament victories; was the 1st female professional golfer to win over $1 million; served as president of LPGA. Was the 1st recipient of the LPGA's Player of the Year Award (1966), receiving it a total of 7 times; named Female Athlete of the Year by Associated Press (1965–66); inducted into LPGA Hall of Fame, World Golf Hall of Fame, Texas Sports Hall of Fame, and International Women's Sports Hall of Fame; won the Vare Trophy (1965–67, 1969–72). ❖ See also Patricia Mulrooney Eldred, *Kathy Whitworth* (1975); and *Women in World History*.

WHYTE, Edna Gardner (1902–1992). American aviator and nurse. Name variations: Edna Marvel Gardner. Born Edna Marvel Gardner, Nov 3, 1902, in Garden City, Minnesota; died in Grapevine, Texas, Feb 15, 1992; dau. of Walter Carl Gardner (farmer and railroad laborer) and Myrtle (Marvel) Gardner (schoolteacher); m. Ray L. Kidd, 1935 (div. 1940); m. George Murphy Whyte, 1946 (div. 1967); children: (adopted) Georgeann. ❖ Pioneer aviator, flight instructor, and nurse who won over 120 racing trophies in the course of a nearly 60-year flying career; began nurses' training, La Crosse (Wisconsin) Hospital (1921); was a staff nurse, University of Wisconsin (1924), Parkland Hospital, Dallas (1925), and Virginia Mason Hospital, Seattle (1925), University of Wisconsin (1927); took 1st flying lesson (1927); received student pilot license (1929); joined US Navy's Nursing Corps (1929); soloed and received pilot's license (1931); joined earliest women's flying sorority, the Ninety-Nines (1931), serving as its president (1956–57); assigned to Newport Naval Hospital (1931), then Naval Hospital Washington, DC (1934); resigned commission (1935); opened Southern Aviation School with husband at Shushan Airport, New Orleans; opened New Orleans Air College, Wedell-Williams Airport (1937); moved to Meacham Field, Fort Worth, as instrument instructor for US Army (1941); joined Army Nursing Corps (1944); became instructor, Roy Taylor Flying School, Meacham Field (1946); built Aero Valley Airport, Roanoke, Texas, and created last flying school (1969); retired (1988); trained over 4,000 aviators to fly a variety of aircraft and logged more than 25,000 hours in the air over her lifetime; was one of the original 10 members of the Whirlygirls. Inducted in Curtiss-Wright Hall of Fame for Pioneer Pilots (1975), Texas Women's Hall of Fame (1984), Oklahoma Aviation and Space Hall of Fame (1985) and Texas State Hall of Fame (1985); received Charles Lindbergh Foundation, Life Time Achievement in Aviation Award (1986). ❖ See also (with Ann L. Cooper) *Rising Above It: An Autobiography* (Orion, 1991); and *Women in World History*.

WHYTE, Kathleen (1909–1996). Scottish embroiderer and teacher. Name variations: Helen Kathleen Ramsay Whyte. Born Aug 1909 in Arbroath, Scotland; died 1996; studied at Gray's School of Art in Aberdeen, 1927–32; studied embroidery with Dorothy Angus, from 1920, and design with James Hamilton; graduated with Diploma of Design and Decorative Arts, 1932; attended Aberdeen Teacher Training College, 1932–33; studied weaving with Ethel Mairet at her Gospels studio in Ditchling, 1942–43. ❖ With family, lived in Jamshedpur, India (1911–13, 1920–23); taught art at Frederick Street School, Central Secondary School, and Aberdeen High School for Girls; was a lecturer in embroidery and weaving in Design and Craft section of Glasgow School of Art (1948–74); revitalized embroidery teaching in Glasgow, with gradual introductions of new techniques, an emphasis on draftsmanship and experimentation, and a stimulating, demanding teaching style; formed Glasgow School of Art Embroidery Group (1957); received a number of commissions from Church of Scotland and worked on the Tay Road Bridge stole, commissioned on behalf of Queen Elizabeth II (1966). Awarded MBE for services to Scottish art education (1969). ❖ See also Liz Arthur, *Kathleen Whyte, Embroiderer* (Batsford, 1989); and *Women in World History*.

WHYTE, Sandra (1970—). American ice-hockey player. Born Aug 24, 1970; Harvard University, degree in bio-anthropology, 1992. ❖ Named Ivy League Player of the Year (1990–91 and 1991–92); won a team gold medal at Nagano (1998), the 1st Olympics to feature women's ice hockey; won a team silver medal at World championships (1997). ❖ See also Mary Turco, *Crashing the Net: The U.S. Women's Olympic Ice Hockey Team and the Road to Gold* (HarperCollins, 1999); and *Women in World History*.

WHYTE, Violet (1856–1911). *See Winter, John Strange.*

WHYTOCK, Janet (1842–1894). *See Patey, Janet Monach.*

WIBERG, Pernilla (1970—). Swedish Alpine skier. Born Oct 15, 1970, in Norkoping, Sweden. ❖ Won a gold medal for giant slalom at World championships (1991); won a gold medal for giant slalom at Albertville Olympics (1992); finished 2nd overall in World Cup standings and 2nd in slalom (1993–94); won a gold medal for combined at Lillehammer Olympics (1994); finished 10th in World Cup downhill standings (1995–96); won gold medals in the slalom and combined at World championships (1996); registered 8 World Cup victories (5 in slalom, 2 in super-G, and 1 in downhill, 1996–97); won 1st overall crown and set a single-season record for most World Cup points in the final World Cup standings—1,960 (1997); won a silver medal for downhill at Nagano Olympics (1998); won a gold medal for combined at World championships (1999); competed at Salt Lake City Olympics but did not medal (2002). ❖ See also *Women in World History.*

WIBERG, Susanne (1963—). *See Gunnarsson, Susanne.*

WICHFELD, Monica (1894–1945). *See Massy-Beresford, Monica.*

WICHFELD-MUUS, Varinka (1922–2002). Danish resistance worker. Name variations: known as Inkie. Born Feb 9, 1922, in Saxkøbing, Denmark; died Dec 18, 2002, in Copenhagen; dau. of Jørgen de Wichfeld (Danish aristocrat) and Monica Massy-Beresford (1894–1945, Danish heroine); m. Flemming Muus (resistance leader), 1944 (died 1982). ❖ One of the heroines of the Danish resistance, helped her mother with arms pickups, hid wanted persons, ran errands, then became a resistance leader in her own right; married the chief agent in Denmark for Britain's Special Operations Executive (SOE). ❖ See also memoirs (in Danish), *Fra Solskin til Tusmoerke* (From Sunshine to Twilight, 1994).

WICHMAN, Sharon (1952—). American swimmer. Born May 13, 1952, in Indiana; m. David Jones, 1973; children: 2 sons. ❖ At Mexico City Olympics, won a bronze medal in the 100-meter breaststroke and a gold medal in the 200-meter breaststroke with Olympic-record time of 2:44.4, the 1st woman to win that event (1968).

WICKENHEISER, Hayley (1978—). Canadian ice-hockey and softball player. Born Aug 12, 1978, in Shaunavon, Saskatchewan; cousin of former NHL player Doug Wickenheiser; attended University of Calgary. ❖ Won a team silver medal at Nagano (1998), the 1st Olympics to feature women's ice hockey; won a team gold medal at World championships (1994, 1997, 1999, 2000); won a team gold medal at Salt Lake City Olympics (2002) and was named MVP; as a softball player, competed at Sydney Summer Games (2000); became the 1st woman to play professional men's hockey in Finland (2003), not as a goalie but as a center; won a team gold medal at Torino Olympics (2006).

WICKES, Mary (1916–1995). American comedic stage, tv, and screen actress. Born Mary Isabelle Wickenhauser, June 13, 1916, in St. Louis, MO; died Oct 22, 1995, in Los Angeles, CA. ❖ Known for sardonic delivery, made NY stage debut in *The Farmer Takes a Wife* (1934); recreated stage role of Miss Preen for film debut in *The Man Who Came to Dinner* (1941); other films include *Now Voyager, On Moonlight Bay, By the Light of the Silvery Moon, The Music Man, The Trouble with Angels, Postcards from the Edge, Sister Act* and *Sister Act 2.*

WICKHAM, Anna (1883–1947). English poet. Name variations: Edith Harper; Edith Harper Hepburn. Born Edith Alice Mary Harper in Wimbledon, Surrey, England, 1883 (some sources cite 1884); committed suicide in London, 1947; dau. of Geoffrey Harper and Alice (Whelan) Harper (both Australians); earned a scholarship to the Tree's Academy of Acting, and studied opera in Paris; m. Patrick Hepburn (English lawyer, later secretary of Astronomical Society), 1905 (sep. 1926, drowned 1929); children: 4, including James, John, and George. ❖ Grew up in Australia, then returned to England as a young adult; became interested in social welfare causes, but husband disapproved of her writing and liberal political views and had her forcibly confined to an asylum for 6 weeks after an argument; privately printed a collection of poems, *Songs for John Oland* (1911), against husband's wishes; under pseudonym Anna Wickham, issued 3 more vols. of poetry, *The Contemplative Quarry, The Man With a Hammer* (1916) and *The Little Old House* (1921); her poetry found a large audience among middle-class women in England and US, and was frequently included in anthologies; left husband and moved to Paris (1922), where she met Natalie Clifford Barney who became a source of financial and emotional support; her letters to Barney, as well as much of her poetry from this period, has erotic undertones and testifies to her growing woman-centered consciousness.

❖ See also *The Writings of Anna Wickham, Free Woman and Poet* (edited by R. D. Smith, Salem House, 1984); and *Women in World History.*

WICKLOW, countess of (c. 1915–1997). *See Butler, Eleanor.*

WICKWIRE, Nancy (1925–1974). American stage and tv actress. Born Nov 20, 1925, in Harrisburg, PA; died July 10, 1974, in San Francisco, CA; m. Basil Langton (div.). ❖ Made NY stage debut in *St. Joan* (1951), followed by *Jane, Dial M for Murder, The Way of the World, Cherry Orchard, Measure for Measure, Girl of the Golden West, As You Like It, Rosmersholm,* and *Here's Where I Belong,* among others; appeared in the original US production of Dylan Thomas' *Under Milk Wood*; performed often at American Conservatory Theatre (ACT) in San Francisco; also appeared on tv.

WIDDECOMBE, Ann (1947—). English politician and writer. Name variations: Rt. Hon. Ann Widdecombe. Born Oct 4, 1947, in Bath, Somerset, England; dau. of Rita Widdecombe and James Murray Widdecombe (OBE, director general in Ministry of Defence); University of Birmingham, BA; Lady Margaret Hall, Oxford, MA. ❖ As an outspoken, controversial Conservative, elected to House of Commons for Maidstone and the Weald (1987, 1992, 1997, 2001, 2005); became Home Office minister in Charge of Prisons in John Major's government; became shadow Health Secretary (1997), then shadow Home Secretary; when the Church of England approved the ordination of women as priests (1993), protested by joining the Roman Catholic Church; also a novelist, wrote *The Clematis Tree* (2000), *An Act of Treachery* (2002) and *An Act of Peace* (2005).

WIDDEMER, Margaret (1884–1978). American writer. Born Sept 30, 1884, in Doylestown, Pennsylvania; died July 14, 1978; dau. of William Barton Widdemer (cleric); attended Drexel Institute of Arts and Sciences. ❖ Pulitzer Prize-winning poet, came to prominence with poem denouncing child labor, which eventually titled her 1st collection, *The Factories and Other Poems* (1915); published bestselling novel, *The Rose Garden Husband* (1915); won Pulitzer Prize for poetry (then called Poetry Society Prize) for *Old Road to Paradise* (1918); published many of best poems in *Collected Works* (1957); also published "Winona" series of books for girls and wrote *Cross Currents* (1921), *Little Girl and Boy Land* (1924), *Ballads and Lyrics* (1925), *Road to Downderry* (1931), *Hill Garden* (1937) and *Dark Cavalier* (1958).

WIDDOP, Elizabeth (1846–1924). *See Parsons, Elizabeth.*

WIDDOWSON, Elsie (1906–2000). English nutritionist. Name variations: Elsie May Widdowson. Born Oct 21, 1906, in Dulwich, London, England; died June 14, 2000; sister of Eva Crane (b. 1911, apiculturalist); studied at Imperial College, London, and at King's College of Household and Social Science (1933–34). ❖ Pioneer in scientific food analysis, nutrition and diet, worked closely throughout career with Robert A. McCance; during WWII, with her nation under wartime rationing, worked out that cabbage, bread and potatoes contained all the nutrients needed for a healthy survival; also advised on what food could be tolerated by victims of the war as they were nursed back to health; with McCance, wrote *The Composition of Foods* (1940), known as the dietitian's bible, which was regularly updated. Made a Commander of the Order of the British Empire (1979).

WIDDOWSON, Eva (b. 1911). *See Crane, Eva.*

WIDEMAN, Lydia (1920—). Finnish cross-country skier. Name variations: Lydia Widemann. Born May 17, 1921, in Finland. ❖ Won a gold medal for 10 km at Oslo (1952), the 1st cross-country skiing medal for women in Olympic history.

WIDNALL, Sheila (1938—). American aeronautical engineer and military leader. Born Sheila Evans, July 13, 1938, in Tacoma, WA; dau. of Genevieve (juvenile probation officer) and Rolland Evans (math professor); Massachusetts Institute of Technology, PhD, 1964; m. William Widnall (engineer), 1960; children: Bill and Ann. ❖ Joined MIT faculty as engineering professor (1964), winning international acclaim for her work in fluid dynamics; became the 1st woman to chair the MIT faculty (1979), then named associate provost (1992); served as secretary of the Air Force (1993–97), the 1st woman to head a branch of US armed forces.

WIECHOWNA, Wanda (1946—). Polish volleyball player. Born May 14, 1946, in Poland. ❖ At Mexico City Olympics, won a bronze medal in team competition (1968).

WIECK, Clara (1819–1896). *See Schumann, Clara.*

WIECK, Dorothea (1908–1986). German stage and screen actress. Born Jan 3, 1908, in Davos, Switzerland; died Feb 20, 1986, in Berlin, Germany. ❖ Trained with Max Reinhardt; became a leading star of the German stage; came to international prominence as Fräulein von Bernburg in film *Mädchen in Uniform* (1931); other films include *Gräfin Mariza* (title role), *Trenck, Ein Toller Einfall, Anna und Elisabeth, Miss Fane's Baby is Stolen, Der student von Prag, Liselotte von der Pfalz* (as Mme de Maintenon), *Liebe kann lügen, Die gelbe flagge, Herz der Welt, Anastasia, A Time to Love and a Time to Die,* and *Die Schachnovelle*; became a baroness on marriage.

WIECZOREK, Teresa (1937—). See Cieply-Wieczorkowna, Teresa.

WIED, Martina (1882–1957). Austrian poet and novelist. Name variations: Martina Weisl; Alexandrine M. Weisl. Born Dec 10, 1882, in Vienna, Austria; died Jan 25, 1957; m. Sigmund Weisl (chemist); children: Hanno. ❖ Works include *Bewegung* (1919), *Das Asyl zum obdachlosen Geist* (1934), *Das Einhorn* (1948, The Unicorn), which she wrote in exile in Scotland during WWII, and *Das Krähennest* (1951).

WIED, princess of.
See Marie of Nassau (1841–1910).
See Elizabeth of Wied (1843–1916).
See Pauline of Wurttemberg (1877–1965).

WIEDERSHEIM, Grace Gebbie (1877–1936). *See Drayton, Grace Gebbie.*

WIEDERSHELM-PAUL, Annette (1944—). *See Av-Paul, Annette.*

WIEGMANN, Bettina (1971—). German soccer player. Born Oct 7, 1971, in Mechernich, Germany. ❖ Midfielder; joined German national team (1989), becoming Germany's 3rd all-time leading scorer; won team European championships (1991, 1995, 1997, 2001); played for FFC Brauweiler-Pulheim; won a team bronze medal at Sydney Olympics (2000); signed with Boston Breakers (2002). Named German Player of the Year (1997).

WIELAND, Gerhard (1878–1967). *See Lask, Berta.*

WIELAND, Joyce (1931–1998). Canadian film director and artist. Born June 30, 1931, in Toronto, Ontario, Canada; died of Alzheimer's disease, age 66, June 27, 1998, in Toronto; educated at Central Technical Vocational High School in Toronto; m. Michael Snow (artist), 1957 (div.). ❖ One of Canada's most significant 20th-century artists, was an animator for Graphic Films (1955–56); with husband, worked on numerous film projects (1957–60); became the only woman to achieve artistic prominence among the new group of Canadian painters influenced by Abstract Expressionism and Pop Art (1950s–60s); in addition to her painting, produced a number of mixed-media assemblages and began making quilts in collaboration with sister Joan Stewart; with husband, relocated to NY (early 1960s), and began making short films, which were soon included in Greenwich Village avant-garde screenings, such as *Patriotism, Part II* (1964), *Rat Life and Diet in North America* (1968) and *Reason Over Passion/La Raison Avant la Passion* (1969); by 1971, had returned to Toronto, where she was the 1st woman to be featured in a solo exhibit at National Gallery of Art; works became increasingly associated with issues of Canadian identity, feminism, and the environment (1970s–80s); working primarily in paints and colored pencils, produced such memorable works as *The one above waits for those below* (1981) and *Experiment with Life* (1983); completed 2 additional short structural documentaries, *Pierre Vallières,* about a French-Canadian revolutionary, and *Solidarity*; co-wrote, co-produced, and directed the feature-length film, *The Far Shore.* ❖ See also *Women in World History.*

WIELEMA, Geertje (1934—). Dutch swimmer. Born July 24, 1934, in Hilversum, Netherlands. ❖ At Helsinki Olympics, won a silver medal in 100-meter backstroke (1952); won European championship (1954).

WIELICZKO, Malgorzata (1958—). *See Dluzewska, Malgorzata.*

WIENHAUSEN, abbess of. *See Hoya, Katherina von (d. around 1470).*

WIENIAWSKA, Irene Regine (1880–1932). Belgian-born composer, pianist and singer. Name variations: Lady Dean Paul; (pseudonym) Mme. Poldowski. Born Irene Regine Wieniawska in Brussels, Belgium, May 16, 1880; died in London, Jan 28, 1932; dau. of Polish violinist and composer Henryk (Henri) Wieniawski (1835–1880), who died 6 weeks before her birth; entered Brussels Conservatory at age 12 to study piano and composition; went to London to complete musical education, studying with Percy Pitt and Michael Hambourg; m. Sir Aubrey Dean Paul, Bt. (who as a baritone gave concerts with his wife in England and the Continent), 1901. ❖ Composed finely crafted orchestral works, chamber music, piano pieces and vocal works, as well as an operetta entitled *Laughter,* but was primarily a composer of songs; excelled in setting the French poets, from Victor Hugo to Paul Verlaine, to music, songs interpreted by herself and a number of noted singers, particularly Gervase Elwes; had several orchestral compositions, considered sufficiently excellent in their day, performed by major London orchestras; her "Nocturne for Orchestra" was presented by Sir Henry Wood at one of his Promenade Concerts (1912). ❖ See also *Women in World History.*

WIESENTHAL, Grete (1885–1970). Austrian dancer and choreographer. Born Margarete Wiesenthal in Vienna, Austria, Dec 9, 1885; died in Vienna, June 22, 1970; dau. of Franz Wiesenthal (painter) and Rosa (Ratkovsky) Wiesenthal; had 1 brother and 5 sisters, including Elsa and Berta (both dancers) and Martha Wiesenthal (leader of a string quartet); trained at Vienna's Hofoper ballet school under Joseph Hassreiter; m. Erwin Lang (painter and son of Austrian feminist Marie Lang), June 1910 (div. 1923, died 1962); m. Nils Silfverskjöld (Swedish physician), in 1923 (div. 1927); children: Martin. ❖ The "ambassador of waltz," began life as a dancer within the traditions of ballet; entered the corps (1901) and advanced to coryphée (1902); with sister Elsa, began choreographing new ways of movement and expression through dance and allied with Secession circle of innovators; with Elsa and sister Berta, came to prominence as the Wiesenthal sisters at Vienna's Cabaret Fledermaus (1908); in Berlin, danced with sisters at Max Reinhardt's Deutsches Theater; danced role of 1st elf in Reinhardt's production of *A Midsummer Night's Dream* at Munich's Artist's Theater (1909); with sisters, performed at London's Hippodrome and at Théâtre du Vaudeville in Paris (1909); made solo debut in Berlin in pantomime *Sumurùn,* produced by Reinhardt (1910); made US debut at Winter Garden in NY (1912); created role of Kitchen Boy in Reinhardt's Stuttgart production of *Der Bürger als Edelmann,* with music by Richard Strauss; appeared in "Grete Wiesenthal Series" of films (1913–14): *Kadra Sâfa, Erlkönigs Tochter* and *Die goldne Fliege*; following WWI, opened dancing school (1919); returned to Vienna stage at Staatsoper (State Opera House), in lead role of her ballet *Der Taugenichts in Wien* (The Ne'er-Do-Well in Vienna, 1927); remained active professionally, appearing in solo dance concerts and tours, including a return to NY (1933); appointed professor of dance at Vienna's Academy for Music and the Performing Arts (1934), then served as director of artistic dance section (1945–52); after WWII, her work enjoyed a renaissance in Austria, especially the dances she created for various Salzburg Festival productions; wrote autobiography, *Der Aufstieg* (The Way Upwards, 1919), which appeared as *Die ersten Schritte* (The First Steps, 1947); also published a novel, *Iffi: Roman einer Tänzerin* (Iffi: Novel of a Dancer, 1951); best remembered for having transformed the Viennese waltz from a monotonous one-two-three movement, performed by smiling dancers laced into corsets, into an ecstatic experience, performed by dancers with unbound hair and swinging dresses. ❖ See also *Women in World History.*

WIESMAN, Linden (1975—). American equestrian. Born Jan 23, 1975, in Columbia, Tennessee. ❖ Won a bronze medal for eventing at Sydney Olympics (2000), on Anderoo.

WIFSTRAND, Naima (1890–1968). Swedish actress and acting school founder. Born Sept 4, 1890, in Stockholm, Sweden; died Oct 23, 1968, in Stockholm. ❖ Joined Anna Lundberg traveling theatrical troupe (1905); appeared in major roles in the operettas of Emmerich Kálmán and Franz Lehár; toured Sweden in Bertolt Brecht's *Threepenny Opera* (1937); translated his play *The Rifles of Senora Carrar* into Swedish and performed in the title role in Stockholm's Odeon Theater (1938); in return, Brecht wrote *Mother Courage* for her; founded an actors' school, engaging Brecht's wife Helene Weigel as a teacher (1940); starred in *Me and My Gal* with Nils Poppe at Södra Teatern (1948); worked at Malmö with Ingmar Bergman and appeared in many of his films, most notably as Mrs. Armfelt in *Sommarnattens leende* (Smiles of a Summer Night, 1955); made over 60 Swedish films.

WIGGIN, Kate Douglas (1856–1923). American educator and writer. Born Kate Douglas Smith, Sept 28, 1856, in Philadelphia, Pennsylvania; died in Harrow, England, Aug 24, 1923; dau. of Robert Noah Smith and Helen Elizabeth (Dyer) Smith; sister of Nora Archibald Smith (educator); graduate of Emma J. C. Marwedel's Kindergarten Training School, Los Angeles, 1878; m. Samuel Bradley Wiggin, Dec 28, 1881 (died 1889); m. George Christopher Riggs, Mar 30, 1895. ❖ Kindergarten pioneer and author of children's books, who is best known for writing the classic *Rebecca of Sunnybrook Farm* (1903); with sister, organized Silver Street Kindergarten in San Francisco (1879) and California Kindergarten Training School (1880); to raise funds for her kindergarten, published

The Birds' Christmas Carol (1887), which was hugely successful; quickly emerged as one of the most popular writers of children's books in US; other writings for children include *The Story of Patsy* (1883), *Timothy's Quest* (1890) and *Mother Carey's Chickens* (1911); also wrote *A Cathedral Courtship* (1893), *Penelope's English Experiences* (1900) and (with Nora Smith) *Kindergarten Principles and Practice* (1896); edited with Nora Smith, a 5-vol. collection of fairy tales and fables: *The Fairy Ring* (1906), *Magic Casements* (1907), *Tales of Laughter* (1908), *Tales of Wonder* (1909), and *The Talking Beasts* (1911). ❖ See also autobiography *My Garden of Memory* (1923); Nora Archibald Smith, *Kate Douglas Wiggin as Her Sister Knew Her* (Houghton, 1925); and *Women in World History*.

WIGGINS, Myra Albert (1869–1956). American artist, photographer, and writer. Born 1869 in Salem, Oregon; died 1956 in Seattle, Washington; educated at Art Students League, 1891–93; m. Fred Wiggins, in 1894; children: 1 daughter. ❖ Was an amateur photographer (1888–1929), with work exhibited internationally; began publishing photographs in periodicals (1903); admitted to Photo-Secession group; had retrospectives of paintings at Seattle Art Museum (1953) and M.H. De Young Memorial Museum in San Francisco (1954); daughter donated 400 of Wiggins' photographs to Portland (Oregon) art museum, and a major exhibition of these works was held in early 1990s. ❖ See also *Women in World History*.

WIGHTMAN, Hazel Hotchkiss (1886–1974). American tennis player. Name variations: Hazel Hotchkiss; Mrs. George W. Wightman; Mrs. Wightie. Born Hazel Hotchkiss in Healdsburg, CA, Dec 20, 1886; died Dec 5, 1974, in Chestnut Hill, MA; m. George William Wightman (lawyer), 1912 (div. 1940). ❖ Won 44 national titles, more than any other player in the history of the game; won gold medals for doubles and mixed doubles at Paris Olympics (1924); played her last national tournament at age 73. The Hazel Hotchkiss Wightman Trophy or Wightman Cup (given to the winner of a match between British and Americans) was named in her honor; inducted into International Tennis Hall of Fame (1957); made honorary Commander of the British Empire by Queen Elizabeth II (1973). ❖ See also *Women in World History*.

WIGMAN, Mary (1886–1973). German dancer. Name variations: Wiegmann. Pronunciation: VEEG-mahn. Born Mary Wiegmann, Nov 13, 1886, in Hannover, Germany; died Sept 18, 1973, in Berlin; dau. of a businessman and Amalie Wiegmann; never married; no children. ❖ Helped create the art form of modern dance with its emphasis on movement as an articulation of personal expression, emotions, and profound truths; enrolled for dance training in school of Emile-Jacques Dalcroze in Dresden-Hellerau (1910); attended summer dance school taught by Rudolf Van Laban in Ascona, Switzerland (1913); made choreographic debut (1914); left Laban school to open own studio (1919); eschewed the principles of ballet to expose the unformulated, natural expression of the human body, and thereby became one of the preeminent founders of the German form of modern dance known as *Ausdruckstanz*; established dance group (1923); dancing with masks, and bringing movement to abstract ideas, aroused public adulation with her riveting solos and innovative choreography; made 1st tour of US under direction of Sol Hurok (1930–31); with Gret Palucca, Harald Kreutzberg and Dorothee Günther, choreographed "Olympic Youth" under Nazi supervision for Berlin Olympics (1936); retired from performing (1942); served as teacher and choreographer (1949–67), until the closing of her school in West Berlin; taught Yvonne Georgi, Gret Palucca and Harald Kreutzberg, all crucial to the development of German modern dance, and Hanya Holm who conveyed her style and methods to America; works choreographed include *Witch Dances Without Music* (1914), *Seven Dances of Life* (1922–23), *Ecstatic Dances* (1919), *Scenes from a Dance Drama* (1924), *Shifting Landscape* (1929), *Choric Movement* (1929), *Totenmal* (1930), *Dance of Silent Joy* (1934), and *Farewell and Thanksgiving* (1942). Received Great Cross of the Order of Merit (Grosses Bundesverdienstkreuz) of German Federal Republic (1957). ❖ See also Susan A. Manning, *Ecstasy and the Demon: Feminism and Nationalism in the Dances of Mary Wigman* (U. of California Press, 1993); Walter Sorell, ed. and trans., *The Mary Wigman Book* (Wesleyan U. Press, 1973); "Mary Wigman 1886–1973: When the Fire Dances Between Two Poles" (documentary by Allegra Fuller Synder and Annette MacDonald, 1991); and *Women in World History*

WIGNELL, Ann Brunton. *See Merry, Ann Brunton.*

WIGNOLLE, Yvonne (1894–1977). *See Printemps, Yvonne.*

WIJENAIKE, Punyakanthi (1935—). Sri Lankan novelist and short-story writer. Born 1935 in Sri Lanka. ❖ Works include *The Third Woman and Other Stories* (1963), *The Waiting Earth* (1966), *Giraya* (1971), *The Rebel* (1979), *Way of Life* (1987), *Amulet* (1994) and *An Enemy Within* (1998); also published stories in Sri Lankan English-language journals and newspapers.

WIJNBERG, Rosalie (1887–1973). Dutch gynecologist. Born 1887 in Netherlands; died 1973. ❖ The Dutch Society of Surgery's 4th female member, studied gynecology with Professor Treub in Amsterdam; established the Dutch Society of Women Doctors (1933); during WWII, because she was Jewish, was transported to the Westerbork concentration camp, where, as the only doctor there, refused to obey orders to sterilize Jewish women involved in mixed marriages.

WIJSMULLER-MEIJER, Truus (c. 1896–1978). Dutch hero. Name variations: Gertrude Wijsmuller; Geertruida or Gertruida Wijsmuller-Mejer; Gertruida Wijsmuller-Meijer; Truus Wijsmuller-Meijer; Truus Wysmuller. Born c. 1896; died in Amsterdam in 1978; married a banker. ❖ A Christian, became a key participant in the Kindertransport system that helped German-Jewish children to safety by finding them temporary and, if at all possible, permanent places of refuge in the Netherlands and United Kingdom; went to Nazi-occupied Vienna on behalf of the Council for German Jewry (1938), a British organization, and negotiated for the release of 600 Viennese-Jewish children through the Kindertransport program; when German troops approached Amsterdam (1940), filled 5 buses with 200 Jewish refuges, then persuaded the captain of the *Bodegraven*, a Dutch freighter set to sail for England, to accept them; took on a leadership role in the underground network that over the next 5 years would find ways to smuggle thousands of endangered Jews across Nazi-occupied Europe into neutral Spain and Switzerland. ❖ See also autobiography in Dutch (with L.C. Vrooland), *Geen tijd voor tranen* (No Time for Tears, 2nd ed., 1963); and *Women in World History*.

WILBER, Doreen (1930—). American archer. Born Jan 8, 1930, in Iowa. ❖ At Munich Olympics, won a gold medal in double FITA round (1972), the 1st woman to win an Olympic gold medal in individual archery championship; placed 2nd in World championships (1969) and was 4-time winner of national championships.

WILBERFORCE, Octavia (1888–1963). British physician. Born 1888 in Lavington, Sussex, England; died 1963 in Brighton; dau. of Reginald Wilberforce and Anna Wilberforce; great-granddau. of William Wilberforce, leader of the anti-slavery movement in England, and granddau. of Samuel Wilberforce, bishop of Winchester; educated at the London School of Medicine, 1913–14. ❖ Pioneer in the field of women's health, was disinherited when she pursued a career against parents' wishes; began treating men who had been injured on the battlefields of World War I at St. Mary's Hospital (1914); with Elizabeth Robins and Louisa Martindale, established the 50-bed New Sussex Hospital for Women (mid-1920s), and served as head physician until 1954; also founded a convalescent home for working women in the country town of Backsettown, near Brighton, that was designed to educate its patients in health practices. ❖ See also *Women in World History*.

WILBURN, Margaret (1935—). *See Matthews, Margaret.*

WILCOX, Ella Wheeler (1850–1919). American poet and journalist. Born Ella Wheeler in Johnstown Center, Rock County, near Madison, Wisconsin, Nov 5, 1850; died in Short Beach, Connecticut, Oct 30, 1919; attended University of Wisconsin, 1867–68; m. Robert Marius Wilcox, 1884 (died 1916); children: 1 son (died at birth). ❖ Following marriage, moved to New York, where she became a successful contributor to magazines and wrote many short essays for the *New York Journal* and *Chicago American*; her populist career was ensured when one Chicago firm refused to publish a collection of her love poems, *Poems of Passion*, calling them immoral; soon dubbed "Poetess of Passion," sold 60,000 copies of the book (1883); produced over 20 vols. of verse and contributed a daily poem for newspaper syndication; writings include *Drops of Water* (1872), *Sweet Danger* (1902), *The Heart of New Thought* (about spiritualism, 1902), and *The Art of Being Alive* (1914). ❖ See also autobiographies, *The Story of a Literary Career* (1905) and *The Worlds and I* (1918); and *Women in World History*.

WILCOX, Elsie Hart (1879–1954). American politician. Born Mar 22, 1879, in Hanalei, Kauai, Hawaii; died June 30, 1954, in Hawaii; dau. of Samuel Whitney Wilcox (businessman) and Emma Washburn (Lyman)

Wilcox; graduate of Wellesley College, 1902. ❖ The 1st woman to serve in the Territory of Hawaii senate, was active in community service, particularly in the area of public education; served as chair of International Institute of the YWCA (1919); served on Commission on Public Instruction (1920–32); helped organize 1st Pan-Pacific Women's Conference (1928); elected to Territorial Senate on Republican ticket (1932), served as vice-president of the senate (1935) and on the judiciary committee and as chair of the health and education committee (1937–39); defeated in 1940 election after several defections from Republican Party eroded her base of political support; active in Hawaiian Evangelical Association and other community organizations. ❖ See also *Women in World History.*

WILCOX, Lisa (1966—). American equestrian. Born Sept 8, 1966, in Thousand Oaks, CA. ❖ Won a bronze medal for team dressage at Athens Olympics (2004).

WILD, Anke (1967—). German field-hockey player. Born Oct 12, 1967. ❖ At Barcelona Olympics, won a silver medal in team competition (1992).

WILD, Eleonora (1969—). Yugoslavian basketball player. Born June 9, 1969. ❖ At Seoul Olympics, won a silver medal in team competition (1988).

WILD, Ute (1965—). East German rower. Born June 14, 1965. ❖ At Seoul Olympics, won a gold medal in coxed eights (1988).

WILDE, Florence M. (1836–1914). *See Leslie, Miriam Folline Squier.*

WILDE, Fran (1948—). New Zealand politician. Born Fran Kitching, Nov 11, 1948, in Wellington, NZ; m. Geoff Wilde, 1968 (div.); children: (adopted) 3. ❖ Served as Labour MP for Wellington Central (1981–92), sponsoring bills on homosexual law reform and adult adoption information; named the 1st woman whip in New Zealand Parliament; became an associate minister (1987); became minister of Disarmament and minister of Tourism, and associate minister of External Relations and Trade (1990); elected mayor of Wellington (1992) and resigned from Parliament.

WILDE, Jane (1821–1896). Irish writer. Name variations: Jane Francesca Elgee; Lady Anna Francesca Wilde; Lady Jane Wilde; (pseudonyms) John Fanshawe Ellis, Albanus or A, and Speranza. Born Jane Francesca Elgee, probably on Dec 27, 1821; died in London, England, Feb 3, 1896; dau. of Charles and Sarah (Kingsbury) Elgee; m. William Wilde (ophthalmic surgeon), Nov 12, 1851 (died 1876); children: William (Willie) Wilde (1852–1899, who was once m. to Miriam Folline Squier Leslie); Oscar Wilde (1854–1900, the writer); Isola Wilde (1857–1867). ❖ Irish nationalist writer who was the mother of Oscar Wilde, wrote 1st poem for *The Nation* (1846); published this and subsequent items under pseudonyms—John Fanshawe Ellis, Albanus or A—before finally settling on the pen name which made her famous, Speranza; between 1846 and 1848, wrote most of her best-known poems, which included "The Lament," "The Stricken Land," "The Exodus" and "The Brothers"; translated Meinhold's *Sidonia the Sorceress* (1849), which greatly influenced the pre-Raphaelites and was one of son Oscar's favorite stories; also wrote regularly for *Dublin University Magazine*; was involved with 2 dramatic court trials (1848 and 1864); began to hold soirées or *conversazioni* at her house in Merrion Square (1860s), which soon became the most celebrated salon in Dublin; when Oscar was charged with homosexual offenses (1895), urged him not to flee the country; also wrote *Ancient Legends, Mystic Charms and Superstitions of Ireland* (1887), *Notes on Men, Women and Books* (1891) and *Social Studies* (1893). ❖ See also Joy Melville, *Mother of Oscar: The Life of Jane Francesca Wilde* (John Murray, 1994); Horace Wyndham, *Speranza: A Biography of Lady Wilde* (Boardman, 1951); and *Women in World History.*

WILDEN, Rita (1947—). West German runner. Name variations: Rita Jahn. Born Rita Jahn, Oct 9, 1947, in Leipzig, Germany. ❖ At Munich Olympics, won a bronze medal in 4 x 400-meter relay and a silver medal in 400 meters (1972).

WILDER, Cherry (1930–2002). *See Grimm, Cherry Barbara.*

WILDER, Laura Ingalls (1867–1957). American writer. Name variations: Bess or Bessie. Born Laura Elizabeth Ingalls, Feb 7, 1867, in Pepin, Wisconsin; died at Rocky Ridge Farm in Mansfield, Missouri, Feb 10, 1957; dau. of Charles Philip Ingalls (frontiersman, farmer, and carpenter) and Caroline Quiner Ingalls (teacher); m. Almanzo James Wilder (farmer), 1885; children: Rose Wilder Lane (1886–1968, writer); and 1 son who died shortly after birth. ❖ Author of the enormously popular

"Little House" books, a series of award-winning children's novels based on her own late 19th-century frontier childhood; traveled with her family on an 11-year migration, zigzagging back and forth across the Midwest and the Great Plains in search of a piece of land that would grant them a living (1868–79); lived in the open prairies of Montgomery County, Kansas (1868–71), Pepin, Wisconsin (1871–74), and Walnut Grove, Minnesota (1874–79); ultimately settled in De Smet, (South) Dakota (1879), where she met and married Almanzo Wilder; moved with him to a farm outside Mansfield, Missouri, in the Ozarks (1894), where she lived until her death; wrote for *The Missouri Ruralist* (1911–24); served as secretary-treasurer of Mansfield Farm Loan Association (1919–27); from a 1930 autobiographical manuscript, "Pioneer Girl," elaborated the stories that would become the 7 "Little House" books published in her lifetime; in the chronicling of her childhood, had the active collaboration of her writer daughter, Rose Wilder Lane; also wrote a book about the childhood of Almanzo Wilder; writings include *Little House in the Big Woods* (1932), *Farmer Boy* (1933), *Little House on the Prairie* (1935), *On the Banks of Plum Creek* (1937), *By the Shores of Silver Lake* (1939), *The Long Winter* (1940), *Little Town on the Prairie* (1941), *These Happy Golden Years* (1943), (with Rose Wilder Lane) *On the Way Home: The Diary of a Trip from South Dakota to Mansfield, Missouri in 1894* (1962), and *The First Four Years* (1971). Received 6 Newbery Honor Awards; was 1st recipient (1954) of Laura Ingalls Wilder Award created by American Library Association. ❖ See also *West From Home: Letters of Laura Ingalls Wilder to Almanzo Wilder—San Francisco 1915* (1974); William Anderson, *Laura Ingalls Wilder: A Biography* (HarperCollins, 1992); William Holtz, *The Ghost in the Little House: A Life of Rose Wilder Lane* (U. of Missouri Press, 1993); John E. Miller, *Laura Ingalls Wilder's Little Town: Where History and Literature Meet* (U. Press of Kansas, 1994); and *Women in World History.*

WILDERMUTH, Ottilie (1817–1877). German short-story and children's writer. Name variations: Ottilie Rooschutz or Rooschütz. Born Ottilie Rooschütz, Feb 22, 1817, in Rottenburg, Germany; died July 12, 1877, in Tübingen; dau. of Eleanore and Gottlob Rooschütz (judge); m. David Wildermuth (teacher); children: 5, including Agnes, Adelheid and Hermann (physician). ❖ Wrote about family life in her native Swabia; writings, which were extremely popular, include *Bilder und Geschichten aus dem schwäbischen Leben* (1852, Portraits and Stories of Life in Swabia) and *Bilder aus einer bürgerlichen Familiengalerie* (1892, Portraits from a Middle-Class Family Album); also wrote a magazine for adolescents, *Der Jugendgarten.* Was the 1st woman to receive a Gold Medal for Arts and Sciences by Charles I, king of Wurttemberg.

WILDING, Cora (1888–1982). New Zealand painter, physiotherapist, health camp organizer, and youth hostel founder. Born Cora Hilda Blanche Wilding, Nov 15, 1888, in Christchurch, New Zealand; died Oct 8, 1982, in Kaikoura, New Zealand; dau. of Frederick Wilding (barrister) and Julia (Anthony) Wilding. ❖ Studied painting at Canterbury College School of Art (1907), and at Bushey School of Painting in Hertfordshire (1910); trained as physiotherapist at Dunedin School of Massage (1917), becoming one of New Zealand's first qualified physiotherapists; influenced by New Health Society and Sunlight League in England, returned home to establish Sunlight League of New Zealand, which encouraged physical fitness; organized health camps (1931–36); instrumental in founding Youth Hostels Association of New Zealand; became women's superintendent of Ford Millton Memorial Home for Children near Rangiora (1946); founded Kaikoura Art Group and was involved in mural painting; published *Murals for New Zealanders* (1946); participated in opening Cora Wilding Youth Hostel in Christchurch (1966). Named MBE (1952). ❖ See also *Dictionary of New Zealand Biography* (Vol. 4).

WILDING, Dorothy (1893–1976). British photographer. Born 1893 in Longford, England; died 1976 in England; m. Walter Portham, 1920 (div. 1932); m. Thomas "Rufus" Leighton-Pearce (designer and architect), 1932 (died 1940). ❖ Began to specialize in theatrical portrait photography in her London studio (1914); work also found its way into magazines such as *Sketch* and *Tatler*; expanded operation to 7 studios within greater London; photographed members of the royal family (1937); admitted to the Royal Photographic Society of Great Britain (1930); opened studio in New York City (1937); photographed coronation of Queen Elizabeth II (1953); retired (1957). ❖ See also *Women in World History.*

WILEY, Lee (1915–1975). American pop and jazz singer and actress. Born Oct 9, 1915, in Fort Gibson, OK; died Dec 11, 1975; m. Jess Stacy (pianist), 1944 (div.); m. Nat Tischenkel (businessman), 1966. ❖ Was featured vocalist on radio show "Kraft Music Hall" (1933–35); hired as dramatic actress for radio dramas; with such sidemen as Eddie Condon, Fats Waller, Pee Wee Russell and Bud Freeman, made groundbreaking series of recordings that were the 1st to spotlight the works of individual composers like George Gershwin, Cole Porter, Rodgers and Hart, and Harold Arlen (c. 1937–40); performed with Condon's orchestra over the Armed Services Radio Network (c. 1939–45); toured with Jess Stacy Orchestra (1944–46); was considered by many to be one of the most talented and underappreciated vocalists in US. ❖ See also *Women in World History.*

WILEY, Mildred (1901–2000). American track-and-field athlete. Name variations: Mildred Wiley Dee. Born Dec 3, 1901; died Feb 7, 2000, in Falmouth, Massachusetts. ❖ At Amsterdam Olympics, won a bronze medal in the high jump (1928).

WILEY, Vickie Orr- (1967 –). See *Orr, Vickie.*

WILHELM, Anja (1968—). German gymnast. Born Sept 26, 1968, in Wolfsburg, Germany. ❖ Won German nationals (1984, 1985, 1990); at European championships, won a bronze medal for balance beam (1987).

WILHELM, Kate (1928—). American science-fiction, mystery and short-story writer. Name variations: Mrs. Damon Knight. Born Katie Gertrude Meredith, June 8, 1928, in Toledo, OH; m. Joseph P. Wilhelm, 1947 (div. 1962); m. Damon Knight (science-fiction writer and founder of Science Fiction Writers of America), 1963 (died April 14, 2002); children: 3. ❖ Taught with husband at the Clarion SF and Fantasy Writer's Workshop for decades; works include *More Bitter Than Death* (1963), *The Clone* (with Ted Thomas, 1965), *Let the Fire Fall* (1969), *Margaret and I* (1971), *The Infinity Box* (1975), *Listen, Listen* (1981), *Huysman's Pets* (1985), *The Hamlet Trap* (1987), *Sweet, Sweet Poison* (1990), *And the Angels Sing* (1992), *For the Defense: or, Malice Prepense* (1996), *The Good Children* (1998), *The Deepest Water* (2000), and *The Clear and Convincing Proof* (2003); stories published in magazines and anthologies. Won Hugo Award for *Where Late the Sweet Birds Sang* (1976); 3-time winner of the Nebula Award.

WILHELM, Kati (1976—). German biathlete. Born Aug 2, 1976, in Schmalkalden, Germany. ❖ At World championships, won a gold meal in the sprint (2001); won gold medals for the 4 x 7.5 km relay and 7.5 km sprint and a silver medal for 10 km pursuit at Salt Lake City (2002); won a gold medal for 10 km pursuit and silver medals for 12.5 km and 4 x 6 km relay at Torino Olympics (2006).

WILHELMI, Jane Russell (1911–1967). See *Russell, Jane Anne.*

WILHELMINA (1709–1758). Margravine of Bayreuth. Name variations: Friederike Sophie Wilhelmine. Born Frederica Sophia Wilhelmina in 1709; died 1758; dau. of Sophia Dorothea of Brunswick-Lüneburg-Hanover (1687–1757) and Frederick William I (1688–1740), king of Prussia (r. 1713–1740); sister of Frederick II the Great (1712–1786), king of Prussia; m. Frederick, margrave of Bayreuth. ❖ Throughout childhood and adult life, was extremely close to brother Frederick II the Great. ❖ See also *Women in World History.*

WILHELMINA (1880–1962). Queen of the Netherlands. Born Wilhelmina Helen Pauline Mary in The Hague, the Netherlands, Aug 31, 1880; died at Het Loo, in Apeldoorn, Gelderland, Nov 28, 1962; dau. of William III (1817–1890), king of the Netherlands (r. 1849–1890) and grand duke of Luxemburg, and his 2nd wife, Emma of Waldeck (1858–1934); m. Henry (or Heinrich) Wladimir Albert Ernst, duke of Mecklenburg-Schwerin, on Feb 7, 1901 (died 1934); children: Juliana (b. April 30, 1909), queen of the Netherlands (r. 1948–1980). ❖ Queen who, during her long reign, won the respect of her people for her intelligence and strength of character and became the living symbol of her country during its occupation in World War II; at 10, became queen of the Netherlands (1890), under the regency of her mother; coming of age, was crowned at Amsterdam (Sept 6, 1898); earnestly desired to better the lives of all her people and was a strong advocate of progressive social doctrines; during WWI, stood firm in her declaration that the Netherlands would maintain its neutrality; was one of the 1st world leaders to condemn Nazi treatment of European Jews; after German troops crossed the Dutch frontier, fled to Britain and sent daughter to Canada (1940); encouraged Dutch resistance through radio broadcasts (1941–45); addressed the US Congress, the 1st reigning queen to do so (1942); returned to the Netherlands (1945); strengthened the link between her people, her government and herself; at 60, abdicated in favor of her daughter, assuming the title Princess of the Netherlands (Sept 4, 1948); throughout her reign, insisted that decency and morality should govern

diplomacy between nations. ❖ See also autobiography *Lonely But Not Alone* (McGraw-Hill, 1960); A. J. Barnouw, *Holland under Queen Wilhelmina* (Scribner, 1923); Philip Paneth, *Queen Wilhelmina: Mother of the Netherlands* (Alliance, 1943); and *Women in World History.*

WILHELMINA CAROLINA (1683–1737). See *Caroline of Ansbach.*

WILHELMINA OF BRUNSWICK (1673–1742). Holy Roman empress of Austria. Name variations: Amalia Wilhelmine of Brunswick-Lüneburg. Born April 21, 1673; died April 10, 1742; dau. of John Frederick (b. 1625), duke of Brunswick-Luneburg, and Benedicte Henriette Philippine (1652–1730); m. Joseph I (1678–1705), Holy Roman emperor (r. 1705–1711); children: Marie Josepha (1699–1757), who m. Augustus III, king of Poland).

WILHELMINA OF PRUSSIA (1751–1820). Princess of Orange. Born Frederica Sophia Wilhelmine on Aug 7, 1751, in Potsdam, Brandenburg, Germany; died June 9, 1820; dau. of Augustus William (brother of Frederick II the Great) and Louise of Brunswick-Wolfenbuttel (1722–1780); m. William V (1748–1806), prince of Orange (r. 1751–1795, though he succeeded to the throne in 1751 did not actually begin ruling until 1766, deposed), on Oct 4, 1767; children: Frederica Louise (1770–1819); William I (1772–1843), king of the Netherlands (r. 1813–1840); Frederick (1774–1799).

WILHELMINA OF PRUSSIA (1774–1837). See *Frederica Wilhelmina of Prussia.*

WILHELMINA ZAHRINGEN (1788–1836). See *Wilhelmine of Baden.*

WILHELMINE (1650–1706). Electress Palatine. Born Wilhelmine Ernestine on June 20, 1650; died April 22, 1706; dau. of Sophie Amalie of Brunswick-Lüneberg (1628–1685) and Frederick III (1609–1670), king of Denmark and Norway (r. 1648–1670); m. Charles II, elector Palatine, on Sept 20, 1671.

WILHELMINE (1747–1820). Electress of Hesse. Born Wilhelmina Caroline on July 10, 1747; died Jan 14, 1820; dau. of Louise of England (1724–1751) and Frederick V (1723–1766), king of Denmark and Norway (r. 1746–1766); m. William IX, elector of Hesse-Cassel, on Sept 1, 1764; children: Marie Frederica of Hesse-Cassel (1768–1839, who m. Alexis Frederick, prince of Anhalt-Bernburg); Caroline Amelia of Hesse-Cassel (1771–1848, who m. Emile Leopold, duke of Saxe-Gotha); Frederick (b. 1772); William II, elector of Hesse (b. 1777).

WILHELMINE (1808–1891). Princess of Schleswig-Holstein. Name variations: Wilhelmine Oldenburg. Born Wilhelmine Marie on June 18, 1808, in Kiel; died May 30, 1891, in Glucksborg; dau. of Marie Sophie of Hesse-Cassel (1767–1852) and Frederick VI, king of Denmark (r. 1808–1839); became 1st wife of Frederick VII (1808–1863), king of Denmark (r. 1848–1863), on Nov 1, 1828 (sep. 1837); m. Charles, prince of Schleswig-Holstein, on May 19, 1838. ❖ Frederick VII's 2nd wife was Caroline of Mecklenburg-Strelitz (1821–1876).

WILHELMINE OF BADEN (1788–1836). Grand duchess of Hesse-Darmstadt. Name variations: Wilhelmina von Baden; Wilhelmina Zahringen. Born Sept 10, 1788; died Jan 27, 1836; dau. of Charles Louis (b. 1755), margrave of Baden, and Amalie of Hesse-Darmstadt (1754–1832); sister of Frederica Dorothea of Baden (1781–1826), queen of Sweden; m. Ludwig also known as Louis II, grand duke of Hesse-Darmstadt, on June 19, 1804; children: (1st m.) Louise III, grand duke of Hesse-Darmstadt (1806–1877); Charles of Hesse-Darmstadt (1809–1877); Alexander of Hesse-Darmstadt (1823–1888); (with August Ludwig Senarclans-Grancy) Marie of Hesse-Darmstadt (1824–1880). ❖ See also *Women in World History.*

WILHELMINE OF DARMSTADT (1765–1796). Bavarian royal. Name variations: Augusta Wilhelmine of Hesse-Darmstadt. Born April 14, 1765, in Darmstadt; died Mar 30, 1796, near Heidelberg, Germany; became 1st wife of Maximilian I Joseph (1756–1825), elector of Bavaria (r. 1799–1805), king of Bavaria (r. 1805–1825), on Sept 30, 1785; children: Ludwig I also known as Louis I Augustus (1786–1868), king of Bavaria (r. 1825–1848); Amalie Auguste (1788–1851); Caroline Augusta of Bavaria (1792–1873); Charles (1795–1875); Amelia (1790–1794).

WILKE, Marina (1958—). East German rower. Born Feb 28, 1958. ❖ Won a gold medal at Montreal Olympics (1976) and a gold medal at Moscow Olympics (1980), both in coxed eights.

WILKER, Gertrud (1924–1984). Swiss poet and novelist. Born Mar 18, 1924, in Solothurn, Switzerland; died Sept 25, 1984, in

Herrenschwanden, Switzerland; grew up in Berne; dau. of Max Hürsch (customs officer); studied in Berne, Paris and Zurich, earning a PhD, 1950. ❖ Spent years dealing with depression caused by an incurable illness; works, which address such themes as nuclear power, modern technology, and consumerism, include *Wolfsschatten* (1966), *Collages USA* (1968), *Altläger* (1971), *Flaschenpost* (1977), *Blick auf meinesgleichen* (1979), and *Nachleben* (1980).

WILKES, Debbi (c. 1947—). Canadian pairs skater. Born c. 1947 in Canada. ❖ With partner Guy Revell, won Canadian nationals (1963, 1964), North American championships (1963) and a bronze medal at Innsbruck Olympics (1964); became a sports columnist, commentator and wrote *Ice Time* (1994) and *The Figure Skating Book* (1999).

WILKIE, Caroline (c. 1832–1857). See Chevalier, Caroline.

WILKINS, Brooke (1974—). Australian softball player. Born June 6, 1974, in Penrith, NSW, Australia. ❖ Won team bronze medals at Atlanta Olympics (1996) and Sydney Olympics (2000) and a team silver medal at Athens Olympics (2004).

WILKINS, Mary Eleanor (1852–1930). See Freeman, Mary E. Wilkins.

WILKINSON, Anne (1910–1961). Canadian poet. Born Anne Gibbons, Sept 21, 1910, in Toronto, Ontario, Canada; died of cancer, May 10, 1961, in Toronto; m. Frederick Robert Wilkinson, 1932 (div. 1954); children: 3. ❖ Attended schools in US and France; was founding editor and patron of *The Tamarack Review*; works include *Counterpoint to Sleep* (1951), *The Hangman Ties the Holly* (1955), *Lions in the Way: A Discursive History of the Oslers* (1956), and *Swan and Daphne* (1960); *The Collected Poems of Anne Wilkinson and a Prose Memoir* published posthumously (1968).

WILKINSON, Dolores (c. 1890–1975). See Dolores.

WILKINSON, Ellen (1891–1947). English trade union organizer, feminist agitator, and politician. Name variations: Red Ellen. Born Ellen Cicely Wilkinson, Oct 8, 1891, in Ardwick district of city of Manchester, England; died in London, Feb 6, 1947; dau. of Richard Wilkinson (insurance agent) and Ellen (Wood) Wilkinson; graduate of University of Manchester, 1913; never married; no children. ❖ Was involved in politics and women's movement in her teens; became Manchester organizer for National Union of Women Suffrage Societies (1913); was a full-time women's organizer for Amalgamated Union of Co-operative Employees (later National Union of Distributive and Allied Workers [NUDAW], 1915–24); served as member of Parliament for Middlesbrough East (1924–31); increasingly known by such terms as the "fiery particle," the "elfin fury," and, most often, "Red Ellen," was heavily involved in the General Strike of May 1926; was made the parliamentary private secretary to Susan Lawrence, a junior minister (1929); was an official of NUDAW (1931–35); served as a member of Parliament for Jarrow (1935–47), an area suffering heavy unemployment; was a leader of the Jarrow Crusade, the single most important aspect of her public life, when the men of Jarrow marched into history, an abiding image of interwar unemployment (1936); served as junior minister in the coalition government (1940–45), 1st at the Ministry of Pensions (May–Oct 1940) and then the Ministry of Home Security (Oct 1940–May 1945); appointed to the Cabinet, only the 2nd woman to rise to this position, serving as minister of Education in the Labour government (1945–47); writings include *Clash* (1929), *Peeps at Politicians* (1930), *The Division Bell Mystery* (1932), (with Edward Conze) *Why Facism?* (1934) and *The Town that was Murdered: The Life-Story of Jarrow* (1939). ❖ See also Betty Vernon, *Ellen Wilkinson* (Croom Helm, 1982); Tom Pickard, *Jarrow March* (Allison & Busby, 1982); and *Women in World History*.

WILKINSON, Iris (1906–1939). New Zealand writer. Name variations: (pseudonyms) Robin Hyde; Novitia. Born Iris Guiver Wilkinson on Jan 19, 1906, in Cape Town, South Africa; at 33, took an overdose of pain medication and died in a hospital in London, England, Aug 23, 1939; dau. of George Edward Wilkinson (English-born civil servant) and Edith Ellinor (Butler) Wilkinson (Australian); attended Victoria University College; never married; children: Derek Challis (b. 1930). ❖ One of the best-known journalists of New Zealand, was also a celebrated poet and novelist; relocated with family to New Zealand (1906); stricken with crippling arthritis (1924), suffered excruciating pain in her legs for the rest of her life and could not walk without crutches; under pen-name Novitia, wrote a women's column on Parliamentary proceedings for *Dominion,* a pro-Conservative Party daily newspaper (1924–26); became pregnant (1926) and gave birth to a stillborn baby; hospitalized several

times as a borderline psychotic, became addicted to morphine and other painkillers; committed herself to a mental institution (1927); began writing under pseudonym Robin Hyde; contributed articles to *Christchurch Press* and the *Sun*; also wrote book reviews and a regular society column for *Auckland Mirror*; was the women's editor for *The Wanganui Chronicle* (1929–30); published 1st book of poetry, *The Desolate Star* (1929), which brought her a national readership; worked for *The New Zealand Observer* in Auckland (1930–33); attempted suicide (1933), after which she was hospitalized as a mental patient; reestablished her writing career, publishing more poetry and her 1st two novels (mid-1930s); in her last few years, wrote autobiographical and historical novels and travel pieces, all of which continue one of the overriding themes of her writings; often wrote against the oppression of the Maori and of the need for economic and social equity for women; while in China (1938), sent back accounts of the destruction caused by the invading Japanese army; published autobiographical *The Godwit's Fly* (1938), followed by book on China, *Dragon Rampant* (1939), which achieved considerable acclaim. Her last book, a collection of poems, was published by her son as *Houses by the Sea* (1952), considered her finest work. ❖ See also Gillian Boddy and Jacqueline Matthews, eds. *Disputed Ground: Robin Hyde, Journalist* (Victoria University Press, 1991); *Dictionary of New Zealand Biography* (Vol. 4); and *Women in World History*.

WILKINSON, Jemima (1752–1819). American religious leader. Born Jemima Wilkinson, Nov 29, 1752, in Cumberland, Rhode Island; died at Jerusalem, near Seneca Lake, New York, July 1, 1819; dau. of Jeremiah Wilkinson (farmer and member of the Colony Council) and Elizabeth Amey (Whipple) Wilkinson; had some public school education; never married; no children. ❖ While suffering a severe illness (1775), believed she died and was "reanimated" by the spirit and power of Jesus; took the name "The Public Universal Friend" and began to speak at open-air meetings where the spirit of her personality rather than the content of her words held her audience captive; preached the elevation of the state of celibacy over marriage, the importance of the church over family, and asserted she was Jesus Christ come again; traveled a circuit through Rhode Island and Connecticut, preaching her message, founding churches in New Milford, Connecticut, and East Greenwich and South Kingston, Rhode Island (1777–82); transferred headquarters to Philadelphia (1783), where she published *The Universal Friend's Advice, to Those of the Same Religious Society, Recommended to be read in their Public Meetings*; on a large parcel of land in Yates County near Seneca Lake in western New York state, established a colony called Jerusalem (1790). ❖ See also Herbert A. Wisbey, *Pioneer Prophetess: Jemima Wilkinson, the Publick Universal Friend* (Cornell U. Press, 1964); and *Women in World History*.

WILKINSON, Laura (1977—). American diver. Born Nov 17, 1977, in Houston, TX; attended University of Texas. ❖ Won a gold medal for platform at Sydney Olympics (2000); was 10-time US national champion.

WILKINSON, Marguerite Ogden (1883–1928). Canadian-born American poet. Born Marguerite Ogden Bigelow, Nov 15, 1883, in Halifax, Nova Scotia, Canada; drowned while swimming in ocean off Coney Island, NY, Jan 12, 1928; dau. of Nathan Kellogg Bigelow and Gertrude (Holmes) Bigelow; educated at Northwestern University; m. James G. Wilkinson (school administrator), 1909. ❖ Published several volumes of poetry, beginning with *In Vivid Gardens* (1911); became poetry reviewer for *The New York Times Book Review* (c. 1915); published *New Voices* (1919), an anthology of modern poetry, to critical acclaim; lectured on modern poetry at schools, library associations, and women's clubs; writings include *By a Western Wayside* (1912), *Golden Songs of the Golden State* (1917), *The Dingbat of Arcady* (1922), *Contemporary Poetry* (1923), *Yule Fire* (1925) and *Citadels* (1928). ❖ See also *Women in World History*.

WILKINSON, Martha (1948—). See Kirouac, Martha Wilkinson.

WILLARD, Emma Hart (1787–1870). American educator, writer and founder. Born Emma Hart, Feb 23, 1787, in Berlin, Connecticut; died April 15, 1870, at Troy, New York; dau. of Samuel Hart (Revolutionary War hero) and Lydia (Hinsdale) Hart; older sister of Almira Lincoln Phelps (1793–1884), educator; m. Dr. John Willard, 1809 (died 1825); m. Christopher Yates (physician), 1838 (div. 1843); children: (1st m.) John Hart Willard (b. 1810). ❖ Founder of Troy Seminary, writer of textbooks, and partisan for the common-school movement who advocated female control of women's education with support from public funds and promoted change while urging stability during a boisterous historical era; studied at one of the 1st academies in Connecticut; began teaching at age 17; opened a boarding school for girls in her home (1814); presented plan for a female seminary to New York State Legislature (1819); opened Troy Seminary in NY (1821); founded the Willard Association for the Mutual Improvement of Female Teachers (1837); wrote history textbooks; attempted, unsuccessfully, to establish seminaries for teachers in Greece; granted a divorce by the Connecticut Legislature (1843); elected superintendent of the common schools in Kensington, Connecticut (1840); toured extensively as a speaker for teachers' institutes (1845–46); without openly rebelling against a culture determined to teach women to "know their place," developed political strategies for enlarging and expanding their dominion under the guise of defending society; writings include *A Plan for Improving Female Education* (1819), *Advancement of Female Education: Or, a series of Addresses in Favor of Establishing at Athens, In Greece, A French Seminary, Especially Designed to Instruct Female Teachers* (1833), *History of the United States or Republic of America* (1830) and *Morals for the Young or, Good Principles Instilling Wisdom* (1857). ❖ See also John Lord, *Life of Emma Willard* (Appleton, 1873); Alma Lutz, *Emma Willard: Daughter of Democracy* (Houghton, 1929); and *Women in World History*.

WILLARD, Frances E. (1839–1898). American reformer. Born Frances Elizabeth Caroline Willard, Sept 28, 1839, in Churchville, New York; died in New York, NY, Feb 17, 1898; dau. of Josiah Willard (farmer) and Mary (Hill) Willard (teacher); attended Milwaukee Normal Institute (1 term), North Western Female College (3 terms, Laureate of Science, 1860); never married; lived with Anna Adams Gordon (1853–1931); no children. ❖ President of the Woman's Christian Temperance Union (WCTU), who actively advocated for the prohibition of alcohol and other reforms affecting women, including the "home protection ballot"; served as president, Northwestern University's Ladies College (1871–74); served as president, Chicago Woman's Christian Temperance Union (1874–76); was secretary, National WCTU (1874–77); as leader of the 1st great organization of American women, served as president, Illinois WCTU (1878), National WCTU (1879–98), and World WCTU (1891–97), expanding the WCTU, founded just 5 years before she became president, into a national and international political force; urged the adoption of a "home protection ballot" so that women could vote against the establishment of saloons in their neighborhoods, and eventually supported women's right to the full franchise; argued for women to be ordained as ministers in churches and included in church government; embraced diet and exercise fads as well as dress reform; worked with WCTU to establish day nurseries for poor working women, and endorsed the free kindergarten movement, federal aid to education to compel Southern states to educate blacks, and a department of hygiene to study municipal sanitation; lobbied for "social evil reform," to raise the age of consent, hold men equally guilty in prostitution offenses, and strengthen and enforce laws against rape; and personally supported the labor movement and Christian socialism; writings include *Nineteen Beautiful Years* (1863), *Woman and Temperance* (1883), *Woman in the Pulpit* (1888), *Glimpses of Fifty Years: The Autobiography of an American Woman* (1889), *Evanston: A Classic Town: The Story of Evanston by an Old-Timer* (1891), *A Wheel Within a Wheel: How I Learned to Ride the Bicycle* (1895) and (ed. with Mary Livermore) *A Woman of the Century* (1893). Inducted into the Women's Hall of Fame at Seneca Falls (2000). ❖ See also Ruth Bordin, *Frances Willard: A Biography* (U. of North Carolina Press, 1986); and *Women in World History*.

WILLARD, Marlene (1934—). See Mathews, Marlene.

WILLARD, Mary (1941—). American diver. Name variations: Patsy Willard. Born May 18, 1941, in Mesa, Arizona. ❖ At Tokyo Olympics, won a bronze medal in springboard (1964); also won 7 national championships.

WILLARD, Patsy (1941—). See Willard, Mary.

WILLCOX, Sheila (1936—). English equestrian. Name variations: Sheila Waddington; Mrs. J. Waddington; Sheila Willcox-Waddington. Born in 1936 in UK; m. John Waddington. ❖ On High and Mighty, became the 1st woman champion rider of all Europe, at age 21 (1957); on High and Mighty, won Badminton 3-day event Horse Trials (1957 and 1958), and was runner-up (1956); on Airs and Graces, won Badminton (1959); also won Little Badminton on Glenamoy (1964). ❖ See also autobiographies *Three Days Running* (1958) and *From the Center of the Ring* (1973) and.

WILLEBRANDT, Mabel Walker (1889–1963). American government official. Born Mabel Walker, May 23, 1889, in Woodsdale, Kansas; died April 6, 1963, in Riverside, California; dau. of David William Walker (newspaper editor) and Myrtle (Eaton) Walker (teacher); graduate of State Normal School in Tempe, Arizona, 1911; University of Southern California, LLB, 1916, LLM, 1917; m. Arthur F. Willebrandt (school administrator), Feb 1910 (div. 1924); children: (adopted) Dorothy Rae. ❖ Career as educator included positions at public schools in Buckley, Michigan, and Phoenix, Arizona, and appointments as principal at Buena Park School in Los Angeles, and Lincoln Park School in Pasadena, California; appointed head of Legal Advisory Board, District 11, Los Angeles (1914–19); admitted to the bar in California (1916); appointed assistant public defender of Los Angeles; appointed assistant attorney general of US (1921), where much of her time was spent enforcing the Prohibition laws decreed by passage of 18th Amendment, despite the fact that she was not personally in favor of the constitutional revision; earning the nickname "Prohibition Portia," argued over 40 cases before US Supreme Court; helped establish the 1st federal prison for women (c. 1925); became 1st woman to chair a committee on the Republican National Convention (1928); returned to private practice (1929); published monograph *The Inside of Prohibition* (1929); obtained pilot's license (c. 1940). ❖ See also *Women in World History*.

WILLEFORD, Mary B. (1900–1941). American nurse-midwife. Born Mary Bristow Willeford, Feb 4, 1900, in Flatonia, TX; died Dec 24, 1941, in New York, NY; dau. of Ellen (Bristow) Willeford and William Willeford; University of Texas at Austin, AB, 1920; Columbia University Teachers College, MA in public health, 1927; Columbia University, PhD, 1932. ❖ One of the 1st nurses in America to earn a doctorate, enrolled in a York Lying-In Hospital midwifery course in London (1926); began work as a district nurse-midwife at Mary Breckinridge's Frontier Nursing Service (Aug 1926); with 16 others, was a charter member of Kentucky State Association of Midwives (1928), later the American Association of Nurse-Midwives; traveled to England (1929) and earned a midwifery teaching certificate; served as the FNS assistant director (1930–38); appointed maternal and child health consultant to California State Board of Health (1938); became public health nursing consultant to the federal Children's Bureau in Washington, DC (1940), and helped to establish the Tuskegee Institute's midwifery school in Alabama.

WILLFRIED, H. (1849–1917). *See Villinger, Hermine.*

WILLIAMS, Ann (d. 1753). English murderer. Burned at the stake in Gloucester, April 13, 1753. ❖ Poisoned husband to death by adding white mercury to his gruel, apparently so that she could pursue affair with her butler.

WILLIAMS, Anna (1706–1783). English poet. Born 1706 in Rosemarket, England; died Sept 6, 1783, in London, England; dau. of Zachariah Williams (a physician and inventor, died 1755). ❖ Supported her impoverished father by taking on embroidery piecework; also assisted Stephen Grey with his rudimentary experimentation with electricity; fluent in several languages, earned much-needed funds with translation of *The Life of the Emperor Julian* (1746) from its original French; by middle age, developed cataracts which led to blindness; was provided support by her father's friend, the eminent Dr. Johnson, and his wife Elizabeth "Tetty" Porter Johnson; developed a close relationship with Johnson, and resided with him, off and on, after his wife died in 1752; when several of her poems were collected and published in *Miscellanies in Prose and Verse* (1766), earned enough money to live in reasonable comfort for the rest of her life. ❖ See also *Women in World History*.

WILLIAMS, Anna Maria (1839–1929). New Zealand teacher and school principal. Born Feb 25, 1839, at Waimate mission station, Northland, New Zealand; died May 5, 1929, in Napier, New Zealand; dau. of William Williams (missionary) and Jane (Nelson) Williams. ❖ Fluent in Maori language and culture, worked as teacher and administrator of Bishop's School, established by her father (1875–99). ❖ See also *Dictionary of New Zealand Biography* (Vol. 2).

WILLIAMS, Anna Wessels (1863–1954). American bacteriologist. Born Mar 17, 1863, in Hackensack, New Jersey; died Nov 20, 1954, in Westwood, New Jersey; dau. of William Williams (teacher) and Jane (Van Saun) Williams; graduate of New Jersey State Normal School, 1883; New York Infirmary Woman's Medical College, MD, 1891. ❖ Scientist who made possible the widespread, cost-effective production of diphtheria antitoxin and also aided in the diagnosis of rabies, joined staff of New York Infirmary upon receiving her MD (1891–1905); together with William Hallock Park, produced successful antitoxin for diphtheria (1894); produced method of determining presence of rabies in pathology (1896); served as assistant director of New York City Research

Laboratories (1905–34); wrote numerous medical papers, articles, and textbooks, including (as co-author) *Pathogenic Microorganisms Including Bacteria and Protozoa* (1905) and *Who's Who among the Microbes* (1929); elected to the laboratory section of American Public Health Association, the 1st woman to be given such office. ❖ See also *Women in World History*.

WILLIAMS, Augusta (1825–1876). See Maywood, Augusta.

WILLIAMS, Barbara. See Roles, Barbara.

WILLIAMS, Betty (1943—). Irish peace activist. Name variations: Betty Williams Perkins. Born Betty Smyth in Belfast, Northern Ireland, May 22, 1943; dau. of a butcher and a housewife; m. Ralph Williams (engineer in merchant marine), June 14, 1961; immigrated to US where she later remarried; children: (1st m.) Paul and Deborah. ❖ With Mairead Corrigan, co-founded the Irish Peace People movement of mid-1970s, the most successful of several early attempts to create a cross-community alliance against terrorism; after witnessing the tragedy of Anne Maguire and her children (see Corrigan, Mairead), organized the petition calling for the Irish Republican Army (IRA) to cease its campaign, a petition signed by many thousands of Belfast people; her courage represented the 1st real threat to the popular support on which the moral position of the terrorists depended. Received Norwegian People Peace Prize (1976) and Nobel Peace Prize (1976). ❖ See also *Women in World History*.

WILLIAMS, Betty (1944—). Welsh politician and member of Parliament. Born July 31, 1944; dau. of Griffith Williams and Elizabeth Williams; m. Evan Glyn Williams. ❖ Representing Labour, elected to House of Commons for Conwy (1997, 2001, 2005).

WILLIAMS, Camilla (1922—). African-American soprano and teacher. Born in Danville, VA, Oct 18, 1922; Virginia State College, BS, 1941; studied with Marion Szekely-Freschl, Hubert Giesen, Sergius Kagen, and Leo Taubman; m. Charles Beavers (attorney), 1950. ❖ Won the Marian Anderson Award (1943 and 1944) and Philadelphia Orchestra Youth Award (1944); made operatic debut at New York City Opera in title role of *Madama Butterfly* (1946), remaining there until 1954; also toured widely as a concert artist; taught at Brooklyn College and City College of New York (1970–73); began teaching at Indiana University School of Music in Bloomington (1977). ❖ See also *Women in World History*.

WILLIAMS, Cara (1925—). American tv and screen actress. Name variations: Bernice Kay. Born Bernice Kamiat, June 29, 1925, in Brooklyn, NY; m. John Drew Barrymore (actor), 1952 (div. 1959). ❖ Made film debut under name Bernice Kay (1941); changed name to Cara Williams (1943); films include *The Saxon Charm, Knock on Any Door, Boomerang!, The Girl Next Door, The Helen Morgan Story, The Man From the Diner's Club, Never Steal Anything Small* and *The White Buffalo*; on tv, starred on "Pete and Gladys" (1960–62) and "The Cara Williams Show" (1964). Nominated for Oscar for *The Defiant Ones* (1958).

WILLIAMS, Catherine Lucy (1839/40–1900). See Innes, Catherine Lucy.

WILLIAMS, Christa (1978—). American softball player. Born Christa Lee Williams, Feb 8, 1978, in Houston, TX. ❖ Won team gold medals at Atlanta Olympics (1996) and Sydney Olympics (2000).

WILLIAMS, Cicely (1893–1992). British physician. Born Cicely Delphine Williams in Kew Park, Jamaica, Dec 2, 1893; died in Oxford, England, July 13, 1992; dau. of Margaret (Farewell) Williams (died 1953) and James Rowland Williams (plantation owner, died 1916); Oxford University, BM, 1920; Oxford University, ChB, 1923; London University, diploma in tropical medicine and hygiene, 1929; never married; no children. ❖ Scientist who discovered kwashiorkor (protein energy malnutrition), a primary cause of early mortality; traveled to England (1906); passed the Oxford University entrance examination (1912); interned at King's College Hospital (1920); appointed house physician, South London Hospital for Women and Children (1923); worked for American Farm School, Salonika, Greece (1927); was 1st woman appointed to British Colonial Service, Gold Coast, Africa (1929); appointed head of Princess Marie Louise Hospital for Children (1930); while working with natives of West Africa, discovered kwashiorkor (1931); transferred to General Hospital, Singapore, Malaya (1936), then to Unfederated State of Trengganu (1941); during WWII, was interned in Changi Prison (1941); appointed commandant of the women's camp (Feb 1943); imprisoned by the Kempe Tai (Oct 1943–Mar 1944); served as head of the child health department, Oxford University (1948); was 1st head of the Section of Maternal and Child Health of World Health Organization (1948); undertook research into

vomiting sickness, Jamaica (1951); was a senior lecturer in nutrition at London University (1953); studied toxaemia of pregnancy, University College (1955); joined faculty of American University of Beirut, Lebanon (1960); appointed advisor in Training Programs for Family Planning Association of Great Britain (1964); joined faculty of University of Tulane (1971). Awarded Companion of the Order of St. Michael and St. George (1968). ❖ See also Sally Craddock, *Retired Except on Demand: The Life of Dr. Cicely Williams* (Green College, 1983); Ann Dally, *Cicely: The Story of a Doctor* (Gollancz, 1968); and *Women in World History*.

WILLIAMS, Clara (1888–1928). American actress. Born May 3, 1888, in Seattle, WA; died May 8, 1928, in Los Angeles, CA. ❖ Contract star with Thomas Ince, films include *The Bargain, The Italian, Hell's Hinges, Paws of the Bear* and *Carmen of the Klondike*.

WILLIAMS, Deniece (1951—). African-American singer. Born June 3, 1951, in Gary, Indiana. ❖ As young girl, sang in gospel choirs, and later was volunteer hospital nurse; auditioned for Stevie Wonder and joined his group, Wonderlove, later touring with him; released 1st solo album, *This Is Niecy* (1976), which included hit, "Free"; had #1 pop and R&B hit with "Too Much, Too Little, Too Late" (1978); released hit cover of Royalettes song, "It's Gonna take a Miracle" (1982); released *Let's Hear It for the Boy* (1984), whose title track went to #1 in pop and R&B charts, and was used in film, *Footloose* (1984); began to record gospel music, and won 2 Grammys for *So Glad I Know* (1986); other albums include *Water Under the Bridge* (1987), *Love Solves It All* (1996), and *This Is My Song* (1998), which won a Grammy; published children's book, *Lullabies to Dreamland* (1991).

WILLIAMS, Eileen Hope (1884–1958). New Zealand golfer. Name variations: Eileen Hope Lewis. Born Oct 16, 1884, in Rotorua, New Zealand; died Oct 13, 1958, in Masterton, New Zealand; dau. of Thomas Hope Lewis (surgeon) and Ellen (Fenton) Lewis; m. Guy Coldham Williams (sheepfarmer), 1905; children: 4. ❖ Learned to golf at early age and became member of Auckland Ladies' Golf Club; won numerous championships, including Australian Women's Championship (1920); managed New Zealand team that won first Tasman Cup match with Australia (1933); helped establish New Zealand Ladies' Golf Union (1911). ❖ See also *Dictionary of New Zealand Biography* (Vol. 3).

WILLIAMS, Elizabeth Sprague (1869–1922). American social worker. Born Aug 31, 1869, in Buffalo, New York; died Aug 19, 1922, in New York, NY; dau. of Frank Williams (businessman) and Olive (French) Williams (teacher); Smith College, BS, 1891; Columbia University, AM, 1896; children: (adopted) 1. ❖ Joined College Settlement as a resident (1896), and served as head worker (1898–1919); founded Mount Ivy (a summer camp for inner-city youth); founded the Lackawanna (NY) Social Center (1911); founded an orphanage in war-torn Serbia (1919). ❖ See also *Women in World History*.

WILLIAMS, Ella Gwendolen Rees (1890–1979). See Rhys, Jean.

WILLIAMS, Esther (1923—). American actress and swimmer. Born Aug 8, 1923, in Inglewood, CA; graduate of Los Angeles City College; attended University of Southern California; m. Leonard Kovner (physician, div.); m. Ben Gage (radio announcer and singer), 1945 (div.); m. Fernando Lamas (actor), 1967 (died 1982); m. Edward Bell (former professor and sometime actor). ❖ As a swimmer, won every race entered at the 1939 Women's Outdoor Swimming nationals (100-meter freestyle, 300-meter and 800-yard relays, and 100-meter breaststroke); made Olympic team (1940) but World War II intervened and summer games in Tokyo were canceled; starred in Billy Rose's Aquacade at Golden Gate International Exposition in San Francisco; as a hugely popular actress, starred in such films as *Andy Hardy's Double Life* (1942), *Bathing Beauty* (1944), *Ziegfeld Follies* (1946), *On an Island With You* (1948), *Take Me Out to the Ball Game* (1949), *Neptune's Daughter* (1948), *Pagan Love Song* (1950), *Skirts Ahoy!* (1952), *Million Dollar Mermaid* (1952), *Dangerous When Wet* (1953), *Easy to Love* (1953), *Jupiter's Darling* (1955), *The Unguarded Moment* (1956), *Raw Wind in Eden* (1958) and *The Big Show* (1961). ❖ See also autobiography *The Million Dollar Mermaid* (Simon & Schuster, 1999); and *Women in World History*.

WILLIAMS, Ethel (1863–1948). English doctor. Name variations: Ethel May Nucella Williams. Born July 8, 1863, in Cromer, Norfolk, England; died Jan 29, 1948; London School of Medicine, MD, 1895; studied at University of Vienna Medical School. ❖ The 1st woman general practitioner in Newcastle upon Tyne (1897–1924), the 1st woman in

Newcastle with a driver's license and the 1st woman in northern England to be seen driving a car (1906), was also the 1st school doctor for Gateshead High School; joined the 1st London suffragist procession (1907) and was involved with North-East Society for Women's Suffrage; served as a secretary of the Newcastle Workers' and Soldiers' Council (1917); elected vice chair and president of Federation of Medical Women; cofounded the Northern Women's Hospital in Newcastle upon Tyne.

WILLIAMS, Fannie Barrier (1855–1944). African-American lecturer and civil-rights leader. Born Feb 12, 1855, in Brockport, New York; died Mar 4, 1944, in Brockport; dau. of Anthony J. Barrier (businessman) and Harriet (Prince) Barrier; graduate of New York State Normal School in Brockport, 1870; attended New England Conservatory of Music and School of Fine Arts in Washington, DC; m. S. Laing Williams (attorney), 1887 (died 1921); no children. ❖ Taught at freedmen's schools throughout the southern US (c. 1880s); co-founded Provident Hospital and Training School for Nurses, Chicago (1891); spoke at World's Columbian Exposition (1893); co-founded National League of Colored Women (1893); inducted into Chicago Woman's Club as 1st black member (1895); co-founded National Association of Colored Women (1896); co-organized Colored Women's Conference of Chicago (1900); appointed director of Frederick Douglass Center (1905); was 1st black and 1st female elected to Chicago Library Board (1924). ❖ See also *Women in World History.*

WILLIAMS, Frances (1903–1959). American musical-comedy star. Name variations: Frances E. Williams. Born Frances Jellineck (also seen as Jellinek), Nov 3, 1901, in St. Paul, MN; died Jan 27, 1959, in New York, NY; m. Frank Malino (div.); m. Lester Clark (div.); m. Baron Miguel de Sousa (div.); m. Robert A. Wachsman (div.); m. Frank Lovejoy (actor, div.). ❖ Popular star of vaudeville and the NY stage, made Broadway debut in *Innocent Eyes* (1924); credits include *Mary, Artists and Models,* George White's *Scandals* (5 editions), *The Cocoanuts, The New Yorkers, Life Begins at 8:40, Panama Hattie, Bright Lights of 1944* and *Toplitsky of Notre Dame;* introduced the song "As Time Goes By" in *Everybody's Welcome.*

WILLIAMS, Grace (1906–1977). Welsh composer. Born Feb 19, 1906, in Barry, Wales; died Feb 10, 1977, in Barry; studied at University of Cardiff, at Royal College of Music, and in Vienna with Egon Wellesz; studied with Ralph Vaughan Williams. ❖ Was heavily influenced by Ralph Vaughan Williams and Egon Wellesz and by the work of Benjamin Britten; most noted works include *Penillion,* an early work for full orchestra based on Welsh barding songs, *Sea Sketches* (1944), a work for strings, and *The Parlour* (1961); also composed a trumpet concerto (1963), a symphony, and several works for both chorus and solo voice. ❖ See also *Women in World History.*

WILLIAMS, Hattie (1872–1942). American musical comedy dancer, actress and singer. Born 1872 in Boston, MA; died Aug 17, 1942, in the Bronx, NY. ❖ Made NY stage debut in *1492;* had soubrette roles in Gus and Max Rodgers productions, including *The Rodgers Brothers in Washington* (1901) and *The Rodgers Brothers at Harvard* (1902); performed as specialty dancer in many productions, most notably doing Spanish dance solo in *The Doll Girl* (1913); starred in *Fluffy Ruffles* (1908).

WILLIAMS, Helen Maria (1762–1827). English poet and correspondent. Born June 17, 1762, in London, England; died Dec 15, 1827, in Paris, France; dau. of Charles Williams (army officer) and Helen (Hay) Williams. ❖ Published 1st work of poetry, the romance *Edwin and Eltruda: A Legendary Tale* (1782); continued to publish both poetry and fiction during her 20s, most notably "Poem on the Slave Trade" (1788), which describes her liberal reaction to the then-legal market in human flesh and firmly cemented her acceptance within London's more radical literary circles; moved to France (1790), funding her 1st year there by translating and reworking Rousseau's novel *Julie;* quickly caught up in the political energy of the French Revolution, began a salon that drew such expatriates as Thomas Paine and Mary Wollstonecraft; also published several vols. of correspondence, among them *Letters Written in France in the Summer of 1790;* arrested as a suspected Girondist and imprisoned by Robespierre during his Reign of Terror (1793), managed to escape to Switzerland, a journey recounted in *A Tour in Switzerland* (1798); also wrote *Sketches of the State of Manners and Opinions in the French Republic* (1801) and *A Narrative of the Events Which Have Taken Place in France* (1815). ❖ See also *Women in World History.*

WILLIAMS, Hope (1897–1990). American stage star. Born Aug 11, 1897, in New York, NY; died May 3, 1990, in New York, NY; m. Dr. R. Bartow Read (div.). ❖ Made NY stage debut as Fanny Shippan in *Paris Bound* (1927), followed by *The New Yorkers, The Passing Present, Strike Me Pink, Too Good to Be True* and *The Importance of Being Earnest,* among others; best known for role of Linda Seton in *Holiday;* appeared in film *The Scoundrel* (1935).

WILLIAMS, Ivy (1877–1966). English lawyer. Born 1877 in England; died 1966 in England; Society of Oxford Home-Students, BCL, 1902, LLD, 1903; Oxford University, DCL, the 1st woman to receive that degree. ❖ Became the 1st woman to be called to the bar in England when she was accepted to the Inner Temple (1922); working as a tutor to aspiring lawyers (beginning 1920), served as a lecturer in law at her alma mater until her retirement (1945); was a delegate to The Hague Conference for the Codification of International Law (1930); wrote several books, among them *The Sources of Law in the Swiss Civil Code* (1923) and the annotated *The Swiss Civil Code: English Version* (1925). ❖ See also *Women in World History.*

WILLIAMS, Jane (c. 1801–1896). New Zealand missionary. Name variations: Jane Nelson. Born Jane Nelson (baptized, April 29, 1801, in Nottingham, England); died Oct 6, 1896, at Napier, Bay of Islands, New Zealand; dau. of James and Anna Maria (Dale) Nelson; m. William Williams, 1825 (died 1878); children: 6 daughters, 3 sons. ❖ Immigrated to New Zealand with husband (1826); established mission station at Turanga, Poverty Bay (1840); with sister-in-law, Marianne Williams, helped to establish boarding school for young Maori women and the 1st English girls' school for daughters of other missionaries; was one of last survivors of the missionary groups of 1820s. ❖ See also *Dictionary of New Zealand Biography* (Vol. 1).

WILLIAMS, Jody (1950—). American political activist. Born Jo-Anne Williams, Oct 9, 1950, in Poultney, Vermont; dau. of John and Ruth Williams; University of Vermont, BA, 1972; School for International Training, MA in Spanish and teaching English as a 2nd language, 1976; Johns Hopkins School of Advanced International Studies, MA, 1984. ❖ Served as co-coordinator for the Nicaragua-Honduras Education Project (1984–86); was deputy director of Medical Aid for El Salvador (1986–1992); drafted by the founder of the Vietnam Veterans of America Foundation to build a coalition to combat the widespread international use of antipersonnel land mines (1991); began serving as coordinator of the International Campaign to Ban Landmines (1992), an effort for which she and her organization were awarded the Nobel Prize for Peace (1997); attended signing of Mine Ban Treaty (Dec 1997), which was entered into force (Mar 1999). ❖ See also *Women in World History.*

WILLIAMS, Kathlyn (1888–1960). American silent-film star. Born May 31, 1888, in Butte, MT; died Sept 23, 1960, in Hollywood, CA; m. 2nd husband Charles Eyton (film producer). ❖ Began career in stock; made film debut (1908) and often appeared opposite Tom Mix; films include *The Spoilers, The Two Orphans, Sweet Lady Peggy, Big Timber, Just a Wife, Clarence, The Spanish Dancer, The City That Never Sleeps, A Single Man, Wedding Rings* and *Road to Paradise;* also played title role in 1st serial, *The Adventures of Kathlyn* (1913); lost leg in an auto accident, effectively ending her career.

WILLIAMS, Lauryn (1983—). African-American runner. Born Sept 11, 1983, in Pittsburgh, PA; graduate of University of Miami, 2004. ❖ Won a silver medal for 100 meters at Athens Olympics (2004); won NCAA 100 meters (2004 and 2005).

WILLIAMS, Lavinia (1916–1989). African-American dancer. Born in Philadelphia, PA, 1916; died July 19, 1989, in Port-au-Prince, Haiti; studied at Art Students League, 1935; m. Shannon Yarborough; children: Sara Yarborough (b. 1950, ballet dancer). ❖ Danced with American Negro Ballet (1936–39), Agnes de Mille's American Ballet Theater (1940), then with Katherine Dunham Company (1940–45), where she was featured in numerous solos in such works as *Rites de Passage, Bolero* and *Rara Tonga;* appeared on Broadway in *Cabin in the Sky, Show Boat, Finian's Rainbow,* and *My Darlin' Aida;* appeared in film *Stormy Weather* (1943); toured Europe in Noble Sissle's revival of *Shuffle Along* (1945–46); founded Haitian Institute of Folklore and Classic Dance (1954) and became director of Haiti's Theatre de Verdure, remaining in Haiti for 26 years; worked to develop national schools of dance in Guyana (1972–76) and Bahamas (1976–80); returned to NY to teach dance at Alvin Ailey School.

WILLIAMS, Lucinda (1937—). African-American runner. Name variations: Lucinda Williams Adams. Born Aug 10, 1937, in Savannah, GA; Tennessee State University, BS, 1959, MS, 1961; m. Floyd Adams, 1959 (died). ❖ A world-class sprinter (1950s–60s) and member of the Tennessee Tigerbelles, won 3 gold medals at Pan American Games (1958); earned a gold medal at Rome Olympics for the 4 x 100-meter relay (1960). Inducted into Georgia Hall of Fame (1994). ❖ See also *Women in World History.*

WILLIAMS, Lucinda (1953—). American guitarist, singer and songwriter. Born Jan 26, 1953, in Lake Charles, LA; dau. of Miller Wiliams (poet and professor); m. Greg Sowders (musician, div. 1980s). ❖ Recorded 1st album, *Ramblin' on My Mind* (1978); released highly praised 3rd album, *Lucinda Williams* (1988), which included "Change the Locks," later covered by Tom Petty, and "Passionate Kisses," later covered by Mary-Chapin Carpenter, which earned Williams a Grammy for Best Country Song (1994); released acclaimed album, *Car Wheels on a Gravel Road* (1998), which included "Still I Long for You," went gold, and won Grammy for Best Contemporary Folk Album; released album, *Essence* (2001), and won Grammy for Best Female Rock Vocal with track, "Get Right With God"; released *World Without Tears* (2003), which debuted in Top 20.

WILLIAMS, Lydia (1906–1969). *See Hall, Lydia E.*

WILLIAMS, Lynn (1960—). Canadian runner. Name variations: Lynn Kanuka. Born Lynn Williams, July 11, 1960, in Regina, Saskatchewan, Canada; children: 4. ❖ At Los Angeles Olympics, won a bronze medal in 3,000 meters (1984), the 1st Canadian woman to win an Olympic track medal since 1936; set 4 Canadian track records (1985); did color commentary for CTV, CBC and ESPN.

WILLIAMS, Marcia (1932—). *See Falkender, Marcia.*

WILLIAMS, Margery (1881–1944). *See Bianco, Margery Williams.*

WILLIAMS, Marianne (1793–1879). New Zealand missionary and letter writer. Name variations: Marianne Coldham. Born Marianne Coldham, Dec 12, 1793, in Yorkshire, England; died Dec 16, 1879, at Pakaraka, New Zealand; dau. of Wright Coldham and Ann (Temple) Coldham; children: 3. ❖ With sister-in-law Jane Williams, helped to establish boarding school for young Maori women, and the 1st English girls' school for daughters of other missionaries; through numerous letters, was among 1st women to record daily interaction among the Maori. ❖ See also *Dictionary of New Zealand Biography* (Vol. 1).

WILLIAMS, Marietta (1911–1987). *See Sullivan, Maxine.*

WILLIAMS, Marion (1927–1994). African-American gospel singer. Born Aug 29, 1927, in Miami, FL; died July 2, 1994, in Philadelphia, PA; married. ❖ Started career with Clara Ward Singers (1947–58); left the group (1958), taking Frances Steadman, Kitty Parham and Henrietta Waddy with her to form another gospel group, the Stars of Faith; sang with Stars of Faith in Langston Hughes' song-play *Black Nativity* (1961), which had a 3-year run in US; debuted as a soloist (1966); appeared in films *Fried Green Tomatoes* and *Mississippi Masala*; recorded 10 albums of gospel and pop music, and experimented with other musical genres, including blues, folk, and calypso; influenced a host of secular artists with her unique traditional gospel style, including Little Richard and Aretha Franklin. Received International Television Award from Princess Grace of Monaco (Grace Kelly); honored for contributions to American culture by President Bill Clinton at Kennedy Center (1993); received a MacArthur Foundation "genius" grant, the 1st singer so honored. ❖ See also *Women in World History.*

WILLIAMS, Mary Lou (1910–1981). African-American jazz pianist, arranger, and composer. Name variations: Mary Elfrieda Scruggs; Mary Elfrieda Winn; Mary Burleigh (or Burley). Born Mary Elfrieda Scruggs, May 8, 1910, in Atlanta, GA; died May 28, 1981, in Durham, NC; dau. of Joe Scruggs and Virginia Burley Winn; m. John Williams (bandleader), 1927 (div. 1942); m. Harold "Shorty" Baker (trumpet player), 1942 (marriage ended c. 1944). ❖ Musician who absorbed and influenced the changing style of jazz—from boogie-woogie to Kansas City swing, bebop, symphonic and avant-garde—through 6 decades; began playing piano professionally at age 6; toured, age 17, with John Williams' Synco Jazzers, and married him (1927); toured with John Williams when he joined Andy Kirk's Twelve Clouds of Joy (1928); made 1st solo recording, "Night Life" (1930); hired as pianist and arranger for Andy Kirk's group (1931); received commissions for arrangements from other bandleaders, including Benny Goodman,

Jimmie Lunceford, Louis Armstrong, Earl Hines and Tommy Dorsey (1930s); div. John Williams and married trumpet player Harold "Shorty" Baker, with whom she led a 6-piece band (1942); composed 1st extended work, *The Zodiac Suite,* which was performed at NY's Town Hall (1945) and a portion of which was performed at Carnegie Hall by NY Philharmonic (1946); appeared with all-woman trio at Carnegie Hall (1947); had several long engagements at Cafe Society (1950s); after 2 years of living in England and France, quit music to devote herself to the study of religion and helping the poor (1954); joined Catholic Church (1956); returned to music, appearing at Newport Jazz Festival with Dizzy Gillespie (1957); founded her own record label, Mary Records (1963); commissioned by the Vatican, wrote *Mary Lou's Mass,* which premiered at Columbia University (1970); rewrote the mass for Alvin Ailey's City Center Dance Theater (1971); played at Jimmy Carter's White House Jazz Party (1978); was artist-in-residence at Duke University (1976). Was the 1st woman instrumentalist inducted into *Down Beat* Hall of Fame (1990). ❖ See also Linda Dahl, *Morning Glory: A Biography of Mary Lou Williams* (Pantheon, 2000); and *Women in World History.*

WILLIAMS, Mary Wilhelmine (1878–1944). American historian. Born May 14, 1878, in Stanislaus Co., California; died Mar 10, 1944, in Palo Alto, California; dau. of Charles and Caroline (Madsen) Williams; graduate of San Jose State Normal School, 1901; Stanford University, AB, 1907, AM, 1908, PhD, 1914; studied at University of Chicago. ❖ Appointed associate professor of history at Goucher College (1916), then associate professor (1919), and professor (1920–40); organized 1st course in Canadian history to be offered in US (1916); retained as a consultant by Honduran government (1918–19); co-founded Baltimore branch of Women's International League for Peace and Freedom (1923), serving as state chair (1934–36); toured 15 Latin American countries for the American Association of University Women (1926–27); wrote several texts and travel books, the most widely read being *The People and Politics of Latin America* (1930). ❖ See also *Women in World History.*

WILLIAMS, Matilda Alice (1875–1973). New Zealand deaconess. Name variations: Matilda Alice Jeffrey, Sister Olive. Born Jan 5, 1875, at Alexandra, Victoria, Australia; died Oct 22, 1973, at Kew, Victoria, Australia; dau. of John (farmer) and Ann (Scale) Jeffrey; m. William James Williams (cleric), 1908 (died 1936). ❖ Trained as deaconess in Melbourne; performed social-welfare work for Australian Home Mission Board; invited to work for Trinity Wesleyan Church in Dunedin (1900); particularly concerned for welfare of underprivileged women and children, the ill and unemployed; worked closely with New Zealand Women's Christian Temperance Union (WCTU); after marriage, became lady superintendent at Deaconess House, Christchurch. ❖ See also *Dictionary of New Zealand Biography* (Vol. 3).

WILLIAMS, Michelle (1980—). American singer. Name variations: Destiny's Child. Born Tenetria Michelle Williams, July 23, 1980, in Houston, TX. ❖ Joined girl-group Destiny's Child, after departure of LeToya Luckett and LaTavia Robertson; with group, released hit singles including "Independent Women, Part 1," from film *Charlie's Angels* soundtrack, and "Bootylicious." Albums with Destiny's Child include *Survivor* (2001).

WILLIAMS, Myrlie Evers- (1933—). *See Evers-Williams, Myrlie.*

WILLIAMS, Natalie (1970—). American basketball and volleyball player. Born Nov 30, 1970, in Taylorsville, UT; dau. of Robyn Gray and Nate Williams (NBA basketball player); graduate of University of California, Los Angeles (1994). ❖ Forward; assigned to ABL's Portland Power (1996); won a team gold medal at World championships (1998) and Sydney Olympics (2000); drafted by Utah Starzz in 1st round (1999); led WNBA in rebounding (2000); acquired by Indiana Fever (2003); also won a team silver (1991) and team bronze (1993) at World University Games for volleyball. Named Pac-10 Female Athlete of the Decade (1987–96); named one of UCLA's 15 greatest women basketball players (1998); named USA Basketball's Female Athlete of the Year (1999).

WILLIAMS, Nesta (c. 1912–1995). *See Toumine, Nesta.*

WILLIAMS, Novlene (1982—). Jamaican runner. Born April 26, 1982, in Saint Ann, Jamaica. ❖ Won a bronze medal for 4 x 400-meter relay at Athens Olympics (2004).

WILLIAMS, Sarah (1841–1868). British poet. Name variations: Sadie Williams. Born 1841 in London, England; died April 25, 1868, in London, England; dau. of a Welsh businessman; graduate of Queen's

College, London. ❖ Published 1st work, *Rainbows in Springtide* (1866); continued publishing, mainly children's verses and religious writings, donating half her earnings to London's poor; also published *Twilight Hours: A Legacy of Verse.* ❖ See also *Women in World History.*

WILLIAMS, Serena (1981—). African-American tennis player. Born Sept 26, 1981, in Saginaw, Michigan; dau. of Richard (her coach) and Oracene Williams; sister of Venus Williams (tennis player). ❖ Turned pro (1995); won mixed doubles at Wimbledon (1998) and US Open (1998); won a gold medal for doubles at Sydney Olympics (2000); with sister Venus, won doubles championships at Wimbledon (2000, 2002), Australian Open (2001, 2003), French Open (1999), and US Open (1999); won singles titles at French Open (2002), US Open (1999, 2002), Wimbledon (2002, 2003), and Australian Open (2003, 2005); was the 1st African-American since Althea Gibson to win the US Open (1999).

WILLIAMS, Sherley Anne (1944–1999). African-American poet, novelist, playwright, educator, and literary critic. Born in Bakersfield, California, Aug 25, 1944; died in San Diego, California, July 6, 1999; dau. of Jessee Winson Williams and Lelia Marie (Siler) Williams (migrant farm workers); California State University at Fresno, BA, 1966; Brown University, MA, 1972; children: John Malcolm (b. 1968). ❖ An important voice in African-American poetry, began career with a short story, "Tell Martha Not to Moan," in the *Massachusetts Review* (1968); became associate professor at California State University in Fresno (1972); joined faculty of University of California at San Diego (1975), where she served as a professor of literature until her death; 1st attracted attention in literary circles with publication of *Give Birth to Brightness: A Thematic Study in Neo-Black Literature* (1972), a work of literary criticism; became known as a poet with publication of *The Peacock Poems* (1975), a nominee for Pulitzer Prize and National Book Award in Poetry (1976), followed by *Some One Sweet Angel Chile* (1982), which was also nominated for a National Book Award in Poetry; made debut as a novelist with *Dessa Rose* (1986); her one-woman play, *Letter from a New England Negro,* was staged at National Black Theater Festival (1991) and her 1st children's book, *Working Cotton* (1992), won Caldecott Award. Received Emmy for a tv performance of poems from *Some One Sweet Angel Chile.* ❖ See also *Women in World History.*

WILLIAMS, Shirley (1930—). British politician. Name variations: Shirley Vivien Teresa Brittain Williams; Baroness Shirley Williams. Born Shirley Vivien Teresa Brittain, July 27, 1930, in Chelsea, England; dau. of Sir George Catlin (professor of political science) and Vera Brittain (1893–1970, the writer); educated at Somerville College, Oxford; attended Columbia University; m. Bernard Williams (philosopher), 1955 (annulled 1974); m. Richard Neustadt (professor of politics at Harvard), 1987; children: (1st m.) Rebecca Clair Williams. ❖ Began career as a journalist for *Daily Mirror* and *Financial Times* (1954–59); ran for election to Parliament in Harwich (1954–55); served as general secretary of Fabian Society (1960–64); served as member of Parliament for Hitchin (1964–74), and Hertford-Stevenage (1974–79); served in numerous government posts in Ministry of Health (1964–66), Ministry of Labor (1966–67), Ministry of Education and Science (1967–69), and Home Office (1969–70); appointed minister of Prices and Consumer Protection (1974–76), and minister for Education and Science and paymaster-general (1976–79); was a member of Labour Party National Executive (1970–81); appointed Professorial Fellow of London Policy Study Institute (1979); co-founded the Social Democratic Party (1981), and served as president (1982–88); as a Social Democrat, served as a member of Parliament for Crosby (1981–84); published *Politics Is for People* (1981). ❖ See also *Women in World History.*

WILLIAMS, Sophie (1896–1939). See Heath, Sophie.

WILLIAMS, Susan (1969—). See Bartholomew, Susan.

WILLIAMS, Tonique (1976—). Bahamian runner. Name variations: Tonique Williams-Darling or Tonique Williams Darling. Born Jan 17, 1976, in the Bahamas; attended St. Johns College, Nassau, Bahamas; attended University of South Carolina; m. Dennis Darling (Bahamian track-and-field athlete). ❖ Won a gold medal in the 400 meters at Athens Olympics (2004), becoming Bahamas 1st individual gold medalist; had 4 1st-place finishes in the Golden League (2004) and placed 1st in the Super Grand Prix (2004).

WILLIAMS, Tonya (1968—). See Sanders, Tonya.

WILLIAMS, Vanessa (1963—). African-American singer. Born Vanessa Lynn Williams, Mar 18, 1963, in Millwood, NY; attended Syracuse University; married; children: 4. ❖ Representing New York, named Miss America (1984), the 1st African-American in pageant history; resigned 10 months later (July 23, 1984), after publication of nude photographs taken several years before, and replaced by Suzette Charles; made frequent appearances on tv and several recordings, including "Save the Best for Last," "Running Back to You" and "Colors of the Wind." Has been nominated for 9 Grammy Awards and honored with 2 NAACP Image Awards.

WILLIAMS, Venus (1980—). African-American tennis player. Born June 17, 1980, in Lynwood, CA; dau. of Richard (her coach) and Oracene Williams; sister of Serena Williams (tennis player). ❖ Won mixed doubles at Australian Open (1998) and French Open (1998); with sister Serena, won doubles championships at Wimbledon (2000, 2002), Australian Open (2001, 2003), French Open (1999), and US Open (1999); won a gold medal for doubles at Sydney Olympics (2000); won singles titles at Wimbledon (2000, 2001, 2005) and US Open (2000, 2001); was the 1st African-American to win a Wimbledon singles title since Althea Gibson in 1958.

WILLIAMS, Victoria (1958—). American folksinger and songwriter. Name variations: Vicky Williams. Born Dec 23, 1958, in Forbing, LA; attended Centenary College; m. Peter Case (musician, div. 1989); m. Mark Olson (musician). ❖ Moved to Los Angeles (1979), and began to perform at Troubadour Club; played with jug-band-style group, Incredibly Strung Out Band (mid-1980s); released debut album, *Happy Come Home* (1987), which included performances by T Bone Burnett and Bernie Worrell; appeared in several films, including *The Rapture* (1991), *Even Cowgirls Get the Blues* (1993), and *Bedrooms and Hallways* (1998); was diagnosed with multiple sclerosis while touring with Neil Young (1992), but did not have health insurance, so musical friends released *Sweet Relief* (1993), a collection of her songs performed by others, including Lou Reed, Michelle Shocked, Lucinda Williams, Pearl Jam and Soul Asylum, to raise money (the album earned over $200,000); set up Sweet Relief Musicians Fund for other uninsured musicians needing medical help (1994); albums include *Loose* (1994), *Musings of a Creekdipper* (1998) and *Water to Drink* (2000).

WILLIAMS, Wendy Lian (1967—). American diver. Born June 14, 1967, in St. Louis, Missouri. ❖ At Seoul Olympics, won a bronze medal in platform (1988); had to retire due to a spinal injury (1992).

WILLIAMS, Wendy O. (1951–1998). American musician. Name variations: Wendy Orleans Williams, W. O. W.; Plasmatics. Born Wendy Orleans Williams in 1951 in Rochester, NY; died April 6, 1998, in Storrs, CT. ❖ Lead singer for heavy-metal band, the Plasmatics, formed in New York City (1978), was best known for her trademark Mohawk cut and stage theatrics, which included chainsawing guitars and blowing up equipment; with group, recorded 4 albums, including *New Hope for the Wretched* (1981) and *Coup d'Etat* (1982); nominated for Grammy for Best Female Rock Vocal (1985); also recorded solo, with such albums as *W. O. W.* (1984), *Kommander of Kaos* (1986), and *Maggots: The Record* (1987); appeared in film, *Reform School Girls* (1986); retired and moved to Storrs, CT, with manager and companion, Rod Swenson (1991); suffering from depression, committed suicide by a self-inflicted gunshot wound to the head.

WILLIAMS, Yvette (1929—). New Zealand track-and-field athlete. Name variations: Yvette Corlett. Born April 25, 1929, in Dunedin, New Zealand; m. Buddy Corlett (basketball and softball player), 1954; children: 4. ❖ At Empire Games, won gold medal for long jump (1950, 1954), discus (1954) and shot put (1954); at Helsinki, took 1st place in the long jump, the 1st New Zealand woman to win an Olympic gold medal (1952). Awarded MBE (1953); inducted into New Zealand Hall of Fame (1990).

WILLIAMSBURG, countess of. See Desmier, Eleanor (1639–1722).

WILLIAMS PERKINS, Betty (b. 1943). See Williams, Betty.

WILLIAMSON, Alison (1971—). English archer. Born Nov 3, 1971, in Melton Mowbray, Leicestershire, England; attended Arizona State University. ❖ At Athens Olympics, won a bronze medal for indiv. round (2004).

WILLIAMSON, Audrey (1926—). English runner. Born Sept 28, 1926, in UK. ❖ At London Olympics, won a silver medal in 200 meters (1948).

WILLIAMSON, Mrs. J. C. (1847–1929). See Moore, Maggie.

WILLIAMSON, Jessie Marguerite (c. 1855–1937). New Zealand feminist and welfare worker. Name variations: Jessie Marguerite McAllan. Born Jessie Marguerite McAllan, between 1855 and 1857, in Dublin, Ireland; died July 26, 1937, in Epsom, New Zealand; dau. of John McAllan (merchant); m. Hugh Bellis Williamson (clerk), 1875; children: 4 daughters. ❖ Immigrated with husband to New Zealand (c. 1877); active in women's issues, was principal member of Wanganui Women's Franchise League (1893); was founding member of National Council of Women of New Zealand (NCW, 1896); named official visitor to Wanganui prison and worked to improve conditions there (1896); appointed to Patea and Wanganui United Charitable Aid Board (1900); proposed reforms to Wanganui's Jubilee Home for elderly, and advocated forcing fathers to provide for their illegitimate children. ❖ See also *Dictionary of New Zealand Biography* (Vol. 2).

WILLIAMSON, Sarah Eileen (1974—). American mayor of Boys Town. Born Sept 22, 1974, in Portland, OR. ❖ Became 1st girl elected mayor of Boys Town (now Girls and Boys Town), the non-sectarian organization which assists troubled girls and boys outside of Omaha, Nebraska (1991).

WILLING, Jennie Fowler (1834–1916). Canadian-born American preacher and temperance reformer. Born Jan 22, 1834, in Burford, Canada; died Oct 6, 1916, in New York, NY; dau. of Horatio and Harriet (Ryan) Fowler; m. William C. Willing (Methodist pastor), 1853 (died 1894); no children. ❖ Raised in farm country, 1st in western Canada and then in Newark, Illinois; encouraged by husband, obtained a preacher's license and presided over a number of services and revival meetings; also wrote fiction and nonfiction, which appeared in church pamphlets, books, and magazines; involved in the founding of the Woman's Christian Temperance Union (WCTU, 1874); served as editor of WCTU's newspaper *Our Union* (1875–76); founded New York Evangelistic Training School to create settlement projects in New York City (1895). ❖ See also *Women in World History*.

WILLIS, Ann (b. 1933). *See Richards, Ann Willis.*

WILLIS, Ann Bassett (1878–1956). *See Bassett, Ann.*

WILLIS, Connie (1945—). American science-fiction and short-story writer. Name variations: Constance E. Willis. Born Dec 31, 1945, in Denver, CO; m. Courtney W. Willis, 1967. ❖ Novels include *Water Witch* (with Cynthia Felice, 1982), *Lincoln's Dreams* (1987), *Impossible Things* (1993), *Bellwether* (1996), *Daisy in the Sun* (1998) and *Passage* (2001); short-fiction collections include *Miracle: And Other Christmas Stories* (1979), *Fire Watch* (1985), *The Pear-Shaped Man* (1991), and *Even the Queen: And Other Short Stories* (1998). Received Nebula and Hugo awards.

WILLIS, Frances (1899–1983). American diplomat. Name variations: Frances Elizabeth Willis. Born May 20, 1899, in Metropolis, Massac Co., Illinois; lived in California. ❖ Foreign service officer, was only the 3rd woman accepted into the US foreign service (1927); began career on the US/Mexican border, as a vice counsel in Valparaiso (1929); posted to Madrid (1943), and Sweden; 1st appointed by Dwight Eisenhower, served as ambassador to Switzerland (1953–57), then Norway (1957–61), then Sri Lanka (1961–64); became the 1st woman in the foreign service to be appointed a career ambassador (Mar 20, 1962); retired (1964).

WILLIS, Olympia Brown (1835–1926). *See Brown, Olympia.*

WILLIS, Sara Payson (1811–1872). *See Fern, Fanny.*

WILLISON, Marjory (1869–1938). *See MacMurchy, Marjory.*

WILLITS, Mary (1855–1902). American physician. Born Oct 16, 1855, in Maidencreek Township, PA; died of cancer, Dec 16, 1902; dau. of Thomas and Susan (Parvin) Willits; graduate of Swarthmore College, 1876, and Woman's Medical College of Pennsylvania, 1881. ❖ The 1st woman physician admitted to the Philadelphia County Medical Society (June 20, 1888); opened a private practice (1882); worked as a part-time instructor at Woman's Medical College and recording secretary at Philadelphia Clinical Society (1886); became assistant to the neurologist at Philadelphia Polyclinic School of Medicine (1887), then staff physician under Dr. Alice Bennett at State Hospital for the Insane in Norristown, PA (1892).

WILLMOTT, Ellen (c. 1859–1934). British horticulturist. Name variations: Ellen Ann Willmott. Born c. 1859; died 1934. ❖ One of Britain's most famous horticulturists and the Linnean Society's 1st female fellow (1904), created an elaborate, 55-acre garden at Warley Place, Essex (at its peak, it held as many as 100,000 species and required 104 gardeners); nurtured another garden in Italy and another in France; wrote *Warley Garden in Spring and Summer* (1909) and *The Genus Rosa* (1910); eventually had to sell possessions to maintain the gardens (1917); died penniless (1934). Received Royal Horticultural Society's Victoria Medal of Honour (jointly awarded to Willmott and Gertrude Jekyll, 1897).

WILLOUGHBY, Catharine (1519–1580). *See Bertie, Catharine.*

WILLOUGHBY, Frances L. (c. 1906–1984). American physician. Born c. 1906 in Harrisburg, PA; died Oct 13, 1984, in Woodbury, NJ. ❖ Enlisted in US Navy but assigned to naval reserve due to gender during WWII; with Women's Armed Services Act, which mandated the dissolution of separate women's branches in the armed forces, became 1st woman physician to hold regular US Navy commission (1948); retired from Navy (1964) and opened private practice in psychiatry (Glassboro, NJ); received Benjamin Rush Award for achievement in psychiatry (1981).

WILLS, Helen Newington (1905–1998). American tennis player. Name variations: Helen Wills; Helen Wills Moody; Mrs. F. S. Moody. Born Helen Newington Wills, Oct 6, 1905, in Centerville, CA; died in Carmel, CA, Jan 1, 1998; attended University of California; m. Frederick S. Moody, 1929 (div. 1937); m. Aidan Roark, 1939 (div. c. 1970). ❖ Eight-time Wimbledon tennis champion who was the outstanding American woman player of her time: won US Girls' championship (1921–22); won American National Singles championship (1923–25, 1927–29), illness had prevented her from competing (1926); won American Doubles championship with Mrs. M. Z. Jessup (1922), with Hazel Hotchkiss Wightman (1924), with Mary K. Browne (1925), and with Hazel Wightman (1928); won Olympic gold medals for singles and doubles at Paris Olympics (1924); won British Singles championship at Wimbledon (1927–30, 1932–33, 1935, and 1938); won French Singles championship (1928–30, and 1932); retired from major competition (1938); devoted rest of life to painting and writing, producing an autobiography and a collection of mystery novels. Inducted into International Tennis Hall of Fame (1959). ❖ See also autobiography, *Fifteen-Thirty: The Story of a Tennis Player* (Scribner, 1937); Larry Engelmann, *The Goddess and the American Girl: The Story of Suzanne Lenglen and Helen Wills* (Oxford U. Press, 1988); and *Women in World History*.

WILLSON, Rini Zarova (d. 1966). Russian-born actress and singer. Name variations: Rini Zarova. Born Ralina Rina Zarova in Russia; died Dec 6, 1966, age 54, in Santa Monica, CA; m. Meredith Willson (playwright, wrote *The Music Man*), 1948. ❖ Age 7, made stage debut in Russia; moved to US (1927); performed with opera companies; won a radio contract, having been seen in the musical *Mistress of the Inn*; also appeared on tv.

WILLUMS, Sigbrit (fl. 1507–1523). Danish counsellor of a king. Name variations: Sigbrit Villoms; Sigbrit Villems; Sibrecht Willumsdatter; Mother Sigbrit. Birth and death dates unknown; born in the Netherlands; children: Dyveke (died 1517). ❖ Powerful figure in Danish history who flourished as counsellor to King Christian II; with young daughter Dyveke, arrived in Norway (early 1500s); obtained a license to sell bakery goods (or fish) from a booth at the harbor; after daughter attracted the attention of crown prince, Christian (1507), was invited to move into a stone house across from the royal palace in Oslo; when Christian became king of Denmark and Norway (1513), moved into a royal manor north of Copenhagen; was often sought out by the king for her counsel, even after Dyveke died suddenly in the summer of 1517—allegedly from eating poisoned cherries, though modern historians have theorized appendicitis; became the king's most prominent and increasingly visible counsellor; at times of his absence, was his representative in negotiations with foreign secretaries of state; considered a clever negotiator, quick of wit, was well acquainted with the questions and problems at issue; became controller of the Sound tolls (1519), the tariffs paid by all ships sailing between Denmark and Sweden for trading in the Baltic, and moved the center for collecting those tariffs from Elsinore to Copenhagen; assumed the role of foster mother of Crown Prince Hans, and from then on was called Mother Sigbrit; ruled with Christian from 1517 to 1523, until he was forced into exile. ❖ See also *Women in World History*.

WILLUMSEN, Dorrit (1940—). Danish novelist. Born Dorrit Kirsten Willumsen, Aug 31, 1940, in Copenhagen, Denmark; dau. of Lilian Addy Adelaide Johansen and Kaj Poul Willumsen, an opera singer who left the family; grew up with maternal grandparents; m. Jess Jørgen

Ärnsbo, 1963; children: Tore (b. 1970). ❖ Works focus on children and women who are alone, absent love; though early works are experimental, later works are more realist in style; writings include *Modellen Coppelia* (1973), *Neonhaven* (1976), *Hvis det virkelig var en film* (1978), *Marie: En roman om Marie Tussauds liv* (1983), *Suk, hjerte* (1986), *Margrethe I* (1992), *Koras Stemme* (2000), and *Bruden fra Gent* (2003). Received the Nordic Council Prize for Literature for *Bang*, a biographical novel about the writer Herman Bang (1997).

WILMAN, Maria (1867–1957). South African botanist and geologist. Born April 29, 1867, in South Africa; died Nov 9, 1957. ❖ An expert on the plants, tribes and archaeology of South Africa, was educated at Good Hope Seminary in Cape Town and Newnham College, Cambridge (1885–88); worked as an assistant at South African Museum in Cape Town; as the 1st director of the Alex McGregor Memorial Museum in Kimberley (1908–46), built collections, had 7,000 plants placed in the herbarium (5 were named after her), and nurtured a famous rock collection; elected life member of Royal Society of South Africa. Writings include *The Rock Engravings of Griqualand West and Bechuanaland* (1933), *Preliminary Checklist of the Flowering Plants and Ferns of Griqualand West* (1946) and (ed.) *The Bushmen Tribes of Southern Africa* (1942).

WILMOT, Barbarina (1768–1854). *See Dacre, Barbarina.*

WILMOT, Olivia (d. 1774). Duchess of Cumberland. Died Dec 5, 1774; dau. of Reverend D. James Wilmot; allegedly m. Henry Frederick (1745–1790), duke of Cumberland (brother of George III of England), Mar 4, 1767; children: Olivia, princess of Cumberland (April 3, 1772–Dec 3, 1834, who m. John Thomas Serres). ❖ Henry Frederick later married Ann Horton (1743–1808). ❖ See also *Women in World History.*

WILSON, Anne Glenny (1848–1930). Australian romance writer and poet. Name variations: Lady Anne Glenny Wilson; Mrs. Glenny Wilson; (pseudonym) Austral. Born Anne Adams, June 11, 1848, in Greenvale, Queensland, Australia; died Feb 11, 1930, at Letheny, Rangitikei, New Zealand; dau. of Jane Adams (a Scot) and Robert Adams (Irish pastoralist); educated in Melbourne; married James Glenny Wilson (farmer), 1874; children: 5. ❖ At 26, married a prosperous Scottish farmer and moved to New Zealand, where they purchased over 6,000 acres and farmed the land; began publishing stories and poems in literary journals throughout Australia and New Zealand (1890s); wrote a collection of poetry, *Themes and Variations* (1889), followed by 2 novels, *Alice Lander, A Sketch* (1893) and *Two Summers* (1900), and a 2nd volume of poems, *A Book of Verses* (1917).

WILSON, Augusta Evans (1835–1909). American writer. Name variations: Augusta Evans. Born Augusta Jane Evans, May 8, 1835, in Wynnton, Georgia; died May 9, 1909, in Mobile, Alabama; dau. of Matt Ryan Evans (merchant) and Sarah Skrine (Howard) Evans; m. Lorenzo Madison Wilson (financier and plantation owner), Dec 2, 1868 (died 1891); children: 4 stepchildren. ❖ Moved with family to Mobile, Alabama (1849), which was to remain her home for the rest of her life; at 20, published anonymously *Inez: A Tale of the Alamo* (1855), a moralizing and anti-Catholic tome that earned her the money to buy her home; came to prominence with *Beulah* (1859); an ardent secessionist, organized a Confederate Army hospital (named Camp Beulah after her book) near Mobile (1860) and worked there throughout Civil War; wrote *Macaria; or, Altars of Sacrifice* (1864), to defend Confederate policy and lift the morale of her fellow Southerners; wrote *St. Elmo* (1866), the 3rd most popular American novel of the 19th century, which concerns the virtuous Edna Earl, whose prayers, righteousness, and affection rescue a dashing hero from his sins; also wrote *Vashti* (1869), *Infelice* (1875), *At the Mercy of Tiberius* (1887), *A Speckled Bird* (1902), which opposed women's suffrage and labor unions, and *Devota* (1907). ❖ See also William Perry Fidler, *Augusta E. Wilson* (U. of Alabama Press, 1951); and *Women in World History.*

WILSON, Bertha (1923—). Canadian jurist. Born Sept 18, 1923, in Kirkcaldy, Scotland; dau. of Archibald Wernham and Christina Noble; University of Aberdeen, MA, 1944; Dalhousie University, LLB, 1957; m. Rev. John Wilson, Dec 1945. ❖ Immigrated to Canada (1949); called to the bar of Nova Scotia (1957), then Ontario (1959); worked at Toronto law firm, Osler, Hoskin & Harcourt, for 16 years, became the 1st woman appointed to the Ontario Appeal Court (1975); appointed to the Supreme Court of Canada (Mar 4, 1982), the 1st woman to sit on the highest court; wrote many major decisions, including the decision to strike down the criminal law on abortion; retired from the court (Jan 4, 1991).

WILSON, Cairine (1885–1962). Canadian politician. Pronunciation: Car-EEN. Born Cairine Reay Mackay, Feb 4, 1885, at Montreal, Quebec, Canada; died Mar 3, 1962, in Ottawa, Canada; dau. of Robert Mackay (Liberal member of Canadian Senate, died 1916) and Jane (Baptist) Mackay; attended Trafalgar Institute, Montreal; m. Norman Wilson (Liberal MP), Feb 1909 (died 1956); children: Olive (b. 1910), Janet (b. 1911), Cairine (b. 1913), Ralph (b. 1915), Anna (b. 1918), Angus (b. 1920), Robert (b. 1922), Norma (b. 1925). ❖ Elected joint president of Eastern Ontario Liberal Association (1921), traveled widely throughout Ontario speaking on behalf of Liberal Party; organized National Federation of Liberal Women of Canada (1923); helped establish Twentieth Century Liberal Association of Canada; appointed the 1st female member of Canadian Senate by Prime Minister Mackenzie King (Feb 15, 1930), due to her leading role in Liberal Party organizations, the fact that she was fluent in French (an important consideration in Canadian politics) and because she was in a position to contribute financially to the party's funds; used her position to advance many socially progressive causes: spoke in favor of liberalizing the (highly restrictive) divorce laws and in favor of legislation designed to limit hours in a work week; elected president of League of Nations Society (1936); publicly denounced the Munich agreement (1938); during WWII, served on the board of Canadian National Committee on Refugees; served as member of Canadian delegation to UN General Assembly in New York (1949–51), the 1st Canadian woman to be accorded this distinction. ❖ See also *Women in World History.*

WILSON, Carnie (1968—). American singer. Name variations: Wilson Phillips. Born April 29, 1968, in Los Angeles, CA; dau. of Brian Wilson (of The Beach Boys) and Marilyn Wilson (member of band, The Honeys); sister of Wendy Wilson (singer); m. Rob Bonfiglio (musician), June 23, 2000. ❖ With sister Wendy and Chynna Phillips, formed the vocal trio, Wilson Phillips (1989); with group, released eponymous debut album (1990), which went to #2, sold 10 million copies, and had hit singles "Hold On," "Release Me" and "You're in Love"; with group, released album, *Shadows and Light* (1992), which, despite going platinum and reaching #4 on charts, failed to deliver any hit singles; after Wilson Phillips disbanded (1993), released albums *Hey Santa!* (1993) and *The Wilsons* (1997), with Wendy, and appeared in documentary about father, *Brian Wilson: I Just Wasn't Made for These Times* (1995); hosted short-lived tv talk show, "Carnie!" (1997); reunited with Wilson Phillips to record *California* (2004).

WILSON, Catherine (1842–1862). English nurse and poisoner. Born 1842; hanged Oct 20, 1862, in London; married a man named Dixon. ❖ Notorious poisoner, lived in London (1853–62), working as housekeeper and nurse to ailing persons who also happened to be wealthy; won their trust, persuaded them to make out new wills bequeathing their assets to her, then poisoned them; killed 8, all told, including her husband. ❖ See also *Women in World History.*

WILSON, Charlotte (1854–1944). English anarchist and feminist. Born Charlotte Mary Martin, May 6, 1854, at Kemerton, near Tewkesbury, England; died at Irvington-on-Hudson, New York, April 28, 1944; dau. of Robert Spencer Martin (physician) and Mary (Edgeworth) Martin; attended Cheltenham Ladies College and Merton Hall (later to become part of Newnham College), Cambridge; m. Arthur Wilson (stockbroker), Sept 1876 (died 1932); no children. ❖ Founder of the Freedom Press and the 1st female executive member of Fabian Society, who played a significant part in facilitating the further work of anarchist refugees and in laying the foundations of the British anarchist movement; began to immerse herself in the works of radical anarchist and socialist theoreticians like Michael Bakunin and Karl Marx; was outraged by the unfairness of the judicial proceedings during the trial of anarchist Peter Kropotkin at Lyons, France (Jan 1883); founded Hampstead Marx Circle (Oct 1884); elected to executive committee of Fabian Society (Dec 1884), a loose alliance of intellectuals (which included George Bernard Shaw) who ranged from moderate socialists to radical anarchists; in a series of articles, provided what was the 1st native British contribution to anarchist theory (1884–86); published 1st edition of *Freedom* (Oct 1886), the earliest publication of what eventually became the Freedom Press, the most important publisher of anarchist literature in Britain; served as chief editor, publisher, translator (of foreign contributions) and financial supporter of *Freedom* (1886–92); wrote "Anarchism and Outrage," her most famous contribution to anarchist thought (1886); for reasons that are not entirely clear, severed all connections with anarchist movement (1895); founded Fabian women's group (Mar 1908); again served on executive committee of Fabian Society (1911–14). ❖ See also *Women in World History.*

WILSON, Dana (1922–2004). *See Broccoli, Dana.*

WILSON, Deborah (1955—). American diver. Name variations: Debbie Wilson. Born Nov 1955. ❖ At Montreal Olympics, won a bronze medal in platform (1976).

WILSON, Debra (c. 1957—). *See Maffett, Debra.*

WILSON, Edith (1896–1981). African-American blues singer and vaudevillian. Born Edith Goodall, Sept 6, 1896, in Louisville, KY; died Mar 30, 1981, in Chicago, IL; m. Danny Wilson (pianist), 1910s (died 1928); m. Millard Wilson, 1947. ❖ Began performing in Chicago and Milwaukee; with husband Danny Wilson at piano, sang with sister-in-law Lena Wilson in Chicago clubs; as a solo, signed with Columbia and recorded "Nervous Blues" and "Vampin' Liza Jane" (1921), followed by "Frankie" and "Old Time Blues" which began to sell; toured with Theater Owners Booking Association (TOBA); was a prominent performer in musical revues and vaudeville and played Cotton Club with comic Doc Straine; sang in Lew Leslie's *Blackbirds* (1926); sang on Cotton Club's weekly radio programs broadcast by CBS; performed with headliners like Louis Armstrong and Thomas "Fats" Waller, the latter of whom wrote the song "(What Did I Do To Be So) Black and Blue" for her and arranged versions of "My Handy Man Ain't Handy No More" and "I'll Get Even With You" for her Victor recordings; became a well-known performer on the East Coast, singing with other renowned performers, including Eubie Blake in his *Shuffle Along* shows; made film debut in Bogart-Bacall classic *To Have and Have Not* (1944); on radio, appeared in stereotypical parts, as a mother-in-law on "Amos 'n' Andy" and Aunt Jemima on "The Breakfast Club"; based on the latter role, hired by Quaker Oats to continue appearing as Aunt Jemima until retiring the character in 1965; returned to NY stage in *Black Broadway* and guest-starred at Newport Jazz Festival (1980). ❖ See also *Women in World History.*

WILSON, Edith Bolling (1872–1961). American first lady. Name variations: Edith Bolling Galt; Edith Galt Wilson. Born Oct 15, 1872, in Wytheville, Virginia; died Dec 28, 1961, in Washington, DC; dau. of William Holcombe Bolling (lawyer and circuit judge) and Sallie (White) Bolling; m. Norman Galt (businessman), April 30, 1896 (died 1908); became 2nd wife of Woodrow Wilson (president of US), Dec 18, 1915 (died 1924); children: (1st m.) 1 son (died in infancy). ❖ Met Woodrow Wilson 7 months after the death of his 1st wife Ellen Axson Wilson (Feb 1915); married him 10 months later; after the Armistice (1919), accompanied him to Europe, where he spent months pushing through an acceptable peace treaty; when husband suffered a life-threatening stroke (Oct 2, 1919), an illness shrouded in secrecy, embarked on what she termed her "stewardship," though it was characterized in the press as "Mrs. Wilson's Regency" (she claimed that her "stewardship" lasted only 6 weeks; some believe that she directed the executive branch of the government for the remaining 17 months of her husband's term). ❖ See also (with Alden Hatch) *My Memoir* (1961); Ishbel Ross, *Power with Grace: The Life Story of Mrs. Woodrow Wilson* (1975); and *Women in World History.*

WILSON, Eileen Hiscock (1909—). *See Hiscock, Eileen.*

WILSON, Eleanora Mary Carus- (1897–1977). *See Carus-Wilson, Eleanora Mary.*

WILSON, Elizabeth (d. 1786). American murderer. Hanged Jan 3, 1786, in Chester, Pennsylvania. ❖ Resident of East Bradford, PA, murdered her 10-week-old illegitimate twins; was hanged, despite the fact that her brother William had obtained a reprieve from the governor and ridden hard over muddy terrain to save her (he arrived 23 minutes too late).

WILSON, Ellen Axson (1860–1914). American first lady. Born Ellen Louise Axson, May 15, 1860, in Savannah, Georgia; died Aug 6, 1914, in Washington, DC; dau. of Margaret (Hoyt) Axson and Samuel E. Axson (Presbyterian minister); graduate of Rome (GA) Female College, 1876; attended Art Students League in NY; m. (Thomas) Woodrow Wilson (president of US), June 24, 1885; children: Margaret Wilson (1886–1944); Jessie Wilson (1887–1933); Eleanor "Nell" Wilson McAdoo (1889–1967), who m. William Gibbs McAdoo). ❖ Had a profound influence on husband's career, acting as his trusted advisor and confidante; supported his political aspirations, becoming active in Democratic affairs; a warm and charming Southern host, preferred modest teas in the White House garden to lavish receptions after husband became president (1913); oversaw 2 White House weddings, that of daughters Jessie (1913) and Nell (1914); with her strong social conscience, was something of an activist—a new role for a first lady; crusaded against housing conditions for African-Americans in Washington DC,

used and promoted the hand-woven products made by women from the poor mountain states in the South, and supported a variety of other social causes and philanthropies. ❖ See also Eleanor Wilson McAdoo, *The Woodrow Wilsons* (1932) and *The Priceless Gift* (1962); and *Women in World History.*

WILSON, Enid (b. 1910). English golfer. Born Mar 15, 1910, in Stonebroon, Derbyshire, England. ❖ One of England's top women players, won British Girls' championship (1925); won the British Women's Amateur 3 years in a row (1931–33); member of the Curtis Cup team (1932); won the English Ladies' title (1928, 1930) and was runner-up (1927). ❖ See also Enid Wilson and Robert A. Lewis *So That's What I Do!* (Donovan & Murdoch, 1935).

WILSON, Ethel (1888–1980). South African-born Canadian novelist and short-story writer. Born Ethel Bryant, 1888, in Port Elizabeth, South Africa; died 1980; received teaching certificate in Vancouver; married a physician, 1921. ❖ Orphaned at 10 (1898), traveled to Vancouver, British Columbia, Canada, to live with maternal grandmother; published 1st article in *The New Statesman and Nation* (1937); wrote 1st novel, *Hetty Dorval* (1947), which established her reputation; wrote the family saga, *The Innocent Traveller* (1949), and 2 novellas, released as *The Equation of Love* (1952); her characters, often ambivalent and unpredictable, are best represented in the novel *The Swamp Angel* (1954), considered her finest work; also wrote *Love and Saltwater* (1956) and *Mrs. Golightly and Other Stories* (1961). ❖ See also *Ethel Wilson: Stories, Essays, and Letters.*

WILSON, Ethel (d. 1980). American stage and radio actress. Born in Baltimore, MD; died April 19, 1980, age 88, in St. Petersburg, FL. ❖ Made stage debut (1914); plays include *Tyranny of Love, So This is Paris, Rain, The Bishop Misbehaves, First Lady, The Doughgirls, You Can't Take It with You* and *My Sister Eileen;* on radio, performed on "Henry Aldrich," "Backstage Wife," "Our Gal Sunday," "Ma Perkins" and "The Goldbergs."

WILSON, Fanny (1874–1958). New Zealand nurse and hospital matron. Born May 25, 1874, at Christchurch, New Zealand; died Sept 11, 1958, at Christchurch; dau. of Samuel Wilson (laborer) and Mary Jane (Whitto) Wilson. ❖ Trained as nurse at Wellington District Hospital (1909), and worked there until 1914; joined nurses accompanying New Zealand Expeditionary Force to German Samoa (1914), then Egypt (1915); became matron at No. 2 New Zealand Hospital, Walton-on-Thames (1917); discharged (1920); helped run private hospital in Wellington (early 1920s); trained as midwife at St. Helens Hospital, Wanganui, and worked at St. Helens Hospital, Christchurch (1925–29); served as matron of Limes Private Hospital, Christchurch (1930–37); became deputy matron in chief, New Zealand Army Nursing Service (1931–33). ❖ See also *Dictionary of New Zealand Biography* (Vol. 3).

WILSON, Fiammetta Worthington (1864–1920). English astronomer. Born 1864 in Lowestoft, Suffolk, England; died 1920; dau. of Helen Till Worthington and F. S. Worthington (physician); studied languages in Lausanne, Switzerland (4 years) and Germany (1 year); studied music in Italy; no formal training in astronomy; married S. A. Wilson. ❖ Joined British Astronomical Association and specialized in astronomical observations of meteors; during WWI, served as acting director (along with A. Grace Cook) of the British Astronomical Society's Meteor Section; observed over 10,000 meteors (1910–20); also became an expert in comets, zodiacal light, and the *aurora borealis*; discovered the return of Westphal's comet (1913); after publishing several papers on meteors, was elected fellow of Royal Astronomical Society (1916). ❖ See also *Women in World History.*

WILSON, Florence (1894–1968). *See Austral, Florence.*

WILSON, Florence Ada Mary Lamb (1877–1941). *See Polson, Florence Ada Mary Lamb.*

WILSON, Harriet E. Adams (c. 1827–c. 1870). African-American writer. Born c. 1827 in Milford, New Hampshire; died c. 1870; married Thomas Wilson, Oct 6, 1851; children: George M. Wilson (died young). ❖ Published only known work, *Our Nig: or Sketches from the Life of a Free Black, in a Two-Story White House, North, Showing That Slavery's Shadows Fall Even There* (1859), the 1st novel by an African-American woman and the 1st novel by an African-American to be published in US. ❖ See also *Women in World History.*

WILSON, Harriette (1786–1855). English courtesan and writer. Born Harriette Dubochet in 1786; died in 1855 (some sources cite 1846). ❖ During long career, was the mistress of the earl of Craven, the duke of Argyll, the marquess of Worcester, the duke of Beaufort, and the duke of Wellington; published what was purported to be the opening chapter of her *Memoirs of Herself and Others* (1825), followed by a highly successful serialization of her memoirs, all 8 vols. ❖ See also Angela Thirkell, *Tribute for Harriette*; and *Women in World History*.

WILSON, Heather (1960—). American politician. Born Dec 30, 1960, in Keene, New Hampshire; graduate of the US Air Force Academy, 1982; Oxford University, MPhil, 1984, and DPhil in international relations, 1985; m. Jay Hone (attorney); children: 3. ❖ Served in US Air Force (1978–87); was a Rhodes Scholar; served as defense planning officer, NATO (1987–89); was director of Defense Policy and Arms Control, National Security Council (1989–91); representing New Mexico as a Republican, was elected to US House of Representatives by special election to fill a vacant seat (1998), the 1st woman veteran to serve in Congress; as of 2005, reelected to 4 succeeding Congresses; served on the Energy and Commerce committee and Armed Services committees; chair of the subcommittee on National Security of the Republican House Policy Committee; spoke out against Congress restricting women in combat zones (2005).

WILSON, Helen Ann (1793/94–1871). New Zealand nurse, social leader, and artist. Name variations: Helen Ann Simpson. Born Helen Ann Simpson, c. 1793 or 1794, at Gibraltar; died June 24, 1871, at New Plymouth, New Zealand; dau. of James Simpson (US consul general at Tangier); m. Peter Wilson (medical practitioner), 1840. ❖ Immigrated to New Zealand with husband (1841); worked with husband as nursing assistant; prominent in social and charitable activities; recorded life through sketches. ❖ See also *Dictionary of New Zealand Biography* (Vol. 1).

WILSON, Helen Hopekirk (1856–1945). See Hopekirk, Helen.

WILSON, Helen Mary (1869–1957). New Zealand teacher, farmer, union activist, and writer. Name variations: Helen Mary Ostler. Born May 4, 1869, at Oamaru, New Zealand; died April 16, 1957, in Hamilton, New Zealand; dau. of William Henry Ostler (runholder) and Emma Brignell (Roberts) Ostler; m. Charles Kendall Wilson (politician), 1892 (died 1934); children: 2 daughters, 1 son. ❖ Helped husband run family farm (1890s); became active in Women's Division of New Zealand Farmers' Union (WDFU); made justice of peace (1939); wrote novels, *Moonshine* (1930s) and *Land of My Children* (1955), and well-received autobiography, *My First Eighty Years* (1950). ❖ See also *Dictionary of New Zealand Biography* (Vol. 3).

WILSON, Ida Lewis (1842–1911). See Lewis, Ida.

WILSON, Jean (1910–1933). Canadian speedskater. Born 1910 in Glasgow, Scotland; died 1933 in Toronto, Ontario, Canada. ❖ Came in 1st all-around, North American championship (1931), winning all four of her events—220, 440, 880, and three-quarter mile; came in 1st in the 500 meters and second in the 1,500 meters at Lake Placid Olympics (1932), though speedskating was considered a demonstration event at Olympics until 1960; died of a degenerative muscle disease the following year.

WILSON, Kaye Lani (c. 1963—). See Rafko, Kaye Lani.

WILSON, Kini (1872–1962). Hawaiian dancer, singer and musician. Name variations: Ana Kini Kuululani; Kini Kapahu; Jennie. Born Ana Kini Kuululani, Mar 4, 1872, in Honolulu, HI; died July 23, 1962, in Honolulu; dau. of John N. McColgan (Irish tailor) and Hawaiian mother; *hanai* (adoptive) dau. of Kapahu Kula O Kamamalu; trained as a hula dancer, ballroom dancer, ukelele player, and singer; m. John Wilson (elected mayor of Honolulu, 1924, 1928, 1948, 1950, 1952), 1909. ❖ Joined the king's royal troupe of hula dancers (c. 1888); toured US, performing at Chicago World's Fair of 1893, and Europe, dancing at Folies-Bergère in Paris, and for Nicholas II in Russia and Wilhelm II in Germany; returned to Hawaii (early 1900s) and became politically active in Democratic Party (1919); was designated by legislature as Hawaii's "Honorary First Lady" (1959); served as one of Hawaii's 1st presidential electors (1960). ❖ See also *Women in World History*.

WILSON, Lois (1894–1988). American stage, tv, and screen actress. Born June 28, 1894, in Pittsburgh, PA; died Mar 3, 1988, in Reno, Nevada; sister of Diana Kane (1901–1977) and Connie Lewis (both actresses). ❖ Starred in films opposite such leading men as John Gilbert and Rudolph Valentino; made screen debut in *The Dumb Girl of Portici* (1915); appeared in more than 100 films, including *Midsummer Madness, What Every Woman Knows, Miss Lulu Bett, Ruggles of Red Gap,*

Monsieur Beaucaire, The Deluge, The Show-Off, Bright Eyes, and most notably as Molly Wingate in *The Covered Wagon* and Daisy Buchanan in *The Great Gatsby.*

WILSON, Mabel (1884–1976). See Whitaker, Mabel.

WILSON, Margaret (1798–1835). See Bayne, Margaret.

WILSON, Margaret Bush (1919—). African-American lawyer and civil-rights leader. Born Margaret Berenice Bush, Jan 30, 1919, in St. Louis, Missouri; dau. of James Thomas Bush (real-estate broker) and Margaret Berenice (Casey) Bush; Talladega College, BA *cum laude*; Lincoln University School of Law, LLB, 1943; m. Robert Edmund Wilson Jr. (lawyer), 1944 (div. 1968); children: Robert Wilson III. ❖ Began practicing civil-rights and real-estate law (1943); helped the Real Estate Brokers Association, the 1st such organization for black brokers in St. Louis, in obtaining a charter (1944); as the association's counsel, led its legal battle against racially restrictive covenants in housing contracts, which culminated in the Supreme Court's landmark decision in *Shelley v. Kraemer* that branded such covenants unconstitutional (1948); with husband, had a private practice (1947–65); ran unsuccessfully for Congress on the Progressive ticket, the 1st black woman from Missouri to run for Congress (1948); served as assistant attorney general for Missouri (1961–62); was the 1st African-American woman to serve as chair of the board of directors of the NAACP (1975–84). ❖ See also *Women in World History*.

WILSON, Margaret Joyce (1934—). See Wilson, Peggy.

WILSON, Margaret Oliphant (1828–1897). See Oliphant, Margaret.

WILSON, Margaret W. (1882–1973). American writer. Name variations: Mrs. G. D. Turner; (pseudonym) An Elderly Spinster. Born Margaret Wilhelmina Wilson, Jan 16, 1882, in Traer, Iowa; died Oct 6, 1973, in Droitwich, Worcester, England; dau. of West Wilson (livestock trader, died 1923) and Agnes (McCornack) Wilson; University of Chicago, AB, 1903, BA in philosophy, 1904; m. George Douglas Turner (assistant commissioner of prisons for England and Wales), 1923 (died 1946). ❖ Pulitzer Prize-winning novelist, joined United Presbyterian Church of North America as a missionary (1904); spent 6 years as missionary in Punjab region of northern India, assisting Dr. Maria White at Sailkot Hospital and teaching at Gujranwala Girls' School; ill with typhoid, forced to return to US (1910); reentered University of Chicago (1912) as divinity student; taught at West Pullman High School (1913–18); under pseudonym "An Elderly Spinster," completed a set of short stories, "Tales of a Polygamous City," some of which appeared in *Atlantic Monthly* (1917); published 1st novel, *The Able McLaughlins* (1923), which examined the influence of religion in a sparse Scottish Presbyterian community and won the Pulitzer Prize; following marriage (1923), settled in England, where she published 2nd novel, *The Kenworthys* (1925); was one of 20th century's early feminist writers; also wrote *The Painted Room* (1927), *Daughters of India* (1928), *Trousers of Taffeta* (1929), *The Law and the McLaughlins* (1936), and *The Devon Treasure Mystery* (juvenile, 1939), among others. ❖ See also *Women in World History*.

WILSON, Margery (1896–1986). American actress, writer, and director. Name variations: Margie Wilson. Born Oct 31, 1896, in Gracey, KY; died Jan 21, 1896, in Arcadia, CA. ❖ Made acting debut in *Intolerance* (1916); films include *The Habit of Happiness, The Primal Lure, Wolf Lowry, Venus in the East* and *That Something*; also wrote and directed. ❖ See also autobiography *I Found My Way* (Lippincott, 1956).

WILSON, Margie (1896–1986). See Wilson, Margery.

WILSON, Marie (1916–1972). American comedic actress. Born Katherine Elizabeth Wilson, Dec 30, 1916, in Anaheim, CA; died Nov 23, 1972, in Hollywood, CA; m. Nick Grinde (director, div.); m. Alan Nixon (actor), 1942 (div. 1950); m. Robert Fallon (producer), 1951. ❖ Comedic actress, best known for portrayal of Irma in "My Friend Irma," on radio (1947–54), tv (1952–54), and in two films; other movies include *Boy Meets Girl, Never Wave at a WAC, Rookies on Parade* and *Mr. Hobbs Takes a Vacation.*

WILSON, Marilyn (1943—). Australian swimmer. Born July 14, 1943, in Australia. ❖ At Rome Olympics, won a silver medal in 4 x 100-meter medley relay (1960).

WILSON, Mary (1916—). British prime-ministerial wife and poet. Name variations: Lady Wilson of Rievaulx. Born Gladys Mary Baldwin in 1916 in Norfolk, England; dau. of a Congregational minister; m. Harold Wilson (later prime minister of Britain, 1964–70, 1974–76), later Baron Wilson of Rievaulx, in 1940 (died 1995); children: sons Robin (b. Dec 1943) and Giles (b. May 1948). ❖ Wife of British Prime Minister Harold Wilson, lived at No. 10 Downing Street in London (1964–70, 1974–76); sought as normal an existence as life in public permitted; though she objected to public speaking, was quick to kill the "timid housewife image" associated with her and adapted well to the grander life and to public appearances, accompanying husband on state visits to Washington, Paris, Rome, Ottawa, and Moscow; was also a poet. ❖ See also *Women in World History.*

WILSON, Mary (1944—). African-American singer. Name variations: The Supremes. Born in Greenville, MS, Mar 6, 1944; dau. of Johnnie Mae Wilson (d. 1999) and Sam Wilson; from age 3 to 9, thought mother's younger sister I. V. Pippin was her mother; at age 57, got her associate's degree in arts, New York University, 2001; m. Pedro Ferrer. ❖ With Florence Ballard, organized a singing group called "The Primettes" (1959); joined by Diana Ross, recorded 1st song for Motown (1964), under group's new name "The Supremes"; saw recording of "Where Did Our Love Go" reach *Billboard*'s Top 100; had 7 #1 hits and was rarely out of the Top 10 (1965–69) with such songs as "Your Heart Belongs to Me" (1964), "Baby Love" (1964), "Come See about Me" (1964), "Stop! In the Name of Love" (1965), "Back in My Arms Again" (1965), "Nothing But Heartaches" (1965), "I Hear a Symphony" (1965), "My World Is Empty Without You" (1966), "You Can't Hurry Love" (1966), "You Keep Me Hangin' On" (1966), "Love Is Here and Now You're Gone" (1967), "Love Child" (1968), "Someday We'll Be Together" (1969); when Ross left the group (1970), continued to tour and record with various replacement singers until the group was disbanded (1977). Inducted into Rock and Roll Hall of Fame (1988). ❖ See also autobiography *Dreamgirl* (St. Martin, 1986); *Dreamgirls*, loosely based on The Supremes, opened on Broadway (1981); and *Women in World History.*

WILSON, Monica Hunter (1908–1982). South African social anthropologist. Born Monica Hunter, Jan 3, 1908, in village of Lovedale, South Africa; died 1982; dau. of David Alexander Hunter and Jessie McGregor Hunter (both missionaries); Girton College, Cambridge, BA, 1930, PhD, 1934; m. Godfrey Wilson (anthropologist, died 1944), 1935; children: 4. ❖ Performed fieldwork among Pondo in Eastern Cape (present-day Tanskei); with husband, conducted research among Nyakyusa in East Africa and published *The Analysis of Social Change*; served as lecturer in social anthropology and warden of women students at University College of Fort Hare, Eastern Cape; became chair of social anthropology and 1st woman professor at Rhodes University College (1947); served as chair of social anthropology and 1st woman professor at University of Cape Town (1952–73); with Leonard Thompson, served as editor of 2-vol. *Oxford History of South Africa* (1969, 1971).

WILSON, Nancy (1937—). African-American song stylist and actress. Born Nancy Wilson, Feb 20, 1937, in Chillicothe, OH; m. Kenny Dennis (drummer), 1960 (div.); m. Wiley Burton (minister), 1970. ❖ Began singing professionally at local clubs at 15; toured with Rusty Bryant Band (1956–59); moved to NY; signed with Capitol Records, recorded 5 albums (1960–62), including *Nancy Wilson/ Cannonball Adderly Quintet*, which is now considered a classic; had 1st major hit with "Tell Me the Truth" (1963); won a Grammy Award for song "How Glad I Am" (1964); began appearing regularly on tv and starred on "The Nancy Wilson Show" (1967–68), which won an Emmy; also acted in such shows as "Hawaii Five-O," "I Spy," "Police Story" and "Room 222"; made over 60 albums, including *With My Lover Beside Me* (1991), *Love, Nancy* (1994), and *If I Had My Way* (1997). Received NAACP Image Award (1986), Whitney Young Award (1992), and Paul Robeson Humanitarian Award. ❖ See also *Women in World History.*

WILSON, Naomi (1940—). Australian politician. Name variations: Naomi Kate Wynn Wilson. Born Jan 27, 1940, in Arusha, Tanganyika, East Africa. ❖ As a member of the National Party, served in the Queensland Parliament for Mulgrave (1995–98).

WILSON, Peggy (1934—). American golfer. Born Margaret Joyce Wilson, Dec 28, 1934, in Lauderdale, Mississippi; attended Mississippi State College for Women. ❖ Joined LPGA tour (1962); won Hollwood Lakes Open (1968); was runner-up at USGA Women's Open (1969).

WILSON, Romer (1891–1930). English novelist. Name variations: Florence Roma Muir Wilson; Florence Roma Muir O'Brien; (pseudonym) Alphonse Marichaud. Born Florence Roma Muir Wilson, Dec 16,

1891, in Sheffield, England; died of TB, Jan 11, 1930, in Lausanne, Switzerland; dau. of Arnold Muir Wilson (solicitor) and Amy Letitia (Dearden) Wilson; studied law at Girton College, Cambridge University, 1911–14; m. Edward Joseph H. O'Brien (American anthologist), 1923; children: 1 son. ❖ Published 1st novel *Martin Schüler* (1918); enjoyed success with novel *If All These Young Men* (1919) and play *The Social Climbers* (1927); in addition, wrote *The Death of Society: A Novel of Tomorrow*, for which she was awarded the Hawthornden Prize (1921); traveled to Paris for 3 weeks, then published *The Grand Tour of Alphonse Marichaud* (1923); also wrote *Dragon's Blood* (1926), *Greenlow* (1927), *Latterday Symphony* (1927), *All Alone: The Life and Private History of Emily Jane Brontë* (1928), *The Hill of Cloves: A Tract on True Love, with a Digression upon an Invention of the Devil* (1929) and *Tender Advice* (published posthumously, 1935); edited 3 collections of fairy tales. ❖ See also *Women in World History.*

WILSON, Ruth (1919–2001). Canadian athlete. Born 1919 in Calgary, British Columbia, Canada; died in 2001 in Vancouver; m. Art Willoughby (killed 1942). ❖ Won the Vancouver junior girls' singles and doubles tennis titles (1936); won four Canadian women's basketball championships as a guard with the Vancouver Hedlunds (1943–46); played catcher in two Women's World Softball Series (1943, 1945); was a four-time member of women's inter-provincial golf championship team; coached women's basketball for 35 years, including the Canadian bronze-medal basketball team at Pan American Games (1967).

WILSON, Sallie (1932—). American ballet dancer. Born April 18, 1932, in Fort Worth, TX; trained with Margaret Craske. ❖ Danced with Ballet Theater in New York City (1949–50); joined Metropolitan Opera Ballet under Antony Tudor, but returned to Ballet Theater (1954) and remained there for most of her long career; created roles for Herbert Ross's *Concerto*, *Metamorphoses*, and *Paean* (all 1958); featured in classical repertory, including *Dim Lustre*, *Gala Performance*, *Giselle* and *Jardin aux Lilas*; created roles for Jerome Robbins' *Les Noces* (1965), Michael Smuin's *Schubertiade* (1970) and Alvin Ailey's *The River* (1971) and *Sea-Change* (1973); celebrated for her portrayal of Hagar in Tudor's *Pillar of Fire*, The Accused in Agnes de Mille's *Fall River Legend* and Emilia in José Limón's *The Moor's Pavanne*; also danced with New York City Ballet and created roles in Graham's *Episodes* and Balanchine's *Panamerica* (1959–60).

WILSON, Sarah (1750–?). English thief, adventurer, and impostor. Name variations: (alias) Susanna (or Sophia) Carolina Matilda, Marchioness de Waldegrave. Born 1750 in a village in Staffordshire, England; date and place of death unknown; m. Captain William Talbot, after 1775. ❖ Journeyed to London, where she found a job as a servant with Caroline Vernon, who was a maid of honor to Queen Charlotte of Mecklenburg-Strelitz, wife of King George III; crept into the queen's boudoir and stole one of Charlotte's miniature portraits, as well as a diamond necklace and a gown (spring 1771); attempting a 2nd episode later that evening, was caught, tried, found guilty of burglary, and sentenced to death; after the queen intervened on her behalf, sentence was commuted to indentured servitude in the British colonies in North America; arrived in Maryland (autumn 1771); escaped and traveled throughout the Colonies styling herself as Susanna (or Sophia) Carolina Matilda, marchioness de Waldegrave, a sister of the queen of England (1771–73); duped several victims by claiming to be able to secure government posts and army commissions—for substantial fees. ❖ See also *Women in World History.*

WILSON, Staci (1976—). American soccer player. Name variations: Staci Nicole Wilson. Born July 8, 1976, in Livingston, NJ; attended University of North Carolina. ❖ Defender; won a gold medal at Atlanta Olympics (1996).

WILSON, Stacy (1965—). Canadian ice-hockey player. Born May 12, 1965, in Salisbury, New Brunswick, Canada. ❖ Won team gold medals at World championships (1990, 1992, 1994) and captained the gold medal team (1997); won a team silver medal at Nagano (1998), the 1st Olympics to feature women's ice hockey.

WILSON, Tracy. Canadian ice dancer. Born in Port Moody, British Columbia, Canada. ❖ With partner Rob McCall, won Canadian nationals in ice dancing (1982–88); at Calgary Olympics, won a bronze medal (1988), the 1st Canadian ice-dancing team to medal at the Olympics; won a bronze medal at World championships (1986–88); toured with Stars on Ice; when Rob McCall died of AIDS (1991), became a figure-skating commentator for Canadian and US tv. Awarded Order of Canada (1988); inducted into Canadian Olympic Hall of Fame.

WILSON, Wendy (1969—). American singer. Name variations: Wilson Phillips. Born Oct 16, 1969, in Los Angeles, CA; dau. of Brian Wilson (of The Beach Boys) and Marilyn Wilson (member of band, The Honeys); sister of Carnie Wilson (singer); m. Dan Knutson (May 24, 2002); children: Leo Evan (b. Sept 14, 2003) and Beau (b. Sept 29, 2004). ❖ With sister Carnie and Chynna Phillips, formed vocal trio, Wilson Phillips in Los Angeles (1989); released debut album (1990), which had hit singles "Hold On," "Release Me" and "You're in Love"; group *Shadows and Light* (1992), which went platinum; after Wilson Phillips disbanded (1993), released albums *Hey Santa!* (1993) and *The Wilsons* (1997), with Carnie, and appeared in documentary *Brian Wilson: I Just Wasn't Made for These Times* (1995); reunited with Wilson Phillips to record *California* (2004).

WILSON, Mrs. Woodrow.
See Wilson, Ellen Axson (1860–1914)
See Wilson, Edith Bolling (1872–1961).

WILSON CARUS, Eleanora (1897–1977). *See Carus-Wilson, Eleanora.*

WILSON PHILLIPS.
See Phillips, Chynna.
See Wilson, Carnie.
See Wilson, Wendy.

WILT, Mary Badham (1952—). *See Badham, Mary.*

WILTON, Emilie Monson (1829/30–1905). *See Malcolm, Emilie Monson.*

WILTON, Marie (1839–1921). *See Bancroft, Lady.*

WILTSHIRE, countess of.
See Stafford, Catherine (d. 1474).
See Howard, Elizabeth (d. 1538).

WIMAN, Anna Deere (1924–1963). American-born producer and manager. Born Mar 17, 1924, in Moline, IL; died Mar 22, 1963; dau. of Dorothea (Stephens) and Dwight Deere Wiman (producing manager). ❖ Made stage debut as one of the dancers in *Rosalinda* (1942); produced tv shows in Hollywood, then moved to England and entered management (1954), producing such plays as *Morning's at Seven, The Reluctant Debutante, Patience, The Iron Duchess, The Head of the Family, Be My Guest, The Grass is Greener, Aunt Edwina* and *A Shred of Evidence*; with Sam Wanamaker, created and ran the New Shakespeare Culture Center in Liverpool (1957–59).

WIMBERSKY, Petra (1982—). German soccer player. Born Nov 9, 1982, in Munich, Germany. ❖ Midfielder, won a team bronze medal at Athens Olympics (2004).

WINA, Princess Nakatindi (c. 1943—). *See Nakatindi, Princess.*

WINANT, Ethel (1922–2003). American tv executive. Born Ethel Wald, Aug 5, 1922, in Worcester, MA; died Nov 29, 2003, in Canoga Park, CA; m. H. M. Wynant, who changed the spelling of his name (div.); children: William, Scott and Bruce Winant. ❖ One of the 1st female executives in network television, became a vice president at CBS (1973); began career as production assistant for *A Streetcar Named Desire* on Broadway; joined staff on "Studio One" (1958); was casting director and associate producer for "Playhouse 90"; was vice president of talent and casting for CBS (1966–73); oversaw casting for such hit shows as "The Waltons," "Mary Tyler Moore Show," "Rhoda" and "Bob Newhart Show." Inducted into Academy of Television Arts and Sciences Hall of Fame (1999).

WINCH, Hope (1895–1944). English pharmacist. Name variations: Hope Constance Monica Winch. Born 1895 in UK; died April 8, 1944, from a fall while climbing Scafell (the highest Lake District peak). ❖ Passed the Apothecaries Hall assistant exam (1913); served as a dispenser to a surgeon in Wigan (1913–16); studied at Pharmaceutical Society School in London (1916–17); qualified as a chemist and druggist (1917); qualified as pharmaceutical chemist (1918); was a Redwood scholar researcher for Pharmaceutical Society (1918–20); lectured at Rutherford Technical College at Newcastle (1920); as the 1st full-time pharmacy lecturer (1921) and head of the Sunderland Technical College's pharmacy department (1930–44), developed pharmaceutical studies.

WINCH, Joan. English tennis player. Born in UK. ❖ At London Olympics, won a bronze medal in singles (1908).

WINCHELSEA, countess of.
See Finch, Ann (1661–1720).
See Seymour, Mary (d. 1673).

WINCHESTER, countess of.
See Matilda (d. 1252).
See Beauchamp, Isabel (fl. 1285).

WINCHESTER, Lady of. *See Emma of Normandy (c. 985–1052).*

WINCKLESS, Sarah (1973—). English rower. Born Oct 18, 1973, in Reading, Berkshire, England. ❖ Won a bronze medal for double sculls at Athens Olympics (2004).

WINDEYER, Mary (1836–1912). Australian reformer. Name variations: Lady Mary Windeyer. Born Mary Elizabeth Bolton at Hove, England, 1836; died in Raymond Terrace, NSW, Australia, Dec 1912; dau. of Robert Thorley Bolton (minister) and Jane (Ball) Bolton; m. William Charles Windeyer (barrister, judge, MP, and government official), Dec 31, 1857 (died 1897); children: 9, including Lucy Windeyer and Margaret Windeyer. ❖ Charity organizer and champion of orphans' welfare and women's suffrage, moved with family to Hexham in NSW, Australia, at a young age; helped to establish a foundling hospital that later became the Ashfield Infants' Home (1874); drafted legislation for a State Children's Relief Board, which assumed responsibility for fostering children from the state-run orphanages and was appointed a member of the board; helped organize a Temporary Aid Society, which helped women make new starts in their lives by advancing them small amounts of money; after daughter Margaret helped organize the 1st meeting of the Women's Literary Society, which had matured into the Womanhood Suffrage League by 1891, became its 1st president; served as secretary for the 2nd Australasian Conference on Charity, helped establish a Women's College at the University of New South Wales, and led the delegation on suffrage that met with Prime Minister Parkes (all 1891); organized a district hospital to care for poor women (1896), which later relocated to larger premises as Crown Street Women's Hospital. ❖ See also *Women in World History.*

WINDSOR, Alice de (d. 1400). *See Perrers, Alice.*

WINDSOR, Claire (1897–1972). American silent-film star. Born Clara Viola Cronk in Crawker City, Kansas, in 1897; died 1972; m. William Boyes (lasted one year); m. Bert Lytell (actor), 1925 (div. 1927); children: (1st m.) Bill Boyes. ❖ Star of silents who worked for nearly every major Hollywood studio, but retired soon after the advent of sound; appeared in such Lois Weber films as *To Please One Woman* (1920), *What's Worth While* (1921), *Too Wise Wives* (1921), *The Blot* (1921), and *What Do Men Want?* (1921); also starred in *Little Church Around the Corner* (1923), *Rupert of Hentzau* (1923), *Dance Madness* (1926), *The Claw* (1927), *Captain Lash* (1929), and many others.

WINDSOR, duchess of. *See Windsor, Wallis Warfield, duchess of (1895–1986).*

WINDSOR, Katherine (b. 1933). *See Worsley, Katherine.*

WINDSOR, Marie (1919–2000). American actress. Born Emily Marie Bertelsen, Dec 11, 1919, in Marysvale, UT; died Dec 10, 2000, in Beverly Hills, CA; studied under Maria Ouspenskaya; m. Ted Steele, 1946 (div.); m. Jack Hupp, 1954. ❖ Named Miss Utah; made film debut (1941); began playing featured parts (1947); films include *The Narrow Margin, The Killing, Dakota Lil, The Jungle, Trouble Along the Way, The Story of Mankind, Paradise Alley, The Day Mars Invaded the Earth, Bedtime Story, Support Your Local Gunfighter* and *Freaky Friday*; served as a director of Screen Actors Guild for 25 years.

WINDSOR, Wallis Warfield, duchess of (1895–1986). American duchess. Name variations: Bessie Wallis Warfield (1895–1916); Wallis Spencer (1916–25); Wallis Simpson (1928–36); Duchess of Windsor (1936–86). Born out of wedlock as Bessie Wallis Warfield in Blue Ridge Summit, Pennsylvania, June 19, 1895; died in France, April 24, 1986; dau. of Teackle Wallis Warfield and Alice Montague Warfield (1869–1929); m. Earl Winfield "Win" Spencer (navy aviator), 1916 (div. 1925); m. Ernest Simpson (Anglo-American shipping entrepreneur), 1928 (div. 1936); m. Edward VIII (1894–1972), king of England (r. 1936–1936) and duke of Windsor, June 1937; no children. ❖ Famous hostess and international celebrity, whose husband abdicated the throne of England to be with her, had a successful debutante season in Baltimore (1914); during 1st marriage, moved to Washington, DC, and had love affairs with an Argentinean diplomat and Prince Gelasio Caetani, ambassador from Mussolini's Italy, who taught her to admire fascism; later had an affair with another Italian fascist, Count Galeazzo Ciano; on 2nd marriage (1928), settled in London, where she soon became a popular host; met Edward (VIII), prince of Wales (1931), and began love affair (early 1934); now found herself being courted by Nazi German diplomatic corps, which were cultivating the prince (these contacts, and the dogged support of the British Union of Fascists which she and the prince enjoyed during the abdication crisis, linked her name with fascism permanently and added to her unpopularity in later years); after Edward assumed the throne (1936), was a frequent visitor to Buckingham Palace; husband's announcement that they were getting a divorce caused a political crisis when Edward told the Conservative prime minister that he intended to marry her and make her queen; fled for south of France, urging the king not to abdicate; was bitterly disappointed when he did (Dec 1936); in most respects, lived rest of life as a protracted, 50-year anticlimax; after 31 years, appeared in public at a British royal function as duchess of Windsor alongside the queen (1967). ❖ See also memoir *The Heart Has Its Reasons* (McKay, 1956); Michael Bloch, ed. *Wallis and Edward: Letters, 1931–1937* (Weidenfeld & Nicolson, 1986); Charles Higham, *The Duchess of Windsor: The Secret Life* (McGraw-Hill, 1988); Ralph G. Martin, *The Woman He Loved* (Simon & Schuster, 1974); Edwina Wilson, *Her Name Was Wallis Warfield* (Dutton, 1936); and *Women in World History*.

WINE-BANKS, Jill (1943—). American attorney. Name variations: Jill Volner. Born Jill Susan Wine, May 5, 1943, in Chicago, IL; dau. of Bert S. and Sylvia Dawn (Simon) Wine; University of Illinois–Champaigne-Urbana, BS, 1964; Columbia University, JD, 1968; m. Ian David Volner, Aug 21, 1965; m. Michael A. Banks, Jan 12, 1980. ❖ Attained prominence as assistant Watergate special prosecutor, general counsel of US Army, and deputy attorney general of Illinois; admitted to NY bar (1969); served as 1st woman executive director of American Bar Association (1987—90); worked in senior management positions at Motorola and Maytag; served as president and chief executive officer of non-profit organization Winning Workplaces.

WINFREY, Oprah (1954—). African-American talk-show host, actress, and entrepreneur. Born out of wedlock, Jan 29, 1954, in Kosciusko, Mississippi; dau. of Vernon Winfrey and Vernita Lee; entered Tennessee State University, 1972. ❖ Television talk-show host, actress, and producer, the 1st African-American woman to helm a national tv program, who became one of the most recognized and influential media personalities in America; raised in poverty on grandparents' farm before moving to Milwaukee to live with mother; during her troubled years, was often threatened with placement in an institution; moved to Nashville to live with father, who introduced strict discipline and a respect for education into her life; entered Tennessee State University as a speech and drama major (1972); became a reporter at a Nashville radio station (1973); offered a job as a weekend tv news anchor on Nashville's CBS affiliate, WTVF, becoming the city's 1st black news anchor (1973); became a co-anchor on Baltimore's WJZ evening newscast (1976), then was teamed as a co-host with one of the station's best-known reporters on "People Are Talking," a half-hour morning chat show meant to challenge top-rated "Phil Donahue Show"; received an offer to host "A. M. Chicago" (1984), where her obvious empathy with whomever she was talking to and her ability to relate her personal experiences to the subject at hand convinced the show's producers that her guests and topics should be drawn from everyday life; show was renamed "The Oprah Winfrey Show" and syndicated nationally (1986); made film debut in *The Color Purple* (1985), receiving an Oscar nomination (1986); after winning 3 daytime Emmy Awards, bought the rights to her show from Capitol Cities/ABC, with which she also negotiated a deal to broadcast her company's 1st major tv film, "The Women of Brewster Place" (1987); began to head her own production company, Harpo, which produces her tv show along with tv mini-series and feature films, becoming the 1st black woman to own a studio, and only the 3rd woman in American history, after Mary Pickford Mary and Lucille Ball; finally managed to bring the film *Beloved* to the screen (1995) after a tortuous process she described in her book *The Road to Beloved*; launched *Oprah,* the magazine; remains one of America's most influential women. ❖ See also George Mair, *Oprah Winfrey: The Real Story* (Carol, 1994); Lois Nicholson, *Oprah Winfrey* (Chelsea House, 1994); and *Women in World History*.

WING, Toby (1915–2001). American dancer and actress. Born Martha Virginia Wing, July 14, 1915, in Amelia Court House, VA; died Mar 22, 2001, in Mathews, VA; m. Henry Tindall "Dick" Merrill (celebrated aviator); children: 2 sons, one died in infancy. ❖ Made film debut at age 8; appeared as Max Sennett bathing beauty at 16; as one of America's favorite pinups, made 38 movies in 10 years, including *The Kid from*

Spain (1933), *Forty-Second Street* (1933), *Baby Face* (1933), *College Humor* (1933), *Come on Marines* (1934), *Rhythmitis* (1936) and *True Confession* (1937); appeared on Broadway in Cole Porter's *You Never Know* (1938).

WINGARD, Lenore (1911–2000). *See Kight-Wingard, Lenore.*

WINGER, Debra (1955—). American actress. Born May 16, 1955, in Cleveland, Ohio, into Orthodox Hungarian-Jewish family; attended California State University; m. Timothy Hutton (actor), 1986 (div. 1990); m. Arliss Howard (actor), 1996; children: Noah Hutton, Babe Howard. ❖ At 6, moved with family to California; spent 1 year working on kibbutz in Israel after high school; made inauspicious movie debut in *Slumber Party '57* (1977); had 1st major success in *Urban Cowboy* (1980), followed by *An Officer and a Gentleman* (1982), and *Terms of Endearment* (1983); other films include *Cannery Row* (1982), *Mike's Murder* (1984), *Black Widow* (1986), *Legal Eagles* (1986), *The Sheltering Sky* (1990), *Shadowlands* (1993) and *A Dangerous Woman*.

WINGO, Effiegene Locke (1883–1962). American politician. Name variations: Effiegene Locke. Born April 13, 1883, in Lockesburg, Arkansas; died Sept 19, 1962, in Burlington, Ontario, Canada; descendant of US Representative Matthew Locke of North Carolina; graduate of Maddox Seminary in Little Rock, Arkansas, 1901; m. Otis Theodore Wingo (US congressional representative, 1912–30, died 1930). ❖ Following husband's death (1930), was nominated to finish his unexpired term in 71st Congress and serve in the 72nd Congress to which he had been nominated prior to his death; won both the special election for the 1st term and the general election for the 2nd (Nov 1930); while in Congress (1930–33), aided her Arkansas district in the Depression years, served on the Committee on Foreign Affairs, and created the Ouachita National Forest game refuge and Ouachita National Park; later co-founded the National Institute of Public Affairs, offering Washington internships to students. ❖ See also *Women in World History*.

WINKEL, Kornelia (1944—). Dutch swimmer. Born Feb 26, 1944, in Netherlands. ❖ At Tokyo Olympics, won a silver medal in 4 x 100-meter medley relay (1964).

WINKELMANN, Maria (1670–1720). *See Kirch, Maria Winkelmann.*

WINKWORTH, Catherine (1827–1878). English poet and translator. Born Sept 13, 1827, in London, England; died July 1, 1878; dau. of Henry Winkworth (silk merchant) and Susanna (Dickenson) Winkworth (died 1841); sister of Susanna Winkworth (1820–1884); tutored by 2 celebrated Unitarian clerics: Reverend William Gaskell (later husband of novelist Elizabeth Gaskell) and Reverend James Martineau (brother of Harriet Martineau); privately studied German language and literature. ❖ Traveled to Dresden (1845), to live with an aunt and act as governess to her cousins; developed a fluency in German and an interest in German literature; published collection of translations of common hymns in *Lyra Germanica* (1855), which went through more than 20 editions; printed a 2nd series of hymns (1858) and a 3rd (1859), then published *The Chorale Book for England* (1862); subsequent writing extended to translations of German prose as well as hymns in *Veni Sancti Spiritus* (1865), and a set of biographical sketches, *Christian Singers of Germany* (1869); back in England, helped found Bristol University College, later Bristol University, and acted as a Cheltenham Ladies College council member; joined Committee on Higher Education for Women (1868), becoming its secretary (1870). ❖ See also *Women in World History*.

WINKWORTH, Susanna (1820–1884). English writer, translator, and social reformer. Born Aug 13, 1820, in London, England; died Nov 25, 1884, in Clifton, Bristol, England; dau. of Henry (silk merchant) and Susanna (Dickenson) Winkworth; sister of Catherine Winkworth (1827–1878); tutored by Unitarian clerics: Reverend William Gaskell (later husband of novelist Elizabeth Gaskell) and Reverend James Martineau (brother of Harriet Martineau); privately studied German language and literature. ❖ Published translation of Barthold Georg Niebuhr's *Life* (1851–52), adding such extensive new material in the form of letters and essays that the biography essentially became an original work; translated *Theologica Germanica*, a text that had been discovered and published by Martin Luther (1854); translated Baron Bunsen's works, *Signs of the Times* (1856) and *God in History* (1868–70); also translated the biography and sermons of theologian John Tauler (1857) and the work *German Love from the Papers of an Alien* (1858), written by Max Muller. ❖ See also *Women in World History*.

WINLOCK, Anna (1857–1904). American astronomer. Born 1857 in Cambridge, Massachusetts; died 1904 in Cambridge; dau. of Joseph

Winlock (astronomer and 3rd director of Harvard College Observatory, died 1875) and Isabella (Lane) Winlock. ❖ Exhibited remarkable abilities in mathematics from a young age; taught herself astronomy and followed in father's career, becoming one of the 1st women to hold a paid position as a staff member at Harvard College Observatory; worked on the star catalogue project, which lasted nearly as long as her life; supervised the preparation of a table listing the relative positions of variable stars in clusters and their comparison stars which was published in Vol. 38 of Observatory's *Annals*; determined the path of the asteroid Eros, one of the largest inner asteroids; also found the circular orbit for asteroid Ocllo, and later assisted in determining its elliptical elements; her most significant independent investigation, a catalogue of the stars near the North and South poles, was the most complete compilation assembled at that time. ❖ See also *Women in World History*.

WINN, Anona (1907–1994). Australian-born radio singer, actress, and revue artist. Born 1907 in Sydney, NSW, Australia; died Feb 2, 1994; dau. of Lilian (Woodgate) and David Winn-Wilkins; m. Frederick Lamport (died). ❖ Trained as a lawyer, made stage debut in Melbourne in *The Merry Widow* and London debut in *Hit the Deck* (1928); found fame as a singer with the help of Nellie Melba; following WWII, was a popular member of the game-show panel on BBC's "Twenty Questions." Named Member of the British Empire (MBE).

WINNEMUCCA, Sarah (1844–1891). Native American activist. Name variations: Sarah Winnemucca Hopkins; Paiute name was Thoc-me-tony, Thocmetony, or Toc-me-to-ne ("Shell-Flower"). Born in 1844 (some sources cite 1842) near Humboldt Lake, in present-day northern Nevada; died of TB at Henry's Lake, Nevada, Oct 17 (some sources cite 16), 1891; dau. of Paiute Chief Winnemucca II and Tuboitonie (Paiute woman and hunter-gatherer); attended St. Mary's Convent in San Jose, California, 1860; spoke English and Spanish as well as 3 Indian dialects; married an unidentified Paiute man, c. 1861 (div.); m. Edward C. Bartlett (first lieutenant), Jan 29, 1871 (div. 1876); m. Joseph Satwaller, Nov 13, 1878; m. Lewis H. Hopkins, Dec 5, 1881 (died 1887); children: none. ❖ Northern Paiute who lectured and wrote about the ill-treatment of her people and campaigned for the rights of American Indians; with her sister, joined the household of Major William Ormsby, stagecoach agent, in Mormon Station, Nevada, now known as Genoa, Nevada (1857), where they worked as domestics and companions to Ormsby's daughter; learned to speak English and read and write; returned home (1859); served as official interpreter for the Army post at Camp McDermitt in northern Nevada (1868); wrote letter to Major Henry Douglass, Indian superintendent to Nevada, relating the plight of the Paiute caused by the reservation system (1870); fame as a spokesperson for her people spread, and several articles about her appeared in various magazines; after the Paiutes were finally given an official home on a large tract of land in southeast Oregon, known as the Malheur Reservation, interpreted for Sam B. Parrish, at Malheur Agency (1875); served US Army as an interpreter, scout, and peacemaker under General Oliver O. Howard, in the Bannock War (1878); following war, lectured in major Western cities on behalf of justice for Indians and, accompanied by her father Chief Winnemucca II, went to Washington to plead for Indians' cause (1880); went East to lecture on Indian rights and became protege of Elizabeth Palmer Peabody and her sister Mary Peabody Mann (1883); wrote *Life Among the Paiutes: Their Wrongs and Claims*, edited by Mary Peabody Mann; wrote a pamphlet, "Sarah Winnemucca's Practical Solution of the Indian Problem"; opened Peabody Indian School for Paiute children; became an important lobbyist for Indian policy reform. ❖ See also Gae Whitney Canfield, *Sarah Winnemucca of the Northern Paiutes* (U. of Oklahoma Press, 1983); Katherine Gehm, *Sarah Winnemucca: Most Extraordinary Woman of the Paiute Nation* (O'Sullivan Woodside, 1975); Dorothy Nafus Morrison, *Chief Sarah: Sarah Winnemucca's Fight for Indian Rights* (Atheneum, 1980); and *Women in World History*.

WINSCOM, Jane (c. 1754–1813). See Cave, Jane.

WINSER, Beatrice (1869–1947). American librarian and museum director. Born Mar 11, 1869, in Newark, New Jersey; died Sept 14, 1947, in Newark, New Jersey; dau. of Henry Jacob Winser (journalist) and Edith (Cox) Winser; educated in French and German languages at schools in Germany; studied at Columbia University Library School. ❖ Lived in Germany as a child; became cataloguer of the French and German archives at Newark Public Library (1889), then promoted to assistant librarian (1894), working 1st under John Cotton Dana, an educational crusader; became his assistant in advocating the open-shelf system; helped Dana with

founding of the Newark Museum (1909), then became assistant director and assistant secretary of the museum (1915), joining its board of trustees as a member (1916); accepted an appointment to Newark Board of Education (1915), the 1st woman to serve on any of the city's governing boards; following Dana's death (1929), succeeded him as both head librarian of Newark Public Library and director of the museum; was a founding member of New Jersey Library Association, serving as president (1907–08, 1921–22); resigned from Newark Public Library (1942), then the museum (1947). ❖ See also *Women in World History*.

WINSLOE, Christa (1888–1944). German playwright, screenwriter, novelist, and sculptor. Born Dec 23, 1888, in Darmstadt, Germany; killed June 10, 1944; m. Baron Ludwig Hatvany (1880–1961, div.); began relationship with writer Dorothy Thompson (1893–1961), in 1933. ❖ Adapted her anti-authoritarian play into the film *Gestern und Heute* (Yesterday and Today), which was then made into the classic German film *Mädchen in Uniform* (Girls in Uniform, 1931), starring Dorothea Wieck and Hertha Thiele, and directed by Leontine Sagan; also wrote scripts for G. W. Pabst; during World War II, lived in exile, helping fellow Germans escape to Switzerland; just before the end of the war, was shot and killed by a French criminal. ❖ See also *Women in World History*.

WINSLOW, Anna Green (1759–1779). American diarist. Born 1759 in Cumberland, Novia Scotia; died 1779; dau. of Joshua Winslow and Anna Green. ❖ Kept diary for parents of life at Boston finishing school (1771–73), published as *Diary of Anna Green Winslow* (1894).

WINSLOW, Catherine Mary Reignolds (1836–1911). See Reignolds, Catherine Mary.

WINSLOW, Kate (1836–1911). See Reignolds, Catherine Mary.

WINSLOW, Ola Elizabeth (c. 1885–1977). American writer and historian. Born c. 1885 in Grant City, Missouri; died Sept 27, 1977, in Damariscotta, Maine; dau. of William Delos Winslow and Hattie Elizabeth (Colby) Winslow; Stanford University, AB, 1906, MA, 1914; University of Chicago, PhD, 1922; pursued special studies at Johns Hopkins University. ❖ Highly regarded in the field of Colonial religious history, was an instructor at College of the Pacific (now University of the Pacific) in San Jose, California (1909–14); as a professor of English, headed English department at Goucher College in Baltimore, where she would remain until 1944; was a professor of English at Wellesley College (1944–50), then professor emeritus until 1977; was also professor of English at Radcliffe College (1950–52); won Pulitzer Prize in biography for *Jonathan Edwards, 1703–1758* (1941); other writings include *Meetinghouse Hill, 1630–1783* (1952), *Master Roger Williams* (1957), *John Bunyan* (1961), *Samuel Sewall of Boston* (1964), *Portsmouth, the Life of a Town* (1966), (editor) *Jonathan Edwards: Basic Writings* (1966), *John Eliot: Apostle to the Indians* (1968), *"And Plead for the Rights of All": Old South Church in Boston, 1669–1969* (1970) and *A Destroying Angel: The Conquest of Smallpox in Colonial Boston* (1974). ❖ See also *Women in World History*.

WINSOR, Kathleen (1919–2003). American writer. Born Oct 16, 1919, in Olivia, Minnesota; died May 26, 2003, in New York, NY; dau. of Myrtle Belle (Crowder) Winsor and Harold Lee Winsor; University of California, BA, 1938; m. Robert J. Herwig, 1936 (div. 1946); m. Artie Shaw (bandleader), 1946 (div.); m. Arnold Robert Krakower (lawyer), 1949 (div. 1953); m. Paul A. Porter (lawyer), 1956 (died 1975). ❖ Began career as a reporter and receptionist for *Oakland Tribune* in Oakland, California (1938); published 1st book, *Forever Amber* (1944), which sold millions of copies and was banned in Boston; also wrote *Star Money* (1950), *The Lovers* (1952), *America, with Love* (1957), *Wanderers Eastward, Wanderers West* (1965), *Calais* (1979), *Jacintha* (1985) and *Robert and Arabella* (1986); served as a story consultant for tv series "Dreams in the Dust" (1971).

WINTER, Alice Ames (1865–1944). American reformer and novelist. Name variations: Alice Vivian Ames Winter. Born Alice Vivian Ames, Nov 28, 1865, in Albany, NY; died April 5, 1944, in Pasadena, CA; dau. of Charles Gordon Ames (Unitarian minister) and Fanny Baker Ames (1840–1931, social activist and reformer); m. Thomas Gerald Winter (grain firm president), June 25, 1892; children: 1 son, 1 daughter. ❖ Was president of Minneapolis Kindergarten Association (1890s); published romantic novels *The Prize to the Hardy* (1905) and *Jewel Weed* (1906); was 1st president of Woman's Club of Minneapolis (1907–15); chaired Department of Literature (1916) and Americanization Division of General Federation of Women's Clubs (1919) and served as president

(1920–24); helped create Women's Joint Congressional Committee (1920); appointed by President Warren Harding to advisory committee of Washington Conference on naval disarmament (1921–22); published *The Business of Being a Club Woman* (1925) and *The Heritage of Women* (1927); worked as liaison between women's groups and movie industry for Motion Picture Producers and Distributors of America (1929–42).

WINTER, Ethel (1924—). American modern dancer and choreographer. Born June 18, 1924, in Wrentham, MA. ❖ Trained with Martha Hill and Martha Graham at Bennington College; joined the Graham company (1945), and created numerous roles throughout career in such Graham works as *Appalachian Spring* (1945), *Dark Meadow* (1946), *Night Journey* (1947), *Clytemnestra* (1958), *Alcestis* (1960), *Phaedra* (1962), and *Cortege of Eagles* (1967); created role of The Bride for Yuriko's *The Ghost* (1960); choreographed for Bat-sheva Dance Company of Israel.

WINTER, Grace (1836–188). *See Blackwell, Ellen Wright.*

WINTER, Joanne (1924—). American baseball player. Born Nov 24, 1924, in IL; never married. ❖ Joined the Racine Belles of the All-American Girls Baseball League (1943); ended the 1946 season with a 22–10 record, striking out 183 batters, and pitched 63 consecutive shutout innings, a record that still stands. ❖ See also *Women in World History.*

WINTER, John Strange (1856–1911). British novelist. Name variations: Henrietta Stannard; Mrs. Arthur Stannard; Henrietta Palmer; (pseudonym) Violet Whyte. Born Henrietta Elizabeth Vaughan Palmer, Jan 13, 1856, in York, England; died Dec 13, 1911, in Putney, London, England; dau. of Henry Vaughan Palmer (rector and former artillery officer) and Emily Catherine (Cowling) Palmer; m. Arthur Stannard (civil engineer), 1884; children: 1 son, 3 daughters. ❖ Popular novelist and journalist, began professional career at 18, contributing a number of short stories and serialized novels to the *Family Herald* under pseudonym Violet Whyte (1874); under pseudonym John Strange Winter, published several novels, including *Cavalry Sketches* (1881) and *Regimental Legends* (1883), which deal with the life of a military family; kept this pen name for the rest of her life; earned national prominence with *Bootles' Baby: A Story of the Scarlet Lancers* (1885), which drew praise for her accurate portrayal of British soldiers; founded magazine, *Golden Gates* (1891), which was renamed *Winter's Weekly* (1892), and served as its editor (1891–95); was president of Society of Women Journalists (1901–03); wrote over 100 novels, including *Army Society* (1886), *Pluck* (1886), *Mignon's Husband* (1887), *Beautiful Jim of the Blankshire Regiment* (1888), *He Went for a Soldier* (1890), *A Soldier's Children* (1892), *That Mrs. Smith* (1893), *Grip* (1896) and *A Summer Jaunt* (1899). ❖ See also *Women in World History.*

WINTER, Liane (1942—). West German marathon runner. Born June 24, 1942, in Wolfsburg, West Germany. ❖ Won Boston Marathon (1975) with a time of 2:42:24, a world, national, and course record.

WINTER, Lucretia van (1721–1789). *See Merken, Lucretia Wilhelmina van.*

WINTERBACH, Ingrid (1948—). South African novelist. Name variations: Ingrid Gouws; Ingrid Scholtz; (pseudonym) Lettie Viljoen. Born Feb 14, 1948, in Johannesburg, South Africa; children: 2. ❖ Studied fine art, Afrikaans, and Dutch at University of Stellenbosch; art work has been exhibited worldwide; writings include *Klaaglied vir Koos* (1984), *Erf* (1986), *Belemmering* (1990), *Karolina Ferreira* (1993), *Landskap met Vroue en Slang* (1996), *Buller se Plan* (1999) and *Niggie* (2002).

WINTER QUEEN, the. *See Elizabeth of Bohemia (1596–1662).*

WINTERS, Kay (1913–1971). *See Comingore, Dorothy.*

WINTERS, Linda (1913–1971). *See Comingore, Dorothy.*

WINTERS, Marian (1924–1978). American actress and playwright. Born April 19, 1924, in New York, NY; died Nov 3, 1978 in New York, NY; m. Jay H. Smolin. ❖ Made stage debut in stock (1940); made NY debut in *Hippolytus* (1948), followed by *King John, Dream Girl, I Am a Camera, Cherry Orchard, Auntie Mame, Tall Story* and *Deathtrap*, among others; played more than 300 roles on tv; also wrote plays, including *A is for All, All Saints Day*, and *All is Bright* and the teleplay "Animal Keepers" (which won 2 Emmys).

WINTERS, Shelley (1920—2006). American actress. Born Shirley Schrift, Aug 18, 1920, in East St. Louis, Illinois; died Jan 14, 2006, in Beverly Hills, California; dau. of Johan Schrift (clothing retailer) and Rose (Winter) Schrift (singer); studied acting at New Theater School and Actors Studio; m. Mack Mayer (textile merchant), Jan 1, 1943 (div. 1948); m. Vittorio Gassman (actor), April 28, 1952 (div. 1954); m. Anthony Franciosa (actor), May 4, 1957 (div. 1960); children: (2nd m.) Vittoria Gassman. ❖ On Broadway, appeared as Fifi in *Rosalinda* (1942), which led to contract with Columbia; played series of bit parts in some 10 films without gaining attention (1942–44), including *Knickerbocker Holiday* and *Cover Girl*; came to prominence as the murder victim in *A Double Life* (1948), which brought her Academy Award Best Supporting nomination; followed with such films as *Cry of the City* (1948), *The Great Gatsby* (1949) and *South Sea Sinner* (1950); abandoned all trappings of glamour for role as the pregnant factory worker who is murdered in *A Place in the Sun* (1951), for which she earned a 2nd Academy Award nomination (as Best Actress) and established her reputation; won a pair of Oscars for work in *The Diary of Anne Frank* (1959) and *A Patch of Blue* (1965), and electrified Broadway with performance in *A Hatful of Rain* (1955); won acclaim as mother of Marx Brothers in Broadway production of *Minnie's Boys* (1970); had recurring role as the dotty mother on tv's "Roseanne"; other films include *Red River* (1948), *Frenchie* (1951), *Phone Call From a Stranger* (1952), *Meet Danny Wilson* (1952), *Executive Suite* (1954), *I Am a Camera* (1955), *The Night of the Hunter* (1955), *Lolita* (1962), *The Balcony* (1963), *Alfie* (1966), *Harper* (1966), *Enter Laughing* (1967), *Bloody Mama* (1970), *What's the Matter with Helen?* (1971), *Who Slew Auntie Roo?* (1971), *The Poseidon Adventure* (1972), *Next Stop Greenwich Village* (1976), *Pete's Dragon* (1977), *The Three Sisters* (1977), *King of the Gypsies* (1979), *The Visitor* (1979), *Fanny Hill* (1983), *Touch of a Stranger* (1990) and *La Bomba* (1999). ❖ See also autobiographies, *Shelley: Also Known as Shirley* (Morrow, 1980) and *Shelley II: The Middle of My Century* (Simon & Schuster, 1989); and *Women in World History.*

WINTERTON, Ann (1941—). English politician and member of Parliament. Born Jane Ann Hodgson, Mar 6, 1941; m. Nicholas Winterton (Tory MP), 1960; children: 2 sons, 1 daughter. ❖ As a Conservative, elected to House of Commons for Congleton (1983, 1887, 1992, 1997, 2001, 2005); was shadow minister for Agriculture and Fisheries (2001–02); became Tory whip; was twice embroiled in controversy for telling jokes, the 1st revolved around Pakistanis, the second around the deaths of 20 Chinese immigrant workers.

WINTERTON, Rosie (1958—). English politician and member of Parliament. Born Aug 10, 1958, in Doncaster, England; dau. of Valerie Winterton and Gordon Winterton, both teachers; Hull University, BA in history. ❖ Representing Labour, elected to House of Commons for Doncaster Central (1997, 2001, 2005); named parliamentary secretary, Lord Chancellor's Deparment (2001); became minister at the Department for Health (2003).

WINTHROP, F. (1888–1960). *See Jacob, Rosamund.*

WINTHROP, Lucy (c. 1600–1679). *See Downing, Lucy Winthrop.*

WINTHROP, Margaret (c. 1591–1647). Colonial American. Born Margaret Tyndal about 1591 in Great Maplestead, Essex County, England; died June 1647 in Boston, Massachusetts; dau. of Sir John Tyndal (master of chancery) and Lady Anne Egerton Tyndal; m. John Winthrop (Colonial governor), on April 24 or 29, 1618; children: 8, 4 of whom survived childhood, Stephen, Adam, Deane, and Samuel. ❖ English-born colonial, wife of the 1st governor of the Massachusetts Bay Colony, who was first lady for the colony's initial 16 years; arrived in the New World on the ship *Lyon* in Boston Harbor (Nov 4, 1631), two years after husband's arrival; her infant daughter had died at sea; during husband's 12 terms as governor, befriended Anne Bradstreet and was troubled by the actions taken against Anne Hutchinson. ❖ See also Alice Morse Earle, *Margaret Winthrop* (Scribner, 1895); Joseph Hopkins Twichell, ed. *Some Old Puritan Love Letters: John and Margaret Winthrop, 1618–1638* (1893); and *Women in World History.*

WINTON, Jane (1905–1959). American stage and screen actress. Born Oct 10, 1905, in Philadelphia, PA; died Sept 22, 1959, in New York, NY; m. Michael T. Gottlieb (NY stockbroker). ❖ Began career in *Ziegfeld Follies*; films include *My Old Dutch, Why Girls Go Back Home, The Fair Co-Ed, Burning Daylight, Melody of Love, Scandal, The Furies, Limelight, The Bridge of San Luis Rey, Hell's Angels* and *Don Juan.*

WINTOUR, Anna (1949—). English-born magazine editor. Born Nov 3, 1949 in London, England; dau. of Charles Wintour (British editor of *Evening Standard*) and Elinor Baker (American); m. David Schaffer (child psychiatrist, div.); children: Charlie and Bee. ❖ Began career working in fashion department at *Harpers & Queen* in London (1970);

moved to NY to join *Harper's Bazaar* as its fashion editor; served as senior editor of *New York* magazine; was creative director of American *Vogue* (1983–86); served as editor-in-chief of British *Vogue* (1986–88), then became editor-in-chief of American *Vogue* (1988), where she has remained for years; wields considerable influence in the world of fashion.

WINWOOD, Estelle (1883–1984). English-born stage, tv, and screen actress. Born Estelle Goodwin, Jan 24, 1883, in Lee, Kent, England; died June 20, 1984, in Woodland Hills, CA; m. Arthur Chesney (brother of Edmund Gwenn, div.); m. Guthrie McClintic (div.); m. Francis Barlow Bradley (died 1929); m. Robert Barton Henderson (English director). ❖ Began career at age 5 (1888) and continued until age 100 (1983); made London debut in *School* (1899), followed by *When Knights Were Bold, Mrs. Skeffington, The Cage, Nan* and *Half Past 8*; made NY debut in *Hush* (1916), followed by *A Successful Calamity, A Little Journey, The Circle, Spring Cleaning, Trelawny of the Wells, The Vortex, Ladies in Retirement* and *Ten Little Indians,* among many others; made film debut (1933), followed by *Quality Street, The Swan, 23 Paces to Baker Street, The Misfits, The Cabinet of Dr Caligari, Camelot, The Producers* and *Murder by Death*.

WIRATTHAWORN, Aree (1980—). Thai weightlifter. Born Feb 26, 1980, in Thailand. ❖ At World championships, placed 2nd in 48 kg and 48 kg clean and jerk (2003); won a silver medal for 48 kg at Athens Olympics (2004).

WIRT SIKES, Mrs. (1839–1909). *See Logan, Olive.*

WISCHNEWETZKY, Florence Kelley (1859–1932). *See Kelley, Florence.*

WISDOM, Saint. *See Sophia (fl. early 2nd c.).*

WISE, Brownie (1913–1992). American entrepreneur. Born Brownie Mae Humphrey, 1913, in Buford, Georgia; died Dec 1992 in Kissimmee, Florida; dau. of Jerome Humphrey (plumber) and Rosabelle Stroud Humphrey (hat maker); married Robert W. Wise (machinist), Dec 15, 1936 (div. 1942); children: Jerry Wise (b. 1938). ❖ When Earl Tupper invented the plastic containers with the famous "Tupper seal" (1947), when sales were flat, was asked to come up with a merchandising strategy; invented the Tupperware party; was made vice president of the company, in charge of sales and distribution, and withdrew the product from stores; deemed a marketing genius, was the 1st woman featured on the cover of *Business Week*. ❖ See also Alison Clarke, *Tupperware: The Promise of Plastic in 1950s America* (Smithsonian, 1999); and *Women in World History*.

WISE, Louise Waterman (1874–1947). American charitable leader and Zionist. Born Louise Waterman, July 17, 1874, in New York, NY; died Dec 10, 1947; dau. of Julius Waterman (artisan) and Justine (Mayer) Waterman; studied painting at Art Students League; m. Stephen Samuel Wise (rabbi and Zionist), Nov 14, 1900 (died 1949); children: James Waterman Wise (b. 1901, writer) and Justine Wise (b. 1903, lawyer and judge). ❖ In Portland, Oregon, established the Free Nurses Association for medical assistance to poor mothers (1902); in NY, improved school buildings and started an adoption agency for Jewish orphans (1909–16); began championing aid to children in Palestine (1923); captured injustice on canvas, with such titles as "Orphanage," "Sacrifice of Abraham" and "Flight from Belgium" (1920s), paintings that were acclaimed and exhibited; translated French books about Judaism, such as *The Unknown Sanctuary* (1928) by Aimé Pallière, and *My Palestine* (1933) and *Why I am a Jew* (1934) by Edmond Fleg; created Women's Division of American Jewish Congress to heighten public awareness of the threats of Nazism and anti-Semitism; began establishing shelters for Eastern European refugees (1933); provided hostels for Allied military personnel; raised funds for wounded Russian and British civilians and for children evacuated during the Blitz in WWII; attempted to assist Holocaust survivors after the war. ❖ See also *Women in World History*.

WISE, Ursula (1885–1948). *See Isaacs, Susan.*

WISELY, Violet Alberta Jessie (1893–1972). *See Burns, Violet Alberta Jessie.*

WISEMAN, Hilda Alexandra (1894–1982). New Zealand bookplate designer, artist, calligrapher, and children's writer. Born April 7, 1894, in Mooroopna, Victoria, Australia; died April 28, 1982, in Auckland, New Zealand; dau. of Alexander Wiseman (architect and music teacher) and Harriot Amanda (Coombes) Wiseman. ❖ Worked for advertising firm of Chandler and Co. (1915); learned lettering at Elam School of Art (1917), and illuminating at Seddon Memorial Technical College (1923–24); designed and printed the 1st of more than 100 linocut bookplates (1925); established Selwyn Studio (1931);

published children's story, *Minna Mantis Gives a Party* (1944). ❖ See also *Dictionary of New Zealand Biography* (Vol. 4).

WISEMAN, Jane (fl. 17th c.). British playwright. Name variations: Jane Holt; Mrs. Wiseman. Born in late 1600s in England; was possibly the actress Mrs. Wiseman who appeared on stage in 1700; married a vintner named Holt. ❖ Was a servant in the family of William Wright; wrote *Antiochus the Great* (1702), which was performed at Lincoln's Inn Fields (c. 1701), and *A Fairy Tale . . . With Other Poems* (1717); used her playwrighting profits to open a tavern in Westminster.

WISKEMANN, Elizabeth Meta (1899–1971). English historian, journalist, and educator. Born in Sidcup, Kent, England, Aug 13, 1899; committed suicide, July 5, 1971, in London, England; dau. of Heinrich Odomar Hugo Wiskemann (German immigrant and merchant) and Emily Myra (Burton) Wiskemann; awarded 1st class degree in history from Newnham College, Cambridge, 1921; Newnham College, MLitt in history, 1927; never married; no children. ❖ Journalist and historian of international renown, who, while living in Berlin, forecasted the impending Nazi threat in articles for the *New Statesman* in the years up to World War II; was expelled from Germany (1936); during war, lived in Berne, Switzerland, and worked as assistant press attaché to British legation (1941–45), responsible for collecting non-military intelligence from Germany and the countries it had conquered; following war, served as an occasional Rome correspondent to *The Economist*; held Montague Burton chair as professor of history, Edinburgh University (1958–61), then tutored in modern European history at Sussex University (1961–64); writings include *Undeclared War* (1939), *The Rome-Berlin Axis* (1949), *A Great Swiss Newspaper, the Story of the Neue Zürcher Zeitung* (1959), *Fascism in Italy* (1969) and *Italy since 1945* (1971). ❖ See also memoir *The Europe I Saw* (1968); and *Women in World History*.

WISTER, Sally (1761–1804). *See Wister, Sarah.*

WISTER, Sarah (1761–1804). American diarist and poet. Name variations: Sally Wister. Born 1761 in Philadelphia, PA; died April 21, 1804, in Philadelphia, PA. ❖ Attended Quaker school run by philanthropist Anthony Benezet; while staying in rural Pennsylvania, wrote journal account of American Revolution for 2 girlfriends which was later published in *The Pennsylvania Magazine of History and Biography* (1885–86); also wrote devotional journal (1796–97), published with other writings in Kathryn Zabelle Derounian, ed., *The Journal and Occasional Writings of Sarah Wister* (1987).

WISTER, Sarah Butler (1835–1908). American socialite. Born 1835; died 1908; dau. of Pierce Butler (d. 1867, plantation owner) and Fanny Kemble (1809–1893, actress); m. Owen Jones Wister (Philadelphia physician); children: Owen Wister (1860–1938, novelist who wrote *The Virginian*). ❖ See also Fanny Kemble Wister (Stokes), *Owen Wister Out West: His Journals and Letters* (1958) and *That I May Tell You. Journals and Letters of the Owen Wister Family* (1979); and *Women in World History*.

WITHBURGA (fl. 7th c.). Princess and nun. Dau. of Saewara and Anna, king of East Anglia (r. 635–654); sister of Elthelthrith and Sexburga and half-sister of Ethelburga (d. 665).

WITHEE, Mabel (d. 1952). American musical-comedy actress. Died Nov 3, 1952, in Bayside, NY. ❖ Appeared in many musicals, including *Sinbad, The Rose of Stamboul, Dew Drop Inn, Artists and Models, The Cocoanuts, Big Boy* and *Bye Bye Bonnie*.

WITHERINGTON, Pearl (1914—). French-born resistance leader. Name variations: Pearl Cornioley; (code names) Marie and Pauline. Born June 24, 1914, in Paris, France; grew up in Hertfordshire; m. Henri Cornioley (1910–1999), 1945. ❖ At the start of WWII, was working in Paris; escaped to England with family (1941), with help from the resistance; became a secretary in the Air Ministry; joined British SOE; parachuted into southern Loire region of occupied France (Sept 22, 1943), where she met up with Maurice Southgate, leader of the Stationer Network; worked as his courier for next 8 months; with arrest of Southgate (May 1944), reorganized the group and became leader of Wrestler Network, running a highly successful sabotage circuit, cutting the railway line to Paris 800 times; with the help of local man Henri Cornioley, built the group to 1,500 members of Maquis; played an important role during the D-Day landings and after. ❖ See also autobiography, *Pauline* (1997).

WITHERS, Googie (1917—). British stage and film actress. Born Georgette Lizette Withers, Mar 12, 1917, in Karachi, India (now

Pakistan); dau. of Edgar Clements Withers (British captain) and Lizette Catarina Wilhelmina (van Wageningen) Withers (Dutch); m. John McCallum (actor), in 1948; children: Joanna McCallum (actress). ❖ Equally at home with comedy and tragedy, made stage debut at 12 in *The Windmill Man* (1929), followed by *Private Lives* (1945), *Hamlet* (1958), *The Constant Wife* (1960), *Woman in a Dressing Gown* (1962), *Exit the King* (1963), *The Cherry Orchard* (1971), *An Ideal Husband* (1971), *The Importance of Being Earnest* (1979), *Time and the Conways* (1983) and *The Chalk Garden* (1986), among others; appeared in 1st film *The Girl in the Crowd* (1934); came to prominence as a Dutch resistance leader in *One of Our Aircraft Is Missing* (1942), then starred as another Dutch woman in *The Silver Fleet* (1943); other films include *The Lady Vanishes* (1938), *Bulldog Sees It Through* (1940), *Once Upon a Dream* (1949), *Night and the City* (1950), *Devil on Horseback* (1954), *Port of Escape* (1955), *Time After Time* (1985), *Country Life* (1995) and *Shine* (1996); appeared on tv in Jane Austen's "Northanger Abbey" (1986) and "Hotel du Lac" (1986). ❖ See also *Women in World History*.

WITHERS, Jane (1926—). American vaudeville, radio, film, and tv actress. Born April 12, 1926, in Atlanta, Georgia; dau. of Walter and Lavinia Ruth Withers; m. William Moss Jr. (oil man), 1947 (div. 1954); m. Kenneth Errair (member of Four Freshmen singing group), 1955 (died 1968); children: (1st m.) Wendy, William III, and Randy; (2nd m.) Kenneth and Kendall. ❖ Made screen debut with a small role in *Handle With Care* (1932), and went on to have an extensive career as one of Hollywood's leading child stars; had 1st major role, opposite Shirley Temple (Black) in *Bright Eyes* (1934); was one of 1937's top-10 box-office draws, appearing in such films as *Little Miss Nobody* (1936), *Pepper* (1936), *The Holy Terror* (1937), *Wild and Woolly* (1937), *Checkers* (1937), *Rascals* (1938), *The Arizona Wildcat* (1939), *Pack Up Your Troubles* (1939), *The Girl from Avenue A* (1940), *The Mad Martindales* (1942), *The North Star* (1943), *My Best Gal* (1944), *Affairs of Geraldine* (1946), *Giant* (1956) and *Captain Newman, M. D.* (1963); retired from films (1947); appeared on tv commercial as "Josephine the Plumber," for Comet Cleanser (1963–75). ❖ See also *Women in World History*.

WITHERSPOON, Cora (1890–1957). American stage and screen actress. Born Jan 5, 1890, in New Orleans, LA; died Nov 17, 1957, in Las Cruces, NM. ❖ Made Broadway debut as Edith Gordon in *The Concert* (1910); other NY appearances include *Daddy Long Legs, The Awful Truth, Grounds for Divorce, Camille, The Constant Wife, Waterloo Bridge, Three Faces East* and *Forsaking All Others*; made film debut (1931); best remembered as W. C. Fields' wife in *The Bank Dick*.

WITHERSPOON, Naomi (b. 1923). See Madgett, Naomi Long.

WITHINGTON, Alfreda (1860–1951). American physician. Born Alfreda Bosworth Withington, Aug 15, 1860, in Germantown, PA; died Oct 1, 1951, in Pittsfield, MA; dau. of Alfreda (Bosworth) Withington and James Harvey Withington; Cornell University, BA, 1881; graduate of Woman's Medical College of the New York Infirmary, 1887. ❖ Pioneering physician who was the 1st woman student admitted to K. K. Allgemeines Krankenhaus teaching hospital in Vienna, Austria, and the 1st woman to perform an autopsy; became the 1st woman resident physician at Czech National Obstetrical Hospital (c. 1889); opened a medical and surgical practice in Pittsfield, MA (1891); played an important role in the creation of a Tuberculosis Society (c. 1907); during WWI, as a chief physician of American Red Cross, traveled to work at the Franco-American Dispensary in Dreux, France (1917); worked and wrote of her experience as a physician in rural (KY) mountains. ❖ See also autobiography *Mine Eyes Have Seen: A Woman Doctor's Saga* (1941).

WITHINGTON, Eliza (1825–1877). American portrait and landscape photographer. Name variations: Elizabeth W. Kirby. Born in New York, NY, 1825 (some sources cite 1823); died 1877 in Ione City (Amador City), California; educated in photographic technique in New York, c. 1857; m. George V. Withington, 1845 (sep. c. 1871); children: Sarah Augusta (b. around 1847); Eleanor B. (b. around 1848); Everett (b. 1861, died 5 months later). ❖ Opened Excelsior Ambrotype Gallery in a rented house in Ione City (1857); made stereographic photographs of people, landscapes, and other subjects; is best known for her stereographs of miners, mining operations, and the rugged landscapes of Sierra Nevada Mountains that she took near Silver Lake (1873); joined San Francisco Photographic Art Society of the Pacific (1875). ❖ See also *Women in World History*.

WITT, Henriette de (1829–1908). French biographer and Protestant writer. Born Henriette Elizabeth Guizot, 1829, in France; died 1908; dau. of prime minister François Guizot (1787–1874) and Marguerite Andree Eliza de la Croix-Dillon; m. Conrad Jacob Cornelis de Witt, Mar 1850; children: 2 daughters. ❖ Works include educational texts for young ladies, such as *Contes d'une mère à ses petits enfants* (1861), *Petites Méditations Chrétiennes* (1862), *Histoire sainte racontée aux enfants* (1863) and *Scènes historiques et religieuses* (1872); also wrote biographical and historical works, including *M. Guizot dans sa famille et avec ses amis* (M. Guizot with His Family and Friends, 1880) and *Les Chroniquers de l'histoire de France* (1882).

WITT, Katarina (1965—). East German skater. Born Katarina Witt, Dec 1965, in Karl-Marx-Stadt (now Chemnitz), German Democratic Republic. ❖ Won her 1st European championship (1982); won 6 European championships and 5 World championships; won a gold medal at Sarajevo Olympics (1984) and a gold medal at Calgary Olympics (1988); became tv sports commentator for Olympics (1992); returned to Olympic competition at Lillehammer (1994); became a major staple of the professional figure-skating circuit; appeared in films, including *Ronin*, and in tv roles. ❖ See also *Women in World History*.

WITTELSBACH, Hedwig (fl. late 1600s). See Hedwig Wittelsbach.

WITTENMYER, Annie Turner (1827–1900). American activist. Born Aug 26, 1827, in Sandy Springs, Ohio; died Feb 2, 1900, in Sanatoga, Pennsylvania; dau. of John G. Turner and Elizabeth (Smith) Turner; educated at a seminary in Ohio; m. William Wittenmyer (merchant), 1847 (died c. 1861); children: son Charles Albert, and 4 others who died in infancy. ❖ War-relief worker, church leader, and charity organizer, organized a Methodist church and a free school for destitute children in Keokuk, Iowa; during Civil War, served as secretary of Keokuk's Soldiers' Aid Society which became the central collection point for relief supplies dispatched throughout Iowa; also nursed the wounded at the front; served as a state sanitary agent (1862–64); directed the establishment of kitchens at army hospitals to provide special diets for patients; moved to Philadelphia (1871), where she established *Christian Woman* magazine, which she edited for 11 years; also wrote hymns and books, including *Woman's Work for Jesus* (1871) and *Women of the Reformation* (1884); elected the 1st president of Woman's Christian Temperance Union (WCTU, 1874), served 3 terms (1874–79) and established the 1st journal of the WCTU, *Our Union*; wrote *History of the Woman's Temperance Crusade* (1878); helped organize the Non-Partisan Woman's Christian Temperance Union (1890), serving as its president (1896–98); also served as president of Woman's Relief Corps (WRC, 1889–90), the women's branch of Grand Army of the Republic; successfully lobbied Congress to pay pensions to former war nurses (1892). ❖ See also memoir *Under the Guns* (1895); and *Women in World History*.

WITTIG, Monique (1935–2003). French feminist writer and literary theorist. Born July 13, 1935, in Dannemarie, Alsace, France; died Jan 3, 2003, in Tucson, AZ; dau. of Maria Wittig and Henri Dubois (poet); sister of Gilberte Wittig; attended the Sorbonne; lived with Sande Zeig. ❖ Lesbian and radical feminist, founded the group Féministes Révolutionnaires; was one of the major players in the movement to reject the social convention that allows women to be marked by gender in language; published 1st novel *L'Opoponax* (1964, English trans. *The Opoponax*, 1966), winning the Prix Médicis; wrote *Les guérillères* (1969, Eng. trans. 1972), a Utopian allegory; other books include *Le Corps lesbien* (1973, Eng. trans. *The Lesbian Body*, 1975), *Virgile, Non* (1984, Eng. trans. *Across the Acheron*, 1987), *La pensée straight* (1980, Eng trans. *The Straight Mind and Other Essays,*); with Sande Zeig, made the film, *The Girl* (2001); moved to US to teach at University of California at Berkeley (1976); taught at the University of Arizona (1990–2002).

WITTKE, Gudrun (1907–1982). See Baudisch-Wittke, Gudrun.

WITTPENN, Caroline Stevens Alexander (1859–1932). American welfare worker. Name variations: Caroline Alexander or Caroline Stevens Alexander; Caroline Bayard Wittpenn. Born Caroline Bayard Stevens, Nov 21, 1859, in Hoboken, NJ; died Dec 4, 1932, in Hoboken; dau. of Edwin Augustus Stevens and Martha Bayard (Dod) Stevens; m. Archibald Alexander (philosophy teacher), June 1879 (sep. c. 1895); H. Otto Wittpenn (mayor of Jersey City, NJ), Jan 6, 1915; children: (1st m.) 1 son. ❖ Assumed presidency of board of managers for Clinton Farms women's reformatory (1913); served as adviser on state welfare issues to NJ governor Woodrow Wilson; was 1st committeewoman for Democratic National Committee in NJ; sat on board of control of New Jersey Department of Institutions and Agencies as part of reorganization of state's charitable and correctional institutions (1918–26, 1929–32); appointed by President Herbert Hoover to International Prison Commission (1929). ❖ See also Joan N. Burstyn, *Caroline Stevens Alexander Wittpenn* (Scarecrow, 1990).

WITTY, Chris (1975—). American speedskater and cyclist. Born June 23, 1975, in West Allis, WI. ❖ Won US Sprint championship (1995, 1996); at World Sprint championship, won a silver medal (1995), gold (1996), and bronze (1997); won 9 medals in World Cup competition, including a sweep of the 1,000 meters in Milwaukee (1996, 1997); won a bronze medal for the 1,500 and a silver medal for the 1,000 meters at Nagano Olympics (1998); competed as a cyclist at Sydney Olympics (2000), the 9th US athlete to vie in Summer and Winter Games; at World Cup, finished 2nd in the 1,000 standings (2000–02); won a gold medal in the 1,000 meters at Salt Lake City Olympics (2002); carried the flag at Torino Olympics but did not medal (2006).

WITZIERS-TIMMER, Jeanette (1923–2005). Dutch runner. Name variations: Netty Timmer. Born Jeannette Josephina Maria Timmer, July 22, 1923, in Amsterdam, Holland, Netherlands; died Jan 25, 2005. ❖ At London Olympics, won a gold medal in 4 x 100-meter relay (1948).

WITZIERS-TIMMER, Netty (1923–2005). *See Witziers-Timmer, Jeanette.*

WIXOM, Emma (1859–1940). *See Nevada, Emma.*

WOBESER, Caroline von (1769–1807). German novelist. Name variations: Wilhelmine Karoline Wobeser; Wilhelmine Caroline von Wobeser; Karoline von Wobeser. Born 1769 in Germany; died 1807. ❖ Wrote the most widely-read women's novel of her time, *Elisa, oder das Weib wie es seyn sollte* (1795, Elisa, or Woman as She Should Be), with a protagonist who responds to hardship with unwavering goodness.

WÖCKEL-ECKERT, Bärbel (1955—). East German track-and-field athlete. Name variations: Baerbel Woeckel, Barbel Wockel, Barbel Eckert. Born Barbel Eckert, Mar 21, 1955, in Leipzig, Germany. ❖ Won Olympic gold medals in 200 meters and 4 x 100-meter relay in Montreal (1976) and Olympic gold medals in 200 meters and 4 x 100-meter relay in Moscow (1980); won a silver medal for 100 meters and gold medal for 200 meters at European championships (1982).

WODARS, Sigrun (1965—). East German runner. Name variations: Sigrun Grau; Sigrun Wodars-Grau. Born Sigrun Ludwigs, Nov 7, 1965, in Neu-Kaliß, Mecklenburg, Western Pomerania; married and divorced; married once more. ❖ Began career as a 400-meter runner in junior meets; at 800 meters, placed 2nd at European championships (1986) and 1st at World championships (1987); at Seoul Olympics, won a gold medal in 800 meters (1988); became a physiotherapist.

WOECKEL, Baerbel (1955—). *See Wöckel-Eckert, Bärbel.*

WOERISHOFFER, Carola (1885–1911). American social activist and philanthropist. Born Emma Carola Woerishoffer, Aug 1885, in New York, NY; died Sept 11, 1911; dau. of Anna (Uhl) Woerishoffer (social reformer) and Charles Frederick Woerishoffer (German-born Wall Street banker); granddau. of Anna Uhl Ottendorfer (1815–1884); graduate of Bryn Mawr College, 1907. ❖ Having inherited a large fortune on father's death (1886), followed the example of her mother and became active as a social reformer; was a founder of New York Women's Trade Union League (WTUL, 1908), serving as its treasurer; became a district leader for New York Woman Suffrage Party; took jobs under an assumed name in a dozen laundries, then reported to the National Consumers' League on the terrible conditions laundresses endured; was appointed investigator to Bureau of Industries and Immigration of New York State Association for Labor Legislation (1910); at 26, died in a car accident near Cannonsville, New York, while driving home from a labor camp investigation; left a bequest of $750,000 to Bryn Mawr, which founded the Carola Woerishoffer Graduate Department of Social Economy and Social Research, the 1st professional school of social work in the world and the 1st American school to offer a doctoral degree in social work. ❖ See also *Women in World History*.

WOERISHOFFER, Sophie (1838–1890). *See Wörishöffer, Sophie.*

WOFTZEL, Mandy (1973—). German pairs skater. Name variations: Mandy Wötzel or Wotzel. Pronunciation: VERT-sul. Born July 21, 1973, in Chemnitz, Germany. ❖ With Ingo Steuer, won a silver medal (1993, 1996) and a gold medal (1997) at World championships; won the European championship (1995); won a bronze medal at Nagano Olympics (1998); will also be remembered for a terrible spill at Lillehammer Olympics, slamming chin and chest on the ice; turned pro (1998).

WOFFINGTON, Peg (c. 1714–1760). Irish actress. Name variations: Margaret Woffington. Born Margaret Woffington, Oct 18, 1714 (some sources cite 1717, 1718, or 1720), in Dublin, Ireland; died at Queen Square, Westminster, Mar 26, 1760; dau. of John Woffington (bricklayer) and Hannah Woffington (some sources give Murphy as the family name, Woffington being adopted later as a stage name); never married; no children. ❖ One of the most celebrated actresses of her century, who delighted audiences by the charm of her personality no less than by the magic of her performances and achieved great success in comedy and in "breeches" parts; made stage debut as a child with Madame Violante, who ran theatrical entertainments in Dublin; appeared as Polly in *The Beggar's Opera* in Dublin and London; played Ophelia, her 1st major role (1737); was cast in the role with which her name was to become synonymous, that of Sir Harry Wildair in Farquhar's *The Constant Couple* (1740); engaged by John Rich for Covent Garden, London (1740), made a sensational debut as Sylvia in *The Recruiting Officer* (1740); returned to Dublin and appeared opposite David Garrick in *Hamlet* (1742); played at Theater Royal, Drury Lane (1743–48), giving her 1st performance as Mistress Ford in *The Merry Wives of Windsor*; performed at Covent Garden (1748–51), winning praise for such roles as Portia in *Julius Caesar*, Andromache in *The Distress'd Mother*, Calista in *The Fair Penitent*, Arpasia in *Tamerlane*, and the Lady in *Comus*, as well as Desdemona, Lady Macbeth, and Cleopatra; returned to Dublin (1751), receiving a record salary at Smock Alley Theater and opening as Lady Townley in *The Provoked Husband*; remained in Dublin until a riot closed Smock Alley (1754), when she returned to Covent Garden; appeared as Maria in *The Nonjuror*, and followed this, among other roles, with Phaedra in *Phaedra and Hippolitus*, Lady Pliant in *The Double Dealer* and Jocasta in *Oedipus*; collapsed on stage while appearing in *As You Like It* (1757); prevented from returning to the theater because of ill health, lived in retirement until her death 3 years later. ❖ See also Janet Dunbar, *Peg Woffington and Her World* (Heinemann, 1968); Janet Camden Lucey, *Lovely Peggy: The Life and Times of Margaret Woffington* (Hurst & Blackett, 1952); and *Women in World History*.

WOHLERS, Eliza (c. 1812–1891). New Zealand missionary, dressmaker, nurse, and teacher. Name variations: Eliza Hanham, Eliza Palmer. Born Eliza Hanham (baptized, Sept 6, 1812), at Bridport, Dorset, England; died Dec 14, 1891, at Thornbury, Southland, New Zealand; dau. of William (laborer) and Hannah (Hinde) Hanham; m. Richard Woodcock Palmer (carpenter), 1838; m. Johann Friedrich Heinrich Wohlers (missionary), 1849 (died 1885). ❖ Immigrated with 1st husband to New Zealand (1841); helped 2nd husband to sustain mission through her domestic and language skills; helped to administer government-funded native school on Ruapuke Island (1870–1884). ❖ See also *Dictionary of New Zealand Biography* (Vol. 1).

WOHMANN, Gabriele (1932—). German writer. Born Gabriele Guyot, May 21, 1932, in Darmstadt, Germany; dau. of Paul Daniel Guyot (parson) and Luise (Lettermann) Guyot; educated at University of Frankfurt; m. Reiner Wohmann, 1953. ❖ With husband, taught for a year at a private school on the North Sea island of Langeroog, then took teaching positions in Darmstadt; published 1st short story, "Ein unwiderstehlicher Mann" (An Irresistible Man, 1956), to critical acclaim; began writing full-time (1957); released 3 vols. of short stories (1958, 1960, and 1963), securely establishing herself as a leading figure in modern German literature; writings include *Abschied für länger* (A Farewell for a Long Time, 1965), *Die grosse Liebe* (True Love, 1966), *Ländliches Fest und andere Erzählungen* (Country Party and Other Stories, 1968), *Paulinchen war allein zu Haus* (Paulinchen Was Home Alone, 1974), *Schönes Gehege* (Beautiful Enclosure, 1975), *Frühherbst in Badenweiler* (Early Fall in Badenweiler, 1978), *Der Flötenton* (Sound of a Flute, 1987), *Aber das war noch nicht das Schlimmste* (But That Was Not Yet the Worst, 1998) and *Frauen machens am späten Nachmittag: Sommergeschichten* (Summer Stories, 2000). Elected to Berlin Academy of Art (1975) and Academy of Language and Literature (1980); awarded West German Order of Merit (1980). ❖ See also *Women in World History*.

WOIZIKOWSKA, Sonia (1919—). Polish-American ballet dancer. Name variations: Sonia Woizikovski, Woicikowska or Wojcikowska. Born Sonia Woizikowska, Dec 17, 1919, in London, England; dau. of Helene Antonova (1898–1974) and Leon Woizikowski (both ballet dancers); children: 2. ❖ Trained with Lyubov Egorova, Carlotta

Brianza, and Ludmilla Schollar, in London, Paris, and New York; made professional debut in London in father's Coliseum Ballet and danced with his Polish Ballet in New York City (1939); joined Ballet Theater in NY and was featured in works of Mikhail Fokine and Mikhail Mordkin; danced with Ballet Russe de Monte Carlo; joined The Foxhole Ballet, founded by Grant Mouradoff, and performed on tour in his *Garden Party* and *Circle* (1946–47); toured with national company of Agnes de Mille's *Oklahoma* before retiring to teach at Ballet Arts.

WOJCIKOWSKA, Sonia (b. 1919). *See Woizikowska, Sonia.*

WOJTULANIS, Barbara (1912–2005). *See Karpinski, Stephanie.*

WOJTULANIS, Stefania (1912–2005). *See Karpinski, Stephanie.*

WOLCOTT, Marion Post (1910–1990). American photographer. Born Marion Post in Montclair, New Jersey, June 7, 1910; died in Santa Barbara, California, Nov 24, 1990; dau. of Walter Post (physician) and Helen (Hoyt) Post (nurse who worked with Margaret Sanger); sister of Helen Post Modley; attended New School for Social Research, New York University and University of Vienna; m. Leon Oliver Wolcott (government official), June 6, 1941; children: Linda Wolcott Moore and Michael Wolcott. ❖ After landing a photo on the cover of *The New York Times Magazine*, joined New York Photo League, where she was mentored by Ralph Steiner and Paul Strand; also assisted on a film about labor organizing in Cumberland Mountains of Tennessee, and worked briefly as full-time staff photographer on Philadelphia *Evening Bulletin*; for Farm Security Administration (FSA), produced a vast body of compelling black-and-white photographs documenting life in rural America during Depression (1938–42), which have found their way into numerous exhibits, publications, and major collections, including those of Metropolitan Museum of Art, Chicago Art Institute and Smithsonian Institution. ❖ See also Paul Hendrickson, *Looking for the Light: The Hidden Life and Art of Marion Post Wolcott* (Knopf, 1992); and *Women in World History*.

WOLF, Christa (1929—). German writer. Pronunciation: VOllff (O as in old). Born Christa Margarete Ihlenfeld, Mar 18, 1929, in Landsberg-Wartha (today Gorzów Wielkopolski, Poland); dau. of Otto Ihlenfeld (merchant); Abitur in Bad Frankenhausen, 1949; studied Germanic languages and literature in Jena and Leibzig, 1949–53; m. Gerhard Wolf (Germanist and essayist), 1951; children: Annette (b. 1952); Katrin (b. 1956). ❖ Writer from the former German Democratic Republic (GDR) whose internationally acclaimed novels and essays advocate the humanistic goals of Marxism while promoting a confrontation with Germany's past and present; was a member of the Socialist Unity Party (SED, 1949–89); moved to Berlin (1953); was on staff of *Neue deutsche Literatur* (1954–59); served as chief editor for publishing company Neues Leben (1956–59); was a member and executive committee member of Writers' Union, GDR (1955–77); published 1st novel, *Moskauer Novelle* (1962); had 1st success with *Divided Heaven* (1963); was a candidate of the Central Committee of the Socialist Unity Party (1963–67); published *The Quest of Christa T.* (1968), which was popular in the West; wrote *A Model Childhood*, a partly autobiographical account of life under fascism and the difficulty of dealing with the fascist past in the present (1976); for signing an open letter protesting the expulsion of the writer Wolf Biermann from the executive committee of Berlin Section of Writers' Union of GDR (1976); published the story of a fictional encounter between writer Heinrich von Kleist and poet Karoline von Günderrode in *No Place on Earth* (1979); was a guest professor in Poetics at the University of Frankfurt am Main (1982) and a guest professor at Ohio State University (1983); wrote *Cassandra* (1983); after Chernobyl, published *Accident/A Day's News* (1987); with the fall of the Berlin Wall, withdrew from Socialist Union Party (1989); received intense attention from the media and faced charges of cowardice after the publication of "What Remains?" (1990), which chronicled her experience of being spied upon by the Stasi, the secret security service of the GDR; was found to be listed as an informer and informal collaborator of the Stasi (1959–62), in a Stasi file that was discovered (1993); her *Auf dem Weg nach Tabou* (1994, trans. and released in US as *Parting from Phantoms: Selected Writings, 1990–1994*, 1997) documents the doubts and uncertainty following the collapse of the GDR and the unification of Germany. ❖ See also Marilyn Sibley Fries, ed. *Responses to Christa Wolf* (Wayne State U. Press, 1989); Anna K. Kuhn, *Christa Wolf's Utopian Vision: From Marxism to Feminism* (Cambridge U. Press, 1988); and *Women in World History*.

WOLF, Hazel (1898–2000). Canadian-born American reformer and conservationist. Born Hazel Anna Cummings Anderson, Mar 10, 1898, in Victoria, British Columbia; died Jan 19, 2000, in Port Angeles, Washington; dau. of Canadian father and American mother; m. Edward Dalziel (div.); m. Herbert Wolf (div.); children: (1st m.) Nydia Levick. ❖ Moved to US (1923); joined Communist Party during Depression, attracted by its social welfare programs, then left it during WWII; was charged with sedition and briefly jailed during McCarthy era (1958); became US citizen (1974); was a frequent public speaker on such issues as the environment, human rights, feminism, labor and peace, and was a strong advocate for the rights of immigrants; helped found more than 20 chapters of the National Audubon Society.

WOLF, Kate (1942–1986). American folksinger and guitarist. Born Kathryn Louise Allen, Jan 27, 1942, in San Francisco, California; died of leukemia, 1986, in California; m. Saul Wolf (architect), 1963 (div.); Dan Coffin (musician) (div. 1979); m. Terry Fowler (owner of natural foods distribution co.); children: Max Wolf and Hannah Wolf. ❖ Formed 1st band, The Wildwood Flower, with future husband Dan Coffin; hosted radio show, "Uncommon Country," on KVRE, then "Sonoma County Singers Circle" on KSRO; formed Owl Records and produced *Back Roads* (1976), singing own songs and those of local artists, followed by *Lines on the Paper* (1977); began touring US and Canada to larger and larger audiences (1977); divorced Coffin, dissolved Wildwood Flower, and hired guitarist and mandolin player Nina Gerber as accompanist (1979); made 1st professional studio album, *Safe at Anchor*, on independent label Kaleidoscope; also released *Close to You* (1981) and *Yourself to Love* (1983); often guested on "A Prairie Home Companion"; memorialized with posthumous release of 10-year retrospective album *Gold in California* (1987) and *The Wind Goes Wild* (1988).

WOLF, Sigrid (1964—). Austrian Alpine skier. Born Feb 14, 1964, in Lechtal, Austria. ❖ Won a gold medal for super-G at Calgary Olympics (1988); won the World championship for super-G (1989).

WOLFE, Catharine L. (1828–1887). American philanthropist. Name variations: Catherine L. Wolfe. Born Catharine Lorillard Wolfe in New York, NY, May 8, 1828; died in New York, NY, April 4, 1887; dau. of John David Wolfe (hardware mogul) and Dorothea Ann (Lorillard) Wolfe (tobacco heir); 1st cousin of Catherine Wolfe Bruce (patron of astronomy); never married; no children. ❖ Inherited a large fortune and devoted her life to works of charity; besides giving generous sums to Grace Church, Union College, the American School at Athens, and St. Luke's Hospital in New York City, founded a newsboys' lodging and a home for incurables; also supplied the funds for Dr. William It. Ward's archaeological expedition to Asia Minor (1884), and gave a valuable collection of paintings to the Metropolitan Museum of Art, with an endowment of $200,000, for its preservation and enlargement.

WOLFE, Elsie de (1865–1950). *See de Wolfe, Elsie.*

WOLFE, Louise Dahl- (1895–1989). *See Dahl-Wolfe, Louise.*

WOLFENSTEIN, Martha (1869–1905). Prussian-born short-story writer. Born 1869 in Insterburg, Prussia; died 1905 in Cleveland, OH; dau. of Samuel Wolfenstein and Bertha Brieger. ❖ After mother's death, looked after siblings and later worked as matron of Cleveland Jewish Orphan Asylum run by father; published short stories in *Lippincott's Magazine* and *Outlook* which were collected as *Idylls of the Gass* (1901); stories from *Cleveland Jewish Review and Observer* published as *The Renegade and Other Stories* (1905).

WOLFF, Elizabeth Betjen (1738–1804). *See Bekker, Elizabeth.*

WOLFF, Helen (1906–1994). German-American publisher. Born Helen Mosel in Üsküb (Skopje), Macedonia, 1906; died Mar 29, 1994, in Hanover, New Hampshire; m. Kurt Wolff (publisher), 1933 (killed in accident, Oct 21, 1963); children: son Christian Wolff (b. 1934). ❖ Publisher, who with partner Kurt Wolff, was responsible for publishing many of the best-known books of this century such as *Doctor Zhivago, The Tin Drum,* and *The Leopard*; after the Balkan War, lived with family in Vienna (1915–16), then Berlin (1916), then Oberammergau in rural Bavaria (1918); went to work for Wolff Verlag in Munich (1927); sent to Paris when Pegasus, part of Wolff Verlag, was sold (1929); because husband was half-Jewish, lived in exile in Italy (1935–37) and France (1937–39); interned with husband by the French as enemy aliens (1940); thanks to Varian Fry, escaped to US (1941); with husband, founded Pantheon Books from their apartment (1942); published the Bollingen Series—handsome volumes on the arts, humanities, and psychology; moved offices to 333 Sixth Avenue, where she was in charge of editing, copy editing, proofreading, advertising, publicity, and also ran the juvenile department; published *Gift from the*

Sea (1955), *Born Free* (1960) and Mary Renault's *The Last of the Wine*; established "A Helen and Kurt Wolff Book" imprint (1960s); after his death, continued as publisher for Konrad Lorenz, Amos Oz, Stanislaw Lem, Umberto Eco, and many others; was the undisputed grande dame of literary publishing in the US. ❖ See also *Women in World History*.

WOLFF, Ingrid (1964—). Dutch field-hockey player. Born Feb 17, 1964. ❖ At Seoul Olympics, won a bronze medal in team competition (1988).

WOLFF, Sister Madeleva (1887–1964). *See Madeleva, Sister Mary.*

WOLFF, Mary Evaline (1887–1964). *See Madeleva, Sister Mary.*

WOLFF, Victoria (1903–1992). German essayist, scriptwriter, novelist, and short-story writer. Name variations: (pseudonym) Claudia Martell. Born Dec 10, 1903, in Heilbronn, Germany; died Sept 16, 1992, in Los Angeles, CA. ❖ Contributed to Swiss and German magazines; banned from working in Germany with the rise of the Nazi Party, traveled through Europe and settled in US (1941); was a scenarist and scriptwriter for 20th Century-Fox and MGM; writings include the novels, *Eine Frau wie du und ich* (1932), *Mutter und Tochter* (1964), and *Der Feuersturm* (1977), and the travelogue *Im Tal de Könige* (In the Valley of the Kings, 1945).

WOLFF-BEKKER, Elizabeth (1738–1804). *See Bekker, Elizabeth.*

WOLFIDA OF SAXONY (c. 1075–1126). Duchess of Bavaria. Born c. 1075; died Dec 29, 1126; dau. of Magnus, duke of Saxony, and Sophie of Hungary; m. Henry the Black (c. 1074–1126), duke of Bavaria (r. 1120–1126), around 1095; children: Henry IV the Proud (c. 1100–1139), duke of Bavaria; Judith of Bavaria (fl. 1120s); Guelph also known as Welf VI (d. 1191); and possibly Sophia of Zahringen.

WOLFSON, Theresa (1897–1972). American labor economist and educator. Born July 19, 1897, in Brooklyn, New York; died May 14, 1972, in Brooklyn; dau. of Adolph Wolfson and Rebecca (Hochstein) Wolfson (Russian-Jewish radical socialists); Adelphi College, AB, 1917; Columbia University, MA, 1923; Brookings Institute, PhD, 1926; m. Iago Galdston (psychiatrist), 1920 (div. 1935); m. Austin Bigelow Wood (psychology professor), 1938; children: (1st m.) Richard (b. 1926); Margaret Beatrice (b. 1930). ❖ Took a job with the Meinhardt Settlement House in New York City (1917), then worked for 2 years as an investigator for the National Child Labor Committee (1918–20); worked for New York Consumers' League and Joint Board of Factory Control in the women's clothing industry (1920–23); became active as an educator, working with trade unions to arrange classes in economics and labor; went to work for International Ladies' Garment Workers' Union (ILGWU) as education director of Union Health Center (1925); accepted teaching position in economics at Brooklyn College (1928) and remained there for rest of career; wrote *The Woman Worker and the Trade Unions* and co-authored *Labor and the N.R.A.* (1934) and *Frances Wright, Free Enquirer: The Study of a Temperament* (1939). ❖ See also *Women in World History*.

WOLLERIN, Cecilie (d. 1341). German wool merchant. Born into a family of urban artisans of Regensburg, Germany; died 1341 in Regensburg; never married; no children. ❖ Inherited parents' wool-weaving company and managed the operation herself for many years; her business acumen and independent status led her company to flourish, and she amassed enormous personal wealth. ❖ See also *Women in World History*.

WOLLEY, Ann (b. 1623). *See Woolley, Hannah.*

WOLLEY, Hannah (b. 1623). *See Woolley, Hannah.*

WOLLSCHLAEGER, Susanne (1967—). German field-hockey player. Name variations: Susanne Wollschläger. Born May 1967 in Germany. ❖ At Barcelona Olympics, won a silver medal in team competition (1992).

WOLLSTEIN, Martha (1868–1939). American pathologist and researcher. Born Nov 21, 1868, in New York, NY; died Sept 30, 1939, in New York, NY; dau. of Lewis and Minna (Cohn) Wollstein; received medical degree from Woman's Medical College of the New York Infirmary, 1889; never married; no children. ❖ After serving a 2-year internship at Babies Hospital in New York, was hired as a pathologist there (1892); spent early years researching malaria, tuberculosis, and typhoid fever; began experimental work on bacteriology of infant diarrhea (1903), which proved important in the diagnosis and treatment of the disease; was assistant researcher at Rockefeller Institute of New York (1906–21), where she studied polio, pneumonia, mumps, and an anti-

meningitis serum; served as a pediatric pathologist at Babies Hospital (1921–35), working on the pathology of influenzal meningitis, tuberculosis, jaundice, congenital defects, and leukemia; named head of the pediatric section of New York Academy of Medicine (1928); became 1st woman elected to American Pediatric Society (1930); over course of career, published 80 scientific papers. ❖ See also *Women in World History*.

WOLLSTONECRAFT, Mary (1759–1797). English writer and feminist. Name variations: Mary Imlay; Mary Godwin; Mary Wollstonecraft Godwin. Born Mary Wollstonecraft, April 21, 1759, London, England; died Sept 10, 1797, in London; dau. of Edward John Wollstonecraft and Elizabeth (Dickson) Wollstonecraft; had liaison with Gilbert Imlay, 1793; m. William Godwin, 1797; children: (with Imlay) Fanny Imlay (b. 1794); Mary Shelley (1797–1851, the writer). ❖ Reformer, radical, and feminist, who is best known for *A Vindication of the Rights of Woman*, an analysis of the injustices and disadvantages women suffered as a result of social, economic, political, and educational inequality; father lost most of a substantial inheritance through incompetence; moved frequently with virtually dysfunctional family; met Fanny Blood (1775), with whom she established a fervent longterm friendship; left home to go to Bath as a paid companion (1778); returned home to nurse her dying mother (1781); after mother's death, lived with the Blood family; "rescued" her sister Eliza from her husband's home following her postpartum breakdown (1784); established schools at Islington, then Newington Green with sisters Eliza and Everina and Fanny Blood; visited Fanny, who married (1785) in Lisbon, and found her dying in childbirth; returned to England to find the school had foundered (1786); wrote *Thoughts on the Education of Daughters*; took a position as governess with Kingsborough family; dismissed by Lady Kingsborough (1787); published her novel, *Mary, A Fiction*, with Joseph Johnson, printer of works by radical writers; hired by Johnson to write for the *Analytical Review*; earned an independent living as a reviewer, translator, and writer of fiction and children's stories (1788–90); wrote *A Vindication of the Rights of Men* (1790), a response to Burke's *Reflections on the Revolution in France*; published *A Vindication of the Rights of Woman* and went to Paris to observe the French Revolution (1792); met and established relationship with Gilbert Imlay; daughter Fanny Imlay born in LeHavre (1793); made 1st suicide attempt (May 1795); visited Scandinavian countries with infant daughter; made 2nd suicide attempt (Oct 1795); renewed acquaintance with William Godwin, radical social and political philosopher (1796); married Godwin (Mar 1797) and died 10 days after the birth of their daughter, Mary (Sept 1797). ❖ See also Eleanor Flexner, *Mary Wollstonecraft* (1972); William Godwin, *Memoirs of Mary Wollstonecraft* (1927); Jennifer Lorch, *Mary Wollstonecraft: The Making of a Radical Feminist* (1990); Emily W. Sunstein, *A Different Face: The Life of Mary Wollstonecraft* (1975); Claire Tomalin, *The Life and Death of Mary Wollstonecraft* (1974); Diane Jacobs, *Her Own Woman: The Life of Mary Wollstonecraft* (2001); Janet Todd, *Mary Wollstonecraft: A Revolutionary Life* (2000); and *Women in World History*.

WOLNICKA, Barbara (1970—). *See Szewczyk, Barbara.*

WOLSTENHOLME-ELMY, Elizabeth (1834–1913). British feminist and suffragist. Name variations: Elizabeth Wolstenholme; Elizabeth Wolstenholme Elmy; E. Ellis; Ellis Ethelmer. Born 1834 in England; died 1913; dau. of a Methodist minister; m. Benjamin Elmy (poet), 1874; children: 1 son. ❖ Pioneer in women's education and the training of teachers, helped form Manchester Schoolmistresses' Association (1865); with Josephine Butler, established North of England Council for the Higher Education of Woman, which provided special lectures and examinations for women schoolteachers; was also an avid suffragist, joining with Lydia Becker as early as 1865 to form Manchester Society for Women's Suffrage; joined the Pankhursts to form Women's Franchise League (1889); later in life, joined Women's Social and Political Union. ❖ See also *Women in World History*.

WOLTER, Charlotte (1834–1897). Austrian actress. Born in Cologne, Germany, Mar 1, 1834; died June 14, 1897, in Vienna, Austria. ❖ Considered one of the great tragic actresses of her time, began career in Budapest (1857); appeared at Victoria Theater in Berlin (1861), where her performance of Hermione in *The Winter's Tale* took the playgoing world by storm; joined the Vienna Hofburg Theater (1862), where she remained until her death; achieved her most brilliant success in the role of Iphigenia.

WOLTERS, Kara (1975—). American basketball player. Born Aug 15, 1975, in Holliston, MA; dau. of Bill Wolters (played center for Boston

College under Bob Cousy); sister of Kristen Wolters (basketball player); graduate of University of Connecticut, 1997. ❖ Center; played in 4 NCAA Tournaments while at UConn (1994–97); drafted by New England Blizzard of ABL (1997); drafted by the Houston Comets of the WNBA (1999); won team gold medals at World championships (1998) and at Sydney Olympics (2000); drafted by Indiana Fever (2000); traded to Sacramento Monarchs (2001). Received Victor Award (1996); named Player of the Year by AP (1997).

WOLZOGEN, Karoline von (1763–1847). German biographer, novelist and salonnière. Name variations: Baroness Karoline von Wolzogen; Karoline von Lengefeld; Mme von Wolzogen. Born Friederike Sophie Karoline Auguste von Lengefeld in 1763 in Rudolstadt, Germany; died 1847 in Jena; sister of Charlotte von Lengefeld who was married to Friedrich Schiller; m. Wilhelm von Wolzogen, 1794. ❖ Headed an important literary salon in Weimar; wrote a biography of Friedrich Schiller and novels *Agnes von Lilien* (1796) and *Cordelia* (1840), among others; also published series of letters from Switzerland in the magazine *Pomona.*

WON HYE-KYUNG. South Korean short-track speedskater. Born in South Korea. ❖ Won a gold medal for 3,000-meter relay at Lillehammer Olympics (1994) and a gold medal for 3,000-meter relay and a bronze medal for 1,000 meters at Nagano Olympics (1998).

WONG, Anna May (1907–1961). Chinese-American actress. Name variations: Wong Liu Tsong. Born Wong Liu Tsong, Jan 3, 1905, in Los Angeles, California; died Feb 3, 1961, in Santa Monica, California; dau. of Sam Wong and Lee Gon Toy (laundry owners). ❖ The 1st successful Chinese-American film actor, popular in both US and Europe, struggled throughout career against racial stereotyping in US movies; as an extra, made 1st film appearance in *The Red Lantern* (1919); had 1st screen credit, as the wife of Lon Chaney Sr. in *Bits of Life* (1921); her talent and beauty led to the leading role of Lotus Flower in one of the 1st Technicolor films, *The Toll of the Sea* (1922); came to prominence in Douglas Fairbanks' *The Thief of Bagdad* (1924); appeared regularly in films, almost always cast as an "oriental villainess"; went to Germany, where her performance in the silent film *Song* brought praise from German critics (1928); over next 2 years, appeared on stage and in several movies in Germany, France and England, and enjoyed a considerably expanded range of roles, most notably in *Piccadilly* (1929); made Broadway debut as a "half-Chinese gangster's moll" in *On the Spot* (late 1930); appeared in more than 80 films, including *Daughter of the Dragon* and *Shanghai Express* (1932), *Limehouse Blues* (1934), *Bombs Over Burma, The Lady from Chungking* and *Portrait in Black*; starred in the tv series, *The Gallery of Madame Liu Tsong* (1951). ❖ See also *Women in World History.*

WONG, Betty Ann (1938—). American composer, pianist, instrumentalist and lecturer. Name variations: Siu Junn. Born in San Francisco, CA, Sept 6, 1938; studied music at Mills College under Morton Subotnick, Nathan Rubin, and Colin Hampton; studied Chinese music under David Liang, Lawrence Lui, and Leo Lew. ❖ Taught piano at San Francisco Music Conservatory and University of California at San Diego; co-managed the Flowing Stream Ensemble, a Chinese silk and bamboo orchestra whose repertoire covered 25 centuries; composed Chinese and Western music; also played banjo, gong, Chinese recorder and zither. ❖ See also *Women in World History.*

WONG, Flossie (1946—). See Wong-Staal, Flossie.

WONG, Jade Snow (1919–2006). Chinese-American writer. Born Jan 21, 1919, in San Francisco, California; died Mar 16, 2006, in San Francisco; dau. of Hong Wong (manufacturer) and Hing Kwai (Tong) Wong; San Francisco Junior College, AA, 1940; Mills College, BA, 1942; married Woodrow Ong (travel agent), Aug 29, 1950; children: Mark Stuart; Tyli Elizabeth; Ellora Louise; Lance Orion. ❖ Chronicled experiences growing up in America with a traditional Chinese family in her 1st book, *Fifth Chinese Daughter* (1945), which met with critical acclaim, had strong sales, and remains a classic of Asian-American literature; published 2nd work, *No Chinese Stranger* (1975), which was a continuation of her memoirs. ❖ See also *Women in World History.*

WONG, Yee-ching (1946—). See Wong-Staal, Flossie.

WONG-STAAL, Flossie (1946—). Asian-American geneticist and medical researcher. Name variations: Yee-ching Wong; Yee Ching Wong; Flossie Wong; Flossie Staal. Born Yee Ching Wong, Aug 27, 1946, in Guangzhou, Kwangtung Province, China; dau. of Sueh-fung Wong (cloth exporter-importer); University of California, Los Angeles,

bachelor's degree in molecular biology, 1969, PhD, 1972; m. Steven Staal, 1971 (div.); children: Stephanie and Caroline Staal. ❖ Leading AIDS researcher, began career working with Robert Gallo at National Cancer Institute (1973), where they investigated the possibility of viruses linked to cancer, and eventually discovered 3 similar viruses: human T-cell leukemia virus (HTLV), the 1st virus proven to cause human cancer (1981), followed by a virus named HTLV-2, and finally HTLV-3, now known as HIV or human immunodeficiency virus, which was discovered simultaneously by France's Pasteur Institute (1983); researched and was 1st to clone and reveal chemical sequence of HIV's genes (1985); moved to University of California, San Diego (1990) and directed its AIDS research center to develop possible treatments, including inserting gene coding to prevent growth and reproduction of AIDS cells; became chief scientific officer and executive vice president of Research for Immusol, a biopharmaceutical company based in San Diego; co-authored *AIDS Vaccine Research* (2002) and *The Control of Human Retrovirus Gene Expression* (1988).

WOO HYUN-JUNG. South Korean field-hockey player. Born in South Korea. ❖ Won a team silver medal at Atlanta Olympics (1996).

WOO SUN-HEE (1978—). South Korean handball player. Born July 1, 1978, in South Korea. ❖ Won a team silver at Athens Olympics (2004).

WOOD, Anna (1966—). Dutch-Australian kayaker. Name variations: Anna Maria Wood. Born July 22, 1966, in Roemund, Netherlands. ❖ Was on the Dutch sprint team (1983–89) and Australian sprint team (1990–93, 1995–2000); won a bronze medal for K2 500 meters at Atlanta Olympics (1996); at World championships, won gold medals for K2 1,000 (1998, 1999), K2 500 meters (1998); won World Cup for K2 1,000 (2000).

WOOD, Audrey (1908–1998). English midwife. Born Aug 19, 1908, in Cambridge, England; died Mar 21, 1998. ❖ Trained in midwifery in Oxford; qualified as a midwife tutor (1941); served as district nursing sister and night sister, Oxford (1937–41); employed as assistant matron and midwifery tutor at Heathfield Maternity Home in Birmingham (1941) and at Royal Maternity Hospital in Belfast (until 1951); was midwifery tutor at Royal College of Midwives in London (1951–52) and the 1st graduate to serve as general secretary there (1952–70); campaigned to have a midwifery officer position appointed by the Ministry of Health; encouraged cooperation between midwives and other healthcare professionals; appointed to the expert committee on maternity care for the World Health Organization (1965); was a lifetime Quaker member and an assistant secretary of the Society of Friends' Social Responsibility Council (1971–78). Made Officer of the Order of the British Empire (1970).

WOOD, Audrey (1905–1985). American theatrical and literary agent. Born Feb 28, 1905, in New York, NY; died Dec 27, 1985, in Fairfield, CT; m. William Liebling. ❖ With husband, founded the theatrical agency International Famous (1937), eventually representing such writers as Tennessee Williams, Carson McCullers, Arthur Kopit, Studs Terkel, Murray Schisgal, William Inge, Robert Anderson, Brian Friel and Eva Le Gallienne; was a major force in the theater world for many years; spent last years in a coma following a stroke (1981–85).

WOOD, Baby Gloria (1919–1994). See Stevens, K. T.

WOOD, Beatrice (1893–1998). American painter, sculptor, and ceramist. Born Mar 3, 1893, in San Francisco, California; died Mar 13, 1998, in Ojai, California; studied drawing at Académie Julien; studied with Viennese master ceramists Otto and Gertrude Natzler; married twice; no children. ❖ Best known for her lustreware ceramic pieces, characterized by their opalescent glazes, was called "Mama of Dada" because of her association with several early 20th-century artists and writers; for several years, was the companion of Marcel Duchamp and Henri-Pierre Roché; became Roché's lover, until he cheated on her, then replaced him with Duchamp (Roché later immortalized the trio in his novel *Jules and Jim,* which became a film starring Jeanne Moreau); moved home and studio to Ojai (1948), where she studied with spiritual guru Krishnamurti and continued to work until her death. ❖ See also autobiography *I Shock Myself* (1985); *Beatrice Wood: Mama of Dada* (60 min. documentary, 1991); and *Women in World History.*

WOOD, Bette Anderson (c. 1929—). See Anderson, Bette B.

WOOD, Carolyn (1922–1982). See Sherif, Carolyn Wood.

WOOD, Carolyn (1945—). American swimmer. Born Dec 18, 1945, in Oregon. ❖ At Rome Olympics, won a gold medal in 4 x 100-meter freestyle relay (1960).

WOOD, Daisey (1877—). English comedian. Name variations: Daisy Wood. Born Sept 15, 1877, in London, England; dau. of John Wood (waiter) and Matilda Mary (Archer) Wood; sister of Alice Lloyd, Grace Lloyd, Rosie Lloyd, and Marie Lloyd (music-hall star, 1870–1922); m. Donald Munro. ❖ Made stage debut with Charles Godfrey at the South London Music Hall in *My Willie* (1890); appeared in all the leading music halls in England and at the Palladium in *The Whirl of the Town*; popularized such songs as "My Diamond Queen," "Saturday Afternoon," "Till Sunday Morning" and "Cupid."

WOOD, Edith Elmer (1871–1945). American housing reformer. Born Sept 24, 1871, in Portsmouth, New Hampshire; died April 29, 1945, in Greystone Park, New Jersey; dau. of Horace Elmer (Civil War veteran and naval officer) and Adele (Wiley) Elmer; Smith College, BL, 1890; Columbia University, in a joint program with the New York School of Philanthropy, MA, 1917, PhD, 1919; m. Albert Norton Wood (naval officer), 1893; children: Horace Elmer (b. 1895); Thurston Elmer (b. 1897); Horace Elmer II (b. 1900); and Albert Elmer (b. 1910). ❖ Began career as a novelist, publishing several books of romantic fiction and travelogues; married a naval officer (1893) and traveled frequently as his assignments changed; in Puerto Rico (1906), started a crusade to improve public-health facilities especially for the poor; founded the Anti-Tuberculosis League of Puerto Rico; when the family moved to Washington, DC, tried to improve housing conditions in the slums, though with limited success; entered Columbia University's graduate school (1915), at 44; published thesis, *The Housing of the Unskilled Wage Earner* (1920); dedicated rest of life to housing-reform advocacy; appointed to numerous housing advisory boards, including Women's Municipal League of Boston (1917–19) and American Association of University Women's committee on housing, of which she was chair (1917–29); taught courses on housing economics and public policy at Columbia (1926–30); was director of the National Public Housing Conference (1932–45); during Roosevelt's tenure, served as a consultant to Public Works Administration (1933–37), and US Housing Authority (1933–45), shaping New Deal housing legislation. ❖ See also *Women in World History*.

WOOD, Ellen Price (1814–1887). English novelist. Name variations: Mrs. Henry Wood; Johnny Ludlow. Born Ellen Price, Jan 17, 1814, in Worcester, England; died Feb 10, 1887, in London; dau. of Thomas Price (prosperous manufacturer) and Elizabeth (Evans) Price; m. Henry Wood (banker), 1836; children: Charles Wood (b. 1850). ❖ Prolific Victorian novelist who wrote the hugely popular *East Lynne*; after developing scoliosis as a child, remained a semi-invalid throughout life, able to write only while lying on a couch; wrote stories which were published in *Bentley's Miscellany* and *New Monthly Magazine*; published 1st novel, *Danesbury House* (1860), followed by *East Lynne* which appeared serially in *New Monthly Magazine* (1861), then in book form (by 1900, it had sold over half a million copies); published the family sagas *Mrs. Halliburton's Troubles* and *The Channings*; wrote in a melodramatic style with a similar theme, a stern Christian morality with severe punishment for those characters who transgress middle-class Victorian values; published over 300 short stories and 30 novels, including *The Shadow of Ashlydyat* (1863), *Lord Oakburn's Daughters* (1864), *Roland Yorke* (1869) and *Edina* (1876), among others; with son Charles, owned and co-edited the literary magazine, *The Argosy*, for which she wrote stories based on her Worcestershire childhood and published under the name "Johnny Ludlow." ❖ See also Charles Wood, *Memorials of Mrs. Henry Wood* (Bentley, 1894); and *Women in World History*.

WOOD, Ethel Mary Reader (1871–1946). *See Shakespear, Ethel Mary Reader.*

WOOD, Evelyn (1909–1995). American entrepreneur. Born Evelyn Nielsen, Jan 8, 1909, in Logan, Utah; died Aug 26, 1995, in Tucson, Arizona; dau. of Elias and Rose (Stirland) Nielsen; University of Utah, BA, 1929, MS in speech, 1947; m. Myron Douglas Wood, June 12, 1929 (died 1987); children: Carol Wood Evans. ❖ Speech and reading specialist, developed and broadcast numerous radio programs on reading skills in Utah (1947); worked with C. Lowell Lees on speech and reading studies at University of Utah (1947–50); as a girls' counselor at Jordan High School in Sandy, Utah (1948–57), began a remedial reading program; developed a speed-reading technique which she further refined by teaching it in schools (1948–59); taught reading skills courses at

University of Utah (1957–59); naming her program Evelyn Wood Reading Dynamics (1959), opened an institute to teach speed-reading in Washington, DC, and published *Reading Skills*, which promised to increase the student's reading speed from the average 250 words per minute to 1,500; also wrote *A Breakthrough in Reading* (1961), *A New Approach to Speed-Reading* (1962), and *Speed Reading for Comprehension* (1962); was appointed assistant professor at University of Delaware (1961); asked by John F. Kennedy to teach Reading Dynamics to joint chiefs of staff (1963); established over 150 Reading Dynamics Institutes and lectured across US, Canada, and in Europe (1960s); retired (1977). ❖ See also *Women in World History*.

WOOD, Florence (c. 1854–1954). English actress. Born c. 1854 in London, England; died April 17, 1954; dau. of John Wood (actor) and Matilda Wood (actress); m. Ralph R. Lumley (barrister and playwright), c. 1890. ❖ Made London stage debut in title role of one-act play *Hermine* (1888); other plays include *A Court Scandal, The Elixir of Youth, The Prodigal Son, The Bondman, Lady Frederick, The Crimson Alibi, The Trial of Mary Dugan* and *These Pretty Things*.

WOOD, Helen Muir- (1895–1968). *See Muir-Wood, Helen.*

WOOD, Mrs. Henry (1814–1887). *See Wood, Ellen Price.*

WOOD, Joan Wentworth (1905–2004). *See Morgan, Joan.*

WOOD, Mrs. John (1831–1915). *See Wood, Matilda.*

WOOD, Madam (1759–1855). *See Wood, Sally Sayward Barrell Keating.*

WOOD, Marjorie (1882–1955). English-born stage and screen actress. Born Sept 5, 1882, in London, England; died Nov 9, 1955, in Hollywood, CA. ❖ Broadway credits include *Call of the North, Baby Mine, The Third Party, The Woman, Chu Chin Chow, Yes and No* and *Yellow*; made 20 films, including *Pride and Prejudice* (1940), *Excuse my Dust* and *Seven Brides for Seven Brothers*.

WOOD, Mary Anne Everett (1818–1895). *See Green, Mary Anne Everett.*

WOOD, Mary Elizabeth (1861–1931). American missionary and librarian. Born Aug 22, 1861, in Elba, New York; died May 1, 1931, in Wuchang, China; dau. of Edward Farmer Wood and Mary Jane (Humphrey) Wood; studied library science at Pratt Institute, New York, and Simmons College, Boston; never married. ❖ Episcopal missionary and librarian in China for 30 years, helped found the National Library of Peking (Beijing) with funds raised in US; worked for 10 years as librarian of the newly founded Richmond Library in Batavia, NY; visited brother Robert Wood, an Episcopal missionary in Wuchang (1899) and decided to stay; was made a lay missionary by Episcopal Church (1904); helped establish a series of branch libraries at state and private colleges in Wuchang and Hankow; founded a school for library science at Boone College in Wuchang (1920), which trained nearly 500 Chinese librarians before its closure after the Communist revolution (it was subsequently reopened as an affiliate of National Wuhan University). ❖ See also *Women in World History*.

WOOD, Matilda (1831–1915). English stage actress and theater manager. Name variations: Mrs. John Wood. Born Matilda Charlotte Vining, Nov 6, 1831, in Liverpool, England; died Jan 11, 1915, on Isle of Thanet, Kent, England; dau. of Henry Vining (actor) and an actress mother; m. John Wood (actor), 1854 (sep. 1858); children: Florence Wood (actress). ❖ At 10, made stage debut (1841); appeared regularly in small theaters outside London (1841–53); with husband, appeared in vaudeville and burlesque at Boston Theater (MA) for 3 seasons, then debuted in NY at Academy of Music (1856); performed at Maguire's Opera House, San Francisco, and separated from husband (1858); remained in San Francisco for a season, then managed the Forrest Theater, Sacramento (1859), followed by San Francisco's American Theater; appeared frequently on stage in NY, Boston, Philadelphia and New Orleans (1860–63); launched her own company at the Olympic (NY), managing and performing to great success; returned to England (1866), appearing there in numerous stage roles at London's best theaters; held a management position at St. James's Theater (1869–79); co-managed New Royal Court Theater (1888–91), while also performing in several productions; retired to Isle of Thanet, off Kent, after final stage appearance in *The Prodigal Son* at Drury Lane (1905).

WOOD, Matilda Alice Victoria (1870–1922). *See Lloyd, Marie.*

WOOD, Natalie (1938–1981). American actress. Born Natasha Gurdin (also seen as Natasha Zakharenko), July 20, 1938, in Santa Rosa, California; died Nov 29, 1981, in a boating accident off California coast; dau. of Maria Nikolaevna Gurdin (later Maria Wood) and Nicholas Gurdin; m. Robert Wagner (actor), 1957 (div. 1962); m. Richard Gregson (actor), 1969 (div. 1971); rem. Robert Wagner, 1972; children: (with Gregson) Natasha Gregson (b. 1970, later Natasha Wagner, actress); (with Wagner) Courtney Wagner (b. 1974); (step-daughter) Katie Wagner. ❖ Best known for her role in the classic *Rebel Without a Cause*, was cast as an extra in *Happy Days*, a film shooting in her hometown when she was 4 (1942); as Natalie Wood, became a popular child star (1940s), coming to prominence with her appearance in *Miracle on 34th Street* (1947); nominated for her 1st Academy Award for *Rebel Without a Cause* (1955), followed by nominations for *Splendor in the Grass* and *Love with the Proper Stranger*; during later career, turned more toward tv films; other films include *The Ghost and Mrs. Muir* (1947), *The Searchers* (1956), *Kings Go Forth* (1958), *Marjorie Morningstar* (1958), *Cash McCall* (1959), *West Side Story* (1961), *Gypsy* (1962), *Sex and the Single Girl* (1964), *The Great Race* (1965), *Inside Daisy Clover* (1965), *This Property Is Condemned* (1966), *Bob & Carol & Ted & Alice* (1969), *Meteor* (1979), *Willie and Phil* (1980) and *Brainstorm* (1983). ❖ See also Lana Wood, *Natalie* (Putnam, 1984); Suzanne Finstad, *Natasha* (Harmony, 2001); and *Women in World History*.

WOOD, Peggy (1892–1978). American actress, singer, playwright, and writer. Born Margaret Wood, Feb 9, 1892, in Brooklyn, NY; died Mar 18, 1978, in Stamford, CT; dau. of journalist Eugene Wood and Mary (Gardner) Wood; m. John van Alstyne Weaver (writer), 1924 (died 1938); m. William H. Walling (executive), 1946 (died 1973). ❖ Studied voice with Arthur Van der Linde and Emma Calvé; made professional singing debut in Broadway chorus of *Naughty Marietta* (1910); began long theater career, including starring roles as Marietta in *Naughty Marietta* (1916), Ottilie in a 2-year run of *Maytime* (1917–19), title role in *Candida* (1925), and Ruth in *Blithe Spirit* (1942); made film debut in Will Rogers' *Almost a Husband* (1919), followed by *Jalna* (1935), *A Star is Born* (1937), *The Bride Wore Boots* (1946) and *Dream Girl* (1948), among others; starred on tv series "Mama" (1949–57); one of the founders of Actors' Equity, was also president of American National Theater and Academy (1959–66); wrote several plays, including *The Flying Prince* and *Miss Quis*, as well as the novel *Star Wagon*. Nominated for Academy Award for Best Supporting Actress for portrayal of Mother Abbess in *The Sound of Music* (1965). ❖ See also memoirs, *How Young You Look* (1941) and *Arts and Flowers* (1963); and *Women in World History*.

WOOD, Sally Sayward Barrell Keating (1759–1855). American novelist. Name variations: Sarah Sayward Barrell Keating Wood; S. S. B. K. Wood; Madam Wood. Born Sally Sayward Barrell, Oct 1, 1759, in York, ME; died Jan 6, 1855, in Kennebunk, ME; dau. of Nathaniel Barrell (merchant) and Sally (Sayward) Barrell; m. Richard Keating (court clerk), Nov 23, 1778 (died June 1783); m. Gen. Abiel Wood, Oct 28, 1804 (died 1811); children: (1st m.) 1 son, 2 daughters. ❖ Maine's 1st female novelist and America's 1st gothic writer, favored the sentimental fiction style established by Susanna Rowson; using pseudonym "A Lady of Massachusetts," published 4 novels, *Julia and the Illuminated Baron* (1800), *Dorval, or the Speculator* (1801), *Amelia; or the Influence of Virtue* (1802), and *Ferdinand and Elmira: A Russian Story* (1804); published *Tales of the Night* in Portland, ME, as "A Lady of Maine" (1927).

WOOD, Sara Bard Field (1882–1974). *See Field, Sara Bard.*

WOOD, Susan (1836–1880). New Zealand writer. Name variations: Susan Lapham, Mrs. Nugent Wood. Born Susan Lapham, Aug 21, 1836, at Lisdillon, Great Swan Port, Van Diemen's Land (Tasmania), Australia; died Nov 30, 1880, at Riverton, New Zealand; dau. of Samuel Lapham and Susan (Butler) Lapham; sister of Henry Lapham (writer); m. John Nugent Wood, 1854; children: 2 sons, probably 3 daughters. ❖ Resided near goldfields of New Zealand and regularly contributed verse, feature articles, and short stories to local newspapers and periodicals; though work is considered sentimental and stylized, provided valuable insight into daily life, emotions, and aspirations of pioneer women; wrote *Women's Work in Australia* (1862), *Bush Flowers* (1867) and *Waiting for the Mail* (1875), among others. ❖ See also *Dictionary of New Zealand Biography* (Vol. 1).

WOOD, Thelma (1901–1970). American artist and sculptor. Born July 3, 1901, in Kansas; grew up in St. Louis, Missouri; died Dec 10, 1970, in Danbury, CT. ❖ Born well to do, arrived in Paris (1920), aged 19; the great love of Djuna Barnes' life, lived with Barnes in the heart of the Left Bank (1920–31). Their affair was fictionalized in Barnes *Nightwood*. ❖ See also *Women in World History*.

WOOD, Yvonne (b. 1914). American costume designer. Born in 1914; educated at Chouinard Art School. ❖ First worked for Fox and Universal studios as a sketch artist; earned initial film credit as a costume designer for *The Gang's All Here* with Carmen Miranda (1943); costumed some 75 films, including *A Bell for Adano* (1945), *L'il Abner* (1959), *One-Eyed Jacks* (1959), *The Cheyenne Social Club* (1969), *The Life and Times of Judge Roy Bean* (1972) and *Zoot Suit* (1981), as well as the tv series "Quincy" (1976).

WOODARD, Lynette (1959—). African-American basketball player. Born Aug 12, 1959, in Wichita, Kansas; graduate of University of Kansas, 1981. ❖ Was a star national player at the University of Kansas; won a team gold medal at World University Games (1979); played for US at Pan American Games (1981, 1983) and World championship (1983, 1990); was the 1st woman signed with the Harlem Globetrotters (1985); captained the 1st American women's basketball team in the Olympics (1984) and won a gold medal; had 9 years of professional play; became a stockbroker for Magna Securities in NY; signed with Cleveland Rockers in WNBA (1997); drafted by Detroit Shock (1998); retired to coach (1999). Wade Trophy winner (1981). ❖ See also Matthew Newman, *Lynette Woodard* (Crestwood, 1986) and Bert Rosenthal, *Lynette Woodard: The First Female Globetrotter* (Children's Press, 1986); and *Women in World History*.

WOODBRIDGE, Louise Deshong (1848–1925). American photographer. Born 1848 in Chester, Pennsylvania; died 1925, possibly in Chester; m. Jonathon Edwards Woodbridge, 1877. ❖ Took up photography (1884); her photographs, primarily landscapes, were featured in the Sixth Joint Annual Exhibition of Photography in Philadelphia and the World's Columbian Exhibition in Chicago (1893).

WOODBRIDGE, Margaret (1902—). American swimmer. Born 1902; trained in Detroit, Michigan. ❖ In Antwerp Olympics, awarded a silver medal in the 300-meter freestyle and a gold in the 4 x 100-meter freestyle relay (1920). Inducted into International Swimming Hall of Fame (1989).

WOODBURY, Clare (c. 1880–1949). American stage actress. Born c. 1880; died Mar 13, 1949, in New York, NY. ❖ Plays include Broadway, *Little Accident, Green Grow the Lilacs, Missouri Legend*, and *Apple of His Eye*; retired from stage (1946).

WOODBURY, Helen Sumner (1876–1933). American historian and public official. Born Helen Laura Sumner, Mar 12, 1876, in Sheboygan, Wisconsin; died Mar 10, 1933, in New York, NY; dau. of George True Sumner (Colorado judge) and Katherine Eudora (Marsh) Sumner; Wellesley College, AB, 1898; University of Wisconsin, PhD, 1908; m. Robert M. Woodbury (economist), Nov 1918. ❖ Studied labor economics with Richard T. Ely and John Commons at University of Wisconsin; contributed to Commons' *Trade Unionism and Labor Problems* (1905) and for next several years was an important figure in his American Bureau of Industrial Research; with Thomas S. Adams, also co-authored a college textbook, *Labor Problems* (1905); conducted a long investigation of women's suffrage in Colorado (1906), which was published as *Equal Suffrage* (1909); wrote thesis, "The Labor Movement in America, 1827–1837" (1911), which appeared revised in Commons' 2-vol. *The History of Labor in the US* (1918), the 1st serious study on the topic; also served as associate editor on Commons' *A Documentary History of American Industrial Society* (1910–11); headed numerous studies on child-labor issues, most of which were published for the US Children's Bureau (1913–18), including *Child Labor Legislation in the US* (1915); promoted to director of investigations for the Bureau (1918). ❖ See also *Women in World History*.

WOODBURY, Joan (1915–1989). American actress. Name variations: Nana Martin. Born Joanne Woodbury, Dec 17, 1915, in Los Angeles, CA; died Feb 22, 1989, in Desert Hot Springs, CA; m. Henry Wilcoxon, 1939 (div.); m. Ray Mitchell. ❖ Began career as a dancer; films include *Eagle's Brood, Anthony Adverse, Algiers, The Ten Commandments*, and the title role in *Brenda Starr* (serial); produced and directed plays and light operas in California.

WOODBY-MCKANE, Alice (1865–1948). *See McKane, Alice Woodby.*

WOODGATE, Margaret (1935—). Australian politician. Born Sept 1, 1935, in Brisbane, Australia. ❖ As a member of the Australian Labor Party, served in the Queensland Parliament for Pine Rivers (1989–92), then Kurwongbah (1992–97); was shadow minister for Families, Community Care and Aboriginal and Islander Affairs (1996).

WOODHAM-SMITH, Cecil (1896–1977). British biographer and historian. Name variations: (pseudonym) Janet Gordon. Born Cecil Blanche FitzGerald April 29, 1896, in Tenby, Wales; died Mar 16, 1977, in London, England; dau. of James FitzGerald (army colonel) and Blanche Elizabeth Philipps FitzGerald; educated at St. Hilda's College, Oxford; m. George Ivon Woodham-Smith (attorney), 1928 (died 1968); children: Elizabeth Sarah Woodham-Smith; Charles James Woodham-Smith. ❖ Published 3 novels under pseudonym "Janet Gordon," beginning with *April Sky* (1938); under own name, published *Florence Nightingale: 1820–1910* (1950), which won the James Tait Black Memorial Prize; continued work on 19th century with next book about the British Light Brigade, *The Reason Why* (1953), then wrote *The Great Hunger: Ireland 1845–1849* (1962), which is still considered a classic; published 1st vol., *Queen Victoria: Her Life and Times,* of her planned multivolume biography (1972), but did not live to complete the work. Named Commander of the Order of the British Empire (1960); received A.C. Benson Medal for contributions to British literature (1969). ❖ See also *Women in World History.*

WOODHEAD, Cynthia (1964—). American swimmer. Name variations: Sippy Woodhead. Born Feb 1964 in Riverside, California; attended University of Southern California. ❖ At World championships, won gold medal in 200-meter freestyle, 4 x 100-meter relay, and 4 x 100-meter medley relay (1978); at Pan American Games, won gold medal in 100-meter, 200-meter and 400-meter freestyle, 4 x 100-meter relay, and 4 x 100-meter medley relay (1979) and 200-meter freestyle (1983); at Los Angeles Olympics, won a silver medal in 200-meter freestyle (1984); held 7 World records; won 18 AAU/US national titles. Inducted into International Swimming Hall of Fame (1994).

WOODHEAD, Florence Marie (1891–1994). *See Harsant, Florence Marie.*

WOODHOUSE, Chase Going (1890–1984). *See Woodhouse, Margaret Chase Going.*

WOODHOUSE, Danielle. Australian water-polo player. Born in Perth, Australia; sister of Bridgette Gusterson (water-polo player). ❖ Goalkeeper, won a team gold medal at Sydney Olympics (2000).

WOODHOUSE, Margaret Chase Going (1890–1984). American educator and politician. Name variations: Chase Woodhouse; Mrs. Chase Going Woodhouse; Margaret Woodhouse. Born Margaret Chase Going in Victoria, British Columbia, Canada, Mar 3, 1890; died Dec 12, 1984, in Sprague, Connecticut; dau. of Seymour Going and Harriet (Jackson) Going; McGill University, BA, 1912, MA, 1913; m. Edward Woodhouse (professor of government), 1917; children: Noel Robert (b. 1921) and Margaret (b. 1925). ❖ Known as Chase, worked as an economics professor at a number of American universities throughout career; served as senior economist with Bureau of Home Economics of US Department of Agriculture (1926–28); acted as founder and managing director of Institute of Women's Professional Relations (1929–46); contributed articles on labor policy to various scholarly journals, and published several books aimed at women, including *Business Opportunities for the Home Economist* (1934); began 12-year tenure as professor of economics at Connecticut College for Women (1934–46); elected secretary of state for Connecticut (1941); as a liberal Democrat, elected to US Congress (1944), becoming the 2nd Connecticut woman to serve in Congress; faced controversy on her 1st roll-call vote when she opposed a bill to make the House Committee on Un-American Activities a standing committee (1945); was assigned to the important Committee on Banking and Currency; failed in reelection bid (1946); became executive director of women's division of Democratic National Committee (1947); won 2nd term in Congress (1948); lost reelection bid (1950); became special assistant to director of Price Stabilization (1951); served as director of Service Bureau for Women's Organizations in Hartford (1952–80). ❖ See also *Women in World History.*

WOODHOUSE, Mary Ann (c. 1832–1910). *See Bibby, Mary Ann.*

WOODHULL, Victoria (1838–1927). American activist. Name variations: Victoria Woodhull-Martin; Victoria Claflin. Born Victoria Claflin, Sept 23, 1838, in Homer, Ohio; died June 9, 1927, in Worcestershire, England; dau. of Reuben Buckman Claflin (gristmill operator) and Roxanna (Hummel) Claflin; sister of Tennessee Claflin (1846–1923) and Utica Claflin Brooker (d. 1873); m. Canning Woodhull, c. 1853; m. Colonel James Harvey Blood, 1866; m. John

Martin, 1882; children: (1st m.) Byron; Woodhull; Zulu Maude Woodhull. ❖ Advocate of free love, women's suffrage and workers' rights and one of the most notorious women of her era, operated a stock brokerage, lectured, ran for the US presidency, precipitated a scandalous adultery trial, and flaunted Victorian social and sexual mores throughout most of her life; promoted by father, toured as a clairvoyant with her sister Tennessee Claflin; moved with husband Canning Woodhull and children to New York City; while touring as a spiritualist, met Colonel Blood, an advocate of free love, whom she married (1866); with sister, opened the 1st women-owned brokerage firm on Wall Street (1870); announced candidacy for presidency (April 1870); founded *Woodhull & Claflin's Weekly* (May 1870); addressed House Judiciary Committee regarding women's right to vote (Jan 1871); publicly declared herself a practitioner of free love (Nov 1871); nominated by the Equal Rights Party as candidate for the US presidency, with Frederick Douglass as vice-president (1872): in a direct challenge to the Victorian standards of morality of the day, revealed the extramarital affair of Elizabeth Tilton and the Reverend Henry Ward Beecher (who had publicly denounced sexual activity outside the institution of matrimony as immoral), leading to charges of criminal libel and mailing obscene literature (Nov 1872); moved with family to England, with probable financial support of the heir of Commodore Cornelius Vanderbilt (1877); married millionaire John Martin (1882); became a philanthropist on behalf of agriculture and education. ❖ See also Johanna Johnston, *Mrs. Satan: The Incredible Saga of Victoria C. Woodhull* (Putnam, 1967); Mary Gabriel, *Notorious Victoria: The Life of Victoria Woodhull, Uncensored* (Algonquin, 1997); Emanie Sachs, *The Terrible Siren* (Harper, 1928); Theodore Tilton, *The Life of Victoria Claflin Woodhull* (1871); and *Women in World History.*

WOODLEY, Erin (1972—). Canadian synchronized swimmer. Born June 6, 1972, in Mississauga, Ontario, Canada. ❖ Placed 1st in duet at Commonwealth Games (1994); won a team silver medal at Atlanta Olympics (1996).

WOODROW, Nancy Mann Waddel (c. 1866–1935). American writer. Name variations: Mrs. Wilson Woodrow, Jane Wade. Born Nancy Mann Waddle (later changed the spelling to "Waddel"), c. 1866 in Chillicothe, OH; died Sept 7, 1935, in New York, NY; dau. of William (physician) and Jane S. (McCoy) Waddle; sister of Charles Carey Waddell (mystery writer), Eleanor Waddel (writer and editor of *Vogue Magazine*); m. James Wilson Woodrow (prospector and cousin of President Woodrow Wilson), Aug 4, 1897 (sep. c. 1900). ❖ Prolific contributor of short stories and articles to magazines such as *McClure's, Cosmopolitan, Life, Harper's, American,* and *Good Housekeeping,* wrote in a masculine voice, leading many editors to believe she was male using a female pseudonym; her style set her apart from sentimental female novelists and earnest feminists of the day; wrote 1 play and 13 novels, including *The New Missioner* (1907), *The Silver Butterfly* (1908), and *The Black Pearl* (1912); published series of satires of popular novels in *Life* (1905–06).

WOODROW, Mrs. Wilson (c. 1866–1935). *See Woodrow, Nancy Mann Waddel.*

WOODS, Doris. English gymnast. Born in UK. ❖ At Amsterdam Olympics, won a bronze medal in team all-around (1928).

WOODS, Katharine Pearson (1853–1923). American novelist. Born Jan 28, 1853, in Wheeling, VA; died Feb 19, 1923, in Baltimore, MD; dau. of Alexander Quarrier Woods (tobacco merchant) and Josephine Augusta (McCabe) Woods. ❖ Secretly wrote and anonymously published 1st novel, *Metzerott, Shoemaker* (1889), which advocated economic reform for working people, based on Christian principals, and was acclaimed; also wrote *Web of Gold* (1890), *From Dusk to Dawn* (1892), *John: A Tale of King Messiah* (1896), *The Son of Ingar* (1897), and *The True Story of Captain John Smith* (1901).

WOODS, Taryn (1975—). Australian water-polo player. Born Aug 12, 1975, in Balmain, Sydney, NSW, Australia; dau. of David Woods (Olympic water-polo player); cousin of Bronwyn Mayer (water-polo player). ❖ Center back, won a team gold medal at Sydney Olympics (2000).

WOODSMALL, Ruth F. (1883–1963). American social activist. Born Ruth Frances Woodsmall, Sept 20, 1883, in Atlanta, Georgia; died May 25, 1963, in New York, NY; dau. of Hubert Harrison Woodsmall (Union soldier and lawyer) and Mary Elizabeth (Howes) Woodsmall (art teacher); educated at Franklin College, Indiana University, Columbia University and University of Heidelberg; University of

Nebraska, BA, 1905; Wellesley College, MA, 1906. ❖ Young Women's Christian Association (YWCA) official whose studies of the condition of women around the world aided in international relief and development efforts; started career with YWCA as a director of hostess houses (1917); worked as a liaison to the American military during the occupation of Germany following World War I, specifically reporting on conditions in Germany, Poland, and the Baltic and Balkan regions; became executive secretary of YWCA in Near East and secretary of YWCA Eastern Mediterranean Federations (1920); published germinal study on changing status of Muslim women (1930); published further research into status of women in Far East (1933); served as specialist on international affairs to national board of YWCA (1932–35); became general secretary of World's YWCA (1935); conducted studies of women in Nazi Germany (1930s) and Latin America during WWII; became chief of Women's Affairs in Germany following the war. ❖ See also *Women in World History.*

WOODSTRA, Susan (1957—). American volleyball player. Name variations: Sue Woodstra. Born May 21, 1957, in Colton, CA; attended University of Southern California. ❖ As team captain at Los Angeles Olympics, won a silver medal in team competition (1984); was on US national team for 8 years; was head volleyball coach at University of Pittsburgh (1989–92) and University of California (1995–2000); became head coach at Humboldt State University (2000).

WOODVILLE, Anne (b. around 1458). Countess of Kent. Born c. 1458; dau. of Richard Woodville, 1st earl Rivers, and Jacquetta of Luxemburg; sister of Elizabeth Woodville (1437–1492), queen of England; m. William Bourchier, Viscount Bourchier; m. George Grey, 2nd earl of Kent; children: (1st m.) Henry Bourchier, 2nd earl of Essex, and Cecily Bourchier; (2nd m.) Richard Grey, 3rd earl of Kent.

WOODVILLE, Mrs. Antony Caton (1884–1966). *See Barton, Dora.*

WOODVILLE, Catherine (c. 1442–1512). *See Woodville, Katherine.*

WOODVILLE, Elizabeth (1437–1492). Queen of England. Name variations: Dame Elizabeth Grey; Elizabeth Wideville. Born Elizabeth Woodville around 1437 in Grafton Regis, Northamptonshire, England; died June 7 or 8, 1492, in Bermondsey Abbey, London; eldest and one of six daughters and seven sons of Sir Richard Woodville, 1st earl Rivers, and Jacquetta of Luxemburg; m. Sir John Grey, 2nd baron Ferrers of Groby (died); m. Edward IV, king of England, on May 1, 1464 (died 1483); children: (1st m.) Thomas Grey, 1st marquess of Dorset (d. 1501) and Richard Grey (c. 1453–1483); (2nd m.) Elizabeth of York (1466–1503, who m. Henry VII); Mary Plantagenet (1467–1482); Cecilia (1469–1507); King Edward V (1470–1483, who was murdered in the Tower of London); Margaret (1472–1472); Richard (1473–1483, who was murdered in the Tower); Anne Howard (1475–1511); George (1477–1479, who died of the plague); Katherine Plantagenet (1479–1527); Bridget (1480–1517, who became a nun at Dartford). ❖ During 1st marriage to a Lancastrian, became a lady of the bedchamber to Henry VI's queen, Margaret of Anjou; when husband was killed in battle and Yorkist Edward IV had himself proclaimed king, lost her husband's estates and was left penniless; set out to petition the new king to provide support for her children; instead, married him and was crowned in a splendid ceremony at Westminster; busied herself with having more babies and situating her many siblings within wealthy marriages, a task made simpler by her ability to favorably influence husband; was not popular among many Yorkist supporters, who were incensed over the favors granted to her upstart relatives, many of whom had Lancastrian connections; after Edward's death (1483), was devastated when her power-hungry brother-in-law, Richard (III) of Gloucester, kept her sons from succeeding to the throne by confining them to the Tower of London where they were eventually murdered; became simply Dame Elizabeth Grey and lived under the king's control in Bermondsey Abbey; her lands were restored by Henry VII. ❖ See also David MacGibbon, *Elizabeth Woodville, 1437–1492* (1938); and *Women in World History.*

WOODVILLE, Jacquetta (fl. 15th c.). English royal. Name variations: Lady Strange of Knockin. Dau. of Richard Woodville, 1st earl Rivers, and Jacquetta of Luxemburg; sister of Elizabeth Woodville, queen of England (1437–1492); m. John, Lord Strange of Knockin.

WOODVILLE, Katherine (c. 1442–1512). English royal. Name variations: Duchess of Buckingham, Duchess of Bedford; Catherine Woodville; Catherine Wydeville. Born c. 1442; died in 1512; dau. of Richard Woodville, 1st earl Rivers, and Jacquetta of Luxemburg; sister of Elizabeth Woodville, queen of England (1437–1492); m. Henry Stafford (1455–1483), 2nd duke of Buckingham (r. 1460–1483), in 1466 (executed on Nov 2, 1483); m. Jasper Tudor, duke of Bedford, in 1485; m. Richard Wingfield; children: (1st m.) Edward Stafford, 3rd duke of Buckingham (1478–1521); Henry Stafford, earl of Wiltshire (c. 1479–1523); Elizabeth Stafford (d. 1532, mistress of Henry VIII).

WOODVILLE, Margaret (fl. 1450s). Countess of Arundel. Dau. of Richard Woodville, 1st earl Rivers, and Jacquetta of Luxemburg; sister of Elizabeth Woodville, queen of England (1437–1492); m. Thomas Fitzalan, 14th earl of Arundel.

WOODVILLE, Mary (c. 1443–c. 1480). Countess of Pembroke. Born c. 1443; died before 1481; dau. of Richard Woodville (b. 1405), 1st earl Rivers, and Jacquetta of Luxemburg; sister of Elizabeth Woodville, queen of England (1437–1492); m. William Herbert (1455–1491), 2nd earl of Pembroke; children: possibly Elizabeth Herbert (c. 1476–c. 1511). ❖ William Herbert's 2nd wife was Katherine Herbert (c. 1471–?).

WOODWARD, Alice (1871–1957). *See Horsley, Alice Woodward.*

WOODWARD, Aubertine (1841–1929). *See Moore, Aubertine Woodward.*

WOODWARD, Danielle (1965—). Australian kayaker. Born Mar 20, 1965, in Wollongong, Australia. ❖ At Barcelona Olympics, won a silver medal in K1 slalom (1992).

WOODWARD, Ellen Sullivan (1887–1971). American government official. Born July 11, 1887, in Oxford, Mississippi; died Sept 23, 1971, in Washington, DC; dau. of William Van Amberg Sullivan (US senator) and Belle (Murray) Sullivan; m. Albert Young Woodward (judge and state legislator), 1906; children: Albert Young Jr. ❖ After husband died (1925), took his place in the next election, winning a decisive victory and thus becoming the 2nd woman to serve in Mississippi House of Representatives; instead of seeking reelection, became director of civic development for Mississippi State Board of Development (1926), serving as executive director (1929–33); during Franklin Roosevelt's tenure as president, was appointed to direct women's work programs of Works Progress Administration (WPA, 1932), then became director of WPA projects for writers, musicians, actors and artists (1936), making her the 2nd-highest ranked woman in the federal government; also served on Social Security board for a number of years; during Truman's administration, served as director of Office of Inter-Agency and International Relations of the Federal Security Administration; retired (1954). ❖ See also *Women in World History.*

WOODWARD, Joanne (1930—). American actress. Born Joan Woodward, Feb 27, 1930, in Thomasville, Georgia; dau. of Wade Woodward (school administrator) and Elinor Woodward; majored in drama at Louisiana State University; m. Paul Newman (actor), Jan 29, 1958; children: Elinor "Nell" Teresa Newman (b. 1959); Melissa "Lissy" Newman (b. 1961); Claire "Clea" Newman (b. 1963); and 3 stepchildren. ❖ One of the most respected actresses of her generation, enrolled in Neighborhood Playhouse (NY), then later studied at Actors Studio; made tv debut on "Robert Montgomery Presents" (1952); made Broadway debut in *The Lovers*; while performing on New York stage and on tv, was given her 1st feature film role, *Count Three and Pray* (1955); won Academy Award for Best Actress for her career-making performance in *The Three Faces of Eve* (1957); was nominated 3 more times for Best Actress, for *Rachel, Rachel* (1969), *Summer Wishes, Winter Dreams* (1973) and *Mr. and Mrs. Bridge* (1990); won 2 Emmy Awards for work in tv films, "See How She Runs" and "Do You Remember Love?"; worked frequently with husband Paul Newman, who not only acted with her but also directed some of her most well-received roles; other films include *The Long, Hot Summer* (1958), *Rally 'Round the Flag, Boys!* (1958), *The Sound and the Fury* (1959), *The Fugitive Kind* (1959), *From the Terrace* (1960), *A Big Hand for the Little Lady* (1966), *A Fine Madness* (1966), *WUSA* (1970), *They Might Be Giants* (1971), *The Effect of Gamma Rays on Man-in-the-Moon Marigolds* (1972), *The Drowning Pool* (1975), *Harry and Son* (1984), *The Glass Menagerie* (1987) and *Philadelphia* (1993). With husband, awarded the Kennedy Center honors for lifetime achievement (1992). ❖ See also Morella and Epstein, *Paul and Joanne* (Delacorte, 1988); and *Women in World History.*

WOODWARD-MOORE, Aubertine (1841–1929). *See Moore, Aubertine Woodward.*

WOOLF, Virginia (1882–1941). English writer. Name variations: Virginia Stephen. Born Adeline Virginia Stephen, Jan 25, 1882, in

Kensington, London; drowned herself in River Ouse near Monk's House in Rodmell, Mar 28, 1941; dau. of Sir Leslie Stephen (editor, critic, historian) and Julia (Jackson Duckworth) Stephen; sister of Vanessa Bell (b. 1879), Thoby Stephen (b. 1880), and Adrian Stephen (b. 1883); stepdaughter of Harriet Thackeray; m. Leonard Woolf (writer, publisher, and editor), Aug 10, 1912; no children. ❖ Major 20th-century British novelist who, besides being one of the chief architects of the modern novel, was a pioneer in the use of the literary technique of stream-of-consciousness; grew up in and around London, in low end of upper-middle-class Victorian household, where she remained throughout life, in addition to regular stays at a country retreat; mother died when she was 13; oldest half-sister and mother-substitute, Stella Duckworth, died 2 years later; experienced the 1st serious signs of mental illness that shadowed and, ultimately, claimed her; began to keep a diary, which she sustained periodically throughout life (1897); had 2nd breakdown and made 1st suicide attempt (1904), following father's death by cancer; became a part of Bloomsbury group and published 1st article in *The Guardian* (1904); after establishing a career in writing through reviews and criticism, embarked on a literary career; published 1st novel, *The Voyage Out* (1915); suffered 2 more breakdowns (1910, 1913), resulting in extended "rest cures" and a 2nd suicide attempt (1913); besides activity in women's suffrage movement, enrolled in Women's Co-operative Guild (1915); established Hogarth House with Leonard Woolf, publishing the work of renowned writers like James Joyce and T. S. Eliot in addition to their own writing (1917); active in the "1917 Club," a resurgence of Bloomsbury intellectuals and antiwar socialists; saw the publication of Hogarth Press' 1st full-length novel, her *Jacob's Room* (1922); published *Orlando*—based on her love affair with Vita Sackville-West—which marked an upward turn in her commercial and critical success (1928); gave famous lectures on "Women and Fiction" at Girton and Newnham Colleges (1928) which became the basis for *A Room of One's Own*; continued writing and publishing throughout middle age, her literary accomplishments alternating with mental breakdowns; works include *Kew Gardens* (1919), *Night and Day* (1919), *Mr. Bennett and Mrs. Brown* (1924), *The Common Reader* (1925), *Mrs. Dalloway* (1925), *To the Lighthouse* (1927), *The Waves* (1931), *Letter to a Young Poet* (1932), *Flush: A Biography* (1933), *Walter Sickert: A Conversation* (1934), *The Years* (1937), *Three Guineas* (1938), *Roger Fry: A Biography* (1940) and *Between the Acts* (1941). Posthumous publications include (ed. by Leonard Woolf) *A Writer's Diary* (1953), *The Death of the Moth and other Essays* (1942), *A Haunted House and other Short Stories* (1943), *The Captain's Death Bed and Other Essays* (1950), *Granite and Rainbow* (1958), *Collected Essays* (4 vols., 1966–67), (ed. by Leonard Woolf and James Strachey) *Virginia Woolf & Lytton Strachey: Letters* (1956). ❖ See also Quentin Bell, *Virginia Woolf: A Biography* (1972); Louise DeSalvo, *Virginia Woolf: The Impact of Childhood Sexual Abuse on Her Life and Work* (1989); Lyndall Gordon, *Virginia Woolf: A Writer's Life* (1984); James King, *Virginia Woolf* (1995); Mitchell Leaska, *Granite and Rainbow: The Life of Virginia Woolf* (1998); Hermione Lee, *Virginia Woolf* (1997); Nigel Nicholson, *Virginia Woolf: A Penguin Life* (2000); and *Women in World History*.

WOOLGAR, Sarah Jane (1824–1909). *See Mellon, Sarah Jane.*

WOOLLEY, Ann (b. 1623). *See Woolley, Hannah.*

WOOLLEY, Hannah (1623–1677). English teacher and cookbook writer. Name variations: Ann Woolley or Wolley; Hannah Wolley, Mrs. Hannah Challinor. Born 1623 in England; died 1677 in England; m. Jeremy Woolley (schoolmaster at Free School in Newport, Essex), 1647 (died 1661); m. Francis Challinor, 1666 (died c. 1669); children: (1st m.) 4. ❖ Was probably orphaned at young age, though little is known about her childhood; ran her own school by age 15; became governess to nobility; published 1st book, *The Ladie's Directory* (1661), followed by *The Cook's Guide* (1664); widowed twice, resented lack of educational and employment opportunities available to women; trained gentlewomen for domestic service, but simultaneously encouraged them to study; wrote *The Queen Like Closet* (1670) and *The Ladie's Delight* (1672); moved in with son Richard and published final work *The Accomplisht Ladie's Delight* (1675).

WOOLLEY, Helen (1874–1947). American psychologist. Born Helen Bradford Thompson, Nov 6, 1874, in Chicago, Illinois; died Dec 24, 1947, in Havertown, Pennsylvania; dau. of David Wallace Thompson (shoe manufacturer) and Isabella Perkins (Faxon) Thompson; University of Chicago, PhB, 1897, PhD, 1900; m. Paul Gerhardt Woolley (physician), 1905 (sep. 1924); children: Eleanor Faxon Woolley; Charlotte Gerhardt Woolley. ❖ One of the 1st to study child development, was

an instructor at Mount Holyoke College (1901), then director of the psychological lab and professor of psychology (1902); married and lived in the Philippines (1905–06) and Thailand (1906); taught at University of Cincinnati; developed the Cincinnati Vocation Bureau (1914), as a part of the public school system, and conducted studies of the impaired physical and mental development of working children compared to non-working children, resulting in *An Experimental Study of Children at Work and in School between the Ages of Fourteen and Eighteen Years* (1926); elected president of National Vocational Guidance Association (1921); appointed staff psychologist (1921), then named associate director at Merrill-Palmer School in Detroit (1922), where she organized one of the 1st nursery schools in the nation and researched children's personality and mental development patterns; taught at University of Michigan; became professor of education and director of the Institute of Child Welfare Research at Columbia University Teachers College (1925). ❖ See also *Women in World History*.

WOOLLEY, Mary E. (1863–1947). American educator, college president, and activist. Born Mary Emma Woolley, July 13, 1863, in South Norwalk, Connecticut; died Sept 5, 1947, in Westport, New York; dau. of Joseph Judah Woolley (Congregational cleric) and Mary Augusta (Ferris) Woolley (schoolteacher); graduate of Wheaton Seminary (now College), 1884; Brown University, AB, 1894, MA in history, 1895, PhD, 1900. ❖ Accepted a position as instructor of Biblical history and literature at Wellesley College (1895), becoming full professor (1899); a popular teacher, introduced new elective courses in church history and headed her department; served as president of Mount Holyoke College for over 3 decades (1901–37) and was crucial in its development as one of the most respected of American women's colleges; was also made chair of Federal Council of Churches (1936), served as honorary moderator for the General Council of the Congregational-Christian Churches, and was vice-president of American Peace Society (1907–13); appointed by President Herbert Hoover to represent the US at the Geneva Conference on Reduction and Limitation of Armaments (1932), the 1st woman to represent the nation at a major diplomatic event; co-founded College Women's Equal Suffrage League (1908); was president of American Association of University Women (AAUW, 1927–33); wrote *Internationalism and Disarmament* (1935). ❖ See also *Women in World History*.

WOOLLIAMS, Anne (1926–1999). English ballet dancer and teacher. Born Aug 3, 1926, in Folkestone, Kent, England; died July 8, 1999, in Canterbury, Kent, England; trained with Judith Espinosa and Vera Volkova; m. Jan Stripling. ❖ In England, danced with Lydia Kyasht troupe, London Ballet, and Russian Opera Ballet (late 1940s); taught for Vera Volkova in Florence and Chicago; served on faculty of Essen Folkwangschule (1958–63); with John Cranko, founded and taught at the Stuttgart Ballet school (1963–75); danced as Lady Capulet in *Romeo and Juliet* and Queen Mother in *Swan Lake*, and became Cranko's assistant artistic director (1969); after Cranko's death (1973), became artistic director at the Stuttgart, and staged his works throughout Europe; was artistic director of Australian ballet (1976–77); was dean of dance at Victorian College of the Arts, Melbourne (1977–87); appointed artistic director of Vienna State Opera Ballet (1993).

WOOLMAN, Mary Schenck (1860–1940). American home economist and vocational educator. Born Mary Raphael Schenck, April 26, 1860, in Camden, NJ; died Aug 1, 1940, in Newton, MA; dau. of John Vorhees Schenck (physician) and Martha (McKeen) Schenck; m. Franklin Conrad Woolman (lawyer), Oct 18, 1883. ❖ Hired as assistant in domestic science at Columbia University Teachers College (1892), then promoted to instructor of sewing (1893), adjunct professor of household arts education (1898), and professor (1903); organized and directed Manhattan Trade School for Girls (1902–10); became acting head of home economics department of Simmons College and president of Women's Educational and Industrial Union in Boston (1912); lectured for Retail Trade Board of Boston Chamber of Commerce (1915–17); improved, broadened and publicized vocational education.

WOOLNOUGH, Kate Emma (1847–1926). *See Clark, Kate Emma.*

WOOLSEY, Abby Howland (1828–1893). American relief worker. Born July 16, 1828, in Alexandria, VA; died April 7, 1893, in New York, NY; dau. of Charles William Woolsey (sugar refiner) and Jane Eliza (Newton) Woolsey; sister of relief workers, Jane Stuart Woolsey (1830–1891) and Georgeanna Muirson Woolsey (1833–1906); cousin of Sarah Chauncey Woolsey (1835–1905, writer). ❖ Was influential in creation of Bellevue Hospital Training School for Nurses (1873); wrote many reports for

State Charities Aid Association, including *A Century of Nursing* (1876) and *Lunacy Legislation in England* (1884); worked as acting clerk and served as temporary executive officer for sister Jane during absences at Presbyterian Hospital in NY (1872–76).

WOOLSEY, Georgeanna Muirson (1833–1906). American relief worker. Name variations: Georgeanna Bacon. Born George Anna Muirson Woolsey Nov 5, 1833, in Brooklyn, NY; died Jan 27, 1906, in New Haven, CT; dau. of Charles William Woolsey (sugar refiner) and Jane Eliza (Newton) Woolsey; sister of relief workers, Abby Howland Woolsey (1828–1893) and Jane Stuart Woolsey (1830–1891); cousin of Sarah Chauncey Woolsey (1835–1905, writer); m. Francis Bacon (professor of surgery at Yale Medical School), June 7, 1866. ❖ Worked as nurse at large for hospital transport service of US Sanitary Commission (1862); tended to wounded and set up relief stations at various hospitals and battlefields during Civil War, including Belle Plain, Fredericksburg, and Gettysburg (1862–64); wrote *Three Weeks at Gettysburg*, for Sanitary Commission (1863); with husband, established Connecticut Training School for Nurses at New Haven Hospital (1873); published *Hand Book of Nursing for Family and General Use* (1879); co-founded Connecticut Children's Aid Society (1892); with sister Eliza, wrote 2-vol. *Letters of a Family during the War for the Union* (1899).

WOOLSEY, Jane Stuart (1830–1891). American relief worker. Born Feb 7, 1830, on ship *Fanny*, en route from Norwich, CT, to New York, NY; died July 9, 1891, in Matteawan, NY; dau. of Charles William Woolsey (sugar refiner) and Jane Eliza (Newton) Woolsey; sister of relief workers, Abby Howland Woolsey (1828–1893) and Georgeanna Muirson Woolsey (1833–1906); cousin of Sarah Chauncey Woolsey (1835–1905, writer). ❖ Took charge of nursing and dietary departments of Fairfax Theological Seminary Hospital in Alexandria, VA (1863–65); wrote about wartime activities in privately published *Hospital Days* (1868); taught at and was director of girls' industries (1869–72) of Hampton Normal and Agricultural Institute in VA; served as resident mistress at Presbyterian Hospital in New York (1872–76).

WOOLSEY, Lynn C. (1937—). American politician. Born Nov 3, 1937, in Seattle, Washington; attended University of Washington, 1955–57; University of San Francisco, BS, 1980; married and divorced; children: 3. ❖ Taught at Marin Community College, then Dominican College; representing California, elected as a Democrat to 103rd Congress of US House of Representatives (1992), the 1st former welfare mother in Congress; became chair of the Democratic Caucus Task Force on Children and Families, and ranking member of the House Education committee's subcommittee on Education Reform; also a senior member on House Science committee's subcommittee on Energy; won 7th term (2004).

WOOLSEY, Sarah Chauncey (1835–1905). American author and poet. Name variations: Sarah Chauncy Woolsey; (pseudonym) Susan Coolidge. Born Jan 29, 1835, in Cleveland, Ohio; died April 9, 1905, in Newport, Rhode Island; dau. of John Mumford Woolsey (land agent and businessman) and Jane (Andrews) Woolsey; niece of Theodore Dwight Woolsey (1801–1889), president of Yale University; cousin of Abby Howland Woolsey (1828–1893), Jane Stuart Woolsey (1830–1891), and Georgeanna Muirson Woolsey (1833–1906), all Civil War relief and hospital workers; never married. ❖ With sisters, attended a private school for girls in New Hampshire, the setting of which later inspired her successful children's stories; during Civil War, worked in different hospitals for the wounded; met and began a lifelong friendship with Helen Hunt Jackson; took up residence in Newport, RI; under pseudonym of Susan Coolidge, published a collection of her children's stories, *The New-Year's Bargain* (1872); published *What Katy Did* (1873), the 1st of the "Katy Did" series, her most popular children's books; also wrote poetry for adults, edited scholarly works, and continued to contribute stories, verse and travel articles to such prominent magazines as *Outlook, Woman's Home Companion* and *Scribner's*. ❖ See also *Women in World History*.

WOOLSON, Abba Gool (1838–1921). American teacher, author, and advocate of dress reform. Born Abba Louisa Goold, April 30, 1838, in Windham, Maine; died Feb 6, 1921, in Portland, Maine; dau. of William Goold (politician) and Nabby Tukey (Clark) Goold; m. Moses Woolson (school principal), 1856; no children. ❖ Began teaching at Portland High School (c. 1857); taught literature at Mount Auburn Young Ladies' Institute in Cincinnati, Ohio (1862–65); wrote essays for the *Home Journal, Portland Transcript* and *Boston Journal*; published 1st collection of essays, *Woman in American Society* (1873), to favorable reviews;

chaired the dress-reform committee of New England Women's Club (1873) and published *Dress-Reform* (1874); also wrote *Browsing Among Books* (1881) and *George Eliot and Her Heroines* (1886).

WOOLSON, Constance Fenimore (1840–1894). American writer. Name variations: (pseudonym) Anne March. Born Mar 5, 1840, in Claremont, New Hampshire; died Jan 24, 1894, in Venice, Italy; dau. of Charles Jarvis Woolson (stove manufacturer) and Hannah Cooper (Pomeroy) Woolson; grandniece of James Fenimore Cooper; graduate of Cleveland Female Seminary, 1858; never married; no children. ❖ Began publishing (1870), and for next few years contributed travel and descriptive sketches to such magazines as *Harper's* and *Putnam's*; also wrote local color stories situated in the Great Lakes region, the Ohio Valley, and Cooperstown, NY; published *Anne: A Novel* (1882), which proved to be one of her biggest successes; becoming ever more familiar with the South during her travels, wrote a series of short works that were collected as *Rodman the Keeper: Southern Sketches* (1886); after mother died (1879), traveled to Europe, where she remained the rest of her life; developed a notable friendship with author Henry James and adopted his introspective, psychological style in her later works of fiction, particularly in *For the Major* (1883), which is considered one of her best; also wrote (as Anne March) *The Old Stone House* (1872), *Castle Nowhere: Lake-Country Sketches* (1875), *Two Women, 1862: A Poem* (1877), *East Angels* (1886), *Jupiter Lights: A Novel* (1889), *Horace Chase: A Novel* (1894), *The Front Yard, and Other Italian Stories* (1895), *Dorothy, and Other Italian Stories* (1896) and *Mentone, Cairo, and Corfu* (1896). ❖ See also *Women in World History*.

WOOTTEN, Bayard (1875–1959). American landscape photographer. Born Mary Bayard Morgan, 1875, in New Bern, North Carolina; died 1959 in New Bern; educated at North Carolina State Normal and Industrial School (later University of North Carolina at Greensboro); m. Charles Thomas Wootten, 1897 (sep. 1901); children: 2 sons. ❖ Began photography career (c. 1904), opening a studio in New Bern and joining the Women's Federation of the Photographers' Association of America (1909 or 1910); became the 1st woman to take aerial photographs in North Carolina (1914); photographed the landscapes of the southeastern US, and also produced a series portraying Appalachian life. ❖ See also *Women in World History*.

WOOTTON, Barbara (1897–1988). English educator and activist. Name variations: Baroness Wootton of Abinger. Born Barbara Frances Adam, April 14, 1897, in Cambridge, England; died in Surrey, July 11, 1988; dau. of James Adam (university teacher) and Adela Marion (Kensington) Adam; attended Girton College, Cambridge, 1915–19; m. John Wesley Wootton (army officer), Sept 7, 1917 (died of wounds during WWI, Oct 11, 1917); m. George Percival Wright, 1935 (died 1964); no children. ❖ Educationalist, social scientist and public servant who advocated liberal and progressive causes; following husband's death during WWI, moved from classics to social inquiry, from Christian faith to agnosticism, and from conservatism to socialism, but always retained the intellectual discipline and sense of purpose with which she was brought up; was on a research scholarship at London School of Economics (1919–20); served as director of studies in economics, Girton College (1920–22); was a researcher for Trades Union Congress and Labour Party Joint Research Department (1922–26); served as principal of Morley College for Working Men and Women (1926–27), then director of studies for tutorial classes, University of London (1927–44); was a reader in social studies, University of London (1944–52), professor from 1948; was Nuffield research fellow, Bedford College, University of London (1952–57); raised to the peerage with title of Baroness Wootton of Abinger (1958), became a member of House of Lords and was eventually made a deputy-speaker, the 1st woman to occupy that post; was made a Companion of Honor (1977); was regularly invited to speak at conferences throughout the world; writings include *London's Burning* (1938), *Lament for Economics* (1938), *The Social Foundations of Wage Policy: A Study of Comparative British Wage and Salary Structure* (1955), *Crime and Criminal Law* (1963) and *Crime and Penal Policy: Reflections on Fifty Years' Experience* (1978). ❖ See also *In a World I Never Made: Autobiographical Reflections* (Allen & Unwin, 1967); Bean and Whynes, eds. *Barbara Wootton, Social Science and Public Policy: Essays in her Honour* (Tavistock, 1986); and *Women in World History*.

WORDSWORTH, Dorothy (1771–1855). English diarist. Born Dec 25, 1771, in Cockermouth, England; died Jan 25, 1855, at Rydal Mount after 20 years of mental and physical illness; dau. of John Wordsworth and Anne (Cookson) Wordsworth; sister of William Wordsworth (the poet, died 1850); never married; no children. ❖ Natural historian who was friends with other influential British Romantics, including Samuel Taylor Coleridge; served as caretaker and companion of brother, even after his marriage to Mary Hutchinson (1802); kept diary in large part as an aid to brother's memory, while he in turn delved into them, borrowing events, descriptions, and even close turns of phrase in such poems as "I Wandered Lonely as a Cloud," "Beggars" and "Resolution and Independence"; published nothing during her lifetime, with the exception of a few poems included by brother in *Poems by William Wordsworth* (1815); grew seriously ill (1829); for rest of life, her physical health deteriorated, confining her to a wheelchair, and her mental capacity diminished, perhaps from arteriosclerosis; entered a private world from which she was less and less able to emerge; died (1855), 5 years after William. Her work is in various collections and editions of her journals, correspondence, poetry and short fiction; these include *Recollections of a Tour Made in Scotland, A.D. 1803* (1874); *Journals of Dorothy Wordsworth* (1941); *George & Sarah Green: A Narrative by Dorothy Wordsworth* (1936); *The Letters of William and Dorothy Wordsworth* (1967–82, 6 vols.). ❖ See also Ernest de Selincourt, *Dorothy Wordsworth: A Biography* (Clarendon, 1933); Gittings and Manton, *Dorothy Wordsworth* (Clarendon, 1985); Susan M. Levin, *Dorothy Wordsworth and Romanticism* (Rutgers U. Press, 1987); Catherine Macdonald Maclean, *Dorothy Wordsworth: The Early Years* (1932); Ernest de Selincourt, ed. *Journals of Dorothy Wordsworth* (2 vols., 1941); Amanda M. Ellis, *Rebels and Conservatives: Dorothy and William Wordsworth and Their Circle* (Indiana U. Press, 1967); Kathleen Jones, *A Passionate Sisterhood: Women of the Wordsworth Circle* (St. Martin, 2000); Mary Moorman, ed. *Journals of Dorothy Wordsworth* (Oxford U. Press, 1971); Pamela Woof, ed. *The Grasmere Journal* (Joseph, 1989); and *Women in World History*.

WORDSWORTH, Elizabeth (1840–1932). British educator. Name variations: (pseudonym) Grant Lloyd. Born June 22, 1840, at Harrow-on-the-Hill, England; died Nov 30, 1932, in Oxford; dau. of Christopher Wordsworth (bishop of Lincoln) and Susanna (Hatley) Wordsworth; sister of John Wordsworth (bishop of Salisbury); great-niece of poet William Wordsworth and diarist Dorothy Wordsworth (1771–1855). ❖ Leader in women's education at Oxford University, became 1st principal of Lady Margaret Hall at Oxford University (1878), serving there for 30 years; opened St. Hugh's Hall (later St. Hugh's College) at Oxford (1886); encouraged the opening of Lady Margaret Hall Settlement in Lambeth (1897); published 2 novels under pseudonym Grant Lloyd; also published *Glimpses of the Past* (1912), *Essays Old and New* (1919), *Poems and Plays* (1931) and a biography of her father (1888). Made a Dame of the British Empire (1928).

WORHEL, Esther (1975—). Dutch rower. Born Mar 18, 1975, in the Netherlands. ❖ Won a bronze medal for coxed eights at Athens Olympics (2004).

WÖRISHÖFFER, Sophie (1838–1890). German novelist. Name variations: Sophie von Worishoffer, Woerishoffer or Woerishoeffer. Born 1838 in Germany; died 1890. ❖ Wrote adventure stories for young people which include *Robert des Schiffsjungen Fahrten und Abenteuer auf der deutschen Handels-und kriegsflotte* (1877), *Gerettet aus Sibirien* (1885), and *Unter Korsaren* (1889).

WORKMAN, Fanny (1859–1925). American explorer and mountaineer. Born Jan 8, 1859, in Worcester, Massachusetts; died in Cannes, France, Jan 22, 1925; dau. of Alexander Hamilton Bullock (Massachusetts governor, 1866–1868) and Elvira (Hazard) Bullock; m. William Hunter Workman (physician), 1881; children: Rachel Workman (1884–1954), later known as Lady Rachel MacRobert (geologist). ❖ Traveled extensively throughout world for nearly 3 decades, exploring mountainous areas, traveling by bicycle (over 17,000 miles), and publishing accounts of travels and exploration which she co-authored with husband, including *Algerian Memories* (1895), *Sketches Awheel in Modern Iberia* (1897), *Through Town and Jungle: 14,000 Miles Awheel among the Temples and People of the Indian Plain* (1904), *In the Ice World of the Himalaya* (1900), *Ice-bound Heights of Mustagh* (1908), *Peaks and Glaciers of Nun Kun* (1909), *The Call of the Snowy Hispar* (1910) and *Two Summers in the Ice Wilds of Eastern Karakorum* (1917); mapped, photographed and recorded scientific data in the Karakorum range in the Himalayas; set an altitude record for women by climbing Mt. Koser Gunga to 21,000 feet (1903); broke her own record by ascending to 23,300 feet on Pinnacle Peak (1906); was a fellow of Royal Geographical Society. ❖ See also *Women in World History*.

WORKMAN, Rachel (1884–1954). *See MacRobert, Rachel.*

WORMELEY, Katharine Prescott (1830–1908). English-born American translator, author and philanthropist. Born Jan 14, 1830, in Ipswich, Suffolk, England; died Aug 4, 1908, in Jackson, New Hampshire; dau. of Ralph Randolph Wormeley (rear admiral, died 1852) and Caroline (Preble) Wormeley (both American born). ❖ Settled in US with family (1852); at onset of Civil War, was one of the 1st to initiate and participate in relief work in Newport, Rhode Island, where family was then living; became a member of the hospital transport service of US Sanitary Commission, caring for the sick and wounded on hospital ships; published letters she had written during this period as *The Other Side of the War* (1889); was lady superintendent of Lowell General Hospital, at Portsmouth Grove, Rhode Island (1862); founded Newport Charity Organization Society (1879) and an industrial school for girls (1887); best known for her translations of the works of noted French writers, particularly Honoré de Balzac's *La Comédie Humaine* (40 vols., 1885–96); also translated Paul Bourget's *Pastels Man* (1891, 1892), various works by Alexander Dumas (1894–1902), plays by Molière (1894–97), *The Works of Alphonse Daudet* (1898–1900), *Memoirs of the Duc de Saint-Simon* (1899), *Letters of Mlle. de Lespinasse* (1901), *Diary and Correspondence of Count Axel Fersen* (1902) and Sainte-Beuve's *Portraits of the Eighteenth Century* (1905); wrote *A Memoir of Honoré de Balzac* (1892). ❖ See also *Women in World History*.

WORMINGTON, H. Marie (1914–1994). American archaeologist. Name variations: Hannah Marie Wormington; Marie Wormington. Born Hannah Marie Wormington, Sept 5, 1914, in Denver, CO; died 1994; dau. of Charles Watkin Wormington and Adrienne Roucolle; University of Denver, BA in anthropology, 1935; Radcliffe College at Harvard University, MA, 1950, PhD, 1954, the 1st Harvard woman PhD to specialize in archaeology; m. George D. Volk (geologist and engineer), 1940. ❖ Worked with Colorado Museum of Natural History (now Denver Museum of Natural History) for 33 years (1935–68), becoming curator of archaeology (1937); performed archaeological excavations in CO and at Fremont village site in UT; taught at University of Denver and University of Colorado at Boulder; published important work of Paleo-Indian studies in New World, *Ancient Man in North America* (1939); was 1st woman elected president of Society for American Archaeology (1967). Other works include *Prehistoric Indians of the Southwest* (1947).

WORMS, Pamela Lee (d. 1852). American murderer. Hanged in Pittsburgh, PA, Jan 30, 1852. ❖ Found guilty of murdering husband Moses with poison, was hanged before a sizable crowd.

WORNS, Eila (1862–1934). *See Almeida, Julia Lopes de.*

WORONTSOVA, Ekaterina (1744–1810). *See Dashkova, Ekaterina.*

WORSLEY, Katherine (1933—). Duchess of Kent. Name variations: Katherine Windsor. Born Katherine Lucy Mary Worsley on Feb 22, 1933, in Hovingham Hall, York, Yorkshire, England; dau. of William Worsley and Joyce Brunner; m. Edward Windsor (b. 1935), 2nd duke of Kent, on June 8, 1961; children: George, Lord St. Andrews (b. 1962); Lady Helen Windsor (b. 1964, who m. Timothy Taylor); Nicholas (b. 1970). ❖ Has been a fixture at Wimbledon for many years, since husband is president of The All England Lawn Tennis Club.

WORTH, Irene (1916–2002). American actress and director. Pronunciation: eye-REENY. Born Harriet Elizabeth Abrams, June 23, 1916, in Lincoln, Nebraska; died Mar 10, 2002, in New York, NY; University of California at Los Angeles, BEdn, 1937; studied for stage in London under Elsie Fogarty, 1944–45. ❖ Made stage debut while touring with Elizabeth Bergner in *Escape Me Never* (1942); made Broadway debut in *The Two Mrs. Carrolls* (1942) and UK debut as Elsie in *The Time of Your Life* in Hammersmith (1946); remaining in England, played a variety of parts, including that of Cella Copplestone in Eliot's *The Cocktail Party*; performed with Old Vic (1951–53), as Desdemona in *Othello*, Helena in *A Midsummer Night's Dream*, Catherine de Vausselles in *The Other Heart* and Portia in *The Merchant of Venice*; co-founded the Stratford Festival in Ontario, Canada (1953); joined Royal Shakespeare Company to play the Marquise de Merteuil in *The Art of Seduction* (*Les liaisons dangereuses*, 1962); originated title role in Albee's *Tiny Alice* (1964), for which she received a Tony Award; received *Evening Standard* Award for Best Actress for *Suite in Three Keys* (1965); at Stratford, was critically acclaimed for performance as *Hedda Gabler* (1970); triumphed as Mrs. Alving in Greenwich Theater's *Ghosts* (1974); won British Film Academy Award for performance as Leonie in *Orders to Kill* (1958); also had a distinguished career as a tv actress, receiving awards for "The Lady from the Lake" and "The Lady from the Sea" (1954). Received Order of the British Empire, and Obie Award for Sustained Achievement in the Theater (1989). ❖ See also *Women in World History.*

WORTHINGTON, Kay (1959—). Canadian rower. Born Dec 21, 1959; graduate of University of Toronto, 1983, then attended University of Pennsylvania. ❖ At Barcelona Olympics, won a gold medal in coxed eights and a gold medal in coxed fours (1992); also competed in 1984 and 1988 Olympics; was a rowing analyst for CBC.

WORTLEY, Emmeline Stuart- (1806–1855). *See Stuart-Wortley, Emmeline.*

WORTLEY-MONTAGU, Lady Mary (1689–1762). *See Montagu, Lady Mary Wortley.*

WOTTON, Margaret (fl. 16th c.). Marquise of Dorset. Dau. of Robert Wotton; m. Thomas Grey (1477–1530), 2nd marquess of Dorset; children: Henry Grey, duke of Suffolk; Katherine Fitzalan (b. around 1520, who m. Henry Fitzalan, 16th earl of Arundel); Elizabeth Grey (who m. Thomas Audley). ❖ Thomas Grey was 1st married to Eleanor St. John.

WÖTZEL, Mandy (1973—). *See Woetzel, Mandy.*

WOXHOLT, Grete (1916–2000). *See Gynt, Greta.*

WRACK, Aileen Anna Maria (c. 1861–1951). *See Garmson, Aileen Anna Maria.*

WRANGEL, Baroness (1850–1912). *See von Essen, Siri.*

WRANGEL, Siri von Essen (1850–1912). *See von Essen, Siri.*

WRATHER, Bonita Granville (1923–1988). *See Granville, Bonita.*

WRAY, Fay (1907–2004). American actress. Born Vina Fay Wray, Sept 15, 1907, near Cardston, in Alberta, Canada; died Aug 8, 2004, in New York, NY; dau. of Joseph Wray; m. John Monk Saunders (playwright and screenwriter), 1928 (div. 1939); m. Robert Riskin (screenwriter), 1942 (died 1953); children: (1st m.) Susan; (2nd m.) Robert and Victoria. ❖ Canadian-born American actress, best known for her performance as the giant ape's love interest in *King Kong,* moved with family to Arizona, then Los Angeles as a young child; at 13, made film debut in the comedy *Blind Husbands* (1919); came to prominence starring in Erich von Stroheim's *The Wedding March* (1926), followed by *The Four Feathers* (1929), *Paramount on Parade* (1930), *The Texan* (1930), *The Conquering Horde* (1931), *The Most Dangerous Game* (1932), *Doctor X* (1932) and *The Bowery* (1933), among others; secured cinematic immortality with *King Kong* (1933); was in retirement (1942–53); appeared on tv in such shows as "Alfred Hitchcock Presents" and "Perry Mason" and tv movie "Gideon's Trumpet"; other films include *The Countess of Monte Cristo* (1934), *Viva Villa* (1934), *Alias Bull Dog Drummond* (1935), *When Knights Were Bold* (1936), *It Happened in Hollywood* (1937), *Murder in Greenwich Village* (1937), *Adam Had Four Sons* (1941), *The Cobweb* (1955), *Queen Bee* (1955), *Hell on Frisco Bay* (1956), *Crime of Passion* (1957) and *Tammy and the Bachelor* (1957). ❖ See also autobiography *On the Other Hand: A Life Story* (1989); and *Women in World History.*

WREDE, Mathilda (1864–1928). Finnish prison reformer. Born Mar 8, 1864, in Vaasa, Finland; died Dec 25, 1928, in Finland; dau. of Baron Carl Gustav Wrede (governor of Finland's Vaasa district) and Baroness Eleonora Glansenstjerna (died 1875). ❖ Prison reformer, peace activist and national heroine, had a long career dedicated to improving Finnish prisons and reforming criminals through religious instruction; worked closely with individual prisoners, earning their respect by respecting them; traveled across Finland, meeting alone with thousands of incarcerated men; during WWI, turned her efforts to helping Finnish soldiers, volunteering as a relief worker for their families; refused to take sides in Finnish War of Liberation (1917), instead aiding the soldiers of both sides of the conflict. ❖ See also *Women in World History.*

WREN, Jenny (c. 1852–1942). *See Harris, Jane Elizabeth.*

WRIGHT, Belinda (1927—). English ballet dancer. Born Brenda Wright, Jan 18, 1927, in Southport, England. ❖ Began performance career in pantomimes in Southport area in England; moved to Paris to train under Olga Preobrazhenska and Rosanne Crotton; danced with range of English companies throughout career, including Ballet Rambert (1945–49) and London Festival Ballet (1951–54, 1955–57, 1959–62); also danced with Roland Petit's Ballet de Paris (1949–51) and Grand Ballet

du Marquis de Cuevas (1954–55); featured in premieres of Petit's *Les Forains* (1945) and Ashton's *Vision of Marguerite* (1952).

WRIGHT, Betty (1953—). African-American singer and songwriter. Born Dec 21, 1953, in Miami, FL. ❖ When young, began singing with family gospel group, Echoes of Joy; at 14, recorded "Girls Can't Do What the Guys Do," which went to #15 on R&B charts; at 15, had #2 R&B hit with "Clean Up Woman," which went gold (1971); albums include *I Love the Way You Love* (1972), *Mother Wit* (1988), and *B-Attitudes* (1994); other hits include "Baby Sitter" (1972), "Let Me Be Your Lovemaker" (1973), and Grammy-winning "Where Is the Love" (1975); co-wrote lyrics to many of her hits; performed with numerous musicians, including Stevie Wonder, Richard "Dimples" Fields, and Peter Brown.

WRIGHT, Camille (1955—). American swimmer. Born Mar 5, 1955. ❖ At Montreal Olympics, won a silver medal in 4 x 100-meter medley relay (1976).

WRIGHT, Cobina (1887–1970). American columnist and singer. Name variations: Cobina Wright Sr. Born Sept 20, 1887, in Bakeview, OR; died April 9, 1970, in Hollywood, CA; children: Cobina Wright Jr. (actress). ❖ Singer and Hollywood columnist, appeared in 3 films, including *The Razor's Edge* (1946).

WRIGHT, Cobina Jr. (1921—). American actress. Name variations: Cobina Wright. Born Aug 14, 1921, in New York, NY; m. Palmer Thayer Beaudette, Nov 3, 1941 (died Sept 7, 1968). ❖ Began career as a model; when Bob Hope used a character named Cobina on his radio program (1939), sued, settled out of court, joined his program, and launched a radio career; films include *Moon Over Miami, Week-End in Havana, Footlight Serenade* and *Something to Shout About.*

WRIGHT, Dana (1959—). Canadian runner. Born Sept 20, 1959; graduate of Old Dominion University, 1983. ❖ At Los Angeles Olympics, won a silver medal in 4 x 400-meter relay (1984).

WRIGHT, Elsa Gress (1919–1989). *See Gress, Elsa.*

WRIGHT, Frances (1795–1852). Scottish-born American social activist. Name variations: Fanny Wright; Frances Wright d'Arusmont; Frances Darusmont. Born Frances Wright, Sept 6, 1795, in Dundee, Scotland; died in Cincinnati, Ohio, Dec 13, 1852; dau. of James Wright (linen merchant) and Camilla (Campbell) Wright; m. William Phiquepal d'Arusmont, July 22, 1831 (div.); children: Frances Sylva d'Arusmont (b. 1832). ❖ Freethinker, writer, and public speaker who advocated radical social reform, abolition of slavery, and women's rights in US, based on her criticism of the superstitions and immorality of Christianity; orphaned at 2, grew up in London and Dawlish, England; age 18, moved to Dundee, Scotland (1813); settled in US (1824); established and lived with emancipation community at Nashoba, Tennessee (1825–29); moved to New Harmony, Indiana (1828); assuming editorship of New Harmony paper, changed its name to *Free Enquirer* and moved with it to New York City (1828–29); purchased Hall of Science for weekly lectures and meetings on freethought subjects (1829); the 1st woman in America to ascend to fame as a public speaker and social reformer, was a frequent lecturer and writer (1828–52); as the most well-known leader of the freethought movement, bore the double stigma of being a religious skeptic and an educated, independent woman; by 1830, her notoriety had reached such a level that the New York City press labeled her "The Red Harlot of Infidelity"; writings include *Altorf: A Tragedy* (1819), *Views of Society and Manners in America* (1821), *A Few Days in Athens* (1822), and *Biography, Notes, and Political Letters* (1844), and *England the Civilizer* (1848). ❖ See also *Life, Letters, and Lectures, 1834–1844* (Arno, 1972); Celia Morris Eckhardt, *Fanny Wright: Rebel in America* (Harvard U. Press, 1984); Alice Perkins and Theresa Wolfson, *Frances Wright, Free Enquirer: The Study of a Temperament* (Harper, 1939); and *Women in World History.*

WRIGHT, Francesca (1897–1985). *See Robins, Denise Naomi.*

WRIGHT, Haidée (1868–1943). English actress. Name variations: Haidee Wright. Born in London, England, Jan 13, 1868; died Jan 29, 1943; dau. of Fred Wright (actor-manager) and Jesse (Frances) Wright (actress); sister of Fred, Huntley, Bertie, and Marie Wright (all actors). ❖ Trained for the stage in father's touring company; debuted as Diamond Wetherwick in *The Hoop of Gold* (1878); made London debut as Esther Forester in *False Lights* (1887) and West End debut as Stephanus in *The Sign of the Cross* (1896), opposite Wilson Barrett; portrayed Miss Kite in *The Passing of the Third Floor Back* at the

St. James (1908) and toured US in the same role (1909–11); played Anna in Gorky's *The Lower Depths* at Kingsway Theater (1911); was Miss Scrotton in *Tante* in NY (1913); back in London, appeared as Mrs. Hilperty in *The Melody of Youth* (1917), Mother Marguerite in *Cyrano de Bergerac* (1919), Madame de Musset in *Madame Sand* (1920), Queen Elizabeth I in *Will Shakespeare* (1921), Mrs. David Garrick (Eva-Maria Veigel) in *Ned Kean of Old Drury* (1923), and Queen Elizabeth in *Dark Lady of the Sonnets* (1923); appeared in New York as Fanny Cavendish in *Royal Family* (1927) and in London as Letizia Bonaparte in *Napoleon* (1932); made last stage appearance as Martha Blackett in *Gentle Rain* (1936); films include *The Blarney Stone, Jew Süss*, and *Tomorrow We Live*.

WRIGHT, Helen (1914–1997). American astronomer and author. Name variations: Helen Wright Greuter. Born Helen Wright in Washington, DC, Dec 20, 1914; died in Washington, DC, Oct 23, 1997; dau. of Frederick Eugene Wright (well-known petrologist and consultant for National Parks) and Kathleen Ethel (Finley) Wright (who graduated from McGill University with governor-general's medal for highest honors in history and languages); graduate of Bennett Junior College, 1934; Vassar College, BA, 1937, MA, 1939; m. John Franklin Hawkins (artist), 1946 (div.); m. Rene Greuter (died early 1970s); no children. ❖ Pioneering American astronomer, founded and directed the great California observatories: Mount Wilson in Pasadena and Mount Palomar; also founded *The Astrophysical Journal*, one of the preeminent journals of astronomy and physics, before turning to freelance writing and editing (1940s); during WWII, was a junior astronomer at US Naval Observatory; best known for her books *Sweeper of the Sky: The Life of Maria Mitchell* (1949) and *Explorer of the Universe: A Biography of George Ellery Hale* (1966); also chronicled the creation of Palomar, then the world's largest telescope (1952).

WRIGHT, Helena (1887–1982). English medical practitioner and author. Name variations: Helena Rosa Lowenfeld. Born Helena Rosa Lowenfeld, Sept 17, 1887, in Brixton, London, England; died Mar 21, 1982; dau. of Heinz Lowenfeld; educated at Cheltenham Ladies' College and London School of Medicine for Women; m. Henry Wardel Snarey Wright (surgeon). ❖ Early advocate of family planning in England, China and India, became a member of Royal College of Surgeons, England, and a Licentiate of Royal College of Surgeons, London (1914); with husband, worked as medical missionary at Shantung Christian University in Tsinan, China (1919–27); was also an associate gynecologist at the university; returning to England, became involved in the movement for birth control; worked as a medical officer of a woman's health-care clinic and as a gynecologist in private practice; helped set up the International Committee on Planned Parenthood (later known as the International Planned Parenthood Federation); published 7 books, including *The Sex Factor in Marriage* (1930) and *Sex and Society* (1968); advocated improvement and reform of women's health care. ❖ See also *Women in World History*.

WRIGHT, Jane Cooke (1919—). African-American cancer researcher. Born Jane Cooke Wright, Nov 30, 1919, in New York, NY; dau. of Louis Tompkins Wright (surgeon) and Corinne Cooke Wright; graduate of Smith College, 1942; New York Medical College, MD with honors, 1945; m. David D. Jones (lawyer), 1947; children: 2. ❖ Raised in family of researchers and doctors, including father, the 1st African-American doctor to work at a New York City hospital and founder of Harlem Hospital's Cancer Research Foundation; after father died, assumed his position as head of Harlem Hospital's Cancer Research Foundation (1952); joined faculty (1955) and later became associate professor of research surgery at New York University; worked as professor of surgery, associate dean, and director of new cancer research laboratory at New York Medical College; collaborated with Jewel Plummer Cobb on the effects of chemotherapy on cancer cells; was the 1st woman elected president of the New York Cancer Society (1972); received Albert Einstein School of Medicine's Spirit of Achievement Award, and American Association for Cancer Research award (1975); retired (1987).

WRIGHT, Jay (1935—). See Wright, Mickey.

WRIGHT, Judith (1915–2000). Australian writer and activist. Born Judith Arundell Wright, May 31, 1915, in Armidale, New South Wales (NSW), Australia; died June 26 (some sources cite June 25), 2000, in Canberra; dau. of Phillip Arundell Wright (pastoralist and businessman) and Ethel (Bigg) Wright (died 1919); educated at University of Sydney, 1934–36, as a non-matriculating student in English honors; m. Jack McKinney (philosopher), 1944 (died 1966 or 1967); children: Meredith McKinney (b. 1950). ❖ Conservationist and campaigner for Aboriginal rights, who is considered the doyenne of Australia's women poets; helped C. B. Christensen with his magazine *Meanjin*; published 1st volume of poetry, *The Moving Image* (1946), which included "South of My Day's Circle," one of her best-known poems; moved to Tambourine Mountain in Queensland (1948); wrote 2nd book, *Woman to Man* (1949); edited a book of Australian verse and gave Commonwealth Literary Fund Lectures at University of Queensland (1956); published the 3-part *The Generations of Men*, a history of her family in New South Wales (1959); co-founded the Wildlife Preservation Society of Queensland (WPSQ, 1962) and held the post of president (1962–76); appointed a fellow of the Australian Academy of Humanities (1970); appointed a member of the Commonwealth Government Committee of Enquiry into the National Estate (1973); awarded a Creative Arts fellowship from the Australian National University and appointed to the University Council (1974); awarded an ANZAC fellowship to visit New Zealand (1976); wrote *The Coral Battleground* (1977), concerning the Great Barrier Reef; became an honorary life member of the Australian Conservation Foundation (1981); lived in Braidwood, NSW; over the years, her work addressed the issues of the day, including subjects like the Vietnam War, as well as ecological causes and the fight for Aboriginal rights; was twice nominated for a Nobel Prize; writings include *The Gateway* (1953), *The Two Fires* (1955), *Australian Bird Poems* (1961), *Birds* (1962), *Judith Wright* (1963), *Five Senses* (1963), *City Sunrise* (1964), *The Nature of Love* (short stories, 1966), *The Other Half* (1966), *Collected Poems, 1942–1970* (1971), *Alive* (1973), *Because I Was Invited* (1975), *Fourth Quarter and Other Poems* (1976), *The Coral Battleground* (1977), *The Double Tree: Selected Poems, 1942–1976* (1978), *Reef, Rainforest, Mangroves, Man* (1980), *Phantom Dwelling* (1985), *We Call for a Treaty* (1985), *A Human Pattern* (1990); also wrote various children's books and literary criticism. Awarded the Robert Frost Medallion of the Fellowship of Australian Writers (1975); awarded the Order of Golden Ark: Degree of Ridder (1980); awarded the ASAN World Prize for Poetry (1984). ❖ See also Alec Derwent Hope, *Judith Wright* (Oxford U. Press, 1975); Bill Scott, *Focus on Judith Wright* (U. of Queensland Press, 1967); Jennifer Strauss, *Judith Wright* (Oxford U. Press, 1995); Shirley Walker, *Judith Wright* (Oxford U. Press, 1981); and *Women in World History*.

WRIGHT, L. R. (1939–2001). Canadian mystery writer, novelist and journalist. Name variations: Laurali Rose Wright; Bunny Wright. Born Laurali Appleby, 1939, in Saskatoon, Canada; died of breast cancer, Feb 2001, in Vancouver, Canada; attended Banff School of Fine Arts. ❖ Worked as journalist on the *Calgary Herald* (1970–77); wrote "Karl Alberg" and "Edwina Henderson" mystery series, as well as mainstream novels; writings include *Neighbours* (1979), *The Favorite* (1982), *Among Friends* (1984), *The Suspect* (1985), *Sleep While I Sing* (1986), *Fall From Grace* (1991), *Acts of Murder* (1997), *Kidnap* (1999), and *Menace* (2001). Received Edgar Allan Poe Award for *The Suspect*; won the Arthur Ellis Award for *A Chill Rain in January* and *Mother Love*; also won Canadian Authors Association Literary Award for Fiction.

WRIGHT, Laura Maria (1809–1886). American missionary and linguist. Name variations: Auntie Wright. Born Laura Maria Sheldon, July 10, 1809, in St. Johnsbury, Vermont; died Jan 21, 1886, near Iroquois, New York; dau. of Solomon Sheldon and Dorothy (Stevens) Sheldon; granddau. of pioneer Willard Stevens; m. Asher Wright (missionary), Jan 21, 1833 (died 1875). ❖ Following marriage, moved with husband to the Buffalo Creek Reservation in western New York State; became a proficient speaker in the Seneca language; with husband, developed a written Seneca language, taught the Seneca how to read, and translated hymns, prayers, and scripture into Seneca; also took many orphaned Seneca children into their newly founded Thomas Asylum for Orphan and Destitute Indian Children. ❖ See also *Women in World History*.

WRIGHT, Lucy (1760–1821). American religious leader. Name variations: Mother Lucy, Lucy Goodrich. Born Feb 5, 1760, in Pittsfield, MA; died Feb 7, 1821, in Watervliet, NY; dau. of John and Mary (Robbins) Wright; m. Elizur Goodrich (merchant), c. 1779. ❖ Was chosen by Father Joseph Meacham as the "first leading character in female line" for Shaker sect (1787); took leadership of Shakers' central ministry (1796); dispatched missions to establish Shaker communities in Midwest (1804); made worship services more animated and created Children's Order schools. Under her leadership, Shakers transitioned from loosely organized group to association of monasticlike, economically self-supporting communities.

WRIGHT, Mabel Osgood (1859–1934). American nature writer, conservationist, and novelist. Name variations: (pseudonym) Barbara. Born Jan 26, 1859, in New York, NY; died July 16, 1934, in Fairfield, Connecticut; dau. of Samuel Osgood (cleric) and Ellen Haswell (Murdock) Osgood; m. John Osborne Wright (English rare-book dealer), Sept 25, 1884 (died 1920). ❖ Highly regarded nature writer and prominent conservationist, contributed "A New England May Day," to New York *Evening Post* (1893); published *The Friendship of Nature* (1894); in the several years that followed, produced books that varied between impressionistic nature writing to actual field manuals for study of birds; also wrote books on plants and mammals, nature stories, and fables for children; was a contributing editor of *Bird-Lore*; helped to found the Connecticut Audubon Society (1898) and served as director of National Association of Audubon Societies (1905–28); was also the author of several romance novels (1901–13), published under her own name or the pseudonym Barbara; published the largely autobiographical *My New York* (1926); writings include *Birdcraft* (1895), (with naturalist Elliot Coues) *Citizen Bird* (1897), *Gray Lady and the Birds* (1907), *The Garden of a Commuter's Wife* (1901), *Poppea of the Post Office* (1904) and *The Stranger at the Gate* (1913). ❖ See also *Women in World History*.

WRIGHT, Maginel (1881–1966). American artist. Name variations: Maginel Wright Barney; Maginel Wright Enright. Born Maginel Wright, June 19, 1881, in Weymouth, Massachusetts; died April 18, 1966, in East Hampton, New York; dau. of William Cary Wright (minister) and Anna (Lloyd-Jones) Wright; sister of architect Frank Lloyd Wright; attended Chicago Art Institute; m. Walter J. Enright (illustrator and cartoonist, div.); m. Hiram Barney (lawyer, died 1925); children: (1st m.) Elizabeth Enright (1909–1968, author). ❖ Known primarily for her illustrations of children's classics, including *Hans Brinker* and *Heidi*, also painted covers for a number of leading magazines, such as *Woman's Home Companion* and *Ladies' Home Journal*; held several exhibitions of her work in New York; as a shoe designer, created high-fashion jeweled and sequined shoes manufactured by Capezio (1940s); also illustrated Ruth Sawyer's *This Way to Christmas* (1924), Caroline D. Snedeker's *Downright Dencey* (1927), Sophie de Ségur's *Sophie: The Story of a Bad Little Girl* (1929), Philip Broughton's *Pandy* (1930) and Ethel Calvert Phillips' *Calico* (1937), as well as books by L. Frank Baum. ❖ See also autobiography *The Valley of the God-Almighty Joneses* (Appleton-Century, 1965); and *Women in World History*.

WRIGHT, Martha Coffin (1806–1875). American women's rights leader. Born Dec 25, 1806, in Boston, Massachusetts; died Jan 4, 1875, in Boston; dau. of Thomas Coffin Jr. (merchant and ship's captain) and Anna (Folger) Coffin (both Quakers); sister of suffragist Lucretia Mott (1793–1880); m. Peter Pelham (army captain), Nov 18, 1824 (died 1826); m. David Wright (lawyer), 1829; children: (1st m.) Marianna Pelham (b. 1825); (2nd m.) Eliza Wright Osborne (b. 1830, suffragist), Matthew Tallman Wright (b. 1832), Ellen Wright (b. 1840, suffragist), William Pelham Wright (b. 1842), Frank Wright (b. 1844), Charles Wright (b. 1848). ❖ Began long career in the women's movement (1848), when she worked with sister Lucretia Mott and Elizabeth Cady Stanton in organizing the 1st convention for women's rights in US; continued to organize and lead women's rights conventions over following years, serving as secretary of a convention in Syracuse (1852), vice-president of a convention in Philadelphia (1854), and then president of 3 different conventions (1855); also presided over New York State Woman's Rights Committee's 10th annual women's rights convention held in New York City (1860); played important role as an advisor to Stanton and Susan B. Anthony; helped organize American Equal Rights Association (1866) and National Women's Suffrage Association (1869), serving as president (1874–75). ❖ See also *Women in World History*.

WRIGHT, Mary Clabaugh (1917–1970). American scholar. Born Mary Oliver Clabaugh on Sept 25, 1917, in Tuscaloosa, Alabama; died June 18, 1970, in Guilford, Connecticut; dau. of Samuel Francis Clabaugh (newspaper publisher) and Mary Bacon (Duncan) Clabaugh; graduate of Vassar College, 1937; Radcliffe College, PhD, 1951; m. Arthur Frederick Wright (1913–1976, scholar of Chinese history), July 6, 1940; children: Charles Duncan (b. 1950) and Jonathan Arthur (b. 1952). ❖ Chinese history scholar, published several academic works, including *The Last Stand of Chinese Conservatism: The T'ung-chih Restoration 1862–1874* (1957), and *China and Revolution: The First Phase, 1900–1913* (1968); founded the Society for Ch'ing Studies; created journal for this society, *Ch'ing-shih wen-t'i*; established prominent collection of Chinese resources for the Hoover Library; became associate professor of history at Yale University (1959), later becoming the 1st woman to be named a

full professor there; worked on the Joint Committee on Contemporary China. ❖ See also *Women in World History*.

WRIGHT, Mary Kathryn (1935—). *See Wright, Mickey.*

WRIGHT, Mickey (1935—). American golfer. Name variations: Jay Wright; Mary Kathryn Wright. Born Mary Kathryn Wright, Feb 14, 1935, in San Diego, CA; attended Stanford University, 1953–54. ❖ Turned pro (1954); won LPGA championship (1958, 1960, 1961, 1963); won U.S. Women's Open (1958, 1959, 1961, 1964); won Titleholders (1961 and 1962); won the Western Women's Open (1962, 1963, 1966); won the Colgate-Dinah Shore championship (1973); only woman to hold all four major titles simultaneously; achieved a record 14 wins (1963); was LPGA all-time leading money winner (1964–68). Inducted into the LPGA Hall of Fame (1964), the World Golf Hall of Fame (1976), and the International Women's Sports Hall of Fame (1981). ❖ See also *Women in World History*.

WRIGHT, Muriel Hazel (1889–1975). Native American writer and historian. Born near Lehigh, Choctaw Nation (later Coal County, Oklahoma), Mar 31, 1889; died in Oklahoma City, Feb 27, 1975; dau. of Eliphalet Nott Wright (physician for Missouri-Pacific Coal Mines, who was half Choctaw and son of the chief of the Choctaw Nation) and Ida Belle (Richard) Wright (Anglo-Scotch Presbyterian missionary); attended Wheaton Seminary, 1906–08, and East Central State Normal School, 1911–12; pursued master's in English and history, 1916–17. ❖ Taught in the Coal County school system (1912–14, 1917–24); served as secretary of the Choctaw Committee (1922–28); began contributing articles to *The Chronicles of Oklahoma*, the journal of the Oklahoma Historical Society, and other periodicals; collaborated with Joseph B. Thoburn on the 4-vol. work, *Oklahoma: A History of the State and Its People* (1929), then published 3 textbooks of Oklahoma history; helped organize the Choctaw Advisory Council (1934), serving as secretary until 1944; was named associate editor of *The Chronicles of Oklahoma* (1943), becoming editor (1955), where she remained until her retirement (1973); published her nationally known reference work, *A Guide to the Indian Tribes of Oklahoma* (1951). Inducted into Oklahoma Hall of Fame (1940). ❖ See also *Women in World History*.

WRIGHT, Patience Lovell (1725–1786). American artist. Born in Bordentown, New Jersey, 1725; died in London, England, Mar 23, 1786; dau. of John and Patience (Townsend) Lovell; sister of Rachel Wright Wells, who ran a wax museum in Philadelphia; m. Joseph Wright (cooper), 1748 (died 1769); children: Mary Wright (who m. Benjamin Van Cleef); Elizabeth Wright (who m. Ebenezer Platt); Joseph Wright (1756–1793, studied with Benjamin West and was the 1st engraver of US mint); Phoebe Wright (b. 1761, modeled for Benjamin West and m. portrait painter John Hoppner); Sarah Wright (b. 1769, died young). ❖ Launched a career as a sculptor, modeling well-known public figures in wax; created a remarkably successful series of portraits, and made them into a traveling exhibit which was the 1st of its kind, charging the public to see them in Charleston, NY, and Philadelphia; traveled to England (1772), where her works and eccentric personality captivated spectators; commissioned to create wax works of many famous figures in America and England; was a good friend of Benjamin Franklin. ❖ See also *Women in World History*.

WRIGHT, Patricia (1945—). American singer. Name variations: Patsy Wright; The Crystals. Born 1945 in Brooklyn, NY. ❖ As an original member of girl-group, the Crystals (formed 1961), had hit singles "There's No Other (Like My Baby)" (1961), "Uptown" (1962), "Da Doo Ron Ron" (1963), and "Then He Kissed Me" (1964); with group, had #1 hit with "He's a Rebel," but it was actually recorded by session singers the Blossoms, not the Crystals.

WRIGHT, Paula Rae (1923–2003). *See Raymond, Paula.*

WRIGHT, Rebecca (1942—). American ballet and modern dancer. Born Dec 5, 1942, in Springfield, OH. ❖ Trained at City Center Joffrey Ballet and American Ballet Center; danced with Joffrey Ballet for over a decade (1966–75), where she created roles for Gerald Arpino's *Confetti* (1970), Margo Sappington's *Weewis* (1971), and Joe Layton's *Double Exposure* (1972), among others; joined American Ballet Theater as a soloist and danced in company's productions of such classics as *The Sleeping Beauty, Don Quixote, The Nutcracker,* and *Swan Lake* (1975–82); starred on Broadway in *Merlin*; was a professor at California State University, Long Beach (1987–93); became director of the Washington School of Ballet (2004).

WRIGHT, Rita (1946–2004). *See Wright, Syreeta.*

WRIGHT, Sarah Elizabeth (1928—). African-American poet and novelist. Born Sarah Elizabeth Wright, 1928, in Wetipquin, MD; dau. of Willis Charles and Mary Amelia Moore Wright. ❖ Moved to New York (1957) and established friendships with important African-American writers; with Maya Angelou and others, organized Cultural Association for Women of African Heritage (1960s); with Lucy Smith, published collection of poetry, *Give Me a Child* (1955); also published the novel *This Child's Gonna Live* (1969).

WRIGHT, Sophie Bell (1866–1912). American educator. Born June 5, 1866, in New Orleans, LA; died June 10, 1912, in New Orleans; dau. of William Haliday Wright (plantation owner) and Mary (Bell) Wright. ❖ Established girls' day school in parents' home (c. 1881); formally named school the Home Institute (1883); opened Free Night School for men and boys (1884); served as president of Louisiana Woman's Club (1897–98); was secretary and president (1906) of Louisiana branch of International Order of the King's Daughters and Sons. ❖ See also Viola Mary Walker, *Sophie Bell Wright: Her Life and Work* (MA thesis, Tulane University, 1939).

WRIGHT, Susanna (1697–1784). American colonial writer and poet. Born in Manchester, England, Aug 4, 1697; died in Columbia, Pennsylvania, Dec 1, 1784; dau. of John (Quaker minister) and Patience (Gibson) Wright (died 1722); educated in England. ❖ Moved with family to US (1714); established friendships with other colonial intellectuals, such as James Logan, Benjamin Franklin, and Charles and Isaac Morris; was celebrated as a witty conversationalist who could discuss poetry and natural philosophy with ease and grace; also drew and wrote verse, though few examples of her work survive. ❖ See also *Women in World History*.

WRIGHT, Sybil Mary (1899–1983). *See Mulvany, Sybil Mary.*

WRIGHT, Syreeta (1946–2004). African-American singer and songwriter. Name variations: Syreeta, Rita Wright. Born Rita Wright, Feb 28, 1946, in Pittsburgh, PA; died of breast cancer, July 6, 2004, in Los Angeles, CA; m. Stevie Wonder (musician), Sept 14, 1970 (div. 1972); Curtis Robertson Jr. (bass player, div.); children: Takiyah, Harmoni, Jamal and Hodari. ❖ Best known for collaborations with Stevie Wonder, began career as a backup singer and receptionist at Motown; released single, "Can't Give Back the Love I Feel for You" (1968); began collaborating with Wonder and contributed lyrics to several of his hits, including "Signed, Sealed, Delivered" and "If You Really Love Me"; co-wrote lyrics for his albums, *Music of My Mind* (1972), *Talking Book* (1972), and *Journey Through the Secret Life of Plants* (1979); released albums, *Syreeta* (1972) and *Stevie Wonder Presents Syreeta* (1974); with Billy Preston, had hit duet, "With You I'm Born Again" (1980); after releasing unsuccessful albums, *Set My Love in Motion* (1981) and *The Spell* (1983), stopped performing; played Mary Magdalene in Broadway tour of *Jesus Christ Superstar* (1995).

WRIGHT, Teresa (1918–2005). American actress. Born Muriel Teresa Wright in Harlem, New York, Oct 27, 1918; died Mar 6, 2005, in New Haven, CT; dau. of Arthur Wright and Martha (Espy) Wright; studied acting at the Wharf Theater, Provincetown, Massachusetts, 1937–38; m. Niven Busch (screenwriter and novelist), 1942 (div. 1952); m. Robert Woodruff Anderson (playwright), 1959 (div.); m. Carlos Pierre (marriage ended); remarried Robert Anderson. ❖ Academy Award-winning actress, best known for her performances in such classics as *Shadow of a Doubt* and *The Little Foxes*, enjoyed a film and stage career which spanned 6 decades; replaced Dorothy McGuire in *Our Town* (1939); landed a role in Broadway production of *Life with Father* (1939), which ran for 2 years; made film debut in *The Little Foxes* (1941), for which she was nominated for Academy Award for Best Supporting Actress; portrayed Eleanor Gehrig opposite Gary Cooper in *The Pride of the Yankees*, which earned her an Oscar nomination for Best Actress (1942); appeared with Greer Garson in *Mrs. Miniver*, winning an Academy Award for Best Supporting Actress (1942); earned critical praise for performance in *The Best Years of Our Lives*, but later roles in Hollywood did not enhance her career, possibly because of her tendency to avoid publicity; nominated for Emmy Awards for performances in tv movies "The Miracle Worker" (1957) and "The Margaret Bourke-White Story" (1960); returned to Broadway, most notably in *Mary, Mary* (1962) and *Death of a Salesman* (1975); earned 3rd Emmy nomination for an episode of "Dolphin Cove" (1989); other films include *Casanova Brown* (1944), *The Men* (1950), *Track of the Cat* (1954), *The Search for Bridey Murphy* (1956), *Roseland* (1977), *Somewhere in Time* (1979) and *The Good Mother* (1988). ❖ See also *Women in World History*.

WRIGHTSON, Patricia (1921—). Australian novelist. Born Alice Patricia Furlonger in Lismore, New South Wales, Australia, June 1921; dau. of Charles Radcliff Furlonger (a solicitor) and Alice (Dyer) Furlonger; attended St. Catherine's College, Stanthrope, Queensland, 1932; State Correspondence School, 1933–34; married 1943 (div. 1953); children: Jennifer Mary Wrightson Ireland; Peter Radcliff. ❖ Published the novel *The Crooked Snake* (1955), which was named Australia's Book of the Year; won award thrice more (1974, 1978, and 1984); became assistant editor of Sydney's *School Magazine* (1964), a publication for elementary school students, serving as editor (1970–75); published a new book every year or two (1955–97); though best known for her realistic books, which were often set in the Australian landscapes of her childhood, also published science fiction and fantasy novels for children, including several series, most notably the "Wirrun" trilogy: *The Ice is Coming* (1977), *The Dark Bright Water* (1979) and *Behind the Wind* (1981); wrote numerous fantasy novels for adults as well, and edited 2 collections of juvenile stories, *Beneath the Sun* (1972) and *Emu Stew* (1976). Awarded the Order of the British Empire (1978); received New South Wales Premier's Award for ethnic literature (1979); won Hans Christian Andersen Medal (1986) and New South Wales Premier's Special Occasion Award (1988). ❖ See also *Women in World History*.

WRINCH, Dorothy (1894–1976). English physicist and philosopher. Name variations: Dorothy Wrinch Nicholson; Dot Wrinch; (pseudonym) Jean Ayling. Born Dorothy Wrinch to English parents in Rosario, Argentina, 1894; died Feb 1976; Girton College, Cambridge, BA and MA, 1918; University of London, MSc and DSc; Oxford University, MA, and was the 1st woman to receive a DSc from Oxford, 1929; m. John Nicholson (Oxford physicist known for his work on atomic structure), 1922 (div. 1938); m. O. C. Glaser (biology professor at Amherst), 1941; children: (1st m.) Pamela Wrinch Schenkman (1928–1975). ❖ Appointed lecturer in pure mathematics, University College, London (1918); was a member of the Executive Committee of the Aristotelian Society (1925–26); moved to US (1939); was a member of the chemistry department, Johns Hopkins University (1940–41); taught at Amherst, Smith, and Mt. Holyoke (1941–44); taught physics at Smith College (1944–71); also taught courses in crystallography at the Marine Biology Laboratory at Woods Hole; labeled variously as a mathematician, biochemist, physicist, and philosopher, her work bridged the disciplines of several fields, and helped to reconcile divergences between the biological and physical sciences; writings include *Chemical Aspects of Polypeptide Chain Structures and the Cyclol Theory* (1965). ❖ See also *Women in World History*.

WRIOTHESLEY, Rachel (1636–1723). *See Russell, Rachel.*

WRIOTHESLY, Elizabeth (d. 1690). Countess of Northumberland. Died in Sept 1690; dau. of Thomas Wriothesly (b. 1607), 5th earl of Southampton, and Elizabeth Leigh; m. Josceline also known as Jocelyn Percy (d. 1670), 11th and last earl of Northumberland, on Dec 23, 1662; m. Ralph Montagu, 1st duke of Montagu; children: (1st m.) Elizabeth Percy (1667–1722).

WROBEL, Agata (1981—). Polish weightlifter. Name variations: Wróbel. Born 1981 in Zywiec, Poland. ❖ Won European championships (1997–2002); won World championships (1998, 2002); won a silver medal at Sydney Olympics (2000) and a bronze medal at Athens Olympics (2004), both for +75 kg.

WROTH, Mary (c. 1587–c. 1651). English poet, prose writer, and literary patron. Born Mary Sydney in Penshurst Place, Kent, England, c. 1587; died c. 1651; dau. of Robert Sidney, 1st earl of Leicester, and Barbara Gamage; niece of Mary Herbert (1561–1621) and poet Sir Philip Sidney; m. Sir Robert Wroth (eldest son of a member of Parliament), in 1604 (died 1614); children: (1st m.) son James (died 1616); (with William Herbert, 3rd earl of Pembroke) 2 illeg. children. ❖ Was prominent at the English court, where she circulated her verses and was a generous supporter of other writers; had works dedicated to her by George Chapman, George Wither, and Ben Jonson, who dedicated *The Alchemist* to her (1610), after she had performed in one of his masques; following death of husband, began a relationship with her cousin, William Herbert, 3rd earl of Pembroke; issued a prose romance, *The Countesse of Montgomerie's Urania* (1621), which is considered the 1st English novel published by a woman; also authored a play, a tragicomedy titled *Love's Victorie*, which was not published until 1853; retired from court and spent final years at her country estates. ❖ See also *Women in World History*.

WU CHAO (624–705). *See Wu Zetian.*

WU, Chien-Shiung (1912–1997). Chinese-American physicist. Name variations: Wu Chien-Shiung. Pronunciation: CHEN-shoong WOO. Born Chien-Shiung Wu, May 29, 1912, in Shanghai, China; died in New York, NY, Feb 16, 1997; dau. of Wu Zhongyi (school principal) and Fuhua H. Fan Wu; National Central University, Nanjing, BS, 1934; University of California, Berkeley, PhD, 1940; m. Luke Cha-Liou Yuan (physicist), May 30, 1942; children: Vincent Weichen Yuan (b. 1947). ❖ Experimental physicist who supplied the proof for the hypothesis that the principle of the conservation of parity was invalid, overthrowing what had been a fundamental concept of physics; was hired as physics instructor at Smith College (1942); became physics instructor at Princeton University (1943); was on the scientific staff, Division of War Research, Manhattan Project, Columbia University (1944–45), designing radiation detectors for the atomic bomb project and perfecting Geiger counters, as well as neutron and uranium enrichment research; studied beta decay; was research physicist, Columbia University (1945–81); received tenure as associate professor at Columbia (1952), an academic rank few women had achieved in universities or research laboratories; became naturalized citizen (1954); determined invalidity of principle of parity (1957); was the 1st woman to receive the Research Corporation Award; was 7th woman elected to the National Academy of Sciences (1958); promoted to full professor at Columbia (1959); was 1st woman to receive National Academy of Sciences Comstock Award (1964); received National Medal of Science, America's highest science award (1975); became the 1st woman to serve as president of American Physical Society (1975); awarded the 1st honorary doctorate in science ever given to a woman by Princeton University; retired from Columbia (1981); writings include (with Luke C. L. Yuan) *Nuclear Physics* (2 vols., 1961–63), (with Steven A. Moszkowski) *Beta Decay* (1966), (edited with Vernon W. Hughes) *Muon Physics* (3 vols., 1975–77). ❖ See also *Women in World History*.

WU DAN (1968—). Chinese volleyball player. Born Jan 13, 1968, in China. ❖ At Seoul Olympics, won a bronze medal in team competition (1988).

WU EMPRESS (624–705). *See Wu Zetian.*

WU HOU (624–705). *See Wu Zetian.*

WU HSING CHÜN FU-JEN (1262–1319). *See Guan Daosheng.*

WU HUI JU (1982—). Chinese Taipei archer. Born Nov 12, 1982, in Taiwan. ❖ Won a bronze medal for team at Athens Olympics (2004).

WU JIANI (1966—). Chinese gymnast. Born April 23, 1966, in Shanghai, China. ❖ Won a silver medal for team all-around and a bronze medal for balance beam at World championships (1981); won a silver medal for uneven bars at World Cup (1982); at Los Angeles Olympics, won a bronze medal in team all-around (1984).

WU LANYING (d. 1929). Chinese revolutionary. Name variations: Wu Lan-ying. Executed in 1929; became 3rd wife of Zhu De (Chu Teh, a general), in 1928. ❖ An educated Hunanese woman, married Zhu De when his forces occupied her home province (1928); was captured by the governor of Hunan and executed (1929). ❖ See also *Women in World History*.

WU MEI (624–705). *See Wu Zetian.*

WU MEILIANG (624–705). *See Wu Zetian.*

WU MINXIA (1985—). Chinese diver. Born Nov 10, 1985, in Shanghai, China; attended Renmin University of China. ❖ At World championships, won gold medals for 3-meter synchronized springboard (2001, 2003) and a silver in 1-meter springboard (2001); in Grand Prix ranking, placed 3rd (2001) and 2nd (2004); won 16 Grand Prix events (2001–04); won a silver medal for 3-meter springboard and a gold medal for 3-meter synchronized springboard at Athens Olympics (2004).

WU TSE-T'IEN (624–705). *See Wu Zetian.*

WU TSO TIEN (624–705). *See Wu Zetian.*

WU WENYING (1932—). Chinese politician. Born 1932 in Nantong, Jiangsu Province, China; children: son Lu. ❖ Worked in textile industry and went on to become deputy secretary of Changzhou Municipal Textile Bureau Party Committee and deputy head of Changzhou Cotton Mill; studied industrial management and was made deputy secretary of Changzhou Municipal Party Committee and head of its Organization Department (1977); was mayor of Changzhou and moved to Beijing (Peking) to become alternate member of Communist Party central committee and then Minister of Textile Industry (1983); became full member of central committee (1985) and led textile delegations to Germany,

Belgium, New Zealand, Burma, Britain and Bulgaria (1985, 1986); was placed on probation within the party because she was said to have used her power to help her son profit illegally (2000).

WU XIAOXUAN (1958—). Chinese shooter. Born Jan 26, 1958, in China. ❖ At Los Angeles Olympics, won a bronze medal in air rifle and a gold medal in smallbore rifle 3 positions (1984).

WU XINGJIANG (1957—). Chinese handball player. Born May 25, 1957, in China. ❖ At Los Angeles Olympics, won a bronze medal in team competition (1984).

WU YI (1938—). Chinese politician. Born 1938 in Wuhan, Hubei, China; graduate of the Beijing Petroleum Institute with a degree in petroleum engineering; never married; no children. ❖ One of China's most beloved and open politicians, joined the Communist Party (1962); worked in the oil industry for years; served as vice mayor of Beijing (1988–91); as China's chief trade negotiator, was vice minister of Foreign Economic Relations and Trade, then minister of Foreign Trade and Economic Cooperation, and member of the 14th and 15th CPC Central committees (1991–98); a protege of Zhu Ronqi, was named a state councillor (1998); became one of four vice premiers of the State Council (2003); appointed health minister during the SARS crisis (2003).

WU YONGMEI (1975—). Chinese volleyball player. Name variations: Wu Yong Mei. Born Jan 1, 1975, in Bao Ding, Hebei Province, China. ❖ Joined national team (1991); won a team silver medal at Atlanta Olympics (1996).

WU ZETIAN (624–705). Chinese empress. Name variations: Wu Ze-tian; Wu Chao, Wu Hou, or Wu Zhao; Wu Mei or Wu Meiliang; Wu Tse-t'ien, Wo Tse-tien, or Wu Tso Tien; Wu of Hwang Ho or Huang He; Empress Wu, Lady Wu. Pronunciation: Woo-jeh-ten. Born née Wu (1st name at birth not known) in 624 in Taiyuan, Shanxi province; died 705 in Luoyang, Henan province; dau. of high-ranking official, Wu Shihuo, and his aristocratic wife; m. Emperor Taizong (r. 626–649), in 640 (died 649); m. Emperor Gaozong (r. 650–683), in 654; children: (2nd m.) Crown Prince Li Hong; Crown Prince Li Xian; Emperor Zhongzong; Emperor Ruizong; Princess Taiping; another daughter (died in infancy). ❖ Controversial ruler of Tang China who dominated Chinese politics for half a century, 1st as empress, then as empress-dowager, and finally as emperor of the Zhou Dynasty (690–705) that she founded; at 13, became concubine to Emperor Taizong (640); entered Buddhist nunnery, as required of concubines of deceased emperors (649); returned to the palace as concubine (654), then as empress (657) to Taizong's son Emperor Gaozong; became empress dowager and regent to her 2 sons (684–89); declared herself emperor after deposing her sons and founding her own dynasty (Zhou, 690–705) and ruled as emperor for 15 years; a decisive, capable ruler, challenged the traditional patriarchical dominance of power, state, sovereignty, monarchy, and political ideology; exhibited strengths traditionally attributed to men, including political ambition, long-range vision, skillful diplomacy, power drive, decisive resolve, shrewd observation, talented organization, hard work, and firm dispensal of cruelty. ❖ See also Richard W. Guisso, *Empress Wu Tse-t'ien and the Politics of Legitimation in T'ang China* (Western Washington University, 1978); Lin Yutang, *Lady Wu* (Putnam, 1965); Tong Su, *Wu Zetian* (Hong Kong: Cosmos, 1994); and *Women in World History*.

WU ZHAO (624–705). *See Wu Zetian.*

WU OF HUANG HE or HWANG HO (624–705). *See Wu Zetian.*

WUERCH, Shawntel (1971—). *See Smith, Shawntel.*

WUJAK, Brigitte (1955—). East German long jumper. Born Mar 6, 1955. ❖ At Moscow Olympics, won a silver medal in the long jump (1980).

WULDETRADA OF THE LOMBARDS (fl. 6th c.). Duchess of Bavaria. Daughter of Wacho, king of the Lombards; m. Garibald I, duke of Bavaria, in 555; children: Theudeline of Bavaria; Gundoald, duke of Asti.

WULFETRUD OF NIVELLES (fl. 7th c.). Abbess of Nivelles. Dau. of Grimoald, mayor of Austrasia (d. 656); sister of Childebert, king of Austrasia and the Franks (r. 656).

WULFHILD (fl. 11th c.). West Saxon princess. Name variations: Wulfhilda. Dau. of Elfgifu (c. 963–1002) and Aethelred or Ethelred II the Unready (c. 968–1016), king of the English (r. 979–1013, deposed, 1014–1016); m. Ulfcytel Snylling, ealdorman of East Anglia; m. Thurchil, earl of East Anglia.

WULFRID (c. 945–1000). *See Wulfthryth.*

WULFTHRYTH (fl. 860s). Queen of the English. Married Ethelred I (c. 843–871), king of the English (r. 865–871), around 868; children: Ethelhelm, archbishop of Canterbury (d. 923); Ethelwald, king of York (c. 868–902).

WULFTHRYTH (c. 945–1000). English royal mistress. Name variations: Wulfrida; Saint Wulfrid. Born c. 945; died in 1000; mistress of Edgar the Peaceful (944–975), king of the English (r. 959–975); children: Edith (c. 961–984).

WULZ, Wanda (1903–1984). Italian photographer. Born 1903 in Trieste, Italy; died in Italy in 1984; dau. of Carlo Wulz and granddau. of Guiseppe Wulz (both portrait photographers). ❖ Often photographed artists in the field of theater, dance, and music; work is usually associated with late Futurists because her experimental photography often incorporated motion and superimposed images; during 10th Anniversary of the Fascist Revolution (1932), established her greatest success, exhibiting experimental work with the "Futurist Collection."

WUNDERLICH, Claudia (1956—). East German handball player. Born Feb 16, 1956, in East Germany. ❖ At Moscow Olympics, won a bronze medal in team competition (1980).

WUNDERLICH, Frieda (1884–1965). German-born American sociologist, feminist and social-political activist. Born Nov 8, 1884, in Germany; died Dec 1965 in New York, NY. ❖ Served as a judge in Berlin (1926–33), during which time she was also a member of both the Berlin City Council (1926–33) and the Prussian Diet (1930–33); fled Nazi Germany for NY (1933); was the 1st woman to be a faculty member of the "University in Exile," the precursor of the New School for Social Research, and became its 1st female dean (Jan 4, 1939); wrote a handbook on labor in Nazi Germany for the Office of Strategic Services during World War II.

WUNDERLICH, Magdalena (1952—). West German kayaker. Born May 16, 1952. ❖ At Munich Olympics, won a bronze medal in K1 slalom (1972).

WUNDERLICH, Pia (1975—). German soccer player. Born Jan 26, 1975, in Bad Berleburg, Germany; sister of Tina Wunderlich (soccer player). ❖ Center; played for FFC Frankfurt; won team European championships (1997, 2001); won FIFA World Cup (2003); won team bronze medal at Athens Olympics (2004).

WUNDERLICH, Tina (1977—). German soccer player. Born Oct 10, 1977, in Bad Berleburg, Germany; sister of Pia Wunderlich (soccer player). ❖ Defender; won a team bronze medal at Sydney Olympics (2000); won team European championships (1995, 2001).

WUOLIJOKI, Hella (1886–1954). Estonian-born Finnish writer, social critic, and unofficial diplomat. Name variations: (pseudonyms) Juhani Tervapää or Juhani Tervapaa; Felix Tuli. Born Ella Maria Murrik, July 22, 1886, in Helme, Estonia; died Feb 20, 1954, in Helsinki, Finland. ❖ At 18, moved to Finland to continue her education, enrolling at University of Helsinki; became intrigued with Finland's rich traditions of epic poetry; arrested by the Finns on charges of treason during Finnish-Soviet conflict and sentenced to death, was saved primarily by Bertolt Brecht, who spoke on her behalf (her play *The Sawdust Princess* had served as model for Brecht's *Herr Puntila und sein Knecht Matti*); on release (1944), became involved in international diplomacy, using her friendship with Alexandra Kollontai to initiate contacts between Helsinki and Moscow that led to an armistice between Finland and USSR; her radical social commentaries and sharp critiques of patriarchal society made her a controversial writer who was often ahead of her time.

WUORNOS, Aileen (1956–2002). American murderer. Name variations: Lee Wuornos. Born Aileen Pittman, Feb 29, 1956, in Rochester, Michigan; executed Oct 9, 2002, in Florida; dau. of Leo (convicted child molester) and Diane (Wuornos) Pittman; brought up by grandparents, Lauri and Britta Wuornos. ❖ Said to have been America's 1st female serial killer (though not true), killed 7 men in Florida; pregnant at 14, became ward of the court; took to the streets; moved to Florida (1976); became involved with Tyria Moore in Daytona Beach (1986); as an alcoholic and prostitute, worked the highways, picking up men; claimed she killed the 1st man in self-defense, after he assaulted her; taken into custody (Jan 1991), received 6 death sentences. ❖ See also (film) *Monster,* starring Charlize Theron (2003).

WURDEMANN, Audrey Mary (1911–1960). American poet. Name variations: Mrs. Joseph Auslander. Born 1911 in Seattle, Washington; died 1960; graduate of University of Washington; m. Joseph Auslander (1896–1965, novelist and lyric poet). ❖ Youngest winner of the Pulitzer Prize for Poetry, published 1st collection, *The House of Silk* (1926), while still in her teens; published prize-winning collection *Bright Ambush* (1934) at 24; also wrote *The Seven Sins* (1935), *Splendor in the Grass* (1936) and *The Testament of Love* (1938); collaborated with husband on 2 books, including *The Islanders* (1951).

WURSTER, Catherine Bauer (1905–1964). *See Bauer, Catherine Krouse.*

WURTTEMBERG, duchess of.
See Gonzaga, Barbara (1455–1505).
See Sabine of Bavaria (1492–1564).
See Maria Augusta A.A. Thurn and Taxis (1706–1756).
See Sophia Dorothea of Brandenburg (1736–1798).
See Elizabeth Frederike of Bayreuth (fl. 1750).
See Antoinette Saxe-Coburg (1779–1824).
See Henrietta of Nassau-Weilburg (1780–1857).
See Catherine Charlotte of Hildburghausen (1787–1847).
See Marie d'Orleans (1813–1839).
See Theodelinde (1814–1857).
See Vera Constantinovna (1854–1912).
See Margaret Sophie (1870–1902).
See Maria Immaculata (1878–1968).
See Nadejda of Bulgaria (b. 1899).
See Helene (1903–1924).
See Rosa (1906–1983).

WURTTEMBERG, queen of.
See Augusta of Brunswick-Wolfenbuttel (1764–1788).
See Catherine of Russia (1788–1819).
See Pauline of Wurttemberg (1800–1873).
See Olga of Russia (1822–1892).

W.W. (fl. 1866–1910). *See Fortune, Mary.*

WYATT, Jane (1911—). American actress. Born August 10, 1911, in Campgaw, New Jersey; dau. of Christopher Billop Wyatt (lawyer) and Eupemia Van Rensselaer (Waddington) Wyatt (writer for *Commonweal* and *Catholic World*); attended Barnard College, 1928–30, and Apprentice School of Berkshire Playhouse, 1930; m. Edgar Bethune Ward, Nov 9, 1935; children: Christopher, Michael. ❖ Best known for role as Margaret Anderson, the quintessential 1950s housewife, in tv series "Father Knows Best" (1954–60), made professional stage debut as a walk-on in *Trade Winds* in Philadelphia (1930); made NY debut as Freda Mannock in A.A. Milne's *Give Me Yesterday* (1931); on Broadway, replaced Margaret Sullivan in *Dinner at Eight* (1933); also appeared in *Save Me the Waltz* (1938), *Night Music* (1940), *Quiet Please* (1940) and *Hope for the Best* (1945); made film debut in *One More River* (1934), followed by *Great Expectations* (1934); came to prominence in *Lost Horizon* (1937); other films include *None but the Lonely Heart* (1944), *Gentlemen's Agreement* (1947), *My Blue Heaven* (1950), *The Man Who Cheated Himself* (1951), *Never Too Late* (1965), *Treasure of Matacumbe* (1976), *Star Trek IV: The Voyage Home* (1986) and *Amityville IV: The Evil Escapes* (1990). Won Emmy Awards for "Father Knows Best" (1958–60). ❖ See also *Women in World History.*

WYATT, Rachel (1929—). Canadian novelist and playwright. Born Oct 14, 1929, in Bradford, England. ❖ Wrote radio dramas for BBC and Canadian Broadcasting Corporation, as well as novels and short stories; became instructor at Banff Centre for the Arts (1986) and then director of writing programs there; works include *The String Box* (1970), *The Rosedale Hoax* (1977), *Foreign Bodies* (1982), *Time in the Air* (1985), *The Day Marlene Dietrich Died* (1996), *The Last We Heard of Leonard* (2002) and *Time's Reach* (2003).

WYATT, Violet (1856–1935). *See Melnotte, Violet.*

WYBORN, Kerry (1977—). Australian softball player. Born Dec 22, 1977, in Sydney, Australia. ❖ Outfielder, won a team silver medal at Athens Olympics (2004).

WYCHERLY, Margaret (1881–1956). English stage and screen actress. Born Margaret De Wolfe, Oct 26, 1881, in London, England; died June 6, 1956, in New York, NY; m. Bayard Veiller, 1901; children: Anthony Veiller (writer). ❖ Had an illustrious career in the theater, most notably as Olivia in *Twelfth Night*, Ada Lester in *Tobacco Road* and Rosalie La Grange in *The 13th Chair*; films include *The Fight*, *The 13th Chair*,

Sergeant York (as Gary Cooper's mother), *The Loves of Carmen, Random Harvest, The Yearling, White Heat* (as James Cagney's mother), *Johnny Angel, Forever Amber* and *The Man with a Cloak.* Nominated for Academy Award for Best Supporting Actress for *Sergeant York* (1941).

WYCHINGHAM, Elizabeth (fl. 15th c.). English royal. Name variations: Lady Hoo. Married Thomas Hoo, Lord Hoo and Hastings; mother of Anne Hoo (c. 1425–1484); great-great-grandmother of Anne Boleyn.

WYDEVILLE. *Variant of Woodville.*

WYETH, Henriette (1907–1997). American artist. Name variations: Henriette Wyeth Hurd. Born Ann Henriette Wyeth, Oct 22, 1907, in Wilmington, Delaware; died April 3, 1997, in Roswell, New Mexico; dau. of N(ewell) C(onvers) Wyeth (the artist) and Carolyn Brenneman (Bockius) Wyeth; sister of Andrew Wyeth, artist; attended Museum of Art, Boston, 1921–23, and Pennsylvania Academy of Fine Arts; m. Peter Hurd (artist), 1929 (died 1984); children: Peter Hurd Jr. (musician), Michael Hurd and Carol Rogers Hurd (both artists). ❖ Trained as an artist by father at home in Chadds Ford, Pennsylvania; remained heavily influenced by his unique realistic style, and rejected painting genres, such as Impressionism and Cubism, which he disliked; received many commissions from wealthy patrons, including Helen Hayes, Paulette Goddard, and Mrs. John D. Rockefeller III (Blanchette Hooker Rockefeller), for which she earned a lasting celebrity; also explored painting still-lifes and the New Mexico landscape and rendered a portrait of Patricia Nixon for the White House; created a portrait of her brother Andrew Wyeth for cover of *Time* magazine (1963). ❖ See also *Women in World History.*

WYLAND, Wendy (1964–2003). American diver. Name variations: Wendy W. VanDerWoude. Born Nov 25, 1964, in Penfield, NY; died Sept 2003, age 38, in Webster, NY; dau. of Vernon and Beth Wyland; m. David VanDerWoude; children: Abigayle. ❖ Won Quayaquil World championship in 10-meter platform (1982); won a gold medal in platform and silver in 3-meter springboard at Pan American Games (1983); at Los Angeles Olympics, won a bronze medal in platform (1984); won a bronze in World championship for 10-meter platform (1986); was head swimming and diving coach at Rochester Instititute of Technology. Inducted into International Swimming Hall of Fame (1991).

WYLIE, Elinor (1885–1928). American writer. Born Elinor Hoyt, Sept 7, 1885, in Somerville, New Jersey; died Dec 16, 1928; dau. of Henry and Anne (McMichael) Hoyt; m. Philip Hichborn (Washington lawyer), 1906 (committed suicide 1916); m. Horace Wiley, 1916 (div. Jan 1923); m. William Rose Benét (poet), Oct 1923. ❖ Poet and novelist, who became a social celebrity as well as a leading literary figure of the post-World War I years, 1st came to public attention with the appearance of her collection of poems *Nets to Catch the Wind* (1921); with impressive social connections, her widely admired beauty, and a well-publicized extramarital affair during her 1st marriage, became a social celebrity as well as a leading literary figure; published 3 more vols. of poetry, *Black Armour* (1922), *Trivial Breath* (1928) and *Angels and Earthly Creatures* (1929), as well as 4 novels, *Jennifer Lorn* (1923), *The Venetian Glass Nephew* (1925), *Orphan Angel* (1926) and *Mr. Hodge and Mr. Hazard* (1928), before her early death at the age of 43 (1928); her poetry is known for the contrast between its meticulous structure and its sensuality, while her novels correspondingly display a classic formality combined with a sense of fantasy. Benét later edited and published her *Collected Poetry* (1932) and *Collected Prose* (1933). ❖ See also Stanley Olson, *Elinor Wylie: A Life Apart* (Dial, 1979); and *Women in World History.*

WYLIE, Ida A. R. (1885–1959). Australian-born English novelist. Name variations: I. A. R. Wylie. Born Ida Alexa Ross Wylie in Melbourne, Australia, 1885; died Nov 4, 1959; dau. of a Scottish barrister; attended Cheltenham Ladies' College and a private school in Karlsruhe, Germany; lived with Louise Pearce (1885–1959). ❖ Moved to England with family soon after her birth; wrote several novels about her experiences in Germany, including *My German Year* (1910) and *Eight Years in Germany* (1914), though she considered her 1st successful novel to be *Towards Morning* (1920); returned to England prior to World War I and participated in the women's suffrage movement there; traveled to US (1917), purchasing a farm near Princeton, New Jersey; also wrote *The Rajah's People* (1910), *Rambles in the Black Forest* (1911), *The Daughter of Brahma* (1912), *The Paupers of Portman Square* (1913), *Tristram Sahib* (1916), *The Duchess in Pursuit* (1918), *Brodie and the Deep Sea* (1920), *The Dark House* (1922), *Ancient Fires* (1924), *Black Harvest* (1925), *To the Vanquished* (1934), *Prelude to Richard* (1935), *A Feather in Her Hat* (1937), *Strangers Are Coming* (1941) and *Keeper of the Flame* (1942),

among others. ❖ See also autobiography *My Life with George* (1940); and *Women in World History.*

WYLIE, Mina (1892—). *See Wylie, Wilhelmina.*

WYLIE, Wilhelmina (1892–1984). Australian swimmer. Name variations: Mina Wylie. Born Wilhelmina Wylie, 1892 (some sources cite 1891), in Australia; died in 1984. ❖ Won the silver medal in the 100-meter freestyle in Stockholm Olympics (1912).

WYLLIE, Elizabeth Jennet (1847–1903). *See McMaster, Elizabeth Jennet.*

WYLLIE, Kate (d. 1913). New Zealand tribal leader. Name variations: Kate Halbert, Keita Waere (Waera), Kate Gannon. Born Kate Halbert, in early 1840s, in Poverty Bay, New Zealand; died Feb 4, 1913, in Auckland, New Zealand; dau. of Thomas Halbert (trader) and Keita Kaikeri (Kaikiri); m. James Ralston Wyllie, 1854 (died 1875); m. Michael Joseph Gannon (interpreter), 1881; children: (1st m.) 6 sons, 3 daughters; (2nd m.) 2 sons, 2 daughters. ❖ An acknowledged authority on Rongowhakaata lore, was effective advocate for her people several times at Native Land Court hearings; lost farm established with 1st husband in tribal warfare (1865); awarded vast amounts of land in Kaiaua block. ❖ See also *Dictionary of New Zealand Biography* (Vol. 2).

WYLUDDA, Ilke (1969—). German discus thrower. Born Mar 28, 1969, in Leipzig, Germany. ❖ Won a gold medal for discus at Atlanta Olympics (1996).

WYMAN, Jane (1914—). American actress. Name variations: Jane Durrell. Born Sarah Jane Fulks, Jan 4, 1914, in St. Joseph, Missouri; dau. of Richard (city official, died 1929) and Emma (Reise) Fulks; m. Myron Futterman (dress manufacturer), 1937 (div.); m. Ronald Reagan (actor and president of US), Jan 26, 1940 (div. 1948); m. Fred Karger (bandleader), Nov 1, 1952 (div. 1955, remarried Mar 1961, div. 1965); children: (2nd m.) Maureen Reagan (1941–2001, singer-actress turned political activist); (adopted) Michael Edward Reagan. ❖ Actress who won an Academy Award for her wordless performance in *Johnny Belinda* and was married to Ronald Reagan long before he became president, began career as a radio vocalist under name Jane Durrell; made film debut in *Gold Diggers of 1937* (1936); following a featured role in *My Man Godfrey* (1936), signed with Warner Bros.; for 8 years, played leads and 2nd leads in a string of light comedies, but came to prominence in *The Lost Weekend* (1945); nominated for Oscar for *The Yearling* (1946); won Academy Award for Best Actress for *Johnny Belinda* (1948); received 2 additional Oscar nominations, for *The Blue Veil* (1951) and *Magnificent Obsession* (1954); other films include *Stage Struck* (1937), *Brother Rat* (1938), *You're in the Army Now* (1941), *Night and Day* (1946), *The Lady Takes a Sailor* (1949), *Stage Fright* (1950), *The Glass Menagerie* (1950), *Here Comes the Groom* (1951), *So Big* (1953), *Lucy Gallant* (1955), *All That Heaven Allows* (1956), *Miracle in the Rain* (1956), *Pollyanna* (1960) and *How to Commit Marriage* (1969); starred on tv in "The Jane Wyman Theater." Won Golden Globe Award (1984), for Best Performance by an Actress in a Dramatic Series, for *Falcon Crest.* ❖ See also *Women in World History.*

WYMORE, Patrice (1926—). American actress. Name variations: Pat Wymore. Born Dec 17, 1926, in Miltonvale, KS; m. Errol Flynn (actor), 1950 (died 1959); children: Arnella Flynn (died 1998). ❖ Began career as a child in vaudeville; made film debut in *Tea for Two* (1950), followed by *I'll See You in My Dreams, She's Working Her Way Through College, The Man Behind the Gun, She's Back on Broadway, The Sad Horse, Ocean's 11* and *Chamber of Horrors,* among others; moved to Jamaica, becoming a successful businesswoman.

WYNDHAM, Esther (1908–1999). *See Lutyens, Mary.*

WYNDHAM, Mary (1861–1931). English actress and founder. Born Mary Moore in London, England, July 3, 1861; died April 6, 1931; dau. of Charles Moore; attended Warwick Hall, Maida Vale; m. James Albery (playwright), 1878 (died 1889); m. Sir Charles Wyndham, 1916 (died 1919); children: (1st m.) Bronson. ❖ Co-founder of Wyndham's Theaters, made stage debut at the Gaiety Theater, under direction of John Hollingshead; retired from acting during most of 1st marriage (1878–85); joined Sir Charles Wyndham's company (1885), appearing as Lady Dorothy in *The Candidate* at Theater Royal, Bradford; was president of Actors' Benevolent Fund; with Sir Charles, managed the Criterion, beginning 1897, and built Wyndham's Theater (1899), on Charing Cross Road in London, opening with their successful *David Garrick;* also partnered to build the New Theater. ❖ See also *Women in World History.*

WYNEKOOP, Alice (1870–1952). American murderer. Name variations: Dr. Alice Wynekoop. Born 1870; died 1952; m. Frank Wynekoop; children: 4. ❖ Was a respected doctor in Chicago; after daughter-in-law Rheta Gardner Wynekoop was found chloroformed and shot to death (Nov 21, 1933), initially speculated that she must have surprised a robber who killed her; later confessed to killing her with an accidental overdose of chloroform, and shooting her to cover up the mistake; eventually recanted confession; in one of the most sensational cases of the day, found guilty of murder (1934) after prosecution asserted that she would have done anything for her son Earle, who was in an unhappy marriage; paroled (1949).

WYNETTE, Tammy (1942–1998). American country singer. Born Virginia Wynette Pugh, May 5, 1942, in Itawamba County, MS; died in Nashville, TN, April 6, 1998; m. Euple Byrd, c. 1959 (div. c. 1965); m. Don Chapel (musician), 1965 (div. 1968); m. George Jones (singer), 1969 (div. 1975); m. Michael Tomlin (real-estate agent), 1978 (div. 6 weeks later); m. George Richey (songwriter and producer), 1978; children: 6, including (1st m.) Gwendolyn Byrd, Jacqueline "Jackie" Byrd Daly, and Tina Byrd; (3rd m.) Georgette Jones. ❖ One of the most famous country music stars of all time, taught herself to play guitar; after separation from 1st husband and a move to Birmingham, Alabama, began singing on local tv programs; signed 1st recording contract with Epic in Nashville (1966) and released "Your Good Girl's Gonna Go Bad," her 1st #1 hit; released "Stand By Your Man" (1968) which became the 1st country music recording by a female artist to sell more than 1 million records; joined Grand Ole Opry (1969); over next 30 years, had 20 #1 hits, including "Till I Can Make It on My Own," "These Days I Barely Get By" and "D-I-V-O-R-C-E"; was a frequent guest on tv variety shows and daytime chat shows and performed at the White House; teamed with Dolly Parton and Loretta Lynn for landmark album *Honky Tonk Angels* (1993); recorded duet, "Two Story House," with George Jones and produced the joint album *One* with him (1995); joined British pop group KLF for song "Justified and Ancient," which became an international dance-pop hit; later career marred by illness and financial difficulties. Named Country Music Association's Female Vocalist of the Year (1968) and twice more; won 2 Grammy Awards; inducted into Country Music Hall of Fame (1998). ❖ See also autobiography (with Joan Dew) *Stand By Your Man* (Simon & Schuster, 1979); Jackie Daly (with Tom Carter) *Tammy Wynette: A Daughter Recalls Her Mother's Tragic Life and Death* (Putnam, 2000); and *Women in World History*.

WYNN, Sally Gilmour (1921–2004). See Gilmour, Sally.

WYNNE, Jean (1921—). See Pearce, Jean.

WYNONNA (1964—). See Judd, Wynonna.

WYNTER, Dana (1927—). American actress. Name variations: Dagmar Wynter. Born Dagmar Spencer-Marcus, June 8, 1927, in Berlin, Germany; dau. of a noted surgeon; m. Greg Bautzer (lawyer). ❖ Brought up in England, then moved with family to Southern Rhodesia; appeared on the English stage before arriving in NY (1953); made film debut in *White Corridors* (1951), followed by *The View from Pompey's Head, D-Day the Sixth of June, Something of Value, Fraulein, In Love and War, Invasion of the Body Snatchers, Shake Hands with the Devil, Sink the Bismarck!, On the Double, The List of Adrian Messenger* and *Airport*; on tv, starred on "The Man Who Never Was" (1966–67); retired from film and moved to Co. Wicklow, Ireland.

WYNTER, Sylvia (1928—). Jamaican novelist, essayist and playwright. Born 1928 in Cuba; London University MA, 1953. ❖ Taught at University of West Indies, University of Michigan, and Stamford, among others; also was a radio and television writer for BBC; works include *Shh . . . it's a Wedding* (1961), *Miracle in Lime Lane* (1962), *1865*

Ballad for a Rebellion (1965), *Maskarade* (1979), and *The Hills of Hebron*; frequently contributed essays to literary journals.

WYNYARD, Diana (1906–1964). English actress. Born Dorothy Isobel Cox, Jan 16, 1906, in London, England; died May 13, 1964, in London; dau. of Edward Cox and Margaret (Thompson) Cox; m. Sir Carol Reed (director), 1943 (div. 1947); m. Tibor Csato (div.). ❖ Made London debut as a walk-on in *The Grand Duchess* (1925); appeared with Liverpool Rep (1927–30), then at the St. Martin's Theater in London in *Sorry You've Been Troubled*; made successful Broadway debut opposite Basil Rathbone in *The Devil Passes* (1932), then made film debut in a supporting role with the Barrymores in *Rasputin and the Empress*, followed by *Reunion in Vienna, Angel Street, The Prime Minister, Kipps, Tom Brown's Schooldays* (as Mrs. Arnold) and *Island in the Sun*; resumed career on British stage, appearing for 2 years with the Stratford Memorial Theater in such roles as Desdemona, Beatrice, and Queen Catherine; other plays include *Sweet Aloes, Pygmalion, Design for Living, No Time for Comedy, Watch on the Rhine, Marching Song, The Bad Seed, Toys in the Attic* and *Camino Real*. Nominated for Academy Award for Best Actress for *Cavalcade* (1933); named Companion of the Order of the British Empire (1953).

WYSE, Marie (1830–1902). See Rute, Mme de.

WYSE POWER, Jennie (1858–1941). Irish suffragist and nationalist. Name variations: Jennie Wyse-Power. Born Jane O'Toole in Baltinglass, Co. Wicklow, Ireland, May 1858; died in Dublin, Ireland, Jan 5, 1941; dau. of Edward O'Toole and Mary (Norton) O'Toole; m. John Wyse Power (journalist), July 5, 1883 (died 1926); children: Maire Wyse Power (died 1916); Nancy Wyse Power (nationalist); Charles Stewart Wyse Power (judge). ❖ Orphaned (1877), lived with brother; became a member of the Ladies' Land League (LLL) executive (1881); married John Wyse Power (1883), a journalist of Fenian sympathies who had been imprisoned during the land agitation; supported Parnell during his divorce scandal (1890) and compiled and edited a book of his speeches, *Words of the Dead Chief* (1892); set up a shop in Dublin, the Irish Farm Produce Co. (1899), which also had its own restaurant and soon became a mecca for various nationalist groups; joined Inghinidhe na hEireann (1900) and became one of its 4 vice-presidents; served as a poor-law guardian for North Dublin (1903–11) and as such had responsibility for social welfare issues affecting the poor; saw her shop destroyed (1916), after the proclamation declaring an Irish Republic on Easter Monday 1916 was signed at the Wyse Power house; as radical nationalism regrouped after the rebellion, was active in most of the key organizations, including Cumann na mBan (the Women's League) and Sinn Fein; with husband, during Irish War of Independence, sheltered people who were on the run from British authorities; won a seat in municipal elections (1920); was also on the executives of Sinn Fein and Cumann na mBan and was a member of the industrial commission set up by the revolutionary parliament, the Dail; was nominated to the senate by the new Irish prime minister, W. T. Cosgrave, one of only 4 women senators (1922); became an independent senator (1926), fighting against legislation which tried to restrict women's employment in the civil service and to prevent them from serving on juries; remained active in the senate until 1934 when her term ended. ❖ See also Marie O'Neill, *From Parnell to de Valera: A Biography of Jennie Wyse Power 1858–1941* (Blackwater, 1991); and *Women in World History*.

WYSMULLER, Truus (c. 1896–1978). See Wijsmuller-Meijer, Truus.

WYSOCZANSKA, Barbara (1949—). Polish fencer. Born Barbara Szeja, Aug 12, 1949, in Poland. ❖ At Moscow Olympics, won a bronze medal in indiv. foil (1980).

WYTHENS, Lady (d. 1708). See Taylor, Elizabeth.

X. *See Exene.*

XANTHIPPE (c. 435 BCE–?). Athenian wife of Socrates. Name variations: Xantippe. Born c. 435 BCE; death date unknown; m. Socrates (the Greek philosopher); children—only sons are known: Lamprocles, Sophroniscus and Menexenus. ❖ Wife of Socrates whose name, thanks to the philosopher's disciples, has for centuries been a byword for a sharp-tongued shrew (it is possible that Socrates was married once before, for a suspect ancient tradition also associates him with a Myrto, reportedly the daughter of the prominent Athenian politician Aristides the Just); is often portrayed as a nag, because she scolded Socrates in public for his failure to shoulder his familial responsibilities; was banished by Socrates from his presence when she could not refrain from bewailing the injustice of his death sentence at the hands of the Athenian people. ❖ See also *Women in World History.*

XENE (fl. 1300s). *See Maria of Armenia.*

XENIA (1582–1622). *See Godunova, Xenia.*

XENIA ALEXANDROVNA (1876–1960). Grand duchess. Name variations: Xenia Romanov or Romanof. Born April 6, 1876 (some sources cite April 18, 1875); died April 20, 1960, in London, England; dau. of Marie Feodorovna (1847–1928) and Alexander III (1845–1894), tsar of Russia (r. 1881–1894); sister of Nicholas II, tsar of Russia (r. 1894–1917); m. Alexander Michaelovitch (1866–1933, grandson of Nicholas I of Russia), grand duke, on July 25, 1894; children: Irina (1895–1970, who m. Felix Yussoupov, count Soumarokov-Elston); Andrew (b. 1897); Theodore (b. 1898); Nikita (b. 1900); Dmitri (b. 1901); Rostislav (b. 1902); Basil (b. 1907).

XENIA CHESTOV or SHESTOV (1560–1631). *See Martha the Nun.*

XI TAIHOU (1835–1908). *See Cixi.*

XIAN DONGMEI (1975—). Chinese judoka. Born Sept 15, 1975, in China. ❖ Won a gold medal for 52 kg at Athens Olympics (2004); placed 1st at 2 Super A Tournaments for 52 kg (2004).

XIANG JINGYU (1895–1928). Chinese revolutionary and women's-rights activist. Name variations: Xiang Jingyu; Hsiang Ching-yu or Hsiang Chin-yu; incorrectly Hsiang Ching Yu and Xiang Chingyu. Pronunciation: SEE-ahng JING-yew. Born in Hunan, China, 1895; captured by Chinese Nationalist Party and executed, May 1, 1928; father was a well-to-do merchant in town of Xupu; received traditional Confucian education and then attended a modern academy, the Zhou-nan Girls' School in Changsha; m. fellow provincial Cai Hesen (1890–1931), 1921; children: daughter Yi-yi (b. 1921); son Bo-bo (b. around 1924). ❖ Most prominent of the earliest leaders of the Chinese Communist Party who became a revolutionary model for the 1st generation of Chinese communist female activists; started a modern co-educational primary school in Xupu; went to France (1919); attended a French women's school and worked part-time in a rubber plant and a textile mill; returned to China (around 1921) and joined Chinese Communist Party, becoming the 1st female member of the Central Committee and head of its women's movement; organized and led strikes in foreign factories in Shanghai (1924) and worked at Shanghai University; went to Moscow for further education and training (1926–27); returned to China and engaged in radical labor activity; captured by the Guomindang and executed (May 1, 1928), was defiant to the last; remembered with great reverence as "the grandmother of the Chinese revolution," dedicated her life to building the Communist Party, particularly among women; also had a strong interest in education and a love of poetry and literature; was both respected and loved by her comrades. ❖ See also *Women in World History.*

XIAO HONG (1911–1942). Chinese author. Name variations: Hsiao Hung; Chang Nai Ying; Zhang Naiying; Chiao Yin. Born Zhang Naiying in a wealthy landholding family in northeast Heilongjiang Province, near Harbin, China, 1911; died Jan 22, 1942, in Hong Kong; attended a girls' school in Harbin, beginning 1926; fled from an arranged marriage, 1928; became common-law wife of Duanmu Hongliang, 1938. ❖ One of the most important modern Chinese writers, published under several names but is best known as Xiao Hong; became a celebrity in Shanghai with novel, *Shengsi Chang* (*The Field of Life and Death,* 1935), which describes life in northeast China during the Japanese occupation; published 2nd novel, *Shangshi Jie* (*Market Street,* 1936); in Chonqwig, collaborated with writer Hu Feng and published a leftist journal, *Qu-yne*; published *Minzu Hun* (*Soul of a Nation,* 1940) to commemorate the life of her friend and mentor Lu Xun, followed by *Hulan He Chuan* (*Tales of Hulan River,* 1941), which describe her unhappy childhood. ❖ See also *Women in World History.*

XIAOJIAO SUN (1984—). Chinese gymnast. Born Dec 18, 1984, in Zhe Jiang, China. ❖ At World championships, was a bronze medal for balance beam (2001).

XIAOQIN XIAN HUANGHOU (1835–1908). *See Cixi.*

XIDE XIE (1921–2000). *See Xie Xide.*

XIE HUILIN (1975—). Chinese soccer player. Born Jan 17, 1975, in Shanghai, China. ❖ Joined the Chinese national team (1992); won a team silver medal at Atlanta Olympics (1996).

XIE WANYING (1900–1999). Chinese essayist, poet, short-story writer and children's writer. Name variations: Hsieh Wan-ying; Hsieh Wang-ying; (pseudonym) Bing Xin (Ping Hsin). Born Oct 5, 1900, in Fuzhou, Fujian Province, China; died 1999; dau. of a naval officer; graduate of Yanjing University, 1923; m. Wu Wenzao (one of the founders of anthropology in China), 1929. ❖ Encouraged by May Fourth Movement (1919), published 1st collection of short stories, *Two Families*; studied in US at Wellesley College (1921–26), receiving MA; taught Chinese literature at Yanjing (1926–36); contributed essays to newspapers and journals about her experience in US, which were collected and published as *Letters to Young Readers,* the beginning of a series that brought her fame; taught at Tokyo University (1947–51); active in Chinese Writers Association and All China Federation of Literary and Art Circles, traveled in Europe, Asia and Africa; served as deputy of Fujian province; despite being a tremendously popular writer, her reputation took a beating during the Cultural Revolution (1967–72), but she was soon held in high esteem once more; other writings include *More Letters to Young Readers, A Maze of Stars and Spring Water, About Women, After the Return* and *We Have Woken up the Spring*; translated poetry of Rabindranath Tagore and Kahlil Gibran.

XIE XIDE (1921–2000). Chinese physicist. Name variations: Hsieh Hsi-teh. Born Mar 19, 1921, in Quanzhou, Fujian Province, China; dau. of a professor of physics; died 2000; Amoy University (now Xiamen University), BSc, 1946; Smith College, MA in physics, 1949; Massachusetts Institute of Technology, PhD, 1951; m. Cao Tianqin, May 17, 1952. ❖ One of China's leading physicists, was a teaching assistant at Shanghai University (1946–47); served as lecturer in physics at Fudan University (1952–56), then associate professor (1956–62) and became professor (1962); during Cultural Revolution (1966–67), lost job and was disgraced; reinstated (1974); founded the Institute of Modern Physics (1977); served as vice president of Fudan University (1978–83), then president (1983–88) and university advisor (1988–94); elected to Chinese Academy of Sciences (1980) and was a member of its presidium (1981–96); chaired the 21st International Conference on Semiconductor Physics in Beijing (1993), among several other conferences. Wrote *Semiconductor Physics* (with K. Huang, 1958), *Group Theory and Its Applications* (1986) and over 90 papers; received over 10 honorary doctorates and the Ho Leung Ho Lee Foundation of Hong Kong's Award for the Advancement of Science and Technology (1997).

XIMENA. *Variant of Jimena.*

XING HUINA (1984—). Chinese runner. Born Feb 25, 1984, in Shangdong Province, China. ❖ Won a gold medal for 10,000 meters at Athens Olympics (2004).

XIRINACS, Olga (1936—). Spanish poet and novelist. Name variations: Olga Xirinacs Diaz. Born 1936 in Tarragona, Spain. ❖ Catalan writer, studied and taught piano; is the only woman who has been awarded the title Mestre en Gai Saber (Master in the Art of Poetry) in the Barcelona Jocs; poetry collections include *Botons de tiges* (1977), *Clau de blau* (1978), *Lençol de noces* (1979), *Preparo el te sota palmeres rogues* (1981), *Marina* (1986), and *Muralla* (1993); novels include *Música de cambra* (1982), *Interior amb difunts* (1983), *Al meu cap una llosa* (1985), *Enteraments lleugers* (1991), *Xocolata* (1994), *La tarda a Venècia* (1999) and *L'escrivent de làpides* (2002).

XIU LIJUAN (1957—). Chinese basketball player. Born Oct 26, 1957, in China. ❖ At Los Angeles Olympics, won a bronze medal in team competition (1984).

XOC, Lady (c. 660–c. 720). Mayan royal. Ritual partner of Shield Jaguar, Mayan king of Yaxchilan, a ceremonial city of Mayan culture. ❖ Performed auto-sacrifice rituals as part of her role as the partner of a king. Her specific actions are recorded on 2 carved lintels, currently housed in the British Museum. ❖ See also *Women in World History.*

XOSTARIA, Anastasia Eristavi (1868–1951). *See Eristavi-Xostaria, Anastasia.*

X-RAY SPEX.
See Logic, Lora.
See Styrene, Poly.

XU JIAN. Chinese softball player. Born in China. ❖ Won a silver medal at Atlanta Olympics (1996).

XU NANNAN (1979—). Chinese aerials skier. Pronunciation: JOO naan-naan. Born Nov 26, 1979, in Benxi City, Liaoning Province, China; attended Shengyang Physical Education College. ❖ Began career as a tumbler; won a silver medal for freestyle aerials at Nagano Olympics with 186.97 points (1998); placed 2nd at Asian Games (1996) and World Cup (1997).

XU YANMEI (1971—). Chinese diver. Born Feb 9, 1971, in Nanchang, Jiangxi Province, China; attended Hainan University. ❖ At Seoul Olympics, won a gold medal in platform (1988); placed 1st in platform at Asian Games (1990) and 1st at FINA World Cup (1987); became an international diving referee. Inducted into International Swimming Hall of Fame (2000).

XU YANWEI (1984—). Chinese swimmer. Born June 14, 1984, in China. ❖ At World championships SC, won 4 x 200-meter freestyle relay (2002); won a silver medal for 4 x 200-meter freestyle relay at Athens Olympics (2004); won 4 World Cup events (2002–03).

XUAN, Bui Thi (d. 1771). *See Bui Thi Xuan.*

XUE SHEN (1978—). Chinese pairs skater. Pronounced SHOO-ee Chen. Born Nov 3, 1978, in Harbin, China. ❖ Began skating with partner Hongbo Zhao (1992); won Chinese nationals (1993–99, 2001), Asian Winter Games (1996, 1999, 2003), NHK Trophy (1997, 2000, 2001), Skate Canada (1998), Nations Cup (2001), Cup of Russia (2002); won a bronze medal at Salt Lake City Olympics (2002) and gold medals at World championships (2002, 2003).

XUE TAO (c. 760–c. 832). Chinese poet. Name variations: Hsueh T'ao; Hsüeh Tao. Born c. 760 in Xian, China; died c. 832; dau. of a minor government official. ❖ Lived during Tang Dynasty; became singer to support mother after father's death; became favorite concubine of Wei Gao, military governor of Sichuan province; met many prominent figures, including poets Bo Juyi and Yuan Zhen; poetry was widely popular and admired by other poets; wrote poems on handmade paper which became known as Xue Tao Stationery; only 100 poems extant.

XUED CONG (1963—). *See Cong Xued.*

YAA AKYAA (c. 1837–c. 1921). Asantehemaa (queenmother) of the Ashanti Empire. Born into the royal matriclan of Oyoko, c. 1837, in Kumasi, Ashanti (later Ghana); died in Seychelles Islands, c. 1921 (some sources cite after 1896); m. Kwasi Gyambibi (advisor to asantehene); children: 13, including Kwaka Dua II (asantehene, 1884); Agyemon Badu; and Agyeman Prempe (also known as Kwaku Dua III or Prempeh I, asantehene, 1888–1896). ❖ Elected asantehemaa (queen-mother) of Ejisu, a state within the Ashanti Empire (1884), during the disarray in the Ashanti Empire; with her people ravaged by war and new diseases, set about resurrecting the Ashanti Empire; as a king was required, placed her sons Kwaka Dua II and Agyemon Badu in the positions of asantehene and heir apparent respectively, but both men died from European-borne chicken pox; alone in ruling the Ashanti, repeatedly requested diplomatic representation from the British government (1884–88); maneuvered 3rd son Prempeh I into power (1888); was arrested on false charges and held without trial by the British, who hoped to finally subdue the troublesome Ashanti; ruled as queenmother until imprisonment (1896); lived out her days exiled on the Seychelles Islands, 1,000 miles off the east coast of Africa. ❖ See also *Women in World History.*

YAA ASANTEWAA (c. 1850–1921). Asantehemaa (queenmother) of the Ashanti Empire. Name variations: Nana Yaa Asantewaa; Yaa Asantewah; Yah Asantiwa; Yaa Asantuah; Yaa Asantewa. Pronunciation: Yaah A-san-TE-waah. Born Yaa Asantewaa between 1840 and 1850 at Besease in the Edweso (Ejisu) state, Ashanti; died Oct 5, 1921, in the Seychelles; dau. of Ataa Po and Ampomah of Ampabame (both farmers); sister of Afrane Panin, Ejisuhene or chief of Ejisu, r. 1884–88; children: daughter, Nana Ama Serwaah of Boankra; grandmother of Kofi Teng, later Ejisuhene. ❖ Queenmother of Ejisu, Ashanti, in Ghana, who resisted British colonialism and incited her people to fight the British in a war that bore her name; enstoolment as queenmother of Ejisu (about 1884); between the period of her brother's death and her grandson's enstoolment (1888–92), became chief of Ejisu, the 16th chief of that state, and again after 1896, when her grandson was deposed and exiled by the British; a courageous and resolute woman, led the war against the British (April 1900), which is often referred to as the Yaa Asantewaa war; became a "wanted person" toward end of 1900; escaped to Ahafo, north of Ashanti; captured (late 1900); subsequently exiled to the Seychelles Islands (1901); converted to Christianity and baptized by British in the Seychelles (1904). ❖ See also *Women in World History.*

YABE, Sayaka. Japanese inline skater. Born in Japan. ❖ Won gold in Women's Street/Park at X Games (1997 and 1999).

YACCO, Sada (d. 1946). *See Yakko, Sada.*

YAEL (fl. 1125 BCE). *See Jael.*

YAKKO, Sada (d. 1946). Japanese actress. Name variations: Madame Sada-yakko; Sada Yacco; Sada Jacco. Born in Tokyo, Japan; died Feb 7, 1946, age 74; m. Kawakami Otojiro (founder and leader of the New School, a new form of theater). ❖ Began career as a Geisha; appeared as Desdemona in the Japanese version of Othello, as well as Ophelia, Monna Vanna, and Tomoye in a farce entitled *The New Othello*; with husband and his company, appeared in London, then at the Paris Exhibition (1900) to rave reviews; performed in America (1903).

YAKOVLEFF, Maria (1898–1980). *See Shabelska, Maria.*

YAKOVLEVA, Olga (1963—). Soviet basketball player. Born Dec 15, 1963, in USSR. ❖ At Seoul Olympics, won a bronze medal in team competition (1988).

YAKUNCHIKOVA, Maria (1870–1901). Russian artist. Name variations: Maria Vasilevna Yakunchikova. Born 1870 in Wiesbaden, Germany; died of TB, 1901, in Chêne Bougerie, Switzerland; grew up in Moscow; sister of Natalya Polenova; niece of the wife of Pavel Tretyakov, a famous art collector, and related by sister's marriage to artist Vasily Polenov; studied painting privately with N. A. Martynov; attended Moscow School of Painting, Sculpture and Architecture; studied at Académie Julian in Paris, 1889. ❖ Developed an interest in Russian history, architecture, and artifacts under the influence of artist Elena Polenova and began to collect Russian arts and crafts (1887); traveled to Europe (1888); studied art in Paris (1889); began experimenting with wood engraving, etching and lithography (1893); helped to create an exhibition of Russian handicrafts for Exposition Universelle in Paris (1900); her work was imbued with the nostalgia and somber mood characteristic of the Symbolist movement; works include *Bois de Boulogne* (1896), *The Window* (1896), *Aspen and Fir-Tree* (1896), *The Flame* (1897), *Fear* (Polenov Estate Museum), *The Unattainable* (1893–95), *Little Girl and Wood Spirit* (embroidered panel, c. 1900). ❖ See also *Women in World History.*

YALE, Caroline A. (1848–1933). American educator. Born Caroline Ardelia Yale, Sept 29, 1848, in Charlotte, Vermont; died July 2, 1933, in Northampton, Massachusetts; dau. of William Lyman Yale (farmer and educator) and Ardelia (Strong) Yale; attended Mt. Holyoke Seminary, 1866–68. ❖ Introduced innovations that influenced how the deaf were taught in US; served as teacher, then principal, at the Clarke Institution for Deaf Mutes, later renamed Clarke School for the Deaf (1870–1922); popularized her new system of phonetic symbols with the booklet *Formation and Development of Elementary English Sounds* (1892); co-founded and elected a director of the American Association to Promote the Teaching of Speech to the Deaf (1890). ❖ See also autobiography *Years of Building: Memories of a Pioneer in a Special Field of Education* (1931); and *Women in World History.*

YALOW, Rosalyn (1921—). American medical physicist. Born Rosalyn Sussman, July 19, 1921, in South Bronx, New York; dau. of Simon Sussman (paper and twine jobber) and Clara (Zipper) Sussman (piece sewer); Hunter College, AB, 1941; University of Illinois, MS, 1942, PhD, 1945; m. Aaron Yalow, June 6, 1943 (died 1992); children: Benjamin Yalow (b. 1952); Elanna Yalow (b. 1954). ❖ Physicist who was awarded the 1977 Nobel Prize in medicine and physiology for her development of radioimmunoassay (RIA); was the only female research engineer at Federal Telecommunications Laboratory, International Telephone and Telegraph Corporation (1945–46); was a lecturer and assistant professor of physics, Hunter College (1946–50); went from part-time consulting physicist to chief of radioisotopic services, Radioimmunoassay Reference Laboratory, and director of the Solomon A. Berson Research Laboratory, Radioisotope Unit, Veterans Administration Hospital, Bronx, New York (1947–91); served as consultant at Lenox Hill Hospital (1956–62); published watershed article about work with insulin antibodies (1956); introduced radioimmunoassay to scientific community (1959); was a research professor at Mt. Sinai School of Medicine (1968–91); elected to National Academy of Sciences (1975); saw the Rosalyn S. Yalow Research and Development Award established by American Diabetes Association (1978), because, as a result of her research, thousands of medical facilities worldwide are able to utilize inexpensive, quick, and sensitive testing to diagnose and detect crucial biomedical substances in the human body, and modern insulin has been genetically engineered to be identical to human insulin, saving many lives; elected to American Academy of Arts and Sciences (1979); appointed distinguished professor-at-large at Albert Einstein College of Medicine, Yeshiva University (1979); served as chair, Department of Clinical Sciences, Montefiore Hospital and Medical Center, the Bronx (1980–85); writings include (edited with Berson) *Peptide Hormones* (2 vols., 1973), (with Luft and Accary) *Radioimmunoassay: Methodology and Applications in Physiology and in Clinical Studies: Commemorative Issue for Solomon A. Berson* (1974). Awarded Albert Lasker Prize for Basic Medical Research (1976), Nobel Prize (1977), and National Medal of Science (1988). ❖ See also Eugene Straus, *Rosalyn Yalow, Nobel Laureate: Her Life and Work in Medicine* (Plenum, 1998); and *Women in World History.*

YAMADA, Eri (1984—). Japanese softball player. Born Mar 8, 1984, in Japan. ❖ Outfielder, won a team bronze at Athens Olympics (2004).

YAMADA, Isuzu (1917—). Japanese stage and screen actress. Born Mitsu Yamada, Feb 5, 1917, in Osaka, Honshu, Japan; dau. of an actor; m. 6 times, including Teinosuke Kinugasa (director); children: Michiko Saga (b. 1934, actress). ❖ At 14, made film debut in *Kokushi Muso* (1932), followed by *Aizo toge, Orizuro Osen* (title role), *Maria no Oyuki* (title role), *Chushingura, Joyu, Takekurabe, Nagareru, Samurai Nippon* and *Giwaku,* among others; best known in the West for *Hiroshima, Throne of Blood, The Lower Depths* and *Yojimbo*; worked with such directors as Kenji Mizoguchi and Teinosuke Kinugasa.

YAMADA, Mitsuye (1923—). Japanese-born American writer. Name variations: Mitsuye May Yamada; Mitsuye Yasutaka Yamada. Born in Fukouka, Japan, July 5, 1923; came to US, 1926, and raised in Seattle, Washington; naturalized citizen, 1955; dau. of Jack Kaichiro Yasutake (interpreter) and Hide (Shiraki) Yasutake (seamstress); New York University, BA, 1947; University of Chicago, MA, 1953; further graduate study at University of Chicago and University of California, Irvine; m. Yoshikazu Yamada (research chemist); children: Jeni, Stephen, Douglas, Hedi. ❖ During WWII, was held with family at the Minidoka Relocation Center in Idaho (1942–44); began teaching as an instructor at Cypress College in California (1966); joined faculty of Fullerton College as an instructor (1970), becoming associate professor (1976) and coordinator of the women's program; served as writer-in-residence at Pitzer College and San Diego University; published *Camp Notes and Other Poems* (1976), about the years spent at the Idaho camp; also published *Desert Run: Poems and Stories* (1989); contributed to various literary magazines, including *Velvet Wings, Willmore City* and *Plexus*; with

Nellie Wong, collaborated on "Mitsuye and Nellie: Two Asian-American Women Poets," a biographical documentary made for public tv (1981); served on national board of Amnesty International USA.

YAMADA, Miyo (c. 1976—). Japanese softball player. Born c. 1976 in Japan. ❖ Won a team silver medal at Sydney Olympics (2000).

YAMADA, Waka (1879–1956). Japanese writer, translator, and social reformer. Born Asaba Waka, Dec 1, 1879, in Kimura, Kanagawa Prefecture, Japan; died Sept 6, 1956; dau. of Asaba Kunihisa (farmer); m. Araki Hichijiro, Aug 20, 1896 (div.); m. Yamada Kakichi (teacher of Western languages, sociology and economics), 1905. ❖ Ardent advocate for underprivileged and abused women, who became one of the most respected women of prewar Japan; to aid family's declining fortunes, sailed for US (c. 1897), but was seized by pimps upon arrival on West Coast and sold to a brothel; known as "Arabian Oyae," remained in forced prostitution in Seattle until a man helped her escape; sought protection from Cameron House, a Methodist home for the rehabilitation of prostitutes in San Francisco (1902), where she received vocational and religious instruction and served as an interpreter; on marriage (1905), returned to Japan where she was introduced to female activists of Seitosha (The Bluestockings) who published a literary feminist journal, *Seito*; began a prolific career as a translator and writer, 1st by translating the essays of South African feminist Olive Schreiner; translated book-length works of Lester Ward, an American sociologist who wrote *Women's Natural Instincts* and *Women's Education,* and the works of Swedish feminist Ellen Key, including *Love and Marriage* and *The Century of the Child*; published a collection of her essays (1920), concerning labor unions, working conditions for women textile workers, female suffrage, and new trends in women's issues; began publishing a popular advice column in the Tokyo *Asahi Shimbun* (1926), a mass-circulation daily; elected chair of Motherhood Protection League (1935); founded Hatagaya House for Mothers and Children and Hatagaya Nursery School (1939). ❖ See also Yamazaki Tomoko, *The Story of Yamada Waka: From Prostitute to Feminist Pioneer* (Kodansha, 1985); and *Women in World History.*

YAMAGUCHI, Kristi (1971—). American figure skater. Born Kristi Tsuya Yamaguchi, July 12, 1971, in Hayward, CA; m. Bret Hedican (hockey player), July 8, 2000. ❖ Captured gold medals in ladies' singles and pairs (with Rudy Galindo) at World Jr. championships (1988); won silver medals at US National championships (1989, 1990, 1991) and a gold medal (1992); won back-to-back World titles (1991, 1992); won the gold medal at Albertville Olympics (1992). Inducted into World and US Figure Skating Hall of Fame (1998). ❖ See also autobiography, *Kristi Yamaguchi: Always Dream*; and *Women in World History.*

YAMAJI, Noriko (1970—). Japanese softball player. Born Sept 17, 1970, in Hyogo, Japan. ❖ Catcher, won a team silver medal at Sydney Olympics (2000) and a team bronze at Athens Olympics (2004).

YAMAMOTO, Hiromi (1970—). Japanese speedskater. Born April 21, 1970, in Japan. ❖ Won a bronze medal for 5,000 meters at Lillehammer Olympics (1994).

YAMAMOTO, Michiko (1936—). Japanese novelist and poet. Born 1936 in Tokyo, Japan. ❖ Lived with husband in Australia and wrote about experiences there; works include *There is a Snake, An Umbrella on Sunday, Trees of People, Magic,* which won the Shincho Prize (1972), and *Betty-san,* which won Akutagawa Prize (1972).

YAMAMOTO, Noriko (1945—). Japanese volleyball player. Born Mar 6, 1945, in Japan. ❖ At Munich Olympics, won a silver medal in team competition (1972).

YAMATO-HIME-MIKOTO (fl. 3rd c.). See Himiko.

YAMAUCHI, Wakako (1924—). Japanese-American playwright. Born Wakako Nakamura, Oct 24, 1924, in Westmoreland, CA. ❖ Wrote *And the Soul Shall Dance* (1974), *Shirley Temple Hotcha-Cha* (1978), *The Music Lesson* (1980), *Songs That Made the Hit Parade* (1985), *The Memento* (1986), *The Trip* (1988), *Not a Through Street* (1990), and *The Chairman's Wife (A Gang of One)* (1990).

YAMA YAMA GIRL, The (1888–1931). See McCoy, Bessie.

YAMAZAKI, Tomoko (1931—). Japanese historian. Born 1931 in Nagasaki prefecture, Japan. ❖ Works often focus on lives of unknown women; wrote *The Eighth House of Japanese Prostitutes in the South Sea Islands* (1973), which was based on oral history and won the Oya Soichi

Prize for Non-Fiction; also wrote *The Graves in Sandakan* and *Love and Blood-History of Interchange of Asian Women.*

YAMAZAKI, Toyoko (1924—). **Japanese novelist.** Born 1924 in Osaka, Japan. ❖ Works include *A Curtain with a Shop Name* (1957), *Hana Noren, Bonchi, A Huge White Tower, The Barren Zone,* and *Two Fatherlands.*

YAMAZAKI, Yaeko (1950—). **Japanese volleyball player.** Born Sept 2, 1950, in Japan. ❖ At Munich Olympics, won a silver medal in team competition (1972).

YAMETSU-HIME (fl. 3rd c.). *See Himiko.*

YAMPOLSKY, Mariana (1925–2002). **American-born Mexican photographer, artist, and writer.** Born Sept 6, 1925, in Chicago, Illinois; died May 3, 2002, in Mexico City; became a Mexican citizen in 1955; University of Chicago, BA in humanities, 1945; studied graphic arts at the Escuela de Artes Gráficos, Mexico City, 1948–49; studied photography with Lola Alvarez Bravo at Academia de Saint Carlos, Mexico City; m. Arjen van der Sluis, 1967. ❖ In Mexico City, worked at the Taller de Gráfica Popular, which designed posters, book illustrations and other commercial art (1946–58); also created illustrations for newspapers, magazines and children's books; began experimenting with photography (1948) both on her own and with Lola Alvarez Bravo; helped found Salón de la Plástica Mexicana (1951); illustrated for several newspapers, including *El Nacional, Excelsior,* and *El Día* (1956–62); co-edited, with Leopold Méndez, *Lo Efímero y lo Eterno del Arte Popular Mexicano* (1970); was an official photographer for Mexico City Olympics (1968); published 1st book dedicated solely to her photographs, *La Casa en la tierra* (1981), followed by *La Casa que canta* (1982), both pertain to Mexican Indian architecture; also published a book on the once-grand haciendas, *Estancias del olvido* (1987). ❖ See also *Women in World History.*

YAN BA (1962—). *See Ba Yan.*

YAN FANG. **Chinese softball player.** Born in China. ❖ Won a silver medal at Atlanta Olympics (1996).

YAN, Mari. *See Yañez, María Flora.*

YANARANOP, Sukanya (1931—). **Thai novelist and short-story writer.** Name variations: (pseudonym) Asokesin Krisan. Born 1931 in Thailand. ❖ Published over 100 novels and many short stories; works include *Rua manut* (1968) and *Tawan Tok Din* (1972). Received National Artist Award for Literature (1988).

YÁÑEZ, María Flora (1898–1982). **Chilean novelist and short-story writer.** Name variations: Maria Flora Yanez; (pseudonym) Mari Yan. Born María Flora Yáñez de Echeverria, Sept 1898, in Santiago, Chile; died April 7, 1982, in Santiago; dau. of Eliodoro Yáñez, founder of *La Nación*; sister of writer Alvaro Yáñez Bianchi, also known as Juan Emar (who m. Inés Echeverria, feminist writer). ❖ Studied at Sorbonne, Paris, and lectured in Spain, Uruguay, and Peru; founded the Pen club of Chile (1936); writings include *El abrazo de la tierra* (1933), *Espejo sin imagen* (1936), *Las Cenizas* (1942), (autobiography) *Visiones de infancia* (1947, Visions of Childhood), *Juan Estrella* (1954), *El último faro* (1968) and *El Peldaño.*

YANG BO (1973—). **Chinese gymnast.** Born Sept 8, 1973, in China. ❖ Won Beijing International (1989) and China Cup (1990); placed 2nd all-around at Australian Grand Prix (1989) and 3rd at French International (1990); at World championships, won a bronze medal in team all-around (1989); came in 4th all-around at World Cup and earned a gold on balance beam (1990); does commentary on Chinese television.

YANG CHIANG (b. 1911). *See Yang Jiang.*

YANG HAO (1980—). **Chinese volleyball player.** Born Mar 21, 1980, in China. ❖ Opposite hitter, won a team gold medal at Athens Olympics (2004).

YANG JIANG (b. 1911). **Chinese critic, memoirist, translator and educator.** Name variations: Yang Chiang. Born 1911 in China; studied at Qinghua University and in England and France; m. Qian Zhongshu (scholar, died 1998); children: daughter Qian Yuan (1937–1997, professor). ❖ Taught university in Beijing and did scholarly work on Spanish, French, and English literature; her translations are regarded as masterpieces; works include *The Slushy School of Spring* (1976), the semi-autobiographical *A Cadre School Life: Six Chapters* (1982), which focuses

on her experiences during the Cultural Revolution and has been praised for its irony and humor, and *The Bath* (1989); translations include Le Sage's *Gil Blas* (1956), Cervantes's *Lazarillo de Tormes* (1951), and *Don Quixote* (1978).

YANG SHAOQI. **Chinese fencer.** Name variations: Yang Shao-qi; Yang Shao Qi. Born in China. ❖ China's top fencer, won a bronze medal for team épée at Sydney Olympics (2000).

YANG WEI (1979—). **Chinese badminton player.** Born Jan 13, 1979, in Guangdong Province, China. ❖ Won a silver medal for doubles at Sydney Olympics (2000) and a gold medal for doubles at Athens Olympics (2004).

YANG WENYI (1972—). **Chinese swimmer.** Born Jan 11, 1972, in Shanghai. ❖ At Seoul Olympics, won a silver medal in 50-meter freestyle (1988); at Barcelona Olympics, won a gold medal in 50-meter freestyle and a silver in 4 x 100-meter freestyle relay (1992).

YANG XIA (1977—). **Chinese weightlifter.** Born 1977 in Hunan Province, China. ❖ Won a gold medal at Asian Games (1998); won a gold medal for 48–53 kg at Sydney Olympics (2000), setting 3 world records.

YANG XIAO (1964—). **Chinese rower.** Born Mar 6, 1964, in China. ❖ At Seoul Olympics, won a bronze medal in coxed eights and a silver medal in coxed fours (1988).

YANG XIAOJUN (1963—). **Chinese volleyball player.** Born May 18, 1963, in China. ❖ Won a gold medal at Los Angeles Olympics (1984) and a bronze medal at Seoul Olympics (1988), both in team competition.

YANG XILAN (1961—). **Chinese volleyball player.** Born Mar 16, 1961, in China. ❖ Won a gold medal at Los Angeles Olympics (1984) and a bronze medal at Seoul Olympics (1988), both in team competition.

YANG YANG (1976—). **Chinese short-track speedskater.** Name variations: Yang Yang (A). Born Aug 24, 1976, in Heilongjiang Province, China. ❖ Known officially as Yang Yang (A) to distinguish from teammate Yang Yang (S), won a silver medal for the 3,000-meter relay at Nagano Olympics (1998); won gold medals for 1,000 meters and 500 meters and a silver medal for 3,000-meter relay at Salt Lake City Olympics, giving China its 1st ever Winter Games gold medal (2002); won a bronze medal for 1,000 meters at Torino Olympics (2006); won 18 World championships (1997–2005).

YANG YANG (1977—). **Chinese short-track speedskater.** Name variations: Yang Yang (S). Born Sept 14, 1977, from Jilin Province, China. ❖ Known officially as Yang Yang (S) to distinguish from teammate Yang Yang (A), won silver medals for the 3,000-meter relay, 500 meters, and 1,000 meters at Nagano Olympics (1998); won a silver medal for 3,000-meter relay and a bronze medal for 1,000 meters at Salt Lake City (2002).

YANG YING (1977—). **Chinese table tennis player.** Born 1977 in Xuzhou, Jiangsu Province, China. ❖ Won World Cup (1995); won WTTC team and doubles championships (1997); won a silver medal for doubles at Sydney Olympics (2000); retired from national team (2001).

YANG YOUNG-JA (1964—). **Korean table tennis player.** Born July 6, 1964, in South Korea. ❖ At Seoul Olympics, won a gold medal in doubles (1988).

YANG YU (1985—). **Chinese swimmer.** Born Feb 6, 1985, in China. ❖ At World championships, placed 1st for 4 x 100-meter medley relay (2003); at World championships SC, won 200-meter freestyle (2000) and 4 x 200-meter freestyle relay (2002); won a silver medal for 4 x 200-meter freestyle relay at Athens Olympics (2004); won 15 World Cup events (2000–04).

YANG YUN (c. 1984—). **Chinese gymnast.** Born c. 1984 in China. ❖ At Sydney Olympics, won bronze medals for team all-around and uneven bars (2000); won gold medal at East Asian Games.

YANJMAA, Sühbaataryn (1893–1962). **Mongolian head of state.** Name variations: Yanjmaa Suhbaataryn. Born 1893; died 1962; m. Nemendeyn Yanjmaa, also known as Sühbaatar (a Mongolian national hero). ❖ Was 1st deputy chair of the Presidium of the People's Great Khural of Mongolia; acted as chair of the Presidium (effectively head of state) during a vacancy in that position (Sept 23, 1953–July 7, 1954); except for queens, was the 1st woman political ruler in contemporary Mongolian history.

YANO, Hiromi (1955—). Japanese volleyball player. Born Jan 5, 1955, in Japan. ❖ At Montreal Olympics, won a gold medal in team competition (1976).

YANOVICH, Irina (1976—). *See Yanovych, Iryna.*

YANOVYCH, Iryna (1976—). Ukrainian cyclist. Name variations: Irina Yanovich. Born July 14, 1976, in Ukraine. ❖ Won a bronze medal for sprint at Sydney Olympics (2000).

YAO FEN (1967—). Chinese badminton player. Born Jan 2, 1967, in China. ❖ At Barcelona Olympics, won a bronze medal in doubles (1992).

YAPING DENG (b. 1973). *See Deng Yaping.*

YARBOROUGH, Sara (1950—). American ballet and modern dancer. Name variations: Sara Yarborough Smith. Born 1950 in New York, NY; raised in Haiti; dau. of Lavinia Williams (ballet dancer). ❖ Trained by mother in New York City and Haiti; studied at Harkness Ballet School and School of American Ballet; danced with Harkness Ballet (1967–71) and Alvin Ailey Dance Theater (1971–75, 1977), where she performed in almost all of Ailey's repertory works, including *Hidden Rites, The Lark Ascending,* and *Revelations,* and created roles for his *La Mooche* (1974); also danced with City Center Joffrey Ballet (1975–76).

YARBRO, Chelsea Quinn (1942—). American science-fiction writer. Name variations: (pseudonyms) Quinn Fawcett; Vanessa Pryor; Terry Nelson Bonner. Born Sept 15, 1942, in Berkeley, CA; m. Donald P. Simpson, 1969 (div. 1982). ❖ Worked as theater manager, playwright, children's counselor, and composer; writings include *Ogilvie, Tallant and Moon* (1976), *Time of the Four Horsemen* (1976), *Hotel Transylvania* (1978), *Dead and Buried* (1980), *Path of the Eclipse* (1981), *Hyacinths* (1983), *The Mortal Glamour* (1985), *Beastnights* (1989), *Michael's People* (1989), *Bad Medicine* (1990), *Out of the House of Life* (1990), *Better in the Dark* (1993), *Against the Brotherhood* (1997), *Monet's Ghost* (1997), *In the Face of Death* (2001) and *Siren Song* (2003). Won World Fantasy, Bram Stoker, and British Fantasy Society awards.

YARD, Molly (1912–2005). American feminist and political activist. Name variations: Mary Alexander Yard. Born Mary Alexander Yard in 1912 in Chengdu, Szechwan province, China; died Sept 21, 2005 in Pittsburgh, PA; dau. of James and Mabelle (Hickok) Yard (both politically liberal American Methodist missionaries); moved to US, 1925; graduate of Swarthmore College, 1933; m. Sylvester Garrett (labor arbitrator), 1938; children: 1 daughter, 2 sons. ❖ In a career that spanned 7 decades, including a term as president of National Organization for Women (NOW), worked as the national secretary (1934), then chair, of the American Student Union (ASU); as a Democrat, made unsuccessful bid for a seat in the Pennsylvania state legislature (1964); worked for passage of the 1964 Civil Rights Act in conjunction with the Leadership Conference on Civil Rights; joined NOW and worked for the ratification of Equal Rights Amendment; was senior staff member on NOW Political Action Committee (1978–84), then served as NOW's national political director (1985–87); at 75, was elected to a 4-year term as president of national NOW (1987), serving until 1991; was part of the successful fight against the nomination of conservative Robert Bork to the Supreme Court. ❖ See also *Women in World History.*

YARDE, Margaret (1878–1944). English actress. Born April 2, 1878, in Dartmouth, England; died Mar 11, 1944, in London. ❖ Made London stage debut as Mrs. Gadband in *Mrs. Ellison's Answer* (1907), followed by *Isaac's Wife, The Thumbscrew, Turandot, Hush, The Purple Mask, Zozo, The Jew of Malta, The Alchemist, Ned Kean of Old Drury, The Way of the World* (as Lady Wishfort), *The Moon and Sixpence* and *Poison Pen;* made NY debut as Mrs. Rosel in *Many Waters* (1929); appeared in over 50 films, including *Madame Recamier* (as Mme de Stael, 1923), *Tiger Bay, No Escape, French Leave, French without Tears* and *Thursday's Child.*

YARMOLINSKY, Babette Deutsch (1895–1982). *See Deutsch, Babette.*

YARMOUTH, Countess of (1704–1765). *See Wallmoden, Amalie Sophie Marianne.*

YARROS, Rachelle (1869–1946). Russian-born physician and educator. Name variations: Rachelle Slobodinsky Yarros. Born May 18, 1869, at Berdechev, near Kiev, Russia; died Mar 17, 1946, in San Diego, CA; dau. of Joachim Slobodinsky and Bernice Slobodinsky; m. Victor S. Yarros (journalist), July 18, 1894; children: 1 daughter (adopted). ❖ Was 1st woman to attend College of Physicians and Surgeons in Boston (1890);

received medical degree from Woman's Medical College of Pennsylvania (1893); named instructor in clinical obstetrics (1897) and promoted to associate professor (1902) at College of Physicians and Surgeons at University of Illinois medical school; lived at social settlement Hull House (1907–27); helped found American Social Hygiene Association (1914); was vice-president of Illinois Social Hygiene League (1915); persuaded Chicago Woman's Club to form birth control committee (later Illinois Birth Control League, of which she was director); published *Modern Woman and Sex* (1933, reissued as *Sex Problems in Modern Society,* 1938). Saw physical health issues, such as venereal disease and rising birth rate, as interwoven with sociological problems such as loosening of divorce laws and juvenile delinquency.

YASODHARA (fl. 547 BCE). Indian princess. Name variations: Yasodhana. Born c. 563 BCE in Lumbini; m. Siddhartha Gautama, c. 547 BCE; children: at least one child (Rahula). ❖ At a young age, married a neighboring youth of 16, a prince named Siddhartha, who would also be known as the Buddha.

YASUI, Kono (1880–1971). Japanese biologist and cytologist. Born Feb 16, 1880, in Sanbonmatsu Ouchicho, Japan; died Mar 24, 1971. ❖ The 1st woman to receive a doctorate from a Japanese University, researched cytology at University of Chicago; studied coal at Harvard University (1915–16); established *Cytologya* magazine (1929); served as a research supervisor at Toyko Imperial University (1918–39); was a professor at the Tokyo Joshi Shihan Gakko (1919–49); began a survey (1945) of plants affected by fallout from the atomic bombs; appointed a professor at the Ochanomizu Women's University (1949–52). Honors include the Medal with Purple Ribbon (1955), the Order of the Precious Crown, Butterfly (1965) and Third Grade, Junior of the Court Rank.

YASUKO NAMBA (b. 1939). *See Namba, Yasuko.*

YATCHENKO, Irina (1965—). Belarusian discus thrower. Name variations: Irina Iattchenko. Born Oct 31, 1965, in Gomel, Belarus; m. Igor Astapkovich. ❖ Won a bronze medal at Sydney Olympics (2000) and a bronze medal at Athens Olympics (2004); placed 1st at World championships (2003).

YATES, Elizabeth (1799–1860). English actress. Born Elizabeth Brunton in 1799; died 1860; m. Frederick Henry Yates, in 1823 (died 1842). ❖ At 16, appeared as Desdemona in *Othello* opposite Charles Kemble (1815); arrived at Covent Garden in London (1817) where, over next several years, appeared as Rosalind in *As You Like It,* Viola in *Twelfth Night,* Beatrice in *Much Ado About Nothing* and Imogen in *Cymbeline;* also performed at Drury Lane (1824); served a year as co-manager of the Adelphi Theater in London after death of husband, who had owned the theater with an associate; retired (1849). ❖ See also *Women in World History.*

YATES, Elizabeth (c. 1844–1918). New Zealand politician. Name variations: Elizabeth Oman. Born Elizabeth Oman, between 1840 and 1848, in Caithness, Scotland; died Sept 6, 1918, in Auckland, New Zealand; dau. of George Oman (laborer) and Eleanor (Lannigan) Oman; m. Michael Yates, 1875 (died 1902). ❖ Immigrated with family to New Zealand (1853); became mayor of Onehunga (1893–94), the 1st woman mayor in British Empire; an effective administrator, despite local opposition, reorganized fire brigade, improved roads, and sanitation. ❖ See also *Dictionary of New Zealand Biography* (Vol. 2).

YATES, Frances Amelia (1899–1981). English scholar. Name variations: Dame Frances Yates. Born Nov 28, 1899, in Portsmouth, England; died Sept 29, 1981; dau. of James Alfred Yates (naval architect) and Hannah (Malpas) Yates; University College, London, BA, 1924, MA, 1926, DLitt, 1967. ❖ Historian of the Renaissance and Shakespearean scholar, devoted life to the Renaissance in 16th-century England, France, and Italy, including the literature and cultural customs of the time; published *John Florio: The Life of an Italian in Shakespeare's England* (1934), which won Rose Mary Crawshay Prize from British Academy; spent most of academic career at Warburg Institute (1941–67); was also a fellow of British Academy and Royal Society of London; writings include *The French Academies of the Sixteenth Century* (1947), *The Valois Tapestries* (1959), *Giordano Bruno and the Hermetic Tradition* (1964), *The Rosicrucian Enlightenment* (1972), *Astraea: The Imperial Theme* (1972), *Shakespeare's Last Plays; A New Approach* (1972), *The Occult Philosophy in the Elizabethan Age* (1979), and *Collected Essays,* Vol. 1· *Lull and Bruno* (1982), Vol. 2: *Renaissance and Reform: The Italian Contribution* (1983), Vol. 3: *Ideas and Ideals in the North European Renaissance* (1984).

Awarded Order of the British Empire (1972); made Dame of the British Empire (1977). ❖ See also *Women in World History*.

YATES, Mary Ann (1728–1787). English actress. Born Mary Ann Graham in 1728; died 1787; m. Richard Yates, around 1756. ❖ One of England's greatest tragic actresses, became known for a powerful dignity that was aptly suited for the role of a tragic heroine; acted in London theaters, in such roles as Medea (1767), Cleopatra in *Antony and Cleopatra*, Imogen in *Cymbeline*, Cordelia in *King Lear*, Desdemona in *Othello*, Constance in *The Life and Death of King John* and Anne Boleyn in *The Life of King Henry VIII* (1753–85); was joint manager of Haymarket Opera House (1774); also originated role of Berinthia in *Trip to Scarborough* by Sheridan (1777); spent more than 30 years on the stage, retiring only 2 years before her death. ❖ See also *Women in World History*.

YATES, Ngawini (1852/53?–1910). New Zealand tribal leader, landowner, and shopkeeper. Name variations: Ngawini Murray, Annie Murray. Born probably in 1852 or 1853, at Pukepoto, near Kaitaia, New Zealand; died July 29, 1910, at Parengarenga, New Zealand; dau. of John Murray (John Boradale) and Kateraina Te Kone; m. Samuel Yates (trader), 1880 (died 1900); children: 5 daughters, 3 sons. ❖ Helped to establish and run trading station at Parengarenga Harbour (early 1900s); husband accumulated vast land holdings because of her tribal affiliation; after his death, assumed control of trading station and store. ❖ See also *Dictionary of New Zealand Biography* (Vol. 3).

YAT-SEN, Madame Sun (1893–1981). *See Song, Qingling.*

YATSENKO, Olena (1977—). Ukrainian handball player. Born Oct 4, 1977, in Ukraine. ❖ Won a team bronze medal at Athens Olympics (2004).

YAVORSKA, Lydia (1869–1921). Russian-born actress and manager. Name variations: Lidia Yavorska, Princess Bariatinsky, Lady Pollock. Born Lidia Borisovna von Hübbenet, July 23, 1869, in Kiev, Russia; died Sept 3, 1921, in Brighton, Sussex, England; m. Prince Vladimir Bariatinsky, 1896 (div. 1916); m. Sir Frederick John Pollock, 4th baronet, 1920. ❖ Made stage debut at the Korsch Theater, Moscow, as Marguerite Gautier in *La Dame aux Camelias* (1894); appeared at the Théâtre Litteraire, St. Petersburg (1895–1900); founded her own theater, the New Theatre Yavorska, St. Petersburg, appearing there in such roles as Madame Sans-Gêne, Nora in *A Doll's House*, Magda, Zaza, L'Aiglon, Hedda, Rebecca in *Rosmersholm*, Ellida Wangel in *The Lady from the Sea*, Candida, Cleopatra, Lady Macbeth, and in leading parts in her 1st husband's plays; toured with her own company throughout Russia and Southern Europe; made London debut (1909), English-language debut (1910), then assumed management of the Royalty Theatre (1911), appearing there as Nora in an English-speaking production.

YAW, Ellen Beach (1868–1947). American singer. Name variations: Lark Ellen. Born Sept 14, 1868, in Boston, New York; died Sept 9, 1947, in West Covina, California; dau. of Ambrose Spencer Yaw (cowbell manufacturer) and Mary Jane (Beach) Yaw; m. Vere Goldthwaite (lawyer), Mar 21, 1907 (died 1912); m. Franklin Cannon (pianist and teacher), Aug 22, 1920 (div. 1935). ❖ Made 1st professional appearance at a concert in Brooklyn (1888); capitalized on her remarkable ability to sing the high note of E above high C to launch her 1st American tour (1894); made 1st European tour (1895); appeared at Carnegie Hall (1896); at the Savoy Theater in London, was lead soprano in the comic opera *The Rose of Persia* (1899–1900), a role written for her by Sir Arthur Sullivan; studied under Mathilde Marchesi in Paris; made grand opera debut in Rome in title role in *Lucia di Lammermoor* (1907); spent a season with the Metropolitan Opera in New York (1908), singing Lucia; established the Lark Ellen Bowl in California (1934). ❖ See also *Women in World History*.

YAYOI AOKI (b. 1927). *See Aoki, Yayoi.*

YAYOI YOSHIOKA (1871–1959). *See Yoshioka, Yayoi.*

YAYORI MATSUI (1934–2002). *Matsui, Yayori.*

YAZOVA, Yana (1912–1974). Bulgarian writer. Name variations: Lyuba Gancheva. Born in 1912; murdered in 1974; studied in Sofia, Bulgaria. ❖ Poet and novelist who wrote the historical trilogy *Balkani*, which was issued after her mysterious death; published 1st vol. of poetry (1931); when the Communists took over Bulgaria (1944), was banned from publishing and disappeared from public life; was murdered in her apartment (1974) and most of her papers and books disappeared, though some of her manuscripts were later found in the Central State Archives.

Thirteen years after her death, her *Balkani* (Balkans) trilogy—*Levski* (1987), *Benkovski* (1988) and *Shipka* (1989)—which looks at the spiritual source of all freedom, was published. ❖ See also *Women in World History*.

YE JIAYIN (1924—). Chinese literary critic and educator. Born 1924 in Beijing, China. ❖ Taught at Taiwan University and universities in US and Canada; published works on Chinese poetry in Chinese and English.

YE QIAOBO (1964—). Chinese speedskater. Born Aug 3, 1964, in Changchun, Jilin, China. ❖ Won a silver medal for overall at World Sprint championships (1991) and became China's 1st World champion (1992); won silver medals in the 500 and 1,000 meters at Albertville Olympics (1992), taking home China's 1st medals of the Winter Games; won a bronze medal for 1,000 meters at Lillehammer Olympics (1994); won 13 World Cup races, 11 on the 500 meters and 2 on the 1,000 meters.

YE WENLING (1942—). Chinese short-story writer. Born 1942 in Zhejiang, China. ❖ Works include *Scenes of Life at Changtan Village*, *Glorious Son of the Sun*, and *The Fig* (1980).

YE ZHAOYING (1974—). Chinese badminton player. Born May 7, 1974, in Hangzhou, China. ❖ Won a bronze medal for singles at Sydney Olympics (2000).

YEAGER, Jeana (1952—). American aviator. Born May 18, 1952, in Fort Worth, Texas; studied energy, aerospace design and commercial engineer drafting; no relation to Chuck Yeager (the test pilot). ❖ Set various records for speed while flying planes designed by Burt Rutan; after 10 years of piloting experience, became the 1st woman to fly around the world nonstop without refueling (Dec 14–23, 1986); received Presidential Citizen's Medal of Honor (1986); co-authored *Voyager* with co-pilot Dick Rutan. ❖ See also *Women in World History*.

YEARSLEY, Ann (1752–1806). English poet and playwright. Name variations: Lactilla; "Milkwoman of Bristol." Born Ann Cromartie in Clifton, near Bristol, England, July 1752 (some sources cite 1753 and 1756); died in Melksham, Wiltshire, May 8, 1806; dau. of John Cromartie (laborer) and Ann Cromartie (milkwoman); m. John Yearsley (illiterate laborer), in 1774; children: 6 (one died young). ❖ Showed her poems to Hannah More who helped publish her 1st book, *Poems on Several Occasions* (1784); garnered praise from such figures as Sir Joshua Reynolds and Horace Walpole; had a falling out with More; published *Poems on Various Subjects* (1787), attempting to overcome rumors that her previous material had been made publishable only through More's editing; issued *Poem on the Inhumanity of the Slave-Trade* (1788); wrote *Stanzas of Woe* (1790) to attack a local mayor who had chastised her children for trespassing on his property; composed *Earl Goodwin* (1791), a tragedy in verse that was staged in both Bath and Bristol; wrote historical novel, *The Royal Captives*; published last collection, *The Rural Lyre* (1796). ❖ See also *Women in World History*.

YEARWOOD, Trisha (1964—). American singer and actress. Born Patricia Lynn Yearwood, Sept 19, 1964, in Monticello, GA; Belmont College, BA in Music Business (1987); m. Christopher Latham, 1987 (div. 1981); m. Robert Reynolds (bassist with band, The Mavericks), May 21, 1994 (div. 1999); m. Garth Brooks (singer). ❖ Moved to Nashville (1985), and sang backup for Garth Brooks; released double-platinum debut album, *Trisha Yearwood* (1991), winning Top New Female Vocalist Award from Academy of Country Music (1992); hits include "She's in Love With the Boy," "The Woman Before Me," "Like We Never Had a Broken Heart" and "That's What I Like About You"; released hit album, *Hearts in Armor* (1992), which included singles "Wrong Side of Memphis" and "Walkaway Joe"; appeared in film, *This Thing Called Love* (1993); won Best Country Vocal Collaboration Grammys for "I Fall to Pieces" (1994), sung with Aaron Neville, and "In Another's Eyes" (1997), sung with Garth Brooks; other albums include *Thinkin' About You* (1995), *Where Your Road Leads* (1998) and *Inside Out* (2001), which included hit, "I Would've Loved You Anyway"; received Oscar nomination and Grammy for song, "How Do I Live," from soundtrack of film, *Con Air* (1997).

YEATS, Elizabeth (1868–1940). Irish printer and publisher. Name variations: Lolly Yeats. Born Elizabeth Corbet Yeats, Mar 11, 1868, in Regent's Park, London, England; died Jan 16, 1940, in Dublin, Ireland; dau. of John Butler Yeats, known as J. B. Yeats, and Susan Pollexfen Yeats; sister of William Butler Yeats (the poet) and Lily Yeats; educated at Metropolitan School of Art, Dublin, and Froebel College, London; never married; no children. ❖ Artisan, printer and publisher whose Cuala Press, co-owned with sister, produced books by such writers as J. M. Synge and their brother W. B. Yeats in editions noted for grace and simplicity; worked for May Morris as a children's art teacher; trained as a Froebel teacher (1890s), then taught in London and Dublin; published the 1st of 4 brushwork manuals (1895), which proved successful; trained as a process engraver; recruited by Evelyn Gleeson to run the printing department of Dun Emer Industries, the arts and crafts cooperative based on the Morris model (1902); with sister, became an independent entity within Dun Emer (1904); published brother's collection of poems *In the Seven Woods*; with sister, severed connection with Dun Emer (1907) and set up the Cuala Press, the only private press run by women. ❖ See also Gifford Lewis, *The Yeats Sisters and the Cuala Press* (1994); and *Women in World History*.

YEATS, Lily (1866–1949). Irish embroiderer, printer and publisher. Born Susan Mary Yeats, Aug 25, 1866, at Enniscrone, Co. Sligo, Ireland; died Jan 5, 1949, in Dublin, Ireland; dau. of John Butler Yeats, known as J. B. Yeats, and Susan Pollexfen Yeats; sister of William Butler Yeats (poet) and Elizabeth Yeats; educated at Notting Hill School, London, and Metropolitan School of Art, Dublin; never married; no children. ❖ Worked as an embroiderer for William Morris' daughter, May Morris, at Kelmscott Manor, gaining a vital introduction to the Arts and Crafts movement, which decisively influenced her future career; left Morris workshop (1894); recruited by Evelyn Gleeson to run embroidery department of Dun Emer Industries, the arts and crafts cooperative based on the Morris model (1902); with sister, became an independent entity within Dun Emer (1904); embroidered sodality banners for Loughrea Cathedral for which she won much acclaim; with sister, severed connection with Dun Emer (1907) and set up the Cuala Press whose 1st publication was a book by brother William, *Poetry and Ireland*; also published works by J. M. Synge and Æ (George Russell), among others. ❖ See also Gifford Lewis, *The Yeats Sisters and the Cuala Press* (1994); and *Women in World History*.

YEGOROVA, Irina (1940—). Russian speedskater. Name variations: Irina Egorova; Irina Pavlova. Born Irina Nikolayevna Yegorova, April 8, 1940, in Ivanovo, near Moscow, USSR. ❖ Won silver medals for the 1,000 meters and 500 meters at Innsbruck Olympics (1964).

YEGOROVA, Ljubov or Lyubov (1966—). See *Egorova, Lyubov*.

YEGOROVA, Lyudmila (1931—). Soviet gymnast. Name variations: Ludmila Egorova. Born Feb 24, 1931, in USSR. ❖ At Melbourne Olympics, won a bronze medal in teams all-around, portable apparatus, and a gold medal in team all-around (1956).

YEGOROVA, Valentina (1964—). Soviet marathon runner. Born Feb 16, 1964, in Chuvash, Russia. ❖ Won a silver medal at European championships (1990); won a gold medal at Barcelona Olympics (1992) and a silver medal at Atlanta Olympics (1996), both for marathon.

YEHONALA (1835–1908). See *Cixi*.

YEHUDIT (fl. 10th c. CE). See *Judith*.

YEKATERINA. *Variant of Catherine*.

YELENA. *Variant of Elena or Helen*.

YELENA GLINSKAYA or GLINSKI (c. 1506–1538). See *Glinski, Elena*.

YELESINA, Yelena (1970—). Russian high jumper. Name variations: Elena Yelesina. Born April 4, 1970, in Chelyabinsk, USSR. ❖ Won silver medals at World championships (1991, 1999) and a bronze at European championships (1990); won a gold medal for high jump at Sydney Olympics (2000).

YELIZA OR YELIZAVETA. *Variant of Eliza or Elizabeth*.

YELTSIN, Tatyana (1960—). See *Dyachenko, Tatyana*.

YEMBAKHTOVA, Tatyana (1956—). Soviet field-hockey player. Born Jan 17, 1956, in USSR. ❖ At Moscow Olympics, won a bronze medal in team competition (1980).

YENER, Aslihan (1946—). Turkish-American archaeologist. Name variations: Kutlu Aslihan Yener; K. Aslihan Yener. Born July 21, 1946, in Istanbul, Turkey; dau. of Reha Turkkan and Eire Guntekin; raised in New Rochelle, NY; studied chemistry at Adelphi University; studied archeology at Robert College (later Bosphorus University) in Istanbul (graduated, 1969); Columbia University, PhD, 1980. ❖ Conducted chemical analyses of ancient Middle East silver and lead objects to reveal the mines from which they originated; studied tin, which was used to make bronze and metal objects during the Bronze Age (3000–1100 BCE); discovered Bronze Age tin mine remains in Taurus Mountains (formerly Anatolia, Turkey, 1987), while working as associate history professor at Bosphorus University (1980–88); discovered Goltepe (1989), a city site where tin ore was refined, near Taurus Mountains site, which confirmed that the area was an important tin site; became associate professor at University of Chicago's Oriental Institute; created new technique to analyze chemical composition of ancient objects using Argonne Laboratories' Advanced Photon Source, a device that reveals how objects were made and fixed (1998). Received Daughters of Ataturk Women of Distinction Award (2000).

YEO KAB-SOON (1974—). Korean shooter. Born May 8, 1974, in South Korea. ❖ At Barcelona Olympics, won a gold medal in air rifle (1992).

YEOMANS, Amelia (1842–1913). Canadian physician. Name variations: Amelia Le Sueur Yeomans. Born Amelia Le Sueur, 1842 in Quebec, Canada; died 1913; dau. of Barbara (Dawson) Le Sueur and Peter Le Sueur; graduate of University of Michigan Department of Medicine, 1883; m. Augustus A. Yeomans (American army surgeon), 1860; children: 3, including Lilian Yeomans (1st practicing woman physician in Winnipeg, Canada). ❖ Social reformer, suffragist and the 2nd practicing woman physician in Winnipeg (the 1st was her daughter), served as president of Dominion Women's Christian Temperance Union; presented graphic speeches about the effects of venereal disease on women, and, rather than condemn prostitutes, encouraged the public to protect young women from the hazardous practice; contributed to the creation of the Equal Franchise Association (1894), which imposed fines and consequences for drunkenness and irresponsible behavior (and ultimately affected prostitution).

YERMOLAYEVA, Galina (1948—). Soviet rower. Born Oct 21, 1948, in USSR. ❖ At Montreal Olympics, won a silver medal in quadruple sculls with coxswain (1976).

YERMOLEVA, Zinaida (1898–1974). See *Ermoleva, Zinaida*.

YERMOLOVA, Maria Nikolaijevna (1853–1928). See *Ermolova, Mariia*.

YERMOLYEVA, Zinaida (1898–1974). See *Ermoleva, Zinaida*.

YEROSHINA, Radya. Russian cross-country skier. Name variations: Radya or Radia Eroshina or Erochina; Radja Jeroschina. Born in USSR. ❖ Won silver medals for 10 km and 3 x 5 km relay at Cortina Olympics (1956); won a bronze medal for 10 km and a silver medal for 3 x 5 km at Squaw Valley Olympics (1960).

YESSAYAN, Zabel (1878–1943). Armenian writer. Born to a prosperous family in 1878 in Scutari, a suburb of Constantinople (now Istanbul); died 1943 in exile from Soviet Armenia; studied at Sorbonne. ❖ While studying in Paris, wrote regularly for French literary journals *Mercure de France*, *L'Humanite nouvelle* and *La grande France*, and in the Armenian periodicals *Anahit*, *Masis* and *Arevelyan Mamoul*; serialized her short novel *Spasman srahin mej* (The Waiting Room) in *Tsaghik*, an Armenian literary magazine (1903); by now a public and literary figure among Armenians, returned to Constantinople after the declaration of the new Turkish constitution (1909) and was sent to Cilicia to distribute food and assist the sick following the massacre there; wrote *Averaknerun mej* (Among the Ruins), based on what she saw, alienating the Young Turks, who added her to their list of Armenian intellectuals to be liquidated, the only woman writer so singled out; wrote a satirical novel, *Keghts Hantarner* (Phony Geniuses, 1910); published a short novel, *Anjkut'yan zhamer* (Hours of Agony, 1911), about an unhappily married woman who induces her husband to commit suicide; returned to this subject in *Verjin Bazkakê*, 1st serialized and later published in book form; escaped from Armenia by crossing the Bulgarian border (1915); visited Soviet Armenia and outlined her impressions in *Promet'eos azatagrvats* (Prometheus Unchained, 1928); moved to Soviet Armenia (1933) and became a Soviet citizen; wrote *Silihtarhi Partezner* (The Gardens of Silihader, 1936) in both French and Armenian, chronicling her early life in Scutari, but was accused of fostering nostalgia by the Soviet government; wrote *Krake Shapik* (Shirt of Fire, 1936); was arrested with some 200 other intellectuals (1937), accused of being a counter-revolutionary and nationalist criminal; died in exile amid questionable circumstances (1943); left unfinished her magnum opus, a lengthy novel based on the life of her Zorba-like uncle, *Barpa Khatchik* (Uncle K.). ❖ See also *Women in World History*.

YEVDOKIMOVA, Irina (1978—). See *Evdokimova, Irina*.

YEVDOKIYA. *Variant of Eudoxia*.

YEVKOVA, Olga (1965—). Soviet basketball player. Born Aug 15, 1965, in USSR. ❖ At Seoul Olympics, won a bronze medal in team competition (1988).

YEVLEVSKAYA-MILCHINA, Lolita. See *Milchina, Lolita.*

YEVONDE (1893–1975). English photographer. Name variations: Yevonde Cumbers; Philonie Yevonde; Madame Yevonde; incorrectly as Edith Plummer. Born Yevonde Cumbers in London in 1893; died in England in 1975; educated at boarding schools; studied at the Sorbonne; married Edgar Middleton (playwright), 1921 (died 1939). ❖ Began career in photography, apprenticing with Lallie Charles (1911–14); worked for and with women her entire career; opened her own studio after World War I, doing portraits of such prominent figures as Lady Nancy Astor, Lady Edwina Ashley Mountbatten, Princess Marina of Greece, Rebecca West and Gertrude Lawrence; also contributed work to the society magazines *Bystander* and *Sketch*; joined Royal Photographic Society of Great Britain (1921); began experimenting with color (1932) and using theatrical props in a satirical style; championed women's suffrage for most of her life. The Royal Photographic Society of Great Britain introduced a significant retrospective of her work, *Sixty Years a Portrait Photographer* (1973). ❖ See also autobiography *In Camera*; and *Women in World History.*

YEZIERSKA, Anzia (c. 1881–1970). American-Jewish writer. Name variations: Anzia Mayer Gordon (1910); Anzia Mayer Levitas (1911–12); Anzia Yezierska to her family; "Hattie Mayer" to US Immigration officials at Ellis Island. Born Anzia Yezierska (she never knew her date of birth so she made one up, Oct 18, 1883, though it was more likely 1880 or 1881) in Plotsk, Russian Poland; died in Ontario, California, Nov 21, 1970; dau. of Bernard Yezierska (Talmudic scholar) and Pearl Yezierska; educated at Rand School and Columbia University; m. Jacob Gordon (attorney), 1910 (div.); m. Abraham "Arnold" Levitas (printer), 1911 (div.); children: Louise Levitas Henriksen. ❖ Novelist whose fiction preserves the spirit, suffering and generational strife of immigrant families on New York's Lower East Side; at 11, migrated as a child to New York City with mother, father, and 7 siblings (1892); taught school (1904–20); won a prize for best story of the year for "The Fat of the Land" (1919); having struggled for years, became an overnight publishing sensation with *Hungry Hearts* (1920); enjoyed 10 years of fame and fortune, for such books as *Salome of the Tenements* (1922), *Children of Loneliness* (1923), *Arrogant Beggar* (1927), *All I Could Never Be* (1932), and her masterpiece, *Bread Givers* (1925), the most overtly autobiographical of her novels, then faded almost as rapidly as she had risen; worked as a screenwriter (1920–21); worked as a short-story writer, novelist, and independent author (1921–70); lived mainly in New York, but spent a year in Hollywood (1920–21), a year in Wisconsin (1929–30), and a year in Vermont (1931–32); also wrote (with introduction by W. H. Auden) *Red Ribbon on a White Horse* (1950). ❖ See also Louise L. Henriksen, *Anzia Yezierska: A Writer's Life* (Rutgers U. Press, 1988); Carol B. Schoen, *Anzia Yezierska* (Twayne, 1982); and *Women in World History.*

YIN JIAN (1978—). Chinese windsurfer. Born Dec 25, 1978, in China. ❖ Won a silver medal for board (Mistral) at Athens Olympics (2004).

YINGCHAO DENG (1903–1992). See *Deng Yingchao.*

YLLA (1911–1955). Austrian-born photographer. Name variations: Camilla Koffler; Ylla Koffler. Born Camilla Koffler, 1911, in Vienna, Austria, to a Yugoslav mother and Hungarian father; killed Mar 30, 1955, in Mysore, India. ❖ Studied sculpture in Belgrade; moved to Paris (1931), where she worked with photographer Ergy Landau as a photo retoucher; opened a studio in Paris specializing in animal portraits; commissioned to do photos for Julian Huxley's *Animal Language* (1938); moved to US (1941) and opened a studio in New York; published 10 books (1944–54), some for children; spent 3 months in Africa photographing animals (1952); traveled to India (1954); while photographing a bullock cart race, fell from the hood of a jeep and was killed. Nine more books of her photos were published after her death.

YOGESHWARI, Lalla (b. 1355). See *Lal Ded.*

YOHÉ, May (1869–1938). American actress. Name variations: Lady Francis Hope; Lady May Hope, May Yohe. Born Mary Augusta Yohé, April 6, 1869, in PA; died Aug 28, 1938; m. Lord Francis Thomas Hope (owner of the Hope diamond), 1894 (div. 1902); m. Captain Putnam B. Strong, 1903 (div. 1910); m. Captain Jan Smuts, 1914 (wounded in WWI and disabled, not to be confused with the South African statesman). ❖ Made stage debut in Chicago in repertory under management of David Henderson (1887); made NY debut in *Natural Gas* (1888) and London debut in *The Magic Opal* (1893), coming to prominence there as Christopher in *Little Christopher Columbus* when she sang "Honey, ma Honey"; hired by William Hammerstein to sing at his NY theater wearing a replica of the famous Hope diamond, a 44.52-carat jewel that had been owned by her husband before he sold it in 1902 to pay off debts (it was later owned by Evalyn Walsh McLean); co-wrote and appeared in film *The Hope Diamond Mystery* as Lady Francis Hope (1921); published *The Mystery of the Hope Diamond* (1929), launching the legend of the curse of the Hope diamond.

YOKEBED. See *Jochebed.*

YOKO (c. 1849–1906). Queen of Seneghun. Name variations: Madam Yoko; Madame Yoko. Born in Sierre Leone, West Africa, 1849; died 1906; married the leader of Sierre Leone (died 1878). ❖ Was the head wife of her 3rd husband, a powerful chieftain for the Mendeland; when husband died (1878), took his place as chief; used her clout to build local alliances and a large confederacy, then negotiated for protection from the British; destroyed her main political rival, Kamanda (late 1880s); after Kamanda's death, officially became queen of Seneghun, then extended her territories; one of only a handful of women who owed their position to the British government; managed to reach that status despite her aversion to missionaries and her refusal to convert to Christianity. ❖ See also *Women in World History.*

YOKO ONO (1933—). See *Ono, Yoko.*

YOKOSAWA, Yuki (1980—). Japanese judoka. Born Oct 29, 1980, in Gunma, Japan. ❖ Won a silver medal for 52 kg at Athens Olympics (2004).

YOKO TSUKASA (1934—). See *Tsukasa, Yoko.*

YOKOYAMA, Juri (1955—). Japanese volleyball player. Born Mar 9, 1955, in Japan. ❖ At Montreal Olympics, won a gold medal in team competition (1976).

YOLANDA. *Variant of Violante and Yolande.*

YOLANDA MARGHERITA OF ITALY (1901–1986). Italian princess. Name variations: Iolande; Iolanda; Yolanda de Savoie; Yolanda of Savoy; Yolanda Marguerite di Savoia-Carignano; Yolanda Calvi. Born June 1, 1901; died Oct 16, 1986, in Rome; dau. of Victor Emmanuel III, king of Italy (r. 1900–1946), and Elena of Montenegro (1873–1952); m. Giorgio Carlo Calvi, count of Bergolo, April 9, 1923; children: Marie Ludovica (b. 1924); Vittoria (1927–1985); Guja Anna (b. 1930); Pier (b. 1933). ❖ See also *Women in World History.*

YOLANDA OF GNESEN (d. 1299). Hungarian saint. Name variations: Helen of Gnesen, duchess of Kalish. Died in 1299; dau. of Bela IV, king of Hungary (r. 1235–1270), and Salome of Hungary ([1201–c. 1270] or possibly Maria Lascaris); niece of Elizabeth of Hungary (1207–1231); m. Boleslaus, duke of Kalish. ❖ Following death of husband (1279), entered the order of St. Clare at Sandeck; later became abbess of the Poor Clares at Gnesen where she died. Feast day is June 15.

YOLANDE DE BAR (fl. 14th c.). Queen of Aragon. Name variations: Yolande of Bar. Descended from John II (1319–1364), king of France (r. 1350–1364); m. Juan I also known as John I the Hunter, king of Aragon (r. 1387–1395); children: Yolande of Aragon (1379–1442).

YOLANDE DE BOURGOGNE (1248–1280). See *Yolande of Burgundy.*

YOLANDE DE COUCY (d. 1222). Countess of Dreux. Died Mar 18, 1222; dau. of Ralph I de Marle, Sir de Coucy; m. Robert II, count of Dreux, in 1184; children: Pierre I, count of Brittany; Adelaide de Dreux (1189–1258, who m. Gaucher IV de Macon); Agnes de Dreux (1195–1258, who m. Etienne III, count of Auxonne); Philippa de Dreux (d. 1240); Yolande de Dreux (d. 1238).

YOLANDE DE COURTENAY (d. 1233). Queen of Hungary. Died 1233; dau. of Yolande of Courtenay (d. 1219) and Peter II (Pierre II) of Courtenay, emperor of Constantinople; became second wife of Andrew II, king of Hungary (r. 1205–1235), in 1215; children: Iolande of Hungary (1215–1251). ❖ Andrew II's 1st wife was Gertrude of Andrechs-Meran (d. 1213); his 3rd wife was Beatrice d'Este (d. 1245).

YOLANDE DE DREUX (d. 1238). Countess of Eu. Died Jan 26, 1238; interred in Fourcarmont Abbey; dau. of Robert II, count of Dreux, and Yolande de Coucy (d. 1222); m. Raoul III de Lusignan, count of Eu; children: Marie of Lusignan (d. 1260), countess of Eu.

YOLANDE DE DREUX (1212–1248). Duchess of Burgundy. Born in 1212; died in 1248; dau. of Robert III, count of Dreux; m. Hugh IV (1213–1272), duke of Burgundy (r. 1218–1272), in 1229; children: Eudes (1230–1266), count of Nevers; Jean or John (b. 1231); Robert II (1248–1306), duke of Burgundy; Adelaide of Burgundy (d. 1273).

YOLANDE DE DREUX (d. 1272). Countess of Marche. Died in 1272; dau. of Peter Mauclerk, count of Brittany; m. Hugh le Lusignan (b. around 1221), count of Marche and Angoulême; children: Hugh XII, count of Marche and Angouleme; Alice de Lusignan (d. 1290); Mary de Lusignan.

YOLANDE DE DREUX (d. 1323). Queen of Scots. Name variations: sometimes referred to as Jolanta or Joleta. Died in 1323 (some sources cite 1322); dau. of Robert IV, count of Dreux (r. 1249–1282); became 2nd wife of Alexander III (d. 1286), king of Scots (r. 1249–1286), Oct 14, 1285; m. Arthur II (d. 1312), duke of Brittany (r. 1305–1312), in May 1294; children: (second marriage) John de Dreux, count of Montfort and earl of Richmond, also known as John III, duke of Brittany; Joan de Dreux (1294–1363, who m. Robert, Lord of Cassel); Beatrice de Dreux (1295–1384, who m. Guy, Lord of Laval); Alice de Dreux (1297–1377, who m. Bouchard VI, count of Vendome); Blanche de Dreux (b. 1300, died young); Mary de Dreux (1302–1371, a nun).

YOLANDE OF ANJOU (1428–1483). See Yolande of Vaudemont.

YOLANDE OF ARAGON (d. 1300). Queen of Castile and Leon. Name variations: Violante. Died in 1300 (some sources cite 1301) in Roncevalles; dau. of Iolande of Hungary (1215–1251) and James or Jaime I, king of Aragon; m. Alphonso X the Wise (1221–1284), king of Castile and Leon (r. 1252–1284), on Nov 26, 1248; children: Berenguela (c. 1253–c. 1313, a nun); Beatrice of Castile (c. 1254–c. 1280, who m. William IX, margrave of Montferrat); Fernando de la Cerda (c. 1255–1275); Leonor (c. 1256–1275); Sancho IV the Fierce (1257–1296), king of Castile and Leon (r. 1258–1295); Constanza (b. around 1259); Pedro of Castile (c. 1261–1283); Juan of Castile (c. 1264–1319); Isabel (b. around 1265, died young); Violante or Yolande (b. around 1277, who m. Diego Lopez de Haro, count of Vizcaya); Jaime (1268–1284). ❖ Another child of Alphonso X, Beatrice of Castile and Leon (1242–1303), who m. Alphonso III of Portugal), was his illegitimate daughter with Mayor Guillen de Guzman (one source also places Sancho IV as son of de Guzman).

YOLANDE OF ARAGON (fl. 14th c.). Queen of Naples. Married Robert the Good, king of Naples (r. 1309–1343); children: Charles of Calabria (who m. Marie of Valois). ❖ Robert the Good also had an illegitimate daughter, Maria dei Conti d'Aquino.

YOLANDE OF ARAGON (1379–1442). Duchess of Anjou and queen and regent of Sicily. Name variations: Yolanda of Anjou; Yolanda of Sicily. Born in 1379 in Saragossa, Aragon; died in Nov 1442 in Paris; dau. of Juan I also known as John I the Hunter, king of Aragon (r. 1387–1395), and Yolande de Bar (who was descended from King John II of France); m. Louis II, duke of Anjou and king of Sicily, in 1400; children: Marie of Anjou (1404–1463, who m. Charles VII of France); Louis III (1403–1434), king of Naples (r. 1417–1434); René I (1408–1480), duke of Lorraine and Bar, duke of Provence, duke of Anjou and Guise, and later king of Naples (b. 1409); Yolande of Anjou (1412–1440); Charles, count of Maine (1414–1472). ❖ An important political figure in France, adopted the interests of Anjou as her own, despite her Spanish upbringing; came to be one of the French monarchy's most loyal defenders in the chaos of the Hundred Years' War against England and the simultaneous civil war which plagued France; when husband left Anjou to try to establish his rule in Naples (1410), remained in their capital of Angers; ruled as regent of Anjou and their smaller provinces, and quelled an insurrection (1411); following this victory, learned that her father had died and that some of her Spanish relatives were disputing her inheritance in Aragon, so she hastened with her army across the Pyrenees to defend her patrimony; became a loving foster mother to young son-in-law, the dauphin Charles (VII), gaining a positive influence over him which would never wane; when husband died (1417), ruled as regent of Anjou for her son, now Louis III, as well as devoting herself to the education of the new dauphin; when Charles VI died (1422) and the infant king Henry VI of England was proclaimed king of France, encouraged the irresolute dauphin to fight for his throne; was also instrumental in the success of Joan of Arc when the girl 1st arrived at Yolande's court at Chinon, asking to lead Charles' troops against the English; even after Charles' coronation (1429), remained active in the struggle to unite the French factions and end the English occupation of France; negotiated a peace treaty with the duke of Brittany (1431), and intervened in the civil war between two of Charles' advisors, presiding over the peace settlement; remained an important advisor to her son-in-law and daughter Marie of Anjou until her death. ❖ See also *Women in World History.*

YOLANDE OF BAVARIA (d. 1731). See Medici, Violante Beatrice de.

YOLANDE OF BRIENNE (1212–1228). Holy Roman empress and titular queen of Jerusalem. Name variations: Yolande de Brienne; Yolanta; Isabella II; Isabel II of Jerusalem. Born in 1212; died in 1228; dau. of Marie of Montferrat (d. 1212) and John I of Brienne, king of Jerusalem (r. 1210–1225); 2nd wife of Frederick II (1194–1250), Holy Roman emperor (r. 1215–1250) and king of Jerusalem (r. 1225–1250); children: Conrad (1228–1254), king of Jerusalem (r. 1250–1254), king of Naples and Sicily (r. 1250–1254), and Holy Roman emperor as Conrad IV (r. 1250–1254). ❖ Died at age 16, following the birth of her son Conrad, later king of Jerusalem, Naples and Sicily, and Holy Roman emperor as Conrad IV. Frederick II's 1st wife was Constance of Aragon (d. 1222); his 3rd was Isabella of England (1214–1241).

YOLANDE OF BURGUNDY (1248–1280). Countess of Nevers and Tonnerre. Name variations: Yolande de Burgundy; Yolande de Bourgogne. Born in 1248; died June 2, 1280; dau. of Mahaut II de Dampierre (1234–1266) and Eudes (1230–1266), count of Nevers; m. Jean Tristan, count of Valois and Nevers, on June 1, 1265; m. Robert III, count of Flanders, in March 1272; children: 1 son.

YOLANDE OF COURTENAY (d. 1219). Latin empress of Constantinople. Name variations: Yolande de Courtenay; Yolande of Alsace; Yolande of Constantinople. Empress from 1217 to 1219; died in 1219; dau. of Baldwin V, count of Hainault (Baldwin VIII of Flanders), and Margaret of Alsace (d. 1194); sister of Baldwin IX, count of Flanders and Hainault (crowned Baldwin I of Constantinople); m. Peter II (Pierre II) of Courtenay (d. 1218), emperor of Constantinople (r. 1216–1218); children: Marie de Courtenay; Yolande de Courtenay (d. 1233).

YOLANDE OF FRANCE (1434–1478). Duchess of Savoy. Born in 1434 (some sources cite 1436); died in 1478; dau. of Marie of Anjou (1404–1463) and Charles VII (1403–1461), king of France (r. 1422–1461); sister of Louis XI, king of France (r. 1461–1483); m. Amedée also known as Amadeus IX, duke of Savoy (r. 1465–1472); children: Philibert I the Hunter, duke of Savoy; Charles I the Warrior, duke of Savoy; Anna of Savoy (1455–1480, who m. Frederick IV, future king of Naples); Louise of Savoy (1461–1503, who m. Hughes of Chateau-Guyon). ❖ Served as regent for her son Philibert I.

YOLANDE OF HUNGARY (1215–1251). See Iolande of Hungary.

YOLANDE OF MONTFERRAT (fl. 1300). See Irene of Montferrat.

YOLANDE OF VAUDEMONT (1428–1483). Duchess of Lorraine and Bar. Name variations: Yolande of Anjou; Yolande de Vaudémont. Born Nov 2, 1428; died Feb 23, 1483; dau. of René I the Good, duke of Anjou and titular king of Sicily, Hungary, and Naples, and Isabelle of Lorraine (1410–1453); sister of Margaret of Anjou (1429–1482); m. Ferry or Ferrey de Vaudemont also known as Frederick (d. 1470 or 1471), count of Vaudemont, in 1445; children: Margaret of Lorraine (1463–1521); Jolanthe of Lorraine (d. 1500); Jeanne of Lorraine (1458–1480); René II (1451–1508), duke of Lorraine (r. 1480–1508, who m. Philippa of Guelders). ❖ See also *Women in World History.*

YOLANDE-IRENE OF MONTFERRAT (fl. 1300). See Irene of Montferrat.

YOLANTE. Variant of Yolande.

YOLI, Lupe (1939–1992). See La Lupe.

YONEDA, Yuko (1979—). Japanese synchronized swimmer. Born Sept 8, 1979, in Osaka, Japan. ❖ Won a team silver medal at Sydney Olympics (2000); at World championships, placed 1st in free routine combination (2003); won a team silver medal at Athens Olympics (2004).

YONGE, Charlotte Mary (1823–1901). English writer. Born in Otterbourne, Hampshire, England, Aug 11, 1823; died in Otterbourne, Mar 24, 1901; dau. of William Yonge (retired Army officer, died 1854) and Frances Mary (Fanny) Bargus Yonge (died 1868); sister of Julian Yonge (b. Jan 13, 1830); never married. ❖ Popular and prolific writer who promoted and defended the quintessential values of the Victorian upper-middle-class and was the "leading novelist of the Anglo-Catholic revival"; came under the influence of John Keble, a leader in the Oxford

Movement; published 1st book, a collection of French short stories (1838); edited *The Monthly Packet* (1851–93); also contributed stories for school-age children to *The Magazine for the Young*, later collected and published as *Langley School* (1852), which was widely read; published *The Heir of Redclyffe* (1853), an immediate success, whose main character, Sir Guy Morville, became a hero for the times; issued *The Little Duke* (1854), written for children about the 10th-century Richard of Normandy, one of her best books; produced 2 or 3 books a year for next 40 years and became "a British institution"; compensated for the lack of plot in her novels by an adroit use of dialogue through which she defined character; moved to Elderfield (1862); brother Julian Yonge died (1892); wrote in a variety of genres, including fiction, stories for children, histories, religion, and biography. ❖ See also Georgina Battiscombe, *Charlotte Mary Yonge: The Story of an Uneventful Life* (Constable, 1943); Alethea Hayter, *Charlotte Yonge* (Northcote House, 1996); Margaret Mare and Alicia C. Percival, *Victorian Best-seller: The World of Charlotte M. Yonge* (Harrap, 1948); Christabel Coleridge, *Charlotte Mary Yonge: Her Life and Letters* (Macmillan, 1903); Barbara Dennis, *Charlotte Yonge (1823–1901): Novelist of the Oxford Movement* (Edwin Mellen, 1992); and *Women in World History*.

YONGMEI CUI (1969—). *See Cui Yongmei.*

YOON BYUNG-SOON (1963—). Korean handball player. Born Nov 27, 1963, in South Korea. ❖ At Los Angeles Olympics, won a silver medal in team competition (1984).

YOON HYE-YOUNG. South Korean archer. Born in South Korea. ❖ Won a gold medal for teams at Atlanta Olympics (1996).

YOON SOO-KYUNG (1964—). Korean handball player. Born Jan 19, 1964, in South Korea. ❖ At Los Angeles Olympics, won a silver medal in team competition (1984).

YOON YOUNG-SOOK (1971—). Korean archer. Born Sept 10, 1971, in South Korea. ❖ At Seoul Olympics, won a bronze medal in double FITA round and a gold medal in team round (1988).

YORDANOVA, Reni (1953—). Bulgarian rower. Born Oct 25, 1953, in Bulgaria. ❖ At Montreal Olympics, won a silver medal in coxed fours (1976).

YORDANOVA, Todorka (1956—). Bulgarian basketball player. Born Jan 3, 1956, in Bulgaria. ❖ At Montreal Olympics, won a bronze medal in team competition (1976).

YORDANOVA, Zdravka (1950—). Bulgarian rower. Born Dec 9, 1950, in Bulgaria. ❖ At Montreal Olympics, won a gold medal in double sculls (1976).

YORGOVA, Diana (1942—). Bulgarian track-and-field athlete. Name variations: Diana Prodanova or Prodanova-Yorgova. Born Dec 9, 1942, in Bulgaria; m. Nikolai Prodanov (Bulgarian athlete), 1964. ❖ At Munich Olympics, won a silver medal in the long jump (1972).

YORGOVA, Diana Vassilleva (1971—). Bulgarian shooter. Name variations: Diana Vassileva Yorgova. Born April 11, 1971, in Russia. ❖ Won a silver medal for 25 m pistol at Atlanta Olympics (1996); broke the world record for sports pistol with 594 points (1994); won World Cups (1995, 1996).

YORK, duchess of.
See Isabel of Castile (1355–1392).
See Holland, Joan (c. 1380–1434).
See Neville, Cecily (1415–1495).
See Mohun, Philippa (d. 1431).
See Hyde, Anne (1638–1671).
See Mary of Modena (1658–1718).
See Frederica of Prussia (1767–1820).
See Mary of Teck (1867–1953).
See Elizabeth Bowes-Lyon (b. 1900).
See Ferguson, Sarah (b. 1959).

YORK, Janice-Lee (b. 1927). *See Romary, Janice-Lee.*

YORK, queen of. *See Edith (d. 937).*

YORK, Susannah (1941—). English actress. Born Susannah Yolande Fletcher, Jan 9, 1941, in London, England; raised in Scotland; graduate of Royal Academy of Dramatic Art; m. Michael Wells, 1960 (div. 1976); children: Orlando Wells (child actor), Sasha Wells (child actor). ❖ Made screen debut in *Tunes of Glory* (1960), followed by *Freud*; on stage, co-starred in *There Was a Crooked Man* (1960) and played 1st

substantial role in *The Greengage Summer* (1961); came to prominence in *Tom Jones* (1963), followed by *A Man for All Seasons* (1966), *Battle of Britain* (1969), *The Killing of Sister George* (1968), *They Shoot Horses, Don't They?* (1969), which earned her Oscar nomination for Best Supporting Actress, as well as the "Superman" series, for which she played Christopher Reeve's mother (1978, 1980), *Sands of the Kalahari* (1965) *Kaleidoscope* (1966), *Oh! What a Lovely War* (1969), *Happy Birthday, Wanda June* (1971), *XY and Zee* (1972), *The Maids* (1975), *Conduct Unbecoming* (1975), *Yellowbeard* (1983), *The Book of Eve* (2002), *Visitors* (2003) and *Love Is a Survivor* (2005); won Best Actress award at Cannes Film Festival (1972) for *Images*; wrote children's books *In Search of Unicorns* (1973) and *Lark's Castle* (1975).

YORKIN, Nicole (1958—). American tv writer and producer. Born Nov 22, 1958, in Los Angeles, California; dau. of Peg Yorkin (feminist and activist) and Bud Yorkin (director and producer); sister of David Yorkin (tv writer and producer); University of California, Berkeley, BA; m. Tim Shaheen, 1989; children: Julian Shaheen (b. June 23, 1994); Natalie Shaheen (b. Mar 12, 1998). ❖ Spent 6 years reporting for *Los Angeles Herald Examiner*, as a journalist, was nominated for a Pulitzer Prize for a series of articles concerning a 12-year-old prostitute; with writing partner Dawn Prestwich, worked on "Chicago Hope," "Ally McBeal," "The Practice," "The Trials of Rosie O'Neill," "Melrose Place," and the critically acclaimed "Judging Amy," for which Yorkin and Prestwich served as writers and executive producers; with Prestwich, also wrote and co-produced "The Education of Max Bickford." ❖ See also *Women in World History*.

YORKIN, Peg (1927—). American feminist and activist. Born in New York, NY, April 16, 1927; dau. of Dora (Lavine) Diem (actress) and Frank Diem (photographer); attended Barnard College and Neighborhood Playhouse; m. Newton Arnold (assistant director), 1950 (div. 1952); m. Bud Yorkin (tv and film director and producer), May 9, 1954 (div. 1986); children: (2nd m.) Nicole Yorkin (b. 1958); David Yorkin (b. 1961). ❖ Theater producer, philanthropist, and feminist leader who was instrumental in bringing RU-486 to the country and has advanced the cause of global equality for women; in early years, ran L. A. Free Shakespeare Festival; elected president of California Theater Council; transformed L. A. Shakespeare Festival into the powerful L. A. Public Theater (LAPT, 1982), then one of only 3 Equity houses in Los Angeles; produced the star-studded *NOW's 20th Anniversary Show* at Dorothy Chandler Pavilion in Los Angeles (1986); with Eleanor Smeal, Katherine Spillar, Toni Carabillo, and Judith Meuli (1987), founded Feminist Majority Foundation (FMF) and the Feminist Majority (FM), of which Yorkin serves as chair of the board; donated $10 million, the largest gift ever made for women's rights, to FMF (1991), for such initiatives as the National Clinic Defense Project, the Campaign for RU-486 and Contraceptive Research, the Campaign to Stop Violence Against Women, the Task Force on Women and Girls in Sports, the National Center for Women and Policing, National Feminist Expositions, the Feminization of Power Campaign, Rock for Choice, Women United for Equality, as well as protecting clinics from anti-abortion violence, and the Campaign to Stop Gender Apartheid in Afghanistan, chaired by Mavis Leno (Leno and the FMF would be nationally recognized for their earlier efforts to make the country aware of the terrorist-inspired nature of the Taliban regime; many would voice profound regret that their warnings had not been heeded). ❖ See also *Women in World History*.

YOSANO, Akiko (1878–1942). Japanese writer and feminist. Pronunciation: Yoe-sah-no Ah-key-koe. Born Ho Sho in Sakai, Japan, in 1878; died in Tokyo in 1942; dau. of Otori (owner of a confectionery shop); m. Yosano Hiroshi (poet and founder of Shinshi Shi [New Poetry Society]); children: 10. ❖ One of the best-known poets in Japan, caused a sensation with publication of 1st book of poems, *Midaregami* (Tangled Hair, 1901), which became an important work of Japanese romanticism; wrote over 20 volumes of poetry and social commentary; essays ranged from feminist tracts to criticism of Japan's foreign aggression, and her poetry reflects some of these concerns as well; also broke social taboos with poems about experiencing labor pains and the birth of her stillborn baby; published translations into modern Japanese of Murasaki Shikibu's classic *Genji monogatari* (*The Tale of Genji*, 1912 and 1939); also published a monumental compilation of 26,783 poems written by 6,675 poets in modern times. ❖ See also *Women in World History*.

YOSHIDA, Mariko (1954—). Japanese volleyball player. Born July 27, 1954, in Japan. ❖ At Montreal Olympics, won a gold medal in team competition (1976).

YOSHIDA, Saori (1982—). Japanese wrestler. Born Oct 5, 1982, in Mie, Japan. ❖ Won World championships (2002, 2003) and Asian championships (2004), all for 55 kg freestyle; won a gold medal for 55 kg freestyle at Athens Olympics (2004).

YOSHIDA, Setsuko (1942—). Japanese volleyball player. Born Nov 4, 1942, in Japan. ❖ At Mexico City Olympics, won a silver medal in team competition (1968).

YOSHIKO (1834–1907). Japanese royal concubine. Name variations: Nakayama Yoshiko; sometimes referred to as Komei empress and empress dowager. Born in 1834; died in 1907; dau. of Nakayama Tadayasu (1809–1888, the great counselor or *dainagon*); concubine of Komei, emperor of Japan (r. 1847–1866, originally Osahito); children: at least 2 sons, including Mutsuhito (1852–1912), emperor of Japan (r. 1867–1912). ❖ A lady in waiting and concubine of Komei.

YOSHIKO KAWASHIMA (1906–1947). See *Kawashima, Yoshiko.*

YOSHIOKA, Yayoi (1871–1959). Japanese physician. Pronunciation: Yoe-she-o-kah Yah-yo-ee. Born Washiama Yayoi in 1871 in Shizuoka Prefecture, Japan; died in Tokyo, Japan, 1959; dau. of Dr. Washiama Yosai (who introduced Western medicine to his home region); m. Yamada Arata (a German-language instructor), in 1895; children: 1 son. ❖ The founder of Japan's 1st medical school for women, merged her medical clinic, where she was training women students, and her husband's German-language academy (1900), into Tokyo Women's Medical Institute (today, Tokyo Women's Medical University); had a 53-year tenure as president, overseeing the education of more than 7,000 women doctors; also operated a hospital (Tokyo Shisei Byoin) and was an active participant in government organizations. Received the Fujin Bunka Sho, the highest award given to women in Japan (1955). ❖ See also *Women in World History.*

YOU JAE-SOOK. South Korean field-hockey player. Born in South Korea. ❖ Won a team silver medal at Atlanta Olympics (1996).

YOUNG, Ann Eliza (b. 1844). American religious reformer. Name variations: Ann Eliza Dee; Ann Eliza Denning. Born Ann Eliza Webb, Sept 13, 1844, in Nauvoo, Illinois; date and place of death unknown; dau. of Chauncy Griswold Webb (wheelwright) and Eliza Jane (Churchill) Webb; m. John L. Dee, April 4, 1863 (div. 1865); m. Brigham Young (pioneer leader of the Church of Jesus Christ of the Latter-day Saints), April 7, 1869 (div. 1874); m. Moses Denning, in 1883; children: (1st m.) James Edward Dee (b. 1864); Leonard Lorenzo Dee (b. 1865). ❖ Plural wife of Brigham Young who divorced him and became an impassioned orator on the lecture circuit against the practice of polygamy and its effects on women; migrated with family to Missouri and then to Salt Lake City, Utah (1846); at 25, married Brigham Young (1869); left Young and Mormonism and started lecturing against polygamy (1873); delivered her message to US Congress (April 1874); lecture crusade ended after passage of the Edmunds Act outlawing polygamy (1882); writings include *Wife No. 19, or the Story of Life in Bondage, Being a Complete Expose of Mormonism, and Revealing the Sorrows, Sacrifices, and Sufferings of Women in Polygamy* (1875). ❖ See also *Women in World History.*

YOUNG, Anna (1756–1780). See *Smith, Anna Young.*

YOUNG, Anne Sewell (1871–1961). American astronomer. Born in Bloomington, Wisconsin, 1871; died in Claremont, California, 1961; dau. of Albert Young (cleric) and Mary (Sewell) Young; niece of Charles Augustus Young, professor of astronomy at Princeton University; Carleton College, BL, 1892, MS, 1897; attended University of Chicago, 1898 and 1902; Columbia University, PhD, 1906. ❖ Served as director of John Payson Williston Observatory, head of astronomy department, instructor, and professor at Mt. Holyoke College (1899–1936); while there supervised an active program of observations, keeping a daily record of sunspots which eventually developed into an international research project; was elected president of American Association of Variable Star Observers (1923); wrote a monthly column on astronomy for the *Springfield Republican.* ❖ See also *Women in World History.*

YOUNG, Annie (1814–1881). See *Dupuy, Eliza Ann.*

YOUNG, Cecilia (c. 1711–1789). English opera singer. Name variations: Cecilia Arne. Born in London, England, c. 1711; died in London, Oct 6, 1789; dau. of Charles Young (organist at All Hallows, in Barking); sister of Isabella Young and Esther Young, both singers; married Thomas Augustine Arne (1710–1778, composer), in 1737 (sep. 1756, reunited 1777, died shortly after). ❖ Studied with Geminiani; began career in opera productions by Lampe and Smith (1732–33) and went on to sing

in Handel's 1735 premieres of *Alcina* and *Ariodante*; later created parts in his oratorios *Saul* and *Alexander's Feast*; performed in Milton's *Comus,* Thomson and Mallet's *Alfred,* and Congreve's *Judgment of Paris,* for which her husband contributed the music; made last appearance in one of his productions in *Eliza* (1754).

YOUNG, Clara Kimball (1890–1960). American silent-film actress. Born Sept 6, 1890, in Chicago, Illinois; died Oct 15, 1960, in Woodland Hills, California; dau. of Edward M. Kimball (stagehand) and Pauline Maddern Garret (actress); m. James Young (director and actor, div. 1916); m. Harry Garson (her agent, early 1920s). ❖ Once named the most popular screen actress in America, made stage debut at 3; became a skilled actress in vaudeville productions and stock; made film debut in *Washington Under the American Flag* for Vitagraph (1909), followed by *A Midsummer's Night Dream* (1909), *Uncle Tom's Cabin* (1910), *Cardinal Wolsey* (1912), *Lincoln's Gettysburg Address* (1912), *Beau Brummel* (1913), *The Little Minister* (1913), *The Fates and Flora Fourflush* (serial, 1915), *Camille* (1915), and *Trilby* (1915), among others; left Vitagraph to become the top name at World Film Productions (1915), a newly formed company created by Lewis J. Selznick; with Selznick, formed the Clara Kimball Young Film Company (1916), which was devoted entirely to her films; career waned when husband Harry Garson became the producer and director of her films (mid-1920s); retired from films for a time, reverting to vaudeville; returned to the screen (1930s), primarily in character parts in low-budget productions; after a career that spanned some 50 films, retired (1941). ❖ See also *Women in World History.*

YOUNG, Connie Anne (1961—). See *Paraskevin-Young, Connie.*

YOUNG, Dannette (1964—). American runner. Name variations: Dannette Young-Stone. Born Oct 6, 1964, in Jacksonville, FL; attended Alabama A&M; m. Curtis Stone (track-and-field athlete), 1993; children: Dyshann. ❖ Won a gold medal at Los Angeles Olympics in 4 x 100-meter relay (1984) and a silver medal at Barcelona Olympics in 4 x 400-meter relay (1992).

YOUNG, Donna Caponi (1945—). See *Caponi, Donna.*

YOUNG, E. H. (1880–1949). English writer. Name variations: Emily Hilda Young; Mrs. Daniell. Born Emily Hilda Young in 1880 in Northumberland, England; died in Bradford-on-Avon, Wiltshire, Aug 8, 1949; dau. of William Michael Young (shipowner) and Frances Jane Young; educated at Penrhos College; m. J. A. H. Daniell (solicitor), 1902 (killed in battle at Ypres, 1917). ❖ Moved to Bristol (1902), where husband was a solicitor; published the 1st of her 13 books, *A Corn of Wheat* (1910) under name E. H. Young; used Bristol and nearby Clifton (renamed Radstowe and Upper Radstowe) as settings for many of her early novels, including *Yonder* (1912) and *Moon Fires* (1916); published *The Bridge Dividing* (1922), the 1st of her London novels, which was reprinted as *The Misses Mallett* (1927); other works include *William* (1925), *Miss Mole* (1930), which won the James Tait Black Memorial Prize, *Jenny Wren* (1932), *The Curate's Wife* (1934) and *Chatterton Square* (1947); also wrote 2 children's books, *Caravan Island* (1940) and *River Holiday* (1942). ❖ See also *Women in World History.*

YOUNG, Elizabeth (fl. 1558). British religious reformer. Born in England; married; children: 3. ❖ Was among the Protestants who fled to the Continent to avoid persecution in the time of Mary I; smuggled John Olde's *Antichrist,* and other Protestant tracts across the English channel; arrested for importing Protestant books, refusal to attend Mass, and rejection of tenets of Catholicism and authority of pope, underwent 13 interrogations before being released; John Foxe records legal examinations of Young in *Actes and Monuments* (1563).

YOUNG, Ella (1867–1951). Irish writer. Born in Fenagh, Co. Antrim, Ireland, Dec 6, 1867; died in California, 1951; dau. of John Young (high sheriff); sister of Rose Maud Young (1865–1947); earned political science and law degree at University College, Dublin. ❖ Poet, mythologist, and children's writer, who immersed herself in the Irish past, then traveled to the west of Ireland where she lived among the peasants and listened to them recite the old poetry; learned the Irish language and the tales of the Gobhan Saor, which she later collected in *The Wonder-Smith and His Son*; began to write verse and poetry for young and old, recounting stories of Irish fairies and ancient Celtic myths; a steadfast Irish republican, also joined Sinn Féin (1912) and smuggled guns for the Irish Republican Army; while sharing a flat with Maud Gonne, became a founding member of Cumann na mBan and was active in the Easter Rising; was eventually imprisoned in Mountjoy Gaol and in North Dublin Union Internment Camp by the Free State; traveled to US (1925), where she lectured at numerous American universities before moving to California, where she held the Phelan Memorial Lectureship on Celtic mythology and literature at University of California; published *The Unicorn with Silver Shoes* (1932), generally considered her finest literary accomplishment; also wrote *The Coming of Lugh* (1909), *Celtic Wonder Tales* (1910), *The Rose of Heaven* (poetry, 1920), *The Weird of Fionavar* (1922), *The Tangle-Coated Horse* (1929), *To the Little Princess* (poetry, 1930), *Marzilian and Other Poems* (1930), *Flowering Dusk* (1945) and *Smoke of Myrrh* (poetry, 1950). ❖ See also memoirs *Seed of the Pomegranate* (1949); and *Women in World History*.

YOUNG, Ella Flagg (1845–1918). American educator. Name variations: Ella Flagg. Born Ella Flagg, Jan 16, 1845, in Buffalo, New York; died Oct 26, 1918, in Washington, DC; dau. of Theodore Flagg (skilled metal worker) and Jane (Reed) Flagg; University of Chicago, undergraduate course work, 1895–99, PhD, 1900; m. William Young (merchant), in 1868 (died 1873); no children. ❖ Educator and theorist who was the 1st female superintendent of a major school district and the 1st female president of National Education Association; moved with family to Chicago (1858); in Chicago, held 1st teaching position in primary grade (1862); promoted to head assistant in grammar school (1863); at 20, named principal of the new School of Practice (teacher training); taught mathematics and was assistant to the principal at the Chicago Normal School (1872); was promoted to 2 consecutive principalships; promoted to district superintendent for Chicago School District (1887); served on the State Board of Education (1889–1909); started taking John Dewey's seminars at University of Chicago (1895); was associate professorial lecturer of pedagogy at University of Chicago (1899–1900), then professor of education (1900–04); published *Contributions to Education* series with John Dewey (1901–02); traveled in Europe, studying educational systems and theories (1904–05); named principal at Chicago Normal School (1905); named superintendent of Chicago School System (1909); elected president of National Education Association (1910); retired (1915) and moved to California; asked by US secretary of the Treasury to assist effort to sell war bonds during WWI with the Women's Liberty Loan Committee (1917); caught influenza while traveling for the war effort and died of pneumonia; fought tirelessly to improve schools; inspired, encouraged, and cajoled teachers to aim higher, use modern methods, and monitor their students' progress; in return, involved them in decisions about educational policy and practice; also fought to increase their pay, elevate their professional standing, and ensure their right to organize as a labor group. ❖ See also John T. McManis, *Ella Flagg Young And a Half-Century of the Chicago Public Schools* (1902); Joan K. Smith, *Ella Flagg Young—Portrait of a Leader* (Educational Studies Press, 1979); and *Women in World History*.

YOUNG, Esther (1717–1795). English soprano. Name variations: Hester Young; Mrs. Jones. Born 1717; died 1795; dau. of Charles Young (organist at All Hallows, in Barking); sister of Cecilia Young and Isabella Young, both singers. ❖ Created Handel's *Semele* (1744) and continued for many years in *The Beggar's Opera*.

YOUNG, Grace Chisholm (1868–1944). English mathematician. Name variations: Grace Chisholm. Born Grace Chisholm, Mar 15, 1868, in Haslemere, England; died 1944 in England; dau. of Anna Louisa (Bell) Chisholm and Henry William Chisholm; educated by tutors; graduate of Cambridge University, 1892, and University of Göttingen, 1895; m. William Henry Young (mathematician), June 1896 (died 1942); children: Francis (b. 1897, killed during WWI), Cecily (b. 1900, mathematician), Janet (b. 1901, physician), Helen (b. 1903), Lawrence (b. 1904), Patrick (b. 1908). ❖ Analytical mathematician and algebraic geometer, passed Cambridge University senior examination at 17 (1885); denied entry to Cambridge, as female students were still a novelty in the English university system (1885); won scholarship to Girton College, Cambridge, then the only institution of higher education for women in England (April 1889); passed the Cambridge Tripos with the equivalent of a 1st (1892); graduated from University of Göttingen (1895), 1st female holder of a formal PhD in Germany's history; returned to England (1895); moved to Switzerland (1897); with husband, published *The First Book of Geometry* (1905) and *The Theory of Sets of Points* (1906); published a paper on continuous non-differentiable functions (1915); awarded the Gamble Prize by Cambridge (1915); published paper, "On the Derivates of a Function" (1916), which delineated what has since become known as the Denjoy-Saks-Young Theorem; returned to England (1940); with husband, published roughly 220 articles and several books. ❖ See also *Women in World History*.

YOUNG, Heather Armitage (1933—). See Armitage, Heather.

YOUNG, Helen May (1867–1957). *See Butler, Helen May.*

YOUNG, Hilda (b. 1912). *See Cameron, Hilda.*

YOUNG, Isabella (d. 1795). English singer. Name variations: Mrs. Lampe. Died 1795; dau. of Charles Young (organist at All Hallows, in Barking); sister of Cecilia Young and Esther Young, both singers; m. J. F. Lampe. ❖ Married to composer J. F. Lampe, performed at Covent Garden in roles composed by him, including Thisbe in *Pyramus and Thisbe* (1745); had a daughter-in-law who also sang as Mrs. Lampe.

YOUNG, Janet (1926–2002). British politician. Name variations: Baroness Young. Born Oct 23, 1926; died Sept 6, 2002; educated at Oxford University; m. Geoffrey Young; children: 3. ❖ Was member of Oxford City Council (1957–72) and leader of Conservative Group; was offered life peerage (1971) and became first conservative woman to be Whip in House of Lords (1972); was under-secretary of State for Education (1973–74) and vice-chair of Conservative Party under Margaret Thatcher; became Cabinet minister of State in Department of Education and Science, the 1st female leader of the House of Lords (1981–83), and minister of State for Foreign Commonwealth office (1983–87).

YOUNG, Katherine (1904–2003). *See Cheung, Katherine.*

YOUNG, Lisa (1960—). *See Walters, Lisa.*

YOUNG, Loretta (1913–2000). American actress. Born Gretchen Michaela Young, Jan 6, 1913, in Salt Lake City, Utah; died Aug 12, 2000, in Los Angeles, California; dau. of John Earl Young (railroad auditor) and Gladys (Royal) Young; sister of Polly Ann Young, Sally Blane (actress), and Georgiana Young (who m. Ricardo Montalban); m. Grant Withers (actor), 1930 (div. 1931); m. Thomas H. A. Lewis (advertising executive), July 31, 1940 (div. 1969); m. Jean Louis (fashion designer), Aug 1993 (died April 1997); children: (2nd m.) Christopher Lewis (b. 1944); Peter Lewis (b. 1945); Judy Lewis (probably b. 1935, adopted 1937, actress). ❖ One of Hollywood's most glamorous actresses, was the 1st to make a successful crossover into tv, producing and starring in "The Loretta Young Show" (1953–61), which ran for 8 years; as a child, appeared as an extra in movies, often with older sisters; at 13, appeared in film *Naughty But Nice* (1927), starring Colleen Moore; made quick transition into leading roles, the 1st of which was opposite Lon Chaney in *Laugh Clown Laugh* (1928); spent 7 years with Warner Bros., then switched to 20th Century-Fox, becoming one of the 1st female stars to command a 6-figure salary; won Academy Award for performance in *The Farmer's Daughter* (1947); also gave notable performances in *Rachel and the Stranger* (1948), *Come to the Stable* (1949), for which she received an Oscar nomination, and *Cause for Alarm* (1951); made last feature film, *It Happens Every Thursday* (1952); though supposedly adopted, daughter Judy wrote an autobiography, *Uncommon Knowledge* (1994), claiming that Young was her biological mother and Clark Gable her father; other films include *Clive of India* (1935), *Call of the Wild* (1935), *The Crusades* (1935), *Ramona* (1936), *The Story of Alexander Graham Bell* (1939), *The Doctor Takes a Wife* (1940), *Bedtime Story* (1942), *A Night to Remember* (1942), *Ladies Courageous* (1944), *And Now Tomorrow* (1944), *The Stranger* (1946), *The Bishop's Wife* (1947), *The Accused* (1949) and *Because of You* (1952). Won 3 Emmy Awards for "The Loretta Young Show," making her the 1st actress to win both an Oscar and an Emmy. ❖ See also Joe Morella and Edward Z. Epstein. *Loretta Young: An Extraordinary Life* (Delacorte, 1986); and *Women in World History*.

YOUNG, Marguerite (1908–1995). American educator and writer. Born in Indianapolis, Indiana, 1908; died Nov 17, 1995, in Indianapolis; dau. of Chester Ellis Young (salesman) and Fay (Knight) Young; attended Indiana University; Butler University, BA, 1930; University of Chicago, MA, 1936; graduate work at University of Iowa. ❖ Published *Miss MacIntosh, My Darling* (1965), 18 years in the writing and 1,200 pages long, which was hailed as a masterpiece and its author was compared to James Joyce and Marcel Proust; served on the faculty at an Indianapolis high school; followed that with stints at University of Iowa (1955–57), New York's New School for Social Research (1958–67), and Fairleigh Dickinson University (1960–62); also wrote (poetry) *Prismatic Ground* (1937), (poetry) *Moderate Fable* (1945), *Angel in the Forest: A Fairy Tale of Two Utopias* (1945), *The Collected Poems of Marguerite Young* (1990), *Nothing But the Truth* (1993), *Inviting the Muses: Stories, Essays, Reviews* (1994) and *Harp Song for a Radical: The Life and Times of Eugene Victor Debs* (published posthumously, 1999). ❖ See also *Women in World History*.

YOUNG, Mary Marsden (1880–1971). American stage and screen actress. Name variations: Mrs. John Dickey Craig; Mary Young. Born June 21, 1880, in New York, NY; died June 23, 1971, in La Jolla, CA; m. John Dickey Craig (actor-manager, died 1932); children: John Craig. ❖ With husband and later her son, co-managed and starred at the Castle Square Theater in Boston for 21 years; appeared on Broadway in *Hamlet, The Outrageous Mrs. Palmer,* and *Dancing Mothers*; also appeared on tv and in films; retired (1968).

YOUNG, Mary Sophie (1872–1919). American botanist and teacher. Born in Glendale, Ohio, in 1872; died of cancer in 1919; dau. of an Episcopal priest; attended Harcourt Place Seminary; Wellesley College, BA, 1895; University of Chicago, PhD, 1910. ❖ Taught school in Kansas, Illinois, Wisconsin, and Missouri (1895–1908); was hired as a botany tutor at University of Texas at Austin (1910), then promoted to instructor (1911) and named curator of the university's herbarium (1912); her collecting trips (1912–18), and numerous trades with other herbaria, resulted in thousands of new specimens of Texas flora for the university; published a definitive guide, *A Key to the Families and Genera of Flowering Plants and Ferns in the Vicinity of Austin, Texas* (1917). ❖ See also *Women in World History.*

YOUNG, Patsy (1910–1985). See Hanshaw, Annette.

YOUNG, Rida Johnson (1869–1926). American playwright, lyricist, and librettist. Born Rida Louise Johnson, Feb 28, 1869, in Baltimore, Maryland; died from breast cancer, May 8, 1926, at her home in Southfield Point, near Stamford, Connecticut; dau. of William A. Johnson and Emma (Stuart) Johnson; attended Wilson College, Chambersberg, Pennsylvania, and Radcliffe College; m. James Young (actor), 1898 (div., 1909 or 1910). ❖ After a few unsuccessful years as an actress, took a job with Witmark music publishers, where for 2 years she wrote music; scored 1st true playwrighting success with *Brown of Harvard* (1906); next play, *The Boys of Company B* (1907), had a 2 year run on Broadway, followed by another success, *Glorious Betsy* (1908); estimated that she wrote a total of 500 songs in her lifetime, including those that she later incorporated into her own plays, including "Mother Machree" from *Barry of Ballymore* (1911), "I'm Falling in Love with Someone" from *Naughty Marietta* (1910) and "Sweethearts" from *Maytime* (1917); other plays include *Little Old New York* (1920), *Macushla* (1920), *The Front Seat* (1921), (with Harold Atteridge) *The Dream Girl* (music by Victor Herbert, 1924), and *Cock o' the Roost* (1924); other songs include "Ah! Sweet Mystery of Life," "'Neath the Southern Moon," "Tramp! Tramp! Tramp!," "The Sweet Bye and Bye," "Italian Street Song," "Will You Remember?" and "The Road to Paradise." ❖ See also *Women in World History.*

YOUNG, Rose Maud (1865–1947). Irish scholar. Name variations: Rose Mabel Young; Róis Ní Ógáin. Born in Galgorm Castle of Ballymena, Co. Antrim, Ireland, 1865; died in Cushendun, Co. Antrim, May 28, 1947; dau. of John Young (high sheriff); sister of Ella Young (1867–1951); trained as a teacher at Cambridge University; lived with Margaret Emmeline Dobbs (1873–1961). ❖ Committed to preserving the Irish language, attended Seán Ó Catháin's Irish College in Belfast, and continued her language studies at Coláiste Uladh in Gort a Choirce; made several lengthy stays in Dublin, where she visited members of the Gaelic League and other Irish scholars; Gaelicized her name, Róis Ní Ógáin, in her writing; also collaborated with Ellen O'Brien and contributed to O'Brien's book *The Gaelic Church,* in an attempt to Gaelicize the Church of Ireland; best remembered for editing and publishing *Duanair Gaedhilge* (Songs and Poems from Gaelic), 3 vols. of Gaelic poetry and songs. ❖ See also *Women in World History.*

YOUNG, Sheila (1950—). American speedskater and cyclist. Name variations: Sheila Young Ochowicz. Born Sheila Young, Oct 14, 1950, in Birmingham, Michigan; m. Jim Ochowicz (cyclist), 1976; children: Katie, Alex and Elli Ochowicz (b. 1983, speedskater). ❖ Was the 1st American woman to win the World Sprint Ladies Speedskating championship (1973), then won again (1975, 1976); won a gold medal in the 500-meter, silver in the 1,500-meter, and bronze in the 1,000-meter at Innsbruck (1976), the 1st American to win 3 medals in the Olympic Winter Games; won both the speedskating overall and sprint cycling World titles (1976), the 1st athlete, male or female, to hold World titles in both speedskating and cycling. Was a founding member of the Women's Sports Foundation; served on the board of US Olympic Committee, US Cycling Federation, and Special Olympics International. ❖ See also (juvenile) Joe Soucheray, *Sheila Young* (Creative Education Society, 1977); and *Women in World History.*

YOUNG, Wanda (1944—). African-American pop singer. Name variations: Wanda Rogers; Marvelettes. Born 1944 in Detroit, Michigan; m. Bobby Rogers (singer with the Miracles). ❖ Was a member of the Marvelettes, a popular Motown group whose songs "Don't Mess With Bill," "Please Mr. Postman," "I Keep Holding On," and "Beachwood 4–5789" reached the top of the charts (early 1960s). Other members included Gladys Horton, Katherine Anderson, Juanita Cowart. ❖ See also *Women in World History.*

YOUNGER, Maud (1870–1936). American labor reformer and suffragist. Born Jan 10, 1870, in San Francisco, California; died June 25, 1936, in Los Gatos, California; dau. of William John Younger and Annie Maria (Lane) Younger; never married; no children. ❖ Known as the "millionaire waitress," organized her co-workers on two coasts and wrote a series of articles exposing the harsh conditions under which women waited table in the early years of 20th century; served as resident, College Settlement House, New York City (1901–06); was an organizer, San Francisco waitress union (1908); was a delegate, San Francisco Central Trades and Labor Council (1908–11); was an organizer, Wage Earners' Equal Suffrage League (1911); served as an organizer for the Congressional Union, later named the National Woman's Party (1913–20); was active in the efforts to secure an Equal Rights Amendment (1923–36). ❖ See also *Women in World History.*

YOUNGHUSBAND, Adela Mary (1878–1969). New Zealand painter, art teacher, and photographer. Name variations: Adela Mary Roche. Born April 3, 1878, at Te Awamutu, New Zealand; died April 3, 1969, in Auckland, New Zealand; dau. of Hungerford Roche (farmer and politician) and Emily Adela (Malcolm) Roche; m. Frank Younghusband (grocer, d. 1921), 1905; children: 2 sons, 1 daughter. ❖ Taught art in Hamilton (Auckland, late 1910s and 1940s); managed photographic studio in Whangarei (1920s); co-established Whangarei Art and Literary Society (1920s); returned to painting and exhibited in Australia and New Zealand; founded Phoenix Group (1952), and Studio Art Group (1957); work represented in numerous private and public collections. ❖ See also *Dictionary of New Zealand Biography* (Vol. 4).

YOUNGHUSBAND, Eileen Louise (1902–1981). English social worker and teacher. Name variations: Dame Eileen Younghusband. Born Jan 1, 1902, in London, England; raised in Kashmir, India; died May 27, 1981, in Raleigh, North Carolina; dau. of Sir Francis Edward Younghusband (diplomat-explorer); attended London School of Economics. ❖ At London School of Economics, began as a tutor (1929), then served as a lecturer (1933–57); developed the school's 1st applied studies course to train professional social workers; helped establish Council for Training in Social Work; also served as a consultant to National Institute for Social Work Training, as president of International Association for Schools of Social Work, and as principal officer for National Association of Girls' Clubs; writings include *Social Work in Britain, 1950–1975* and *Social Work and Social Change*; named a fellow of London School of Economics (1961). Made a Member of Order of the British Empire (1946), Commander of Order of the British Empire (1955) and Dame of Order of the British Empire (1964); awarded the René Sand Prize (1976). ❖ See also *Women in World History.*

YOUNGS, Elaine (1970—). American volleyball player. Born Feb 14, 1970, in Orange, CA; attended University of California, Los Angeles. ❖ Played professional volleyball in Europe and represented US volleyball in Atlanta Olympics (1996); placed 2nd overall in World Tour ranking (2004); with Holly McPeak, won a bronze medal for beach volleyball at Athens Olympics (2004). Named WPVA Rookie of the Year (2003).

YOUNKER, Jenna (1967—). See Johnson, Jenna.

YOURCENAR, Marguerite (1903–1987). French writer. Name variations: Marguerite de Crayencour. Born Marguerite Antoinette Jeanne Marie Ghislaine Cleenewerckx de Crayencour in Brussels, Belgium, June 8, 1903; died in Bar Harbor, Maine, Dec 17, 1987; dau. of Michel-René Cleenewerckx de Crayencour (aristocrat, died 1929) and Fernande de Cartier de Marchienne (died 1903); passed her baccalauréat in Nice, France, 1919; never married; lived with Grace Frick (died Nov 18, 1979); no children. ❖ Novelist, poet, essayist, playwright, and translator who was the 1st female member of the Académie Française; published 1st work, *Le Jardin des Chimères* (*The Garden of Chimerae*), under pen name Marguerite Yourcenar (1921); published 1st novel, *Alexis or The Treatise of Vain Combat* (1928), followed by *The New Eurydice* (1931); translated Virginia Woolf's *The Waves* into French (1937); in Paris, met Grace

Frick, an American academic who became her companion for the rest of Frick's life (Feb 1937); published *Coup de Grâce* and moved to US (1939); taught part-time at Sarah Lawrence College (1941–53); became US citizen (1947); awarded Prix Fémina for *Memoirs of Hadrian* (1952); saw her play *Electra* staged in Paris (1953); wrote *Render unto Caesar* (1959), a theatrical adaptation of her novel *A Coin in Nine Hands*; also published a book on African-American spirituals, *Deep River, Dark River* (1964); awarded Prix Combat (France, 1962) for her collection of essays, *The Dark Brain of Piranesi*; awarded Prix Fémina for *The Abyss* (1968); elected to Académie royale belge de Langue et de Littérature françaises (1971); elected to the Académie Française (1980), the 1st woman ever; wrote 1st vol. of family trilogy, *Dear Departed*; elected to American Academy of Arts and Letters (1982); published 1st vol. of her novelistic works in the *Bibliothèque de la Pléiade* series, Paris (1982). ❖ See also Josyane Savigneau, *Marguerite Yourcenar: Inventing a Life* (trans. by Joan E. Howard, U. of Chicago Press, 1993); and *Women in World History*.

YOURIEVSKI, Princess (1847–1922). *See Dolgorukova, Ekaterina.*

YOUSHKEVITCH, Nina (c. 1921–1998). Ukrainian ballet dancer and teacher. Name variations: Yushkevich; Nina Youshkevitch Johnson. Born Dec 7, c. 1921, in Odessa, Ukraine; died Nov 3, 1998, in New York, NY; raised in Paris. ❖ Trained with Olga Preobrazhenska and Lyubov Egorova in Paris; danced with Bronislava Nijinska's Ballet Russe companies (1934), in such works as *Les Biches, Variations,* and *Baiser de la Fée;* created roles in Nijinska's *Chopin Concerto* (1937), *Apollo Through the Ages* (1937), and *Le Chant de la Terre* (1937), among others; also danced with Polish National Ballet and Ballet Russe de Monte Carlo; moved to US (1942) and became ballerina at Metropolitan Opera Ballet in New York City; danced Aurora in America's 1st full-length *The Sleeping Beauty,* for San Francisco Russian Opera (1945); appeared on final tour to Canada before retiring from performance career (1946); was a ballet teacher at Nijinska's Los Angeles studio; opened her own studio in New York (1973); created works of her own, including *The Infinite* (1951), *Light and Shadow* (1953), *Les Cinq Petites Variations* (1969), and *The Nightingale and the Rose* (1969).

YOUSKEVITCH, Maria (c. 1946—). American ballet dancer. Born c. 1946 in New York, NY; dau. of Igor Youskevitch and Anna Scarpova Youskevitch (soloist with Ballet Russe de Monte Carlo and ballet teacher, died 1997). ❖ Received original training from parents; danced in father's Ballet Romantique and performed with Metropolitan Opera Ballet in New York City; danced with American Ballet Theater for 7 years (1967–74) in works by Agnes de Mille, Antony Tudor, Frederick Ashton, and Eugene Loring; joined The Maryland Ballet and performed there in classical as well as modern works.

YOUSSOUPOFF, Irina (1895–1970). *See Irina.*

YOUVILLE, Marie Marguerite d' (1701–1771). Canadian nun, founder and saint. Name variations: Marie Marguerite Dufrost de Lajemmerais, Marie-Marguerite d'Youville, Marie Margaret Dufrost de Lajemmerais d'Youville. Born Marie Marguerite Dufrost de Lajemmerais, Oct 15, 1701, in Varennes, Quebec, Canada; died Dec 23, 1771, in Montreal; dau. of Christophe Dufrost de Lajemmerais and Marie-Renée Gaultier; studied under Ursuline nuns (1711–1713); m. François-Madeleine d'Youville (gambler, bootlegger), 1722; children: 6 (only 2 sons survived and both became priests). ❖ Grew up in poverty after losing father at 7; spent 2 years studying with Ursuline nuns in Quebec; married at 21 (1722), was widowed after unhappy marriage (1730); cleared husband's debts and supported 2 surviving sons by running small shop; devoted much time to Confraternity of Holy Family charitable activities; despite resistance from family and community, founded Sisters of Charity (Grey Nuns of Montreal) with 3 companions (1737), to care and advocate for poor; was asked to restore derelict Hôpital Général (1749) and opened refuge to the elderly, insane, incurable, foundlings, orphans and disabled soldiers; as mother superior of Grey Nuns, established schools, hospitals and orphanages throughout Canada, US, Africa and South America; was beatified by Pope John XXIII (1959) and canonized (1990), the 1st native Canadian to be elevated to sainthood.

YOW, Kay (1942—). American basketball coach. Born Mar 14, 1942, in Gibsonville, North Carolina; graduate of East Carolina University, 1964. ❖ Coached at Elon College (1972–75) and won 2 state titles; became coach at North Carolina State (1976), where she compiled a 579–266 record by the 2002–03 season; won her 600th game (Jan 11, 2001); coached US Olympic team (1988), which won a gold medal. Inducted into Naismith Memorial Basketball Hall of Fame (2002).

YPOLLITA. *Variant of Ippolita.*

YRENES. *Variant of Irene.*

YSABEAU. *Variant of Elisabeth or Elizabeth, Isabel or Isabella.*

YSABEL or YSABELLA. *Variant of Elisabeth or Elizabeth, Isabel or Isabella.*

YU HONGQI. Chinese soccer player. Born in China. ❖ Won a team silver medal at Atlanta Olympics (1996).

YU JUNG-HYE (1954—). Korean volleyball player. Born Feb 10, 1954, in South Korea. ❖ At Montreal Olympics, won a bronze medal in team competition (1976).

YU KYUNG-HWA (1953—). Korean volleyball player. Born Dec 22, 1953, in South Korea. ❖ At Montreal Olympics, won a bronze medal in team competition (1976).

YU LIHUA (1932—). Chinese novelist and short-story writer. Born 1932 in Shanghai, China; moved to US. ❖ Works include *Witness to an Academic Conference* (1972), *The Women of New China* (1977), and *Sons and Daughters of the Fu Family* (1978).

YU MANZHEN (fl. 1900). Chinese reformer. Name variations: Yü Man-chen. Married Jiang Yufeng (Confucian scholar); children: Ding Ling (writer, 1904–1985). ❖ Was an early female political activist.

YU SUN-BOK (1970—). North Korean table tennis player. Born Aug 2, 1970, in North Korea. ❖ At Barcelona Olympics, won a bronze medal in doubles (1992).

YUAN HUA (1974—). Chinese judoka. Born 1974 in Liaoning Province, China. ❖ Won debut title at World Jr. championships (1992); won International Judo championship (1997) and World University championship (1999); won a gold medal for heavyweight +78 kg at Sydney Olympics (2000); won World championship (2001).

YUAN JING (b. 1914). Chinese novelist and scriptwriter. Born 1914 in China; educated in Beijing. ❖ Joined Communist-led resistance against the Japanese invasion (1937); worked in women's movement and addressed social and political issues in novels and plays; works include (play) *Liu Jiaoer Seeks Justice* and (novel) *Sons and Daughters.*

YUAN SHU CHI (1984—). Chinese Taipei archer. Born Nov 9, 1984, in Taiwan. ❖ Won a bronze medal for team at Athens Olympics (2004).

YUAN, Tina (c. 1950—). Chinese modern dancer. Name variations: Tina Yuan Lems. Born c. 1950 in Shanghai, China. ❖ Moved to New York City to train at Juilliard School and at studio of Martha Graham; was a principal dancer with Alvin Ailey Dance Theater, appearing in a range of Ailey's works, as well as in works by Talley Beatty, Pearl Primus, and James Truitte; created roles in Janet Collins *Canticle of the Elements* (1974), Jennifer Muller's *Crossword* (1977), and Yuriko's *Events I and II;* founded East-West Contemporary Dance Company which she also co-directed; created range of works for that company, often in collaboration with Richard Ornellas; served as director of Chinese Dance Company in NY, an innovative group that integrated modern dance with traditional Chinese and Taiwanese movements. Works of choreography include *Suite of Taiwanese Dances* (1972), *The Peacock* (1972), *Martian Dances* (1972), *Dances of the Border Provinces* (1972), *Legend of the White Snake Lady* (1972) and *Trilogy* (1975).

YUASA, Toshiko (1909–1980). Japanese nuclear physicist. Born Dec 11, 1909, in Tokyo, Japan; died Feb 1, 1980. ❖ Prominent physicist who was considered Japan's Marie Curie, attended Tokyo Bunrika University (1931–34) and the Laboratoire de Chimie Nucléaire du Collège de France in Paris (1940–44); earned DSc (1962) from Kyoto University for her dissertation; researched at University of Berlin's Physics Institute (1944); developed a double-focus spectroscope (1945); investigated nuclear spectroscopy as a Centre National de la Recherche Scientifique (CNRS) researcher at the Laboratoire de Physique Nucléaire du Collège de France (1949–52); at CNRS, worked as a researcher (1952–57), research head (1957–74) and became honorary research head (1975); taught at several universities in Japan, including the Ochanomizu Women's University (1952–55).

YUDINA, Maria (1899–1970). Soviet pianist. Born Maria Veniaminovna Yudina in Nevel, Russia, Sept 10, 1899; died in Moscow, Nov 20, 1970. ❖ Studied at St. Petersburg Conservatory with Annette Essipova and others; made concert debut (1921); taught at the Petrograd (later Leningrad) Conservatory (1921–31); moved to Moscow, where she was a professor at the Moscow Conservatory (1936–51); produced Taneyev's

Orestes at the Moscow Conservatory (1939), repeating this work with the Soviet Opera Ensemble (1946); championed the works of composers whose style was not always approved by the Soviet musical establishment, these being compositions by Shostakovich, Stravinsky and Hindemith.

YUGOSLAVIA, queen of.
See Marie (1900–1961).
See Alexandra (1921–1993).

YUN MI-JIN (1983—). South Korean archer. Born April 30, 1983, in Daejeon, South Korea; attended Kyounghee University. ❖ Won a gold medal for teams and a gold medal for indiv. FITA round at Sydney Olympics (2000), insuring Korea's 5th successive indiv. Olympic medal in the women's division; at World championships, placed 1st in indiv. and team (2003); at Athens Olympics, won a gold medal for team round (2004).

YUN YOUNG-NAE (1952—). Korean volleyball player. Born Sept 26, 1952, in South Korea. ❖ At Montreal Olympics, won a bronze medal in team competition (1976).

YURCHENKO, Natalia (1965—). Soviet gymnast. Born Jan 26, 1965, in Norilsk, USSR; m. Viktor Sklyarov (Olympic soccer player). ❖ Won USSR nationals (1981, 1982), Moscow News (1982, 1983), USSR Cup (1982), World Cup (1982), University Games (1983, 1985); at World championships, won gold medals in all-around (1983) and team all-around (1983 and 1985); was the 1st to perform a Korbut loop on beam, the 1st to do a layout mount on beam, and the 1st female to perform the round-off entry vault; immigrated to US (1999).

YURCHENYA, Marina (1959—). Soviet swimmer. Born Nov 1959 in USSR. ❖ At Montreal Olympics, won a silver medal in 200-meter breaststroke (1976).

YURIC, Dragica (1963—). Yugoslavian handball player. Born Mar 26, 1963, in Yugoslavia. ❖ At Los Angeles Olympics, won a gold medal in team competition (1984).

YURIESKY, Princess (1847–1922). See Dolgorukova, Ekaterina.

YURIKO (b. 1920). American modern dancer and choreographer. Name variations: Yuriko Kikuchi. Born Yuriko Kikuchi, Feb 2, 1920, in San Jose, CA; raised in Japan; children: Susan Kikuchi. ❖ Danced with company of Konami Ishii during adolescence in Tokyo; returned to US and danced in Dorothy Lyndall's Junior Dance Company until 1941; following bombing of Pearl Harbor (1941), was interned at the Gila River Reservation Center in Arizona, along with 13,000 Japanese-American; started a dance school for the prisoners; released to study with Martha Graham in NY (1944); began a 50-year association with the Graham Company, creating roles in *Primitive Mysteries* (1944), *Appalachian Spring* (1944), *Imagined Wing* (1944), *Ardent Song* (1954), *Clytemnestra* (1958), *Embattled Garden* (1958) and *Equatorial* (1978); took over Graham's roles in numerous works, including *Appalachian Spring*; also created role of Eliza for *The King and I* on Broadway (1951); founded and directed Yuriko Dance Company (1967–74) for which she choreographed many works; formed Martha Graham Dance Ensemble to recreate Graham dances from the 1930s.

YURINA, Esfir (1923—). Soviet spy. Name variations: Esfir Grigoryevna Yurina; Rita Elliott (also seen as Rita Elliot). Born 1923 in Moscow, USSR; dau. of Grigoriy Ivanovich Yurin (circus artist). ❖ Attended Graczyna spy school (1945) where she became known as Rita Elliott and perfected cover as tightrope walker; smuggled into Australia (1955),

worked as variety artiste in several cities, including Sydney and Canberra, while entertaining men involved in nuclear research; methods included drugging and hypnotizing; after coming under observation, ceased espionage activities; left Australia (1961) and worked in variety and circus shows in India and Pakistan.

YURKA, Blanche (1887–1974). American actress and writer. Name variations: Blanche Jurka. Born June 19, 1887, in Czechoslovakia; died June 6, 1974, in New York, NY; dau. of Anton and Karolina (Novak) Jurka; attended Metropolitan Opera School, 1903–05, Institute of Musical Art (now Juilliard School of Music), 1905–07; m. Ian Keith (actor), Sept 1922 (div. 1928). ❖ Brought to US as an infant; spent early years in St. Paul, Minnesota; moved to NY (1900); studied for a career in opera but injured voice; toured for years with stock companies, and finally achieved some recognition with *Daybreak* (1917); became one of the most well-known stage actresses of the day, known for playing strong-willed women in such plays as *The Warrens of Virginia* (1907), *The Wild Duck* (1925), *Hedda Gabler* (1929), *Lady from the Sea* (1929), *Electra* (1932), *Romeo and Juliet* (1935) and *The Madwoman of Chaillot* (1969); also played Queen Gertrude to John Barrymore's Hamlet (1922) for 125 performances; made film as Madame Defarge in *A Tale of Two Cities* (1935), followed by more than 20 films, including *Queen of the Mob* (1940), *Escape* (1940), *Lady for a Night* (1942), *A Night to Remember* (1942), *Keeper of the Flame* (1942), *Tonight We Raid Calais* (1943), *The Song of Bernadette* (1943), *The Bridge of San Luis Rey* (1944), *The Cry of the Werewolf* (1944), *The Southerner* (1945), *13 Rue Madeleine* (1947) and *Dinner at Eight* (1966). ❖ See also autobiography, *Bohemian Girl: Blanche Yurka's Theatrical Life* (1970); and *Women in World History*.

YURKINA, Olga (1976—). Belarusian gymnast. Born Sept 21, 1976, in Belarus; twin sister of Yulia Yurkina (gymnast). ❖ Won Belarusian nationals (1992, 1993); won a bronze medal for uneven bars at Cottbus (1994); placed 3rd at Gymnix Invitational (1995) and 6th for team all-around at Atlanta Olympics (1996).

YUSOVA, Zoya (1948—). Soviet volleyball player. Born April 1948 in USSR. ❖ At Montreal Olympics, won a silver medal in team competition (1976).

YUSSOUPOV, Irina (1895–1970). See Irina.

YUSUF, Fatima (1971—). Nigerian runner. Name variations: Fatima Yusuf-Olukoju. Born May 2, 1971, in Nigeria. ❖ Won a silver medal for the 4 x 400-meter relay at Atlanta Olympics (1996).

YUSUPOV, Irene (1895–1970). See Irina.

YVA (1900–1942). German photographer. Name variations: Else Simon; Elsa Simon; Else Neuländer-Simon. Born Else Ernestine Neuländer, Jan 26, 1900, in Berlin, Germany, of Jewish parents; died in the Majdanek concentration camp during WWII (death date uncertain); m. Alfred Simon (Jewish). ❖ Ran a photo studio in Berlin (1925–38), specializing in advertising; did fashion shoots for large publishing houses and reaped worldwide attention; with the rise of the Nazis, was banned from practising her profession; deported to concentration camp with husband (1942). Helmut Newton apprenticed with her.

YVETTA or YVETTE. *Variant of Joveta, Ivetta or Ivette.*

YVETTA OF JERUSALEM (b. 1120). See Joveta of Jerusalem.

YVETTE OF HUY (1158–1228). See Ivetta of Huy.

Z

❖

ZABAINA (r. 267–272). *See Zenobia.*

ZABAR, Lillian (1905–1995). Ukranian-born American entrepreneur. Born Lillian Teit, Dec 22, 1905, in the Ukraine; died Dec 22, 1995; m. Louis Zabar (died 1950); m. Louis Chartoff (died c. 1980); children: Saul, Stanley, and Eli. ❖ Co-founder of the famous New York City delicatessen, came to US (1920s); opened Zabar's gourmet delicatessen in Brooklyn (1934), and later moved the business to Broadway and 80th Street in Manhattan. ❖ See also *Women in World History.*

ZABEL (b. around 1210). Queen of Lesser Armenia. Name variations: Isabella; Zabel the Rupenid. Born c. 1210 in Sis, Lesser Armenia (Cilicia in modern-day Turkey); younger dau. of Leo the Great, king of Lesser Armenia (died 1219), and his 2nd wife Sibylla of Cyprus; m. Andrew of Hungary (div. 1219); m. Philip of Antioch, later king of Lesser Armenia, in 1222 (died 1225); m. Hetoum (Hayton) I of Baberon, later king of Lesser Armenia, on June 14, 1226; children: (3rd m.) Leo II, king of Lesser Armenia; Thoros; Sybilla; Euphemia; Maria. ❖ At 9, named heir by father before he died (1219), the 1st woman to succeed to the throne in Cilicia; though married to prince Andrew of Hungary as part of a political alliance, saw marriage annulled by regent, her cousin Prince Constantine of Baberon (1219); was next married to her cousin Philip of Antioch, son of the French crusader-king Bohemond IV of Antioch (1222), but he was arrested and executed (1225); forced to marry Constantine's 11-year-old son Hetoum, was coerced into a double coronation with him (1225); while co-reigning, was allowed little authority; son became king as Leo II on his father Hetoum's abdication (1269). ❖ See also *Women in World History.*

ZABELINA, Aleksandra (1937—). Soviet fencer. Born Mar 11, 1937, in USSR. ❖ Won a gold medal at Rome Olympics (1960), gold medal at Mexico City Olympics (1968), and gold medal at Munich Olympics (1972), all in team foil.

ZABELL, Theresa (1965—). Spanish-English yacht racer. Name variations: Theresa Zabell Lucas. Born May 22, 1965, in Ipswich, England. ❖ At Barcelona Olympics, won a gold medal in 470 class (1992); won World championships for 470 (1992, 1994, 1995, 1996); won European championship (1991, 1994); won a gold medal for double-handed dinghy (470) at Atlanta Olympics (1996); as a member of the European People's Party (Christian Democrats) and European Democrats, elected to 5th European Parliament (1999–2004); served as vice-chair of the Committee on Culture, Youth, Education, the Media and Sport. Named IYRU Sperry Top-Sider World Sailor of the Year (1994); awarded Grand Cross of Sporting Merit (Spain).

ZABELLE, Flora (1880–1968). Turkish-born actress, singer, and designer. Born April 1, 1880, in Constantinople, Ottoman Empire (now Istanbul, Turkey); died Oct 7, 1968, in New York, NY; dau. of Rev. M. M. Mangasarian; m. Raymond Hitchcock (actor). ❖ Made Broadway debut as Poppy in *San Toy* (1900), then took over title role; with husband, appeared in *King Dodo, The Yankee Consul, Easy Dawson,* and *A Yankee Tourist;* films include *The Savage Tiger* and *The Red Widow;* launched a 2nd career as a designer (1920).

ZABIROVA, Zulfia (1973—). Russian cyclist. Name variations: Zulfiya. Born Dec 19, 1973, in Tashkent, Uzbekistan. ❖ Won a gold medal for indiv. time trial at Atlanta Olympics (1996); won Tour de Suisse (1996); placed 2nd (1997) and 1st (2002) at World championships.

ZABOLOTNAIA, Natalia (1985—). Russian weightlifter. Born Aug 15, 1985, in USSR. ❖ Won a silver medal for 75 kg at Athens Olympics (2004).

ZABOLUYEVA, Svetlana (1966—). Soviet basketball player. Born Aug 20, 1966, in USSR. ❖ At Barcelona Olympics, won a gold medal in team competition (1992).

ZABRISKIE, Louise (1887–1957). American nurse. Born 1887 in Preston City, CT; died Dec 12, 1957, in New York, NY; graduate of New York Hospital School of Nursing, 1913. ❖ Maternity educator, was the founder (1939) and director (1939–57) of the Maternity Consultation Service (NYC), the 1st center in America to offer classes for expectant fathers; wrote *Nurses Handbook of Obstetrics* (1929), *Baby Care in Pictures* (1935) and a regular column for *My Baby Magazine,* among others.

ZACHRISSON, Vendela (1978—). Swedish yacht racer. Born June 11, 1978, in Norrköping, Sweden. ❖ Won World championship for 470 class (2004); won a bronze medal for double-handed dinghy (470) at Athens Olympics (2004).

ZACHRY, Caroline B. (1894–1945). American educational psychologist. Born Caroline Beaumont Zachry, April 20, 1894, in New York, NY; died Feb 22, 1945, in New York, NY; dau. of James Greer Zachry (attorney) and Elise Clarkson (Thompson) Zachry; Columbia University Teachers College, BS, 1924, MS, 1925, PhD, 1929; never married; children: (both adopted) Stephen Beaumont and Nancy Greer. ❖ Worked in the English and psychology departments of the New Jersey State Teachers College, assuming the directorship of its Mental Hygiene Institute (1930); studied with Carl Jung in Vienna; incorporated developments in the field of psychology in her improvements of educational practices, specifically focusing on the role of the school in a child's social development; published *Emotion and Conduct in Adolescence* (1940); for 2 years, served as director of the Institute for the Study of Personality Development; became director of Bureau of Child Guidance for New York City Board of Education (1942). ❖ See also *Women in World History.*

ZACZKIEWICZ, Claudia (1962—). West German hurdler. Born July 1962. ❖ At Seoul Olympics, won a bronze medal in 100-meter hurdles (1988).

ZAGONI-PREDESCU, Marlena (1951—). Romanian rower. Born Jan 22, 1951. ❖ At Moscow Olympics, won a bronze medal in coxed eights (1980).

ZAGORKA, Maria Jurić (1873–1957). Croatian author. Name variations: Maria Juric; Marija Juric Zagorka. Born in 1873; died in 1957; forced to marry a wealthy Hungarian, whom she fled three years later. ❖ As Croatia's 1st political journalist, expressed her intellectual and feminist ideas, which made her the target of attack in southeastern Europe, a region with virtually no evidence of feminist expression at the time; also wrote adventure novels and dramas.

ZAGUNIS, Mariel (1985—). American fencer. Born Mar 3, 1985, in Portland, OR; sister of Marten Zagunis (fencer); attended Notre Dame University. ❖ At World championship, won a gold medal for team sabre (2000); won a gold medal for indiv. sabre at Athens Olympics (2004).

ZAHARIA, Noemi (1968—). *See Lung, Noemi Ildiko.*

ZAHARIAS, Babe Didrikson (1911–1956). American golfer, softball player, and track-and-field athlete. Name variations: Mildred Didrikson; Mildred Didrikson Zaharias. Born Mildred Ella Didriksen, June 26, 1911, in Port Arthur, TX; died in Galveston, TX, Sept 26, 1956; m. George Zaharias (professional wrestler), 1938; lived with Betty Dodd. ❖ Premiere woman athlete of 20th century, was chosen two-time All-American in basketball (1931–32); won AAU javelin toss (1930) with a throw of 133′6 (AAU-US record); won Women's National AAU championship with a broad jump of 17′11¾ (1931); as a one-woman "team," won the championship of Amateur Athletic Union Track and Field Meet (1932) in following 5 events: shot put with a throw of 39′6¼ (AAU-US record), baseball throw, 272′2 (a record she would break at 296′ which still stands since the event was phased out), javelin with 139′3 (world record), 80-meter hurdles in 12.1 seconds, high jump with 17′6, and 4th in the discus; at Olympic Games in Los Angeles (1932), won a gold medal in 80-meter hurdles in 11.7 seconds (world and American record), and javelin toss, 143'4 (world and Olympic record), also received controversial gold-silver medal for high jump, 5'5¼ (denied a pure gold because of her "unorthodox" jumping style); won 13 (claimed 17) consecutive amateur golf tournaments (1945–47); was the 1st American woman to win British Women's Open (1947); co-founded LPGA (late 1940s); was a member of Walker Cup Team that defeated British players (1948–49); served as president of LPGA. Inducted into LPGA Hall of Fame, National Track and Field Hall of Fame, International Women's Sports Hall of Fame, Helms Athletic Foundation Hall of Fame (for basketball), and Professional Golfers' Hall of Fame; given the Graham McNamee Memorial Award as the greatest woman athlete in history by the Sports Broadcasters' Association; given the Associated Press' Woman of the Half Century Award; voted "Woman Athlete of the Year" 6 times by Associated Press; named the Greatest Woman Athlete of the Past 50 Years, by the nation's Associated Press Sports Writers'; honored on US commemorative stamp (1981). ❖ See also *This Life I've Led* (with Harry Paxton, 1955); Johnson and Williamson, *"Whatta-Gal": The Babe Didrikson Story* (Little, Brown, 1975); Susan E. Cayleff, *The "Golden Cyclone": The Life and Legend of Babe Didrikson Zaharias, 1911–1956* (U. of Illinois Press, 1995) and "Babe," fictionalized tv movie, starring Susan Clark (1975).

ZAHOUREK, Berta (1896–1967). Austrian swimmer. Born Jan 3, 1896, in Austria; died June 14, 1967. ❖ At Stockholm Olympics, won a bronze medal in 4 x 100-meter freestyle relay (1912).

ZAIDA (d. 1107). Moorish mistress of Alphonso VI. Name variations: Isabella. Died in 1107; dau. of Abul-Kasim Muhammad be Abbad, emir of Seville, and Itamid (a former slave); m. Al Ma'mun, prince of Seville; mistress of Alphonso VI (c. 1030–1109), king of Leon (r. 1065–1070, 1072–1109) and Castile (r. 1072–1109); children: (with Alphonso VI) illeg. son Sancho (b. around 1093); Sancha of Castile (who m. Rodrigo "El Franco," count of Liebana); Elvira (d. 1135, who m. Robert II the Great, king of Sicily).

ZAINAB. *Variant of Zaynab.*

ZAINAB BINT DJAHSH (c. 590–640). *See Zaynab bint Jahsh.*

ZAINAB BINT JAHSH (c. 590–640). *See Zaynab bint Jahsh.*

ZAKARIAS, Maria (1952—). Hungarian kayaker. Born Sept 28, 1952, in Hungary. ❖ At Moscow Olympics, won a bronze medal in K2 500 meters (1980).

ZAKHAROVA, Galina (1947—). Soviet handball player. Born Mar 22, 1947, in USSR. ❖ At Montreal Olympics, won a gold medal in team competition (1976).

ZAKHAROVA, Nadezhda (1945—). Soviet basketball player. Born Feb 1945 in USSR. ❖ At Montreal Olympics, won a gold medal in team competition (1976).

ZAKHAROVA, Olga (1973—). Ukrainian climber. Born May 3, 1973, in Kramatorsk, Ukraine; married. ❖ Won silver (1999 and 2001) and bronze (2000) in Speed Climbing at X Games; received UIAA World year-end rankings of 2nd (2000) and 1st (2001); other 1st-place finishes include World Cup, Kuala Lampur in Speed (2001) and World Cup, Yekaterinburg, Russia, in Speed (2002).

ZAKHAROVA, Stella (1963—). Soviet gymnast. Born July 12, 1963, in Odessa, Ukraine, USSR; m. Viktor Khuls (football player). ❖ Won American Cup (1979) and Moscow News (1979, 1980); at World championships, won silver medals for team all-around and vault (1979) and a gold medal for team all-around and a silver for vault (1981); won World Cup (1979, 1980); at Moscow Olympics, won a gold medal in team all-around (1980); was the 1st female to perform 3 double back somersaults in floor exercise.

ZAKHAROVA, Svetlana (1970—). Russian marathon runner. Born Sept 15, 1970, in Attayevo, Chuvashiya Republic, USSR; trained with Valentina Yegorova. ❖ Won Honolulu Marathon (1997); placed 2nd in London Marathon (2001) and 3rd in World championships (2001); won Boston Marathon (2003).

ZAKHAROVA, Tatyana (1951—). Soviet basketball player. Born Jan 29, 1951, in USSR. ❖ Won a gold medal at Montreal Olympics (1976) and a gold medal at Moscow Olympics (1980), both in team competition.

ZAKRZEWSKA, Marie (1829–1902). German-American doctor. Name variations: Dr. Zak. Pronunciation: zuk-SHEF-ska. Born Marie Elizabeth Zakrzewska of Polish parents in Berlin, Germany, in 1829;

died 1902; dau. of a midwife; immigrated to US, 1853; Cleve[...] Medical College at Western Reserve University, MD, 1856. ❖ Joi[...] the Blackwell sisters in founding the New York Infirmary for Women a[...] Children, the 1st hospital in America to be staffed by women, and was it[...] 1st resident physician and general manager; moved to Boston to teach at New England Female Medical College (1859); founded her own teaching hospital in Roxbury section of Boston (1862), which would become the New England Hospital for Women and Children, adding a training school for nurses the following year; served as resident physician from its inception until 1902; also championed the poor and African-Americans. ❖ See also *Women in World History*.

ZALAFFI, Margherita (1966—). Italian fencer. Born April 7, 1966, in Siena, Italy. ❖ Won a silver medal at Seoul Olympics (1988) and a gold medal at Barcelona Olympics (1992), both in team foil; won a silver medal for épée team at Atlanta Olympics (1996); at World championships, won team gold (1982, 1983, 1990, 1991).

ZALAINE-KOEVI, Maria (1923—). Hungarian gymnast. Born Oct 20, 1923, in Hungary. ❖ At London Olympics, won a silver medal in team all-around (1948); at Helsinki Olympics, won a silver medal in team all-around and a bronze medal in teams all-around, portable apparatus (1952).

ZALESKA, Katherine (1919—). Polish-Jewish resistance fighter. Name variations: also seen as Katherina Zalenska. Born 1919 in Lvov, Poland; attended Rockefeller Nursing School, Warsaw; studied medicine at Poznan and Stettin universities in Poland; served as registrar of St. James's Hospital, London; married in 1959 (div.). ❖ During World War II, was a courier with her sister for the Polish resistance, carrying messages to Hungary through German-occupied territory; worked as a nurse in a hospital in Cracow until it closed in 1941, after which she enrolled in nursing studies at the Rockefeller Nursing School in Warsaw, while also acting as a courier for the Warsaw resistance movement (the Home Army), using the codename "Juka"; twice earned decorations for valor, which included helping Jews escape from the besieged Warsaw Ghetto in 1944; married a fellow Pole (1959) and moved with him to Lagos, Nigeria, where she secured work as an ENT Specialist in the General Hospital. ❖ See also *Women in World History*.

ZALOGAITYTE, Birute (b. 1934). *See Kalediene, Birute.*

ZAMBA, Frieda (1965—). American surfer. Born Oct 24, 1965, in Flagler Beach, Fl; m. Flea Shaw (her coach), 1987. ❖ Won Mazda Women's Pro tournament (1982), finishing 6th in the world in her rookie year; won World championship (1984), the youngest titleholder ever at 19; won World championship (1985–86, 1988). Inducted into Surfing Hall of Fame (1998).

ZAMBELLI, Carlotta (1875–1968). Italian ballet dancer. Born Nov 4, 1875, in Milan, Italy; died Jan 28, 1968 in Milan. ❖ Studied at La Scala; made debut at Paris Opéra (1894); became principal dancer (1898) and remained at the Opéra for her entire career; created roles in *Faust* (1894), *Le Cid* (1900), *Bacchus* (1902), *La Ronde de Saisons* (1905), *Namouna* (1908), *España* (1911), *La Roussalka* (1911), *Les Abeilles* (1917) and *Impressions de Music-hall* (1927), among others; served as director of the school (1930–55). Was made Chevalier (1926) and then Officier (1956) of Légion d'Honneur, becoming 1st person to enter Légion for dance.

ZAMBRANO, María (1904–1991). Spanish philosopher and essayist. Name variations: Maria Zambrano. Born April 25, 1904, in Vélez Málaga, Spain; died Aug 1991, in Madrid, Spain; dau. of teachers. ❖ Moved with family to Madrid (1926), where she completed her studies in philosophy and letters; influenced by philosopher José Ortega y Gasset, also studied with Xavier Zubiri and Manuel García Morente; while working on doctorate (1930), lectured in philosophy and joined the Republic's Cultural Missions; published *Nuevo liberalismo* (New Liberalism, 1930), which built on the utopian socialist thoughts of her father; published *El hombre y lo divino* (Man and Divinity, 1955), considered her masterpiece; forced into exile following Spanish Civil War of 1936–39, taught in Mexico, Cuba, and Puerto Rico, spending 11 years in Rome (1952–63), and 16 in France (1964–80); returned to Madrid (1984), among the last exiles repatriated; was the 1st woman and 1st philosopher to receive the Spanish language's premier award, the Cervantes Prize (1988); other writings include *Hacia un saber sobre el alma* (Toward a Knowledge of the Soul, 1937), *El freudismo: Testimonio del hombre actual* (Freudianism: Testimony to Contemporary Man, 1940), *El pensamiento vivo de Séneca* (Seneca's Living Thought, 1944), *España, sueño y verdad* (Spain, Dream and Truth, 1965), *Claros del bosque* (Forest Clearings,

1977), *Delirio y destino* (Delirium and Destiny, 1989) and *Los sueños y el tiempo* (Dreams and Time, 1992). Awarded Prince of Asturias literary prize (1981). ❖ See also memoir, *Los intelectuales en el drama de España* (1937); and *Women in World History*.

ZAMOLODCHIKOVA, Elena (1982—). Russian gymnast. Name variations: Yelena Zamolodtchikova. Born Sept 19, 1982, in Moscow, Russia. ❖ At World championships, won a gold medal for vault, silver for team all-around, and bronze for all-around (1999) and gold medal for vault (2002); at European championships, won a gold medal for team all-around, silver for all-around and vault, and bronze for beam (2000); at Sydney Olympics, won a gold medal for vault and floor exercises and silver for team all-around (2000); won Visa Cup and Russian nationals (2001); won a bronze medal for team all-around at Athens Olympics (2004).

ZAMOLODTCHIKOVA, Elena (1982—). *See Zamolodchikova, Elena.*

ZAMOLODTCHIKOVA, Yelena (1982—). *See Zamolodchikova, Elena.*

ZAMORA, Daisy (1950—). Nicaraguan revolutionary, government official, and poet. Born 1950 in Managua, Nicaragua; attended University of Central America in Managua, beginning 1967; m. Dionisio Marenco (engineer, div. c. 1990); m. Oscar-Rene Vargas (sociologist and writer, div. 1997); children: (adopted) Maria Denise Marenco. ❖ Father taken prisoner after being involved in a coup against regime of Anastasio Somoza (1954); married and settled in Chinandega, where husband worked as an engineer at a sugar mill and she taught at the mill's school; with husband, began to organize the mill workers for growing socialist Sandinista guerrilla movement (1972); when this became dangerous, moved back to Managua, where her political cell executed a successful attack on the National Palace (Aug 22, 1978), and later participated in a series of raids on state police stations, in which she was in the lead attack vehicle; fled the country; in Costa Rica, became an announcer at the revolutionary Radio Sandino, where she created a program called "The Sandinist Women"; when civil war ended (July 1979), became vice-minister of culture in the new National Reconstruction government; later served as director of Institute of Economic and Social Research, and was Nicaragua's representative to UNESCO; also founded and edited the economic and social science journal *Pensamiento Propio*; was also one of a group of Nicaraguan women poets active during the revolution known as Las Seis (The Six); writings include *Riverbed of Memory, Clean Slate: New and Selected Poems* and *Life for Each.* ❖ See also *Women in World History*.

ZAMUDIO, Adela (1854–1928). Bolivian poet and novelist. Name variations: (pseudonym) Soledad. Born 1854 in La Paz, Bolivia; died 1928. ❖ Worked as primary school teacher in Cochabamba, Bolivia; works include *Ensayos poéticos* (1887), *Violeta o la princesa azul* (1890), *El castillo negro* (1906), *Intimas* (1913), *Ráfagas* (1914), *Peregrinando* (1943), and *Cuentos breves* (1943).

ZANCHI, Manuela (1977—). Italian water-polo player. Born Oct 17, 1977, in Italy. ❖ Driver, won a team gold medal at Athens Olympics (2004).

ZANE, Betty (c. 1766–c. 1831). American frontier heroine. Born Elizabeth Zane, c. 1766, in Virginia (now West Virginia); died c. 1831 in Martins Ferry, Ohio; dau. of William Zane; attended school in Philadelphia, Pennsylvania; m. John (or Henry) McGloughlin, McGlaughlin, or McLaughlin (died); m. Jacob (or John) Clark; children: (1st m.) Mary, Rebecca, Nancy, Catherine, and Hannah; (2nd m.) Catherine and Ebenezer. ❖ Known for her daring display of bravery during a British-inspired Indian attack on Fort Henry (Sept 11, 1782), when she volunteered to retrieve a powder magazine in a house less than 50 yards from the fort. ❖ See also *Women in World History*.

ZANFRETTA, Francesca (1862–1952). Italian ballet dancer and teacher. Born 1862 in Milan, Italy; died June 4, 1952, in London, England; m. Charles Lauri (acrobat). ❖ Important teacher of Italian ballet technique, made performance debut at Deutschtheater in Prague, Czechoslovakia (c. 1878); appeared at Théâtre de la Monnaie in Brussels, Belgium; appeared at London's Covent Garden, presumably with Royal Italian Opera, which was then in residence; remained in London, performing at The Empire and The Prince of Wales Theatre, often *en travestie*; danced role of Mephistopheles in Katti Lanner's *Faust* opposite Malvina Cavallazzi; on retirement (1915), taught classes in London for many years.

ZANFRETTA, Marietta (c. 1837–1898). Italian tightrope dancer. Born c. 1837 in Venice, Italy; died Mar 1898 in New York, NY. ❖ Grew up in family of tightrope performers in northern Italy; appeared early on at Franconi's Theater in Paris; toured US with Carine troupe and appeared at Niblo's in New York City (1858); danced in Martinelli and Manzetti family troupes and was highly acclaimed throughout performance career for performing on point on tightrope, a feat rarely repeated by others; formed own family troupe with daughter and adopted sons.

ZANGE-SCHÖNBRUNN, Gabi (1961—). East German speedskater. Name variations: Gabi Schönbrunn or Schoenbrunn; Gabi Zange Schönbrunn; Gabi Zange. Born Gabriele Schönbrunn, June 1, 1961, in East Germany. ❖ Won the Olympic bronze medal for the 3,000 meters at Sarajevo Olympics (1984); won a gold medal for allround at European championships (1984); at World championships, won a bronze medal for allround (1984), silver for allround (1985); won bronze medals for the 3,000 meters and 5,000 meters at Calgary Olympics (1988).

ZANGRANDI, Giovanna (1910–1988). *See Bevilacqua, Alma.*

ZANI, Giselda (1909–1975). Uruguayan journalist, poet and short-story writer. Born 1909 in Uruguay; died 1975. ❖ Worked as diplomat in Buenos Aires; wrote fiction, poetry, and art criticism; writings include *La costa despierta* (1930) and *Por vínculos sutiles* (1958).

ZANOTTO, Kendra (1981—). American synchronized swimmer. Born Oct 30, 1981, in Los Gatos, CA. ❖ Won a team bronze medal at Athens Olympics (2004).

ZAPATA OLIVELLA, Delia (1926–2001). Colombian dancer, choreographer and educator. Born Delia Zapata Olivella, April 1, 1926, in Santa Cruz de Lorica, Colombia; died of malaria, May 24, 2001, in Bogotá, Colombia; dau. of Antonio Zapata Vásquez (educator and actor); sister of Manuel Zapata Olivella (doctor, writer, folklorist); Juan Zapata Olivella (poet, educator, founder of Cartagena's Museum of Black Culture); children: 1 daughter. ❖ Accomplished Afro-Colombian dancer and choreographer who pioneered study and preservation of Colombian traditional dances and Afro-Colombian culture and history, demanded enrollment in Cartagena's exclusive and previously all-male high school system, graduating with 24 other women in city's 1st co-ed class; traveled with brother Manuel to research traditional Afro-Colombian dances and culture (1955), then toured Colombia, Europe and China with her troupe Danzas Folklóricas Colombianas (Colombian Folk Dance); became main choreographer for Institute of Popular Culture in Cali (1963); awarded fellowship (1964), studied African dance with Katherine Dunham in US; returned to Bogotá, where she taught, danced and directed at National University (1967–83); founded Institute for Colombian Folklore (1974); served as director of Latin America's 1st university program in dance, theater and popular tradition at Antonio Nariño University in Bogotá (1983–2001); published *Manual de danzas de la costa Pacífica de Colombia* (Manual of Dances of the Pacific Coast of Colombia, 1998); while traveling to Africa with daughter, contracted malaria (2001). Received Medalla de Oro (Gold Medal) from Colombian Society of Authors and Composers (1964) and Orden del Mérito (Order of Merit) General José María Cordoba from Colombian government (1997).

ZAPOLSKA, Gabriela (1857–1921). Polish actress, playwright, and novelist. Name variations: Gabryela Zapolska; Gabriela Korwin-Piotrowska or Kerwin-Piotrowska. Born Maria Gabriela Stefania Korwin-Piotrowska, Mar 30, 1857, in Podhajce, Poland; died Dec 17, 1921, in Lvov, Poland; dau. of Wncentry Korwin Piotrowski (landowner) and Józefa Karska Piotrowska (ballet dancer and opera singer); studied at Sacré Cour convent and the private Institute of Education and Science in Lvov; m. Konstanty Śnieżko-Błocki (lieutenant in the tsar's guards), 1876 (marriage annulled 1888); m. Stanisław Janowski (div. 1904). ❖ Lived in Warsaw (1879–80); worked professionally with a theater in Cracow (1882), changing name to Gabriela Zapolska; spent next several years performing in Galician theaters and traveling with troupes throughout the country; after an attempted suicide (Oct 1888), left Poland for Paris (1889), where she played minor roles in small theaters and joined Antoine's Théâtre Libre; returned to Poland, establishing a drama school in Cracow (1902); also worked as a journalist and theater reviewer; moved to Lvov (1904), where she served as patron of Gabriela Zapolska Theater, established by 2nd husband; began writing extensively (1880s); published 1st story, "A Day in the Life of a Rose," in *Gazeta Krakowska* (1881); wrote novels, which she frequently adapted for the stage, and later plays, most of which concerned women and the circumstances in which they found themselves; portrayed marital infidelity in *Żabusia* (My Darling, 1897) and *Ich czworo* (The Four of Them, 1907), a subject that merited the condemnation of the clergy, but later brought in full houses for the theater; wrote her most respected play *Moralność pani Dulskiej* (*The Morals of Mrs. Dulska*, 1906). ❖ See also *Women in World History*.

ZAPOLYA, Barbara (fl. 1500). *See Barbara Zapolya.*

ZAPPI, Faustina Maratti (c. 1680–1745). *See Maratti Zappi, Faustina.*

ZAPPIS, Lavinia Fontana de (1552–1614). *See Fontana, Lavinia.*

ZARCEZNY, Teresa (1966—). *See Bell, Teresa Z.*

ZARDOYA, Concha (1914–2004). Spanish poet and literary critic. Name variations: María Concepción Zardoya González. Born Nov 14, 1914, in Valparaíso, Chile; died April 21, 2004, in Madrid, Spain; dau. of Alfonso Zardoya Francés and Concepción González Ortiz (both Spanish); attended University of Madrid, 1934–36. ❖ Moved with family to Spain (1932), eventually settling in Madrid; during siege of Madrid, moved to Valencia, where she read her poetry on the radio; published 1st book of poetry, *Pájaros del Nuevo Mundo* (1946), followed by *Dominio del llanto* (1947); wrote a screenplay about Goya, published multivolume compilations of Hispanic legends and stories, and translated works of Walt Whitman and Charles Morgan; began teaching Spanish at University of Illinois (1948), then at Tulane, Yale, Indiana and Berkeley; as an academic, wrote surveys of modern Spanish poetry, a biography of poet Miguel Hernández, and a Spanish-language survey of American literature; returned to Spain upon retirement (1977); in all, published more than 2 dozen vols. of poetry, several winning literary prizes. ❖ See also *Women in World History*.

ZARIA, queen of.
See Turunku, Bakwa (fl. 1530s).
See Amina (c. 1533–c. 1598).

ZARIPOVA, Amina (1976—). Uzbekistan rhythmic gymnast. Born Aug 10, 1976, in Tchirtchik, Uzbekistan; m. Alexei Kortnev (singer), 2002. ❖ At World championships, won a bronze medal for team and indiv. all-around (1993) and silver in all-around (1994, 1995); placed 3rd at European championships (1994); won Goodwill Games (1994); placed 4th in all-around at Atlantic Olympics (1996).

ZAROVA, Rini (d. 1966). *See Willson, Rini Zarova.*

ZASIPKINA, Maria (1985—). Russian gymnast. Born Dec 19, 1985, in Tula, Russia. ❖ At World championships, won a silver medal in team all-around (2001).

ZASLAVSKAYA, Tatyana (1924—). Ukrainian economist and sociologist. Name variations: Tatiana Ivanovna Zaslavskaya. Born 1924 in Kiev, Ukraine; attended Moscow University. ❖ Was a member of the Communist Party (1954–90); became a full member of Russian Academy of Sciences (1981); wrote the Novosibirsk Memorandum, criticizing the Soviet economic system, and was one of the academic supporters of the Gorbachov reform plan of perestroika during the final years of the USSR; was president of Sociological Association of USSR (1989–91) and USSR People's Deputy (1989–91).

ZASPA, Larysa (1971—). Ukrainian handball player. Born Sept 22, 1971, in Ukraine. ❖ Won a team bronze medal at Athens Olympics (2004).

ZASUL, Vera (1849–1919). *See Zasulich, Vera.*

ZASULICH, Vera (1849–1919). Russian revolutionary. Name variations: Zasul. Born Vera Ivanovna Zasulich, Aug 8, 1849, on her parents' estate at Mikhailovka, in Smolensk, Russia; died in Petrograd, May 8, 1919; dau. of Ivan Petrovich Zasulich (petty noble and former army officer) and Feoktista Mikhailovna Zasulich; never married, but had a longtime liaison with Lev Deich, a fellow revolutionary. ❖ Revolutionary whose 1878 attempt to assassinate the governor of St. Petersburg followed by her acquittal in a sensational jury trial made her a popular heroine and influential figure in the Russian radical movement during late 19th and early 20th centuries; sent to live with relatives on neighboring estate (1852); attended school for governesses in Moscow (1866–67); falsely arrested for revolutionary activity and imprisoned in St. Petersburg (1869); over next 6 years, was imprisoned, exiled to the provinces, arrested a 2nd time, and exiled once again (1869–75); released from exile, joined revolutionary group in Kiev (1875), by now a committed revolutionary; for attempted assassination of governor-general of St. Petersburg, Feodor Trepov, was tried and acquitted, then fled to Western Europe (1878); returned to Russia (1879–80); lived in Switzerland, France, and Britain (1880–1906); founded Liberation of Labor group in Geneva (1883); companion Lev Deich arrested and exiled

to Siberia (1884); returned to Russia (1899–1900); was considered the chief peacemaker and architect of compromise on the Russian Left; after Second Russian Marxist Congress (1903), sympathies came to rest with the Mensheviks; permanently returned to Russia (1906); defended Russian participation in World War I (1914–17); criticized Bolshevik Revolution (1918). ❖ See also Jay Bergman, *Vera Zasulich: A Biography* (Stanford U. Press, 1983); and *Women in World History*.

ZASULSKAYA, Natalya (1969—). Soviet basketball player. Born May 28, 1969, in USSR. ❖ Won a bronze medal at Seoul Olympics (1988) and a gold medal at Barcelona Olympics (1992), both in team competition.

ZATOPEK, Dana (1922—). Czech javelin thrower and political dissident. Name variations: Dana Ingrova; Dana Ingrova Zatopkova; Dana Zatopkova. Born Dana Ingrova, Sept 19, 1922, in Tryskat, Moravia, Czechoslovakia; m. Emil Zatopek (also born Sept 19, 1922–2000, distance runner). ❖ One half of a famous sporting couple, won a gold medal for javelin at Helsinki Olympics (1952); took 1st place for javelin at European championships (1954, 1958); broke world record for javelin held by Soviet athlete Nadezhda Konyayeva (1958); won a silver medal at Rome Olympics (1960); with husband, signed Alexander Dubcek's "Manifesto of 2,000 Words," backing the reforms of "Prague Spring" (1968); when Soviet troops invaded Czechoslovakia, initiating a two-decade period of repression, her husband was stripped of his army rank and lost his job; both grew old in obscurity until the fall of communism in 1989. ❖ See also *Women in World History*.

ZATOPKOVA, Dana (1922—). *See Zatopek, Dana.*

ZATURENSKA, Marya Alexandrovna (1902–1982). Russian-born American poet. Born Sept 12, 1902, in Kiev, Russia; died Jan 19, 1982, in Shelburne Falls, Massachusetts; dau. of Avram Alexander and Johanna (Lupovska) Zaturensky; attended Valparaiso University, 1922–23; graduate of University of Wisconsin, 1925; m. Horace Gregory (poet and critic), 1925; children: Joanna and Patrick. ❖ Immigrated to US with family (1909); won John Reed Memorial Award from *Poetry* magazine (1922); won Shelley Memorial Award for *Threshold and Hearth* (1935); won Guarantors Award from *Poetry* magazine (1937); won Pulitzer Prize for *Cold Morning Sky* (1938); other poetry collections include *The Listening Landscape* (1941), *The Golden Mirror* (1944), (with husband) *A History of American Poetry, 1900–1940* (1946), (ed. with husband) *The Mentor Book of Religious Verse* (1957), *Terraces of Light* (1960), (ed. with husband) *The Crystal Cabinet: An Invitation to Poetry* (1962), *Collected Poems of Marya Zaturenska* (1965), (comp.) *The Silver Swan: Poems of Romance and Mystery* (1966), (ed.) *Collected Poems of Sara Teasdale* (1967), (ed.) *Selected Poems of Christina Rossetti* (1970) and *The Hidden Waterfall* (1974); also wrote *Christina Rossetti: A Portrait with Background* (1970). ❖ See also *Women in World History*.

ZAUDITU (1876–1930). Ethiopian empress. Name variations: Judith (Zauditu means Judith in English); Waizero. Born 1876; died 1930; dau. of Menelik II (1844–1913), king of Shoa (r. 1865–1889), emperor of Ethiopia (r. 1889–1913), and possibly Altash (1st of four wives of Menelik II); m. Aria Selassi (died 1888); married and widowed a 2nd time; m. Ras Gugsa Wolie, in 1902 (died 1930). ❖ Became empress of Ethiopia (1916); as a condition of her rule, had to renounce her marriage to Ras Gugsa Wolie and share her power with Ras Tafari (later known as Haile Selassie), a cousin of Emperor Menelik; was quickly eclipsed by the pro-Western, liberal Ras Tafari as ruler; came under pressure to concede even more power to him, as Ethiopia's economy prospered under his policies; reluctantly crowned him king (1928), a move that effectively made her ruler in title alone. ❖ See also *Women in World History*.

ZAUNEMANN, Sidonia Hedwig (1714–1740). German poet. Name variations: Sidonia Hedwig Zäunemann or Zaeunemann. Born 1714 in Ilmenau, Erfurt, Germany; died 1740. ❖ Often traveled about on horseback in men's clothing; wrote about ordinary life, nature, and experiences on travels; became Poet Laureate at University of Göttingen at 24; works include *Das Bergwerk in Ilmenau* (1737) about mines in hometown; also wrote social satires.

ZAYAK, Elaine (1965—). American figure skater. Born April 12, 1965, Paramus, NJ; m. John Berg, 1998. ❖ Won US championships (1981) and World championship (1982); was a bronze medalist at World championships (1984); placed 6th at Sarajevo Olympics (1984); known for the Zayak Rule which limits the repetitions of triples in the freestyle skating program.

ZAYAS Y SOTOMAYOR, María de (1590–c. 1650). Spanish poet and short-story writer. Born in Madrid, Spain, Sept 1590; died c. 1650; dau. of Fernando de Sayas y Sotomayor and Catalina Barrasa. ❖ Gained renown 1st as a poet, then as a novelist, but achieved greatest fame for 2 collections of short stories: *Novelas amorosas y ejemplares* (*Amorous and Exemplary Tales*, 1637) and *Novelas* (1647); integrated in her work a concern for women, calling for better education and greater respect for their rights. ❖ See also Lena E. V. Sylvania, *Doña María de Zayas y Sotomayor; a Contribution to the Study of Her Works* (AMS, 1966); and *Women in World History*.

ZAYAT, Latifa al- (b. 1923). *See Zayyat, Latifa al-.*

ZAYNAB. *Variant of Zainab.*

ZAYNAB BINT JAHSH (c. 590–c. 640). Wife of the Prophet Muhammad. Name variations: Zainab bint Djahsh; also known as Umm al-Hakam and Barra. Born c. 590 in Arabia, probably in Mecca, to the tribe of Quraysh; died in Mecca, 640 or 641; dau. of Jahsh and Umayma or Umaimah (who was the dau. of the Prophet Muhammad's paternal grandfather 'Abd al-Muttalib); given in marriage by the Prophet Muhammad to his adopted son Zayd Ibn Haritha (in 624, Zayd div. her so that she could marry the Prophet); m. Muhammad, in 627; children: no information. ❖ Legendary for her generosity, was nearly 30 and according to some traditions a widow, when she married Prophet Muhammad's adopted son Zayd Ibn Haritha, who was a former slave of his 1st wife Khadijah; her marriage to Zayd was not destined to last, and the events surrounding her divorce and subsequent marriage to Muhammad inspired one of the most colorful stories from the life of the Prophet. ❖ See also *Women in World History*.

ZAYYAT, Latifa al- (1923–). Egyptian writer and feminist. Name variations: Zayat; az-Zayyat, as-Zayyat. Born in Damietta, Egypt, in 1923; Cairo University, BA, MA, and PhD. ❖ Writer and novelist who worked for greater emancipation for Egyptian women, came to Cairo to be educated (1936); became a Marxist after she began studying at University of Cairo (1942); taught English at Women's College of Ain Shams University; writings include *The Open Door* (1960) and *Old Age and Other Stories* (1980); also wrote extensive literary criticism. ❖ See also *Women in World History*.

ZAZDRAVNYKH, Valentina (1954–). Soviet field-hockey player. Born Nov 24, 1954, in USSR. ❖ At Moscow Olympics, won a bronze medal in team competition (1980).

ZBYSLAWA (fl. 1100). Russian princess. Dau. of Sviatopolk II, grand prince of Kiev (r. 1093–1113); m. Boleslaus III the Wrymouthed (Bloeslaw III Krzywousty), king of Poland (r. 1102–1138); children: Wladyslaw or Ladislas II the Exile of Silesia, king of Poland (r. 1138–1146). Boleslaus' 2nd wife was Salomea (d. 1144).

ZDUNKIEWICZ, Jaroslawa (1937–). *See Jozwiakowska, Jaroslawa.*

ZEB-UN-NISSA (1639–1702). Indo-Persian poet and literary patron. Name variations: Zeb-un-Nisa, Zeb-un-Nissar, Zebunnisa; (pseudonym) Makhfi ("the hidden one"). Born 1639 in Delhi, India; died 1702 in Delhi; eldest dau. of Aurangzeb (1618–1707), Mughal emperor (r. 1658–1707); her mother was his 1st wife who died in 1657; studied Arabic, Persian, mathematics and astronomy; never married. ❖ In early years, had sway over her father, had her own court, which attracted scholars and poets, and established a library; influenced by her paternal aunt Jahanara, became a Sufi; when her brother Akbar tried to usurp the throne (1681), was imprisoned for 21 years in Salimgarh Fort, an island prison, accused by father of being part of the conspiracy; wrote some of her poetry under the name Makhfi, using elements of Hinduism, Islam, and Zoroastrianism. Years after her death, over 400 of her poems were collected and published in Persian as *Diwan-i-Makhfi* (1724, English translation published as *The Divan of Zeb-un-Nisa* [1913]).

ZEDONG, Madame Mao (1914–1991). *See Jiang Qing.*

ZEGHERS, Margriet (1954–). Dutch field-hockey player. Born April 29, 1954, in the Netherlands. ❖ At Los Angeles Olympics, won a gold medal in team competition (1984).

ZEHRT, Monika (1952–). East German runner. Name variations: Monika Landgraf. Born Sept 29, 1952, in Riesa, Saxony. ❖ At Munich Olympics, won a gold medal in 400 meters and a gold medal in 4 x 400-meter relay (1972).

ZEI, Alki (1925–). Greek novelist and children's writer. Born 1925 in Athens, Greece; niece by marriage of Dido Sotiriou (writer). ❖ Studied literature, drama, and music; traveled to Moscow (1954) and remained 10 years; works, which have been translated into many languages, include *The Tiger in the Shop Window* (1963), *Peter's Great Walk* (1971), *Achilles' Fiancée* (1987), *Uncle Plato*, and *Hannibal's Shoes*; also translated works from Russian into Greek. Awarded Mildred L. Batchelder Award (1973) in US for best foreign children's book translated into English.

ZEIDLER, Judith (1968–). German rower. Born May 11, 1968. ❖ Won a gold medal at Seoul Olympics (1988) and a bronze medal at Barcelona Olympics (1992), both in coxed eights.

ZEIDLER, Susanna Elisabeth (1657–1706). German poet. Born Mar 16, 1657, in Fienstedt, Germany; died 1706; dau. of Gottfried Zeidler and Margarethe Zeidler; m. Andreas Haldensleben, 1684. ❖ Wrote *Jungferlicher Zeitvertreiber* (1686), proclaiming right of women to be poets.

ZEILE, Julianne (1966–). *See McNamara, Julianne.*

ZEISEL, Eva (b. 1906). Hungarian-born American ceramist and designer. Name variations: Eva Polanyi Stricker. Born Nov 11, 1906, in Budapest, Hungary; studied painting under Vaszari at Royal Academy of Fine Arts, Budapest, 1923–25; m. Hans Zeisel (sociologist and lawyer), in 1938; children: John and Jean. ❖ Apprenticed at Yakob Karpanscik's pottery, Budapest (1924–25); worked for several ceramic manufacturers in Budapest (1925–32); was freelance designer and art director for 3 companies in Leningrad (1932–37); arrested and expelled to Germany under Stalin's orders (1937); escaped to Great Britain (1938), then traveled to US; freelanced out of New York and Chicago for a variety of manufacturers, including Red Wing Pottery, Hall China Company, Rosenthal Porcelain, Loza Gina, Manioli, Noritake, Nikkon Toki, Zsolnay Factory, and others; also taught industrial design at Pratt Institute (1939–53) and Rhode Island School of Design (1954); was commissioned by Museum of Modern Art (1946) to design a set of china called "Museum Shape," for the Castleton China firm, the 1st contemporary, translucent, porcelain dinnerware produced in the US for a general audience. ❖ See also *Women in World History*.

ZEISLER, Fannie Bloomfield (1863–1927). Austrian pianist. Born July 16, 1863, in Bielitz, Austria; died Aug 20, 1927, in Chicago IL; m. Sigmund Zeisler, 1885. ❖ Moved with family to US (1867) and made debut in one of Carl Wolfsohn's Beethoven Society concerts (1875); joined faculty of School of Lyric and Dramatic Art, Chicago (1884), and made New York debut (1885); toured Europe (1894, 1898, 1902, 1911–12, 1914) and US; appeared with Chicago Symphony Orchestra for 19 seasons from 1891.

ZELDA (1914–1984). *See Mishkowsky, Zelda Shneurson.*

ZELEPUKINA, Svetlana (1980–). Ukrainian gymnast. Born Aug 16, 1980, in Kirovograd, Ukraine. ❖ Won Ukraine Cup (1996); came in 5th in team all-around at Atlanta Olympics (1996).

ZELIDE (1740–1805). *See Charrière, Isabelle de.*

ZELIKOVICH-DUMCHEVA, Antonina (1958–). Soviet rower. Born Feb 18, 1958, in USSR. ❖ At Barcelona Olympics, won a bronze medal in quadruple sculls without coxswain (1992).

ZELINOVÁ, Hana (b. 1914). Slovak prose writer and dramatist. Name variations: Hana Zelinova. Born July 20, 1914. ❖ Influenced by the Scandinavian saga and the Slovak social novel, writings deal with tragic love and self-sacrifice; published 1st collection of short stories, *Zrkadlový most* (The Bridge of Mirrors, 1941); wrote and staged 3 Ibsenesque plays dealing with the position of women in an urban society (1940s); wrote a brief novel, *Diablo čardáš* (The Devil's Csardas, 1958), and a trilogy: *Alžbetin dvor* (Elizabeth's Court, 1971), *Volanie vetra* (The Call of the Wind, 1974), and *Kvet hrôzy* (The Flower of Fright, 1977). ❖ See also *Women in World History*.

ZELKOWITZ, Goldie (1942–). *See Ravan, Genya.*

ZELL, Katharina Schütz (c. 1497–1562). German religious reformer. Name variations: Katherine, Catherina or Catherine Zell; Zell-Schütz or Zell-Schutz or Schuetz-Zell; Maister Mathis frauw; Katharina Schützin or Schützinn or Zellin or Zellen. Born 1497 or 1498 in Strassburg (now Strasbourg, France); died in Strassburg, Sept 5, 1562; dau. of Jacob Schütz (cabinetmaker) and Elisabeth (Gerster) Schütz; m. Matthew Zell (leading priest in Strassburg), Dec 3, 1523 (1548); children: 2, who died young, one by 1527, the other probably by 1534. ❖ Outstanding lay reformer in the early Protestant Reformation who wrote, preached, and spoke to teach her faith, welcomed refugees and everyone in need, and provided a remarkable model of women's leadership in the Christian Church; lived in Strassburg all her life, though traveled in Germany and Switzerland; converted to Protestant teachings (probably 1521–22); became the 1st respectable Strassburg woman to marry a priest, then established one of the 1st Protestant parsonages (1523); wrote a letter to the bishop in defense of clerical marriage: *Apologia of Katharina Schütz for Her Husband, Master Matthew Zell, a Pastor and Servant of the Word of God in Strassburg, Because of the Great Lies About Him* (1524); during husband's lifetime, shared in the work of his teaching and preaching to an unusual degree; following husband's death, was viewed by some as a troublemaker, and even a heretic, for befriending and encouraging dissenters. ❖ See also *Women in World History*.

ZELLE, Margaretha (1876–1917). Dutch courtesan, dancer and accused spy. Name variations: Margarida Zelle; Mata Hari; Baroness von der Linden; Clara Benedix or Benedict; Red Dancer. Born Margaretha Gertrud Zelle, Aug 7, 1876, in Leeuwarden, Holland; died Oct 15, 1917, by execution, at Château de Vincennes, France; dau. of Adam and Antje (van der Meulen) Zelle; m. Captain John MacLeod, July 11, 1895 (sep. 1902); children: Norman (b. 1897); Juana-Luisa MacLeod (1898–1919). ❖ Courtesan and erotic dancer who would be accused of espionage by French authorities and executed; sailed for Dutch East Indies with husband (1897); returned to Holland and left husband (1902); then known as Lady MacLeod, made dancing debut in Paris under the exotic name of Mata Hari, meaning "Eye of the Morning" (Mar 13, 1905); garnered a large and appreciative following in the French capital among the fashionable and famous, graduating from the drawing rooms of Paris to the stage, until she was packing in audiences at theaters across the city; performed in Berlin, where she become the darling of high society and involved in a romance with an officer of the 11th Regiment of Hussars; fled Germany at outbreak of World War I; performed in Holland (1914–16); received 20,000 francs to spy for Germany; recruited by French Intelligence as a double agent (1916); convinced she was still spying for the Germans, was detained by British authorities and deported to Spain (1916), where she rapidly become the mistress of the German military attaché and French military attaché; returned to Paris and was arrested for espionage by the French (Feb 12, 1917); tried by Military Tribunal, maintained her innocence throughout (July 27–28, 1917); a high-profile personality of infamous repute, became the scapegoat of a disillusioned nation, during the last year of a savage conflict. ❖ See also Thomas Coulson, *Mata Hari: Courtesan and Spy* (1930); Bernard Newman, *Inquest of Mata Hari* (Hale, 1956); Russell Howe, *Mata Hari: The True Story* (Dodd, 1986); Erika Ostrovsky, *Eye of Dawn: The Rise & Fall of Mata Hari* (Dorset, 1978); and *Women in World History*.

ZELLER, Eva (1923—). German poet and novelist. Born 1923 in Eberswalde, Germany; children: 4. ❖ Lived until 1956 in East Germany; novels include *Lampenfieber* (1974), *Hauptfrau* (1977), and the autobiographical *Solange ich denken kann: Roman einer Jugend* (1981, As Long as I Can Think: Novels of a Childhood); poetry collections include *Fliehkraft* (1975) and *Auf dem Wasser* (1979).

ZELLIN, Katherina (c. 1497–1562). See Zell, Katharina Schütz.

ZELLNER, Martina (1974—). German biathlete. Born Feb 26, 1974, in Traunstein, Germany. ❖ Won a gold medal for 4x7.5 km relay at Nagano Olympics (1998); won World sprint championship (1998).

ZEMINA, Kathryn (1968—). American swimmer. Name variations: Kathryn Paige Zemina; Paige Zemina. Born Feb 15, 1968; attended University of Florida. ❖ At Seoul Olympics, won a bronze medal in 4x100-meter freestyle relay (1988).

ZENAIDA R—VA. See Gan, Elena.

ZENG XIAOYING (1929—). Chinese conductor. Born 1929 in China; studied medicine at Jinling Girls' College, Nanjing. ❖ The 1st woman conductor in China, spent 4 years in song and dance troupe and taught theory of music, conducting, and composition; was chosen to study at Central Conservatory of Music (1952) and then sent to Moscow Conservatory; became nationally recognized in China as teacher and conductor; became Principal Conductor at Central Opera Theater, Beijing (1977).

ZENGER, Anna Catharina (c. 1704–1751). American printer. Name variations: Anne Catharine Zenger; Anna Catharina Maul; Anna Catharina Maule; Anna Catherine Maule; Anna Catharina Maulin; Anna Catherine Maulin; Anna Maul Zenger. Born Anna Catharina Maul, place unknown, c. 1704; died 1751; m. John Peter Zenger (1697–1746, printer), Sept 11, 1722; children: 5. ❖ Printer who ran

the *New-York Weekly Journal*, the 1st woman to publish a newspaper in America, when her husband John Peter Zenger was imprisoned and tried for seditious libel in one of the most important political trials in American history (1734); continued to print and publish the *New-York Weekly Journal* after husband's death (1746); produced a number of other imprints, including a yearly almanac by "John Nathan, Philomath"; also sold books and stationery, the only woman bookseller in New York City (1746–48); retired (1748), after having passed her responsibilities on to her son. ❖ See also Kent Cooper, *Anna Zenger, Mother of Freedom* (Farrar, 1946); and *Women in World History*.

ZENOBIA (r. 267–272). Queen of Palmyra. Name variations: (Latin) Septimia Zenobia; (Aramaic) Bat Zabbai or Bath-Zabbai; Zabaina. Born probably between 230–240 CE and died c. 300 CE in Palmyra (northeast Syria); married 1st husband, name unknown; m. Septimius Odenathus (Odainat, Odenath); married an unnamed Roman senator; children: (1st m.) at least one son, Vaballathus Athenodorus (Vaballath, Wahballat); (2nd marriage) stepson Hairun, sons Herennius and Timolaus, and at least two daughters, names unknown. ❖ One of the most illustrious and captivating women of ancient times, became a warrior queen and challenged the might of the Roman Empire; was well educated, having been tutored by a famous Greek, Cassius Longinus; chose to marry Odenathus, Palmyran military leader and Roman consul (probably late 250s); accompanied husband on military expeditions against the Persians, forgoing a more comfortable chariot for a horse; after Odenathus, along with his son Hairun, was assassinated (267), stepped in as regent and proclaimed Vaballathus, her young son by her 1st marriage, heir; immediately became effective ruler of Palmyra; sent her chief general Zabdas to conquer the province of Syria (269); negotiated with an Egyptian military leader named Timagenes who was willing to help overthrow Roman rule in Egypt and hand the province over to Palmyra; her troops also spread north throughout 270 CE, entering Asia Minor; ruled the eastern portion of the Roman Empire for several years and claimed the region for her own; attacked by the forces of Roman emperor Aurelian (272), fought a successful final large-scale pitched battle in the plains before Emesa with an army estimated at about 70,000; ultimately captured, lived out her days respected and in comfort in the homeland of her conquerors. ❖ See also Antonia Fraser, *The Warrior Queens* (Knopf, 1989); and *Women in World History*.

ZENZ, Therese (1932—). West German kayaker. Born Oct 15, 1932. ❖ At Melbourne Olympics, won a silver medal in K1 500 meters (1956); at Rome Olympics, won silver medals in K1 500 meters and K2 500 meters (1960).

ZETKIN, Clara (1857–1933). German feminist and political activist. Name variations: Klara Zetkin. Born Clara Eissner, July 5, 1857, at Niederlau, Saxony, Germany; died June 20, 1933, in Moscow; eldest dau. of Gottfried and Josephine (Vitale) Eissner (both teachers); attended Van Steyber Institute, Leipzig, Germany, graduated as teacher; m. Ossip Zetkin (Marxist), 1871 (died 1889); children: Maxim (b. 1883) and Konstantin (b. 1885). ❖ Feminist and Marxist, whose political activities made an important contribution to the development of European socialism, as she demanded that the rights of women become an integral part of the socialist agenda; though, as a woman, legally prohibited by the German authorities from membership of the German Social Democratic Party (SPD, 1869), attended the political meetings; delivered 1st clandestine speech on women's issues (1886); lived in exile; began to acquire a reputation as one of the party's most forceful and dynamic speakers; attended the 2nd International (1889), where she gave her famous speech on working women (known as "For the Liberation of Women"); became the acknowledged leader of the international socialist women's movement; when anti-socialist legislation in Germany lapsed (1890), returned home and openly pursued political activities; appointed editor of *Die Gleichheit* (Equality, 1891), a position she was to hold for the next quarter of a century; appointed to executive committee of the SPD (1895), the 1st woman to be elected to the executive committee; attended 1st International Socialist Women's conference (1907); saw outbreak of WWI (1914); after organizing an antiwar conference (1915), was arrested, charged with sedition, and held in prison for almost a year; in support of the Bolshevik cause, resigned from the SPD and joined the German Communist Party (KPD, 1919); represented the party as a deputy in the Wurttemberg Provincial Constituent Assembly; in Oct 1919, was one of two Communist deputies elected to the Reichstag, where she continued to sit as a member until that assembly's final dissolution by Hitler's Nazis in 1933. ❖ See also *Women in World History*.

ᴢETTERLING, Mai (1925–1994). Swedish stage and screen actress, film director and author. Born Mai Elisabeth Zetterling in Vasterås, Sweden, May 24, 1925; died in London, England, Mar 15, 1994; dau. of Lina Zetterling; attended Royal Dramatic Theater School in Stockholm, 1942–45; m. Isaac Samuel "Tutte" Lemkow, 1944 (div.); m. David Hughes, 1958; children: (1st m.) 2. ❖ Actress and director, made her most important contribution to Swedish cinema as an advocate of women's rights and a critic of contemporary society; acted in films in Sweden, England and US before settling in England; after a commendable career on stage and screen with major roles in plays by Shakespeare, Lorca, Sartre, Ibsen, Strindberg and Anouilh, turned director and made documentaries for BBC before moving on to feature films; acted in such films as *Lasse-Maja* (1941), *Frieda* (1947), *Quartet* (1948), *Desperate Moment* (1953), *Knock on Wood* (1954), *The Truth About Women* (1958), *Only Two Can Play* (1961), *The Vine Bridge* (1965), *Hidden Agenda* (1990), *The Witches* (1990); directed such films as *Lords of Little Egypt* (docu., 1961), (and co-screenwriter) *Loving Couples* (1964), (and co-screenwriter from her novel) *Night Games* (1966), (and co-screenwriter) *The Girls* (1968), (and screenwriter) *Love* (1981), (and screenwriter) *Scrubbers* (1983), (and screenwriter) *Amorosa* (1986). ❖ See also memoir *All Those Tomorrows* (Grove, 1985); and *Women in World History*.

ZETTERLUND, Monica (1937 2005). Swedish jazz singer and actress. Born Monical Nilsson, Sept 20, 1937, in Sweden; died in a fire in her apartment, May 12, 2005, in Stockholm, Sweden; married 3 times; children: Eva-Lena Zetterlund (actress). ❖ One of Sweden's best-known performers, began career as a singer in her father's band; recorded more than 20 albums (1958–2000); also acted in plays, on tv, and in Swedish films, including *The Emigrants* and *The New Land*; had scoliosis, a disabling disease that twists the spine, making it difficult to move.

ZETTERLUND, Yoko (1969—). Japanese-American volleyball player. Born Mar 24, 1969, in San Francisco, CA; raised in Japan; attended Waseda University in Tokyo, Japan. ❖ Setter, joined US national team (1991); won a bronze medal in team competition at Barcelona Olympics (1992).

ZETTS, Anita (1926—). *See Simonis, Anita.*

ZGURIŠKA, Zuska (1900–1984). Slovak novelist. Name variations: Zuska or Zuzka Zguriska. Born 1900; died 1984; attended Bratislava University. ❖ Studied sociology, was an actress with the Slovak National Theater, and worked as scriptwriter for Czechoslovak State Film; works, which focus on life in small towns and villages in Slovakia, include *Bičianka z Doliny* (1938), *Metropola pod slamou* (1949), *Mestečko na predaj* (1953), *Zbojnícke chodníčky* (1959), *Husitská nevesta* (1962), and *Strminou liet* (1972).

ZHADOVSKAIA, Iuliia Valerianovna (1824–1883). Russian poet and short-story writer. Name variations: Iuliia Valerianovna Zhádovskaia. Born 1824 in Russia; died 1883. ❖ Works include lyric poems, some of which were set to music and became popular romances; also wrote fiction, including *Apart from the Great World* (1857), *Woman's Story* (1861), and *Behind the Times* (1861).

ZHAN SHUPING (1964—). Chinese basketball player. Born April 25, 1964, in China. ❖ At Barcelona Olympics, won a silver medal in team competition (1992).

ZHANG, Ailing (1920–1995). *See Chang, Eileen.*

ZHANG CHUNFANG. Chinese softball player. Born in China. ❖ Won a silver medal at Atlanta Olympics (1996).

ZHANG DI (1968—). Chinese judoka. Born July 4, 1968, in China. ❖ At Barcelona Olympics, won a bronze medal in half-middleweight 61 kg (1992).

ZHANG HUI (1959—). Chinese basketball player. Born Sept 29, 1959, in China. ❖ At Los Angeles Olympics, won a bronze medal in team competition (1984).

ZHANG JIE (1937—). Chinese novelist and short-story writer. Name variations: Chang Chieh. Born April 27, 1937, in Beijing, China; graduate of People's Univerisity of Beijing. ❖ Studied economics and worked as National Bureau of Mechanical Equipment; works, which address constraints facing women in Chinese society and condemn sexual and social discrimination, include *Love Must Not be Forgotten* (1979), *Leaden Wings* (1981), *The Ark* (1982), *Emerald* (1984), *If Nothing Happens, Nothing Will* (1986), and *My Mother* (1998).

ZHANG JIEWEN (1981—). Chinese badminton player. Born Jan 4, 1981, in Guangzhou, China. ❖ With Wei Yang, won a gold medal for doubles at Athens Olympics (2004).

ZHANG JUANJUAN (1981—). Chinese archer. Born Jan 2, 1981, in Qingdao, China. ❖ Placed 1st for team at World championships (2001); won a silver medal for team at Athens Olympics (2004).

ZHANG MEIHONG (1963—). Chinese handball player. Born Jan 31, 1963, in China. ❖ At Los Angeles Olympics, won a bronze medal in team competition (1984).

ZHANG NA (1980—). Chinese volleyball player. Born April 19, 1980, in China. ❖ Won a team gold medal at Athens Olympics (2004). Voted Best Receiver at Asian championships (2003).

ZHANG NAN (1986—). Chinese gymnast. Born April 30, 1986, in Guizhou, China. ❖ Won a bronze medal for indiv. all-around at Athens Olympics (2004).

ZHANG NING (1975—). Chinese badminton player. Born May 19, 1975, in Shenyang, China. ❖ At World championships, won singles (2003); won a gold medal for singles at Athens Olympics (2004).

ZHANG OUYING (1975—). Chinese soccer player. Born Nov 2, 1975, in Heibei, China. ❖ Forward; played for Heibei in China for 11 years, scoring 90 goals in 175 games; played for Chinese national team 5 years and was a member of the Olympic team (2000); signed with San Diego Spirit (2002).

ZHANG PEIJUN (1958—). Chinese handball player. Born April 29, 1958, in China. ❖ At Los Angeles Olympics, won a bronze medal in team competition (1984).

ZHANG PING (1982—). Chinese volleyball player. Born Mar 23, 1982, in China. ❖ Second spiker, won a team gold medal at Athens Olympics (2004).

ZHANG RONGFANG (1957—). Chinese volleyball player. Born April 15, 1957, in China. ❖ At Los Angeles Olympics, won a gold medal in team competition (1984).

ZHANG RUIFANG (1918—). Chinese actress. Name variations: Chang Jui-fang. Born 1918 in China; studied in Beijing. ❖ Joined drama troupe and became member of Communist Party; starred in feature films (1949–66), including *Nieh Erh* (1959), *Li Shuang-shuang* (1962); was delegate to Afro-Asia Solidarity Conference (1957) and visited Japan; was blacklisted and imprisoned (1967) but after policy change was elected to National Committee and returned to acting (1973); headed Shanghai Drama Troupe and delegation to First Manila Film Festival; represented China at New Youth International Film Festival (1983) and was elected vice chair of Shanghai Branch of Chinese Communist Party (1985).

ZHANG SHAN (1968—). Chinese shooter. Born Mar 23, 1968, in China. ❖ At Barcelona Olympics, won a gold medal in skeet shooting (1992).

ZHANG XIANGHUA (1968—). Chinese rower. Born May 10, 1968, in China. ❖ At Seoul Olympics, won a bronze medal in coxed eights and a silver medal in coxed fours (1988).

ZHANG XIAODONG (1964—). Chinese yacht racer. Born Jan 4, 1964, in China. ❖ At Barcelona Olympics, won a silver medal in Lechner (boardsailing, 1992).

ZHANG XIUYUN (1976—). Chinese rower. Born Feb 25, 1976, in Hubei, China. ❖ Won a silver medal for double sculls at Atlanta Olympics (1996).

ZHANG YALI (1964—). Chinese rower. Born Feb 24, 1964, in China. ❖ At Seoul Olympics, won a bronze medal in coxed eights (1988).

ZHANG YANMEI. Chinese short-track speedskater. Born in China. ❖ Won a silver medal for the 500 meter at Lillehammer Olympics (1994).

ZHANG YINING (1981—). Chinese table tennis player. Born Oct 5, 1981, in Beijing, China. ❖ At World championships, won a team gold medal (2000, 2001, 2004) and placed 2nd in singles (1999, 2003); placed 1st in ITTF Pro Tour ranking for singles (2002, 2003); won gold medals for table tennis singles and doubles (with Wang Nan) at Athens Olympics (2004).

ZHANG YUEHONG (1975—). Chinese volleyball player. Born Nov 9, 1975, in China. ❖ Chief spiker, won a team gold medal at Athens Olympics (2004).

ZHANG YUEQIN (1960—). Chinese basketball player. Born Jan 27, 1960, in China. ❖ At Los Angeles Olympics, won a bronze medal in team competition (1984).

ZHAO KUN (1973—). Chinese swimmer. Born Jan 10, 1973, in China. ❖ At Barcelona Olympics, won a silver medal in 4 x 100-meter freestyle relay (1992).

ZHAO LIHONG (1972—). Chinese soccer player. Born Dec 4, 1972, in Guangdong Province, China. ❖ Midfielder and captain of the Chinese national team; won Asian championships (1993, 1995); won a team silver medal at Atlanta Olympics (1996); placed team 2nd at World Cup (1999); played for WUSA's Philadelphia Charge (2001). Named MVP of Asian championship (1993, 1995).

ZHAO LUORUI (b. 1912). Chinese poet, translator and educator. Born 1912 in China; University of Chicago, PhD, 1949. ❖ Taught literature at Beijing University; translations include T. S. Eliot's *The Wasteland* (1922), Longfellow's *The Song of Hiawatha* (1855), and Whitman's *Leaves of Grass* (1855); co-edited first *History of European Literature* (1979) in Chinese.

ZHAO RUIRUI (1981—). Chinese volleyball player. Born Oct 8, 1981, in Jiangshu, China. ❖ Second spiker, won a team gold medal at Athens Olympics (2004).

ZHAO YUFEN (1948—). Chinese biochemist. Born 1948 in Qi County, Hunan Province, China; grew up in Taiwan; studied chemistry at Tsinghua University in Taiwan; State University of New York at Stony Brook, PhD in organic chemistry, 1975. ❖ Worked as industrial chemist in US; returned to mainland China with family (1979) and taught and researched organic chemistry at Chemistry Research Institute of the Chinese Academy of Sciences; contributed discoveries about phosphorus in organic and biological compounds, as well as its potential role in origin of life; announced that phosphorus controls and regulates biological elements and activities (1988) at an international scientific meeting; introduced method to create new organic compounds which contain phosphorus, including anti-cancer drug substance; established phosphorus laboratory at Tsinghua University in Beijing (1991), where she worked as a professor, then vice dean of School of Life Science and Engineering; was the youngest person elected to Chinese Academy of Sciences; holds 5 patents; published more than 120 papers.

ZHELEZNIAK, Yocheved (1901–1980). *See Bat-Miriam, Yocheved.*

ZHENG DONGMEI (1967—). Chinese basketball player. Born Dec 23, 1967, in China. ❖ At Barcelona Olympics, won a silver medal in team competition (1992).

ZHENG HAIXIA (1967—). Chinese basketball player. Born Mar 10, 1967, in central Henan Province, China. ❖ Won a bronze medal at Los Angeles Olympics (1984) and a silver medal at Barcelona Olympics (1992), both in team competition; with Chinese national team, won gold medals in the Asian championships (1994, 1995) and a silver medal at the Sydney World championships (1994); was a member of WNBA Los Angeles Sparks for 2 seasons (1997–98); won the WNBA Sportsmanship Award (1997).

ZHENG MEIZHU (1962—). Chinese volleyball player. Born Nov 5, 1962, in China. ❖ Won a gold medal at Los Angeles Olympics (1984) and a bronze medal at Seoul Olympics (1988), both in team competition.

ZHENG MIN (1920—). Chinese poet and educator. Born 1920 in Beijing, China; studied philosophy in China; University of Illinois, MA in literature. ❖ Was professor of Western literature at Beijing Teachers' University; writings include *The Nine Leaves* (1980) and *Shiji: 1942–1947.*

ZHENGYING QIAN (b. 1923). *See Qian Zhengying.*

ZHINGA (c. 1580s–1663). *See Njinga.*

ZHIRKO, Yelena (1968—). Soviet basketball player. Born Feb 16, 1968, in USSR. ❖ At Barcelona Olympics, won a gold medal in team competition (1992).

ZHIRKOVA, Lyudmila (1942–1981). *See Zhivkova, Lyudmila.*

ZHIROVA, Marina (1963—). Soviet runner. Born June 6, 1963, in USSR. ❖ At Seoul Olympics, won a bronze medal in 4 x 100-meter relay (1988).

ZHIVANEVSKAYA, Nina (1977—). Russian-Spanish swimmer. Born June 24, 1977, in Moscow, Russia. ❖ At Barcelona Olympics, won a bronze medal in 4 x 100-meter medley relay (1992); moved to Spain and began representing that nation in competition (1999); at SC and LC European championships, won a gold medal for 100-meter backstroke (1999, 2000), 50-meter backstroke (2000, 2002), and 200-meter backstroke (2000); won a bronze medal for 100-meter backstroke at Sydney Olympics (2000).

ZHIVKOVA, Lyudmila (1942–1981). Bulgarian political leader. Name variations: Liudmila or Ludmilla Zhivkova; Lyudmila Zhirkova. Born Lyudmila Todorova Zhivkova in Sofia, Bulgaria, July 26, 1942; died in Sofia, July 21, 1981; dau. of Todor Christov Zhivkov (1st secretary of Communist Party of Bulgaria and chair of State Council) and Mara Malleeva Zhivkova; studied history and philosophy at University of Sofia and art history in Moscow; also attended Oxford; m. Ivan Slavkov (director-general of Bulgarian State television); children: Zheni; Todor; Lyudmila Zhivkova. ❖ One of the few women in Eastern Europe to achieve significant political influence during the Communist era, directed virtually all aspects of cultural and educational affairs in Bulgaria in the years before her early death; a woman of considerable intelligence, spent several years as a scientific assistant at Bulgarian Academy of Sciences; when mother died (1971), was thrust into role of Bulgaria's first lady; became deputy chair of Committee of Art and Culture (1972), which gave her Cabinet rank; voted a full member of BCP Party's Central Committee (1976), then a full member of the ruling BCP Politburo (1979), taking charge of a commission on culture, education and science; wielded enormous power over Bulgaria's intelligentsia, and usually ignored the political views of gifted artists; playing an increasingly significant role in her country's politics (1971–81), was responsible for the building of the ornate Palace of Culture which was named in her honor. ❖ See also *Women in World History.*

ZHONG HONGLIAN. Chinese soccer player. Born in China. ❖ Goalkeeper; won a team silver medal at Atlanta Olympics (1996).

ZHOSEFINA or ZHOZEFINA. *Variant of Josephina.*

ZHOU, Guanghu (b. 1917). *See Han, Suyin.*

ZHOU JIHONG (1965—). Chinese diver. Born Jan 1, 1965, in China. ❖ At Los Angeles Olympics, won a gold medal in platform (1984).

ZHOU MI (1979—). Chinese badminton player. Born Feb 18, 1979, in Guangxi Zhuang, China. ❖ Won a bronze medal for singles at Athens Olympics (2004).

ZHOU PING (1968—). Chinese gymnast. Born Feb 18, 1968, in China. ❖ At Los Angeles Olympics, won a bronze medal in team all-around (1984).

ZHOU QIURUI (1967—). Chinese gymnast. Born Aug 10, 1967, in China. ❖ At Los Angeles Olympics, won a bronze medal in team all-around (1984).

ZHOU SHOUYING (1969—). Chinese rower. Born Sept 11, 1969, in China. ❖ At Seoul Olympics, won a bronze medal in coxed eights and a silver medal in coxed fours (1988).

ZHOU SUHONG (1979—). Chinese volleyball player. Born April 23, 1979, in China. ❖ Middle blocker, won a team gold medal at Athens Olympics (2004).

ZHOU XIAOLAN (1957—). Chinese volleyball player. Born Oct 9, 1957, in China. ❖ At Los Angeles Olympics, won a gold medal in team competition (1984).

ZHOU XIUHUA (1966—). Chinese rower. Born Dec 8, 1966, in China. ❖ At Seoul Olympics, won a bronze medal in coxed eights (1988).

ZHU, Bailan (1904–1971). *See Blum, Klara.*

ZHU JUEFENG (1964—). Chinese handball player. Born May 5, 1964, in China. ❖ At Los Angeles Olympics, won a bronze medal in team competition (1984).

ZHU LING (1957—). Chinese volleyball player. Born July 10, 1957, in China. ❖ At Los Angeles Olympics, won a gold medal in team competition (1984).

ZHU YINGWEN (1981—). Chinese swimmer. Born Oct 9, 1981, in China. ❖ At World championships, placed 1st for 4 x 200-meter freestyle relay (2002); won a silver medal for 4 x 200-meter freestyle relay at Athens Olympics (2004).

ZHU YUNYING (1978—). Chinese volleyball player. Born Jan 15, 1978, in Shanghai, China. ❖ Setter, joined the national team (1995); won a team silver medal at Atlanta Olympics (1996).

ZHUANG XIAOYAN (1969—). Chinese judoka. Born May 4, 1969, in China. ❖ At Barcelona Olympics, won a gold medal in +72 kg heavyweight (1992).

ZHUANG YONG (1972—). Chinese swimmer. Born Aug 10, 1972, in China. ❖ At Seoul Olympics, won a silver medal in 100-meter freestyle (1988); at Barcelona Olympics, won a gold medal in 100-meter freestyle and silver medals in 50-meter freestyle and 4 x 100-meter freestyle relay (1992).

ZHUCHENKO, Mariia (1834–1907). See Vilinska, Mariya.

ZHUK, Tatiana. Russian pairs skater. Name variations: Tatyana or Tatjana Zhuk. Born in USSR. ❖ With Aleksandr Gavrilov, placed 3rd at World championships (1963); with partner Aleksandr Gorelik, won silver medals at World championships (1966, 1968) and a silver medal at Grenoble Olympics (1968).

ZHUKOVA, Maria (1804–1855). Russian prose writer. Name variations: Márya Semyónovna Zhúkova; Mariia Semenovna Zhúkova. Born 1804 in Nizhegorod, Russia; died April 13, 1855 (one source cites 1851), in Saratov, Russia; dau. of a government clerk; married a landowner but left him sometime after 1830. ❖ Together with Elena Gan and Nadezhda Durova, was among the 1st Russian women to publish a significant amount of fiction; wrote several books and short stories, which reflect the Russian transition from romanticism to realism; earliest stories, compiled in *Evenings on the Karpovka,* humorously provide details of Russian noble life and refreshingly atypical heroines; most popular work appeared in *Sketches of Southern France and Nice* (1844), conversational travel notes about her lengthy trips abroad due to ill health from 1838 to 1842. ❖ See also *Women in World History.*

ZHULINA, Valentina (1953—). Soviet rower. Born June 15, 1953, in USSR. ❖ At Moscow Olympics, won a silver medal in coxed eights (1980).

ZHUPINA, Olena (1973—). Ukrainian diver. Name variations: Olena Zhupyna. Born Aug 23, 1973, in Zaporozhye, Ukraine. ❖ Won European championship for synchronize springboard (1999); won a bronze medal for synchronized 3-meter springboard at Sydney Olympics (2000).

ZHUPIYEVA, Yelena (1960—). Soviet long-distance runner. Born April 18, 1960, in USSR. ❖ At Seoul Olympics, won a bronze medal in the 10,000 meters (1988).

ZHUPYNA, Olena (1973—). See Zhupina, Olena.

ZHUROVA, Svetlana (1972—). Russian speedskater. Name variations: Svetlana Boyarkina-Zhurova. Born Jan 7, 1972, in Kirovsk, Russia. ❖ At World Single Distance championships, won a gold medal (1996), silver medals (1999, 2000), and a bronze medal (2001), all for the 500 meters; won a gold medal in the 500 meters at World championships (1996); won a gold medal for 500 meters at Torino Olympics (2006).

ZI Zhongji (1262–1319). See Guan Daosheng.

ZI Xi (1835–1908). See Cixi.

ZIA, Khaleda (1946—). Bangladeshi politician and prime minister. Name variations: Begum Khaleda Zia. Born Aug 15, 1946 (some sources cite 1944 or 1945), in Dinajpur, East Bengal; dau. of Iskander and Taiyaba Majumder; attended Surendranath College, Dinajpur; m. Ziaur Rahman (president of Bangladesh), early 1960s (assassinated 1981); children: 2 sons. ❖ Following assassination of husband (1981), joined the Bangladesh National Party (BNP), which he had founded; became leader of BNP (1984), a position in which she coordinated repeated agitations against the autocratic regime of General Hossain Mohammad Ershad, which led to his resignation (1990); became the 1st woman prime minister of Bangladesh (Mar 20, 1991); focused on the advancement of women, ending illiteracy, and economic reform; resigned in the face of strong opposition (1996); worked as an opposition leader, continuing with the BNP; was returned to power as prime minister when her 4-party coalition gained a two-thirds majority in Parliament (Oct 2001). ❖ See also *Women in World History.*

ZIADAH, Mayy (1886–1941). See Ziyada, Mayy.

ZIDE, Rochelle (1938—). American ballet dancer. Born April 21, 1938, in Boston, MA. ❖ Danced with Ballet Russe de Monte Carlo in Massine's *Gaité Parisienne,* Ruthanna Boris' *Cirque de Deux,* and company productions of *Swan Lake* and *Coppélia,* among others (mid-1950s); danced for Robert Joffrey in his Joffrey Ballet (1958–62) and New York City Opera Ballet (1962–64), and was his ballet master for City Center Joffrey Ballet (c. 1965–68); appeared on tv, dancing as a regular on "Ed Sullivan Show" and in ballet specials; taught at universities and New York studios upon retiring from performance career.

ZIEGELMEYER, Nikki (c. 1975—). American short-track speedskater. Name variations: Nicole Ziegelmeyer. Born c. 1975 in Imperial, MO; m. Brad Brown. ❖ Won a silver medal at Albertville Olympics (1992) and a bronze medal at Lillehammer Olympics (1994), both for the 3,000-meter relay.

ZIEGLER, Anne (1910–2003). English actress and singer. Born Irene Frances Eastwood, June 22, 1910, in Liverpool, England; died Oct 13, 2003, in Colwyn Bay, Wales; m. Webster Booth (singer, 1902–1984). ❖ With husband, appeared as the singing duo Ziegler and Booth on radio and records, becoming a household name in the 1930s with signature tune "Only a Rose"; appeared on London stage and Broadway, and as Marguerite in the film *Faust* (1934); later immigrated to South Africa; settled in northern Wales (1978).

ZIEGLER, Christiane Mariane von (1695–1760). German poet. Name variations: Christiana Mariana von Ziegler; Christiana Mariana von Steinwehr. Born Christiane Mariane Romanus, June 28, 1695 in Leipzig, Germany; died May 1, 1760, in Frankfurt, Germany; dau. of Franz Conrad Romanus (mayor of Leipzig); m. Heinrich Levin (died); m. Georg Friedrich von Ziegler (died 1722); m. Balthasar von Steinwehr, 1741; children: 2 (died young). ❖ Opened literary salon in Leipzig and gained fame for poetry, some of which was set to music by J. S. Bach; became 1st woman member of poet Johann Christoph Gottsched's literary society, Deutsche Gesellschaft; published anthology *Versuch in gebundener Schreib-Art* (1728), which contain the texts of the 9 cantatas composed by Bach; was poet laureate of University of Wittenberg (1733).

ZIGANSHINA, Natalia (1985—). Russian gymnast. Name variations: Natalya Zighanshina. Born Dec 24, 1985, in St. Petersburg, Russia; sister of Gulnara Ziganshina (gymnast). ❖ At World championships, won a silver medal for all-around (2001); won a bronze medal for team all-around at Athens Olympics (2004).

ZIGGY MARLEY AND THE MELODY MAKERS.
See Marley, Cedella.
See Prendergast, Sharon Marley.

ZIGHANSHINA, Natalia or Natalya (1985—). See Ziganshina, Natalia.

ZIJLAARD, Leontien (1970—). See van Moorsel, Leontien.

ZILBER, Irina (c. 1980—). Russian rhythmic gymnast. Born c. 1980 in USSR. ❖ Won a team World championship (1999) and a team gold medal at Sydney Olympics (2000).

ZILIUTE, Diana (1976—). Lithuanian cyclist. Born May 28, 1976, in Rietavas, Lithuania. ❖ Won World championship (1998); won a bronze medal for indiv. road race at Sydney Olympics (2000).

ZILLMAN, Bertha (d. 1893). German murderer. Beheaded at Plötzensee prison, Germany, Oct 1893. ❖ After she and her children were beaten by husband, poisoned him to death with arsenic; quickly condemned for the crime.

ZILPAH. Biblical woman. Name variations: Zelpha. Concubine of Jacob; children: Gad and Asher. ❖ One of the female slaves of Laban (the father of Rachel and Leah); became Leah's handmaiden, when Leah was given in marriage to Jacob; later became the concubine of Jacob, with whom she gave birth to Gad and Asher, the 7th and 8th of Jacob's 12 sons.

ZILPORITE, Laima (1967—). Soviet cyclist. Born April 1967 in USSR. ❖ At Seoul Olympics, won a bronze medal in indiv. road race (1988).

ZIMBALIST, Mary Louise Curtis (1876–1970). American music patron and philanthropist. Name variations: Mary Louise Curtis; Mary Louise Curtis Bok. Born Mary Louise Curtis, Aug 6, 1876, in Boston, Massachusetts; died Jan 4, 1970, in Philadelphia, Pennsylvania; dau. of Cyrus Hermann Kotzschmar, known as Cyrus Curtis (publisher) and Louisa (Knapp) Curtis (editor); m. Edward William Bok (editor of *Ladies' Home Journal*), Oct 22, 1896 (died 1930); m. Efrem Zimbalist (violinist), July 6, 1943; children: (1st m.): William Curtis (b. 1897), and

Cary William (b. 1905). ❖ Founder and president of the Curtis Institute of Music in Philadelphia, donated a building to house the Settlement School of Music (1910), which served the children of a disadvantaged neighborhood in Philadelphia; established a separate conservatory branch of the school (1924), which she called the Curtis Institute of Music; relocated the Curtis Institute to 2 mansions in downtown Philadelphia's Rittenhouse Square (1925); also established one of the most outstanding music libraries in US, and created a summer music colony in Rockport, Maine. ❖ See also *Women in World History.*

ZIMETBAUM, Mala (1920–1944). Jewish escapee from Auschwitz-Birkenau. Born in Brzesko, Poland, 1920; grew up in Belgium; committed defiant suicide at Auschwitz, Aug 22, 1944. ❖ One of the most extraordinary prisoners to pass through Auschwitz, arrived there from Belgium (Sept 1942); fluent in several languages, was chosen by the Germans to be a messenger and interpreter, which allowed her to move more freely than other prisoners; carried out assignments for camp resistance, smuggled in food and medicine, and managed to switch identity cards of those women selected for the gas chambers with those who had already died; escaped with Polish political prisoner Edward Galinski (June 24, 1944), but was caught 2 weeks later; brought before the assembled women prisoners to be hanged, pulled out a razor blade and slit her wrists; when one of the SS tried to snatch the blade from her, slapped his face with her bloody hand; was trampled to death by the guards; became a hero for fellow prisoners. ❖ See also *Women in World History.*

ZIMMERMAN, Jillana (1934—). See *Jillana.*

ZIMMERMAN, Mary Beth (1960—). American golfer. Born Dec 11, 1960, in Mt. Vernon, IL; attended Florida International University. ❖ Won Broadmoor (1980); Florida State Collegiate champion (1983); named All-American (1983); won Standard Register/Samaritan Tourquoise Classic and Uniden Invitational (1986); won Henredon Classic (1987); won State Farm Rail Classic (1995).

ZIMMERMAN, Suzanne (1925—). American swimmer. Name variations: Suzanne Zimmerman-Edwards. Born July 13, 1925, in Oregon. ❖ At London Olympics, won a silver medal in the 100-meter backstroke (1948).

ZIMMERMANN, Agnes (1847–1925). English pianist. Born in Cologne, Germany, July 5, 1847; died in London, England, Nov 14, 1925. ❖ Moved to England as a child with family (1847); after studies at Royal Academy of Music with Cipriani Potter and others, made debut at Crystal Palace (1863); her tours of the British Isles were vastly popular; gave the 1st performance in England of Beethoven's piano transcription of his violin concerto (1872); edited the sonatas of Mozart and Beethoven, and the complete piano works of Schumann; also composed, producing a number of lyrical and well-constructed compositions, including a piano trio, several violin sonatas, a piano sonata, and a cello sonata.

ZIMMERMANN, Edith. Austrian Alpine skier. Born in Austria. ❖ Won a silver medal for downhill at Innsbruck Olympics (1964).

ZIMMERMANN, Gerda (1927—). German ballet dancer. Born Mar 26, 1927, in Cuxhaven, Germany. ❖ Trained in modern, ballet, and ethnic dance forms; performed with Rheinische Oper in Duesseldorf; danced with Ballet of Landestheater in over 40 works of Yvonne Georgi, including *Carmina Burana, Four Temperaments, Apollon Musagète, Evolution,* and *Orpheus and Eurydice*; moved to US (1960) to train with José Limón, Donald McKayle, Alwin Nikolais, Ethel Winter, Yuriko, and Helen McGehee; created many works of her own; a major importer of German expressionist dance, taught throughout US.

ZIMMERMANN, Heidi (1946—). Austrian Alpine skier. Born May 1, 1946, in Hohenhems, Austria. ❖ Won a silver medal for giant slalom and a bronze for combined at World championships (1966).

ZIMMERMANN, Kathrin (1966—). East German swimmer. Born Dec 22, 1966. ❖ At Seoul Olympics, won a silver medal in 200-meter backstroke (1988).

ZIMMERMANN-WEBER, Annemarie (1940—). West German kayaker. Born June 10, 1940. ❖ Won a gold medal at Tokyo Olympics (1964) and a gold medal at Mexico City Olympics (1968), both in K2 500 meters.

ZINAIDA R—VA. See *Gan, Elena.*

ZINDERSTEIN, Marion (b. 1896). See *Jessup, Marion.*

ZINDKA (c. 1890–c. 1919). See *Zintkala Nuni.*

ZINDLER, Petra (1966—). West German swimmer. Born Feb 11, 1966. ❖ At Los Angeles Olympics, won a bronze medal in 400-meter indiv. medley (1984).

ZINGA (c. 1580s–1663). See *Njinga.*

ZINKEISEN, Doris (1898–1991). Scottish costume designer and painter. Name variations: Doris Grahame Johnstone. Born Doris Clare Zinkeisen, 1898, in Kilcreggan, Scotland; died 1991; sister of Anna Zinkeisen (painter); m. Capt E. Grahame Johnstone; children: (twins) Janet and Anne Grahame-Johnstone (illustrators). ❖ Designed scenes and costumes for such London plays as *The Insect Play* (1924), *The Way of the World, Cochran's Revues, Evergreen, Waltzes from Vienna, Words and Music, Wild Violets, The Taming of the Shrew, Under Your Hat, Nymph Errant, Lights Out, Black Vanities, The Belle of New York, Arms and the Man, After the Ball* and *Cinderella*; also designed for ballet and such films as *Bitter Sweet, Nell Gwyn, Show Boat* (1936) and *Sixty Glorious Years*; painted and held exhibitions; was commissioned by British Red Cross as a war artist (1945), with paintings displayed at the National Gallery; wrote the book *Designing for the Stage* (1938); was briefly engaged to director James Whale.

ZINN, Elfi (1953—). East German runner. Born Aug 24, 1953. ❖ At Montreal Olympics, won a bronze medal in 800 meters (1976).

ZINNER, Hedda (1902–1990). German novelist, playwright, and political writer. Name variations: Heda. Born 1902 in Vienna, Austria; died 1990; studied acting at the Schauspielakemie. ❖ Developing an interest in the workers' movement, moved to Berlin (1924), where she joined Communist Party (1929); worked as a reporter for *Rote Fahne* and contributed short stories, poems, and satirical political songs to leftwing journals; with rise of Hitler, left Germany for Prague (1933), where she founded the subversive cabaret *Studio 1934*; migrated to USSR (1935) and lived in Moscow for remainder of WWII; worked as a reporter, served on the editorial board of *Das Wort*, and wrote radio plays; after war, moved to East Berlin; wrote of Luise Otto-Peters in her novel *Nur eine Frau* (Only a Woman, 1954); also wrote *Die Schwestern* (Sisters, 1970), and various modern history plays, including *Tesufelskreis* (The Devil's Circle, 1953) and *General Landt.* ❖ See also autobiography (in German) *Ahnen und Erben* (Ancestors and Inheritors, 1968); and *Women in World History.*

ZINÓVEVA-ANNIBAL, Lidiia Dmitrievna (1866–1907). Russian playwright and short-story writer. Name variations: Lydia Zinoveva-Annibal; Lidiia Zinoveva. Born 1866 in Russia; died 1907; m. Viacheslav Ivanon. ❖ With husband, established famous literary salon called Tower; also established literary salon for women only; works, which were criticized by contemporaries for overt sensuality and negative characterization of men, include *Rings* (1904), *Thirty-Three Abominations* (1907), *The Tragic Menagerie* (1907) and *No!* (1918).

ZINTKALA NUNI (c. 1890–c. 1919). Lakota survivor of Wounded Knee massacre. Name variations: Lost Bird; Zindka. Born c. 1890; died c. 1919; adopted dau. of Leonard Wright Colby (leader of NE National Guard and state senator) and Clara Colby (suffragist). ❖ After Lakota mother's death at Wounded Knee massacre, SD (1890), was taken by Leonard Wright Colby and adopted by him and wife Clara Colby to be raised as a white child; performed in Wild West shows and early Western movies; died at age 30 (c. 1919); became symbol of American Indian children taken from their tribes. Her remains were returned to Wounded Knee on Pine Ridge Reservation (1991) and her story inspired founding of Lost Bird Society at Pine Ridge, SD, which assists American Indians with finding their roots. ❖ See also Renee Sansom Flood, *Lost Bird of Wounded Knee: Spirit of the Lakota* (DaCapo, 1998).

ZINZENDORF, Benigna (1725–1789). See *Watteville, Benigna von.*

ZIPPORAH. Biblical woman. Pronunciation: zip-POE-rah. One of the daughters of Jethro, priest of Midian; m. Moses; children: Gershom and Eliezer. ❖ Married Moses' during his 40-year exile in the desert of Midian, and gave birth to sons Gershom and Eliezer; when the Lord threatened to kill Moses because his 2nd son Eliezer had not been circumcised, grabbed a stone and circumcised the boy herself; did not accompany Moses back to Egypt, but was ordered by him to return to her own people, the Midianites; along with her father and sons, was later reunited with Moses during his years in the wilderness.

ZIPPRODT, Patricia (1925–1999). American costume designer. Born in Chicago, Illinois, 1925; died in New York, NY, July 17, 1999; graduate of Wellesley College; attended the New School and the Fashion Institute of Technology, both in New York City; m. Robert O'Brien Jr. (retired), 1993 (died 1998); no children. ❖ Apprenticed with Irene Sharaff; created costumes for the American Ballet Theater, New York City Ballet, Houston Ballet and Ballet Hispanico; designed for musical theater, winning Tony Awards for *Fiddler on the Roof* (1964), *Cabaret* (1966) and *Sweet Charity* (1985); in addition, designed for *1776* (1969), *Pippin* (1972), *Chicago* (1975), and co-designed *Sunday in the Park with George* (1984); created costumes for non-musical plays as well, such as *Plaza Suite* (1968), *Brighton Beach Memoirs* (1983) and *The Glass Menagerie* (1983); also designed for the Boston Opera, New York City Opera, and Metropolitan Opera. ❖ See also *Women in World History.*

ZIRIMU, Elvania Namukwaya (1938–1979). Ugandan poet and playwright. Born 1938 in Uganda; died 1979. ❖ Studied at Makerere University and University of Leeds; worked as producer and actor and published plays for theater and radio; works, which often focus on erosion of traditional values, include *Keeping up with the Mukasas* (1975), *When the Hunchback Made Rain* (1975), and *Snoring Strangers* (1975).

ZIRKOWA, Elisaveta Ivanovna (1888–1949). See Bichovsky, Elisheva.

ZIRZOW, Carola (1954—). East German kayaker. Born Sept 15, 1954. ❖ At Montreal Olympics, won a bronze medal in K2 500 meters and a gold medal in K1 500 meters (1976).

ZISKE, Joyce (c. 1935—). See Malison, Joyce.

ZISSENER, Sabine (1970—). German politician. Born Nov 1, 1970, in Gebhardshain, Germany. ❖ As a member of the European People's Party (Christian Democrats) and European Democrats, elected to 5th European Parliament (1999–2004).

ZITA OF LUCCA (1218–1275). Italian saint of Lucca. Name variations: Sitha. Born 1218 in Lucca, Italy; died 1275 in Lucca; never married; no children. ❖ At 10, was sent to work as a serving girl; quiet and reserved, served her employers, the Faytinelli family, for almost 50 years; spent her spare time in service for the poor, helping out at local hospitals, caring for the ill; became well known and respected. Feast day is April 27.

ZITA OF PARMA (1892–1989). Empress of Austria and queen of Hungary. Name variations: Zita of Bourbon-Parma; Zita von Bourbon-Parma; Zita von Habsburg; Zita Habsburg; Zita von Parma. Reigned from Nov 1916 to Nov 1918. Born Zita Maria Grazia Adelgonda Michela Raffaella Gabriella Giuseppina Antonia Luisa Agnese of Bourbon-Parma in Pianore near Lucca, Italy, May 9, 1892; died in Zizers, Switzerland, Mar 14, 1989, and was buried on April 1, 1989, in the Habsburg crypt in Vienna's Capuchin Church; dau. of Maria Antonia of Portugal (1862–1959) and Robert I, duke of Bourbon-Parma; had 18 brothers and sisters; m. Karl von Habsburg-Lothringen or Karl Franz Josef (1887–1922), also known as Charles I of Austria or Carol, Karoly, or Charles IV of Hungary, on Oct 21, 1911; children: Otto (b. 1912, who m. Regina of Saxe-Meiningen); Adelheid or Adelaide (b. 1914); Robert (b. 1915, who m. Margarita of Savoy); Felix (b. 1916, who m. Anna von Arenberg); Karl Ludwig or Charles Louis (b. 1918, who m. Yolande de Ligne); Rudolf (b. 1919, who m. Xenia Chernicheva); Charlotte (b. 1921, who m. George Alexander, duke of Mecklenburg); Elisabeth or Elizabeth (b. 1922, who m. Henry of Liechtenstein). ❖ A key participant in the Austrian monarchist movement in both Austria and Hungary until the end of the 1930s, served for more than 2 generations as a symbol of the ideals of monarchists and political-cultural traditionalists in Central Europe; during WWI, tried to bring about a separate peace between Austria-Hungary and France, but failed; when husband abdicated (Nov 11, 1918), went into exile in Switzerland (Mar 24, 1919); planned for a coup in Hungary to restore husband to the throne (1921), one that was backed by military force in the form of Hungarian legitimists led by Colonel Anton Lehár; with husband, entered Hungary, but was surrounded by police and formally arrested two days later; exiled to Funchal, on the Portuguese island of Madeira in the Atlantic, where husband died; now a widow with 8 children, moved her family to a château near Brussels, Belgium (1929); escaped the advancing German forces when Belgium was invaded (May 1940) and moved to US, where she had several meetings with President Franklin Roosevelt; returned to Europe (1962), settling in Zizers, a village in eastern Switzerland; was finally permitted to return to Austria for a visit (1982). ❖ See also Bogle and Bogle, *A Heart for Europe: The Lives of Emperor Charles and Empress Zita of Austria-Hungary* (Gracewing,

1993); Gordon Brook-Shepherd, *The Last Empress: The Life and Times of Zita of Austria-Hungary, 1892–1989* (HarperCollins, 1991); and *Women in World History.*

ZITKALA SA (1876–1938). See Bonnin, Gertrude Simmons.

ZITZ, Kathinka (1801–1877). German short-story writer. Name variations: Kathinka Zitz-Halein. Born Kathinka Halein, Nov 11, 1801, in Mainz, Germany; died Mar 8, 1877, in Mainz; m. Franz Zitz, 1837. ❖ Was involved with Humania Association, women's group founded to support 1849 revolt to defend Frankfurt Assembly's constitution; wrote stories about German society and fictional biographies of Byron, Goethe, Heine and Rahel Varnhagen, among others.

ZIYADA, Mayy (1886–1941). Lebanese feminist and activist. Name variations: May or Mai; Ziada, Ziadah, Ziyadah, or Ziyadeh; published 1st work under pseudonym Isis Copia. Born Mari Ilyas Ziyada, Feb 11, 1886, in Nazareth; died in Cairo, Oct 19, 1941; father was a Lebanese Christian teacher and journalist; mother was a housewife from a village near Nazareth in Galilee; educated at French language schools, 1st at St. Joseph's School in Nazareth (1892–99), later in Lebanon at Ayn Tura (1900–04) and Lazarist school in Beirut (1904–08); never married; no children. ❖ Early 20th-century Lebanese intellectual, active in literary and feminist circles in Egypt and Lebanon, who advocated the education and employment of women and celebrated the accomplishments of 19th-century female Arab writers; immigrated with family to Cairo (1908), where she established a literary salon (1914); entered Egyptian University to study literature and philosophy (1916); lived in Cairo for rest of life except for a short period (1935–38) when, following the deaths of her parents, she grew increasingly depressed and relatives persuaded her to return to Beirut (there, they admitted her to a mental hospital for 9 months, while her friends published essays in the journal *al-Makshuf* calling for her release); returned to Cairo (1938); lectured extensively and published in Arabic, English and French; work appeared in various journals, including *al-Mahrusa* (The Protected One), *al-Ahram* (The Pyramids), *Sphynx, Le Progrès Égyptien,* and *The Egyptian Mail*; lectures were collected in *Kalimat wa-isharat* (Words and signs, Cairo, 1922), and articles on important French and Arab figures were published in *al-Saha'if* (Pages, Cairo, 1924); renowned for her biographies of the female Arab writers Bahithat al-Badiyya (Cairo, 1920) and A'isha al-Taymuriyya (Cairo, 1924). Most of her prose works, which were collected during her lifetime in 10 vols., were republished in 2 vols. compiled by Salma al-Haffar al-Kuzbari, *al-Muallafat al-kamila: May Ziyada* (The Complete Works: May Ziyada, Beirut, 1982). ❖ See also *Women in World History.*

ZLATA (b. around 1981). See Filipovic, Zlata.

ZLATIN, Sabina (1907–1996). Polish rescuer. Name variations: Sabine Zlatin. Born Sabina Chwast in Warsaw, Poland, Jan 13, 1907; died in Paris, Sept 21, 1996; immigrated to France; m. Miron or Myron Zlatin (killed in Auschwitz, July 1944). ❖ Polish-born rescuer during the Holocaust who, along with husband, hid a group of Jewish children in the remote village of Izieu; was a licensed military nurse; after the defeat of France by Nazi Germany (June 1940), moved with husband to Montpellier in the zone not occupied by the Germans; found work in the local military hospital and a three-story farmhouse in Izieu to house Jewish children (1942); by 1943, was in charge of several dozen Jewish children whose parents had been arrested or deported; while she was in Montpellier (April 6, 1944), her husband and 44 children were taken from the farmhouse by Nazis led by Klaus Barbie; went to Paris and became active in the resistance. ❖ See also memoir (in French), *Mémoires de la "Dame d'Izieu": Avant propos be François Mitterand* (Gallimard, 1992); Serge Klarsfeld, *The Children of Izieu* (1985); and *Women in World History.*

ZMESKAL, Kim (1976—). American gymnast. Born Feb 6, 1976, in Houston, TX; m. Chris Burdette, Oct 1999. ❖ Won American Classic and Arthur Gander Memorial (1988), and US nationals (1990–92); at World championships, was the 1st American woman to win a gold medal in all-around (1991) and won gold medals in floor exercise and balance beam (1992); at Barcelona Olympics, won a bronze medal in team all-around (1992); won the Rock and Roll Gymnastics (1997); retired from competition (2000). Inducted into USA Gymnastics Hall of Fame (2001). ❖ See also *Women in World History.*

ŻMICHOWSKA, Narcyza (1819–1876). Polish novelist and reformer. Name variations: Narcyza Zmichowska; (pseudonym) Gabryella. Born Mar 4, 1819, in Warsaw, Poland; died Dec 25, 1876, in Warsaw; dau. of Jan Żmichowski and Wiktoria z Kiedrzyńskych, educated at the school of Zuzanna Wilczyńska and the Institut Guwernantek in Warsaw, 1835. ❖ Taught at Institut Guwernantek in Warsaw; following an unsuccessful uprising against Russian domination (1830), presided over a group of intellectual women; moved to Paris (1838) and reunited with brother in Reims, who had previously fled Poland for political reasons; supported herself as a tutor; became active in a political group that committed illegal acts to aid Polish prisoners and teach Polish workers (1839); aligned herself with a group of women, including Anna Skimborowicz, Kazimiera Ziemiecka, and Wincentyna Zablocka, as part of a women's emancipation movement that was later called the Enthusiasts; as a writer, became best known of the Enthusiasts; returning to Warsaw (1846), resumed illegal activities, but was arrested and spent 3 years in a nunnery at Lublin; upon release, once again taught courses for young women and advocated for women's schools; though her work went largely unread in 20th century, was a leader of her contemporary literary circles and a prolific, though highly self-critical, writer; later work, *Poganka* (The Pagan Woman, 1846), is classified as one of her finest examples of romantic fiction; also wrote the novels *Książa pamiąstek* (Book of Remembrances, 1847), *Biala róża* (White Rose, 1858), *Kasia i Marynka* (Kasia and Marynka, 1869), and *Czy to powieść?* (Is this a novel?, 1876). ❖ See also *Women in World History.*

ZNAK, Marina (1961—). Belarusian rower. Born May 17, 1961, in Minsk, Belarus. ❖ Won a bronze medal for coxed eights at Atlanta Olympics (1996); won a world championship for quadruple sculls (1999, 2000).

ZOBELT, Roswietha (1954—). East German rower. Born Nov 24, 1954. ❖ Won a gold medal at Montreal Olympics (1976) and a gold medal at Moscow Olympics (1980), both in quadruple sculls with coxswain.

ZOBER, Hannelore (1946—). East German handball player. Born Nov 6, 1946. ❖ Won a silver medal at Montreal Olympics (1976) and a bronze medal at Moscow Olympics (1980), both in team competition.

ZOCH, Jacqueline (1949—). American rower. Born June 1949 in US. ❖ At Montreal Olympics, won a bronze medal in coxed eights (1976).

ZOË CARBOPSINA (c. 890–920). Byzantine empress. Name variations: Carbonopsina or Carbonupsina; Carbonopsina means "with the coal-black eyes." Born c. 890; died in 920 CE; became 4th wife of Leo VI the Wise, Byzantine emperor (r. 886–912); children: Constantine VII Porphyrogenitus (c. 906–959), Byzantine emperor (r. 913–959); possibly Anna of Byzantium (who m. Louis III the Blind, Holy Roman emperor). ❖ Was a member of an established Byzantine aristocratic family among whose numbers was her contemporary Himerius, an influential admiral; an eye-catching beauty, attracted the attention of Leo VI, whose mistress she became (probably) after the death of his 3rd wife, Eudocia Baiane; gave birth to Leo's long-awaited son (905), but most of the clergy, especially the powerful patriarch of Constantinople, Nicholas I Mystikos, were firmly set against Leo taking a 4th wife; her marriage and elevation split both the ecclesiastical establishment and the general population of the Byzantine Empire into warring camps; after Leo died, was exiled from the palace by Leo's younger brother, Alexander (III), and her son Constantine VII co-reigned with Alexander; when Alexander died and Nicholas I Mystikos became regent, engineered a coup which transferred the regency of her son from Nicholas to herself (914); eventually had to yield the running of the empire to Romanus I Lecapenus (919); retired from court to take up residence in the convent of St. Euthymia, where she died shortly thereafter. ❖ See also *Women in World History.*

ZOE DUCAS (fl. 11th c.). Byzantine princess. Dau. of Eudocia Macrembolitissa (1021–1096) and Constantine X Ducas (d. 1067), Byzantine emperor (r. 1059–1067). ❖ See *Women in World History.*

ZOE PALAEOLOGUS OR PALEOLOGA (1448–1503). See *Sophia of Byzantium.*

ZOË PORPHYROGENITA (980–1050). Byzantine empress. Name variations: Zoe Prophyrogenita; Zoe of Byzantium. Pronunciation: ZOE-ee por-fear-o-GEN-i-tuh. Co-empress of Byzantium (r. 1028–1050). Born in 980 in Constantinople, capital of the Byzantine Empire; died in Constantinople in 1050 of illness; 2nd dau. of Constantine VIII, Byzantine emperor (r. 1025–1028), and Helena of Alypia; sister of Theodora Porphyrogenita (c. 989–1056); m. Romanus III Argyrus, Byzantine emperor (r. 1028–1034), in Nov 1028 (died April 12, 1034); m. Michael IV the Paphlagonian, Byzantine emperor (r. 1034–1041), on April 12, 1034 (died Nov 1042); m. Constantine IX

Monomachus, Byzantine emperor (r. 1042–1055), on June 1042; children: (adopted) Michael V Kalaphates or Calaphates, Byzantine emperor (r. 1041–1042). ❖ Byzantine empress, one of only four women to rule the empire in her own name, who was crucial in establishing the principal of dynastic succession in Byzantium; was the daughter of Constantine VIII of Constantinople, the last male heir of the great Macedonian Dynasty; was betrothed to Holy Roman Emperor Otto III (1002), but he died; became heir to the Byzantine throne upon the death of her uncle, Basil II (1025); married Romanus Argyrus (1028) and became empress that same year upon her father's death; widowed, married Michael the Paphlagonian (Nov 1034), who died (Nov 1041); deposed and forced into a convent by adopted son Michael V (April 1042), causing the citizens of Constantinople to rise in anger and riot; reinstated as ruling co-empress with her younger sister Theodora Porphyrogenita, and Michael was sent into exile (April 1042). This was the 1st time the Byzantine Empire had been ruled by 2 empresses and only the 2nd time an empress held supreme power. Though the Byzantines allowed women to inherit power, position, wealth, and land from their fathers, no emperor's daughter had followed him to the throne as ruling empress before Zoë; before this, the only way a new family could come to power was through marriage to the female heir or by overthrowing the ruling dynasty; this broader interpretation of dynastic succession became a part of the Byzantine political system. ❖ See also *Women in World History.*

ZOË ZAUTZINA (c. 870–c. 899). Byzantine empress. Name variations: Zoe Zautza or Zaütza. Born c. 870; died in 899 or 900 CE; dau. of Stylianus Zaoutzes; became the 2nd wife of Leo VI the Wise, Byzantine emperor (r. 886–912). ❖ Was the daughter of a prominent adviser of the Byzantine emperor Leo VI; became Leo's mistress while he was still married to Theophano; after Theophano died of natural causes (897), wed Leo (early 898) and was elevated to the status of Augusta (empress); died shortly after without giving birth to the longed-for heir. ❖ See also *Women in World History.*

ZOFDJA. *Variant of Sofia, Sophia or Zofia.*

ZOFIA. *Variant of Sofia or Sophia.*

ZOFJA. *Variant of Zofia and Sophia.*

ZOFF, Marianne (1893–1984). Austrian opera singer and actress. Name variations: Marianne Brecht. Born 1893 in Austria; died 1984; became 1st wife of Bertolt Brecht, Nov 3, 1922 (div. 1927); m. Theo Lingen (actor), 1928; children: (1st m.) daughter Hanne (b. 1923, later known as Hanne Hiob); (2nd m.) Ursula Lingen (actress).

ZOGRAPHOU, Lili. Greek novelist and essayist. Born in Crete, Greece. ❖ Lived unconventional life in Athens; novels, which enjoyed success in Greece, include *Loves* (1949), *Job: Whore* (1979), and *The Woman Lost Riding a Horse* (1981); also wrote essays on Greek writers.

ZOLNER, Urska (1982—). Slovenian judoka. Born Oct 9, 1981, in Slovenia. ❖ Won a bronze medal for 63 kg at Athens Olympics (2004).

ZOLOTOW, Charlotte (b. 1915). American children's writer and publisher. Name variations: (pseudonyms) Sarah Abbott; Charlotte Bookman. Born June 26, 1915, in Norfolk, Virginia; dau. of Louis and Ella (Bernstein) Shapiro; attended University of Wisconsin; m. Maurice Zolotow (writer), April 14, 1938 (div. 1969); children: Stephen Zolotow; Ellen Zolotow. ❖ Entered the publishing field (1930s), rising to become senior editor of children's literature at Harper & Row (1940), a position she held until 1944; turned to writing her own stories for children, beginning with *The Park Book* (1944); received Caldecott award for *The Storm Book* (1953), an honor repeated for *Mr. Rabbit and the Lovely Present* (1963), for which she also received the Newbery award; regularly published illustrated children's books, over 70 in all, through the 1980s; served as senior editor at Harper (1962–76), was vice-president and associate publisher of Junior Books (1976–82), then returned to Harper to establish a new imprint, Charlotte Zolotow Books, serving as its editorial director and launching the careers of numerous successful writers and book illustrators. ❖ See also *Women in World History.*

ZONG PU (1928—). Chinese short-story writer. Name variations: Feng Zhongpu. Born Feng Zhongpu, 1928, in Peking, China; studied at Qinghua University. ❖ Works, which were often concerned with inner lives of women and difficulties of life during Cultural Revolution, include "The Red Beans" (1957), "Melody in Dreams" (1978), *The Everalasting Stone* (1980), "Who Am I?" (1983), "A Head in the Marshes" (1985), and *Heading South.*

ZORACH, Marguerite Thompson (1887–1968). American painter and tapestry designer. Born Marguerite Thompson in 1887 in Santa Rosa, California; died 1968; studied at La Palette in Paris; m. William Zorach (sculptor and lithographer), 1912; children: son Tessim (b. 1915); daughter Dahlov Ipcar (b. 1917, writer and illustrator). ❖ Exhibited paintings at Royar Galleries in Los Angeles (1912); married and moved to Greenwich Village (1912); with husband, created pioneering works of art and exhibited them in the Armory Show (1913), where she received scorching criticism; eventually turned to the design and embroidery of tapestries and was able to incorporate both her Fauvist and Cubist ideas in them; founded and became the 1st president of the New York Society of Women Artists (1925), the avant-garde wing of women painters. Only after her death did the art world realize the singularity of her paintings and the fine artistry of her tapestries. ❖ See also *Women in World History.*

ZORBA, Myrsini (1949—). Greek publisher and politician. Born Feb 7, 1949, in Athens, Greece; University of Athens, law degree (1973); University of Rome, postgraduate diploma in philosophy of law (1975). ❖ Worked as translator (1972–78), publisher (1973–92), consultant at the Ministry of Culture (1992–93), and director of the National Book Centre (1994–99); as a European Socialist, elected to 5th European Parliament (1999–2004).

ZORINA, Vera (1917–2003). German-born Norwegian-American ballet dancer and actress. Name variations: Eva Brigitta Hartwig; Brigitta Hartwig. Born Eva Brigitta Hartwig, Jan 2, 1917, in Berlin, Germany; became US citizen, 1943; died April 9, 2003; dau. of Fritz Hartwig (a German) and Billie Wimpel (Mann) Hartwig of Kristiansund, Norway; studied dance with Eugenie Eduardova in Germany, Olga Preobrazhenska in Paris, and Nicholas Légat in London; m. George Balanchine (director and choreographer), Dec 24, 1938 (div. 1947); m. Goddard Lieberson (president of Columbia Records), 1948 (died 1977); m. Paul Wolfe (harpsichordist), 1991; children: (2nd m.) Peter and Jonathan. ❖ Made stage debut in Kristiansund, Norway (where she grew up), as a butterfly in a Flower Ballet (1923); partnered with Anton Dolin in *Ballerina* and danced in Max Reinhardt's *Midsummer Night's Dream* (1931); danced with Ballets Russes (1934–36), reluctantly changing name to Vera Zorina (since all their dancers had Russian names), and had great success in Massine's *Symphonie fantastique*; left Ballets Russes to appear in role of Vera Baranova in British version of *On Your Toes* (1937); subsequently appeared in film version (1939), followed by *The Goldwyn Follies*; on Broadway, starred in *I Married an Angel* (1938) and *Louisiana Purchase* (1941), among others; after 7 films, career in Hollywood came to an abrupt end when replaced by Ingrid Bergman in *For Whom the Bell Tolls* (1943); returned to stage as Ariel in *The Tempest* (1945); later became narrator-performer in such works as Stavinsky's *Persephone*, Milhaud's *Les Choëphores*, and Debussy's *The Martydom of St. Sebastian*; took active role at Lincoln Center in NY, as advisor and director, and directed operas at Santa Fe Opera in New Mexico; also contributed to the raising of $1.7 million for a theater in the hills of New Mexico. ❖ See also autobiography *Zorina* (1986).

ZORKA OF MONTENEGRO (1864–1890). Princess of Montenegro. Name variations: Zorka Petrovitch-Njegos or Petrovic-Njegos. Born Dec 23, 1864; died Mar 16, 1890; dau. of Milena (1847–1923) and Nicholas I (b. 1841), king of Montenegro (r. 1910–1918); m. Peter I (1844–1921), king of Serbia (r. 1903–1921), Aug 11, 1883; children: Helen Karadjordjevic (1884–1962, who m. grand duke Ivan of Russia); Milena (1886–1888); George Karadjordjevic (b. 1887, renounced right to throne in 1909, after kicking a groom to death and being declared insane); Alexander I (1888–1934), king of Yugoslavia.

ZORLUTUNA, Halidé Nusret (1901–1984). Turkish poet and novelist. Name variations: Halide Nusret Zorlutuna. Born 1901 in Istanbul, Turkey; died 1984. ❖ Lived in exile with father and later traveled with army officer husband; worked for rights of women and children; writings include poetry, collection of short stories, novels, and memoirs *The Novel of an Era* (1973).

ZOZULA, Vera. Russian luge athlete. Name variations: Zozulya; Vera Sosulja. Born in Latvia. ❖ Won a gold medal for singles at Lake Placid (1980); won World championships (1978).

ZRIHEN, Olga (1953—). Belgian politician. Born Jan 10, 1953, in Casablanca, Morocco. ❖ Founded the La Louvière contraception collective and was chair of the La Louvière Socialist Union; served as head of department in the Directorate-General for Cultural Affairs in Hainaut; as a European Socialist, elected to 5th European Parliament (1999–2004).

ZRINSKA, Ana Katarina (1625–1673). Croatian noble and translator. Name variations: Ana Katarina Frankopan-Zrinska; Katalin Frangepán (Frankopan) Zrinyi; Ana Zrinyi. Born 1625; died in Graz, Austrian Styria, in 1673; dau. of Countess Ursula Inkofer; sister of Franjo Krsto Frankopan (1643–1671); m. Péter or Petar Zrinyi or Zrinski (1621–1671); children: daughter Ilona Zrinyi (1643–1703). ❖ Found a place in the history of Croatian literature by translating a prayer book from German into fluent and persuasive Croatian prose, *Putni tovarus* (Traveler's Prayer-Book, 1661); was involved with the ill-fated Ferenc Wesselényi conspiracy against Habsburg rule in Hungary, Croatia and Transylvania (1660s); after the conspiracy was crushed (1670), her husband and brother were executed (April 30, 1671). ❖ See also *Women in World History.*

ZRINYI, Ana Katarina (1625–1673). *See Zrinska, Ana Katarina.*

ZRINYI, Ilona (1643–1703). Hungarian hero. Name variations: Helena Zrinyi; Ilona Rákóczi or Rakoczi; Ilona Thököly or Thokoly or Thoekoely. Born in 1643; died in exile in Nicomedia (Izmit), Turkey, Feb 18, 1703; dau. of Péter or Petar Zrinyi or Zrinski (1621–1671) and Ana Katarina Zrinska (1625–1673); niece of poet Miklós Zrinyi (1620–1664); m. Prince Ferenc Rákóczi I of Transylvania (1645–1676); m. Imre Thököly (1657–1705), in 1681; children: son, Prince Ferenc Rákóczi II (1676–1735). ❖ Hungarian national hero of Croatian ancestry whose involvement in anti-Habsburg activities made her an equal to the most renowned members of her illustrious noble family; married 2nd husband who had become the acknowledged leader of a large-scale uprising against the Austrian emperor (1678); placed at the disposal of the anti-Habsburg struggle the immense wealth she had inherited from 1st husband; fully backed husband's plans, including his alliance with the only reliable anti-Habsburg state in the region, that of the Ottoman Turks; husband was captured in battle (1683); with her young son Ferenc, was at the head of the struggle to defend the fortress of Munkács (modern-day Mukacevo, Ukraine, Nov 1685), and defied the emperor's forces for more than 2 years; taken as a prisoner to a convent in Vienna (1688), was released (1691); with husband, was forced into exile in Turkey. One of the greatest heroes in Hungarian history, was depicted in the Romantic paintings of Viktor Madarász (1830–1917), as well as on postage stamps issued in 1944, 1952 and 1976. ❖ See also *Women in World History.*

ZSAK, Marcela (1956—). Romanian fencer. Born June 3, 1956. ❖ At Los Angeles Olympics, won a silver medal in team foil (1984).

ZSCHERPE, Iris (1967—). West German swimmer. Born Jan 7, 1967. ❖ At Los Angeles Olympics, won a bronze medal in 4 x 100-meter freestyle relay (1984).

ZSEMBERY, Tamasne (1967—). Hungarian handball player. Name variations: Tamasné. Born Sept 28, 1967, in Hungary. ❖ Won a team silver medal at Sydney Olympics (2000).

ZSOFIA. *Variant of Sophia.*

ZUBAREVA, Olga (1958—). Soviet handball player. Born Jan 27, 1958, in USSR. ❖ At Moscow Olympics, won a gold medal in team competition (1980).

ZUBEIDA (d. 831). Arabian queen. Name variations: Zubaidah; Zubaydah. Died in 831; granddau. of Abu Jafar (known as al-Mansur), 2nd Abbasid caliph; cousin-wife of Harun al-Rashid; stepmother to al-Mamun who m. Buran, dau. of his vizier; children: son al-Amin. ❖ Reigned with her husband during the golden age of the Abbasid dynasty. ❖ See also *Women in World History.*

ZUBKO, Yelena (1953—). Soviet rower. Born May 1953 in USSR. ❖ At Montreal Olympics, won a silver medal in coxed eights (1976).

ZUCCA, Mana (1887–1981). *See Mana-Zucca.*

ZUCCARI, Anna Radius (1846–1918). Italian novelist and poet. Name variations: Neera. Born 1846 in Italy; died June 19, 1918, in Milan, Italy; dau. of Fermo Zuccari; m. Emilio Radius, 1871; children: 2. ❖ Lived solitary, independent life; expressed concern for women's issues but disavowed any feminist leanings; works include *Vecchie catene* (1878), *Dizionario d'igiene per la famiglie* (1881), *Il marito dell'amica* (1885), *Anima sola* (1894), *La vecchia casa* (1900), *Conchiglie* (1905), *Una giovinezza del XIX secolo* (1919), and *Fiori* (1921); collected works appeared 1943.

ZUCCHI, Virginia (1849–1930). Italian ballet dancer. Born Feb 10, 1849 in Parma, Italy; died 1930 in Nice, France; studied in Milan. ❖ After performance in Padua (1873), was engaged at La Scala (1874), where she danced in the revival of Manzotti's *Excelsior*; visited St Petersburg with touring production of *Le Voyage dans la Lune* (1885); an enthusiastic reception, led to engagement by Imperial Theater, where she performed in Petipa's *Le Roi l'a Dit* (1886) and *La Fille du Pharon*; numerous appearances in Russia helped to establish Italian influence over Russian ballet; returned to France (1889) and later opened school in Monte Carlo, where she taught until her death; was renowned for superior technique and passionate interpretation of work of Petipa. ❖ See also I. Guest, *The Divine Virginia* (1977).

ZUCHOLD, Erika (1947—). East German gymnast. Born Mar 19, 1947. ❖ At Mexico City Olympics, won a silver medal in vault and a bronze medal in team all-around (1968); at Munich Olympics, won silver medals in team all-around, vault, and uneven bars (1972).

ZUCKERMAN, Kathy Kohner (1941—). *See Kohner, Kathy.*

ZUCKERMAN, Ruth (1908–1984). *See Taylor, Ruth.*

ZUCKERMAN, Zivia Lubetkin (1914–1978). *See Lubetkin, Zivia.*

ZULUS, queen of the. *See Nandi (c. 1760s–1827).*

ZUREK, Natasza (1978—). Canadian snowboarder. Born Mar 4, 1978, in Zakopane, Poland. ❖ Immigrated to Canada (1985); was an X Games Superpipe silver medalist (2001); won US Open (2000, 2001) and Vans Triple Crown (2001), all for halfpipe.

ZUR MÜHLEN, Hermynia (1883–1951). Austrian novelist, translator and playwright. Name variations: Hermynia Zur Muhlen. Born Dec 12, 1883, in Austria; died 1951; dau. of a high-ranking Austrian count. ❖ Joined Communist Party (1919) and wrote for left-wing journals; was accused of high treason for novella, *Schupomann Karl Müller* (1924); after writing analysis of women's role in Nazism, *Unsere Töchter, die Nazzinen* (1935), went into exile in England; other works include *We Poor Shadows* (1943) and *Came the Stranger* (1946); was also well known for her stories and fairytales for children.

ZÜRN, Unica (1916–1970). German poet, playwright and short-story writer. Name variations: Unica Zurn or Zuern. Born 1916 in Berlin, Germany; died 1970. ❖ Moved with Surrealist artist Hans Bellmer to Paris (1953); mixed poetry with Surrealist illustration in *Hexentexte* (1954); suffered from mental illness and committed suicide; other works include *Dunkler Frühling* (1970) and *Der Mann in Jasmin* (1977).

ZUZORIC, Cvijeta (c. 1555–1600). Croatian poet and salonnière. Born in Dubrovnik, c. 1555 (some sources cite 1550 and 1552); died in Florence, Italy, 1600; m. Bartolomeo Pescioni. ❖ Moved with family from Dubrovnik to Italian port city of Ancona; a noted beauty, met and married Florentine aristocrat Bartolomeo Pescioni; in Florence, presided over an influential salon that attracted many of the city's most gifted writers and artists, including Torquato Tasso (1544–1595), who wrote a number of sonnets and madrigals in her honor, Croatian writers Miho Bunic Babulinov and Miho Monaldi, philosopher Niko Vitov Gucetic, who dedicated his *Dialogo d'amore* to her, and Dominko Zlataric (1558–1613), whose name was linked romantically to her by some contemporaries, and who dedicated his poem *Smrt Pirama i Tizbe* (Death of Pyramus and Thisbe) to her; also wrote works herself in Croatian and Italian. ❖ See also *Women in World History.*

ZVEREVA, Ellina (1960—). Belarusian discus thrower. Born Nov 16, 1960, in Dolgoprudny, Belarus. ❖ Won a bronze medal at Atlanta Olympics (1996) and a gold medal at Sydney Olympics (2000); won a silver medal at World championships (2001).

ZVEREVA, Natasha (1971—). Belarusian tennis player. Name variations: Natalya Zvereva. Born April 16, 1971, in Minsk, Russia. ❖ At Barcelona Olympics, won a bronze medal in doubles (1992); won Australian Open for mixed doubles (1990, 1995); won three of the four Grand Slam doubles titles in the same year 4 times (1992–94, 1997); won 20 Grand Slam titles.

ZWANZIGER, Anna (1760–1811). Bavarian poisoner. Born 1760; beheaded 1811. ❖ Widow, used arsenic to poison numerous people, including a baby, in early 19th century.

ZWEHL, Julia (1976—). German field-hockey player. Born Mar 20, 1976, in Hannover, Germany. ❖ Won bronze medal at World Cup (1998) and European championships (2003); won a team gold medal at Athens Olympics (2004).

ZWI, Rose (1928—). South African novelist. Born May 8, 1928, in Oaxaca, Mexico. ❖ Arrived in South Africa with family (1930) and lived in Johannesburg; lived in Israel (1949–53) and moved to Australia (1988); received Olive Schreiner Prize and Australian Human Rights Award for Literature (1994); works explore Communist Party politics, fascism, Afrikaner Nationalism, Zionism, and tension between personal and political; writings include *Another Year in Africa* (1980), *The Inverted Pyramid* (1981), *Exiles* (1984), and *Safe Houses* (1994).

ZWICKY, Fay (1933—). Australian poet, literary critic and short-story writer. Born 1933 in Melbourne, Australia. ❖ Began career as concert pianist; became lecturer in English at University of Western Australia; was writer-in-residence at Rollins College, FL; works include *Isaac Babel's Fiddle* (1975), *Kaddish and Other Poems* (1982), *Ask Me* (1990), *A Touch of Ginger* (1992), and *The Gatekeeper's Wife* (1997); essays published as *The Lyre in the Pawnshop: Essays on Literature and Survival 1974–1984* (1985). Received New South Wales Premier's Award (1982) and Western Australian Premier's Award for poetry (1991).

ZWIERS, Claudia. Dutch judoka. Born in the Netherlands. ❖ Won a bronze medal for 61–66 kg middleweight at Atlanta Olympics (1996); won European championship (1996).

ZWILICH, Ellen Taaffe (1939—). American composer. Born April 30, 1939, in Miami, Florida; adopted daughter of Edward Taaffe (airline pilot) and Ruth (Howard) Taaffe; Florida State University, bachelor of music, 1960, MA in music, 1962; Juilliard School of Music, DMA in composition (1975); m. Joseph Zwilich (violinist), June 22, 1969 (died 1979); no children. ❖ Pulitzer Prize-winning composer whose works are widely performed and appreciated for their accessibility to audiences of all levels of musical sophistication; taught at Converse College in Spartanburg, SC (1963–64); moved to New York to study violin with Ivan Galamian; worked as an usher at Carnegie Hall; taught theory and music at Mannes College of Music and Hunter High School; awarded position in the violin section of the American Symphony Orchestra (1965–72); began work on doctorate of musical arts in composition at Juilliard (1970), studying under Elliott Carter and Roger Sessions; wrote *Symposium,* a work for orchestra, premiered by the Juilliard orchestra under the direction of Pierre Boulez (1973); inducted into the American Academy and Institute of Arts and Letters (1974); wrote *String Quartet* (1974); was the first woman to be awarded a DMA in composition from the Juilliard School of Music (1975); won the Pulitzer Prize for *Symphony No. 1* (1983), the first woman to receive this award; wrote *Cello Symphony* (1984) and *Symbolon* (1988). ❖ See also *Woman in World History.*

ZWINGLI, Anna Reinhard (1487–c. 1538). Swiss Protestant leader. Name variations: Anna Reinhard. Born 1487 in Switzerland; died c. 1538 in Zurich, Switzerland; dau. of Oswald Reinhard (landlord of the Little Horse Inn) and Elizabeth (Wynzuern) Reinhard; m. Hans Meyer van Knonau (died); m. Ulrich Zwingli, also seen as Huldreich or Huldrych Zwingli, in 1522 (died 1531); children: (1st m.) Margaret, Agatha, Gerrold; (2nd m.) Regula, Anna, Wilhelm, Huldrych. ❖ Widowed with 3 children, began attending the church of Ulrich Zwingli and was attentive to his message; married him privately (1522), while he was still considered a Roman Catholic priest; when husband became leader of the Protestant Reformation in Switzerland, publicly celebrated their marriage (1524), a year before Martin Luther's marriage to former nun Katharina von Bora; supported her husband's views, and her home became a center for people who opposed the pope and who broke with the Roman Catholic Church. ❖ See also *Women in World History.*

ZWINK, Tara (1973—). American snowboarder. Born Feb 13, 1973, in Edmonds, WA. ❖ Won silver (1997) and bronze (1998) in Big Air at Winter X Games.

ZYBINA, Galina (1931—). Soviet track-and-field athlete. Born Jan 22, 1931, in USSR. ❖ Won a gold medal at Helsinki Olympics (1952), silver medal at Melbourne Olympics (1956), and bronze medal at Tokyo Olympics (1964), all in the shot put.

ZYKINA, Olesya (1980—). Russian runner. Born Oct 7, 1980, in Kaluga, USSR. ❖ Placed 1st for 4 x 400-meter relay at World Indoor championships; won a bronze medal for 4 x 400-meter relay at Sydney Olympics (2000) and a silver medal for 4 x 400-meter relay at Athens Olympics (2004).

ZYUSKOVA, Nina (1952—). Soviet runner. Born May 1952 in USSR. ❖ At Moscow Olympics, won a gold medal in 4 x 400-meter relay (1980).